Encyclopedia of Medical Organizations and Agencies

Explore your options!
Gale databases offered in
a variety of formats

DISKETTE/MAGNETIC TAPE

Many Gale databases are available on diskette or magnetic tape, allowing systemwide access to your most-used information sources through existing computer systems. Data can be delivered on a variety of mediums (DOS-formatted diskette, 9-track tape, 8mm data tape) and in industry-standard formats (comma-delimited, tagged, fixed-field). Retrieval software is also available with many of Gale's databases that allows you to search, display, print and download the data.

ONLINE

For your convenience, many Gale databases are available through popular online services, including DIALOG, NEXIS (Mead Data Central), Data-Star, Orbit, Questel, OCLC, I/Plus Direct, Prodigy, HOOVER and Telebase Systems.

CD-ROM

A variety of Gale titles are available on CD-ROM, offering maximum flexibility and powerful search software.

The information in this Gale publication is also available in some or all of the formats described here. Your Gale Representative will be happy to fill you in.

For information, call

GALE

ISSN 0743-4510

Encyclopedia of Medical Organizations and Agencies

SIXTH EDITION
1996-97

A Subject Guide to Organizations, Foundations,
Federal and State Government Agencies, Research Centers,
and Medical and Allied Health Schools

Karen Boyden, Editor

Gale Research

An ITP Information/Reference Group Company

I(T)P
Changing the Way the World Learns

NEW YORK • LONDON • BONN • BOSTON • DETROIT
MADRID • MELBOURNE • MEXICO CITY • PARIS
SINGAPORE • TOKYO • TORONTO • WASHINGTON
ALBANY NY • BELMONT CA • CINCINNATI OH

Karen Boyden, *Senior Editor*
Pamela Proffitt, *Assistant Editor*
Nicole Beatty, Kristine Binkley, Sheila Dow, Christine B. Jeryan,
Paul Lewon, and Robyn Young, *Contributing Editors*

Mary Beth Trimper, *Production Director*
Deborah Milliken, *Production Assistant*

Benita L. Spight, *Manager, Data Entry Services*
Gwendolyn S. Tucker, *Data Entry Supervisor*
Civie Ann Green, *Senior Data Entry Associate*
Johnny Carson, Sr. and Arlene Ann Kevonian, *Data Entry Associates*

Sherrell Hobbs, *Macintosh Artist*

Theresa Rocklin, *Manager, Technical Support Services*
Charles Beaumont, *Programmer/Analyst*

∞™ The paper used in this publication meets the minimum requirements of American National Standard for Information Sciences--Permanence Paper for Printed Library Materials, ANSI Z39.48-1984.

♲ This book is printed on recycled paper that meets Environmental Protection Agency standards.

ISBN 0-8103-9119-8
ISSN 0743-4510
Library of Congress Catalog Card Number 84-640206

Printed in the United States of America

I(T)P™ Gale Research, an International Thomson Publishing Company.
ITP logo is a trademark under license.

Contents

Continues . . .

Continues . . .

Continues . . .

Continues . . . .

Continues . . .

Highlights

The sixth edition of the *Encyclopedia of Medical Organizations and Agencies (EMOA)* is a comprehensive guide to medical and health-related organizations, agencies, and institutions, including:

- National, International, and State & Regional Organizations
- Foundations & Other Funding Organizations
- U.S. Federal & State Government Agencies
- Research Centers
- Medical & Allied Health Schools

Entries in *EMOA* are carefully selected from a wide array of resources to provide a convenient, one-stop source of information on a broad range of topics relating to clinical medicine, basic biomedical sciences, and the technological and socioeconomic aspects of health care. Subjects covered in *EMOA* include:

- Aging
- Biomedical Engineering
- Child Abuse & Family Violence
- Death & Dying
- Environmental Health
- Family Planning
- Genetics & Genetic Disorders
- Health Care Administration & Financing
- Infectious Diseases
- Mental Health

- Neurology
- Nursing
- Nutrition
- Occupational Health
- Radiology
- Respiratory Diseases
- Sports Medicine
- Substance Abuse
- Transplantation
- and more...

Features of *EMOA*

- More than **13,800** entries arranged within **69** subject-specific chapters, ranging from Aging to Vision.

- Some **1,200** entries new to this edition.

- **Entry cross-references** direct users to key entries appearing in other chapters.

- **Easy-to-read page design**. Catchwords at the top of each page and headings throughout the text help the user quickly locate desired information.

- The **Subject Cross-Index** provides a quick overview of all topics covered in *EMOA*.

- The **Alphabetical Name and Keyword Index** contains citations to all organizations listed in *EMOA*, as well as to subject keywords appearing in organization names.

Introduction

The *Encyclopedia of Medical Organizations and Agencies (EMOA)*, now in its sixth edition, is a convenient single-volume resource to subject-classified information on medical and health-related organizations, agencies, and institutions. *EMOA* directs health care professionals and the public alike to a wide variety of organizations, including:

- National & International Organizations
- State & Regional Organizations
- Foundations & Other Funding Organizations
- U.S. Federal Government Agencies
- U.S. State Government Agencies
- Research Centers
- Medical & Allied Health Schools

EMOA provides contact and descriptive information on more than 13,800 such organizations–including some 1,200 new to this edition–active in clinical medicine, the basic biomedical sciences, or the technological and socioeconomic aspects of health care. The book covers 69 subject areas representing a wide range of contemporary medical interests, including:

- diseases and disorders (birth defects, communicative disorders, infectious diseases, respiratory diseases, etc.);
- medical disciplines (dermatology, neurology, orthopedics, radiology, etc.);
- social health concerns (aging, child abuse, family planning, substance abuse, etc.);
- special aspects of medicine (health care administration, health care financing, the health care industry, and information and communications).

New to this Edition

The sixth edition of *EMOA* features:

- Some 1,200 organizations, agencies, and institutions not previously listed.
- Enhanced coverage of foundations, including arrangement of entries by foundation type and expanded information on the funding programs of private and corporate foundations.
- Additional contact information. E-mail addresses now provided for many research centers.

Content and Arrangement

EMOA consists of descriptive listings and indexes.

- The **descriptive listings** are organized within 69 chapters that are arranged alphabetically by subject name. (Consult the "Contents" pages for a complete list of subjects.) Key entries appearing in other chapters are identified through cross-references appearing throughout the descriptive listings.

- The **Subject Cross-Index**, immediately preceding the descriptive listings, provides thorough access to the subject content of *EMOA* via chapter names and numbers, synonyms, related terms, and more specific subjects included but not reflected in chapter titles.
- The **Alphabetical Name and Keyword Index** speeds access to *EMOA* entries through a single alphabetical listing of all organizations, agencies, and institutions included in the book, as well as to significant keywords appearing in organization titles.

For additional information on the content, arrangement, and indexing of *EMOA*, consult the "User's Guide" following this introduction.

Method of Compilation

Many sources were used in compiling the sixth edition of *EMOA*. Entries relevant to the medical and allied health fields were carefully selected from Gale Research directories, federal government documents, state government publications, and lists and directories supplied by numerous national organizations. Telephone inquiries were also employed to gather data and/or verify information.

Available in Electronic Form and Mailing Labels

Diskette/Magnetic Tape. The information in *EMOA* is available for licensing on magnetic tape or diskette in a fielded format. Either the complete database or a custom selection of entries may be ordered. The database is available for internal processing and nonpublishing purposes only. For more information call 800-877-GALE.

Mailing Labels. *EMOA* is available in mailing list format on either labels or magnetic tape. Selections may be made from specific sections or based upon geographical criteria. List rental is for one-time use only. For more information call 800-877-GALE.

Comments Welcome

We encourage users to bring new or unlisted organizations to our attention. Every effort will be made to include them in subsequent editions of *EMOA*. Comments and suggestions for improving the directory are also welcome. Please contact:

Encyclopedia of Medical Organizations and Agencies
Gale Research
835 Penobscot Bldg.
Detroit, MI 48226-4094
Telephone: (313)961-2242
Toll-Free: 800-347-GALE
Fax: (313)961-6741

User's Guide

EMOA is organized into 3 parts: **descriptive listings** and **entry cross-references**, which are arranged within subject chapters; a **Subject Cross-Index**, which provides further subject access to the content of *EMOA*; and an **Alphabetical Name and Keyword Index**, which provides a convenient alphabetical listing of all organizations, agencies, and institutions included in *EMOA*.

Each part is described below.

Descriptive Listings

Listings are numbered sequentially within 69 subject chapters, as outlined on the "Contents" pages. With the exception of the General Medical section, which is presented first, chapters are arranged alphabetically by subject names.

Entries within subject chapters are grouped according to functional categories. An individual chapter may contain all or only some of the categories, as appropriate to the subject. Consult the "Contents" pages for a listing of the entry categories included in each chapter. Specific information on the content, arrangement, and indexing of each functional category is provided in the following descriptions.

Federal Government Agencies

Scope: Some 120 units of the federal government concerned with medicine and health.
Entries include: Agency name, address, telephone number, fax number (when available), and, in many cases, a brief description of the agency's programs and purposes.
Arrangement: Alphabetical by agency names.
Indexed by: Parent agency and specific unit names, as well as significant intermediate agency names and keywords within names.
Source: *United States Government Manual* (published by the U.S. National Archives and Records Administration and available from the U.S. Government Printing Office) and original research by the *EMOA* editorial staff.

Foundations and Other Funding Organizations

Scope: More than 1,200 U.S. funding organizations, including major private and corporate foundations that provide charitable support to nonprofit organizations, as well as professional associations and special interest groups that administer scholarship, fellowship, and grant programs, and provide other financial assistance for a variety of medical and health-related interests.
Entries include: Organization name, address, telephone number, toll-free and fax numbers (when available), contact name, and descriptive information on the funding program, including foundation philosophy, giving priorities, typical health-related recipients, and geographic distribution of funds.
Arrangement: Alphabetical by organization names within three sections: 1) Private Foundations, 2) Corporate Foundations, and 3) Other Funding Organizations.
Indexed by: Organization names and significant keywords within names.
Source: *Foundation Reporter*, 27th Edition and *Corporate Giving Directory*, 16th Edition (both published by the Taft Group, 12300 Twinbrook Parkway, Ste. 520, Rockville, MD 20852), and *Encyclopedia of Associations*, Volume 1: *National Organizations of the U.S.*, 30th Edition (published by Gale Research).

Medical and Allied Health Schools

Scope: More than 2,300 educational institutions and training programs in 28 occupational categories. Coverage is limited primarily to baccalaureate and advanced degree programs. To obtain information on related educational programs at other levels, consult the section description referred to under the "Arrangement" heading below. Information on schools and programs is also available from the Commission on Accreditation of Allied Health Education Programs (515 N. State St., Ste. 7530, Chicago, IL 60610, 312-464-4623), which accredits educational programs in some 29 allied health professions.
Entries include: Institution name, address, telephone number, and fax number (when available).
Arrangement: Geographical by states, then alphabetical by institution names within states. Each section of schools is accompanied by a brief description of the programs listed there, along with references to professional organizations that may be contacted for general information concerning accreditation or careers in that field.
Indexed by: Sponsoring institution names.
Source: Lists provided by national organizations and original research by the *EMOA* editorial staff.

National and International Organizations

Scope: Nearly 4,200 primarily nonprofit membership groups, including national organizations of the United States, as well as organizations that are international in scope, membership, or interest and are headquartered outside the United States.
Entries include: Organization name, address, telephone number, toll-free and fax numbers (when available), name and title of the chief official, and a brief description, including founding date, number of members, purpose, publications, and former/alternate organization names (if applicable). In non-U.S. entries, the principal foreign-language name is listed in parentheses following the English-language version of the organization name.
Arrangement: Alphabetical by organization names.
Indexed by: Organization names, both English- and foreign-language, as well as significant keywords within names.
Source: *Encyclopedia of Associations*, Volume 1: *National Organizations of the U.S.*, 30th Edition, and *Encyclopedia of Associations: International Organizations*, 30th Edition (published by Gale Research).

Research Centers

Scope: More than 3,200 research organizations, including: 1) university-related and other nonprofit research centers in the U.S. and Canada that are engaged in medical and health-related research on a continuing basis, and 2) U.S. government research centers and programs, including federal agencies and bureaus that are themselves research organizations, research facilities owned and operated by the federal government, government-owned/contractor-operated facilities, test centers and facilities, cooperative research programs, data collection and analysis activities, and offices that support research by awarding grants and/or contracts.
Entries include: Organization or agency name, address, telephone number, toll-free and fax numbers (when available), E-mail address (when available) director name, a brief description of principal activities and fields of research, and a listing of publications issued by the research unit.
Arrangement: Alphabetical by organization or agency names.
Indexed by: Parent organization names, research unit names, significant intermediate organization names, and significant keywords within names.
Source: *Research Centers Directory*, 20th Edition and *Government Research Directory*, 8th Edition (both published by Gale Research).

State Government Agencies

Scope: Some 1,400 agencies that function in 27 areas relating to medicine and health.
Entries include: Agency name, address, telephone number, and fax number (when available).

Arrangement: Geographical by states.
Indexed by: State designations (Michigan Department of Public Health, Alabama State Board of Pharmacy, etc.) and other keywords within agency names.
Source: Lists provided by organizations and federal government agencies, as well as original research by the *EMOA* editorial staff.

State and Regional Organizations

Scope: More than 1,300 entries representing state and regional affiliates of 25 national organizations. For the most part, only those with paid staff have been selected for inclusion. Affiliates of some national groups do not maintain executive offices; they are instead managed by chapter presidents that change on an annual basis. In these cases, the national organizations often prefer to serve as central contacts and will provide current information on the state or regional group of interest. Readers should consult the National and International Organizations category of appropriate *EMOA* chapters for contact and descriptive information on national organizations.
Entries include: Organization name, address, telephone number, and fax number (when available).
Arrangement: Geographical by states, then alphabetical by organization names within states.
Indexed by: Organization names, as well as geographic designations and other keywords within names.
Source: Lists provided by national organizations and original research by the *EMOA* editorial staff.

Entry Cross-References

In a subject-classified compilation such as *EMOA*, there are many entries that are appropriate for listing in more than one subject chapter. For example, the International Society for Pediatric Neurosurgery applies to three *EMOA* chapters: Child Health, Neurology, and Surgery. The use of text cross-references in these cases allows the user to locate the names of all organizations concerned with a subject area, while eliminating the need to duplicate complete entries in multiple chapters. In the example cited above, the full entry appears in the Child Health Chapter and cross-references, with the organization name only, are listed in the Neurology and Surgery chapters, referring the user to the full entry in the Child Health Chapter.

Subject Cross-Index

The **Subject Cross-Index** provides access to the subject content of *EMOA* by listing chapter names as well as *See* and *See Also* references for synonyms, related terms, and more specific subjects included but not reflected in chapter titles. References are to chapter names and their corresponding chapter numbers.

Alphabetical Name and Keyword Index

The **Alphabetical Name and Keyword Index** provides access to all entries included in *EMOA*, as well as to former or alternate names that appear within the text of entries. Each organization, agency, and institution is indexed by the name listed and, when appropriate, by significant keywords that are a part of that name. Index references are to book **entry numbers** rather than page numbers. Entry numbers appear in the index in **boldface** type if the reference is to a main entry, and in lightface type if the reference is to a former or alternate name included within the text of the cited entry.

Many of the entries in *EMOA* use a hierarchical organization name structure, with a parent organization and often intermediate subunits preceding the specific unit name. The Alphabetical Name and Keyword Index offers access to all multiple-part organization names via the parent organization name. Many entries are also referenced under the specific unit name and some under a significant intermediate unit name. Multiple parts of names are separated in index citations by a bullet (•). If several entries have the same parent organization, as is the case with many of the government and university groups listed in *EMOA*, the related units appear as a group under the name of the parent organization. The parent agencies of most federal government organizations are indexed under "U.S." (e.g., U.S. House of Representatives, U.S. Department of Health and Human Services, etc.).

Indexing Sample

Following is a typical entry in *EMOA*:

★2884★ Boston University
Whitaker Cardiovascular Institute
700 Albany St.
Boston, MA 02118
Phone: (617)638-4890
Fax: (617)638-4066

The index provides the following citations to the above entry:

Boston University • Whitaker Cardiovascular Institute **2884**
Cardiovascular Institute; Whitaker • Boston University **2884**
Whitaker Cardiovascular Institute • Boston University **2884**

Alphabetizing Rules

In both the descriptive listings chapters and the index, organization names are sorted on a word-by-word basis, so that "New York Easter Seal Society" comes before "Newbury College". Initial articles ("A," "An," or "The") are ignored for sorting purposes. Conjunctions, articles, and most prepositions elsewhere in the names are also not considered in alphabetizing. In addition:

- Numbers are sorted as if spelled-out and interfiled alphabetically with other non-number words.

- Abbreviations such as "U.S.," "St.," "Mt.," "Ft.," and "Dr.," are sorted as if spelled-out and interfiled with names in which the full version of those words are used.

- Personal names are sorted under the first name, or initial, within the descriptive listings chapters. In the index, they can be accessed under both the first and last names.

Key to Abbreviations

&	And	Fwy.	Freeway
Act.	Acting	GA	Georgia
Adj.	Adjutant	Gen.	General
Admin.	Administrator	GU	Guam
AFB	Air Force Base	Hd.	Head
AK	Alaska	HI	Hawaii
AL	Alabama	Hwy.	Highway
Apt.	Apartment	IA	Iowa
AR	Arkansas	ID	Idaho
Asst.	Assistant	IL	Illinois
Assoc.	Associate	IN	Indiana
Ave.	Avenue	Inc.	Incorporated
AZ	Arizona	Info.	Information
Bldg.	Building	KS	Kansas
Blvd.	Boulevard	KY	Kentucky
Br.	Branch	LA	Louisiana
CA	California	Lib.	Library
CEO	Chief Executive Officer	Libn.	Librarian
Chf.	Chief	Ln.	Lane
Chm.	Chairman	MA	Massachusetts
Cir.	Circle	MD	Maryland
Clghse.	Clearinghouse	ME	Maine
c/o	Care of	Med.	Medical
CO	Colorado	Mgr.	Manager
Co.	Company	MI	Michigan
Coll.	Collection	MN	Minnesota
Comdr.	Commander	MO	Missouri
Commun.	Communication	MS	Mississippi
Coord.	Coordinator	MT	Montana
Corp.	Corporation	Mt.	Mount
Couns.	Counselor	N.	North
CT	Connecticut	Natl.	National
Ct.	Court	NC	North Carolina
Ctr.	Center	ND	North Dakota
DC	District of Columbia	NE	Nebraska, Northeast
DE	Delaware	NH	New Hampshire
Dept.	Department	NJ	New Jersey
Dir.	Director	No.	Number
Dr.	Drive	NV	Nevada
E.	East	NW	Northwest
Educ.	Education	NY	New York
Exec.	Executive	Off.	Officer
Expy.	Expressway	OH	Ohio
Ext.	Extension	OK	Oklahoma
Fl.	Floor	OR	Oregon
FL	Florida	PA	Pennsylvania
Ft.	Fort	Pkwy.	Parkway

Pl.	Place		Spec.	Specialist
Plz.	Plaza		Sq.	Square
PO Box	Post Office Box		Sr.	Senior
PR	Puerto Rico		St.	Saint, Street
Pres.	President		Sta.	Station
Prog.	Program		Ste.	Suite, Sainte
Rd.	Road		Supv.	Supervisor
RD	Rural Delivery		SW	Southwest
Ref.	Reference		Ter.	Terrace
Reg.	Regional		TN	Tennessee
Res.	Research		Tpke.	Turnpike
RFD	Rural Free Delivery		Trl.	Trail
RI	Rhode Island		TX	Texas
Rm.	Room		Univ.	University
RR	Rural Route		U.S.	United States
Rte.	Route		UT	Utah
S.	South		VA	Virginia
SC	South Carolina		VI	Virgin Islands
Sci.	Science		VP	Vice President
SD	South Dakota		VT	Vermont
SE	Southeast		W.	West
Sec.	Secretary		WA	Washington
Sect.	Section		WV	West Virginia
Serv.	Service		WY	Wyoming
Soc.	Social			

Subject Cross Index

This index provides alphabetical subject access to *EMOA* by listing chapter names as well as *See* and *See Also* references for synonyms, related terms, and more specific subjects included but not reflected in chapter titles. References are to chapter names and their corresponding chapter numbers.

Encyclopedia of Medical Organizations and Agencies

Chapter 1
General Medical

Federal Government Agencies

★1★ Executive Office of the President
Office of Management and Budget
Health Division
Health Programs and Social Services
Bureau
725 17th St. NW
Washington, DC 20503
Phone: (202)395-4926

★2★ Smithsonian Institution
National Museum of American History
Department of the History of Science and
Technology
Science, Medicine, and Society Division
14th St. & Constitution Ave. NW
Washington, DC 20560
Phone: (202)357-2145
Fax: (202)347-7757

Description: Division is concerned with the history of public health and pharmacy, 17th-20th century history of medical and dental technology, and 20th century health sciences.

★3★ Tennessee Valley Authority
Vice President of Human Resources
Health Services
11th and Market Sts.
Chattanooga, TN 37402
Phone: (615)751-2091

★4★ U.S. Department of Health and
Human Services (HHS)
200 Independence Ave. SW
Washington, DC 20201
Phone: (202)619-0257

Description: The Department of Health and Human Services is the cabinet-level department of the federal executive branch most concerned with people and most involved with the nation's human concerns. The Secretary of HHS advises the President on health, welfare, and income security plans, policies, and programs of the federal government. Principal operating components of the Department are: 1) Administration for Children and Families, 2) the Health Care Financing Administration, 3) the Public Health Service, and 4) the Social Security Administration.

★5★ U.S. Department of Health and
Human Services
Administration for Children and Families
(ACF)
901 D St. SW
Washington, DC 20447
Phone: (202)619-0257

Description: The Administration for Children and Families provides national leadership and direction to plan, manage, and coordinate comprehensive support services for vulnerable children and families, Native Americans, people with disabilities, refugees and legalized aliens. The mission of ACF is to promote stability, economic security, responsibility and self-sufficiency. There are seven major program offices: Administration for Children, Youth and Families (ACYF), Administration for Developmental Disabilities, Administration for Native Americans (see separate entries), Office of Family Assistance, Office of Child Support Enforcement, Office of Community Service, and Office of Refugee Resettlement.

★6★ U.S. Department of Health and
Human Services
Administration for Children and Families
(ACF)
Administration on Children, Youth and
Families (ACYF)
330 C St. SW
Washington, DC 20201
Phone: (202)205-8347

Description: The Administration for Children, Youth, and Families advises on matters relating to sound development of children, youth, and families. It oversees and finances a broad range of programs to help children and families develop and grow toward more independent and self-reliant lives. It also supports and encourages services which prevent or remedy the effects of abuse and/or neglect of children and youth.

★7★ U.S. Department of Health and
Human Services
Administration for Children and Families
(ACF)
Administration for Native Americans (ANA)
200 Independence Ave. SW
Washington, DC 20201
Phone: (202)690-7776

Description: The Administration for Native Americans represents the concerns of American Indians, Alaska Natives, Native Hawaiians, and other Native American Pacific Islanders (including American Samoan Natives) and advises the Assistant Secretary for Human Development Services on their behalf. ANA has primary responsibility for the social and economic development and self-sufficiency of Native Americans; serves as departmental liaison with other federal agencies on Native American affairs; administers a grant program to promote the social and economic development of Native Americans; and explores new program concepts and methods.

★8★ U.S. Department of Health and
Human Services
Public Health Service
Health Resources and Services
Administration (HRSA)
5600 Fishers Ln.
Rockville, MD 20857
Phone: (301)443-2216

Description: The mission of the Administration has responsibility for general health services and resource issues relating to access, equity, quality, and cost of care. Provides information on programs for the distribution, supply, use, quality, and cost-effectiveness of health resources, and on health services programs for certain segments of the population. Specific areas of concentration are health professions training, health services for Hansen's disease patients, community/migrant health centers, maternal and child health, migrant health, health facilities, and the National Health Service Corps. HRSA also administers programs relating to pediatric AIDS service demonstration projects, regional AIDS education and training centers, long-term and intermediate care facilities for AIDS patients, HIV services planning, and AIDS drug reimbursement. HRSA also adminsters programs relating to organ transplantation, federal employee occupational health, rural health issues, and the National Practitioner Data Bank. Major components of HRSA include: 1) Bureau of Health Care Delivery and Assistance, 2) Bureau of Health Professions, 3) Bureau of Maternal and Child Health, and 4) Bureau of Health and Resources Development.

★9★ U.S. Department of Health and Human Services
Public Health Service
Health Resources and Services Administration
Bureau of Health Professions
5600 Fishers Ln.
Rockville, MD 20857
Phone: (301)443-5794
Free: 800-767-6732

Description: The Bureau of Health Professions provides national leadership in coordinating, evaluating, and supporting the development and utilization of the nation's health personnel.

★10★ U.S. Department of Health and Human Services
Public Health Service
Indian Health Service (IHS)
5600 Fishers Ln.
Rockville, MD 20857
Phone: (301)443-1083

Description: The Indian Health Service assures a comprehensive health services delivery system for American Indians and Alaska Natives, with sufficient options to provide for maximum tribal involvement in meeting their health needs. The goal of the Service is to raise the health level of the Indian and Alaska Native people to the highest possible level.

★11★ U.S. Department of Justice
Office of the Deputy Attorney General
Federal Bureau of Prisons
Health Services Division
320 1st St. NW
Washington, DC 20534
Phone: (202)307-3055

Description: The Health Services Division has oversight responsibility for all medical and environmental, health, safety, and sanitation services in Bureau institutions. The Division is also responsible for food service, farm operations, and inmate accident compensation programs.

★12★ U.S. Department of State
Under Secretary for Management
Office of Medical Services
2201 C St. NW
Washington, DC 20520
Phone: (202)647-3484
Fax: (202)647-0029

Description: The Office develops, manages, and staffs a worldwide primary health care system for U.S. citizen employees, and their eligible dependents, residing abroad.

★13★ U.S. Department of Transportation
Coast Guard
Office of Health and Safety
400 7th Ave. SW
Washington, DC 20590
Phone: (202)267-1098

★14★ U.S. House of Representatives
Committee on Appropriations
Subcommittee on Labor, Health and Human Services, Education, and Related Agencies
2358 Rayburn House Office Bldg.
Washington, DC 20515
Phone: (202)225-3508

★15★ U.S. House of Representatives
Committee on Commerce
Subcommittee on Health and Environment
2125 Rayburn House Office Bldg.
Washington, DC 20515-6115
Phone: (202)225-2927

★16★ U.S. House of Representatives
Committee on Government Operations
Subcommittee on Human Resources and Intergovernmental Relations
B372 Rayburn House Office Bldg.
Washington, DC 20515
Phone: (202)225-2548
Fax: (202)225-2382

★17★ U.S. House of Representatives
Committee on Science
Subcommittee on Basic Research
B-374 Rayburn House Office Bldg.
Washington, DC 20515
Phone: (202)225-9662
Fax: (202)225-7815

★18★ U.S. House of Representatives
Committee on Ways and Means
Subcommittee on Human Resources
B-317 Rayburn House Office Bldg.
Washington, DC 20515
Phone: (202)225-1025

★19★ U.S. Senate
Committee on Appropriations
Subcommittee on Labor, Health and Human Services, Education, and Related Agencies
SD-186 Dirksen Senate Office Bldg.
Washington, DC 20510
Phone: (202)224-7230

★20★ U.S. Senate
Committee on Indian Affairs
SH-838 Hart Senate Office Bldg.
Washington, DC 20510-6450
Phone: (202)224-2251
Fax: (202)224-5429

Foundations & Other Funding Organizations

Private Foundations

★21★ A. E. Finley Foundation
PO Box 27785
Raleigh, NC 27611
Phone: (919)782-0529
Robert C. Brown, President

Foundation Philosophy: The A. E. Finley Foundation "contributes to and supports charitable, scientific, literary, religious, and educational organizations. It endeavors to contribute to soundly managed and operated qualifying organizations which fundamentally give service with a broad scope and impact, aid all kinds of people, and contribute materially to the general welfare." **Giving Priorities:** In fiscal 1992, approximately 64% of funding went to educational

institutions in North Carolina. Health care received about 15% of contributions, with major support to Northampton Memorial Hospital, Northampton, NC. Social services received 12% of grants. Religion received 8% of funding, and the arts and civic concerns each received about 1% of total grants. **Typical Health-Related Recipients:** Hospices, Hospitals, Medical Education, People with Disabilities. **Geographic Distribution:** Focus on North Carolina.

★22★ A. L. Mailman Family Foundation
707 Westchester Ave.
White Plains, NY 10604
Phone: (914)681-4448
Fax: (914)681-5182
Luba H. Lynch, Executive Director and Secretary

Foundation Philosophy: The A. L. Mailman Family Foundation is "committed to strengthening families and enhancing their ability to support the development and well-being of their children, committed to the restructuring of social systems to incorporate a family-focused approach in the delivery of human services, interested in developmental approaches to early childhood education that are responsive to individual needs and differences, and interested in promoting the ideals of social justice and the development of moral responsibility in children and youth." **Giving Priorities:** In 1993, the foundation gave approximately 55% of funding to social services. Health groups received about 27% of total contributions. Educational institutions were awarded about 7% of funding; religious institutions, 6%; civic concerns, 3%; and the arts and humanities, 1%. **Typical Health-Related Recipients:** Cancer, Children's Health/Hospitals, Clinics/Medical Centers, Domestic Violence, Family Planning, Health Organizations, Medical Education, Mental Health, People with Disabilities, Prenatal Health Issues, Research/Studies Institutes. **Geographic Distribution:** National.

★23★ A. V. Hunter Trust
55 Madison St., Ste. 225
Denver, CO 80206
Phone: (303)399-5450
Fax: (303)399-5499
Sharon Siddons, Executive Director and Secretary

Foundation Philosophy: The Trust generally funds established non-sectarian, charitable institutions or projects or endeavors whose objects or purposes are to give aid, comfort, support or assistance to children, or aged persons or indigent adults. **Giving Priorities:** In 1993, approximately 54% of funding went to social servive organizations, including the highest grant of $85,000 to Planned Parenthood of Aurora, CO. Health organizations received about 27% of funding; civic concerns, 10%; educational institutions, 6%; and religious institutions, 3%. **Typical Health-Related Recipients:** Children's Health/Hospitals, Clinics/Medical Centers, Domestic Violence, Emergency/Ambulance Services, Family Planning, Hospices, Hospitals, Medical Rehabilitation, Multiple Sclerosis, Nursing Services, People with Disabilities, Prenatal Health Issues, Sexual Abuse, Single-Disease Health Associations,

Substance Abuse. **Geographic Distribution:** Limited to Colorado, with an emphasis on Denver.

★24★ **Aaron Diamond Foundation**
1270 Avenue of the Americas, Ste. 2624
New York, NY 10020
Phone: (212)757-7680
Vincent McGee, Executive Director

Foundation Philosophy: The Aaron Diamond Foundation was created to have an ''impact on three fields of importance in the life of New York City: medical research, minority education and culture.'' The foundation has committed continued funding for AIDS research and drug abuse programs. **Giving Priorities:** In 1994, the foundation gave approximately 45% of contributions to education, while 34% of funding went to health organizations, primarily those specializing in AIDS research and drug abuse research. Cultural concerns were given 12%, and civic causes, 9%. **Typical Health-Related Recipients:** AIDS/HIV, Children's Health/Hospitals, Health Organizations, Home-Care Services, Medical Research, Outpatient Health Care, Substance Abuse. **Geographic Distribution:** New York City.

★25★ **Aaron and Lillie Straus Foundation**
101 W Mount Royal Ave.
Baltimore, MD 21201
Phone: (410)539-8308
Fax: (410)752-1177
Jan Rivitz, Executive Director

Foundation Philosophy: The foundation has two main program areas--early childhood initiatives, and programs that foster the growth and well-being of the nonprofit sector. Giving priorities are Jewish social services, programs that support families with very young children, and projects which address public policy. The foundation reports a growing emphasis on family planning. **Giving Priorities:** In 1993, the foundation awarded 43% of its total contributions to religious organizations, primarily Jewish concerns. About 39% of funds went to social services. The arts received 6% of support; health care, 5%; civic groups, 3%; and educational institutions, 3%. **Typical Health-Related Recipients:** AIDS/HIV, Diabetes, Emergency/Ambulance Services, Family Planning, Heart, Hospitals, Kidney, Medical Research, Multiple Sclerosis, People with Disabilities, Public Health, Single-Disease Health Associations, Substance Abuse. **Geographic Distribution:** Primarily Baltimore, MD.

★26★ **Abbot and Dorothy H. Stevens Foundation**
PO Box 111
N Andover, MA 01845
Phone: (508)688-7211
Fax: (508)686-1620
Elizabeth A. Beland, Administrator

Foundation Philosophy: The purpose of the Abbot and Dorothy Stevens Foundation is to assist local charitable organizations. Grants are made across the major categories of support. Specific interests include the arts, law and justice, colleges, hospitals, churches, and social services. **Giving Priorities:** In 1993, the foundation gave about 40% of total contributions to the

arts and humanities. Social services received about 16% of funding. Civic concerns received about 14% of funding. Health concerns received about 9% of total funding. Educational institutions in Massachusetts received approximately 9% of giving; religion, 6%; and environmental programs, 5%. **Typical Health-Related Recipients:** Children's Health/Hospitals, Clinics/Medical Centers, Home-Care Services, Hospitals, Nursing Services, People with Disabilities, Substance Abuse. **Geographic Distribution:** Limited to Massachusetts, with an emphasis on Greater Lawrence area.

★27★ **Abell-Hanger Foundation**
PO Box 430
Midland, TX 79702
Phone: (915)684-6655
Fax: (915)684-4474
David. L. Smith, Executive Director

Foundation Philosophy: Since its inception, the foundation has focused its funding in the arts, community and social services, health, social sciences, and education. **Giving Priorities:** In fiscal 1994, the foundation reported that approximately 26% of its contributions supported education. The arts received about 25% of funding; human services, 24%; and health care, 13%. Approximately 11% went to civic groups, and the remainder supported religious organizations. **Typical Health-Related Recipients:** AIDS/HIV, Alzheimers Disease, Cancer, Child Abuse, Domestic Violence, Emergency/Ambulance Services, Family Planning, Health Funds, Health Organizations, Hospices, Hospitals, Medical Education, Medical Research, Medical Training, Multiple Sclerosis, Nursing Services, People with Disabilities, Public Health, Single-Disease Health Associations, Substance Abuse. **Geographic Distribution:** Primarily Texas.

★28★ **Abercrombie Foundation**
5005 Riverway, Ste. 500
Houston, TX 77056
Phone: (713)627-2500
D. Merril Cummings, Manager and Vice President

Foundation Philosophy: The focus of the Abercrombie Foundation is education, mostly professional medical training. The other leading areas of interest are health and social services. The foundation also places a priority on child-related projects. **Giving Priorities:** In 1992, the foundation gave 71% of total contributions to education, including the foundation's highest grant of $185,000, which went to the Baylor College of Medicine. Social services received 18% of funding. Civic concerns received 8% of giving, and one health grant of $15,000 accounted for 3% of total funding. **Typical Health-Related Recipients:** Cancer, Domestic Violence, Family Planning, Medical Education. **Geographic Distribution:** Primarily Texas and Kentucky.

★29★ **Achelis Foundation**
767 Third Ave, 4th Fl
New York, NY 10017
Phone: (212)644-0322
Fax: (212)755-4476
Joseph S. Dolan, Secretary and Executive Director

Foundation Philosophy: The foundation was created to distribute funds for ''charitable, benevolent, educational, and religious uses and purposes.'' **Giving Priorities:** In 1993, the foundation gave approximately 44% of its funds to youth and social service agencies, about 18% to educational institutions, 14% to civic and public affairs programs, 9% to hospitals and health organizations, 6% to science, 6% to the arts and humanities, 3% to environmental causes, and the remainder to religious organizations. **Typical Health-Related Recipients:** AIDS/HIV, Cancer, Children's Health/Hospitals, Clinics/Medical Centers, Domestic Violence, Emergency/Ambulance Services, Health Funds, Health Organizations, Hospitals, Medical Education, Medical Rehabilitation, Medical Training, Mental Health, Nursing Services, Outpatient Health Care, People with Disabilities, Speech & Hearing, Substance Abuse. **Geographic Distribution:** Primarily New York City.

★30★ **Addison H. Gibson Foundation**
Ste. 860, Six PPG Pl.
Pittsburgh, PA 15222
Phone: (412)261-1611
Fax: (412)261-5733
Rebecca Wallace Sapiente, Director

Foundation Philosophy: The foundation's primary interests are health care and higher education. It continues the tradition established by its founder of providing direct assistance on behalf of individuals in need of medical care for which they, and their families, cannot pay. **Giving Priorities:** In 1994, loans for higher education accounted for approximately 70% of total funding. Grants to hospitals and health professionals for individuals' medical expenses accounted for the remaining 30% of the foundation's support. **Typical Health-Related Recipients:** Children's Health/Hospitals, Eyes/Blindness, Health Funds, Health Organizations, Hospitals, Medical Education, Medical Rehabilitation, Medical Research, People with Disabilities. **Geographic Distribution:** Western Pennsylvania.

★31★ **Adolph Coors Foundation**
3773 Cherry Creek N Dr., No. 955
Denver, CO 80209-3829
Phone: (303)388-1636
Fax: (303)388-1684
Linda S. Tafoya, Executive Director

Foundation Philosophy: The foundation traditionally has funded a variety of organizations. In the area of health, emphasis has been on programs that are preventive in nature and that can demonstrate a reduction in health-care costs. Educational grants usually are directed to private independent four-year colleges and universities that do not receive a significant amount of tax-derived funding. Preservation of historic sites and buildings is funded when there is evidence that a facility will be used by a variety of organizations. Limited grants are made to cultural organizations for capital or special projects. Human service funding targets organizations that help people become self-sufficient and realize their potential. **Giving Priorities:** In fiscal 1993, the foundation gave approximately 38% of its contributions to educational institutions. Social services received 25% of funding. Civic affairs received 19%. The arts received 14%. The remaining funds supported religious organizations. **Typical Health-Related Recipients:** Clinics/Medical Centers, Domestic Violence, Health Organizations, Hospitals, Medical Rehabilitation, Medical Research, People with Disabilities, Substance Abuse. **Geographic Distribution:** Colorado only.

★ 32 ★ Adrian and Jessie Archbold Charitable Trust
150 E 58th St., 32nd Fl.
New York, NY 10155
Phone: (212)371-1152
Myra Mahon, Director

Foundation Philosophy: The trust makes most of its grants in the areas of education, health, and civic affairs. Health support includes single disease associations, medical centers, health foundations, and hospitals. **Giving Priorities:** In fiscal 1993, approximately 47% of funding went to education, including the highest grant of $250,000 to the Partnership for Quality Education. Health care received 26% of gifts. Civic groups received 14% of support; social services, 7%; international organizations, 3%; scientific institutions, 3%; and the arts, 1%. The remainder went to religious concerns. **Typical Health-Related Recipients:** Clinics/Medical Centers, Emergency/Ambulance Services, Family Planning, Health Funds, Health Organizations, Hospitals, Medical Education, Medical Research, Mental Health, People with Disabilities, Single-Disease Health Associations, Substance Abuse. **Geographic Distribution:** Eastern United States, with emphasis on New York.

★ 33 ★ Agnes M. Lindsay Trust
95 Market St.
Manchester, NH 03101
Phone: (603)669-4140
Fax: (603)669-6018
Robert L. Chiesa, Managing Trustee

Foundation Philosophy: The Agnes M. Lindsay Trust supports colleges, universities, and private secondary schools through scholarship funds. It makes grants for capital needs to certain elementary and secondary schools, especially those schools that serve a special need (for example, to blind, deaf, or learning disabled children). In addition, the foundation supports a number of social welfare organizations, many of which work with special needs populations, health projects, children's hospitals, homes, and youth organizations. **Giving Priorities:** In 1993, the trust reported that it gave approximately 68% of its contributions to education including support for colleges, private secondary schools, and special education. Social service organizations received 17% of the trust's funds for shelters, repairs and renovations. Civic and public affairs received 8% and religious causes, 7%. The highest grant was awarded to the Commonwealth of Massachusetts, Boston, MA. **Typical Health-Related Recipients:** Children's Health/Hospitals, Clinics/Medical Centers, Health Organizations, Heart, Hospices, Hospitals, Medical Education, Mental Health, Nursing Services, Outpatient Health Care, People with Disabilities, Prenatal Health Issues, Substance Abuse. **Geographic Distribution:** Maine, Massachusetts, New Hampshire, and Vermont.

★ 34 ★ Ahmanson Foundation
9215 Wilshire Blvd.
Beverly Hills, CA 90210
Phone: (310)278-0770
Lee E. Walcott, Jr., Vice President and Managing Director

Foundation Philosophy: "The Foundation concentrates its funding on cultural projects supporting the arts, education at the collegiate and precollegiate levels, medicine and delivery of health care services, specialized library collections, programs related to homelessness and low-income populations, preservation of the environment, and a wide range of human service projects." **Giving Priorities:** In fiscal 1993, the foundation gave approximately 30% of its contributions to the arts. Health care received 21% of funds; education, 15%; social services, 11%; religious causes, 9%; environmental concerns, 5%; and civic groups, 4%. Scientific organizations and international institutions received the remainder. **Typical Health-Related Recipients:** Adolescent Health Issues, AIDS/HIV, Alzheimers Disease, Cancer, Children's Health/Hospitals, Clinics/Medical Centers, Domestic Violence, Emergency/Ambulance Services, Eyes/Blindness, Family Planning, Health Organizations, Heart, Hospitals, Long-Term Care, Medical Education, Medical Research, Mental Health, Nursing Services, People with Disabilities, Prenatal Health Issues, Research/Studies Institutes, Single-Disease Health Associations, Speech & Hearing, Substance Abuse. **Geographic Distribution:** Primarily in Southern California, with emphasis on Los Angeles County.

★ 35 ★ Albert and Ethel Herzstein Charitable Foundation
6131 Westview
Houston, TX 77055
Phone: (713)681-7868
Fax: (713)681-3652
Albert H. Herzstein, Manager

Foundation Philosophy: The foundation gives to a variety of organizations in several fields, but the majority of its donations support education, social services, international affairs, and religion. **Giving Priorities:** In 1993, the foundation gave approximately 41% to religious institutions. Civic concerns received about 38% of contributions. Educational institutions received about 9% of funding. Social services and international affairs each received 4% of total funds, while the arts and health care each received 3%. Science programs received the remainder of funds. **Typical Health-Related Recipients:** Cancer, Children's Health/Hospitals, Clinics/Medical Centers, Diabetes, Emergency/Ambulance Services, Eyes/Blindness, Health Organizations, Heart, Hospitals, Medical Education, Multiple Sclerosis, People with Disabilities, Prenatal Health Issues, Substance Abuse. **Geographic Distribution:** Focus on Texas.

★ 36 ★ Albert Pick, Jr. Fund
30 N Michigan Ave.
Chicago, IL 60602
Phone: (312)236-1192
Nadine Van Sant, Executive Director and Secretary

Foundation Philosophy: The Albert Pick, Jr. Fund makes grants across the major categories

of support. In health and human services interests include programs in wellness, community-based health-care delivery, youth, family planning, or geriatric services. Also included is mental health, physical rehabilitation, and crisis care services. Funding for the arts goes to a wide spectrum of organizations. Educational support includes early childhood education and at-risk intervention, universities, and post-secondary institutions. Civic and community funding supports neighborhood development, environmental affairs, human relations, and minority. **Giving Priorities:** In 1992, the fund contributed 27% of its total giving to social services. Health care received about 21% of funds, and the arts received 18%. Educational institutions, civic groups, religious causes, and scientific organization each received 8% of support. The remainder went to environmental concerns. **Typical Health-Related Recipients:** AIDS/HIV, Children's Health/Hospitals, Clinics/Medical Centers, Domestic Violence, Emergency/Ambulance Services, Family Planning, Health Organizations, Hospitals, Long-Term Care, People with Disabilities, Preventive Medicine/Wellness Organizations, Public Health, Sexual Abuse, Single-Disease Health Associations, Substance Abuse. **Geographic Distribution:** Focus on Chicago, IL.

★ 37 ★ Alex Hillman Family Foundation
630 Fifth Ave.
New York, NY 10111
Phone: (212)265-3115
Rita K. Hillman, President

Foundation Philosophy: The Alex Hillman Family Foundation makes most of its grants in the areas of arts and education. The foundation's major priority is funding the arts. Educational funding supports nursing schools. **Giving Priorities:** In 1993, educational institutions received approximately 73% of funding, primarily supporting nursing programs at colleges and universities. Health received 12%, principally supporting Lenox Hill Hospital in New York, NY. The arts also received 12% and international organizations received 2%. The remaining funds supported civic affairs, religious organizations, and social services. **Typical Health-Related Recipients:** Emergency/Ambulance Services, Hospitals, Medical Education, Nursing Services, People with Disabilities. **Geographic Distribution:** Focus on the New York, NY, metropolitan area.

★ 38 ★ Alfred I. duPont Foundation
PO Box 1380
Jacksonville, FL 32201
Phone: (904)396-6600
Rosemary C. Wills, Asst. Sec. and Asst. Treas.

Foundation Philosophy: The Alfred I. duPont Foundation makes most of its grants in the areas of education, social services, and the arts. Educational funding favors medical and religious education and college funds. Social service funding favors homes, while the support for the arts focuses on galleries and preservation societies. The foundation will also support health services, civic affairs, and churches. **Giving Priorities:** In 1994, approximately 39% of funding went to secondary and higher education. Health organizations received 28%, while social services received 9%. The arts, civic causes, and religious concerns each received 7%. The remaining 3% supported an international organization. **Typical Health-Related Recipients:** Alzheimers Disease, Arthritis, Children's Health/Hospitals, Emergency/Ambulance Services, Health Organizations, Hospices, Medical Education, Nursing Services, Public Health, Single-Disease Health Associations. **Geographic Distribution:** Southeastern United States, focus on Florida.

★39★ Altman Foundation
220 E 42nd St., Ste. 411
New York, NY 10017
Phone: (212)682-0970
John S. Burke, President

Foundation Philosophy: The foundation supports a variety of organizations and programs in social welfare, health, education, and the arts. Health interests include private voluntary hospitals and health centers, and improving access to care for underserved populations. **Giving Priorities:** In 1993, the foundation awarded 25% of its total giving to health care. Religious organizations received 24% of funding. Educational institutions and social services each received 17%. About 9% went to civic groups and about 8% went to the arts. **Typical Health-Related Recipients:** AIDS/HIV, Cancer, Children's Health/Hospitals, Clinics/Medical Centers, Domestic Violence, Geriatric Health, Health Funds, Health Organizations, Hospitals, Medical Education, Outpatient Health Care, People with Disabilities. **Geographic Distribution:** New York State, with emphasis on the five boroughs of New York City.

★40★ Ambrose Monell Foundation
1 Rockefeller Plz., Ste. 301
New York, NY 10020
Phone: (212)586-0700
George Rowe, Jr., President

Foundation Philosophy: The foundation was set up to support health, the arts, education, social services, science, and civic causes. **Giving Priorities:** In 1993, the foundation gave approximately 29% of funding to educational institutions, including the highest grant of $1,500,000 to the Harvard School of Public Health. About 21% of contributions to health care; 18% to the arts; 18% to science institutions; and 9% to civic affairs. The remaining funds supported international affairs and social services. **Typical Health-Related Recipients:** AIDS/HIV, Alzheimers Disease, Arthritis, Cancer, Emergency/Ambulance Services, Eyes/Blindness, Geriatric Health, Hospitals, Medical Education, Medical Rehabilitation, Medical Research, Mental Health, Research/Studies Institutes, Speech & Hearing. **Geographic Distribution:** National, with emphasis on the New York City metropolitan area.

★41★ Amelia Peabody Foundation
30 Western Ave.
Gloucester, MA 01930
Phone: (508)283-0643
Fax: (508)283-1642
Bayard D. Waring, Trustee

Foundation Philosophy: The foundation funds only charitable organizations in Massachusetts.

The foundation's focus is on youth and inner-city organizations. It also supports hospitals and educational institutions. **Giving Priorities:** In 1993, the foundation gave approximately 33% of its total contributions to health concerns, including its highest grant of $333,333 to Massachusetts General Hospital. Educational institutions received about 29%; social services, 24%; civic affairs, 10%; and the arts received the remaining funds. **Typical Health-Related Recipients:** Clinics/Medical Centers, Diabetes, Health Organizations, Hospitals, Medical Education, Medical Research, People with Disabilities, Public Health, Single-Disease Health Associations, Substance Abuse. **Geographic Distribution:** Massachusetts only.

★42★ Amon G. Carter Foundation
500 W Seventh St., Ste. 1212
PO Box 1036
Ft. Worth, TX 76101
Phone: (817)332-2783
Fax: (817)332-2787
Bob J. Crow, Executive Director

Foundation Philosophy: The foundation supports visual and performing arts, education, health, and social services in Ft. Worth and Tarrant County, TX. Contributions in the health field are made to hospitals and to local and national single-disease health organizations. Social service grants emphasize programs that benefit youth, the aged, and the disabled. **Giving Priorities:** In 1993, the foundation reported that approximately 54% of funding went to arts organizations. Social services received 19% of the contributions. Education received 15%, and health care, 9%. The remaining grants went to civic and public affairs with 2%, and religious organizations with 1%. **Typical Health-Related Recipients:** Children's Health/Hospitals, Emergency/Ambulance Services, Family Planning, Health Organizations, Health Policy/Cost Containment, Hospitals, Medical Education, Medical Rehabilitation, Medical Research, Mental Health, Nursing Services, People with Disabilities, Public Health, Research/Studies Institutes, Single-Disease Health Associations, Substance Abuse. **Geographic Distribution:** Primarily Ft. Worth/Tarrant County, TX, area.

★43★ Andersen Foundation
100 Fourth Ave., N
Bayport, MN 55003
Phone: (612)439-5150
Fax: (612)430-5107
Mary Gillstrom, Assistant Secretary

Foundation Philosophy: The foundation traditionally contributes a significant portion of its funding to education, with emphasis on colleges and higher education. Medical funding is directed toward hospitals and single disease health organizations. Contributions also have been made in the areas of social services, youth, and the arts. **Giving Priorities:** In 1991, the foundation gave approximatley 56% of its contributions to education. Health care received 20%; primary recipients were pediatrics, health organizations, and cancer research programs. Social services received 14%; the arts received 5%; and religious organizations, 5%. The remaining funds supported civic affairs, environmental efforts, and a science museum. **Typical Health-**

Related Recipients: Cancer, Children's Health/Hospitals, Clinics/Medical Centers, Domestic Violence, Emergency/Ambulance Services, Health Organizations, Heart, Hospices, Hospitals, Kidney, Medical Research, Mental Health, People with Disabilities, Research/Studies Institutes, Single-Disease Health Associations, Substance Abuse. **Geographic Distribution:** Emphasis on Minnesota, with some national giving.

★44★ Annenberg Foundation
St. Davids Center, Ste. A-200
150 Radnor-Chester Rd.
St. Davids, PA 19087
Phone: (610)341-9066
Fax: (610)964-8688
Dr. Gail C. Levin, Senior Program Officer

Foundation Philosophy: The Annenberg foundation's current focus is on primary and secondary education. The foundation also has interests in the areas of arts and culture, health care, civic causes, and international institutions. **Giving Priorities:** In fiscal 1994, the foundation reported that it gave approximately 82% of its contributions to education. Civic and public affairs received about 14% and health care received 3%. The remaining funds went to other foundation interests. **Typical Health-Related Recipients:** Cancer, Clinics/Medical Centers, Emergency/Ambulance Services, Family Planning, Health Funds, Health Organizations, Hospitals, Medical Education, Medical Research, People with Disabilities, Research/Studies Institutes, Substance Abuse. **Geographic Distribution:** Principally to national organizations.

★45★ Anschutz Family Foundation
2400 Anaconda Tower
555 17th St.
Denver, CO 80202
Phone: (303)293-2338
Fax: (303)298-8881
Sue Anschutz-Rodgers, President and
Executive Director

Foundation Philosophy: The Anschutz Family Foundation's mission is to support efforts to assist the elderly, the young, and the economically disadvantaged. **Giving Priorities:** In fiscal 1994, the foundation reported that it gave approximately 36% of funding to social services. Civic and public affairs received 25%; health care, 14%; religions causes, 10%; the arts, 7%; education, 5%; and international organizations, 3%. **Typical Health-Related Recipients:** Alzheimers Disease, Cancer, Children's Health/Hospitals, Clinics/Medical Centers, Domestic Violence, Emergency/Ambulance Services, Family Planning, Geriatric Health, Health Organizations, Heart, Home-Care Services, Hospices, Hospitals, Medical Research, People with Disabilities, Research/Studies Institutes, Single-Disease Health Associations, Substance Abuse. **Geographic Distribution:** Metropolitan Denver area and other communities in Colorado.

★46★ Applebaum Foundation
441 W End Ave.
New York, NY 10024
Phone: (212)595-3839
Warren Weiss, Vice President

Foundation Philosophy: The Applebaum Foundation makes most of its grants in the areas of education and religion. The foundation also supports health services and some civic affairs. **Giving Priorities:** In fiscal 1991, educational institutions received 45% of total contributions. Religious organizations received 36%, including the highest grant of $250,000 to the Ohr Torah Institution for Israel. Of the remainder, civic affairs received 10%; health care, 5%; and international organizations, 3%. **Typical Health-Related Recipients:** Hospitals, Medical Education, Medical Research, People with Disabilities, Single-Disease Health Associations. **Geographic Distribution:** Focus on New York and Florida; also nationally.

★ 47 ★ Arcadia Foundation
105 E Logan St.
Norristown, PA 19401-3058
Phone: (610)275-8460
Marilyn L. Steinbright, President

Foundation Philosophy: The foundation generally supports art, civic, human service, health, and educational organizations working to improve the quality of life in Pennsylvania. **Giving Priorities:** In fiscal 1993, the foundation gave approximately 35% of total contributions to the arts and humanities; educational institutions received 27%; civic concerns received 13%; science, 8%; social services and health each received 6%; and religion, 5%. **Typical Health-Related Recipients:** Arthritis, Diabetes, Emergency/Ambulance Services, Health Organizations, Hospices, Hospitals, Medical Education, Nursing Services, People with Disabilities. **Geographic Distribution:** Limited to Eastern Pennsylvania with zip codes of 18000 and 19000.

★ 48 ★ Arcana Foundation
1401 Eye St., NW, Ste. 530
Washington, DC 20005
Phone: (202)789-7280
Fax: (202)842-2298
Joan Kennan, Executive Director

Foundation Philosophy: The foundation supports programs in Washington, DC that work to alleviate poverty and enhance cultural activities. It also makes grants to organizations that Mr. and Mrs. von Hoffman have been actively involved with in the past. **Giving Priorities:** In fiscal 1993, approximately 27% of the foundation's funds were awarded to arts groups. Social Services received 26%; civic and public affairs, 20%; health care organizations, 9%; education, 8%; international organizations 6%; and religious causes 3%. **Typical Health-Related Recipients:** Clinics/Medical Centers, Domestic Violence, Health Organizations, Hospices, Mental Health, People with Disabilities, Substance Abuse. **Geographic Distribution:** Focuses primarily on Washington, DC.

★ 49 ★ Arie and Ida Crown Memorial
222 N LaSalle St., Ste. 2000
Chicago, IL 60601
Phone: (312)236-6300
Fax: (312)899-5038
Rebecca Stimson, Executive Director

Foundation Philosophy: The foundation gives in the designated areas of community and social organizations; cultural groups; hospitals and medical institutions; colleges and universities; other educational concerns; synagogues, churches, and religious organizations; and other (including philanthropic umbrella) organizations. **Giving Priorities:** In 1992, Arie and Ida Crown Memorial contributed 37% of its total grants to educational institutions. Health care and international organizations each received 14% of funds; civic groups, 13%; religious organizations, 8%; and social services, 7%. The remaining 6% went to the arts. **Typical Health-Related Recipients:** Alzheimers Disease, Children's Health/Hospitals, Clinics/Medical Centers, Diabetes, Domestic Violence, Hospitals, Mental Health, People with Disabilities, Single-Disease Health Associations. **Geographic Distribution:** Metropolitan Chicago, IL.

★ 50 ★ Arkell Hall Foundation
66 Montgomery St.
Canajoharie, NY 13317
Phone: (518)673-5417
Joseph A. Santangelo, Vice President, Treasurer, Administrator

Foundation Philosophy: "The primary mission of the Arkell Hall Foundation is the operation and maintenance of a home for elderly ladies. Funds which may become available above the needs of the Home may be distributed annually to organizations providing services within the Western Montgomery County of New York community, with preference given to those active in service to senior citizens, education, and health care." **Giving Priorities:** In fiscal 1993, the foundation awarded 77% of its funds to social service organizations. Health care concerns received 12%; educational institutions, 9%; civic and public affairs and religious causes each received 1%. **Typical Health-Related Recipients:** Cancer, Children's Health/Hospitals, Clinics/Medical Centers, Domestic Violence, Emergency/Ambulance Services, Health Funds, Heart, Hospitals, Long-Term Care, Medical Education, Medical Research, People with Disabilities, Single-Disease Health Associations. **Geographic Distribution:** Limited to the Canajoharie, NY, area.

★ 51 ★ Arnold and Mabel Beckman Foundation
100 Academy Dr.
Irvine, CA 92715
Phone: (714)721-2222
Fax: (714)721-2288
Ron Henderson, Administrator

Foundation Philosophy: "The Arnold and Mabel Beckman Foundation makes grants to nonprofit research institutions to promote research in chemistry and the life sciences, broadly interpreted, and particularly to foster the invention of methods, instruments and materials that will open up new avenues of research in science. The Beckman Young Investigators Program is intended to provide research support to the most promising young faculty members in the early stages of academic careers in the chemical and life sciences." **Giving Priorities:** In fiscal 1993, the foundation reported that it gave approximately 87% of its contributions to scientific research in chemistry and life sciences. Education received 9% of funding, for research in colleges and universities; medical research was given 4%. **Typical Health-Related Recipients:** Medical Research, Speech & Hearing. **Geographic Distribution:** United States at recognized research and academic institutions.

★ 52 ★ Arthur Vining Davis Foundations
111 Riverside Ave., Ste. 130
Jacksonville, FL 32202-4921
Phone: (904)359-0670
Dr. Max King Morris, Executive Director

Foundation Philosophy: The foundations will continue their commitment to Mr. Davis' ideals in 1995, again concentrating their funding in the area of private higher education, and, to a lesser extent, to hospice programs, medicine, religion, public television, and secondary education. The foundations are interested in hospice projects seeking to solve problems common to programs for the terminally ill. The trustees hope that involvement in the hospice movement will strengthen the concept of care. Funding encourages the establishment of hospices in rural areas and small towns which presently do not have such services. Grants are awarded as challenge grants for varying amounts, not to exceed $30,000. The trustees prefer to give grants in the medical field for projects heightening national interest in the delivery of health care. Projects should have the potential for a wide application, rather than a local effect. Proposals related to nursing and physician education receive favorable attention. **Giving Priorities:** In 1994, the foundation reported that it gave approximately 42% of funding to education. Arts received 24%. Religious education accounted for 15% of all funding. Medical centers and hospices received 10%. Conservation, philanthropic organizations, secondary education, and other non-profits received the remaining 9%. **Typical Health-Related Recipients:** Children's Health/Hospitals, Health Organizations, Hospices, Hospitals, Mental Health. Research Studies Institutes. **Geographic Distribution:** National; no grants outside the United States.

★ 53 ★ Atran Foundation
23-25 E 21st St., 3rd Fl.
New York, NY 10010
Phone: (212)505-9677
Diane Fischer, Corporate Secretary

Foundation Philosophy: The Atran Foundation makes most of its grants in support of Jewish religious organizations, education, and civic affairs. Educational support goes to Jewish universities, medical education, and social science education. The foundation supports other recipient areas on a limited basis. **Giving Priorities:** In fiscal 1993, the foundation gave approximately 53% of giving to Jewish religious organizations. Educational institutions received about 38% of funding, including the foundation's highest grant of $150,000 to the Albert Einstein College of Medicine of Yeshiva University. Health groups received about 4% of contributions, and civic concerns, about 3%. The remainder of funding went to the arts(1%), international affairs(1%), and social services(1%). **Typical Health-Related Recipients:** Clinics/Medical Centers, Emergency/Ambulance Services, Geriatric Health, Hospitals, Long-Term Care, Medical Education, Medical Research, People with Disabilities. **Geographic Distribution:** Focus on New York.

★54★ **Audrey and Sydney Irmas Charitable Foundation**
2029 Century Pk.
East Tower, Ste. 3250
Los Angeles, CA 90067
Phone: (310)557-8444
Fax: (310)312-9405
Robert Irmas, Administrator and Manager

Foundation Philosophy: The foundation distributes its giving evenly between Jewish religious organizations, civic affairs with international interests, and social services. The foundation also supports health services. **Giving Priorities:** In 1992, the foundation gave 26% of its contributions to religious organizations, primarily Jewish organizations. International organizations received 23% of funding, including $200,000 to Operation Exodus, Los Angeles, CA. Social services received 15%; health care, 12%; the arts, 11%; and civic groups, 8%. The remaining 4% went to educational institutions. **Typical Health-Related Recipients:** AIDS/HIV, Cancer, Children's Health/Hospitals, Clinics/Medical Centers, Health Organizations, Hospitals, Medical Research, Single-Disease Health Associations, Substance Abuse. **Geographic Distribution:** Focus on Los Angeles, CA.

★55★ **Ball Brothers Foundation**
PO Box 1408
Muncie, IN 47308
Phone: (317)741-5500
Fax: (317)741-5518
Douglas A. Bakken, Executive Director

Foundation Philosophy: The Ball Brothers Foundation built the Minnetrista Cultural Center, which houses many artistic projects. Because this center is a foundation venture, it will receive a certain amount of funding priority in the next few years. The foundation also supports the Ball State University Foundation. **Giving Priorities:** In 1993, the foundation gave approximately 50% of funding to the arts, including the foundation's highest grant of $1,400,044 to the Minnetrista Cultural Foundation. Educational institutions received about 33% of giving. Civic concerns received 7% of funding; health, 5%; social services, 4%; and religion and environment, less than 1% each. **Typical Health-Related Recipients:** AIDS/HIV, Heart, Hospitals, People with Disabilities, Preventive Medicine/Wellness Organizations. **Geographic Distribution:** Indiana.

★56★ **Banbury Fund**
Box 479
Huntington, NY 11743-0479
William S. Robertson, President

Foundation Philosophy: The fund places an emphasis on civic and environmental causes, educational institutions, and scientific and health care organizations. **Giving Priorities:** In 1993, approximately 33% of funding went to educational institutions, including a grant of $130,000 to Columbia University. Civic and public affairs received 16%; scientific organizations, 15%; the environment, 15%; and health care, 8%. International affairs received 6%; social services, 5%; and religious organizations, 1%. **Typical Health-Related Recipients:** Cancer, Eyes/Blindness, Family Planning, Health Orga-

nizations, Hospices, Hospitals, Hospitals (University Affiliated), Medical Education. **Geographic Distribution:** Primarily New York state.

★57★ **Barker Welfare Foundation**
Box 2
Glen Head, NY 11545
Phone: (516)759-5592
Fax: (516)759-5497
Sarane H. Ross, President

Foundation Philosophy: The Barker Welfare Foundation gives the majority of its support in the areas of social service and the arts. The foundation also gives some support to civic causes, health organizations, and educational institutions. **Giving Priorities:** In fiscal 1993, the foundation gave approximately 37% of its contributions to social services. The arts received 23%. Civic organizations received 19% of grants; health care, 9%; scientific organizations, 6%; and educational insitutions, 4%. The remainder went to religious social services. **Typical Health-Related Recipients:** Cancer, Clinics/Medical Centers, Emergency/Ambulance Services, Family Planning, Hospitals, Long-Term Care, Mental Health, Nursing Services, People with Disabilities, Substance Abuse. **Geographic Distribution:** Mainly New York, NY; Chicago, IL; and Michigan City, IN, metropolitan areas.

★58★ **Barra Foundation**
8200 Flourtown Ave., Ste. 12
Wyndmoor, PA 19038
Phone: (215)233-5115
Robert L. McNeil, Jr., President

Foundation Philosophy: The Barra Foundation seeks to advance knowledge and education, particularly "in the fields of American art history and material culture from the colonial period to 1900." To this end, the foundation supports innovative pilot studies and projects not supported by other agencies or individuals. **Giving Priorities:** In 1993, the foundation awarded 42% of its total contributions to the arts. About 18% of support went to health care. Educational institutions received 13% of funds; civic groups, 10%; social services, 8%; and environmental concerns, 6%. The remainder went to religious organizations. **Typical Health-Related Recipients:** Children's Health/Hospitals, Emergency/Ambulance Services, Family Planning, Health Organizations, Home-Care Services, Hospices, Hospitals, Medical Education, Medical Rehabilitation, Medical Research, People with Disabilities, Single-Disease Health Associations. **Geographic Distribution:** Primarily the Philadelphia, PA, area.

★59★ **Baughman Foundation**
PO Box 1356
Liberal, KS 67905-1356
Phone: (316)624-1371
Eugene W. Slaymaker, President

Foundation Philosophy: The foundation gives to local municipalities and local organizations, primarily providing scholarships and capital or special project support. **Giving Priorities:** In 1993, approximately 38% of funding went to educational institutions. Social service organizations received 20%, health care received 18%, and the arts and civic affairs each received

11%. The remainding funds supported religion and science. **Typical Health-Related Recipients:** Diabetes, Domestic Violence, Emergency/Ambulance Services, Health Organizations, Hospitals, People with Disabilities, Sexual Abuse, Single-Disease Health Associations. **Geographic Distribution:** Emphasis on Liberal, KS.

★60★ **Beatrice Fox Auerbach Foundation**
25 Brookside Blvd.
West Hartford, CT 06107
Phone: (203)232-5854
Dorothy A. Schiro, Vice President and Treasurer

Foundation Philosophy: The foundation stresses improving the quality of life in the Hartford, CT, area with its charitable contributions. Civic groups, social services, education, health care, and the arts all received support from the foundation in 1992. **Giving Priorities:** In 1993, approximately 67% of funding went to religious causes. Health care organizations received 13%; civic and public affairs, 7%; the arts, 3%; educational institutions, 2%; and environmental and international organizations each received 1% of the foundation's funds. **Typical Health-Related Recipients:** AIDS/HIV, Children's Health/Hospitals, Emergency/Ambulance Services, Family Planning, Health Funds, Heart, Hospices, Hospitals, Nursing Services, People with Disabilities, Prenatal Health Issues, Public Health, Research/Studies Institutes, Single-Disease Health Associations, Substance Abuse. **Geographic Distribution:** Focus on the Hartford, CT area.

★61★ **Beatrice P. Delany Charitable Trust**
c/o Chase Manhattan Bank, 34th Fl.
1211 Avenue of the Americas
New York, NY 10036
Phone: (212)789-5374
John H. F. Enteman, Administrator

Foundation Philosophy: The foundation traditionally supports programs and organizations in the areas of education, religion, civic groups, health, social services, and the arts. **Giving Priorities:** In fiscal 1993, the foundation contributed 40% of its giving to education. Social services received 21% of funding. Health care and religious organizations each received 17% of support. The remaining gifts went to civic groups and the arts. **Typical Health-Related Recipients:** Children's Health/Hospitals, Clinics/Medical Centers, Hospitals, Medical Education, Medical Research, Multiple Sclerosis. **Geographic Distribution:** Broad geographic distribution, with some emphasis on metropolitan Chicago, IL.

★62★ **Beazley Foundation/Frederick Foundation**
3720 Brighton St.
Portsmouth, VA 23707
Phone: (804)393-1605
Fax: (804)393-4708
Lawrence W. I'Anson, Jr., President and Executive Director

Foundation Philosophy: Current charitable interests include a community center for senior citizens, operated by the foundation. Additionally, the foundation fully funds a Portsmouth Dental Clinic operated by the city. In the area of education, the foundation focuses its funding to public and private schools, colleges and universities, and scholarships. In health care, the foundation funds hospitals, a dental clinic, and single-disease associations. Support for social services includes crime prevention, youth development, and recreation, and support for civic groups include job training and philanthropic organizations. **Giving Priorities:** In 1993, the foundation awarded 39% of its grants to educational institutions. About 23% of funds went to health care. Social service organizations received 19% of support; civic groups, 17%; and the arts, 1%. **Typical Health-Related Recipients:** Cancer, Children's Health/Hospitals, Clinics/Medical Centers, Domestic Violence, Emergency/Ambulance Services, Geriatric Health, Health Organizations, Hospitals, Medical Education, People with Disabilities, Single-Disease Health Associations, Substance Abuse. **Geographic Distribution:** Primarily Portsmouth, VA, and the South Hampton Roads area.

★ 63 ★ Belfer Foundation
767 5th Ave., 46th Fl.
New York, NY 10153-0002
Phone: (212)644-2257
Elise Owens, Administrator

Foundation Philosophy: The foundation supports U.S.-based organizations that distribute funds in Israel, primarily to higher education institutions and other Jewish projects and programs. It provides limited support to New York area arts organizations and hospitals. **Giving Priorities:** In 1994, the foundation gave approximately 46% of its contributions to religious organizations. International organizations received 22%. Educational institutions, primarily medical schools, colleges, and universities, received 21%. Health care and the arts each received 5%, and civic affairs and social services received the remaining funds. **Typical Health-Related Recipients:** Clinics/Medical Centers, Diabetes, Emergency/Ambulance Services, Eyes/Blindness, Health Organizations, Hospitals, Medical Education, Medical Research. **Geographic Distribution:** Emphasis on New York, NY, and, to a lesser extent, Palm Beach, FL.

★ 64 ★ Ben B. Cheney Foundation
1201 Pacific Ave. South
Ste. 1600
Tacoma, WA 98402
Phone: (206)572-2442
William O. Rieke, MD, Executive Director

Foundation Philosophy: Under its program guidelines, the foundation states that it seeks to disburse funds to civic projects, culture, education, health, social services, youth, and the elderly. **Giving Priorities:** The foundation reported that in 1993 about 28% of funding went to social services. Elderly and youth organizations received about 24% of contributions. Civic groups received approximately 13% of support; health care, 9%; educational institutions, 15%. The remaining 11% of contributions supported the arts. **Typical Health-Related Recipients:** Cancer, Children's Health/Hospitals, Clinics/Medical Centers, Emergency/Ambulance Services, Hospitals, Medical Training, Mental

Health, People with Disabilities, Single-Disease Health Associations. **Geographic Distribution:** Southwest Washington, southern Oregon, and northern California.

★ 65 ★ Ben B. and Joyce E. Eisenberg Foundation
11999 San Vicente Blvd., Ste. 300
Los Angeles, CA 90049
Phone: (310)471-4220
Fax: (213)627-1187
Richard Bender, Secretary and Treasurer

Foundation Philosophy: The foundation primarily supports Jewish organizations in several fields including health, social services, and education. **Giving Priorities:** In fiscal 1993, the foundation gave about 40% of funding to religious institutions. International affairs received about 31% of contributions. Health groups received about 26% of funding. Social services, the arts and humanities, civic concerns, and educational institutions each received about 1% of total funding. **Typical Health-Related Recipients:** AIDS/HIV, Cancer, Children's Health/Hospitals, Clinics/Medical Centers, Diabetes, Emergency/Ambulance Services, Family Planning, Health Organizations, Hospitals, Medical Research, Multiple Sclerosis, Preventive Medicine/Wellness Organizations, Single-Disease Health Associations. **Geographic Distribution:** Focus on Los Angeles, CA.

★ 66 ★ Benjamin and Mary Siddons Measey Foundation
PO Box 258
Media, PA 19063
Phone: (610)566-5800
Fax: (610)566-8197
James C. Brennan, Esq., Member of the Board of Managers

Foundation Philosophy: The Benjamin and Mary Siddons Measey Foundation supports two areas of giving: education and health. Educational support favors universities and their medical schools. In health care, interests include university hospitals and health consortiums. **Giving Priorities:** In 1993, the foundation gave approximately 94% of its funding to higher education, mostly supporting medical education. Health organizations received 4% of contributions; international concerns received 2%. **Typical Health-Related Recipients:** Clinics/Medical Centers, Geriatric Health, Health Funds, Health Organizations, Hospitals, Hospitals (University Affiliated), Medical Education, Public Health. **Geographic Distribution:** Focus on Philadelphia, PA.

★ 67 ★ Benwood Foundation
1600 American National Bank Bldg.
736 Market St.
Chattanooga, TN 37402
Phone: (615)267-4311
Fax: (615)267-9049
Jean McDaniel, Executive Director

Foundation Philosophy: A broad range of organizations receive funding. A significant number of grants go to organizations in Chattanooga that are involved with early childhood education. **Giving Priorities:** In 1993, the foundation gave approximately 47% of its contributions to education, including its highest grant of $1,200,000

for the McCallie School, Chattanooga, TN. The arts received 35%. Health received 8% of funding. Social services received 7%; civic affairs, 2%; and religion received the remainder. **Typical Health-Related Recipients:** Clinics/Medical Centers, Health Organizations, Mental Health, Substance Abuse. **Geographic Distribution:** Primarily Tennessee, principally Chattanooga.

★ 68 ★ Blandin Foundation
100 N Pokegama Ave.
Grand Rapids, MN 55744
Phone: (218)326-0523
Fax: (218)327-1949
Paul M. Olson, President

Foundation Philosophy: The foundation holds special interest in the area of education, where it strives to increase opportunities for residents in rural Minnesota. Funding for economic development is geared to create economic opportunities for people living in rural communities. Support for health and human services focuses on children and youth at risk. Arts and humanities grants provide cultural opportunities for rural communities of Minnesota. Support for the environment focuses on projects which improve Minnesota's freshwater resources and on experimental environmental education opportunities. The foundation also plans to initiate a "Global Education Statewide Program" and support a planning assistance program for rural hospitals in crisis to ensure quality health care. **Giving Priorities:** In fiscal 1994, the foundation awarded 82% of its total contributions to environmental concerns. Educational institutions received 10% of funds. Civic groups and health care each received 3% of support. The remainder went to the arts and social services. **Typical Health-Related Recipients:** Domestic Violence, Emergency/Ambulance Services, Health Organizations, Hospices, Medical Education, Medical Research, Nursing Services, Outpatient Health Care, People with Disabilities, Substance Abuse. **Geographic Distribution:** Grand Rapids, Itasca County, and rural areas of Minnesota.

★ 69 ★ Blum-Kovler Foundation
919 N Michigan Ave., Ste. 2800
Chicago, IL 60611
Phone: (312)664-5050
Fax: (312)664-8983
H. Jonathan Kovler, Treasurer

Foundation Philosophy: The foundation gives to a wide variety of agencies in the arts, civic affairs, education, health, and welfare. **Giving Priorities:** In 1994, the foundation gave 50% of its support to cultural and civic concerns. Health received 20% of the funding for support of hospitals, pediatrics, and diabetes treatment and research; education received 13%; general welfare, 11%; children's welfare, 3%; and religion, principally Jewish organizations, 2%. **Typical Health-Related Recipients:** Children's Health/Hospitals, Clinics/Medical Centers, Diabetes, Health Funds, Hospices, Hospitals, Medical Education, Medical Rehabilitation, Medical Research, Mental Health, People with Disabilities, Single-Disease Health Associations, Substance Abuse. **Geographic Distribution:** Primarily in the Chicago, IL, metropolitan area; also Washington, DC, and New York, NY.

★ 70 ★ **Blumenthal Foundation**
PO Box 34689
Charlotte, NC 28234
Phone: (704)377-6555
Fax: (704)377-9237
Philip Blumenthal, Trustee

Foundation Philosophy: According to the foundation's literature, it considers grant requests, primarily in North Carolina, in several fields including the following: religious and interfaith groups, social services, education, the arts and humanities, health care, the environment, and Jewish institutions and philanthropies. **Giving Priorities:** In fiscal 1994, the foundation gave approximately 46% of its contributions to social services. Educational institutions received 25%. The arts received 12%, while religious organizations received 10%. Civic affairs receive 5%, primarily to support philanthropic organizations and environmental affairs. Health care received the remainder. **Typical Health-Related Recipients:** Family Planning, Mental Health, Single-Disease Health Associations. **Geographic Distribution:** Near headquarters only with a focus on North Carolina, especially on the Charlotte area. **Formerly:** Blumenthal Foundation for Charity, Religion and Education.

★ 71 ★ **Bodman Foundation**
767 Third Ave.
Fourth Floor
New York, NY 10017
Phone: (212)644-0322
Fax: (212)755-4476
Joseph S. Dolan, Secretary and Executive Director

Foundation Philosophy: The foundation was set up to reflect the philanthropic interests of both Mr. and Mrs. Bodman, including religious, educational, and charitable organizations "for the moral, ethical, and physical well-being and progress of mankind." The foundation maintains a strong local orientation. **Giving Priorities:** In 1993, the foundation gave approximately 32% of giving to social services, including the foundation's highest grant of $70,000 to the Children's Aid Society of New York, NY. Health groups received about 21% of total contributions; educational institutions, 19%; civic concerns, 9%; science groups, 8%; the arts and humanities, 6%; environmental programs, 5%; and international affairs, 1%. **Typical Health-Related Recipients:** Cancer, Clinics/Medical Centers, Domestic Violence, Emergency/Ambulance Services, Eyes/Blindness, Health Funds, Health Organizations, Hospices, Hospitals, Medical Education, Medical Rehabilitation, Medical Research, People with Disabilities, Speech & Hearing, Substance Abuse. **Geographic Distribution:** Primarily metropolitan New York City, and Monmouth County, NJ.

★ 72 ★ **Boettcher Foundation**
600 Seventeenth St., Ste. 2210 S
Denver, CO 80202
Phone: (303)534-1937
William A. Douglas, President and Executive Director

Foundation Philosophy: The foundation typically supports education, civic, health, cultural, and community groups. In recent years, the foundation's health priorities have focused on programs enhancing cost containment efforts and preventative services, especially in rural areas of Colorado. **Giving Priorities:** In 1993, the foundation gave approximately 39% of its contributions to educational institutions, primarily to colleges and universities. The arts, with a focus on music, received 26%; social services, 17%; civic groups, 7%; and scientific groups, 6%. Health care and environmental concerns received the remainder. **Typical Health-Related Recipients:** AIDS/HIV, Children's Health/Hospitals, Clinics/Medical Centers, Domestic Violence, Emergency/Ambulance Services, Family Planning, Hospices, Long-Term Care, Mental Health, People with Disabilities. **Geographic Distribution:** Colorado only.

★ 73 ★ **Booth-Bricker Fund**
830 Union St., Ste. 200
New Orleans, LA 70112
Phone: (504)581-2430
Gray S. Parker, Trustee

Foundation Philosophy: The Booth-Bricker Fund supports a variety of local organizations, "and makes contributions for the purposes of promoting, developing, and fostering religious, charitable, scientific, literary, or educational programs." Educational support is provided to universities, day schools, and private schools. Health care favors both general care and specialty hospitals in New Orleans. Museums, theater, and public broadcasting are favored areas of support for the arts. The fund also gives to local church organizations and provides general support for social service organizations. **Giving Priorities:** In 1993, 28% of funding went to educational institutions. The arts received 23%; social services, 16%; civic affairs, 15%; health care, 11%; and religious organizations, 7%. **Typical Health-Related Recipients:** Children's Health/Hospitals, Clinics/Medical Centers, Health Organizations, Hospitals, People with Disabilities. **Geographic Distribution:** Focus on New Orleans, LA.

★ 74 ★ **Bothin Foundation**
873 Sutter St., Ste. B
San Francisco, CA 94109
Phone: (415)771-4300
Fax: (415)771-4064
Lyman H. Casey, Executive Director and Treasurer

Foundation Philosophy: With limited funds available, "the foundation traditionally has supported charitable organizations promoting youth, the elderly, the environment, the disabled, health care, minorities, community social services and the arts." The fund generally prefers to make grants for capital or building and equipment needs. **Giving Priorities:** In 1993, the foundation reported that it gave approximately 38% of its contributions to social service organizations, 11% to health care, 11% to civic organizations, 10% to education, 9% to the arts, 9% to religious organizations, 8% to environmental concerns, 2% to international causes, and 1% to science. **Typical Health-Related Recipients:** Health Organizations, Hospitals, Kidney, Medical Rehabilitation, Mental Health, People with Disabilities, Sexual Abuse, Substance Abuse. **Geographic Distribution:** Focus on metropolitan San Francisco area (San Francisco, Marin, San Mateo, Sonoma, and Santa Barbara counties).

★ 75 ★ **Bradley-Turner Foundation**
PO Box 140
Columbus, GA 31902
Phone: (706)571-6040
Stephen T. Butler, Chairman and Trustee

Foundation Philosophy: The foundation generally funds higher educational institutions, the arts and cultural organizations, religious associations, and social services. **Giving Priorities:** In 1993, the foundation gave approximately 43% of its contributions to educational institutions. About 23% of funding went to health care, including the highest grant of $813,585 to the Bradley Center, Columbus, GA; 12% to civic affairs; 12% to social services; 6% to religious organizations; and 4% to the arts. **Typical Health-Related Recipients:** Cancer, Child Abuse, Children's Health/Hospitals, Clinics/Medical Centers, Health Organizations, Hospitals, Medical Education, Medical Research, People with Disabilities. **Geographic Distribution:** Primarily Georgia.

★ 76 ★ **Brown Foundation**
PO Box 130646
2217 Welch Ave.
Houston, TX 77219-0646
Phone: (713)523-6867
Fax: (713)523-2917
Katherine B. Dobelman, Executive Director and Treasurer

Foundation Philosophy: Major areas of giving include education, the arts and humanities, health and medicine, and community service. **Giving Priorities:** In fiscal 1994, the foundation gave approximately 51% of its funding to educational institutions. The arts received about 31% of funds. Social and community service organizations received 11% of support, and health organizations received the remaining 7%. **Typical Health-Related Recipients:** Adolescent Health Issues, Clinics/Medical Centers, Domestic Violence, Family Planning, Health Organizations, Hospices, Hospitals, Medical Education, Medical Research, Mental Health, Single-Disease Health Associations. **Geographic Distribution:** National, with emphasis on Texas.

★ 77 ★ **Broyhill Family Foundation**
PO Box 500
Golfview Park
Lenoir, NC 28645
Phone: (704)758-6120
Fax: (704)754-7335
Paul H. Broyhill, Chairman and Manager

Foundation Philosophy: The Broyhill Family Foundation, formerly the Broyhill Foundation, originally was established to help needy individuals obtain a college education through loans. The foundation also funds civic organizations, community and human services, hospitals and health organizations, and the arts. **Giving Priorities:** In 1994, the foundation reported that it gave approximately 49% of its contributions to colleges and schools. Health and hospitals received 16%. Youth development programs and civic groups each received 10% of the foundation's total giving. Public policy groups that support free enterprise received 4%. Parks and recreation, as well as churches and religious organizations, each received 3%. Scholarships, and the arts and museums each received 2%. The remainder was given to social services to assist indigent people. **Typical Health-Related Recipients:** Hospitals, Medical Research, People with Disabilities, Substance Abuse. **Geographic Distribution:** Primarily North Carolina.

★78★ **Bunbury Company**
169 Nassau St.
Princeton, NJ 08542
Phone: (609)683-1414
Samuel W. Lambert, III, President

Foundation Philosophy: The foundation makes numerous smaller grants across the major categories of giving. In education, preference is given to private secondary education and Princeton University. In social services, the emphasis is on family and youth services and programs. The Windham Foundation and environmental affairs make up the bulk of civic contributions. Arts support goes to various museums, theaters, arts councils, and dance organizations. **Giving Priorities:** In 1992, approximately 47% of funding went to educational institutions. Civic affairs received 24%. Social services received 12% of funding, and the arts and health care each received 8%. **Typical Health-Related Recipients:** AIDS/HIV, Clinics/Medical Centers, Domestic Violence, Emergency/Ambulance Services, Family Planning, Hospitals, Medical Research, People with Disabilities, Substance Abuse. **Geographic Distribution:** Most grants are distributed in the Princeton, NJ, area; to a lesser degree in Vermont.

★79★ **Burnett-Tandy Foundation**
801 Cherry St., Ste. 1400
Ft. Worth, TX 76102
Phone: (817)877-3344
Fax: (817)338-0448
Thomas F. Beech, Executive Vice President

Foundation Philosophy: The foundation supports organizations in the areas of education, health, community affairs, human services, and the arts. The foundation is anticipating more funding for youth-related causes in the near future, and is focusing on implementing site-based management in secondary schools, as well as summer school scholarships, tutoring, enrichment and mentoring programs, and summer employment opportunities for at-risk youth. **Giving Priorities:** In 1993, the foundation awarded approximately 58% of its total contributions to the arts. Civic affairs received about 20%; social services, 8%; educational institutions and programs, 5%; health concerns, 5%; religious causes, 3%; and scientific interests received the remaining funds. **Typical Health-Related Recipients:** AIDS/HIV, Alzheimers Disease, Clinics/Medical Centers, Family Planning, Health Policy/Cost Containment, Hospitals, Medical Education, Mental Health, People with Disabilities, Single-Disease Health Associations, Substance Abuse. **Geographic Distribution:** Primarily Texas, with an emphasis on the Ft. Worth metropolitan area. **Formerly:** Anne Burnett and Charles Tandy Foundation.

★80★ **Burton D. Morgan Foundation**
PO Box 1500
Akron, OH 44309-1500
Phone: (216)258-6512
Fax: (216)867-3020
John V. Frank, President

Foundation Philosophy: The Burton D. Morgan Foundation primarily supports education, including private Episcopal schools and universities. Other interests include churches, arts centers, art associations, civic affairs, and social services. **Giving Priorities:** In 1993, the foundation awarded approximately 81% of its contributions to educational institutions. Health care organizations received 6% of the distributed funds, while civic affairs and religious affairs each received about 4%. The arts received 3% of distributed funds. The remaining 2% was split between social services and international affairs. **Typical Health-Related Recipients:** Children's Health/Hospitals, Domestic Violence, Emergency/Ambulance Services, Family Planning, Hospices, Mental Health, People with Disabilities. **Geographic Distribution:** Focus on Summit County, OH.

★81★ **Burton G. Bettingen Corporation**
9777 Wilshire Blvd., Ste. 611
Beverly Hills, CA 90212
Phone: (310)276-4115
Fax: (310)276-4693
Patricia A. Brown, Executive Director

Foundation Philosophy: The current focus of the corporation is child welfare including assistance to child prostitutes, runaways, and abandoned children. The corporation has two separate giving funds: the Haven Fund is committed to supporting child welfare; the General Fund includes support for youth but also supports organizations in several fields including education, health, environment, and welfare. **Giving Priorities:** In fiscal 1993, the corporation gave approximately 53% of its total charitable contributions to social service organizations. Religious institutions received 22% of support. About 9% of the distributed funds were given in support of education, while health care organizations received 7% of the funds. Civic affairs received 5% of support, environmental affairs received 3%, and the arts received the remaining 1%. **Typical Health-Related Recipients:** Children's Health/Hospitals, Emergency/Ambulance Services, Family Planning, Health Organizations, Hospitals, Medical Education, Medical Research, People with Disabilities, Preventive Medicine/Wellness Organizations, Research/Studies Institutes, Single-Disease Health Associations. **Geographic Distribution:** Focus on, but not limited to, Los Angeles, CA.

★82★ **Bush Foundation**
E-900 First National Bank Bldg.
332 Minnesota St.
St. Paul, MN 55101
Phone: (612)227-0891
Fax: (612)297-6485
Humphrey Doermann, President

Foundation Philosophy: The foundation was incorporated with the broadest possible statement of purpose. It concentrates its grants in the areas of education, humanities and the arts, community and social welfare, health, and lead-ership development. In the area of health, the foundation supports programs to improve the quality, accessibility, and efficiency of health care services within its geographic region. Grants are concentrated on training programs for health professionals, efforts to improve access to health care in rural and underserved areas, and the promotion of minority career development in the health field. In 1989, the foundation helped support an AIDS prevention program on Indian reservations in North Dakota. Human services funding supports programs for troubled and disadvantaged youth; emergency housing and employment counseling services for homeless women with children; programs to assist victims of domestic violence; and programs that provide rehabilitation services for developmentally disabled adults. The Bush Medical Fellows Program seeks to develop physicians' potential for increased competence and leadership in clinical medicine, health care delivery, administration, and education. **Giving Priorities:** In fiscal 1994, the foundation reported that it gave approximately 50% of its contributions to education. Human services received 20%, with support for youth programs, the United Way, adult rehabilitation, law and corrections, and domestic violence. Education fellowship programs received 11%. The arts received 10%. The foundation also awarded 5% of its total contributions to miscellaneous organizations. Health care received 4% with support for nursing services and AIDS prevention. **Typical Health-Related Recipients:** AIDS/HIV, Children's Health/Hospitals, Clinics/Medical Centers, Domestic Violence, Family Planning, Health Organizations, Medical Education, Medical Rehabilitation, Medical Training, Mental Health, People with Disabilities, Substance Abuse. **Geographic Distribution:** Primarily Minnesota, North Dakota, and South Dakota; faculty development grants are made to tribally controlled colleges both inside and outside the primary geographic region.

★83★ **Callaway Foundation**
PO Box 790
209 Broome St.
La Grange, GA 30241
Phone: (706)884-7348
Fax: (706)884-7349
J. T. Gresham, President

Foundation Philosophy: The foundation is intended for religious, charitable, and educational benefits to the people in Troup County and La-Grange, GA. The foundation prefers to provide capital funds for established and active community organizations, especially those that offer lasting benefit to the community. **Giving Priorities:** In fiscal 1994, the foundation reported that it gave 68% of its total giving to educational institutions, primarily colleges and universities. Approximately 13% of funding went to civic affairs, 7% to religious organizations, 6% to health care; and 4% to the arts and humanitites. Social service organizations were awarded the remaining funds. **Typical Health-Related Recipients:** Alzheimers Disease, Cancer, Clinics/Medical Centers, Emergency/Ambulance Services, Health Organizations, Heart, Hospitals, Medical Education, Medical Rehabilitation, People with Disabilities, Single-Disease Health Associations, Substance Abuse, Transplant Networks/Donor Banks. **Geographic Distribution:** Georgia, primarily in the city of LaGrange and Troup County.

★84★ Carl J. Herzog Foundation
c/o Bentley, Lane, Mosher, and Babson
20 Dalton Ave.
Greenwich, CT 06830
Phone: (203)629-2424
David F. Babson, Jr., President, Treasurer, and Director

Foundation Philosophy: The Carl J. Herzog Foundation is primarily interested in supporting colleges and universities around the country. A secondary interest is health, specifically dermotology, cancer, and prosthetic research organizations. **Giving Priorities:** In 1993, the foundation awarded 93% of its total giving to educational institutions, including a single $2,000,000 grant to Rockefeller University, New York, NY. About 6% of funds went to health care. The remaining 1% went to the Americas Foundation, an international organization. **Typical Health-Related Recipients:** Cancer, Clinics/Medical Centers, Health Funds, Health Organizations, Hospitals, Medical Education, Medical Research, Research/Studies Institutes. **Geographic Distribution:** National.

★85★ Carl and Lily Pforzheimer Foundation
650 Madison Ave., 23rd Fl.
New York, NY 10022
Phone: (212)223-6500
Carl H. Pforzheimer, III, President

Foundation Philosophy: The foundation supports scholarly works by leading university presses of books dealing with fields in which the foundation has a major interest, such as English and American literature. In general, the foundation provides limited support to ongoing programs in education, health care, the arts, and organizations with which the foundation is familiar. **Giving Priorities:** In 1993, the foundation gave approximately 51% of its total contributions to educational institutions. The arts received about 23%; health concerns, 16%; social services, 6%; and civic affairs and international organizations received the remaining funds. **Typical Health-Related Recipients:** Clinics/Medical Centers, Emergency/Ambulance Services, Hospitals, Nursing Services. **Geographic Distribution:** National, with a focus on New York, NY.

★86★ Carolyn Foundation
4800 First Bank Pl.
Minneapolis, MN 55402-4320
Phone: (612)339-7101
Fax: (612)338-2084
Carol J. Fetzer, Foundation Administrator

Foundation Philosophy: The Carolyn Foundation is interested principally in health and welfare, education, culture, the environment, and programs for the disadvantaged. It is a regional foundation and limits funding to Minneapolis and St. Paul, MN, and New Haven, CT, and to some national environmental organizations with programs affecting these areas. **Giving Priorities:** In 1993, the foundation gave approximately 38% of total contributions to environmental causes. Civic and public affairs received 23%.

Social service organizations received 12%; the arts and educational institutions each received 8%; religious causes, 7%; health care organizations, 3%; and international groups, 1%. **Typical Health-Related Recipients:** Children's Health/Hospitals, Clinics/Medical Centers, Domestic Violence, Family Planning, Health Organizations, Hospitals, Nursing Services, People with Disabilities, Substance Abuse. **Geographic Distribution:** Metropolitan New Haven, CT; and Minneapolis and St. Paul, MN.

★87★ Carrie Estelle Doheny Foundation
911 Wilshire Blvd., Ste. 1750
Los Angeles, CA 90017
Phone: (213)488-1122
Fax: (213)488-1544
Robert A. Smith, III, President

Foundation Philosophy: The foundation supports a variety of local organizations, with emphasis on Roman Catholic groups, medical research, hospital care, education, child health and welfare, and assistance to the sick and needy. **Giving Priorities:** In 1994, the foundation gave approximately 54% of total funding to health care. Religious organizations received 27% of giving with emphasis on Catholic services. Educational institutions were awarded 14%; social services, 5%; and the remaining funds supported civic affairs. **Typical Health-Related Recipients:** Clinics/Medical Centers, Eyes/Blindness, Family Planning, Health Organizations, Heart, Hospitals, Long-Term Care, Medical Research, Medical Training, Nutrition, People with Disabilities, Single-Disease Health Associations, Speech & Hearing. **Geographic Distribution:** Primarily Los Angeles, CA.

★88★ Catherine and Henry J. Gaisman Foundation
PO Box 277
Hartsdale, NY 10530-0277
Phone: (914)948-0666
Catherine V. Gaisman, President

Foundation Philosophy: The foundation is primarily interested in supporting health care services and makes regular contributions to the Mount Sinai Medical Center. The foundation's secondary interest is religious organizations. Minor grants are also given to other recipient areas. **Giving Priorities:** In 1993, the foundation awarded 86% of its giving to health care, including a $570,000 grant to the Mount Sinai Medical Center. Religious organizations received 8%; educational institutions, 6%; and civic causes, 1%. **Typical Health-Related Recipients:** Clinics/Medical Centers, Eyes/Blindness, Hospitals, Medical Education, Medical Research. **Geographic Distribution:** Focus on New York.

★89★ Champlin Foundations
410 S Main St.
Providence, RI 02903
Phone: (401)421-3719
David A. King, Executive Director

Foundation Philosophy: The aim of the foundations is to provide funds to Rhode Island organizations helping the broadest possible segment of the population. The foundations are interested in preserving land for recreation and open space. Although cultural projects involving

libraries and library services receive considerable support, the foundations generally do not support the arts. Capital funding is offered to educational institutions other than elementary schools. They also have an interest in social service agencies, facilities for youth, hospitals, and health care agencies. **Giving Priorities:** In 1994, the foundation gave approximately 27% of its contributions to health care, with the majority of funds going to hospitals. Social services received 22%. The arts received 17%; education, 16%; the environment, 14%; and civic affairs, 3%. The remaining funds supported religion and a natural history museum. **Typical Health-Related Recipients:** Clinics/Medical Centers, Emergency/Ambulance Services, Family Planning, Health Organizations, Hospices, Hospitals, Medical Rehabilitation, Nursing Services, Transplant Networks/Donor Banks. **Geographic Distribution:** Almost exclusively Rhode Island.

★90★ Charles A. Dana Foundation
745 Fifth Ave., Ste. 700
New York, NY 10151
Phone: (212)223-4040
Fax: (212)593-7623
Stephen A. Foster, Executive Vice President

Foundation Philosophy: In health, the foundation will concentrate on neuroscience, and identify programs and investigators that can apply recent discoveries in neuroscience research to the treatment of the problems of memory loss, genetic basis of manic-depression, and language-based learning disorders. In addition, the foundation will support centers with advanced neuroimaging capability to train the neuroscience leadership needed to promote the application of such technologies to neuroscience research. Most of the foundation's resources in health will support these efforts. Applicants should be aware that funds for other initiatives will be quite limited. The foundation's education program will seek projects that have an impact on key developments in precollege education. The Charles A. Dana Awards for Pioneering Achievements in Health and Education call attention to innovative ideas with demonstrated potential for promoting health, preventing disease, or strengthening education. **Giving Priorities:** In 1993, the foundation awarded 70% of its total contributions to health care, including a single $5,167,080 grant to the Dana Farber Cancer Institute, Boston, MA. About 14% of funds went to educational institutions. Civic groups and the arts received 10% of funds; the Dana Award program, 5%; and public affairs program, 1%. **Typical Health-Related Recipients:** AIDS/HIV, Cancer, Clinics/Medical Centers, Geriatric Health, Health Organizations, Hospitals, Medical Education, Medical Research, Medical Training, Mental Health, People with Disabilities, Substance Abuse. **Geographic Distribution:** United States, no international giving.

★91★ Charles A. Frueauff Foundation
307 E 7th Ave.
Tallahassee, FL 32303
Phone: (904)561-3508
Zoe Cole Golloway, Assistant Executive Director

Foundation Philosophy: The foundation favors education, social services, and health causes. **Giving Priorities:** In 1993, the foundation contributed 41% of its total giving to educational institutions, primarily to private colleges and universities. Social service organizations received about 26% of support, including community service organizations and programs for people with disabilities. Health care received 18% of funds, the arts were granted 10%, and religion received the remaining 5%. **Typical Health-Related Recipients:** Children's Health/Hospitals, Clinics/Medical Centers, Health Organizations, Hospices, Hospitals, Medical Education, People with Disabilities, Substance Abuse. **Geographic Distribution:** Broad geographic distribution.

★92★ **Charles Edison Fund**
101 S Harrison St.
East Orange, NJ 07018
Phone: (201)675-9000
Fax: (201)675-3345
Paul J. Christiansen, President and Trustee

Foundation Philosophy: The Charles Edison Fund borders on being an operating foundation because of its formation and makeup, yet also serves a broad range of charitable needs. Grants primarily support historic preservation, education, medical research, hospitals, churches, and recreational groups. **Giving Priorities:** The fund reports that in 1993 it gave approximately 59% of its total contributions to educational institutions. About 21% of giving went to historic preservation. Health care received 20% of funds, and miscellaneous organizations recieved 1%. **Typical Health-Related Recipients:** Hospitals, Medical Education, Medical Research, Medical Training. **Geographic Distribution:** Primarily northeastern states (mainly at the local level); largely in New York/New Jersey metropolitan area.

★93★ **Charles Engelhard Foundation**
PO Box 427
Far Hills, NJ 07931
Phone: (908)935-2430
Joan D. Ricci, Secretary

Foundation Philosophy: The foundation gives to a variety of cultural, civic, and educational organizations. Less emphasis is placed on religion and social services. **Giving Priorities:** In fiscal 1992, the foundation gave approximately 35% of its contributions to the arts. Health care, mainly hospitals, received 17%. Education received 13%. Environmental preservation organizations received about 11%. International affairs and religion each received 9% of the giving, science received 3%, and civic affairs and social services received the remainder. **Typical Health-Related Recipients:** AIDS/HIV, Clinics/Medical Centers, Family Planning, Health Organizations, Hospices, Hospitals, Medical Education, Medical Research, People with Disabilities, Public Health, Single-Disease Health Associations, Substance Abuse. **Geographic Distribution:** Broad geographic distribution, with emphasis on New York, NY; Washington, DC; Houston, TX; and New Jersey.

★94★ **Charles J. Strosacker Foundation**
PO Box 471
Midland, MI 48640-0471
Phone: (517)832-0066
Patricia E. McKelvey, Secretary

Foundation Philosophy: The foundation was established "to assist and benefit political subdivisions of the State of Michigan, and religious, charitable, benevolent, scientific or educational organizations." A majority of foundation giving in 1992 went to educational institutions and social service agencies, primarily in Midland, MI. Remaining support went to a variety of activities. **Giving Priorities:** In 1993, the foundation gave approximately 41% of its contributions to education. Social services received 31% of giving. Civic and public affairs concerns received about 20% of the foundation's donations. Health care and the arts each received about 3% of total grants. Environmental concerns received 1% of funds, with the remaining small amount going to religious organizations. **Typical Health-Related Recipients:** Emergency/Ambulance Services, Family Planning, Health Organizations, Hospices, Medical Education, Mental Health, Substance Abuse, Transplant Networks/Donor Banks. **Geographic Distribution:** Focus on Michigan, with emphasis on the city of Midland.

★95★ **Charles and M. R. Shapiro Foundation**
200 N LaSalle St., Ste. 2100
Chicago, IL 60601
Phone: (312)346-3100
Norman Shubert, President

Foundation Philosophy: The Charles and M. R. Shapiro Foundation makes most of its grants to Jewish religious organizations. A secondary interest is Jewish education. Minor grants go to civic affairs, health, social services, and the arts. **Giving Priorities:** In fiscal 1993, the foundation contributed 74% of its funds to Jewish religious organizations. The foundation's largest gift, $150,000, went to the Jewish United Fund. International affairs received 10%; health care, 8%; the arts, 3%. The remaining funds supported education, civic affairs, and social services. **Typical Health-Related Recipients:** Emergency/Ambulance Services, Geriatric Health, Hospices, Hospitals, Medical Research, Multiple Sclerosis, People with Disabilities. **Geographic Distribution:** Some nationally, with a focus on Chicago, IL.

★96★ **Chatlos Foundation**
PO Box 915048
Longwood, FL 32791-5048
Phone: (407)862-5077
William J. Chatlos, President

Foundation Philosophy: The Chatlos Foundation gives funding priority to Bible colleges, religious causes, medical issues, liberal arts colleges, and social concerns. The foundation prefers to provide program support. As a result, the foundation makes fewer grants to capital funds, conference expenses, administrative costs, multiyear grants or computer projects. **Giving Priorities:** In 1993, approximately 36% of funding went to health care. Religion received 30%; international affairs, 20%; and education, 8%. The arts and civic affairs each received 2% and

social services received 1%. **Typical Health-Related Recipients:** AIDS/HIV, Arthritis, Cancer, Clinics/Medical Centers, Emergency/Ambulance Services, Eyes/Blindness, Health Organizations, Hospitals, Medical Research, Nursing Services, People with Disabilities, Trauma Treatment. **Geographic Distribution:** National; no geographic restrictions.

★97★ **Chauncey and Marion Deering McCormick Foundation**
410 North Michigan Ave., Rm. 590
Chicago, IL 60611
Phone: (312)644-6720
Charles E. Schroeder, Secretary and Treasurer

Foundation Philosophy: The foundation primarily concentrates on local giving to organizations such as arts institutions, hospitals, universities, museums, wildlife conservation groups, private secondary schools, churches, and social services agencies. The foundation supports capital campaigns, art purchases, library funds, and building funds. **Giving Priorities:** In fiscal 1991, about 48% of funding went to civic and public affairs. Approximately 21% was allocated to arts and humanities. About 16% went to education. Another 9% went to social services, and remaining funds to health organizations and religion. **Typical Health-Related Recipients:** Health Organizations, Medical Research, Single-Disease Health Associations. **Geographic Distribution:** Primarily metropolitan Chicago area.

★98★ **Chichester duPont Foundation**
3120 Kennett Pke.
Wilmington, DE 19807
Phone: (302)658-5244
Gregory F. Fields, Secretary

Foundation Philosophy: The foundation is primarily interested in supporting today's youth. A majority of the giving goes to social service organizations for the direct benefit of children. Most of the support is for operating budgets and capital campaigns. Another interest is education at the primary and secondary levels. Giving has been for endowment funds and youth recreation facilities in schools. The foundation also gives to civic affairs and organization's building funds and operating budgets. The arts and health are minimally supported. **Giving Priorities:** In 1993, approximately 48% of funding went to social service organizations. Environmental causes received 22% of funding; education, 12%; health organizations, 10%; the arts, 5%; and religious organizations, 3%. **Typical Health-Related Recipients:** Arthritis, Child Abuse, Emergency/Ambulance Services, Family Planning, Health Organizations, Heart, Hospices, Hospitals, Medical Rehabilitation, Medical Research, People with Disabilities, Public Health, Substance Abuse. **Geographic Distribution:** Mid-Atlantic and northeastern United States.

★99★ **Chiles Foundation**
111 SW Fifth Ave., Ste. 4050
Portland, OR 97204
Phone: (503)222-2143
Fax: (503)228-7079
Earle M. Chiles, President and Trustee

Foundation Philosophy: "The foundation's principal purposes are to assist and support education, medical advancement, youth, and community activities." **Giving Priorities:** In 1992, the foundation gave approximately 53% of its contributions to educational institutions, including its highest grant of $335,565 for Stanford University. Health organizations received 21% of giving, with a grant of $219,500 going to the Saint Vincent Medical Foundation, Portland, OR. The arts received 16%; international affairs, 5%; and social services received 3%. Religion (1%), civic affairs (1%), and science (1%) received the remainder. **Typical Health-Related Recipients:** Health Funds, Hospitals, Medical Research, Nursing Services, Prenatal Health Issues, Single-Disease Health Associations. **Geographic Distribution:** Primarily Oregon and the Pacific Northwest.

★ 100 ★   **China Medical Board of New York**
750 Third Ave., 23rd Fl.
New York, NY 10017
Phone: (212)682-8000
William D. Sawyer, M.D., President

Foundation Philosophy: The board's primary interest is supporting medical, nursing, and public health education and research. Contributions are made to eleven different countries and territories in East and Southeast Asia, as directed by its charter. "The Board is especially interested in grants to advance the recipient institution's pursuit of excellence and for the enhancement of the academic and professional content of medical, nursing, and public health education and training." The board reports that it has started a new program for higher education in nursing. **Giving Priorities:** In fiscal 1994, 100% of funding went to medical universities and colleges in the People's Republic of China, Mongolia, Myanmar, and Vietnam. **Typical Health-Related Recipients:** Health Organizations, Medical Education, Medical Research. **Geographic Distribution:** Limited to East and Southeast Asia, the People's Republic of China, Hong Kong, Indonesia, Korea, Malaysia, the Philippines, Singapore, Taiwan, and Thailand.

★ 101 ★   **Christy-Houston Foundation**
1296 Dow St.
Murfreesboro, TN 37130
Phone: (615)898-1140
Fax: (615)895-9524
James R. Arnhart, Executive Director

Foundation Philosophy: The foundation is dedicated to the "improvement of the quality of life for the citizens and residents of Rutherford County, TN, with an emphasis on the promotion and enhancement of health care." The foundation has reported that it will place a greater focus on social services in Rutherford County, TN, and that it plans in the future to fund a Boys and Girls Club, a YMCA, and a senior citizen's center. **Giving Priorities:** In fiscal 1994, the foundation awarded 47% of its total contributions to educational institutions. Another 47% of support went to social services. Health care received 4% of funds, and the arts received 2%. **Typical Health-Related Recipients:** Health Organizations, Hospices, Hospitals, Medical Education. **Geographic Distribution:** Rutherford County, TN.

★ 102 ★   **Clara Blackford Smith and W. Aubrey Smith Charitable Foundation**
c/o NationsBank
300 W Main St.
Denison, TX 75020
Phone: (903)465-2131
Jane Ayres, Trust Officer

Foundation Philosophy: The foundation makes most of its grants to health care organizations. Interests include the Texoma Medical Center, cancer treatment and research, and rehabilitation facilities. Secondary interests include education, civic affairs, and social services. Social service support includes counseling and youth organizations. **Giving Priorities:** In fiscal 1994, the foundation reported that it gave approximately 70% of its contributions to health services. Education received about 11% of the funding. Civic affairs received 9%; social services, 8%; and the arts received the remaining funds. **Typical Health-Related Recipients:** Health Funds, Hospitals, Medical Education, Medical Research, Nursing Services. **Geographic Distribution:** Focus on Denison, TX.

★ 103 ★   **Clark-Winchcole Foundation**
4550 Montgomery Ave., Ste. 345N
Bethesda, MD 20814
Phone: (301)654-3607
Laura E. Phillips, President and Trustee

Foundation Philosophy: The foundation gives to broad purposes in the Washington, DC, area with emphasis on social services and the arts. **Giving Priorities:** In 1993, the foundation awarded 34% of its total contributions to the arts in the metropolitian Washington, DC, area. About 20% of funds went to health care. Social services and educational institutions each received 16% of support, and religious causes received 11%. The remainder went to civic groups and international affairs. **Typical Health-Related Recipients:** Children's Health/Hospitals, Clinics/Medical Centers, Emergency/Ambulance Services, Health Organizations, Hospitals, Long-Term Care, Medical Rehabilitation, Mental Health, Nursing Services, People with Disabilities, Single-Disease Health Associations, Speech & Hearing, Substance Abuse. **Geographic Distribution:** Primarily the Washington, DC, area.

★ 104 ★   **Claude Worthington Benedum Foundation**
1400 Benedum-Trees Bldg.
Pittsburgh, PA 15222
Phone: (412)288-0360
Fax: (412)288-0366
Paul R. Jenkins, President and Trustee

Foundation Philosophy: The foundation's regional grants program is shaped by its desire to maintain flexibility in grant making and its commitment to enhance the life quality of the region's people through education, health care, community and economic development, social services, and the arts. This precludes it from making long-term grant commitments. **Giving Priorities:** In 1993, the foundation awarded 40% of total funding to educational institutions. About 16% of contributions went to environment concerns. Health care received 15% of support; social services, 12%; civic groups, 11%; and the arts, 5%. The remainder went to

the religious organizations. **Typical Health-Related Recipients:** Children's Health/Hospitals, Emergency/Ambulance Services, Health Organizations, Hospitals, Medical Education, Nursing Services, Nutrition, People with Disabilities, Preventive Medicine/Wellness Organizations, Public Health. **Geographic Distribution:** West Virginia and Pittsburgh, PA.

★ 105 ★   **Clay Foundation**
1426 Kanawha Blvd., E
Charleston, WV 25301
Phone: (304)344-8656
Charles M. Avampato, President

Foundation Philosophy: The Clay Foundation was established "to promote and enhance the quality of life of the citizens of West Virginia." The foundation's goal is to fund innovative projects or support services which best serve the residents of the state. Although the foundation considers requests from a broad range of organizations, it currently has a special interest in programs in the field of aging; health care research and education; vocational education programs; and services to disadvantaged youth and their families. **Giving Priorities:** In fiscal 1993, the foundation awarded 30% of its total contributions to social services. About 24% of funding went to the arts. Educational institutions received 22% of support; health care, 9%; religious organizations, 7%; and civic groups, 7%. The remainder went to scientific organizations. **Typical Health-Related Recipients:** Health Organizations, Health Policy/Cost Containment, Hospices, Hospitals, Medical Education, Mental Health, People with Disabilities, Preventive Medicine/Wellness Organizations. **Geographic Distribution:** Primarily West Virginia, with emphasis on Kanawha Valley.

★ 106 ★   **Clayton Fund**
c/o Texas Commerce Bank
PO Box 2558
Houston, TX 77252-8037
Phone: (713)216-3447
William Askey, Secretary and Treasurer

Foundation Philosophy: "The trust was created for charitable or educational purposes. These purposes include provision of scholarships; promotion, aid, and contribution to farm contests and educational activities, as well as educational institutions and organizations, especially in the agricultural field; and financial aid and assistance to needy persons who because of age, sickness, physical disability, misfortune, or mishap may require such aid and assistance." The foundation also shows interest in medical research, population control, and arts and music. **Giving Priorities:** In 1993, the Clayton Fund gave 31% of funding to medical concerns. Education received 29% of giving; social services, 17%; environmental causes, 13%; arts, 9%. **Typical Health-Related Recipients:** Health Organizations, Medical Education, People with Disabilities, Single-Disease Health Associations. **Geographic Distribution:** Primarily Texas, with emphasis on Houston; limited support elsewhere.

★ 107 ★ Clipper Ship Foundation

Grants Management Association
230 Congress St., 3rd Fl.
Boston, MA 02110
Phone: (617)426-7172
Fax: (617)439-3580
Suzanne Sack

Foundation Philosophy: The foundation's principal objective is to assist nonprofit, operating organizations serving the Boston community. Special attention will be given to those organizations involved with "the homeless, the destitute, the handicapped, children and the aged, or supplying the special needs of minority, low-income individuals and families." Worldwide disaster relief is also an occasional concern of the foundation. **Giving Priorities:** In fiscal 1993, the foundation gave approximately 38% of funding to social services, with major support going to child welfare. Civic affairs organizations received 37% of grants. Health care received 10% of giving, education received 8%, and the arts received 4%. International concerns were awarded about 2% of funds. **Typical Health-Related Recipients:** AIDS/HIV, Clinics/Medical Centers, Emergency/Ambulance Services, Family Planning, Hospices, Hospitals, Medical Rehabilitation, Mental Health, People with Disabilities, Substance Abuse. **Geographic Distribution:** Boston, MA, area.

★ 108 ★ Clowes Fund

250 E 38th St.
Indianapolis, IN 46205
Phone: (317)923-3264
Allen W. Clowes, President and Treasurer

Foundation Philosophy: The fund typically supports higher educational institutions, the performing arts, and social services, primarily in Indiana and Massachusetts. **Giving Priorities:** In 1993, the fund gave approximately 33% of its contributions to educational institutions. The arts received 29%. Social services received 13% of total contributions. Civic and public affairs received 8% and religious causes, 7%. Science received 6%. Health care organizations received 3%, and environmental concerns received the remaining 1%. **Typical Health-Related Recipients:** Diabetes, Family Planning, Health Funds, Health Organizations, Hospitals, Hospitals (University Affiliated), Medical Education, Medical Research, People with Disabilities, Substance Abuse. **Geographic Distribution:** Primarily Indiana and Massachusetts.

★ 109 ★ Cockrell Foundation

1600 Smith, Ste. 4600
Houston, TX 77002-7348
Phone: (713)651-1271
Fax: (713)651-7811
Nancy Williams, Executive Vice President

Foundation Philosophy: The foundation is required by the last will and testament of Ernest Cockrell, Jr., to give one-half of annual funding to the University of Texas at Austin School of Engineering. It outlines no giving priorities for remaining funds and gives to a variety of areas. **Giving Priorities:** In 1993, the foundation awarded 42% of its charitable contributions to support health care, including a $1,575,000 grant to the M.D. Anderson Cancer Center. The Houston Museum of Natural Science received

27% of support, while education received 24%, including an $850,000 grant to the University of Texas Austin Engineering Foundation. Civic affairs and social service organizations received 3% each. The remaining 1% was given in support of the arts. **Typical Health-Related Recipients:** Adolescent Health Issues, Alzheimers Disease, Cancer, Children's Health/Hospitals, Clinics/Medical Centers, Emergency/Ambulance Services, Eyes/Blindness, Family Planning, Health Organizations, Heart, Hospices, Hospitals, Medical Research, Mental Health, People with Disabilities, Single-Disease Health Associations. **Geographic Distribution:** Primarily Houston, TX.

★ 110 ★ Coleman Foundation

575 W Madison St.
Ste. 4605
Chicago, IL 60661
Phone: (312)902-7120
Fax: (312)902-7124
Jean D. Thorne, Executive Director

Foundation Philosophy: The foundation traditionally supports secondary and higher educational institutions, hospitals, medical training, and health organizations concerned with a single disease. Community and youth-oriented human service organizations are also supported. Limited funding goes to civic and cultural organizations. Program areas funded by the foundation include entrepreneurship awareness education, cancer research in the Midwest, housing and education of the handicapped, and education. The foundation has endowed chairs in entrepreneurship ($1 million or more) at colleges, professorships at colleges, and medical chairs for cancer at hospitals and rehabilitation institutes. **Giving Priorities:** In 1992, the foundation awarded 63% of its contributions to educational organizations and institutions. Social services, health care, and civic organizations each received approximately 12% of the funds. These grants included separate awards of $100,000 to three Chicago institutions: the Misericorda Heart of Mercy, the Mount Sinai Hospital Medical Center, and the Providence St.-Mel Development Corporation. The remaining funds supported the arts. **Typical Health-Related Recipients:** AIDS/HIV, Clinics/Medical Centers, Health Organizations, Hospitals, Medical Rehabilitation, Medical Research, People with Disabilities, Single-Disease Health Associations. **Geographic Distribution:** United States with focus on the Midwest, particularly Illinois.

★ 111 ★ Collins Foundation

1618 SW 1st Ave., Ste. 305
Portland, OR 97201-5708
Phone: (503)227-7171
William C. Pine, Vice President and Executive Director

Foundation Philosophy: The foundation was established to use its funds for religious, charitable, and educational purposes within the state of Oregon. It looks favorably on small, creative programs that can serve the community. **Giving Priorities:** In 1994, the foundation reports that it gave approximately 33% of funding to education/science institutions. About 15% went to health concerns, and about 14% went to the arts. Welfare/youth organizations received

10%, religious causes, 9%, and environmental concerns, 3%. Other miscellaneous organizations received 16%. **Typical Health-Related Recipients:** Alzheimers Disease, Emergency/Ambulance Services, Family Planning, Health Funds, Health Organizations, Hospices, Hospitals, People with Disabilities, Trauma Treatment. **Geographic Distribution:** Oregon only.

★ 112 ★ Colorado Trust

1600 Sherman St.
Denver, CO 80203
Phone: (303)837-1200
Fax: (303)839-9034
Mae C. Brooks, Grants Administrator

Foundation Philosophy: "The mission of the Colorado Trust is to promote and enhance the health and well-being of the people of Colorado. To fulfill its mission, the foundation supports innovative projects, conducts studies, develops services and provides education to produce long-lasting benefits for all Coloradans. Within the framework of human development, the Colorado Trust advances its goals of accessible and affordable health care programs and the strengthening of families." **Giving Priorities:** In 1993, the trust awarded 46% of its giving to health care. Social services received 33%; education, 9%; religion, 7%; and civic affairs, 5%. **Typical Health-Related Recipients:** AIDS/HIV, Children's Health/Hospitals, Clinics/Medical Centers, Domestic Violence, Emergency/Ambulance Services, Family Planning, Geriatric Health, Health Organizations, Health Policy/Cost Containment, Hospices, Hospitals, Long-Term Care, Medical Education, Mental Health, Nursing Services, Nutrition, People with Disabilities, Prenatal Health Issues, Preventive Medicine/Wellness Organizations, Sexual Abuse, Single-Disease Health Associations, Substance Abuse. **Geographic Distribution:** Colorado.

★ 113 ★ Commonwealth Fund

1 E 75th St.
New York, NY 10021-2692
Phone: (212)535-0400
Fax: (212)249-1276
Adrienne A. Fisher, Grants Manager

Foundation Philosophy: The five themes of the fund's domestic programs are improving health care services, advancing the well-being of elderly people, developing the capacities of young people, promoting healthier lifestyles, and bettering the health of minorities. Internationally, since 1925, the fund has also awarded Harkness Fellowships to enable citizens of the United Kingdom, Australia, and New Zealand to study and travel in the United States. **Giving Priorities:** In fiscal 1993, the fund gave approximately 54% of its contributions to health services, including the fund's highest grant of $400,000 to Beth Israel Hospital in Boston. Social services received 18% of funds; civic concerns, 14%; educational institutions, 9%; international affairs, 3%; and science organizations, 2%. **Typical Health-Related Recipients:** Cancer, Clinics/Medical Centers, Family Planning, Geriatric Health, Health Funds, Health Organizations, Health Policy/Cost Containment, Heart, Hospitals, Long-Term Care, Medical Education, Medical Research, Medical Training,

Mental Health, Nursing Services, Prenatal Health Issues, Preventive Medicine/Wellness Organizations, Public Health, Substance Abuse. **Geographic Distribution:** National; some emphasis on New York City.

★ 114 ★ **Comstock Foundation**
819 Washington Trust Financial Ctr.
Spokane, WA 99204
Phone: (509)747-1527
Horton Herman, Trustee

Foundation Philosophy: The foundation is best characterized by the number and diversity of projects and organizations that it supports. The foundation prefers to make grants for capital projects rather than contribute to operating expenses. Whenever possible, the foundation prefers to join with other donors in funding a project, rather than assuming a major portion of the amount needed. **Giving Priorities:** In 1993, the foundation gave 35% of its funds to religious organizations. Educational institutions received 29% of support; social services, 22%; and health care, 5%. Civic groups and the arts each received 4%. **Typical Health-Related Recipients:** AIDS/HIV, Cancer, Children's Health/Hospitals, Eyes/Blindness, Health Organizations, Hospitals, Medical Education, Medical Rehabilitation, Nursing Services, People with Disabilities, Single-Disease Health Associations, Substance Abuse. **Geographic Distribution:** Metropolitan Spokane County, WA, and its environs.

★ 115 ★ **Connelly Foundation**
One Tower Bridge, Ste. 1450
West Conshohocken, PA 19428
Phone: (610)834-3222
Fax: (610)834-0866
Victoria K. Flaville, Vice President and Secretary

Foundation Philosophy: The Connelly Foundation primarily supports educational institutions and organizations in the medical, civic, and cultural fields and encourages them to improve the quality of life. Each year a sizeable amount of funding is directed toward organizations affiliated with the Catholic Church. **Giving Priorities:** In 1993, approximately 46% of the foundation's contributions supported education. Health care received about 18% of support, and religious organizations received 12%. International affiars received 8% of distributed funds, social service organizations received 6%, while civic affairs received 5%. About 3% of contributions were distributed to arts organizations, with 2% supporting science. The remaining funds supported environmental affairs. **Typical Health-Related Recipients:** AIDS/HIV, Alzheimers Disease, Cancer, Child Abuse, Children's Health/Hospitals, Clinics/Medical Centers, Domestic Violence, Emergency/Ambulance Services, Family Planning, Geriatric Health, Health Organizations, Heart, Hospices, Hospitals, Long-Term Care, Medical Education, Medical Rehabilitation, Nursing Services, Outpatient Health Care, People with Disabilities, Prenatal Health Issues, Preventive Medicine/Wellness Organizations, Research/Studies Institutes, Substance Abuse, Transplant Networks/Donor Banks. **Geographic Distribution:** Primarily Pennsylvania and the surrounding Delaware Valley, with emphasis on Philadelphia.

★ 116 ★ **Conrad N. Hilton Foundation**
100 W Liberty St., Ste. 840
Reno, NV 89501
Phone: (702)323-4221
Fax: (702)323-4150
Donald H. Hubbs, President

Foundation Philosophy: A showcase project for the foundation is the Rand Corporation's long-term substance abuse education research project, currently being implemented by the Best Foundation for a Drug-Free Tomorrow. In addition, the foundation has identified the needs of the blind as a priority, and is funding a $40 million long term project, including a program related investment with the Perkins School for the Blind to meet these needs. The foundation is conducting research in the areas of early childhood development and the homeless and has made some initial grants in these areas. The foundation prefers to initiate and develop major long-term projects and then to seek out organizations to implement them. This proactive approach leaves very little for smaller scale miscellaneous grants. **Giving Priorities:** In fiscal 1994, the foundation gave approximately 48% of total contributions to various foundation interests, including education and international water development. More than 22% of funds supported the worldwide work of Catholic Sisters. Programs to aid the handicapped received about 17%, and 13% of contributions supported the drug prevention program, BEST Campaign for a Drug Free Tomorrow. **Typical Health-Related Recipients:** Children's Health/Hospitals, Diabetes, Domestic Violence, Emergency/Ambulance Services, Eyes/Blindness, Family Planning, Health Organizations, Heart, Hospitals, Medical Research, Multiple Sclerosis, People with Disabilities, Research/Studies Institutes, Single-Disease Health Associations, Substance Abuse, Transplant Networks/Donor Banks. **Geographic Distribution:** National; no geographic restrictions.

★ 117 ★ **Cooke Foundation**
222 Merchant St.
Honolulu, HI 96813
Phone: (808)537-6333
Susan Jones, Grants Administrator

Foundation Philosophy: The foundation is dedicated primarily to culture and the arts; education; social services, including programs for youth; health; and the environment. The foundation is interested in directing financial support to organizations responding to new needs or changing conditions. **Giving Priorities:** In fiscal 1993, the foundation awarded 25% of its total gifts to educational institutions. About 22% of funds went to social service organizations. The arts received 20% of support; civic groups, 16%; environmental concerns, 7%; religion organizations, 6%; and health care, 5%. **Typical Health-Related Recipients:** AIDS/HIV, Domestic Violence, Family Planning, Health Organizations, Heart, Hospices, Hospitals, Mental Health, People with Disabilities, Single-Disease Health Associations, Substance Abuse. **Geographic Distribution:** Only in Hawaii, with emphasis on Oahu.

★ 118 ★ **Corella and Bertram Bonner Foundation**
22 Chambers St., Box 712
Princeton, NJ 08542
Phone: (609)924-6663
Wayne Meisel, President

Foundation Philosophy: The foundation is primarily interested in directing financial assistance to the basic needs of food, education, and health care. It focuses on several major areas: crisis ministry, education, medical services, aid to the handicapped, and general relief. In addition to its contributions to numerous food banks throughout the United States, the foundation also supports education. The foundation will also consider requests from organizations serving those communities who are in need of emergency or continuing assistance. **Giving Priorities:** In fiscal 1993, the foundation gave approximately 48% of its total funds to educational institutions through the Bonner Scholars Program. About 45% of funds went to the foundation's Food Bank Program. Grants to food banks averaged approximately $10,000. The remaining 6% of funds went to health care and religious organizations. **Typical Health-Related Recipients:** Clinics/Medical Centers, Health Funds, Hospitals, Medical Research, Research/Studies Institutes. **Geographic Distribution:** National; emphasis on the East Coast.

★ 119 ★ **Cowles Charitable Trust**
630 Fifth Ave., Ste. 1612
New York, NY 10111
Phone: (212)765-6262
Mary Croft, Secretary and Treasurer

Foundation Philosophy: The Cowles Charitable Trust makes most of its grants in the areas of education, arts, health, and environment. The trust also will fund civic groups, social services, and health organizations. **Giving Priorities:** In 1993, the trust awarded 42% of its total giving to support the arts. Education received 24% of the support. About 15% of donations went to social service organizations, with major support going to Planned Parenthood. Health care received 9% of distributed funds, while science received 6%. About 2% went to civic affairs, while international affairs and religious institutions each received about 1%. **Typical Health-Related Recipients:** AIDS/HIV, Cancer, Clinics/Medical Centers, Emergency/Ambulance Services, Family Planning, Health Organizations, Hospitals, Medical Research, Mental Health, People with Disabilities, Single-Disease Health Associations, Substance Abuse. **Geographic Distribution:** National, with emphasis in New York City.

★ 120 ★ **Crestlea Foundation**
1004 Wilmington Trust Center
Wilmington, DE 19801
Phone: (302)654-2477
Stephen A. Martinenza, Treasurer

Foundation Philosophy: The foundation has three main areas of interest, but does not limit giving to these areas specifically. Secondary and higher education are major interests, followed by support for libraries and museums in Pennsylvania and Delaware. The third main interest is youth activities and family planning. In addition, the foundation varies the remainder of its support to community affairs, nature conservation, and churches. **Giving Priorities:** In 1993, the foundation contributed approximately 48% of its total funding went to support the arts. About 27% of its total funding to educational institutions. Social service organizations received 14% of support. Environmental affairs, religion, and civic affairs each received about 3% of donations. The remaining 2% went to health care organizations. **Typical Health-Related Recipients:** Cancer, Clinics/Medical Centers, Family Planning, Geriatric Health, Health Organizations, Hospices, Hospitals, Long-Term Care, Medical Education, People with Disabilities, Single-Disease Health Associations. **Geographic Distribution:** Majority of grants given to organizations within 50 miles of Wilmington, DE.

★ 121 ★   Crystal Trust
1088 du Pont Bldg.
Wilmington, DE 19898
Phone: (302)774-8421
Stephen C. Doberstein, Executive Director

Foundation Philosophy: The trust has no specific mandate other than that of serving the Wilmington community. It supports a wide variety of causes. Emphasis is on gifts for capital and other one-time special purposes, and against gifts for continuing expenses of operations or deficits. **Giving Priorities:** In 1993, education received 57% of total funds awarded. Social services and the arts were each given 14%, while civic and public affairs shared 8% of the giving with environmental organizations. The remaining funds went to health-related concerns, 3%, religious groups, 2%, and science interests, 1%. **Typical Health-Related Recipients:** Cancer, Domestic Violence, Family Planning, Health Organizations, Hospices, Hospitals, People with Disabilities, Single-Disease Health Associations. **Geographic Distribution:** The state of Delaware.

★ 122 ★   Cullen Foundation
PO Box 1600
Houston, TX 77251
Phone: (713)651-8600
Fax: (713)651-8663
Alan M. Stewart, Executive Director

Foundation Philosophy: The foundation supports a variety of educational and health institutions, social service programs, and arts groups. **Giving Priorities:** In fiscal 1994, the foundation reported that it gave approximately 56% of its contributions to educational institutions, including its highest grant of $6,000,000 to the University of Houston for an endowment fund. Health care, primarily hospitals, received 27%. The arts, including support for ballet and opera, received 10% and science received 3%. Social services, civic affairs, and religion received the remainder. **Typical Health-Related Recipients:** Cancer, Children's Health/Hospitals, Clinics/Medical Centers, Family Planning, Heart, Hospices, Hospitals, Medical Education, Medical Rehabilitation, Medical Research. **Geographic Distribution:** Texas, primarily Houston.

★ 123 ★   Daisy Marquis Jones Foundation
500 Granite Bldg.
130 E Main St.
Rochester, NY 14604
Phone: (716)263-3331
Roger L. Gardner, President and Trustee

Foundation Philosophy: The foundation encourages preventive programs and focuses on projects involving the disadvantaged. The foundation makes grants primarily to improve the quality of health care in Monroe and Yates counties. Other areas of support include senior citizens, youth, women, and improving the administration of justice. **Giving Priorities:** The foundation approved in 1993 approximately 38% of its total grants to support health care. About 28% of funds were awarded to children and youth groups. Public affairs received 11% of support; women's issues, 11%; community development, 6%; and justice received the remaining funds. **Typical Health-Related Recipients:** Adolescent Health Issues, AIDS/HIV, Alzheimers Disease, Children's Health/Hospitals, Clinics/Medical Centers, Domestic Violence, Emergency/Ambulance Services, Family Planning, Geriatric Health, Health Organizations, Hospitals, Medical Education, Medical Rehabilitation, Mental Health, Nursing Services, Nutrition, Outpatient Health Care, People with Disabilities. **Geographic Distribution:** Monroe and Yates counties, NY.

★ 124 ★   Dale J. Bellamah Foundation
PO Box 36600, Sta. D
Albuquerque, NM 87176
Phone: (505)293-1098
Frank A. Potenziani, Vice President and Director

Foundation Philosophy: The foundation's interests include higher education scholarships, business school programs in international business and law in Eastern Europe, research in diabetes, hospitals, the U.S. Olympic Committee, youth programs, and care of the mentally retarded. **Giving Priorities:** In 1993, educational institutions received 50% of the funding, including five grants totaling $351,400 to the University of Notre Dame for various programs and projects. Social service organizations received 26%, and health care received 24%. **Typical Health-Related Recipients:** Arthritis, Diabetes, Hospitals, Medical Education, People with Disabilities, Single-Disease Health Associations. **Geographic Distribution:** Focus on New Mexico.

★ 125 ★   Dan Murphy Foundation
PO Box 711267
Los Angeles, CA 90017
Phone: (213)623-3120
Daniel J. Donohue, President

Foundation Philosophy: The Dan Murphy Foundation's primary concerns are the charities and activities of the Roman Catholic church, in the Archdiocese of Los Angeles. Organizations of interest include religious orders, higher education, high schools and elementary schools, social services (especially religious welfare), and medical institutions. **Giving Priorities:** In 1993, The foundation awarded approximately 57% of its total contributions to Roman Catholic religious organizations. About 23% of funds went to educational institutions. Social services

received 15% of support; health care, 3%; and civic groups, 2%. The remainder went to the arts. **Typical Health-Related Recipients:** Cancer, Children's Health/Hospitals, Clinics/Medical Centers, Emergency/Ambulance Services, Family Planning, Hospices, Hospitals, Medical Research, Nursing Services, People with Disabilities, Substance Abuse. **Geographic Distribution:** Primarily California, with emphasis on the Los Angeles metropolitan area; limited support elsewhere.

★ 126 ★   Dane G. Hansen Foundation
PO Box 187
Logan, KS 67646
Phone: (913)689-4832
Fax: (913)689-4833
Dane G. Bales, Vice President and Trustee

Foundation Philosophy: Support is provided to a variety of organizations and programs in the arts, civic and public affairs, education, health, and social services. **Giving Priorities:** In 1993, the foundation gave approximately 28% of its contributions to civic and public affairs. Educational institutions received 23% of funding; health care, 22%; and social services, 18%. The arts received 8% of total giving and religious organizations were given the remaining funds. **Typical Health-Related Recipients:** Cancer, Children's Health/Hospitals, Clinics/Medical Centers, Emergency/Ambulance Services, Eyes/Blindness, Hospices, Hospitals, Long-Term Care, Medical Education, Medical Research, People with Disabilities, Single-Disease Health Associations. **Geographic Distribution:** Primarily Kansas, with emphasis on northwestern area of state.

★ 127 ★   Danforth Foundation
231 S Bemiston Ave., Ste. 1080
St. Louis, MO 63105
Phone: (314)862-6200
Bruce J. Anderson, President

Foundation Philosophy: The foundation welcomes proposals that identify and have the potential to eliminate the barriers to school success. Grant proposals are accepted in three focus areas. A Good Beginning for Every Child focuses support for projects that promote prenatal care, early childhood education, and parenting skills with emphasis on pregnant teens, parenting teens, and their children. School and Community Partnerships supports projects which create or improve collaboration among schools, families, and agencies that provide comprehensive services to students in need. Leadership for Schools focuses on projects which provide improved preparation and development opportunities for educational and lay leaders. **Giving Priorities:** In fiscal 1994, the foundation gave approximately 77% of its contributions to education. Interests included colleges and universities, professional development, and public education. Civic affairs received 13%. Social services received 7%, with the remaining 3% supporting health organizations. **Typical Health-Related Recipients:** Clinics/Medical Centers, Domestic Violence, Health Organizations, Mental Health, Research/Studies Institutes. **Geographic Distribution:** National, with some emphasis on St. Louis, MO.

★ 128 ★ **Daniel Foundation of Alabama**
820 Shades Creek Pkwy.
Ste. 1200
Birmingham, AL 35209
Phone: (205)879-0902
Fax: (205)879-0906
S. Garry Smith, Foundation Manager

Foundation Philosophy: The concerns of the Daniel Foundation encompass a wide variety of educational, social service, cultural, and community interests in the state of Alabama, particularly in Birmingham. **Giving Priorities:** In 1992, the foundation gave approximately 42% of contributions to education. Health organizations received 17%, while the arts also received 17%. Social services, principally those supporting youth organizations, received 13%. The remainder went to scientific organizations, 5%; religious causes, 4%; and civic concerns received the remainder. **Typical Health-Related Recipients:** Cancer, Clinics/Medical Centers, Eyes/Blindness, Health Organizations, Hospices, Medical Research, Mental Health, Research/Studies Institutes, Single-Disease Health Associations, Substance Abuse. **Geographic Distribution:** Primarily Alabama and other southeastern states.

★ 129 ★ **Danner Foundation**
2 International Dr., Ste. 510
Nashville, TN 37217
Phone: (615)367-9092
Mr. Francis Guess, Executive Director

Foundation Philosophy: "The Danner Foundation's mission is to foster the improvement of human welfare in education, health, civic, social and cultural areas." **Giving Priorities:** In 1993, the foundation gave approximately 46% of funding to education with the largest grant of $89,250 going to Franklin Road Academy in Nashville, TN. Civic affairs received 16%; the arts, 13%; social services, 10%; and religion, 8%. Health care received the remaining 7% of funds. **Typical Health-Related Recipients:** Arthritis, Children's Health/Hospitals, Clinics/Medical Centers, Medical Education, Single-Disease Health Associations, Substance Abuse, Transplant Networks/Donor Banks. **Geographic Distribution:** Primarily Tennessee.

★ 130 ★ **Davenport-Hatch Foundation**
c/o Fleet Investment Services
45 East Ave.
Rochester, NY 14638
Phone: (716)546-9822
Laura Weisenfluh, Contact

Foundation Philosophy: The foundation makes grants across the major categories of support. In the area of health care, interests include hospitals, single-disease health associations, and mental health. Social services support goes to community service organizations, children and families, and youth organizations. Educational support includes nursing scholarships and capital support to a variety of schools. Arts interests include history and theater, and the remainder goes to civic affairs and churches. **Giving Priorities:** In fiscal 1993, the foundation awarded 33% of its total contributions to educational institutions. About 25% of funds supported health care. Social services and religious organizations each received 13% of support. The arts received 11% and scientific organizations received 5%. **Typical Health-Related Recipients:** Cancer, Clinics/Medical Centers, Emergency/Ambulance Services, Family Planning, Health Organizations, Hospices, Hospitals, Kidney, Long-Term Care, Medical Education, Medical Rehabilitation, Medical Research, Multiple Sclerosis, Nursing Services, People with Disabilities, Single-Disease Health Associations. **Geographic Distribution:** Focus on the Rochester, NY, area.

★ 131 ★ **David M. Whitney Fund**
150 W Jefferson, Ste. 2500
Detroit, MI 48226
Phone: (313)963-6420
Peter P. Thurber, President and Treasurer

Foundation Philosophy: The David M. Whitney Fund makes most of its grants in the areas of social services and the arts. The fund also supports higher education and private secondary schools. Many minor grants are given to other recipient areas. **Giving Priorities:** In 1993, the fund supported social services with 29% of its giving. Major contributions were made to Crossroads of Michigan, Planned Parenthood League, and other youth organizations. The arts received 27% of the giving. Education accounted for 20% of the total funding, including gifts to universities, colleges, and secondary schools. The remainder of the funding went to civic affairs, 13%; health, 6%; religious causes, 3%; environment, 2%. **Typical Health-Related Recipients:** Children's Health/Hospitals, Emergency/Ambulance Services, Family Planning, Hospitals, Single-Disease Health Associations. **Geographic Distribution:** Focus on southeastern Michigan.

★ 132 ★ **David W. and Sadie Klau Foundation**
c/o Lipsky, Goodkin & Company
120 W 45th St.
New York, NY 10036
Phone: (212)840-6444
Sadie K. Klau, President

Foundation Philosophy: The foundation primarily supports educational institutions, health concerns, religious groups, and social services, with an overall emphasis on Jewish organizations. Secondary interests include the arts and civic affairs. **Giving Priorities:** In 1993, the foundation gave approximately 40% of its total contributions to educational institutions. Religious organizations received about 27% of funding, and health concerns received 19%. Social services received 13%; and civic affairs and environmental causes received the remaining funds. **Typical Health-Related Recipients:** Cancer, Children's Health/Hospitals, Clinics/Medical Centers, Emergency/Ambulance Services, Family Planning, Geriatric Health, Hospitals, Medical Research, People with Disabilities, Single-Disease Health Associations, Transplant Networks/Donor Banks. **Geographic Distribution:** Northeastern United States, with an emphasis on New York, NY.

★ 133 ★ **Davidson Family Charitable Foundation**
310 W Texas, Ste. 709
Midland, TX 79701
Phone: (915)687-0995
Steve Davidson, Vice Chairman

Foundation Philosophy: The foundation favors health and human service causes in the state of Texas. Limited funding has been directed toward civic issues, education, and the arts. The foundation also maintains a minor scholarship program at school financial offices. **Giving Priorities:** In fiscal 1993, the foundation gave approximately 51% of total contributions to social services. Educational institutions received about 19% of funding, including the foundation's highest grant of $50,000 to the Bynum School Development Disabilities Center. Health concerns received about 13% of contributions; the arts, 11%; religion, 4%; and civic concerns, 2%. **Typical Health-Related Recipients:** Cancer, Diabetes, Eyes/Blindness, Hospices, Hospitals, People with Disabilities, Sexual Abuse, Single-Disease Health Associations, Substance Abuse. **Geographic Distribution:** Primarily west Texas.

★ 134 ★ **Del E. Webb Foundation**
2023 W Wickenburg Way
PO Box 20519
Wickenburg, AZ 85358
Phone: (602)684-7223
Robert H. Johnson, President and Director

Foundation Philosophy: "The foundation primarily applies its resources to preserve and enrich the benefits to be derived by residents of Arizona, Nevada, and California from improved and expanded medical services and medical research." Traditional areas of support include health care, health facilities, medical education, and medical research. **Giving Priorities:** In 1993, the foundation awarded 62% of its total contributions to health care. About 36% of funds went to educational institutions. The remaining funds went to social services. **Typical Health-Related Recipients:** Cancer, Children's Health/Hospitals, Clinics/Medical Centers, Diabetes, Health Organizations, Hospitals, Medical Education, Medical Research, Medical Training, People with Disabilities, Research/Studies Institutes, Single-Disease Health Associations. **Geographic Distribution:** Arizona, Nevada, and California.

★ 135 ★ **Dellora A. and Lester J. Norris Foundation**
PO Box 1081
St. Charles, IL 60174
Phone: (708)584-2500
Eugene W. Butler, Treasurer

Foundation Philosophy: The foundation gives primarily to higher and secondary education; health institutions, especially hospitals; and social service organizations, where the emphasis is on child welfare, family services, and youth organizations. The foundation also provides funding to the arts, civic organizations, and churches. Funding is generally limited to organizations started by or supported by Mr. and Mrs. Norris during their lifetimes. **Giving Priorities:** In 1992, precollege education and educational programs received approximately 47% of funding. Health care received 21% with support for single-disease associations and medical foundations. The arts were awarded 14% of giving and civic affairs received 11%. The remaining funds were given to social service organizations (6%) and a chapel (1%). **Typical Health-Related Recipients:** AIDS/HIV, Cancer, Children's Health/Hospitals, Diabetes, Health Funds, Health Organizations, Heart, Hospices, Hospitals, Medical Rehabilitation, Medical Research, People with Disabilities, Respiratory, Single-Disease Health Associations. **Geographic Distribution:** National, with some emphasis on Illinois, Colorado, and Florida.

★ 136 ★ **Dickson Foundation**
2000 Two First Union Center
Charlotte, NC 28282
Phone: (704)372-5404
Fax: (704)372-6409
Colleen S. Colbert, Secretary-Treasurer

Foundation Philosophy: The Dickson Foundation makes most of its grants in the areas of education, civic affairs, and the arts, with education being the major priority. Other recipient areas are supported on a limted basis. **Giving Priorities:** In 1994, approximately 54% of funding went to educational institutions. Civic affairs, exclusively in North Carolina, received 17%. The arts received 10%; social service organizations, 9%; health care services, 8%; and religious organizations, 3%. **Typical Health-Related Recipients:** Hospices, Hospitals, Medical Education, Medical Research, Single-Disease Health Associations. **Geographic Distribution:** Focus on Charlotte, NC, South Carolina, and Virginia.

★ 137 ★ **Dr. Scholl Foundation**
11 S La Salle St., Ste. 2100
Chicago, IL 60603
Phone: (312)782-5210
Pamela Scholl Mahaffee, President

Foundation Philosophy: The foundation supports private education at all levels including elementary, secondary, and post-secondary schools; colleges and universities; and medical education. Support is also available for general charitable programs including grants to hospitals, programs for senior citizens, children, and the developmentally disabled. The foundation also shows an interest in civic, cultural, religious, and social welfare projects. **Giving Priorities:** In 1992, approximately 42% of giving went to education, with major support to Dr. William M. Scholl College, Chicago, IL, and Loyola University, Chicago, IL. International affairs received 15% of donations. Social services received about 13% of funding, especially in support of disabled youth programs and family services. Health care received 12% of grants; the arts, 9%; civic concerns, 8%; and science, 1%. **Typical Health-Related Recipients:** Cancer, Eyes/Blindness, Health Organizations, Heart, Hospitals, Medical Education, Medical Research, People with Disabilities, Research/Studies Institutes, Single-Disease Health Associations. **Geographic Distribution:** No geographic restrictions; an emphasis on Illinois.

★ 138 ★ **Dr. W.C. Swanson Family Foundation**
1104 Country Hills
Suite 411
Ogden, UT 84401
Phone: (801)399-5837
Lew Costley, Trustee and Manager

Foundation Philosophy: The majority of donations given by the Dr. W. C. Swanson Family Foundation are in the areas of education, civic and public affairs, and social services, with most of the grants falling in the $5,000 to $30,000 range. **Giving Priorities:** In 1993, the foundation gave 28% of its donations in support of education, including its largest grant of $195,000 to the Ogden City School. Civic and public affairs received 25% of contributions, including a $100,000 grant to the Ogden City Downtown Civic Center, for building expenses. Social services received 22% of donations, while arts and humanities received 20%. Support for health care programs was 5%. **Typical Health-Related Recipients:** Cancer, Children's Health/Hospitals, Domestic Violence, Hospices, Hospitals, People with Disabilities. **Geographic Distribution:** Giving primarily in Utah, with primary emphasis on Weber County, then northern Utah.

★ 139 ★ **Dodge Jones Foundation**
PO Box 176
Abilene, TX 79604
Phone: (915)673-6429
Fax: (915)673-2028
Lawrence Gill, Grants Administrator

Foundation Philosophy: The foundation focuses its activity in the areas of education, community services, health, civic affairs, historic preservation, and youth organizations. **Giving Priorities:** In 1992, the foundation contributed approximately 39% of giving to social services, including the highest grant of $420,022 to the Ben Richey Boys Ranch in Abilene, TX. Educational institutions received 26% of funding with support for school programs, renovation, and building funds. Health services received 16% and civic affairs were given about 13% of funding. The arts received 4% of total giving and religious organizations and a science group received the remaining funds. **Typical Health-Related Recipients:** AIDS/HIV, Alzheimers Disease, Clinics/Medical Centers, Emergency/Ambulance Services, Health Organizations, Hospices, Hospitals, Medical Education, Medical Rehabilitation, People with Disabilities. **Geographic Distribution:** Principally Texas.

★ 140 ★ **Dolan Family Foundation**
c/o William A. Frewin, Jr.
One Media Crossways
Woodbury, NY 11797
Phone: (516)496-1136
Marianne Dolan Weber, President

Foundation Philosophy: The foundation generally supports educational institutions and health and medical research organizations. **Giving Priorities:** In fiscal 1991, the foundation directed approximately 71% of its giving to educational causes with substantial contributions to Cold Spring Harbor Laboratory. Health concerns received 27% of funding, primarily supporting the National Center for Disabilities. Reli-

gious causes and social services received about 1% each. **Typical Health-Related Recipients:** Hospitals, Medical Research, People with Disabilities. **Geographic Distribution:** No geographic restrictions, with emphasis on New York.

★ 141 ★ **Don and Sybil Harrington Foundation**
801 S Fillmore, Ste. 700
Amarillo, TX 79101
Phone: (806)373-8353
Fax: (806)373-3656
Jim Allison, President and Executive Director

Foundation Philosophy: The foundation has a wide range of funding interests including health, human services, and education in the Panhandle area of Texas. **Giving Priorities:** In 1992, the foundation reported that it gave approximately 49% of its contributions to support health care organizations, including a grant of $1,685,293 to the Harrrington Cancer Center. Social services received 20%. Education received 11%. The remaining contributions of the foundation supported the arts and humanites with 7%, science and religion each received 6% of funds, and civic affairs less than 1%. **Typical Health-Related Recipients:** Arthritis, Cancer, Children's Health/Hospitals, Clinics/Medical Centers, Domestic Violence, Emergency/Ambulance Services, Eyes/Blindness, Geriatric Health, Health Organizations, Hospices, Hospitals, Medical Education, Medical Rehabilitation, Medical Research, People with Disabilities. **Geographic Distribution:** The northernmost 26 counties of the Texas Panhandle.

★ 142 ★ **Donald E. and Delia B. Baxter Foundation**
PO Box 449
Rancho Santa Fe, CA 92067
Phone: (619)759-9181
Fax: (619)759-0203
Donald B. Haake, President

Foundation Philosophy: The foundation provides major support to university-related medical research on the West Coast. **Giving Priorities:** In 1994, the foundation gave 100% of its contributions to schools of medicine. Stanford University School of Medicine received the highest grant, in the amount of $349,500, which went to support research programs. **Typical Health-Related Recipients:** Medical Research. **Geographic Distribution:** Focus on California.

★ 143 ★ **Donald W. Reynolds Foundation**
7130 S Lewis Ave.
Ste. 900
Tulsa, OK 74136
Phone: (918)496-0033
Fax: (918)496-1777
Donald E. Pray, Executive Director

Foundation Philosophy: "The trustees have indicated a preference for capital investment in the construction of new buildings and facilities, the cost of which will be no less than five million dollars nor more than fifteen million dollars. The trustees will consider grant proposals made in any of the following areas of interest: arts and culture, civic and public affairs, education, health, and human services. Generally, grants will not be made to religious institutions, annual fundraising appeals, program support, or for elementary and secondary education programs." **Giving Priorities:** In fiscal 1993, the foundation gave approximately 38% of its total contributions to social services organizations. About 37% of donations were given in support of education. Civic and public affairs organizations received 13% of support, while 7% went to the arts. The remaining 5% went to support health care. **Typical Health-Related Recipients:** Emergency/Ambulance Services, Health Funds, Health Organizations, Hospitals, Single-Disease Health Associations, Substance Abuse. **Geographic Distribution:** National.

★ 144 ★ Dora Roberts Foundation

PO Box 2050
Ft. Worth, TX 76113
Phone: (817)884-4442
Rick Piersall, Vice President

Foundation Philosophy: The Dora Roberts Foundation makes grants across the major categories of support. Most of the giving goes to social services. Health support favors rehabilitation, hospitals, and medical centers. Educational interests include junior colleges, high schools, and foundations for education. **Giving Priorities:** In fiscal 1993, the foundation gave approximately 25% of funds to social services. Civic concerns received about 18% of funding. Education received 17% of total contributions; the arts, 15%; religion, 13%; and health, 12%. **Typical Health-Related Recipients:** Hospices, Hospitals, Medical Education, Medical Rehabilitation, Sexual Abuse. **Geographic Distribution:** Limited to Texas, with a focus on Big Spring.

★ 145 ★ Dorothy U. Dalton Foundation

c/o Arcadia Bank and Trust Company
251 E Michigan Ave.
Kalamazoo, MI 49007
Phone: (616)349-0900
Ronald N. Kilgore, Secretary-Treasurer

Foundation Philosophy: The Dorothy U. Dalton Foundation primarily supports social service organizations. Secondary interests include museums, civic centers, and health clinics in Kalamazoo, MI. **Giving Priorities:** In 1993, the foundation gave approximately 31% of its total contributions to social service programs, with major funding going to United Way, YMCA, and YWCA. Health care received 27% of the contributions, including the largest grant, $88,000 to aid a paitient assistance fund at the Borgess Medical Center in Kalamazoo. About 19% of the donations went to the arts, with much of the support going to the performing arts. Civic affairs received 10% of funds, and education received 7%. Religious institutions, primarily ministries and missions, received 5%, while the remaining 1% supported scientfic interests. **Typical Health-Related Recipients:** AIDS/HIV, Clinics/Medical Centers, Domestic Violence, Emergency/Ambulance Services, Hospitals, Mental Health, Nursing Services, People with Disabilities, Substance Abuse. **Geographic Distribution:** Primarily Kalamazoo County, MI.

★ 146 ★ Dover Foundation

PO Box 208
Shelby, NC 28151
Phone: (704)487-8890
Fax: (704)482-6818
Hoyt Q. Bailey, President

Foundation Philosophy: The Dover Foundation is primarily interested in supporting higher education in North Carolina. Most of the support is for scholarships. Secondary interests include religious organizations, the environment, medical foundations and hospitals, human services, arts and humanities, and youth organizations. **Giving Priorities:** In fiscal 1994, educational institutions received 45% of giving. Religious organizations received approximately 20% of total contributions. Health care received 15% of funds. Other miscellaneous interests, including social services, civic affairs, the arts, and the environment received 20% of total giving. **Typical Health-Related Recipients:** Family Planning, Health Funds, Hospices, Mental Health. **Geographic Distribution:** Almost exclusively North Carolina.

★ 147 ★ Duke Endowment

100 N Tryon St., Ste. 3500
Charlotte, NC 28202-4012
Phone: (704)376-0291
Fax: (704)376-9336
Jere W. Witherspoon, Executive Director

Foundation Philosophy: Funds are directed to Duke University, Davidson College, Furman University, and Johnson C. Smith University; nonprofit hospitals for operations programs and for improving and expanding facilities; nonprofit child care institutions; retired ministers; widows and dependent children of ministers; and rural United Methodist Churches in North Carolina. The endowment currently addresses health issues that include health care financing, small and rural hospitals, access and primary care, community affiliations, children's health, and care of the indigent. **Giving Priorities:** In 1994, the endowment reported that its primary beneficiary was health care, particularly hospitals and medical research, which received approximately 82% of the total contributions. Social service organizations received about 16%. Duke University Divinity School in Durham, NC, and various religious interests received the remaining funds. **Typical Health-Related Recipients:** Adolescent Health Issues, AIDS/HIV, Alzheimers Disease, Cancer, Children's Health/Hospitals, Clinics/Medical Centers, Diabetes, Emergency/Ambulance Services, Family Planning, Geriatric Health, Health Organizations, Health Policy/Cost Containment, Heart, Home-Care Services, Hospices, Hospitals, Hospitals (University Affiliated), Long-Term Care, Medical Rehabilitation, Medical Research, Nursing Services, Nutrition, Outpatient Health Care, People with Disabilities, Prenatal Health Issues, Preventive Medicine/Wellness Organizations, Respiratory. **Geographic Distribution:** North Carolina and South Carolina.

★ 148 ★ Dunspaugh-Dalton Foundation

9040 Sunset Dr., Ste. 30
Miami, FL 33173
Phone: (305)596-6951
Fax: (305)595-3294
William A. Lane, Jr., President and Trustee

Foundation Philosophy: The primary focus of the foundation's grant making is education. Other areas of interest include social services, health, and the arts. **Giving Priorities:** In 1991, the foundation reported that it gave 56% of its contributions to education, including support for private education and colleges, which received the foundation's highest grant of $175,000 for Duke University. Social services received 22%. Interests included youth organizations. The arts received 11%, and health care received 5%. Civic affairs received 5%; and religion, 1%. **Typical Health-Related Recipients:** Family Planning, Health Organizations, Hospices, Hospitals, Medical Education, People with Disabilities. **Geographic Distribution:** National; emphasis on Dade County, FL; California; and North Carolina.

★ 149 ★ Dyson Foundation

740 Union St.
Schenectady, NY 12305
Phone: (518)377-1576
Diana M. Gurieva, Executive Director

Foundation Philosophy: The Dyson Foundation supports a wide variety of organizations in the arts, higher education, health care, and social services; however its current priority for new grant applications revolves around organizations and projects that make significant differences in the lives of poor and disadvantaged children. The foundation also makes grants to social services, health, and arts-related organizations. **Giving Priorities:** In 1993, the foundation gave approximately 47% of funding to health concerns, including the foundation's highest grant of $650,000 to the New York Hospital Cornell Medical Center. Four educational institutions in New York received about 27% of total contributions. The arts received about 19% of total contributions; the environment, 3%; social services, 3%; and the remainder went to religious and civic concerns. **Typical Health-Related Recipients:** AIDS/HIV, Cancer, Children's Health/Hospitals, Family Planning, Health Funds, Health Organizations, Hospitals, Medical Research, People with Disabilities. **Geographic Distribution:** Primarily to national organizations, also to organizations in Dutchess County, NY.

★ 150 ★ E. L. Wiegand Foundation

Wiegand Center
165 W Liberty St.
Reno, NV 89501
Phone: (702)333-0310
Fax: (702)333-0314
Kristen A. Avansino, President and Executive Director

Foundation Philosophy: The foundation funds "programs and projects...at educational institutions in the academic areas of science, business, fine arts, law and medicine; and...at health and medical research institutions in the areas of heart, eye, and cancer surgery, treatment, and research, with priority given to programs and projects that benefit children." To a lesser degree, the foundation considers applications from civic and community affairs organizations, public affairs institutions, and cultural institutions. The foundation shows a strong preference for organizations affiliated with the Roman Catholic Church. **Giving Priorities:** In fiscal 1993, the foundation gave 57% of its contributions to education. Social services received 16%; health care, 10%; the arts, 9%; civic affairs, 7%; and religion, 1%. **Typical Health-Related Recipients:** Cancer, Children's Health/Hospitals, Clinics/Medical Centers, Diabetes, Heart, Hospitals, Long-Term Care, Medical Education, Medical Research. **Geographic Distribution:** Nevada, California, Oregon, Idaho, Utah, Arizona, District of Columbia, and New York City.

★ 151 ★ E. M. Lynn Foundation
2501 N Military Trail
Boca Raton, FL 33431
Phone: (407)994-1900
Christine Lynn, Executive Director

Foundation Philosophy: The foundation generally supports a variety of charitable organizations; however, recent giving has been devoted to the College of Boca Raton and Lynn University. **Giving Priorities:** In fiscal 1993, the foundation gave approximately 48% of funding to educational institutions. Health groups received about 32% of total contributions; religious programs, 9%; the arts and humanities, 5%; and social services, 4%. Environmental groups, civic concerns, and international affairs each received 1% of total funding. **Typical Health-Related Recipients:** Arthritis, Cancer, Clinics/Medical Centers, Diabetes, Emergency/Ambulance Services, Family Planning, Heart, Hospices, Hospitals, Hospitals (University Affiliated), Kidney, Medical Research, People with Disabilities, Research/Studies Institutes, Respiratory, Single-Disease Health Associations, Substance Abuse. **Geographic Distribution:** Focus on southern Florida.

★ 152 ★ Earl C. Sams Foundation
101 N Shoreline Dr., Ste. 602
Corpus Christi, TX 78401
Phone: (512)888-6485
Dorothy P. Tate, President

Foundation Philosophy: The Earl C. Sams Foundation makes most of its grants to civic affairs organizations, focusing primarily on the needs of south Texas. The foundation's primary interests are zoos and aquariums. Social services are a secondary interest, with an emphasis on homes. Other recipient areas are supported on a limited basis. **Giving Priorities:** In 1993, the foundation awarded approximately 44% of its total contributions to civic affairs. Social services received 23%; the arts, 11%; health care, 10%; and religion, 8%. Scientific interests, education, and environmental causes received the remaining funds. **Typical Health-Related Recipients:** Arthritis, Cancer, Children's Health/Hospitals, Emergency/Ambulance Services, Heart, Medical Research, Mental Health, People with Disabilities, Substance Abuse. **Geographic Distribution:** Focus on south Texas.

★ 153 ★ Eden Hall Foundation
600 Grant, Ste. 3232
Pittsburgh, PA 15219
Phone: (412)642-6697
Edward M. Pierson, General Manager

Foundation Philosophy: The foundation has four primary areas of interest: "social welfare and the improvement of conditions of the poor and needy; educational programs dedicated to the advancement and dissemination of useful knowledge, and support and maintenance of private colleges, universities, and other educational institutions; the advancement of better health through support and maintenance of hospitals or organizations whose primary purpose is the prevention and alleviation of sickness and disease." **Giving Priorities:** In 1993, the foundation awarded approximately 54% of its total contributions in support of education. Social service organizations received about 15% of funds, while health care organizations received about 13%. Civic affairs organizations received 8% of support, the arts received 6%, and religious interests received 4%. **Typical Health-Related Recipients:** Arthritis, Cancer, Children's Health/Hospitals, Clinics/Medical Centers, Domestic Violence, Emergency/Ambulance Services, Health Funds, Health Organizations, Hospitals, Medical Education, Medical Rehabilitation, Mental Health, Nursing Services, People with Disabilities, Single-Disease Health Associations, Substance Abuse. **Geographic Distribution:** Primarily western Pennsylvania.

★ 154 ★ Edna McConnell Clark Foundation
250 Park Ave., Rm. 900
New York, NY 10177-0026
Phone: (212)551-9100
Fax: (212)986-4558
Carol B. Einiger, Vice President & Chief Financial Officer

Foundation Philosophy: The trustees concentrate on five areas of funding: children, justice, disadvantaged youth, tropical disease research, and homeless families. The foundation also maintains a small special projects category to respond to important initiatives that fall outside the five program areas. The Program For Tropical Disease Research seeks to improve health in the developing world by advancing the means to control schistosomiasis (snail fever), as well as the two major infectious causes of blindness, onchocerciasis and trachoma. The current emphasis of the program is on the development of a vaccine for each disease, but grants also support operational research to strengthen national programs to control schistosomiasis and trachoma. **Giving Priorities:** In fiscal 1993, the foundation contributed $20,000,504 in grants. Approximately 20% of the total was contributed to each of the four following program area: Children, Justice, Tropical Disease Research, and Disadvantaged Youth. The Program for Homeless Families received approximately 15%. The foundation also contributed appoximately 3% of funding to Special Projects. The foundation used the remaining 2% for publications and public education focused on the issues of its five program areas. **Typical Health-Related Recipients:** Domestic Violence, Eyes/Blindness, Hospitals, Medical Research, Nursing Services. **Geographic Distribution:** No geographic restrictions on giving.

★ 155 ★ Educational Foundation of America
35 Church Ln.
Westport, CT 06880
Phone: (203)226-6498
Fax: (203)227-0424
Diane M. Allison, Executive Director

Foundation Philosophy: In general, the foundation makes grants for specific projects in the areas of population issues, the arts, education, the environment, Native American issues, and other interests including medicine and peace. Other civic concerns focus on problems of energy use, conservation, and nonprofit management. **Giving Priorities:** In 1993, the foundation reported that environmental concerns received 39% of total giving. Population affairs received 20% of funding, and educational programs and schools received 15%. Native American issues were awarded 12% of giving and the arts and humanities received 10% of contributions. The remaining funds were given to medicine and peace efforts. **Typical Health-Related Recipients:** Family Planning, Geriatric Health, Medical Education, Medical Research, Substance Abuse. **Geographic Distribution:** National.

★ 156 ★ Edward C. Johnson Fund
82 Devonshire St., S3
Boston, MA 02109
Phone: (617)563-6806
Anne-Marie Soulliere, Foundation Director

Foundation Philosophy: The Edward C. Johnson Fund has made grants to educational institutions, museums, historic preservation and other cultural organizations, for the protection and improvement of the environment, and to community organizations. Purposes include capital campaigns, program support, and special projects. **Giving Priorities:** In 1993, the foundation gave approximately 46% of its total contributions to the arts. Educational institutions received about 27%; health concerns, 19%; and civic affairs, 6%. Environmental causes and social services received the remaining funds. **Typical Health-Related Recipients:** Alzheimers Disease, Cancer, Emergency/Ambulance Services, Eyes/Blindness, Hospitals, Medical Research, Preventive Medicine/Wellness Organizations. **Geographic Distribution:** Focus on New England.

★ 157 ★ Edward D. and Anna Mitchell Family Foundation
6310 San Vicente Blvd, Ste. 500
Los Angeles, CA 90048
Phone: (213)935-6222
Joseph N. Mitchell, President

Foundation Philosophy: The foundation's primary interest is Jewish religious organizations and education. Nearly all support is devoted to the Jewish faith, either directly or indirectly. Other interests include foreign policy, health relief, and career development. **Giving Priorities:** In 1993, the foundation supported education with approximately 45% of its donated funds. Religious organizations received about 34% of the contributions. Civic affairs received 8%, health care received 7%, and social services received 4%. About 2% of giving went to international affairs, while the remaining 1% supported the arts. **Typical Health-Related Recipients:**

AIDS/HIV, Children's Health/Hospitals, Clinics/Medical Centers, Diabetes, Emergency/Ambulance Services, Family Planning, Health Organizations, Heart, Hospitals, Long-Term Care, Medical Research, Medical Training, Single-Disease Health Associations. **Geographic Distribution:** Focus on New York, NY, and Los Angeles, CA.

★ 158 ★ Edward G. Schlieder Educational Foundation
313 Carondlet St.
New Orleans, LA 70130
Phone: (504)533-5727
Donald J. Nalty, President

Foundation Philosophy: The foundation primarily supports higher education in Louisiana. **Giving Priorities:** In 1993, the foundation gave approximately 67% of funding to educational institutions, primarily in New Orleans. Health concerns received about 29% of grants, including a the foundation's highest grant of $250,000 to Tulane University to establish a Chair in Medical Oncology. Religious institutions received approximately 4% of total contributions. **Typical Health-Related Recipients:** Cancer, Medical Education, Medical Research. **Geographic Distribution:** Limited to educational institutions in Louisiana.

★ 159 ★ Edward Mallinckrodt, Jr. Foundation
One N Jefferson
St. Louis, MO 63103
Phone: (314)289-3000
Fax: (314)289-4707
Oliver M. Langenberg, President and Treasurer

Foundation Philosophy: The foundation supports medical research at universities or research hospitals. **Giving Priorities:** In fiscal 1993, the foundation gave 100% of its total contributions to health care and research in major medical universities. The highest grant of $120,000 was awarded to Duke University in Durham, NC, for its scholar program. **Typical Health-Related Recipients:** Cancer, Emergency/Ambulance Services, Medical Research, Speech & Hearing. **Geographic Distribution:** National.

★ 160 ★ Edward S. Moore Foundation
47 Arch St.
Greenwich, CT 06830
Phone: (203)629-4591
John W. Cross III, President

Foundation Philosophy: The foundation distributes donations to a variety of organizations primarily in New York and Connecticut. The foundation typically supports educational institutions, the arts, hospitals and health organizations, and social services, particularly those organizations concerned with the welfare of young people. **Giving Priorities:** In 1992, the foundation gave approximately 30% of its contributions to the arts. Social services received 23%, primarily supporting child welfare and youth organizations. Health organizations received 20%, while educational institutions received 15%. The remainder went to religious causes, 7%, civic concerns, 3%, and a scientific institute, 2%. **Typical Health-Related Recipi-**

ents: Health Organizations, Hospitals, Medical Education, Medical Research, Mental Health, People with Disabilities. **Geographic Distribution:** Focus on New York and Connecticut.

★ 161 ★ Edyth Bush Charitable Foundation
199 E Welbourne Ave.
PO Box 1967
Winter Park, FL 32790
Phone: (407)647-4322
Fax: (407)647-7716
David A. Odahowski, President

Foundation Philosophy: The foundation's original goal was to support charitable, religious, educational, and literary purposes; with special consideration to organizations that help underprivileged or needy people. The foundation adheres to the intent of Edyth Bush in its giving patterns, supporting organizations in the areas of education, human services, health, and the arts. **Giving Priorities:** In fiscal 1994, the foundation gave 31% of its contributions to social services, including $250,000 grant to Health Care for the Homeless in Orlando, FL. Science received 27% of the support. Religious affairs received 14% of funding, while education received 13%. Health care programs received 11% of contributions. Civic affairs received 3% of the donations, with the remaining 1% supporting the arts. **Typical Health-Related Recipients:** Alzheimers Disease, Clinics/Medical Centers, Eyes/Blindness, Health Organizations, Hospitals, Nursing Services, People with Disabilities. **Geographic Distribution:** Central Florida (100 mile radius from Winter Park) with special emphasis on organizations from Orange, Seminole, Lake, and Osceola counties; limited giving in Arizona and California at the interest of one or more board members.

★ 162 ★ Effie and Wofford Cain Foundation
4131 Spicewood Springs Rd., Ste. A-1
Austin, TX 78759
Phone: (512)346-7490
Fax: (512)346-7491
Harvey L. Walker, Exec. Dir., Sec., and Treas.

Foundation Philosophy: The foundation traditionally focuses its support on educational institutions and programs, social service organizations, medical institutions, and medical research programs. The foundation is now placing more emphasis on medical research and less on higher education. **Giving Priorities:** In fiscal 1993, the foundation gave approximately 39% of total contributions to educational institutions. Health groups received about 33% of funding, including the foundation's highest grant of $300,000 to the University of Texas Southwestern Medical Center. Social services received about 10% of giving; religious institutions, 10%; the arts and humanities, 5%; environmental concerns, 2%; and civic concerns, 1%. **Typical Health-Related Recipients:** Alzheimers Disease, Arthritis, Cancer, Children's Health/Hospitals, Clinics/Medical Centers, Domestic Violence, Emergency/Ambulance Services, Heart, Hospitals, Medical Education, Medical Research, Medical Training, People with Disabilities, Single-Disease Health Associations, Substance Abuse. **Geographic Distribution:** Texas.

★ 163 ★ El Pomar Foundation
10 Lake Circle
Colorado Springs, CO 80906
Phone: (719)633-7733
Fax: (719)577-5702
William J. Hybl, Chairman and Chief Executive Officer

Foundation Philosophy: In general, the foundation supports educational and health institutions; civic, community, and social services; and the arts in Colorado. The foundation places greater emphasis on civic, community, and emergency needs of the poor. In the future, the foundation plans to concentrate on programs designed to promote excellence in nonprofit organizations. **Giving Priorities:** In 1992, the foundation reported that it gave approximately 38% of its contributions to education, while health concerns received 23%. Civic and public affairs received 18%; social services, 10%; and the arts, 8%. The remaining 3% supported other miscellaneous causes. **Typical Health-Related Recipients:** Alzheimers Disease, Arthritis, Cancer, Clinics/Medical Centers, Domestic Violence, Emergency/Ambulance Services, Health Organizations, Hospitals, Medical Rehabilitation, Medical Research, Mental Health, Nursing Services, People with Disabilities, Substance Abuse. **Geographic Distribution:** Colorado only.

★ 164 ★ Elis Olsson Memorial Foundation
PO Box 311
West Point, VA 23181
Phone: (804)843-5354

Foundation Philosophy: The foundation makes most of its grants to educational institutions. Interests include private high schools, seminaries, universities, medical colleges, and literacy institutes. Secondary interests include family services, historical preservation, and various other charitable organizations. **Giving Priorities:** In 1993, the foundation gave 50% of total contributions to education. Religious interests received 20%. The arts and humanities received approximately 14% of gifts; health concerns, 7%; and social service institutions, 5%. The remaining funds supported environmental and civic concerns and science institutions. **Typical Health-Related Recipients:** Cancer, Children's Health/Hospitals, Clinics/Medical Centers, Emergency/Ambulance Services, Health Organizations, Hospitals, Long-Term Care, Medical Education, Medical Rehabilitation, Medical Research, People with Disabilities, Respiratory, Single-Disease Health Associations. **Geographic Distribution:** Focus on Virginia.

★ 165 ★ Elisabeth Severance Prentiss Foundation
c/o National City Bank
PO Box 5756
Cleveland, OH 44101
Phone: (216)575-2761
Fax: (216)575-3008
Mr. Richard Mack, Secretary

Foundation Philosophy: "The Elisabeth Severance Prentiss Foundation is a charitable trust dedicated to the support and advancement of health care services in the greater Cleveland community. The foundation awards monetary grants to qualifying institutions and agencies for medical research and programs designed to improve the method of health care services." The trust agreement's five objectives are to promote medical and surgical research; to promote public health; to aid hospitals and health institutions in Cuyahoga County, OH, with support for capital and operating expenses; to improve methods of hospital administration; and to promote equitable health care delivery and cost-containment programs. **Giving Priorities:** In 1993, approximately 98% of funding was awarded to health concerns, primarily to hospitals and other health care delivery organizations, and to medical training and research. The remaining funds supported social services, education institutions, and civic affairs. **Typical Health-Related Recipients:** AIDS/HIV, Alzheimers Disease, Cancer, Children's Health/Hospitals, Clinics/ Medical Centers, Family Planning, Health Organizations, Health Policy/Cost Containment, Heart, Hospices, Hospitals, Medical Education, Medical Research, Medical Training, Mental Health, Nursing Services, Outpatient Health Care, People with Disabilities, Research/ Studies Institutes, Single-Disease Health Associations, Substance Abuse, Transplant Networks/Donor Banks. **Geographic Distribution:** Greater Cleveland, OH, area.

★ 166 ★ **Ellen Browning Scripps Foundation**
Union Bank, Trust Dept.
PO Box 109
San Diego, CA 92112
Phone: (619)230-3676
E. Douglas Dawson, Vice President and Manager

Foundation Philosophy: The Ellen Browning Scripps Foundation makes most of its grants in the areas of education, the arts, health, and civic affairs. Health interests include research, medical centers, and hospitals. The foundation also supports a variety of social service interests. **Giving Priorities:** In fiscal 1994, the foundation gave 33% of its funding to education, mainly to support colleges and private schools. Health care received 20% of the contributions, including the highest grant of $54,000 to Scripps Clinic and Research Foundation. The arts and civic affairs also received 20% of the funding each. Arts interests included historic preservation, museums, and libraries. Civic affairs funding went to zoos and women's affairs. Social services received 7% of the funding, with emphasis on youth organizations and community centers. **Typical Health-Related Recipients:** Hospices, Hospitals, Medical Research. **Geographic Distribution:** Focus on San Diego County, CA.

★ 167 ★ **Ellison Foundation**
c/o David L. Babson Co.
One Memorial Dr.
Cambridge, MA 02142-1300
Phone: (617)225-3830
Elton F. Drew, Trustee

Foundation Philosophy: The foundation was formed for the purposes of disbursing funds solely and exclusively for religious, charitable, scientific, literary, or educational purposes, and for the prevention of cruelty to children or ani-

mals. **Giving Priorities:** In 1993, the foundation awarded approximately 78% of total contributions to health care, including its highest grant of $1,475,000 for the Massachusetts General Hospital in Boston, MA. Civic affairs received about 8%; the arts, 4%; education, 4%; and environmental interests, 3%. Social services (2%) and religion (1%) received the remaining funds. **Typical Health-Related Recipients:** Cancer, Children's Health/Hospitals, Clinics/Medical Centers, Health Organizations, Hospitals, Medical Rehabilitation, Nursing Services, Speech & Hearing. **Geographic Distribution:** Primarily Massachusetts.

★ 168 ★ **Ellwood Foundation**
PO Box 52482
Houston, TX 77052
Phone: (713)652-0613
H. Wayne Hightower, Trustee

Foundation Philosophy: The Ellwood Foundation primarily makes grants in the areas of health services and social services. Health support goes to hospitals, health foundations, single-disease associations, and health organizations. In social services, funding favors homes, child welfare, the disabled, and youth centers. Grants are made to other recipient areas on a limted basis. **Giving Priorities:** In fiscal 1993, the foundation gave approximately 66% of its total contributions to health care, including its two highest grants of $100,000 each, which were awarded to Brown University Medical School and University of Texas Medical School. Educational institutions received about 18%; social service organizations, 15%; and religious causes received the remaining funds. **Typical Health-Related Recipients:** Alzheimers Disease, Cancer, Children's Health/Hospitals, Eyes/Blindness, Health Organizations, Heart, Hospices, Hospitals, Hospitals (University Affiliated), Medical Rehabilitation, Medical Research, Mental Health, People with Disabilities, Prenatal Health Issues, Speech & Hearing. **Geographic Distribution:** Focus on Houston, TX.

★ 169 ★ **Elmer and Mamdouha Bobst Foundation**
c/o Elmer Holmes Bobst Library, New York Univ.
70 Washington Sq. S
New York, NY 10012
Phone: (212)998-2440
Fax: (212)995-4070
Mamdouha S. Bobst, President

Foundation Philosophy: The foundation's interests include the promotion of health and cancer research, Islamic organizations in the United States and abroad, youth and community service organizations, and the arts. **Giving Priorities:** In 1993, the foundation gave 62% of its funding to social services. Health care organizations received 20%, with several grants made to cancer centers and the American Cancer Society in New York City. Educational institutions received 7%; international causes, 6%; and religious groups, 2%. The remaining funds were awarded to various arts, civic, and environmnetal organizations. **Typical Health-Related Recipients:** AIDS/HIV, Cancer, Clinics/Medical Centers, Health Organizations, Heart, Hospices,

Hospitals, Single-Disease Health Associations. **Geographic Distribution:** New York, NY, and Israel.

★ 170 ★ **Ethel Wilson Bowles and Robert Bowles Memorial Fund**
301 E Colorado Blvd., No. 900
Pasadena, CA 91101
Phone: (818)796-9123
Emrys J. Ross, Trustee

Foundation Philosophy: The foundation funds medical research and medical schools in California. **Giving Priorities:** In 1993, the fund gave approximately 51% of funding to education, especially medical education. Health concerns, including two hospitals, received about 49% of total contributions. **Typical Health-Related Recipients:** Children's Health/Hospitals, Hospitals, Hospitals (University Affiliated), Medical Education, Medical Research, Single-Disease Health Associations. **Geographic Distribution:** Typically limited to California.

★ 171 ★ **Eugene and Agnes E. Meyer Foundation**
1400 Sixteenth St., NW, Ste. 360
Washington, DC 20036
Phone: (202)483-8294
Julie L. Rogers, President

Foundation Philosophy: The foundation hopes to improve the quality of life in Washington, by supporting community efforts and promoting community responsibility. Innovation in problem solving is one of the foundation's special interests. Other interests include low- and moderate-income housing, AIDS, immigrant services, and creative approaches to human needs. **Giving Priorities:** In 1994, the foundation gave approximately 70% of total contributions to civic and public affairs. The arts received about 13% of funding; health concerns, 11%; and education, 6%. **Typical Health-Related Recipients:** AIDS/HIV, Children's Health/ Hospitals, Clinics/Medical Centers, Domestic Violence, Hospices, Mental Health, People with Disabilities, Public Health, Substance Abuse. **Geographic Distribution:** Washington, DC, metropolitan area.

★ 172 ★ **Eugene B. Casey Foundation**
800 S Frederick Ave.
Ste. 100
Gaithersburg, MD 20877-1701
Phone: (301)948-4595
Betty Brown Casey, Chairman, President, and Treasurer

Foundation Philosophy: Major support goes to organizations directly affiliated with the foundation, including the Casey Family Foundation at Washington College and the Eugene B. Casey Center for Diagnostic Cardiololgy. Other foundation interests include hospices, mental health, family services, shelters, arts for the disabled and youth, and Washington, D.C., area colleges and universities. **Giving Priorities:** In fiscal 1993, the foundation awarded 52% of its total contributions to the arts. About 20% of support went to educational institutions. Social services received 18% of funds; health care, 8%; civic groups, 2%; and religious organizations, 1%. **Typical Health-Related Recipients:** Cancer, Children's Health/Hospitals, Clinics/

Medical Centers, Domestic Violence, Emergency/Ambulance Services, Family Planning, Health Funds, Health Organizations, Hospices, Hospitals, Medical Education, Medical Research, Mental Health, Nutrition, People with Disabilities. **Geographic Distribution:** Focus on the metropolitan Washington, DC, area.

★ 173 ★ **Eugene McDermott Foundation**
3808 Euclid Ave.
Dallas, TX 75205
Phone: (214)521-2924
Eugene McDermott, President

Foundation Philosophy: The foundation traditionally has supported medical facilities, science, schools, the arts, educational programs, and cultural organizations. **Giving Priorities:** In fiscal 1993, the foundation awarded approximately 53% of its total contributions to the arts. Health care received about 37%, including the foundation's highest grant of $500,000 to the University of Texas Southwestern Medical Center in Dallas, TX. Civic affairs received 4%; educational institutions, 3%; and social services, environmental interests, religious causes, and scientific institutions received the remaining funds. **Typical Health-Related Recipients:** Cancer, Clinics/Medical Centers, Domestic Violence, Hospitals, Hospitals (University Affiliated), Medical Education, People with Disabilities, Substance Abuse. **Geographic Distribution:** Predominantly Dallas, TX, with some national giving.

★ 174 ★ **Eva L. and Joseph M. Bruening**
     Foundation
1422 Euclid Ave.
627 Hanna Bldg.
Cleveland, OH 44115
Phone: (216)621-2632
Fax: (216)621-8198
Janet E. Narten, Executive Director

Foundation Philosophy: Priority is given to initiatives designed to educate youth, comfort the aged, and provide encouragement and support to the disabled and disadvantaged. The foundation supports practical programs that meet clearly defined community needs in a creative and efficent manner. **Giving Priorities:** In 1993, the foundation reported that it awarded 51% of its contributions to social services. More than one-third of these social service grants went to programs and services specifically for the elderly. Approximately 28% of the giving went to educational organizations and institutions. Health care for the physically and mentally impaired received 22% of the funds. **Typical Health-Related Recipients:** AIDS/HIV, Clinics/Medical Centers, Domestic Violence, Emergency/Ambulance Services, Eyes/Blindness, Geriatric Health, Hospitals, Long-Term Care, Nursing Services, People with Disabilities, Preventive Medicine/Wellness Organizations, Speech & Hearing, Substance Abuse. **Geographic Distribution:** Limited to the greater Cleveland, OH, area as well as Cuyahoga County.

★ 175 ★ **F. M. Kirby Foundation**
17 DeHart St.
PO Box 151
Morristown, NJ 07963-0151
Phone: (201)538-4800
F. M. Kirby, II, President

Foundation Philosophy: The foundation provides funds to organizations in areas where family members live and work, and to organizations in which Fred M. Kirby, the original donor, had an interest. **Giving Priorities:** In 1992, the foundation gave 44% of its giving to health concerns, including the highest grant of $5,000,000 to the Scheie Eye Institute. Approximately 28% of its contributions went to education. Social services received 16%; the arts and humanities, 8%; civic affairs, 4%; and science, religion, and international organizations all received less than 1% of contributions. **Typical Health-Related Recipients:** AIDS/HIV, Alzheimers Disease, Arthritis, Cancer, Domestic Violence, Emergency/Ambulance Services, Eyes/Blindness, Family Planning, Geriatric Health, Health Funds, Heart, Hospices, Hospitals, Medical Education, Medical Rehabilitation, Nursing Services, People with Disabilities, Respiratory, Single-Disease Health Associations, Substance Abuse. **Geographic Distribution:** Geographic areas where the Kirby family has lived and worked, primarily New Jersey, Pennsylvania, and North Carolina; some national funding.

★ 176 ★ **F. R. Bigelow Foundation**
600 Norwest Ctr.
St. Paul, MN 55101
Phone: (612)224-5463
Fax: (612)224-8123
Paul A. Verret, Secretary and Treasurer

Foundation Philosophy: In 1986, the foundation revised its giving program. Grant making in 1987 and 1988 reflected this revision, as over half of the grants supported the new priority areas of low-income populations, minority populations, and employment opportunities. Program efforts in these three areas focus on social services and education. Primary social service programs include child-care alternatives; prevention of teen pregnancy; prevention of child abuse and incest; health and nutritional needs of young people; and programs providing food and other needs for the disadvantaged. An additional foundation interest is the Pacific Basin geographical region. **Giving Priorities:** In 1991, the foundation gave approximately 40% of its contributions to social services, with the United Way receiving grants totaling more than $507,000. Education received 22%, and the arts and health care each received 16% of the foundation's total giving. About 5% went to civic groups and 1% to environmental organizations. **Typical Health-Related Recipients:** Single-Disease Health Associations. **Geographic Distribution:** Primarily metropolitan St. Paul, MN.

★ 177 ★ **Fan Fox and Leslie R. Samuels**
     Foundation
630 Fifth Ave., Ste. 2255
New York, NY 10111
Phone: (212)315-2940
Fax: (212)765-3319
Eva M. Burt, Program Assistant

Foundation Philosophy: The foundation is generally interested in funding organizations in the metropolitan New York area dealing with the performing arts and health. **Giving Priorities:** In fiscal 1993, the foundation reported that about 50% of giving went to arts organizations, while 45% went to health. Foundation service organizations and the director's discretionary funds received 3%. Educational institutions and social services each received 1% of funding. **Typical Health-Related Recipients:** AIDS/HIV, Children's Health/Hospitals, Clinics/Medical Centers, Diabetes, Geriatric Health, Health Organizations, Hospitals, Medical Rehabilitation, Prenatal Health Issues. **Geographic Distribution:** New York, NY, metropolitan area.

★ 178 ★ **Fannie E. Rippel Foundation**
The Concourse at Beaver Brook
PO Box 569
Annandale, NJ 08801-0569
Phone: (908)735-0990
Edward W. Probert, President

Foundation Philosophy: In recent years, the foundation has supported medical research in the fields of cancer and heart disease. It also provides grants for purchasing equipment for hospitals and renovating or constructing hospital facilities. **Giving Priorities:** In fiscal 1994, the foundation reported that it gave 100% of its contributions to health care including support for hospitals and research concerning cancer and heart disease. **Typical Health-Related Recipients:** Cancer, Heart, Hospitals, Medical Research, Research/Studies Institutes. **Geographic Distribution:** Wide geographic distribution, with emphasis on New Jersey and New York.

★ 179 ★ **Faye McBeath Foundation**
1020 N Broadway
Milwaukee, WI 53202
Phone: (414)272-2626
Fax: (414)272-6235
Sarah M. Dean, Executive Director

Foundation Philosophy: Under the terms of the trust, grants are made to organizations for the following purposes: to promote research and education in the fields of medical science and public health; to provide medical, nursing, and hospital care for the sick and disabled; to promote child welfare; to promote research in civic and government affairs directed toward improved efficiency of local government; and to disseminate the results of the research. Funding is made to promote improvement in the health of high-risk populations, especially infants, the elderly, and the poor through projects designed to improve prenatal care, encourage healthy lifestyles, and prevent disease; to provide and expand alternatives to institutional and inpatient care; to facilitate access to comprehensive medical care for elderly, youth, minorities, and the indigent; to enhance the development of the Milwaukee Regional Center as a viable resource for the community and state; and to improve the capability of local universities and colleges to educate health-care providers. **Giving Priorities:** In 1993, the foundation gave approximately 49% of its contributions to social services, including major funding to youth programs, housing, and elderly and handicapped services. Health care received about 21% of grants; civic affairs, 17%; and education, 11%. The arts received 2% of giving, with a sole grant of $20,000 to the Milwaukee Symphony Orchestra. Religious organizations received the remaining 1% of support. **Typical Health-Related Recipients:** AIDS/HIV, Children's Health/Hospitals, Clinics/Medical Centers, Domestic Violence, Eyes/Blindness, Family Planning, Health Organizations, Health Policy/Cost Containment, Long-Term Care, Medical Education, Mental Health, People with Disabilities, Public Health, Substance Abuse. **Geographic Distribution:** Wisconsin, particularly the Milwaukee metropolitan area.

★ 180 ★ Field Foundation of Illinois
200 S Wacker Ste. 28
Chicago, IL 60606
Phone: (312)831-0910
Mr. Handy Lindsey, Jr., Executive Director

Foundation Philosophy: The foundation has initiated a grants program in primary and secondary education that supports schools' efforts to improve education and to help children succeed in academics. The foundation continues to maintain its general grant program which gives to broad purposes primarily in the Chicago, IL, area. **Giving Priorities:** In fiscal 1993, the foundation reported that it gave approximately 24% of funding to social services. Health care and civic affairs each received 20%. Educational institutions were awarded 18% of funding and the arts and humanities were given 17%. **Typical Health-Related Recipients:** Health Organizations, Hospitals, Medical Rehabilitation, People with Disabilities, Substance Abuse. **Geographic Distribution:** Primarily the Chicago metropolitan area.

★ 181 ★ Flagler Foundation
The Heritage Bldg., Ste. 601
PO Box 644
Richmond, VA 23205
Phone: (804)648-5033
Lawrence Lewis, Jr., President

Foundation Philosophy: The Flagler Foundation makes most of its grants in the areas of education, civic affairs, and social services. Educational support goes to Flagler College, college funds, and numerous private schools. The foundation will make grants to other recipient areas on a limted basis. **Giving Priorities:** In 1993, the foundation gave about 42% of funding to religious groups. Educational institutions received approximately 27% of funds. Civic concerns received about 14% of total contributions; the arts, 11%; health groups, 3%; social services, 2%; and environmental concerns, 1%. **Typical Health-Related Recipients:** Cancer, Children's Health/Hospitals, Emergency/Ambulance Services, Family Planning, Health Organizations, Hospitals, Nursing Services, People with Disabilities, Single-Disease Health Associations. **Geographic Distribution:** Eastern United States, with emphasis on Virginia. **Formerly:** Clisby Charitable Trust.

★ 182 ★ Fletcher Jones Foundation
One Wilshire Bldg., Ste. 1210
624 S Grand Ave.
Los Angeles, CA 90017
Phone: (213)689-9292
John W. Smythe, Executive Director

Foundation Philosophy: According to the foundation, "the trustees of the foundation give consideration to charitable, scientific, literary, and educational areas, plus a minor portion to general-purpose grants. However, from time to time, the trustees may give special emphasis to any one of the above-listed areas. At present, grants are given primarily to private colleges and universities, particularly those in California." **Giving Priorities:** In 1993, education received approximately 76% of foundation funding. The arts received 13% of giving; health organizations, 9% and the remaining funds supported civic and public affairs, international concerns, religion, science, and social services. **Typical Health-Related Recipients:** Children's Health/Hospitals, Clinics/Medical Centers, Health Organizations, Hospitals, Nursing Services, People with Disabilities, Research/Studies Institutes. **Geographic Distribution:** Primarily California.

★ 183 ★ Flinn Foundation
3300 N Central Ave., Ste.2300
Phoenix, AZ 85012
Phone: (602)274-9000
Fax: (602)274-3194
John W. Murphy, Executive Director

Foundation Philosophy: The Flinn Foundation supports a diverse array of projects in health, education, and the cultural arts. The foundation seeks to strengthen the state's medical education and biomedical research programs and enhance the effectiveness of health care services. **Giving Priorities:** In 1993, the foundation awarded about 64% of its total grants to health care. About 20% of funds went to educational institutions. The arts received 10% of gifts, and philanthropic organizations received 6%. **Typical Health-Related Recipients:** AIDS/HIV, Alzheimers Disease, Child Abuse, Family Planning, Geriatric Health, Health Organizations, Health Policy/Cost Containment, Heart, Hospitals, Medical Education, Medical Research, Public Health. **Geographic Distribution:** Funding is limited to Arizona.

★ 184 ★ Florence V. Burden Foundation
10 E. 53rd St., 32nd Floor
New York, NY 10022
Phone: (212)872-1150
Fax: (212)332-1150
Eliza Rossman, Executive Director

Foundation Philosophy: The foundation is interested in issues of broad national importance, looking for projects on the cutting edge of social innovation that will demonstrate new ways to solve basic or enduring problems. The foundation's overall theme is to strengthen families and communities. It has changed priorities replacing crime and justice with a focus on children while continuing its focus on the elderly with its aging program area. For children, the foundation addresses the following: to intervene early in children's lives and to prevent abuse and violence. The foundation will focus on children and youth up to 18 years of age. **Giving Priorities:** In 1993, the foundation awarded approximately 35% of its charitable giving to social service organizations. Education received about 29% of the foundation's support. Health care interests were awarded 19% of funds, while 11% sup-

ported civic affairs. Religion and the arts each received about 3% of the foundation's support. The remaining amount went to environmental affairs. **Typical Health-Related Recipients:** AIDS/HIV, Alzheimers Disease, Clinics/Medical Centers, Domestic Violence, Family Planning, Geriatric Health, Health Organizations, Hospices, Hospitals, Long-Term Care, Single-Disease Health Associations, Substance Abuse, Transplant Networks/Donor Banks. **Geographic Distribution:** National, with emphasis on New York.

★ 185 ★ Foellinger Foundation
520 E Berry
Ft. Wayne, IN 46802
Phone: (219)422-2900
Harry V. Owen, President

Foundation Philosophy: The foundation has a broad range of interests that include youth, education, culture, health and welfare, and civic and community development. **Giving Priorities:** In fiscal 1993, the foundation gave 31% of its contributions to civic and public affairs, 31% to education, 15% to social services, 15% to the arts, 6% to health care, and the remaining funds supported religion and the environment. **Typical Health-Related Recipients:** AIDS/HIV, Clinics/Medical Centers, People with Disabilities, Substance Abuse. **Geographic Distribution:** Primarily Allen County, IN.

★ 186 ★ Fondren Foundation
c/o Texas Commerce Bank
PO Box 2558
Houston, TX 77252-8037
Phone: (713)236-4403
Melanie Boone Scioneaux, Assistant
  Secretary/Treasurer

Foundation Philosophy: Traditionally, the foundation has focused on education, including higher education and private schools, and health. Major past health recipients have been the Ella F. Fondren Building, a part of Methodist Hospital, as well as university and community hospitals. The foundation also has given generously to the social services, the arts and humanities, and civic and public affairs. **Giving Priorities:** In fiscal 1993, the foundation awarded educational institutions with 33% of its total contributions. About 28% of funds went to health care. The arts received 17% of support; civic groups, 8%; social services, 6%; religious organizations, 5%; and scientific organizations, 3%. The remainder went to environmental concerns. **Typical Health-Related Recipients:** AIDS/HIV, Cancer, Children's Health/Hospitals, Clinics/Medical Centers, Emergency/Ambulance Services, Hospices, Hospitals, Medical Education, Medical Rehabilitation, Medical Research, Mental Health, Prenatal Health Issues, Research/Studies Institutes, Single-Disease Health Associations, Substance Abuse. **Geographic Distribution:** Texas, particularly Houston.

★ 187 ★ Ford Foundation
320 E 43rd St.
New York, NY 10017
Phone: (212)573-5000
Fax: (212)599-4584
Barron M. Tenny, VP, Sec. & Gen. Couns.

Foundation Philosophy: Grants are given primarily to institutions for experimental, demonstration, and developmental efforts that are likely to produce significant advances within the foundation's seven major fields of interest: The Urban Poverty Program; The Rural Poverty and Resources Program; The Rights and Social Justice Program; The Governance and Public Policy Program; Education and Culture; International Affairs Program; and its Reproductive Health and Population Program. The foundation's principal areas of interest include social science research and training; women's empowerment; policy, ethics, and law; and AIDS. **Giving Priorities:** The foundation reported in its latest annual report for 1993 about 18% of contributions went to Urban Poverty. Approximately 18% of funding went to Education and Culture. Rural Poverty and Resources received 16% of funding. Another 13% went to Rights and Social Justice. Interntional Affairs received approximately 11%. Governance and Public Policy received 13%. About 7% went to other activities, including the Reproductive Health and Population Program for social science research and training; family planning and reproductive health, including AIDS prevention and dissemination of information; special program actions; and grants to individuals. The foundation also allocated an additional $13.6 million to program-related investments to advance its philanthropic purposes. **Typical Health-Related Recipients:** AIDS/HIV, Family Planning, Health Organizations, Medical Research, Nutrition, Public Health, Substance Abuse. **Geographic Distribution:** Nationally and internationally.

★188★ Forest Foundation
820 A St., Ste. 345
Tacoma, WA 98402
Phone: (206)627-1634
Frank D. Underwood, Executive Director

Foundation Philosophy: The foundation focuses on these specific program areas: community improvement, culture and the arts, education, the environment, and social services, which includes child welfare, day care, the disabled, drug rehabilitation, hunger/emergency shelter, senior adults, and youth. **Giving Priorities:** In fiscal 1992, civic organizations received 41% of total funding, with major support to community associations in Washington. Health care organizations received 22%, including the highest grant of $100,000 to the Fred Hutchinson Cancer Research Center in Dayton, OH. The arts in Washington received 18%, and social services and community programs were given 15%. The remainder went to a science center, educational institutions, and religious organizations. **Typical Health-Related Recipients:** Cancer, Clinics/Medical Centers, Domestic Violence, Family Planning, Health Funds, Health Organizations, Medical Research, People with Disabilities, Single-Disease Health Associations. **Geographic Distribution:** Southwest Washington with a focus on Pierce County.

★189★ Forest Lawn Foundation
1712 S Glendale Ave.
Glendale, CA 91205
Phone: (213)254-3131
Frederick Eaton Llewellyn, Chairman and President

Foundation Philosophy: The foundation's interests are chiefly focused on social sevices around Los Angeles. Youth organizations, the Braille Institute, and services for the needy are generally funded. Although the foundation has other interests, most of the giving goes to community interests and health, including hospitals and hospices. **Giving Priorities:** In 1993, the foundation contributed 51% of its total giving to social service organizations, including a single $300,000 grant to the Boy Scouts of America, Los Angeles, CA. About 24% of funds went to health care, primarily to hospitals and hospices. Religious organizations received 14% of support, while educational groups and the arts each received 5%. The final 1% of funds went to civic groups. **Typical Health-Related Recipients:** Clinics/Medical Centers, Emergency/Ambulance Services, Heart, Hospices, Hospitals, Nursing Services, People with Disabilities, Single-Disease Health Associations. **Geographic Distribution:** Focus on California.

★190★ Forrest C. Lattner Foundation
777 E Atlantic Ave., Ste. 317
Delray Beach, FL 33483
Phone: (407)278-3781
Susan L. Lloyd, President and Secretary

Foundation Philosophy: The Forrest C. Lattner Foundation makes most of its grants in the areas of health care, civic affairs, and the arts. Health service funding favors hospitals, mental health, pediatrics, and single-disease associations. Minor support is given to education and social services. **Giving Priorities:** In 1992, the foundation gave approximately 44% of its contributions to health, with emphasis on hospitals and the Alzheimer's Association in Boca Raton, FL. Social services received 33%, while educational institutions received 11%. The arts received 7%; civic causes, 4%; and religious concerns, 1%. **Typical Health-Related Recipients:** AIDS/HIV, Alzheimers Disease, Cancer, Children's Health/Hospitals, Clinics/Medical Centers, Domestic Violence, Eyes/Blindness, Family Planning, Health Funds, Hospices, Hospitals, Medical Education, Medical Research, Mental Health, People with Disabilities, Research/Studies Institutes, Single-Disease Health Associations. **Geographic Distribution:** Focus on midwestern United States and Florida.

★191★ Foster Foundation
1201 Third Ave., Ste. 2101
Seattle, WA 98101
Phone: (206)624-5200
Jill Goodsell, Administrator

Foundation Philosophy: The Foster Foundation makes most of its grants in the areas of education, social services, and health. Health interests include hospitals, cancer research, and nursing. The foundation makes grants in other areas of support as well. **Giving Priorities:** In 1992, the foundation gave approximately 47% of its contributions to education, including the highest grant of $500,000 to the University of

Washington, Seattle, WA. Literacy projects also received major support. Social service organizations received 26%, and health concerns received 13% of giving. Civic affairs received 6%; the arts, 4%; religion, 2%; and science received the remainder. **Typical Health-Related Recipients:** AIDS/HIV, Cancer, Children's Health/Hospitals, Clinics/Medical Centers, Emergency/Ambulance Services, Family Planning, Health Organizations, Hospitals, Nursing Services, Public Health. **Geographic Distribution:** Focus on Seattle, WA.

★192★ Foundation for Child Development
345 E 46th St.
New York, NY 10017
Phone: (212)697-3150
Fax: (212)697-2258
Barbara Blum, President

Foundation Philosophy: "The board of directors believes the foundation should continue its broad mission to understand, document, and intervene in the lives of children and families at risk." **Giving Priorities:** In fiscal 1994, the foundation gave approximately 43% of its contributions to social service organizations, with an emphasis on family support services. Civic concerns received 28% of funding. Educational institutions received approximately 13% of support; health care, 11%; the arts, 3%; and scientific organizations, 2%. **Typical Health-Related Recipients:** Child Abuse, Children's Health/Hospitals, Domestic Violence, Family Planning, Health Funds, Hospitals, Medical Education, Medical Rehabilitation, Medical Research, Mental Health, People with Disabilities, Research/Studies Institutes. **Geographic Distribution:** Policy, research, and advocacy programs are nationwide; direct charitable activities are in New York City only.

★193★ Foundation for New Era Philanthropy
c/o Grants Review Committee
3 Radnor Corp. Ctr.
100 Matsonford Rd., Ste. 150
Radnor, PA 19087
Phone: (610)989-9778
Fax: (610)989-9766

Foundation Philosophy: In addition to traditional giving and philanthropic interests in global, cultural, religious, environmental, educational, or health-related affairs, the foundation has six major programs that represent its specific interests in nonprofits. The New Era Fellows Program supports 501(c)(3) organizations. The Youth in Philanthropy Program was developed "to encourage young people to learn the commitment and process of giving." The Templeton Institute Prize for Excellence honors graduate organizations from the foundation's Templeton Institutes. The New Era Spiritual Leadership Prize was created in 1994 "to identify individuals who will be the spiritual leaders for tomorrow and support, encourage, and make the world aware of their special spiritual significance." The foundation's International Expansion effort funds and trains organizations throughout the world. The New Concepts in Philanthropy Fund is a "unique program that provides the opportunity for matching funds to augment the philanthropic giving of selected individuals throughout the world." **Giving Priorities:** The foundation gives to organizations which have a positive impact on society. Funds are distributed according to the foundation's and their clients' decisions. Giving spans all categories of recipients, including the arts, civic and public affairs, educational institutions and programs, the environment, health care, international affairs, religion, science, and social services. The percentages vary greatly from year to year, therefore a percentage breakdown of giving is not available. **Typical Health-Related Recipients:** Cancer, General, Medical Education, Trauma Treatment. **Geographic Distribution:** Nationally and internationally.

★ 194 ★ **Frances and Benjamin Benenson Foundation**
708 Third Ave., 28th Fl.
New York, NY 10017
Phone: (212)867-0990
Fax: (212)983-1952
Charles B. Benenson, President

Foundation Philosophy: The foundation has two primary interests: the arts and education. Funding for the arts favors museums, the performing arts, and libraries. Funding for education emphasizes educational foundations and universities. Secondary interests include religious organizations and social services. **Giving Priorities:** In fiscal 1993, the foundation awarded 44% of contributions to education, including a $200,000 gift to Yale University. The arts received 16% of total contributions made. Religious causes received 16% of support, with some emphasis on Jewish organizations. Social services was awarded 9% of giving. International affairs received 6% of donations, and health care received 5% of funds awarded. Civic and public affairs received the remaining 4% of funds. **Typical Health-Related Recipients:** AIDS/HIV, Cancer, Children's Health/Hospitals, Clinics/Medical Centers, Diabetes, Emergency/Ambulance Services, Health Organizations, Hospitals, People with Disabilities, Single-Disease Health Associations, Substance Abuse. **Geographic Distribution:** Focus on New York, NY.

★ 195 ★ **Frances L. & Edwin L. Cummings Memorial Fund**
501 Fifth Ave., Ste. 708
New York, NY 10017-6103
Phone: (212)286-1778
Fax: (212)682-9458
Elizabeth Costas, Administrative Director

Foundation Philosophy: The major fields of interest are as follows: social welfare, especially programs addressing child abuse, homelessness, teenage pregnancy, parenting education, and youth employment and job training; education, with a focus on students from disadvantaged backgrounds, especially efforts to reform the public education system or programs that serve public school children; health care, especially institutions and programs serving economically and socially disadvantaged populations; and medical research, with an emphasis on AIDS and cancer, which has been pre-screened and prioritized by an objective, national scientific advisory committee. (The fund does not generally support research requests from in-

dividual researchers or private institutions.) **Giving Priorities:** In fiscal 1994, the foundation gave approximately 29% of funding to social services, with major support to organizations supporting youth. Civic concerns received about 26% of total contributions. The remainder of funds went to health projects, 22%; educational institutions, 19%; and religious organizations, 5%. **Typical Health-Related Recipients:** AIDS/HIV, Cancer, Children's Health/ Hospitals, Clinics/Medical Centers, Family Planning, Home-Care Services, Hospitals, Medical Rehabilitation, Mental Health, People with Disabilities, Substance Abuse. **Geographic Distribution:** Primarily the New York metropolitan area.

★ 196 ★ **Frances Wood Wilson Foundation**
PO Box 33188
Decatur, GA 30033
Phone: (404)634-3363
Fax: (404)634-3365
W. T. Wingfield, President

Foundation Philosophy: The foundation generally awards its grants to programs and institutions involved in child welfare, religious, civic, health, or educational activities in Georgia, except for programs carried on by Chestnut Hill Benevolent Association in Boston, MA. **Giving Priorities:** The foundation reports that in fiscal 1992 it gave approximately 46% of its overall giving to education, including its largest grant of $650,000 to the Young Harris College, Young Harris, GA. Civic and public affairs received 20%, and health care received 19%. About 11% went to child welfare, and 4% to religion. **Typical Health-Related Recipients:** Hospitals, Single-Disease Health Associations. **Geographic Distribution:** Georgia.

★ 197 ★ **Francis Families Foundation**
800 W 47th St., Ste. 604
Kansas City, MO 64112
Phone: (816)531-0077
Linda K. French, Secretary-Treasurer

Foundation Philosophy: The foundation supports medical fellowships in pulmonary medicine and anesthesiology, and educational and cultural institutions in the greater Kansas City metropolitan area. **Giving Priorities:** In 1993, the foundation reported that approximately 55% of its giving went to medical education in the form of fellowships to doctors in various medical departments at universities, and at health organizations and hospitals. General educational support made up 35% of the funds distributed, while the arts and humanities received the remaining 10% of funding. **Typical Health-Related Recipients:** Children's Health/ Hospitals, Health Organizations, Hospitals, Medical Education, Medical Research, Respiratory, Single-Disease Health Associations. **Geographic Distribution:** National for medical funding; Kansas City, MO, for education and cultural concerns. **Formerly:** Parker B. Francis Foundation.

★ 198 ★ **Frank E. and Seba B. Payne Foundation**
c/o Bank of America
231 S LaSalle St.
Chicago, IL 60697
Phone: (312)987-0806
M. Catherine Ryan, Second Vice President

Foundation Philosophy: Grants are made solely at the discretion of the trustees for any "religious, charitable, scientific, literary, or educational purposes, and in addition, for the prevention of cruelty to children or animals." **Giving Priorities:** In fiscal 1993, the foundation gave approximately 39% of giving to health concerns, including the foundation's highest grant of $1,300,000 to St. Lukes Hospital in Bethlehem, PA. Educational institutions received 35% of total contributions; the arts and humanities, 10%; religious institutions, 8%; social services, 7%; and civic concerns, 1%. **Typical Health-Related Recipients:** AIDS/HIV, Clinics/ Medical Centers, Domestic Violence, Emergency/Ambulance Services, Hospitals, Nursing Services, People with Disabilities, Speech & Hearing, Substance Abuse, Transplant Networks/Donor Banks. **Geographic Distribution:** Principally Chicago, IL, and Bethlehem, PA, areas.

★ 199 ★ **Frank Loomis Palmer Fund**
c/o Shawmut Bank
250 State St.
New London, CT 06320
Phone: (203)447-6133
Mildred E. Devine, Vice President and
  Administrator

Foundation Philosophy: The Frank Loomis Palmer Fund distributes its income "to corporations, societies, institutions, and trusts which are devoted exclusively to religious, charitable, scientific, literary, historical, or educational purposes, including the encouragement of art." **Giving Priorities:** In fiscal 1993, the foundation gave 36% of its contributions to social service organizations. Support went to family services, youth organizations, and planned parenthood programs. The arts and humanities received 19% of funds, and education and health-related organizations each received 15%. The remainder went to civic and public affairs with 8%, science with 4%, religion with 1%, and the environment with 1%. **Typical Health-Related Recipients:** AIDS/HIV, Children's Health/Hospitals, Emergency/Ambulance Services, Family Planning, Health Organizations, Hospices, Hospitals, Mental Health, Nursing Services, People with Disabilities, Single-Disease Health Associations, Substance Abuse. **Geographic Distribution:** Primarily limited to New London, CT.

★ 200 ★ **Frank Stanley Beveridge Foundation**
301 Yamato Rd., Ste. 1130
Boca Raton, FL 33431-4929
Phone: (407)241-8388
Fax: (407)241-8332
Philip Caswell, President and Director

Foundation Philosophy: The foundation was organized "to aid and provide for the benefit of such poor and needy persons...and to aid and provide for the advancement or promotion of science, learning, medicine, surgery, literature, music, art or human welfare." The foundation annually sets aside approximately one-third of funds for the general maintenance of Stanley Park in Westfield, MA, one-third for organizations in Hampden and Hampshire Counties, and one-third for nonprofits located in regions where Beveridge family members reside, namely the Tampa and Palm Beach, FL, areas. **Giving Priorities:** In 1991, the foundation gave about 50% of funding to civic causes, primarily supporting Stanley Park of Westfield, MA. Social services received 22%, while educational institutions received 13%. Health organizations received 8%, and the arts, 5%. The remainder supported religious concerns. **Typical Health-Related Recipients:** Geriatric Health, Health Organizations, Hospices, Hospitals, Mental Health, People with Disabilities, Single-Disease Health Associations. **Geographic Distribution:** Primarily Hampden and Hampshire counties, MA; and the Tampa and Palm Beach, FL, areas.

★201★ **Frankel Foundation**
c/o Harris Trust & Savings Bank, 7W
111 W Monroe St.
Chicago, IL 60690
Phone: (312)461-2613
Ellen A. Bechtold, Contact Person

Foundation Philosophy: The foundation principally supports the arts, concentrating on music and dance; higher education; hospitals and health organizations; and social welfare groups. **Giving Priorities:** In fiscal 1994, the foundation reported that it gave approximately 30% of funding went to educational institutions. The arts received 27%; health organizations, 22%; social services, 15%; and civic causes received the remaining 6%. **Typical Health-Related Recipients:** Hospices, Hospitals, Medical Rehabilitation, People with Disabilities. **Geographic Distribution:** Primarily Illinois.

★202★ **Fred L. Emerson Foundation, Inc.**
PO Box 276
Auburn, NY 13021
Phone: (315)253-9621
Fax: (315)253-5235
Ronald D. West, Executive Director and Secretary

Foundation Philosophy: "Among the foundation's interests are hospital and health programs, education (primarily private higher education), community agencies, local churches, cultural institutions, youth and community service programs, and social welfare agencies." **Giving Priorities:** In 1993, the foundation gave approximately 39% of total contributions to educational institutions and social services received about 22% of funding. Civic concerns received about 17% of funding, including the foundation's highest grant of $350,000 to the E. John Garvas Center of Auburn, NY. Another 17% of support went to the arts. Health groups received about 3% of funding, and the remainder of funding went to religious institutions (2%) and environmental programs (1%). **Typical Health-Related Recipients:** Cancer, Emergency/Ambulance Services, Eyes/Blindness, Health Organizations, Hospices, Hospitals, Medical Rehabilitation, Medical Research, Single-Disease Health Associations. **Geographic Distribution:** Primarily Auburn, Cayuga County, and central New York.

★203★ **Fred Maytag Family Foundation**
200 First St. S
PO Box 426
Newton, IA 50208
Phone: (515)792-1800
Fax: (515)792-4291
Mr. Francis C. Miller, Foundation Manager

Foundation Philosophy: The foundation focuses its funding primarily on higher educational institutions, the arts, health and human service organizations, and civic groups. **Giving Priorities:** In 1993, approximately 37% of giving went to social services, including the highest grant of $250,000 to Wesley Retirement Services in Des Moines, IA. Education received 23%; the arts, 16%; health care, 11%; and environmental concerns, 5%. Religion received 4%; and civic organizations and international affairs each received 2%. **Typical Health-Related Recipients:** Cancer, Clinics/Medical Centers, Family Planning, Health Organizations, Hospices, Hospitals, Medical Education, Medical Rehabilitation, Mental Health, People with Disabilities, Single-Disease Health Associations, Substance Abuse. **Geographic Distribution:** Exclusively the Des Moines and Newton, IA, area.

★204★ **Frederick S. Upton Foundation**
100 Ridgeway
St. Joseph, MI 49085
Phone: (616)982-0272
Stephen E. Upton, Chairman of the Board of Trustees

Foundation Philosophy: The foundation's primary purpose is local giving, with emphasis on higher education, religion, cultural programs, community funds, and youth organizations. **Giving Priorities:** In 1993, the foundation gave approximately 38% of funding to the arts. Educational institutions received 30%. Social services, primarily youth and family interests, received 16%, including the highest grant of $75,190 to the YWCA of Southwestern Michigan. Religion received 10%; health care, 6%; and environmental efforts, 1%. **Typical Health-Related Recipients:** Family Planning, Health Organizations, Hospitals, People with Disabilities. **Geographic Distribution:** Primarily Michigan.

★205★ **Frost Foundation**
314 McKenzie St.
Santa Fe, NM 87501
Phone: (505)986-0208
Fax: (505)986-0430
Mary Amelia Whited-Howell, President and Director

Foundation Philosophy: The focus of the Frost Foundation has expanded over the years to include health groups, social services, humanitarian needs, the environment, and education. Social service projects will include, but not be limited to, street and domestic violence, child abuse, specific public health issues such as alcohol and drug abuse, homelessness, and problems of the elderly. **Giving Priorities:** In 1993, the foundation gave approximately 42% of its charitable contributions in support of education, including a $75,000 grant to Texas Christian University. Social services, the arts, and health care each received about 12% of overall support. Civic affairs received 10% of foundation

support, while environmental affairs received about 9%. The remaining 3% of funds supported religious concerns and organizations. **Typical Health-Related Recipients:** Cancer, Children's Health/Hospitals, Domestic Violence, Hospices, Hospitals, Medical Research, Single-Disease Health Associations. **Geographic Distribution:** No geographic restrictions.

★206★ **Fuller E. Callaway Foundation**
209 Broome St.
La Grange, GA 30241
Phone: (706)884-7348
Fax: (706)884-7349
J. T. Gresham, General Manager

Foundation Philosophy: The foundation traditionally devotes significant resources to nursing scholarships, the West Georgia Medical Center, and two foundation-sponsored scholarship programs. The remainder goes to LaGrange area schools and the college, local community service organizations, and churches. **Giving Priorities:** In 1993, the foundation reported that 59% of its funding went to health care, including the highest grant of $475,000 to the George E. Sims, Jr., Nursing Scholarship. Education received 24% of the award money. Scholarships to individuals account for approximately two-thirds of the grants in this category; the remaining one-third of the education grants went to educational institutions. Civic affairs received 10%, with primary funding to Troup County. Social service organizations received 7% of the contributions. **Typical Health-Related Recipients:** Arthritis, Cancer, Children's Health/Hospitals, Domestic Violence, Health Organizations, Heart, Hospitals, Medical Education, Multiple Sclerosis, Respiratory, Single-Disease Health Associations. **Geographic Distribution:** Focus on the city of LaGrange as well as Troup County, GA.

★207★ **Fullerton Foundation**
PO Box 2208
Gaffney, SC 29342
Phone: (803)489-6678
Walter E. Cavell, Executive Director

Foundation Philosophy: The Fullerton Foundation makes grants in the areas of education, health, and social services. All of the educational funding supports university-level medical training. Health care support goes to medical centers, hospitals, and health associations. Social service funding favors children's homes and community centers. **Giving Priorities:** In fiscal 1992, the foundation gave approximately 70% of its contributions to health care, including its highest grant of $200,000 for the Memorial Mission Medical Center, Asheville, NC. Education, primarily scholarship programs for colleges and universities, received 23%. Social services, including support for youth organizations, received 6%. Science and civic affairs received the remainder. **Typical Health-Related Recipients:** Children's Health/Hospitals, Clinics/Medical Centers, Emergency/Ambulance Services, Family Planning, Geriatric Health, Health Organizations, Health Policy/Cost Containment, Hospitals, Hospitals (University Affiliated), Medical Education, Medical Research, Nursing Services, Nutrition, Outpatient Health Care, Preventive Medicine/Wellness Organizations, Trauma Treatment. **Geographic Distribution:** Focus on South Carolina and North Carolina.

★ 208 ★ G. Harold and Leila Y. Mathers Charitable Foundation
103 S Bedford Rd.
Ste. 101
Mt. Kisco, NY 10549-3440
Phone: (914)242-0465
James H. Handelman, Executive Director

Foundation Philosophy: The foundation typically focuses its giving in the field of medical research performed at various hospitals, medical research institutes, and universities throughout the country. **Giving Priorities:** In 1993, the foundation gave approximately 66% of its total contributions to health care, including its highest grant of $424,284 to the Dana-Farber Cancer Institute. Educational institutions received about 26% and scientific interests received 5%. The arts, international organizations, and social services received the remaining funds. **Typical Health-Related Recipients:** Cancer, Children's Health/Hospitals, Clinics/Medical Centers, Emergency/Ambulance Services, Hospitals, Medical Education, Medical Research, Public Health, Research/Studies Institutes. **Geographic Distribution:** National.

★ 209 ★ GAR Foundation
50 S Main St.
PO Box 1500
Akron, OH 44309
Phone: (216)376-5300
Richard A. Chenoweth, Executive Director

Foundation Philosophy: The foundation supports higher and secondary educational institutions. It also contributes to a variety of programs in the arts. Religious organizations, medical institutions, civic groups, and social service agencies are funded on a lesser scale. The foundation also shows a preference for organizations in areas where Roadway Express or an affiliate conducts business. **Giving Priorities:** In 1993, the foundation awarded approximately 37% of its total contributions to educational institutions. About 30% of funds went to civic groups. The arts received 17% of support; social services, 9%; health care, 5%; and religious concerns, 2%. **Typical Health-Related Recipients:** Alzheimers Disease, Children's Health/Hospitals, Emergency/Ambulance Services, Family Planning, Health Funds, Hospices, Hospitals, Medical Education, Mental Health, Multiple Sclerosis, Nursing Services, People with Disabilities, Substance Abuse. **Geographic Distribution:** Akron and the northeastern Ohio area.

★ 210 ★ Gebbie Foundation
308 Hotel Jamestown Office Bldg.
PO Box 1277
Jamestown, NY 14702-1277
Phone: (716)487-1062
Fax: (716)484-6401
John D. Hamilton, President and Director

Foundation Philosophy: The foundation has initiated an Early Childhood Development Initiative as part of its focus on the welfare of children in particular and, in general, the religious, educational, and charitable fields that concerned the donors. Foundation support includes aid to

the United Way and its member agencies, hospitals, libraries, historical centers, and cultural organizations. The foundation also supports some medical research. Current interests include bone metabolism, particularly Paget's Disease. The development of programs for the detection and improvement of hearing and visual deficiencies in both children and adults has also received foundation support. **Giving Priorities:** In fiscal 1994, the foundation gave approximately 48% of its contributions to education including a $500,000 grant to Jamestown Community College, Jamestown, NY for construction and renovations. Social service organizations, including the YMCA, YWCA, and the United Way of Southern Chautauqua County, NY, received approximately 29% of the foundation's funds. Arts organizations received 11%, and civic and public affairs received 10%. The funds went to environmental causes. **Typical Health-Related Recipients:** Children's Health/Hospitals, Domestic Violence, Heart, Hospices, Hospitals, Medical Research, Nursing Services, People with Disabilities, Prenatal Health Issues, Research/Studies Institutes, Substance Abuse. **Geographic Distribution:** Jamestown/Chautauqua County, NY.

★ 211 ★ George B. Storer Foundation
PO Box 1270
Saratoga, WY 82331
Phone: (307)326-8308
Peter Storer, President

Foundation Philosophy: The foundation traditionally gives to education, conservation efforts, social services, and health organizations. **Giving Priorities:** In 1991, about 37% of foundation support went to civic affairs, primarily to conservation concerns. Education received about 29% of contributions, with emphasis on colleges, universities, and scholarship funds. Health organizations received 15%; social services, 10%; and the arts, 9%. **Typical Health-Related Recipients:** Hospitals, People with Disabilities, Single-Disease Health Associations. **Geographic Distribution:** Emphasis on the Miami, FL, area.

★ 212 ★ George D. Smith Fund
805 Third Ave., 20th Fl.
New York, NY 10022
Phone: (212)832-0508
Lawrence W. Milas, Vice President

Foundation Philosophy: The George D. Smith Fund primarily supports health care services and medical research. Other interests include universities, civil rights, family planning, and public broadcasting. **Giving Priorities:** In 1993, about 71% of the foundation's giving went to health-related research, including a $734,138 gift to the Stanford University Medical Center and a $380,543 donation to the Foundation for Medicine in San Francisco. Educational institutions received an additional 18% of funding, while the social services were granted 5%. Religion received 4%, and the arts received the remaining 2%. **Typical Health-Related Recipients:** Clinics/Medical Centers, Family Planning, Health Funds, Health Organizations, Medical Education. **Geographic Distribution:** Focus on California, New York, and Utah.

★ 213 ★ George F. Baker Trust
767 Fifth Ave., Ste. 2850
New York, NY 10153
Phone: (212)755-1890
Rocio Suarez, Executive Director

Foundation Philosophy: Grants from the trust are for general charitable giving, largely to institutions in the New York area that have received continuous support over the years from the donor and his family. Special consideration is given to education, hospitals, social services, youth agencies, conservation, and historic preservation. **Giving Priorities:** In 1992, the foundation gave approximately 71% of its contributions to the arts including the largest grant of $3,000,000 to Dartmouth University for renovation of their Baker Library. Private education and universities received 17% of funding. Civic concerns were awarded 7%; health care organizations and hospitals, 3%; and the remaining funds were split among social services, science, religious organizations, and international affairs. **Typical Health-Related Recipients:** Children's Health/Hospitals, Diabetes, Emergency/Ambulance Services, Family Planning, Hospitals, Medical Rehabilitation, Medical Research, People with Disabilities, Substance Abuse. **Geographic Distribution:** National, with emphasis on New York City.

★ 214 ★ George F. and Sybil H. Fuller Foundation
730 Main St.
PO Box 8
Boylston, MA 01505
Phone: (508)869-2106
Fax: (508)869-6516
Russell E. Fuller, Chairman, Treasurer, and Trustee

Foundation Philosophy: The foundation generally supports higher educational organizations, cultural institutions, hospitals, historic preservation efforts, and social services. **Giving Priorities:** In 1993, the foundation gave approximately 37% of its total contributions to educational institutions, including its highest grant of $210,000 to the Worcester Polytechnic Institute. The arts received about 27%; social services, 11%; scientific interests, 8%; civic affairs, 6%; health concerns, 6%; religious organizations, 4%; and environmental causes received the remaining funds. **Typical Health-Related Recipients:** Children's Health/Hospitals, Diabetes, Health Organizations, Hospices, Hospitals, Medical Education, Medical Research, Nursing Services, People with Disabilities, Single-Disease Health Associations, Substance Abuse. **Geographic Distribution:** Primarily Worcester County, MA.

★ 215 ★ George Foundation
PO Drawer C
207 S Third St.
Richmond, TX 77406-0076
Phone: (713)342-6109
Fax: (713)341-7635
Roland Adamson, Executive Director

Foundation Philosophy: The foundation limits its giving to Ft. Bend County, TX, with emphasis on hospitals, educational institutions, social service agencies, and local arts groups. **Giving Priorities:** In 1993, the foundation gave approximately 31% of funding to social services, supporting a variety of causes, including children's centers, United Ways, and drug and alcohol rehabilitation centers. Health organizations and educational institutions each received 25%, while the arts received 13%, primarily supporting museums. The remaining 6% was split between civic concerns and religion. **Typical Health-Related Recipients:** AIDS/HIV, Alzheimers Disease, Child Abuse, Children's Health/Hospitals, Clinics/Medical Centers, Domestic Violence, Emergency/Ambulance Services, Family Planning, Geriatric Health, Hospitals, Long-Term Care, Medical Education, Mental Health, People with Disabilities, Prenatal Health Issues, Research/Studies Institutes, Single-Disease Health Associations, Speech & Hearing, Substance Abuse. **Geographic Distribution:** Primarily Ft. Bend County, TX.

★216★ George Frederick Jewett Foundation

The Russ Bldg.
235 Montgomery St., Ste. 612
San Francisco, CA 94104
Phone: (415)421-1351
Theresa A. Mullen, Executive Director

Foundation Philosophy: The foundation continues to support the philanthropic interests of its donor, making grants in a variety of areas, including the arts, conservation and preservation, education, health, religion, social welfare, public affairs, and population. **Giving Priorities:** In 1993, the foundation gave approximately 41% of its contributions to the arts, including its highest grant of $200,000 for the Mary Cooper Jewett Arts Center at Wellesley College, Wellesley, MA. Educational institutions, mainly colleges and universities, received 15%. Health organizations received 11%, with major support for cancer concerns. International affirs, 9%; social services received 8%; environmental concerns, 7%; religious causes, 5%; and civic affairs, 4%. **Typical Health-Related Recipients:** Cancer, Diabetes, Family Planning, Hospitals, Medical Education, People with Disabilities, Substance Abuse. **Geographic Distribution:** Primarily eastern Washington and the city of San Francisco.

★217★ George Gund Foundation

45 Prospect Ave. W, Ste. 1845
1845 Guildhall Bldg.
Cleveland, OH 44115
Phone: (216)241-3114
Fax: (216)241-6560
David Bergholz, Executive Director

Foundation Philosophy: The foundation funds education, human services, economic revitalization, arts, environmental quality, and civic affairs. **Giving Priorities:** In 1993, the foundation awarded 35% of its total contributions to economic development and community revitalization. Educational institutions received about 19% of funds. The majority of education funding went to support educational improvement and organziational change in Cleveland Public Schools. About 17% went to human services, including child and family welfare, reproductive health, summer youth programs, and AIDS services. Environmental concerns receved 11% of support; retinal degeneration research, 7%; the

arts, 6%; and civic affairs, 5%. The foundation reports that it regularly gives about 8% of its yearly budget for retinitis pigmentosa research. **Typical Health-Related Recipients:** Family Planning, Single-Disease Health Associations. **Geographic Distribution:** Primarily northeastern Ohio, with emphasis on Cleveland.

★218★ George H. Deuble Foundation

PO Box 2288
North Canton, OH 44720
Phone: (216)494-4199
Andrew H. Deuble, Trustee

Foundation Philosophy: The George H. Deuble Foundation makes grants across the major categories of support. In civic affairs, interests include municipalities, foundations, and community interests. Social service support goes to family planning, child welfare, community centers, and employment. Support for education includes scholarships, universities, technical education, and funds. Health support includes brain research, nursing, and single-disease associations. The foundation also will fund churches, libraries, and other arts. **Giving Priorities:** In 1993, the foundation gave 30% of its total contributions to support social services. About 25% of contributions went in support of the arts. Educational institutions received 25% of funds. Health care received 9% of giving, including the largest grant of $66,800 to Aultman Hospital. Religious programs received 8%. Civic causes received approximately 3% of funds. **Typical Health-Related Recipients:** Adolescent Health Issues, Children's Health/Hospitals, Emergency/Ambulance Services, Family Planning, Health Funds, Heart, Hospitals, Medical Education, Medical Research, People with Disabilities, Single-Disease Health Associations, Substance Abuse. **Geographic Distribution:** Focus on the Stark County, OH, area.

★219★ George I. Alden Trust

370 Main St.
Worcester, MA 01608
Phone: (508)798-8621
Fax: (508)791-1201
Francis H. Dewey, III, Chairman

Foundation Philosophy: The primary interest of the George I. Alden Trust is education. The focus is on higher education, although projects in secondary education are also supported. **Giving Priorities:** In 1993, the foundation gave 73% of total funding to higher education, primarily supporting colleges and universities in New England. About 12% of support was awarded to social service organizations. Health care received 8% of support; the arts, 3%; science, 3%; and civic affairs, 1%. **Typical Health-Related Recipients:** Clinics/Medical Centers, Emergency/Ambulance Services, Family Planning, Medical Education. **Geographic Distribution:** No geographic restrictions; some emphasis on New England, in particular Worcester, MA.

★220★ George Link, Jr. Foundation

c/o Emmet, Marvin & Martin
120 Broadway, Ste. 3200
New York, NY 10271
Phone: (212)422-2974
Bernard F. Joyce, Vice President, Secretary, and Director

Foundation Philosophy: The foundation typically supports health organizations, educational institutions, religious causes, and social services. **Giving Priorities:** In 1993, the foundation gave approximately 37% of its contributions to health care. Education received 29% of giving, mainly to secondary schools and colleges. Religious organizations received 26% of support; international concerns, 4%; the arts and humanities, 3%; and social services, 2%. **Typical Health-Related Recipients:** Clinics/Medical Centers, Health Funds, Health Organizations, Heart, Hospitals, Medical Education, Medical Research, Mental Health, People with Disabilities, Single-Disease Health Associations. **Geographic Distribution:** Primarily New York and New Jersey.

★221★ George and Mary Josephine Hamman Foundation

910 Travis St., No. 1990
Houston, TX 77002-5816
Phone: (713)658-8345
Stephen I. Gelsey, Administrator

Foundation Philosophy: The foundation makes grants across the major categories of support: health care (interests include single-disease associations, hospices, health organizations, and hospitals), the arts, educational funding, and social service (interests include family planning, the homeless, homes, child welfare, and the disabled). Other interests include churches and religious groups. **Giving Priorities:** In fiscal 1994, the foundation contributed 25% of its funding to the arts. Scholarships received 24% of funding. Civic groups received 21%; health care, 14%; educational institutions, 8%; and about 5% went to social services. The remaining funds went to religious groups. **Typical Health-Related Recipients:** Cancer, Clinics/Medical Centers, Eyes/Blindness, Family Planning, Health Organizations, Heart, Hospices, Hospitals, Medical Rehabilitation, Medical Research, Mental Health, Single-Disease Health Associations. **Geographic Distribution:** Limited to Texas, primarily the Houston area.

★222★ George S. and Dolores Dore Eccles Foundation

Deseret Bldg.
79 S Main St., Ste. 1201
Salt Lake City, UT 84111
Phone: (801)246-5336
Dr. David P. Gardner, Chairman of the Board

Foundation Philosophy: ''The Foundation's field of interest includes the arts, community organizations, education and health.'' **Giving Priorities:** In 1993, the foundation contributed 43% of its total giving to educational institutions. About 24% of funds went to the arts. Environmental concerns and social services each received 9% of gifts. Health care and religious organizations each received 6%. About 3% went to civic concerns. **Typical Health-Related Recipients:** Clinics/Medical Centers, Eyes/

Blindness, Health Organizations, Hospitals, Medical Education, Medical Research, Nursing Services, Outpatient Health Care, People with Disabilities, Public Health, Single-Disease Health Associations, Speech & Hearing. **Geographic Distribution:** Preference for the "Intermountain area," with emphasis on the State of Utah.

★ 223 ★ George W. Brackenridge Foundation

711 Navarro St., Ste. 535
San Antonio, TX 78205
Phone: (210)224-1011
Fax: (210)223-3657
Gilbert M. Denman, Jr., Trustee

Foundation Philosophy: Foundation support goes to accredited Texas educational organizations for individual scholarhips, scholarship programs, and educational facilities and programs. The foundation also supports the arts and zoos. **Giving Priorities:** In 1993, the foundation awarded 75% of its total contributions to educational institutions. About 18% of contributions went to the arts. Health care received 5% of support, and civic groups received 2%. **Typical Health-Related Recipients:** Clinics/Medical Centers, Medical Education, Medical Training. **Geographic Distribution:** Limited to Texas.

★ 224 ★ Gheens Foundation

One Riverfront Plz., Ste. 705
Louisville, KY 40202
Phone: (502)584-4650
Fax: (502)584-4652
James N. Davis, Executive Director and Treasurer

Foundation Philosophy: The foundation favors educational institutions. Other recipients of funding have been health institutions, community development groups, arts centers, and human service agencies. **Giving Priorities:** In fiscal 1993, the foundation gave approximately 42% of its contributions to education. Social Services received 25%. The arts received 21%. The highest grant of $250,000 was awarded to Bellarmine College for a new library. Religious organizations received 6%; civic affairs, 3%; and health care, 3%. **Typical Health-Related Recipients:** Cancer, Children's Health/Hospitals, Diabetes, Eyes/Blindness, Family Planning, Geriatric Health, Medical Education, Medical Rehabilitation, Mental Health, People with Disabilities, Single-Disease Health Associations, Substance Abuse. **Geographic Distribution:** Emphasis on Louisville, KY, and Louisiana.

★ 225 ★ Gladys and Roland Harriman Foundation

63 Wall St., 13th Fl.
New York, NY 10005
Phone: (212)493-8182
Fax: (212)493-5570
William F. Hibberd, Secretary

Foundation Philosophy: The foundation generally gives a majority of funding to educational institutions, primarily to private secondary schools and colleges and universities. Hospitals and medical research organizations, as well as the arts, are also major beneficiaries. **Giving Priorities:** In 1993, the foundation gave approx-

imately 45% of its contributions to health care, including its highest grant of $750,000 to the New York Hospital. Other health-care recipients included the American Red Cross and medical centers and institutes. Educational institutions received 23%; the arts, 16%; social services, 10%; and civic and public affairs, 3%. The remaining funds went to science, religion, and the environment. **Typical Health-Related Recipients:** Cancer, Clinics/Medical Centers, Diabetes, Domestic Violence, Emergency/Ambulance Services, Geriatric Health, Health Organizations, Hospitals, Medical Education, Medical Research, Speech & Hearing, Substance Abuse. **Geographic Distribution:** Nationally, with an emphasis on New York, NY.

★ 226 ★ Gordon and Mary Cain Foundation

Eight Greenway Plz., Ste. 702
Houston, TX 77046
Phone: (713)960-9283
James D. Weaver, President

Foundation Philosophy: The foundation makes grants across the major categories of support. In health services, interests include children's hospitals, health science centers, and single disease associations. Social service support goes to homes, aid to the homeless, youth organizations, and united funds. Educational funding favors colleges and universities. Various programs also are supported in the arts and civic affairs. **Giving Priorities:** In 1994, approximately 31% of funding went to health care services. Educational institutions and programs received 25%. Civic concerns received 17% of funding, and social service organizations were given 15%. A science museum received 5%; religious organizations were given 4%; and the arts, 3%. The remaining funds supported international affairs. **Typical Health-Related Recipients:** AIDS/HIV, Cancer, Children's Health/Hospitals, Eyes/Blindness, Family Planning, Hospices, Hospitals, Medical Rehabilitation, Medical Research, Single-Disease Health Associations, Substance Abuse. **Geographic Distribution:** National, with a focus on Houston, TX.

★ 227 ★ Gordon / Rousmaniere / Roberts Fund

10 Hanover Sq.
New York, NY 10005
Phone: (212)510-4690
Mary G. Roberts, Trustee

Foundation Philosophy: The foundation makes grants across the major categories of support. The foundation's primary interest is education, with an emphasis on Harvard University and other colleges. Support for civic affairs includes environmental concerns and foreign relations. Health support favors public health and cancer research and treatment. Religious giving focuses on Catholic churches and organizations. Other support goes to social services and the arts. **Giving Priorities:** In 1994, the foundation reported that approximately 37% of funding went to education. Civic affairs received 16%, and 15% went to health care. The arts, religious organizations, and social service organizations each received approximately 11%. **Typical Health-Related Recipients:** Hospitals, Medical Education, Single-Disease Health Associations. **Geographic Distribution:** Focus on New York, Massachusetts, and Connecticut.

★ 228 ★ Gottesman Fund

1818 N St., NW, Ste. 200
Washington, DC 20036
Phone: (202)785-2727
Fax: (202)331-9306
Milton M. Gottesman, Vice President

Foundation Philosophy: The fund primarily supports the Jewish religion and higher education, including teaching and medicine. Other interests include organizations involved with Israel and civic foundations. **Giving Priorities:** In 1993, the fund gave approximately 42% of total contributions to religious institutions. About 36% of funding went to health concerns, including the fund's highest grant of $310,200 to the Mt. Sinai Medical Center. Educational institutions received about 11% of support; the arts and humanities, 5%; and international affairs, 3%. Social services, science groups, and civic concerns each received 1% of total funding. **Typical Health-Related Recipients:** AIDS/HIV, Clinics/Medical Centers, Family Planning, Hospitals, Medical Education, Medical Rehabilitation, Single-Disease Health Associations. **Geographic Distribution:** Eastern United States; focus on New York.

★ 229 ★ Grace and Franklin Bernsen Foundation

15 W 6th St.
Ste. 1308
Tulsa, OK 74119
Phone: (918)584-4711
Fax: (918)584-4713

Foundation Philosophy: The foundation traditionally has placed emphasis on the arts, education, and social services. **Giving Priorities:** In fiscal 1993, the foundation gave approximately 29% of its contributions to arts organizations, including a grant of $75,000 to the Tulsa Ballet Theater Building program. Health organizations received 20% of funding; social service organizations, 19%; civic organizations, 10%; religious concerns, 10%; and educational institutions, 8%. The remaining funds went to scientific and environmental organizations. **Typical Health-Related Recipients:** Children's Health/Hospitals, Clinics/Medical Centers, Domestic Violence, Health Organizations, Heart, Hospices, Hospitals, Medical Education, Medical Research, People with Disabilities, Sexual Abuse, Single-Disease Health Associations, Substance Abuse. **Geographic Distribution:** Focus on in the Tulsa, OK, area.

★ 230 ★ Grayce B. Kerr Fund

101 Bay St.
Easton, MD 21601
Phone: (410)822-6652
Fax: (410)822-4546
Sheryl V. Kerr, President

Foundation Philosophy: The trustees of the Grayce B. Kerr Fund are primarily interested in supporting projects that further educational excellence. The fund is also interested in supporting cultural activities and "improving the information base available for public policy-making." **Giving Priorities:** In 1993, the fund gave approximately 29% of its total contributions to educational institutions, including its highest grant of $200,000. The arts received about 28%; civic organizations, 14%; science, 13%; health, 9%;

environmental concerns, 7%; and social service organizations received the remaining funds. **Typical Health-Related Recipients:** Family Planning, Hospitals, Medical Research. **Geographic Distribution:** Focus on Maryland's Eastern Shore.

★ 231 ★   **Green Fund**
14 E 60th St., Ste. 702
New York, NY 10022
Phone: (212)755-2445
Fax: (212)755-0021
Bruce Rosenblatt, Contact

Foundation Philosophy: Because the fund initiates its grants program, it will not respond to solicitations. The fund concentrates its donations in the New York metropolitan area, providing general support for social service groups, especially to Jewish welfare organizations, health-related institutions, education, and the arts. **Giving Priorities:** In fiscal 1994, the foundation gave approximately 28% of its total contributions to religious organizations, including its highest grant of $288,780 to the United Jewish Appeal Federation. Educational institutions received about 27%; the arts, 17%; health concerns, 14%; civic affairs, 8%; social services, 4%; and international organizations received the remaining funds. **Typical Health-Related Recipients:** Cancer, Clinics/Medical Centers, Family Planning, Health Funds, Health Organizations, Hospices, Hospitals, Medical Education, Medical Rehabilitation, Medical Research, Nursing Services, People with Disabilities, Prenatal Health Issues, Single-Disease Health Associations. **Geographic Distribution:** Primarily New York City.

★ 232 ★   **Greenwall Foundation**
2 Park Ave., 24th Fl.
New York, NY 10016-9301
Phone: (212)679-7266
Fax: (212)679-7269
William C. Stubing, President

Foundation Philosophy: The foundation primarily supports work in medical research, education, and the arts. Medical funding targets areas of special interest to the foundation, namely bone tumors, insulin-dependent diabetes mellitus, geriatrics, and the moral dilemmas of medical decision making. In 1988, the foundation officers decided that medical grants should emphasize basic medical research as compared to the delivery of health services. **Giving Priorities:** In 1993, the foundation awarded 52% of total grants to education, including the highest grant of $150,000 to Stanford University. Health care received approximately 16%; civic affairs, 12%; and the arts, 10%. Science received 9% and social services received 2% of funding. **Typical Health-Related Recipients:** Clinics/Medical Centers, Diabetes, Health Organizations, Hospitals, Medical Education, Medical Research, Public Health. **Geographic Distribution:** Primarily in New York for arts and humanities; to national organizations for medical research and education.

★ 233 ★   **Gregg-Graniteville Foundation**
PO Box 418
Graniteville, SC 29829
Phone: (803)663-7552
Fax: (803)663-6435
Joan F. Phibbs, Administrator and Secretary-Treasurer

Foundation Philosophy: The purposes of the foundation are to make contributions or to render financial aid to the churches, schools, colleges, public libraries, and other educational and religious organizations located in Aiken County, SC, and Richmond County, GA; to provide scholarships or to finance other educational training; and to construct, own, operate, and maintain parks, gymnasiums, swimming pools, and other facilities for the benefit of the health and welfare of the people who work in the Graniteville, SC, area. **Giving Priorities:** In 1993, the foundation gave about 51% of total contributions to education. About 17% of funding went to religious institutions. Health concerns received approximately 13% of funds; civic, 7%; social services, 6%; and the arts, 5%. **Typical Health-Related Recipients:** Cancer, Domestic Violence, Geriatric Health, Health Organizations, Hospitals, Hospitals (University Affiliated), Medical Rehabilitation, Mental Health, People with Disabilities, Research/Studies Institutes, Single-Disease Health Associations. **Geographic Distribution:** Aiken County, SC, and Richmond County, GA.

★ 234 ★   **Grover Hermann Foundation**
7200 Sears Tower
233 South Wacker Dr.
Chicago, IL 60606
Phone: (312)876-1000
Fax: (312)258-5600
Paul K. Rhoads, President and Director

Foundation Philosophy: "The Grover Hermann Foundation funds education, health, community, public policy and religious programs throughout the United States. Its major interests are in higher education and health." In the health category, the foundation considers grants for facilities, basic research, disease-specific organizations, and other health programs having demonstrable significance. **Giving Priorities:** In 1993, the foundation gave approximately 38% of its total contributions to civic affairs, including its highest grant of $375,000 to the Pacific Legal Foundation in Sacramento, CA. Education, mainly colleges, universities, and student aid programs, received 24%. International affairs received about 16%; social services, 14%; and health care, 4%. The arts (2%) and religion (2%) received the remaining funds. **Typical Health-Related Recipients:** Domestic Violence, Health Organizations, Hospices, Hospitals, Medical Rehabilitation, Mental Health, Nursing Services, People with Disabilities, Single-Disease Health Associations, Speech & Hearing. **Geographic Distribution:** Broad geographic distribution, with grants for community-related activities favoring Chicago, IL, and Monterey County, CA.

★ 235 ★   **Grundy Foundation**
680 Radcliffe St.
PO Box 701
Bristol, PA 19007
Phone: (215)788-5460
Roland H. Johnson, Executive Director

Foundation Philosophy: The foundation considers scientific, literary, educational, and charitable projects in the Commonwealth of Pennsylvania. **Giving Priorities:** In 1993, the foundation gave approximately 31% of its contributions to the arts. Social services received 30%, including the highest grant of $100,000 to the United Way of Bucks County. Civic causes received 20% of funding; health care, 10%; the environment, 5%; and educational institutions, 4%. **Typical Health-Related Recipients:** Cancer, Children's Health/Hospitals, Family Planning, Hospitals, Long-Term Care, People with Disabilities, Respiratory, Substance Abuse. **Geographic Distribution:** Bucks County, PA.

★ 236 ★   **H. A. and Mary K. Chapman
Charitable Trust**
One Warren Pl., Ste. 1816
6100 S Yale
Tulsa, OK 74136
Phone: (918)496-7882
Fax: (918)496-7887
Ralph L. Abercrombie, Trustee

Foundation Philosophy: The trust typically supports higher and secondary educational institutions, social services, hospitals and health organizations, and the arts. **Giving Priorities:** In 1993, approximately 34% of the trust's financial support was awarded to health care, including a $298,900 grant to the Children's Medical Center, Tulsa, OK. Educational institutions received 32% of distributed funds. Social services received 14% of support. Religious interests received 8% of donations, while environmental affairs groups received 5%. The arts received 3% of support, while science and civic affairs organizations each received 2%. **Typical Health-Related Recipients:** Cancer, Children's Health/Hospitals, Clinics/Medical Centers, Domestic Violence, Hospices, Hospitals, Medical Research, People with Disabilities, Single-Disease Health Associations, Substance Abuse. **Geographic Distribution:** Primarily Tulsa, OK.

★ 237 ★   **H.C.S. Foundation**
1801 E 9th St., Ste. 1035
Cleveland, OH 44114-3103
Phone: (216)781-3502
Fax: (216)781-3504
L. Thomas Hiltz, Trustee

Foundation Philosophy: The foundation's priorities are education and social services. Educational support goes to university level capital improvements. Social service funding favors child welfare and homes. Other interests include conservation, health care, and the arts. **Giving Priorities:** In 1993, the foundation gave 32% of contributions to health organizations. Educational institutions received about 30% of funding. The arts and humanities received about 21% of total contributions, which consisted of the foundation's highest grant of $500,000 to the Cincinnati Art Museum. About 17% of funding went to religious institutions. **Typical**

Health-Related Recipients: Cancer, Eyes/ Blindness, Family Planning, Health Funds, Health Organizations, Hospitals, Medical Rehabilitation, People with Disabilities, Prenatal Health Issues. **Geographic Distribution:** Limited to Ohio, with a focus on Cleveland.

★ 238 ★ **H. Leslie Hoffman and Elaine S. Hoffman Foundation**
225 S Lake Ave., Ste. 1150
Pasadena, CA 91101
Phone: (818)793-0043
Fax: (818)793-0047
Eugene P. Carver, Trustee

Foundation Philosophy: The H. Leslie Hoffman and Elaine S. Hoffman Foundation's main focus is educational institutions in the Los Angeles, CA, area. The foundation also supports social service organizations, health concerns; and the arts. **Giving Priorities:** In 1993, the foundation awarded approximately 76% of its total contributions to educational institutions. Social service groups received 12% of support; health care, 5%; civic affairs, 3%; religion, 2%; and the arts, 2%. **Typical Health-Related Recipients:** Cancer, Children's Health/Hospitals, Diabetes, Emergency/Ambulance Services, Medical Education, Medical Research, People with Disabilities. **Geographic Distribution:** Los Angeles, CA, area only.

★ 239 ★ **H. N. and Frances C. Berger Foundation**
PO Box 661178
Arcadia, CA 91006-1178
Phone: (818)447-3551
Fax: (818)447-9524
Ronald M. Auen, President

Foundation Philosophy: The foundation maintains a long-term commitment to the support of education, especially colleges and universities where the foundation has established scholarships and endowments. Besides its support of education, the foundation generally limits its support of charitable organizations to California. **Giving Priorities:** In 1992, approximately 58% of contributions went to education, with special emphasis on colleges and universities. Health organizations received 27%, with a large grant going to the Methodist Hospital Foundation in Arcadia, CA. Social services received 13%. The arts, civic causes, and religious concerns received the remaining funds. **Typical Health-Related Recipients:** AIDS/HIV, Alzheimers Disease, Cancer, Children's Health/Hospitals, Clinics/Medical Centers, Domestic Violence, Emergency/Ambulance Services, Heart, Hospices, Hospitals, Medical Research, Nursing Services, Single-Disease Health Associations, Substance Abuse. **Geographic Distribution:** Emphasis on California.

★ 240 ★ **Hagedorn Fund**
c/o Chemical Bank
270 Park Ave., 23rd Fl.
New York, NY 10017
Phone: (212)270-9107
Robert C. Rosenthal, Vice President

Foundation Philosophy: The Hagedorn Fund makes most of its grants in two areas: social services and health care. In social services, interests include children, religious charities, homes, and domestic violence. Health care support favors single disease associations and hospitals. Other areas of interest include religious and legal education, community colleges, minority college funds, libraries, civic affairs, and churches. **Giving Priorities:** In 1992, health care, including major support for hospitals, received 29%. Educational institutions received 22% of total contributions. Religious concerns received 21%. Social service organizations received 18% of giving. Civic and public affairs received 6% of donations, while the arts received 3%. The remainder went to fund international concerns, with a donation to CARE. **Typical Health-Related Recipients:** AIDS/HIV, Arthritis, Cancer, Clinics/Medical Centers, Diabetes, Emergency/Ambulance Services, Eyes/ Blindness, Family Planning, Health Organizations, Health Policy/Cost Containment, Heart, Hospices, Hospitals, Medical Rehabilitation, Mental Health, People with Disabilities. **Geographic Distribution:** Northeastern United States, with a focus on New York, NY.

★ 241 ★ **Haggar Foundation**
6113 Lemmon Ave.
Dallas, TX 75209
Phone: (214)956-4241
Marty Vaughn Rumble, Executive Director

Foundation Philosophy: The main purpose of the foundation is to support civic and other charitable projects that have a wide community appeal. Except for ten national projects the foundation has traditionally supported, it supports projects only in communities where Haggar Apparel Company operates facilities. In addition to its general giving program, the foundation also offers a scholarship program to relatives of employees of Haggar Apparel Company. **Giving Priorities:** In fiscal 1992, the foundation gave approximately 55% of its total contributions to educational institutions and organizations. Health care organizations received 12% of the funds while religious organizations were granted 11%. Awards to social service organizations accounted for 8% of the giving; these included support for religious welfare and youth organizations. Civic organizations and the arts each received approximately 6% of the funds. The remaining contributions funded a science exhibit. (Grants analysis derived from a 1992 partial grants list.) **Typical Health-Related Recipients:** Alzheimers Disease, Cancer, Children's Health/Hospitals, Health Organizations, Heart, Hospitals, Nursing Services, Prenatal Health Issues, Public Health, Substance Abuse. **Geographic Distribution:** Focus on southern Texas communities with Haggar Apparel facilities.

★ 242 ★ **Hall Foundation**
115 3rd St. SE, No. 803
Cedar Rapids, IA 52401-1222
Phone: (319)362-9079
John G. Lidvall, Executive Director and Vice President

Foundation Philosophy: "The foundation is interested in assisting local tax-exempt public institutions and organizations dedicated to the solution of problems of people of all ages. The foundation has a particular interest in all areas of health care. It also has a concern for the advancement of education, seeks to support projects to resolve social problems, and is interested in the encouragement and maintenance of community cultural activities." **Giving Priorities:** In 1993, the foundation gave approximately 29% of funding to social services. The arts and education each received 24% of total giving. Health care received 17%; civic affairs, 4%; religion, 1%; and environmental efforts, 1%. **Typical Health-Related Recipients:** Domestic Violence, Emergency/Ambulance Services, Family Planning, Geriatric Health, Health Organizations, Hospitals, People with Disabilities, Substance Abuse. **Geographic Distribution:** Cedar Rapids, IA, community and surrounding Linn County area.

★ 243 ★ **Harden Foundation**
PO Box 779
Salinas, CA 93902-0779
Phone: (408)442-3005
Fax: (408)443-1429
Patricia Tynan-Chapman, Secretary

Foundation Philosophy: The foundation distributes its support among a variety of organizations in different fields. While social services generally receive the largest measure of support from the foundation, its largest grant of $1,050,000 was awarded to the Salinas Valley Memorial Hospital Foundation in fiscal 1992. **Giving Priorities:** In fiscal 1993, the foundation gave 41% of total contributions to social services. Health concerns in Monterey County received 35% of the foundation's funds. Civic concerns received 13% of support. The arts and humanities received 10%. Two educational foundations received the remaining funds. **Typical Health-Related Recipients:** AIDS/HIV, Children's Health/Hospitals, Clinics/Medical Centers, Domestic Violence, Family Planning, Health Funds, Home-Care Services, Hospices, Hospitals, Long-Term Care, Mental Health, Nursing Services, Nutrition, People with Disabilities, Respiratory, Single-Disease Health Associations. **Geographic Distribution:** Limited to Monterey County, CA, with a focus on the Salinas Valley area.

★ 244 ★ **Harold K. L. Castle Foundation**
146 Hekili St., Ste. 203A
Kailua, HI 96734
Phone: (808)262-9413
Fax: (808)261-6918
Katherine F. Braden, Vice President and Treasurer

Foundation Philosophy: The foundation favors higher education, the environment, health and human services, and the arts, in Hawaii. The foundation places more emphasis on programs that can effect true systemic change rather than programs which do not address the cause of the problem. **Giving Priorities:** In 1993, education received approximately 38% of funding. Social services, primarily youth organizations, received 30%. Health care was awarded 14% of funds; environment received 7%; and approximately 6% supported the arts. The remaining funds supported other foundation interests. **Typical Health-Related Recipients:** Clinics/Medical Centers, Domestic Violence, Health Organizations, Hospitals, Medical Rehabilitation, People with Disabilities, Single-Disease Health Associations, Substance Abuse. **Geographic Distribution: Primarily Hawaii, particularly Windward Oahu.

★245★ **Harold McAlister Charitable Foundation**
4801 Wilshire Blvd., Ste. 232
Los Angeles, CA 90010
Phone: (213)937-0927
Virginia Gilbert, Contact

Foundation Philosophy: Health services are a major interest of the foundation, although no specific health care field is supported uniformly. Social services organizations also receive regular support, with primary interests in child welfare, animal protection, services for the disabled, and other community support organizations. Higher education in California also is a major priority. **Giving Priorities:** In fiscal 1992, the foundation gave approximately 57% of its total contributions to health concerns, including its highest grant of $236,000 for the Los Angeles Heart Institute. Educational institutions, mainly colleges and universities, received 24%. Social service organizations received 15%; the arts, 3%; and religion and civic affairs received the remaining funds. **Typical Health-Related Recipients:** Arthritis, Children's Health/Hospitals, Clinics/Medical Centers, Geriatric Health, Health Organizations, Heart, Hospitals, Kidney, Medical Research, Nutrition, People with Disabilities, Research/Studies Institutes, Respiratory, Sexual Abuse, Single-Disease Health Associations, Speech & Hearing, Substance Abuse. **Geographic Distribution:** Focus on the Los Angeles, CA, area.

★246★ **Harriett Ames Charitable Trust**
St. Davids Center, Ste. A-200
150 Radnor-Chester Rd.
St. Davids, PA 19087
Phone: (215)341-9270
Fax: (215)964-8688
L. Dianne Lomonaco, Trust Administrator

Foundation Philosophy: The trust's primary funding interests include hospitals and organizations engaged in medical research, educational institutions, and Jewish welfare organizations. The trust also supports cultural and youth programs. **Giving Priorities:** In 1993, the trust contributed 53% of its total funding to health care. The highest grant of $72,000 was awarded to United Cerebral Palsy of New York. Educational institutions received 30% of giving, and the arts received 14%. Social services received 2% of giving and the remaining funds supported civic groups, religious organizations, and international concerns. **Typical Health-Related Recipients:** Alzheimers Disease, Cancer, Clinics/Medical Centers, Diabetes, Eyes/Blindness, Health Funds, Health Organizations, Hospitals, Medical Education, Medical Research, Multiple Sclerosis, People with Disabilities, Research/Studies Institutes, Single-Disease Health Associations, Trauma Treatment. **Geographic Distribution:** Emphasis on New York State, with some national giving.

★247★ **Harris and Eliza Kempner Fund**
PO Box 119
Galveston, TX 77553-0119
Phone: (409)765-6671
Fax: (409)765-9098
Elaine Perachio, Executive Director

Foundation Philosophy: The fund intends to focus on the needs of children and youth including education, health care, and human services, as well as access to social, spiritual, and cultural enrichment. A second priority is addressing the need for affordable housing for low- to moderate-income families. Finally, economic development will receive particular attention in the coming years. **Giving Priorities:** In 1994, the fund gave approximately 32% of its contributions to social service organizations, while religious causes received 20%. Health organizations received 13%. Other areas receiving support included civic and public affairs, 10%; international, 9%; education, 8%; environment, 5%; and the arts, 3%. **Typical Health-Related Recipients:** Adolescent Health Issues, AIDS/HIV, Alzheimers Disease, Domestic Violence, Emergency/Ambulance Services, Family Planning, Health Organizations, Heart, Medical Education, People with Disabilities, Research/Studies Institutes, Single-Disease Health Associations, Substance Abuse. **Geographic Distribution:** Focus on Galveston, TX.

★248★ **Harry A. and Margaret D. Towsley Foundation**
3055 Plymouth Rd., Ste. 200
Ann Arbor, MI 48105
Phone: (313)662-6777
Fax: (313)994-0165
Margaret Ann Riecker, President and Trustee

Foundation Philosophy: The foundation generally focuses its philanthropic work on the problems and needs of private higher education and health education and services. Cultural arts, religion, community services, and innovative projects also receive considerable funding. **Giving Priorities:** In 1993, approximately 70% of funding went to educational institutions. Civic and public affairs received 11% of total giving. Health organizations received 7% of giving; the arts, 6%; social services, 5%; and religious organizations, 2%. **Typical Health-Related Recipients:** AIDS/HIV, Cancer, Children's Health/Hospitals, Family Planning, Hospitals, Medical Education, Medical Rehabilitation, Medical Research, Nursing Services, Public Health, Single-Disease Health Associations, Substance Abuse. **Geographic Distribution:** Michigan, especially Ann Arbor and Washtenaw County.

★249★ **Harry C. Moores Foundation**
100 S 3rd St.
Columbus, OH 43215
Phone: (614)227-8884
Fax: (614)227-2390
Mary Cummings, Foundation Contact

Foundation Philosophy: The Harry C. Moores Foundation is primarily interested in supporting social services, education, and health. Health funding goes to hospitals, health organizations, and single-disease associations. The foundation also supports the arts, civic affairs, and religion. **Giving Priorities:** In 1993, the foundation gave approximately 31% of funding to social services, including the foundation's highest grant of $100,000. Health groups and educational institutions each received about 24% of total contributions, while religious concerns received 13% of funds. The arts and humanities were granted 7%, and the remaining contributions went to science and civic affairs. **Typical Health-Related Recipients:** Alzheimers Disease, Arthritis, Cancer, Children's Health/Hospitals, Clinics/Medical Centers, Diabetes, Emergency/Ambulance Services, Eyes/Blindness, Health Funds, Health Organizations, Hospitals, People with Disabilities, Single-Disease Health Associations. **Geographic Distribution:** Focus on the Columbus, OH, area.

★250★ **Harry C. Trexler Trust**
33 S Seventh St., Ste. 205
Allentown, PA 18101
Phone: (610)434-9645
Fax: (610)437-5721
Thomas H. Christman, Secretary to the Trustees

Foundation Philosophy: Following the wishes of the donors, the trustees look to fund organizations which are "of the most benefit to humanity" in Allentown or Lehigh County. Areas of funding are not rigid, but will continually change in response to the needs of the area. Present areas of concern are culture and parks, education, youth, the elderly, and the disadvantaged. **Giving Priorities:** In fiscal 1994, civic and public affairs organizations received about 30% of giving. About 18% of funding supported social services. The arts received 17% of giving, and educational institutions received 14%. Religious concerns were given 12%; health organizations, 7%; and environmental affairs, 3%. **Typical Health-Related Recipients:** Long-Term Care, Medical Rehabilitation, Nursing Services, People with Disabilities. **Geographic Distribution:** Allentown and Lehigh County, PA, only.

★251★ **Harry Frank Guggenheim Foundation**
527 Madison Ave., 15th Fl.
New York, NY 10022-4304
Phone: (212)644-4909
Fax: (212)644-5110
Joel Wallman, Program Officer

Foundation Philosophy: Highest priority is given to research that can increase understanding and amelioration of urgent problems of violence, aggression, and dominance in the modern world. "Particular questions that interest the Foundation concern violence, aggression, and dominance in relation to social change, the socialization of children, intergroup conflict, drug trafficking and use, family relationships, and investigations of the control of aggression and violence." **Giving Priorities:** In 1992, the foundation gave approximately 68% of funding to educational institutions. The arts and humanities received about 17% of total contributions; health concerns, 9%; science programs, 3%; religious institutions, 1%; social services, 1%; and civic concerns, 1%. **Typical Health-Related Recipients:** Health Funds, Medical Education, Medical Research, People with Disabilities. **Geographic Distribution:** No geographic restrictions.

★ 252 ★ Harry and Grace Steele Foundation
441 Old Newport Blvd., Ste. 301
Newport Beach, CA 92663
Phone: (714)631-9158
Marie F. Kowert, Assistant Secretary

Foundation Philosophy: Grant making is concentrated in four main fields of interest: education, health, humanities, and welfare. **Giving Priorities:** In fiscal 1993, the foundation gave approximately 46% of its contributions to social service organizations, including its highest grant of $1,815,000 to the Planned Parenthood Federation of America, New York, NY. Educational institutions received 18% of funding and the arts received 15%. International affairs, mainly health care and peace and security issues, received 10%. Health concerns received 9%, and civic affairs and religion received the remainder. **Typical Health-Related Recipients:** Cancer, Children's Health/Hospitals, Domestic Violence, Family Planning, Hospitals, Outpatient Health Care, People with Disabilities. **Geographic Distribution:** Primarily Orange County, CA.

★ 253 ★ Harry and Maribel G. Blum Foundation
919 N Michigan Ave., Ste. 2800
Chicago, IL 60611
Phone: (312)664-5050
H. Jonathan Kovler, President

Foundation Philosophy: The foundation's primary interest is Jewish organizations, including religious and social service organizations. It also supports health care, child welfare, and educational institutions. **Giving Priorities:** In 1994, the foundation reported that it gave approximately 39% of its total contributions to religious groups, primarily to Jewish organizations. Health care received 35% of funds; the arts, 22%; and educational institutions, 3%. The remainder went to civic and social service organizations. **Typical Health-Related Recipients:** Clinics/Medical Centers, Diabetes, Hospitals, Medical Research, Single-Disease Health Associations, Transplant Networks/Donor Banks. **Geographic Distribution:** National, with emphasis on Illinois.

★ 254 ★ Harry S. and Isabel C. Cameron Foundation
Nations Bank of Texas
PO Box 298502
Houston, TX 77298-0502
Phone: (713)787-4553
Fax: (713)787-4585
Carl W. Schumacker, Jr., Senior Vice President and Trust Officer

Foundation Philosophy: The foundation, following the interests of its donors, supports educational institutions in Texas. It also shows an interest in religious organizations and social service agencies. **Giving Priorities:** In fiscal 1993, religious organizations and churches received approximately 33% of giving. Colleges, universities, and private schools received 31% of total funding. Social services were awarded 19% of giving, with support for drug rehabilitation programs. Civic affairs received 9%; health care, 7%; and international services, 1%. **Typical Health-Related Recipients:** Cancer, Clinics/

Medical Centers, Emergency/Ambulance Services, Eyes/Blindness, Health Organizations, Hospices, Hospitals, Medical Rehabilitation, Mental Health, Nursing Services, People with Disabilities, Single-Disease Health Associations, Substance Abuse. **Geographic Distribution:** Texas, primarily Houston.

★ 255 ★ Harry S. Moss Heart Trust
PO Box 830241
Nations Bank, 19th Fl.
Dallas, TX 75283-0242
Phone: (214)508-1936
Connie Rogers, Trust Officer

Foundation Philosophy: The Harry S. Moss Heart Trust supports health education and health care organizations. Most of the recent funding goes to medical schools. Health care is supported through medical centers and nursing. The foundation also supports community centers. **Giving Priorities:** In fiscal 1993, the trust awarded 91% of its total contributions to health care, including a single $750,000 grant to the University of Texas Southwestern Medical Center, Dallas, TX. The remaining 9% went to social services organizations. **Typical Health-Related Recipients:** Children's Health/Hospitals, Clinics/Medical Centers, Heart, Hospitals, Medical Education, Medical Research, Nursing Services, People with Disabilities, Single-Disease Health Associations. **Geographic Distribution:** Focus on Dallas, TX.

★ 256 ★ Harvey Randall Wickes Foundation
4800 Fashion Sq. Blvd.
Plaza North, Rm. 472
Saginaw, MI 48604
Phone: (517)799-1850
James V. Finkbeiner, President

Foundation Philosophy: The main purpose of the foundation is to provide buildings and equipment to educational, health, and social service organizations in the Saginaw, MI, area. Support for the area's three hospitals is also given. The foundation also supports the United Way, and parks and recreation facilities in Saginaw Township. **Giving Priorities:** In 1993, the foundation gave 28% of its total contributions to local civic organizations and public affairs. Educational institutions received 27%. Health care was awarded 16%; social services, 13%; religious welfare organizations, 10%; and the arts received 6% of support. **Typical Health-Related Recipients:** Clinics/Medical Centers, Health Funds, Health Organizations, Hospitals, Medical Rehabilitation, People with Disabilities, Substance Abuse. **Geographic Distribution:** Saginaw County, MI.

★ 257 ★ Hawn Foundation
5956 Sherry Ln., Ste. 1210
Dallas, TX 75225
Phone: (214)265-8435
William R. Hawn, President

Foundation Philosophy: The Hawn Foundation primarily makes grants in the areas of education and health care. In health care, interests include health and research foundations, nursing, single-disease associations, and hospitals. Other recipient areas receive support from the foundation on a limited basis. **Giving Priorities:**

In fiscal 1993, the foundation gave approximately 49% of funding to health organizations, including a $100,000 grant to the Texas Scottish Rite Hospital in Dallas. The arts and humanities received about 23% of total contributions. The remainder of funds went to religious organizations, 14%; social services, 10%; educational institutions, 3%; international affairs, 1%; and civic concerns, 1%. **Typical Health-Related Recipients:** Arthritis, Child Abuse, Children's Health/Hospitals, Clinics/Medical Centers, Diabetes, Eyes/Blindness, Health Funds, Health Organizations, Heart, Hospitals, Long-Term Care, Medical Rehabilitation, Medical Research, Multiple Sclerosis, Nursing Services, People with Disabilities, Single-Disease Health Associations, Substance Abuse. **Geographic Distribution:** Focus on Texas, with emphasis on Dallas.

★ 258 ★ HCA Foundation
One Park Plz.
PO Box 550
Nashville, TN 37202-0550
Phone: (615)320-2165
Fax: (615)320-2017
Kenneth L. Roberts, President and Executive Director

Foundation Philosophy: The HCA Foundation makes most of its grants in the areas of education, social services, and the arts. Most of its resources are funnelled through its initiatives, the best-known of which include The Center for Nonprofit Management; The Young Leaders Council; The HCA Fund for Collaboration; The HCA Awards of Achievement; and The HCA Teacher Awards. **Giving Priorities:** In 1993, the foundation awarded approximately 35% of total contributions to educational institutions. Social services received 32%. The arts received about 24% of funding. Health concerns received 5%; and civic affairs received the remaining 4%. **Typical Health-Related Recipients:** Domestic Violence, Family Planning, Health Organizations, Health Policy/Cost Containment, Medical Education, Medical Training, Mental Health, Nursing Services, People with Disabilities, Public Health, Substance Abuse. **Geographic Distribution:** Restricted to Nashville, TN organizations.

★ 259 ★ Hearst Foundation
888 Seventh Ave., 45th Fl.
New York, NY 10106
Phone: (212)586-5404
Robert M. Frehse, Jr., Executive Director and Vice President

Foundation Philosophy: The foundation continues to reflect the philanthropic interests of William Randolph Hearst: education, human services, health, and culture. Priority areas include programs to aid poverty-level and minority groups; education programs, with emphasis on private secondary and higher education; health care and medical research; and publicly supported cultural programs. **Giving Priorities:** In 1994, the foundation reported that it gave approximately 50% of its contributions to education. The arts and humanities received 20%; social services, 16%; and health care, 14%. The remaining funds supported miscellaneous projects. **Typical Health-Related Recipients:**

AIDS/HIV, Clinics/Medical Centers, Emergency/Ambulance Services, Home-Care Services, Hospitals, Medical Education, Medical Rehabilitation, Nursing Services, People with Disabilities, Prenatal Health Issues, Substance Abuse. **Geographic Distribution:** National, including Puerto Rico and other United States possessions.

★260★ Helen Brach Foundation
55 W Wacker Dr., Ste. 701
Chicago, IL 60601
Phone: (312)372-4417
Raymond F. Simon, President and Director

Foundation Philosophy: The foundation's grants have not been limited to any single area, but "areas of interest, among others, have included efforts to save wildlife, curtail the abuse of children and animals, provide funding for education at the secondary and college level, and help for those serving the physically and mentally disabled, the poor, the blind, the homeless, the teenaged unwed mother, and the elderly." **Giving Priorities:** In fiscal 1993, approximately 64% of giving went to social services, primarily supporting youth organizations, human services, and animal protection groups. Education received 25% with a majority of grants funding colleges and universities. Religious organizations received 6%; health concerns, 3%; and the arts, 2%. **Typical Health-Related Recipients:** AIDS/HIV, Children's Health/Hospitals, Clinics/Medical Centers, Geriatric Health, Health Funds, Health Organizations, Hospices, Hospitals, Nursing Services, Nutrition, People with Disabilities, Public Health. **Geographic Distribution:** National, with emphasis on Illinois.

**★261★ Helen K. and Arthur E. Johnson
       Foundation**
1700 Broadway, Ste. 2302
Denver, CO 80290
Phone: (303)861-4127
Fax: (303)861-0607
Stan Kamprath, Vice President and Executive Director

Foundation Philosophy: The foundation supports a wide variety of creative efforts to solve human problems and to enrich the quality of life. It concentrates its efforts on health, education, youth, civic and cultural affairs, community and social services, and senior citizens. **Giving Priorities:** In 1993, foundation gave approximately 25% of its contributions to community and social services, including funding for drug abuse programs and community service organizations. Educational institutions received 24%; religion, 17%; health care, 16%; civic affairs, 11%; and the arts, 6%. **Typical Health-Related Recipients:** AIDS/HIV, Alzheimers Disease, Cancer, Clinics/Medical Centers, Family Planning, Health Organizations, Hospitals, Medical Research, Nursing Services, People with Disabilities, Single-Disease Health Associations, Speech & Hearing, Substance Abuse. **Geographic Distribution:** Colorado only.

★262★ Helena Rubinstein Foundation
405 Lexington Ave., 15th Fl.
New York, NY 10174
Phone: (212)986-0806
Diane Moss, President

Foundation Philosophy: The foundation has developed and broadened its original philanthropic concepts to meet the changing needs of society and continues to support an increasing number of innovative programs in education, the arts, arts-in-education, women's issues, and community services. **Giving Priorities:** In fiscal 1993, about 28% of the foundation's contributions went to religious affiliations. Education received 22% of giving. International concerns received about 15% of funding, and the arts, about 14%. Health care received approximately 13% of total grants; social services, 5%; and civic affairs, 3%. **Typical Health-Related Recipients:** AIDS/HIV, Cancer, Family Planning, Geriatric Health, Health Organizations, Hospitals, Medical Education, Medical Rehabilitation, Medical Research, Medical Training, Nursing Services, Prenatal Health Issues, Public Health, Single-Disease Health Associations, Substance Abuse. **Geographic Distribution:** Primarily New York, NY; minimal support nationally and internationally.

★263★ Helmerich Foundation
1579 E 21st St.
Tulsa, OK 74114
Phone: (918)742-5531
Walter H. Helmerich, III, Trustee

Foundation Philosophy: The Helmerich Foundation makes the majority of its grants in the arts. The foundation prefers to make large grants that have an impact on projects. Therefore, other recipient areas are funded on a limited basis. **Giving Priorities:** In fiscal 1993, the foundation awarded 55% of its total contribution to the arts. About 18% of funds went to religious organizations. Educational institutions received 11% of support; social services, 7%; health care, 7%; and environmental concerns, 1%. **Typical Health-Related Recipients:** Children's Health/Hospitals, Clinics/Medical Centers, Domestic Violence, Eyes/Blindness, Health Organizations, People with Disabilities. **Geographic Distribution:** Limited to the Tulsa, OK, area.

★264★ Henry Ford II Fund
100 Renaissance Center, 34th Fl.
Detroit, MI 48243
Phone: (313)259-7777
Pierre V. Heftler, Secretary and Trustee

Foundation Philosophy: The fund's designated areas of support are the arts, churches, community chests and other related organizations, hospitals and medical research, and education. The fund reports that awards "are generally limited to charitable organizations already favorably known to, and of interest to, the substantial contributors of the foundation." **Giving Priorities:** In 1993, the fund donated about 54% of funds to educational institutions. Health concerns received approximately 17% of funding; social services, 16%. Religious groups received 8% of total contributions. Civic causes received about 4% of funding. The arts and humanities received the remainder of funds. **Typical Health-Related Recipients:** Children's Health/

Hospitals, Emergency/Ambulance Services, Eyes/Blindness, Health Organizations, Hospitals, Medical Rehabilitation, Medical Research, People with Disabilities. **Geographic Distribution:** Emphasis on Detroit, MI.

★265★ Henry J. Kaiser Family Foundation
2400 Sand Hill Rd.
Menlo Park, CA 94025
Phone: (415)854-9400
Fax: (415)854-4800
Bruce W. Madding, VP of Finance and Admin.

Foundation Philosophy: The foundation supports efforts to make government more responsive to the health needs of the American people, to improve the health of low-income and minority groups, to help make the foundation's home state of California a leader in innovation and reform, and to develop a more equitable and effective health care system in South Africa. **Giving Priorities:** In 1993, health and health-related programs received 98% of the foundation's new grant commitments including universities and policy research groups, as well as conventional health organizations. International concerns received 18% of new commitments (most of which is included in the foundation's 98% which goes to health-related programs) through the foundation's Health and Development in South Africa program. The foundation's three categories of contributions are reproductive health, HIV/AIDS policy, and medicaid. **Typical Health-Related Recipients:** AIDS/HIV, Cancer, Clinics/Medical Centers, Family Planning, Geriatric Health, Health Organizations, Health Policy/Cost Containment, Heart, Hospitals, Long-Term Care, Medical Education, Nursing Services, Nutrition, Prenatal Health Issues, Preventive Medicine/Wellness Organizations, Public Health, Substance Abuse. **Geographic Distribution:** Some emphasis on California; also South Africa.

★266★ Henry L. Hillman Foundation
2000 Grant Bldg.
Pittsburgh, PA 15219
Phone: (412)338-3466
Ronald W. Wertz, President

Foundation Philosophy: The foundation contributes to multiple interests based on the single principle of helping people and organizations to improve themselves mainly in the Pittsburgh and Southwestern Pennsylvania area. The foundation annually contributes to the Carnegie Institute. **Giving Priorities:** In 1990, the foundation gave approximately 37% of its contributions to education. The arts received 21%. Civic and public affairs also received 21%. Churches received 15%; health care, 5%; and social services, 1%. **Typical Health-Related Recipients:** Hospitals, Medical Rehabilitation. **Geographic Distribution:** Primarily Pittsburgh and southwestern Pennsylvania.

★267★ Henry and Lucy Moses Fund
c/o Moses and Singer
1301 Avenue of the Americas, 40th Fl.
New York, NY 10019
Phone: (212)554-7800
Fax: (212)554-7700
Henry Schneider, President

Foundation Philosophy: The foundation's major concern is hospitals and health-related causes. Other areas which receive support are higher education, Jewish welfare activities, youth, social services, and music. **Giving Priorities:** In 1993, the foundation gave 48% of its funding to Jewish service organizations. Civic affairs received 15% and health care was awarded 14% of funding. The arts received 9% of contributions. Social services received 8% of contributions; education received 5%; and international concerns were given 1%. **Typical Health-Related Recipients:** Cancer, Clinics/Medical Centers, Family Planning, Health Organizations, Hospitals, Medical Education, Medical Research, Nursing Services, People with Disabilities, Single-Disease Health Associations. **Geographic Distribution:** Primarily New York City metropolitan area, some national funding.

★ 268 ★ Henry and Marilyn Taub Foundation
c/o Wiss and Co.
354 Eisenhower Pkwy.
Livingston, NJ 07039
Phone: (201)994-9400
Henry Taub, President

Foundation Philosophy: The Henry and Marilyn Taub Foundation provides funds for Jewish religious organizations. The arts, civic affairs, health services and social services also are supported by the foundation, particularly when they are affiliated with the Jewish faith. **Giving Priorities:** In 1993, the foundation gave approximately 38% of funding to educational institutions. Religious institutions received about 37% of funding. International affairs received about 12% of funding; the arts and humanities, 7%; health groups, 5%; civic concerns, 1%; and social services, 1%. **Typical Health-Related Recipients:** Clinics/Medical Centers, Hospitals, Medical Education, Medical Rehabilitation, People with Disabilities, Single-Disease Health Associations, Substance Abuse. **Geographic Distribution:** Eastern United States; focus on New York and New Jersey.

★ 269 ★ Henry Nias Foundation
Ste. 226
540 W Boston Post Rd.
Mamaroneck, NY 10543
Phone: (914)969-9707
Albert J. Rosenberg, President

Foundation Philosophy: The Henry Nias Foundation makes grants across the major categories of support. In health care, interests include geriatric care, hospitals, and medical centers. Social service support goes to the disabled, the aged, youth organizations, and family planning. Support for the arts favors public broadcasting, museums, and the performing arts. Funding for education goes to continuing education, scholarships, and medical schools. Other recipient areas also are supported. **Giving Priorities:** In fiscal 1993, the foundation gave 24% of its funds to religious organziations. Social services, with emphasis on services for the handicapped, the homeless, and the elderly, also claimed 24% of the giving. Health centers and hospitals received 23% and the arts received 15% of contributions. Educational institutions received 10%; international organizations, 2%; and the remaining 2% was split between civic affairs and science. **Typical Health-Related Recipients:** Clinics/Medical Centers, Family Planning, Geriatric Health, Health Organizations, Hospitals, Long-Term Care, Medical Education, Medical Rehabilitation, People with Disabilities, Single-Disease Health Associations, Speech & Hearing. **Geographic Distribution:** New York City only.

★ 270 ★ Herbst Foundation
3 Embarcadero Ctr., 21st Fl.
San Francisco, CA 94111
Phone: (415)951-7508
Fax: (415)296-0628
John T. Seigle, President

Foundation Philosophy: The foundation's primary purpose is to provide capital support (bricks-and-mortar) to organizations in the city and county of San Francisco. Primary concerns include education and social services. **Giving Priorities:** In fiscal 1993, the foundation gave approximately 27% of its total contributions to educational institutions. Civic affairs received about 20% of giving. Scientific interests received 17%, including the foundation's highest grant of $250,000 to the California Academy of Sciences. Religious organizations received 15%; health care, 9%; social services, 9%; and the arts, 3%. Environmental causes and international affairs received the remaining funds. **Typical Health-Related Recipients:** Alzheimers Disease, Clinics/Medical Centers, Geriatric Health, Hospitals, Medical Research, People with Disabilities. **Geographic Distribution:** Primarily within city and county of San Francisco, CA.

★ 271 ★ Herman Goldman Foundation
61 Broadway, 18th Fl.
New York, NY 10006
Phone: (212)797-9090
Richard K. Baron, Executive Director

Foundation Philosophy: Program guidelines emphasize education, social development and justice, health, and the arts. **Giving Priorities:** In fiscal 1994, the foundation gave approximately 37% of contributions to health care, including hospitals, single-disease health associations, and health-related programs at colleges and universities. Education received 18% of support. Civic affairs received 15%. Social services received 14% of funds. The arts received 7%; international organizations, 5%; and religious organizations, 4%. **Typical Health-Related Recipients:** Health Funds, Health Organizations, Hospitals, Medical Education, Medical Research, Mental Health, People with Disabilities, Single-Disease Health Associations. **Geographic Distribution:** Primarily New York City metropolitan area and surrounding counties.

★ 272 ★ Herman T. and Phenie R. Pott Foundation
PO Box 4503
Chesterfield, MO 63006-4503
Phone: (314)537-0016
James Collins, Member of Advisory Committee

Foundation Philosophy: The foundation makes most of its grants in the areas of social services and education. Social service funding favors shelters, family resource centers, children's services, and united funds. Funding in education emphasizes universities and college funds in St. Louis. The trust also will fund civic affairs, libraries, and health services. **Giving Priorities:** In 1990, the foundation gave 37% of its contributions to social service organizations. Education received 21% of the contributions. Civic affairs received 15% of the giving. The foundation contributed 14% of its funds to the arts. The remainder went to health, 10%, and religious causes, 3%. **Typical Health-Related Recipients:** Domestic Violence, Family Planning, Health Organizations, Hospitals, Medical Research, Mental Health. **Geographic Distribution:** Focus on Missouri, with an emphasis on St. Louis.

★ 273 ★ Herrick Foundation
150 W Jefferson, Ste. 2500
Detroit, MI 48226
Phone: (313)963-6420
Fax: (313)496-8462
Kenneth G. Herrick, Chm., Pres., Treas., & Trustee

Foundation Philosophy: The foundation traditionally supports educational projects, churches, hospitals, health organizations, civic groups, social service agencies, and cultural organizations in Michigan. **Giving Priorities:** In fiscal 1992, the foundation gave about 52% of funding to educational concerns principally to colleges and universities. Health agencies and civic concerns each received approximately 16%, while social services received 9%. The arts received 5%; religious causes, 2%. **Typical Health-Related Recipients:** Children's Health/Hospitals, Health Funds, Health Organizations, Hospices, Hospitals, Medical Education, People with Disabilities, Single-Disease Health Associations, Substance Abuse. **Geographic Distribution:** No geographic restrictions; some emphasis in Michigan.

★ 274 ★ Hess Foundation
1185 Avenue of the Americas
New York, NY 10036
Phone: (212)536-8421
Leon Hess, President

Foundation Philosophy: The foundation concentrates its giving in the areas of higher and secondary education, hospitals, medical research, temples, and social services. **Giving Priorities:** In fiscal 1993, the foundation gave approximately 33% of its contributions to social services, including the foundation's highest grant of $630,000 for the Hurricane Allen St. Lucia Rebuilding Fund, New York, NY. Religious organizations received 23% of funds. Education received 19% of contributions, primarily in support of colleges and universities. The arts and international affairs each received 7% of support, while health care received 6%. Civic affairs organizations received 5% of contributions. **Typical Health-Related Recipients:** Emergency/Ambulance Services, Health Organizations, Hospitals, Medical Education, People with Disabilities, Prenatal Health Issues, Single-Disease Health Associations. **Geographic Distribution:** National, with emphasis on the New York City area.

★275★ Hillcrest Foundation
c/o NationsBank Texas
PO Box 830241
Dallas, TX 75283
Phone: (214)508-1965
Daniel J. Kelly, Trust Officer

Foundation Philosophy: The Hillcrest Foundation was created to help alleviate poverty problems, to aid the advancement of education, and to promote health care in Texas. The grant applicant must be a charitable organization located in Texas, with a purpose compatible with the principles of the foundation. **Giving Priorities:** In fiscal 1993, the foundation reported that it gave approximately 40% of its total contributions to social services. Education received 25%. Health care received 25%, including support for medical research, pediatric health, and single-disease health associations. The arts received 5%, and civic and public affairs, 5%. **Typical Health-Related Recipients:** Arthritis, Children's Health/Hospitals, Clinics/Medical Centers, Domestic Violence, Emergency/Ambulance Services, Heart, Hospitals, Long-Term Care, Medical Research, Mental Health, Nursing Services, Outpatient Health Care, People with Disabilities, Respiratory, Single-Disease Health Associations, Substance Abuse. **Geographic Distribution:** Texas, emphasis on Dallas.

★276★ Hillsdale Fund
PO Box 20124
Greensboro, NC 27420
Phone: (910)274-5471
Ruth Forest, Sec. to Admin. VP

Foundation Philosophy: The Hillsdale Fund makes most of its grants in the areas of civic affairs, education, and social services. The arts are a secondary interest with support to public broadcasting and historical preservation. Other recipient areas also are supported. **Giving Priorities:** In 1991, the fund gave 38% of its support to educational institutions. About 18% of funding went to the arts. Civic groups and social service organizations each received 14% of contributions, and religious and health organizations each received 8%. The remaining funds went to scientific organizations. **Typical Health-Related Recipients:** AIDS/HIV, Alzheimers Disease, Cancer, Children's Health/Hospitals, Family Planning, Health Organizations, Hospices, Hospitals, People with Disabilities, Preventive Medicine/Wellness Organizations, Public Health, Substance Abuse. **Geographic Distribution:** Primarily eastern United States, with a focus on North Carolina.

★277★ Hobby Foundation
2131 San Felipe
Houston, TX 77019-5620
Phone: (713)521-1163
Fax: (713)521-3950
Peggy C. Buchanan, Treasurer

Foundation Philosophy: The Hobby Foundation primarily supports education and the arts. Other grants are made in the areas of family planning, youth organizations, religious welfare, hospitals, single-disease associations, and a variety of other recipient areas. **Giving Priorities:** In 1993, the foundation awarded 53% of its total giving to education. The arts received approximately 17% of the funds. Health care received about 13% of support, while social service organizations received about 8%. Religious and civic affairs organizations each received about 3% of support, while environmental affairs received 2%. The remaining 1% went to the sciences. **Typical Health-Related Recipients:** AIDS/HIV, Alzheimers Disease, Cancer, Children's Health/Hospitals, Emergency/Ambulance Services, Eyes/Blindness, Family Planning, Health Funds, Health Organizations, Heart, Hospitals, Mental Health, People with Disabilities, Single-Disease Health Associations. **Geographic Distribution:** Focus on Texas, with an emphasis on Houston.

★278★ Hoblitzelle Foundation
5956 Sherry Ln., Ste. 901
Dallas, TX 75225-6522
Phone: (214)373-0462
Fax: (214)750-7412
Paul W. Harris, Executive Vice President

Foundation Philosophy: The foundation supports educational, scientific, literary, and charitable organizations. The foundation seeks "to provide the basic tools for people to improve the quality of life in Texas." **Giving Priorities:** In fiscal 1994, the foundation gave approximately 42% of funding to health care organizations, including the foundation's highest grant of $500,000 to the Southwestern Medical Foundation. Social services received about 20% of total giving. Educational institutions received about 12% of funding; religious groups, 11%; the arts and humanities, 8%; civic concerns, 6%; and environmental programs, 1%. **Typical Health-Related Recipients:** AIDS/HIV, Children's Health/Hospitals, Clinics/Medical Centers, Diabetes, Emergency/Ambulance Services, Health Funds, Health Organizations, Hospitals, Medical Education, Medical Research, Medical Training, Nursing Services, People with Disabilities, Prenatal Health Issues, Single-Disease Health Associations, Substance Abuse, Transplant Networks/Donor Banks, Trauma Treatment. **Geographic Distribution:** Limited to Texas, primarily Dallas.

★279★ Homeland Foundation
412 N Pacific Coast Hwy., Ste. 345
Laguna Beach, CA 92651
Glenda S. Menges, Contact

Foundation Philosophy: The Homeland Foundation makes most of its grants in the areas of environmental affairs and social services. Social service funding favors women's programs and programs that assist the homeless. **Giving Priorities:** In 1992, the foundation contributed 42% of its funding to environmental efforts. International affairs received 21%. Health organizations were given 8%. The arts, civic affairs, and religious organizations each received 6% of contributions. Social services were awarded 5%, and education and science both received 3% of funding. **Typical Health-Related Recipients:** Clinics/Medical Centers, Domestic Violence, Emergency/Ambulance Services, Family Planning. **Geographic Distribution:** Focus on Southern California for social services; and the U.S. West Coast, Latin America, and Caribbean for environmental issues.

★280★ Homer and Martha Gudelsky Family Foundation
11900 Tech Rd.
Silver Spring, MD 20904
Phone: (301)622-0100
Medda Gudelsky, Secretary and Director

Foundation Philosophy: The foundation's major interests are education and the arts. Educational funding favors secondary and higher education in suburban Maryland. Social service organizations also receive support, with emphasis on handicapped services. The foundation has minor interests in the arts and health care. **Giving Priorities:** In 1992, the foundation gave approximately 94% of its contributions to educational institutions, including its highest grant of $1,000,500 to the University of Maryland Medical School, Baltimore, MD. Jewish interests received about 4%. The arts received the remaining 2% of funds. **Typical Health-Related Recipients:** Cancer, Hospitals, Medical Education, Substance Abuse. **Geographic Distribution:** Focus on suburban Maryland, particularly Silver Spring, MD.

★281★ Horace W. Goldsmith Foundation
375 Park Ave.
Ste. 1602
New York, NY 10152
Phone: (212)308-9832
Fax: (212)750-2455
James C. Slaughter, Esq., Chief Executive Officer and Director

Foundation Philosophy: The foundation is interested in the support of higher education, the performing arts and cultural groups, and social welfare programs. Funding by the foundation is generally self-initiated. **Giving Priorities:** In 1993, approximately 30% of foundation funding went to education. Health organizations received 25%, and the arts received 19% of giving. International affairs received 8%; religion, 7%; social services, 6%; and civic affairs, 4%. **Typical Health-Related Recipients:** AIDS/HIV, Cancer, Clinics/Medical Centers, Family Planning, Geriatric Health, Heart, Hospitals, Hospitals (University Affiliated), Medical Education, Medical Rehabilitation, Medical Research, Nursing Services, People with Disabilities, Public Health, Research/Studies Institutes, Single-Disease Health Associations, Substance Abuse. **Geographic Distribution:** No geographic restrictions; emphasis on the New York City metropolitan area.

★282★ Houston Endowment
600 Travis, Ste. 6400
Houston, TX 77002-3007
Phone: (713)238-8120
Fax: (713)238-8101
H. Joe Nelson, III, President

Foundation Philosophy: The purpose of the endowment "is the support of any charitable, educational or religious undertaking." Support is given to a wide variety of charitable activities, including those in the areas of education, health, the arts, culture, civic, and human services. **Giving Priorities:** In 1993, the endowment gave about 41% of funding to education. Health concerns received 24%; the arts, 22%; social services, 8%; and civic affairs, 3%. The remaining funds supported the environment, religion, and science. **Typical Health-Related Recipients:** AIDS/HIV, Cancer, Children's Health/ Hospitals, Clinics/Medical Centers, Domestic Violence, Emergency/Ambulance Services, Family Planning, Geriatric Health, Health Organizations, Health Policy/Cost Containment, Heart, Hospices, Hospitals, Medical Education, Medical Training, Mental Health, People with Disabilities, Research/Studies Institutes, Single-Disease Health Associations, Substance Abuse, Transplant Networks/Donor Banks. **Geographic Distribution:** Texas, primarily the Houston area.

★ 283 ★ **Howard Heinz Endowment**
30 CNG Tower
625 Liberty Ave.
Pittsburgh, PA 15222-3199
Phone: (412)281-5777
Fax: (412)281-5788
Frank Tugwell, Executive Director

Foundation Philosophy: The endowment generally makes one-time, nonrenewable grants for new programs, seed money, and capital projects in Pittsburgh and Allegheny County. In addition, operating grants are made to certain types of visual and performing arts groups, human service organizations, and urban programs. In cooperation with other Pittsburgh foundations, the endowment has tried to lessen the impact of financial cutbacks by participating in the establishment of an emergency fund, known as the Forbes Fund. In the field of education, the endowment supports projects designed to strengthen educational institutions and leadership, and to produce new knowledge on educational issues. A major concern of the endowment is the early intervention in the lives of at-risk children, including those most likely to suffer abuse or neglect, to drop out of school, or to develop behavioral and emotional problems. The foundation pays special attention to the elderly and to the problems they face. Housing and health care delivery systems are major concerns. **Giving Priorities:** In 1993, the foundation awarded 32% of its charitable donations to arts organizations. Civic affairs received 18% of the foundation's support. Social services received 17% of total giving, education received 16%, and health care received 15%. Environmental affairs received 2% of distributed funds. The remining funds were given in support of science. **Typical Health-Related Recipients:** Child Abuse, Children's Health/Hospitals, Clinics/Medical Centers, Domestic Violence, Family Planning, Health Policy/Cost Containment, Hospitals, Medical Education, Medical Rehabilitation, Medical Research, Mental Health, Nursing Services, Nutrition, Prenatal Health Issues, Substance Abuse. **Geographic Distribution:** Pittsburgh and Allegheny County, PA.

★ 284 ★ **Howard Hughes Medical Institute**
4000 Jones Bridge Rd.
Chevy Chase, MD 20815-6789
Phone: (301)215-8890
Fax: (301)215-8888
Joseph G. Perpich, M.D., J.D., VP for Grants & Special Prog.

Foundation Philosophy: The Howard Hughes Medical Institute is a nonprofit scientific and philanthropic organization whose principal pur-

pose is the direct conduct of medical research. The institute is qualified as a medical research organization, not as a private foundation, under the federal tax code. It administers a medical research program for the direct conduct of medical research and a grants program for support of science education. Under the Medical Research Program, the institute currently employs about 275 scientific investigators in the fields of cell biology and regulation, genetics, immunology, neuroscience, and structural biology. These investigators conduct fundamental biomedical research at over sixty academic medical centers, hospitals, and universities, and other research institutes throughout the United States. In each program, special emphasis is placed on the institute's research areas, namely, cell biology and regulation, genetics, immunology, neuroscience, and structural biology. **Giving Priorities:** In fiscal 1994, the Howard Hughes Medical Institute awarded 95% of its grants to science education. The remaining 5% of funds supported the research of outstanding scientists in selected countries abroad. **Typical Health-Related Recipients:** Medical Education. **Geographic Distribution:** National and international.

★ 285 ★ **Hugh J. Andersen Foundation**
c/o Baywood Corporation
287 Central Ave.
Bayport, MN 55003
Phone: (612)439-1557
Fax: (612)439-9480
Sarah J. Andersen, President

Foundation Philosophy: The board of directors at the foundation have prioritized general areas of interest which include the following: human services; children and youth; literacy and local (St. Croix Valley) educational enrichment opportunities; and health-related programming. **Giving Priorities:** In fiscal 1994, the foundation reported that it gave approximately 44% of contributions to social services. About 22% of the funding went to the arts. Civic groups and educational institutions received 12%. Health care received 10% of support. **Typical Health-Related Recipients:** AIDS/HIV, Cancer, Clinics/Medical Centers, Domestic Violence, Emergency/Ambulance Services, Family Planning, Health Organizations, Hospitals, People with Disabilities, Substance Abuse. **Geographic Distribution:** Primarily Washington County, MN; and Pierce, Polk, and St. Croix Counties, WI; secondarily St. Paul, MN.

★ 286 ★ **Hunt Alternatives Fund**
500 E Eighth Ave.
Denver, CO 80203
Phone: (303)839-1933
Fax: (303)839-1013
Lauren Y. Casteel, President

Foundation Philosophy: The board gives primary consideration to organizations serving women and girls most affected by economic, social, mental, and physical oppression, especially women of color, lesbians, and economically disadvantaged, aged, and/or disabled women. **Giving Priorities:** In fiscal 1993, the fund awarded 31% of its total contributions to social service organizations, with an emphasis on youth-assistance programs, including teen

pregnancy and violence prevention. About 30% of support went to civic affairs. About 16% of donations supported education. The arts received about 13% of support. Health care received about 5% of donations, while religious organizations received 3%. The remaining 2% supported environmental affairs. **Typical Health-Related Recipients:** AIDS/HIV, Cancer, Clinics/Medical Centers, Domestic Violence, Family Planning, Health Organizations, Mental Health, People with Disabilities, Prenatal Health Issues, Public Health, Respiratory, Single-Disease Health Associations, Substance Abuse. **Geographic Distribution:** Limited primarily to metropolitan Denver, CO; Dallas, TX; and New York, NY.

★ 287 ★ **Huston Foundation**
Ste. 910, One Tower Bridge
100 Front St.
West Conshohocken, PA 19428
Phone: (610)832-4949
Susan B. Heilman, Administrative Assistant

Foundation Philosophy: Grants are primarily made in the categories of health, human services, education, civic affairs, the arts, and science. The foundation reports that at least 51% of the funding each year supports evangelical Christian organizations. **Giving Priorities:** In 1992, approximately 19% of funding went to religious causes. The arts received 18%, while social services received 17%. Educational institutions received 16%, and health organizations, 13%. International organizations received 7%; civic causes, 6%; and scientific academies received the remaining 4%. **Typical Health-Related Recipients:** Children's Health/ Hospitals, Clinics/Medical Centers, Emergency/Ambulance Services, Eyes/Blindness, Family Planning, Health Organizations, Hospices, Hospitals, Medical Education, Medical Rehabilitation, Sexual Abuse. **Geographic Distribution:** Eastern United States; emphasis on Pennsylvania.

★ 288 ★ **Hyams Foundation**
One Boston Pl., 32nd Fl.
Boston, MA 02108
Phone: (617)720-2238
Fax: (617)720-2434
Susan Perry, Administrative Assistant

Foundation Philosophy: The Hyams Foundation supports new and continuing programs in human services and community development in the Boston area. Recently, the major beneficiary of the foundation's giving has been the youth of Boston with support for programs from health care to job training to day care. **Giving Priorities:** In 1992, the foundation reported that it contributed 63% of its total giving to social services. Interests included youth programs, senior services, substance abuse, and homelessness. Civic groups received 20% of funds. About 10% went to educational institutions. The remaining support went to health and cultural programs. **Typical Health-Related Recipients:** Adolescent Health Issues, Children's Health/ Hospitals, Domestic Violence, Family Planning, Health Organizations, Hospitals, Mental Health, Substance Abuse. **Geographic Distribution:** Boston, Cambridge, Chelsea, Lynn, and Somerville, MA.

★ 289 ★ Hyde and Watson Foundation
437 Southern Blvd.
Chatham, NJ 07928
Phone: (201)966-6024
Fax: (201)966-6404
Robert W. Parsons, Jr., President

Foundation Philosophy: The foundation supports projects in the broad fields of education, health, social services, the arts and humantities, and religion. Typical projects of interest include the purchase, relocation, renovation, or improvement of facilities; purchase of capital equipment; construction; development of materials; and certain areas of medical research. **Giving Priorities:** In 1993, the Hyde and Watson Foundation gave approximately 26% of its contributions to health care organizations, including a $100,000 grant for the Foundation of the University of Medicine and Dentistry of New Jersey in Newark, NJ. The arts received about 19%. Religion received 16%; education, 15%; civic affairs, 12%; and social services received 10%. Environmental causes and scientific interests each received 1% of the remaining funds. **Typical Health-Related Recipients:** Cancer, Children's Health/Hospitals, Clinics/Medical Centers, Emergency/Ambulance Services, Eyes/Blindness, Health Organizations, Hospitals, Medical Education, Medical Rehabilitation, Medical Research, People with Disabilities, Prenatal Health Issues, Single-Disease Health Associations, Speech & Hearing, Substance Abuse. **Geographic Distribution:** Restricted to the United States; primarily metropolitan New York City and Essex, Union, and Morris counties in New Jersey.

★ 290 ★ International Foundation
1700 Rt. 23 N
Ste. 170
Wayne, NJ 07470
Phone: (201)598-0894
Fax: (201)598-5436
Edward A. Holmes, Grants Chairman

Foundation Philosophy: The International Foundation makes most of its grants in the areas of health care, social services, agriculture, education, and international interests. Health interests include medical missions, international medical training exchange programs, and a variety of other international health services in combination with relief organizations. Social service support favors entrepreneurial projects, family services, and international family planning. International organizations receiving funding are involved in social development, health, education, environment, and agricultural projects. Grants to other recipient areas are limited. **Giving Priorities:** In 1992, about 98% of funding went to international organizations, supporting social services, education, and health concerns worldwide. Environmental and health concerns in the United States received the remaining funds. **Typical Health-Related Recipients:** Clinics/Medical Centers, Emergency/Ambulance Services, Family Planning, Health Funds, Hospitals, Medical Rehabilitation, Medical Training, Nutrition, People with Disabilities, Single-Disease Health Associations. **Geographic Distribution:** Only international.

★ 291 ★ Ira W. DeCamp Foundation
c/o Donovan Leisure Newton & Irvine
30 Rockefeller Plaza, 40th floor
New York, NY 10112
Phone: (212)632-3336
Carolyn Handler, Contact Person

Foundation Philosophy: The chief purpose of the foundation is to support health care organizations, medical research, and medical education. **Giving Priorities:** In fiscal 1992, the foundation allocated approximately 44% of funding to health, primarily supporting medical research. Education received 42%, with an emphasis on science and health education. Social service organizations received 4%; religious organizations and scientific centers each received 3%; and civic affairs and the arts received the remaining funds. **Typical Health-Related Recipients:** AIDS/HIV, Alzheimers Disease, Cancer, Children's Health/Hospitals, Clinics/Medical Centers, Emergency/Ambulance Services, Eyes/Blindness, Geriatric Health, Health Organizations, Heart, Hospices, Hospitals, Medical Education, Medical Rehabilitation, Medical Research, Medical Training, Mental Health, Nursing Services, People with Disabilities, Single-Disease Health Associations, Substance Abuse. **Geographic Distribution:** National, with some emphasis on New York.

★ 292 ★ Irene W. and C. B. Pennington Foundation
c/o Robert R. Casey
PO Box 1267
Baton Rouge, LA 70821
Phone: (504)383-3412
Claude Bernard Pennington, Trustee

Foundation Philosophy: The foundation primarily favors social service organizations, with emphasis on youth organizations and community centers. In the past, large grants were given to universities in Louisiana. Minor grants are given to other recipient areas. **Giving Priorities:** In 1992, the foundation gave approximately 60% of funding to the arts and humanities. About 26% of total contributions supported health care organizations. Education received 6% of giving. Social services and religious concerns each received approximately 3% of giving. The remainder of funds supported civic causes. **Geographic Distribution:** Baton Rouge, LA.

★ 293 ★ Irvine Health Foundation
18301 Von Karman Ave.
Ste. 440
Irvine, CA 92715-1009
Phone: (714)253-2959
Fax: (714)253-2962
Edward B. Kacic, Executive Director

Foundation Philosophy: "The mission of the Irvine Health Foundation is to sponsor, promote and support activities related to health care and the health of the greater Irvine Community. The foundation is also interested in supporting activities addressing the needs of specific population groups, including youth, the elderly and various other segments of the population. Categorically, areas of interest of the foundation include, but are not limited to, health promotion, education, direct services, mental health, substance abuse and research." **Giving Priorities:** In fiscal 1993,

the foundation gave 38% of its funds to health care, including the largest grant of $127,400 to the Wellness Community. Social services received 36% of contributions, with a particular emphasis on child welfare organizations. Education received 25% of contributions. Civic concerns received about 1% of total giving. **Typical Health-Related Recipients:** AIDS/HIV, Alzheimers Disease, Child Abuse, Children's Health/Hospitals, Clinics/Medical Centers, Domestic Violence, Emergency/Ambulance Services, Health Organizations, Mental Health, People with Disabilities, Preventive Medicine/Wellness Organizations, Public Health, Respiratory, Sexual Abuse, Single-Disease Health Associations, Speech & Hearing, Substance Abuse. **Geographic Distribution:** Orange County, CA.

★ 294 ★ Irving S. Gilmore Foundation
136 E Michigan Ave.
Old Kent Bank Bldg., Ste. 615
Kalamazoo, MI 49007-3912
Phone: (616)342-6411
Fax: (616)349-3831
S. W. Freund, Executive Director

Foundation Philosophy: The foundation concentrates on sustaining and improving the cultural, social, and economic life of greater Kalamazoo, MI. Priorities of the foundation, in rank order, focus on the performing and visual arts, human services, health care, education and youth, and community development. The foundation emphasizes specific initiatives within its priorities, rather than operational funding or specific research. **Giving Priorities:** In 1992, the foundation gave approximately 42% of its contributions to the arts. Social service organizations received 28%, with a grant of $250,000 going to Kalamazoo Child Guidance Clinic, Kalamazoo, MI. Education and civic affairs each received 11%; health concerns, 5%; and religious causes received the remaining funds. **Typical Health-Related Recipients:** Clinics/Medical Centers, Emergency/Ambulance Services, Eyes/Blindness, Nursing Services, People with Disabilities, Single-Disease Health Associations, Substance Abuse. **Geographic Distribution:** Kalamazoo, MI.

★ 295 ★ J. E. and L. E. Mabee Foundation
3000 Mid-Continent Tower
401 S Boston Ave.
Tulsa, OK 74103
Phone: (918)584-4286
John H. Conway, Jr., Vice Chm., Sec.-Treas. and Trustee

Foundation Philosophy: The general objectives of the foundation are to assist religious, charitable, and educational organizations. Youth issues are also an important foundation focus. Grants in this area generally fund building programs. In the health field, the foundation funds capital projects for hospitals, health agencies, and institutions engaged in the discovery, treatment, and care of diseases. **Giving Priorities:** In fiscal 1994, the foundation reported that it gave approximately 41% of its contributions to social services; education received 25%; health care, 17%; the arts and humanities, 11%; and religious institutions, 6%. **Typical Health-Related Recipients:** Children's Health/

Hospitals, Clinics/Medical Centers, Domestic Violence, Health Organizations, Hospitals, Long-Term Care, Medical Education, Medical Rehabilitation, Nursing Services, People with Disabilities, Research/Studies Institutes, Substance Abuse. **Geographic Distribution:** Limited to Arkansas, Kansas, Missouri, New Mexico, Oklahoma, and Texas.

★ 296 ★ J.E. and Z.B. Butler Foundation
122 E 42nd St., Ste. 2500
New York, NY 10168

Foundation Philosophy: The foundation is commiteed to supporting social service, health, education, civic, religious, and environmental organizations. The foundation takes a special interest in Jewish causes. **Giving Priorities:** In 1993, the foundation gave approximately 52% of its contributions to social services, including support to youth organizations, aid to the disabled, and family services. Health organizations received 18% of contributions, including children's hospitals and geriatric centers. About 17% of support went to education. Religion, mainly Jewish concerns, received 5%. Civic and public affairs organizations received 5%. Environmental concerns received 2%. **Typical Health-Related Recipients:** Cancer, Children's Health/Hospitals, Family Planning, People with Disabilities, Prenatal Health Issues, Single-Disease Health Associations. **Geographic Distribution:** New York, NY, area.

★ 297 ★ J. L. Bedsole Foundation
PO Box 1137
Mobile, AL 36633
Phone: (205)432-3369
Mabel B. Ward, Executive Director

Foundation Philosophy: The J. L. Bedsole Foundation's primary interest is the support of educational institutions in Alabama. Funding of educational institutions accounted for approximately 30% of the foundation's giving in 1993. The arts, social services, health, and civic groups also received grants from the foundation. While the foundation has a wide variety of interests, it strictly limits awards on a geographical basis. **Giving Priorities:** In 1993, the foundation reported that approximately 30% of contributions went to civic and economic causes, while another 30% went to education. Social services received 15% of funding; medical and health organizations, about 8%; and arts and humanities, about 8%. The remaining 10% supported other miscellaneous causes. **Typical Health-Related Recipients:** Clinics/Medical Centers, Eyes/Blindness, Health Organizations, Hospitals, Medical Education, Public Health, Single-Disease Health Associations. **Geographic Distribution:** Alabama, with primary emphasis in Mobile and the southwest part of the state.

★ 298 ★ J. M. Kaplan Fund
30 Rockefeller Plz., Ste. 4250
New York, NY 10112
Phone: (212)767-0630
Fax: (212)767-0639, Director

Foundation Philosophy: The fund continues to focus most of its support on local nonprofit organizations, community grassroots efforts, and social policy interests in New York City. Grants are made primarily in three program areas. Within the environmental area, the fund is concerned with conservation; historic preservation; improving neighborhoods; and enhancing public parks, farmlands, and open space. Within the social programs and public policy area, the fund supports efforts to promote civil rights, ensure legal protection, provide basic public services, and promote human rights. The fund also supports a variety of cultural interests in its third program area, arts and education. The fund reports that it is undergoing a major revamping of program priorities and governance structure. **Giving Priorities:** In fiscal 1992, the fund reported that it gave 33% of its contributions to arts and education, 33% to social programs and public policy, and 33% to environmental concerns. **Typical Health-Related Recipients:** AIDS/HIV, Children's Health/Hospitals, Family Planning. **Geographic Distribution:** Primarily New York.

★ 299 ★ J. M. McDonald Foundation
Box 470
Cortland, NY 13045
Phone: (607)756-9283
Reed L. McJunkin, Secretary and Trustee

Foundation Philosophy: The foundation reflects Mr. McDonald's concerns in greater educational opportunity and educational institutions, the problems of the physically and mentally handicapped and the aged, and the potential for research to improve human conditions. The foundation supports established organizations. Colleges generally receive grants for facilities. The foundation makes grants to social service organizations and has a particular interest in child welfare and care of the aged and needy. The foundation also makes grants to hospitals for facilities. **Giving Priorities:** In 1993, the foundation gave 46% of funding to education. Social services received 26% of funding; health concerns received 11%; the arts received 8%; science received 4%; religious organizations received 3%; and civic organizations received 2%. **Typical Health-Related Recipients:** Cancer, Clinics/Medical Centers, Domestic Violence, Geriatric Health, Health Organizations, Hospitals, Medical Education, Mental Health, People with Disabilities, Single-Disease Health Associations. **Geographic Distribution:** Primarily in the Northeast.

★ 300 ★ J. S. Bridwell Foundation
807 8th St., Ste. 500
Wichita Falls, TX 76301-3381
Phone: (817)322-4436
Clifford G. Tinsley, Vice President and Treasurer

Foundation Philosophy: While recent grants have primarily been addressed to social services, in 1989 the foundation contributed $2,000,000 to Southern Methodist University in Dallas, TX, for the renovation of the Bridwell Library. The foundation has demonstrated a giving pattern of ongoing support to certain established charities, such as the Salvation Army, United Way, and Easter Seals. While the foundation gives to many organizations, it has shown a particular interest in organizations that address the concerns of disadvantaged youth, such as the Methodist Home in Waco, TX. **Giving Priorities:** In 1993, the foundation gave approximately 74% of its total charitable contributions to social services organizations, including its largest donation, a $100,00 grant to Harmony Family Services, a boys residential treatment center. The foundation also gave 8% of its contributions to religious causes, 7% to health organizations, and 6% to education institutions. Civic and public affairs organizations received 3% of giving, and arts organizations received 1%. **Typical Health-Related Recipients:** Cancer, Children's Health/Hospitals, Emergency/Ambulance Services, Heart, Hospices, Medical Rehabilitation, Medical Research, People with Disabilities, Single-Disease Health Associations, Substance Abuse. **Geographic Distribution:** Limited to Texas.

★ 301 ★ J. W. Kieckhefer Foundation
PO Box 1151
Prescott, AZ 86302
Phone: (602)445-4010
Fax: (602)445-4012
Eugene P. Polk, Administrative Officer, Trustee

Foundation Philosophy: The foundation is a general purpose charity which emphasizes social services. **Giving Priorities:** In 1993, the foundation gave approximately 41% of its contributions to the arts. Social services received 18%, including support for youth oranizations, families, and the homeless. Civic organizations and community development received 15% of funding. Health care and medical research received 13%. Scientific organizations received 4%, international affairs, 3%; education, 2%; religion, 2%; and the remaining funds supported the environment. **Typical Health-Related Recipients:** Children's Health/Hospitals, Clinics/Medical Centers, Eyes/Blindness, Family Planning, Health Funds, Hospitals, Medical Research, People with Disabilities, Research/Studies Institutes, Single-Disease Health Associations. **Geographic Distribution:** Nationwide with emphasis on Arizona.

★ 302 ★ J. Willard Marriott Foundation
One Marriott Dr.
Washington, DC 20058
Phone: (301)380-7523
Kay Bodeen, Administrator

Foundation Philosophy: The foundation primarily awards grants to local organizations. It also gives to a few general scholarship funds. The majority of funding, however, goes to previously supported organizations. **Giving Priorities:** In 1992, the foundation gave approximately 29% of its contributions to educational institutions. Social services received 25%, which consisted of the foundation's two highest grants totaling $1,500,000 to the Marriott Foundation for People with Disabilities. Health concerns received 16%, with a grant of $300,000 awarded to the Massachusetts General Hospital. Religion received 11% of giving. The arts received 9%. Civic affairs received 6%, and international organizations received the remaining funds. **Typical Health-Related Recipients:** Eyes/Blindness, Health Organizations, Hospitals, Hospitals (University Affiliated), People with Disabilities, Prenatal Health Issues. **Geographic Distribution:** National, with emphasis on Utah and the Washington, DC, area.

★303★ **Jacob and Annita France Foundation**
1122 Kenilworth Dr., Ste. 118
Baltimore, MD 21204
Phone: (410)832-5700
Fredrick W. Lafferty, Executive Director

Foundation Philosophy: The foundation provides most of its support to higher education, social services, the arts, health, historic preservation, conservation, and civic issues. **Giving Priorities:** In fiscal 1993, the foundation gave approximately 67% of its contributions to education, focusing on colleges and universities, arts education, and a scholarship fund. The arts received 11%, primarily supporting museums. Social service organizations received 6%; health care, 5%; and civic affairs and a science center each received 4%. The remaining funds were given to religious and international organizations. **Typical Health-Related Recipients:** Hospices, Hospitals, Medical Education, People with Disabilities, Trauma Treatment. **Geographic Distribution:** Maryland, primarily the metropolitan Baltimore area.

★304★ **Jacob G. Schmidlapp Trust No. 1**
Charitable Foundations Screening Committee
Fifth Third Bank, MD 1090 C7
Cincinnati, OH 45263
Phone: (513)579-5476
Fax: (513)744-6997
Carolyn F. McCoy, Foundation Officer

Foundation Philosophy: The Jacob G. Schmidlapp Trust No. 1 believes that funds should be used "for relief in sickness, suffering and distress, the care of young children, or the helpless and afflicted." To this purpose, the trust concentrates on social services, health facilities, and educational institutions that directly or indirectly benefit children, the sick, and the disadvantaged. **Giving Priorities:** In 1993, the foundation gave approximately 35% of its total contributions to social service organizations. Civic affairs received about 19%; the arts, 17%; educational institutions, 13%; health concerns, 10%; and religious causes received the remaining 6% of funds. **Typical Health-Related Recipients:** Adolescent Health Issues, Children's Health/Hospitals, Clinics/Medical Centers, Diabetes, Domestic Violence, Family Planning, Geriatric Health, Health Funds, Health Organizations, Hospices, Hospitals, Long-Term Care, Medical Rehabilitation, Mental Health, Nursing Services, People with Disabilities, Single-Disease Health Associations, Speech & Hearing, Substance Abuse. **Geographic Distribution:** Greater Cincinnati area.

★305★ **Jacob and Hilda Blaustein Foundation**
Blaustein Bldg.
PO Box 238
Baltimore, MD 21203
Phone: (410)347-7204
Diana Morris

Foundation Philosophy: Jewish issues and higher education are the foundation's two primary interests, with limited funding in the areas of health, the arts, and social services. **Giving Priorities:** In 1993, the foundation awarded 41% of its contributions to educational institutions, including a $770,000 grant to the Ameri-

can Associates of Ben Gurion University of the Negev, New York, NY. Approximately 32% of the funds went to religious organizations. International concerns received 17%; health care organizations and the arts each received 4%. The remainder went to civic and public affairs and social services. **Typical Health-Related Recipients:** Children's Health/Hospitals, Clinics/Medical Centers, Emergency/Ambulance Services, Eyes/Blindness, Health Organizations, Hospitals, Medical Education, People with Disabilities, Single-Disease Health Associations. **Geographic Distribution:** Mainly Baltimore, MD, and New York, NY.

★306★ **James H. Cummings Foundation**
1807 Elmwood Avenue, Rm. 112
Buffalo, NY 14207
Phone: (716)874-0040
Fax: (716)874-0040
William J. McFarland, Executive Director and Secretary

Foundation Philosophy: The foundation was created "to further medical science, medical research and medical education... to provide services for under--privileged boys ad girls" and "to assist aged and infirm persons." Grants are generally for capital expenditures, in particular for the purchase of medical research equipment. The foundation prefers to support organizations that do not receive government funding. **Giving Priorities:** In fiscal 1994, the foundation gave 51% of its charitable contributions to support health care, including and $83,000 grant to Buffalo General Hospital. Education received 32% of the foundation's support. Social service organizations received 15% of distributed funds. The remaining 2% went to support the arts. **Typical Health-Related Recipients:** Cancer, Children's Health/Hospitals, Clinics/Medical Centers, geriatric Health, Health Organizations, Heart, Hospices, Hospitals, Medical Research, Medical Training, People with Disabilities, Respiratory. **Geographic Distribution:** Support Limited to the cities of Buffalo, NY; Toronto, Ontario; and Hendersonville, NC.

★307★ **James Irvine Foundation**
One Market Plz.
Spear Tower, Ste. 1715
San Francisco, CA 94105
Phone: (415)777-2244
Fax: (415)777-0869
Craig E. McGarvey, Director of Administration

Foundation Philosophy: Foundation giving has traditionally been concentrated in five major areas: community services, culture, health, higher education, and youth. Health care grant making is designed to increase access to basic health care for traditionally underserved populations including the economically disadvantaged, people of color, children, and residents of rural areas of California. **Giving Priorities:** In 1992, the foundation gave approximately 41% of its contributions to education. Civic concerns received about 20% of funding, and health care, 18%. The arts received 13% of support. The remaing 8% of grants were made to social services. **Typical Health-Related Recipients:** AIDS/HIV, Children's Health/Hospitals, Organizations, Health Policy/Cost Containment, Hospitals, Prenatal Health Issues, Public Health.

Geographic Distribution: Exclusively California.

★308★ **James M. Cox, Jr. Foundation**
c/o Cox Enterprises, Inc.
PO Box 105357
Atlanta, GA 30348
Carl R. Gross, Trustee and Treasurer

Foundation Philosophy: The foundation continues to support environmental affairs through major support to the Nature Conservancy and other environmental organizations. Education interests include journalism and medicine. Arts support goes to major Atlanta arts institutions with interests in history and historic preservation. Limited grants are made in other recipient areas. **Giving Priorities:** In 1993, the foundation awarded 34% of its total contributions to educational institutions. About 25% of funds went to environmental concerns. Civic groups received 12% of support; health care, 11%; the arts, 7%; and international organizations, 5%. The remaining funds went to social services and scientific organizations. **Typical Health-Related Recipients:** Arthritis, Cancer, Children's Health/Hospitals, Clinics/Medical Centers, Domestic Violence, Emergency/Ambulance Services, Eyes/Blindness, Health Organizations, Heart, Hospices, Hospitals, Medical Education, Medical Rehabilitation, Medical Research, Mental Health, Nursing Services, People with Disabilities. **Geographic Distribution:** Emphasis on Georgia and Ohio.

★309★ **James M. Johnston Trust for Charitable and Educational Purposes**
1101 Vermont Ave., NW
Ste. 403
Washington, DC 20005
Phone: (202)289-4996
Julia G. Sanders, Office Manager

Foundation Philosophy: The trust, following the interests of its donor, concentrates its grant-making program on education, particularly at the University of North Carolina at Chapel Hill. Support is directed toward scholarship programs, nursing education, and faculty development. **Giving Priorities:** In 1993, education received approximately 87% of the foundation's charitable support. Health care received 7% of the foundation's support, while social services received 3% and religious causes were awarded 2%. Civic affairs received the remaining 1% of support. **Typical Health-Related Recipients:** Cancer, Children's Health/Hospitals, Emergency/Ambulance Services, Hospices, Hospitals, Long-Term Care, Medical Education, Medical Rehabilitation, Medical Research, Medical Training, Mental Health, Nursing Services, People with Disabilities, Single-Disease Health Associations. **Geographic Distribution:** Emphasis on North Carolina and Washington, DC.

★310★ **Janirve Foundation**
PO Box 3276
82 Patton Ave.
Asheville, NC 28802
Phone: (704)258-1877
Met R. Poston, Chairman of the Advisory Committee

Foundation Philosophy: The foundation supports a wide range of charities with emphasis on social services, health, and education. Support also goes to the arts and humanities and environmental causes. The foundation "encourages the submission of proposals which set forth new or different and innovative approaches toward dealing with a problem affecting a significant sector of society." **Giving Priorities:** In 1993, the foundation gave approximately 33% of its contributions to health care. Education received 25%; social services, 17%; the arts, 13%; and civic affairs, 10%. The remaining funds supported the environment and religious organizations. **Typical Health-Related Recipients:** Adolescent Health Issues, Clinics/Medical Centers, Domestic Violence, Family Planning, Geriatric Health, Health Organizations, Hospices, Hospitals, People with Disabilities, Preventive Medicine/Wellness Organizations. **Geographic Distribution:** North Carolina, South Carolina, and Florida.

★ 311 ★ **Jay and Rose Phillips Family Foundation**
2345 Kennedy St., NE
Minneapolis, MN 55413
Phone: (612)331-6230
Fax: (612)623-1644
Patricia A. Cummings, Executive Director

Foundation Philosophy: Of particular interest to the foundation are health, higher education, programs for people with disabilities, and programs that address issues of discrimination. Also, during times of severe economic hardship and financial distress, the foundation reports that its primary concern is providing support for projects addressing unmet human and social needs. **Giving Priorities:** In 1993, the foundation awarded 46% of total funding to Jewish organizations. Educational institutions received 20% of giving. Medical centers received 15% of contributions, including another $200,000 grant to the Mayo Clinic. Social services received 12%, and civic affairs were given 4%. The remaining funds supported international concerns, science, and the arts. **Typical Health-Related Recipients:** Clinics/Medical Centers, Health Organizations, Hospitals, Long-Term Care, Medical Education, Medical Research, Multiple Sclerosis, People with Disabilities, Research/Studies Institutes, Sexual Abuse, Single-Disease Health Associations. **Geographic Distribution:** Primarily metropolitan Minneapolis/St. Paul, MN.

★ 312 ★ **Jean and Louis Dreyfus Foundation**
c/o Decker, Hubbard, and Weldon
30 Rockefeller Plz., Ste. 4340
New York, NY 10112
Phone: (212)581-7575
Fax: (212)649-5998
Edmee de Montmollin Firth, Executive Director

Foundation Philosophy: The foundation makes grants across the major categories of support. In social services, interests include community and neighborhood centers, crime prevention, and family and children's services. Educational support goes to medical and private education, educational funds, and art education. Museums and other art organizations, civic affairs, and health services are also supported. The foundation no longer gives medical re-

search grants. **Giving Priorities:** In 1994, the foundation reported that social services received 36% of the contributions. The arts received 30% of the funds. Approximately 19% went to support health care services, especially those concerned with the aging. Educational organizations and institutions received 15%. **Typical Health-Related Recipients:** AIDS/HIV, Alzheimers Disease, Cancer, Clinics/Medical Centers, Family Planning, Geriatric Health, Health Funds, Hospitals, Medical Education, Medical Training, Mental Health, Nursing Services, Substance Abuse. **Geographic Distribution:** Eastern United States, focus on New York, NY.

★ 313 ★ **Jessie B. Cox Charitable Trust**
c/o Grants Management Associates
230 Congress St.
Boston, MA 02110
Phone: (617)426-7172
Katherine S. McHugh, Administrator

Foundation Philosophy: "The purpose of the trust is to increase significantly the ability of nonprofit organizations to carry out their stated missions in the fields of health, education, the environment, and the development of philanthropy in the community. "In the health field, the trust is particularly interested in supporting primary health care, advocacy projects, and research which will have a positive effect on the prevention and treatment of illness, particularly among children and youth, increased access to appropriate levels of care for New England's underserved populations, and delivery of health services to the poor. **Giving Priorities:** In 1993, the trust gave approximately 34% to health care, including support for health care reform advocacy and primary care for children. Environmental concerns received 30%. Education received 25%. Family grants received 7%; and development of philanthropy and special projects received 4%. **Typical Health-Related Recipients:** Adolescent Health Issues, Children's Health/Hospitals, Diabetes, Health Organizations, Health Policy/Cost Containment, Hospitals, Mental Health, Nursing Services, Nutrition, People with Disabilities, Preventive Medicine/Wellness Organizations, Substance Abuse. **Geographic Distribution:** New England.

★ 314 ★ **Jessie Ball duPont Fund**
225 Water St., Ste. 1200
Jacksonville, FL 32202-5176
Phone: (904)353-0890
Fax: (904)353-3870
Sherry P. Magill, PhD, Executive Director

Foundation Philosophy: In 1991 the foundation launched several new programs. The trustees established the Jessie Ball duPont Fund Award to honor selected individuals at the Fund's eligible institutions. The fund also began the Clergy Professional Development Initiative, which is designed to respond to the needs of ordained clergy at the fund's eligible religious institutions and includes a sabbatical program and a professional development fund. The other program, the Nonprofit Initiative, is a six-year program that addresses the needs of eligible nonprofits with discretionary funds, technical assistance, and a leadership developmental institute. In 1990, the fund launched the Jessie Ball

du Pont Fund Small Liberal Arts College Initiative. The fund has application guidelines for a People-In-Need program and a Feasability Grant program. **Giving Priorities:** In fiscal 1994, the fund gave approximately 42% of its total contributions to civic affairs, 26% of which supported community development and 16% supported institutional development initiatives. Educational institutions received about 23%; health concerns, 11%; arts, culture, and humanities, 10%; and social and human services, 5%. Other foundation interests received about 5% of giving. Religious organizations received the remaining 4%. **Typical Health-Related Recipients:** Cancer, Clinics/Medical Centers, Health Organizations, Hospitals, Medical Education, Mental Health, People with Disabilities, Sexual Abuse, Single-Disease Health Associations. **Geographic Distribution:** No geographic restrictions. **Formerly:** Jessie Ball duPont Religious, Charitable and Educational Fund.

★ 315 ★ **Jewish Healthcare Foundation of Pittsburgh**
Ctr. City Tower, Ste. 2550
650 Smithfield St.
Pittsburgh, PA 15222
Phone: (412)261-1400
Fax: (412)232-6240
Karen Wolk Feinstein, PhD, President

Foundation Philosophy: The Jewish Healthcare Foundation of Pittsburgh serves both the Jewish and general community in western Pennsylvania. It is currently concentrating grant making towards women's health concerns, the health of children at risk, and the special needs of the elderly and the chronically ill. The foundation pays special attention to programs that improve health care systems, provide new information and fresh perspectives, build partnerships among community institutions, or contain a community education component. While addressing ongoing concerns, the foundation will also address emerging health care concerns. **Giving Priorities:** In 1993, the foundation gave approximately 50% of total contributions to religious organizations. Health concerns received about 26% of funding; social service organizations, 16%; educational institutions, 6%; and civic concerns, 2%. **Typical Health-Related Recipients:** Adolescent Health Issues, AIDS/HIV, Alzheimers Disease, Cancer, Children's Health/Hospitals, Clinics/Medical Centers, Domestic Violence, Geriatric Health, Health Funds, Health Organizations, Health Policy/Cost Containment, Home-Care Services, Hospitals, Hospitals (University Affiliated), Kidney, Long-Term Care, Medical Education, Medical Research, Mental Health, Nutrition, People with Disabilities, Prenatal Health Issues, Public Health, Substance Abuse, Transplant Networks/Donor Banks. **Geographic Distribution:** Western Pennsylvania.

★ 316 ★ **JM Foundation**
60 E 42nd St., Ste. 1651
New York, NY 10165
Phone: (212)687-7735
Fax: (212)697-5495
Chris K. Olander, Exec. Dir. and Asst. Treas.

Foundation Philosophy: The JM Foundation grants program encompasses several related fields, including rehabilitation of people with disabilities, prevention and wellness with an emphasis on individual responsibility for health, health-related policy research, and prevention or early intervention in alcohol and drug abuse. The foundation also has a strong interest in educational activities. In addition, the foundation directors recognize the importance of the American family and support organizations that reinforce the role of parents; enhance the quality of family life; and provide youth with jobs, healthy lifestyles, and positive character development. **Giving Priorities:** In fiscal 1993, the foundation gave approximately 37% of its contributions to social service organizations, including four grants totaling $267,500 for the International Center for the Disabled (ICD), New York, NY. Civic affairs received 29%, with substantial support going to policy research organizations. Health concerns received 27% of giving; education, 5%; and the arts received the remaining funds. **Typical Health-Related Recipients:** Cancer, Clinics/Medical Centers, Family Planning, Geriatric Health, Health Organizations, Health Policy/Cost Containment, Heart, Hospitals, Medical Education, Medical Rehabilitation, Medical Research, People with Disabilities, Prenatal Health Issues, Public Health, Substance Abuse. **Geographic Distribution:** No geographic restrictions.

★317★ **Joe and Emily Lowe Foundation**
249 Royal Palm Way
Palm Beach, FL 33480
Phone: (407)655-7001
Bernard Stern, President and Treasurer

Foundation Philosophy: The foundation funds a wide variety of causes in the arts, civic and public affairs, education, health, religion, and social services. **Giving Priorities:** In 1992, the foundation gave approximately 43% of its contributions to religious concerns, primarily supporting Jewish causes. Health organizations received 19% of funding, while educational institutions received 15%. Social services received 8%, the arts, 8%, civic causes, 6%, and international agencies, 1%. **Typical Health-Related Recipients:** Cancer, Children's Health/Hospitals, Emergency/Ambulance Services, Eyes/Blindness, Family Planning, Heart, Hospices, Medical Education, Medical Rehabilitation, People with Disabilities, Single-Disease Health Associations, Substance Abuse. **Geographic Distribution:** Primarily New York and Florida.

★318★ **John Edward Fowler Memorial Foundation**
1725 K St. NW, Ste. 1201
Washington, DC 20006
Phone: (202)728-9080
Fax: (202)728-9082
Richard H. Lee, President

Foundation Philosophy: The Fowler Foundation is interested in supporting "smaller, well managed, non-profit organizations that have innovative ideas about how to help people help themselves." Most grants are limited to grassroots programs in the Washington, DC, area. **Giving Priorities:** In 1993, the foundation gave approximately 59% of its contributions to social service organizations, primarily in support of

inner city and other special projects. Educational institutions, particularly nontraditional education, received 21%. Health care received 12%; religious organizations, 3%; and the arts and civic groups received the remainder. **Typical Health-Related Recipients:** AIDS/HIV, Alzheimers Disease, Cancer, Emergency/Ambulance Services, Hospices, Hospitals, Long-Term Care, Mental Health, Multiple Sclerosis, Outpatient Health Care, People with Disabilities, Prenatal Health Issues, Public Health. **Geographic Distribution:** Focus on metropolitan Washington, DC, area.

★319★ **John G. and Marie Stella Kenedy Memorial Foundation**
1700 First City Tower II, Ste. 1020
Corpus Christi, TX 78478
Phone: (512)887-6565
Judy Gilbreath, General Director

Foundation Philosophy: A majority of the foundation's funding supports dioceses and religious organizations in Texas. Educational institutions and social services also receive funding. **Giving Priorities:** In fiscal 1993, the foundation gave approximately 75% of its donations to religious organizations. Social services received about 8% of grants, with primary support to day care centers, youth organizations, and drug prevention programs. The arts received 7% of contributions and educational institutions received 5% of giving, mainly for scholarship programs. Civic affairs and health care received the remaining funds. **Typical Health-Related Recipients:** AIDS/HIV, Hospitals, People with Disabilities, Substance Abuse. **Geographic Distribution:** Primarily South Texas.

★320★ **John M. Hopwood Charitable Trust**
c/o Charitable and Endowment Managment
PNC Bank
One Oliver Plz., 27th Fl.
Pittsburgh, PA 15265
Phone: (412)762-3412
Bruce Bickel, Vice President and Manager

Foundation Philosophy: The trust makes grants across the major categories of support. In health services, interests include hospital foundations, health programs, and hospitals. Art support favors museums, libraries, festivals, theater, and other performing arts. Support for education includes giving to colleges, universities, and private schools. Social service support goes to united funds, community centers, and community activities. The trust also places emphasis on environmental concerns. **Giving Priorities:** In 1993, the trust contributed 37% of its total funding to health concerns, including its largest grant of $50,000 to the Shadyside Hospital Foundation, Pittsburgh, PA. The arts received 26% of support; educational institutions, 20%; the environment, 5%; social services, 5%; and religious organizations, 4%. About 3% went to civic affairs. **Typical Health-Related Recipients:** Cancer, Children's Health/Hospitals, Domestic Violence, Emergency/Ambulance Services, Health Organizations, Hospices, Hospitals, Kidney, Long-Term Care, Medical Education, Medical Rehabilitation, Multiple Sclerosis, Nursing Services, People with Disabilities, Single-Disease Health Associations. **Geographic**

Distribution: Focus on western Pennsylvania (75%) and Florida (25%).

★321★ **John and Mary Franklin Foundation**
PO Box 4387-MC 678
Atlanta, GA 30302
Phone: (404)989-6106
Virlyn B. Moore, Jr., Secretary

Foundation Philosophy: In 1955, John Franklin wrote that the foundation was to be organized solely for charitable, religious, scientific, and educational purposes. He listed fifteen charities which he and his wife had supported in the preceding year as an indication of their personal preferences. These consisted of health care institutions and social service organizations, primarily for young people. Mr. Franklin also described his and his wife's charitable interests in the fields of science, religion, and education. In the field of science, they were particularly interested in medical research, and listed the Heart Fund, Cancer Fund, and March of Dimes as typical recipients. In education, their primary interest was in educating the disabled so that they might lead fuller lives, listing the Atlanta Speech School and the Muscular Dystrophy Fund as examples. **Giving Priorities:** In 1993, approximately 58% of funding went to educational institutions. About 14% went to arts organizations; 13%, to social services; 9%, to civic and public affairs; and 6%, to health institutions. **Typical Health-Related Recipients:** Family Planning, Hospitals, Medical Education, Medical Research, Medical Training, People with Disabilities, Single-Disease Health Associations. **Geographic Distribution:** Primarily Atlanta, GA.

★322★ **John P. McGovern Foundation**
6969 Brompton
Houston, TX 77025
Phone: (713)661-1444
John P. McGovern, M.D., President

Foundation Philosophy: The foundation primarily supports medical research organizations and medical funds, with some focus on prevention of allergies. **Giving Priorities:** In fiscal 1993, more than 99% of foundation giving went to health concerns, including the largest grant to the McGovern Fund for the Behavioral Sciences in Houston, TX. Education and civic organizations received less than 1%. **Typical Health-Related Recipients:** Children's Health/Hospitals, Health Funds, Medical Research. **Geographic Distribution:** Primarily Houston, TX, area; some national giving.

★323★ **John P. Murphy Foundation**
Tower City Center
924 Terminal Tower
50 Public Sq.
Cleveland, OH 44113-2203
Phone: (216)623-4770
Fax: (216)623-4773
Herbert E. Strawbridge, President, Secretary, and Treasurer

Foundation Philosophy: The foundation's articles of incorporation state that the foundation will distribute its grants for "charitable, educational, scientific, literary, and religious purposes." Artistic and cultural grants generally range from $1,000 to $50,000 and focus on the field of music. Grants to social service organizations typically are below $5,000, and are given to a wide variety of needs. Community service grants also are given to numerous types of organizations. Most of the foundation's health grants are given to hospital building programs. **Giving Priorities:** In 1993, the foundation gave approximately 40% of funding to the arts. Education received 23%; health care, 16%; civic affairs, 10%; social services, 7%; religious concerns, 3%; and science, 2%. **Typical Health-Related Recipients:** Cancer, Clinics/Medical Centers, Family Planning, Health Funds, Health Organizations, Heart, Hospices, Hospitals, Hospitals (University Affiliated), Long-Term Care, Medical Education, Medical Research, People with Disabilities, Preventive Medicine/Wellness Organizations, Substance Abuse. **Geographic Distribution:** Metropolitan Cleveland and adjacent counties in northeastern Ohio.

★ 324 ★ **John S. Dunn Research Foundation**
3355 W Alabama, Ste. 720
Houston, TX 77098
Phone: (713)626-0368
Milby Dow Dunn, President

Foundation Philosophy: The foundation typically funds organizations "whose primary efforts are medically related to educational and research activities." **Giving Priorities:** In 1993, the foundation awarded 84% of its contributions to health care organizations, including its largest grant of $1,300,000 to the Methodist Hospital Foundation. Social service organizations received 10% of support, while education received 4%. Science and religion each received 1% of support. **Typical Health-Related Recipients:** Cancer, Clinics/Medical Centers, Eyes/Blindness, Health Funds, Health Organizations, Heart, Hospices, Hospitals, Medical Education, Medical Rehabilitation, Medical Research, People with Disabilities. **Geographic Distribution:** Generally limited to the state of Texas.

★ 325 ★ **John S. and James L. Knight Foundation**
2 S Biscayne Blvd., Ste. 3800
Miami, FL 33131-1803
Phone: (305)539-0009
Creed Black, President

Foundation Philosophy: To heighten the impact of their grant making, the trustees have elected to focus on four programs, each with its own eligibility requirements: Community Initiatives, Journalism, Education, and Arts and Culture. The foundation considers requests from a broad range of community organization and institutions. Current priority areas of interest are: (1) arts and culture; (2) education; (3) children/social welfare; (4) citizenship; (5) community development; (6) homelessness; and (7) literacy. While retaining the flexibility to consider the diversity of needs in each community, the foundation encourages grant proposals in these areas of special interest. **Giving Priorities:** In 1993, the foundation reported that it awarded approximately 35% of its contributions to health and human services. These awards supported child welfare, delinquency, homelessness, and food/clothing distribution. Health awards went to hos-

pitals for capital campaigns only. Education received 24% of the funds. Grants in journalism accounted for 22% of the money awarded. The arts received 19% of the foundation's funding. **Typical Health-Related Recipients:** Cancer, Children's Health/Hospitals, Emergency/Ambulance Services, Hospices, Hospitals, Prenatal Health Issues. **Geographic Distribution:** Selected areas in California, Colorado, Florida, Georgia, Indiana, Kansas, Kentucky, Michigan, Minnesota, Mississippi, North Carolina, North Dakota, Ohio, Pennsylvania, South Carolina, and South Dakota. **Formerly:** Knight Foundation.

★ 326 ★ **John W. Anderson Foundation**
402 Wall St.
Valparaiso, IN 46383
Phone: (219)462-4611
Paul G. Wallace, Secretary and Trustee

Foundation Philosophy: The largest concentration of giving by the foundation traditionally supports the social services. A second area of interest is education. In addition, special education, educational associations, minority education, and secondary education are supported. The foundation also funds a number of youth organizations. **Giving Priorities:** In 1992, the foundation reported 50% of its funding went to social services, while 38% went to education. Health groups received 8%; the remainder was given to arts, civic, and religious groups. **Typical Health-Related Recipients:** Cancer, Children's Health/Hospitals, Clinics/Medical Centers, Emergency/Ambulance Services, Family Planning, Health Organizations, Hospices, Medical Education, Mental Health, Nursing Services, People with Disabilities, Research/Studies Institutes, Single-Disease Health Associations. **Geographic Distribution:** Mainly Lake and Porter counties area of Northwestern Indiana.

★ 327 ★ **John W. and Effie E. Speas Memorial Trust**
c/o Boatmen's First National Bank of Kansas City
PO Box 419038
Kansas City, MO 64183
Phone: (816)221-2800
David P. Ross, Senior Vice President

Foundation Philosophy: The Speas Memorial Trust supports a variety of health and social service organizations, with some focus on mental health and substance abuse programs. Recently, it has initiated services for the elderly in the Kansas City metropolitan area, with emphasis on helping the elderly to continue to reside in their own homes, and on providing respite care. The trust also contributes to university medical schools. **Giving Priorities:** In 1993, the trust awarded 65% of its total contributions to health care, including a single $137,115 grant to Midwest Research Institute, Kansas City, MO. About 17% of funds went to social services. Educational institutions recevied 15% of support; civic groups, 2%; and religious organizations, 1%. **Typical Health-Related Recipients:** Cancer, Clinics/Medical Centers, Eyes/Blindness, Health Organizations, Heart, Hospitals, Kidney, Medical Education, Medical Rehabilitation, Medical Research, Medical Training, Mental Health, Multiple Sclerosis, Nursing Services,

People with Disabilities, Prenatal Health Issues, Public Health, Substance Abuse. **Geographic Distribution:** Jackson, Clay, Platte, and Cass counties, MO; and Wyandotte and Johnson counties, KS.

★ 328 ★ **John and Wilhelmina D. Harland Charitable Foundation**
Two Piedmont Center, Ste. 106
Atlanta, GA 30305
Phone: (404)264-9912
John A. Conant, Secretary

Foundation Philosophy: The Harlands had a particular interest "in causes that serve children and higher education." These remain primary concerns of the foundation, but consideration is given to grant requests that fall within the following categories: religion, education, health, community services, and culture. **Giving Priorities:** In 1993, the foundation contributed 29% of its total giving to support health care, including a $244,375 grant to Eagleston Hospital for Children in Atlanta. Social service organizations received 21% of the donations, with support going to child welfare and people with disabilities. Civic affairs was awarded 18% of distributed funds, while 16% supported religious affairs. Educational institutions received 13%, and the remaining 3% supported the arts. **Typical Health-Related Recipients:** Children's Health/Hospitals, Clinics/Medical Centers, Domestic Violence, Emergency/Ambulance Services, Health Organizations, Hospitals, Long-Term Care, Mental Health, People with Disabilities, Single-Disease Health Associations. **Geographic Distribution:** Focus on metropolitan Atlanta, GA.

★ 329 ★ **Joseph Alexander Foundation**
400 Madison Ave., Ste. 906
New York, NY 10017
Phone: (212)355-3688
Robert M. Weintraub, Vice President, Director

Foundation Philosophy: The Joseph Alexander Foundation makes most of its grants in the areas of health, education, and social services. Health funding favors cancer and AIDS research and treatment, hospitals, and geriatric care. Educational support primarily goes to Jewish universities, medical education, and legal education. In social services, interests include the aged, the disabled, homes for children, family services, and community centers. The foundation also makes grants to other recipient areas. **Giving Priorities:** In fiscal 1993, the foundation gave 24% of its contributions to religious causes relating to Judaism. International affairs received 20% of funds. Health care received 15% of contributions, primarily for disease research. Educational institutions were the beneficiaries of 14% of donations, while the arts were given 13% of total support. Social service organizations received 10% support, while civic concerns received 3%. The remainder, about 1%, supported science. **Typical Health-Related Recipients:** AIDS/HIV, Cancer, Children's Health/Hospitals, Diabetes, Emergency/Ambulance Services, Eyes/Blindness, Family Planning, Geriatric Health, Health Organizations, Hospitals, Medical Education, Medical Rehabilitation, Medical Research, Mental Health, Nursing Services, People with Disabilities, Single-Disease Health Associations, Substance Abuse, Transplant Networks/Donor Banks, Trauma Treatment. **Geographic Distribution:** National, with emphasis on New York, NY.

★ 330 ★ Joseph B. Whitehead Foundation
50 Hurt Plz., Ste. 1200
Atlanta, GA 30303
Phone: (404)522-6755
Fax: (404)522-7026
Charles H. McTier, President

Foundation Philosophy: The foundation was established with a particular interest in benefitting children. Its primary areas of giving include human services, particularly for children and youth; elementary and secondary education; health care; economic development and civic affairs; literacy and vocational training; art and cultural activities; and the environment. **Giving Priorities:** In 1993, the foundation awarded approximately 48% of its total contributions to social service organizations. Educational institutions and programs received about 20%; religious causes, 9%; health care, 7%; scientific interests, 6%; civic affairs, 4%; international organizations, 4%; and the arts and environmental projects received the remaining funds. **Typical Health-Related Recipients:** Arthritis, Child Abuse, Health Organizations, Health Policy/Cost Containment, Hospitals, Kidney, Mental Health, People with Disabilities, Prenatal Health Issues, Respiratory, Substance Abuse, Trauma Treatment. **Geographic Distribution:** Limited to metropolitan Atlanta, GA.

★ 331 ★ Joseph Drown Foundation
1999 Avenue of the Stars, Ste. 1930
Los Angeles, CA 90067
Phone: (310)277-4488
Norman C. Obrow, President

Foundation Philosophy: The foundation's focus remains education and medical research. The focus on medical and scientific research remains broad, but no unsolicited grant requests in this area are accepted. The grantmaking in community health and social services is geared towards improving the life in the local community. The focus is on programs that deal with issues such as high drop-out rates, teen pregnancy, lack of sufficient health care, substance abuse, and violence. The funding in the arts and humanities is limited to outreach and education. **Giving Priorities:** In fiscal year 1994, the foundation gave about 39% of its contributions to education and 36% of its funding to health-related organizations. Social services received 22% of giving, and the remaining funds were divided between civic and public affairs and international organizations. **Typical Health-Related Recipients:** Arthritis, Cancer, Clinics/Medical Centers, Diabetes, Emergency/Ambulance Services, Eyes/Blindness, Family Planning, Health Organizations, Heart, Medical Education, Medical Research, Mental Health, People with Disabilities, Preventive Medicine/Wellness Organizations, Research/Studies Institutes, Single-Disease Health Associations, Speech & Hearing, Substance Abuse. **Geographic Distribution:** Primarily California.

★ 332 ★ Josiah Macy, Jr. Foundation
44 E 64th St.
New York, NY 10021
Phone: (212)486-2424
Fax: (212)644-0765
Thomas H. Meikle, Jr., MD, President

Foundation Philosophy: Traditionally, the Macy Foundation has focused on medicine and health. The foundation's interests currently are focused on conferences that explore critical issues in medical education and on projects that demonstrate new educational directions and evaluate their effectiveness. The foundation is currently assisting projects that: recruit and retain medical students from underrepresented racial, ethnic, geographic, and socioeconomic backgrounds; strengthen the clinical education of physicians by instituting performance-based evaluations of students' and residents' competencies throughout their training; and enhance the training of physicians and non-physician professionals for primary care practices. **Giving Priorities:** In fiscal 1994, the foundation reported that it gave approximately 80% of its contributions to education including support for colleges and universities, medical education, and minority education. Health care received 17% including support for medical training, nursing, and health policy organizations. The remaining 3% was distributed to other organizations including support for foreign health personnel training. **Typical Health-Related Recipients:** Health Organizations, Health Policy/Cost Containment, Medical Education, Medical Training, Nursing Services. **Geographic Distribution:** No geographic restrictions.

★ 333 ★ Josiah W. and Bessie H. Kline Foundation
42 Kline Village
Harrisburg, PA 17104
Phone: (717)232-0266
Harry R. Bughman, Secretary

Foundation Philosophy: The foundation makes most of its grants in the areas of education, health, and social services. Health interests include medical centers, health foundations, and hospitals. The foundation also makes grants to the arts and civic affairs. **Giving Priorities:** In 1993, the foundation gave 48% of its funds to higher education. Health services received 28% of the contributions; the arts received 15%; social services received 7%; civic concerns received 2%. **Typical Health-Related Recipients:** Alzheimers Disease, Cancer, Children's Health/Hospitals, Clinics/Medical Centers, Emergency/Ambulance Services, Family Planning, Health Organizations, Heart, Hospices, Hospitals, Medical Research, Multiple Sclerosis, Outpatient Health Care, People with Disabilities, Public Health, Single-Disease Health Associations, Substance Abuse. **Geographic Distribution:** Limited to central Pennsylvania.

★ 334 ★ Joukowsky Family Foundation
111 Broadway, 14th Fl.
New York, NY 10006
Nina Joukowsky Koprulu, Executive Director

Foundation Philosophy: The Joukowsky Family Foundation makes most of its grants in the areas of education. Additional funding is available for civic affairs, the arts, health care, international affairs, religion, and social services. The foundation supports preselected organizations and they do not have specific funding priorities. **Giving Priorities:** In fiscal 1993, the foundation gave approximately 76% of its contributions to educational institutions. Civic affairs received 5%; health care, 4%; religion, 4%; and social services, 4%. International organizations received 3%; the arts, 2%; and environmental efforts, 1%. **Typical Health-Related Recipients:** Diabetes, Domestic Violence, Family Planning, Hospices, Hospitals, People with Disabilities. **Geographic Distribution:** National.

★ 335 ★ Jules and Doris Stein Foundation
PO Box 30
Beverly Hills, CA 90213
Phone: (310)276-2101
Fax: (310)276-0126
Linda L. Valliant, Program Officer

Foundation Philosophy: Organized in 1981, the foundation has provided grant support to a variety of worthy causes with emphasis on educational, medical, and artistic programs. The foundation is fulfilling the Doris Stein Research Center pledge, and is not soliciting new grant applications or programs through 1995. **Giving Priorities:** In 1994, health received approximately 46% of funding; art, 24%; social services, 14%; education, 9%; civic, 6%; and religious organizations, 1%. Health funding includes support of the Jules Stein Eye Institute and the Don Stein Eye Research Center. **Typical Health-Related Recipients:** Cancer, Diabetes, Family Planning, Health Organizations, Medical Rehabilitation, Medical Research. **Geographic Distribution:** Primarily in Los Angeles, CA; Kansas City, MO; and New York, NY.

★ 336 ★ Julia R. and Estelle L. Foundation
3600 Marine Midland Ctr.
Buffalo, NY 14203
Phone: (716)856-9490
Fax: (716)856-9493
Richard L. Wolf, Vice President

Foundation Philosophy: The foundation typically supports social services, educational institutions, and health organizations in New York. **Giving Priorities:** In 1993, the foundation awarded 25% of its total contributions to social services. Another 25% of funds supported educational institutions. Health care received 23% of gifts; religious organizations, 18%; and the arts, 10%. **Typical Health-Related Recipients:** Children's Health/Hospitals, Emergency/Ambulance Services, Hospices, Hospitals, Long-Term Care, Medical Research, People with Disabilities. **Geographic Distribution:** Primarily Buffalo and the greater western New York State area.

★ 337 ★ June Rockwell Levy Foundation
136 Ridgeway Rd.
Weston, MA 02193
Phone: (617)237-4037
James W. Noonan, Secretary

Foundation Philosophy: The June Rockwell Levy Foundation supports a variety of charitable organizations. Health care support favors general hospitals and medical foundations. Private education and colleges are favored for educational support. All areas of social services and civic affairs are supported by the foundation. The arts and international organizations receive minor support. **Giving Priorities:** In 1993, the foundation gave approximately 38% of its contributions to health concerns. Educational institutions received about 20% of giving. Social service organizations received 17%; the arts, 10%; civic affairs, 7%; international organizations, 4%; and environmental organizations, 2%. Religion and science received the remainder. **Typical Health-Related Recipients:** Cancer, Children's Health/Hospitals, Emergency/Ambulance Services, Family Planning, Geriatric Health, Health Funds, Health Organizations, Hospices, Hospitals, Medical Education, Medical Research, Nursing Services, People with Disabilities, Single-Disease Health Associations, Substance Abuse. **Geographic Distribution:** Focus on Rhode Island and Massachusetts.

★338★ **Jurodin Fund**
630 Fifth Ave., Rm. 1418
New York, NY 10111
Phone: (212)247-5060
Julius Silver, President

Foundation Philosophy: The Jurodin Fund primarily supports education and religious organizations. Education funding favors colleges and legal education. Jewish religious organizations are also a major priority. Secondary interests include medical centers, civic affairs, and the arts. **Giving Priorities:** In 1993, the fund donated 30% of its total giving to educational institutions. Religious organizations received 24% of funding. Health care received 20% of support, including a single $50,000 grant to the Greenwich Hospital Association, for cancer research. International organizations received 13% of support, while arts and humanities received 7%. Social services were supported with 4% of giving, and civic and public affairs received 2%. The remaining funds, just under 1%, went to environmental organizations. **Typical Health-Related Recipients:** Cancer, Clinics/Medical Centers, Emergency/Ambulance Services, Family Planning, Health Organizations, Hospitals, Medical Education, Medical Rehabilitation, Medical Research, People with Disabilities, Single-Disease Health Associations. **Geographic Distribution:** Northeastern United States, with a focus on New York, NY.

★339★ **Justin and Valere Potter Foundation**
c/o Waller, Lansden, Dortch and Davis
511 Union St., Ste. 2100
Nashville, TN 37219
Phone: (615)244-6380
Justin P. Wilson, Chairman and Trustee

Foundation Philosophy: The purpose of the foundation is to benefit the Nashville area by funding institutions of secondary and higher education, including medical education and medical research, as well as scholarship funds. Other priorities include the arts and humanities, particularly libraries and historic preservation programs, and social services, especially those that benefit youth. **Giving Priorities:** In 1991, the foundation gave approximately 34% of total funding to educational institutions, primarily colleges and universities, with the Vanderbilt University School of Medicine receiving the foundation's highest grant of $245,000. The arts received 29%. Social services received 13%; religious organizations, 10%; civic groups, 8%; and health organizations, 5%. **Typical Health-Related Recipients:** Medical Education. **Geographic Distribution:** Focus on metropolitan Nashville, TN.

★340★ **Kate B. Reynolds Charitable Trust**
128 Reynolda Village
Winston-Salem, NC 27106-5123
Phone: (910)723-1456
Fax: (910)723-7765
E. Ray Cope, Executive Director

Foundation Philosophy: One-quarter of the total income from the trust is disbursed through the Poor and Needy Division and the remaining three-quarters of the total income from the trust is expended through the Health Care Division, which supports innovative health care programs throughout North Carolina. The Health Care Division funds are used to encourage and support innovative programs that increase the availability of health services to underserved groups, address the problems of health services in rural areas, reduce the rate of infant mortality/morbidity, and promote good health and prevent illness. This division also provides support for well-conceived studies that clearly define health care problems in North Carolina and that will assist the trust and others in developing viable solutions to these problems. The Poor and Needy Division funds are used to support organizations which provide for basic needs, such as food, clothing, shelter, and health care. **Giving Priorities:** In fiscal 1994, the trust gave 75% of its income to health groups. Organizations that assist the poor and needy received 25% of the foundation's funding. **Typical Health-Related Recipients:** Adolescent Health Issues, Alzheimers Disease, Cancer, Children's Health/Hospitals, Clinics/Medical Centers, Diabetes, Domestic Violence, Emergency/Ambulance Services, Family Planning, Geriatric Health, Health Organizations, Health Policy/Cost Containment, Heart, Hospices, Hospitals, Long-Term Care, Medical Education, Medical Rehabilitation, Mental Health, People with Disabilities, Prenatal Health Issues, Public Health, Single-Disease Health Associations, Speech & Hearing, Substance Abuse. **Geographic Distribution:** Health care grants are limited to North Carolina; grants for the poor and needy are limited to Winston-Salem, NC, and Forsyth County, NC.

★341★ **Kathleen Price and Joseph M. Bryan Family Foundation**
One North Pointe, Ste. 170
3101 N Elm St.
Greensboro, NC 27408
Phone: (910)288-5455
Fax: (910)288-5458
William P. Massey, Executive Director

Foundation Philosophy: The foundation seeks to improve conditions and opportunities in North Carolina, primarily through support of nonprofit organizations working to build community in the broad fields of arts and culture, education, health care, human service, public interest and youth. Emphasis is placed on helping the economically disadvantaged in rural North Carolina, and the majority of funding is given on a challenge basis. Within the coming year, the foundation anticipates more program-related investments in its areas of interest. **Giving Priorities:** In 1993, the foundation contributed 55% of its total giving to civic affairs. Education received 16% of funds. About 15% of support went to health care; 11% to social services, especially to organizations supporting children; and 3% to the arts. **Typical Health-Related Recipients:** AIDS/HIV, Alzheimers Disease, Clinics/Medical Centers, Domestic Violence, Health Organizations, People with Disabilities, Single-Disease Health Associations, Substance Abuse. **Geographic Distribution:** Only in North Carolina; primarily in Guilford County and in North Carolina's rural area and to projects with statewide impact.

★342★ **Kenneth T. and Eileen L. Norris Foundation**
11 Golden Shore, Ste. 450
Long Beach, CA 90802
Phone: (310)435-8444
Fax: (310)436-0584
Ronald R. Barnes, Executive Director

Foundation Philosophy: The foundation supports organizations which directly and indirectly affect positive change in the community. This support generally is directed to medicine and medical research, private educational institutions, youth and social service agencies, and cultural programs. **Giving Priorities:** In 1993, health-related concerns received approximately 42% of foundation support. About 25% of contributions went to education. Socials services received 19% of grants awarded, with youth organizations receiving 10% of social service grants made. Support to the arts comprised 14% of contributions made. **Typical Health-Related Recipients:** Hospitals, Medical Research, People with Disabilities, Substance Abuse. **Geographic Distribution:** Los Angeles County area.

★343★ **Kentland Foundation**
PO Box 837
Berryville, VA 22611
Phone: (703)955-1268
Helene Walker, Secretary

Foundation Philosophy: The Kentland Foundation makes most of its grants to education and religion. Funding favors literacy, religious education, universities, and parochial education. Other significant interests include youth organizations, housing, churches, and health services. **Giving Priorities:** In 1993, approximately 30% of the foundation's charitable giving went to education. Religious organizations received 27% of funding. Social Service organizations were awarded 24% of giving, including a single, $20,000 grant to the Boy Scouts of America. Civic affairs received 9% of the distributed funds, health care received 6%, while 2% went to support environmental concerns. The arts received 2% of the total support. **Typical Health-Related Recipients:** Children's Health/Hospitals, Domestic Violence, Emergency/Ambulance Services, Family Planning, Hospices, Hospitals, Nutrition, People with Disabilities, Prenatal Health Issues, Preventive Medicine/Wellness Organizations, Sexual Abuse. **Geographic Distribution:** Mid-Atlantic United States.

★ 344 ★ Kettering Fund
1440 Kettering Tower
Dayton, OH 45423
Phone: (513)228-1021
Fax: (513)449-8644
Richard F. Beach, Administrator

Foundation Philosophy: The fund supports groups furthering "general philanthropy with an emphasis in higher education and cultural development." **Giving Priorities:** In fiscal 1993, the fund awarded approximately 59% of its total contributions to health concerns, including its highest grant of $2,000,000 to the Kettering Medical Center in Kettering, OH. Educational institutions received about 27%; social services, 6%; the arts, 4%; scientific interests, 2%; and civic affairs, international organizations, and religious causes received the remaining funds. **Typical Health-Related Recipients:** Clinics/ Medical Centers, Emergency/Ambulance Services, Family Planning, Health Organizations, Hospitals, Nursing Services, People with Disabilities. **Geographic Distribution:** Limited to Ohio, principally Dayton.

★ 345 ★ Kirkpatrick Foundation
PO Box 268822
Oklahoma City, OK 73126
Phone: (405)840-2882
Marilyn B. Myers, Director and Assistant
  Secretary

Foundation Philosophy: The Kirkpatrick Foundation makes most of its grants in the areas of civic affairs, the arts and cultural programs, education, and social services. In social services, interests include youth organizations, family planning, and child welfare. **Giving Priorities:** In 1993, the foundation awarded approximately 65% of its total contributions to civic affairs. Health concerns received about 9% of funds. Social services, mainly those supporting women and youth, received 8%. The arts, education, and religious organizations each received 6% of the remaining funds. **Typical Health-Related Recipients:** Children's Health/Hospitals, Clinics/Medical Centers, Domestic Violence, Emergency/Ambulance Services, Family Planning, Hospitals, Medical Research, Single-Disease Health Associations. **Geographic Distribution:** Focus on the Oklahoma City area.

★ 346 ★ Kresge Foundation
3215 W Big Beaver Rd.
PO Box 3151
Troy, MI 48007-3151
Phone: (810)643-9630
Fax: (810)643-0588
John E. Marshall, III, President and Secretary

Foundation Philosophy: The foundation is one of the few large foundations concentrating exclusively on bricks-and-mortar campaigns, providing construction funds to recipient institutions, or assisting with the renovation of existing facilities. The foundation has no predetermined grants budget by field, geography, or type of project. The foundation primarily makes challenge grants to four-year colleges and universi-

ties; and to organizations concerned with health and long-term care, human services, science, the environment, public policy, and the arts. **Giving Priorities:** In 1993, the foundation gave approximately 31% of its contributions to educational institutions. Health organizations and social services each received 16% of funds. The arts, including support for libraries, museums, and galleries, received 15% of giving. Civic affairs received 12%; environmental efforts, 5%; religious organizations, 3%; and science and international affairs received the remainder. **Typical Health-Related Recipients:** AIDS/ HIV, Cancer, Children's Health/Hospitals, Clinics/Medical Centers, Domestic Violence, Emergency/Ambulance Services, Eyes/Blindness, Family Planning, Health Organizations, Hospices, Hospitals, Medical Education, Medical Rehabilitation, Medical Research, Nursing Services, Outpatient Health Care, People with Disabilities, Preventive Medicine/Wellness Organizations, Research/Studies Institutes, Sexual Abuse, Substance Abuse. **Geographic Distribution:** No geographic restrictions.

★ 347 ★ L. K. Whittier Foundation
1260 Huntington Dr., Ste. 204
South Pasadena, CA 91030
Phone: (213)259-0484
Fax: (213)259-0462
Linda J. Blinkenberg, Secretary and Chief
  Financial Officer

Foundation Philosophy: The foundation assists in the establishment and development of innovative endeavors in the areas of health and medicine, the sciences, and education. **Giving Priorities:** In fiscal 1993, the foundation gave approximately 40% of its contributions to the arts. Health care received 28% of contributions made, including a $119,500 grant to the Huntington Medical Research Institute to support research on non-invasive brain examination. Education received 26% of funds; social services, 4%; civic affairs, 2%; and religion less than 1% of funds. **Typical Health-Related Recipients:** Children's Health/Hospitals, Clinics/Medical Centers, Eyes/Blindness, Health Organizations, Medical Education, Medical Research, Research/Studies Institutes, Single-Disease Health Associations. **Geographic Distribution:** Primarily Southern California area, particularly Los Angeles.

★ 348 ★ L. and S. Milken Foundation
c/o Foundations of the Milken Family
1250 Fourth St., Sixth Fl.
Santa Monica, CA 90401
Phone: (310)998-2800
J. Lesner, Vice President

Foundation Philosophy: Support primarily goes to social service organizations and education. The Milken foundations were established "to discover and advance inventive ways to build human resources through programs aimed at rewarding educational inventors, stimulating creativity among students, involving parents and other citizens in our schools, and offering opportunities to the disadvantaged student; making the benefits of both basic and highly advanced health care available to those who need them, and supporting medical research." **Giving Priorities:** In fiscal 1994, the foundation

gave 36% of total contributions to religious needs. International affairs received approximately 24% of funding. Educational programs received 17% of total funds. Health care received 11% of gifts, including contributions to several single-disease foundations. Civic concerns received 8% of funds, and social services received approximately 4%. The remaining funds went to support the arts and humanities. **Typical Health-Related Recipients:** Cancer, Children's Health/Hospitals, Clinics/Medical Centers, Eyes/Blindness, Heart, Hospitals, Medical Research, People with Disabilities, Single-Disease Health Associations. **Geographic Distribution:** Focus on the Los Angeles, CA, area.

★ 349 ★ Laffey-McHugh Foundation
PO Box 2207
Wilmington, DE 19899-2207
Phone: (302)658-9141
Thomas S. Lodge, Secretary

Foundation Philosophy: The foundation continues to reflect the interests of the original donors by supporting Roman Catholic churches and church-related institutions, including schools, child welfare agencies, and religious welfare groups. The foundation also makes grants to institutions of higher education, both sectarian and nonsectarian; and to local hospitals, cultural organizations, and nonsectarian welfare agencies. **Giving Priorities:** In 1993, the foundation gave approximately 30% of funding to religious services and programs. Education received 28%, primarily supporting capital campaigns at private colleges and secondary schools. Social services received 20%, including the highest grant of $165,000 to the United Way of Delaware. The arts received 10% of giving; health care organizations and civic and public affairs each received 6%. **Typical Health-Related Recipients:** Cancer, Child Abuse, Family Planning, Geriatric Health, Hospices, Hospitals, People with Disabilities, Single-Disease Health Associations, Substance Abuse. **Geographic Distribution:** Primarily Delaware.

★ 350 ★ Leighton-Oare Foundation
112 W Jefferson Blvd., Ste. 603
South Bend, IN 46601
Phone: (219)232-5977
Judd C. Leighton, Secretary-Treasurer

Foundation Philosophy: The Leighton-Oare Foundation is primarily interested in health services, education, and the arts. Health service funding heavily favors health foundations. interests include civic affairs, religion, and social services. **Giving Priorities:** In 1993, the foundation gave approximately 51% of its contributions to support the arts. Educational institutions received about 24% of donations. Health care received 16% of giving, while 7% went to civic affairs. The remaining 2% went to social services. **Typical Health-Related Recipients:** Children's Health/Hospitals, Geriatric Health, Health Funds, Multiple Sclerosis, Research/Studies Institutes. **Geographic Distribution:** National, with a focus on Indiana.

★351★ Leland Fikes Foundation

3050 Lincoln Plz.
500 N Akard, Ste. 3060
Dallas, TX 75201
Phone: (214)754-0144
Nancy Solana, Vice President and Secretary

Foundation Philosophy: The Fikes Foundation offers support to a wide variety of cultural, civic, educational, health, scientific, and social service organizations. A preference is shown toward local projects and organizations. **Giving Priorities:** In 1993, the foundation awarded approximately 29% of its total contributions to health concerns. Educational institutions received about 20%. Social services received 14%; religious causes, 13%; international organizations, 8%; civic affairs, 6%, the arts, 5%; environmental projects, 3%; and scientific interests received the remaining funds. **Typical Health-Related Recipients:** AIDS/HIV, Cancer, Children's Health/Hospitals, Domestic Violence, Eyes/Blindness, Family Planning, Health Organizations, Heart, Hospitals, Medical Education, Medical Research, Mental Health, Nursing Services, People with Disabilities, Public Health, Substance Abuse, Trauma Treatment. **Geographic Distribution:** Primarily in Dallas, TX.

★352★ Leon Lowenstein Foundation

126 E 56th St., 28th Fl.
New York, NY 10022
Phone: (212)319-0670
Robert Austin Bendheim, President

Foundation Philosophy: The foundation provides funding "to higher education and health for the benefit of New York City." **Giving Priorities:** In 1993, the foundation gave approximately 55% of its total contributions to educational institutions. Health concerns received about 26%; social service organizations, 9%; religious interests, 8%; and the arts and civic affairs received the remaining funds. **Typical Health-Related Recipients:** Cancer, Clinics/Medical Centers, Emergency/Ambulance Services, Eyes/Blindness, Health Organizations, Hospitals, Medical Education, Medical Research, Nursing Services, People with Disabilities, Single-Disease Health Associations, Substance Abuse. **Geographic Distribution:** Emphasis on New York City metropolitan area.

★353★ Lettie Pate Whitehead Foundation

50 Hurt Plz., Ste. 1200
Atlanta, GA 30303
Phone: (404)522-6755
Fax: (404)522-7026
Charles H. McTier, President

Foundation Philosophy: As specified under the will of Conkey Pate Whitehead, the foundation is limited to providing funds for needy female Christian students in Alabama, Florida, Georgia, Louisiana, Mississippi, North Carolina, South Carolina, Tennessee, and Virginia. Grants are made directly to institutions of higher education which, in turn, allocate scholarship funds to individual students. Scholarships are based on financial need. This educational program accounts for more than 90% of giving. The remainder of support is given to homes for needy elderly Christian women. Grants awarded in 1993 and 1994 include: $59,000 to Lynchburg College, VA, for nursing scholarships; $45,000

to Presbyterian College, SC, for general scholarships; $42,000 to Columbia College, SC, for general scholarships; $35,000 to Judson College, AL, for student aid; and $25,000 to King College, TN, also for general scholarships. **Giving Priorities:** In 1993, the foundation reported that education received 100% of its contributions through scholarships for needy female Christian students in southern states. **Typical Health-Related Recipients:** Medical Education. **Geographic Distribution:** Alabama, Florida, Georgia, Louisiana, Mississippi, North Carolina, South Carolina, Tennessee, and Virginia.

★354★ Lied Foundation Trust

3965 W Charleston Blvd.
Las Vegas, NV 89102
Phone: (702)878-1559
Christina M. Hixson, Trustee

Foundation Philosophy: The Lied Foundation Trust traditionally funds three main areas: higher education, the Omaha Zoological Society, and youth organizations in Las Vegas. Major contributions are made to higher education, particularly to Kansas University, the Lied Institute for Real Estate Studies, and the University of Nebraska. The Boys and Girls Club of Las Vegas also is a main interest. The foundation also funds other organizations primarily in the areas of social services and education. **Giving Priorities:** In 1993, the foundation gave approximately 37% of its contributions to educational institutions. Civic affairs received 22% of funding. Environmental concerns received 11%. Health care received 9%; social service organizations, 8%; religious organizations, 7%; the arts, 5%; and a science museum, 1%. **Typical Health-Related Recipients:** People with Disabilities, Research/Studies Institutes, Speech & Hearing, Transplant Networks/Donor Banks. **Geographic Distribution:** Focus on Las Vegas, NV, Nebraska, Kansas, and Los Angeles, CA.

★355★ Lightner Sams Foundation

11811 Preston Rd., Ste. 200
Dallas, TX 75230
Phone: (214)458-8811
Larry Lightner, Trustee

Foundation Philosophy: The Lightner Sams Foundation makes grants across the major categories of giving. In civic affairs, interests include zoos, business and economics, conservation, and philanthropic organizations. Educational funding favors colleges and universities, special education, and private schools. The arts are supported in the areas of festivals and the performing arts. Social service support includes recreation, child welfare, youth organizations, and counseling. The foundation will make grants in other recipient areas also. **Giving Priorities:** In 1993, the foundation gave approximately 37% of its contributions to civic affairs. Educational institutions received 21%. The arts received 14%; social services, 10%; environmental causes, 8%; health care, 8%; and religion received the remainder. **Typical Health-Related Recipients:** Cancer, Children's Health/Hospitals, Domestic Violence, Emergency/Ambulance Services, Family Planning, Health Organizations, Heart, Hospitals, Medical Rehabilitation, Mental Health, People with Disabilities, Single-Disease Health Associations.

Geographic Distribution: Focus on Texas and Wyoming.

★356★ Lincy Foundation

4045 Spencer St., Ste. A57
Las Vegas, NV 89109
Phone: (702)737-8060
James D. Aljian, President

Foundation Philosophy: The Lincy Foundation is primarily interested in aiding Armenian interests through its support of the United Armenian Fund and other organizations. The foundation has also supported care for the elderly with two large grants going to homes for the aged in Southern California. **Giving Priorities:** In fiscal 1993, the foundation gave approximately 48% of its total contributions to civic affairs. Educational institutions received about 20%. Social services received 14%; health care, 11%; the arts, 5%; and religious causes received the remaining funds. **Typical Health-Related Recipients:** AIDS/HIV, Arthritis, Clinics/Medical Centers, Diabetes, Geriatric Health, Health Organizations, Hospices, Hospitals, Medical Education, Medical Research, People with Disabilities, Public Health, Single-Disease Health Associations, Transplant Networks/Donor Banks. **Geographic Distribution:** Nationally, with an emphasis on Southern California.

★357★ Lloyd A. Fry Foundation

135 S LaSalle St., Ste. 1910
Chicago, IL 60603
Phone: (312)580-0310
Fax: (312)580-0980

Foundation Philosophy: The foundation focuses its philanthropic efforts in the areas of education, health, civic affairs, social services, and the arts. In the area of health, the foundation continues to focus on health education and disease prevention among low-income and minority populations, as well as on efforts to improve health care for the medically indigent in Chicago. Improving health services for low-income children is a special emphasis in this area. **Giving Priorities:** In fiscal 1993, the foundation gave approximately 33% of its funding to educational organizations primarily supporting inner-city education projects. Social services and civic causes each received 19% of giving. The arts benefited from 15% of giving, while health concerns received 14%. **Typical Health-Related Recipients:** AIDS/HIV, Clinics/Medical Centers, Domestic Violence, Geriatric Health, Health Organizations, Health Policy/Cost Containment, Hospitals, Mental Health, Nursing Services, People with Disabilities, Prenatal Health Issues, Public Health, Single-Disease Health Associations, Substance Abuse. **Geographic Distribution:** Metropolitan Chicago, IL.

★358★ Lon V. Smith Foundation

9440 Santa Monica Blvd., Ste. 300
Beverly Hills, CA 90210-4201
Phone: (310)276-9306
Marguerite M. Murphy, Secretary and Treasurer

Foundation Philosophy: The primary focus of the foundation is on social services in the Los Angeles area. A variety of organizations are supported, including services for the disabled, child welfare programs, youth organizations, family services, shelters, and homes. The foundation also is interested in supporting health services. A variety of health organizations are supported by the foundation, including hospitals, single-disease associations, family clinics, counseling, and pediatrics. **Giving Priorities:** In 1993, the foundation gave 45% of its funding to social service organizations. Health services received 22% of giving, with emphasis on single-disease health associations and hospitals. Civic affairs accounted for 13% of the funds. Religious organizations received 9% and educational programs were given 6%. The remaining funds went to international affairs (3%) and the arts (3%). **Typical Health-Related Recipients:** Cancer, Children's Health/Hospitals, Clinics/Medical Centers, Diabetes, Emergency/Ambulance Services, Health Organizations, Hospitals, Long-Term Care, Medical Research, Nutrition, Outpatient Health Care, People with Disabilities, Prenatal Health Issues, Research/Studies Institutes, Single-Disease Health Associations, Speech & Hearing, Substance Abuse. **Geographic Distribution:** Focus on Los Angeles, CA.

★359★ Longwood Foundation
1004 Wilmington Trust Ctr.
Wilmington, DE 19801
Phone: (302)654-2477
David Wakefield, Executive Secretary

Foundation Philosophy: One of the foundation's primary interests has been to support and develop Longwood Gardens, once the home of Pierre du Pont. The foundation also has supported educational institutions for the construction of scientific, engineering training, and library facilities. Local conservation and horticultural groups, hospitals, and a variety of social service agencies have received substantial funding from the foundation. **Giving Priorities:** In fiscal 1993, the foundation reported that it gave 35% of its contributions to social services. Longwood Gardens received 25%. Education received 15%; the arts and health care each received 10%; and civic and public affairs, 5%. **Typical Health-Related Recipients:** Children's Health/Hospitals, Clinics/Medical Centers, Emergency/Ambulance Services, Family Planning, Health Organizations, Hospices, Hospitals, Long-Term Care, People with Disabilities, Substance Abuse. **Geographic Distribution:** Limited to Delaware, primarily the greater Wilmington area.

★360★ Loren M. Berry Foundation
3055 Kettering Blvd., Ste. 418
Dayton, OH 45439
Phone: (513)293-0398
William T. Lincoln, Treasurer, Trustee

Foundation Philosophy: The foundation supports a variety of youth organizations, social and family service organizations, and united funds. The foundation prioritizes higher education and educational foundations. Community affairs, the arts, and health concerns are also important. **Giving Priorities:** In 1993, the Loren M. Berry Foundation focused on education with 56% of their giving. Social services received 15%; the arts, 12%; civic affairs, 6%; and health care received 5%. Science received 3%; environmental efforts, 2%; and the remaining funds supported religion and international affairs. **Typical Health-Related Recipients:** Alzheimers Disease, Cancer, Eyes/Blindness, Family Planning, Health Organizations, Hospitals, Single-Disease Health Associations. **Geographic Distribution:** Primarily in Dayton, OH.

★361★ Louis Calder Foundation
230 Park Ave., Rm. 1525
New York, NY 10169
Phone: (212)687-1680
Barbara Sommer, Grant Program Manager

Foundation Philosophy: Foundation grants reflect a high level of social awareness, with particular attention to the problems and needs of those in New York City. The current policy of the foundation is to promote health, education, and welfare through grants to established organizations. Current priorities include health, welfare, and educational programs designed to enhance the potential and increase the self-sufficiency of New York City's disadvantaged children, youth, and their families. **Giving Priorities:** The foundation reported that in fiscal 1994, the foundation gave 31% of its funding to support a variety of social services; 27% to education projects; 7% to support medical research; 5% to support arts and cultural education projects; 21% to colleges and universities for student aid programs; 8% to building and renovation funds; and 1% other. **Typical Health-Related Recipients:** AIDS/HIV, Children's Health/Hospitals, Heart, Research/Studies Institutes. **Geographic Distribution:** New York City.

★362★ Louis E. Wolfson Foundation
One Financial Center
Boston, MA 02111
Phone: (617)542-6000
Paul Bishop, Manager

Foundation Philosophy: The Louis E. Wolfson Foundation supports medical schools at Harvard, Boston University, and Tufts University. The funds are used to provide low-interest loans to medical students. **Giving Priorities:** In fiscal 1993, the foundation gave 100% of its contributions to university medical schools. The medical schools of Boston University, Harvard, and Tufts each received large gifts. **Typical Health-Related Recipients:** Medical Education. **Geographic Distribution:** Cambridge, Medford, and Boston, MA.

★363★ Louis and Harold Price Foundation
654 Madison Ave., Ste. 2005
New York, NY 10021
Phone: (212)753-0240
Fax: (212)752-9338
Harold Price, Chairman

Foundation Philosophy: The foundation supports a business institute, Jewish welfare funds, hospitals, community funds, and higher education, including scholarship funds. Grants also are given to youth agencies, camps for children, temple support, medical research, the arts, and services for the blind and other disabled persons. The foundation reports that in the future it will place an emphasis on organizations in California and Colorado. **Giving Priorities:** In 1992, the foundation gave approximately 67% of funds to education. Approximately 12% went to international organizations. About 8% went to

civic causes, while social services and health organizations received 5% each. The remainder supported the arts and religious causes. **Typical Health-Related Recipients:** Hospitals, Medical Rehabilitation, Medical Research, Mental Health, Single-Disease Health Associations. **Geographic Distribution:** Primarily in metropolitan New York and Los Angeles; also in Israel.

★364★ Louis R. Lurie Foundation
555 California St., Ste. 5100
San Francisco, CA 94104
Phone: (415)392-2470
Robert A. Lurie, President

Foundation Philosophy: The foundation gives to a wide range of local interests in the San Francisco and Chicago areas. While there is no specific area of focus, the foundation does give substantially to organizations concerned with civic and community issues, the social sciences, education, the arts and humanities, and a variety of health issues. **Giving Priorities:** In 1994, the foundation reports that they gave approximately 44% of its contributions to religious organizations. Educational institutions received 15%, and social service organizations received 11%. Arts interest groups, primarily located in San Francisco, received 10%. Health concerns received 9%; civic affairs, 7%; and science received the remaining 4%. **Typical Health-Related Recipients:** Clinics/Medical Centers, Domestic Violence, Emergency/Ambulance Services, Geriatric Health, Health Funds, Health Organizations, Hospitals, Medical Research, Mental Health, People with Disabilities, Single-Disease Health Associations, Substance Abuse. **Geographic Distribution:** Primarily metropolitan San Francisco, CA; and Chicago, IL.

★365★ Louis and Rachel Rudin Foundation
345 Park Ave., 33rd Fl.
New York, NY 10154
Phone: (212)407-2400
Susan H. Rapaport, Administrator

Foundation Philosophy: The purpose of the foundation is to aid medical and nursing schools in the education and training of doctors and nurses. **Giving Priorities:** In fiscal 1993, the foundation solely funded medical and nursing schools. **Typical Health-Related Recipients:** Cancer, Children's Health/Hospitals, Medical Education, Medical Training. **Geographic Distribution:** Primarily New York.

★366★ Louise H. and David S. Ingalls Foundation
301 Tower E
20600 Chagrin Blvd.
Shaker Heights, OH 44122
Phone: (216)921-6000
Louise Ingalls Brown, President and Trustee

Foundation Philosophy: The foundation makes most of its grants in the areas of education, health, and the arts. Health care interests include hospital building campaigns, research, and pediatrics. Secondary interests include youth organizations and civic affairs. **Giving Priorities:** In 1993, the foundation contributed 38% of its contributions to education. The arts received 37% of total giving, including a $118,000 grant to the Naval Aviation Museum. Health services received 13%; science institutions, 6%; and international affairs, 3%. The remaining funds supported environmental concerns, civic affairs, and social services. **Typical Health-Related Recipients:** Eyes/Blindness, Family Planning, Health Organizations, Hospitals, Long-Term Care, Medical Education, Medical Rehabilitation, Nursing Services, Single-Disease Health Associations, Transplant Networks/Donor Banks. **Geographic Distribution:** Focus on Ohio, Connecticut, Virginia, and New York.

★ 367 ★ **Luke B. Hancock Foundation**
360 Bryant St.
Palo Alto, CA 94301
Phone: (415)321-5536
Fax: (415)321-0697
Ruth Ramel, Administrator

Foundation Philosophy: "The selection of funding areas has recently been a major focus of study by the board. Family poverty and disruption of the family unit, increased violence already at a very early age, and a perceived lack of values in our society are three areas of consideration at this time." The foundation previously funded cultural grants and special projects. **Giving Priorities:** In fiscal 1994, the foundation contributed 59% of its total funding to social service organizations, primarily to support youth organizations. Civic affairs received 10% and education received 9%. Health care received 7%; international affairs, 5%; religion, 5%; the arts, 4%; science, 1%; and the environment, 1%. **Typical Health-Related Recipients:** Children's Health/Hospitals, Emergency/Ambulance Services, Health Organizations, People with Disabilities, Transplant Networks/Donor Banks. **Geographic Distribution:** Primarily the San Francisco Bay area.

★ 368 ★ **M. D. Anderson Foundation**
c/o Texas Commerce Bank
PO Box 2558
Houston, TX 77252-8037
Elizabeth Calvert, Secretary and Treasurer

Foundation Philosophy: The foundation provides funding for the "improvement of working conditions among workers generally, as well as among particular classes of unskilled, skilled, and agricultural workers; to the establishment, support and maintenance of hospitals, homes and institutions for the care of the sick, the young, the aged, the incompetent and the helpless among the people; to the improvement of living conditions among people generally as well as in particular sections or localities; and to the promotion of health, science, education, and advancement and diffusion of knowledge and understanding among people." **Giving Priorities:** In 1992, the foundation gave 40% of its total support to health and medical institutions, including a single $245,000 grant to Texas Medical Center, TX. Educational concerns received 32% of funds; the arts, 14%; and social services, 7%. Approximately 4% went to civic groups. The remaining funds went to a science museum. **Typical Health-Related Recipients:** Children's Health/Hospitals, Clinics/Medical Centers, Emergency/Ambulance Services,

Eyes/Blindness, Health Organizations, Hospices, Hospitals, Medical Education, Medical Rehabilitation, Medical Research, Nursing Services, People with Disabilities, Research/Studies Institutes, Single-Disease Health Associations, Transplant Networks/Donor Banks. **Geographic Distribution:** Primarily Houston area and Harris County, TX.

★ 369 ★ **M. G. and Lillie A. Johnson Foundation**
PO Drawer 2269
Victoria, TX 77902
Phone: (512)575-7970
Robert Halepeska, Executive Vice President

Foundation Philosophy: The foundation's stated priority is support for health and higher education institutions in the Gulf Coast area of Texas. **Giving Priorities:** The foundation reported that in fiscal 1994 it donated approximately 42% of its giving to health care. Educational institutions received 25% of funds; social services, 18%; and civic groups, 15%. **Typical Health-Related Recipients:** Clinics/Medical Centers, Domestic Violence, Emergency/Ambulance Services, Hospices, Hospitals, Nursing Services, People with Disabilities, Substance Abuse, Transplant Networks/Donor Banks. **Geographic Distribution:** Primary emphasis on the state of Texas; priority is given to organizations in the Gulf Coast area located between San Patricio and Wharton counties.

★ 370 ★ **M. J. Murdock Charitable Trust**
PO Box 1618
Vancouver, WA 98668
Phone: (360)694-8415
Ford A. Anderson, II, Executive Director

Foundation Philosophy: The trust favors programs aimed at solutions for and the prevention of social problems, either through research or the application of existing knowledge and capabilities. Science continues to be a major interest of the trust, reflecting Mr. Murdock's own scientific bent. The trust is taking an increasingly informed, active role in improving science and science education in the Pacific Northwest. **Giving Priorities:** In 1993, the trust gave approximately 45% to education. The arts received 15% of funding; religious organizations, 11%; health care, 9%; civic affairs, 6%; and social services, 5%. Scientific research received 4%; international affairs, 3% and environmental efforts, 2%. **Typical Health-Related Recipients:** Cancer, Children's Health/Hospitals, Clinics/Medical Centers, Health Policy/Cost Containment, Medical Education, Medical Rehabilitation, Medical Research, People with Disabilities, Preventive Medicine/Wellness Organizations. **Geographic Distribution:** Regional, with emphasis on the Pacific Northwest, including Alaska, Idaho, Montana, Oregon, and Washington.

★ 371 ★ **M. R. Bauer Foundation**
208 S LaSalle St., Ste. 1750
Chicago, IL 60604
Phone: (312)372-1947
Fax: (312)372-2389
Kent Lawrence, President and Director

Foundation Philosophy: The foundation typically supports colleges and universities, hospitals and health organizations, civic and public

affairs causes, cultural concerns, and social welfare organizations. **Giving Priorities:** In 1993, the foundation gave 29% of its funds to educational institutions, primarily college and universities. The arts received 17%; civic and public affairs, 16%; health-care organizations, 15%; social services, 15%; and religious causes, 9%. **Typical Health-Related Recipients:** Cancer, Children's Health/Hospitals, Clinics/Medical Centers, Family Planning, Health Organizations, Hospitals, Medical Education, Medical Rehabilitation, Medical Research, Mental Health, Research/Studies Institutes, Single-Disease Health Associations. **Geographic Distribution:** Principally Southern California and the metropolitan Chicago, IL, area.

★ 372 ★ **M. S. Doss Foundation**
PO Box 1677
Seminole, TX 79360-1677
Phone: (915)758-2770
Joe K. McGill, President

Foundation Philosophy: The M. S. Doss Foundation primarily supports social service organizations. Recipients include children's homes and youth organizations. The foundation makes grants to other recipient areas, with an emphasis on building funds. **Giving Priorities:** In 1993, the foundation gave approximately 58% of contributions to social services, especially services supporting youth, including the foundation's highest grant of $550,133 to the M.S. Doss Youth Center. Religious institutions in Texas and New Mexico received about 34% of funding; civic concerns, 4%; educational institutions, 3%; and health programs, 1%. **Typical Health-Related Recipients:** Child Abuse, Diabetes, Hospices, People with Disabilities. **Geographic Distribution:** Focus on eastern New Mexico and west Texas.

★ 373 ★ **Mahadh Foundation**
287 Central Ave.
Bayport, MN 55003
Phone: (612)439-1557
Fax: (612)439-9480
Peggie Scott, Grants Consultant

Foundation Philosophy: The MAHADH Foundation, formerly known as Mary Andersen Hulings Foundation, makes most of its grants in the areas of the arts and education. Other interests include conservation and social services, and support for municipalities. The foundation reports that it will be shifting the focus of its grant-making from the arts to environmental concerns and social services. **Giving Priorities:** In fiscal 1993, the arts received 40% of total funding. Educational institutions received 26%, including the highest grant of $200,000 to Lakeview Community College. Health care received 16%; social services, 10%; civic affairs and environmental concerns, 6%; and religious organizations, 3%. **Typical Health-Related Recipients:** Clinics/Medical Centers, Emergency/Ambulance Services, Health Funds, Hospitals, Mental Health, People with Disabilities, Single-Disease Health Associations, Substance Abuse, Transplant Networks/Donor Banks. **Geographic Distribution:** Focus on Minnesota, with emphasis in St. Paul, the Bayport area, and western Wisconsin. **Formerly:** Mary Andersen Hulings Foundation.

★374★ Mardag Foundation
600 Norwest Ctr.
St. Paul, MN 55101
Phone: (612)224-5463
Fax: (612)224-8123
Paul A. Verret, Executive Director and
Secretary

Foundation Philosophy: The foundation primarily funds organizations benefiting senior citizens, children and youth, education, conservation of natural resources, social services, cultural heritage, and the arts. **Giving Priorities:** In 1994, the foundation gave approximately 41% to arts and humanities, 39% to social services, 8% to education, 7% to health care, 3% to civic affairs, and 2% to environmental causes. **Typical Health-Related Recipients:** Domestic Violence, Geriatric Health, Health Organizations, Hospices, Hospitals, Mental Health, People with Disabilities, Single-Disease Health Associations, Substance Abuse. **Geographic Distribution:** Minnesota.

★375★ Margaret L. Wendt Foundation
40 Fountain Plz., Ste. 277
Buffalo, NY 14202-2220
Phone: (716)855-2146
Fax: (716)855-2149
Robert J. Kresse, Secretary and Trustee

Foundation Philosophy: The foundation makes grants in the following designated areas: schools, religious organizations, hospitals and health organizations, youth programs, the arts, and social and community welfare organizations. **Giving Priorities:** In fiscal 1994, approximately 28% of funding went to the arts and humanities. Health services received 26%, including the highest grant of $300,000 to Children's Hospital of Buffalo. Social service organizations received 19%; educational institutions, 8%; civic affairs, 6%; religious concerns, 6%; and science organizations, 5%. The remaining funds supported environmental efforts and international affairs. **Typical Health-Related Recipients:** AIDS/HIV, Alzheimers Disease, Children's Health/Hospitals, Emergency/Ambulance Services, Health Funds, Health Organizations, Hospices, Hospitals, Medical Research, Mental Health, Nursing Services, People with Disabilities, Single-Disease Health Associations, Substance Abuse. **Geographic Distribution:** Primarily Buffalo, and Western New York.

★376★ Margaret T. Morris Foundation
PO Box 592
Prescott, AZ 86302
Phone: (602)445-4010
Eugene P. Polk, Trustee

Foundation Philosophy: The foundation supports all areas of philanthropy equally. Acceptable proposals have included arts associations, libraries, community development, support for educational programs at the primary and secondary levels, single-disease health organizations, hospitals, churches and religious community living, youth clubs, shelters, homes, and food and clothing distributors. **Giving Priorities:** In 1993, the foundation contributed 33% of its total giving to social services, including a $70,000 grant to Children's Action Alliance in Phoenix, AZ. Additionally, educational institu-

tions received 18% of funds. Health institutions received 16% of funds, arts and humanities received 15%, while civic and public affairs concerns received 13%. Science organizations received 3%, while international and environmental causes received 1% each. **Typical Health-Related Recipients:** AIDS/HIV, Cancer, Clinics/Medical Centers, Emergency/Ambulance Services, Family Planning, Health Organizations, Health Policy/Cost Containment, Hospices, Hospitals, Medical Education, Medical Research, People with Disabilities, Single-Disease Health Associations. **Geographic Distribution:** Focus on New York and Arizona.

★377★ Margaret W. and Herbert Hoover, Jr. Foundation
200 S Los Robles Ave., Ste. 520
Pasadena, CA 91101
Phone: (818)796-4014
Sara K. Bond, Vice President

Foundation Philosophy: The Margaret and Herbert Hoover, Jr. Foundation makes most of its grants in the area of health care. Funding favors medical education, and supports research and eye and ear institutes. The foundation also supports the Hoover Institution of War, Revolution and Peace. Grants to other recipient areas are limited. **Giving Priorities:** In 1993, the foundation awarded 72% of its total giving to support health care, primarily medical and disease research. International affairs received 13% of funds, and educational support totaled 7%. Social service organizations received 3% of giving, while science and civic affairs both received 2%. The remaining 1% went to environmental affairs. **Typical Health-Related Recipients:** Cancer, Diabetes, Emergency/Ambulance Services, Eyes/Blindness, Hospitals, Medical Education, Medical Research, Multiple Sclerosis, Single-Disease Health Associations, Speech & Hearing, Transplant Networks/Donor Banks. **Geographic Distribution:** National.

★378★ Marion I. and Henry J. Knott Foundation
3904 Hickory Ave.
Baltimore, MD 21211
Phone: (410)235-7068
Fax: (410)889-2577
Robin Platts, Executive Director

Foundation Philosophy: The Marion I. and Henry J. Knott Foundation makes grants to "further Roman Catholic activities and other charitable, cultural, educational, health care, and human service activities." Other interests include housing assistance, public and mental health, hospitals, religious organizations, and a variety of social services. **Giving Priorities:** In 1993, educational organizations and Catholic schools received 50% of the total contributions. Social service organizations were granted 14% of the funds, and health care organizations were granted 13%. Religious organizations and civic concerns each received approximately 10% of the grant money. The remaining 3% went to support the arts. **Typical Health-Related Recipients:** Alzheimers Disease, Children's Health/Hospitals, Eyes/Blindness, Health Funds, Health Organizations, Mental Health, Multiple Sclerosis, People with Disabilities, Prenatal Health Issues, Preventive Medicine/

Wellness Organizations, Single-Disease Health Associations, Trauma Treatment. **Geographic Distribution:** Limited to Baltimore City and the following counties in Maryland: Allegheny, Anne Arundel, Baltimore, Carroll, Frederick, Garrett, Harford, Howard, and Washington.

★379★ Marriner S. Eccles Foundation
701 Deseret Bldg.
79 S Main St.
Salt Lake City, UT 84111
Phone: (801)322-0116
Erma E. Hogan, Manager

Foundation Philosophy: The foundation's giving is restricted to private, nongovernmental charitable, scientific, and educational organizations located in Utah for the benefit of the citizens of that state. **Giving Priorities:** In fiscal 1994, the foundation gave approximately 28% of its charitable contributions in support of the arts. Health care and education were each awarded about 22% of the foundation's support. About 20% of the funds went to social services organizations. Civic affairs received 5% of the support, while religious interests received 3%. **Typical Health-Related Recipients:** AIDS/HIV, Arthritis, Cancer, Children's Health/Hospitals, Eyes/Blindness, Family Planning, Geriatric Health, Health Organizations, Hospices, Hospitals, Mental Health, Nursing Services, People with Disabilities, Single-Disease Health Associations, Substance Abuse. **Geographic Distribution:** Limited to Utah.

★380★ Mars Foundation
6885 Elm St.
Mc Lean, VA 22101
Phone: (703)821-4900
Robert C. Cargo, Secretary

Foundation Philosophy: Grantees include: educational organizations; fine art associations; public health organizations including groups concerned with population problems and medical care and assistance; and conservation and wildlife organizations. **Giving Priorities:** In 1993, the foundation gave approximately 51% of its contributions to education. The foundation also gave 11% each in support of the arts, and health care organizations. Environmental causes received 8% of funds, social services 6%, religious concerns 5%, and international organizations 4%. Civic and public affairs causes, and science organizations each received 2 % of support. **Typical Health-Related Recipients:** Cancer, Children's Health/Hospitals, Family Planning, Health Funds, Hospices, Medical Education, Medical Research, Nursing Services, People with Disabilities, Single-Disease Health Associations, Substance Abuse. **Geographic Distribution:** National.

★381★ Mary and Daniel Loughran Foundation
c/o NationsBank Trust Co., N.A., Trustee
1501 Pennsylvania Ave., NW
Washington, DC 20005
Phone: (202)624-4198
Fax: (202)347-4866
Adrian Nelson, Trust Officer

Foundation Philosophy: The foundation primarily supports higher education in Washington, DC, and Virginia. The trustees also support agricultural education and schools for handicapped children. Youth organizations also are a primary focus, with emphasis on infant homes and maternity care. The foundation supports other charitable organizations in addition to its main interests. **Giving Priorities:** In fiscal 1993, the foundation gave approximately 40% of its contributions to educational institutions. Social service organizations, primarily youth groups, received 20%. The arts and health care organizations received 13% of giving; religion, 9%; civic and public affairs, 3%; international organizations, 3%. The remainder of funds supported science organizations. **Typical Health-Related Recipients:** Children's Health/Hospitals, Emergency/Ambulance Services, Eyes/Blindness, Family Planning, Hospitals, Medical Research, Prenatal Health Issues, Single-Disease Health Associations. **Geographic Distribution:** Limited to Washington, DC, Virginia, and Maryland.

★382★ **Mary Hillman Jennings Foundation**
One PNC Plaza, Ste. 2325
Fifth Ave. & Wood St.
Pittsburgh, PA 15222
Phone: (412)566-2510
Fax: (412)566-1008
Paul Euwer, Jr., Director

Foundation Philosophy: The foundation's principal areas of interest are education, social services, and health. In addition, the foundation funds civic, arts, and religious organizations. **Giving Priorities:** In 1992, the foundation awarded about 29% of its contributions to educational institutions. Health care received 27% of giving. The arts, including the foundation's highest grant of $100,000 for the Carnegie Second Century Fund, Pittsburgh, PA, received 16%. Social services received 15%; civic affairs, 9%; and religion received the remainder. **Typical Health-Related Recipients:** Alzheimers Disease, Cancer, Children's Health/Hospitals, Domestic Violence, Family Planning, Health Organizations, Hospitals, Medical Rehabilitation, Medical Research, People with Disabilities, Sexual Abuse. **Geographic Distribution:** Primarily Pittsburgh and surrounding areas.

★383★ **Mary Ranken Jordan and Ettie A. Jordan Charitable Foundation**
One Mercantile Ctr., Ste. 3400
St. Louis, MO 63101
Phone: (314)425-2525
Fred E. Arnold, Chairman, Advisory Committee

Foundation Philosophy: The foundation makes most of its grants in the areas of education, the arts, and children's health and welfare. Educational support favors colleges, universities, special education for the disabled, private secondary education, and art education. In social services, support goes to homes, youth organizations, food and clothing distribution, united funds, and community centers. Other recipient areas are funded on a limited basis. **Giving Priorities:** In 1993, the foundation gave approximately 32% of total contributions to educational institutions. Social services received about 22%; the arts, 21%; health concerns, 12%; civic affairs, 11%; and religious organizations received the remaining funds. **Typical Health-**

Related Recipients: Children's Health/Hospitals, Diabetes, Emergency/Ambulance Services, Hospitals, People with Disabilities. **Geographic Distribution:** Limited to Missouri, with emphasis on St. Louis.

★384★ **Mary W. Harriman Foundation**
63 Wall St., 13th Fl.
New York, NY 10005
Phone: (212)493-8182
William F. Hibberd, Secretary

Foundation Philosophy: Board and family members directly involved with the distribution of funds give to groups that provide "a solid philanthropic benefit to the New York area." **Giving Priorities:** In 1993, the foundation awarded approximately 27% of its contributions to educational institutions, including a $50,000 grant to the Kennan Institute for Advanced Russian Studies. The arts received 19% of giving, and civic affairs received 17% of the donations. Social services received 13% of support, while environmental affairs received 9% of support. International affairs and health interests each received 7%. The remaining 1% was given in support of science. **Typical Health-Related Recipients:** AIDS/HIV, Cancer, Children's Health/Hospitals, Emergency/Ambulance Services, Family Planning, Hospices, Hospitals, Medical Education, Mental Health, People with Disabilities. **Geographic Distribution:** Primarily New York City metropolitan area.

★385★ **Massey Charitable Trust**
PO Box 1178
Coraopolis, PA 15108
Phone: (412)262-5992
Walter J. Carroll, Executive Director and Trustee

Foundation Philosophy: The trust makes grants across the major categories of support. In education, funding favors colleges, minority education, and special education for the handicapped. Social service support goes to living services, family services, counseling, youth organizations, and food and clothing distribution. Health support favors single-disease associations, rehabilitation services, and specialty hospitals. In the arts, interests include opera, art centers, historic preservation, and public broadcasting. **Giving Priorities:** In 1993, the trust gave 40% of its contributions to educational organizations. Health services received 21%, concentrated in the Pittsburgh area. Social service organizations received 14% of funding, supporting youth organizations and women's shelters. The arts received 13%; civic affairs, 6%; religion, 4%; and science, 1%. **Typical Health-Related Recipients:** Alzheimers Disease, Arthritis, Cancer, Children's Health/Hospitals, Diabetes, Emergency/Ambulance Services, Health Organizations, Hospitals, Kidney, Medical Rehabilitation, Medical Research, People with Disabilities, Sexual Abuse, Single-Disease Health Associations, Substance Abuse. **Geographic Distribution:** Focus on Pennsylvania, with an emphasis on Pittsburgh and southwestern Pennsylvania.

★386★ **Massey Foundation**
Four N. Fourth St.
PO Box 26765
Richmond, VA 23219
Phone: (804)288-9500
Fax: (804)288-9502
William E. Massey, Jr., President

Foundation Philosophy: The foundation has traditionally directed its philanthropy to medical, civic, and education activities in the southeastern United States. In addition to educational institutions, the foundation supports religious and charitable organizations. The foundation supports hospitals and selected health care facilities with both capital and program grants. Symphonies, museums, and special arts organizations receive consideration, particularly regional facilities open to the general public. **Giving Priorities:** In fiscal 1993, the foundation gave approximately 51% of funding to education. Health care received 29% of funding including the highest grant of $420,000 to the Medical College of Virginia Massey Cancer Center. The arts received 9%; religion, 4%; civic affairs, 3%; science, 2%; and the remaining funds supported the environment and social services. **Typical Health-Related Recipients:** Cancer, Emergency/Ambulance Services, Health Organizations, Hospitals, Medical Education, Mental Health, Single-Disease Health Associations. **Geographic Distribution:** Primarily Virginia, West Virginia, and Kentucky.

★387★ **Matilda R. Wilson Fund**
100 Renaissance Ctr., Ste. 3400
Detroit, MI 48243
Phone: (313)259-7777
Pierre V. Heftler, President

Foundation Philosophy: The foundation generally contributes to Michigan organizations offering services in the folowing areas: the arts, youth services, education, health, and human services. **Giving Priorities:** In 1993, the foundation awarded approximately 26% of its total giving to civic groups, including a $125,000 grant to the Greater Detroit Chambers Foundation. About 25% of support went to educational institutions. The arts received 22% of funds; health care, 12%; social services, 11%; and religious organizations, 2%. The remaining funds went to international organizations and environmental concerns. **Typical Health-Related Recipients:** Children's Health/Hospitals, Emergency/Ambulance Services, Eyes/Blindness, Hospitals, People with Disabilities. **Geographic Distribution:** National, with emphasis on Michigan.

★388★ **Max Kade Foundation**
100 Church St., Rm. 1604
New York, NY 10007
Phone: (212)964-7980
Dr. Erich H. Markel, President

Foundation Philosophy: The foundation's primary interest lies in higher education, particularly at the graduate and postdoctoral level. Grants are generally made to universities, colleges, and other educational and research institutions. The foundation seeks to promote international understanding and sharing of knowledge, through the exchange of young postdoctoral research scholars and visiting faculty members between U.S. and European universities. Research scholars are nominated by their home institutions. The foundation's major fields of interest are research and training in medicine or the natural and physical sciences (math, physics, chemistry, and biochemistry), and the study of foreign languages, literature, and culture. **Giving Priorities:** In 1993, the foundation gave approximately 60% of its contributions to health-related research. An additional 32% of funding went to education, while 6% went to the arts and humanities. The remaining funds supported civic and public affairs. **Typical Health-Related Recipients:** Cancer, Children's Health/ Hospitals, Diabetes, Eyes/Blindness, Geriatric Health, Heart, Hospitals, Medical Education, Medical Research, Medical Training, Nutrition, Research/Studies Institutes. **Geographic Distribution:** National.

★ 389 ★ **Max and Victoria Dreyfus Foundation**
50 Main St., Ste. 1000
White Plains, NY 10606
Phone: (914)682-2008
Fax: (914)682-2187
Lucy Gioia, Office Administrator

Foundation Philosophy: The foundation supports a variety of organizations in the arts, education, social services, health, and civic areas. **Giving Priorities:** In 1993, the foundation gave 32% of its contributions to education. The arts received 27% of funding; social services, 20%; and civic affairs, 8%. Health and religion each received 5% and environmental efforts received 2%. **Typical Health-Related Recipients:** Cancer, Emergency/Ambulance Services, Family Planning, Hospices, Hospitals, Hospitals (University Affiliated), Medical Education, Medical Rehabilitation, Medical Research, Mental Health, People with Disabilities, Single-Disease Health Associations, Substance Abuse. **Geographic Distribution:** National.

★ 390 ★ **Maximilian E. and Marion O. Hoffman Foundation**
970 Farmington Ave., Ste. 203
West Hartford, CT 06117
Phone: (203)521-2949
Doris C. Chaho, President

Foundation Philosophy: The foundation primarily supports health care, public policy, and environmental concerns; however, education, social services, and the arts also receive support from the foundation. **Giving Priorities:** In fiscal 1993, the foundation gave approximately 36% of funding to health concerns, including its highest grant of $300,000 to the St. Francis Hospital and Medical Center in Hartford, CT. Educational institutions and programs received about 22% of total contributions. Civic concerns received approximately 12% of giving; international affairs, 11%; social services, 8%; the arts, 5%; environmental concerns, 4%; and scientific interests received the remaining 2%. **Typical Health-Related Recipients:** Adolescent Health Issues, Children's Health/Hospitals, Emergency/Ambulance Services, Geriatric Health, Health Organizations, Heart, Hospitals, Hospitals (University Affiliated), Medical Education, Medical Rehabilitation, Nursing Services, Nutrition, People with Disabilities. **Geographic Distribution:** No geographic restrictions, with an emphasis on the Northeast.

★ 391 ★ **Mazza Foundation**
225 W Washington, Ste. 1300
Chicago, IL 60606-3405
Phone: (312)444-9300
Mary Jane Rubinelli, Secretary-Treasurer

Foundation Philosophy: The Mazza Foundation primarily supports social service organizations. Most of the funding goes to Catholic charities, homes for children, and missions. A secondary interest is supporting Catholic religious organizations and Catholic education. Health and civic affairs are minor interests. **Giving Priorities:** In fiscal 1991, the foundation gave 53% of giving to religious services. Social service organizations received 20% of funding and educational institutions were awarded 19%. Health care was given 5% of total contributions, and the remaining funds were given to civic concerns. **Typical Health-Related Recipients:** Clinics/Medical Centers, Health Organizations, Hospitals, Medical Rehabilitation, People with Disabilities, Single-Disease Health Associations, Substance Abuse. **Geographic Distribution:** Focus on Chicago, IL.

★ 392 ★ **McCasland Foundation**
PO Box 400
Duncan, OK 73534
Phone: (405)252-5580
Fax: (405)255-1471
Monica McCasland, Executive Director

Foundation Philosophy: The foundation funds colleges and universities, mostly within Oklahoma, as well as a variety of other organizations. **Giving Priorities:** In 1993, the foundation gave approximately 29% of its total contributions to educational institutions. The arts received about 22% of giving. Scientific interests received 18%. Health concerns received 10%; social services, 9%; religious organizations, 8%; civic affairs, 2%; and environmental causes received the remaining funds. **Typical Health-Related Recipients:** Alzheimers Disease, Clinics/ Medical Centers, Emergency/Ambulance Services, Health Organizations, Hospices, Hospitals, Medical Education, Medical Research, People with Disabilities, Single-Disease Health Associations, Substance Abuse. **Geographic Distribution:** Primarily Oklahoma.

★ 393 ★ **McCune Foundation**
1104 Commonwealth Bldg.
316 Fourth Ave.
Pittsburgh, PA 15222
Phone: (412)644-8779
Fax: (412)644-8059
Henry S. Beukema, Executive Director

Foundation Philosophy: Grants are made primarily to organizations in Pittsburgh and southwestern Pennsylvania, with emphasis on education and human services. The foundation is interested in innovative approaches that contribute directly to community vitality and promote human and institutional capabilities. The foundation is interested in helping to reverse the effects of social and economic dysfunction while creating a stronger base for future growth. **Giving Priorities:** In fiscal 1993, education, primarily colleges, received 31% the total contributions; the arts, 26%; and social services, 23%. Health care was awarded 11% of funding and civic and public affairs received 9%, including

support for community development, conservation, and economic development. **Typical Health-Related Recipients:** AIDS/HIV, Cancer, Clinics/Medical Centers, Domestic Violence, Geriatric Health, Health Organizations, Hospitals, Medical Rehabilitation, Nutrition, People with Disabilities, Prenatal Health Issues, Substance Abuse. **Geographic Distribution:** Focus on Pittsburgh and southwestern Pennsylvania.

★ 394 ★ **McGregor Fund**
333 W Fort Bldg., Ste. 2090
Detroit, MI 48226
Phone: (313)963-3495
Fax: (313)963-3512
C. David Campbell, Executive Director/ Assistant Secretary

Foundation Philosophy: "Concern for the needs of the homeless and hungry remains a priority of the fund." In addition, "partnerships and cooperative endeavors which address the critical issues facing greater Detroit continue to be a key element." To these ends, the fund supports a broad range of civic, health, and human service programs in the Detroit area. It also has expanded its interest in the environment and in the arts and humanities. In keeping with Mr. McGregor's belief that education was an essential prerequisite to solving society's ills, the fund supports private liberal arts colleges and universities, and private elementary and secondary schools. The fund is no longer supporting national or local chapters of disease-specific organizations. **Giving Priorities:** In fiscal 1994, the fund reported that it gave approximately 40% of its contributions to educational institutions. Social services, including support for shelters, food distribution, and substance abuse treatment received 33%. Civic and public affairs were given 10% of funding; the arts, 9%; health care, 7%; and the remainder went to other interests. **Typical Health-Related Recipients:** Hospitals. **Geographic Distribution:** Primarily Michigan (metropolitan Detroit area); educational grants in Michigan and Ohio.

★ 395 ★ **McInerny Foundation**
Hawaiian Trust Company, Ltd.
PO Box 3170
Honolulu, HI 96802
Phone: (808)528-4944
Fax: (808)538-4647
Lois C. Loomis, Contact Person

Foundation Philosophy: Under the terms of the deed of trust creating the foundation, the income is to be used for "charitable, scientific or educational purposes, or for the prevention of cruelty to children or animals." Grants currently are made in five fields: education, social services, environment, the arts, and health. **Giving Priorities:** In fiscal 1993 the foundation reported that approximately 38% of funding went to educational institutions. About 34% was allocated to social and community service organizations. The arts and humanities, including public broadcasting, received about 13% of funding. About 13% went to health organizations. The remaining funding went to the environment, 2%, and general purposes, 1%. **Typical Health-Related Recipients:** AIDS/HIV, Cancer, Children's Health/Hospitals, Clinics/Medical Centers, Emergency/Ambulance Services, Family Planning, Health Organizations, Hospices, Hospitals, Medical Rehabilitation, Mental Health, People with Disabilities, Prenatal Health Issues, Single-Disease Health Associations. **Geographic Distribution:** Exclusively Hawaii.

★396★ **McIntosh Foundation**
215 Fifth St., Ste. 300
West Palm Beach, FL 33401
Phone: (407)832-8845
Michael A. McIntosh, President and Director

Foundation Philosophy: Recently the foundation has begun to direct its energies toward support of environmental and civil rights litigation initiated by public interest groups. Other areas of interest include university-level education and other educational issues, and a wide range of projects in civic and public affairs. **Giving Priorities:** In 1993, the foundation gave approximately 38% of its contributions to historic preservation organizations. About 19% of funding supported the environment and conservation efforts. Educational institutions received 15%; health care, 13%; and civic affairs, 11%. The remaining funds supported international affairs, social services, a church, and a scientific institution. **Typical Health-Related Recipients:** Cancer, Clinics/Medical Centers, Geriatric Health, Health Organizations, Hospitals, People with Disabilities. **Geographic Distribution:** Primarily New York and Florida.

★397★ **McLean Contributionship**
945 Haverford Rd.
Bryn Mawr, PA 19010
Phone: (610)527-6330
William L. McLean, III, Chairman and Trustee

Foundation Philosophy: The foundation makes most of its grants in the areas of education, health care, and social services. Health care interests include hospitals, nursing homes, research, cancer treatment, and rehabilitation. Funding for social services goes to senior centers, homes, united funds, youth services, and job training. Other recipient areas also are supported. **Giving Priorities:** In 1993, the foundation contributed 20% of its charitable giving to support health care, including a $70,000 grant to the Hospital of the University of Pennsylvania, Rodebaugh Diabetes center. The arts also received about 20% of distributed funds. Civic and public affairs received 17% of support, while social services organizations were awarded 13%. Education was given 12% of contributions, and environmental concerns received about 11%. Scientific organizations received 4% of support, and religious causes about 3% of support. **Typical Health-Related Recipients:** Children's Health/Hospitals, Diabetes, Family Planning, Geriatric Health, Hospitals, Long-Term Care, Medical Rehabilitation, Medical Research, People with Disabilities, Public Health, Single-Disease Health Associations, Transplant Networks/Donor Banks. **Geographic Distribution:** Focus on the Philadelphia, PA, metropolitan area.

★398★ **McMillen Foundation**
6610 Mutual Dr.
Ft. Wayne, IN 46825
Phone: (219)484-8631
John F. McMillen, President

Foundation Philosophy: The McMillen Foundation makes most of its grants in the areas of social services and education. Social service funding favors recreational support for the benefit of youth. Educational support is directed at health education and outreach programs. Minor grants are given to other recipient areas. **Giving Priorities:** In 1993, the foundation gave approximately 70% of funding to social services. Educational recipients were awarded 14% of total contributions. Health concerns received about 7% of funding; civic causes, 6%; and the arts, 4%. **Typical Health-Related Recipients:** Clinics/Medical Centers, Domestic Violence, Family Planning, Geriatric Health, Health Organizations, People with Disabilities, Public Health, Substance Abuse. **Geographic Distribution:** Limited to Allen County and Fort Wayne, IN.

★399★ **Meadows Foundation**
3003 Swiss Ave.
Wilson Historic District
Dallas, TX 75204-6090
Phone: (214)826-9431
Fax: (214)827-7042

Foundation Philosophy: The foundation continues its tradition of balanced giving in basic areas of human activity and need: the arts, social services, health, education, and civic programs. Grants for health services are especially targeted towards disadvantaged or rural citizens. **Giving Priorities:** In 1993, the foundation gave approximately 23% of its total contributions to health concerns. Social service organizations also received about 23% of giving. The arts received 18%; civic affairs, 14%; educational institutions and programs, 12%; religious organizations, 6%; and environmental causes received the remaining funds. **Typical Health-Related Recipients:** AIDS/HIV, Alzheimers Disease, Cancer, Children's Health/Hospitals, Clinics/Medical Centers, Domestic Violence, Emergency/Ambulance Services, Eyes/Blindness, Geriatric Health, Health Organizations, Health Policy/Cost Containment, Heart, Home-Care Services, Hospices, Hospitals, Long-Term Care, Medical Education, Medical Training, Mental Health, Outpatient Health Care, People with Disabilities, Preventive Medicine/Wellness Organizations, Speech & Hearing, Substance Abuse, Transplant Networks/Donor Banks. **Geographic Distribution:** Texas only.

★400★ **Mericos Foundation**
1260 Huntington Dr., Ste. 204
South Pasadena, CA 91030
Phone: (213)259-0484
Fax: (213)259-0412
Linda J. Blinkenberg, Director and Secretary

Foundation Philosophy: The Mericos Foundation makes grants across the major categories of support. Educational funding favors universities and public school systems. Social services support includes family planning, child welfare, and youth organizations. Arts interests include historic preservation, museums, and art organi-

zations. Health care support goes to medical rehabilitation, nursing services, and hospices. In civic affairs, interests include the environment, other foundations, and zoos and botanical gardens. **Giving Priorities:** In 1993, the foundation gave about 33% of total contributions to the arts. Educational institutions also received approximately 33% of giving. Social services received approximately 13% of giving; science received 9%; and health, religion, and civic each received about 4% of funding. **Typical Health-Related Recipients:** Children's Health/Hospitals, Clinics/Medical Centers, Domestic Violence, Hospices, Medical Research. **Geographic Distribution:** Focus on Southern California, primarily Santa Barbara.

★401★ **Mervin Bovaird Foundation**
c/o Boesche, McDermott and Eskridge
100 W. 5th St., Ste. 800
Tulsa, OK 74103-4216
Phone: (918)583-1777
Fax: (918)592-5809
T. H. Eskridge, President, Treasurer, and Trustee

Foundation Philosophy: The foundation primarily supports scholarship programs at the University of Tulsa. Funding also is provided for social services, civic causes, and health organizations in the Tulsa area. **Giving Priorities:** In 1994, the foundation reported that it gave approximately 37% of its contributions to social service organizations. Health concerns received 23% of giving. Educational institutions received 18%. Civic affairs received 13%; religion, 8%; and the arts received the remainder. **Typical Health-Related Recipients:** Arthritis, Cancer, Children's Health/Hospitals, Clinics/Medical Centers, Emergency/Ambulance Services, Family Planning, Health Organizations, Health Policy/Cost Containment, Hospices, Hospitals, Medical Rehabilitation, Medical Research, Mental Health, People with Disabilities, Single-Disease Health Associations, Substance Abuse. **Geographic Distribution:** Metropolitan Tulsa, OK, area only.

★402★ **Meyer Memorial Trust**
1515 SW Fifth Ave., Ste. 500
Portland, OR 97201
Phone: (503)228-5512
Charles S. Rooks, Executive Director

Foundation Philosophy: The trust conducts two types of grant-making activities. General purpose grants are made within Oregon to a broad range of causes, including culture and the arts, education, health, and social services. As part of the General Purpose Program, the trust operates a Small Grants Program, initiated in 1988, under which grants of $500 to $8,000 are awarded for small projects. The trust also makes grants for special purposes like the Support for Teacher Initiatives. The trust also operates a Special Purpose program in Alaska, Idaho, Montana, Oregon, and Washington: Support for Children at Risk. **Giving Priorities:** In fiscal 1994, the trust gave approximately 27% of its contributions to educational institutions. The arts received 19% of funding; social services, 16%; and science organizations received 13%. Civic affairs were given 11%; health care, 9%; and the remaining funds supported religious organizations and environmental concerns. **Typical Health-Related Recipients:** AIDS/HIV, Alzheimers Disease, Cancer, Child Abuse, Children's Health/Hospitals, Clinics/Medical Centers, Domestic Violence, Family Planning, Geriatric Health, Health Organizations, Health Policy/Cost Containment, Hospices, Hospitals, Long-Term Care, Medical Education, Medical Rehabilitation, Medical Research, Medical Training, Mental Health, Nursing Services, People with Disabilities, Prenatal Health Issues, Public Health, Sexual Abuse, Substance Abuse. **Geographic Distribution:** Oregon; and Alaska, Idaho, Montana, Oregon, and Washington for the children at-risk program.

★403★ Middendorf Foundation
5 E Read St.
Baltimore, MD 21202
Phone: (410)752-7088
E. Phillips Hathaway, President and Trustee

Foundation Philosophy: The foundation's primary interest is supporting health care, specifically the establishment of health clinics. Arts funding favors historical preservation in Maryland. Civic affairs, the Boys Latin School in Baltimore, and family services also are supported. **Giving Priorities:** In fiscal 1994, the foundation awarded 31% of its total contributions to educational institutions. About 29% went to health care. Religious organizations received 14% of funds; social services, 12%; civic groups, 10%; and the arts, 2%. The remaining support went to environmental concerns and international organizations. **Typical Health-Related Recipients:** Cancer, Clinics/Medical Centers, Eyes/Blindness, Family Planning, Geriatric Health, Health Organizations, Hospitals, Medical Education, Mental Health, People with Disabilities, Prenatal Health Issues, Preventive Medicine/Wellness Organizations, Single-Disease Health Associations. **Geographic Distribution:** Focus on Maryland.

★404★ Milken Family Medical Foundation
1250 Fourth St., Sixth Fl.
Santa Monica, CA 90401
Phone: (310)998-2800
Fax: (310)998-2828
Cammie R. Cohen, Program Administrator

Foundation Philosophy: The Milken Family Medical Foundation is one of the Foundations of the Milken Families. The specific purpose of the medical foundation is aimed at "making the benefits of both basic and highly advanced health care available to those who need them, and supporting medical research." **Giving Priorities:** In fiscal 1992, approximately 73% of funding went to health care services, including the largest grant of $671,627 to the American Epilepsy Society of Hartford, CT. Other donations in this category went mainly to single-disease associations as well. Education received 10% of contributionss. Religious organizations and international affairs each received about 6% of giving; social services, 5%; and civic concerns, 1%. **Typical Health-Related Recipients:** AIDS/HIV, Alzheimers Disease, Cancer, Children's Health/Hospitals, Clinics/Medical Centers, Diabetes, Eyes/Blindness, General, Health Organizations, Hospices, Hospitals, Medical Rehabilitation, Medical Re-

search, Nursing Services, People with Disabilities, Preventive Medicine/Wellness Organizations, Single-Disease Health Associations, Speech & Hearing, Substance Abuse. **Geographic Distribution:** Focus on the Los Angeles, CA, area.

★405★ Monfort Family Foundation
PO Box 890
Greeley, CO 80632
Phone: (303)356-3611
Fax: (303)356-7646
Dave Evans, Administrator

Foundation Philosophy: The foundation primarily supports student programs at the university level. Other educational interests include technical training and support. "Funds are earmarked primarily for projects and/or groups promoting access to education, development of the arts and humanities, conducting scientific research into the causes and/or prevention of life-threatening diseases and the treatment thereof, and providing various forms of aid to the disadvantaged." **Giving Priorities:** In 1993, the foundation gave approximately 39% of funding to education. Social services organizations received about 28% of total contributions. Health organizations received about 23% of funding; civic concerns, 6%; and the arts, 4%. **Typical Health-Related Recipients:** AIDS/HIV, Arthritis, Cancer, Children's Health/Hospitals, Clinics/Medical Centers, Medical Rehabilitation, Multiple Sclerosis, Prenatal Health Issues, Single-Disease Health Associations, Speech & Hearing, Substance Abuse. **Geographic Distribution:** Focus on Greeley, CO. **Formerly:** Monfort Charitable Foundation.

★406★ Montgomery Street Foundation
235 Montgomery St., Ste. 1107
San Francisco, CA 94104
Phone: (415)398-0600
Carol K. Elliott, Secretary-Treasurer

Foundation Philosophy: The foundation primarily supports colleges and universities with moderate grants. Grants to higher education focus on economic education and business schools. Civic interests include law and justice, conservation, and better business. The foundation also supports a number of social service and arts interests. **Giving Priorities:** In 1993, the foundation gave 36% of its contributions to education. Health care received 31% of total funds awarded. Social services received 17% of the funding, supporting the disabled, family affairs, and youth organizations. Civic affairs received 7% of contributions. The arts received 7%, international affairs received 2%. **Typical Health-Related Recipients:** Cancer, Child Abuse, Children's Health/Hospitals, Domestic Violence, Emergency/Ambulance Services, Family Planning, Health Organizations, Hospices, Hospitals, Medical Education, Medical Research, People with Disabilities, Public Health, Single-Disease Health Associations, Substance Abuse. **Geographic Distribution:** Focus on California and some national giving.

★407★ Moody Foundation
2302 Postoffice St., Ste. 704
Galveston, TX 77550
Phone: (409)763-5333
Fax: (409)763-5564
Peter M. Moore, Grants Officer

Foundation Philosophy: In recent years, much of the foundation's funding has supported foundation-initiated projects, primarily through the Transitional Learning Community, a comprehensive head-injury rehabilitation facility, and through Moody Gardens. The entire complex has been designed with special attention to the needs of persons with disabilities, both for recreation and employment. The foundation's remaining grants support a wide variety of programs benefiting the people of Texas (mainly in Galveston) in the areas of education, health, social service, law enforcement, civic and public affairs, performing arts and medical research. **Giving Priorities:** In 1993, the foundation reported that 33% of its giving went to education. Civic causes received 25%; health care, 18%; social services, 12%; and the arts, 10%. The remaining funds were given to religion, 2%, and nonmedical science, 1%. **Typical Health-Related Recipients:** AIDS/HIV, Children's Health/Hospitals, Emergency/Ambulance Services, Eyes/Blindness, Geriatric Health, Health Organizations, Health Policy/Cost Containment, Hospitals, Medical Rehabilitation, Medical Research, Nursing Services, People with Disabilities, Prenatal Health Issues, Respiratory, Single-Disease Health Associations, Speech & Hearing, Substance Abuse, Transplant Networks/Donor Banks. **Geographic Distribution:** Texas.

★408★ Morris and Gwendolyn Cafritz Foundation
1825 K St., NW
Washington, DC 20006
Phone: (202)223-3100
Fax: (202)296-7567
Calvin Cafritz, Chm., Pres., CEO

Foundation Philosophy: The foundation's areas of concern have been the arts and humanities, education, community services, and health in Washington, DC. The foundation supports the arts and humanities, gives money for scholarships to local students, and supports education, local health, and community services. This emphasis on the Washington, DC, community is expected to continue. **Giving Priorities:** In fiscal 1993, educational institutions received 33% of support. The arts and social services each received 27% of funds awarded, while health associations received 13%. **Typical Health-Related Recipients:** Adolescent Health Issues, AIDS/HIV, Children's Health/Hospitals, Domestic Violence, Emergency/Ambulance Services, Family Planning, Geriatric Health, Health Organizations, Hospices, Hospitals, Medical Education, Medical Rehabilitation, Mental Health, Nursing Services, People with Disabilities, Single-Disease Health Associations, Substance Abuse. **Geographic Distribution:** Washington, DC, metropolitan area only.

★409★ Nathan Cummings Foundation

1926 Broadway, Ste. 600
New York, NY 10023
Phone: (212)787-7300
Fax: (212)787-7377
Charles R. Halpern, President

Foundation Philosophy: The foundation has made two changes in its funding areas during the last year. First, the foundation's interest in the environment now focuses on transportation and sustainable agriculture instead of farms, forestry, and waste. Secondly, the foundation also supports the emerging field of mind/body and behavioral medicine and in particular patient-centered responses to cancer instead of biomedical ethics. The foundation maintains attention to ethical issues in practical contexts, such as the quality of doctor-patient relations and the promotion of humane values in the health field. Traditional concern over health care and health delivery systems for the poor continues to be a priority. The foundation's Jewish Life Program focuses on social justice programs, Jewish renewal and spirituality, initiatives in culture and the arts, on enhancing understanding between Jews and non-Jews, and on the emerging Jewish communities in the former Soviet Union. **Giving Priorities:** In 1994, the foundation contributed 22% of its total giving to environmental affairs. Health care received 19%; religious organizations, 17%; international concerns, 16%; and the arts, 11%. Approximately 9% of funding was awarded to civic and public affairs; 4% to educational institutions; and 2% to social services. **Typical Health-Related Recipients:** Cancer, Children's Health/Hospitals, Clinics/Medical Centers, Family Planning, Geriatric Health, Health Organizations, Health Policy/Cost Containment, Medical Education, Medical Research, Mental Health, People with Disabilities, Preventive Medicine/Wellness Organizations, Public Health. **Geographic Distribution:** National.

★410★ New-Land Foundation

1114 Avenue of the Americas, 46th fl.
New York, NY 10036
Phone: (212)479-6000
Fax: (212)841-6275
Robert Wolf, President

Foundation Philosophy: The foundation is currently interested in funding programs in the following areas: civil rights/justice, the environment (other than hazardous waste), population control, child development, and peace and arms control. The foundation does not typically fund programs in medicine, religion, educational institutions, or general social programs. **Giving Priorities:** In 1993, the foundation awarded 36% of total contributions to civic and public affairs, including a single $40,000 grant to the Institute for Policy Studies, Washington, DC. Approximately 30% went to environmental affairs. Health care received 17% of funds; educational institutions, 8%; the arts, 4%; and international groups, 3%. The remaining funds went to social services. **Typical Health-Related Recipients:** Clinics/Medical Centers, Family Planning, Hospitals, Medical Education, Medical Research, Mental Health, Research/Studies Institutes. **Geographic Distribution:** Principally to national organizations.

★411★ New York Foundation

350 Fifth Ave., Rm. 2901
New York, NY 10118
Phone: (212)594-8009
Madeline Lee, Executive Director

Foundation Philosophy: The foundation supports groups in New York city that are working on problems of urgent concern to disadvantaged communities and neighborhoods. **Giving Priorities:** In 1993, the foundation gave approximately 42% of its funds to civic affairs. About 26% of funds supported social service organizations, 18% went to health, religion received 10%, and the remaining 4% went to education-related projects. **Typical Health-Related Recipients:** Adolescent Health Issues, AIDS/HIV, Cancer, Domestic Violence, Geriatric Health, Health Organizations, Health Policy/Cost Containment, Hospitals, Mental Health, Nutrition, People with Disabilities, Prenatal Health Issues, Preventive Medicine/Wellness Organizations. **Geographic Distribution:** New York City metropolitan area.

★412★ Norman Foundation

147 E 48th St.
New York, NY 10017
Phone: (212)230-9830
Fax: (212)230-9849
Florence Lastique, Administrative Assistant

Foundation Philosophy: The foundation has identified two main areas of interest: economic justice and civil rights/individual liberties. In 1992, a third major priority, environmental justice, was added to the foundation's agenda. "Other grants have gone to projects addressing government and corporate abuses of power, particularly those that create threats to the environment, human health and safety." **Giving Priorities:** In 1993, approximately 73% of the foundation's contributions went to civic affairs, including such concerns as violence prevention, minority programs, legal aid, and community housing. Social services received about 10% of giving, health care, 9%, and international concerns, 6%. Education received 2% of total grants. **Typical Health-Related Recipients:** AIDS/HIV, Domestic Violence, Family Planning, Health Policy/Cost Containment, Mental Health. **Geographic Distribution:** Nationally.

★413★ Norman and Rosita Winston Foundation

1740 Broadway
New York, NY 10019
Phone: (212)757-0707
Fax: (212)956-2223
Julian S. Perlman, Director

Foundation Philosophy: The foundation focuses its funding on higher education, the arts, health and medical research, civic organizations, and social services. **Giving Priorities:** In 1992, education received about 41% of giving, with institutions of higher education the primary beneficiaries. Approximately 33% of the contributions went to the arts, chiefly to museums and the performing arts. Scientific and biomedical organizations received approximately 13%, while civic and public affairs received 10%. The remainder went to social services and science. **Typical Health-Related Recipients:** Hospitals, Medical Education, Medical Research. **Geographic Distribution:** Principally New York.

★414★ Northwest Area Foundation

E-1201 First National Bank Bldg.
332 Minnesota St.
St. Paul, MN 55101-1373
Phone: (612)224-9635
Fax: (612)225-3881
Terry Tinson Saario, President

Foundation Philosophy: "The Foundation's grantmaking this year reflects its continuing commitment to alleviating poverty among the region's most disadvantaged citizens and promoting sustainable development of the region's natural resources." **Giving Priorities:** In fiscal 1994, the foundation reported that programs targeted at alleviating rural and urban poverty received 74% of its contributions. Sustainable development programs received 25%, and miscellaneous grants accounted for 1%. **Typical Health-Related Recipients:** AIDS/HIV, Clinics/Medical Centers, Family Planning, Health Organizations, Health Policy/Cost Containment, Outpatient Health Care. **Geographic Distribution:** Idaho, Iowa, Minnesota, Montana, North Dakota, Oregon, South Dakota, and Washington.

★415★ Offield Family Foundation

400 N Michigan Ave., Rm. 470
Chicago, IL 60611
Phone: (312)467-5480
Marie Larson, Secretary

Foundation Philosophy: The foundation supports a wide variety of charitable organizations. Most of the support goes to civic affairs, including conservation issues and women's affairs. Health is also a major priority, mainly supporting hospitals. Public broadcasting and family planning are consistently supported, while public education remains a minor interest. **Giving Priorities:** In fiscal 1993, the foundation awarded 44% of its total contributions to environmental concerns. About 31% of funds went to the arts. Social services received 9% of support; educational institutions, 6%; civic groups, 5%; and health care, 4%. Religious and scientific organizations received the remainder. **Typical Health-Related Recipients:** Children's Health/Hospitals, Clinics/Medical Centers, Emergency/Ambulance Services, Family Planning, Health Funds, Health Organizations, Hospitals, Medical Education, Medical Research, People with Disabilities, Substance Abuse, Transplant Networks/Donor Banks, Trauma Treatment. **Geographic Distribution:** Nationally.

★416★ Ohrstrom Foundation

540 Madison Ave.
New York, NY 10022
Phone: (212)759-5380
George F. Ohrstrom, President

Foundation Philosophy: The Ohrstrom Foundation makes most of its grants in the areas of civic affairs and education. Civic affairs funding favors the Little River Foundaton, other philanthropic organizations, and environmental affairs. In education, interests include technical training, universities, and private schools. The foundation also supports social services, religion, health, and the arts. **Giving Priorities:** In fiscal 1992, the foundation gave 53% of its funds to civic affairs. The Little River Foundation received grants totaling $330,000. Other recipients included conservation projects and wildlife councils. Educational institutions received 29% of the contributions. Health services received 6%; social services, 6%; the arts, 4%; and Episcopal churches, 2%. **Typical Health-Related Recipients:** Hospices, Hospitals, Medical Research, People with Disabilities, Single-Disease Health Associations, Substance Abuse. **Geographic Distribution:** Nationally, with a focus on Virginia.

★ 417 ★ Oppenstein Brothers Foundation
PO Box 13095
Kansas City, MO 64199-3095
Phone: (816)234-8671
Sheila Rice, Program Officer

Foundation Philosophy: The foundation makes most of its grants in the areas of social services, religion, civic affairs, and the arts. In social services, interests include family planning, children's centers, united funds, and community foundations. **Giving Priorities:** In fiscal 1994, the foundation reported that social service organizations received 32% of total funding. Religious organizations received 25%. Health care received 21% of funding; civic affairs, 12%; and the arts, 7%. The remaining funds supported educational institutions. **Typical Health-Related Recipients:** AIDS/HIV, Children's Health/Hospitals, Clinics/Medical Centers, Emergency/Ambulance Services, Family Planning, Health Organizations, Heart, Hospices, Hospitals, Medical Rehabilitation, Mental Health, People with Disabilities, Single-Disease Health Associations. **Geographic Distribution:** Limited to Kansas City, MO.

★ 418 ★ Ordean Foundation
501 Ordean Bldg.
Duluth, MN 55802
Phone: (218)726-4785
Fax: (218)726-4848
Antoinette Poupore-Haats, Executive Director

Foundation Philosophy: The foundation's mission concentrates on the funding of services and facilities for the needy, treatment of the chronically or temporarily mentally ill, the care and rehabilitation of the physically impaired, and the support of youth guidance programs. **Giving Priorities:** In 1994, the foundation gave approximately 61% to social services. Health care received 23% of contributions, and education received 16% of support. **Typical Health-Related Recipients:** Domestic Violence, Medical Education, Medical Rehabilitation, Mental Health, People with Disabilities, Single-Disease Health Associations. **Geographic Distribution:** Only in Duluth, MN, and contiguous cities and townships in St. Louis County, MN.

★ 419 ★ Otho S. A. Sprague Memorial Institute
PO Box 806214
Chicago, IL 60680-4123
James N. Alexander, Consultant

Foundation Philosophy: The institute's mandate is "the investigation of the causes of disease and the prevention and relief of human suffering in the city of Chicago, IL." The directors annually solicit proposals from nonprofit organizations with programs of bio-medical research, direct service, and policy research. **Giving Pri-**

orities: In 1994, the foundation reported that it gave 50% of its funds to bio-medical research. Medical education and social services each received 25% of the funding. Remaining funds went to health care agencies. **Typical Health-Related Recipients:** Adolescent Health Issues, Children's Health/Hospitals, Clinics/Medical Centers, Emergency/Ambulance Services, Health Organizations, Health Policy/Cost Containment, Hospices, Medical Education, Medical Research, Nursing Services, Prenatal Health Issues, Preventive Medicine/Wellness Organizations. **Geographic Distribution:** Limited to Chicago, IL.

★ 420 ★ Otto Bremer Foundation
445 Minnesota St., Ste. 2000
St. Paul, MN 55101-2107
Phone: (612)227-8036
Fax: (612)227-2522
John Kostishack, Executive Director

Foundation Philosophy: Principal grant recipients are "agencies which address the needs of children, single parent families, battered women, the disabled, and individuals affected by poverty; activities which address general community needs and encourage citizen participation; educational internships; promotion of individual and community health; and activities of religious organizations which address community needs." **Giving Priorities:** In 1994, the foundation reported that 33% of funding went to social services. Approximately 18% of funding went to programs that addressed the problems of racism and discrimination. Health concerns received 15% of gifts. Civic concerns received approximately 14% of total contributions. Programs for the eradication of rural poverty received 10% of funding. Educational institutions received 6% of funding. Religion received approximately 1% of funding. The remainder supported foundation initiatives. **Typical Health-Related Recipients:** AIDS/HIV, Clinics/Medical Centers, Domestic Violence, Emergency/Ambulance Services, Geriatric Health, Health Organizations, Hospices, Hospitals, Medical Education, Mental Health, Nursing Services, People with Disabilities, Substance Abuse. **Geographic Distribution:** Specific rural communities in Minnesota, North Dakota, and Wisconsin.

★ 421 ★ Overbrook Foundation
521 Fifth Ave., Rm. 1501
New York, NY 10175
Phone: (212)661-8710
Sheila McGoldrick, Corresponding Secretary

Foundation Philosophy: Foundation support is often given on a continuing basis. Although the foundation makes some large grants, it prefers to make smaller grants to a variety of institutions. Many of the recipient organizations have a national or international orientation. Major interests of the foundation include Jewish welfare funds, higher and secondary education, hospitals, international relations, cultural programs, and community funds. **Giving Priorities:** In 1993, the foundation gave approximately 36% of total contributions to educational institutions. Civic concerns received about 15% of funding; social services, 13%; the arts and humanities, 9%; religious institutions and environmental

programs, 8% each; international affairs, 7%; and health groups, 4%. **Typical Health-Related Recipients:** AIDS/HIV, Emergency/Ambulance Services, Family Planning, Health Organizations, Hospices, Hospitals, Medical Research, Nursing Services, People with Disabilities, Single-Disease Health Associations, Substance Abuse. **Geographic Distribution:** National, with emphasis on New York metropolitan area and Connecticut.

★ 422 ★ Oxford Foundation
55 S Third St.
Oxford, PA 19363
Phone: (610)932-2000
Marian S. Ware, Chairman and President

Foundation Philosophy: The Oxford Foundation makes grants across the major categories of support. In education, interests include colleges, universities, public school districts, private education, medical training, and day schools. Health support goes to medical centers, health organizations, and Alzheimer's research. Social service support includes community centers, family services, shelters, and youth organizations. Funding for civic affairs favors foundations, agricultural support, and zoos. **Giving Priorities:** In 1993, the foundation gave 27% of its funding to education. Social services received 21% of total giving. Health care received 16%, including support for medical centers and single-disease associations. The arts received 14%; civic affairs, 11%; environmental concerns, 7%; religious organizations, 4%; and science institutions, 1%. **Typical Health-Related Recipients:** Alzheimers Disease, Children's Health/Hospitals, Clinics/Medical Centers, Diabetes, Emergency/Ambulance Services, Family Planning, Hospices, Hospitals, Medical Education, Medical Research, Mental Health, Nursing Services, People with Disabilities, Sexual Abuse, Single-Disease Health Associations, Substance Abuse. **Geographic Distribution:** Focus on Pennsylvania.

★ 423 ★ Pauline Allen Gill Foundation
8111 Preston Rd., No. 605
Dallas, TX 75225
Phone: (214)696-3336
Nancy Seay, Vice President

Foundation Philosophy: The Pauline Allen Gill Foundation primarily supports social services and health care with a majority of its grants. In social services, support goes to child welfare, united funds, and family services. Health funding favors hospitals. The foundation also supports education, religion, and the arts with minor grants. **Giving Priorities:** In 1993, the foundation gave approximately 37% of funding to health groups, including the foundation's highest grant of $250,000 to University of Texas Southwestern Medical Center Fund for Molecular Research. The arts received approximately 27% of funding, which consisted of five grants to groups in Dallas, Texas. Educational institutions received about 20% of funding; social services, 10%; and religion, 5%. The environment and civic each received 1% of total contributions. **Typical Health-Related Recipients:** Children's Health/Hospitals, Clinics/Medical Centers, Domestic Violence, Emergency/Ambulance Services, Family Planning, Health

Organizations, Hospitals, Medical Research, Nutrition, People with Disabilities, Research/ Studies Institutes, Substance Abuse. **Geographic Distribution:** Primarily Texas, with emphasis on Dallas.

★ 424 ★ Penzance Foundation
237 Park Ave., 21st Fl.
New York, NY 10017-3412
Phone: (212)551-3559
John M. Emery, Vice President

Foundation Philosophy: The foundation's giving program generally supports the preferences of Mrs. Clark, with the majority of funding going to educational institutions and social service organizations, principally to youth groups. Medical facilities are also beneficiaries of the foundation's grant-making program. **Giving Priorities:** In fiscal 1993, the foundation gave approximately 45% of total contributions to health concerns. Science received 23% of gifts. Education and social services each received approximately 13% of total contributions. International affairs received 3% of funds. The remaining funds supported religious concerns, the arts and humanities, and civic affairs. **Typical Health-Related Recipients:** Family Planning, Health Organizations, Hospitals, Kidney, Medical Rehabilitation, Medical Research. **Geographic Distribution:** Primarily New York and Massachusetts.

★ 425 ★ Perkins-Prothro Foundation
PO Box 360
Wichita Falls, TX 76307
Phone: (817)691-7770
Charles N. Prothro, President

Foundation Philosophy: The Perkins-Prothro Foundation makes endowments to several universities in Texas in support of higher education. Health services is a secondary interest, with emphasis on hospice care and medical rehabilitation. Other recipient areas are supported on a limited basis. **Giving Priorities:** In 1993, the foundation gave approximately 75% of total contributions to educational institutions, including the foundation's highest grant of $250,000 to Sweet Briar College in Virginia. Religious institutions received about 22% of giving, primarily to Methodist churches in Texas. Social services received the remaining 3% of funding. **Typical Health-Related Recipients:** Cancer, Emergency/Ambulance Services, Health Policy/Cost Containment, Hospices. **Geographic Distribution:** Focus on Texas.

★ 426 ★ Perot Foundation
12377 Merit Dr., Ste. 1700
Dallas, TX 75251
Phone: (214)788-3068
Fax: (214)788-3091
Margaret B. Perot, Vice President

Foundation Philosophy: The majority of contributions made by the Perot Foundation in 1993, were to the Salvation Army. Additional funding supports medical education in Texas universities, particularly for the University of Texas Southwestern. Social services are a secondary interest. Grants to other recipient areas are made on a limited basis. **Giving Priorities:** In 1993, the foundation gave 48% of its funds to religious welfare and churches. Educational institutions received 24% and health care ser-

vices received 22%. Social service organizations received 5% of funding and the arts received less than 1%. **Typical Health-Related Recipients:** Cancer, Children's Health/Hospitals, Family Planning, Health Organizations, Medical Education, Medical Research, Single-Disease Health Associations. **Geographic Distribution:** Focus on Texas; with an emphasis on Dallas.

★ 427 ★ Peter Kiewit Foundation
1200 Woodmen Tower
Farnam at Seventeenth
Omaha, NE 68102
Phone: (402)344-7890
Lyn L. Wallin Ziegenbein, Executive Director and Secretary

Foundation Philosophy: The foundation makes charitable contributions in the designated areas of education, community development and service, culture, social welfare, health, and character building and physical improvement. The foundation also maintains a scholarship program for graduating high school seniors in the Omaha area. **Giving Priorities:** In fiscal 1992, the foundation awarded 27% of its funding to the arts. Social services received about 26% of giving, with major support for youth and senior citizens. Education also received 26% of funding. Civic and public affairs received 20%, with a $1 million award to the Omaha Zoological Society. The remainder of the funds supported health care. **Typical Health-Related Recipients:** AIDS/HIV, Emergency/Ambulance Services, Family Planning, Health Organizations, Hospitals, Nutrition, People with Disabilities. **Geographic Distribution:** Nebraska; the part of Iowa which is within a 100-mile radius of Omaha, NE; Sheridan, WY; and Rancho Mirage, CA.

★ 428 ★ Pew Charitable Trusts
One Commerce Sq.
2005 Market St., Ste. 1700
Philadelphia, PA 19103-7017
Phone: (215)575-9050
Fax: (215)575-4939
Deidra A. Lyngard, Communications Manager

Foundation Philosophy: "The Pew Charitable Trusts support the work of nonprofit organizations in the fields of culture, education, the environment, health and human services, public policy and religion. Through their grantmaking, the Trusts seek to encourage individual development and personal achievement, cross-disciplinary problem solving, and innovative, practical approaches to meeting the changing needs of a global community." The health and human services program's goal is to promote the health and well-being of the American people and our neighbors in Mexico, Central America, and the Caribbean. The Trusts seek to strengthen the ability of health centers and other educational institutions to train health practitioners to be more responsible to the needs of the public, and to promote research in the biomedical and behavioral sciences. Additionally, the Trusts seek to improve prenatal and postnatal care. And, in Mexico, Central America, and the Caribbean, it seeks to increase the capacity of institutions to meet the health needs of at-risk women, children, and other disadvan-

taged populations. **Giving Priorities:** In 1994, the Trusts categorized charitable appropriations as follows: health and human services, 31%; education, 18%; interdisciplinary fund, 14%; culture, 13%; the environment, 12%; public policy, 6%; and religion, 6%. **Typical Health-Related Recipients:** Adolescent Health Issues, AIDS/HIV, Cancer, Children's Health/Hospitals, Domestic Violence, Emergency/Ambulance Services, Family Planning, Geriatric Health, Health Organizations, Health Policy/Cost Containment, Home-Care Services, Medical Education, Nutrition, Prenatal Health Issues, Public Health, Substance Abuse. **Geographic Distribution:** Nationally, with a special commitment to Philadelphia, PA; some international giving.

★ 429 ★ Philip L. Graham Fund
1150 15th St., NW
Washington, DC 20071
Phone: (202)334-6640
Fax: (202)334-4536
Mary Bellor, President and Secretary

Foundation Philosophy: Areas of funding priority reflect the interests of the late Mr. Graham and include: programs enriching the lives of children; projects aiding needy citizens in the community; cultural organizations, especially those promoting the visual or dramatic arts; programs improving pre-college and public education; and journalism and communications organizations promoting minority interests and freedom of the press worldwide. **Giving Priorities:** In 1993, the fund gave approximately 46% of its contributions to human service organizations. Education, including institutions of higher learning and special educational projects, received 22% of giving. The arts, mainly museums and the theater, received 13%. Civic and public affairs received about 10%, with grants supporting community foundations, housing projects, and advocacy programs. Journalism and communications received 9% of funds. **Typical Health-Related Recipients:** AIDS/HIV, Children's Health/Hospitals, Clinics/Medical Centers, Domestic Violence, Health Organizations, Home-Care Services, Hospices, Mental Health, People with Disabilities, Substance Abuse. **Geographic Distribution:** Emphasis on metropolitan Washington, DC.

★ 430 ★ Philip L. Van Every Foundation
c/o Lance, Inc.
PO Box 32368
Charlotte, NC 28232
Phone: (704)554-1421
Zean Jamison, Jr., Executive Director

Foundation Philosophy: The foundation's primary interests are health-related organizations, social welfare causes, and civic concerns in North Carolina. **Giving Priorities:** In 1994, the foundation reported that approximately 45% of giving went to health organizations and hospitals. Social services received 33%, while civic causes received 12%. The arts and religious causes received 4% each, with the remainder supporting educational institutions. **Typical Health-Related Recipients:** Hospices, Hospitals, Medical Research, Single-Disease Health Associations. **Geographic Distribution:** Primarily North Carolina.

★ 431 ★ **Pinewood Foundation**
3 Manhattenville Rd.
Purchase, NY 10577-2110
Phone: (914)696-9002
Celeste G. Bartos, President

Foundation Philosophy: The foundation typically funds arts organizations, museums, and cultural programs, and also supports health organizations. **Giving Priorities:** In fiscal 1993, the foundation awarded approximately 59% of its total contributions to the arts, including its highest grant of $1,224,600 to the Museum of Modern Art in New York, NY. Civic affairs received about 17%; education, 8%; international organizations, 8%; health concerns, 3%; social services, 3%; and environmental causes and religion each received 1% of the remaining funds. **Typical Health-Related Recipients:** Clinics/ Medical Centers, Eyes/Blindness, Family Planning, Health Organizations, Hospitals, Medical Education, Multiple Sclerosis, Prenatal Health Issues, Single-Disease Health Associations. **Geographic Distribution:** Primarily New York, NY.

★ 432 ★ **Plough Foundation**
6077 Primacy Pkwy., Ste. 230
Memphis, TN 38119
Phone: (901)761-9180
Fax: (901)761-0237
Noris R. Haynes, Jr., Executive Director and Trustee

Foundation Philosophy: The foundation is planning to provide more funding for elementary public school programs, the homeless, low income housing and youth programs in Shelby County, TN. The foundation also plans to place more emphasis on public school reform. The foundation supports a variety of causes. In the area of social services, it has emphasized education reform, Jewish Federations, united funds, and youth organizations. Grants to local educational institutions continue to receive primary consideration. The foundation reports that its current special interests include: public education, specifically early intervention programs for children; substance abuse early intervention, particularly programs dealing with prevention, as opposed to rehabilitation; families in crisis, preferably programs and ideas that take a realistic approach to the problems and offer avenues for the participants to become self-sufficient; youth programs, mainly programs which specifically address the needs of and opportunities for young people; stretching the non-profit dollar, particularly programs and activities that demonstrate unique, innovative ways to maximize resources. **Giving Priorities:** In 1993, the foundation awarded approximately 43% of its total contributions to social services organizations, including its highest grant of $1,000,000 to the United Way in Memphis, TN. Education received about 23%; religion, 13%; the arts, 11%; civic affairs, 6%; and health care received the remaining 4% of funds. **Typical Health-Related Recipients:** Cancer, Clinics/Medical Centers, Medical Education, Mental Health, Outpatient Health Care, Substance Abuse. **Geographic Distribution:** Primarily in Shelby County and Memphis, TN.

★ 433 ★ **Pritzker Foundation**
200 W Madison St., 38th Fl.
Chicago, IL 60606
Phone: (312)750-8400
Fax: (312)750-8545
Jay A. Pritzker, President

Foundation Philosophy: The Pritzker Foundation supports Jewish organizations, the arts, health, education, and social services in the Chicago metropolitan area, by providing small grants, ranging from $25 to $1,000, to a large number of organizations. Significant grants are made to a limited number of recipients that include the Jewish United Fund, Crusade of Mercy, several Jewish organizations and synagogues, and programs in support of Israel. In addition, the foundation awards the annual Pritzker Architecture Prize of more than $100,000, administered through the Hyatt Foundation. **Giving Priorities:** In 1992, the foundation gave approximately 52% of its total contributions to civic affairs, including major support for philanthropic organizations, particularly the Hyatt Foundation. International organizations received about 18%, including the foundation's highest grant of $250,000 to the Jerusalem Foundation in New York City. Health concerns received 12% of giving; the arts, 10%; educational institutions, 5%; social services, 2%; and religious causes received the remaining funds. **Typical Health-Related Recipients:** Cancer, Children's Health/Hospitals, Domestic Violence, Family Planning, Health Organizations, Hospitals, Medical Education, Medical Research, People with Disabilities, Public Health, Single-Disease Health Associations, Substance Abuse. **Geographic Distribution:** Focus on the Chicago, IL, metropolitan area.

★ 434 ★ **Prospect Hill Foundation**
420 Lexington Ave., Ste. 3020
New York, NY 10170-0087
Phone: (212)370-1144
Constance Eiseman, Executive Director

Foundation Philosophy: The areas for which the foundation is most interested in receiving proposals are nuclear weapons control, environmental conservation, and population. The population program is concerned with programs in Latin America which encourage access to family planning services. **Giving Priorities:** In fiscal 1994, the foundation gave approximately 24% of funding to the arts and humanities, including the foundation's highest grant of $180,000 to the New York Philharmonic. International affairs also received about 24% of total contributions. Environmental programs received about 18% of total contributions. Educational institutions received 12% of giving. Civic organizations received about 8% of funding; health institutions, 7%; science, 3%; and religious and social services, 2% each. **Typical Health-Related Recipients:** Emergency/ Ambulance Services, Family Planning, Hospitals. **Geographic Distribution:** Nationally, with emphasis on New York.

★ 435 ★ **R. C. Baker Foundation**
PO Box 6150
Orange, CA 92613-6150
Phone: (714)750-8987
Frank L. Scott, Chairman

Foundation Philosophy: The foundation supports organizations and projects concerned with the arts, education, community services, health, and social services. **Giving Priorities:** In 1993, the foundation awarded 37% of its total contributions to educational institutions, including a single $122,000 grant to Harvey Mudd College, Claremont, CA. Approximately 33% of funds went to social services. Civic groups received 12% of gifts; health care, 10%; and the arts, 3%. Environmental concerns and religious groups each received 2% of support. **Typical Health-Related Recipients:** Cancer, Children's Health/Hospitals, Clinics/Medical Centers, Emergency/Ambulance Services, Eyes/ Blindness, Health Organizations, Hospitals, Medical Rehabilitation, Medical Research, Mental Health, Nursing Services, People with Disabilities, Preventive Medicine/Wellness Organizations, Research/Studies Institutes, Single-Disease Health Associations, Substance Abuse. **Geographic Distribution:** National, with some emphasis on California and Texas.

★ 436 ★ **R. Dee and Joan Dale Hubbard Foundation**
PO Box 1679
Ruidoso Downs, NM 88346
Phone: (505)378-4431
James A. Stoddard, Executive Director

Foundation Philosophy: The foundation's two major categories of support are the arts and humanities and education. **Giving Priorities:** In 1992, more than 90% of contributions, totaling $2.93 million, went to the Hubbard Museum to begin renovation of the Chaparral Convention Center, which houses the Anne C. Stradling Museum of the Horse. Education received approximately 8%. The remainder was divided among other art recipients, health, and social services. **Typical Health-Related Recipients:** Medical Training, Single-Disease Health Associations. **Geographic Distribution:** Major emphasis on Kansas, Nebraska, New Mexico, Oklahoma, and Texas. **Formerly:** R. Dee # Hubbard Foundation

★ 437 ★ **Ralph M. Parsons Foundation**
1055 Wilshire Blvd., Ste. 1701
Los Angeles, CA 90017
Phone: (213)482-3185
Christine Sisley, Executive Director and Secretary

Foundation Philosophy: The foundation's primary areas of interest include the following Higher Education; Social Impact; Civic and Cultural Affairs; Health--with emphasis on services to disadvantaged elderly, families, and youth, through support of programs and medical equipment associated with these services; and Special Projects--response to emerging societal needs or to projects related to the broad purposes of the foundation. **Giving Priorities:** The foundation reported that in 1993 about 35% of its total contributions funded programs concerned with social impact, primarily assistance to social or disadvantaged groups. Civic groups and the arts received 28% of funds; health care, 21%; higher education, 13%; and special projects, 2%. **Typical Health-Related Recipients:** AIDS/HIV, Alzheimers Disease, Cancer, Child Abuse, Children's Health/Hospitals, Clinics/

Medical Centers, Domestic Violence, Family Planning, Health Organizations, Hospitals, Long-Term Care, Medical Research, Mental Health, People with Disabilities, Prenatal Health Issues, Trauma Treatment. **Geographic Distribution:** Primarily Los Angeles County, CA, with the exception of higher education grants distributed to a few select national institutions in engineering education.

★ 438 ★ Raskob Foundation for Catholic Activities
Kennett Pke. and Montchanin Rd.
PO Box 4019
Wilmington, DE 19807
Phone: (302)655-4440
Fax: (302)655-2332
Gerard S. Garey, President

Foundation Philosophy: The foundation's purpose is to "engage in such exclusively religious, charitable, literary, and educational activities as will aid the Roman Catholic Church and institutions and organizations identified with it." **Giving Priorities:** In 1993, the foundation gave approximately 38% of its total contributions to religious organizations. Educational institutions received about 32%, including the foundation's highest grant of $90,000 to the Salesianum School in Wilmington, DE. International organizations received 14%; civic affairs, 6%; health concerns, 5%; and social services received the remaining 5% of funds. **Typical Health-Related Recipients:** AIDS/HIV, Clinics/ Medical Centers, Domestic Violence, Family Planning, Health Organizations, Hospices, Hospitals, Medical Education, Medical Rehabilitation, Mental Health, Nursing Services, People with Disabilities, Substance Abuse. **Geographic Distribution:** National and international.

★ 439 ★ Ray C. Fish Foundation
2001 Kirby Dr., Ste. 1005
Houston, TX 77019
Phone: (713)522-0741
Barbara F. Daniel, President

Foundation Philosophy: The foundation's first large grant, $5 million, was made in 1966 as seed money for the Texas Heart Institute. Other health interests include the American Heart Association, the Living Bank, and various Houston hospitals. Educational interests include colleges, universities, and schools located in Texas. The foundation supports a broad range of community service programs and organizations. The foundation also supports various Houston museums and performing arts groups. **Giving Priorities:** In fiscal 1993, the foundation gave 28% of total contributions to education, including the foundation's highest grant of $55,000, which went to Schreiner College in Kerrville, TX. Social services received 25% of funding. Civic concerns in Texas received approximately 16% of funds. The arts and humanities received 13% of gifts, including a $50,000 grant to the George Bush Presidential Library. Health care programs in Texas received 12% of giving. Religious groups in Houston received 4% of contributions. Science received 2% of total contributions, in the form of $17,500 to the Houston Museum of Natural Science. **Typical Health-Related Recipients:** Cancer, Clinics/ Medical Centers, Emergency/Ambulance Ser-

vices, Family Planning, Health Organizations, Heart, Hospitals, Medical Rehabilitation, Medical Research, People with Disabilities, Single-Disease Health Associations. **Geographic Distribution:** Texas, primarily the metropolitan Houston area, Kerrville, and Galveston..

★ 440 ★ Raymond John Wean Foundation
PO Box 760
Warren, OH 44482
Phone: (216)394-5600
Fax: (216)394-5601
Raymond J. Wean, Jr., Chairman

Foundation Philosophy: Grants from the foundation primarily support higher and secondary education. Some support is given to health facilities, such as hospitals, medical centers, and rehabilitation centers, as well as to mental health and medical research. The foundation has interests in social services, including Goodwill Industries and religious welfare agencies. In the arts and humanities, the foundation makes grants to symphonies, historical societies, and opera associations. **Giving Priorities:** In 1993, the foundation awarded approximately 80% of funding to educational institutions, including the foundation's two highest grants of $250,000, which went to Miss Porter's School in Farmington, CT and Palm Beach Day School in Palm Beach, FL. Health care facilities, specifically hospitals, received 6% of total contributions. Social service programs received 5%; arts organizations, 4%; civic and public affairs, 3%; and religious causes, 2%. **Typical Health-Related Recipients:** Family Planning, Health Organizations, Hospices, Hospitals, Medical Education, Medical Rehabilitation, Mental Health, Nursing Services, People with Disabilities, Single-Disease Health Associations, Substance Abuse. **Geographic Distribution:** National, emphasis on Ohio and the eastern states.

★ 441 ★ Reinberger Foundation
27600 Chagrin Blvd.
Cleveland, OH 44122
Phone: (216)292-2790
Robert N. Reinberger, Co-Director

Foundation Philosophy: The foundation does not place any restrictions on the types of organizations which may request a grant; nor does it have a fixed pattern of giving. Priorities are apt to change from year to year. All giving, however, is limited strictly to the greater Cleveland and Columbus areas. The foundation prefers to provide funds for operating purposes and capital improvements. It usually does not provide seed money or fund new projects, preferring to help well-established, traditional organizations. **Giving Priorities:** In 1992, the foundation contributed 55% of its total funding to the arts, including $166,667 to Cleveland Orchestra, the first payment of an $1 million pledge. Health care received 15% of support; civic groups, 14%; and religious organizations, 5%. Educational institutions and scientific organizations each received 4%. The remaining 3% went to social services. **Typical Health-Related Recipients:** Alzheimers Disease, Cancer, Children's Health/ Hospitals, Clinics/Medical Centers, Family Planning, Health Organizations, Hospitals, Medical Education, Medical Research. **Geographic Distribution:** Primarily Cleveland and Columbus, OH.

★ 442 ★ RGK Foundation
2815 San Gabriel
Austin, TX 78705-3596
Phone: (512)474-9298
Gregory A. Kozmetsky, President

Foundation Philosophy: The foundation reports that grants for research have generally been made to education or medicine. In medical research, the foundation has placed major emphasis on connective tissue diseases, particularly scleroderma. The foundation has also sponsored studies in the areas of health, corporate governance, energy, and economic analysis. In addition to grants, the foundation supported and sponsored conferences examining the role of business in American society. **Giving Priorities:** In 1994, the foundation reported that it gave approximately 42% of its funding to health care organizations, 33% to educational institutions, and 14% to civic and public affairs. The remaining 11% of funds was distributed between the arts and miscellaneous programs. **Typical Health-Related Recipients:** Arthritis, Cancer, Domestic Violence, Geriatric Health, Health Organizations, Heart, Hospices, Medical Education, Medical Research, Mental Health, People with Disabilities, Prenatal Health Issues, Public Health, Respiratory, Single-Disease Health Associations, Transplant Networks/ Donor Banks. **Geographic Distribution:** Nationally, with emphasis on Texas, particularly Austin; also to international organizations.

★ 443 ★ Rhodebeck Charitable Trust
575 Lexington Ave.
New York, NY 10022-6102
Huyler C. Held, Trustee

Foundation Philosophy: The Rhodebeck Charitable Trust makes most of its grants in the area of social services. Interests include homes, the homeless, food distribution, and children's services. **Giving Priorities:** In fiscal 1993, health concerns received 53% of total funding, including a $1,000,000 gift to the Fountain House of New York, New York. Civic affairs received 32% of contributions. Both religious and social services received 7% of total gifts. Arts and humanities received 2% of total gifts. A majority of the gifts given by the Rhodebeck Charitable Trust were received by organizations located in the New York city area. **Typical Health-Related Recipients:** Health Organizations, Mental Health, Nursing Services, Substance Abuse. **Geographic Distribution:** Limited to New York, NY.

★ 444 ★ Rice Foundation
8600 Gross Point Rd.
Skokie, IL 60077-2151
Phone: (708)581-9999
Arthur A. Nolan, Jr., President and Director

Foundation Philosophy: The foundation generally supports the arts and civic organizations in the Chicago metropolitan area. **Giving Priorities:** In 1992, the foundation gave approximately 33% of its contributions to the arts. Science received 26% of giving; health care, 20%; civic affairs and education, each 9%; social services, 2%; and religion received the remainder. **Typical Health-Related Recipients:** Arthritis, Cancer, Clinics/Medical Centers, Geriatric Health, Health Organizations, Hospitals, Medical Education, Medical Rehabilitation, Mental Health, People with Disabilities, Single-Disease Health Associations. **Geographic Distribution:** Focus on Illinois, primarily Chicago.

★445★ **Rich Foundation**
10 Piedmont Center, Ste. 802
Atlanta, GA 30305
Phone: (404)266-2123
Anne Berg, Grant Consultant

Foundation Philosophy: The foundation typically supports human service organizations, health associations, educational institutions, and the arts and humanities. Funding is limited to the metropolitan Atlanta area. **Giving Priorities:** In fiscal 1992, health organizations received approximately 36% of funding. Educational institutions received 24% of giving; social services, 23%; and the arts, 17%. Percentages do not include a single $175,000 grant to the United Way of Atlanta, GA. **Typical Health-Related Recipients:** Hospitals, Medical Research, People with Disabilities, Single-Disease Health Associations. **Geographic Distribution:** Metropolitan Atlanta, GA.

★446★ **Richard and Helen DeVos Foundation**
126 Ottowa NW, Ste. 500
Grand Rapids, MI 49503
Phone: (616)454-4114
Fax: (616)454-4654
Richard M. DeVos, President

Foundation Philosophy: The foundation primarily funds religious programs and associations, as well as some churches. Education (largely religious) is also a major focus. **Giving Priorities:** In 1992, the foundation gave approximately 45% of funding to religious organizations. Health concerns received about 19% of contributions, including the foundation's highest grant of $1,141,000 to Butterworth Hospital in Grand Rapids, Michigan. The arts and humanities received about 12% of total funds. Educational institutions received about 8% of total funds; civic concerns, 5%; social services, 5%; environmental projects, 4%; and international affairs, 3%. **Typical Health-Related Recipients:** Health Funds, Health Organizations, Hospitals, Long-Term Care, People with Disabilities, Single-Disease Health Associations. **Geographic Distribution:** National.

★447★ **Richard King Mellon Foundation**
PO Box 2930
Pittsburgh, PA 15230-2930
Phone: (412)392-2800
Fax: (412)392-2837
George H. Taber, Vice President and Director

Foundation Philosophy: The Foundation has two distinct areas of interests: 1) Pittsburgh and Southwestern Pennsylvania -- programs that relate to education, human services, medicine and health care, civic affairs, and cultural activities; and 2) National programs -- American Land Conservation Program, and conservation of natural areas. "1993 also saw the introduction of new priorites for the Foundation's Human Services Program. We are seeking ways to provide comprehensive services for children--who are among western Pennsylvania's poorest citizens--and their families....The Foundation is fo-

cusing its efforts on programs which work toward reducing the risks our children face." The Foundation concentrates its efforts on programs addressing drugs, sex, violence, and abuse in the lives of children. **Giving Priorities:** In 1993, the foundation awarded 59% of its total contributions to environmental conservation programs. Human services programs received 15% of the total donations. Medical programs received 10% of overall support, with donations to hospitals, medical centers, and medical foundations. Education received 7% of support, while civic affairs received 5%. The remaining 4% of distributed funds supported cultural affairs programs. **Typical Health-Related Recipients:** AIDS/HIV, Cancer, Children's Health/ Hospitals, Clinics/Medical Centers, Emergency/Ambulance Services, Family Planning, Geriatric Health, Health Organizations, Health Policy/Cost Containment, Hospices, Hospitals, Long-Term Care, Medical Education, Medical Research, Medical Training, Mental Health, People with Disabilities, Sexual Abuse, Single-Disease Health Associations, Substance Abuse. **Geographic Distribution:** Pittsburgh, PA, and western Pennsylvania; nationally for conservation programs.

★448★ **Richard Lounsbery Foundation**
159-A E 61st St.
New York, NY 10021
Phone: (212)319-7033
Martha Norman, Executive Director

Foundation Philosophy: The Richard Lounsbery Foundation makes most of its grants in the area of education. Educational funding favors higher education, with emphasis on scientific research at universities. Other interests include medical and scientific research, international concerns, civic and environmental causes, and the arts. **Giving Priorities:** In 1993, educational institutions received approximately 40% of funding, while scientific organizations received 18%. International affairs received about 13% of distributed funds, while health care concerns received 12%. Civic affairs received 8% of support, the arts received 5%, and environmental affairs received 4%. The remaining amount went to support social services. **Typical Health-Related Recipients:** Hospitals, Medical Education, Medical Research, Nutrition, People with Disabilities, Single-Disease Health Associations. **Geographic Distribution:** National and some international; focus on New York.

★449★ **Richard and Rhoda Goldman Fund**
One Lombard St., Ste. 303
San Francisco, CA 94111
Phone: (415)788-1090
Duane Silverstein, Executive Director

Foundation Philosophy: The fund's current priorities include support for programs that "focus on protecting and restoring the environment, addressing global population growth, helping the elderly and at-risk youth." **Giving Priorities:** In 1993, the arts received approximately 32% of total contributions, including support for museums, theater, ballet, symphony, and arts associations. Civic affairs, primarily philanthropic organizations and women's concerns, received 16% of funding. Educational institutions received about 15%, including the

foundation's highest grant of $400,000 to Stanford University for its undergraduate honors program in environmental studies. Environmental concerns received 14%, with grants supporting general support programs, air/water quality, forestry, and resource conservation. Social services, mainly United Way and family services, received 7%. International affairs and religious groups each received 6%; and health concerns received the remaining 4% of funds. **Typical Health-Related Recipients:** AIDS/HIV, Alzheimers Disease, Children's Health/Hospitals, Domestic Violence, Family Planning, Health Organizations, Health Policy/Cost Containment, Hospices, Long-Term Care, Medical Training, Nursing Services, Public Health. **Geographic Distribution:** Focus on the San Francisco Bay Area.

★450★ **Richard S. Reynolds Foundation**
6601 W Broad St.
Richmond, VA 23230
Phone: (804)281-4801
David P. Reynolds, President

Foundation Philosophy: The foundation gives to a variety of groups mainly in the Richmond, VA, area. Education, the arts, and health care generally receive a majority of the foundation's giving. **Giving Priorities:** In fiscal 1994, the foundation gave approximately 63% of its total contributions to educational institutions, including its highest grant of $425,000 to St. Christopher's School in Richmond, VA. Religious organizations received about 19%; the arts, 8%; health concerns, 6%; social services, 4%; and civic affairs received the remaining funds. **Typical Health-Related Recipients:** Health Funds, Heart, Hospitals, Medical Education, Medical Rehabilitation, Medical Research, People with Disabilities. **Geographic Distribution:** Focus on Richmond, VA.

★451★ **Robert E. Brennan Foundation**
c/o Mortenson & Associates, P.C.
340 North Ave.
Cranford, NJ 07016-2435
Phone: (908)272-7000
Fax: (908)272-7101
Ronald J. Riccio, Treasurer and Trustee

Foundation Philosophy: The foundation's highest priority is religion, including Jewish and Roman Catholic organizations. Religious-affiliated human service providers, private secondary education, and universities are also supported. **Giving Priorities:** In 1992, the foundation contributed 74% of its total giving to religious organizations, including a single $1,000,000 grant to Yeshiva Imrei Yosef Building Fund, Brooklyn, NY. The foundation also funds Roman Catholic religious organizations. Educational institutions received approximately 17% of support; the arts, 5%; and social services, 2%. Civic and health concerns received the remainder. **Typical Health-Related Recipients:** Cancer, Clinics/Medical Centers, Health Funds, Health Organizations, Hospitals, People with Disabilities, Prenatal Health Issues, Single-Disease Health Associations. **Geographic Distribution:** Focus on New Jersey and New York.

★452★ Robert G. Cabell III and Maude Morgan Cabell Foundation
PO Box 85678
Richmond, VA 23285
Phone: (804)780-2050
Fax: (804)780-2054
John B. Werner, Executive Director

Foundation Philosophy: The foundation makes grants across the major categories of support. In education, interests include colleges and universities in Virginia. Social service support goes to shelters, food banks, senior centers, and youth organizations. Funding for the arts favors historic preservation, and ballet. Civic affairs funding includes housing and philanthropic organizations. Grants also are made to other recipient areas. **Giving Priorities:** In 1993, the foundation gave approximately 36% of its total contributions to educational institutions, including its three highest grants of $100,000 each, awarded to Randolph-Macon College, Randolph-Macon Women's College, and Sweet Briar College. The arts received about 17%; religious organizations, 14%; health concerns, 11%; civic affairs, 9%; social services, 9%; and environmental projects received the remaining funds. **Typical Health-Related Recipients:** Children's Health/Hospitals, Clinics/Medical Centers, Diabetes, Emergency/Ambulance Services, Family Planning, Health Organizations, People with Disabilities. **Geographic Distribution:** Virginia, with a preference for Richmond area.

★453★ Robert J. Kleberg, Jr. and Helen C. Kleberg Foundation
700 N St. Mary's, Ste. 1200
San Antonio, TX 78205
Phone: (210)271-3691
Robert L. Washington, Grants Coordinator

Foundation Philosophy: The foundation's goal is to support organizations reflecting the interests of the late donors. The greatest emphasis has been on medical research. Other areas supported by the foundation include veterinary science, wildlife research and preservation, health services, higher education, community organizations, and the arts and humanities. **Giving Priorities:** In 1993, the foundation gave approximately 54% of its contributions to medical research including the foundation's largest grant of $309,024 to the Southwest Foundation for Biomedical Research. Approximately 20% of funding went to the arts; 8% to civic affairs; 8% to social services; and 8% to environmental efforts. Educational institutions received the remaining 2%. **Typical Health-Related Recipients:** Cancer, Children's Health/Hospitals, Clinics/Medical Centers, Domestic Violence, Eyes/Blindness, Family Planning, Hospitals, Medical Education, Medical Research, Nursing Services, People with Disabilities, Research/Studies Institutes, Transplant Networks/Donor Banks. **Geographic Distribution:** No specific geographic preference, some emphasis on the southern Texas region.

★454★ Robert R. McCormick Tribune Foundation
435 N Michigan Avenue, Ste. 770
Chicago, IL 60611
Phone: (312)222-3510
Fax: (312)222-3523
Nicholas Goodban, Vice President of Philanthropy

Foundation Philosophy: At the end of 1993, the foundation expected a large percentage of its grant-making capacity to be liberated after having fulfilled $59 million in grant commitments made in 1989. The foundation has shifted its giving program to emphasize its intention to improve the social and economic environment, to encourage a free and responsible discussion of national issues, to improve American education, and to stimulate responsible citizenship. **Giving Priorities:** In 1993, the foundation awarded 34% of its total contributions to civic groups. About 25% of funds went to educational institutions. Social services received 17% of support; health care, 14%; and religious organizations, 8%. The remainder went to the arts and international affairs. **Typical Health-Related Recipients:** Children's Health/Hospitals, Clinics/Medical Centers, Domestic Violence, Emergency/Ambulance Services, Health Organizations, Hospitals, Medical Education, Medical Rehabilitation, Medical Research, Mental Health, People with Disabilities, Public Health, Single-Disease Health Associations, Substance Abuse. **Geographic Distribution:** Varies by program area; some emphasis on metropolitan Chicago, IL. **Formerly:** Robert R. McCormick Charitable Trust.

★455★ Robert R. Meyer Foundation
AmSouth Bank, N.A., Trust Dept.
PO Box 11426
Birmingham, AL 35202
Phone: (205)326-4696
Fax: (205)581-7433
Leah Scalise, Vice President

Foundation Philosophy: The foundation provides a broad base of support to all types of charitable organizations in the Birmingham area. **Giving Priorities:** In 1993, the foundation gave approximately 23% of its total contributions in support of education, including significant donations to several Alabama universities and colleges. Social service organizations received about 20% of support, including contributions to several youth-oriented organizations such as Boy Scouts of America and Big Brothers and Big Sisters. Arts organizations received 15% of funds, including a $100,000 grant, the largest given, to the Birmingham Museum of Art. Health care institutions and religious organizations each received 14% of funds. Science organizations received 7% of support, while civic and public affairs received 6%. The remaining amount, less than 1%, went to support environmental causes. **Typical Health-Related Recipients:** Clinics/Medical Centers, Domestic Violence, Eyes/Blindness, Family Planning, Health Organizations, Hospitals, Mental Health, Nursing Services, People with Disabilities, Research/Studies Institutes, Substance Abuse. **Geographic Distribution:** Limited to Birmingham, AL, metropolitan area.

★456★ Robert R. Young Foundation
PO Box 1423
Greenwich, CT 06836
David W. Wallace, President

Foundation Philosophy: The foundation generally supports colleges and universities, hospitals, and social services in New York and New England. **Giving Priorities:** In 1993, about 72% of giving went to health care, including grants of $937,000 to the New York Hospital and $501,000 to the Greenwich Hospital. Education received 19% of contributions, with major support to the Greenwich Academy Annual Fund, Greenwich, CT. Social service organizations received 5% of grants, while religion and the arts and humanities each received 2% of giving. The remaining funds went to the Greenwich Fire and Police Departments in the form of a $600 grant. **Typical Health-Related Recipients:** Arthritis, Cancer, Children's Health/Hospitals, Clinics/Medical Centers, Diabetes, Emergency/Ambulance Services, Family Planning, Heart, Hospices, Hospitals, Medical Research, Mental Health, Multiple Sclerosis, People with Disabilities, Single-Disease Health Associations, Substance Abuse. **Geographic Distribution:** New York and New England.

★457★ Robert Stewart Odell and Helen Pfeiffer Odell Fund
c/o Wells Fargo Bank Trustee
PO Box 63002
San Francisco, CA 94163
Phone: (415)396-3226
Fax: (415)834-0604
Thomas N. Neville, Trustee

Foundation Philosophy: The foundation makes most of its grants to benefit youth in California. The primary interest is social services, specifically child welfare programs and youth organizations. Other interests include funding for schools, health care, and the arts. **Giving Priorities:** In 1993, social service organizations received approximately 30% of total funding, with major support to youth activities and the disabled. Educational institutions received 26%. Religious organizations received 21%, while health care received 10% of support. About 5% of funding supported the arts, with civic affairs receiving 4%, and science receiving 3%. The remaining 1% supported international affairs. **Typical Health-Related Recipients:** Children's Health/Hospitals, Clinics/Medical Centers, Health Organizations, Hospitals, Medical Research, People with Disabilities. **Geographic Distribution:** Focus on northern California, with emphasis on San Francisco.

★458★ Robert W. Woodruff Foundation
50 Hurt Plz., Ste. 1200
Atlanta, GA 30303
Phone: (404)522-6755
Fax: (404)522-7026
Charles H. McTier, President

Foundation Philosophy: The foundation's principal giving interests include education, health care, human services, the arts, civic affairs, and the environment. **Giving Priorities:** In 1993, the foundation awarded approximately 42% of its total contributions to educational institutions and programs, including its two highest grants of $5,000,000 each to Emory University in Atlanta, GA. The arts received about 21%; scientific interests, 19%; civic and public affairs, 11%; international organizations, 5%; and environmental causes, health concerns, and social services received the remaining funds. **Typical Health-Related Recipients:** Health Organizations, Health Policy/Cost Containment, Medical Education. **Geographic Distribution:** Limited to Georgia, primarily the metropolitan Atlanta area.

★459★ **Robert Wood Johnson Foundation**
Rte. 1 and College Rd. E
PO Box 2316
Princeton, NJ 08543-2316
Phone: (609)452-8701
Fax: (609)452-1865
Edward H. Robbins, Proposal Manager

Foundation Philosophy: For the 1990s, the foundation's four objectives are the following: to assure that Americans of all ages have access to basic health care; to improve the way services are organized and provided to people with chronic health conditions; to address the issue of rising health care costs; and to promote health and prevent disease by reducing harm caused by substance abuse. **Giving Priorities:** In 1994, the foundation gave 100% to health care. **Typical Health-Related Recipients:** Adolescent Health Issues, AIDS/HIV, Alzheimers Disease, Cancer, Children's Health/Hospitals, Clinics/Medical Centers, Family Planning, Geriatric Health, Health Organizations, Health Policy/Cost Containment, Heart, Home-Care Services, Hospitals, Long-Term Care, Medical Education, Medical Training, Mental Health, Nursing Services, People with Disabilities, Prenatal Health Issues, Public Health, Research/Studies Institutes, Single-Disease Health Associations, Substance Abuse. **Geographic Distribution:** National.

★460★ **Rockefeller Foundation**
420 Fifth Ave.
New York, NY 10018-2702
Phone: (212)869-8500
Fax: (212)764-3468
Lynda Mullen, Secretary

Foundation Philosophy: The foundation was established "to promote the well-being of mankind throughout the world," and is dedicated to identifying and attacking the underlying causes of human suffering and need at their source. The foundation carries out its mission through grants and fellowships to individuals and institutions in five areas: international science-based development (in agriculture, health, population sciences, and global environment); arts and humanities; equal opportunity; international security; and school reform. The Health Sciences program concentrates on vaccinological and pharmacological research and the development of cost-effective ways to treat and prevent the most serious health problems in developing nations. The Population Sciences program concentrates on scientific research in reproductive biology; developing new contraceptives; evaluating how available contraceptive methods can be changed to improve their acceptance, safety, and effectiveness; and studying the connection between fertility and social factors, such as the status of women. **Giving Priorities:** In 1993, the

foundation reported the percentages of total giving awarded to specific foundation programs. The foundation's international science-based development programs were awarded a total of $58,050,722 and 53% of funding and consisted of agricultural sciences, 15%; health sciences, 15%; population sciences, 12%; the global environment, 8%; and the African initiatives program, 3%. The foundation's equal opportunity program received $24,411,572 and 22% of funding. The arts and humanities received 13% of giving and school reform efforts received 7%. Special international initiatives and special interests received 5%, including grants for international security and international philanthropy. **Typical Health-Related Recipients:** AIDS/HIV, Family Planning, Health Organizations, Medical Education, Medical Research, Medical Training, Public Health, Research/Studies Institutes. **Geographic Distribution:** International and national.

★461★ **Rockwell Fund**
1360 Post Oak Blvd., Ste. 780
Houston, TX 77056
Phone: (713)629-9022
Fax: (713)629-7702
Martha Vogt, Program Officer

Foundation Philosophy: The fund supports a broad range of activities, with preference for causes in the Houston area. **Giving Priorities:** In 1993, the foundation gave 27% of its total contributions to social service organizations in Texas. Educational institutions received 23% of the funds. The highest grant amount of $50,000 was awarded to three separate colleges and universities. Health concerns received 17%, the arts and humanities received 16%; religious groups, 13%; civic and public affairs and environmental organizations each received 2% of total funding. **Typical Health-Related Recipients:** Cancer, Children's Health/Hospitals, Clinics/Medical Centers, Emergency/Ambulance Services, Eyes/Blindness, Family Planning, Health Organizations, Hospices, Hospitals, Medical Rehabilitation, Medical Research, Mental Health, Nursing Services, People with Disabilities, Prenatal Health Issues, Single-Disease Health Associations, Substance Abuse. **Geographic Distribution:** Texas, primarily the Houston area; limited giving out of Houston area.

★462★ **Rollin M. Gerstacker Foundation**
Box 1945
Midland, MI 48641-1945
Phone: (517)631-6097
Carl A. Gerstacker, Vice President, Treasurer, and Trustee

Foundation Philosophy: The foundation traditionally has given to homes for the elderly, colleges and universities, youth, and community services particularly in Midland, MI. These areas of interest remain the focus of foundation giving. Human services also receive strong support from the foundation. These include focuses on children and youth, family services, mental health, and the disabled. **Giving Priorities:** In 1993, the foundation gave approximately 56% of its contributions to education, including the highest grant of $1,510,000 to the University of Michigan. Civic affairs received 20% and social

services received 13%. The arts, health, and religion each received 3%. The remaining funds supported science and the environment. **Typical Health-Related Recipients:** Domestic Violence, Emergency/Ambulance Services, Eyes/Blindness, Medical Research, Mental Health, People with Disabilities, Single-Disease Health Associations, Substance Abuse, Transplant Networks/Donor Banks. **Geographic Distribution:** Primarily Michigan and Ohio.

★463★ **RosaMary Foundation**
PO Box 51299
New Orleans, LA 70151-1299
Phone: (504)895-1984
Fax: (504)895-1988
Louis McDaniel Freeman, Chairman

Foundation Philosophy: The foundation supports organizations working toward the betterment of the New Orleans community. Educational institutions and the United Way for the Greater New Orleans Area are the major recipients of foundation giving. The foundation also has an interest in the arts and supports various cultural organizations in New Orleans. **Giving Priorities:** In 1994, the foundation gave approximately 53% of its contributions to social service organizations in Louisiana, including a $400,000 grant to the Kingsley House and a $200,000 grant to the United Way of Greater New Orleans. The foundation gave 17% of its gifts for education, 13% to civic and public affairs, 7% to religious groups, and 6% to health care. The remaining funds supported the arts. **Typical Health-Related Recipients:** AIDS/HIV, Clinics/Medical Centers, Eyes/Blindness, Family Planning, Health Organizations, Hospitals, People with Disabilities, Research/Studies Institutes, Transplant Networks/Donor Banks. **Geographic Distribution:** New Orleans, LA.

★464★ **Rosamond Gifford Charitable Corporation**
731 James St., Rm. 404
Syracuse, NY 13203
Phone: (315)474-2489
Dean A. Lesilinski, Executive Director

Foundation Philosophy: The corporation's major priority is supporting social service organizations. Interests include united funds, children's welfare, youth organizations, homes, food and clothing distribution, and community centers. Other interests include hospitals, health organizations, religious organizations for clergy counseling, education, and the arts. **Giving Priorities:** In 1993, about 36% of funding went to social service organizations, including the highest grant of $97,500 to the United Way of Central New York. The arts received 21% of total contributions; religious services, 16%; health organizations, 9%; educational and scientific institutions, 7% each; and civic causes, 4%. **Typical Health-Related Recipients:** Alzheimers Disease, Emergency/Ambulance Services, Health Organizations, Heart, Hospices, Hospitals, Kidney, Medical Research, Mental Health, People with Disabilities, Sexual Abuse, Single-Disease Health Associations, Substance Abuse. **Geographic Distribution:** Limited to organizations serving the residents of Syracuse and Onondaga counties, NY.

★ 465 ★ Rose M. Badgeley Residuary Charitable Trust

c/o Marine Midland Bank, N.A.
250 Park Ave., 4th Fl.
New York, NY 10177
Phone: (212)503-2786
Eleanor D. Kress, Administrative Vice President

Foundation Philosophy: The trust traditionally supports organizations and programs in the areas of social welfare, health, education, and the arts, primarily in the metropolitan New York City area. **Giving Priorities:** In fiscal 1993, approximately 31% of overall giving went to social services, including religious welfare, child welfare, youth organizations, and the disabled. Another 31% of funding went to health care, including a single $65,000 grant to the New York Hospital Cornell Medical Center. Arts and education each received about 17% of total contributions. Religion received about 4%. **Typical Health-Related Recipients:** Health Organizations, Hospitals, Medical Research, People with Disabilities, Single-Disease Health Associations, Substance Abuse. **Geographic Distribution:** Primarily New York metropolitan area.

★ 466 ★ Rosenstiel Foundation

c/o Rosenman & Colin
575 Madison Ave., 11th Fl.
New York, NY 10022
Phone: (212)940-8837
Maurice C. Greenbaum, Secretary

Foundation Philosophy: The Rosenstiel Foundation primarily supports the arts, civic affairs, and health care. Secondary interests include education with gifts to universities and science education. The foundation also will fund social service organizations. **Giving Priorities:** In 1993, the foundation gave 37% of funding to civic and public affairs. The arts and humanities received 25% and education received 17%. Health care was awarded 14%; international affairs, 4%; and social services, 3%. **Typical Health-Related Recipients:** AIDS/HIV, Cancer, Children's Health/Hospitals, Health Organizations, Hospitals, Kidney, Medical Education, Medical Research, Nursing Services, Public Health, Single-Disease Health Associations, Substance Abuse. **Geographic Distribution:** Eastern United States, with a focus on New York, NY.

★ 467 ★ Ross Foundation

PO Box 335
Arkadelphia, AR 71923
Phone: (501)246-9881
Fax: (501)246-9674
Ross M. Whipple, President

Foundation Philosophy: The Ross Foundation has two primary interests: promoting the economic, cultural, and educational interests of Arkadelphia and Clark County through various projects and programs, and promoting conservation and the management of natural resources. The foundation's funding is generated through the timber industry, therefore grants are made to support the environment and conservation. **Giving Priorities:** In 1994, the foundation gave approximately 55% to educational institutions, including the foundation's highest grant of $62,495 to the Joint Educational Consortium of Arkadelphia, AR. Two health programs in Arkansas received about 16% of total contributions; social services, 12%; civic groups, 8%; environmental concerns, 3%; religious institutions, 3%; and the arts and humanities, 3%. **Typical Health-Related Recipients:** AIDS/HIV, Child Abuse, Domestic Violence, Emergency/Ambulance Services, Hospitals, Substance Abuse. **Geographic Distribution:** Limited to Arkadelphia and Clark County, AR.

★ 468 ★ Roy A. Hunt Foundation

One Bigelow Sq., Ste. 630
Pittsburgh, PA 15219-3030
Phone: (412)281-8734
Fax: (412)281-9463
Torrence M. Hunt, Jr., President and Trustee

Foundation Philosophy: The foundation primarily supports the institutions with which Mr. and Mrs. Hunt were involved. **Giving Priorities:** In fiscal 1992, the foundation gave approximately 49% of its funding to educational institutions, primarily to Carnegie-Mellon University, with specified grants going to fund the Hunt Institute for Botanical Documentation. About 23% went to the arts. Civic and public affairs received 10%; social services, 7%; health concerns, 7%; international affairs, 3%; and science, about 1%. **Typical Health-Related Recipients:** Alzheimers Disease, Children's Health/Hospitals, Hospitals, Medical Rehabilitation, Mental Health, Single-Disease Health Associations. **Geographic Distribution:** Primarily Pittsburgh, PA, and Boston, MA.

★ 469 ★ Roy and Christine Sturgis Charitable and Educational Trust

c/o Nations Bank
PO Box 830241
Dallas, TX 75283
Phone: (214)508-1965
Fax: (214)508-1997
Daniel J. Kelly, Trust Officer

Foundation Philosophy: The trust's main priorities include education, the arts, health, science, and "the relief of human suffering." **Giving Priorities:** In fiscal 1992, about 38% of giving went to educational institutions, including a single $575,000 grant to the University of Arkansas, Fayetteville, AR. Social services received approximately 32% of contributions primarily supporting youth organizations. Civic groups received about 10% of support; health care, 9%; and the arts, 9%. The remainder funded religious organizations. **Typical Health-Related Recipients:** Cancer, Children's Health/Hospitals, Clinics/Medical Centers, Diabetes, Domestic Violence, Health Organizations, Medical Education, Nursing Services, Single-Disease Health Associations, Substance Abuse. **Geographic Distribution:** Primarily Arkansas and Texas.

★ 470 ★ Roy J. Carver Charitable Trust

PO Box 76
Muscatine, IA 52761
Phone: (319)263-4010
Roger A. Hughes, Executive Administrator

Foundation Philosophy: Roy J. Carver's "commitment to helping young people through educational opportunities and to building a better world through medical and scientific research are cornerstones of the charitable trust. As a matter of policy, the trust favors grants that make its participation a vital factor in the success of the project. Such projects should promote the ethical, intellectual, and physical development of young men and women; establish, equip, or provide for the maintenance of institutions of learning; or contribute to the advancement of knowledge and its practical applications through medical and scientific research." **Giving Priorities:** In fiscal 1994, the trust gave approximately 27% of its contributions to science, math, and technology. General educational affairs received about 22%; scholarships, 15%; medical and scientific research, 14%; and youth and recreation received about 11%. General youth programs (6%) and various other interests (5%) received the remaining funds. **Typical Health-Related Recipients:** Medical Education, People with Disabilities. **Geographic Distribution:** Primarily in the state of Iowa, and organizations outside Iowa with which the founder had a significant association.

★ 471 ★ Ruth and Vernon Taylor Foundation

1670 Denver Club Bldg.
Denver, CO 80202
Phone: (303)893-5284
Friday A. Green, Trustee

Foundation Philosophy: The foundation's charter decrees the areas of giving to be educational, religious, charitable, and scientific causes. Over the years, the foundation has expanded its interests to include the arts and humanities. **Giving Priorities:** In fiscal 1993, the foundation gave approximately 28% of its contributions to education. The arts received 25%; civic affairs, 21%; social services, 11%; health, 8%; science, 6%; and international, 1%. **Typical Health-Related Recipients:** Cancer, Emergency/Ambulance Services, Family Planning, Health Funds, Health Organizations, Hospitals, Medical Rehabilitation, Medical Research, People with Disabilities, Research/Studies Institutes, Single-Disease Health Associations, Substance Abuse. **Geographic Distribution:** National, with some preference for Texas, Colorado, Wyoming, Montana, Illinois, and the Mid-Atlantic states.

★ 472 ★ S. H. Cowell Foundation

120 Montgomery St., No. 2570
San Francisco, CA 94111
Phone: (415)397-0285
Fax: (415)986-6786
Thomas G. David, Director of Grants Programs

Foundation Philosophy: The foundation's interests include aiding organizations concerned with the welfare of children and minorities; promoting the relative self-sufficiency of physically or mentally handicapped persons; providing general improvement in basic social programs in needy areas; assisting family planning organizations; supporting programs for the prevention of alcoholism; promoting job training programs; and providing for low-income housing. **Giving Priorities:** In 1993, the foundation gave approximately 31% of its total contributions to civic affairs, with major support for community foundations and programs. Educational institutions received about 29% of giving, including the foundation's two highest grants of $400,000 each, which were awarded to the Brentwood Union School District and the Redwood City School District. Social services received 21%; the arts, 10%; health concerns, 4%; environmental causes, 2%; international organizations, 2%; and scientific interests received the remaining funds. **Typical Health-Related Recipients:** AIDS/HIV, Clinics/Medical Centers, Domestic Violence, Family Planning, People with Disabilities, Public Health, Substance Abuse. **Geographic Distribution:** Mainly Northern California.

★473★ Sage Foundation
10315 E Grand River, Ste. 204
Brighton, MI 48116
Melissa Sage Booth, Chairman, President, and Treasurer

Foundation Philosophy: The objective of the Sage Foundation is to make contributions and grants that further charitable, religious, scientific, literary, and educational purposes. **Giving Priorities:** In 1992, the foundation gave approximately 62% of its contributions to the arts, including a $350,000 grant to Hillsdale College, MI, to construct a cultural and performing arts center. Education received 10% of total contributions awarded; health care, 9%; civic affairs, 8%; religion, 7%; and social services, 3%. **Typical Health-Related Recipients:** AIDS/HIV, Clinics/Medical Centers, Health Organizations, Heart, Hospices, Hospitals, Medical Research, Mental Health, People with Disabilities, Single-Disease Health Associations, Substance Abuse. **Geographic Distribution:** No geographic restrictions.

★474★ Samuel Goldwyn Foundation
10203 Santa Monica Blvd., Ste. 500
Los Angeles, CA 90067
Phone: (310)552-2255
Meyer Gottlieb, Treasurer

Foundation Philosophy: The foundation's trustees generally support all areas of philanthropy. In the past, large grants have been given to the arts. Libraries, theaters, museums, and public broadcasting have all received funding. Other interests include support for police academies, public education, the aged, child care, and a variety of health concerns. **Giving Priorities:** In 1991, health-related organizations received 95% of total funding, including the highest grant of $3,672,872 to the Motion Picture and TV Relief Fund. Educational institutions received 3%, while the arts received 1%. The remainder supported civic concerns, social services, and Jewish causes. **Typical Health-Related Recipients:** AIDS/HIV, Cancer, Children's Health/Hospitals, Clinics/Medical Centers, Family Planning, Health Funds, Hospitals, People with Disabilities, Research/Studies Institutes. **Geographic Distribution:** Some national; focus on Los Angeles, CA, metropolitan area.

★475★ Samuel I. Newhouse Foundation
c/o Paul Scherer & Co.
330 Madison Ave.
New York, NY 10017
Phone: (212)661-9300
Edward Laminsky, Asst. Sec. and Asst. Treas.

Foundation Philosophy: The foundation principally supports the arts, social services, higher education, and civic concerns. **Giving Priorities:** In fiscal 1993, arts and humanities organizations and educational institutions each received about 28% of total contributions. Religious institutions received about 13% of funding. Social services received about 12% of giving. Health groups and international affairs each received about 7% of contributions. Civic concerns received about 4% of funding and environmental programs were awarded 1% of giving. **Typical Health-Related Recipients:** Cancer, Clinics/Medical Centers, Health Organizations, Heart, Hospitals, Medical Education, Medical Research, Mental Health, People with Disabilities, Single-Disease Health Associations, Substance Abuse. **Geographic Distribution:** Broad geographic distribution, with emphasis on New York City.

★476★ Samuel Roberts Noble Foundation
PO Box 2180
Ardmore, OK 73402
Phone: (405)223-5810
Fax: (405)221-7362
Michael A. Cawley, President and Trustee

Foundation Philosophy: By combining inhouse research and traditional grant making, the foundation seeks to improve the quality of life in rural and urban communities. The foundation conducts research in the areas of plant biology and agriculture. The foundation continues to focus its grants program on the general areas of education, including scientific research, and in health research and delivery systems. The foundation has an interest in the arts, as well as the promotion and preservation of traditional western culture and landmarks. The foundation also supports organizations which study methods to improve the quality and effectiveness of government. **Giving Priorities:** In 1993, the foundation reported that it gave 55% of its contributions to health and research; 22% to Quality of Life and Community Affairs programs; 11% to public affairs and information; 10% to education; and 2% to miscellaneous programs. **Typical Health-Related Recipients:** Cancer, Diabetes, Emergency/Ambulance Services, Family Planning, Health Organizations, Health Policy/Cost Containment, Hospices, Hospitals, Medical Rehabilitation, Medical Research, Mental Health, People with Disabilities, Research/Studies Institutes, Single-Disease Health Associations, Substance Abuse, Transplant Networks/Donor Banks. **Geographic Distribution:** Southwestern United States, primarily Oklahoma.

★477★ Samuel S. Fels Fund
1616 Walnut St.
Ste. 800
Philadelphia, PA 19103
Phone: (215)731-9455
Helen Cunningham, Executive Director

Foundation Philosophy: The fund seeks "to initiate and/or to assist any activities or projects of a scientific, educational, or charitable nature which tend to improve human daily life and to bring to the average person greater health, happiness, and a fuller understanding of the meaning and purposes of life." **Giving Priorities:** In

1993, the foundation gave 28% of its total giving to educational institutions, including multiple grants to Parents Union for Public Schools in Philadelphia. Civic groups received 24% of funds; social services, 20%; health care, 12%; and the arts, 11%. The remaining 4% went to environmental concerns. **Typical Health-Related Recipients:** Adolescent Health Issues, AIDS/HIV, Cancer, Children's Health/Hospitals, Diabetes, Domestic Violence, Emergency/Ambulance Services, Family Planning, People with Disabilities, Prenatal Health Issues. **Geographic Distribution:** Philadelphia, PA, only.

★478★ Sandra Atlas Bass and Edythe and Sol G. Atlas Fund
185 Great Neck Rd.
Great Neck, NY 11021
Phone: (516)487-9030
Sandra Atlas Bass, President

Foundation Philosophy: The fund makes most of its grants in the areas of social services, health, and religion. Social service funding favors programs for the blind and disabled. Health support primarily funds single disease associations, while major support for religion goes to the United Jewish Federation Appeal. Other areas of interest include education, the arts, and international organizations. **Giving Priorities:** In 1992, the fund gave approximately 36% of its contributions to social service organizations, including support for animal protection groups, people with disabilities, and child welfare programs. Health care received 30% of giving. Religious organizations received 22%, including the fund's highest grant of $125,000 for the United Jewish Appeal Federation. International affairs received 7%; civic organizations, 3%; and education received the remainder. **Typical Health-Related Recipients:** Cancer, Children's Health/Hospitals, Emergency/Ambulance Services, Hospitals, Kidney, Medical Research, Multiple Sclerosis, People with Disabilities, Single-Disease Health Associations, Trauma Treatment. **Geographic Distribution:** Focus on Long Island, NY, and the New York, NY, metropolitan area.

★479★ Sarkeys Foundation
116 S Peters, Rm. 219
Norman, OK 73069
Phone: (405)364-3703
Fax: (405)364-8191
Cheri D. Cartwright, Executive Director

Foundation Philosophy: The foundation's mission is "to improve the quality of life in Oklahoma and the Southwest." Major areas of support include higher education, health care and medical research, and cultural and humanitarian programs of regional significance. **Giving Priorities:** In 1994, the foundation reports that they gave approximately 53% of total contributions to educational organizations. Social services received about 21% of funding; health groups, 12%; environmental programs, 8%; and the arts and humanities, 7%. **Typical Health-Related Recipients:** AIDS/HIV, Alzheimers Disease, Child Abuse, Family Planning, Health Organizations, Hospitals, Medical Education, Medical Rehabilitation, People with Disabilities, Sexual Abuse, Single-Disease Health Associations,

Substance Abuse. **Geographic Distribution:** Oklahoma.

★ 480 ★ Scaife Family Foundation
3 Mellon Bank Ctr.
525 William Penn Pl., Ste. 3900
Pittsburgh, PA 15219-1708
Phone: (412)392-2900
Joanne B. Beyer, Vice President

Foundation Philosophy: "The Scaife Family Foundation grant awards will support and develop programs that address the well-being of the family and its members and that enhance traditional values." **Giving Priorities:** In 1992, the foundation gave approximately 27% of funding to civic concerns. Social services received 20% of funding. The arts and humanities received 19% of funding, including the foundation's highest grant of $1,000,000, which went to support The Carnegie. Health care received 18% of total contributions. Educational institutions received 14% of funding. Religious needs received less than 2% of giving. **Typical Health-Related Recipients:** Children's Health/Hospitals, Eyes/Blindness, Family Planning, Health Funds, Health Organizations, Hospices, Hospitals, Medical Education, Medical Rehabilitation, Medical Research, Mental Health, People with Disabilities, Prenatal Health Issues, Single-Disease Health Associations, Substance Abuse. **Geographic Distribution:** Focuses on Pittsburgh and western Pennsylvania areas.

★ 481 ★ Schultz Foundation
PO Box 98
Essex Fells, NJ 07021
Phone: (201)857-9303
Margaret F. Schultz, President

Foundation Philosophy: The Schultz Foundation is primarily interested in supporting health care and educational institutions. Health support favors health foundations, medical schools, and hospitals for cancer treatment and research. A majority of the educational support goes to medical training and research at the university level. Social services, the arts, and civic affairs are also supported by the foundation, but are secondary interests. **Giving Priorities:** In fiscal 1992, the foundation gave 45% of its funding to health services, including grants totaling $136,512 to the University of Medicine and Dentistry of New Jersey. Contributions to education accounted for 34% of the giving. Major contributions were made to Loyola University, Marquette University, and the College of Physicians and Surgeons of Columbia University. Social services received 12% of the funds; civic affairs, 5%; and the arts, 4%. **Typical Health-Related Recipients:** Family Planning, Health Organizations, Hospices, Hospitals, Medical Education, Medical Research. **Geographic Distribution:** Focus on eastern United States.

★ 482 ★ Seabury Foundation
208 S LaSalle St., Ste. 1224
Chicago, IL 60604
Phone: (312)372-1808
Fax: (312)372-1809
Deborah Seabury Holloway, Executive
 Director and Trustee

Foundation Philosophy: "The Seabury Foundation is a family foundation which funds projects in the areas of education, social services, health, conservation, and the arts in the Chicago metropolitan area. Particular emphasis is placed on programs which nurture strong family relationships and promote self-sufficiency." **Giving Priorities:** In 1994, the foundation gave approximately 27% of its total contributions to educational organizations. Social services also received about 27% of giving. Social service grants focused on child care and parent training, emergency and long-term housing solutions, substance abuse treatment, and family resource centers. The trustees have a particular interest in programs serving Native Americans. Approximately 25% of the funds were given to health care organizations, including visiting nurses associations, other health care delivery organizations, and programs for the disabled. Cultural organizations received about 15%, with support for major institutions, out-reach programs, and mid-size and small arts organizations. Religion received 4% of the funds, mainly in support of education for the Epicopal priesthood. Civic affairs and environmental causes, including conservancies and wildlife rescue and reintroduction, received the remaining funds. **Typical Health-Related Recipients:** Children's Health/Hospitals, Clinics/Medical Centers, Emergency/Ambulance Services, Family Planning, Hospices, Hospitals, Medical Rehabilitation, Medical Research, Mental Health, Nursing Services, People with Disabilities, Single-Disease Health Associations. **Geographic Distribution:** Focus on the greater Chicago, IL, area.

★ 483 ★ Self Foundation
Drawer 1017
Greenwood, SC 29648
Phone: (803)941-4036
Fax: (803)229-1111
Frank J. Wideman, III, Executive Director

Foundation Philosophy: The foundation funds health care and higher education organizations primarily. Funds are also available for civic and community service activities for youth and the elderly, as well as for cultural and historical activities. These latter areas of interest are usually confined to the Greenwood, SC, area. **Giving Priorities:** In 1993, the foundation gave approximately 44% to science, which is only one grant, the foundation's highest grant of $568,500, to the J.C. Self Institute of Human Genetics. Educational institutions received about 32% of funding, primarily to colleges and universities in South Carolina. Health programs received 16% of total contributions; social services, 4%; arts and humanities, 4%; and civic, approximately 1%. **Typical Health-Related Recipients:** Clinics/Medical Centers, Heart, Home-Care Services, Hospitals, Sexual Abuse. **Geographic Distribution:** South Carolina, with emphasis on Greenwood area.

**★ 484 ★ Seth Sprague Educational and
 Charitable Foundation**
U.S. Trust Company of New York
114 W. 47th St.
New York, NY 10036
Phone: (212)852-3686
Ms. Maureen O. Augusciak, Senior Vice
 President

Foundation Philosophy: The foundation gives to a broad range of interests, with a focus on education, social services, community affairs, and health. **Giving Priorities:** In 1992, about 34% of the foundation's total contributions supported education, mostly for colleges, universities, and preparatory schools including a $48,000 grant to the Woodberry Forest School in Virginia. Civic affairs received 21% of distributed funds, while health care organizations received 17%. Social service organizations and the arts each received 11% of support. Science, environmental affairs, and religious concerns each received about 2% of contributions. **Typical Health-Related Recipients:** Domestic Violence, Emergency/Ambulance Services, Family Planning, Geriatric Health, Health Funds, Health Organizations, Hospices, Hospitals, Medical Education, Medical Rehabilitation, Medical Research, Medical Training, Mental Health, Nursing Services, People with Disabilities, Single-Disease Health Associations, Substance Abuse. **Geographic Distribution:** Nationally, with a primary focus on New York and Massachusetts.

★ 485 ★ Seymour H. Knox Foundation
3750 Marine Midland Ctr.
Buffalo, NY 14203
Phone: (716)854-6811
James F. Wendell, Asst. Sec. and Asst. Treas.

Foundation Philosophy: The Seymour H. Knox Foundation makes most of its grants in the areas of education, the arts, and civic affairs. Funding for education favors universities and private education. Support for the arts goes to arts academies, museums, and historic preservation. Funding for civic affairs supports environmental affairs, the natural sciences, and community development. The foundation also supports hospitals, churches, and social services. **Giving Priorities:** In 1993, the foundation contributed about 52% of its giving to educational institutions, including a single $150,000 grant to the University of Buffalo Foundation. Health care was given 14%; social services, 11%; and the arts, 9%. Environmental efforts received 7% of funds; religious organizations, 4%; and civic groups, 3%. **Typical Health-Related Recipients:** Cancer, Children's Health/Hospitals, Family Planning, Health Funds, Hospices, Hospitals, Medical Rehabilitation, Medical Research, People with Disabilities. **Geographic Distribution:** Eastern United States, with a focus on Buffalo, NY, area.

★ 486 ★ Share Foundation
11901 Grandview Rd.
Grandview, MO 64030
Phone: (816)966-2222
Harry J. Lloyd, President and Treasurer

Foundation Philosophy: The Share Foundation makes most of its grants in the areas of social services, religion, and education. Social service funding favors youth groups and religious homes. Funding for religion emphasizes a number of denominational organizations. Educational funds favor religious universities, colleges, and high schools. The foundation will also fund health care organizations and civic affairs. **Giving Priorities:** In 1993, the foundation gave approximately 28% of its total contributions to health concerns, including a $150,000 grant to the Mayo Foundation in Rochester, MN, and a $150,000 grant to the National Center for Human Genome Research. Religious organizations received about 25%; education, 24%; civic affairs, 8%; international organizations, 7%; science, 5%; and social services received 3%. **Typical Health-Related Recipients:** Family Planning, Health Organizations, Medical Research, Mental Health, Research/Studies Institutes, Single-Disease Health Associations. **Geographic Distribution:** National, with an emphasis on Kansas City, MO.

★487★ **Shelby Cullom Davis Foundation**
70 Pine St.
New York, NY 10270
Phone: (212)425-3212

Foundation Philosophy: The foundation typically focuses on public policy and economic research organizations and higher educational institutions. **Giving Priorities:** In fiscal 1993, the foundation awarded 66% of its total contributions to educational institutions. About 19% of funds went to civic groups. Health care received 6% of support; social services, 3%; the arts, 2%; scientific organizations, 2%; and religious concerns, 1%. **Typical Health-Related Recipients:** Children's Health/Hospitals, Clinics/Medical Centers, Domestic Violence, Family Planning, Health Policy/Cost Containment, Hospitals, Medical Research, Research/Studies Institutes. **Geographic Distribution:** National, with emphasis on New York.

★488★ **Sherman Fairchild Foundation**
71 Arch St.
Greenwich, CT 06830
Phone: (203)661-9360
Patricia A. Lydon, Vice President

Foundation Philosophy: The foundation generally emphasizes the following areas: grants to education, particularly colleges and universities; health and medical research; and, to a lesser extent, the arts and social services. **Giving Priorities:** In 1993, about 53% of foundation giving went to education. Primary recipients were colleges and universities with emphasis on science and technical education. Case Western Reserve University received a large grant of $750,000. The arts received 25% including the two highest grants of $1,000,000 each to the Metropolitan Museum of Art and the Pierpont Morgan Library. Social services received 8%; religion, 8%; and health care, 6%. The remaining funds went to scientific institutions. **Typical Health-Related Recipients:** Cancer, Hospitals, Medical Education, Medical Research. **Geographic Distribution:** No geographic restrictions; emphasis on New York City metropolitan area.

★489★ **Sid W. Richardson Foundation**
309 Main St.
Ft. Worth, TX 76102
Phone: (817)336-0494
Fax: (817)332-2176
Valleau Wilkie, Jr., Exec. VP and Exec. Dir.

Foundation Philosophy: The foundation believes it can best serve the state of Texas through its support of both tax-supported groups and nonprofit organizations. In education, it emphasizes support to public elementary

and secondary schools, and faculty development programs. Health interests include preventive medicine and efforts to improve the delivery of efficient health care. In the areas of the arts, human services, and community projects, the foundation focuses on the needs of the Ft. Worth area. **Giving Priorities:** In 1993, the foundation gave approximately 46% of its total contributions to the arts, including the highest grant of $6,000,000 (part of an $18 million grant payable over 3 years). About 24% was awarded to educational institutions; 15% to health care; 7% to social services; 3% to civic affairs; 3% to science; and 2% to religion. **Typical Health-Related Recipients:** Cancer, Clinics/Medical Centers, Diabetes, Emergency/Ambulance Services, Eyes/Blindness, Family Planning, Health Policy/Cost Containment, Hospitals, Medical Education, Medical Research, Nursing Services, Outpatient Health Care, People with Disabilities, Research/Studies Institutes, Substance Abuse. **Geographic Distribution:** Texas, especially Ft. Worth area.

★490★ **Sidney Stern Memorial Trust**
Board of Advisory, PO Box 893
Pacific Palisades, CA 90272
Peter H. Hoffenberg, Member of the Board of
Advisors

Foundation Philosophy: The Board gives priority to the following areas: education, health and science, community service projects, youth, services to the physically and mentally disabled, the arts, and organizations and activities serving California. **Giving Priorities:** In fiscal 1993, the trust awarded approximately 27% of its total contributions to health concerns, including its highest grant of $60,000 to the Yale New Haven Hospital in New Haven, CT. Educational institutions received about 26%; social services, 20%; civic affairs, 10%; the arts, 8%; religious groups, 5%; and international organizations received the remaining funds. **Typical Health-Related Recipients:** AIDS/HIV, Arthritis, Clinics/Medical Centers, Domestic Violence, Emergency/Ambulance Services, Family Planning, Health Organizations, Hospitals, Kidney, Medical Education, Medical Research, Mental Health, Multiple Sclerosis, People with Disabilities, Prenatal Health Issues, Public Health, Research/Studies Institutes, Single-Disease Health Associations, Substance Abuse. **Geographic Distribution:** National, with an emphasis on California.

★491★ **Sierra Health Foundation**
2525 Natomes Pk. Dr., Ste. 200
Sacramento, CA 95833
Phone: (916)922-4755
Fax: (916)922-4024
Len McCandliss, President

Foundation Philosophy: The foundation focuses all funding on health-related programs in a twenty-six county region in Northern California. Although it funds a variety of projects, the foundation gives preference to three types of projects: ones which have a long-term impact on underserved populations; ones which provide a positive change in health care delivery; and ones which cause a positive change in the use of health care. During fiscal 1994, the foundation commenced a ten-year initiative focusing on improving children's health through strength-

ening families and communities. **Giving Priorities:** During fiscal 1994, the foundation gave all of its funding to health and health-related organizations. **Typical Health-Related Recipients:** Adolescent Health Issues, AIDS/HIV, Children's Health/Hospitals, Clinics/Medical Centers, Domestic Violence, Eyes/Blindness, Health Organizations, Health Policy/Cost Containment, Hospitals, Long-Term Care, Mental Health, Nursing Services, Outpatient Health Care, People with Disabilities, Prenatal Health Issues, Research/Studies Institutes, Single-Disease Health Associations, Trauma Treatment. **Geographic Distribution:** Focus on Northern California.

★492★ **Skillman Foundation**
333 W Fort St., Ste. 1350
Detroit, MI 48226
Phone: (313)961-8850
Leonard W. Smith, President

Foundation Philosophy: The foundation's purpose is to improve the well-being of residents of Southeastern Michigan and, in particular, the Detroit metropolitan area. Developing children and youth to their maximum potential is the foundation's primary goal. A central concern is meeting the needs of the disadvantaged. **Giving Priorities:** The foundation reports that in 1993 it gave 84% of its total contributions to its Children, Youth and Families program area, with major support to child and family welfare, child and family health, and education. Culture and the Arts program area received 8% of support, and Basic Human Needs program area received 6%. Strengthening Major Community Institutions and Out-Of-Program program areas each received 1% of funds. **Typical Health-Related Recipients:** Child Abuse, Children's Health/Hospitals, Domestic Violence, Family Planning, Health Organizations, Mental Health, Nursing Services, People with Disabilities, Public Health, Respiratory, Substance Abuse, Trauma Treatment. **Geographic Distribution:** Detroit area and Southeastern Michigan metropolitan.

★493★ **Smart Family Foundation**
15 Benders Dr.
Greenwich, CT 06831
Phone: (203)531-1474
Fax: (203)531-1558
Raymond Smart, President

Foundation Philosophy: The foundation funds a wide variety of projects across all major categories. **Giving Priorities:** In 1993, the foundation gave approximately 54% of total funding to education, including the foundation's highest grant of $500,000 to the Hyde Foundation. The arts and humanities received about 14% of giving. Health groups were awarded about 12% of funding; social services, 9%; religion, 5%; the environment, 3%; civic concerns, 1%; international affairs, 1%; and science, 1%. **Typical Health-Related Recipients:** Eyes/Blindness, Health Organizations, Hospitals, Medical Research, People with Disabilities, Research/Studies Institutes. **Geographic Distribution:** Broad geographic distribution.

★494★ Smith Richardson Foundation
60 Jesup Rd.
Westport, CT 06880
Phone: (203)222-6222
Fax: (203)222-6282
Peter L. Richardson, President

Foundation Philosophy: The foundation's main objective is to support public affairs programs promoting a vigorous economy and free society, primarily through funding public policy research projects and educational programs focusing on business and economics. The primary area of support for domestic public policy affairs continues to be law, law-related, and regulatory affairs. The foundation initiated a program concerned with children and families at risk of damage from persistent poverty. Funding is designed to "improve the lives and enhance development of these at-risk children and their families, through research, public policy, and direct action." **Giving Priorities:** In 1992, the foundation contributed 43% of its total funding to educational institutions, including a single $1.63 million grant to the Center for Creative Leadership. Civic groups received about 28% of support, primarily for public policy research. Health-care organizations, primarily the Cystic Fibrosis Foundation, received 17%. About 10% went to social services. The remaining funds went to religious organizations and international affairs. **Typical Health-Related Recipients:** Cancer, Domestic Violence, Health Policy/Cost Containment, Medical Education, Single-Disease Health Associations. **Geographic Distribution:** Primarily to national organizations; limited international giving.

★495★ Solon E. Summerfield Foundation
270 Madison Ave., Rm. 1201
New York, NY 10016
Phone: (212)685-5529
Clarence R. Treeger, President

Foundation Philosophy: Education receives the majority of support from the Solon E. Summerfield Foundation. Jewish organizations and groups concerned with blindness and visual impairment also receive large grants from the foundation. Almost 80% of the foundation's funds are set aside for these and other preselected organizations. Generally, for new proposals, the foundation makes smaller contributions to many organizations with a wide variety of interests. **Giving Priorities:** In 1992, the foundation gave 51% of its contributions to education, including the highest grant of $450,466 to Kansas State University, Lawrence, KS. Approximately 19% of support went to social services, with an emphasis on children's programs. Religious organizations received 14% of grants; health care, 12%; and the arts, 2%. The remaining 1% of support went to civic concerns. **Typical Health-Related Recipients:** Clinics/Medical Centers, Emergency/Ambulance Services, Eyes/Blindness, Hospitals, Long-Term Care, Medical Education, Mental Health, Nursing Services, People with Disabilities. **Geographic Distribution:** Nationally; emphasis on the Northeast, especially New York, NY.

★496★ Sosland Foundation
4800 Main St., No. 100
Kansas City, MO 64112-2504
Phone: (816)756-1000
Fax: (816)756-0494
Morton I. Sosland, President

Foundation Philosophy: The foundation supports a wide range of institutions, with at least half of the total awards going to Jewish philanthropies. The purpose of each grant "is to further the causes, whether they be civic, cultural, or religious, of each organization." **Giving Priorities:** In fiscal 1994, the foundation directed approximately 47% of total contributions to cultural organizations. Religious affairs, primarily Jewish concerns, received about 31%. Social welfare received 10%; health concerns, 7%; matching gifts, 3%; civic affairs, 2%. **Typical Health-Related Recipients:** AIDS/HIV, Children's Health/Hospitals, Clinics/Medical Centers, Emergency/Ambulance Services, Family Planning, Hospitals, Medical Rehabilitation, Mental Health. **Geographic Distribution:** Restricted to the metropolitan Kansas City, MO, area.

★497★ South Texas Charitable Foundation
PO Box 2549
Victoria, TX 77902
Phone: (512)573-4383
Rayford L. Keller, Secretary-Treasurer

Foundation Philosophy: The South Texas Charitable Foundation makes most of its grants to Christian religious organizations and social service organizations. Other interests include hospitals, religious education, community emergency services, and counseling. **Giving Priorities:** In fiscal 1993, the foundation gave approximately 41% of its total contributions to social service organizations, including its highest grant of $150,000 to the Covenant House Texas in Houston, TX. Religious interests received 23%; health concerns, 18%;; civic affairs, 16%; and educational institutions received the remaining funds. **Typical Health-Related Recipients:** Cancer, Children's Health/Hospitals, Domestic Violence, Emergency/Ambulance Services, Heart, Hospices, Hospitals, Long-Term Care, Sexual Abuse, Single-Disease Health Associations. **Geographic Distribution:** Focus on Texas.

★498★ Springs Foundation
PO Drawer 460
Lancaster, SC 29721
Phone: (803)286-2196
Fax: (803)286-3295
Charles A. Bundy, President

Foundation Philosophy: The foundation was established to improve the lives of people in areas where Springs Industries plants were located. Colonel Springs was particularly interested in young people and helping them develop their greatest potential. The categories the founder determined to be the most basic to the well-being of individuals were recreation, health care, education, community service, and religion. The foundation continues to give in these five areas. **Giving Priorities:** In 1993, the foundation gave approximately 74% of total contributions to social services, including the founda-

tion's highest grant of $725,000 to Leroy Springs and Company. Health concerns in South Carolina received about 12% of giving. Educational institutions received about 8% of funding. Environmental projects received about 2% of total funding; the arts and humanities, 2%; religion, 1%; civic concerns, 1%. **Typical Health-Related Recipients:** Cancer, Clinics/Medical Centers, Emergency/Ambulance Services, Health Organizations, Hospitals, Medical Education, Mental Health, Prenatal Health Issues, Substance Abuse. **Geographic Distribution:** Lancaster County, Chester Township of Chester County, and Fort Mill Township of York County, SC.

★499★ Stackpole-Hall Foundation
44 S Saint Marys St.
St. Marys, PA 15857
Phone: (814)834-1845
William C. Conrad, Executive Secretary

Foundation Philosophy: The foundation emphasizes local giving, with major priorities in the fields of education, social services, youth programs, and religious organizations. Educational support includes in-state universities, private education, and minority education funds. Some funding is given to civic causes, medical facilities, and the arts. **Giving Priorities:** In 1993, the foundation gave 37% of giving to civic causes, including the foundation's highest grant of $150,000, which went to the Elk County Development Foundation in St. Mary's, PA. Religion received 18% of giving; educational institutions, 14%; health care, 14%; social services, 13%; and the arts, 3%. **Typical Health-Related Recipients:** Emergency/Ambulance Services, Family Planning, Hospices, Hospitals, Medical Education, Mental Health, Nursing Services, People with Disabilities, Substance Abuse. **Geographic Distribution:** Focus on Elk County, PA, area.

★500★ Starr Foundation
70 Pine St.
New York, NY 10270
Phone: (212)770-6882
Fax: (212)425-6261
Mr. Ta Chun Hsu, President and Director

Foundation Philosophy: The foundation's initial activities "focused on education, particularly the provision of scholarships in the United States and Asia, and local assistance for international studies, community funds, and other civic organizations." This focus continued and grew through the 1970s. In 1980, the foundation added another area of funding: hospitals and health groups. The foundation's current interests are educational institutions and student aid. The foundation also funds health concerns, civic organizations, and cultural activities. **Giving Priorities:** In 1993, the foundation gave approximately 29% of its total contributions to health organizations, including its two highest grants of $6,250,000 each for New York Hospital and Cornell University Medical College. International organizations received about 23%; educational institutions, 19%; the arts, 16%; civic affairs, 7%; social services, 3%; religious causes, 2%; and environmental projects received the remaining funds. **Typical Health-Related Recipients:** AIDS/HIV, Cancer, Emergency/Ambulance Services, Family Planning, Geriatric Health, Health Organizations, Hospices, Hospitals, Medical Education, Medical Research, Medical Training, Nursing Services, People with Disabilities, Single-Disease Health Associations, Substance Abuse, Transplant Networks/Donor Banks. **Geographic Distribution:** National and international, with emphasis on metropolitan New York City.

★501★ Steele-Reese Foundation
c/o Davidson, Dawson and Clark
330 Madison Ave., 35th Fl.
New York, NY 10017
Phone: (212)557-7700
William T. Buice, III, Co-Trustee

Foundation Philosophy: The foundation has a strong preference for projects benefiting rural areas and those directly affecting the people served. **Giving Priorities:** In fiscal 1993, the foundation gave approximately 53% of giving to educational institutions, including the foundation's highest grant of $275,072 to Gonzaga University. Hospitals and health centers received about 13% of funding. Social services in Montana and Kentucky received approximately 12% of total contributions. Environmental projects received about 10% of total funding; civic concerns, 5%; science, 4%; the arts and humanities, 2%; and religion, 1%. **Typical Health-Related Recipients:** AIDS/HIV, Clinics/Medical Centers, Family Planning, Heart, Hospices, Hospitals, People with Disabilities, Single-Disease Health Associations, Substance Abuse, Transplant Networks/Donor Banks. **Geographic Distribution:** Primarily Southern Appalachia, particularly Kentucky; and the Northwest, particularly Idaho and surrounding states.

★502★ Stella and Charles Guttman Foundation
445 Park Ave., 19th Fl.
New York, NY 10022
Phone: (212)371-7082
Fax: (212)371-8936
Elizabeth Olofson, Executive Director

Foundation Philosophy: The foundation makes most of its grants in the areas of religion, social services, education, and health. Funding for health care favors breast diagnostic institutes, medical centers, and single-disease associations. **Giving Priorities:** In 1992, the foundation gave approximately 27% of its contributions to health concerns, including four grants totaling $100,000 for the Stella and Charles Guttman Breast Diagnostic Institute, New York, NY. Religion, mainly Jewish causes, received 24%. Educational institutions and social service organizations each received 19%. The arts received 7%, and civic and international affairs received the remaining funds. **Typical Health-Related Recipients:** AIDS/HIV, Alzheimers Disease, Cancer, Diabetes, Family Planning, Hospitals, Medical Education, Medical Research, People with Disabilities, Public Health, Single-Disease Health Associations. **Geographic Distribution:** Focus on the New York, NY, metropolitan area.

★503★ Stephen and Mary Birch Foundation
3650 Silverside Rd., Rm. 1048
Wilmington, DE 19810-5118
Patrick J. Patek, President

Foundation Philosophy: The foundation's support is focused on the areas of education, youth, culture, health, the arts, and social services. **Giving Priorities:** In 1991, the foundation gave 35% of funding to the Roman Catholic Bishop of San Diego, CA, in one grant of $600,000. The arts received about 29% of giving, with emphasis on the performing arts. Social services received 18%; health concerns, 10%; and educational institutions, 7%. The remaining funds were given to scientific organizations and civic causes. **Typical Health-Related Recipients:** Diabetes, Domestic Violence, Emergency/Ambulance Services, Heart, Hospitals, Hospitals (University Affiliated), Medical Education, Mental Health, Nursing Services, People with Disabilities, Single-Disease Health Associations, Substance Abuse. **Geographic Distribution:** No geographic restrictions.

★504★ Stewart Huston Charitable Trust
76 S First Ave.
Coatesville, PA 19320
Phone: (610)384-2666
Louis J. Beccaria, Executive Director

Foundation Philosophy: Forty percent of the foundation's funds are distributed to charitable organizations within a one hundred mile radius of Coatsville, PA. The balance is awarded to Trinitarian evangelical activities. **Giving Priorities:** In fiscal 1993, the foundation gave approximately 22% of its total contributions in support of the arts. Religious concerns received 19% of total giving, while social services received 18%. Educational programs were awarded about 17% of the distributed funds. Health care and international affairs each received 9% of the foundation's support, while civic affairs received 6%. **Typical Health-Related Recipients:** AIDS/HIV, Child Abuse, Family Planning, Medical Rehabilitation, Mental Health, Substance Abuse. **Geographic Distribution:** Pennsylvania and Georgia.

★505★ Stoddard Charitable Trust
370 Main St., 12th Fl.
Worcester, MA 01608
Phone: (508)798-8621
Fax: (508)791-1201
Warner S. Fletcher, Chairman

Foundation Philosophy: The trust does not have a fixed policy regarding the distribution of its funds. It makes grants to organizations in the areas of education, medicine, religion, science, social services, the arts, and civic affairs. Priorities among these areas are apt to vary significantly from year to year. **Giving Priorities:** In 1993, approximately 35% of total contributions went to educational institutions, including the foundation's highest grant of $325,000 to the Worchester Polytechnic Institute. Social services received about 30% of funding; the arts and humanities, 10%; civic concerns, 8%; science groups, 8%; health programs, 6%; environmental organizations, 3%; and religious institutions, 1%. **Typical Health-Related Recipients:** Children's Health/Hospitals, Clinics/

Medical Centers, Diabetes, Emergency/Ambulance Services, Family Planning, Health Organizations, People with Disabilities, Substance Abuse. **Geographic Distribution:** Worcester, MA, area.

★506★ Strake Foundation
712 Main St., Ste. 3300
Houston, TX 77002-3291
Phone: (713)216-2400
Fax: (713)216-2401
George W. Strake, Jr., President

Foundation Philosophy: The foundation makes grants "for public charitable, religious, educational and/or literary uses and purposes for the public good," in Texas. Grants are usually made for a brief period of time. They are frequently made to projects whose funding is shared with other contributors. **Giving Priorities:** In 1993, the foundation gave approximately 29% of its charitable contributions in support of education. Health care received about 26% of the support, including a $105,000 grant to St. Joseph Hospital Fund. The arts were awarded 13% of overall support, while religious affairs received 11%. Social service organizations received 9% of distributed funds, civic affairs received 8%. Science received 3% of support, while international affairs received 1%. **Typical Health-Related Recipients:** Cancer, Children's Health/Hospitals, Clinics/Medical Centers, Health Organizations, Hospices, Hospitals, Medical Education, Medical Rehabilitation, Medical Research, Mental Health, People with Disabilities, Single-Disease Health Associations, Substance Abuse. **Geographic Distribution:** Primarily Texas.

★507★ Stranahan Foundation
4149 Holland-Sylvania Rd.
Toledo, OH 43623
Phone: (419)882-6575
Fax: (419)882-2072
Charles G. Yeager, Director and Trustee

Foundation Philosophy: The foundation primarily supports educational institutions, social service organizations, and health organizations in Ohio. **Giving Priorities:** In 1993, the foundation awarded 44% of its contributions to educational institutions and organizations, primarily in higher education and in secondary education. Health concerns received 17% of funding; social services, 16%; religious organizations, 9%; civic and public affairs, 9%; arts and humanities, 6%. **Typical Health-Related Recipients:** Children's Health/Hospitals, Emergency/Ambulance Services, Geriatric Health, Hospitals, Medical Education, People with Disabilities. **Geographic Distribution:** Toledo, OH, area; some national giving.

★508★ Strauss Foundation
c/o Fildelity Bank, N.A.
Broad and Walnut Streets
Philadelphia, PA 19109
Phone: (215)985-8031
Judy Prendergast, Administrator

Foundation Philosophy: The Strauss Foundation makes grants across the major categories of support. In social services, interests include youth camps and youth organizations. Art support favors museums and art institutes. Healthcare funding supports medical centers, pediatrics, and research. Religious giving supports Jewish organizations and temples. The foundation also supports civic affairs. **Giving Priorities:** In 1993, the foundation gave approximately 36% of its contributions to religious organizations, including the highest grant of $75,000 to the Federation of Jewish Agencies. Social service organizations received 30%, including three grants totaling $100,000 to Camp Max Straus Foundation in Los Angeles, CA. Health care received 17% of funding; education, 7%; environmental concerns, 5%; the arts, 3%; and the remaining funds supported civic and international affairs. **Typical Health-Related Recipients:** AIDS/HIV, Alzheimers Disease, Cancer, Clinics/Medical Centers, Diabetes, Health Organizations, Hospitals, Medical Research, People with Disabilities, Single-Disease Health Associations, Transplant Networks/Donor Banks. **Geographic Distribution:** Focus on New York and California and, to a lesser extent, Pennsylvania.

★ 509 ★ **Sulzberger Foundation**
229 W 43rd St.
New York, NY 10036
Phone: (212)556-1750
Marian S. Heiskell, President

Foundation Philosophy: The Sulzberger Foundation makes most of its grants to environmental organizations, zoos and botanical gardens, the arts, and education. The foundation makes grants to other recipient areas on a limited basis. **Giving Priorities:** In 1993, the foundation gave approximately 22% of giving to educational institutions. The arts and humanities received about 18% of funding, primarily supporting museums and the performing arts. Environmental groups received about 14% of funds, including the foundation's highest grant of $86,500 to the Council on the Environment of New York City. Civic groups in New York City and Washington, DC, received about 12% of funding. International affairs received about 10% of total contributions; health centers, 9%; social services, 7%; religion, 6%; and science, 2%. **Typical Health-Related Recipients:** AIDS/HIV, Clinics/Medical Centers, Family Planning, Hospitals, Medical Education, Medical Research, Single-Disease Health Associations. **Geographic Distribution:** National.

★ 510 ★ **Swalm Foundation**
8707 Katy Fwy., Ste. 300
Houston, TX 77024
Phone: (713)464-1321
Jo Beth Camp Swalm, President

Foundation Philosophy: The Swalm Foundation makes most of its grants in the areas of social services and health care. Social service interests include youth organizations, retirement centers, family services, and drug counseling and rehabilitation. Funding for health care favors rehabilitation centers, mental health, and hospices. The foundation also provides scholarships for dyslexic students. **Giving Priorities:** In fiscal 1993, the foundation gave approximately 67% of its total contributions to social services, including its highest grant of $77,850 to the Wesley Community Center. Health concerns received about 17%; educational institutions and

programs, 14%; and civic affairs and international organizations received the remaining funds. **Typical Health-Related Recipients:** Clinics/Medical Centers, Emergency/Ambulance Services, Hospices, Hospitals, Mental Health, People with Disabilities, Substance Abuse. **Geographic Distribution:** Focus on Texas.

★ 511 ★ **T. L. L. Temple Foundation**
109 Temple Blvd.
Lufkin, TX 75901
Phone: (409)639-5197
Fax: (409)634-3333
Phillip M. Leach, Executive Director

Foundation Philosophy: The T. L. L. Temple Foundation looks favorably upon educational institutions located in the East Texas Pine Timber Belt area. The foundation also supports healthcare and human services, civic and public affairs, and provides limited funding for the arts. **Giving Priorities:** In fiscal 1993, the foundation awarded 38% of its funding to health care organizations, including grants of $1,000,000 each to St. Michael's Hospital Foundation and the University of Texas M.D. Anderson Cancer Center. Educational institutions received 26% of funds, including a $1,250,000 grant to the Diboll Independent School District. Support to social services totaled 16%. The arts and civic and public affairs each received 7% of support, while religious organizations received 4%. The remaining amount, less than 1%, went to support environmental concerns. **Typical Health-Related Recipients:** Alzheimers Disease, Cancer, Children's Health/Hospitals, Clinics/Medical Centers, Domestic Violence, Emergency/Ambulance Services, Eyes/Blindness, Family Planning, Health Organizations, Hospices, Hospitals, Hospitals (University Affiliated), Kidney, Medical Education, Medical Rehabilitation, Medical Research, Mental Health, People with Disabilities, Substance Abuse, Transplant Networks/Donor Banks. **Geographic Distribution:** Primarily to the East Texas Pine Timber Belt area.

★ 512 ★ **Ted Mann Foundation**
10100 Santa Monica Blvd., Ste. 900
Los Angeles, CA 90067
Phone: (310)284-8528
Fax: (310)551-0604
David Sarver, Financial Advisor

Foundation Philosophy: The foundation gives to broad purposes, with emphasis on educational organizations, health care, and youth welfare. **Giving Priorities:** In fiscal 1993, the foundation gave approximately 25% to the arts, including the highest grant of $500,000 awarded to the University of Minnesota Foundation School of Music. Health care received 23% of total contributions. The Rhonda Fleming Mann Resource Center for Women with Cancer at the University of California at Los Angeles received a $450,000 grant. Civic and public affairs received 13%, and international organizations received 12% of giving. Educational institutions received 11% of funding and religious organizations received 9%. About 7% of contributions were awarded to social services. **Typical Health-Related Recipients:** Cancer, Clinics/Medical Centers, Diabetes, Hospitals, Medical Re-

search, Preventive Medicine/Wellness Organizations, Single-Disease Health Associations, Speech & Hearing. **Geographic Distribution:** No geographic restrictions.

★ 513 ★ **Temple Hoyne Buell Foundation**
2700 E Hampden Ave.
Englewood, CO 80110
Phone: (303)761-1717
Fax: (303)761-2408
Richard P. Koeppe, Executive Director

Foundation Philosophy: "The foundation's principal purposes are enhancing the education of youth, research for improving treatment of diseases, and assistance for organizations whose goals are to provide continuing and long-term solutions for the welfare of the citizens of Colorado." **Giving Priorities:** In fiscal 1993, the arts, including the performing arts and architecture, received 48% of the grants. Health foundations were given 16%. Colleges and universities received 31%; the remaining funds went to civic and social concerns. **Typical Health-Related Recipients:** Children's Health/Hospitals, Heart, Hospitals, Preventive Medicine/Wellness Organizations, Single-Disease Health Associations. **Geographic Distribution:** Focus on Colorado.

★ 514 ★ **Thelma Doelger Charitable Trust**
950 John Daly Blvd., Ste. 300
Daly City, CA 94015
Phone: (415)755-2333
Edward M. King, Trustee

Foundation Philosophy: The trust traditionally supports California zoos and humane societies with large grants. **Giving Priorities:** In fiscal 1993, the trust gave approximately 50% of its contributions to scientific research projects, including its highest grant of $400,000 for Primarily Primates, San Antonio, TX. Social service organizations, including senior services and animal protection groups, received 34%. Health concerns received 9% of giving. The arts received 6%, in the form of a single grant of $50,000 for the Coyote Point Museum, San Francisco, CA. Religion and civic affairs received the remainder. **Typical Health-Related Recipients:** Clinics/Medical Centers, Hospitals. **Geographic Distribution:** Focus on the San Francisco Bay area, CA.

★ 515 ★ **Theodore H. Barth Foundation**
45 Rockefeller Plaza, 20th Fl.
New York, NY 10111
Irving P. Berelson, President

Foundation Philosophy: The foundation's interests focus on higher education, including scholarships, health and hospitals, conservation, Lutheran churches, youth organizations, and the arts. **Giving Priorities:** In 1993, the foundation gave approximately 40% of its funding to the arts, including support for opera, ballet, symphony, libraries, and museums. Health care received 24% of giving; social services, 12%; civic affairs, 9%; education, 9%; and religious organizations, 4%. The remaining funds supported international and environmental affairs. **Typical Health-Related Recipients:** Clinics/Medical Centers, Health Funds, Health Organizations, Hospices, Hospitals, Nursing Services, People with Disabilities, Research/Studies Institutes, Single-Disease Health Associations, Speech & Hearing, Transplant Networks/Donor Banks. **Geographic Distribution:** Primarily New York and Massachusetts.

★516★ **Thomas and Agnes Carvel Foundation**
35 E Grassy Sprain Rd.
Yonkers, NY 10710
Phone: (914)793-7300
Fax: (914)793-7381
Robert Davis, President

Foundation Philosophy: The Thomas and Agnes Carvel Foundation makes most of its grants in the areas of health care and education. Health-care funding favors cancer research, hospitals, and pediatric care. Funding for education emphasizes private secondary schools and religious education. **Giving Priorities:** In fiscal 1993, the foundation gave 62% of its funding to health concerns, including the highest grant of $540,000 to St. Josephs Hospital. The arts received 16% of funding. A local school district received about 13% of support. The remaining 9% of funds supported a religious diocese scholarship fund. **Typical Health-Related Recipients:** Children's Health/Hospitals, Clinics/Medical Centers, Emergency/Ambulance Services, Hospitals, Medical Research, Nutrition, Single-Disease Health Associations, Transplant Networks/Donor Banks. **Geographic Distribution:** New York, with a focus on Westchester County.

★517★ **Thomas Anthony Pappas Charitable Foundation**
PO Box 463
Belmont, MA 02178-0463
Phone: (617)862-2802
Betsy Pappas, Vice President, Clerk

Foundation Philosophy: The foundation makes most of its grants in the areas of health, education, and the arts. Health interests include hospitals and single disease associations. Educational funding favors dental schools, universities, technology, and law. Arts support goes to performing arts centers. **Giving Priorities:** In 1993, the foundation gave 35% of its funding to education, including support for colleges and specialized schools. About 21% went to health services, including hospitals, nursing, and single-disease health associations. The arts received 17% with major support to the Kravis Center for Performing Arts with a grant of $50,000. Social services received 12%; civic affairs, 8%; religious organizations, 4%; and science, 3%. **Typical Health-Related Recipients:** Alzheimers Disease, Cancer, Children's Health/Hospitals, Clinics/Medical Centers, Eyes/Blindness, Health Organizations, Hospices, Hospitals, Kidney, Medical Education, Nursing Services, People with Disabilities, Research/Studies Institutes, Single-Disease Health Associations, Substance Abuse. **Geographic Distribution:** Focus on Massachusetts.

★518★ **Thomas and Dorothy Leavey Foundation**
4680 Wilshire Blvd.
Los Angeles, CA 90010
Phone: (213)930-4252
J. Thomas McCarthy, Chairman and Trustee

Foundation Philosophy: The foundation originally was established to provide college scholarships. They have broadened their grant-making program to include medical research, churches, and civic groups. **Giving Priorities:** In 1993, the foundation awarded 48% of its total contributions to educational institutions. About 21% of funds went to religious organizations. Health care received 18% of support; civic groups, 5%; social services, 4%; and the arts, 2%. The remaining funds went to international groups and scientific organizations. **Typical Health-Related Recipients:** Children's Health/Hospitals, Clinics/Medical Centers, Domestic Violence, Family Planning, Health Funds, Health Organizations, Hospitals, Medical Education, Nursing Services, People with Disabilities, Prenatal Health Issues, Substance Abuse. **Geographic Distribution:** Primarily California, with special emphasis on the Los Angeles metropolitan area.

★519★ **Thomas F. and Kate Miller Jeffress Memorial Trust**
c/o NationsBank, N.A., Trust Div.
PO Box 26903
Richmond, VA 23261
Phone: (804)788-2964
Fax: (804)788-2700
J. Samuel Gillespie, Jr., Director

Foundation Philosophy: "The purpose of the Jeffress Trust is to support research in chemical, medical, and other scientific fields through grants to non-profit educational and research institutions in the Commonwealth of Virginia. Grants are given to assist scientists in such institutions to conduct investigations in the natural sciences." **Giving Priorities:** In fiscal 1992, the foundation gave 100% of its funds to scientific research. Those funded included Virginia colleges, universities, and research institutes. **Typical Health-Related Recipients:** Medical Education. **Geographic Distribution:** Virginia institutions only.

★520★ **Thomas J. Emery Memorial**
c/o Frost and Jacobs
2500 PNC Center
Cincinnati, OH 45202
Phone: (513)621-3124
Fax: (513)651-6981
Henry W. Hobson, Jr., President

Foundation Philosophy: The memorial makes grants across the major categories of support. In social services, interests include united funds, homes, youth organizations, the disabled, child welfare, and community centers. Educational funding favors universities, high schools, day schools, and nursery schools in Cincinnati. Arts support goes to art institutes, museums, and public broadcasting. Health funding includes children's hospitals and hospices. The memorial also makes grants to other recipient areas. **Giving Priorities:** In 1993, the memorial awarded 28% of its total contributions to educational institutions, including its largest gift of $125,000 to Cincinnati Scholarship Foundation. The arts in Cincinnati, OH, received 26% of funding; social services, 19%; civic groups, 14%; and health care, 7%. About 5% went to religious organizations. The remaining funds went to environmental concerns. **Typical Health-Related Recipients:** Diabetes, Domestic Violence, Family Planning, Health Organizations, Hospices,

Hospitals, Medical Rehabilitation, Mental Health, People with Disabilities, Research/Studies Institutes, Transplant Networks/Donor Banks. **Geographic Distribution:** Focus on Ohio.

★521★ **Thompson Charitable Foundation**
PO Box 10516
Knoxville, TN 37939-0516
Phone: (615)588-0491
Monica Luke, Administrative Manager

Foundation Philosophy: The foundation's primary focus is health and human services, including hospitals and clinics. Major funding also supports capital campaigns and renovation projects for educational institutions. In addition, support is also given to religious and civic concerns. **Giving Priorities:** In fiscal 1993, the foundation gave approximately 52% of total funding to educational institutions, including the highest grant of $536,875 to the Oneida Special School District for the completion of a high school, gym, middle school, and cafeteria. Health services received 24%; religious organizations, 10%; and civic affairs and social services each received 7%. **Typical Health-Related Recipients:** Cancer, Children's Health/Hospitals, Clinics/Medical Centers, Geriatric Health, Hospitals, Nursing Services, Prenatal Health Issues. **Geographic Distribution:** Focus on Knox, Anderson, Scott, and Blount Counties in Tennessee; Bell, Clay, Laurel, and Leslie Counties in Kentucky; and Buchanan and Tazewell Counties in Virginia.

★522★ **Tisch Foundation**
667 Madison Ave.
New York, NY 10021
Phone: (212)545-2930
Fax: (212)545-2983
E. Jack Beatus, Secretary and Treasurer

Foundation Philosophy: The foundation emphasizes higher education and research programs. It supports Jewish organizations and welfare funds, museums, and secondary schools. It also supports institutions in Israel. **Giving Priorities:** In 1993, approximately 51% of giving went to health organizations, with the highest grant of $2,000,000 awarded to New York University's Tisch Hospital. About 18% went to religious causes, while 11% went to the arts. International concerns received 9% of total funding; social services, 5%; educational institutions, 4%; and civic and environmental affairs received the remaining funds. **Typical Health-Related Recipients:** AIDS/HIV, Cancer, Children's Health/Hospitals, Clinics/Medical Centers, Diabetes, Emergency/Ambulance Services, Family Planning, Health Funds, Hospitals, Medical Education, Medical Research, People with Disabilities, Single-Disease Health Associations. **Geographic Distribution:** National, with emphasis on New York City.

★523★ **Trull Foundation**
404 Fourth St.
Palacios, TX 77465
Phone: (512)972-5241
Colleen Claybourn, Executive Director

Foundation Philosophy: During the approximately forty years of its existence, the Trull Foundation has funded a wide range of educational, religious, cultural, and social programs. It has an affinity for organizations supporting Presbyterian interests and projects within Texas. The foundation strives to improve the quality of life for individuals, especially the disadvantaged. Three current priorities established to forward its mission are the needs of the Palacios area, advocacy of good conditions for pre-adolescents, aid for Mexican-Americans oppressed by discrimination, and help for those with chemical or alcohol dependencies. **Giving Priorities:** In 1993, the foundation reported that it gave approximately 40% of its funding to social service groups. Educational institutions received 21% of giving. International projects received 15%; the arts and humanities, 9%; and religious organizations, 8%. The remaining funds were given to health care, 5%, and civic policy, 1%. **Typical Health-Related Recipients:** AIDS/HIV, Cancer, Domestic Violence, Family Planning, Medical Education, Mental Health, Nutrition, Preventive Medicine/Wellness Organizations, Substance Abuse. **Geographic Distribution:** Primarily Texas area, but no geographic restrictions.

★ 524 ★ Tull Charitable Foundation
Hurt Bldg.
50 Hurt Plz., Ste. 1245
Atlanta, GA 30303
Phone: (404)659-7079
Barbara Cleveland, Executive Director

Foundation Philosophy: The primary focus of the foundation is to respond to needs, particularly in the Atlanta metropolitan area, and in Georgia. The foundation's areas of primary interest are education, health and human services, youth development, and the arts. **Giving Priorities:** In 1994, approximately 42% of funding went to educational institutions; 18% to social services; and 15% to civic and public affairs; 11% to the arts; 10% to health organizations; 4% to religious organizations. The remaining funds went to international concerns. **Typical Health-Related Recipients:** Children's Health/Hospitals, Emergency/Ambulance Services, Eyes/Blindness, Health Organizations, Hospitals, Long-Term Care, Medical Research, Nursing Services, People with Disabilities, Single-Disease Health Associations, Substance Abuse. **Geographic Distribution:** Restricted to Georgia.

★ 525 ★ Turner Charitable Foundation
811 Rusk, Ste. 205
Houston, TX 77002
Phone: (713)237-1117
Fax: (713)223-4638
Eyvonne Moser, Asst. Sec. and Asst. Treas.

Foundation Philosophy: The Turner Charitable Foundation makes grants primarily in the areas of social services, the arts, and civic affairs. Social service funding favors recreation, youth organizations, the disabled, and child welfare. Funding for the arts includes opera, ballet, theater, and music. Civic affairs interests include housing, zoos, and emergency services. The foundation funds other recipient areas on a limited basis. **Giving Priorities:** In fiscal 1994, the foundation gave 31% of funding to the arts, including the highest grant of $166,667 to the Museum of Fine Arts in Houston, TX. About 23%

of contributions were given to educational institutions, primarily in Texas. Social services received 19%; religious organizations, 17%; health care, 7%; and civic and international affairs received the remainder. **Typical Health-Related Recipients:** Cancer, Children's Health/Hospitals, Clinics/Medical Centers, Emergency/Ambulance Services, Eyes/Blindness, Family Planning, Hospices, Hospitals, Medical Education, Medical Research, Mental Health, People with Disabilities, Single-Disease Health Associations, Substance Abuse. **Geographic Distribution:** Restricted to Texas.

★ 526 ★ Valley Foundation
16450 Los Gatos Blvd., Ste. 210
Los Gatos, CA 95032
Phone: (408)292-1124
Fax: (408)971-7107
Ervie L. Smith, Executive Director

Foundation Philosophy: Medical services and health care for lower income households within Santa Clara County, CA, are the foundation's highest priorities. More than one-half of its grants will primarily fund research, social services, and higher education in the medical and health care field. Other areas that receive funding from the foundation include youth, the arts, seniors, and general medical care. **Giving Priorities:** In fiscal 1994, the foundation reported that health care received 33% including support for research on Parkinson's disease, pediatric health, and a capital grant for a medical center's expansion. Approximately 28% of contributions were awarded to social services. Interests included the disabled, community centers, food for the needy, and youth organizations. Education received 20% of contributions, with support going to health-related education. The arts and humanities received 18%, primarily in the areas of music, theater, and arts organizations. **Typical Health-Related Recipients:** Adolescent Health Issues, Children's Health/Hospitals, Clinics/Medical Centers, Emergency/Ambulance Services, Health Funds, Health Organizations, Hospices, Medical Education, Medical Research, Mental Health, People with Disabilities, Public Health, Single-Disease Health Associations, Substance Abuse. **Geographic Distribution:** Restricted to Santa Clara County, CA.

★ 527 ★ Van Houten Memorial Fund
c/o First Fidelity Bank, N.A.
765 Broad St.
Newark, NJ 07102
Phone: (201)430-4533
Fax: (201)430-4519
James S. Hohn, Vice President

Foundation Philosophy: The Van Houten Memorial Fund makes most of its grants in the areas of health, education, social services, and children's services. Health care funding favors hospitals and health foundations. Funding for education supports scholarships for medicine and dentistry training. In social services, interests include children's homes, child welfare, and youth organizations. Health and human services are funded in Bergen and Passaic counties only. Children's services and organizations and medical and dental scholarships and fund-

ed statewide. **Giving Priorities:** In fiscal 1993, the foundation contributed 60% of its funds to health services. The foundation's largest gift in the health services, $75,000, went to St. Joseph's Hospital in Paterson, NJ. Other recipients included hospitals and health foundations. Higher education received 25% of the giving, including a contribution of $134,910 to the University of Medicine and Dentistry Foundation. Social services received 10% of the funds, with emphasis on children's aid. The remaining 5% supported religious organizations and civic affairs. **Typical Health-Related Recipients:** Cancer, Children's Health/Hospitals, Clinics/Medical Centers, Family Planning, Geriatric Health, Hospitals, Hospitals (University Affiliated), Medical Education, Medical Rehabilitation, Medical Research, Mental Health, Multiple Sclerosis, Prenatal Health Issues, Respiratory, Single-Disease Health Associations. **Geographic Distribution:** Bergen and Passaic counties, NJ, only; except children's programs are funded statewide. **Formerly:** Van Houten Charitable Trust.

★ 528 ★ Victor E. Speas Foundation
c/o Boatmen's First National Bank of Kansas City
PO Box 419038
Kansas City, MO 64183
Phone: (816)221-2800
David P. Ross, Senior Vice President

Foundation Philosophy: The foundation focuses on health and social service programs. It emphasizes the improvement of health-related services in the greater Kansas City metropolitan area. **Giving Priorities:** In 1993, the foundation awarded 56% of its total contributions to social service organizations, including a single $100,000 grant to Open Options, Kansas City, MO. About 14% of funds went to civic groups. Health care received 12% of support; educational institutions, 10%; religious organizations, 6%; and the arts, 2%. **Typical Health-Related Recipients:** Cancer, Children's Health/Hospitals, Emergency/Ambulance Services, Geriatric Health, Health Funds, Health Organizations, Hospitals, Medical Education, Medical Rehabilitation, Mental Health, Nursing Services, Nutrition, People with Disabilities, Public Health, Single-Disease Health Associations, Speech & Hearing, Substance Abuse, Trauma Treatment. **Geographic Distribution:** Metropolitan Kansas City, MO.

★ 529 ★ Vira I. Heinz Endowment
30 CNG Tower
625 Liberty Ave.
Pittsburgh, PA 15222
Phone: (412)281-5777
Fax: (412)281-5788
Frank Tugwell, Executive Director

Foundation Philosophy: The Vira I. Heinz Endowment supports initiatives in the broad areas of human services, arts and humanities, economic development, education, health, nutrition, and religion. The endowment is particularly concerned with providing aid to the victims in society, including the victims of domestic violence and child abuse; children at risk of becoming school dropouts; and young potential candidates for delinquency, drug and alcohol abuse, teen pregnancy, and suicide. The endowment also supports programs for the elderly, especially programs that link health care to social services, that exhibit innovative ways to deliver needed services, and that explore the problems of caring for the elderly by their families. **Giving Priorities:** In 1993, the endowment gave approximately 30% of its contributions to the arts, including the largest grant of $850,000 to the Carnegie Institute's Museum of Art in Pittsburgh, to support the Andy Warhol Museum. Civic affairs programs received 27% of giving, including a grant for $750,000 to the Forbes Fund. Education programs received 14% of support, while social services received 12%. Environmental affairs and health care programs each received 6% of support, with 3% going to international affairs. Religious organizations and science programs each received 1% of funding. **Typical Health-Related Recipients:** Cancer, Children's Health/Hospitals, Domestic Violence, Family Planning, Geriatric Health, Health Policy/Cost Containment, Hospitals, Medical Education, Medical Research, Mental Health, Sexual Abuse, Single-Disease Health Associations, Substance Abuse. **Geographic Distribution:** Primarily western Pennsylvania.

★ 530 ★ **W. K. Kellogg Foundation**
c/o Manager of Grant Proposals
One Michigan Ave. E
Battle Creek, MI 49017-4058
Phone: (616)968-1611
Fax: (616)968-0413

Foundation Philosophy: Most foundation grants are awarded in the areas of higher education; youth development; leadership; philanthropy and volunteerism; integrated, comprehensive health care systems; food systems; and rural development. **Giving Priorities:** In fiscal 1994, the foundation reported that it gave approximately 25% to health care. Higher education and youth development received 20%; philanthropy and volunteerism, 19%; and agriculture and rural development received 11%. Leadership was awarded 11%; special opportunities, 7%; foundation-administered programs, 4%; general programs, 1%; emergent programming, 1%; and economic development in Michigan, 1%. **Typical Health-Related Recipients:** Clinics/Medical Centers, Geriatric Health, Health Organizations, Health Policy/Cost Containment, Hospices, Hospitals, Medical Education, Medical Training, Mental Health, Nursing Services, Nutrition, People with Disabilities, Prenatal Health Issues, Public Health, Research/Studies Institutes. **Geographic Distribution:** International (primarily Latin America, the Caribbean, and Southern Africa) and national.

★ 531 ★ **W. M. Keck Foundation**
555 S Flower St., Ste. 3230
Los Angeles, CA 90071
Phone: (213)680-3833
Fax: (213)614-0934
Joan F. DuBois, Program Vice President

Foundation Philosophy: The foundation has designated four specific areas of funding: the Science and Engineering in Higher Education Program; the Medical Research, Medical Education, and Liberal Arts Program; the Southern California Program; and the Law and Legal Ad-

ministration Program. Concentration is placed upon strengthening studies and programs in institutions of higher education in the areas of earth science, engineering, general science, medical education, medical research, law, and the liberal arts. Some consideration, focused primarily in Southern California, is given to organizations in the categories of arts and culture, civic and community affairs, health care and hospitals, and precollegiate education. **Giving Priorities:** In 1993, the foundation reported that it gave approximately 42% of its total funding to the Science and Engineering in Higher Education Program. The Medical Research/Education and Liberal Arts Program received 35%, the Southern California Program received about 15%, and the Law and Legal Administration Program received 8%. Approximately 57% of the grants supported capital projects, such as equipment, construction, and renovation. Education and research institutions received about 85% of total funding, the majority of which went to science and medical research. Arts and cultural groups received 6%; community services agencies, 4%; precollegiate education, 3%; and health organizations, 2%. **Typical Health-Related Recipients:** Clinics/Medical Centers, Geriatric Health, Hospitals, Medical Education, Medical Rehabilitation, Medical Research, People with Disabilities, Speech & Hearing. **Geographic Distribution:** National for scientific and medical programs, and law and liberal arts; Southern California for arts, hospitals, precollegiate education, and human services.

★ 532 ★ **W. W. Smith Charitable Trust**
101 Bryn Mawr Ave., Ste. 200
Bryn Mawr, PA 19010
Phone: (610)525-9667
Fax: (610)525-1239
Camie A. Morrison, Administrator

Foundation Philosophy: The trust supports four specific programs in the Delaware Valley: research projects for heart disease, cancer, and AIDS; hospital indigent medical care; food, clothing, and shelter for children and the aged; and college finanical aid. The trust funds research projects for heart disease, cancer, and AIDS that are new or are conducted by investigators before they have qualified for larger National Institutes of Health grants. In its program to provide medical care for the poor and needy, the trust supports hospitals in the cities of Chester and Philadelphia, with an explicit policy of accepting patients with no ability to pay. **Giving Priorities:** In fiscal 1993, the trust gave approximately 40% of its contributions to basic medical research for heart disease, cancer, and AIDS, and 30% to college financial aid. Programs that provide food, clothing, and shelter for children and the aged received 20% of the foundation's grants, and hospital indigent medical care received 10%. **Typical Health-Related Recipients:** Geriatric Health, Health Organizations, Hospitals, Medical Research, Nursing Services, People with Disabilities. **Geographic Distribution:** Delaware Valley area.

★ 533 ★ **Wallace Alexander Gerbode Foundation**
470 Columbus Avenue, Ste. 209
San Francisco, CA 94133-3930
Phone: (415)391-0911
Thomas C. Layton, Executive Director

Foundation Philosophy: Major interests and priorities include the arts and culture, the environment, population, reproductive rights, citizen participation in the building of communities, the strength of the philanthropic process, and media projects relating to these issues. **Giving Priorities:** In 1993, the foundation reported that approximately 36% of total giving went to community affairs. About 22% of giving was awarded to the arts and humanities, while environmental concerns received 14%. Education was given about 11%, health-related organizations were awarded 7%, and international and social services giving each constituted 5% of total giving. **Typical Health-Related Recipients:** Children's Health/Hospitals, Family Planning, Long-Term Care, People with Disabilities. **Geographic Distribution:** In Alameda, Contra Costa, Marin, San Francisco, and San Mateo counties, CA, and the state of Hawaii.

★ 534 ★ **Wallace Genetic Foundation**
4900 Massachusetts Ave., NW, Ste. 220
Washington, DC 20016
Phone: (202)966-2932
Polly Lawrence, Research Secretary

Foundation Philosophy: Grants are almost entirely limited to organizations associated with the personal interests of present or former trustees which include agricultural research, preservation of farmland, ecology, conservation and sustainable development. **Giving Priorities:** As in years past, each of the three trustees gave approximately one-third of the grant money according to their individual interests: women, population, and environment; sustainable agriculture, farmland preservation, and other environmental issues; agricultural, health, and cancer research. Where these interests overlap, the trustees consult and coordinate giving. Actual 1993 percentages are as follows: international affairs, 27%; the environment, 27%; education, 21%; health care, 13%; civic affairs, 7%; science, 4%; and less than 1% was awarded to social services and religion. **Typical Health-Related Recipients:** Cancer, Clinics/Medical Centers, Health Organizations, Heart, Medical Education, Medical Research, Nutrition, Respiratory, Single-Disease Health Associations. **Geographic Distribution:** National, international; no geographic restrictions.

★ 535 ★ **Walter and Elise Haas Fund**
One Lombard St., Ste. 305
San Francisco, CA 94111
Phone: (415)398-4474
Fax: (415)986-4779
Bruce R. Sievers, Exec. Dir., Sec. and Treas.

Foundation Philosophy: The fund supports a wide variety of programs and activities, primarily in the San Francisco Bay area. According to Rhoda H. Goldman, daughter of Walter and Elise Haas and president of the fund, "we are interested in local programs which promise expansion of access to human services and public affairs, to the arts, humanities, and education."

Giving Priorities: The fund reported that in 1994 it gave about 30% of its total contributions to support education, with 24% of support to the arts; and 19% to special projects. Human services programs received 14% of funds, the humanities received 6%, and civic affairs groups received 3%. Health care programs received 2% of donations, while the remaining support was divided between environmental affairs and citizenship programs. **Typical Health-Related Recipients:** Children's Health/Hospitals, Diabetes, Domestic Violence, Family Planning, Health Organizations, Hospitals, Mental Health, People with Disabilities, Prenatal Health Issues, Public Health, Substance Abuse. **Geographic Distribution:** Primarily San Francisco, with consideration given to projects in Alameda, Marin, and San Mateo counties.

★ 536 ★ **Washington Square Health Foundation**
875 N Michigan Ave., Ste. 3516
Chicago, IL 60611
Phone: (312)664-6488
Fax: (312)664-7787
Howard Nochumson, Executive Director

Foundation Philosophy: The Washington Square Health Foundation makes grants and program related investments "in order to promote and maintain access to adequate health care for all people in the Chicagoland area regardless of race, sex, creed, or financial need. The foundation meets this goal through its grants for medical and nursing scholarships, medical research, and direct health care services." The foundation plans to place an increased emphasis on primary care and alternate health-care delivery systems. **Giving Priorities:** In fiscal 1994, the foundation reported that it awarded all of its contributions to health care. Specifically, 31% of the funds went to health services; 28% supported purchases of medical equipment; 24% funded medical and nursing education; and 17% went to medical research. **Typical Health-Related Recipients:** AIDS/HIV, Clinics/Medical Centers, Health Organizations, Hospitals, Medical Education, Medical Research, People with Disabilities, Sexual Abuse. **Geographic Distribution:** Focus on the Chicago, IL, area.

★ 537 ★ **Wasserman Foundation**
c/o Musick, Peeler & Garrett
One Wilshire Blvd., No. 2000
Los Angeles, CA 90017
Phone: (213)629-7635
William J. Bird, Vice President

Foundation Philosophy: The foundation generally supports arts groups, educational institutions, religious groups, and medical research. **Giving Priorities:** In 1992, the foundation gave approximately 36% of its contributions to education, including its largest grant of $1,035,754 to the University of California at Los Angeles. Approximately 20% of support was awarded to the arts, including a grant of $498,750 to the Motion Picture and Television Fund. Health, civic affairs, and religion each received 14% of total donations made. Social services and international affairs each received approximately 1% of funds awarded. **Typical Health-Related Recipients:** AIDS/HIV, Emergency/Ambulance

Services, Eyes/Blindness, Hospitals, Medical Education, Medical Research, Multiple Sclerosis, People with Disabilities, Single-Disease Health Associations, Speech & Hearing. **Geographic Distribution:** Primarily Los Angeles, CA, and New York, NY, areas.

★ 538 ★ **Wayne and Gladys Valley Foundation**
1939 Harrison St. No. 510
Oakland, CA 94612
Phone: (510)466-6060
Fax: (510)466-6067
Stephen M. Chandler, President and Executive Director

Foundation Philosophy: The foundation has established four areas of interest. The areas include the following: Education, including public and private universities' research programs in oceanography, eye diseases, vascular defects, learning disabilities, and physical or mental afflictions affecting children and young adults; Medical Research concerning the above mentioned health-related programs; Community and Social Services (generally limited to smaller grants to East Bay area projects serving youth or provided by Catholic hospitals, social services, or health care groups); and Special Projects, which provides the foundation with flexibility in its grant program for worthy projects. **Giving Priorities:** In fiscal 1993, the foundation gave approximately 72% of its contributions to education, including support for Catholic primary and secondary schools in the East Bay, CA, area. Education also received the foundation's highest grant of $2,000,000, which was awarded to the University of California Berkeley. Health care received 12%. Interests included hospital foundations and medical research. Religious organizations were awarded 9% of total giving; social services, 3%; the arts, 2%; and civic affairs, 2%. Science received less than 1%. **Typical Health-Related Recipients:** Alzheimers Disease, Eyes/Blindness, Health Organizations, Hospitals, Medical Research, Mental Health, People with Disabilities, Research/Studies Institutes. **Geographic Distribution:** Focus on East Bay, CA, which includes Alameda, Contra Costa, and Santa Clara counties.

★ 539 ★ **Weingart Foundation**
PO Box 17982
Los Angeles, CA 90017-0982
Phone: (213)688-7799
Fax: (213)481-1004
John G. Ouellet, Pres. and Chief Admin. Off.

Foundation Philosophy: Overall, the foundation emphasizes programs and projects that address the prevention rather than the consequences of social problems affecting children and youth. The foundation generally has supported organizations and programs involved in education, social services, health care, and public policy. The degree of emphasis in each area is reviewed annually; the foundation is anticipating an increased emphasis on grants for youth under the age of 18. **Giving Priorities:** In fiscal 1994, the foundation gave approximately 32% of its contributions to education, primarily to support colleges and universities, including those institutions participating in the Weingart student loan program. Health care received

about 28%, including the foundation's highest grant of $2,500,000 to the American Red Cross, Los Angeles Chapter, for Northridge earthquake relief. Social services, mainly youth organizations such as the YMCA and the Boy Scouts, received 23% of giving. The arts received 9%, with major support for libraries, museums, and galleries. Religious concerns (7%) and civic affairs (1%) received the remaining funds. **Typical Health-Related Recipients:** Cancer, Child Abuse, Children's Health/Hospitals, Clinics/Medical Centers, Emergency/Ambulance Services, Health Organizations, Hospices, Hospitals, Medical Education, Medical Research, Nursing Services, Outpatient Health Care, People with Disabilities, Prenatal Health Issues, Substance Abuse. **Geographic Distribution:** Nine counties in Southern California.

★ 540 ★ **Welfare Foundation**
1004 Wilmington Trust Center
Wilmington, DE 19801
Phone: (302)654-2477
David Wakefield, Executive Secretary

Foundation Philosophy: The foundation supports social welfare organizations, civic associations, the arts, and educational institutions. **Giving Priorities:** In 1993, the foundation gave approximately 41% of its contributions in support of social services, including $100,000 grants to Special Olympics and the YMCA. Environmental organizations received 16% of funds, while educational and institutions and health care organizations received 12% each. The arts received 10% of donations, and civic and public affairs 5%. Religious organizations received 3% of contributions, and the remaining 1% went to support the sciences. **Typical Health-Related Recipients:** Health Organizations, Hospices, People with Disabilities, Prenatal Health Issues, Substance Abuse. **Geographic Distribution:** Delaware, with emphasis on the greater Wilmington area.

★ 541 ★ **Willard L. Eccles Charitable Foundation**
PO Box 45385
Salt Lake City, UT 84145-0385
Phone: (801)532-1500
Fax: (801)532-7543
Clark P. Giles, Secretary

Foundation Philosophy: The Willard L. Eccles Charitable Foundation makes most of its grants in the areas of health care and medical research. In health care, interests include state departments of health, health centers, hospitals, and hospices. Research funding favors medical research at the University of Utah and Utah State University. The foundation will make grants to other recipient areas on a limited basis. Proposals for such grants are not solicited. **Giving Priorities:** In fiscal 1994, the foundation awarded approximately 62% of its charitable giving to health care organizations, including a $130,000 grant to the University of Utah Health Sciences Department, for a magnetic resonance research center. Scientific research received 12% of donations, while social service organizations received 10%. Approximately 9% of the foundation's support was for education, while the arts received 3%. Religious interests received 2% of support, while environmental and civic affairs received about 1% each. **Typical Health-Related Recipients:** AIDS/HIV, Alzheimers Disease, Cancer, Children's Health/Hospitals, Emergency/Ambulance Services, Eyes/Blindness, Family Planning, Health Organizations, Hospices, Hospitals, Medical Education, Medical Research, Medical Training, People with Disabilities, Prenatal Health Issues, Preventive Medicine/Wellness Organizations, Respiratory, Single-Disease Health Associations. **Geographic Distribution:** Primarily Utah, with a focus on Salt Lake City.

★542★　**Willard T. C. Johnson Foundation**
c/o The Johnson Co.
630 Fifth Ave., Ste. 1510
New York, NY 10111
Phone: (212)332-7500
Robert W. Johnson, IV, President and Director

Foundation Philosophy: The foundation primarily supports an opera festival and the Liberty Science Center and Hall of Technology. Other recipients include Planned Parenthood, support for AIDS research, and pediatric health organizations. **Giving Priorities:** In 1992, the foundation gave 62% of funding to health concerns, including the highest grant of $850,000 to the Juvenile Diabetes Foundation International. About 16% of funding went in a single $250,000 grant to the Black Youth Organization. Social services received 13%; and the arts received about 8% of funds. **Typical Health-Related Recipients:** AIDS/HIV, Diabetes, Emergency/Ambulance Services, Family Planning, Hospitals. **Geographic Distribution:** Primarily New York City and New Jersey.

★543★　**William Bingham Second Betterment Fund**
330 Madison Ave., Rm. 3500
New York, NY 10017
Phone: (212)557-7700
Fax: (212)286-8513

Foundation Philosophy: The foundation is interested in the welfare of the residents of Maine. Charitable giving is concentrated in the areas of education, health, conservation, and community support. **Giving Priorities:** In 1993, the fund reported that educational institutions received 37% of total funding, including support for colleges, private secondary education and educational reform efforts. Civic affairs also received 37%, with major support to the Maine Community Foundation and environmental concerns. Health care received 21%, and other interests, including social services, received 5%. **Typical Health-Related Recipients:** Cancer, Clinics/Medical Centers, Diabetes, Family Planning, Health Funds, Health Organizations, HomeCare Services, Long-Term Care, Preventive Medicine/Wellness Organizations, Substance Abuse. **Geographic Distribution:** Maine only.

★544★　**William E. and Carol G. Simon Foundation**
c/o William E. Simons & Sons
310 South St., PO Box 1913
Morristown, NJ 07962-1913
Phone: (201)898-0293
Fax: (201)898-0078
William E. Simon, Chairman

Foundation Philosophy: While the foundation supports a large number of organizations that

have a wide variety of interests, it displays three main areas of interest: education; social services and health care; and civic and public affairs. One of the foundation's main area of interest is higher education. Another area of interest is social services and health care organizations that seek to assist and contribute to the relief of the unfortunate. The foundation awarded almost one-quarter of its total contributions to these two areas in 1993 including multiple grants totaling $150,000 to the Morristown Memorial Health Foundation. The foundation also supports civic and public affairs. **Giving Priorities:** In 1993, the foundation gave approximately 59% of its total contributions in support of education, including a $166,667 grant for a scholarship fund at the archdiocese of New York. Health care received 15% of overall support, including $150,000 in grants to the Morristown Memorial Health Foundation. About 9% of contributions were awarded to the arts, while civic affairs groups received 8%. Social service organizations received 6% of distributed funds, and international affairs received 2% of support. The remaining funds, about 1% of the total giving, supported environmental affairs. **Typical Health-Related Recipients:** Cancer, Clinics/Medical Centers, Family Planning, Health Funds, Health Organizations, Hospices, Hospitals, Multiple Sclerosis, Nursing Services, People with Disabilities, Public Health, Single-Disease Health Associations, Substance Abuse. **Geographic Distribution:** Nationally, with emphasis on the Northeast particularly New York and New Jersey.

★545★　**William and Flora Hewlett Foundation**
525 Middlefield Rd., Ste. 200
Menlo Park, CA 94025-3495
Phone: (415)329-1070
Fax: (415)329-9342
Mr. David P. Gardner, President

Foundation Philosophy: In defining programs and establishing "objectives that show promise of realizing the aspirations of the founders," the foundation has restricted its attention to the fields of education, population, environment, performing arts, and family and community development. A special projects category was also established to provide the foundation with flexibility to respond to proposals of special interest to the board. A large portion of funding has been for the general support of institutions, rather than for project support. **Giving Priorities:** In 1993, according to programs designated by the foundation, it gave approximately 29% of its contributions to population concerns, including support for domestic and international family planning and social science research and training. Educational institutions received 24%, including support for public education and liberal arts colleges. The foundation's conflict resolution program received 11% of funding; performing arts, 9%; special projects, 9%; and children, youth, and families received 8%. The remaining funds supported regional grants (6%) and environmental efforts (4%). **Typical Health-Related Recipients:** Adolescent Health Issues, Family Planning, Health Policy/Cost Containment, Research/Studies Institutes. **Geographic Distribution:** National, with emphasis in the

San Francisco Bay area; some international giving for population issues.

★546★　**William G. Baker, Jr. Memorial Fund**
2 E Read St., Latrobe Bldg., 9th Fl.
Baltimore, MD 21202
Phone: (410)332-0486
Martha K. Johnston, Program Officer

Foundation Philosophy: The William G. Baker, Jr., Memorial Fund makes most of its grants in the areas of social services, the arts, civic affairs, health care, and education. **Giving Priorities:** In 1993, the foundation gave approximately 27% of its total contributions to civic groups, including three grants totaling $65,000 to the Baltimore Community Foundation. The arts received 23% of support; social service organizations, 21%; and educational institutions, 13%. About 12% of funds were awarded to health care organizations. The remainder went to religious and environmental groups. **Typical Health-Related Recipients:** Clinics/Medical Centers, Emergency/Ambulance Services, Health Funds, Health Organizations, Heart, Hospitals, Mental Health, People with Disabilities, Substance Abuse. **Geographic Distribution:** Limited to the Baltimore, MD, metropolitan area.

★547★　**William G. Irwin Charity Foundation**
235 Montgomery St.
711 Russ Bldg.
San Francisco, CA 94104
Phone: (415)362-6954
Michael R. Gorman, Executive Director

Foundation Philosophy: "The foundation is particularly interested in medical facilities, secondary schools, and cultural and community projects." **Giving Priorities:** In 1992, the foundation gave 44% of its funds to educational institutions, primarily colleges and universities in California. Health care received 29% of support; religious organizations, 12%; the arts, 10%; and social services, 3%. Civic groups received the remainder. **Typical Health-Related Recipients:** Cancer, Clinics/Medical Centers, Geriatric Health, Health Organizations, Hospitals, Medical Rehabilitation, Medical Research, People with Disabilities, Research/Studies Institutes, Single-Disease Health Associations. **Geographic Distribution:** Only in the states of California and Hawaii.

★548★　**William G. Selby and Marie Selby Foundation**
1800 Second St., Ste. 905
Sarasota, FL 34236
Phone: (813)957-0442
Fax: (813)957-3135
Dr. Robert E. Perkins, Executive Director

Foundation Philosophy: The purpose of the foundation is to "make grants which will result in the improvement of life in the Sarasota community." Emphasis is placed on social services and education. Organizations and programs serving youth, and programs for the handicapped and the elderly are stressed. The foundation also maintains an extensive scholarship program. Funds are provided to Florida colleges and universities which grant scholarships to individuals on the basis of academic excellence. Other than scholarships, most grants are for capital expenditures. **Giving Priorities:** In fiscal 1993, about 33% of funding went to educational foundations, colleges, and secondary schools. About 29% of funding went to social service agencies, with a focus on the aged, animal protection, and youth programs. The arts and civic causes each received 11%; health care, 8%; science, 7%; and religious organizations, 1%. **Typical Health-Related Recipients:** Children's Health/Hospitals, Domestic Violence, Emergency/Ambulance Services, Family Planning, Hospices, Medical Research, Mental Health, People with Disabilities, Single-Disease Health Associations. **Geographic Distribution:** Sarasota, FL, and adjoining counties.

★ 549 ★ **William H. Donner Foundation**
500 Fifth Ave., Ste. 1230
New York, NY 10110
Phone: (212)719-9290
Fax: (212)302-8734
William T. Alpert, Senior Program Officer

Foundation Philosophy: In general, the foundation supports grants in three program areas: U.S.-Canadian relations, Education, and Human Capital Development. **Giving Priorities:** In fiscal 1993, the foundation awarded 34% of contributions to civic organizations. Approximately 30% of funding went to educational institutions, including the foundation's highest grant of $233,694 to John Hopkins University. International affairs received about 16% of contributions; the arts and humanities received 7% of support; science, 7%; health, 4%; social services, 2%. **Typical Health-Related Recipients:** Adolescent Health Issues, Clinics/Medical Centers, Geriatric Health, Hospitals, Mental Health, People with Disabilities, Prenatal Health Issues. **Geographic Distribution:** Principally to national organizations.

★ 550 ★ **William K. Warren Foundation**
PO Box 470372
Tulsa, OK 74147-0372
Phone: (918)492-8100
Fax: (918)481-7935
W. R. Lissau, President

Foundation Philosophy: The foundation reports that it gives preference to "local Catholic health care facilities." Its designated areas of interest are hospitals and medical research centers; churches and related organizations; educational institutions; and other (including youth-related causes, substance abuse prevention, human services, and single disease health associations). **Giving Priorities:** In 1992, the foundation contributed 96% of its total funding to health concerns. The majority of funding went in three large grants to Laureate Mental Health Corporation, Saint Francis Hospital, and William K. Warren Medical Research Center. Religious organization received 3% of support. The remaining funds went to arts, education, and social service organizations. **Typical Health-Related Recipients:** Arthritis, Cancer, Children's Health/Hospitals, Diabetes, Emergency/Ambulance Services, Health Organizations, Heart, Hospitals, Medical Research, Mental Health, Multiple Sclerosis, People with Disabilities, Respiratory, Single-Disease Health Associ-

ations, Substance Abuse. **Geographic Distribution:** Emphasis on Tulsa, OK.

★ 551 ★ **William Penn Foundation**
1630 Locust St.
Philadelphia, PA 19103
Phone: (215)732-5114
Fax: (215)735-7920
Harry E. Cerino, President

Foundation Philosophy: The main goal of the foundation is to help improve the quality of life in Philadelphia and the Delaware Valley. A major portion of the foundation's giving program is directed toward human development. This broad classification encourages an integrated approach to solving the problems of individuals and families; it includes programs that address the need for education, human services, and health care. Because different age groups face different problems, separate programs have been developed for children, adolescents, and the elderly. Programs for children include prevention of child abuse, summer day camp enrichment, and arts education. Programs for adolescents include a major drive to prevent teen pregnancy aimed at male as well as female teenagers. Programs for the elderly address physically appropriate, safe, and supportive housing at affordable rates. The foundation also supports a variety of projects designed to strengthen institutions upon which people rely to make society function, including housing, community-based primary health care, and community institutions. **Giving Priorities:** In 1993, the foundation awarded approximately 35% of funding to projects aimed at maximizing human development, including children, adolescents, and the elderly. Projects to strengthen community fabric, including housing, essential institutions, and neighborhood health care, accounted for 27% of funding. Cultural grants, including historic preservation, amounted to 16% of funding. Approximately 8% went to the foundation-initiated program to help maintain the Philadelphia Ranger Corps. Environmental programs also received about 8%. Roughly 4% of funds was spent in areas for which the foundation does not accept proposals, including national and international grants, and the remaining 2% was dispersed through matching gifts. **Typical Health-Related Recipients:** Domestic Violence, Family Planning, Geriatric Health, Health Organizations, Prenatal Health Issues, Public Health. **Geographic Distribution:** Mostly restricted to regional giving; some national and international giving.

★ 552 ★ **William Randolph Hearst Foundation**
888 Seventh Ave., 45th Fl.
New York, NY 10106-0057
Phone: (212)586-5404
Robert M. Frehse, Jr., Executive Director and Vice President

Foundation Philosophy: The foundation reflects the philanthropic interests of William Randolph Hearst: human services, education, health, and culture. Specific priorities include: "programs to aid poverty-level and minority groups; education programs, with emphasis on private secondary and higher education; health care delivery systems; and cultural programs

with records of public support." The foundation also fully funds two programs for youth: the Journalism Awards Program and the United States Senate Youth Program. **Giving Priorities:** In 1994, approximately 39% of funding went to educational institutions, including colleges, universities, private secondary schools, and educational associations. Arts groups and museums received 27%. Health organizations received approximately 19% of funding; social services received 13%; and miscellaneous organizations were given the remaining funds. **Typical Health-Related Recipients:** Cancer, Children's Health/Hospitals, Geriatric Health, Health Funds, Health Organizations, Hospitals, Medical Education, Medical Rehabilitation, Medical Research, Medical Training, People with Disabilities, Prenatal Health Issues, Substance Abuse, Transplant Networks/Donor Banks. **Geographic Distribution:** United States and its possessions.

★ 553 ★ **William Rosenwald Family Fund**
122 E 42nd St., 24th Fl.
New York, NY 10168
Phone: (212)697-2420
David P. Steinmann, Secretary

Foundation Philosophy: The William Rosenwald Family Fund primarily supports Jewish religious organizations. The fund also supports Jewish education and various other interests on a limited basis. **Giving Priorities:** In 1992, the fund gave approximately 59% of its funding to religious organizations, including the highest grant of $840,000 to United Jewish Appeal Federation of Jewish Philanthropies, New York. Education received 23% of giving, including a $209,250 donation to the Kirksville College of Osteopathic Medicine in Kirksville, MO. Civic affairs received 10% of contributions; the arts and health care each received 3%; and social services, science, and international concerns received the remaining funds. **Typical Health-Related Recipients:** AIDS/HIV, Clinics/Medical Centers, Hospitals, Medical Education, People with Disabilities. **Geographic Distribution:** Focus on New York.

★ 554 ★ **William Stamps Farish Fund**
1000 Memorial Dr., Ste. 920
Houston, TX 77024
Phone: (713)757-7300
Fax: (713)655-9124
William Stamps Farish, President

Foundation Philosophy: The fund primarily gives to local primary education, arts and humanities, and medical research. **Giving Priorities:** During fiscal 1993, the fund gave approximately 36% of its contributions to education. Health organizations received 24% of funding; social services, 18%; and the arts, 7%. Civic interests and scientific organizations each received 6%. The remaining funds went to religious organizations. **Typical Health-Related Recipients:** Cancer, Child Abuse, Clinics/Medical Centers, Emergency/Ambulance Services, Eyes/Blindness, Family Planning, Health Organizations, Hospices, Medical Education, Medical Research, People with Disabilities, Single-Disease Health Associations, Substance Abuse. **Geographic Distribution:** Near headquarters only.

★555★ **William T. Kemper Foundation**
Commerce Bank, Trustee
PO Box 13095
Kansas City, MO 64199-3095
Phone: (816)234-2985

Foundation Philosophy: The foundation is "dedicated to continuing Mr. Kemper's lifelong interest in improving the human condition and quality of life." The foundation concentrates on education, health and human services, the arts, and civic improvements, as well as, organizations and projects that "offer multiple solutions, both short and long term, to a problem." **Giving Priorities:** In fiscal 1993, the foundation awarded 28% of its total funding to health care. About 21% of support went to educational institutions. The arts received 18% of contributions; civic groups, 15%; religious concerns, 14%; and social services, 2%. The remainder went to scientific organizations. **Typical Health-Related Recipients:** Cancer, Children's Health/Hospitals, Clinics/Medical Centers, Eyes/Blindness, Health Organizations, Hospitals, Medical Research, Nursing Services. **Geographic Distribution:** The Midwest, with a focus on Missouri.

★556★ **William T. Morris Foundation**
230 Park Ave., Ste. 622
New York, NY 10169-0622
Phone: (212)986-8036
Fax: (212)370-1962
Edward A. Antonelli, President, Chief
 Executive Officer, and

Foundation Philosophy: The foundation supports general philanthropy, particularly in the areas of education, health, culture, and youth. The foundation also administers a scholarship program for West Pittston, PA, residents. **Giving Priorities:** In fiscal 1991, the foundation gave approximately 41% of its contributions to education, including support for colleges, universities, and education funds. The arts received 26%, including the foundation's highest grant of $250,000. Health care received 20%, primarily to support hospitals and health funds. Social services received 7%, with grants awarded to youth groups, community service organizations, and the United Way. Civic and public affairs received 5%, including support for the environment and botanical gardens. **Typical Health-Related Recipients:** Arthritis, Cancer, Clinics/Medical Centers, Health Funds, Hospitals, Medical Education, Medical Rehabilitation, Medical Research, People with Disabilities, Respiratory. **Geographic Distribution:** Emphasis on New York, Connecticut, and Pennsylvania.

★557★ **Windham Foundation**
Grafton, VT 05146
Phone: (802)843-2211
Fax: (802)843-2205
Stephan A. Morse, President

Foundation Philosophy: "The Windham Foundation, Inc. provides for the restoration and preservation of rural or village areas of Vermont in order to preserve existing charm and historic or native features of such areas for the general benefit of the communities concerned. Its activities have centered on the Village of Grafton, Windham County, Vermont." **Giving Priorities:** In fiscal 1994, the foundation gave approximately 27% of its total funding in support of educa-

tion, with $10,000 going to the Stratton Mountain School. About 23% of its charitable donations were awarded to civic and public affairs organizations, including its largest grant of $25,000 to the town of Grafton, VT for repairs to a bridge. Arts and humanities received 16% of distributed funds, which included a $10,000 gift to the Vermont Symphony Orchestra. Religious causes received 16% of funds, with a $20,000 grant to the Grafton church. Social service organizations received 10%, while 7% went to health concerns. The remaining 1% of support went to science. **Typical Health-Related Recipients:** Arthritis, Cancer, Diabetes, Domestic Violence, Emergency/Ambulance Services, Family Planning, General, Health Organizations, Hospitals, Kidney, Prenatal Health Issues, Trauma Treatment. **Geographic Distribution:** Limited to Vermont, in particular to Windham County.

★558★ **Wyomissing Foundation**
1015 Penn Ave., Ste. 201
Wyomissing, PA 19610
Phone: (610)376-7494
Fax: (610)372-7626
Alfred G. Hemmerich, Secretary

Foundation Philosophy: The Wyomissing Foundation makes most of its grants in the areas of education, the arts, civic affairs, and social services. Educational funding favors colleges and universities, special education, and literacy. Support for the arts goes to museums, festivals, ballet, libraries, and public broadcasting. Civic affairs support includes environmental affairs and zoos. The majority of the social service funding goes to united funds. Other recipient areas are also supported. **Giving Priorities:** In 1993, the foundation gave approximately 27% of its funds to social services, including the largest grant, $83,000, to the United Way. The arts received 21% of the funding, with major support going to music programs. Education received 20% of support, including a $50,000 grant to Pennsylvania State University. Environmental organizations received 14% of funds, while civic and public affairs was given 12%. Health care organizations received 5%, while religious organizations and the sciences each received 1%. The remaining amount, less than 1%, went to international organizations. **Typical Health-Related Recipients:** AIDS/HIV, Emergency/Ambulance Services, Family Planning, Hospitals, Medical Rehabilitation, Nursing Services, People with Disabilities. **Geographic Distribution:** Focus primarily on Berks County, PA, and contiguous counties.

★559★ **Zale Foundation**
3102 Maple Ave., Ste. 110
Dallas, TX 75201-1233
Phone: (214)855-0627
Fax: (214)220-0633
Dr. Michael F. Romaine, President

Foundation Philosophy: Since 1983, the foundation has been involved in a long-term project with the University of Texas Southwestern Medical Center in Dallas. Major funding has been given toward this project. The trustees of the foundation recently expressed strong interest in supporting programs which would address the needs of the children of homeless families.

"These needs would ideally, but not necessarily be directed to daytime care, education, medical or psychological care. The foundation wishes to encourage the development of such programs where there has been community involvement and commitment to help the homeless family unit." **Giving Priorities:** In 1993, the foundation awarded 41% of its contributions to religious organizations, including $121,000 to the South Palm Beach Jewish Foundation. About 32% of funding went to health care. International organizations received 11% of support; educational institutions, 9%; and social services, 3%. The remaining funds went to the arts and civic groups. **Typical Health-Related Recipients:** Children's Health/Hospitals, Clinics/Medical Centers, Emergency/Ambulance Services, Geriatric Health, Health Organizations, Hospitals, Mental Health, Nutrition. **Geographic Distribution:** No geographic restrictions.

★560★ **Zellerbach Family Fund**
120 Montgomery St., Ste. 2125
San Francisco, CA 94104
Phone: (415)421-2629
Fax: (415)421-6713
Edward A. Nathan, Executive Director

Foundation Philosophy: In recent years, high priority areas have included early intervention to assist in family stability, and efforts to improve private sector collaboration and integration with public services. Specifically, such interests are programs supporting community arts projects and self-help programs for mental health. Grants also promote language and reading development, as well as increased understanding of diverse cultures through curriculum development. **Giving Priorities:** In 1992, the fund reported that it contributed 28% of its overall giving to the arts and humanities, including a gift of $271,135 to the Community Arts Distribution Committtee in San Francisco. Approximately 25% of its contributions funded social service concerns, 22% went to education, and 14% went to health-related organizations and projects. Religious concerns and civic and public affairs each received 6%. **Typical Health-Related Recipients:** AIDS/HIV, Health Organizations, Mental Health, People with Disabilities, Public Health. **Geographic Distribution:** Emphasis on San Francisco Bay Area.

Corporate Foundations

★561★ **A.O. Smith Foundation**
PO Box 23975
Milwaukee, WI 53223
Phone: (414)359-4100
Fax: (414)359-4064
Edward J. O'Connor, Secretary

Giving Priorities: *Social Welfare/United Way:* 50% to 55% of contributions. The remainder, in grants generally less than $5,000, support youth activities, child welfare, family services, and a variety of community service organizations. *Education:* About 20% of total. *Arts & Humanities:* About 10%. *Civic & Cultural:* 5% to 10% of contributions. *Health & Hospital:* 5% to 10% of giving, primarily to hospitals, pediatric health, and emergency services in plant locations. **Typical Health-Related Recipients:** Emergency/

Ambulance Services, Hospitals, Medical Education, Medical Rehabilitation, Mental Health, People with Disabilities, Public Health, Substance Abuse. **Geographic Distribution:** Primarily in communities where company has manufacturing facilities.

★ 562 ★ Abbott Laboratories Fund
One Abbott Park Rd.
Abbott Park, IL 60064-3500
Phone: (708)937-8686
Fax: (708)938-5824
Cindy Schwab, Vice President

Giving Priorities: *Health & Social Services:* About 50% of total fund contributions, much of which supports united funds and community drives funding local institutions, or other specific, well-defined programs in communities in which the company has significant numbers of employees. Supports agencies working with disadvantaged youth and senior citizens and agencies seeking to improve the socioeconomic position of women, minorities, and immigrant populations. Also supports individual hospitals and health care institutions used frequently by company employees. *Education:* About 30% of contributions. Concentrates on colleges and universities having the potential to benefit the health-care industry, including basic research programs in physical and biological sciences, medicine, pharmacy, nutrition, and diagnostics. Also supports institutions that are potential sources of personnel for the health-care industry. *Civic & Public Affairs:* About 10%. *Culture & the Arts:* About 10% of funding. *International:* Contributes limited amount of funds to U.S.-based nonprofits with an international focus. **Typical Health-Related Recipients:** Children's Health/ Hospitals, Clinics/Medical Centers, Emergency/Ambulance Services, Geriatric Health, Health Organizations, Heart, Hospices, Hospitals, Kidney, Medical Education, Medical Rehabilitation, Medical Research, Medical Training, Nursing Services, Nutrition, People with Disabilities, Public Health, Sexual Abuse, Single-Disease Health Associations, Substance Abuse. **Geographic Distribution:** In communities where company has significant operations or number of employees.

★ 563 ★ Acushnet Foundation
21 Francis St.
Fairhaven, MA 02719
Phone: (508)992-0820
Edward Powers, Foundation Manager

Giving Priorities: *Social Services:* 35% to 40% of total contributions. United Way receives one-half. Also supports child welfare, community centers, youth organizations, family services, and drug and alcohol counseling. *Health:* About 25%. More than four-fifths supports hospital capital campaign. Other recipients include pediatrics, medical rehabilitation, and health organizations. *Education:* 20% to 25%. *Arts & Humanities:* 5% to 10%. *Civic & Public Affairs:* About 5%. **Typical Health-Related Recipients:** Health Organizations, Hospitals, Medical Rehabilitation, Substance Abuse. **Geographic Distribution:** Generally limited to the greater New Bedford, MA, area.

★ 564 ★ Aetna Foundation
151 Farmington Ave., RE1B
Hartford, CT 06156-3180
Phone: (203)273-1932
Fax: (203)273-4764
Michael C. Alexander, Vice President & Executive Director

Giving Priorities: *Social Services:* 30% to 35% of contributions. In 1993, a $1.6 million grant was awarded to the United Way in Hartford, CT. Other interests include child welfare and volunteer programs. *Health:* 25% to 30% of total giving. In 1993, the foundation contributed more than $1.8 million to organizations working with child immunization issues and have committed to donate more than $15 million within the next five years. Aetna's main objective under this initiative is to help meet the Surgeon General's goal for immunizing children and to use immunization as a point of entry to a more durable health care system by: funding selected programs that overcome the economic, social, and institutional barriers to health care; promoting education and outreach efforts at national and local levels, with emphasis on field offices and the company's headquarters area; and encouraging creative, cost-effective methods to deliver health care to children who otherwise would not receive care. *Minority Education:* About 15% of giving. *Civic & Public Affairs:* About 15% of funding. *Arts & Humanities:* 5% to 10% of contributions. *International:* Less than 5%. In 1993, the company gave $250,000 to UNICEF for an immunization/child health program. **Typical Health-Related Recipients:** Children's Health/ Hospitals, Emergency/Ambulance Services, Nursing Services. **Geographic Distribution:** National, emphasizing the Hartford, CT, metropolitan area and cities selected under the FOCUS program; also supports international organizations.

★ 565 ★ Air Products Foundation
7201 Hamilton Blvd.
Allentown, PA 18195-1510
Phone: (610)481-6349
William J. Kendrick, Chairman

Giving Priorities: *Education:* 50% to 55% of contributions budget. *Health & Welfare:* 25% to 30%, primarily supporting the United Way. Also supports youth organizations, programs for the disabled, and for the prevention of drug and alcohol abuse. Health interests include single-disease health associations. *Community Investment:* 10% to 15%. *Culture & Art:* 5% to 10%. *International:* Company donates an unspecified amount of money to international organizations through foreign subsidiaries. **Typical Health-Related Recipients:** Domestic violence, Emergency/Ambulance Services, Nutrition, People with Disabilities, Single-Disease Health Associations, Substance Abuse. **Geographic Distribution:** Near headquarters and operating locations.

★ 566 ★ Alabama Power Foundation
PO Box 2641, 600 N 18th St.
Birmingham, AL 35291
Phone: (205)250-2508
Fax: (205)250-1860
Jera G. Stribling, Executive Director

Giving Priorities: *Education:* 40% to 45%. *Social Services:* 30% to 35% of total contributions.

Majority of support funds the United Way. Also supports the aged, community service organizations, counseling, drug and alcohol rehabilitation, family services, athletics, shelters, and volunteer services. *Arts & Humanities:* 10% to 15% of funds. *Health:* About 10% of gifts. About two-thirds of gifts go to pediatric health. Mental health associations receive about two-fifths of funds. Also supports health funds and single-disease health associations. *Civic & Public Affairs:* 5% to 10%. **Typical Health-Related Recipients:** Health Organizations, Mental Health, People with Disabilities, Single-Disease Health Associations, Substance Abuse. **Geographic Distribution:** Primarily at headquarters and operating locations.

★ 567 ★ Alcoa Foundation
1501 Alcoa Bldg.
Pittsburgh, PA 15219
Phone: (412)553-2348
Fax: (412)553-4532
F. Worth Hobbs, President

Giving Priorities: *Education:* 40% to 45% of contributions. *Health & Welfare:* 25% to 30%. Emphasis on United Ways (about one-third of this support), hospitals, and medical organizations. Other organizations of particular interest include those dealing with drug and alcohol abuse, battered women, abused children, homelessness, and unemployment. In addition, the foundation supports single-disease health associations, medical research, and community service organizations. *Arts & Humanities:* 10% to 15%. *Civic & Community Development:* About 10%. *Youth Organizations:* Less than 5%. *Other:* Less than 5%, to local, national, and international organizations. **Typical Health-Related Recipients:** Cancer, Children's Health/Hospitals, Domestic Violence, Emergency/Ambulance Services, Family Planning, Geriatric Health, Health Funds, Health Organizations, Health Policy/Cost Containment, Hospices, Hospitals, Medical Education, Medical Rehabilitation, Medical Research, Medical Training, Mental Health, People with Disabilities, Single-Disease Health Associations, Substance Abuse. **Geographic Distribution:** National and international (near corporate operating facilities).

★ 568 ★ Alex. Brown and Sons Charitable Foundation Inc.
135 E Baltimore St.
Baltimore, MD 21202
Phone: (410)234-3636
Fax: (410)347-2913
Walter W. Brewster, Secretary

Giving Priorities: *Health:* 40% to 45%. Foundation gives to hospitals, hospices, general and single-disease health groups, and research organizations. *Education:* 30% to 35% of contributions. *Civic & Public Affairs:* 20% to 25%. *Social Services:* About 10%. Grants go to youth organizations including recreational groups and organizations concerned with child abuse, organizations that provide food and shelter, the United Way, and Junior Achievement. *Arts & Humanities:* 5% to 10%. **Typical Health-Related Recipients:** Children's Health/Hospitals, Clinics/Medical Centers, Domestic Violence, Health Organizations, Hospitals, Medical Education,

People with Disabilities, Preventive Medicine/Wellness Organizations. **Geographic Distribution:** Mostly Maryland, with emphasis on the company's headquarters city of Baltimore.

★569★ **Alexander & Baldwin Foundation**
822 Bishop St.
PO Box 3440
Honolulu, HI 96801
Phone: (808)525-6642
Fax: (808)525-6677
Linda Howe, Manager, Community Relations

Giving Priorities: *Health & Human Services:* 45% to 50% of contributions. Support for hospitals, health services, single-disease organizations. Youth organizations, child welfare, and the United Way also receive funding. *Arts & Humanities:* 25% to 30%. *Civic & Public Affairs:* 10% to 15%. *Education:* 10% to 15% of funding. **Typical Health-Related Recipients:** Health Organizations, Hospitals, Single-Disease Health Associations. **Geographic Distribution:** Organizations in Hawaii and Bay area in California.

★570★ **Allegheny Ludlum Foundation**
1000 Six PPG Pl.
Pittsburgh, PA 15222
Phone: (412)394-2836
Fax: (412)394-3010
Jon D. Walton, VP, Sec. and General Counsel

Giving Priorities: *Social Services:* 45% to 50% of annual contributions. *Arts & Humanities:* 15% to 20%. *Education:* 15% to 20% of funding. *Civic & Public Affairs:* 10% to 15% of contributions. *Health:* 5% to 10%. Supports medical rehabilitation, hospitals, and single-disease health associations. *Other:* Also contributes to religious organizations. **Typical Health-Related Recipients:** Children's Health/Hospitals, Hospitals, Medical Rehabilitation, Mental Health, Nursing Services, People with Disabilities, Sexual Abuse, Single-Disease Health Associations. **Geographic Distribution:** Near operating locations only, with emphasis on the Pittsburgh, PA, area.

★571★ **Allendale Insurance Foundation**
PO Box 7500
Johnston, RI 02919
Phone: (401)275-3000
Fax: (401)275-3029
Robert R. Gardner, Sr. VP of Finance, and Treasurer

Giving Priorities: *Education:* 45% to 50% of total giving. *United Way:* 35% to 40%. *Civic and Cultural:* 10% to 15% of funding. *Health:* Less than 5%. Emphasis is on single disease health associations. Other interests include hospitals and medical research. **Typical Health-Related Recipients:** Emergency/Ambulance Services, Health Organizations, Hospices, Hospitals, Medical Education, Medical Research, Mental Health, Nursing Services, People with Disabilities, Single-Disease Health Associations. **Geographic Distribution:** Nationwide, with emphasis on Rhode Island.

★572★ **AlliedSignal Foundation**
PO Box 2245
Morristown, NJ 07962-2245
Phone: (201)455-5876
Fax: (201)455-3632
Alan S. Painter, Vice President & Executive Director

Giving Priorities: *Education:* About 50% of contributions, primarily to colleges and universities; interests include business, technical, engineering, and science education. *Health & Human Services:* About 40% of funding. Major support to United Ways, hospitals, and medical research programs, including programs on aging. Other health interests include single-disease health associations and various health services. Human service interests include the disabled, employment and job training, youth organizations, and child welfare groups. Also matches employee gifts to hospitals and first aid squads. *Cultural:* Between 5% and 10% of contributions. *Civic & Community Affairs:* Less than 5%. **Typical Health-Related Recipients:** Cancer, Children's Health/Hospitals, Clinics/Medical Centers, Diabetes, Domestic Violence, Geriatric Health, Health Organizations, Heart, Hospitals, Medical Education, Medical Rehabilitation, Medical Research, Multiple Sclerosis, Nursing Services, People with Disabilities, Sexual Abuse, Single-Disease Health Associations, Substance Abuse, Transplant Networks/Donor Banks. **Geographic Distribution:** Principally near operating locations and to national organizations.

★573★ **Allstate Foundation**
2775 Sanders Rd., Ste. F-4
Northbrook, IL 60062-6127
Phone: (708)402-5502
Fax: (708)402-5142
Ron Morrie

Giving Priorities: *General Support:* The Allstate Foundation focuses its grants to achieve general accord with Allstate's mission to partner customers and the community in the management of the risks they face. As with other foundations, focus areas change to keep pace with present needs. For 1993, the Foundation's focus areas included: --Automobile and Highway Safety --Homes and Housing --Safety and Security **Typical Health-Related Recipients:** Emergency/Ambulance Services, Health Organizations, Health Policy/Cost Containment, Medical Education, Prenatal Health Issues, Public Health, Substance Abuse. **Geographic Distribution:** Nationwide.

★574★ **American National Bank & Trust Co. of Chicago Foundation**
33 N LaSalle St.
Chicago, IL 60690
Phone: (312)661-6115
Fax: (312)661-3562
Joan Klaus, Trustee

Giving Priorities: *United Way:* 35% to 40% of total contributions annually. *Civic & Social Welfare:* About 20%. A new focus in this area is economic development; also supports youth organizations, employment programs, and drug rehabilitation. *Education:* About 15%. *Health:* About 10%. Majority of support funds hospitals and medical research. Local and national health or-

ganizations and single-disease health associations are also supported, in addition to an employee-matching gift program in this category. *Arts & Humanities:* 10% to 15%. *Other:* Less than 5%. Supports additional foundation interests in religion and science. **Typical Health-Related Recipients:** Alzheimers Disease, Cancer, Clinics/Medical Centers, Diabetes, Domestic Violence, Eyes/Blindness, Health Funds, Hospices, Hospitals, Medical Rehabilitation, Medical Research, People with Disabilities, Single-Disease Health Associations. **Geographic Distribution:** Within the six-county Chicago metropolitan area.

★575★ **Ameritech-Ohio Foundation**
45 Erieview Plz., Rm. 850
Cleveland, OH 44114
Phone: (216)822-2423
Fax: (216)822-5522
William W. Boag, Jr., Executive Director

Giving Priorities: *Education:* About 40% of giving. *Health & Human Services:* 35% of contributions. The foundation participates in the maintenance and development of local health and human services programs through the United Way and other programs. Support is considered for health care agencies addressing specific health problems such as alcohol and drug prevention programs as well as family services, senior citizens groups, and special need organizations. Support is not provided for United Way member agencies' annual operating campaigns, nursing or retirement homes and national health organizations. *Culture & the Arts:* About 20%. *Civic & Community:* Less than 5%. **Typical Health-Related Recipients:** Health Policy/Cost Containment. **Geographic Distribution:** Limited to company's service area, except for educational matching gifts. **Formerly:** Ohio Bell Foundation.

★576★ **AMETEK Foundation**
Station Sq.
Paoli, PA 19301
Phone: (215)647-2121
Fax: (215)647-0211
Robert W. Yannarell, Secretary and Treasurer

Giving Priorities: *Education:* 30% to 35%, primarily supporting colleges and universities and technical and engineering institutions and organizations. Other interests include student aid, private secondary education, education funds, and literacy. *Social Services:* 25% to 30%. *Health:* 10% to 15%. Supports hospitals and medical research organizations. Other interests include rehabilitation, mental health, and cancer research. *Civic Affairs:* About 5%. *Arts & Humanities:* Less than 5%. **Typical Health-Related Recipients:** Cancer, Health Funds, Health Organizations, Hospitals, Medical Education, Medical Rehabilitation, Medical Research, Mental Health, People with Disabilities. **Geographic Distribution:** To national organizations and near plant locations.

★577★ **Amoco Foundation**
200 E Randolph Dr.
Chicago, IL 60601
Phone: (312)856-6306
Fax: (312)616-0826
Patricia Wright, Executive Director

Giving Priorities: *Education:* 50% to 55% of annual foundation contributions. *Community Service:* Between 25% and 30% of giving. Emphasis on neighborhood organizations working to improve their own communities. Other interests include youth organizations including a five-year, $1 million grant to support a youth program in Texas City, TX, where the company has its largest refinery; child welfare; and hospitals that serve communities designated as medically underserved. *Arts & Culture:* 5% to 10%. *Civic & Environment:* 5% to 10%. *Foreign:* About 5% of giving. In 1993, foreign grants totaled $917,084. Support went to hospitals, schools, museums, and other institutions in Amoco's overseas operating locations. Also contributed to local and national groups dedicated to improving conditions for the citizens in the host country. **Typical Health-Related Recipients:** Children's Health/Hospitals, Clinics/Medical Centers, Emergency/Ambulance Services, Hospitals, People with Disabilities, Single-Disease Health Associations. **Geographic Distribution:** Near operating locations, nationally, and internationally.

★ 578 ★ **Amon G. Carter Star Telegram Employees Fund**
PO Box 17480
Ft. Worth, TX 76102
Phone: (817)332-3535
Nenetta Tatum, President

Giving Priorities: *Social Services:* 55% to 60% of total contributions. Includes community centers, community service organizations, counseling, and youth organizations. One-half goes to the YMCA. *Health:* 15% to 20%. Interests include children's hospitals and single-disease health associations. *Arts & Humanities:* 10% to 15%. *Education:* 5% to 10%. *Civic & Public Affairs:* Less than 5%. Favors community affairs, public safety associations, and community funds. **Typical Health-Related Recipients:** Cancer, Children's Health/Hospitals, Domestic Violence, Eyes/Blindness, Family Planning, Hospitals, Research/Studies Institutes, Single-Disease Health Associations, Substance Abuse. **Geographic Distribution:** Focus on Texas.

★ 579 ★ **AMP Foundation**
PO Box 3608 (176-042)
Harrisburg, PA 17105-3608
Phone: (717)780-6708
Fax: (717)780-7111
Merrill A. Yohe, Jr., Chm., Corp. Contributions Comm.

Giving Priorities: *Education:* About 40% of total annual contributions. *Social Services:* About 20% of contributions. *Health:* About 15%. Primary support goes to hospitals. Special consideration is given to health-care institutions that are working to contain health-care costs while maintaining high levels or service. Other interests include health-related organizations such as the American Heart Association and United Cerebral Palsy, hospices, and outpatient health facilities. *Civic:* About 15%. *Culture and Arts:* Less than 10%. **Typical Health-Related Recipients:** Cancer, Children's Health/Hospitals, Clinics/Medical Centers, Emergency/Ambulance Services, Health Organizations,

Hospices, Hospitals, People with Disabilities, Single-Disease Health Associations. **Geographic Distribution:** Within a 50-mile radius of Harrisburg, PA, and in operating locations.

★ 580 ★ **AMR / American Airlines Foundation**
PO Box 619616
Mail Drop 5575
DFW Airport, TX 75261-9616
Phone: (817)967-3545
Fax: (817)967-9784
Kathy Andersen, Administrator, Corporate Contributions

Giving Priorities: *Health & Welfare:* 40% to 45% of funds. United Way receives highest percent of foundation grants. Company is also a corporate partner with Cystic Fibrosis Foundation and Susan B. Komen Foundation and other organizations that support breast cancer research. *Education:* About 30% of total contributions. *Community & Civic:* 10% to 15% of total annual giving. *Arts & Culture:* 10% to 15%. **Typical Health-Related Recipients:** Children's Health/Hospitals, Clinics/Medical Centers, Health Funds, Hospitals, Public Health, Single-Disease Health Associations. **Geographic Distribution:** Nationwide and international.

★ 581 ★ **Anheuser-Busch Foundation / Anheuser-Busch Charitable Trust**
One Busch Pl.
St. Louis, MO 63118
Phone: (314)577-2453
Fax: (314)577-3251
Sylvia Morris, Contributions Specialist

Education and social services are highest priorities for Charitable Trust giving, with colleges and United Ways near operating locations receiving the most support. Also gives to civic, arts, and health organizations. Highest priorities for Foundation giving are united funds and social service organizations, including youth organizations, programs for the disabled, and child welfare organizations. Education interests include colleges and universities, with major support to Washington University (St. Louis), St. Louis University, and the University of California (Berkely). Interests include arts, business, vocational, technical, and medical education. Health grants support hospitals, medical centers, medical research, and public health instruction. Also gives to international emergency relief, environmental protection, and public policy research organizations. **Typical Health-Related Recipients:** Children's Health/Hospitals, Health Organizations, Health Policy/Cost Containment, Heart, Hospitals, Medical Research, People with Disabilities, Public Health, Single-Disease Health Associations, Substance Abuse. **Geographic Distribution:** Primarily in communities in which company has major production facilities.

★ 582 ★ **ANR Foundation**
One Woodward Ave.
Detroit, MI 48226
Phone: (313)496-3781
Bernard V. Quinlan, Director, Corporate & Community Affairs

Giving Priorities: *Civic & Public Affairs:* About 30%. *Arts & Humanities:* 20% to 25%. *Educa-

tion: 20% to 25%. *Health & Social Services:* About 20%. Major support goes to United Ways in operating locations. Also supports capital programs of health and welfare agencies that benefit employees, emergency health care programs, programs that help alleviate unemployment and hunger, child welfare organizations, volunteer services, and medical rehabilitation. **Typical Health-Related Recipients:** Emergency/Ambulance Services, Health Organizations, Health Policy/Cost Containment, Hospices, Hospitals, Medical Rehabilitation, Medical Research, People with Disabilities, Public Health, Single-Disease Health Associations. **Geographic Distribution:** Operating locations.

★ 583 ★ **AON Foundation**
123 N Wacker Dr.
Chicago, IL 60606
Phone: (312)701-3035
Fax: (312)701-4580
Carolyn E. Labutka, Director, AON Foundation

Giving Priorities: *Social Services:* About 45% of contributions. *Arts & Humanities:* 15% to 20%. *Civic & Public Affairs:* 15% to 20%. *Education:* 10% to 15%. *Health:* 5% to 10%. Primarily supports hospitals and single-disease health organizations including research. Also supports pediatric health and health funds. **Typical Health-Related Recipients:** AIDS/HIV, Alzheimers Disease, Children's Health/Hospitals, Clinics/Medical Centers, Emergency/Ambulance Services, Health Funds, Hospitals, Medical Rehabilitation, Medical Research, People with Disabilities, Single-Disease Health Associations. **Geographic Distribution:** Primarily in operating locations; also internationally.

★ 584 ★ **Armco Foundation**
300 Interpace Pkwy.
Parsippany, NJ 07054
Phone: (201)316-5200
Loyce A. Martin, Foundation Administrator

Giving Priorities: *Education:* About 40% of contributions. Grants go mostly to higher education. *Health & Welfare:* 35% to 40%. United Way receives major support. Other recipients include youth organizations and hospitals. *Culture & the Arts:* 15% to 20%. *Civic & Public Affairs:* 5% to 10%. **Typical Health-Related Recipients:** Emergency/Ambulance Services, Health Funds, Health Organizations, Hospices, Hospitals, Medical Education, Medical Rehabilitation, Medical Training, Nursing Services, People with Disabilities, Public Health, Single-Disease Health Associations, Trauma Treatment. **Geographic Distribution:** Areas where major company operations exist.

★ 585 ★ **Armstrong Foundation**
Liberty & Charlotte Sts.
Box 3001
Lancaster, PA 17604
Phone: (717)397-0611
M. William Jones, Assistant to the President

Giving Priorities: *Social Services:* 35% to 40% of total contributions. *Civic & Public Affairs:* 20% to 25%. *Education:* 20% to 25%. *Arts & Humanities:* Less than 10%. *Health:* Less than 10%. Funding supported health-care associations and hospitals. *Other:* Less than 5% of funding supported religious and scientific organizations.

Typical Health-Related Recipients: Cancer, Clinics/Medical Centers, Emergency/Ambulance Services, Eyes/Blindness, Family Planning, Hospitals, Medical Education, People with Disabilities, Public Health, Single-Disease Health Associations, Substance Abuse. **Geographic Distribution:** Focus on Lancaster, PA.

★586★ **Arthur D. Little Foundation**
25 Acorn Pk.
Cambridge, MA 02140
Phone: (617)498-5524
Fax: (617)498-7119
Ann Farrington, Secretary for the Trustees

Giving Priorities: *Education:* About 70%. *Social Services:* 20% to 25%. *Civic & Public Affairs:* 5% to 10%. *Arts & Humanities:* Less than 5% of total contributions. *Other:* Support also goes to international organizations, science institutions, and health care. **Typical Health-Related Recipients:** Adolescent Health Issues, AIDS/HIV, Hospices, Hospitals, Medical Research, Mental Health, People with Disabilities, Sexual Abuse. **Geographic Distribution:** Primarily in areas of company operations, particularly in home-office community, Cambridge, MA.

★587★ **Arvin Foundation**
One Noblitt Plz.
PO Box 3000
Columbus, IN 47202-3000
Phone: (812)379-3285
Fax: (812)379-3285
William Kendall, Contributions Committee
  Chairman

Giving Priorities: *Education:* About 60% of total contributions. *Social Services:* About 20% of funding. *Health:* 5% to 10% of contributions. Grants were made to several research institutes and projects, as well as support for hospice and home care. *Civic & Public Affairs:* About 5% of total giving. *Arts & Humanities:* Less than 5% of giving. *Other:* Less than 5% of giving. The remainder of funds went to support international affairs (1%) and religious organizations (1%). **Typical Health-Related Recipients:** Cancer, Clinics/Medical Centers, Hospices, Hospitals, People with Disabilities, Single-Disease Health Associations. **Geographic Distribution:** Principally near operating locations, especially in Indiana; and to some state and national organizations.

★588★ **Ashland Oil Foundation**
1000 Ashland Dr.
PO Box 391
Ashland, KY 41114
Phone: (606)329-4525
Fax: (606)329-3758
Judy B. Thomas, President

Giving Priorities: *Education:* 60% to 65% of total annual contributions. *Health & Welfare:* 10% to 15% of contributions. United funds receive most of this, primarily through matching gifts. Other recipients include youth organizations, groups concerned with the aged and child welfare, community centers and service agencies, and hospitals and health groups. *Culture & Art:* 5% to 10%. *Civic Causes:* Less than 5%. *Public Policy & Economic Education:* Less than 5% of contributions. *Other:* Less than 5%. Supports minority affairs organizations, environmen-

tal concerns, professional associations, and think tanks. **Typical Health-Related Recipients:** Cancer, Clinics/Medical Centers, Health Organizations, Hospitals, People with Disabilities, Single-Disease Health Associations, Speech & Hearing. **Geographic Distribution:** Near corporate facilities.

★589★ **AT&T Foundation**
1301 Avenue of the Americas
Rm. 3124
New York, NY 10019
Phone: (212)841-4747
Fax: (212)841-4683
Laura M. Abbott, Secretary

Giving Priorities: *Education:* About 50% of total annual contributions. *Health & Human Services:* 30% to 35% of foundation giving, two-thirds of which supports United Way. Also supports programs with national application for addressing socioeconomic problems in urban areas with major company presence. Special interest in supporting model projects that strengthen families. Interest in health is in AIDS prevention through education and maternal and child health. Does not consider AIDS research projects. Limited support available to local hospitals that offer emergency care services in communities where AT&T has a substantial number of employees and that serve a substantial portion of the underprivileged. In general, does not make grants to organizations formed to combat specific diseases or for medical research. *Arts & Culture:* About 15% of foundation giving. *International:* Less than 5% of foundation giving. **Typical Health-Related Recipients:** Children's Health/Hospitals, Emergency/Ambulance Services, Hospitals, Medical Education, People with Disabilities, Speech & Hearing, Substance Abuse. **Geographic Distribution:** Principally near operating locations and to national organizations.

★590★ **AUL Foundation**
PO Box 368
Indianapolis, IN 46206-0368
Phone: (317)263-1613
Fax: (317)263-1979
Jim Hetherington, Chm., Corp. Contributions
  Comm.

Giving Priorities: *Health:* 40% to 45% of total contributions. Recipients include hospitals, medical research, and health organizations. *Education:* About 30% of foundation and direct corporate contributions combined. *Social Services:* 10% to 15% of foundation and direct corporate contributions combined. *Arts & Humanities:* 5% to 10% of foundation and direct corporate contributions combined. Provides grants for arts associations, libraries, music, and theater, among other interests. *Civic & Public Affairs:* 5% to 10% of foundation and direct corporate giving combined. **Typical Health-Related Recipients:** Domestic Violence, Health Organizations, Hospitals, Medical Education, Medical Research, Medical Training, Mental Health, Nursing Services, People with Disabilities, Single-Disease Health Associations, Substance Abuse. **Geographic Distribution:** Near operating location, with emphasis on Indiana.

★591★ **Avon Products Foundation**
9 W 57th St.
New York, NY 10019
Phone: (212)546-6731
Fax: (212)546-7695
Glenn S. Clarke, President

Giving Priorities: *Education:* 35% to 40% of total annual contributions. *Social Services:* 15% to 20%. *Arts & Humanities:* About 15%. *Civic & Public Affairs:* About 15%. *Health:* 5% to 10% of annual contributions. Also supports women's health organizations and programs that deal with early detection of breast cancer. *Religion:* About 5%. Funds religious welfare organizations. *Note:* Foundation reports that major focus of its giving program is women's issues. **Typical Health-Related Recipients:** Emergency/Ambulance Services, Health Funds, Health Organizations, Hospices, Hospitals, Medical Education, Medical Rehabilitation, Medical Research, Mental Health, People with Disabilities, Single-Disease Health Associations, Substance Abuse. **Geographic Distribution:** Near headquarters and operating locations.

★592★ **Badger Meter Foundation**
PO Box 23099
Milwaukee, WI 53223-0099
Phone: (414)355-0400
Mary George, Manager

Giving Priorities: *Education:* 35% to 40% of total contributions. *Community Service Contributions:* 25% to 30%. *Dependent Citizens:* about 10% to 15%. Recipients include rescue missions, aid for the mentally retarded, and food and clothing distribution. Almost one-fifth goes to Goodwill Industries. *Health:* 10% to 15%. Support favors single-disease health associations and hospitals. More than one-third of contributions go to American Heart Association. Two-fifths go to pediatric health care. The remainder goes to emergency services, community hospitals, and health organizations. *Conservation:* 5% to 10%. *Arts & Humanities:* About 5% to 10%. **Typical Health-Related Recipients:** Hospitals, Medical Education, Medical Research, People with Disabilities, Single-Disease Health Associations. **Geographic Distribution:** Primarily in Milwaukee, WI.

★593★ **Baltimore Gas & Electric Foundation**
Gas & Electric Bldg.
PO Box 1475
Baltimore, MD 21203
Phone: (410)234-7481
Fax: (410)234-7426
Malinda B. Small, Chairman, Corporate
  Contributions

Giving Priorities: *General Support Program:* Foundation and direct giving programs support a wide variety of charitable organizations, without fixed contribution priorities. In the area of health, contributions emphasize hospitals and medical centers in the Baltimore area. *Note:* The company reported that in 1993 about 39% of its total giving went to healthcare and welfare organizations; 23% to education; 21% to civic groups; and 17% to the arts. **Typical Health-Related Recipients:** Hospices, Hospitals. **Geographic Distribution:** Primarily near company headquarters.

★594★ Banc One Wisconsin Foundation
111 E Wisconsin Ave.
PO Box 481
Milwaukee, WI 53201
Phone: (414)765-3000
Frances Smyth, Secretary

Giving Priorities: *Social Services:* 55% to 60% of total contributions. *Arts & Humanities:* Generally 20% to 25% of contributions. *Education:* About 10% of funding. *Civic & Public Affairs:* About 5% of giving. *Health:* About 5%. Supports single-disease health associations, hospitals, outpatient health care delivery, and health funds. **Typical Health-Related Recipients:** Hospitals, People with Disabilities, Single-Disease Health Associations. **Geographic Distribution:** Near headquarters and operating locations only.

★595★ Bancorp Hawaii Charitable
Foundation
PO Box 2900
Honolulu, HI 96846
Phone: (808)537-8580
Pauline Worsham, Vice President

Giving Priorities: *Education:* 35% to 40% of total contributions. *Social Services:* 20% to 25%. *Civic & Public Affairs:* About 20%. *Health:* 10% to 15%. Recipients include hospitals and medical centers. *Arts & Humanities:* 5% to 10%. **Typical Health-Related Recipients:** Health Organizations, Hospitals. **Geographic Distribution:** Limited to Hawaii, with a focus on Honolulu.

★596★ Banfi Vintners Foundation
1111 Cedar Swamp Rd.
Old Brookville, NY 11545
Phone: (516)626-9200
John G. Troiano, Executive Director

Giving Priorities: *Education:* About 60% of total funding. *International:* About 20%. *Health:* About 5%. Primarily supporting hospitals and disease research and prevention. *Civic & Public Affairs:* Less than 5%. *Religion:* Less than 5%. *Arts & Humanities:* Less than 5% of gifts. *Social Services:* Less than 1%. **Typical Health-Related Recipients:** Cancer, Eyes/Blindness, Health Organizations, Hospitals, Medical Research, Multiple Sclerosis, People with Disabilities, Single-Disease Health Associations, Substance Abuse. **Geographic Distribution:** No geographic restrictions; focus on New York City. **Formerly:** Villa Banfi Foundation.

★597★ Bank of Boston Corp. Charitable
Foundation
Government & Community Affairs Department
PO Box B2016
01-17-04
Boston, MA 02106-2016
Phone: (617)434-2171
Fax: (617)434-8905
Michele Courton Brown, Director, Corporate Contributions

Giving Priorities: *Social Services:* About 30% of total contributions. Over half awarded to united funds. Other interests include programs for the aged, refugees, minorities, and youth, as well as family and community services, dependent care, job training and employment, and

food and shelter assistance. *Civic & Community Affairs:* About 30% of contributions. *Education:* 20% to 25% of funding. *Culture & the Arts:* 5% to 10%. *Health:* 5% to 10%. Emphasis on delivery of health care services to underserved populations such as the poor, the elderly, those who do not speak English, and adolescents. Support offered to hospitals, usually through capital or endowment campaigns, and substance abuse prevention programs. Also provides ongoing support to community health centers and organizations that help families with health care planning and treatment. *Other:* Matching gifts to cultural organizations and education comprise about 6% of total giving. **Typical Health-Related Recipients:** AIDS/HIV, Clinics/Medical Centers, Health Organizations, Hospitals, People with Disabilities. **Geographic Distribution:** Only in New England; branches located outside of New England may make small grants locally.

★598★ Bank IV Charitable Trust
PO Box 4
Wichita, KS 67201
Phone: (316)261-4433
Gary Sherrer, Senior Vice President

Giving Priorities: *Social Services:* Around 40% of total contributions. About one-third of the total foundation giving typically goes to the United Way of Wichita and other United Ways throughout the state, and more than one-quarter supports youth organizations. Other interests include drugs and alcohol rehabilitation, and food and clothing distribution. *Education:* Around 25% of total giving. *Health:* 10% to 15%, with most benefiting medical research. Another major interest is single disease health associations. *Arts & Humanities:* 10% to 15%. *Other:* In 1989, foundation gave 2% to a zoological society and less than 1% to religious organizations. **Typical Health-Related Recipients:** Clinics/Medical Centers, Domestic Violence, Health Organizations, Hospitals, Medical Rehabilitation, People with Disabilities, Single-Disease Health Associations, Substance Abuse. **Geographic Distribution:** Throughout Kansas and Oklahoma.

★599★ BankAmerica Foundation
PO Box 37000
Dept. 3246
San Francisco, CA 94137
Phone: (415)953-3175
Fax: (415)622-3469
Caroline Boitano, President & Executive Director

Giving Priorities: *Health & Human Services:* About 60% of annual contributions, most of which is disbursed through United Ways in operating locations. Also supports hospitals, youth and family service organizations, and various other health, community service, civic, and social service organizations. *Education:* About 20% of funding. Interests include economic, medical, and minority education. *Arts & Humanities:* About 10% of giving. *Environment:* About 10% of giving. **Typical Health-Related Recipients:** Children's Health/Hospitals, Health Organizations, Hospitals, Medical Education, People with Disabilities, Prenatal Health Issues. **Geographic Distribution:** Nationally, with emphasis

on California; some international giving where corporation operates.

★600★ Barden Foundation
200 Park Ave.
Danbury, CT 06810
Phone: (203)336-0121
Thomas Loughman, Controller

Giving Priorities: *Social Services:* 35% to 40%. *Health:* About 45% of funds. Supports hospitals, hospices, and health centers. Also funds American Cancer Society. *Education:* About 10%. *Civic & Public Affairs:* Less 5%. *Other:* Less than 5%. Contributes to the arts and religious groups. **Typical Health-Related Recipients:** Cancer, Children's Health/Hospitals, Health Organizations, Hospices, Hospitals, Medical Rehabilitation, Nursing Services, Single-Disease Health Associations. **Geographic Distribution:** Focus on Danbury, CT.

★601★ Baxter Foundation
One Baxter Pkwy.
Deerfield, IL 60015
Phone: (708)948-4604
Fax: (708)948-2887
Patricia A. Morgan, Executive Director

Giving Priorities: *Health:* 50% to 55% of total contributions. Supports health care access, improving the quality of the health-care delivery system, and increasing the availability of resources to health-care providers. Also supports improved cost effectiveness of the delivery system and sponsors employee matching gifts to hospitals. The foundation also awards three prizes in the health-care field. The Foster McGraw Prize honors hospitals that have demonstrated a commitment to public service and that enhance the lives of community members, particularly the poor. The Baxter Health Services Research Prize is awarded to and individual researcher who has significantly improved the delivery of medical care through innovative health services research. The Baxter Foundation Episteme Award recognizes an individual for significant research in nursing. *Education:* About 20% of funding. Generally does not support educational institutions except when funding will help achieve other health care goals. *Social Services:* 20% to 25% of contributions. *Civic & Public Affairs:* Less than 5%. *Culture:* About 2% of total. *Note:* Foundation reports that, overall, more than three-fifths of contribution dollars support health-related programs. **Typical Health-Related Recipients:** AIDS/HIV, Clinics/Medical Centers, Emergency/Ambulance Services, Health Organizations, Health Policy/Cost Containment, Home-Care Services, Hospitals, Medical Education, Medical Rehabilitation, Medical Research. **Geographic Distribution:** Nationally for health-related issues; other grants concentrated in northern Illinois.

★602★ Bayport Foundation
100 Fourth Ave. N
Bayport, MN 55003-1096
Phone: (612)430-7395
Fax: (612)430-7419
Keith D. Olson, Secretary & Treasurer

Giving Priorities: *Social Services:* Between 45% and 50% of total annual contributions, with over one-third benefiting youth organizations. Major grants also awarded to the United Way and the Salvation Army. Other interests include the aged, community service organizations, recreation and athletics, drug and alcohol treatment programs, and volunteer services. *Health:* 25% to 30% yearly, with majority of support going to hospitals, medical research, and single-disease health organizations. *Education:* 10% to 15% of annual total. *Religion:* 5% to 10%. *Arts & Humanities:* Less than 5%. *Civic & Public Affairs:* Less than 5%. **Typical Health-Related Recipients:** Clinics/Medical Centers, Emergency/Ambulance Services, Family Planning, Health Organizations, Hospitals, Kidney, Medical Research, People with Disabilities, Single-Disease Health Associations, Substance Abuse. **Geographic Distribution:** Predominantly in Minnesota, especially the Twin Cities area; also in St. Croix, WI, area, and to national organizations.

★603★ **Bemis Company Foundation**
222 S 9th St.
Ste. 2300
Minneapolis, MN 55402-4099
Phone: (612)376-3000
Fax: (612)376-3180
Lawrence E. Schwanke, Trustee

Giving Priorities: *Social Welfare & Health:* 50% to 55% of total contributions. Over half supports united fund drives. Of the remainder, the highest priority is food shelves and food banks. Other social welfare interests include child welfare and youth organizations, the aged, employment, and community service organizations. Health interests include hospitals and single-disease health organizations. *Education:* 35% to 40%. *Cultural & Civic:* About 10%. *Note:* Foundation's reported giving goals are: 50% to education, 40% to social welfare and health, and 10% to cultural and civic organizations. **Typical Health-Related Recipients:** Emergency/Ambulance Services, Family Planning, Health Funds, Health Policy/Cost Containment, Hospitals, Medical Education, People with Disabilities, Single-Disease Health Associations, Substance Abuse. **Geographic Distribution:** In areas where company has facilities, with emphasis on Minneapolis, MN.

★604★ **Benjamin Jacobson & Sons Foundation**
61 Broadway, Rm. 2800
New York, NY 10006
Phone: (212)952-1012
Robert J. Jacobson, Sr., President

Giving Priorities: *Civic & Public Affairs:* About 30% to 35% of total contributions. *Health:* 25% to 30%. More than two-fifths supports cancer research. Also funds hospitals, single-disease health associations, and health organizations. *Social Services:* 10% to 15%. *Religion:* 10%. *Arts & Humanities:* About 10%. *Education:* About 5%. **Typical Health-Related Recipients:** Health Organizations, Hospitals, Medical Research, People with Disabilities, Single-Disease Health Associations. **Geographic Distribution:** Nationally, with a focus on New York, NY.

★605★ **Betz Foundation**
200 Witmer Rd.
Horsham, PA 19044
Phone: (215)355-3300
Fax: (215)355-2869
Edward Ross, President

Giving Priorities: *Education:* Supports selected colleges and universities operating specific academic disciplines or programs that are considered important to Betz; programs that provide educational opportunities for members of minority groups, women, and the disabled; literacy training; and scholarship program for employees. *Arts & Humanities:* Supports performing arts programs and institutions that have established community acceptance and support. *Health Care & Human Services:* Interests include United Way, health care organizations providing direct services to Betz employees, and research programs considered important to Betz operations, such as those dealing with toxic substance and environmental health. *Civic:* Supports adult job training and youth employment programs. *Environment:* Favors environmental issues that impact on Betz, its employees, and the community. Also supports projects which promote awareness and create technological solutions for environmental issues. **Typical Health-Related Recipients:** General. **Geographic Distribution:** Headquarters area.

★606★ **BFGoodrich Foundation**
3925 Embassy Pkwy.
Akron, OH 44333-1799
Phone: (216)374-2000
Fax: (216)374-3401
Gary L. Habegger, President

Giving Priorities: *Health & Welfare:* 20% to 25% of contributions. Emphasis on United Ways in communities where company has operating facilities. Also supports privately financed agencies directed to basic human needs, such as youth development and family care. Gifts to hospitals are for capital grants only and are given in communities in which company has operating facilities. *Education:* 30% to 35% of total giving. *Culture:* About 5% of giving. *Civic:* 20% to 25%. *Other:* About 15% of contributions for public information. **Typical Health-Related Recipients:** Emergency/Ambulance Services, Geriatric Health, Health Organizations, Hospitals, People with Disabilities, Substance Abuse. **Geographic Distribution:** Foundation gives priority to organizations in Northeast Ohio; limited giving to national organizations: company gives near headquarters and operating locations.

★607★ **BHP Petroleum Americas (HI) Foundation**
PO Box 3379
Honolulu, HI 96842
Phone: (808)547-3225
Fax: (808)547-5084
Sherelee Saneishi-Kim, Secretary

Giving Priorities: *Health, Youth & Social Services:* 40% of contributions. Interests include united funds, community service organizations, shelters, and family services. Health support is directed primarily toward hospitals and single-disease associations. Other interests include public health, nutrition, and health maintenance. Supports youth organizations and groups concerned with child welfare. *Education:* 25% of contributions. *Culture & Arts:* 25% of contributions. *Environment* 5% to 10% of contributions support environmental education. *International:* Contributions are made on an international level to nonprofit organizations in the company's international marketplaces. **Typical Health-Related Recipients:** Hospices, Hospitals, Nutrition, Substance Abuse. **Geographic Distribution:** The state of Hawaii and near operating locations. **Formerly:** PRI Foundation.

★608★ **Boatmen's Bancshares Charitable Trust**
PO Box 236
St. Louis, MO 63166
Phone: (314)466-7565
Fax: (314)466-7333
Carol A. Gruen, Administrative Officer

Giving Priorities: *Health and Human Services:* 45% to 50% of total annual funding. Supports united funds and youth organizations. Recipients also include community service organizations and family services groups. *Education:* Between 20% and 25%. *Arts & Humanities:* 10% to 15%. *Civic & Public Affairs:* 5% to 10%. *Other:* Less than 1% supports scientific and religious organizations. **Typical Health-Related Recipients:** Health Organizations, Hospitals. **Geographic Distribution:** Only near operating locations.

★609★ **Boatmen's First National Bank of Oklahoma Foundation**
PO Box 25189
Oklahoma City, OK 73125-4000
Phone: (405)272-5216
Sheila Mayberry, Secretary

Giving Priorities: *Education:* 30% to 35%. Main priority of giving. *Health:* 20% to 25% of gifts. Funding supports single-disease health associations and medical research, including a $20,000 grant to Oklahoma Medical Research Foundation. One-fifth of support is contributed to hospitals. Mental health organizations also receive funds. *Arts & Humanities:* About 15% of contributions. *Civic & Public Affairs:* 10% to 15%. **Typical Health-Related Recipients:** Cancer, Children's Health/Hospitals, Clinics/Medical Centers, Diabetes, Domestic Violence, Emergency/Ambulance Services, Eyes/Blindness, Health Organizations, Hospitals, Medical Research, Mental Health, Nutrition, People with Disabilities, Public Health, Research/Studies Institutes, Single-Disease Health Associations, Substance Abuse. **Geographic Distribution:** Limited to the state of Oklahoma. **Formerly:** First Interstate Foundation.

★610★ **Borden Foundation**
180 East Broad St.
Columbus, OH 43215-3799
Phone: (614)225-4340
Fax: (614)225-3410
Judy Barker, President

Giving Priorities: *Social Services:* 40% to 45%. Considerable support goes to united funds, youth organizations, and religious welfare organizations. Special consideration given to nutrition education and food programs for children and projects that improve living conditions for children or provide them with adequate shelter and/or health care. *Education:* 25% to 30%. *Civic & Public Affairs:* 10% to 15%. *Health:* 5% to 10%. Supports hospitals and single-disease health associations. *Arts & Humanities:* Less than 5%. *International:* Less than 5% to international organizations. *Religion:* Less than 5% to religious organizations and churches. **Typical Health-Related Recipients:** Cancer, Eyes/Blindness, Hospitals, Mental Health, People with Disabilities, Prenatal Health Issues, Single-Disease Health Associations. **Geographic Distribution:** Preference given to locations where Borden Inc. maintains facilities.

★611★ Borg-Warner Foundation
200 S Michigan Ave.
Chicago, IL 60604
Phone: (312)322-8659
Donald Charles Trauscht, President

Giving Priorities: *Education:* 50% to 55% of contributions. *Social Services:* 20% to 25%. *Civic Affairs & Economic Development:* 10% to 15% of contributions. *Culture:* 5% to 10% of giving. *Health:* 5% to 10% Supports hospitals and medical centers, geriatric health, a program for the disabled, and various other health organizations. **Typical Health-Related Recipients:** Emergency/Ambulance Services, Health Organizations, Hospitals, Kidney, Single-Disease Health Associations, Substance Abuse. **Geographic Distribution:** Primarily in Chicago, IL.

★612★ The Borman Fund
20500 Civic Center Dr., Ste. 2750
Southfield, MI 48076
Phone: (313)353-3772
Fax: (313)350-2920
Gilbert Borman, Secretary-Treasurer

Giving Priorities: *Religion:* About 50% of total contributions. *Civic & Public Affairs:* 20% to 25%. *Education:* 5% to 10%. *Health:* 5% to 10%. Largest contribution went to the Michigan Cancer Foundation. Additional funding is awarded to single-disease health organizations and national health societies. *Arts & Humanities:* About 5%. *Other:* Less than 5%. Contributes limited funds to social services in Michigan and international organizations. **Typical Health-Related Recipients:** AIDS/HIV, Alzheimers Disease, Cancer, Children's Health/Hospitals, Domestic Violence, Emergency/Ambulance Services, Family Planning, Geriatric Health, Health Organizations, Hospices, Hospitals, Mental Health, Multiple Sclerosis, People with Disabilities, Single-Disease Health Associations, Substance Abuse. **Geographic Distribution:** Focus on southeastern Michigan area.

★613★ Boston Edison Foundation
800 Boylston St. P203
Boston, MA 02199-2599
Phone: (617)424-2235
Fax: (617)424-2736
Frank A. Chiaravalloti, Director

Giving Priorities: *Health:* About 40%, more than three-quarters of which went to hospitals. Other interests included health centers, nursing services, and hospices. *Education:* About 20% of annual total. *Civic & Public Affairs:* 15% to 20%. *Matching gifts:* About 10%. Employee contributions to higher education, secondary

schools, and member organizations of the Massachusetts Cultural Alliance, are matched. *Other:* 5% to 10%. Gives special consideration to unique programs not included in the above categories if they are consistent with company's interests, generally improve the quality of life, or make other significant positive contributions to the operating region. *Arts & Humanities:* About 5%. **Typical Health-Related Recipients:** AIDS/HIV, Alzheimers Disease, Cancer, Clinics/Medical Centers, Emergency/Ambulance Services, Health Organizations, Hospices, Hospitals, Nursing Services, Single-Disease Health Associations. **Geographic Distribution:** In greater Boston and eastern Massachusetts areas.

★614★ Boston Globe Foundation
135 Morrissey Boulevard
Boston, MA 02107-2378
Phone: (617)929-3194
Fax: (617)929-2041
Suzanne W. Maas, Executive Director

Giving Priorities: *Community Services:* About 50% of total contributions. *Culture & the Arts:* 20% to 25%. *Education:* 15% to 20% of contributions. *Hospitals & Health Care:* 5% to 10%. Supports community-based health centers and grassroots organizing and advocacy efforts for increased access to healthcare in the Boston area. *Summer Camps:* Less than 5%. Grants in this category support a variety of inner-city youth summer programs. **Typical Health-Related Recipients:** AIDS/HIV, Children's Health/Hospitals, Clinics/Medical Centers, Domestic Violence, Hospitals, Medical Research, Mental Health, Nutrition, People with Disabilities, Substance Abuse. **Geographic Distribution:** Boston, Cambridge, Somerville, Chelsea, and Billerica, MA.

★615★ Bristol-Myers Squibb Foundation
345 Park Ave.
New York, NY 10154
Phone: (212)546-4331
Fax: (212)546-9574
Cindy Johnson, Grants Administrator

Giving Priorities: *Education:* 35% to 40%. Directs support toward advancement of higher education. Also emphasizes support for secondary education, particularly programs that focus on math, science, and health education; and the shortage of qualified teachers in these subjects. *Medical Research & Health:* 30% to 35%. Most grants support unrestricted medical research in cancer, nutrition, orthopedics, cardiovascular medicine, pain, infectious diseases, and the neurosciences. Funding also goes to research into alternatives to the use of animals in testing. Other health interests include hospitals, and organizations working to solve administrative, economic, and public policy problems in health care. *Civic & Community Services:* 20% to 25%. *Cultural Activities:* 5% to 10%. **Typical Health-Related Recipients:** AIDS/HIV, Cancer, Children's Health/Hospitals, Diabetes, Emergency/Ambulance Services, Health Organizations, Heart, Hospitals, Medical Education, Medical Rehabilitation, Medical Research, Medical Training, Nutrition, People with Disabilities, Substance Abuse. **Geographic Distribution:** Principally near operating locations, nationally and internationally.

★616★ Brunswick Foundation
One N Field Ct.
Lake Forest, IL 60045
Phone: (708)735-4700
Wendy L. Fuhs, President

Giving Priorities: *Education:* Generally about 50% to 55% of annual funding. *Welfare & Civic:* Approximately 20% to 25%. *Cultural:* About 15% to 20% of contributions. *Health:* 10% to 15%, major support goes to hospitals in plant cities. Remaining grants support local health organizations. **Typical Health-Related Recipients:** Family Planning, Health Organizations, Hospices, Hospitals, Mental Health, Nursing Services, People with Disabilities, Substance Abuse. **Geographic Distribution:** Emphasis on areas where company has major facilities.

★617★ Bucyrus-Erie Foundation
PO Box 500
South Milwaukee, WI 53172-0500
Phone: (414)768-5005
Dennis L. Strawderman, Manager & Secretary

Giving Priorities: *Social Services:* Between 30% and 35% of total contributions. Interests include the handicapped, domestic violence prevention, homes, employment programs, and family service organizations. *Education:* 25% to 30% of funding. *Health:* 10% to 15%, most going to hospitals. Also supports pediatric health and single-disease health associations. *Arts & Humanities:* 10% to 15%. *Civic & Public Affairs:* 5% to 10%, **Typical Health-Related Recipients:** Domestic Violence, Health Organizations, Hospitals, Medical Education, Medical Rehabilitation, Medical Research, People with Disabilities, Single-Disease Health Associations. **Geographic Distribution:** Primarily Milwaukee, WI, and communities where company has business operations or subsidiaries.

★618★ C. R. Bard Foundation
730 Central Ave.
Murray Hill, NJ 07974
Phone: (908)277-8182
Fax: (908)277-8098
Linda A. Hrevnack, Secretary/Contributions Coordinator

Giving Priorities: *Health and Welfare:* 45% to 50%. Major support goes to health-related united funds. Clinics and research institutes also receive substantial funding. Other interests include health care associations, hospitals, and emergency services. *Education:* About 25%. Emphasis on colleges, universities, and independent college funds, and medical education. *Social Services:* 15% to 20% of contributions. *Arts & Humanities:* 5% to 10%. *Civic & Public Affairs:* Less than 5%. **Typical Health-Related Recipients:** Domestic Violence, Emergency/Ambulance Services, Health Funds, Health Organizations, Hospitals, Medical Education, Medical Research. **Geographic Distribution:** Principally near operating locations.

★619★ Campbell Soup Foundation
Campbell Pl.
Camden, NJ 08103-1799
Phone: (609)342-6433
Fax: (609)541-8185
Bertram C. Willis, Secretary

Giving Priorities: *Education:* 20% to 25% of total contributions. The foundation supports education on many levels. *Arts & Humanities:* 20% to 25% of funding. *The Young:* 15% to 20% of giving. *Nutrition & Health:* 15% to 20% of contributions. Supports programs that advance the linkage between diet and health. Recipients include the National Kidney Foundation, the American Heart Association, Oregon Health Sciences University, and the Strang Cancer Prevention Center. *Camden Aquarium:* About 15% of funding. The New Jersey State Aquarium in Camden received $250,000, as the final installment on a $500,000 challenge grant from the foundation. *Other:* About 5% of giving. **Typical Health-Related Recipients:** Cancer, Heart, Hospitals, Kidney, Medical Education, Medical Research, Nutrition, Single-Disease Health Associations. **Geographic Distribution:** Near company headquarters and operating facilities in the United States only.

★620★ **Capital Cities / ABC Foundation**
77 W 66th St.
16th Fl.
New York, NY 10023
Phone: (212)456-7011
Fax: (212)456-6202
Bernadette Williams, Contributions
   Administrator

Giving Priorities: *Civic & Public Affairs:* 30% to 35%. *Arts & Humanities:* 20% to 25%. *Education:* 15% to 20% of total contributions. Major support goes to colleges and universities. Interests include medical, education. *Social Services:* 10% to 15%, with emphasis on youth organizations. Child welfare, family services, community service organizations, employment, the aged, and religious welfare are also supported. *Health:* 10% to 15%, to single-disease health associations, health centers, and hospitals. **Typical Health-Related Recipients:** Clinics/Medical Centers, Health Organizations, Hospitals, Medical Education, Medical Research, Medical Training, People with Disabilities, Single-Disease Health Associations, Substance Abuse. **Geographic Distribution:** Near headquarters and operating locations only.

★621★ **Cargill Foundation**
PO Box 9300
Minneapolis, MN 55440
Phone: (612)475-6213
Fax: (612)475-6301
James S. Hield, Sec., Cargill Contributions
   Comm.

Giving Priorities: *Social Services:* About 30% of total giving. *Education:* About 25% of funding. *Civic:* About 15% of total funding. *Health:* About 15% of total support. Major interests include organizations that provide health-care services to a broader community and projects seeking the causes and methods of control of health conditions and diseases. Primarily administered by the foundation. *Culture:* About 15% of total giving. *Environment:* Less than 5%. **Typical Health-Related Recipients:** Hospitals, People with Disabilities. **Geographic Distribution:** Concentrated in Minneapolis and St. Paul, MN and the seven-county metropolitan area.

★622★ **Caring Foundation**
450 Riverchase Pkwy. East
Birmingham, AL 35298
Phone: (205)988-2120
Phillip Pope, Treasurer

Giving Priorities: *Social Services:* 60% to 65% of total contributions. *Civic & Public Affairs:* About 20%. *Health:* 15% to 20%. Favors children's hospitals and community health programs. Also supports single-disease health associations. *Other:* Less than 5%. Gives to orchestras, choirs, and historical preservation. **Typical Health-Related Recipients:** Health Organizations, Hospitals, Single-Disease Health Associations. **Geographic Distribution:** Limited to Alabama, with a focus on Birmingham.

★623★ **Carpenter Technology Corp.**
   Foundation
P.O. Box 14662
Reading, PA 19612-4662
Phone: (610)208-3182
Fax: (610)208-3242
Robert W. Lodge, Vice President

Giving Priorities: *Health & Welfare:* Over 50% of total contributions. More than three-fifths support united funds. Capital campaigns, including contributions to boys and girls clubs, account for one-fifth. The remainder supports various human service programs, including homes, single-disease health associations, chemical abuse counseling, and health organizations. Also supports hospitals. *Education:* 30% to 35%. *Civic, Community, & Public Activity:* Less than 5%. *Culture & the Arts:* 5% to 10%. *Other:* Less than 5%. Recipients include professional executive, industrial, and materials science associations. **Typical Health-Related Recipients:** AIDS/HIV, Emergency/Ambulance Services, Health Funds, Health Organizations, Heart, Hospitals, Substance Abuse. **Geographic Distribution:** Principally near operating locations and to national organizations.

★624★ **Carter-Wallace Foundation**
1345 Avenue of the Americas
New York, NY 10105
Phone: (212)339-5000
Fax: (212)339-5086
Mr. James L. Wagar, Vice-President and
   Treasurer

Giving Priorities: *Education:* 35% to 40% of contributions. Medical and dental education among highest priorities. *Health:* About 30% of giving. Priority given to hospitals and medical centers. Single-disease health associations also of considerable interest. *Arts & Humanities:* 10% to 15% of funds. *Civic & Public Affairs:* 5% to 10%. *Social Services:* 5% to 10%. *Science:* Less than 5%. **Typical Health-Related Recipients:** Cancer, Clinics/Medical Centers, Family Planning, Health Organizations, Hospitals, Medical Education, Medical Research, Mental Health, People with Disabilities, Single-Disease Health Associations, Substance Abuse. **Geographic Distribution:** Primarily in New York, New Jersey, Connecticut tri-state area, with limited support to Decatur, IL, area.

★625★ **Caterpillar Foundation**
100 NE Adams St.
Peoria, IL 61629-1480
Phone: (309)675-4418
Fax: (309)675-5815
Henry Holling, Vice President & Manager

Giving Priorities: *Education:* 45% to 50% of total contributions. *Health & Human Services:* 30% to 35% of contributions. United Ways in plant communities receive about three-fourths. Also makes capital grants to local health institutions and human service agencies, including youth and religious welfare organizations, homes, and programs for drug and alcohol abuse prevention. *Civic:* 5% to 10%. *Culture:* 5% to 10%. *Other:* Less than 5%. Chiefly to support international economic development organizations such as the International Executive Service Corps. **Typical Health-Related Recipients:** Emergency/Ambulance Services, Health Organizations, Hospitals, People with Disabilities, Sexual Abuse, Single-Disease Health Associations, Substance Abuse. **Geographic Distribution:** Generally only to communities where company has a facility; Educational Matching Gifts Program is national.

★626★ **CBI Foundation**
800 Jorie Blvd.
Oak Brook, IL 60521-2268
Phone: (708)572-7000
Susan E. Marks, Secretary

Giving Priorities: *United Way:* 60% to 65% of funds. *Education:* 15% to 20%. *Civic & Cultural:* About 15%. *Health:* About 5% of gifts. Funds hospices, hospitals, cancer research, and single-disease health associations. **Typical Health-Related Recipients:** Health Organizations, Hospices, Hospitals, Medical Rehabilitation, Medical Research, People with Disabilities, Single-Disease Health Associations. **Geographic Distribution:** Primarily in the Chicago, IL, area.

★627★ **Centerior Energy Foundation**
6200 Oaktree Blvd.
Independence, OH 44131
Phone: (216)479-1530
Fax: (216)479-4826
Jackie K. Hauserman, Chairman Contributions
   Committee

Giving Priorities: *Health & Welfare:* 50% to 55% of total contributions, more than four-fifths of which supports the United Way. Also support for community centers, youth organizations, community service organizations, religious charities, and the aged. Small percentage to health, primarily supporting hospitals. *Education:* 25% to 30%. *Arts & Culture:* 10% to 15%. *Civic & Public Affairs:* 10% to 15%. *Voluntarism:* Employees volunteer for a number of community events. **Typical Health-Related Recipients:** Health Organizations, Hospitals, Medical Training, Mental Health, People with Disabilities. **Geographic Distribution:** Exclusively in northeastern and northwestern Ohio: does not give out of service area.

★628★ Central Fidelity Banks Foundation
PO Box 27602
Richmond, VA 23261
Phone: (804)697-7038
Fax: (804)697-7078
Charles Tysinger, Foundation Manager

Giving Priorities: *Education:* About 50% of giving. *Civic:* About 25%. *Social Services:* 15% to 20%. *Arts:* 5% to 10%. *Health:* 5% to 10%. Supports hospitals, single-disease health associations, and clinics in market locations. *Voluntarism:* The company sponsors an employee volunteer Adopt-A-School program. **Typical Health-Related Recipients:** Cancer, Clinics/Medical Centers, Health Organizations, Hospitals, Single-Disease Health Associations. **Geographic Distribution:** In locations served by their facilities.

★629★ Central Soya Foundation
PO Box 1400
Ft. Wayne, IN 46801
Phone: (219)425-5500
Mack Wootton, Vice President

Giving Priorities: *Social Services:* 35% to 40%. *Education:* 30% to 35%. *Civic & Public Affairs:* About 10%. *Arts & Humanities:* 5% to 10%. *Health:* 5% to 10%. Supports hospitals and health organizations. *Other:* Less than 5% of funding supports religious organizations. **Typical Health-Related Recipients:** Children's Health/Hospitals, Emergency/Ambulance Services, Health Organizations, Hospitals, Medical Rehabilitation, People with Disabilities. **Geographic Distribution:** Primarily in operating areas.

★630★ CertainTeed Corp. Foundation
PO Box 860
Valley Forge, PA 19482
Phone: (610)341-7000
Fax: (610)341-7777
Janet Weber, Communications Coordinator

Giving Priorities: *Social Services:* Support goes to United Way, homes, community centers, community service organizations, and youth services. *International:* Supports organizations affiliated with France. *Civic & Public Affairs:* Emphasis on international business management and development, public policy, housing, safety organizations, and economic development. *Arts & Humanities:* Supports museums, theater, and music centers. *Education:* Emphasis on colleges and universities. *Health:* Supports health organizations, hospitals, pediatric health, and single-disease associations. *Other:* Less than 5% of total contributions goes to religion. *Note:* Approximately 30% of contributions are for matching gifts across all categories of support. **Typical Health-Related Recipients:** Cancer, Children's Health/Hospitals, Domestic Violence, Emergency/Ambulance Services, Health Organizations, Hospitals, Medical Education, Medical Research, Multiple Sclerosis, Single-Disease Health Associations, Substance Abuse. **Geographic Distribution:** Principally near operating locations and to national organizations.

★631★ Cessna Foundation
PO Box 7706
Wichita, KS 67277-7706
Phone: (316)941-6488
Fax: (316)941-7812
David M. Franson, Secretary & Treasurer

Giving Priorities: *Social Services:* About 40% of total contributions. *Education:* About 35% of contributions. *Arts & Humanities:* 5% to 10%. *Civic & Public Affairs:* 5% to 10%. *Health/Other:* About 5% of giving. Limited support for health, including mental health and single disease association. Also supports religious organizations. *Voluntarism:* The company supports food drives, the Cessna United Friendship Fund, and the Special Olympics volunteers. **Typical Health-Related Recipients:** Cancer, Health Funds, Health Organizations, Heart, Hospitals, Medical Education, Multiple Sclerosis, People with Disabilities, Single-Disease Health Associations. **Geographic Distribution:** Operating locations; primarily the Wichita, KS, area.

★632★ Chambers Development Charitable Foundation
10700 Frankstown Rd.
Pittsburgh, PA 15235
Phone: (412)244-6958
Jill Rangos

Giving Priorities: *Education:* 30% to 35% of total contributions. Support includes medical education. *Arts & Humanities:* 25% to 30%. *Social Services:* About 15%. *Religion:* About 15%. *Civic & Public Affairs:* 5% to 10%. *Health:* About 5%. Supports single-disease health associations, health organizations, and hospitals. **Typical Health-Related Recipients:** Health Organizations, Hospitals, Medical Education, Medical Rehabilitation, Single-Disease Health Associations. **Geographic Distribution:** Focus on Pittsburgh, PA.

★633★ Charles Schwab Corp. Foundation
101 Montgomery St.
San Francisco, CA 94104
Phone: (415)627-8415
Fax: (415)627-7112
Karen Ens, Manager, Community Relations

Giving Priorities: *Health and Human Services:* About 50% of total funding. Primary support to health care and human service organizations, with the exception of hospitals. Major interests in youth groups and AIDS education and information. *Education:* About 20%. *Arts & Humanities:* About 20%. *Civic & Public Affairs:* About 10%. **Typical Health-Related Recipients:** People with Disabilities, Single-Disease Health Associations. **Geographic Distribution:** Primarily headquarters and in geographic areas where there are Schwab branch offices (approximately 200 locations nationwide).

★634★ Chatam Inc.
Liberty Ln.
Hampton, NH 03842
Phone: (603)926-5911
Spencer Stokes, President

Giving Priorities: *Education:* 35% to 40%. *Arts & Humanities:* About 25%. *Health:* 20% to 25%. Concerns supported include medical foundations, single-disease health associations, medi-

cal centers, and hospitals. Funding also goes to help disabled veterans. *Civic & Public Affairs:* 5% to 10%. *Social Services:* 5% to 10%. *Religion:* Less than 5%. **Typical Health-Related Recipients:** Cancer, Clinics/Medical Centers, Diabetes, Emergency/Ambulance Services, Health Organizations, Hospitals, Medical Education, Medical Research, People with Disabilities, Research/Studies Institutes, Single-Disease Health Associations, Speech & Hearing, Transplant Networks/Donor Banks. **Geographic Distribution:** Near operating locations.

★635★ CIT Group Foundation
650 CIT Drive
Livingston, NJ 07039
Phone: (201)740-5395
Albert R. Gamper, Jr., President & Chief Executive Officer

Giving Priorities: *General Support Program:* Company reports 62% of contributions support health and human services, 30% support education, 5% support community services, and 3% support arts and culture. Recipients include health organizations, medical research, single-disease health associations, community service organizations, and united funds. **Typical Health-Related Recipients:** Cancer, Children's Health/Hospitals, Clinics/Medical Centers, Emergency/Ambulance Services, Health Organizations, Hospitals, Medical Research, People with Disabilities, Single-Disease Health Associations, Transplant Networks/Donor Banks, Trauma Treatment. **Geographic Distribution:** Nationally, with an emphasis on headquarters area.

★636★ Citizens Charitable Foundation
One Citizens Plaza
Providence, RI 02903-1339
Phone: (401)456-7285
Fax: (401)456-7366
D. Faye Sanders, Senior Vice President

Giving Priorities: *Social Services:* About 70% of total contributions. *Education:* 15% to 20%. *Health:* 5% to 10%. Primarily supports hospitals and ambulatory health care centers. *Civic & Public Affairs:* About 5%. *Other:* Less than 5%. Recipient areas include museums, libraries, and religious organizations. **Typical Health-Related Recipients:** Emergency/Ambulance Services, Health Organizations, Hospitals, Medical Education, Medical Rehabilitation, Medical Research, Single-Disease Health Associations, Substance Abuse. **Geographic Distribution:** Focus on Rhode Island.

★637★ CLARCOR Foundation
PO Box 7007
Rockford, IL 61125
Phone: (815)962-8867
Fax: (815)962-0417
William Knese, Chairman

Giving Priorities: *Social Services:* 40% to 45% of total funding. *Arts & Humanities:* 10% to 15% of total contributions. *Civic & Public Affairs:* 10% to 15% of funding. *Health:* 10% to 15%. Recipients include health organizations and hospitals. *Education:* 5% to 10% of funds. *Other:* 5% to 10% of funding. Mainly grants of $500 or less. Limited support for civic and religious organizations. **Typical Health-Related Recipients:**

Health Organizations, Hospitals. **Geographic Distribution:** Operating locations only.

★638★ Cleveland-Cliffs Foundation
1100 Superior Ave.
Cleveland, OH 44114
Phone: (216)694-5407
Fax: (216)694-5382
David L. Gardner, VP, Assistant Treasurer

Giving Priorities: *Education & Other:* 50% to 55% of total contributions. *Health & Human Services:* 20% to 25%. Two-fifths of categorical support goes to United Way services. Other recipients include health foundations, community child care services, cancer society, hospitals, the aged, youth organizations, athletics, and community service organizations. *Civic:* 10% to 15%. *Culture:* 10% to 15%. **Typical Health-Related Recipients:** Cancer, Clinics/Medical Centers, Emergency/Ambulance Services, Health Organizations, Heart, Hospitals, People with Disabilities, Preventive Medicine/Wellness Organizations. **Geographic Distribution:** Headquarters and operating locations.

★639★ Clorox Company Foundation
1221 Broadway
PO Box 24305
Oakland, CA 94623
Phone: (510)271-7751
Fax: (510)832-1463
Carmella J. Johnson, Contributions Manager

Giving Priorities: *Youth:* 25% to 30%. *Social Services:* 25% to 30%. United campaigns account for majority of contributions in this category. Emphasis is on programs for the elderly, the homeless, and persons with disabilities. Other interests include family services, battered men's and women's shelters, and food distribution programs. *Education/Employment Training/Economic Development:* 15% to 20% of total contributions. *Culture & the Arts:* 5% to 10%. *Civic:* 5% to 10% of giving. *Health:* 5% to 10%. Gives to agencies that help to improve the overall health care delivery system. Supports health funds, community clinics, hospices, hospitals, outpatient health care delivery, AIDS education and support programs, and other health organizations. *Voluntarism:* The company reports that more than one-third of employees in its General Offices and its Technical Center volunteer time at more than 375 agencies. **Typical Health-Related Recipients:** Clinics/Medical Centers, Domestic Violence, Family Planning, Geriatric Health, Health Funds, Health Organizations, Hospices, Hospitals, Mental Health, People with Disabilities, Single-Disease Health Associations, Substance Abuse. **Geographic Distribution:** Primarily to organizations located in Oakland; the San Francisco East Bay area; communities where Clorox has operating facilities; a few major national causes.

★640★ Collins & Aikman Holdings Foundation
8320 University Executive Pk., Ste. 102
Charlotte, NC 28262
Phone: (704)548-2389
Fax: (704)548-2391
Susan E. Simpson, Administrator

Giving Priorities: *Social Services:* Between 65% and 70% of total annual contributions. *Education:* About 20% of annual total. *Civic & Public Affairs:* 5% to 10% annually. *Arts & Humanities:* Less than 5%. *Health:* Less than 5%. Almost all funds assisted single-disease health organizations, with preference toward groups conducting cancer research. **Typical Health-Related Recipients:** Hospitals, Medical Research, Nursing Services, People with Disabilities, Single-Disease Health Associations, Substance Abuse. **Geographic Distribution:** Near company operating locations. **Formerly:** Wickes Foundation.

★641★ Coltec Industries Charitable Foundation
430 Park Ave.
New York, NY 10022
Phone: (212)940-0400
Terry Bellew, Secretary

Giving Priorities: *Social Services:* 55% to 60% of total contributions. *Arts & Humanities:* 10% to 15%. *Civic & Public Affairs:* About 10%. *Health:* 5% to 10%. Primarily to support hospitals. Other recipients include medical research, hospices, and medical clinics. *Education:* 5% to 10%. **Typical Health-Related Recipients:** Health Funds, Health Organizations, Hospices, Hospitals, Medical Research, Medical Training. **Geographic Distribution:** Nationally where company has plants or facilities. **Formerly:** Colt Industries Charitable Foundation.

★642★ Columbia/HCA Healthcare Foundation
201 W Main St.
PO 740033
Louisville, KY 40201-7433
Phone: (502)572-2000
Fax: (502)572-2002
Ann Boyd Hancock, Manager, Marketing and Public Affairs

Giving Priorities: *General Support Program:* Supports a variety of nonprofit organizations, including the arts, education, and health and social services. **Typical Health-Related Recipients:** General. **Geographic Distribution:** National programs; Louisville, KY, organizations; and organizations near operating locations.

★643★ Compaq Computer Foundation
20555 SH 249
Houston, TX 77070
Phone: (713)374-0527
Fax: (713)378-7379
Marti Branch, Manager, Community Relations

Giving Priorities: *CASH CONTRIBUTIONS:* Approximately 50% of all giving, distributed as follows: *Education:* 45% to 50%. Recipients include literacy and drug education programs. *Health & Human Services:* 35% to 40% of total cash contributions. Most health recipients are research facilities or single-disease health organizations. Cancer research also receives strong support. *Arts & Humanities:* 15% to 20%. **Typical Health-Related Recipients:** Medical Rehabilitation, Medical Research, Single-Disease Health Associations. **Geographic Distribution:** In the Houston area.

★644★ Compass Bank Foundation
PO Box 10566
Birmingham, AL 35296
Phone: (205)933-3571
Fax: (205)933-3336
Dick Tindol

Giving Priorities: *General Support Program:* Makes grants to charitable, educational, and scientific organizations. Major support to United Way and colleges and universities. Remainder spread among traditional categories, including social services, the arts, and health and welfare, including youth organizations. *Note:* In 1992, the foundation gave 41% of giving to education, 31% of contributions to social services, 15% to arts and humanities, 5% each to health and civic concerns, less than 5% to religious concerns. **Typical Health-Related Recipients:** Children's Health/Hospitals, Clinics/Medical Centers, Health Funds, Health Organizations, Hospitals, Mental Health, People with Disabilities. **Geographic Distribution:** Focus on Alabama and Texas.

★645★ Connecticut Mutual Life Foundation
140 Garden St.
Hartford, CT 06154
Phone: (203)727-6500
Fax: (203)987-6532
Bertina Williams, Corporate Responsibility Officer

Giving Priorities: *Education:* 35% to 40% of foundation contributions. *Federated Campaigns:* Roughly 25% of giving, awarded to the United Way/Combined Health Appeal in Hartford. *Health Care:* About 15%. Special consideration given to increasing efficiency and effectiveness of health care in such areas as health education and disease prevention, alternative modes of health care delivery, and programs for cost containment. Almost three-fifths of health funds given to a pediatric health organization that works to combat infant mortality and reduce teen pregnancy. *Communities:* 5% to 10%. *Culture:* 5%. *Economic/Government Understanding:* 5%. *Employment & Training:* 5%. *Other:* About 2% of contributions supports special foundation programs, including the CMA Volunteer program, which encourages employee voluntarism. **Typical Health-Related Recipients:** AIDS/HIV, Children's Health/Hospitals, Clinics/Medical Centers, Health Funds, Health Organizations, Health Policy/Cost Containment, Hospitals, Medical Education, Prenatal Health Issues, Public Health, Single-Disease Health Associations, Substance Abuse. **Geographic Distribution:** Primarily giving is reserved for the greater Hartford area and to Connecticut..

★646★ Consolidated Natural Gas Co. Foundation
CNG Tower
625 Liberty Ave.
Pittsburgh, PA 15222-3199
Phone: (412)227-1185
Fax: (412)227-1306
Sarah Banda Purvis, Manager

Giving Priorities: *General Support Program:* Primary interests are education, cultural programs, civic groups, and health and human services organizations. Percentages are generally around 40% for health and human services, 30% for education, 15% for civic groups, and 15% for cultural programs. **Typical Health-Related Recipients:** Clinics/Medical Centers, Domestic Violence, Emergency/Ambulance Services, Health Organizations, Hospitals, People with Disabilities. **Geographic Distribution:** Principally in company's service areas of western Pennsylvania, Ohio, Virginia, and West Virginia, but also in Louisiana, Oklahoma, and Washington, D.C., with limited national giving.

★ 647 ★ Consolidated Papers Foundation
PO Box 3
Wisconsin Rapids, WI 54495-0003
Phone: (715)424-3004
Susan Feith, Vice President and Executive Director

Giving Priorities: *Civic:* 40% to 45% of total support. *Education:* 25% to 30% of contributions. *Health & Human Services:* 15% to 20%. Supports united funds, youth, recreation, the aged, and community services. Awards matching gifts to social service organizations. Limited support goes to hospitals and other health interests. Also matches employee gifts to a variety of health organizations. *Arts & Humanities:* 10% to 15%. *Voluntarism:* Company reports employees volunteer in the United Way campaign. **Typical Health-Related Recipients:** Family Planning, Health Organizations, Hospices, Hospitals, Medical Education, People with Disabilities, Trauma Treatment. **Geographic Distribution:** Primarily near headquarters and operating locations in central Wisconsin.

★ 648 ★ Cooper Industries Foundation
PO Box 4446
Houston, TX 77210
Phone: (713)739-5400
Fax: (713)739-5555
Virginia Weiler, Assistant Secretary

Giving Priorities: *Education:* 30% to 35% of annual foundation contributions. *United Way:* 25% to 30%. *Civic & Community:* 10% to 15%. *Health & Welfare:* 10% to 15%. Gives to youth organizations, child and welfare groups, and other community service organizations, as well as hospitals, health funds, and miscellaneous health organizations. *Cultural:* 5% to 10% of contributions. **Typical Health-Related Recipients:** Health Funds, Health Organizations, Hospitals, Mental Health, People with Disabilities, Single-Disease Health Associations. **Geographic Distribution:** Locations where company maintains facilities.

★ 649 ★ Cooper Tire & Rubber Foundation
Lima and Western Ave.
Findlay, OH 45840
Phone: (419)424-4320
J. Alec Reinhardt, Trustee

Giving Priorities: *General Support Program:* The foundation accepts applications from nonprofit organizations in the categories of arts and humanities, civic and public affairs, education, health and hospitals, and social services. Proposals are reviewed on a case-by-case basis. **Typical Health-Related Recipients:** General. **Geographic Distribution:** Focus on Ohio and where manufacturing facilities are located.

★ 650 ★ Crane and Co. Fund
30 South St.
Dalton, MA 01226
Phone: (413)684-2600
David W. Crane, Treasurer, Chief Financial Officer

Giving Priorities: *Social Services:* 50% to 55% of total contributions. *Arts & Humanities:* 15% to 20% of giving. *Education:* 10% to 15%. *Civic & Public Affairs:* 5% to 10%. *Health:* 5% to 10%. A local medical center, health organizations, and emergency services are supported. *Environment:* Less than 5%. *Religion:* Less than 1%. **Typical Health-Related Recipients:** Cancer, Clinics/Medical Centers, Diabetes, Emergency/Ambulance Services, Eyes/Blindness, General, Health Funds, Health Organizations, Heart, Hospices, Hospitals, Hospitals (University Affiliated), Kidney, People with Disabilities, Respiratory, Single-Disease Health Associations. **Geographic Distribution:** Massachusetts, primarily near headquarters.

★ 651 ★ Cranston Foundation
1381 Cranston St.
Cranston, RI 02920
Phone: (401)943-4800
Fax: (401)943-3971
Frederic L. Rockefeller, Trustee

Giving Priorities: *Education:* About 60% of total contributions. *Health & Welfare:* 25% to 30%. Focus on community service organizations, homes for the elderly, and health foundations and associations. One-third goes to the United Jewish Appeal. Other interests include community centers and municipal funds for community needs and health. *Hospitals:* 5% to 10%. Supports operating funds at various hospitals, mostly in Rhode Island. *Civic & Community:* About 5%. *Culture:* Less than 5%. **Typical Health-Related Recipients:** Hospitals. **Geographic Distribution:** Nationally, with a focus on areas where company has operations.

★ 652 ★ Crestar Foundation
Box 26665
Richmond, VA 23261
Phone: (804)782-7906
J. Thomas Vaughan, President

Giving Priorities: *Health & Human Services:* 30% to 35% of total annual contributions. Awards capital and other grants to hospitals, religious welfare organizations such as the Salvation Army, homes, and youth organizations. *Education:* 25% to 30%. Primarily supports private colleges and universities through independent college funds. *Culture & the Arts:* 15% to 20% of total. *Civic & Community:* 25% to 30% of total. **Typical Health-Related Recipients:** Domestic Violence, Health Funds, Health Organizations, Hospitals, Medical Education, Mental Health, Multiple Sclerosis, People with Disabilities. **Geographic Distribution:** Near headquarters and operating locations only.

★ 653 ★ Crown Central Petroleum Foundation
One North Charles St.
Baltimore, MD 21201
Phone: (410)539-7400
Edward L. Rosenberg, President

Giving Priorities: *Social Services:* 45% to 50% of total contributions. *Education:* About 30%.

Civic & Public Affairs: About 5%. *Health:* About 5%. More than half goes to the American Red Cross. Also supports single-disease health associations. *Other:* Less than 5%. Supports arts festivals, museums, and public broadcasting. **Typical Health-Related Recipients:** Health Organizations, Mental Health, People with Disabilities. **Geographic Distribution:** Primarily in Maryland and Texas; emphasis on Baltimore, MD.

★ 654 ★ CS First Boston Foundation Trust
55 E 52nd St.
New York, NY 10055
Phone: (212)909-4571
Fax: (212)318-1105
Larry Reno, VP Mktg. & Dir. Corp. Contributions

Giving Priorities: *Education:* 60% to 65% of contributions. *Social Services:* Approximately 20% of total. *Civic & Public Affairs:* 5% to 10%. *Arts & Humanities:* Less than 5%. *Health:* Less than 5%. Support to medical research and single-disease health organizations. *Other:* Limited support to international relief and scientific organizations. **Typical Health-Related Recipients:** Cancer, Children's Health/Hospitals, Clinics/Medical Centers, Emergency/Ambulance Services, Medical Research, Mental Health, People with Disabilities, Single-Disease Health Associations. **Geographic Distribution:** Nationally and near operating locations. **Formerly:** First Boston Foundation Trust.

★ 655 ★ CUNA Mutual Charitable Foundation
5910 Mineral Point Rd.
PO Box 391
Madison, WI 53705
Phone: (608)231-7908
Fax: (608)238-2449
Terry J. Fiez, Assistant Secretary-Treasurer

Giving Priorities: *Social Services:* About 55% of total contributions. *Education:* 15% to 20%. *Civic & Public Affairs:* 10% to 15%. *Health:* 5% to 10%. Focuses on health organizations, medical research, and health care cost containment. *Arts & Humanities:* Less than 5%. *Other:* Less than 5%. Supports credit union activities and religious organizations. **Typical Health-Related Recipients:** AIDS/HIV, Children's Health/Hospitals, Emergency/Ambulance Services, Health Organizations, Medical Rehabilitation, Medical Research, Prenatal Health Issues, Public Health. **Geographic Distribution:** Focus on Wisconsin, with an emphasis on Madison.

★ 656 ★ Curtice-Burns / Pro-Fac Foundation
PO Box 681
Rochester, NY 14603
Phone: (716)383-1850
Fax: (716)383-1281
Marilyn T. Helmer, Vice President

Giving Priorities: *Social Services:* 35% to 40% of total annual contributions. Most goes to united funds. Other interests include youth organizations, child welfare, organizations for the handicapped, recreation and athletics, and community service organizations. *Education:* Between 15% and 20%. *Health:* 15% to 20%. Grants primarily support hospitals and single-disease health associations. *Civic & Public Affairs:* Between 15% and 20%. *Arts & Humanities:* 5% to 10%. **Typical Health-Related Recipients:** Children's Health/Hospitals, Domestic Violence, Emergency/Ambulance Services, Family Planning, Geriatric Health, Health Organizations, Heart, Hospices, Hospitals, Medical Rehabilitation, Mental Health, Nursing Services, People with Disabilities, Public Health, Single-Disease Health Associations, Substance Abuse. **Geographic Distribution:** Near headquarters and operating locations.

★657★ D.B. Reinhart Family Foundation
636 L. Hauser Rd.
Onalaska, WI 54650
Phone: (608)782-4999
Nancy Hengel, Director

Giving Priorities: *Education:* 25% to 30% of total funding. *Religion:* About 25%. *Health:* 20% to 25%. Major support to the Children's Hospital Foundation of Milwaukee, WI, and the Department of Ophthalmology in Madison, WI, each receiving grants of $25,000. *Social Services:* About 10%. *Other:* The foundation also supports a library, an orchestra, and community affairs. **Typical Health-Related Recipients:** Hospitals, Medical Research, Single-Disease Health Associations. **Geographic Distribution:** Focus on Wisconsin.

★658★ Dana Corp. Foundation
PO Box 1000
Toledo, OH 43697
Phone: (419)535-4601
Fax: (419)535-4756
Don M. Decker, Administrator, Dana Foundation

Giving Priorities: *Social Services:* 45% to 50%. Most of this supports united funds. Other interests include youth organizations, child welfare, community centers, community service organizations, drug and alcohol programs, and emergency relief. *Education:* 15% to 20%, primarily supporting colleges and universities. Also supports medical education. *Arts & Humanities:* 15% to 20%. *Civic & Public Affairs:* 5% to 10%. *Health:* About 5%, to hospitals, hospices, health organizations, pediatric health, and medical research. **Typical Health-Related Recipients:** Alzheimers Disease, Emergency/Ambulance Services, Family Planning, Health Organizations, Hospitals, Medical Education, People with Disabilities, Single-Disease Health Associations, Substance Abuse. **Geographic Distribution:** Primarily where company maintains operating facilities and to national organizations.

★659★ Davis Foundation, Inc.
One National Dr.
Atlanta, GA 30336
Phone: (404)696-9440
Fax: (404)691-0364
Alfred A. Davis, President

Giving Priorities: *Cultural Institutions:* Approximately 30% of total contributions. *Medical Institutions:* 25% to 30%. Focus on research centers and hospitals. Nearly one-half goes to medical research. Also supports pediatric health care and health organizations. *Community Service Organizations:* 20% to 25%. *Academic Institutions:* 15% to 20%. *Other:* Less than 5%

supports religion. **Typical Health-Related Recipients:** Medical Education. **Geographic Distribution:** Nationally, with an emphasis on Atlanta, GA.

★660★ Dayton Power and Light Co. Foundation
PO Box 1247
Dayton, OH 45402
Phone: (513)259-7131
Fax: (513)259-7382
Sharon Tolliver, Foundation Administrator

Giving Priorities: *Youth & Education:* 40% to 45% of total giving. *Health & Welfare:* 30% to 35% of annual contributions. Major support goes to united funds and other health related organizations. *Arts & Humanities:* 10% to 15%. *Civic & Public Affairs:* 5% to 10% of support. **Typical Health-Related Recipients:** Domestic Violence, Substance Abuse. **Geographic Distribution:** Principally near operating locations.

★661★ Deluxe Corp. Foundation
PO Box 64399
St. Paul, MN 55164-0399
Phone: (612)483-7842
Fax: (612)483-7821
Jennifer A. Anderson, Director of Foundations

Giving Priorities: *Human Services:* 45% to 50% of total annual contributions. *Education:* 35% to 40% of total. *Arts & Humanities:* 15% to 20%. **Typical Health-Related Recipients:** AIDS/HIV, Clinics/Medical Centers, Domestic Violence, Health Organizations, Medical Rehabilitation, People with Disabilities, Single-Disease Health Associations, Substance Abuse. **Geographic Distribution:** In areas where company has production facilities and where employees live and work.

★662★ Demoulas Foundation
875 East St.
Tewksbury, MA 01876
Phone: (508)851-8000
Fax: (508)851-3942
Elizabeth Miliotis

Giving Priorities: *Health:* 30% to 35% of giving. The majority of support funds hospitals. Also supports medical rehabilitation for burn victims, pediatric health, and single-disease health associations. *Religion:* 30% to 35% of total gifts. *Education:* 10% to 15% of contributions. A large portion of gifts support colleges and universities in the New England area. Medical education also receives support. *Civic & Public Affairs:* 5% to 10%. *Social Services:* 5% to 10% of giving. *Arts & Humanities:* Less than 5%. **Typical Health-Related Recipients:** Cancer, Children's Health/Hospitals, Hospitals, Long-Term Care, Medical Education, Medical Rehabilitation, Medical Research, People with Disabilities, Respiratory, Single-Disease Health Associations, Substance Abuse. **Geographic Distribution:** Primarily New England.

★663★ Deutsch Foundation
2444 Wilshire Blvd.
Ste. 600
Santa Monica, CA 90403
Phone: (310)453-0055
Fax: (310)453-6467
Lester Deutsch, Executive Vice President

Giving Priorities: *Education:* 60% to 65% of total annual contributions. *Civic & Public Affairs:* 10%% to 15%. *Social Services:* Between 10% and 15%. *Health:* About 5% total. Major interests include single-disease health organizations, pediatric medicine, and health centers. *Arts & Humanities:* Less than 5%. **Typical Health-Related Recipients:** Family Planning, Geriatric Health, Hospitals, Medical Rehabilitation, Medical Research, Mental Health, People with Disabilities, Public Health, Single-Disease Health Associations, Substance Abuse. **Geographic Distribution:** In Southern California.

★664★ Dickson Foundation
2000 Two First Union Ctr.
Charlotte, NC 28282
Phone: (704)372-5404
Colleen Colbert, Secretary-Treasurer

Giving Priorities: *Education:* Almost 55% of total contributions, primarily in the form of support for colleges and universities in North Carolina. Other support in this area went to education funds, faculty development, medical education, and secondary schools. *Civic & Public Affairs:* About 15%. *Health:* 10% to 15%. Primary support in this area went to the Arthritis Research Center in Chapel Hill, NC, with a grant of $17,500. Cancer research and hospitals and hospices also received support. *Arts & Humanities:* About 10%. *Other:* Social service organizations and religious organizations each received less than 10% of contributions. **Typical Health-Related Recipients:** Health Organizations, Hospices, Hospitals, Medical Education, Medical Research, Single-Disease Health Associations. **Geographic Distribution:** Focus on North Carolina.

★665★ Donaldson Foundation
PO Box 1299
Minneapolis, MN 55440
Phone: (612)887-3010
Raymond F. Vodovnik, Trustee & Secretary

Giving Priorities: *Social & Human Services:* About 60% of total contributions. Three-fifths supports general charities. About one-tenth goes to health services, including hospitals, pediatric care, and volunteer health services. Counseling and rehabilitation accounts for one-tenth. Interests include opportunity workshops, homes, family planning, religious charity groups, and resources for women. *Education:* About 29%. *Arts & Humanities:* Approximately 11%. **Typical Health-Related Recipients:** Domestic Violence, Family Planning, Health Funds, Hospices, Hospitals, Mental Health, People with Disabilities, Substance Abuse. **Geographic Distribution:** Focus on Minnesota.

★666★ Dresser Foundation
PO Box 718
Dallas, TX 75221
Phone: (214)740-6741
Fax: (214)740-6960
Libby McClarren, Contact

Giving Priorities: *Health & Social Services:* 55% to 60% of annual contributions. Main priority is united funds. Other interests include religious welfare, youth and community service organizations, child welfare, recreation and athletics, and the disabled. Health interests include hospitals, single-disease health associations, and pediatric health. *Education:* 30% to 35% of funding, much of which is awarded to colleges and universities. Other interests include medical education. *Civic & Public Affairs:* Less than 5% of total contributions. *Arts & Humanities:* Less than 5% of contributions. *Other:* Less than 5% goes to scientific and international organizations. **Typical Health-Related Recipients:** Clinics/Medical Centers, Emergency/Ambulance Services, Family Planning, Health Organizations, Heart, Hospices, Hospitals, Medical Education, Medical Research, Mental Health, Nursing Services, People with Disabilities, Single-Disease Health Associations, Substance Abuse. **Geographic Distribution:** In operating communities.

★ 667 ★ **Duchossois Foundation**
845 Larch Ave.
Elmhurst, IL 60126
Phone: (708)870-2202
Fax: (708)870-1891
Kimberly D. Lenczuk, President

Giving Priorities: *Education:* 30% to 35%. *Civic & Public Affairs:* 25% to 30%. *Health:* 15% to 20% of contributions, supporting hospitals and medical research especially cancer research in Illinois. Contributions to health programs include research, education, and advocacy in the fields of AIDS, cancer, and mental health. *Social Services:* 10% to 15%. Supports youth organizations and united funds. Also supports community service organizations and the disabled. *Arts & Humanities:* About 5% of contributions. *Other:* Less than 5%. Additional foundation interests include religious organizations and a science foundation. **Typical Health-Related Recipients:** Cancer, Clinics/Medical Centers, Health Funds, Hospitals, Medical Research, Mental Health, People with Disabilities, Research/Studies Institutes, Single-Disease Health Associations, Speech & Hearing, Substance Abuse. **Geographic Distribution:** Primarily in Chicago, IL.

★ 668 ★ **Dun & Bradstreet Corp. Foundation**
299 Park Ave.
New York, NY 10171
Phone: (212)593-6746
Fax: (212)593-4151
Juliann Gill, Administrator

Giving Priorities: *Social Services:* 50% to 55%. *Education:* 15% to 20% of contributions. *Health:* 5% to 10%. Supports the American Red Cross, AIDS research, and single-disease health associations. *Civic & Public Affairs:* 5% to 10%. *Science:* About 5%. *Arts & Humanities:* Less than 5%. **Typical Health-Related Recipients:** AIDS/HIV, Cancer, Emergency/Ambulance Services, Health Organizations, Hospitals, Mental Health, People with Disabilities, Single-Disease Health Associations. **Geographic Distribution:** Nationwide.

★ 669 ★ **Dynamet Foundation**
195 Museum Rd.
Washington, PA 15301
Phone: (412)228-1000
Viola G. Taboni, Treasurer, Assistant
  Secretary, Trustee

Giving Priorities: *Education:* About 70% of total contributions. *Social Services:* 5% to 10%. *Health:* About 10%. Recipients include single-disease health associations, cancer research, health organizations, hospitals, and hospices. *Arts & Humanities:* 5%. *Other:* Less than 5%. Funds philanthropic organizations, community celebrations, and international affairs. **Typical Health-Related Recipients:** Cancer, Clinics/Medical Centers, Diabetes, Emergency/Ambulance Services, Eyes/Blindness, Health Organizations, Hospices, Kidney, Medical Rehabilitation, Medical Research, People with Disabilities, Single-Disease Health Associations, Substance Abuse. **Geographic Distribution:** Focus on Pennsylvania, with an emphasis on Pittsburgh.

★ 670 ★ **Eastman Kodak Charitable Trust**
343 State St.
Rochester, NY 14650-0517
Phone: (716)724-1980
Fax: (716)724-5786
Essie L. Calhoun, President

Giving Priorities: *Education:* 45% to 50% of total contributions. *Health & Human Services:* 30% to 35%, principally in support of United Way. Youth groups, local and national health organizations, job training, homes and shelters, child welfare, and services for the aged and the handicapped also supported. *Community Revitalization:* 15% to 20%. *International:* In 1994, company budgeted $383,500 (not included in above totals) for contributions to international nonprofit organizations through foreign subsidiaries. Foreign subsidiaries maintain autonomous giving programs. *Other:* Less than 5% of support. Supports organizations which fall outside the company's primary areas of interests and that make a strong case for the company's involvement. **Typical Health-Related Recipients:** Health Organizations. **Geographic Distribution:** Education grants made nationwide; others made in main corporate locations.

★ 671 ★ **Eaton Charitable Fund**
1111 Superior Ave.
Cleveland, OH 44114
Phone: (216)523-4822
Frederick B. Unger, Director, Community
  Affairs

Giving Priorities: *Health & Human Services:* About 45% of total contributions. Main priority is united funds. Health funding goes almost entirely to hospitals near company operating locations and to single-disease health associations. *Education:* 35% to 40%. *Civic & Public Affairs:* 10% to 15%. *Arts & Culture:* About 5%. **Typical Health-Related Recipients:** Cancer, Health Funds, Health Organizations, Health Policy/Cost Containment, Hospices, Hospitals, People with Disabilities, Single-Disease Health Associations. **Geographic Distribution:** Corporate operating locations.

★ 672 ★ **Eli Lilly and Co. Foundation**
Lilly Corporate Ctr.
Indianapolis, IN 46285
Phone: (317)276-5342
Fax: (317)276-9249
Steve Twait, Secretary, Contributions
  Committee

Giving Priorities: *Health & Welfare:* 35% to 40% of annual contributions. Primary support goes to united funds in corporate communities. Also supports the disabled and working to prevent and treat alcoholism. Health grants support medical research, medical centers, and local health organizations. Funds national health organizations concerned with mental health and diabetes research. *Education:* 35% to 40%. Majority of grants goes to pharmaceutical and medical education, colleges and universities, and higher education associations. *Cultural:* 15% to 20%. *Civic:* 5% to 10%. *Note:* Percentages are based on cash grants only. **Typical Health-Related Recipients:** Children's Health/Hospitals, Emergency/Ambulance Services, Health Organizations, Health Policy/Cost Containment, Medical Education, Medical Research, Mental Health, Prenatal Health Issues, Single-Disease Health Associations, Trauma Treatment. **Geographic Distribution:** Principally near operating locations and to national organizations.

★ 673 ★ **Emerson Charitable Trust**
PO Box 4100
8000 W Florissant Ave.
St. Louis, MO 63136
Phone: (314)553-3722
Jo Ann Harmon, Vice President, Corporate
  Administration

Giving Priorities: *Health & Welfare:* 35% to 40%, with strong emphasis on united funds and youth organizations. Other areas of interest include community centers, homes, animal welfare, recreation and athletics, and substance abuse prevention and treatment. *Education:* 35% to 40% of total contributions. *Arts & Humanities:* 10% to 15%. *Civic & Public Affairs:* Between 10% to 15%. *Other:* Less than 5%. Supports related foundation interests. **Typical Health-Related Recipients:** Hospitals, Medical Education, Single-Disease Health Associations, Substance Abuse. **Geographic Distribution:** Nationally, emphasizing operating locations.

★ 674 ★ **Employers Mutual Charitable Foundation**
PO Box 712
Des Moines, IA 50303
Phone: (515)280-2450
Richard Hoffmann, General Counsel

Giving Priorities: *General Support Program:* Company supports civic and public affairs, education, the arts, and health and welfare. There is no real priority within the giving program. Each proposal is reviewed on a case-by-case basis. Company declined to provide additional information on its charitable contributions. **Typical Health-Related Recipients:** General. **Geographic Distribution:** Headquarters area and operating locations.

★ 675 ★ **Enron Foundation**
PO Box 1188
Houston, TX 77251-1188
Phone: (713)853-5400
Fax: (713)853-6790
Rebecca King, Contributions Representative

Giving Priorities: *Education:* 30% to 35%. Supports colleges, universities, institutes of technology, private secondary education, and education associations (typically with business, economics, public policy, or engineering orientations). *Health & Welfare:* 20% to 25%. Health interests include major disease research organizations, hospitals, and health funds. Areas of interest in the welfare category include united funds and youth and community service organizations. *Culture & the Arts:* 15% to 20%. *Civic:* 10% to 15%. *Other:* 5%. Foundation reserves limited funding for organizations not fitting into above categories. Has supported research to advance technology, American competitiveness, and economic diversification. **Typical Health-Related Recipients:** Geriatric Health, Health Organizations, Hospitals, Medical Education, Medical Research, Mental Health, Nursing Services, Public Health, Single-Disease Health Associations. **Geographic Distribution:** In headquarters and operating locations only.

★676★   **Enterprise Leasing Foundation**
35 Hunter Ave.
St. Louis, MO 63124
Phone: (314)863-7000
Fax: (314)863-9003
Van-Lear Black, III, Secretary

Giving Priorities: *Civic & Public Affairs:* About 45% of total contributions. *Welfare:* 20% to 25%. *Education:* About 15% of total contributions. *Arts & Humanities:* 10% to 20%. *Health:* 5% to 10%. Gives to single-disease health associations. Limited support goes to hospitals. *Science:* Less than 5%. *Religion:* Less than 5%. *Voluntarism:* All employees are encouraged to participate in community and national programs. **Typical Health-Related Recipients:** Hospitals, Single-Disease Health Associations. **Geographic Distribution:** Emphasis on organizations where Enterprise employees are volunteers or board members, organizations where customers are volunteers, and areas that receive Enterprise services.

★677★   **Equifax Foundation**
c/o Equifax
PO Box 4081
Atlanta, GA 30302
Phone: (404)885-8000
Fax: (404)888-5452
John A. Ford, Vice President, Corporate Public
   Affairs

Giving Priorities: *Health & Social Services:* About 50% of total annual giving. Primarily supports the United Way of Metropolitan Atlanta. Also funds youth organizations, disabled, child welfare programs, and homes. Health contributions are to single disease health associations. *Education:* About 25%. *Arts & Culture:* 10% and 15%. *Civic/Community:* About 5% of contributions. *International:* Contributes to U.S.-based nonprofits with an international focus. *Voluntarism:* In Fall 1992, the company founded ECAV (Equifax Council for Activities & Volunteerism), which is a formal company-sponsored employee program. **Typical Health-Related Recipients:** Health Organizations, Hospices, Medical Rehabilitation, People with Disabilities, Single-Disease Health Associations, Substance Abuse. **Geographic Distribution:** Primarily in the southeastern states and to some national organizations.

★678★   **Exxon Education Foundation**
225 E John W. Carpenter Fwy., Rm. 1429
Irving, TX 75062-2298
Phone: (214)444-1000
Fax: (214)444-1405
Edward F. Ahnert, Manager, Contributions

Giving Priorities: *Health, Welfare and Civic & Community Services:* Approximately half of corporate contributions. United appeals and federated drives account for about 16% of this funding. Civic and Community Services represents 13%. Health organizations receive about 11% of U.S. giving. Grants support programs on substance abuse, medical education, environmental health, risk analysis, and the disabled. Approximately 6% goes to local and national groups concerned with improving the social and economic environment for women and minorities. *Education:* About 20% of U.S. corporate donations. *Arts, Museums & Historical Associations & Public Broadcasting:* 16% of corporate giving. *Environment:* 10% of corporate U.S. contributions. *Public Information & Policy Research:* Approximately 8% of corporate U.S. donations. **Typical Health-Related Recipients:** Cancer, Clinics/Medical Centers, Health Organizations, Hospitals, Medical Education, Medical Rehabilitation, Medical Research, Medical Training, Nursing Services, Public Health, Substance Abuse. **Geographic Distribution:** Nationally and internationally.

★679★   **Farmers Group Safety Foundation**
4680 Wilshire Blvd.
Los Angeles, CA 90010
Phone: (213)932-3018
Fax: (213)964-8095
Diane Tasaka, Community Relations Manager

Giving Priorities: *General Support Program:* The company reports that 75% to 80% of contributions support education. Also concentrates efforts in five areas: (1) Youth; (2) Education; (3) Health & Safety, funding medical research organizations and treatment programs to improve the quality of life until cures are discovered, as well as safety-related programs that seek to reduce the incidence of injury and death on the nation's highways, in the home, and in the workplace; (4) The Arts; (5) Civic Organizations. Company reports that in 1993, about 79% of contributions went to education, 7% to health, approximately 7% to civic and public affairs, 5% to social services, and about 2% to the arts. **Typical Health-Related Recipients:** General. **Geographic Distribution:** Headquarters and operating locations.

★680★   **Federal-Mogul Corp. Charitable Trust Fund**
Corporate Communications
PO Box 1966
Detroit, MI 48235
Phone: (810)354-8663
Fax: (810)354-8103
Christine Cusmano, Secretary, Contributions
   Committee

Giving Priorities: *Social Services:* 35% to 40%, the majority of which supports united funds. Organizations concerned with the disabled and youth also are supported. *Civic & Community:* 20% to 25% of funds. *Health:* 15% to 20%. Recipients include medical research,

single-disease health organizations, hospitals, and pediatric health. *Education:* 10% to 15% of giving. *Arts & Culture:* 10% to 15%. *Other:* Less than 5% of contributions support scientific and international organizations. **Typical Health-Related Recipients:** Cancer, Children's Health/Hospitals, Clinics/Medical Centers, Health Funds, Health Organizations, Hospices, Hospitals, Medical Research, People with Disabilities, Single-Disease Health Associations, Substance Abuse. **Geographic Distribution:** Near corporate operating locations; a relatively small portion of the budget goes to regional and national activities.

★681★   **Fidelity Foundation**
82 Devonshire St. S3
Boston, MA 02109
Phone: (617)570-6806
Anne-Marie Soulliere, Foundation Director

Giving Priorities: *Community Development & Social Services:* 50% to 55%. *Arts & Humanities:* About 20%. *Education:* 10% to 15%. *Health:* 5% to 10%. Interests include health organizations and hospitals. **Typical Health-Related Recipients:** Health Organizations, Hospitals, Medical Research. **Geographic Distribution:** Operation locations.

★682★   **First Hawaiian Foundation**
165 S King St.
Honolulu, HI 96813
Phone: (808)525-8144
Fax: (808)525-6204
Herbert E. Wolff, Director/Secretary

Giving Priorities: *Social Services:* Between 30% and 35% of total annual contributions. *Education:* About 25%. *Health:* 15% to 20%, mostly toward modernization of facilities. *Arts & Humanities:* 10% to 15%. *Civic & Public Affairs:* 10% to 15% of annual total. *Other:* 5% to 10%. Additional funding supports religious organizations and a scientific center. **Typical Health-Related Recipients:** Clinics/Medical Centers, Emergency/Ambulance Services, Hospitals, Substance Abuse. **Geographic Distribution:** Primarily in Hawaii, with emphasis on Honolulu, but sometimes makes gifts in Guam and the continental United States.

★683★   **First Interstate Bank of Arizona Charitable Foundation**
PO Box 29743
Phoenix, AZ 85038-9743
Phone: (602)229-4544
Fax: (602)229-4409
Dianne E. Stephens, Sec., Corp. Contributions
   Comm.

Giving Priorities: *Health & Human Services:* 55% to 60% of total contributions. Highest priorities are united funds and youth organizations. Other recipients include community service organizations, child welfare, aid to the aged and the handicapped, community service organizations, and food and clothing distribution. Health interests include hospitals, hospices, health funds, and medical rehabilitation. *Education:* 15% to 20%. *Culture & Arts:* 15% to 20%. *Civic:* 5% to 10%. *Other:* Company also supports economics education, the Special Olympics, and volunteer efforts of employees. **Typical Health-Related Recipients:** Domestic Violence, Hospices, Hospitals, People with Disabilities, Single-Disease Health Associations, Substance Abuse. **Geographic Distribution:** In Arizona only.

★684★ First Interstate Bank of California Foundation
633 W Fifth St.
T11-55
Los Angeles, CA 90071
Phone: (213)614-3068
Fax: (213)614-4614
Ruth Jones-Saxey, Secretary & Treasurer

Giving Priorities: *Social Services:* 45% to 50% of total contributions, primarily supporting California united funds. Other areas of interest include child welfare, youth-oriented organizations, the elderly, and the handicapped. *Education:* 15% to 20%. *Arts & Humanities:* 10% to 15%. *Health:* 10% to 15%, primarily supporting hospitals for purposes including capital improvements, pediatric care, and building funds. *Civic & Public Affairs:* 5% to 10% of funding. **Typical Health-Related Recipients:** Health Organizations, Hospices, Hospitals, Medical Rehabilitation, People with Disabilities, Substance Abuse. **Geographic Distribution:** In California communities.

★685★ First Interstate Bank of Oregon Charitable Foundation
PO Box 3131
Portland, OR 97208
Phone: (503)225-2167
Fax: (503)225-3206
Harleen Katke, Administrator

Giving Priorities: *Social Services & Health:* About 55% of contributions, primarily supporting United Ways organizations. Health interests include hospitals, health campaigns, pediatric health, single-disease health associations, hospices, and local health centers. *Education:* 25% to 30%. *Arts & Humanities:* 15% to 20%. *Civic & Public Affairs:* Less than 5%. **Typical Health-Related Recipients:** Clinics/Medical Centers, Health Funds, Health Organizations, Heart, Hospices, Hospitals, Medical Education, Medical Rehabilitation, Medical Research, Mental Health, People with Disabilities, Substance Abuse. **Geographic Distribution:** Matching gifts to colleges and universities are given nationwide; all other giving is within the state of Oregon.

★686★ First Interstate Bank of Texas Foundation
PO Box 3326
MS 519
Houston, TX 77253-3326
Phone: (713)250-1633
Fax: (713)250-7924
Alice King, Community Project Coordinator

Giving Priorities: *Social Services:* About 50% to total annual contributions. *Arts & Humanities:* 15% to 20%. *Education:* 15% to 20%. *Civic & Public Affairs:* 5% to 10%. *Health:* 5% to 10%. Recipients include single-disease health associations, focusing on diabetes, cancer, and the heart. Medical centers and hospitals also receive funding for contruction projects. **Typical Health-Related Recipients:** Cancer, Clinics/Medical Centers, Diabetes, Emergency/Ambulance Services, Heart, Hospitals, Medical Education, Mental Health, People with Disabilities, Research/Studies Institutes, Single-Disease Health Associations.

★687★ First Union Foundation
First Union Plz.
Charlotte, NC 28288-0143
Phone: (704)374-6649
Fax: (704)374-2484
Ann D. Thomas, Vice President, Corporate Contributions

Giving Priorities: *Health & Welfare:* 35% to 40%. Primary emphasis is on united funds and youth, community service, and local affiliates of national welfare organizations. Interests include programs for youth, children, and the disadvantaged; hospitals; and health organizations. *Education:* About 40%. *Culture:* About 10%. *Civic:* 10% to 15%. **Typical Health-Related Recipients:** Children's Health/Hospitals, Domestic Violence, Emergency/Ambulance Services, Family Planning, Geriatric Health, Health Funds, Health Organizations, Hospices, Hospitals, Medical Education, Medical Rehabilitation, Mental Health, People with Disabilities, Research/Studies Institutes, Single-Disease Health Associations, Substance Abuse. **Geographic Distribution:** In headquarters and operating locations only.

★688★ Firstar Milwaukee Foundation
777 E Wisconsin Ave.
Milwaukee, WI 53202
Phone: (414)765-4579
Fax: (414)765-6108
Dennis Fredrickson, Secretary-Treasurer

Giving Priorities: *Health and Welfare:* 50% to 55% of annual giving. Primarily supports united fund campaigns. Other recipients include youth organizations, religious welfare groups, community centers, child welfare, and programs for the aged. Funds also went to single-disease health associations, medical research, nursing services, and health funds. *Education:* 20% to 25%. *Arts & Humanities:* About 10% of contributions. *Civic & Public Affairs:* Under 5% of funding. *Religion:* About 1%. **Typical Health-Related Recipients:** Children's Health/Hospitals, Clinics/Medical Centers, Heart, Hospitals, Medical Education, Nursing Services, People with Disabilities, Single-Disease Health Associations, Substance Abuse, Transplant Networks/Donor Banks. **Geographic Distribution:** Wisconsin, with emphasis on Milwaukee. **Formerly:** First Wisconsin Foundation.

★689★ FirsTier Bank Omaha Charitable Foundation
1700 Farnam St.
Omaha, NE 68102
Phone: (402)348-6000
David A. Rismiller, Chairman, Pres., CEO

Giving Priorities: *General Support Program:* Foundation has no specific priorities. Committee decides which organizations to support. Interests include libraries and theater, business and free enterprise, traditional educational institutions, hospitals, and community services. **Typical Health-Related Recipients:** Hospitals. **Geographic Distribution:** Limited to Nebraska, with an emphasis on Omaha. **Formerly:** Omaha National Bank Charitable Trust.

★690★ Fisher Brothers Foundation
299 Park Ave.
New York, NY 10017
Phone: (212)752-5000
Fax: (212)940-6207
Richard Fisher, Director

Giving Priorities: *Social Services:* 70% and 75% of total annual contributions. *Civic & Public Affairs:* Less than 5% of annual total. *Arts & Humanities:* 10% to 15%. *Health:* 5% to 10%. Most grants go to hospitals and single-disease health organizations. Also interested in medical rehabilitation and research. *Education:* Less than 5%. **Typical Health-Related Recipients:** Diabetes, Hospitals, Medical Education, People with Disabilities, Single-Disease Health Associations. **Geographic Distribution:** Primarily in metropolitan New York City.

★691★ Fleet Bank of Upstate New York Foundation Trust
69 State St.
Albany, NY 12201
Phone: (518)346-2491
Fax: (518)346-2496

Giving Priorities: *Social Services:* Between 45% and 50% of total annual contributions. *Health:* 25% to 30% of annual total, with highest priority given to hospitals and hospices. Single-disease health organizations also receive limited support. *Education:* About 10% annually. *Civic & Public Affairs:* 5% to 10%. *Arts & Humanities:* 5% to 10%. **Typical Health-Related Recipients:** Health Organizations, Hospices, Hospitals, Medical Rehabilitation, People with Disabilities, Single-Disease Health Associations. **Geographic Distribution:** Throughout Upstate New York.

★692★ Fleet Charitable Trust
111 Westminster St.
Providence, RI 02903
Phone: (401)278-6242
Fax: (401)278-3685
Sheila McDonald, Secretary

Giving Priorities: *Education:* About 50% of total giving. *Health and Social Services:* Approximately 35% of contributions. Majority of support to United Way. The remainder supports youth organizations, child welfare, religious and community service organizations. In the area of health, support goes to hospitals and health organizations. *Civic & Public Affairs:* About 10% of funds. *Arts & Humanities:* 5% to 10%. *Voluntarism:* Company sponors Team Fleet--an all employee-directed volunteer program to assist local nonprofits. **Typical Health-Related Recipients:** AIDS/HIV, Cancer, Children's Health/Hospitals, Clinics/Medical Centers, Hospitals, Medical Research, People with Disabilities, Research/Studies Institutes, Substance Abuse. **Geographic Distribution:** Primarily within areas where parent company maintains a major business presence. **Formerly:** Fleet/Norstar Charitable Trust.

★693★ Forbes Foundation
60 5th Ave.
New York, NY 10011
Phone: (212)620-2248
Leonard H. Yablon, President

Giving Priorities: *Education:* 50% to 55% of total annual funding, primarily to colleges, universities, and private precollege education. *Health:* 15% to 20%, with major support to Memorial Sloan-Kettering Cancer Center. Remaining funds support other hospitals, medical education, and pediatric health. *Religion:* 10% to 15%. *Arts & Humanities:* 5% to 10%. *Social Services:* About 5%. *Civic & Public Affairs:* About 5%. *Other:* Limited support to international organizations. **Typical Health-Related Recipients:** AIDS/HIV, Cancer, Clinics/Medical Centers, Emergency/Ambulance Services, Family Planning, Health Organizations, Hospices, Hospitals, Medical Education, Medical Research, Mental Health, Nursing Services, Single-Disease Health Associations, Substance Abuse. **Geographic Distribution:** Giving is primarily in the New York, NY, area.

★ 694 ★   **Ford Family Foundation**
PO Box 1088
Roseburg, OR 97470
Phone: (503)679-3311
Ronald C. Parker, Treasurer

Giving Priorities: *Education:* About 40%. *Science:* About 25%. *Health:* 15% to 20%. Health services, hospital foundations, clinics, and single-disease health organizations receive funding. *Social Services:* 10% to 15%. *Civic & Public Affairs:* Less than 5%. *Religion:* Less than 5%, with primary support going to religious welfare organizations. *Other:* Limited support is provided to the arts. **Typical Health-Related Recipients:** Cancer, Children's Health/Hospitals, Clinics/Medical Centers, Domestic Violence, Emergency/Ambulance Services, General, Health Organizations, People with Disabilities, Prenatal Health Issues, Substance Abuse. **Geographic Distribution:** In headquarters and operating communities. **Formerly:** Kenneth W. Ford Foundation.

★ 695 ★   **Ford Motor Co. Fund**
The American Rd., Rm. 949
PO Box 1899
Dearborn, MI 48121
Phone: (313)845-8711
Fax: (313)323-2683
Leo J. Brennan, Jr., Executive Director

Giving Priorities: *Education:* 50% to 55% of total annual fund contributions. *Arts & Humanities:* About 15%. *Civic & Public Policy:* about 15% of total. *Health & Welfare:* About 15% of giving. Most of this supports united fund drives. Other significant interests include hospitals, substance abuse programs, and other health organizations. The remainder supports other social service groups. *United States-International Relations:* Less than 5% of giving. **Typical Health-Related Recipients:** Emergency/Ambulance Services, Health Organizations, Health Policy/Cost Containment, Hospitals, Kidney, Substance Abuse. **Geographic Distribution:** Near headquarters and operating locations and to national organizations.

★ 696 ★   **Franklin Mint Foundation for the Arts**
US Route 1
Franklin Center, PA 19063
Phone: (215)459-7494
Fax: (215)459-6880
Jack Wilkie, Vice President, Corporate Communications

Giving Priorities: *General Support Program:* Primary focus is national visual arts organizations (70% of contributions), with limited support to health and human service (10%), civic (10%) organizations, and social services (10%) in operating communities. **Typical Health-Related Recipients:** Hospitals, Mental Health, People with Disabilities, Single-Disease Health Associations. **Geographic Distribution:** Headquarters and operating locations.

★ 697 ★   **Gallo Foundation**
PO Box 1130
Modesto, CA 95353
Phone: (209)579-3111
Fax: (209)579-3324
Ouida McCullough, Director

Giving Priorities: *Social Services:* 60% to 65%. *Education:* 15% to 20% of total funding. *Civic & Public Affairs:* 10% to 15% of giving. *Health:* 5% to 10% of contributions. Primarily supports hospitals and medical centers. Other interests include single-disease health associations and medical research. *Arts & Humanities:* Less than 5%. **Typical Health-Related Recipients:** Alzheimers Disease, Cancer, Children's Health/Hospitals, Diabetes, Domestic Violence, Emergency/Ambulance Services, Heart, Hospices, Hospitals, Medical Research, People with Disabilities, Single-Disease Health Associations, Substance Abuse. **Geographic Distribution:** Nationally; with emphasis on California.

★ 698 ★   **GEICO Philanthropic Foundation**
c/o GEICO Corp.
Geico Plz.
Washington, DC 20076
Phone: (301)718-5239
Kathy Allen

Giving Priorities: *Social Services:* 40% to 45% of contributions, primarily supporting united funds. Other major recipients include child welfare and recreation groups, programs for the mentally retarded and disabled, and family services. *Civic & Public Affairs:* 35% to 40%. *Health:* About 10% to 15%. Funds go primarily to hospitals and single-disease research organizations. Some support to hospices and other facilities. *Education:* 5% to 10%. *Arts & Humanities:* Less than 5%. **Typical Health-Related Recipients:** Emergency/Ambulance Services, Heart, Hospices, Hospitals, Medical Rehabilitation, Medical Research, Mental Health, People with Disabilities, Single-Disease Health Associations, Substance Abuse. **Geographic Distribution:** Priority to organizations serving the geographic areas of office locations.

★ 699 ★   **General American Charitable Foundation**
700 Market St.
PO Box 396
St. Louis, MO 63101
Phone: (314)444-0681
Charles L. Larance, President

Giving Priorities: *Health:* Highest priority. Percentage varies widely from year to year according to amount of solicitation. Gives primarily to cancer and AIDS research and support services in an effort to help cure disease. Also interested in wellness programs. Additional interests include single-disease health associations, medical education, hospitals, medical organizations, health centers, and mental health. *Social Services:* Support depends on demand for health-related grants, much of which goes to support united funds. Other interests include youth organizations, the aged, religious welfare, the disabled, and counseling. *Arts & Humanities:* Support again depends on the health-related dollar demands. *Education:* Support depends on demand for health-related grants, with an emphasis on colleges and universities. Interests include medical education. *Civic & Public Affairs:* About 5%. **Typical Health-Related Recipients:** AIDS/HIV, Alzheimers Disease, Diabetes, Domestic Violence, Emergency/Ambulance Services, Family Planning, Hospitals, Hospitals (University Affiliated), Medical Education, Medical Rehabilitation, Medical Research, People with Disabilities, Single-Disease Health Associations, Substance Abuse. **Geographic Distribution:** Primarily in the St. Louis, MO, area.

★ 700 ★   **General Mills Foundation**
PO Box 1113
Minneapolis, MN 55440
Phone: (612)540-7890
Fax: (612)540-4925
Dr. Reatha Clark King, President & Executive Director

Giving Priorities: *Health & Social Action:* 45% to 50% of total funding. Emphasizes services that strengthen families and assist the development of children and youth. Interests include hospitals and substance abuse programs. *Education:* 25% to 30% of funding. *Arts & Culture:* 20% to 25%. *Other:* Less than 5%. Supports a variety of organizations which do not fall within above categories, including public policy, economic development, and nonprofit management. *Voluntarism:* General Mills sponsors the Volunteer Connection. **Typical Health-Related Recipients:** Cancer, Domestic Violence, Emergency/Ambulance Services, Family Planning, Geriatric Health, Health Organizations, Health Policy/Cost Containment, Hospitals, Medical Education, Medical Rehabilitation, Medical Research, Mental Health, Nutrition, People with Disabilities, Substance Abuse. **Geographic Distribution:** Primarily in communities where the company has a substantial number of employees.

★701★ **General Motors Foundation**
3044 W Grand Blvd.
Ste. 11-128
Detroit, MI 48202
Phone: (313)556-6517
Fax: (313)974-4451
Deborah I. Dingell, President

Giving Priorities: *Education:* 45% to 50% of total annual contributions. *Social Services:* About 25%. Approximately 5% to 10% of total contributions support annual United Way campaigns in North American cities in which the company operates. *Civic & Public Affairs:* About 10%. *Arts & Humanities:* 5% to 10%. *Health:* 5% to 10%. Supports American Red Cross, hospital capital camapigns, and numerous health organizations. **Typical Health-Related Recipients:** Alzheimers Disease, Cancer, Emergency/Ambulance Services, Health Organizations, Hospices, Hospitals, Medical Rehabilitation, Medical Training, Mental Health, People with Disabilities, Public Health, Single-Disease Health Associations, Substance Abuse. **Geographic Distribution:** Nationally, with local contributions awarded primarily in communities with significant numbers of GM employees.

★702★ **Georgia Power Foundation**
333 Piedmont Ave.
20th Fl.
Atlanta, GA 30308
Phone: (404)526-6784
Fax: (404)526-2945
Judy M. Anderson, Executive Director

Giving Priorities: *Health and Social Services:* About 45% of contributions, with the major portion awarded to the United Way. Interests also include the YMCA and YWCA, hospitals and clinics, national health organizations, medical research, and the American Red Cross. *Education:* Between 25% and 30% of annual contributions. Interests include medical education. *Civic & Public Affairs:* 15% to 20%. *Arts & Humanities:* 5% and 10%. *International:* In 1991, company made $3,750 in contributions to U.S.-based nonprofit organizations with an international focus. *Other:* Less than 5% to religious organizations, sports and miscellaneous. **Typical Health-Related Recipients:** Family Planning, Geriatric Health, Health Organizations, Hospices, Hospitals, Medical Rehabilitation, Medical Research, Mental Health, People with Disabilities, Single-Disease Health Associations, Substance Abuse. **Geographic Distribution:** In Georgia, with emphasis on Atlanta.

★703★ **Giant Food Foundation**
PO Box 1804, D-593
Washington, DC 20013
Phone: (301)341-4301
Fax: (301)341-3954
David W. Rutstein, Secretary

Giving Priorities: *Community Service:* 75% to 80% of total giving. *Arts:* 5% to 10%. *Health:* 5% to 10%. Primarily supporting medical research for single diseases, hospitals, health and mental health organizations, and organizations concerned with the handicapped. *Education:* About 5%. *Other:* Less than 5%. Includes grants to civil rights and public policy organizations. **Typical Health-Related Recipients:** Cancer, Heart, Hospitals, Medical Education,

Mental Health, People with Disabilities, Single-Disease Health Associations. **Geographic Distribution:** Maryland, District of Columbia, and Virginia.

★704★ **Gillette Charitable & Educational Foundation**
Prudential Tower Bldg.
48th Fl.
Boston, MA 02199
Phone: (617)421-7722
James Furlong, Director, Civic Affairs

Giving Priorities: *Social Services:* 60% to 65% of contributions. *Civic & Public Affairs:* 5% to 10%. *Health:* 5% to 10%. Major support goes to hospitals and other facilities in Boston. Nationally, areas of giving include health funds, single-disease health organizations, and mental health. *Education:* Less than 5%. *Religion, Art & International:* Less than 5%. *Note:* Priorities for 1992 to new organizations will be for low income housing, shelters, food distribution programs, and domestic and women's violence counseling. **Typical Health-Related Recipients:** Health Organizations, Hospitals, Medical Rehabilitation, Medical Research, Mental Health, Nursing Services, Single-Disease Health Associations. **Geographic Distribution:** Primarily in Boston and other operating locations.

★705★ **Glaxo Foundation**
5 Moore Dr.
Research Triangle Park, NC 27709
Phone: (919)248-2100
Marilyn Foote-Hudson, Contributions Administrator

Giving Priorities: *General Support Program:* Giving extends to social services, health programs, education, the arts, and civic activities. Health care recipients include national relief organizations, hospitals, and health care cost containment programs. Priority programs are aimed at youth, minorities, women, and the disabled. **Typical Health-Related Recipients:** Health Organizations, Health Policy/Cost Containment, Hospitals, Medical Research, People with Disabilities, Single-Disease Health Associations, Substance Abuse. **Geographic Distribution:** Principally near headquarters and operating locations.

★706★ **Glickenhaus Foundation**
6 E 43rd St.
New York, NY 10017
Phone: (212)953-7800
Nancy G. Pier, President

Giving Priorities: *Education:* About 30% of total contributions. Primarily supports colleges and universities, but also makes grants to educational foundations and funds. *Arts & Humanities:* 25% to 30% of giving. *Health:* About 15% of contributions. Funding supported single-disease health associations, medical research, and medical centers throughout New York. *Civic & Public Affairs:* 10% to 15% of total funds. *Social Services:* About 5% of total funds. Funding supported Planned Parenthood, as well as child care organizations. *International:* Less than 5% of giving. *Religion:* Less than 5% of total contributions. **Typical Health-Related Recipients:** Cancer, Clinics/Medical Centers, Emergency/

Ambulance Services, Family Planning, Geriatric Health, Health Organizations, Hospitals, Medical Education, Mental Health, People with Disabilities, Single-Disease Health Associations. **Geographic Distribution:** Nationally, with an emphasis on New York.

★707★ **Globe Foundation**
3634 Civic Center Blvd.
Scottsdale, AZ 85251
Phone: (602)947-7888
Fax: (602)945-1912
Clifton L. Lux, Vice President and Treasurer

Giving Priorities: *Civic & Public Affairs:* 40% to 45%. *Health:* 35% to 40% of total contributions. Majority of funds went in a single $210,000 grant in 1992 to the Children's Memorial Hospital, Chicago, IL. Funding also goes to a variety of causes including health organizations and medical research and education. *Education:* 10% to 15%. Support generally funds colleges and universities, religious education, and medical education. *Other:* Less than 10% of total contributions. Funds organizations involved with family services, religious welfare, the disabled, family planning, united funds, and youth organizations. Emphasis is also placed on museums, historical organizations, arts associations, dance, and music. **Typical Health-Related Recipients:** Children's Health/Hospitals, Clinics/Medical Centers, Domestic Violence, Family Planning, Hospitals, Medical Education, Medical Research, Nursing Services, People with Disabilities, Research/Studies Institutes. **Geographic Distribution:** Primarily Arizona.

★708★ **Golub Foundation**
PO Box 1074
Schenectady, NY 12301
Phone: (518)356-9450

Giving Priorities: *Religion:* 55% to 60% of total contributions. *Social Services:* 15% to 20%. *Civic & Public Affairs:* 5% to 10%. *Health:* 5% to 10% of support. Contributes to hospitals, medical centers, children's health, and single-disease health associations. *Education:* 5% to 10%. *Arts & Humanities:* 5% to 10%. **Typical Health-Related Recipients:** Cancer, Children's Health/Hospitals, Clinics/Medical Centers, Eyes/Blindness, Health Organizations, Hospices, Hospitals, People with Disabilities, Single-Disease Health Associations. **Geographic Distribution:** Limited to New York area.

★709★ **Goodyear Tire & Rubber Company Fund**
1144 E Market St.
Akron, OH 44316-0001
Phone: (216)796-2121
Patricia A. Kemph, Assistant Secretary

Giving Priorities: *Education:* 40% to 45%. *Health & Human Services:* 35% to 40%. Majority of support funds United Ways in corporate operating locations. Generally, does not give to organizations receiving United Way support. Other interests include community service organizations and youth groups. *Civic & Public Affairs:* 10% to 15%. *Arts & Culture:* 5% to 10%. *Note:* Percentages are based on a three year average. **Typical Health-Related Recipients:** Health Organizations, Hospitals, Medical Education. **Geographic Distribution:** Primarily where company maintains manufacturing facilities or to schools active in scientific areas of interest to the company.

★710★ Grace Foundation, Inc.
One Town Center Rd.
Boca Raton, FL 33486-1010
Phone: (407)362-1487
W. Brian McGowan, Chairman

Giving Priorities: *Education:* About 55% of total contributions, with emphasis on colleges and universities with undergraduate and graduate schools of business and major departments of chemistry. *Community Chests:* 15% to 20% of total giving. *Health, Science & Social Welfare:* About 15%. Foundation interests include primary health-care facilities that serve the communities in which the company operates; hospitals whose activities are national in scope or unique in type of care delivered; major national medical research programs deemed vital to social welfare; major national organizations whose objective is the betterment of societal welfare; and a variety of community service organizations. *Urban & Minority Affairs:* 5% to 10% of contributions. *Culture:* Less than 5%. **Typical Health-Related Recipients:** Health Funds, Health Organizations, Hospices, Hospitals, Medical Education, Medical Rehabilitation, Medical Research, People with Disabilities, Substance Abuse. **Geographic Distribution:** Nationally with emphasis on corporate operating locations.

★711★ Graco Foundation
PO Box 1441
Minneapolis, MN 55440-1441
Phone: (612)623-6684
Fax: (612)623-6650
Elizabeth M. Jaros, Executive Director

Giving Priorities: *Health & Human Services:* Generally 60% to 65% of total giving, with primary support going to the United Way. Other areas of interest include youth organizations, care for the elderly, community centers, community service organizations, recreation and athletics, child welfare, and health associations. *Education:* Between 25% and 30%. *Civic & Public Affairs:* About 5% of contributions. *Arts & Humanities:* Less than 5%. **Typical Health-Related Recipients:** Domestic Violence, People with Disabilities. **Geographic Distribution:** Focuses on Minnesota, particularly Minneapolis, where the foundation places special emphasis on grants serving the northeast and near-north neighborhoods; limited support goes to communities where the company has a large number of employees; some international giving.

★712★ Groves Foundation
PO Box 1267
Minneapolis, MN 55440
Phone: (612)546-6943
Elfriede M. Lobeck, Executive Director

Giving Priorities: *Education:* About 50%. *Social Services:* 30% to 35%. Recipients include programs for the disabled, teen suicide prevention, neighborhood services, and food banks. *Health:* 15%. Supports state medical foundation, health organizations, and single-disease associations. *Other:* Less than 5% goes to music, philanthropic organizations, and conser-

vation. **Typical Health-Related Recipients:** AIDS/HIV, Children's Health/Hospitals, Health Funds, Health Organizations, Hospitals, Multiple Sclerosis, People with Disabilities, Single-Disease Health Associations. **Geographic Distribution:** Primarily in the Minneapolis, MN, area.

★713★ H. J. Heinz Co. Foundation
PO Box 57
Pittsburgh, PA 15230
Phone: (412)456-5772
Fax: (412)456-7859
Loretta M. Oken, Manager

Giving Priorities: *Education:* 30% to 35% of contributions. Principal support to colleges and universities in a variety of areas, including business, nutrition, economic, legal, health, and medical education. *International Affairs:* About 20%. *Social Services:* About 15% to 20%. *Health & Welfare:* About 15% of total. Major support to united fund drives and hospitals. Also supports child welfare and nutrition organizations. Other interests include community and family services, single-disease health associations, the handicapped, medical rehabilitation and research, and community centers. Also sponsors employee matching gifts program for nonprofit hospitals or medical rehabilitation. *Civic & Public Affairs:* 5% to 10%. *Arts & Humanities:* About 5%. **Typical Health-Related Recipients:** AIDS/HIV, Children's Health/Hospitals, Family Planning, Health Organizations, Home-Care Services, Hospices, Hospitals, Medical Education, Medical Rehabilitation, Medical Research, Nutrition, People with Disabilities, Single-Disease Health Associations, Substance Abuse. **Geographic Distribution:** Where company maintains facilities.

★714★ Habig Foundation
1600 Royal St.
Jasper, IN 47549
Phone: (812)482-1600
Fax: (812)482-8803
Douglas A. Habig, President

Giving Priorities: *Educational Institutions:* 45% to 50%. *Civic Organizations & Charities:* 20% to 25% total contributions. *Health & Human Services:* 10% to 15%. Supports the aged, child welfare, community service organizations, family services, and the United Way. *Religious Institutions:* 10% to 15%. *Arts & Humanities:* Less than 5%. **Typical Health-Related Recipients:** Hospices, Hospitals, Mental Health. **Geographic Distribution:** Headquarters area only.

★715★ Hallmark Corporate Foundation
PO Box 419580
Mail Drop 323
Kansas City, MO 64141-6580
Phone: (816)274-8515
Fax: (816)274-8547
Jeanne M. Bates, Community Development Manager

Giving Priorities: *Education:* 45% to 50% of total giving. *Health & Human Services:* 20% to 25%. Support includes contributions to human service programs and/or agencies which serve minorities, low income, homeless, disadvantaged youth, infant care, the disabled, AIDS patients, and others; primary support of programs

is through United Way campaigns. *Civic & Public Affairs:* 15% to 20%. *Arts & Culture:* About 15% of giving. *Other:* About 1%. Funds miscellaneous programs. *Product Donations:* Company makes charitable donations of its products to programs which serve the needy, the mentally or physically ill, and youths. *Volunteer Involvement Pays:* A nominal $200 grant is contributed to 501(c)(3) charitable organizations that have benefited from Hallmark employee volunteers. *Note:* Company prefers to respond to requests on a case-by-case basis and has not established target levels for contribution categories. **Typical Health-Related Recipients:** AIDS/HIV, Domestic Violence, Emergency/Ambulance Services, Health Organizations, Hospices, Hospitals, Long-Term Care, Mental Health, People with Disabilities, Sexual Abuse. **Geographic Distribution:** In their headquarters community of Kansas City, MO, and in other areas where company has a plant facility.

★716★ Hamilton Bank Foundation
PO Box 3959
Lancaster, PA 17604
Phone: (717)291-3508
Thomas H. Bamford, Chairman

Giving Priorities: *Social Services:* 50% to 55%. *Education:* 10% to 15%. *Health:* 10% to 15%. In 1990, ten hospitals and providers of health care received grants from the foundation. Other areas of interest include medical research, mental health, nursing services, and single-disease health associations. *Arts & Humanities:* 10% to 15% of contributions. *Civic & Public Affairs:* 5% to 10%. *Religion:* Less than 5%. **Typical Health-Related Recipients:** Children's Health/Hospitals, Emergency/Ambulance Services, Hospices, Hospitals, Medical Research, Mental Health, Nursing Services, People with Disabilities, Single-Disease Health Associations. **Geographic Distribution:** Limited to Berks, Cumberland, Dauphin, Lancaster, Lebanon, and York counties, PA.

★717★ Handleman Charitable Foundation
500 Kirts Blvd.
Troy, MI 48007
Phone: (313)362-4400
Louis A. Kircos, Treasurer

Giving Priorities: *Arts & Humanities:* About 55% of total contributions. *Social Services:* 20% to 25% of giving. *Health:* About 10% of funds. Support to hospitals and single-disease health associations. *Education:* 5% to 10% of contributions. *Religion:* Less than 5% of giving. *Civic & Public Affairs:* Less than 5% of giving. **Typical Health-Related Recipients:** Cancer, Children's Health/Hospitals, Diabetes, Heart, Hospitals, Medical Research, Transplant Networks/Donor Banks. **Geographic Distribution:** Nationally, with an emphasis on Detroit, MI.

★718★ H & R Block Foundation
4410 Main St.
Kansas City, MO 64111
Phone: (816)753-6900
Fax: (816)753-5346
Lin Dunlap, Administrative Assistant

Giving Priorities: *Education:* 30% to 35% of contributions. *Arts & Culture:* 15% to 20%. *Corporate Social Responsibility:* 15% to 20% of funding. *Health & Mental Health:* 5% to 10%. Considers requests for special projects from hospitals and neighborhood health centers, especially programs focused on indigent care and adolescent pregnancy. Capital requests generally are not considered. Also interested in mental health centers and educational programs to prevent mental illness. 5% to 10% of funds go to programs for high-risk, vulnerable, or emotionally disturbed youth. Priority given to programs dealing with prevention and treatment of child and alcohol abuse, and prevention of teenage pregnancy. *Associate Involvement:* About 5% to 10%. *Neighborhood Development:* Less than 5%. **Typical Health-Related Recipients:** Cancer, Children's Health/Hospitals, Clinics/Medical Centers, Domestic Violence, Family Planning, Geriatric Health, Health Funds, Health Organizations, Hospices, Hospitals, Medical Rehabilitation, Mental Health, People with Disabilities, Public Health, Substance Abuse. **Geographic Distribution:** Major emphasis on Kansas City, MO, and Columbus, OH.

★719★ **Harcourt General Charitable Foundation**
27 Boylston St.
Chestnut Hill, MA 02167
Phone: (617)232-8200
Fax: (617)731-2354
Kay M. Kilpatrick, Contributions Administrator

Giving Priorities: *General Support:* General Cinema operates four funding programs: Major Grants, Institutional Impact, National Impact, and Matching Gifts. The Major Grants Program focuses its support on organizations within the Greater Boston area. It emphasizes organizations which deal with the special needs of children. Also interested in the areas of education, health, medical research, and the arts. **Typical Health-Related Recipients:** Children's Health/Hospitals, Diabetes, Health Funds, Hospices, Hospitals, Medical Education, Medical Research, People with Disabilities. **Geographic Distribution:** Only in Greater Boston area. **Formerly:** General Cinema Foundation.

★720★ **Harold Simmons Foundation**
5430 LBJ Fwy., Ste. 1700
Dallas, TX 75240-2697
Lisa K. Simmons, President

Giving Priorities: *Social Services:* 40% to 45% of total contributions. *Health:* About 30%. Recipients are medical facilities and research centers. In 1992, the foundation gave more than $3.3 million to the University of Texas Southwestern Medical Center at Dallas. Support was also given to the Visiting Nurse Association's Children's Food Program in Dallas, a total of $172,290 from seven grants. *Education:* 10% to 15%. *Arts & Humanities:* 5% to 10% of contributions. *Other:* 5% to 10%. Support for civic policy-making groups, religious groups, and matching gifts. *International:* In 1993, the foundation contributed $50,000 to U.S.-based nonprofit organizations with an international focus. **Typical Health-Related Recipients:** Cancer, Children's Health/Hospitals, Clinics/Medical Centers, Domestic Violence, Health Organizations, Kidney, Medical Education, Medical Research, Nursing Services, Prenatal Health Issues, Public Health, Substance Abuse, Trans-

plant Networks/Donor Banks. **Geographic Distribution:** Only in the Dallas, TX, area.

★721★ **Harris Foundation**
1025 W NASA Blvd.
Melbourne, FL 32919
Phone: (407)727-9272
Fax: (407)727-9648
W. Peter Carney, Secretary

Giving Priorities: *Computer Grants Program:* About 55% of annual contributions. Company donates technical equipment to colleges and universities for research in the communications field. *Other:* Approximately 45%. Company administers a direct giving program and a foundation. Both programs direct funds to eligible nonprofit organizations primarily through united funds, civic organizations, and various communities service organizations. Also supports selected groups at the national level. Other interests include arts organizations and health organizations, including pediatric health and hospitals. **Typical Health-Related Recipients:** Emergency/Ambulance Services, Health Organizations, Hospitals. **Geographic Distribution:** Primarily in Florida and in other plant locations.

★722★ **Harsco Corp. Fund**
PO Box 8888
Camp Hill, PA 17001-8888
Phone: (717)763-7064
Robert Yocum, Secretary

Giving Priorities: *Social Services:* 40% to 45% of total contributions. *Education:* 30% to 35% of contributions. Most grants go to colleges, universities, and other organizations associated with higher education. *Health:* 5% to 10%. Most contributions support hospitals in Pennsylvania. Other recipients include single-disease and general health organizations. *Civic & Public Affairs:* 5% to 10%. *Arts & Humanities:* 5% to 10%. **Typical Health-Related Recipients:** Children's Health/Hospitals, Emergency/Ambulance Services, Family Planning, Health Organizations, Hospices, Hospitals, Medical Education, Medical Research, Mental Health, People with Disabilities, Sexual Abuse, Single-Disease Health Associations, Substance Abuse. **Geographic Distribution:** Near headquarters and operating locations only.

★723★ **Harvey Hubbell Foundation**
584 Derby-Milford Rd.
Orange, CT 06477
Phone: (203)799-4100
Harry B. Rowell, Trustee

Giving Priorities: *Social Services:* 60% to 65% of total contributions. *Education:* 15% to 20%. Almost three-fifths goes to University of Bridgeport. Also supports medical education and a scholarship program. *Health:* 10% to 15%. Interests include hospitals, emergency services, and medical rehabilitation. *Civic & Public Affairs:* Less than 5%. *Other:* Less than 5%. Supports foundation interests in the arts, religion, and science. **Typical Health-Related Recipients:** Children's Health/Hospitals, Domestic Violence, Emergency/Ambulance Services, Health Organizations, Hospitals, Medical Education, Medical Rehabilitation, Mental Health, Nursing Services, People with Disabilities, Single-Disease Health Associations. **Geographic Dis-

tribution:** Primarily in areas of company operations.

★724★ **Hasbro Charitable Trust**
1027 Newport Ave.
Pawtucket, RI 02861
Phone: (401)727-5429
Mary Louise Fazzano, Director

Giving Priorities: *Project-Oriented Support:* Hasbro reviews requests on a case-by-case basis. Highest priority is funding organizations concerned with the health and welfare of children. Also supports other human service organizations. Arts and civic organizations are lesser priorities. In fiscal 1993, approximately 54% of the trust's giving went to health, 18% to education, 18% to social services, 3% to civic and public affairs, 2% to the arts and humanities, and 5% to other miscellaneous causes. *International:* Giving outside the U.S. is minimal and handled on a case-by-case basis. **Typical Health-Related Recipients:** Clinics/Medical Centers, Family Planning, Geriatric Health, Hospitals, Prenatal Health Issues, Research/Studies Institutes, Sexual Abuse. **Geographic Distribution:** Headquarters and operating locations only.

★725★ **Hershey Foods Corp. Fund**
100 Crystal A Dr.
Hershey, PA 17033-0810
Phone: (717)534-7574
Fax: (717)534-7038
Andrea Bowerman, Corporate Contributions Administrator

Giving Priorities: *Education:* 45% to 50%. *Health & Human Services:* Approximately 25%, with emphasis on local United Way campaigns and food bank donations. Also supports youth groups, community service centers, and organizations serving minority and disadvantaged groups. *Civic & Community:* 10% to 15%. *Culture & the Arts:* About 10%. *Other:* Less than 5%. Limited support is provided for organizations that fall outside above guidelines or plant sites, including environmental programs. *Voluntarism:* The fund has an employee volunteer recognition program. **Typical Health-Related Recipients:** Clinics/Medical Centers, Hospitals, Nutrition, People with Disabilities, Substance Abuse. **Geographic Distribution:** Strongly prefers areas where Hershey Foods maintains facilities.

★726★ **Heublein Foundation**
PO Box 388
Farmington, CT 06034-0388
Phone: (203)231-5000
Fax: (203)678-6612
Moira E. Burke, Treasurer

Giving Priorities: *Education:* 35% to 40% of total contributions. *Social Services:* 30% to 35%. *Arts & Humanities:* 10% to 15%. *Health:* About 10%, primarily supporting community health care centers. Also supports hospitals and health organizations. Company plans to increase giving in this area. *Civic & Public Affairs:* About 10%. **Typical Health-Related Recipients:** Health Funds, Health Organizations, Hospitals, People with Disabilities. **Geographic Distribution:** Only in areas where company has operating locations.

★727★ **High Meadow Foundation**
30 Main St.
Stockbridge, MA 01262
Phone: (413)243-1474
Fax: (413)243-1067
Tamara Stevens, Administrator

Giving Priorities: *Arts & Humanities:* About 60% of total gifts. *Education:* 10% to 15%. *Health:* 5% to 10% of contributions. Over one-fourth of support funds pediatric health and about one-fourth funds medical research. One-fifth of gifts go to hospitals, hospices, and medical centers. Single-disease health associations and outpatient health care also receive support. *Social Services:* 5% to 10%. *Civic & Public Affairs:* About 5% of all giving. **Typical Health-Related Recipients:** Emergency/Ambulance Services, Family Planning, Hospices, Hospitals, People with Disabilities, Public Health. **Geographic Distribution:** Primarily in Berkshire County, MA.

★728★ **Hoechst Celanese Foundation**
Rte. 202-206 N
PO Box 2500
Somerville, NJ 08876-1258
Phone: (908)231-2880
Fax: (908)231-2431
Lewis F. Alpaugh, President

Giving Priorities: *Education:* About 55% of total annual contributions. Emphasis on institutions of higher education. Priority to colleges and universities that specialize in scientific research and that supply corporate staffing needs. *Civic & Public Affairs:* About 20%. *Health & Human Services:* About 15% of total giving. Supports hospitals, youth programs, and federated drives. Emphasis on hospitals serving significant numbers of employees, engaged in research, operating as teaching facilities, or affiliated with medical schools. Also supports youth organizations and united funds only in communities where company has significant number of employees. *Culture & the Arts:* About 5%. *Equal Opportunity:* About 5%. Supports programs and institutions that promote equal opportunity for minorities and the disadvantaged. *Science:* Less than 5%. Supports scientific centers. **Typical Health-Related Recipients:** Cancer, Clinics/Medical Centers, Health Organizations, Health Policy/Cost Containment, Hospitals, Medical Education, People with Disabilities, Substance Abuse. **Geographic Distribution:** Principally near operating locations and to national organizations.

★729★ **Hubbard Foundation**
3415 University Ave.
St. Paul, MN 55114
Phone: (612)642-4300
Gerald D. Deeney, Secretary

Giving Priorities: *Social Services:* 40% to 45%. *Arts & Humanities:* Between 25% and 30% of total contributions. *Education:* 10% to 25%. *Health:* About 10%. Primarily suports hospitals. Grants also made to single-disease health associations and health organizations. *Civic & Public Affairs:* Less than 5%. *Other:* Less than 5% each to religion and science. **Typical Health-Related Recipients:** Children's Health/Hospitals, Family Planning, Health Funds, Health Organizations, Hospitals, Kidney, Medi-

cal Education, Medical Rehabilitation, Medical Research, Mental Health, People with Disabilities, Research/Studies Institutes, Single-Disease Health Associations, Substance Abuse. **Geographic Distribution:** Near areas of company operations and to national, state, and local organizations.

★730★ **Huffy Foundation, Inc.**
PO Box 1204
Dayton, OH 45401
Phone: (513)865-5498
Fax: (513)865-5470
W. Anthony Huffman, Secretary

Giving Priorities: *Social Services:* 60% to 65% of total contributions. *Education:* 10% to 15% of gifts. *Arts & Humanities:* 5% to 10% of total giving. *Health:* 5% to 10% of contributions. Recipients included a hospital, a single-disease health association, and Fund 2003. *Science:* Less than 5%. Included one grant of $8,750 to the National Aviation Hall of Fame. **Typical Health-Related Recipients:** Alzheimers Disease, Family Planning, General, Health Funds, Health Organizations, Hospices, Hospitals, People with Disabilities, Substance Abuse. **Geographic Distribution:** Limited to Dayton, OH, (headquarters) and operating locations.

★731★ **Humana Foundation**
500 W Main St.
PO Box 1438
Louisville, KY 40201
Phone: (502)580-3041
Virginia Lewman, Foundation Manager

Giving Priorities: *Arts & Humanities:* Almost exclusively in major grants to arts groups in Louisville, KY. *Education:* Major support goes to colleges and universities, including medical education programs. *Social Services:* Major support goes to the Metro United Way of Louisville, KY. Other recipients include youth organizations, recreation and athletics, child welfare, the aged, and community services. *Civic & Public Affairs:* Supports economic development, business and free enterprise, philanthropic organizations, and urban and community affairs. *Health:* Recipients include hospitals, single-disease health associations, and mental health organizations. **Typical Health-Related Recipients:** Children's Health/Hospitals, Clinics/Medical Centers, Emergency/Ambulance Services, Family Planning, Heart, Hospitals, Medical Education, Medical Research, Mental Health, Nursing Services, People with Disabilities, Single-Disease Health Associations. **Geographic Distribution:** Emphasis on Louisville, KY.

★732★ **IFF Foundation**
521 W 57th St.
New York, NY 10019
Phone: (212)765-5500
Thomas H. Hoppel, Treasurer

Giving Priorities: *Arts & Humanities:* 30% to 35%. *Health & Science:* 20% to 25% of total funding. About two-thirds of health contributions go to cancer research. Also funds hospitals, medical centers, and single-disease health associations. The foundation is ongoing sponsor of Monell Chemical Senses Center for research on mechanisms of taste and smell. *Civic & Public Affairs:* 10% to 15%. *Social Services:* 10% to

15% of overall giving. *Education:* About 10%. *International:* 5% to 10%. Supports an international hospital foundation and a Japan society. **Typical Health-Related Recipients:** Cancer, Clinics/Medical Centers, Domestic Violence, Emergency/Ambulance Services, Health Policy/Cost Containment, Heart, Hospitals, Medical Research, People with Disabilities, Single-Disease Health Associations, Substance Abuse. **Geographic Distribution:** Focus on New York City; with some interest in New Jersey.

★733★ **Inland Container Corp. Foundation**
4030 Vincennes Rd.
Indianapolis, IN 46268-0937
Phone: (317)879-4308
Fax: (317)879-4234
Frank F. Hirschman, President

Giving Priorities: *Health & Welfare:* 45% to 50% of contributions, with half generally awarded to united funds. Also supports youth groups, the disabled, community service organizations, and the elderly. Health interests include hospitals, health organizations, and single-disease health associations. *Education:* 30% to 35% of total contributions. *Civic & Public Affairs:* 5% to 10%. *Arts & Humanities:* 5% to 10%. **Typical Health-Related Recipients:** Health Organizations, Hospitals, People with Disabilities, Single-Disease Health Associations, Substance Abuse. **Geographic Distribution:** Near company operating locations.

★734★ **Inman-Riverdale Foundation**
Inman Mills
Inman, SC 29349
Phone: (803)472-2121
Fax: (803)472-9674
W. Marshall Chapman, Chairman

Giving Priorities: *Education:* 55% to 60%. *Social Services:* 25% to 30%. *Arts & Humanities:* 5% to 10%. *Health:* About 5%. Supports Red Cross and single-disease health associations. *Other:* Less than 5%. Recipients include churches, civic institutes, and professional associations. **Typical Health-Related Recipients:** Health Organizations, Medical Research, People with Disabilities, Single-Disease Health Associations. **Geographic Distribution:** Focus on South Carolina.

★735★ **Interco Inc. Charitable Trust**
101 S Hanley Rd.
St. Louis, MO 63105
Phone: (314)863-1100
Fax: (314)863-5306
Robert T. Hensley, Jr., Treasurer

Giving Priorities: *Social Services:* 30% to 35% of funding. *Education:* 25% to 30%. *Civic & Public Affairs:* About 15% to 20%. *Arts & Humanities:* About 10%. *Health:* 5% to 10% of contributions. Most of this supports children's hospitals, with the remainder going to single-disease health associations and medical education. **Typical Health-Related Recipients:** Hospices, Hospitals, Medical Research, Mental Health, People with Disabilities, Single-Disease Health Associations. **Geographic Distribution:** Mainly in areas where company maintains facilities, with particular emphasis on St. Louis, MO.

★ 736 ★ International Paper Co.
Foundation
Two Manhattanville Rd.
Purchase, NY 10577
Phone: (914)397-1581
Fax: (914)397-1909
Sandra C. Wilson, Vice President

Giving Priorities: *Education:* About 65% of total annual contributions. *Community & Civic:* 10% to 15% of giving. *Arts & Culture:* 10% to 15%. *Health and Welfare:* Between 10% and 15%, with an emphasis on hospitals and community centers. **Typical Health-Related Recipients:** Clinics/Medical Centers, Emergency/Ambulance Services, Health Organizations, Hospitals, Substance Abuse. **Geographic Distribution:** Mainly in areas where company facilities are located, and limited giving to national organizations.

★ 737 ★ ITT Hartford Insurance Group
Foundation
Hartford Plz.
690 Asylum Ave.
Hartford, CT 06115
Phone: (203)547-4972
Richard Madden, Director, Corporate
Communications

Giving Priorities: *Health & Human Services:* 55% to 60% of giving, principally to United Way programs. Also supports hospitals, health centers, hospices, programs that teach preventive care, family medicine clinics, health care cost containment, and child care. *Education & Equal Opportunity:* About 20% to 25% of funding. *Greater Hartford Area:* About 20%, aimed at maintaining and improving the vitality of the headquarters city, the state, and the region as a whole. **Typical Health-Related Recipients:** Children's Health/Hospitals, Clinics/Medical Centers, Domestic Violence, Geriatric Health, Health Organizations, Health Policy/Cost Containment, Hospices, Hospitals, Medical Education, Medical Rehabilitation, Medical Research, People with Disabilities, Prenatal Health Issues, Public Health, Substance Abuse. **Geographic Distribution:** Mainly in Hartford, CT; company also considers requests from organizations in the 42 office communities in which it operates.

★ 738 ★ ITT Rayonier Foundation
1177 Summer St.
Stamford, CT 06904
Phone: (203)348-7000
Jay A. Fredericksen, Vice President

Giving Priorities: *Education:* 45% to 50% of total gifts. *Social Services:* 20% to 25%. *Civic & Culture:* 15% to 20% of funding. *Health:* 5% to 10%. Contributes to hospitals and health care organizations. *Discretionary Grants:* 5% to 10%. Funds a variety of organizations which fall into traditional giving categories; majority of grants are less than $500. **Typical Health-Related Recipients:** Domestic Violence, Hospices, Hospitals, Substance Abuse. **Geographic Distribution:** Primarily in areas of company operations in Florida, Georgia, and Washington.

★ 739 ★ J.P. Morgan Charitable Trust
60 Wall St.
New York, NY 10260
Phone: (212)648-9673
Fax: (212)648-5082
Roberta A. Ruocco, VP, Community Relations
& Public Affairs

Giving Priorities: *Education:* About 30% of contributions. *Urban Affairs & Housing:* About 30% of contributions. *Arts:* About 15%. *Health & Related Services:* 10% to 15% of funding. Supports major medical centers in New York, health care cost containment programs, programs addressing the challenges posed by an aging population, programs addressing the needs of disadvantaged young mothers and infants, and outreach support programs for catastrophic public health problems such as AIDS. In 1993, about one-third was matching grants. *International Affairs:* Between 5% and 10%. *Other:* In l993, less than 5% went as a single grant to the Tri-State United Way, and less than 5% to environmental groups. *Voluntarism:* Employee volunteers work with social service agencies, educational institutions, arts organizations, and hospitals. **Typical Health-Related Recipients:** Cancer, Clinics/Medical Centers, Domestic Violence, Emergency/Ambulance Services, Family Planning, Geriatric Health, Health Organizations, Health Policy/Cost Containment, Hospitals, Medical Education, People with Disabilities, Sexual Abuse, Transplant Networks/Donor Banks. **Geographic Distribution:** Primarily New York City; supports relief and development programs internationally.

★ 740 ★ J. T. Tai and Co. Foundation
18 E 67th St.
New York, NY 10021
Phone: (212)288-5242
Ping Y. Tai, Co-President, Co-Treasurer

Giving Priorities: *Education:* 60% to 65% of total funding. Primarily to colleges, universities, and medical schools throughout the country. In 1992, New York University School of Medicine received $100,000. *Health:* 20% to 25%. Primary funding went to cancer research. The China Health Clinic also received support. *Religion:* 5% to 10%. *Other:* Less than 5%. The foundation also supports public affairs and social services. **Typical Health-Related Recipients:** Cancer, Clinics/Medical Centers, Emergency/Ambulance Services, Health Organizations, Heart, Hospitals, Medical Education, Medical Research, People with Disabilities. **Geographic Distribution:** Northeastern United States, focus on New York.

★ 741 ★ Jack Eckerd Corp. Foundation
PO Box 4689
Clearwater, FL 34618
Phone: (813)399-6000
James M. Santo, Chairman

Giving Priorities: *United Funds:* About 45% of total contributions. *Education:* 25% to 30%. Most contributions support colleges and universities; other interests include medical education, especially pharmaceutical programs. *Health:* 10% to 15%, much of which supports medical research organizations. Other interests include hospitals and mental and pediatric health. *Civic & Cultural:* 5% to 10%. **Typical Health-Related**

Recipients: Health Funds, Health Organizations, Hospices, Hospitals. **Geographic Distribution:** Near market areas only.

★ 742 ★ James S. Copley Foundation
7776 Ivanhoe Ave.
PO Box 1530
La Jolla, CA 92038-1530
Phone: (619)454-0411
Fax: (619)454-5014
Anita A. Baumgardner, Secretary, Trustee

Giving Priorities: *Social Services:* About 50% of total contributions. *Arts & Humanities:* Around 20%. *Education:* 15% to 20%. *Health:* 5% to 10%. Funds hospitals and hospices. Also gives to single-disease health associations. *Civic & Public Affairs:* Less than 5%. **Typical Health-Related Recipients:** AIDS/HIV, Hospices, Hospitals, Mental Health, People with Disabilities, Substance Abuse. **Geographic Distribution:** Near headquarters and operating locations only.

★ 743 ★ Jefferson-Pilot Foundation
One Julian Price Pl.
Charlotte, NC 28208
Phone: (704)374-3500
Linda Scott, Assistant to the President

Giving Priorities: *Education:* 60% to 65% of total contributions. *Social Services:* 10% to 15%. *Health:* 10% to 15% of funds. Supports a hospice, medical training, and single-disease health associations. *Civic & Public Affairs:* About 5%. *Arts & Humanities:* Less than 5%. *Religion:* Less than 5%. **Typical Health-Related Recipients:** Heart, Medical Education. **Geographic Distribution:** Primarily headquarters and operating locations.

★ 744 ★ JELD-WEN Foundation
PO Box 1329
Klamath Falls, OR 97601
Phone: (503)882-3451
Fax: (503)885-7454
R.C. Wendt, Trustee

Giving Priorities: *Social Services:* About 45% of contributions. *Education:* About 15%. *Civic & Public Affairs:* 10% to 15%. *Health & Welfare:* 5% to 10% of contributions. Primary recipients include family and child medical centers and national health organizations such as the Red Cross. *Religion:* 5% to 10%. *Science:* About 5%. **Typical Health-Related Recipients:** Emergency/Ambulance Services, Health Organizations, Hospices, Hospitals, People with Disabilities. **Geographic Distribution:** In communities where company plants exist, or areas where a sufficient number of company employees reside.

★ 745 ★ Jochum-Moll Foundation
P. O. Box 368022
Cleveland, OH 44136
Phone: (216)225-2600
Theo Moll, President

Giving Priorities: *Religion:* 65% to 70%. *Education:* 10% to 15%. *Health:* 5% to 10%. Favors hospitals. Also supports single-disease health associations. *Social Services:* 5% to 10% of total contributions. *Arts & Humanities:* Less than 5%. *Other:* Less than 5% of total contributions.

Includes support for scientific and environmental interests. **Typical Health-Related Recipients:** Clinics/Medical Centers, Diabetes, Hospitals, People with Disabilities. **Geographic Distribution:** Focus on Ohio.

★746★   **John Deere Foundation**
John Deere Rd.
Moline, IL 61265
Phone: (309)765-5030
Fax: (309)765-5772
Donald R. Margenthaler, President

Giving Priorities: *Health & Human Services:* 45% to 50% of total grants, with major support to united funds. Also supports health and youth organizations, and programs for drug and alcohol abuse, child welfare, and the handicapped. *Education:* About 30% of total contributions. *Civic & Community Development:* 10% to 15%. *Cultural:* Less than 5% of donations. *International:* In 1993. **Typical Health-Related Recipients:** Health Organizations, People with Disabilities, Substance Abuse. **Geographic Distribution:** In areas where company has facilities and to some national organizations.

★747★   **Johnson Controls Foundation**
5757 N Green Bay Ave.
Box 591
Milwaukee, WI 53201-0591
Phone: (414)228-3155
Fax: (414)228-3200
Denise M. Zutz, Secretary, Advisory Board

Giving Priorities: *Social Services:* 45% to 50% of total contributions. About one-half goes to the United Way. Other interests include child welfare, the disabled, homes, the aged, and family and community centers. *Education:* 25% to 30%, primarily supporting public and private colleges and universities. *Arts & Humanities:* 15% to 20%, primarily to Milwaukee-based arts organizations. *Health:* 5% to 10%, primarily supporting hospitals and single-disease health associations. Will consider grants to capital fund programs supporting hospitals only if programs have been approved by appropriate health planning agencies. *Civic & Public Affairs:* About 5%. **Typical Health-Related Recipients:** Hospitals, Medical Education, People with Disabilities, Public Health, Single-Disease Health Associations, Substance Abuse. **Geographic Distribution:** In Wisconsin and nationally.

★748★   **Johnson & Johnson Family of**
         Cos. Contribution Fund
One Johnson & Johnson Plz.
New Brunswick, NJ 08933
Phone: (908)524-3255
Fax: (908)524-3300
Helen M. Hughes, Manager, Corporate Contributions

Giving Priorities: *Targeted Programs:* Main Emphasis is on health. Conducts several major programs on request for proposal basis (no unsolicited appeals). Programs include: (1) Johnson & Johnson - Wharton Fellows Program in Management for Nurses; (2) Johnson & Johnson Community Health Care Program (improved access to care for medically underserved); (3) Johnson & Johnson Bridge to Employment Program (employment training for at-risk youth); (4) Johnson & Johnson Hospital Support Program;

(5) Head Start - Johnson & Johnson Management Fellows Program; (6) Johnson & Johnson New Brunswick Revitalization Project; (7) Johnson & Johnson Focused Giving Program (basic medical and science research grants). Many of the contributions to health-related causes are categorized under "Major Programs." *International:* In 1993, company donated $3.9 million in products and cash to U.S.-based nonprofit organizations with an international focus and $5.0 million to international organizations through foreign subsidiaries. **Typical Health-Related Recipients:** Cancer, Geriatric Health, Health Organizations, Hospitals, Medical Research, People with Disabilities, Single-Disease Health Associations, Substance Abuse. **Geographic Distribution:** Nationally and internationally, with an emphasis on operating locations.

★749★   **Johnson's Wax Fund**
1525 Howe St., Mail Sta. 11
Racine, WI 53403
Phone: (414)631-2267
Reva Holmes, Vice President & Secretary

Giving Priorities: *Education:* Generally 50% to 55% of annual contributions. *Medical, Health, & Environmental Protection:* About 20% to 25%. Major support goes to the Children's Hospital of Wisconsin as payment on a 5-year pledge. In the health field, also supports single-disease health associations. In the area of environmental protection, co-sponsors research on the red-crowned crane and contributed a major grant to the Wisconsin chapter of the Nature Conservancy. Smaller grants went to a variety of environmental affairs organizations. *Social & Community Concerns:* Approximately 10% to 15%. *Cultural:* Typically about 5% to 10%. *New Programs:* About 2%. The fund provided seed funding to Child Care Resources and Referral of Racine to establish a child care information service. Also supported the Children's Audit Project to assist low income parents involved in the Head Start program and the Racine YWCA Teen Parenting Program. **Typical Health-Related Recipients:** Hospitals, Medical Education, Medical Training, Nutrition, Single-Disease Health Associations. **Geographic Distribution:** Nationally, but primarily in Wisconsin and the Midwest.

★750★   **Journal Gazette Foundation**
701 South Clinton St.
Ft. Wayne, IN 46802
Phone: (219)461-8202
Richard G. Inskeep, President

Giving Priorities: *Social Services:* 35% to 40% of funding. Other support goes to food banks, Planned Parenthood, and a Lutheran social services organization. *Education:* 25% to 30%. *Health:* 15% to 20%, primarily to the Lutheran Hospital Foundation. Also supports health services and an AIDS task force. *Civic & Public Affairs:* 5% to 10%. *Arts & Humanities:* less than 5% of funding. **Typical Health-Related Recipients:** AIDS/HIV, Children's Health/Hospitals, Emergency/Ambulance Services, Family Planning, Health Organizations, Hospitals, Mental Health, People with Disabilities, Research/Studies Institutes, Single-Disease Health Associations, Substance Abuse. **Geographic Distribution:** Primarily in northeastern IN.

★751★   **Julius and Ray Charlestein**
         Foundation
1710 Romano Dr.
Norristown, PA 19401
Phone: (215)277-3800
Morton Charlestein, President

Giving Priorities: *Religion:* 50% to 55% of total contributions. *Education:* 30% to 35%. *Health:* 5% to 10%. Supports single-disease health associations, medical centers and health foundations. *Arts & Humanities:* About 5%. *Other:* Less than 5%. Supports Jewish international organizations, civic affairs in Philadelphia, PA, and community service organizations. **Typical Health-Related Recipients:** Alzheimers Disease, Children's Health/Hospitals, Diabetes, Eyes/Blindness, Family Planning, Geriatric Health, Health Organizations, Medical Rehabilitation, Nursing Services, People with Disabilities, Single-Disease Health Associations. **Geographic Distribution:** National, with emphasis on Pennsylvania.

★752★   **Kennametal Foundation**
PO Box 231
Rt. 981 S.
Latrobe, PA 15650
Phone: (412)539-5203
Richard P. Gibson, Secretary-Treasurer

Giving Priorities: *Health:* 35% to 40%. Major support to the Latrove Area Hospital with a $200,000 grant in fiscal 1993. Additional support for a health foundation and the American Cancer Society. *Education:* 30% to 35% of total contributions. *Arts & Humanities:* 15% to 20%. *Social Services:* 10% to 15%. *Civic & Public Affairs:* 5% to 10%. **Typical Health-Related Recipients:** Cancer, Health Organizations, Hospitals, Medical Research, Mental Health, Single-Disease Health Associations. **Geographic Distribution:** Eastern United States.

★753★   **Kiewit Cos. Foundation**
1000 Kiewit Plz.
Omaha, NE 68131
Phone: (402)342-2052
Fax: (402)271-2989
Michael L. Faust, Assistant to the Chairman

Giving Priorities: *Arts & Humanities:* About 45% of total contributions. *Education:* Between 20% to 25% of total annual contributions. *Social Services:* Between 15% to 20%. *Health:* Between 5% to 10%, primarily to hospitals and health centers. *Civic & Public Affairs:* Less than 5%. *Note:* Approximately 90% of grants are made to organizations in Omaha, NE. The other 10% supports higher education, engineering, and welfare where company branch offices are located. **Typical Health-Related Recipients:** Health Organizations, Hospitals, Medical Rehabilitation, People with Disabilities, Single-Disease Health Associations. **Geographic Distribution:** Omaha, locations where the company has significant operations, very few outside Nebraska; company only makes contributions in areas where it has permanent locations.

★754★   **Kimberly-Clark Foundation**
PO Box 619100
Dallas, TX 75261-9100
Phone: (214)830-1200
Colleen B. Berman, Vice President

Giving Priorities: *General Support Program: Social Welfare:* Major emphasis on United Ways in operating communities. Other recipients include youth and the aged, services for the handicapped, and programs for the treatment and prevention of alchohol and drug abuse. *Education:* Major support to colleges and universities as capital and operating grants, and to minority education programs. *Medicine & Health:* Support includes hospitals and health agencies such as single-disease health associations. *Civic, Cultural & Miscellaneous:* Interests include municipalities, music, and arts associations. **Typical Health-Related Recipients:** Cancer, Domestic Violence, Emergency/Ambulance Services, Geriatric Health, Hospitals, Medical Education, Medical Research, Multiple Sclerosis, Nursing Services, People with Disabilities, Single-Disease Health Associations, Substance Abuse. **Geographic Distribution:** In areas where the company maintains facilities; limited number of contributions to national organizations.

★ 755 ★ **La-Z-Boy Foundation**
1284 North Telegraph Rd.
PO Box 713
Monroe, MI 48161
Phone: (313)242-1444
Fax: (313)241-4424
Donald E. Blohm, Administrator

Giving Priorities: *Human & Social Services:* Typically between 40% and 45% of total annual giving. *Education:* 15% to 20% annually. *Health:* 10% to 15%. Major grants benefit hospitals and single disease health organizations. *Arts & Culture:* less than 5%. *Civic & Public Affairs:* Less than 5% of total annual support. **Typical Health-Related Recipients:** Diabetes, Emergency/Ambulance Services, Hospices, Hospitals, Single-Disease Health Associations. **Geographic Distribution:** Near plant operating locations and corporate offices in the United States.

★ 756 ★ **Lance Foundation**
PO Box 32368
Charlotte, NC 28232
Phone: (704)554-1421
Zean Jamison, Director

Giving Priorities: *Education:* 30% to 35% of total contributions. *Civic & Public Affairs:* 25% to 30%. *Social Services:* 20% to 25%. *Arts & Humanities:* 10% to 15%. *Health:* 5% to 10%. The American Red Cross, Juvenile Diabetes Foundation, and American Cancer Society all received support. **Typical Health-Related Recipients:** Health Organizations, Medical Research, Single-Disease Health Associations. **Geographic Distribution:** Focus on NC.

★ 757 ★ **Leo Burnett Co. Charitable Foundation**
35 W Wacker Dr.
Chicago, IL 60601
Phone: (312)220-5959
Fax: (312)220-6533
Kristin Anderson, VP and Dir. Community Affairs

Giving Priorities: *Social Services:* 30% to 35% of contributions. *Education:* 30% to 35%. *Arts & Humanities:* 15% to 20%. *Civic & Public Af-*

fairs: 5% to 10%. *Other:* 5% to 10%. Most contributions go to health organizations such as single-disease research groups, hospitals, and hospices. A small number of grants have also gone to religious groups and international programs. **Typical Health-Related Recipients:** Cancer, Clinics/Medical Centers, Health Organizations, Hospices, Hospitals, Single-Disease Health Associations. **Geographic Distribution:** Almost exclusively in the Chicago area.

★ 758 ★ **Levi Strauss Foundation**
1155 Battery St., 7th Fl.
San Francisco, CA 94111
Phone: (415)544-6579
Fax: (415)544-1693
Judy Belk, Executive Director

Giving Priorities: *Community Partnership Grants:* 45% to 50% of contributions. Support is provided in three areas: Community-Based Economic Development, AIDS Prevention and Care, and Social Justice. In AIDS, priorities are direct assistance to persons with HIV/AIDS and their caregivers; risk reduction education for those with high-risk behaviors; and services targeted to populations severly affected by HIV/AIDS. *Community Involvement Teams (CIT):* 20% to 25% of funding. Supports a broad range of programs and concerns selected by employees, including the handicapped, domestic violence, alcohol and drug abuse, and aging. *Social Benefits Program:* Between 10% and 15%, disbursed primarily as matching gifts. *United Way:* Receives 5% to 10% of budget. *Scholarships:* About 5% supports scholarships for dependents of company employees. *Other:* About 5% of giving awarded in directed, general support grants to a variety of arts, civic, education, health, and welfare organizations. **Typical Health-Related Recipients:** AIDS/HIV, Cancer, Clinics/Medical Centers, Domestic Violence, Emergency/Ambulance Services, People with Disabilities, Public Health. **Geographic Distribution:** Emphasis on communities where Levi Strauss & Co. maintains production or distribution facilities; also gives limited support to national and regional organizations providing technical assistance to those communities.

★ 759 ★ **Liz Claiborne Foundation**
1441 Broadway Ave.
New York, NY 10018
Phone: (212)626-5424
Fax: (212)626-5608
Melanie Lyons, Director

Giving Priorities: *Social Services:* About 30% of total annual contributions. Major support for programs in AIDS education, outreach, and services. Other interests include organizations concerned with child and family welfare, homelessness, poverty, and violence. *Nature:* Approximately 30% of giving. *Education:* About 15% of contributions. *Health & Safety:* 10% to 15%, primarily to healthcare for the disadvantaged and to local hospitals. In 1992, a grant of $109,360 was awarded to the National Alliance of Breast Cancer. *Arts & Humanities:* 5% to 10%. *Other:* Less than 10% goes to a variety of groups, chiefly through an employee matching-gifts program. **Typical Health-Related Recipients:** AIDS/HIV, Cancer, Clinics/Medical Centers, Domestic Violence, Eyes/Blindness, Hospitals,

Medical Education, Prenatal Health Issues, Single-Disease Health Associations. **Geographic Distribution:** New York City and Hudson County, NJ.

★ 760 ★ **Loews Foundation**
667 Madison Ave.
New York, NY 10021
Phone: (212)545-2950
Roy Edward Posner, Sr. VP, Chief Financial Officer

Giving Priorities: *Religion:* About 40% of total contributions. *Arts & Humanities:* 30% to 35%. *Health:* 20% to 25%. Supports hospitals, single-disease associations, and medical research. *Other:* 5% to 10%. Supports a variety of educational, civic, international, and social service organizations. **Typical Health-Related Recipients:** AIDS/HIV, Cancer, Children's Health/Hospitals, Diabetes, Emergency/Ambulance Services, Hospitals, Medical Research, Multiple Sclerosis, Nutrition, People with Disabilities, Single-Disease Health Associations. **Geographic Distribution:** Primarily New York, also in operating locations.

★ 761 ★ **Louisiana Land & Exploration Co. Foundation**
PO Box 60350
New Orleans, LA 70160
Phone: (504)566-6500
Fax: (504)566-6891
Betty Hoag, Contributions Coordinator

Giving Priorities: *Education:* Approximately 35% to 40% of annual contributions. *Cultural & Civic:* 30% to 35%. *Health & Welfare:* 25% to 30%, nearly nine-tenths of which supporting united funds. Youth organizations also receive significant support. Other interests include drug and alcohol rehabilitation, religious welfare organizations, and single-disease health associations. *Religion & Other:* Less than 2%. Supports religious organizations and churches in order to benefit needy parishoners. Also has supported science exhibits and fairs. *Note:* Priorities include foundation and direct giving. **Typical Health-Related Recipients:** Health Organizations, Hospices, Medical Research, Single-Disease Health Associations, Substance Abuse. **Geographic Distribution:** Company operating locations.

★ 762 ★ **Lubrizol Foundation**
29425 Chagrin Blvd.
Ste. 303
Pepper Lake, OH 44122
Phone: (216)943-4200
Fax: (216)591-1533
Martha L. Berens, Foundation Manager and Secretary

Giving Priorities: *Education:* 50% to 55% of annual contributions. *Health & Human Services:* Typically 25% to 30% of funding, with major support to united funds. Other interests include hospitals and single-disease health organizations. *Cultural & Civic:* 5% to 10%. *Youth Activities:* Less than 5%. **Typical Health-Related Recipients:** Clinics/Medical Centers, Emergency/Ambulance Services, Eyes/Blindness, Health Organizations, Hospices, Hospitals, Medical Rehabilitation, Nursing Services, People with Disabilities, Single-Disease Health Associations. **Geographic Distribution:** Near headquarters and operating locations only.

★763★ **Lukens Foundation**
50 S First Ave.
Coatesville, PA 19320-0911
Phone: (610)383-2159
Fax: (610)383-2684
Katherine G. Pella, Secretary & Administrator

Giving Priorities: *Social Services:* 60% to 65%. *Education:* About 20%. *Health:* About 10%. Gives to a variety of causes, including hospitals, pediatrics, and single-disease health associations. *Arts & Humanities:* 5% to 10%. Grants are generally $5,000 or less. **Typical Health-Related Recipients:** Domestic Violence, Family Planning. **Geographic Distribution:** Only in communities where Lukens has facilities.

★764★ **Marcus Corp. Foundation**
250 E Wisconsin Ave.
Suite 1700
Milwaukee, WI 53202-4220
Phone: (414)272-6020
Stephen Howard Marcus, President

Giving Priorities: *Civic & Public Affairs:* 45% to 50% of total annual contributions. *Arts & Humanities:* 10% to 15% of funding. *Social Services:* 10% to 15% of contributions. *Health:* 10% to 15% of giving. Primarily support for hospitals and single disease health organizations. *Education:* 5% to 10% of contributions. *Religion:* About 5% of giving. **Typical Health-Related Recipients:** Alzheimers Disease, Arthritis, Cancer, Children's Health/Hospitals, Clinics/Medical Centers, Domestic Violence, Heart, Hospitals, Medical Education, Medical Research, Single-Disease Health Associations. **Geographic Distribution:** Focus on Milwaukee, WI.

★765★ **Marion Merrell Dow Foundation**
9300 Ward Pkwy.
Kansas City, MO 64114
Phone: (816)966-4000
Lynda Norris, Coordinator Community Affairs

Giving Priorities: *Health and Welfare:* About 55% of total annual contributions. Primary areas of focus include medical care for the medically indigent and the needy. A recent grant of $250,000 also went to provide medical training for minorities and to encourage certain physicians to practice at Swope Parkway Health Center. Company manufactures products specifically to be used for disaster relief and to aid residents of impoverished nations. *Education:* 20% to 25%. A recent grant of $8 million went to the University of Cincinnati College of Medicine in a collaborative effort to assist in education and research, primarily in the area of cardiovascular disease. *Community Enhancement:* Note: Giving to arts organizations is estimated to be between 5% and 10% of total annual contributions. **Typical Health-Related Recipients:** Geriatric Health, Hospices, Medical Education, Medical Research, Medical Training, Single-Disease Health Associations.

★766★ **Martin Marietta Corp. Foundation**
6801 Rockledge Dr.
Bethesda, MD 20817
Phone: (301)897-6284
Fax: (301)897-6252
Donna S. Price, Coord., Gifts and Grants

Giving Priorities: *Education:* 55% to 60% of contributions. *Health & Human Resources:* 20% to 25% of contributions. United funds are a major priority. Interests also include recreation and athletics, youth organizations, community service organizations, child welfare, and aid to the disabled. Hospitals, medical research, single-disease health organizations, and hospices are also included in this category. *Cultural:* About 15% of contributions. *Civic & Public Affairs:* Less than 5%. **Typical Health-Related Recipients:** Cancer, Emergency/Ambulance Services, Family Planning, Hospices, Hospitals, Medical Education, Medical Research, People with Disabilities, Single-Disease Health Associations. **Geographic Distribution:** Near headquarters and operating locations only.

★767★ **Masco Corp. Charitable Trust**
21001 Van Born Rd.
Taylor, MI 48180
Phone: (313)274-7400
Fax: (313)374-6134
Karyn L. Wells, Director, Corporate Contributions

Giving Priorities: *Education:* 35% to 40% of annual funding. Majority of education support funds colleges and universities. Some funds go to medical education. *Arts & Humanities:* 30% and 35% of contributions. *Health:* 10% to 15%. Interests include children's hospitals and medical research. *Social Services:* 10% to 15%. *Civic & Public Affairs:* Less than 5%. Funds environmental and philanthropic organization. *Other:* Less than 5% supports a scientific organization and a religious organization. **Typical Health-Related Recipients:** Hospitals, Medical Education, Medical Research. **Geographic Distribution:** Nationally, with emphasis on the Detroit, MI, area.

★768★ **Matlock Foundation**
1201 Third Ave., Ste. 4900
Seattle, WA 98101-3045
Phone: (206)224-5196
Fax: (206)224-5060
Lin Smith, Public Affairs Assistant

Giving Priorities: *Social Services:* 25% to 35% of annual giving. *Education:* 20% to 25% of contributions. *Arts & Humanities:* 20% to 25%. *Civic:* 10% to 15%. *Health:* About 5% to 10%, mostly awarded to hospitals. Hospices, emergency ambulance and nursing services, pediatric health, and single disease health organizations also receive support. *Other:* Limited support to scientific, religious, and other miscellaneous organizations. **Typical Health-Related Recipients:** Emergency/Ambulance Services, Hospices, Hospitals, Nursing Services. **Geographic Distribution:** Washington, Oregon, California, Michigan, Pennsylvania, Texas, Vermont, Iowa, New York.

★769★ **Mattel Foundation**
333 Continental Blvd.
El Segundo, CA 90245
Phone: (310)524-3530
Fax: (310)524-4443
Janice Nakayama, Foundation Manager

Giving Priorities: *Education:* About 40%. *Social Services:* 25% to 30% of contributions. Areas of interest include aid for the handicapped, family counseling, and substance abuse prevention programs. *Health:* About 25% of contributions. Majority of funds support activities at local health clinics. *Arts & Humanities:* Less than 5% of giving. *Civic & Public Affairs:* Less than 5%. **Typical Health-Related Recipients:** AIDS/HIV, Cancer, Clinics/Medical Centers, Multiple Sclerosis, Research/Studies Institutes, Substance Abuse. **Geographic Distribution:** Nationally.

★770★ **May Stores Foundation**
611 Olive St.
St. Louis, MO 63101
Phone: (314)342-6300
Fax: (314)342-4461
James Abrams, Vice President, Corporate Communications

Giving Priorities: *Health & Welfare:* 50% to 55% of contributions. Supports the United Way, hospitals, single-disease health associations, and federated organizations. *Education:* 25% to 30% of total giving. *Arts & Humanities:* 5% to 10% of contributions. *Other:* 5% to 10%. Foundation interests include scientific and religious organizations. *Civic & Public Affairs:* Less than 5%. **Typical Health-Related Recipients:** AIDS/HIV, Cancer, Children's Health/Hospitals, Health Funds, Health Organizations, Heart, Hospitals, Medical Education, Multiple Sclerosis, People with Disabilities, Substance Abuse. **Geographic Distribution:** In cities where company operates.

★771★ **MCA Foundation**
100 Universal City Plz.
Ste. 500/3
Universal City, CA 91608
Phone: (818)777-1208
Fax: (818)777-6202
Helen D. Yatsko, Administrator

Giving Priorities: *Arts & Humanities:* About 35% of total contributions. *Social Services:* 20% to 25%. *Health:* About 20%. Supports single-disease health associations, with interests in cancer and cystic fibrosis. Also supports hospitals and out-patient health care delivery. *Education:* 15% to 20%. *Civic & Public Affairs:* 10% to 15%. **Typical Health-Related Recipients:** Cancer, Clinics/Medical Centers, Emergency/Ambulance Services, Family Planning, Hospitals, Medical Education, Medical Research, Mental Health, Multiple Sclerosis, People with Disabilities, Single-Disease Health Associations. **Geographic Distribution:** Principally near operating locations and to national organizations.

★772★ **McDonald & Co. Securities Foundation**
800 Superior Ave. Ste. 2100
Cleveland, OH 44114
Phone: (216)443-2981
Fax: (216)443-3865
Thomas G. Clevidence, Secretary

Giving Priorities: *General Support Program:* Company supports a variety of interests, including community funds, community services, community arts programs, medical research, health services, and youth organizations. **Typical Health-Related Recipients:** Children's Health/Hospitals, Domestic Violence, Emergency/Ambulance Services, Family Planning, General, Hospices, Hospitals, Medical Research, Mental Health, Multiple Sclerosis, Nursing Services, People with Disabilities, Sexual Abuse, Single-Disease Health Associations, Speech & Hearing, Substance Abuse. **Geographic Distribution:** In headquarters and operating communities.

★773★ **McGraw-Hill Foundation**
1221 Avenue of the Americas
New York, NY 10020
Phone: (212)512-6113
Susan A. Wallman, Vice President

Giving Priorities: *Education:* About 60% of contributions. *Arts & Humanities:* 20% to 25%. *Health & Welfare:* 15% to 20% of contributions. Primary support to social service organizations, principally united funds. Interests in the health category include national and local health organizations. *Civic & Public Affairs:* Less than 5%. **Typical Health-Related Recipients:** Health Organizations, Substance Abuse. **Geographic Distribution:** Principally near operating locations, with emphasis on New York City, and to national organizations.

★774★ **MCI Foundation**
1801 Pennsylvania Ave., NW
Washington, DC 20006
Phone: (202)887-3247
Fax: (202)887-2106
Rolf Preisendorfor, Executive Director

Giving Priorities: *Arts & Humanities:* 35% to 40% of total contributions. *Education:* 20% to 25% of total contributions. *Civic & Public Affairs:* 15% to 20%. *Health:* About 10% of contributions. Interests include health organizations, hospitals, single-disease health associations and pediatric health. *Social Services:* 5% to 10% of giving. *Other Interests:* Less than 5%. Interests include scientific institutes. **Typical Health-Related Recipients:** Arthritis, Cancer, Emergency/Ambulance Services, Family Planning, Health Organizations, Hospitals, Medical Education, Medical Training, People with Disabilities, Single-Disease Health Associations. **Geographic Distribution:** Headquarters and operating locations.

★775★ **Mellon Bank Foundation**
One Mellon Bank Ctr.
Corporate Affairs
Rm. 1830
Pittsburgh, PA 15258-0001
Phone: (412)234-2732
Fax: (412)236-1662
James P. McDonald, Vice President & Secretary

Giving Priorities: *Cash Grants:* 40% to 45% of corporate charitable support, disbursed as follows: *Neighborhood & Economic Development:* About 35% of cash funding. *Health & Human Services:* 30% to 35%. Awarded largely to united funds, which receive more than three-quarters of these funds. Health grants given to hospitals, health centers, special care facilities, and health cost containment programs. Human service grants include organizations concerned with the disabled, drug and alcohol abuse, and food distribution. *Arts & Culture:* About 15%. *Education:* 10% to 15% of cash contributions. *Other:* Less than 5%. Limited funding supports additional foundation-related interests. *IN-KIND SUPPORT & COMMUNITY ACTIVITIES:* 60% to 65% of corporate support to charitable organizations. **Typical Health-Related Recipients:** Health Organizations, People with Disabilities. **Geographic Distribution:** Pennsylvania, Maryland, and Delaware and Boston, MA; in retail locations.

★776★ **Merck Co. Foundation**
One Merck Dr.
PO Box 100
Whitehouse Station, NJ 08889-0100
Phone: (908)423-2042
Fax: (908)423-1987
John R. Taylor, Executive Vice President

Giving Priorities: *PRODUCT DONATIONS:* 60% to 70% of total annual contributions. Merck contributes its health-related products to U.S. organizations serving the needy in Third World nations and Eastern European countries, and for emergency disaster relief programs. *CASH CONTRIBUTIONS:* 30% to 40% of total contributions, including donations made directly by the company and those made through the foundation. Cash contributions are made in the following areas. *Medical and Science Education:* 45% to 50% of annual cash contributions. Supports programs designed to increase knowledge of medicine and related disciplines. *Health:* About 20%. Primarily supports hospitals and medical centers. Major recipients in 1992 were the Children's Health Fund in Washington, DC and Massachusetts General Hospital in Boston, MA. *Social Services:* 15% to 20% of cash contributions. *International:* 5% to 10%. *Arts & Humanities:* Less than 5% of giving. *Civic & Public Affairs:* Less than 5% of cash contributions, mostly to groups concerned with health policy issues. Also supports organizations dealing with the pharmaceutical business, economics, medical research, and health care cost containment. In 1991, Merck announced $1 million in funding for the next two years for the Instituto Nacional de Beiodiversidad de Costa Rica (INBio), a national institute that screens plant and animal species for development into potential medicines. *Science:* Less than 5%, with principal support going to laboratories and science

centers. **Typical Health-Related Recipients:** Cancer, Children's Health/Hospitals, Clinics/Medical Centers, Emergency/Ambulance Services, Geriatric Health, Health Policy/Cost Containment, Hospitals, Medical Education, Medical Research, Medical Training. **Geographic Distribution:** Principally near operating locations and nationally.

★777★ **Merrill Lynch & Co. Foundation**
World Headquarters, South Tower
World Financial Ctr.
New York, NY 10080-6106
Phone: (212)236-4319
Fax: (212)236-8005
Westina L. Matthews, Vice President, Philanthropic Programs

Giving Priorities: *Education:* About 30% of total annual giving. *Arts & Humanities:* 20% to 25% of total. *Social Services:* About 15%. Gives to a variety of local and national organizations, with emphasis on youth and community service organizations. Other interests include employment, the disabled, and child welfare. Company also founded in 1990 Deaf/Head-of-Hearing Grants Initiative. *Civic & Public Affairs:* 10% to 15%. *Health:* 10% to 15%. The majority goes to hospitals, with other interests including medical research and rehabilitation, pediatric health, and single-disease health organizations. Grants made primarily in New York and New Jersey, ranging from $5,000 to $25,000. In 1988, foundation implemented an annual AIDS grants initiatives, which targets provision and referral services, AIDS education and advocacy, housing, and research. *United Way:* 5% to 10%. **Typical Health-Related Recipients:** AIDS/HIV, Cancer, Clinics/Medical Centers, Emergency/Ambulance Services, Geriatric Health, Health Organizations, Hospitals, Medical Research, People with Disabilities, Single-Disease Health Associations, Substance Abuse, Transplant Networks/Donor Banks. **Geographic Distribution:** Primarily in areas where Merrill Lynch & Co. maintains offices with priority given to organizations in greater New York metropolitan area; also to national organizations.

★778★ **Metropolitan Life Foundation**
One Madison Ave.
New York, NY 10010
Phone: (212)578-6272
Sibyl C. Jacobson, Vice President

Giving Priorities: *Education:* 20% to 25% of annual contributions. *Health:* 20% to 25% of total contributions, with emphasis on health and safety programs, substance abuse prevention for youth, wellness programs, and medical career opportunities for minorities. In 1993, a $635,237 grant was awarded to the Health and Safety Education Program. Other priorities include medical research for Alzheimers and AIDS education programs. Remaining funds go to health care planning and cost containment, as well as medical education for minorities. *Civic & Public Affairs:* About 15%. *Culture:* 10% to 15%. *Public Broadcasting:* 10% to 15%. *United Ways:* 10% to 15% of yearly funding. **Typical Health-Related Recipients:** AIDS/HIV, Children's Health/Hospitals, Health Funds, Health Organizations, Health Policy/Cost Containment, Hospitals, Medical Education, Medical

Research, Medical Training, Nursing Services, Nutrition, Substance Abuse, Transplant Networks/Donor Banks. **Geographic Distribution:** Special consideration to communities in which Metropolitan has a major presence, and to programs that are national in scope.

★779★ Miles Inc. Foundation
One Mellon Ctr.
500 Grant St.
Pittsburgh, PA 15219-2502
Phone: (412)394-6725
Fax: (412)349-5586
Sande Deitch, Executive Director

Giving Priorities: *Education:* About 55% of total contributions. *Health:* Between 25% and 30%. Most benefits single-disease health organizations, especially those dealing with AIDS and cancer. Hospitals and hospices also receive support. *Arts & Humanities:* Between 10% and 15%. *Social Services:* Less than 5% of total contributions. *Civic & Public Affairs:* Less than 5%. **Typical Health-Related Recipients:** Clinics/Medical Centers, Health Funds, Health Organizations, Hospitals, Medical Education, People with Disabilities, Single-Disease Health Associations. **Geographic Distribution:** Near manufacturing plants and headquarters.

★780★ Milliken Foundation
PO Box 1926, M-416
Spartanburg, SC 29304
Phone: (803)573-2904
Fax: (803)573-2073
Lawrence Heagney, Secretary

Giving Priorities: *Education:* About 35%. *Social Services:* About 25%. *Civic and Political Affairs:* 10% to 15%. *Science:* 5% to 10%. *Arts & Humanities:* 5% to 10%. *Health:* 5% to 10%, mostly to hospitals and single-disease health organizations. *Religion:* About 5%. **Typical Health-Related Recipients:** Clinics/Medical Centers, Emergency/Ambulance Services, Family Planning, Hospitals, Medical Education, People with Disabilities, Prenatal Health Issues, Single-Disease Health Associations. **Geographic Distribution:** Nationally and near operating locations.

★781★ Millipore Foundation
80 Ashby Rd.
Bedford, MA 01730
Phone: (617)275-9200
Fax: (617)275-3236
Charleen Johnson, Executive Director

Giving Priorities: *Education:* 35% to 40% of total. *Social Services:* 30% to 35%. *Health:* 10% to 15% of total. Supports hospitals, mental health associations and single-disease health associations. *Culture:* About 15% of total. *Public Policy:* Less 5% of total. *International:* Gives limited to U.S. based nonprofits with an international focus. **Typical Health-Related Recipients:** AIDS/HIV, Clinics/Medical Centers, Emergency/Ambulance Services, Home-Care Services, Hospitals, Medical Training, Mental Health. **Geographic Distribution:** Cash grants made primarily in Massachusetts; matching gifts awarded throughout the country.

★782★ Mine Safety Appliances Co. Charitable Trust
PO Box 426
Pittsburgh, PA 15230
Phone: (412)967-3000
Fax: (412)967-3452
James E. Herald, Secretary

Giving Priorities: *Social Services:* 40% to 45% of contributions. *Arts & Humanities:* 30% to 35%. *Health:* About 15%, primarily in support of hospitals. Other interests include pediatric health, rehabilitation centers, and single-disease health associations. *Education:* 5% to 10% of contributions. *Civic & Public Affairs:* Less than 5%. **Typical Health-Related Recipients:** Health Funds, Health Organizations, Hospitals, Medical Rehabilitation, Mental Health, People with Disabilities, Single-Disease Health Associations. **Geographic Distribution:** Primarily in Pittsburgh, PA, and in other areas where company has operations.

★783★ Mobil Foundation
3225 Gallows Rd.
Fairfax, VA 22037-0001
Phone: (703)846-3381
Richard G. Mund, Secretary & Executive Director

Giving Priorities: *Education:* About 40% of annual contributions. *Arts & Culture:* 15% to 20%. *Community Funds:* 15% to 20% of total contributions. *Civic:* About 15% of total contributions. *Hospitals:* 10% to 15%. Contributions to hospitals are restricted to company communities. Grants also are made to selected research hospitals. Average grant is in the range of $5,000 to $10,000. Also matches employee gifts to hospitals. *Health Agencies:* Less than 5% of annual contributions, to such agencies as the American Red Cross, National Council on Alcoholism, and Visiting Nurse Service of New York. Does not make grants to local or national organizations concerned with specific diseases. *Note:* Above percentages reflect foundation giving only. **Typical Health-Related Recipients:** Domestic Violence, Emergency/Ambulance Services, Geriatric Health, Health Funds, Health Organizations, Hospices, Hospitals, Medical Education, Medical Rehabilitation, Medical Research, Nursing Services, People with Disabilities, Substance Abuse. **Geographic Distribution:** Primarily in communities where company has operations; some emphasis on corporate headquarters.

★784★ Morrison Knudsen Corp. Foundation Inc.
PO Box 73
Boise, ID 83729
Phone: (208)345-5000
Mary Cunningham Agee, Chairman

Giving Priorities: *Civic & Public Affairs:* About 55% of total contributions. *Arts & Humanities:* About 15%. *Social Services:* About 15% of funding. *Education:* About 10%. *Health:* About 5%. Supports medical rehabilitation, medical centers and hospitals, emergency services, and single-disease health associations. **Typical Health-Related Recipients:** Emergency/Ambulance Services, Health Organizations, Medical Rehabilitation, Single-Disease Health Associations. **Geographic Distribution:** Nationally, with a focus on Idaho and operating locations.

★785★ Motorola Foundation
1303 E Algonquin Rd.
Schaumburg, IL 60196
Phone: (708)576-6200
Fax: (708)576-6846
Pamela Cox, Program Administrator

Giving Priorities: *Education:* 55% to 60% of contributions. *Health & Human Services:* 25% to 30%; primarily supports united funds, community chests, and youth groups. Remaining grants go to a variety of interests, including capital expansion programs at select community service organizations, aid to the handicapped, recreation, employment, hospitals, and single-disease health organizations. *Civic & Public Affairs:* 5% to 10%. *Arts & Humanities:* Less than 5%. *Other:* Limited support for science fairs and science organizations. **Typical Health-Related Recipients:** Hospices, Hospitals, People with Disabilities, Single-Disease Health Associations, Substance Abuse. **Geographic Distribution:** Primarily near headquarters and major plant locations; also to select national organizations.

★786★ MPCo/Entech Foundation
40 E Broadway
Butte, MT 59701
Phone: (406)723-5454
Pamela K. Merrell, Vice President, Secretary

Giving Priorities: *Health and Human Services:* About 48% of total contributions, including a grant of $44,038 to the United Way in Silver Bow County, MT. Various United Ways received grants totaling $96,093. Also supported traditional youth organizations and family services. *Education:* 25% to 30%. *Arts & Humanities:* About 19%. *Civic and Community:* Less than 5%. *International:* Alberta, Canada **Typical Health-Related Recipients:** Cancer, Clinics/Medical Centers, Diabetes, Domestic Violence, Health Organizations, Hospitals. **Geographic Distribution:** Primarily in areas of company operations.

★787★ Nabisco Foundation Trust
7 Campus Dr.
Parsippany, NJ 07054
Phone: (201)682-7098
Fax: (201)682-6265
Henry Sandbach, Vice President, Public Relations

Giving Priorities: *Social Services:* 45% to 50%. *Education:* About 15%. Supports colleges and universities, particularly for medical education and programs related to food marketing. *Health:* 10% to 15%. Supports hospitals and health foundations. In 1992, the Desert Hospital Foundation in Palm Springs, CA, received a $60,000 grant. *Science:* 10% to 15%. *Religion:* About 5%. *Civic & Public Affairs:* Less than 5%. *Arts & Humanities:* Less than 5% of total contributions. **Typical Health-Related Recipients:** Health Organizations, Hospitals, Medical Education, Nutrition. **Geographic Distribution:** Areas where Nabisco Brands maintains corporate facilities.

★788★ Nalco Foundation
One Nalco Center
Naperville, IL 60563-1198
Phone: (708)305-1556
Fax: (708)305-2985
Joanne C. Ford, President

Giving Priorities: *Education:* Generally about 35% of foundation contributions. *Community & Civic Affairs:* Approximately 30% of funding. *Health:* Usually about 25% of funds, with major support to hospitals and single-disease health associations. Interests include medical research and rehabilitation, pediatric health, and health-care cost containment. *Culture & Arts:* Typically about 10%. *International:* 5% to 10%. Support for U.S.-based nonprofit organizations with an international focus comes from health and/or education budgets. This is included in the totals above. **Typical Health-Related Recipients:** Domestic Violence, Emergency/ Ambulance Services, Health Organizations, Health Policy/Cost Containment, Hospices, Hospitals, Medical Education, Medical Rehabilitation, Mental Health, People with Disabilities, Single-Disease Health Associations, Substance Abuse. **Geographic Distribution:** Towns where Nalco has major manufacturing facilities or subsidiaries; emphasis on Chicago metropolitan area, including DuPage County; few to U.S.-based nonprofit organizations with an international focus.

★789★ National City Corporation Charitable Foundation Trust
c/o Corporate Public Affairs Department
National City Bank
PO Box 5756
Cleveland, OH 44101
Phone: (216)575-2000
Fax: (216)575-2670
Allen C. Waddle, Senior Vice President

Giving Priorities: *Health & Human Services:* 45% to 50% of annual contributions. Primarily supports united funds, community service and religious welfare organizations, community centers, food and clothes distribution, and a range of organizations that provide services for the elderly, families, youth, and children. Has supported groups devoted to research in diseases including cancer, arthritis, cystic fibrosis, and kidney ailments. *Education:* 20% to 25%. *Arts & Humanities:* 15% to 20% of contributions. *Civic & Public Affairs:* 10% to 15% of contributions. *Other:* 1%. Bank reserves limited funds for other concerns generally falling into the traditional civic and social services areas. Interests have included benefits, charitable organizations, women's affairs, scouting organizations, and professional associations. **Typical Health-Related Recipients:** Geriatric Health, Hospitals, Mental Health, Substance Abuse. **Geographic Distribution:** Mainly in Cleveland, OH, and northeastern Ohio operating locations; parts of Kentucky and Indiana; and considers national organizations on an individual basis.

★790★ National Machinery Foundation
161 Greenfield St.
Tiffin, OH 44883
Phone: (419)447-5211
Don B. Bero, Assistant Secretary

Giving Priorities: *Social Services:* 45% to 50% total contributions. *Education:* 20% to 25%. *Health:* About 15%. Recipients include rehabilitation centers, hospitals, nursing homes, hospices, and single-disease health associations. *Civic & Public Affairs:* 10%. *Arts & Humanities:* 5% to 10%. **Typical Health-Related Recipients:** Geriatric Health, Health Organizations, Hospices, Hospitals, Medical Rehabilitation, Nursing Services, Single-Disease Health Associations, Substance Abuse. **Geographic Distribution:** Limited to Seneca County, OH.

★791★ National Starch & Chemical Foundation
10 Finderne Ave.
Bridgewater, NJ 08807
Phone: (908)685-5201
Mary Gagliardi, Human Resources

Giving Priorities: *Social Services:* 45% to 50% of contributions. *Education:* 15% to 20% of contributions. *Civic & Public Affairs:* 15% to 20%. *Health:* 10% to 15%. Most grants in this category go to hospitals. Contributions also support research, single-disease organizations, and general health organizations such as the Red Cross. *Arts & Humanities:* Less than 5%. **Typical Health-Related Recipients:** Clinics/ Medical Centers, Emergency/Ambulance Services, Health Funds, Hospitals, Medical Training, Nursing Services, Substance Abuse. **Geographic Distribution:** Primarily in company operating areas.

★792★ Nationwide Insurance Enterprise Foundation
One Nationwide Plz.
Columbus, OH 43216
Phone: (614)249-5095
Stephen A. Rish, Vice President

Giving Priorities: *Health & Welfare:* 50% to 55% of total annual contributions, most of which goes to united funds. Other areas of interest include youth and community service organizations, and programs for the elderly and child welfare. Health support goes primarily to hospitals, but mental health and other health groups also are of interest. *Education:* 25% to 30%. *Arts & Humanities:* 10% to 15% of contributions. *Civic & Public Affairs:* About 5%. *Voluntarism:* Company sponsors an informal employee volunteer program. **Typical Health-Related Recipients:** Alzheimers Disease, Cancer, Children's Health/Hospitals, Emergency/ Ambulance Services, Eyes/Blindness, Family Planning, Health Organizations, Hospitals, Long-Term Care, Medical Research, Mental Health, People with Disabilities, Single-Disease Health Associations, Substance Abuse. **Geographic Distribution:** Principally near operating locations.

★793★ Nestle USA Foundation
Corporate Public Service
800 N Brand Blvd.
Glendale, CA 91203
Phone: (818)549-6000
Fax: (818)549-6534
Betty A. Dumas, Philanthropy & Gov't Relations Coord.

Giving Priorities: *Education:* 25% to 30%. *Arts & Humanities:* 20% to 25%. *Social Services:* 15% to 20%. *Civic & Public Affairs:* About 15%. *Health:* About 15%. Supports health organizations, medical centers, and hospitals. *Voluntarism:* Company employees volunteer at an Adopt-A-School program. **Typical Health-Related Recipients:** Clinics/Medical Centers, Emergency/Ambulance Services, Hospitals, Preventive Medicine/Wellness Organizations. **Geographic Distribution:** Near company's manufacturing facilities. **Formerly:** Carnation Company Foundation.

★794★ New York Life Foundation
51 Madison Ave.
New York, NY 10010
Phone: (212)576-7000
Carol J. Reuter, President and Executive Director

Giving Priorities: *Social Services:* 30% to 35% of contributions. *Civic & Public Affairs:* 30% to 35%. *Health:* 15% to 20%. Medical research is a priority. Also funds single-disease health organizations, AIDS, hospitals, medical rehabilitation, and mental health. *Education:* 15% to 20% of contributions. *Arts & Humanities:* Less than 5%. **Typical Health-Related Recipients:** AIDS/HIV, Domestic Violence, Emergency/ Ambulance Services, Geriatric Health, Health Organizations, Hospitals, Medical Education, Medical Rehabilitation, Medical Research, Medical Training, Mental Health, Nursing Services, People with Disabilities, Single-Disease Health Associations, Substance Abuse. **Geographic Distribution:** Nationally.

★795★ Newman's Own Foundation
246 Post Rd. E
Westport, CT 06880-3615
Phone: (203)222-0136
Aaron E. Hotchner, Director

Giving Priorities: *International:* 100% of total contributions. Primarily concerned with international child welfare organizations, including hospitals, child abuse prevention, and pediatric health. Also supports the disabled, particularly the blind or deaf; community centers; and other social service agencies in Australia and Canada. **Typical Health-Related Recipients:** Domestic Violence, Health Funds, Hospitals, People with Disabilities, Single-Disease Health Associations.

★796★ Norfolk Southern Foundation
PO Box 3040
Norfolk, VA 23514-3040
Phone: (804)629-2652
William J. Romig, Vice President and Executive Director

Giving Priorities: *Education:* 30% to 35%. *Arts & Humanities:* 25% to 30% of total contributions. *Health & Social Services:* About 20%. Contributes mainly to united funds. Funds health organizations and hospitals. Grants also support volunteer services, community centers such as YMCAs, and some other community service organizations. Other interests include mental health and health funds. *Civic & Public Affairs:* 15% to 20% of support. *Other:* Less than 1%. Recent grants include a small number to science institutes. **Typical Health-Related Recipients:** Cancer, Children's Health/Hospitals, Emergency/Ambulance Services, Health Organizations, Heart, Hospitals, Medical Education, Medical Research. **Geographic Dis-**

tribution: Primarily near major employment centers and along Norfolk Southern rail systems.

★ 797 ★ **Northern Trust Co. Charitable Trust**
50 S LaSalle St., M-5
Chicago, IL 60675
Phone: (312)444-3538
Fax: (312)444-3108
Marjorie W. Lundy, Vice President

Giving Priorities: *Social Welfare:* 30% to 35% of contributions. *Education:* 25% to 30%. *Arts & Culture:* 10% to 15%. *Community Revitalization:* 10% to 15%. *Health:* 5% to 10%. Priorities are health care cost containment and new models of health service delivery. Also emphasizes health care accessible to low-income communities in Chicago. Medical rehabilitation and hospitals also receive support. Sponsors an employee matching gifts program for accredited hospitals. *Other:* Less than 5%. Supports various community organizations that do not fall within categories above. *Voluntarism:* Company sponsors an employee volunteer program. **Typical Health-Related Recipients:** Domestic Violence, Family Planning, Health Organizations, Hospices, Hospitals, Mental Health, Nutrition, People with Disabilities, Public Health, Substance Abuse. **Geographic Distribution:** Exclusively in the Chicago area, except matching gifts.

★ 798 ★ **Northwestern National Life Foundation**
20 Washington Ave. S
Minneapolis, MN 55401
Phone: (612)342-7443
Fax: (612)342-3002
Teresa K. Egge, Mgr. Community Relations & NWNL Found.

Giving Priorities: *Education:* About 40% of annual giving. *United Way:* About 25% of giving. *Urban & Civic Affairs:* About 15% of giving. *Health:* 5% to 10% of giving, emphasis on health education and wellness; supports health clinics, cost-containment programs, and AIDS education. Generally does not support hospitals. *Culture:* 5% to 10% of giving. **Typical Health-Related Recipients:** Health Funds. **Geographic Distribution:** Near headquarters, subsidiaries, and to a limited number of national organizations in the health field.

★ 799 ★ **Norton Co. Foundation**
1 New Bond St.
PO Box 15008
Worcester, MA 01615-0008
Phone: (508)795-2605
Fax: (508)795-5535
Judi Cutts, Contributions Coordinator

Giving Priorities: *Health & Human Services:* 45% to 50% of total contributions. Supports primarily United Way chapters. Other interests include child welfare, community service and youth organizations, and programs concerned with counseling, drugs and alcohol rehabilitation, family services, the aged and the handicapped, and recreation. Also supports various health interests, including hospices, emergency/ambulance services, and single-disease health organizations. *Education:* 25% to 30% of

contributions. *Civic & Community Activities:* 10% to 15% of contributions. *Arts & Humanities:* 5% to 10% of contributions. *Memberships:* Less than 5%. Includes membership in a number of organizations, including Associated Grantmakers of Massachusetts, Council on Foundations, and Worcester Municipal Research Bureau. **Typical Health-Related Recipients:** Children's Health/Hospitals, Clinics/Medical Centers, Domestic Violence, Emergency/Ambulance Services, Family Planning, Geriatric Health, Health Organizations, Health Policy/Cost Containment, Hospices, Hospitals, Medical Rehabilitation, Medical Research, Mental Health, Nursing Services, Nutrition, People with Disabilities, Public Health, Substance Abuse. **Geographic Distribution:** Communities where Norton Co. maintains facilities.

★ 800 ★ **NutraSweet Co. Charitable Trust**
1751 Lake Cook Rd.
Box 730
Deerfield, IL 60015
Phone: (708)405-6804
Fax: (708)405-7680
Max Downham, Vice President

Giving Priorities: *General* Priority will be given to organizations that are dedicated to nutrition, hunger, health, fitness, education and crisis intervention. These organizations should service the communities where employees live and work. *Community Enrichment Fund:* Foundation maintains this fund to encourage and support employee-volunteer efforts. **Typical Health-Related Recipients:** Hospitals, Nutrition, Single-Disease Health Associations. **Geographic Distribution:** Operating locations.

★ 801 ★ **Occidental Petroleum Charitable Foundation**
10889 Wilshire Blvd.
Los Angeles, CA 90024
Phone: (213)879-1700
Evelyn Wong, Assistant Secretary-Treasurer

Giving Priorities: *Education:* 30% to 35% of total giving. *Arts & Humanities:* 25% to 30% of contributions. *Social Services:* About 20%. *Civic & Public Affairs:* 5% to 10%. *Health:* 5% to 10%. Supports hospitals and related health organizations. **Typical Health-Related Recipients:** Health Organizations, Hospitals, Medical Education, Single-Disease Health Associations. **Geographic Distribution:** Communities where Occidental Petroleum maintains facilities.

★ 802 ★ **Oklahoma Gas & Electric Co. Foundation**
Box 321
Oklahoma City, OK 73101
Phone: (405)272-3196
Fax: (405)272-3760
James G. Harlow, Jr., President

Giving Priorities: *Education:* 40% to 45% of total giving. *Civic:* 30% to 35%. *Arts:* 10% to 15% of funding. *Health:* 10% to 15% of funding. Grants usually range from $2,500 to $6,000 and are awarded primarily to hospitals, medical research, and pediatric health. *Social Services:* Less than 5%. Most grants are between $1,000 and $5,000. Usually about one-half goes to youth organizations. Other interests include community services, family planning, recreation

and athletics, and organizations concerned with the elderly and children. **Typical Health-Related Recipients:** Clinics/Medical Centers, Emergency/Ambulance Services, Family Planning, Health Organizations, Heart, Hospitals, People with Disabilities. **Geographic Distribution:** Areas of corporate operations; primarily Oklahoma.

★ 803 ★ **Olin Corp. Charitable Trust**
120 Long Ridge Rd.
Stamford, CT 06904
Phone: (203)356-3301
Fax: (203)356-3065
Carmella V. Piacentini, Administrator

Giving Priorities: *Education:* About 40% of total contributions. *Health & Human Services:* About 30%. Primary interests are hospitals and united funds. Other areas of interest include organizations for the handicapped, drug and alcohol education, child welfare, and community service. Limited support to medical research and rehabilitation and pediatric health. *Civic & Public Affairs:* About 10% annually. *Arts & Humanities:* About 5%. *Note:* About 10% of contributions go to social service organizations. Information on social service organizations is not available. Another 15% of contributions in the category of "other" is also made. **Typical Health-Related Recipients:** Emergency/Ambulance Services, Health Organizations, Hospices, Hospitals, Medical Rehabilitation, Mental Health, Single-Disease Health Associations, Substance Abuse. **Geographic Distribution:** Principally near operating locations and to national organizations.

★ 804 ★ **Orscheln Industries Foundation**
PO Box 698
Moberly, MO 65270
Phone: (816)263-4335
Gerald A. Orscheln, President

Giving Priorities: *Religion:* 35% to 40% of total contributions. *Social Services:* 15% to 20%. *Education:* 15% to 20%. *Civic & Public Affairs:* 10% to 15%. *Health:* 5% to 10% of contributions. Funds support hospitals, single-disease health organizations, and similar health groups. **Typical Health-Related Recipients:** Health Organizations, Hospitals, Single-Disease Health Associations. **Geographic Distribution:** Primarily in Missouri, especially Randolph County.

★ 805 ★ **OSG Foundation**
511 Fifth Ave.
New York, NY 10017
Phone: (212)953-4100
Fax: (212)578-1832
Michael A. Recanati, Exec. VP, Sec., Treas.

Giving Priorities: *Health:* Between 45% and 50% of total annual contributions, almost four-fifths of which supports hospitals. Remaining funds benefit medical research, with small grants also going to various single-disease health organizations. *Social Services:* 20% to 25% of annual total. Priorities include aid to the handicapped and child welfare. *Education:* 10% to 15% annually. Substantial interest shown in medical education. *Civic & Public Affairs:* 10% to 15%. *Arts & Humanities:* About 5%. **Typical Health-Related Recipients:** AIDS/HIV, Clinics/Medical Centers, Hospitals, Medical Education, Medical Research, Mental Health, People with Disabilities, Single-Disease Health Associations, Substance Abuse. **Geographic Distribution:** Primarily in New York City area.

★806★ **Owens-Corning Fiberglas Foundation**
Fiberglas Tower
Toledo, OH 43659
Phone: (419)248-8315
Fax: (419)248-5337
Emerson J. Ross, Secretary, Corporate Contibutions

Giving Priorities: *Health & Human Services:* 40% to 45% of annual contributions, with most of this going to human service organizations in communities with major employee populations. Major support goes to united funds, community centers, and organizations concerned with domestic violence and substance abuse. Other interests include youth organizations, family services, the aged, and deliquency and crime. In health, supports health organizations, hospitals, and health care cost containment. *Education:* About 40% of funding. *Civic & Public Affairs:* 10% to 15% of annual giving. *Arts & Humanities:* 5% to 10%. *International:* Companies foreign subsidiaries also make contributions to international organizations. Contributions in 1992 totaled $300,060. *Other:* About 5% goes to miscellaneous groups, including science organizations. **Typical Health-Related Recipients:** Substance Abuse. **Geographic Distribution:** Near headquarters and operating locations only.

★807★ **Oxy USA Charitable Foundation**
PO Box 300
Tulsa, OK 74102
Phone: (918)561-2212
Fax: (918)561-2427
Ronald G. Peters, Director, Public Affairs

Giving Priorities: *Health and Human Services:* 50% to 55% Major support has gone to Domestic Violence Intervention Services, Little Light House, and Project Get Together. Other interests include drug abuse programs, handicapped services, food and clothing distribution, family services, and youth organizations. Health interests include major support to single-disease health associations. *Education:* 30% to 35% of total contributions. *Arts & Humanities:* 5% to 10%. *Civic & Public Affairs:* 5% to 10%. **Typical Health-Related Recipients:** Domestic Violence, Hospices, Hospitals, Medical Rehabilitation, Mental Health, People with Disabilities, Single-Disease Health Associations, Substance Abuse. **Geographic Distribution:** Near operating locations. **Formerly:** Occidental Oil & Gas Charitable Foundation.

★808★ **Pacific Mutual Charitable Foundation**
700 Newport Center Dr.
Newport Beach, CA 92660
Phone: (714)640-3787
Fax: (714)640-7614
Robert G. Haskell, President

Giving Priorities: *United Way:* 30% to 35% of total annual contributions. *Education:* About 20% of contributions. Recipients include minority, medical, economic, and health education, as well as precollegiate public education. *Health & Welfare:* 60% to 65% of contributions. Priority in this area is to improve public understanding of and participation in health education programs, and to promote healthier lifestyles. Other interests include hospitals, Hispanic issues, youth agencies, drug and alcohol rehabilitation programs, shelters, and organizations concerned with the disabled, the aged, counseling, and children and families. *Arts:* 5% to 10% of funding. *Civic:* 5% to 10%. **Typical Health-Related Recipients:** AIDS/HIV, Children's Health/Hospitals, Emergency/Ambulance Services, Family Planning, Geriatric Health, Health Organizations, Health Policy/Cost Containment, Hospices, Hospitals, Medical Education, Medical Research, Medical Training, Mental Health, Nutrition, People with Disabilities, Public Health, Single-Disease Health Associations, Substance Abuse. **Geographic Distribution:** Primarily to local organizations in areas with large concentrations of company employees; some state and national funding.

★809★ **Paramount Communications Foundation**
15 Columbus Circle
New York, NY 10023
Phone: (212)373-8250
Pat Colon, Director

Giving Priorities: *Arts & Humanities:* 50% to 55% of total contributions. *Education:* 20% to 25%. *Health:* 10% to 15% of total contributions. Interests include single-disease associations, medical research, and medical centers. *Social Services:* 5% to 10%. *Civic & Public Affairs:* 5% to 10% of total contributions. **Typical Health-Related Recipients:** Cancer, Clinics/Medical Centers, Diabetes, Domestic Violence, Hospices, Medical Education, Medical Research, Mental Health, Multiple Sclerosis, Nursing Services, People with Disabilities, Single-Disease Health Associations, Substance Abuse, Transplant Networks/Donor Banks. **Geographic Distribution:** Primarily in corporate operating locations.

★810★ **PemCo. Foundation**
325 Eastlake Ave. E
Seattle, WA 98109
Phone: (206)628-4027
Stanley O. McNaughton, Secretary & Treasurer

Giving Priorities: *Social Services:* 40% to 45%. *Education:* 35% to 40%. *Health:* 5% to 10%. Primary support to Visiting Nurse Service, the American Lung Association, and Community Home Health Care. Other support to various health organizations in Seattle, WA. *Civic & Public Affairs:* 5% to 10%. *Other:* The foundation also supports arts organizations and a church. **Typical Health-Related Recipients:** Cancer, Children's Health/Hospitals, Clinics/Medical Centers, General, Health Funds, Home-Care Services, Hospices, Hospitals, Medical Rehabilitation, Multiple Sclerosis, People with Disabilities, Respiratory. **Geographic Distribution:** Focus on Washington state.

★811★ **Persis Hawaii Foundation**
605 Kapiolani Blvd.
Honolulu, HI 96813
Phone: (808)525-8050
Kenneth Uemura, Treasurer

Giving Priorities: *Arts & Humanities:* About 40% of total contributions. *Education:* About 25% of giving. *Social Services:* 20% to 25% of total giving. *Civic & Public Affairs:* 5% to 10% of contributions. *Health:* About 5% of giving. Supports hospitals and health centers in Hawaii. Other recipients include two health care foundations. **Typical Health-Related Recipients:** Clinics/Medical Centers, General, Health Organizations, Hospices, Hospitals, Medical Rehabilitation, Nursing Services, People with Disabilities, Substance Abuse. **Geographic Distribution:** In headquarters and operating locations.

★812★ **Pfizer Foundation**
235 E 42nd St.
New York, NY 10017-5755
Phone: (212)573-5936
Fax: (212)573-2883
Linda B. Gornitsky, Director, Corporate Support Programs

Giving Priorities: *Education:* About 20% to 25% of contributions. Preference given to educational programs that relate to the company's business operations in medicine, agriculture, chemistry, pharmacology, and other science-based disciplines. *Health and Human Services:* 30% to 35% of giving. Program supports selected health care organizations, including hospitals, hospices, alcohol and drug rehabilitation centers, mental health institutions, rehabilitation programs for the handicapped and other community health projects. Also supports United Ways. Funding of health associations fighting diseases such as cancer, tuberculosis, heart disease, diabetes, hypertension, and muscular dystrophy are handled by the appropriate health-related division of the company. *Civic & Community Services:* 20% to 25% of cash contributions. *Culture:* 15% to 20% of contributions. *International Affairs:* Less than 5% of contributions. *Matching Gifts & Pfizer Volunteer Program:* About 15%. **Typical Health-Related Recipients:** Adolescent Health Issues, Emergency/Ambulance Services, Geriatric Health, Health Organizations, Hospices, Hospitals, Medical Education, Medical Rehabilitation, Medical Research, Mental Health, People with Disabilities, Single-Disease Health Associations, Substance Abuse, Transplant Networks/Donor Banks. **Geographic Distribution:** Nationally and in communities where Pfizer and its subsidiaries operate; some emphasis on New York City.

★813★ **Phelps Dodge Foundation**
2600 N Central Ave.
Phoenix, AZ 85004
Phone: (602)234-8100
William C. Tubman, President

Giving Priorities: *Education:* 60% to 65% of total annual contributions. Interests include medical education. *Culture & Art:* 25% to 30% of giving. *Health & Welfare:* 5% to 10%, with nearly half going to federated drives. Significant support also goes to youth organizations and national health organizations. Also supports hospitals. *Civic & Public Affairs:* 5% to 10%. *International:* About 5%. *Note:* Matching gifts, which comprise 25% to 30% of annual grants, are made to educational, not-for-profit voluntary hospitals, and cultural organizations and institutions. **Typical Health-Related Recipients:** Family Planning, Health Funds, Health Organizations, Hospitals, Medical Education, Medical Training. **Geographic Distribution:** Where company maintains major operating facilities.

★814★ PHH Foundation
11333 McCormick Rd.
Hunt Valley, MD 21031
Phone: (410)771-2733
Fax: (410)771-2841
Pilar M. Page, Vice President

Giving Priorities: *Health & Human Services:* 45% to 50% of total contributions. In fiscal 1992, the United Way of Central Maryland received the highest grant of $120,000. Other interests include national health organizations, national human service organizations, youth organizations, local health and human service agencies, safety, recreation, family planning, drug abuse, and disaster relief. Major support to United Way. Emphasis on neighborhood health agencies and public education programs for nutrition and health. *Education:* About 35%. *Arts & Culture:* About 10%. *Civic & Community:* 5% to 10%. *Other:* Less than 5%. Supports employee assistance program. **Typical Health-Related Recipients:** Children's Health/ Hospitals, Clinics/Medical Centers, Domestic Violence, Emergency/Ambulance Services, General, Health Organizations, Hospitals, Medical Research, Multiple Sclerosis, People with Disabilities, Respiratory, Single-Disease Health Associations, Substance Abuse. **Geographic Distribution:** Limited to community where corporation headquarters is located; Baltimore, MD, area. **Formerly:** PHH Group Foundation.

★815★ Phillips Petroleum Foundation
Phillips Bldg., 16th Fl.
Bartlesville, OK 74004
Phone: (918)661-9072
John C. West, Executive Manager

Giving Priorities: *Education:* 55% to 60% of total annual contributions. *Civic:* 15% to 20%. *Health & Welfare:* 10% to 15%. Supports united funds, community services, and substance abuse prevention. Health interests included health agencies, including children's and community hospitals. Emphasis on Oklahoma and Texas. Also supports traditional youth organizations and athletic events. *Culture & the Arts:* 5% to 10%. *Youth:* 5% to 10%. **Typical Health-Related Recipients:** Clinics/Medical Centers, Domestic Violence, Health Organizations, Hospitals, Medical Rehabilitation, Medical Research, Mental Health, Nutrition, People with Disabilities, Substance Abuse. **Geographic Distribution:** Nationally, with emphasis on corporate operating locations.

★816★ Phillips-Van Heusen Foundation
1290 Avenue of the Americas
New York, NY 10104
Phone: (212)541-5200
Lawrence S. Phillips, Chairman

Giving Priorities: *Religion:* About 30%. *Education:* 15% to 20%. *International:* 15% to 20%.

Social Services: 15% to 20%. *Health:* About 15%. Cancer centers, children's hospitals, medical centers, and hearing and speech are primary interests. *Other:* The foundation also supports art centers, museums, and civic concerns. **Typical Health-Related Recipients:** Cancer, Clinics/Medical Centers, Health Organizations, Hospitals, Medical Research, People with Disabilities, Respiratory, Speech & Hearing. **Geographic Distribution:** Focus on New York.

★817★ Piper Jaffray Cos. Foundation
222 S Ninth St.
Minneapolis, MN 55402
Phone: (612)342-6082
Fax: (612)342-6085
Marina Lyon, Community Affairs Manager

Giving Priorities: *General Support Program:* 31% of total contributions went to human services. Education received 30%. The arts received approximately 13% of giving. Other interests included health care, which received 13%. Civic and public affairs organizations received 11%. **Typical Health-Related Recipients:** Cancer, Domestic Violence, Medical Rehabilitation, Multiple Sclerosis, People with Disabilities. **Geographic Distribution:** Near headquarters and branch locations; also to national organizations.

**★818★ Pittsburgh National Bank
Foundation**
5th Ave. & Wood St.
Pittsburgh, PA 15222
Phone: (412)762-4222
Fax: (412)762-8392
D. Paul Beard, Secretary, Distribution
 Committee

Giving Priorities: *Social Services:* 40% to 45% of annual contributions. Most of this supports united funds in southwestern Pennsylvania. Also contributes to organizations concerned with youth, the elderly, the disabled, food distribution, community and family services, religious welfare, and emergency relief. *Education:* 15% to 20% of contributions. *Civic & Public Affairs:* 15% to 20% of giving. *Arts & Humanities:* 10% to 15%. *Health:* 5% to 10%, primarily to local hospitals. Other interests include single-disease health associations, health funds and organizations, medical rehabilitation, and pediatric health. *Other:* Limited support to religious and scientific organizations. **Typical Health-Related Recipients:** Cancer, Children's Health/Hospitals, Domestic Violence, Health Organizations, Hospices, Hospitals, Long-Term Care, Medical Rehabilitation, People with Disabilities, Single-Disease Health Associations. **Geographic Distribution:** Metropolitan Pittsburgh; surrounding communities of Allegheny County.

**★819★ Pittway Corp. Charitable
Foundation**
200 S Wacker St., Ste. 700
Chicago, IL 60606
Phone: (312)831-1070
Fax: (312)831-0808
King Harris, Vice President, Director

Giving Priorities: *Health:* 45% to 50% of contributions. Funds support hospitals, various single-disease health organizations, mental health,

and other facilities. *Social Services:* About 25% of contributions. *Education:* 10% to 15% of contributions. *Civic & Public Affairs:* 5% to 10%. *Arts & Humanities:* 5% to 10%. *Other:* Less than 1%. Primarily funding to science organizations. **Typical Health-Related Recipients:** Family Planning, Health Funds, Hospices, Hospitals, Medical Education, Medical Research, Mental Health, Nursing Services, Single-Disease Health Associations, Substance Abuse. **Geographic Distribution:** Emphasis on communities near company's manufacturing sites.

★820★ Polaroid Foundation
750 Main St., 2nd Fl.
Cambridge, MA 02139
Phone: (617)577-3470
Fax: (617)577-5770
Donna Furlong, Associate Director

Giving Priorities: *Social Services:* 30% to 35%. An additional 17% goes to united funds. Other areas of interest include services for families and children, employment, legal services, the handicapped, and substance abuse rehabilitation. *Education:* 20% to 25% of total funding. *Arts & Humanities:* About 10%. *Civic & Public Affairs:* 5% to 10%. *Health:* 5% to 10%. Interests include mental health, hospices, outpatient health care, and geriatric health. Also sponsors employee matching gifts to hospitals. **Typical Health-Related Recipients:** AIDS/HIV, Diabetes, Hospices, Hospitals, Medical Education, Mental Health, Nursing Services, Public Health. **Geographic Distribution:** Primarily greater Boston and New Bedford, MA area; small number of grants awarded in areas where distribution centers are located; considers funding outside of Massachusetts in areas of minority higher education and photographic acquisition and exhibition; donates products nationwide.

★821★ PPG Industries Foundation
One PPG Pl.
Pittsburgh, PA 15272
Phone: (412)434-2962
Roslyn Rosenblatt, Executive Director

Giving Priorities: *Health & Human Services:* 40% to 45%. Prefers to support United Way campaigns, funding programs through employee volunteer allocations, capital projects, and special programs to provide support for new facilities and changing services. Health grants fund improved patient care, effective delivery of services, and educational programs. *Education:* 35% to 40% of total contributions. *Arts & Humanities:* 10% to 15%. *Civic & Community Affairs:* 5% to 10% of contributions. **Typical Health-Related Recipients:** Clinics/Medical Centers, Health Organizations, Health Policy/ Cost Containment, Hospitals, Long-Term Care, Medical Rehabilitation, Mental Health, Nursing Services, People with Disabilities, Single-Disease Health Associations. **Geographic Distribution:** Nationally, with emphasis on corporate operating locations; special interest in Pittsburgh, PA, area.

★822★ Presto Foundation
3925 N Hastings Way
Eau Claire, WI 54703
Phone: (715)839-2119
Norma Jaenke, Executive Director

Giving Priorities: *Arts & Humanities:* 35% to 40% of contributions. *Social Services:* 20% to 25% of total contributions. *Health:* About 20%, most of which goes to single-disease health organizations. Also supports hospitals and other health associations. *Education:* 10% to 15%. *Other:* About 5%. Limited contributions to civic groups, with emphasis on environmental and beautification projects. Additional funding for religious organizations. **Typical Health-Related Recipients:** Cancer, Health Funds, Hospitals, Medical Research, Multiple Sclerosis, People with Disabilities, Single-Disease Health Associations. **Geographic Distribution:** Northwestern Wisconsin, especially Eau Claire and Chippewa County, and operating locations.

★ 823 ★   **Principal Financial Group**
          Foundation
711 High St.
Des Moines, IA 50392-0150
Phone: (515)247-5209
Fax: (515)248-8469
Mary Gesiriech, Assistant Director, Corporate Relations

Giving Priorities: *Health and Human Services:* About 40% of total contributions. Contributions are made to local organizations and local chapters of national organizations as well as a few targeted national groups. Areas of primary interest include AIDS, affordable housing, and children at risk. Other recipients include organizations concerned with medical research, the disabled, and health care cost containment. Community and family service groups and substance abuse prevention programs are also supported. United Way grants comprise between 15% and 20% of these contributions. *Education:* Approximately 30%. *Civic & Public Affairs:* 10% to 15%. *Arts & Humanities:* About 10%. *Disaster Relief:* 5% to 10%. **Typical Health-Related Recipients:** AIDS/HIV, Cancer, Emergency/ Ambulance Services, Family Planning, Health Organizations, Health Policy/Cost Containment, Hospices, Medical Research, Mental Health, People with Disabilities, Single-Disease Health Associations, Substance Abuse. **Geographic Distribution:** Primarily in Iowa; occasional consideration to national request.

★ 824 ★   **Procter & Gamble Cosmetic &**
          Fragrance Foundation
11050 York Rd.
Hunt Valley, MD 21030
Phone: (410)785-7300
Veronica Mouring, Contact

Giving Priorities: *Culture & the Arts:* About 15% of total annual giving. *Health & Welfare:* 30% to 35%. Major interests include united funds and institutes and foundations concerned with dermatology. Hospitals, medical centers, and community service organizations also receive support. Matches employee gifts. *Education:* 40% to 45%. *Civic:* About 5%. **Typical Health-Related Recipients:** AIDS/HIV, Cancer, Children's Health/Hospitals, Clinics/ Medical Centers, Diabetes, Domestic Violence, Emergency/Ambulance Services, Health Organizations, Hospitals, Medical Education, Medical Rehabilitation, Mental Health, Nursing Services, People with Disabilities, Public Health, Respiratory, Single-Disease Health Associa-

tions, Substance Abuse. **Geographic Distribution:** Emphasis on Baltimore, MD, metropolitan area; some support to national organizations. **Formerly:** Noxell Foundation.

★ 825 ★   **Procter & Gamble Fund**
PO Box 599
Cincinnati, OH 45201
Phone: (513)945-8486
Robert R. Fitzpatrick, Jr., Vice President & Secretary

Giving Priorities: *Education:* About 60% of annual fund contributions. *Health & Human Services:* About 20%, the bulk of which is awarded to united funds. Other concerns include youth organizations and groups concerned with family and community services, hospitals and health organizations, the aged, and the disabled. *Civic & Public Affairs:* About 10%. *Arts & Humanities:* About 10% of giving. **Typical Health-Related Recipients:** Cancer, Emergency/Ambulance Services, Health Organizations, Hospitals, Nutrition, People with Disabilities, Substance Abuse. **Geographic Distribution:** Communities where Procter & Gamble maintains facilities.

★ 826 ★   **Providence Journal Charitable**
          Foundation
75 Fountain St.
Providence, RI 02902
Phone: (401)277-7514
John Columbo, Trustee

Giving Priorities: *Social Services:* Top priority with 30% to 35% of total giving. *Health:* About 20% of annual giving. Largest grants go to hospitals, although hospices and single-disease health organizations also receive funding. *Arts & Humanities:* 10% to 15% of total. *Civic & Public Affairs:* 10% to 15% of total giving. *Education:* 10% to 15% of total giving. *Religion:* 5% to 10%. *International:* Less than 5%. **Typical Health-Related Recipients:** Emergency/ Ambulance Services, Family Planning, Health Organizations, Hospices, Hospitals, People with Disabilities, Sexual Abuse, Single-Disease Health Associations, Substance Abuse. **Geographic Distribution:** Throughout Rhode Island and nearby Massachusetts.

★ 827 ★   **Prudential Foundation**
Prudential Plz.
751 Broad St.
15th Fl.
Newark, NJ 07102-3777
Phone: (201)802-7354
Fax: (201)802-3345
Barbara L. Halaburda, Secretary

Giving Priorities: *Education:* About 30% of annual contributions. *United Way Federated Drives:* 15% to 20% of annual contributions. *Health & Human Services:* 15% to 20%. Focuses on health care cost containment; health policy development and health issues exploration; medical education and training for minorities; family health programs, with emphasis on reducing teenage pregnancy, increasing health care services for disadvantaged children, and providing counseling and guidance for parents; enhancing the distribution of primary-care physicians and facilities; promoting wellness concepts; medical research when potential breakthrough for cost effectiveness seems imminent;

and community-based efforts to provide human services and to improve the local environment. Major support has gone to AIDS prevention programs, drug and alcohol abuse treatment, hospitals, youth and local health organizations, and family services. *Urban & Community Development:* 10% to 15%. *Focus on Children:* 5% to 10%. Concentrates on programs that improve and expand successful policies and programs and that coordinate services for at-risk children under age six and pregnant women. *Culture & the Arts:* About 5%. **Typical Health-Related Recipients:** AIDS/HIV, Children's Health/ Hospitals, Clinics/Medical Centers, Emergency/Ambulance Services, Family Planning, Geriatric Health, Health Organizations, Health Policy/Cost Containment, Hospitals, Medical Education, Medical Rehabilitation, Medical Training, Mental Health, People with Disabilities, Substance Abuse. **Geographic Distribution:** Near operating locations, with special emphasis on New Jersey and the city of Newark; also nationally.

★ 828 ★   **Prudential Securities Foundation**
One Seaport Plz.
New York, NY 10292
Phone: (212)214-4884
Fax: (212)214-5541
Elizabeth Longley, Vice President, Corporate Affairs

Giving Priorities: *Welfare:* 25% to 30%. *Arts & Humanities:* 25% to 30%. *Health:* 15% to 20%. Most contributions go to hospitals and single-disease health associations. Foundations involved with mental health, children, cancer, general health, emergency relief, and fitness also receive funding. *Education:* 10% to 15%. *Religion:* 5% to 10%. *Civic & Public Affairs:* 5% to 10%. *International:* Less than 5%. **Typical Health-Related Recipients:** Health Organizations, Hospitals, Mental Health, People with Disabilities, Single-Disease Health Associations. **Geographic Distribution:** Focus on New York.

★ 829 ★   **PSI Foundation**
251 N Illinios St., Ste. 1400
Indianapolis, IN 46204
Phone: (317)488-3532
Connie Carter, Foundation Assistant

Giving Priorities: *Education:* 30% to 35%. *Community Development:* 20% to 25%. *Health and Human Services:* 20% to 25%. Supports health, human, and social service programs that provide essential services and enhance the quality of life. United Way campaigns are included in this category. *Arts and Culture:* About 20%. **Typical Health-Related Recipients:** General. **Geographic Distribution:** Company service area, comprised of 69 counties in Indiana.

★ 830 ★   **Quaker Chemical Foundation**
Elm and Lee Streets
Conshohocken, PA 19428
Phone: (215)832-4119
Fax: (215)832-4494
Mary Lou McClain, Corporate Administrative Assistant

Giving Priorities: *Education:* 45% to 50%. *Health and Welfare:* 15% to 20%. One-third of the health and welfare contributions were in the form of employee matching gifts. VNA Community Services of Ambler, PA, and Montgomery Health Foundation of Norristown, PA, each received grants of $4,000. *Cultural:* 15% to 20%. *Civic and Community:* 15% to 20%. *Other:* The foundation also supports outreach and special projects. **Typical Health-Related Recipients:** Health Organizations, Hospitals, Medical Research, Nutrition, People with Disabilities, Single-Disease Health Associations. **Geographic Distribution:** Primarily in operating areas.

★831★ Quaker Oats Foundation
321 N Clark St.
Ste. 27-5
P.O. Box 049001
Chicago, IL 60610
Phone: (312)222-7377
Charles E. Curry, Assistant Secretary

Giving Priorities: *Social Services:* 40% to 45%, with over two-fifths going to united funds. Other recipients include programs for the aged and handicapped, family planning and services, and child welfare. *Education:* About 40% of contributions. *Arts & Humanities:* 5% to 10% of annual contributions. *Health:* 5% to 10% with most of this going as matching gifts to hospitals and health care associations. Foundation focuses on organizations located in company communities and whose projects deal with health cost containment. *Other:* Less than 5% goes to "Dollars for Doers," a program that encourages and supplements the volunteer efforts of company employees in areas of the arts, civic involvement, education, health, social services, and youth. About 1% of funding goes to public and urban affairs. **Typical Health-Related Recipients:** Domestic Violence, Family Planning, Health Organizations, Health Policy/Cost Containment, Hospices, Hospitals, Medical Education, Medical Rehabilitation, Medical Research, Mental Health, Nutrition, People with Disabilities, Single-Disease Health Associations, Substance Abuse. **Geographic Distribution:** Principally near operating locations and to national organizations.

★832★ Reilly Foundation
1510 Market Sq. Center
151 N Delaware St.
Indianapolis, IN 46204
Phone: (317)248-6468
Lorraine D. Schroeder, Trustee

Giving Priorities: *Education:* 40% to 45% of total funding. *Social Services:* 20% to 25%. *Arts & Humanities:* 15% to 20%. *Civic & Public Affairs:* 10% to 15%. *Health:* 10% to 15%. Funding went to a health center, community hospitals, and the Indianapolis Campaign for Healthy Babies. **Typical Health-Related Recipients:** Hospitals. **Geographic Distribution:** Limited to areas of company operations.

★833★ Reily Foundation
640 Magazine St.
New Orleans, LA 70130
Phone: (504)524-6131
Robert D. Reily, President

Giving Priorities: *Social Services:* 30% to 35% of total contributions. Including major support to Planned Parenthood, with a grant of $25,000. *Education:* About 30%. *Civic & Public Affairs:*

15% to 20%. *Arts & Humanities:* About 10%. *Health:* About 10%. The Touro Infirmary received primary support with a grant of $51,000. The American Red Cross and the Multiple Sclerosis society also received funding. **Typical Health-Related Recipients:** Family Planning, Health Organizations, People with Disabilities, Single-Disease Health Associations. **Geographic Distribution:** Focus on Louisiana.

★834★ Reliance Electric Co. Charitable, Scientific and Educational Trust
6065 Parkland Blvd.
Cleveland, OH 44124
Phone: (216)266-5826
Fax: (216)266-7666
Edward R. Towns, Secretary

Giving Priorities: *Health & Welfare:* 50% to 55% of total, primarily supporting united funds. Other interests include employment, volunteer services, and child welfare groups. Also matches employee gifts to United Ways. Health interests are primarily directed to miscellaneous health organizations. *Education:* 35% to 40% of total contributions. *Arts & Humanities:* 5% to 10%. *Civic & Public Affairs:* Less than 5%. **Typical Health-Related Recipients:** Domestic Violence, Emergency/Ambulance Services, People with Disabilities, Substance Abuse. **Geographic Distribution:** Operating locations, emphasis on Cleveland, OH; U.S.-based nonprofit organizations with an international focus.

★835★ Revlon Foundation
625 Madison Ave.
New York, NY 10153
Phone: (212)572-5000
Fax: (212)527-6977
Phyllis Orta, Director, Community Relations

Giving Priorities: *Health:* 40% to 45%. Primary support to medical centers and hospitals. In 1992, a $2,000,000 grant went to the New York University Medical Center. *Religion:* About 35% of total annual contributions. *Education:* 15% to 20% of total contributions. Major support to University of California Los Angeles School of Medicine. Matching grants are also made in the area of education. *Arts:* Less than 5% of funding. *Other:* 5% to 10%. Also supports ethnic and minority organizations and international causes. **Typical Health-Related Recipients:** Clinics/Medical Centers, Hospitals, Medical Education, People with Disabilities, Single-Disease Health Associations. **Geographic Distribution:** Nationally and locally, where company has operating divisions.

★836★ Reynolds & Reynolds Company Foundation
PO Box 2608
Dayton, OH 45401
Phone: (513)449-4375
Fax: (513)449-4211
Rosalyn Lake, Administrator

Giving Priorities: *Arts & Humanities:* About 40% of total contributions. *Social Services:* About 25% of funding. *Education:* About 20%. *Community Betterment:* 5% to 10%. *Health:* About 5%. Supports Hospice of Dayton, Miami Valley Health Foundation, and Hipple Cancer Research Center. Also funds single-disease health associations. *Voluntarism:* Company

sponsors an "Employee Spirit Award," providing a $200 grant to organizations where employees have donated 50-plus hours per year. **Typical Health-Related Recipients:** Arthritis, Cancer, Children's Health/Hospitals, Emergency/Ambulance Services, Health Organizations, Hospices, Trauma Treatment. **Geographic Distribution:** Focus on Ohio.

★837★ Rockwell International Corp. Trust
625 Liberty Ave.
Pittsburgh, PA 15222-3123
Phone: (412)565-5803
Fax: (412)565-7156
William R. Fitz, Assistant Secretary

Giving Priorities: *Education:* 55% to 60% of total annual giving. *United Way:* 15% to 20%. *Health & Human Services:* 10% to 15%. Support for organizations in company operating locations. Funding for community service groups, youth organizations, and health foundations. *Arts & Humanities:* 5% to 10%. *Civic & Public Affairs:* 5% to 10% of contributions. *International:* About 5% to 10% of above contributions. **Typical Health-Related Recipients:** Domestic Violence, Health Organizations, Health Policy/Cost Containment, Hospices, Hospitals, Medical Rehabilitation, Mental Health, People with Disabilities, Single-Disease Health Associations, Substance Abuse. **Geographic Distribution:** Primarily where company maintains facilities; nationally to education.

★838★ Rubbermaid Foundation
1147 Akron Rd.
Wooster, OH 44691
Phone: (216)264-6464
Fax: (216)287-2864
Karen Houser, Administrator

Giving Priorities: *General Support Program Education:* Majority of support goes toward education. Most grants go to colleges and universities. Other recipients include educational funds, local schools, and educational programs such as Junior Achievement. *Health:* Primarily supports hospitals, with the foundation's largest grant of of 1992 going to Wooster Community Hospital. Also supports health organizations such as the American Red Cross. *Social Services:* Grants go primarily to united funds, substance abuse programs, youth organizations, and community centers. *Civic & Public Affairs:* Contributions go to a range of areas, including business and advertising councils, organizations for minorities, law and justice groups, and philanthropic organizations. *Arts & Humanities:* Recipients include arts centers and arts committees, historical societies and museums. Current focus is on education and early child care development. **Typical Health-Related Recipients:** Cancer, Clinics/Medical Centers, Emergency/Ambulance Services, Health Organizations, Hospitals, People with Disabilities, Substance Abuse. **Geographic Distribution:** Only in communities where it has facilities.

★839★ **Ryder System Charitable Foundation**
3600 NW 82nd Ave.
Miami, FL 33166
Phone: (305)593-3642
Fax: (305)470-7971
Ross Roadman, Executive Director

Giving Priorities: *Health & Human Services:* 50% to 55% of total annual giving. More than three-quarters generally supports the Dade County United Way, Ryder Trauma Center, and We Will Rebuild (Hurricane Andrew Recovery). Remaining funds support food and clothing distribution, organizations concerned with minority advancement, volunteer organizations and family self-sufficiency programs. *Education:* 20% to 25%. *Cultural Organizations:* 10% to 15% of contributions. *Civic Activities:* 10% to 15% of contributions. **Typical Health-Related Recipients:** Hospitals, Substance Abuse. **Geographic Distribution:** Primarily greater Miami and Dade County, FL, and through community initiative programs in Dallas, Atlanta, Cincinnati, St. Louis, and Los Angeles.

★840★ **Salomon Foundation**
7 World Trade Ctr.
New York, NY 10048
Phone: (212)783-7434
Jane E. Heffner, Vice President, Corp.
  Communications

Giving Priorities: *Education:* 40% to 45% of total annual giving. *Community:* About 25% of contributions. *Cultural:* About 15% to 20% of giving. *Medical:* 5% to 10% primarily supporting hospitals, medical research, and pediatric health. *Other:* 5% to 10% of giving supports civic and international affairs organizations. *International:* Company makes international contributions through foreign subsidiaries. *Note:* Matching gifts, comprising 15% to 20% of contributions, are disbursed through the matching gifts program. **Typical Health-Related Recipients:** Family Planning, Hospitals, Medical Research, Single-Disease Health Associations, Substance Abuse. **Geographic Distribution:** Nationally, with emphasis on cities where company operates.

★841★ **Sanford C. Bernstein and Co. Foundation**
767 Fifth Ave.
New York, NY 10153-0001
Phone: (212)486-5800
Fax: (212)756-4574
Zalman C. Bernstein, Trustee

Giving Priorities: *Religion:* 30% to 35% of total contributions. *Health:* About 25% to 30%. Support favors hospitals, medical research, single-disease associations, and pediatric health. *Education:* 15% to 20%. *Social Services:* 5% to 10%. *Arts & Humanities:* 5% to 10%. *International:* 5% to 10%. *Civic & Public Affairs:* Less than 5%. **Typical Health-Related Recipients:** AIDS/HIV, Diabetes, Eyes/Blindness, Geriatric Health, Health Organizations, Hospitals, Medical Research, Nursing Services, People with Disabilities, Prenatal Health Issues, Preventive Medicine/Wellness Organizations, Single-Disease Health Associations. **Geographic Distribution:** Focus on New York.

★842★ **Santa Fe Pacific Foundation**
1700 E Golf Rd.
Schaumburg, IL 60173-5860
Phone: (708)995-6000
Catherine A. Westphal, President

Giving Priorities: *United Way:* 35% to 40%. *Education:* About 25% of total contributions. *Health & Human Services:* About 10% of total annual giving. Interests include aid to the hungry, homeless, and elderly; youth training and development; self-help services for the mentally and physically disabled; programs for the blind and visually impaired; job training and employment assistance; and crisis aid for abused women and children. Generally does not consider national single- disease health organizations. Grants typically range between $500 and $5,000. *Civic & Community Affairs:* 5% to 10% of giving. *Culture & Art:* Between 5% and 10%. *Employee Matching Gifts:* 5% to 10%. Gifts are matched to education, cultural organizations, and hospitals. **Typical Health-Related Recipients:** Domestic Violence, Medical Education, Medical Rehabilitation, Medical Training, Mental Health, People with Disabilities, Substance Abuse. **Geographic Distribution:** Company service areas, principally the midwestern, southwestern, and western United States.

★843★ **Schering-Plough Foundation**
One Giralda Farms
Madison, NJ 07940-1000
Phone: (201)822-7412
Fax: (201)822-7447
Rita Sacco, Assistant Secretary

Giving Priorities: *Medical & Allied Education:* 40% to 45% of foundation giving. Interests include medical and pharmaceutical schools, medical research, and public health education. *Social/Civic Welfare & Public Policy:* Around 20%. *Health Care:* 15% to 20%. Supports hospitals and health care programs most used by employees and their families. *Matching Gifts:* 10% to 15% of foundation giving awarded to match employee contributions to universities, colleges, secondary schools, hospitals, and educational or hospital funds and associations. Minimum gift matched is $25; maximum is $10,000 per employee for one year. *Culture & Arts:* 10% to 15%. **Typical Health-Related Recipients:** Cancer, Clinics/Medical Centers, Hospitals, Long-Term Care, Medical Education, Medical Research, Medical Training, Public Health, Single-Disease Health Associations, Substance Abuse, Transplant Networks/Donor Banks. **Geographic Distribution:** Emphasizes locations in which corporation has major facilities, and national organizations.

★844★ **Schlumberger Foundation**
277 Park Ave.
New York, NY 10172-0266
Phone: (212)350-9455
Fax: (212)350-9457
Arthur W. Alexander, Secretary-Treasurer

Giving Priorities: *Education:* 50% to 55% of contributions. *Social Services:* About 15%. *Arts & Humanities:* 10% to 15%. *Civic & Public Affairs:* 5% to 10%. *Science:* 5% to 10%. *Health:* About 5%. Interests include geriatric health, single-disease health associations, and hospitals. **Typical Health-Related Recipients:** AI-

zheimers Disease, Hospitals, Medical Education, Medical Research, People with Disabilities, Single-Disease Health Associations. **Geographic Distribution:** Nationally to education; other contributions concentrated in New York City area.

★845★ **Searle Charitable Trust**
PO Box 5110
Chicago, IL 60680
Phone: (708)982-7000
Charles L. Fry, Corporate Vice President,
  Public Affairs

Giving Priorities: *Social Services:* About 30% of total annual contributions. *Education:* Approximately 25% of annual total. *Arts & Humanities:* About 15%. *Civic & Public Affairs:* About 10%. *Health:* Approximately 10%. Most funding goes to single-disease health organizations and medical research, often through special fundraising events. Hospitals and medical education also receive support. *Science:* About 10%. **Typical Health-Related Recipients:** Health Organizations, Nursing Services, Public Health, Single-Disease Health Associations. **Geographic Distribution:** Nationally, with emphasis on operating communities.

★846★ **Security Benefit Life Insurance Co. Charitable Trust**
700 Harrison St.
Topeka, KS 66636
Phone: (913)295-3000
Howard R. Fricke, Trustee

Giving Priorities: *Education:* About 30% of total funding. *Social Services:* About 25% of contributions. *Health:* 15% to 20%. Major support to the Menninger Foundation of Topeka, KS, with a grant of $25,000. *Civic & Public Affairs:* About 15%. *Arts & Humanities:* About 10%, all of which went to arts organizations in Topeka. **Typical Health-Related Recipients:** Health Organizations, Single-Disease Health Associations. **Geographic Distribution:** Primarily Kansas, specifically Topeka.

★847★ **Shawmut Charitable Foundation**
777 Main St.
MSN 988
Hartford, CT 06115
Phone: (203)728-2274
Maxine Dean, Asst. VP, Community Relations

Giving Priorities: *United Way:* Contributions support United Ways in operating communities. *Community Services:* Operating and capital support to community-based organizations. *Education:* Supports colleges and universities, minority education programs, scholarship funds, and adult basic literacy projects and programs. *Health:* Hospitals, health funds, pediatric care, and outpatient health care delivery receive funding. *Culture:* Supports libraries, museums, and performing arts. *Other:* Also supports a special program for community organizations serving disadvantaged or low- to moderate-income populations in Massachusetts, Connecticut, and Rhode Island. **Typical Health-Related Recipients:** AIDS/HIV, Clinics/Medical Centers, Domestic Violence, Emergency/Ambulance Services, Family Planning, Health Funds, Health Organizations, Hospices, Hospitals, Medical Rehabilitation, Medical Training, Mental Health,

Nutrition, People with Disabilities, Public Health, Substance Abuse. **Geographic Distribution:** Throughout Massachusetts, Connecticut, and Rhode Island.

★848★ **Shell Oil Co. Foundation**
Two Shell Plz.
Box 2099
Houston, TX 77252
Phone: (713)241-3617
Fax: (713)241-3329
J. N. Doherty, Senior Vice President

Giving Priorities: *Education:* 50% to 55% of total contributions. *Health & Welfare:* 30% to 35% of giving. Primary support goes to united funds. The remainder is distributed to health and welfare agencies and community hospital campaigns in areas where Shell employees live. Support also goes to youth organizations and child welfare agencies. Other areas of interest include the aged, the handicapped, minorities, and research and treatment of major diseases. *Civic & Public Affairs:* 5% to 10%. *Arts & Culture:* About 5% to 10% of contributions. *International:* In 1992, foundation donated $97,500 to U.S.-based nonprofit organizations with an international focus. *Other:* About 1% of giving awarded to various other interests, including international relief and science fairs. **Typical Health-Related Recipients:** Children's Health/Hospitals, Clinics/Medical Centers, Health Funds, Health Organizations, Heart, Hospices, Hospitals, Medical Education, Medical Rehabilitation, Medical Research, Mental Health, People with Disabilities, Single-Disease Health Associations, Substance Abuse. **Geographic Distribution:** Nationally, with emphasis on communities where Shell employees are located.

★849★ **Shelton Foundation**
3600 One First Union Ctr.
301 S. College St.
Charlotte, NC 28202
Phone: (704)348-2200
James E. Harris, Secretary-Treasurer

Giving Priorities: *Education:* 60% to 65% of total contributions. *Civic & Public Affairs:* About 20%. *Social Services:* About 10%. *Health:* About 5%. Favors single-disease health associations and medical centers. *Other:* Less than 5%. Recipients include the arts and churches. **Typical Health-Related Recipients:** Hospitals, Medical Education, Single-Disease Health Associations. **Geographic Distribution:** Primarily North Carolina, with an emphasis on the Charlotte area.

★850★ **Sherwin-Williams Foundation**
101 Prospect Ave. NW
Cleveland, OH 44115
Phone: (216)566-2511
Fax: (216)566-3266
Barbara Gadosik, Director, Corporate Contributions

Giving Priorities: *Health & Human Services:* 40% to 45% of total giving. More than half of health and human services funding supports United Way chapters. Other interests include youth, the disabled, single-disease health associations, food distribution and shelters, and other human services organizations. *Education:* About 35% of contributions. *Civic & Public Af-*

fairs: 10% to 15%. *Arts & Humanities:* 5% to 10%. **Typical Health-Related Recipients:** People with Disabilities, Single-Disease Health Associations. **Geographic Distribution:** In areas of headquarters office and plant locations.

★851★ **Signet Bank/Maryland Charitable Trust**
PO Box 1077
Baltimore, MD 21203
Phone: (410)332-5878
Fax: (410)783-6043
Gail H. Sanders, Vice President, Public Affairs

Giving Priorities: *General Support Program:* Supports a variety of cultural and arts, civic and community, educational, health, and human service organizations. In 1991, about 40% went to civic and community affairs; 25%, health and human services; 20%, education; and 15%, the arts. *Voluntarism:* Supports an active volunteer organization which promotes several group and individual projects, including food and clothing drives. Presently, Signet has a Signet Volunteer Organization and all volunteer projects are sponsored by the bank. **Typical Health-Related Recipients:** Hospitals. **Geographic Distribution:** Baltimore metropolitan area; the Maryland Eastern Shore.

★852★ **Slant/Fin Foundation**
100 Forest Dr.
Greenvale, NY 11548
Phone: (516)484-2600
Fax: (516)484-6994
Ray Blaquiere, Controller

Giving Priorities: *Religion:* 75% to 80% of total contributions. *Health:* About 10%. Supports hospitals, medical centers, and cancer research. *International:* Less than 5%. Funds educational institutions and medical centers in Israel. *Arts & Humanities:* Less than 5%. *Other:* Less than 5% of giving. Supports educational, civic, and social service organizations. **Typical Health-Related Recipients:** Cancer, Clinics/Medical Centers, Hospices, Hospitals, Medical Education, Medical Research, People with Disabilities, Single-Disease Health Associations. **Geographic Distribution:** Nationally, with emphasis on New York.

★853★ **SmithKline Beecham Foundation**
One Franklin Plz.
PO Box 7929
Philadelphia, PA 19101
Phone: (215)751-3574
Fax: (215)751-7655
Elizabeth A. Tyson, Chairperson

Giving Priorities: *Focused Giving Program:* In 1993, foundation realigned its giving program to focus funding on the promotion and advancement of health care and science education. *Other:* Company also matches employee contributions to educational and arts organizations, and hospitals. **Typical Health-Related Recipients:** Cancer, Emergency/Ambulance Services, Health Funds, Health Organizations, Long-Term Care, Medical Education, Single-Disease Health Associations, Substance Abuse. **Geographic Distribution:** Where company has major facilities.

★854★ **Sonat Foundation**
PO Box 2563
Birmingham, AL 35202
Phone: (205)325-7460
Fax: (205)326-2050
Darlene O'Donnell, Secretary

Giving Priorities: *Education:* 45% to 50% of total contributions. Primarily supports higher education, mostly for capital campaigns, but also for scholarships, general support, business and medical education, endowment funds, and education funds. *Social Services:* 35% to 40% of funding. Support goes to United Way agencies, disaster relief groups, youth and community service organizations, child welfare, and athletics. *Arts & Culture:* 10% to 15% of giving. *Community & Civic Affairs* Less than 5% of contributions. **Typical Health-Related Recipients:** Health Funds, Health Organizations, Health Policy/Cost Containment, Hospitals, Medical Education, People with Disabilities, Single-Disease Health Associations, Substance Abuse. **Geographic Distribution:** Communities where company operates, with emphasis on Birmingham, AL.

★855★ **Sony USA Foundation**
1 Sony Dr., MD 3E2
Park Ridge, NJ 07656
Phone: (201)833-6870
Fax: (201)833-6869
Shelley Moore, Commun. Spec.

Giving Priorities: *Health & Social Welfare:* 35% to 40% of total contributions. Major support goes to the United Way, including a grant of $79,348 in 1992 to the United Way-Chad (San Diego). Additional funding supports health associations and social service organizations. *Arts & Culture:* 25% to 30%. *Education:* 25% to 30%. *Civic & Public Affairs:* 5% to 10%. **Typical Health-Related Recipients:** Emergency/Ambulance Services, Eyes/Blindness, Health Organizations, Hospitals, Multiple Sclerosis, People with Disabilities. **Geographic Distribution:** Nationally, with emphasis on communities where Sony has a presence. **Formerly:** Sony Corp. of America Foundation.

★856★ **Sooner Pipe & Supply Corp. Foundation**
PO Box 1530
Tulsa, OK 74101
Phone: (918)587-3391
Fax: (918)587-0863
J. W. Kerby, Secretary-Treasurer

Giving Priorities: *Health:* 30% to 35%. Interests include single-disease health associations, a medical center, hospices, and a mental health foundation. *Social Services:* 25% to 30%. *Religion:* 15% to 20% of total contributions. *Education:* 10% to 15%. *Arts & Humanities:* 5% to 10%. **Typical Health-Related Recipients:** Cancer, Children's Health/Hospitals, Clinics/Medical Centers, Emergency/Ambulance Services, Eyes/Blindness, Geriatric Health, Health Funds, Health Organizations, Hospices, Hospitals, Medical Education, Medical Research, Mental Health, People with Disabilities, Prenatal Health Issues, Single-Disease Health Associations, Substance Abuse. **Geographic Distribution:** Primarily in Tulsa, OK.

★ 857 ★ Southwest Gas Corp. Foundation
PO Box 98510
Las Vegas, NV 89193-8510
Phone: (702)876-7299
Delores Nielsen, Assistant to the CEO

Giving Priorities: *Social Services:* 30% to 35%. *Education:* 30% to 35%. *Arts & Humanities:* 10% to 15%. *Civic & Public Affairs:* 10% to 15%. *Health:* 5% to 10%. Funds single-disease associations, hospitals, and university medical centers. **Typical Health-Related Recipients:** Clinics/Medical Centers, Diabetes, Heart, Hospitals, People with Disabilities, Respiratory, Single-Disease Health Associations. **Geographic Distribution:** In headquarters and operating locations.

★ 858 ★ Southwestern Bell Foundation
175 E Houston, Ste. 200
San Antonio, TX 78205
Phone: (210)351-2210
Fax: (210)351-2205
Charles O. DeRiemer, Executive Director

Giving Priorities: *Education:* 40% to 45% of contributions. *Health & Welfare:* About 30% to 35% of contributions. More than two-thirds of health and welfare contributions is awarded to more than 200 United Way, United Fund, and Community Chest fund drives in the corporation's operating areas. Primary emphasis is on organizations that seek to meet pressing community needs. *Community & Civic Development:* 10% to 15% of giving. *Arts & Culture:* 10% to 15% of giving. **Typical Health-Related Recipients:** Cancer, Emergency/Ambulance Services, Hospitals, Medical Education, Mental Health, People with Disabilities. **Geographic Distribution:** Nationally, with emphasis on corporate operating locations.

★ 859 ★ Square D Foundation
1415 S Roselle
Palatine, IL 60067
Phone: (708)397-2600
Fax: (708)397-8814
Charlie Hutchinson, Secretary

Giving Priorities: *Human Services & Civic Affairs* 45% to 50% of contributions. *Education:* 40% to 45% of total funding. *Health:* 5% to 10%. Primarily supports capital grants to hospitals. Other interests include single-disease health associations, medical research, and emergency and ambulance services. *Arts & Humanities:* Generally about 5%. **Typical Health-Related Recipients:** Emergency/Ambulance Services, Health Funds, Hospitals, Medical Research, Mental Health, People with Disabilities, Single-Disease Health Associations. **Geographic Distribution:** Areas where Square D Co. maintains manufacturing facilities.

★ 860 ★ Stanley Works Foundation
1000 Stanley Dr.
New Britain, CT 06053
Phone: (203)225-5111
Ronald F. Gilrain, Vice President, Public Affairs

Giving Priorities: *Social Services:* 35% to 40% of contributions. *Health:* 25% to 30% of total contributions, primarily to hospitals and capital programs that promote high-quality, affordable, and cost-efficient health care, in communities where Stanley is resident. *Civic & Public Affairs:* 15% to 20%. *Education:* 5% to 10% of contributions. *Arts & Humanities:* 5% to 10%. *International:* Company's foreign subsidiaries also make contributions to international organizations. **Typical Health-Related Recipients:** Cancer, Children's Health/Hospitals, Emergency/Ambulance Services, Hospitals, Medical Research, People with Disabilities, Substance Abuse. **Geographic Distribution:** Primarily in communities in which company has operating locations.

★ 861 ★ State Street Foundation
225 Franklin St.
12th Fl.
Boston, MA 02101
Phone: (617)654-3381
Fax: (617)451-6315
George A. Bowman, Jr., Vice President, Community Affairs

Giving Priorities: *Education:* 40% to 45%. Supports colleges and universities, largely through the matching grants program. In 1992, Harvard Medical School received a $400,000 gift. *Health & Human Services:* 25% to 30% of total giving, primarily supporting the United Way. Other areas of interest include youth programs, hospitals, and other social service organizations. *Civic & Public Affairs:* Between 20% to 25%. *Arts & Humanities:* 5% to 10%. *Other:* Less than 5%. Funding for single-disease health associations, health centers, and science. **Typical Health-Related Recipients:** Adolescent Health Issues, Diabetes, Domestic Violence, Health Organizations, Health Policy/Cost Containment, Hospitals, Medical Education, Mental Health. **Geographic Distribution:** Priority to greater Boston area, emphasis on Suffolk County.

★ 862 ★ Steelcase Foundation
PO Box 1967
Grand Rapids, MI 49501
Phone: (616)246-4695
Kate Pew Wolters, Executive Director

Giving Priorities: *Environment:* 30% to 35% of total contributions. *Social Services:* 25% to 30% of giving. *Education:* 10% to 15% of total funds. *Arts & Humanities:* 10% to 15%. *Health:* About 5% of funding. Gifts supported groups that provide medical support for the homeless and the transient. Other recipients include Planned Parenthood and the National Kidney Foundation. *Community & Economic Development:* Less than 5% of giving. *Other:* Less than 5%. The remainder of funds went to support broadcasting, YMCA, the United Way, and the Salvation Army. **Typical Health-Related Recipients:** Domestic Violence, Family Planning, Health Organizations, Health Policy/Cost Containment, Hospices, Medical Rehabilitation, Mental Health, Nutrition, People with Disabilities, Single-Disease Health Associations, Substance Abuse. **Geographic Distribution:** Exclusively in communities in which company has manufacturing operations.

★ 863 ★ StorageTek Foundation
2270 S 88th St., MS-4310
Louisville, CO 80028-4310
Phone: (303)673-6833
Fax: (303)673-8876
Arlyce K. Lewis, Manager, Community Relations

Giving Priorities: *Education:* About 40% of total contributions. *Arts & Humanities:* About 20%. *Health and Human Services:* Funding hospices, nutrition/health maintenance programs, drug and alcohol abuse prevention, food and clothing distribution, and traditional youth organizations. *United Way:* About 10% of funding. **Typical Health-Related Recipients:** General, Hospices, Nutrition, Substance Abuse. **Geographic Distribution:** In headquarters and operating locations.

★ 864 ★ Stride Rite Charitable Foundation
400 Atlantic Ave.
Boston, MA 02110
Phone: (617)574-4169
Fax: (617)574-4112
Ellen Sahl, Assistant to the Chairman

Giving Priorities: *Education:* 70% to 75% of contributions. Other interests include higher education through Stride Rite's own programs. *Health and Human Services:* 10% to 15%. Most funds go to child welfare organizations. Recipients also include child recreational groups, including volunteer groups and community centers; United Way organizations. *Arts & Humanities:* 5% to 10%. *Civic and Community:* 5% to 10%. **Typical Health-Related Recipients:** Hospitals, Nursing Services, People with Disabilities, Substance Abuse. **Geographic Distribution:** To organizations in Boston and Cambridge, Massachusetts.

★ 865 ★ Sundstrand Corp. Foundation
4949 Harrison Ave.
PO Box 7003
Rockford, IL 61125
Phone: (815)226-6310
Carolyn Thomas, Secretary

Giving Priorities: *Health & Welfare:* 55% to 60% of contributions. Almost four-fifths support united funds and youth organizations. Remaining grants, generally between $500 and $5,000, support community centers and service organizations, homes, programs for the disabled, welfare, health organizations, child welfare, family planning and services, and food and clothing distribution. *Education:* 25% to 30% of support. *Arts & Humanities:* About 5%. *Civic & Public Affairs:* About 5%. **Typical Health-Related Recipients:** Clinics/Medical Centers, Hospices, Hospitals, Long-Term Care, Medical Education, Mental Health, Nursing Services, People with Disabilities, Transplant Networks/Donor Banks. **Geographic Distribution:** Primarily Illinois, with emphasis on the Rockford area; areas where Sundstrand has a significant presence.

★ 866 ★ Superior-Pacific Fund
Seven Wynnewood Rd.
Wynnewood, PA 19096
Phone: (215)647-2701
Fax: (215)649-5475
Paul E. Kelly, Jr., President

Giving Priorities: *Education:* 40% to 45% of total contributions. *Health:* 25% to 30%. Major support to Bryn Mawr Hospital in Bryn Mawr, PA, with a grant of $90,000. Other support went to health care organizations in Pennsylvania. *Arts & Humanities:* 15% to 20%. *Social Services:* About 5%. *Civic & Public Affairs:* Less than 5%. *Other:* The foundation also distributes small amounts of support to religious organizations. **Typical Health-Related Recipients:** Cancer, Clinics/Medical Centers, Eyes/Blindness, Heart, Hospitals, Long-Term Care. **Geographic Distribution:** Focus on Pennsylvania.

★ 867 ★ **Synovus Charitable Trust**
PO Box 120
Columbus, GA 31902
Phone: (706)649-2679
William L. Slaughter, Jr., Trust Officer

Giving Priorities: *Social Services:* 45% to 50% of total contributions. *Civic & Public Affairs:* About 25%. *Health:* 10% to 15%. Favors medical centers and single-disease health associations. Also contributes to hospice care. *Education:* About 10%. *Other:* Supports museums, churches, and a religious organization. **Typical Health-Related Recipients:** Geriatric Health, Health Organizations, Hospices, Hospitals, Mental Health, Single-Disease Health Associations. **Geographic Distribution:** Limited to Columbus, GA. **Formerly:** CB & T Charitable Trust.

★ 868 ★ **T. Rowe Price Associates Foundation**
100 E Pratt St., 9th Fl.
Baltimore, MD 21202
Phone: (410)547-2100
Brenda K. Ashworth, Administrator

Giving Priorities: *Education:* 45% to 50% of total contributions. *Arts & Humanities:* 25% to 30%. *Health & Human Services:* 15% to 20% of gifts. Supports United Way chapters, community centers, and community service organizations. Also funds child welfare, shelters for abused women and children, and food distribution. Health interests include hospitals, hospices, and medical centers. *Civic & Public Affairs:* 5% to 10%. *Other:* Less than 5%. Supports foundation interests including the natural sciences and religious welfare. **Typical Health-Related Recipients:** Health Organizations, Hospitals, People with Disabilities, Single-Disease Health Associations. **Geographic Distribution:** Focus on headquarters and operating locations.

★ 869 ★ **Taco Bell Foundation**
17901 Von Karman Ave.
Irvine, CA 92714
Phone: (714)863-4500
Fax: (714)863-2858
Michele Myszka, Executive Director

Giving Priorities: *Aid to Youths:* The foundation funds nonprofit organizations that aid young people. It focuses its funding on nonprofits, which provide youth-oriented services in the areas of health care, homelessness, hunger relief, substance abuse, and education. Also of interest to the foundation are innovative 'breakthrough' and special emergency projects. **Typical Health-Related Recipients:** Emergency/Ambulance Services, Health Organizations. **Geographic Distribution:** Primarily Southern California.

★ 870 ★ **Temple-Inland Foundation**
303 S Temple Dr.
PO Box N
Diboll, TX 75941
Phone: (409)829-1314
James R. Wash, Secretary & Treasurer

Giving Priorities: *General Support Program:* Recipients include united funds, municipalities, colleges and universities, museums, libraries, health-related programs, and youth organizations in company's headquarters area. Foundation also operates an employee matching gifts program and a scholarship program for the children of company employees. *Note:* Grant awards comprise 55% to 60% of total foundation giving; employee scholarships and other scholastic awards, 20% to 25%; and matching gifts, 15% to 20%. **Typical Health-Related Recipients:** Clinics/Medical Centers, Health Organizations, Hospices, Hospitals, People with Disabilities, Substance Abuse. **Geographic Distribution:** Primarily near company headquarters.

★ 871 ★ **Tension Envelope Foundation**
819 E 19th St., 5th Fl.
Kansas City, MO 64108
Phone: (816)471-3800
Eliot S. Berkley, Secretary

Giving Priorities: *Jewish Organizations:* 35% to 40% of total contributions. *United Way:* About 20%. *Education:* 15% to 20% of donations. *Community Affairs:* 10% to 15%. Wide range of recipients including Planned Parenthood. *Medicine, Health, and Science:* 5% to 10%. Medical centers, clinics, and hospices all receive support from the foundation. *Arts & Humanities:* About 5%. *Youth Organizations* Less than 5%. Supports Junior Achievement, YMCA, and an outdoor education center. **Typical Health-Related Recipients:** Domestic Violence, Family Planning, Health Organizations, Hospices, Hospitals, People with Disabilities, Substance Abuse. **Geographic Distribution:** Focus on Missouri.

★ 872 ★ **Texaco Foundation**
2000 Westchester Ave.
White Plains, NY 10650
Phone: (914)253-4655
Carl Barry Davidson, President

Giving Priorities: *Arts & Culture:* About 30% to 35% of contributions. *Education:* 30% to 35% of annual contributions, primarily in direct grants to colleges and universities. Interests also include medical, special, and minority education. *Civic, Public, & Environmental Interests:* About 15% of giving. *Social Enrichment:* Between 10% and 15%, with united funds and the American Red Cross receiving most support. Also supports drug and alcohol abuse prevention programs and agencies for the disabled. *Health & Hospitals:* About 5%. Committed to hospitals, especially teaching hospitals, and health facilities serving communities where Texaco has an operating presence. Other interests include occupational health, toxicology, cancer research, and screening programs. *International:* About 10% and is included in all categories above. **Typical Health-Related Recipients:** Children's Health/Hospitals, Diabetes, Emergency/Ambulance Services, Hospices, Hospitals, Medical Education, Medical Rehabilitation, Medical

Research, Medical Training, People with Disabilities, Public Health, Substance Abuse, Transplant Networks/Donor Banks. **Geographic Distribution:** National organizations and organizations near operating locations.

★ 873 ★ **Texas Commerce Bank Houston Foundation**
PO Box 2558
Houston, TX 77252-8050
Phone: (713)216-4004
Fax: (713)216-5486
Belinda Griffin, Secretary

Giving Priorities: *Social Services:* 60% to 65% of total annual contributions. *Education:* 10% to 15%. *Art & Humanities:* 10% to 15%. *Civic & Public Affairs:* 5% to 10%. *Health:* About 5%. Supports hospitals, pediatric health, substance abuse, and single-disease health associations. **Typical Health-Related Recipients:** Cancer, Children's Health/Hospitals, Clinics/Medical Centers, Diabetes, Family Planning, Health Organizations, Heart, Hospices, Hospitals, Medical Education, Medical Research, Medical Training, Mental Health, People with Disabilities, Prenatal Health Issues, Single-Disease Health Associations, Substance Abuse. **Geographic Distribution:** Limited to Houston, TX.

★ 874 ★ **Texas Instruments Foundation**
PO Box 650311, M/S 3906
Dallas, TX 75265
Phone: (214)917-4505
Fax: (214)995-8787
L. M. Rice, Jr., President

Giving Priorities: About 50% to 55% of foundation funding goes to education. Contributions include medical education. Health and social services generally receive about 25% of foundation contributions. Most of this goes to the United Way. Other interests include youth and community service organizations, hospitals, and medical research. Additional funding, 5% to 10%, supports the arts and humanities. International organizations receive 5% to 10%; civic concerns are supported by 5% to 10% of funding. **Typical Health-Related Recipients:** Hospitals, Medical Education, Medical Research, Substance Abuse. **Geographic Distribution:** Nationally, with emphasis on Texas-based groups.

★ 875 ★ **Textron Charitable Trust**
PO Box 878
Providence, RI 02901
Phone: (401)457-2430
Elizabeth W. Monahan, Contributions Coordinator

Giving Priorities: *Education:* 30% to 35% of total contributions. *United Way:* 25% to 30% of giving. *Culture:* 10% to 15%. *Health:* About 10%. Hospitals receive the largest amount of health care funds, through both general support and matching grants. Health organizations, single-disease health associations, hospices, and pediatric health also are supported. *Youth Groups:* About 5%. *Urban/Minority/Women:* Less than 5%. *Other:* About 15% of total annual contributions support environmental affairs, law and justice, public policy, science, and international affairs. **Typical Health-Related Recipients:** Family Planning, Health Organizations,

Health Policy/Cost Containment, Hospices, Hospitals, Medical Education, People with Disabilities, Single-Disease Health Associations, Substance Abuse. **Geographic Distribution:** Primarily in areas where company operates.

★876★ Thomas & Betts Charitable Trust
1555 Lynnfield Rd.
Memphis, TN 38119
Phone: (901)680-5933
Fax: (901)685-1988
Janice H. Way, Trust Administrator

Giving Priorities: *Social Services:* About 50% of the total contributions. Interests include youth organizations, community service organizations, and assistance for the disabled. *Education:* About 20%. *Health:* 15% to 20%. Supports hospital foundations, blood services, hospices, a visiting nurse association, and the Red Cross. *Science:* 5% to 10%. *Other:* Less than 5%. Recipients include economic development in Puerto Rico, museums, symphonies, arts associations, and art centers. **Typical Health-Related Recipients:** Clinics/Medical Centers, Emergency/Ambulance Services, Health Funds, Health Organizations, Hospices, Hospitals, Nursing Services, Transplant Networks/Donor Banks. **Geographic Distribution:** Primarily headquarters and operating locations, some nationally.

★877★ Thomas J. Lipton Foundation
800 Sylvan Ave.
Englewood Cliffs, NJ 07632
Phone: (201)894-7778
Fax: (201)871-8181
Helen Siegle, Administrator

Giving Priorities: *Health & Human Services:* 30% of contributions. Emphasis is on nutrition programs. Primary recipients include united funds, youth organizations, legal aid agencies, family planning, recreation and athletics, and community service organizations. Funds also support hospitals, single-disease health organizations, and medical research groups. *Education:* About 30%. *Civic & Public Affairs:* About 30%. *Arts & Humanities:* 5% to 10%. *Other:* Less than 5%. In 1991, giving included small grants to the Business Council of the U.N. and UNICEF. Funds from international grants must be used in the United States. **Typical Health-Related Recipients:** Family Planning, Health Funds, Health Organizations, Hospices, Hospitals, Medical Education, Medical Rehabilitation, Medical Research, Medical Training, Mental Health, Nutrition, People with Disabilities, Single-Disease Health Associations, Substance Abuse. **Geographic Distribution:** Primarily near corporate headquarters and plant locations.

★878★ Times Mirror Foundation
Times Mirror Sq.
Los Angeles, CA 90053
Phone: (213)237-3936
Fax: (213)237-3800
Cassandra Malry, Treasurer

Giving Priorities: *Cultural & Art:* 25% to 30% of total funding. *Health & Human Services:* 25% to 30%. About one-third of this goes to united funds. Other community service concerns include youth agencies, shelters for homeless women and youth, child welfare, community centers, religious welfare, services for the disabled, and family planning. Health interests include hospitals, mental health, medical schools, and health organizations. *Education:* 20% to 25% of total annual contributions. *Civic & Community:* About 20% of total. **Typical Health-Related Recipients:** Cancer, Diabetes, Domestic Violence, Emergency/Ambulance Services, Eyes/Blindness, General, People with Disabilities, Respiratory. **Geographic Distribution:** Primarily nonprofits located in southern California, and in communities where there is a significant employee presence.

★879★ TJX Foundation
770 Cochituate Rd.
Framingham, MA 01701
Phone: (508)390-3199
Fax: (508)390-2828
Carla Bertonazzi, Community Affairs
 Administrator

Giving Priorities: *Social Services:* 30% to 35% of total annual contributions. The major recipient is Save the Children. Other recipients include the United Way, youth and child welfare organizations, and homeless assistance groups. *Civic & Public Affairs:* 25% to 30% of funding. *Health:* 20% to 25% of giving. Major support to Beth Israel Hospital in Boston. Also supports single-didease health associations and health centers. *Education:* About 15% of giving. *Arts & Humanities:* Less than 5% of total annual giving. **Typical Health-Related Recipients:** AIDS/HIV, Children's Health/Hospitals, Clinics/Medical Centers, Diabetes, Domestic Violence, Health Organizations, Hospices, Hospitals, Medical Education, Medical Rehabilitation, Mental Health, Nursing Services, People with Disabilities, Public Health, Single-Disease Health Associations, Substance Abuse. **Geographic Distribution:** Limited to geographical area of TJX operations.

★880★ Tomkins Industries Foundation
4801 Springfield St.
Dayton, OH 45431
Phone: (513)253-7171
Fax: (513)253-5809
William R. Winkler, Vice President

Giving Priorities: *Social Services:* 45% to 50%. *Education:* 35% to 40%. *Health:* About 5%. Funds a variety of health care groups, including the American Cancer Society, the March of Dimes, and the Memorial Sloan-Kettering Cancer Center. *Civic & Public Affairs:* Less than 5%. Supports community affairs and safety organizations. *Other:* Less than 5%. Funds a variety of arts, science, and religious organizations. **Typical Health-Related Recipients:** Alzheimers Disease, Cancer, Children's Health/Hospitals, Clinics/Medical Centers, Emergency/Ambulance Services, Health Organizations, Hospices, Hospitals, Prenatal Health Issues, Single-Disease Health Associations. **Geographic Distribution:** Primarily in the Dayton, OH, area. **Formerly:** Philips Industries Foundation.

★881★ Transamerica Foundation
600 Montgomery St.
San Francisco, CA 94111
Phone: (415)983-4333
Fax: (415)983-4234
Mary Sawai, Assistant Secretary

Giving Priorities: *Health & Welfare:* Approximately 45% to 50% of total annual contributions. Primarily supports homelessness and housing, food distribution programs, and shelters. Other interests include community service organizations and groups concerned with child welfare and drug abuse prevention. *Education:* 30% to 35% of total contributions. *Culture & the Arts:* 10% of funding. *Civic:* 5% to 10% of gifts. **Typical Health-Related Recipients:** Cancer, Clinics/Medical Centers, Health Funds, Hospices, Hospitals, Mental Health, People with Disabilities, Single-Disease Health Associations. **Geographic Distribution:** Primarily in operating areas.

★882★ Travelers Foundation
65 E 55th St.
New York, NY 10022
Phone: (212)891-8884
Fax: (212)891-8908
Dee Topol, President

Giving Priorities: *General Grants:* The contribution program's highest priority is to improve public education. Grants are also awarded to nonprofit organizations that address needs in the area of human services, health, civic development, and culture. *Local Contributions Program:* Grants to meet the needs of communities where Travelers has offices are administered locally by employees. *Volunteer Incentive Program:* Company supports employee volunteer efforts. *Note:* The company reported that in 1993, 50% of its contributions went to education. The arts, civic and public affairs, and social services each received 15% of total giving. The remaining 5% went to health care. **Typical Health-Related Recipients:** AIDS/HIV, Clinics/Medical Centers, Domestic Violence, Substance Abuse. **Geographic Distribution:** Near headquarters and operating locations only. **Formerly:** Primerica Foundation.

★883★ TRINOVA Foundation
3000 Strayer
PO Box 50
Maumee, OH 43537-0050
Phone: (419)867-2294
Fax: (419)867-2395

Giving Priorities: *Education:* About 30% of total funding. *Social Services:* About 30%. *Health:* About 20%. Supports hospitals and community health organziations. *Arts & Humanities:* About 15%. *Civic & Public Affairs:* About 5%. **Typical Health-Related Recipients:** Health Organizations, Hospitals, People with Disabilities, Substance Abuse. **Geographic Distribution:** Near headquarters and operating locations only.

★884★ TRW Foundation
1900 Richmond Rd.
Cleveland, OH 44124
Phone: (216)291-7160
Fax: (216)291-0620
Alan F. Senger, Vice President

Giving Priorities: *Education:* About 50% of total contributions. *United Way:* About 20%. *Health, Welfare, & Youth:* About 15% to non-United Way agencies, primarily youth organizations. Other social service recipients include community service organizations and groups concerned with child welfare, the handicapped, and employment. Limited support goes to health organizations; hospitals are the primary recipients. *Civic & Culture:* Approximately 15%. **Typical Health-Related Recipients:** Alzheimers Disease, Clinics/Medical Centers, Emergency/Ambulance Services, Health Organizations, Health Policy/Cost Containment, Hospitals, Medical Rehabilitation, Research/Studies Institutes. **Geographic Distribution:** In plant communities; to a select number of educational institutions with engineering, science, or business administration programs; and to selected national and international organizations.

★885★ 21 International Holdings Foundation
375 Park Ave.
New York, NY 10152
Phone: (212)230-0400
Fax: (212)593-1363
Judith G. Hershon, Vice President

Giving Priorities: *Arts & Humanities:* 20% to 25% of total contributions. *Social Services:* 15% to 20% of funding. *International:* 15% to 20% of total annual giving. *Religion:* 10% to 15% of giving. *Civic & Public Affairs:* 10% to 15% of contributions. *Education:* About 10% of total contributions. *Health:* 5% to 10% of giving. Grants concentrate on medical research with some support also going to single-disease health organizations. **Typical Health-Related Recipients:** Cancer, Emergency/Ambulance Services, Hospitals, Medical Education, Medical Research, People with Disabilities, Single-Disease Health Associations. **Geographic Distribution:** Primarily in New York City area.

★886★ Union Bank Foundation
Terminal Annex
PO Box 3100
Los Angeles, CA 90051
Phone: (213)236-5823
Fax: (213)236-6982
Christopher I. M. Houser, President

Giving Priorities: *Health & Human Services:* 35% and 40% of annual contributions. Supports hospitals and medical centers, as well as youth, child welfare, and family service organizations. *Civic & Public Affairs:* 20% to 25%. *Culture:* About 20%. *Education:* 10% and 15%. **Typical Health-Related Recipients:** Domestic Violence, Emergency/Ambulance Services, Hospitals, Medical Rehabilitation, Medical Research, People with Disabilities, Single-Disease Health Associations. **Geographic Distribution:** Primarily in California.

★887★ Union Camp Charitable Trust
1600 Valley Rd.
Wayne, NJ 07470
Phone: (201)628-2248
Fax: (201)628-2848
Sydney N. Phin, Director, Human Resources

Giving Priorities: *Health & Welfare:* Approximately 50%. Major support to united funds, youth organizations, children's and community hospitals, and single-disease health associations. The remainder is disbursed among employment and job training, children's homes, medical rehabilitation, emergency and ambulance services, delinquency and crime councils, the disabled, and religious welfare. *Education:* 25% to 30% of total contributions. *Civic & Public Affairs:* 10% to 15%. *Other:* 10% to 15% to miscellaneous organizations. **Typical Health-Related Recipients:** Clinics/Medical Centers, Domestic Violence, Emergency/Ambulance Services, Family Planning, Geriatric Health, Health Funds, Health Organizations, Hospices, Hospitals, Medical Education, Medical Rehabilitation, Medical Research, Medical Training, Mental Health, Nursing Services, People with Disabilities, Single-Disease Health Associations, Substance Abuse. **Geographic Distribution:** Principally near operating locations and to national organizations.

★888★ Union Carbide Foundation
39 Old Ridgebury Rd.
L4-507
Danbury, CT 06817
Phone: (203)794-6484
Deborah Surat, Manager, Corporate Contributions

Giving Priorities: *General Support Program:* Education is highest priority. In the area of health and human services, primarily supports the United Way, hospitals, clinics, hospices, families, children, and minorities. Limited funding to civic organizations promoting environmental preservation, public policy research, and safety organizations. In 1993, percentage distribution among categories of interest was education, 59%; health and human services, 15%; environment, 8%; diversity, 7%; civic affairs, 5%; the arts, 3%; and other, 3%. **Typical Health-Related Recipients:** Clinics/Medical Centers, Home-Care Services, Hospices, People with Disabilities. **Geographic Distribution:** Foundation has six geographic priority areas, which include Danbury, CT; Taft, LA; Texas City, TX; central NJ; Kanawah Valley, WV; and Seadrift, TX. They also provide funding for national organizations.

★889★ Union Pacific Foundation
Martin Tower
8th & Eaton Ave.
Bethlehem, PA 18018
Phone: (215)861-3225
Fax: (215)816-3111
Judy L. Swantak, President

Giving Priorities: *Social Welfare:* About 40% of annual giving. Supports united funds, youth organizations and child welfare groups, as well as services for the handicapped and the disadvantaged, and a variety of other community service agencies. *Education:* About 30% of giving. *Arts & Culture:* About 20%. *Health:* About 10%. Grants awarded largely to hospitals for building, equipment, or project support. Also supports hospices and rehabilitation facilities. **Typical Health-Related Recipients:** Domestic Violence, Hospices, Hospitals, Medical Rehabilitation, People with Disabilities, Substance Abuse. **Geographic Distribution:** In communities served by Union Pacific's operating companies, principally in the western United States.

★890★ United States Sugar Corp. Charitable Trust
PO Box 1207
Clewiston, FL 33440
Phone: (813)983-8121
Fax: (813)983-4804
Atwood Dunwody, Trustee

Giving Priorities: *Social Services:* 40% to 45%. *Education:* About 35% of contributions. *Civic & Public Affairs:* 15% to 20% of giving. *Health:* About 5%. Support goes to hospitals and single-disease health associations. **Typical Health-Related Recipients:** Emergency/Ambulance Services, Health Organizations, Hospices, Hospitals, People with Disabilities, Single-Disease Health Associations. **Geographic Distribution:** In geographic areas near operating locations.

★891★ Universal Leaf Foundation
PO Box 25099
Richmond, VA 23260
Phone: (804)359-9311
Nancy G. Powell, Manager, Corporate Relations

Giving Priorities: *Social Services:* 35% to 40% of total contributions. *Education:* 25% to 30%. *Civic & Public Affairs:* 15% to 20%. *Arts & Humanities:* 10% to 15%. *Health:* About 5%. Supports Red Cross, National Multiple Sclerosis Society, and health organizations. **Typical Health-Related Recipients:** Health Funds, Health Organizations, People with Disabilities, Single-Disease Health Associations. **Geographic Distribution:** Focus on VA and NC.

★892★ USF&G Foundation
100 Light St.
Baltimore, MD 21202
Phone: (410)547-3752
Fax: (410)547-3700
Sue Lovell, Corporate Foundation Administrator

Giving Priorities: *Education:* About 50%. *Health & Social Services:* About 45% of total annual contributions. Supported media campaign to reduce adolescent pregnancy. Provided health care to low-income children. Assisted in the comprehensive educational, rehabilitative, vocational, and residential services to disabled children and adults. Provided "extra care" homeless shelter for the physically ill. Supported the fight against drugs. Improved housing for the elderly as well as low and moderate income families. Provided capital construction help to health care and service facilities. Supported United Way activities. *Arts & Culture:* About 5%. **Typical Health-Related Recipients:** Cancer, Clinics/Medical Centers, Emergency/Ambulance Services, Heart, Hospitals, People with Disabilities, Prenatal Health Issues, Single-Disease Health Associations, Substance Abuse. **Geographic Distribution:** Primarily in operating locations and to national organizations; also through their 34 branch offices throughout the United States.

★ 893 ★ USG Foundation
125 S Franklin
Chicago, IL 60606
Phone: (312)606-4594
Fax: (312)606-5316
Harold Pendexter, Jr., President

Giving Priorities: *Education:* Between 35% and 40% of total annual contributions. *Social Services:* Between 35% and 40%, the majority of which supports united funds. Also supports youth and child welfare, community and family services, and the handicapped. *Health:* Between 20% and 25%, with principal support to hospitals and medical centers. Also supports national health organizations and their local affiliates, mental health, and medical research. *Arts & Humanities:* About 10%. *Civic & Public Affairs:* Between 5% and 10%. *International:* Gives a small amount of support in Canada, primarily around company's subsidaries. **Typical Health-Related Recipients:** Health Organizations, Hospices, Hospitals, Medical Research, Mental Health, People with Disabilities. **Geographic Distribution:** Nationally, with emphasis on Illinois and corporate operating locations.

★ 894 ★ USX Foundation
USX Tower
600 Grant St., Rm. 2640
Pittsburgh, PA 15219-4776
Phone: (412)433-5237
Fax: (412)433-6847
James L. Hamilton, III, General Manager

Giving Priorities: *Education:* 50% to 55% of total annual giving. *Health & Human Services:* About 35% of total contributions. About two-third of human services funding supported local United Ways. Other interests include community service organizations, alcohol and drug rehablitation, shelters, services to unemployed and dislocated workers, and low-income housing. Health funding supported hospital, rehabilitation centers, and single-disease associations. *Arts & Humanities:* 5% to 10%. *Civic & Public Affairs:* Less than 5%. *Science:* Less than 5%. **Typical Health-Related Recipients:** Health Organizations, Medical Rehabilitation, Mental Health, People with Disabilities, Single-Disease Health Associations, Substance Abuse, Trauma Treatment. **Geographic Distribution:** U.S., with emphasis on communities where USX Corp. and its subsidiaries operate.

★ 895 ★ Valley Bank Charitable Foundation
PO Box 71
Phoenix, AZ 85001
Phone: (602)221-2230
Fax: (602)221-1535
Lydia Lee, Chairperson, Contributions Committee

Giving Priorities: *Health and Human Services* 35% to 40% of total annual contributions. Primary support goes to united funds and community programs. Also supports hospitals, with some contributions to research organizations, single-disease health groups, and outpatient care programs. *Civic & Public Affairs:* 25% to 30%. *Arts & Humanities:* 15% to 20%. *Education:* 10% to 15% of contributions. **Typical Health-Related Recipients:** Health Funds, Hospitals, Single-Disease Health Associations, Substance Abuse. **Geographic Distribution:** Arizona.

★ 896 ★ Vulcan Materials Co. Foundation
PO Box 530187
Birmingham, AL 35253-0187
Phone: (205)877-3229
Fax: (205)877-3094
Mary S. Russom, Administrator, Community Affairs

Giving Priorities: *Education:* About 45% of total contributions. *Health & Welfare:* 25% to 30%, primarily to united funds. Also interested in programs for unemployed youth, employment, youth organizations, local health organizations, and mental health agencies. *Arts & Community Services:* 20% to 25%. *Civic & Public Affairs:* 5% to 10%. **Typical Health-Related Recipients:** Health Organizations, Mental Health, People with Disabilities, Substance Abuse. **Geographic Distribution:** In states where company has operations.

★ 897 ★ Walt Disney Co. Foundation
500 S Buena Vista St.
Burbank, CA 91521-0987
Phone: (818)560-1006
Tilly J. Baptie, Executive Director

Giving Priorities: *Education:* About 60% of total annual contributions. *Social Services:* 15% to 20%. *Health:* 10% to 15%. Grants go to hospitals and other facilities in company operating areas. *Arts & Humanities:* About 10%. **Typical Health-Related Recipients:** Clinics/Medical Centers, Diabetes, Hospitals, Medical Education, Medical Rehabilitation, People with Disabilities, Single-Disease Health Associations. **Geographic Distribution:** Nationally to company operating areas, with emphasis on California (Los Angeles and Orange Counties) and Florida (Orange and Osceola Counties).

★ 898 ★ Warner-Lambert Charitable Foundation
201 Tabor Rd.
Morris Plains, NJ 07950
Phone: (201)540-2243
Fax: (201)540-3320
Evelyn Self, Secretary

Giving Priorities: *Education:* Approximately 45% to 50% of total contributions. Major recipients include scientific, medical, pharmaceutical, dental, and health-related education programs. Also contributes to higher education funds and associations. *Health:* 20% to 25%. Principal recipients are health organizations, university medical centers, single disease research, and hospitals. Areas of interest also include pediatric health, health funds, medical education and rehabilitation, and mental health. *Social Services:* 10% to 15%. Areas of interest include youth organizations, the aged, and aid to the handicapped. *Civic & Public Affairs:* About 10%. *Arts & Humanities:* 5% to 10%. *Note:* Company reports educational and direct contributions priorities are similar. **Typical Health-Related Recipients:** Alzheimers Disease, Cancer, Children's Health/Hospitals, Clinics/Medical Centers, Domestic Violence, Health Funds, Health Organizations, Heart, Hospitals, Medical Education, Medical Rehabilitation, Medical Research, People with Disabilities, Single-Disease Health Associations. **Geographic Distribution:** Primarily where company maintains corporate facilities, especially near headquarters in Morris Plains, NJ.

★ 899 ★ Washington Trust Bank Foundation
c/o Washington Trust Bank, PO Box 2127
Spokane, WA 99210
Phone: (509)353-3820
F. W. Scammell, Administrator and Trustee

Giving Priorities: *Education:* 35% to 40% of total contributions. *Social Services:* 30% to 35% of funding. *Arts & Humanities:* 10% to 15%. *Civic & Public Affairs:* About 10%. *Health:* 5% to 10%. The foundation also supports hospitals and medical centers, hospices, and health funds, with the largest portion of support going to Sacred Heart Medical center. **Typical Health-Related Recipients:** Cancer, Children's Health/Hospitals, Clinics/Medical Centers, Heart, Hospitals, Multiple Sclerosis, Nursing Services. **Geographic Distribution:** Emphasis on the greater Spokane, WA, area.

★ 900 ★ Westinghouse Foundation
11 Stanwix St.
Pittsburgh, PA 15222-1384
Phone: (412)642-6033
Fax: (412)642-4874
Cheryl Kubelick, Mgr., Contributions & Commun. Affairs

Giving Priorities: *Education:* 45% to 50% of contributions. *Health & Welfare:* 30% to 35% of giving, over half of which is awarded to united funds in communities where Westinghouse operates. Hospitals are excluded. Health contributions center on upgrading the conditions of the blind, homeless, handicapped, aged, abused, disabled, and minorities. Also supports youth organizations and recreation. *Culture & the Arts:* About 10%. *Civic & Social:* 5% to 10%. **Typical Health-Related Recipients:** Emergency/Ambulance Services, Medical Rehabilitation, People with Disabilities. **Geographic Distribution:** Principally near operating locations and to national organizations.

★ 901 ★ Westvaco Foundation Trust
299 Park Ave.
New York, NY 10171
Phone: (212)688-5000
Fax: (212)318-5070
Roger Holmes, Secretary, Contributions Committee

Giving Priorities: *Social Services:* About 35% of contributions, primarily supporting united funds. Recipients of smaller amounts include youth organizations and drug and alcohol programs. *Education:* 20% to 25%. *Health:* 10% to 15%, primarily supporting hospitals and medical centers. Other interests include single-disease health associations, health organizations, and medical research. *Civic & Public Affairs:* 5% to 10%. *Arts & Humanities:* Less than 5%. *Note:* Information on the remaining percentage of grants given is not available. **Typical Health-Related Recipients:** Health Funds, Health Organizations, Hospitals, Medical Education, Medical Rehabilitation, Medical Research, People with Disabilities, Single-Disease Health Associations, Substance Abuse. **Geographic Distribution:** Near headquarters and operating locations only.

★902★   **Wheat, First Securities/Butcher and Singer Foundation**

P. O. Box 1357
Richmond, VA 23211
Phone: (804)649-2311
Fax: (804)782-3384
William V. Daniel, Vice President and Treasurer

Giving Priorities: *Education:* 60% to 65% of contributions. *Arts & Humanities:* 10% to 15%. *Civic & Public Affairs:* 5% to 10%. *Health:* 5% to 10%. Primarily supports health funds and hospitals. *Social Services:* 5% to 10%. **Typical Health-Related Recipients:** Children's Health/Hospitals, Emergency/Ambulance Services, Eyes/Blindness, Health Organizations, Hospitals, Medical Education, Medical Research, People with Disabilities, Single-Disease Health Associations. **Geographic Distribution:** In headquarters and operating communities. **Formerly:** Wheat Foundation.

★903★   **White Consolidated Industries Foundation**

11770 Berea Rd.
Cleveland, OH 44111
Phone: (216)252-8385
Fax: (216)252-8158
Daniel R. Elliott, Jr., Chairman

Giving Priorities: *Social Services:* About 50% of total funding. *Education:* 15% to 20% of annual contributions. *Arts & Humanities:* Generally 10% to 15%. *Civic & Public Affairs:* About 10%. *Health:* 5% to 10%. Supporting hospitals and health centers, and single-disease health associations. **Typical Health-Related Recipients:** Hospitals, Nutrition. **Geographic Distribution:** Primarily Cleveland and Columbus, OH, areas; other operating locations receive local requests.

★904★   **Whitman Corp. Foundation**

3501 Algonquin Rd.
Rolling Meadows, IL 60008
Phone: (708)818-5000
Charles H. Connolly, President

Giving Priorities: *Education:* About 75% of contributions. *Social Services, Health, & Welfare:* About 20%, mostly to hospitals, medical research institutes, and single-disease health organizations. *Civic & Public Affairs:* About 5%. **Typical Health-Related Recipients:** People with Disabilities. **Geographic Distribution:** Nationwide, with emphasis the Chicago area.

★905★   **WICOR Foundation**

626 East Wisconsin Ave.
Milwaukee, WI 53202
Phone: (414)291-6565
Fax: (414)291-6361
Carolyn Simpson, Foundation Coordinator

Giving Priorities: *Health & Human Services:* About 50% of total funding. Supports children's hospitals of Wisconsin, blood centers, and other community hospitals. Major contributions are made to various United Ways. Other interests include traditional youth organizations, child welfare, community services, and Milwaukee inner-city agencies. In 1992, 4 grants totaling $138,000 went to the United Way of Greater Milwaukee. *Education:* About 25%. Primary support to higher education and medical education

in Milwaukee. *Civic & Public Affairs:* About 15%. *Arts & Humanities:* About 10%. **Typical Health-Related Recipients:** Clinics/Medical Centers, Domestic Violence, Emergency/Ambulance Services, General, Health Policy/Cost Containment, Hospitals, Medical Education, People with Disabilities, Substance Abuse, Transplant Networks/Donor Banks. **Geographic Distribution:** Giving largely limited to WICOR plant locations and service territory.

★906★   **Williams Cos. Foundation**

PO Box 2400
Tulsa, OK 74102
Phone: (918)588-2106
Fax: (918)588-2334
Hannah Davis Robson, Managing Director

Giving Priorities: *Education:* 50% to 60% of contributions. *Civic & Public Affairs:* 20% to 25%. *Health & Human Services:* 10% to 15% of total contributions. More than three-fourths goes to united funds, American Red Cross, and family service organizations. Other interests include youth organizaions, drug and alcohol abuse, the disabled, and child welfare organizations. Health interests include medical centers, medical research, and single-disease health associations. *Arts & Humanities:* About 10%. *Other:* Less than 1% each to international organizations, religion, and science funds. **Typical Health-Related Recipients:** Domestic Violence, Family Planning, Health Funds, Health Organizations, Hospitals, People with Disabilities, Single-Disease Health Associations, Substance Abuse. **Geographic Distribution:** Exclusively in areas near company headquarters and operating locations.

★907★   **Winn-Dixie Stores Foundation**

Box B
Jacksonville, FL 32203
Phone: (904)783-5000
Larry H. May, President

Giving Priorities: *Employee Matching Gifts:* About 65% of giving consists of matching gifts to United Ways, Hope Lodge, and other nonprofit organizations. The remainder of funds support a variety of organizations in operating areas. In 1992, the foundation gave a major grant to the American Red Cross for Hurricane Andrew relief efforts. *Education:* 15% to 20% of support. *Health:* 10% to 15%. Gives primarily to single-disease health associations. Other interests include hospitals, hospices, and mental health organizations. *Youth Organizations:* Less than 5% of funds. *Other:* 5% to 10%. Gives to a variety of organizations, including community and urban affairs, minority organizations, social services, and arts groups. **Typical Health-Related Recipients:** Alzheimers Disease, Cancer, Emergency/Ambulance Services, Heart, Hospices, Hospitals, Medical Education, Mental Health, People with Disabilities, Prenatal Health Issues, Single-Disease Health Associations. **Geographic Distribution:** Primarily in the company's 13-state trade area; generally within the southeastern United States.

★908★   **Wisconsin Energy Corp. Foundation**

231 W Michigan St.
PO Box 2046
Milwaukee, WI 53201
Phone: (414)221-2105
Fax: (414)221-2594
Jerry G. Remmel, Treasurer

Giving Priorities: *Social Services:* Generally 30% to 35% of total annual contributions. *Education:* Typically 20% to 25% of total. *Civic & Public Affairs:* About 15% to 20% of contributions. *Arts & Humanities:* Approximately 15% of funding. *Health:* About 10%, with an emphasis on hospitals. Also supports nursing services, single-disease health associations, and other health organizations. **Typical Health-Related Recipients:** Health Organizations, Hospitals, Medical Rehabilitation, Medical Research, Mental Health, People with Disabilities, Single-Disease Health Associations. **Geographic Distribution:** Almost exclusively in company's service area, but grants may be made in other states.

★909★   **Wisconsin Power and Light Foundation**

PO Box 192
Madison, WI 53701
Phone: (608)252-5545
Fax: (608)252-3479
Jo Ann Healy, Vice President

Giving Priorities: *Education:* About 35% of contributions. *Health & Welfare:* 25% to 30% of contributions. Most support goes to social services, with about one-third awarded to united fund drives in local communities. Also supports youth organizations, family services, nursing services, and hospitals. *Civic:* 20% to 25%. *Culture & Art:* 10% to 15%. **Typical Health-Related Recipients:** Children's Health/Hospitals, Emergency/Ambulance Services, Health Organizations, Hospitals, Nursing Services, People with Disabilities, Single-Disease Health Associations. **Geographic Distribution:** Principally near headquarters and service areas (Central and South-Central WI).

★910★   **Wisconsin Public Service Foundation**

700 North Adams St.
PO Box 19001
Green Bay, WI 54307-9001
Phone: (414)433-1464
Fax: (414)433-1526
D. A. Bollom, President & CEO

Giving Priorities: *Health & Human Services:* Approximately 41%. Substantial support goes to united funds. Health interests include hospitals, and health organizations. *Education:* About 34% of total annual contributions. Major support for colleges and universities. Also funds health education. *Civic & Public Affairs:* 15%. *Arts & Humanities:* 10%. **Typical Health-Related Recipients:** Hospitals, Substance Abuse. **Geographic Distribution:** Northeast Wisconsin and parts of upper Michigan.

★911★ Wm. Jr. Wrigley Co. Foundation
410 N Michigan Ave.
Chicago, IL 60611
Phone: (312)645-3950
Fax: (312)644-4911
William M. Piet, President

Giving Priorities: *Health & Welfare:* Highest priority, with major support going to the United Way. Major interest in national basic health and welfare organizations and their local affiliates. Major health concern is dental health. Other interests include youth and community service organizations and groups concerned with food distribution, child welfare, domestic violence, employment, and substance abuse. *Education:* Second priority, with major contributions going to groups concerned with minority education. Other interests include education funds, and nursing scholarships. *Other:* Also gives to civic groups, especially those concerned with civil rights, and occasionally to arts organizations. **Typical Health-Related Recipients:** Domestic Violence, Health Funds, Health Organizations, Nursing Services, People with Disabilities, Single-Disease Health Associations, Substance Abuse. **Geographic Distribution:** Nationally, with an emphasis on the Chicago area.

★912★ Wyman-Gordon Foundation
244 Worcester St.
North Grafton, MA 01536-8001
Phone: (508)839-4441
Fax: (508)839-7500
Wallace F. Whitney, Jr., Secretary-Treasurer

Giving Priorities: *Health & Social Services:* 70% to 75% of total funding, almost all of which went to United Ways. The remainder went to traditional youth organizations and disease research and prevention. *Education:* 10% to 15%. *Civic & Public Affairs:* About 5%. *Arts & Humanities:* Less than 5%. *Other:* Less than 5%. Supports related foundation interests. **Typical Health-Related Recipients:** AIDS/HIV, Cancer, Children's Health/Hospitals, Emergency/Ambulance Services, General, Health Organizations, Hospitals, Multiple Sclerosis. **Geographic Distribution:** New operating locations and nationally.

Other Funding Organizations

★913★ American Academy of Family Physicians
8880 Ward Pkwy.
Kansas City, MO 64114
Phone: (816)333-9700
Robert Graham, M.D., Exec. VP

Description: The foundation, which is the Academy's funding arm, presents awards to practicing physicians and students for research on subjects affecting health care delivery in family practice; Mead Johnson awards for graduate training in family practice; and Parke-Davis teacher development awards; Resident Repayment Program in which the foundation assists residents with the interest on their student loans; Offers research externships in which medical students are paired with a family physician.

★914★ American College of Physicians
Independence Mall W
6th St. at Race
Philadelphia, PA 19106-1572
Phone: (215)351-2400
Free: 800-523-1546
Fax: (215)351-2448
John R. Ball, M.D., Exec. VP

Description: Presents 10 annual awards and sponsors teaching and research scholarship competition for physicians specializing in internal medicine and related specialties, such as dermatology, cardiology, gastroenterology, neurology, psychiatry, and public health.

★915★ American Health Assistance Foundation
15825 Shady Grove Rd., Ste. 140
Rockville, MD 20850
Phone: (301)948-3244
Free: 800-437-2423
Fax: (301)258-9454
Eugene H. Michaels, Pres.

Description: Foundation supports medical research on heart disease, glaucoma, and Alzheimer's disease, as well as an Alzheimer's Family Relief Program.

★916★ American Medical Association Education and Research Foundation
515 N. State St.
Chicago, IL 60610
Phone: (312)464-5000
Fax: (312)464-5833
James S. Todd, M.D., Exec. VP

Description: Receives and distributes funds to benefit medical education in U.S. medical schools and to support medical research and innovative pilot programs in health care.

★917★ Foundation for Hand Research
310 E. 30th St.
New York, NY 10016
Phone: (212)685-3834
Fax: (212)545-1646
Dr. Robert Beasley, Dir.

Description: Grants clinical fellowships for development of special skills in care of the hand; provides visiting professorships.

★918★ Institute for Advanced Research in Asian Science and Medicine
PO Box 67336
Chestnut Hill, MA 02167
Phone: (617)739-1182
Fax: (617)739-1183
Dr. John J. Kao, Contact

Description: Offers research fellowships for the humanistic study of Asian scientific and medical traditions; gives grants for scientific research in comparative physiology and medicine.

★919★ National Foundation for Research in Medicine
c/o Jeanette Baptiste
2296-83 Caminito Pajarito
San Diego, CA 92107
Jeanette Baptiste, Pres.

Description: Supports medical research in areas where other aid is not available; is particularly interested in the independent medical research investigator.

★920★ National Medical Fellowships
254 W. 31st St., 7th Fl.
New York, NY 10001
Phone: (212)714-0933
Fax: (212)239-9718
Leon Johnson, Jr., Pres.

Description: Awards fellowships to medical students from minority groups.

★921★ National Organization for Rare Disorders
PO Box 8923
New Fairfield, CT 06812-8923
Phone: (203)746-6518
Free: 800-999-NORD
Fax: (203)746-6481
Abbey S. Meyers, Exec. Dir.

Description: Offers grants to scientists for clinical research on new treatments for rare diseases.

★922★ Pan American Health Organization
525 23rd St. NW
Washington, DC 20037
Phone: (202)861-3200
Fax: (202)223-5971
Dr. Carlyle Guerra de Macedo, Dir.

Description: Awards fellowships for training health services personnel.

Medical & Allied Health Schools

Medicine

The following are accredited U.S. medical schools. Professional associations to contact for further information on medical education include the Association of American Medical Colleges, 2450 N St. NW, Washington, DC 20037, (202) 828-0400 and the American Medical Association, 515 N. State St., Chicago, IL 60610, (312) 464-5000.

Alabama

★923★ University of Alabama at Birmingham School of Medicine
1813 6th Ave. S.
Birmingham, AL 35233
Phone: (205)934-4011
Fax: (205)934-0333

★924★ University of South Alabama College of Medicine
307 University Blvd.
Mobile, AL 36688
Phone: (205)460-7174
Fax: (205)460-6073

Arizona

★925★ **University of Arizona**
College of Medicine
Arizona Health Sciences Center
1501 N. Campbell Ave.
Tucson, AZ 85724
Phone: (602)626-6214
Fax: (602)626-4884

Arkansas

★926★ **University of Arkansas at Little Rock**
College of Medicine
4301 W. Markham St.
Little Rock, AR 72205
Phone: (501)686-5000
Fax: (501)686-8160

California

★927★ **Loma Linda University**
School of Medicine
Loma Linda, CA 92350
Phone: (909)824-4462
Fax: (909)824-4146

★928★ **Stanford University**
School of Medicine
300 Pasteur Dr.
Stanford, CA 94305
Phone: (415)725-3900
Fax: (415)725-7368

★929★ **University of California, Davis**
School of Medicine
Davis, CA 95616
Phone: (916)752-0331
Fax: (916)752-3517

★930★ **University of California, Irvine**
College of Medicine
Irvine, CA 92717
Phone: (714)856-6119
Fax: (714)725-2083

★931★ **University of California, Los Angeles**
UCLA School of Medicine
10833 Le Conte Ave.
Los Angeles, CA 90024
Phone: (310)825-9111
Fax: (310)206-5046

★932★ **University of California, San Diego**
School of Medicine
La Jolla, CA 92093
Phone: (619)534-3713
Fax: (619)534-6573

★933★ **University of California, San Francisco**
School of Medicine
513 Parnassus Ave.
San Francisco, CA 94143-0410
Phone: (415)476-9000
Fax: (415)476-0689

★934★ **University of Southern California**
School of Medicine
1975 Zonal Ave.
Los Angeles, CA 90033
Phone: (213)342-1544
Fax: (213)342-2722

Colorado

★935★ **University of Colorado—Denver**
School of Medicine
4200 E. 9th Ave.
Denver, CO 80262
Phone: (303)399-1211
Fax: (303)270-8494

Connecticut

★936★ **University of Connecticut**
School of Medicine
263 Farmington Ave.
Farmington, CT 06030
Phone: (203)679-2000
Fax: (203)679-1282

★937★ **Yale University**
School of Medicine
333 Cedar St.
PO Box 208055
New Haven, CT 06520
Phone: (203)432-4771
Fax: (203)785-7437

District of Columbia

★938★ **George Washington University**
School of Medicine and Health Sciences
2300 Eye St. NW
Washington, DC 20037
Phone: (202)994-3501

★939★ **Georgetown University**
School of Medicine
3900 Reservoir Rd. NW
Washington, DC 20007
Phone: (202)687-1612
Fax: (202)687-2792

★940★ **Howard University**
College of Medicine
520 W St. NW
Washington, DC 20059
Phone: (202)806-6270
Fax: (202)806-7934

Florida

★941★ **University of Florida**
College of Medicine
J. Hillis Miller Health Center
Box 100215
Gainesville, FL 32610
Phone: (904)392-5397
Fax: (904)392-6482

★942★ **University of Miami**
School of Medicine
1600 NW 10th Ave.
PO Box 016099
Miami, FL 33101
Phone: (305)547-6545
Fax: (305)548-4888

★943★ **University of South Florida**
College of Medicine
Box 66
12901 Bruce B. Downs Blvd.
Tampa, FL 33612-4799
Phone: (813)974-2196
Fax: (813)974-5556

Georgia

★944★ **Emory University**
School of Medicine
Woodruff Health Sciences Center Admin. Bldg.
1440 Clifton Rd. NE
Atlanta, GA 30322
Phone: (404)727-5640
Fax: (404)727-0473

★945★ **Medical College of Georgia**
School of Medicine
1120 15th St.
Augusta, GA 30912
Phone: (706)721-0211
Fax: (706)721-7035

★946★ **Mercer University**
School of Medicine
1550 College St.
Macon, GA 31207
Phone: (912)752-2600
Fax: (912)752-2547

★947★ **Morehouse School of Medicine**
720 West View Dr. SW
Atlanta, GA 30310
Phone: (404)752-1500
Fax: (404)752-8443

Hawaii

★948★ **University of Hawaii at Manoa**
John A. Burns School of Medicine
1960 East-West Rd.
Honolulu, HI 96822
Phone: (808)956-8287
Fax: (808)956-5506

Illinois

★949★ **Finch University of Health Sciences / Chicago Medical School**
3333 Green Bay Rd.
North Chicago, IL 60064-3095
Phone: (708)578-3000
Fax: (708)578-3320

★950★ **Loyola University of Chicago**
Stritch School of Medicine
2160 S. 1st Ave.
Maywood, IL 60153
Phone: (708)216-9000
Fax: (708)216-4305

★951★ **Northwestern University**
Medical School
303 E. Chicago Ave.
Chicago, IL 60611-3008
Phone: (312)503-8649

★952★ Rush University
Rush Medical College
600 S. Paulina St.
Chicago, IL 60612
Phone: (312)942-6913
Fax: (312)942-2828

★953★ Southern Illinois University at
Springfield
School of Medicine
801 N. Rutledge
PO Box 19230
Springfield, IL 62794-9230
Phone: (217)782-3318
Fax: (217)524-0786

★954★ University of Chicago
Pritzker School of Medicine
5841 S. Maryland Ave.
Chicago, IL 60637
Phone: (312)702-1000
Fax: (312)702-1897

★955★ University of Illinois
College of Medicine at Peoria
1 Illini Dr.
PO Box 1649
Peoria, IL 61656
Phone: (309)671-3000

★956★ University of Illinois
College of Medicine at Rockford
1601 Parkview Ave.
Rockford, IL 61107
Phone: (815)395-5600

★957★ University of Illinois
College of Medicine at Urbana-Champaign
190 Medical Sciences Bldg.
506 S. Mathews
Urbana, IL 61801
Phone: (217)333-9285

★958★ University of Illinois at Chicago
College of Medicine
1853 W. Polk St. (M/C 784)
Chicago, IL 60680
Phone: (312)996-3500
Fax: (312)996-9006

Indiana

★959★ Indiana University
School of Medicine
1120 South Dr.
Indianapolis, IN 46202-5114
Phone: (317)274-8157

Iowa

★960★ University of Iowa
College of Medicine
200 Medical Admin. Bldg.
Iowa City, IA 52242-1101
Phone: (319)335-8050
Fax: (319)335-8049

Kansas

★961★ University of Kansas
School of Medicine
3901 Rainbow Blvd.
Kansas City, KS 66160-7300
Phone: (913)588-5200
Fax: (913)588-5259

★962★ University of Kansas
School of Medicine at Wichita
1010 N. Kansas
Wichita, KS 67214
Phone: (316)261-2600

Kentucky

★963★ University of Kentucky
College of Medicine
A.B. Chandler Medical Center
800 Rose St.
Lexington, KY 40536-0084
Phone: (606)323-5000
Fax: (606)323-2039

★964★ University of Louisville
School of Medicine
Health Sciences Center
Louisville, KY 40292
Phone: (502)852-5184
Fax: (502)852-6849

Louisiana

★965★ Louisiana State University
School of Medicine in New Orleans
1542 Tulane Ave.
New Orleans, LA 70112-2822
Phone: (504)568-4007
Fax: (504)568-4008

★966★ Louisiana State University
School of Medicine in Shreveport
PO Box 33932
Shreveport, LA 71130-3932
Phone: (318)675-5000
Fax: (318)675-5244

★967★ Tulane University
School of Medicine
1430 Tulane Ave.
New Orleans, LA 70112
Phone: (504)588-5263
Fax: (504)584-2495

Maryland

★968★ Johns Hopkins University
School of Medicine
720 Rutland Ave.
Baltimore, MD 21205
Phone: (410)955-5000
Fax: (410)955-0497

★969★ Uniformed Services University of
the Health Sciences
F. Edward Hebert School of Medicine
4301 Jones Bridge Rd.
Bethesda, MD 20814-4799
Phone: (301)295-3016
Fax: (301)295-3542

★970★ University of Maryland
School of Medicine
655 W. Baltimore St.
Baltimore, MD 21201
Phone: (410)706-7410
Fax: (410)706-0235

Massachusetts

★971★ Boston University
School of Medicine
80 E. Concord St.
Boston, MA 02118
Phone: (617)638-8000
Fax: (617)638-5258

★972★ Harvard Medical School
25 Shattuck St.
Boston, MA 02115
Phone: (617)432-1000
Fax: (617)432-3907

★973★ Tufts University
School of Medicine
136 Harrison Ave.
Boston, MA 02111
Phone: (617)956-7000
Fax: (617)956-0375

★974★ University of Massachusetts
Medical School
55 Lake Ave. N.
Worcester, MA 01655
Phone: (508)856-0011
Fax: (508)856-8181

Michigan

★975★ Michigan State University
College of Human Medicine
A-110 E. Fee Hall
East Lansing, MI 48824
Phone: (517)353-1730
Fax: (517)355-0342

★976★ University of Michigan
Medical School
Medical Science Bldg. I
1301 Catherine Rd.
Ann Arbor, MI 48109-0624
Phone: (313)763-9600
Fax: (313)763-4936

★977★ Wayne State University
School of Medicine
540 E. Canfield
Detroit, MI 48201
Phone: (313)577-1460
Fax: (313)577-8777

Minnesota

★978★ Mayo Medical School
200 1st St. SW
Rochester, MN 55905
Phone: (507)284-3671
Fax: (507)284-2634

★979★ University of Minnesota
Medical School
420 Delaware St. SE
UMHC Box 293
Minneapolis, MN 55455
Phone: (612)624-1188
Fax: (612)626-6800

★980★ University of Minnesota, Duluth
School of Medicine
10 University Dr.
Duluth, MN 55812
Phone: (218)726-7571
Fax: (218)726-6235

Mississippi

★981★ University of Mississippi
School of Medicine
2500 N. State St.
Jackson, MS 39216
Phone: (601)984-1000
Fax: (601)984-1011

Missouri

★982★ St. Louis University
School of Medicine
1402 S. Grand Blvd.
St. Louis, MO 63104
Phone: (314)577-8200
Fax: (314)577-8214

★983★ University of Missouri—Columbia
School of Medicine
MA204 Medical Sciences Bldg.
1 Hospital Dr.
Columbia, MO 65203
Phone: (314)882-2923
Fax: (314)884-4808

★984★ University of Missouri—Kansas
City
School of Medicine
2411 Holmes St.
Kansas City, MO 64108-2792
Phone: (816)235-1800
Fax: (816)235-5277

★985★ Washington University
School of Medicine
660 S. Euclid Ave.
St. Louis, MO 63110
Phone: (314)362-5000
Fax: (314)362-9862

Nebraska

★986★ Creighton University
School of Medicine
California at 24th St.
Omaha, NE 68178
Phone: (402)280-2900
Fax: (402)280-2599

★987★ University of Nebraska at Omaha
College of Medicine
600 S. 42nd St.
Omaha, NE 68198
Phone: (402)559-4000
Fax: (402)559-4148

Nevada

★988★ University of Nevada, Reno
School of Medicine
332 Savitt Medical Bldg.
Reno, NV 89557-0046
Phone: (702)784-6001
Fax: (702)784-6096

New Hampshire

★989★ Dartmouth College
Medical School
Hanover, NH 03755-3833
Phone: (603)650-1481
Fax: (603)650-1614

New Jersey

★990★ University of Medicine and
Dentistry of New Jersey
New Jersey Medical School
185 S. Orange Ave.
Newark, NJ 07103-2714
Phone: (201)982-4300
Fax: (201)982-7104

★991★ University of Medicine and
Dentistry of New Jersey
Robert Wood Johnson Medical School
675 Hoes Lane
Piscataway, NJ 08854-5635
Phone: (908)235-5600
Fax: (908)235-4006

★992★ University of Medicine and
Dentistry of New Jersey
Robert Wood Johnson Medical School at
Camden
401 Haddon Ave.
Camden, NJ 08103
Phone: (609)757-7877

New Mexico

★993★ University of New Mexico
School of Medicine
Albuquerque, NM 87131
Phone: (505)277-2413
Fax: (505)277-6851

New York

★994★ Columbia University
College of Physicians and Surgeons
630 W. 168th St.
New York, NY 10032
Phone: (212)305-3592
Fax: (212)305-3545

★995★ Cornell University
Medical College
1300 York Ave.
New York, NY 10021
Phone: (212)746-5454
Fax: (212)746-0931

★996★ Mt. Sinai School of Medicine of
City University of New York
1 Gustave L. Levy Pl.
New York, NY 10029-6574
Phone: (212)241-6500
Fax: (212)410-6111

★997★ New York Medical College
Administration Bldg.
Valhalla, NY 10595
Phone: (914)993-4000
Fax: (914)993-4565

★998★ New York University
School of Medicine
550 1st Ave.
New York, NY 10016
Phone: (212)263-7300
Fax: (212)725-2140

★999★ State University of New York at
Buffalo
School of Medicine and Biomedical
Sciences
3435 Main St.
Buffalo, NY 14214
Phone: (716)829-2775
Fax: (716)829-3395

★1000★ State University of New York
Health Science Center at Brooklyn
College of Medicine
Box 97
450 Clarkson Ave.
Brooklyn, NY 11203
Phone: (718)270-1000
Fax: (718)270-4074

★1001★ State University of New York
Health Science Center at Syracuse
College of Medicine
750 E. Adams St.
Syracuse, NY 13210
Phone: (315)464-5540
Fax: (315)464-5564

★1002★ State University of New York at
Stony Brook
School of Medicine
Health Sciences Center
Stony Brook, NY 11794-8430
Phone: (516)444-2080
Fax: (516)444-2202

★1003★ Union University
Albany Medical College
47 New Scotland Ave.
Albany, NY 12208
Phone: (518)262-5582
Fax: (518)262-5029

★1004★ University of Rochester
School of Medicine and Dentistry
601 Elmwood Ave.
Rochester, NY 14642
Phone: (716)275-7181
Fax: (716)256-1131

★1005★ Yeshiva University
Albert Einstein College of Medicine
1300 Morris Park Ave.
Bronx, NY 10461
Phone: (212)430-2000
Fax: (212)430-2488

North Carolina

★ 1006 ★ Duke University
School of Medicine
PO Box 3005
Durham, NC 27710
Phone: (919)684-8111
Fax: (919)684-2593

★ 1007 ★ East Carolina University
School of Medicine
Greenville, NC 27858-4354
Phone: (919)816-2201
Fax: (919)816-3192

★ 1008 ★ University of North Carolina at
Chapel Hill
School of Medicine
Chapel Hill, NC 27599
Phone: (919)966-4161
Fax: (919)966-7564

★ 1009 ★ Wake Forest University
Bowman Gray School of Medicine
Medical Center Blvd.
Winston-Salem, NC 27157-1040
Phone: (910)716-2011
Fax: (910)716-5139

North Dakota

★ 1010 ★ University of North Dakota
School of Medicine
Box 9037
501 N. Columbia Rd.
Grand Forks, ND 58202-9037
Phone: (701)777-2514
Fax: (701)777-3527

Ohio

★ 1011 ★ Case Western Reserve University
School of Medicine
10900 Euclid Ave.
Cleveland, OH 44106-4915
Phone: (216)368-2000
Fax: (216)368-3013

★ 1012 ★ Medical College of Ohio
PO Box 10008
Toledo, OH 43699-0008
Phone: (419)381-4172
Fax: (419)382-1319

★ 1013 ★ Northeastern Ohio Universities
College of Medicine
4209 State Rte. 44
PO Box 95
Rootstown, OH 44272-0095
Phone: (216)325-2511
Fax: (216)325-7943

★ 1014 ★ Ohio State University
College of Medicine
200 Meiling Hall
370 W. 9th Ave.
Columbus, OH 43210
Phone: (614)292-5674
Fax: (614)292-1544

★ 1015 ★ University of Cincinnati
College of Medicine
PO Box 670555
Cincinnati, OH 45267
Phone: (513)558-7391
Fax: (513)558-3512

★ 1016 ★ Wright State University
School of Medicine
PO Box 927
Dayton, OH 45401-0927
Phone: (513)873-3010
Fax: (513)873-3672

Oklahoma

★ 1017 ★ University of Oklahoma
College of Medicine
PO Box 26901
Oklahoma City, OK 73190
Phone: (405)271-2265
Fax: (405)271-3032

★ 1018 ★ University of Oklahoma
Tulsa Medical College
2808 S. Sheridan
Tulsa, OK 74129-1077
Phone: (918)838-4600
Fax: (918)838-4899

Oregon

★ 1019 ★ Oregon Health Sciences
University
School of Medicine
3181 SW Sam Jackson Park Rd.
Portland, OR 97201-3098
Phone: (503)494-8311
Fax: (503)494-3400

Pennsylvania

★ 1020 ★ Medical College of Pennsylvania
and Hahnemann University
School of Medicine
2900 Queen Lane
Philadelphia, PA 19129
Phone: (215)842-6000
Fax: (215)991-8202

★ 1021 ★ Pennsylvania State University
College of Medicine
500 University Dr.
PO Box 850
Hershey, PA 17033
Phone: (717)531-8521
Fax: (717)531-5351

★ 1022 ★ Temple University
School of Medicine
3400 N. Broad St.
Philadelphia, PA 19140
Phone: (215)204-7000
Fax: (215)707-2940

★ 1023 ★ Thomas Jefferson University
Jefferson Medical College
1025 Walnut St.
Philadelphia, PA 19107-5083
Phone: (215)955-6000
Fax: (215)923-6939

★ 1024 ★ University of Pennsylvania
School of Medicine
Edward J. Stemler Hall, Ste. 100
3450 Hamilton Walk
Philadelphia, PA 19104-6087
Phone: (215)898-8034
Fax: (215)898-5607

★ 1025 ★ University of Pittsburgh
School of Medicine
Alan Magee Scaife Hall of the Health
  Professions
Pittsburgh, PA 15261
Phone: (412)648-9891
Fax: (412)648-1236

Puerto Rico

★ 1026 ★ Ponce School of Medicine
PO Box 7004
Ponce, PR 00732
Phone: (809)844-3710
Fax: (809)840-9756

★ 1027 ★ Universidad Central Del Caribe
School of Medicine
PO Box 60-327
Bayamon, PR 00960-6032
Phone: (809)798-3001
Fax: (809)798-6836

★ 1028 ★ University of Puerto Rico
School of Medicine
Medical Sciences Campus
PO Box 365067
San Juan, PR 00936-5067
Phone: (809)758-2525
Fax: (809)751-6389

Rhode Island

★ 1029 ★ Brown University
School of Medicine
97 Waterman St.
Providence, RI 02912
Phone: (401)863-3330
Fax: (401)863-3431

South Carolina

★ 1030 ★ Medical University of South
Carolina
College of Medicine
171 Ashley Ave.
Charleston, SC 29425
Phone: (803)792-2300
Fax: (803)792-2967

★ 1031 ★ University of South Carolina
School of Medicine
Columbia, SC 29208
Phone: (803)733-3200
Fax: (803)733-3335

South Dakota

★ 1032 ★ **University of South Dakota**
School of Medicine
1400 W. 22nd
Sioux Falls, SD 57105-1570
Phone: (605)357-1300
Fax: (605)357-1311

Tennessee

★ 1033 ★ **East Tennessee State University**
James H. Quillen College of Medicine
PO Box 70694
Johnson City, TN 37614
Phone: (615)929-4112
Fax: (615)929-6433

★ 1034 ★ **Meharry Medical College**
School of Medicine
1005 Dr. D.B. Todd, Jr. Blvd.
Nashville, TN 37208
Phone: (615)327-6337
Fax: (615)327-6568

★ 1035 ★ **University of Tennessee,**
Memphis
College of Medicine
800 Madison Ave.
Memphis, TN 38163
Phone: (901)448-5529
Fax: (901)448-7683

★ 1036 ★ **Vanderbilt University**
School of Medicine
21st Ave. S. at Garland Ave.
Nashville, TN 37232
Phone: (615)322-2145
Fax: (615)343-7286

Texas

★ 1037 ★ **Baylor College of Medicine**
1 Baylor Plaza
Houston, TX 77030
Phone: (713)798-4951
Fax: (713)790-0055

★ 1038 ★ **Texas A&M University**
College of Medicine
147 Joe H. Reynolds Medical Bldg.
College Station, TX 77843-1114
Phone: (409)845-7743
Fax: (409)847-8663

★ 1039 ★ **Texas Tech University**
Health Sciences Center
School of Medicine
3601 4th St.
Lubbock, TX 79430
Phone: (806)743-1000
Fax: (806)743-3021

★ 1040 ★ **Texas Tech University**
Health Sciences Center at Amarillo
School of Medicine
1400 Wallace Blvd.
Amarillo, TX 79106
Phone: (806)354-5401

★ 1041 ★ **Texas Tech University**
Health Sciences Center at El Paso
School of Medicine
4800 Alberta Ave.
El Paso, TX 79905
Phone: (915)545-6510

★ 1042 ★ **Texas Tech University**
Health Sciences Center at Odessa
School of Medicine
800 W. 4th St.
Odessa, TX 79763
Phone: (915)335-5113

★ 1043 ★ **University of Texas Health**
Science Center at Houston
School of Medicine
6431 Fannin
Houston, TX 77030
Phone: (713)792-5000
Fax: (713)796-8570

★ 1044 ★ **University of Texas Health**
Science Center at San Antonio
School of Medicine
7703 Floyd Curl Dr.
San Antonio, TX 78284-7790
Phone: (210)567-4420
Fax: (210)567-6962

★ 1045 ★ **University of Texas Medical**
Branch at Galveston
School of Medicine
301 University Blvd.
Galveston, TX 77555
Phone: (409)772-1011
Fax: (409)772-9598

★ 1046 ★ **University of Texas**
Southwestern Medical Center at Dallas
Southwestern Medical School
5323 Harry Hines Blvd.
Dallas, TX 75235
Phone: (214)648-3111
Fax: (214)648-8690

Utah

★ 1047 ★ **University of Utah**
School of Medicine
50 N. Medical Dr.
Salt Lake City, UT 84132
Phone: (801)581-7201
Fax: (801)585-3300

Vermont

★ 1048 ★ **University of Vermont**
College of Medicine
Burlington, VT 05405
Phone: (802)656-2150
Fax: (802)656-8584

Virginia

★ 1049 ★ **Medical College of Hampton**
Roads
Eastern Virginia Medical School
PO Box 1980
Norfolk, VA 23501
Phone: (804)446-5600
Fax: (804)640-0311

★ 1050 ★ **University of Virginia**
School of Medicine
Box 395
Medical Center, McKim Hall
Charlottesville, VA 22908
Phone: (804)924-0211
Fax: (804)982-0874

★ 1051 ★ **Virginia Commonwealth**
University
Medical College of Virginia
School of Medicine
Box 565, MCV Sta.
Richmond, VA 23298
Phone: (804)786-9793
Fax: (804)371-7628

Washington

★ 1052 ★ **University of Washington**
School of Medicine
Seattle, WA 98195
Phone: (206)543-1060
Fax: (206)543-3639

West Virginia

★ 1053 ★ **Marshall University**
School of Medicine
1801 6th Ave.
Huntington, WV 25755-9000
Phone: (304)696-7000
Fax: (304)696-7243

★ 1054 ★ **West Virginia University**
School of Medicine
Morgantown, WV 26506
Phone: (304)293-4511
Fax: (304)293-4973

Wisconsin

★ 1055 ★ **Medical College of Wisconsin**
8701 Watertown Plank Rd.
Milwaukee, WI 53226
Phone: (414)456-8296
Fax: (414)257-0449

★ 1056 ★ **University of Wisconsin—**
Madison
Medical School
1300 University Ave.
Madison, WI 53706
Phone: (608)263-4900
Fax: (608)262-2327

Physician Assistant

*The physician assistant educational programs
listed in this section are accredited by the Commission on Accreditation of Allied Health Education Programs, 515 N. State St., Ste. 7530, Chicago, IL 60610, (312)464-4623. For information
on the profession, contact the Association of
Physician Assistant Programs, 950 N. Washington St., Alexandria, VA 22314, (703) 548-5538,
or the American Academy of Physician Assistants, 950 N. Washington St., Alexandria, VA
22314 (703) 836-2272.*

Alabama

★ 1057 ★ University of Alabama at
 Birmingham
School of Health Related Professions
Surgeon's Assistant Program
222 Sharp Bldg.
1714 9th Ave. S.
Birmingham, AL 35294-1270
Phone: (205)934-4407

California

★ 1058 ★ Charles R. Drew University of
 Medicine and Science
College of Allied Health
Physician Assistant Program
1621 E. 120th St.
Los Angeles, CA 90059
Phone: (213)563-5879

★ 1059 ★ College of Osteopathic Medicine
 of the Pacific
Physician Assistant Program
College Plaza
Pomona, CA 91766-1889
Phone: (909)469-5390

★ 1060 ★ Naval School of Health Sciences
Physician Assistant Program
San Diego, CA 92134-5291
Phone: (619)532-7938

★ 1061 ★ Naval School of Health Sciences
Physician Assistant Program
San Diego, CA 92134-6000
Phone: (619)532-7938

★ 1062 ★ Stanford University Medical
 Center / Foothill Community College
School of Medicine
Primary Care Associate Program
703 Welch Rd., Ste. F-1
Palo Alto, CA 94304-1760
Phone: (415)723-7043

★ 1063 ★ University of California, Davis
School of Medicine
Department of Family Practice
Physician Assistant Program
2270 Stockton Blvd.
Sacramento, CA 95817
Phone: (916)734-3550

★ 1064 ★ University of Southern California
School of Medicine
Primary Care Physician Assistant Program
1975 Zonal Ave., KAM B-29
Los Angeles, CA 90033
Phone: (213)342-1328

Colorado

★ 1065 ★ University of Colorado—Denver
School of Medicine
Child Health Associate Program
4200 E. 9th Ave.
PO Box C-219
Denver, CO 80262
Phone: (303)270-7963

Connecticut

★ 1066 ★ Yale University
School of Medicine
Physician Associate Program
47 College St., Ste. 220
New Haven, CT 06510
Phone: (203)785-4252

District of Columbia

★ 1067 ★ George Washington University
School of Medicine and Health Sciences
Physician Assistant Program
Himmelfarb 307
2300 Eye St. NW
Washington, DC 20037
Phone: (202)994-4034

★ 1068 ★ Howard University
College of Allied Health Sciences
Physician Assistant Program
2041 Georgia Ave. NW
Washington, DC 20001
Phone: (202)806-7536

Florida

★ 1069 ★ Nova Southeastern University
Physician Assistant Program
1750 NE 167th St.
North Miami Beach, FL 33162-3017
Phone: (305)949-4000

★ 1070 ★ University of Florida
College of Medicine
Physician Assistant Program
Box 100176
J. Hillis Miller Health Center
Gainesville, FL 32610-0176
Phone: (904)395-7955

Georgia

★ 1071 ★ Emory University
School of Medicine
Physician Assistant Program
1462 Clifton Rd. NE, Ste. 280
Atlanta, GA 30322
Phone: (404)727-7825

★ 1072 ★ Medical College of Georgia
Physician Assistant Program
AE 1032
Augusta, GA 30912
Phone: (706)721-3246

Illinois

★ 1073 ★ Finch University of Health
 Sciences / Chicago Medical School
Physician Assistant Program
3333 Green Bay Rd.
North Chicago, IL 60064-3095
Phone: (708)578-3312

★ 1074 ★ Malcolm X College / Cook
 County Hospital
Physician Assistant Program
CCSN 801
1900 W. Polk St.
Chicago, IL 60612
Phone: (312)633-8030

★ 1075 ★ Midwestern University
Physician Assistant Program
555 31st St.
Downers Grove, IL 60515
Phone: (708)515-6034

Iowa

★ 1076 ★ University of Iowa
College of Medicine
Physician Assistant Program
2333 Steindler Bldg.
Iowa City, IA 52242
Phone: (319)335-8922

★ 1077 ★ University of Osteopathic
 Medicine and Health Sciences
Physician Assistant Program
3200 Grand Ave.
Des Moines, IA 50312
Phone: (515)271-1415

Kansas

★ 1078 ★ Wichita State University
College of Health Professions
Physician Assistant Program
Campus Box 43
Wichita, KS 67208
Phone: (316)689-3011

Kentucky

★ 1079 ★ University of Kentucky
College of Medicine
Physician Assistant Program
Albert B. Chandler Medical Center, Annex 2,
 Rm. 113
Lexington, KY 40536-0080
Phone: (606)233-5743

Maryland

★ 1080 ★ Essex Community College
Physician Assistant Program
7201 Rossville Blvd.
Baltimore, MD 21237
Phone: (410)780-6579

Massachusetts

★ 1081 ★ Northeastern University
Physician Assistant Program
202 Robinson Hall
Boston, MA 02115
Phone: (617)337-3195

Michigan

★ 1082 ★ **University of Detroit Mercy**
Physician Assistant Program
8200 W. Outer Dr.
Detroit, MI 48219
Phone: (313)993-6177

★ 1083 ★ **Western Michigan University**
Physician Assistant Program
Kalamazoo, MI 49008-5138
Phone: (616)387-5314

Missouri

★ 1084 ★ **St. Louis University**
School of Allied Health Professions
Physician Assistant Program
1504 S. Grand Blvd.
St. Louis, MO 63104
Phone: (314)577-8521

Nebraska

★ 1085 ★ **University of Nebraska at Omaha**
College of Medicine
Physician Assistant Program
600 S. 42nd St.
Omaha, NE 68198-4300
Phone: (402)559-5266

New Jersey

★ 1086 ★ **University of Medicine and**
Dentistry of New Jersey / Rutgers
University
Robert Wood Johnson Medical School
Physician Assistant Program
675 Hoes Lane
Piscataway, NJ 08854-5635
Phone: (908)235-4444

New York

★ 1087 ★ **Albany Medical College / Hudson**
Valley Community College
Physician Assistant Program
47 New Scotland Ave.
Albany, NY 12208
Phone: (518)262-5251

★ 1088 ★ **Bayley Seton Hospital**
Physician Assistant Program
75 Vanderbilt Ave.
Staten Island, NY 10304
Phone: (718)390-5570

★ 1089 ★ **Cornell University**
Medical College
Surgeon's Assistant Program
1300 York Ave.
New York, NY 10021
Phone: (212)746-5133

★ 1090 ★ **D'Youville College**
Physician Assistant Program
320 Porter Ave.
Buffalo, NY 14201
Phone: (716)881-7713

★ 1091 ★ **Long Island University /**
Brooklyn Hospital Center
Physician Assistant Program
121 De Kalb Ave.
Brooklyn, NY 11201
Phone: (718)403-8144

★ 1092 ★ **Mt. Sinai School of Medicine of**
City University of New York
Physician Assistant Program at Harlem
Hospital Center
506 Lenox Ave., WP-619
New York, NY 10037
Phone: (212)939-2525

★ 1093 ★ **Rochester Institute of**
Technology
Department of Allied Health
Physician Assistant Program
85 Lomb Memorial Dr.
Rochester, NY 14623-5603
Phone: (716)475-2978

★ 1094 ★ **State University of New York**
Health Science Center at Brooklyn
Physician Assistant Program
450 Clarkson Ave.
Brooklyn, NY 11203
Phone: (718)270-2324

★ 1095 ★ **State University of New York at**
Stony Brook
School of Health Technology and
Management
Physician Assistant Program
L2-052 Health Sciences Center
Stony Brook, NY 11794-8202
Phone: (516)444-3190

★ 1096 ★ **Touro College**
Barry Z. Levine School of Health Sciences
Physician Assistant Program
135 Carman Rd., Bldg. 14
Dix Hills, NY 11746
Phone: (516)673-3200

North Carolina

★ 1097 ★ **Duke University**
School of Medicine
Physician Assistant Program
Box CFM-2914
Durham, NC 27710
Phone: (919)286-8234

★ 1098 ★ **Wake Forest University**
Bowman Gray School of Medicine
Physician Assistant Program
1990 Beach St.
Winston-Salem, NC 27103-2696
Phone: (910)716-4356

North Dakota

★ 1099 ★ **University of North Dakota**
Department of Community Medicine and
Rural Health
Physician Assistant Program
501 N. Columbia Rd.
Grand Forks, ND 58203
Phone: (701)777-2344

Ohio

★ 1100 ★ **Cuyahoga Community College**
Physician Assistant and Surgeon's
Assistant Programs
11000 Pleasant Valley Rd.
Parma, OH 44130
Phone: (216)987-5363

★ 1101 ★ **Kettering College of Medical Arts**
Physician Assistant Program
3737 Southern Blvd.
Kettering, OH 45429
Phone: (513)296-7238

Oklahoma

★ 1102 ★ **University of Oklahoma**
Physician Associate Program
Health Sciences Center
PO Box 26901
Oklahoma City, OK 73190
Phone: (405)271-2047

Pennsylvania

★ 1103 ★ **Duquesne University**
John G. Rangos Sr. School of Health
Sciences
Physician Assistant Program
123 Health Sciences Bldg.
Pittsburgh, PA 15282
Phone: (412)396-5000

★ 1104 ★ **Gannon University**
Physician Assistant Program
University Sq.
Erie, PA 16541
Phone: (814)871-7606

★ 1105 ★ **King's College**
Physician Assistant Program
133 N. River St.
Wilkes Barre, PA 18711
Phone: (717)826-5853

★ 1106 ★ **Medical College of Pennsylvania**
and Hahnemann University
School of Health Sciences and Humanities
Physician Assistant Program
Broad and Vine Sts., MS504
Philadelphia, PA 19102
Phone: (215)762-7135

★ 1107 ★ **St. Francis College**
Physician Assistant Program
Loretto, PA 15940
Phone: (814)472-3131

South Dakota

★ 1108 ★ **University of South Dakota**
School of Medicine
Physician Assistant Program
414 E. Clark St.
Vermillion, SD 57069-2390
Phone: (605)677-5128

Tennessee

★ 1109 ★ Trevecca Nazarene College
Physician Assistant Program
333 Murfreesboro Rd.
Nashville, TN 37210-2877
Phone: (615)248-1225

Texas

★ 1110 ★ Baylor College of Medicine
Department of Community Medicine
Physician Assistant Program
1 Baylor Plaza, Rm. 633E
Houston, TX 77030
Phone: (713)798-4619

★ 1111 ★ U.S. Air Force
Physician Assistant Program
381 MTS/CSP
917 Missile Rd.
Sheppard AFB, TX 76311-2246
Phone: (817)676-6575

★ 1112 ★ U.S. Army
Physician Assistant Program
HSHA-MM
Academy of Health Sciences
Ft. Sam Houston, TX 78234
Phone: (210)221-8004

★ 1113 ★ University of Texas Medical
  Branch at Galveston
School of Allied Health Sciences
Physician Assistant Program
301 University Blvd.
Galveston, TX 77550-1028
Phone: (409)772-3046

★ 1114 ★ University of Texas
  Southwestern Medical Center at Dallas
Physician Assistant Program
6011 Harry Hines Blvd.
Dallas, TX 75235-9090
Phone: (214)648-1700

Utah

★ 1115 ★ University of Utah
School of Medicine
Physician Assistant Program
50 N. Medical Dr., Bldg. 528
Salt Lake City, UT 84132
Phone: (801)581-7764

Washington

★ 1116 ★ University of Washington
School of Public Health and Community
  Medicine
Physician Assistant Program
4245 Roosevelt Way NE
Seattle, WA 98105
Phone: (206)548-2600

West Virginia

★ 1117 ★ Alderson-Broaddus College
Physician Assistant Program
PO Box 578
Philippi, WV 26416
Phone: (304)457-1700

Wisconsin

★ 1118 ★ University of Wisconsin—
  Madison
Department of Family Medicine and
  Practice
Physician Assistant Program
1300 University Ave., Rm. 1050 MSC
Madison, WI 53706
Phone: (608)263-5620

National & International Organizations

★ 1119 ★ Accreditation Association for
  Ambulatory Health Care (AAAHC)
9933 Lawler Ave.
Skokie, IL 60077-3708
Phone: (708)676-9610
Fax: (708)676-9628
Christopher Damon, Exec.Dir.

Founded: 1979. **Members:** 13. **Description:** Operates a voluntary, peer-based accreditation and consulting program for ambulatory health care organizations as a means of assisting them in efficiently providing a high level of care for patients. Distributes free lists of accredited organizations. **Publications:** *Accreditation Handbook for Ambulatory Health Care*, biennial. Standards for accreditation of ambulatory health care centers. Includes subject index. *Price:* $50/copy prepaid. Also publishes related survey materials.

★ 1120 ★ Accreditation Council for
  Continuing Medical Education (ACCME)
515 N. State St., Ste. 7340
Chicago, IL 60610
Phone: (312)464-2500
Fax: (312)464-2586
John J. Fauser, Ph.D., Interim Sec.

Founded: 1981. **Description:** Acts as an accrediting agency for sponsors of continuing medical education for physicians. Sponsoring participants are: American Board of Medical Specialties; American Hospital Association; American Medical Association; Association of American Medical Colleges; Association for Hospital Medical Education; Council of Medical Specialty Societies; Federation of State Medical Boards of the United States. **Formerly:** Liaison Committee on Continuing Medical Education.

★ 1121 ★ Accreditation Council for
  Graduate Medical Education (ACGME)
515 N. State St., Ste. 2000
Chicago, IL 60610
Phone: (312)464-4920
Fax: (312)464-4098
John C. Geinapp, Exec. Dir.

Founded: 1974. **Description:** Representatives from the American Board of Medical Specialties, American Hospital Association, American Medical Association, Association of American Medical Colleges, and Council of Medical Specialty Societies. Accredits postgraduate medical education programs; recommends and conducts studies aimed at improving programs in postgraduate medical education; reviews and approves proposals for new programs in graduate medical education; provides information to the public and government relating to the evaluation and accreditation of graduate medical education programs. Maintains 25 residency review committees including: Allergy and Immunology; Anesthesiology; Colon and Rectal Surgery; Dermatology. **Publications:** *ACGME Bulletin*, 3-4/year. Includes meeting dates. • *ACGME Report.* • *Manual of Policies and Procedures for Graduate Medical Education Review Committees.* **Formerly:** (1981) Liaison Committee on Graduate Medical Education.

★ 1122 ★ Accreditation Review Committee
  on Education for Physician Assistants
  (ARC-PA)
1000 N. Oak Ave.
Marshfield, WI 54449-5788
Phone: (715)389-3785
Fax: (715)389-3131
John E. McCarty, Exec.Dir.

Founded: 1971. **Members:** 13. **Description:** Serves as an accrediting review body for physician assistant education nationwide. Makes recommendations to Commission on Accreditation of Allied Health Education Programs. **Formerly:** (1972) Joint Review Committee on Educational Programs for Physician's Assistants; (1987) Joint Review on Educational Programs for Physician Assistants; (1989) Accreditation Committee on Education for Physicians Assistants.

★ 1123 ★ Ad Hoc Group for Medical
  Research Funding (AHGMRF)
c/o Association of American Medical Colleges
2450 N St. NW
Washington, DC 20037-1126
Phone: (202)828-0525
Fax: (202)828-1125
Richard M. Knapp, Ph.D., Exec.Officer

Founded: 1982. **Members:** 180. **Description:** Organizations engaged in or supporting biomedical and behavioral research. Goals are to assess federal funding for biomedical and behavioral research and to develop alternatives to proposed budgets. Advocates appropriate funding for the National Institutes of Health. **Publications:** Annual Report. *Price:* Free. • Brochure, annual.

★ 1124 ★ **Aesculapius International Medicine (AIM)**
c/o John Fitzpatrick
731 8th St. SE
Washington, DC 20003
Phone: (202)547-3800
Fax: (202)546-4784
John Fitzpatrick, Contact

Founded: 1978. **Description:** Facilitates the involvement of U.S. health professionals in international health projects, including the operation of such projects when the usual response mechanisms fail. Works in conjunction with local private organizations. Upholds no political or religious ideology beyond a strong concern for human rights. Current projects include health projects in Guatemala and El Salvador. Group is named for Aesculapius, the ancient Greek god of healing. Maintains speakers' bureau. **Also Known As:** Aesculapius.

★ 1125 ★ **African Medical and Research Foundation (AMREF)**
PO Box 2773
Upanga Rd.
Dar es Salaam, United Republic of Tanzania
Phone: 51 31981
Fax: 51 46440
John Male-Mukasa, Country Dir.

Founded: 1957. **Description:** Works to develop health programs among communities in Africa. Conducts research; compiles and disseminates information on health issues. Networks with other organizatins with similar objectives, providing a forum for information exchange and cooperation in projects and research.

★ 1126 ★ **African Medical and Research Foundation**
(Stichting AMREF - Nederland)
Jan van Brakelplantsoen 5
NL-2253 TD Voorschoten, Netherlands
Phone: 71 762480
Fax: 71 763777
Dr. J.T. Braaksma, Chm.

Founded: 1962. **Languages:** English. **Description:** Coordinates activities of the African Medical and Research Foundation in the Netherlands. Works to improve health and living standards among east Africans. **Publications:** Newsletter, quarterly.

★ 1127 ★ **African Medical and Research Foundation (AMREF - Sw)**
Jakobsbergsgatan 2
S-103 75 Stockholm, Sweden
Phone: 8 7885001
Fax: 8 7885010
Vera Axson Johnson, Chairman

Description: Aims to improve the health of people in eastern Africa. Seeks to identify health needs and develop, implement, and evaluate methods and programmes to meet those needs through service, training and research. Programmes include: primary health care; training of community health workers; training of rural health staff through continuing education, teacher training, and correspondence courses; development, printing, and distribution of training manuals, medical journals, and health education materials; application of behavioral and social sciences to health improvement; airborne support for remote health facilities, including surgical, medical, and public health services; ground mobile health services for nomadic pastoralists; medical research into the control of hydatid disease, malaria, and sleeping sickness.

★ 1128 ★ **African Medical and Research Foundation (AMREF - It)**
(Fondzione Africana per la Medicina e la Ricerca)
P.za. Hartiri di Belfiore 4
I-00195 Rome, Italy
Phone: 6 3202222
Fax: 6 3202227
Thomas Simmons, Exec.Dir.

Founded: 1988. **Members:** 6,000. **Languages:** Italian. **Description:** Provides health care services to people in eastern Africa. Identifies health needs and evaluates and implements methods and programs to meet those needs. Maintains projects which emphasize affordable health care for people in underdeveloped, rural areas. Operates mobile health service facilities, airborn support for health centers in remote areas, and radio communication services with over 100 two-way radio stations. Conducts training programs for rural health care workers and research into the control of hydatid disease, malaria, and sleeping sickness. Applies knowledge from the behavioral and social sciences to health care improvement initiatives. Writes articles and information for training manuals, health education materials, and medical journals. Disseminates information. Offers consultancy services.

★ 1129 ★ **African Medical and Research Foundation (AMREF - Ge)**
(Gesellschaft fur Medizin und Forschung in Afrika)
Maurkircherstr. 155
81925 Munich, Germany
Phone: 89 981129
Fax: 89 981189
Leonore Semler, Chm.

Founded: 1957. **Languages:** English, German. **Description:** Works towards improving the health of those residing in East Africa, identifying health needs and striving to meets those needs through evaluation and implementation of methods and programs; aims to provide low-cost health care for people living in rural areas. Operates health care and health care training facilities. Provides medical and surgical supplies to remote health care facilities through air and ground transport, utilizing medical radio communication with over 100 two-way stations. Disseminates information, promoting health care awareness. Conducts medical research into the controlling hydatid disease, malaria, and sleeping sickness. Maintains a behavioral scientific view to health improvement. Offers consultancy services. Receives funding from government and nongovernment aid agencies and private donors. **Publications:** Afya. • Cobasheca. • Defender.

★ 1130 ★ **African Medical and Research Foundation (AMREF)**
PO Box 30125
Nairobi, Kenya
Phone: 2 501301
Fax: 2 506112
Dr. Michael S. Gerber, Dir.Gen.

Founded: 1957. **National Groups:** 4. **Languages:** English. **Description:** Purpose is to improve the health of people living in 5 east African countries. Focuses efforts on developing low-cost healthcare for people in rural areas. Program includes: training of community health workers; planning and evaluation of health projects; consulting services; primary healthcare education; operation of a medical radio communication network within the region; ground mobile health services for nomadic and pastoral peoples; the Flying Doctor Service (funded by the Flying Doctors' Society of Africa), which provides airborne support for remote medical, surgical, and public health facilities. Conducts medical research, particularly into the control of malaria, sleeping sickness, and hydatid disease; applies behavioral and social sciences in health improvement. Offers computerized services. **Publications:** Afya, quarterly. • AMREF-in-Action, annual. • AMREF News, quarterly. • Cobasheca, quarterly. • Defender, quarterly. • Reports. • Research Papers, periodic. • Training Manuals, periodic. **Formerly:** Flying Doctors Service.

★ 1131 ★ **African Medical and Research Foundation, U.S.A. (AMREF)**
19 W. 44th St., Ste. 1707-8
New York, NY 10036
Phone: (212)986-1835
Fax: (212)599-5064
Lewis B. Heyman, Contact

Founded: 1957. **Regional Groups:** 9. **Description:** U.S. branch of the African Medical and Research Foundation (see separate entry, International Organizations). Voluntary organization providing medical services to aid and augment health programs in developing nations and in rural areas of East Africa. Attempts to reach isolated peoples and outlying medical facilities through a network of 100 two-way radios, clinic-equipped mobile units, and a ''Flying Doctor Service.'' Undertakes research programs in the field of medicine and general health surveys. Engages in national surveys. Designs and implements primary health care projects. Provides health education courses through its training center to train health educators and is implementing a program of continuing education for health workers. **Publications:** AFYA, bimonthly. Journal. • Defender: Health Journal for Africa, bimonthly. Journal. • Rural Health Series, periodic. **Formerly:** African Research Foundation; (1973) African Medical and Research Foundation; (1981) International Medical and Research Foundation.

★1132★ Aga Khan Health Service Pakistan (AKHSP)
516 Gold St.
Garden East
Karachi 74550, Pakistan
Phone: 21 7216903
Fax: 21 7225850
Noor Mohammad Bhamani

Founded: 1924. **Languages:** English. **Description:** Medical professionals and individuals in Pakistan. Promotes preventive and rehabilitative health care for all Pakistani citizens. Provides diagnostic services; organizes polio treatment programs. Operates day care centers and child welfare clinics. Maintains large volunteer staff. **Publications:** *Handbook for Lady Health Visitors and Midwives.* Also publishes flip charts and booklets on health education; distributes posters and pamphlets. **Formerly:** (1986) His Royal Highness Prince Aga Khan Cetral Health Board for Pakistan.

★1133★ Alpha Epsilon Delta
c/o Dr. Thomas Pearce
University of Virginia
Garrett Hall of Medicine
Charlottesville, VA 22904
Phone: (804)924-3601
Dr. Thomas Pearce, Pres.

Founded: 1926. **Members:** 88,600. **Regional Groups:** 5. **Description:** Honor society of men and women in the field of premedical study. **Publications:** Newsletter, bimonthly. • *The Scalpel*, semiannual.

★1134★ Alpha Omega Alpha Honor Medical Society
525 Middlefield Rd., Ste. 130
Menlo Park, CA 94025
Phone: (415)329-0291
Fax: (415)329-1618
Robert J. Glaser, M.D., Exec.Sec.

Founded: 1902. **Members:** 72,000. **Regional Groups:** 123. **Description:** Honor society for men and women studying medicine at graduate and postgraduate levels. Sponsors "Leaders in American Medicine" videotape series; underwrites visiting professorships. **Publications:** *The Pharos*, quarterly. Journal. Contains nontechnical articles of medical interest. **Formerly:** Alpha Omega Alpha.

★1135★ AMER Medical Division (AMER) American Near East Refuge Aid
1522 K St. NW, Ste. 202
Washington, DC 20005
Phone: (202)347-2558
Fax: (202)682-1637
Nina Dodge, Dir.

Founded: 1948. **Description:** Has operated since 1971 as a division of American Near East Refugee Aid . Solicits and ships medical supplies and pharmaceuticals for use by Palestinians, Lebanese and Jordanians in the Middle East. **Formerly:** (1963) American Middle East Relief; (1978) American Middle East Rehabilitation.

★1136★ American Academy of Family Physicians (AAFP)
8880 Ward Pky.
Kansas City, MO 64114
Phone: (816)333-9700
Free: 800-274-2237
Fax: (816)822-0580
Robert Graham, M.D., Exec.VP

Founded: 1947. **Members:** 79,000. **State Groups:** 55. **Local Groups:** 200. **Description:** Professional society of family physicians who provide continuing comprehensive care to patients. Maintains placement services. **Publications:** *AAFP Reporter*, monthly. Newsletter. Covers socioeconomic issues and legislative news affecting medicine; includes member news. Available to selected media. • *American Academy of Family Physicians*, annual. Membership Directory. • *American Family Physician*, 16/year. Journal. Includes book reviews, newsletter, calendar of events, and therapeutic, product, and subject indexes. *Price:* Free to qualified recipients; $50/year for nonmembers. • Annual Report. • *Family Practice Management*, 10/year. Covers practice management and socioeconomic issues. **Formerly:** (1971) American Academy of General Practice.

★1137★ American Academy of Physician Assistants (AAPA)
950 N. Washington St.
Alexandria, VA 22314
Phone: (703)836-2272
Fax: (703)684-1924
Stephen C. Crane, Exec.VP

Founded: 1968. **Members:** 18,500. **Local Groups:** 59. **Description:** Physician assistants who have graduated from an American Medical Association accredited program and/or are certified by the National Commission on Certification of Physician Assistants; individuals who are enrolled in an accredited PA educational program. Purposes are to: educate the public about the physician assistant profession; represent physician assistants' interests before Congress, government agencies, and health-related organizations; assure the competence of physician assistants through development of educational curricula and accreditation programs; provide services for members. Organizes annual National PA Day. Develops research and education programs; compiles statistics. **Publications:** *AAPA Bulletin*, monthly. Bulletin. • *AAPA News*, monthly. Newsletter. Includes academy news and member profiles. *Price:* Included in membership dues; $75/year for nonmembers. • *Career Magazine*, monthly. Magazine. Provides nationwide listing of employment opportunities for physician assistants. *Price:* Included in membership. • *Journal of the American Academy of Physician Assistants*, 11/year. Journal. Covers clinical and scholarly research. Includes book reviews. *Price:* Included in membership dues; $32/year for nonmembers; $45/year for institutions. • *Legislative Watch*, monthly. • Membership Directory, annual.

★1138★ American Alliance for Health, Physical Education, Recreation and Dance (AAHPERD)
1900 Association Dr.
Reston, VA 22091
Phone: (703)476-3400
Fax: (703)476-9527
A. Gilson Brown, Exec.VP

Founded: 1885. **Members:** 42,000. **Regional Groups:** 6. **State Groups:** 54. **Description:** Students and educators in physical education, dance, health, athletics, safety education, recreation, and outdoor education. Purpose is to improve its fields of education at all levels through such services as consultation, periodicals and special publications, leadership development, determination of standards, and research. Operates Information and Resource Utilization Center devoted to physical education and recreation for the handicapped and programs for senior citizens. Sponsors placement service. **Publications:** *AAHPERD Update*, bimonthly. Newsletter. *Price:* Included in membership dues; $40/year for institutions. • *Health Education*, bimonthly. Journal. For health educators. Includes advertisers' index and book reviews. *Price:* Included in membership dues; $50/year for institutions. • *Journal of Physical Education Recreation and Dance*, 9/year. Journal. • *Leisure Today*, semiannual. • *News Kit on Programs for the Aging*, semiannual. • *Research Quarterly*. • *Strategies*, bimonthly. *Price:* $10. Also publishes manuals and handbooks. **Formerly:** (1903) American Association for Advancement of Physical Education; (1938) American Physical Education Association; (1974) American Association for Health, Physical Education and Recreation; (1979) American Alliance for Health, Physical Education and Recreation.

★1139★ American Association of Anatomists (AAA)
c/o Dr. Robert D. Yates
Tulane Med. Center
1430 Tulane Ave.
New Orleans, LA 70112
Phone: (504)584-2727
Fax: (504)584-1687
Dr. Robert D. Yates, Sec.-Treas.

Founded: 1888. **Members:** 2,500. **Description:** Professional society of anatomists and scientists in related fields. **Publications:** *Anatomical News*, quarterly. Includes list of employment opportunities. *Price:* Included in membership dues. • *Anatomical Record*, monthly. • *Developmental Dynamics*, monthly. • *Directory, Departments of Anatomy, U.S. and Canada*, triennial. Directory.

★1140★ American Association for the History of Medicine (AAHM)
Boston University School of Medicine
80 E. Concord St.
Boston, MA 02118-2394
Phone: (617)638-4328
Fax: (617)638-4329
J. Worth Estes, M.D., Sec.-Treas.

Founded: 1925. **Members:** 1,400. **Local Groups:** 35. **Description:** Physicians and others with professional or vocational interest in the history of medicine. Promotes research, study, interest, and writing in history of medicine, including public health, dentistry, pharmacy, nursing, medical social work, and allied sciences and professions. **Publications:** *Bulletin of the History of Medicine*, quarterly. Bulletin. • Directory, biennial. Provides information on membership activities. • Newsletter, 3/year. • *Research-in-Progress*, biennial.

★ 1141 ★ **American Association of Medical Assistants (AAMA)**
20 N. Wacker Dr., Ste. 1575
Chicago, IL 60606-2903
Phone: (312)899-1500
Fax: (312)899-1259
Donald A. Balasa, Exec.Dir.

Founded: 1956. **Members:** 14,000. **State Groups:** 47. **Local Groups:** 500. **Description:** Assistants, receptionists, secretaries, bookkeepers, nurses, and laboratory personnel employed in the offices of physicians and other medical facilities. Activities include a certification program consisting of study and an examination, passage of which entitles the individual to a certificate as a Certified Medical Assistant. Conducts accreditation of one- and two-year programs in medical assisting in conjunction with the Committee on Allied Health Education and Accreditation of the American Medical Association (see separate entries). Provides assistance and information to institutions of higher learning desirous of initiating courses for medical assistants. Offers continuing education to assistants who cannot return to school and home study courses. Awards continuing education units for selected educational programs. **Publications:** *A User's Guide to the Resource Based Relative Value Scale. Price:* $15 for members; $25 for nonmembers. • *Accounts Receivable and Collection for the Medical Practice. Price:* $20 for members; $30 for nonmembers. • *AIDS Concepts for Medical Assistnts -- Part I. Price:* $15 for member; $25 for nonmember. • *Brochures.* • *Human Relations for the Medical Office. Price:* $30 for member; $50 for nonmember.* • *Law for the Medical Office. Price:* $30 for member; $50 for nonmember.* • *Managing Managed Care. Price:* $15 for member; $25 for nonmember.* • *Medical Office Management -- Part I. Price:* $22 for member; $32 for nonmember.* • *Pamphlets.* • *PMA*, bimonthly. Journal. Includes association news, index of advertisers, continuing education articles, and calendar of events. *Price:* Included in membership dues; $30/year for nonmembers and students. • *Urinalysis Today. Price:* $30 for member; $50 for nonmember.

★ 1142 ★ **American Association of Medical Society Executives (AAMSE)**
515 N. State St.
Chicago, IL 60610
Phone: (312)464-2555
Fax: (312)464-2467
Robin Kriegel, CAE, Exec.Dir.

Founded: 1947. **Members:** 1,000. **Description:** Professional society of executives of national, state, regional, or county medical and specialty societies. Conducts continuing education seminars. Makes available management resources and operational evaluations. **Publications:** *Hotline*, monthly. • *The Medical Execu-*

tive, quarterly. • *Who's Who in Medical Society Management*, annual. **Formerly:** Medical Society Executives Association.

★ 1143 ★ **American Association for World Health (AAWH)**
1129 20th St. NW, Ste. 400
Washington, DC 20036
Phone: (202)466-5883
Fax: (202)466-5896
Richard L. Wittenberg, Exec. Officer

Founded: 1953. **Members:** 1,200. **Description:** Individuals and organizations interested in strengthening U.S. commitment to world health. To inform Americans about world health issues and to strengthen public support for activities and programs that improve health conditions worldwide. Supports programs of the World Health Organization, Pan American Health Organization, and other agencies. Maintains speakers' bureau. Sponsors: World Health Day in U.S.; World AIDS Day, and World No-Tobacco Day. **Publications:** *AAWH Quarterly.* Newsletter. Covering international health policy issues; includes news of the AAWH and WHO. *Price:* Included in membership dues. • *World AIDS Day Action Kit*, annual. Booklet. *Price:* Free. • *World Health*, semimonthly. Magazine. *Price:* Included in membership dues. • *World Health Day Planning Kit*, annual. Booklet. *Price:* Free. **Also Known As:** U.S. Committee for the World Health Organization. **Formerly:** (1966) National Citizens Committee for the World Health Organization.

★ 1144 ★ **American Baptist Homes and Hospitals Association (ABHHA)**
PO Box 851
Valley Forge, PA 19482-0851
Phone: (215)768-2254
Fax: (215)768-2470
Milton E. Owens, Jr., Exec.Dir.

Founded: 1935. **Members:** 112. **Description:** Retirement facilities (69), nursing homes and hospitals (24), and children's homes and special services (19). Provides special programs and educational events for member institutions. Offers consulting network program for member facilities. Compiles statistics. **Publications:** *Directory of American Baptist Retirement Homes, Hospitals and Nursing Homes, Children's Homes and Special Services*, annual. Directory. • *Perspective*, quarterly. Newsletter. **Formerly:** (1954) Association of Baptist Homes and Hospitals.

★ 1145 ★ **American Board of Family Practice (ABFP)**
2228 Young Dr.
Lexington, KY 40505
Phone: (606)269-5626
Fax: (606)266-9699
Paul R. Young, M.D., Exec.Dir.

Founded: 1969. **Description:** Certifying board for physicians specializing in family practice. Conducts certification examinations.

★ 1146 ★ **American Board of Internal Medicine (ABIM)**
3624 Market St.
Philadelphia, PA 19104
Phone: (215)243-1500
Fax: (215)382-4702
Harry R. Kimball, Pres.

Founded: 1936. **Members:** 25. **Description:** Certification board established to determine the qualifications of, administer examinations to, and certify as specialists in internal medicine those doctors meeting its standards of clinical competence. Board members are elected from certified leaders in internal medicine. The board has certified approximately 121,000 internists and 54,000 subspecialist diplomates and issued 10,000 recertification certificates. **Publications:** *Policies and Procedures*, annual.

★ 1147 ★ **American Board of Medical Specialties (ABMS)**
1007 Church St., Ste. 404
Evanston, IL 60201-5913
Phone: (708)491-9091
Fax: (708)328-3596
J. Lee Dockery, M.D., Exec.VP

Founded: 1970. **Members:** 30. **Description:** Primary medical specialty boards and conjoint boards; organizations with related interests are associate members. Acts as spokesman for approved medical specialty boards as a group; is actively concerned with the establishment, maintenance, and elevation of standards for the education and qualification of physicians recognized as specialists through the certification procedures of its members; cooperates with other groups concerned in establishing standards, policies, and procedures for ensuring the maintenance of continued competence of such physicians. Compiles statistics. **Publications:** *ABMS Directory of Board Certified Medical Specialists*, annual. Directory. Four volumes listing over 400,000 specialists certified by 24 U.S. medical specialty boards. Arranged by specialty, name, and location. *Price:* $425/copy. • *ABMS Record*, quarterly. Newsletter. Reports on legislative-judicial events related to medical education. Includes meeting reports. *Price:* Free. • *American Board of Medical Specialties-- Annual Report and Reference Handbook*, annual. Guide to medical specialty bo ards and specialty certification. *Price:* $5. Also publishes text publications on evaluating physicians.

★ 1148 ★ **American Board of Quality Assurance and Utilization Review Physicians (ABQAURP)**
4890 W. Kennedy Blvd., Ste. 260
Tampa, FL 33609
Phone: (813)286-4411
Fax: (813)286-4387
Carla T. Murrill, Exec.VP

Founded: 1977. **Members:** 6,351. **Description:** Established to recognize the expertise of physicians, registered nurses, and other healthcare professionals involved in quality assurance and utilization review. Seeks to maintain and improve the process of quality assurance and utilization review through development, administration, and supervision of a certification program in the field. Provides evaluation services in connection with certification examinations for physicians and coordinators and makes available study material. **Publications:** Books. • *Computers in the Healthcare Industry.* • *Diplomate Focus Newsletter.* Newsletter. • *Quality Assurance and Utilizations Review: Current Readings in Concept and Practice.* • *Risk Management Trends and Applications.*

★1149★ American Bureau for Medical Advancement in China (ABMAC)
1216 5th Ave.
New York, NY 10029
Phone: (212)860-1990
Fax: (212)860-1994
Hope N. F. Phillips, Exec. Dir.

Founded: 1937. **Members:** 52. **Description:** Cooperates with medical and health personnel to support a broad program of medical and health services for the Chinese people. Provides, upon request from Republic of China institutions, consultants for development projects and visiting specialists for longer term teaching and clinical assignments in Taiwan. Sponsors Republic of China postgraduate fellowships for study, research, and observation in the U.S. Organizes research projects for treatment of diseases prevalent in Southeast Asia. Offers placement services for Chinese doctors and nurses interested in postgraduate study in the U.S. **Formerly:** (1978) American Bureau for Medical Aid to China.

★1150★ American Center for Chinese Medical Sciences (ACCMS)
c/o Yng-Shiuh Sheu
4623 Rosedale Ave.
Bethesda, MD 20814
Yng-Shiuh Sheu, Ph.D., Pres.

Founded: 1974. **Members:** 200. **Description:** Medical and scientific professionals from the U.S. and China working to develop medical contacts, share experience, and promote exchange of scientific information between America and China. Sponsors meetings and tours to China; promotes joint research; conducts lectures. Maintains biographical archives. Conducts symposium. **Publications:** *ACCMS Bulletin*, semiannual. Newsletter. Includes obituaries. *Price:* Included in membership dues; $5/issue for nonmembers. • *American Journal of Chinese Medical Sciences*, annual. Journal. • Membership Directory, biennial. **Formerly:** (1980) American Center for Chinese Medicine.

★1151★ American Clinical and Climatological Association (ACCA)
Mayo Clinic
200 1st St. SW
1601 Guggenheim Bldg.
Rochester, MN 55905
Phone: (507)284-3320
Fax: (507)284-2053
Dr. Lynwood H. Smith, Sec.

Founded: 1884. **Members:** 375. **Description:** Internists interested in the clinical study of disease. **Publications:** *Transactions*, annual.

★1152★ American College Health Association (ACHA)
PO Box 28937
Baltimore, MD 21240-8937
Phone: (410)859-1500
Fax: (410)859-1510
Charles H. Hartman, Exec.Dir.

Founded: 1920. **Members:** 3,800. **Local Groups:** 11. **Description:** Institutions (900) and individuals (2900). Provides an organization in which institutions of higher education and interested individuals may work together to promote health in its broadest aspects for students and all other members of the college community. Offers continuing education programs for health professionals. Maintains placement listings for physicians and other personnel seeking positions in college health. Compiles statistics. Conducts seminars and training programs. **Publications:** *ACHA Action*, bimonthly. Newsletter. Includes calendar of events, employment opportunities, college health resource listings, annual report, and leadership directory. *Price:* Included in membership dues. • Catalog. Lists publications. • *Health Information Series.* Pamphlets. • *Membership Profile Directory*, periodic. Directory. • Monographs. • Reports. Also publishes guidelines. **Formerly:** American Student Health Association.

★1153★ American College of International Physicians (ACIP)
711 2nd St. NE, Ste. 200
Washington, DC 20002
Phone: (202)544-7498
Fax: (202)546-7105
Dale Dirks, Admin.

Founded: 1975. **Members:** 1,500. **Description:** Physicians and surgeons interested in initiatives to promote national efforts in international health, education, research, training, and welfare. Promotes the betterment of the health of all peoples and seeks to advance the art and science of medicine. Emphasizes the international character of medicine and the education of international physicians. Seeks parity for foreign medical graduates. Supports relief programs to areas struck by natural calamities or epidemic diseases. **Publications:** *International Medical Journal*, semiannual. Newsletter. • *The International Physician*, quarterly. Newsletter.

★1154★ American College of Medical Quality (ACMQ)
9005 Congressional Ct.
Potomac, MD 20854
Phone: (301)365-3570
Fax: (301)365-3202
Russell E. Barker, Exec.VP

Founded: 1973. **Members:** 2,600. **Description:** Physicians, affiliates, and institutions seeking to set standards of competence in the field of quality assurance and utilization review. Conducts educational seminars and workshops in quality assurance and utilization review. Compiles statistics on numbers of physicians and allied health personnel working in quality assurance and utilization review. Offers placement services. Maintains speakers' bureau. **Publications:** *American College of Medical Quality Newsletter - Focus*, monthly. Newsletter. Includes college and chapter news and obituaries.

Price: Included in membership dues; $75/year for nonmembers. • *Journal of the American College of Medical Quality*, quarterly. Journal. Covers topics concerning evaluation of quality in health care, DRGs, Medicare and Medicaid, risk management, and other areas of interest. *Price:* Included in membership dues; $55/year for nonmembers. • *Study Guide in Quality Assurance and Utilization Review*, annual. Study guide for the certification examination of the American Board of Quality Assurance and Utilization Review Physicians. *Price:* $69.95/copy prepaid; $75/copy invoiced. • *Washington Update*, monthly.

★1155★ American College of Medicine (ACM)
4711 W. Golf Rd., Ste. 408
Skokie, IL 60076
Phone: (312)951-1400
Fax: (708)568-1527
Randall T. Bellows, M.D., Dir.

Founded: 1981. **Description:** Promotes and recognizes the specific needs of general practitioners and provides continuing medical education programs for maintaining competence in the practice of medicine. **Publications:** *Comprehensive Therapy*, monthly. **Formerly:** (1984) American College of General Practice.

★1156★ American College of Physicians (ACP)
Independence Mall West
6th St. at Race
Philadelphia, PA 19106-1572
Phone: (215)351-2400
Free: 800-523-1546
Fax: (215)351-2448
Joseph Johnson, III, Acting V.P.

Founded: 1915. **Members:** 80,000. **Description:** Professional society of medical doctors specializing in internal medicine and closely related specialties such as dermatology, neurology, psychiatry, cardiology, gastroenterology, and public health. Sponsors annual postgraduate courses for practicing physicians. Sponsors teaching and research scholarship competition. **Publications:** *Annals of Internal Medicine*, bimonthly. • Directory, periodic. • *Medical Knowledge Self-Assessment*, triennial. • *Observer*, monthly.

★1157★ American Correctional Health Services Association (ACHSA)
PO Box 2307
Dayton, OH 45401-2307
Phone: (513)223-9630
Fax: (513)223-6307
Francine W. Rickenbach, CAE, Exec.Dir.

Founded: 1975. **Members:** 1,600. **State Groups:** 14. **Description:** Health care providers, individuals, or organizations interested in improving the quality of correctional health services. Aims are: to promote the provision of health services to incarcerated persons consistent in quality and quantity with acceptable health care practices; to promote and encourage continuing education and provide technical and professional guidance for correctional health care personnel; to establish a forum for the sharing and discussion of correctional health care issues. Conducts conferences on correctional health care management, nursing, mental health, juvenile corrections, dentistry, and related subjects. Maintains placement service. **Publications:** Brochures. Provides information on policy matters. • *CORHEALTH*, bimonthly. Newsletter. Includes book reviews, conference calendar, list of new members, and chapter news. *Price:* Included in membership dues.

★1158★ American Council for Health Care Reform (ACHCR)
4200 Wilson Blvd., Ste. 750
Arlington, VA 22203
Phone: (703)908-9220
Free: 800-240-6423
Fax: (703)908-9467
William Shaker, Pres.

Founded: 1982. **Members:** 500,000. **Description:** Organized to eliminate what the council terms unnecessary and costly federal and state health care regulations and laws, such as certificate of public need restrictions that limit public choice in the selection of health care providers. Supports health care reform, based on Consumer choice. Testifies before congressional and state legislative committees. Coordinates grass roots support for free market approaches to health care delivery and health, safety, and consumer-oriented projects. Works to achieve public access to medical practice information. Supports medical savings accounts.

★1159★ American Electrology Association (AEA)
106 Oak Ridge Rd.
Trumbull, CT 06611
Phone: (203)374-6667
Fax: (203)372-7134
Teresa E. Petricca, Pres.

Founded: 1958. **Members:** 2,000. **State Groups:** 27. **Description:** Electrologists united for education, professional advancement, and to protect the public welfare. Promotes uniform legislative standards throughout the states. Coordinates efforts of affiliated associations in dealing with problems of national scope. Sponsors the International Board of Electrologist Certification. Maintains referral, reference, advisory, and consulting services. **Publications:** *American Electrology Association--Roster*, annual. Membership Directory. Arranged geographically. Includes modalities used. *Price:* Included in membership dues. • Brochures. • *Direct Line*, periodic. Bulletin. Provides communication between AEA executives and board members. Includes meeting minutes, committee reports, and program status reports. *Price:* Available to board members and committee chairs. • *Electrolysis World*, quarterly. Newsletter. Includes calendar of events. *Price:* Available to members only. • *Infection Control Standards for the Practice of Electrology*. • *Journal of the American Electrology Association*, semiannual. Journal. Includes case studies. *Price:* $10/issue. • *Medical/Professional News*, semiannual. **Formerly:** (1986) American Electrolysis Association.

★1160★ American Federation of Home Health Agencies (AFHHA)
1320 Fenwick Ln., Ste. 100
Silver Spring, MD 20910
Phone: (301)588-1454
Fax: (301)588-4732
Ann B. Howard, Exec.Dir.

Founded: 1980. **Members:** 325. **Description:** Agencies providing therapeutic services such as nursing, speech therapy, and physical therapy in the home; associate members are corporations and individuals that support the federation. Promotes home health by influencing public policy. Presents the concerns of home health agencies to Congress and the Health Care Financing Administration; helps members work with their fiscal intermediary. **Publications:** *Insider*, semimonthly. Newsletter. *Price:* Included in membership dues.

★1161★ American Federation of Medical Accreditation (AFMA)
522 Rossmore Dr.
Las Vegas, NV 89110-4123
Phone: (702)452-9538
Fax: (702)452-1031
Bartholomew A. Sinatra, M.D., Chm.

Founded: 1979. **Members:** 70. **Description:** Medical associations that have primary certifying boards; scientific organizations. Accredits medical and scientific organizations and continuing medical education for member organizations. Also credits those organizations having primary certifying board examinations and nonprofit, charitable schools, colleges, and medical schools.

★1162★ American Foundation for Health (AFH)
Box 1249
Berkeley, CA 94701
Phone: (510)644-3366
Leonard Stryker, Exec.Dir.

Founded: 1979. **Members:** 2,000. **Description:** Individuals interested in improving the delivery of health care services. Encourages recording of personal medical data. Conducts educational research projects and activities. Plans to hold period conference. **Publications:** *Health Features*, periodic. Newsletter.

★1163★ American Group Practice Association (AGPA)
1422 Duke St.
Alexandria, VA 22314-3430
Phone: (703)838-0033
Fax: (703)548-1890
Dr. Donald W. Fisher, Exec.VP & CEO

Founded: 1949. **Members:** 261. **Description:** Private group practice medical and dental clinics representing more than 26,000 physicians. Fosters accreditation of medical clinics; compiles statistics on group practice; sponsors research, patient education, and insurance programs. Conducts symposia; makes available consulting services. **Publications:** *American Group Practice Association--Executive News Service*, 22/year. Newsletter. Covers federal health care legislation and regulations affecting physician and hospital reimbursement under Medicare. *Price:* Included in membership dues.

• Books. Topics include administration and operation of clinics. • Directory, annual. *Price:* $150/year, available to members only. • *Executive News Service*, biweekly. *Price:* Available to members only. • *Group Practice Journal*, bimonthly. Journal. Covers market trends, health care policy and legislation, and management topics affecting the medical profession. Includes advertiser index. *Price:* Included in membership dues; $65/year for nonmembers. • *Quality Source*, quarterly. Covers quality measurement and outcomes information. *Price:* Included in membership dues. **Formerly:** (1974) American Association of Medical Clinics.

★1164★ American Health Care Advisory Association (AHCAA)
433 E. Las Colinas Blvd., Ste. 800
Irving, TX 75039
Phone: 800-232-4222
Tom Coston, Pres.

Founded: 1982. **Members:** 25,000. **Description:** Acts as an advisory organization promoting improved health care and reduction in medical costs. Gathers information concerning medical and insurance costs. **Publications:** *Vitality Health Gram*, quarterly.

★1165★ American Health Decisions (AHD)
1445 Market St., Ste. 380
Denver, CO 80202
Phone: (303)820-5635
Fax: (303)534-8774
Judy Hutchison, M.A., Exec.Off.

Founded: 1989. **Members:** 21. **Description:** Confederation of state health programs. Assists in establishing public education programs about health care and policy; works to increase availability of quality medical care. Promotes personal autonomy on ethical issues, such as patients making the decision to refuse or accept treatment. Addresses problems arising from ethical conflicts over new medical technologies and disease prevention. Maintains research and educational programs; disseminates information.

★1166★ American Indian Health Care Association (AIHCA)
1550 Larimer St., No. 225
Denver, CO 80202-1602
Carol Marquez-Baines, Contact

Founded: 1975. **Members:** 35. **Regional Groups:** 9. **State Groups:** 22. **Local Groups:** 35. **Description:** Urban Indian health programs; staff and support persons from member programs and other concerned persons. Develops and assists in the implementation of improved management techniques for urban Indian health care centers including quality community education programs and quality health care delivery systems responsive to community needs. Provides training, technical assistance, health care delivery management, research, and evaluation for Indian health programs and organizations. Compiles statistics on health services provided by programs of clinical, and fiscal training and information exchange; maintains speakers' bureau. **Publications:** Brochures. • *Health Promotion and Disease Prevention Bibliography.* • Monographs. • *Native AIDS Briefs*, quarterly. Newsletter. *Price:* Free. • Reports. • *Summary Program Publication*, annual.

★1167★ American Jewish Joint Distribution Committee (AJJDC)
711 3rd Ave.
New York, NY 10017
Phone: (212)687-6200
Fax: (212)370-5467
Michael Schneider, Exec.VP
Founded: 1914. **Description:** Maintains health, welfare, relief assistance, and rehabilitation programs for needy Jews in over 40 countries in Asia, Africa, Europe, the former Soviet Union, and Latin America. Provides funds for secular and religious education, feeding and medical programs, economic aid, summer camps, community development, manpower training, and aid to the aged and handicapped. The JDC program in Israel, in addition to education, provides a broad range of services for the aged, ill, and handicapped and participates with local agencies in developing health, welfare, and rehabilitation services, vocational training and placement, social integration, and community center programs. Financially supported by Jewish federations and welfare funds through the United Jewish Appeal. **Publications:** *American Jewish Joint Distribution Committee--Annual Report.* Annual Report. Provides information on the JDC, its programs, and countries where the organization operates. Includes budget information. *Price:* Free. • Brochures. **Also Known As:** Joint Distribution Committee. **Formerly:** Joint Distribution Committee for Relief of Jewish War Sufferers.

★1168★ American Medical Association (AMA)
515 N. State St.
Chicago, IL 60610
Phone: (312)464-5000
Fax: (312)464-4184
James S. Todd, M.D., Exec.VP
Founded: 1847. **Members:** 297,,000. **State Groups:** 54. **Description:** County medical societies and physicians. Disseminates scientific information to members and the public. Informs members on significant medical and health legislation on state and national levels and represents the profession before Congress and governmental agencies. Cooperates in setting standards for medical schools, hospitals, residency programs, and continuing medical education courses. Offers physician placement service and counseling on practice management problems. Operates library which lends material and provides specific medical information to physicians. Ad-hoc committees are formed for such topics as health care planning and principles of medical ethics. **Publications:** *American Medical News,* weekly. Newspaper. Covers news and opinions on key issues of political, social, and economic significance concerning the practice and delivery of medical care. *Price:* Included in membership dues; $99/year for nonmembers; $49.50/year for medical students, interns, and residents. • *Archives of Dermatology,* monthly. Journal. Oriented to the dermatologic clinician. Includes book reviews, employment opportunity listings, annual index, and index of advertisers. *Price:* $67.50/year for members; $135/year for nonmembers; $67.50/year for residents and medical students. • *Archives of Family Medicine,* monthly. Oriented to physicians in family

and general practice. *Price:* $47.50 for members; $95 for nonmembers. • *Archives of General Psychiatry,* monthly. Journal. Oriented toward the psychiatric clinician. Includes employment opportunity listings, book reviews, annual index, and index of advertisers. *Price:* $47.50/ year for members; $95/year for nonmembers; $47.50/year for residents and medical students. • *Archives of Internal Medicine,* semimonthly. Journal. Oriented toward physicians in internal medicine. Includes employment opportunity listings, annual index, and index of advertisers. *Price:* $57.50/year for members; $115/year for nonmembers; $57.50/year for residents and medical students. • *Archives of Neurology,* monthly. Journal. Oriented toward the neurologic clinician. Includes employment opportunity listings, annual index, and index of advertisers. *Price:* $72.50/year for members; $145/year for nonmembers; $72.50/year for residents and medical students. • *Archives of Ophthalmology,* monthly. Journal. Includes employment opportunity listings, case reports, book reviews, annual index, and index of advertisers. *Price:* $55/ year for members; $110/year for nonmembers; $55/year for residents and medical students. • *Archives of Otolaryngology--Head and Neck Surgery,* monthly. Journal. Oriented toward the otolaryngolic clinician. Includes employment opportunity listings, annual index, and index of advertisers. *Price:* $62.50/year for members; $125.00/year for nonmembers; $62.50/year for residents and medical students. • *Archives of Pediatrics & Adolescent Medicine,* monthly. Journal. Oriented toward the pediatric clinician. Includes book reviews, employment opportunity listings, annual index, and index of advertisers. *Price:* $50.00/year for members; $100.00/year for nonmembers; $50.00/year for residents and medical students. • *Archives of Surgery,* monthly. Journal. Oriented toward general surgeons. Includes employment opportunity listings, calendar of events, book reviews, index of advertisers, and annual index. *Price:* $50.00/year for members; $100.00/year for nonmembers; $50.00/year for medical sudents and residents. • *Journal of the American Medical Association,* weekly. Covers topics in general medicine; includes employment opportunity listings, book reviews, calendar of events, case reports, and obituaries. *Price:* Included in membership dues; $120.00/year for nonmembers; $60.00/year for medical students and residents.

★1169★ American Medical Association Alliance (AMAA)
515 N. State St.
Chicago, IL 60610-0174
Phone: (312)464-4470
Fax: (312)464-5839
Hazel J. Lewis, Exec.Dir.
Founded: 1922. **Members:** 70,000. **State Groups:** 46. **Local Groups:** 815. **Description:** Physicians' spouses. Serves as the volunteer arm of the American Medical Association. Promotes the goals of the medical profession and works to meet public health needs. Raises more than $2 million annually for the American Medical Association Education and Research Foundation, which provides assistance to medical schools and students. Sponsors the Shape Up for Life Campaign, a nationwide auxiliary program to promote good health. Maintains Project

Bank, an information clearinghouse of community projects initiated by auxiliaries across the country. Implements community health projects on such concerns as child abuse prevention, adolescent health, family violence, AIDS education, seatbelt usage, pre- and postnatal care, drug abuse, suicide prevention, proper nutrition, drunk driving prevention, venereal disease awareness, and services to the aging. Works with the AMA to promote sound health legislation; conducts public education programs, letter-writing campaigns, and personal interviews with legislators involved in health matters. **Publications:** *Facets Magazine,* bimonthly. Magazine. Includes information on community health projects, public health issues, socioeconomic health care issues, and physician family concerns. *Price:* Included in membership dues; $7/ year for nonmembers. • *Horizons Newsletter,* bimonthly. Newsletter. Covers topics of concern to the families of resident physicians and medical students. *Price:* Free to resident physicians and medical students. • *Newsline,* bimonthly. Includes information on health periodicals and health projects. *Price:* Included in membership dues. **Formerly:** (1975) Women's Auxilliary to the American Medical Association; (1993) American Medical Association Auxilliary.

★1170★ American Medical Peer Review Association (AMPRA)
1140 Conneticut Ave. NE, Ste. 1050
Washington, DC 20036
Phone: (202)331-5790
Fax: (202)833-2047
Andrew H. Webber, Exec.VP
Founded: 1973. **Members:** 1,400. **Description:** Institutions and individuals. Purpose is to develop communications programs for physicians, institutions, and others interested in peer review organizations (PROs). Provides a national forum for the interchange of ideas, techniques, and information relating to medical quality assessment. Conducts courses and on-site educational programs to increase physicians' involvement and leadership in PROs, improve practice patterns through review, understand and use PRO data to improve service delivery, pre-admission review, profile analysis, retrospective review, and organizational development. Sponsors placement service; maintains a speakers' bureau and a library. **Publications:** *AMPRA Bulletin,* periodic. Bulletin. Covers medical regulatory and legislative developments. *Price:* Included in membership dues. • *AMPRA Review,* quarterly. Newsletter. Includes Policy Outlook, Innovation, Washington Update, Legislative Update, AMPRA Calendar of Events columns and job announcements. *Price:* Included in membership dues; $75/year for nonmembers. • *Legislative Monitor,* periodic. *Price:* Free, available to members only. • Membership Directory, annual. • *Physician Advisor Manual.* • *Resource Document and Private Review Manual.* • Tapes of Conference Programs. **Formerly:** (1982) American Association of Professional Standards Review Organizations.

★1171★ American Medical Student Association (AMSA)
1902 Association Dr.
Reston, VA 22091
Phone: (703)620-6600
Free: 800-767-2266
Fax: (703)620-5873
Paul R. Wright, Exec.Dir.

Founded: 1950. **Members:** 30,000. **Local Groups:** 140. **Description:** Medical students; local, state, and national organizations; premedical students, interns, and residents. Seeks to improve medical education by making it relevant to today's needs and by making the process by which physicians are trained more humanistic. Contributes to the improvement of health care of all people; involves its members in the social, moral, and ethical obligations of the profession of medicine. Serves as a mechanism through which students may actively participate in the fields of community health through various student health programs. Addresses political issues relating to the nation's health care delivery system and other medical and health issues. Offers specialized education and placement services; conducts research; operates speakers' bureau. Maintains 18 task forces and standing committees which publish newsletters, organize educational workshops, and initiate special projects. **Publications:** *The New Physician*, monthly. **Formerly:** (1975) Student American Medical Association.

★1172★ American Medical Women's Association (AMWA)
801 N. Fairfax St., Ste. 400
Alexandria, VA 22314
Phone: (703)838-0500
Fax: (703)549-3864
Eileen McGrath, Exec.Dir.

Founded: 1915. **Members:** 11,000. **Local Groups:** 160. **Description:** Women holding a M.D. or D.O. degree from approved medical colleges; women interns, residents, and medical students. Seeks to find solutions to problems common to women studying or practicing medicine, such as career advancement and the integration of professional and family responsibilities. Provides student members with educational loans and personal counseling. Accredited to sponsor continuing medical education programs. Maintains Friends of American Medical Women's Association, an auxiliary organization for husbands, relatives, and supporters of AMWA. **Publications:** Journal, bimonthly. • Newsletter, quarterly. • *What's Happening in AMWA*, semiannual. Newsletter. *Price:* Included in membership dues.

★1173★ American Osler Society (AOS)
c/o Lawrence D. Longo
Loma Linda University School of Medicine
Division of Perinatal Biology
Loma Linda, CA 92350
Phone: (909)824-4325
Fax: (909)824-4029
Lawrence D. Longo, Sec.-Treas.

Founded: 1970. **Members:** 116. **Description:** Physicians, librarians, and scientists united to further a humanistic approach to the study and practice of medicine as exemplified in the life work of Sir William Osler (1849-1919). **Publica-**tions: *Osler Biographical Directory*, periodic. Directory. • *The Persisting Osler*. Book. • *The Persisting Osler II*. Book. Also publishes books on Sir William Osler, medical humanism, and the history of medicine.

★1174★ American Physicians Association of Computer Medicine (APACM)
10 N. Main St.
Pittsford, NY 14534
Phone: (716)586-8159
Lawrence B. Tilis, M.D., Pres.

Founded: 1984. **Members:** 350. **Description:** Physicians, interns, and medical students. Encourages the use of computers in medicine. Seeks to inform physicians about the computer and its applications in patient care, education, and research. Conducts lectures. Is developing a database of programs and a certifying board of computer medicine.

★1175★ American Physicians Fellowship for Medicine in Israel (APF)
2001 Beacon St.
Brookline, MA 02146
Phone: (617)232-5382
Daniel Goldfarb, Exec.Dir.

Founded: 1950. **Members:** 5,000. **Description:** American doctors whose goals are to foster and aid medical progress in Israel. Major activities include: fellowship assistance for Israeli physicians; support for Israel's trauma program; funding important medical research projects; Israel's first podiatry programs; emergency help for Israel; CME seminars in Israel; excellence awards; support for Russian immigrant physicians; intensive specialty training for Israeli nurses; establishment of the Dr. Manuel M. Glazier Institute of the History of Medicine; and assistance to Israel's medical schools. **Publications:** *Koroth, Periodical of Medical History*, semiannual. • *News*, semiannual. Also publishes multi-language medical dictionary and other books. **Formerly:** (1979) American Physicians Fellowship for the Israel Medical Association.

★1176★ American Professional Practice Association (APPA)
292 Madison Ave., 4th Fl.
New York, NY 10017
Phone: (212)949-5900
Free: 800-221-2168
Fax: (212)949-5910
Ms. Pat Arden, Exec.Dir.

Founded: 1959. **Members:** 70,000. **Description:** Provides physicians with economic benefits and services including the following: unsecured loan plans; equipment, furniture, and automobile leasing; seminars and information programs; low-cost group insurance; group purchase discounts; investment opportunities; local, travel, and personal service programs. **Publications:** *APPA Digest*, quarterly. Newsletter. Provides business advice on private practice; also covers APPA activities. *Price:* Included in membership dues.

★1177★ American Red Cross National Headquarters (ARC)
431 18th St. NW
Washington, DC 20006
Elizabeth Dole, Pres.

Founded: 1881. **Description:** Operating under congressional charter and fulfilling America's obligations under certain international treaties, the American Red Cross serves members of the armed forces and veterans and their families, aids disaster victims, and assists other Red Cross societies in times of emergency. Other activities include: blood services; training of volunteers for chapters, hospitals, and other community agencies; community services; international activities; service opportunities for youth. Maintains 46 regional blood centers. Conducts research programs. Local chapters provide speakers. **Publications:** *Annual Report*. • Also publishes service-related booklets and other materials. **Formerly:** (1893) American Association of the Red Cross; (1978) American National Red Cross.

★1178★ American Red Magen David for Israel (ARMDI)
888 7th Ave., Ste. 403
New York, NY 10106
Phone: (212)757-1627
Fax: (212)757-4662
Benjamin Saxe, Exec.VP

Founded: 1941. **Members:** 125,000. **Local Groups:** 167. **Description:** U.S. support arm for Magen David Adom (MDA), Israel's equivalent of the Red Cross Society. Supports the MDA emergency medical, ambulance, blood, and disaster services which benefit Israel's entire population. Contributions are used to: supply and equip ambulances, bloodmobiles, and cardiac rescue ambulances serving all hospitals and communities throughout Israel; provide supplies and equipment for the MDA Blood Bank and MDA Fractionation Institute, and for MDA's emergency medical clinics; provide education funds to train paramedics, laboratory technicians, and scientists. Funds are raised from individual donors, ARMDI Chapters, foundation grants, and legacy programs. Maintains speakers' bureau. **Publications:** *Chapter News*, semiannual. • *Lifeline*, semiannual. **Also Known As:** Red Magen David.

★1179★ American Refugee Committee (ARC)
2344 Nicollet Ave. S., Ste. 350
Minneapolis, MN 55404
Phone: (612)872-7060
Fax: (612)872-4309
Anthony J. Kozlowski, Pres. & CEO

Founded: 1979. **State Groups:** 2. **Local Groups:** 1. **Description:** Nonsectarian, international refugee assistance organization. Works to ensure the survival, health, and well-being of refugees, displaced persons, and others affected by mass population movements, particularly those resulting from social and political unrest, civil wars, and famine. Works with refugees, displaced persons, and host country citizens to provide basic medical and health care training as well as direct care. **Publications:** Annual Report. • *Bridges Newsletter*, 4/year. Newsletter.

★1180★ American Registry of Medical Assistants (ARMA)
69 Southwick Rd., Ste. A
Westfield, MA 01085-4729
Phone: (413)562-7336
Free: 800-527-2762
Annette H. Heyman, Dir.

Founded: 1950. **Members:** 4,000. **Description:** Medical assistants who have completed an accredited medical assistant training course or who have trained with a physician. Objectives are to: establish and maintain high training standards for medical assistants; promote greater efficiency within the profession; raise awareness of medical assistants within the medical community. **Publications:** Brochures. • *The Medical Assistant*, annual. Journal. • *Registry Connection*, quarterly.

★1181★ American School Health Association (ASHA)
7263 State Rte. 43
PO Box 708
Kent, OH 44240
Phone: (216)678-1601
Fax: (216)678-4526
Dana A. Davis, Exec.Dir.

Founded: 1927. **Members:** 4,000. **State Groups:** 16. **Description:** School physicians, school nurses, dentists, nurses, nutritionists, health educators, dental hygienists, school-based professionals, and public health workers. Promotes comprehensive and constructive school health programs including the teaching of health, health services, and promotion of a healthful school environment. Offers a professional referral service, classroom teaching aids, and professional reference materials. Conducts research programs; maintains placement service; compiles statistics. Sponsors foreign travel study tour. **Publications:** *A Pocketguide to Health and Health Problems in School Physical Activities*. Book. • *ASHA Newsletter*, periodic. Newsletter. • *Building Effective Coalitions to Prevent the Spread of HIV*. Book. • *Health Counseling*. Book. • *Healthy Students 2000: An Agenda for Continuous Improvement in America's Schools*. Book. • *Journal of School Health*, 10/year. Journal. Includes articles, research papers, reports, commentaries, teaching techniques, and health service application. *Price:* $85/year; $95/year for institutions; $110/year outside U.S.; $8.50/copy for members. • *The PULSE*, quarterly. *Price:* Included in membership. • *The Role of the Nurse in the School Setting: A Historical Perspective*. Book. • *School-Based HIV Prevention: A Multidisciplinary Approach*. Book. • *School Health in America*. Survey. • *Science and Health Experiments and Demonstrations in Smoking Education*. Book. • *Sexuality Education Within Comprehensive School Health Education*. Book. • *Standards of School Nursing Practice*. Book. • *Teaching Human Sexuality*. Book. • *Topical Index of Articles From the Journal*, annual. Journal. **Formerly:** (1936) American Association of School Physicians.

★1182★ American Society of Bariatric Physicians (ASBP)
5600 S. Quebec, Ste. 109-A
Englewood, CO 80111
Phone: (303)779-4833
Fax: (303)779-4834
James F. Merker, CAE, Exec. Officer

Founded: 1950. **Members:** 700. **Description:** Physicians with a special interest in the study and treatment of obesity and associated conditions. Encourages excellence in the practice of bariatric medicine through exchange of information, research, and continuing education. Implements research programs in conjunction with The Obesity Foundation. Sponsors regional courses and clinical research programs. Offers Dial-A-Tape and physician referral service. **Publications:** *The Bariatrician*, quarterly. Journal. Includes articles on health, fitness, nutrition, and current treatments for obesity. *Price:* $40/year in U.S.; $50/year outside U.S. • Manuals. • Membership Directory, annual. • *News from ASBP*, bimonthly. *Price:* Available to members only. • Pamphlets. **Formerly:** (1961) National Glandular Society; (1972) American Society of Bariatrics.

★1183★ American Society for Clinical Investigation (ASCI)
6900 Grove Rd.
Thorofare, NJ 08086
Phone: (609)848-1000
Free: 800-257-8290
Fax: (609)848-5274
Andrew Schafer, M.D., Sec.-Treas.

Founded: 1909. **Members:** 2,400. **Description:** Physicians living in the United States or Canada who have accomplished meritorious original investigations in the clinical or allied sciences of medicine. Active members are doctors under age 48; emeritus members are those over age 48. Promotes cultivation of clinical research by methods of natural sciences, correlation of science with the art of medical practice, encouragement of scientific investigation by medical practitioners, and publication of papers on the methods and results of clinical research. **Publications:** *By-Laws and Membership*, annual. • *Journal of Clinical Investigation*, monthly. Journal.

★1184★ American Society of Directors of Volunteer Services (ASDVS)
American Hospital Association
840 N. Lake Shore Dr.
Chicago, IL 60611
Phone: (312)422-3939
Fax: (312)442-4575
Nancy A. Brown, Dir.

Founded: 1968. **Members:** 1,700. **Regional Groups:** 2. **State Groups:** 45. **Local Groups:** 3. **Description:** Members are persons who are employed or recognized by the administration of a health care institution as having major or continuing responsibility for managing and coordinating the volunteer services program within that institution and who are eligible for personal membership in the American Hospital Association. Purposes are: to develop the knowledge and increase the competence of the individual member; to provide a means of intercommunication for directors of volunteer services and health care institutions; to conduct periodical surveys; to provide consultation and guidance on matters relating to health care volunteer services management; to establish and maintain professional standards and ethics; to cooperate with appropriate organizations in activities relating to volunteer services management that will be beneficial to the society; to cooperate with institutions of higher education in the development of programs in volunteer services management. Offers course on basic principles of volunteer services management. **Publications:** *Membership Roster*, annual. • *Volunteer Services Administration*, bimonthly. Newsletter. • *Volunteer Services Department in a Health Care Institution*.

★1185★ American Society of Internal Medicine (ASIM)
2011 Pennsylvania Ave. NW, Ste. 800
Washington, DC 20006-1808
Phone: (202)835-2746
Fax: (202)835-0443
Alan R. Nelson, M.D., Exec.VP

Founded: 1956. **Members:** 26,000. **State Groups:** 51. **Description:** Professional society of physicians specializing in internal medicine. Is concerned with the social, economic, and political factors affecting the delivery of high quality care. Focuses on the delivery and financing of medical care in areas including access to care, appropriate reform of American health care system, medical and public education, issues affecting the elderly, private and public sector, health insurance and reimbursement, managed care, documentation of physician performance, and medical technology and computerization aimed at maintaining and promoting high quality medical care at a reasonable cost. **Publications:** *The Internist: Health Policy in Practice*, 10/year. Magazine. *Price:* $24/year for nonmembers. • *Internist's Intercom*, monthly. Newsletter. Covers regulatory and legislative actions, socioeconomic issues and trends, and society news. *Price:* Included in membership dues. Also publishes a series of practice management guides on administrative aspects of medical practice and literature for internists' patients.

★1186★ American Subacute Care Association (ASCA)
PO Box 545939
Surfside, FL 33154
Phone: (305)864-0396
Fax: (305)868-0905
Laura Hyatt, Exec.Dir.

Founded: 1993. **Members:** 300. **Description:** Executives of subacute care companies, vendors, and allied legal and financial professionals; physicians, nurses, physical therapists, occupational therapists, and other healthcare professionals involved in subacute care. Dedicated to advancing the field of subacute care. **Publications:** *ASCA Quarterly*, quarterly. Newsletter. *Price:* Included in membership dues.

★ 1187 ★ **Americans for Medical Progress**
   Educational Foundation (AMPEF)
Crystal Sq. 3
421 King St., Ste. 401
Alexandria, VA 22314-3121
Phone: (703)836-9595
Susan E. Paris, Pres.

Founded: 1990. **Members:** 2,500. **Description:** Works to educate the American people about the benefits of using animals in medical research and counters the "disinformation" spread by the animal rights movement. Endorses the belief that regulated animal testing is a vital and irreplaceable aspect of medical research and is necessary for continued medical progress. Conducts advertising campaigns; produces television programs and a nationally distributed newspaper column. Bestows annual Sabin Award for contribution to human health through medical research. Maintains speakers' bureau; conducts educational programs. **Publications:** *Breakthrough and Progress*, bimonthly. Newsletter. *Price:* Included in membership dues. • Brochures. • *Progress*, bimonthly. *Price:* Included in membership dues. • *Students for Medical Progress*. Brochure. Also publishes glossies of advertisements, research fact sheets, and talking-point cards.

★ 1188 ★ **Americares Foundation (AF)**
161 Cherry St.
New Canaan, CT 06840
Phone: (203)966-5195
Free: 800-486-HELP
Fax: (203)972-0116
Robert C. Macauley, CEO

Founded: 1979. **Description:** Private relief organization dedicated to saving lives and fulfilling emergency medical needs worldwide. Sponsors airlifts and sea shipments of food, medicine, and medical supplies to provide immediate relief whenever and wherever needed. Responds to disasters caused by earthquakes, famines, floods, political upheavals, and wars. Welcomes cooperation and support of other groups from both the public and private sectors. Dedicated to providing the greatest possible measure of assistance per dollar contributed. Since 1982, the organization has sent more than $1 billion in medical and pharmaceutical aid.

★ 1189 ★ **Amigos de las Americas**
   (AMIGOS)
5618 Star Ln.
Houston, TX 77057
Phone: (713)782-5290
Margaret Guerriero, Pres.

Founded: 1965. **State Groups:** 20. **Description:** Purpose is to send young U.S. volunteers above the age of 16 on 4-, 6-, and 8-week public health work assignments in Latin American countries that have requested AMIGOS projects. Provides opportunities for young people to explore their own potential and to enrich their lives and the lives of others. Volunteer parents, leaders, and professionals raise funds, recruit, and train young Amigos in medical procedures, human relations, Spanish language, and Latin American culture. During their term of duty abroad, Amigos give inoculations, perform eye and dental examinations, distribute eyeglasses, conduct nutrition studies, provide paramedical services such as oral rehydration therapy education, immunize dogs and cats against rabies, establish community sanitation facilities, and other services related to health care. **Publications:** Annual Report. • *La Carta*, semiannual. • *Resource*, 4/year. • *Volunteer Directory*, annual. Directory. Also publishes fact sheet and brochure.

★ 1190 ★ **Appropriate Health Resources**
   and Technologies Action Group
   (AHRTAG)
1 London Bridge St.
London SE1 9SG, England
Phone: 171 3781403
Fax: 171 4036003
K. Attawell, Co-Dir.

Founded: 1977. **Members:** 70. **Languages:** English. **Description:** Primary health care specialists in developing countries. Addresses the problems of disease, disability, and high infant mortality. Promotes better primary health care in developing countries through the dissemination of information to health workers and the establishment of advisory services. Participates in the design and development of low-cost health equipment. Conducts courses and surveys. **Publications:** *AIDS Action*, quarterly. Newsletter. • *Annual Report*. • *ARI News*, 3/year. Newsletter. • *Community Based Rehabilitation News*, quarterly. Newsletter. • *Dialogue on Diarrhoea*, quarterly. Newsletter. • *Health Action*, quarterly. Newsletter.

★ 1191 ★ **Arab American Medical**
   Association (AAMA)
1025 E. Maple, Ste. 210
Birmingham, MI 48009
Phone: (810)646-3661
Fax: (810)646-0617
Ellen R. Potter, Exec.Dir.

Founded: 1974. **Members:** 1,200. **State Groups:** 20. **Description:** Medical professionals of Arab descent. Fosters exchange of scientific information. Encourages continuing education for members. Provides financial and technical support for medical students and institutions in the United States and in Arab countries. Offers medical assistance to needy individuals of Arab descent. **Publications:** Newsletter, quarterly. *Price:* Included in membership dues.

★ 1192 ★ **Arise**
718 State St.
Springfield, MA 01109
Phone: (413)734-4948
Fax: (413)781-3712
Sherri Marshall, Pres.

Founded: 1985. **Members:** 200. **Description:** Works to empower low-income individuals and those on entitlement programs through education on their social and economic rights, including health care, housing, and voting. Encourages political and social participation; promotes self-esteem and a sense of efficacy. Maintains speakers' bureau. **Publications:** *Our Voices Heard*, semiannual. Newsletter. On events facing low-income individuals; includes calendar of events. *Price:* Free.

★ 1193 ★ **Asociacion Apostol de la Salud**
   (AAS)
Col. Miraflores
Hospital y Clinica
San Roque
Tegucigalpa, DC, Honduras
Phone: 312919
Fax: 354849
Jesus Orlando Molina, Dir.

Founded: 1984. **Members:** 70. **National Groups:** 84. **Local Groups:** 38. **Languages:** Spanish. **Description:** Promotes better health care in Honduras through the dissemination of information. Works to develop low cost health care.

★ 1194 ★ **Association of Academic Health**
   Centers (AHC)
1400 16th St. NW, Ste. 410
Washington, DC 20036
Phone: (202)265-9600
Fax: (202)265-7514
Roger J. Bulger, M.D., Pres.

Founded: 1969. **Members:** 104. **Description:** Chief executive officers of university-based health centers in the U.S. Interdisciplinary in focus, with a primary interest in total health manpower education. Sponsors task forces. Is developing research and education programs. **Publications:** Directory, periodic. • *General Meetings*, periodic. • Reports. On special projects. **Formerly:** Organization of University Health Center Administrators.

★ 1195 ★ **Association for the Advancement**
   of Health Education (AAHE)
1900 Association Dr.
Reston, VA 22091
Phone: (703)476-3437
Fax: (703)476-6638
Becky J. Smith, Ph.D., Exec.Dir.

Founded: 1937. **Members:** 11,000. **Description:** Professionals who have responsibility for health education in schools, colleges, communities, hospitals and clinics, and industries. Purposes are advancement of health education through program activities and federal legislation; encouragement of close working relationships between all health education and health service organizations; achievement of good health and well-being for all Americans automatically, without conscious thought and endeavor. Member of the American Alliance for Health, Physical Education, Recreation and Dance. **Publications:** Books. • *Directory of Institutions Offering Specialization in Health Education*, biennial. Directory. • Handbooks. • *HE-XTRA*, 6/year. Reports on health education programs across the nation. Includes association news and research updates. *Price:* Included in membership dues. • *Journal of Health Education*, bimonthly. Journal. • Reports. • Videos. Also publishes guides and educational packets, and produces microcomputer software. **Formerly:** (1974) School Health Division of American Association for Health, Physical Education and Recreation.

★ 1196 ★ Association of American Indian Physicians (AAIP)
1235 Sovereign Row, Ste. C-7
Oklahoma City, OK 73108
Phone: (405)946-7072
Fax: (405)946-7651
Founded: 1971. **Members:** 220. **Description:** Physicians (M.D. or D.O.) of American Indian descent. Encourages American Indians to enter the health professions. Provides a forum for the interchange of ideas and information of mutual interest to physicians of Indian descent. Establishes contracts with government agencies to provide consultation and other expert opinion regarding health care of American Indians and Alaskan Natives; receives contracts and grant monies and other forms of assistance from these sources. Supports and encourages all other agencies and organizations, Indian and non-Indian, working to improve health conditions of American Indians and Alaskan Natives. Locates scholarship funds for Indian professional students; provides counseling assistance; preserves American Indian culture. Conducts seminars for students interested in health careers and for counselors in government and other schools where American Indian children are taught. **Publications:** Newsletter, semiannual.

★ 1197 ★ Association of American Medical Colleges (AAMC)
2450 N St. NW
Washington, DC 20037
Phone: (202)828-0400
Fax: (202)828-1125
Jordan J. Cohen, M.D., Pres.
Founded: 1876. **Members:** 2,200. **Description:** Medical schools, graduate affiliate medical colleges, academic societies, teaching hospitals, and individuals interested in the advancement of medical education, biomedical research, and healthcare. Provides centralized application service. Offers management education program for medical school deans, teaching hospital directors, department chairmen, and service chiefs of affiliated hospitals. Develops and administers the Medical College Admissions Test (MCAT). Operates student loan program. Maintains information management system and institutional profile system. Compiles statistics. **Publications:** *Academic Medicine*, monthly. *Price:* $60/year in U.S. and Canada. • *Curriculum Directory*, annual. Directory. • *Directory of American Medical Education*, annual. Directory. • *Medical School Admission Requirements*, annual. • Reports, annual. • Reports, semiannual. • *Weekly Report*.

★ 1198 ★ Association of American Physicians (AAP)
PO Box 4000
Princeton, NJ 08543
Phone: (609)252-4404
Founded: 1886. **Members:** 1,200. **Description:** Medical school faculty and clinical investigators. **Publications:** *Transactions of the Association of American Physicians*, annual. Proceedings. Proceedings of the annual meeting; includes membership list and obituaries. *Price:* Included in membership dues; $50/copy for nonmembers.

★ 1199 ★ Association of American Physicians and Surgeons (AAPS)
1601 N. Tucson Blvd., Ste. 9
Tucson, AZ 85716
Phone: (602)327-4885
Free: 800-635-1196
Fax: (602)326-3529
Jane M. Orient, M.D., Exec.Dir.
Founded: 1943. **Members:** 4,500. **Description:** Physicians dedicated to preserving and promoting quality medical care. Represents physicians in the socioeconomic and legal aspects of medical practice such as medical economics, public relations, and legislation. Makes available legal consultation services. **Publications:** *A Letter to My Colleagues: The Solution to Today's Health Economic Crisis*. • *AAPS News*, monthly. Newsletter. Covers developments affecting health care and the profession. Includes legislative news, calendar of events, and health law commentary. *Price:* Included in membership dues; $35/year for nonmembers. • Audiotapes. • *The Canadian Model: Could it Work Here?*. • *How to Challenge Health Insurers Who Refuse to Pay Legitimate Claims: A Guide for Patients*. • *John Q. Privatepractice, RIP*. • *The Political Fallacy that Medical Care is a Right*. • *Relative Value Scales: Fundamental Economic Principles*. • Videos.

★ 1200 ★ Association of Asian / Pacific Community Health Organizations (AAPCHO)
1212 Broadway, No. 730
Oakland, CA 94612
Phone: (510)272-9536
Stephen P. Jiang, Contact
Founded: 1987. **Members:** 10. **Description:** Works to improve access to culturally and linguistically appropriate health care in order to improve the health status of Asians and Pacific Islanders with a special focus on the medically underserved. **Publications:** *Behind the Mask: AIDS. . .It Affects All of Us*. Video. • *Community Health Watch*, quarterly. • *Hepatitis B*. Brochure. • *Parent's Guide to Common Childhood Illnesses*. Brochure. • *Thalassemia Among Asians*. Brochure.

★ 1201 ★ Association de Conjoints de Medecins (ACMED)
22, rue Garnier
F-92200 Neuilly, France
Phone: 1 46403240
Fax: 1 46403240
Mme. Mazzoni
Founded: 1971. **Languages:** English, French. **Description:** Individuals in the medical field in France. Works towards an increased awareness of the rights of dependents of doctors. Supports their representation and participation in activities of the medical cabinet. Works to develop improved policies and practices and influence attitudes related to the rights of doctors' families. **Publications:** Articles. • Brochures. • *Lettre aux Adherents*, quarterly.

★ 1202 ★ Association for Faculty in the Medical Humanities (AFMH)
6728 Old McLean Village Dr.
Mc Lean, VA 22101
Phone: (703)556-9222
Fax: (703)556-8729
George K. Degnon, Exec.Dir.
Founded: 1983. **Members:** 350. **Description:** A section of the Society for Health and Human Values. Faculty in the humanities at medical schools. Promotes teaching and research in the humanities in the context of medical education; closer links among scholars in the humanities who work in medical education; interdisciplinary teaching and research among humanities scholars, scientists, and clinicians; alliances with colleagues who relate in a scholarly way to the humanities in contexts other than medical education. **Publications:** Membership Directory, annual.

★ 1203 ★ Association of Haitian Physicians Abroad (AMHE)
60 Plaza St.
Brooklyn, NY 11238
Phone: (718)783-0701
Claude Manigat, Pres.
Founded: 1972. **Members:** 900. **State Groups:** 8. **Description:** Haitian doctors. Purpose is to unite Haitian doctors abroad and to organize professional activities among them. Provides charitable assistance to the Haitian community. Sponsors educational programs. **Publications:** *Directory of Haitian Physicians in N.Y.*, biennial. Directory. • *Journal des Medecins Haitien a l'Etranger*, 6/year. Journal. Also publishes educational materials. **Formerly:** (1986) Haitian Medical Association Abroad.

★ 1204 ★ Association for Health-Care Institutions (Verbond der Verzorgingsinstellingen — VVI)
Guimardstraat 1
B-1040 Brussels, Belgium
Phone: 2 5118008
Fax: 2 5135269
A. Aernoudt, Adm.Dir.
Founded: 1938. **Members:** 325. **Languages:** Dutch, English, French. **Description:** Hospitals; psychiatric hospitals; nursing homes; homes for elderly people. Promotes high standards of health service. Fosters exchange and cooperation; offers consultative services; makes recommendations to government authorities. **Publications:** *Hospitalia*, quarterly. • *VVI-Information*, 11/year.

★ 1205 ★ Association of Health Occupations Teacher Educators (AHOTE)
c/o University of Louisville
School of Education Rm. 346
Louisville, KY 40292
Phone: (502)852-0608
Dr. Patricia K. Leitsch, Pres.
Founded: 1978. **Members:** 28. **Description:** Educators of health occupations education teachers; graduate students preparing to teach health occupations. Purposes are: to plan and implement professional development of health

occupations teachers; to facilitate sharing of teacher education curriculum materials; to investigate and disseminate innovative strategies for health occupations teacher education delivery systems; to attempt to impact national issues relating to health occupations teacher education personnel and programs. Identifies needed research relating to health occupations and encourages dissemination of findings that have implications for the field. Cooperates with other organizations engaged in the preparation of health personnel and programs. Operates speakers' bureau. **Publications:** *Health Occupations Personnel in Teacher Education*, annual. • *Journal of Health Occupations Education*, semiannual. Journal. • *Membership List*, annual.

★1206★ Association for Health Services Research (AHSR)
1350 Connecticut Ave. NW, Ste. 1100
Washington, DC 20036
Phone: (202)223-2477
Fax: (202)835-8972
Alice S. Hersh, Exec.VP & CEO

Founded: 1981. **Members:** 2,500. **Description:** Individuals and organizations concerned with health services research. Objectives are to educate the public concerning the need for and contribution of health services research in improving health care in the U.S.; to foster productive cooperation among researchers, public and private funding agencies, health professionals, policymakers, and the public; to represent the views of members in the development and implementation of national legislative and administrative policies concerning health services research. Disseminates research findings to public and private sector officials. **Publications:** *HSR Reports*, quarterly. Newsletter. Covers legislative news and association activities. Includes conference calendar, employment listings, and information on new publications.

★1207★ Association of International Health Researchers (AIHR)
2665 Pleasant Valley Rd.
Mobile, AL 36606
Phone: (205)473-3946
Dr. Roy E. Kadel, Pres.

Founded: 1982. **Members:** 123. **Regional Groups:** 5. **Description:** Individuals interested in quality health research. Works to: promote a better understanding of scientifically effective research techniques and methodologies; encourage interaction among individuals in international health research. Compiles statistics.

★1208★ Association of Medical Research Charities (AMRC)
29-35 Farringdon Rd.
London EC1M 3JB, England
Phone: 171 4046454
Fax: 171 4046448
Diana A. Garnham, Gen.Sec.

Founded: 1987. **Members:** 79. **Languages:** English. **Description:** Medical research charities. Furthers the advancement of medical research in the United Kingdom. Focuses attention on the collective effectiveness of members. Monitors the administration of government contracts and quotas for contracted researchers. **Publications:** *Handbook*, annual.

★1209★ Association of Medical Schools in Europe (AMSE)
Group for Clinical Medicine
University of Oslo
Oyeacdelingen
Rikshospitlat
N-0027 Oslo, Norway
Phone: 47 22867863
Fax: 47 22867848
Ivar Horven, Contact

Founded: 1979. **Languages:** English. **Description:** Deans of medical schools; representatives of medical deans in 25 countries. Provides a forum for the exchange of ideas and information. Objectives are: to address important questions concerning medical education, with special emphasis on policies affecting the future of medical education in Europe; to discuss practical issues such as admission criteria and organizational problems; to analyze the relationship between medical schools and health service organizations; to assess the impact of medical science on medical education. **Publications:** *AMSE Newsletter*, quarterly. Newsletter. **Formerly:** (1992) Association of Medical Deans in Europe.

★1210★ Association of Minority Health Professions Schools (AMHPS)
711 2nd St. NE, Ste. 200
Washington, DC 20002
Phone: (202)544-7499
Fax: (202)546-7105
Dale P. Dirks, Wash.Rep.

Founded: 1978. **Members:** 8. **Description:** Predominantly black health professions schools. Seeks to: increase the number of minorities in health professions; improve the health of blacks in the U.S.; increase the federal resources available to minority schools and students. Provides information to the U.S. Congress; conducts educational programs. **Publications:** *Study of the Health Status of Minorities in the U.S.*, periodic.

★1211★ Association Mondiale des Medecins Francophones (AMMF)
805-545, blvd. St. Laurent
Ottawa, ON, Canada K1K 4H9
Phone: (613)749-4001
Dr. Pierre Sarda, Sec.Gen.

Founded: 1973. **Members:** 400. **Languages:** French. Does not correspond in English. **Publications:** *AMMF Bulletin*, semiannual. Bulletin.

★1212★ Association of Pakistani Physicians (APPNA)
6414 S. Cast Ave., Ste. L2
Westmont, IL 60559
Phone: (708)968-8585
Fax: (708)968-8677
Waheed Akbar, M.D., Pres.

Founded: 1976. **Members:** 1,200. **Description:** Physicians and dentists who are native to Pakistan but now live and practice in North America. Purposes are: to support medical education and research and advance the interests of medicine and medical organizations; to foster scientific development and education in order to improve the quality of medicine and health care; to facilitate better relations among Pakistani

physicians and between them and the people of North America. Assists Pakistani physicians newly arrived in North America in orientation and adjustment. Arranges for donation of medical literature and medical supplies to Pakistan, and for lecture tours, medical conferences, and seminars to be held there. Participates in medical relief and charitable activities in Pakistan and North America; cooperates with other medical organizations in North America. Offers scientific programs for which continuing medical education credits are awarded. **Publications:** Bulletin, monthly. • Newsletter, quarterly.

★1213★ Association of Philippine Physicians in America (APPA)
2717 W. Olive Ave., Ste. 200
Burbank, CA 91505
Phone: (818)843-8616
Dr. Fred Quevedo, M.D., Exec.Dir.

Founded: 1972. **Members:** 3,000. **Description:** Individuals from the Philippines who are licensed to practice medicine in the U.S. Seeks to: render free medical care to indigent persons; establish a continuing medical education program for physicians; provide aid for education of physicians; support medical research. Sends medical missions to the Philippines. Provides medical residency program placement service. Maintains speakers' bureau; compiles statistics. **Publications:** *Directory of Physicians*, biennial. Directory. • *Leadership Roster of Officers*, annual. • *Philippine Physician*, periodic. Association and professional newsletter. *Price:* Free. Also publishes CME abstracts; plans to publish journal of medicine. **Formerly:** (1986) Association of Philippine Practicing Physicians in America.

★1214★ Association of Physician Assistant Programs (APAP)
950 N. Washington St.
Alexandria, VA 22314
Phone: (703)548-5538
Ron Garcia, Pres.

Founded: 1972. **Description:** Educational institutions with training programs for assistants to primary care and surgical physicians. Assists in the development and organization of educational curricula for physician assistant (PA) programs to assure the public of competent PAs; contributes to defining the roles of PAs in the field of medicine to maximize their benefit to the public; serves as a public information center on the profession; coordinates program logistics such as admissions and career placements. Sponsors Annual Survey of Physician Assistant Educational Programs in the United States. Conducts research projects; compiles statistics. **Publications:** *Annual Report on Physician Assistant Education in the U.S.*, annual. Report. Provides data on physician assistant education, employment, and trends affecting the profession. Includes statistics. *Price:* $25/copy. • *APAP Update*, monthly. Newsletter. For physician assistant program faculty and others concerned with curricula and government/legislative developments affecting the profession. *Price:* Included in membership dues. • *National Directory of Physician Assistant Programs*, annual. Directory. Describes curriculum, university and institutional affiliations, entrance requirements, selection factors, credentials awarded, and financial aid. *Price:* $25/copy.

★1215★ Association of Professors of Medicine (APM)
1200 19th St. NW, Ste. 300
Washington, DC 20036
Phone: (202)857-1158
Fax: (202)223-4579
James Terwilliger, Exec.Dir.

Founded: 1954. **Members:** 125. **Description:** Heads of departments of medicine in medical schools. Conducts educational programs; compiles statistics. **Publications:** *APM Update*, quarterly. Newsletter. • Directory, annual. • *Federal Health Policy Update*, quarterly. **Formerly:** Academic Medicine Club.

★1216★ Association of Program Directors in Internal Medicine (APDIM)
700 13th St. NW, Ste. 250
Washington, DC 20005
Phone: (202)393-1658
Free: 800-622-4558
Fax: (202)783-1347
Dema Daley, Exec.Dir.

Founded: 1977. **Members:** 1,150. **Description:** Physicians in internal medicine including departmental chairmen and directors of internal medicine, directors of residency training programs, associate program directors, medical education directors, and chiefs of medical service. Advances medical education through assisting accredited hospital internal medicine residency training programs in the United States and Puerto Rico. Conducts annual course for chief residents and program directors. Offers consulting services. **Publications:** *APDIM Directory*, annual. Membership Directory. • *Careers in Internal Medicine*, quarterly. • Membership Directory, annual. • Newsletter, quarterly. Profiles successful residency programs and summarizes developments in the field of internal medicine. *Price:* Included in membership dues; $60/year for individuals; $600/year for institutions.

★1217★ Association for the Study of Obesity (ASO)
DMAS
Univ. of Bristol
Churchill Buildings
Langford
Bristol, Avon BS18 7DY, England
Phone: 1934 852581
Fax: 1934 852741
Dr. Michael Enser, Sec.

Members: 200. **Languages:** English. **Description:** Scientists, researchers, dieticians, health education workers, and students in England. Promotes information exchange between members. **Publications:** *International Journal of Obesity*, bimonthly. Journal.

★1218★ Auxiliary to the National Medical Association (ANMA)
1012 10th St. NW
Washington, DC 20001
Phone: (202)371-1674
Fax: (202)289-ANMA
D. Darcell McDonald, Sec.

Founded: 1935. **Regional Groups:** 6. **State Groups:** 14. **Local Groups:** 40. **Description:**

Spouses of active members of the National Medical Association; widows and widowers of former members. Purposes are to: create a greater interest in the NMA; assist and encourage the medical profession in its efforts to educate and serve the public in matters of sanitation and health; develop and promote a national program on health and education with subcategories in community needs, legislation, and human relations. Conducts workshops on teenage pregnancy, breast self-examinations, high blood pressure screening, and sickle cell anemia screening. Plans and implements an annual youth forum under the auspices of the March of Dimes Birth Defects Foundation. Provides youth with professional guidance and the opportunity for peer exchange in the areas of mental and physical health; deals with the health of newborns, health services, nutrition, and teenage pregnancy. Also conducts programs for youth on parenting, socially transmitted diseases, nutrition, birth defects, and continued education after pregnancy. **Publications:** Book. Covers standard procedures. • Membership Directory, periodic. *Price:* Available to members only. • Newsletter, quarterly. **Formerly:** (1975) Women's Auxiliary to the National Medical Association.

★1219★ AVEHI - Audio Visual Resource Center
Raoli Camp, S.M. Rd.
Sardar Nagar 4
Sion Koliwada
Bombay 400 037, Maharashtra, India
Phone: 22 4072188
Chandita Mukherjee, Dir.

Founded: 1981. **Members:** 305. **Languages:** English, Gujarati, Hindi, Marathi. **Description:** Operates audio-visual resource center in India for members and the public at large. Areas of concentration include rural and urban development, health, and education. Conducts educational programs. **Publications:** *AVEHI Catalogue of Audio-Visual Materials*, periodic. Directory. • *Perspectives*, periodic. Newsletter.

★1220★ Bangladesh Medical Association of North America (BMA)
c/o S. Hasan
1575 Woodward Ave., Ste. 212
Bloomfield Hills, MI 48304
Phone: (810)338-8182
F. Hasan, M.D., Pres.

Founded: 1982. **Members:** 200. **Description:** Physicians who are from Bangladesh or have graduated from a medical college in Bangladesh. Seeks to bring together and improve communication between physicians who are of Bangladeshi origin or have trained in Bangladesh, and are currently residents of the United States or Canada, and other physicians. Assists medical students and physicians in obtaining specialized medical training and in post-training job placement in North America.

★1221★ Bangladesh Medical Studies and Research Institute (BMSRI)
35 H Rd., No. 14 A
Dhanmondi Residential Area
Dacca, Bangladesh
Phone: 2 318202
Dr. Anis Waiz, Dir.

Founded: 1984. **Members:** 14. **Languages:** Bengali, English. **Description:** Promotes medical studies and research with the object of raising the standard of medical education in Bangladesh. Encourages growth in Bangladesh's pharmaceutical, medical, and surgical instrument industries. Conducts research in disease prevention and treatment and on medical applications of indigenous plants and herbs. Offers refresher courses and monthly academic seminar; organizes conferences, lectures, seminars, and study groups. Operates speakers' bureau. Maintains the Bangladesh Medical College which grants degrees in medicine and surgery. **Publications:** *Annual Report and Prospectus*, annual. Journal. • *Bangladesh Medical College*, biennial. Directory. **Also Known As:** Bangladesh Medical College.

★1222★ British Medical Association (BMA)
Tavistock Sq.
London WC1H 9JP, England
Phone: 171 3874499
Fax: 171 3836400
Dr. E. McAlpine Armstrong, Sec.

Founded: 1832. **Members:** 101,174. **Languages:** English. **Description:** British medical societies and physicians. Represents members' interests before the government. Stimulates discussion on ethical and sociological issues; keeps members abreast of developments in medicine; disseminates scientific information. **Publications:** *British Medical Journal*, weekly. Journal. Scientific Journal.

★1223★ British Support Group - Inter-African Committee Against Harmful Traditional Practices
Severn Trow Cottage
21 Dunn's Ln.
Upton-upon-Severn
Worcester, Hereford and Worcester WR8 0HZ, England
Phone: 1684 592563
Joan Higman Davies

Founded: 1990. **Languages:** English. **Description:** Expresses solidarity with African women who struggle against traditional health practices which are harmful to their lives, health, and personal dignity. Raises funds and conducts research. Arouses public awareness through the media. Offers educational programs related to the population in Africa and African immigrants in Britain. **Publications:** Newsletter, bimonthly.

★1224★ Canadian Medical Association
1867 Alta Vista Dr.
Ottawa, ON, Canada K1G 3Y6
Phone: (613)731-9331
Fax: (613)731-9013

Description: Seeks to improve medical care for persons living in Canada. Works to maintain high standards of hospital care and health related services. Encourages constant improvement in the medical profession.

★1225★ Canberra Women's Health Centre
Box 1492
Woden, ACT 2606, Australia
Phone: 6 2902166
Fax: 6 2864742
Ms. Dorothy Broom, Contact

Founded: 1989. **Languages:** English. **Description:** Lobbies government on women's health issues. Promotes eqitable access to health care for all people; works to eliminate discrimination in health care on the basis of ethnicity, age, sexual orientation, or disability. Supports a woman's ability to control her reproductive choices. Fosters development of women's health groups and services. Provides a national forum for discussion of women's health care issues.

★1226★ Catholic Health Association of Canada
1247 Kilborn Pl.
Ottawa, ON, Canada K1H 6K9
Phone: (613)731-7797

Description: Works to administer Christian principles within the Canadian medical profession. Fosters competent and efficient health care services. Disseminates health information.

★1227★ Catholic Health Association of the United States (CHA)
4455 Woodson Rd.
St. Louis, MO 63134-3797
Phone: (314)427-2500
Fax: (314)427-0029
John E. Curley, Jr., Pres. & CEO

Founded: 1915. **Members:** 1,200. **Description:** Catholic hospitals, health care facilities, religious orders, health care systems, and extended care facilities. Aims to: participate in the life of the Church by advancing the healthcare ministry; assert leadership within the Church and society through programs of advocacy, facilitation, and education. Conducts surveys; compiles statistics. **Publications:** *Catholic Health Association Members*, periodic. Directory. Provides descriptive and statistical information on over 900 hospitals and long-term care facilities, 200 religious institutes, and archdioceses. *Price:* $40/copy for members; $200/copy for nonmembers. • *Catholic Health Association of the U.S.--Law Reports*, periodic. Newsletter. Reports on federal and state legislation, regulation, and court decisions affecting general health care and the ministry in the United States. *Price:* Included in membership dues. • *Catholic Health World*, bimonthly. Newspaper. Reports on the health care ministry. Includes *Catholic Health Association Assembly. Price:* Included in membership dues; $30/year for nonmembers. • *Health Progress*, 10/year. Journal. Addresses the administrative, ethical, financial, legal, and political problems faced by Catholic health care administrators. *Price:* Included in membership dues; $40/year for nonmembers. **Formerly:** Catholic Hospital Association of U.S. and Canada; (1979) Catholic Hospital Association.

★1228★ Catholic Medical Mission Board (CMMB)
10 W. 17th St.
New York, NY 10011-5765
Phone: (212)242-7757
Fax: (212)807-9161
Rev. Edward J. McMahon, SJ, Pres. & Dir.

Founded: 1928. **Description:** Provides health care assistance to clinical facilities in developing and transitional countries. Financial aid granted to students matriculated in accredited health care education programs in their own mission countries. Placement program assists health providers interested in volunteering for short- and long-term tours of service at selected clinical sites around the world. Conducts charitable programs. **Publications:** Annual Report. *Price:* Free. • *Medical Mission News*, quarterly. Magazine. Provides information on CMMB's programs. Recipients of shipments and health care placement opportunities are features. *Price:* Free.

★1229★ Cayman Islands Medical and Dental Society
PO Box 273
George Town, Cayman Islands
Phone: (809)949-6066
Fax: (809)949-8190
Dr. S.A. Tomlinson, Pres.

Languages: English. **Description:** Medical doctors, dentists, residents, and students. Promotes effective practice of medicine and dentistry in the Cayman Islands. Conducts public and continuing professional education programs. Encourages development of medical science and technology; serves as a forum for exchange of information among members.

★1230★ Center for Health Action (CHA)
49 Deepfield Rd.
Springfield, MA 01118-1911
Phone: (413)782-2115
Susan I. Pare, Pres.

Founded: 1982. **Members:** 6,000. **Description:** Individuals who oppose the fluoridation of drinking water in the U.S. Seeks to implement "individual, controlled, and supervised programs in place of this compulsory addition of a known contaminant to our fragile drinking water." Acts as a clearinghouse of information regarding what the group believes are the adverse effects of low levels of fluoride on the human body. Maintains speakers' bureau. **Publications:** *Fluoride: The Aging Factor*. Book. • *Update*, quarterly. **Formerly:** (1984) Safe Water Foundation.

★1231★ Center for Medical Consumers and Health Care Information (CMC)
237 Thompson St.
New York, NY 10012
Phone: (212)674-7105
Fax: (212)674-7100
Arthur A. Levin, Dir.

Founded: 1976. **Description:** Encourages individuals to make a critical evaluation of all information received from health professionals, to use medical services more selectively, and to understand the limitations of modern medicine. Promotes awareness that lifestyle choices such as smoking, exercise habits, and nutritional practices have more effect on health than access to medical care. **Publications:** *HealthFacts*, monthly. Newsletter. Helps consumers determine the risks and effectiveness of common medical procedures. Presents all treatment options, including nonmedical. *Price:* $21/year. • Reports.

★1232★ Central Society for Clinical Research (CSCR)
c/o Dr. John P. Phair
Northwestern University Med. School
Department of Medicine
303 E. Chicago Ave.
Chicago, IL 60611
Phone: (312)951-5610
Dr. John P. Phair, Sec.-Treas.

Founded: 1928. **Members:** 1,294. **Description:** Individuals who have accomplished a meritorious original investigation in the clinical or allied sciences of medicine and who enjoy an unimpeachable moral standing in the profession. Objectives are: the advancement of medical science; the cultivation of clinical research; the correlation of science with the art of medical practice; the encouragement of scientific investigation by the medical practitioner; the diffusion of a scientific spirit among the members of the society; the sponsorship of scientific meetings; the publication of papers on the methods and results of clinical research. **Publications:** *Journal of Laboratory and Clinical Medicine*, monthly. Journal. • *Roster*, quinquennial.

★1233★ Chatter Box
c/o Cupar St. Clinic
91 Cupar St.
Belfast, Antrim BT13 2LJ, Northern Ireland
Phone: 1232 327613
Fax: 1232 240362
Pat McConville, Contract

Description: Promotes improvement of women's general health and well-being. Offers counselling to depressed women. Disseminates information.

★1234★ Chi Delta Mu
c/o Tracy M. Walton, Jr.
1012 10th St. NW
Washington, DC 20001-4402
Phone: (202)842-1111
Fax: (202)842-0222
Tracy M. Walton, Jr., M.D., Sec.

Founded: 1913. **Members:** 650. **Local Groups:** 7. **Description:** To improve relationships among physicians, dentists, and pharmacists so that they may better serve their respective communities. Maintains revolving loan funds. **Publications:** *Dragon*, annual. Magazine. • Newsletter, quarterly. • Proceedings, annual.

★1235★ China Rural Health Association
10 Tiantan Xili
Beijing 100050, People's Republic of China
Phone: 1 5114358
Zhao Fu-tian, Sec.Gen.

Founded: 1986. **Members:** 41. **Languages:** Chinese. **Description:** Public health organizations comprised of 700,000 individuals promoting adequate health care among the rural Chinese populations. Works to improve current health care practices. Conducts studies on rural health conditions and educational programs. Bestows awards. **Publications:** *Rural Health*, monthly. • *Snake Treatment*, quarterly.

★ 1236 ★ **China Women's Health Care Society**
17 Qihe Bldg.
Dongcheng District
Beijing 100006, People's Republic of China
Phone: 1 5121620
Xiaoying Xiang, Sec.

Founded: 1989. **Members:** 3,000. **Languages:** Chinese. **Description:** Works to improve accessibility of preventative physical and mental health care for women in China. Conducts scientific research; sponsors academic exchange and professional training in the area of women's medicine. Participates in international conventions regarding women's health care. **Publications:** *Maternal Health Journal of Abroad Medicine*, quarterly. Journal.

★ 1237 ★ **Chinese American Medical Society (CAMS)**
c/o Dr. H.H. Wang
281 Edgewood Ave.
Teaneck, NJ 07666
Phone: (201)833-1506
Fax: (201)833-8252
Dr. H. H. Wang, Exec. Officer

Founded: 1962. **Members:** 600. **Regional Groups:** 4. **Description:** Physicians of Chinese origin residing in the U.S. and Canada. Seeks to advance medical knowledge, scientific research, and interchange of information among members and to promote the health status of Chinese Americans. Conducts educational meetings; supports research. Maintains placement service. Sponsors limited charitable program. **Publications:** *Chinese American Medical Society--Newsletter*, 3-4/year. Newsletter. Includes membership news, annoucements, and calendar of events. *Price:* Included in membership dues. • Membership Directory, biennial. **Formerly:** (1985) American Chinese Medical Society.

★ 1238 ★ **Chinese Medical Association**
42 Dongsi W St.
Beijing 100710, People's Republic of China
Phone: 1 5133311
Fax: 1 5123754
Min-Zhang Chen, Pres.

Founded: 1915. **Members:** 250,000. **Description:** Physicians in the People's Republic of China. Promotes the advancement of medical science and technology. Conducts information exchanges among physicians in China and in other countries. Conducts and analyzes medical research programs. Gathers and disseminates medical data. Develops and approves medical terminology. Offers training programs to members.

★ 1239 ★ **CHOSEN**
3642 W. 26th St.
Erie, PA 16506
Phone: (814)833-3023
Fax: (814)833-4091
Carl C. Eldred, Exec.Dir.

Founded: 1969. **Members:** 160. **Description:** Interdenominational organization supporting overseas Christian medical mission work. Procures new and used medical equipment for mission hospitals in economically deprived nations; repairs and modifies equipment; prepares equipment for shipping. Provides training in infection control (operating room and sterile departments) and in the proper use and maintenance of equipment for all mission hospital staffs. **Publications:** *CHOSEN Mission Project Newsletter*, quarterly. Newsletter. *Price:* Free. **Also Known As:** Christian Hospitals Overseas Secure Equipment Needs. **Formerly:** (1988) CHOSEN Mission Project.

★ 1240 ★ **Christian Health Association of Kenya (CHA)**
PO Box 30690
Nairobi, Kenya
Phone: 2 445542
J. Khalhiea, Exec. Dir.

Description: Fosters improved health in Kenya through offering programs in health education. Compiles statistics on youth and population. Disseminates information.

★ 1241 ★ **Christian Medical and Dental Society (CMDS)**
1616 Gateway Blvd.
PO Box 830689
Richardson, TX 75083-0689
Phone: (214)783-8384
Fax: (214)783-0921
David Stevens, M.D., Exec.Dir.

Founded: 1931. **Members:** 9,000. **Description:** Physicians, dentists, and medical and dental students who share a belief in the necessity of satisfying man's spiritual as well as physical needs. Approximately one out of every five members is actively engaged in foreign medical missionary work. Seeks to strengthen the spiritual lives of members and gain mutual strength and encouragement by meeting together for prayer, Bible study, and fellowship. Hopes to extend the reality of the Christian faith through the members' daily contacts and, through the active support of medical missions, to extend this faith around the world. Sponsors Medical Group Missions, a project sending health teams to underdeveloped countries. Also provides a health insurance program for missionaries in groups. Offers continuing medical education program. **Publications:** *Christian Medical & Dental Society--Journal*, bimonthly. Journal. Contains book reviews. *Price:* Included in membership dues. • *Christian Medical & Dental Society--Membership Directory*, biennial. Membership Directory. *Price:* Available to members only. • *CMDS Newsletter*, bimonthly. Newsletter. Contains calendar of events, group mission news, and obituaries. Contained with journal. *Price:* Included in membership dues. **Formerly:** (1988) Christian Medical Society.

★ 1242 ★ **Christian Medical Foundation International (CMF)**
7522 N. Himes Ave.
PO Box 152136
Tampa, FL 33684-2136
Phone: (813)932-3688
Fax: (813)932-3767
William Standish Reed, M.D., Pres.

Founded: 1962. **Members:** 4,854. **State Groups:** 4. **Description:** Physicians, nurses, clergy, and laity. Seeks to: investigate and promote the Christian spiritual care of those who are ill; educate doctors, nurses, and medical students regarding Christian medical and ethical principles. Bestows awards. Maintains speakers' bureau, placement service, biographical archives, and 2500 volume library; sponsors charitable programs. **Publications:** *Progress Notes*, bimonthly. Also publishes books and monographs.

★ 1243 ★ **Church World Service Aids for the Horn of Africa (CWSAHA)**
c/o Church World Service
National Council of Churches of Christ in the USA
Africa Office, Rm. 612
475 Riverside Dr.
New York, NY 10115-0050
Phone: (212)870-2645
Fax: (212)870-2056
Willis Logan, Dir.

Founded: 1980. **Description:** Purpose is to aid refugees in Somalia through Forest Station, a project to revitalize Somalian forestland, and Healthcare, a project promoting health in Somalian refugee centers and surrounding areas. **Publications:** Report, annual. **Formerly:** (1985) Interchurch Response for the Horn of Africa.

★ 1244 ★ **Churches' Action for Health (CMC)**
World Council of Churches
(L'Action des Eglises pour la Sante)
BP 2100
150, rte. de Ferney
CH-1211 Geneva 2, Switzerland
Phone: 22 7916111
Fax: 22 7910361
Margareta Skold, Coord.

Founded: 1967. **Languages:** English, French, Portuguese, Spanish. **Description:** A department of the World Council of Churches. Promotes more effective use of resources for health care through the establishment of structures for joint planning and action between all Christian churches and between churches, other voluntary agencies, and governments. Undertakes and encourages the study of the nature of healing and the problems that confront it in a changing world. Coordinates church-related medical programs at international, national, and regional levels; directs previously hospital-centered church medical work towards a more broad-based community health approach; assists church-related hospitals to plan more closely with government health services; advises health workers about new approaches. **Publications:** *AIDS: Sharing the Challenge*. Book. Contains resource material for the Asia-Pacific region. • *Contact*, bimonthly. Includes selected issues in Arabic, Portuguese, and Swahili. • *Financing Primary Health Care*. Monograph. • *Guide to HIV/AIDS Pastoral Counseling*. • *Learning About AIDS*. Monograph. • *What is AIDS?*. Monograph. **Formerly:** (1993) Christian Medical Commission.

★1245★ **City of Hope (COH)**
1500 E. Duarte Rd.
Duarte, CA 91010
Phone: (818)359-8111
Fax: (818)301-8115
Dr. Sanford M. Shapero, CEO

Founded: 1913. **Description:** Supports the National Pilot Medical Center and the Beckman Research Institute, which are engaged in treatment, research, and medical education in catastrophic diseases including cancer; leukemia; blood, heart and lung diseases; certain hereditary maladies; and metabolic disorders, such as diabetes. Patient care is available on a national and nonsectarian basis. Provides physician referrals. Offers free consulting service to doctors and hospitals. Seeks to influence medicine and science through 80 pilot research programs. From its staff and 200 laboratories, during the past decade over 3000 original findings have emerged in diseases treated as well as studies in diabetes, Alzheimer's disease, AIDS, Huntington's disease, genetics, and brain and nerve function. Receives nationwide support from nearly 500 chartered auxiliaries in over 230 cities, 32 states and Washington, DC, and from management, labor, fraternal and benevolent organizations, individuals, and special campaigns.

★1246★ **Colectivo Mujer y Salud**
Calle Elvira de Mendoza No. 59
Altos
Zona Universitaria
Santo Domingo, Dominican Republic
Fax: (809)530-8829
J. Garcia

Languages: Spanish. **Description:** Works to bring about public awareness of women's health issues. Supports means of preventative health care. Disseminates information.

★1247★ **College of Family Physicians of Canada (CFPC)**
(College des Medecins de Famille du Canada — CMFC)
2630 Skymark Ave.
Mississauga, ON, Canada L4W 5A4
Phone: (905)629-0900
Free: 800-387-6197
Fax: (905)629-0893
Dr. Reg L. Perkin, Exec.Dir.

Founded: 1954. **Members:** 12,080. **State Groups:** 10. **Languages:** English, French. **Description:** National medical association of family physicians and general practitioners. Members must maintain a minimum of 50 hours of continuing medical education credits annually. Works to maintain standards of family medicine training in the 16 Canadian medical schools through support of the Departments of Family Medicine and the accreditation of family practice residency programs. Administers certification examinations in emergency medicine and family medicine. Runs practice assessment program. Offers public education programs on fami-

ly medicine topics. **Publications:** *Canadian Family Physician*, monthly. Journal. • *CFPC-Liaison Newsletter*, quarterly. Newsletter. • *Self-Evaluation*, bimonthly. Home study program. • *Stress Without Distress: A Guide to the Management of Stress in Family Physicians*..

★1248★ **Command Trust Network (CTN)**
PO Box 17082
Covington, KY 41017
Phone: (606)331-0055
Fax: (606)331-0055
Kathleen Anneken, Exec. Officer

Founded: 1988. **Description:** Individuals concerned with the effects of silicone breast implants. Seeks to inform the public and motivate women with implants to consider all possible options. Disseminates information on medical studies, legal referrals, research, choosing a doctor, implant removel procedures, and other related topics. Maintains speakers' bureau for consumer, medical, or legal meetings on breast implants. **Publications:** *Elective Surgery Booklet*. Booklet. • *Legal Guide*. Booklet. • Newsletter, quarterly.

★1249★ **Commission on Accreditation of Allied Health Education Programs (CAAHEP)**
515 N. State St., Ste. 7530
Chicago, IL 60610
Phone: (312)464-4636
Fax: (312)464-5830
Mr. L.M. Detmer, MHA, Contact

Founded: 1976. **Members:** 70. **Description:** Serves as an accrediting agency for allied health programs in 19 occupational areas. **Formerly:** (1994) Committee on Allied Health Education and Accreditation.

★1250★ **Committee of Interns and Residents (CIR)**
386 Park Ave. S., Rm. 1502
New York, NY 10016
Phone: (212)725-5500
Fax: (212)779-2413
John Ronches, Exec.Dir.

Founded: 1957. **Members:** 5,000. **Description:** Medical and dental interns, residents, chief residents, and fellows (collectively referred to as house staff officers) at 50 member hospitals located in New York, New Jersey, and Washington, DC. Purposes include representing house staff in matters pertaining to compensation, benefits, hours, working conditions, and other issues affecting their employment, education, training, and the quality of health services and patient care. **Publications:** *News*, monthly. **Formerly:** (1974) Committee of Interns and Residents in New York City.

★1251★ **Committee for the Promotion of Medical Research**
191 Hayward St.
Yonkers, NY 10704
Phone: (914)968-0262
Ellen M. Cosgrove, Exec.Sec.

Founded: 1944. **Description:** Is concerned with the administration of medical research grants.

★1252★ **Commonwealth Medical Association (CMA)**
BMA House
Tavistock Sq.
London WC1H 9JP, England
Phone: 171 3836095
Fax: 171 3836195
Dr. J.D.J. Havard, Hon.Sec.

Founded: 1962. **Members:** 38. **National Groups:** 38. **Regional Groups:** 6. **Languages:** English. **Description:** National medical associations in Commonwealth countries. Provides technical assistance and cooperation to the national medical associations of Commonwealth developing countries. Offers educational programs and conducts projects in areas such as reproductive health, AIDS/HIV, medical ethics, and human rights. Conducts studies; acts as a clearinghouse for news and information. **Publications:** *Common Health*, quarterly. Bulletin. • *Medical Ethics in the Protection of Human Rights*. • *Prescribing and Health Education*. • *Problems of Professional Practice in Small Member States*. • *Women and Aids*.

★1253★ **Commonwealth Regional Health Secretariat (CRHS)**
PO Box 1009
Arusha, United Republic of Tanzania
Phone: 57 2961
Fax: 57 8292
Prof. A.M. Nhonoli, Regional Sec.

Founded: 1974. **Members:** 12. **Languages:** English. **Description:** Ministries of health from the Commonwealth countries of Botswana, Kenya, Lesotho, Malawi, Mauritius, Namibia, Seychelles, Swaziland, Tanzania, Uganda, Zambia, and Zimbabwe. Seeks better health for the people of eastern, central, and southern Africa; promotes cooperation among members to achieve this goal and coordinates health activities of member ministries. Conducts health research and training courses. Disseminates health information. **Publications:** Annual Report. • *CRHCS News*, semiannual. Newsletter. • *Inventory of Training Institutions and Courses*, periodic.

★1254★ **Community for Creative Non-Violence (CCNV)**
425 2nd St. NW
Washington, DC 20001
Phone: (202)393-1909
Fax: (202)783-3254

Founded: 1970. **Members:** 70. **Description:** Individuals working to combat homelessness and poverty in the U.S. Serves as a nonpartisan advocate to influence federal legislation relevant to the homeless; sponsors and participates in public demonstrations protesting homelessness. Operates Federal City Shelter, which provides social services including medical and mental health care, substance abuse rehabilitation, and recreational opportunities to 1500 homeless people in Washington, DC. **Publications:** *Housing and Homelessness: A Teaching Guide*. Book. • *Managing the Media: A Guide for Activists*. • Pamphlets.

★ 1255 ★ Community Systems Foundation (CSF)
1130 Hill St.
Ann Arbor, MI 48104
Phone: (313)761-1357
Fax: (313)761-1356
William D. Drake, Exec. Officer

Founded: 1963. **Members:** 10. **Description:** Organization committed to improving the quality of life through applied research and direct assistance to communities, governmental agencies, and service-oriented entities in the private sector. Focuses on community learning and encourages citizen involvement. Is working to develop systems for evaluating, monitoring, and implementing programs of nutrition and family planning. **Publications:** *Research Reports.* Reports.

★ 1256 ★ Comprehensive Health Education Foundation (CHEF)
22323 Pacific Hwy. S.
Seattle, WA 98198
Phone: (206)824-2907
Fax: (206)824-3072
Carl J. Nickerson, Ed.D., Pres.

Founded: 1974. **Description:** Encourages and supports improvement of health through education. Seeks to improve health education in the schools and community, enhance the public image of health educators, and stimulate community support of health education. Produces and disseminates health education information and materials. Initiates and supports innovations in health education. Supports the Health Education Fund, which sponsors pilot programs, offers scholarships for health education studies, and bestows leadership/recognition and professional enrichment awards.

★ 1257 ★ Council on Electrolysis Education (CEE)
46 S. Holmes St.
Memphis, TN 38111
Phone: (901)458-1431
Dorothy Graves, Pres.

Founded: 1972. **Description:** Professional electrologists. Sponsors educational programs and research in the field of electrolysis. Establishes criteria for accreditation and certification. Maintains speakers' bureau. Compiles statistics.

★ 1258 ★ Council for Health and Human Services Ministries, United Church of Christ (CHHSM)
700 Prospect Ave.
Cleveland, OH 44115
Phone: (216)736-2250
Fax: (216)736-2251
Bryan W. Sickbert, Exec.Dir.

Founded: 1939. **Members:** 191. **Description:** Health and human service institutions related to the United Church of Christ. Seeks to study, plan, and implement a program in health and human services; assist members in developing and providing quality services and in financing institutional and noninstitutional health and human service ministries; stimulate awareness of and support for these programs; inform the UCC of policies that affect the needs, problems,

and conditions of patients; cooperate with interdenominational agencies and others in the field. Maintains placement service and hall of fame. Compiles statistics; provides specialized education programs. **Publications:** *Directory of Services*, biennial. Directory. • *Employment Opportunities*, monthly. • *President's Newsletter*, 2-3/year. Newsletter. • *Shoptalk*, monthly. **Formerly:** (1961) Commission on Benevolent Institutions; (1983) Council for Health and Welfare Services, United Church of Christ; (1993) Council for Health and Human Services.

★ 1259 ★ Council for International Organizations of Medical Sciences (CIOMS)
(Conseil des Organisations Internationales des Sciences Medicales)
World Health Org.
Ave. Appia
CH-1211 Geneva 27, Switzerland
Phone: 22 7913406
Fax: 22 7910746
Dr. Zbigniew Bankowski, Sec. Gen.

Founded: 1949. **Members:** 103. **Languages:** English, French. **Description:** International organizations of medical sciences. Promotes and coordinates medical and scientific activities of member associations and national institutions affiliated with the council. Maintains collaborative relations with the World Health Organization and United Nations Educational, Scientific and Cultural Organization (see separate entries). Serves the scientific interests of the international biomedical community. **Publications:** *Calendar of International and Regional Congresses of Medical Sciences*, annual. • Directory, periodic. • *International Nomenclature of Diseases*. • *Proceedings of Round Table Conferences*.

★ 1260 ★ Council on Medical Education of the American Medical Association (CME-AMA)
515 N. State St.
Chicago, IL 60610
Phone: (312)464-4804
Fax: (312)464-5830
Dr. Carlos J. M. Martini, Sec.

Founded: 1847. **Members:** 12. **Description:** A council of the American Medical Association. Participates in the accreditation of and provides consultation to medical school programs, graduate medical educational programs, and educational programs for several allied health occupations. Provides information on medical and allied health education at all levels. **Publications:** *Allied Health Education Directory*, annual. Directory. • *Annual Report of Medical Education in the Journal of the AMA*. Annual Report. • *Continuing Education Courses for Physicians Supplement to the Journal of the AMA*, semiannual. Journal. • *Directory of Graduate Medical Education Programs*, annual. Directory.

★ 1261 ★ Council of Medical Specialty Societies (CMSS)
51 Sherwood Ter., Ste. Y
Lake Bluff, IL 60044
Phone: (708)295-3456
Fax: (708)295-3759
Rebecca R. Gschwend, MA, MB, Exec.VP

Founded: 1965. **Members:** 18. **Description:** National medical specialty societies represent-

ing 350,000 physicians. Purpose is to improve the quality of medical care in the United States and to foster excellence in the education of physicians. Provides a forum for discussion by specialty societies of national issues affecting the practice and teaching of medicine. Promotes communication among specialty organizations involved in the principal disciplines of medicine. **Formerly:** Tri-College Council.

★ 1262 ★ CPK Mothers' Union (CPKMU)
Box 40502
Nairobi, Kenya
Phone: 2 714752
Fax: 2 714750

Languages: English. **Description:** Mothers in Kenya. Promotes issues that affect the welfare of women and their children.

★ 1263 ★ Czech Medical Association (CMS)
Sokolska 31
PO Box 88
CS-120 26 Prague, Czech Republic
Phone: 2 24915195
Fax: 2 24216836

Founded: 1968. **Description:** Physicians, pharmacists, and other medical personnel. **Publications:** *Medical Congresses and Symposia*, annual.

★ 1264 ★ Delta Psi Kappa
PO Box 90264
Indianapolis, IN 46290
Phone: (317)255-4379
Fax: (317)253-5067
Harriet Rodenberg, Exec.Dir.

Founded: 1916. **Members:** 20,000. **Regional Groups:** 30. **State Groups:** 8. **Description:** Professional fraternity - health, physical education, recreation, and dance. **Publications:** *Foil*, semiannual.

★ 1265 ★ Direct Relief International (DRI)
27 S. La Patera Ln.
Santa Barbara, CA 93117
Phone: (805)964-4767
Fax: (805)681-4838
Ann Wyckoff Carlos, Pres. & CEO

Founded: 1948. **Description:** Donates contributed pharmaceuticals, medical supplies, and equipment to health facilities and locally coordinated health projects in medically underdeveloped areas of the world. Provides emergency assistance to victims of natural disasters, refugees, and others. **Publications:** *Presidents' Report*, annual. Report. • *Program Reports*, periodic. Reports. • *Response*, 3/year. Newsletter. **Formerly:** (1982) Direct Relief Foundation.

★ 1266 ★ DOC (Doctors Ought to Care) (DOC)
5615 Kirby Dr., No. 440
Houston, TX 77005
Phone: (713)528-1487
Fax: (713)528-2146
Luke Burchard, M.D., Chm.

Founded: 1977. **Members:** 2,000. **Local Groups:** 150. **Description:** A physician-led organization of medical students, teachers, parents, and other concerned individuals working to prove that doctors do care about health issues. Works through school programs, health professionals' offices, hospitals, media, and Super Health 2000, a health promotion effort which attempts to counter the effects of advertising unhealthy products. Seeks to launch a broad health promotion effort aimed at educating the public, particularly teenagers and children, on the "lethal" lifestyles of cigarette smoking, alcohol dependency, drug abuses, poor nutrition, and teenage pregnancy. Campaigns through television commercials, newspaper comic strips, radio, sports events, posters and t-shirts, and its speakers' bureau to promote the image of good health through community-wide reinforcement of the positive role model of the health professional and to emphasize nutrition, contraception, and moderation. Sponsors competitions; maintains library, biographical archives, and the International Tobacco Archive. Conducts children's services and research programs. **Publications:** *The Journal of Medical Activism*, quarterly. Newsletter. Fights advertising and promotion of unhealthy products by the tobacco and alcohol industry. Includes information on the pro-health community. *Price:* $25/year.

★1267★ DOCARE International (DI)
1750 NE 168th St.
North Miami Beach, FL 33162
Phone: (305)949-4000
Anslie M. Stark, Exec.Sec.

Founded: 1961. **Members:** 150. **Description:** Volunteer organization of medical doctors, osteopathic physicians, nurses, dentists, veterinarians, pharmacists, optometrists, podiatrists, and laypersons with special skills. Serves as a medical outreach program providing health care services to people in remote areas of Mexico, Central America, and the Caribbean. Is concerned with those deprived of medical care due to terrain, language, and cultural barriers. Conducts two to three one-week medical missions per year to areas in need until physicians or health care specialists are provided by the host country government. Has provided care to the Tarahumara Indians of northern Mexico, the Tepehuan Indians of Central Mexico, Mayan Indians in the Yucatan jungle, and an orphanage in Honduras. **Publications:** *DOCARE Flyer*, quarterly. Newsletter. Includes stories about members, meetings, planned missions, and election of officers. *Price:* Included in membership dues.

★1268★ Doctors for Artists (DFA)
105 W. 78th St.
New York, NY 10024
Phone: (212)496-5172
Dr. Lambert Macias, Dir.

Founded: 1984. **Members:** 20. **Description:** Doctors in New York directly or indirectly involved with the arts. Established to provide performing and visual artists with specialized health care at a reduced rate, and treatment especially sympathetic to their needs. Artists receive a 20% discount on medical services, including office visits and surgery; membership is represented in some 23 areas of specialized medicine. Although there are no plans to expand outside New York, assistance is offered to individuals wishing to establish similar groups in other parts of the country.

★1269★ Doctors Without Borders (DWB) (Medecins Sans Frontieres — MSF)
8, rue St. Sabin
F-75544 Paris Cedex 11, France
Phone: 1 40212929
Fax: 1 48066868
Dr. Philippe Biberson, Pres.

Founded: 1971. **Members:** 3,500. **National Groups:** 5. **Regional Groups:** 12. **Languages:** English, French. **Description:** Physicians and other members of the medical profession. Provides medical assistance to victims of war or natural disasters. Is presently rendering aid in the crisis-stricken areas of Africa. Sponsors professional training for physicians. **Publications:** *Medecins Sans Frontieres*, quarterly. • *Medical and Surgical Guidelines*, periodic. • *MSF Info*, 10/year.

★1270★ Dooley Foundation / INTERMED
420 Lexington Ave., Rm. 2428
New York, NY 10170
Phone: (212)687-3620
Fax: (212)599-6137
Verne Chaney, M.D., Founder & Pres.

Founded: 1961. **Description:** Assists Third World countries in the development of medical care systems through self-help projects in disease prevention, health education, personnel development, and research and medical aid to refugees. Presently operates programs in El Salvador, Honduras, Nepal, and Nicaragua. **Publications:** Brochure. • *INTERMED Journal*, quarterly. Journal. **Formerly:** Dooley Foundation/INTERMED - U.S.A.; (1962) Dr. Thomas A. Dooley Foundation; (1978) Thomas A. Dooley Foundation; (1980) Thomas A. Dooley Foundation/INTERMED U.S.A..

★1271★ East Coast Migrant Health Project Inc. (ECMHP)
1234 Massachusetts Ave. NW, Ste. C-1017
Washington, DC 20005
Phone: (202)347-7377
Fax: (202)347-6385
Jennifer Schmidt, Exec.Dir.

Founded: 1970. **Description:** Health and social care delivery system for migrant and seasonal farm workers and their families. Provides health and social services to migrant workers through outreach health and parahealth professionals associated with existing community health clinics/departments in Delaware, Florida, Georgia, Maine, Maryland, New York, New Jersey, North Carolina, Pennsylvania, South Carolina, Tennessee, Virginia, and West Virginia. Goals are: empowerment of migrant and seasonal farmworkers and their families through practical health and social education. Activities include: staff orientation; in-service education; community liaison work; health education and cultural awareness. Maintains placement service. **Publications:** *Farmworker Outreach Manual*, annual. Manual. Guidelines for conducting outreach and health education to farm workers. Extensive list of resources and organizations dealing with farmworkers. *Price:* $30.

★1272★ Ecological Physicians Association (Okologischer Arztebund)
Sauerbruchstr. 31
32049 Herford, Germany
Phone: 5221 270063
Fax: 5221 270130
Raymund Munster, Contact

Founded: 1987. **Members:** 500. **Description:** Promotes the return to a natural life existence as well as the preservation of human health. Provides information and treatment. Seeks to contribute to building ecological awareness.

★1273★ Educational Commission for Foreign Medical Graduates (ECFMG)
3624 Market St.
Philadelphia, PA 19104
Phone: (215)386-5900
Marjorie P. Wilson, M.D., VP

Founded: 1956. **Members:** 20. **Description:** Organizational members are American Board of Medical Specialties; American Hospital Association; American Medical Association; Association of American Medical Colleges; Association for Hospital Medical Education; Federation of State Medical Boards of U.S.; National Medical Association. Aims to provide information to foreign medical graduates regarding entry into graduate medical education and the U.S. health care system; evaluate their qualifications; identify foreign medical graduates' cultural and professional needs; assist in the establishment of educational policies and programs. Distributes to foreign medical graduates around the world information about U.S. conditions and requirements in the area of medicine. Acts as a screening agency for hospitals, state licensing boards, and specialty boards. Selects items for two-day examinations annually from National Board of Medical Examiners' questions. Sponsors exchange visitor program to enable physicians from other countries to participate in graduate medical education or training. Gathers and disseminates data about foreign medical graduates. **Publications:** *Educational Commission for Foreign Medical Graduates--Annual Report*. Annual Report. *Price:* Free. • *Educational Commission for Foreign Medical Graduates--Information Booklet*, annual. Booklet. Provides procedures for fulfilling ECFMG examination and certification requirements. *Price:* Free. **Formerly:** (1974) Educational Council for Foreign Medical Graduates.

★1274★ Estonian Doctors' Association (Eesti Arstide Liit)
Puusepa St. 2
EE-2400 Tartu, Estonia
Phone: 7 428575
Vaino Sinisalu, Pres.

Description: Promotes the educational and professional interests of physicians.

★1275★ Estonian Family Doctors' Association (Eesti Perearstide Selts)
Puusepa St. 1a
EE-2400 Tartu, Estonia
Phone: 7 428706
Rein Kermes, Chm.

Description: Family physicians and general practitioners in Estonia.

★ 1276 ★ European Calcified Tissue Society (ECTS)

Vakgroup Orale CelBiologie
van der Boechorstast 7
NL-1081 BT Amsterdam, Netherlands
Phone: 20 5484574
Fax: 20 6610741
Prof.Dr. Elisabeth H. Burger, Pres.

Founded: 1981. **Members:** 450. **Languages:** English. **Description:** Scientists in 21 countries interested in tissue calcification, a process wherein organic tissue becomes hardened as a result of lime salt deposits. Objectives are to: expand scientific knowledge of tissue calcification and related phenomena; promote fundamental and clinical research; encourage a multidisciplinary approach to scientific inquiry; provide authoritative advice on aspects of tissue calcification research that have a wide professional and public significance. **Publications:** *Abstracts of Symposium Proceedings.* • *List of Members,* periodic.

★ 1277 ★ European Health Policy Forum (EHPF)

(Forum Europeen de Politique de Sante — EHPF)
School of Public Health
Leuven University
PO Box 214
B-3000 Louvain, Belgium
Phone: 16 336978
Fax: 50 220541
Prof. Mia Defever, Dir.

Founded: 1981. **Languages:** English. **Description:** Leading policymakers in a broad range of health care fields and industries representing 25 countries. Purposes are: to inform members of new developments in health care policy and research; to facilitate communication between policymakers in different fields; to draw attention to new research and its implications for health policy. Sponsors the development and transfer of health information systems. Collaborates with the World Health Organization. **Publications:** *Health Policy,* monthly. Journal. • Papers, periodic. • Proceedings, periodic.

★ 1278 ★ European Medical Research Councils (EMRC)

1, quai Lezay Marnesia
F-67080 Strasbourg Cedex, France
Phone: 88 767119
Fax: 88 370532
Dr. J.H. Kock, Sec.

Founded: 1971. **Members:** 25. **Languages:** English. **Description:** National medical research councils or equivalent organizations. Promotes public medical and biomedical research. Exchanges information on topics including scientific policies of various research organizations, and information on planned or undertaken but unpublished research programs in specific fields of interdisciplinary and priority research. Encourages the creation of research projects through the coordination and cooperation of research groups on an international level. Identifies and defines research problems in member countries and prompts members to influence national policies pertaining to research grants in those areas. A committee of the European Science Foundation . *Human Genome Re-search: A Review of European and International Contributions, Report on Genome Research,* and *Clinical Research Training in Europe.*

★ 1279 ★ European Union of General Practitioners (UEMO)

(Europaische Vereinigung der Allgemeinartze — UEMO)
Trondhjemsgade 9
DK-2100 Copenhagen 0, Denmark
Phone: 35261460
Fax: 31385507
Ole Asbjorn Jensen, M.D.

Founded: 1967. **Languages:** English, French, German, Italian, Spanish. **Description:** National European medical organizations. Promotes the educational and professional interests of general practitioners and defends their professional independence. Fosters unity among general practitioners. Advocates high standards in medical training and patient care.

★ 1280 ★ European Union of Medical Specialists (UEMS)

20, ave. de la Couronne
B-1050 Brussels, Belgium
Phone: 2 6495164
Fax: 2 6403730
Dr. R. Peiffer, Gen.Sec.

Founded: 1958. **Members:** 12. **Languages:** English, French. **Description:** Medical specialists in 15 countries. Works to ensure high quality care for patients. Fosters communication among members; promotes members' interests. **Publications:** *Bulletin,* semiannual. Bulletin.

★ 1281 ★ Ev. Lutheran Good Samaritan Society (ELGSS)

PO Box 5038
Sioux Falls, SD 57117
Phone: (605)336-2998
Fax: (605)336-0673
Dr. Mark A. Jerstad, Pres.

Founded: 1922. **Description:** Owns, operates, and manages 240 Christian institutions in 26 states, including nursing homes and homes for the elderly and the handicapped. Provides each center with computerized accounting, comparative data, administrator and staff training programs, a regional director, special purchasing agreements, life enrichment programming, emergency financial backing, and specialists in other fields. Conducts meetings to provide administrators with credits for continuing education. **Publications:** Directory, periodic. • *The Good Samaritan,* quarterly.

★ 1282 ★ Ezer Metzion

13 Frankfurter St.
Petach Tikva, Israel
Phone: 3 9218849
Fax: 3 5744030
Rabbi Chananya Tzolek

Languages: Hebrew. **Description:** Provides guidance and counseling in medical matters. Assists hospitalized patients and their families. Makes available medical and children's services; conducts educational and charitable programs.

★ 1283 ★ Family and Health

Vesnina str. 24, Bldg. 3
121002 Moscow, Russia
Phone: 95 2411436
Fax: 95 2410421
Irina Manuilova, Gen.Dir.

Founded: 1991. **Description:** Promotes improved health conditions for women and their families. Conducts educational programs on health. Offers counseling services.

★ 1284 ★ Family and Health Section of the National Council on Family Relations (FHS)

3989 Central Ave. NE, Ste. 550
Minneapolis, MN 55421
Phone: (612)781-9331
Fax: (612)781-9348

Founded: 1984. **Description:** A section of the National Council on Family Relations. Health and education professionals. Serves as a forum for all professionals involved in interdisciplinary work in the family and health fields. Presents clinical research and educational programs at NCFR conferences. **Publications:** *Family Health News,* periodic. Newsletter. **Formerly:** (1991) Family and Health Section.

★ 1285 ★ Family Research Institute (FRI)

PO Box 2091
Washington, DC 20013
Phone: (703)690-8536
Dr. Paul Cameron, Exec. Officer

Founded: 1982. **Members:** 6,400. **Description:** Promotes information about sexual, family, and substance abuse issues. Conducts research and educational programs. Maintains speakers' bureau; compiles statistics. **Publications:** *Family Research Report,* bimonthly. Newsletter. *Price:* $20/year.

★ 1286 ★ Federal Physicians Association (FPA)

PO Box 45150
Washington, DC 20026
Phone: (703)455-5947
Fax: (703)455-8282
Dennis W. Boyd, Exec.Dir.

Founded: 1978. **Members:** 400. **State Groups:** 1. **Description:** Civil service physicians employed by or retired from the federal government. Objectives are: to improve the health care of patients served by federal civil service physicians; to advance the practice of medicine within the federal government; to better the working conditions and benefits of federal civil service physicians. Conducts specialized education programs. **Publications:** *The Federal Physician,* bimonthly. Newsletter. *Price:* $37.50/year. **Formerly:** (1982) American Academy of Federal Civil Service Physicians.

★ 1287 ★ Federation of Associations of Regulatory Boards (FARB)

400 S. Union St., Ste. 295
PO Box 4389
Montgomery, AL 36103-4389
Phone: (205)834-2415
Fax: (205)269-6379
Randolph P. Reaves, Contact

Founded: 1973. **Members:** 9. **Description:** National associations of regulatory boards united to exchange information and engage in programs and joint activities relating to the education and licensing of professionals and to cooperate in solving the mutual problems of members. Conducts attorney certification course. **Publications:** *FARB Facts*, periodic. **Formerly:** (1985) Federation of Associations of Health Regulatory Boards.

★ 1288 ★ Federation of Feminist Women's Health Centers (FFWHC)
633 E. 11th Ave.
Eugene, OR 97401
Phone: (503)344-0966
Fax: (503)344-1993
Beverly Whipple, Pres.

Founded: 1975. **Members:** 163. **Description:** Women's health clinics; interested individuals. Works to secure reproductive rights for women and men, educate women about the normal functions of their bodies, and improve the quality of women's health care. Coordinates activities of women's health centers. **Publications:** *A New View of a Woman's Body.* • *How to Stay Out of the Gynecologist's Office.* Book. • *Woman-Centered Pregnancy and Birth.* Book.

★ 1289 ★ Federation of Hungarian Medical Societies (MOTESZ)
(Magyar Orvostudomanyi Tarsasagok es Egyesuletek Szovetsege — MOTESZ)
Nador utca 36
H-1051 Budapest, Hungary
Phone: 1 1123807
Fax: 1 1837918
Dr. Bela Szalma, Exec.Dir.

Founded: 1966. **Members:** 72. **Languages:** English, German, Hungarian. **Description:** Medical, dental and natural scientific societies comprising 32,000 individuals. Works to enhance the medical and sciences in Hungary. Promotes the development of international relations in the field of health. Conducts educational programs; bestows awards. **Publications:** *MOETSZ Calendar*, annual. • *MOETSZ Magazin*, quarterly. Scientific journal.

★ 1290 ★ Federation of State Medical Boards of the United States (FSMB)
6000 Western Pl., Ste. 707
Fort Worth, TX 76107
Phone: (817)735-8445
Fax: (817)738-6629
Dr. James Winn, M.D., Exec.VP

Founded: 1912. **Members:** 67. **Description:** State medical examining and licensing boards (including twelve osteopathic boards). **Publications:** *Federation Bulletin*, quarterly. Bulletin. • *FSMB NewsLine*, monthly. • *Handbook*, annual. Directory. • *Legislative and Regulatory Exchange*, biennial.

★ 1291 ★ Federation of Women's Health Councils—New Zealand
CPO Box 853
27 Gilles Ave, 2nd Fl
Newmarket
Auckland, New Zealand
Phone: 9 5205175
Fax: 9 5204152
Judi Strid, Contact

Founded: 1990. **Languages:** English. **Description:** Women's health councils united to devel-

op a national health policy for women. Coordinates information sharing and networking among member organizations. Monitors the provision of women's health care services to ensure that doctors and health professionals are accountable to consumers. Defends women's rights to control their bodies; supports access to free abortions. Fosters research activities. **Publications:** *Accident Compensation: A Women's Issue.* Monograph. • *Consumer Consultation, Representation and Participation.* Monograph. • *Ensuring the Cervical Screening Programme Survives the Health Changes.* Monograph. • Newsletter, bimonthly.

★ 1292 ★ Flying Physicians Association (FPA)
PO Box 677427
Orlando, FL 32867
Phone: (407)359-1423
Fax: (407)359-1167
Patricia A. Nodecker, Exec.VP

Founded: 1954. **Members:** 1,200. **Regional Groups:** 5. **Description:** Doctors of medicine who have a current pilot certificate and are members of an ethical medical organization. Promotes the interests of medicine in aviation, safety, and education. **Publications:** *Flying Physician*, 3/year. Newsletter. For physicians with pilot's certificates covering medical and aviation topics; also includes association activities, book reviews, and calendar. *Price:* Included in membership dues; $15/year for nonmembers. • *Flying Physicians Association--Bulletin*, monthly. Bulletin. Membership activities newsletter. *Price:* Included in membership dues. • *Flying Physicians Association--Directory*, annual. Directory. *Price:* Included in membership dues.

★ 1293 ★ Forum for Medical Affairs (FORUM)
c/o Med. Society of the State of New York
420 Lakeville Rd.
Lake Success, NY 11042
Phone: (516)488-6100
Charles N. Aswad, Exec.VP

Founded: 1944. **Members:** 800. **Description:** Presidents, presidents-elect, and past presidents of state medical associations, members of the American Medical Association and the House of Delegates, editors of state medical association journals, executive directors of state medical associations, and representatives of AMA-recognized medical specialty societies. **Formerly:** (1972) Conference of Presidents and Officers of State Medical Associations.

★ 1294 ★ Foundation for Advances in Medicine and Science (FAMS)
PO Box 832
Mahwah, NJ 07430-0832
Phone: (201)818-1010
Fax: (201)818-0086
Tony Bourgholtzer, Bd.Chm.

Founded: 1983. **Members:** 400. **Description:** Clinical cardiologists, scientists, and scanning electron microscopists. Disseminates resource information in clinical medicine and science. Funds research projects. **Publications:** *Clinical Cardiology*, monthly. Journal. Contains peer-reviewed articles for practicing cardiologists. *Price:* $80/year in U.S.; $126.50/year outside

U.S.; $15.50/single copy. • *Scanning*, 7/year. *Price:* $163/year in U.S.; $187/year outside U.S.; $260.50/year, institutional in the U.S.; $40/single copy. **Formerly:** (1990) Foundation for Advances in Clincal Medicine and Science.

★ 1295 ★ Foundation for Church Related Health Institutions in Rwanda (Bureau des Formations Medicales Agrees au Rwanda — BUFMAR)
BP 716
Kigali, Rwanda
Phone: 83008
Fax: 86176
C. Lydsmau

Languages: French. **Description:** Promotes improved health among individuals living in Rwanda. Provides health and medical services. Offers training in medical technology. Operates emergency care activities. Monitors health and medical care programs and projects.

★ 1296 ★ Foundation for Health (FFH)
337 East Ave.
Watertown, NY 13601-3829
Phone: (315)782-6664
Free: 800-724-7460
George Bonadio, Exec.Dir.

Founded: 1972. **Description:** Gathers and disseminates information regarding health; seeks to publicize "natural" laws of health in an effort to make excellent health and long, useful lives common throughout the world. Proclaims the simplicity and inexpensiveness of maintaining one's health in contrast to the complexity and expense of disease. Researches and develops nutrition and health related projects and programs. **Publications:** *Ask the Nutritionist*, weekly. Newspaper. • *Seven Disciplines of Health*. Also contributes weekly health column to newspapers; plans to publish book.

★ 1297 ★ Foundation for Health Care Evaluation (FHCE)
2901 Metro Dr., Ste. 400
Bloomington, MN 55425
Phone: (612)854-3306
Free: 800-444-3423
Fax: (612)853-8503
David M. Ziegenhagen, CEO

Founded: 1971. **Members:** 3,500. **Description:** Physicians interested in ensuring the availabilty of quality health care at reasonable costs. Evaluates health care services at hospitals, retirement homes, and other facilities. Develops health care standards for hospitals and offers consultation services to operators of health care facilities to improve efficiency in services. Conducts research and development on latest treatments and medical technologies. Tests new medical technologies.

★ 1298 ★ Foundation for Health Services Research (FHSR)
1350 Connecticut Ave. NW, Ste. 1100
Washington, DC 20036
Phone: (202)223-2477
Fax: (202)835-8972
Alice S. Hersh, Exec.VP & CEO

Founded: 1981. **Description:** Conducts professional and educational activities beneficial to the field of health services research. **Publications:** *Bridge*, 3/year. Newsletter. • *Connection*, semiannual. Newsletter. • *Focus*, semiannual. Newsletter. • *Forum*, semiannual. Newsletter. Also publishes informational materials.

★ **1299** ★ **Foundation for Hospice and Homecare (FHH)**
519 C St. NE
Stanton Park
Washington, DC 20002
Phone: (202)547-6586
Fax: (202)546-8968
Bill Halamandaris, CEO

Founded: 1985. **Description:** Established to improve the quality of life of American citizens, with particular emphasis on the needs of the dying, the disabled, the disadvantaged, and the elderly. Promotes high standards of patient care for hospice and home care services; develops and fosters mechanisms for assuring the proper preparation of hospice and home care staff and volunteers; conducts research related to health services, aging, and social policies; develops and promotes innovative and efficient alternatives to current health and social policies. Promotes the development of a comprehensive continuum of health care; provides a forum for public comment on social and health policy issues; educates and informs the public concerning matters of health and social policy. Seeks to reverse negative stereotypes associated with age and physical impairment. Accredits homemaker-home health aides; sponsors projects on subjects of importance to health care including Alzheimer's Disease, cancer care, and chronic pediatric health problems. **Publications:** *All About Homecare--A Consumer's Guide*. Booklet. • Annual Report, annual. • Brochures. • *Directory of Accredited Homemaker-Home Health Aide Services*, semiannual. Directory. *Price:* Free. • *Foundation News*, quarterly. Newsletter. *Price:* Free. • Manuals. • *Model Curriculum and Teaching Guide for the Instruction of the Homemaker-Home Health Aide*. Published in conjunction with the U.S. Public Health Service. Also produces documentaries.

★ **1300** ★ **Foundation for Informed Medical Decision Making**
PO Box C-17
Hanover, NH 03755
Phone: (603)650-1180
Fax: (603)650-1125

Founded: 1989. **Description:** Develops and produces interactive videos for patient use in hospitals, so they can make informed decisions about their medical care. The videos are made available for use in hospitals and medical facilities. **Publications:** Video.

★ **1301** ★ **Foundation for Innovation in Medicine (FIM)**
411 North Ave. E.
Cranford, NJ 07016
Phone: (908)272-2967
Fax: (908)272-4583
Stephen L. DeFelice, M.D., Chm.

Founded: 1976. **Description:** Seeks to regenerate interest in medical discovery and innovation, which the foundation believes flourished in the U.S. in the 1940s and 1950s, but has since

declined despite "vastly increased public and private expenditures in research and development." Intends to monitor the state of innovation by conducting seminars and conferences. Encourages clinical research on natural substances and substances with little commercial value. **Publications:** *From Oysters to Insulin: Nature and Medicine at Odds*. Book. *Price:* $15.95. • *Nutraceutical White Paper*. *Price:* $10.

★ **1302** ★ **Foundation for the Support of International Medical Training (FSIMT)**
417 Center St.
Lewiston, NY 14092
Mrs. M. A. Uffer, Pres.

Founded: 1960. **Members:** 6000,000. **Description:** Individuals and corporations organized to provide information regarding the availability of competent medical care overseas and information concerning sanitary conditions, health hazards, and climatic conditions in various parts of the world. Offers detailed guidance on vaccination and immunization requirements and tropical diseases. **Publications:** *Be Aware of Schistosomiasis*. • Brochure, annual. • Directory, annual. • *How to Protect Yourself Against Malaria*. • *Immunization Chart*, annual. • *Malaria Risk Chart*, annual. • *Schistosomiasis Risk Chart*. • *Set of 24 World Climate Charts*, annual. • *Traveller Clinical Chart*, annual.

★ **1303** ★ **Foundation for Women's Health Research and Development (FORWARD)**
Africa Centre
38 King St.
Covent Garden
London WC2E 8JT, England
Phone: 171 3796889
Fax: 171 3796889

Languages: English. **Description:** Promotes the studies of women's health research and development throughout Europe and other western countries. Supports the rights of women and children. Protects women and children from becoming victims of abuse. Opposes and fights for the elimination of the practice of genital mutilation of young girls. Disseminates information. Conducts training programs. **Publications:** *Another Form of Physical Abuse: Prevention of Female Genital Mutilation in the United Kingdom*. Video. • *Child Protection and Female Genital Mutilation: Advice for Health, Education, and Social Work Professionals*. Book. • *Working Together: A Guide to Arrangement for Inter-Agency Protection of Children from Abuse*. Book.

★ **1304** ★ **French-Language Society for Reanimation (FLSR)**
(Societe de Reanimation de Langue Francaise — SRLF)
Gustave Roussy
F-94805 Villejuif Cedex, France
Phone: 1 45594506
Fax: 1 45596444
Dr. G. Nitenberg, Sec.

Founded: 1970. **Members:** 800. **Languages:** French. Does not correspond in English. **Description:** Medical doctors in 25 countries who specialize in intensive care. Encourages production of scientific papers on intensive care treatment of patients. Conducts Annual sympo-

sium and postgraduate course. Bestows awards. Compiles statistics. **Publications:** *Actualites en Reanimation et Urgences*, annual. • *Perspectives en Reanimation*, annual. • *Reanimation - Urgences*, bimonthly. Also publishes *Recommendations from Conferences de Consensus en Reanimation et Medicine et Urgence*.

★ **1305** ★ **Fundacao Instituto Integrado de Saude**
Rua Solon Pinheira No. 1330 centro
60050-041 Fortaleza, Ceara, Brazil
Phone: 85 2260830
Antonio Beserra Veras, Pres.

Founded: 1992. **Languages:** Portuguese, Spanish. **Description:** Works to improve the quality of life and the availability of health care available to people living in rural areas of Brazil. Constructs hospital facilities; provides dental and medical care staff to underserved areas; makes legal assistance available to individuals and communities in need. Promotes cultural development through creation of study centers and libraries.

★ **1306** ★ **Fundacion Salvadorena para el Desarrollo de la Mujer y el Nino (FUNDEMUN)**
Ave. Santa Monica y Calle Aurora
Edificio Carisma 4
Apartado Postal 0583
San Salvador, El Salvador
Phone: 253518
Fax: 269194
Sara Ventura

Founded: 1989. **Languages:** Spanish. **Description:** Seeks to: safeguard the rights of women, families, and communities; promote development based on belief in equality; achieve full access of women to the land, water, and other natural resources. Provides educational programs such as: literacy, preventive medicine, dress making, and money management. Maintains a center for research and documentation.

★ **1307** ★ **German Women Physicians Association**
(Deutscher Arztinnenbund)
Herbert-Lewin-Str. 5
50931 Cologne, Germany
Phone: 221 4004540
Rosmarie Hennings, Contact

Founded: 1924. **Members:** 1,800. **Description:** Promotes solidarity among women doctors. Represents members' interests in the medical sphere. Cultivates international contacts.

★ **1308** ★ **Global Health Action (GHA)**
1712 Clifton Rd. NE
Atlanta, GA 30329
Phone: (404)634-5748
Fax: (404)634-9685
Robin C. Davis, Exec.Dir.

Founded: 1972. **Description:** Supported by churches, organizations, foundations, businesses, government agencies, and individuals. Conducts continuing education programs for health and development professionals and community health care workers from developing countries. Seeks to educate Americans about the role they can play in improving world health. Holds international health management and leadership courses in Atlanta, GA, for health professionals from emerging countries and the former Soviet Union. Designs and conducts special health workshops and courses when requested and funded by other agencies. Operates Community Health Worker Training Program in Haiti and Village Health Worker Trainers' Program and AIDS Education Program in India. Consultation services available. Maintains speakers' bureau. **Publications:** *A Great and Mighty Tree.* Video. • *Global Health Action Newsletter*, semiannual. Newsletter. Primarily for donor education and publicity. • Videos. **Formerly:** (1985) International Nursing Services Association; (1993) INSA, The International Service Association for Health.

★ 1309 ★ **Grupo Nacional Mujer, Salud y Desarrollo**
Ministerio de Salud
Ave. 5, calle 35
Apartado Postal 2048
Panama 1, Panama
Phone: 253540

Languages: Spanish. **Description:** Works to improve the health and development conditions of women in Panama. Coordinates and evaluates women's health and development programs. Coordinates efforts with similar organizations.

★ 1310 ★ **Guam Lytico and Bodig Association**
PO Box 1458
Agana, Guam 96910
Phone: 4772293
Fax: 4772294
Madeleine Z. Bordallo

Description: Provides supportive services and information to individuals stricken with disease.

★ 1311 ★ **Hadassah, The Women's Zionist Organization of America (HWZOA)**
50 W. 58th St.
New York, NY 10019
Phone: (212)355-7900
Free: 800-664-JOIN
Fax: (212)303-8282
Beth Wohlgelernter, Exec.Dir.

Founded: 1912. **Members:** 385,000. **Regional Groups:** 36. **Local Groups:** 1500. **Description:** Conducts many community services in the U.S. and Israel. Provides "basic Jewish education as a background for intelligent and creative Jewish living in America." Organizes programs in Jewish education, Zionist and American affairs, leadership development, singles, young leaders, health care professionals, seniors, and Young Judaea clubs and camps. Built and maintains Hadassah Medical Organization encompassing the Hadassah University Hospital on Mt. Scopus, Israel and the Hadassah Hebrew University Medical Center at Ein Karem, Israel. Maintains Hadassah College of Technology in Jerusalem, Israel, providing courses in computer science, medical and dental technology, electro-optics, printing, hotel managment and graphics; operates Hadassah Career Counseling Institute for high school students, young adults, and new immigrants. Is the principal

agency in the U.S. for support of Youth Aliyah villages and day-centers for immigrant and deprived youth. Participates in land purchase and reclamation programs of the Jewish National Fund. Maintains Hadassah International, which works worldwide to raise funds and support for medical activities and to encourage cooperation in public health and community medicine. Sponsors Young Judaea for American Jewish young people, ages 9 through 30. Conducts three month live-in program for adults wishing to volunteer their services in Israel. Operates speakers' bureau; sponsors seminars and workshops. **Publications:** *The American Scene*, 3/year. Focuses on Hadanah's domestic agenda. *Price:* Included in membership dues. • *Hadassah Associates Medbriefs*, quarterly. • *Hadassah Headlines*, quarterly. Newsletter. Contains medical news. *Price:* Included in membership dues. • *Hadassah Magazine*, monthly, except combined June/July and August/September issues. Magazine. Contains articles on art, medicine, parenting, Hadassah projects, and Hebrew education. *Price:* Included in membership dues; $25/year for nonmembers. • *Textures: Hadassah National Jewish Studies Bulletin*, 3/year. Bulletin. Contains articles on Jewish art, culture, and thought. Examines daily life in Israel; discusses Hebrew texts, literature, and poetry. *Price:* Free to presidents, VPs, and education chairs; $3/year for others. • *Zionist Affairs Update*, 20/year. Also publishes Jewish education study guides. **Formerly:** (1914) Daughters of Zion.

★ 1312 ★ **Haitian and Co-Arts Association**
165 Park Row, Ste. 8-D
New York, NY 10038
Phone: (212)732-9735
Andre Letellier, Pres. & Exec.Dir.

Founded: 1956. **Members:** 450. **Description:** Professionals, business executives, clergy, artists, and others both in the U.S. and Haiti. Serves as a charitable educational assistance program to voluntarily contribute to the elimination of hunger, eradication of disease, and promotion of literacy of deprived children of the peasants in rural areas of Haiti. Establishes rural and mobile free clinics to provide community-wide vaccination against polio, diphtheria, whooping cough, tuberculosis, yaws, malaria, and tetanus to needy children in remote villages. Provides villagers with advice on common tropical diseases, prenatal care, hygiene, and birth control. Promotes the self-sufficiency of small peasant farmers by encouraging cooperative rural agroforestry and aquaculture programs and new irrigation and far ming techniques. Promotes literacy, with primary emphasis on modern industrial technology and advanced vocational trade schools. Provides medical and dental care, food, and shelter to needy schoolchildren enrolled in the five geographic departments of Haiti's rural areas. U.S. corporations and individuals donate funds, medical and dental supplies, drugs, seeds, and educational materials for distribution by the association. Also attempts to develop public interest in Haiti by sponsoring cultural endeavors in such fields as folklore, dance, music, history, literature, art, theater, photography, and wood sculpture; sponsors sports events and trade exhibits.

Formerly: (1973) Haiti Voluntary Central Committee.

★ 1313 ★ **Harvey Society (HS)**
c/o DR. Paul Lazarow
Mt. Sinai School of Medicine
Department of Cell Biology and Anatomy
1 Gusgaze Levy Pl., Box 1107
New York, NY 10029
Phone: (212)241-1505
Dr. Paul Lazerow, Ph.D.

Founded: 1905. **Members:** 1,600. **Description:** Persons with a Ph.D. or M.D. degree active or interested in making contributions to the literature of medical and biological science. Seeks to disseminate knowledge and promote the development of the medical sciences. Sponsors a series of public lectures delivered by persons active in the field. Society is named after William Harvey (1578-1657), who identified the circulation of blood. **Publications:** *Harvey Lectures*, annual.

★ 1314 ★ **Health Action Foundation (Fundacja Akcja dla Zdrowia)**
Nowogrodzka St. 25-3
PL-00-511 Warsaw, Poland
Phone: 22 287723
Fax: 22 286509
Michal Pawelek, Chm.

Description: Works to improve the quality of health care available.

★ 1315 ★ **Health Action International (HAI)**
Jac. van Lennepkade 334 T
NL-1053 NJ Amsterdam, Netherlands
Phone: 20 6833684
Fax: 20 6855002
Catherine Hodgkin, Coordinator

Founded: 1981. **Languages:** English. **Description:** Nongovernmental organizations addressing consumer health questions, especially those concerning developing countries. Campaign goals are: to further safe and economically rational use of pharmaceuticals throughout the world; to find nondrug solutions to problems related to sanitation and nutrition; to implement the World Health Organization Action Programme on Essential Drugs and Vaccines. Seeks to halt export of hazardous pharmaceutical products. Sponsors consumer education and research; maintains clearinghouse. Lobbies as a consumer advocate before the World Health Organization, the general assembly of the United Nations and the European Economic Community. Conducts seminars. **Publications:** *HAI News*, bimonthly.

★ 1316 ★ **Health First International, Inc. (HFI)**
508 N. 1st St.
Sartell, MN 56377
Phone: (612)252-5857
Elsie Harper, Exec.Dir.

Founded: 1989. **Members:** 250. **Regional Groups:** 1. **State Groups:** 3. **Local Groups:** 1. **Description:** Disseminates information on low-cost health care. Offers classes in nutrition, diet management, stress and anger control, family life, drug abuse recognition, and how to stop smoking; holds well-baby clinics. Compiles statistics. Plans to conduct cooking, physical therapy, and exercise classes.

★ 1317 ★ Health Occupations Students of America (HOSA)

6309 N. O'Connor Rd., Ste. 215, LB-117
Irving, TX 75039-3510
Phone: (214)506-9780
Free: 800-321-HOSA
Fax: (214)506-9919
Dr. Jim Koeninger, Exec.Dir.

Founded: 1975. **Members:** 52,000. **State Groups:** 36. **Local Groups:** 2100. **Description:** Secondary and postsecondary students enrolled in health occupations education programs; health professionals and others interested in assisting and supporting the activities of HOSA; alumni of health occupations education programs and individuals who have made significant contributions to the field. Primary aim is to improve the quality of healthcare for all Americans by urging members to develop self-improvement skills. Operates within health occupation education programs in public high schools and postsecondary institutions. Encourages members to develop an understanding of current healthcare issues, environmental concerns, and survival needs worldwide. Conducts programs to help individuals improve their occupational skills and develop leadership qualities. Conducts exhibits, management workshops, and medical facility tours; provides social and recreational activities. Maintains speakers' bureau; compiles statistics. **Publications:** Brochure. • Handbook. • *HOSA Leaders Directory*, annual. Directory. • *HOSA Leaders' Update*, quarterly. • *HOSA News Magazine*, quarterly. Magazine. • *Story of HOSA*. Video. Also publishes recruitment package. **Also Known As:** National HOSA.

★ 1318 ★ Health Research Council of New Zealand (HRC)

PO Box 5541
Wellesley St.
Auckland, New Zealand
Phone: 9 3798227
Fax: 9 3779988
Dr. Bruce A. Scoggins, Dir.

Founded: 1937. **Description:** Initiates and supports general health-related research, including the medical, dental, biological, and public health fields in New Zealand. Coordinates health research on a national basis and administers and disburses government research funding. Collects and disseminates scientific information. Bestows awards. **Publications:** *AIDS Newsletter*, periodic. Newsletter. • Annual Report. • *HRC Newsletter*, quarterly. Newsletter. Contains information on health research in New Zealand. • *Madri Health Research Newsletter*, semiannual. Newsletter. **Formerly:** (1990) Medical Research Council of New Zealand.

★ 1319 ★ Health and Social Policy Corporation

(Corporacion de Salud y Politicas Sociale — CORSAPS)

Vina del Mar 12
Apartado Postal 296-22
Providencia
Santiago, Chile
Phone: 2 2225520
Fax: 2 6353967
Teresa Marshall, Contact

Founded: 1990. **Languages:** English, Spanish. **Description:** Promotes health reform and the development of related social policy for the citizens of Chile. Focuses primarily on the health concerns young people and women. Supports applied research.

★ 1320 ★ Health Volunteers Overseas (HVO)

PO Box 65157, Washington Sta.
Washington, DC 20035-5157
Phone: (202)296-0928
Fax: (202)296-8018
Kate Skillman, Coord.

Founded: 1986. **Members:** 1,500. **Description:** Physicians, dentists, nurses, and physical therapists. Works to improve health care in developing countries through the participation of trained health and medical volunteers. Programs include Anesthesia, Dentistry, General Surgery, Oral and Maxillofacial Surgery, Internal Medicine, Orthopaedics, and Pediatrics. HVO has program sites in St. Lucia, Uganda, Brazil, Guyana, India, Jamaica, Trinidad, Mexico, Philippines, Malawi, Indonesia, South Africa, Eritrea, Guyana, Vietnam, Kenya, Bangladesh, Bhutan, Pakistan, and China. **Publications:** *A Guide for Short-Term Volunteer Medical Workers in Developing Countries.* • *The Volunteer Connection*, quarterly. Newsletter.

★ 1321 ★ Hesperian Foundation (HF)

PO Box 1692
Palo Alto, CA 94302
Phone: (415)325-9017
Fax: (415)325-9044
Thomas G. Kelly, Admin.Dir.

Founded: 1973. **Description:** Promotes good health in Third World countries through community-based, informed self-care. Fosters constructive dialogue on health care and social change. Originally established to help launch Project Piaxtla, a health care network, and Project Projimo, a community-based rehabilitation center for spinal cord injuries, in western Mexico. The foundation now focuses on community-based rehabilitation and the state of health and health care throughout the rural areas of Latin America and in Third World countries. Analyzes and criticizes existing social, political, and economic systems that prevent the poor from obtaining adequate standards of life and health. Operates gratis book fund, in which third world health care workers recieve Hesperian publications at no charge. **Publications:** *A Manual for Midwives.* Book. • *Disabled Village Children.* Book. • *Helping Health Workers Learn.* Book. • *There Is No Doctor.* Book. • *Where There Is No Dentist.* Book.

★ 1322 ★ Human Biology Council (HBC)

c/o Dr. Gary D. James
Cardiovascular Center
The New York Hospital - Cornell Medical Center
520 E. 70th St.
New York, NY 10021
Phone: (212)746-2191
Fax: (212)746-8451
Dr. Gary James, Ph.D., Sec.-Treas.

Founded: 1974. **Description:** Individuals who are involved in fields related to human biology, including physical anthropology, sports medicine, genetics, nutrition, physiology, and pediatrics. Promotes study of human biology and related topics; encourages communication and utilization of results from such studies; aids in education of persons involved in such studies. Seeks to stimulate discussions of common goals and problems among scientists in the field. Assists with scholarly research in human biological sciences. Sponsors courses. **Publications:** *American Journal of Human Biology*, bimonthly. Journal. Contains information on human population biology; includes papers, articles, and book reviews. *Price:* $90/year (inside US); $114/year (outside U.S.). • Directory, annual.

★ 1323 ★ Incurably Ill for Animal Research (IIFAR)

PO Box 27454
Lansing, MI 48909
Phone: (517)887-1141
Fax: (517)887-1550
Gregory A. Maas, CEO

Founded: 1985. **Members:** 2,500. **Local Groups:** 18. **Description:** Persons who have health problems and are concerned that animal research for medical purposes will be stopped or severely limited due to the efforts of animal rights activists; interested individuals. Supports the use of animals for the purpose of medical research, teaching, and testing. Seeks to educate the public regarding the role animals serve in biomedical research and improving human and animal health. Maintains speakers' bureau; conducts fundraising. **Publications:** *Have You Benefited?.* Brochure. • *How Can You Show Your Support?.* Brochure. • *iiFAR Update*, monthly. Includes local chapter news and information on legislation and the activities of animal rights activists. • *iiFARsighted Report*, quarterly. Report. • *Why Should You Care?.* Brochure. Also distributes educational literature and student information packets.

★ 1324 ★ Independent Citizens Research Foundation for the Study of Degenerative Diseases (ICRFSDD)

PO Box 97
Ardsley, NY 10502
Phone: (914)478-1862
Dorothea P. Seeber, Exec.Dir.

Founded: 1957. **Description:** Individuals united to seek and publish information of aid to those affected by degenerative diseases. Makes available in bulletin form documented information on the multiple and contributing causes of degenerative diseases, testing procedures for their early detection, and possible approaches to therapy and prevention. Seeks out factors in the environment that are detrimental to health. Supports research on calibrated transcutaneous electric nerve stimulation and preventive medicine techniques. Maintains 400 volume library on maintenance of health and prevention of disease. Seeks out factors in the environment that are detrimental to health. **Publications:** Newsletter, bimonthly. Also publishes authorized transcripts of radio lectures on nutrition.

★ 1325 ★ Independent Physicians Association of Germany (Unabhangiger Arzteverband Deutschland)
Hohenstaufenring 39
50674 Cologne, Germany
Phone: 221 235562
Fax: 221 231234
Dr. Klaus Menten, Contact

Founded: 1961. **Description:** Represents the interests of independent physicians. Provides advice and help on all matters concerning the medical profession.

★ 1326 ★ Indians Into Medicine (INMED)
University of North Dakota
School of Medicine
501 N. Columbia Rd.
Grand Forks, ND 58203
Phone: (701)777-3037
Fax: (701)777-3277
Eugene DeLorme, J.D.Dir.

Founded: 1973. **Description:** Support program for American Indian students. Seeks to: increase the awareness of and interest in healthcare professions among young American Indians; recruit and enroll American Indians in healthcare education programs; place American health professionals in service to Indian communities. Coordinates financial and personal support for students in healthcare curricula. Provides referral and counseling services. Maintains 2000 volume library. **Publications:** *Serpent, Staff and Drum*, quarterly. Newsletter. *Price:* Free. Also publishes program information and motivational materials.

★ 1327 ★ Indonesian Medical Association (IMA)
Jalan Sam Ratulangi 29
Jakarta, Indonesia
Phone: 21 3150679
Fax: 21 3900473
Dr. Pudjiastuti Arsadi

Founded: 1950. **Description:** Medical doctors in Indonesia. Promotes effective practice of medicine in Indonesia; conducts public education programs; represents members' interests before government agencies and regulatory bodies. Fosters the development of medical science and technology. Serves as a forum fo the exchange of ideas and information among members. **Publications:** *Indonesian Family Physician's Journal*, bimonthly. Journal. • *Majalah Kedokteran Indonesia*, monthly. Journal. • Newsletter, biweekly.

★ 1328 ★ Institute for Social Studies and Action (ISSA)
QCC PO Box 1078
Quezon City, Metro Manila 1104, Philippines
Phone: 2 997396
Fax: 2 9240717
Rowena Ong Alvarez, Exec.Dir.

Founded: 1983. **Languages:** English, Filipino. **Description:** Filipino women and health organizations working to increase public awareness of women's health needs. Seeks to improve maternal health; fertility management and contraceptive practices; techniques for prevention of sexually transmitted diseases; and government action on violence against women. Monitors and lobbies the legislative and executive levels of government on women's issues. Organizes informational and educational activities on women's health and reproductive rights issues. Maintains clinics which offer OB/GYN, pediatric, family planning, general medicine, and counseling services for disadvantaged citizens. Trains members of like-minded organizations in health care and helps them organize clinics. Refers clients to resource, counseling, legal, and medical centers. **Publications:** *Medium for the Advancement and Achievement of Reproductive Rights, Health Information and Advocacy*, quarterly. Bulletin. Address the issues surrounding the reproductive health rights of Filipino women. Disseminates information on women's health to raise consciousness.

★ 1329 ★ Instituto Costarricense de Acueductors y Alcantarrillados Oficina de la Mujer y la Familia para el Desarrollo
Calle 5 avenida central y 1
Edificio La Llacuna
Apartado 5120-1000
San Jose, Costa Rica
Phone: 2332155
Fax: 2222259
Laura Chen

Founded: 1990. **Languages:** Spanish. **Description:** Works to educate Costa Rican women on sanitation, nutrition, health, and development. Investigates the social, legal, and employment status of women. Provides educational and training programs on legal issues, community leadership, and job skills. Coordinates activities with similar organizations. Disseminates research findings in order to increase public awareness of women's concerns. **Publications:** *Mujer, Agua y Salud*, quarterly. Bulletin.

★ 1330 ★ Intensive Care Society (ICS)
Tavistock House
Tavistock Sq.
London WC1H 9HX, England
Phone: 171 3882856
Fax: 171 3883759
Dr. Alasdair Short, Hon.Sec.

Founded: 1971. **Members:** 1,000. **Languages:** English. **Description:** Medical and scientific specialists in the field of intensive care. Seeks to provide the scientific and professional basis necessary for the research activities related to intensive care issues, and to make advice and information available to interested parties. Promotes communication among related organizations. **Publications:** *Fire Safety in the Intensive Care Unit*. Book. • *Future of Intensive Care in the U.K.*. Book. • *ICS Newsletter*, semiannual. Newsletter. • *Intensive Care Audit*. Book. • *The Organ Donor*. • *Standards for Intensive Care Units*. Book.

★ 1331 ★ Interamerican College of Physicians and Surgeons (ICPS)
915 Broadway, Ste. 1105
New York, NY 10010
Phone: (212)777-3642
Fax: (212)505-7984
Dr. Rene F. Rodriguez, Pres.

Founded: 1979. **Members:** 4,000. **Description:** Physicians in countries of the Americas. Encourages understanding and communication among members concerning all aspects of medical practice. Promotes health education in Hispanic communities in the Western Hemisphere. Maintains library of Spanish language medical books. **Publications:** *Interamerican Medical Directory*, biennial. Directory. • *Medico Interamericano*, monthly.

★ 1332 ★ Interamerican Medical and Health Association (IMHA)
3025 St. James Dr.
Boca Raton, FL 33434
Phone: (407)483-6573
Fax: (407)483-3239
Dr. Maurizio Luca-Moretti, Pres.

Founded: 1989. **Members:** 4,000. **Description:** Academicians of national academies of medicine, deans of medical facilities, and professors of medical science. Promotes the work of biomedical and health scientists and the effectiveness of science in the promotion of human welfare. Facilitates networking among members and their institutions. Conducts research programs on medical and public health issues; current research focuses on nutrition and AIDS. **Publications:** *Journal of the Interamerican Medical and Health Association*, 3/year. Journal. *Price:* $60/year for institutions in North America; $60/year for insititutions in Europe and Japan; $30/year for individuals in North America; $30/year for individuals in Europe and Japan.

★ 1333 ★ Interchurch Medical Assistance (IMA)
College Ave. at Blue Ridge
Box 429
New Windsor, MD 21776
Phone: (410)635-8720
Fax: (410)635-8726
Paul Derstine, Exec.Dir.

Founded: 1961. **Members:** 14. **Description:** Denominational-founded autonomous organization for the solicitation, collection, and distribution of pharmaceutical, medical, dental, and hospital supplies for use in the overseas charity medical programs of American Protestant churches, relief agencies, and other American charitable organizations. **Publications:** Annual Report, annual. • *Interchurch Medical Newsletter*, quarterly. Newsletter.

★ 1334 ★ International Academy of Health Care Professionals (IAHCP)
70 Glen Cove Rd., Ste. 209
Roslyn Heights, NY 11577
Phone: (516)621-0620
Dr. Henry H. Reiter, Pres.

Founded: 1984. **Members:** 41. **Description:** Nurses, psychologists, social workers, and medical and health care professionals. Provides for educational exchange among members. Offers research and educational materials to Third World health care institutions.

★ 1335 ★ International Association for Accident and Traffic Medicine (IAATM) (Association Internationale de Medecine des Accidents et du Trafic)
Postfack 1644
S-751 46 Uppsala, Sweden
Phone: 18 175025
Fax: 18 175031
Kjell Roos, M.D., Exec.Dir.

Founded: 1960. **Regional Groups:** 7. **Languages:** English. **Description:** Physicians and other professionals in 56 countries who are interested in motor vehicle and traffic related accidents; national associations for accident and traffic medicine. Fosters communication among governments and other organizations concerned with traffic problems. Conducts research; disseminates information. **Publications:** Brochure, periodic. • *Congress Proceedings.* Proceedings. • *Journal of Traffic Medicine,* quarterly. Journal.

★ 1336 ★ International Association for Medical Assistance to Travellers (IAMAT)
417 Center St.
Lewiston, NY 14092
Phone: (716)754-4883
Fax: (519)836-3412
Mrs. M. A. Uffer-Marcolongo, Pres.

Founded: 1960. **Members:** 9500,000. **Description:** A division of the Foundation for the Support of International Medical Training. Seeks to make competent 24 hour-a-day medical care available to the traveller around the world by doctors who usually speak English or French and have medical training in Europe or North America. Is establishing the International Center for Study of the Medical Aspects of Travel and Geographical Health. **Publications:** *Be Aware of Schistosomiasis.* • *Directory of Participating Physicians and Medical Institutions Abroad,* annual. Directory. • *How to Protect Yourself Against Malaria.* Also issues world climate charts, world malaria risk chart, world immunization chart, and world schistosomiasis risk chart.

★ 1337 ★ International Association for Medical Research and Cultural Exchange (AIRMEC) (Association Internationale pour la Recherche Medicale et les Echanges Culturels — AIRMEC)
2, blvd. du Montparnasse
F-75015 Paris, France
Phone: 1 45669115
Fax: 1 45665072

Founded: 1956. **Members:** 2,000. **Languages:** French. **Description:** Medical and pharmaceutical professionals. Fosters and participates in the development of medical research. Initiates scientific exchange among members throughout the world. Organizes activities such as conferences, conventions, and workshops to facilitate medico-pharmaceutical comparison. Promotes and contributes to postgraduate medical and pharmaceutical study. **Publications:** *Medecine d'Afrique Noire,* monthly.

★ 1338 ★ International Community for the Relief of Starvation and Suffering (ICROSS)
PO Box 1649
Southampton, NY 11969
Phone: (516)288-3807
Mary A. Hogarty, Pres.

Founded: 1980. **Members:** 1,000. **Description:** Raises funds to operate a mobile medical unit that provides inoculations, primary health care, and health education to people in areas of East Africa affected by drought and starvation.

★ 1339 ★ International Council for Health, Physical Education, Recreation, Sport, and Dance (ICHPERSD)
1900 Association Dr.
Reston, VA 22091
Phone: (703)476-3486
Fax: (703)476-9527
Dr. Dong Ja Yang, Sec.Gen.

Founded: 1958. **Members:** 1,500. **Description:** National groups and professional organizations concerned with programs, policies, and the educational aspects of health, physical education, sports, recreation, and dance; institutions of higher education, libraries, and HPERD departments and professional individuals in 114 countries. Serves as a clearinghouse for exchange of information and ideas; represents members' interests in the field. Sponsors consultations and seminars. Prepares exhibits of books, photographs, films, pictures, and other materials. Compiles statistics; conducts study and research in cooperation with national groups and governmental organizations such as UNESCO. **Publications:** *Congress Proceedings,* biennial. Proceedings. • *Journal of the International Council for Health, Physical Education, Recreation, Sport, and Dance,* quarterly. Journal. Contains association news, coverage of developments in international athletic competition, and information about new techniques in physical education. • Report. Covers physical education and games in curriculum. Published in conjunction with UNESCO. • Report. Covers teacher preparation for physical education. Published in conjunction with UNESCO. • Report. Covers the status of teachers in physical education. Published in conjunction with UNESCO.

★ 1340 ★ International Council of Homehelp Services (ICHS) (Conseil International des Services d'Aide Familiale — CISAF)
Postbus 100
NL-3980 GB Bunnik, Netherlands
Phone: 3405 96211
Fax: 3405 63994
Mr. R. Kalfsbeek, Exec.Sec.

Founded: 1959. **Members:** 85. **National Groups:** 11. **Languages:** English, French. **Description:** National homehelp organizations, governmental agencies organizing homehelp services, and interested individuals in 20 countries. Purpose is to support the development of care services provided in the home. (Homehelp is a service rendered by qualified persons to assist in achieving or maintaining an independently functioning household.) Works to prevent, shorten, or delay institutional care. Trains family members in the care of children and the handi-

capped, household management, and personal hygiene; encourages research in the field. Serves as liaison among members worldwide and facilitates the exchange of knowledge and ideas among them. Aids in the planning of exchange visits between member agencies. Organizes congresses and biennial seminar. **Publications:** *Congress Proceedings,* quadrennial. • *ICHS Information,* quarterly. • *Newsletter,* periodic. Newsletter. • *Public Relations Commission,* periodic. Directory. • *Seminar Proceedings,* quadrennial. Also publishes national reports.

★ 1341 ★ International Council of Prison Medical Services (ICPMS) (Conseil International des Services Medicaux Penitentiaires)
750 W. Broadway, Ste. 1417
Vancouver, BC, Canada V5Z 1J4
Phone: (604)872-8719
Chunilal Roy, M.D., Sec.Gen.

Founded: 1976. **Members:** 200. **National Groups:** 1. **Languages:** English, French, Spanish. **Description:** Medical and health care professionals; associate members are administrators of prison health care agencies. Promotes discussion among prison health professionals. Strives to improve health care worldwide; encourages postgraduate training for doctors working in prison settings. **Publications:** Proceedings.

★ 1342 ★ International Electrology Educators (IEE)
c/o SCME
132 Great Rd., No. 200
Stow, MA 01775
Phone: (617)431-7263
Fax: (617)237-9039
Wallace A. Roberts, Pres.

Founded: 1979. **Members:** 55. **Description:** Electrology schools and teachers. Purposes are to instruct teachers and standardize the curriculum and teaching of electrology. Conducts educational programs and regional educational conferences for electrology educators. **Publications:** *IEE Directory of Schools,* periodic. Directory. • *Perspectives,* quarterly. **Formerly:** (1982) National Electrology Educators; (1985) International Electrology Educators; (1993) Institute of Electrology Educators.

★ 1343 ★ International Federation of Catholic Medical Associations (FIAMC) (Federation Internationale des Associations Medicales Catholiques — FIAMC)
Palazzo San Calisto
00120 Vatican City, Vatican City
Phone: 6 69887372
Prof. Walter Osswald, Pres.

Founded: 1950. **Members:** 44. **National Groups:** 39. **Regional Groups:** 5. **Languages:** English, French. **Description:** National associations and guilds of Catholic physicians. Seeks to: coordinate the efforts of Catholic medical associations worldwide; promote Christian principles throughout the medical profession; discuss and find new ethical approaches to biotechnological problems. Encourages the development of Catholic medical associations globally to assist in the moral, spiritual, and technical advancement of the Catholic physician; participates in the development of the medical profession. Maintains speakers' bureau. **Publications:** *Catholic Medical Quarterly.* • *Decisions,* quarterly. • *Journal,* quarterly. • *Linacre Bulletin,* quarterly. • Newsletter, quarterly.

★ 1344 ★　International Federation of Health Funds (FHF)
39 Friar St.
Reading, Berks. RG1 1DZ, England
Phone: 1734 566544
Fax: 1734 393464
Kenneth N. Groom, Sec.Gen.

Founded: 1968. **Members:** 205. **Languages:** English. **Description:** Organizations involved in the coordination and execution of voluntary nonprofit health services (170); other interested nonprofit organizations (12) and individuals (23) in 20 countries. Promotes the study and development of voluntary nonprofit health care services. Encourages research and the exchange of information. Operates speakers' bureau. Offers study tours and staff exchange program; sponsors seminars. Compiles and disseminates statistics. **Publications:** *Basic Data Tabulations,* annual. Annual Report. • Booklets, periodic. • *Conference Proceedings,* biennial. • *Membership Directory,* annual. Directory. • *National Commentaries,* biennial. • *Newsletter,* quarterly. Newsletter. • *Survey of Hot Topics,* annual. **Formerly:** (1989) International Federation of Voluntary Health Service Funds.

★ 1345 ★　International Federation of Medical Students Associations (IFMSA) (Federacion Internacional de Asociaciones de Estudiantes de Medicina)
Academisch Medisch Centrum
Faculteit der Geneeskunde
Meibergdreef 15
NL-1105 AZ Amsterdam, Netherlands
Phone: 20 5665366
Fax: 20 6972316
Mrs. Mia Hilhorst, Contact

Founded: 1951. **Members:** 50. **Regional Groups:** 4. **Languages:** English, French, Spanish. **Description:** National medical student associations in 50 countries. Objectives are: to provide an international forum for medical students to discuss topics of interest and to formulate policies from such discussions; to provide a professional exchange for medical students; to facilitate contacts with other worldwide organizations; to enhance members' influence in fundraising activities for IFMSA-recognized projects. Trains medical personnel to meet the health needs of their societies. Organizes clerkships and study tours. Places students in hospitals worldwide through its Professional Exchange Committee. Promotes practical teaching in primary health care. Has established relations with the European Economic Community, and organizations of the United Nations and the World Health Organization. **Publications:** *Newsletter,* quarterly. Newsletter.

★ 1346 ★　The International Foundation (TIF)
1700 Route 23N, Ste. 170
Wayne, NJ 07470
Phone: (201)633-6993
Fax: (201)633-7796
Dr. Edward A. Holmes, Chm.

Founded: 1948. **Description:** Supports agricultural, environmental, nutritional, medical, public health, educational, and cultural projects throughout the Third World. Encourages projects that will provide the greatest promise of solid accomplishment in preserving resources, expanding educational awareness, and providing health and medical services in foreign countries. **Formerly:** (1966) China International Foundation.

★ 1347 ★　International Guild of Professional Electrologists (IGPE)
202 Boulevard, Ste. B
High Point, NC 27262
Phone: (910)841-6631
Fax: (910)841-5187
Trudy Brown, Pres.

Founded: 1978. **Members:** 2,200. **Regional Groups:** 5. **Languages:** English. **Description:** Electrologists; electrology schools; manufacturers and suppliers of electrolysis equipment. Works to improve the image of electrolysis and promote it as an acceptable allied health profession. Promotes licensing of electrologists. Provides referral service. Conducts seminars and research programs. **Publications:** *A Complete Guide to Hair Removal.* Brochure. • *A Doctor Answers Questions About Hair Removal.* Brochure. • *Everything You Ever Wanted to Know About Hair Removal But Were Afraid to Ask.* Brochure. • *International Directory,* annual. Directory. • *International Guild of Professional Electrologists,* quarterly. Newsletter. Includes biennial conference reports. • *Official Health Guidelines.* Brochure. • *Physical Methods for the Management of Hirsutism.* Brochure. • *Selecting an Electrologist: Thermolysis for Permanent Hair Removal.* Brochure.

★ 1348 ★　International Health Center (IHC)
505 Beach St.
San Francisco, CA 94133
Phone: (415)776-0502
Barbara Bernie, CEO

Founded: 1992. **Description:** Works to promote Global Human Health through creating services and healing environments that demonstrate practices and teachings of the world's systems of health and healing. Creates exhibits on health and healing from different world cultures; educates individuals regarding different approaches to health and healing through classes, seminars, and international conferences; educates individuals so they may better participate in their own healthcare decisions; creates a New World Model for health and healing that uses principles and practices from the world's cultures; provides primary healthcare services demonstrating the New World Model of health and healing. By incorporating traditional Chinese, Western, and other medicines at this center, patients will have available a wide variety of diagnosis and treatment options which will result in reducing the cost of healthcare.

★ 1349 ★　International Health Foundation (IHF)
116, ave. de Broqueville
BP 9
B-1200 Brussels, Belgium
Phone: 2 7719598
Fax: 2 7719287
Dr. A.P. Visser, M.D., Dir.Gen.

Founded: 1969. **Languages:** Dutch, English, French. **Description:** Works to advance the health of humankind by defining human, mental, physical, and social problems, and by contributing to their solutions. Promotes research and education in the field of biomedicine and its related sciences. Conducts and publishes comparative studies on aspects of aging, contraception, infertility, menopause, menstruation, premenstrual syndrome, social relationships, and sexuality. Conducts research; sponsors educational programs. **Publications:** *Information Bulletin,* quarterly. Bulletin.

★ 1350 ★　International Health Foundation
6501 Bright Mountain Rd.
McLean, VA 22101
Fax: (703)356-4143
Kenneth D. Hansen, MD, Exec.Dir.

Founded: 1972. **Description:** Provides governmental organizations and health providers with methods for improving health services. Focuses on medical systems and medical and legal affairs. Offers assistance to developing countries. Sponsors educational programs; conducts research. Maintains speakers' bureau. Distinct from organization of same name listed in index.

★ 1351 ★　International Medical Association for Radio and Television (IMART)
52, blvd. Auguste Reyers
B-1040 Brussels, Belgium
Phone: 2 7374177
Fax: 2 7369566
Dr. Jacques Sporcq, Pres.

Founded: 1980. **Members:** 18. **Languages:** English, French. **Description:** Broadcasting corporations; organizations and individuals interested in the radio and television fields. Seeks to: improve the physical and mental health of radio and television employees in 18 countries; promote safety, hygiene, and preventive medicine as well as better working facilities for radio and television personnel; advance ergonomics, rehabilitation for the handicapped, and the disciplines of industrial medicine. Encourages the collection of statistical and nosological information on the health of television and radio personnel. Conducts research on ergonomics and occupational therapy and medicine. **Publications:** *Newsletter,* semiannual. Newsletter. • Papers, periodic. Containing information on science and applied medical and paramedical technology.

★ 1352 ★　International Medical Corps (IMC)
12233 W. Olympic Blvd., Ste. 280
Los Angeles, CA 90064-1052
Phone: (310)826-7800
Free: 800-481-4IMC
Fax: (310)442-6622
Nancy A. Aossey, Pres. & CEO

Founded: 1984. **Members:** 8,000. **Description:** Physicians, surgeons, nurses, physician assistants, and persons with expertise in administration, management, logistics, and finances. Provides medical training and emergency relief to devastated areas of the world. Provides the knowledge to rebuild lives and healthcare systems. Conducts worldwide self-sufficiency and independence programs. Assumes an active role in creating public awareness of human suffering and acts of atrocity throughout the world through testimony, published reports, and visual images. **Publications:** Annual Report. • Brochure. • *Expat Exchange*, bimonthly. Newsletter. *Price:* Free. • Also publishes fact sheet. **Formerly:** World Medical Corps.

★ 1353 ★ International Medical Relief Fund / Salvadoran Medical Relief Fund (IMRF/ SMRF)
PO Box 1194
Salinas, CA 93902
Phone: (408)758-4001
Fax: (408)422-1808
Joan Condon, Exec.Dir.

Founded: 1983. **Description:** Provides health care, medicines, and medical supplies to needy rural and urban communities in El Salvador and Mexico. Projects in clinical care, preventive care, public health, and health promoter education are supported through grants to nongovernmental, grassroots, and church organizations. Sponsors PROSES, a community and medicine education and training project between U.S. and Salvadoran health professionals. Conducts research into violations of medical neutrality; maintains speakers' bureau. **Publications:** Brochure. • *Quarterly Report to Contributors*, quarterly. Report. • *SMRF Newsletter*, quarterly. Newsletter. Includes updates and photos from projects. *Price:* Free to donors. Also publishes monthly sustainer mailings. **Formerly:** Committee for Health Rights in El Salvador; Salvadoran Medical Relief Fund.

★ 1354 ★ International Organization for Cooperation in Health Care (IOCHC) (Medicus Mundi Internationalis — MMI)
19, rue du Marteau
B-1040 Brussels, Belgium
Phone: 2 2199588
Fax: 2 2311852
Frieda Wijckmans, Exec.Sec.

Founded: 1962. **Members:** 11. **National Groups:** 8. **Languages:** English, French. **Description:** National branches and organizations of physicians and paramedical personnel. Promotes the fields of health care and disease prevention as a necessary part of development of all nations. Encourages primary health care through comprehensive, integrated, long-term health programs. Documents socio-medical information on developing countries to assess the medical needs and demands of those countries. Other aims include: encouraging dialogue with the Third World; strengthening relations between national branches and European governments; profiling experts serving IOCHC; providing field workers with practical conclusions, recommendations, and moral support regarding new strategies, methods, or operations. Offers training programs. **Publications:** *Developement et Sante*, periodic. Journal. • Newsletter, quarterly. • Proceedings, periodic. Contains meeting reports.

★ 1355 ★ International Patient Education Council (IPEC)
4826 Briarbend Dr.
Houston, TX 77035-4936
Maryanne Biddison, COAP, Exec.Dir.

Founded: 1988. **Members:** 608. **Languages:** English, French, Spanish. **Description:** Hospitals, regisered nurses, physcians, dentists, pharmaceutical and diagnostic product manufacturers, patient education committees, and others with an interest in patient education. Promotes patient education as a means of improving patient adherence to medical advice, enhancing patient self-care capabilities, and reducing inappropriate use of health care services. Conducts professional development programs, patient education demonstrations, and research. Encourages development of local chapters. Sponsors annual Patient Education Week in November. Sponsors competitions; bestows awards. **Publications:** *Patient Education and Counseling Journal*, bimonthly. Journal. • *Patient Education Rx*, bimonthly. Newsletter. • *Who's Who in Patient Education*, annual.

★ 1356 ★ International Physicians for the Prevention of Nuclear War (IPPNW)
126 Rogers St.
Cambridge, MA 02142
Phone: (617)868-5050
Fax: (617)868-2560
Barry Levy, M.D., Exec.Dir.

Founded: 1980. **Members:** 81. **Description:** Federation of national physicians' organizations representing 200,000 physicians in 81 countries dedicated to mobilizing the influence of the medical profession against the threat of war and its weapons. Seeks to focus international attention on the medical consequences of nuclear or conventional war. Works to delegitimize, and therefore abolish, all forms of nuclear weaponry. Promotes alternatives to violence and armed conflict. Educates the public, world leaders, and the medical profession about the link between militarism, underdevelopment, and the destruction of the environment. Works with the United Nations and World Health Organization on projects related to world health and the arms race. Sponsors educational campaigns; prepares curricula on nuclear war at leading medical schools; conducts continued research on the medical, psychological, and biospheric effects of nuclear war. Coordinates regional symposia. **Publications:** *Affiliate Directory*, semiannual. Directory. • Annual Report. • Booklets. • Brochures. • *Opportunities for International Control of Weapons-Usable Fissile Materials*. Report. • *Plutonium: Deadly Gold of the Nuclear Age*. Book. • *Radioactive Heaven and Earth: The Health and Environmental Effects of Nuclear Weapons Testing In, On, and Above the Earth*. Book. • *Vital Signs*, quarterly. *Price:* $25. • *The War in Nicaragua: The Effects of Low-Intensity Conflict on an Underdeveloped Country*. Report.

★ 1357 ★ International Society of General Practice (Societas Internationalis Medicinae Generalis — SIMG)
Bahnhofstrasse 27
28816 Stuhr, Germany
Phone: 421 895089
Fax: 421 808801
Edith Jysch

Founded: 1959. **Members:** 705. **Languages:** English, French, German. **Description:** General practitioners and national general practice institutes and societies in 26 countries. Objectives are to: promote systematic research into the scientific basis underlying the general practitioner's work; develop new methods of improving the treatment of the patient by the family doctor; include general practice in the curriculum at all universities, exchange information about the content and methods of teaching used, and test the effectiveness of this teaching; provide postgraduate training programs and teaching practice models to be developed and exchanged; facilitate the exchange of ideas about new forms and content of permanent continuing education geared to the needs of the general practitioner. Sponsors exchange students, trainees, and research fellows.

★ 1358 ★ International Society of Internal Medicine (ISIM) (Societe Internationale de Medecine Interne)
Regionalhospital
CH-4900 Langenthal, Switzerland
Phone: 63 293102
Fax: 63 293112
Dr. Rolf A. Streuli, Sec.Gen.

Founded: 1948. **Members:** 2,000. **National Groups:** 42. **Description:** Internal medicine specialists in 42 countries. Promotes scientific knowledge in internal medicine; furthers the education of young internists; encourages friendship among physicians in all countries.

★ 1359 ★ International Travelers Health Institute (ITHI)
c/o B.H. Kean, M.D.
435 E. 70th St., No. 34D
New York, NY 10021-5351
Phone: (212)737-7380
B. H. Kean, M.D., Pres.

Description: Physicians, researchers, and others interested in certain aspects of medical protection for travelers. Studies and supports investigations related to the health problems of travelers, including diarrhea and similar illnesses. Publishes studies in medical journals. **Formerly:** (1979) Travelers Health Institute.

★ 1360 ★ International Union for Health Promotion and Education (IUHPE) (Union Internationale de Promotion de la Sante et d'Education pour la Sante — UIPES)
2, rue Auguate Comte
F-92170 Vanves, France
Phone: 46450059
Fax: 46450045
Marie-Claude Lamarre, Contact

Founded: 1951. **Members:** 1,500. **National Groups:** 32. **Regional Groups:** 5. **Languages:**

English, French. **Description:** National organizations, educational institutions, foundations, and individuals working to promote worldwide health promotion and education activities. Objectives are: to promote disease control and develop the biological, psychological, and social potentials of humans; to improve health by strengthening the participation of communities, individuals, and families in promoting their own health; to improve professional training in health education; to foster the worldwide exchange of information and experiences among members. Conducts scientific research. Maintains study group on information exchange and communication. **Publications:** Brochure, periodic. • *Conference Proceedings*, triennial. • Monographs, periodic. On research and health education. • Newsletters, periodic. • *Promotion and Education*, quarterly. Journal. • *Scientific Reports*, periodic.

**★ 1361 ★   Interstate Postgraduate Medical
    Association of North America (IPMANA)**
PO Box 5474
Madison, WI 53705
Phone: (608)257-1401
Fax: (608)257-1401
H. B. Maroney, Exec.Dir.

Founded: 1916. **Description:** Presents annual four-day teaching program in various branches of medicine and medical research, aimed at the family practitioner who must keep up with new developments in a short time away from his practice.

★ 1362 ★   Islamic Medical Association (IMA)
4121 Fairview, Ste. 203
Downers Grove, IL 60515
Phone: (708)852-2122
Fax: (708)969-9237
Khursheed Mallick, M.D., Exec.Dir.

Founded: 1967. **Members:** 6,000. **Description:** Muslim physicians and allied health professionals. Unites Muslim physicians and allied health professionals in the U.S. and Canada for the improvement of professional and social contact; provides assistance to Muslim communities worldwide. Charitable programs include: donation of books, journals, and educational and research materials to medical institutions; donation of medical supplies and equipment to charity medical institutions in Muslim countries. Maintains speakers' bureau to present Islamic viewpoints on medical topics; sponsors placement service; offers assistance in orientation. **Publications:** Journal, quarterly. • Newsletter, quarterly.

**★ 1363 ★   Italian Society of Anatomy (ISA)
(Societa Italiana di Anatomia — SIA)**
Istituto di Anatomia Umana Normale
Via A. Borelli No. 50
I-00161 Rome, Italy
Phone: 5 4462623
Fax: 6 4452349
Prof. Pietro Motta, Pres.

Founded: 1929. **Members:** 800. **Languages:** English, Italian. **Description:** Fosters the study of anatomy, histology, and embryology in Italy. **Publications:** *Italian Journal of Anatomy and Embriology*, quarterly. Journal. • Papers, periodic.

**★ 1364 ★   Japan Medical Women's
    Association
(Nihon Joi Kai)**
3rd Floor, Aoyama-Miyano Bldg.
Shibuya 2-8-7
Shibuya-ku
Tokyo 150, Japan
Phone: 3 34980571
Fax: 3 34988769

Description: Women working in the medical profession. Works to maintain high standards.

**★ 1365 ★   Japan Overseas Christian
    Medical Cooperative Service (JOCMCS)**
2-3-18-23 Nishiwaseda
Shinjuku-ku
Tokyo 169, Japan
Phone: 3 32082416
Fax: 3 32326922
Rev.Dr. Katsuji Kosugi, Gen.Sec.

Founded: 1960. **Languages:** English, Japanese. **Description:** Works to coordinate the efforts of Christian sects providing medical services in Bangladesh, Cambodia, India, Indonesia, Nigeria, Pakistan, and Taiwan. Organization believes that Japan is indebted to the rest of Asia due to atrocities committed during World War II. Does not conduct evangelical programs, providing medical services without reference to a patients race, religion, color, or creed.

**★ 1366 ★   Joint Commission on
    Accreditation of Healthcare
    Organizations (JCAHO)**
1 Renaissance Blvd.
Oakbrook Terrace, IL 60181
Phone: (708)916-5600
Fax: (708)916-5644
Dennis S. O'Leary, M.D., Pres.

Founded: 1951. **Description:** Participants include representatives from the American Hospital Association, the American Medical Association, the American College of Surgeons, the American College of Physicians, the American Dental Association and the public. Establishes standards and conducts voluntary accreditation programs for more that 5,300 hospitals as well as 3,000 other health care organizations that provide home care, mental health care, ambulatory care, and long term care services. Works to improve the quality of health care provided to the public. Sponsors continuing education programs; maintains speakers' bureau and lists of accredited organizations. **Publications:** *Abstracts of Clinical Care Guidelines*, 10/year. *Price:* $95. • Books. Covers performance improvement. • *Home Care Bulletin*, quarterly. Newsletter. Covers the home care accreditation programs. Includes information about survey processes, standards, and programs for home care providers. *Price:* Free. • *JCAHO Perspectives*, bimonthly. Newsletter. Covers changes in accreditation standards, policies, and procedures. *Price:* Free to JCAHO accredited organizations; $80/year to others. • *Joit Commission Journal on Quality Improvement*, monthly. Journal. Provides information about quality assurance approaches, activities, theory, and research and related aspects of quality care of hospitals. *Price:* $115/year. • *LTC Update*, quarterly. Newsletter. Covers the long term care accreditation program. Includes information

about survey processes, standards, and programs for long term providers. *Price:* Free. • Manuals. • *MHC News*, quarterly. Newsletter. Covers the mental health care accreditation program. Includes information about survey processes for mental health care and substance abuse treatment. *Price:* Free. • *Plant, Technology, and Safety Management Series*, quarterly. Provides health care organizations with extensive clarification of the plant, technology, and safety management standards. *Price:* $140/year; $95/year for renewal. Also publishes educational materials. **Formerly:** (1987) Joint Commission on Accreditation of Hospitals.

**★ 1367 ★   Kiribati Family Health
    Association**
PO Box 275
Bikenibeu
Tarawa, Kiribati
Rubenteiti Neeti, Chair

Founded: 1992. **Members:** 56. **Description:** Promotes family planning and general health care. Offers health education programs for new mothers.

**★ 1368 ★   Korean Medical Association of
    America (KMAA)**
162 Deer Run
Watchung, NJ 07060-5532
Phone: (908)755-5262
Fax: (908)755-5622
Joseph Sirh, Pres.

Founded: 1974. **Members:** 4,300. **Description:** Korean-American physicians. Purpose is to provide a social and scientific forum for the exchange of scholarly information among members and between Korean-Americans and Korean physicans. Plans to offer scholarship program and to form liaisons with other health care professional societies. **Publications:** Membership Directory, quinquennial. • Newsletter, 3/year.

**★ 1369 ★   Latin American Association of
    Medical Schools and Faculties (LAAMSF)
(Asociacion Latinoamericana de
    Facultades y Escuelas de Medicina de
    America Latina — ALAFEM)**
Casilla de Correos 8105
Sucursal 8
Quito, Ecuador
Phone: 2 528810
Fax: 2 502399
Dr. Dimitri Barreto, Contact

Founded: 1984. **Members:** 56. **Languages:** Portuguese, Spanish. **Description:** Medical schools and faculties of medicine in Latin American countries. Represents the interests of medical faculties. Provides speakers' bureau. **Publications:** *Boletin*, semiannual.

**★ 1370 ★   Latin American Association of
    National Academies of Medicine
    (ALANAM)**
1200 Mariposa Ave., E-201
Coral Gables, FL 33146
Phone: (305)665-7341
Fax: (305)446-3340
Alberto Cardenas-Escovar, M.D., Sec.

Founded: 1967. **Members:** 11. **Description:** National academies of medicine in Argentina,

Brazil, Bolivia, Chile, Colombia, Ecuador, Mexico, Paraguay, Peru, Uruguay, and Venezuela. Coordinates research on problems of public health, social security, medical research and education, and related topics. **Publications:** *Memoirs*, biennial.

★1371★ Latin American and Caribbean Women's Health Network
Casilla 2067
Correo Central
Santiago, Chile
Phone: 2 44150
Fax: 2 490271
Ampara Claro, Dir.

Founded: 1984. **Members:** 1,700. **Languages:** English, Spanish. **Description:** Members include groups and organizations working directly or indirectly in fields related to women's health. Seeks to establish contacts among women and organizations active in women's health issues at the local, regional, and national levels. Promotes the sharing of information, experiences, and ideas through the development of communication networks. Coordinates common activities. Encourages informational campaigns on such subjects as reproductive rights, medicine, the environment, and other health topics of interest to women. Participates in conferences, seminars, and meetings. **Publications:** *Revista de Salud*, quarterly. Magazine. • *Women's Health Journal*, quarterly. Magazine.

★1372★ Liga International (LI)
19531 Campus Dr., Ste. 20
Santa Ana, CA 92707
Phone: (714)852-8611
Fax: (714)852-8739
Dr. David S. Lawson, D.D.S., Pres.

Founded: 1948. **Members:** 700. **Regional Groups:** 6. **State Groups:** 4. **Local Groups:** 5. **Description:** Physicians, dentists, nurses, pilots, technicians, assistants, educators, and laypeople interested in providing medical and educational assistance to impoverished people of rural Mexico. Liga (Spanish word for "league") seeks to stimulate interest and support for establishing and maintaining educational, charitable, and medical programs among underprivileged inhabitants of Mexico; exchange scientific information between medical and educational groups; promote the etablishment of institutions of hygiene and research, schools, and clinics. Sponsors monthly trips to clinics in Loma de Bacum, Ocoroni, El Fuerte, San Blas, and Ruiz Cortinez, Mexico. Established and supports Colegio del Pacifico, a school near Navojoa, Mexico. Operates speakers' bureau. **Publications:** Brochure. • *Liga High Flying Times*, quarterly. Newsletter. **Also Known As:** Flying Doctors of Mercy.

★1373★ Machne Israel
770 Eastern Pky.
Brooklyn, NY 11213
Phone: (718)774-4000
Rabbi Yehuda Krinsky, Exec.Dir.

Founded: 1942. **Members:** 600,000. **Description:** Social service arm of the Lubavitch Movement. To materially and spiritually aid Jewish and non-Jewish persons. Provides clubs for senior citizens; relieves the hungry and homeless;

assists the sick in hospitals; cooperates in the establishment of drug rehabilitation centers; and engages in other community social services.

★1374★ MADRE
121 W. 27th St., Rm. 301
New York, NY 10001
Phone: (212)627-0444
Fax: (212)675-3704
Vivian Stromberg, Exec.Dir.

Founded: 1983. **Members:** 23,000. **Description:** Seeks to further the possibilities for peace through a women's human rights agenda in the U.S. and abroad. Conducts health campaign to raise funds for improved health care for women and children, including delivery of medical supplies and training workshops by midwives and health professionals. Addresses the effects of U.S. policies on women and children in the U.S. and abroad; conducts educational tours in the U.S. on issues related women's human rights throughout the world. ("Madre" is Spanish for "mother.") **Publications:** Brochures. • *MADRE*, quarterly. Newsletter. Also publishes fact sheets.

★1375★ MAP International (MAP)
PO Box 215000
Brunswick, GA 31521-5000
Phone: (912)265-6010
Fax: (912)265-6170
Larry E. Dixon, Pres.

Founded: 1954. **Description:** Global health organization which provides concerned individuals, organizations, churches, and companies the opportunity to respond to world needs. Works with Christian mission organizations and churches "in a ministry to the whole man, physical and spiritual." Coordinates programs providing medical supplies, community health development, and emergency relief. Conducts health promotion and community health training in East Africa, South America, and the United States. **Publications:** Annual Report. • *MAP International REPORT*, bimonthly. Newsletter. **Formerly:** (1976) Medical Assistance Programs.

★1376★ Medecins du Monde (MOM)
67, ave. de la Republique
F-75005 Paris, France
Phone: 1 49291515
Fax: 1 43559122
Michel Brugiere, Exec.Dir.

Founded: 1980. **Members:** 3,000. **National Groups:** 8. **Regional Groups:** 24. **Description:** International humanitarian medical aid organization. Raises public awareness on health issues in rural communities. Provides a network for the exchange of information on rural health issues. **Publications:** *Ingerences*, 3/year. • *Les Nouvelles*, monthly. Magazine.

★1377★ Medic Alert Foundation International (MAFI)
1735 N. Lynn St., Ste. 950
Arlington, VA 22209-2022
Phone: (703)524-7710
R.S. Wilbur, M.D., Chm.

Founded: 1956. **Members:** 350,000. **Description:** Individuals with medical or health problems who wear a descriptive warning bracelet or neck chain to alert medical or law enforcement personnel in an emergency. Medic Alert emblems are worn by diabetics, epileptics, hemophiliacs, persons with severe allergies to various drugs, and others to insure prompt and proper treatment should they be unconscious or otherwise unable to communicate with others. Membership provided without charge to individuals whose physicians indicate that they are unable to pay the membership fee themselves. The foundation maintains a central database with additional medical information on each member if n eeded, and accepts emergency collect calls 24 hours a day from doctors and public safety officials. Conducts continuous public and professional education program. **Publications:** *Medic Alert Foundation International--Newsletter*, quarterly. Newsletter. **Also Known As:** Medic Alert.

★1378★ Medical Aid for El Salvador (MAES)
6030 Wilshire Blvd., Ste. 400
Los Angeles, CA 90036
Phone: (213)937-3596
Fax: (213)935-7404
Mario Velasquez, Exec.Dir.

Founded: 1981. **Description:** Raises funds for direct medical relief for Salvadorans who have little or no access to health care; provides medicines and equipment to clinics, hospitals, and other health care providers in El Salvador. Operates Prosthetics Project, which provides artificial arms and legs to individuals who have lost limbs. Plans fundraisers; conducts direct mail fundraising campaigns. Encourages groups, committees, and individuals nationwide to raise funds; offers fundraising advice and direction. **Publications:** *Report of Medical Fact-Finding Delegation to El Salvador*.

★1379★ Medical Association of Thailand
105/4 Soi Theveevorayart
Luang Rd.
Bangkok 10100, Thailand
Phone: 2 2237780
Mr. Tak Sai Li, Pres.

Description: Physicians, medical practitioners, and other professionals working in or related with the medical field in Thailand. Promotes the medical profession; represents members' interests. Fosters improved health standards for the Thai population. Conducts educational programs.

★1380★ Medical Council of Zimbabwe
PO Box 422
Harare, Zimbabwe
Phone: 4 705139

Languages: English. **Description:** Scientists engaged in medical and related research. Promotes and coordinates members' activities; facilitates communication among members and between members and international biomedical and research organizations.

★1381★   Medical Group Missions of the Christian Medical and Dental Society (MGM)
1616 Gateway
PO Box 830689
Richardson, TX 75083-0689
Phone: (214)783-8384
Fax: (214)783-0921
David Stevens, M.D., Exec.Dir.
Founded: 1968. **Description:** A mission of the Christian Medical and Dental Society. Conducts 35 short-term mission outreach projects annually, which send medical and nonmedical personnel to supply medical, dental, and spiritual assistance in 12 Third World countries. Promotes fellowship among participants. Sponsors Eye Project, which collects used eyeglasses and distributes them to needy individuals. **Publications:** Brochure. • *The Happening*, quarterly. Newsletter. *Price:* Free.

★1382★   Medical Mission Sisters (MMS)
8400 Pine Rd.
Philadelphia, PA 19111
Phone: (215)742-6100
Fax: (215)342-3948
Rita Syron, MMS, Soc.Coor.
Founded: 1925. **Members:** 700. **Regional Groups:** 6. **Description:** International women's religious community that combines religious life with practice of medicine, surgery, and obstetrics. Maintains 30 health centers and hospital in India, Pakistan, Ghana, Uganda, Venezuela, Indonesia, the Philippines, Kenya, Malawi, Ethiopia, Zaire, Brazil, Peru, Nicaragua, U.S., England, Netherlands, Belgium, Germany, Italy, and Mexico. Conducts local training programs for professional, managerial, and grassroots level staffs. **Publications:** *Medical Mission Sisters News*, quarterly. Newsletter. *Price:* Free.

★1383★   Medical Outreach for Armenians (MOA)
33-00 Broadway, Ste. 201
Fair Lawn, NJ 07410
Phone: (201)796-0050
Fax: (201)796-3305
Arthur Halvajian, Dir.
Description: Health care professionals and other individuals wishing to improve delivery of medical services to needy Armenians and to upgrade medical facilities in Armenia. Gathers monetary donations, medical supplies and medications, and technological equipment for distribution to hospitals in Armenia; sponsors transportation to America for Armenian children in need of complex surgical procedures. Plans to construct a children's heart center in Yerovan, Armenia. **Publications:** *Activities of Medical Outreach for Armenians*, periodic. Newsletter. Includes financial reports. • *Pediatric Intensive Care Unit and Pediatric Cardiac Surgery Center for Yerevan, Armenia.*

★1384★   Medical Research Modernization Committee (MRMC)
PO Box 2751, Grand Central Sta.
New York, NY 10163
Phone: (212)832-3904
Fax: (212)283-6702
Stephen R. Kaufman, M.D., Chair
Founded: 1978. **Members:** 1,500. **Description:** Individuals, primarily scientists and clini-
cians, who evaluate the medical and/or scientific merit of research modalities in an effort to identify outdated research methods and to promote sensible, reliable, and efficient methods. Represents positions to the public, health care professionals, and government officials. Maintains speakers' bureau; distributes literature to the public. **Publications:** *Perspectives on Medical Research*, annual. Monograph. Includes essays and commentary. *Price:* $10/paperback; $16/hardback.

★1385★   Medical Society of the United States and Mexico
634 S. Spring St., 11th Fl.
Los Angeles, CA 90014
Phone: (213)489-3765
Fax: (213)629-8016
Abelardo de la Pena, Jr., Dir. of Communications
Founded: 1968. **Members:** 65. **Description:** Protects and promotes the civil rights of Latin Americans in the United States. Offers educational programs, leadership development programs, and parent organizations. Litigates on behalf of Hispanics. **Publications:** *Leading Hispanics*, biennial. Newsletter. • *Maltef*, biennial. Newsletter.

★1386★   Medical Society of the United States and Mexico (MSUSM)
810 W. Bethany Home Rd.
Phoenix, AZ 85013
Phone: (602)246-8901
Fax: (602)242-6283
Founded: 1954. **Members:** 400. **Languages:** English, Spanish. **Description:** Doctors of medicine in the United States (200) and in Mexico (200). Promotes scientific and international goodwill; sponsors research and educational programs; fosters interchange of doctors. Conducts scientific program. **Publications:** Directory, annual.

★1387★   Medical Women's International Association (MWIA)
Herbert-Lewin-Strasse 1
50931 Cologne, Germany
Phone: 221 4004558
Fax: 221 4004557
Dr. Carolyn Motzel, Sec.Gen.
Founded: 1919. **Members:** 20,000. **National Groups:** 44. **Regional Groups:** 8. **Languages:** English. **Description:** Women involved in or interested in medicine in 70 countries. Provides women with an opportunity to exchange information about medical problems with worldwide implications; promotes friendship and understanding between women; secures members' cooperation in matters relating to international health. Seeks to encourage women to enter the field of medicine and allied sciences and to overcome discrimination against female physicians. Aids women in developing countries in obtaining fellowships and grants for research and travel; offers information and advice to members visiting other countries. **Publications:** *Circular Letter*, quarterly. • *Congress Report*, triennial. • *Newsletter*, semiannual. Newsletter. • *Women Physicians of the World*. Book.

★1388★   Medico-Social Association of French-Speaking Protestants (Association Medico-Sociale Protestante de Langue Francaise)
95, rue de Reuilly
F-75012 Paris, France
Phone: 1 48992783
Yves Ravaud, Pres.
Founded: 1948. **Members:** 900. **Languages:** French. **Description:** Doctors, nurses, social workers, aides, hospital administrators, and chaplains professing faith in the Gospel of Jesus Christ who are concerned with professional ethics and quality of international health care. Promotes exchange and affiliation among professional medical and paramedical groups. Encourages interaction between the public and health care professionals. Conducts continuing education programs for health professionals. **Publications:** *Ouvertures*, quarterly. Magazine.

★1389★   Medicus Mundi (MM)
rue du Marteau, 19
B-1040 Brussels, Belgium
Phone: 2 2199588
M. Vandermeulen, Contact
Founded: 1961. **Members:** 56. **Languages:** English. **Description:** Member association of the International Organization for Cooperation in Health Care . Works with local authorities in Benin, Mali, Senegal, and Zimbabwe to operate health development projects. Provides personnel and scientific support to existing health programs; offers consulting services. **Formerly:** Medicus Mundi Belgium.

★1390★   Melpomene Institute for Women's Health Research (MIWHR)
c/o Judy Mahle Lutter
1010 University Ave.
St. Paul, MN 55104
Phone: (612)642-1951
Fax: (612)642-1871
Judy Mahle Lutter, Pres.
Founded: 1982. **Members:** 1,653. **Description:** Individuals professionally trained in healthcare, physical activity, and sports for girls and women. Researches and disseminates information on issues such as body image, osteoporosis, athletic amenorrhea, exercise and pregnancy, and aging. Offers undergraduate and graduate internships, and volunteer programs. Provides consulting services for program evaluations. Sponsors competitions and physical activities. Operates speakers' bureau. **Publications:** *The Bodywise Woman*. Book. Provides information for women on physical activity and health. • *Breast Cancer: A Handbook*. Book. • Brochures. • *Heroes*. Video. Concerns self-esteem in adolescent girls. • *Melpomene Journal*, 3/year. Journal. Examines the relationship between physical activity and lifestyles. Features research reports, scientific bibliographies, and personal profiles. *Price:* Included in membership dues; $5/issue for nonmembers. • Newsletter, quarterly. • *One in Nine: One Woman's Response to Breast Cancer*. • Video. Covers osteoporosis.

★1391★ Mercy Medical Airlift (MMA)
PO Box 1940
Manassas, VA 22110
Phone: (703)361-1191
Free: 800-296-1217
Fax: (703)361-1792
Edward R. Boyer, Pres.

Founded: 1984. **Regional Groups:** 3. **Description:** Provides long-distance air ambulance service to patients whose physicians prescribe recovery or special treatment at a distant location. Beneficiaries include patients in need of medical and nursing care enroute to hospitals or other places of continuing care, especially in the case of low-income and medically indigent families. Operates information clearinghouse and air transportation referral service. Although operations are based regionally, group plans to expand nationwide. Conducts educational program on medical air transportation.

★1392★ Mission Doctors Association (MDA)
1531 W. 9th St.
Los Angeles, CA 90015
Phone: (818)285-8868
Fax: (818)309-1716
Timothy Lefevre, M.D., Pres.

Founded: 1957. **Description:** Recruits, trains, and supports volunteer Catholic physicians and sends them to serve in Third World hospitals or clinics for a period of 2-3 years. Mission doctors accepted in the program must display a genuine spirit of sacrifice and must participate in a 9-month course on theology, missiology, scripture, and Third World culture. Provides for complete support of doctors and their families while overseas; also provides small monthly stipend. Screens and trains physicians' spouses to be part-time lay missionaries.

★1393★ Musu Lako
34 Regiant Rd.
African Development Foundation
Freetown, Sierra Leone
Phone: 22 9262
Neneba Jalloh, P

Founded: 1985. **Members:** 25. **Languages:** English. **Description:** Women and non-governmental organizations working to improve the quality of life for women and children living in developing areas of Sierra Leone. Offers educational programs for young women, training for illiterate women, and employment facilities. Sponsors daycare programs.

★1394★ National Association of Advisors for the Health Professions (NAAHP)
PO Box 1518
Champaign, IL 61824-1518
Phone: (217)355-0063
Fax: (217)355-1287
Julian M. Frankenberg, Exec.Dir.

Founded: 1974. **Members:** 1,275. **Regional Groups:** 4. **Description:** College and university faculty who advise and counsel students on health careers. Seeks to improve and preserve advisement at all educational levels of the health professions. Fosters and coordinates communication among the health professions and advisers. Marshalls resources; provides services concerning health professions advisement. Goals include: informed counseling for students seeking careers in the health professions; proper preparation of student evaluations for the professional schools; participation of advisers in curriculum development; improved communication between secondary and undergraduate institutions; coordination of record keeping and information exchange among undergraduate schools and local, state, and regional preprofessional programs. Makes available Advisor's Supplementary Student Evaluation Tool software program; conducts surveys. **Publications:** Audiotapes. • *Directory of the National Association of Advisors for the Health Professions*, annual. Directory. Includes health professional school announcements and order forms. *Price:* $25/issue. • *The Medical School Interview.* • *National Association of Advisors for the Health Professions--The Advisor*, quarterly. Focuses on manpower statistics, financial aid, admission procedures, curriculum, advising, recruitment, counseling practice, and ethics. *Price:* $70/year. • *Plan for Success.* • *Special Edition of the Advisor*, annual. • *Strategy for Success: A Handbook for Prehealth Students.* Handbook. • Videos. • *Write for Success.*

★1395★ National Association for Ambulatory Care (NAFAC)
18665 Rutledge Rd.
Wayzata, MN 55391
Phone: (612)476-0015
Fax: (612)476-0646
William H. Wenmark, Pres.

Founded: 1981. **Members:** 600. **State Groups:** 6. **Description:** Representatives of hospital, corporate, and independently owned ambulatory care centers. Seeks to: establish operational standards for such centers; provide lower cost and more convenient outpatient medical care; make the public aware of the concept of ambulatory care centers and their usefulness in primary and episodic care. Cooperates with medical organizations; conducts public relations activities and studies on the industry. Sponsors a bank card program. **Publications:** *Ambulatory Care*, quarterly. Newsletter. Contains research updates. *Price:* Included in membership dues; $96/year for nonmembers. **Formerly:** (1981) National Association of Centers for Urgent Treatment; (1984) National Association of Freestanding Emergency Centers.

★1396★ National Association of Community Health Centers (NACHC)
1330 New Hampshire Ave. NW, Ste. 122
Washington, DC 20036
Phone: (202)659-8008
Fax: (202)659-8519
Thomas Van Coverden, Pres. & CEO

Founded: 1970. **Members:** 950. **Description:** Advocacy organization of ambulatory healthcare centers, administrators, clinicians, and consumers. Works to assure the continued growth and development of community-based healthcare delivery programs for medically underserved populations by providing technical assistance and education and training opportunities for health center staff and board members. Disseminates information and research data and provides representation in legislative and professional arenas. Sponsors educational institutes, workshops, and seminars throughout the year. **Publications:** *NACHC Link.* Newsletter. *Price:* Included in membership dues. • *The Vanguard*, quarterly. Newsletter. • *Washington Update*, monthly. Newsletter. **Formerly:** National Association of Directors and Administrators; (1977) National Association of Neighborhood Health Centers.

★1397★ National Association of Health Authorities and Trusts (NAHAT)
Birmingham Research Park
Vincent Dr.
Edgbaston
Birmingham, W. Midlands B15 2SQ, England
Phone: 121 4714444
Fax: 121 4141120
Mrs. E.A. Mason

Founded: 1990. **Members:** 298. **Languages:** English. **Description:** Regional and local health authorities and family health authorities. Provides a forum for the exchange of views and information among members. **Publications:** *Health Direct*, monthly. Newsletter. • Pamphlets, periodic.

★1398★ National Association for Healthcare Quality (NAHQ)
5700 Old Orchard Rd., 1st Fl.
Skokie, IL 60077
Phone: (708)965-2776
Fax: (708)966-9418
Anne M. Cordes, Exec.Dir.

Founded: 1976. **Members:** 6,800. **Regional Groups:** 6. **State Groups:** 47. **Description:** Healthcare professionals in quality assessment and improvement, utilization and risk management, case management, infection control, managed care, nursing, and medical records. Objectives are: to encourage, develop, and provide continuing education for all persons involved in health care quality; to give the patient primary consideration in all actions affecting his or her health and welfare; to promote the sharing of knowledge and encourage a high degree of professional ethics in health care quality. Offers accredited certification in the field of healthcare quality, utilization, and risk management. Facilitates communication and cooperation among members, medical staff, and health care government agencies. Conducts educational seminars and conferences. **Publications:** *Journal for Healthcare Quality*, bimonthly. Journal. *Price:* $100/year. • *Membership Directory*, annual. • *NAHQ Guide to Quality Management.* • *NAHQ News*, quarterly. Newsletter. **Formerly:** (1979) National Association of Utilization Review Coordinators; (1991) National Association of Quality Assurance Professionals.

★1399★ National Association of Health Career Schools (NAHCS)
10963 St. Charles Rock Rd.
St. Louis, MO 63114
Phone: (314)739-4450
Larkin Hicks, Contact

Founded: 1980. **Description:** Private, vocational, technical, and junior colleges training allied health personnel. Objectives are to: promote the interests and general welfare of health career training schools and their students accredited by the Accrediting Bureau of Health Education Schools; conduct and promote research for the advancement of the educational offerings of such schools; cooperate with local, state, and federal authorities and organizations engaged in the healing arts and the allied health sciences and with business, commerce, and industry in the maintenance of proper standards and sound policies in the field of health career training. Compiles statistics; develops curricula for allied health programs. **Publications:** Bulletin, weekly. • Newsletter, quarterly.

★ 1400 ★ National Association for Home Care (NAHC) ✓
519 C St. NE
Stanton Park
Washington, DC 20002
Phone: (202)547-7424
Fax: (202)547-3540
Val J. Halamandaris, Pres.

Founded: 1982. **Members:** 6,000. **Description:** Providers of home health care, hospice, and homemaker-home health aide services; interested individuals and organizations. Develops and promotes high standards of patient care in home care services. Seeks to affect legislative and regulatory processes concerning home care services; gathers and disseminates home care industry data; develops public relations strategies; works to increase political visibility of home care services. Interprets home care services to governmental and private sector bodies affecting the delivery and financing of such services. Provides legal and accounting consulting services; conducts market research and compiles statistics. Offers members insurance discounts. Sponsors educational programs for organizations and individuals concerned with home care services. **Publications:** *Caring*, monthly. Magazine. *Price:* Included in membership dues; $45/year in U.S.; $65/year outside U.S. • *Homecare News*, monthly. Tabloid covering association news; serves as an information exchange between state associations and providers/suppliers to the industry. *Price:* Included in membership dues; $18/year for nonmembers. • *Hospice Forum*, biweekly. Newsletter. Covers legislative and research news. *Price:* Included in membership dues; $105/year for nonmembers. • *NAHC Report*, weekly. Newsletter. Covers legislative and regulatory issues related to the home health care industry. Contains employment opportunity listings. *Price:* Included in membership dues; $325/year for nonmembers. • *National Home Care and Hospice Directory*, annual. Directory.

★ 1401 ★ National Association for Human Development (NAHD)
1424 16th St. NW, Ste. 102
PO Box 100
Washington, DC 20036
Phone: (202)328-2191
Free: (202)296-8134
Anne Radd, Exec.VP

Founded: 1974. **Description:** Seeks to help people establish and maintain physical and emotional health and vigor. Operates model demonstration projects and evaluation, research and training programs; conducts multimedia community awareness activities; spon-

sors "Active People Over 60" campaign. Provides specialized education in motivational communications; develops and implements employment training programs. Develops drug prevention educational programs, activities, and materials for minority populations; advocates on behalf of troubled children and youth. Offers resource development and technical assistance to other organizations. **Publications:** Booklets. • *Digest*, quarterly. • Manuals. Also publishes evaluation sheets and audiovisual and media-oriented materials.

★ 1402 ★ National Association of Local Boards of Health (NALBOH)
c/o Ned Baker
1021 Melrose
Bowling Green, OH 43402
Phone: (419)352-0370
Ned Baker, MPH, Pres.

Founded: 1992. **Members:** 2,600. **State Groups:** 6. **Local Groups:** 54. **Description:** Represents the interests of local boards of health throughout the United States and relates their concerns to individuals responsible for developing public health policy at the national level. Offers educational programs and speakers' bureau. **Publications:** *News Brief*, quarterly. Newsletter.

★ 1403 ★ National Association for Maternal and Child Welfare
Strode House, Ste. 25
46/48 Osnaburgh St.
London NW1 3ND, England
Phone: 171 3834117
Edna Llewellyn, Contact

Founded: 1911. **Members:** 200. **Languages:** English. **Description:** Health authorities, schools, and voluntary organizations concerned with improving the health and well-being of mothers and children. Offers health education programs; conducts research. **Publications:** *Annual Review*, semiannual. Newsletter.

★ 1404 ★ National Association of Residents and Interns (NARI)
292 Madison Ave.
New York, NY 10017
Phone: (212)949-5900
Free: 800-221-2168
Fax: (212)949-5910
Mrs. Patricia Arden, Exec.Dir.

Founded: 1959. **Members:** 18,000. **Description:** Medical and dental students, interns, residents, and fellows. Contributes to the economic welfare of members through unsecured loan plans, low-cost group insurance, group purchase discounts, physician search service, and special financial planning services. **Publications:** *NARI Stethoscope*, quarterly. Newsletter. Provides advice on business interests and benefits news. *Price:* Included in membership dues.

★ 1405 ★ National Black Women's Health Project (NBWHP)
1237 Ralph David Albernathy Blvd. SW
Atlanta, GA 30310
Phone: (404)758-9590
Free: 800-ASK-BWHP
Fax: (404)758-9661
Cynthia Newbille, Dir.

Founded: 1981. **Members:** 2,000. **Regional Groups:** 5. **State Groups:** 26. **Local Groups:** 150. **Description:** Encourages mutual and self-help advocacy among women to bring about a reduction in health care problems prevalent among black women. Urges women to communicate with health care providers, seek out available health care resources, become aware of selfhelp approaches, and communicate with other black women to minimize feelings of powerlessness and isolation, and thus realize they have some control over their physical and mental health. Points out the higher incidence of high blood pressure, obesity, breast and cervical cancers, diabetes, kidney disease, arteriosclerosis, and teenage pregnancy among black women than among other racial or socioeconomic groups. Also notes that black infant mortality is twice that of whites and that black women are often victims of family violence. Offers seminars outlining demographic information, chronic conditions, the need for health information and access to services, and possible methods of improving the health status of black women. Sponsors Center for Black Women's Wellness. Maintains library, database, and speakers' bureau. Conducts gender and race specific health research programs. Plans to: establish black women's wellness centers; develop Empowerment Through Wellness curriculum. **Publications:** Annual Report. • *On Becoming a Woman: Mothers and Daughters Talking Together*. Video. • *Vital Signs*, quarterly. Newsletter. *Price:* Included in membership dues. Also publishes conference reports, brochures, and health fact sheets. Makes available educational films. **Formerly:** (1984) Black Women's Health Project.

★ 1406 ★ National Board of Medical Examiners (NBME)
3930 Chestnut St.
Philadelphia, PA 19104
Phone: (215)590-9500
Fax: (215)590-9555
L. Thompson Bowles, M.D., Pres.

Founded: 1915. **Members:** 75. **Description:** Purposes are: to prepare and administer qualifying examinations either independently or in conjunction with other organizations, of such high quality that legal agencies governing the practice of medicine within each state may, in their discretion, grant a license without further examination for those who have successfully completed such examinations; to establish requirements for certification of Diplomates of the NBME; to cooperate with and, where appropriate, to make its specialized services available to the examining boards of the states, specialty boards, and other organizations concerned with the education and qualification of personnel in the fields of health; to assist medical schools, hospitals and related organizations and institutions in evaluation of the effectiveness of their educational programs; to initiate, develop, and participate in research designed to evaluate the effectiveness of educational programs and techniques, and to assess ever more precisely the knowledge, competence, and qualification of professionals in public health care; to provide educational opportunities for professional personnel in the methods, techniques, and values of testing methods related to knowledge and competence in the broad field of medicine. **Publications:** Annual Report. • *National Board Examiner*, quarterly. Newsletter. Reports on new medical evaluation programs and new directions in the research and development of examinations. *Price:* Free. Also publishes information bulletins and policy statements.

★ 1407 ★ **National Center for the Advancement of Blacks in the Health Professions (NCABHP)**
PO Box 21121
Detroit, MI 48221
Phone: (313)345-4480
Free: 800-NCA-BHP6
Della McGraw Goodwin, Pres.

Founded: 1988. **Description:** Participants belong to organizations including the American Public Health Association, National Urban League, National Black Nurses Association, and the American Hospital Association. Promotes the advancement of blacks in the health professions. Publicizes the disparity between the health of black and white Americans and its relationship to the underrepresentation of blacks in the health professions. (According to the National Center for Health Statistics, blacks have a higher death rate from cancer, heart disease, stroke, and diabetes than whites; blacks also have a higher infant mortality rate.) Acts as clearinghouse. Conducts skills development seminars for college recruiters and employers and empowerment seminars for new graduates. Demonstrates recruitment projects. Bestows Pathfinder Award. **Publications:** *Improving the Health Status of Black Americans*, annual. Lists priorities and agenda for the coming year. *Price:* $8. • *Pathways to Parity*, 8/year. Newsletter. Contains updates on programs of interest; announces recipient of Pathfinder of the Month award. *Price:* $15. • Proceedings, periodic. Also publishes career information brochures; issues Strategies to Achieve Parity in the Health Professions (videotape and plan document), and other videotapes.

★ 1408 ★ **National Center for Health Education (NCHE)**
72 Spring St., Ste. 208
New York, NY 10012-4019
Phone: (212)334-9470
Fax: (212)334-9845
David J. Andrews, Pres.

Founded: 1975. **Description:** Professionals promoting health education in schools, communities, and family settings. Aims to "extend the reach and power of education for health." Advocates health education and health promotion; builds coalitions of private and public sector groups; documents, develops, and disseminates model programs. Manages Growing Healthy, a comprehensive school health education curriculum.

★ 1409 ★ **National Central America Health Rights Network (NCAHRN)**
775 E. 19th St.
Brooklyn, NY 11230-1807
Phone: (212)732-4790

Founded: 1983. **Local Groups:** 40. **Description:** Doctors, nurses, public health professionals, psychologists, medical students, nutrition-

ists, mental health workers, and others in the health field. Promotes health and provides medical assistance to projects in Central America. Sponsors health-oriented educational tours to Central America. Undertakes fundraising activities; disseminates information about Central America. **Publications:** *LINKS*, quarterly. Journal. • *Salud y Paz Bulletin*, quarterly. Newsletter. Covers group activities and Central American news.

★ 1410 ★ **National Coalition of Hispanic Health and Human Services Organizations (COSSMHO)**
1501 16th St. NW
Washington, DC 20036
Phone: (202)387-5000
Fax: (202)797-4353
Jane L. Delgado, Ph.D., Pres.-CEO

Founded: 1973. **Members:** 1,000. **Description:** National coalition of health, mental health, and human service agencies and organizations and professional individuals serving Hispanics. Primary mission is to improve health and human services to Hispanic communities throughout the United States, including Puerto Rico. Works to help Hispanic community-based organizations to develop new model programs, strengthen local infrastructures, and conduct studies. Does not accept funds from alcohol or tobacco companies. Activities focus on: identifying and coordinating research; producing and disseminating key findings; increasing awareness among decision-makers of emerging issues; increasing funding for community-based programs; providing direct funding and technical assistance to community-base d organizations; maintaining a coordinated system among members; developing prevention and intervention programs and materials; conducting community-based demonstration programs. **Publications:** Bibliographies. • Books. • *The COSSMHO Reporter*, quarterly. Newsletter. Includes funding leads, updates on activities, and stories of interest. *Price:* $40/year. • Manuals. • Papers. • Report, annual. • Videos. **Formerly:** (1976) Coalition of Spanish Speaking Mental Health Organizations.

★ 1411 ★ **National Commission on Certification of Physician Assistants (NCCPA)**
2845 Henderson Mill Rd. NE
Atlanta, GA 30341
Phone: (404)493-9100
Fax: (404)493-7316
David L. Glazer, Exec.VP & Mng.Dir.

Founded: 1975. **Description:** Certifies physician assistants at the entry level and for continued competence. Has certified 22,750 physician assistants. **Publications:** *Directory of Physician Assistants - Certified*, annual. Directory. **Formerly:** (1987) National Commission on Certification of Physician's Assistants.

★ 1412 ★ **National Commission on Correctional Health Care (NCCHC)**
2105 N. Southport, Ste. 200
Chicago, IL 60614
Phone: (312)528-0818
Fax: (312)528-4915
Edward A. Harrison, Pres.

Founded: 1983. **Members:** 37. **Description:** Professional organizations in the fields of medical and health care. Works to improve the quality of and set standards for medical care in correctional institutions in the U.S. including prisons, jails, and detention and juvenile facilities. Acts as an accrediting body for such facilities; develops training programs and conducts seminars; provides technical assistance; organizes special task forces on issues such as suicide and AIDS; annually bestows Award of Merit for achievement in the field of correctional health care. Compiles statistics; conducts research; disseminates information. **Publications:** *CorrectCare*, quarterly. Newspaper. • Films. • *Journal of Correctional Health Care*, semiannual. Journal. Contains articles on correctional health care topics including law, medicine, and ethics. *Price:* $30/year for individuals; $65/year for institutions. • Monographs. • *Prison Health Care: Guidelines for the Management of an Adequated Delivery System*. Manuals. • Proceedings.

★ 1413 ★ **National Commission for Electrologist Certification (NCEC)**
132 Great Rd., No. 200
Stow, MA 01775
Phone: (508)461-0313
Fax: (508)897-5442
Aaron S. Bernstein, R.Ph., Chm.

Founded: 1983. **Members:** 1,200. **Description:** Conducts certification program for individuals practicing electrolysis (a method of permanent hair removal). Establishes and promotes safety and proficiency in the practice of permanent hair removal. Conducts research in occupational credentialing and develops and administers credentialing examinations. Seeks to enhance public confidence in electrolysis and electrolysis practitioners. Compiles statistics. **Publications:** *NCEC Directory of Certified Clinical Electrologists*, 2/year. Directory. • *NCEC Handbook for Candidates*, annual. Handbook.

★ 1414 ★ **National Council on Alternative Health Care Policy (NCAHCP)**
1029 K St., No. 48
Sacramento, CA 95814-3816
Phone: (916)447-1641
Fax: (916)447-9281
R. EuGene Lokey, Exec.Dir.

Founded: 1976. **Description:** Offers technical assistance to organizations interested in developing alternative health care models, policies, and programs directed toward low-income individuals. Provides policy analyses; monitors legislative policies and trends; conducts educational sessions in national, state, and regional health policy. Acts as information clearinghouse for health-related programs.

★ 1415 ★ **National Council for International Health (NCIH)**
1701 K St. NW, Ste. 600
Washington, DC 20006
Phone: (202)833-5900
Fax: (202)833-0075
Frank Lospumbo, Pres.

Founded: 1971. **Members:** 1,800. **Description:** Membership organization made up of private voluntary organizations, health and medical associations, universities, government agencies, foundations, corporations, consulting firms, and individuals interested in promoting greater and more effective U.S. participation in practical international health and development programs. Seeks to strengthen U.S. public and private sector participation in international health activities. Areas of concern include: AIDS; women's health; improving primary health care worldwide; environmental health; population and family planning; tropical and preventive medicine; appropriate health technology. Supports improved health and development legislation. Conducts a job placement service in conjunction with annual conference. **Publications:** *Career Network*, monthly. Bulletin. *Price:* $10/ issue for members; $60/year for members; $20/issue for nonmembers; $120/year for nonmembers. • *Directory of U.S.-Based Agencies Involved in International Health Assistance*, periodic. Directory. Lists geographical areas served and types of workers sought BY U.S. health agencies. • *Healthlink*, 10/year. Contains information on international health policy issues and calendar of events. *Price:* Available to members only. • *Membership Directory*, periodic. • *Proceedings of Workshops and Conferences*. Proceedings.

★ 1416 ★ **National Federation of Catholic Physicians Guilds (NFCPG)**
850 Elm Grove Rd.
Elm Grove, WI 53122
Phone: (414)784-3435
Fax: (414)782-8788
Robert H. Herzog, Exec.Sec.

Founded: 1932. **Members:** 3,500. **Local Groups:** 90. **Description:** Catholic physicians and dentists with a priest-moderator for each local group. **Publications:** *The Linacre Quarterly*.

★ 1417 ★ **National Flotation Health Care Foundation (WH2O)**
5757 W. Century Blvd., Ste. 512
Los Angeles, CA 90045
Phone: (310)417-8077
Free: 800-925-3874
Fax: (310)417-8078
Raymond P. Delrich, CAE, Exec. Officer

Founded: 1983. **Description:** Provides flotation systems (waterbeds) to medically and financially needy individuals upon the recommendation of a physician or other health care professional. Sponsors research into the benefits of flotation systems for physical ailments such as arthritis.

★ 1418 ★ **National Health Council (NHC)**
1730 M St. NW, Ste. 500
Washington, DC 20036
Phone: (202)785-3910
Fax: (202)785-5923
Joseph C. Isaacs, Pres.

Founded: 1920. **Members:** 130. **Description:** National membership association of voluntary and professional societies in the health field; national organizations and business groups with strong health interests. Seeks to improve the health of the nation. Holds annual National Health Forum. Distributes printed material on health careers and related subjects. Promotes

standardization of financial reporting for voluntary health groups. **Publications:** *Congress and Health*. Book. • *Council Currents*, bimonthly. Books. *Price:* Free. • *Directory of Health Groups in Washington*. Directory. • *Guide to America's Voluntary Health Agencies*. Directory. • *Long-Term Care*. Book. • *Standards of Accounting and Reporting for Voluntary Health and Welfare Organizations (The Black Book)*. Book. • *200 Ways to Put Your Talent to Work in the Health Field*. Book.

★ 1419 ★ **National Health Federation (NHF)**
PO Box 688
Monrovia, CA 91017
Phone: (818)357-2181
Fax: (818)303-0642
Dr. Jonathan Wright, Pres.

Founded: 1955. **Members:** 55,000. **Local Groups:** 123. **Description:** Persons interested in individual freedom of choice in matters relating to health. Represents belief "that organized medicine, the pharmaceutical industry, and other special interests have been responsible for many laws, rules, and regulations which very often better serve the interests of these groups than the interests of the American public. . .that through the activities of these groups monopolies in the field of health have been created and thus, that American free enterprise is threatened." Seeks to serve as a "watch dog" and to institute corrective measures through investigation, education, legislation, and coordination of organizations with similar purposes. Supports research in areas such as laetrile testing; supports numerous educational foundation programs. Conducts lobbying activities. **Publications:** *Health Freedom News*, periodic. Journal. *Price:* $3.95.

★ 1420 ★ **National Health and Medical Research Council (NHMRC)**
GPO Box 9848
Canberra, ACT 2601, Australia
Phone: 6 2897019
Fax: 6 2897802
Joe Corcoran, Chm.

Founded: 1936. **Members:** 30. **Languages:** English. **Description:** Representatives from state and territory health authorities, professional and scientific colleges and associations, unions, universities, industry, business and consumer groups, welfare organizations, and the commonwealth administration. Evaluates reports from committees, expert panels, working parties and disseminates results. **Publications:** Reports, periodic. Contains research results.

★ 1421 ★ **National Health Policy Forum (NHPF)**
2021 K St. NW, Ste. 800
Washington, DC 20052
Phone: (202)872-1390
Judith Miller Jones, Dir.

Founded: 1971. **Description:** Senior level health policymakers from Congress and the executive branch of the federal government; subscribers to issue papers are health policy professionals from academia and industry. Primary goal is to improve the process of federal decision-making in health policy. Provides continuing education for health policymakers in small,

"off-the-record" settings to encourage the free and candid exchange of ideas. Does not lobby for or against legislative proposals, but emphasizes the discussion of underlying issues and concepts in such areas as health finance, manpower, child health and development, access to health care, aging, and preventive health care. Furthers cooperation and understanding among the numerous government agencies and bureaus involved in health policy. Sponsors technical briefings; conducts site visits to observe the problems and successes of exemplary health programs across the country. **Publications:** *Issue Briefs*, 25-30/year.

★ 1422 ★ **National Indian Health Board (NIHB)**
1385 S. Colorado Blvd., Ste. A-708
Denver, CO 80222
Phone: (303)759-3075
Fax: (303)759-3674
Levi Mestegh, II, Exec.Dir.

Founded: 1969. **Members:** 12. **Regional Groups:** 12. **Description:** Indians of all tribes and natives of Alaskan villages. Advocates the improvement of health conditions which directly or indirectly affect American Indians and Alaskan Natives. Seeks to inform the public of the health condition of Native Americans; represents Indians and their interests. Conducts seminars and workshops on health subjects. Provides technical assistance to members and Indian organizations. **Publications:** *Conference Report*, annual. • *NIHB Health Reporter*, quarterly. Newsletter. *Price:* Free. Also publishes special reports on health issues and produces audiotapes.

★ 1423 ★ **National Medical Association (NMA)**
1012 10th St. NW
Washington, DC 20001
Phone: (202)347-1895
Fax: (202)842-3293
Dr. Clifton Peay, Int.VP

Founded: 1895. **Members:** 14,500. **Regional Groups:** 6. **State Groups:** 32. **Local Groups:** 62. **Description:** Professional society of black physicians. Maintains 19 sections representing major specialties of medicine. Plans to establish library and physician placement service. Conducts symposia and workshops. **Publications:** *Journal of the National Medical Association*, monthly. Journal. • *National Medical Association Newsletter*, quarterly. Newsletter.

★ 1424 ★ **National Medical Fellowships (NMF)**
254 W. 31st St., 7th Fl.
New York, NY 10001
Phone: (212)714-0933
Fax: (212)239-9718
Leon Johnson, Jr., Pres.

Founded: 1946. **Regional Groups:** 2. **Description:** Promotes education of minority students in medicine. Conducts financial assistance program for first- and second-year minority medical students who are U.S. citizens. Conducts workshops in financial planning and management for medical and premedical students, administrators, and parents. **Publications:** Annual Report. • Brochure, annual. • *Informed Decision Mak-*

ing. • *NMF Update,* biennial. Newsletter. • *Special Report,* annual. **Formerly:** (1952) Provident Medical Associates.

★**1425★ National Migrant Resource Program (NMRP)**
c/o E. Roberta Ryder
1515 Capital of Texas Hwy. S, Ste. 220
Austin, TX 78746
Phone: (512)328-7682
Fax: (512)328-8559
E. Roberta Ryder, Exec.Dir.

Founded: 1975. **Description:** Seeks to make quality primary health care accessible to migrant and seasonal farm workers. Supports the establishment of a national network of migrant health centers through the production, processing, and distribution of information, including information on health problems specific to or more prevalent in the migrant community. Works to provide technical assistance for health development and research. Develops collaborative working relationship between agencies serving migrant farmworkers. Disseminates portable health referral cards, which contain English/Spanish health records designed to assist migrants in the transfer of medical information. Maintains job/resume bank, biographical archives, library, and speakers' bureau. Bestows awards; operates placement service; compiles statistics. **Publications:** Books. • Catalogs. • Directory. • *Migrant Health Newsline,* bimonthly. Includes clinical supplement. • *Migrant Health Referral Directory,* annual. Directory. • Videos. **Formerly:** (1989) National Migrant Referral Project.

★**1426★ National Migrant Workers Council (NMWC)**
502 W. Elm Ave.
Monroe, MI 48161
Phone: (313)243-0711
Fax: (313)243-0435
Kimberly Kratz, Exec.Dir.

Founded: 1983. **Members:** 280. **Description:** Provides, coordinates, and oversees the provision of health, educational, and social services for migratory families. Sponsors the East Coast Migrant Health Project and the Midwest Migrant Health Information Office. Implements community-based health education programs for migrant farmworkers. **Publications:** Brochures. • *Camp Health Aide.* Manual. • *Directory for Migrant Health Services-Midwest Regional,* annual. Directory. • *Health for the Nation's Harvesters: A History of the Migrant Health Program in its Economic and Social Setting.* • *Membership List,* annual. **Formerly:** National Migrant Workers Council; (1979) Sisters Concerned for the Rural Poor.

★**1427★ National Minority Health Association (NMHA)**
PO Box 11876
Harrisburg, PA 17108
Phone: (717)763-1323
Leroy Robinson, Exec.Dir.

Founded: 1987. **Members:** 1,500. **State Groups:** 1. **Description:** Health care providers and associations, consumers, executives and administrators, educators, pharmaceutical and health insurance companies, and other corporations with an interest in health care. Seeks to

identify and focus attention on the health needs of minorities. Promotes: more effective research in minority health issues; better training of health care practitioners; development of programs that encourage minorities to pursue careers in the health care industry and educate minority communities on the importance of good health. Initiates discussions with professional health organizations, academic institutions, state and federal governments, and health departments to develop strategies to improve the quality and availability of health care, health delivery systems, and health professionals to minority communities. Maintains speakers' bureau, conducts research and educational programs; sponsors children's programs; complies statistics. **Publications:** *The National Minority Health Association News,* quarterly.

★**1428★ National Organization for Competency Assurance (NOCA)**
1200 19th St. NW, Ste. 300
Washington, DC 20036-2401
Phone: (202)857-1165
Fax: (202)223-4579
Michael S. Hamm, Exec.Dir.

Founded: 1977. **Members:** 93. **Description:** Nonprofit organizations conducting certification programs for occupations and professionals and trade associations representing these professionals. Seeks to increase public awareness, understanding, and acceptance of private sector credentialing as an alternative to licensure; promotes nonlicensed but certified practitioners as a means to achieving high quality and cost containment. **Publications:** *Professional Regulation News,* monthly. **Formerly:** (1989) National Commission for Health Certifying Agencies.

★**1429★ National Organization for Rare Disorders (NORD)**
PO Box 8923
New Fairfield, CT 06812-8923
Phone: (203)746-6518
Free: 800-999-NORD
Fax: (203)746-6481
Abbey S. Meyers, Pres.

Founded: 1983. **Members:** 65,000. **National Groups:** 130. **Description:** Doctors, professionals, academics, voluntary health organizations, and individuals interested in rare disorders. Serves as a clearinghouse for information concerning rare disorders. Objectives are: to monitor the Orphan Drug Act; to link individuals with rare disorders together for mutual support; to stimulate research on rare diseases; to foster communication among voluntary agencies, health-related industries, and government bodies. (Orphan drugs are used in the treatment of rare disorders. Since their use is not widespread, most drug companies cannot expect to profit from the development and manufacture of these drugs. The Orphan Drug Act gives financial assistance and tax incentives to drug companies that develop these drugs.) Provides information on rare disorders and referrals to organizations. **Publications:** *NORD On-Line Bulletin,* monthly. Updating service for voluntary health agency members on legislation and other issues related to orphan drugs and diseases. Includes meeting schedule. *Price:* Included in membership dues, for organizations. • *Orphan*

Disease Update, 3/year. Newsletter. For individual members updating information on orphan diseases and orphan drug research; discusses legislative issues related to health. *Price:* Included in membership dues. • *Physician Guide to Rare Diseases.* Book.

★**1430★ National Resident Matching Program (NRMP)**
2450 N St. NW, Ste. 201
Washington, DC 20037-1141
Phone: (202)828-0676
Edward Stemmler, Exec.Dir.

Founded: 1951. **Description:** National clearinghouse for matching the preferences of applicants for residencies with the hospitals' choice of applicants, in order to assist, to the extent possible, their choices of residencies. Conducts studies relating to medical education. **Publications:** *NRMP Data,* annual. **Formerly:** (1953) National InterAssociation Committee on Internships; (1968) National Intern Matching Program; (1978) National Intern and Resident Matching Program.

★**1431★ National Rural Health Association (NRHA)**
301 E. Armour Blvd., Ste. 420
Kansas City, MO 64111
Phone: (816)756-3140
Fax: (816)756-3144
Walter P. Pidgeon, Jr., Exec.Dir.

Founded: 1987. **Members:** 1,700. **Description:** Administrators, physicians, nurses, physician assistants, health planners, academicians, and others interested or involved in rural health care. Purpose is to create a better understanding of health care problems unique to rural areas; utilize a collective approach in finding positive solutions; articulate and represent the health care needs of rural America; supply current information to rural health care providers; serve as a liaison between rural health care programs throughout the country. Offers continuing education credits for medical, dental, nursing, and management courses. Provides placement services. **Publications:** *Journal of Rural Health,* quarterly. Journal. Includes book reviews, abstracts of published research, and research reviews. *Price:* Included in membership dues; $35 for nonmembers; $90 for institutions. • *Rural Health Care,* bimonthly. Newsletter. Includes listing of employment opportunities, information on new members, and legislative and state news. *Price:* Included in membership dues. • *Rural Mental Health and Substance Abuse Resources Directory--1993.* Directory. Divided into federal, national, regional, state and private agencies and programs. *Price:* $5/copy. Also publishes many other resources.

★**1432★ National Society for Shut-Ins (NSFS)**
PO Box 1392
Reading, PA 19603
Phone: (215)374-2930
Fax: (215)372-0130
Michael Shiedy, Pres.

Founded: 1970. **Local Groups:** 3. **Description:** Persons united to organize chapters throughout the country in order to educate people to care for and visit shut-ins. Seeks to promote a sense of emotional and spiritual well-being and self-worth in individuals who are confined to their homes or institutions, due to age, sickness, handicap, or imprisonment (inclusively, "shut-ins"). Designates third Sunday in October each year as National Shut-In Day and encourages people to visit the sick, elderly, and imprisoned on that day. Activities include: annual Sunshine Day, providing a day of entertainment and recreation for shut-ins away from the home or institution; National Shut-In Day and Sunshine Week, fostering public recognition of the plight of shut-ins; Sunshine Productions, producing amateur musical performances for the enjoyment and benefit of shut-ins; treating shut-ins to various programs of entertainment. Sponsors Project SUNSHINE, promoting visitation and performance of service by volunteer high school and college students, civic clubs, and church groups to institutionalized and homebound shut-ins. **Publications:** *Sunshine News*, quarterly. **Formerly:** (1982) National Shut-In Day Society.

★ 1433 ★　National Voluntary Health Agencies (NVHA)
1660 L St. NW, Ste. 601
Washington, DC 20036-5603
Phone: (202)467-5913
Free: 800-654-0845
James L. Barr, Exec.Dir.

Founded: 1956. **Members:** 62. **State Groups:** 44. **Description:** Nonprofit corporation of national health agencies. Purpose is to receive funds generated by the Combined Federal Campaign and to distribute them to member agencies. Encourages donations to member agencies. **Formerly:** (1975) National Committee of the Federal Service Campaign for National Health Agencies; (1985) National Health Agencies Committee for the Combined Federal Campaign.

★ 1434 ★　National Women's Health Network (NWHN)
514 10th St. NW, Ste. 400
Washington, DC 20004
Phone: (202)347-1140
Fax: (202)347-1162
Beverly Baker, Exec.Dir.

Founded: 1976. **Members:** 15,000. **Local Groups:** 500. **Description:** Individual consumers, organizations, and health centers. Represents the women's health movement. Monitors federal health policy as it affects women; testifies before Congress and federal agencies. Supports feminist health projects. Sponsors the Women's Health Clearinghouse, a national resource file on all aspects of women's health care. Operates speakers' bureau. **Publications:** *National Women's Health Network--Network News*, bimonthly. Newsletter. Provides health information and medical alerts for women. *Price:* Included in membership dues. • *Newsalerts*, periodic. Also publishes health information packets, booklets, and brochures.

★ 1435 ★　National Women's Health Resource Center (NWHRC)
2440 M St. NW, Ste. 325
Washington, DC 20037
Phone: (202)293-6045
Fax: (202)293-7256
Heidi Rosvolo-Brenholtz, Prog. Coord.

Founded: 1988. **Description:** Dedicated to improving the health of women throughout the nation. Disseminates information about women's health. Serves as a national clearinghouse for women's health information. **Publications:** *National Women's Health Report*, bimonthly. Newsletter. Contains features on current women's health issues. *Price:* $25 for individuals; $50 for organizations and institutions.

★ 1436 ★　New Frontiers of Medicine (NFM)
PO Box 1423
Eaton Park, FL 33840
Phone: (813)682-1247
Fax: (813)683-2054
Ben H. McConnell, M.D., Dir.

Founded: 1985. **Description:** Volunteers who seek to raise funds and commodities to aid specific medical clinics in Egypt, Ethiopia, and Sudan. Organizes person-to-person projects to link academic theory with hands-on experience. Maintains speakers' bureau and book collection. **Publications:** *Manna in the Desert*, periodic. **Formerly:** (1987) Friends of Sudan.

★ 1437 ★　New Professionals Section of the American Public Health AssociatioN (NPSAPHA)
c/o Ruth Scarborough
Temple Family Planning
Hudson Bldg., Lower Level
3425 N. Carlisle St.
Philadelphia, PA 19140
Phone: (215)707-3061
Fax: (215)707-7918
Ruth Scarborough, Chairperson

Founded: 1969. **Members:** 300. **Description:** A section of the American Public Health Association. Professionals and paraprofessionals in the human service areas. Offers specialized education and forum for health advisors. **Publications:** Newsletter, quarterly. **Formerly:** (1982) National New Professional Health Workers.

★ 1438 ★　New Zealand Medical Women's Organisation
PO Box 55-074
Auckland, New Zealand
Dr. Elizabeth Steele, Pres.

Languages: English. **Description:** Women physicians. Works to increase public awareness of the medical profession. Promotes unity among members. Encourages the entry of women into the medical profession; represents members' interests before government agencies and the public. Makes available charitable programs.

★ 1439 ★　Nicaragua Medical Aid (NMA)
1400 Shattuck Ave., Ste. 7-125
Berkeley, CA 94709
Phone: (510)841-1644
Fax: (510)644-2923
Dr. Paul Kranz, Exec.Dir.

Founded: 1986. **Members:** 10,000. **Description:** A project of the Inter-American Health Foundation. Supports community-based health care organizations in Nicaragua. Provides medical supplies and equipment for primary and preventative care; promotes accessiblity of quality health care to the Nicaraguan poor. **Publications:** Brochure.

★ 1440 ★　Nordic Council for Arctic Medical Research (NCAMR)
(Nordiska Samarbetskommitten for Arktisk Medicinsk Forskning)
Aapistie 1
SF-90220 Oulu 22, Finland
Phone: 81 5376202
Fax: 81 5376203
Mikael Knip, Sec.Gen.

Founded: 1969. **Members:** 13. **Languages:** English, Finnish, Swedish. **Description:** Individuals appointed by Nordic governments. Promotes research into arctic medicine; encourages cooperation among researchers. Disseminates reports and other information to persons engaged in arctic medicine. **Publications:** *Arctic Medical Research*, quarterly. Journal. • Monographs. • Proceedings.

★ 1441 ★　Nordic Council on Medicines (NCM)
(Nordiska Lakemedelsnamnden — NLN)
Box 26
S-751 03 Uppsala, Sweden
Phone: 18 174700
Fax: 18 541580
Ulf Janzon, Gen.Sec.

Founded: 1975. **Members:** 10. **Languages:** Danish, English, Finnish, Icelandic, Norwegian, Swedish. **Description:** Heads of regulatory agencies and doctors, lawyers, and pharmacists in Denmark, Finland, Iceland, Norway, and Sweden. Works for harmonization of legislation and administrative procedures concerning medicines within the Nordic countries. Sets guidelines for legislation; coordinates statistics on medicines; works for better reporting of adverse reactions and drug information. Serves as advisory body to health authorities. **Publications:** *NLN News*, quarterly. Newsletter. • *Nordic Statistics on Medicines*, triennial. • *Registration Guidelines*. • Reports.

★ 1442 ★　Nordic Federation for Medical Education (NFME)
(Nordisk Federation for Medicinsk Undervisning)
Rigshospitalet
Tagensvej 18
DK-2200 Copenhagen N, Denmark
Phone: 35375252
Fax: 31357043
Jorgen Nystrup, M.D., Sec.Gen.

Founded: 1966. **Members:** 92. **Languages:** Danish, English, Finnish, Icelandic, Norwegian, Swedish. **Description:** Organizations in 5 countries involved in medical education. Promotes medical education in the Nordic countries; encourages Nordic cooperation. Sponsors teacher-training program and quarterly symposia. **Publications:** Articles. • *Newsletter*, 3-4/year. Newsletter. • Reports.

★1443★ North American Medical / Dental Association (NAMDA)
PO Box 1982
Newport Beach, CA 92663
Phone: (714)642-7689
Free: 800-346-2632
Dorene M. Christensen, Pres.

Founded: 1968. **Members:** 10,000. **Description:** Dentists and physicians who promote medical education combined with recreation for membership. Fosters professional education through lecture series featuring nationally known educators in the dental and medical fields. Offers recreational skiing program as a means of healthful recreation and physical fitness for membership. **Publications:** Brochure, annual. Publicizes seminars for the following season.

★1444★ North American Primary Care Research Group (NAPCRG)
Med. College of Virginia
PO Box 251
Richmond, VA 23298
Phone: (804)786-9625
Fax: (804)786-5856
Robert B. Williams, M.D., Exec.Dir.

Founded: 1972. **Members:** 500. **Description:** Physicians and other individuals interested in primary care research. (Primary care is the type of medicine practiced by physicians who do not require patient referrals from other physicians.) Promotes research on primary care topics. Maintains 11 special interest groups including: Ambulatory Sentinel Practice; Clinical Decision Making; Health Status Group. Disseminates information and serves as a forum for exchange of ideas on research projects. Maintains speakers' bureau. **Publications:** Family Medicine, bimonthly. Journal. • Glossary of Primary Care Terms. • Newsletter, quarterly. • Proceedings. • Process Classification for Family Care. • Reports.

★1445★ The Obesity Foundation (TOF)
5600 S. Quebec, Ste. 109-A
Englewood, CO 80111
Phone: (303)850-0328
Fax: (303)779-4834
James F. Merker, CAE, Exec.Dir.

Founded: 1950. **Members:** 700. **Description:** Philanthropic organization that seeks to control, and ultimately cure, the disease of obesity. Encourages children to be aware of good nutrition. Sponsors research programs. Operates Dial-A-Tape service. Encourages health insurance plans to cover obesity treatment; improves communications between bariatric physicians and the public. Holds "Gone with the Weight" Fun Walk at annual meeting of American Society of Bariatric Physicians. **Publications:** Bearly Any Fat. Book. Cookbook. • Bearly AnyFat Too. Book. Cookbook. • Trim and Fit, quarterly. Newsletter. Price: $5/year.

★1446★ ODPHP National Health Information Center (NHIC)
PO Box 1133
Washington, DC 20013-1133
Phone: (301)565-4167
Free: 800-336-4797
Fax: (301)984-4256
Andrew Lefton, Dir.

Founded: 1979. **Description:** A referral service to aid consumers and health professionals in locating health information. Funded by the Office of Disease Prevention and Health Promotion, Public Health Service, U.S. Department of Health and Human Services. **Publications:** Health Information Resources in the Federal Government, periodic. • HealthFinders. • Locating Funds for Health Promotion Projects, periodic. **Formerly:** (1986) National Health Information Clearinghouse; (1987) ODPHP Health Information Center.

★1447★ Operation U.S.A. (OPUSA)
8320 Melrose Ave., No. 200
Los Angeles, CA 90069
Phone: (213)658-8876
Free: 800-678-7255
Fax: (213)653-7846
Richard Walden, Pres. & Founder

Founded: 1979. **Description:** Provides relief aid to crisis areas in the U.S. and worldwide; makes available financial and material support to clinics, hospitals, and orphanages. Maintains speakers' bureau. **Publications:** OP USA Newsletter, semiannual. Newsletter. Price: Free. **Formerly:** (1988) Operation California.

★1448★ OPTIONS Service of Project Concern (OSPC)
PO Box 85323
San Diego, CA 92138
Phone: (619)279-6990
Fax: (619)694-0294
Dan Shaughnessy, Contact

Founded: 1963. **Description:** Nonsectarian, nonpolitical agency serving worldwide areas of health care shortage. Functions in matching health care and development personnel with domestic and overseas clinics, hospitals, and agencies where their services are needed. Assignments are volunteer as well as stipend by the participating programs. Some voluntary assignments offer room, board, subsistance allowances, and travel assistance. Long-term assignments usually offer subsistence allowance. Recruits health care personnel through medicine magazines and other sources. **Publications:** OPTIONS, bimonthly. Newsletter. Lists employment opportunities in areas in need of health professionals, especially rural America and the Third World. **Also Known As:** Options. **Formerly:** (1972) American Doctors; (1973) AmDoc; (1976) Options/AmDoc; (1989) AmDoc/Option Agency; (1990) AMDOC/Option; (1993) Project Concern's Options Service.

★1449★ Organisation Mondiale de la Sante - Congo
BP 6
Brazzaville, Congo
Coleman A.A. Quenum

Languages: French. **Description:** Promotes health and nutrition in the Congo. Provides edu-

cational programs. Monitors healthcare programs. Conducts research.

★1450★ Organizacion Panamericana de la Salud - Programa Mujer, Salud y Desarrollo (OPS-MSD)
Ministerio de Salud, Piso 3
Apartado 3745-1000
San Jose, Costa Rica
Phone: 2337354
Fax: 2338061
Lea Guido

Founded: 1986. **Languages:** Spanish. **Description:** Advises government and private organizations on women's health issues. Works to change laws relating to women and health. Supports more integrated health services for women. Researches the legal and medical situation of women. Trains workers for the Health Ministry. Conducts workshops on self-help medical procedures. Disseminates information about women's health issues. Encourages formation of women's groups.

★1451★ Organization Internationale de Cooperation pour la Sante
153, rue de Charonne
F-75011 Paris, France
Phone: 1 43732904
Philippe Lamy, Dir.

Description: Promotes health care and disease prevention efforts in developing nations. Conducts research.

★1452★ PanAmerican Federation of Associations of Medical Schools (PAFAMS) (Federacion Panamericana de Asociaciones de Facultades y Escuelas de Medicina — FEPAFEM)
Apartado 60411
Caracas 1060-A, Venezuela
Phone: 2 936271
Fax: 2 936346
Dr. Pablo A. Pulido, Exec.Dir.

Founded: 1962. **Members:** 357. **National Groups:** 22. **Regional Groups:** 6. **Languages:** English, Portuguese, Spanish. **Description:** National and regional associations, international institutions, medical school faculties, and individuals in 22 countries. Purposes are to improve the quality of medical education and meet the medical service needs of Pan American countries. Sponsors seminars on medical education. Operates an information and documentation center on medical education and health. **Publications:** Bulletin, quarterly. Bulletin. • Guide to Pan American Medical Schools, annual. • Newsletter, 6/year. Newsletter.

★1453★ Pan American Health and Education Foundation (PAHEF)
525 23rd St. NW
Washington, DC 20037
Phone: (202)861-3416
Fax: (202)861-8878
Richard Marks, Exec.Sec.

Founded: 1968. **Description:** Seeks to mobilize financial and human resources for the improvement of health and education, particularly in Latin America; to advance the objectives of the Pan American Health Organization and World Health Organization. Cosponsors Program for Textbooks and Instructional Materials, which makes needed items available for the training of health personnel at all levels, including professional, technical, and auxiliary. Works cooperatively with organizations and governmental bodies which share the same objectives. **Publications:** *Boletin de Medicamentos y Terapeutica*, quarterly. • Manuals. Provides information for primary health care workers.

★ 1454 ★ Pan American Health Organization (PAHO)
525 23rd St. NW
Washington, DC 20037
Phone: (202)861-3200
Fax: (202)223-5971
Dr. George Alleyne, Dir.

Founded: 1902. **Members:** 41. **Languages:** English, Spanish. **Description:** Governments of Western Hemisphere nations united to improve physical and mental health in the Americas. Coordinates regional activities combating disease including exchange of statistical and epidemiological information, development of local health services, and organization of disease control and eradication programs. Encourages development in health systems and technology; provides consulting services; conducts educational courses on public health topics including environmental health, food and nutrition, and tropical diseases. Has established Emergency Preparedness and Disaster Relief Coordination Program in order to increase the ability of health institutions to effectively handle emergencies. Operates the Natural Disaster Relief Voluntary Fund to support disaster relief activities. Maintains the Pan American Sanitary Bureau, the regional office for the Americas of the World Health Organization. Develops health documentaries and coordinates teleconferences. **Publications:** *Boletin de la Oficina Sanitaria Panamericana*, monthly. Serves as a reference source regarding health problems in the Americas and progress made toward solutions. Includes book reviews and results. • *Bulletin of the Pan American Health Organization*, quarterly. Bulletin. Features original articles on medical research, preventive medicine, public health administration, and other information. • *Disaster Preparedness in the Americas*, quarterly. Newsletter. PAHO Emergency Preparedness and Disaster Relief Coordination Program. Includes news items about studies and programs in the countries of America. • *Educacion Medica y Salud*, quarterly. Journal. Covers curriculum planning, development, and evaluation of new educational methods and research in medical education and human resources development. • *EPI Newsletter*, bimonthly. Newsletter. Provides information on immunization programs in the Americas. Covers new technologies available for the execution of programs. • *Epidemiological Bulletin*, bimonthly. Bulletin. Disseminates epidemiological information regarding communicable and noncommunicable diseases of public health importance. • *Health Conditions in the Americas*, quadrennial. Each edition, different price. • Manuals. • Monographs. • Reports. Also publishes textbooks.

★ 1455 ★ Pan American Health Organization
PO Box 384
Cross Roads
Kingston 5, Jamaica

Description: National branch of international organization. Promotes good health and physical and mental well-being for individuals in Jamaica. Sponsors educational programs dealing with health-related issues.

★ 1456 ★ Pan American Health Organization
Apartado Postal 105-34
Mexico City, DF, Mexico

Description: Promotes the well-being and health of individuals in Mexico. Sponsors health education programs.

★ 1457 ★ Pan American Health Organization
Apartado Postal No. 728
Tegucigalpa, Honduras

Description: Promotes health education and awareness programs. Works to increase the standard of living in Honduras. **Publications:** *Boletin de la Oficina Sanitaria Panamericana*, monthly. • *Bulletin*, monthly.

★ 1458 ★ Pan American Health Organization
Apartado Postal 8982
Sucursal 7
Quito, Ecuador

Description: Promotes quality health care for individuals in Ecuador. Sponsors public health educational programs. Works to improve the standard of living for those living in Ecuador. **Publications:** *Boletin de la Oficina Sanitaria Panamericana*, monthly. • *Bulletin*, quarterly.

★ 1459 ★ Pan American Health Organization (Organizacion Panamericana de la Salud - Costa Rica)
Apartado 3745
San Jose, Costa Rica

Description: Works to improve the health and standard of living for individuals in Costa Rica. **Publications:** *Boletin de la Oficina Sanitaria Panamericana*, monthly. • *Bulletin*, quarterly.

★ 1460 ★ Pan American Health Organization
Apartado Aereo 253367
Bogota, Colombia

Description: Promotes the health and well-being of individuals in Colombia. Educates the public about disease. Works to increase the average life expectancy in Colombia. **Publications:** *Boletin de la Oficina Sanitaria Panamericana*, monthly. • *Bulletin*, quarterly.

★ 1461 ★ Pan American Health Organization (Organizicion Panamerican de la Salud - Chile)
Monjitas 689
Santiago, Chile

Description: Promotes the aims of the Pan American Health Organization. Seeks to edu-

cate Chileans about the importance of good health. **Publications:** *Boletin de la Oficina Sanitaria Panamericana*, monthly. • *Bulletin of the PAHO*, quarterly.

★ 1462 ★ Pan American Medical Association (PAMA)
c/o Frederic C. Fenig, M.D.
745 5th Ave., Ste. 403
New York, NY 10151
Phone: (212)753-6033
Fax: (212)308-6847
Frederic C. Fenig, M.D., Sec.

Founded: 1925. **Members:** 6,000. **Description:** Fosters the exchange of medical information and research results among physicians in Western Hemisphere countries. **Also Known As:** Associacion Medica Pan Americana.

★ 1463 ★ Participaction
40 Dundas St. W, Ste. 220
Box 64
Toronto, ON, Canada M5G 2C2
Phone: (416)954-1212
Fax: (416)954-4949

Founded: 1971. **Languages:** English. **Description:** Promotes increased physical activity among Canadians. Provides educational materials and films.

★ 1464 ★ PEF Israel Endowment Funds (PEF)
41 E. 42nd St., Rm. 607
New York, NY 10017
Phone: (212)599-1260
Abraham J. Kremer, Pres.

Founded: 1922. **Members:** 4,000. **Description:** Provides charitable, scientific, educational, cultural, and social aid to institutions and organizations in Israel. Works to provide relief for and to minister to needy persons in Israel; to support and maintain public hospitals and clinics; to assist all types of social service agencies; to help support and maintain various universities and other educational and religious institutions in Israel; and to promote scientific research. **Publications:** Annual Report. **Formerly:** Palestine Endowment Funds.

★ 1465 ★ People-to-People Health Foundation (HOPE)
Project HOPE Health Sciences
Educ. Center
Carter Hall
Millwood, VA 22646
Phone: (703)837-2100
Free: 800-544-HOPE
Fax: (703)837-1813
William B. Walsh, Jr., Pres.&CEO

Founded: 1958. **Description:** Promotes better world health and understanding through the training of medical, nursing, dental, and allied health personnel in developing areas of the world. Operates the Center for Health Affairs, which provides research and policy analysis to help develop solutions to problems in worldwide health systems. Develops programs which include the use of volunteer doctors, nurses, and allied health professionals to teach modern techniques in health sciences education, health services delivery systems, health facilities management, and health-related humanitarian assistance. Programs are currently operating in 37 countries, located in Africa, Asia, Eastern Europe, and North, Central, and South America. **Publications:** Annual Report. • *Health Affairs*, quarterly. Journal. Covers domestic and international health policies; annual and five-year indexes available. *Price:* $45/year for individuals; $75/year for institutions. • *HOPE News*, quarterly. Newsletter. Covers Project HOPE's international and domestic programs. Includes calendar of events and news of fundraising activities. *Price:* Free. **Also Known As:** Project HOPE.

★ 1466 ★ **Peoples Health Care Foundation (Narodowy Fundusz Ochrony Zdrowia)**
Wspolna St. 1/3
PL-00-529 Warsaw, Poland
Phone: 22 284628
Jan Kostrzewski, Pres.

Description: Works to ensure that needy individuals receive proper health care.

★ 1467 ★ **People's Medical Society (PMS)**
462 Walnut St.
Allentown, PA 18102
Phone: (610)770-1670
Free: 800-624-8773
Fax: (610)770-0607
Charles B. Inlander, Pres.

Founded: 1982. **Members:** 80,000. **Description:** Promotes citizen involvement in the cost, quality, and management of the American health care system. Seeks to: train and encourage individuals to study local health care systems, practitioners, and institutions and promote preventive health care and medical cost control by these groups; address major policy issues and control health costs; encourage more preventive practice and research; promote self-care and alternative health care procedures; launch an information campaign to assist individuals in maintaining personal health and to prepare them for appointments with medical professionals. **Publications:** *Arthritis: Questions You Have, Answers You Need.* • *Asthma: Questions You Have, Answers You Need.* • Bibliographies. • Bulletins. • *Depression: Questions You Have, Answers You Need.* • *Good Operations--Bad Operations.* • *Healthy Body Book.* Book. • *Hearing Loss: Questions, You Have, Answers You Need.* • *Medicine Made Easy.* • *Medicine on Trial.* • *Misdiagnosis: Woman as a Disease.* • *150 Ways to Be a Savvy Medical Consumer.* • *People's Medical Society Newsletter*, bimonthly. Newsletter. Includes membership activities information. *Price:* Included in membership dues. • *77 Ways to Beat Colds and Flu.* • *Take This Book to the Gynecologist With You.* • *Take This Book to the Hospital With You.* • *Take This Book to the Obstetrician With You.* • *Vitamins & Minerals: Questions You Have, Answers You Need.* • *Your Complete Medical Record.*

★ 1468 ★ **Phi Alpha Sigma**
313 S. 10th St.
Philadelphia, PA 19107
Phone: (215)627-6638
Paul J. Antal, Pres.

Founded: 1886. **Members:** 120. **Description:** Professional fraternity - medicine. **Publications:**

Bubbling Rales, annual. Newsletter. for Alumni. *Price:* Free to alumni.

★ 1469 ★ **Phi Chi Medical Fraternity (PCMF)**
1201 E. Spring St.
New Albany, IN 47150
Phone: (812)948-0581
Free: 800-800-7442
Daniel H. Cannon, M.D., Chm., Exec. Trustees

Founded: 1889. **Members:** 40,818. **Local Groups:** 12. **Description:** Professional fraternity - medicine. Maintains Phi Chi Welfare Association, which accepts voluntary contributions to a student loan fund and other services. **Publications:** *Constitution and Statutes.* • *Officers' Manual.* Manual. • *PC Chronicles*, semiannual. Magazine. Provides chapter news and information. *Price:* Included in membership dues. • *Phi Chi Directory.* Directory. • *Psi Chi History, 1889-1989.* • *Psi Chi Songs.* **Formerly:** (1989) Phi Chi.

★ 1470 ★ **Phi Delta Epsilon Medical Fraternity**
2565A US Hwy. 23 S
Alpena, MI 49707-4617
Phone: 800-347-3713
S. M. Greenstone, Exec.Dir.

Founded: 1904. **Members:** 25,000. **Local Groups:** 41. **Description:** Professional fraternity - medicine. **Publications:** *Phi Delta Epsilon News and Scientific Journal*, quarterly. Journal.

★ 1471 ★ **Phi Epsilon Kappa**
901 W. New York St.
Indianapolis, IN 46202
Phone: (317)637-8431
Jeffery Vessely, Ed.D., Exec.Sec.

Founded: 1913. **Members:** 2,000. **Regional Groups:** 5. **Local Groups:** 30. **Description:** Professional fraternity - physical and health education. **Publications:** *Black and Gold Bulletin*, semiannual. Newsletter. *Price:* Included in membership dues. • *The Physical Educator*, quarterly. Journal. *Price:* $25/year.

★ 1472 ★ **Phi Lambda Kappa Medical Fraternity**
Bucks County Office Center
1200 New Rodgers Rd.
Box 805
Bristol, PA 19007
Phone: (215)785-2325
Eleanor G. Halprin, Exec.Sec.

Founded: 1907. **Members:** 4,800. **Regional Groups:** 17. **Local Groups:** 20. **Description:** Professional fraternity - medicine. **Publications:** *Quarterly.*

★ 1473 ★ **Phi Rho Sigma Medical Society**
PO Box 90264
Indianapolis, IN 46290
Phone: (317)255-4379
Fax: (317)253-5067
Martin B. Wice, M.D., Sec.-Treas.

Founded: 1890. **Members:** 31,260. **Regional Groups:** 13. **State Groups:** 12. **Description:** Professional society - medicine. **Publications:** *Journal of Phi Rho Sigma*, quarterly. Journal.

★ 1474 ★ **Philippine Medical Women's Association (PMWA)**
PMWA Bldg., No. 70
V. Luna Rd., Cor. Malakas St.
Quezon City, Metro Manila, Philippines
Phone: 2 9213947
Dr. Ninde Sanico Castro, Pres. Officer

Founded: 1949. **Members:** 3,500. **Regional Groups:** 56. **Languages:** English. **Description:** Filipino women physicians. Works to increase public awareness of the medical profession. Promotes unity among members. Encourages women in the medical profession to participate in national issues affecting women and children. Operates medical and dental clinics and laboratories and the PMWA Learning Center, a kindergarten and daycare center. Conducts charitable activities; offers scholarships and grants. **Publications:** *Philippine Medical World*, 1-2/year. Journal. Includes research papers. • *PMWA Newsette*, quarterly.

★ 1475 ★ **Physicians Committee for Responsible Medicine (PCRM)**
PO Box 6322
Washington, DC 20015
Phone: (202)686-2210
Fax: (202)686-2216
Neal D. Barnard, M.D., Pres.

Founded: 1985. **Members:** 60,000. **Description:** Physicians, scientists, healthcare professionals, and interested others. Increases public awareness about the importance of preventive medicine and nutrition, and raises scientific and ethical questions pertaining to the use of animals in medical research. Supports research into U.S. agricultural and public health policies. Promotes the New Four Food Groups, a no-cholesterol, low-fat alternative to U.S.D.A. dietary recommendations. Maintains the Gold Plan program which includes information on low-fat, cholesterol-free entrees and nutrition for institutional food services. Provides legislative testimony on alternatives to animal tests for consumer product marketing, and evaluates federal requirements for animal tests to identify cancer-and birth defect-causing chemicals. Offers fact sheets on nutrition, preventive medicine, and non-animal research topics. Is establishing a coalition of environmental and public health groups which will encourage regulators and other environmental policymakers to adopt new requirements for short-term non-animal tests, and to eliminate those mandating animal tests. Maintains speakers' bureau. **Publications:** *Alternatives in Medical Education.* • Brochures. • *Food for Life.* • *Good Medicine*, quarterly. Magazine. Provides information about preventive medicine, nutrition, public health policy, medical/nutrition research updates, and AIDS research. *Price:* Included in membership dues. • *The Power of Your Plate.* Also publishes fact sheets.

★ 1476 ★ **Physicians for Social Responsibility (PSR)**
1101 14th St., 7th Fl.
Washington, DC 20005
Phone: (202)898-0150
Fax: (202)898-0172
Julia Moore, Dir.

Founded: 1961. **Members:** 19,000. **Local Groups:** 90. **Description:** Medical professionals and others with doctoral degrees and medical students concerned with the threat of nuclear war, environmental degradation, and violence in our society; others supporting the work of PSR. Educates the public on the medical effects of nuclear war and nuclear weapons and on the implications of national policy and legislative actions on arms control and environmental issues. Conducts media outreach and voter education programs. Supports the negotiation of comprehensive test ban treaty and opposes nuclear attack-related civilian defense. Engages in lobbying; researches legislative alternatives and disseminates legislative information. PSR became inactive in 1977, but was reactivated in 1979. **Publications:** *Briefing Papers*, periodic. Annual Report. • *Dead Reckoning: A Critical Review of the Department of Energy's Epidemiologic Research.* • *PSR Annual Report.* • *PSR Report*, quarterly. Newsletter. Informs the public of the medical consequences of nuclear war and the testing of nuclear weapons. Focuses on environmental issues and disarmament. *Price:* Included in membership dues.

★1477★ Physicians Who Care (PWC)
215 E. Quincy, Ste. 305
San Antonio, TX 78215
Phone: (210)226-1400
Free: 800-545-9305
Fax: (210)225-6159
Stephen C. Cohen, M.D., Pres.

Founded: 1985. **Members:** 3,500. **Regional Groups:** 4. **Description:** Devoted to protecting the traditional doctor-patient relationship and ensuring quality health care. Believes the responsibility for medical care belongs to physicians, as provider of care, and patients, who have the choice of determining the type of treatment received. Promotes communication between members and their patients on health care issues. **Publications:** Brochure. • *Patients Who Care Newsletter*, quarterly. Newsletter. • *Physicians Who Care Newsletter*, bimonthly. Newsletter. **Also Known As:** (1989) National Organization of Physicians Who Care.

★1478★ Polish Medical Association (Polski Towarzystwo Lekarskie)
Al. Ujazdowskie St. 24
PL-00-478 Warsaw, Poland
Phone: 22 288699
Fax: 22 288699
Jerzy Wojciechowski, Pres.

Description: Aims to maintain high professional and ethical standards in the medical profession.

★1479★ Presbyterian Health, Education and Welfare Association (PHEWA)
Presbyterian Center, Rm. 3B-3041
100 Witherspoon St.
Louisville, KY 40202
Phone: (502)569-5794
Fax: (502)569-5034
Rev. Mark W. Wendorf, Exec.Dir.

Founded: 1955. **Members:** 1,800. **Regional Groups:** 100. **Description:** Health, education, and welfare agencies and programs related to the United Presbyterian Church, U.S.A.; individuals with a variety of professional skills who are concerned about issues in the health, education, and welfare fields. Among member agencies are children's homes and services, hospital and health services, homes and services for the aging, community centers, and neighborhood houses. Coordinates HEW programming; establishes standards for the effectiveness of services; organizes social action and research; provides consultative services to community ministries; prepares and distributes materials on critical issues. Is organizing regional councils for policy and program development. Maintains library of periodicals from government, religious, social, welfare, and other agencies. **Publications:** Annual Report. • *Directory of Presbyterian Related Agencies*, periodic. Directory. • *PHEWA Newsletter*, quarterly. Newsletter. **Formerly:** (1969) National Presbyterian Health and Welfare Association; (1979) United Presbyterian Health, Education and Welfare Association.

★1480★ Professional Association of German Internists (Berufsverband Deutscher Internisten)
Schone Aussicht 5
65193 Wiesbaden, Germany
Phone: 611 525010
Fax: 611 599279
Max Broglie, Contact

Founded: 1959. **Members:** 26,000. **Description:** Protects and represents the interests of internal medicine specialists in Germany. Promotes continuing education. **Publications:** *Der Internist*, monthly. Magazine. • Newsletter, monthly.

★1481★ Program for Appropriate Technology in Health (PATH)
4 Nickerson St., Ste. 300
Seattle, WA 98109-1699
Phone: (206)285-3500
Fax: (206)285-6619
Gordon W. Perkin, M.D., Pres.

Founded: 1981. **Description:** Works to improve reproductive and child health, immunization programs, and diagnostic technologies in developing countries. Focuses on the effectiveness, availability, safety, and appropriateness of technologies for health and family planning. Conducts research and development, field assessment, communications, and technology transfer programs. Offers loans to assist developing countries in producing the essential health products. **Publications:** *Global Access to STD Diagnostics*, 3/year. • *Global Perspectives on Hepatitis*, semiannual. • *Health Technology Directions*, semiannual. • *Outlook*, quarterly.

★1482★ Project Concern International (PCI)
3550 Afton Rd.
San Diego, CA 92123
Phone: (619)279-9690
Fax: (619)694-0294
Daniel E. Shaughnessy, Exec.Dir.

Founded: 1961. **Description:** Works with communities worldwide to ensure low-cost, basic health care for those most in need, particularly mothers and children. Provides education, training, and medical assistance to safeguard the world's impoverished children. Works with volunteers to prepare local communities to care for their own children with long-term, self-sustaining projects. Maintains programs in Bolivia, Guatemala, El Salvador, Mexico, Nicaragua, Indonesia, Papua New Guinea, Romania, and the United States. Operates OPTIONS recruitment and referral service. **Publications:** *OPTIONS Newsletter*, bimonthly. Newsletter. Lists volunteer opportunities available to members. *Price:* $25/year. • *Project Concern International--Annual Report.* Annual Report. Contains financial statements. *Price:* Free. • *Project Concern International--Concern News*, quarterly. Provides information on Project Concern health and education programs and activities worldwide. *Price:* Free. **Formerly:** (1978) Project Concern, Inc..

★1483★ Project Concern International - Indonesia (PCII)
Kotak Pos 56, Mekar 11
Kendari, Sulawesi
93001 Tengarra, Indonesia
Phone: 401 21633
Fax: 21 3800717
Dr. Stephen Robinson, Dir.

Description: National branch of the international organization. Works to reduce morbidity and mortality, particularly among children, through immunization and proper care of preventable and treatable diseases. Integrates local governing bodies into the provision of public health services; conducts training programs for local public healt service providers.

★1484★ Project: Hearts and Minds (PHAM)
Veterans for Peace
33 Portola Ave.
Monterey, CA 93940
Phone: (408)649-5599
Fax: (408)646-8376
Gordon Smith, Exec. Officer

Description: A project of Veterans for Peace. Collects surplus medical supplies and equipment for delivery to hospitals in Vietnam, Cambodia, and Cuba.

★1485★ Project Hope
Republic Rehabilitation Center
Hin Echmiadzni Khjughi, 109
Yerevan, Armenia
Phone: 885 2151061
Fax: 885 2151061
Laura Movsessian, Contact

Founded: 1988. **Description:** Aims to ensure reliable health care programs in Armenia. Conducts educational programs. Provides measles vaccinations.

★1486★ Public Responsibility in Medicine and Research (PRIM&R)
132 Boylston St., 4th Fl.
Boston, MA 02116
Phone: (617)423-4112
Fax: (617)423-1185
Joan Rachlin, Exec.Dir.

Founded: 1974. **Description:** Researchers, clinicians, nurses, research/health care administrators, subjects/patients, attorneys, and laypersons interested in research, primarily with human subjects and animals. Formed to educate the health care community about the development of procedures regulating research and to constructively sterm the growth of increasingly hostile public sentiment towards the scientific field. Has established and perpetuated a forum where concerned groups and individuals who are involved with research-related activities can meet. Acts as an information and resource center. Aids members in assembling data they might require for testimony before legislative and other hearings. Plans to systematically monitor, analyze, and address nationwide research-related activities. Offers specialized education program. **Publications:** *Conference Report*, semiannual. Proceedings. Includes educational materials from conferences. • *Guidebook on Institutional Animal Care and Use Committees.* Book. Also publishes volumes on research and the protection of human subjects.

★ 1487 ★ **Raigarh Ambikapur Health Association**
BTI Chowk - Ambikapur Rd.
PO Pathalgaow
Raigarh DT, Madhya Pradesh, India
Phone: 7765 22420

Founded: 1969. **Members:** 85. **Regional Groups:** 3. **Local Groups:** 73. **Languages:** English, Hindi. **Description:** Works to improve the quality of health care in rural India. Conducts health and educational programs. Offers medical insurance.

★ 1488 ★ **Red de Grupos por la Salud de la Mujer y del Nino (REGSAMUNI)**
Revolucion 1133-3, Col. Mixcoac
Apartado Postal 22-443
03910 Mexico City, DF, Mexico
Phone: 5 5935336
Fax: 5 5935336
Dra. Leticia Quesnel Galvan

Founded: 1987. **Members:** 6. **Languages:** English, Spanish. **Description:** Women working to improve the health of women and children in Mexico. Seeks to empower women and improve their standard of living. Conducts educational and informational courses for women and women's organizations on nutrition, sexuality, lactation and breastfeeding, and other women's health issues. Trains health workers; conducts research. **Publications:** *Dialogos de Salud Popular*, quarterly. Bulletin.

★ 1489 ★ **Refugee Relief International (RRI)**
PO Box 693
Boulder, CO 80306
Phone: (303)449-3750
Fax: (303)444-5617
Alexander M. S. McColl, Pres.

Founded: 1982. **Description:** Physicians, paramedics, and nurses with prior military experience. Provides medical and other help to refugees and other victims of war and oppression throughout the world. Major efforts have been in Central America, although significant contributions to multi-national, multi-agency relief efforts have been made in Afghanistan, Azerbaijan, and in support of the Karens in Burma. Transports and distributes medical supplies and equipment. Conducts classes on first aid, hygiene, public health and sanitation for indigenous paramedics, refugees and others.

★ 1490 ★ **Registered Medical Assistants of American Medical Technologists (RMAAMT)**
710 Higgins Rd.
Park Ridge, IL 60068-5765
Phone: (708)823-5169
Free: 800-275-1268
Fax: (708)823-0458
Gerard P. Boe, Ph.D., Exec.Dir.

Founded: 1976. **Members:** 12,000. **State Groups:** 40. **Description:** A program of the American Medical Technologists. Certified assistants to physicians in office practice, clinics, hospitals, and private health care facilities. Works to establish standards of training; provides continuing education and home study programs; promotes quality care in allied health. Works with the Accrediting Bureau of Health Education Schools in regard to certification examinations and student societies. Offers group insurance programs. **Publications:** *AMT Events*, quarterly. Includes state chapter news, legislative updates, and book reviews. *Price:* Included in membership dues; $35 nonmembers. • *AMT Events Continuing Education Supplement*, 3/ year. *Price:* Included with AMT Events fees. • *Medical Assisting - A Career for Today and Tomorrow.* Brochure. **Formerly:** (1991) Registered Medical Assistants.

★ 1491 ★ **Religious Coalition for a Moral Drug Policy**
3421 M St. NW, Ste. 351
Washington, DC 20007
Fr. Joseph Ganssle, OFM, Pres.

Founded: 1990. **Members:** 700. **Description:** Maintains speakers' bureau and library of materials on drug legalization. Has published a book by clergy which calls the current drug policy immoral.

★ 1492 ★ **Rephael Society (RS)**
c/o Assn. of Orthodox Jewish Scientists
3 W. 16th St.
New York, NY 10011
Phone: (212)229-2340
Fax: (718)338-8593
Joel Schwartz, Exec.Dir.

Founded: 1966. **Members:** 600. **Description:** A section of the Association of Orthodox Jewish Scientists. Jewish Orthodox doctors, dentists, physical therapists, nurses, and others in the health care field. Objectives are to study medical issues and problems as they relate to Orthodox Jewish law and to promote the welfare of Orthodox Jews in the health care field. Sponsors lectures and seminars. Compiles listing of residency programs recommended for Orthodox Jewish medical students. **Publications:** *Practical Medical Halacha*, periodic. Reports on studies and meetings.

★ 1493 ★ **Research! America**
1522 King St.
Alexandria, VA 22314
Phone: (703)739-2577
Free: 800-366-CURE
Fax: (703)739-2372
Mary Woolley, Pres. & CEO

Founded: 1989. **Members:** 270. **Description:** Academia, voluntary health organizations, professional and scientific societies, colleges and universities, businesses and industries, and foundations and philanthropists. Believes that an informed public is the key to greater public and private investment in medical research. Works to increase awareness of the benefits to humankind of medical research and to build a strong base of citizen support for research into the cure, treatment, and prevention of physical and mental disorders. Seeks to stimulate interest in medical research careers. Appeals to institutions and the government to provide essential funding for medical research. Engages in multimedia communications programs and serves as a clearinghouse and source of information to members, the media, the general public, and elected officials. **Publications:** *Membership Matters*, monthly. Newsletter. *Price:* Included in membership dues.

★ 1494 ★ **RHEMA International (RI)**
PO Box 82085
Rochester, MI 48308-2085
Phone: (810)652-2450
Fax: (810)650-9642
Patricia Gruits, Pres.

Founded: 1977. **Description:** Participants are individuals concerned about the quality of life in Haiti. Seeks to afford to Haitians the opportunity to live better lives by providing educational and medical services and establishing selfhelp programs. Operates medical and dental clinics; conducts paramedical training courses in areas including prenatal care and physical hygiene. Maintains Hope Academy International, which trains Haitians to organize medical, health education, and spiritual enlightenment programs for the benefit of rural villages. Accepts donated funds, equipment, and medicine; cooperates with other non-profit charities and organizations to distribute aid to needy Haitians. Conducts job training courses to teach young Haitians marketable skills. Offers seminars for pastors, ministers, and Christian educators. Plans to construct a hospital, memorial chapel, housing for visiting medical teams, and an administrative headquarters in Haiti. **Publications:** *Rhema Newsletter*, monthly. Newsletter. *Price:* Free. • *Understanding God and His Covenants.* • *Understanding the Master's Voice.* **Also Known As:** Restoring Hope through Educational and Medical Aid.

★ 1495 ★ **Royal College of Physicians (RCP)**
11 St. Andrew's Pl.
London NW1 4LE, England
Phone: 171 9351174
Fax: 171 4875218
Mr. D.B. Lloyd, Sec.

Founded: 1518. **Languages:** English. **Description:** Individuals in 64 countries. Establishes standards and quality controls for the medical practice. Advises the government, public, and members of the profession on health and medical issues. Conducts educational and training programs; organizes examinations; operates research unit. **Publications:** *Annual Report.* • *College List*, annual. • Journal, bimonthly. • *Working Party Reports.*

★ 1496 ★ Royal College of Physicians and Surgeons of Canada (RCPSC)
774 Echo Dr.
Ottawa, ON, Canada K1S 5N8
Phone: (613)730-6201
Fax: (613)730-8252
Gilles D. Hurteau, M.D., Exec.Dir.

Founded: 1929. **Members:** 28,000. **Languages:** English, French. **Description:** Medical fellows (18,300); surgical fellows (9,300). Founded by the Canadian Medical Association, the College works to: further the excellence of professional training and standards; contribute to the improvement of health care in Canada by providing medical specialty designations; maintain high standards of professional ethics and conduct; promote and assist in continuing medical education via its MOCOMP Program; encourage the study of quantitative and qualitative aspects of specialized health care in Canada. Maintains the McLaughlin Centre for Evaluation of Clinical Competence for the conduct of specialty examinations. Issues policy statements and guidelines. **Publications:** *Annals RCPSC*, 8/year, always 1st Friday of the month of publication. Journal. Peer reviewed scientific articles • *Annual Meeting Scientific Programme*, annual. • *Annual Report.* • *Bulletin*, 8/year. Bulletin.

★ 1497 ★ Royal College of Physicians and Surgeons (of United States of America) (RCPS)
16126 E. Warren
PO Box 24224
Detroit, MI 48224
Phone: (313)882-0641
Ben Allie, M.D., Exec. Officer

Founded: 1984. **Members:** 2,100. **National Groups:** 32. **Regional Groups:** 30. **State Groups:** 4. **Description:** Physicians and allied health professionals interested in tropical medicine. Provides postgraduate continuing medical education; confers certificates and diplomas. Maintains speakers' bureau and hall of fame and provides placement services. Conducts research and educational programs; compiles statistics. **Publications:** *Journal of the Royal College of Physicians and Surgeons*, semiannual. Journal. Focuses on continuing medical education. *Price:* $50 for members; $75 for nonmembers; $110 institutions. • *Newsletter*, periodic. • *Proceedings of the Royal College of Physicians and Surgeons*, semiannual. *Price:* $145.

★ 1498 ★ Royal Society of Medicine Foundation (RSMF)
150 E. 58th St., 32nd Fl.
New York, NY 10155-0002
Phone: (212)371-1150
Fax: (212)371-1151
William G. O'Reilly, Exec. Officer

Founded: 1967. **Members:** 3,500. **Description:** Serves as a forum for the discussion of topics relevant to the medical community in the U.S. and the United Kingdom. Sponsors conference series and exchange programs in conjunction with the Royal Society of Medicine. **Publications:** *Digest*, quarterly.

★ 1499 ★ St. Jude Express (SJE)
PO Box 5333
Albuquerque, NM 87185
Phone: (505)268-5051
Angelo Tomedi, Pres.

Founded: 1968. **Members:** 20. **Description:** An interdenominational group of medical personnel, pilots, and other volunteers. Provides airborne medical missionary service to remote areas of the Sierra Madre Mountains of Mexico. Collects and donates food, clothing, medical supplies, and used school equipment to needy communities. Supports missions in the southwest U.S. and northern Mexico. Offers health care seminar in Spanish for rural Mexican health-care providers. **Publications:** Brochure. • *St. Jude Expression*, quarterly.

★ 1500 ★ The Salvation Army (SA)
National Headquarters
615 Slaters Ln.
PO Box 269
Alexandria, VA 22313
Phone: (703)684-5500
Fax: (703)684-3478
Commissioner Kenneth L. Hodder, Natl.Cmdr.

Founded: 1880. **National Groups:** 1. **Regional Groups:** 4. **Local Groups:** 1173. **Description:** Commissioned officers are ordained ministers devoting full time to religious and social welfare activities; members of local church or corps community centers are known as soldiers. An international Christian religious and charitable movement, organized on a paramilitary pattern, dedicated to meeting the physical, spiritual, and emotional needs of mankind. Work is carried out through local centers of operation which include adult rehabilitation centers, hospitals, clinics, homes and outpatient programs for unwed mothers, recreation centers, camping programs for children and adults, senior and children's day care, senior housing and activity centers, and emergency feeding and shelter stations; and through service extension units located in communities not supporting a full Salvation Army program, which extend aid in emergencies. Maintains speakers' bureau and 38 divisions; compiles statistics. Offers placement and referral services at local level. Provides officers' training schools. **Publications:** Annual Report. • *Marching to Glory.* Book. • *ProgramAids*, quarterly. Contains weekly in-house programs for women, including ideas for decorations, games, refreshments, and devotionals. *Price:* $6/year. • *War Cry*, biweekly. Magazine. Features articles on Christian topics; includes association news and Bible studies. *Price:* $7.50/year. • *What Is The Salvation Army?*. Booklet. • *Young Salvationist*, 10/year. Magazine. For high-school age volunteers of The Salvation Army; covers issues confronting teenagers from a Christian perspective. Also includes fiction. *Price:* $4/year.

★ 1501 ★ Salvation Army Medical Fellowship (SAMF)
101 Queen Victoria St.
London EC4P 4EP, England
Phone: 171 2365222
Mrs.Gen. Kay Rader, World Pres.

Founded: 1943. **Members:** 13,879. **Languages:** English, French, German, Norwegian, Swedish. **Description:** Purpose is to support members of the International Headquarters of the Salvation Army involved in the field of medicine, particularly those involved in nursing.

★ 1502 ★ Save Lebanon (SL)
918 16th St. NW, No. 901
Washington, DC 20006
Phone: (202)429-2505
Fax: (202)466-3464
Khatmeh Osseiran-Hanna, Exec.Dir.

Founded: 1982. **State Groups:** 14. **Local Groups:** 20. **Description:** Contributors are individuals in the U.S., Canada, and Lebanon interested in assisting individuals in Lebanon. Provides medical aid and emergency help to people displaced from their homes. Assists social and economic development projects undertaken by Lebanese organizations. Maintains Save Lebanon's Children Project, whereby injured, financially needy Lebanese children receive medical care in Lebanon. Through a monthly sponsor program, provides children in Lebanon with school tuition. Operates speakers' bureau. **Publications:** *Our Hope for Lebanon*, quarterly. Newsletter. Includes profiles, studies, and reports. • *Save Lebanon Update*, annual. • *Special Report*, annual.

★ 1503 ★ Seva Foundation (SF)
8 N. San Pedro Rd.
San Rafael, CA 94903
Phone: (415)492-1829
Free: 800-223-7382
Fax: (415)492-8705
Amy Somers, Exec.Dir.

Founded: 1978. **Members:** 27,000. **Local Groups:** 22. **Description:** Health-related social scientists and others. Seeks to improve health and environmental conditions on a worldwide basis. (The name Seva comes from the Sanskrit word meaning service to humankind.) Provides relief services to Mayan refugees living in southern Mexico and Guatemala. Sponsors Nepal Blindness Program which: establishes eye care centers and camps, and trains ophthalmic assistants to work in remote areas and to identify and treat early stages of blinding conditions; provides medical supplies and equipment, and support for eye care in Nepal's Lumbini Zone. Supports the Aravind Eye Hospital in India. Maintains speakers' bureau. **Publications:** *Epidemiology of Blindness in Nepal: Report of the 1981 Nepal Blindness Survey.* Book. • *Gift of Service Catalog*, annual. Catalog. Describes gifts that individuals can give to needy communities, including traditional gifts and gifts of training. *Price:* Free. • *Seva Foundation--Progress Report*, annual. Includes achievements, goals, and financial statement. • *Special Project Reports*, periodic. • *Spirit of Service*, annual. Newsletter. Reports on national and international humanitarian activities. Includes project updates and annual gift catalog. *Price:* Free.

★ 1504 ★ Slovak Medical Society (SMS) (Slovenska Ledarska Spolocnost — SLS)
Legionarska 4
813 22 Bratislava, Slovakia
Phone: 7 212363
Fax: 7 212363
Sona Kozakova

Founded: 1969. **Members:** 31,125. **Local Groups:** 67. **Languages:** English, French, German. **Description:** Chemical engineers, doctors, medical workers, and pharmacists. Member organization of the Czechoslovak Medical Society. **Publications:** *Avicennum*, periodic. Directory.

★ 1505 ★ Society for Ambulatory Care Professionals (SACP)
American Hospital Association
1 N. Franklin, 31st Fl.
Chicago, IL 60606
Phone: (312)422-3900
Fax: (312)422-4577
Tod N. Tappert, Exec.Dir.

Founded: 1986. **Members:** 2,400. **Description:** Works to advance the development of ambulatory care and advocates issues that enhance the value, .role, delivery, and management of ambulatory care services. **Publications:** *Issue Briefings.* • *The Legislative and Regulatory Monitor.* • *Megatrends.* • *Outreach*, bimonthly. Newsletter. *Price:* Included in membership dues; $85/year for nonmembers. • *Trendlines.* Also publishes books.

★ 1506 ★ Society of Clinical and Medical Electrologists (SCME)
132 Great Rd., No. 200
Stow, MA 01775
Phone: (508)461-0313
Fax: (508)897-5442
Wallace Roberts, Pres.

Founded: 1985. **Members:** 1,000. **Regional Groups:** 10. **Description:** Professional society of electrologists (persons engaged in the removal of superfluous hair by galvanic blend or short wave methods for cosmetic and medical purposes). Conducts continuing education and leadership development seminars. **Publications:** *Perspectives*, periodic. • *SCME Directory of Membership*, annual. Membership Directory. • *SCME Newsletter*, quarterly. Newsletter.

★ 1507 ★ Society for Clinical Trials (SCT)
600 Wyndhurst Ave.
Baltimore, MD 21210
Phone: (410)433-4722
Fax: (410)435-8631
Sylvan B. Green, Pres.

Founded: 1978. **Members:** 1,450. **Description:** Persons with training and expertise in behavioral science, bioethics, biostatistics, computer science, dentistry, epidemiology, law, management, medicine, nursing, and pharmacology. To promote the development and dissemination of knowledge about the design and conduct of clinical trials and other research employing similar methods. **Publications:** *Controlled Clinical Trials*, bimonthly.

★ 1508 ★ Society of General Internal Medicine (SGIM)
700 13th St. NW, Ste. 250
Washington, DC 20005
Phone: (202)393-1662
Free: 800-822-3060
Fax: (202)783-1347
Elnora M. Rhodes, Exec.Dir.

Founded: 1978. **Members:** 2,300. **Regional Groups:** 8. **Description:** Faculty members of medical schools in the U.S. and Canada. Seeks to promote improved patient care, teaching, and research in primary care and general internal medicine. **Publications:** *Directory of Primary Care Internal Medicine Residency and Fellowship Training Programs*, biennial. Directory. • *Journal of General Internal Medicine*, monthly. Journal. • *SGIM Newsletter*, monthly. Newsletter. **Formerly:** (1987) Society of Research and Education in Primary Care Internal Medicine.

★ 1509 ★ Society for Health and Human Values (SHHV)
6728 Old McLean Village Dr.
McLean, VA 22101
Phone: (703)556-9222
Fax: (703)556-8729
George K. Degnon, Exec. Officer

Founded: 1969. **Members:** 900. **Description:** Educators in the health professions united to develop new understandings, concepts, and programs in the area of human values and medicine with special emphasis on the education of health professionals. Conducts programs at national association meetings. Acts as resource service for educational institutions. **Publications:** *Advance Directives in Medicine.* Book. • *Literature and Medicine: A Claim for a Discipline.* Book. • *The Meaning of AIDS: Implications for Medical Science, Clinical Practice and Public Health Policy.* Book. • *Medicine & Religion: Strategies of Care.* Book. • *Ministers in Medical Education.* Book. • *Nurshing the Humanities in Medicine: Interactions with the Social Sciences.* Book. • *Of Value*, quarterly. • *The Teaching of Humanities and Human Values in Primary Care Residency Training.* Book. • Video. • *The Visual Arts and Medical Education.* Book.

★ 1510 ★ Society for Life History Research (SLHR)
Temple University
Philadelphia, PA 19122
Phone: (215)204-8080
Joan McCord, Exec.Off.

Founded: 1970. **Members:** 700. **Description:** Members are drawn from a wide range of disciplines, including behavior genetics, medicine, statistics, psychology, psychiatry, and sociology. Research programs are carried out by individual members; the society reports and publishes research results. **Publications:** *Human Functioning in Longitudinal Perspective.* • *Life History Research in Psychopathology.* • *Origins and Course of Psychopathology.* • *Origins of Psychopathology.* • *Proceedings*, every 18 months. • *Research and Public Policy.* • *Straight and Devious Pathways from Childhood to Adulthood.* **Formerly:** (1984) Society for Life History Research in Psychopathology.

★ 1511 ★ Society for the Social History of Medicine (SSHM)
Centre for Cultural History
University of Aberdeen
The Spittal
Aberdeen, Scotland
Phone: 1224 273676
David Smith, Chm.

Founded: 1969. **Members:** 800. **Languages:** English. **Description:** Professionals and interested amateurs in medical, historical, sociological, and related disciplines. Promotes the study of the social history of medicine as it relates to patients, doctors, disease, and health. Topics of interest include national health service, mental handicaps, occupational health, general practice, and health and town planning. **Publications:** Books. • *The Gazette*, 3/year. Newsletter. • *Membership List.* • *Social History of Medicine*, 3/year. Journal.

★ 1512 ★ Society of Teachers of Family Medicine (STFM)
8880 Ward Pky.
Kansas City, MO 64114
Phone: (816)333-9700
Free: 800-274-2237
Fax: (816)333-3884
Roger A. Sherwood, CAE, Exec.Dir.

Founded: 1967. **Members:** 3,800. **Description:** Physicians involved in teaching or promoting family medicine; individuals in related fields. Organized to promote public welfare by maintaining and improving standards and practices of medical service, especially in the field of family medicine. Promotes these objectives by: supporting and expressing the tenets of family medicine as an academic discipline; maintaining and continually improving the quality of instructional and scientific skills and knowledge in the field of family medicine; providing a forum for the interchange of experience and ideas among its members and other interested persons; and encouraging research and teaching in family medicine. **Publications:** *Family Medicine*, monthly. Journal. Includes annual index, book reviews, and employment opportunities. Published in conjunction with the North American Primary Care Research Group. *Price:* Included in membership dues; $10/copy for nonmembers; $75/year for individual nonmembers; $100/year for institutions. • *Monographs.* • *STFM Membership Directory*, biennial. Membership Directory. Arranged alphabetically and geographically. *Price:* Included in membership dues; $25/year for nonmembers. • *STFM Messenger*, bimonthly. Newsletter. Covers federal government information related to family medicine issues. Includes research and education columns. *Price:* Included in membership dues.

★ 1513 ★ SOS Corpo - Grupo de Saude da Mulher
Rua do Hospicio 859, Apto. 14
50050 Recife, Pernambuco, Brazil
Phone: 81 2213018
Fax: 81 4290992
Angeles M. Texera de Freitus, Contact

Languages: Portuguese. **Description:** Works towards raising awareness of women's health issues. Disseminates information and provides education on women's health care and health risks.

★ 1514 ★ South Pacific Underwater Medicine Society (SPUMS)
Australian College of Occupational Medicine
PO Box 2090
St. Kilda West, VIC 6050, Australia
Phone: 3 2485950
Fax: 6 2485950
Dr. D. Wallner, Contact

Founded: 1972. **Members:** 1,000. **Languages:** English. **Description:** Physicians and interested individuals in 10 countries. Serves to promote diving medicine. Organizes Project Stickybeak. **Publications:** *SPUMS Journal*, quarterly. Journal.

★ 1515 ★ Student National Medical Association (SNMA)
1012 10th St. NW
Washington, DC 20001
Phone: (202)371-1616
Sharon D. Allison, Chm.

Founded: 1964. **Members:** 3,300. **Regional Groups:** 10. **Local Groups:** 155. **Description:** Medical students, residents, and undergraduates of color. Seeks to help students in recruitment, admission, and retention in medical school and publishes information on problems and achievement in this area. Conducts research forums and community health projects. **Publications:** *SNMA Journal*, quarterly. Journal. • *SNMA News*, quarterly.

★ 1516 ★ Sudan Medical Students Association (SMSA)
Khartoum Faculty of Medicine
PO Box 102
Khartoum, Sudan
Phone: 79741
Fax: 80308
Elmotaz Mustafa Ahmed, Sec.Gen.

Founded: 1924. **Members:** 2,820. **Local Groups:** 3. **Languages:** Arabic, English. **Description:** Medical societies and students in Sudan. Promotes the interests of members. Works to improve the state of public health in Sudan. Conducts cultural and social activities; supports exchange programs and offers training seminars. Conducts research on refugee camps. Provides children's services; maintains museum; compiles statistics. **Publications:** *El Hakeem*, semiannual. Magazine. • *Journal*, periodic. Journal. • *SMSA Directory*, periodic. Directory.

★ 1517 ★ Swedish Alliance Mission
PO Box 35
Mankayane, Swaziland
Phone: 88326

Description: Promotes improved health care in Swaziland.

★ 1518 ★ Swedish Medical Association (Sveriges Laekarfoerbund)
Villagatan 5
PO Box 5610
S-114 86 Stockholm, Sweden
Phone: 8 7903300
Fax: 8 205718
Dr. Anders Milton, CEO

Founded: 1903. **Members:** 34,000. **Regional Groups:** 29. **Description:** Union of physicians in Sweden. Advocates collective negotiations on physicians' employment conditions, health policy, and medical education issues. Maintains professional and specialist groups. **Publications:** *Laekartidningen*, weekly. Journal.

★ 1519 ★ Thank-You Research
818 Conneticut Ave. NW, Ste. 30
Washington, DC 20006
Phone: (202)872-0315
Fax: (202)457-0659
Lenore M. Rumpf, Exec.Dir.

Founded: 1992. **Description:** Voluntary health organizations. Promotes communication among medical researchers and patients by facilitating a system for patients to send the researchers thank you letters. Maintains speakers' bureau.

★ 1520 ★ TOPS Club
c/o Susan Trones
4575 S. 5th St.
PO Box 07360
Milwaukee, WI 53207
Phone: (414)482-4620
Free: 800-932-8677
Esther Manz, Pres.

Founded: 1948. **Members:** 300,000. **Description:** Weight control selfhelp association using group dynamics, competition, and recognition to help members lose weight. TOPS is medically oriented, requiring physician-approved individual diet programs, and physician-set weight goals. **Publications:** *TOPS News*, monthly. Magazine. Contains member news, success stories, inspirational materials, features on diet-related subjects, chapter news, medical questions and answers. *Price:* Included in membership dues. Also publishes monograph on nutrition and other membership literature. **Also Known As:** Take Off Pounds Sensibly; TOPS.

★ 1521 ★ Turkish American Physicians Association (TAPA)
c/o Dr. Cemil Bikmen
222 Middle County Rd.
Smithtown, NY 11787
Phone: (516)724-0777
Dr. Cemil Bikmen, Exec. Officer

Founded: 1969. **Members:** 1,260. **Regional Groups:** 4. **Description:** To develop closer relationships among physicians of Turkish origin, facilitate the exchange of information, and develop cultural and medical exchange with physicians in Turkey. **Publications:** *Membership Roster*, biennial.

★ 1522 ★ Ukrainian Medical Association of North America (UMANA)
2247 W. Chicago Ave.
Chicago, IL 60622
Phone: (312)278-6262
Andrew Lincky, Dir.

Founded: 1950. **Members:** 1,000. **Local Groups:** 17. **Description:** Physicians, surgeons, dentists, and persons in related professions who are of Ukrainian descent. Provides assistance to members; sponsors lectures. Maintains placement service, museum, biographical and medical archives, and library of 1800 medical books and journals in Ukrainian. **Publications:** *Medical Journal*, quarterly. Journal. • *Newsletter to Membership*, quarterly. Newsletter. • *Ukrainian Medical Dictionary*. **Formerly:** American Ukrainian Medical Society.

★ 1523 ★ Undersea and Hyperbaric Medical Society (UHMS)
10531 Metropolitan Ave.
Kensington, MD 20895
Phone: (301)942-2980
Fax: (301)942-7804
Leon J. Greenbaum, Jr., Exec.Dir.

Founded: 1967. **Members:** 2,500. **Regional Groups:** 4. **Description:** Diving physiologists, physicians, biologists, and bioengineers with subsea or hyperbaric interests. Seeks to: develop and advance undersea and hyperbaric medicine and its supporting sciences; provide channels of scientific communication among researchers dedicated to the safe penetration of the oceans by man; disseminate information on diving problems. Conducts courses on diving medicine for physicians. **Publications:** *Case Histories of Diving and Hyperbaric Accidents*. • *Directory of Hyperbaric Chambers*. • *Diving Accident Management*. • *Fitness to Dive*. • *Flying After Diving*. • *Handbook and Membership Directory*, biennial. Directory. • *Hyperbaric Oxygen Therapy*. • *Journal: Undersea & Hyperbaric Medicine*, quarterly. Journal. *Price:* $85. • *Key Documents of the Biomedical Aspects of Deep Diving*. • *Physicians Guide to Diving Medicine*. • *Pressure*, bimonthly. Newsletter. Includes book reviews and obituaries. *Price:* $25/year. • *Underwater and Hyperbaric Medicine: Abstracts from the Literature*, bimonthly. *Price:* $100. • *Women in Diving*.

★ 1524 ★ Union of American Physicians and Dentists (UAPD)
1330 Broadway, Ste. 730
Oakland, CA 94612
Phone: (510)839-0193
Robert Weinmann, M.D., Pres.

Founded: 1972. **Members:** 10,000. **Description:** Independent national labor organization consisting of state federations made up of self-employed medical doctors and dentists as well as those employed by hospitals, teaching institutions, counties, and municipalities. Seeks to: provide optimum medical care for the people; ensure quality facilities for the provision of medical care; enable physicians to give of themselves, unhindered by extraneous forces, for the welfare of their patients; ensure reasonable compensation for physicians commensurate with their training, skill, and the responsibility they bear for the life and health of their fellow human beings. **Publications:** *UAPD Report*, monthly. Also publishes materials on socioeconomic issues. **Formerly:** Union of American Physicians.

★ 1525 ★ Union Nationale des Associations de Soins et Service a Domicile (UNASSAD)
108-110 rue St. Maur
F-75011 Paris, France
Phone: 1 43552626
Fax: 1 43385533
C. Martel, Gen.Dir.

Founded: 1970. **Members:** 1,000. **Languages:** English, French. **Description:** Organizations providing home health care for the elderly or disabled and their families. Promotes high industry standards. **Publications:** *Information Paper*, monthly. **Also Known As:** National Organisation for Home Care.

★ 1526 ★ United Jewish Appeal - Federation of Jewish Philanthropies of New York (UJAFJP)
130 E. 59th St.
New York, NY 10022
Phone: (212)980-1000
Fax: (212)888-7538
Stephen D. Solender, Exec.VP

Founded: 1986. **Description:** Federation of agencies that provide hospital, health, geriatric, vocational, family and child care services, and Jewish education to individuals in the greater New York area, Israel, and 34 countries. Conducts fundraising and communal planning programs; maintains biographical archives. **Publications:** *Focus on UJA - Federation*, quarterly. Newsletter. Includes profiles of leaders and calendar of events. *Price:* Free. • *Jewish Information and Referral Service Directory*, annual. Lists Jewish and non-Jewish social service programs. *Price:* $30/year to member agencies; $40/year to nonmembers. • *UJA - Federation Network Directory*, biennial. Directory. Lists agency services. • *United Jewish Appeal - Federation of Jewish Philanthropies of New York-- Annual Report*. Annual Report. *Price:* Free.

★ 1527 ★ United Methodist Association of Health and Welfare Ministries (UMA)
601 W. Riverview Ave.
Dayton, OH 45406-5543
Phone: (513)227-9494
Fax: (513)227-9493
Dean W. Pulliam, Pres.

Founded: 1940. **Members:** 300. **Description:** Membership association for 400 United Methodist affiliated hospitals, retirement homes, community based ministries, youth and family service organizations, children's homes, and individuals. Offers communications and church relations guidance. Provides leadership development training for health and human service professionals in United Methodist related organizations and agencies. Develops ethical and theological statements on institutional care. Operates Educational Assessment Guidelines Leading Toward Excellence (EAGLE), a self-assessment and peer review program. Operates a field Consultation Program; members may access skilled professionals to assist with governance questions. Offers audiovisual services to members. Maintains speakers' bureau; compiles statistics. **Publications:** Directory. • *Directory of United Methodist Related Health and Welfare Ministries*, semiannual. *Price:* $17/year for members; $27/year for nonmembers. • *The UMA Journal*, monthly. Journal. **Formerly:** (1968) Board of Hospitals and Homes of the Methodist Church; (1972) Division of Health and Welfare Ministries of the United Methodist Church; (1983) National Association of Health and Welfare Ministries of the United Methodist Church.

★ 1528 ★ University of Calcutta Medical Association of America (UCMAA)
4700 Pickering Rd.
Bloomfield Hills, MI 48301
Phone: (810)246-6946
Fax: (810)246-6918
Dr. Sajal P. Choudhury, CEO

Founded: 1976. **Members:** 120. **Description:** Disseminates recent medical research to those

in India and other interested parties. Gives lectures. **Publications:** *UCMAA Newsletter*, semiannual. Newsletter.

★ 1529 ★ Village Education Programme
PO Box 520
Honiara, Solomon Islands
Phone: 23130
Fax: 21339

Founded: 1909. **Description:** Works to improve living conditions in the villages through educational programs on nutrition, food resource management, and health.

★ 1530 ★ Volunteers of America (VOA)
3939 N. Causeway Blvd.
Metairie, LA 70002
Phone: (504)837-2652
Free: 800-899-0089
Fax: (504)837-4200
Clint Cheveallier, Pres.

Founded: 1896. **Regional Groups:** 5. **Local Groups:** 54. **Description:** A Christian human services organization offering over 400 programs in 300 communities across the U.S. for the elderly, youth, families, alcoholics, drug abusers, and the disabled. Compiles statistics; maintains speakers' bureau. **Publications:** Annual Report, annual. • *History of Volunteers of America*. Book. • *Something Wonderful*. Brochure. • *Spirit*, quarterly. Magazine. *Price:* $8/year. • *The Volunteers Gazette*, monthly.

★ 1531 ★ West African Health Community (WAHC)
6 Taylor Dr., Edmund Crescent
Medical Compound
Private Mail Bag 2023
Yaba, Lagos, Nigeria
Phone: 1 862324
Fax: 1 862324
Dr. Kabba T. Joiner, Exec. Dir.

Founded: 1971. **Members:** 5. **Languages:** English. **Description:** Medical, pharmaceutical, and nursing professionals and senior health administrators. Encourages cooperation among member countries in matters of public health, education, and research. Emphasizes the importance of developing adequate, effective means of addressing the health service needs of the region. Conducts seminars, workshops, and professional training. **Publications:** *WAHC Bulletin*, quarterly. Bulletin. • *WAHC Calendar of Events*, annual. • *WAHC Information Booklet*, annual. • *West African Journal of Medicine*, quarterly. Journal. • *West African Journal of Nursing*, quarterly. Journal. • *West African Journal of Pharmacy*, quarterly. Journal.

★ 1532 ★ Wilderness Medical Society (WMS)
PO Box 2463
Indianapolis, IN 46206
Phone: (317)631-1745
Fax: (317)259-8150
D. M. Simpkins, Exec.Sec.

Founded: 1983. **Members:** 2,800. **Description:** Persons with advanced degrees in the biomedical or life sciences with an interest in the medical, behavioral, and life sciences aspects of wilderness environments. Objectives are to

promote research and educational activities that increase scientific knowledge about human activities in wilderness environments; stimulate interest and research in health consequences of wilderness activities; serve as central information source. Areas of interest include treatment of overpressure accident victims and victims of bites and stings, exotic infectious diseases and toxic plants, desert survival, avalanche control, and search and rescue. **Publications:** *Journal of Wilderness Medicine*, quarterly. • *Wilderness Medicine*, quarterly. Newsletter. *Price:* Included in membership dues.

★ 1533 ★ Williams Syndrome Association (WSA)
PO Box 297
Clawson, MI 48017-0297
Phone: (810)541-3630
Terry Monkaba, Pres.

Founded: 1983. **Members:** 2,500. **Regional Groups:** 10. **State Groups:** 50. **Description:** Individuals with Williams Syndrome and their families; medical and health care professionals; educators. (Williams Syndrome is characterized by elfin facial features, low birth weight, heart disorders, hearing sensitivity, talkative personality, mild mental retardation, and developmental delays.) Provides support and assistance to families with a WS child. Conducts networking in the medical, scientific, educational, and professional communities for referral and study of newly-diagnosed WS individuals; encourages medical and behavioral research to improve methods of social integration. Compiles statistics. **Publications:** Brochures. • Handbook. For parents and professionals. • *Williams Syndrome Association National Newsletter*, quarterly. Newsletter. Includes research updates and parent and professional forums. *Price:* $15/year.

★ 1534 ★ Women in Crisis (WIC)
360 W. 125th St.
New York, NY 10027
Phone: (212)316-5200
Mari DaSilza, Dir.

Founded: 1979. **Description:** National conference participants concerned with the plight of "women in crisis," including victims of sexual discrimination and poverty, battered wives, rape and incest victims, women offenders, and female drug abusers and alcoholics. Focuses efforts on women and work, mental health, women in leadership positions, drugs and alcohol, and justice. Seeks to create a network of professionals in these areas.

★ 1535 ★ Women's Health
52-54 Featherstone St.
London EC1Y 8RT, England
Phone: 171 2516580
Fax: 171 6080928
Blanca Fernandez

Founded: 1982. **Members:** 150. **Languages:** English. **Description:** Feminist women in the United Kingdom. Works to empower women to make informed decisions about health and reproductive issues. Promotes a pro-choice perspective on women's health issues, including abortion. Informs women of their reproductive rights; provides information about women's health issues. Develops and promotes a feminist perspective of women's health and reproductive rights. **Publications:** *Annual Report.* • *Black Women and Hypertension.* Article. • *Ectopic Pregnancy.* Article. • *Fertility Awareness Chart.* Booklet. • *Women's Health*, quarterly. Newsletter. Covers information about women's health and reproductive issues. • *Women's Health & Food Broadsheet.* Article. • *Women's Health Work & Stress Broadsheet.* Article.

★ 1536 ★ Women's Health and Economic Development Association (WHEDA)
44A Etuk St.
Akwa Ibom
Uyo, Nigeria
Phone: 85 20427
Fax: 85 204964
Mrs. Fidela Etim Ebuk, National Coord.

Founded: 1988. **Members:** 4,000. **National Groups:** 3. **State Groups:** 15. **Local Groups:** 45. **Languages:** English. **Description:** Works to prevent health problems of women in rural Nigerian communities. Provides education and counseling on nutritional and family planning issues. Encourages economic independence for women through supportive programs and activities. **Publications:** Articles. **Formerly:** (1988) Rural Women Health Association.

★ 1537 ★ Women's Health Research Network in Nigeria (WHERNIN)
Ahmadu Bello University
c/o Counselling Centre
Zaria, Kaduna, Nigeria
Phone: 69 51064
Mrs. V.T. Aidiy, Coord.

Languages: English. **Description:** Promotes the health of women in Nigeria through action-oriented advocacy, research, and coordination of grassroots projects. Works in close collaboration with health professionals and women's organizations.

★ 1538 ★ World Federation of Doctors Who Respect Human Life (WFDWRHL) (Federacion Mundial de Medicos que Respectan la Vida Humana)
Serruyslaan 76-3
B-8400 Ostend, Belgium
Phone: 59 234616
Fax: 59 707446
Dr. Philippe Schepens, Sec.Gen.

Founded: 1974. **Members:** 350,000. **National Groups:** 70. **Regional Groups:** 4. **Languages:** English, French, Spanish. **Description:** Associations of medical doctors and others. Purpose is to obtain additional signatures for and to publicly uphold and promote adherence to the Medical Code of Ethics/Declaration of Geneva 1948, to article 3 of the Universal Declaration of Human Rights, and to the Helsinki Declaration. Provides moral and public support to doctors and health professionals who are discriminated against because of their adherence to the declarations. Advocates implementation of measures designed to eliminate conditions worldwide that are detrimental to human mental and physical development. Seeks further legal protection for all human beings from conception to natural death. Operates information center. **Publications:** *News Exchange of the WFDWRHL*, quarterly.

★ 1539 ★ World Federation for Medical Education (WFME) (Federation Mondiale pour l'Enseignement Medical — FMEM)
Univ. of Edinburgh
11 Hill Sq.
Edinburgh EH8 9DR, Scotland
Phone: 131 6506209
Fax: 131 6506537
Prof. H.J. Walton, Pres.

Founded: 1972. **Languages:** English. **Description:** Regional medical associations and associations of medical schools. Promotes the integrated study of medical education worldwide. Evaluates the effectiveness of medical education in meeting the needs of contemporary society. Acts as international representative of medical education before the World Health Organization, UNICEF, UNESCO, United Nations Development Programme, and the World Bank . **Publications:** *Report of the World Conference on Medical Education, Edinburgh, 1988.* Report. • *World Summit on Medical Education, Edinburgh, 1994.* Proceedings.

★ 1540 ★ World Health Organization (WHO) (Organisation Mondiale de la Sante — OMS)
20, ave. Appia
CH-1211 Geneva 27, Switzerland
Phone: 22 7912111
Fax: 22 7910746
Hiroshi Nakajima, M.D., Dir.Gen.

Founded: 1948. **Members:** 170. **Regional Groups:** 6. **Languages:** Arabic, Chinese, English, French, Russian, Spanish. **Description:** International health agency of the United Nations consisting of countries working toward the goal of "health for all by the year 2000," seeking to obtain the highest level of health care for all people. Believes health is a fundamental right of every human being without distinction of race, religion, political belief, economic situation, or social conditions and holds that all people deserve equal access to health services to enable them to lead socially and economically productive lives. Objectives are to: act as directing and coordinating authority on international health work; ensure valid and productive technical cooperation; promote research; prevent and combat diseases; generate and transfer information. Strives to eliminate poverty. Emphasizes the health needs of developing countries lacking resources and funds for modern medical technologies; works toward developing new techniques that will fulfill these needs by utilizing available resources, integrating educational, agricultural, town planning, and sanitation programs with health programs, combining peripheral health services and existing health systems, and applying appropriate technologies at reasonable costs. Establishes standards for food, biological, and pharmaceutical needs, develops standardized diagnostic procedures, and determines environmental health criteria. Promotes 8 elements of primary health care including: health education on prevention and cures; proper food supply and nutrition; adequate supply of safe water and sanitation; maternal and child health care; immunization; control of endemic diseases; and provisions of essential drugs. Acts as clearinghouse; coordinates activities

with the United Nations on health and socioeconomic development; works with international nongovernmental organizations in the health sector. Supports International Agency for Research on Cancer. Maintains expert and scientific committees. Recognizes April 7th as World Health Day, May 31 as World No-Tobacco Day, and December 1 as World AIDS Day. **Publications:** *Bulletin of WHO*, bimonthly. Bulletin. • *International Digest of Health Legislation*, quarterly. • *Weekly Epidemiological Record.* • *WHO Drug Information*, quarterly. • *World Health*, 10/year. Magazine. • *World Health.* • *World Health Forum*, quarterly. • *World Health Statistics Annual.* • *World Health Statistics Quarterly.* Includes summaries in Arabic, Chinese, Russian, and Spanish. Also publishes *WHO Technical Report Series, WHO Environmental Health Criteria Series, WHO AIDS Series, WHO Health and Safety Guidelines*, directories, and nonserial publications.

★ 1541 ★ World Health Organization (AFRO)
Regional Office for Africa
PO Box 6
Brazzaville, Congo
Phone: 833860
Fax: 839400

Languages: Arabic, English, French. **Description:** Regional branch of the World Health Organization. Works to ensure that WHO programs effectively meet the particular public health needs of Africa; serves as a liaison between national and local public health agencies and the WHO.

★ 1542 ★ World Health Organization (EMRO)
Regional Office for the Eastern Mediterranean
PO Box 1517
Alexandria 21511, Egypt
Phone: 3 4820223
Fax: 3 4838916

Description: Regional branch of the World Health Organization. Works to ensure that WHO programs effectively meet the particular public health needs of the eastern Mediterranean; serves as a liaison between national and local public health agencies and the WHO.

★ 1543 ★ World Health Organization (EURO)
Regional Office for Europe
8 Schefigesvej
DK-2100 Copenhagen O, Denmark
Phone: 39171717
Fax: 39171818

Languages: Danish, English. **Description:** Regional branch of the World Health Organization. Works to ensure that WHO programs effectively meet the particular public health needs of Europe; serves as a liaison between national and local public health agencies and the WHO.

★ 1544 ★ World Health Organization (SEARO)
Regional Office for South-East Asia
World Health House
Indraprastha Estate
Mahatma Gandhi Rd.
New Delhi 110 002, Delhi, India
Phone: 11 3317804
Fax: 11 3318607

Description: Regional branch of the World Health Organization. Works to ensure that WHO programs effectively meet the particular public health needs of southeast Asia; serves as a liaison between national and local public health agencies and the WHO.

★ 1545 ★ World Health Organization (WPRO)
Regional Office for the Western Pacific
PO Box 2932
Manila 1099, Philippines
Phone: 2 5218421
Fax: 2 5211036

Description: Regional branch of the World Health Organization. Works to ensure that WHO programs effectively meet the particular public health needs of the western Pacific; serves as a liaison between national and local public health agencies and the WHO.

★ 1546 ★ World Medical Association (WMA)
(Association Medicale Mondiale — AMM)
28, ave. des Alpes
F-01210 Ferney-Voltaire, France
Phone: 50 407575
Fax: 50 405937
Dr. Andre Wynen, Sec.Gen.

Founded: 1947. **Members:** 58. **Languages:** English, French, German, Japanese, Spanish. **Description:** Federation of national medical associations throughout the world. Goal is to achieve the highest international standards in medical education, medical science, medical ethics, and health care for people worldwide. Promotes closer ties and better communication among medical organizations and doctors of the world; studies professional problems in different countries. Represents and protects the rights and interests of physicians and people internationally. Encourages proper nutrition in developing countries; urges the teaching of human values in the practice of medicine. Seeks to improve maternal and child health care. Issues declarations on ethical topics including: abortion; AIDS; abuse of children and the elderly; euthanasia; genetic engineering; organ transplantation; the use and misuse of psychotropic drugs; torture; biomedical research on human subjects; medical care in rural areas; an international code of medical ethics. **Publications:** *World Medical Journal*, bimonthly. Journal.

★ 1547 ★ World Medical Mission (WMM)
PO Box 3000
Boone, NC 28607
Phone: (704)262-1980
Fax: (704)262-0175
W. Franklin Graham, III, Pres.

Founded: 1977. **Description:** Coordinates medical activities of the evangelical group Sa-

maritan's Purse. Places Christian physicians who serve voluntarily in evangelical mission hospitals overseas and conducts emergency medical relief. Provides assistance in refurbishing and equipping mission hospitals and conducts training sessions. **Publications:** Brochures. • *On Call*, quarterly. • *The PaceMaker*, quarterly. • *World Medical Mission Newsletter*, 6/year. Newsletter.

★ 1548 ★ World Medical Relief (WMR)
11745 Rosa Parks Blvd.
Detroit, MI 48206
Phone: (313)866-5333
Fax: (313)866-5588
Carolyn E. George, Exec.Dir.&CEO

Founded: 1953. **Description:** Nonsectarian, philanthropic organization contributing medical supplies and equipment for the care of the world's destitute sick. Instruments, equipment, and pharmaceuticals are donated to WMR, which in turn sends them to relief agencies and charitable medical clinics and hospitals worldwide. Provides prescriptions and medical supplies to needy senior citizens in the Detroit, MI, area. **Publications:** *Annual Report*. Brochure. • *World Medical Relief News*, quarterly.

★ 1549 ★ World Mercy Fund (WMF)
121 S. St. Asaph St.
Alexandria, VA 22314
Phone: (703)548-4646
Fax: (703)548-6963
Fr. Patrick Leonard, Pres. & CEO

Founded: 1969. **Description:** Builds hospitals and provides medical facilities and water for less fortunate peoples of the world, particularly those in Africa. Has built hospitals and clinics in Africa that are equipped with mobile units. Has initiated projects to bring fresh water to places where it is most urgently needed. Conducts child and adult education programs in nutrition and agriculture; provides on-the-spot education in villages to raise the standard of food production.

★ 1550 ★ World Organization of National Colleges, Academies and Academic Associations of General Practitioners / Family Physicians (WONCA)
(Organisation Mondiale des Colleges Nationaux, Academies et Associations Academiques des Generalistes et des Medecins de Famille)
PO Box 790
Shatin, Hong Kong
Phone: 6036902
Fax: 6036926
Dr. W.E. Fabb

Founded: 1972. **Members:** 42. **Regional Groups:** 4. **Languages:** English, French, German, Spanish. **Description:** Colleges, academies, or organizations in 38 countries concerned with the academic aspects of general family practice. Objectives are to: promote and maintain high standards of general family practice through education and research; foster worldwide communication and understanding among general practitioners; represent the academic and research activities of general practitioners to other worldwide bodies concerned with health or medical care. **Publications:** *The*

Family Doctor, semiannual. Journal. • *International Classification of Health Problems in Primary Care*. Book. • *Membership Directory*, annual. Directory. • *WONCA News*, quarterly.

★ 1551 ★ World Research Foundation (WRF)
15300 Ventura Blvd., Ste. 405
Sherman Oaks, CA 91403
Phone: (818)907-5483
Fax: (818)907-6044
Steven A. Ross, Pres.

Founded: 1980. **Description:** Informs the public of the latest developments in health and environmental issues. Provides health care professionals and the public with information on health tools and technologies currently available outside the U.S. but which have been overlooked or are unavailable in the U.S. Acts as a depository of public information. **Publications:** Journal, quarterly. Contains traditional and nontraditional international health news. *Price:* $20. • Proceedings, annual. • Reports. • *World Research News*, quarterly. Newsletter.

★ 1552 ★ Zimbabwe Medical Association
PO Box 3671
Harare, Zimbabwe
Phone: 4 720731

Languages: English. **Description:** Registered medical doctors and residents. Represents and promotes the interests of the medical profession in Zimbabwe; promotes advancement in medicine and related sciences. Sponsors continuing professional education courses of members.

Research Centers

★ 1553 ★ Allegheny-Singer Research Institute
320 E. North Ave.
Pittsburgh, PA 15212-9986
Phone: (412)359-1500
Fax: (412)359-1525
James H. McMaster, M.D., Pres./CEO

Research Activities and Fields: Cardiovascular and pulmonary genetics, human genetics, cancer, neurosciences, musculoskeletal and trauma issues. Staff specializations include molecular biology, radiobiology, cell biology, immunology, genetics, biochemistry, surgery, mechanical engineering, electrical engineering, psychology, child development, physics, and special education. **Publications:** *Scientific Report* (bienially); Monographs. **E-mail Address:** shuttlew@asri.edu.

★ 1554 ★ Alton Ochsner Medical Foundation
1516 Jefferson Hwy.
New Orleans, LA 70121
Phone: (504)842-3135
Fax: (504)842-3899
Richard N. Re, M.D., Dir., Division of Research

Research Activities and Fields: Hypertension, oncology, cardiovascular research, immunology, orthopedics, renal stones, gastrointestinal physiology (motility and perfusion), depression, and clinical pharmacology.

★ 1555 ★ **American Council on Science and Health**
1995 Broadway, 2nd Fl.
New York, NY 10023-5860
Phone: (212)362-7044
Fax: (212)362-4919
Elizabeth Whelan, Pres.

Research Activities and Fields: Relationship between human health and chemicals, foods, nutrition, lifestyle factors, including cigarette smoking, the environment and human health. Activities include studies on animal-to-man extrapolation in laboratory testing, smoking cessation, Lyme disease, Reye's syndrome, hay fever, microwave ovens, infant mortality, life expectancy, AIDS, and automobile occupant restraint systems. **Publications:** *Media Update; Priorities* (quarterly magazine).

★ 1556 ★ **Aultman Hospital Community Health Research Institute**
2600 6th St. SW
Canton, OH 44710
Phone: (216)452-9911
Fax: (216)438-6356
Jere M. Boyer, Ph.D., Dir.

Research Activities and Fields: Clinical and health services, hypertension, and human papilloma virus testing and epidemiology. Also conducts cancer and perinatal research. **Publications:** *Research Grants Information Facts Sheet* (monthly); also publishes a peer-reviewed journal.

★ 1557 ★ **Battelle Memorial Institute**
505 King Ave.
Columbus, OH 43201
Phone: (614)424-6424
Fax: (614)424-5263
Dr. Douglas E. Olesen, Pres./CEO

Research Activities and Fields: Commercial and industrial technology, environment, health, transportation, technology transfer, and national security. Conducts marine research at three coastal locations: Florida Marine Research Facility (Daytona Beach), Northwest Marine Research Laboratory (Sequim, Washington), and the Ocean Sciences Laboratory (Duxbury, Massachusetts). Specialized facilities and units include: Center for High-Speed Commercial Flight, Aviation Safety Reporting System Project Office, Advanced Materials Center for the Commercial Development of Space, Health and Population Center, Human Factors and Organizational Effectiveness Research Center, Technology and Society Research Center, Battelle Pressure Vessel and Piping Test Facility, and Battelle Center for Materials Fabrication. **Publications:** *Battelle Today* (four times per year); Annual Report; Published Papers and Articles (annually).

★ 1558 ★ **Baylor College of Medicine General Clinical Research Center—Adults**
1 Baylor Plaza
Houston, TX 77030
Phone: (713)790-4306
Fax: (713)793-1298
Dr. Robert R. Rich, M.D., Prin. Investigator

Research Activities and Fields: Cardiology, endocrinology, gastroenterology, genetics, gynecology, hypertension and clinical pharmacology, immunology, infectious diseases, lipid metabolism, neurology, ophthalmology, and pulmonary diseases. The Center functions as a per diem unit within the Hospital; it accommodates inpatients as well as outpatients. **E-mail Address:** gailj@bcm.tmc.edu.

★ 1559 ★ **Boston University General Clinical Research Center**
Boston City Hospital, Thorndike 2
818 Harrison Ave.
Boston, MA 02218
Phone: (617)534-4834
Fax: (617)638-8882
Michael F. Holick, M.D., Program Dir.

Research Activities and Fields: Cardiovascular disease, collagen vascular disease, diabetes, gastrointestinal disease, nephrology, pediatrics, dermatology, AIDS, psoraisis, amyloidosis, and drug abuse.

★ 1560 ★ **Boston University Robert Dawson Evans Memorial Department of Clinical Research**
75 E. Newton St.
Boston, MA 02118
Phone: (617)638-7250
Fax: (617)638-8728
Dr. Norman G. Levinsky, Dir.

Research Activities and Fields: Peripheral vascular system, arthritis and connective tissue, medical respiratory, hematology, hypertension and atherosclerosis, cardiovascular disease, gastroenterology, infectious diseases, endocrinology, metabolism, nephrology, nutrition, computers in medicine, health care, biomolecular medicine, immunology, geriatrics, oncology, and health services research.

★ 1561 ★ **Brigham and Women's Hospital Clinical Research Center**
221 Longwood Ave., 3rd. Fl.
Boston, MA 02115
Phone: (617)732-5661
Dr. Gordon Williams, Program Dir.

Research Activities and Fields: Support facility for clinical investigation of diseases in humans.

★ 1562 ★ **Brigham Young University Ezra Taft Benson Agriculture and Food Institute**
110 B-49
Provo, UT 84602
Phone: (801)378-2607
N. Paul Johnston, Dir.

Research Activities and Fields: Quality of life in developing countries, including studies on health, nutrition, food production, agronomy, animal science, and technology. **Publications:** *Benson Institute Newsletter; Benson Institute Information Series.*

★ 1563 ★ **California Institute for Medical Research**
2260 Clove Dr.
San Jose, CA 95128
Phone: (408)998-4554
Fax: (408)998-2723
Jada Lin, Mgr.

Research Activities and Fields: Medical research, including infectious diseases, stroke, cancer, analytical tools for pharmacokinetic study of anticoagulant drugs, Parkinson's disease and other neurological disorders, tumor biology, and AIDS. Also serves as a model regional center for traumatic head injury. **Publications:** *Discovery Newsletter* (biannual). **Formerly:** Institute for Medical Research, San Jose (1990).

★ 1564 ★ **California Pacific Medical Center Research Institute**
2330 Clay St., Stern Bldg.
San Francisco, CA 94115
Phone: (415)561-1700
Fax: (415)561-1753
David R. Fielder, Vice.Pres.

Research Activities and Fields: Medical sciences, including basic clinical research on heart and lung disease, organ transplantation, neurology, laboratory medicine, cancer, epidemiology, alcohol use and abuse, arthritis, behavioral medicine, juvenile diabetes, neonatology, and pediatric gastroenterology. **Publications:** *California Pacific Quarterly.* **Formerly:** Institutes of Medical Sciences (1982); Medical Research Institute of San Francisco (1993).

★ 1565 ★ **California State University, Bakersfield Applied Research Center**
9001 Stockdale Hwy.
Bakersfield, CA 93311-1099
Phone: (805)664-2173
Fax: (805)664-3194
Kenneth L. Nyberg, Dir.

Research Activities and Fields: Performs applied research, program evaluation, needs assessment, computer-aided telephone interviewing, data management, and data analysis on education, higher education, public health, gerontology, economics, social welfare, and drugs and alcohol. **Formerly:** Center for Scientific and Educational Research.

★ 1566 ★ **Case Western Reserve University Center for Practice Innovations**
Mandel School for Applied Social Science
10900 Euclild Ave.
Cleveland, OH 44106-7164
Phone: (216)368-3611
Fax: (216)368-8670
David E. Biegel, Ph.D., Codir.

Research Activities and Fields: Human services, including social work and service delivery to at-risk populations. Major research projects include accessibility of services to minority caregivers of the mentally impaired, the mental health consequences of violence on inner-city youth, studies of the support systems of incarcerated women with chemical dependencies, and research on children and adolescents with serious emotional disorders and adults with chronic mental illness. **Publications:** *Center for Practice Innovations Newsletter*, *Family Caregiver Applications* (book series). **E-mail Address:** pxk5@po.cwru.edu.

★ 1567 ★ **Case Western Reserve University Clinical Research Center**
2074 Abington Rd.
Cleveland, OH 44106
Phone: (216)844-1589
Fax: (216)844-8216
E. Regis McFadden, Jr., M.D., Dir.

Research Activities and Fields: Clinical investigations in humans, including specific, carefully planned studies of illnesses of voluntarily participating adult and pediatric patients. **E-mail Address:** db821@cleveland.freenet.edu. **Formerly:** Metabolic Research Unit (1962).

★ 1568 ★ **Center for Health Research**
3800 N. Kaiser Center Dr.
Portland, OR 97227-1098
Phone: (503)335-2400
Fax: (503)335-2424
Mary Durham, Dir.

Research Activities and Fields: Research is divided into nine major areas: 1) health status and the use of medical care services, 2) demonstration projects and testing of innovations in health care organization, financing, and delivery for geriatric, adolescent, and other special populations, 3) organized health care systems (HMOs) and the organization, financing, and costs of medical care, 4) health behavior and health behavior intervention, 5) biometry and research methods, 6) epidemiological studies and clinical trials, 7) social and economic studies, 8) studies in oncology, and 9) organizational studies. Studies include hypertension treatment, cardiovascular risk reduction, and cardiovascular, smoking, and health services epidemiology. **Publications:** Research Report Series (monographs); *CHR Newsletter* (three times per year). **Formerly:** Medical Care Research Unit (1968), Health Services Research Center (1984).

★ 1569 ★ **Center for Medical Consumers and Health Information**
237 Thompson St.
New York, NY 10012
Phone: (212)674-7105
Fax: (212)674-7100
Arthur Levin, Dir.

Research Activities and Fields: Center focuses on medicine, health, and nutrition. **Publications:** *HEALTHFACTS* (monthly).

★ 1570 ★ **Center for Public Representation, Inc.**
121 S. Pinckney St.
Madison, WI 53703
Phone: (608)251-4008
Fax: (608)251-1263
Louise G. Trubek, Clinical Dir.

Research Activities and Fields: Health cost containment, elderly, open government, children's rights, consumer issues, and advocacy. **Publications:** *Public Eye* (quarterly newsletter).

★ 1571 ★ **Centers for Health, Education and Social Systems Studies (CHESS)**
Park Plaza
128 N. Craig St.
Pittsburgh, PA 15213-2713
Phone: (412)681-3000
Fax: (412)681-1471
Dr. Melvin H. Rudov, Pres.

Research Activities and Fields: Investigation, analysis, and evaluation of health care, education, industry, and other social systems. Operates computer service bureau for research projects. **Formerly:** Center for Health and Social Systems Research.

★ 1572 ★ **Chiles Research Institute**
4805 NE Glisan
Portland, OR 97213
Phone: (503)230-6593
Fax: (503)230-6857
David N. Gilbert, M.D., Dir.

Research Activities and Fields: Clinical and basic investigations in cancer immunology, cardiovascular diseases, infectious diseases, and diabetes and metabolism. **Publications:** Annual Report.

★ 1573 ★ **City of Hope National Medical Center**
1500 E. Duarte Rd.
Duarte, CA 91010
Phone: (818)359-8111
Fax: (818)301-8115
Dr. Sanford M. Shapero, Pres./CEO

Research Activities and Fields: Metabolism, diabetes, genetics, cytology, hematology, physiology, pharmacology, neurology, cancer, cancer diagnosis and therapy, bone marrow transplantation, surgery, respiratory diseases, pathology, radiology, nuclear medicine, gene therapy, and developmental biology. **Publications:** Biennial Report, summarizing all research activities.

★ 1574 ★ **Clinical Research Center**
Northwestern University
Northwestern Memorial Hospital
250 E. Superior St., Wesley Pavilion
Chicago, IL 60611
Phone: (312)908-3192
Fax: (312)908-8450
Gary L. Robertson, M.D., Program Dir.

Research Activities and Fields: Diabetes insipidus, malabsorption in AIDS, occular complications of AIDS, cardiac arrhythmias, effects of diabetes on pregnancy, pituitary tumors, tumoral calcinosis, hypophosphatemic rickets, congenital adrenal hypoplasia, allergic pulmonary disease, sickle cell vaso-occlusive crises, chronic liver disease, vasculitis, renal insufficiency, gastrointestinal malabsorption of carbohydrates and other nutrients, monoclonal antibodies in diagnosis and therapy of cancer, and Phase I and II drug trials. **Publications:** Annual Report.

★ 1575 ★ **College of Physicians of Philadelphia**
Francis Clark Wood Institute for the History of Medicine
19 S. 22nd St.
Philadelphia, PA 19103
Phone: (215)563-3737
Fax: (215)561-6477
Thomas A. Horrocks, Dir.

Research Activities and Fields: Supports research in the history and culture of medicine. **Publications:** *Transactions & Studies of the College of Physicians of Philadelpia* (annually); Monograph Series in the History of Medicine (occasionally).

★ 1576 ★ **Colorado State University Hypo-Hyperbaric Chamber Facility**
Dept. of Physiology
Fort Collins, CO 80523
Phone: (303)491-6106
Fax: (303)491-7569
Dr. Alan Tucker, Dir.

Research Activities and Fields: High altitude physiology, altitude illness, pulmonary hypertension, human performance at various altitudes, hyperbaric physiology, and human and animal studies.

★ 1577 ★ **Columbia University Irving Center for Clinical Research**
Columbia-Presbyterian Medical Center
622 W. 168th St., PH-10
New York, NY 10032
Phone: (212)305-2071
Fax: (212)305-3213
Robert E. Canfield, M.D., Program Dir.

Research Activities and Fields: Multidisciplinary studies of human disease and clinical pharmacology. Areas include arrhythmia control, heart failure, atherosclerosis, nutrition, metabolism, clinical pharmacology, dermatology, endocrinology, hypertension, immunology, mineral metabolism and skeletal disease, neuromuscular disease, physiology, pulmonary disease, pulmonary physiology, reproductive research studies, neurology (including dementia, stroke, and seizure disorders), oncology, AIDS/infectious disease, geriatrics, epidemiology, and substance abuse.

★ 1578 ★ **Columbia University New York Obesity Research Center**
St. Luke's-Roosevelt Hospital
114th St. & Amsterdam Ave.
New York, NY 10025
Phone: (212)523-4161
Fax: (212)523-5376
Dr. Xavier Pi-Sunyer, M.D., Dir.

Research Activities and Fields: Obesity, including molecular genetics, regulation of food intake, nutrient uptake and oxidation, body composition, stable isotope methodology, exercise physiology, diabetes, and insulin resistance. **Formerly:** Obesity Research Center.

★ 1579 ★ **Commonweal**
Box 316
Bolinas, CA 94924
Phone: (415)868-0970
Fax: (415)868-2230
Michael Lerner, Contact

Research Activities and Fields: Health, education, and environmental research, with special interest in nutrition, chronic disease, and alternative health care techniques, including health promotion, disease prevention, and alternative and adjunct cancer therapies. Also studies conditions of confinement in the California Youth Authority (CYA) state correctional facilities for juvenile offenders. **Publications:** Reports. **Formerly:** Commonweal Research Institute.

★ 1580 ★ **Consumer Health Information Research Institute**
Medical Information Retrieval Center
3521 Broadway
Kansas City, MO 64111
Phone: (816)753-8850
Fax: (816)753-6706
Dr. George X. Trimble, Dir.

Research Activities and Fields: Clinical medicine, health fraud and quakery, patient education, toxicology, history of medicine, medicine in art, and therapeutics. **Publications:** Reports and Critical Reviews (irregularly); Medical Literature Critiques (irregularly).

★ 1581 ★ **Dorothea Dix Hospital**
Clinical Research Unit
S. Boylan Ave.
Raleigh, NC 27611
Phone: (919)733-5228
Fax: (919)733-5351
James C. Garbutt, M.D., Dir.

Research Activities and Fields: Conducts inpatient and outpatient clinical research on the neuroendocrinology, neurobiology, and psychopharmacology of affective disorders, alcoholism, and schizophrenia. Examines behavioral and endocrine effects of neuropeptides in healthy human subjects and investigates biological risk factors of alcoholism using young adults without the disease but with a history of familial alcoholism.

★ 1582 ★ **Duke University**
F.G. Hall Hyper-Hypo-Baric Center
Medical Center
Box 3823
Durham, NC 27710
Phone: (919)684-5514
Fax: (919)684-6002
Dr. Peter B. Bennett, Senior Dir.

Research Activities and Fields: Hypobaric and hyperbaric medicine and physiology, including studies of how increased hydrostatic pressure affects cells, tissues, organs, and intact organisms; investigations into mechanism of inert gas narcosis and its antagonism by pressure; studies of morphological and metabolic effects of oxygen pressures; clinical investigations of use of hyperbaric oxygen therapy; study of effects of pressure on respiratory and cardiovascular systems and thermal homeostasis; and investigations of causes, mechanisms, and prevention of effects of decompression sickness. **Formerly:** Hyperbaric Program (1967).

★ 1583 ★ **Duke University**
General Clinical Research Center
Medical Center
Box 3854
Durham, NC 27710
Phone: (919)684-3806
Fax: (919)684-5041
M. Louise Markert, M.D., Prog.Dir.

Research Activities and Fields: Multidisciplinary, clinical research into the cause, progression, prevention, control, and cure of human disease. Sample projects have studied immunodeficiency diseases, Alzheimer's disease, food allergy, X-linked hypophosphatemic rickets, and cardiovascular disease. **Formerly:** Rankin Clinical Research Unit.

★ 1584 ★ **Dwight David Eisenhower Army Medical Center**
Department of Clinical Investigation
Fort Gordon, GA 30905-5650
Phone: (706)787-4273
Fax: (706)787-5216
Col. Kent M. Plowman, MC, Chief

Research Activities and Fields: Osteomyelitis in rat tibias, fibroblast attachment to teeth, periodontal implants, pharmacotherapy in burns, hormonal influence of bone growth, synthetic bone grafting materials, wound healing, and markers for malignancy. **Publications:** Annual Progress Report.

★ 1585 ★ **ECRI**
5200 Butler Pike
Plymouth Meeting, PA 19462
Phone: (215)825-6000
Fax: (215)834-1275
Dr. Joel J. Nobel, Pres.

Research Activities and Fields: Improvement of safety, performance, reliability, and cost effectiveness of health care technology; quality of health care; health care environmental management; and risk management. **Publications:** *Health Devices Alerts* (weekly); *Health Devices* (monthly); *Health Technology Trends* (monthly); *Hospital Risk Control* (monthly); *Hospital Product Comparison System* (monthly); *Clinical Laboratory Product Comparison System* (monthly); *Diagnostic Imaging and Radiology Product Comparison System* (monthly); *Executive Briefings on Technology Assessment* (monthly); *Health Care Technology* (bimonthly); *Health Devices Sourcebook* (annually); *Health Standards Directory* (annually); *Health Care Hazardous Materials Management* (monthly); *Health Care Environmental Management*.

★ 1586 ★ **Emory University**
W. Dean Warren Clinical Research Center
School of Medicine
Atlanta, GA 30322
Phone: (404)727-7258
Fax: (404)727-5563
W. Dallas Hall, M.D., Dir.

Research Activities and Fields: Disorders of amino acid, and protein metabolism; branch-chain ketoacid abnormalities; mitochondrial myopathies; clinical nutrition; energy metabolism; metabolic consequences of diabetes and obesity; effects of low protein diets and blood pressure control on the progression of renal disease; and growth disorders.

★ 1587 ★ **Florida Institute of Technology**
Life Science Research Complex
3325 W. New Haven Ave.
Melbourne, FL 32904-3521
Phone: (407)768-8000
Fax: (407)984-8461
John Thomas, Contact

Research Activities and Fields: Comparative mammalogy and biochemistry, infectious diseases, medicinal chemistry, and reproductive biology. Major research missions include the following: armadillo-leprosy animal model program and related laboratory studies; armadillo physiology and reproduction in captivity; development of antimicrobial and medicinal agents; continued development and evaluation of specialty products and techniques for rapidly diagnosing infectious agents, disease states, and microbial antibiotic susceptibility; study of nutrition and physiology of causative agents of leprosy that will lead to their successful in vitro cultivation; conversion of biomass to fuels; development of marketable products from phosphate wastes; and reproductive biology involving studies on the surface transformation of spermatozoa during epididymal maturation and capacitation in the female reproductive tract. **Formerly:** Medical Research Institute.

★ 1588 ★ **Frontier Science and Technology Research Foundation**
303 Bolyston St.
Brookline, MA 02146
Phone: (617)632-2000
Fax: (617)632-2444
Marvin Zelen, Contact

Research Activities and Fields: Conducts joint research projects with cooperative clinical trial groups and other organizations. Provides biostatistical support and collaboration, data management and processing, project management, and administrative support to researchers.

★ 1589 ★ **General Clinical Research Center**
Scripps Research Institute
10666 N. Torrey Pines Rd.
La Jolla, CA 92037
Phone: (619)554-8925
Fax: (619)554-6230
Francis V. Chisari, M.D., Dir.

Research Activities and Fields: Develops and evaluates new and experimental therapeutic procedures, including therapies for cancer, vascular disease, thrombotic disease, sleep disorders, multiple sclerosis, hepatitis, inflammatory bowel disease, asthma, alcoholism and depression, and autoimmune diseases such as rheumatoid arthritis and systemic lupus erythematosus. **E-mail Address:** bieger@scripps.edu.

★ 1590 ★ **General Clinical Research Center at Beth Israel Hospital**
330 Brookline Ave., Rm. GZ 800
Boston, MA 02215
Phone: (617)735-4269
Fax: (617)735-5953
Alan Moses, M.D., Prog. Dir.

Research Activities and Fields: Biomedicine, cardiology, endocrinology, gastroenterology, gerontology, hematology, nephrology, neurology, nutrition, obstetrics, pulmonary physiology, psychiatry, and surgery. **E-mail Address:** jordan@bih.harvard.edu.

★ 1591 ★ **General Clinical Research Center at Harbor-UCLA Medical Center**
1000 W. Carson St.
Box 16
Torrance, CA 90509-2910
Phone: (310)222-2503
Fax: (310)533-6972
Christina Wang, M.D., Program Dir.

Research Activities and Fields: Biomedicine, endocrinology, reproductive physiology, gastroenterology, genetics, immunology and infectious disease, nephrology, obstetrics and gynecology, labor and delivery, diabetes, metabolism, oncology, pediatrics, nutrition, psychiatry, and neonatology. **E-mail Address:** norton%csc@humc.edu.

★ 1592 ★ **General Clinical Research Center at Mayo Foundation**
St. Mary's Hospital
200 1st St. SW
Rochester, MN 55905
Phone: (507)255-6122
Fax: (507)255-7445
Lawrence Riggs, Dir.

Research Activities and Fields: Allergy, endocrinology, gastrointestinal disease, lipid disorders, osteoporosis, pediatrics, pharmacology, renal disease, surgery, cardiovascular disease, oncology, neurology, hypertension, and nutrition. **E-mail Address:** andresen@mayo.edu. **Formerly:** Nutrition Unit.

★ 1593 ★ **Georgetown University Research Resources Facility**
3950 Reservoir Rd. NW, Rm. G05
Washington, DC 20007
Phone: (202)687-2488
Fax: (202)687-6256
Stephen P. Schiffer, D.V.M., Dir.

Research Activities and Fields: Medical sciences, with particular reference to surgical aspects, including basic studies of tissue transplantation, neuroscience, techniques of extracorporeal circulation, magnetic resonance imaging (MRI) techniques, and technique of perfusion of orbital artery and heart/lung transplantation. Also designs and develops valvular devices and other cardiac instrumentation and evaluates vascular prosthetic devices. **Formerly:** Surgical Research Laboratory.

★ 1594 ★ **Graduate Hospital Research Center**
1 Graduate Plaza
Philadelphia, PA 19146
Phone: (215)893-7497
Robert H. Cox, Ph.D., Dir.

Research Activities and Fields: Major health problems, including heart disease, lung disease, neurological disorders, and cancer. Studies include hypertension, emphysema, Parkinson's disease, epilepsy, psychological evaluations, and gene therapy. **Publications:** *Graduate Hospital Research Notes.*

★ 1595 ★ **Hamot Medical Center Research Department**
201 State St.
Erie, PA 16550
Phone: (814)877-6026
Phyllis Joan Kuhn, Ph.D., Dir.

Research Activities and Fields: Drug evaluations, medical devices and diagnostic products, orthopedics, infection control, and microbiology.

★ 1596 ★ **Harbor-UCLA Research and Education Institute**
1124 W. Carson St.
Torrance, CA 90502
Phone: (310)222-3601
Fax: (310)320-6515
Frank J. De Santis, CAE, Pres.

Research Activities and Fields: Cardiology, reproductive endocrinology, neuroscience (psychiatry, neurology, neurosurgery, and radiology), pathology, respiratory physiology, oncology, rheumatology, medical genetics, perinatology, laser surgery, sleep disorders, Alzheimer's disease, and depression. Also studies infectious diseases, including AIDS. Conducts clinical research studies using volunteers to determine the effectiveness of new drugs and therapies, including vaccines. **Publications:** *REI Report* (newsletter, 3-4 times per year); Annual Report. **E-mail Address:** santis@harbor3.humc.edu. **Formerly:** Research and Education Institute, Inc.

★ 1597 ★ **Harvard University Physicians' Health Study Research Group**
Brigham Women's Hospital
900 Commonwealth Ave.
Boston, MA 02215
Phone: (617)732-4965
Fax: (617)734-1437
Dr. Charles Hennekens, Dir.

Research Activities and Fields: Investigates the effect of aspirin on reducing heart attack risk and the effect of beta-carotene on reducing cancer risk and risk of cardiovascular disease.

★ 1598 ★ **Heimlich Institute**
2368 Victory Pkwy., Ste. 410
Cincinnati, OH 45206
Phone: (513)221-0002
Fax: (513)221-0003
Henry J. Heimlich, M.D., Pres.

Research Activities and Fields: Malaria therapy for cancer and Lyme disease, rehabilitation of swallowing, and transtracheal oxygen therapy for chronic lung diseases, including oxygen-dependent emphysema, black lung, cystic fibrosis, and interstitial fibrosis. Developments include Heimlich Maneuver for choking and drowning, Heimlich chest drainage valve, Heimlich Micro-Trach, and Heimlich operation for esophageal replacement. **Publications:** Newsletter. **Formerly:** Dysphagia Foundation (1982).

★ 1599 ★ **Hektoen Institute for Medical Research**
627-637 S. Wood St.
Ste. 201
Chicago, IL 60612-3810
Phone: (312)738-3100
Morris T. Friedell, M.D., Chm.

Research Activities and Fields: Medicine and surgery, including laboratory and clinical studies

in cancer metabolism, kidney disease, virology, hematology, microbiology, bacteriology, endocrinology, pediatric cardiology, neurology, immunology, pathology, gastroenterology, orthopedic surgery, congenital heart diseases, infectious diseases, and hypertension. Specific investigations include treatment of cancer by new modalities, incidence of perinatal mortality and effect of neonatal care, metabolic aspects of renal disease, cell surface alterations in cancer and their effects on metastasis, effects of different hormones in breast carcinoma, influence of hormone receptors on several varieties of soft tissue sarcomas and malignant melanomas, and the immunological aspects of prostatic cancer. **Publications:** Biennial Report.

★ 1600 ★ **Howard Hughes Medical Institute**
4000 Jones Bridge Rd.
Chevy Chase, MD 20815-6789
Phone: (301)215-8550
Fax: (301)215-8558
Purnell W. Choppin, M.D., Pres.

Research Activities and Fields: Genetics, immunology, cell biology and regulation, structural biology, and neuroscience. Conducts research with scientists and staff at over 60 academic medical centers, hospitals, and universities. **Publications:** Annual Report.

★ 1601 ★ **Human Life Center**
Franciscan Univ. of Steubenville
Steubenville, OH 43952
Phone: (614)282-9953
Fax: (614)282-0769
Mike Marker, Dir.

Research Activities and Fields: Marriage and family issues, sexuality, family planning, abortion, infanticide, euthanasia, and related subjects. **Publications:** *Human Life Issues* (quarterly); *International Review of Natural Family Planning* (quarterly).

★ 1602 ★ **Independent Citizens Research Foundation for Study of Degenerative Diseases, Inc.**
PO Box 97
Ardsley, NY 10502
Phone: (914)478-1862
Dorothea Seeber, Exec.Dir.

Research Activities and Fields: Causes and treatment of degenerative diseases. Current activities include the study of Acquired Immune Deficiency Syndrome (AIDS) and evaluation and development of calibrated Transcutaneous Electrical Nerve Stimulation (TENS), with focus on pain as related to degenerative diseases.

★ 1603 ★ **Indiana University Bloomington Center for Health and Safety Studies**
Bloomington, IN 47405
Phone: (812)855-3627
Fax: (812)855-3936
Dr. James W. Crowe, Dir.

Research Activities and Fields: Health behavior, quantitative and qualitative evaluation of instructional materials, and human behavior and attitudes relating to safety and driver education, including studies on industrial safety, health and safety practices in industry and recreational settings, childhood accident prevention and injury control, nutrition, family life, and human development. **E-mail Address:** crowe@indiana.edu. **Formerly:** Center for Safety and Traffic Education (1979).

★ 1604 ★ Indiana University Northwest Northwest Center for Medical Education
School of Medicine
3400 Broadway
Gary, IN 46408
Phone: (219)980-6550
Fax: (219)980-6566
Panayotis G.G. Iatridis, M.D., Dir.

Research Activities and Fields: Diabetes, mitochondria enzymes, lymphocyte activation microvessels, corneal innervation, autonomic nervous system, blood coagulation, neuroglial-neuron interactions, membrane-bound transport enzymes, erthrocyte membrane skeletal proteins, avian musculoskeletal funtional morphology, bacterial growth, immunoglobulin molecular biology.

★ 1605 ★ Indiana University-Purdue University at Indianapolis
General Clinical Research Center
926 W. Michigan St., 5595
Indianapolis, IN 46223
Phone: (317)274-4356
Fax: (317)274-7346
Dr. Doris H. Merritt, Prin. Investigator

Research Activities and Fields: Clinical pharmacology, metabolic bone disease, AIDS, alcoholism, diabetes, hypertension, oncologic diseases, cardiac arrhythmias, neuroendocrinology, arthritis, and neonatal metabolism.

★ 1606 ★ Institute for Alternative Futures
100 N. Pitt St., Ste. 205
Alexandria, VA 22314
Phone: (703)684-5880
Fax: (703)684-0640
Dr. Clement Bezold, Exec.Dir.

Research Activities and Fields: Conducts legislative foresight work with states and Congress, consults with state and local governments on anticipatory democracy, offers strategic planning assistance to voluntary organizations and corporations, and conducts future research on information, communications, bioengineering, health care, nutrition, pharmaceuticals, work and the environment. **E-mail Address:** futures@delphi.com.

★ 1607 ★ Institute of Applied Physiology and Medicine
701 16th Ave.
Seattle, WA 98122
Phone: (206)553-7330
Fax: (206)553-1717
Merrill P. Spencer, M.D., Exec.Dir.

Research Activities and Fields: Basic sciences and applied medical physiological research divided among two departments: 1) the Department of Physical Sciences conducts basic and applied research in Doppler ultrasound, signal processing, and pattern recognition in cardiovascular ultrasound and cardiac outflow monitoring, multi-modality imaging technologies, and expert systems in artificial intelligence for medical applications and therapeutic

radiological physics; 2) the Department of Physiology investigates new techniques in the clinical diagnosis and treatment of cardiovascular diseases, especially vascular Doppler ultrasound.

★ 1608 ★ Institute for Scientific Research, Inc.
33 Bedford, Ste. 19A
Lexington, MA 02173
Phone: (617)861-7900
Dr. Steven L. Guberman, Pres.

Research Activities and Fields: Conducts fundamental studies in theoretical quantum chemistry with applications to atmospheric, interstellar, laser, and combustion phenomena. Sociological studies focus on the areas of rehabilitation, medicine, and education. Performs evaluations of social programs.

★ 1609 ★ Institutes of Religion and Health
3 W. 29th St.
New York, NY 10001
Phone: (212)725-7850
Anne E. Impellizzeri, Pres.

Research Activities and Fields: Conducts policy studies related to pastoral care and counseling and the dialogue among theology, medicine and the social sciences. **Publications:** *Journal of Religion and Health* (quarterly).

★ 1610 ★ Jackson Foundation for Medical Research & Education
345 W. Washington Ave.
Madison, WI 53701-2596
Phone: (608)258-2280
Fax: (608)258-2296
Dorothy Adams, Exec.Dir.

Research Activities and Fields: Cardiovascular disease, hypertension, rheumatology, gastroenterology, diabetes, urology, cancer, and pain. Conducts medical and clinical investigations in areas of interest to multispecialty group physicians.

★ 1611 ★ Johns Hopkins University Division of Comparative Medicine
720 Rutland Ave.
Baltimore, MD 21205
Phone: (410)955-3273
Fax: (410)681-5392
Dr. John D. Strandberg, Dir.

Research Activities and Fields: Comparative pathology, laboratory animal medicine, retrovirus biology, transgenic biology, infectious diseases, and oncology. Research activities focus on naturally occurring diseases of animals as models of human disease, molecular biology and pathogenesis of lentiviral infections, aquatic toxicology, and benign prostatic hyperplasia. **E-mail Address:** jstrand@welchlink.welch.jhu.edu. **Formerly:** Division of Laboratory Animal Medicine (1976).

★ 1612 ★ Johns Hopkins University Outpatient General Clinical Research Center
John Hopkins Hospital
Carnegie 284
Baltimore, MD 21205
Phone: (410)955-5888
Paul Whelton, M.D., Dir.

Research Activities and Fields: Funds 40-50 clinical research projects, involving 175-200 investigators, covering a wide variety of medical interests.

★ 1613 ★ Lahey Clinic Foundation
41 Mall Rd.
Burlington, MA 01805
Phone: (617)273-5100
Fax: (617)273-8999
Nancy L. Rizzo, V.Pres. of Ambulatory Operations

Research Activities and Fields: Medical, surgical, and radiological techniques, with special emphasis on clinical applications, including studies on high and mega voltage radiation, treatment of cancer with drugs and immunotherapy, cancer cell kinetics, electronic measurement of bacterial growth, pancreatic and renal transplantation, cardiac surgery, diagnostic radiology, amino acid absorption, treatment of pancreatitis, and hospital and prolonged storage by freezing of blood for transfusion. Maintains a clinic for patient care and application of research results and an educational division for postgraduate medical training and residency, both at the clinic and at local hospitals and medical schools. **Publications:** *Lahey Clinic Foundation Bulletin* (quarterly). **Formerly:** Formed from merger of Lahey Clinic established in 1923 and Lahey Foundation established in 1943; formerly known as LCF Foundation, Inc.

★ 1614 ★ Lankenau Medical Research Center
100 Lancaster Ave., W.
Wynnewood, PA 19096
Phone: (215)645-3475

Research Activities and Fields: Cancer, including premalignancy of cells, oncogenetics, and how cells recognize each other during embryo development; cardiology; ophthalmology; sleep disorders; infectious diseases; arthritis; diabetes; and kidney disease. Center is also involved in testing a new excimer laser system.

★ 1615 ★ Laval University Medical Research Centre
2705, boulevard Laurier
Ste. Foy, PQ, Canada G1V 4G2
Phone: (418)654-2129
Fax: (418)654-2714
Dr. Fernand Labrie, Dir.

Research Activities and Fields: Family medicine, rheumatology and immunology, infectious diseases, health and environment, genetics and molecular medicine, ontogeny and reproduction, molecular endocrinology, hypertension, diabetes, lipids, ophthalmology, pediatrics, hormonal bioregulation, and public health.

★ 1616 ★ Laval University Medical Research Centre Family Medicine Research Group
2705, boulevard Laurier
Ste. Foy, PQ, Canada G1V 4G2
Phone: (418)654-2701
Fax: (418)654-2138
Lucie Baillargeon, Dir.

Research Activities and Fields: Causes of, and therapeutic alternatives to, overuse of hypnotic and anxiolytic drugs; family physicians treatment of patients who are facing domestic violence; evaluation of validity of international prostatic symptoms scale; physicians knowledge of diabetic retinopathy; risk of severe perineal tears in relation to median episiotomy; clinical trials on antibiotherapy for various infectious diseases; and smoking cessation.

★1617★ Laval University
Saint-Sacrement Hospital Research Centre
1050, chemin Ste-Foy
Quebec, PQ, Canada G1S 4L8
Phone: (418)682-7838
Fax: (418)682-7949
Jean R. Joly, M.D., Dir.

Research Activities and Fields: Epidemiology and public health, experimental organogenesis, hematology, and clinical research in gynecology, obstetrics, respiratory diseases, and breast cancer.

★1618★ Lehigh University
Center for Social Research
516-520 Brodhead Ave.
Bethlehem, PA 18015
Phone: (610)758-3800
Dr. Diane T. Hyland, Dir.

Research Activities and Fields: Interdisciplinary studies in social and behavioral sciences, including health and human development, families and children, aging, and program evaluation, with particular emphasis on family dynamics and child rearing practices, family responses to perinatal loss, social influences on health, and evaluation of technology transfer and educational programs. Collaborates with local corporations and private and governmental agencies on some projects. Formerly: Center for Business and Economics; Center for Business, Economics, and Urban Studies (1972).

★1619★ Los Amigos Research and
Education Institute, Inc.
PO Box 3500, Los Amigos Sta.
Downey, CA 90242
Phone: (310)940-8111
Fax: (310)803-5569
Chester W. Palmer, Exec.Dir.

Research Activities and Fields: Clinical medicine, including multidisciplinary study of severe chronic disabilities in pulmonary and respiratory functions, cardiology, spinal cord injury, orthopedic disabilities, environmental health, stroke, pathokinesiology, liver disease, neuromuscular stimulation and control, rehabilitation of severely disabled persons, cerebral palsy, problem amputations, arthritis, and diabetes. Treats effects of atmospheric pollutants on human lung function, investigates possible causes of Alzheimer's disease, and explores new methods and procedures for care and treatment of gerontology patients. Formerly: Rancho Los Amigos Medical Center (1990).

★1620★ Louisiana State University
Public Administration Institute
3200 CEBA Bldg.
Baton Rouge, LA 70803
Phone: (504)388-6743
Fax: (504)334-1719
James A. Richardson, Dir.

Research Activities and Fields: Public administration, including studies on health policy, mi-

nority health care, economics and taxes, state and local governments, and public finance.

★1621★ The Lovelace Institutes
2425 Ridgecrest Dr. SE
Albuquerque, NM 87108
Phone: (505)262-7155
Fax: (505)262-7043
David J. Ottensmeyer, M.D., Pres. and CEO

Research Activities and Fields: Environmental health research, including basic research in cardiopulmonary and secretory physiology, photobiology and immunotoxicology; additional research in nuclear magnetic resonance and Doppler acoustics; clinical research in renal disease and substance abuse and in clinical information systems; research and education in health services and health economics and in community intervention programs. Publications: Advances (semiannually). Formerly: Lovelace Medical Foundation.

★1622★ Maharishi International University
Laboratory for Health and Aging Studies
1000 N. 4th St., FB 1028
Fairfield, IA 52557-1028
Phone: (515)472-1129
Fax: (515)472-1167
Robert H. Schneider, M.D., Dir.

Research Activities and Fields: Behavioral cardiology, minority health, preventive cardiology, behavioral and preventive gerontology, and traditional and alternative medicine. Conducts controlled clinical trials on cardiovascular disease treatment and prevention in community settings with behavioral methods; research into methods to slow or retard aging processes; research and development in traditional natural medicine; and programs with African American populations. Publications: Collected Papers.

★1623★ Maine Medical Center Research
Institute
22 Bramhall St.
Portland, ME 04102
Phone: (207)871-2163
Fax: (207)761-4294
Peter W. Rand, M.D., Assoc. V.P. for Research

Research Activities and Fields: Laboratory, clinical, and epidemiologic research, and molecular genetics, hematology, infectious diseases, endocrinology, cardiology and nephrology. Provides research, instruction, and consultation for medical staff of the 598-bed Medical Center. Publications: Inquiry (newsletter). Formerly: Maine Medical Center Research Department.

★1624★ Mallinckrodt General Clinical
Research Center
Massachusetts General Hospital
Boston, MA 02114
Phone: (617)726-3294
Fax: (617)724-3423
David Nathan, M.D., Dir.

Research Activities and Fields: Cardiology, dermatology, diabetes, endocrinology, orthopedics, pediatrics, neuropsychiatry, reproductive endocrinology, neurology, gynecology, and rheumatology. Provides medical scientists opportunity for clinical research in all aspects of biomedicine.

★1625★ Marshfield Medical Research and
Education Foundation
1000 N. Oak Ave.
Marshfield, WI 54449-5790
Phone: (715)387-5241
Fax: (715)389-3131
Paul Gunderson, Ph.D., Dir.

Research Activities and Fields: Diagnosis and treatment of human disease, including basic and/or applied studies on farmer's lung, cancer clonogenic testing, plasma proteinase inhibitors in diabetes, human angiotensinogen and renin in hypertension, complement in hypersensitivity pneumonitis, estrogen receptors in breast cancer, infertility, human genome mapping, epidemiology and biostatistics, and clinical drug trials. Provides research service for area physicians. Operates National Farm Medicine Center program designed to improve the quality of life, health, and well-being of individuals and families engaged in agribusiness. Also operates Health Policy Research Institute which conducts research relevant to rural health care and legislative policy's impact on rural health care. Publications: Annual Report. E-mail Address: gundersp@mfldclin.edu. Formerly: Marshfield Clinic Foundation for Medical Research and Education; Marshfield Medical Research Foundation (1990).

★1626★ Mary Imogene Bassett Medical
Research Institute
1 Atwell Rd.
Cooperstown, NY 13326
Phone: (607)547-3045
Fax: (607)547-3061
Thomas A. Pearson, M.D., Dir.

Research Activities and Fields: Basic, clinical, and population studies in the following areas: biochemistry of serum albumin; molecular biology of autoimmune diseases; experimental pathology of cancer; immunology and antigen processing; salt sensitivity in African Americans; fecal fermentation and colon neoplasia; cardiovascular epidemiology of black and white populations; physician practice strategies in management of elevated cholesterol; rural health education; neuroendocrine regulation of breast cancer; and physiology of gut hormones. E-mail Address: tpearson@scsns.com.

★1627★ Masonic Medical Research
Laboratory
Bleecker St.
Utica, NY 13504
Phone: (315)735-2217
Fax: (315)735-5648
Dr. Charles Antzelevitch, Dir.

Research Activities and Fields: Cardiac electrophysiology as related to cardiac arrhythmias, cellular immunology, cancer, and hypertension.

★1628★ Massachusetts Health Research
Institute, Inc.
18 Tremont St.
Boston, MA 02108
Phone: (617)523-6565
Fax: (617)523-2070
Jonathan Spack, Exec.Dir.

Research Activities and Fields: Conducts research in biotechnology and public health and human services. Sponsors interorganizational demonstration projects in the areas of infant mortality, violence prevention, genetics, and intervention strategies with substance abusers. Collaborates with and assists public and private agencies and institutions in the management and administration of research projects, including collaborative and time limited start-up projects.

★ 1629 ★ **Massachusetts Institute of Technology**
Clinical Research Center
50 Ames St.
Cambridge, MA 02142
Phone: (617)253-6731
Fax: (617)253-6882
Richard J. Wurtman, M.D., Program Dir.

Research Activities and Fields: Normal human metabolism, physiology, and behavior, including studies on hormones (melatonin and sleep), fates of deuterated amino acids, behavioral and neuroendocrine effect of foods (carbohydrate, protein, and caffeine), effects of drugs on memory and other behaviors, and endocrine and metabolic effects on aging. Also studies human diseases such as obesity, Alzheimer's disease, brain injury, Parkinson's disease, seasonal depression, use of brain imaging techniques to follow metabolic events, and facilitation of smoking withdrawal by psychopharmacologic agents.

★ 1630 ★ **McGill University**
Centre for Nonlinear Dynamics in Physiology and Medicine
McIntyre Medical Sciences Bldg.
3655 Drummond St.
Montreal, PQ, Canada H3G 1Y6
Phone: (514)398-4336
Fax: (514)398-7452
Michael C. Mackey, Dir.

Research Activities and Fields: Centre focuses on understanding the origin of dynamic behavior in health and disease,focusing on cyclical hematopoiesis, neurological tremor, and cardiac arrythmias.

★ 1631 ★ **Medical College of Wisconsin**
Clinical Research Center
9200 W. Wisconsin Ave.
Milwaukee, WI 53226
Phone: (414)259-3010
Fax: (414)259-1529
Ahmed H. Kissebah, M.D., Dir.

Research Activities and Fields: Physiology and pathophysiology of disease in areas of metabolism, endocrinology, gastroenterology, kidney, central nervous system, connective tissues, hematopietic system, and bone, respiratory, and cardiovascular disorders.

★ 1632 ★ **Medical University of South Carolina**
General Clinical Research Center
171 Ashley Ave.
Charleston, SC 29425
Phone: (803)792-3256
Fax: (803)792-3260
L. Lyndon Key, Jr., M.D., Program Dir.

Research Activities and Fields: Bone and mineral metabolism, cardiology, diabetes, endo-

crinology, gastroenterology, hypertension, nutrition, obstetrics and gynecology, pharmacology, pulmonary medicine, and rheumatology and immunology. Provides medical scientists with the opportunity for clinical research in all aspects of biomedicine. **E-mail Address:** sisco@lp.musc.edu.

★ 1633 ★ **Meharry Medical College**
Clinical Research Center
1005 D.B. Todd Blvd.
PO Box 115-A
Nashville, TN 37208
Phone: (615)327-6353
Fax: (615)327-5835
Ernest A. Turner, M.D., Dir.

Research Activities and Fields: Clinical research, including pulmonary studies, AIDS, sickle cell disease, hypertension, body composition, coronary artery disease, infectious diseases, and oncology. **E-mail Address:** clinres93@ccvax.mmc.edu.

★ 1634 ★ **Methodist Hospital**
Department of Medical Research
1701 N. Senate Blvd.
PO Box 1367
Indianapolis, IN 46206
Phone: (317)929-8226
Fax: (317)929-5954
Dr. Richard Kovacs, Med. Dir. of Research

Research Activities and Fields: Basic, clinical, and applied medical and health services research. Studies include health care delivery, cost analysis, and pharmaceutical and device clinical trials. Coordinates special projects, including heart, kidney, lung, pancreas, and liver transplants; biliary and renal extracorporeal shock wave lithotripsy; and clot lysis programs.

★ 1635 ★ **Michigan State University**
Institute of International Health
West Fee Hall, B-301
East Lansing, MI 48824-1316
Phone: (517)353-8992
Fax: (517)355-1894
Evangelos A. Petropoulos, M.D., Dir.

Research Activities and Fields: Promotes, supports, and coordinates research on world health problems, including overseas health studies. Specific projects include Sudan Project, which conducts studies on tropical parasitic diseases in the Sudan; Cerebral Malaria in Children Project, which conducts studies in tropical medicine in Malawi; Medical Anthropology Program, which conducts health research projects in Asia, Africa, and Latin America on problems related to nutrition, childbirth, infant mortality, traditional health care delivery, and migrant worker health; and High Blood Pressure Research Project, which conducts collaborative studies in Zimbabwe. Conducts collaborative research program on maternal and child health and the role of midwives in Zimbabwe; conducts research and training on schistosomiasis with Egyptian scientists (USAID) and the management and prevention of cardiovascular diseases in Bulgaria (USAID); and helps develop country background information on health in Sub-Saharan Africa for the World Bank. **Publications:** Newsletter (bimonthly). **E-mail Address:** 20565iih@msu.edu.

★ 1636 ★ **Michigan State University**
Office of Medical Education Research and Development (OMERAD)
College of Human Medicine
E. Fee Hall, Rm. A-217
East Lansing, MI 48824
Phone: (517)353-7791
Fax: (517)353-8926
William A. Anderson, Ph.D., Actg.Dir.

Research Activities and Fields: Medical education evaluation and research including evaluation of innovative educational programs, measures of physician competence, health policy forums, and faculty development. Utilizes an interdisciplinary faculty representing the fields of psychology, anthropology, statistics, and education. Office capabilities include research design and analysis support, faculty development, and program evaluation. **E-mail Address:** 15718waa@msu.edu.

★ 1637 ★ **Midwest Research Institute (MRI)**
425 Volker Blvd.
Kansas City, MO 64110-2299
Phone: (816)753-7600
Fax: (816)753-8420
John C. McKelvey, Pres. and CEO

Research Activities and Fields: Conducts research, development, and engineering, activities in the major areas of health, chemistry, the environment, and technology. Specific interests in the health area are pharmaceutical development and regulatory support, preclinical toxicology, metabolism studies, integrated clinical and preclinical drug development support, phytochemicals and designer foods, pesticide product registration support, chemistry support for toxicology, biotechnology, immunoassay development, antibody production, biosensor development, electromagnetic field effects, neurobehavioral toxicology, reversal theory, and health risk behavior. In the field of chemistry, MRI focuses on analytical chemistry methods, including method development, improvement, validation, and application for programs involving immunoanalytical chemistry, exposure assessment, biological monitoring, industrial hygiene, environmental monitoring, chemical surety, site remediation, demilitarization, atmospheric chemistry, and product analysis of foods, consumer and commercial products, drinking water, and other materials. Environmental programs address environmental measurements, emission inventory development, emission factor development, modeling, water quality, waste minimization, pollution prevention, environmental control strategy development, process analysis and industry profiling, nonpoint source pollution, ambient air toxics, indoor air quality, industrial hygiene, multimedia environmental sampling and analysis, environmental impact assessment, facility assessment, environmental audits, waste processing and characterization, waste combustion, solar soil detoxification, risk analysis, regulatory support, policy analysis, cooling tower performance testing, permitting assistance, and tank and pipeline management. Technology areas include thermoelectrics, microclimate conditioning systems, industrial systems evaluation, safety engineering, engineering design, prototype development, bench-scale testing, technology testing, dental biomaterial formulation, dental polymer development, pipeline coating technology, deicing chemical evaluation, traffic engineering, economic impact assessment, financial and business analysis, economic development, strategic planning, international programs, instructional material development, training program design and presentation, technology transfer, multivariate statistical analysis, geostatistics, geographic information systems, database design and implementation, experimental design, quality assurance, and total quality management. **Publications:** Midwest Research Institute Annual Report; *Innovations.*

★ 1638 ★ **Minneapolis Medical Research Foundation**
825 S. 8th St., Ste. M-50
Minneapolis, MN 55404
Phone: (612)347-5099
William F. Keane, M.D., Pres.

Research Activities and Fields: Medicine, surgery, pediatrics, neurology, urology, renal transplant, endocrinology, nephrology, dialysis, anesthesia, hyperbaric medicine, program evaluation and outcomes research, addiction, AIDS, Alzheimer's disease, trauma, and health care policy.

★ 1639 ★ **Minnesota Public Interest Research Group**
2512 Delaware St. SE
Minneapolis, MN 55414-3432
Phone: (612)627-4035
Fax: (612)627-4050
Heather Cusick, Exec.Dir.

Research Activities and Fields: Social problems in Minnesota, including studies on environmental quality, consumer protection, occupational safety and health, energy, food and nutrition, health care, housing, and job discrimination. Also provides opportunity for student participation in research teams and in follow-up action. **Publications:** Project Reports; Handbooks; *Statewatch.*

★ 1640 ★ **Mount Sinai School of Medicine of City University of New York**
General Clinical Research Center
100th St. & 5th Ave.
Box 1027
New York, NY 10029
Phone: (212)241-6045
Fax: (212)348-5811
Dr. Robert Desnick, Dir.

Research Activities and Fields: Nature and treatment of human diseases through clinical investigation, including studies on Gaucher disease, Parkinson's disease, Fabry's disease, Alzheimer's disease, nutrition, energy expenditure, AIDS, lipid metabolism, peptide and steroid hormones, and lead poisoning. **E-mail Address:** system@vaxa.crc.mssm.edu.

★ 1641 ★ **National Public Services Research Institute**
8201 Corporate Dr., Ste. 220
Landover, MD 20785
Phone: (301)731-9891
Fax: (301)731-6649
Dr. A. James McKnight, Pres.

Research Activities and Fields: Safety and health including substance abuse prevention and treatment, alcohol consumption and traffic and water safety, driver education and licensing, motorcycle and truck safety, and safety research methods. **Publications:** Technical Reports. **E-mail Address:** npsri@iia.org.

★ 1642 ★ **Naylor Dana Institute for Disease Prevention**
American Health Foundation
Dana Rd.
Valhalla, NY 10595
Phone: (914)592-2600
Fax: (914)592-2339
Noreen T. Sweeney, Libn.

Research Activities and Fields: Medicine, science, and social science, focusing on smoking and health, nutrition, and biology and chemistry.

★ 1643 ★ **Nemours Research Programs of the Nemours Foundation**
PO Box 269
Wilmington, DE 19899
Phone: (302)651-6800
Fax: (302)651-6888
Charles R. Hartzell, Ph.D., Dir. of Research

Research Activities and Fields: Programs are composed of four research departments: the Department of Applied Science and Engineering, which applies technology to the development of communication, mobility, robotic, and therapeutic interactive devices to aid in independent living, education, and employment of disabled children; the Department of Clinical Investigation, which studies metabolic diseases, endocrinology, health services research, clinical pharmacology and pharmacodynamics, and other diseases of chidren; the Department of Medical Cell Biology, which performs interdisciplinary research on the musculoskeletal and central nervous systems, autoimmune diseases, epithelial cell biology, developmental cell biology, and cellular pharmacology, with particular emphasis on childhood diseases; and the Department of Clinical Research, which supports research in investigating, diagnosing, treating, and preventing children's diseases. Research emphasizes rehabilitation research in the U.S. Office of Education-funded centers in Augmentative Communication and in Robotics. **Formerly:** Alfred I. duPont Institute of the Nemours Foundation.

★ 1644 ★ **New England Medical Center**
General Clinical Research Center
750 Washington Ave.
Box 268
Boston, MA 02111
Phone: (617)956-5692
Fax: (617)956-4719
Dr. Aubrey E. Boyd, III, M.D., Prog.Dir.

Research Activities and Fields: Biomedicine, including endocrinology and metabolism, hematology, neurology, nutrition, oncology, immunology, and infectious disease. **Formerly:** New England Medical Center, Clinical Study Unit.

★ 1645 ★ **New York University**
General Clinical Research Center
NYU Medical Center
550 1st Ave.
New York, NY 10016
Phone: (212)263-7900
Fax: (212)263-8501
William N. Rom, M.D., Dir.

Research Activities and Fields: The unit is a hospital within a hospital that allows investigators to observe patients for extended lengths of time. Projects include studies in endocrinology and metabolism, rheumatology, immunology, genetics, hypertension, hematology, neurology, neurosurgery, respiratory medicine, and infectious diseases. Focuses on cancer, AIDS, and tuberculosis research. Maintains a nursing staff and laboratories to facilitate research.

★ 1646 ★ **Northeastern University**
Center for Medical Economics Studies
360 Huntington Ave.
Boston, MA 02115
Phone: (617)373-2884
Dr. Harold M. Goldstein, Dir.

Research Activities and Fields: Health manpower, national health insurance, unionization of health workers, computerization of medical records, and medical malpractice. **Publications:** Annotated Bibliography in Area of Health Manpower (semiannually). **Formerly:** Center for Medical Manpower Studies (1986).

★ 1647 ★ **Ohio State University**
Clinical Research Center
410 W. 10th Ave.
Columbus, OH 43210
Phone: (614)293-8749
Manuel Tzagournis, Prin. Investigator

Research Activities and Fields: Provides facilities and financial support for most inpatient and outpatient clinical investigations of the College, including studies on diabetes, heart disease, endocrine and metabolic disorders, nutrition, neuroendocrine tumors, osteoporosis, cancer, eating disorders, affective disorders and depression, and renal disease. The Center's core laboratory performs high pressure liguid chromatography assays and radioimmunoassays for 17 different peptides and hormones.

★ 1648 ★ **Ohio University**
Health Promotion and Research Division
415 Tower
Athens, OH 45701
Phone: (614)593-1217
Fax: (614)593-0555
Dr. Margaret Christensen, Dir.

Research Activities and Fields: Primary cancer prevention, cancer epidemiology, motor vehicle accident epidemiology; use of tobacco and smokeless tobacco by adolescents; effect of school health education projects on substance use, self-esteem, and adolescent stress; implementing and evaluating worksite health promotion for corporate employees; and retention of health care workers in rural health care facilities utilizing distance learning. Conducts prevalence surveys on tobacco use, cancer epidemiology and prevention. Explores management concern in Health Care Facilities and Researches Retirement Accommodations and Activities for members of the Academic and town residents.

★ 1649 ★ **Omaha Department of Veteran Affairs Medical Center**
Research and Development Service
4101 Woolworth Ave.
Omaha, NE 68105
Phone: (402)346-8800
Fax: (402)449-0604
Lynell W. Klassen, M.D., Assoc. Chief of Staff
Research Activities and Fields: Immunology, infectious disease, oncology, liver disease, diabetes, orthopedics, pulmonary disease, gastroenterology, and endocrinology. Utilizes rats, mice, guinea pigs, rabbits, and dogs as animal models.

★ 1650 ★ **Oregon Health Sciences University**
General Clinical Research Center
3181 SW Sam Jackson Park Rd., OP11
Portland, OR 97201-3098
Phone: (503)494-7593
Fax: (503)494-4324
John M. Porter, M.D., Program Dir.
Research Activities and Fields: Cardiovascular disease, collagen vascular disease and immunology, endocrinology, hematology, hypertension, metabolism, neurology, oncology, pediatric nephrology, pharmacology, psychiatry, renal disease, and rheumatology. Testing services include steroid receptor analysis, membrane receptor analysis, radioimmunoassay, and spectrophotometric analyses.

★ 1651 ★ **Pacific Health Research Institute**
Thomas Sq. Centre
846 S. Hotel St., Ste. 303
Honolulu, HI 96813
Phone: (808)524-4411
Fax: (808)524-5559
Dr. Robert A. Nordyke, Med.Dir.
Research Activities and Fields: Health services research, including breast cancer, hypertension, osteoporosis, diabetes, heart attacks, drug studies, effects of chemical exposure, and cost-effectiveness analysis. Specific studies focus on risk factors associated with breast cancer, methods of delaying or preventing postmenopausal osteoporosis, isolated systolic hypertension among the elderly, outcomes research, leprosy, interactive videodiscs, geriatrics, and prostate, lung, colorectal, and ovarian cancer screening. Participates in a statewide consortium of hospitals to address quality and cost of care. Hawaii MEDTEP (Medical Treatment Effectiveness Program) Research Center, outcomes research with a focus on minority populations. **Formerly:** Straub Medical Research Institute.

★ 1652 ★ **Pennsylvania State University**
Center for Special Populations and Health
106 Henderson Bldg.
University Park, PA 16802
Phone: (814)863-9794
Fax: (814)863-9950
Dr. Toni P. Miles, M.D., Dir.
Research Activities and Fields: Populations that have been historically underrepresented in human health research, focusing on the Black Elderly Twin Study, which identifies the contribution of genetic and environmental factors for disability in physical function. Other research interests include alcohol use and physical health in older twins, and women's health and reproductive experience in the U.S.

★ 1653 ★ **Pennsylvania State University**
Doctors Kienle Center for Humanistic Medicine
Hershey Medical Center
Hershey, PA 17033-0850
Phone: (717)531-8037
David J. Hufford, Ph.D., Dir.
Research Activities and Fields: Developing programs in humanistic medicine, including medical curriculum concerning the patients experience of care, phenomonology of care, and human diversity and medicine. **Formerly:** Center for Humanistic Medicine.

★ 1654 ★ **Queen's University at Kingston**
Social Program Evaluation Group
Kingston, ON, Canada K7L 3N6
Phone: (613)545-6256
Fax: (613)545-2556
Dr. Alan J.C. King, Dir.
Research Activities and Fields: Evaluates social programs related to business, criminal justice, education, law, rehabilitation, health promotion, and physical and health education, seniors, child welfare, and HIV/AIDS education. **E-mail Address:** warrenw@qucdn.queensu.ca.

★ 1655 ★ **Rees-Stealy Research Foundation**
2001 4th Ave.
San Diego, CA 92101
Phone: (619)235-8744
Fax: (619)234-8190
H.D. Peabody, Jr., M.D., Dir.
Research Activities and Fields: Basic cardiac research involving cardio myocyte contractility studies. Research includes the analysis of recording heart cell function, utilizing the video camera technique of living motion using electronic devices for computer transfer, heart cell preparation, and cell culture.

★ 1656 ★ **Research Institute of Palo Alto Medical Foundation**
860 Bryant St.
Palo Alto, CA 94301
Phone: (415)326-8120
Fax: (415)329-9114
Dr. Allen D. Cooper, Dir.
Research Activities and Fields: Clinical and general medical sciences, including immunology, infectious diseases, medical economics, cardiac physiology, metabolism, atherosclerosis, and cancer cell biology. **Publications:** News (quarterly). **Formerly:** Palo Alto Medical Research Foundation (1980).

★ 1657 ★ **Research Triangle Institute**
3040 Cornwallis Rd.
PO Box 12194
Research Triangle Park, NC 27709-2194
Phone: (919)541-6000
Fax: (919)541-7004
F. Thomas Wooten, Pres.
Research Activities and Fields: Research focuses on public health, medicine, environmental protection, electronic technology, and public policy. Disciplines include chemical analysis, chemical synthesis, polymer science, life sciences and toxicology, environmental sciences and engineering, physics and aerosol technology, earth sciences, policy analysis and public sector management, economics, social sciences, statistical science and survey research, computer sciences, engineering, health care and pharmaceuticals, medical devices, public health research, health effects, environmental protection, social issues, public services, digital systems and computer architecture, semiconductors, energy, and industrial processes. **Publications:** Hypotenuse (quarterly); Annual Report (January). **E-mail Address:** crm@rti.org.

★ 1658 ★ **Rockefeller University**
Clinical Research Center
Rockefeller Univ. Hospital
1230 York Ave.
New York, NY 10021
Phone: (212)327-8000
Richard Galbraith, M.D., Med.Dir.
Research Activities and Fields: Chronic immune disorders, dermatology, gastrointestinal motility, lipid metabolism, metabolic disorders, medical biochemistry, cystic fibrostic, AIDS, tuberculosis, neurological disorders, and obesity and nutrition. **E-mail Address:** galbrth@rockvax.rockefeller.edu.

★ 1659 ★ **Rutgers University**
Institute for Health, Health Care Policy, and Aging Research
30 College Ave.
New Brunswick, NJ 08903
Phone: (908)932-8413
Fax: (908)982-6872
Dr. David Mechanic, Dir.
Research Activities and Fields: Research divisions include and focus on the following activities: 1) the Division of Health studies the impact of stress on emotional states and health and risk behaviors and how these latter factors influence the immune system and morbidity and mortality, studies how stress and emotional states affect symptom appraisal and the decision to use health care, and sponsors a Center for Promoting Health Among Elderly Black Americans; 2) the Division of Health Care Policy analyzes the health and cost outcomes of the current allocation of health and resources, with emphasis on preventive care and children's health; 3) the Division on Aging measures income inequality, investigates the role of instrumental and social support as buffers against stress, and identifies predictors of chronic pain and poor self-assessments of health among the elderly; 4) the AIDS Policy Research Group measures health care utilization and cost among patients with HIV illness; 5) the Center for Research on the Organization and Financing of Care for the Severely Mentally Ill provides a structure for interdisciplinary research and training on mental health services and policy as they pertain to persons with severe and persistent mental illness and examines the human services and family support systems that shape outcomes for patients and their families. Multi-investigator research teams work in the areas of successful community living, organization and

financing incentives in treatment programs, service systems integration, and managed care and rationing. **Formerly:** Aging Institute (1985).

★ 1660 ★ **St. Francis Research Institute, Inc.**
1100 N. St. Francis
Wichita, KS 67214
Phone: (316)291-4900
Fax: (316)291-7704
Dr. James L. Gumnick, Pres.

Research Activities and Fields: Psychiatry; phase I, II, and III clinical drug studies; orthopedic research; biomedical device and materials research and development; heart, lung, and vascular drug and device development and evaluation; technology transfer and product development; hospital operations research; and pharmaco economic research.

★ 1661 ★ **Sansum Medical Research Foundation**
2219 Bath St.
Santa Barbara, CA 93105
Phone: (805)682-7638
Fax: (805)682-3332
Charles M. Peterson, M.D., Dir. of Research

Research Activities and Fields: Cancer, obesity, diabetes mellitus, vascular disease, immunology, AIDs, coagulation, alcoholism, muscle disease, chemical metabolism, and physiology. **Publications:** *The Quest* (quarterly). **Formerly:** Sansum Clinic Research Foundation (1975).

★ 1662 ★ **Scripps Research Institute**
10666 N. Torrey Pines Rd.
La Jolla, CA 92037
Phone: (619)554-8265
Fax: (619)554-9899
Richard A. Lerner, M.D., Pres.

Research Activities and Fields: Immunology and immunopathology, biochemistry, cell biology, molecular biology, structural biology, oncology, autoimmune diseases, cardiopulmonary diseases, hematology, diabetes and endocrinology, virology, preclinical neuroscience, neuropharmacology, vascular biology, synthetic bioorganic chemistry, biocatalysis and protein design, plant biology, and synthetic and vaccine development. **Publications:** Scientific Report. **Formerly:** Research Institute of Scripps Clinic.

★ 1663 ★ **Sigfried and Janet Weis Center for Research**
Geisinger Clinic 26-01
Danville, PA 17822
Phone: (717)271-6659
Fax: (717)271-6701
Howard E. Morgan, M.D., Senior V.Pres. for Research

Research Activities and Fields: Cardiovascular disease and developmental biology at the cellular and molecular biology level; clinical research in areas of cancer and cardiovascular disease; and investigational drug studies. **Publications:** *Geisinger* (quarterly magazine of the Geisinger system). **Formerly:** Institute for Medical Education and Research (1981).

★ 1664 ★ **Southern Research Institute**
PO Box 55305
Birmingham, AL 35255
Phone: (205)581-2000
Fax: (205)581-2726
John W. Rouse, Pres.

Research Activities and Fields: Chemistry, biochemistry, and chemotherapy of cancer, AIDS, and other viral diseases, including studies on bacteriological, tissue culture, and small animal screening; new treatment concepts; pharmacology; toxicology and carcinogenesis; engineering and physics; metallurgy, including physical and process metallurgy of ferrous, nonferrous, and new refractory metals; physical and thermal properties of nonmetallic and brittle materials in extreme conditions; industrial chemistry and technology, including plastics and synthetic textiles; product and process development; air toxics measurements, hot gas filtration, infrared radiation spectroscopic measurements, and particulate control applications; microencapsulation; controlled release of drugs and agrichemicals; development of biomaterials and biomedical devices; development and application of analytical chemistry methods; and protein crystallography. **Publications:** Annual Report.

★ 1665 ★ **SRI International**
333 Ravenswood Ave.
Menlo Park, CA 94025-3493
Phone: (415)326-6200
Fax: (415)326-5512
Dr. William Sommers, Pres., CEO

Research Activities and Fields: Conducts research in more than 100 disciplines in the physical and life sciences, engineering, industrial management, business, social sciences, and public policy. Engages in 2,000 projects per year involving scientists, engineers, industry experts, and management consultants from hundreds of fields. Areas of research and consulting include economics, energy, engineering and development, environment, health, industry consulting, information sciences, management consulting, public policy, national security, and physical, life, and social sciences. **Publications:** Annual Report. **Formerly:** Stanford Research Institute (SRI) (1977).

★ 1666 ★ **Stanford University General Clinical Research Center**
Stanford Hospital, Rm. H136
Rte. 6
Stanford, CA 94305
Phone: (415)723-7496
Fax: (415)725-6698
Branimir I. Sikic, M.D., Program Dir.

Research Activities and Fields: Clinical research on nutrition, diabetes, growth hormone deficiencies and growth hormone therapies, oncology, monoclonal antibodies, lupus nephritis, epidermolysis bullosa, pharmokinetics of drugs, interferon, infectious diseases, human immunodeficiency virus (HIV), and sleep disorders; physiological and pathophysiological adaptations of prematurely born infants, critically ill term infants, and normal infants. Also focuses on computer modelling of pressure-limited mechanical ventilation, infant heme catabolism, modulation of circadian rhythmicity in preterm

infants, treatment of perinatal infectious diseases such as neonatal herpes simplex infection and AIDS, markers of basement membrane disruption, late pulmonary sequelae of BPD, treatment of newborn skin, cystic fibrosis, and extra corporeal membrane oxygenation (ECMO).

★ 1667 ★ **State University of New York Health Science Center at Brooklyn General Clinical Research Center**
Box 123
Brooklyn, NY 11203
Phone: (718)270-1542
Harold E. Lebovitz, M.D., Program Dir.

Research Activities and Fields: Diabetes, endocrinology, immunology and metabolism, nephrology, and carcinoid syndrome.

★ 1668 ★ **State University of New York Health Science Center at Syracuse Clinical Research Center**
Univ. Hospital
750 E. Adams St., Rm. 8330
Syracuse, NY 13210
Phone: (315)464-9000
Arnold M. Moses, M.D., Program Dir.

Research Activities and Fields: Endocrinology, gastroenterology, metabolism, nephrology, oncology, and nutrition.

★ 1669 ★ **Temple University General Clinical Research Center**
3401 N. Broad St.
Philadelphia, PA 19140
Phone: (215)221-3088
Fax: (215)221-1560
Guenther Boden, M.D., Program Dir.

Research Activities and Fields: Gastroenterology, cardiology, metabolism, nephrology, neurology, AIDS, pulmonary research, and cystic fibrosis.

★ 1670 ★ **Thomas Jefferson University Center for Research in Medical Education and Health Care**
Jefferson Medical College
1025 Walnut St., Rm. 119 College
Philadelphia, PA 19107-5083
Phone: (215)955-8907
Fax: (215)923-6939
Joseph S. Gonnella, M.D., Dir.

Research Activities and Fields: Medical education process and factors affecting the quality of cost of health care. Medical education research focuses on the following areas: 1) measurement of physician competence, 2) long-term follow-up study of graduates, 3) program evaluation, 4) specialty choice, and 5) refinement of evaluation methods. Health services research focuses on the concept and system of disease staging for classification of severity of illness, AIDS patients, and cost and quality of care. **Publications:** *ABSTRACTS: Longitudinal Study of Medical Students and Graduates*; Annual Report. **E-mail Address:** louisd@jefflin.tju.edu. **Formerly:** Succeeded Jefferson's Office of Medical Education established in 1969.

★1671★ Totts Gap Medical Research Laboratories, Inc.
RD 1, Box 1120G
Bangor, PA 18013
Phone: (215)588-0572
Fax: (215)588-8452
Stewart Wolf, M.D., Dir.

Research Activities and Fields: Neural regulation of visceral function, emphasizing current focus on the cardiovascular system. Specific projects involve the study of the mechanisms of cardiac arrhythmia and sudden death and other aspects of neurocardiology. **Formerly:** Stewart Wolf Medical Research Foundation.

★1672★ U.S. Congress
Office of Technology Assessment
Health, Education, and Environment Division
600 Pennsylvania Ave. SE, 5th Fl.
Washington, DC 20003
Phone: (202)224-3695
Fax: (202)228-6218
Clyde Behney, Director

Research Activities and Fields: Division's activities include data collection and analysis on major public policy issues in the areas of health, biology, agriculture, food science, and biomedicine. Specific interests include: 1) food and renewable resources, including control of non-indigenous species in the U.S., agricultural biotechnology, control of coca crops in producing areas of the hemisphere, and forest service planning; 2) biological applications, including national screening programs for cystic fibrosis, research on risk assessment of chemical carcinogens, root causes of substance abuse, and new developments in neuroscience; and 3) health, including monitoring of mandated veterans studies, drug labelling in developing countries, cost of pharmaceutical R&D, federal response to AIDS (congressional issues), osteoporosis, evaluation of the Oregon Medicaid proposal, defensive medicine, health insurance, and home drug infusion therapy.

★1673★ U.S. Department of Defense
Wilford Hall USAF Medical Center
Clinical Investigation Facility
ATTN: WHMC/RD
1255 Wilford Hall Loop
Lackland Air Force Base, TX 78236-5319
Phone: (512)670-7141
Col. John H. Cissik, Ph.D., Director

Research Activities and Fields: Medical research includes biological, behavioral, and psychological studies. Investigative efforts have contributed to improved disease prevention, diagnosis, and treatment modalities, including: advances in the application of hyperbaric oxygen therapy in a variety of conditions; better biochemical characterization of disease leading to enhanced understanding of underlying mechanisms in a spectrum of non-cancer diseases; improved procedures for cancer chemo-, immuno-, radiotherapy, and surgical techniques; pioneer development of extra-corporeal membrane oxygenation, high frequency ventilation, and organ transplantation techniques; and selection of improved dental procedures through critical evaluation of safety and effectiveness.

★1674★ U.S. Department of Energy
Brookhaven National Laboratory
Medical Department
Bldg. 490
Upton, NY 11973-5000
Phone: (516)282-3568
Fax: (516)282-3100
Darrel Joel, Contact

Research Activities and Fields: The Medical Department carries out basic and applied research aimed at improving health and prevent disease. Studies range from the cellular function of unusual biochemicals to nuclear medicine and the development of radiopharmaceuticals to aid in the diagnosis of disease. Principal areas of research interest include cancer, respiratory diseases, hematological disorders, bone diseases, and radiation effects.

★1675★ U.S. Department of Health and Human Services
National Institute of Child Health and Human Development
Intramural Research Division
NIH Bldg. 31
9000 Rockville Pike
Bethesda, MD 20892
Phone: (301)496-2133
Fax: (301)402-0105
Dr. Arthur S. Levine, Scientific Director

Research Activities and Fields: Plans and conducts laboratory and clinical research at the National Institutes of Health in Bethesda. The Division is broadly concerned with the biological and neurobiological, medical, and behavioral aspects of normal and abnormal human development. In addition to five major clinical research and training programs in the areas of genetics, perinatology, and endocrinology, a diversity of developmental models are under study in fundamental research laboratories drawing upon observations in bacteria, Drosophila, yeasts, viruses, mollusks, frogs, rodents, and non-human primates. Disciplines employed in these studies include biochemistry, virology, molecular biology, immunology, pharmacology, genetics, cell and neuronal biology, biophysics, mathematical and theoretical biology, reproductive physiology, and developmental psychology. **Publications:** Annual Report (available on request).

★1676★ U.S. Department of Health and Human Services
National Institute of General Medical Sciences
Westwood Bldg., Rm. 922
Bethesda, MD 20892
Phone: (301)594-7817
Fax: (301)594-7701
Dr. Marvin Cassman, Acting Director

Research Activities and Fields: Supports non-disease-targeted research and research training in the basic biomedical sciences; maintains no intramural (in-house) research. Program focuses on six major areas: four (Biophysics and Physiological Sciences, Cellular and Molecular Basis of Disease, Genetics, and Pharmacology and Biorelated Chemistry areas) fund grants for research projects and research training; two (Minority Access to Research Careers (MARC) and Minority Biomedical Research Support

(MBRS) areas) promote minority individuals engaged in biomedical research and teaching by funding research (MBRS) and training (MARC) at colleges and universities with substantial minority enrollments. The Institute fosters multidisciplinary approaches to research and employs the full range of support mechanisms--research project grants, program-project grants, research center grants, research career development awards, awards to new investigators, and institutional and individual fellowships.

★1677★ U.S. Department of Health and Human Services
National Institutes of Health
9000 Rockville Pike
Bethesda, MD 20892
Phone: (301)496-2433
Harold Varmus, Director

Research Activities and Fields: NIH is the principal medical research arm of the federal government, with a mission to improve the health of the nation by increasing understanding of the processes underlying human health and by acquiring new knowledge to help prevent, detect, diagnose, and treat disease. NIH accomplishes this mission by: 1) supporting research in universities, medical schools, hospitals, and research institutions in this country and abroad; 2) conducting research in its own laboratories and clinics; 3) supporting training for promising young researchers; 4) helping to develop and maintain research resources; 5) identifying research findings that can be applied to the care of patients and helping to transfer such advances to the health care system; 6) promoting effective ways to communicate biomedical information to scientists, health practitioners, and the public; and 7) developing and recommending policies related to the conduct and support of biomedical research. To carry out these functions, NIH is organized into 13 research Institutes (National Cancer Institute; National Eye Institute; National Heart, Lung and Blood Institute; National Institute on Aging; National Institute of Allergy and Infectious Diseases; National Institute of Arthritis and Musculoskeletal and Skin Diseases; National Institute of Child Health and Human Development; National Institute on Deafness and Other Communicative Disorders; National Institute of Dental Research; National Institute of Diabetes and Digestive and Kidney Diseases; National Institute of Environmental Health Sciences; National Institute of General Medical Sciences; National Institute of Neurological Disorders and Stroke; two divisions (Computer Research and Technology, and Research Grants); National Center for Nursing Research; the Warren Grant Magnuson Clinical Center; the John E. Fogarty International Center for Advanced Study in the Health Sciences; the National Center for Research Resources; and the National Library of Medicine.

★1678★ U.S. Department of Health and Human Services
National Institutes of Health
Fogarty International Center for Advanced Study in the Health Sciences

NIH Bldg. 31-B2C02
9000 Rockville Pike
Bethesda, MD 20892
Phone: (301)496-2075
Dr. Philip E. Schambra, Director

Research Activities and Fields: Center's primary mission is to promote international cooperation in biomedical and behavioral research through advanced studies, conferences and seminars, and fellowship and exchange programs.

**★ 1679 ★   U.S. Department of Health and
    Human Services**
National Institutes of Health
Warren Grant Magnuson Clinical Center
NIH Bldg. 10
9000 Rockville Pike
Bethesda, MD 20892
Phone: (301)496-2563
Fax: (301)402-2984

Research Activities and Fields: The Clinical Center is designed to place patient care facilities close to research laboratories to promote the quick transfer of new findings of basic and clinical scientists to the treatment of patients. The Center provides high-quality patient care necessary for intramural clinical research conducted at the National Institutes of Health; performs research on methods and systems involved in patient care and study; disseminates information to professionals and to the public relevant to clinical investigation; develops and maintains training programs in the techniques and ethics of biomedical and clinical research; and interacts with scientists and physicians, nationally and internationally, on such mutual problems of clinical research as policy, education, ethics, and priorities. To be considered for admission to the Clinical Center, patients must be referred by their private physician and they can be admitted only if their medical condition meets the precise requirements of a specific research protocol.

**★ 1680 ★   University of Alabama at
    Birmingham**
General Clinical Research Center
3 W. Jefferson Tower
UAB Sta.
Birmingham, AL 35294-6909
Phone: (205)934-4852
John J. Curtis, M.D., Program Dir.

Research Activities and Fields: Patient care and laboratory support of clinical investigations for all departments and divisions of the Medical Center, including the Schools of Medicine and Dentistry. Studies are conducted on metabolism, cardiology, hematology, rheumatology, infectious diseases, virology, immunology, pulmonary medicine, renal medicine, gastroenterology, oncology, neurosurgery, AIDS, and the mechanisms of disease. **Formerly:** Clinical Research Center.

**★ 1681 ★   University of Alaska Anchorage
Institute for Circumpolar Health Studies
(ICHS)**
3211 Providence Dr.
Anchorage, AK 99508
Phone: (907)786-4020
Fax: (907)786-4019
Dr. John M. Booker, Dir.

Research Activities and Fields: Health care issues in Alaska and the Circumpolar North, including dentistry, trauma care, nursing, orthopedics, emergency medical service, Fetal Alcohol Syndrome, Native health issues, mental health, radiology, and anesthesiology. **E-mail Address:** siberia@orion.alaska.edu.

**★ 1682 ★   University of Alaska Fairbanks
Institute of Arctic Biology**
Fairbanks, AK 99775
Phone: (907)474-7648
Fax: (907)474-6967
Dr. Robert G. White, Dir.

Research Activities and Fields: Animal physiology, plant physiology, biochemistry, molecular biology, population genetics, microbiology, ecosystem ecology, human biology and health, freshwater ecology, and veterinary science. Conducts research on interrelations of plants and animals (including humans) with their environment, with particular reference to specializations that allow them to survive in arctic or boreal habitats. Animal disease studies focus on rabies, brucellosis, the warble fly, and medical and surgical care of large animals. Health-related studies focus on Alzheimer's, seasonal affective disorders, and other neurological disorders. Molecular biological studies focus on: analysis of the phylogenetics of diverse species, interrelationships of indigenous human populations, cold adaptation, and the control over non-shivering thermogenesis, developpnent of new tests for Paralytic Shellfish Poisoning, and analysis of the evolutionary origins of different developmental modes. Paleobiological studies include the **E-mail Address:** fyiabdo@aurora.alaska.edu.

**★ 1683 ★   University of Arizona
Native American Research and Training
Center**
1642 E. Helen
Tucson, AZ 85719
Phone: (520)621-5075
Fax: (520)621-9802
Jennie R. Joe, Ph.D., Dir.

Research Activities and Fields: Health and rehabilitation of disabled and chronically ill Native Americans. Core areas include the following: 1) needs assessment, service delivery, and evaluation as determined by or in cooperation with the disabled; 2) empowerment that is sensitive to Indian values and needs; and 3) vocational rehabilitation, including preventive, restorative, and occupational processes for the disabled that lead to self-sufficiency. Also studies the impact of government policy on the delivery of health care. Promotes self determination and parity among Native Americans in health and rehabilitation. Serves as a national resource for all North American tribes and Alaska natives.

**★ 1684 ★   University of British Columbia
Jack Bell Research Centre**
Vancouver General Hospital
2660 Oak St.
Vancouver, BC, Canada V6H 3Z6
Phone: (604)875-4810
Fax: (604)875-4497
Dr. Jim McKeown, Dir.

Research Activities and Fields: Steroid hormone receptors, cancer chemotherapy, microsurgical procedures for repairing the bladder and uretha after an injury, and lung hazards in the work place and their effects on workers. Research also focuses on improving patient care, determining causes and treatments of diseases, detecting cancer at an early stage, and improving facilities for specialized surgery.

**★ 1685 ★   University of California, Los
    Angeles**
Center for the Study of Women
276 Kinsey Hall
405 Hilgard Ave.
Los Angeles, CA 90024-1504
Phone: (310)825-0590
Fax: (310)206-7700
Kathryn Norberg, Dir.

Research Activities and Fields: Women's studies in areas such as women and health, including prenatal care and birth outcomes and health and women's work; violence involving women, including rape, spouse abuse, child abuse, and victimization; women in history and literature; psychology of sex differences; women and science; women and the law; women and the arts; women of color; women and the media; women in the professions; and women in education, including women in higher education and developing and implementing an inclusive, multicultural curriculum. **Publications:** Newsletter (quarterly); Calendar of Events (annually); Conference Proceedings; Working Papers. **E-mail Address:** ikj5mkn@mvs.oac.ucla.edu.

**★ 1686 ★   University of California, Los
    Angeles**
General Clinical Research Center
Center for Health Sciences
27-066CHS
10833 LC Conte Ave.
Los Angeles, CA 90024
Phone: (310)825-7117
Fax: (310)206-9440
Isidro B. Salusky, M.D., Program Dir.

Research Activities and Fields: Cardiovascular system, dermatology, endocrinology and metabolism, gastroenterology, genetic disease, gynecology, hematology, immunology and rheumatology, nephrology, neurology, oncology, and pulmonary physiology.

**★ 1687 ★   University of California, Los
    Angeles**
**Laboratory of Biomedical and
    Environmental Sciences**
900 Veteran Ave.
Los Angeles, CA 90024-1786
Phone: (213)825-8741
Gabriella Grey, Dir.

Research Activities and Fields: Biochemistry, nuclear medicine, environmental science, and cell biology. **Publications:** Annual Report.

★ 1688 ★ University of California, San Diego
General Clinical Research Center
UCSD Medical Center, 8203
200 W. Arbor Dr.
San Diego, CA 92103-8203
Phone: (619)543-6180
Fax: (619)543-5536
Michael G. Ziegler, M.D., Dir.

Research Activities and Fields: Cardiovascular disease, endocrinology, gastroenterology, genetic disease, immunology, infectious disease, metabolism, neurological disease, oncology, pulmonary medicine, renal disease, reproductive endocrinology, rheumatology, hypertension, and gene therapy. **E-mail Address:** mziegler@ucsd.edu.

★ 1689 ★ University of California, San Francisco
General Clinical Research Center
San Francisco General Hospital
Box 1352
San Francisco, CA 94143
Phone: (415)206-8239
Fax: (415)826-3381
Morris Schambelan, M.D., Dir.

Research Activities and Fields: Human disorders, including interdisciplinary clinical studies of aldosterone and renin activity in hypertension and chronic renal insufficiency. Investigates the effect of diet in patients with lipid disorders. Explores the regulation of potassium metabolism by renal and adrenal hormones, the nature and extent of adrenal defects in AIDS, and the mechanisms of wasting in AIDS. Examines drug interactions and the effects of nicotine on cardiovascular response. Coordinates effectiveness of new treatment modalities in AIDS and HIV patients. **Formerly:** Clinical Study Center.

★ 1690 ★ University of California, San Francisco
General Clinical Research Center—Adults
1202 Moffitt Hospital
San Francisco, CA 94143-0126
Phone: (415)476-1241
Fax: (415)476-0986
R. Curtis Morris, Jr., M.D., Program Dir.

Research Activities and Fields: Cardiovascular disease, hypertension, clinical pharmacology, diabetes mellitus, vitamin D metabolism, genetic disease, lipid metabolism, nephrology, nutrition, oncology, acid-base physiology, dermatology, infectious diseases, reproductive endocrinology, AIDS, potassium metabolism, osteoporosis, recombinant human hemoglobin, liver disease, cardiac function and smoking, and interferon gamma, aging, psychopharmacology, hereditary fructose intolerance, gene theraphy, and wound healing. **E-mail Address:** tobin@gcrc.uscf.edu.

★ 1691 ★ University of Chicago
General Clinical Research Center
5841 S. Maryland Ave.
MC 1027
Chicago, IL 60637
Phone: (312)702-6980
Fax: (312)702-6952
Murray J. Favus, Actg.Prog.Dir.

Research Activities and Fields: Endocrinology, including insulin metabolism in health and disease, evaluation and treatment of hormonal disorders of growth and puberty, and polycystic ovary syndrome; psychiatry, including substance abuse; nutrition in health, obesity, and disease states; pharmacology; characterization of lipid production and treatment of idiopathic hyperlipidemias; oncological research chemotherapies in the treatment of malignancies; investigations into human circadian rhythms; and genetics of diabetes, osteoporosis, and asthma. **E-mail Address:** vwald@medicine.bsd.uchicago.edu.

★ 1692 ★ University of Chicago
Morris Fishbein Center for the History of Science and Medicine
1126 E. 59th St.
Chicago, IL 60637
Phone: (312)702-8391
Fax: (312)702-7550
Robert Richards, Dir.

Research Activities and Fields: History of science and medicine with emphasis on ancient and early modern science and medicine, history of biology and evolutionary theory, history of astronomy and physics, history of mathematics and statistics, history of chemistry, and history of the human sciences.

★ 1693 ★ University of Cincinnati
Cincinnati Medical Heritage Center
121 Wherry Hall
Eden & Bethesda Aves.
Cincinnati, OH 45267-0574
Phone: (513)558-5120
Fax: (513)558-0412
Billie Broaddus, Dir.

Research Activities and Fields: Center focuses on the history of medicine and pharmacy. **E-mail Address:** billie.broaddus@uc.edu.

★ 1694 ★ University of Colorado
General Clinical Research Center—Adults
Health Sciences Center
4200 E. 9th Ave., B-141
Denver, CO 80262
Phone: (303)270-8383
Fax: (303)270-5610
Robert H. Eckel, M.D., Program Dir.

Research Activities and Fields: Cardiovascular disease, connective tissue disease, dermatology, endocrinology, gastroenterology, hematology, immunology, metabolism, nephrology, neurology, oncology, psychiatry, and pulmonary disease.

★ 1695 ★ University of Florida
General Clinical Research Center
JHMHC, Box J-322
Gainesville, FL 32610
Phone: (904)395-0032
Fax: (904)338-9843
Peter W. Stacpoole, M.D., Program Dir.

Research Activities and Fields: Allergy, immunology, rheumatology, cardiology, endocrinology, gastroenterology, hematology, metabolism, obstetrics and gynecology, oncology, and surgery.

★ 1696 ★ University of Florida
Human Development Center
1600 SW Archer Rd., Rm. H102
PO Box 100014
Gainesville, FL 32610-0014
Phone: (904)392-2761
Fax: (904)392-9395
Dr. David R. Challoner, V.Pres. Health Affairs

Research Activities and Fields: Human development, with particular interest in emotional and neurological disease, cardiac hematology, and immunology.

★ 1697 ★ University of Illinois
Health Systems Research
College of Medicine
1601 Parkview Ave.
Rockford, IL 61107
Phone: (815)395-5639
Fax: (815)395-5687
Joel B. Cowen, Asst. Dean

Research Activities and Fields: Community health, including primary care, public health, geriatrics, substance abuse, evaluation of delivery of health services, survey research, focus groups, demographic studies, health care planning, program evaluation, and feasibility studies. **E-mail Address:** joelc@uic.edu. **Formerly:** Office of Community Health Research (1982); Health Services Research.

★ 1698 ★ University of Illinois at Chicago
Department of Medical Education
M/C 591
808 S. Wood St.
Chicago, IL 60612
Phone: (312)996-3590
Fax: (312)413-2048
Prof. Leslie J. Sandlow, M.D., Interim Head

Research Activities and Fields: Issues related to the development, implementation, and evaluation of undergraduate, graduate, and continuing education programs in the health professions, including curriculum, clinical education and evaluation, medical humanities and ethics, processes of innovation in health professions education, clinical decision-making and medical informatics, and community based health programs. Competence Assessment unit staffs a Clinical Performance Center and investigates new techniques of student and program evaluations. **Publications:** Newsletter; Annual Report. **Formerly:** Office of Research in Medical Education, Center for Educational Development.

★ 1699 ★ University of Iowa
Center for International Rural and Environmental Health (CIREH)
350 International Center
Iowa City, IA 52242
Phone: (319)335-1443
Fax: (319)335-0280
Dr. Burton Kross, Dir.

Research Activities and Fields: International rural and environmental health, including occupational exposures to pesticides, groundwater and surface water, contamination by agrichemicals, impact of occupational and social conditions on health, agricultural respiratory disease, medical and environmental health surveillance, air pollution assessment and health effects, birth defects and adverse reproductive outcomes, women's health and development, injury epidemiology and prevention, AIDS and other infectious disease epidemiology, environmental and health assessment of contaminated grain, health care delivery models and systems and location of medical and dental services in rural areas, rural aging epidemiology and care models, and the history of medicine science and public health.

★ 1700 ★ University of Manitoba
St. Boniface General Hospital Research
    Center
351 Tache Ave.
Winnipeg, MB, Canada R2H 2A6
Phone: (204)235-3206
Fax: (204)231-1918
Harry Schultz, Dir.

Research Activities and Fields: Cardiovascular sciences, magnetic resonance imaging, and degenerative disorders associated with aging, including surgical research, sleep apnea, nursing, microbiology/infectious diseases, psychiatry, epidemiology, anaesthesia, nephrology, health care economics, and pharmaceutics.

★ 1701 ★ University of Michigan
Center for Human Growth and
    Development
300 N. Ingalls Bldg., 10th Level
Ann Arbor, MI 48109-0406
Phone: (313)764-2443
Fax: (313)936-9288
Dr. Betsy Lozoff, Dir.

Research Activities and Fields: Human growth and development through childhood and adolescence, including interdisciplinary studies on normal and abnormal behavioral, physical, and mental development, focusing especially on the challenges to children who grow up in adverse conditions. Publications: Biennial Report; Craniofacial Growth Monograph Series (annually). E-mail Address: kathleen.restrick@um.cc.umich.edu.

★ 1702 ★ University of Michigan
Center for Population Planning
School of Public Health
Ann Arbor, MI 48109
Phone: (313)764-7516
Fax: (313)936-8199
Arnold S. Monto, M.D., Dir.

Research Activities and Fields: Population planning and international health, including policy-related research, particularly in conjunction with institutions of developing nations. Collaborates with international agencies and national governments in their efforts to implement health programs and to limit population growth through development as well as through more direct interventions such as family planning programs.

★ 1703 ★ University of Michigan
General Clinical Research Center
Univ. Hospital
A7119 Box 0108
Ann Arbor, MI 48109-0108
Phone: (313)936-8080
Dr. Paul B. Watkins, Dir.

Research Activities and Fields: Conducts multicategorical research program geared to re-

search on humans in support of clinical studies at department or subspecialty sectional level throughout the Medical School and the Hospital. E-mail Address: paul.watkins@med.umich.edu. Formerly: Clinical Research Center.

★ 1704 ★ University of Michigan
Office of Educational Resources and
    Research
G1111 Towsley Center
Box 0201
Ann Arbor, MI 48109-0201
Phone: (313)763-1153
Fax: (313)936-1641
Dr. Wayne K. Davis, Dir.

Research Activities and Fields: Medical education research and behavioral sciences applied to health education and health care. Disseminates medical information and evaluates educational effectiveness and instrument design. E-mail Address: wayne.davis@med.umich.edu.

★ 1705 ★ University of Minnesota
Center to Study Human-Animal
    Relationships and Environments
    (CENSHARE)
284 McNeal Hall
St. Paul, MN 55108
Phone: (612)625-5741
Dr. Geraldine Gage, Dir.

Research Activities and Fields: Human-animal relationships and environments and their effects on health, quality of life, and economics. Publications: CENSHARE Reports; Bulletins; The Pet Connection.

★ 1706 ★ University of Minnesota
Clinical Research Center
Mayo Memorial Bldg., Box 504
Minneapolis, MN 55455
Phone: (612)626-1960
Dr. R. Paul Robertson, Prog.Dir.

Research Activities and Fields: Human disease, including normal and abnormal physiology and biochemistry in the human being, AIDS, cystic fibrosis, organ transplantation, human growth, carbohydrate metabolism, and a broad range of other medical areas. Provides opportunities for interdepartmental collaboration between surgery, and medicine in relation to pancreas and isbet transplantation.

★ 1707 ★ University of Missouri—Columbia
John M. Dalton Cardiovascular Research
    Center
Research Park
Columbia, MO 65211
Phone: (314)882-7586
Fax: (314)884-4232
Edward H. Blaine, Ph.D., Dir.

Research Activities and Fields: Multidisciplinary research in health science and related areas, emphasizing cardiovascular studies. Formerly: John M. Dalton Research Center (1993).

★ 1708 ★ University of Montreal
Montreal Research Centre
Hospital du Sacre-Coeur

5400, boulevard Gouin Ouest
Montreal, PQ, Canada H4J 1C5
Phone: (514)338-2172
Fax: (514)338-2694
Reginald Nadeau, Dir.

Research Activities and Fields: Biomedical modelling, pharmacology, and clinical studies of cardiac arrhythmias, with the aim of describing the spatial distribution of cardiac arrhythmias, their relationship to the nervous system, and their treatment by pharmacologic and noninvasive surgical methods. Centre also studies occupational respiratory diseases, biology of asthma, sleep disorders and neuropsychobiology, and molecular genetics of kidney diseases.

★ 1709 ★ University of Montreal
Montreal Research Centre, Hotel-Dieu
Pavillon Marie-de-la-Ferre, 2e etage
3850, rue Saint-Urbain
Montreal, PQ, Canada H2W 1T8
Phone: (514)843-2700
Fax: (514)843-2715
Dr. Pavel Hamet, Dir.

Research Activities and Fields: Cardiovascular diseases and hypertension, AIDS, cancer, diabetes and nutrition, pulmonary dieases and anesthesia, major burns, and gene therapy, including cardiovascular biochemistry, cellular biology of hypertension, moleculer biology of growth, experimental surgery, oncology surgery, molecular targetting, metabolism and diabetes, respiratory electrophysiology, molecular endocrinology, epidemiology, nuclear medicine, neurobiology, nutrition and cancer, oncology, molecular oncopathology, molecular medicine, clinical pharmacology, pharmacoepidemiology and pharmacoeconomy, respiratory physiology, physiopathology of burns and related aftereffects, pain, and microbiology. E-mail Address: hamethdm@ere.umontreal.ca.

★ 1710 ★ University of Montreal
Notre-Dame Hospital Research Centre
Pavillion Mailloux, 5e etage
1560, rue Sherbrooke Est
Montreal, PQ, Canada H2L 4M1
Phone: (514)876-6670
Fax: (514)876-6630
Eugenio Rasio, Dir.

Research Activities and Fields: Oncology, neurological sciences, endocrinology and nephrology, rheumatology, tissue transplantion and regeneration, and immunology. Publications: 150 per year.

★ 1711 ★ University of New Mexico
General Clinical Research Center
2211 Lomas Blvd. NE
5 E. Wing, UNMH
Albuquerque, NM 87106
Phone: (505)843-2366
Fax: (505)272-0266
Katherine M. Legoza, Prog. Mgr.

Research Activities and Fields: Diabetes, renal diseases, arthritis, premature infants, asthma, depression, hypertension, and pituitary tumors. Provides inpatient, outpatient, and neonatal facilities (including laboratory, dietary, and nursing support) in support of clinical research.

★1712★ **University of New Mexico**
Institute of Public Law
1117 Stanford NE
Albuquerque, NM 87131
Phone: (505)277-5006
Fax: (505)277-7064
Paul S. Nathanson, Dir.

Research Activities and Fields: IPL conducts research on all areas of public law and assists government officials and others in their policy-making roles. Prepares rules, regulations, legal manuals, issue papers, opinions, and proposed legislation on topics ranging from narrow legal questions to broad policy issues. Develops methods to convey occupant protection methods to culturally distinct groups in New Mexico. Prepares curriculum materials for use in secondary and higher education in New Mexico regarding issues affecting the aging population. Drafts regulations for topics such as procedures for the rate cases of small water utilities, rural electric cooperatives, and water and sanitation districts; medical malpractice reform; telecommunications; University regulations governing student grievances, discrimination allegations, and sexual harassment complaints; and revisions of the New Mexico Criminal Code. IPL also conducts research on DWI and traffic related issues; wildlife laws, legislation, regulations, and case law affecting the field; the availability and affordability of pollution liability insurance for underground storage tanks; and the feasibility of and design of a state-sponsored insurance program for owners and operators of petroleum underground storage tanks. IPL recently developed a program of town meetings to create intergenerational dialogue about public policy issues involving high school students and community elders. Special emphasis is placed on intergenerational policy questions, such as allocation of health care, social security, and fam ily and government responsiblity with regard to the elderly. **Publications:** *The Traffic Safety Newsletter* (monthly); *Tank Notes* (published quarterly for storage tank owners); *IPL Bulletin* (weekly newsletter); *Case Indexing Service* (monthly index of New Mexico judicial opinions).

★1713★ **University of North Carolina at**
Chapel Hill
General Clinical Research Center
UNC Hospital
CB 7600
Chapel Hill, NC 27599
Phone: (919)966-1435
Fax: (919)966-1576
Eugene P. Orringer, M.D., Dir.

Research Activities and Fields: Human physiology and pharmacology, including research on growth hormone and somatomedin-C physiology, hemophilia, AIDS and other sexually transmitted diseases, stress and cardiovascular physiology, cystic fibrosis, drug metabolism and disposition in patients with hepatic and renal dysfunction, glomerular diseases, the neuropsychopharmacologic correlates of depression and other mental illnesses, cancer chemotherapy and immunotherapy, sickle cell anemia and related red blood cell diseases, infants with the "failure to thrive" syndrome, and cardiac diseases such as congestive failure and arrhyth-

mias. **Publications:** *GCRC Newsletter* (12 per year).

★1714★ **University of North Dakota**
UND Center for Rural Health
PO Box 9037
Grand Forks, ND 58202-9037
Phone: (701)777-3848
Fax: (701)777-2389
Jack M. Geller, Ph.D., Dir.

Research Activities and Fields: Rural health care delivery, especially in the areas of health manpower, the viability of rural health facilities, gerontology, Native American health care, and uncompensated care. Collaborates with other research organizations throughout the nation. **Publications:** *Focus on Rural Health* (semiannually) **E-mail Address:** jack.geller@medicine.und.nodak.edu. **Formerly:** Office of Rural Health (1986); Center for Rural Health Services, Policy and Research (1990); Center for Rural Health (1993).

★1715★ **University of North Texas Health**
Science Center at Fort Worth
Wound Healing Research Institute (WHRI)
3500 Camp Bowie Blvd.
Ft. Worth, TX 76107-2699
Phone: (817)735-2125
Fax: (817)735-2113
S. Dan Dimitrijevich, Ph.D., Actg.Dir.

Research Activities and Fields: Biochemical, biological, physiological, and clinical aspects of tissue repair in humans and the effects of aging on wound healing. Studies include the development and character of in vitro models of human tissue (normal and pathological); the effects of hyperbaric oxygen on wound healing; the effects of aging on growth factor expression; and the role of growth factors on wound healing, cutaneous, ocular, and vascular tissues.

★1716★ **University of Pennsylvania**
Clinical Research Center
3400 Spruce St.
Philadelphia, PA 19104-4283
Phone: (215)662-2641
Fax: (215)662-2643
Garret A. FitzGerald, M.D., Dir.

Research Activities and Fields: AIDS, cardiovascular research, chemical senses, chronobiology and sleep, dermatology, endocrinology, gene therapy, metabolism, neonatal medicine, neurology, oncology, psychiatry, and women and minority health issues.

★1717★ **University of Pennsylvania**
Weight and Eating Disorders Program
Dept. of Psychiatry
3600 Market St., Ste. 734
Philadelphia, PA 19104-2648
Phone: (215)898-7314
Fax: (215)898-2878
Dr. Thomas Wadden, Dir.

Research Activities and Fields: Obesity and bulimia, including behavioral treatment of obesity, genetics of obesity, body fat distribution as predictor of disease, and predictors of adiposity in infancy. **Formerly:** Obesity Research Group.

★1718★ **University of Pittsburgh**
General Clinical Research Center
8N Montefiore University Hospital
200 Lothrop St.
Pittsburgh, PA 15261
Phone: (412)648-6691
Fax: (412)648-6697
Robert A. Branch, M.D., Program Dir.

Research Activities and Fields: Cardiology, connective tissue disease, diabetes, endocrinology, hematology and oncology, hypertension, infectious disease, pulmonary physiology, nephrology, transplantation, and behavioral medicine.

★1719★ **University of Puerto Rico**
Outpatient Unit for Clinical Research
Univ. District Hospital
Puerto Rico Medical Center
San Juan, PR 00936
Phone: (809)758-2525
Fax: (809)751-6242
Dr. Reynold Lopez, Dir.

Research Activities and Fields: Parasitic and renal diseases, nutritional deficiencies, and malabsorption. Maintains a 6-bed unit where patients and subjects can be hospitalized for observation under ideal conditions for multidisciplinary clinical studies by faculty members of various departments of the School. **Formerly:** Clinical Research Center (1979).

★1720★ **University of Rochester**
Clinical Research Center
601 Elmwood Ave.
Box MED
Rochester, NY 14642
Phone: (716)275-5295
Fax: (716)461-4737
John E. Gerich, M.D., Prog.Dir.

Research Activities and Fields: Studies of normal and deranged tissue and organ function in humans, including endocrinology, metabolism, neurology, gastroenterology, immunology, pulmonary disease, cardiology, hematology, psychiatry, dermatology, infectious disease, oncology, and pediatrics. Functions as a resource for Medical Center faculty. **E-mail Address:** 74364.2371@compuserve.com.

★1721★ **University of South Dakota**
Sioux Falls Medical Research Center
2501 W. 22nd St.
Sioux Falls, SD 57105
Phone: (605)336-3230
Fax: (605)333-6878
Dr. Angelina Trujillo, Research Coord.

Research Activities and Fields: Oncology, endocrinology, hypertension, muscle disease, microbiology/virology, trace minerals, fertility, nephrology, gastroenterology, cardiology, pulmonary, critical care, and geriatrics.

★1722★ **University of Southern California**
Clinical Research Center
2025 Zonal Ave.
Los Angeles, CA 90033
Phone: (213)226-4632
Fax: (213)226-2796
Dr. John T. Nicoloff, Program Dir.

Research Activities and Fields: Clinical endocrinology, infectious diseases, cancer, cardiology, rheumatology, neurology, obstetrics and gynecology, surgery, pediatrics, psychiatry, and radiology, including studies on thyroid hormone metabolism, reproductive endocrinology, role of aldosterone and renin in system, growth hormone metabolism, calcium and bone metabolism, water and electrolyte metabolism, androgen metabolism, obesity, hypertension, diabetes, fasting, and neuromuscular disease. Specific research includes a study on the mechanism by which smoking and contraceptive pills combine to produce cardiovascular disease in women, and the thyroid function, association of obesity, diabetics, and hypertension in fasting and nonthyroidal illnesses. **Publications:** Annual Report.

★ 1723 ★ University of Southwestern Louisiana
New Iberia Research Center
4401 W. Adviral Ave., Doyle Dr.
New Iberia, LA 70560
Phone: (318)365-2411
Fax: (318)373-0057
Dr. William E. Greer, Dir.

Research Activities and Fields: Human disease research, animal models development, and pharmacology/toxicology research. **Formerly:** Gulf South Research Institute, Life Science Division (1984).

★ 1724 ★ University of Tennessee
Clinical Research Center
951 Court Ave., Rm. 326B
Memphis, TN 38163
Phone: (901)528-5802
Williams B. Applegate, M.D., Program Dir.

Research Activities and Fields: Provides general clinical research facilities for controlled inpatient and outpatient studies on human subjects with various disorders, including sickle cell anemia, diabetes mellitus, hyperandrogenism and other endocrine disorders, kidney disease, liver disorders, hypertension, brain tumors, muscular dystrophy, obesity, metabolic bone diseases, psychiatric disorders, osteoporosis, Reye's syndrome, hirsutism, sexual disorders, reproduction problems, thyroid disorders, breast cancer, and leukemia. Also studies the physiology of hypertension and the metabolic effect of exercise. **Publications:** Annual Report. **E-mail Address:** jkaras@utmem1.utmem.edu.

★ 1725 ★ University of Texas at Arlington
Human Performance Institute
Box 19180
Arlington, TX 76019
Phone: (817)273-2335
Fax: (817)273-2548
Dr. George Kondraske, Dir.

Research Activities and Fields: Methods of measurement of human performance, including performance theory, human performance conceptual framework, and specialized instrumentation; studies have broad applications in the fields of space, rehabilitation, the military, and industry. Fundamental focus is on the human system-task interface. Projects include development of a computer-automated system to measure basic elements of human performance, testing of both normal and impaired individuals, and the development of methods for auto-

mated, objective disability determination. Conducts longitudinal studies of patients to characterize disease history. Also studies human performance in relation to spasmodic dysphonia, athletes, post-polio syndrome, and head injuries. Develops software tools for automated assessment of complex sets of measurements. **Publications:** Progress Report (annually); Newsletter (semiannually).

★ 1726 ★ University of Texas Health Science Center at San Antonio
General Clinical Research Center
7703 Floyd Curl Dr.
San Antonio, TX 78284-7877
Phone: (210)567-4900
Fax: (210)567-6693
Gregory R. Mundy, M.D., Program Dir.

Research Activities and Fields: Diabetes, endocrinology, infectious disease, metabolism, nephrology, oncology, pharmacology, and psychiatry. **E-mail Address:** schulz@uthscsa.edu.

★ 1727 ★ University of Texas Medical Branch at Galveston
Clinical Research Center
301 University Blvd., Rte. C31
Galveston, TX 77555-0331
Phone: (409)772-1950
Fax: (409)772-8097
Charles A. Stuart, M.D., Program Dir.

Research Activities and Fields: Research is performed in disease-related areas including studies of sleep apnea and respiratory control; insulin action in endocrine disorders and other altered metabolic states; extensive stable isotope technology-based studies of the regulation of substrate utilization and energy expenditure in normal and diseased states; endocrinology of the gastrointestinal tract, growth disorders, regulation of hypertension, depression, and appetite control; renal function in diabetes; regulators of asthmatic responses; absorption and lipid abnormalities in cholestatic disorders; and aplastic anemia. **E-mail Address:** stuart@crcvax.utmb.edu.

★ 1728 ★ University of Texas Medical Branch at Galveston
Institute for the Medical Humanities
Galveston, TX 77555-1311
Phone: (409)772-2376
Fax: (409)772-5640
Prof. Ronald A. Carson, Dir.

Research Activities and Fields: The Institute integrates humanities into medical education through programs in art and medicine, philosophy of medicine, medical ethics, religion and medicine, history of medicine, literature and medicine, law and medicine, and politics and medicine. Research projects include studies in images of healers in literature, history of professional medical ethics, phenomenology of aging, iconography of the life cycle, confidentiality in the doctor-patient relationship, women in medicine, visual representations in scientific practice, ethics of research in clinical medicine, and empathy in medical practice. **Publications:** *Medical Humanities Chronicle*; *Literature and Medicine*; *Medical Humanities Review*.

★ 1729 ★ University of Texas Southwestern Medical Center at Dallas
General Clinical Research Center
5323 Harry Hines Blvd.
Dallas, TX 75235-8891
Phone: (214)648-2100
Fax: (214)648-2526
Charles Pak, M.D., Prin. Investigator

Research Activities and Fields: Calcium metabolism, cardiopulmonary system, endocrinology, liver diseases, lipid disorders, rheumatology, neurology, oncology, and pharmacology.

★ 1730 ★ University of Utah
Clinical Research Center
50 N. Medical Dr.
Salt Lake City, UT 84132
Phone: (801)581-6736
Fax: (801)581-5393
James P. Kushner, M.D., Dir.

Research Activities and Fields: Provides facilities for School of Medicine faculty conducting clinical investigations in the areas of renal and cardiac failure, cardiac transplantation, genetic diseases, nutrition and cancer, atherosclerosis, diabetes and obesity, psychiatric and neuromuscular disorders, disorders of intermediary metabolism (porphyrins, carbohydrates, lipids, trace elements), diseases of the endocrine system (adrenal, pituitary, gonad, thyroid, and pancreas), infectious disease, and drug therapy of human diseases. **E-mail Address:** blong@crc_gw.med.utah.edu.

★ 1731 ★ University of Vermont
General Clinical Research Center
Medical Center Hospital of Vermont
Baird 7
Burlington, VT 05401
Phone: (802)656-3920
Fax: (802)656-5371
Dr. K. Sree Nair, Dir.

Research Activities and Fields: Various medical and surgical problems. Provides research facility for individual research studies.

★ 1732 ★ University of Virginia
General Clinical Research Center
School of Medicine
Box 410
Charlottesville, VA 22908
Phone: (804)924-3160
Fax: (804)979-4967
Dr. Michael O. Thorner, Dir.

Research Activities and Fields: Endocrinology, neurology, surgery, gastroenterology, ophthalmology, cardiology, obstetrics/gynecology, immunology, renal diseases, and ear, nose, and throat studies. Special interests include neuroendocrinology, hypertension, vascular disease, juvenile diabetes mellitus, genetic disorders, fertility disorders, digestive and growth disorders, sleep disorders, asthma and pulmonary disorders, congestive heart failure, arrhythmias, and epilepsy. Personnel are trained in rapid blood sampling and blood processing and a biostatistician is available to assist in research protocol design. Serves as a general clinical center for use by entire faculty of the School for any type of clinical investigation. **E-mail Address:** pfs2h@virginia.edu.

★ 1733 ★ University of Washington
Clinical Research Center
Univ. Hospital
Seattle, WA 98195
Phone: (206)548-4700
Fax: (206)548-6987
Dr. John W. Ensinck, Program Dir.

Research Activities and Fields: Conducts a diversified research program designed to make possible precise, laboratory-type measurements of patients' disease states and their progress under various types of treatment.

★ 1734 ★ University of Wisconsin—
Madison
Office of International Health Affairs
107 Bradley Memorial Hospital
1300 Univ. Ave.
Madison, WI 53706
Phone: (608)263-4150
Fax: (608)262-2327
Dr. Judith L. Ladinsky, Dir.

Research Activities and Fields: Conducts and coordinates international health research, teaching, and other activities for medical students, staff, and international agencies. **Publications:** Newsletter. **E-mail Address:** preve-health@macc.wisc.edu.

★ 1735 ★ URSA Institute
China Basin Bldg., Ste. 6400
185 Berry St.
San Francisco, CA 94107
Phone: (415)777-1922
Fax: (415)512-9625
Ernest Fazio, Adm.

Research Activities and Fields: Social policies, including AIDS prevention and education, crime and justice, aging, economic development, health care, housing, mental health, substance abuse, public education, public media, and public advertising.

★ 1736 ★ Vanderbilt University
Center for Health Services
Sta. 17
Nashville, TN 37232
Phone: (615)322-4773
Barbara Clinton, Dir.

Research Activities and Fields: The relationship of health care to community change, health care in rural communities, grass roots fund raising, rural activism, community environmental struggles, and comparison of health care in the U.S. and other countries. Compiles statistics on program participants. **Publications:** Newsletter (semiannually); Annual Report.

★ 1737 ★ Vanderbilt University
Clinical Research Center
21st Ave. S.
Nashville, TN 37232-2195
Phone: (615)343-6499
Fax: (615)343-8649
Dr. David Robertson, Dir.

Research Activities and Fields: Human physiology and diseases, including studies in medicine, neuroscience, molecular biology, pharmacology, hematology, cardiovascular diseases, genetics, obstetrics and gynecology, pediatrics, psychiatry, surgery, and psychology. Activities

focus on hypertension, hypotension, arrhythmias, carcinoid syndrome, and disorders of the autonomic nervous system. **Publications:** *Elliot Newman Handbook.* **E-mail Address:** david.robertson@mcmail.vanderbilt.edu.

★ 1738 ★ Veterans Affairs Medical Center
Research and Development Service
1900 E. Main St.
Danville, IL 61832
Phone: (217)442-8000
Fax: (217)431-6523
Mukund Prabhudesai, M.D., R&D Coord.

Research Activities and Fields: Alcoholism, rehabilitation, psychology, drugs, and nutrition. Also studies health care management and psychiatry.

★ 1739 ★ Veterans Affairs Medical Center
Research and Development Service
700 S. 19th St.
Birmingham, AL 35233
Phone: (205)933-8101
Fax: (205)933-4484
Jerry G. Spenney, M.D., Assoc. Chf. of Staff

Research Activities and Fields: Cancer, gastroenterology, rheumatology and arthritis, muscular dystrophy, neurology, and spinal cord injury and repair systems.

★ 1740 ★ Veterans Affairs Medical Center
Research Service
500 Foothill Dr.
Salt Lake City, UT 84148
Phone: (801)584-1271
Fax: (801)583-9624
Andrew Deiss, M.D., Assoc. Chief of Staff for Research

Research Activities and Fields: Diabetes, cancer, arthritis, aging and alcoholism, stroke and rehabilitation, dermatitis, neuroimmunological diseases, myasthenia gravis, tumors, dementia, laser medicine and surgery, herpes, genetics, cardiology, immunology, basic science, molecular biology, national cooperative drug studies, and rehabilitation research and development of artificial limbs.

★ 1741 ★ Veterans Affairs Medical Center
Research Service
3710 SW U.S. Veterans Hospital Rd.
PO Box 1034
Portland, OR 97207
Phone: (503)273-5123
Fax: (503)273-5351
Michael P. Davey, M.D., Assoc. Chf. of Staff, Research

Research Activities and Fields: Genetics of alcoholism and substance abuse, osteoporosis in men, virology (CMV, HIV), immunology, diabetes, multiple sclerosis, hematology-oncology, spinal cord regeneration, tardive dyskinesia, health services research, hypertension, dermatology (malignant melanoma), etiology of rheumatoid arthritis, Alzheimer's disease, audiology, and colon cancer.

★ 1742 ★ Veterans Affairs Medical Center
Research Service
1000 Locust St.
Reno, NV 89520
Phone: (702)328-1486
Fax: (702)328-1464
Aaron Smith, Ph.D., Dir. of Research

Research Activities and Fields: Alzheimer's disease, bone marrow transplantation, cancer, clinical trials of investigational drugs, diabetes, geriatric rehabilitation, in utero transplantation of blood-forming cells, stress in employment, health services, and surgery.

★ 1743 ★ Veterans Affairs Medical Center
Research Service
Univ. Dr. C
Pittsburgh, PA 15240
Phone: (412)683-3000
Fax: (412)692-3497
Martin Sax, Research Dir.

Research Activities and Fields: Oncogene expression in colon cancer, immunochemical targeting of tumors, dermatology, vascular surgery, three-dimensional structure of bacterial toxins, and transplantation. Neurosciences studies focus on epilepsy, hypertension, and neural control of bladder function.

★ 1744 ★ Virginia Commonwealth
University
General Clinical Research Center
Box 155, MCV Sta.
Richmond, VA 23298
Phone: (804)786-9228
Fax: (804)371-5002
William Griffith Blackard, M.D., Program Dir.

Research Activities and Fields: Endocrinology, gastroenterology, infectious disease, metabolism, neurology, pediatrics, pharmacology, psychiatry, pulmonary physiology, and surgery.

★ 1745 ★ Virginia Mason Research Center
1000 Seneca St.
Seattle, WA 98101
Phone: (206)583-6525
Fax: (206)223-7543
Gerald T. Nepom, M.D., Dir.

Research Activities and Fields: Immunology, diabetes and clinical research. **Publications:** *Bulletin of the Virginia Mason Clinic.*

★ 1746 ★ Wake Forest University
Comparative Medicine Clinical Research
Center
Bowman Gray Sch. of Med.
Dept. of Comparative Med.
Medical Ctr. Blvd.
Winston-Salem, NC 27157-1040
Phone: (910)716-7045
Fax: (910)764-5818
Thomas B. Clarkson, D.V.M., Dir.

Research Activities and Fields: Animal models of human disease studies, including research in heart disease, osteoporosis, women's health, and arteriosclerosis. Also studies relationship between aggression and low cholesterol levels.

★ 1747 ★ **Wake Forest University**
Overseas Research Center (ORC)
PO Box 7807, Reynolda Sta.
Winston-Salem, NC 27109
Phone: (910)759-5276
Fax: (910)759-9831
Dr. David K. Evans, Dir.

Research Activities and Fields: Problems facing emerging and newly developing nations, including interdisciplinary studies in anthropology, nutrition, ecology, comparative education, economics, folklore, geography, history, psychology, political science, public health, medical behavioral sciences, and sociology. **Publications:** *ORC Developing Nations Monograph Series* (irregularly); *Medical Behavioral Science* (irregularly). **E-mail Address:** dkevans@ac.wfu.edu.

★ 1748 ★ **Washington University**
Clinical Research Center
School of Medicine
660 S. Euclid
St. Louis, MO 63110
Phone: (314)362-7617
Fax: (314)362-7989
Dr. Philip E. Cryer, Dir.

Research Activities and Fields: Provides clinical research facilities for faculty members of the School.

★ 1749 ★ **Wayne State University**
Center for Health Research
College of Nursing
5557 Cass Ave.
Detroit, MI 48202
Phone: (313)577-4134
Fax: (313)577-5777
Dr. Darlene W. Mood, Assoc. Dean for Research

Research Activities and Fields: Nursing, pain reduction in hospitalized children, adolescent health, teen pregnancy, aging, chronicity, health education and promotion (e.g. smoking cessation), community health, psychosocial oncology, health behavior, self care, stress and coping, parent/child health, family health, caregivers of aged individuals, drug use, violence and abuse, sleep patterns, risk-taking with respect to teen pregnancy and sexually transmitted diseases (including HIV), and transcultural nursing. Multidisciplinary studies involve health professionals and faculty members from disciplines such as nursing, psychology, sociology, anthropology, medicine, and epidemiology. **Formerly:** Center for Nursing Research (1975).

★ 1750 ★ **Welfare Research, Inc.**
112 State St.
Albany, NY 12207
Phone: (518)432-2563
Fax: (518)432-2564
Virginia H. Sibbison, Exec.Dir.

Research Activities and Fields: Child welfare, AIDS, human services, health services, mental hygiene, nutrition assistance, public housing, employment and training, and nonprofit organization management. **Publications:** Annual Report.

★ 1751 ★ **Wesley Medical Research**
Institutes
3306 E. Central
Wichita, KS 67208
Phone: (316)686-7172
Fax: (316)688-7390
Dr. Sechin Cho, M.D., Scientific Dir.

Research Activities and Fields: Maternal and fetal medicine, respiratory distress syndrome in neonates, obstetrical and gynecologic oncology, infant nutrition, genetics, sickle cell anemia, heart disease, cancer, birth defects, infertility, and hypertension. **Publications:** Research Reports (twice a year). **Formerly:** Wesley Medical Research Foundation (1979).

★ 1752 ★ **Wright State University**
Cox Institute
3525 Southern Blvd.
Kettering, OH 45429
Phone: (513)873-5300
D. Diane Myers, Operations Mgr.

Research Activities and Fields: Myocardial infarction in coronary arteries, biomedical/biochemical applications of nuclear magnetic resonance spectroscopy and imaging, in vivo evaluation of catheter materials thrombogenicity, cerebral edema, cardiac arrest, childhood epilepsy, and cerebral ischemia.

★ 1753 ★ **Wright State University**
Fels Research Institute
Division of Human Biology
School of Medicine
1005 Xenia Ave.
Yellow Springs, OH 45387-1695
Phone: (513)767-6915
Fax: (513)767-6922
Dr. Roger M. Siervogel, Dir.

Research Activities and Fields: Physical growth, body composition, and genetic epidemiology, including a long-term longitudinal study. Other projects are conducted in the areas of aging and nutritional assessment. Utilizes a population of over 1,100, most of whom have been studied since birth and many of whom had been studied prenatally. Studies groups from the community at large.

★ 1754 ★ **Yale University**
General Clinical Research Center
333 Cedar St.
New Haven, CT 06510
Phone: (203)785-4796
Fax: (203)785-7273
Henry J. Binder, M.D., Dir.

Research Activities and Fields: Endocrinology, gastroenterology, mineral metabolism, oncology, psychology and pharmacology, respiratory psychology, and rheumatology.

★ 1755 ★ **Yeshiva University**
General Clinical Research Center
Nathan Van Etten Hospital, Rm. 230
Eastchester Rd. & Morris Park Ave.
Bronx, NY 10461
Phone: (718)430-8514
Harriet S. Gilbert, M.D., Program Dir.

Research Activities and Fields: Cardiovascular disease, infectious diseases, endocrinology, hematology, metabolism, nephrology, neurology, oncology, pharmacology, psychiatry, rheumatology, and nutrition.

State Government Agencies

Medical Boards

★ 1756 ★ **Alabama State Board of Medical**
Examiners
848 Washington Ave.
PO Box 946
Montgomery, AL 36101-0946
Phone: (334)242-4116
Fax: (334)242-4155

★ 1757 ★ **Alaska State Medical Board**
3601 C St., Ste. 722
Anchorage, AK 99503
Phone: (907)561-2878
Fax: (907)562-5781

★ 1758 ★ **Arizona State Board of Medical**
Examiners
1651 E. Morten Ave., Ste. 210
Phoenix, AZ 85020
Phone: (602)255-3751
Fax: (602)255-1848

★ 1759 ★ **Arkansas State Medical Board**
2100 Riverfront Dr., Ste. 200
Little Rock, AR 72202
Phone: (501)296-1802
Fax: (501)296-1805

★ 1760 ★ **California Medical Board**
1426 Howe Ave., Ste. 54
Sacramento, CA 95825-3236
Phone: (916)263-2388
Fax: (916)263-2387

★ 1761 ★ **Colorado State Board of Medical**
Examiners
1560 Broadway, Ste. 1550
Denver, CO 80202
Phone: (303)894-7719
Fax: (303)894-7885

★ 1762 ★ **Connecticut State Board of**
Medical Quality Assurance
150 Washington St.
Hartford, CT 06106
Phone: (203)566-7398
Fax: (203)566-6606

★ 1763 ★ **Delaware Board of Medical**
Practice
Cannon Bldg., Ste. 203
861 Silver Lake Blvd.
PO Box 1401
Dover, DE 19903
Phone: (302)739-4522
Fax: (302)739-2711

★ 1764 ★ **District of Columbia Board of**
Medicine
605 G St. NW, Rm. 202
PO Box 37200
Washington, DC 20013-7200
Phone: (202)727-5365
Fax: (202)727-4087

★ 1765 ★ **Florida Board of Medicine**
Northwood Centre, No. 60
1940 N. Monroe St.
Tallahassee, FL 32399-0750
Phone: (904)488-9849
Fax: (904)922-3040

★ 1766 ★ **Georgia Composite State Board of Medical Examiners**
166 Pryor St. SW
Atlanta, GA 30303-3465
Phone: (404)656-3913
Fax: (404)656-9723

★ 1767 ★ **Guam Board of Medical Examiners**
PO Box 2816
Agana, GU 96910
Phone: (671)734-7296
Fax: (671)734-2066

★ 1768 ★ **Hawaii Board of Medical Examiners**
1010 Richards St.
PO Box 3469
Honolulu, HI 96801
Phone: (808)586-2708
Fax: (808)586-2689

★ 1769 ★ **Idaho State Board of Medicine**
280 N. 8th St., No. 202
PO Box 83720
Boise, ID 83720-0058
Phone: (208)334-2822
Fax: (208)334-2801

★ 1770 ★ **Illinois Department of Professional Regulation Board of Medicine**
320 W. Washington St.
Springfield, IL 62786
Phone: (217)785-0800
Fax: (217)524-2169

★ 1771 ★ **Indiana Health Professions Bureau Medical Licensing Board**
402 W. Washington, Rm. 041
Indianapolis, IN 46204
Phone: (317)232-2960
Fax: (317)233-4236

★ 1772 ★ **Iowa State Board of Medical Examiners**
State Capitol Complex
Executive Hills West
1209 E. Court Ave.
Des Moines, IA 50319-0180
Phone: (515)281-5171
Fax: (515)242-5908

★ 1773 ★ **Kansas State Board of Healing Arts**
235 SW Topeka Blvd.
Topeka, KS 66603
Phone: (913)296-7413
Fax: (913)296-0852

★ 1774 ★ **Kentucky Board of Medical Licensure**
Hurstbourne Office Park
310 Whittington Pkwy., Ste 1B
Louisville, KY 40222
Phone: (502)429-8046
Fax: (502)429-9923

★ 1775 ★ **Louisiana State Board of Medical Examiners**
830 Union St., Ste. 100
New Orleans, LA 70112
Phone: (504)524-6763
Fax: (504)568-8893

★ 1776 ★ **Maine Board of Licensure in Medicine**
State House, Sta. 137
2 Bangor St.
Augusta, ME 04333
Phone: (207)287-3601
Fax: (207)287-6590

★ 1777 ★ **Maryland Board of Physician Quality Assurance**
4201 Patterson Ave., 3rd Fl.
PO Box 2571
Baltimore, MD 21215
Phone: (410)764-4777
Fax: (410)764-2478

★ 1778 ★ **Massachusetts Board of Registration in Medicine**
10 West St., 3rd Fl.
Boston, MA 02111
Phone: (617)727-3086
Fax: (617)451-9568

★ 1779 ★ **Michigan Board of Medicine**
611 W. Ottawa St., 4th Fl.
PO Box 30018
Lansing, MI 48909
Phone: (517)373-6873
Fax: (517)373-2179

★ 1780 ★ **Minnesota Board of Medical Practice**
2700 University Ave. W., Ste. 106
St. Paul, MN 55114-1080
Phone: (612)642-0538
Fax: (612)642-0393

★ 1781 ★ **Mississippi State Board of Medical Licensure**
2688-D Insurance Center Dr.
Jackson, MS 39216
Phone: (601)354-6645
Fax: (601)987-4159

★ 1782 ★ **Missouri State Board of Registration for the Healing Arts**
3605 Missouri Blvd.
PO Box 4
Jefferson City, MO 65102
Phone: (314)751-0098
Fax: (314)751-3166

★ 1783 ★ **Montana Board of Medical Examiners**
111 N. Jackson
PO Box 200513
Helena, MT 59620-0513
Phone: (406)444-4284
Fax: (406)444-1667

★ 1784 ★ **Nebraska State Board of Examiners in Medicine and Surgery**
301 Centennial Mall S.
PO Box 95007
Lincoln, NE 68509-5007
Phone: (402)471-2115
Fax: (402)471-0383

★ 1785 ★ **Nevada State Board of Medical Examiners**
1105 Terminal Way, Ste. 301
PO Box 7238
Reno, NV 89510
Phone: (702)688-2559
Fax: (702)688-2321

★ 1786 ★ **New Hampshire Board of Registration in Medicine**
Health and Welfare Bldg.
6 Hazen Dr.
Concord, NH 03301
Phone: (603)271-4501
Fax: (603)271-3745

★ 1787 ★ **New Jersey State Board of Medical Examiners**
140 E. Front St., 2nd Fl.
Trenton, NJ 08608
Phone: (609)826-7100
Fax: (609)984-3930

★ 1788 ★ **New Mexico State Board of Medical Examiners**
Lamy Bldg., 2nd Fl.
491 Old Santa Fe Trail
Santa Fe, NM 87501
Phone: (505)827-5022
Fax: (505)827-7377

★ 1789 ★ **New York State Board for Medicine**
Empire State Plaza
Cultural Education Center, Rm. 3023
Albany, NY 12230
Phone: (518)474-3841
Fax: (518)473-0578

★ 1790 ★ **North Carolina Board of Medical Examiners**
1203 Front St.
PO Box 20007
Raleigh, NC 27619
Phone: (919)828-1212
Fax: (919)828-1295

★ 1791 ★ **North Dakota State Board of Medical Examiners**
City Center Plaza
418 E. Broadway, Ste. 12
Bismarck, ND 58501
Phone: (701)223-9485
Fax: (701)223-9756

★ 1792 ★ **Ohio State Medical Board**
77 S. High St., 17th Fl.
Columbus, OH 43266-0315
Phone: (614)466-3934
Fax: (614)728-5946

★ 1793 ★ **Oklahoma State Board of Medical Licensure and Supervision**
5104 N. Francis, Ste. C
PO Box 18256
Oklahoma City, OK 73154-0256
Phone: (405)848-2189
Fax: (405)848-8240

★ 1794 ★ **Oregon Board of Medical Examiners**
Crown Plaza, No. 620
1500 SW 1st Ave.
Portland, OR 97201-5826
Phone: (503)229-5770
Fax: (503)229-6543

★ 1795 ★ **Pennsylvania State Board of Medicine**
Po Box 2649
Harrisburg, PA 17105-2649
Phone: (717)787-2381
Fax: (717)772-1892

★ 1796 ★ Puerto Rico Board of Medical Examiners
Call Box 13969
San Juan, PR 00908
Phone: (809)782-8989
Fax: (809)782-8733

★ 1797 ★ Rhode Island Board of Medical Licensure and Discipline
3 Capitol Hill, Rm. 205
Providence, RI 02908-5097
Phone: (401)277-3855
Fax: (401)277-2158

★ 1798 ★ South Carolina Board of Medical Examiners
Salvda Bldg., Ste. 120
101 Executive Center Dr.
PO Box 212269
Columbia, SC 29221-2269
Phone: (803)731-1650
Fax: (803)731-1660

★ 1799 ★ South Dakota State Board of Medical and Osteopathic Examiners
1323 S. Minnesota Ave.
Sioux Falls, SD 57105
Phone: (605)336-1965
Fax: (605)336-0270

★ 1800 ★ Tennessee State Board of Medical Examiners
283 Plus Park Blvd.
Nashville, TN 37217
Phone: (615)367-6231
Fax: (615)367-6210

★ 1801 ★ Texas State Board of Medical Examiners
1812 Centre Creek, Ste. 300
PO Box 149134
Austin, TX 78714-9134
Phone: (512)834-7728
Fax: (512)834-4597

★ 1802 ★ Utah Physicians Licensing Board
Heber M. Wells Bldg., 4th Fl.
160 East 300 South
Po Box 45805
Salt Lake City, UT 84145-0805
Phone: (801)530-6628
Fax: (801)530-6511

★ 1803 ★ Vermont Board of Medical Practice
109 State St.
Montpelier, VT 05609-1101
Phone: (802)828-2363
Fax: (802)828-2496

★ 1804 ★ Virgin Islands Board of Medical Examiners
48 Sugar Estate
St. Thomas, VI 00802
Phone: (809)776-8311
Fax: (809)777-4001

★ 1805 ★ Virginia Board of Medicine
6606 W. Broad St., 4th Fl.
Richmond, VA 23230-1717
Phone: (804)662-9908
Fax: (804)662-9943

★ 1806 ★ Washington Quality Medical Assurance Commission
1300 SE Quince St.
PO Box 47868
Olympia, WA 98504-7866
Phone: (206)753-2287
Fax: (206)586-4573

★ 1807 ★ West Virginia Board of Medicine
101 Dee Dr.
Charleston, WV 25311
Phone: (304)558-2921
Fax: (304)558-2084

★ 1808 ★ Wisconsin Medical Examining Board
1400 E. Washington Ave.
PO Box 8935
Madison, WI 53708
Phone: (608)266-2811
Fax: (608)267-0644

★ 1809 ★ Wyoming Board of Medicine
Barrett Bldg., Rm. 208
2301 Central Ave.
Cheyenne, WY 82002
Phone: (307)777-6463
Fax: (307)777-6478

State & Regional Organizations

Medicine

Listed below are state medical associations. The national organization is the American Medical Association, 515 N. State St., Chicago, IL 60610, (312) 464-5000.

Alabama

★ 1810 ★ Medical Association of the State of Alabama
19 S. Jackson St.
Montgomery, AL 36102-1900
Phone: (205)263-6441
Fax: (205)269-5200

Alaska

★ 1811 ★ Alaska State Medical Association
4107 Laurel St.
Anchorage, AK 99508
Phone: (907)562-2662
Fax: (907)561-2063

Arizona

★ 1812 ★ Arizona Medical Association
810 W. Bethany Home Rd.
Phoenix, AZ 85013
Phone: (602)246-8901
Fax: (602)242-6283

Arkansas

★ 1813 ★ Arkansas Medical Society
10 Corporate Hill Dr., Ste. 300
PO Box 5776
Little Rock, AR 72215-5776
Phone: (501)224-8967
Fax: (501)224-6489

California

★ 1814 ★ California Medical Association
221 Main St.
PO Box 7690
San Francisco, CA 94120-7690
Phone: (415)541-0900
Fax: (415)882-5116

Colorado

★ 1815 ★ Colorado Medical Society
7800 E. Dorado Pl.
Englewood, CO 80111-2306
Phone: (303)779-5455
Fax: (303)771-8657

Connecticut

★ 1816 ★ Connecticut State Medical Society
160 St. Ronan St.
New Haven, CT 06511
Phone: (203)865-0587
Fax: (203)865-4997

Delaware

★ 1817 ★ Medical Society of Delaware
1925 Lovering Ave.
Wilmington, DE 19806
Phone: (302)658-7596
Fax: (302)658-9669

District of Columbia

★ 1818 ★ Medical Society of the District of Columbia
1707 L St. NW, Ste. 400
Washington, DC 20036
Phone: (202)466-1800
Fax: (202)452-1542

Florida

★ 1819 ★ Florida Medical Association
760 Riverside Ave.
PO Box 2411
Jacksonville, FL 32203
Phone: (904)356-1571
Fax: (904)353-1247

Georgia

★ 1820 ★ Medical Association of Georgia
938 Peachtree St. NE
Atlanta, GA 30309
Phone: (404)876-7535
Fax: (404)874-8651

Guam

★1821★ Guam Medical Society
850 Governor Camacho Rd.
Tamuning, GU 96911
Phone: (671)646-5801

Hawaii

★1822★ Hawaii Medical Association
1360 S. Beretania St., 2nd Fl.
Honolulu, HI 96814
Phone: (808)536-7702
Fax: (808)528-2376

Idaho

★1823★ Idaho Medical Association
305 W. Jefferson
PO Box 2668
Boise, ID 83701
Phone: (208)344-7888
Fax: (208)344-7903

Illinois

★1824★ Illinois State Medical Society
20 N. Michigan, Ste. 700
Chicago, IL 60602
Phone: (312)782-1654
Fax: (312)782-2023

Indiana

★1825★ Indiana State Medical Association
322 Canal Walk, Canal Level
Indianapolis, IN 46202
Phone: (317)261-2060
Fax: (317)261-2076

Iowa

★1826★ Iowa Medical Society
1001 Grand Ave.
West Des Moines, IA 50265
Phone: (515)223-1401
Fax: (515)223-8420

Kansas

★1827★ Kansas Medical Society
623 SW 10th Ave.
Topeka, KS 66612-1627
Phone: (913)235-2383
Fax: (913)235-5114

Kentucky

★1828★ Kentucky Medical Association
301 N. Hurstbourne Pkwy., Ste. 200
Louisville, KY 40222-8512
Phone: (502)426-6200
Fax: (502)426-6877

Louisiana

★1829★ Louisiana State Medical Society
3501 N. Causeway Blvd., Ste. 800
Metairie, LA 70002-3673
Phone: (504)832-9815
Fax: (504)833-7685

Maine

★1830★ Maine Medical Association
PO Box 190
Manchester, ME 04351
Phone: (207)622-3374
Fax: (207)622-3332

Maryland

★1831★ Medical and Chirurgical Faculty of the State of Maryland
1211 Cathedral St.
Baltimore, MD 21201
Phone: (410)539-0872
Fax: (410)547-0915

Massachusetts

★1832★ Massachusetts Medical Society
1440 Main St.
Waltham, MA 02154-1649
Phone: (617)893-4610
Fax: (617)893-3481

Michigan

★1833★ Michigan State Medical Society
120 W. Saginaw
East Lansing, MI 48823
Phone: (517)337-1351
Fax: (517)337-2490

Minnesota

★1834★ Minnesota Medical Association
2221 University Ave. SE, Ste. 400
Minneapolis, MN 55414
Phone: (612)378-1875
Fax: (612)378-3875

Mississippi

★1835★ Mississippi State Medical Association
735 Riverside Dr.
Jackson, MS 39202
Phone: (601)354-5433
Fax: (601)352-4834

Missouri

★1836★ Missouri State Medical Association
113 Madison St.
PO Box 1028
Jefferson City, MO 65102
Phone: (314)636-5151
Fax: (314)636-8552

Montana

★1837★ Montana Medical Association
2021 11th Ave., Ste. 1
Helena, MT 59601
Phone: (406)443-4000
Fax: (406)443-4042

Nebraska

★1838★ Nebraska Medical Association
233 S. 13th St., Ste. 1512
Lincoln, NE 68508-2091
Phone: (402)474-4472
Fax: (402)474-2198

Nevada

★1839★ Nevada State Medical Association
3660 Baker Ln., Ste. 101
Reno, NV 89509
Phone: (702)825-6788
Fax: (702)825-3202

New Hampshire

★1840★ New Hampshire Medical Society
7 N. State St.
Concord, NH 03301-4018
Phone: (603)224-1909
Fax: (603)226-2432

New Jersey

★1841★ Medical Society of New Jersey
2 Princess Rd.
Lawrenceville, NJ 08648
Phone: (609)896-1766
Fax: (609)896-1368

New Mexico

★1842★ New Mexico Medical Society
7770 Jefferson NE, Ste. 400
Albuquerque, NM 87109
Phone: (505)828-0237
Fax: (505)828-0336

New York

★1843★ Medical Society of the State of New York
420 Lakeville Rd.
Lake Success, NY 11042
Phone: (516)488-6100
Fax: (516)488-1267

North Carolina

★1844★ North Carolina Medical Society
222 N. Person St.
PO Box 27167
Raleigh, NC 27611-7167
Phone: (919)833-3836
Fax: (919)833-2023

North Dakota

★ 1845 ★ North Dakota Medical Association
PO Box 1198
Bismarck, ND 58502-1198
Phone: (701)223-9475
Fax: (701)223-9476

Ohio

★ 1846 ★ Ohio State Medical Association
1500 Lake Shore Dr.
Columbus, OH 43204-3824
Phone: (614)486-2401
Fax: (614)486-3130

Oklahoma

★ 1847 ★ Oklahoma State Medical Association
601 Northwest Expwy.
Oklahoma City, OK 73118
Phone: (405)843-9571
Fax: (405)842-1834

Oregon

★ 1848 ★ Oregon Medical Association
5210 SW Corbett Ave.
Portland, OR 97201
Phone: (503)226-1555
Fax: (503)241-7148

Pennsylvania

★ 1849 ★ Pennsylvania Medical Society
777 E. Park Dr.
PO Box 8820
Harrisburg, PA 17105-8820
Phone: (717)558-7750
Fax: (717)558-7830

Puerto Rico

★ 1850 ★ Puerto Rico Medical Association
PO Box 9387
San Juan, PR 00908
Phone: (809)721-6969
Fax: (809)722-1191

Rhode Island

★ 1851 ★ Rhode Island Medical Society
106 Francis St.
Providence, RI 02903
Phone: (401)331-3207
Fax: (401)751-8050

South Carolina

★ 1852 ★ South Carolina Medical Association
PO Box 11188
Columbia, SC 29211
Phone: (803)798-6207
Fax: (803)772-6783

South Dakota

★ 1853 ★ South Dakota State Medical Association
1323 S. Minnesota Ave.
Sioux Falls, SD 57105
Phone: (605)336-1965
Fax: (605)336-0270

Tennessee

★ 1854 ★ Tennessee Medical Association
PO Box 120909
Nashville, TN 37212-0909
Phone: (615)385-2100
Fax: (615)383-5918

Texas

★ 1855 ★ Texas Medical Association
401 W. 15th St.
Austin, TX 78701-1680
Phone: (512)370-1300
Fax: (512)370-1633

Utah

★ 1856 ★ Utah Medical Association
540 East 500 South
Salt Lake City, UT 84102
Phone: (801)355-7477
Fax: (801)531-0381

Vermont

★ 1857 ★ Vermont State Medical Society
136 Main St., Box 1457
Montpelier, VT 05601
Phone: (802)223-7898
Fax: (802)223-1201

Virgin Islands

★ 1858 ★ Virgin Islands Medical Society
PO Box 5986
St. Croix, VI 00823
Phone: (809)778-5305

Virginia

★ 1859 ★ Medical Society of Virginia
4205 Dover Rd.
Richmond, VA 23221-3267
Phone: (804)353-2721
Fax: (804)355-6189

Washington

★ 1860 ★ Washington State Medical Association
2033 6th Ave., Ste. 1100
Seattle, WA 98121
Phone: (206)441-9762
Fax: (206)441-5863

West Virginia

★ 1861 ★ West Virginia State Medical Association
4307 MacCorckle Ave., SE
PO Box 4106
Charleston, WV 25364
Phone: (304)925-0342
Fax: (304)925-0345

Wisconsin

★ 1862 ★ State Medical Society of Wisconsin
330 E. Lakeside St.
PO Box 1109
Madison, WI 53701
Phone: (608)257-6781
Fax: (608)283-5401

Wyoming

★ 1863 ★ Wyoming Medical Society
PO Drawer 4009
Cheyenne, WY 82003
Phone: (307)635-2424
Fax: (307)632-1973

Chapter 2
Aging

Federal Government Agencies

★ 1864 ★ **U.S. Department of Health and Human Services**
National Institute on Aging
9000 Rockville Pike
Bethesda, MD 20892
Phone: (301)496-9265

Description: The Institute conducts and supports biomedical and behavioral research to increase the knowledge of the aging process and associated physical, psychological, and social factors resulting from advanced age. Incontinence, menopause, susceptibility to diseases, and memory loss are among the areas of special concern.

★ 1865 ★ **U.S. Department of Health and Human Services**
Office of the Secretary
Administration on Aging (AOA)
330 Independence Ave. SW
Washington, DC 20201
Phone: (202)401-4634
Fax: (202)619-3759

Description: The Administration on Aging is the principal federal organization for identifying the needs, concerns, and interests of older persons; for promoting coordination of federal resources available to meet the needs of older persons; and for carrying out the programs of the Older Americans Act. Under this Act, AOA administers a program of formula grants to state agencies on aging to serve as advocates for the elderly and to assist in the establishment of comprehensive, coordinated service systems for older persons at the community level.

★ 1866 ★ **U.S. Department of Health and Human Services**
Office of the Secretary
Federal Council on the Aging
330 Independence Ave. SW
Washington, DC 20201
Phone: (202)619-2451

Description: Council was created to advise the President, Secretary of Health and Human Services, Commissioner on Aging, and Congress on matters relating to the special needs of older Americans. It is composed of 15 members appointed by the President, with the approval of the Senate. Members are representatives of older Americans, national organizations with an interest in aging, business, labor, and the general public. At least five members must themselves be older persons.

★ 1867 ★ **U.S. Senate**
Committee on Labor and Human Resources
Subcommittee on Aging
SH-615 Hart Senate Office Bldg.
Washington, DC 20510
Phone: (202)224-0136

★ 1868 ★ **U.S. Senate**
Special Committee on Aging
SD-G31 Dirksen Senate Office Bldg.
Washington, DC 20510-6400
Phone: (202)224-5364
Fax: (202)224-8660

Foundations & Other Funding Organizations

Private Foundations

★ 1869 ★ **A. C. Buehler Foundation**
c/o Bank of America-Illinois
231 S LaSalle St.
Chicago, IL 60697
Phone: (312)828-1785
Kathy Ryan, Administrator

Foundation Philosophy: The foundation is primarily interested in supporting health care and hospitals. Recently, the foundation has supported health education, specifically the Northwestern University Center on Aging. Minor support is given to the arts. **Giving Priorities:** In 1990, the Northwestern University Center on Aging received 55% of total funding. Health care received 36%, with major funding to Children's Memorial Hospital in Chicago, IL. Civic affairs received 7%. The remainder went to the arts. **Typical Health-Related Recipients:** Hospitals, Medical Research. **Geographic Distribution:** Focus on Chicago, IL.

Commonwealth Fund
See: Entry 113

Florence V. Burden Foundation
See: Entry 184

Harry C. Trexler Trust
See: Entry 250

J.E. and Z.B. Butler Foundation
See: Entry 296

Jean and Louis Dreyfus Foundation
See: Entry 312

John A. Hartford Foundation
See: Entry 5718

Joseph Alexander Foundation
See: Entry 329

★ 1870 ★ **Marty and Dorothy Silverman Foundation**
150 E 58th St., 26th Fl.
New York, NY 10155
Phone: (212)832-9170
Lorin Silverman, Secretary-Treasurer and Director

Foundation Philosophy: The foundation provides grants to programs that address the needs of indigent senior citizens including nursing homes and hospitals. Additionally, grants may be made to other educational, scientific, cultural, and health and welfare agencies. **Giving Priorities:** In fiscal 1993, the foundation gave approximately 48% of its contributions to Jewish causes. Social services received 17%, while health organizations received 16%. Educational institutions also received 16%, with the remainder supporting civic and international causes. **Typical Health-Related Recipients:** Alzheimers Disease, Clinics/Medical Centers, Geriatric Health, Health Organizations, Heart, Hospitals, Medical Education, Medical Research, Nursing Services, Single-Disease Health Associations. **Geographic Distribution:** New York, NY.

★1871★ Max Factor Family Foundation
9777 Wilshire Blvd., Ste. 1015
Beverly Hills, CA 90212
Phone: (310)274-8193
Barbara Factor Bentley, Trustee

Foundation Philosophy: The foundation's primary concerns lie in geriatric health, research grants for doctors, Jewish welfare organizations, and children's diseases. **Giving Priorities:** In 1993, the foundation gave approximately 34% of total contributions to health organizations. Religious institutions received about 32% of funding, including the foundation's highest grant of $225,000 to the United Jewish Fund. The remainder of funding went to social services, 28%; educational institutions, 5%; and the arts and humanities, 1%. **Typical Health-Related Recipients:** Cancer, Children's Health/Hospitals, Clinics/Medical Centers, Diabetes, Emergency/Ambulance Services, Eyes/Blindness, Geriatric Health, Health Organizations, Heart, Hospitals, Medical Research, Mental Health, People with Disabilities, Public Health, Single-Disease Health Associations, Substance Abuse. **Geographic Distribution:** Primarily Southern California.

★1872★ Ramapo Trust
126 E 56th St., 10th Fl.
New York, NY 10022
Phone: (212)308-7355
Fax: (212)750-0132
Stephen L. Schwartz, Trustee

Foundation Philosophy: The trust "is a charitable institution whose resources have centered on gerontology and geriatrics. The trust will consider innovative projects which serve the aging, or increase knowledge in the field of aging." Recently, the trust has placed more emphasis on services for families of Alzheimer's disease patients. Grants are made nationally. **Giving Priorities:** In fiscal 1994, the trust gave approximately 34% of its contributions to education. Health care received 29%, including the highest grant of $371,797 to the Picower Institute for Medical Research. Religion received 24%; social services, 8%; and civic affairs, 4%. **Typical Health-Related Recipients:** Alzheimers Disease, Clinics/Medical Centers, Geriatric Health, Health Organizations, Hospitals, Long-Term Care, Medical Education, Medical Research, Mental Health, Nursing Services, Public Health. **Geographic Distribution:** No geographic restrictions.

★1873★ Retirement Research Foundation
8765 W Higgins Rd., No. 401
Chicago, IL 60631
Phone: (312)714-8080
Fax: (312)714-8089
Marilyn Hennessy, President

Foundation Philosophy: Currently the foundation conducts the National Media Awards Program, an annual competition for films and videotapes on aging, and the Community Awards Program (ENCORE Program) to identify exemplary programs run by not for profit agencies in the metropolitan Chicago area. Programs are judged on their ability to provide the services promised, the real benefit they provide to the elderly, the involvement of the elderly and their families, and use of available resources and ability to solve problems. **Giving Priorities:** In 1994, approximately 64% of contributions was awarded to health concerns, principally hospitals, nursing homes, and health care agencies. Social service organizations received 24%; religion, 5%; civic affairs, 4%; the arts, 2%; and education, 1%. **Typical Health-Related Recipients:** Clinics/Medical Centers, Diabetes, Emergency/Ambulance Services, Geriatric Health, Health Organizations, Health Policy/Cost Containment, Home-Care Services, Hospices, Hospitals, Long-Term Care, Medical Research, Mental Health, Nursing Services, People with Disabilities, Single-Disease Health Associations. **Geographic Distribution:** U.S. only.

Vira I. Heinz Endowment
See: Entry 529

Corporate Foundations

AlliedSignal Foundation
See: Entry 572

Other Funding Organizations

★1874★ AARP Andrus Foundation
American Association of Retired Persons
601 E St. NW
Washington, DC 20049
Phone: (202)434-6190
Dr. Kenneth G. Cook, Admin.

Description: The Foundation's purpose is to encourage research in gerentology through grants to college and universities for applied gerentology research projects.

★1875★ American Federation for Aging Research
1414 Avenue of the Americas, 18th Fl.
New York, NY 10019
Phone: (212)752-2327
Fax: (212)832-2298
Stephanie Lederman, Exec. Dir.

Description: Awards grants for research on aging and associated diseases.

★1876★ American Foundation for Aging Research
North Carolina State University
Biochemistry Dept.
128 Polk Hall
Raleigh, NC 27695-7622
Phone: (919)737-5679
Fax: (919)515-2047
Paul F. Agris, Pres.

Description: Awards undergraduate scholarships and graduate fellowships to support basic research and educational opportunities for the study of age-related diseases and the biology of aging.

★1877★ National Council on the Aging
409 3rd St. SW
Washington, DC 20024
Phone: (202)479-1200
Fax: (202)479-0735
Dr. David Thursz, Pres.

Description: Offers fellowships to medical and pharmacy students for projects in geriatrics.

National & International Organizations

★1878★ Aging in America (AIA)
1500 Pelham Pky. S
Bronx, NY 10461
Phone: (718)824-4004
Fax: (212)597-1524
Ralph Hall, Pres.

Founded: 1979. **Description:** Research and service organization for professionals in gerontology. Objectives are: to produce, implement, and share effective and affordable programs and services that improve the quality of life for the elderly community; to better prepare professionals and students interested in, or currently involved with, aging and the aged. Conducts research projects, educational and training seminars, and in-service curricula for long-term and acute care facilities. Operates: Education and Training Program to educate professionals and para-professionals; Projects With Industry Program to help both able-bodied and disabled elderly individuals enter into the work force. Conducts local programs in New York City including: In-Home Services, which provides Meals-on-Wheels, transportation, and housekeeping; Alzheimer's Day Care; Respite and Long-Term Residence; Self-Governing Senior Centers. Provides social services, including case management, information, referral, and advocacy; Research. Maintains speakers' bureau; compiles statistics. **Publications:** Brochure. Outlines various programs. • *Sharing Newsletter*, quarterly. Newsletter. **Formerly:** (1952) Morningside House.

★1879★ Alliance for Aging Research (AAR)
2021 K St. NW, Ste. 305
Washington, DC 20006
Phone: (202)293-2856
Fax: (202)785-8574
Daniel Perry, Exec.Dir.

Founded: 1986. **Description:** Gerontologists and other medical professionals, executives, and members of Congress are participants. Works to increase private and public research into aging. Supports policies concerning: productive aging; independence for older Americans; successful aging; human genome initiative. Operates speakers' bureau; compiles statistics. **Publications:** *Aging Research on the Threshold of Discovery.* • *Alliance Reports.* Reports. • *Americans' View on Aging.* • *Independence for Older Americans: Task Force for Aging Research Funding.* • *Investing in Older Women's Health.* • *Issue Reports*, periodic. • *Meeting the Medical Needs of the Senior Boom: The National Shortage of Geriatricians.* • *Report on Public Opinion.* Report. • *The Research Gap.*

★1880★ American Aging Association (AGE)
2129 Providence Ave.
Chester, PA 19013-5506
Phone: (610)874-7550
Fax: (610)876-7715
Arthur K. Balin, M.D., Exec.Dir.

Founded: 1970. **Members:** 500. **Description:** Laymen and scientists primarily in the biomedical field. Dedicated to "helping people live better, longer" by promoting biomedical aging studies directed toward slowing down the aging process, informing the public of the progress of aging research and of practical means of achieving a long and healthy life, and increasing knowledge of gerontology among physicians and other health workers. **Publications:** *AGE*, quarterly. Journal. Covers biomedical aging research. *Price:* $30/year for members; $55/year for nonmembers.

★ **1881** ★ **American Association for Geriatric Psychiatry (AAGP)**
7910 Woodmont Ave., 7th Fl.
Bethesda, MD 20814
Phone: (301)654-7850
Fax: (301)654-4137
Janet L. Pailet, J.D., Exec.Dir.

Founded: 1978. **Members:** 1,468. **Description:** Psychiatrists interested in promoting better mental health care for the elderly. Maintains placement service and speakers' bureau. **Publications:** *AAGP Membership Directory*, annual. Membership Directory. • *American Association for Geriatric Psychiatry--Newsletter*, bimonthly. Newsletter. Provides brief articles on psychiatric topics and case reports pertaining to elderly patients; includes association news, and employment listings.

★ **1882** ★ **American Association of Homes and Services for the Aging (AAHSA)**
901 E St. NW, Ste. 500
Washington, DC 20004-2037
Phone: (202)783-2242
Fax: (202)783-2255
Sheldon L. Goldberg, Pres.

Founded: 1961. **Members:** 4,500. **Regional Groups:** 4. **State Groups:** 39. **Description:** Voluntary not-for-profit nursing homes, housing, retirement communities, and health-related facilities and services for the elderly; state associations; interested individuals. Provides a unified means of identifying and solving problems in order to protect and advance the interests of the residents served. Believes that long-term care should be geared toward individual needs and provided in a spectrum ranging from nursing care to independent living and community-based care. Is committed to community involvement in the home to ensure the highest quality of care for residents. Maintains liaison with Congress and federal agencies. Provides educational programs, publications, group purchasing program, capital financing, and in surance programs. **Publications:** *AAHA Provider News*, monthly. Newsletter. Includes job listings. *Price:* Included in membership dues. • *American Association of Homes for the Aging Publications Catalog*, 2/year. Catalog. • Membership Directory, annual. • *Washington Report*, biweekly. Report. Provides legislative and regulatory highlights. *Price:* Included in membership dues. **Formerly:** American Association of Homes for the Aging.

★ **1883** ★ **American Disabled for Attendant Program Today (ADAPT)**
201 S. Cherokee St.
Denver, CO 80223-1836
Phone: (303)733-9324
Fax: (303)733-6211
Wade Blank, Founder

Founded: 1983. **Members:** 1,500. **State Groups:** 26. **Local Groups:** 33. **Description:** Promotes federal funding of in-home support services for the elderly and disabled in an effort to decrease the number of individuals being placed in nursing homes. **Publications:** *Incitement*, 6/year. Newsletter. **Formerly:** (1991) American Disabled for Accessible Public Transit.

★ **1884** ★ **American Federation for Aging Research (AFAR)**
1414 Avenue of the Americas, 18th Fl.
New York, NY 10019
Phone: (212)752-2327
Fax: (212)832-2298
Stephanie Lederman, Exec.Dir.

Founded: 1979. **State Groups:** 2. **Description:** Physicians, scientists, and other individuals involved or interested in research in aging and associated diseases. Purpose is to stimulate and fund research on aging. Facilitates communication among scientists in the field. Fosters public education regarding the need for support of related research. **Publications:** *AFAR Newsletter*, quarterly. Newsletter. Includes profiles of members. *Price:* Free. • *American Federation for Aging Research--Newsletter*, quarterly. Newsletter. Includes profiles of members. *Price:* Free.

★ **1885** ★ **American Foundation for Aging Research (AFAR)**
North Carolina State University
Biochemistry Dept.
128 Polk Hall
Raleigh, NC 27695-7622
Phone: (919)737-5679
Fax: (919)515-2047
Paul F. Agris, Pres.

Founded: 1979. **Members:** 295. **Description:** Supports basic research and educational opportunities for the study of age-related diseases and the biology of aging. Supports projects emphasizing modern biological, genetic, biochemical, and biophysical techniques and approaches to the problems of age-associated diseases and the understanding of aging. **Publications:** *News From AFAR*, quarterly. Newsletter. *Price:* Included in membership dues.

★ **1886** ★ **American Geriatrics Society (AGS)**
770 Lexington Ave., Ste. 300
New York, NY 10021
Phone: (212)308-1414
Free: 800-247-4779
Fax: (212)832-8646
Linda Hiddemen Barondess, Exec.VP

Founded: 1942. **Members:** 6,022. **Regional Groups:** 3. **State Groups:** 13. **Description:** Professional society of physicians and other health care professionals interested in problems of the aged. Encourages and promotes the study of geriatrics; stresses the importance of medical research in the field of aging. Conducts seminars. **Publications:** *AGS Newsletter*, bimonthly. Newsletter. Includes information on public policy issues of concern to members, upcoming courses, events, publications, and annual meeting. *Price:* Free. • *Directory of Fellowship Programs in Geriatric Medicine*, every 18-24 months. Directory. Describes programs in the United States and Canada. *Price:* $28/copy for members; $35/copy for nonmembers; $50/copy for institutions. • *Geriatrics Review Syllabus: A Core Curriculum in Geriatric Medicine*. Brochure. • *Journal of the American Geriatrics Society*, monthly. Journal. Includes original articles, abstracts of geriatric literature, book reviews, employment listings, and notices of meetings, courses, and symposia. *Price:* Included in membership dues; $92/year for nonmembers; $130/year for institutions; $48/year for nonmember residents and interns.

★ **1887** ★ **American Society on Aging (ASA)**
833 Market St., Ste. 511
San Francisco, CA 94103-1824
Phone: (415)974-9600
Fax: (415)882-4280
Gloria H. Cavanaugh, Exec.Dir.

Founded: 1954. **Members:** 10,000. **Description:** Health care and social service professionals, educators, researchers, administrators, businesspersons, students, and senior citizens. Works to enhance the well-being of older individuals and to foster unity among those working with and for the elderly. Offers 25 continuing education programs for professionals in aging-related fields. **Publications:** *Aging Today*, bimonthly. Newspaper. Tabloid covering critical events and issues in the field of aging, including legislative news, new products and designs, and research. *Price:* Included in membership dues; $30/year for nonmembers. • *Generations*, quarterly. Journal. Provides practical, current information in the field of aging, with emphasis on medical and social practice, research, and policy. *Price:* Included in membership dues; $35/year for nonmember individuals; $40 for institutions. **Formerly:** (1985) Western Gerontological Society.

★ **1888** ★ **American Society for Geriatric Dentistry (ASGD)**
211 E. Chicago Ave., 17th Fl.
Chicago, IL 60611
Phone: (312)440-2661
John S. Rutkauskas, D.D.S., Exec.Dir.

Founded: 1965. **Members:** 500. **Regional Groups:** 3. **Description:** Devoted to the maintenance and improvement of the oral health of the elderly. Promotes the continuing education of the practitioner of geriatric dentistry; auxiliary and nursing home administrators and personnel; hygienists, nurses, and students. Maintains speakers' bureau. **Publications:** *ASGD - Interface*, quarterly. Newsletter. Includes book reviews and calendar of events. *Price:* Included in membership dues; $25/year for nonmembers. • *Special Care in Dentistry*, bimonthly. Published in cooperation with American Association of Hospital Dentists and Academy of Dentistry for the Handicapped.

★ 1889 ★ Association of Brethren Caregivers (ABC)
1451 Dundee Ave.
Elgin, IL 60120
Phone: (708)742-5100
Free: 800-323-8039
Fax: (708)742-6103
Jay A. Gibble, Exec.Dir.

Founded: 1968. **Members:** 650. **Description:** Develops resources, leadership, and programs within the Church of the Brethren and the wider community. **Publications:** *Caregiver*, quarterly. Newsletter. Contains information for deacons of the Church of the Brethren. • *Update*, quarterly. Newsletter. Contains information for members of the association. **Formerly:** (1989) Church of the Brethren Homes and Hospitals Association; (1990) Board of Brethren Homes and Older Adult Ministries; (1993) Brethren Homes and Older Adult Ministries.

★ 1890 ★ Association for Gerontology in Higher Education (AGHE)
1001 Connecticut Ave. NW, Ste. 410
Washington, DC 20036
Phone: (202)429-9277
Elizabeth B. Douglass, Exec.Dir.

Founded: 1974. **Members:** 320. **Description:** Higher education institutions which offer, on a national level, gerontological education and research programs. Promotes and encourages education and training of persons preparing for research or careers in gerontology, and works to increase public awareness of the needs of such training. Provides base for continuing cooperation with public officials, voluntary organizations, national associations, and others interested in aging and education. **Publications:** *AGHE Exchange*, quarterly. Newsletter. Includes program resources, public policy update, research reports, calender of workshops and seminars, association news, and new member profiles. *Price:* Included in membership dues; $25/year for nonmembers. • *Brief Bibliographies*, periodic. Bibliographies. Covers 29 different titles. *Price:* $10. • *Determining the Impact of Gerontology Preparation on Personnel in the Aging Network.* • *Diversity and Change in Gerontology, Geriatrics, and Aging Studies Programs in Institutions of Higher Education.* • *Meeting Abstracts*, annual. • *National Directory of Educational Programs in Gerontology and Geriatrics*, biennial. Directory. *Price:* Included in membership dues; $85/year for nonmembers. • *Standards and Guidelines for Gerontology Programs.* • *State-of-the-Art Research Papers*, periodic. Papers. Includes three titles. *Price:* $10.

★ 1891 ★ Beverly Foundation (BF)
70 S. Lake Ave., Ste. 750
Pasadena, CA 91101
Phone: (818)792-2292
Fax: (818)792-6117
Carroll Wendland, Ph.D., Pres.

Founded: 1978. **Description:** Develops education and research programs and policy studies to facilitate long-term health care and supportive services and life quality of people with chronic-care needs, particularly older adults, their families, and caregivers. The focus is on optimal functional independence and an informed public. Unrestricted income is derived from product

sales, interest, dividends, donations, and grants. Restricted funds are sought to support new program developments which focus on improving service systems and methods of long-term care. Sells educational materials to health care industry. Maintains library. **Publications:** *Geriatric Nutrition.*

★ 1892 ★ Brazilian Society of Geriatrics and Gerontology
Avenida Indianapolis 2343
04063-004 Sao Paulo, SP, Brazil
Phone: 11 5782425
Fax: 11 5785625
Dr. Norton Sayeg, Contact

Languages: English, Portuguese, Spanish. **Description:** Gerontologists, other health care professionals, and others with an interest in the care of geriatric patients. Seeks to improve the quality of gerontology in Brazil. Works to increase public awareness of gerontological issues; promotes continued professional development of members.

★ 1893 ★ British Society for Research on Ageing (BSRA)
University of Manchester
School of Biological Sciences
1124 Stopford Bldg.
Oxford Rd.
Manchester M13 9PT, England
Phone: 161 2755252
Fax: 161 2755363
Dr. I. Davies, Hon.Sec.

Founded: 1945. **Members:** 150. **Languages:** English. **Description:** Biological scientists and clinicians involved in the study of aging. Promotes knowledge of the biology of aging and effective treatment of age-related diseases. Works to increase public awareness of the aging process. Sponsors annual postgraduate award competition. **Publications:** *Lifespan*, semiannual. Newsletter. • *Newsletter*, periodic. Newsletter.

★ 1894 ★ The Center for Social Gerontology (TCSG)
2307 Shelby Ave.
Ann Arbor, MI 48103
Phone: (313)665-1126
Fax: (313)665-2071
Penelope A. Hommel, Exec.Dir.

Founded: 1971. **Description:** Purpose is to advance the well-being of older people in the U.S. through research, education, technical assistance, and training. Focuses primarily on legal rights, guardianship and alternative protective services, and delivery of legal services. Provides consulting services. Develops and researches standards for the provision of guardianship services for older people; works to improve the court processes for determining the need for guardianship through development and evaluation of a new model. Conducts periodic training on Legal rights and Legal resources, for legal advocates, nonlawyers who work with the elderly, and older consumers. **Publications:** *Age Discrimination in Employment Law, The ADEA of 1967: A Compendium for Training and Practice.* • *Audiotapes.* • *Best-Practice Notes on Delivery of Legal Services to Older Persons*, quarterly. Bulletin. • *Comprehensive Guide to*

Delivery of Legal Assistance to Older Persons. • *Guardianship and Alternative Legal Interventions: A Compendium for Training and Practice.* • *Guidelines for Planning and Evaluating Legal Assistance Programs Funded Under the Older Americans Act.* • *Headnotes on Critical Legal Issues Affecting Older Persons*, quarterly. Bulletin. • Manuals. • Reports. • *Social Security Disability Law: A Compendium for Training and Practice.* • Videos. **Formerly:** (1985) International Center for Social Gerontology.

★ 1895 ★ Center for the Study of Pharmacy and Therapeutics for the Elderly (CSPTE)
c/o Peter P. Lamy, Ph.D.
School of Pharmacy
20 N. Pine St., Rm. 352
Baltimore, MD 21201
Phone: (410)706-3011
Fax: (410)328-4012
Peter P. Lamy, Ph.D., Dir.

Founded: 1978. **Description:** Conducts research in geriatrics and gerontology, particularly as they relate to pharmacotherapy and pharmacodynamics. Offers educational programs; maintains speakers' bureau; compiles statistics. **Publications:** *Elder Care News*, quarterly. Newsletter.

★ 1896 ★ Center for Understanding Aging (CUA)
200 Executive Blvd, Ste. 201
PO Box 246
Southington, CT 06489
Phone: (203)621-2079
Fax: (203)621-2989
Dr. Donna P. Couper, Exec.Dir.

Founded: 1983. **Members:** 250. **Description:** Professionals in gerontology, education, health care, and other fields interested in developing aging education and intergenerational programming. Seeks to dispel myths about aging and old age; encourages communication among generations and works to create a social environment where people of all ages can live together. Serves as a clearinghouse of information on issues of aging and intergenerational programs; provides consultation and presentation services to individuals or groups that wish to develop aging education programs. Maintains resources for aging education and intergenerational programming. **Publications:** *AgeShare.* • *LINK-AGES*, quarterly. Newsletter. *Price:* $25. • *Schools in an Aging Society.* Six interrelated curriculum guides which provide education, for, with, and about older adults. *Price:* $55. **Formerly:** (1989) Understanding Aging.

★ 1897 ★ Children of Aging Parents (CAPS)
Woodbourne Office Campus, Ste. 302A
1609 Woodbourne Rd.
Levittown, PA 19057-1511
Phone: (215)945-6900
Fax: (215)945-8720
Louise Fradkin, Dir. of Oper.

Founded: 1977. **Members:** 1,300. **Regional Groups:** 10. **Local Groups:** 5. **Description:** Devoted to the education, support, guidance, and development of coping skills of caregivers of the elderly. Holds in-house training for social workers and for nurses and health aides in hospitals, nursing homes, and rehabilitation centers. Conducts outreach programs for hospitals and for gerontology classes in colleges; encourages development of support groups for the elderly. Provides referrals to appropriate professionals. Although most of the organization's activities are centered in Pennsylvania and New Jersey, CAPs acts as a national clearinghouse for information, guidance, advice, and networking to groups and individuals. Plans to organize seminars and additional workshops; has made television and radio appearances. **Publications:** Bibliographies. • *CAPSule*, bimonthly. Newsletter. Reports on concerns of elderly persons and their families. Includes publications listing, book reviews, and research news. *Price:* Included in membership dues. • *Care-Share*, periodic. Directory. • *Guide to Selecting a Nursing Home.* • *How to Start A Self Group for Caregivers.* • *Instant Aging--Sensory Deprivation Manual.* Manual. Publishes fact sheets on caregiving issues.

★ 1898 ★ **Daughters of the Elderly Bridging the Unknown Together (DEBUT)**
c/o Pat Meier
710 Concord St.
Ellettsville, IN 47429
Phone: (812)876-5319
Pat Meier, Facilitator

Founded: 1981. **Members:** 15. **Local Groups:** 1. **Description:** Women involved in caring for elderly parents; individuals preparing for future roles as caregivers. Provides: nonjudgmental support; education in all areas of caring, coping, and in the complex process of aging. Stresses the importance of nursing center advocacy, community outreach, and intergenerational dialogue between adult children and their parents. Delivers presentations at local gerontological functions. Educates the public through radio and television. **Publications:** *Daughters of the Elderly: Building Partnerships in Caregiving.* Book.

★ 1899 ★ **Ebenezer Society (ES)**
2722 Park Ave. S.
Minneapolis, MN 55407
Phone: (612)879-1400
Fax: (612)879-1473
Mark Thomas, Pres.

Founded: 1917. **Members:** 45. **Description:** Lutheran congregations and their delegates. Works to provide quality services and facilities for older people with varying needs; to make their lives more healthful, meaningful, and secure. Services are not limited to Lutheran clients. Offers nursing home care for low-income elderly; provides home services, including medical treatment, to help persons remain in their own homes as long as possible. Sponsors Ebenezer Center for Aging and Human Development which provides consultative services, conducts educational events and applied research, and issues publications. Maintains Ebenezer Foundation as the support arm of the society. Compiles research statistics; offers placement service. Ebenezer means "stone of help."

★ 1900 ★ **Gerontological Society of America (GSA)**
1275 K St. NW, Ste. 350
Washington, DC 20005
Phone: (202)842-1275
Fax: (202)842-1150
Ms. Carol Schutz, Contact

Founded: 1945. **Members:** 7,000. **Description:** Physicians, physiologists, psychologists, anatomists, biochemists, sociologists, social workers, psychiatrists, pharmacologists, nurses, geneticists, zoologists, endocrinologists, economists, administrators, and other professionals interested in improving the well-being of older people by promoting scientific study of the aging process, publishing information for professionals about aging, and bringing together groups interested in aging research. Encourages research and education on the aging process. **Publications:** *Aging and Sensory Change: An Annotated Bibliography.* Bibliography. • *CommonStake.* • *The Gerontologist*, bimonthly. Journal. Includes book and media reviews and abstracts of papers to be presented at the annual meeting. *Price:* Included in membership dues; $55/year for nonmembers; $89/year for institutions. • *Gerontology News*, monthly. Newsletter. Includes employment listings, information on fellowship opportunities and new books, and conference calendar. *Price:* Included in membership dues; $50/year for nonmembers. • *Journals of Gerontology*, bimonthly. Journal. Contains four individual journals entitled *Biological Sciences*, *Medical Sciences*, and *Psychological Sciences*. *Price:* Included in membership dues; $65/year for nonmembers; $99/year for institutions. • *Membership Directory*, periodic. • *Where Do We Come From? What Are We? Where Are We Going?*. **Formerly:** (1980) Gerontological Society.

★ 1901 ★ **Health Promotion Institute (HPI)**
c/o National Council on the Aging
409 3rd St. SW, 2nd Fl.
Washington, DC 20024
Phone: (202)479-1200

Founded: 1985. **Members:** 700. **Description:** A program of the National Council on the Aging. Seeks to aid professionals who are interested in developing and implementing health promotion programs for senior citizens and serving older consumers. Promotes optimal quality of life for older adults, including physical, emotional, and mental health as well as social and spiritual well-being. Advocates for and empowers older adults to achieve health and well-being through a multidisciplinary approach. Provides information and materials on\health promotion programs. **Formerly:** (1991) National Center for Health Promotion and Aging.

★ 1902 ★ **Hispanic American Geriatrics Society (HAGS)**
1 Cutts Rd.
Durham, NH 03824-3102
Phone: (603)868-5757
Dr. Eugene E. Tillock, Pres.

Founded: 1980. **Description:** Long-term care service providers and professionals. Provides advocacy for older Hispanic Americans; offers advice, health care services, and health education programs. **Publications:** *Hispanic Aging*

and Health, periodic. Newsletter. Contains subjects of concern to health service providers serving elderly Hispanic Americans.

International Menopause Society
See: Entry 9667

★ 1903 ★ **International Psychogeriatric Association (IPA)**
5700 Old Orchard Rd.
Skokie, IL 60077
Phone: (708)966-9418
Fax: (708)866-6984
Fern Finkel, Exec.Dir.

Founded: 1981. **Members:** 1,000. **Regional Groups:** 2. **Description:** Health care professionals and scientists with an interest in the behavioral and biological aspects of mental health in the elderly. Works to keep members abreast of developments in research and clinical practice in the field of geriatric mental health. Conducts research programs. **Publications:** Books. • *International Psychogeriatric Association Newsletter*, semiannual. Newsletter. • *International Psychogeriatrics*, semiannual. Journal. *Price:* Available to members only. • Pamphlets.

★ 1904 ★ **Jewish Association for Services for the Aged (JASA)**
40 W. 68th St.
New York, NY 10023
Phone: (212)724-3200
Fax: (212)769-1218
David J. Stern, Exec.VP

Founded: 1968. **Local Groups:** 61. **Description:** Social welfare organization whose objective is to provide the services necessary to enable the older adult to remain in the community. Maintains 18 community service offices and 24 local senior citizens centers in New York City and Nassau and Suffolk Counties, NY. Services include: case management; information and referral to appropriate health, welfare, educational, social, recreational, and vacation services, and on government benefits and entitlements; personal counseling; financial assistance; health and medical service counsel; counsel on housing and long-term care; homemaker service; group educational and recreational activities through senior citizens centers; information and guidance for social action on legislative issues affecting the elderly; hot lunch programs; referral to summer camps; legal services; protective services; reaching out to the isolated; programs for independent senior clubs; volunteer service opportunities. Conducts programs for elderly Soviet Jewish immigrants. Sponsors housing for the elderly: Friendset Apartments, Brookdale Village; Scheuer Houses of Coney Island, Brighton Beach, and Manhattan Beach; Green Residences at Far Rockaway and Cooper Square, NY. Operates home attendant agencies in Brooklyn and Queens, NY. Trains students from the New York University School of Social Work, Hunter College School of Social Work, Yeshiva University School of Social Work, and Adelphi University School of Social Work. **Publications:** *JPAC Action Memo/Senior Citizens Advocate*, 10/year. Newspaper addressing issues of interest to senior citizens, especially those with low income. *Price:* Free.

★ 1905 ★ **Jewish Association for Services for the Aged (JASA)**
97-45 Queens Blvd.
Rego Park, NY 11374
Phone: (718)263-4700
Fax: (718)275-1774
Gloria Sprung, Exec.Dir.

Founded: 1945. **Members:** 75. **Formerly:** Central Bureau for the Jewish Aged.

Lutheran Hospitals and Homes Society (LHHS)
See: Entry 6456

★ 1906 ★ **National Asian Pacific Center on Aging (NAPCA)**
Melbourne Tower
1511 3rd Ave., Ste. 914
Seattle, WA 98101
Phone: (206)624-1221
Fax: (206)624-1023
Don Watanabe, Exec.Dir.

Founded: 1979. **Regional Groups:** 4. **Description:** Goals are to: ensure and improve the delivery of health and social services to elderly Pacific/Asians; increase the capabilities of community-based services by expanding their information and technical base; include Pacific/Asians in planning and organizational activities, thus maintaining a strong link between the center and the community. Provides technical assistance to the generic service delivery system on program development and organizational capacity building and training. Compiles statistics. **Publications:** *Asian Pacific Affairs*, quarterly. Newsletter. • *Directory of Pacific/Asian Media Sources*. Directory. • *Pacific/Asian Elderly Bibliography*. Directory. • *Registry of Services for Pacific/Asian Elderly*, biennial. Directory. **Formerly:** (1993) National Pacific/Asian Resource Center on Aging.

National Association of Activity Professionals (NAAP)
See: Entry 4513

★ 1907 ★ **National Association of Nutrition and Aging Services Programs (NANASP)**
2675 44th St. SW, Ste. 305
Grand Rapids, MI 49509
Phone: (616)531-9909
Free: 800-999-6262
Fax: (616)531-3103
Connie Benton Wolfe, Exec.Dir.

Founded: 1977. **Members:** 1,000. **Description:** Directors and staff of congregate and home-delivered nutrition services programs for the elderly. Objectives are: to promote professional growth and raise the standards of the profession among members; to encourage communication between aging services programs and federal agencies and governmental bodies; to promote the development of resources supportive to aging service programs. Informs members of national legislation that affects nutrition and aging programs; testifies at congressional hearings. Has developed national standards for congregate and home-delivered services programs. Conducts research and national surveys. **Publications:** Annual Report, annual. • *Collection of Innovative Models*. • *Many Hats*, quarterly. Newsletter. Contains tips on professional site

management and activity updates. *Price:* Included in membership dues. • *Monthly Membership Updates*, monthly. • *NANASP News*, quarterly. Newsletter. Contains legislative and membership updates, and new product information. *Price:* Included in membership dues. • *National Standards for Congregate Meals*. • *National Standards for Home-Delivered Meals*. • *Preparing Nutrition Programs for the Nineties*. • *Special Bulletins*, monthly. Bulletin. • *Special Report to Members*, quarterly. Newsletter. *Price:* Included in membership dues. **Formerly:** (1978) National Association of Title Seven Directors.

★ 1908 ★ **National Association of Professional Geriatric Care Managers (NAPGCM)**
1604 N. Country Club Rd.
Tucson, AZ 85716
Phone: (602)881-8008
Fax: (602)325-7925
Laury L. Adsit, Exec.Dir.

Founded: 1985. **Members:** 550. **Description:** Promotes quality services and care for elderly citizens. Provides referral service and distributes information to individuals interested in geriatric care centers. Operates speakers' bureau; maintains referral network. **Publications:** *Geriatric Care Manager*, quarterly. Journal. • Membership Directory, annual. *Price:* $35.

★ 1909 ★ **National Association of State Units on Aging (NASUA)**
1225 Eye St. NW, Ste. 725
Washington, DC 20005
Phone: (202)898-2578
Free: 800-989-2243
Fax: (202)898-2583
Daniel A. Quirk, Ph.D., Exec.Dir.

Founded: 1964. **Members:** 57. **Description:** Public interest organization that provides information, technical assistance, and professional development support to State Units on Aging. (A state unit is an agency of state government designated by the governor and state legislature to administer the Older Americans Act and to serve as a focal point for all matters relating to older people.) Serves as organized channel for officially designated state leadership in aging to exchange information and mutual experiences, and to join together for appropriate action on behalf of the elderly. Services include: information on federal policy and program developments in aging; training and technical assistance on a wide range of program and management issues; liaison with organizations representing the public and private sectors. **Publications:** Books. • *Directory of State Units on Aging*, periodic. Directory. • Manuals. • Reports. Also publishes materials on aging policy and programs, policy briefs, legislative updates, and technical assistance documents.

★ 1910 ★ **National Caucus and Center on Black Aged (NCBA)**
1424 K St. NW, Ste. 500
Washington, DC 20005
Phone: (202)637-8400
Fax: (202)347-0895
Samuel J. Simmons, Pres.

Founded: 1970. **Members:** 3,000. **Local Groups:** 45. **Description:** Seeks to improve living conditions for low-income elderly Americans, particularly blacks. Advocates changes in federal and state laws in improving the economic, health, and social status of low-income senior citizens. Promotes community awareness of problems and issues effecting low-income aging population. Operates an employment program involving 2000 older persons in 14 states. Sponsors, owns, and manages rental housing for the elderly. Conducts training and intern programs in nursing home administration, long-term care, housing management, and commercial property maintenance. **Publications:** Bulletin. • *Golden Page*, quarterly. Newsletter. Reports developments concerning elderly blacks; includes association news and legislative update. *Price:* Included in membership dues.

★ 1911 ★ **National Council on the Aging (NCOA)**
409 3rd St. SW, 2nd Fl.
Washington, DC 20024
Phone: (202)479-1200
Fax: (202)479-0735
Dr. James Firman, Pres.

Founded: 1950. **Members:** 8,000. **Description:** Individuals and organizations who work on behalf of older Americans, including individuals in business and industry, organized labor, and the health professions; social workers, librarians, the clergy, and educators; housing, research, and government agencies; state and local agencies on the aging. Cooperates with other organizations to promote concern for older people and develop methods and resources for meeting their needs. Provides a national information and consultation center; holds conferences and workshops. Operates Family Friends Program, which recruits and trains older volunteers to work with families with chronically ill or disabled children. Conducts research and demonstration programs on issues important to older people such as: training and placement of older workers; economic security; services for the frail elderly living in their own homes; access to health and social services; increasing opportunities for socialization and participation in artistic, cultural, and educational programs and services; corporate programs; senior centers. Maintains the National Association of Older Worker Employment Services, Health Promotion Institute, National Center on Rural Aging, National Institute on Adult Daycare, National Institute on Community-Based Long-Term Care, National Institute of Senior Centers, National Institute of Senior Housing, National Interfaith Coalition on Aging, National Voluntary Organizations for Independent Living for the Aging and National Institute on Financial Issues and Services for Elders and National Center for Voluntary Leadership in Aging. **Publications:** *Abstracts in Social Gerontology: Current Literature on Aging*, quarterly. Journal. Features books, reports, and articles on a variety of aging issues. Includes author and subject index. *Price:* Free to members. • Books. • Brochures. • *NCOA Networks*, bimonthly. Newspaper. Contains highlights of activities, legislative reports, and new developments in the field. *Price:* Available to members only. • Pamphlets. • *Perspective on Aging*, quarterly. Magazine. Covers issues and developments in the field of aging. *Price:* Available to members only. **Formerly:** (1960) National Committee on Aging of National Social Welfare Assembly.

★ **1912** ★ **National Council of Senior Citizens (NCSC)**
1331 F St. NW
Washington, DC 20004-1171
Phone: (202)347-8800
Fax: (202)624-9595
Lawrence T. Smedley, Exec.Dir.

Founded: 1961. **Members:** 5000,000. **Description:** Organization of autonomous senior citizens clubs, associations, councils, and other groups with a combined membership of over 5,000,000 persons. Educational and action group which supports the preservation of Medicare and Social Security, the enactment of a national health plan which includes long-term care, reduced costs on drugs, better housing, and other programs to aid senior citizens. Sponsors mass rallies, educational workshops and leadership training institutes; provides speakers on issues concerning senior citizens; helps organize and develop programs for local and state groups. Encourages participation in social and political action activities. Endorses candidates for political office. Sponsors National Senior Citizens Education and Research Center. **Publications:** *Congressional Directory*, biennial. Directory. • *Retirement Newsletter*, monthly. Newsletter. • *Senior Citizens News*, monthly. *Price:* Free to members. **Formerly:** National Council of Senior Citizens for Health Care Through Social Security.

National Eye Care Project (NECP)
See: Entry 13534

★ **1913** ★ **National Institute on Adult Daycare (NIAD)**
c/o National Council on the Aging
409 3rd St. SW, 2nd Fl.
Washington, DC 20024
Phone: (202)479-6682
Fax: (202)479-0735
Betty Ransom, Program Mgr.

Founded: 1979. **Members:** 1,200. **Regional Groups:** 10. **Description:** Adult daycare practitioners; health and social service planners; individuals involved in planning and providing services for older persons. (Daycare centers offer services in a group setting ranging from active rehabilitation to social and health care.) Promotes and enhances adult daycare programs; provides services and activities for disabled older persons on a long-term basis; provides training and technical assistance and consultation services for daycare personnel; organizes funding; develops standards and guidelines for adult daycare programs; encourages adult daycare centers to participate in local area health planning activities to heighten the effectiveness of adult daycare. Plans and conducts training events for annual meeting and related conferences; maintains annotated bibliography; lobbies for approved public policy positions; surveys state adult daycare regulations and legislation. **Publications:** *Developing Adult Day Care: An Approach to Maintaining Independence for Impaired Older Persons.* • *NCOA Networks*, bimonthly. Newsletter. Reports on adult day care and other aging issues with a focus on public

policy. *Price:* Free, for members only. • *Standards for Adult Day Care.*

★ **1914** ★ **National Institute on Community-Based Long-Term Care (NICLC)**
c/o National Council on the Aging
409 3rd St. SW, 2nd Fl.
Washington, DC 20024
Phone: (202)479-1200
Fax: (202)479-0735
Jennifer L. Taylor, Mgr.

Founded: 1984. **Members:** 1,100. **Description:** A unit of the National Council on the Aging. Seeks to promote and develop a comprehensive long-term care system that will integrate home-and community-based services, enabling older adults to live in their own homes as long as possible. Serves as information clearinghouse for long-term care professionals. Advocates public policies that support home and community-based services. Maintains speakers' bureau; offers educational sessions; compiles statistics. **Publications:** *Care Management Standards*. Book. • *NCOA Networks*, bimonthly. Newsletter. • *Perspective on Aging*, periodic. Journal. Deals with aging issues.

★ **1915** ★ **National Voluntary Organizations for Independent Living for the Aging (NVOILA)**
c/o National Council on the Aging
409 3rd St. SW
Washington, DC 20024
Phone: (202)479-6682
Fax: (202)479-0735
Betty Ransom, Program Manager

Founded: 1971. **Members:** 100. **Description:** A constituent unit of the National Council on the Aging. National voluntary organizations seeking to improve the lives of older persons. Emphasizes the need for in-home and community-based health and social services designed to help older persons remain in or return to their homes and live independently; works to educate and assist national voluntary organizations to help develop such services. Encourages cooperation between voluntary organizations and the public; provides forum for organizations, government agencies, and consumer groups to share ideas and develop a network of services for the aged. Informs members on matters concerning aging; assists members in planning projects and conferences. Sponsors projects. **Formerly:** (1973) Steering Committee of National Voluntary Organizations for Service to Older Persons in Their Own Homes or Other Places of Residence.

★ **1916** ★ **North American Association of Jewish Homes and Housing for the Aging (NAJHHA)**
10830 N. Central Expwy., Ste. 150
Dallas, TX 75231-1022
Phone: (214)696-9838
Fax: (214)360-0753
Dr. Herbert Shore, Exec.VP

Founded: 1960. **Members:** 225. **Description:** Nonprofit charitable Jewish homes and nursing homes; retirement and housing units; independent and assisted living, geriatric hospitals, and special facilities for Jewish aged and chronically ill. Conducts institutes and conferences; undertakes legislative activities; compiles statistics. **Publications:** Directory, biennial. • *From the Housing Home Front*, bimonthly. • *Perspectives*, quarterly. **Formerly:** (1982) National Association of Jewish Homes for the Aged.

PRIDE Foundation - Promote Real Independence for the Disabled and Elderly
See: Entry 12710

★ **1917** ★ **Retired Persons Services (RPS)**
500 Montgomery St.
Alexandria, VA 22314-1563
Phone: (703)684-0244
Fax: (703)684-0246
Brian Frid, Pres.

Founded: 1959. **Description:** Mail service pharmacy for members of the American Association of Retired Persons. Provides prescription and nonprescription drugs, vitamins, and other health care items through mail service and walk-in facilities in California, Texas, Missouri, Oregon, Indiana, Connecticut, Florida, Pennsylvania, Nevada, Virginia, and Washington, DC. Encourages consumer awareness, comparison shopping, and use of generic drugs.

★ **1918** ★ **Re'uth Women's Social Service (WSSI)**
130 E. 59th St., Ste. 900
New York, NY 10022
Phone: (212)836-1570
Fax: (212)836-1114
Rosa Strygier, Pres.

Founded: 1951. **Members:** 1,500. **Description:** Raises funds for OHN hospital and homes for the aged in Israel by means of subscription social functions. **Publications:** Journal, annual. **Formerly:** (1988) Women's Social Service for Israel.

★ **1919** ★ **Sandoz Foundation for Regional Gerontological Research in Latin America**
(Fundacio Sandoz para Investigacion en Gerontologia Regional para Latin America)
Rua Henri Dunant 500
04709 Sao Paulo, SP, Brazil

Languages: Portuguese, Spanish. **Description:** Health care professionals, medical researchers, and others with an interest in gerontology. Promotes improved understanding of gerontological issues among health care providers in Latin America; supports gerontology research programs in the region.

★ **1920** ★ **Society of Geriatric Ophthalmology (SGO)**
63 2nd St.
South Orange, NJ 07079
Phone: (201)763-1381
Fax: (201)762-9449
John Norris, Exec.Dir.

Founded: 1975. **Members:** 80. **Description:** Ophthalmologists interested in the vision problems of the elderly. Works to disseminate information regarding the problems of geriatric patients and to stimulate research. Provides speakers and programs dealing with the needs of the elderly. **Publications:** *Society of Geriatric Ophthalmology--Newsletter*, 2-3/year. Newsletter.

Special Constituency Section for Aging and Long Term Care Services
See: Entry 6472

Research Centers

★ 1921 ★ Auburn University
Center on Aging
100 Mell Hall
Auburn, AL 36849-5609
Phone: (334)844-5165
Fax: (334)844-3101
Dr. Gene Bramlett, Dir.

Research Activities and Fields: Studies problems associated with aging, including decubital ulcers, speech and hearing disorders, and experimental drug therapy; identifies creative initiatives to assist older adults to fulfill personal needs, such as nutritious food, exercise, shelter, medical services, knowledge and skills, satisfying personal relationships, reading, writing, reasoning, travel, recreation, artistic endeavors, and development of second careers.

★ 1922 ★ Ball State University
Center for Gerontology
Muncie, IN 47306
Phone: (317)285-1293
Fax: (317)285-1624
Royda Crose, Ph.D., Coord.

Research Activities and Fields: Aging, including mental health and Alzhemier's disease research. **Publications:** *Kirkpatrick Proceedings.* **Formerly:** Institute of Gerontology (1992).

★ 1923 ★ Baylor College of Medicine
Roy M. and Phyllis Gough Huffington
Center on Aging
One Baylor Plaza, M-320
Houston, TX 77030-3498
Phone: (713)798-4453
Fax: (713)798-4161
Robert J. Luchi, M.D., Dir.

Research Activities and Fields: Cell and molecular biology of aging, cardiovascular disease, and ethics in long-term care. **E-mail Address:** jsmith@bcm.tmc.edu.

★ 1924 ★ Baylor University
Institute for Gerontological Studies
PO Box 97292
Waco, TX 76798-7292
Phone: (817)755-1164
Fax: (817)755-1175
Dr. Ben E. Dickerson, Dir.

Research Activities and Fields: Physical, emotional, social, and spiritual needs of older persons, including family solidarity in later life, geriatric dentistry, problems of the older offender, and life-long learning.

★ 1925 ★ Boston University
Gerontology Center
53 Bay State Rd.
Boston, MA 02215
Phone: (617)353-5045
Fax: (617)353-5047
Patricia P. Barry, M.D., Dir.

Research Activities and Fields: Gerontology, including biological, psychological, social, medical, and humanistic concerns relating to aging and the elderly. Identifies socially relevant problems in the fields of gerontology and human development, socioeconomic factors impinging upon the lives and well-being of older adults, historical context in which values and attitudes toward the aging have been defined and redefined, and the medical and social services developed to serve the older person in American society. **Publications:** Newletter.

Brandeis University
Policy Center on Aging
See: Entry 5612

★ 1926 ★ Brown University
Center for Gerontology and Health Care
Research
Box G
Providence, RI 02912
Phone: (401)863-3490
Fax: (401)863-3489
Vincent Mor, Ph.D., Dir.

Research Activities and Fields: Fundamental and applied research relating to aging, chronic disease, and long-term care with particular emphasis on the assessment of function and health status and its application to diagnosis, prognosis and monitoring of long-term care. Offers data collection and teaching and training services. **Publications:** *Long Term Care Quality* (newsletter); Monograph series. **E-mail Address:** rls@chcrvi.chcr.brown.edu. **Formerly:** New England Long Term Gerontology Center (1985).

★ 1927 ★ Case Western Reserve University
Elderly Care Research Center (ECRC)
Mather Memorial, 226
Cleveland, OH 44106
Phone: (216)368-5247
Fax: (216)368-2676
Dr. Eva Kahana, Dir.

Research Activities and Fields: Aging, health, and mental health, including public policy issues, predictors of wellness and vulnerability, environmental and social influences on well-being of the elderly, cross-national and cross-cultural comparisons, and health and mental health outcomes of stress, coping, and adaptation. **Publications:** Brochure. **E-mail Address:** exk@po.cwru.edu.

★ 1928 ★ Case Western Reserve University
University Center on Aging and Health
10900 Euclid Ave.
Cleveland, OH 44106-7131
Phone: (216)368-2692
Fax: (216)368-6389
May L. Wykle, Ph.D., R.N., Dir.

Research Activities and Fields: Conducts, supports, and facilitates research at the University on aging and health, including black vs. white caregivers' formal/informal service use, and effects of stress on persons over 85 years of age. Emphasizes prevention, diagnosis, treatment, management of illness or disability, and service utilization of care giver. **Publications:** Newsletter (semiannually); cosponsors publication of the *Journal of Cross-Cultural Gerontology.*

★ 1929 ★ Center for Senility Studies:
Alzheimer's Disease Treatment Research
161 N. Dithridge St.
Pittsburgh, PA 15213
Phone: (412)683-7111
Arthur C. Walsh, M.D., Pres.

Research Activities and Fields: Senility, Alzheimer's disease, and hypochondriasis in the elderly, particularly brain dysfunction related to impaired circulation, psychiatric aspects of senility, treatment of chronic schizophrenia, and the effect of anticoagulant therapy. **Publications:** *Mental Capacity: Medical and Legal Aspects of Aging* (annual supplement of research findings). **Formerly:** Center for Senility Studies (1991).

★ 1930 ★ Center for the Study of Aging,
Inc.
706 Madison Ave.
Albany, NY 12208
Phone: (518)465-6927
Fax: (518)462-1339
Sara Harris, Exec.Dir.

Research Activities and Fields: Social and medical research on aging, including physical activity and aging, housing for the elderly, geriatric cardiology, nutrition, mental health, oral history, public policy, caregiving, prevention and respite care for the frail elderly. **Publications:** *Physical Activity, Aging and Sports*(volume i-iv); *Environment and Aging* (second edition); *Safe Therapeutic Exercise for the Frail Aged, an Introduction.*

★ 1931 ★ Cleveland State University
Center on Applied Gerontological
Research
1983 E. 24th St.
Cleveland, OH 44115
Phone: (216)687-3762
Fax: (216)687-9294
Dr. Boaz Kahana, Dir.

Research Activities and Fields: Aging, post-retirement relocation, and coping with caregiving among the elderly; long-term effects of post-traumatic stress syndrome, focusing on war veterans, prisoners of war, Holocaust survivors, and Cambodian refugees.

★ 1932 ★ Columbia University
Center for Geriatrics, Gerontology
100 Haven Ave., Tower 3-30F
New York, NY 10032
Phone: (212)781-0600
Fax: (212)795-7696
Dr. Barry Gurland, Dir.

Research Activities and Fields: Methodological, epidemiological and clinical research in geriatrics/gerontology and long-term care. Specific studies are directed toward mental disorders, psychosocial problems, and funtional impairments of the elderly. The Center has developed model projects using a comprehensive assessment instrument that has been refined for use in various settings. The Center is also active in cross-national research with a collaborating group in London. **Formerly:** Long-Term Care Gerontology Center.

Dallas Geriatric Research Institute
See: Entry 9272

★ 1933 ★ **Duke University**
Center for Study of Aging and Human
   Development
Medical Center
Box 3003
Durham, NC 27710
Phone: (919)660-7500
Fax: (919)684-8569
Harvey Jay Cohen, M.D., Dir.

Research Activities and Fields: Human and animal physiology, immunology, neuroendocrinology, pharmacology, carcinogenesis, enzyme biochemistry, free radical effects, membrane and receptor function, bone metabolism and osteoporosis, central nervous system structure and function, Alzheimer's disease, dementia, cognitive processes, psychometrics, human personality and behavior, family structure and intergenerational relationships, and the demographics and economics of aging populations. The Aging Center coordinates research, training, and clinical services in aging for the University. The Division of Geriatrics focuses research on the basic and clinical aspects of aging, emphasizing neoplasia, bone and musculoskeletal disorders and rehabilitation involved, immunology, cardiovascular diseases, cerebrovascular dis ease/dementia, enzymatic and cellular basis for aging, and health services delivery for the aged. **Publications:** *Long Term Care Advances*; *Center Report* (quarterly).

★ 1934 ★ **Edward and Esther Polisher**
   Research Institute
Philadelphia Geriatric Center
5301 Old York Rd.
Philadelphia, PA 19141
Phone: (215)456-2000
Fax: (215)456-2017
Dr. Robert Rubinstein, Dir.

Research Activities and Fields: Social, cultural, psychological, medical, and biological aspects of aging and services to the aged. Conducts basic and applied research on caregivers of impaired elderly and treatments for depression. Also conducts studies of housing, ethnicity and aging, Alzheimer's disease, and biomarkers of depression. **Publications:** *Research Highlights* (occasionally). **Formerly:** Gerontological Research Institute (1988).

★ 1935 ★ **Georgia Consortium on the**
   Psychology of Aging
Univ. of Georgia
Gerontology Center
100 Candler Hall
Athens, GA 30602
Phone: (706)542-3954
Fax: (706)542-4805
Leonard W. Poon, Ph.D., Consortium Coord.

Research Activities and Fields: Psychology of aging, including basic studies in cognition, and clinical diagnosis and treatment of behavioral dysfunctions most often found with the aged. The Consortium was formed to share training and research resources and to foster interaction between psychologists and other scientists.

★ 1936 ★ **Gerontology Research Center**
4940 Eastern Ave.
Baltimore, MD 21224
Phone: (410)558-8110
Fax: (410)558-8137
Dr. Edward Lakatta, Dir.

Research Activities and Fields: Gerontology research, including molecular genetics, human physiology, personality, behavioral research, and Alzheimer's disease studies. **Formerly:** Gerontology Research Institute.

★ 1937 ★ **J. Paul Sticht Center on Aging**
   and Rehabilitation
North Carolina Baptist Hospitals, Inc.
Winston-Salem, NC 27157
Phone: (910)716-4722
Fax: (910)716-2067
Steven C. Snelgrove, V.Pres., Operations

Research Activities and Fields: Metabolic and biomedical research in aging and rehabilitation, focusing on nutritional deficiencies and problems in the elderly.

★ 1938 ★ **Kent State University**
Gerontology Center
College of Continuing Studies
PO Box 5190
Kent, OH 44242
Phone: (216)672-2002
Fax: (216)672-2079
David Hefling, Coord.

Research Activities and Fields: All facets of aging and related issues. Works with the School of Family and Consumer Studies and the Northeastern Ohio Universities College of Medicine on a continual basis. **Publications:** *Gerontology Center News and Information Bulletin* (several times annually).

Loyola University Chicago
Neuroscience and Aging Institute
See: Entry 8388

Maharishi International University
Laboratory for Health and Aging Studies
See: Entry 1622

★ 1939 ★ **Medical College of Pennsylvania**
   and Hahnemann University
Center for Gerontological Research
2900 Queen Lane
Philadelphia, PA 19129
Phone: (215)991-8460
Fax: (215)843-1192
Dr. Vincent J. Cristofalo, Dir.

Research Activities and Fields: Cell cycle kinetics and dynamics, growth factor regulatory mechanisms, growth/senescence regulatory genes, cellular transformation and immortalization, and regulation of gene expression. **Publications:** Annual Status Report.

★ 1940 ★ **Memorial University of**
   Newfoundland
Gerontology Centre
St. John's, NF, Canada A1B 3X9
Phone: (709)737-4381
Fax: (709)737-4510
Dr. Albert Kozma, Dir.

Research Activities and Fields: Gerontology, focusing on quality of life studies, including determinants of subjective well-being in the elderly, loneliness, pursuits of the creative elderly, and adjustment after bereavement; prevention of later life illness, including longitudinal investigation of health behavior consequences; determinants and treatment of later life illness, including hypertension, immune system function, Alzheimer's disease and cognitive disorders, and medication use; aging and behavior change, including learning and memory, hearing loss, and cognitive and physical performance; and the social context of aging, including abuse and victimization of the elderly, detection of dysfunction by physicians, social networks, and resource requirements of the ill.

★ 1941 ★ **Mount Sinai School of Medicine**
   of City University of New York
International Leadership Center on
   Longevity and Society
Dept. of Geriatrics & Adult Development
Box 1070
New York, NY 10029-1070
Phone: (212)241-1472
Fax: (212)860-9737
Robert N. Butler, M.D., Dir.

Research Activities and Fields: Health, long-term care, and productive aging, emphasizing policy implications for future generations and institutions. **Publications:** *Productive Aging News*, (newsletter); Annual Report.

★ 1942 ★ **Multidisciplinary Center for the**
   Study of Aging
VA Medical Center
111T 3495 Bailey Ave.
Buffalo, NY 14215
Phone: (716)862-3421
Fax: (716)862-3414
Dr. John Edwards, Head

Research Activities and Fields: Mental health in later life, including quality of geriatric care in HMO settings, service utilization by minority elderly, epidemiology of Alzheimer's disease and Down's syndrome, and the use of tests in assessment of dementia. Supports training caregivers of frail and dependent elders, particularly those with Alzheimer's disease, and the continuing education of geriatric health care and social service professionals in New York State. **Publications:** Monographs.

★ 1943 ★ **Old Dominion University**
Center for Gerontology
College of Health Sciences
Norfolk, VA 23529
Phone: (804)683-4989
Fax: (804)683-5674
Raymond M. Leinbach, Dir.

Research Activities and Fields: Gerontology.

Oxford Gerontology Center
See: Entry 9273

★ 1944 ★ Pennsylvania State University Gerontology Center
S-210 Henderson Bldg.
University Park, PA 16802
Phone: (814)865-1710
Fax: (814)863-9423
Dr. K. Warner Schaie, Dir.

Research Activities and Fields: Broad interdisciplinary approach to questions on aging. Major areas of research are cognition in aging, developmental methodology, family and informal supports, and animal models of aging. Specific topics include reversing cognitive decline, human services for the elderly, caregiving, urinary incontinence, and the use of pharmaceutical products. **Publications:** Biannual Newsletter; Annual preprint/reprint catalog. **E-mail Address:** arhi@psuvm.psu.edu.

★ 1945 ★ Portland State University Institute on Aging
Box 751
Portland, OR 97207
Phone: (503)725-3952
Fax: (503)725-5199
Elizabeth A. Kutza, Ph.D., Dir.

Research Activities and Fields: Adult development and aging, including health and social care systems, social and economic life maintenance, political behavior, age status, economic behavior, social and psychological phenomena, and communication. **Publications:** Discussion Paper Series. **E-mail Address:** beth@upa.pdx.edu.

Research Institute of the Hebrew Home of Greater Washington
See: Entry 9274

★ 1946 ★ Sun Health Research Institute
10515 W. Santa Fe
Sun City, AZ 85351
Phone: (602)876-5328
Fax: (602)876-5461
Dr. Joseph Rogers, Dir.

Research Activities and Fields: Alzheimer's disease, Parkinson's disease, and arthritis and other age-related diseases. Research focuses on molecular genetics of aging, immune dysfunctions in the elderly, and neural-tissue transplantation. **Formerly:** Institute for Biogerontology Research.

★ 1947 ★ Temple University Institute on Aging
1601 N. Broad St.
Philadelphia, PA 19122
Phone: (215)204-6834
Fax: (215)204-6733
Dr. Albert Finestone, Exec.Dir.

Research Activities and Fields: Changes in adaptive capabilities during aging, anti-aging effects of dehydroepiandrosterone (DHEA), the influences of characteristics of elderly disabled clients on their experiences in case management, minority/ethnic aging research, and service management and services to the frail elderly. **E-mail Address:** bitnet.v2226a. **Formerly:** Outgrowth of the Aging Research Center.

U.S. Department of Agriculture Agricultural Research Service Human Nutrition Research Center on Aging
See: Entry 9538

★ 1948 ★ U.S. Department of Health and Human Services National Institute on Aging
Bldg. 31., Rm. 5C27
9000 Rockville Pike
Bethesda, MD 20892
Phone: (301)496-1752
Fax: (301)496-1072
Dr. Richard J. Hodes, Director

Research Activities and Fields: NIA conducts and supports research and training relating to the biomedical, social, and behavioral aspects of aging. The Intramural Research Program is primarily conducted at the Gerontology Research Center in Baltimore, MD. In addition, the Institute's Neurosciences Laboratory operates basic and clinical research programs from the NIH Clinical Center in Bethesda, MD. The principal NIA extramural programs are the Behavioral and Social Research Program, the Biology of Aging Program, the Geriatrics Program, and the Neuroscience and Neuropsychology of Aging Program. The Institute also funds 28 Alzheimer's Disease Research Centers (ARDC's). ARDC studies include the basic mechanisms of Alzheimer's Disease, what can be done to treat it, and helping families to cope. In addition, the NIA Teaching and Nursing Home Awards program supports research by academic medical centers and nursing homes on geriatric health problems in nursing homes and other clinical settings. Areas included in the program are: diagnostic assessment of the geriatric patient, dementia, incontinence, fall injuries, and musculoskeletal disorders producing functional disability in the geriatric population, among others.

★ 1949 ★ U.S. Department of Health and Human Services National Institute on Aging Behavioral and Social Research Program
Gateway Bldg., Rm 2C-234
7201 Wisconsin Ave.
Bethesda, MD 20892
Phone: (301)496-3136
Fax: (301)402-0051
Dr. Ronald P. Abeles, Acting Associate Director

Research Activities and Fields: Program supports research and research training concerned with social, psychological, cultural, and economic factors that affect both the process of growing old and the place of older people in society as well as the ways in which behavioral and social processes interacting with biomedical processes influence particular aspects of health and functioning as people age. Its goals are to prolong the productive, healthy, middle years of life and to prevent or reverse such decrements of old age as memory loss, chronic ill health, sensory deficits, low self-esteem, and withdrawal from active participation in social and economic roles. The program focuses primarily on three broad categories: 1) adult psychological development, with research supported that investigates social and behavioral influences upon cognitive functioning, personal-

ity, attitudes, and interpersonal relations over the adult life course, with emphasis on research relevant to maintaining and improving well being and independent functioning; 2) social science research on aging, which is directed at understanding the social and environmental conditions influencing health, well being, and functioning of people in their middle and later years as well as the influence of social structures on aging and the interactions among psychosocial and biological processes on health and functioning; and 3) demography and population epidemiology, involving research on the dynamics and consequences of population aging and aims to describe and understand the older population in terms of its social, demographic, economic, health, and functional characteristics and the impact of these changes on society as a whole.

★ 1950 ★ U.S. Department of Health and Human Services National Institute on Aging Biology of Aging Program
7201 Wisconsin Ave., Ste. 2C-231
Bethesda, MD 20892
Phone: (301)496-4996
Fax: (301)402-0010
Dr. Richard L. Sprott, Associate Director

Research Activities and Fields: Program supports research focusing on basic mechanisms involved in aging processes and age-related disease. It funds research and training in ten main areas: 1) biochemistry; 2) genetics; 3) endocrinology; 4) immunology; 5) nutrition and metabolism; 6) molecular biology; 7) pathobiology; 8) cell biology; 9) physiology; and 10) biomarkers of aging. The Program also supports facilities that provide investigators with aging animals and cell cultures for use in aging research.

★ 1951 ★ U.S. Department of Health and Human Services National Institute on Aging Biology of Aging Program Biology Branch
Gateway Bldg., Ste. 2C231
7201 Wisconsin Ave.
Bethesda, MD 20892
Phone: (301)496-6402
Fax: (301)402-0010
Dr. Anna McCormick, Contact

Research Activities and Fields: Branch currently supports research in four main areas: 1) cellular aging research, which involves research using differentiated human cells in culture and the study of age-associated alterations in differentiated functions that are expressed by cells in vitro; 2) fundamental molecular and genetics research and research training on the biology and mechanisms of aging at the cellular level and on vertebrate and invertebrate organisms, with particular interest in research that emphasizes the use of mammalian and human models; 3) immunological research on the effects of aging on the various functions of the immune system; and 4) research on age-related changes in endocrine function.

★ 1952 ★ **U.S. Department of Health and Human Services**
National Institute on Aging
Biology of Aging Program
Geriatrics Branch
NIH Bldg. 31, Rm. 5C27
9000 Rockville Pike
Bethesda, MD 20892
Phone: (301)496-1033
Dr. Evan Hadley, Chief

Research Activities and Fields: Areas of research currently supported through the Geriatrics Program include studies on the epidemiology, etiology, pathophysiology, diagnostic evaluation, and treatment of urinary incontinence in the elderly; studies on obesity, with particular interest in the effects of obesity on health and longevity, treatment of obesity, and contribution of overnutrition to aging of organ systems; research on infectious diseases in the elderly (cosponsored with the National Institute of Allergy and Infectious Diseases); studies on aspects of diabetes mellitus related to aging and the elderly and studies on the epidemiology of diabetes; and nutrition in relation to health of the aged and the aging process. Research also includes investigation of the function of the aging musculoskeletal system (including support for animal models or clinical studies in exercise physiology or orthopedic research); studies on enteral and parenteral nutritional support in elderly patients in acute and long-term care facilities (announced with five other institutes); research on the causes of age-related cardiovascular changes (and changes in risk factors for cardiovascular disease) and on the role of cardiovascular factors in age-related physiologic and pathologic changes; and studies on exercise physiology and aging.

★ 1953 ★ **U.S. Department of Health and Human Services**
National Institute on Aging
Epidemiology, Demography, and Biometry Program
7201 Wisconsin Ave., Ste. 3C-309
Bethesda, MD 20892
Phone: (301)496-1178
Fax: (301)496-4006
Richard J. Havlick, M.D., Associate Director

Research Activities and Fields: Health and illness in older populations, including hip fractures and osteoporosis, dementia and other cognitive impairments, sleep disorders, predictive factors of mortality, bereavement behaviors, and events and conditions common among older persons prior to death. Gathers demographic information on the current and projected health, economic, social, and occupational status of older people.

★ 1954 ★ **U.S. Department of Health and Human Services**
National Institute on Aging
Intramural Research Program
Gerontology Research Center
4940 Eastern Ave.
Baltimore, MD 21224
Phone: (301)558-8114
Fax: (301)558-8103
Dr. George R. Martin, Scientific Director

Research Activities and Fields: NIA intramural laboratories conduct quantitative and qualitative research on the process of aging in animals and man. Projects include the Baltimore Longitudinal Study of Aging, which involves the biennial observation of the same human subjects to determine changes and elucidate mechanisms underlying these changes. Program components include: 1) Behavioral Sciences Laboratory; 2) Biological Chemistry Laboratory; 3) Cardiovascular Science Laboratory; 4) Cellular and Molecular Biology Laboratory; 5) Clinical Physiology Laboratory; 6) Longitudinal Studies Branch; 7) Molecular Genetics Laboratory; 8) Neurosciences Laboratory; and 9) Personality and Cognition Laboratory.

★ 1955 ★ **U.S. Department of Health and Human Services**
National Institute on Aging
Intramural Research Program
Longitudinal Studies Branch
Gerontology Research Center
4940 Eastern Ave.
Baltimore, MD 21224
Phone: (301)550-1766
Fax: (301)550-1704
James L. Fozard, Ph.D., Chief

Research Activities and Fields: Branch conducts research on aging, particularly physiological and psychological aspects.

★ 1956 ★ **U.S. Department of Health and Human Services**
National Institute on Aging
Laboratory of Behavioral Sciences
Gerontology Research Center
4940 Eastern Ave.
Baltimore, MD 21224
Phone: (410)558-8210
Dr. Bernard T. Engel, Chief

Research Activities and Fields: Laboratory conducts clinical research on the application of behavioral methods and principles in the assessment, control, and treatment of age-related medical disorders. Activities of the Laboratory's Behavioral Medicine Section include laboratory and field studies of the interactions between behavioral or psychological factors such as mobility and depression, and clinical disorders such as incontinence, heart disease, emphysema, and high blood pressure. The interactions between behavioral and psychological factors (such as work activity or mood) and physiological or biochemical responses in normal human subjects are also studied. The Behavioral Physiology Section conducts basic studies in appropriate animal models on the mechanisms mediating the interactions between behavioral factors (e.g., learning or dissemination) and physiological or biochemical factors (e.g., the cardiovascular or pulmonary adjustments to exercise or to cold stress). The influence of aging on the interaction between behavioral and physiological processes is also studied.

★ 1957 ★ **U.S. Department of Health and Human Services**
National Institute on Aging
Laboratory of Cardiovascular Science

Gerontology Research Center, Rm. 3D09
4940 Eastern Ave.
Baltimore, MD 21224
Phone: (410)558-8202
Fax: (410)558-8150
Dr. Edward G. Lakatta, Chief

Research Activities and Fields: Scientists conceptualize and implement original research to identify and characterize the basic mechanisms that control myocardial and vascular function. Studies are extended to describe the influence of age and age-related chronic pathologic conditions in studies conducted in human and animal models. In humans, laboratory seeks to identify the adaptive changes in cardiovascular structure and function that occur with normative aging as well as those changes which predict or accompany the development of cardiovascular disease. Studies in animal models involve isolated cardiac and vascular cells and subcellular organelles. The biophysical mechanisms that govern excitation and contraction of myocardial cells are investigated with techniques that allow the simultaneous recording of contractility, cytosolic and membrane potential or current in a single myocyte. Current research includes a program to study molecular mechanisms of vascular cell functions and pathology using molecular and tissue culture techniques. Also studies whether the blood vessels of adults and animals respond differently to injury by altered gene expression of growth factors and extracellular matrix proteins, and whether age alters endothelial cell growth and differentiation of in vivo systems. Also investigates the effects produced by cytokines, second messengers, aging, and cell cycle of in vitro models for angiogenesis.

★ 1958 ★ **U.S. Department of Health and Human Services**
National Institute on Aging
Laboratory of Cardiovascular Science
Membrane Biology Section
Gerontology Research Center, Rm. 1B04
4940 Eastern Ave.
Baltimore, MD 21224
Phone: (410)558-8202
Fax: (410)558-8150
Dr. Jeffrey Froehlich, Chief

Research Activities and Fields: Investigates mechanisms of ion and metabolite transport across biological membranes; studies how the translocation mechanisms are regulated by hormones, pharmacological agents, diet, and other pathophysiological effectors; and explores the mechanisms by which these systems are modified during the aging process and in age-associated disease. Also studies angiogenesis and smooth muscle function with special emphasis on intracellular ion metabolism. intracellular and extracellular environment and metabolism (involving identification, characterization, and regulation of membrane transport systems largely, but not exclusively, in the kidney).

★ 1959 ★ **U.S. Department of Health and Human Services**
National Institute on Aging
Laboratory of Cellular and Molecular Biology

Gerontology Research Center
4940 Eastern Ave.
Baltimore, MD 21224
Phone: (410)558-8172
Fax: (410)558-8173
Dr. Gunther L. Eichhorn, Chief

Research Activities and Fields: Laboratory conducts research on the biochemistry of aging, focusing on studies on the mechanisms of fundamental biochemical events that are important in the aging process. Activities include research into the mechanism of RNA synthesis, age changes in hormonal receptors, age changes in molecular dynamics, and non-invasive magnetic resonance studies of aging in animals and humans. Four sections make up the Laboratory: 1) Inorganic Biochemistry Section; 2) Macromolecular Chemistry Section; 3) Molecular Dynamics Section; and 4) Molecular Physiology and Genetics Section.

★ 1960 ★ U.S. Department of Health and Human Services
National Institute on Aging
Laboratory of Clinical Physiology
Gerontology Research Center
4940 Eastern Ave.
Baltimore, MD 21224
Phone: (410)558-8193
Fax: (410)558-8113
Dr. Reubin Andres, Chief

Research Activities and Fields: Laboratory is concerned primarily with studies on physiologic changes occurring over the entire adult lifespan. The Laboratory comprises sections on Applied Physiology, Clinical Immunology, Endocrinology, and Metabolism. The Applied Physiology Section studies age changes in specific human systems, including renal, bone, and musculoskeletal. Investigations are concerned with interrelationships between age effects in different organ systems and in overall physiological changes in individuals, and efforts are made to differentiate between pathological disease changes and those secondary to pure age effects. In addition, Section develops and adapts computer techniques for kinetic modeling of physiological systems for the analysis of longitudinal data. In the Clinical Immunology Section, studies are conducted on the decline in host immune responsiveness that is seen in aging. These studies involve the development of diagnostic procedures for the detection of relative immunodeficiencies in humans and the investigation of the mechanisms of these deficiencies in humans and experimental animals. The Endocrinology Section conducts studies on the molecular basis of age-related changes of hormone responses, especially those related to the biochemistry of the adenylate cyclase system and hormone receptors, aging and the endocrinology of the reproductive system, and neuroendocrinology. Clinical studies are conducted on subjects from the Baltimore Longitudinal Study of Human Aging; and studies on rodents are done on tissues from a variety of organs. The Metabolism Section emphasizes clinical research on such metabolic variables as: glucose-insulin homeostatic mechanisms and diabetes mellitus; obesity, patterns of fat distribution, and body composition; acute and sustained effects of physical activity; dietary and nu-

tritional evaluation; and the interactive effects of these variables on rates of aging, disease developments, and longevity. (There is close collaboration of this Laboratory with the Research Program of the Geriatric Division at the Francis Scott Key Medical Center.)

★ 1961 ★ U.S. Department of Health and Human Services
National Institute on Aging
Laboratory of Molecular Genetics
Gerontology Research Center
4940 Eastern Ave.
Baltimore, MD 21224
Phone: (410)558-8162
Fax: (410)558-8157
Dr. Uilhelm A. Bohr, Chief

Research Activities and Fields: Laboratory conducts research on the fundamental nature of aging at the molecular level, including studies on changes in gene structure and function with aging. Researchers utilize the techniques of molecular genetics to examine age-related alterations in cellular function and identify, isolate, and characterize genes involved in aging processes and in age-dependent disorders.

★ 1962 ★ U.S. Department of Health and Human Services
National Institute on Aging
Laboratory of Neurosciences
NIH Bldg. 10, Rm. 6C103
9000 Rockville Pike
Bethesda, MD 20892
Phone: (301)496-8970
Fax: (301)402-0074
Dr. Stanley Rapoport, Chief

Research Activities and Fields: Laboratory studies the function, structure, physiology, biochemistry, and pharmacology of the central and peripheral nervous system. Laboratory also examines changes that take place in these systems during development and aging in animal models and humans. The Laboratory comprises the Brain Aging and Dementia Section, the Cerebral Physiology and Metabolism Section, and the Neurochemistry and Brain Transplant Section. The Brain Aging and Dementia Section operates an eight-bed Patient Care Unit at the Clinical Center as well as an outpatient Dementia and Aging Clinic. Clinical methods involve positron emission tomography. Research activities focus primarily on aging of the central nervous system and on dementia and associated neurological diseases as these relate to the elderly. Subject groups include outpatient healthy men and women between 18 and 90 years of age, with syndrome and chronic hypertension. The Cerebral Physiology and Metabolism Section conducts fundamental research on animal models of human brain aging and disease using molecular biology, clinical in vivo brain imaging, neurochemistry involving phospholipid metabolism, electrophysiology, and cell culture techniques. The Neurochemistry and Brain Transport Section studies transport and regulation at the blood-brain and blood-nerve barriers, focusing on amino acids, toxic metals, and fatty acids.

★ 1963 ★ U.S. Department of Health and Human Services
National Institute on Aging
Laboratory of Personality and Cognition
Gerontology Research Center
4940 Eastern Ave.
Baltimore, MD 21224
Phone: (410)558-8216
Fax: (410)558-8316
Dr. Paul T. Costa, Chief

Research Activities and Fields: Laboratory emphasizes basic and clinical studies of individual differences in cognitive and personality processes and traits. Also investigated are the influence of age on these variables and their reciprocal influence on health, well-being, and adaptation. Studies employ longitudinal, experimental, and epidemiological methods in the analysis of psychological and psychosocial issues of aging, including health and health care needs, predictors of intellectual competence and decline, models of adult personality, and correlates of disease risk factors. Laboratory comprises sections on: Cognition and Personality, Stress, and Coping. The Cognition Section studies the psychological mechanisms underlying age-related changes in memory, learning, problem solving, and information processing. In addition, the roles of psychological and physiological characteristics in age differences and age changes in cognitive performance are analyzed. The Personality, Stress, and Coping Section deals with the dimensions of personality and their influence on processes of adaptation in adult men and women. The objective is to determine methods and strategies for coping with the stresses of adult life and evaluate the effects of different coping mechanisms and personality dispositions on such outcomes as subjective well-being, social functioning, physical and psychiatric health and personality and psychological processes.

★ 1964 ★ U.S. Department of Health and Human Services
National Institute on Aging
Neuroscience and Neuropsychology of Aging Program
NIH Gateway Bldg., Ste. 3C307
7201 Wisconsin Ave.
Bethesda, MD 20892-9914
Phone: (301)496-9350
Fax: (301)496-1494
Dr. Zaven Khachaturian, Associate Director

Research Activities and Fields: Program provides support for research projects to elucidate the etiology or pathogenesis of Alzheimer's disease, improve diagnosis, and eventually provide a sound basis for effective therapy. Areas of particular interest are: differential diagnosis; clinical and basic studies of cerebral circulation, metabolism, neurochemistry, and neuroendocrinology; genetics; population studies; immunology-virology; and animal and other model systems. Other areas of interest include: research on role of infectious agents in causing degeneration process in the aging brain; identification of biological markers in the diagnosis of diseases, such as Alzheimer's; epidemiological investigations of Alzheimer's disease and other dementing disorders of older age; research on diagnostic screening; development and validation of new measures for the diagnosis of Alzheimer's disease; studies designed to examine the nature and extent of age-related changes in older people's hearing and understanding of everyday speech; research on the nature of age-related changes in visual perception as they relate to the effective functioning of older people in everyday contexts; neurobiological processes as they relate to the aging nervous system; and neuropsychological processes in aging animals and humans.

★ 1965 ★ U.S. Department of Health and Human Services
National Institute on Aging
Office of Extramural Affairs
Gateway Bldg. 2C218
7201 Wisconsin Ave.
Bethesda, MD 20892
Phone: (301)496-9373
Fax: (301)402-2945
Dr. Miriam F. Kelty, Associate Director

Research Activities and Fields: The Office of Extramural Affairs administers the funding programs through which NIA supports research and research training. Specific NIA funding mechanisms include: Research Project Grants; Research Program Project Grants; Research Career Development Awards; Clinical Investigator Awards; Academic Awards; Special Emphasis Research Career Awards; National Research Service Awards; Physician Scientist Awards; Geriatric Leadership Academic Awards; Small Business Innovative Research Program; and Academic Research Enhancement Awards.

U.S. Department of Health and Human Services
National Institute of Mental Health
Clinical Research Division
Mental Disorders of the Aging Research Branch
See: Entry 7621

★ 1966 ★ University of Akron
Institute for Life-Span Development and Gerontology
Akron, OH 44325-4307
Phone: (216)972-7243
Fax: (216)972-6990
Dr. Harvey L. Sterns, Dir.

Research Activities and Fields: Improving older adult cognitive functioning, aging and work, mental retardation and aging, training and retraining adult older workers, gender identity, human development, health and aging, and family and aging. Programs concentrate on aging changes in perception, perceptual style, selective attention, and learning and memory. Other studies focus on performance appraisal and selection of older adult workers. **Publications:** *Continuum* (newsletter).

★ 1967 ★ University of Alabama
Center for the Study of Aging
Box 870326
University, AL 35487-0326
Phone: (205)348-1345
Fax: (205)348-6544
Dr. Lorin A. Baumhover, Dir.

Research Activities and Fields: Gerontology, including public perceptions of programs for older people, needs assessment of the elderly, evaluation of programs, health promotion and maintenance, long-term care, abuse of the elderly, caregiving stress and support, gerontology education research, demographic characteristics of the older population, housing needs of the elderly, developmental disabilities in the elderly, and community-based structures for the provision of services for older people. Coordinates research activities of researchers of aging in a variety of disciplines at the University. **Publications:** Technical Papers; Research Reports; and Monographs. **E-mail Address:** sbeall@ua1vm.ua.edu.

★ 1968 ★ University of Alabama at Birmingham
Center for Aging
Community Health Services Building, Ste. 201
933 S. 19th St.
Birmingham, AL 35294-2041
Phone: (205)934-9261
Fax: (205)934-7354
Richard M. Allman, M.D., Dir.

Research Activities and Fields: Primary research areas include immobility and its complications, urinary incontinence, and the social-behavioral aspects of Alzheimer's disease. Collaborative research is conducted in the areas of atherosclerosis, muscoskeletal disease, and age-related cancer. **Publications:** *Insight on Aging: An Alzheimer's Family Program Newsletter.*

★ 1969 ★ University of Alberta
Centre for Gerontology
P-581 Biological Sciences Bldg.
Edmonton, AB, Canada T6G 2E9
Phone: (403)492-4718
Allen R. Dobbs, Ph.D., Dir.

Research Activities and Fields: Aging, including retirement, health, supply of labor, effects of large-scale migration of the elderly population on local economies, effects of aging on human performance, memory in normal aging, health care services, Alzheimer's disease, and diet, nutrition, dental health, and bone loss in the elderly. **Publications:** Newsletter (quarterly). **E-mail Address:** adob@ualta.mts.

★ 1970 ★ University of Arizona
Arizona Center on Aging
1807 E. Elm
Tucson, AZ 85719
Phone: (520)626-4854
Fax: (520)626-3746
Prof. Theodore H. Koff, Dir.

Research Activities and Fields: Long-term care, retirement communities, minority elderly, health and long-term care policy, and aging. Conducts applied research in service delivery system development and provides technical assistance and research dissemination. **Publications:** Papers; Monographs. **Formerly:** Arizona Long Term Care Gerontology Center.

★ 1971 ★ University of Bridgeport
Center for the Study of Aging
Division of Human & Community Services
136 Lafayette St.
Bridgeport, CT 06601
Phone: (203)576-4175
Fax: (203)576-4200
Joseph E. Nechasek, Dir.

Research Activities and Fields: Aging, including studies on such topics as elderly Hispanics, housing options for low income elderly, Medicare and Medicaid, mental health of the elderly, family assessment, and individuals working with elderly.

University of California, Los Angeles
Center for Research on Aging Project
See: Entry 7655

★ 1972 ★ University of California, San Diego
Sam and Rose Stein Institute for Research on Aging
0664 School of Medicine
9500 Gilman Dr.
La Jolla, CA 92093-0664
Phone: (619)534-6299
Fax: (619)534-5475
Dennis A. Carson, M.D., Dir.

Research Activities and Fields: Aging and Alzheimer's disease, arthritis, osteoporosis, cardiovascular disease, sleep disorders, genetics, and mind, body, and health relationships. Investigates the relationships between the deterioration of the central nervous system and speech, hearing, and sleep problems; studies the effects of aging on production of hormones; evaluates alternatives to nursing home confinement; investigates immune system deteriorations; and studies the genetic and biochemical basis for long and healthy lifespans and the genetic basis of human diseases of accelerated aging. Also conducts studies of the elderly's susceptibility to infections, loss of bone minerals, changes in the vascular system and the development of glaucoma. **Publications:** Newsletter (monthly). **E-mail Address:** steininstitute@ocsd.edu.

★ 1973 ★ University of California, San Francisco
Center for Clinical and Aging Services Research
3330 Geary Blvd., 2nd Fl.
San Francisco, CA 94118
Phone: (415)750-4170
Fax: (415)750-4179
Meryl Brod, Ph.D., Dir.

Research Activities and Fields: Geriatrics and gerontology, including testing and improvement of medical and social interventions; drug efficacy studies and medication compliance in the elderly; outcomes of long-term care interventions in the areas of Alzheimer's disease, respite care, and home care; and ethical issues arising from the extended life cycle.

★ 1974 ★ **University of California, San Francisco**
Institute for Health & Aging
School of Nursing
San Francisco, CA 94143-0612
Phone: (415)476-3236
Fax: (415)476-1253
Carroll L. Estes, Ph.D., Dir.

Research Activities and Fields: Aging health policy issues and policy alternatives; state discretionary policies in long-term care, social services, and income maintenance; private sector involvement in supporting health and social services for the elderly; effects of intergovernmental relations and state and federal fiscal conditions on services to the elderly; coordination between state and local aging programs and health planning, financing, and regulatory programs; special health and social service needs of the low-income, isolated elderly; enrollment of the elderly in health maintenance and social/health organizations; gender issues; Alzheimers' disease resources and program evaluation; AIDS; international alcohol; health promotion and injury and disease prevention; disability statistics; and health status of the elderly, with special emphasis on selected acute and chronic health conditions. **Publications:** *Institute for Health and Aging Research Briefs*; Policy Papers. Also publishes resource guides, case studies, syntheses, reports, and reprints. **Formerly:** Aging Health Policy Center.

★ 1975 ★ **University of Connecticut**
Travelers Center on Aging
348 Mansfield Rd., Box U-58
Storrs, CT 06269-2058
Phone: (203)486-4049
Fax: (203)486-3452
Nancy W. Sheehan, Ph.D., Dir.

Research Activities and Fields: Geriatrics and gerontology, including: housing; improved linkage between the University, the community, and at-risk elderly; different aspects of retirement; public policy on aging; Alzheimer's disease and other health issues; death and bereavement; and coping with various lifestyle changes.

★ 1976 ★ **University of Florida**
Center for Gerontological Studies
3355 Turlington Hall
Gainesville, FL 32611
Phone: (904)392-2116
Fax: (904)392-8524
Dr. Otto von Mering, Dir.

Research Activities and Fields: Faculty associates conduct interdisciplinary studies on family economic status, labor force participation and survivorship in life course perspective, alternative living environments for older people, biology of aging, political attitudes and policy issues in aging, preventive health self-care learning for intergenerational groups, nutritional status of elderly, memory fitness and intelligence in adulthood and old age, training needs of counselors and physician assistants, age-sensitive counseling and self-help resource development, geriatric dentistry, older driver fitness and transportation safety, and ambulatory health care case mix management for older persons. **Publications:** Occasional Papers in *Outlook on Aging: Florida*; *Gerofiles Newsletter*; Research Pro-

files; Conference Proceedings. **Formerly:** Institute of Gerontology (1971).

University of Florida
Center for the Neurobiology of Aging
See: Entry 8498

★ 1977 ★ **University of Florida**
Claude D. Pepper Center for Research on Oral Health in Aging
Box 100416, JHMHSC
Gainesville, FL 32610
Phone: (904)392-6796
Fax: (904)392-3070
Dr. Marc Heft, Dir.

Research Activities and Fields: Health services research and basic oral-health functions of the elderly, including the development of periodontal disease, the effects of medications on saliva production, and the effects of aging on the senses. **Formerly:** Research Center on Oral History in Aging.

★ 1978 ★ **University of Georgia**
Gerontology Center
100 Candler Hall
Athens, GA 30602
Phone: (706)542-3954
Fax: (706)542-4805
Dr. Leonard W. Poon, Dir.

Research Activities and Fields: Aging, focusing on applied gerontology, demography as it relates to the aged, mental and physical health of the oldest-old, Alzheimer's disease and other dementia in the aged, and cognitive aging, especially memory for pictures. **E-mail Address:** lpoon@uga.cc.uga.edu.

★ 1979 ★ **University of Kansas**
Center on Aging
Medical Center, Rm. 5021B
39th & Rainbow Blvd.
Kansas City, KS 66103
Phone: (913)588-1265
Fax: (913)588-1201
Stephanie A. Studenski, M.D., Dir.

Research Activities and Fields: Provides support for interdisciplinary research on issues of age and aging. **Formerly:** Absorbed the Long-Term Care Gerontology Center (1986).

★ 1980 ★ **University of Kentucky**
Sanders-Brown Center on Aging
101 Sanders-Brown Bldg.
Lexington, KY 40536-0230
Phone: (606)323-6040
Fax: (606)323-2866
William Markesbery, M.D., Dir.

Research Activities and Fields: Biology of aging, including studies on aging nervous systems, Alzheimer's disease, stroke, hypertension in the elderly, immunology, geriatrics, and social-behavioral science. **Publications:** *Sounding Board* (four per year); *Kentucky Atlas of the Elderly*. **Formerly:** Multidisciplinary Center on Gerontology.

★ 1981 ★ **University of Manitoba**
Centre on Aging
338 Isbister Bldg.
Winnipeg, MB, Canada R3T 2N2
Phone: (204)474-8754
Fax: (204)261-7977
Laurel Strain, Ph.D., Dir.

Research Activities and Fields: Aging, interpreted within a lifespan perspective. Research includes basic and applied studies of the elderly, health and aging, informal and formal care, living arrangements, products and services to promote independence, and methodology. Seeks to provide a focus, impetus, and direction to University and regional activities in population aging, encourage multidisciplinary research, and bridge the gap between basic and applied research. The Centre also seeks to centralize the collection, collation, and dissemination of information relevant to the aged, ensuring that existing data are more readily accessible to decision makers in both the University and the community. **Publications:** *Centre on Aging News* (triennially); Working Papers. **E-mail Address:** coaman@ccm.umanitoba.ca.

★ 1982 ★ **University of Maryland**
Center on Aging
College Park, MD 20742
Phone: (301)405-2469
Fax: (301)314-9167
Susan Nippes, Contact

Research Activities and Fields: Gerontology, including exercise and aging, long-term care financing, service credit banking, informal caregiving, aging and developmental disabilities, intergenerational relations, mid-life and career transitions, and health care cost containment. Conducts health assessment and longitudinal data base projects on aging in the Interdisciplinary Health Research Laboratory. **Publications:** National Eldercare Institution on Employment and Volunteerism Product List available upon request.

University of Maryland
Center for the Study of Pharmacy and Therapeutics for the Elderly
See: Entry 10475

University of Maryland
Division of Infectious Diseases
See: Entry 6846

★ 1983 ★ **University of Massachusetts Boston**
Gerontology Institute and Center
100 Morrissey Blvd.
Boston, MA 02125-3393
Phone: (617)287-7300
Fax: (617)287-7080
Dr. Scott A. Bass, Dir.

Research Activities and Fields: Aging social policy, including health care, economics, demographics, long-term care, productive aging, systems delivery, older women's issues, and minority issues. **Publications:** *Journal of Aging & Social Policy* (quarterly).

★1984★ **University of Miami**
Center on Adult Development and Aging
Univ. of Miami Medical School (D-101)
1425 NW 10th Ave., Ste. 200
Miami, FL 33136
Phone: (305)548-4782
Fax: (305)548-4414
Carl Eisdorfer, Ph.D., Dir.

Research Activities and Fields: Biochemistry, neuropsychiatry, and clinical treatment of Alzheimer's disease and related disorders, including brain reactive antibodies and autoimmune responses. Also studies ethnicity and aging, human factors and aging, aging and developmental disabilities, biology of aging, osteoporosis, social and behavioral patterns of older persons and families, stress and aging, nutrition and aging, and demographics of elderly population in Florida and specific areas in Florida, including studies relating to the migration of elderly persons around the U.S., and the improvement of the quality of life for the elderly. Recently, awarded 11-year contract for the Women's Health Intiative, a 45-site national longitudinal clinical trial which follows the health of postmenopausal women. **Formerly:** Absorbed the Center for Social Research in Aging (1988).

★1985★ **University of Michigan**
Institute of Gerontology
300 N. Ingalls
Ann Arbor, MI 48109-2007
Phone: (313)764-3493
Fax: (313)936-2116
Richard C. Adelman, Ph.D., Dir.

Research Activities and Fields: Gerontological research studies in the behavioral, biological, clinical, and social sciences and the humanities. **Publications:** Annual Report.

★1986★ **University of Missouri—Columbia**
Center for the Study of Aging
314 Clark Hall
Columbia, MO 65211
Phone: (314)882-6011
Fax: (314)882-6158
James A. Irvin, Ph.D., Dir.

Research Activities and Fields: Gerontology, including management across continuum of care, geriatric assessment by allied health professionals, respite care, care of patients with Alzheimer's disease, and home health care. Special project supported by the Bureau of the Blind aims to introduce low vision and blindness aids to nursing homes. **E-mail Address:** hsmirvin@mizzou1.missouri.edu.

★1987★ **University of Missouri—Kansas City**
Center for Aging Studies
5245 Rockhill Rd.
Kansas City, MO 64110
Phone: (816)235-1747
Fax: (816)235-5193
Linda M. Breytspraak, Ph.D., Dir.

Research Activities and Fields: Caregiving to the elderly, health care systems and costs, health promotion/disease prevention, public perceptions of Social Security, voluntarism among the elderly, the care of Chinese elderly, and rural elderly. Rural studies include program assessment and testing in areas of health promotion/disease prevention, caregiving intergenerational relationships and the elderly, transportation, and housing. **E-mail Address:** breytspraak@vax1.umkc.edu.

★1988★ **University of Missouri—Rolla**
Center for Aging Studies
221 Humanities-Social Sciences
Rolla, MO 65401
Phone: (314)341-4680
Dr. Nicholas Knight, Dir.

Research Activities and Fields: Senior adult education, especially in humanities and arts, psychology of aging, economics of aging, computers, transportation and management, and arterial flow of elderly. **Publications:** *Missouri Gerontology Institute Newsletter.*

★1989★ **University of Montreal**
Centre hospitalier Cote-des-Neiges Research Centre
4565, chemin de la Reine-Marie
Montreal, PQ, Canada H3W 1W5
Phone: (514)340-3540
Fax: (514)340-3548
Andre Roch Lecours, Dir.

Research Activities and Fields: Gerontology and geriatrics, including neuropsychology, neurolinguistics, and electrophysiology of normal and pathological aging; nutrition and epidemiology of illness in old age; and genetics, pathology, and epidemiology of Alzheimer's disease.

★1990★ **University of Nebraska at Omaha**
Department of Gerontology
Omaha, NE 68182
Phone: (402)554-2272
Fax: (402)554-4871
Dr. James A. Thorson, Dir.

Research Activities and Fields: Gerontology, including psychosocial aspects of aging. Past projects include national study on gerontology instruction in U.S., adaptation on the part of the aged to natural disasters, developmental disabilities and the elderly, problem-solving strategies and the aged, drug use and the elderly, barriers to the use of health maintenance organizations on the part of the aged, attitudes toward old people, attitudes toward death, and spiritual well-being of the elderly. **Formerly:** Gerontology Program (1989).

★1991★ **University of North Texas**
Center for Studies in Aging
PO Box 13438
Denton, TX 76203-6438
Phone: (817)565-2765
Fax: (817)565-4370
Richard A. Lusky, Dir.

Research Activities and Fields: Social gerontology, including employee job performance in nursing homes, impact of leadership on culture of nursing homes and retirement communities, the Native American elderly, development of databases and models for community services planning, geriatric programs in community health centers, aging and developmental disability, and the low-income minority elderly. Conducts demographic, social-psychological, and evaluation studies and surveys for cities, labor unions, churches, and other client groups. **Publications:** Center Studies.

★1992★ **University of North Texas Health Science Center at Fort Worth**
Texas Institute for Research and Education on Aging (TIREA)
3500 Camp Bowie Blvd.
Fort Worth, TX 76107-2699
Phone: (817)735-2403
Fax: (817)735-2283
Stanley R. Ingman, Ph.D., Dir.

Research Activities and Fields: Biology of aging, including fundamental chemical and molecular biological changes that may cause aging; health promotion in older adults, including health programs that promote the physical, psychological, and social well-being of older populations; geriatric care and practice, including evaluations of new clinical programs and their effectiveness in improving physical and mental functions; and long-term care system development, focusing on case management, minority needs assessment, adult day health care, the developmentally disabled, and the quality of nursing home care. Other projects include studies on Alzheimer's Disease, the health and social needs of older adults, methods for improving older patients' compliance with medical prescriptions, the effects of water aerobics on older people, the impact of custodial grandparenting, and problem-solving and reasoning skills for the elderly. **Publications:** *Southwest Journal on Aging.*

University of Pennsylvania
Aging Skin Clinic
See: Entry 4270

★1993★ **University of Pennsylvania**
Institute on Aging
3615 Chestnut St.
Philadelphia, PA 19104-6006
Phone: (215)898-3163
Fax: (215)573-8684
Risa Lauizzo-Mourey, M.D., Act.Dir.

Research Activities and Fields: Biomedical and social science research on aging, including cellular mechanisms of aging, Alzheimer's disease, sleep disturbances, arthritis, population demographics of aging, organization and structure of life care communities, social security, and social support systems for the aged. **Publications:** Newsletter (quarterly). **Formerly:** Center for the Study of Aging (1990).

★1994★ **University of Southern California**
Ethel Percy Andrus Gerontology Center
Univ. Park
MC 0191
Los Angeles, CA 90089-0191
Phone: (213)740-6060
Fax: (213)740-8241
Dr. Edward L. Schneider, Exec.Dir.

Research Activities and Fields: Gerontology, including interdisciplinary studies on biological, behavioral, social, and environmental aspects of aging process. Develops and evaluates curricula for training scientific and professional personnel specializing in study of aging processes and for improving associated personal, medical and social disorders, cognitive behavior, employment and retirement, state politics of aging, Alzheimer's disease, income maintenance, neurobiology, and reproductive aspects of aging. Also responsible for coordination of graduate and postgraduate instruction and research training in gerontology conducted within academic disciplines of architecture, biology, economics, education, linguistics, pharmacy, political science, psychology, psychiatry, public administration, urban and regional planning, social work, and sociology at the University. **E-mail Address:** eschneid@mizar.usc.edu. **Formerly:** Gerontology Center.

★ 1995 ★ University of Toronto
Centre for Studies of Aging
455 Spadina Ave., Ste. 305
Toronto, ON, Canada M5S 2G8
Phone: (416)978-7910
Fax: (416)978-4771
Victor W. Marshall, Ph.D., Dir.

Research Activities and Fields: Health promotion, healthcare and aging, family and intergenerational studies, ethnic and cross-cultural studies in aging, memory and cognition with aging, demographics and economics of an aging population, and work and aging. **Publications:** *Focus on Aging* (occasional newsletter). **E-mail Address:** carnet@vm.utcc.utoronto.ca. **Formerly:** Programme in Gerontology (1979).

★ 1996 ★ University of Utah
University Gerontology Center
316 College of Nursing
Salt Lake City, UT 84112
Phone: (801)581-8198
Fax: (801)581-4642
Dale A. Lund, Ph.D., Dir.

Research Activities and Fields: Basic and applied research in both health and social sciences as they relate to the aged, including longterm care, gerontology curriculum and standards, bereavement of the elderly, in-home and respite care services, the family as a support system, family caregiving, and intergenerational families. **Formerly:** Rocky Mountain Gerontology Program.

★ 1997 ★ University of West Florida
Center on Aging
Dept. of Social Work
11000 Univ. Pkwy.
Pensacola, FL 32514-5751
Phone: (904)474-2381
Michael Beechem, Ph.D., Admin.Dir.

Research Activities and Fields: Gerontology, including rural elderly, housing, and death. Develops and evaluates training material for aging services.

★ 1998 ★ University of Wisconsin—
Madison
Institute on Aging
2245 Medical Sciences Center
1300 Univ. Ave.
Madison, WI 53706
Phone: (608)262-1818
Fax: (608)263-6211
William B. Ershler, M.D., Dir.

Research Activities and Fields: Aging, including lifespan development, clinical geriatrics, so-

cial gerontology, and biology of aging. Specific areas of study include caloric restriction and aging, relocation of older women, influenza, osteoporosis, Alzheimer's disease, prostate cancer and aging on rhesis monkeys, midlife parenting, and housing for older adults. **E-mail Address:** smithk@ssc.wisc.edu. **Formerly:** Faye McBeath Institute on Aging and Adult Life (1983); Institute on Aging and Adult Life.

Veterans Affairs Medical Center (GRECC)
Geriatric Research, Education and Clinical
center
See: Entry 10493

★ 1999 ★ Virginia Commonwealth
University
Virginia Center on Aging
Medical College of Virginia Campus
Richmond, VA 23298-0229
Phone: (804)828-1525
Fax: (804)828-7905
Edward F. Ansello, Ph.D., Dir.

Research Activities and Fields: Mental and physical health of the elderly, focusing on community-living and health-related factors of aging. Studies include: eldercare responsibilities of employed amily caregivers, staffing requirements in residential care facilities, impact of aging of adults with developmental disabilities, minority healthcare utilization, caregiving of demented elders, research and documentation project on rural geropharmacy. **Publications:** *AGE In Action* (quarterly newsletter). **E-mail Address:** ccoogle@gems.vcu.edu.

Washington University
Alzheimer's Disease Research Center
See: Entry 8536

★ 2000 ★ Wayne State University
Institute of Gerontology
226 Knapp Bldg.
87 E. Ferry
Detroit, MI 48202
Phone: (313)577-2297
Fax: (313)875-0127
Jeffrey W. Dwyer, Ph.D., Dir.

Research Activities and Fields: Gerontology, including studies on public policy, acute and long-term health care, service delivery, aging process, family relations, and work and retirement. **Publications:** Newsletter. **E-mail Address:** IOG@WAYNEST1.

★ 2001 ★ Western Kentucky University
Gerontology Program
College of Education & Behavioral Sciences
Bowling Green, KY 42101
Phone: (502)745-2921
Fax: (502)745-6588
Dr. Lois Layne, Dir.

Research Activities and Fields: Gerontology, including studies on care givers and visual perception in the aged.

★ 2002 ★ Yeshiva University
Resnick Gerontology Center
Albert Einstein College of Medicine
Bldg. F, Rm. G9
1300 Morris Park Ave.
Bronx, NY 10461
Phone: (718)892-4300
Fax: (718)824-1223
Dr. Howard Crystal, Dir.

Research Activities and Fields: Alzheimer's disease and other dementia. Conducts the Bronx Aging Study, a ten-year longitudinal study of the Bronx elderly. Also conducts a teaching nursing project, a biochemical research assessment program, and drug studies.

State Government Agencies

Aging

★ 2003 ★ Alabama Commission on Aging
770 Washington Ave., Ste. 470
Montgomery, AL 36130
Phone: (334)242-5743
Fax: (334)242-5594

★ 2004 ★ Alaska Department of
Administration
Senior Services Division
PO Box 110209
Juneau, AK 99811-0209
Phone: (907)465-3250
Fax: (907)465-4716

★ 2005 ★ Arizona Department of Economic
Security
Aging and Community Services Division
PO Box 6123
Phoenix, AZ 85005
Phone: (602)542-6572
Fax: (602)542-5339

★ 2006 ★ Arkansas Department of Human
Services
Aging and Adult Services Division
Donaghey Plaza S.
PO Box 1437
Little Rock, AR 72203
Phone: (501)682-8521
Fax: (501)686-6836

★ 2007 ★ California Health and Welfare
Agency
Aging Department
1600 K St.
Sacramento, CA 95814
Phone: (916)322-5290
Fax: (916)324-1903

★ 2008 ★ Colorado Department of Human
Services
Aging and Adult Services Division
1575 Sherman St.
Denver, CO 80203-1714
Phone: (303)620-4147
Fax: (303)866-4214

★ 2009 ★ Connecticut Department of
  Social Services
Elderly Services Division
25 Sigourney St.
Hartford, CT 06106
Phone: (203)424-5274
Fax: (203)424-4960

★ 2010 ★ Delaware Department of Health
  and Social Services
Aging Division
Delaware State Hospital
1901 N. Dupont Hwy.
New Castle, DE 19720
Phone: (302)577-4660
Fax: (302)577-4510

★ 2011 ★ District of Columbia Diversity
  and Special Services Office
Aging Office
441 4th St. NW, Ste. 900
Washington, DC 20001
Phone: (202)724-5622
Fax: (202)724-4979

★ 2012 ★ Florida Department of Health and
  Rehabilitative Services
Aging and Adult Services Office
1317 Winewood Blvd.
Tallahassee, FL 32399-0700
Phone: (904)488-8922
Fax: (904)922-2993

★ 2013 ★ Georgia Department of Human
  Resources
Aging Services Office
2 Peachtree St. NW
Atlanta, GA 30303
Phone: (404)894-2023
Fax: (404)657-5255

★ 2014 ★ Hawaii Office of the Governor
Aging Office
335 Merchant St., Rm. 241
Honolulu, HI 96813
Phone: (808)586-0100
Fax: (808)586-0185

★ 2015 ★ Idaho Office on Aging
PO Box 83720
Boise, ID 83720-0007
Phone: (208)334-3833
Fax: (208)334-3033

★ 2016 ★ Illinois Department on Aging
421 E. Capitol Ave., No. 100
Springfield, IL 62701-1789
Phone: (217)785-2870
Fax: (217)785-4477

★ 2017 ★ Indiana Family and Social
  Services Administration
**Disability, Aging and Rehabilitative
Services Division**
402 W. Washington St., Rm. W341
Indianapolis, IN 46204
Phone: (317)232-1147
Fax: (317)233-4693

★ 2018 ★ Iowa Department of Elder Affairs
914 Grand Ave., Ste. 236
Des Moines, IA 50309
Phone: (515)281-5188
Fax: (515)281-4036

★ 2019 ★ Kansas Department on Aging
915 SW Harrison St., Rm. 150
Topeka, KS 66612-1500
Phone: (913)296-4986
Fax: (913)296-0256

★ 2020 ★ Kentucky Human Resources
  Cabinet
Social Services Department
Aging Services Division
275 E. Main St.
Frankfort, KY 40621
Phone: (502)564-6930
Fax: (502)564-5002

★ 2021 ★ Maine Department of Human
  Services
Elder and Adult Services Bureau
State House Sta. 11
Augusta, ME 04333
Phone: (207)624-5335
Fax: (207)287-3005

★ 2022 ★ Maryland Office on Aging
301 W. Preston St., Rm. 1004
Baltimore, MD 21201-2374
Phone: (410)225-1102
Fax: (410)333-7943

★ 2023 ★ Massachusetts Department of
  Elder Affairs
1 Ashburton Pl., 5th Fl.
Boston, MA 02108
Phone: (617)727-7750
Fax: (617)727-9368

★ 2024 ★ Michigan Office on Aging
PO Box 30026
Lansing, MI 48909
Phone: (517)373-8230
Fax: (517)373-4092

★ 2025 ★ Minnesota Department of Human
  Services
Social Services Administration
Aging and Adult Services Program Division
444 Lafayette Rd.
St. Paul, MN 55155
Phone: (612)296-1531
Fax: (612)297-1949

★ 2026 ★ Mississippi Department of Human
  Services
Aging and Adult Services Division
PO Box 352
Jackson, MS 39205-0352
Phone: (601)359-4480
Fax: (601)359-4477

★ 2027 ★ Missouri Department of Social
  Services
Aging Division
0615 Howerton Ct.
PO Box 1337
Jefferson City, MO 65109
Phone: (314)751-8535
Fax: (314)751-3203

★ 2028 ★ Montana Family Services
  Department
Aging Services Bureau
Box 8005
Helena, MT 59604
Phone: (406)444-5900
Fax: (406)444-5956

★ 2029 ★ Nebraska Department on Aging
PO Box 95044
Lincoln, NE 68509
Phone: (402)471-2306
Fax: (402)471-4619

★ 2030 ★ Nevada Department of Human
  Resources
Aging Services Division
505 E. King St., Rm. 600
Carson City, NV 89710
Phone: (702)687-4400
Fax: (702)687-4733

★ 2031 ★ New Hampshire Department of
  Health and Human Services
Elderly and Adult Services Division
115 Pleasant St., Annex Bldg. 1
Concord, NH 03301-3843
Phone: (603)271-4394
Fax: (603)271-4643

★ 2032 ★ New Jersey Department of
  Community Affairs
Aging Division
101 S. Broad St., CN 800
Trenton, NJ 08625-0800
Phone: (609)292-4833
Fax: (609)392-4339

★ 2033 ★ New Mexico State Agency on
  Aging
228 E. Palace Ave.
Santa Fe, NM 87501
Phone: (505)827-7640
Fax: (505)827-7649

★ 2034 ★ New York State Office on Aging
Empire State Plaza, Bldg. 2
Albany, NY 12223-0001
Phone: (518)474-4425
Fax: (518)474-0608

★ 2035 ★ North Carolina Department of
  Human Resources
Aging Division
PO Box 29526
Raleigh, NC 27626-0526
Phone: (919)733-3983
Fax: (919)715-4645

★ 2036 ★ North Dakota Department of
  Human Services
Aging Services Division
600 E. Boulevard Ave.
Bismarck, ND 58505
Phone: (701)328-2577
Fax: (701)328-2359

★ 2037 ★ Ohio Department on Aging
50 W. Broad St., 9th Fl.
Columbus, OH 43215-5928
Phone: (614)466-7246
Fax: (614)466-5741

★ 2038 ★ Oklahoma Department of Human
  Services
Aging Services Division
PO Box 25352
Oklahoma City, OK 73125
Phone: (405)521-2327
Fax: (405)521-6458

★ 2039 ★ **Oregon Department of Human Resources**
Senior and Disabled Services Division
500 Summer St. NE
Salem, OR 97310-1015
Phone: (503)945-5811
Fax: (503)373-7823

★ 2040 ★ **Pennsylvania Department on Aging**
MSSOB, 6th Fl
400 Market St.
Harrisburg, PA 17101-2301
Phone: (717)783-1550
Fax: (717)772-3382

★ 2041 ★ **Rhode Island Department of Elderly Affairs**
160 Pine St.
Providence, RI 02903
Phone: (401)277-2894
Fax: (401)277-1490

★ 2042 ★ **South Carolina Office of the Governor**
Aging Division
PO Box 11369
Columbia, SC 29211
Phone: (803)734-9818
Fax: (803)734-1598

★ 2043 ★ **South Dakota Department of Social Services**
Program Management Division
Adult Services on Aging Office
700 Governors Dr.
Pierre, SD 57501
Phone: (605)773-3656
Fax: (605)773-4855

★ 2044 ★ **Tennessee Commission on Aging**
500 Deaderic St., 9th Fl.
Nashville, TN 37243-0860
Phone: (615)741-2056
Fax: (615)741-3309

★ 2045 ★ **Texas Department on Aging**
Box 12786
Austin, TX 78711
Phone: (512)444-2727
Fax: (512)440-5290

★ 2046 ★ **Utah Department of Human Services**
Aging and Adult Services Division
PO Box 45500
Salt Lake City, UT 84145-0500
Phone: (801)538-3910
Fax: (801)538-4016

★ 2047 ★ **Vermont Agency of Human Services**
Aging and Disability Department
State Complex
103 S. Main St.
Waterbury, VT 05671-0204
Phone: (802)241-2220
Fax: (802)241-2979

★ 2048 ★ **Virginia Department of Health and Human Resources**
Aging Department
700 E. Franklin St., 10th Fl.
Richmond, VA 23219-2327
Phone: (804)225-2271
Fax: (804)371-8381

★ 2049 ★ **Washington Department of Social and Health Services**
Aging and Adult Services Office
PO BOX 45040
Olympia, WA 98504-5040
Phone: (360)586-3768
Fax: (360)586-5874

★ 2050 ★ **West Virginia Department of Health and Human Resources**
Aging Commission
State Capitol Complex
1900 Kanawha Blvd.
Charleston, WV 25305
Phone: (304)558-3317
Fax: (304)558-0004

★ 2051 ★ **Wisconsin Department of Health and Social Services**
Community Services Division
Aging Bureau
PO Box 7850
Madison, WI 53707-7850
Phone: (608)266-3840
Fax: (608)266-2579

★ 2052 ★ **Wyoming Department of Health**
Aging Division
139 Hathaway Bldg.
Cheyenne, WY 82002-0710
Phone: (307)777-7986
Fax: (307)777-5340

Chapter 3
Allergy & Immunology

Federal Government Agencies

★2053★ U.S. Department of Health and Human Services
National Institute of Allergy and Infectious Diseases
9000 Rockville Pike
Bethesda, MD 20892
Phone: (301)496-2263
Fax: (301)496-4409

Description: NIAID conducts and supports broadly based research and research training on the causes, characteristics, prevention, control, and treatment of a wide variety of diseases believed to be attributable to infectious agents, including bacteria, viruses, and parasites; to allergies; or to other deficiencies or disorders in the responses of the body's immune mechanisms. Among areas of special emphasis are: asthma and allergic disease, clinical immunology, disease control measures, research and development, antiviral substances, and hospital-associated infections.

Foundations & Other Funding Organizations

Private Foundations

John P. McGovern Foundation
See: Entry 322

Other Funding Organizations

★2054★ American Academy of Otolaryngic Allergy
8455 Colesville Rd., Ste. 745
Silver Spring, MD 20910-9998
Phone: (301)588-1800
Fax: (301)588-2454

Description: Offers research fellowship in allergy related to the head and neck.

★2055★ Asthma and Allergy Foundation of America
1125 15th St. NW, Ste. 502
Washington, DC 20005
Phone: (202)466-7643
Free: 800-7-ASTHMA
Fax: (202)466-8940

Description: Awards postdoctoral fellowships to support research and clinical training in allergy and immunology.

National & International Organizations

Academy of Veterinary Allergy (AVA)
See: Entry 13018

★2056★ Action Against Allergy (AAA)
24-26 High St.
Hampton Hill
Middlesex, Greater London TW12 1PD, England
Fax: 181 9433631
Mrs. Amelia Nathan Hill, Chm.

Founded: 1978. Members: 1,200. Languages: English, French, German, Italian. Description: Campaigns for diagnosis and treatment of allergies through the British national health service institutions and physicians. Raises funds for research into the causes and treatment of allergic illness. Provides information to chronic allergy sufferers. Coordinates medical reference center. Publications: Brochures, periodic. • Directory, periodic. Information on suppliers of additive-free and non-allergenic foods and materials. • Newsletter, 3/year. Newsletter.

African AIDS Project
See: Entry 6614

AIDS Counseling Trust (ACT)
See: Entry 6617

AIDS Information Support Centre
See: Entry 6621

AIDS Task Force for the American College Health Association
See: Entry 6623

★2057★ Allergy / Asthma Information Association (AAIA)
30 Eglinton Ave. W., Ste. 750
Mississauga, ON, Canada L5R 3E7
Phone: (905)712-2242
Fax: (905)712-2245
Susan Daglish, Exec.Dir.

Founded: 1964. Members: 6,000. Regional Groups: 5. Local Groups: 70. Description: Seeks to develop societal awareness of the seriousness of allergic disease, including asthma, and to enable allergic individuals, their families, and caregivers to increase control over allergy symptoms. Provides leadership in information, education, and advocacy through partnership with healthcare professionals, businesses, industry, and government. Maintains speakers' bureau. Publications: Quarterly, quarterly. Magazine. Also publishes letters on allergies and asthma.

Allergy and Asthma Network / Mothers of Asthmatics (AAN/MA)
See: Entry 3154

Alliance for the Arts
See: Entry 6625

★2058★ American Academy of Allergy and Immunology (AAAI)
611 E. Wells St.
Milwaukee, WI 53202
Phone: (414)272-6071
Fax: (414)276-3349
Donald L. McNeil, Exec.Dir.

Founded: 1943. Members: 5,000. Description: Professional society of physicians specializing in allergy and allergic diseases. Sponsors annual two-day postgraduate course and three-day scientific session. Conducts research and educational programs. Maintains speakers' bureau; operates placement service; compiles statistics. Publications: American Academy of Allergy and Immunology--Abstract Book, annual. Journal. Contains abstracts of papers presented at annual meeting. Price: $30/copy. • American Academy of Allergy and Immunology-

-*Membership Directory*, annual. Membership Directory. *Price:* Included in membership dues; $125/copy for nonmembers. • *American Academy of Allergy and Immunology--News and Notes*, quarterly. Newsletter. *Price:* Included in membership dues. • *Asthma and Allergy Advocate: Practical Information and Health Tips from Your Allergist, a Specialist in Patient Care*, quarterly. Newsletter. For asthma and allergy sufferers. Focuses on current trends in treatment and medication. *Price:* $70/year for 100 copies of each quarterly issue. • *Journal of Allergy and Clinical Immunology*, monthly. Journal. *Price:* Included in membership dues. **Formerly:** (1982) American Academy of Allergy.

★ 2059 ★ **American Academy of Otolaryngic Allergy (AAOA)**
8455 Colesville Rd., Ste. 745
Silver Spring, MD 20910-9998
Phone: (301)588-1800
Fax: (301)588-2454
Donald J. Clark, Exec.Dir.

Founded: 1941. **Members:** 1,900. **Description:** Otolaryngologists who are interested in the study, research, and practice of otolaryngic allergy. Offers research fellowship in allergy related to the head and neck. Sponsors scientific meetings and continuing medical education programs. **Publications:** *AAOA News*, quarterly. *Price:* Free. • *Directory*, annual. Also publishes pamphlets. **Formerly:** American Society of Ophthalmologic and Otolaryngologic Allergy.

★ 2060 ★ **American Allergy Association (AAA)**
PO Box 7273
Menlo Park, CA 94026
Phone: (415)322-1663
Carol Rudoff, Pres.

Founded: 1978. **Description:** Allergy patients and others interested in problems created by foods, allergies, and asthma. Disseminates information on diet, environmental control, and other facets of allergy advice. **Publications:** *Living With Allergies*, annual. Handbook. Includes articles on maintaining an allergen-free diet and enviroment, allergen-free recipes, book reviews, and pollen data. *Price:* Free with a $15 donation. • Pamphlets.

★ 2061 ★ **American Association of Certified Allergists (AACA)**
85 W. Algonquin Rd. Ste. 550
Arlington Heights, IL 60005
Phone: (708)427-8111
Joseph J. Lotharius, Exec.Dir.

Founded: 1968. **Members:** 510. **Description:** Physicians specializing in allergy and clinical immunology. Objectives are to: improve expertise in allergy treatment; disseminate information pertaining to undergraduate and graduate education in allergology; promote improved standards for the practice and teaching of allergy; exchange information between physicians facing similar problems under different circumstances. **Publications:** Newsletter, 3/year. *Price:* Included in membership dues.

★ 2062 ★ **American Association of Immunologists (AAI)**
9650 Rockville Pike
Bethesda, MD 20814
Phone: (301)530-7178
Fax: (301)571-1816
Joann Scichilane, Acting Exec.Dir.

Founded: 1913. **Members:** 5,500. **Description:** Scientists engaged in immunological research including aspects of virology, bacteriology, biochemistry, genetics, and related disciplines. Goals are to advance knowledge of immunology and related disciplines and to facilitate the interchange of information among investigators in various fields. Promotes interaction between laboratory investigators and clinicians. Conducts training courses, symposia, workshop, and lectures. Compiles statistics. **Publications:** *AAI Newsletter*, bimonthly. Newsletter. • *Journal of Immunology*, semimonthly. Journal. Reports on original research efforts on cellular immunology; clinical immunology and immunopathology; cytokines, mediators, and regulatory molecules. *Price:* Included in membership dues.

★ 2063 ★ **American Board of Allergy and Immunology (ABAI)**
University City Science Center
3624 Market St.
Philadelphia, PA 19104
Phone: (215)349-9466
Fax: (215)222-8669
Herbert C. Mansmann, Jr.,MD, Exec.Sec.

Founded: 1972. **Description:** Conjoint board of the American Board of Internal Medicine and the American Board of Pediatrics. Internists and pediatricians with special competency in treating problems of allergy and immunology. Establishes qualifications and examines physician candidates for certification as specialists in allergy and immunology.

★ 2064 ★ **American College of Allergy and Immunology (ACAI)**
85 W. Algonquin Rd., Ste. 550
Arlington Heights, IL 60005
Phone: (708)427-1200
Free: 800-842-7777
Fax: (708)427-1294
James R. Slawny, Exec.Dir.

Founded: 1942. **Members:** 3,800. **Description:** Practicing allergists, educators, researchers, and clinical immunologists united to: encourage the study, improve the practice, and advance the cause of clinical immunology and allergy; promote association of and highest possible standards among medical scientists and physicians specializing in clinical immunology and in research, teaching, and treatment of allergy; promote dissemination of information regarding clinical immunology and allergy. Maintains a special program for allergy assistants such as nurses, technologists, and clinic aides of lectures, conferences, seminars, participatory workshops, peer-group discussions, poster programs, and technical and scientific exhibits. **Publications:** *Annals of Allergy*, 13/year. Journal. Includes original articles by experts in the field, abstracts, reviews, and editorials. *Price:* $42.50/year for individuals; $55/year for institutions; $58/year outside the U.S. • *Immunology*

and Allergy Practice, monthly. Journal. • Membership Directory, biennial. • Newsletter, bimonthly.

American Dermatologic Society of Allergy and Immunology (ADSAI)
See: Entry 4215

American Foundation for AIDS Research (AmFAR)
See: Entry 6629

★ 2065 ★ **American In-Vitro Allergy / Immunology Society**
c/o Gloria Boyajian
PO Box 5423
Englewood, NJ 07631
Phone: (201)816-1289
Fax: (201)816-1289
Gloria Boyajian, Admin.

Founded: 1988. **Members:** 300. **Description:** Physicians, scientists, and other health professionals who study or use in-vitro technology in the diagnosis and treatment of allergic and immunologic disorders; individuals engaged in activities related to the treatment of allergies or the advancement of immunological science. Promotes the appropriate use of in-vitro procedures in allergy and immunology; explores and refines allergy and immunology in-vitro techniques; fosters research in and development of in-vitro procedures that enhance the diagnosis and management of allergy or immune dysfunction. Acts as forum on information regarding new scientific information, research, and application of in-vitro techniques in allergy and immunology practice; represents members in professional and public relations; operates physician referral service. Offers services in third party payer negotiation and in-vitro testing standardization. Conducts continuing medical education. **Publications:** Brochure. • Newsletter.

American Osteopathic College of Allergy and Immunology (AOCAI)
See: Entry 9986

★ 2066 ★ **American Society for Histocompatibility and Immunogenetics (ASHI)**
PO Box 15804
Lenexa, KS 66285-5804
Phone: (913)541-0009
Fax: (913)541-0156
Debbie J. Elder, CMP, Exec.Dir.

Founded: 1968. **Members:** 1,000. **Description:** Scientists, physicians, and technologists involved in research and clinical activities related to histocompatibility testing (a state of mutual tolerance that allows some tissues to be grafted effectively to others). Conducts proficiency testing and educational programs. Maintains liaison with regulatory agencies; offers placement services and laboratory accreditation. Has developed histocompatability specialist certification program. **Publications:** *ASHI Quarterly*, quarterly. Includes calendar of events, employment listings, certification data, and notices of awards. *Price:* Included in membership dues; $30/year for nonmembers. • *Human Immunology*, monthly. Journal. • Manual. Covers laboratory procedures. • Membership Directory. • Papers. • Proceedings. **Formerly:** American Association for Clinical Histocompatibility Testing.

★2067★ Association of Latin Languages Allergologistes and Immunologists (LLSA)
(Groupement des Allergologistes et Immunologistes de Langues Latines — GAILL)
Rua Sampaio e Pina 16-4
P-1000 Lisbon, Portugal
Phone: 1 3874201
Fax: 1 658202
Maria Laura Palma-Carlos, Ph.D., Pres.

Founded: 1969. **Members:** 300. **Languages:** English, French, Italian, Portuguese, Spanish. **Description:** Latin-language-speaking medical doctors and holders of doctoral and master's degrees in 14 countries. Promotes and disseminates information on allergic and immunologic diseases. Facilitates personal contacts between scientists. Sponsors charitable program. Provides research and travel grants. Operates speakers' bureau and placement service; bestows awards. Holds biennial symposium and training seminars. **Publications:** *Allergie et Immunologie*, quarterly. Journal. • *Cadernos Luso-Brasileiros de Alergia e Imunologia*, quarterly. Journal. • *GAILL Directory*, annual. Directory.

Association of Nurses in AIDS Care (ANAC)
See: Entry 9071

★2068★ Asthma and Allergy Foundation of America (AAFA)
1125 15th St. NW, Ste. 502
Washington, DC 20005
Phone: (202)466-7643
Free: 800-7-ASTHMA
Fax: (202)466-8940
Mary Worstell, Exec.Dir.

Founded: 1953. **Local Groups:** 25. **Description:** National voluntary health agency established to unite the public, the medical profession, research scientists, and public health workers in a campaign to solve the health problems posed by the allergic diseases; such diseases include hay fever, asthma, skin disorders, and allergic reactions to drugs, foods, molds, and insect stings. Supported by individual contributions and funds from foundations, industries, and physician groups. Supports research and clinical training in allergy and immunology through postdoctoral fellowships. Provides information and educational materials to the public, the medical profession, and health workers. Cooperates with medical institutions, hospitals, and other health organizations in the development of programs for treatment and prevention of allergic diseases. Maintains speakers' bureau. **Publications:** *ADVANCE*, monthly. Newsletter. Also publishes educational pamphlets. **Formerly:** (1957) American Foundation for Allergic Diseases; (1978) Allergy Foundation of America.

Australian National Council on AIDS (ANCA)
See: Entry 6643

Body Positive
See: Entry 6644

Brazilian Interdisciplinary AIDS Association (ABIA)
See: Entry 6645

★2069★ Bulgarian Society of Immunology (BSI)
Oborishte Strada
BG-1504 Sofia, Bulgaria
Phone: 2 430128
Prof. Assen Toshkov, Pres.

Founded: 1979. **Members:** 88. **Languages:** Bulgarian, English. **Description:** Immunologists and other scientists in Bulgaria. Evaluates and publicizes achievements in the field of immunology. Conducts training program. **Publications:** *Proceedings of the Congress of Microbiology - Section Immunology*, quadrennial.

Canadian Public Health Association AIDS Program
(Sante Canada par la Strategie Nationale sur la Sida)
See: Entry 6647

Cancer Federation, Inc. (CFI)
See: Entry 5932

CAVDA-Citizens AIDS Project (CAP)
See: Entry 6648

CDC National AIDS Clearinghouse (NAC)
See: Entry 6649

Cides-Centroamerica
See: Entry 6653

★2070★ Clinical Immunology Society (CIS)
6900 Grove Rd.
Thorofare, NJ 08086
Phone: (609)848-1000
Fax: (609)848-5274
Susan J. Nelson, Admin.

Founded: 1986. **Members:** 1,000. **Description:** Investigators and clinicians concerned with immunologic diseases. Promotes research on: the causes and mechanisms of immunologic diseases; improved treatment, evaluation, and prevention of diseases related to immunity. Facilitates exchange of ideas and findings; fosters excellence in research and medical practice. Works to increase public awareness and knowledge of immunologically-mediated diseases. Conducts scientific, educational programs. **Publications:** *Clinical Immunology Spectrum*, bimonthly. Newsletter. • *Clinical Immunology Spectrum*, bimonthly. Includes summary of recent advances, overview of relevant topics, meeting reports, editorials, and debates. *Price:* Free to members.

Cure Foundation
See: Entry 5216

Design Industries Foundation Fighting AIDS (DIFFA)
See: Entry 6664

★2071★ Dutch Society of Immunology (NSI)
(Societe Hollandaise d'Immunologie)
PO Box 2215
2301 - CE
NL-2280 AA Leyden, Netherlands
Phone: 71 181818
Fax: 15 181901
Dr. C.J. Lucas, Sec.

Founded: 1964. **Members:** 1,050. **Languages:** Dutch, English. **Description:** Health professionals working in the field of immunology. Conducts courses. **Publications:** *Directory*, annual. Directory. • *Nieuwsbrief*, bimonthly.

★2072★ European Academy of Allergology and Clinical Immunology (EAACI)
(Academie Europeenne d'Allergologie et d'Immunologie Clinique)
I Clinico Medico
Policlinico Umberto 1
I-00161 Rome, Italy
Phone: 6 35346840
Fax: 6 35403017
Prof. S. Bonini, Gen.Sec.-Treas.

Founded: 1950. **Members:** 1,500. **National Groups:** 27. **Languages:** English, French, German. **Description:** Medical doctors in 27 countries. Facilitates the exchange of ideas and information in the field of allergy and clinical immunology; assists and promotes international initiatives among European workers in related fields. Conducts training courses. **Publications:** *Allergy - The European Journal of Allergy and Clinical Immunology*, bimonthly. Journal.

European Society for Paediatric Haematology and Immunology (ESPHI)
(Europese Vereniging voor Pediatrische Hematologie en Immunologie — EVPHI)
See: Entry 3224

Evans Syndrome Research and Support Group
See: Entry 7875

Foundation of Pharmacists and Corporate America for AIDS Education (FPCA)
See: Entry 6669

Gay Men's Health Crisis (GMHC)
See: Entry 6670

Global Network of People Living with HIV / AIDS
See: Entry 6672

Haitian Coalition on AIDS (HCA)
See: Entry 6673

Health Education Resource Organization (HERO)
See: Entry 6994

★ 2073 ★ Immune Deficiency Foundation (IDF)
25 W. Chesapeake Ave.
Towson, MD 21204
Phone: (410)321-6647
Free: 800-296-4433
Fax: (410)321-9165
Jane Thompson, Contact

Founded: 1980. **Members:** 5,600. **State Groups:** 19. **Local Groups:** 14. **Description:** Immune deficiency patients, their families, and medical professionals. Promotes education and research in primary immune deficiency diseases. Supports education and research fellowship for physicians. Disseminates educational materials for patients and family members. Holds medical symposia; bestows patient scholarship and research awards. **Publications:** *Guide for Nurses*. • *IDF Newsletter*, quarterly. Newsletter. Contains announcements of patient scholarship and research awards. Includes health insurance information and calendar of events. *Price:* Free. • *Our Immune System*. • *Overview of Primary Immune Deficiencies*. • *Patient and Family Handbook*. • *Primer for Physicians*.

★ 2074 ★ International Association of Allergology and Clinical Immunology (IAACI)
611 E. Wells St.
Milwaukee, WI 53202
Phone: (414)276-6445
Fax: (414)276-3349
Rick Iber, Exec.Sec.

Founded: 1945. **Members:** 17,000. **Description:** Medical practitioners in allergology (the study of allergies and their treatment) and immunology, from 40 national allergology societies in 34 countries. Conducts research; increases awareness of completed and in-progress research programs; develops world standardization of categorization of allergies; establishes criteria for and monitors training of allergists; assesses world environmental conditions. **Publications:** *Allergy and Clinical Immunology News*, bimonthly. Journal. Includes research updates. *Price:* $38/year for members; $49/year for nonmembers. • Proceedings, triennial. **Formerly:** (1951) International Association of Allergists; (1980) International Association of Allergology.

International Association of Asthmology (INTERASMA)
(Asociacion Internacional de Asmologia — INTERASMA)
See: Entry 11596

★ 2075 ★ International Correspondence Society of Allergists (ICSA)
5811 Outlook Dr.
Shawnee Mission, KS 66202
Phone: (913)432-0625
Fax: (913)432-5833
Jeremy E. Baptist, M.D., Ph.D., Exec.Dir.

Founded: 1936. **Members:** 415. **Description:** Physicians who specialize in research and treatment of allergies. Exchanges of technical information and experiences are conducted via letters. **Publications:** *Allergy Letters*, monthly. Newsletter. Includes case reports, comments, questions and answers, and related material. *Price:* Included in membership dues.

★ 2076 ★ International Nutritional Immunology Group (INIG)
Janeway Child Health Centre
St. John's, NF, Canada A1A 1R8
Phone: (709)778-4519
Fax: (709)737-6400
Dr. R.K. Chandra, Convenor

Founded: 1982. **Members:** 110. **Languages:** English. **Description:** Scientists and physicians from 8 countries interested in nutritional immunology. Acts as a forum for the exchange of information on topics pertaining to nutritional immunology. Sponsors competitions; bestows awards.

International Society for AIDS Education (ISAE)
See: Entry 6682

★ 2077 ★ International Society of Developmental and Comparative Immunology (ISDCI)
Wageningen Agricultural University
Dept. of Experimental Animal Morphology
Postbus 338
Wageningen NL-6700 AH, England
Phone: 18370 83509
Fax: 18370 83962
Prof. Michael Balls, Sec.-Treas.

Founded: 1978. **Members:** 500. **Languages:** English. **Description:** Immunologists, zoologists, and biologists in 36 countries. Fosters scientific cooperation and communication among individuals, scientists, regional groups, and national societies interested in the study of developmental and comparative immunology. Conducts annual workshop. **Publications:** *Developmental and Comparative Immunology*, quarterly. Journal.

International Society for Immunology of Reproduction (ISIR)
See: Entry 11227

★ 2078 ★ International Society for Thymology and Immunotherapy (Internationale Gesellschaft fur Thymologie und Immuntherapie)
Am Stadtpark 18
38667 Bad Harzburg, Germany
Phone: 5322 6520
Fax: 5322 3017
Hildegarde Rieger, Contact

Founded: 1975. **Description:** Promotes the study of thymology and immunotherapy treatment. Disseminates information on the different areas of thymus research and the therapeutic applications of thymus elements.

★ 2079 ★ International Union of Immunological Societies (IUIS)
Dept. of Surgery
University of Edinburgh Medical School
Teviot Place
Edinburgh EH8 9AG, Scotland
Phone: 131 6503557
Fax: 131 6676190
Keith James, Sec.Gen.

Founded: 1969. **Members:** 44. **Regional Groups:** 4. **Languages:** English. **Description:** National professional societies of basic and ap-

plied immunologists. Encourages the orderly development and utilization of the science of immunology. Promotes the application of new developments to clinical and veterinary problems and standardizes reagents and nomenclature. Conducts educational symposia and scientific meetings. **Publications:** *International Union of Immunological Societies*, triennial. Proceedings.

★ 2080 ★ International Union of Reticuloendothelial Societies (IURES)
c/o Dr. Sherwood M. Reichard
Med. College of Georgia
1120 15th St.
Augusta, GA 30912
Phone: (706)721-2601
Fax: (706)721-3048
Dr. Sherwood M. Reichard, Exec.Dir.

Founded: 1975. **Members:** 3,000. **Description:** Reticuloendothelial and related research societies concerned with the body's defenses against disease and cancer. Works to advance research and understanding of the reticuloendothelial system. (RES is a diffuse system of cells arising from mesenchyme and comprising all phagocytic cells of the body excluding circulating leukocytes.) Fosters and maintains scientific cooperation and communication among individual scientists and regional and national societies worldwide. Maintains liaison with the International Council of Scientific Unions, World Health Organization, and similar organizations to facilitate the appropriate representation of RES research. Sponsors international scientific conferences, seminars, workshops, and training courses. **Publications:** *Proceedings of International Meetings*, biennial.

★ 2081 ★ Joint Council of Allergy and Immunology (JCAI)
PO Box 4620
Arlington Heights, IL 60006
Phone: (708)427-8100
Joseph J. Lotharius, Exec.Dir.

Founded: 1975. **Members:** 2,850. **Description:** Physicians specializing in allergy or clinical immunology. Members must belong to the American Academy of Allergy and Immunology or the American College of Allergy and Immunology. Serves as political and socioeconomic arm for these organizations. **Publications:** *JCAI Reports*, periodic. **Formerly:** (1977) Joint Council of Socio-Economics of Allergy.

★ 2082 ★ Latin American Association of Immunology (Associacion Latinoamericana de Imunologia)
Academia Nacional de Medidina
Las Heras 3092
1425 Buenos Aires, Argentina
Dr. Pasqualini, Sec.

Description: Promotes the study of immunology in Latin America. Fosters communication between immunologists to exchange information about the science.

Mobilization Against AIDS (MAA)
See: Entry 6696

Names Project Foundation (NPF)
See: Entry 6697

Namibia Network of AIDS Service Organisations
See: Entry 6698

National AIDS Control Programme
See: Entry 6726

National AIDS Prevention and Control Program
See: Entry 6727

National Association of People With AIDS (NAPWA)
See: Entry 6730

★ 2083 ★ National Foundation for the Chemically Hypersensitive (NFCH)
PO Box 222
Ophelia, VA 22530
Phone: (517)697-3989
Fred Nelson, Dir.

Founded: 1986. **Members:** 5,000. **Regional Groups:** 40. **State Groups:** 40. **Description:** Individuals suffering from chemical hypersensitivity, their families, and friends; health care professionals; interested others. Promotes public awareness of chemical hypersensitivity disorders, such as multiple chemical sensitivities, environmental illness, food intolerance, total allergy syndrome, candida, and chronic fatigue. Disseminates information on symptoms of chemical hypersensitivity and the potential sources of exposure to the toxic substances that can result in hypersensitivity. Facilitates networking among those afflicted with chemical hypersensitivity. Compiles case histories and statistics; conducts research and educational programs; operates health care and legal referral services. Provides assistance in handling Social Security and worker's compensation claims and locating low-cost housing resources. Maintains speakers' bureau. **Publications:** *Cheers*, quarterly. Newsletter. Covers selfhelp and networking activities. *Price:* $15/year.

National Jewish Center for Immunology and Respiratory Medicine
See: Entry 11605

National Minority AIDS Council (NMAC)
See: Entry 6737

★ 2084 ★ National Sjogren's Syndrome Association (NSSA)
3201 W. Evans Dr.
Phoenix, AZ 85023
Phone: (602)516-0787
Free: 800-395-6772
Fax: (602)516-0111
Barbara Henry, Exec.Dir.

Founded: 1990. **Members:** 4,500. **Description:** Promotes public awareness of Sjogren's Syndrome; encourages research into the cause and cure of the disorder. (Sjogren's Syndrome is an autoimmune disorder characterized by dryness of all mucous membranes resulting from deficient secretion of the glands. Approximately 50% of Sjogren's Syndrome patients also have rheumatoid arthritis.) Sponsors chapters and offers information to the medical community. Conducts educational and research programs; maintains speakers' bureau. **Publications:**

Learning to Live with Sjogren's Syndrome. Video. *Price:* $25. • *Patient Education Series*, quarterly. • *Sjogren's Digest*, quarterly. Newsletter. *Price:* Included in membership dues.

National Vaccine Information Center
See: Entry 3273

★ 2085 ★ Netherlands Society of Allergology (NAA)
(Nederlandse Vereniging voor Allergologie — NVA)
G.V. Voornestraat 145-147
NL-3232 BE Brielle, Netherlands
Phone: 1010 17320
Fax: 1010 15628
I.F. Simon-Licht, Sec.

Founded: 1948. **Members:** 180. **Languages:** Dutch, English. **Description:** Allergists interested in the clinical and practical aspects of allergology and related fields. Furthers information exchange on topics including clinical chemistry, dermatology, immunology, and prescription drugs.

★ 2086 ★ Norwegian Immune Deficiency Foundation (NIDF)
(Norsk Immunsviktforening — NI)
Brunholmgt. 3A
N-6004 Alesund, Norway
Phone: 71 28388
Fax: 71 28388
Eva Brox, Pres.

Founded: 1983. **Members:** 120. **National Groups:** 1. **Languages:** Norwegian. **Description:** Persons with immunological disorders and their families; private companies. Acts as support group. Disseminates information. **Publications:** *Immunsvikt hos Voksne og Barn*, periodic.

★ 2087 ★ Pan-American Allergy Society (PAAS)
PO Box 947
Fredericksburg, TX 78624
Phone: (210)997-9853
Fax: (210)997-8625
Ann Brey, Exec.Sec.

Founded: 1956. **Members:** 600. **Description:** Physicians who include allergy diagnosis and management in their practice. Purpose is to serve as a forum for physicians who actively participate in the diagnosis and treatment of allergic disorders. Seeks to provide a means of social communication among members, thereby promoting interspecialty cooperation and an increase in individual excellence. Sponsors continuing medical education programs. **Publications:** Membership Directory, biennial. • *Pan American Allergy Society Report*, semiannual. Newsletter. **Formerly:** (1976) Gulf Coast Allergy Study Group.

Pediatric AIDS Foundation
See: Entry 3280

★ 2088 ★ Polish Society for Immunology (PSI)
(Polskie Towarzystwo Immunologiczne — PTI)
Department of Pathophysiology
Institute of Basic Medical Sciences
Military Medical Academy
Pl. Hallera 1
PL-90-647 Lodz 39, Poland
Phone: 42 324273
Fax: 42 324273
Prof. K. Zeman, Sec.Gen.

Founded: 1969. **Members:** 298. **Local Groups:** 9. **Languages:** English, Polish. **Description:** Researchers. Encourages, coordinates, and supervises immunological research activities in Poland. Assists instruction at universities and medical centers. Disseminates scientific information. Conducts educational and research programs. Bestows awards. **Publications:** *Bulletin*, periodic. Bulletin. • *Polish Journal of Immunology*, quarterly.

★ 2089 ★ Practical Allergy Research Foundation (PARF)
PO Box 60
Buffalo, NY 14223
Phone: (716)875-5578
Free: 800-787-8780
Fax: (716)875-5399
Doris J. Rapp, M.D., Pres.

Description: Seeks to enhance public awareness of allergies, their symptoms, and remedies; fosters research in allergy. Produces and distributes teaching aids; participates in allergy teaching programs and seminars worldwide. Maintains speakers' bureau. **Publications:** *Allergies and the Hyperactive Child.* Book. • *Allergies and Your Family.* Book. • *Allergies Do Alter Activities and Behavior.* Video. • *Audiotapes.* • *Catalog.* • *The Impossible Child.* Book. • *Impossible Child or Allergic Child?.* Video. • *Recognize and Manage Your Allergies.* Book. • *Why An Environmentally Clean Classroom?.* Video. • *Why Some Children Can't Learn or Behave.* Video.

Remdios AIDS Foundation
See: Entry 6746

Romanian Anti-AIDS Association
See: Entry 6747

Ryan White National Teen Education Program (RWNTEP)
See: Entry 3285

San Francisco AIDS Foundation (SFAF)
See: Entry 6749

Shanti Project (SP)
See: Entry 6750

Sjogren's Syndrome Foundation (SSF)
See: Entry 7910

★2090★ Society for Leukocyte Biology (A Reticuloendothelial Society) (SLB)

c/o Debbie Stoutamire
9650 Rockville Pike
Bethesda, MD 20814
Phone: (301)530-7120
Fax: (301)530-7049
Debbie Stoutamire, Exec. Officer

Founded: 1954. **Members:** 1,025. **Description:** Persons holding M.D. and/or Ph.D. degrees who conduct research with universities; private, industrial, and government institutes; hospital clinics; members of the pharmaceutical industry. Facilitates the association of persons studying the reticuloendothelial system; fosters research in the field. (The reticuloendothelial system comprises all the cells of the blood and body tissues, including macrophages, lymphocytes, and granulocytes. It is involved in the immune response and in inflammation and functions in host defense against such problems as malignancies, infection, and environmental pathogens.) Sponsors workshop on macrophage methodology. **Publications:** Books. • *Directory and Constitution*, annual. Directory. • *Journal of Leukocyte Biology*, monthly. Journal. • Newsletter, quarterly. **Formerly:** (1988) Reticuloendothelial Society.

Task Force for Child Survival and Development (TFCSD)
See: Entry 3302

Teens Teaching AIDS Prevention (TEENS TAP)
See: Entry 6751

Treatment Action Group (TAG)
See: Entry 6752

Tuvalu National AIDS Committee (TUNAC)
See: Entry 6753

Ugandan AIDS Project
See: Entry 6754

World Association of Veterinary Microbiologists, Immunologists, and Specialists in Infectious Diseases (WAVMI)
(Association Mondiale des Veterinaires Microbiologistes, Immunologistes et Specialistes des Maladies Infectieuses — AMVMI)
See: Entry 13120

World Hemophilia AIDS Center (WHAC)
See: Entry 6759

Research Centers

Aaron Diamond Aids Research Center
See: Entry 6760

★2091★ Allergy / Immunology Service

Rush Medical College
1725 W. Harrison, Ste. 207
Chicago, IL 60612
Phone: (312)942-6296
Fax: (312)563-2201
Anita Gewurz, Contact

Research Activities and Fields: Allergies, immunology, and product testing, including therapeutic agent evaluation, allergenic extract developments, laboratory assay development, adverse food reaction pathogensis, Samter Syndrome etiology and pathogenesis, urticaria/angiodema etiology, and hypogammaglobulinemia treatment. **Formerly:** Max Samter Institute of Allergy and Clinical Immunology.

American Auto Immune Related Diseases Association
See: Entry 7859

★2092★ Armand-Frappier Institute Immunology Research Center

531, boulevard des Prairies
Laval, PQ, Canada H7N 4Z3
Phone: (514)686-5332
Fax: (514)686-5501
Suzanne Lemieux, Dir.

Research Activities and Fields: Nutritional and environmental factors of cancer and genetics; cancer epidemiology and anti-tumor immunity; cellular and molecular analysis of immunological effectors, their regulations and mechanisms, and characterization of cellular and molecular interactions; immunomodulation; and therapeutic tools.

★2093★ Baylor College of Medicine Center for Allergy and Immunological Disorders

1 Baylor Plaza
Houston, TX 77030
Phone: (713)770-1319
Fax: (713)770-1260
William T. Shearer, M.D.,, Dir.

Research Activities and Fields: Allergy and immunological disorders, including basic and clinical projects in cancer immunology, immunoreconstitution of immunodeficient children, immunoregulation of cellular and humoral immune responses, immune complex diseases, immunotherapy of neoplastic diseases, pulmonary immunology, rheumatic diseases, allergic diseases of children, and AIDS. Facilities available for specialty training of pre- and postdoctoral students on either a research or clinical level.

Bone Marrow Transplant Laboratory
See: Entry 12883

★2094★ Brigham and Women's Hospital Asthma & Allergic Disease Cooperative Research Center

75 Francis St.
Boston, MA 02115
Phone: (617)432-1995
Fax: (617)432-0979
K. Frank Austen, M.D., Contact

Research Activities and Fields: Clinical areas include allergy, clinical immunology, rheuma-

tology, nephrology, immunodermatology, and infectious diseases; pre-clinical areas include mast cell biology, biology of human peripheral blood, leukocytes including eosinophils, neutrophils and monocytes, arachidonic acid metabolism by the 5-lipoxygenase pathway, and complement biology.

Brigham and Women's Hospital Center for Neurologic Diseases
See: Entry 8344

★2095★ Bucknell University Immunobiology Research Laboratory

Dept. of Biology
Lewisburg, PA 17837
Phone: (717)524-1135
Dr. David D. Pearson, Dir.

Research Activities and Fields: Autoimmune diseases, particularly the causes of rheumatoid arthritis. Studies techniques to detect the disease, including protein blotting on nitrocellulose, binding of oligosaccharides to lectins, and enzyme-linked immunoabsorbent assay tests. Also studies methods to detect small quantities of antibodies secreted from single cells and a small number of immunoassays in developmental stages for small amounts of proteins.

California Collaborative Treatment Group
See: Entry 6764

★2096★ Center for Molecular Medicine and Immunology / Garden State Cancer Center

1 Bruce St.
Newark, NJ 07103
Phone: (201)982-4600
Fax: (201)982-7047
David M. Goldenberg, Sc.D., M.D., Pres.

Research Activities and Fields: Molecular immunology, nuclear medicine, immunobiology, and molecular genetics. Seeks to advance cancer detection techniques and translate them into methods of treatment and control. **Formerly:** Center for Molecular Medicine and Immunology.

★2097★ Center for Reproduction and Transplantation Immunology

Methodist Hospital
1701 N. Senate Blvd.
Indianapolis, IN 46202
Phone: (317)929-5195
W. Page Faulk, M.D., Dir.

Research Activities and Fields: Reproduction and transplantation immunology, including development of vaccines and vaginal suppositories to prevent miscarriages caused by abnormal immune responses in pregnant women.

City of Hope National Medical Center National Cooperative Drug Discovery Group for the Treatment of AIDS
See: Entry 6765

Comprehensive AIDS Center
See: Entry 6767

★2098★ Creighton University
Allergic Disease Center
2500 California
Omaha, NE 68178
Phone: (402)280-2940
Fax: (402)280-1843
Robert G. Townley, M.D., Chief

Research Activities and Fields: Multidisciplinary research in asthma, allergic rhinitis, allergic diseases, clinical and basic immunology, clinical and basic pharmacology and physiology, airway reactivity in patients with asthma, and allergies. Laboratory research consists of studies of human lung, eosinophils, mast cells, lymphocytes, and platelets to correlate adrenergic and cholinergic receptors and receptor mechanisms; and role of leukotrienes and platelet activating factor on airway reactivity and in asthma and animal models of asthma. Focuses on mechanisms of immediate hypersensitivity. **Publications:** *Allergy Principles & Practice* (quadrennially).

★2099★ Donald Guthrie Foundation for Education and Research
1 Guthrie Square
Sayre, PA 18840
Phone: (717)882-4620
Fax: (717)882-5151
Pauline Stamp, Sr.Admin.

Research Activities and Fields: Basic laboratory research in cell communication and signal transduction and clinical research in immunology, virology, cancer biology, lung cancer, and neuroscience. **Publications:** *Guthrie Medical Journal* (quarterly). **Formerly:** Donald Guthrie Foundation for Medical Research.

★2100★ Duke University
Asthma and Allergic Disease Center
Medical Center
Box 2898
Durham, NC 27710
Phone: (919)684-2922
Fax: (919)681-7979
Rebecca H. Buckley, Chief of Division

Research Activities and Fields: As a unit of NIAID, the Center seeks to integrate the concepts of immunology, genetics, biochemistry, and pharmacology into clinical investigations of patients with asthma and allergic diseases. Specific projects include studies on immunoregulation in atopic eczema and in vitro studies of human immunoglobulin E (IgE) synthesis, including lymphocyte phenotypes and their function in humans with allergic diseases and excessively high IgE antibody production. Functional studies include proliferative responses, in vitro IgE production and the effects of various cytokines on it, and epidermal T cell interactions in atopic dermatitis.

★2101★ Georgetown University
International Center for Interdisciplinary Studies of Immunology at Georgetown
3800 Reservoir Rd. NW
G-1034
Washington, DC 20007
Phone: (202)687-8227
Fax: (202)784-3597
Joseph A. Bellanti, M.D., Dir.

Research Activities and Fields: Immunobiology, immunochemistry, immunogenetics, immunopharmacology, and immunopathology, including the clinical disciplines of allergy and immunology, infectious diseases, respiratory diseases, and disorders of immune regulation. The Center's research program emphasizes pediatrics.

★2102★ Harvard University
Laboratory of Immunology
Harvard Medical School
200 Longwood, 5th Fl., D-530
Boston, MA 02115
Phone: (617)432-1978
Fax: (617)432-2789
Dr. Martin Dorf, Dir.

Research Activities and Fields: Prokaryotic and eukaryotic gene transcription in studying the regulation of class II major histocompatibility complex genes in the immune system. **E-mail Address:** dorf@warren.med.harvard.edu.

Human Immunodeficiency Virus Center for Clinical and Behavioral Studies
See: Entry 6772

★2103★ Irvington Institute for Medical Research
120 E. 56th St., Ste. 340
New York, NY 10022
Phone: (212)758-8250
Fax: (212)758-8968
Gail Freeman, Exec.Dir.

Research Activities and Fields: Diseases and dysfunctions involving the immune system, including AIDS, cancer, diabetes, rheumatoid arthritis, allergies, organ rejection, and systemic lupus erythematosus.

James N. Gamble Institute of Medical Research
See: Entry 6773

★2104★ Jane Forbes Clark Surgical Research Laboratories
St. Luke's-Roosevelt Hospital Center
Amsterdam Ave. at 114th St.
New York, NY 10025
Phone: (212)870-1143
Dr. George A. Hashim, Dir.

Research Activities and Fields: Cell-mediated immunity, immunochemistry, transplantation, and tumor immunobiology. **Formerly:** Autoimmune Disease Laboratories; Experimental Immunology Laboratories.

★2105★ Johns Hopkins University
Asthma and Allergy Center
5501 Hopkins Bayview Circle
Baltimore, MD 21224
Phone: (410)550-2101
Fax: (410)550-2090
Dr. Lawrence M. Lichtenstein, Dir.

Research Activities and Fields: Allergic diseases and individuals with allergic diseases, pulmonary diseases and individuals with pulmonary diseases, and diseases involving inflammation and immunological processes.

Johns Hopkins University
Center for Immunization Research
See: Entry 6774

★2106★ Johns Hopkins University
Immunologic Disease Cooperative Research Center
Asthma & Allergy Center
5501 Hopkins Bayview Circle
Baltimore, MD 21224
Phone: (410)550-2581
Fax: (410)550-2090
Dr. P.S. Norman, Head

Research Activities and Fields: Causes, prevention, and treatment of immunologically mediated diseases. Studies focus on the release of mediators in asthma, allergic rhinitis, and urticaria; mechanisms of pollen immunotherapy in persons with allergic rhinitis and asthma; the natural history of food allergy; immunology of anaphylactic reaction in lungs and other organs; and control of asthma in adolescents. **Formerly:** Center for Interdisciplinary Research on Immunologic Diseases.

Laboratory of Tumor Antigen Immunochemistry
See: Entry 6064

★2107★ Laval University
Medical Research Centre
Inflammation, Immunology, and Rheumatology Research Group
2705, boulevard Laurier
Ste. Foy, PQ, Canada G1V 4G2
Phone: (418)654-2240
Fax: (418)654-2765
Andre Beaulieu, Dir.

Research Activities and Fields: Tissue damage in rheumatoid arthritis, regulation of leukotriene synthesis, arachidonic acid metabolism, regulation of antibody production, identification of major surface antigens, and importance of cellular compatibility.

Loyola University Chicago
Cardiac Transplant Program
See: Entry 12884

★2108★ Mayo Clinic and Foundation
Allergic Diseases Research Laboratory
200 1st St. SW
Rochester, MN 55905
Phone: (507)284-2789
Fax: (507)284-1086
Gerald J. Gleich, M.D., Dir.

Research Activities and Fields: Provides a focus for research into the causes, prevention, and management of allergic diseases such as asthma, allergies, contact hypersensitivity, immune deficiencies and infection, and autoimmune disorders plus related studies of fundamental immune mechanisms involving immune cells, antibodies, genetic factors, and immune regulatory systems. Projects focus on functions of the eosinophilic leukocyte, immunotherapy of patients with pollen allergies, and clinical studies of passive immunotherapy in patients allergic to honeybee stings who fail to respond to venom immunotherapy and who are members of beekeeping families.

McGill University
McGill AIDS Center
See: Entry 6777

National Cooperative Drug Discovery Group for the Treatment of AIDS
See: Entry 6779

★2109★ National Jewish Center for Immunology and Respiratory Medicine
1400 Jackson St.
Denver, CO 80206
Phone: (303)388-4461
Lynn M. Taussig, M.D.

Research Activities and Fields: Basic and clinical research in etiology, progression, manifestation, treatment, rehabilitation, and prevention of pulmonary, allergic, and immunologic diseases. Studies encompass cellular and molecular biology. **Publications:** *New Directions Newsletter, Lung Line Newsletter, Update Newsletter, National Jewish Center Scientific Annual Report.* **Formerly:** National Jewish Hospital and Research Center/National Asthma Center (1985).

New York Society for the Relief of the Ruptured and Crippled
See: Entry 7925

★2110★ Northwestern University
Ernest S. Bazley Asthma and Allergic Disease Center
303 E. Chicago Ave.
Chicago, IL 60611
Phone: (312)908-8172
Fax: (312)908-0205
Roy Patterson, M.D., Head

Research Activities and Fields: Basic and clinical investigation of the etiology, mechanisms, diagnosis, and treatment of allergic diseases. Studies focus on idiopathic anaphylaxis, potentially fatal asthma, IgE mediated disease, drug allergy, hypersensitivity pneumonitis, allergic bronchopulmonary aspergillosis, anaphylaxis, occupational immunologic lung disease, polymerized allergens for treatment of IgE mediated disease, and animal models of allergic disease. **Formerly:** Allergy Diseases Center.

★2111★ Ohio State University
Pulmonary Laboratories
Means Hall, N325
1654 Upahm Dr.
Columbus, OH 43210
Phone: (614)293-4925
Fax: (614)293-4799
James E. Gadek, M.D., Dir.

Research Activities and Fields: Mechanisms of allergic, immunologic, and inflammatory diseases, including ventilatory control and respiratory failure, inflammatory mechanisms in adult respiratory distress syndrome, cystic fibrosis, emphysema, staging and therapy of pulmonary neoplasms, and occupational lung diseases. Collaborates with the departments of physiology and exercise physiology and with the cardiopulmonary unit of the School of Veterinary Medicine at the University. **Formerly:** Established in 1982 through merger of Pulmonary Function Laboratories and Allergy/Immunology Laboratories.

★2112★ Ohio State University
Therapeutic Immunology Laboratories
357 Means Hall
1654 Upham Dr.
Columbus, OH 43210
Phone: (614)293-3212
Fax: (614)293-4541
Dr. Charles Orosz, Dir.

Research Activities and Fields: Transplantation related immunobiology, inflammation, clinical histocompatibility testing and post-transplant immunologic monitoring, and clinical and experimental immunosuppression.

Oklahoma Medical Research Foundation
Arthritis / Immunology Research Program
See: Entry 7927

Oklahoma Medical Research Foundation
Immunology and Cancer Research Program
See: Entry 6098

Oregon Health Sciences University
Transplant and Immunogenetics Laboratory
See: Entry 12885

Purdue University
Center for AIDS Research
See: Entry 6783

★2113★ Rockefeller University
Laboratory of Bacterial Pathogenesis and Immunology
1230 York Ave.
New York, NY 10021
Phone: (212)327-8155
Fax: (212)327-7584
Dr. John B. Zabriskie, Dir.

Research Activities and Fields: Microbe-induced autoimmunity and human genetics, including molecular biology emphasizing eukaryotic systems, protein chemistry, and immunology.

Rockefeller University
Laboratory of Bacteriology and Immunology
See: Entry 6784

★2114★ Rockefeller University
Laboratory of Cellular Physiology and Immunology
1230 York Ave.
New York, NY 10021-6399
Phone: (212)327-8000
Fax: (212)327-8875
Ralph Stiman, Head

Research Activities and Fields: Functional properties of eukaryotic cells and their role in physiologic and pathologic events. Using the tools of immunology, cell biology, and biochemistry, the Lab studies problems of inflammation, the immune response, and host defense against parasites and tumor cells.

★2115★ Rockefeller University
Laboratory of Immunology
1230 York Ave.
New York, NY 10021-6399
Phone: (212)327-8157
Fax: (212)327-8960
Emil C. Gotschlich, Head

Research Activities and Fields: Fundamental problems of immunology and their relevance to human diseases. Specific emphasis is placed on the role of the lymphocyte cell in the analysis of diseases, especially the basic molecular mechanisms involved in lymphocyte cellular recognition, activation, differentiation, and immunoregulation.

Rutgers University
AIDS Research Group
See: Entry 6786

★2116★ Scripps Research Institute
Autoimmune Disease Center
10666 N. Torrey Pines Rd.
La Jolla, CA 92037
Phone: (619)554-8686
Fax: (619)554-6805
Eng Tan, M.D., Dir.

Research Activities and Fields: Immunologic studies on the development of allergic disorders, especially aspirin and related drug sensitivities, bisulfite-sensitivity in asthma, and hereditary angioedema. Investigates the role of leukotrienes in the development of allergic disorders and conducts studies on drug-induced lupus reactions and the role specific autoantibodies may play in the development of the disease. Emphasizes immunology and molecular biology of autoimmunity related to lupus, scleroderma, Sjogren's syndrome, dermatomyositis, and polymyositis. **Formerly:** Scripps Clinic and Research Foundation, Autoimmune Disease Center; Scripps Clinic and Research Foundation, Asthma and Allergic Disease Center.

★2117★ Sherbrooke University
Immunobiology Research Unit
Faculte de medecine
3001, 12e Avenue Nord
Sherbrooke, PQ, Canada J1H 5N4
Phone: (819)563-5555
Fax: (819)564-5215
Dr. Marek Rola-Pleszczynski, Dir.

Research Activities and Fields: Immunoglobulin gene expression and control, lymphocyte activation pathways and second messangers, stem cell biology, cytokine receptor physiology, structure-function studies of lipid mediator receptors, natural cytotoxicity against tumor cells, ultraviolet-irradiation and immune functions, and immune interactions in atherosclerosis. **E-mail Address:** mrolaple@courrier.usherb.ca.

Spellman Center for HIV-Related Disease
See: Entry 6789

Stanford University
Center for AIDS Research
See: Entry 6790

Stanford University
Laboratory for Transplantation
Immunology
See: Entry 12886

★ 2118 ★ State University of New York at Buffalo
Ernest Witebsky Center for Immunology
School of Medicine & Biomedical Sciences
Buffalo, NY 14214
Phone: (716)829-2848
Fax: (716)829-2158
Dr. Roger K. Cunningham, Dir.

Research Activities and Fields: Provides a basis for collaboration among immunologists working in various departments of the University and local University-affiliated hospitals. **Publications:** *Immunological Investigations* (bimonthly). **E-mail Address:** rcunning@ubmed.buffalo.edu. **Formerly:** Center for Immunology (1967).

★ 2119 ★ State University of New York
Health Science Center at Stony Brook
Asthma and Allergic Diseases Center
Stony Brook, NY 11794
Phone: (516)444-2272
Fax: (516)444-2493
Prof. Allen P. Kaplan, Head

Research Activities and Fields: One of a network of NIAID centers studying the cause, pathogenesis, diagnosis, prevention, and treatment of both naturally occurring and acquired allergic diseases. Examines the biochemical and immunologic mechanisms by which inflammation occurs in allergic diseases, including urticaria (hives), angioedema, asthma, vasculitis, Lyme disease, arthritis, and other rheumatic diseases.

★ 2120 ★ Surgical Immunology Research
Laboratory
West Haven Veterans Hospital
950 Camel Ave.
West Haven, CT 06516
Phone: (203)932-5711
Fax: (203)937-3883
Dr. Marvin A. McMillen, Dir.

Research Activities and Fields: Immunology, including lymphocyte signal transduction, neuroenteric mediators of immune functions, and the effects of immunosuppressives on second messengers and activation events.

Thomas Jefferson University
Lupus Study Center
See: Entry 7934

Thomas Jefferson University
Scleroderma and Arthritis Research Center
See: Entry 7935

★ 2121 ★ Trudeau Institute, Inc.
PO Box 59
Saranac Lake, NY 12983
Phone: (518)891-3080
Fax: (518)891-5126
Dr. Robert J. North, Dir.

Research Activities and Fields: Cellular immunology, emphasizing lymphocyte physiology and the effector mechanisms of cell-mediated immunity and antimicrobial and antitumor immunity. **Publications:** *Focus* (newsletter); Annual Report. **Formerly:** Trudeau Laboratory; Trudeau Sanitorium (1954).

★ 2122 ★ Tulane University
School of Medicine
Clinical Immunology Section
1700 Perdido St., 3rd Fl.
New Orleans, LA 70112
Phone: (504)588-5578
Prof. Manuel Lopez, M.D., Dir.

Research Activities and Fields: Provides a focus for research into the causes, prevention, and management of diseases such as asthma, allergies, immune deficiencies and infections, and autoimmune disorders, plus related studies of fundamental immune mechanisms involving immune cells, antibodies, genetic factors, and immune regulatory systems, especially as they relate to the lung. Investigates tobacco smoke products as possible allergens, mechanisms of AIDS, and immunologic mechanisms of occupational and environmental lung disease.

U.S. Department of Defense
Armed Forces Institute of Pathology
Infectious and Parasitic Disease Pathology
Department
AIDS Pathology Division
See: Entry 10168

U.S. Department of Defense
Armed Forces Institute of Pathology
Infectious and Parasitic Disease Pathology
Department
Microbiology Division
See: Entry 10170

U.S. Department of Defense
Armed Forces Institute of Pathology
Scientific Laboratory Department
Immunopathology Division
See: Entry 10177

U.S. Department of Defense
Armed Forces Radiobiology Research
Institute
Experimental Hematology Department
See: Entry 11077

U.S. Department of Health and Human
Services
National Cancer Institute
Division of Cancer Biology, Diagnosis, and
Centers
Cancer Immunology Branch
See: Entry 6131

U.S. Department of Health and Human
Services
National Cancer Institute
Division of Cancer Biology, Diagnosis, and
Centers
Metabolism Branch
See: Entry 6135

U.S. Department of Health and Human
Services
National Cancer Institute
Laboratory of Immunobiology
See: Entry 6189

U.S. Department of Health and Human
Services
National Cancer Institute
Laboratory of Molecular Biology
See: Entry 6192

U.S. Department of Health and Human
Services
National Cancer Institute
Laboratory of Molecular Immunoregulation
See: Entry 6194

U.S. Department of Health and Human
Services
National Cancer Institute
Laboratory of Tumor Immunology and
Biology
See: Entry 6200

U.S. Department of Health and Human
Services
National Center for Infectious Diseases
Division of HIV / AIDS
Immunology Branch
See: Entry 6798

U.S. Department of Health and Human
Services
National Center for Prevention Services
Immunization Division
Surveillance, Investigations, and Research
Branch
See: Entry 10878

★ 2123 ★ U.S. Department of Health and
Human Services
National Institute of Allergy and Infectious
Diseases
NIH Bldg. 31, Rm. 7A50
9000 Rockville Pike
Bethesda, MD 20892
Phone: (301)496-5717
Fax: (301)402-0120
Anthony S. Fauci, M.D., Director

Research Activities and Fields: NIAID conducts and supports research contributing to a better understanding of causes of allergic, immunologic, and infectious diseases and to the development of better means of preventing, diagnosing, and treating illnesses. Its mission involves studies on: genetic control, maturation, characteristics, and manipulation of the immune system; disorders of the immune system, including asthma and other allergies, immunodeficiency states, and autoimmunity; the role of the immune system in the pathogenesis of chronic diseases such as arthritis, chronic glomerulonephritis, and lupus erythematosus; the etiology, epidemiology, and pathogenesis of all types of infections (including those caused by viruses, mycoplasma, bacteria, fungi, and parasites) involving a variety of organ systems; the diagnosis, treatment, and prevention of all types of infections (including research on antimicrobial, antifungal, and antiviral therapy, and vaccines); and the role and mechanism of nucleic acid recombination in microbial agents. Fields of research include microbiology, parasitology, virology, bacteriology, genetics and transplantation biology, and mycology. The Institute is also concerned with enteric diseases and tropical diseases research. NIAID's program includes both in-house (intramural) research and research conducted through grants, contracts, and interagency agreements (extramural). NIAID's extramural divisions are the Division of Acquired Immunodeficiency Syndrome (DAIDS), Division of Allergy/Immunology, and Transplantation (DAIT), and the Division of Microbiology and Infectious Diseases. NIAID's Division of Intramural Research (DIR) comprises 17 laboratories in Bethesda, MD, and the Rocky Mountain Laboratories in Hamilton, MT. Also supports a 52-bed inpatient service and outpatient research facility on the NIH campus.

U.S. Department of Health and Human Services
National Institute of Allergy and Infectious Diseases
Division of Acquired Immunodeficiency Syndrome (AIDS)
See: Entry 6816

U.S. Department of Health and Human Services
National Institute of Allergy and Infectious Diseases
Division of Acquired Immunodeficiency Syndrome (AIDS)
Basic Research and Development Program
See: Entry 6817

U.S. Department of Health and Human Services
National Institute of Allergy and Infectious Diseases
Division of Acquired Immunodeficiency Syndrome (AIDS)
Biostatistics Research Branch
See: Entry 6818

U.S. Department of Health and Human Services
National Institute of Allergy and Infectious Diseases
Division of Acquired Immunodeficiency Syndrome (AIDS)
Vaccine Research and Development Branch
See: Entry 6821

★ 2124 ★ U.S. Department of Health and Human Services
National Institute of Allergy and Infectious Diseases
Division of Allergy, Immunology, and Transplantation
Control Data Bldg., Rm. 4A16
9000 Rockville Pike
Bethesda, MD 20892
Phone: (301)496-1886
Fax: (301)402-2571
Dr. Lawrence Prograis, Deputy Director

Research Activities and Fields: Focuses on the immune system as it functions in the maintenance of health and as it malfunctions in the production of disease. The Division provides leadership in the identification, design, and implementation of basic and clinical research initiatives encompassing a wide range of disorders including: autoimmune diseases such as childhood diabetes, rheumatoid arthritis and multiple sclerosis, allergic diseases such as asthma and occupational and environmental disorders and organ transplant rejection.

★ 2125 ★ U.S. Department of Health and Human Services
National Institute of Allergy and Infectious Diseases
Division of Allergy, Immunology, and Transplantation
Asthma and Allergy Branch
Solar Bldg., Rm. 4A23
Bethesda, MD 20892
Phone: (301)496-8973
Fax: (301)402-2571
Marshall Plaut, Chief

Research Activities and Fields: Branch supports (through grants, contracts, fellowships, and other mechanisms) studies on the etiology, pathogenesis, diagnosis, prevention, and treatment of allergic diseases and asthma; it also supports research on mucosal immunity and complement. Basic investigations include a study of the regulation of IgE antibody synthesis and IgE interactions with IgE receptors and other IgE binding molecules; studies of the epitopes of allergens and T cells that mediate allergic reactions; assessment of the role of cytokines and adhesion molecules in regulating IgE synthesis and allergic inflammation in vitro and in vivo; and molecular and biochemical characterization of molecules expressed on, and in, mast cells, basophils and eosinophils. The diseases studied include asthma, allergic rhinitis, otitis, atopic dermatitis, and urticaria/angioedema. Also studies diseases induced by immune responses to specific antigens, notably IgE-mediated and T cell-mediated reactions to insect venoms, foods, industrial chemicals, contact sensitizers, airborne allergens, and drug hypersensitivity. The Asthma and Allergy Branch supports eight centers for the National Cooperative Inner City Asthma Study (NCICAS), which focuses on determining the mechanisms for the high morbidity and mortality from asthma of African American and Hispanic children ages 4-9 living in inner cities, and defining effective interventions to reduce that high morbidity and mortality. In addition, the Branch supports 15 (of 21) Asthma, Allergic and Immunologic Diseases Cooperative Research Center, which integrate investigations of basic and clinical research related to human asthma, allergic diseases, and other immunologic diseases.

★ 2126 ★ U.S. Department of Health and Human Services
National Institute of Allergy and Infectious Diseases
Division of Allergy, Immunology, and Transplantation
Basic Immunology Branch
Solar Bldg., Rm. 4A22
9000 Rockville Pike
Bethesda, MD 20892
Phone: (301)496-7551
Fax: (301)402-0175
Dr. Michele Hogan, Chief

Research Activities and Fields: Branch is concerned with the biology and chemistry of the immune system and its products. Immunobiologic studies include: the origin, maturation, localization, and interactions of immunocyte (lymphocyte, plasmocyte, macrophage) populations and subpopulations; the cellular and biochemical mechanisms responsible for antigen process-

ing, tolerance, and enhancement; research in the mechanisms responsible for induction and regulation of the immune response; and studies on lymphokines and other substances produced by immunocytes and other cells that regulate the immune system. Immunochemical studies include: the chemical structure and function of the immunoglobulin components of body fluids; the chemical structure, function, and biologic importance of naturally occurring antigens; the mechanisms of antigen-antibody reactions and the chemical basis of immunologic specificity; the regulation of immunoglobulin synthesis; the chemistry and function of immunopharmacologic agents; and chemical characterization of the molecular components and the function of accessory systems that participate in the immune response.

★ 2127 ★ U.S. Department of Health and Human Services
National Institute of Allergy and Infectious Diseases
Division of Allergy, Immunology, and Transplantation
Clinical Immunology Branch
Solar Bldg. 4A19
9000 Rockville Pike
Bethesda, MD 20892
Phone: (301)496-7104
Howard Dickler, Director

Research Activities and Fields: Supports research to investigate the underlying cellular and molecular mechanisms responsible for the pathogenesis of immunologic diseases, as well as the application of basic knowledge to the etiology, prevention, and management of immunologic disorders, including autoimmune, immune complex, and immunodeficiency diseases and immunoregulatory dysfunctions. A special feature of this program is the support of Asthma, Allergic and Immunologic Disease Cooperative Research Centers (AAIDCRCs). An objective of AAIDCRCs is to accelerate the clinical application of new knowledge of the immune system. Programs are designed to integrate and coordinate research projects in clinical immunology that are being pursued in clinical specialties with those in basic research. AAIDCRC grants are awarded to an institution on behalf of a program director for support of a broadly based, multidisciplinary long-term research program that has a specific objective or basic theme. An AAIDCRC generally involves the organized efforts of groups of investigators who conduct research projects related to the overall program objective. The grant can provide support for the projects and for certain basic resources shared by individuals in a program where the sharing facilitates the total research effort. NIAID currently supports five AAIDCRCs.

★ 2128 ★ U.S. Department of Health and Human Services
National Institute of Allergy and Infectious Diseases
Division of Allergy, Immunology, and Transplantation
Genetics and Transplantation Branch

Solar Bldg., Rm. 4A14
Bethesda, MD 20892
Phone: (301)496-5598
Fax: (301)402-2571
Dr. Stephen Rose, Chief

Research Activities and Fields: The goal of studies in immunogenetics and transplantation biology is to understand and control the genetic and immunologic mechanisms that are involved in responses to foreign substances such as infecting microorganisms and engrafted tissues. These mechanisms determine susceptibility or resistance to various diseases and the success or failure of organ or tissue grafts. The program supports investigations in animal species ranging from invertebrates to man, and the development of technologies and reagents. Research in genetics and transplantation is supported through the award of both grants and contracts. The research grant program supports studies on the molecular genetics of the immune system. The contract program in transplantation immunology supports the acquisition and distribution of reagents useful in research in immunogenetics and transplantation, evaluation of methodologies currently in use at the laboratory and the clinical level in those fields, development of new and more effective technologies for histocompatibility testing and immunologic manipulation, and collection and analysis of data to permit assessment of the efficacy of various transplant procedures.

★2129★ U.S. Department of Health and Human Services
National Institute of Allergy and Infectious Diseases
Division of Extramural Activities
Solar Bldg., Rm 3C20
6003 Executive Blvd.
Rockville, MD 20892
Phone: (301)496-7291
Fax: (301)402-0369
Dr. John J. McGowan, Director

Research Activities and Fields: Coordinates and provides administrative support for all NIAID program activities in the extramural area. The DEA staff work closely with scientific program staff, grantees, and potential grantees in providing management information, advice, and consultation as needed to fulfill the broad objectives of the NIAID research grants and contracts programs. DEA also directs and carries out the scientific and technical merit review of proposals and applications for research contracts, program projects, special research grants, and research training. Activities are organized in branches for contract management, grants management, program and project review, and research manpower development.

★2130★ U.S. Department of Health and Human Services
National Institute of Allergy and Infectious Diseases
Division of Intramural Research
NIH Bldg. 10, Rm. 4A-31
9000 Rockville Pike
Bethesda, MD 20892
Phone: (301)496-3006
Fax: (301)402-0166
John I. Gallin, M.D., Director

Research Activities and Fields: Program is responsible for basic or clinical research on the causes of allergic, immunologic, and infectious diseases; however, research that has developed to the point of clinical application is pursued through clinical trials, performed at The Clinical Center of NIH or in collaboration with university centers. The NIAID Intramural Program has many diverse components covering most of the basic fields of medical research and includes laboratories for: Biological Resources; Cellular and Molecular Immunology; Clinical Investigation; Host Defense; Immunogenetics; Immunology; Immunopathology; Immunoregulation; Infectious Diseases; Microbial Immunity; Molecular Microbiology; Parasitic Diseases; Viral Diseases; Microbial Structure and Function Laboratory; and Persistant Viral Diseases.

★2131★ U.S. Department of Health and Human Services
National Institute of Allergy and Infectious Diseases
Division of Intramural Research
Laboratory of Molecular Structure
NIH Bldg. 4, Rm. 413
9000 Rockville Pike
Bethesda, MD 20892
Phone: (301)496-3213
Fax: (301)402-0284
John E. Coligan, Ph.D., Chief

Research Activities and Fields: Molecular basis of the immune response. Also studies structural biology of immunologically relevent molecules.

U.S. Department of Health and Human Services
National Institute of Allergy and Infectious Diseases
Division of Microbiology and Infectious Diseases
Epidemiology and Biometry Branch
See: Entry 6828

★2132★ U.S. Department of Health and Human Services
National Institute of Allergy and Infectious Diseases
Laboratory of Cellular and Molecular Immunology
NIH Bldg. 4, Rm. 111
9000 Rockville Pike
Bethesda, MD 20892
Phone: (301)496-1257
Fax: (301)496-0877
Ronald H. Schwartz, M.D., Ph.D., Chief

Research Activities and Fields: Cellular and molecular immunology.

★2133★ U.S. Department of Health and Human Services
National Institute of Allergy and Infectious Diseases
Laboratory of Clinical Investigation
NIH Bldg. 10, Rm. 11N228
9000 Rockville Pike
Bethesda, MD 20892
Phone: (301)496-5807
Fax: (301)496-7383
Dr. Stephen E. Straus, Chief

Research Activities and Fields: Laboratory conducts clinical investigations into allergic, im-

munologic, and infectious diseases. Specific areas of research interest are: the molecular biology, pathogenesis, and antiviral treatment of herpes virus infections in humans; the role of host defense mechanisms in prevention of infections; the pathogenesis, treatment, and prevention of cryptococcal and candida infections; the molecular basis of macrophage responses to infection; identification of genes that contribute to virulence in E. coli; mechanisms of regulation of immune reactivity in normal individuals and patients with immunologically mediated diseases; the biochemical response in lymphoid cells following antigenic stimulation in normal and immunologically impaired subjects; the immunologic abnormalities of asthma and other allergic disease mechanisms of regulation of mucosal immune responses; pathogenesis of inflammatory bowel diseases; the pathogenesis of immunodeficiency diseases; the biology of the mast cell; and the diagnosis and effective management of systemic mastocytosis.

★2134★ U.S. Department of Health and Human Services
National Institute of Allergy and Infectious Diseases
Laboratory of Immunogenetics
NIAID Twinbrook Facility
12441 Parklawn Dr.
Rockville, MD 20852
Phone: (301)496-9589
Fax: (301)402-0259
Thomas J. Kindt, Ph.D., Chief

Research Activities and Fields: The Immunogenetics Laboratory studies the multigene families that are involved in the control of immune function. Research emphasizes the structure and function of the genes and their products as well as mechanisms for gene regulation. Studies involve structural, serologic, and molecular genetic investigations. Techniques used include quantitative radioimmunoassays, protein structure determinations, recombinant DNA technologies (gene cloning and nucleotide sequencing) assays for DNA regulatory elements, and DNA-mediated gene transfer into mammalian cells; preparation and study of T- and B-cell hybridomas; and a variety of immunologic assays for cellular and humoral components of the immune response.

★2135★ U.S. Department of Health and Human Services
National Institute of Allergy and Infectious Diseases
Laboratory of Immunology
NIH Bldg. 10, Rm. 11N311
9000 Rockville Pike
Bethesda, MD 20892
Phone: (301)496-5046
Fax: (301)496-0222
William Paul, M.D., Chief

Research Activities and Fields: Laboratory studies various aspects of cellular, molecular, and developmental biology of lymphocytes; the regulation of immune responses; immunogenetics; and immunochemistry. Emphasis is on developing an understanding of how the various elements of the immune system function normally and of the role of immune mechanisms in the prevention and pathogenesis of diseases.

Studies utilize a variety of techniques, including production and use of monoclonal antibodies, cloning and long-term growth of lymphocyte lines; molecular genetic analysis of cells of the immune system; and cell biological analysis of lymphocyte activation and differentiation.

★ 2136 ★ U.S. Department of Health and Human Services
National Institute of Allergy and Infectious Diseases
Laboratory of Immunology
Experimental Pathology Section
NIH Bldg. 7, Rm. 300
9000 Rockville Pike
Bethesda, MD 20892
Phone: (301)496-4600
Richard Asofsky, M.D., Chief

Research Activities and Fields: Basic mechanisms in the responses of lymphocytes to antigens, including microbial antigens. Emphasizes mechanisms of induction, control, and ontogeny of immunoglobulin synthesis; in vivo and in vitro examinations of the development of T lymphocytes from early precursors to reactive cells; cellular and genetic factors controlling the amplitude and duration of the response to certain bacterial antigens; and development of methods for the physical separation of lymphoid cells to obtain purified subpopulations.

★ 2137 ★ U.S. Department of Health and Human Services
National Institute of Allergy and Infectious Diseases
Laboratory of Immunopathology
NIH Bldg. 7, Rm. 304
9000 Rockville Pike
Bethesda, MD 20892
Phone: (301)496-1150
Fax: (301)402-0077
Dr. Herbert C. Morse III, Chief

Research Activities and Fields: Conducts studies primarily focused on the mechanisms by which retroviruses and adenoviruses induce disease. Activities involve: 1) evaluation of the genetic organization of viruses in relation to their pathogenic properties; 2) definition of the characteristics of normal target cell population and the effects of viruses on these cells; and 3) identification of host characteristics that influence the outcome of virus infections. Methods involve molecular technology as well as in vivo analyses of viral pathogenicity in mice and hamsters, and immunologic studies of cells from normal, mutant, and virus-infected mice.

★ 2138 ★ U.S. Department of Health and Human Services
National Institute of Allergy and Infectious Diseases
Laboratory of Immunoregulation
NIH Bldg. 10, Rm. 11B13
9000 Rockville Pike
Bethesda, MD 20892
Phone: (301)496-1124
Fax: (301)402-0070
Dr. Anthony S. Fauci, Chief

Research Activities and Fields: Laboratory conducts basic research and clinical studies on the mechanisms of activation and immunoregulation of human immune responses in normal individuals and in a variety of disease states characterized by abnormalities of immune function. Recent areas of research interest have included: acquired immunodeficiency syndrome (AIDS); immunoregulation of human lymphocyte function in normal and disease states; immunopathogenic features of immune-mediated diseases; clinical, immunopathogenic, and therapeutic studies in the spectrum of vasculitis; molecular biologic approach to the immune system; and immunopathogenesis of *Chlamydia trachomatis* infection.

★ 2139 ★ U.S. Department of Health and Human Services
National Institute of Child Health and Human Development
Laboratory of Developmental and Molecular Immunity
NIH Bldg. 6, Rm. 145
9000 Rockville Pike
Bethesda, MD 20892
Phone: (301)496-1185
Dr. John B. Robbins, Chief

Research Activities and Fields: Laboratory conducts research into the developmental and molecular biology of "natural" and immunization-induced immunity to bacterial and other antigens. Emphasis is on the study of pathogenic mechanisms, MHC and other antigenic molecules (including their purification and characterization), and the immunoregulatory mechanisms of the host. Areas of interest include: development of new vaccines to bacterial pathogens using cloned genes; the modification of transplantation antigen genes at the DNA level in order to determine the structural basis for immunological polymorphism and the function of gene products; and the development of expression of histocompatibility and immune response molecules in cultured mouse embryos. Laboratory comprises the: Bacterial Disease Pathogenesis and Immunity Section, Immunoregulation and Cellular Control Section, and Molecular Genetics of Immunity Section.

U.S. Department of Health and Human Services
National Institute of Dental Research
Laboratory of Immunology
See: Entry 4021

U.S. Department of Health and Human Services
National Institute of Diabetes and Digestive and Kidney Diseases
Division of Digestive Diseases and Nutrition
Gastrointestinal Motility Program
See: Entry 5243

U.S. Department of Health and Human Services
National Institute of Neurological Disorders and Stroke
Neuroimmunology Branch
See: Entry 8470

University of California, Davis
AIDS Virus Diagnostic Laboratory
See: Entry 6839

★ 2140 ★ University of California, Davis
Allergy-Clinical Immunology Program
School of Medicine
TB 192
Davis, CA 95616
Phone: (916)752-2884
Fax: (916)752-4669
Dr. M. Eric Gershwin, Dir.

Research Activities and Fields: Cellular immunology and immunochemistry. Explores the immunopathogenesis of systemic rheumatic diseases and autoimmune disorders.

University of California, Los Angeles
UCLA Center for Clinical AIDS Research and Education / AIDS Clinical Trials Unit
See: Entry 6840

University of California, San Francisco
AIDS Clinical Research Center
See: Entry 6841

★ 2141 ★ University of California, San Francisco
Immunogenetics and Transplantation Laboratory
Health Sciences E., Rm. 520
513 Parnassus Ave.
San Francisco, CA 94143
Phone: (415)476-3883
Fax: (415)476-0379
Marvin R. Garovoy, M.D., Dir.

Research Activities and Fields: Immunogenetics and transplantation, including immunopharmacology of immunosuppressive agents.

University of California, San Francisco
Liver Transplant Division
See: Entry 12889

University of Chicago
Gwen Knapp Center for Lupus and Immunology Research
See: Entry 7947

★ 2142 ★ University of Colorado
Allergy & Immunology Center
Division of Immunology
4200 E. 9th Ave., B164
Denver, CO 80262
Phone: (303)270-7601
Fax: (303)270-7642
Dr. Henry Claman, Dir.

Research Activities and Fields: Provides a focus for research into the causes, prevention, and management of diseases such as asthma, allergies, contact hypersensitivity, immune deficiencies and infection, and autoimmune disorders, plus related studies of fundamental immune mechanisms involving immune cells, antibodies, genetic factors, and immune regulatory systems. Specific studies are to develop better assays for detecting circulating, injurious antigen-antibody complexes (immune complexes) in patients with inflammation of the blood vessels and improve treatment of chronic urticaria (hives).

University of Florida
Center for Transplantation Biology
See: Entry 12890

**★2143★ University of Illinois at Chicago
Institute for Tuberculosis Research**
840 W. Taylor St.
M/C 964 (2014 SEL)
Chicago, IL 60607
Phone: (312)996-3906
Fax: (312)996-4689
Michael J. Groves, Ph.D., Dir.
Research Activities and Fields: Cellular immunology, including tuberculosis immunity with special reference to use of Bacillus Calmette-Guerin (BCG) vaccine. Active in evaluating BCG vaccine as nonspecific stimulant for immune system in prevention and treatment of cancer in animals and man. Research also encompasses biotechnology and drug delivery based on immunological principles. **Publications:** Annual Reports; *Chicago Symposium Proceedings* (1973-82, seven volumes to date). **Formerly:** Prior to 1986, the Institute was a separately incorporated organization located at the University and known as Institution for Tuberculosis Research (1973); (ITR).

**★2144★ University of Kansas
Allergy and Immunology Clinic**
3901 Rainbow Blvd.
Kansas City, KS 66160-7317
Phone: (913)588-6008
Fax: (913)588-3995
Dr. Daniel J. Stechschulte, Dir.
Research Activities and Fields: Studies of the normal mechanism that attract and inhibit the accumulation of WBG (type of defense cells) in the lungs and synovial membranes, clinical trials to evaluate the effectiveness of less toxic drugs in the treatment of systemic lupus erythematosus and rheumatoid arthritis, and studies on the role of mediators in the disease course of asthma. **Formerly:** Allergy Clinic (1982).

**University of Kansas
Center for Neurobiology and Immunology
   Research (CNIR)**
See: Entry 8502

**University of Michigan
Immunology Laboratory**
See: Entry 4037

**★2145★ University of Michigan
Montgomery Allergy Research Laboratory**
6621 Kresge Medical Research Bldg. I, Box
   0529
Ann Arbor, MI 48109-0529
Phone: (313)764-0227
Fax: (313)936-8898
William R. Solomon, M.D., Dir.
Research Activities and Fields: Allergic diseases of humans, including studies in immunology, botany, nasal physiology and pharmacology, aerobiology of fungi and pollen, mediators of immediate hypersensitivity, enzyme inhibitors, hypersensitivity to drugs, and indoor microbial air pollution.

**University of North Carolina at Chapel Hill
Thurston Arthritis Research Center**
See: Entry 7958

**University of Puerto Rico
Arthritis Research Unit**
See: Entry 7960

**★2146★ University of Southern California
Division of Rheumatology and Immunology**
2011 Zonal Ave., HMR 711
Los Angeles, CA 90033
Phone: (213)342-1946
Fax: (213)342-2874
David A. Horwitz, M.D., Dir.
Research Activities and Fields: Basic and clinical immunology, tumor immunology, rheumatology, autoimmune disease, connective tissue disease, and biochemistry, including studies of immune mechanisms, immunologic diseases in man, immunologic and biochemical aspects of rheumatic diseases, and related areas of medicine. **Formerly:** Clinical Immunology and Rheumatology Research Unit.

**University of Tennessee, Knoxville
Human Immunology and Cancer Program
   (HICP)**
See: Entry 6252

**★2147★ University of Virginia
Beirne Carter Center for Immunology
   Research**
Health Sciences Center
Box MR-4-4012
Charlottesville, VA 22908
Phone: (804)924-1219
Fax: (804)924-1221
Thomas J. Braciale, M.D., Dir.
Research Activities and Fields: Basic and clinical immunology, infectious diseases, cancer, autoimmune diseases, and cell signaling in the immune system. **Publications:** Annual Report. **E-mail Address:** ehh2e@galen.med.virginia.edu.

**★2148★ Washington University
Center for Interdisciplinary Research on
   Immunological Diseases**
660 S. Euclid Ave., Box 8045
St. Louis, MO 63110
Phone: (314)362-9049
Dr. Loh, Dir.
Research Activities and Fields: Human immune response, including cell surface receptors, lymphocyte activation, control of immunoglobulin E (IgE) synthesis, major histocompatibility complex, cellular cytotoxicity, complement system, and isolation, characterization, and clinical investigation of allergenic proteins.

**Webb-Waring Institute for Biomedical
   Research**
See: Entry 2705

**Worcester Foundation for Experimental
   Biology**
See: Entry 2709

Chapter 4
Alternative Medicine

National & International Organizations

★2149★ Acupuncture Research Institute (ARI)
313 W. Andrix St.
Monterey Park, CA 91754
Phone: (213)722-7353
Louis Gasper, Ph.D., Exec.Sec.

Founded: 1972. **Members:** 750. **Description:** Acupuncturists, medical doctors, homoeopathic physicians, podiatrists, dentists, physical therapists, nurses, naturopaths, other persons in other healing practices, herbologists, nutritionists, including scholars and researchers. Works with Chinese Medical Academy to investigate the validity and American application of acupuncture; to establish a means of exchange of information and experience in acupuncture; to provide basic study courses in acupuncture concerning theory and methods including clinical training and continuing education for licensed acupuncturists; offers seminars and international conferences to bring acupuncturists from China and other countries thereby improving the abilities and status of locally licensed acupuncturists; supports and cooperates with acupuncture schools, providing assistance in improving acupuncture curriculum and clinical experience. **Publications:** *The Meridian*, quarterly. Newsletter. Includes book reviews and research updates. *Price:* Included in membership dues.

★2150★ Advocate Health Care (AHC)
2025 Windsor Dr.
Oak Brook, IL 60521-0222
Phone: (708)572-9393
Stephen Ummel, Pres.

Founded: 1995. **Members:** 10. **Description:** Health care corporations. Promotes the philosophy that good health care involves an understanding of human ecology and must meet the emotional and spiritual as well as the physical needs of patients. (Human ecology is the "understanding and care of human beings as whole persons in light of their relationships to God, themselves, their families, and the society in which they live.") Supports the concept of holistic health care. Sponsors teaching programs at hospitals; maintains support groups. Sponsors

the Park Ridge Center, an institute for the study of health, faith, and ethics; and Parkside Alcoholic Research Foundation, which studies the cause and course of alcoholism and substance abuse. Maintains speakers' bureau. **Publications:** Annual Report. • Bulletin, bimonthly. • *Human Ecology Booklet*, semiannual. Booklet. • *Ounce of Prevention*, quarterly. • *Second Opinion: Health, Faith, and Ethics*, 3/year. Journal. *Price:* $35/year.

★2151★ AIDS Prevention League (APPLE)
c/o Saiom Lehman
291 Crosby St.
Akron, OH 44303
Phone: (216)535-5567
Saiom Lehman, Exec. Officer

Founded: 1987. **Description:** Coalition promoting non-dairy vegetarianism as a deterrent to AIDS. Works to educate the public about the alleged correlation between animal products and AIDS. Believes that ingesting animal products weakens the immune system, making it vulnerable to the AIDS virus. (Group believes that out of all AIDS patients, not a single one is vegetarian.) Promotes the use of intravenous vitamin C and a raw fruit diet as a possible cure for or means of causing remission of AIDS. **Publications:** *AIDS News*, periodic.

★2152★ All India Nature Cure Federation
15 Rajghat Colony
New Delhi 110 002, Delhi, India
Phone: 3317396

Languages: English, Hindi. **Description:** Promotes use of natural medical treatments including herbs and meditation, particularly in cases of acute and chronic disorders. Gathers and disseminates information on effective natural remedies; conducts educational and training programs.

★2153★ Alliance for Alternatives in Healthcare (AAH)
PO Box 6279
Thousand Oaks, CA 91359-6279
Phone: (805)494-7818
Fax: (805)494-8528
Steve Gorman, Pres.

Founded: 1983. **Members:** 1,000. **Description:** Holistic physicians; employers; interested

individuals. Seeks to enhance public recognition of holistic, homeopathic, naturopathic, chiropractic, and acupuncture treatments. (Holistic medicine focuses on the treatment of the entire body, rather than on any one organ or system; homeopathic medicine treats diseases by administering minute quantities of a substance that would produce the disease's symptoms in a healthy person; naturopathic medicine avoids the use of surgery and drugs, focusing instead on natural agents, such as sunshine and fresh air, or on physical means, such as manipulation or acupuncture.) Encourages health insurance systems to cover holistic, homeopathic, and naturopathic treatments in their policies. Attends exhibitions to disseminate information on holistic, homeopathic, and naturopathic medicine to health care providers and the public. Offers group medical, dental, and vision plans to members. Manages network of holistic and natural providers who offer discounts to subscribers of the Holistic Health Network. **Publications:** *Natural Marketing News*, periodic. • *Press Releases*, periodic. **Formerly:** Alternative Health Insurance Services; (1989) Natural Marketing Association.

★2154★ Alliance for Cannabis Therapeutics (ACT)
PO Box 21210
Washington, DC 20009
Phone: (202)483-8595
Robert Randall, Pres.

Founded: 1980. **Description:** Alliance of lay persons, medical professionals, and policymakers concerned with the medical use of cannabis (marijuana) in treating the side effects of chemotherapy experienced by persons with cancer, and in aiding persons with glaucoma, AIDS, and multiple sclerosis. Works to end federal prohibition of cannabis in medicine and to "construct a medically meaningful, ethically correct and compassionate system of regulation which permits the seriously ill to legally obtain cannabis." **Publications:** *Cancer Treatment and Marijuana Therapy*. Book. • *Marijuana and Aids: Pot, Politics, and PWAs in America*. Book. • *Marijuana, Medicine and the Law, Vols I and II*. Book. • *Muscle Spasm, Pain and Marijuana Therapy*. Book. • Newsletter, periodic.

★2155★ American Academy of Medical Acupuncture
5820 Wilshire Blvd., Ste. 500
Los Angeles, CA 90036
Phone: (213)937-5514
Fax: (213)937-0959
C. James Dowden, Exec.Admin.

Founded: 1987. **Members:** 600. **Description:** Professional society of physicians and osteopaths who utilize acupuncture in their practices. Provides ongoing training and information related to the Chinese practice of puncturing the body at specific points to cure disease or relieve pain. Offers educational and research programs. **Publications:** *AAMA Review*, semiannual. Journal.

★2156★ American Acupuncture Association (AAA)
4262 Kissena Blvd.
Flushing, NY 11355
Phone: (718)886-4431
Fax: (718)463-0808
Dr. David P. J. Hung, Chm.

Founded: 1972. **Members:** 400. **Description:** Physicians, nurses, acupuncturists, physical therapists, and herbologists. Promotes acceptance of acupuncture as a viable medical method. Works to legalize acupuncture on the state level. Offers continuing education course. Maintains speakers' bureau. Conducts lectures to educate public on acupuncture. **Publications:** *Journal of Chinese Acupuncture*, annual. Journal.

★2157★ American Apitherapy Society (AAS)
c/o Dr. Christopher Kim
252 Broad St.
Red Bank, NJ 07701
Phone: (908)842-5700
Fax: (908)530-7220
Dr. Christopher Kim, Pres.

Founded: 1989. **Members:** 2,500. **Regional Groups:** 9. **Description:** Beekeepers, physicians, scientists, and others interested in apitherapy, the therapeutic use of honey bee products. Purpose is to collect and disseminate information in the field and to provide a forum for researchers to present the results of their work. Encourages investigation of hive products in order to provide a scientific foundation for their curative properties and use in human medicine. Seeks to prove the effectiveness of bee venom in treating inflammatory diseases such as arthritis and rheumatism. Gains funding for clinical laboratory studies through contributions. Supports selected research and fundraising projects for the investigation of apitherapeutic agents. Compiles statistics. **Publications:** *Bee-Well Newsletter*, quarterly. Newsletter. *Price:* Free. • Brochures. Contains information on bee venom, honey, pollen, and beeswax. • Journal, annual. *Proceedings*, annual. *Price:* Free. **Formerly:** (1989) North American Apio-Therapy Society.

★2158★ American Association for Acupuncture and Oriental Medicine (AAAOM)
433 Front St.
Catasauqua, PA 18032-2506
Phone: (610)266-1433
Fax: (610)264-2768
David Molony, Exec.Dir.

Founded: 1981. **Members:** 1,200. **Regional Groups:** 4. **State Groups:** 32. **Description:** Professional acupuncturists and other interested individuals. Seeks to: elevate the standards of education and practice of acupuncture and oriental medicine; establish laws governing acupuncture; provide a forum to share information on acupuncture techniques; increase public awareness of acupuncture; support research in the field. Conducts educational programs; compiles statistics. Operates speakers' bureau. **Publications:** *AAAOM Membership Directory*, annual. Membership Directory. Contains listing of U.S. acupuncture and oriental medicine practitioners. • *American Acupuncturist Newsletter*, semiannual. Newsletter. Contains political and educational news and information.

★2159★ American Association of Ayurvedic Medicine (WMAFPH)
c/o Stuart Rothenberg
PO Box 282
Fairfield, IA 52556
Phone: (515)472-8477
Dr. Deepak Chopra, Pres.

Founded: 1978. **Description:** Physicians; auxiliary members are students and nonphysician health care professionals; honorary members are outstanding scientists elected by the board. Encourages physicians to develop within themselves the highest ideal of the perfect physician. Assists physicians in: encouraging patients to utilize transcendental meditation (TM) programs to prevent disease and improve health; improving doctor-patient relationships; bringing "perfect" health to society. Acts as clearinghouse for information exchange among physicians and professionals; makes information available to the medical community and the public; operates physician referral service. Promotes research into physiological effects of TM programs. Maintains speakers' bureau; offers specialized education; compiles statistics. **Publications:** Directory, quarterly. • *MAAA Newsletter*, quarterly. Newsletter. Latest developments in research on Maharishi Ayur-Veda. *Price:* Free to members. • *Scientific Research on the Transcendental Meditation Program, Collected Papers: Volume One*. Also makes available patient education materials, brochures, books, and papers; produces software programs and videotapes. **Also Known As:** United States Association of Physicians. **Formerly:** (1983) American Association of Physicians Practicing the Transcendental Meditation and TM-Sidhi Programs; (1986) American Association of Physicians Practicing the Transcendental Meditation Program; (1990) World Medical Association for Perfect Health.

★2160★ American Board of Chelation Therapy (ABCT)
70 W. Huron
Chicago, IL 60610
Free: 800-356-2228
Fax: (312)266-7291
Jack Hank, Exec.Dir.

Founded: 1982. **Description:** Purpose is to define and establish qualifications required of licensed physicians and surgeons for certification in the field of chelation therapy. (Chelation therapy is used in cases of blood poisoning and involves the use of metal binding and bioinorganic agents intravenously infused into the bloodstream to "pick up" and remove calcium, lead, or other toxic heavy metals and restore cellular homeostasis. Because of lack of controlled studies for conditions other than calcinosis, digitalis toxicity, and excessive body storage of heavy metals, chelation therapy is not considered standard medical procedure.) Stresses that proper use of chelation therapy requires knowledge of nutrition and exercise and expertise in assisting patients in implementing lifestyle changes. Refers candidate physicians to sponsoring organizations for teaching workshops, audio and video learning aids, and reading and study materials. Has created series of testing procedures designed to be comprehensive and unbiased. Administers oral and written examinations and conducts reviews of candidates' background experience and patient records. Maintains standards through process of recertification and reexamination. Sponsored by the American Holistic Medical Association and American College of Advancement in Medicine.

★2161★ American College of Orgonomy (ACO)
PO Box 490
Princeton, NJ 08542
Phone: (908)821-1144
Fax: (908)821-0174
Peter A. Crist, M.D., Pres.

Founded: 1968. **Members:** 12. **Description:** Physicians and social scientists seeking to promote and advance the science of orgonomy. (Orgonomy is derived from the theory formulated by Wilhelm Reich, M.D. "that all space is filled with a specific form of energy called orgone energy which accounts for life and living functions.") Provides training in medical orgonomy and character analysis for physicians. Sponsors training and research for physicians and scientists in orgone physics, orgone biology, and weather control. Holds laboratory workshops for physicians and scientists. Offers referral service. Conducts specialized education. **Publications:** *A Book of Dreams*. • *Fury on Earth*. • *Journal of Orgonomy*, semiannual. Journal. Contains articles on scientific topics related to Orgonomy. *Price:* $40/year in the U.S. and Canada; $45/year outside the U.S. and Canada. • *Man in the Trap*. • *Orgonomic Medicine*. • *The Work of Wilhelm Reich: An Introduction to Orgonomy*.

★ 2162 ★ **American Foundation for Alternative Health Care, Research and Development (AFAHCRD)**
25 Landfield Ave.
Monticello, NY 12701
Phone: (914)794-8181
Fax: (914)794-5861
Edwin M. Field, Exec.Dir.

Founded: 1978. **Description:** Serves as an alternative health care information resource center. Compiles data. **Formerly:** (1985) American Foundation for Alternative Health Care.

★ 2163 ★ **American Foundation of Traditional Chinese Medicine (AFTCM)**
505 Beach St.
San Francisco, CA 94133
Phone: (415)776-0502
Fax: (415)776-9053
Barbara Bernie, Pres., Chrm. and CEO

Founded: 1982. **Description:** Practitioners and individuals interested in contributing to the advancement of traditional Chinese medicine for the improvement of health care. (Traditional Chinese medicine is a holistic form of medicine that offers additional insights into how the human body functions relative to the disease process. Diagnosis is obtained by taking 6 wrist pulses, one for each major organ of the body; the abnormal pulse indicates the organ affected. Treatment is administered by treating the causes instead of the symptoms. Forms of treatment include acupuncture, herbs, exercise and diet regulation.) Seeks to: encourage the use of Eastern and Western medicine in hospitals and clinics providing more treatment options for patients; improve standards and regulations of the profession; increase communication between East and West for cooperative research. Offers masters' teaching workshops and continuing education courses for practitioners in techniques, theory, and methods; provides referral service. Maintains clinic for administering traditional Chinese medicine. Is currently working to establish an International Health Center that will bring medical experts of different backgrounds together for exchange of information and exploration of complementary forms of medical treatment. **Publications:** *Gateways*, quarterly. Newsletter. Includes developments in traditional Chinese medical research. *Price:* Included in membership dues; $3/copy for nonmembers. **Formerly:** (1992) International Health Center.

★ 2164 ★ **American Herbalists Guild (AHG)**
Box 1683
Soquel, CA 95073
Phone: (408)464-2441
Fax: (408)464-2441
Roy Upton, Pres.

Founded: 1989. **Members:** 300. **Description:** Promotes research and education in the field of herbal medicine. Works to establish high standards for the professional practice of herbalism; and to increase "interdependence of all life, especially between plants and humans". Provides a forum for the exchange of information in the field. **Publications:** *American Herbalism*. • Newsletter, quarterly. *Price:* $35/year.

★ 2165 ★ **American Holistic Medical Association (AHMA)**
4101 Lake Boone Trl., Ste. 201
Raleigh, NC 27607
Phone: (919)787-5146
Fax: (919)787-4916
Susan Kruse, Exec.Dir.

Founded: 1978. **Members:** 600. **Regional Groups:** 11. **Description:** Licensed medical doctors, doctors of osteopathy, and students enrolled in medical or osteopathic programs who are interested in furthering the practice of holistic health care, a concept that stresses the integration of physical, mental, emotional, and spiritual concerns with environmental harmony. Medical education is provided in these areas through the association's conference. **Publications:** *AHMA Member Directory*, annual. Membership Directory. *Price:* Available to members only. • Brochures. • *Fitness Guidelines*. Book. • *Holistic Medicine*, bimonthly. Magazine. Contains information for holistic health care professionals, technical and scientific articles, book reviews, and research reports. *Price:* $5/issue; $40/year. • *National Referral Directory of Holistic Practitioners*. Directory. *Price:* $8. • *Nutritional Guidelines*. Book.

★ 2166 ★ **American Holistic Medical Foundation (AHMF)**
4101 Lake Boone Trl., Ste. 201
Raleigh, NC 27607
Phone: (919)787-5146
Fax: (919)787-4916
Susan Kruse, Exec.Dir.

Founded: 1974. **Members:** 450. **Description:** Educational and research foundation of American Holistic Medical Association. Supports research and educational concepts related to holistic health and medicine. **Formerly:** (1981) Biogenic Institutes of America; (1983) American Holistic Medical Institute.

★ 2167 ★ **American Holistic Nurses Association (AHNA)**
4101 Lake Boone Trl., Ste. 201
Raleigh, NC 27607
Phone: (919)787-5181
Fax: (919)787-4916
Cathy Young, Exec.Dir.

Founded: 1981. **Members:** 2,700. **Regional Groups:** 7. **Local Groups:** 63. **Description:** Registered, licensed practical, vocational, and student nurses. Objectives are: to promote education for nurses and the public on the concept of holistic health care; to examine new directions of health care delivery, especially within nursing; to serve as a network for persons interested in holistic nursing. **Publications:** *Beginnings*, monthly. Newsletter. Covers membership activities. Includes calendar of events, tape and book reviews, and regional reports. *Price:* Included in membership dues; $16/year for nonmembers. • Brochure. • *Journal of Holistic Nursing*, quarterly. Journal. Presents academic and scholarly works from the field of holistic nursing practice; includes research news. *Price:* Included in membership dues; $28.80/year for nonmembers; $60/year for institutions. Also publishes membership printout.

★ 2168 ★ **American Holistic Veterinary Medical Association (AHVMA)**
2214 Old Emmorton Rd.
Bel Air, MD 21015
Phone: (410)569-0795
Fax: (410)515-7774
Dr. Carvel G. Tiekert, Exec.Dir.

Founded: 1982. **Members:** 425. **Description:** Veterinarians and others interested in exploring alternative approaches in veterinary medicine, including clinical nutrition, homeopathy, and herbal medicine. **Publications:** Journal, quarterly. Includes association news and book reviews. *Price:* Included in membership dues. **Formerly:** (1985) American Veterinary Holistic Medical Association.

★ 2169 ★ **American Institute of Homeopathy (AIH)**
1585 Glencoe St., Ste. 44
Denver, CO 80220-1338
Phone: (303)898-5477
Karen Kaiser Nossaman, Exec.Sec.

Founded: 1844. **Members:** 160. **Description:** Professional society of medical doctors, osteopaths, and dentists practicing homeotherapeutics according to the three natural laws of cure propounded by German physician Samuel C. F. Hahnemann (1755-1843). Promotes research and quality homeopathic health care. **Publications:** *Homeopathy Notes*, monthly. Newsletter. • *Journal of the American Institute of Homeopathy*, quarterly. Journal. *Price:* $12/each; $35/year (inside North America); $45/year (outside North America).

★ 2170 ★ **American Naprapathic Association (ANA)**
c/o Roy P. Krueger, D.N.
5913 W. Montrose Ave.
Chicago, IL 60634
Phone: (312)685-6020
Roy P. Krueger, D.N., Corr.Sec.

Founded: 1909. **Members:** 300. **Description:** Professional society of naprapathic physicians. (Naprapathy is the science and system of therapeutic manipulation of tissue structures that have become damaged due to stress and strain.) Promotes and publishes the principles of natural healing; seeks to further legislation and recognition of the system of treatment based on the belief that many functional disorders are caused by abnormal connective tissue and ligamentous changes and can be corrected by manipulation. Sponsors Naprapathic Education and Research Foundation. Conducts seminars and educational programs. Maintains speakers' bureau. **Publications:** *Back Pain*. • Directory, periodic. • *Headache: A Warning*. • *Naprapathy: A Scientific Approach to Natural Healing*. • *The Three Facets of Naprapathy*. • *Voice of Naprapathy*. Booklet. Includes articles on nutrition and health topics. *Price:* Free. • *Why Manipulation?*.

★ 2171 ★ **American Natural Hygiene Society (ANHS)**
PO Box 30630
Tampa, FL 33630
Phone: (813)855-6607
James Michael Lennon, Exec.Dir.

Founded: 1948. **Members:** 6,500. **Description:** Public health education organization dedicated to teaching and preserving a tradition of health freedom and independence. Promotes health maintenance through natural means such as natural foods, fresh air, pure water, sunshine, fasting, exercise, and rest. Emphasizes a lifestyle that encourages people to maximize their health by living in harmony with their physiological needs. Operates Natural Hygiene Press; maintains Herbert Shelton Library on fasting, natural hygiene, and related subjects. **Publications:** *Health Science*, bimonthly. Journal. *Price:* Included in membership dues. Also publishes and distributes books and tapes. **Formerly:** American Physiological and Natural Hygiene Society.

★2172★ **American Naturopathic Association**
1377 K St. NW, Ste. 852
Washington, DC 20005
Phone: (202)682-7352
Fax: (202)448-2657
Dr. George A. Freibott, Pres.

Founded: 1896. **Members:** 5,000. **Regional Groups:** 7. **State Groups:** 32. **Local Groups:** 15. **Description:** Students, laypeople, and naturopathic physicians. Promotes the practice and education of naturopathy. Operates a national training center and university; offers public awareness and wellness programs. Conducts research; provides statistics; maintains a museum, Hall of Fame, and speakers' bureau. **Publications:** *Naturopath and Herald of Health*, monthly. Journal.

★2173★ **American Oriental Bodywork Therapy Association (AOBTA)**
6801 Jericho Tpke.
Syosset, NY 11791
Phone: (516)364-5533
Fax: (516)364-5559
Steven Schenkman, Pres.

Founded: 1984. **Members:** 1,000. **Regional Groups:** 3. **Description:** Professional oriental bodyworkers and teachers; interested individuals. (Oriental bodywork is a form of massage which includes soft tissue and myofascial manipulation and techniques used in acupuncture.) Identifies qualified practitioners; serves as a legal entity representing members when dealing with the government, especially in terms of establishing professional status. Sets teaching standards for all styles of oriental bodywork including acupressure, five element shiatsu, macrobiotic shiatsu, nippon, and zen. Sponsors speakers' bureau; conducts educational programs. **Publications:** *AOBTA Directory*, annual. Membership Directory. Lists members of the association. • *AOBTA Newsletter*, quarterly. Newsletter. **Formerly:** (1990) American Shiatsu Association; (1991) American Association of Oriental Healing Arts.

★2174★ **American Phyto Aromatherapy Association**
7436 SW 117 Ave., Ste. 188
Miami, FL 33183
Phone: (305)460-3392
Fax: (305)598-9544
Miguel Angel Cisneros, Co-Founder

Description: Promotes awareness and use of aromatherapy as an alternative method of medi-

cine. (Aromatherapy seeks to prevent and treat ailments and conditions such as headaches, stress, open sores, and stress with essential oils and plants.) Works to set standards in education and practice of the therapy. Seeks to fund laboratories to conduct research in areas such as cancer, immune systems, and arthritis. **Publications:** *Making Scents*, quarterly. Newsletter. Published in two versions, for professional licensing members and for nonlicensing members.

★2175★ **American Podiatric Circulatory Society (APCS)**
c/o Dr. Stanley Goldstein
5704 18th Ave.
Brooklyn, NY 11204
Phone: (718)236-7952
Dr. Stanley Goldstein, Pres.

Founded: 1979. **Members:** 900. **Description:** Podiatrists. Disseminates information on the Suffuse Osmotic Chemisorb Asphyxiation (SOCA) therapy, now known as the Tereno Method, devised by Dr. Isaac Tereno for treatment of geriatric patients suffering from arterial blockage in their limbs. (The Tereno Method uses vitamins to enrich the blood and enlarge subcutaneous capillaries and lymph vessels, thus creating an alternate circulatory network which bypasses blocked arteries. It is an alternative to major surgery and/or amputation in geriatric patients with poor circulation in their limbs.) Conducts research; maintains speakers' bureau. **Publications:** *American Podiatric Circulatory Society Bulletin*, quarterly. Bulletin. Contains case studies of patients treated using the Tereno Method.

★2176★ **Archaeus Project (AP)**
PO Box 7079
Kamuela, HI 96743
Phone: (808)885-6773
Fax: (808)885-9863
Dennis Stillings, Dir.

Founded: 1981. **Description:** Business, medical, academic, and engineering professionals, scientists, psychologists, psi researchers, and interested others. Investigates the effects of ordinary and altered states of consciousness on conditions of health and disease; studies the relationships between the mind, body, and matter, and the implications of these relationships for medicine. Sponsors lecture series, seminars, and workshops; conducts cyberphysiology (science of self-regulation in physiology) research. **Publications:** *Chronobiology: A Science in Tune With the Rhythms of Life.* • *Cyberphysiology: The Science of Self-regulation.* • *Healing Island*, quarterly. Journal. Contains items on health care, health care costs, and the integration of alternative with mainstream medicine, Hawaii as a health/healing destination. *Price:* Included in membership dues; $20/year for subscribers. • *Project 2010.* Monograph. • *Tape Catalog.* Catalog.

The Arlin J. Brown Information Center (TAJBIC)
See: Entry 6974

★2177★ **Associated Bodywork and Massage Professionals (ABMP)**
28677 Buffalo Park Rd.
Evergreen, CO 80439-7347
Phone: (303)674-8478
Free: 800-458-2267
Fax: (303)674-0859
Sherri L. Williamson, Intl.Dir.

Founded: 1986. **Members:** 17,000. **Description:** Professional massage therapists and bodyworkers, sports massage therapists, reflexologists, orthobionomists, and infant massage instructors; massage therapy schools; affiliated organizations. Promotes the art and science of massage and bodywork. Seeks to improve the image of massage therapy and bodywork, and to educate the public about its benefits. Fosters greater credibility and cooperation with the medical profession. Encourages ethical practices, high standards of professional conduct, and continuing education. Provides members with low-cost liability insurance coverage and product discounts. **Publications:** *ABMP Massage and Bodywork Yellow Pages.* Directory. • *ABMP Successful Business Handbook.* Handbook. • *ABMP Touch Training Directory.* Directory. • *Massage and Bodywork Quarterly. Price:* Included in membership dues. **Formerly:** (1988) Associated Professional Massage Therapists and Allied Health Practitioners International; (1990) Associated Professional Massage Therapists and Bodyworkers.

Association for Dance Movement Therapy—United Kingdom (ADMT)
See: Entry 12664

★2178★ **Association for Health Without Vaccination (AHWV) (Association pour la Sante sans Vaccination — ASSVAN)**
6, rue Jean Perrin
F-94400 Vitry-sur-Seine, France
Phone: 1 46816109
Mrs. Staffalo, Dir.

Founded: 1987. **Members:** 800. **Languages:** French. Does not correspond in English. **Description:** Professionals in France who believe that illness is related to mental state and that harmony between mind and body is the key to health. Advocates the patient's freedom of choice in medical treatment and the cessation of obligatory human and animal vaccination. Works to influence public policy and obtain favorable legislation; provides individual legal and practical assistance. Offers cost reductions on a broad range of products. Disseminates information. Organizes classes, debates, and roundtables.

Australian Music Therapy Association (AMTA)
See: Entry 12669

★2179★ **Australian Natural Hygiene Society**
31 Cobar Rd.
Arcadia, NSW 2159, Australia
Phone: 2 6531115

Languages: English. **Description:** Health care practitioners advocating supervised therapeutic fasting as part of a regime of natural hygiene. Promotes drug-free health care.

★ 2180 ★ **Austrian Society of Acupuncture and Auricular Therapy (ASAAT) (Osterreichische Gesellschaft fur Akupunktur — OGA)**
Kaiserin-Elisabeth Hospital
Huglgasse 1-3
A-1150 Vienna, Austria
Phone: 1 98104261
Fax: 1 98104460
Manfred Richart, Sec.

Founded: 1954. **Members:** 2,147. **Languages:** Chinese, English, French, Italian. **Description:** Promotes the acceptance of acupuncture as a recognized healing method in the western medical world. Works in conjunction with the World Health Organization to disseminate and standardize nomenclature. Offers training course.

★ 2181 ★ **British Acupuncture Association and Register (BAAR)**
34 Alderney St.
Westminster
London SW1V 4EU, England
Phone: 181 9732309
E. Welton Johnson, Exec. Officer

Founded: 1962. **Members:** 320. **Languages:** English. **Publications:** *BAAR Journal*, semiannual. Journal. • Books, periodic. • *Directory*, periodic. Directory. • Papers, periodic. **Also Known As:** British Acupuncture Association.

★ 2182 ★ **Center for Attitudinal Healing (CAH)**
33 Buchanan Dr.
Sausalito, CA 94965
Phone: (415)331-6161
Fax: (415)331-4545
Don Goewey, Exec.Dir.

Founded: 1975. **Description:** Nonsectarian organization established to supplement traditional health care by offering free services in attitudinal healing for both children and adults with life-threatening illnesses, or other crises. (The concept of attitudinal healing is based on the belief that it is possible to choose peace rather than conflict, and love rather than fear; the center defines health as inner peace and healing as the process of letting go of fear.) Offers support groups and arranges home and hospital visits for children, youth, and adults. Offers volunteer training program. Maintains speakers' bureau; conducts educational programs and charitable activities. **Publications:** *Advice to Doctors and Other Big People*. Book. • *Another Look at the Rainbow*. Book. • Audiotapes. • *Rainbow Connection*, 3/year. Newsletter. • *There is a Rainbow Behind Every Dark Cloud*. Book. • Videos.

★ 2183 ★ **China Association of Research and Development of Traditional Chinese Medicine and Pharmacy**
9 Xizongbu Ln.
Dongcheng District
Beijing 100005, People's Republic of China
Phone: 1 4652265
Yan Lin, Sec.Gen.

Founded: 1984. **Members:** 1,072. **Languages:** Chinese, English. **Description:** Promotes research and development projects associated with traditional Chinese medicine and pharmacy techniques. Fosters the application of traditional Chinese medicine prescriptions. Offers educational programs.

★ 2184 ★ **China Association of Traditional Chinese Medicine and Pharmacology (CAYCMP)**
A4 Ying Hua Yuan Dong St.
Chaoyang District
Beijing 100027, People's Republic of China
Phone: 1 4218316
Fax: 1 4218316
Yue-li Cui, Chm.

Founded: 1979. **Members:** 60,000. **Description:** Promotes the practice of traditional Chinese medicine. Fosters communication between medical students of Chinese and Western schools. Sponsors research and academic discussions in traditional Chinese medicine. Provides consulting services. **Publications:** *Bone Injury Therapy*, periodic. • *Chinese Qigong*, periodic. • *Journal of Traditional Chinese Medicine*, periodic. Journal.

★ 2185 ★ **Chinese Association for the Integration of Traditional Chinese and Western Medicines**
18 Beixincang Ln.
Dongzhimennei
Beijing 100700, People's Republic of China
Phone: 1 4014411
Fax: 1 4016387
Wen-cheng Dong, Sec.Gen.

Founded: 1981. **Members:** 27,013. **Description:** Individuals (27,000) and organizations (13) in the People's Republic of China. Promotes cooperation between traditional Chinese and Western medicines. Organizes studies and research. Conducts educational programs. Disseminates information. **Publications:** *Chinese Journal of Integrated Traditional and Western Medicine*, monthly. Journal.

★ 2186 ★ **Chinese Association for Research and Advancement of Traditional Chinese Medicine**
66 Xin'anli
Gulou
Beijing 100009, People's Republic of China
Phone: 1 4035950
Shen Qi-zhen, Pres.

Founded: 1989. **Members:** 348. **Description:** Promotes the practice of traditional Chinese medicine in the People's Republic of China. Conducts research programs to develop improved traditional medicinal methods. Sponsors educational programs and seminars. Offers consulting services.

★ 2187 ★ **Citizens for Health**
PO Box 1195
Tacoma, WA 98401
Phone: (206)922-2457
Free: 800-357-2211
Fax: (206)922-7583
Dee Christoff, Contact

Founded: 1991. **Local Groups:** 150. **Description:** Lobbies government to assure continued access to dietary supplements and herbs, as well as truthful information on their benefits. Seeks to protect the right of individuals to make informed health care choices from a range of traditional and alternative therapies. Holds public forums; organizes rallies. **Publications:** *Action Alert*, periodic. Bulletin. • *Citizens for Health Digest*, bimonthly. Newsletter. *Price:* Included in full member dues. • *FAX Hotline*.

★ 2188 ★ **Committee for Freedom of Choice in Medicine (CFCM)**
1180 Walnut Ave.
Chula Vista, CA 91911
Phone: (619)429-8200
Free: 800-227-4473
Fax: (619)429-8004
Mike Culbert, Chm. Emeritus

Founded: 1972. **Members:** 30,000. **Local Groups:** 30. **Description:** Purpose is to support freedom of choice for any therapy which shows clear evidence of efficacy and to prohibit the interference of government or any third party in the relationship between an informed patient and his or her physician. Activities include: publishing information to keep members apprised of the latest developments in research and treatment; directing people with questions concerning alternative therapy to physicians in their areas; maintaining an information service for physicians interested in expanding their knowledge of metabolic/nutritional treatment; providing educational exhibits for programs and seminars being conducted by various medical groups. Conducts research; compiles statistics on people with degenerative diseases who have been treated with metabolic therapy. Operates speakers' bureau. **Publications:** Audiotapes. • Books. • Brochures. • *Choice Magazine*, quarterly. Magazine. Includes science corner and heart, cancer, drug, and court watch sections. *Price:* Included in membership dues. • Pamphlets. • Reprints. • Videos. **Formerly:** (1985) Committee for Freedom of Choice in Cancer Therapy.

★ 2189 ★ **Council of Colleges of Acupuncture and Oriental Medicine (CCAOM)**
8403 Colesville Rd., Ste. 370
Silver Spring, MD 20910
Phone: (301)608-9175
Fax: (301)608-9576
Anthony Abbate, Pres.

Founded: 1982. **Members:** 14. **Description:** Schools and colleges of acupuncture that offer a minimum two-year accredited training program. Purposes are: to advance the status of acupuncture and oriental medicine through educational programs; to provide high-quality classroom and clinical instruction; to promote the improvement of research and teaching methods. **Formerly:** (1992) National Council of Acupuncture Schools and Colleges.

★ 2190 ★ **Dinshah Health Society (DHS)**
PO Box 707
Malaga, NJ 08328
Phone: (609)692-4686
Darius Dinshah, Pres.

Founded: 1976. **Members:** 775. **Description:** Health professionals and other interested individuals who use and promote chromopathy as a therapy. (Chromopathy, or color therapy, involves the use of projected colors of light to treat specific health problems.) Seeks to stimulate interest in and knowledge of chromopathy and other lesser-known methods of health restoration and maintenance such as vegetarianism and mind-power. Maintains speakers' bureau. **Publications:** Booklets. • Brochures. • *Let There Be Light*. Book. • Manuals. • Newsletter, 2-4/year.

★2191★ East West Academy of Healing Arts (EWAHA)
450 Sutter, Ste. 2104
San Francisco, CA 94108
Phone: (415)788-2227
Fax: (415)788-2242
Dr. Effie Chow, Pres.

Founded: 1973. **Description:** Promotes holistic health, Qigong, and Oriental medicine. Sponsors educational and research programs; provides clinical services.

★2192★ Floatation Tank Association (TANK)
PO Box 1396
Grass Valley, CA 95945
Phone: (916)477-1319
Fax: (916)477-1953
Lee Perry, Chairperson

Founded: 1982. **Members:** 200. **Description:** Medical and other health professionals using floatation tanks in conjunction with other patient treatments; academicians and scientific researchers studying the effect of using tanks; tank manufacturers and proprietors of public tank facilities; private tank owners, frequent tank users, journalists, students, and other interested individuals. Tanks known as sensory deprivation tanks, relaxation tanks, floatation tanks, and isolation tanks, are used for relaxation and to treat such problems as smoking, hypertension, chronic pain, and obesity. The tanks are believed to be capable of bringing about actual changes in physiology and providing access to the unconscious mind. Purposes are to: promote and publicize floatation internationally; define and make known ethical practices for commercial tank usage; research the psychology, productivity, and efficiency of the tank, and coordinate and index the findings; establish standards for safety and sanitary conditions in commercial and private installations; act as clearinghouse for news on tanks and tanking. Cooperates with environmental protection agencies, the media, and public health officials. **Publications:** *FLOATING*, quarterly. Newsletter. *Price:* Included in membership dues. • *International Directory of Floatation Facilities*, annual. Directory. • *International Directory of Tank Centers and Manufacturers*, periodic. Directory. **Formerly:** (1983) International Tanking Association.

★2193★ Flower Essence Society (FES)
PO Box 459
Nevada City, CA 95959
Phone: (916)265-9163
Free: 800-548-0075
Fax: (916)265-6467
Patricia A. Kaminski, Pres.

Founded: 1979. **Members:** 30,000. **Description:** Project of Earth-Spirit Inc. Health centers, holistic health practitioners, and interested individuals. Purpose is to increase public awareness of Nature and the evolving spiritual relationship between human beings and the earth. Promotes the use of flower essences as catalysts to health and important tools "for personal and planetary evolution." Seeks to establish a worldwide network among health practitioners and others using flower essences. Encourages intuitive and scientific investigation of the es-

sences and the creation of a center for educational and research programs. Organizes introductory weekends and annual week-long intensives for professional and lay health practitioners. Sponsors lectures and research, educational, and experimental activities on topics concerning scientific and spiritual approaches to nature, preparation and use of flower essences, practical skills for flower essence practitioners, and recent developments in the field. Maintains library and referral service. Conducts nine-day professional training seminar and wildflower preservation and naturalist program. Distributes photographs and slides of flowers of the FES essences; makes slide shows available for rental. **Publications:** *Flower Essence Repertory*. Books. *Price:* $19.95. • *Flower Essence Society--Members' Newsletter*, 1-2/year. Newsletter. Includes book reviews, calendar of events, and research updates. *Price:* Included in membership dues. Also publishes informational flyer series.

★2194★ Foundation for Advancement in Cancer Therapy (FACT)
Box 1242, Old Chelsea Sta.
New York, NY 10113
Phone: (212)741-2790
Ruth Sackman, Pres.

Founded: 1971. **Members:** 2,500. **Regional Groups:** 1. **Description:** Believes that cancer is a symptom of imbalance in body chemistry; thus, to control the disease, not only must any tumors be destroyed, but the body must also be regenerated through the "total person approach" which emphasizes nutrition, detoxification, and mind-body cohesion. Asserts the right of the public to be informed of the "nontoxic biological" adjuncts and alternatives to surgery, chemotherapy, and radiotherapy, but cautions that patients be discriminating; disseminates information concerning only those preventive schemes and nontoxic therapies that have been verified as "safe" by long-term clinical tests. Does not intend to discredit traditional therapies, but to complement them; works cooperatively with established practitioners and institutions. Seeks the elimination of carcinogens from the environment; supports cancer and nutrition research and compiles statistics; maintains speakers' bureau. **Publications:** *Cancer Forum*, bimonthly. Magazine. **Formerly:** (1988) Foundation for Alternative Cancer Therapies.

★2195★ G-Jo Institute
4950 SW 70th Ave.
Davie, FL 33314
Phone: (305)791-1562
Michael Blate, Exec.Dir.

Founded: 1977. **Members:** 3,000. **Description:** People interested in "self-health" techniques that are natural, require no drugs or medications, and are based on traditional Oriental healing philosophies, especially acupuncture and acupressure. Objective is to promote the use of self-health techniques. Makes available charts and teaching guides. Provides classes in self-health methods and natural (vegetarian) cooking. Conducts radio program and research on natural health and healing. Sponsors Vegetarian Gourmet Society. Institute derives name from G-Jo, the easiest form of acupressure. It is

commonly used for headaches, indigestion, menstrual cramps, and athletic injuries; when used regularly, the group maintains it provides long-term healing benefits. Publishes self-health reports.

★2196★ German Association of Non-Medical Practitioners (Verband Deutscher Heilpraktiker)
Ernst-Grote-Str. 13
30916 Isernhagen, Germany
Phone: 511 618289
Fax: 511 6151320
Ekkehard S. Scharnick, Contact

Founded: 1963. **Members:** 2,800. **Description:** Promotes and protects the interests of non-medical health practitioners. Seeks to raise public awareness of holistic medicine.

★2197★ Gerson Institute (GI)
PO Box 430
Bonita, CA 91908-0430
Phone: (619)472-7450
Fax: (619)267-6441
Charlotte Gerson, Pres.

Founded: 1977. **Members:** 3,000. **Description:** Individuals interested in health information. Purpose is to educate the public on nutritional health and to disseminate information about the Gerson therapy for healing. (The Gerson therapy was developed by Max Gerson, M.D., and seeks to prevent disease as well as to restore the natural healing mechanism in patients suffering from cancer and other degenerative diseases without the use of standard toxic therapies. Therapy includes a detoxification program to help the body eliminate toxins and waste materials that interfere with metabolism and healing and an intensive nutrition program.) Acts as consultant to operating physicians at hospital near Tijuana, Mexico; assists and trains physicians who want to learn the Gerson therapy. Presents lectures on health; conducts medical and nutritional research. **Publications:** *A Cancer Therapy - Results of 50 Cases*, bimonthly. Newsletter. *Price:* $25/year inside U.S.; $30/year outside U.S.. • *Censored for Curing Cancer.* • *Healing Newsletter*, quarterly. Newsletter. Includes historical review. • Videos.

★2198★ Health Optimizing Institute (HOI)
PO Box 1233
Del Mar, CA 92014
Phone: (619)481-7751
Gail Slavin, Exec. Officer

Founded: 1978. **Description:** Disseminates information on holistic and alternative health therapies aimed at building the human immune system and reversing the aging process. Conducts research and training programs in energy medicine. **Publications:** *Chronicle of Holistic Health*. Journal. **Formerly:** National Center for the Exploration of Human Potential.

★ 2199 ★ Himalayan International Institute of Yoga Science and Philosophy of the U.S.A.
RR 1, Box 400
Honesdale, PA 18431
Phone: (717)253-5551
Free: 800-822-4547
Fax: (717)253-9078
John Clarke, M.D., Pres.

Founded: 1971. **Members:** 1,500. **Regional Groups:** 23. **Description:** Aims to teach meditation, philosophy, and holistic health care based on a synthesis of Eastern and Western knowledge and techniques; benefit mankind and society. Sponsors scientific research to explore the different facets of yoga and meditation and to clarify their application in the areas of health and the evolution of consciousness. Conducts courses on the philosophy and practice of "Superconscious Meditation," a systematic method for developing each level of one's consciousness; believes that everyone has the power to recreate his life and realize his inner potential through study and practice. Imparts techniques for regulation of the body, mind, and emotions; conducts research to establish scientific basis for these techniques. Offers stress management programs, training programs for counselors, therapists, and physicians, diet and nutrition programs, and training in combined therapy. Maintains speakers' bureau; operates a children's school. Has established the Eleanor N. Dana Research Laboratory and the Himalayan Institute Teachers Association, which certifies yoga teachers. Administers charitable program. **Publications:** Audiotapes. • Books. • *Himalayan Institute quarterly Guide to Programs*, quarterly. Newsletter. Contains course descriptions. *Price:* Included in membership dues. • Videos. • *Yoga International*, bimonthly. Magazine. *Price:* $3.50/issue; $14.97/year; $23.97/ two years; Included in membership.

Holistic Dental Association (HDA)
See: Entry 3943

★ 2200 ★ Holistic Health Havens (HHH)
5020 Spring Mountain Rd., No. 2
Las Vegas, NV 89102-8704
Phone: (702)873-4542
Dr. Joseph M. Kadans, Pres.

Founded: 1980. **Description:** Works to: establish standards for public retreats for the study of health practices; operate health havens as pilot studies; approve and supervise retreats operated by others. **Publications:** *Holistic Health Quarterly*, quarterly. Journal.

★ 2201 ★ Homeopathic Council for Research and Education (HCRE)
c/o William Bergman, M.D.
50 Park Ave.
New York, NY 10016
Phone: (212)684-2290
William Bergman, M.D., Contact

Founded: 1965. **Members:** 5. **Description:** Physicians and scholars united to encourage research and education in homeopathy. Endows and supervises homeopathic research and education.

★ 2202 ★ HUNA Research (HUNA)
1760 Anna St.
Cape Girardeau, MO 63701
Phone: (314)334-3478
Fax: (314)334-3478
Dr. E. Otha Wingo, Pres.

Founded: 1945. **Members:** 19,016. **Regional Groups:** 10. **State Groups:** 22. **Local Groups:** 163. **Description:** Teachers of Huna and others from the healing professions; individuals wishing to develop and improve their lives; others interested in Huna. (Huna is a system of psychology used by the Kahunas of ancient Hawaii to remedy emotional and physical problems. The system is based on the knowledge of how the physical, mental, and spiritual levels of consciousness function effectively when used properly.) Works to assist members and others in taking charge of their own destiny and making a better life for themselves and their friends. Offers self-development program and classes. Conducts research; sponsors Certified Huna Teacher Program. **Publications:** *The Aka Cord*, 8/year. Newsletter. Contains information about group meetings, classes, seminars, research projects, books, and related activities of Huna Research. *Price:* Included in membership dues. • *Huna, The Ancient Religion of Positive Thinking*. Book. • *The Huna Work*, quarterly. Newsletter. Devoted to the distribution of information and instruction of Huna. Includes book reviews. *Price:* Included in membership dues. • *Recovering the Ancient Magic*. Book. • *Tarot Card Symbology*. Book.

★ 2203 ★ Hygienic Community Network (HCN)
c/o Helen Jean Story
PO Box 277
Boulder Creek, CA 95006-0277
Helen Jean Story, Newsletter Editor

Founded: 1980. **Members:** 125. **Regional Groups:** 1. **Description:** Individuals interested in gaining the healthful benefits of a lifestyle, known as natural hygiene, which includes: diets of mostly raw fruits, vegetables, nuts, and seeds; pursuit of fulfilling jobs and relationships; beneficial fasting; adequate rest, sunshine, and clean air and water; enjoyment of natural phenomena. Supports cooperative living and develops communities where natural hygiene is practiced; disseminates information on existing and proposed communities; provides networking services for individuals wishing to meet others with similar interests who are practicing natural hygiene. **Publications:** *Hygienic Community Network News*, bimonthly. Newsletter. Includes book reviews and letters from readers. *Price:* Included in membership dues.

★ 2204 ★ Institute for Advanced Research in Asian Science and Medicine (IARASM)
PO Box 67336
Chestnut Hill, MA 02167
Phone: (617)739-1182
Fax: (617)739-1183
Dr. John J. Kao, MD, Contact

Founded: 1972. **Description:** Purpose is to advance international understanding between Asia and the West in the areas of science, medical systems, and health care delivery. Serves as a clearinghouse for international scholarly efforts in the comparative study of science and medicine. Provides consulting services and mediation of scientific and biomedical exchange with Asian countries. Assists in generating innovative curricula in medical education; translates contemporary and classical Asian scientific and medical literature; provides training for medical professionals in acupuncture therapeutics. **Publications:** *American Journal of Chinese Medicine*, 3/year. Journal.

★ 2205 ★ Institute for Complementary Medicine (ICM)
PO Box 194
London SE16 1QZ, England
Phone: 171 2375165
Fax: 171 2375175
Anthony Baird, Sec.

Founded: 1982. **Members:** 6,000. **Languages:** English. **Description:** Individuals united to promote the practice of alternative medicine. Seeks to establish educational standards for practitioners and to establish ties between therapy groups, organizations, teachers, and practitioners. Cooperates with the British government to develop natural therapy curricula. Maintains British Register of Complementary Practitions. Conducts research; disseminates information. Advises groups establishing healing practices on legal, organizational, and practical matters. **Publications:** *Journal for Complementary Medicine*, semiannual. Journal. • *Newsletter*, quarterly. Newsletter. Supplement to journal.

★ 2206 ★ Institute for Gravitational Strain Pathology (IGSP)
PO Box 526
Rangeley, ME 04970-0526
Phone: (207)864-5511
Gertrude Jungmann, Sec.-Treas.

Founded: 1957. **Description:** Medical institute organized to study the ill effects of terrestrial gravity upon man and to develop ways and means to counteract pathology of gravitational strain. Provides instruction on clinical work with patients by means of a special research tool, known as the "antigravity leverage technique," designed to modify and reduce the harmful consequences of gravity. Is especially concerned with relationship of backaches, postural decline, aging, and gravity-strain. Presents papers on results of institute's work at medical meetings and to the public. **Publications:** Handbook. • *The Jungmann Concept of Gravitational Strain Pathology*. • Papers. • *Vevral*. Booklet.

★ 2207 ★ International Acupuncture Institute
301 Nathan Rd., 1113A
Kowloon, Hong Kong
Phone: 7711066
Fax: 3888835
Dr. Lo Chi Kwong, Dir.

Languages: Chinese, English. **Description:** Acupuncturists and other health care professionals; individuals with an interest in acupuncture. Promotes effective practice of acupuncture; devises and maintains standards of practice. Conducts research and educational programs.

★ 2208 ★ **International Alliance of**
   Nutrimedical Associations (IANA)
PO Box 225
Long Prairie, MN 56347-0225
Phone: (612)671-5557
Dr. G. Guevara, Exec. Officer

Founded: 1983. **Members:** 127. **Regional Groups:** 5. **State Groups:** 32. **Description:** Chiropractors, naturopathic doctors, nutritionists, and other medical personnel promoting natural health care. Serves as umbrella group for nutrimedical associations worldwide. Encourages the recognition of natural health care as a legitimate form of health-care. Disseminates information; approves guidelines, procedures, and regulatory codes of nutrimedical associations. Bestows nutrimedical fellowships; conducts educational, charitable, and research programs. Maintains biographical archives and speakers' bureau. **Publications:** *Holistic Hotline*, quarterly.

★ 2209 ★ **International Association of**
   Holistic Health Practitioners (IAHHP)
5020 Spring Mt. Rd.
Las Vegas, NV 89121
Phone: (702)873-4542
Fax: (702)873-9221
Dr. A. B. Kadans, Pres. & CEO

Founded: 1970. **Members:** 2,000. **Description:** Holistic health practitioners. Encourages the improvement of public, mental, physical, and spiritual health. Conducts research program on natural methods of improving health. **Publications:** *Journal of Holistic Health Practitioners--Newsletter*, periodic. Newsletter. *Price:* Included in membership dues. **Formerly:** (1981) International Naturopathic Association.

★ 2210 ★ **International Association of**
   Professional Natural Hygienists (IAPNH)
204 Stambaugh Bldg.
Youngstown, OH 44503
Phone: (216)746-5000
Fax: (216)746-1836
Mark A. Huberman, Sec.-Treas.

Founded: 1978. **Members:** 45. **Description:** Doctors of medicine, osteopathy, chiropractic, and naturopathy who specialize in the supervision of therapeutic fasting as part of a natural hygiene regimen. Promotes clinical advancement and ethical responsibility. Works for the health freedom of members. Provides certification for professionals and accreditation for schools and training programs; offers internship programs. Funds research. **Publications:** *IAPNH Newsletter*, quarterly. Newsletter. Includes association news, bibliography, book reviews, case studies, medical journal reviews, and reports from foreign countries. *Price:* Included in membership dues; $12/year for nonmembers.

★ 2211 ★ **International College of Applied**
   Kinesiology (ICAK)
Box 905
Lawrence, KS 66044-0905
Phone: (913)542-1801
Fax: (913)542-1746
Terry Kay Underwood, Contact

Members: 1,000. **Description:** Promotes the science of kinesiology. Kinesiology is the system of evaluating the structural, chemical, and mental aspect of human heath, involving muscle health, nutrition, manipulation, diet, acupressure, and exercise. Conducts educational programs, research programs, and training seminars. Provides placement service. **Publications:** *A.K. Review*, semiannual. *Price:* $15/issue. • *Health Capsule*, 6/year. *Price:* $10/year.

★ 2212 ★ **International Committee of**
   Homeopathic Pharmacists
   (Comite International des Pharmaciens
   Homeopathiques — CIPH)
LPH Dolisos
5, rue Carli
B-1140 Brussels, Belgium
Phone: 2 2160544
Fax: 2 2426241
Yvan Dierckxsens, Gen.Sec.

Founded: 1955. **Members:** 73. **Languages:** English, French, German. **Description:** Homeopathic pharmacists in 21 countries. **Publications:** *Annual Report.* • *Circular Letter*, semiannual. • *Draft of an International Homeopathic Pharmacopeia.*

★ 2213 ★ **International Federation for**
   Health
   (Federation Internationale pour la Sante —
   FEDIS)
BP 19
F-75680 Paris Cedex 18, France
Phone: 1 46660327
Fax: 1 46745270
Yves Machelard, Dir.

★ 2214 ★ **International Foundation for**
   Homeopathy (IFH)
2366 Eastlake Ave. E., No. 301
Seattle, WA 98102
Phone: (206)324-8230
Fred Bishop, Exec.Dir.

Founded: 1978. **Members:** 2,000. **Description:** Medical professionals (700) and laypersons (1300) interested in homeopathy. Promotes homeopathy and provides the public with a better understanding of health and diseases through homeopathy. (The word "homeopathy" is taken from the Greek "homeos", meaning "similar", and "pathos", meaning "suffering." Homeopathy therefore means "to treat with something that produces an effect similar to the suffering.") Works to: increase public and professional education; promote acceptance and teaching of homeopathy in medical schools. Maintains 500 volume library on homeopathic literature and resources. Sponsors research; conducts annual introductory seminar and postgraduate courses for licensed medical professionals. **Publications:** *Directory of Classical Homeopaths*, periodic. Directory. • *International Foundation for Homeopathy--Resonance*, bimonthly. Magazine. Contains information on case histories and clinical advances in research, medicine, and technology. Includes book reviews and calendar of events. *Price:* Included in membership dues. **Formerly:** (1981) International Foundation for the Promotion of Homeopathy.

★ 2215 ★ **International Foundation of**
   Oriental Medicine
PO Box 640625
Oakland Gardens, NY 11364
Phone: (718)886-4431
Fax: (718)463-0808
Dr. David P. J. Hung, Pres.

Founded: 1989. **Description:** Conducts research and public education programs on the use of oriental medicine (acupressure, acupuncture, chi-kong, and herbs). Offers fellowships and scholarships in oriental arts, medicine, and philosophy and Christian religion. Promotes East/West exchange. Conducts lectures and seminars; maintains speakers' bureau. Bestows awards; operates library and referral service. Plans to issue publications.

★ 2216 ★ **International Institute for**
   Bioenergetic Analysis (IIBA)
144 E. 36th St., Ste. 1A
New York, NY 10016
Phone: (212)532-7742
Fax: (212)532-5331
Alexander Lowen, M.D., Exec.Dir.

Founded: 1956. **Members:** 1,000. **Regional Groups:** 50. **Description:** Works to promote research and education in the fields of mental and physical health as they relate to biological energy processes. Areas of interest include: the role of muscle tension in emotional and physical illness, relationship of body structure and body movement, energy dynamics, disturbances in motility as a factor in illness, genetic factors, principles and methods of therapy, and growth and development of the child in response to patterns of child rearing. Conducts lectures, 1-day patient workshops, professional weekend workshops, seminars, and exercise classes. **Publications:** *Bioenergetic Analysis*, periodic. Journal. • Books. • Brochures. • Membership Directory, periodic. • Papers. **Formerly:** (1979) Institute for Bioenergetic Analysis.

★ 2217 ★ **International Laser Acupuncture**
   Society (ILAS)
228 E. Stadium
Stockton, CA 95204
Brian Foust, Exec. Officer

Founded: 1990. **Description:** Seeks to exchange information on laser acupuncture techniques and educate the public concerning the benefits of laser acupuncture and holistic medicine. Conducts research program on bioenergetic measurement and meridian system balancing for tissue regeneration.

★ 2218 ★ **International Society for the**
   Study of Subtle Energies and Energy
   Medicine
c/o C. Penny Hiernu
356 Goldco Cir.
Golden, CO 80403
Fax: (303)279-3539
C. Penny Hiernu, Exec.Dir.

Founded: 1989. **Members:** 1,400. **Description:** Individuals interested in the study of human capacities of the role of consciousness in Nature. Offers educational programs. **Publications:** *Bridges*, quarterly. Magazine. • *Subtle Energies*, 3/year. Journal.

★2219★ International Society for
Vibroacoustics (ISVA)
Hovdingveien 98
N-7700 Steinkjer, Norway
Phone: 77 763803
Olav Skille, Pres.

Founded: 1985. Members: 20. Languages:
English, French, German, Norwegian. Description: Therapists, scientists, and interested individuals working in the medical field. Promotes
the study and use of vibroacoustic therapy for
stress alleviation, blood flow stimulation, and relief to the nervous system. (Vibroacoustic therapy uses a series of vibrations that is transmitted
to the patient through a reclining chair.) Offers
tutoring. Publications: ISVA Bulletin, semiannual. Bulletin. Also publishes Manual of Vibroacoustic Therapy (monograph).

International Veterinary Acupuncture
Society (IVAS)
See: Entry 13091

★2220★ Israeli Association of Creative-
Expressive Therapy (ICET)
PO Box 18388
91183 Jerusalem, Israel
Phone: 2 817232
Shmuel Ben Dov, Sec.

Founded: 1971. Members: 560. Local
Groups: 4. Languages: Hebrew. Description:
Music, dance movement, and art therapists.
Fosters public awareness of the use of art therapy in the treatment and prevention of various
dysfunctions. Provides educational and growth
opportunities for therapy professionals. Establishes training standards; conducts workshops
and lectures; maintains placement service; offers childrens' services. Publications: Brochure. • ICET Information Bulletin, periodic. Bulletin. Includes directory. • Therapy Through
Arts, 2-3/year.

★2221★ Jin Shin Do Foundation for
Bodymind Acupressure (JSDF)
366 California Ave., Ste. 16
Palo Alto, CA 94306
Phone: (415)328-1811
Iona Marsaa Teeguarden, Dir.

Founded: 1982. Members: 500. Description:
A referral and educational organization of teachers and practitioners of the Jin Shin Do acupressure method. (Jin Shin Do acupressure integrates a traditional Japanese acupressure technique with classical Chinese acu-theory, Taoist
philosophy and breathing methods, and Western psychology.) Outlines tension points associated with common physical problems and distressing feelings, and teaches points and exercises that help release physical and emotional
tensions. Conducts continuing education classes, practicums, and workshops for students.
Publications: Acupressure Way of Health: Jin
Shin Do. • Audiotapes. • Booklets. • Directory
of Registered Practitioners and Authorized
Teachers, periodic. Directory. Includes listing of
authorized basic, intermediate, and advanced
teachers. Price: Free. • Jin Shin Do Acupressure Handbook. • Jin Shin Do Acupressure
Newsletter, annual. Newsletter. Includes association information and catalog. • Joy of Feeling: Bodymind Acupressure. • Videos.

★2222★ Lok Swasthya Parampara
Samvardhan (LSPSS)
Ayurbedic Trust Complex
Trichy Rd.
PO Box 7102
Ramanathapuram
Coimbatore 641 045, Tamil Nadu, India
Phone: 422 23188
Fax: 422 214953
Dr. G.G. Gangadharan, Exec.Dir.

Founded: 1985. Members: 875. Languages:
English, Hindi. Description: Village healers,
midwives, folk practitioners, and other individuals interested in traditional healing methods.
Seeks to revitalize folk traditions in areas including: childcare, nutrition, and home remedies for
common ailments. Encourages the integration
of folk medicine and organized health care systems in India. Cultivates medicinal gardens, forests, and nurseries. Fosters communication
among members; gathers and disseminates information. Publications: Newsletter, quarterly.
Formerly: Lok Swasthya Parampara Samuardhan Samithi.

★2223★ National Accreditation
Commission for Schools and Colleges of
Acupuncture and Oriental Medicine
(NACSCAOM)
8403 Colesville Rd., Ste. 370
Silver Spring, MD 20910
Phone: (301)608-9680
Fax: (301)608-9576
Penelope Ward, Dir.-Prof.Serv.

Founded: 1982. Members: 9. Description:
Members of the acupuncture educational and
professional communities and interested others. Evaluates schools and colleges of acupuncture and Oriental medicine to establish and
maintain high educational standards and ethical
business practices. Established by Council of
Colleges of Acupuncture and Oriental Medicine
(CCAOM). Publications: Accreditation Handbook. Handbook. • Brochure. • Manuals. •
Newsletter, semiannual. Price: Free.

★2224★ National Association for Holistic
Aromatherapy
PO Box 17622
Boulder, CO 80308-7622
Phone: (303)564-6785
Fax: (303)564-6799
Jeanne Rose, Chair

Founded: 1988. Members: 75. Regional
Groups: 5. Description: Seeks to establish and
promote the art and science of aromatherapy as
a health care alternative. Works to elevate and
maintain high standards of aromatherapy education. Works to raise public awareness of the
benefits of aromatherapy. Fosters communication and exchange among members. Offers educational programs. Maintains speakers' bureau. Publications: Directory, annual. • Scentsitivity, quarterly. Newsletter. Price: $20/year.

★2225★ National Board of Naturopathic
Examiners
1377 K St. NW, Ste. 852
Washington, DC 20005
Phone: (202)682-7352
Fax: (202)448-2657
Dr. George A. Freibott, Trustee

Founded: 1919. Members: 5,000. Description: Naturopathic physicians. Acts as a national testing association/board for diplomate status in naturopathic medicine. Compiles statistics. Conducts research, educational, and charitable programs. Maintains speakers' bureau.

★2226★ National Center for Homeopathy
(NCH)
801 N. Fairfax St., Ste. 306
Alexandria, VA 22314
Phone: (703)548-7790
Fax: (703)548-7792

Founded: 1974. Members: 3,500. Description: Comprises: National Center for Instruction
in Homeopathy and Homeotherapeutics, and
Homeopathic Information Service. Purposes
are: to promote the art of healing according to
the natural laws of cure from a strictly homeopathic standpoint; to facilitate the study of homeopathy by the medical and allied health professions; to implement the study of homeopathic philosophy and principles among laypersons;
to fund scientific research in the field. Sponsors
introductory courses in homeopathy to licensed
health care practitioners and laypersons; maintains speakers' bureau and library. Publications: Brochures. • Directory of Homeopathic
Practitioners, biennial. Directory. Price: $6. •
Homeopathy Today, monthly. Newsletter. Covers membership activities. Includes calendar of
events, employment opportunity and new member listings, and book reviews. Price: $40 in U.S.;
$55 outside U.S. • Pamphlets. • Reprints. Also
distributes Homeopathic Household Kit.

★2227★ National Commission for the
Certification of Acupuncturists (NCCA)
1424 16th St. NW, Ste. 501
Washington, DC 20036
Phone: (202)232-1404
Fax: (202)462-6157
Colleen F. Prasil, Dir.

Founded: 1982. Members: 9. Description:
Representatives of: National Accreditation
Commission for Schools and Colleges of Acupuncture and Oriental Medicine; Council of Colleges of Acupuncture and Oriental Medicine;
National Alliance of Acupuncture and Oriental
Medicine. Works to establish standards of competence for the safe and effective practice of
acupuncture and Oriental medicine; to evaluate
an applicant's qualifications in relation to these
established standards through the administration of national board examinations; to certify
practitioners who meet these standards. Acts as
consultant to state agencies in regulation, certification, and licensing of the practice of acupuncture and Oriental medicine. Publications:
Clean Needle Technique Manual. • NCCA Directory of Diplomates, annual. Directory. • State
Acupuncture Laws.

★2228★ National Iridology Research
Association
c/o William Caradonna
PO Box 31013
Seattle, WA 98103
Phone: (206)282-6604
William Caradonna, Dir.

Founded: 1982. Description: Researches iridology, the study of the iris of the eye for indications of bodily health and disease. Offers educational programs. **Publications:** Article, quarterly. • *Iridology Review.* Newsletter.

★ 2229 ★ Norwegian Association for Classical Acupuncture (NFKA) (Norsk Forening for Klassisk Akupunktur)
Munchsgate 7
N-0165 Oslo 1, Norway
Phone: 22361774
Fax: 22361853
Mr. Bergt Rognleien, Pres.

Founded: 1978. **Members:** 210. **Languages:** English, Norwegian. **Description:** Doctors, nurses, dentists, and physiotherapists; students. Encourages the practice of acupuncture in Norway. Operates training institute for members. Conducts educational programs. **Publications:** *Tidsskrift for Norsk Forening for Klassisk Akupunktur,* 3/year. Journal. Includes information on acupuncture and Chinese medicine. Also publishes brochure.

★ 2230 ★ Nurse Healers—Professional Association (NHPA)
175 5th Ave., Ste. 2755
New York, NY 10010

Founded: 1977. **Members:** 1,100. **Description:** Healthcare professionals united to promote a holistic approach to healing and health maintenance and nontraditional healing methods. Disseminates information. Maintains speakers' bureau; conducts research and educational programs. **Publications:** *Cooperative Connection,* quarterly. *Price:* $15/year.

★ 2231 ★ Ohashi Institute (OI)
12 W. 27th St., 9th Fl.
New York, NY 10001
Phone: (212)684-4190
Free: 800-810-4190
Fax: (212)447-5819
Wataru Ohashi, Dir.

Founded: 1974. **National Groups:** 7. **Description:** Professionals and laypeople interested in studying preventive health methods of the Japanese culture and Oriental philosophy. Promotes the understanding of the Oriental healing arts, particularly Ohashiatsu. Ohashiatsu is a combination of shiatsu technique, exercise, and meditation. Ohashiatsu is a technique of applying pressure with the hands and body to the tsubos (pressure points) and meridians (energy channels) to release stagnated energy. Ohashiatsu, claims the Institute, can be administered as a form of manipulation in order to rebalance human energy. Offers courses in beginning, intermediate, and advanced Ohashiatsu. Operates programs in the United States, Europe, and Japan. **Publications:** *Ohashiatsu News.* Newsletter. **Formerly:** (1983) Shiatsu Education Center of America.

★ 2232 ★ Pacific Women's Traditional Medicine Association
PO Box 1168
Suva, Fiji

Members: 23. **Languages:** English. **Description:** Women practitioners of traditional medicine in Fiji, the Cook Islands, Tonga, Vanuatu, Papua New Guinea, the Solomon Islands, and Tahiti. Encourages: conservation of medicinal plants and their habitats; dissemination of information on traditional healing practices; communication among members; establishment of national traditional medicine centers.

★ 2233 ★ Physicians Association for Anthroposophical Medicine (PAAM)
PO Box 66609
Portland, OR 97290
Phone: (503)234-1531
Fax: (503)234-2367
Joan Takacs, DO, Sec.

Members: 250. **Description:** Physicians, nurses, and therapists promoting the use of anthroposophical medicine. Sponsors educational programs. Studies the legal issues involving the use of anthroposophical medical treatment. **Publications:** *Directory of Physicians.* Directory. • *Journal of Anthroposophical Medicine,* quarterly. Journal. *Price:* $50/year. • Newsletter, 3/year. *Price:* $10.

★ 2234 ★ The Radiance Technique Association International (TRTAI)
PO Box 40570
St. Petersburg, FL 33743-0570
Phone: (813)347-3421
Maralyn Rose, Exec.Dir.

Founded: 1980. **Description:** Students of The Official Reiki Program - The Radiance Technique, a "science of universal energy which harmonizes and aligns the mind-body-spirit dynamic." Provides a network for those interested in The Radiance Technique. Maintains speakers' bureau. Compiles statistics and conducts research on the effectiveness of The Radiance Technique. **Publications:** *The Radiance Technique Journal,* quarterly. Newsletter. Includes book reviews, and calendar of regional and international activities. *Price:* Included in membership dues. **Formerly:** American Reiki Association; (1988) American-International Reiki Association.

★ 2235 ★ Radionic Association (RA)
Baerlein House
Goose Green
Deddington
Banbury, Oxon. OX15 0SZ, England
Phone: 1869 38852
Pat Golby, Sec.

Founded: 1943. **Members:** 501. **Description:** Individuals who have trained in radionics and are qualified to practice professionally and laymen who are interested in radionics and wish to support the association. (Radionics is described as "a method of healing at a distance through the medium of a specially designed instrument using the faculty of extra-sensory perception.") Main objectives of the association are to promote knowledge and understanding of radionics and to maintain the highest standards of competence and conduct among its practicing members. Maintains School of Radionics which provides professional training. **Publications:** Monograph, periodic. • Pamphlets, periodic. • *Radionic Quarterly.*

★ 2236 ★ The Rolf Institute (RI)
PO Box 1868
Boulder, CO 80306
Phone: (303)449-5903
Free: 800-530-8875
Fax: (303)449-5978

Founded: 1971. **Members:** 850. **Regional Groups:** 14. **Description:** Purposes are to: train and certify Rolfers and Movement Teachers; serve the professional needs of members; inform the public about the benefits of Rolfing and Rolfing Movement Integration. (Rolfing is a technique devised by Dr. Ida P. Rolf, an American biochemist, for reordering the body to bring its major segments toward a vertical alignment.) Conducts research activities; maintains speakers' bureau. **Publications:** Books. • *Expressive Movement.* • Films. • *Healing Through Touch.* • *Ida Rolf Talks.* • Pamphlets. • *The Power of Balance.* • Reprints. • *Rolf Lines,* quarterly. *Price:* Available by subscription. • *Rolfing.* • *Rolfing and Physical Reality.* • *The Rolfing Experience.* • *Rolfing Stories of Personal Empowerment.* • Videos. **Formerly:** (1975) Ida P. Rolf Foundation for Structural Integration.

★ 2237 ★ Scandinavian Association of Zone Therapeutists (SFFF) (Skandinavisk Forening for (Fodreflexologer) Zoneterapeutes — SFFF)
Krogholmgardsvej 50
DK-2950 Vedbek, Denmark
Phone: 42890188
Birgitte Bendjellal, Contact

Founded: 1975. **Members:** 500. **Languages:** Danish, English, German, Norwegian, Swedish. **Description:** Zone therapy practitioners and students. (Zone therapy involves the division of the body into parts or zones. Certain zones are then studied and/or manipulated in order to maintain health or treat particular health problems.) Examines the impact of vitamins, minerals, and diet on health. Studies related therapeutic procedures. **Publications:** *Fodnoten.* Magazine. • *SFFF Medlemsblad,* periodic.

★ 2238 ★ Serendipity Association for Research and Implementation of Holistic Health and World Peace (SARIHHWP)
c/o Bob Hemstreet
3605 S. Granada
Spring Valley, CA 92077
Phone: (619)455-9052
Dr. Doug Hemstreet, Contact

Founded: 1973. **Description:** Individuals and professionals interested in or working with holistic health care, world peace, and concepts involved with a"How to Make the World Work Project." Proposes reinventing our world to create a happy, healthy home for humanity, so that "all children everywhere are loved, housed, and well fed." Works to: reform educational system based on "correcting 14 vested Interest Distortions"; stop "government lies, deceit, and cover-ups in health, agriculture, education, defense, and waste." Promotes herbs, natural healing systems, and energy medicine for healing problems such as cancer and AIDS. Supports scientific research in the field of holistic medicine. Sponsors speakers, workshops, and training programs. Offers consulting services on designing and starting Holistic Health Centers and for government and corporations on reducing health care costs. **Publications:** *Serendipity News*, semiannual. Newsletter. *Price:* Included in membership dues. Also publishes library information packages ($45). **Also Known As:** Serendipity Association.

★ 2239 ★ **Swiss Society of Holistic Medicine (SSHM) (Schweizerische Aerztegesellschaft fur Holistische Medizin — SAGHOM)**
Hus am Sportplatz
CH-8134 Adliswil, Switzerland
Phone: 1 7109070
Fax: 1 7109091
K. Imhof, Contact

Founded: 1986. **Languages:** English, German. **Description:** Holistic health practitioners. Encourages improvement of mental, physical, and spiritual health. Conducts educational programs; represents members' interests.

★ 2240 ★ **Swiss Society of Homeopathy (SHG/SGKH) (Schweiz Homoopathie Gesellschaft — SHG/SGKH)**
Hus am Sportplatz
CH-8134 Adliswil, Switzerland
Phone: 1 7109070
Fax: 1 7109091
K. Imhof, Exec. Officer

Founded: 1980. **Languages:** German. **Description:** Medical doctors organized to promote the development of homeopathy in Switzerland. Conducts educational programs. **Formerly:** Schweizerische Arztegesellschaft fur Akupunktur; Swiss Medical Society of Acupuncture.

★ 2241 ★ **Touch for Health Foundation (THF)**
11194 Spruce Ave.
Bloomington, CA 92316
Phone: (909)873-8292
Fax: (909)873-8320
John Thie, Pres.

Founded: 1974. **Members:** 1,500. **Local Groups:** 50. **Description:** International network of independent instructors comprising medical doctors, chiropractors, osteopaths, nurses, teachers, physical therapists, massage therapists, and interested individuals. Promotes techniques for restoring natural energies and improving postural balance through muscle testing using applied kinesiology and acupressure points to improve muscle function and balance the body's energy, stimulates trained professionals to utilize natural health care research techniques with laypeople and their associates, and disseminates information on research plans, methodology, and results of self-development programs in health care, both mental and physical. Increases the level of professional confidence and keeps interested instructors, trainers, laypeople, and those in the health care profession regularly and reliably informed on development in natural health care. Conducts research projects on Touch for Health methods and results. **Publications:** *Touch for Health Book.* Book. • *Touch for Health Chart.* • *Touch for Health Directory*, annual. Directory. •

Touch for Health Folios. • *Touch for Health Newsletter*, bimonthly. Newsletter. Includes coverage of research developments, book reviews, calendar of events, and statistics. *Price:* $24.95.

★ 2242 ★ **Traditional Acupuncture Society (TAS)**
1 The Ridgeway
Stratford upon Avon, Warwickshire CV37 9JL, England
Phone: 1789 298798
Yvonne Matthews, Coun.Sec.

Founded: 1976. **Members:** 500. **Languages:** English. **Description:** Practitioners of acupuncture. Promotes the use of traditional Chinese acupuncture. Encourages exchange of ideas. Organizes seminars, study tours of China, and educational courses. Maintains charitable program. **Publications:** Journal, semiannual. • *Register of Members*, semiannual. Membership Directory. • *TAS Newsletter*, quarterly. Newsletter.

★ 2243 ★ **Traditional Healers Organisation for Africa**
PO Box 1070
Manzini, Swaziland
Phone: 52141

Description: Promotes the use of traditional healing methods. Aims to establish an herbal factory for the manufacture, bottling, and preserving of traditional herbal medicine throughout Africa.

★ 2244 ★ **World Federation of Acupuncture-Moxibustion Societies**
3 Haiyuncang
Dongcheng District
Beijing 100700, People's Republic of China
Phone: 1 4014411
Deng Liang-yue, Sec.Gen.

Founded: 1987. **Members:** 65. **Languages:** Chinese, English. **Description:** Members in 34 countries promoting the practice of acupuncture-moxibustion medicinal practices. Conducts research and educational programs; fosters exchange among members. **Publications:** *WFAS Communication*, periodic. Newsletter. • *World Journal of Acupuncture-Moxibustion*, quarterly. Journal.

★ 2245 ★ **World Society of Medical Qigong**
9 Hepingjie Beikou
Chaoyang District
Beijing 100013, People's Republic of China
Phone: 1 4211591
He-ting Gao, Sec.Gen.

Founded: 1989. **Members:** 577. **Description:** Physicians and interested individuals in 19 countries promoting the use of qigong, deep breathing exercises, as a medicinal practice. Promotes the study of medical qigong. Fosters cooperation and exchange with medical qigong organizations in other countries. Sponsors seminars. **Publications:** *World Qigong*, periodic.

★ 2246 ★ **Zimbabwe National Traditional Healers Association (ZINATHA)**
PO Box 116
Reliance House
Corner of Takcawira and Speke Ave.
Harare, Zimbabwe
Phone: 4 751902
B. Makoni, Mgr

Founded: 1980. **Members:** 45,000. **Description:** Promotes public awareness of alternative medicine. Coordinates actions of the Ministry of Health of Zimbabwe and traditional healers. Disseminates information. **Publications:** *ZINATHA.* Booklet.

Research Centers

★ 2247 ★ **Acupuncture Research Institute (ARI)**
313 W. Andrix St.
Monterey Park, CA 91754-6408
Phone: (213)722-7353
Harry A. Lusk, Exec.Dir.

Research Activities and Fields: Validity and American application of the ancient Chinese traditional healing art of acupuncture homoeopathy, including its modern innovations and international modifications. **Publications:** *MERIDIAN* (quarterly newspaper that disseminates new research and treatment data on acupuncture and related information); *Hahnemannian* (quarterly publication).

★ 2248 ★ **Hahnemannian Research Center, Inc.**
18818 Teller Ave., Ste. 230
Irvine, CA 92715
Phone: (714)852-9038
Fax: (714)852-1353
Kattunilathu Oommen George, M.D., Dir.

Research Activities and Fields: Homeopathic medicine and education, including biochemical analysis, micronutrition, Mother Tincture development, structural and degenerative studies, and deficiency detection (electromagnetic disturbances) with attention given to the emotional, mental, and physical aspects. **Publications:** *Hahnemannian Quarterly Publication.*

Heart Disease Research Foundation

★ 2249 ★ **Holos Institutes of Health**
1328 E. Evergreen
Springfield, MO 65803
Phone: (417)865-5940
C. Norman Shealy, M.D., Pres.

Research Activities and Fields: Conducts clinical studies in holistic medicine with emphasis on neurochemical profiles and management of biochemical aspects of pain and stress.

★ 2250 ★   Institute for Gravitational Strain
  Pathology, Inc.
S. Shore Dr.
PO Box 526
Rangeley, ME 04970
Phone: (207)864-5511
Gertrude Jungmann, Exec.Dir.

Research Activities and Fields: Effects of
gravity on humans and the effect of special
countermeasures to gravity strain.

★ 2251 ★   Institute of Noetic Sciences
475 Gate Five Rd., Ste. 300
Sausalito, CA 94965
Phone: (415)331-5650
Fax: (415)331-5673
Willis Harman, Pres.

Research Activities and Fields: Supports research on the nature and potential of the human
mind and consciousness, particularly in the
areas of exceptional human abilities, the mind/
body link and healing, the role of consciousness, positive global change, and creative altru-
ism. **Publications:** *Noetic Sciences Review*
(quarterly); *Bulletin* (quarterly); *Investigations*
(periodically); Special Reports (periodically);
*Noetic Sciences Book, Audiotape, and Video-
tape Catalog* (three times per year).

★ 2252 ★   International Institute of Integral
  Human Sciences
1974 de Maisonneuve W.
Montreal, PQ, Canada H3H 1K5
Phone: (514)937-8359
Fax: (514)937-8359
Rene Egli, Libn.

Research Activities and Fields: East-West
world religions, comparative religions and philosophy, ancient religions and cultures, science
of consciousness, new sciences, healing research, oriental medicine, comparative mysti-
cism, and esoteric traditions.

★ 2253 ★   Mankind Research Foundation,
  Inc.
1315 Apple Ave.
Silver Spring, MD 20910
Phone: (301)587-8686
Fax: (301)585-8959
Dr. Carl Schleicher, Pres.

Research Activities and Fields: Scientific development and the application of humanistic
psychology, biocommunication, biocybernetics,
biophysics, psychophysiology, AIDS research
educational development, cancer research,
mind/body development, and other activities
which affect the health, education, and welfare
of mankind. **Publications:** Newsletter.

★ 2254 ★   Naturopathy Institute
PO Box 56
Malverne, NY 11565
Dr. Edgar A. Kinon, Dir.

Research Activities and Fields: Naturopathy,
nutrition, natural healing sciences, radiesthesia
and radionics, botanical medicine, anatomy,
physiology, osteopathy, and chiropractic medicine.

★ 2255 ★   Research Institute of
  Acupuncture and Chinese Medicine
66 Skyline Dr.
Middlebury, CT 06762
Phone: (203)758-9900
Fax: (203)758-9900
Dr. Sung J. Liao, Pres.

Research Activities and Fields: Thermography as an objective measurement of chronic
pain and the measurement of acupuncture in
the management of chronic pain; clinical investigation of acupuncture as an alternative healing
modality. **Publications:** *Questions and Answers
of Acupuncture* (monograph); *Chinese-English
Terminology of Traditional Chinese Medicine*
(monograph). Also publishes brochures and videos.

★ 2256 ★   Rolf Institute of Structural
  Integration
PO Box 1868
Boulder, CO 80306
Phone: (303)449-5903
Fax: (303)449-5978
James Schuelke, Dir.

Research Activities and Fields: Studies the
Rolfing (registered trademark) technique of connective tissue manipulation and its effect on integration of human physical structure and physical, emotional, and psychological functioning,
including studies on human imbalance and its
correction and/or improvement by a technique
for reordering of the body to bring its major segments, head, shoulders, thorax, pelvis, and legs,
toward a vertical alignment. **Publications:**
ROLF Lines.

★ 2257 ★   World Research Foundation
15300 Ventura Blvd., Ste. 405
Sherman Oaks, CA 91403
Phone: (818)907-5483
Fax: (818)907-6044
Steven Ross, Ph.D., Pres.

Research Activities and Fields: Encourages
and supports scientific research to evaluate the
phenomenon of healing as it occurs beyond the
boundaries of traditional medicine. Projects at
major universities funded by the Center have included the following: the existence of a measur-
able healing energy, the healing potential of
lucid dreaming, the positive effects of self-help
groups for persons suffering from catastrophic
illness, the therapeutic effects of meditation and
imagery as stress reducing factors in elementary school children, suggestion and psychic healing in human surgical patients, good humor and
good health, and behavioral approaches to reduce pain and nausea of cancer treatments.
Publications: Research Report Series; *Research Reporter* (quarterly).

Chapter 5
Anesthesiology

Foundations & Other Funding Organizations

Private Foundations

Francis Families Foundation
See: Entry 197

Medical & Allied Health Schools

Nurse Anesthesia

Listed below are nurse anesthesia educational programs accredited by the Council on Accreditation of Nurse Anesthesia Educational Programs, 222 South Prospect Ave., Ste. 304, Park Ridge, IL 60068-4010, (708) 692-7050.

Alabama

★2258★ Manley L. Cummins School of Nurse Anesthesia
Southeast Alabama Medical Center
PO Drawer 6987
Dothan, AL 36302-6987
Phone: (205)793-8104

★2259★ University of Alabama at Birmingham
School of Health Related Professions
Nurse Anesthetist Program
247 SHRP Bldg.
1714 9th Ave., S.
Birmingham, AL 35294-1270
Phone: (205)934-3209

California

★2260★ Kaiser Permanente / California State University, Long Beach
School of Anesthesia for Nurses
100 S. Los Robles, Ste. 550
Pasadena, CA 91101
Phone: (818)564-3000

★2261★ Samuel Merritt College
Graduate Program of Nurse Anesthesia
370 Hawthorne Ave.
Oakland, CA 94609-3108
Phone: (510)874-8026

★2262★ University of California, Los Angeles / Olive View Medical Center
Nurse Anesthesia Program
Nursing Education Center, Ste. 205
14445 Olive View Dr.
Sylmar, CA 91342
Phone: (818)364-3277

★2263★ University of California, San Francisco
School of Nursing
Department of Physiological Nursing
Program in Nurse Anesthesia
Box 0610
N611Y
San Francisco, CA 94143-0610
Phone: (415)476-2685

Connecticut

★2264★ Hospital of St. Raphael
School of Nurse Anesthesia
1423 Chapel St.
New Haven, CT 06511
Phone: (203)789-3538

★2265★ New Britain School of Nurse Anesthesia
100 Grand St.
New Britain, CT 06050
Phone: (203)224-5612

★2266★ Southern Connecticut State University / Bridgeport Hospital
Nurse Anesthesia Program
267 Grant St.
Bridgeport, CT 06610-2870
Phone: (203)384-3280

Florida

★2267★ Barry University / Mt. Sinai Medical Center
Master of Science in Anesthesiology Program
1300 NE 2nd Ave.
Miami Shores, FL 33161-6695
Phone: (305)899-3199

★2268★ Bay Medical Center
Gooding Institute of Nurse Anesthesia
615 N. Bonita Ave.
PO Box 2515
Panama City, FL 32401
Phone: (904)747-6918

Illinois

★2269★ Decatur Memorial Hospital / Bradley University
Nurse Anesthesia Program
2300 N. Edward St.
Decatur, IL 62526-4193
Phone: (217)876-2578

★2270★ Ravenswood Hospital Medical Center / DePaul University
School of Nurse Anesthesia
4550 N. Winchester
Chicago, IL 60641-5205
Phone: (312)878-4300

★2271★ Rush University
College of Nursing
Nurse Anesthesia Program
1653 Congress Pkwy.
401 Jones
Chicago, IL 60612-3833
Phone: (312)942-7100

★2272★ Southern Illinois University at Edwardsville
School of Nursing
Nurse Anesthesia Specialization
Box 1066
Edwardsville, IL 62026-1066
Phone: (618)692-3906

Iowa

★ 2273 ★ Drake University
Department of Nursing
Clinical Specialization in Nurse Anesthesia
2507 University
Des Moines, IA 50311-4505
Phone: (515)271-4181

★ 2274 ★ University of Iowa
College of Nursing
Anesthesia Nursing Program
101 F NB
Iowa City, IA 52242-1121
Phone: (319)335-7009
Free: 800-553-4692

Kansas

★ 2275 ★ University of Kansas
Nurse Anesthesia Education Program
3901 Rainbow Blvd.
Kansas City, KS 66160-7604
Phone: (913)588-6612

Kentucky

★ 2276 ★ Trover Clinic Foundation /
Murray State University
Nurse Anesthesia Program
435 N. Kentucky Ave., Ste. A
Madisonville, KY 42431-1698
Phone: (502)824-3460

Louisiana

★ 2277 ★ Charity Hospital / Xavier
University
School of Nurse Anesthesiology
1532 Tulane Ave.
New Orleans, LA 70112-2860
Phone: (504)568-2816

Maine

★ 2278 ★ Eastern Maine Medical Center
School of Nurse Anesthesia
489 State St.
Bangor, ME 04401-6674
Phone: (207)945-8137

★ 2279 ★ University of New England
School of Nurse Anesthesia
11 Hills Beach Rd.
Biddeford, ME 04005-9599
Phone: (207)283-0171
Free: 800-477-4863

Maryland

★ 2280 ★ Uniformed Services University of
the Health Sciences
Graduate School of Nursing
Nurse Anesthesia Program
11426 Rockville Pike
Rockville, MD 20852
Phone: (301)295-1990

★ 2281 ★ U.S. Navy
Nurse Corps Anesthesia Program
Naval School of Health Sciences
8901 Wisconsin Ave.
Bethesda, MD 20889-5611
Phone: (301)295-1250

Massachusetts

★ 2282 ★ Berkshire Medical Center
School of Anesthesia
725 North St.
Pittsfield, MA 01201
Phone: (413)447-2555

★ 2283 ★ Northeastern University Graduate
School of Nursing at New England
Medical Center
School of Nurse Anesthesia
750 Washington St., Box 298
Boston, MA 02111
Phone: (617)636-6209

Michigan

★ 2284 ★ Henry Ford Hospital / University
of Detroit Mercy
Graduate Program of Nurse
Anesthesiology
Henry Ford Hospital
2799 W. Grand Blvd., Rm. 303 CFP
Detroit, MI 48202-2689
Phone: (313)876-2934

★ 2285 ★ Oakland University
Beaumont Graduate Program of Nurse
Anesthesia
3601 W. 13 Mile Rd.
Royal Oak, MI 48073-6769
Phone: (810)551-8075

★ 2286 ★ St. Joseph Mercy Hospital /
University of Detroit Mercy
Graduate Program in Nurse
Anesthesiology
900 N. Woodward
PO Box 600
Pontiac, MI 48341-2985
Phone: (810)858-6595

★ 2287 ★ University of Michigan—Flint
Hurley Medical Center
Anesthesia Program
1 Hurley Plaza
Flint, MI 48502
Phone: (810)257-9264

★ 2288 ★ Wayne State University
College of Pharmacy and Allied Health
Professions
Department of Nurse Anesthesia
Detroit Receiving Hospital
4201 St. Antoine
Detroit, MI 48201
Phone: (313)745-3610

Minnesota

★ 2289 ★ Abbott-Northwestern Hospital
School of Anesthesia
800 E. 28th St. at Chicago Ave.
Minneapolis, MN 55407-3799
Phone: (612)874-9877

★ 2290 ★ Mayo Foundation
School of Health-Related Sciences
Nurse Anesthesia Program
1108 Siebens Bldg.
200 1st St. SW
Rochester, MN 55905
Phone: (507)284-8331

★ 2291 ★ Minneapolis School of
Anesthesia
6715 Minnetonka Blvd.
St. Louis Park, MN 55426-3499
Phone: (612)925-5222

★ 2292 ★ Minneapolis VA School of
Anesthesia
1 Veterans Dr., 112A
Minneapolis, MN 55417
Phone: (612)725-2000

Missouri

★ 2293 ★ Southwest Missouri School of
Anesthesia
1900 S. National, Ste. 1900
Springfield, MO 65804
Phone: (417)887-7457

★ 2294 ★ Truman Medical Center
School of Nurse Anesthesia
2301 Holmes St.
Kansas City, MO 64108
Phone: (816)556-3216

Nebraska

★ 2295 ★ Bryan Memorial Hospital /
University of Kansas
School of Anesthesia
1600 S. 48th St.
Lincoln, NE 68506-1299
Phone: (402)483-3135

New Jersey

★ 2296 ★ Our Lady of Lourdes Medical
Center
Nurse Anesthesia Program
1600 Haddon Ave.
Camden, NJ 08103
Phone: (609)757-3897

New York

★ 2297 ★ Albany Medical College
Nurse Anesthesiology Program
43 New Scotland Ave., Rm. A-131
Albany, NY 12208
Phone: (518)262-4303

★ 2298 ★ Columbia University
School of Nursing
Program of Nurse Anesthesia
630 W. 168th St.
New York, NY 10032
Phone: (212)305-5756

★ 2299 ★ Harlem Hospital Center / Herbert
H. Lehman College of the City University
of New York
Nurse Anesthesia Program
MLK Pavillion
506 Lenox Ave., Rm. 6177A
New York, NY 10037-1801
Phone: (212)939-3575

★ 2300 ★ Kings County Hospital Center
School of Anesthesia for Nurses
441 Clarkson Ave., Bldg. T, Rm. 608
Brooklyn, NY 11203
Phone: (718)245-3259

★ 2301 ★ State University of New York at
Buffalo
Adult Health-Nurse Practitioner Programs
Nurse Anesthesia Option
1116 Kimball Tower
Buffalo, NY 14214-3079
Phone: (716)829-2410

North Carolina

★ 2302 ★ Carolinas Medical Center /
University of North Carolina at Charlotte
Nurse Anesthesia Program
1000 Blythe Blvd.
PO Box 32861
Charlotte, NC 28232
Phone: (704)355-2375

★ 2303 ★ Durham Regional Hospital
School of Anesthesia for Nurses
3643 N. Roxboro St.
Durham, NC 27704-2763
Phone: (919)470-6187

★ 2304 ★ North Carolina Baptist Hospital /
University of North Carolina at
Greensboro
Bowman Gray School of Medicine
Nurse Anesthesia Program
Medical Center Blvd.
Winston-Salem, NC 27157-1118
Phone: (910)777-3086

★ 2305 ★ University of North Carolina at
Greensboro
Raleigh School of Nurse Anesthesia
2500 Blue Ridge Rd., Ste. 200-H
Raleigh, NC 27607-6454
Phone: (919)787-8870

North Dakota

★ 2306 ★ University of North Dakota
College of Nursing
Nurse Anesthesiology Program
PO Box 9025
Grand Forks, ND 58202-9025
Phone: (701)777-4526

Ohio

★ 2307 ★ Cleveland Clinic Foundation /
Case Western Reserve University
Frances Payne Bolton School of Nursing
School of Nurse Anesthesia
9500 Euclid Ave., M-26
Cleveland, OH 44195-5154
Phone: (216)444-6547

★ 2308 ★ Mt. Sinai Medical Center / Case
Western Reserve University
Frances Payne Bolton School of Nursing
School of Nurse Anesthesia
2121 Abington Rd.
Cleveland, OH 44106-4904
Phone: (216)368-5253

★ 2309 ★ St. Elizabeth Hospital Medical
Center / La Roche College
School for Nurse Anesthetists
1044 Belmont Ave.
Youngstown, OH 44501-1790
Phone: (216)480-3444

★ 2310 ★ University of Akron
College of Nursing
Nurse Anesthesia Program
209 Carroll St.
Canton, OH 44325-3701
Phone: (216)972-7551

★ 2311 ★ University of Cincinnati
College of Nursing and Health
Nurse Anesthesia Program
Cincinnati, OH 45221-0038
Phone: (513)558-3600

Pennsylvania

★ 2312 ★ Allegheny Valley Hospital / La
Roche College
School of Anesthesia
Nurse Anesthesia Program
1301 Carlisle St.
Natrona Heights, PA 15065-9989
Phone: (412)226-7012

★ 2313 ★ Altoona Hospital
School of Anesthesia for Nurses
620 Howard Ave.
Altoona, PA 16601-4899
Phone: (814)946-2762

★ 2314 ★ Geisinger Medical Center
School of Nurse Anesthesia
100 N. Academy Ave.
Danville, PA 17822-2025
Phone: (717)271-6587

★ 2315 ★ Hamot Medical Center / Gannon
University
School of Anesthesia
201 State St.
Erie, PA 16550
Phone: (814)877-6000

★ 2316 ★ Lankenau Hospital
School of Nurse Anesthesia
100 Lancaster Ave.
Wynnewood, PA 19096-3430
Phone: (610)645-2145

★ 2317 ★ Medical College of Pennsylvania
and Hahnemann University
Graduate Program of Nurse Anesthesia
201 N. 15th St., Rm. 517
Philadelphia, PA 19102-1192
Phone: (215)762-1336

★ 2318 ★ Montgomery Hospital
Frank J. Tornetta School of Anesthesia
1301 Powell St.
PO Box 992
Norristown, PA 19401-0992
Phone: (215)270-2139

★ 2319 ★ Nazareth Hospital
School of Nurse Anesthesiology
2601 Holme Ave.
Philadelphia, PA 19152-2096
Phone: (215)335-6217

★ 2320 ★ Pennsylvania Hospital
School of Nurse Anesthesia
800 Spruce St.
Philadelphia, PA 19107-6192
Phone: (215)829-3320

★ 2321 ★ St. Francis Medical Center / La
Roche College
School of Anesthesia
400 45th St.
Pittsburgh, PA 15201-1198
Phone: (412)622-4369

★ 2322 ★ University of Pittsburgh
School of Nursing
Graduate Nurse Anesthesia Program
314 Victoria Bldg.
3500 Victoria St.
Pittsburgh, PA 15261
Phone: (412)624-4700

★ 2323 ★ Washington Hospital
School of Anesthesia
155 Wilson Ave.
Washington, PA 15301-3398
Phone: (412)223-3134

★ 2324 ★ Westmoreland-Latrobe Hospitals
/ La Roche College
School of Anesthesia for Nurses
532 W. Pittsburgh St.
Greensburg, PA 15601
Phone: (412)832-4144

★ 2325 ★ Wilkes Barre General Hospital /
Wyoming Valley Health Care System
Hospital
School of Anesthesia
575 N. River St.
Wilkes Barre, PA 18764-0001
Phone: (717)820-2299

Puerto Rico

★ 2326 ★ University of Puerto Rico
College of Health Related Professions
School of Nursing
Box 365067
San Juan, PR 00936-5067
Phone: (809)758-2525

Rhode Island

★ 2327 ★ Memorial Hospital of Rhode
Island
School of Nurse Anesthesia
111 Brewster St.
Pawtucket, RI 02860
Phone: (401)729-2000

★ 2328 ★ St. Joseph Hospital
School of Anesthesia for Nurses
200 High Service Ave.
North Providence, RI 02904-5113
Phone: (401)456-3639

South Carolina

★ 2329 ★ Medical University of South
Carolina
**College of Health Related Professions
Anesthesia for Nurses Program**
171 Ashley Ave.
Charleston, SC 29425-2701
Phone: (803)792-3785

★ 2330 ★ Richland Memorial Hospital /
University of South Carolina
Graduate Program in Nurse Anesthesia
5 Richland Medical Park
Columbia, SC 29203
Phone: (803)434-6344

South Dakota

★ 2331 ★ McKennan Hospital / University
of South Dakota
**School of Anesthesiology for Registered
Nurses**
800 E. 21st St.
Sioux Falls, SD 57117-5045
Phone: (605)339-8095

★ 2332 ★ Mt. Marty College
**Graduate Program in Nurse
Anesthesiology**
3100 W. 41st St.
Sioux Falls, SD 57105
Phone: (605)357-9802

Tennessee

★ 2333 ★ Erlanger Medical Center /
University of Tennessee at Chattanooga
Nurse Anesthesia Program
975 E. 3rd St.
Chattanooga, TN 37403
Phone: (615)778-7760

★ 2334 ★ Middle Tennessee School of
Anesthesia
Nurse Anesthesia Program
PO Box 6414
Madison, TN 37116
Phone: (615)868-6503

★ 2335 ★ University of Tennessee,
Knoxville
School of Nurse Anesthesia
Drawer U 109
1924 Alcoa Hwy.
Knoxville, TN 37920-6999
Phone: (615)544-9222

Texas

★ 2336 ★ Baylor College of Medicine
Graduate Program in Nurse Anesthesia
6550 Fannin, Ste. 1003
Houston, TX 77030
Phone: (713)793-2860

★ 2337 ★ Texas Wesleyan University
Graduate Program of Nurse Anesthesia
1201 Wesleyan St.
Ft. Worth, TX 76105-1536
Phone: (817)531-4406

★ 2338 ★ U.S. Air Force / University of
Texas Health Science Center at San
Antonio
**School of Nursing
Nurse Anesthesia Program**
7703 Floyd Curl Dr.
San Antonio, TX 78284-7943
Phone: (210)567-5832

★ 2339 ★ U.S. Army / University of Texas
Health Science Center at Houston
Program in Anesthesia Nursing
Army Medical Dept. Center and School
2250 Stanley Rd.
Ft. Sam Houston, TX 78234-6100
Phone: (210)221-8095

★ 2340 ★ University of Texas Health
Science Center at Houston
Program in Nurse Anesthesia Education
1100 Holcombe Blvd.
Houston, TX 77030
Phone: (713)792-7890

Virginia

★ 2341 ★ DePaul Medical Center
School of Anesthesia
150 Kingsley Lane
Norfolk, VA 23505-4602
Phone: (804)889-5183

★ 2342 ★ Sentara-Norfolk General Hospital
Graduate Program of Nurse Anesthesia
600 Gresham Dr.
Norfolk, VA 23507-1999
Phone: (804)668-2909

★ 2343 ★ Virginia Commonwealth
University
**Medical College of Virginia
Nurse Anesthesia Program**
PO Box 980226, MCV Campus
Richmond, VA 23298-0226
Phone: (804)828-9808

Washington

★ 2344 ★ Sacred Heart Medical Center /
Gonzaga University
**Master of Anesthesiology Education
Program**
101 W. 8th Ave.
PO Box 2555
Spokane, WA 99220-2555
Phone: (509)455-4971

West Virginia

★ 2345 ★ Charleston Area Medical Center
School of Nurse Anesthesia
Robert C. Byrd Bldg., Rm. 2041
3110 MacCorkle Ave. SE
Charleston, WV 25304
Phone: (304)348-4125

★ 2346 ★ United Hospital Center / La
Roche College
Nurse Anesthesia Program
PO Box 1680
Clarksburg, WV 26302-1680
Phone: (304)624-2300

Wisconsin

★ 2347 ★ St. Francis Medical Center
School of Anesthesia
700 West Ave., S.
La Crosse, WI 54601-4783
Phone: (608)785-0940

National & International Organizations

★ 2348 ★ American Association of Nurse
Anesthetists (AANA)
222 S. Prospect
Park Ridge, IL 60068-4001
Phone: (708)692-7050
John F. Garde, Exec.Dir.

Founded: 1931. **State Groups:** 52. **Description:** Active registered professional nurses who have successfully completed an accredited program in nurse anesthesia and passed a national examination for certification. Advances the art and science of anesthesiology; promotes research in anesthesia; develops educational standards and techniques for the administration of anesthesia. Sponsors continuing education; promotes biennial recertification. **Publications:** *AANA Journal*, bimonthly. Journal. Contains clinical, practical, theoretical, and research articles. Includes advertisers' index, and alphabetical index by organization. *Price:* Included in membership dues; $24/year for nonmembers. • *AANA News Bulletin*, monthly. Bulletin. Contains legislative news, president's message, calendar of events, and employment listings. *Price:* Included in membership dues. • *American Association of Nurse Anethestists List of Recognized Educational Programs*, semiannual. Arranged by state.

★ 2349 ★ American Board of
Anesthesiology (ABA)
100 Constitution Plz.
Hartford, CT 06103
Phone: (203)522-9857
Fax: (203)522-6626
Francis P. Hughes, Ph.D., Exec.Sec.

Founded: 1938. **Members:** 12. **Description:** Certification board which seeks to elevate and maintain the standards of the practice of anesthesiology and to establish criteria of fitness for the designation of a specialist in this field. Advises the Accreditation Council for Graduate Medical Education of the American Medical Association concerning training of individuals seeking certification. Arranges and conducts examinations to determine the competence of physicians who apply; issues certificates to those who meet the required standards. **Publications:** *American Board of Anesthesiology-- Booklet of Information*, annual. Booklet. Describes the examination system and the policies and regulations governing the board's examination and certification process. *Price:* Free.

★ 2350 ★　**American Board of Post Anesthesia Nursing Certification (ABPANC)**
11512 Allecingie Pky.
Richmond, VA 23235
Phone: (804)378-4936
Free: 800-622-7262
Fax: (804)379-1386
Susan Fetzer-Fowler, R.N., Pres.

Founded: 1985. **Description:** Administers examination to individuals wishing to attain post-anesthesia nursing certification. **Publications:** *CPAN Newsletter*, quarterly. Newsletter. *Price:* Free.

★ 2351 ★　**American Dental Society of Anesthesiology (ADSA)**
211 E. Chicago Ave., Ste. 948
Chicago, IL 60611
Phone: (312)664-8270
Free: 800-722-7788
Fax: (312)642-9713
Christopher LoFrisco, DMD, Exec.Dir.

Founded: 1953. **Members:** 3,200. **State Groups:** 21. **Description:** Dentists and physicians. Encourages study and progress in dental anesthesiology. **Publications:** *ADSA Directory*, annual. Directory. • *ADSA Pulse*, bimonthly. Newsletter. Includes society news, calendar of events, and research updates. *Price:* Included in membership dues; $5/year for nonmembers. • *Anesthesia Progress*, bimonthly. *Price:* $30/ year for members; $35/year for nonmembers; $55/year for institutions.

American Osteopathic College of Anesthesiologists (AOCA)
See: Entry 9987

★ 2352 ★　**American Society for Advancement of Anesthesia in Dentistry (ASAAD)**
c/o Dr. Louis L. Zall
11245 W. Atlantic Blvd., Apt. 301
Coral Springs, FL 33071-5112
Phone: (305)584-5600
Fax: (305)584-5601
Dr. Louis L. Zall, Editor

Founded: 1929. **Members:** 400. **Description:** Dentists and physicians interested in dental anesthesia. Studies new anesthetics and chemicals; researches pain control methods. Organized and sponsored international congresses on modern pain control in dentistry in Latin America, Europe, and Japan. Maintains speakers' bureau. **Publications:** *Modern Anesthesia in Dentistry*. Book. • *Modern Dental Anesthesia*. Book. • *Modern Pain Control*, biennial. • *Pain*

Control in Dentistry, semiannual. Journal. Covers and promotes the use of dental anesthesia. *Price:* Included in membership dues. • *Transcripts*, semiannual. **Formerly:** (1975) American Society for Advancement of General Anesthesia in Dentistry.

★ 2353 ★　**American Society of Anesthesiologists (ASA)**
520 N. Northwest Hwy.
Park Ridge, IL 60068-2573
Phone: (708)825-5586
Fax: (708)825-1692
Glenn W. Johnson, Exec.Dir.

Founded: 1905. **Members:** 33,000. **State Groups:** 48. **Description:** Professional society of physicians specializing or interested in anesthesiology. Seeks "to develop and further the specialty of anesthesiology for the general elevation of the standards of medical practice." Encourages education, research, and scientific progress in anesthesiology. Conducts refresher courses and other postgraduate educational activities. Maintains placement service. **Publications:** *Anesthesiology*, monthly. Journal. • *ASA Newsletter*, monthly. Newsletter. Reports on the educational and scientific work of ASA. Contains calendar of events. *Price:* Included in membership dues; $12/year for nonmembers. • Membership Directory, annual. **Formerly:** (1911) Long Island Society of Anesthetists; (1936) New York Society of Anesthetists; (1945) American Society of Anesthetists.

★ 2354 ★　**American Society of Regional Anesthesia (ASRA)**
1910 Byrd Ave., No. 100
PO Box 11086
Richmond, VA 23230
Phone: (804)282-0010
Fax: (804)282-0090
John A. Hinckley, Exec.Sec.

Founded: 1974. **Members:** 8,000. **Description:** Physicians and research Ph.D.s. Conducts educational workshops. Sponsors annual refresher course. **Publications:** *ASRA Newsletter*, quarterly. Newsletter. *Price:* Included in membership dues. • *Regional Anesthesia*, quarterly. Journal. *Price:* Included in membership dues.

★ 2355 ★　**Anaesthetic Research Society (ARS)**
Royal Liverpool University Hospital
Prescot St.
Liverpool, Merseyside L69 3BX, England
Phone: 151 7064008
Fax: 151 7065815
Dr. J.M. Hunter, Hon.Sec.

Founded: 1958. **Languages:** English. **Description:** Facilitates the presentation of members' research in anesthesiology (clinical or experimental, completed or in progress). **Publications:** *Proceedings*, 3/year. Journal. Included in the *British Journal of Anaesthesia*.

★ 2356 ★　**Association of Paediatric Anaesthetists of Great Britain and Ireland (APA)**
Royal Hospital for Sick Children
Yorkhill
Glasgow G3 8SJ, Scotland
Phone: 141 3398888
Fax: 141 3340972
Dr. D.S. Arthur, Contact

Founded: 1973. **Members:** 225. **Languages:** English. **Description:** Pediatric anesthetists practicing in Great Britain and Ireland and outside the British Isles. Promotes the study of pediatric anesthesiology. Collects and disseminates information; conducts research; advises other professional bodies on matters pertaining to pediatric anesthesiology. Bestows awards. Sponsors seminars. **Publications:** *Yearbook*.

★ 2357 ★　**Association of University Anesthesiologists (AUA)**
c/o Michael J. Bishop, M.D.
2033 6th Ave., No. 804
Seattle, WA 98121
Phone: (206)441-6020
Fax: (206)441-8262
Michael J. Bishop, M.D., Sec.

Founded: 1953. **Members:** 600. **Description:** Academic anesthesiologists from medical school faculties. Encourages members to pursue original investigations in the clinic and the laboratory; develops methods of teaching anesthesiology. **Publications:** Directory, annual. **Formerly:** (1990) Association of University Anesthetists.

★ 2358 ★　**Associazione Italiana di Anestesia Odonto-Stomatologica (AINOS)**
Casella Postale 1630
I-40100 Bologna, Italy
Phone: 51 247784
Fax: 51 247784
Dr. Luigi Baldinelli, Gen.Sec.

Founded: 1972. **Members:** 60. **Languages:** Italian. **Description:** Physicians concerned with dental anesthesiology. Sponsors educational and research programs. **Publications:** *Giornale di Anestesia Stomatologica*, quarterly. Magazine.

★ 2359 ★　**Canadian Anaesthetists' Society (CAS) (Societe Canadienne des Anesthesistes — SCA)**
1 Eglinton Ave. E., Ste. 208
Toronto, ON, Canada M4P 3A1
Phone: (416)480-0602
Fax: (416)480-0320
Ann Andrews, Exec.Dir.

Founded: 1920. **Members:** 2,250. **Local Groups:** 10. **Languages:** English, French. **Description:** Professional anesthesiologists and students. Promotes the art and science of anesthesiology in Canada. Advocates measures designed to improve health care in Canada and hospital standards regarding anesthesiology. Works in conjunction with the Canadian Medical Association. Conducts discussion sessions, panels, refresher courses, and workshops. Maintains C.A.S. International Education Fund for aid to developing countries. **Publications:** *Canadian Journal of Anaesthesia*, monthly. Journal. • *CAS Members' Guide*, annual. Directory. • *CAS-SCA Newsletter*, quarterly. Newsletter. • *CJA Annual Meeting Supplement*, annual. Report. **Formerly:** (1924) Canadian Society of Anaesthetists; (1943) Anaesthesia Section of the Canadian Medical Association.

★ 2360 ★ Council on Accreditation of Nurse Anesthesia Educational Programs / Schools
222 Prespect Ave.
Park Ridge, IL 60068-4010
Phone: (708)692-7050
Fax: (708)692-7137
Betty Horton, Exec. Officer

Founded: 1975. **Members:** 100. **Description:** Nurse anesthesia programs. To provide accreditation and to evaluate the education offered by educational institutions and programs. Functions within the framework of the American Association of Nurse Anesthetists. Conducts on-site reviews and educational workshops. Compiles statistics. **Publications:** *Educational Standards and Guidelines*. • *List of Accredited Nurse Anesthesia Educational Program/Schools*, semiannual. Directory. • *Policies and Procedures Manual*.

★ 2361 ★ Council on Certification of Nurse Anesthetists (CCNA)
222 S. Prospect Ave.
Park Ridge, IL 60068
Phone: (708)692-7050
Fax: (708)692-7082
Susan S. Caulk, Contact

Founded: 1975. **Members:** 11. **Description:** Sets certification standards and policies; confers certification upon entry-level nurse anesthetists. Conducts research. Works within the framework of the American Association of Nurse Anesthetists.

★ 2362 ★ Dannemiller Memorial Educational Foundation (DMEF)
12500 Network Blvd., Ste. 101
San Antonio, TX 78249
Phone: (210)641-8311
Free: 800-328-2308
Fax: (210)641-8329
Larry Vervack, Exec. Dir

Founded: 1971. **Members:** 30. **Description:** Conducts annual Anesthesia Review Course in June for M.D. anesthesiologists and in the fall for nurse anesthesiologists, and review course of current concepts in anesthesiology. Sponsors weekend anesthesia workshops. **Publications:** *AnalgesiaFile*. • *Anesthesia File*, monthly. Journal. Abstracting service. • *Developments in Cardiology*. • *Progress In Anesthesiology*. **Formerly:** (1984) Society of Air Force Anesthesiologists.

★ 2363 ★ European Academy of Anaesthesiology (EAA)
Service d'Anesthesie
Hopital de Hautepierre
F-67200 Strasbourg, France
Phone: 88 289000
Fax: 88 285464
Prof. J.C. Otteni, Exec. Officer

Founded: 1978. **Members:** 500. **Languages:** English. **Description:** Works to raise professional standards of anesthesiology throughout Europe and to introduce unified European criteria for the profession. Conducts research and training courses; audits training; administers postgraduate examinations leading to the European Diploma in Anaesthesiology. Organizes seminars. **Publications:** *European Journal of Anaesthesiology*, quarterly. Journal.

★ 2364 ★ European Association of Cardiothoracic Anaesthesiologists (EACTA)
rue Washington, 129
B-1050 Brussels, Belgium
Phone: 2 3465643
Fax: 2 3463637
Mary Roe, Mgr.

Founded: 1986. **Members:** 500. **Languages:** English. **Description:** Physician anesthesiologists. Provides a forum for scientific discussion of issues in cardiothoracic anesthesiology.

★ 2365 ★ European Society of Regional Anaesthesia (ESRA) (Societe Europeenne d'Anesthesie Loco-Regionale)
Kempenlaan 12
B-2300 Turnhout, Belgium
Phone: 14 422773
Fax: 14 439284
Dr. A. Van Zundert, Contact

Founded: 1980. **Members:** 1,700. **Regional Groups:** 7. **Languages:** English, French. **Description:** Doctors of medicine specializing in anesthesiology in 30 countries. Seeks to reduce the risks and heighten the effectiveness of anesthesia by improving techniques of anesthesiology. Provides professional training; conducts workshops and seminars. **Publications:** *International Monitor on Regional Anesthesia*, quarterly. • *Newsletter*, annual. Newsletter. • *Yearbook*.

★ 2366 ★ German Society of Anaesthesiology and Intensive Medicine (GSAIM) (Deutsche Gesellschaft fur Anasthesiologie und Intensivmedizin — DGAI)
Obere Schmiedgasse 11
90403 Nuremberg, Germany
Phone: 911 22046
Fax: 911 232340
Prof. H.W. Opderbecke, Contact

Founded: 1953. **Members:** 5,500. **Description:** Promotes scientific advancement and high standards of practice in anesthesiology and intensive care medicine. **Publications:** *Anasthesie, Intensivmedizin, Notfallmedizin, Schmerztherapie*, periodic. • *Anasthesiologie und Intensivmedizin*, periodic. • *Der Anaesthesist*, periodic.

★ 2367 ★ International Anesthesia Research Society (IARS)
2 Summit Park Dr., Ste. 140
Cleveland, OH 44131-2553
Phone: (216)642-1124
Fax: (216)642-1127
Anne F. Maggiore, Exec.Dir.

Founded: 1922. **Members:** 15,000. **Description:** Anesthesiologists and other doctors of

medicine and dentistry in 50 countries interested in the specialty of anesthesiology; associate members are registered nurses, physician assistants, and respiratory therapists. Fosters progress and research in all phases of anesthesiology. **Publications:** *Anesthesia & Analgesia*, monthly. Journal. Contains research articles and clinical reports on anesthesia and anesthesia-related subjects. Includes book reviews and employment listings. *Price:* $95/year for members; $110/year for nonmembers; $150/year for nonmember institutions.

★ 2368 ★ International Federation of Dental Anesthesiology Societies (IFDAS)
Wilmington Lodge
19 Dunstable St.
Ampthill
Bedford MK45 2NJ, England
Phone: 1525 405008
Fax: 1525 405008
Dr. Peter Sykes, Sec.Gen.

Founded: 1982. **Members:** 10. **Languages:** English. **Description:** Societies of dental and medical practitioners in 7 countries. Promotes and encourages the study and practice of improved methods for administering anesthesia, analgesia, and sedation in dentistry and its related branches. Works to bring the benefits of these methods to people throughout the world. Facilitates the international exchange of information, research, and technology in the field. **Publications:** *IFDAS Newsletter*, semiannual. Newsletter.

★ 2369 ★ International Trauma Anesthesia and Critical Care Society (ITACCS)
PO Box 4826
Baltimore, MD 21211
Phone: (410)235-7697
Fax: (410)235-8084
Christopher M. Grande, MD, MPH, Exec.Dir.

Founded: 1988. **Members:** 600. **Description:** Healthcare professionals involved in trauma and critical care anesthesiology. Works to gain recognition for trauma anesthesiology as a discipline within critical care medicine. Promotes cooperation and information sharing among healthcare professionals. Sponsors seminars and workshops; conducts research and educational programs; provides children's services; holds competitions; maintains speakers' bureau and placement service. **Publications:** *ITACCS Newsletter*, 3/year. Newsletter. *Price:* Free. • *Textbook of Trauma Anesthesia and Critical Care*. Book.

★ 2370 ★ Latin American Confederation of Societies of Anesthesia (Confederacion Latinoamericana de Sociedades de Anestesia)
Fco Solano Antuna 2970/801
Montevideo, Uruguay
Prof. D. Martin Marx, Sec.Gen.

Description: Promotes the advancement of anesthesiology in Latin American. Maintains standards for the use of anesthesia. Fosters the exchange of information between anesthesiologists. **Publications:** *Noticios de la CLASA*.

★ 2371 ★ Romanian Society for Anaesthesia Intensive Care (RSAIC) (Societatea Romana de Anestezie Terapie Intensiva — SRATI)
PO Box 11-86
72400 Bucharest, Romania
Prof. Iurie Acalovschi, Pres.

Founded: 1973. **Members:** 980. **Languages:** English, French, German. **Description:** Anesthesiologists. Promotes new techniques in anesthesia and intensive care. Conducts symposia and scientific events; offers postgraduate educational courses. **Publications:** *Journal of the Romanian Society for Anaesthesia and Intensive Care*, quarterly. Journal.

★ 2372 ★ Slovak Society of Anesthesiology and Intensive Care Medicine
Hodska cesta 373/38
SK-924 22 Galanta, Slovakia
Phone: 707 2441
Fax: 707 4572
Milan Ondercanin, M.D., Contact

Languages: English, Slovak. **Description:** Health care professionals working in the fields of anesthesiology and intensive care medicine. Works to enhance members' professional development and to advance the quality of practice in the fields. Represents members' interests.

★ 2373 ★ Societe Francaise d'Anesthesie et de Reanimation (SFAR)
74, rue Raynouard
F-75016 Paris, France
Phone: 1 45258225
Fax: 1 40503522
Prof. M.C. Laxenaire, Pres.

Founded: 1936. **Members:** 2,764. **Languages:** French. Does not correspond in English. **Description:** Anesthesiologists; interested others in France. Promotes scientific research and high standards of practice in the field. **Publications:** *Annales Francaises d'Anesthesie et de Reanimation*, bimonthly. Journal.

★ 2374 ★ Society of Anaesthetists of West Africa (SAWA)
University of Lagos, College of Medicine
Department of Anaesthesia
Private Mail Bag
Lagos, Nigeria
Dr. Dorothy J.O. Ffoulkes-Crabbe, Contact

Founded: 1966. **Members:** 150. **Regional Groups:** 1. **Languages:** English, French. **Description:** Physicians and anesthetists (100); anesthetists in training (50). Promotes improved anesthetic services in African countries. Organizes seminars, workshops, and scientific conferences aimed at developing better services and professional ability; sponsors competitions. **Publications:** *African Journal of Anaesthesia and Intensive Care*, semiannual. Journal. • *SAWA Newsletter*, semiannual. Newsletter.

★ 2375 ★ Society of Cardiovascular Anesthesiologists (SCA)
1910 Byrd Ave., No. 100
PO Box 11086
Richmond, VA 23230-1086
Phone: (804)282-0084
Fax: (804)282-0090
John A. Hinckley, Exec.Sec.

Members: 6,000. **Description:** Anesthesiologists who specialize in cardiovascular surgical conditions. Purpose is to further medical education of cardiovascular anesthesiologists. Establishes goals and objectives for education of trainees in cardiovascular anesthesia; promotes personnel exchange between the U.S. and other countries; reviews related literature; maintains workshops; conducts research competitions. Sponsors Anesthesia Grand Rounds: Case Presentations as a section of the annual meeting. **Publications:** *Society of Cardiovascular Anesthesiologists--Newsletter*, bimonthly. Newsletter. Contains discussions of major issues within the cardiovascular anesthesiology field and reviews of related literature being published. *Price:* Included in membership dues. Also publishes monographs.

Society of Neurosurgical Anesthesia and Critical Care (SNACC)
See: Entry 8309

Society for Obstetric Anesthesia and Perinatology (SOAP)
See: Entry 9696

★ 2376 ★ World Federation of Societies of Anaesthesiologists (WFSA) (Federation Mondiale des Societes d'Anesthesiologistes)
Pantai Medical Centre
8 Jalan Bukit Pantai
59100 Kuala Lumpur, Malaysia
Phone: 3 2825077
Fax: 3 2558148
Say Wan Lim, M.D., Exec. Officer

Founded: 1955. **Members:** 86. **Languages:** English, French, German, Spanish. **Description:** Societies of anesthesiologists. Objectives are to: promote research in anesthesiology; disseminate scientific information; encourage the establishment of safety measures including equipment standardization; recommend suitable standards for training in anesthesiology. Provides information regarding opportunities for postgraduate training and research. **Publications:** *Annual Report.* • *Directory of Member Societies.* • *International Congress Calendar.* • *WFSA Newsletter*, semiannual. Newsletter. Also publishes specialty manuals.

Research Centers

★ 2377 ★ American Society for the Advancement of Anesthesia in Dentistry
475 White Plains Rd.
Eastchester, NY 10708
Phone: (914)961-8136
Dr. Antonio Reyes-Guerra, Exec.Sec.

Research Activities and Fields: Anesthesia in dentistry, including the study of sedation and its relation to physiologic sleep and the use of sedatives in dentistry. **Publications:** *Pain Control in Dentistry* (semiannual journal).

★ 2378 ★ Medical College of Pennsylvania and Hahnemann University Malignant Hyperthermia Research Center
Dept. of Anesthesiology
Broad & Vine Sts.
Mailstop 310
Philadelphia, PA 19102
Phone: (215)762-7960
Fax: (215)762-8656
Dr. Henry Rosenberg, Dir.

Research Activities and Fields: Malignant hyperthermia, neuromuscular blocking agents, natural toxins, and general anesthetic agents. Studies focus on diagnosis of malignant hyperthermia susceptibility and basic research in mechanisms underlying malignant hyperthermia, anesthetic action, and drug mechanisms; and bleeding after cardiac surgery and its causes and control, especially focusing on the role of antifibrinolytics.

U.S. Department of Health and Human Services National Institute of Dental Research Intramural Research Program Neurobiology and Anesthesiology Branch
See: Entry 4020

★ 2379 ★ University of Arizona Advanced Biotechnology Laboratory
Dept. of Anesthesiology
1501 N. Campbell
Tucson, AZ 85724
Phone: (520)626-2116
Fax: (520)626-6943
Richard Watt, Dir.

Research Activities and Fields: Implementation of advanced technology to anesthesia, including utilization of computers for automation of monitoring and data collection, development of improved anesthesia delivery and monitoring equipment, basic research and development of new monitoring parameters, and ergonomic approaches to anesthesia tasks. Pharmacologic research is also conducted with emphasis on molecular mechanisms of anesthetics. **E-mail Address:** rcw@ccit.arizona.edu.

Chapter 6
Aviation & Space Medicine

Federal Government Agencies

★2380★ U.S. Department of
Transportation
Federal Aviation Administration (FAA)
**Associate Administrator for Regulation
and Certification**
Office of Aviation Medicine
800 Independence Ave. SW
Washington, DC 20591
Phone: (202)267-3535

Description: The Office is responsible for the medical certification of all airmen. It maintains the Civil Aeromedical Institute at the FAA Aeronautical Center in Oklahoma City.

National & International Organizations

★2381★ Aerospace Medical Association
(AsMA)
320 S. Henry St.
Alexandria, VA 22314
Phone: (703)739-2240
Fax: (703)739-9652
Russell B. Rayman, M.D., Exec.Dir.

Founded: 1929. **Members:** 4,200. **Description:** Medical and scientific personnel engaged in clinical, operational, and research activities in aviation, space, and environmental medicine. Sponsors continuing professional education programs. **Publications:** *Aviation, Space, and Environmental Medicine*, monthly. Journal. Covers the medical aspects of survival in aviation, space, and undersea exploration. Includes annual index; book reviews; meetings calendar. *Price:* Included in membership dues; $80/year for nonmembers; $90/year foreign (agency discount available). • Membership Directory, annual. • *Scientific Papers*, annual. **Formerly:** (1959) Aero Medical Association.

★2382★ Airline Medical Directors
Association (AMDA)
c/o Nestor B. Kowalsky, M.D.
American Airlines Med. Department
PO Box 66033
Chicago, IL 60666
Phone: (312)686-4192
Fax: (312)686-6393
Nestor B. Kowalsky, M.D., Sec.

Founded: 1946. **Members:** 130. **Description:** Medical directors and assistants of commercial airlines.

★2383★ Civil Aviation Medical
Association (CAMA)
PO Box 23864
Oklahoma City, OK 73123-3864
Phone: (405)840-0199
Fax: (405)848-1053
James L. Harris, Contact

Founded: 1948. **Members:** 700. **Description:** Aviation medical examiners, physicians who are pilots, aviation medical educators, flight instructors, fixed base operators, NASA physicians, and airline medical department physicians. Purposes are to: ascertain the basic mental and physical requirements of civil airmen and the proper methods for the physical assessment of airmen engaged in civil aviation; review continuously the scientific status of civil aviation medicine and advance and disseminate the information by which civil aviation medicine safeguards public safety; sponsor basic and advanced training in civil aviation medicine; foster international fellowship among members, allied medical and technical groups, and students of aviation medicine; unite the designated civil aviation medical examiners of the world into an effective medical body dedicated to the promotion and practice of aviation safety for the public benefit. Maintains speakers' bureau; compiles statistics. **Publications:** *Bulletin of the Civil Aviation Medical Association*, quarterly. Newsletter. Covers membership activities. Contains meetings calendar and promotion of members. **Formerly:** (1955) Airline Medical Examiners Association.

★2384★ European Association for
Aviation Psychology (EAAP)
(Europaische Gesellschaft fur Luftfahrt
Psychologie — EAAP)
Flugplatz
31675 Buckeburg, Germany
Phone: 5722 71354
Fax: 5722 71354
Frank Fehler, Sec.

Founded: 1956. **Members:** 196. **Languages:** English, French, German. **Description:** Societies of aviation psychologists (civilian and military), aviation research institutes, airlines, industries connected with aviation, defense agencies, and individuals in 22 countries. Promotes psychology as it applies to the field of aviation. **Publications:** *Conference Report*, biennial. • *Members Bulletin*, semiannual. Bulletin. • *Members Directory*, annual. Directory.

★2385★ German Society for Aviation and
Space Medicine (DGLRM)
(Deutsche Gesellschaft fur Luft- und
Raumfahrtmedizin)
Universitatsaugenklinik
Martinistrasse 52
20246 Hamburg, Germany
Phone: 40 47172301
Fax: 40 47174906
Dr. R. Schwartz, Sec.

Founded: 1963. **Members:** 700. **Languages:** English, German. **Description:** Scientists and physicians. Supports scientific work in the fields of aviation and space medicine. Conducts work group studies on ergonomics, the history of aviation medicine, and related subjects. Participates in the presentation of educational courses in aviation medicine for physicians. **Publications:** *Mitteilungen*, bimonthly.

★2386★ Latin American Association of
Aviation and Space Medicine
(Asociacion Latinoamericana de Medicina
de Aviacion y del Espacio)
8631 Las Condes Ave.
Santiago, Chile
Sergio Olmedo, Pres.

Description: Promotes the study of aviation and space medicine throughout Latin America. Works to develop advanced techniques and procedures.

Society of United States Air Force Flight
  Surgeons
See: Entry 7811

Research Centers

★2387★ **Brandeis University**
Ashton Graybiel Spatial Orientation Lab
415 South St.
Waltham, MA 02254-9110
Phone: (617)736-2033
Fax: (617)736-2031
James R. Lackner, Dir.

Research Activities and Fields: Human spatial
orientation, effects of gravity on vestibulo-ocular
reflex, the role of vestibular and cervical sensory
and motor activity in hand movement control,
oculomotor stability, and effects of different G
levels. Also studies human sensorimotor adaptation to unusual force environments.

★2388★ **Columbia University**
Eye Radiation and Environmental Research
  Laboratory
Columbia-Presbyterian Medical Center
635 W. 165th St., Rm. 218
New York, NY 10032-3784
Phone: (212)305-2724
Dr. Basil Worgul, Dir.

Research Activities and Fields: Cellular
mechanisms of radiation cataract, cataracto-
genesis, the effects of heavy particles on ocular
tissue, and potential risks to the eyes of astro-
nauts during extended manned flight in the hostile radiational environment of space. **E-mail
Address:** basil.worgul@columbia.edu.

★2389★ **National Aeronautics and Space**
  Administration
Ames Research Center
Space Human Factors Office
Mail Code N239-2
Moffett Field, CA 94035
Phone: (415)604-5000
Richard F. Haines, Ph.D., Chief

Research Activities and Fields: Office conducts basic and applied aerospace human factors research, particularly in the areas of experimental psychology, environmental psychology,
architecture, industrial design, and life support
technology.

★2390★ **National Aeronautics and Space**
  Administration
Lyndon B. Johnson Space Center
Medical Sciences Division
Mail Code SD
2101 NASA Rd. 1
Houston, TX 77058
Phone: (713)483-4461
Fax: (713)483-6227
Dr. Sam Pool, Chief

Research Activities and Fields: Principal area
of research interest is human response to
microgravity and space flight. Emphasis is on
medical care; vestibular, cardiovascular, and
endocrine studies; toxicology; laboratory medicine hematology; and bioreactor development.

★2391★ **National Aeronautics and Space**
  Administration
Lyndon B. Johnson Space Center
Space Biomedical Research Institute
2101 NASA Rd. 1
Houston, TX 77058
Phone: (713)483-7212
Fax: (713)483-6227
Dr. Michael W. Bungo, Director

Research Activities and Fields: SBRI conducts basic and applied research on the physiologic changes that accompany humans in
microgravity. Investigations are performed on
astronaut crewmembers preflight, postflight,
and during shuttle missions in the following laboratories: Bone and Muscle, Neurophysiology,
Cardiovascular, Exercise, and Environmental
Physiology laboratories.

★2392★ **Pennsylvania State University**
Center for Cell Research
117 Research Office Bldg.
University Park, PA 16802
Phone: (814)865-2407
Fax: (814)865-2413
W.C. Hymer, Ph.D., Dir.

Research Activities and Fields: Provides
space-flight opportunities for commercial projects in space and ground-based expertise for
sponsored programs on earth in three focus
areas: physiological testing, bioseparations, and
illumination. Physiological testing focuses on
spaceflown animals, tissues, and cells in pharmaceutical product testing, and development
and discovery research for aging, osteoporosis,
anemia, cardiovascular deconditioning, muscle
wastage, secretion disorders, immune suppression, gene regulation, bone development, regulation of cell function, protein crystal growth,
and other macromolecular assembly. Bioseparation focuses on continous flow electrophoresis and aqueous two phase partitioning. Illumination projects focus on developing photomet-
ric equipment for biological experimentation and
lighting for space and ground-based environments. **Publications:** Quarterly Newsletter.

★2393★ **U.S. Department of Defense**
Air Force Materiel Command
Air Force School of Aerospace Medicine
Brooks Air Force Base, TX 78235
Phone: (512)536-3207
Fax: (512)536-2371
Col. Kenneth R. Hart, Commander

Research Activities and Fields: Conducts
business in three areas: science and technology
divisions (Clinical Sciences, Crew Technology,
and Radiation Sciences); operational support;
and aeromedical education and training divisions (Education, Epidemiology, and Hyperbaric
Medicine). Technical and Veterinary Sciences
provide support. Products and services provided by the USAFSAM impact the USAF in crew
protection and performance enhancement; occupational, safety and health by making sure appropriate standards are followed to protect the
work force; and medical readiness in combat
casualty care and aeromedical evacuation.

★2394★ **U.S. Department of Defense**
Air Force Materiel Command
Crew Systems Directorate
Bioacoustics and Biocommunications
  Branch
AL/CFBB, Bldg. 441
2610 7th St.
Wright-Patterson AFB, OH 45433-7901
Phone: (513)255-3607
Dr. Charles Nixon, Chief

Research Activities and Fields: Branch conducts research and provides technical consultation on the broad category of effects on personnel of the wide variety of acoustic energy encountered in Air Force environments, with emphasis on biocommunications and audio
communications effectiveness. Present research and development efforts are centered on
audio communications effectiveness, with emphasis on auditory information processing,
voice control and voice warning, analog and digital speech systems, enhancement of vocoded
speech communications, chemical defense
communications, C3 audio communications,
audio communications countermeasures/
counter-countermeasures, and auditory mod-
els/neural nets. The Branch is active in major
programs such as the Speech Technology portion of the DARPA Strategic Computing Program, which provides voice control for strategic
functions; the voice channel of the Joint Tactical
Information Distribution System, which provides
battlefield information in essentially real time;
and is the field office of primary responsibility for
the Project Forecast II, Robotic Telepresence
Initiative.

★2395★ **U.S. Department of Defense**
Air Force Materiel Command
Crew Systems Directorate
Biodynamics and Biocommunications
  Division
ATTN: AL/CFB
Wright-Patterson AFB, OH 45433-6508
Phone: (513)255-3602
Fax: (513)255-2781
Dr. Thomas J. Moore, Chief

Research Activities and Fields: Division conducts a multidisciplinary research and development program to protect man against mechanical force environments, provide him with the
best protective equipment, and guarantee his
full performance capability. The Division's program includes basic research, exploratory development, advanced development, and operational systems support in the areas of: noise, impact, acceleration, vibration, locomotion, microgravity, pilot performance, aircraft operations,
communication effectiveness, aircrew protection, and emergency escape. Activities are carried out in these branches: Bioacoustics and
Biocommunications, Vulnerability Assessment,
Escape and Impact Protection, and Combined
Stress.

★2396★ **U.S. Department of Defense**
Air Force Materiel Command
Crew Systems Directorate
Combined Stress Branch

ATTN: AL/CFBS
Wright-Patterson AFB, OH 45433-6573
Phone: (513)255-5742
Fax: (513)255-9687
Dr. William Albery, Chief

Research Activities and Fields: The mission of the Combined Stress Branch is to study the effects of complex, sustained accelerations of air combat maneuvering on pilot performance and weapon system effectiveness. Research in the Branch has been concerned with the acceleration environments of high performance USAF aircraft. Subjects of interest include spatial disorientation, human operator workload, restraint and ejection system design, and the development of pilot-vehicle interface in future aircraft; especially human factors concerns of helmet-mounted displays and reclined seats. Currently, the major program of the Branch are the performance/mental workload evaluation of positive pressure breathing systems for acceleration protection and spatial disorientation research. The development of advanced acceleration protection systems (anti-G suits and their control valves), advanced oxygen systems, and systems for the monitoring of pilot physiological status is also a branch activity.

★2397★　U.S. Department of Defense
Air Force Materiel Command
Crew Systems Directorate
Escape and Impact Protection Branch
ATTN: AL/CFBE
Wright-Patterson AFB, OH 45433-6573
Phone: (513)255-3602
Fax: (513)255-2019
Dr. Francis S. Knox, III, Branch Chief

Research Activities and Fields: Branch develops crew protection technology for future Air Force systems development programs. Research efforts are aimed at crew protection against mechanical stress environments such as those encountered during emergency escape from aerospace vehicles. Branch's research spans a wide range of basic science issues, exploratory development efforts, and support for aeronautical systems engineering programs. Specific research programs include: establishment of design criteria for new protection equipment, exploration of new principles and techniques of impact and windblast protection, development of acceleration exposure-limit standards, experimental validation of mathematical models of human impact response, and test and evaluation of advanced as well as operational protection systems.

★2398★　U.S. Department of Defense
Air Force Materiel Command
Crew Systems Directorate
Human Engineering Division
2255 H St.
Wright-Patterson AFB, OH 45433-7022
Phone: (513)255-7580
Fax: (513)255-7596
Kenneth R. Boff, Chief

Research Activities and Fields: Division's programs are aimed at learning more about man's physical and mental performance capabilities as an element in modern complex systems. Specific areas of research interest in human engineering include vision, night vision, displays, design

support, simulation, work load, ergonomics, crewstations, chemical defense, and other human performance issues. Division comprises these units: Crew-Centered Cockpit Design Office (AL/CFA); Crew Station Integration Branch (AL/CFHI); Design Technology Branch (AL/CFHD); Ergonomics Analysis Branch (AL/CFHA); Performance Assessment and Interface Technology Branch (AL/CFHP); and Visual Display Branch (AL/CFHV).

★2399★　U.S. Department of Defense
Air Force Materiel Command
Crew Systems Directorate
Vulnerability Assessment Branch
ATTN: AL/CFBV
Wright-Patterson AFB, OH 45433-7901
Phone: (513)255-3665
Fax: (513)255-2781
Dr. Jnts Kaleps, Chief

Research Activities and Fields: Investigates human response to mechanical force exposures using predictive analytical modeling, mechanical human surrogates, and experimental studies. Modeling projects include predictive simulations of body motion during ejection into an airstream, aircraft crash landings, escape through an aircraft emergency escape chute, and automobile rollover crashes. A crew casualty assessment program addresses the danger to humans as a result of penetrating injuries from fragments, burn injuries from fires and explosions, toxicological effects from combustion gases, and hearing loss and organ damage from blast overpressures that may hinder or incapacitate aircraft personnel as a consequence of enemy combat fire. Mannequin development efforts include an advanced mannequin for testing ejection systems, research on the development of more biofidelic mannequin neck, the use of composite materials in mannequin segments for improved inertial and deformation properties, and the development of appropriate criteria for injury likelihood prediction as a function of measured mannequin responses. Also being developed is a floatation mannequin for testing and evaluating personal flotation devices.

★2400★　U.S. Department of Defense
Air Force Materiel Command
Occupational and Environmental Health
**　Directorate**
Noise Effects Branch
ATTN: AL/OEBN
2610 7th St.
Wright-Patterson AFB, OH 45433-7901
Phone: (513)255-3605
Fax: (513)476-7680
Maj. Robert Kull, Chief

Research Activities and Fields: The Noise Effects Branch develops the technology required to assess the environmental impact of noise and sonic booms produced in communities by Air Force aircraft operations. This includes: investigations to determine the noise radiation characteristics of aircraft during both flight and ground operations; studies on the effects of atmosphere, ground cover, and terrain on sound propagation; the development of computer-based models that can predict community exposure using psychophysical acoustic metrics; and the development of prototype instruments and

procedures to monitor exposure around Air Force installations. Branch also studies the effects of noise and boom exposure on humans, animals, and structure, including annoyance, startle, interference with sleep, and various other possible health effects; and develops response functions, criteria, and guidelines for human, animal, and structural exposure.

★2401★　U.S. Department of Defense
Air Force Materiel Command
Occupational and Environmental Health
**　Directorate**
Toxicology Division
OL AL HSC/OET, Bldg. 79
2856 G St.
Wright-Patterson AFB, OH 45433-7400
Phone: (513)255-3423
Fax: (513)255-1474
Lt. Col. Terry A. Childress, Director

Research Activities and Fields: Division has sole responsibility within the Air Force for identifying and quantitating toxic hazards created by chemical environments characteristic of advanced Air Force systems and operational situations. The ultimate purpose of the Division's research program is to provide valid medical guidelines for the prevention of and protection against such health hazards as may be encountered by Air Force personnel in the performance of their military duties.

U.S. Department of Defense
Armed Forces Institute of Pathology
Office of the Armed Forces Medical
**　Examiner**
Forensic and Aerospace Pathology
**　Division**
See: Entry 10171

U.S. Department of Defense
Armed Forces Institute of Pathology
Scientific Laboratories Department
Altitude and Hyperbaric Physiology
**　Division**
See: Entry 10176

★2402★　U.S. Department of Defense
Army Medical Research and Development
**　Command**
Army Aeromedical Research Laboratory
PO Box 577
Fort Rucker, AL 36362-5292
Phone: (205)255-6917
Fax: (205)255-6937
Col. David H. Karney, Commander

Research Activities and Fields: Activities of USAARL include: 1) conducting research and development on health hazards of Army aviation, tactical combat vehicles, and selected weapon systems; 2) assessing stress and fatigue in personnel operating these systems and developing countermeasures; and 3) assisting in the development of criteria upon which to base standards for entry and retention in Army aviation specialties. Principal areas of interest include medical study of visual/auditory functions, man-machine integration, physiological responses to operational environments, impact of continuous operations on individual and crew performance, medical defense against chemical agents, testing of aeromedical evacuation life support equipment, development of improved means of patient evacuation, and airworthiness.

★ 2403 ★ U.S. Department of Defense
**Naval Medical Research and Development
Command
Naval Aerospace Medical Research
Laboratory**
Naval Air Station
Pensacola, FL 32508-5700
Phone: (904)452-3286
Fax: (904)452-4479
Capt. Alfred J. Mateczun, Commanding Officer

Research Activities and Fields: NAMRL's mission is to conduct research, development, testing, and evaluation in aerospace medicine and allied sciences to enhance the health, safety, and readiness of Navy and Marine Corps personnel.

★ 2404 ★ U.S. Department of Transportation
**Federal Aviation Administration
Civil Aeromedical Institute**
PO Box 25082
AAM-3
Oklahoma City, OK 73125-5060
Phone: (405)954-1000
Fax: (405)954-4813
Dr. William E. Collins, Director

Research Activities and Fields: CAMI conducts research in civil aviation medicine directed toward: 1) preventing aircraft accidents; and 2) increasing survival rates associated with aircraft accidents. Studies are primarily in the fields of human factors, psychology, physiology, toxicology, cabin safety, restraint, ditching, and protective breathing equipment. Other areas of study include vision, human performance, and veterinary medicine. Institute also conducts programs in aircraft accident investigation; medical certification (more than 700,000 airmen); statistical studies from the airman data bank; occupational health; and medical education of physicians, pilots, flight inspectors, accident investigators, and flight attendants. **Additional Contact Information:** CAMI is located at the FAA Mike Moroney Aeronautical Center in Oklahoma City.

★ 2405 ★ U.S. Department of Transportation
**Federal Aviation Administration
Civil Aeromedical Institute
Aeromedical Research Division**
Mail Code AAM-600
PO Box 25082
Oklahoma City, OK 73125-5066
Phone: (405)954-4808
Fax: (405)954-4813
Dr. Jerry R. Hordinsky, Manager

Research Activities and Fields: Division provides the Federal Aviation Administration (FAA) and the Federal Air Surgeon with the capability to: resolve operational, regulatory, and administrative problems related to medical certification of pilots; define and optimize workload and performance in aviation-related activities; and improve protection and survival in hostile and adverse aspects of general and commercial aviation. Division comprises the Toxicology and Accident Research Laboratory, Protection and Survival Laboratory, and Aviation Physiology Laboratory.

★ 2406 ★ U.S. Department of Transportation
**Federal Aviation Administration
Civil Aeromedical Institute
Data Analysis Staff**
Mail Code AAM-601
6500 S. MacArthur Blvd.
PO Box 25082
Oklahoma City, OK 73125
Phone: (405)954-4108
Fax: (405)954-4813
Dr. Earl Folk, Research Mathematical Statistician

Research Activities and Fields: Studies involve the use of nonlinear models for toxicological data, probability models for identification of aircraft accident victims, and models of canine response to temperature and humidity factors; and analyses of data on various aspects of aviation and aviation safety (includes a cabin safety data bank and analyses of sled impact test data on various seat structures).

★ 2407 ★ U.S. Department of Transportation
**Federal Aviation Administration
Civil Aeromedical Institute
Human Resources Research Division**
Mail Code AAM-500
PO Box 25082
Oklahoma City, OK 73125
Phone: (405)954-6825
Fax: (405)954-4813
Dr. David J. Schroeder, Manager

Research Activities and Fields: Division conducts research on human factors and industrial and organizational research. Field and laboratory studies focus on human performance enhancement, human factors of complex systems and selection and training criteria for air traffic control and other critical positions. Also studies the performance impacts of automated ATC systems; the effects of aviation stressors and age on performance; general aviation simulations to improve aircraft displays and procedures; workforce performance optimization; and the performance impacts of organizational and technological change.

★ 2408 ★ U.S. Department of Transportation
**Federal Aviation Administration
Civil Aeromedical Institute
Protection and Survival Laboratory**
Mail Code AAM-630
6500 S. MacArthur Blvd.
PO Box 25082
Oklahoma City, OK 73125
Phone: (405)954-5555
Fax: (405)954-4813
Jeff Marcus, Director

Research Activities and Fields: Laboratory investigates problems concerning civil airmen and equipment in emergency conditions, such as function of oxygen systems, protective visual/breathing systems, seat/restraint/interior crash injury protection, emergency evacuation, flotation, and cabin safety. Principal areas of research interest are respiratory physiology, biomechanics of impact, human factors, and physical anthropology. Laboratory comprises the Biodynamics Research, Evacuation Research, Survival Research, and Cabin Safety Research units and the Physical Anthropology Support Staff.

★ 2409 ★ U.S. Department of Transportation
**Federal Aviation Administration
Civil Aeromedical Institute
Toxicology and Accident Research
Laboratory**
6500 S. MacArthur Blvd.
PO Box 25082
Oklahoma City, OK 73125-5066
Phone: (405)954-4866
Fax: (405)954-4813
Jerry R. Hordinsky, M.D., Division Manager

Research Activities and Fields: The Toxicology and Accident Research Laboratory conducts research to promote human factor safety in civilian aviation. Studies are concerned with: 1) medical evidence available from aircraft accidents, including the genesis of the injuries experienced in those accidents; and 2) effects of toxicants that may be present in post-crash fires or that may be otherwise introduced into the aviation environment.

★ 2410 ★ U.S. Department of Transportation
**Federal Aviation Administration
Medical Specialties Division**
400 7th St. SW
Washington, DC 20591
Phone: (202)366-6350
Fax: (202)366-6603
Dr. Robert S. Poole, Acting Dir.

Research Activities and Fields: Division functions as a program office for medical standards, certification policy, and aeromedical research and development. Principal area of research interest is clinical medicine.

★ 2411 ★ U.S. Department of Transportation
**Federal Aviation Administration
Medical Specialties Division
Biomedical and Behavioral Sciences
Branch**
800 Independence Ave. SW
Washington, DC 20591
Phone: (202)366-6910
Fax: (202)366-6603
Dr. William T. Shepherd, Manager

Research Activities and Fields: Branch's primary function is to develop research programs related to the requirements of other FAA organizations, including the Office of Flight Standards and the Office of Airworthiness. Research is typically conducted in-house by the Biomedical and Behavioral Sciences Branch or at the FAA's Civil Aeromedical Institute in Oklahoma City. Principal areas of research interest are aviation physiology, aviation psychology, aviation toxicology, and passenger and crew protection and survival.

★2412★ University of Illinois
Institute of Aviation Research Laboratory
1 Airport Rd., Bldg. Q5
Savoy, IL 61874
Phone: (217)244-8617
Fax: (217)244-8647
Dr. Christopher D. Wickens, Head

Research Activities and Fields: Examines human factors in aviation system design and operation and investigates issues of workload and effects of automation on pilot performance, including use of advanced display techniques such as color, motion, three-dimensional representation, and speech synthesis for presenting complex information related to decision making, navigation, and control. Develops computer-assisted instruction materials for pilot training and investigates the design and use of simulators for flight training. **Publications:** *ARL Technical Report* (irregularly); *Engineering Psychology Research Laboratory Technical Report* (irregularly). **E-mail Address:** cwickens@s.psych.uiuc.edu. **Formerly:** Institute of Aviation.

★2413★ Vanderbilt University
Center for Space Physiology and Medicine
AA-3228 Medical Center North
Nashville, TN 37232-2195
Phone: (615)343-6499
Fax: (615)343-8649
David Robertson, M.D., Dir.

Research Activities and Fields: Space physiology and medicine. Specific research activities include cardiovascular homeostasis in space, neuroendocrine control of intravascular volume, physiologic and pharmacologic influences on neural control of blood pressure, influence of mechanical deformation on electrophysiologic properties of the heart, pathophysiology of orthostatic hypotension, neurovestibular disturbances and impaired sympathetic activity in space flight, cause and treatment of anemia in space travel, muscle adaptation in weightlessness, in-flight pharmacokinetics, prevention of bone loss during space flight, effects of space travel on energy balance and body weight regulation, mathematical modeling of physiological responses, and equipment design for space application.

Chapter 7
Biomedical Engineering

Foundations & Other Funding Organizations

Private Foundations

★2414★ **Whitaker Foundation**
901 15th St., N.W. Ste. 1000
Washington, DC 20005
Phone: (202)408-1505
Fax: (202)408-1506
Miles J. Gibbons, Jr., President

Foundation Philosophy: The foundation supports six biomedical engineering research and education programs and a regional program of grants supporting Harrisburg, PA, area. Its Biomedical Engineering Research Grants program funds medical research projects which substantially involve the innovative use of engineering techniques or principles. Graduate Fellowships in Biomedical Engineering are awarded to assist talented engineering students to develop the skills necessary for a biomedical career. Biomedical Engineering Development Awards are designed to create centers of excellence in biomedical engineering education by establishing or enhancing academic programs at selected universities and medical schools in the U.S. The foundation also gives Special Opportunity Awards in in Biomedical Engineering. These awards are made for educational and research programs that emphasize educational innovations, interdisciplinary collaboration, institutional commitment, and national impact on the field of biomedical engineering. The Cost-Reducing Health Care Technologies program is administered jointly with the National Science Foundation and its purpose is to address the problem of escalating health care costs. Grants are awarded for innovative and multidisciplinary research that will contribute to the containment or reduction of health care costs without compromising the quality, effectiveness, or accessibility of the health care system. The Bioengineering for Disease Prevention and Control program is administered with the National Institutes of Health's National Center for Research Resources to support research on drug delivery systems, miniature sensors, and new methods of physiological monitoring. The Harrisburg Re-

gional Program grants are made in two areas: to improve science and math education from elementary school through higher education, and to help economically disadvantaged individuals become self-sufficient. **Giving Priorities:** In 1993, the foundation awarded 97% of its funding to support health programs, primarily biomedical engineering programs. Support includes research and development grants and graduate fellowships. The foundation awarded the remaining funds to other programs. **Typical Health-Related Recipients:** Cancer, Children's Health/Hospitals, Eyes/Blindness, Geriatric Health, Heart, Hospitals, Medical Education, Medical Rehabilitation, Medical Research, Mental Health, Research/Studies Institutes, Respiratory, Speech & Hearing. **Geographic Distribution:** US and Canada for research program; Harrisburg, PA, area for regional program; US only for other grant programs.

National & International Organizations

American Academy of Maxillofacial Prosthetics (AAMP)
See: Entry 3863

★2415★ **American Association of Electrodiagnostic Medicine (AAEM)**
21 2nd St. SW, Ste. 103
Rochester, MN 55902
Phone: (507)288-0100
Fax: (507)288-1225
Shirlyn A. Adkins, Exec.Dir.

Founded: 1953. **Members:** 3,500. **Description:** Practicing physicians who are active in electromyography and electrodiagnosis and who have made contributions to this field. Objective is to increase and extend knowledge of electromyography and electrodiagnostic medicine, and to improve patient care. **Publications:** *AAEM Case Reports*, periodic. Monograph. *Price:* Included in membership dues; $8/issue for nonmembers. • *AAEM Minimonographs*, 2-3/year. Monograph. *Price:* Included in membership dues; $10/issue for nonmembers. • *American Association of Electrodiagnostic Medicine--*

Membership Directory, annual. Membership Directory. *Price:* Included in membership dues; $15 for nonmembers. • *Guidelines*, periodic. *Price:* Included in membership dues; $8 for nonmembers. • *Muscle and Nerve*, monthly. *Price:* Included in membership. Also publishes course syllabi. **Formerly:** (1990) American Association of Electromyography and Electrodiagnosis.

★2416★ **American Institute for Medical and Biological Engineering (AIMBE)**
1200 G St. NW
Washington, DC 20005
Phone: (202)434-8737
Fax: (202)434-8707
Kevin W. O'Connor, Exec.Dir.

Founded: 1989. **Description:** Individuals with an interest in medical and biological engineering. Fosters exchange of ideas and information among members; works to establish a clear identity for the field and improve public awareness of members' activities; serves as liaison between members and government agencies. Conducts educational programs; promotes public interest in science and science education. **Publications:** *AIMBE News*, quarterly. Newsletter.

American Institute of Ultrasound in Medicine (AIUM)
See: Entry 11090

★2417★ **American Lithotripsy Society (ALS)**
13 Elm St.
Manchester, MA 01944
Phone: (508)526-8330
Fax: (508)526-4018
Wesley E. Harrington, CAE

Founded: 1987. **Members:** 900. **Description:** Promotes public awareness of Lithotripsy. (Lithotripsy is a non-invasive procedure to treat kidney stones and gall stones.) Disseminates information; conducts educational programs. **Publications:** *ALS Quarterly*, quarterly. Newsletter.

American Registry of Diagnostic Medical Sonographers (ARDMS)
See: Entry 11092

American Society of Echocardiography (ASE)
See: Entry 11095

★2418★ Association for the Advancement of Medical Instrumentation (AAMI)
3330 Washington Blvd., Ste. 400
Arlington, VA 22201
Phone: (703)525-4890
Free: 800-332-2264
Fax: (703)276-0793
Michael J. Miller, Pres.
Founded: 1965. **Members:** 6,500. **Description:** Clinical engineers, biomedical equipment technicians, physicians, hospital administrators, consultants, engineers, manufacturers of medical devices, nurses researchers and others interested in medical instrumentation. Purpose is to improve the quality of medical care through the application, development, and management of technology. Maintains placement service. Offers certification programs for biomedical equipment technicians and clinical engineers. Produces numerous standards and recommended practices on medical devices and procedures. Offers educational programs. **Publications:** *AAMI News*, monthly. Newsletter. Informs members on legislative and regulatory proposals, proposed and final AAMI standards, and association policies and programs. *Price:* Included in membership dues; $75/year for nonmembers. • *Biomedical Instrumentation & Technology*, bimonthly. Includes advertisers and annual subject indexes, book reviews, statistics, association news, information on medical instrumentation. *Price:* Included in membership dues; $60 for nonmembers. • *Directory of Members*, annual. Membership Directory. • *Medical Device Research Report*, bimonthly. Newsletter. Informs members of latest medical research information. *Price:* Included in membership dues. Also publishes technology analyses and reviews and medical device standards and recommended practices.

★2419★ Association for Applied Psychophysiology and Biofeedback (AAPB)
10200 W. 44th Ave., Ste. 304
Wheat Ridge, CO 80033
Phone: (303)422-8436
Free: 800-477-8892
Fax: (303)422-8894
Francine Butler, Ph.D., Exec.Dir.
Founded: 1969. **Members:** 2,000. **State Groups:** 35. **Description:** Persons interested in the "interrelationship of external feedback systems, states of consciousness, and the physiological mechanisms involved." Promotes rapid interchange of ideas and information among members. Offers Continuing Education Training Programs. Maintains numerous committees. **Publications:** *Biofeedback and Self Regulation*, quarterly. • Newsletter, 3/year. • *Proceedings of Annual Meeting*. Proceedings. **Formerly:** (1976) Biofeedback Research Society; (1988) Biofeedback Society of America.

★2420★ Biomedical Engineering Society (BMES)
PO Box 2399
Culver City, CA 90231
Phone: (310)618-9322
Rita M. Schaffer, Ph.D., Exec.Dir.
Founded: 1968. **Members:** 1,900. **Description:** Biomedical, chemical, electrical, and mechanical engineers, physicians, managers, and university professors representing all fields of biomedical engineering; students and corporations. Encourages the development, dissemination, integration, and utilization of knowledge in biomedical engineering. **Publications:** *Annals of Biomedical Engineering*, bimonthly. Journal. • *Biomedical Engineering Careers*. Brochure. • *BMES Bulletin*, quarterly. Bulletin. • *BMES Membership Directory*, annual. Membership Directory. *Price:* $75.

British Medical Ultrasound Society (BMUS)
See: Entry 11105

European Laser Association (ELA) (Association Europeenne du Laser — AEL)
See: Entry 11112

Foundation for Hand Research (FHR)
See: Entry 7877

★2421★ IEEE Engineering in Medicine and Biology Society (EMBS)
c/o Institute of Electrical and Electronics Engineers
345 E. 47th St.
New York, NY 10017
Phone: (212)705-7900
Fax: (212)705-4929
Members: 7,026. **Local Groups:** 37. **Description:** A society of the Institute of Electrical and Electronics Engineers. Concerned with concepts and methods of the physical and engineering sciences applied in biology and medicine, including formalized mathematical theory, experimental science, technological development, and practical clinical application. Disseminates information on current methods and technologies used in biomedical and clinical engineering. **Publications:** *Engineering in Medicine and Biology Magazine*, quarterly. Magazine. • *Transaction on Biomedical Engineering*, monthly.

IIT Research Institute
See: Entry 10436

★2422★ International Association of Orthotists and Prosthetists (Union Internationale des Techniciens Orthopedistes — INTERBOR)
108, rue Prince Baudouin
B-1080 Brussels, Belgium
Phone: 2 2525449
Fax: 2 2840782
Jacques Van Rolleghem, Admin.Gen.
Founded: 1958. **Members:** 70. **Languages:** English, French, German. **Description:** Organizations and individuals in 19 countries working to develop the science of orthotics and prosthetics. Conducts research and educational programs.

★2423★ International Conference on Mechanics in Medicine and Biology (ICMMB)
University of Michigan
2150 G.G. Brown Bldg.
Ann Arbor, MI 48109
Phone: (313)764-9910
Fax: (313)747-3170
Wen-Jei Yang, Coord.
Founded: 1977. **Description:** Organizes conferences and disseminates information on mechanics in medicine and biology worldwide. Conducts research; offers seminars and short courses. **Publications:** *Advances in Cardiovascular Physics*. • *Digest*, biennial. • *Directory of Conference Participants*, biennial. Directory. • *Proceedings of the International Conference on Mechanics in Medicine and Biology*, biennial.

★2424★ International Society of Electrocardiology (ISE)
University Department of Medical Cardiology
Royal Infirmary
10 Alexandra Parade
Glasgow G31 2ER, Scotland
Phone: 141 5523535
Fax: 141 5526114
Prof. Peter W. Macfarlane, Sec.
Founded: 1994. **Members:** 300. **Languages:** English. **Description:** Researchers and physicians in 25 countries in cardiovascular physiology and pathology, cardiology, biomathematics, biophysics, and computer science who are interested in electrocardiology. Sponsors International Committee on Electrocardiology to develop professional programs. **Publications:** *Proceedings*, annual.

★2425★ International Society of Electrophysiological Kinesiology (ISEK) (Societe Internationale de Kinesiologie Electrophysiologique)
Concordia Univ.
Psychology Dept.
7141 Surebrook St. W
Montreal, PQ, Canada H4B 1R6
Phone: (514)848-2231
Fax: (514)848-4545
Dr. H.W. Ladd, Pres.
Founded: 1965. **Members:** 500. **Languages:** English. **Description:** Experts in health and life sciences, biomedical engineering, and biophysics. Organizes meetings and carries out activities to advance research and teaching in the areas of electrophysiology, kinesiology, and bioengineering. Maintains placement service; conducts research programs; operates speakers' bureau. **Publications:** *Newsletter*, quarterly. Newsletter.

★2426★ International Society for Peritoneal Dialysis (ISPD)
GeorgeTown University Med. Center
3800 Resevoir Rd. NW, Ste. F6003-PHC
Washington, DC 20007
Phone: (202)784-3662
Fax: (202)687-2808
Dr. James F. Winchester, Sec.-Treas.
Founded: 1984. **Members:** 1,200. **Description:** Physicians, nurses, and biomedical engineers involved in peritoneal dialysis, a proce-

dure similar to artificial kidney machine dialysis but involving insertion of a tube into the abdomen to cleanse blood within the body. Seeks to advance knowledge of peritoneal dialysis through exchange and research. **Publications:** *Peritoneal Dialysis International*, bimonthly. *Price:* $10/year in addition to membership dues.

★2427★　International Society for Pharmaceutical Engineering (ISPE)
3816 W. Linebaugh Ave., No. 412
Tampa, FL 33624
Phone: (813)960-2105
Fax: (813)264-2816
Robert P. Best, Exec.Dir.

Founded: 1980. **Members:** 7,200. **Description:** Pharmaceutical, biotechnological, medical device, diagnostic, and cosmetic engineers and technicians in 40 countries who are responsible for designing, supervising, and maintaining process equipment, systems, and instrumentation in health care materials manufacturing facilities. Promotes information exchange between members and regulatory agencies; enhances productivity. Gathers and disseminates information; sponsors continuing education programs and seminars. Maintains speakers' bureau. **Publications:** Brochures, biweekly. • *International Society for Pharmaceutical Engineering--Newsletter*, monthly. Newsletter. *Price:* Included in membership dues. • *ISPE By-Laws and Membership*, annual. Membership Directory. Arranged alphabetically by name, by country, and by company. *Price:* Included in membership dues. • *Pharmaceutical Engineering*, bimonthly. Journal. Includes legislative, association, and membership news. Also contains new product information, buyers' directory, research reports, and case studies. **Formerly:** (1990) International Society of Pharmaceutical Engineers.

International Society for Prosthetics and Orthotics (ISPO)
(Societe Internationale de Prothese et Orthese)
See: Entry 4498

★2428★　International Union for Physical and Engineering Sciences in Medicine (IUPESM)
IUPESM Secretariat
National Research Council
Bldg. M-55, Rm. 393
Ottawa, ON, Canada K1A 0R8
Phone: (613)993-1686
Fax: (613)954-2216
Mr. O.Z. Roy, Sec.Gen.

Founded: 1982. **Members:** 2. **National Groups:** 35. **Languages:** English. **Description:** A joint project of the International Organization for Medical Physics and the International Federation of Medical and Biological Engineering. Promotes the application of engineering and physics to medicine. Represents the professional interests and views of engineering and physical scientists in the health care community. Coordinates and seeks backing for technology transfer to developing countries. Seeks to promote the coordination of IOMP and IFMBE activities on national and international levels. Promotes cooperation among members, related organizations, and governments. Organizes sci-

entific conferences and seminars. Sponsors regional support programs; maintains working groups.

★2429★　Medical Cybernetics Foundation (MCF)
Med. Design Center
3804 Arrow Lake Dr.
Jacksonville, FL 32257
Phone: (904)730-6916
Bob Frost, CEO

Founded: 1985. **Members:** 1,000. **Description:** Medical and medically affiliated professionals. Works to assist members in researching, developing, and marketing new medical machinery such as monitoring equipment and robotics systems; to improve life through medical cybernetics. (Medical cybernetics refers to the relationship between machinery and medical practices and procedures.) Sponsors charitable program. Compiles statistics.

★2430★　National Institute of Electromedical Information (NIEI)
PO Box 4633
Bay Terrace, NY 11360-4633
Phone: (212)696-9020
Fax: (212)447-1633
Stanley H. Kornhauser, Ph.D., Exec.Dir.

Founded: 1984. **Members:** 1,423. **Description:** Health care practitioners, medical educators, research scientists, and electromedical device manufacturers. Disseminates information on research, case histories, new and proposed theories, and clinical applications of electromedicine to professionals, laypersons, federal agencies, U.S. industry, and universities. (Electromedicine deals with the application of diagnostic, monitoring and prosthetic electromedical devices used in research and clinical settings as well as the application of therapeutic electric currents in the prevention and treatment of diseases.) Supports the development of programs and materials for the preparation of those studying electromedicine; fosters the establishment of programs and creation of partnerships that provide resource-sharing networks and professional linkage among clinicians, researchers, colleges and universities, health care institutions, electromedical equipment manufacturers, and other scientific and educational organizations. Encourages exchange of information through an interdisciplinary forum between researchers and clinicians and advises and coordinates matters of mutual interest between members and other organizations. Enhances the career awareness of secondary or postsecondary students in the emerging fields of electromedical technology. Funds research and educational projects. Develops standards and certification systems for determining the efficacy of electromedical devices. Offers tutorials. Maintains consulting service and speakers' bureau; compiles statistics. Operates placement service, hall of fame, and professional speciality programs. Administers the American College of Electromedicine, including an experimental external graduate degree program at City University Los Angeles/Graduate School of Electromedical Sciences. **Publications:** *American Journal of Electromedicine*, bimonthly. Journal. Includes case studies, original research docu-

mentation, interviews on state-of-the-art topics in electromedicine and product reports. • Books. • Bulletin, periodic. • *National Institute of Electromedical Information--Membership Directory*, annual. Membership Directory. *Price:* Included in membership dues. • *National Institute of Electromedical Information--Newsletter: What's New in Electromedicine*, monthly. Newsletter. Includes member news, abstracts, book reviews, and calendar of events. *Price:* Included in membership dues. • Proceedings, periodic. Also publishes book reviews and educational materials.

★2431★　National Institute for Rehabilitation Engineering (NIRE)
PO Box T
Hewitt, NJ 07421
Phone: (201)853-6585
Free: 800-736-2216
Donald Selwyn, Exec.VP

Founded: 1967. **Description:** Multidisciplinary research, training, and service organization providing custom-designed and custom-made tools and devices, along with intensive personal task-performance and driver training, to aid the handicapped person in becoming more self-sufficient and independent. Often an organization of "last resort" for permanently, severely, or multihandicapped persons, the NIRE is staffed by electronics engineers, physicists, psychologists, optometrists, and other volunteers who work as a team with the handicapped person. These specialists review the handicapped person's abilities, disabilities, and task-performance goals and are thus able to help advise, plan, and implement programs to increase the person's abilities to perform desired tasks, using a combination of methods involving different practitioners and disciplines. Staff members also adapt, modify, and construct equipment specially suited to the individual client's need. No handicapped person is denied the institute's services due to an inability to pay, and fees for others are based on each person's income and means. Conducts occasional seminars for the handicapped and for professionals serving the handicapped. Provides speakers and seminar participants for other agencies' programs. Compiles statistics. **Publications:** *Rehabilitation Newsletter*, quarterly. Newsletter. Features announcements of upcoming seminars. *Price:* Included in membership dues.

North American Society of Pacing and Electrophysiology (NASPE)
See: Entry 2869

★2432★　Society for Biomaterials (SFB)
6518 Walker St., Ste. 215
Minneapolis, MN 55426
Phone: (612)927-8108
Fax: (612)927-8127
Rosealee M. Lee, Business Mgr.

Founded: 1974. **Members:** 1,200. **Description:** Bioengineers and materials scientists; dental, orthopedic, cardiac, and other surgeons and scientists interested in developing biomaterials as tissue replacements in patients; corporations interested in the research manufacture of biomaterials. Provides an interdisciplinary forum for research in biomaterials. Promotes research, development, and education in the biomaterials sciences. **Publications:** *Bio-Materials Forum*, periodic. Newsletter. Reports on developments in the science of biomaterials; includes society news. *Price:* Free to members. • *International Directory-Biomaterials Education Programs*, biennial. • *Journal of Applied Biomaterials*, quarterly. Journal. *Price:* Included in membership dues. • *Journal of Biomedical Materials Research*, monthly. Journal. *Price:* Included in membership dues.

Society of Computed Body Tomography and Magnetic Resonance (SCBT/MR)
See: Entry 11133

Society of Magnetic Resonance
See: Entry 11135

Society for Psychophysiological Research (SPR)
See: Entry 7518

★2433★ Special Interest Group on Biomedical Computing (SIGBIO)
c/o William E. Hammond
Duke University Med. Center
Box 2914
Durham, NC 27710
Phone: (919)684-6421
Fax: (919)684-8675
William E. Hammond, Chairperson

Founded: 1967. **Members:** 1,006. **Description:** A special interest group of the Association for Computing Machinery. Biological, medical, behavioral, and computer scientists; hospital administrators; programmers and others interested in application of computer methods to biological, behavioral, and medical problems. Stimulates understanding of the use and potential of computers in the biosciences; encourages presentation of papers at medical and computer conferences and conventions. **Publications:** Newsletter, 4/year.

Research Centers

★2434★ Arizona State University Biomedical Engineering Laboratories
College of Engineering
COB, B-338
Tempe, AZ 85287
Phone: (602)965-3676
Fax: (602)965-8296
Eric J. Guilbeau, Prof./Chm.

Research Activities and Fields: Biomechanics and bioinstrumentation, including medical devices, artificial organs, biosensors, analysis of motion, and nuclear imaging. Studies cardiovascular, biochemical, and physiological systems in relation to biomedical engineering. Conducts an industrial associate program, develops F.D.A. protocols, provides industrial development support, and offers continuing medical education. **Publications:** Transactions; Proceedings.

Baylor College of Medicine NMR Laboratories
See: Entry 11142

★2435★ Boston University Design Laboratory
NeuroMuscular Research Center
44 Cummington St.
Boston, MA 02215
Phone: (617)353-9637
L. Donald Gilmore, Supvr.

Research Activities and Fields: Develops instrumentation for other NMRC laboratories. Provides researchers with electronic hardware and software technologies used to investigate neuromuscular performance in both the lab and clinical environment. Activities also include design of a surface electrode, and development of a system for evaluating the performance characteristics of back muscles.

★2436★ California State University, Sacramento Assistive Device Center
5025 ECS
6000 J St.
Sacramento, CA 95819-6027
Phone: (916)278-6422
Fax: (916)278-5949
Colette L. Coleman, Ph.D., Dir.

Research Activities and Fields: Aids for the handicapped, particularly augmentative communication devices and assessment techniques for matching the handicapped client with available devices, including assistive devices for communication, mobility, interfaces, and educational access. Specific research includes motor perfomance in disability, speech synthesis and recognition applied to individuals with disabilities, and technological approaches to severe disability.

★2437★ Carnegie Mellon University Biomedical Engineering Program
5000 Forbes Ave.
Pittsburgh, PA 15213
Phone: (412)268-2521
Fax: (412)268-7139
Michael M. Domach, Dir.

Research Activities and Fields: Molecular biophysics and cellular dynamics, biomaterials and biomechanics, signal processing and bioinstrumentation.

★2438★ Carnegie Mellon University Science and Technology Center
4400 5th Ave.
Pittsburgh, PA 15213
Phone: (412)268-3461
Fax: (412)268-6571
Dr. Lansing Taylor, Dir.

Research Activities and Fields: Interdisciplinary applications of fluorescence spectroscopy to basic research in cell biology, biophysics, and biochemistry, and to medical diagnostics. Specific interests include cell motility, stimulus-response coupling, development of fluorescence methods for medical diagnosis, development of digital imaging microscope workstations for quantification and three-dimensional analysis and a display of biological samples, multi-parameter flow cytometric analysis, and laser spectroscopy of biological molecules. **Formerly:** Center for Flurescence Research in Biomedical Sciences.

★2439★ Case Western Reserve University Rehabilitation Engineering Center
Cleveland Metro General Hospital
3395 Scranton Rd., Rm. H-611
Cleveland, OH 44109
Phone: (216)459-3480
P. Hunter Peckham, Ph.D., Dir.

Research Activities and Fields: Functional electrical stimulation (FES) in the restoration of muscle control or sensory function, particularly in the areas of lower and upper extremity deficits, scoliosis, spasticity, respiratory insufficiency, and bladder function. Studies focus on computer-controlled and implanted FES systems for paraplegic and quadraplegic users, patients with hemiplegia due to cerebral trauma or stroke, and patients with spinal cord injuries.

★2440★ Case Western Reserve University Resource for Biomedical Sensor Technology
Bingham Bldg., Rm. 112
10900 Euclid Ave.
Cleveland, OH 44106-7200
Phone: (216)368-2934
Fax: (216)368-8738
Prof. Chung-Chiun Liu, Dir.

Research Activities and Fields: Biomedical sensor and related instrumentation, including 1) development, fabrication, and characterization of microelectronic-based electrochemical sensors for biomedical applications; 2) application of microelectronic and micromachining technologies for the development of three-dimensional miniature physical and chemical sensors; and 3) development of packaging methods and biological assays to evaluate biocompatibility of biomedical sensors.

Center for Imaging and Pharmaceutical Research
See: Entry 10428

★2441★ Drexel University Biomedical Engineering and Science Institute
32nd & Chestnut Sts.
Philadelphia, PA 19104
Phone: (215)895-2215
Fax: (215)895-4983
Dr. Dov Jaron, Ph.D., Dir.

Research Activities and Fields: Medical ultrasound, biomaterials and biotechnology, sensors and bioelectrodes, biomechanics, cardiovascular dynamics and instrumentation, biomedical signal processing, and neural networks and systems. A close research relationship exists with schools in the Philadelphia area. **E-mail Address:** qmbiomed@dunx1.ocs.drexel.edu.

★2442★ Drexel University Fibrous Materials Research Center
Dept. of Materials Engineering
31st & Market Sts.
Philadelphia, PA 19104
Phone: (215)895-1640
Fax: (215)895-6684
Dr. Frank K. Ko, Dir.

Research Activities and Fields: Tough structural composites; engineering of textile structures for medical, geotechnical, and aerospace applications; and mathematical modeling, computer-aided design, and characterization of engineering properties of fibers and fibrous structures. Studies in textile structural composites include structural toughening of composites by 3-dimensional fiber architecture, fabric geometry models, 2- and 3-dimensional braided ceramic, metal matrix, thermoplastic and thermoset composites, aligned short fiber composites, multiaxial warp knit composites, CAD-CAM, and development of very complex shape (VCS) composites. Medical textile research is concerned with artificial ligaments, finger joint prostheses, orthopedic casts, fiber reinforced composites for bone fixation plates, and artificial tendons. Studies in engineering design and analysis of fibrous materials include the development of a database for high modulus linear fiber assemblies, CAD of non-woven fabrics, design curves for industrial fibers, objective assessment of conformability and aesthetics of fibrous structures, and geotextiles. **E-mail Address:** fko@cbis.ece.drexel.edu.

★ 2443 ★ Duke University
Engineering Research Center for Emerging Cardiovascular Technologies
237 Levine Science Research Ctr.
Box 90295
Durham, NC 27708-0295
Phone: (919)660-5137
Fax: (919)684-8886
Olaf T. Von Ramm, Ph.D., Codir.

Research Activities and Fields: Cardiovascular devices and technologies, including biosensors, implantable defibrillators, real-time 3-D ultrasound imaging equipment, custom integrated electronics, and systems design and simulation. Facilitates technology transfer and promotes interaction between engineering students and industrial investigators.

★ 2444 ★ Emory-Georgia Tech Biomedical Technology Research Center
Georgia Institute of Technology
Dept. of Chemical Engineering
Atlanta, GA 30332-0100
Phone: (404)894-2849
Fax: (404)894-2291
Dr. Ajit P. Yoganathan, Codir.

Research Activities and Fields: Cardiovascular mechanics, corneal mechanics, medical imaging, biomedical artificial intelligence, biomedical instrumentation, vascular biology, tissue engineering, telemedicine. **Publications:** Newsletter (three per year).

★ 2445 ★ Georgia Institute of Technology Bioengineering Center
Atlanta, GA 30332-0100
Phone: (404)894-7063
Fax: (404)894-2291
Prof. Ajit P. Yoganathan, Codirector

Research Activities and Fields: Biomechanics research, including biaxial mechanical properties in tissue, biomechanical design, cardiovascular fluid mechanics, cellular engineering and non-invasive blood flow measurement; tissue engineering; and bioelectrical research, including electromagnetic systems for measuring the electrical properties of tissue, medical device/systems for diagnostic and therapeutic applica-

tions, and the applications of either air- or wire-coupled electromagnetic energy to stimulate biofunction; rehabilitation research, which entails developing orthotic devices for patients with lower body dysfunction, evaluating functional electrostimulation, and observance of the parvocellular division of the red nucleus for analyzing movement control; and computer applications research, which involves signal processing, image processing, and visualization, medical informatics, and simulation techniques to assist in making decisions regarding diagnostic and therapeutic strategies.

★ 2446 ★ Georgia Institute of Technology Biomechanics Laboratory
Dept. of Mechanical Engineering
Atlanta, GA 30332-0405
Phone: (404)894-2768
Fax: (404)894-2291
Dr. Robert M. Nerem, Contact

Research Activities and Fields: Application of mechanics to biology and medicine, emphasizing cardiovascular research and problems that occur on the cellular level. Also studies implantable parts and devices, industrial bioprocessing, tissue engineering, and noninvasive diagnostics.

★ 2447 ★ Georgia Institute of Technology Georgia Tech Research Institute (GTRI)
400 Tenth St.
Atlanta, GA 30332
Phone: (404)894-3400
Fax: (404)853-0061
Adm. Richard Truly, V. Pres. and Dir.

Research Activities and Fields: Performs engineering, scientific, and economic research in the following broad areas: antennas, electromagnetics, and optics; artificial intelligence; biomedical engineering; chemical and mechanical sciences; computer research, including robotics, command, and control; economic research and business development assistance; electronic components and techniques, including microelectronics; electronic countermeasures; electronic systems; energy; environmental health sciences; material sciences; millimeter and submillimeter waves; radar; and systems analysis. Alternate energy research includes studies of solar, biomass, conservation, and applications. Conducts surveys to determine a community's strengths and weaknesses for attracting industry and targets industries best suited to them, u sing a computer-assisted decision technique. **Publications:** Annual Report, *GTRI Connector* (monthly), and *Research Horizons* (quarterly). **Formerly:** Engineering Experiment Station (1984).

★ 2448 ★ Illinois Institute of Technology Pritzker Institute of Medical Engineering
10 W. 32nd St.
Chicago, IL 60616
Phone: (312)567-5324
Fax: (312)567-5707
Dr. Robert Arzbaecher, Dir.

Research Activities and Fields: Neuromuscular studies, implantable systems for detection and control of cardiac arrhythmias, and closed-loop drug infusion systems, including a neuromuscular engineering program for re-enabling

paralyzed muscle. **Publications:** *Annual Report of Research*.

★ 2449 ★ Indianapolis Center for Advanced Research
Barn Hill Dr., MS. 313
Indianapolis, IN 46202-5120
Phone: (317)274-3745
Fax: (317)274-3318
Sid Johnson, CEO

Research Activities and Fields: Diagnostic and therapeutic applications of ultrasound, medical instrumentation, and advanced electronics. **Publications:** Newsletter (quarterly).

Institute for Applied Laser Surgery
See: Entry 12321

★ 2450 ★ Iowa State University of Science and Technology
Biomedical Engineering Program
1132 Veterinary Medicine Bldg.
Ames, IA 50011
Phone: (515)294-6520
Fax: (515)294-3932
Mary Helen Greer, In Charge

Research Activities and Fields: Biomedical instrumentation, surgical engineering, including interdisciplinary studies on instrumentation, surgical implant materials, mathematical modeling of biological systems, sensors for biomedical research, computer medical diagnostic programs, and applied physiology. **Formerly:** Biomedical Electronics Program.

★ 2451 ★ Johns Hopkins University
Middle Atlantic Mass Spectrometry Laboratory
725 N. Wolfe St.
Baltimore, MD 21205
Phone: (410)955-3022
Fax: (410)955-3420
Prof. Robert J. Cotter, Dir.

Research Activities and Fields: Maintains a Kratos CONCEPT 1H high resolution mass spectrometer, a UV-laser desorption mass spectrometer and a Bio-Ion plasma desorption mass spectrometer as a collaborative resource for researchers from the University, from other academic institutions, or from industry and government laboratories who have need of special instrumentation and assistance in mass spectral measurement, sample preparation, chemical derivatization, and interpretation of spectra. The facility emphasizes analysis of ions of high mass (greater than 2,000 amu) and analysis of non-volatile compounds. The high resolution mass spectrometer is equipped with an inhomogeneous high mass magnet and interfaced to a DS-90 data system, based upon the Data General Eclipse S-120 CPU with 256K MOS memory. The Laboratory also conducts in-house research focusing on the development of new instrumentation and instrumental techniques for mass spectral measurement.

Kettering-Scott Magnetic Resonance Laboratory
See: Entry 11147

Laser Technology Center
See: Entry 11148

Laval University
Saint-Francois-d'Assise Hospital Research
  Centre
See: Entry 11274

★2452★ **Louisiana Tech University**
Center for Rehabilitation Science and
  Biomedical Engineering
Biomedical Engineering Dept.
PO Box 3185
Ruston, LA 71272
Phone: (318)257-4562
Fax: (318)255-4175
Dr. Paul N. Hale, Jr., Dir.

Research Activities and Fields: Studies conditions leading to disabilities (systems physiology), develops and applies technology to assist disabled people, and develops expert systems in systems physiology and rehabilitation services. **E-mail Address:** phale@engr.latech.edu.

Massachusetts Institute of Technology
Center for Magnetic Resonance
See: Entry 11150

★2453★ **Massachusetts Institute of**
  Technology
Eric P. and Evelyn E. Newman Laboratory
  for Biomechanics and Human
  Rehabilitation
77 Massachusetts Ave., Rm. 3-146
Cambridge, MA 02139
Phone: (617)253-2277
Fax: (617)258-7018
Prof. Neville Hogan, Contact

Research Activities and Fields: Amputation prostheses, normal and pathological human neuromuscular systems, and diagnosis and therapy of muscular, skeletal, and joint malfunctions using an engineering approach. Studies include cybernetic limb and sensory prostheses, mobility aids for the blind, suppression of tremor, functional electrical stimulation, instrumentation for and kinematic studies of human movement, synovial joint mechanics, pathogenesis of osteoarthritis, biomechanics of the hip, knee, and ankle, musculoskeletal models for pathological diagnosis, and computer-aided surgical simulation. **Publications:** Excerpt from the Department of Mechanical Engineering Triennial Report; Bibliography. **E-mail Address:** neville@athena.mit.edu. **Formerly:** Technology and Human Rehabilitation Program (1975), Laboratory for Human Mechanics and Rehabilitation (1979). Laboratory absorbed MIT's Sensory Aids Evaluation & Development Center in 1986.

Massachusetts Institute of Technology
Laser Biomedical Research Center
See: Entry 11151

★2454★ **Mayo Biomedical Imaging**
  Resource
Mayo Clinic
200 1st St. SW
Rochester, MN 55901
Phone: (507)284-4937
Fax: (507)284-1632
Richard A. Robb, Ph.D., Dir.

Research Activities and Fields: Provides expertise and technology related to biomedical imaging, scientific visualization, computer graphics, computer workstations, and computer networks. Through professional consultation, advanced software and hardware systems, and technical support, investigators use the Resource for ongoing research studies, ad hoc projects, feasibility testing, and/or development of applications and systems to be subsequently installed in the user's library. Provides services in six major categories: 1) consultation on biomedical imaging and scientific visualization problems, needs and applications; 2) software packages (ANALYZE) for interactive display and quantitative analysis of multimodality, and multidimensional biomedical images; 3) drop-in center containing several computer workstations connected to a powerful network providing image processing software and computer graphics hardware; 4) hardware systems, including design and configuration of both standard and customized workstations for biomedical image processing; 5) network support for connectivity to the Resource and/or within the investigative laboratory; and 6) training and education in the use of Resource facilities and in biomedical imaging, scientific visualization and computer science. **E-mail Address:** rar@mayo.edu. **Formerly:** Mayo Biomedical Imaging Computer Resource (1991).

Medical College of Wisconsin
Biophysics Research Institute
See: Entry 11152

★2455★ **Michigan Consortium for**
  Enabling Technology
Michigan State Univ.
B241 W. Fee Hall
East Lansing, MI 48824-1316
Phone: (517)353-1940
Dr. William C. Hinds, Dir.

Research Activities and Fields: Design, development, and evaluation of enabling technology, or technology of relevance to the handicapper community. Specific interests in this area are 1) mobility devices; 2) communication devices that are not computer-related, such as speech aids, tactile aids, artificial hearing aids, and screen readers; 3) computer-aided systems to facilitate communication, including informational databases, computer switch interfaces, voice recognition devices for computer access and programming, and augmentation of communication hardware and software; 4) environmental design and control devices for worksite modification, recreation, home management systems, and building design; 5) manipulation devices for daily living activities and employment, including grip apparatus, orthotic systems, mouthpieces, and prostheses; and 6) robotics.

★2456★ **Milwaukee School of Engineering**
Biomedical Research Institute
PO Box 644
Milwaukee, WI 53201-1195
Phone: (414)277-7331
Dr. Vincent R. Canino, Dir.

Research Activities and Fields: Biomedical instrumentation systems, including the design and evaluation of extra-corporeal perfusion instrumentation. **E-mail Address:** canino@kirk.msoe.edu.

★2457★ **National Institute for**
  Rehabilitation Engineering
Box T
Hewitt, NJ 07421
Phone: (201)853-6585
Donald Selwyn, Dir.

Research Activities and Fields: Invention, design, construction, fitting, and servicing of special devices for individuals with any specific physical disability or combination of disabilities; time/motion analyses; job modification engineering; task-performance mobility; driver training; computer software adapted for people with handicapping conditions. **Formerly:** The Rehabilitation Engineering Institute.

★2458★ **National Science Foundation**
Directorate for Engineering
Division of Bioengineering and
  Environmental Systems
Bioengineering and Aiding Persons with
  Disabilities Program
4201 Wilson Blvd., Rm. 567
Arlington, VA 22203
Phone: (703)306-1319
John Enderle, Program Director

Research Activities and Fields: Program provides funding for fundamental and applied academic engineering research relevant to medical needs. To qualify for support, investigations should be directed toward engineering research associated with the characterization, restoration, or substitution of human structure, function, or control. Emphasis is on fundamental and applied research with a potential to produce medical-engineering technologies, especially those that could become medically valuable within 10 years. (Normally this medical-oriented research should have such a strong engineering component that direct clinical input to its activities is not required; however, clinicians may supply data or specimens necessary to conduct the engineering effort.)

New England Medical Center
Electromyography Laboratory
See: Entry 8405

★2459★ **New England Medical Center**
Image Analysis Laboratory
750 Washington St.
NEMC 854
Boston, MA 02111
Phone: (617)956-6178
Fax: (617)350-8350
William D. Selles, Mgr.

Research Activities and Fields: Image measurement and computer-assisted image analysis for use in patient care and in basic and applied research. Develops quantitative techniques to improve patient management and to facilitate the detection of diseases and their underlying mechanisms. Activities include automated analysis of muscle and nerve fibers, retinal image analysis for detection of glaucoma, and three-dimensional modeling of anatomy, especially models of the brain and spinal cord for use in medical instruction. Conducts extensive work in "remote consultation" with images for pathology and cardiology. **E-mail Address:** bill@amber.ial.nemc.org.

★2460★ New Jersey Institute of Technology
Center for Biomedical Engineering
323 Martin Luther King, Jr. Blvd.
Newark, NJ 07102
Phone: (201)596-3584
Fax: (201)596-8436
David Kristol, Dir.

Research Activities and Fields: Design of prosthetic devices (including knee joints, hip joints, and voice prostheses), measurement of fatigue using EMG signal processing, heart rate variability studies, hemorrhagic shock, echo cardiography, visual-evoked response, noninvasive measurement of burn areas, cardiac assist devices, clotting properties of human blood, intracranial pressure sensing, design and testing of prosthetic heart valves, modelling of circadian rhythm, modelling of the histamine H1 receptor, rehabilitation engineering, and modelling of the cardiovascular system.

★2461★ New York Institute of Technology
Science and Technology Research Center
8000 N. Ocean Dr.
Dania, FL 33004
Kenneth R. Solomon, Dir.

Research Activities and Fields: Ultrasonic techniques, nondestructive testing, high definition television systems, bandwidth compression techniques, medical application, medical instrumentation, and psychophysical studies and instrumentation.

New York Society for the Relief of the Ruptured and Crippled
See: Entry 7925

★2462★ Ohio State University
Biomedical Engineering Center
270 Bevis Hall
1080 Carmack Rd.
Columbus, OH 43210
Phone: (614)292-5570
Fax: (614)292-7301
J. Fredrick Cornhill, Ph.D., Dir.

Research Activities and Fields: Bioengineering developments of significance in the life and physical sciences, including studies in artificial organs, atherosclerosis, biofluid mechanics, biomaterials, biomechanics and gait analysis, biomolecular spectroscopy, database systems, functional muscle stimulation, image processing with cardiovascular, computer vision, and neuroscience applications, instrumentation, laser applications, mass transport, medical physics, modeling, molecular biology, neurosciences, orthopedics, psychophysiology, radiation therapy, rehabilitation engineering, sensory aids, and signal processing. **Publications:** Annual Report. **Formerly:** Outgrowth of Bio-Medical Engineering Program initiated in 1965.

Ohio State University
George C. Paffenbarger Dental Research Laboratory
See: Entry 4005

Orthopaedic Institute
Department of Bioengineering
See: Entry 9944

Orthopaedic Research Institute
See: Entry 9945

Orthopedic Engineering and Research Center
See: Entry 9946

Pennsylvania State University
Artificial Heart Research Project
See: Entry 2919

Pittsburgh NMR Institute
See: Entry 11153

★2463★ Polytechnical School of Montreal
Research Group in Biomechanics and Biomaterials
Institut de genie biomedical
2900, boulevard Edouard-Montpetit
C.P. 6079, succursale A
Montreal, PQ, Canada H3C 3A7
Phone: (514)340-4378
Fax: (514)340-4611
L'Hocine Yahia, Dir.

Research Activities and Fields: Biomechanical behavior of the musculoskeletal system, including the following: modelling of the behavior of human joints and biological tissues; graphic representation of biological structures; biomechanics and microstructure of biological tissues and artificial substitutes; computer-aided design and manufacturing of orthopedic and rehabilitation devices; and stress analysis of knee implants.

★2464★ Prosthetics Research Study
720 Broadway, 3rd Fl.
Seattle, WA 98122
Phone: (206)328-3116
Dr. Ernest M. Burgess

Research Activities and Fields: Wound healing and limb viability, prosthesis research and development, mobility aids and artificial limbs, functional electrical physiological response, pain control, neuromuscular assist devices, electrical osteogenesis, mechanical engineering and automated fabrication of prosthetic components and mobility aids, and amputation surgery and post-surgical management.

★2465★ Purdue University
Center for Biomolecular Nuclear Magnetic Resonance, Structure, and Design
Dept. of Chemistry
West Lafayette, IN 47907
Phone: (317)494-5200
Fax: (317)494-0239
Patricia Lodi, Dir.

Research Activities and Fields: Provides nuclear magnetic resonance (NMR) instrumentation, computers, and molecular modeling graphics workstations to biomedical researchers in the Midwest. Core research and development is conducted to improve and extend capabilities and to find new biomedical applications for NMR instrumentation. The facility's areas of specialization include high-resolution NMR studies of the structure and dynamics of biopolymers and other biological macromolecules, investigation of enzyme mechanisms, and noninvasive studies of viruses, bacteria, tissues, living cells, and intact organisms. **Publications:** Annual Report. **E-mail Address:** david@chem.purdue.edu.

★2466★ Purdue University
William A. Hillenbrand Biomedical Engineering Center
A.A. Potter Engineering Center, Rm. 204
West Lafayette, IN 47907
Phone: (317)494-2995
Fax: (317)494-0811
W.A. Tacker, Jr., Act.Dir.

Research Activities and Fields: Cardiology, cancer therapy, and biomedical engineering, including preservation of the heart during and following an attack, emergency cardiac pacing, ventricular fibrillation, electrosurgery, heat therapy for cancer, cardiopulmonary resuscitation, automatic control of blood pressure, vascular graft prothesis materials, and skeletal muscle assistance of left ventricular failure. Research emphasis is on the creation and development of medical devices and procedures. **Formerly:** Biomedical Engineering Center.

Radiation Oncology Research & Development Center
See: Entry 11154

Rancho Rehabilitation Engineering Program
See: Entry 12742

★2467★ Regenstrief Institute for Health Care Research
1001 W. 10th St.
Indianapolis, IN 46202
Phone: (317)630-7604
Fax: (317)630-6962
Dr. Charles Clark, Codirector

Research Activities and Fields: Health care, including use of computers in health care delivery, use of industrial engineering methods in analyzing medical systems, and use of engineering and computer techniques to improve medical diagnosis and therapy.

★2468★ Rice University
Bioengineering Research Institute
PO Box 1892
Houston, TX 77251
Phone: (713)527-4954
Fax: (713)285-5154
Dr. Larry V. McIntire, Dir.

Research Activities and Fields: Application of engineering skills to problems in biology and medicine, including cellular and tissue engineering, studies on circulation assistance devices, cardiovascular tissue mechanics, blood proteins, effects of physical forces on various components of blood, fluid mechanics and transport processes related to cardiovascular system, hematologic complications with prostheses, rheology, fluid mechanics of blood and blood flow, tissue culture reactor evaluation, biochemical reactor engineering, applications of artificial intelligence in bioreactor control and dynamics, plant cell bioreactors, bioseparation systems, and development of in vitro methods for studying cellular mechanisms of thrombosis and atherogenesis. **E-mail Address:** ibb@rice.edu.

★ 2469 ★ **Rockefeller University**
Laboratory of Electronics
1230 York Ave.
New York, NY 10021
Phone: (212)327-8613
Fax: (212)327-7974
Dr. Robert L. Schoenfeld, Head

Research Activities and Fields: Applies computer engineering capabilities (microprocessor-based technology combined with programming methodology and software tools) to biomedicine, including medical diagnosis, prosthesis, and rehabilitation medicine. Conducts with biomedical investigators collaborative experiments involving computer-based measurements of activity: food and drink ingestion, heart rate, nerve and muscle activity, spectral analysis and stimulus patterning in nerve and muscle recording, neurophysiological and psychological experiments, control and data acquisition in analytical chemistry and mass spectrometry, and visual, postural, and neuromuscular research. Develops new technologies in the use of biological laboratory computers.

★ 2470 ★ **Sela, Inc.**
545 W. End Ave.
New York, NY 10024
Phone: (212)787-7925
Fax: (212)580-2731
Jon Speller, Dir.

Research Activities and Fields: Metals extraction and medical electronics. Conducts new product development for a variety of clients.

★ 2471 ★ **Smith-Kettlewell Eye Research**
Institute
Rehabilitation Engineering Center
2232 Webster St.
San Francisco, CA 94115
Phone: (415)561-1619
Fax: (415)561-1610
Dr. John A. Brabyn, Codirector

Research Activities and Fields: Design and development of sensory aids for blind, visually-impaired, and deaf-blind persons. **Publications:** Annual Report; *Smith-Kettlewell Technical File* (quarterly do-it-yourself journal published in braille, IBM diskette, and cassette).

★ 2472 ★ **Texas A&M University**
Human Systems Engineering Laboratory
College Station, TX 77843-3120
Phone: (409)845-5532
Fax: (409)845-4450
Dr. Gerald E. Miller, Dir.

Research Activities and Fields: Rehabilitation engineering, man-machine interfacing, artificial organs, biomedical sensors, physiological simulation, and physiological control systems analysis, including development of devices to aid handicapped individuals, development of artificial heart designs, development of neurological sensors, and development of voice, brain wave, and eye tracking controlled robotic and computer systems. **Publications:** Laboratory Report (annually).

Texas Scottish Rite Hospital for Children
Research Department
See: Entry 8433

★ 2473 ★ **Tulane University**
Biomaterials Laboratory
School of Medicine
1430 Tulane Ave.
S.L. 32
New Orleans, LA 70112-2699
Phone: (504)588-2273
Fax: (504)584-2722
Steven Cook, Dir.

Research Activities and Fields: Biomaterials, including study of the properties of porous materials and materials-bone interfaces; surface studies of tissue-implant interactions; and corrosion resistance analysis, especially degradation characteristics of materials in an in vivo environment. Conducts histological and microradiographic evaluations of bone and implant composites.

UCI / AMI Magnetic Resonance Imaging
Center
See: Entry 11156

U.S. Department of Defense
Air Force Materiel Command
Crew Systems Directorate
Biodynamics and Biocommunications
Division
See: Entry 2395

U.S. Department of Health and Human
Services
National Heart, Lung, and Blood Institute
Division of Heart and Vascular Diseases
Devices and Technology Branch
See: Entry 2937

U.S. Department of Health and Human
Services
National Institute for Occupational Safety
and Health
Physical Sciences and Engineering Division
See: Entry 9831

U.S. Department of Health and Human
Services
National Institute for Occupational Safety
and Health
Physical Sciences and Engineering Division
Engineering Control Technology Branch
See: Entry 9832

★ 2474 ★ **University of Akron**
Institute for Biomedical Engineering
Research
Engineering Research Center
Akron, OH 44325-0302
Phone: (216)972-6610
Fax: (216)374-8834
Dr. Stanley E. Rittgers, Dir.

Research Activities and Fields: Biomedical engineering, using and coordinating expertise and resources of biological, medical, engineering, and other scientific disciplines in greater Akron area for conducting research and promoting educational programs at the University, area hospitals, and the College of Medicine. **Publications:** *IBER Update* (quarterly newsletter). **E-mail Address:** iber@guts.biomed.uakron.edu.

★ 2475 ★ **University of Alabama at**
Birmingham
Regional Maxillofacial Prosthetics
Treatment and Training Center
1813 6th Ave. S., B-50
Univ. Sta.
Birmingham, AL 35294
Phone: (205)934-3356
Fax: (205)975-6519
Dr. Kirk Gardner, Dir.

Research Activities and Fields: Methods and materials for maxillofacial prostheses, also clinical aspects of fabrication techniques and basic industrial and laboratory research and testing of new and improved materials in polymers, silicones, and rubbers to be used as skin substitutes. **Publications:** Annual Project Reports to sponsors. **Formerly:** Feasibility Study for Maxillofacial Prosthetics (1968).

★ 2476 ★ **University of Arizona**
Clinical / Biomedical Engineering
Dept. of Electrical & Computer Engineering
Engineering Bldg. 104, Rm. 504
Tucson, AZ 85721
Phone: (520)621-4462
Fax: (520)621-8076
Prof. Kenneth Mylrea, Contact

Research Activities and Fields: Collection, analysis, and display of patient data in the operating room.

University of California, Irvine
Beckman Laser Institute and Medical Clinic
See: Entry 11160

University of California, Irvine
Laser Microbeam Program (LAMP)
See: Entry 11162

★ 2477 ★ **University of California, Los**
Angeles
Crump Institute for Biological Imaging
23-138 CHS
UCLA Sch. of Med.
10833 LeConte Ave., Rm. 23
Los Angeles, CA 90095-1735
Phone: (310)825-6539
Fax: (310)825-6267
Dr. Michael E. Phelps, Dir.

Research Activities and Fields: Biological imaging technologies, including positron emmision tomography; autoradiographic images for in viro and in vitro assays of biochemical and biological process in tissue preparations; fluorescent microscopy to provide images of changing chemical environments in tissue and isolated cell preparations; and image based communication and educational systems using game strategies, expert systems, knowledge navigators, and personal computers. **Formerly:** Crump Institute for Medical Engineering.

★2478★ University of California, Los Angeles
Man-Machine-Environment Systems Laboratory
Dept. of Materials Science & Engineering
5731 Boelter Hall
405 Hilgard Ave.
Los Angeles, CA 90024
Phone: (310)825-5534
Fax: (310)206-7353
Dr. John Lyman, Head

Research Activities and Fields: Man-task, man-environment, and biomedical engineering and system theory, including experimental and mathematical studies of human information processing, man-computer interfacing, skilled neuromuscular performance, effects of stress environments, and self-organizing processes. **Publications:** *Biotechnology Laboratory Reports.*

★2479★ University of California, San Diego
Institute for Biomedical Engineering
9500 Gilman Dr., 0412
La Jolla, CA 92093-0412
Phone: (619)534-4272
Fax: (619)534-5722
Dr. Shu Chien, Dir.

Research Activities and Fields: Biomedical engineering, emphasizing structure-function relationships in normal and pathological tissues and the development of biological substitutes to restore, maintain, or improve tissue functions. Tissue studies focus on the heart, blood, lung, kidney, liver, pancreas, muscle, bone, cartilage, tendon, ligament, skin, nerve, brain, retina, and cochlea. **E-mail Address:** schien@ucsd.edu.

University of California, San Francisco
Mass Spectrometry Facility
See: Entry 2666

★2480★ University of Cincinnati
Herman Schneider Laboratory of Basic and Applied Research
College of Engineering
PO Box 210018
Cincinnati, OH 45221-0018
Phone: (513)556-5438
Fax: (513)556-3626

Research Activities and Fields: Interdisciplinary studies involving aerospace, biomedical, chemical, civil, electrical, environmental, mechanical, metallurgical, and nuclear engineering, materials science, and applied mechanics.

★2481★ University of Colorado
Clinical Mass Spectrometry Research Resource
4200 E. 9th Ave.
Denver, CO 80262
Phone: (303)270-7286
Fax: (303)270-8067
Dr. P.V. Fennessey, Codirector

Research Activities and Fields: Clinical applications of mass spectrometry, including gas chromatograph mass spectrometry, high resolution mass spectrometry, bioactive substances, and application of fast atom bombardment mass spectrometry to biomolecules. Emphasizes methods for synthesis of internal standards for the quantitative analysis of bioactive molecules found in physiological fluids, identification of steroid profiles in patients with biochemical and pathological irregularities, and stable isotope studies for measuring the utilization of important metabolic intermediates in humans. **E-mail Address:** fennessey-p@titania.hsc.colorado.edu.

★2482★ University of Florida
Bioglass Research Center
JHMHC, J-413
Gainesville, FL 32610
Phone: (904)462-0805
Fax: (904)462-0806
Dr. Larry L. Hench, Dir.

Research Activities and Fields: Development and clinical trials of devices made from Bioglass materials in medical and dental applications and basic investigations into the mechanisms of tissue response to bioactive materials.

★2483★ University of Florida
Biomedical Engineering Center
Dept. of Materials Science
MAE 317
PO Box 6400
Gainesville, FL 32611
Phone: (904)392-4907
Fax: (904)392-3771
Dr. Eugene P. Goldberg, Dir.

Research Activities and Fields: Biomaterials and biomedical engineering, with emphasis on biopolymer studies. Current projects include surface modification of ocular implants, viscoelastic polymer solutions for opthalmic surgery, hydrogel synthesis and properties, microsphere and antibody targeted drug delivery biopolymers, biomimetic surfaces, radiation polymerization, polymer implant biocompatibility studies, mammary implants, vascular grafts and stents, surface modified catheters, polymer and viscosurgical polymer solutions to prevent surgical trauma, polymer gels and films to prevent surgical adhesions, endoscopic devices, stimulated wound healing, and polymer matrices for cell regeneration. **Publications:** Project Summary Research Reports.

University of Florida
Cardiovascular Laser Lab
See: Entry 11166

★2484★ University of Florida
Center for Ambulatory Studies
930 NW 8th Ave.
Gainesville, FL 32601
Phone: (904)375-0607
Fax: (904)375-6111
Dr. Mark Kane Goldstein, Dir.

Research Activities and Fields: Behavioral and biomedical engineering, including remote monitoring of ambulatory patients and behavioral aspects of chronically ill outpatients, precision measurement of health-related behaviors, and study of simulated breast with lumps for training in breast self-examination for cancer detection.

★2485★ University of Florida
NMR Imaging and Spectroscopy In Vivo Resource
Dept. of Biochemistry & Molecular Biology
Box 100245
Gainesville, FL 32610-0245
Phone: (904)392-3375
Fax: (904)392-2953
Thomas H. Mareci, Ph.D., Prin. Investigator

Research Activities and Fields: Development of techniques and instrumentation for nuclear magnetic resonance imaging and in vivo spectroscopy. Projects include radio frequency coil and gradient coil development, localization techniques for spectroscopy, and development of image methodology. Biological applications of in vivo are concerned with spectroscopy in tumor detection, tumor response to therapy, imaging and spectroscopy of spinal cord injury and repair, and optic neuritis. **E-mail Address:** thmareci@ufnmr.health.ufl.edu.

★2486★ University of Illinois at Chicago
Research Resources Center
901 S. Wolcott Ave., Rm. E102
Chicago, IL 60612-7341
Phone: (312)996-7600
Fax: (312)996-0539
Dr. C.E. Brown, Dir.

Research Activities and Fields: Electronic and mechanical instrumentation, environmental stress, biostatistics, micro and mini computer programming and databases, atomic force/tunneling microscopy, electron microscopy, atomic absorption spectrometry, nuclear magnetic resonance spectrometry, mass spectrometry, flow cytometry, and protein sequencing/peptide synthesizing. **Publications:** Annual Users Report. **E-mail Address:** charlieb@uicvm.uic.edu.

★2487★ University of Kentucky
Graduate Center for Biomedical Engineering
208 Wenner-Gren Research Lab
Rose St.
Lexington, KY 40506-0070
Phone: (606)257-2894
Fax: (606)257-1856
Charles F. Knapp, Dir.

Research Activities and Fields: Applies engineering principles and practices to medical and biological problems in such areas as mechanics, fluids, mass transfer, instrumentation, and laboratory experimentation.

★2488★ University of Kentucky
Wenner-Gren Research Laboratory
Graduate Center for Biomedical Engineering
Lexington, KY 40506-0070
Phone: (606)257-2894
Fax: (606)257-1856
Dr. Charles F. Knapp, Dir.

Research Activities and Fields: Biodynamics of cardiopulmonary and musculoskeletal systems, biocontrol systems analysis, biosignal processing, and biomaterial and tissue responses to electrical stimulation.

**★ 2489 ★ University of Michigan
Bioelectrical Sciences Laboratory**
3304 GG Bldg.
Ann Arbor, MI 48109-2125
Phone: (313)764-9588
Fax: (313)936-1905
Prof. Charles Cain, Dir.

Research Activities and Fields: Bioelectrical sciences, including bioinstrumentation, data acquisition, signal analysis applied to speech, eye movements, hearing, and neurological systems. Develops biosensors in conjunction with the microcircuits laboratory. Also performs clinical studies on techniques developed from the above studies.

**★ 2490 ★ University of Michigan
Bioengineering Laboratory**
3010 H.H. Dow Bldg.
Ann Arbor, MI 48109
Phone: (313)763-5267
Fax: (313)763-0959
Henry Wang, Dir.

Research Activities and Fields: Sensor probes for the measurement of biochemicals in vivo and in process streams, evaluation of compatibility of materials in contact with blood, and development of procedure for measuring rate of thrombus development on artificial materials in living animals, including facilitation of transport across membranes containing reactive species, with applications in water purification by dialysis and reverse osmosis and in transport of nutrients of drugs in biological tissues.

**University of Michigan
Biomaterials Research Center**
See: Entry 4033

**★ 2491 ★ University of Michigan
Experimental Pathology Laboratory**
5223 School of Dentistry
1101 N. University Ave.
Ann Arbor, MI 48109
Phone: (313)747-4326
Dr. Carl T. Hanks, Contact

Research Activities and Fields: Biocompatibility of materials meant for use in the human body. Current studies include diffusion of molecules in various biological environments, cellular chemotaxis and adhesion to synthetic substrates, cytotoxicity to eukaryotic cells by materials, differentiation of various cell types on synthetic and natural substrates, and macrophage-assisted lymphocytic transformation.

**University of Michigan
Orthopaedic Research Laboratories**
See: Entry 9948

**★ 2492 ★ University of Montreal
Biomedical Modeling Research Group
(BMRG)**
Institut de genie biomedical
C.P. 6128, succursale A Centre-Ville
Montreal, PQ, Canada H3C 3J7
Phone: (514)343-7515
Fax: (514)343-6112
Fernand A. Roberge, Dir.

Research Activities and Fields: Computer simulation and mathematical modeling in cardiac electrophysiology and biomechanics of joints. **E-mail Address:** roberge@igb.umontreal.ca.

**★ 2493 ★ University of Montreal
institute of Biomedical Engineering**
Faculte de medicine
C.P. 6128 succursale A
Montreal, PQ, Canada H3C 3J7
Phone: (514)343-6357
Fax: (514)343-6112
Prof. A.-Robert LeBlanc, Dir.

Research Activities and Fields: Cardiac electrophysiology, biomechanics, electrocardiology, biomedical modelling, neuromuscular physiology, and clinical engineering. **Publications:** Annual Report. **E-mail Address:** leblanc@igb.umontreal.ca.

**★ 2494 ★ University of New Hampshire
Biomedical Engineering Center**
Dept. of Electrical & Computer Engineering
Durham, NH 03824
Phone: (603)862-1357
Fax: (603)862-2030
Dr. John R. LaCourse, Dir.

Research Activities and Fields: Medical instrumentation, including studies of surgical electrotechnology, ocular pulse, fiber optic-based sensors, prosthetic devices, applications of robots, rehabilitation engineering and instrumentation, workplace assessment instrumentation, and blood vessel transfer properties. **E-mail Address:** john.lacourse@unh.edu. **Formerly:** Clinical Engineering Center (1985).

**University of Pennsylvania
Metabolic Magnetic Resonance Research
and Computing Center**
See: Entry 11172

**University of Quebec at Trois-Rivieres
Research Group in Membrane
Biotechnology**
See: Entry 2735

**University of Rochester
Rochester Center for Biomedical
Ultrasound**
See: Entry 11174

**★ 2495 ★ University of Texas at Austin
Biomedical Engineering Program**
Engineering Science Bldg. 610
Austin, TX 78712-1084
Phone: (512)471-3604
Fax: (512)471-0616
Dr. Lee E. Baker, Dir.

Research Activities and Fields: Application of scientific and engineering knowledge to the solution of medical problems. Past projects have dealt with electrical impedance to measure cardiac function and to detect microbubbles in blood and tissue during decompression, a device for measuring visual contrast sensitivity at various spatial frequencies, a totally implantable transducer for measurement of epidural pressure, the use of microthermocouples to measure the safety of laser radiation, diagnostic applications of tissue fluorescence, image analysis by computer, cryopreservation of blood and tissues, quantitative thermographic imaging, electrosurgical safety, thrombosis on injured vessel and atherosclerotic surfaces and on polymeric biomaterials, pulsatile-flow cardiopulmonary bypass, chromatographic features of polar and nonpolar cardiac glycosides, hyperthermia in cancer therapy, effects of coenzyme Q-10 on cardiac function, biodegradable polymer implants for use in surgery, computer graphics analysis of sport biomechanics, rheology of synovial fluids, robotic surgical lasers, laser-tissue interaction, structure and function of hybrid proteins, and microvascular analysis of burn wounds. **E-mail Address:** burks@ece.utexas.edu. **Formerly:** Biomedical Engineering Laboratory.

**★ 2496 ★ University of Texas
Southwestern Medical Center at Dallas
Joint Program in Biomedical Engineering**
5323 Harry Hines Blvd., Rm. G8.248
Dallas, TX 75235-9130
Phone: (214)648-2052
Fax: (214)648-2979
Prof. Robert C. Eberhart, Ph.D., Chm.

Research Activities and Fields: Biomedical engineering, including studies in magnetic resonance, gamma and ultrasound image analysis, orthopedics, human performance, biocompatible materials, biomechanics, artificial organs, biosensors, soft tissue biomechanics, neurological signal acquisition and analysis, and recombinant DNA technology. **Publications:** *BME Information* brochure; *BME Student Activity Reports.* UTA offers master's and doctoral programs in biomedical engineering and internships in clinical engineering and local bioengineering industry.

**University of Texas Southwestern Medical
Center at Dallas
Mary Nell and Ralph B. Rogers Magnetic
Resonance Center**
See: Entry 11175

**University of Utah
Artificial Heart Research Laboratory**
See: Entry 2979

**★ 2497 ★ University of Utah
Center for Biopolymers at Interfaces**
2220 Merrill Engineering Bldg.
Salt Lake City, UT 84112
Phone: (801)581-5455
Fax: (801)585-5151
Dr. Karin D. Caldwell, Dir.

Research Activities and Fields: Adsorption or binding of proteins and other biomolecules onto surfaces, including studies of comprehension and control of protein adhesion to polymeric surfaces, biocompatability, surface modification, analysis of protein conformational changes, and emulsion and particle characterization. Activities focus on tear protein deposits on contact lenses, novel materials and surfaces for protein separation, sensor coatings for medical and biotechnological applications, new surface treatments for medical devices and diagnostic products, surface treatments for improving acceptance of intraocular lenses, and immobilized enzymes for the biotechnology industry. **Publications:** *Biopolymers at Interfaces* (quarterly newsletter).

★2498★ University of Utah
Center for Engineering Design
3176 Merrill Engineering Bldg.
Salt Lake City, UT 84112
Phone: (801)581-6499
Dr. Stephen C. Jacobsen, Dir.

Research Activities and Fields: Robotic design and control, including teleoperated and entertainment robots; actuator technology; touch sensors; micro-electromechanical systems; biomechanics; bioengineering; rehabilitation research, including projects in artificial limb design; and micro pumps and fluid delivery systems. **Formerly:** Center for Biomedical Design.

University of Utah
Dixon Laser Institute
See: Entry 11176

★2499★ University of Utah
Institute for Biomedical Engineering
803 N., 300 W.
Salt Lake City, UT 84112
Phone: (801)581-6991
Fax: (801)581-4044
Don B. Olsen, Dir.

Research Activities and Fields: Design, development, and fabrication of cardiac assist devices, cardiac replacement devices with animal implantation and complete follow-up studies, basic physiologic and psychophysical studies of the effects of electrical stimulation in the scala tympani of deaf human volunteers, testing of new artificial kidneys, peritoneal access devices for peritoneal dialysis, drug metabolism in patients with end state renal disease, dialysis with high flux dialysers, research with chemical effect field transistors, research into the efficacy of insulin administered by intraperitoneal route, new access routers for peritoneal dialysis and peritoneal access routes for diabetes, artificial hearing and arms, implantation of a totally artificial heart in a human patient, and biomaterials research. Cooperates with Department of Biomedical Design for design and manufacture of compact hemodialysis machines and peritoneal access devices. **Publications:** Research Reports; *Institute for Biomedical Engineering--Some of its Projects--Some of its People.*

University of Vermont
Vermont Rehabilitation Engineering Center
for Low Back Pain
See: Entry 12764

★2500★ University of Virginia
Department of Biomedical Engineering
Medical Center, Box 337
Charlottesville, VA 22908
Phone: (804)924-5101
Fax: (804)982-3870
Dr. Jen-shih Lee, Chm.

Research Activities and Fields: Biomedical engineering, including studies in microcirculation, cardio-vascular and pulmonary mechanics, CO2 transport, neuromuscular transmission, membrane biophysics, cellular engineering, pattern recognition and processing of medical images, design for mobility and seating technology, and motion analysis. **E-mail Address:** jl@virginia.edu.

★2501★ University of Washington
Center for Bioengineering
Harris Laboratory WD-12
Seattle, WA 98195
Phone: (206)685-2000
Dr. Lee L. Huntsman, Dir.

Research Activities and Fields: Multidisciplinary program of research and education applying the concepts and techniques of the physical sciences and engineering to challenges in the health sciences and medicine, including studies in biomaterials, biomathematics, biomechanics, imaging, controlled drug release systems, microrheology, hearing, laser applications, microcirculatory exchange, muscles, bioelectromagnetics, molecular design, and molecular assemblies.

University of Washington
Diagnostic Imaging Sciences Center
See: Entry 11177

★2502★ University of Washington
National ESCA and Surface Analysis
Center for Biomedical Problems
Dept. of Chemical Engineering, BF-10
Seattle, WA 98195
Phone: (206)685-1005
Fax: (206)543-3778
Buddy D. Ratner, Ph.D., Dir.

Research Activities and Fields: Surface analysis of biomaterial, polymer, and biological surfaces. Research directed toward integrating electron spectroscopy for chemical analysis (ESCA) and other surface analysis methods into standard analytical tools for biomedical sciences. Provides electron spectroscopy for chemical analysis of organic, metallic, and inorganic materials. Activities focus on understanding the nature of interactions that occur at biological interfaces such as tissue-body fluid, synthetic material-blood, and tooth-saliva. **Publications:** *Photoemissions* (newsletter). **E-mail Address:** ratner@cheme.washington.edu.

★2503★ University of Wisconsin—Madison
Medical Instrumentation Laboratory
1415 Johnson Dr.
Madison, WI 53706
Phone: (608)263-1574
Fax: (608)265-2614
Prof. John G. Webster, Head

Research Activities and Fields: Medical electrodes, medical amplifiers, and bioimpedance techniques. Activities focus on measurement of ventilation using impedance and inductance. **E-mail Address:** webster@engr.wisc.edu.

★2504★ Washington University
Biomedical Computer Laboratory
700 S. Euclid
St. Louis, MO 63110
Phone: (314)362-2135
Fax: (314)362-0234
Dr. Lewis J. Thomas, Jr., Dir.

Research Activities and Fields: Develops applications of computers to biomedical research, including quantitative imaging. **Publications:** Annual Progress Report; Papers.

★2505★ Washington University
Institute for Biomedical Computing
School of Medicine
700 S. Euclid Ave.
St. Louis, MO 63110
Phone: (314)362-2135
Fax: (314)362-0234
David States, Actg.Dir.

Research Activities and Fields: Develops advanced mathematical techniques and computer systems for applications in biomedicine. Current research areas include computational optical-sectioning microscopy, image-estimation for positron-emission tomography, development of advanced analysis techniques for electron-microscopic autoradiography, gel-electrophoretic analysis for physical (restriction) and restriction fragment length polymorphism (RFLP) mapping of DNA, stereo-image analysis for studies of the pathophysiology of glaucoma, development and testing of quantitative models for the encoding of acoustic stimuli as spike discharges in the auditory nerve, cochlear mechanical modeling, computer-aided molecular design and computational chemistry, systematic studies of conformational hyperspace, three-dimensional quantitative structure-activity relationships, interactive dose calculation and presentation for radiation treatment planning, automated segmentation of biomedical images, parallel processing for computationally intensive biomedical requirements, design methodologies for delay-insensitive digital systems, mathematical modeling applied to estimation of physiological paramaters from positron emission tomography, automated summarization and display of temporal information, and information retrieval and large scale databases.

★2506★ Wayne State University
Bioengineering Center
818 W. Hancock St.
Detroit, MI 48202
Phone: (313)577-1344
Fax: (313)577-8333
Dr. Albert I. King, Dir.

Research Activities and Fields: Automotive and aircraft safety, injury mechanisms, and spinal function, including lower back pain, orthopedic biomechanics, and head injury. **E-mail Address:** king@rrb.eng.wayne.edu. **Formerly:** Biomechanics Research Center (1970).

★2507★ Wayne State University
Gurdjian-Lissner Biomechanics Laboratory
Bioengineering Center
818 W. Hancock
Detroit, MI 48202
Phone: (313)577-1344
Fax: (313)577-8333
Dr. Albert I. King, Dir.

Research Activities and Fields: Bioengineering sciences, including studies on head/neck injury mechanisms and prevention of such injuries.

★ 2508 ★ Worcester Polytechnic Institute
Applied Bioengineering Center
Biomedical Engineering Dept.
100 Institute Rd.
Worcester, MA 01609
Phone: (508)831-5447
Fax: (508)831-5541
Dr. Robert Peura, Dir.

Research Activities and Fields: Biomedical engineering, human and animal medicine, biological science, biochemistry, and biotechnology, focusing on improving the practice of medicine and health care, promoting disease prevention, developing new diagnostic and therapeutic modalities, and addressing the economies of biotechnology, pharmaceutical, and medical devices. Specific areas of research include noninvasive diagnosis, biosensors, bioprocess, innovation management, cell and molecular biology, and evaluation of development studies.

Chapter 8
Biomedicine

Federal Government Agencies

★ 2509 ★ U.S. Department of Health and
Human Services
National Center for Research Resources
12 South Dr.
Bethesda, MD 20892-5662
Phone: (301)496-5793

Description: Formed in 1990 by a merger of the
Division of Research Services and Division of
Research Resources, the Center administers,
fosters, and supports research for the development and support of various research resources
needed on an institutional, regional, or national
basis for health-related research. It also oversees a centralized program of intramural research resources through the planning, performance, and reporting of research projects.

★ 2510 ★ U.S. Department of Health and
Human Services
**National Institute of General Medical
Sciences**
45 Center Dr.
Bethesda, MD 20892-6500
Phone: (301)594-2172
Fax: (301)402-0156

Description: NIGMS supports research and research training in basic biomedical sciences. Institute activities range from cell biology to genetics to pharmacology and systemic response to
trauma and anethesia.

★ 2511 ★ U.S. Department of Health and
Human Services
National Institutes of Health
9000 Rockville Pike
Bethesda, MD 20892
Phone: (301)496-2433

Description: The National Institutes of Health
is the principal biomedical research arm of the
federal government. Its programs are oriented
primarily toward basic and applied scientific
studies on the causes, diagnosis, prevention,
treatment, and rehabilitation of human diseases
and disabilities; the fundamental biological process of growth, development, and aging; and
the biological effects of the environment. NIH

conducts research in its own laboratories; supports research in universities, hospitals, and research institutions in this country and abroad;
helps nonprofit institutions build and equip
biomedical research facilities; supports the
training of young, promising career researchers;
and promotes effective ways to communicate
biomedical information to scientists, health
practitioners, and the public. NIH is organized
into 13 research institutes: 1) National Cancer
Institute; 2) National Eye Institute; 3) National
Heart, Lung, and Blood Institute; 4) National Institute on Aging; 5) National Institute of Allergy
and Infectious Diseases; 6) National Institute of
Arthritis and Musculoskeletal and Skin Diseases; 7) National Institute of Child Health and
Human Development; 8) National Institute on
Deafness and Other Communications Disorders; 9) National Institute of Dental Research;
10) National Institute of Diabetes and Digestive
and Kidney Diseases; 11) National Institute of
Environmental Health Sciences; 12) National Institute of General Medical Sciences; and 13)
National Institute of Neurological Disorders and
Stroke. It also includes two divisions: Computer
Research and Technology Division, and Research Grants Division, as well as the National
Center for Research Resources, the National Library of Medicine, the Warren Grant Magnuson
Clinical Center, the John E. Fogarty International Center for Advanced Study in the Health Sciences, the National Center for Nursing Research, and the National Center for Human Genome Research. (For all components, see separate entries that follow or consult Chapter 17,
Federal Government Research Agencies, Facilities, and Programs.)

★ 2512 ★ U.S. Department of Health and
Human Services
National Institutes of Health
**Division of Computer Research and
Technology**
9000 Rockville Pike
Bethesda, MD 20892
Phone: (301)496-5703

Description: Division conducts an integrated
research, developmental, and service program
in computer-related physical and life sciences in
support of NIH biomedical research programs.

★ 2513 ★ U.S. Department of Health and
Human Services
National Institutes of Health
Fogarty International Center
9000 Rockville Pike
Bethesda, MD 20892
Phone: (301)496-1415
Fax: (301)594-1211

Description: The Fogarty International Center
promotes discussion, study, and research on
the development of science internationally as it
relates to health and administers a number of international programs for advanced study in the
health sciences.

★ 2514 ★ U.S. Department of Health and
Human Services
National Institutes of Health
Research Grants Division
6701 Rockledge Dr.
Bethesda, MD 20892
Phone: (301)435-1106

Description: Division provides staff support to
the Office of the Director, NIH, in the formulation
of grant and award policies and procedures,
central receipt of all Public Health Service applications for research training support, and
makes initial referral to Service components.

★ 2515 ★ U.S. Department of Health and
Human Services
Warren Grant Magnuson Clinical Center
9000 Rockville Pike
Bethesda, MD 20892
Phone: (301)496-4114

Description: The Clinical Center is the research
hospital of the National Institutes of Health, the
Federal government's primary medical research
agency. The hospital provides the facilities and
support services for physicians who conduct the
NIH clinical research programs. It was specially
designed to place patient care facilities close to
research laboratories to promote the quick
transfer of new findings of basic and clinical scientists to the treatment of patients. Institutes
admit to their units only those patients (upon referral by their personal physicians) who have the
precise kind or stage of illness under investigation by scientist-clinicians. In addition to
biomedical research and patient care, the Clinical Center offers opportunities for advanced

training to young physicians, medical students, nursing students, and members of the paramedical professions. This training includes a graduate and postgraduate program, a clinical electives program, and many lecture series.

Foundations & Other Funding Organizations

Private Foundations

★2516★ Charles H. Revson Foundation
444 Madison Ave., 30th Fl.
New York, NY 10022
Phone: (212)935-3340
Fax: (212)688-0633
Eli N. Evans, President

Foundation Philosophy: The foundation has four principal areas of interest: urban affairs with an emphasis on New York City; education; biomedical research policy; and Jewish philanthropy. Related to each of these interests are concerns for governmental accountability, the development of public leadership, the changing role of women, and the impact of modern communications on education. In general, foundation grants are public policy-oriented. **Giving Priorities:** In 1992, the foundation gave 25% of giving to international affairs. Educational institutions and civic causes both received 24% of total contributions. Jewish organizations received 20%. The remaining funds went to the arts, 3%; health care, 2%; and social service organizations, 2%. **Typical Health-Related Recipients:** Cancer, Medical Research. **Geographic Distribution:** Emphasis on New York City, with some national giving.

★2517★ Eleanor Naylor Dana Charitable Trust
c/o Trustees
375 Park Ave.
38th Floor
New York, NY 10152
Phone: (212)754-2890

Foundation Philosophy: The trust gives funding priority in two areas: biomedical research, where it supports clinical investigation and "innovative projects designed to improve medical practice and prevent disease;" and the performing arts. **Giving Priorities:** In fiscal 1993, the trust reported that it gave 49% to medical research, 33% to the arts, and 18% to other organizations, representing health care, international affairs and social services. **Typical Health-Related Recipients:** AIDS/HIV, Cancer, Children's Health/Hospitals, Clinics/Medical Centers, Diabetes, Family Planning, Hospitals, Medical Education, Medical Research, Transplant Networks/Donor Banks. **Geographic Distribution:** Emphasis on the East Coast, with primary focus on New York City area.

★2518★ Helen Hay Whitney Foundation
450 E 63rd St.
New York, NY 10021-7928
Phone: (212)751-8228
Barbara M. Hugonnet, Administrative Director

Foundation Philosophy: "The Helen Hay Whitney Foundation supports early postdoctoral training in all basic biomedical sciences." **Giving Priorities:** In fiscal 1992, the foundation made sixty-eight grants for postdoctoral fellowships to individuals at institutions of higher learning and health science facilities. About 81% of contributions went to individuals affiliated with universities, medical schools, and institutes of technology; the remaining 19% went to individuals affiliated with biomedical research, health, and cancer research institutes. **Typical Health-Related Recipients:** Medical Education, Medical Research. **Geographic Distribution:** North America.

Howard Hughes Medical Institute
See: Entry 284

★2519★ James S. McDonnell Foundation
1034 S Brentwood Blvd.
Ste. 1610
St. Louis, MO 63117
Phone: (314)721-1532
Fax: (314)721-7421
Dr. Susan M. Fitzpatrick, Program Officer

Foundation Philosophy: The foundation currently concentrates its efforts in three major areas: biomedical research, research and innovation in education, and international programs. The foundation currently supports research integrating cognitive science and neuroscience to advance our understanding of human mental function, research in the cognitive, behavioral, and social sciences to improve K-12 education, and international activities related to the foundation's programs in science and education. Current programs include the Cognitive Studies for Educational Practice (CSEP), the McDonnell-Pew Program in Cognitive Neuroscience, Molecular Medicine in Cancer Research, and the Partnership for Child Development. **Giving Priorities:** In 1993, the foundation reported that it gave approximately 65% of its contributions to scientific research. Education received 27%, and international organizations were given 5%. The remaining funding was distributed in small one-time gifts to projects of special significance to the foundation or the St. Louis community. **Typical Health-Related Recipients:** Cancer, Medical Education, Medical Research. **Geographic Distribution:** Nationally and internationally.

John D. and Catherine T. MacArthur Foundation
See: Entry 7230

★2520★ Lucille P. Markey Charitable Trust
3250 Mary St., Ste. 405
Miami, FL 33133
Phone: (305)445-5612
Fax: (305)445-6153
Nancy W. Weber, Director for Program Administration

Foundation Philosophy: The major commitment of the trust is its research grant program which supports, in whole or in part, interdisciplinary efforts of investigators who are addressing fundamental scientific questions. Fields of inquiry include cellular and molecular biology, developmental biology, structural biology, neurobiology, immunology, genetics, and virology. The trust also supports general organizational programs aimed at more effective training in the basic biological sciences and the more timely and productive utilization of such knowledge in clinical research. Grants may support a reorganization or restructuring of present training and research programs at applicant institutions, the creation of new intra-institutional programs, or the development of new cooperative programs between institutions. **Giving Priorities:** In fiscal 1992, the trust awarded approximately 87% of its total contributions to educational institutions, mainly for scientific research projects. Health care, including hospitals conducting research, received about 8%. Other scientific interests received the remaining 5% of funds. **Typical Health-Related Recipients:** Hospitals, Medical Education, Medical Research. **Geographic Distribution:** National.

Otho S. A. Sprague Memorial Institute
See: Entry 419

National & International Organizations

★2521★ American Association of Physicists in Medicine (AAPM)
1 Physics Ellipse
College Park, MD 20740-3846
Phone: (301)209-3350
Fax: (301)209-0862
Sal Trofi, Jr., Exec.Dir.

Founded: 1958. **Members:** 3,900. **Regional Groups:** 20. **Description:** Persons professionally engaged in application of physics to medicine and biology in medical research; educational institutions. Encourages interest and training in medical physics and related fields; promotes high professional standards; disseminates technical information. Maintains placement service. Conducts research programs. Member of American Institute of Physics. **Publications:** *AAPM Report Series*, periodic. *Price:* $10/issue. • *American Association of Physicists in Medicine-Membership Directory*, annual. Membership Directory. *Price:* Included in membership dues. • *Medical Physics*, monthly. Journal. Includes information on Diagnostic radiology, Radiation Therapy, and nuclear medicine and program of annual meeting. *Price:* Included in membership dues; $390/year for nonmembers. • Monographs. • Proceedings.

★2522★ American Board of Health Physics (ABHP)
1313 Dolley Madison Blvd., Ste. 402
Mc Lean, VA 22101-3926
Phone: (703)790-1745
Fax: (703)790-9063
Richard J. Burk, Jr., Exec.Sec.

Founded: 1960. **Members:** 8. **Description:** Certifying body. Promotes the health physics profession by establishing standards and procedures for certification and conducting certification examinations. Issues written proof of certification.

★2523★ **American College of Medical Physics**
1891 Preston White Dr.
Reston, VA 22091
Phone: (703)648-8966
Fax: (703)648-9176
Laura Fleming Jones, Exec.Dir.

Founded: 1982. **Members:** 400. **Regional Groups:** 9. **Description:** Covers socioeconomic aspects of practice, management issues, reimbursement, licensure, and practice standards. **Publications:** *Diagnostic Radiology.* Report. *Price:* $25 for nonmembers. • *Magnetic Resonance Imaging.* Report. *Price:* $25 for nonmembers. • *Mammography.* Report. *Price:* $25 for nonmembers. • *Medical Laser Systems.* Report. *Price:* $25 for nonmembers. • Newsletter, 3-4/year. • *Nuclear Medicine.* Report. *Price:* $25 for nonmembers. • *Radiation Oncology.* Report. *Price:* $25 for nonmembers.

★2524★ **Anatomical Society (AS)**
(Anatomische Gesellschaft — AG)
Institut fur Anatomie
Medizinische Universitat zu Lubeck
Ratzeburger Allee 160
23538 Lubeck, Germany
Phone: 451 5004030
Fax: 451 5004034
Dr. Wolfgang Kuhnel, M.D., Sec.

Founded: 1886. **Members:** 1,000. **Languages:** English, French, German. **Description:** Anatomists, histochemists, histologists. **Publications:** *Verhandlungen der Anatomischen Gesellschaft,* annual. Includes proceedings.

★2525★ **Anatomical Society of Great Britain and Ireland**
Department of Anatomy and Cell Biology
St. Mary's Hospital Medical Center
London W2 1PG, England
Phone: 171 7231252
Fax: 171 7247349
Prof. J.A. Firth, Sec.

Founded: 1887. **Members:** 650. **Languages:** English. **Description:** Individuals involved in anatomical science. Promotes development and advancement in anatomy and related science through research and education. Offers program for students. **Publications:** *Journal of Anatomy,* bimonthly. Contains research information in the anatomical sciences.

★2526★ **Anatomical Society of Southern Africa (ASSA)**
(Anatomiese Vereniging van Suider-Afrika)
Faculty of Veterinary Science
Private Bag X04
Onderstepoort 0110, Republic of South Africa
Phone: 12 5298330
Fax: 12 5298300
Prof. A.J. Bezuidenhout, Sec.

Founded: 1969. **Members:** 160. **Languages:** Afrikaans, English. **Description:** Individuals from 5 countries interested in the study of anatomy. Aims to: promote the study of anatomy;

encourage anatomical research; represent anatomists of Southern Africa at the international level. Organizes seminars and workshops. Bestows awards. **Publications:** *Newsletter of the ASSA,* semiannual. Newsletter. • *Proceedings,* annual.

Association of Biomedical Communication Directors (ABCD)
See: Entry 6976

★2527★ **Association of Independent Research Institutes (AIRI)**
c/o Karen E. Campbell
1899 Gaylord St.
Denver, CO 80206
Karen E. Campbell, Sec.

Founded: 1975. **Members:** 77. **Description:** Nonprofit research institutes that primarily conduct independent scientific investigation in biomedical science. Provides mutual assistance for common problems; apprises members of federal government issues affecting research institutes.

★2528★ **Biochemical Society (BS)**
59 Portland Pl.
London W1N 3AJ, England
Phone: 171 5805530
Fax: 171 6377626
G.D. Jones, Exec.Sec.

Founded: 1911. **Members:** 9,000. **Regional Groups:** 6. **Languages:** English. **Description:** Biochemists in 70 countries working in industrial production, health services, and industrial and higher education research. Objectives are to promote biochemistry and to provide a forum for information exchange and discussion of teaching and research in biochemistry. Maintains 16 specialized biochemical groups. **Publications:** *Biochemical Journal,* semimonthly. • *Biochemical Society Transactions,* bimonthly. • *Biochemist,* bimonthly. • *Clinical Science,* monthly. • *Essays in Biochemistry,* annual. • *Symposium Proceedings,* annual.

★2529★ **Bio-Electro-Magnetics Institute (BEMI)**
2490 W. Moana Ln.
Reno, NV 89509-3936
Phone: (702)827-9099
Dr. John T. Zimmerman, Pres. & Founder

Founded: 1986. **Members:** 450. **Description:** Medical professionals, alternative health practitioners, and interested others. Scientific research organization that studies the relationship between living organisms and electromagnetic fields and various frequencies of electromagnetic radiation ranging from ultralow frequencies to ultraviolet light frequencies. Fosters research, education, service, and technical support in matters relating to bioelectromagnetics. Promotes the emerging fields of energy field medicine and bioenergetics. Investigates health hazards that may result from exposure to common sources of electromagnetic fields (e.g., electric power lines, video display terminals, and sources of radio frequency radiation, such as radar and microwaves). Maintains speakers' bureau. **Publications:** *BEMI Currents.* Journal. Contains information on the health hazards and beneficial healing aspects of electromagnetic fields. Back issues. *Price:* $40/year.

★2530★ **Biological Stain Commission (BSC)**
Box 626
Rochester, NY 14642
Phone: (716)275-3202
Fax: (716)273-1027
James M. Powers, M.D., Sec.

Founded: 1922. **Members:** 75. **Description:** Professional scientists in biology, medicine, and related fields. Works for the establishment of standards for the identification, purity, performance, and labeling of the more important biological stains, in order that they may be relied upon as standard tools in biological research. In cooperation with manufacturers and distributors, conducts program of stain certification. Conducts and promotes research in the improvement and applications of biological stains. **Publications:** *Biological Stains.* Book. • *Biotechnic and Histochemistry,* bimonthly. Covers all aspects of the pathological preparation of biological specimens; contains articles on new dyes and staining methods. *Price:* Included in membership dues; $40/year for nonmember individuals; $60/year for institutions; $25/year for students. • *Staining Procedures.* Book. **Formerly:** (1944) Commission on Standardization of Biological Stains.

★2531★ **British Society for Antimicrobial Chemotherapy (BSAC)**
Public Health Laboratory, 8th Fl.
Bristol Royal Infirmary
Marlborough St.
Bristol, Avon BS2 8HW, England
Phone: 117 9282879
Fax: 117 9299162
Dr. R.C. Spencer, Contact

Founded: 1971. **Members:** 700. **Languages:** English. **Description:** Individuals in 33 countries working in the field of antimicrobial chemotherapy. Furthers research and understanding of chemotherapy. **Publications:** *Journal of Antimicrobial Chemotherapy,* monthly. Journal.

★2532★ **European Cell Biology Organization (ECBO)**
University of Milan
Via Vanvitelli 32
I-20129 Milan, Italy
Phone: 2 70146254
Fax: 2 7490574
Prof. Francesco Clementi, Sec.Gen.

Founded: 1977. **Members:** 18. **Languages:** English. **Description:** European national cell biology societies in 18 countries. Promotes the study of cell biology and its applications. Encourages cooperation among individual cell biologists and their respective national societies.

★2533★ **European Society of Biomechanics (ESB)**
Arbeitsbereich Biomechanik
Denickestrasse 15
21073 Hamburg, Germany
Phone: 40 77183053
Fax: 40 77182996
Prof. E. Schneider, Contact

Founded: 1976. **Members:** 250. **Languages:** English. **Description:** Engineers, surgeons, and physicians interested in the mechanics (musculoskeletal, cardiovascular, dental, and athletic) of the human body; universities and research institutions. Promotes biomechanics research; organizes courses, symposia, and seminars. Bestows awards. **Publications:** Proceedings, biennial.

★ 2534 ★ **European Underwater and Baromedical Society (EUBS)**
6 Parkhill Ave.
Dyce
Aberdeen AB2 0FP, Scotland
Phone: 1224 770209
Fax: 1224 770209
Mrs. A. Randell, Membership Sec.
Members: 310. **Languages:** English. **Description:** Professionals and students interested in undersea medicine and related fields. Provides a forum for scientific communication among those interested in undersea medicine; encourages cooperation with related scientific disciplines. Strives to improve the safety of underwater activities by providing expert advice and educational programs; promotes undersea medicine. Holds workshops on topics concerning medical aspects of diving. **Publications:** *Long Term Neurological Consequences of Deep Diving.* • *Newsletter,* quarterly. Newsletter.

★ 2535 ★ **Foundation for Biomedical Research (FBR)**
818 Connecticut Ave. NW, Ste. 303
Washington, DC 20006
Phone: (202)457-0654
Ms. Frankie L. Trull, Pres.
Founded: 1981. **Description:** Individuals and organizations supporting humane animal research. Serves as public information and education program on what the foundation sees as the necessary and important role of laboratory animals in biomedical research and testing. Maintains speakers' bureau and public relations program. **Publications:** *Caring for Laboratory Animals.* • *Caring for Life.* Video. • *Fact vs. Myth.* Brochure. • *Foundation for Biomedical Research--Newsletter,* bimonthly. Newsletter. Includes foundation news and calendar of events. *Price:* Free. • *Hope!.* Film. • *The New Research Environment.* Video. • *The Use of Animals in Biomedical Research and Testing.* • *Why I Should Stay Awake in Science Class.* Video.

★ 2536 ★ **Histochemical Society (HCS)**
PO Box 294
Woods Hole, MA 02543
Phone: (508)457-7680
Fax: (508)548-9053
Morton D. Maser, Bus. Office Mgr.
Founded: 1950. **Members:** 550. **Description:** Physicians and scientists who employ hisotchemical and cytochemical techniques in their research. **Publications:** *The Journal of Histochemistry and Cytochemistry,* monthly. Journal. • Newsletter, semiannual.

Institute of Laboratory Animal Resources (ILAR)
See: Entry 13081

★ 2537 ★ **International Federation of Societies for Histochemistry and Cytochemistry (IFSHC) (Federation Internationale des Societes d'Histochimie et de Cytochimie — FISHC)**
University of Heidelburg
Institute for Anatomy and Cell Biology
Im Neuenheimer Feld 307
69120 Heidelberg, Germany
Prof. H.D. Fahimi, Sec.Gen.
Founded: 1960. **Members:** 19. **Languages:** English, French, German, Italian, Russian, Spanish. **Description:** National societies for histochemistry and cytochemistry. Seeks to promote communication and cooperation among scientists throughout the world and establish histochemistry and cytochemistry institutes. Promotes histochemistry and cytochemistry as basic, independent sciences and advocates their teaching in universities. Appoints committees for the study of scientific matters requiring international collaboration. Organizes symposia. **Publications:** *Proceedings,* quadrennial. Also publishes scientific journals.

★ 2538 ★ **International Organization for Medical Physics (IOMP)**
c/o Prof. Hans Svensson
Radiation Physics Department
University Hospital
90185 UMEA
Phone: 49 90103891
Fax: 49 90101588
Prof. Hans Svensson, Sec.Gen.
Founded: 1963. **Members:** 56. **Description:** A member of the International Union of Physical and Engineering Sciences in Medicine. National organizations of medical physics representing 10,000 individuals. Fosters international cooperation in medical physics; promotes communication between various branches of medical physics and allied subjects. Conducts training programs. Has established 43 libraries in developing countries. **Publications:** *Clinical Physics and Physiological Measurement,* bimonthly. • *Medical Physics World,* semiannual. • *Physics in Medicine and Biology,* monthly.

International Society for Biomedical Research on Alcoholism (ISBRA)
See: Entry 12044

★ 2539 ★ **Latin American Association for Medical Physics (Asociacion Latinoamericana de Fisica Medica)**
Avenida de los Arcos Poniente 362
Jardines del Sur
16050 Mexico City, DF, Mexico
Victor M. Tovar Munoz
Description: Medical physicists throughout Latin America. Promotes study and research in medical physics. Fosters communication and information exchange between members.

★ 2540 ★ **Latin American Confederation of Clinical Biochemistry (LACCB) (Confederacion Latinoamericana de Bioquimica Clinica — CLBC)**
Calle 49, Numero 15-47
Bogota, Colombia
Phone: 1 2323681
Argelia Montoya de Gonzalez, Sec.
Founded: 1964. **Members:** 20. **Languages:** Spanish. **Description:** National clinical chemistry associations representing 19,450 individuals. Seeks to foster professional advancement in the field of biochemistry through informal education, congresses, and courses. Maintains speakers' bureau; sponsors competitions. **Publications:** *Acta Bioquimica Clinica Latinoamericana,* quarterly. • *Acta de Fecodel,* quarterly. • *Faba Informa,* bimonthly. • *Perodico de Fecodel,* bimonthly.

★ 2541 ★ **National Association for Biomedical Research (NABR)**
818 Connecticut Ave. NW, Ste. 303
Washington, DC 20006
Phone: (202)857-0540
Fax: (202)659-1902
Ms. Frankie L. Trull, Pres.
Founded: 1985. **Members:** 400. **Description:** Universities, medical and veterinary schools, teaching hospitals, professional societies, voluntary health agencies, pharmaceutical companies and other research-related firms that use laboratory animals for biomedical research, education, and testing. Monitors and, when appropriate, attempts to influence legislation and regulations on behalf of members who are dependent on animals for biomedical research, education, and testing. **Publications:** Brochure. • *NABR Alert,* 6-10/year. Newsletter. Covers regulatory and legislative action related to the use of animals in biomedical research, research, and testing. *Price:* Included in membership dues. • *NABR Update,* 18-26/year. Bulletin. Covers national, state, and local regulatory and legislative activities affecting biomedical research. *Price:* Included in membership dues. • *National Association for BioMedical Research.* Annual Report. Describes the previous year's activities. *Price:* Included in membership dues. • *State Laws Concerning the Use of Animals in Research,* biennial. *Price:* Included in membership dues; $25/year for nonmembers.

★ 2542 ★ **Polish Anatomical Society (PAS) (Polskie Towarzystwo Anatomiczne — PTA)**
Chalubinskiego 5
PL-02-004 Warsaw, Poland
Phone: 22 298013
Fax: 22 295282
Prof. Ryszard Aleksandrowicz, Pres.
Founded: 1926. **Members:** 500. **Local Groups:** 12. **Languages:** English, French. **Description:** Encourages scientific activities dealing with the morphological sciences, including anatomy, cell biology, embryology, histochemistry, histology, and zoology. Promotes modernization of educational methods. Conducts research. **Publications:** *Advances in Cell Biology,* quarterly. • *Folia Morphologica,* quarterly. **Formerly:** Polish Anatomical and Zoological Society.

Registry of Comparative Pathology (RCP)
See: Entry 10137

Society of Biological Psychiatry (SBP)
See: Entry 7511

★2543★ Society of Biomedical Equipment Technicians (SBET)
3330 Washington Blvd., Ste. 400
Arlington, VA 22201
Phone: (703)525-4890
Free: 800-332-2264
Fax: (703)276-0793
Jane Brookstein, Liaison

Founded: 1976. **Members:** 1,100. **Description:** Biomedical equipment technicians, hospital maintenance engineers, managers of hospital medical equipment departments, sales representatives, and others involved with the repair or installation of biomedical hospital machinery. Seeks to recognize biomedical equipment technicians and engineers as a specialty group. Supports certification programs including CBET (Certified Biomedical Equipment Technician), CRES (Certified Radiologic Equipment Specialist), and CLES (Certified Laboratory Equipment Specialist). Works with local biomedical organizations. Maintains speakers' bureau and placement service; compiles statistics. **Publications:** *AAMI News*, bimonthly. Newsletter. *Price:* $60. • *Biomedical Instrumentation & Technology*, bimonthly. Journal. *Price:* $75. • *Medical Device Research Report*, bimonthly. Newsletter. *Price:* $75. Also publishes reference series, study guides for certification programs, and career information for high school and college students. **Formerly:** (1987) Society of Biomedical Equipment Technicians; (1992) National Society of Biomedical Equipment Technicians.

★2544★ Society for Cryobiology (SC)
c/o Dept of Mechanical Engineering
University of Texas
Austin, TX 78712
Phone: (512)471-7167
Fax: (301)530-7001
Kenneth Diller, Pres.

Founded: 1964. **Members:** 450. **Description:** Basic and applied research in the field of low temperature biology and medicine. Promotes interdisciplinary approach to freezing, freeze-drying, hypothermia, hibernation, physiological effects of low environmental temperature on animals and plants, medical applications of reduced temperatures, cryosurgery, hypothermic perfusion and cryopreservation of organs, cryoprotective agents and their pharmacological action, and pertinent methodologies. Operates charitable program and placement service. **Publications:** *Cryobiology: International Journal of Low Temperature Biology and Medicine*, bimonthly. Journal. • *Medicine*, bimonthly. • Membership Directory, semiannual. • *News Notes*, quarterly. Includes bibliographic citations.

★2545★ Society for Experimental Biology and Medicine (SEBM)
162 W. 56th St., Ste. 203
New York, NY 10022
Felice O'Grady, Admin.

Founded: 1903. **Members:** 1,800. **Regional Groups:** 5. **Description:** Workers actively engaged in research in experimental biology and experimental medicine. Cultivates the experimental method of investigation in the sciences of biology and medicine. **Publications:** Proceedings, 11/year. Includes annual membership directory.

★2546★ Society for InVitro Biology (SIVB)
8815 Centre Park Dr., Ste. 210
Columbia, MD 21045
Phone: (410)992-0946
Fax: (410)992-0949
Marietta W. Ellis, Business Mgr.

Founded: 1946. **Members:** 2,500. **Description:** Professional society of individuals using mammalian, invertebrate, plant cell tissue, and organ cultures as research tools in chemistry, physics, radiation, medicine, physiology, nutrition, and cytogenetics. Aims are to foster collection and dissemination of information concerning the maintenance and experimental use of tissue cells in vitro and to establish evaluation and development procedures. Operates placement service. **Publications:** *In Vitro Cellular and Developmental Biology - Animal*, monthly. Journal. Peer-reviewed; covers in vitro cultivation and characterization of cells, tissues, and tumors. *Price:* Included in membership dues; $240 for nonmembers. • *In Vitro Cellular and Developmental Biology - Plant*, quarterly. Journal. Peer-reviewed; covers in vitro cultivation of tissues, organs, or cells from plants. *Price:* Included in membership dues; $105 for nonmembers. • *In Vitro Report*, bimonthly. Newsletter. Includes national and international news relevant to the field. *Price:* Included in membership dues; $25/year for nonmembers. • *TCA Membership Roster*, annual. Membership Directory. *Price:* Included in membership dues; $150 for nonmembers. **Formerly:** Tissue Culture Association; (1949) Tissue Culture Commission.

★2547★ Society for Physical Regulation in Biology and Medicine
PO Box 64
Dresher, PA 19025
Phone: (215)659-5180
Fax: (215)659-1314
Ethel S. Pollack, Exec.Sec.

Founded: 1980. **Members:** 230. **Description:** Medical professionals, engineers, biological and physical scientists, and representatives of industry. Purpose is to further international and interdisciplinary research, communication, cooperation, and education in the study and clinical applications of the effects of electricity and magnetism in growth, repair, and regeneration of human cells and tissues. **Publications:** *Transactions*, annual. Abstracts of works presented at the annual meeting. *Price:* Included in membership dues; $45/year for nonmembers. **Formerly:** (1993) Bioelectrical Repair and Growth Society.

★2548★ World Federation of the Societies of Biological Psychiatry (WFSBP)
Francisco de Vittoria 2324
1425 Buenos Aires, Argentina
Fax: 1 8037419
Dr. J. Coprian Ollirier, Contact

Founded: 1974. **Members:** 38. **Languages:** English. **Description:** National biological psychiatry societies. Fosters development of biological psychiatry and education in the field. (Biological psychiatry is the study of the biological basis of behavior and behavioral disorders.) Encourages research; promotes improvement in the quality of instruction in related professions. Serves as an information and advisory resource for groups and individuals concerned with biological psychiatry. **Publications:** *Biological Psychiatry*, every 3-6 years.

★2549★ Yugoslav Association of Anatomists (YAA)
(Drustvo Anatoma Jugoslavije — DAJ)
Medical Faculty
Hajduk Veljkova 3
YU-21000 Novi Sad, Yugoslavia
Phone: 21 624138
Fax: 11 644349
Vasilije Devecerski, M.D., Sec.Gen.

Founded: 1956. **Members:** 120. **Languages:** English, French, German, Russian, Serbian. **Description:** Exchanges scientific information. Organizes courses in methodology. **Publications:** *Folia Anatomica*, annual. **Formerly:** (1994) Union of the Yugoslav Association of Anatomists.

Research Centers

★2550★ Bay Medical Research Foundation
425 Divisadero St., Ste. 305
San Francisco, CA 94117
Phone: (415)431-8744
R. Dale Kobler, Exec.Dir.

Research Activities and Fields: Biomedicine, including studies of computed radiography, immunochemistry, cytogerontology, and cell biology. Conducts medical ozone studies and clinical trials and evaluations. **Formerly:** Bay Medical Research and Education Foundation.

Baylor College of Medicine Biochemical Genetics Laboratory
See: Entry 4880

★2551★ Baylor University Baylor Research Institute
3812 Elm St.
Dallas, TX 75226
Phone: (214)820-2687
Fax: (214)820-4952
John Fordtran, M.D., Pres.

Research Activities and Fields: Biomedicine, including digestive diseases, oncology, photobiology, organ transplants, muscle physiology, and metabolic diseases. **Publications:** *Baylor Proceedings* (quarterly). **E-mail Address:** lgibson@tins.technology.org. **Formerly:** Baylor Research Foundation.

★ 2552 ★ Biomechanics Institute, Inc.
25 Bay State Rd.
PO Box 429, Kenmore Sta.
Boston, MA 02215
Phone: (617)236-1448
Fax: (617)236-1449
Jeffrey Fredburg, Dir.

Research Activities and Fields: Respiratory biology and microcirculation for medical applications. **Publications:** *Journal of Applied Physiology.*

★ 2553 ★ Biomedical Research Foundation of Northwest Louisiana
1505 Kings Way Hwy.
Shreveport, LA 71103
Phone: (318)675-4100
Fax: (318)675-4120
Thomas M. Tierney, Exec.Dir.

Research Activities and Fields: Cardiovascular disease, molecular biology, neurobiology and stroke. Focuses on R&D management and supports research, education, and patient care at the University.

Biomedical Research Institute
See: Entry 6763

★ 2554 ★ Blood CARE
9000 Harry Hines Blvd.
Dallas, TX 75235
Phone: (214)351-8111
Fax: (214)351-9803
Dr. William Miller, Dir.

Research Activities and Fields: Genetic engineering, chemistry, immunology, microbiology, and hematology. **Publications:** *Cancer Review* (semiannually). **Formerly:** Wadley Institute of Molecular Medicine; Blood Center.

★ 2555 ★ Boston Biomedical Research Institute (BBRI)
20 Staniford St.
Boston, MA 02114
Phone: (617)742-2010
Fax: (617)523-6649
Dr. Kathleen Morgan, Dir.

Research Activities and Fields: Biological and medical sciences, including fundamental biomedical studies on cell metabolism, developmental biology, gene regulation, recombinant DNA, monoclonal antibodies, intercellular matrix biology, muscle diseases, connective tissue diseases, and muscular dystrophy. **Publications:** *Messenger* (semiannual newsletter). **Formerly:** Institute of Biological and Medical Sciences.

★ 2556 ★ Brigham and Women's Hospital Diagnostic Molecular Biology Laboratory
75 Francis St.
Boston, MA 02115
Phone: (617)732-7446
Fax: (617)732-7449
Dr. Jeffrey Sklar, Dir.

Research Activities and Fields: Molecular biology, human genetics, and molecular oncology, including nucleic acid analysis for the diagnosis of cancer, inherited conditions, and infectious disorders.

★ 2557 ★ Brown University International Health Institute
Box G
Providence, RI 02912
Phone: (401)863-3330
Dr. Charles Carpenter, Dir.

Research Activities and Fields: Clinical and basic biomedical research focusing on the health problems of developing nations, including infectious diseases and nutrition. Activities include ongoing field projects and the transfer of biomedical technology.

★ 2558 ★ Carnegie Institution of Washington
Carnegie Laboratories of Embryology, Davis Division
Univ. of California, Davis
C.P.R.C.
Davis, CA 95616
Phone: (916)752-0210
Prof. R. O'Rahilly, M.D., Dir.

Research Activities and Fields: Developmental neurobiology of primates, including embryonic development of the human brain.

★ 2559 ★ Case Western Reserve University Developmental Biology Center
2109 Adelbert Rd.
Cleveland, OH 44106-4901
Phone: (216)368-2428
Fax: (216)368-3182
Dr. Urs Rutishauser, Dir.

Research Activities and Fields: Developmental biology, genetics, neuroscience, molecular biology, regeneration, regulation of normal and neoplastic growth, biophysics, and biochemistry.

★ 2560 ★ Catholic University of America Center for Advanced Training in Cell and Molecular Biology
School of Arts & Sciences
Washington, DC 20064
Phone: (202)319-6161
Fax: (202)319-4467
Roland M. Nardone, Ph.D., Dir.

Research Activities and Fields: Focuses on new and established biomedically related concepts and technologies for research, industrial applications, and diagnostic laboratory techniques. Established as a national center providing training for scientists and technicians.

Center for Biomedical Research
See: Entry 11262

★ 2561 ★ Center for Crystallographic Research
Roswell Park Cancer Institute
Elem & Carlton Sts.
Buffalo, NY 14263
Phone: (716)845-3135
Fax: (716)845-8899
Dr. Harold C. Box, Dir.

Research Activities and Fields: Conformational studies of nucleotides, peptides, and carbohydrates to determine interatomic arrangements in biological substances using nuclear magnetic resonance and electron spin resonance. Research is oriented to the field of cancer.

★ 2562 ★ City College of City University of New York
Center for the Study of the Cellular and Molecular Basis of Development
Science Bldg., Rm. 423
138th St. & Convent Ave.
New York, NY 10031
Phone: (212)650-8300
Fax: (212)650-7989
Dr. Guyden, Dir.

Research Activities and Fields: Molecular biology, including biomolecular structure and function, gene expression and regulation, cellular and organismic function, and neurobiology.

★ 2563 ★ City of Hope Beckman Research Institute
1450 E. Duarte Rd.
Duarte, CA 91010
Phone: (818)357-9711
Dr. Sanford Shapero, Pres./CEO

Research Activities and Fields: Conducts studies in the following three areas: 1) biology, including cell biology, molecular biology, developmental biology, molecular genetics, molecular immunology, gene regulation, and theoretical biology; 2) immunology, including protein chemistry, peptide chemistry, mass spectrometry, and immunobiology; and 3) neurosciences, including behavioral and neural genetics, cell physiology, cellular neurochemistry, cellular neurophysiology, membrane biochemistry, membrane neurochemistry, neuroanatomy and ultrastructure, neuropharmacology, neurophysiology, receptor physiology, biochemical genetics, and neurobiochemistry. **Formerly:** City of Hope Medical Research Institute (1980); City of Hope Research Institute (1983).

★ 2564 ★ City of Hope Beckman Research Institute
Division of Biology
1450 E. Duarte Rd.
Duarte, CA 91010
Phone: (818)357-9711
Dr. Sanford Shapero, Pres./CEO

Research Activities and Fields: Molecular mechanisms of living systems. Research activities are carried out in Departments of Biology, Molecular Biochemistry, Molecular Genetics, and Theoretical Biology. Department of Biology focuses on dynamic and temporal properties of cell growth and proliferation as it is manifested in cultured cells and intact organisms, including cellular clocks, circadian rhythms, and chemical oscillators; mammalian genes and gene control mechanisms and defining the biological function of postreplication DNA modifications that occur in mammalian cells; the mechanisms of gene repression and its relationship to DNA replication time; the role of amino acid sequence in determining protein function and folding patterns; mammalian chromosome inactivation mechanisms; mutational generation and repair mechanisms; genetic imprinting; and embryonic stem cell biology. Department of Molecular Biochemistry studies the use of synthetic oligodeoxyribonucleotides in the study of human disease, including diagnosis of genetic disease and the analysis of bone marrow transplant patients; the role of genetically engineered antibodies for cancer therapy; the biological function of nucleic acids studied by chemical synthesis; genetic mechanisms of imprinting; and isolation and characterization of genes important to immune function and cancer. Department of Molecular Genetics examines gene expression sequence requirements in eukaryotic systems, diagnosis of viral diseases (including HIV and HCMV), biochemistry of RNA splicing, catalytic RNA function and applications in HIV infection and cancer, control of gene expression, isolation of biologically active pure insulin and insulin-like growth factor receptors, mitochondrial-nuclear interactions and mitochondrial biogenesis, and homologous DNA recombinations. Theoretical Biology examines origins of genetic information and patterns in coding regions of gene families.

★2565★ **City of Hope Beckman Research Institute**
Division of Immunology
1450 E. Duarte Rd.
Duarte, CA 91010
Phone: (818)357-9711
Dr. Sanford M. Shapero, Pres./CEO

Research Activities and Fields: The Division is divided into five sections: Protein Chemistry, Immunobiology, Structural Biochemistry, Mass Spectrometry and NMR Spectroscopy. Sections collaborate on projects in cancer, virology, endocrinology, and immunology. Protein Chemistry Section research activities include development of sequencing strategies and structural studies on tumor markers, fibronectin, viral proteins, lymphokines, peptide hormones and neuroactive peptides. The Immunobiology Section studies the carcinoembryonic gene family, use of monoclonal antibodies in imaging and therapy of tumors, the transfer of antibody genes to tumor cells for enhanced immune response, regulation of the human interferon gene and production of a cytomegalovirus vaccine. The Structural Biochemistry Section performs active site st ud ies on NAD enzymes and aromatase. The Mass Spectrometry Section analyzes peptides, protein glycoconjugates, and nucleotides using time of flight, magnetic sector, and quadruple mass spectrometers. A new NMR Section has been set up for solution phase determination of three dimensional structure of peptides and proteins.

Columbia University
Biochemistry and Molecular Biology
Laboratory
See: Entry 13583

★2566★ **Columbia University**
Biochemistry and Molecular Biophysics
Program
630 W. 168th St.
New York, NY 10032
Phone: (212)305-3881
Fax: (212)305-7932
Dr. David Hirsh, Chr.

Research Activities and Fields: Biochemistry, molecular biology, biophysics, and biochemical genetics, including X-ray diffraction studies of biological macromolecules, structure and function of membrane receptors and transport proteins, computer studies of protein and nucleic acid structure and function, NMR spectroscopy, neutron and electron diffraction, enzymology, regu-

lation of transcription and translation in prokaryotic and eukaryotic cells, molecular virology, genomic and cDNA cloning in prokaryotes and eukaryotes, recombinant DNA technology, gene transfer and somatic-cell genetics, DNA sequencing, in vitro site-specific mutagenesis of cloned DNA, the role of oncogenes in neoplasia, control of gene expression in development, role of growth factors, regulation of oxygen transport by hemoglobin, hormonal regulation of ion transport, immunochemical properties of membrane antigens, structure and composition of synaptic components, metabolism of neurotransmitters, neurotoxic proteins and protein hormones, and chemical carcinogenesis.

Columbia University
Molecular Urology Laboratory
See: Entry 12917

★2567★ **Connective Tissue Research Institute**
Univ. City Science Center
3624 Market St.
Philadelphia, PA 19104
Phone: (215)387-2255
Dr. Nicholas A. Kefalides, Dir.

Research Activities and Fields: Biochemistry, cell biology, immunology, and molecular biology of connective tissues, including characterization and study of basement membranes, blood vessels, cornea and lens capsule of the eye, and cell virus interaction. Research is applied toward problems in cardiovascular disease, kidney disease, ocular disease, and genetic disease.

★2568★ **Coriell Institute for Medical Research**
401 Haddon Ave.
Camden, NJ 08103
Phone: (609)757-4820
Fax: (609)964-0254
David P. Beck, Ph.D., Pres.

Research Activities and Fields: Cell and molecular biology, microbiology, genetics, aging, cancer and cancer immunology, tumor virology, antibodies, genetic disorders, vascular disorders, infectious diseases and virus/chromosome relationships, environmental mutagenesis, and genetic probes. Studies utilization of cells grown in tissue culture for isolation and characterization of tumor cell antigens, viruses, genetic abnormalities, tumor viruses, and chromosomes. **Publications:** *Discover; In Passing* (quarterly newsletter); Biennial Report. **E-mail Address:** dabeck@umdnj.edu. **Formerly:** South Jersey Medical Research Foundation; Institute for Medical Research (1986).

★2569★ **Duke University**
Laboratory of Cell and Molecular Biology
of Leukocytes
PO Box 3712
Durham, NC 27710
Phone: (919)684-5709
Fax: (919)684-5215
Dolph O. Adams, M.D., Dir.

Research Activities and Fields: Cell and leukocyte biology, including macrophages, second messengers, gene regulation, cyclic nucleotides, kinases, and ion fluxes.

★2570★ **Duke University**
Marine Biomedical Center
Sch. of the Env. Marine Lab
135 Duke Marine Lab Rd.
Beaufort, NC 28516-9721
Phone: (919)504-7508
Fax: (919)728-2514
Dr. Joseph Bonaventura, Dir.

Research Activities and Fields: Marine organisms and marine systems as they relate to human health and the health of the environment. Research conducted in the fields of oceanography, chemistry, biochemistry, developmental and behavioral biology, and physiology has led to specific studies on the continental shelf, trace metals in marine and estuarine ecosystems, photosynthetic physiology of marine plants, maritime and pelagic birds, and behavioral toxicology. **Publications:** Annual Report; *Environs* (bimonthly).

★2571★ **Eleanor Roosevelt Institute**
1899 Gaylord St.
Denver, CO 80206
Phone: (303)333-4515
Fax: (303)333-8423
David Patterson, Ph.D., Pres.

Research Activities and Fields: Biochemistry and mammalian genetics. Investigates human and other mammalian cell systems, biosynthetic pathways of purines and pyrimidines, biochemical structure and function of cell surface membranes, cytogenetics, cancer genetics, genetic biochemistry, mutagenesis, carcinogenesis, and regulation of cholesterol metabolism. Identifies and conducts genetic studies of cell surface antigens and analyzes action of cyclic AMP and hormones. Results of studies applied to problems in malignancy, birth defects, and other diseases. **E-mail Address:** davepatt@druid.hsc.colorado.edu.

★2572★ **Emory University**
Yerkes Regional Primate Research Center
Atlanta, GA 30322
Phone: (404)727-7707
Dr. Frederick A. King, Dir.

Research Activities and Fields: Primate studies, including neurobiology, behavioral biology, reproductive biology and conservation of endangered species, pathobiology, and immunobiology. Specialty areas within the foregoing fields include neuroanatomy, neurophysiology, neuropsychology, psychophysics, neuroendocrinology, radioimmunoassays, sexual behavior and autonomic nervous system activities, cardiovascular studies related to coronary disease, effects of drugs on behavior, social behavior, language capacities, in vitro fertilization, fertility and infertility, endocrine studies of reproductive cycles, treatment of physiological impotency, artificial insemination, composition of cervical mucus, adrenarche and chromosome studies in great apes, diseases of nonhuman primates, primate models of human diseases and disorders, long-term effects of irradiation, cell and virus antigens, infectious and degenerative diseases (including AIDS and retroviral immunodeficiency disorders), vision and ophthalmic disorders (glaucoma, lens prostheses, cataract, strabismus, keratoplasty, and amblyopia), oncology, and parasitology. **Publi-**

cations: *Inside Yerkes* (four times yearly). **E-mail Address:** king@rmy.emory.edu. **Formerly:** Yale Laboratories of Primate Biology (1941).

★ 2573 ★ Endocrinology Research Laboratory

Dept. of Veterans Affairs Med. Ctr.
Dept. of Med. (151F), Med. Srvc. III
150 Muir Rd.
Martinez, CA 94553
Phone: (510)372-2076
Fax: (510)372-2501
Arthur Swislocki, Chief, Med. Srvc.

Research Activities and Fields: Basic and clinical diabetes and hypertension related research. **Formerly:** Enzymology Research Laboratory (1994).

★ 2574 ★ Federation of American Societies for Experimental Biology

Life Sciences Research Office
9650 Rockville Pike
Bethesda, MD 20814-3998
Phone: (301)530-7030
Fax: (301)571-1876
Kenneth D. Fisher, Dir.

Research Activities and Fields: Biomedical science, focusing on nutrient-disease relationships, such as folic acid and neural tube defects, omega-3 fatty acids and heart disease, zinc and immune function in the elderly, vitamin A and cancer, calcium and osteoporosis, vitamin C and cancer, sodium and hypertension, vitamin E and cancer, dietary fiber and cancer, lipids and cardiovascular disease, dietary fiber and cardiovascular disease, and lipids and cancer. Other areas of research include the analysis of adverse reactions to monosodium glutamate, the metabolic basis of animal carcinogenicity of butylated hydroxyanisole, and an evaluation of the benefits of biomedical research.

Florida State University
Center for Biomedical Toxicological Research and Hazardous Waste Management
See: Entry 10432

★ 2575 ★ GI Research Laboratory

4150 Clement St.
151-M2
San Francisco, CA 94121
Phone: (415)750-2095
Fax: (415)750-2177
Dr. Young S. Kim, Dir.

Research Activities and Fields: Molecular biology and cell biology, including studies on DNA cloning and sequencing, PCR, vector construction, site-directed mutagenesis, eukaryotic gene transfection, and oncogene and tumor suppressor gene molecular biology.

★ 2576 ★ H.L. Snyder Memorial Research Foundation

1407 Wheat Rd.
Winfield, KS 67156
Phone: (316)221-4080
Larry D. Smith, Dir.

Research Activities and Fields: Biochemical and molecular biological studies of diseases, especially cancer. Develops clinical assays for early cancer detection.

★ 2577 ★ Harbor Branch Oceanographic Institution, Inc.

5600 U.S. 1 North
Fort Pierce, FL 34946
Phone: (407)465-2400
Fax: (407)465-5415
Richard J. Herman, Mng.Dir.

Research Activities and Fields: Marine biology and botany, including environmental, coastal, and ocean sciences; aquaculture and mariculture; marine science; biomedical marine research, including marine pharmaceuticals; physical oceanography; environmental chemistry; ocean and materials engineering; mechanical and electro-optical engineering; and marine operations, including research vessels, manned submersibles, autonomously operated and remotely operated vehicles, and submersible support. **Publications:** *Harbor Branch News* (semimonthly newsletter). **E-mail Address:** harbomet@class.org.

★ 2578 ★ Harvard Medical School
Laboratory of Viral Pathogenesis

Dana-Farber Cancer Institute
44 Binney St.
Boston, MA 02115
Phone: (617)632-3719
Fax: (617)632-3112
Dr. Ruth M. Ruprecht, Chf.

Research Activities and Fields: Molecular biology and immunology, focusing on the interaction of retroviruses with cells and host organisms. **E-mail Address:** ruth_ruprecht@dfci.harvard.edu.

★ 2579 ★ Harvard University
Laboratory for Cell and Molecular Biology

New England Deaconess Hospital, Dept. of Medicine
Burl Bldg., 5th Fl.
185 Pilgrim Rd.
Boston, MA 02215
Phone: (617)632-9982
Fax: (617)632-9992
Dr. Arthur J. Sytkowski, Dir.

Research Activities and Fields: Biology of blood cell production, control mechanisms involved in normal cell growth and development, and identification of factors responsible for malignant transformation and neoplastic or cancerous growth. Ongoing studies include identifying the structural and functional properties of the erythropoietin molecule and the mechanisms of interaction with its receptor on the cell surface, identifying the role of cellular oncogenes in blood cell growth and differentiation, characterizing erythropoietin early response genes, and investigating gene therapy and erythroid burst promoting activity. Studies have direct applications to clinical syndromes accompanied by disordered blood cell production, leukemia, lymphoma, and cancer.

★ 2580 ★ The Hastings Center

255 Elm Rd.
Briarcliff Manor, NY 10510-9974
Phone: (914)762-8500
Fax: (914)762-2124
Dr. Daniel Callahan, Dir.

Research Activities and Fields: Multifaceted research program with an average of 10-12 research projects yearly on ethical issues in medicine, biology, the social and environmental sciences, and the professions, including health policy, research on human subjects, reproductive and genetic technologies, contraception, health care for the elderly, care of the terminally ill, AIDS, chronic illness, hospital ethics committees, rationing health care, environmental ethics, and applied and professional ethics. **Publications:** *The Hastings Center Report* (bimonthly); *IRB: A Review of Human Subjects Research* (bimonthly). **Formerly:** Institute of Society, Ethics and the Life Sciences (1985).

★ 2581 ★ Helicon Foundation

4622 Santa Fe St.
San Diego, CA 92109
Phone: (619)272-3884
Fax: (619)272-1621
Dr. Charles A. Thomas, Jr., Pres.

Research Activities and Fields: Conducts basic biological research in biochemistry, molecular biology, and genetics, including studies on oxidative damage to cellular DNA, structure of chromosomal telomeres, chromatin structure, and role of lipids in radical formation. Seeks to define the biochemical basis of disease prevention through antioxidant diagnostics. **E-mail Address:** cathomas@metcom.com.

Hoffman Heart Institute of Connecticut
See: Entry 2903

★ 2582 ★ Institute for Biophysical and Biomedical Research

Univ. City Science Center
3624 Market St., Ste. 508
Philadelphia, PA 19104
Phone: (215)243-2225
Fax: (215)387-6959
Dr. Britton Chance, Dir.

Research Activities and Fields: Biophysics, physical biochemistry, molecular biology, cellular plant and animal physiology, enzyme kinetics, reaction rates, and development of sensitive physical techniques (absorption and fluorescence, magnetic resonance, temperature-jump, and rapid stopped flow) for application to biological processes at cellular and subcellular levels. Also studies digital and analog computer simulation of biological problems and conducts biochemical studies of cellular respiration and energy conservation in plant and animal material, photon diffusion in tissues, medical optical imaging, brain oximetry, and breast tumor detection. **Publications:** *Johnson Research Foundation Colloquia.* **Formerly:** Institute for Structural and Functional Studies (1990).

★ 2583 ★ John L. McClellan Memorial Veterans' Hospital
Research Office

4300 W. 7th St.
Little Rock, AR 72205
Phone: (501)661-1202
Fax: (501)671-2510

Research Activities and Fields: Biomedicine, including studies of the molecular biology of tuberculosis and other mycobacterial diseases, radiation damage to DNA, molecular mechanisms of hyperthermia effects on tumors, toxic effects of antitumor drugs, and nephrology. Also conducts clinical studies in cardiology, stroke, and infectious diseases.

★ 2584 ★ Kansas State University
University Biochemistry Facility
Dept. of Biochemistry
Willard Hall
Manhattan, KS 66506-3702
Phone: (913)532-6121
Fax: (913)532-7278
Dr. Thomas Roche, Head

Research Activities and Fields: Biochemistry research, including protein sequencing, peptide sequencing, and oligonucleotide synthesis.

★ 2585 ★ Laboratory for Comparative
Biochemistry
4620 Santa Fe St.
San Diego, CA 92109
Phone: (619)274-5401
Dr. David Bartlett, Dir.

Research Activities and Fields: Biomedical sciences, especially comparative biochemistry, including studies on nature of living cells and organisms with special attention directed to a comparison between different species, red blood cell metabolism and function, improvement of blood storage methods, and carbohydrate-phosphate-nucleotide energy metabolic pathways and control.

★ 2586 ★ Laboratory of Molecular
Immunobiology
Memorial Sloan-Kettering Cancer Center
1275 York Ave.
Box 82
New York, NY 10021
Phone: (212)639-8252
Fax: (212)794-4019
Janet S. Lee, Ph.D., Head

Research Activities and Fields: Regulation of HLA Class II gene expression, genetic defects in immunodeficiencies, and aberrant expression on tumors. Studies genes controlling transcription and alternative splicing of the Class II and CD45 genes.

Laval University
Medical Research Centre
Ontogenesis and Molecular Genetics
Research Group
See: Entry 5336

Laval University
Molecular Microbiology and Protein
Engineering Group
See: Entry 5337

★ 2587 ★ Lehigh University
Institute for Health Sciences
Bethlehem, PA 18015
Phone: (610)758-3484
Fax: (610)758-5851
Jack A. Alhadeff, Dir.

Research Activities and Fields: Biological chemistry, biophysics, and molecular biology, including studies on microbiology, toxicology, immunology, virology, biochemistry, diseases of genetic origin, medicinal chemistry, radiation biophysics, clinical chemistry, diagnostic radio-

pharmaceuticals, natural products chemistry, neurophysiology, site-directed drug delivery, physiological basis of behavior, immunodiagnostics, chemical modification of monoclonal antibodies, targeted delivery of drugs, cell-surface interaction, biochemical markers of cancer, DNA/RNA structure and function, and gonadotrophin receptor isolation and characterization. Interdisciplinary research projects include design and synthesis of radiation sensitizer monoclonal antibodies for treatment of cancer, bacterial manipulation to produce a new strain designed to improve production of desired chemicals from fermentations, development of tumor imaging agents, and improvement of reagents for immunological testing.

★ 2588 ★ Linus Pauling Institute of Science
and Medicine
440 Page Mill Rd.
Palo Alto, CA 94306
Phone: (415)327-4064
Fax: (415)327-8564
Dr. Linus Pauling, Jr., Pres. and Board Chm.

Research Activities and Fields: Cardiovascular disease, nutritional biochemistry, cancer, genetics, virology, and viral immunodeficiency, emphasizing prevention and treatment of disease by nutritional means. **Publications:** Newsletter; Fact Sheets; Annual Report.

★ 2589 ★ Mailman Research Center
115 Mill St.
Belmont, MA 02178
Phone: (617)855-3227
Bruce M. Cohen, M.D., Contact

Research Activities and Fields: Neuropharmacology, neurochemistry, neuropathology, molecular neurogenetics, neuroregeneration, and molecular neurobiology with emphasis on psychiatric neurosciences.

★ 2590 ★ McLaughlin Research Institute
for Biomedical Sciences
1520 23rd St. S.
Great Falls, MT 59405-4900
Phone: (406)452-6208
Fax: (406)454-6019
Dr. George A. Carlson, Dir.

Research Activities and Fields: Genetics, immunogenetics, and cancer immunology, including studies of mouse histocompatibility genes and antigens, immunoregulatory gene family diversity and divergence, genetic basis of susceptibility to transmissible neurodegenerative disease, and mitotic recombination in mammalian cells.

★ 2591 ★ Medical Biology Institute
11077 N. Torrey Pines Rd.
La Jolla, CA 92037
Phone: (619)450-3033
Fax: (619)453-5845
Dr. David H. Katz, Pres.

Research Activities and Fields: Immunology, membrane and molecular biology, and developmental biology. Specific diseases being studied include allergy and asthma, rheumatoid arthritis, juvenile-onset diabetes, cancer, lupus, multiple sclerosis, and AIDS.

★ 2592 ★ Medical University of South
Carolina
Marine Biomedical and Environmental
Sciences
221 Ft. Johnson Rd.
Charleston, SC 29412
Phone: (803)762-5530
Fax: (803)762-5535
Dr. Donald Dibona, Dir.

Research Activities and Fields: Basic and applied biomedical research involving the use of marine organisms and their cells as models, particularly in toxicology, immunology, pathology, parasitology, and microbiology studies. **Formerly:** Marine Biomedical Research Program.

★ 2593 ★ Meharry Medical College
Research Center of Excellence in Cell and
Molecular Biology
Division of Biomedical Sciences
1005 D.B. Todd Blvd.
Nashville, TN 37208
Phone: (615)327-6193
Fax: (615)321-2999
Dr. George C. Hill, Program Dir.

Research Activities and Fields: Research emphasizes membrane biology, molecular biology, biochemistry, and immunology. Projects include an investigation of DNA replication mechanisms in normal and abnormal cell growth, viral infection, and the process of mutation; and biophysical analysis of enzyme cytochrome b5 activity in fat metabolism. Other interests include mitochondrial biogenesis, molecular biology of mammalian chromatin, immunobiology and immunogenetics, developmental neurobiology with an emphasis on neuronal plasticity, molecular biology of neuropeptides, cellular immunology and host-parasite interactions, molecular genetics, mechanisms of hormone action, gene therapy, and biochemistry of wound healing. **Publications:** *RCE Report.* **E-mail Address:** HILLGC@VUCTRVAX (Bitnet). **Formerly:** Center of Excellence in Cell and Molecular Biology.

★ 2594 ★ Mount Sinai School of Medicine
of City University of New York
Brookdale Center for Molecular Biology
1 Gustave Levy Pl.
Box 1126
New York, NY 10029-6574
Phone: (212)241-4272
Fax: (212)860-9279
Dr. Robert Lazzarini, Dir.

Research Activities and Fields: Molecular biology and medicine, including molecular neurobiology; developmental molecular biology; receptor and channel structure, function, and regulation; hormone, oncogene, and growth factor actions; the molecular and genetic basis of disease; cytokine action; and control of gene transcription.

★ 2595 ★ Mouse Mutant Resource
600 Main St.
Bar Harbor, ME 04609
Phone: (207)288-3371
Fax: (207)288-5079
Dr. Muriel T. Davisson, Staff Supv.

Research Activities and Fields: Identifies, characterizes, and genetically maps new inherited endocrine, neurological, immunological, skeletal, and other mutations of the laboratory mouse. **Formerly:** Formed by merger of two former units, the Mouse Mutant Gene Resource and Mouse Mutant Stock Center.

★ 2596 ★ National Biomedical Research Foundation
3900 Reservoir Rd. NW
Washington, DC 20007
Phone: (202)687-2121
Fax: (202)687-1662
Dr. Robert S. Ledley, Pres.

Research Activities and Fields: Application of computers and electronic technology to medical research, including biomedical picture pattern analysis, biology, biochemistry, origins of life, and computer technology. Specific research projects include studies on automatic chromosome analysis, biomedical instrumentation, computer aid to medical diagnosis, and genetics, evolution, and function of proteins and nucleic acids. **Publications:** *Newsletter of the Protein Information Resource*; *Pattern Recognition* (monthly journal); *Computers in Biology and Medicine* (bimothly); *Journal of Computerized Medical Imaging & Graphics* (bimonthly); *Journal of Computer Languages* (quarterly).

New York University
Center for Neural Science
See: Entry 8407

★ 2597 ★ Oak Ridge Institute for Science and Education (ORISE)
Oak Ridge Associated Universities
PO Box 117
Oak Ridge, TN 37831-0117
Phone: (615)576-3146
Fax: (615)576-4643
Dr. James E. Drewry, Dir./Exec.V.Pres.

Research Activities and Fields: Research and development in the areas of education and training, environmental and safety evaluation and analysis, occupational and environmental health, and enabling research. ORISE is composed of four research divisions. The Science/ Engineering Education Division seeks to increase the nation's supply of scientists and engineers; to broaden the participation of minorities, women, and the disabled in science and engineering careers; to enhance teacher preparation and faculty development; to strengthen cooperation within the academic community and federal laboratories; and to provide work force analysis, program evaluation, and technical assistance to federal agencies and laboratories. The Training and Management Systems Division designs, delivers, and manages training programs for the U.S. Department of Energy, other federal and state agencies, industries and industrial trade groups, and the private sector; manages widespread dissemination of training systems and information; conducts needs analyses; and finds solutions for training and human resource management problems. The Medical Sciences Division carries out basic research; develops beneficial applications to human health from science and technology; implements approaches to avoid, moderate, or reverse negative health impacts; analyzes the health risks and outcomes to society from appli-

cations of various industrial technologies; and provides information systems and management operations primarily for the U.S. Department of Energy, federal and international agencies, and industries such as utilities and pharmaceutical companies. The Energy and Environment Systems Division develops, analyzes, and evaluates policies and regulations affecting energy and environmental issues; carries out field surveys and assessments of hazardous materials sites; develops techniques for resource protection and enhancement; reviews safety analysis reports and participates in technical safety appraisals; and develops and implements energy systems application programs. **Publications:** Annual Report; *Express* (monthly newsletter); *Medical Research Report* (annually); *REAC/TS Newsletter* (periodically). Also publishes reports related to medical sciences, energy, education, and training.

★ 2598 ★ Oklahoma Center for Molecular Medicine
PO BOX 26901
Oklahoma City, OK 73190
Phone: (405)271-6655
Fax: (405)271-3910
Phillip C. Comp, M.D., Dir.

Research Activities and Fields: Molecular and cellular biology as related to human medicine. Specific research of the Center includes structure, function, and synthesis of macromolecules, structure, function, and behavior of cells, and molecular and cellular basis of disease.

★ 2599 ★ Oklahoma Medical Research Foundation
825 NE 13th St.
Oklahoma City, OK 73104
Phone: (405)271-7210
Fax: (405)271-3980
William G. Thurman, M.D., Pres.

Research Activities and Fields: Basic and clinical investigations in cardiovascular disease, cancer, arthritis, and thrombosis/hematology, including fundamental studies carried out in individually organized laboratories in the areas of molecular biology, biomembranes, lipoproteins, protein chemistry, intermediate metabolism, and genetics.

★ 2600 ★ Oklahoma Medical Research Foundation
Molecular Toxicology Research Group
825 NE 13th St.
Oklahoma City, OK 73104
Phone: (405)271-6673
Fax: (405)271-3980
William G. Thurman, M.D., Pres.

Research Activities and Fields: Seeks to provide new methods of diagnosing and treating diseases and health problems that may be caused by or are associated with normal metabolic processes of the cell, such as lipid peroxidation. Specific studies focus on determining the role of peroxistatin and glutathione in inhibiting lipid peroxidation. **Formerly:** Biomembrane Research Laboratory.

★ 2601 ★ Oklahoma Medical Research Foundation
Protein Studies Program
825 NE 13th St.
Oklahoma City, OK 73104
Phone: (405)271-7291
Fax: (405)271-7249
Dr. Jordan Tang, Dir.

Research Activities and Fields: Protein structure and function, including cloning, expression and mutagenesis of protease genes, mechanisms of proteases, proteolysis by lysosomal enzymes, and streptokinase interaction with plasminogen fibrinolysis. A major interest is the role of proteins in chemical carcinogenesis, particularly the role of proteins responsible for the intracellular transport of the carcinogen, benzopyrene.

★ 2602 ★ Oregon Health Sciences University
Vollum Institute for Advanced Biomedical Research
3181 SW Sam Jackson Park Rd., L474
Portland, OR 97201-3098
Phone: (503)494-5042
Fax: (503)494-4353
Richard Goodman, M.D., Dir.

Research Activities and Fields: Molecular biology, protein chemistry, virology, and immunology of the endocrine system and brain and nervous system. Also conducts studies in electrophysiology and pharmacology. **Formerly:** Institute for Advanced Biomedical Research (1986).

★ 2603 ★ Orentreich Foundation for the Advancement of Science, Inc.
Biomedical Research Station
Rd. 2, Box 375
Cold Spring, NY 10516
Phone: (914)265-4200
Fax: (914)265-4210
Norman Orentreich, Pres. and Dir.

Research Activities and Fields: Conducts biomedical research on dermatology, aging, endocrinology, and serum markers for human diseases. **Publications:** Report of the Director. **E-mail Address:** orentrch@acfcluster.nyu.edu.

★ 2604 ★ Pacific Northwest Research Foundation
720 Broadway
Seattle, WA 98122
Phone: (206)726-1210
Fax: (206)726-1217
William B. Hutchinson, M.D., Pres./Dir.

Research Activities and Fields: Medical sciences, including environmental biochemistry, membrane biochemistry, virus behavior in feline leukemia, biochemical oncology, immunology and limb transplantation, effects of radiation exposure, automation of certain laboratory chemical tests, natural products and acupuncture, prostate evaluation for cancer using ultrasound imaging, molecular epidemiology, and cell and molecular biology.

★2605★ Palo Alto Institute of Molecular Medicine
2462 Wyandotte St.
Mountain View, CA 94043
Phone: (415)694-1420
Fax: (415)694-7717
Dr. James W. Larrick, Dir.

Research Activities and Fields: Cellular and molecular biology, cancer, and immunoinflammatory diseases. **E-mail Address:** paimm@aol.com.

★2606★ Pearlman Biomedical Research Institute
Mt. Sinai Medical Center
4300 Alton Rd.
Miami Beach, FL 33140
Phone: (305)674-2790
Fax: (305)674-2198
Dr. William Abraham, Dir.

Research Activities and Fields: Pulmonary medicine, sleep disorders, pharmacology, dermatology, obstetrics and gynecology, infectious diseases, nuclear medicine, arthritis, and tumor biology.

★2607★ Philadelphia Biomedical Research Institute
100 Ross & Royal Rds.
King of Prussia, PA 19406
Phone: (610)962-0615
Fax: (610)962-0614
S. Tsuyoshi Ohnishi, Ph.D., Dir.

Research Activities and Fields: Mechanisms, methods of diagnosis, and pharmacological treatment of membrane-linked diseases through investigation of structure-function relationship in normal and abnormal biological membranes. Studies focus on the role of calcium ions in membrane structure and function; development of drugs to prevent ischemia-related membrane damages in the heart, liver, and brain; renal manifestations of ischemia during alcohol ingestation; sickle cell anemia; malignant hyperthermia; development of chemotherapies for malaria, cancer, and AIDS. Also develops techniques for biochemical assay, separation/fractionation, and spectrophotometry. **Publications:** *Brain Research*; *Cancer Letters*; *Free Radicals in Biology and Medicine*; *Prostaglandins Leucotrienes and Essential Fatty Acids*; *Arzneimittel Forschung/Drug Research*.

★2608★ Picower Institute for Medical Research
350 Community Dr.
Manhasset, NY 11030
Phone: (516)365-4200
Fax: (516)365-5090
Prof. Anthony Cerami, Ph.D., Pres.

Research Activities and Fields: Uses chemistry to study the pathogenesis of diseases and to develop drugs to treat them. Major areas of investigation include metabolic diseases and parasitology. **Formerly:** Laboratory of Medical Biochemistry, Rockefeller University.

★2609★ Princeton University Department of Molecular Biology
Princeton, NJ 08544
Phone: (609)258-5990
Fax: (609)258-3980
Dr. Arnold J. Levine, Chm.

Research Activities and Fields: Investigation of the molecular basis of cancer analysis of a number of viral and cellular oncogenes capable of subverting a cell from normal growth to transformed behavior, including studies on the oncogenic agents of adenovirus type 5, Simian Virus 40, and Epstein Barr virus and the activation and properties of cellular oncogenes ras, myc, and p53. Also conducts ongoing research on the structure and internal dynamics of DNA and chromatin and their complexes and interactions with carcinogens. **Formerly:** Department of Biology.

★2610★ Public Health Research Institute
455 1st Ave.
New York, NY 10016
Phone: (212)578-0800
Fax: (212)578-0804
Lewis M. Weinstein, Pres.

Research Activities and Fields: Biomedical research with a focus on infectious diseases and public health issues. **Publications:** Annual Report; Symposium Proceedings.

Rockefeller University Laboratory of Cellular Physiology and Immunology
See: Entry 2114

★2611★ Rosenstiel Basic Medical Sciences Research Center
Brandeis Univ.
415 S. St.
Waltham, MA 02254
Phone: (617)736-2400
Dr. Gregory Petsko, Dir.

Research Activities and Fields: Genetics and molecular biology, biochemistry, structural biology, protein crytallography, microbiology, biophysics, and cellular immunology. **E-mail Address:** ira@auriga.rose.brandeis.edu.

★2612★ Roswell Park Cancer Institute Laboratory of Flow Cytometry
Elm and Carlton Sts.
Buffalo, NY 14263
Phone: (716)845-8471
Fax: (716)845-8806
Dr. Carleton Stewart, Dir.

Research Activities and Fields: Licensed reference laboratory for the classification by immunophenotyping of leukemias and lymphomas, monitoring of transplant patients, and evaluation of DNA in solid tumors. Also uses multiparameter flow cytometry to study normal myeloid cell differentiation and the development of molecular phenotyping. Provides clinical research support for protocols that require specific immunophenotyping follow-up to monitor the progress of therapy and develops new tests to improve cancer management. **E-mail Address:** stewart@sc310.med.buffalo.edu.

★2613★ Rutgers University Bureau of Biological Research
PO Box 1059
Piscataway, NJ 08855-1059
Phone: (908)932-3972
Fax: (908)932-5870
Dr. David T. Denhardt, Dir.

Research Activities and Fields: Neurobiology and physiology, cell and developmental biology, and ecology and evolutionary biology.

★2614★ Rutgers University Cell and Cell Products Fermentation Facility
Waksman Institute
PO Box 759
Piscataway, NJ 08855-0759
Phone: (908)932-2925
Fax: (908)932-5735
Kenneth R. Callanan, Mgr.

Research Activities and Fields: Cell fermentation and production of primary and secondary metabolites such as recombinant proteins, hormones, enzymes, regulatory proteins, and antiviral, antibacterial, and antifungal compounds. **E-mail Address:** callanan@mbcl.rutgers.edu.

★2615★ Rutgers University Waksman Institute
PO Box 759
Piscataway, NJ 08855
Phone: (908)445-4257
Fax: (908)445-5735
Dr. Joachim Messing, Dir.

Research Activities and Fields: Microbial, developmental, and plant molecular genetics, and structural and computational biology. Studies focus on certain classes of organisms amenable to genetic analysis, such as bacteria and fungi, animal systems, and plants. **Publications:** Annual Report. **E-mail Address:** messing@mbcl.rutgers.edu.

★2616★ St. Francis Hospital and Medical Center Department of Research
114 Woodland St.
Hartford, CT 06105
Phone: (203)548-4068
Fax: (203)548-5415
Dr. Ernesto Canalis, Dir.

Research Activities and Fields: Cell and molecular biology, protein biochemistry, and coagulation/thrombosis research.

★2617★ St. Louis University Institute for Molecular Virology
3681 Park Ave.
St. Louis, MO 63110
Phone: (314)577-8403
Fax: (314)577-8406
Dr. Maurice Green, Chm.

Research Activities and Fields: Molecular biology, virology, cell bioliogy, oncology, and AIDS, including structure and function of human viruses and mechanism of virus replication and cell transformation by ribonucleic and deoxyribose acid tumor viruses. **Formerly:** Molecular Virology Institute.

★2618★ Salk Institute for Biological Studies
PO Box 85800
San Diego, CA 92186-5800
Phone: (619)453-4100
Fax: (619)552-8285
Dr. Brian E. Henderson, Pres.

Research Activities and Fields: Cellular and molecular biology and neuroscience with particular emphasis on immunology, cancer, molecular genetics, tumor virology, reproductive biology, neurobiology, neuroendocrinology, growth control, prebiotic chemistry, and neurotransmitter/neuroreceptor structure and function; research aimed toward the discovery of cause, prevention, control, and cure of disease. **Publications:** Newsletters; Research Reports; also publishes annual list of staff publications.

★2619★ San Francisco State University
Center for Advanced Medical Technology
1600 Holloway Ave.
San Francisco, CA 94132
Phone: (415)338-1696
Fax: (415)338-6136
Dr. William N. Bigler, Dir.

Research Activities and Fields: Clinical chemistry, immunology, microbiology, hematology, and virology. **E-mail Address:** wbigher@mercurysfsu.edu.

★2620★ Sherbrooke University
Cellular Mechanisms of Action and Ontogenesis Research Group
Faculte de medecine
Sherbrooke, PQ, Canada J1H 5N4
Phone: (819)564-5282
Fax: (819)564-5340
Jean-Guy Lehoux, Contact

Research Activities and Fields: Control of aldosterone secretion, gene expression in adrenal glands, and paracrine control of hormonal synthesis in placenta; regulation and development of hormone receptors in embryo; role of angiotensin II and calcium; study of chitosan and hypocholesterolemia and of ANF and gene expression in adrenal glands; and characterization of an androgen-independent prostate tumor cell line. **E-mail Address:** j.lehoux@courrier.usherb.ca.

★2621★ Sherbrooke University
Fundamental Electrophysiology Research Group
Department de physiologie et de biophysique
Faculte de medecine
Sherbrooke, PQ, Canada J1H 5N4
Phone: (819)564-5302
Fax: (819)564-5399
Elena Ruiz-Petrich, Dir.

Research Activities and Fields: Laser effects on the chorio-retinal interface, electrophysiology and neuropharmacology in visual perception, excitation contraction coupling, involvement of ionic channels in the stimulus-secretion process, control of body fluid volumes, maturation of prenatal control of ventilation, antiepileptic effects of adenosine, function and regulation of ionic channels of sarcoplasmic reticulum in skeletal and cardiac muscles, physiopathology of cardiac electrical alterations, electrophysiological basis of normal and pathological automaticity, production of tactile illustration for the visually impaired, automatic recognition of fingerprints, and electrophysiopharmacology and pathology of vascular, cardiac, and skeletal muscles.

★2622★ Southern Illinois University at Carbondale
Comparative Physiology Lab
243 Life Science II
Carbondale, IL 62901
Phone: (618)453-1518
Fax: (618)453-1517
Prof. Donald M. Miller, Head

Research Activities and Fields: Separation and characterization of small particulates and toxins, neuromuscular physiology of parasites, and tests of toxic substances. **E-mail Address:** miller@qm.c-som.siu.edu.

★2623★ Southern University and Agricultural and Mechanical College
Health Research Center
Lee Hall, Rm. 128
Southern Branch
PO Box 9921
Baton Rouge, LA 70813
Phone: (504)771-4240
Fax: (504)771-3607
Dr. Frederick A. Christian, Dir.

Research Activities and Fields: Biomedical research, including projects in immunology, bacteriology, parasitology, organic chemistry, biochemistry, textile chemistry, virology, cell physiology, molecular biology, physical chemistry, mechanical engineering, inorganic chemistry, reproductive physiology, and mycology.

Southwest Biomedical Research Institute
See: Entry 5349

★2624★ Southwest Foundation for Biomedical Research
PO Box 28147
San Antonio, TX 78228
Phone: (210)674-1410
Fax: (210)670-3301
Dr. Frank F. Ledford, Jr., M.D, Pres.

Research Activities and Fields: Arteriosclerosis, hypertension, cancer, pulmonary disease, aging, genetics, endocrinology, reproductive physiology, virology, neuropharmacology, behavioral science, and organic chemistry. **Publications:** Annual Report; *Progress in Medical Research* (quarterly). **E-mail Address:** dmoreno@darwin.sfbrorg. **Formerly:** Southwest Foundation for Research and Education.

Stanford University
Beckman Center for Molecular and Genetic Medicine
See: Entry 5351

★2625★ State University of New York College at Plattsburgh
Biochemistry Program
Plattsburgh, NY 12901
Phone: (518)564-3159
Dr. Roger L. Heintz, Chm.

Research Activities and Fields: Genetic engineering in plants and control of ultimate gene expression by intracellular and extracellular effectors, including studies in photosynthesis, interferon, mechanism of insulin action, nuclear thyroid hormone binding protein, insect hemocyte development, mechanism of learning, noise induced hearing loss, neuroacoustics, biological thermoregulation, biolistic delivery of transforming DNA, mitochondrial genetics as related to aging, environmental influence on microbial physiology, and molecular aspects of Alzheimer's disease.

★2626★ Tampa Bay Research Institute
10900 Roosevelt Blvd.
St. Petersburg, FL 33716
Phone: (813)576-6675
Fax: (813)577-9862
Dr. Meihan Nonoyama, Pres.

Research Activities and Fields: Molecular genetics, virology, cellular biochemistry, AIDS, gene therapy, cytokines, and cancer. **Publications:** Newsletter (quarterly). **E-mail Address:** tbri@intnet.net. **Formerly:** Showa University Research Institute (1989).

Texas A&M University
Center for Cellular and Molecular Nutrition
See: Entry 9527

★2627★ Texas A&M University
Center for Extracellular Matrix Biology
Alkek Institute of Biosciences and Technology
2121 W. Holcombe Blvd.
Houston, TX 77030-3303
Phone: (713)677-7725
Fax: (713)677-7700
Dr. Magnus Hook, Dir.

Research Activities and Fields: Composition and structural organization of the extracellular matrix in normal physiological and disease processes. Specific research areas include cell adhesion, migration, proliferation, and differentiation; genetic diseases involving connective tissue such as bone and cartilage, metabolic diseases such as diabetes, inflammatory diseases such as rheumatoid arthritis and arteriolosclerosis, and cancer metastasis; matrix interactions at the molecular level; replacement of normal genes with mutated ones; and molecular mechanisms of microbial adhesion to the extracellular matrix.

★2628★ Texas A&M University
Center for Macromolecular Design
College Station, TX 77843-2128
Phone: (409)845-1782
Fax: (409)845-9274
Dr. Thomas O. Baldwin, Dir.

Research Activities and Fields: Structure and activity of biological macromolecules, with emphasis on proteins. **E-mail Address:** baldwin@mail.msen.com.

★2629★ Texas A&M University
Institute of Biosciences & Technology
2121 W. Holcombe Blvd.
Houston, TX 77030-3303
Phone: (713)677-7700
Fax: (713)677-7725
Robert D. Walls, Ph.D., Dir.

Research Activities and Fields: Genome research, mammalian DNA and RNA viruses, eucaryotic gene expression, neurobiology, human nutrition, matrix biology, plant molecular biology, and cancer biology.

★ 2630 ★ Texas A&M University
Laboratory Animal Resources and
Research Facility
Agronomy Rd.
College Station, TX 77801
Phone: (409)845-7433
Dr. Gary N. Joiner, Dir.

Research Activities and Fields: Supports a wide variety of research conducted by faculty members from many disciplines, including cardiovascular physiology, immunology, nutrition, embryo transfer, and industrial toxicology. **Publications:** *TAMU Guide for Laboratory Animal Care.*

★ 2631 ★ Thomas Jefferson University
Daniel Baugh Institute
Jefferson Alumni Hall
1020 Locust St.
Philadelphia, PA 19107
Phone: (215)955-7820
Fax: (215)923-2218
Dr. Emanuel Rubin, Chm.

Research Activities and Fields: Biochemical, physiologic, and anatomic basis for abnormal development in vivo and in vitro, including molecular and genetic mechanisms of teratogenesis, experimental embryology and morphology, normal and abnormal developmental biology, lipid metabolism, tissue and embryo culture, cytology, molecular biology, and cell biology.

★ 2632 ★ Thomas Jefferson University
Jefferson Institute of Molecular Medicine
350 BLSB
233 S. 10th St.
Philadelphia, PA 19107
Phone: (215)955-4830
Fax: (215)955-5393
Darwin Prockop, M.D., Dir.

Research Activities and Fields: Institute conducts studies in biochemistry and molecular medicine.

U.S. Department of Defense
Armed Forces Institute of Pathology
Environmental Pathology Department
Biochemistry Division
See: Entry 10165

U.S. Department of Defense
Army Medical Research and Development
Command
Walter Reed Army Institute of Research
Biochemistry Division
See: Entry 7829

★ 2633 ★ U.S. Department of Energy
Argonne National Laboratory
9700 S. Cass Ave.
Argonne, IL 60439-4832
Phone: (312)252-3872
Alan Schriesheim, Ph.D., Chief Executive Officer

Research Activities and Fields: Primary focus is on energy related issues. Programs in the physical sciences include research in high energy physics, nuclear physics, chemical sciences, materials sciences, engineering, geosciences, mathematics, and computer science. Engineering research programs focus on integral fast reactor technology, including fuel performance demonstration, pyroprocessing development, safety analyses, reactor core design, fuel cycle demonstration, and liquid-metal technology and development. Other engineering programs include new production reactors, advanced reactor research, fusion energy, nuclear fuel cycle, nuclear waste repositories, remedial action programs, and waste management (commercial and defense). Energy, environmental, and biological research includes studies in biochemistry of metals, biostatistics, carcinogenesis, cellular biology, electromagnetic fields, environmental health, gene expression, human genome, low-level radiation effects, molecular biology mutagenesis (heritable and somatic), neurobehavioral chronobiology, nuclear medicine, oncogenes, photobiology, protein mapping, radiation biology and genetics, radiation protection standards, structural biology, energy conservation, fossil energy, renewable energy, advanced energy systems programs, atmospheric physics, biotechnology, ecological models, environmental effects, environmental geoscience and engineering, fundamental molecular physics and chemistry, global climate change, integrated assessments, site characterization and remedial action, and waste minimization. In addition, Argonne's Technology Transfer Center is responsible for transferring Argonne-developed technologies to private firms that can develop them for national, state, and local marketplaces. The Laboratory also has one of the largest programs in support of mathematics and science education at every level from elementary school through postdoctoral studies. **Publications:** *Logos* (quarterly); *Research Highlights* (annually).

U.S. Department of Energy
Lawrence Berkeley Laboratory
Life Science Division
See: Entry 6124

★ 2634 ★ U.S. Department of Energy
Lawrence Livermore National Laboratory
PO Box 808
Livermore, CA 94550
Phone: (510)422-1100
Fax: (510)423-2224
Dr. John H. Knuckolls, Director

Research Activities and Fields: LLNL's mission is to conduct research, development, and educational activities in physics, energy, biomedical and environmental sciences, and materials development. Part of the Laboratory's work is in nuclear weapons, including detailed designing of nuclear warheads, stockpile surveillance, non-proliferation analysis, treaty verification technology, and allied matters. (Some defense-related work in nonnuclear fields is done also.) Other LLNL activities involve research on energy and in biological and environmental science. Energy programs are devoted mainly to research in fusion energy, including magnetic fusion and laser fusion. (The LLNL laser fusion program is the largest in the United States.) Some research is conducted in energy conservation and resource recovery, with emphasis on in situ resource recovery (gas from coal, oil from shale); solar energy applications; and new approaches to old ideas (batteries and flywheels for automotive propulsion). Environmental programs include studies in aquatic and terrestrial ecology; pollutant transport processes; development of field instrumentation; and analyses of the implications of national energy policies. Biomedical research is concerned with gene mutation and cancer induction. LLNL also has a program in advanced isotope separation, which has a number of potential applications, including uranium enrichment. Also assists the Nuclear Regulatory Commission with technical problems related to reactor safety safeguards and waste management; engages in educational programs in coordination with University of California; and performs testing activities at the high explosives facility near Livermore and at the Nevada Test Site.

★ 2635 ★ U.S. Department of Energy
Oak Ridge National Laboratory
Environmental, Life, and Social Sciences
Directorate
Biology Division
PO Box 2009
Oak Ridge, TN 37831
Phone: (615)574-0212
Fax: (615)574-9297
F.C. Hartman, Director

Research Activities and Fields: Division comprises: 1) the Molecular, Cellular, and Cancer Biology Section, which studies protein engineering and chemistry, RNA metabolism, structural biology, genome structure and organization, membrane biology, molecular immunology, radiation carcinogenesis, molecular genetics of cancer, chromosome chemistry, and fundamental and applied cryobiology; and 2) the Mammalian Genetics and Development Section, which is concerned primarily with genetics and mutagenesis, developmental genetics and genome analysis, chromosomal damage, insertional mutagenesis, organismic effects, mammalian biochemical genetics, and DNA sequencing technology.

U.S. Department of Health and Human
Services
National Cancer Institute
Division of Cancer Biology, Diagnosis, and
Centers Extramural Research Program
Cancer Biology Branch
See: Entry 6136

U.S. Department of Health and Human
Services
National Cancer Institute
Laboratory of Biochemistry
See: Entry 6175

U.S. Department of Health and Human
Services
National Cancer Institute
Laboratory of Biological Chemistry
See: Entry 6176

U.S. Department of Health and Human
  Services
National Cancer Institute
Laboratory of Biology
See: Entry 6177

U.S. Department of Health and Human
  Services
National Cancer Institute
Laboratory of Cellular Carcinogenesis and
  Tumor Promotion
See: Entry 6179

U.S. Department of Health and Human
  Services
National Cancer Institute
Laboratory of Cellular and Molecular
  Biology
See: Entry 6180

U.S. Department of Health and Human
  Services
National Cancer Institute
Laboratory of Cellular Oncology
See: Entry 6181

U.S. Department of Health and Human
  Services
National Cancer Institute
Laboratory of Experimental
  Carcinogenesis
See: Entry 6184

U.S. Department of Health and Human
  Services
National Cancer Institute
Laboratory of Human Carcinogenesis
See: Entry 6188

U.S. Department of Health and Human
  Services
National Cancer Institute
Laboratory of Mathematical Biology
See: Entry 6190

U.S. Department of Health and Human
  Services
National Cancer Institute
Laboratory of Medicinal Chemistry
See: Entry 6191

U.S. Department of Health and Human
  Services
National Cancer Institute
Laboratory of Molecular Biology
See: Entry 6192

U.S. Department of Health and Human
  Services
National Cancer Institute
Laboratory of Molecular Carcinogenesis
See: Entry 6193

U.S. Department of Health and Human
  Services
National Cancer Institute
Laboratory of Molecular Oncology
See: Entry 6195

U.S. Department of Health and Human
  Services
National Cancer Institute
Laboratory of Molecular Virology
See: Entry 6197

U.S. Department of Health and Human
  Services
National Cancer Institute
Laboratory of Tumor Cell Biology
See: Entry 6199

U.S. Department of Health and Human
  Services
National Cancer Institute
Laboratory of Tumor Immunology and
  Biology
See: Entry 6200

U.S. Department of Health and Human
  Services
National Cancer Institute
Laboratory of Tumor Virus Biology
See: Entry 6201

U.S. Department of Health and Human
  Services
National Cancer Institute
Laboratory of Viral Carcinogenesis
See: Entry 6202

★ 2636 ★ U.S. Department of Health and
  Human Services
National Center for Research Resources
12 South Dr.
Bethesda, MD 20892-5662
Phone: (301)496-5793
Fax: (301)402-0218
Robert A. Whitney, Jr., D.V.M., Director

Research Activities and Fields: Center provides resources necessary for the conduct of
basic and clinical research. Specifically, it provides financial support (through grants and contracts) to: 1) a network of centralized, cost-
effective General Clinical Research Centers for
interdisciplinary, multicategorical research conducted primarily by NIH-supported investigators; 2) enhance primate research centers and
other valuable animal colonies where laboratory
models of human disease are developed and
studied, upgrade laboratory animal facilities,
and develop nonmammalian models for
biomedical research; 3) provide institutions with
discretionary funds for the development of resources used in biomedical research; 4) develop shared resources such as biomedical computing, biomedical engineering, and biomedical
instrumentation centers that provide collaborating scientists with the latest tools from the physical sciences, mathematics, and engineering; 5)
increase the number of ethnic minorities that become biomedical scientists; 6) develop and enhance scientific infrastructure at minority institutions that offer doctorates in the health professions or health related sciences; 7) construct,
renovate, modernize, and expand existing facilities; 8) promote interest in biomedical research
careers among minority high school students
through experience in professional research
laboratories; and 9) provide professional services to the NIH campus through the NIH library
and the Medical Arts and Photography Branch.

Principal Center components are the: Biological
Models and Materials Research Program;
Biomedical Engineering and Instrumentation
Program; Biomedical Research Support Pro-
gram; Biomedical Research Technology Pro-
gram; Comparative Medicine Program; General
Clinical Research Centers Program; Medical
Arts and Photography Branch; NIH Library
Branch; Research Centers in Minority Institu-
tions Program; and Veterinary Resources Pro-
gram. **Publications:** Center publishes *Research
Resources Reporter* (monthly); and *Program Di-
rectories* and *Program Highlights* (annually).

U.S. Department of Health and Human
  Services
National Eye Institute
Laboratory of Molecular and
  Developmental Biology
See: Entry 13641

U.S. Department of Health and Human
  Services
National Eye Institute
Laboratory of Retinal Cell and Molecular
  Biology
See: Entry 13642

U.S. Department of Health and Human
  Services
National Heart, Lung, and Blood Institute
Division of Intramural Research
Molecular Disease Branch
See: Entry 2942

U.S. Department of Health and Human
  Services
National Heart, Lung, and Blood Institute
Laboratory of Biochemical Genetics
See: Entry 2944

U.S. Department of Health and Human
  Services
National Heart, Lung, and Blood Institute
Laboratory of Biochemistry
See: Entry 2945

U.S. Department of Health and Human
  Services
National Heart, Lung, and Blood Institute
Laboratory of Biophysical Chemistry
See: Entry 2946

U.S. Department of Health and Human
  Services
National Heart, Lung, and Blood Institute
Laboratory of Cell Biology
See: Entry 2948

U.S. Department of Health and Human
  Services
National Heart, Lung, and Blood Institute
Laboratory of Cellular Metabolism
See: Entry 2949

U.S. Department of Health and Human
  Services
National Heart, Lung, and Blood Institute
Laboratory of Molecular Cardiology
See: Entry 2952

U.S. Department of Health and Human Services
National Institute on Aging
Biology of Aging Program
See: Entry 1950

U.S. Department of Health and Human Services
National Institute on Aging
Biology of Aging Program
Biology Branch
See: Entry 1951

U.S. Department of Health and Human Services
National Institute on Aging
Laboratory of Cellular and Molecular Biology
See: Entry 1959

U.S. Department of Health and Human Services
National Institute on Aging
Laboratory of Molecular Genetics
See: Entry 1961

★2637★ U.S. Department of Health and Human Services
National Institute of Child Health and Human Development
Intramural Research Program
Cell Biology and Metabolism Branch
NIH Bldg. 18T
9000 Rockville Pike
Bethesda, MD 20892
Phone: (301)496-6368
Dr. Richard D. Klausner, Chief

Research Activities and Fields: Branch investigates aspects of intracellular structure and function. Activities include: 1) utilizing various methods to study receptor biosynthesis, dynamics, and regulation using the human transferrin receptor as a model; 2) conducting clinical research on the fundamental mechanisms and treatment of patients with genetic disorders of iron metabolism to learn how the intracellular traffic of iron is controlled; 3) examining mechanisms by which intracellular architecture is maintained, providing the basis for the function and dynamics of cellular organelles; and 4) studying the biochemistry and ultrastructure of gametes, with emphasis on cell biological aspects of fertilization and the initiation of embryonic development. A principal component is the Organelle and Receptor Structure and Function Section.

★2638★ U.S. Department of Health and Human Services
National Institute of Child Health and Human Development
Intramural Research Program
Viruses and Cellular Biology Section
9000 Rockville Pike
Bethesda, MD 20892
Phone: (301)496-2133
Fax: (301)402-0105
Dr. Arthur S. Levine, Head

Research Activities and Fields: Section uses DNA viruses to probe the developmental program of macromolecules (e.g., onc gene products) that regulate changes in the phenotypes of normal and transformed animal cells. The DNA viruses are also used as models in studies on mammalian mutagenesis and DNA repair/replication. Techniques of virology, tissue culture, somatic cell hybridization, molecular biology, and immunology are used.

★2639★ U.S. Department of Health and Human Services
National Institute of Child Health and Human Development
Laboratory of Theoretical and Physical Biology
NIH Bldg. 10, Rm. 10D-14
9000 Rockville Pike
Bethesda, MD 20892
Phone: (301)496-6571
Dr. Joshua Zimmerberg, Chief

Research Activities and Fields: Laboratory conducts multidisciplinary and theoretical studies, applying mathematical, statistical, and computer-based techniques to the analysis of complex clinical, biological, biochemical, and pharmacological problems. Experimental work involves the study of receptors for drugs, hormones, and neurotransmitters; the pharmacokinetics of calcium, cortisol, glucose, carnitine, and amino acids in humans; and the physical-chemical characterization of peptide hormones using polyacrylamide gel electrophoresis and related approaches. Activities are carried out in Laboratory's Macromolecular Analysis Section, Metabolic Analysis and Mass Spectroscopy Section, and Theoretical Biology Section.

★2640★ U.S. Department of Health and Human Services
National Institute of Dental Research
Laboratory of Cellular Development and Oncology
NIH Bldg. 30
9000 Rockville Pike
Bethesda, MD 20892
Phone: (301)496-3695
Fax: (301)402-0823
Keith C. Robbins, Chief

Research Activities and Fields: Conducts basic research on the normal and aberrant functions of tissues, cells, and molecules as they relate to oral disease and other disease states, placing a special emphasis on the etiology, diagnosis, treatment, and prevention of oral tumors. Fields of study include cell biology, molecular biology, developmental biology, enzymology, immunochemistry, and protein chemistry.

★2641★ U.S. Department of Health and Human Services
National Institute of Dental Research
Laboratory of Developmental Biology
NIH Bldg. 30, Rm. 421
9000 Rockville Pike
Bethesda, MD 20892
Phone: (301)496-5974
Fax: (301)402-0897
Kenneth M. Yamada, M.D., Director

Research Activities and Fields: Laboratory conducts research on the structure, function, and regulation of extracellular matrix molecules, their receptors, and other cell interaction systems. Research focuses on examining the functions and regulation of these systems in: 1) normal and abnormal development of craniofacial and other tissues; 2) connective tissue remodeling; 3) tumor metastasis and invasion; and 4) other diseases and disorders involving extracellular molecules. Information on cell-matrix interaction mechanisms is applied to the development of biological and biochemical reagents for the understanding and therapy of oral and other diseases.

U.S. Department of Health and Human Services
National Institute of Diabetes and Digestive and Kidney Diseases
Division of Intramural Research
Genetics and Biochemistry Branch
See: Entry 5364

U.S. Department of Health and Human Services
National Institute of Diabetes and Digestive and Kidney Diseases
Laboratory of Analytical Chemistry
See: Entry 4924

★2642★ U.S. Department of Health and Human Services
National Institute of Diabetes and Digestive and Kidney Diseases
Laboratory of Biochemical Pharmacology
NIH Bldg. 8, Rm. 223
9000 Rockville Pike
Bethesda, MD 20892
Phone: (301)496-4193
Herbert Tabor, Chief

Research Activities and Fields: The work of this Laboratory includes a large variety of biochemical, genetic, and molecular biological investigations. Included are studies on polyamine synthesis and action, nucleic acid and protein biosynthesis, tryptophan biosynthesis, and yeast and *Escherichia coli* genetics. Studies are also carried out on developmental biology and genomic structure and aim at identifying and isolating those genes that must be expressed to attain or maintain a particular state of cell differentiation.

★2643★ U.S. Department of Health and Human Services
National Institute of Diabetes and Digestive and Kidney Diseases
Laboratory of Biochemistry and Metabolism
NIH Bldg. 10
9000 Rockville Pike
Bethesda, MD 20892
Phone: (301)496-4391
Fax: (301)496-0839
William B. Jakoby, Chief

Research Activities and Fields: Laboratory's program is directed toward an understanding of the basic biochemical mechanisms involved in both normal and abnormal biological processes. Principal fields of interest include enzymology, molecular biology, cell biology, and toxicological aspects of cell activities.

★ 2644 ★ U.S. Department of Health and Human Services
National Institute of Diabetes and Digestive and Kidney Diseases
Laboratory of Bioorganic Chemistry
NIH Bldg. 8A, Rm. 1A17
9000 Rockville Pike
Bethesda, MD 20892
Phone: (301)496-4024
Fax: (301)402-0008
John W. Daly, Chief

Research Activities and Fields: Laboratory's research mission is to elucidate the mechanism of interaction of pharmacologically active substances with biological systems. Research is designed to develop new chemical agents as tools for the study of membrane and cytosol functions of cells. New mechanisms of action or metabolism of such agents are also investigated for their potential use as therapeutics. Emphasis is on development and application of modern techniques of organic chemistry for the synthesis, separation, and spectral investigation of these chemical agents and their interactions with macromolecules. The goal is to provide insights into the normal and pathologic function of biological systems and to delineate the metabolic formation, fate, and action of physiologically active agents such as amino acids, biogenic amines, cyclic nucleotides, hormones, neurotransmitters, and steroids. Studies include pharmacologically active agents such as natural products, central stimulants, depressants, tranquilizers, anxiolytics, and other therapeutic agents, toxins, carcinogens, and mutagens.

U.S. Department of Health and Human Services
National Institute of Diabetes and Digestive and Kidney Diseases
Laboratory of Cell Biology and Genetics
See: Entry 4925

★ 2645 ★ U.S. Department of Health and Human Services
National Institute of Diabetes and Digestive and Kidney Diseases
Laboratory of Cellular and Developmental Biology
NIH Bldg. 6, Rm. B1-26
9000 Rockville Pike
Bethesda, MD 20892
Phone: (301)496-6125
Robert T. Simpson, Chief

Research Activities and Fields: Laboratory conducts biochemical and physiological investigations in four main areas: 1) endocrinology, including research on hormonal regulation of enzymes involved in chylomicron uptake and metabolism in adipose and mammary tissues, the influence of hormones on cellular development and metabolism, and the disposition of fat and metabolites in the cell as viewed from ultrastructural studies; 2) nutritional biochemistry, including studies on the structural and functional aspects of dihydrofolic reductase and other enzymes involved in folic acid metabolism and the intermediary metabolism of lipids, carbohydrates, and amino acids in the small intestine; 3) membrane regulation, including studies on the mechanism of action of hormones on adenylate cyclase and other membrane regulatory pro-

cesses; and 4) developmental biochemistry, including studies on the structure and function of chromatin and the regulation of gene function during development.

★ 2646 ★ U.S. Department of Health and Human Services
National Institute of Diabetes and Digestive and Kidney Diseases
Laboratory of Chemical Biology
NIH Bldg. 10, Rm. 9N307
9000 Rockville Pike
Bethesda, MD 20892
Phone: (301)496-5408
Fax: (301)402-0101
Dr. Alan N. Schechter, Chief

Research Activities and Fields: Laboratory conducts basic research in: 1) chemical biology, including protein chemistry; and 2) molecular genetics, including genetic diseases and AIDS. Research focuses on the control of gene expression, folding of proteins, and therapy of genetic diseases.

★ 2647 ★ U.S. Department of Health and Human Services
National Institute of Diabetes and Digestive and Kidney Diseases
Laboratory of Chemical Physics
NIH Bldg. 2
9000 Rockville Pike
Bethesda, MD 20892
Phone: (301)496-1024
Fax: (301)496-0825
William A. Eaton, Chief

Research Activities and Fields: Research in this laboratory is characterized by the application of modern physical techniques to the study of a wide range of biological problems. Much of the research involves the use of a variety of spectroscopic methods (e.g., nuclear and electron magnetic resonance, laser-Raman and resonance Raman spectroscopy), electric-field-induced dichroism, ultraviolet and visible microspectrophotometry, and time-resolved absorption spectroscopy with nanosecond lasers.

★ 2648 ★ U.S. Department of Health and Human Services
National Institute of Diabetes and Digestive and Kidney Diseases
Laboratory of Molecular Biology
NIH Bldg. 2, Rm. 319
9000 Rockville Pike
Bethesda, MD 20892
Phone: (301)496-1490
Dr. Nancy Nossal, Acting Chief

Research Activities and Fields: Laboratory is concerned with understanding biological processes in terms of structure and reaction at the molecular level. Research includes direct investigations of biological processes, such as genetic recombination, DNA replication, and protein synthesis; studies of the mechanism of transformation by SV40 (a virus causing tumors in hamsters); and studies of the mechanism of hemoglobin S gelation, the phenomenon that causes sickling of red blood cells in sickle cell anemia. Other investigations are concerned with the structure and chemical properties of biologically important materials.

★ 2649 ★ U.S. Department of Health and Human Services
National Institute of Diabetes and Digestive and Kidney Diseases
Laboratory of Molecular and Cellular Biology
NIH Bldg. 2, Rm. 310
9000 Rockville Pike
Bethesda, MD 20892
Phone: (301)496-3356
Dr. Barrie J. Carter, Chief

Research Activities and Fields: Laboratory conducts biomedical research in molecular and cellular biology. Principal areas of research interest include: molecular virology; gene regulation in humans; viruses; function of oncogene; development of virus vectors for genetic engineering and gene therapy; endocrine regulation of mammary gland development and tumors; growth factors; and genetic diseases.

U.S. Department of Health and Human Services
National Institute on Drug Abuse
Basic Research Division
Biomedical Research Branch
See: Entry 12123

U.S. Department of Health and Human Services
National Institute of Environmental Health Sciences
Laboratory of Molecular Biophysics
See: Entry 5107

★ 2650 ★ U.S. Department of Health and Human Services
National Institute of General Medical Sciences
Biophysics and Physiological Sciences Program
5333 Westbard Ave., Rm. 909
Bethesda, MD 20892
Phone: (301)594-7800
Fax: (301)594-7700
James Cassatt, Acting Director

Research Activities and Fields: The Biophysics and Physiological Sciences (BPS) Program has three major objectives: 1) to apply the physical, chemical, physiological, and engineering sciences to solve significant biomedical problems; 2) to develop new and improved instruments and techniques for research at the molecular, cellular, and organismic levels; and 3) to broaden and strengthen the scientific base in those areas of clinical and physiological research for which the Institute is responsible. Supported research ranges from studies on the structure of proteins to clinical investigations and includes certain aspects of the behavioral sciences. BPS support in bioengineering research includes the development of instruments in the areas of spectroscopy, X-ray and other scattering techniques, microscopy, and cell separation methods; the development of biomaterials and prostheses; and the application of control theory and mathematical modeling to the analysis of physiological systems. The BPS program also funds studies in physiology, biochemistry, and immunology as they relate to trauma and burns. This includes the biochemical and physiological changes induced by trauma and fundamental aspects of wound healing and biological repair. The program encourages research on the systemic response to post-traumatic infection and on the metabolic response of the injured patient in both the acute and convalescent states. In addition, the program funds pre- and postdoctoral research training in selected areas such as structural biology systems and integrative biology and trauma and burns.

★ 2651 ★ U.S. Department of Health and Human Services
National Institute of General Medical Sciences
Cellular and Molecular Basis of Disease Program
903 Westwood Bldg.
5333 Westbard Ave.
Bethesda, MD 20892
Phone: (301)496-7021
Fax: (301)402-0019
Charles A. Miller, Ph.D., Director

Research Activities and Fields: Program supports extramural research concerned with the biophysical and biochemical description and analysis of molecular events in normal and diseased cells and with the structure and function of cell organelles and membranes at molecular and subcellular levels as well as the cellular level. The Program's goal is to develop better understanding of the structure and function of human cells and cells of other species, with the basic premise that many forms of human disease occur ultimately as the direct result of disturbed or abnormal function of cells. Research is concerned with: 1) detailed submolecular structure and function of enzymes, other proteins, and other biological substances; 2) development of knowledge of subcellular organelles and their constituents into more precise concepts of how the cell functions as a unit; 3) cell-cell interactions during morphogenesis and other processes; 4) mechanisms by which enzymes bring about their catalytic effects; and 5) elucidation of the relationship between chemical structure and biological activity. Support is provided for studies on basic biological and biochemical principles, regardless of the particular experimental system being used. A broad array of genetic and highly quantitative methods and instruments is essential to this research. The Program also supports predoctoral research training in the fields of biochemistry, cell and molecular biology, and genetics which encompasses these research areas.

★ 2652 ★ U.S. Department of Health and Human Services
National Institute of General Medical Sciences
Medical Scientist Training Program
5333 Westbard Ave., Rm. 905
Bethesda, MD 20892
Phone: (301)594-7744
Fax: (301)594-7700
Lee Van Lenten, M.D., Director

Research Activities and Fields: The objective of the Medical Scientist Training Program (MSTP) is to assist universities and their medical schools in developing special programs of combined scientific and medical training leading to the M.D.-Ph.D. degree in order to meet the need for clinical investigators who have been trained in basic research in biomedical science research. Using an integrated scientific and medical curriculum, the Program seeks to prepare its graduates to undertake careers in biomedical research and academic medicine. Candidates for admission to MSTP must show evidence of high academic performance and significant prior research experience. Up to six years of support, including a stipend, tuition, and limited sums for travel, equipment, and supplies are provided by the program. Universities that administer the programs are responsible for trainee selection. Continued MSTP support is subject to annual renewal based on satisfactory performance of the individual in the program and successful competition of the institution for funds at the time of grant renewal every three to five years.

★ 2653 ★ U.S. Department of Health and Human Services
National Institute of General Medical Sciences
Minority Access to Research Careers Program
5333 Westbard Ave.
Bethesda, MD 20892
Phone: (301)496-7941
Fax: (301)402-0021
Elward Bynum, Director

Research Activities and Fields: MARC is a minority institutional fellowship and traineeship program for faculty members and students of minority institutions interested in health-related research. It is composed of a Predoctoral and Postdoctoral Faculty Fellowship Program, a Visiting Scientist Program, an Honors Undergraduate Research Training Program, and a Predoctoral Fellowship Program. MARC faculty fellowships are awarded to selected full-time faculty members of four-year colleges, universities, and health professional schools in which student enrollment is drawn substantially from ethnic minority groups. Applicants must be nominated by their institutions and are expected to return to the sponsoring institution after completion of the fellowship. MARC visiting scientist fellowships are awarded to outstanding scientist-teachers to serve as visiting scientists at eligible minority institutions. Under the MARC Honors Undergraduate Research Training Program, awards are made to minority schools for support of 8-10 honors students in college, in order to increase the number of minority students who can compete successfully for entry into graduate programs leading to the Ph.D. degree in a biomedical science. The fourth support method, the MARC Predoctoral Fellowship Program, provides awards to selected graduates of the MARC Honors Undergraduate Research Training Program to help provide living expenses and tuition while the students pursue studies in biomedical sciences leading to the Ph.D. degree. Established in 1991 is a National Postdoctoral Fellowship Program for minority students at any institution in the U.S.

★ 2654 ★ U.S. Department of Health and Human Services
National Institute of General Medical Sciences
Minority Biomedical Research Support Program
Westwood Bldg., Rm. 952
5333 Westbard Ave.
Bethesda, MD 20892
Phone: (301)594-7949
Fax: (301)594-7733
Dr. Ciriaco Q. Gonzales, Director

Research Activities and Fields: Seeks to increase the number and quality of minority research scientists, faculty, and institutional involvement in biomedical research through grants to eligible minority institutions, with emphasis on undergraduate participation in all aspects of biomedical research. Funding provides support to: 1) strengthen the capability of eligible institutions to conduct quality research in the health sciences; 2) enable faculty at eligible institutions to initiate and/or expand their biomedical research interests and capabilities through release time from teaching for the conduct of research and travel to attend scientific meetings; and 3) help students engage in research projects at the undergraduate and graduate level and to motivate and prepare them for careers in biomedical research. In addition, funding provides for the purchase of scientific equipment, facility renovations, and improvement of animal care facilities.

U.S. Department of Health and Human Services
National Institute of Mental Health
General and Comparative Biochemistry Laboratory
See: Entry 7633

U.S. Department of Health and Human Services
National Institute of Mental Health
Intramural Research Programs Division
See: Entry 7634

U.S. Department of Health and Human Services
National Institute of Mental Health
Molecular Biology Laboratory
See: Entry 7643

U.S. Department of Health and Human Services
National Institute of Neurological Disorders and Stroke
Biophysics Section
See: Entry 8443

U.S. Department of Health and Human Services
National Institute of Neurological Disorders and Stroke
Laboratory of Molecular Biology
See: Entry 8460

U.S. Department of Health and Human
Services
National Institute of Neurological Disorders
and Stroke
Laboratory of Molecular and Cellular
Neurobiology
See: Entry 8461

U.S. Department of Health and Human
Services
National Institute of Neurological Disorders
and Stroke
Laboratory of Neurobiology
See: Entry 8463

U.S. Department of Health and Human
Services
National Institute of Neurological Disorders
and Stroke
Laboratory of Neurochemistry
See: Entry 8464

U.S. Department of Health and Human
Services
National Institute of Neurological Disorders
and Stroke
Laboratory of Neurophysiology
See: Entry 8465

U.S. Department of Health and Human
Services
National Institute for Occupational Safety
and Health
Biomedical and Behavioral Science
Division
Applied Biology Branch
See: Entry 9827

★2655★ U.S. Department of Health and
Human Services
National Institutes of Health
Division of Computer Research and
Technology
NIH Bldg. 12A, Rm. 3033
9000 Rockville Pike
Bethesda, MD 20892
Phone: (301)496-5703
David Rodbard, Director

Research Activities and Fields: Division's activities cover a broad spectrum, ranging from
conducting research in biology, statistics, mathematics, and computer science to providing
computer facilities and services for NIH. These
activities are carried out in laboratories for Applied Studies, Computer Systems, Physical Sciences, and Statistical and Mathematical Methodology. In addition, the Computer Center
Branch designs, implements, and operates the
NIH Computer Center and provides assistance,
training, and technical communications to
users. The Data Management Branch serves as
a central resource of systems analysis, design,
and programming for data processing projects
relating to scientific, technical management,
and administrative data; and the Office of ADP
Policy coordinates the complex federal policies
and procedures that govern and the acquisition/
use of computers at NIH. The Office of Administrative Management provides general administrative management support for the Division's
work.

★2656★ U.S. Department of Health and
Human Services
National Institutes of Health
Division of Computer Research and
Technology
Applied Studies Laboratory
NIH Bldg. 12A, Rm. 2041
9000 Rockville Pike
Bethesda, MD 20892
Phone: (301)496-1121
Fax: (301)402-0007
Dr. John Fletcher, Chief

Research Activities and Fields: Laboratory
collaborates with biomedical scientists to apply
mathematical theory and computing science to
the development, testing, and improvement of
mathematical models of physiological processes; collaborates with investigators to develop
and apply mathematical or statistical theory and
special-purpose computing procedures to facilitate research projects aimed at improving the diagnosis of disease and assessment of treatment; and conducts independent research in
applied mathematics, statistics, and computer
systems necessary to provide a sound theoretical basis for collaborative studies. Core research projects within the Laboratory in recent
years have involved the mathematical modeling
of physiological processes.

★2657★ U.S. Department of Health and
Human Services
National Institutes of Health
Division of Computer Research and
Technology
Physical Sciences Laboratory
NIH Bldg. 12A, Rm. 2007
9000 Rockville Pike
Bethesda, MD 20892
Phone: (301)496-1135
George Weiss, Chief

Research Activities and Fields: Activities of
PSL include: 1) basic biomedical research (in
support of NIH programs) in physics, physical
chemistry, applied mathematics, and applied
computer technology; 2) consultation; 3) development of theory; and 4) development of instrumentation for biomedical experiments. Research focuses on the study of biological phenomena such as the electrostatic forces acting
between cells, the cell's active transport mechanism, and the structure of macromolecules in
terms of theoretical chemistry and physics.

U.S. Department of Health and Human
Services
National Institutes of Health
Lister Hill National Center for Biomedical
Communications
See: Entry 7029

U.S. Department of Health and Human
Services
National Institutes of Health
Lister Hill National Center for Biomedical
Communications
Audiovisual Program Development Branch
See: Entry 7030

U.S. Department of Health and Human
Services
National Institutes of Health
Lister Hill National Center for Biomedical
Communications
Communications Engineering Branch
See: Entry 7031

U.S. Department of Health and Human
Services
National Institutes of Health
Lister Hill National Center for Biomedical
Communications
Educational Technology Branch
See: Entry 7033

U.S. Department of Health and Human
Services
National Institutes of Health
Lister Hill National Center for Biomedical
Communications
Information Technology Branch
See: Entry 7034

★2658★ University of Alabama at
Birmingham
Laboratory of Molecular Biophysics
Univ. Sta., VH 300
Birmingham, AL 35294-0019
Phone: (205)934-4177
Fax: (205)934-4256
Dr. Dan Urry, Dir.

Research Activities and Fields: Elastic and
plastic protein-based polymers with elastic
moduli ranging from 10,000 to 100,000 dynes/
square centimeter for the hydrogels, to
1,000,000 to 100,000,000 dynes/square centimeter for the elastomers, and greater for the
plastics, with the potential for related applications with varied design and exact composition
through genetic engineering using the living cell
without employing hazardous and noxious solvents and chemicals; designable, to catalyze
free energy transduction involving the intensive
variables of mechanical force, temperature,
pressure, chemical potential, electrochemical
potential, and electromagnetic radiation; and
biodegradable. Biocompatibility allows for medical applications ranging from the prevention of
postsurgical adhesions and tissue reconstruction to programmed drug delivery. Nonmedical
applications include transducers, molecular machines, superabsorbents, and controlled release of agricultural crop enhancement agents,
such as herbicides, pesticides, growth factors,
and fertilizers.

★2659★ University at Albany, State
University of New York
Center for Biological Macromolecules
Chemistry Dept.
1400 Washington Ave.
Albany, NY 12222
Phone: (518)442-4454
Fax: (518)442-3462
Prof. Ramaswamy Sarma, Exec.Dir.

Research Activities and Fields: Fundamental
studies of the structure, function, and interactions of biologically significant macromolecules,
including studies of the spatial configuration of
nucleic acid structures and dynamics, regulation
of gene expression, heme proteins and bioener-

getics, copper oxidases and oxygenases, and the statistical mechanics of macromolecules. Center associates are interested in the effects of chemical and physical agents used in food processing on the bioavailability of nutrients and on human health, also in the enzymology and biochemistry of bacterial proteins with insecticidal activity. Promotes collaborative research and interaction among faculty researchers from the departments of biological sciences, chemistry, and physics, in addition to adjunct research associates from other academic and industrial research laboratories. **Publications:** Newsletter (biweekly).

★ 2660 ★ **University of Calgary**
Cell Regulation Group
Medical Biochemistry
Faculty of Medicine
3330 Hospital Dr. NW
Calgary, AB, Canada T2N 4N1
Phone: (403)220-3019
Fax: (403)283-4841
Dr. David Waisman, Dir.

Research Activities and Fields: Identifies the principles underlying the complex interaction of the intracellular communications system. Major studies focus on intracellular messengers, such as cyclic AMP and calcium, and secondary messengers such as the protein calmodulin. Studies focus on how normal regulation of cell function is altered in diseases including cancer and diabetes and how living cells regulate their own function, both metabolically and physiologically.

★ 2661 ★ **University of California, Irvine**
Developmental Biology Center
Irvine, CA 92717
Phone: (714)856-5957
Fax: (714)856-7399
Prof. Peter J. Bryant, Dir.

Research Activities and Fields: Developmental biology, molecular biology, neurobiology, cell biology, and genetics, emphasizing analysis of pattern formation, growth control, cancer, and regeneration in both invertebrates and vertebrates. Also carries out collaborative programs with scientists from overseas who spend extended periods of time at the Center through support from their own governments. **Publications:** Annual Report.

★ 2662 ★ **University of California, Irvine**
Hitachi Chemical Research Center
1003 Health Science Rd. W.
Irvine, CA 92175
Phone: (714)725-2721
Fax: (714)725-2727
Dr. Jack Jacobs, Dir.

Research Activities and Fields: Molecular biology and biotechnology, focusing on neurobiology, and cell and developmental biology.

University of California, Los Angeles
Institute for Toxicology
See: Entry 10469

★ 2663 ★ **University of California, Los Angeles**
UCLA-DOE Laboratory of Structural Biology and Molecular Medicine
900 Veteran Ave.
Los Angeles, CA 90024-1786
Phone: (310)825-9431
Fax: (310)825-9433
Dr. David Eisenberg, Dir.

Research Activities and Fields: Biomolecular and cellular biology, environmental biology, structural biology, and nuclear medicine, including supporting fields of physics and engineering and radiopharmacology. **Formerly:** Laboratory of Nuclear Medicine and Radiation Biology (1981); Laboratory of Biomedical and Environmental Sciences.

★ 2664 ★ **University of California, San Diego**
Center for Molecular Genetics
9500 Gilman Dr.
La Jolla, CA 92093-0634
Phone: (619)534-0396
Fax: (619)534-7073
Richard A. Dirtel, Act.Dir.

Research Activities and Fields: Promotes basic and applied research in biological and biomedical areas utilizing molecular genetic techniques, especially in the areas of developmental biology, human heredity, plant molecular biology, and applied microbiology. **E-mail Address:** pcarpenter@ucsd.edu. **Formerly:** Center for Developmental Biology.

★ 2665 ★ **University of California, San Francisco**
Cardiovascular Research Institute
San Francisco, CA 94143-0130
Phone: (415)476-1707
Fax: (415)476-2283
Dr. Richard Havel, Interim Dir.

Research Activities and Fields: Physiology, biochemistry, pharmacology, cell biology, molecular biology, and immunology of the cardiovascular, pulmonary, respiratory, and renal systems; circulation, respiration, lung development, and metabolism of the fetus and newborn; membrane transduction systems; lipoprotein metabolism; growth factors and atherosclerosis; water and electrolyte transport; physical chemistry of contraction/relaxation of muscle; lung injury and repair; myocardial growth and development; macromolecular conformation; and mathematical analysis of biological systems.

★ 2666 ★ **University of California, San Francisco**
Mass Spectrometry Facility
Dept. of Pharmaceutical Chemistry
San Francisco, CA 94143
Phone: (415)476-5641
Fax: (415)476-0688
Prof. A.L. Burlingame, Dir.

Research Activities and Fields: Molecular identification problems in human health and disease and biological chemistry, including studies in chemical and biochemical structure and mechanism. Conducts investigations of the structure of covalently modified informational

biopolymers, drug metabolism, chemical carcinogenesis, signal transduction, proteins in cancer biology, irreversible inhibitors of cytochrome P-450, various genetic diseases, and membrane-bound glycoproteins, such as acetylcholine receptor and esterase, and scrapie glycoprotein. Develops techniques of computerized mass spectrometry. **Publications:** Annual Report. **E-mail Address:** alb@itsa.ucsf.edu.

★ 2667 ★ **University of Chicago**
EM Core Facility for Biological Research
920 E. 58th St.
Chicago, IL 60637
Phone: (312)702-2184
Fax: (312)702-4047
Dr. Anthony P. Mahowald, Dir.

Research Activities and Fields: Biomedical research, including cell biology and molecular imaging. **E-mail Address:** am29@midway.uchicago.edu.

★ 2668 ★ **University of Hawaii at Manoa**
Kewalo Marine Laboratory
41 Ahui St.
Honolulu, HI 96813
Phone: (808)539-7300
Fax: (808)599-4817
Dr. Ian Gibbons, Dir.

Research Activities and Fields: Biomedical research, including molecular, cell, and developmental biology using marine animals (primarily invertebrate gametes) as experimental material.

★ 2669 ★ **University of Hawaii at Manoa**
Pacific Biomedical Research Center
1993 East-West Rd.
Honolulu, HI 96822
Phone: (808)956-7401
Fax: (808)956-4768
Dr. Fredrick C. Greenwood, Dir.

Research Activities and Fields: Conducts interdisciplinary research in cell biology, neurobehavioral biology, molecular biology, biotechnology, Hawaiian evolutionary and conservation biology, molecular endocrinology, retrovirology (HIV and HTLV-1), and native Hawaiian health research.

★ 2670 ★ **University of Illinois at Chicago**
Biomedical Visualization Laboratory
College of Associated Health Professions
1919 W. Taylor, RM 211
Chicago, IL 60612
Phone: (312)996-7337
Fax: (312)996-8342
Dr. Lewis Sadler, Dir.

Research Activities and Fields: Biomedical software technologies development including complex and dynamic biological structure visualization, surface and tissue boundary definition within volume-based models, modular package creation for discipline specific applications, and specialized software, hardware, and networking for basic research. Also serves as a technology transfer center within academic disciplines and between academia and industry.

**★2671★ University of Illinois at Chicago
Laboratory for Molecular Biology**
Dept. of Biological Sciences, MC 067
840 W. Taylor St.
Chicago, IL 60607-7020
Phone: (312)996-9239
Brian Nichols, Coord.

Research Activities and Fields: Regulatory mechanisms involving signal transduction pathways and eukaryotic developmental systems.

**★2672★ University of Iowa
Flow Cytometry Facility**
College of Medicine
48 EMRB
Iowa City, IA 52242
Phone: (319)335-8103
Justin Fishbaugh, Technical Dir.

Research Activities and Fields: Cytometry research in the biomedical sciences, including cell biology, cancer biology, immunology, neurology, hepatology, pathology, tumor biology, and genetics.

**★2673★ University of Kansas
Center for Biomedical Research**
Smissman Research Laboratories
2099 Constant Ave.
Lawrence, KS 66047
Phone: (913)864-5140
Fax: (913)864-3578
Elias K. Michaelis, M.D., Dir.

Research Activities and Fields: Integration of various aspects of drug design currently directed at several specific diseases such as epilepsy, cancer, heart and lung disease, and various mental disorders. Conducts biomedical and chemical projects in neurotransmitter receptors, ion transport mechanisms, phase transport kinetics, metabolism as a barrier to drug delivery, and development of highly sensitive bioanalytical techniques. **Formerly:** Center for Drug Design (1982).

**★2674★ University of Kansas
Laboratory of Biological Anthropology**
Twente Hall
Lawrence, KS 66045
Phone: (913)864-4170
Fax: (913)864-5224
Prof. Michael H. Crawford, Dir.

Research Activities and Fields: Cancer etiology, twin research, aging and longevity, genetic epidemiology, anthropological genetics in Saint Vincent, Hungary, Mexico, Siberia, Belize, rural and urban U.S. ethnic enclaves, dental anthropology, forensic medicine, and skeletal identification. **Publications:** *Human Biology* (journal).

**★2675★ University of Massachusetts Dartmouth
Southeastern New England Clinical Microbiology Research Group**
North Dartmouth, MA 02747-2300
Phone: (508)999-8328
Prof. James T. Griffith, Dir.

Research Activities and Fields: Clinical microbiology, including investigations of practical problems of diagnostic bacteriology, mycology, parasitology, and virology. **E-mail Address:** jgriffith@umassd.edu.

**University of Michigan
Biochemistry Laboratory**
See: Entry 4032

**★2676★ University of Michigan
Laboratory of Experimental Cytology**
Dept. of Anatomy & Cell Biology
Medical Science II
Ann Arbor, MI 48109-0616
Phone: (313)763-5032
Fax: (313)763-1166
Dr. Donald K. MacCallum, Codirector

Research Activities and Fields: Biology of normal and diseased oral and ocular tissues and skin using cell cultures, electron microscopy, and biochemistry.

**★2677★ University of Michigan
Molecular Biology Laboratory**
1198 School of Dentistry
1101 N. University Ave.
Ann Arbor, MI 48109
Phone: (313)763-0017
Donald B. Clewell, Dir.

Research Activities and Fields: Gene expression in bacteria, focusing on antibiotic resistance, pathogenicity, gene translocation between DNA molecules and bacterial cells, and mobile genetic elements including plasmids and transposons.

**★2678★ University of Minnesota
Hormel Institute**
801 16th Ave. NE
Austin, MN 55912
Phone: (507)433-8804
Fax: (507)437-9606
Dr. Harald H.O. Schmid, Exec.Dir.

Research Activities and Fields: Biochemistry, bio-organic chemistry, biophysics, and molecular biology relating to biological membranes and cellular signal transduction. Topics include membrane assembly and packing properties, regulation of lipolytic enzymes, and the role of membrane lipids in heart disease and cancer. **Publications:** Annual Report.

**★2679★ University of Mississippi
Molecular Modeling Laboratory**
School of Pharmacy
University, MS 38677
Phone: (601)232-7101
Fax: (601)232-5118
Robert D. Sindelar, Ph.D., Dir.

Research Activities and Fields: Molecular research, including graphics-assisted structure activity relationships, small molecule/large molecule interactions, and computer-aided drug design.

**★2680★ University of Nevada, Reno
Natural Products Lab**
Dept. of Biochemistry
Reno, NV 89557
Phone: (702)784-6031
Fax: (702)784-6096
Dr. Ronald S. Pardini, Dir.

Research Activities and Fields: Cancer, biochemical pharmacology, and oxidative stress, including investigations of biochemical mechanisms of antitumor drugs and evaluations of the role of oxidative stress in the anticancer activity of drugs. **E-mail Address:** pardini@fs.cs.unr.edu.

**★2681★ University of New Hampshire
Marine Biomedical Research Group**
Spaulding
Durham, NH 03824
Phone: (603)862-2100
Fax: (603)862-3784
Dr. Chuck Walker, Dir.

Research Activities and Fields: Agricultural molecular science, cell biology and physiology, environmental physiology, and drug development.

**★2682★ University of North Dakota
Ireland Research Laboratory**
Dept. of Biochemistry,
Medical Science Bldg., N. Unit
PO Box 9037
Grand Forks, ND 58202
Phone: (701)777-3937
Fax: (701)772-0405
Dr. Robert Nordlie, Chm.

Research Activities and Fields: Medical sciences, including studies on intermediary metabolism of amino acids, carbohydrates, bacterial and mammalian enzymology, mechanism of hormone action, transport mechanisms, biological energetics, natural products, and experimental leukemia. Also studies circulation, tissue culture, molecular biology of transformed cells, and impact of tumors on hepatic glucose-6-phosphatose.

**★2683★ University of Notre Dame
Lobund Laboratory**
Notre Dame, IN 46556
Phone: (219)239-7564
Fax: (219)239-7595
Dr. Morris Pollard, Dir.

Research Activities and Fields: Germfree technology, microbiology, immunology, gerontology, biochemistry, physiology, pathology, and experimental surgery, including studies on carcinogenesis; environmental pollution; radiation effects; cardiovascular diseases; cancer, particularly prostate cancer and benign prostate hyperplasia model systems; nutrition, particularly diet restriction and longevity; histopathology; host-parasite relationships; genetic diseases; bone marrow transplantation; and environmental stress, with emphasis on use of germfree animals as experimental tools and model systems. **Publications:** *Bibliography of Germfree Research* (annually).

**★2684★ University of Pennsylvania
Protein Chemistry Laboratory**
Dept. of Pathology & Lab Medicine
410 Johnson Pavilion
Philadelphia, PA 19104-6079
Phone: (215)662-6697
Fax: (215)573-2059
Dr. John D. Lambris, Dir.

Research Activities and Fields: Protein chemistry, including peptide synthesis, purification and modification; protein purification; peptide coupling to proteins; tryptic peptide preparation; capillary electrophoresis; protein and peptide microsequencing; and mass spectroscopic analysis. **E-mail Address:** labris@mscf.med.upenn.edu.

★ 2685 ★ **University of Pennsylvania**
William Pepper Laboratory
Hospital of Univ. of Pennsylvania
Philadelphia, PA 19104
Phone: (215)662-3435
Fax: (215)349-5090
Donald S. Young, M.D., Dir.

Research Activities and Fields: Microbiology, immunology, clinical chemistry, hematology, toxicology, therapeutic drug monitoring characterization and specificity of blood group, characterization and specificity of blood group antibodies, clinical correlation of disturbances of endocrine metabolism, coagulation disorders, and clinical enzymology. Conducts complete histocompatability evaluations, blood component therapy, therapeutic plasma exchange, therapeutic red cell exchange procedures, tumor receptor-site studies, as well as basic research in cancer biology, endocrine biochemistry, and membrane biology.

University of Southern California
Center for Craniofacial Molecular Biology
See: Entry 4046

★ 2686 ★ **University of Southern California**
Laboratory for Developmental Biology
Dept. of Basic Sciences
School of Dentistry
Univ. Park
Los Angeles, CA 90089-0191
Phone: (213)740-1091
Dr. Harold C. Slavkin, Dir.

Research Activities and Fields: Cellular, molecular, and developmental biology issues associated with craniofacial and lung morphogenesis, including studies of tooth, mandible, secondary palate, and muscle development, birth defects, enamel genes, dentine phosphoprotein genes, cementum genes, craniofacial genetics, and evolutionary biology.

★ 2687 ★ **University of Tennessee**
Memorial Research Center
Graduate School of Medicine
1924 Alcoa Hwy.
Knoxville, TN 37920
Phone: (615)544-9290
Dr. I. Reid Collmann, Actg. Dean

Research Activities and Fields: Conducts research in areas related to hematology, oncology, and the molecular processes of disease, including cellular and humoral immunity, colon cancer and colitis, cytogenetics, experimental and comparative pathology, platelet function, immunobiology, and membrane transport.

★ 2688 ★ **University of Texas at Arlington**
Center for Medicinal Chemistry Research
Dept. of Chemistry
PO Box 19065
Arlington, TX 76019
Phone: (817)273-3818
Fax: (817)273-3808
Dr. A.L. Ternay, Jr., Dir.

Research Activities and Fields: Studies antimicrobial/viral agents, medicaments used in the

field of mental health, and substances to protect individuals from exposure to nuclear radiation. Encourages students interested in careers in medicine to conduct research in the basic sciences, especially chemistry and biochemistry.

★ 2689 ★ **University of Texas at Austin**
Biochemical Institute
Experimental Science Bldg. 442
Austin, TX 78712
Phone: (512)471-1181
Fax: (512)471-5680
Dr. Lester Reed, Dir.

Research Activities and Fields: Drug metabolism, mechanism and regulation of protein synthesis, structure, function, and regulation of enzymes and other proteins, nutritional aspects of human disease, and cloning, sequencing, and site specific mutagenesis of genes, their regulation, and repair. **Formerly:** Clayton Foundation Biochemical Institute.

★ 2690 ★ **University of Texas at Austin**
Center for Fast Kinetics Research
Austin, TX 78712
Phone: (512)471-7583
Fax: (512)471-6095
John Sessler, Dir.

Research Activities and Fields: Biomedical kinetics involving photon and high-energy electron methods, including research on nanosecond and subnanosecond techniques for chemical kinetics in solution, initial effects of radiation on biological materials, fluorescence decay as a monitor of membrane structure and function, and primary processes in vision photosynthesis and photodynamic action. Experimental apparatus and staff assistance are available to qualified researchers. **Publications:** Brochure.

★ 2691 ★ **University of Texas at Austin**
Institute for Biomedical Research
WEL 4.304
Austin, TX 78712
Phone: (512)471-7174
Fax: (512)471-7784
Dr. Karl Folkers, Dir.

Research Activities and Fields: Biomedical and general clinical research, including studies of the B-vitamins, coenzymes, and carpal tunnel syndrome.

★ 2692 ★ **University of Texas at Dallas**
Molecular and Cell Biology Program
Mail Stop FO3.1
PO Box 830688
Richardson, TX 75083-0688
Phone: (214)690-2500
Dr. Donald Gray, Program Head

Research Activities and Fields: Biochemistry, macromolecular physical chemistry, microbial and molecular genetics, and cell biology. **Publications:** Research Reports.

★ 2693 ★ **University of Texas Health**
Science Center at Houston
Analytical Chemistry Center
PO Box 20708
Houston, TX 77225
Phone: (713)792-5612
Fax: (713)794-4226
Dr. Richard M. Caprioli, Dir.

Research Activities and Fields: Seeks to meet the needs of the biomedical research community by offering access to analytical instrumentation and methodology. Specialties include structural analysis and molecular weight determination of peptides and other organic compounds by mass spectrometry, amino acid analysis, protein sequencing, peptide synthesis, chromatographic separations and quantitative measurements, and stable isotope applications. Conducts core research to develop new applications and improved technology and encourages collaborative research between investigators in basic sciences and clinical fields. **E-mail Address:** caprioli@utmmg.med.uth.tmc.edu.

★ 2694 ★ **University of Texas Health**
Science Center at San Antonio
Center for the Enhancement of the Biology
/ Biomaterials Interface
7703 Floyd Curl Dr.
San Antonio, TX 78284-7823
Phone: (210)567-2023
Fax: (210)567-2052
Barbara D. Boyan, Ph.D., Dir.

Research Activities and Fields: Basic research in cell function regulation, including studies on immunologic regulation, microbial pathogenesis, skeletal tissues, cell biology, and mediators. Fields of application include biomedicine, biology/biomaterial interfaces, wear debris, and nutrition. **Publications:** Newsletter; *Biomedical Prospectives*; *UTechnologies*. **Formerly:** Center for Cell Regulation and Enhancement of Biology/Biomaterials Interface; Center for Cell Regulation (1986).

★ 2695 ★ **University of Texas Medical**
Branch at Galveston
Marine Biomedical Institute
200 Univ. Blvd.
Galveston, TX 77555-0843
Phone: (409)772-2101
Fax: (409)762-9382
Dr. William D. Willis, Dir.

Research Activities and Fields: Studies on problems in comparative neurobiology, marine medicine and biology, and biophysics. **Publications:** Project Reports; Bulletin.

★ 2696 ★ **University of Texas Medical**
Branch at Galveston
Sealy Center for Molecular Science
301 University Blvd.
5.104 Medical Research Bldg., Rte. 1068
Galveston, TX 77555-1068
Phone: (409)772-3367
Fax: (409)772-6334
Dr. Samuel Wilson, Dir.

Research Activities and Fields: Molecular biology and biochemistry. Specialized research includes eukaryotic DNA repair, HIV molecular biology, and molecular oncology. **Formerly:** John Sealy Molecular Sciences Center.

★ 2697 ★   University of Texas Southwestern Medical Center at Dallas

Neuroscience Program
Southwestern Grad. Sch. of Biomedical
 Sciences
5323 Harry Hines Blvd.
Dallas, TX 75235-9039
Phone: (214)648-2352
Fax: (214)648-6324
Dr. A. James Hudspeth, Dir.

Research Activities and Fields: Neurobiology, including molecular biology, genetics, biochemistry, neuropharmacology, electrophysiology, neuroanatomy, and neurocytology. Specializes in membrane biophysics, including the operation and modulation of ion channels; neuronal organelle traffic, including the synthesis, axonal transport, mobilization, and release of synaptic and secretory vesicles; and neurogenetics, including both invertebrate and vertebrate experimental systems.

★ 2698 ★   University of Virginia

Markey Center
Box 577
Health Sciences Center
Charlottesville, VA 22908
Phone: (804)924-1235
Fax: (804)924-1236
Dr. David L. Brautigan, Ph.D., Dir.

Research Activities and Fields: Molecular biology of cellular signaling processes, including membranes, receptors, transduction, genome-level signals, and molecular structure. **E-mail Address:** nl9q@virginia.edu.

★ 2699 ★   University of Washington

Biomembrane Institute
201 Elliott Ave. W., Ste. 305
Seattle, WA 98119-4237
Phone: (206)285-1309
Fax: (206)281-9893
Dr. Sen-itiroh Hakomori, Dir.

Research Activities and Fields: Molecular biology, including recombinant bioengineering, cloning, gene expression for membrane-associated receptors, carbohydrate-binding proteins, glycosyltransferases, and tumor immunology.

★ 2700 ★   University of Wisconsin—Milwaukee

Marine and Freshwater Biomedical Sciences Center
PO Box 413
Milwaukee, WI 53201
Phone: (414)382-1735
Fax: (414)382-1705
Dr. David Petering, Dir.

Research Activities and Fields: Aquatic models in biomedicine and comparative toxicology. Studies transformation and metabolism of toxic organic chemicals and metals and investigates genetic, neurobehavioral, and immunological responses of organisms to such chemicals. **Publications:** Annual Report. **Formerly:** Aquatic Biomedical Research Center; Marine and Freshwater Biomedical Core Center.

★ 2701 ★   Veterans Affairs Medical Center

Research Administration Office
150 Muir Rd.
Martinez, CA 94553
Phone: (510)372-2000
Robert Efron, M.D., Assoc. Chief of Staff

Research Activities and Fields: Basic and clinical biomedical research.

★ 2702 ★   W. Alton Jones Cell Science Center, Inc.

10 Old Barn Rd.
Lake Placid, NY 12946-1009
Phone: (518)523-1250
Fax: (518)523-1849
James L. Stevens, Dir.

Research Activities and Fields: Molecular and cellular regulation of growth and development, including cancer. Specific interests include intracellular and intercellular signalling pathways and growth factors; protein chemistry and visual cycle proteins; role of protein kinases in cell signalling; adipocyte, thymocyte, and endothelial cell and molecular biology; molecular regulation of wound repair; and regulation of molecular stress responses. **Publications:** Annual Report.

★ 2703 ★   W.M. Keck Center for Computational Biology

6100 S. Main St.
Houston, TX 77005-1892
Phone: (713)527-4752
Fax: (713)285-5154
Marc Archambault, Exec.Dir.

Research Activities and Fields: Biological research, including chemistry and molecular biology of DNA binding, molecular genetics of inborn errors of metabolism, electron crystallography and tomography of macromolecular assemblies, DNA sequence information and human disease, computational neuroscience, parallel computation and language, high resolution NMR spectroscopy of macromolecular structure and dynamics, computation in molecular genetics, computation in image reconstruction and biofluid mechanics, structure and metabolism of lipoproteins, rapid kinetics of heme-protein-ligand reactions, structure and function of electron transport proteins, nicotonic synaptic transmission in the central nervous system, X-ray crystallography, molecular dynamics of proteins and nucleic acids, a tomic structures and functions of proteins, artificial intelligence, and design and analysis of algorithms. **Publications:** *Keck Center Newsletter* (bienially). **E-mail Address:** march@rice.edu.

★ 2704 ★   Wake Forest University

MICROMED
Bowman Gray School of Medicine
Medical Center Blvd.
Winston-Salem, NC 27157-1092
Phone: (910)716-2675
Fax: (910)716-6174
Dr. W. Gray Jerome, Dir.

Research Activities and Fields: Biomedicine with emphasis on atherosclerosis, microbiology, immunology, pediatrics, and biochemistry. Ongoing projects include receptor localization during leukocyte and platelet activation as they relate to fibrinogen binding and procoagulant activity, and cytochemical and immunochemical studies of lysosomes in arterial cells and macrophages, ultrastructural correlates of lipid metabolism, binding and cytoplasmic translocation of plasma lipoproteins, spatial organization of proteoglycans, collagen, other extracellular matrix proteins during progression of cardiovascular disease, and 3-D computer imaging and quantitation of cells and organelles. **E-mail Address:** jjerome@isnet.is.wfu.edu.

★ 2705 ★   Webb-Waring Institute for Biomedical Research

4200 E. 9th Ave.
Denver, CO 80262
Phone: (303)270-8231
John E. Repine, M.D., Pres. and Dir.

Research Activities and Fields: Research focuses on the role of oxygen radicals in health and diseases, oxidants and antioxidants, air pollution, basic immunology, biochemistry, genetics, cell biology, pathology, and physiology. **Publications:** Annual Report. **Formerly:** Colorado Foundation for Research in Tuberculosis; Webb-Waring Institute for Medical Research; Webb-Waring Lung Institute; Webb-Waring (1992).

★ 2706 ★   West Virginia University

Genetics and Developmental Biology Program
College of Agriculture
Division of Plant & Soil Science
Morgantown, WV 26506
Phone: (304)293-6256
Fax: (304)293-3740
Dr. J. Nath, Chm.

Research Activities and Fields: Genetics and developmental biology, including biochemical genetics, developmental genetics, cytogenetics, quantitative genetics, human genetics, forest genetics, molecular aspects of development, experimental morphogenesis, teratology, mutagenesis, regeneration, oncology, descriptive embryology, and life cycles of animals and plants.

★ 2707 ★   Whitehead Institute for Biomedical Research

9 Cambridge Center
Cambridge, MA 02142
Phone: (617)258-5215
Fax: (617)258-9872
Dr. Gerald Fink, Dir.

Research Activities and Fields: Molecular processes underlying biological development as related to developmental and molecular biology, cancer, membranes, virology, AIDS, vaccine development, plant biology, and yeast. **Publications:** Research Summaries (annually in October); Director's Report (biannually); *BiologyWeek* (weekly newsletter for the Cambridge/Boston biomedical community).

★ 2708 ★   Wistar Institute of Anatomy and Biology

3601 Spruce St.
Philadelphia, PA 19104
Phone: (215)898-3926
Fax: (215)573-2097
Giovanni Rovera, Dir.

Research Activities and Fields: Virology and immunology using a molecular-based approach to a variety of diseases such as cancer, virus-induced diseases, degenerative diseases such as Alzheimer's, and autoimmune diseases including multiple sclerosis, rheumatoid arthritis, lupus, scleroderma, and phemphigo. Specific areas of research include structural biology emphasing the structure of viruses and the interaction of a variety of ligands to cell surface receptors; developmental biology emphasizing early embryonic development, including the development of the immune and cardiovascular systems; molecular genetics, focusing on suppressor genes and oncogenes in leukemias, lymphomas, childhood cancers, melanomas, breast carcinomas, bladder carcinomas, and tumors of the gastrointestinal tract; and experimental therapeutics particularly emphasizing on gene therapy and imune therapy. **Publications:** Research Report (annual); Administrative Report; Wistar Symposia; Newsletters.

★2709★ **Worcester Foundation for Experimental Biology**
222 Maple Ave.
Shrewsbury, MA 01545-2795
Phone: (508)842-8921
Fax: (508)842-7762
Thoru Pederson, Ph.D., Pres. & Scientific Dir.

Research Activities and Fields: Molecular and cellular aspects of growth and development as related to cancer biology, endocrine and reproductive biology, and neurobiology. **Publications:** Annual Report; Scientific Report (biennially); *Research Reporter* (quarterly).

★2710★ **Worcester Foundation for Experimental Biology**
Cancer Center
222 Maple Ave.
Shrewsbury, MA 01545-2795
Phone: (508)842-8921
Fax: (508)842-7762
Thoru Pederson, Ph.D., Codirector

Research Activities and Fields: Cell biology, focusing on normal cell growth and metabolism regulation. Seeks to understand cancer cell abberations through analysis of normal cell processes.

★2711★ **Worcester Foundation for Experimental Biology**
Male Fertility Program
222 Maple Ave.
Shrewsbury, MA 01545
Phone: (508)842-8921
Fax: (508)842-3915
George B. Witman, Ph.D., Dir.

Research Activities and Fields: Male reproductive biology, focusing on the maturation of nonmoving progenitor cells in the testis to actively swimming sperm, control of sperm function in the female reproductive tract, prevention of sperm motility, sperm-egg fusion, and conception, and correction of sperm defects that cause infertility.

Chapter 9
Biotechnology

National & International Organizations

★2712★ **Biotechnology Industry Organization (BIO)**
1625 K St. NW, Ste. 1100
Washington, DC 20006
Phone: (202)857-0244
Free: 800-255-3304
Fax: (202)857-0237
Carl Feldbaum, Pres.

Founded: 1993. **Members:** 520. **Description:** Firms utilizing recombinant DNA, hybridoma, and immunological technologies in areas such as human health care (drugs, biologics, and medical devices), animal husbandry, environmental and specialty industrial chemical and fermentation production; biotechnology equipment manufacturers and service groups. Provides information on biotechnology issues pertaining to U.S. and international regulations, patents, finance, and other problems confronting members. Organizes workshops and seminars; maintains educational dialogue with Congress, non-U.S. governmental bodies, regulatory agencies, and the public. **Publications:** *BIO Bulletin*, bimonthly. Newsletter. Focuses on federal regulatory and legislative developments affecting the biotechnology industry; also covers association news. *Price:* Included in membership dues. • *BIO News*, periodic. *Price:* For members only. • *Biotech for All.* • *Issue Briefs.* • *What is Biotechnology.* Also prepares monthly columns for biotechnology journals.

★2713★ **Council for Responsible Genetics (CRG)**
5 Upland Rd., Ste. 3
Cambridge, MA 02140
Phone: (617)868-0870
Fax: (617)491-5344
Wendy McGoodwin, Acting Exec.Dir.

Founded: 1983. **Members:** 1,000. **Description:** Monitors and analyzes the biotechnology industry and discusses the social implications of new genetic technologies developments. Areas of interest include military uses of biological research, genetic discrimination, and genetically engineered food. Maintains resource center and speakers' bureau. **Publications:** *GeneWatch*, bimonthly. Newsletter. Covers the social and ethical issues of genetic engineering and biotechnology. Includes legislative news. *Price:* Included in membership dues; $24/year for non-members; $30/year for organizations. **Formerly:** (1989) Committee for Responsible Genetics.

International Institute of Dental Ergonomics and Technology (IIDET) (Institut International d'Ergonomie et Technology Dentaire — IIDET)
See: Entry 3962

★2714★ **International Society for Plastination (ISP)**
c/o Harmon Bickley
Mercer University School of Medicine
Department of Pathology
1550 College St.
Macon, GA 31207
Phone: (912)752-4071
Harmon Bickley, Ph.D., Exec.Sec.

Founded: 1984. **Members:** 200. **Description:** Anatomists, pathologists, and technologists. Seeks to share information about plastination, a means of infiltrating biological specimens with curable polymers. **Publications:** *Journal of the International Society for Plastination*, semiannual. Journal. *Price:* $5/issue.

Research Centers

★2715★ **Baylor College of Medicine Center for Biotechnology**
4000 Research Forest Dr.
The Woodlands, TX 77381
Phone: (713)363-8400
Fax: (713)363-8475
Robert R. Rich, M.D., Dir.

Research Activities and Fields: Conducts research to develop new drugs and devices for the prevention and treatment of certain human disorders, as well as other biomedical products to improve the quality of human life. Areas of study include bio-organic chemistry, recombinant DNA technology, oncology, immunology, vision research, and cellular and molecular neurobiology. Seeks to support and foster the biotechnology industry in the area. **Formerly:** Center for Biotechnology.

★2716★ **Biomedical Technology Center**
665 N. Riverpoint Blvd.
Spokane, WA 99202-1665
Phone: (509)456-7091
Fax: (509)456-7097
John Ryan, Asst. Dir.

Research Activities and Fields: New technology development, products, and services that decrease the cost of health care, including facilities and services requiring custom sterile filling, diagnostic tools that utilize advanced computer technologies, and information and network technologies that reduce the cost of healthcare and improve its quality and accessibility. Center applies computer technologies and medical imaging techniques to diagnose patient problems, and demonstrates and tests information and network technologies concerning both defense and civilian health care systems in an effort to improve data-capture, management, sharing, and analysis, cost control, quality of patient care, and reduce administration cost. **E-mail Address:** jryan@sirti.org.

Blood CARE
See: Entry 2554

★2717★ **Center for Advanced Biotechnology and Medicine**
679 Hoes Ln.
Piscataway, NJ 08854-5638
Phone: (908)235-5300
Fax: (908)235-4815
Dr. Aaron J. Shatkin, Dir.

Research Activities and Fields: Cell and developmental biology, molecular pharmacology, molecular genetics, and structural biology. Collaborates with biopharmaceutical firms in New Jersey on technology transfer and research and development. **E-mail Address:** namovicz@mbcl.rutgers.edu.

★2718★ **Center for Biotechnology**
SUNY at Stony Brook
130 Life Sciences Bldg.
Stony Brook, NY 11794-5208
Phone: (516)632-8521
Fax: (516)632-8577
Dr. Glenn D. Prestwich, Dir.

Research Activities and Fields: Supports biomedical research in New York, and facilitates collaborations between small businesses and the research community within the state. Conducts sponsored research projects in biochemistry, immunology, microbiology, pharmacology, and chemistry. **E-mail Address:** glenn.prestwich@sunysb.edu.

★ 2719 ★ Cornell University
Center for Advanced Biotechnology
Ithaca, NY 14853-2703
Phone: (607)255-2300
Fax: (607)255-2428
Dr. Lynn W. Jelinski, Dir.

Research Activities and Fields: Biotechnology, including the following areas of Thrust: environment, focusing on bioremediation; agriculture, including biologically based pest management, breeding for enhanced traits, and waste management; food science and nutrition, focusing on food safety and nutritional quality; and healthcare, including structure-based drug design and diagnostics for human and animal applications. **Publications:** *Research Directory*; Newsletter (quarterly). **Formerly:** Cornell University Biotechnology Program.

★ 2720 ★ Medical Technology and Practice
Patterns Institute, Inc.
2121 Wisconsin Ave. NW, Ste. 220
Washington, DC 20007
Phone: (202)333-8841
Fax: (202)333-5586
Dennis J. Cotter, Exec.Dir.

Research Activities and Fields: New and emerging medical technologies and their implications for national policy. The Institute manages three major research activities: the National Health Services and Practice Patterns Survey performs independent surveys and other forms of research and analysis on health services issues such as the costs, cost-effectiveness, patient outcome, and quality of health care delivery, coverage and reimbursement policies, access to care, and regulation; the Medical Technology Forum involves sponsorship of workshops, conferences, and seminars; and the Hospital Stay Charge Profile investigates public and private health care costs and service utilization databases. Technologies under study include magnetic resonance imaging, extracorporeal shockwave lithotripsy, endocardial electrical stimulation, implantable cardiac defibrillators, percutaneous transluminal coronary angioplasty, percutaneous lithotripsy, heart transplantation, ambulatory blood pressure monitoring, total parenteral nutrition, liver transplantation, bone marrow transplantation, and dialysis treatment for end-stage renal disease. **Publications:** *NHSPPS Public Policy Reports*.

★ 2721 ★ Michigan State University
Biotechnology Research Center
178 Giltner Hall
East Lansing, MI 48824-1101
Phone: (517)355-6465
Jerry Dodgson, Dir.

Research Activities and Fields: Stimulates (through competitive grants to campus investigators) basic and applied research in molecular biology, chemical engineering, genetic engineering, and the development of new biological processes. Current projects approved by the

Center include improvement of NMR analysis of large biomolecules; studies of endocrine functions in appetite, fat production, and aging; genetic manipulation of woody plants; cloning of the genes for enzymes that degrade lignin; and medical applications of enzymes immobilized in hollow fibers.

★ 2722 ★ Northwestern University
Center for Biotechnology and Applied
Science
2153 Sheridan Rd.
Evanston, IL 60208-3500
Phone: (708)467-1453
Fax: (708)467-2180
Dr. Catherine Propst, Exec.Dir.

Research Activities and Fields: Biotechnology in the fields of health, food/agriculture, and environmental protection (bioremediation). Cooperates with industry on issues of national and international significance. **Publications:** *Biotechnology News* (monthly). **E-mail Address:** rloerzel@merle.acns.nwu.edu.

★ 2723 ★ Ohio State University
Biotechnology Center
Rightmire Hall
1060 Carmack Rd.
Columbus, OH 43210
Phone: (614)292-5670
Fax: (614)292-5379
Dr. P.E. Kolattukudy, Dir.

Research Activities and Fields: Serves campus-wide research efforts in agricultural, medical, and industrial biotechnology. Conducts plant biotechnology, neurobiotechnology, and macromolecular structure and function studies. **Publications:** *Ohio State Biotechnology Newsletter* (semiannually).

★ 2724 ★ Ohio University
Edison Biotechnology Institute (EBI)
Tech. & Enterprise Bldg. 20, Rm. 190
The Ridges
Athens, OH 45701
Phone: (614)593-4713
Fax: (614)593-4795
David N. Allen, Ph.D., Dir.

Research Activities and Fields: Genetic engineering, focusing on cloning of novel recombinant DNA molecules, gene transfer in laboratory animals to produce animal models of human diseases, and the development of new pharmaceuticals for humans; gene transfer in agricultural animals to increase growth rates, efficiencies of feed utilization and disease resistance characteristics; development of methods to deliver genetic instructions into living animals for the production of protein pharmaceuticals within livestock; production of protein biologicals as a production method to replace commercial animal cell culture production; embryonic stem cell culture and gene delivery for gene therapy applications; and clonal animal research and development. **E-mail Address:** ma-lott.@ouvaxa.cats.edu. **Formerly:** Institute of Recombinant & Mammalian Genetics (1984); Edison Animal Biotechnology Center (1993).

★ 2725 ★ Oregon State University
Center for Gene Research and
Biotechnology
Agricultural and Life Sciences Bldg., 3021
Corvallis, OR 97331-7303
Phone: (503)737-3347
Fax: (503)737-3045
Prof. Russel H. Meints, Dir.

Research Activities and Fields: Faculty interests include plant growth control, biological nitrogen fixation, plant genetics, prokaryotic genetics, neurochemistry, reproductive endocrinology, antibiotic biosynthesis, molecular plant pathology, carcinogenesis, molecular virology, vaccine development, eukaryotic genetics, gene regulation and differentiation, biological pest control, and cereal crop breeding. **Publications:** Annual Research Report. **E-mail Address:** meintsr@ava.bcc.orst.edu.

★ 2726 ★ State University of New York at
Buffalo
Center for Advanced Molecular Biology
and Immunology
653 Cooke Hall
Buffalo, NY 14260-1300
Phone: (716)645-2164
Fax: (716)645-3776
Bruce Nicholson, Codir.

Research Activities and Fields: Biotechnology, including genetic engineering of fungus resistant plants and development of monoclonal antibodies, vaccine products, and new immunodiagnostic reagents to combat infectious diseases and malignancy. **E-mail Address:** cambjn@ubums.cc.buffalo.edu. **Formerly:** Center for Applied Molecular Biology and Immunology.

U.S. Department of Defense
Air Force Materiel Command
Crew Systems Directorate
Human Engineering Division
See: Entry 2398

U.S. Department of Defense
Naval Medical Research and Development
Command
Naval Biodynamics Laboratory
See: Entry 7838

U.S. Department of Defense
Naval Medical Research and Development
Command
Naval Health Research Center
Operational Performance Department
See: Entry 7843

★ 2727 ★ U.S. Department of Health and
Human Services
National Center for Biotechnology
Information
Bldg. 38A
8600 Rockville Pike
Bethesda, MD 20894
Phone: (301)496-1936
Fax: (301)480-9241
David J. Lipman, M.D., Director

Research Activities and Fields: Supports and develops biotechnology databases. Operates GenInfo Backbone Database.

University of Arizona
Advanced Biotechnology Laboratory
See: Entry 2379

★2728★ University of California, Los Angeles
Harbor-UCLA Medical Center
Division of Medical Genetics
1000 W. Carson St.
Torrance, CA 90509
Phone: (310)222-3663
Fax: (310)328-9921
Dr. Pauline Yen, Ph.D, Adjunct Prof.

Research Activities and Fields: Human genome project and mammalian X-chromosome inactivation. **E-mail Address:** yen@humc.edu.

★2729★ University of Cincinnati
Center for Biomechanics Studies and Research
2900 Reading
Cincinnati, OH 45221-0048
Phone: (513)556-4171
Fax: (513)556-4162
Dr. David L. Butler, Ph.D., Dir.

Research Activities and Fields: Promotes graduate student involvement in biomechanics research, including human body dynamics, joint mechanics and kinematics, soft tissue mechanics, robotics, ergonomics, mechanical stresses in the work place, and sports medicine.

★2730★ University of Florida
Interdisciplinary Center for Biotechnology Research
Box 110580
Gainesville, FL 32611
Phone: (904)392-8408
Fax: (904)392-8598
Dr. Sheldon Schuster, Dir.

Research Activities and Fields: Biotechnology, including flow cytometric analysis, DNA sequencing and synthesis, hybridoma technologies, protein microisolation, peptide synthesis, electron microscopy, biological computing, and genetics and reproductive analyses. Research activities include biotechnologies for ecological, evolutionary, and conservation sciences.

★2731★ University of Florida
Interdisciplinary Center for Biotechnology Research
Box 110580
Gainesville, FL 32611
Phone: (904)392-8408
Fax: (904)392-8598
Dr. Sheldon Schuster, Dir.

Research Activities and Fields: Biotechnology, including flow cytometric analysis, DNA sequencing and synthesis, hybridoma technologies, protein microisolation, peptide synthesis, electron microscopy, biological computing, and genetics and reproductive analysis. Research activities include biotechnologies for ecological, evolutionary, and conservation sciences.

University of Illinois at Chicago
Center for Pharmaceutical Biotechnology
See: Entry 10471

★2732★ University of Illinois at Urbana-Champaign
Biotechnology Center
105 Observatory
901 S. Mathews Ave.
Urbana, IL 61801
Phone: (217)333-1695
Fax: (217)244-0466
Dr. Janet H. Glaser, Assoc.Dir.

Research Activities and Fields: Conducts biotechnological studies in three main areas: 1) medicine, including therapeutics, pharmaceuticals, and diagnostics; 2) agriculture, including herbicide and pesticide mechanisms and plant and molecular genetics; and 3) bioprocessing, including fermentation and biomass conversion. Additional interests include protein biotechnology, molecular biology, and immunology. **Publications:** *Biotechnology Newsletter* (quarterly).

★2733★ University of Louisville
Center for Industrial Ergonomics
James B. Speed Scientific School
Louisville, KY 40292
Phone: (502)852-7173
Fax: (502)852-7397
Dr. Waldemar Karwowski, Dir.

Research Activities and Fields: Consumer product design, manual materials handling, prevention of low-back injuries, ergonomics task analysis, human factors in advanced manufacturing systems and robotics safety, and cumulative trauma disorders of the hand and arm. Seeks to improve human-machine interactions. **E-mail Address:** w0karw03@ulkyvm.louisville.edu.

★2734★ University of Maryland
Medical Biotechnology Center
618 W. Lombard St., 2nd Fl.
Baltimore, MD 21201
Phone: (410)706-8181
Fax: (410)706-8184
Dr. Edmund C. Tramont, Dir.

Research Activities and Fields: Vaccinology, AIDS, immunology, bioimaging, biosensing, bioanalysis, molecular neurobiology, and molecular genetics and gene therapy.

★2735★ University of Quebec at Trois-Rivieres
Research Group in Membrane Biotechnology
C.P. 500
Trois-Rivieres, PQ, Canada G9A 5H7
Phone: (819)376-5052
Fax: (819)376-5012
Claude Gicquaud, Dir.

Research Activities and Fields: Fundamental research on the use of artificial membrane systems applied to biophysical and medical problems. Research includes the study of cytoskeleton-membrane interactions, pharmacological use of liposomes, and physiochemical basis of membrane interactions with physiologically active substances. **E-mail Address:** claudegicquaud@uqtr.uquebec.ca.

University of Tennessee
Molecular Resource Center
See: Entry 5381

★2736★ University of Texas at Austin
Center for Biotechnology
Rm. WEL 4.260C
Austin, TX 78712-1159
Phone: (512)471-3279
Fax: (512)471-8696
Barrie Kitto, Ph.D., Dir.

Research Activities and Fields: Biotechnology.

★2737★ University of Wisconsin—Madison
Human Factors Research Laboratory
1513 Univ. Ave.
Madison, WI 53706
Phone: (608)263-6329
Fax: (608)262-8454
Prof. Michael J. Smith, Head

Research Activities and Fields: Human behavior, including studies on workstation design, human/machine interactions, human/computer interfaces, rehabilitative engineering, hand tool design, human performance, and design of assistive devices.

Utah State University
Biotechnology Center
See: Entry 13243

Chapter 10
Birth Defects

Foundations & Other Funding Organizations

Other Funding Organizations

★ 2738 ★ **March of Dimes Birth Defects Foundation**
1275 Mamaroneck Ave.
White Plains, NY 10605
Phone: (914)428-7100
Fax: (914)428-8203
Dr. Jennifer L. Howse, Pres.

Description: Makes basic and clinical research grants to hospitals and universities, medical service grants for improved perinatal and genetic services, health personnel development grants to professionals concerned with prevention of birth defects, and awards "starter" funds to promising young scientists and medical students.

★ 2739 ★ **National Association for the Craniofacially Handicapped**
PO Box 11082
Chattanooga, TN 37401
Phone: (615)266-1632
Free: 800-332-2373
Fax: (615)267-3124
Margaret C. Culpepper, Pres.

Description: Provides financial assistance for travel expenses to persons with severe facial deformities resulting from congenital defects or accidents.

United Cerebral Palsy Research and Educational Foundation
See: Entry 8140

National & International Organizations

★ 2740 ★ **American Cleft Palate- Craniofacial Association (ACPA)**
1218 Grandview Ave.
Pittsburgh, PA 15211
Phone: (412)481-1376
Fax: (412)481-0847
Nancy Smythe, Exec.Dir.

Founded: 1943. **Members:** 2,500. **Description:** Physicians, dentists, speech pathologists, audiologists, psychologists, nurses and others actively engaged in the care of individuals with cleft lip and palate and associated craniofacial deformities. Works to extend and improve the understanding of the scientific and clinical problems involved in the habilitation of patients with cleft lip and palate, and to stimulate professional and public interest in the field. Conducts educational programs. **Publications:** *American Cleft Palate-Craniofacial Association Membership and Team Directory*, annual. Membership Directory. *Price:* Available to members only. • *American Cleft Palate-Craniofacial Association Newsletter*, quarterly. Newsletter. *Price:* Included in membership dues. • *Cleft Palate-Craniofacial Journal*, bimonthly. Journal. Includes research reports, book reviews, and commentaries. *Price:* Included in membership dues; $100 for nonmembers; $135 for institutions. **Formerly:** American Association for Cleft Palate Rehabilitation; (1949) American Academy of Cleft Palate Prosthesis; (1988) American Cleft Palate Association.

★ 2741 ★ **Association of Birth Defect Children (ABDC)**
827 Irma St.
Orlando, FL 32803
Phone: (407)245-7035
Free: 800-313-ABDC
Fax: (407)245-7035
Betty Mekdeci, Exec.Dir.

Founded: 1980. **Members:** 10,000. **Description:** Parents, health professionals, educators, members of Congress, hospitals, libraries, organizations and services for the handicapped, and individuals united to prevent birth defects, especially those associated with drugs, chemicals, radiation, and other environmental substances. Provides parents, educators, and professionals in medical- and health-related fields with information on birth defects and research in prosthetics. Acts as a support group for those afflicted with birth defects and offers help in adjusting to the problems faced by individuals with physical malformations. Seeks to inform the medical community and the public about the risk involved with prenatal environmental exposures. Conducts studies and compiles statistics. Monitors and takes part in legislative activities; sponsors petitions. Sponsors National Birth Defect Registry and parent matchup service. Accesses data from world medical literature. **Publications:** *ABDC*, quarterly. Newsletter. Includes parent-to-parent column and a birth defects registry. *Price:* $12/year; $5 for low-income members. • *Association of Birth Defect Children-- Newsletter*, quarterly. Provides information on environmental mental causes of birth defects and services for the handicapped. *Price:* Donation requested. • Videos. **Formerly:** (1982) Association of Benedictin Children.

★ 2742 ★ **Avenues—National Support Group for Arthrogryposis Multiplex Congenita**
c/o Mary Anne Schmidt
PO Box 5192
Sonora, CA 95370
Phone: (209)928-3688
Mary Anne Schmidt, Dir.

Founded: 1980. **Members:** 1,200. **Description:** Individuals with arthrogryposis multiplex congentia (AMC), their families and friends, and interested professionals. (AMC, a birth defect, is a muscle and/or nerve syndrome affecting some or all of the body's limbs.) Purpose is to share positive attitudes and selfhelp ideas for the handicapped and for all who deal with them. **Publications:** Audiotapes. • *Avenues*, semiannual. Newsletter. Lists doctors and families interested in corresponding with others about arthrogryposis. *Price:* Included in membership dues; $7.50 annual donation requested for members in U.S.; $10 annual donation requested for members outside U.S. • Bibliography. • Pamphlet. *Price:* $1.

AVM Support Group
See: Entry 8193

★2743★ Beckwith-Wiedemann Support
Network (BWSN)
3206 Braeburn Cir.
Ann Arbor, MI 48108
Phone: (313)973-0263
Free: 800-837-2976
Fax: (313)973-9721
Susan Fettes, Pres.

Founded: 1989. Members: 300. Description:
Patients with Beckwith-Wiedemann Syndrome
and their families; health care professionals; interested others. Works to provide information
and peer support to individuals and families affected by Beckwith-Wiedemann Syndrome
(BWS). (BWS is a congenital growth-related disorder. Patients are at risk for developing hypoglycemia and various tumors.) Seeks to increase public and professional awareness of
BWS. Encourages research on the cause, early
detection, and treatment of BWS. Publications:
Beckwith Wiedeman Support Network Newsletter, 3/year. Newsletter. • Directory. Lists parents. • What Is Beckwith-Wiedemann Syndrome. Brochure.

Cerebral Palsy International Sports and
Recreation Association (CP-ISRA)
See: Entry 4472

★2744★ Children's Craniofacial
Association (CCA)
10210 N. Central Expy., Ste. 230
Lockbox 37
Dallas, TX 75231
Phone: (214)368-3590
Free: 800-535-3643
Fax: (214)368-3599
Charlene Smith, Exec.Dir.

Founded: 1989. Description: Participants include craniofacial surgeons and others wishing
to aid individuals with craniofacial deformities.
Promotes increased awareness of craniofacial
deformities and their treatment among health
care professionals and the public. Provides financial assistance to craniofacially deformed
patients for costs related to treatment such as
food, travel and lodging. Functions as a networking and referral service for patients. Makes
referrals to qualified centers. Conducts craniofacial family workshops. Publications: Booklets.
On craniofacial conditions and their treatment.
• Films. • Videos. Also publishes materials for
health care professionals, government officials,
and parents of craniofacially deformed children.
Formerly: (1992) International Craniofacial
Foundations.

★2745★ Cornelia de Lange Syndrome
Foundation (CdLSF)
60 Dyer Ave.
Collinsville, CT 06022-1273
Phone: (203)693-0159
Free: 800-223-8355
Fax: (203)693-6819
Julie Mairano, Exec.Dir.

Founded: 1977. Members: 5,000. Description: Families of Cornelia de Lange Syndrome
children, friends, and professionals. (Cornelia
de Lange Syndrome is a rare birth defect of unknown cause resulting in babies who continue
to develop, mentally and physically, at a slower
rate.) Seeks to ensure early and accurate diag-

nosis of the syndrome and to enable families,
friends, and professionals to make informed decisions and plans for the affected person. Provides updates on the medical aspects of CdLS
and responds to correspondences and members' inquiries on an individual basis. Support research programs. Publications: CdLS Foundation - Album. Lists families and professionals interested in providing mutual support. Price: $20.
• Facing the Challenges: A Parent's Guide to
CdLS. Book. • Facts About Cornelia de Lange
Syndrome. Pamphlet. • Reaching Out, bimonthly. Newsletter. Provides articles of general interest dealing with the complexities of raising a
handicapped child. Includes medical column.
Formerly: (1981) Cornelia de Lange Parents
Group.

★2746★ Forward Face
317 E. 34th St.
New York, NY 10016
Phone: (212)263-6656
Free: 800-422-FACE
Fax: (212)263-7534
Betsy Old, Pres.

Founded: 1978. Members: 600. Description:
Individuals with craniofacial disorders, their families and friends, and health care professionals.
Provides medical, psychological, and financial
support services. Facilitates communication
and cooperation between patients and health
care professionals; operates referral service.
Offers workshops; conducts networking activities and children's services; Also includes a support group, Inner Faces, specifically for teenagers and young adults; activities include communications workshops theatre productions
and social functions. Publications: Brochures.
• Forward Face Newsletter, quarterly. Newsletter. Price: $20/year. • Videos. Parent Handbook
& Patient Cookbook to be published late 1994

★2747★ Foundation for Nager and Miller
Syndromes
2525 Conklin Dr., Apt. 14
Rockford, IL 61101-1873
Pam LeBaron, Dir.

Founded: 1989. Description: Families affected
by Nager or Miller Syndromes, and interested individuals. (Nager syndrome is characterized by
underdevelopment of the cheeks and lower jaw,
and other craniofacial abnormalities; Miller syndrome is characterized by limb anomalies and
craniofacial deformities including cleft palate
and slanted lower eyelids.) Provides support to
those affected by these rare genetic conditions.
Seeks to increase awareness of the syndromes,
and disseminates information to professionals,
laypeople, and hospitals. Encourages the development of research and diagnostic testing procedures. Publications: Newsletter, biennial. Includes resource list, helpful hints, biographical
information, research updates, articles on
Nager/Miller Syndromes, and book reviews.
Price: Free.

★2748★ Freeman-Sheldon Parent Support
Group (FSPSG)
509 E. Northmont Way
Salt Lake City, UT 84103
Phone: (801)364-7060
Joyce Dolcourt, Exec.Dir.

Founded: 1981. Members: 70. Description:
Families affected by Freeman-Sheldon Syndrome; interested health professionals. (Freeman-Sheldon Syndrome, also known as Whistling Face Syndrome and Cranio-Carpo-Tarsal
Dysplasia, is a disorder characterized by a flat,
stiff, immobile face with excessively bulging
cheeks, resembling that seen when whistling;
retarded growth, flexion contraction of the fingers and thumbs, walking difficulties, and
speech impairment may also be experienced.
The syndrome is believed to be transmitted genetically.) Compiles information on the growth
and development of individuals with Freeman-Sheldon Syndrome; disseminates information
for parents of afflicted children. Operates referral services; promotes medical research. Publications: FSPSG Newsletter, semiannual.
Newsletter. Updates members on research and
news.

International Cerebral Palsy Society (ICPS)
See: Entry 8237

★2749★ March of Dimes Birth Defects
Foundation (MDBDF)
1275 Mamaroneck Ave.
White Plains, NY 10605
Phone: (914)428-7100
Fax: (914)428-8203
Dr. Jennifer L. Howse, Pres.

Founded: 1938. Regional Groups: 3. Local
Groups: 104. Description: Founded by President Franklin D. Roosevelt as the National
Foundation for Infantile Paralysis. Promotes
prevention of birth defects by focusing on maternal and child health issues including low birthweight, infant mortality, prenatal care, and maternal substance abuse. Offers public and professional health education and community service programs to improve maternal and
newborn health. Works with other national and
local organizations to initiate and implement
community programs of prenatal care education
and service. Operates Campaign for Healthier
Babies to support research and educational programs. Develops and distributes educational
materials for health professionals and the public. Publications: Genetics in Practice, quarterly. Newsletter. Reports on current clinical research in genetics and on improving prenatal
services. Formerly: (1958) National Foundation
for Infantile Paralysis; (1979) National Foundation - March of Dimes.

National Association for the Craniofacially
Handicapped (FACES)
See: Entry 4514

National Vascular Malformations
Foundation
See: Entry 8286

★2750★ Prader-Willi Foundation
223 Main St.
Port Washington, NY 11050
Phone: (516)944-8136
Free: 800-253-7993
Fax: (516)944-3173

Founded: 1994. Description: Devoted to serving individuals with Prader-Willi Syndrome. Provides information on subjects related to Prader-

Willi Syndrome. Finances related projects such as residential development, family support, behavioral research, and awareness. Works with other Prader-Willi organizations.

**★2751★ Prader-Willi Syndrome
     Association U.S.A. (PWS)**
2510 S. Brentwood Blvd., Ste. 220
St. Louis, MO 63144
Phone: (314)962-7644
Free: 800-926-4797
Fax: (314)962-7869
Russ Myler, Exec.Dir.

Founded: 1975. **Members:** 1,500. **State Groups:** 30. **Description:** Parents, physicians, educators, dieticians, group homes, and others interested in the Prader-Willi Syndrome, an uncommon condition resulting from a birth defect. (The significant manifestations of the syndrome are obesity, if not controlled; short stature, lack of muscle tone, hypogonadism, and central nervous system performance dysfunction.) Works to provide a forum for communication about the syndrome, particularly the means to cope with it; to promote research and the establishment of treatment facilities. Has been the catalyst for the formation of summer camps and group homes; conducts educational programs; compiles statistics. **Publications:** Brochures. • *Gathered View*, bimonthly. Newsletter. Provides information on education, learning problems, and new resources for individuals with PWS. Includes book reviews and research updates. *Price:* Included in membership dues. • Handbooks. For parents. • *Management of Prader-Willi Syndrome*. Book. • *Overview*. Booklet. Also publishes information packets. **Formerly:** (1977) Prader-Willi Syndrome Parents and Friends; (1992) Prader-Willi Syndrome Association.

**★2752★ Prader-Willi Syndrome
     International Information Forum**
40 Holly Ln.
Roslyn Heights, NY 11577
Phone: (516)621-2445
Free: 800-358-0682
Fax: (516)484-7154

Founded: 1993. **Members:** 2,500. **Description:** Parents, families, professionals, and agencies interested in Prader-Willi Syndrome. Links individuals with information and services. Assists parents in seeking out others who share the same concerns. **Publications:** Booklets. • Brochures. • *Prader-Willi Perspectives*, quarterly. Journal. • *PW Inforum*, periodic. Newsletter. Contains current issues related to Prader-Willi Syndrome.

**★2753★ Rubinstein-Taybi Parent Group
     (RTSPG)**
PO Box 146
Smith Center, KS 66967
Phone: (913)697-2984
Lorrie Baxter, Coord.

Founded: 1984. **Members:** 253. **Description:** Families with children diagnosed with Rubinstein-Taybi Syndrome. Provides information and support. **Publications:** *Rubinstein-Taybi Syndrome*. Pamphlet. • *Rubinstein-Taybi Syndrome: A Book for Families*. Booklet. *Price:* $3.

**★2754★ Society for Research into
     Hydrocephalus and Spina Bifida (SRHSB)**
Dept. of Microbial Disease
City Hospital
Hucknall Rd.
Nottingham NG5 1PB, England
Phone: 115 9691169
Fax: 115 9627766
Dr. Roger Bayston, Hon.Sec.

Founded: 1957. **Members:** 340. **Languages:** English. **Description:** Nursing, psychology, social work, scientific, and medical professionals from 25 countries with a common interest in hydrocephalus (an abnormal accumulation of fluid in the cranium) and spina bifida (a defect in the closing of the bony spinal canal). Object is to advance education and research on hydrocephalus and spina bifida. Brings together members to aid them in their endeavors to prevent, cure, and alleviate the conditions. **Publications:** *Zeitschrift fur Kinder Chirurgie*, annual. Journal.

**★2755★ Spina Bifida Association of
     America (SBAA)**
4590 MacArthur Blvd. NW, Ste. 250
Washington, DC 20007-4226
Phone: (202)944-3285
Free: 800-621-3141
Fax: (202)944-3295
Larry Pencak, Exec.Dir.

Founded: 1972. **Members:** 6,000. **Local Groups:** 75. **Description:** Individuals with spina bifida; their parents, relatives, and friends; concerned professionals. (Spina bifida, or "open spine," is the second most common disabling birth defect and results in muscle weakness or paralysis and incontinence. Its cause is unknown and there is no complete cure.) Purposes are to: develop an information service of materials relating to spina bifida; conduct research into the causes of the birth defect; improve vocational training of individuals with spina bifida; monitor development of legislation applying to disabled persons. Promotes public awareness and action through national media; provides referral services; participates in appropriate legislative activities; holds seminars on scientific, social, medical, and educational programs. Provides training of competent personnel to aid in the treatment, care, education, adjustment, and rehabilitation of individuals with spina bifida. **Publications:** Booklets. • Pamphlets. • Reports. • *Spina Bifida Insights*, bimonthly. Newsletter. Reports on the developments in medicine, education, and legislation affecting the problems and needs of persons with spina bifida. *Price:* Included in membership dues; $25/year for nonmembers; $40/year for professionals; $50/year outside U.S.

Sturge-Weber Foundation (SWF)
See: Entry 8315

United Cerebral Palsy Associations (UCPA)
See: Entry 8320

United States Cerebral Palsy Athletic Association (USCPAA)
See: Entry 8323

Research Centers

**★2756★ Baylor College of Medicine
Birth Defects Center**
6621 Fannin St.
Houston, TX 77030
Phone: (713)770-4280
Fax: (713)770-4294
Dr. Arthur Beaudet, Actg.Chm.

Research Activities and Fields: Etiology and treatment of birth defects and genetic disorders.

**★2757★ Craniofacial Anomalies Research
     Center**
437 BB
Iowa City, IA 52242
Phone: (319)335-1035
Fax: (319)335-2077
Dr. Michael Solursh, Dir.

Research Activities and Fields: Seeks to identify human genes and other risk factors in the etiology of craniofacial anomalies. Conducts five interrelated projects: 1) collection and analysis of epidemiological data; 2) genetic mapping of specific genes involved in craniofacial defects; 3) cloning and sequencing of genes; 4) differentiation between specific DNA isolated from a neural crest cell line; and 5) study of normal functions in craniofacial development.

★2758★ Lancaster Cleft Palate Clinic
223 N. Lime St.
Lancaster, PA 17602
Phone: (717)396-7415
Fax: (717)396-7409
Kathlyn C. McElliott, Ph.D., Pres./CEO

Research Activities and Fields: Plastic surgery, dentistry, orthodontics, prosthodontics, craniofacial morphology, speech, hearing, otolaryngology, genetics, and behavioral science, particularly in regard to children with craniofacial anomalies. Conducts interdisciplinary study of problems of oral/facial growth, orthognathic surgery, and communicative disorders. **Formerly:** H.K. Cooper Institute for Oral-Facial Anomalies and Communicative Disorders; H.K. Cooper Clinic (1985).

**★2759★ U.S. Department of Health and
     Human Services**
National Center for Environmental Health
**Birth Defects and Developmental
     Disabilities Division**
4770 Buford Hwy, F34
Atlanta, GA 30341-3724
Phone: (404)488-7150
Fax: (404)488-7156
Dr. Godfrey P. Oakley, Jr., Director

Research Activities and Fields: Division's interests and activities include surveillance research, intervention methods, and technical consultations leading to the design, conduct, analysis, and evaluation of epidemiologic studies of adverse reproductive outcomes (i.e., birth defects, developmental disabilities, genetic abnormalities, mental retardation, and spontaneous abortion). Activities include population-based surveillance, use of case-control methods, and randomized controlled trials. In addition, cooperative agreements with states have been developed in an effort to increase the Division's research capacity into prevention effectiveness.

U.S. Department of Health and Human Services
National Institute of Neurological Disorders and Stroke
Division of Convulsive, Developmental, and Neuromuscular Disorders
Developmental Neurology Branch
See: Entry 8447

★2760★ **University of Florida**
Craniofacial Center
JHMHC, Box 100424
Gainesville, FL 32610
Phone: (904)392-4370
Fax: (904)392-3070
Dr. W.N. Williams, Dir.

Research Activities and Fields: Studies the efficacy of specific surgical, prosthetic, and health-related professional management and therapy procedures in the early treatment of cleft palate and related craniofacial anomalies; prevention of communicative disorders in children from birth to three years; relationship between craniofacial abnormalities, speech, and hearing disorders; studies on craniofacial, cleft lip, and palate surgery; facial growth and disfigurement; psychological effects of craniofacial disfigurement; and the efficacy of a coordinated, interdisciplinary, team approach in health care delivery. Maintains records on clinical research and graduate or professional education within the three colleges. **Publications:** *Communicative Disorders Related to Cleft Lip and Palate.*

★2761★ **University of Illinois at Chicago**
Craniofacial Center
College of Medicine
808 S. Wood St., M/C 588
Chicago, IL 60612
Phone: (312)996-6979
Fax: (312)413-1157
Dr. Allen S. Goldman, Dir.

Research Activities and Fields: Craniofacial biology, growth, and genetics, including mechanisms of cleft palate and psychological and speech development of children with cleft palate and other craniofacial anamolies. **Formerly:** Cleft Palate Center; Center for Craniofacial Anomalies (1991).

★2762★ **University of Iowa**
Birth Defects and Genetic Disorders Unit
2614 JCP
Iowa City, IA 52242
Phone: (319)335-9901
Fax: (319)356-3347
Dr. James M. Smith, Contact

Research Activities and Fields: Conducts research on the causes, prevention, and treatment of birth defects and genetic disorders. Coordinates University clinical service programs and related educational programs throughout the state of Iowa with afflicted individuals. Service and research fields include biochemical and molecular genetics, teratology, dysmorphology, genetic counseling, management of inborn errors of metabolism, epidemiology of birth defects and genetic screening, and neuromuscular disorders.

★2763★ **University of Pennsylvania**
Craniofacial Anomaly Clinic
Center for Human Appearance
Penn Tower Hotel, 10th Fl.
3400 Spruce St.
Philadelphia, PA 19104
Phone: (215)662-2048
Fax: (215)349-5895
Linton A. Whitaker, M.D., Chief of Plastic Surgery

Research Activities and Fields: Craniofacial anomalies, focusing on developing methods for evaluating human facial form, developing methods for controlling facial growth, evaluating bone replacement material, investigating aging skeletal and support structures, and studying aging skin.

★2764★ **University of Pittsburgh**
Cleft Palate-Craniofacial Center
School of Dental Medicine
Pittsburgh, PA 15261
Phone: (412)648-8400
Fax: (412)648-8779
Dr. Mary L. Marazita, Dir.

Research Activities and Fields: Cleft palate, cleft lip, and craniofacial anomalies, including interdisciplinary, basic, clinical, genetic, embryological, and teratology studies. Also studies ear diseases, velopharyngeal valving, laryngeal characteristics and motor control for speech, computer reconstruction of nasal capsule, and anatomy of pharyngeal walls. **E-mail Address:** mlm3@vms.cis.pitt.edu.

★2765★ **Wayne State University**
C.S. Mott Center for Human Growth and Development
275 E. Hancock St.
Detroit, MI 48201
Phone: (313)577-1068
Fax: (313)577-8554
Dr. Ernest L. Abel, Dir.

Research Activities and Fields: Human growth and development, including causative factors, identification, prevention, and remedy of birth defects. Uses mechanical, chemical, and hormonal devices as well as acceptable social, psychological, ethical, and moral approaches. Identifies environmental pollutants, drugs, infections, and other teratogens responsible for increasing incidence of birth defects and studies the relationships between environmental deterioration, dwindling natural resources, population density, and quality of human existence. Develops and implements population controls. **Publications:** Annual Report.

Chapter 11
Burns

Foundations & Other Funding Organizations

Other Funding Organizations

★ 2766 ★ **American Burn Association**
c/o Cleon W. Goodwin
New York Hospital
Cornell Medical Center
525 E. 68th St., Rm. L-706
New York, NY 10021
Phone: (212)746-5078
Free: 800-548-2876
Fax: (212)746-8991
Andrew M. Munster, M.D., Sec.

Description: Awards research grants for the improvement of care and treatment of the burn patient.

National & International Organizations

★ 2767 ★ **American Burn Association**
(ABA)
c/o Cleon W. Goodwin, M.D.
New York Hospital - Cornell Medical Center
525 E. 68th St., Rm. L-706
New York, NY 10021
Phone: (212)746-5078
Free: 800-548-2876
Fax: (212)746-8991
Cleon W. Goodwin, M.D., Sec.

Founded: 1967. **Members:** 3,500. **Description:** Physicians, nurses, physical therapists, occupational therapists, dietitians, biomedical engineers, social service workers, and researchers interested in the care of burn injuries. Objective is the improvement of the care and treatment of burns, which includes a program of prevention of burn injuries. Sponsors visiting professorship. **Publications:** *American Burn Association--Book of Abstracts*, annual. Journal. *Price:* Included in membership dues; $15/copy for nonmembers. • *American Burn Association--Membership Directory*, annual. Directory.

Price: Included in membership dues. • *Burn Care Services in North America*, annual. Directory. Lists specialized burn care facilities in the United States and Canada. *Price:* Included in membership dues; $50/copy for nonmembers. • *Journal of Burn Care and Rehabilitation*, bimonthly. Journal. Covers burn injuries and their treatment. Includes a list of employment opportunities, research reports, and statistics. *Price:* Included in membership dues; $35/year for nonmembers; $52/year for institutions.

★ 2768 ★ **Burns United Support Groups**
(BUSG)
441 Colonial Ct.
Grosse Pointe Farms, MI 48236
Phone: (313)881-5577
Donna Schneck-Smorol, Exec. Officer

Founded: 1986. **Members:** 80. **Regional Groups:** 3. **State Groups:** 3. **Local Groups:** 3. **Description:** Burn survivors and their families. Provides support services and information on burn care and prevention. Conducts educational programs and childrens' services. Operates speakers' bureau.

★ 2769 ★ **Children's Burn Foundation**
100 Nakhodka Pr
Nakhodka, Russia
Phone: 42366 42641
Liudmila Sukhova, Pres.

Description: Promotes prevention and treatment of childhood burn injuries. Offers assistance to children who have suffered burns and their families.

★ 2770 ★ **International Society for Burn**
Injuries (ISBI)
Keio University Hospital
35 Shinanomachi Shinjuko
Tokyo 160, Japan
Phone: 813 32269877
Fax: 813 32269877
Naoki Aikawa, M.D., Sec. Treas.

Founded: 1965. **Members:** 1,570. **Languages:** English. **Description:** Physicians, surgeons, nurses, scientists, and other interested medical and non-medical personnel who are engaged in the care and research of burns. Seeks to disseminate knowledge and stimulate prevention in the field of burns. Promotes and coordinates

scientific, clinical, and social research in burns; promotes first aid, nursing, and other types of education in all phases of burn care. **Publications:** *BURNS*, 8/year. Journal. • Membership Directory, annual.

★ 2771 ★ **Israeli Burn Association (IBA)**
Hadassah Ein Kerem
Burn Unit
91120 Jerusalem, Israel
Phone: 2 776610
Fax: 2 434434
Dr. A. Eldad, Chair

Founded: 1990. **Members:** 75. **Languages:** English. **Description:** Promotes prevention and treatment of burn injuries in Israel. Conducts research and educational programs. Bestows awards; sponsors competitions. Compiles statistics. **Publications:** *Abstracts of Annual Meeting.*

★ 2772 ★ **National Burn Victim Foundation**
(NBVF)
32-34 Scotland Rd.
Orange, NJ 07050
Phone: (201)676-7700
Fax: (201)673-6353
Prof. Harry J. Gaynor, Pres.

Founded: 1974. **Members:** 1,155. **Description:** Supporters are physicians specializing in burn treatment and care, fire services prevention personnel, nurses, communications experts, health and chemical industry representatives, and others interested in burn treatment and care. Maintains 24-hour emergency burn referral service and crisis intervention team of professionals that provide counseling for burn victims and their families, addressing psychological problems and physical handicaps remaining after treatment. Provides free blood services to burn victims. Sponsors Burns Recovered, a self-help group. Conducts medical emergency burn care seminars and workshops for physicians, nurses, EMTs, and emergency rescue personnel. Operates Medical Disaster Response System, which utilizes private helicopters for transporting medical teams to disaster sites where large numbers of survivors have been burned. Collects burn data from New Jersey hospitals daily. Program currently provides direct professional services in New Jersey and information and referral services nationally. Offers consultation and evaluation services to the Division of Youth and Family Services and law enforcement agencies in cases involving suspected child abuse or neglect. Presents burn awareness and prevention programs to schools, civic organizations, and day-care centers. Maintains speakers' bureau; conducts specialized education, children's services, and research programs; compiles statistics. **Publications:** *Child Abuse? Think Again.* Video. *Price:* $269.95. • *Disaster Medical Response.* Video. *Price:* $49. • *General Burn Awareness.* Video. • *National Burn Victim Foundation--Update,* quarterly. Newsletter. Covers news on membership activities. *Price:* Free. • Pamphlets. • *Training Professionals - Child Abuse/Neglect Investigation.* Video.

★ 2773 ★ **National Institute for Burn Medicine (NIBM)**
909 E. Ann St.
Ann Arbor, MI 48104
Phone: (313)769-9000
Fax: (313)769-9009
Claudella A. Jones, Dir.

Founded: 1968. **Description:** Participants are dedicated to preventing burn injuries; improving the survival rate of and developing the quality of life for burn victims. Provides consultation for development of specialized burn care facilities; prevention programs and materials; education, information, and statistics in burn treatment and care. Maintains International Burn Library containing over 35,000 citations. **Publications:** Books. • Brochures. • Films. Also publishes poster. **Formerly:** (1968) American Burn Research Corporation; (1971) Institute for Burn Medicine.

★ 2774 ★ **Phoenix Society for Burn Survivors (PSBS)**
11 Rust Hill Rd.
Levittown, PA 19056
Phone: (215)946-BURN
Free: 800-888-BURN
Fax: (215)946-4788
Alan Jeffry Breslau, Exec.Dir.

Founded: 1977. **Members:** 6,500. **Local Groups:** 300. **Description:** Selfhelp service organization for burn survivors and their families. Works to ease the psychosocial adjustment of severely burned and disfigured persons during and after hospitalization so they may return to normal and satisfactory lives within their communities. Former burn survivors work as volunteers on a one-to-one basis with other burn survivors and their families. Offers a training program for volunteers; seeks to educate the public about the nature and problems of disfigurement; discourages concealment of disfigurement, which the society believes compounds the difficulty of adjustment; conducts research on psychological ramifications of burn disfigurement and disseminates information on burns and trauma and their treatment. Conducts school programs for burned children returning to classes. Maintains speakers' bureau and contains books on burn recovery, films, and videocassettes. **Publications:** *Audiovisual Materials on Burns, Disfigurement, and Related Subjects,* annual. List of audiovisual materials; includes educational and inspirational materials on coping

with burns and disfigurement. *Price:* $7. • *Bibliographic References--Burns in Children,* annual. Bibliography. Lists reading material for the education and inspiration of parents, siblings, and professionals involved wiht burned children. *Price:* $5. • *Coping Strategies for Burn Survivors and Their Families.* • *Guidelines for Burn Volunteers.* • *Icarus File,* quarterly. Newsletter. Provides news items on burn prevention, cosmetology for burn survivors, and other topics of interest; includes member news and book reviews. *Price:* Included in membership dues; $4/year for nonmembers; $10 outside U.S. **Formerly:** (1991) Phoenix Center.

Shriners Hospitals for Crippled Children (SHCC)
See: Entry 6470

Research Centers

★ 2775 ★ **Burn Trauma Center**
Massachusetts General Hospital
Boston, MA 02114
Phone: (617)726-2809
Fax: (617)726-4217
Ronald G. Tompkins, M.D., Head

Research Activities and Fields: Burns and burn trauma.

★ 2776 ★ **National Institute for Burn Medicine**
909 E. Ann St.
Ann Arbor, MI 48104
Phone: (313)769-9000
Fax: (313)769-9009
Irving Feller, M.D., Pres.

Research Activities and Fields: Burn prevention. Studies etiology of burn injuries and evaluates high risk populations. Organizes and delivers burn care.

★ 2777 ★ **Shriners Burns Institute**
815 Market St.
Galveston, TX 77550-2725
Phone: (409)770-6731
Fax: (409)770-6749
David N. Herndon, M.D., Chief of Staff

Research Activities and Fields: Thermal injuries, wound healing, and scar formation, including treatment of burned children, cardiopulmonary complications, microcirculatory changes, nutritional and metabolic status, epidemiology and ideology of burn injuries, host responsiveness to secondary infections, and lung injuries.

★ 2778 ★ **Shriners Burns Institutes**
51 Blossom St.
Boston, MA 02114
Phone: (617)722-3000
Fax: (617)523-1684
Richard Roderer, Contact

Research Activities and Fields: Prevention of scar formation, burned childrens' reactions to drugs, nutrition, lung function after burn injuries, infections in burns, and development of artificial skin. Specializes in treating children with acute, fresh burns; children needing plastic recon-

structive or restorative surgery as a result of healed burns; and children with severe scarring, resulting in contractures or interference of proper mobility of the limbs, and deformity of the face.

★ 2779 ★ **University of Cincinnati Shriners Burns Institute**
3229 Burnet Ave.
Cincinnati, OH 45229-3095
Phone: (513)872-6000
Fax: (513)872-6999
Glenn D. Warden, M.D., Dir.

Research Activities and Fields: Burns, including nutrition, infection, coverage (autografts/allografts), conversion (topical antimicrobials), pain, scar formation, and care and treatment of children who have suffered from thermal injuries and resulting problems.

★ 2780 ★ **University of Michigan Burn Center**
1500 E. Medical Center Dr.
Ann Arbor, MI 48109-0033
Phone: (313)936-9666
Fax: (313)936-9657
Dr. Jorge Rodriguez, Dir.

Research Activities and Fields: Conducts clinical research, standards review, and vaccine and plasma preparation to combat growth of gram negative organisms in burns. **Publications:** *International Bibliography on Burns,* in collaboration with National Institute for Burn Medicine.

Chapter 12
Cardiology & Cardiovascular Diseases

Federal Government Agencies

★2781★ **U.S. Department of Health and Human Services**
National Heart, Lung, and Blood Institute
9000 Rockville Pike
Bethesda, MD 20892
Phone: (301)496-5166
Fax: (301)402-0818

Description: NHLBI provides leadership for a national program in diseases of the heart, blood vessels, blood, lungs, and in the use of blood and the management of blood resources. It plans, conducts, fosters, and supports an integrated and coordinated program of research, investigations, clinical trials, and demonstrations relating to the causes, prevention, methods of diagnosis and treatment of heart, blood vessel, lung, and blood diseases through research performed in its own laboratories and through contracts and grants to scientific institutions and to individual scientists. The Institute also supports training of manpower in fundamental science and clinical disciplines and collects and disseminates educational materials for health professionals and the lay public.

Foundations & Other Funding Organizations

Private Foundations

★2782★ **Bugher Foundation**
c/o Davis, Polk and Wardwell
450 Lexington Ave.
New York, NY 10017
Phone: (212)450-4082
D. Nelson Adams, Trustee

Foundation Philosophy: The foundation is dedicated to cardiovascular disease research. **Giving Priorities:** In fiscal 1993, 100% of the foundation's funding went to cardiovascular disease research in university medical schools and medical research centers. **Typical Health-**

Related Recipients: Heart, Medical Education, Medical Research. **Geographic Distribution:** National.

E. L. Wiegand Foundation
See: Entry 150

Fannie E. Rippel Foundation
See: Entry 178

★2783★ **Nora Eccles Treadwell Foundation**
239 Joaquin Ave.
San Leandro, CA 94577
Phone: (415)775-2879
Patricia Canepa, President and Director

Foundation Philosophy: The foundation's principal concerns are medical research, primarily in the areas of cardiovascular disease, diabetes, and arthritis. Currently, its major priority is the Nora Eccles Treadwell Cardiovascular Research and Training Institute at the University of Utah's Medical Center. **Giving Priorities:** In 1992, about 98% of funding supported health. The majority went to hospitals and universities for medical research, including the foundation's highest grant of $800,000 for the University of Utah's research on cardiovascular electrophy. The remainder supported social services, the arts, international affairs, and religion. **Typical Health-Related Recipients:** Arthritis, Children's Health/Hospitals, Diabetes, Emergency/Ambulance Services, Family Planning, Health Funds, Health Organizations, Heart, Hospitals, Medical Education, Medical Research, Mental Health, People with Disabilities, Prenatal Health Issues, Single-Disease Health Associations. **Geographic Distribution:** Utah and California only.

Ray C. Fish Foundation
See: Entry 439

Other Funding Organizations

★2784★ **American College of Chest Physicians**
3300 Dundee Rd.
Northbrook, IL 60062
Phone: (708)498-1400
Free: 800-343-ACCP
Alvin Lever, Exec. Dir.

Description: Awards fellowships to support advanced training and research in cardiopulmonary medicine and surgery.

★2785★ **American Heart Association**
7272 Greenville Ave.
Dallas, TX 75231-4596
Phone: (214)373-6300
Free: 800-242-1793
Fax: (214)706-1341
Dudley H. Hafner, Exec. VP

Description: Association's program of support for basic and clinical research includes: Established Investigatorships to assist young physicians and scientists in developing independent cardiovascular research careers; Clinician-Scientist Awards to encourage young physicians to undertake careers in clinical investigation; Research Grants-in-Aid; and Medical Student Research Fellowships.

★2786★ **Heart Disease Research Foundation**
50 Court St.
Brooklyn, NY 11201
Phone: (718)649-6210
Dr. Yoshiaki Omura, Med. Research Dir.

Description: Supports and conducts research, both basic and clinical, in the early diagnosis, prevention, and treatment of cardiovascular diseases. Sponsors postgraduate continuing medical education courses for physicians, dentists, and medical researchers.

★2787★ **International Cardiology Foundation**
c/o American Heart Association
7272 Greenville Ave.
Dallas, TX 75231-4599
Phone: (214)373-6300
Rodman Starke, M.D., Exec. Off.

Description: Funds a program of visiting teachers to foreign countries. In certain situations, the foundation will provide additional limited support for short-term specialized training of younger physicians, technicians, and educators in the U.S.

★2788★ National Heart Council
306 W. Joppa Rd.
Baltimore, MD 21204
Phone: (410)494-0300
Fax: (410)494-0725
Frederick C. Ruof, Pres.

Description: Awards grants to organizations and individuals for the purpose of conducting research, meetings, or other activities which gather and disseminate information on traumatic medicine, particularly cardiac disorders.

★2789★ North American Society of Pacing and Electrophysiology
Natick Executive Park
2 Vision Dr.
Natick, MA 01760-2059
Phone: (508)647-0100
Fax: (508)647-0124
Carol G. McGlinchey, Exec. Dir.

Description: Awards fellowships in cardiac pacing and electrophysiology; bestows Young Investigator awards for original clinical or basic research in the field of cardiac pacing and/or cardiac electrophysiology.

Medical & Allied Health Schools

Perfusion

The following perfusion training programs are accredited by the Commission on Accreditation of Allied Health Education Programs of the American Medical Association, 515 N. State St., Ste. 7530, Chicago, IL 60610, (312) 464-4623. For information on careers in this field, contact the American Society of Extra-Corporeal Technology, 11480 Sunset Hills Rd., Ste. 210E, Reston VA 22090, (703) 435-8556.

Arizona

★2790★ University of Arizona
College of Medicine
Perfusion Sciences
Tucson, AZ 85724
Phone: (602)626-6339
Fax: (602)626-4042

Connecticut

★2791★ Quinnipiac College
Cardiovascular Perfusion Program
555 New Rd./Mt. Carmel Ave.
Hamden, CT 06518-0569
Phone: (203)288-5251
Fax: (203)281-8706

District of Columbia

★2792★ Walter Reed Army Medical Center
Cardiovascular Perfusion Technology Program
Washington, DC 20307-5001
Phone: (202)576-1433
Fax: (202)576-3420

Florida

★2793★ Barry University
Cardiovascular Perfusion Program
11300 NE 2nd Ave.
Miami Shores, FL 33161-6695
Phone: (305)899-3214
Fax: (305)899-3845

Illinois

★2794★ Loyola University of Chicago
Foster G. McGaw Hospital
School of Perfusion
2160 S. 1st Ave.
Maywood, IL 60153
Phone: (708)216-4648
Fax: (708)216-5897

★2795★ Malcolm X College / City College of Chicago
Program of Extracorporeal Perfusion
1900 W. VanBuren
Chicago, IL 60612
Phone: (312)850-7359
Fax: (312)850-7457

★2796★ Rush University
College of Health Science
School of Perfusion Technology
1653 W. Congress Parkway
Chicago, IL 60612
Phone: (312)942-2305
Fax: (312)942-4048

Iowa

★2797★ University of Iowa
Department of Surgery
Perfusion Technology Program
CT 1601JCP
Iowa City, IA 52242
Phone: (319)356-8496
Fax: (319)356-3891

Kansas

★2798★ St. Joseph Medical Center / Kansas Newman College
Perfusion Technology Program
3600 E. Harry
Wichita, KS 67218
Phone: (316)689-6017
Fax: (316)689-5297

Louisiana

★2799★ Alton Ochsner Medical Foundation
Extracorporeal Technology Program
880 Commerce Rd. W.
New Orleans, LA 70123-3335
Phone: (504)842-3267
Fax: (504)842-9129

Maryland

★2800★ Johns Hopkins Hospital
School of Perfusion Technology
814 Blalock
600 N. Wolfe St.
Baltimore, MD 21287-4814
Phone: (410)955-5168
Fax: (410)955-4163

Massachusetts

★2801★ Northeastern University
Perfusion Technology Program
360 Huntington Ave.
Boston, MA 02115
Phone: (617)373-3666
Fax: (617)373-2968

Missouri

★2802★ St. Louis University
Perfusion Technology Program
1504 S. Grand Blvd.
St. Louis, MO 63104
Phone: (314)577-8525
Fax: (314)577-8503

Nebraska

★2803★ University of Nebraska Medical Center
Division of Clinical Perfusion Education
600 S. 42nd St.
Omaha, NE 68105
Phone: (402)559-6386
Fax: (402)559-6913

New Jersey

★2804★ Cooper Hospital / University Medical Center
School of Cardiovascular Perfusion
Sarah Cooper Bldg., Rm. 310
1 Cooper Plaza
Camden, NJ 08103
Phone: (609)342-3277
Fax: (609)365-7582

★2805★ Eastern Heart Institute
School of Perfusion Technology
350 Blvd.
Passaic, NJ 07055
Phone: (201)365-4492
Fax: (201)916-2041

New York

★2806★ Montefiore Medical Center
Jack D. Weiler Hospital of the Albert
Einstein College of Medicine
School of Perfusion Technology
1825 Eastchester Rd.
Bronx, NY 10461
Phone: (718)904-3248
Fax: (718)904-2340

★2807★ State University of New York
Health Science Center at Brooklyn
Perfusion Training Program
450 Clarkson Ave., Box 93
Brooklyn, NY 11203
Phone: (718)270-7703

★2808★ State University of New York
Health Science Center at Syracuse
Cardiovascular Perfusion Program
750 E. Adams St.
Syracuse, NY 13210
Phone: (315)464-6933
Fax: (315)464-6914

Ohio

★2809★ Christ Hospital
School of Perfusion Science
2139 Auburn Ave.
Cincinnati, OH 45219
Phone: (513)369-1106

★2810★ Cleveland Clinic Foundation
School of Cardiovascular Perfusion
1 Clinic Center
9500 Euclid Ave.
Cleveland, OH 44195-5001
Phone: (216)444-3895
Fax: (216)444-0777

★2811★ Ohio State University
Division of Circulation Technology
1583 Perry St.
Columbus, OH 43210
Phone: (614)292-7261
Fax: (614)292-0210

Oregon

★2812★ St. Vincent Hospital and Medical
Center
Heart Institute
Perfusion Training Program
9205 SW Barnes Rd., Ste. 230
Portland, OR 97225
Phone: (503)291-2088
Fax: (503)291-2488

Pennsylvania

★2813★ Duquesne University
John G. Rangos School of Health Sciences
Department of Perfusion Technology
215 Health Science Bldg.
Pittsburgh, PA 15282
Phone: (412)396-5555
Fax: (412)396-5554

★2814★ Episcopal Hospital
School of Perfusion Science
100 E. Lehigh Ave.
Philadelphia, PA 19125
Phone: (215)427-7748
Fax: (215)427-7567

★2815★ Hahnemann University Hospital
Program in Cardiovascular Perfusion
Technology
Broad and Vine Sts., Mail Stop 508
Philadelphia, PA 19102-1192
Phone: (215)762-7895
Fax: (215)241-5347

★2816★ Pennsylvania State University
Milton S. Hershey Medical Center
CV Perfusion Technology Training
Program
PO Box 850
Hershey, PA 17033
Phone: (717)531-8550
Fax: (717)531-4017

★2817★ Shadyside Hospital
School of Cardiovascular Perfusion
5230 Centre Ave.
Pittsburgh, PA 15232
Phone: (412)623-2482
Fax: (412)683-3783

South Carolina

★2818★ Medical University of South
Carolina
College of Health Professions
ECT Educational Program
101 Doughty St., 2nd Fl.
Charleston, SC 29425
Phone: (803)792-2298
Fax: (803)792-4417

Tennessee

★2819★ Vanderbilt University
Department of Cardiothoracic Surgery
Perfusion Training Program
Vanderbilt Clinic, Rm. 2986
Nashville, TN 37232-5734
Phone: (615)343-9192
Fax: (615)343-9194

Texas

★2820★ Baylor College of Medicine
School of Perfusion Technology
1 Baylor Plaza
Houston, TX 77030
Phone: (713)798-6093
Fax: (713)798-7655

★2821★ Texas Heart Institute
Cardiovascular Perfusion Program
PO Box 20345
Houston, TX 77225-0708
Phone: (713)791-4026
Fax: (713)791-4993

National & International
Organizations

Academy of Veterinary Cardiology (AVC)
See: Entry 13019

★2822★ American Association of
Cardiovascular and Pulmonary
Rehabilitation (AACVPR)
7611 Elmwood Ave., Ste. 201
Middleton, WI 53562
Phone: (608)831-6989
Fax: (608)831-5122
Jane C. Shepard, Exec.Dir.

Founded: 1985. Members: 2,500. Description: Allied health professionals involved in the field of cardiovascular and pulmonary rehabilitation. Fosters the improvement of clinical practice in CVPR; promotes scientific CVPR research; seeks the advancement of CVPR education for health care professionals and the public. Publications: AACVPR Directory, annual. Directory. • Directory of Cardiovascular and Pulmonary Rehabilitation Programs, annual. Directory. • Journal of Cardiopulmonary Rehabilitation, bimonthly. Journal. Provides theoretical and practical information on cardiovascular and pulmonary rehabilitation. Includes reviews and calendar of events. Price: Included in membership dues; $120/year for nonmembers. • Newsletter, quarterly.

American Association for Thoracic Surgery
(AATS)
See: Entry 12215

★2823★ American Board of
Cardiovascular Perfusion (ABCP)
207 N. 25th Ave.
Hattiesburg, MS 39401
Phone: (601)582-3309
Drs. Mark and Beth Richmond, Exec.Dirs.

Founded: 1975. Members: 2,066. Description: Certified clinical perfusionists. Seeks to protect the public through the establishment and maintenance of standards in the field. Has established qualifications for examination and procedures for recertification. Administers annual board examinations.

★2824★ American College of Angiology
(ACA)
1044 Northern Blvd., Ste. 103
Roslyn, NY 11576
Phone: (516)484-6880
Fax: (516)625-1174
H. E. Shaftel, M.D., Contact

Founded: 1954. Members: 1,900. Description: Physicians; basic scientists in health care industries. Objective is to support and advance the study and research of vascular diseases. Conducts colloquia. Publications: American College of Angiology Membership Directory, biennial. Membership Directory.

★ 2825 ★ **American College of Cardiology (ACC)**
9111 Old Georgetown Rd.
Bethesda, MD 20814-1699
Phone: (301)897-5400
Free: 800-253-4636
Fax: (301)897-9745
David J. Feild, Exec.VP

Founded: 1949. **Members:** 21,561. **State Groups:** 24. **Description:** Professional society of physicians, surgeons, and scientists specializing in cardiology (heart) and cardiovascular (circulatory) diseases. Operates Heart House Learning Center. Maintains numerous committees. **Publications:** *ACC Current Journal Review*, bimonthly. Journal. Provides abstracts and reviews of pertinent clinical articles. *Price:* Included in membership dues; $56 for individuals; $115 for institutions; $42 for interns. • *ACCEL*, monthly. Journal. On audiocassette. Contains 12 to 16 interviews with leaders in the field of cardiovascular medicine. *Price:* $125/year for members; $150/year for nonmembers. • *Affiliates in Training*, bimonthly. Newsletter. Provides information of the association pertinent to the Affiliate-In-Training category. Includes list of employment opportunities. *Price:* Included in membership dues; $10/year for nonmembers. • *Cardiology*, monthly. Newsletter. Contains information on clincal cardiology practice. Covers health system reform, legislative and socioeconomic activities, and updates. *Price:* Included in membership dues; $59/year. • *Journal of the American College of Cardiology*, monthly. Journal. Covers original clinical and experimental papers on cardiovascular disease featuring reports on medical and surgical therapy, and other subjects. *Price:* Included in membership dues; $107/year for nonmember individuals; $165/year for institutions; $66/year for interns, residents, health professionals. Also publishes self-study materials.

American College of Cardiovascular Administrators (ACCA)
See: Entry 5544

★ 2826 ★ **American College of Chest Physicians (ACCP)**
3300 Dundee Rd.
Northbrook, IL 60062
Phone: (708)498-1400
Free: 800-343-ACCP
Alvin Lever, Exec.Dir.

Founded: 1935. **Members:** 15,000. **Description:** Professional society of physicians and surgeons specializing in diseases of the chest (heart and lungs). Promotes undergraduate and postgraduate medical education and research in the field. Sponsors forums. Maintains placement service; conducts educational programs. **Publications:** *American College of Chest Physicians Membership Directory*, annual. Membership Directory. Arranged geographically and by specialty. *Price:* Included in membership dues. • Books. • Brochures. On smoking and health. • *Chest: For Pulmonologists, Cardiologists, Cardiothoracic Surgeons, and Related Specialists*, monthly. Journal. Presents clinical investigations and case reports in cardiopulmonary medical and surgical specialties. Contains author and subject indexes. *Price:* Included in member-

ship dues; $102/year for nonmembers; $114/year for institutions. • Films. • Reports. Also publishes self-teaching series on coronary care.

★ 2827 ★ **American Heart Association (AHA)**
7272 Greenville Ave.
Dallas, TX 75231-4596
Phone: (214)373-6300
Free: 800-242-1793
Fax: (214)706-1341
Dudley H. Hafner, Exec.VP

Founded: 1924. **Members:** 26,000. **State Groups:** 56. **Description:** Physicians, scientists, and laypersons. Supports research, education, and community service programs with the objective of reducing premature death and disability from cardiovascular diseases and stroke; coordinates the efforts of physicians, nurses, health professionals, and others engaged in the fight against heart and circulatory disease. Financed entirely by voluntary contributions of the public, principally during the Heart Campaign held in February. **Publications:** *Arteriosclerosis and Thrombosis: A Journal of Vascular Biology*, monthly. Journal. Covers research on the biology, prevention, and impact of vascular diseases relating to arteriosclerosis. Includes association news. *Price:* $146/year for individuals; $180/year for institutions. • *Cardiovascular Nursing*, bimonthly. Concise review of new developments in health care for patients with heart disease with particular emphasis on nursing. *Price:* $6/year for individuals; $11/year for institutions. • *Circulation*, monthly. Journal. Covers clinical research and advances in cardiovascular medicine including clinical and laboratory investigations. *Price:* $124/year for individuals; $172/year for institutions. • *Circulation Research*, monthly. Journal. Covers basic cardiovascular research in the areas of anatomy, biology,biochemistry, biophysics, microbiology, and physiology. *Price:* $172/year for individuals; $251/year for institutions. • *Currents in Emergency Cardiac Care*, quarterly. Newsletter. Offers scientific information about ideas, development, and trends in emergency cardiac care; published in conjunction with the Citizen CPR Foundation. *Price:* $12/year for individuals; $20/year for institutions. • *Heart Disease and Stroke*, bimonthly. Provides reviews on diagnosis, treatment, and management of cardiovascular and cerebrovascular diseases. Highlights new research. *Price:* $20/year for individuals; $30/year for institutions. • *Hypertension*, monthly. Journal. Reports clinical and laboratory investigations in hypertension. Includes association news, case studies, and semiannual author/subject index. *Price:* $124/year for individuals; $172/year for institutions. • *Stroke--A Journal of Cerebral Circulation*, monthly. Journal. Provides information on the prevention, diagnosis, treatment, and rehabilitation of cerebral circulation disease. Includes annual indexes. *Price:* $124/year for individuals; $159/year for instituti.

★ 2828 ★ **American Society of Cardiovascular Professionals (ASCP)**
120 Falcon Dr.
Fredericksburg, VA 22408
Phone: (703)891-0079
Free: 800-683-NSCT
Fax: (703)898-2393
Peggy McElgunn, Exec.Dir.

Founded: 1993. **Description:** Dedicated to determining educational needs, developing programs to meet those needs, and providing a structure to offer the cardiovascular and pulmonary technology professional a key to the future as a valuable member of the medical team. Seeks advancement for members through communication and education. Provides coordinated programs to orient the newer professional to his field and continuing educational opportunities for technologist personnel. Has established guidelines for educational programs in the hospital and university setting. Works with educators and physicians to provide basic, advanced, and in-service programs for technologists. Sponsors registration and certification programs which provide technology professionals with further opportunity to clarify their level of expertise. Compiles statistics. **Publications:** *ASCP Membership Directory*, annual. Membership Directory. Arranged alphabetically; includes field specialty, geographical location, and chapter affiliation. *Price:* Included in membership dues; $25/year for nonmembers. • Books. • *CP Digest*, bimonthly. Newsletter. Includes employment opportunity listings, legislative reports, and new member information. *Price:* Included in membership dues; $35/year for nonmembers. • *Journal of Cardiovascular Technology*, semiannual. Journal. Includes book reviews, new product information, computer hardware and software updates, and abstracts. *Price:* Included in membership dues; $45/year for nonmembers. • Monographs. • *Pulmonary News*, quarterly. **Formerly:** (1980) National Society of Cardiopulmonary Technologists; (1986) National Society for Cardiopulmonary Technology; (1988) National Alliance of Cardiovascular Technologists; (1989) American Cardiology Technologists Association.

American Society of Echocardiography (ASE)
See: Entry 11095

★ 2829 ★ **American Society of Extra-Corporeal Technology (AmSECT)**
11480 Sunset Hills Rd., No. 210E
Reston, VA 22090
Phone: (703)435-8556
Fax: (703)435-0056
George M. Cate, Exec.Dir.

Founded: 1964. **Members:** 3,000. **Regional Groups:** 11. **Description:** Perfusionists, technologists, doctors, nurses, and others actively employed and using the applied skills relating to the practice of extracorporeal technology (involving heart-lung machines); student members. Disseminates information necessary to the proper practice of the technology. Conducts programs in continuing education and professional-public liaison and hands-on workshops. Maintains placement service. **Publications:** *Journal of Extra-Corporeal Technology*, quarterly. Journal. Covers dialysis, hemodynamics, organs and tissues, oxygenation, and research. Includes book reviews, case studies and membership directory. *Price:* Included in membership dues; $40/year for nonmembers. • *Perfusion Life*, 11/year. Magazine. Includes calendar of events, reading and employment opportunities lists, and reports of regional events. *Price:* Included in membership dues; $35/year for nonmembers. Also publishes self-study modules, monographs, and clinical simulation series. **Formerly:** (1968) American Society of Extracorporeal Circulation Technicians.

★2830★ American Society of Hypertension (ASH)
515 Madison Ave., Ste. 1515
New York, NY 10022
Phone: (212)644-0650
Fax: (212)644-0658
Sandy Kuhach, Exec.Dir.

Founded: 1985. **Members:** 4,000. **Description:** Medical professionals, paraprofessionals, and post-graduate students interested in hypertension and related cardiovascular diseases. Promotes the development, advancement, and exchange of information on diagnosis and treatment of hypertension; encourages research. **Publications:** *American Journal of Hypertension*, monthly. Journal. • *Membership Directory*, biennial. Also produces educational materials.

★2831★ Association of Black Cardiologists (ABC)
13404 SW 128th St., No. A
Miami, FL 33186-5800
Phone: (305)641-2224
Fax: (305)641-1034
B. Waine Kong, Ph.D., Exec.Dir.

Founded: 1974. **Members:** 500. **Description:** Physicians and other health professionals interested in lowering mortality and morbidity resulting from cardiovascular diseases. Seeks to improve prevention and treatment of cardiovascular diseases. Conducts educational and research programs; bestows awards; maintains speakers' bureau.

★2832★ Association of Estonian Cardiologists (Eesti Kardioloogide Selts)
Sutiste Tee 19
EE-0108 Tallinn, Estonia
Phone: 2 525384
Fax: 2 525908
Jaan Eha, Chm.

Description: Physicians and scientists interested in the field of cardiology.

Association of Physician Assistants in Cardiovascular Surgery (APACVS)
See: Entry 12254

★2833★ Association of Professors of Cardiology (APC)
9111 Old Georgetown Rd.
Bethesda, MD 20814-1699
Phone: (301)493-2330
Fax: (301)897-9745
Donald J. Jablonski, CAE, Contact

Founded: 1990. **Members:** 114. **Description:** Directors or acting directors of divisions of cardi-

ology in accredited medical schools in the U.S. and Puerto Rico. Conducts educational and scientific programs with respect to cardiology.

Association for Research in Vascular Surgery (ARVS) (Association de Recherche en Chirurgie Vasculaire — ARCV)
See: Entry 12256

★2834★ Benelux Phlebology Society (BPS) (Societe Beneluxienne de Phlebologie — SBP)
180, ave. Roi Albert
B-1080 Brussels, Belgium
Phone: 2 4659913
Fax: 2 4659202
Dr. Leon Thiery, Pres.

Founded: 1957. **Members:** 140. **National Groups:** 3. **Languages:** Dutch, French. **Description:** Physicians from 3 countries specializing in vascular and lymphatic disorders. Purpose is to further the field of phlebology by exchanging information and ideas on pathology and treatment. Offers professional training programs. **Publications:** *Phlebology*, bimonthly.

★2835★ British Heart Foundation (BHF)
14 Fitzhardinge St.
London W1H 4DH, England
Phone: 171 9350185
Fax: 171 4865820
Maj.Gen. L.F.H. Busk, CB, Dir.Gen.

Founded: 1961. **Regional Groups:** 9. **Languages:** English. **Description:** Organizes and finances research into the causes and prevention of cardiovascular disease and encourages improvement in diagnosis and treatment. Sponsors postgraduate medical education; distributes fellowships and research funds. Organizes lectures, symposia, and workshops for health care and research professionals. Provides cardiac equipment for hospitals and ambulance services. Conducts fundraising events. Compiles statistics. **Publications:** Annual Report. • Catalog, annual. • *Grant Regulations*. Booklet. • *Medical Reports*, periodic. • *Newsletter*, periodic. Newsletter. • Pamphlets, periodic. • *Take Heart*, quarterly. Newsletter. • *Teenage Newsletter*, periodic. Newsletter. • Videos, periodic.

★2836★ British Microcirculation Society (BMS)
Dept. of Physiology
St. George's Hospital Medical School
Cranmer Terrace
London SW17 ORE, England
Phone: 181 6729944
Fax: 181 6823698
Dr. J.R. Levick, Hon.Sec.

Founded: 1963. **Members:** 190. **Languages:** English. **Description:** Individuals interested in the study of microcirculation and endothelium. Conducts clinical and scientific research.

★2837★ Canadian Adult Congential Heart Network
The Toronto Hospital
200 Elizabeth St., Rm. 12NU-118
Toronto, ON, Canada M5G 2C4
Phone: (416)340-3872
Fax: (416)340-5014
Dr. Gary Webb, Pres.

Founded: 1992. **Members:** 59. **Regional Groups:** 14. **Languages:** English, French. **Description:** Represents the interests of Canadian adults who were born with heart defects. Encourages efforts to educate the public on the problems and treatment of heart disease. Works as a support network for congenital heart patients. **Publications:** *CACH News*, quarterly. Newsletter. **Also Known As:** CACH Network.

★2838★ Canadian Cardiovascular Society (CCS) (Societe Canadienne de Cardiologie — SCC)
360 Victoria Ave., Rm. 401
Westmount, PQ, Canada H3Z 2N4
Phone: (514)482-3407
Fax: (514)482-6574
Dolores Lourenco, Exec.Sec.

Founded: 1949. **Members:** 966. **Languages:** English, French. **Description:** Physicians, surgeons, and scientists practicing or conducting research in cardiology and related fields. Promotes the growth and collection of current cardiology information and facilitates its dissemination for the improvement of public health. **Publications:** *Abstract Program*, annual. **Formerly:** (1962) Canadian Heart Association.

Cardiothoracic Research and Education Foundation (CREF)
See: Entry 12264

★2839★ Cardiovascular Credentialing International (CCI)
4456 Corporation Ln., Ste. 120
Virginia Beach, VA 23462
Phone: (804)497-3380
Free: 800-326-0268
Fax: (804)497-3491
Julia Dow, Exec.Dir.

Founded: 1988. **Members:** 15,000. **Description:** Cardiovascular technologists involved in the allied health professions. Conducts testing of allied health professionals throughout the U.S. and Canada. Provides study guides and reliability and validity testing. Compiles statistics. **Publications:** Directory, annual. • *Pulse*, quarterly. Newsletter. For Level II registered cardiovascular technologists. *Price:* Included in membership dues; $15/year for nonmembers. **Formerly:** (1984) National Board for Cardiopulmonary Credentialing; (1986) National Board for Cardiovascular and Pulmonary Credentialing; (1991) Cardiovascular Credentialing International/Board of Cardiovascular Technology.

★ 2840 ★ **Citizens for Public Action on Blood Pressure and Cholesterol (CPABPC)**
PO Box 30374
Bethesda, MD 20824
Phone: (301)770-1711
Fax: (301)770-1113
Gerald Wilson, Dir.

Founded: 1973. **Members:** 16,000. **State Groups:** 50. **Description:** Public education and advocacy organization. Seeks to instruct health policy officials, the medical profession, and individuals on the importance of public policy and services to treat high blood pressure and high cholesterol and prevent heart attacks and strokes. **Publications:** *Cholesterol and Kids.* Brochure. • *Cholesterol Blood Pressure Update*, quarterly. Newsletter. Covers current events, public services available, and publications. Includes research reports, legislative update, and book reviews. • *Living with High Blood Pressure.* Brochure. • *Understanding Your Blood Cholesterol.* Brochure. **Formerly:** (1989) Citizens for the Treatment of High Blood Pressure; (1991) Citizens for the Treatment of High Blood Pressure - for Public Action on Cholesterol.

★ 2841 ★ **Coronary Club (CC)**
9500 Euclid Ave.
Mailcode EE-37
Cleveland, OH 44106
Phone: (216)444-3690
Free: 800-478-4255
Fax: (216)444-9385
Kathryn E. Ryan-Muldoon, Adm.Asst.

Founded: 1969. **Members:** 9,000. **Description:** Heart patients, doctors, nurses, therapists, educators, and other health professionals involved in cardiac care. **Publications:** *Heartline*, monthly. Newsletter. Covers heart care and rehabilitation. Includes surgery, medication, diet, exercise, depression, stress management, and new research developments. *Price:* $29/year.

★ 2842 ★ **Council on Arteriosclerosis of the American Heart Association (CAAHA)**
7320 Greenville Ave.
Dallas, TX 75231
Phone: (214)706-1293
Fax: (214)706-1341
Dr. Scott Grundy, Exec.Dir.

Founded: 1946. **Members:** 1,014. **Description:** Professional society of physicians and others interested in cardiovascular diseases, especially arteriosclerosis (hardening of the arteries). **Publications:** *Arteriosclerosis and Thrombosis - A Journal of Vascular Biology*, bimonthly. Journal. • Newsletter, semiannual. **Formerly:** (1959) American Society for the Study of Arteriosclerosis.

★ 2843 ★ **Dutch Society of Cardiology (DSC)**
(Nederlandse Vereniging voor Cardiologie — NVVC)
Medisch Spectrum Twente
PO Box 50000
NL-7500 KA Enschede, Netherlands
Dr. G.P. Molhoek, Exec. Officer

Description: Promotes the profession of cardiology, cardiological research, and cardiac care

in the Netherlands. Defends the professional interests of members. **Publications:** *Cardiologie*, monthly. Journal.

European Association of Cardiothoracic Anaesthesiologists (EACTA)
See: Entry 2364

★ 2844 ★ **European Atherosclerosis Society (EAS)**
St. Bartholomew's Hospital
W. Smithfield
London EC1A 7BE, England
Phone: 171 6018431
Fax: 171 6018042
D.J. Galton, M.D., Sec.

Founded: 1964. **Members:** 127. **Languages:** English. **Description:** Researchers in 24 countries of atherosclerosis (a disease characterized by the accumulation of fatty substances that have hardened inside the arteries). Purposes are to: exchange information concerning atherosclerosis and its causes and history; advance understanding of the treatment and prevention of atherosclerosis in humans and animals.

European Society for Cardiovascular Surgery (ESCVS)
(Societe Europeenne de Chirurgie Cardiovasculaire)
See: Entry 12269

★ 2845 ★ **European Society for Microcirculation (ESM)**
Dept. of Vascular Medicine
Postgraduate Med. School
Barrack Rd.
Exeter, Devon EX2 5AX, England
Phone: 1392 403064
Fax: 1392 403027
Prof. J.E. Tooke, Sec.Gen.

Founded: 1960. **Members:** 366. **Languages:** English. **Description:** Individuals from 27 countries involved in education, clinical medicine, and the pharmaceutical industry interested in the study of microcirculation. (Microcirculation is the flow of blood and other tissue fluids into small vessels.) Coordinates research among participating laboratories in areas directly affecting the development, application, and promotion of microcirculation methods that will benefit health care. **Publications:** *European Society for Microcirculation*, biennial. Directory. • *International Journal of Microcirculation: Clinical and Experimental*, quarterly. Journal. • *Newsletter*, semiannual. Newsletter.

★ 2846 ★ **European Society for Noninvasive Cardiovascular Dynamics (ESNICVD)**
Institute of Physiology
Faculty of Medicine
Zaloska 4
SLO-61105 Ljubljana, Slovenia
Phone: 61 317152
Fax: 61 311540
Dr. Susara Juznic, Sec.

Founded: 1960. **Members:** 34. **Languages:** English. **Description:** Scientists and professionals in 17 countries active in fields such as bi-

ology, cardiology, physiology, sports science, hydraulics, and physics who seek better knowledge of the cardiovascular system. Promotes the exchange of ideas in noninvasive cardiovascular research. Fosters the study of cardiovascular function from a mechanical point of reference to gain knowledge applicable to medical practice and technical disciplines. Works to standardize methods used to study the mechanical activity of the cardiovascular system. **Publications:** *Bibliotheca Cardiologica*, periodic. • *Cardiovascular*, annual. Newsletter. Includes information on conferences and meetings. • *Proceedings of Congress*, biennial. **Formerly:** (1970) European Society for Ballisto Cardiographic Research; (1978) European Society for Ballisto Cardiographic and Cardiovascular Dynamics.

★ 2847 ★ **Finnish Cardiac Society (FCS)**
(Suomen Kardiologinen Seura — SKS)
Oulu University Hospital
Department of Cardiology
Kajaanintie 50
SF-90220 Oulu, Finland
Phone: 81 3154447
Fax: 81 3155423
Heikki Huikuri, Contact

Founded: 1969. **Members:** 480. **Languages:** English, Finnish, Swedish. **Description:** Physicians practicing in Finland. Encourages contact between cardiology specialists and doctors interested in the field. Organizes educational courses. Bestows awards. **Publications:** *Sydanaani (Cardiac Sound)*, periodic. Newsletter.

★ 2848 ★ **French Atherosclerosis Society (FAS)**
Hopital Hendri Mondor
F-94010 Creteil, France
Phone: 1 49813586
Fax: 1 48991167
Prof. Ladislas Robert, Contact

Founded: 1973. **Members:** 100. **Languages:** English, French. **Description:** Promotes research in atherosclerosis and the clinical application of findings.

★ 2849 ★ **Heart Foundation of Zimbabwe**
Parirenyatwa Hospital, B. Fl.
Mazowe St.
Harare, Zimbabwe
Phone: 4 739483
Prof. Charles Marks, Chair

Members: 12. **Description:** Organizes and finances research into the causes and prevention of cardiovascular diseases. Operates training programs for medical personnel. Conducts research in and offers education on heart conditions.

★ 2850 ★ **Heart Rhythm Foundation**
(Fundacja Rytm Serca)
Al. Jerozolimskie St. 65/79
PL-00-697 Warsaw, Poland
Phone: 22 306457
Fax: 22 300575
Malgorzata Przesmycka, Chm.

Description: Organizes and finances research into the causes and prevention of cardiovascular disease and encourages improvement in diagnoses and treatment.

★2851★ HHT Foundation International
PO Box 8087
New Haven, CT 06530
Phone: (313)561-2537
Free: 800-448-6389
Fax: (313)561-4585
Rita Van Bergeijk, Pres.

Founded: 1991. **Members:** 300. **Regional Groups:** 3. **State Groups:** 3. **Description:** Patients and their families; physicians, counselors, and health administrators; interested others. Promotes research into the treatment, causes, and cure of hereditary hemmorrhagic telangiectasia (HHT), also known as Osler-Weber-Rendu Syndrome. A rare genetic blood vessel disorder, HHT causes malformations of arteries and veins; hemorrhaging from the nose and intestine is also common. Malformations in the lungs cause shortness of breath, stroke, and brain abscess. Provides information exchange. Raises funds for research and patient service programs. Sponsors support groups. **Publications:** Brochures. • *HHT Newsletter*, quarterly. Newsletter. • Newsletter, semiannual. • *Our Blood Vessels*. Pamphlet.

★2852★ Hungarian Society of Cardiology (HSC)
(Magyar Kardiologusok Tarsasaga — MKT)
Hungarian Institute of Cardiology
Hallerutca 29
Postafiok 88
H-1450 Budapest, Hungary
Phone: 1 2151220
Fax: 1 2155217
Joseph Borbola, M.D., Gen.Sec.

Founded: 1955. **Members:** 700. **Local Groups:** 15. **Languages:** English, Hungarian. **Description:** Cardiologists and other medical specialists. Promotes development of cardiology; facilitates scientific exchanges of information among members. Monitors standards in cardiology training programs; provides cardiologists with ethical advice. Conducts educational, research, and public service programs. Sponsors competitions and bestows awards. **Publications:** *Cardiologia Hungarica*, quarterly. Journal.

★2853★ Icelandic Cardiac Society (ICS)
(Hjartasjukdomafelag Islenskra Laekna — HIL)
Sidumula 37
IS-105 Reykjavik, Iceland
Phone: 1 686200
Gizur Gottskalksson, Exec. Officer

Founded: 1968. **Members:** 45. **Languages:** Danish, English, Finnish, Icelandic, Norwegian, Swedish. **Description:** Physicians and scientists interested in the field of cardiology.

★2854★ Inter-American Society of Cardiology (ISC)
(Sociedad Interamericana de Cardiologia)
Juan Badiano 1
Colonia Seccion XVI
Tlalpan
14080 Mexico City, DF, Mexico
Phone: 5 5732911
Fax: 5 5730994
Dr. Eduardo Salazar, Sec.-Treas.

Founded: 1944. **Languages:** English, French, Portuguese, Spanish. **Description:** National societies of cardiology from the Americas; medical doctors; individuals who have made outstanding contributions in the cardiovascular and allied fields. Purpose is to unite members for the development and advancement of cardiology and related fields, particularly by promoting the association of physicians, surgeons, and scientists with cardiovascular specialties. Fosters cooperation and exchange of information, medical specialists, and scientists at national, regional, and world levels; provides advice to governments seeking counsel. Sponsors exchange programs. **Publications:** *News Bulletin*, periodic. Bulletin.

★2855★ International Atherosclerosis Society (IAS)
c/o Barbara Gordin
6550 Fannin, No. 1423
Houston, TX 77030
Phone: (713)790-4226
Fax: (713)793-1080
Barbara Gordin, Exec.Dir.

Founded: 1979. **Members:** 5,036. **National Groups:** 28. **Description:** Scientists and other professionals involved in research in the field of atherosclerosis; corporations and firms supporting aims of the IAS. Promotes the advancement of science, research, and teaching in the field of atherosclerosis throughout the world. (Atherosclerosis is a form of arteriosclerosis characterized by the deposition of fatty substances in and fibrosis of the inner layer of the arteries.) Advocates an interdisciplinary approach to the study of atherosclerosis and related diseases. Facilitates international communication and exchange of knowledge among scientists in the field. Assists in the organization of exchange visits among scientists at various research centers. Fosters and encourages young researchers by arranging contacts, and offering travel support to world gatherings in the field. Coordinates activities in atherosclerosis research. **Publications:** Newsletter, semiannual. • *Proceedings of Symposia*, triennial. Proceedings. • *Roster of Member Societies*.

★2856★ International Bundle Branch Block Association (IBBBA)
6631 W. 83rd St.
Los Angeles, CA 90045-2899
Phone: (310)670-9132
Rita Kurtz Lewis, Exec.Dir.

Founded: 1979. **Description:** Individuals with bundle branch block (BBB), concerned professionals, and laypersons. (BBB is a rare heart condition caused by an "electrical malfunction".) Objectives are: to increase public awareness of BBB; to disseminate information on the disease; to answer inquiries of members; to serve as a forum for sharing information and experiences; to maintain a bank of information to aid professional research on BBB. Compiles statistics. Plans to conduct specialized education and research programs. **Publications:** *Heartbeat*, quarterly. Provides professional replies to readers' medical questions, reprints from other publications, and names and addresses of members. *Price:* Included in membership dues.

★2857★ International College of Angiology (ICA)
1044 Northern Blvd., Ste. 103
Roslyn, NY 11576
Phone: (516)484-6880
Fax: (516)625-1174
H. E. Shaftel, M.D., Meeting Chmn.

Founded: 1959. **Members:** 2,500. **Languages:** English. **Description:** Scientists from 17 countries interested in the field of vascular medicine and surgery and dedicated to scientific advancement and continued education in angiology (the study of the circulatory, or vascular system). Seeks to: define, represent, and foster the growth and development of the specialty practice of angiology; improve patient care by advising physicians on recent developments in the field; provide a common forum for the exchange of ideas, technical research, and clinical experiences. Conducts continuing medical education programs. Disseminates original research findings related to cerebrovascular, cardiovascular, and peripheral vascular diseases, diagnostic methods, therapeutic procedures, clinical and laboratory research, and case reports. Holds clinical, diagnostic, and therapeutic symposia, seminars, and workshops. **Publications:** *Angiology, The Journal of Vascular Diseases*, monthly. Journal. Includes listing of employment opportunities and research reports. • *Vascular Surgery*, 9/year. Journal. Reports the latest progress in operative surgical techniques, research findings, and clinical experiences. Also publishes abstracts and convention programs.

★2858★ International Society for Cardiovascular Research
(Societe Internationale de Recherches Cardiaques)
Rayne Institute
St. Thomas' Hospital
London SE1 7EH, England
Phone: 171 9289292
Fax: 171 9280658
Prof. David J. Hearse, Sec.Gen.

Founded: 1967. **Members:** 2,000. **Description:** Professionals and investigators in the field of experimental cardiology united to foster multidisciplinary approaches for finding solutions to the problems of heart disease. Conducts research in cardiac metabolism. **Publications:** *Advances in Myocardiology*. • *Journal of Molecular and Cellular Cardiology*, monthly. Journal.

★2859★ International Society for Cardiovascular Surgery (ISCVS)
13 Elm St.
PO Box 1565
Manchester, MA 01944
Phone: (508)526-8330
Fax: (508)526-4018
William T. Maloney, Exec.Dir.

Founded: 1951. **Members:** 2,500. **Description:** Encourages exchange and cooperation between cardiovascular specialists. Promotes discussion of ideas pertinent to the cardiovascular disease field and stimulates investigation and study of cardiovascular diseases. **Publications:** *Cardiovascular Surgery*. Journal. **Formerly:** (1983) International Cardiovascular Society.

International Society of Electrocardiology (ISE)
See: Entry 2424

★ 2860 ★ International Society and Federation of Cardiology (ISFC) (Societe et Federation Internationale de Cardiologie — SFIC)
Case Postale 117
CH-1211 Geneva 12, Switzerland
Phone: 22 3476755
Fax: 22 3471028
Marianne B. de Figueiredo, Exec.Sec.

Founded: 1978. **Members:** 64. **Languages:** English, French, German, Spanish. **Description:** Societies of cardiology and heart foundations. Promotes international study, prevention, and treatment of cardiovascular diseases; encourages, coordinates, and assists the development of educational and scientific programs focusing on cardiovascular problems. **Publications:** *Heartbeat*, quarterly.

International Society for Heart and Lung Transplantation (ISHLT)
See: Entry 12871

★ 2861 ★ Mended Hearts (MH)
7272 Greenville Ave.
Dallas, TX 75231-4596
Phone: (214)706-1442
Darla Bonham, Exec.Dir.

Founded: 1951. **Members:** 24,000. **Local Groups:** 200. **Description:** Persons who have heart disease; their families and friends. Works to: provide advice, encouragement, and services to heart disease patients and to their families; establish programs of assistance to surgeons, physicians, and hospitals. Conducts and assists in research programs designed to benefit heart patients. **Publications:** *Heartbeat*, quarterly. **Formerly:** (1955) Mended Hearts Club.

Michael E. DeBakey International Surgical Society (MEDISS)
See: Entry 12288

★ 2862 ★ Microcirculatory Society (MCS)
Department of Veterinary and Biomedical Sciences
University of Missouri
Columbia, MO 65211
Phone: (314)882-7012
Dr. Bruce Klitzman, Sec.

Founded: 1955. **Members:** 450. **Description:** Bestows awards. **Publications:** *Microcirculatory Society Directory*, annual. Membership Directory. • *Microcirculatory Society Newsletter*, 3/year. Newsletter.

★ 2863 ★ Moscow Association of Cardiologists (Moskovskaya Assotsiatsiya Kardiologov — MAK)
ulitsa 3-aya Cherepkovskaya 15A
121552 Moscow, Russia
Phone: 95 1492802
Fax: 95 4152962
A.P. Yurenev

Founded: 1990. **Members:** 120. **Description:** Works to improve cardiology in the Commonwealth of Independent States and lower levels of illness and death from heart disease. Protects the social and legal rights of cardiologists.

National Foundation for Non-Invasive Diagnostics (NFNID)
See: Entry 11127

★ 2864 ★ National Heart Council (NHC)
306 W. Joppa Rd.
Baltimore, MD 21204
Phone: (410)494-0300
Fax: (410)494-0725
Howard H. Farrington, Pres.

Founded: 1982. **Description:** A project of the National Emergency Medicine Association. Seeks to further advances made in the field of emergency medicine, particularly as related to heart trauma. Awards grants to organizations and individuals for the purpose of conducting research, meetings, or other activities that gather and disseminate information on traumatic medicine, particularly cardiac disorders. **Publications:** *Heart Research Newsletter*, quarterly. Newsletter. Also publishes guides, reports, and brochures; plans to produce videotapes on first aid for household accidents, heart attacks, and choking. **Formerly:** (1994) National Heart Research.

★ 2865 ★ National Heart Savers Association (NHSA)
9140 W. Dodge Rd.
Omaha, NE 68114
Phone: (402)398-1993
Fax: (402)398-1994
Phil Sokolof, Pres.

Founded: 1985. **Description:** Promotes cardiac health care by informing the public of the dangers of a high-cholesterol diet. Conducts public cholesterol screening program; secured congressional designation of September as National Cholesterol Education Month. Has been successful in persuading major food processing and fast food restaurants companies to stop using palm and coconut oil, lard, and beef tallow, which are high in saturated fats, as ingredients in prepared foods. Promotes nutrition education in public schools and lobbies for more healthful school lunches. **Publications:** Books. • Pamphlets.

★ 2866 ★ National Hypertension Association (NHA)
324 E. 30th St.
New York, NY 10016
Phone: (212)889-3557
Fax: (212)447-7032
William M. Manger, M.D., Chm.

Founded: 1977. **Description:** Physicians, medical researchers, and business professionals dedicated to the prevention of the complications of hypertension. Seeks to combat hypertension by developing, directing, and implementing effective programs to educate physicians and the public about the severe, life-threatening dangers of this health disorder. Conducts research on the cause of hypertension through basic laboratory studies. Provides school children with basic information on hypertension; conducts hypertension and hypercholesterol detection programs. Offers medical consulting to those found to have high blood pressure or hypercholesterolemia. Develops educational materials and participates in radio and television programs. **Publications:** Books. • Monographs. •

News Report, annual. Newsletter. Also publishes medical journal periodicals.

★ 2867 ★ National Institute of Hypertension Studies - Institute of Hypertension School of Research (NIHS)
295 Mt. Vernon
Detroit, MI 48202
Phone: (313)872-0505
Fax: (313)872-0505
Dr. H. R. Lockett, Exec.Dir.

Founded: 1975. **Description:** Purposes are to: help find causes of and to help prevent essential hypertension; to educate people concerning essential hypertension; to diagnose, counsel, and refer afflicted individuals for treatment and follow-up activities; to conduct research on hypertension and to extend that research into the areas of crime and drug addiction and psychosocial and occupational stress. Sponsors hypertension detection clinics. Offers youth leadership courses. Compiles statistics and disseminates educational materials. Conducts research programs on psychosocial and occupational stress which offer diplomas to those completing the programs; survey project with Pharmaceutical Research and Manufacturers of America; also conducts research on drugs and hypertension. **Publications:** *IHS 1992 Report*, annual. Research report on causes of essential hypertension. • Magazine, periodic. • *OHRST Assessment Report Series*, annual. **Formerly:** (1971) Institute of Hypertension Studies; (1981) Institute of Hypertension Studies - Institute of Hypertension School of Research.

★ 2868 ★ Nordic Federation of Heart and Lung Associations (NHL)
Box 9090
S-102 72 Stockholm, Sweden
Phone: 8 6690960
Fax: 8 6682385
Bo Mansson, Sec.Gen.

Founded: 1948. **Members:** 130,000. **Regional Groups:** 126. **Languages:** Danish, Finnish, Icelandic, Norwegian, Swedish. **Description:** Lung and heart disease specialists in 5 countries. Addresses medical issues in the context of social welfare. Engages in political activities; operates vocational and training centers. **Publications:** *BM-Bladet*, monthly. • *Silmu*, monthly. • *Status*, monthly. • *Trygd og Arbeid*, monthly.

★ 2869 ★ North American Society of Pacing and Electrophysiology (NASPE)
Natick Executive Park
2 Vision Dr.
Natick, MA 01760-2059
Phone: (508)647-0100
Fax: (508)647-0124
Carol J. McGlinchey, Exec.Dir.

Founded: 1979. **Members:** 1,900. **Description:** Physicians, technicians, nurses, engineers, and individuals involved in pacemaker implantation and cardiac electrophysiology. Seeks to recommend standards for electrophysiologic device testing and the training of electrophysiologists and pacemaker-implanting physician. Informs members and interested nonmembers of new developments in the field by sponsoring educational meetings. **Publications:** Brochure. • Membership Directory, periodic. Includes geographic index. • *NASPE News*, quarterly. Newsletter. Covers membership activities. Includes calendar of events and informattion updates. • *NASPETAPES.* Audiotapes. • *North American Society of Pacing and Electrophysiology Annual Scientific Session Program.* • *PACE: The Journal of Pacing and Clinical Electrophysiology*, monthly. Journal. • Videos. Contains self-assessment programs.

★2870★ **Norwegian Society of Cardiology (NSC)**
(Norsk Cardiologisk Sekskap — NCS)
Rikshospitalet
Oslo, Norway
Phone: 2 867010
Otto A. Smiseth

Founded: 1970. **Members:** 300. **Languages:** English, Norwegian. **Description:** Scientific organization of Norwegian cardiologists. **Publications:** *Hjerteforum*, quarterly.

★2871★ **Peruvian Heart Association (PHA)**
100 S Greenleaf Ave.
Gurnee, IL 60031-3378
Phone: (708)249-2111
Free: 800-367-7378
Fax: (708)249-2772
Luis Vasquez, M.D., Intl.Dir.

Founded: 1967. **Members:** 400. **Regional Groups:** 6. **Description:** Peruvian physicians, nurses, and other health care professionals specializing in cardiology who are devoted to research, training, teaching, and patient care. Offers continuing education courses for Peruvian physicians, enabling them to fulfill coursework required by Peruvian law for continuance of medical practice. Provides community health care information to residents of Lima, Peru concerning heart attacks, high blood pressure, cholesterol, diabetes, diet, and exercise. Conducts programs in conjunction with the American College of Cardiology and the American Heart Association, providing printed information and speakers on health care. Also provides information to U.S. doctors who wish to study and assist with Peruvian health care.

★2872★ **Raynaud's and Scleroderma Association (RSAT)**
112 Crewe Rd.
Alsager, Cheshire ST7 2JA, England
Phone: 1270 872776
Fax: 1270 883556
Anne H. Mawdsley, Dir.

Founded: 1982. **Members:** 8,000. **National Groups:** 1. **Regional Groups:** 4. **Languages:** English. **Description:** Individuals afflicted with Raynaud's Disease or scleroderma; concerned medical professionals. (Raynaud's Disease is marked by interruption of blood flow to the extremities, primarily the toes and fingers but can include the ears and nose, due to spasmodic contraction of the arteries, resulting in a gangrenous condition; this phenomenon is often noted in individuals suffering from scleroderma, a hardening of the skin, Systemic Lupus Erythematosus, an inflammatory disease of the blood vessels and connective tissues, polyvinyl chloride poisoning, and those who work with a vibrating tool.) Encourages better communication among doctors and patients and provides for

mutual support among those with the condition. Strives to heighten public awareness on Raynaud's Disease and scleroderma. Conducts fundraising activities to help finance research. **Publications:** Books, periodic. • Handbooks, periodic. • *Raynaud's Association Newsletter*, quarterly. Newsletter. **Formerly:** (1990) Raynaud's Association Trust.

★2873★ **Romanian Society of Cardiology (SRC)**
(Societatea de Cardiologie — SC)
Sos. Fundeni 258, Sec. 2
72435 Bucharest, Romania
Phone: 1 2402360
Fax: 1 2402360
Dr. Costin Carp, Pres.

Founded: 1947. **Members:** 250. **National Groups:** 3. **Languages:** English, Romanian. **Description:** Cardiologists. Promotes investigation into cardiovascular diseases. Areas of research include: clinical physiopathology; epidemiology; physiopathology; prophylaxy; therapeutics. Bestows awards; maintains educational programs. **Publications:** *Romanian Heart Journal*, quarterly. **Formerly:** (1991) Society of Cardiology.

Scandinavian Association for Thoracic Surgery (SATS)
(Nordisk Thoraxkirurgisk Forening — NTF)
See: Entry 12301

★2874★ **Slovak Society of Angiology**
Mickiewiczova 13
SK-813 69 Bratislava, Slovakia
Phone: 7 410511
Viera Stvrtinova, M.D., Contact

Languages: English, Slovak. **Description:** Angiologists and other health care professionals with an interest in the human vascular system and its diseases. Seeks to advance members' professional standing; represents members' interests.

★2875★ **Slovak Society of Cardiology**
F.D. Roosevelt Hospital
SK-975 17 Banska Bystrica, Slovakia
Phone: 88 713059
Fax: 88 712134
Gabriela Kaliska, M.D., Contact

Languages: English, Slovak. **Description:** Cardiologists and other health care professionals with an interest in the human heart and its diseases. Seeks to enhance the professional standing and skill of members; represents members' interests before government agencies and the public.

★2876★ **Societe Francaise d'Angeiologie (SFA)**
145, rue de la Pompe
F-75116 Paris, France
Phone: 1 47551433
Fax: 1 47272147
Dr. Cazaubon, Exec. Officer

Founded: 1947. **Members:** 400. **Languages:** English, French. **Description:** Individuals in France interested in angiology (the study of blood vessels and lymphatics). **Publications:** *Angeiologie*, bimonthly. Journal.

★2877★ **Society for Cardiac Angiography and Interventions (SCA&I)**
PO Box 7849
Breckenridge, CO 80424
Phone: (303)453-1773
Fax: (303)453-2636
Justine J. Parker, Exec.Dir.

Founded: 1978. **Members:** 1,050. **Description:** Angiographers united to foster excellence in the field of cardiac catheterization, especially coronary arteriography and interventional angiography. (Angiography involves injecting substances opaque to radiation into blood vessels so that diagnostic X-rays of those blood vessels may be made.) Conducts clinical research. **Publications:** *Catheterization and Cardiovascular Diagnosis*, monthly. Journal. • *News Highlights*, quarterly. Newsletter. Includes calender of events and committee reports. *Price:* Free.

Society of Cardiovascular Anesthesiologists (SCA)
See: Entry 2375

Society of Cardiovascular and Interventional Radiology (SCVIR)
See: Entry 11132

Society of Thoracic Radiology (STR)
See: Entry 11140

Society of Thoracic Surgeons (STS)
See: Entry 12309

Society for Vascular Nursing (SVN)
See: Entry 9137

Society for Vascular Surgery (SVS)
See: Entry 12312

★2878★ **Society of Vascular Technology (SVT)**
4601 Presidents Dr., Ste. 260
Lanham, MD 20706-4365
Phone: (301)459-7550
Free: 800-SVT-VEIN
Fax: (301)459-5651
Patricia I. Horner, Exec.Dir.

Founded: 1977. **Members:** 4,300. **Local Groups:** 40. **Description:** Medical technologists and others in the field of noninvasive vascular technology. (Noninvasive vascular technology is a highly technical and specialized method of monitoring the blood flow in arms and legs in order to better diagnose disease and blood clots.) Seeks to establish an information clearinghouse providing reference and assistance in matters relating to noninvasive vascular technology; facilitate cooperation among noninvasive vascular facilities and other health professions; provide continuing education for individuals in the field. **Publications:** Brochures. • *Glossary of Terms. Price:* $7 for members; $10 for nonmembers. • *Journal of Vascular Technology*, 6/year. Journal. *Price:* Included in membership dues; $75/year for nonmembers; $100/year (outside the U.S. and Canada). • Membership Directory, biennial. Includes listings by state and alphabetically. *Price:* Included in membership dues. • *Patient Education Pamphlets.* Pamphlets. Covers peripheral arterial, venous, and cerebrovascular diseases. • *Refer-*

enced *Study Outline. Price:* $10 for members; $15 for nonmembers. • *Spectrum,* quarterly. Newsletter. *Price:* Included in membership dues; $20/year for nonmembers in the U.S. and Canada; $25/year overseas. • *Training Centers Directory.* Directory. *Price:* $10 for members; $15 for nonmembers. • *Vascular Registry Review.* Two-volume (three-ring binder) set. *Price:* $55 for members; $75 for nonmembers. • Videos. Also publishes information kits. **Formerly:** (1988) Society of Non-Invasive Vascular Technology.

★ 2879 ★   **Turkish Society of Cardiology (TSC)**
(Turk Kardiyoloji Dernegi — TKD)
Nisbetiye Caddesi 37/24
Etiler
TR-80630 Istanbul, Turkey
Phone: 1 2576335
Fax: 1 2573787
Dr. Altan Onat, Pres.

Founded: 1963. **Members:** 370. **National Groups:** 5. **Languages:** English, Turkish. **Description:** Cardiologists and specialists in related fields. Promotes increased public and professional awareness of cardiovascular diseases. Encourages cardiological research; gathers and disseminates information to members. Offers postgraduate course in cardiology. Has conducted survey on heart disease and risk factors. **Publications:** *Archives of the Turkish Society of Cardiology,* bimonthly. Journal. Contains research work, reviews, and case reports. English summaries available. • *Congress Supplement for Abstracts,* annual. • Directory, biennial.

★ 2880 ★   **United Patients Association for Pulmonary Hypertension (UPAPH)**
PO Box 061556
Palm Bay, FL 32906-1556
Phone: (407)597-4962
Judy Simpson, RN, Pres.

Founded: 1990. **Members:** 354. **Regional Groups:** 3. **State Groups:** 4. **Local Groups:** 4. **Description:** Patients with pulmonary hypertension (PH) and primary pulmonary hypertension (PPH); families and physicians of patients; researchers. Provides fellowship and educational support for members and the public on PH and PPH, including current research and findings, early detection, resource organizations, organ transplantation, and support networks. Conducts support group meetings. **Publications:** Directory. • *Pathlight,* quarterly. Newsletter. *Price:* Free for members; $1/back issues.

Research Centers

★ 2881 ★   **Arizona Heart Institute**
2632 N. 20th St.
Phoenix, AZ 85006
Phone: (602)266-2200
Fax: (602)240-6160
L. Kent Smith, M.D., Dir. of Drug Research

Research Activities and Fields: Ambulatory cardiovascular drugs, including medications for hypertension, angina pectoris, cholesterol re-

duction, congestive heart failure, and peripheral vascular occlusive disease. Also investigates cardiovascular diagnostic testing procedures and nonpharmacological interventions. **Publications:** Newsletter (quarterly).

★ 2882 ★   **Baylor College of Medicine DeBakey Heart Center**
Texas Medical Center
1 Baylor Plaza
Houston, TX 77030
Phone: (713)797-9353
Fax: (713)793-1192
Dr. Michael E. DeBakey, Dir.

Research Activities and Fields: Atherosclerosis with an emphasis on lipoprotein structure and function and cholesterol metabolism; cardiovascular studies on calcium metabolism, fatty acid metabolism, and cellular ultrastructure; cardiology and cardiovascular surgery, including therapeutic intervention in heart failure, ischemic cardiomyopathy, and role of complement in myocardial infarction; transplantation; and hypertension studies that focus on aldosteronerenin ratio antihypertensive agents. Community outreach studies include control of blood pressure, diabetes, and diet modification. **Publications:** *The DeBakey Health Letter.* **Formerly:** Cardiovascular Research and Training Center; National Heart and Blood Vessel Research and Demonstration Center.

★ 2883 ★   **Bockus Research Institute**
Graduate Hospital
415 S. 19th St.
Philadelphia, PA 19146
Phone: (215)893-2375
Dr. Robert H. Cox, Dir.

Research Activities and Fields: Cardiovascular physiology with specific emphasis on excitation-contraction coupling in smooth and cardiac muscle. Activities include signal transduction mechanisms involving inositol lipids; regulation of contraction in intact and skinned preparations; laser photolysis of caged compounds; whole cell and patch clamp electrophysiological studies of ion channels in cardiac and vascular muscle; and studies of regulation of cytoplasmic calcium using ratiometric fluorescence probes. Applications of these studies include the areas of hypertension, atherosclerosis, and aging. Research also includes studies of gene therapy and cell biology of coronary restenosis following coronary angioplasty. **Publications:** Annual Report.

★ 2884 ★   **Boston University Whitaker Cardiovascular Institute**
700 Albany St.
Boston, MA 02118
Phone: (617)638-4890
Fax: (617)638-4066
Joseph Loscalzo, M.D., Dir.

Research Activities and Fields: Basic and clinical research relating to cardiovascular diseases, including studies on hypertension, atherosclerosis, lipoprotein metabolism, thrombosis, ischemic heart disease, vascular biology, cardiac surgery, and cardiovascular epidemiology. **Publications:** *Reports of Whitaker Cardiovascular Institute* (annually); Newsletter (quarterly).

★ 2885 ★   **Center for Cardiovascular Health Services Research**
New England Medical Center, Box 63
750 Washington St.
Boston, MA 02111
Phone: (617)956-5009
Fax: (617)350-8023
Harry P. Selker, M.D., Dir.

Research Activities and Fields: Cardiovascular health services, particularly in the development and testing of predictive instruments for acute cardiac ischemia, thrombolytic therapy, and the use of cardiac care units in hospitals. **Formerly:** Multicenter Cardiology and Health Services Research Unit (1989).

★ 2886 ★   **Charles R. Drew University of Medicine and Science Hypertension Research Center**
1621 E. 120th St., MP 11
Los Angeles, CA 90059
Phone: (213)563-5927
Harry Ward, M.D., Dir.

Research Activities and Fields: Epidemiology, causes, and treatment of high blood pressure in blacks. Analyzes twin studies to assess genetic and environmental factors in blood pressure variations. Conducts cross-cultural studies in Barbados and Nigeria.

★ 2887 ★   **Children's Heart Institute of Texas**
PO Box 3966
Corpus Christi, TX 78463
Phone: (512)887-4505
Fax: (512)887-0539
Dr. Syed R. Kalamuddin, CEO

Research Activities and Fields: Pediatric cardiology. Projects include investigations of the prevalence of developmental disabilities and heart disease risk factors in various counties, coronary disease among Hispanic children, arterial sclerotic heart disease, hypertension, and prevention.

★ 2888 ★   **Cleveland Clinic Foundation Research Institute**
9500 Euclid Ave.
Cleveland, OH 44195
Phone: (216)444-3900
Fax: (216)444-3279
George R. Stark, Ph.D., Chm.

Research Activities and Fields: Molecular biology; structure and function in regulation of viral and cellular genes and (proto)oncogenes, and interferon signaling mechanisms; cancer biology and genetics, including Wilms' tumor, cellular gene regulation, transgenic models, and use of newly patented 2-5A antisense technology; cell biology, including vessel wall pathophysiology, lipoprotein oxidation, regulation of gene expression and intracellular signaling pathways. Studies also include immunology, biologic response modifiers in tumor growth and regression, chemokines, nitric oxide synthase; neurosciences emphasizing cellular and genetic mechanisms in multiple sclerosis, effects of AIDS; epilepsy; neuronal signaling in cardiovascular neurobiology and diagnostic methods in cerebrovascular disease and hypertrophy, studies of lipoprotein(a), computerized modeling of protein structures, G-proteins, and study of the basis of hypertension; biomedical engineering, including musculoskeletal biology, imaging research, biomaterials and biocompatibility, and total artificial heart and heart assist devices; and biostatistics and epidemiology. **E-mail Address:** starkg@ccsmtp.ccf.org.

★ 2889 ★ **Cornell University**
Hypertension and Cardiovascular Center
New York Hospital-Cornell Medical Center
520 E. 70th St.
New York, NY 10021
Phone: (212)746-2200
Fax: (212)746-8451
Dr. John Laragh, Dir.

Research Activities and Fields: Research into causation, diagnosis, and treatment of hypertension and related disorders of the heart, kidneys, and adrenal glands. Research also includes pathogenesis and treatment of heart attacks, congestive heart failure, renal failure, and stroke.

★ 2890 ★ **Creighton University**
Cardiac Center
3006 Webster St.
Omaha, NE 68131
Phone: (402)280-4566
Fax: (402)280-4938
Dr. Michael Sketch, Med.Dir.

Research Activities and Fields: Cardiology, including drug research, medical care, valvular diseases, invasive and noninvasive treatment techniques, electrocardiogram tests, pacemakers, implants, and ventricular assist devices.

★ 2891 ★ **Creighton University**
Midwest Hypertension Research Center
601 N. 30th St., Ste. 6730
Omaha, NE 68131
Phone: (402)280-4336
Fax: (402)280-4101
Dr. William Pettinger, Dir.

Research Activities and Fields: Causes and treatment of hypertension and related medical problems. Current research focuses on the molecular genetics of hypertension.

Duke University
Engineering Research Center for Emerging
Cardiovascular Technologies
See: Entry 2443

Duke University
Pediatric Cardiac Catheterization
Laboratory
See: Entry 3333

★ 2892 ★ **Duke University**
Specialized Center of Research in
Ischemic Heart Disease
Dept. of Medicine
Division of Cardiology
Box 3845
Durham, NC 27710
Phone: (919)681-5392
Fax: (919)681-5392
Harold C. Strauss, M.D., Adm.

Research Activities and Fields: Ischemic heart disease. Specific projects include tissue

cultured heart cell model for studying myocardial ischemia, pharmacology of ischemic myocardium, computerized mapping of ventricular tachycardia, prognosis of ischemic heart disease, coronary artery vasomotor activity in conscious dogs, radionuclide studies in patients with coronary artery disease, adrenergic receptor and reperfusion dysrhythmias, basic studies of cardiac surgical ischemia, recovery from reversible ischemic myocardial injury, evaluation of central and peripheral cardiovascular function at rest and during exercise in ambulatory patients with coronary artery disease and left ventricular dysfunction, evaluation and application of a QRS scoring system for estimating myocardial infarct size.

★ 2893 ★ **Emory University**
Cardiac Catheterization Laboratory
1364 Clifton Rd. NE
Atlanta, GA 30322
Phone: (404)616-4453
Dr. Charles Treasure, Contact

Research Activities and Fields: Cardiovascular hemodynamics and coronary circulation.

★ 2894 ★ **Framingham Heart Study**
5 Thurber St.
Framingham, MA 01701
Phone: (508)935-3400
Fax: (508)626-1262
Dr. William Castelli, Dir.

Research Activities and Fields: Constitutional and conditioning factors in atherosclerotic, hypertensive, and cardiovascular diseases based on a long-term study of a section of the population of Framingham, Massachusetts. Approximately 5,000 cohorts originally participated in the study, begun in 1948, and subsequent studies have focused on 5135 descendents and spouses of descendents in the second generation. One hundred families of its third and fourth generations are also under study.

★ 2895 ★ **George Washington University**
Lipid Research Clinic
908 New Hampshire Ave. NW, Ste. 500
Washington, DC 20037
Phone: (202)676-5150
Fax: (202)785-2881
Valery T. Miller, M.D., Dir.

Research Activities and Fields: Clinical trials of cholesterol and prevention of heart disease, including cholesterol lowering food and fibers, products, and medication. Also studies cholesterol lowering in senior citizens and trials of postmenopausal hormone replacement and heart disease risk factors in women.

★ 2896 ★ **Gladstone Institute of**
Cardiovascular Disease
San Francisco General Hospital
PO Box 419100
San Francisco, CA 94141-9100
Phone: (415)826-7500
Robert W. Mahley, M.D., Dir.

Research Activities and Fields: Lipoprotein metabolism and biochemistry, cell biology and arterial wall metabolism, molecular biology, and clinical nutrition and metabolism, including studies of the molecular structures of various li-

proteins and their function in transporting blood cholesterol, the relationship of diet to cholesterol levels, and the role of platelets and white blood cells in thrombosis and atherosclerosis. **Publications:** *SPIN*; *Gladstone Focus Newsletter*. **Formerly:** Gladstone Foundation Laboratories for Cardiovascular Disease.

★ 2897 ★ **Harvard Thorndike Laboratory**
Harvard Medical School
330 Brookline Ave.
Boston, MA 02215
Phone: (617)735-3020
Fax: (617)735-4833
Dr. James P. Morgan, Dir.

Research Activities and Fields: Effects of drugs and disease on cardiac hypertrophy and failure; cardiovascular effects of drug abuse. Specific areas of research include cardiac and vasculary pharmacology, physiology, and biochemistry.

★ 2898 ★ **Heart Disease Research**
Foundation
50 Court St.
Brooklyn, NY 11201
Phone: (718)649-6210
Yoshiaki Omura, M.D., Dir. of Medical Research

Research Activities and Fields: Early diagnosis, prevention, and treatment of cardiovascular diseases and related medical and social problems. Studies include the effects of acupuncture and electro-therapeutics on blood chemistry and the cardiovascular system and clinical approaches of these methods directed toward the treatment of abnormal brain circulation and blood pressure and lower extremity circulatory disturbances.

★ 2899 ★ **Heart Research Foundation of**
Sacramento
3900 J St.
Sacramento, CA 95819
Phone: (916)456-3365
Patti Gantenbein, Exec.Dir.

Research Activities and Fields: Clinical and pathological studies of atherosclerosis, experimental cardiovascular pharmaceutical testing, and coronary, myocardial, and conduction system morphology. **Publications:** Newsletter (Three times a year for the lay public, focusing on risk factor reduction).

★ 2900 ★ **Heart and Vascular Institute**
Henry Ford Hospital
2799 W. Grand Blvd.
Detroit, MI 48202
Phone: (313)876-2695
Fax: (313)876-2687
Dr. Norman A. Silverman, Cochairman

Research Activities and Fields: Diagnosis, treatment, and prevention of heart and vascular disease, with components in cardiovascular medicine, cardiac and thoracic surgery, hypertension research, and vascular surgery. Projects include the study of heart sounds as clues to early degenerative processes; medications to decrease susceptibility to second heart attacks, dissolve blood clots, and to address rhythm disorders; heart transplant and implantations of artificial heart valves; heart bypass procedures; ultrafiltration during heart surgery; arteriosclerosis and vascular dysfunctions; aneurysm repair; prostheses; and use of lasers to vaporize cardiac lesions.

★2901★ **Heineman Medical Research**
PO Box 35457
Charlotte, NC 28235
Phone: (704)374-0505
Fax: (704)342-5763
Francis Robicsek, M.D., Pres.

Research Activities and Fields: Diseases of heart, lungs, and great vessels, with special interest in organ preservation, electrophysiology, and laser applications to arrhythmias and vascular diseases. **Publications:** *Heineman Report*; *Bulletin of Cardiopulmonary Disease.*

★2902★ **Henry Ford Hospital**
Hypertension and Vascular Research
Division
7123 E&R Bldg.
2799 W. Grand Blvd.
Detroit, MI 48202
Phone: (313)876-2010
Fax: (313)876-1479
Dr. Oscar A. Carretero, Division Head

Research Activities and Fields: Etiology and pathogenesis of hypertension, vasoactive hormones, and vascular disease.

★2903★ **Hoffman Heart Institute of**
Connecticut
Saint Francis Hospital and Med. Ctr.
114 Woodland St.
Hartford, CT 06105
Phone: (203)481-1548
Robert Jeresaty, Dir.

Research Activities and Fields: Molecular and cellular biology of vascular cells. **Formerly:** Research and Heart Institute.

★2904★ **Honolulu Heart Program**
Kuakini Medical Center
347 N. Kuakini St.
Honolulu, HI 96817
Phone: (808)536-7283
Fax: (808)536-3385
Dan S. Sharp, M.D., Dir.

Research Activities and Fields: Long-term prospective epidemiologic study of cardiovascular diseases and stroke among 8,000 Japanese-American men born between 1900 and 1919 and living in Hawaii. Follow-up data is obtained by repeat examinations and by mortality and morbidity surveillance. Also conducts studies on aging at the Honolulu--Aging Study program. **E-mail Address:** dan@hhs.cba.hawaii.edu.

★2905★ **Hope Heart Institute**
528 18th Ave.
Seattle, WA 98122
Phone: (206)320-2001
Fax: (206)323-2300
Lester R. Sauvage, M.D., Dir.

Research Activities and Fields: Heart and blood vessel research. Develops new grafts to replace diseased artery tissue. Conducts thrombosis research in an effort to identify patients

who will succeed with artificial grafts. Conducts basic endothelial cell research and studies tissue culture, graft porosity, and surgical implantation techniques. Develops diagnostic methods to identify predispositions to clinical atherosclerosis and develops pharmacologic agents to decrease predispositions to clinical atherosclerosis. **Publications:** *Hope HealthLetter*, available to the public. **Formerly:** Bob Hope International Heart Research Institute.

★2906★ **Indiana University-Purdue**
University at Indianapolis
Hypertension Research Center
632 Clinical Bldg.
541 Clinical Dr.
Indianapolis, IN 46202-5111
Phone: (317)274-8153
Fax: (317)274-7700
Dr. Myron H. Weinberger, Dir.

Research Activities and Fields: Hypertension, including a broad-based, multidisciplinary research program of clinical studies involving genetics of hypertension, pathophysiology of hypertension with plasma renin suppression, role of renin and aldosterone in toxemia of pregnancy, causes of childhood hypertension, and role of renin and aldosterone in heart failure. Also studies myocardial metabolism and cyclic AMP system in spontaneously hypertensive rats, role of sympathetic nervous system in human experimental forms of hypertension, control of renin release in vitro and of renal sodium handling, role of sodium in blood pressure, sodium restriction in the treatment of hypertension, and role of calcium and potassium in blood pressure. **E-mail Address:** mweinbe@indyvax.iupui.edu. **Formerly:** Specialized Center for Research in Hypertension (1981).

★2907★ **Johns Hopkins University**
Ischemic Heart Disease Specialized Center
of Research
Johns Hopkins Hospital
600 N. Wolfe St.
Baltimore, MD 21205
Phone: (410)955-5997
Fax: (410)955-0852
Lewis C. Becker, M.D., Dir.

Research Activities and Fields: Basic and clinical studies of reperfusion injury and other aspects of ischemic heart disease, including cellular, physiological, engineering, and patient studies. Conducts a cardiology fellows program. **Formerly:** Myocardial Infarction Research Unit.

★2908★ **Johns Hopkins University**
Lipid Research Atherosclerosis Unit
University Hospital
CMSC, Rm. 604
600 N. Wolfe St.
Baltimore, MD 21287-3654
Phone: (410)955-3197
Fax: (410)955-1276
Dr. Peter Kwiterovich, Contact

Research Activities and Fields: Lipids, lipoproteins, apolipoproteins, atherosclerosis, genetics, coronary artery diseases, and basic serum proteins. **Formerly:** Lipid Research Clinic.

★2909★ **Krannert Institute of Cardiology**
1111 W. 10th St.
Indianapolis, IN 46202-4800
Phone: (317)630-7261
Fax: (317)274-9697
Dr. Charol Sisch, Dir.

Research Activities and Fields: Conducts basic and clinical studies of electrophysiology, cardiac membrane biology, echocardiography, vascular biology, exercise physiology, and cardiovascular transgenics.

★2910★ **Laval University**
Cardiac Rehabilitation Research Group
Ecole des sciences infirmieres
Quebec, PQ, Canada G1K 7P4
Phone: (418)656-3356
Fax: (418)656-7747
Jean Jobin, Dir.

Research Activities and Fields: Group studies the interactions of psychological, biological, and social factors in cardiac rehabilitation.

★2911★ **Laval University**
Laval Hospital Research Centre
2725, chemin Ste-Foy
Ste. Foy, PQ, Canada G1V 4G5
Phone: (418)656-4760
Fax: (418)656-4509
Yvon Cormier, Dir.

Research Activities and Fields: Cardiology and pneumology, including basic clinical, epidemiologic, and animal research.

★2912★ **Laval University**
Medical Research Centre
Hypertension Research Group
2705, boulevard Laurier
Ste. Foy, PQ, Canada G1V 4G2
Phone: (418)654-2107
Fax: (418)654-2759
Yves Lacourciere, Dir.

Research Activities and Fields: Cause and prevention of cardiovascular disease. Research includes physical exercise, arterial hypertension, the relationship between type II diabetes and hypertension, the anatomy and physiology of neurotransmisison circuits of stress and hypertension, the efficacy of new drugs, and the effects of exercise and weight loss on controlling hypertension in obese patients.

★2913★ **Laval University**
Medical Research Centre
Research Centre on Lipid Disorders
2705, boulevard Laurier
Ste. Foy, PQ, Canada G1V 4G2
Phone: (418)654-2106
Fax: (418)654-2134
Dr. Paul J. Lupien, Dir.

Research Activities and Fields: Pharmacological studies on hypolipidemic agents, lipoproteins, apoproteins, LDL receptors, lipoprotein lipase and hepatic lipase activity, abdominal and visceral obesity, metabolism and genetic polymorphism, nutritional studies on polysaturated and omega fatty acids, and epidemiology of ischemic heart disease in the region of Quebec City.

Loyola University Chicago
Cardiac Transplant Program
See: Entry 12884

★2914★ Medical College of Pennsylvania
and Hahnemann University
Center for the Study of Atherosclerosis
2900 Queen Ln.
Philadelphia, PA 19129
Phone: (215)991-8300
Fax: (215)843-8849
Dr. Michael Phillips, Dir.

Research Activities and Fields: Etiology, maintenance, and reduction of lipoproteins in atherosclerosis. **Formerly:** Center for the Study of Lipoproteins.

★2915★ Medical College of Pennsylvania
and Hahnemann University
Likoff Cardiovascular Institute
Broad & Vine Sts.
Philadelphia, PA 19102
Phone: (215)762-7803
Fax: (215)762-1858
Stanley K. Brockman, Dir.

Research Activities and Fields: Diseases of the heart and great vessels, including studies in myocardial metabolism, physioloy, electrophysiology, cardiac surgery, echocardiography, pharmacology, and nuclear cardiology. Initiates research in causes, diagnosis, and treatment of cardiac and pulmonary disease.

★2916★ Miami Heart Research Institute
4701 N. Meridian Ave.
Miami Beach, FL 33140
Phone: (305)674-3160
Fax: (305)674-3009
David J. Crutchley, Ph.D., Research Dir.

Research Activities and Fields: General cardiovascular research, including clinical trials, cell biology, hemodynamics, electrophysiology, and instrumentation development.

★2917★ Oklahoma Medical Research
Foundation
Cardiovascular Biology Research Program
825 NE 13th St.
Oklahoma City, OK 73104
Phone: (405)271-6673
Fax: (405)271-3980
William G. Thurman, M.D., Pres.

Research Activities and Fields: Heart disease, particularly the mechanism of injury to the heart muscle during a heart attack, including studies of metabolic changes in affected cells; metabolite activity; and the anatomy, physiology, and biochemistry of the myocyte in isolated individual heart cells. Studies aim to discover new methods of preserving areas of cardiac tissue affected by heart attacks, and to provide alternative treatment approaches to surgery and invasive procedures.

★2918★ Oklahoma Medical Research
Foundation
Lipid and Lipoprotein Laboratory
825 NE 13th St.
Oklahoma City, OK 73104
Phone: (405)271-7703
Fax: (405)271-8575
Dr. Petar Alaupovic, Head

Research Activities and Fields: Chemistry and metabolism of plasma lipid transport, pathophysiology and treatment of dyslipoproteinemias, and model systems of atherosclerosis, including studies on the chemistry and interaction of lipoprotein particles, formation and lipolytic degradation of lipoprotein particles, dietary and drug treatment of dyslipoproteinemias, and determination of apolipoprotein profiles in dyslipoproteinemias. **E-mail Address:** margo-french@omrf.oukhsc.edu.

Oregon Health Sciences University
Institute for Nutrition and Cardiovascular
Research
See: Entry 9521

★2919★ Pennsylvania State University
Artificial Heart Research Project
Milton S. Hershey Medical Center
500 Univ. Dr.
Hershey, PA 17033
Phone: (717)531-8328
Fax: (717)531-3664
William S. Pierce, M.D., Dir.

Research Activities and Fields: Development of an implantable, long-term, motor-driven left ventricular assist pump, an implantable, pneumatically-driven total artificial heart, and an implantable, motor-driven electric artificial heart, including all aspects of design of implantable blood pumps, implantable energy convertors, bench testing and evaluation, and animal implantation studies.

★2920★ Philadelphia Heart Institute
39th & Market Sts.
Philadelphia, PA 19104
Phone: (215)662-9022
Fax: (215)662-8577
Bernard L. Segal, M.D., Dir.

Research Activities and Fields: Cardiovascular disease and treatments, including the causes of sudden death, magnetic resonance imaging (MRI), single photon emission computerized tomography (SPECT), alternative heart visualization methods, and "cold" excimer laser investigations. **Publications:** *PHI Update* (quarterly newsletter for cardiologists, internists, and physicians); *On The Beat* (quarterly newsletter); Research Report (semiannually).

Preventive Medicine Research Institute
See: Entry 10869

Purdue University
William A. Hillenbrand Biomedical
Engineering Center
See: Entry 2466

Rockefeller University
Laboratory of Biochemical Genetics and
Metabolism
See: Entry 5346

★2921★ Rocky Mountain Heart
Consortium
1601 Milwaukee St., No. 626
Denver, CO 80206
Phone: (303)393-3951
Fax: (303)393-3955
Ann Fenton, Exec.Dir.

Research Activities and Fields: Clinical heart and cardiovascular research, clinical drug trials, and the development of new diagnostic techniques. **Publications:** Newsletter. **Formerly:** Rocky Mountain Heart Research Institute, Inc. (1993).

★2922★ San Francisco Heart Institute
1900 Sullivan Ave.
Daly City, CA 94015
Phone: (415)991-6712
Fax: (415)755-7315
Richard K. Myler, M.D., Medical Dir.

Research Activities and Fields: Analysis of success, complications, and long-term outcome of coronary angioplasty and cardiac surgery; technological advances applied to angioplasty, including new dilatation balloons, lasers, and coronary stents; transdermal therapies in treatment of hypertension; and atherectomy (rotational and directional) research.

★2923★ Stanford University
Stanford Cardiac Rehabilitation Program
780 Welch Rd., Ste. 106
Palo Alto, CA 94304-1517
Phone: (415)723-6463
Fax: (415)723-6798
Robert F. DeBusk, M.D., Dir.

Research Activities and Fields: Recovery from heart attack and coronary heart surgery, systems to facilitate risk factor modification in healthy individuals and patients with heart disease, and systems to enhance the cost-effectiveness of care provided to patients with heart disease. Coordinates random clinical trials in Kaiser foundation hospitals.

★2924★ Temple University
Sol Sherry Thrombosis Research Center
3400 N. Broad St.
Philadelphia, PA 19140
Phone: (215)221-4665
Fax: (215)221-2783
Robert W. Colman, M.D., Dir.

Research Activities and Fields: Thrombotic hemorrhage disorders, biochemistry and molecular biology of blood coagulation, platelet structure and function, and vessel wall interaction with blood cells. Clinical studies are conducted. Core laboratories are established for cell culture, protein sequencing, peptide synthesis, monoclonal antibody production, and molecular modeling. **E-mail Address:** colmanr@vm.temple.edu. **Formerly:** Thrombosis Research Center.

★2925★ Texas A&M University
Microcirculation Research Institute
College of Medicine
College Station, TX 77843
Phone: (409)845-7816
Fax: (409)847-8635
Dr. Harris J. Granger, Dir.

Research Activities and Fields: Applies high technology to analysis of normal and diseased microscopic blood vessels, including studies on bloodflow in both normal and diseased states, basic control and exchange processes in microcirculation, role of microcirculation in hypertension, edema, stroke, and diabetes, computer analysis of microscopic images, cellular and molecular bases of endothelial and vascular smooth muscle functions, and pathobiology of inflammation and ischemic injury.

★ 2926 ★ Texas Heart Institute
PO Box 20345
Houston, TX 77225-0345
Phone: (713)791-4011
Fax: (713)791-3089
James Cuthbertson, Pres./CEO

Research Activities and Fields: Diseases of the heart and cardiovascular system. Specific areas of study include cardiovascular surgery, including coronary artery bypass surgery, valve replacement, transplantation, and mechanical circulatory support and replacement/assist devices; invasive and non-invasive cardiology, including molecular biochemistry; cardiovascular anesthesiology and pathology; and biostatistics and epidemiology. Publications: Texas Heart Institute Journal (quarterly).

★ 2927 ★ Thomas Jefferson University
Ischemia-Shock Research Center
Dept. of Physiology
1020 Locust St.
Philadelphia, PA 19107-6799
Phone: (215)955-7760
Fax: (215)955-2073
Dr. Allan M. Lefer, Dir.

Research Activities and Fields: Basic and clinical studies of myocardial, splanchnic, and cerebral ischemia and circulatory shock, particularly pathophysiology and therapeutics. Promotes collaborative research among members, facilitates basic science and joint research efforts, and provides research opportunities to fellows.

★ 2928 ★ Tulane University
Tulane Center for Cardiovascular Health
1430 Tulane Ave., S1 29
New Orleans, LA 70112
Phone: (504)585-7197
Fax: (504)585-7194
Gerald S. Berenson, M.D., Dir.

Research Activities and Fields: Cardiovascular disease risk factors in children, including a descriptive epidemiology study (Bogalusa Heart Study), laboratory investigations on the mechanisms of arteriosclerosis, structural studies of proteoglycans, and health education and promotion in elementary school children (Health School/Heart Smart). E-mail Address: berenson@bhs.sph.tulane.edu. Formerly: Specialized Center of Research--Arteriosclerosis (1984); National Research and Demonstration Center--Arteriosclerosis (1990); National Center for Cardiovascular Health.

U.S. Department of Defense
Armed Forces Institute of Pathology
Center for Advanced Pathology
Cardiovascular Pathology Department
See: Entry 10148

★ 2929 ★ U.S. Department of Health and Human Services
National Heart, Lung, and Blood Institute
NIH Bldg. 31, Rm. 5A52
9000 Rockville Pike
Bethesda, MD 20892
Phone: (301)496-5166
Fax: (301)402-0818
Claude Lenfant, Director

Research Activities and Fields: NHLBI is responsible for a national program of research leading to the prevention and treatment of heart, lung, and blood diseases. The scope of the Institute's effort encompasses all forms of heart and vascular disease (except the consequences of cerebrovascular disease), most forms of pulmonary disease (except cancers), many blood diseases (including sickle cell disease), and the utilization of blood resources. Research scope is primarily basic and clinical but also includes applied research and clinical trials as well as demonstration and education research. The Institute plans and directs research in the development, trial, and evaluation of drugs and devices relating to the prevention and treatment of these diseases and the rehabilitation of patients suffering from them; conducts studies into the clinical uses of blood and all aspects of the management of blood resources and supports training in basic and clinical research programs relating to heart, blood vessel, blood, and lung disease; conducts educational activities (including collection and dissemination of educational materials), with emphasis on prevention, for health professionals and the public and maintains relationships with various institutions, agencies, and organizations working in these areas; and awards pre- and postdoctoral fellowships and training grants to develop adequate research investigators. The NHLBI program also includes support for Specialized Centers of Research (SCORs), which are research units within institutions focusing on studies of a specific disease or group of diseases. Principal components of the Institute include divisions of: Blood Diseases and Resources, Epidemiology and Clinical Applications, Extramural Affairs, Heart and Vascular Diseases, Intramural Research, and Lung Diseases.

★ 2930 ★ U.S. Department of Health and Human Services
National Heart, Lung, and Blood Institute
Division of Epidemiology and Clinical Applications
7550 Wisconsin Ave.
Bethesda, MD 20892
Phone: (301)496-2533
Fax: (301)496-0075
Lawrence Friedman, M.D., Director

Research Activities and Fields: The Division plans and directs a program of epidemiological studies, clinical trials, basic and applied behavioral research, demonstration and education research, and projects for disease prevention and health promotion in heart, vascular, pulmonary, and blood diseases and blood resources. It maintains surveillance over developments in its program area and assesses the national need for research on the prevention, diagnosis, and treatment of these diseases by maintaining the necessary scientific management capability to

foster and guide an effective attack upon them. Activities are carried out in the Clinical Applications and Prevention Program and Epidemiology and Biometry Program.

★ 2931 ★ U.S. Department of Health and Human Services
National Heart, Lung, and Blood Institute
Division of Epidemiology and Clinical Applications
Clinical Applications and Prevention Program
7550 Wisconsin Ave.
Bethesda, MD 20892
Phone: (301)496-1706
Fax: (301)402-0517
Dr. Jeffrey Cutler, Acting Associate Director

Research Activities and Fields: Program supports clinical trials, demonstration and educational research, basic and applied behavioral research, and projects for the prevention of cardiovascular, lung, and blood diseases as well as therapeutic measures. Principal areas of research are preventive medicine, nutrition, behavioral medicine, cardiology, and community demonstration and education projects.

★ 2932 ★ U.S. Department of Health and Human Services
National Heart, Lung, and Blood Institute
Division of Epidemiology and Clinical Applications
Epidemiology and Biometry Program
7550 Wisconsin Ave.
Bethesda, MD 20892
Phone: (301)496-2327
Dr. Millicent W. Higgins, Associate Director

Research Activities and Fields: Program supports and conducts studies that identify and evaluate risk factors (e.g., elevated cholesterol and blood pressure, smoking, diabetes, type A personality, lack of physical activity) for coronary heart disease, hypertension, stroke, and peripheral vascular disease as well as for lung and blood diseases. Research interests include causes and predictors associated with the onset and course of heart disease, hypertension, stroke, peripheral vascular disease, and lung and blood diseases. Principal components are the Clinical and Genetic Epidemiology Branch, Field Studies and Biometry Branch, and Social and Environmental Epidemiology Branch.

★ 2933 ★ U.S. Department of Health and Human Services
National Heart, Lung, and Blood Institute
Division of Heart and Vascular Diseases
Federal Building, Rm. 416
Bethesda, MD 20892
Phone: (301)496-2553
Fax: (301)402-3508
Dr. Michael J. Horan, Director

Research Activities and Fields: Division plans and directs a program of fundamental research, clinical research, clinical trials, research training, and prevention, education, and demonstrations for the control of heart and vascular diseases. Major program areas are: arteriosclerosis, hypertension, cerebrovascular disease, coronary heart disease, peripheral vascular diseases, arrhythmias, heart failure and shock, congenital and rheumatic heart diseases, cardiomyopathies and infections of the heart, circulatory assistance including artificial hearts, and cardiac complications of AIDS.

★2934★ U.S. Department of Health and Human Services
National Heart, Lung, and Blood Institute
Division of Heart and Vascular Diseases
Arteriosclerosis, Hypertension, and Lipid Metabolism Program
7550 Wisconsin Ave., Rm. 4C12
Bethesda, MD 20892
Phone: (301)496-1613
Michael Horain, M.D., Contact

Research Activities and Fields: Program supports basic and clinical research relating to arteriosclerosis, lipid metabolism, and hypertension. This includes support for: 1) research grants; 2) Specialized Centers of Research (SCORs) in arteriosclerosis and hypertension; 3) National Research and Demonstration Centers in cardiovascular disease; and 4) nonhuman primate resources to facilitate study of disease states. Principal areas of research interest are: fundamental and metabolic research relating to the etiology, pathogenesis, and prevention of atherosclerosis; etiology, pathogenesis, and prevention of coronary artery and peripheral vascular arteriosclerosis; causes, development, complication, and prevention of cerebrovascular diseases that affect the vessels of the head and neck; the relationship of lipids and lipoproteins to coronary heart disease; and causes, mechanisms of development, treatment, and prevention of hypertension.

★2935★ U.S. Department of Health and Human Services
National Heart, Lung, and Blood Institute
Division of Heart and Vascular Diseases
Cardiac Functions Branch
7550 Wisconsin Ave., Rm. 304
Bethesda, MD 20892
Phone: (301)496-1627
Fax: (301)440-6282
Peter M. Spooner, Ph.D., Chief

Research Activities and Fields: Branch is responsible for administering research grants and implementing new research programs in the basic medical sciences as related to cardiology, physiology, anatomy, pharmacology, biochemistry, and bioengineering.

★2936★ U.S. Department of Health and Human Services
National Heart, Lung, and Blood Institute
Division of Heart and Vascular Diseases
Cardiology Program
7550 Wisconsin Ave.
Bethesda, MD 20892
Phone: (301)496-5421
Fax: (301)480-6282
Frank D. Altieri, Acting Associate Director for Cardiology

Research Activities and Fields: The Cardiology Program supports basic, applied, and clinical research relating to: 1) heart function; 2) normal and abnormal mechanisms of heart action; 3) advanced diagnostic methods; and 4) therapies for cardiac and vascular disorders. Research includes studies on myocardial infarction (MI); angina pectoris; arrhythmias; cardiac resuscita-

tion; quantification of infarct size; heart muscle changes during ischemia; effectiveness of thrombolytic therapy in patients with acute MI; effects of coronary bypass grafts on morbidity and mortality in chronic coronary heart disease patients with stable angina pectoris; the effects of PTCA in patients with coronary disease; prototype cardiovascular devices for partial or total replacement of heart function; and development of devices and techniques for noninvasive detection and measurement of arteriosclerotic plaques within the carotid, coronary, and larger arteries of the limbs. Principal components are the Cardiac Functions Branch, Devices and Technology Branch, and Cardiac Diseases Branch.

★2937★ U.S. Department of Health and Human Services
National Heart, Lung, and Blood Institute
Division of Heart and Vascular Diseases
Devices and Technology Branch
7550 Wisconsin Ave., Rm. 312A
Bethesda, MD 20814
Phone: (301)496-1586
Fax: (301)496-9882
John T. Watson, Ph.D., Chief

Research Activities and Fields: Branch supports extramural research in mechanical circulatory support, biomaterials (blood-material interactions), and diagnostic and therapeutic devices, as well as technology transfer through Small Business Innovation Research Grants.

★2938★ U.S. Department of Health and Human Services
National Heart, Lung, and Blood Institute
Division of Heart and Vascular Diseases
Research Training and Development Branch
7550 Wisconsin Ave.
Bethesda, MD 20892
Phone: (301)496-1724
Fax: (301)402-4023
Dr. John L. Fakunding, Chief

Research Activities and Fields: RTDB administers training grants, fellowships, and career program awards to individuals and academic institutions for research training relating to cardiovascular disease.

★2939★ U.S. Department of Health and Human Services
National Heart, Lung, and Blood Institute
Division of Intramural Research
NIH Bldg. 10, Rm. 7N214
9000 Rockville Pike
Bethesda, MD 20892
Phone: (301)496-2116
Fax: (301)402-0013
Dr. Edward Korn, Director

Research Activities and Fields: The Division plans, conducts, and directs a program of: 1) basic laboratory and clinical research in heart, blood vessel, and lung diseases and certain blood diseases (such as sickle cell anemia and hemophilia); and 2) development of technology related to cardiovascular, pulmonary, and hematologic disorders. Division maintains communication with other programs of the Institute to facilitate early practical application of basic research findings. Areas of major interest include

the biology of experimental and clinical arteriosclerosis and its manifestations; the pathophysiology of hypertensive vascular disease; functions of the lung; clinical and experimental studies on physiological and pharmacological aspects of heart, blood, and lung diseases; and a broad program of other basic research and technical developments.

★2940★ U.S. Department of Health and Human Services
National Heart, Lung, and Blood Institute
Division of Intramural Research
Cardiology Branch
NIH Bldg. 10
9000 Rockville Pike
Bethesda, MD 20892
Phone: (301)496-5817
Fax: (301)402-0888
Dr. Stephen Epstein, Chief

Research Activities and Fields: Branch is involved in a broad range of clinical and basic research efforts, including: 1) studies into the genetic causes and pathophysiologic mechanisms responsible for hypertrophic cardiomyopathy; 2) development of approaches to revascularize the ischemic heart, including the promotion of angiogenesis; 3) studies into pathogenesis and treatment of coronary artery disease and of myocardial ischemia secondary to microvascular disease; 4) elucidation of the mechanisms responsible for Syndrome X (chest pain in the presence of normal coronary arteries); 5) elucidation of the molecular mechanisms responsible for restenosis; 6) development of gene therapy for the treatment of restenosis and atherosclerosis; 7) studies into the potential viral role in the pathogenesis of restenosis and atherosclerosis; and 8) development of techniques to detect stunned and hibernating myocardium and the elucidation of responsible mechanisms.

★2941★ U.S. Department of Health and Human Services
National Heart, Lung, and Blood Institute
Division of Intramural Research
Hypertension-Endocrine Branch
NIH Bldg. 10, Rm. 8C103
9000 Rockville Pike
Bethesda, MD 20892
Phone: (301)496-1518
Fax: (301)402-0013
Dr. H.R. Keiser, Chief

Research Activities and Fields: Branch conducts basic and clinical research on the causes of hypertension and the development of better forms of therapy. Activities are carried out in two main areas: 1) a wide spectrum of research, ranging from basic biochemistry, physiology, and pharmacology to the study of chemical factors in disease and clinical response to drugs, with major emphasis on hypertension; and 2) a broad research program on the molecular mechanism of neuronal function (studies relate primarily to the properties and regulation of enzymes responsible for the biosynthesis of neurohumoral amines). Investigations are extended from the molecular level to experimental animals to humans.

★2942★ U.S. Department of Health and Human Services
National Heart, Lung, and Blood Institute
Division of Intramural Research
Molecular Disease Branch
NIH Bldg. 10, Rm. 7N115
9000 Rockville Pike
Bethesda, MD 20892
Phone: (301)496-5095
Dr. H. Bryan Brewer, Chief

Research Activities and Fields: Research activities of this Branch are directed toward elucidation of the molecular mechanisms involved in lipid transport and metabolism in normal individuals and patients with disorders of lipid metabolism and atherosclerosis. Biochemical studies involve protein chemistry, immunology, tissue culture, molecular biology, and enzymology. Clinical research focuses on the effects of drugs and therapeutic diets on dyslipoproteinemia and on kinetic analysis of the metabolic defects in patients with these diseases.

★2943★ U.S. Department of Health and Human Services
National Heart, Lung, and Blood Institute
Division of Intramural Research
Pathology Branch
NIH Building 10, Rm.2N258
9000 Rockville Pike
Bethesda, MD 20892
Phone: (301)496-5203
Fax: (301)402-2387
Dr. William C. Roberts, Chief

Research Activities and Fields: Branch is concerned with the study of morphologic aspects of cardiovascular and pulmonary diseases and their correlation with functional derangements. Morphologic analyses include transmission and scanning electron microscopy.

★2944★ U.S. Department of Health and Human Services
National Heart, Lung, and Blood Institute
Laboratory of Biochemical Genetics
NIH Bldg. 36, Rm. 1C-06
9000 Rockville Pike
Bethesda, MD 20892
Phone: (301)496-2401
Marshall Nirenberg, Ph.D., Chief

Research Activities and Fields: Activities are carried out in two sections: Molecular Biology and Macromolecules. The Molecular Biology Section studies basic problems in molecular biology and biochemistry, particularly those that pertain to the development of the nervous system. Current research focuses on elucidating mechanisms that regulate gene expression using recombinant DNA techniques; and on cyclic nucleotides, ion channels, and cell recognition. The Macromolecules Section studies cellular control in *Escherichia coli*. Areas of interest include: the control of the synthesis and metabolism of cyclic AMP in bacterial cells; the regulation of expression of the gene for adenylate cyclase as well as the factors that regulate enzyme activity, using biological and recombinant DNA approaches; and analyses of structure, function, and repression mechanisms involving the *E. coli* cycle AMO receptor protein.

★2945★ U.S. Department of Health and Human Services
National Heart, Lung, and Blood Institute
Laboratory of Biochemistry
NIH Bldg. 3, Rm. 222
9000 Rockville Pike
Bethesda, MD 20892
Phone: (301)496-4096
Fax: (301)496-0599
Dr. Earl R. Stadtman, Chief

Research Activities and Fields: Laboratory conducts research in biochemistry, primarily as related to control of metabolic processes; amino acid metabolism; vitamin B-12 metabolism; selenium biochemistry; and aging (specifically, the role of post-translational modifications of enzymes in protein turnover and aging).

★2946★ U.S. Department of Health and Human Services
National Heart, Lung, and Blood Institute
Laboratory of Biophysical Chemistry
NIH Bldg. 10, Rm. 7N318
9000 Rockville Pike
Bethesda, MD 20892
Phone: (301)496-2135
Fax: (301)496-9984
Dr. Henry M. Fales, Chief

Research Activities and Fields: Laboratory investigates the physical and chemical properties of molecules with a view to elucidating their biochemical functions. Specialties are nuclear magnetic resonance, mass spectrometry, X-ray crystallography, chromatography, and laboratory computer techniques. A special concern is the development of new techniques and their application to problems of current interest.

★2947★ U.S. Department of Health and Human Services
National Heart, Lung, and Blood Institute
Laboratory of Cardiac Energetics
NIH Bldg. 10, Rm. B1D 161
9000 Rockville Pike
Bethesda, MD 20892
Phone: (301)496-3658
Fax: (301)402-2389
Dr. Robert Balaban, Chief

Research Activities and Fields: Cardiology, nuclear magnetic resonance imaging/spectrography, cardiac energetics, and optical spectroscopy.

★2948★ U.S. Department of Health and Human Services
National Heart, Lung, and Blood Institute
Laboratory of Cell Biology
NIH Bldg. Rm. B1-22
9000 Rockville Pike
Bethesda, MD 20892
Phone: (301)496-1001
Edward Korn, Ph.D., Chief

Research Activities and Fields: Laboratory's research is concerned with regulation of the polymerization and enzymatic activity of actin and myosin, the two major cytoskeletal proteins of the membrane-cytoskeleton complex of non-muscle cells. Activities involve studying the ways in which ATP hydrolysis regulates actin polymerization and how myosin phosphorylation regulates myosin polymerization, actomy-osin ATP-ase activity, and contractile activity. Studies include active site sequence determination and structure-function relationships (studied through a variety of protein physical-chemical methods). Research also involves isolating and sequencing myosin genes, with plans to undertake site-directed mutagenesis to explore further the chemical basis of actin and myosin function. Laboratory also investigates the action of such drugs as cytochalasin D in order to understand at the molecular level their effects on the membrane-cytoskeleton complex.

★2949★ U.S. Department of Health and Human Services
National Heart, Lung, and Blood Institute
Laboratory of Cellular Metabolism
NIH Bldg. 10, Rm. 5N307
9000 Rockville Pike
Bethesda, MD 20892
Phone: (301)496-4554
Fax: (301)402-1610
Dr. Martha Vaughan, Chief

Research Activities and Fields: Laboratory conducts research in molecular biology, membrane chemistry, cell biology, and protein chemistry. Techniques of molecular genetics, biochemistry, and cell biology are used to study mechanisms of transmembrane signalling by guanyl nucleotide-binding (G) proteins that regulate many critical cellular processes.

★2950★ U.S. Department of Health and Human Services
National Heart, Lung, and Blood Institute
Laboratory of Chemical Pharmacology
NIH Bldg. 10, Rm. 8N117
9000 Rockville Pike
Bethesda, MD 20892
Phone: (301)496-2593
Fax: (301)402-0171
Dr. James R. Gillette, Chief

Research Activities and Fields: Principal areas of research are drug metabolism; mechanisms of allergic responses; and mechanisms of drug-induced cellular damage.

★2951★ U.S. Department of Health and Human Services
National Heart, Lung, and Blood Institute
Laboratory of Kidney and Electrolyte Metabolism
NIH Bldg. 10, Rm. 6N307
9000 Rockville Pike
Bethesda, MD 20892
Phone: (301)496-3187
Fax: (301)402-1443
Dr. Maurice B. Burg, Chief

Research Activities and Fields: Laboratory conducts research on the mechanism and regulation (hormonal and otherwise) of a variety of transport processes in systems, including the intact kidney, isolated perfused segments of renal tubules, and epithelial cell cultures. Emphasis is on electrophysiology, quantitative microscopy, nuclear magnetic resonance, and intermediary metabolism as related to transport.

★2952★ U.S. Department of Health and Human Services
National Heart, Lung, and Blood Institute
Laboratory of Molecular Cardiology

NIH Bldg. 10, Rm. 8N-202
9000 Rockville Pike
Bethesda, MD 20892
Phone: (301)496-1865
Fax: (301)402-1542
Dr. Robert S. Adelstein, Chief

Research Activities and Fields: Laboratory conducts research on the regulation function and expression of the contractile proteins in muscle and nonmuscle cells. The role of calcium, calmodulin, and phosphorylation in regulating actin-myosin interaction is of particular interest. Projects include studies of the mechanism by which phosphorylation alters contractile activity in smooth muscle and nonmuscle cells, regulation of contractile protein expression in cultured smooth muscle cells, and cloning the genes for selected contractile proteins. Current interest is the role these proteins and their genes play in cellular development, differentiation, and tumorigenicity.

U.S. Department of Health and Human Services
National Institute on Aging
Laboratory of Cardiovascular Science
See: Entry 1957

U.S. Department of Health and Human Services
National Institute on Aging
Laboratory of Cardiovascular Science
Membrane Biology Section
See: Entry 1958

★ 2953 ★   **University of Alabama at**
             Birmingham
Alabama Congenital Heart Disease
    Diagnosis and Treatment Center
Dept. of Surgery
Univ. Sta.
Birmingham, AL 35294
Phone: (205)934-2344
Fax: (205)934-7514
Dr. Albert D. Pacifico, Dir.

Research Activities and Fields: Seeks to improve the results of surgery on patients with congenital heart disease. Performs heart catheterizations and other operations to correct congenital heart defects.

★ 2954 ★   **University of Alabama at**
             Birmingham
Cardiovascular Research and Training
    Center
THT, Rm. 311
Birmingham, AL 35294
Phone: (205)934-3624
Fax: (205)934-5596
Gerald M. Pohost, M.D., Dir.

Research Activities and Fields: Heart and blood vessels, including interdisciplinary and crossdisciplinary studies of basic function of cardiovascular system in normal and abnormal states. Studies include nuclear magnetic resonance imaging and spectroscopy of myocardial damage, radionuclide assessment of myocardial perfusion and left ventricular function, molecular biology of the myocardial contractile proteins, mechanism of cardiac homograft rejection, and basic and clinical investigations of hypertension, including vascular smooth muscle,

neural factors, renal function abnormalities and post-renal-transplantation, and essential hypertension. **Publications:** *Hypertension* (bimonthly).

★ 2955 ★   **University of Alabama at**
             Birmingham
Specialized Center of Research in
    Ischemic Heart Disease (SCOR)
Univ. Sta.
Birmingham, AL 35294
Phone: (205)934-3624
Fax: (205)975-5150
Gerald M. Pohost, M.D., Program Dir.

Research Activities and Fields: Coronary artery disease. Conducts studies on patients, experimental animals, heart cells, and cellular components.

★ 2956 ★   **University of Arizona**
University Heart Center
Arizona Health Sciences Center
1501 N. Campbell Ave.
Tucson, AZ 85724
Phone: (520)626-6221
Fax: (520)626-2666
Dr. Gordon A. Ewy, Dir.

Research Activities and Fields: Multidisciplinary studies of the heart, including basic, preclinical and clinical research. Basic research focuses on cell growth and development, including genetics, biochemistry, and molecular biology; preclinical research focuses on the microvascular, pharmacologic, and physiologic aspects of heart disease; and clinical research focuses on new drugs, techniques, devices, and interventions. Specific areas of study include cardiac elecrtrical instability, molecular biology and genetics, end-stage heart disease (including heart and lung transplantation and the use of mechanical assist devices and the artificial heart), atherosclerotic heart and vascular disease, detection and diagnosis of cardiovascular disorders, congenital heart disorders, microvascular and vascular disorders, heart disease prevention, cardiovascular diseases specific to Hispanics and Native Americans, and cardiovascular diseases in women and the elderly. **Publications:** Newsletter.

★ 2957 ★   **University of California at**
             Berkeley
Sequoia Hospital Lipid Institute
170 Alameda de las Pulgas
Redwood City, CA 94062-2799
Phone: (415)367-5830
Fax: (415)365-4220
Dr. Robert Superko, Dir.

Research Activities and Fields: Atherosclerosis and lipidology. **Formerly:** Center for Progressive Atherosclerosis Management.

★ 2958 ★   **University of California, Los**
             Angeles
Cardiovascular Research Laboratory
MRL Bldg., No. 3645
UCLA Medical Center
Los Angeles, CA 90024-1760
Phone: (310)825-6824
Fax: (310)206-5777
Dr. Glenn A. Langer, Dir.

Research Activities and Fields: Cellular and subcellular aspects of cardiac contraction,

including ultrastructure, ion exchange and compartmentation, and studies in electrophysiology, mechanics, and biochemistry. **E-mail Address:** glenn@cvrl.ucla.edu. **Formerly:** Originally established by Los Angeles County Heart Association and later known as American Heart Association Greater Los Angeles Affiliate Cardiovascular Research Laboratories (1987).

★ 2959 ★   **University of California, San**
             Diego
Specialized Center of Research in
    Arteriosclerosis
Dept. of Medicine, 0682
La Jolla, CA 92093-0682
Phone: (619)534-0569
Fax: (619)546-9828
Dr. Daniel Steinberg, Codirector

Research Activities and Fields: Arteriosclerosis and atherogenesis, including studies of lipoprotein metabolism, oxidation of low density lipoprotein molecules, and molecular basis of arteriosclerosis.

★ 2960 ★   **University of California, San**
             Diego
Specialized Center of Research in Heart
    Failure
Dept. of Medicine, 0613B
La Jolla, CA 92093-0613
Phone: (619)534-3347
Fax: (619)534-1626
Dr. John Ross, Jr., Dir.

Research Activities and Fields: Causes and treatment of coronary heart disease, including studies of beta-adrenergic receptors and post-receptor components in ischemia; tests of drugs for efficacy in reversing contraction abnormalities of ischemic heart induced by exercise and hypertrophy in myocardium; and investigations of the link between ischemia and leukocyte kinetics in the heart. Also studies molecular events in the heart muscle after ischemia, including specific proteins, mRNAs, and sodium channel genes; and conducts clinical studies on coronary reactivity after cholesterol lowering. **Formerly:** Specialized Center of Research in Coronary Heart Disease.

★ 2961 ★   **University of Chicago**
Specialized Center of Research in
    Atherosclerosis
Dept. of Pathology
MC 6079
5841 S. Maryland Ave.
Chicago, IL 60637
Phone: (312)702-1265
Fax: (312)702-3778
Dr. Peter F. Davies, Dir.

Research Activities and Fields: Molecular mechanisms of hyperlipemia and the localized development of atherosclerotic plaques; arterial wall biology and pathology; the biogenesis, function, and interactions of lipoproteins; role of hemodynamics in atherogenesis; and role of cholesterol homeostasis in regulation of expression of selected genes.

★ 2962 ★ **University of Cincinnati**
Cardio-Vascular Laboratory
University Hospital
234 Goodman Ave.
Cincinnati, OH 45267-0756
Phone: (513)558-5148
Fax: (513)558-3515
David Eppert, Mgr.

Research Activities and Fields: Computerized vascular research, including ultrasound, instrumentation, and pharmaceutical research.

University of Florida
Cardiovascular Laser Lab
See: Entry 11166

★ 2963 ★ **University of Florida**
Hypertension Center
Department of Physiology
College of Medicine
PO Box 100274
Gainesville, FL 32610-0274
Phone: (904)392-3791
Fax: (904)392-8340
Dr. M. Ian Phillips, Ph.D., D.Sc., Act. Dir.

Research Activities and Fields: Hypertension, including renal mechanisms of hypertension and brain control of blood pressure, epidemiological studies in African Americans, models of hypertension in animals, and cellular and molecular studies in vitro. Focuses particularly on the study of the renin-angiotensin system and antisense oligodeoxynucleotides and viral vectors in an effort to develop gene therapy for cardiovascular disease.

★ 2964 ★ **University of Houston**
Institute for Cardiovascular Studies
4800 Calhoun Blvd., SR2
Houston, TX 77204-5515
Phone: (713)743-1218
Fax: (713)743-1237
Dr. B.S. Jandhyala, Dir.

Research Activities and Fields: Cardiovascular research, including central and peripheral control of the cardiovascular system and renal functions, central mechanisms of endogenous opiates and other polypeptides, antihypertensive compounds, pharmacology of compounds affecting cardiovascular function, microcirculation and physiology of exercise, biomedical pharmacology, ischemia-reperfusion injury, oxygen free radicals, anti-oxidants, and organ protection. **E-mail Address:** jandhyala@uh.edu.

★ 2965 ★ **University of Iowa**
Iowa Cardiovascular Center
College of Medicine
616 MRC
Iowa City, IA 52242-1182
Phone: (319)335-8588
Fax: (319)335-6969
Prof. Francois M. Abboud, Dir.

Research Activities and Fields: Coronary and vascular disease, hypertension, lipid arteriosclerosis, the regulation of circulation in pathological states, neurovascular control, clinical management of lipid disorders, lipoproteins, cerebral blood vessels, occupational and immunologic lung disease, cystic fibrosis, and cardiovascular research training program.

★ 2966 ★ **University of Iowa**
Lipid Research Clinic
Dept. of Internal Medicine
Westlawn S-219
Iowa City, IA 52242
Phone: (319)335-8201
Dr. Helmut Schrott, Dir.

Research Activities and Fields: Lipids, including the relationship of cholesterol and other blood lipids to heart disease. Conducts studies on cholesterol reducing effects of lipid lowering drugs. Also studies community cholesterol screening and educational programs for physicians. Awarded a clinical lipid disorders treatment program. Other activities include studies in post-menopausal women (PEPI Trial and HRS Trial).

★ 2967 ★ **University of Kansas**
Lipid Laboratory
Medical Center
3800 Cambridge
Kansas City, KS 66160-7418
Phone: (913)588-6025
Fax: (913)588-6040
William Harris, Ph.D., Dir.

Research Activities and Fields: Measures lipids in blood, including level of cholesterol, triglycerides, and lipoproteins. Tests ability of drugs and other substances to lower levels of lipids in humans, especially for preventing cholesterol absorption.

★ 2968 ★ **University of Kentucky**
Sanders-Brown Center on Aging
Stroke Program
101 Sanders-Brown Bldg.
800 S. Limestone St.
Lexington, KY 40536-0230
Phone: (606)257-5560
Fax: (606)257-8990
Dr. Robert J. Dempsey, M.D., Dir.

Research Activities and Fields: Clinical studies of warfarin versus aspirin in recurrent stroke treatment, changes in the blood-brain barrier under ischemic conditions, and carotid artery plaque lipoprotein content and its oxidation state.

★ 2969 ★ **University of Louisville**
Center for Applied Microcirculatory
Research
School of Medicine
Health Sciences Center, Rm. 1115
Louisville, KY 40292
Phone: (502)588-5373
Frederick N. Miller, Ph.D., Dir.

Research Activities and Fields: Measurements of small blood vessel behavior in humans and animals during various clinical situations and human feasibility studies for application of microcirculatory science in clinical surgery and medicine. Also involved with computer hardware and software engineering development and animal studies.

★ 2970 ★ **University of Michigan**
Division of Cardiology
1500 E. Medical Center Dr.
Ann Arbor, MI 48109-0119
Phone: (313)936-5255
Fax: (313)936-5256
Izumo, M.D., Dir.

Research Activities and Fields: Diagnosis, treatment, and prevention of cardiovascular disease, including new therapeutic approaches to patients with heart failure and development of digital coronary and left ventricular angiography and digital echocardiography, myocardial reperfusion with thrombolytic agents and acute PTCA, and electrophysiology with emphasis on catheter ablation techniques. Also studies molecular biology of myocardial proteins and vascular adhesion molecules as well as new approaches to gene transfer into specific vascular beds. **Formerly:** Heart Station of University Hospital.

★ 2971 ★ **University of Michigan**
Division of Hypertension
3918 Taubman Center
Ann Arbor, MI 48109-0356
Phone: (313)936-4790
Fax: (313)936-8898
Dr. S. Julius, Chief

Research Activities and Fields: Hypertension and hyperlipidemia, including pathophysiology of various forms of human hypertension, epidemiology, mechanism of action of drugs, and improvement of health care delivery. **Formerly:** Hypertension Unit.

University of Michigan
Thoracic Surgery Research Lab
See: Entry 12326

★ 2972 ★ **University of Missouri—Columbia**
Division of Cardiothoracic Surgery
School of Medicine
Medical Sciences Bldg., MA 204
1 Hospital Dr.
Columbia, MO 65212
Phone: (314)882-1566
Dr. Jack Curtis, Contact

Research Activities and Fields: Cardiac physiology and cardiothoracic surgery.

University of Missouri—Columbia
John M. Dalton Cardiovascular Research
Center
See: Entry 1707

★ 2973 ★ **University of Montreal**
Montreal Research Centre
Cardiology Institute
5000, rue Belanger Est
Montreal, PQ, Canada H1T 1C8
Phone: (514)593-2508
Fax: (514)376-1355
Stanley Nattel, Dir.

Research Activities and Fields: Basic studies in cardiovascular disease, including therapeutic effects of exercise, nuclear medicine, angiography, electrophysiology, and clinical pharmacology.

★ 2974 ★ **University of Pennsylvania**
Pennsylvania Muscle Institute
D700 Richards Bldg.
3100 Hamel Walk
School of Medicine
Philadelphia, PA 19104-6085
Phone: (215)898-4017
Fax: (215)898-2653
Yale E. Goldman, M.D., Dir.

Research Activities and Fields: Studies muscle tissue as it relates to heart disease using specialized techniques developed by the Institute, including rapid spectroscopic methods for measurement of cytoplasmic ions, electron energy loss analysis, and electron probe X-ray analysis for obtaining compositional information about cells. Serves as a regional interdisciplinary center for collaborative studies on development, molecular organization, and function of contractile and regulatory proteins and on mechanics, energetics, excitation/contraction coupling mechanism, and intracellular ion movements in cardiac, smooth, and skeletal muscle.

University of Pittsburgh
Safar Center for Resuscitation Research
See: Entry 4766

★ 2975 ★ **University of Southern California**
Coronary Care Research
1200 N. State St., Box 305
Los Angeles, CA 90033
Phone: (213)226-7116
Fax: (213)226-2195
Dr. L. Julian Haywood, Dir.

Research Activities and Fields: Clinical pathophysiology and management of myocardial infarction and other cardiovascular disorders, rhythm disturbances of the heart, computer-based monitoring techniques, vectorcardiography, and related investigations of electrophysiology, with emphasis on noninvasive methods, the use of radioisotopes in nuclear cardiology, and other radiological techniques.

★ 2976 ★ **University of Tennessee**
Division of Cardiovascular Diseases
951 Ct. Ave.
Memphis, TN 38163
Phone: (901)528-5759
Dr. Jay M. Sullivan, Chief

Research Activities and Fields: Cardiovascular system in health and disease, including investigations of hypertension, hemodynamics, electrophysiology, cardiac imaging, and cardiovascular pharmacology.

★ 2977 ★ **University of Texas Medical**
Branch at Galveston
Cardiovascular Surgical Research
Laboratory
J17
Galveston, TX 77555
Phone: (409)772-1203
Fax: (409)772-1421
Dr. Vincent R. Conti, Dir.

Research Activities and Fields: Myocardial metabolism with ischemia using the isolated working rat heart and isolated cardiac mitochondria. Also conducts laboratory and clinical studies of the physiologic effects of cardiopulmonary bypass.

★ 2978 ★ **University of Texas**
Southwestern Medical Center at Dallas
Cardiology Division
5323 Harry Hines Blvd., Rm. NB11.200
Dallas, TX 75235-8573
Phone: (214)648-1400
Fax: (214)648-1450
R. Sanders Williams, M.D., Chf.

Research Activities and Fields: Cardiology, including 1) molecular biology of the cardiovascular system, 2) clinical and basic studies of heart disease, and 3) clinical and basic studies of congestive heart failure.

★ 2979 ★ **University of Utah**
Artificial Heart Research Laboratory
803 North 300 West, NW Wing
Salt Lake City, UT 84103
Phone: (801)581-6991
Fax: (801)581-4044
Dr. Don B. Olsen, Dir.

Research Activities and Fields: Cardiac replacement, cardiac assist devices, and artificial organs, including investigations into acute and chronic ventricular assist and total replacement, cardiac valves, total artificial hearts (pneumatic, electrohydraulic, and electromechanical), and associated pathophysiology. Experiments concern the introduction of such devices in sheep and calves.

★ 2980 ★ **University of Utah**
Cardiovascular Genetic Research Clinic
410 Chipeta Way, Rm. 161
Salt Lake City, UT 84108
Phone: (801)581-3888
Fax: (801)581-6862
Dr. Roger Williams, Dir.

Research Activities and Fields: Cardiovascular genetics, focusing on the correlations between environment, genetics, and the incidence of early heart disease.

★ 2981 ★ **University of Utah**
Nora Eccles Harrison Cardiovascular
Research and Training Institute
Nora Eccles Harrison Bldg. 500
Salt Lake City, UT 84112
Phone: (801)581-8183
Fax: (801)581-3128
Dr. Robert L. Lux, Dir.

Research Activities and Fields: Cardiac electrophysiology, electrocardiography, pharmacology, and biochemistry, including animal experimentation, observations on patients, and computer modeling. **Publications:** Monographs. **E-mail Address:** robert_lux@gatormail.curti.utah.edu. **Formerly:** Cardiovascular Research & Training Institute (1976).

★ 2982 ★ **University of Virginia**
Vascular Medicine and Preventive
Cardiology Unit
Medical Center, Box 146
Charlottesville, VA 22908
Phone: (804)924-2765
Fax: (804)924-9604
Dr. Carlos R. Ayers, Dir.

Research Activities and Fields: Cardiovascular problems, including hypertension, hyperlipidemia, renal blood flow, xenon washout technique, renin-angiotension-aldosterone metabolism, catecholamine metabolism, plethysmography, peripheral vascular physiology and disease, and cardiovascular risk reduction. **Formerly:** Virginia Heart Laboratory (1978); Hypertension/Atherosclerosis Unit.

University of Wisconsin—La Crosse
Human Performance Laboratory
See: Entry 11995

★ 2983 ★ **University of Wisconsin—**
Madison
Biodynamics Laboratory
2000 Observatory Dr., Rm. 1149
Madison, WI 53706-1189
Phone: (608)262-7944
Fax: (608)262-1656
Dr. Greg Carter, Dir.

Research Activities and Fields: Mechanisms associated with the response and adaptation of humans and animals to exercise and environmental stress, focusing on cardiorespiratory and musculoskeletal systems.

★ 2984 ★ **Vanderbilt University**
Autonomic Dysfunction Center
AA-3228 Medical Center North
Medical Center
Nashville, TN 37232-2195
Phone: (615)343-6499
Dr. David Robertson, Dir.

Research Activities and Fields: Pathophysiology of orthostatic hypotension, including dopamine-B-hydroxylase deficiency, a syndrome characterized by congenital absence of norepinephrine and epinephrine. Other areas of research focus on therapeutic modalities for the management of orthostatic hypotensive patients and consequences of baroreflex failure in human subjects.

★ 2985 ★ **Vanderbilt University**
Specialized Center of Research in
Hypertension
Garland Ave.
Nashville, TN 37232
Phone: (615)322-4347
Fax: (615)343-0704
Dr. Tadashi Inagami, Dir.

Research Activities and Fields: Molecular biological studies on hypertensinogenic genes, angiotensin receptors and other new vasoactive substances. Studies include vascular cell function and disease, renal arterial stenosis, carotid arterial stenosis, and carotidarterial stenosis in hypertensive patients with regard to progression of renal arterial lesions and resultant effects on renal function. Also studies hormonal mechanisms in hypertension; structure, cell biology, histochemistry, and molecular biology of renin and low renin or suppressed renin hypertension; antihypertensive action of adrenergic agonists and antagonists; adrenergic recept ors in hypertension; role of prostaglandins in renin release and hypertension; central hypertensive action of adenosin; angiotensin/aldosterone system atrial natriuretic factor; endothelin; endogenous sodium pump inhibitor in hypertension; identification of hypertensinogenic gene; and genetic analysis of dopamine beta hydroxylase. Studies are conducted on clinical and experimental hypertension involving endocrinology, clinical pharmacology, surgery, radiology, biochemistry, and pharmacology.

★ 2986 ★ Vascular Research Laboratory
Akron City Hosptial
525 E. Market St.
Akron, OH 44309
Phone: (216)375-3693
Fax: (216)375-4648
Dr. Steven Schmidt, Dir.

Research Activities and Fields: Vascular cells, focusing on cell and molecular biology, hyperplasia, and pancreatic islet research.

★ 2987 ★ Wake Forest University Hypertension Center
Bowman Gray School of Medicine
Medical Center Blvd.
Winston-Salem, NC 27157-1032
Phone: (910)716-9623
Fax: (910)716-2456
Dr. John Flack, Dir.

Research Activities and Fields: Hypertension. Activities include a clinical hypertension drug trial to treat high blood pressure on individuals 70 years or older and two clinical hypertension drug trials to treat high blood pressure on individuals 21 years or older. **Formerly:** Hypertensive Research Group (at University of Minnesota).

★ 2988 ★ Washington University Atherosclerosis, Nutrition, and Lipid Research Division
4566 Scott Ave.
Box 8046
St. Louis, MO 63110
Phone: (314)362-7038
Fax: (314)362-7657
Gustav Schonfeld, M.D., Dir.

Research Activities and Fields: Atherosclerosis and lipid disorders, including research on genetic lipid disorders, atherogenesis and the roles of growth factors, cytokines, and chemically modified oxidized lipoproteins. Uses chemical, molecular, biologic, immunologic and cell culture techniques for studies of lipogenesis, lipoprotein structure and function. Performs clinical trials to determine optimum diagnostic and treatment modalities for dyslipoproteinemias. Operates the Core Lipid and Lipoprotein Laboratory, which acts as a central laboratory in multicenter clinical trials. **E-mail Address:** schonfel@visa.wustl.edu. **Formerly:** Lipid Research Center, Atherosclerosis, Nutrition and Lipid Research Division.

State & Regional Organizations

Heart

State affiliates of the American Heart Association are listed below. The Association's national center is located at 7272 Greenville Ave., Dallas, TX 75231-4596, (214) 373-6300, 800-242-8721.

Alabama

★ 2989 ★ American Heart Association Alabama Affiliate
1449 Medical Park Dr.
Birmingham, AL 35213
Phone: (205)592-7100
Fax: (205)592-0727

Alaska

★ 2990 ★ American Heart Association Alaska Affiliate
2330 E. 42nd Ave.
Anchorage, AK 99508
Phone: (907)563-3111
Fax: (907)563-5321

Arizona

★ 2991 ★ American Heart Association Arizona Affiliate
2929 S. 48th St.
Tempe, AZ 85282
Phone: (602)414-5353
Fax: (602)414-5355

Arkansas

★ 2992 ★ American Heart Association Arkansas Affiliate
909 W. 2nd St.
Little Rock, AR 72201
Phone: (501)375-9148
Fax: (501)375-9066

California

★ 2993 ★ American Heart Association California Affiliate
1710 Gilbreth Rd.
Burlingame, CA 94010
Phone: (415)259-6700
Fax: (415)259-6891

★ 2994 ★ American Heart Association Greater Los Angeles Affiliate
3550 Wilshire Blvd., 5th Fl.
Los Angeles, CA 90010
Phone: (213)385-4231
Fax: (213)386-4057

Colorado

★ 2995 ★ American Heart Association Colorado Affiliate
1280 S. Parker Rd.
Denver, CO 80231-2128
Phone: (303)369-5433
Fax: (303)369-8087

Connecticut

★ 2996 ★ American Heart Association Connecticut Affiliate
5 Brookside Dr.
Wallingford, CT 06492
Phone: (203)294-0088
Fax: (203)294-3329

Delaware

★ 2997 ★ American Heart Association Delaware Affiliate
1096 Old Churchmans Rd.
Newark, DE 19713
Phone: (302)633-0200
Fax: (302)633-3964

District of Columbia

★ 2998 ★ American Heart Association Nation's Capital Affiliate
5335 Wisconsin Ave. NW, Ste. 940
Washington, DC 20015
Phone: (202)686-6888
Fax: (202)686-6162

Florida

★ 2999 ★ American Heart Association Florida Affiliate
1213 16th St. N.
St. Petersburg, FL 33705-1092
Phone: (813)894-7400
Fax: (813)894-8561

Georgia

★ 3000 ★ American Heart Association Georgia Affiliate
1685 Terrell Mill Rd.
Marietta, GA 30067
Phone: (404)952-1316
Fax: (404)952-2208

Hawaii

★ 3001 ★ American Heart Association Hawaii Affiliate
245 N. Kukui St., Ste. 204
Honolulu, HI 96817
Phone: (808)538-7021
Fax: (808)538-3443

Idaho

★ 3002 ★ American Heart Association Idaho/Montana Affiliate
270 S. Orchard, Ste. B
Boise, ID 83705
Phone: (208)384-5066
Fax: (208)336-5867

Illinois

★ 3003 ★ American Heart Association Illinois Affiliate
1181 N. Dirksen Pkwy.
Springfield, IL 62708
Phone: (217)525-1350
Fax: (217)525-6970

★ 3004 ★ American Heart Association Metropolitan Chicago Affiliate
208 S. LaSalle St., Ste. 900
Chicago, IL 60604-1197
Phone: (312)346-4675
Fax: (312)346-7375

Indiana

★3005★ American Heart Association
Indiana Affiliate
8645 Guion Rd., Ste. H
PO Box 681550
Indianapolis, IN 46268
Phone: (317)876-4850
Fax: (317)876-4859

Iowa

★3006★ American Heart Association
Iowa Affiliate
1111 9th St., Ste. 280
Des Moines, IA 50314
Phone: (515)244-3278
Fax: (515)244-5164

Kansas

★3007★ American Heart Association
Kansas Affiliate
5375 SW 7th St.
Topeka, KS 66606
Phone: (913)272-7056
Fax: (913)272-2425

Kentucky

★3008★ American Heart Association
Kentucky Affiliate
333 Guthrie St., Ste. 207
Louisville, KY 40202-1899
Phone: (502)587-8641
Fax: (502)585-7001

Louisiana

★3009★ American Heart Association
Louisiana Affiliate
105 Campus Dr. E.
Destrehan, LA 70047
Phone: (504)764-8711
Fax: (504)764-8712

Maine

★3010★ American Heart Association
Maine Affiliate
20 Winter St.
Augusta, ME 04330
Phone: (207)623-8432
Fax: (207)626-3213

Maryland

★3011★ American Heart Association
Maryland Affiliate
415 N. Charles St.
Baltimore, MD 21201-4441
Phone: (410)685-7074
Fax: (410)539-5049

Massachusetts

★3012★ American Heart Association
Massachusetts Affiliate
20 Speen St.
Framingham, MA 01701-4680
Phone: (508)620-1700
Fax: (508)620-6157

Michigan

★3013★ American Heart Association
Michigan Affiliate
16310 W. 12 Mile Rd.
Lathrup Village, MI 48076
Phone: (810)557-9500
Fax: (810)569-3353

Minnesota

★3014★ American Heart Association
Minnesota Affiliate
4701 W. 77th St.
Minneapolis, MN 55435
Phone: (612)835-3300
Fax: (612)835-5828

Mississippi

★3015★ American Heart Association
Mississippi Affiliate
4830 McWillie Circle
Jackson, MS 39204
Phone: (601)981-4721
Fax: (601)981-7536

Missouri

★3016★ American Heart Association
Missouri Affiliate
4643 Lindell Blvd.
St. Louis, MO 63108
Phone: (314)367-3383
Fax: (314)367-8605

Montana

★3017★ American Heart Association
Idaho/Montana Affiliate
270 S. Orchard, Ste. B
Boise, ID 83705
Phone: (208)384-5066
Fax: (208)336-5867

Nebraska

★3018★ American Heart Association
Nebraska Affiliate
3624 Farnam
Omaha, NE 68131
Phone: (402)346-0771
Fax: (402)346-1717

Nevada

★3019★ American Heart Association
Nevada Affiliate
6370 W. Flamingo, Ste. 1
Las Vegas, NV 89103
Phone: (702)367-1366
Fax: (702)367-1975

New Hampshire

★3020★ American Heart Association
New Hampshire Affiliate
309 Pine St.
Manchester, NH 03103
Phone: (603)669-5833
Fax: (603)669-6745

New Jersey

★3021★ American Heart Association
New Jersey Affiliate
2550 Rte. 1
North Brunswick, NJ 08902
Phone: (908)821-2610
Fax: (908)821-2736

New Mexico

★3022★ American Heart Association
New Mexico Affiliate
1330 San Pedro NE, Ste. 105
Albuquerque, NM 87110
Phone: (505)268-3711
Fax: (505)268-7680

New York

★3023★ American Heart Association
New York City Affiliate
122 E. 42nd St., 18th Fl.
New York, NY 10168
Phone: (212)661-5335
Fax: (212)697-7232

★3024★ American Heart Association
New York State Affiliate
100 Northern Concourse
North Syracuse, NY 13212
Phone: (315)454-8166
Fax: (315)454-8778

North Carolina

★3025★ American Heart Association
North Carolina Affiliate
300 Silver Cedar Ct.
Chapel Hill, NC 27515
Phone: (919)968-4453
Fax: (919)968-7229

North Dakota

★3026★ American Heart Association
Dakota Affiliate
1005 12th Ave. SE
Jamestown, ND 58401-1287
Phone: (701)252-5122
Fax: (701)251-2092

Ohio

★ 3027 ★ American Heart Association
Northeast Ohio Affiliate
1689 E. 115th St.
Cleveland, OH 44106
Phone: (216)791-7500
Fax: (216)791-5202

★ 3028 ★ American Heart Association
Ohio Affiliate
5455 N. High St.
Columbus, OH 43216
Phone: (614)848-6676
Fax: (614)848-4227

Oklahoma

★ 3029 ★ American Heart Association
Oklahoma Affiliate
3545 NW 58th St., Ste. 400C
Oklahoma City, OK 73112
Phone: (405)942-2444
Fax: (405)942-6616

Oregon

★ 3030 ★ American Heart Association
Oregon Affiliate
1425 NE Irving, No. 100
Portland, OR 97232-4201
Phone: (503)233-0100
Fax: (503)233-4464

Pennsylvania

★ 3031 ★ American Heart Association
Pennsylvania Affiliate
1019 Mumma Rd.
PO Box 8835
Camp Hill, PA 17011-8835
Phone: (717)975-4800
Fax: (717)975-5597

★ 3032 ★ American Heart Association
Southeastern Pennsylvania Affiliate
625 West Ridge Pike, Bldg. A, Ste. 100
Conshohocken, PA 19428
Phone: (610)940-9540
Fax: (610)940-9541

Puerto Rico

★ 3033 ★ Puerto Rico Heart Association
Cabo Alverio 554
Hato Rey, PR 00995
Phone: (809)751-6569
Fax: (809)250-0281

Rhode Island

★ 3034 ★ American Heart Association
Rhode Island Affiliate
40 Broad St.
Pawtucket, RI 02860
Phone: (401)728-5300
Fax: (401)728-5376

South Carolina

★ 3035 ★ American Heart Association
South Carolina Affiliate
400 Percival Rd.
Columbia, SC 29260
Phone: (803)738-9540
Fax: (803)787-0804

Tennessee

★ 3036 ★ American Heart Association
Tennessee Affiliate
1200 Division St., Ste. 201
Nashville, TN 37203
Phone: (615)726-0108
Fax: (615)242-9727

Texas

★ 3037 ★ American Heart Association
Texas Affiliate
1700 Rutherford Ln.
Austin, TX 78754
Phone: (512)836-7220
Fax: (512)832-5880

Utah

★ 3038 ★ American Heart Association
Utah Affiliate
645 East 400 South
Salt Lake City, UT 84102
Phone: (801)322-5601
Fax: (801)364-6732

Vermont

★ 3039 ★ American Heart Association
Vermont Affiliate
12 Hurricane Ln.
PO Box 485
Williston, VT 05495
Phone: (802)878-7700
Fax: (802)878-7850

Virginia

★ 3040 ★ American Heart Association
Virginia Affiliate
4217 Park Place Ct.
Glen Allen, VA 23060
Phone: (804)747-8334
Fax: (804)346-8567

Washington

★ 3041 ★ American Heart Association
Washington Affiliate
4414 Woodland Park Ave. N.
Seattle, WA 98103
Phone: (206)632-6881
Fax: (206)632-8478

West Virginia

★ 3042 ★ American Heart Association
West Virginia Affiliate
211 35th St. SE
Charleston, WV 25304
Phone: (304)346-5381
Fax: (304)346-5560

Wisconsin

★ 3043 ★ American Heart Association
Wisconsin Affiliate
795 Van Buren St. N.
Milwaukee, WI 53202
Phone: (414)271-9999
Fax: (414)271-3299

Wyoming

★ 3044 ★ American Heart Association
Wyoming Affiliate
200 W. 17th St., Ste. 10
Cheyenne, WY 82001
Phone: (307)632-1746
Fax: (307)634-7292

Chapter 13
Child Abuse & Family Violence

Federal Government Agencies

★3045★ **U.S. Department of Health and Human Services**
Administration for Children and Families (ACF)
National Center on Child Abuse and Neglect (ACYF)
330 C St. SW
Washington, DC 20201
Phone: (202)205-8646

Description: The National Center on Child Abuse and Neglect was established to compile, analyze, publish, and disseminate information on research, programs, and training materials addressing the identification, prevention, and treatment of child and spouse abuse and neglect. NCCAN also funds research, demonstration, and service improvement projects; provides technical assistance; and makes grants directly to states and territories to help improve their child and spouse protective services systems.

Foundations & Other Funding Organizations

Private Foundations

Ross Foundation
See: Entry 467

Skillman Foundation
See: Entry 492

William Penn Foundation
See: Entry 551

Corporate Foundations

Intelligent Electronics Foundation
See: Entry 3148

National & International Organizations

★3046★ **Batterers Anonymous (BA)**
8485 Tamarind, Ste. D
Fontana, CA 92335
Phone: (714)355-1100
Jerry M. Goffman, Ph.D., Founder

Founded: 1980. **Local Groups:** 31. **Description:** Selfhelp program designed to rehabilitate men who are abusive toward women. Aims to achieve the complete elimination of physical and emotional abuse and seeks positive alternatives to abusive behavior. Batterers attend weekly informal meeting with other persons who have similar difficulties. Each group is aided by a professional or paraprofessional sponsor and a group leader. A "Buddy System" is encouraged to provide reassurance and support to the batterer. It is believed that through increased awareness of their problem, batterers are better able to cope with abuse issues and develop skills for handling stress. **Publications:** *National Directory*, annual. Directory. • *Self-Help Counseling for Men Who Batter Women*. Also publishes handbook for members.

★3047★ **Child Abuse Institute of Research (CAIR)**
PO Box 1217
Cincinnati, OH 45201
Lou Torok, Founder & Dir.

Founded: 1988. **Members:** 1,000. **Description:** Volunteers and professionals working to improve the quality of life for children by focusing on the problems of child abuse. Promotes education and research into the cause and prevention of child abuse. Works to identify exemplary counseling programs; plans to offer counseling programs to help convicted child abusers recognize their problem and stop the abusive behavior. Believes children should be given the opportunity for a safe and happy childhood in which they can develop to their fullest potential as good citizens. Compiles statistics; operates speakers' bureau. **Publications:** *Child Abuse Institute*, quarterly. Pamphlet. Contains research information, statistics, and self-help resources. *Price:* Free.

★3048★ **Child Abuse Listening and Mediation (CALM)**
PO Box 90754
Santa Barbara, CA 93190-0754
Phone: (805)965-2376
Anna M. Kokotovic, Ph.D., Contact

Founded: 1970. **Description:** Social service program to prevent and treat child sexual abuse, physical abuse, and emotional abuse, and offer early intervention for stressed families. Objective is to reach parents "who feel that they cannot cope with their problems and frustrations and who may be in danger of taking out their feelings against their children." Offers referrals to other organizations and resources. Provides short- and long-term counseling regarding parent-child problems. CALM's volunteers are available to go into the home as family aides, to act as "compassionate listeners and friendly neighbors" and help in situations of crisis. Provides emergency child care for parents under stress. Maintains speakers' bureau and resource library on the batte red child syndrome, child sexual abuse, and parenting problems. Conducts program of public information and education and an in-school education program for students, parents, and teachers on prevention and recognition of child maltreatment. Other services include: individual, marital, and family counseling for high risk families and families involved in physical, emotional, or sexual abuse and neglect; support treatment groups for parents of sexually abused children, for adults who were molested as children, and for children sexually abused within the family; parent support groups focusing on parent education and child development and improving parent/child interaction. Conducts weekly Parental Support Groups (one bilingual). Offers counseling groups for adult offenders legally ordered to seek counseling. **Publications:** Bibliography. Covers battered child syndrome, child sexual abuse, and a report of CALM's work. • *CALM-WORD*, quarterly. Newsletter. • *Chronicle*, monthly. Newsletter. **Formerly:** Children's Protective Society.

★3049★ **Child Welfare League of America (CWLA)**
440 1st St. NW, Ste. 310
Washington, DC 20001
Phone: (202)638-2952
Fax: (202)638-4004
David S. Liederman, Exec.Dir.

Founded: 1920. **Members:** 760. **Regional Groups:** 5. **Description:** Works to improve care and services for abused, dependent, or neglected children, youth, and their families. Maintains the Child Welfare League of America Children's Campaign, a grass roots advocacy network of individuals committed to acting on behalf of children. Provides consultation; conducts research; maintains information service; develops standards for child welfare practice; administers special projects. **Publications:** Books. • *Child Welfare*, bimonthly. Journal. Provides articles for policy makers, researchers, and professionals who work with children. *Price:* $35/year for students; $55/year for individuals; $70/year for institutions. • *Child Welfare League of America-Children's Monitor*, 10/year. Newsletter. Presents information on children's policy decisions at the federal level. *Price:* Free to member agencies; $55/year for nonmembers. • *Children's Voice*, quarterly. Magazine. Reports on program and policy developments in child welfare services. Covers congressional, federal, and state news, and contains articles. *Price:* Included in membership dues; $35/year for individual nonmembers; $50/year for institutional nonmembers. • *CWLA Directory of Member Agencies*, biennial. Directory. Includes calendar of events. *Price:* Included in membership dues; $14 for nonmembers. • Monographs. • *Washington Social Legislation Bulletin*, semimonthly. Newsletter. Provides review of federal social legislation and the activities of federal agencies affecting children, the elderly, the disabled, and delinquents. *Price:* Included in membership dues; $65/year for nonmembers.

★3050★ **Childhelp U.S.A., Inc. (CUI)**
6463 Independence Ave.
Woodland Hills, CA 91370
Phone: (818)347-7280
Fax: (818)593-3257
Sara O'Meara, Bd.Chm.

Founded: 1959. **Members:** 1,100. **State Groups:** 6. **Description:** Works toward research, prevention, and treatment of child abuse. Has established the Village of Childhelp, a residential center devoted to the care and treatment of abused and neglected children. Maintains an aftercare program utilizing professional counseling services and therapeutic foster homes. Operates group homes with professional counseling services. Promotes public awareness of child abuse issues via media campaigns, interviews, and panel discussions. Conducts research; operates speakers' bureau; maintains library. Member of International Alliance on Child Abuse and Neglect, National Council on Child Abuse and Family Violence, and Child Welfare League of America. **Publications:** *Child Abuse and You.* • *Child Help Newsletter*, periodic. Newsletter. • *Report*, 3/year. Newsletter. **Also Known As:** Childhelp U.S.A./International. **Formerly:** Children's Village U.S.A.; International Orphans.

★3051★ **Daughters and Sons United (DSU)**
c/o Giarretto Institute
232 E. Gish Rd., 1st Fl.
San Jose, CA 95112
Phone: (408)453-7616
Fax: (408)453-9064
Brian R. Abbott, Ph.D., Exec.Dir.

Founded: 1972. **Members:** 120. **Local Groups:** 1. **Description:** Counseling program for sexually abused children and their families. Focuses on intra-familial child molestation cases (incest). Self-help program designed to increase leadership and self-assertiveness skills and decrease social isolation and shame for victims of abuse.

★3052★ **Family Therapy Network (FTN)**
7705 13th St. NW
Washington, DC 20012
Phone: (202)829-2452
Fax: (202)726-7983
Richard Simon, Dir.

Founded: 1976. **Members:** 65,000. **Description:** Promotes the exchange of ideas and information among family therapists. **Publications:** *Family Therapy Networker*, bimonthly. Magazine. Contains case studies, calendar of events, listing of employment opportunities, and book and movie reviews. *Price:* $22/year for individuals; $28 outside U.S.

★3053★ **Illusion Theater (IT)**
528 Hennepin Ave., Ste. 704
Minneapolis, MN 55403
Phone: (612)339-4944
Fax: (612)337-8042
Michael H. Robins, Exec. Producing Dir.

Founded: 1974. **Regional Groups:** 5. **State Groups:** 5. **Description:** Educational and theatrical organization known for its work in child sexual abuse prevention education; participants include professionals in theatre, human services, and arts administration. Works to research, create, perform, and distribute new collaborative theatrical productions that address major social issues such as sexual abuse, interpersonal violence, and AIDS. Creates prevention education public service announcements. Maintains speakers' bureau; compiles statistics. **Publications:** Brochures. • *Licensing Newsletter*, semiannual. Newsletter. • *No Easy Answers*. Video. • *No Easy Answers Curriculum.* Adolescent sexual abuse prevention curriculum. • *Sponsor Information Packet, Licensing Summary and Procedures.* • *Touch Video*. Video. • Video. • Video.

★3054★ **Incest Survivors Anonymous**
PO Box 17245
Long Beach, CA 90807-7245

Founded: 1980. **Description:** A spiritually-based self-help, mutual-help recovery program for men, women, and teens who are victims of incest or other forms of sexual abuse. Applies the twelve-step and twelve-tradition programs of Alcoholics Anonymous World Service. Does not accept initiators of sexual abuse, professionals or students who are not victims, and victims who have become perpetrators. **Publications:** *I.S.A. Talks to Friends, Survivors, and Professionals.* Price: $4. • *The Nightmare of Incest.* Price: $4. • *Welcome to the Newcomer.* 4.

★3055★ **Incest Survivors Resource Network, International (ISRNI)**
PO Box 7375
Las Cruces, NM 88006
Phone: (505)521-4260
Anne-Marie Eriksson, Pres.

Founded: 1983. **Description:** Serves as a Quaker witness educational resource dedicated to the primary prevention of incest. Functions as a consultant and participates in committees of national and international organizations. Incest survivors from various professions offer awareness on the intergenerational transmission of verbal and physical violence associated with incest. Offers awareness of Post-traumatic Stress Disorder (PTSD) as a component of intergenerational transmission of verbal and physical violence, especially regarding overt and emotional incest. Through programs such as Parents United, seeks resolution of incest trauma via education, professional therapeutic intervention, and selfhelp. Encourages the local development of Parents United chapters. Members of Friends Association for Higher Education, International Peace Research Association, National Committee for Prevention of Child Abuse, National Organization for Victim Assistance, and World Federation for Mental Health.

★3056★ **International Society for Prevention of Child Abuse and Neglect (ISPCAN)**
332 S. Michigan Ave., Ste. 1600
Chicago, IL 60604
Phone: (312)663-3520
Fax: (312)939-8962
Nancy Peddle, Exec.Dir.

Founded: 1977. **Members:** 2,125. **Description:** Individuals and organizations concerned with alleviating the problems of child abuse including neglect and sexual abuse. Encourages discussion on the subject of child abuse and provides a forum for sharing knowledge and experience. **Publications:** *Child Abuse and Neglect: The International Journal*, monthly. Journal. Covers all aspects of child abuse and neglect including sexual abuse, with special emphasis on prevention and treatment. *Price:* Included in membership dues.

Molesters Anonymous (M.AN)
See: Entry 11701

★3057★ **National Center for Assault Prevention**
606 Delsea Dr.
Sewell, NJ 08080
Phone: (609)582-7000
Free: 800-258-3189
Fax: (609)582-3588
Pat Stanislaski, Exec.Dir.

Founded: 1985. **Regional Groups:** 200. **Description:** Purpose is to prevent interpersonal violence against vulnerable populations through education, prevention training, and research. Provides services to children aged two and one half years through adolescence, children and adults with mental retardation and developmental disabilities, and older citizens. Conducts research on the causes, consequences, and prevention of interpersonal violence. Provides three-day training sessions in the Child Assault

Prevention model; sponsors workshops. Compiles statistics; operates speakers' bureau. **Publications:** *Strategies for Free Children.* Manual. For training. **Formerly:** National Assault Prevention Center.

★ 3058 ★ National Clearinghouse on Child Abuse and Neglect Information (NCCANI)
PO Box 1182
Washington, DC 20013-1182
Phone: (703)385-7565
Free: 800-394-3366
Fax: (703)385-3206
Caroline Hughes, Project Dir.

Founded: 1975. **Description:** A government-sponsored clearinghouse that is a support service of the National Center on Child Abuse and Neglect. Facilitates research by compiling and disseminating information and materials on child abuse and neglect. Provides information to states and communities wishing to develop programs and activities related to the prevention, identification, and treatment of child abuse and neglect. **Publications:** Bibliographies. • Brochures. • Catalogs. • Manuals. • Pamphlets. • Reports. **Formerly:** (1994) Clearinghouse on Child Abuse and Neglect Information.

★ 3059 ★ National Coalition Against Domestic Violence (NCADV)
PO Box 18749
Denver, CO 80218
Phone: (303)839-1852
Fax: (303)831-9251
Rita Smith, Coord.

Founded: 1978. **Members:** 1,300. **State Groups:** 56. **Local Groups:** 2000. **Description:** Grass roots coalition of battered women's service organizations and shelters. Supplies technical assistance and makes referrals on issues of domestic violence. Provides training personnel; offers child advocacy training. Maintains speakers' bureau. Compiles statistics. **Publications:** *Alert,* 3-6/year. *Price:* Included in membership dues. • *Guidelines for Mental Health Practitioners in Domestic Violence Cases.* • *Naming the Violence: Speaking Out About Lesbian Battering.* • *National Coalition Against Domestic Violence--Voice,* quarterly. Newsletter. *Price:* Included in membership dues. • *National Directory of Domestic Violence Programs,* periodic. Directory. • *Rural Task Force Resource Packet.*

★ 3060 ★ National Committee for Prevention of Child Abuse (NCPCA)
332 S. Michigan Ave., Ste. 1600
Chicago, IL 60604-4357
Phone: (312)663-3520
Fax: (312)939-8962
Anne Harris Cohn Donnelly, Exec.Dir.

Founded: 1972. **State Groups:** 67. **Description:** Seeks to stimulate greater public awareness of the incidence, origins, nature, and effects of child abuse. Serves as a national advocate to prevent the neglect and physical, sexual, and emotional abuse of children. Facilitates communication about program activities, public policy, and research related to the prevention of child abuse. Fosters greater cooperation between existing and developing resources in the

area of prevention. Operates the National Center on Child Abuse Prevention Research; conducts annual national media campaigns and child abuse prevention programs. Provides training and technical assistance. **Publications:** Booklets. • Monographs. • *Monthly Memorandum,* monthly. • Pamphlets. **Formerly:** (1974) Family Life Achievement Center.

★ 3061 ★ National Council on Child Abuse and Family Violence (NCCAFV)
1155 Connecticut Ave. NW, Ste. 400
Washington, DC 20036
Phone: (202)429-6695
Free: 800-222-2000
Fax: (818)914-3616
Alan Davis, Pres.

Founded: 1984. **Description:** Supports community-based prevention and treatment programs that provide assistance to children, women, the elderly, and families who are victims of abuse and violence. Is concerned with the cyclical and intergenerational nature of family violence and abuse. Seeks to increase public awareness of family violence and promote private sector financial support for prevention and treatment programs. Collaborates with similar organizations to form an informal network; organized National Alliance on Family Violence. Provides technical assistance program to aid community-based organizations in obtaining nonfederal funding. Collects and disseminates information regarding child abuse, domestic violence, and elder abuse. **Publications:** Brochures. • *IN-FORUM,* periodic. Newsletter. **Also Known As:** American Campaign for Prevention of Child Abuse and Family Violence.

★ 3062 ★ Parents Anonymous (PA)
675 W. Foothill Blvd., Ste. 220
Claremont, CA 91711-3416
Phone: (909)621-6184
Fax: (909)625-6304
Linda Faber, Pres.

Founded: 1970. **Regional Groups:** 4. **State Groups:** 31. **Local Groups:** 1200. **Description:** Works for the prevention and treatment of child abuse. Believes that "parenting falls on a continuum and that parents should not be labeled as 'good,' 'bad,' 'abusive,' or 'non-abusive,' but rather that all parents will experience problems at some time in their parenting careers, and all parents are deserving of help." The treatment model blends traditional support groups with selfhelp. Support groups encourage peer leadership, and include a volunteer professional sponsor who attends all meetings. Maintains speakers' bureau; operates educational programs. **Publications:** *Insider,* quarterly. Newsletter. **Formerly:** (1971) Mothers Anonymous.

★ 3063 ★ Parents United International (PU)
615 15th St.
Modesto, CA 95354-2510
Phone: (408)453-7616
Fax: (408)453-9064
Henry Giarretto, Ph.D., Exec.Dir.

Founded: 1972. **Members:** 6,000. **Regional Groups:** 4. **Description:** Individuals and families who have experienced child sexual molestation. Works to provide assistance to families affected by incest and other types of child sexual

abuse by providing crisis and long-term support. Provides weekly professional counseling and conducts self-help type therapy groups; promotes self-awareness and responsibility to self, family, and community. Compiles information and arranges medical, vocational, and legal counseling for families. Encourages the affected child to meet with other children in self-help sessions through Daughters and Sons United for children ages five to 18, and Adults Molested as Children United. Works in conjunction with the Child Sexual Abuse Treatment Program, which provides coordination and professional counseling support. Conducts educational programs; maintains speakers' bureau. **Publications:** *The PUN,* quarterly. Newsletter. Contains calendar of events. *Price:* $10/year. Also distributes tapes and printed materials. **Formerly:** Parents United.

★ 3064 ★ Paul and Lisa (P&L)
PO Box 348
Westbrook, CT 06498
Phone: (203)399-5338
Susan Breault, Asst. Program Dir.

Founded: 1980. **State Groups:** 2. **Description:** Serves as national program for the prevention and rehabilitation of sexually abused and exploited children. Organization's name is derived from St. Paul's church in Westbrook, CT which gave seed money to the program, and from Lisa, a young girl who died after being sexually abused. Believes that "sexual abuse and exploitation of children is a silent but virulent epidemic that must be brought to the attention of the public"; educates children, the public, and professionals in the dangers of sexual abuse and the problems of sexual abuse in children. Provides training for professionals through conferences, seminars, and workshops. Sponsors educational presentations to schools and private and civic clubs, religious organizations, business and industry associations, and concerned citizen action groups; presentations for children are designed to show children proper ways to cope with sexual advances by adults. Works with local, state, and federal officials in promoting laws dealing with the sexual abuse and exploitation of children. Is planning to open a treatment center with professionals specially trained to address problems faced by sexually abused children. Maintains library of brochures, pamphlets, and films. **Publications:** *The P&L Connection,* quarterly. Newsletter. Includes calendar of events and profiles of volunteer activities. *Price:* Free. **Formerly:** (1982) Paul and Lisa Foundation.

People Against Rape (PAR)
See: Entry 3283

★ 3065 ★ Society's League Against Molestation (SLAM)
c/o Women Against Rape/Childwatch
PO Box 346
Collingswood, NJ 08108
Phone: (609)858-7800
Fax: (609)858-7063
Rita Unger, Dir.

Founded: 1980. **Members:** 100,000. **Local Groups:** 100. **Description:** Works to: prevent sexual abuse and exploitation of children; educate the public through media programs and speeches about child molestation; counsel and assist victims and their families. Researches the social, psychological, and legal aspects of child molestation; monitors court cases and verdicts and suggests introduction of stricter legislation. Offers tips for prevention and awareness of child molestation. **Publications:** *Guardian*, periodic. Newsletter. Also publishes brochures and coloring books. **Formerly:** (1982) Concerned Citizens for Stronger Legislation Against Molesters.

★3066★ **Survivors of Incest Anonymous (SIA)**
PO Box 26870
Baltimore, MD 21212
Phone: (410)433-2365
Linda L. Davis, Public Info. Officer

Founded: 1982. **Members:** 100,000. **Local Groups:** 800. **Description:** Serves as a support group and selfhelp recovery program for any adult who was a victim of sexual abuse as a child. Follows a 12-step approach, modeled after the program espoused by Alcoholics Anonymous World Services, to assist members in their recovery. Sponsors educational programs; maintains speakers' bureau. **Publications:** Directory, bimonthly. • *Information Packet*. Includes 42 of the association's publications. *Price:* $29.75 plus shipping and handling. • *S.I.A. World Service Bulletin*, bimonthly. Bulletin. *Price:* $12.50/year. • *The Slogans of S.I.A.*. *Price:* $1.50 plus shipping and handling. • *Survivors of Incest Anonymous: Survivors Reaching Out to Survivors*. Brochure. Provides the group's definition of incest; explains the purpose of the group. • *The Twelve Steps of S.I.A.*. • *World Service Directory of S.I.A. Meetings*. Directory. *Price:* $1 plus shipping and handling.

★3067★ **Voices in Action**
PO Box 148309
Chicago, IL 60614
Phone: (312)327-1500
Free: 800-7-VOICE-A
Nina Corwin, Pres.

Founded: 1980. **Members:** 1,300. **Description:** Adult survivors of incest and childhood sexual abuse; relatives, concerned citizens, and human service, health care and legal professionals working to eradicate the incidence and alleviate the effects of incest and sexual abuse of children. Purpose is to provide a communication and peer support network for survivors of incest and those affected by it. Seeks to increase public understanding of the prevalence of incest, its consequences, and the possibility of prevention through the dissemination of information. Serves as liaison among survivors, medical and legal professionals, and social service agencies. Advocates the development of outreach, public education, and therapy programs; provides selfhelp and volunteer advocacy. Maintains speakers' bureau. Compiles statistics. Sponsors "rap" group leadership training and special interest groups. **Publications:** *The Chorus*, bimonthly. Newsletter. *Price:* $20. • *How to Choose a Therapist*. Pamphlet. • *How to Confront Your Perpetrator: Dead of Alive, What Helps?*. Pamphlet. • *How to File a Civil Suit for Sexual Abuse*. • *How to Organize Your*

Group. • *Solos*. Creative anthology. • *Survival Kits I and II*. • *Surviving Social Situations*. **Formerly:** (1982) Victims of Incest Concerned Effort; (1984) Victims of Incest Can Emerge; (1985) Victims of Incest Can Emerge Survivors.

Women in Crisis (WIC)
See: Entry 1534

Women in Transition (WIT)
See: Entry 7528

Research Centers

Center on Children and the Law
See: Entry 7197

★3068★ **Domestic Abuse Project**
Evaluation and Research Unit
204 W. Franklin Ave.
Minneapolis, MN 55404
Phone: (612)874-7063
Fax: (612)874-8445
Jeffrey L. Edleson, Ph.D., Dir.

Research Activities and Fields: Evaluation of social service and criminal justice interventions in cases of domestic violence, particularly adult-to-adult abuse in intimate relationships. **Publications:** *DAP Research Update* (annually). **E-mail Address:** magd@maroon.tc.umn.edu.

Emanuel Research Center
See: Entry 8365

★3069★ **Miami University**
Family and Child Studies Center
109 McGuffey Hall
Oxford, OH 45056
Phone: (513)529-5734
Fax: (513)529-7270
Tim Brubaker, Dir.

Research Activities and Fields: Family and children, including projects on families with disabilities, day-care, family violence, child abuse, cross-cultural roles, marriage, and grandparenthood. **E-mail Address:** brubaker@msmail.muohio.edu.

★3070★ **Oregon Social Learning Center, Inc.**
207 E. 5th Ave., Ste. 202
Eugene, OR 97401
Phone: (503)485-2711
Fax: (503)485-7087
Dr. Gerald R. Patterson, Senior Research Scientist

Research Activities and Fields: Family aggression, child abuse, antisocial behavior, resistance in therapy, longitudinal studies on juvenile delinquency, development of delinquent lifestyles, adolescent drug abuse, multiple offending youths, treatment programs for multiple offending youths, specialized foster homes, early gender identity, effects of fathering, and prevention and intervention processes. **Formerly:** Evaluation Research Group, Inc. (1984).

Portland State University
Regional Research Institute for Human Services
See: Entry 11873

★3071★ **State University of New York at Buffalo**
Research Center for Children and Youth
231 Park Hall
Buffalo, NY 14260
Phone: (716)636-3661
Fax: (716)636-2893
Dr. Murray Levine, Codirector

Research Activities and Fields: Child abuse, delinquency, foster care, adolescent substance abuse, children as witnesses, and corporal punishment. **Formerly:** Center for Research on Children and Youth.

★3072★ **U.S. Department of Health and Human Services**
Administration for Children and Families
National Center on Child Abuse and Neglect
PO Box 1182
Washington, DC 20013
Phone: (202)245-0910
David W. Lloyd, Director

Research Activities and Fields: Conducts research; collects, analyzes, and disseminates information; provides assistance to States and communities in developing programs and activities related to the prevention, identification, and treatment of child abuse and neglect; coordinates Federal efforts to combat child maltreatment through an Inter-Agency Task Force on Child Abuse and Neglect. Center awards grants for research in priority areas.

University of California at Berkeley
Berkeley Child Welfare Research Center
See: Entry 11875

★3073★ **University of Colorado**
C. Henry Kempe National Center for the Prevention and Treatment of Child Abuse and Neglect
1205 Oneida St.
Denver, CO 80220
Phone: (303)321-3963
Fax: (303)329-3523
David Olds, Ph.D., Dir.

Research Activities and Fields: Child abuse and neglect, including studies of the primary prevention of child abuse and neglect, longitudinal follow-up of abused children, maternal-infant interactions, safety and day care and other placements, and juvenile sexual offenders. **Formerly:** National Center for the Prevention and Treatment of Child Abuse and Neglect (1984).

University of Montreal
Mental Disorders and Crime Research Group
See: Entry 7676

★3074★ University of New Hampshire Family Research Laboratory
126 Horton Social Science Center
Durham, NH 03824
Phone: (603)862-1888
Fax: (603)862-1122
Dr. Murray A. Straus, Codirector
Research Activities and Fields: Serves as the administrative location for the Family Violence Research Program and other projects, including a program of research on Family Measurement Techniques, and the State and the Regional Indicators Archive. Projects include a national survey of family violence, abuse of elderly family members, parents who never spank, rape in American states and regions, treatment of batterers, characteristics of fathers who commit incest, incidence of missing children, and professional knowledge and attitudes about sexual abuse. **E-mail Address:** mas2@christa.unh.edu.

University of Quebec at Montreal Laboratory of Research in Human and Social Ecology
See: Entry 11001

★3075★ University of Texas at Austin Institute of Human Development and Family Studies
2300 Main Bldg.
Austin, TX 78712
Phone: (512)471-1017
Fax: (512)471-5935
Ira Iscoe, Ph.D., Dir.
Research Activities and Fields: Child policy, child abuse and family violence, child development, and life span development. **Publications:** Newsletter (quarterly). **E-mail Address:** hdinstitute@mail.utexas.edu.

Women's Research Centre
See: Entry 9723

State & Regional Organizations

Domestic Violence

The following are state affiliates of the National Coalition Against Domestic Violence, PO Box 18749, Denver, CO 80218, (303) 839-1852 (national office); PO Box 34103, Washington, DC 20043, (202) 638-6388 (membership/public policy office).

Alabama

★3076★ Alabama Coalition Against Domestic Violence
PO Box 4762
Montgomery, AL 36101
Phone: (334)832-4842
Fax: (334)832-4803

Alaska

★3077★ Alaska Network on Domestic Violence and Sexual Assault
130 Seward St., Rm. 501
Juneau, AK 99801
Phone: (907)586-3650
Fax: (907)463-4493

Arizona

★3078★ Arizona Coalition Against Domestic Violence
100 W. Camelback, No. 109
Phoenix, AZ 85013
Phone: (602)279-2900
Free: 800-782-6400
Fax: (602)279-2980

Arkansas

★3079★ Arkansas Coalition Against Domestic Violence
523 S. Louisiana, Ste. 230
Little Rock, AR 72201
Phone: (501)399-9486
Fax: (501)371-0450

California

★3080★ California Alliance Against Domestic Violence
619 13th St., Ste. I
Modesto, CA 95354
Phone: (209)524-1888
Fax: (209)524-2045

Colorado

★3081★ Colorado Domestic Violence Coalition
PO Box 18902
Denver, CO 80218
Phone: (303)573-9018
Fax: (303)573-9023

Connecticut

★3082★ Connecticut Coalition Against Domestic Violence
135 Broad St.
Hartford, CT 06105
Phone: (203)524-5890
Fax: (203)249-1408

Delaware

★3083★ Delaware Coalition Against Domestic Violence
PO Box 847
Wilmington, DE 19899
Phone: (302)658-2958
Fax: (302)658-2958

District of Columbia

★3084★ DC Coalition Against Domestic Violence
513 U St. NW
Washington, DC 20001
Phone: (202)783-5332
Fax: (202)347-2510

Florida

★3085★ Florida Coalition Against Domestic Violence
1521-A Killearn Center Blvd.
Tallahassee, FL 32308
Phone: (904)668-6862
Free: 800-500-1119
Fax: (904)668-0364

Georgia

★3086★ Georgia Advocates for Battered Women and Children
250 Georgia Ave. SE, Ste. 308
Atlanta, GA 30312
Phone: (404)524-3847
Free: 800-643-1212
Fax: (404)524-5959

Hawaii

★3087★ Hawaii State Committee on Family Violence
98-939 Moanalua Rd.
Aiea, HI 96701
Phone: (808)486-5072
Fax: (808)486-5169

Idaho

★3088★ Idaho Coalition Against Sexual and Domestic Violence
200 N. 4th, Ste. 10
Boise, ID 83702
Phone: (208)384-0419
Fax: (208)384-0419

Illinois

★3089★ Illinois Coalition Against Domestic Violence
730 E. Vine St., No. 109
Springfield, IL 62703
Phone: (217)789-2830
Free: 800-241-8456
Fax: (217)789-1939

Indiana

★3090★ Indiana Coalition Against Domestic Violence
2511 E. 46th St., Ste. N-3
Indianapolis, IN 46205
Phone: (317)543-3908
Free: 800-332-7385
Fax: (317)568-4045

Iowa

★3091★ **Iowa Coalition Against Domestic Violence**
1540 High St., No. 100
Des Moines, IA 50309-3123
Phone: (515)244-8028
Free: 800-942-0333
Fax: (515)244-7417

Kansas

★3092★ **Kansas Coalition Against Sexual and Domestic Violence**
820 SE Quincy, No. 416B
Topeka, KS 66612
Phone: (913)232-9784
Fax: (913)232-9937

Kentucky

★3093★ **Kentucky Domestic Violence Association**
PO Box 356
Frankfort, KY 40602
Phone: (502)875-4132
Fax: (502)875-4268

Louisiana

★3094★ **Louisiana Coalition Against Domestic Violence**
PO Box 3053
Hammond, LA 70404-3053
Phone: (504)542-4446
Free: 800-837-5400
Fax: (504)542-7661

Maine

★3095★ **Maine Coalition for Family Crisis Services**
359 Main St.
Bangor, ME 04402
Phone: (207)941-1194

Maryland

★3096★ **Maryland Network Against Domestic Violence**
11501 Georgia Ave., No. 403
Silver Spring, MD 20902
Phone: (301)942-0900
Free: 800-634-3577
Fax: (301)929-2589

Massachusetts

★3097★ **Massachusetts Coalition of Battered Women Service Groups**
210 Commercial St., 3rd Fl.
Boston, MA 02109
Phone: (617)248-0922
Fax: (617)248-0902

Michigan

★3098★ **Michigan Coalition Against Domestic Violence**
PO Box 16009
Lansing, MI 48901
Phone: (517)484-2924
Fax: (517)372-0024

Minnesota

★3099★ **Minnesota Coalition for Battered Women**
450 N. Syndicate St., Ste. 122
St. Paul, MN 55104
Phone: (612)646-6177
Free: 800-646-0994
Fax: (612)646-1527

Mississippi

★3100★ **Mississippi Coalition Against Domestic Violence**
PO Box 4703
Jackson, MS 39296-4703
Phone: (601)981-9196
Fax: (601)982-7372

Missouri

★3101★ **Missouri Coalition Against Domestic Violence**
331 Madison
Jefferson City, MO 65101
Phone: (314)634-4161
Fax: (314)636-3728

Montana

★3102★ **Montana Coalition Against Domestic Violence**
1236 N. 28th St., No. 103
Billings, MT 59101
Phone: (406)256-6334
Fax: (406)256-6334

Nebraska

★3103★ **Nebraska Domestic Violence and Sexual Assault Coalition**
315 S. 9th, No. 18
Lincoln, NE 68508
Phone: (402)476-6256

Nevada

★3104★ **Nevada Network Against Domestic Violence**
2100 Capurro Way, Ste. E
Sparks, NV 89431
Phone: (702)358-1171
Free: 800-500-1556
Fax: (702)358-0546

New Hampshire

★3105★ **New Hampshire Coalition Against Domestic and Sexual Violence**
PO Box 353
Concord, NH 03302-0353
Phone: (603)224-8893
Free: 800-852-3388
Fax: (603)228-6096

New Jersey

★3106★ **New Jersey Coalition for Battered Women**
2620 Whitehorse/Hamilton Square Rd.
Trenton, NJ 08690-2718
Phone: (609)584-8107
Free: 800-572-7233
Fax: (609)584-9750

New Mexico

★3107★ **New Mexico State Coalition Against Domestic Violence**
PO Box 25363
Albuquerque, NM 87125
Phone: (505)246-9240
Free: 800-773-3645
Fax: (505)246-9434

New York

★3108★ **New York State Coalition Against Domestic Violence**
Women's Bldg.
79 Central Ave.
Albany, NY 12206
Phone: (518)432-4864
Free: 800-942-6906
Fax: (518)432-4864

North Carolina

★3109★ **North Carolina Coalition Against Domestic Violence**
PO Box 51875
Durham, NC 27717-1875
Phone: (919)956-9124
Fax: (919)682-4629

North Dakota

★3110★ **North Dakota Council on Abused Women's Services**
418 E. Rosser Ave., Ste. 320
Bismarck, ND 58501
Phone: (701)255-6240
Free: 800-472-2911
Fax: (701)255-1904

Ohio

★3111★ **Ohio Domestic Violence Network**
4041 N. High St., No. 101
Columbus, OH 43214
Phone: (614)784-0023
Free: 800-934-9840
Fax: (614)784-0033

Oklahoma

★3112★ **Oklahoma Coalition on Domestic Violence and Sexual Assault**
2200 Classen Blvd., No. 610
Oklahoma City, OK 73106
Phone: (405)557-1210
Free: 800-522-9054
Fax: (405)557-1296

Oregon

★3113★ **Oregon Coalition Against Domestic and Sexual Violence**
520 NW Davis, Ste. 310
Portland, OR 97209
Phone: (503)223-7411
Fax: (503)223-7490

Pennsylvania

★3114★ **Pennsylvania Coalition Against Domestic Violence**
6400 Flank Dr., No. 1300
Harrisburg, PA 17112
Phone: (717)545-6400
Free: 800-932-4632
Fax: (717)545-9456

Puerto Rico

★3115★ **Romision para los Asuntos de la Mujer**
Calle San Francisco, 151-153
Viejo San Juan
Bayamon, PR 00905
Phone: (809)722-2907
Fax: (809)723-3611

Rhode Island

★3116★ **Rhode Island Council on Domestic Violence**
422 Post Rd., No. 104
Warwick, RI 02888
Phone: (401)467-9940
Free: 800-494-8100
Fax: (401)467-9943

South Carolina

★3117★ **South Carolina Coalition Against Domestic Violence and Sexual Assault**
PO Box 7776
Columbia, SC 29202-7776
Phone: (803)254-3699
Free: 800-260-9293
Fax: (803)583-9611

South Dakota

★3118★ **South Dakota Coalition Against Domestic Violence and Sexual Assault**
3220 S. Hwy. 281
Aberdeen, SD 57401
Phone: (605)225-5122

Tennessee

★3119★ **Tennessee Task Force Against Domestic Violence**
PO Box 120972
Nashville, TN 37212-0972
Phone: (615)386-9406
Free: 800-356-6767
Fax: (615)383-2967

Texas

★3120★ **Texas Council on Family Violence**
8701 N. Mopac, No. 450
Austin, TX 78759
Phone: (512)794-1133
Fax: (512)794-1199

Utah

★3121★ **Utah Domestic Violence Advisory Council**
120 North 200 West, 2nd Fl.
Salt Lake City, UT 84145
Phone: (801)538-4100
Fax: (801)538-3993

Vermont

★3122★ **Vermont Network Against Domestic Violence and Sexual Assault**
PO Box 405
Montpelier, VT 05601
Phone: (802)223-1302
Fax: (802)223-3751

Virgin Islands

★3123★ **Women's Coalition of St. Croix**
PO Box 2734
Christiansted
St. Croix, VI 00822
Phone: (809)773-9272
Fax: (809)773-9062

★3124★ **Women's Resource Center**
8 Kongens Gade
St. Thomas, VI 00802
Phone: (809)776-3966

Virginia

★3125★ **Virginians Against Domestic Violence**
2850 Sandy Bay Rd., No. 101
Williamsburg, VA 23185
Phone: (804)221-0990
Free: 800-838-8238
Fax: (804)229-1553

Washington

★3126★ **Washington State Coalition Against Domestic Violence**
2101 4th Ave. E., No. 103
Olympia, WA 98506
Phone: (360)352-4029
Free: 800-562-6025
Fax: (360)352-4078

West Virginia

★3127★ **West Virginia Coalition Against Domestic Violence**
PO Box 85
181B Main St.
Sutton, WV 26601-0085
Phone: (304)765-2250
Fax: (304)765-5071

Wisconsin

★3128★ **Wisconsin Coalition Against Domestic Violence**
1400 E. Washington Ave., No. 103
Madison, WI 53703
Phone: (608)255-0539
Fax: (608)255-3560

Wyoming

★3129★ **Wyoming Coalition Against Domestic Violence and Sexual Assault**
341 E. E St., No. 135A
Casper, WY 82601
Phone: (307)266-4334
Free: 800-990-3877
Fax: (307)235-4796

Chapter 14
Child Health

Federal Government Agencies

★3130★ U.S. Department of Health and Human Services
National Institute of Child Health and Human Development
9000 Rockville Pike
Bethesda, MD 20892
Phone: (301)496-3454
Fax: (301)402-1104

Description: The Institute conducts and supports biomedical and behavioral research on child health and maternal health; on problems of human development, with special reference to mental retardation; and on family structure, the dynamics of human population, and the reproductive process. Information related to these research findings is disseminated to other researchers, medical practitioners, and the general public to improve the health of children and their families.

★3131★ U.S. Department of Health and Human Services
Public Health Service
Health Resources and Services Administration
Bureau of Maternal and Child Health
5600 Fishers Ln.
Rockville, MD 20857
Phone: (301)443-2170
Fax: (301)443-0695

Description: The Bureau develops, administers, directs, coordinates, monitors, and supports federal policy and programs pertaining to health care facilities; health care promotion of mothers and children; a national network of activities associated with organ donations, procurements, and transplantation; and activities related to AIDS.

Foundations & Other Funding Organizations

Private Foundations

★3132★ Alexander and Margaret Stewart Trust u/w/o Helen S. Devore
c/o First Union Bank, N.A., Trust Department
740 15th St., NW
Washington, DC 20005
Phone: (202)637-7887
Fax: (202)637-7923
Ruth C. Shaw, Secretary

Foundation Philosophy: The primary concern of the trust is the well-being of children. To this end, the trust makes funds available for the care of children, the enhancement of hospital facilities, and the treatment of pediatric illnesses. Related social services for the benefit of children are also funded, including programs for disabled and autistic children, and for those recovering from drug abuse. Priorities in the field of education include medical education and special education for children. **Giving Priorities:** In 1993, the foundation gave approximately 74% of its total contributions to health concerns, including its highest grant of $365,787 to Children's Hospital National Medical Center in Washington, DC. Social services received about 19%; religious organizations, 6%; and educational institutions received the remaining funds. **Typical Health-Related Recipients:** AIDS/HIV, Cancer, Children's Health/Hospitals, Eyes/Blindness, Family Planning, Health Organizations, Hospitals, Medical Education, Medical Rehabilitation, Mental Health, Nursing Services, People with Disabilities, Prenatal Health Issues, Speech & Hearing, Substance Abuse. **Geographic Distribution:** Primarily the Washington, DC, area.

★3133★ Annie E. Casey Foundation
701 St. Paul St.
Baltimore, MD 21202
Phone: (410)547-6600
Fax: (410)223-2956
Ralph Smith, Director, Planning & Development

Foundation Philosophy: The primary mission of the Annie E. Casey Foundation is to foster public policies and human service reforms that better meet the needs of today's vulnerable children and families. In pursuit of this goal, the foundation makes grants that help states, cities, and communities fashion more innovative, cost-effective responses to those needs. **Giving Priorities:** In 1993, the foundation gave approximately 80% of its contributions to social services. Health care received 8%; educational institutions, 7%; and civic affairs, 5%. **Typical Health-Related Recipients:** Children's Health/Hospitals, Family Planning, Health Organizations, Mental Health, Nutrition, People with Disabilities, Preventive Medicine/Wellness Organizations, Substance Abuse. **Geographic Distribution:** United States.

Anschutz Family Foundation
See: Entry 45

Benson and Edith Ford Fund
See: Entry 6333

★3134★ Carnegie Corporation of New York
437 Madison Ave.
New York, NY 10022
Phone: (212)371-3200
Dorothy Wills Knapp, Secretary

Foundation Philosophy: It is the corporation's policy to select a few broad subject areas on which to focus its financial resources over a period of several years. There are three such areas at the present time: education and healthy development of children and youth, including science education and education reform; strengthening human resources in developing countries; and preventing deadly conflict. Grants which do not fall into one of these three categories may be made under the corporation's special project grants. The first program, the education and healthy development of children and youth, is based on Carnegie Corporation's long-term interest in education and the concerns of the young. Within the early childhood program, special attention is paid to the health, development and education of children ages three and under, with the hopes of ensuring children's success in the transition to the early elementary grades. The young adolescents program seeks not only to improve the educational achievement and to reduce the health problems of young adoiescents, but also supports more comprehensive approaches to the prevention of adolescent health problems. **Giving Priorities:** In 1993, the corporation gave 45% of total funding to international affairs. Education received approximately 40% of total contributions. Social services received 7% of funding, including a $1,000,000 grant to Columbia University for support of the National Center for Children in Poverty. Civic concerns received 6% of funding. The remaining funds went to support the arts and humanities and health care. **Typical Health-Related Recipients:** Adolescent Health Issues, Children's Health/Hospitals, Clinics/Medical Centers, Family Planning, Health Organizations, Health Policy/Cost Containment, Medical Education, Medical Research, Mental Health, Prenatal Health Issues, Public Health, Substance Abuse. **Geographic Distribution:** National, many British Commonwealth nations, and Mexico.

Carrie Estelle Doheny Foundation
See: Entry 87

★3135★ Charles H. Hood Foundation
95 Berkeley St., Ste. 201
Boston, MA 02116
Phone: (617)695-9439
Fax: (617)451-0062
Raymond Considine, Secretary and Executive Director

Foundation Philosophy: The foundation is predominantly interested in supporting research projects concerned with child health in New England. Emphasis is placed on the initiation or furtherance of medical research and related projects undertaken by independent junior faculty in health-oriented tax-exempt institutions in New England, which contribute to a reduction of the health problems and needs of large numbers of children. Its child health research grant program focuses on start-up projects and promising younger investigators. Emphasis is also placed on research which may lead to practical clinical applications. Support is normally limited to one year. **Giving Priorities:** In 1993, the foundation awarded 100% of its funding to pediatric health research. Recipients of support included medical schools, hospitals, and health centers. **Typical Health-Related Recipients:** Adolescent Health Issues, Cancer, Children's Health/Hospitals, Hospitals, Medical Research, Medical Training. **Geographic Distribution:** New England.

Conrad N. Hilton Foundation
See: Entry 116

David, Helen, Marian Woodward Fund-Atlanta
See: Entry 6342

★3136★ David and Lucile Packard Foundation
300 2nd St., Ste. 200
Los Altos, CA 94022
Phone: (415)948-7658
Fax: (415)948-5793
Colburn S. Wilbur, Executive Director

Foundation Philosophy: The foundation traditionally makes grants in the following catego-

ries: child health; community; education; conservation; the arts; the municipality of Pueblo, CO; and public policy. Giving to ancient studies has been discontinued. The main interests of child health grants are programs regarding pregnancy, child development, and population and family planning services. The special interests of the community grants program are child care, families, youth employment, and emergency services in San Mateo, Santa Clara, Santa Cruz, and Monterey counties. **Giving Priorities:** In 1993, the foundation gave approximately 35% of its total contributions to scientific interests. Health concerns received about 33%; educational institutions, 27%; and the arts, 3%. Civic affairs and international organizations received the remaining funds. **Typical Health-Related Recipients:** Children's Health/Hospitals, Clinics/Medical Centers, Family Planning, Health Organizations, Health Policy/Cost Containment, Hospitals, Long-Term Care, Medical Education, Nursing Services, Nutrition, People with Disabilities, Prenatal Health Issues, Public Health. **Geographic Distribution:** National, with an emphasis on San Mateo, Santa Clara, Santa Cruz, and Monterey counties, CA; Pueblo, CO; also Mexico and Columbia.

Duke Endowment
See: Entry 147

Dyson Foundation
See: Entry 149

E. J. Grassmann Trust
See: Entry 6346

★3137★ E. K. and Lillian F. Bishop Foundation
c/o Seafirst Bank Charitable Dept.
PO Box 24565, CSC-23
Seattle, WA 98124
Phone: (206)358-0806
Tom Nevers, Grant Manager

Foundation Philosophy: The foundation makes most of its grants to social service organizations, with an emphasis on projects for the benefit of youth, from infancy to age 23. Interests include recreation and athletics, community centers, and homes, and youth organizations. The arts and civic affairs in Seattle are also priorities. **Giving Priorities:** In fiscal 1993, the foundation gave approximately 33% of its contributions to educational institutions, including two grants to Grays Harbor College and one to Grays Harbor Public Schools, Aberdeen, WA. Civic and public affairs received 23%; social services, 16%; the arts, 10%; health care organizations, 9%; religious causes, 6% and science centers, 3%. **Typical Health-Related Recipients:** Children's Health/Hospitals, Clinics/Medical Centers, Family Planning, Health Funds, Hospitals, Medical Research, Nursing Services, Single-Disease Health Associations, Substance Abuse. **Geographic Distribution:** Focus on Washington State.

E. L. Wiegand Foundation
See: Entry 150

Edna McConnell Clark Foundation
See: Entry 154

Forrest C. Lattner Foundation
See: Entry 190

★3138★ Foundation for Seacoast Health
PO Box 4606
Portsmouth, NH 03802-4606
Phone: (603)433-4001
Fax: (603)433-4091
Susan Bunting, Executive Director

Foundation Philosophy: The Foundation for Seacoast Health supports Seacoast area nonprofit organizations and scholarships for students pursuing health-related fields of study. The foundation has recently shifted its funding focus, concentrating resources on improving health care delivery systems, rather than on particular services; and focusing on prevention rather than intervention through a gradual shift in funding from the elderly and adolescent populations to the earlier childhood years, focusing on the child's health in relation to the family unit. The Foundation for Seacoast Health will continue to focus its resources on programs which have a prevention orientation and which address the systemic issues of health care access and utilization. **Giving Priorities:** In 1993, the foundation gave approximately 73% of funding to health care sevices, primarily in New Hampshire, including the highest grant of $187,500 to the Portsmouth School Department's Clipper Health Center. Social service organizations received 14%, with major support for counseling services. Education received 6%; civic affairs, 5%; and the remaining funds supported the arts, the environment, and religion. **Typical Health-Related Recipients:** AIDS/HIV, Children's Health/Hospitals, Clinics/Medical Centers, Diabetes, Domestic Violence, Emergency/Ambulance Services, Family Planning, Geriatric Health, Health Funds, Health Organizations, Home-Care Services, Hospices, Hospitals, Medical Rehabilitation, Mental Health, Nursing Services, Prenatal Health Issues, Sexual Abuse, Single-Disease Health Associations, Substance Abuse. **Geographic Distribution:** Portsmouth, NH, and Portland, Sanford, and York, ME, and Boston, MA. **Formerly:** Portsmouth Hospital Foundation.

★3139★ Hall Family Foundations
PO Box 419580
Kansas City, MO 64141-6580
Phone: (816)274-8516
Fax: (816)274-8547
Peggy Collins, Vice President

Foundation Philosophy: The five main interests of the foundations are education, the arts, community development, children and families, and additional interests. The foundations also have an interest in improving the lives of children, youth, and families. In this area, programs which help prevent family violence, improve child well-being, expand youth services, and respond to families' physical and emotional health needs are funded. **Giving Priorities:** In 1993, the foundations contributed 71% of its total funding to organizations concerned with children, youth, and family. The majority of funding in this category went to Children's Mercy Hospital for a capital grant to construct an ambulatory care facility. The arts received about 12% of support. Educational institutions received 10%

of gifts; community development, 5%; and miscellaneous organizations, 2%. **Typical Health-Related Recipients:** Domestic Violence, Substance Abuse. **Geographic Distribution:** Limited to metropolitan Kansas City, MO.

★3140★ Heckscher Foundation for Children
17 E 47th St.
New York, NY 10017
Phone: (212)371-7775
Fax: (212)371-7787
Virginia Sloane, President

Foundation Philosophy: The foundation promotes the health and general welfare of children, and makes grants in a number of different areas within this framework. **Giving Priorities:** In 1993, the foundation gave approximately 31% of its total contributions to social service organizations. Educational institutions and programs received about 21%. The arts received 14%; health concerns, 14%; civic affairs, 12%; and religious organizations, 8% of funding. **Typical Health-Related Recipients:** Cancer, Children's Health/Hospitals, Clinics/Medical Centers, Emergency/Ambulance Services, Family Planning, Health Organizations, Hospitals, Medical Education, Medical Rehabilitation, Medical Research, Mental Health, Nursing Services, People with Disabilities, Preventive Medicine/Wellness Organizations, Single-Disease Health Associations, Substance Abuse, Transplant Networks/Donor Banks. **Geographic Distribution:** Primarily New York City.

J.E. and Z.B. Butler Foundation
See: Entry 296

Jacob G. Schmidlapp Trust No. 1
See: Entry 304

Jessie B. Cox Charitable Trust
See: Entry 313

John Merck Fund
See: Entry 4449

John R. McCune Charitable Trust
See: Entry 6367

John S. and James L. Knight Foundation
See: Entry 325

John and Wilhelmina D. Harland Charitable Foundation
See: Entry 328

Joseph B. Whitehead Foundation
See: Entry 330

Lon V. Smith Foundation
See: Entry 358

Louise H. and David S. Ingalls Foundation
See: Entry 366

Mary Ranken Jordan and Ettie A. Jordan Charitable Foundation
See: Entry 383

Max Factor Family Foundation
See: Entry 1871

★3141★ Morris Stulsaft Foundation
100 Bush St., Ste. 825
San Francisco, CA 94104
Phone: (415)986-7117
Joan Nelson Dills, Administrator

Foundation Philosophy: The foundation, in accordance with its stated goal, has traditionally funded organizations in the broad categories of social services and recreation, education, health, and the arts. Social service funding includes support for child welfare (including adoption services and child abuse prevention); programs for disadvantaged and mentally and physically disabled youth; prevention of substance abuse; family planning and parental services. Health funding includes mental health and child development; pediatric nursing services and in-house care for sick children; respite care; hospitals; and single-disease health associations. The foundation is now emphasizing programs for the social problems that face families today. The new focus in grant-making is on organizations that work with homeless families, and with children born with AIDS or to crack-addicted parents. **Giving Priorities:** In 1992, the foundation gave approximately 51% of its contributions to social services, including major support for child welfare and family services, youth programs, and drug abuse prevention. Education received 13% of giving; health care, 11%; religious organizations, 11%; and civic affairs, 7%. The arts received the remaining 7% of grants. **Typical Health-Related Recipients:** Adolescent Health Issues, Children's Health/Hospitals, Domestic Violence, Emergency/Ambulance Services, Family Planning, Hospitals, Medical Research, Mental Health, Nursing Services, People with Disabilities, Prenatal Health Issues, Single-Disease Health Associations, Substance Abuse. **Geographic Distribution:** Six counties of the San Francisco Bay Area (Alameda, Conta Costa, Marin, San Francisco, San Mateo, and Santa Clara).

Robert Stewart Odell and Helen Pfeiffer Odell Fund
See: Entry 457

★3142★ St. Giles Foundation
420 Lexington Ave.
New York, NY 10170
Phone: (212)338-9001
Richard T. Arkwright, President

Foundation Philosophy: The St. Giles Foundation has a special interest in medical science. It also funds hospitals and child services. **Giving Priorities:** In fiscal 1994, the foundation gave 100% of its contributions to health care, specifically supporting children's health and hospitals. The highest grant of $300,000 was awarded to Columbia University in New York, NY, to support the establishment of the endowment fund of the John H. Livingston Professorship Fund. **Typical Health-Related Recipients:** Children's Health/Hospitals, Hospitals, Medical Education, Medical Research, People with Disabilities. **Geographic Distribution:** Focus on New York. **Formerly:** The House of St. Giles the Cripple.

Sidney J. Weinberg, Jr. Foundation
See: Entry 6380

Skillman Foundation
See: Entry 492

Strauss Foundation
See: Entry 508

Thomas and Agnes Carvel Foundation
See: Entry 516

★3143★ Turrell Fund
21 Van Vleck St.
Montclair, NJ 07042
Phone: (201)783-9358
Fax: (201)783-9283
E. Belvin Williams, Exec. Dir. and Sec.

Foundation Philosophy: The foundation makes grants in the following program areas: youth organizations, day programs, welfare programs, programs for the handicapped, residential programs, inner-city programs, state institutions, alcohol and drug abuse, schools, special education, and college scholarships under institutional sponsorship. **Giving Priorities:** In 1993, the foundation gave approximately 48% of its contributions to education including support for scholarships, private education, and education alternatives. Social services received 46%. Interests included community service organizations, youth programs, and family services. Religious welfare causes recived 3% of funding and civic organizations and the arts received the remaining funds. **Typical Health-Related Recipients:** AIDS/HIV, Clinics/Medical Centers, Family Planning, Medical Education, People with Disabilities, Substance Abuse. **Geographic Distribution:** New Jersey and Vermont.

Valley Foundation
See: Entry 526

Van Houten Memorial Fund
See: Entry 527

★3144★ Victoria Foundation
40 S Fullerton Ave.
Montclair, NJ 07042
Phone: (201)783-4450
Catherine M. McFarland, Secretary and Executive Officer

Foundation Philosophy: Within Newark, NJ, the foundation seeks to strengthen and increase opportunities for upward mobility for disadvantaged youth and their families, and to strengthen the neighborhoods in which they live by supporting programs working to overcome social and economic problems that limit access to education, employment, and housing. A secondary focus for the foundation is to further the wise use of land, water, and energy, and to promote rational strategies for their development and use. Priority is given to proposals stressing conservation, preservation, and renewable energy sources. **Giving Priorities:** In 1993, the foundation awarded 24% of its total contributions to educational institutions. About 23% of support went to civic groups. The arts received 19% of funds; social services, 16%; environmental concerns, 12%; and health care, 3%. The remaining funding went to science groups. **Typical Health-Related Recipients:** Children's Health/Hospitals, Clinics/Medical Centers, Family Planning, Medical Education, Substance

Abuse. **Geographic Distribution:** Newark, NJ; with support for statewide environmental programs.

Vira I. Heinz Endowment
See: Entry 529

★3145★ William T. Grant Foundation
c/o Grants Coordinator
515 Madison Ave.
New York, NY 10022
Phone: (212)752-0071
Fax: (212)752-1398

Foundation Philosophy: The foundation aims to develop greater collaborative efforts in research by promoting interdisciplinary studies on the psychological and behavioral problems of children and youth. In general, the foundation focuses on five major areas of research on school-age children's mental health issues: stress and coping, problem behavior and mental health, the psychological consequences of chronic physical disease, school-age pregnancy, and school-related programs. The foundation is committed to supporting research that aims to improve the mental health and functioning of school-age children. In addition, the foundation has an interest in research projects that address the problems of adolescents' transition to adulthood. **Giving Priorities:** In 1993, 294 active research grants were being supported. The foundation sponsors a broad range of social science research, both on a short-term and longitudinal basis. All grants are classified under scientific investigation. The foundation's major areas of interest are children at risk, including the problems of divorce, mental illness, child abuse and adolescent suicide; adolescent pregnancy, including studies on prevention, social and psychological aspects and the role of fathers; prevention in mental health, including programs focusing on children under stress, problem behaviors and teaching social skills; school and learning; social-emotional development; stress, health and illness; and the psychological aspects of physical disorders. **Typical Health-Related Recipients:** Adolescent Health Issues, Cancer, Children's Health/Hospitals, Family Planning, Mental Health, Prenatal Health Issues, Research/Studies Institutes. **Geographic Distribution:** International, national.

Corporate Foundations

Aetna Foundation
See: Entry 564

Alabama Power Foundation
See: Entry 566

Amon G. Carter Star Telegram Employees Fund
See: Entry 578

Caring Foundation
See: Entry 622

Connecticut Mutual Life Foundation
See: Entry 645

D.B. Reinhart Family Foundation
See: Entry 657

GenCorp Foundation
See: Entry 6399

★3146★ Gerber Cos. Foundation
445 State St.
Fremont, MI 49413
Phone: (616)928-2759
Grace J. Deur, Administrator & Secretary

Giving Priorities: *Health:* 55% to 59%. Funds hospitals, research in the area of infant nutrition, pediatric health, and others. Major support in fiscal 1993 went to the Pediatric AIDS Foundation in Alexandria, VA. *Social Services:* 15% of 20% of contributions. *Civic & Public Affairs:* 10% to 15%. *Education:* 5% to 10% of giving. *Arts & Humanities:* Less than 5%. *Science:* Less than 5%. *International:* Provides limited support to U.S.-based nonprofits with an international focus. **Note:** Objective is to support programs that promote health and welfare of infants and young children. **Typical Health-Related Recipients:** AIDS/HIV, Cancer, Children's Health/Hospitals, Domestic Violence, General, Health Organizations, Hospices, Hospitals, Medical Education, Medical Rehabilitation, Medical Training, Nursing Services, Nutrition, People with Disabilities, Preventive Medicine/Wellness Organizations. **Geographic Distribution:** In most cases, support is for programs and activities in cities where company maintains major facilities.

Hasbro Charitable Trust
See: Entry 724

High Meadow Foundation
See: Entry 727

★3147★ Hofmann Foundation
PO Box 907
Concord, CA 94522
Phone: (510)682-4830
Bess Stagner, Exec. Dir.

Giving Priorities: *Education:* 35% to 40%. Supports a variety of institutions ranging from high schools and vocational training, to colleges and universities. In fiscal 1993, the highest grant of $556,297 was awarded to the University of California Berkley Foundation. *Civic & Public Affairs:* 30% to 35%. *Health:* About 10%. Primarily funds children's health issues. Funding supports the Make-A-Wish Foundation and single-disease health associations including diabetes, epilepsy, cancer, cerebral palsy, heart/lung, and paralysis. Funding also went to hospitals and medical centers. *Social Services:* About 10%. *Religion:* 5% to 10%. *Arts & Humanities:* About 5%. **Typical Health-Related Recipients:** AIDS/HIV, Cancer, Children's Health/Hospitals, Clinics/Medical Centers, Diabetes, Domestic Violence, Emergency/Ambulance Services, Health Organizations, Heart, Hospices, Hospitals, Medical Education, Medical Research, People with Disabilities, Preventive Medicine/Wellness Organizations, Respiratory, Single-Disease Health Associations. **Geographic Distribution:** Primarily in northern California, with a concentration on Bay Area organizations. **Formerly:** K. H. Hofmann Foundation.

★3148★ Intelligent Electronics Foundation
411 Eagleview Blvd.
Exton, PA 19341
Phone: (610)458-6606
Fax: (610)458-6805
Tara Sanford, Program Officer

Giving Priorities: *Child Health:* Supports programs designed to give all children access to comprehensive, quality health care, regardless of their families' income level, and programs focused on the prevention of child abuse. Provides support for pediatric health care centers. *Community Development:* Supports programs that encourage the empowerment of residents through the support of programs that concentrate on job development, housing and coordinated delivery of human services. *Education:* Provides children with the opportunity to participate in programs that provide a rich educational environment and to support youth employment and adult literacy programs for those populations that affect disadvantaged children. *Recreation:* Promotes programs that give children the chance to develop self-esteem and life-long skills through artistic, sport, and recreational activities. **Typical Health-Related Recipients:** Children's Health/Hospitals. **Geographic Distribution:** Chester County, PA and Denver, Co.

Interco Inc. Charitable Trust
See: Entry 735

PACCAR Foundation
See: Entry 6414

Other Funding Organizations

★3149★ American Academy of Pediatrics
141 Northwest Point Blvd.
PO Box 927
Elk Grove Village, IL 60009-0927
Phone: (708)228-5005
Fax: (708)228-5097
James E. Strain, M.D., Exec. Dir.

Description: Awards scholarships and grants for pediatric residents and an annual award for research relating to nutrition of infants and children.

Association for Research of Childhood Cancer
See: Entry 5898

★3150★ Foundation for Exceptional Children
1920 Association Dr.
Reston, VA 22091
Phone: (703)620-1054
Ken Collins, Exec. Dir.

Description: Awards scholarships and grants for innovative programs concerned with the education of gifted or disabled children.

★3151★ National Children's Eye Care
Foundation
PO Box 795069
Dallas, TX 75379-5069
Phone: (214)407-0404
Fax: (214)407-0616
Suzanne C. Beauchamp, Exec. Dir.

Description: Provides post-residency fellowships for pediatric ophthalmology and grants for research in children's eye disorders and diseases.

★3152★ National Reye's Syndrome
Foundation
426 N. Lewis
Bryan, OH 43506
Phone: (419)636-2679
Free: 800-233-7393
Fax: (419)636-3366

Description: Raises and provides funds for research into the cause, treatment, cure, and prevention of Reye's Syndrome through research grants to individual scientists.

★3153★ SIDS Alliance
10500 Little Patuxent Pkwy., No. 420
Columbia, MD 21044
Phone: (410)964-8000
Free: 800-221-SIDS
Fax: (410)964-8009
Thomas L. Moran, Pres.

Description: Supports research into sudden infant death syndrome.

National & International
Organizations

★3154★ Allergy and Asthma Network /
Mothers of Asthmatics (AAN/MA)
3554 Chain Bridge Rd., Ste. 200
Fairfax, VA 22030-2709
Phone: (703)385-4403
Free: 800-878-4403
Fax: (703)352-4354
Nancy Sander, Pres.

Founded: 1985. **Members:** 5,000. **Description:** Professional associations, physicians, patients, parents, and educators. Dedicated to the education and support of people with allergies and asthma. **Publications:** *Asthma Organizer.* Includes daily symptom diary, form for tracking medications and doctor visits, information on peak flow monitoring and managing asthma. *Price:* $25. • *Breathing Easy with Day Care.* • *Consumer Update on Asthma.* • *I'm a Meter Reader.* Book. • *I'm a Meter Reader.* Video. • *MA Report,* monthly. Newsletter. Provides patients and families of children with asthma and allergies with coping strategies, medical information, and moral support. *Price:* $25/year. • *So You Have Asthma Too!.* Book. • *So You Have Asthma Too!.* Video. **Formerly:** (1991) Mothers of Asthmatics; (1993) National Allergy and Asthma Network.

★3155★ Alliance to End Childhood Lead
Poisoning
227 Massachusetts Ave. NE, Ste. 200
Washington, DC 20002
Don Ryan, Exec.Dir.

Founded: 1990. **Description:** Public interest organization dedicated to the elimination of childhood lead poisoning. Seeks to inform health professionals, the general public, and policy makers of the hazards posed by lead and the need for prevention of lead poisoning. Works to strengthen federal policies and programs developing cost-effective strategies for protecting children and targeting resources where most needed and ensuring the development of a national infrastructure for reducing lead hazards. Strives to accelerate national action by keeping pressure on federal agencies, overcoming private sector obstacles, and mobilizing other resources. Conducts lobbying activities. **Publications:** *Alliance Alert,* bimonthly. Newsletter. Update on important national developments related to lead poisoning prevention. *Price:* $35. • Brochures. Also publishes technical, policy, and program guides.

★3156★ ALSAC - St. Jude Children's
Research Hospital
501 St. Jude Pl.
PO Box 3704
Memphis, TN 38105
Phone: (901)522-9733
Free: 800-USS-JUDE
Richard C. Shadyac, Exec.Dir.

Founded: 1957. **Members:** 2,000. **Regional Groups:** 8. **Local Groups:** 60. **Description:** Fundraising organization maintaining St. Jude Children's Research Hospital and laboratories in Memphis, TN. Conducts research and children's services and provides patient care in children's catastrophic diseases. Incorporated as American Lebanese Syrian Associated Charities, ALSAC was organized through the auspices of Danny Thomas, television and theatre personality. **Publications:** *ALSAC News,* quarterly. Tabloid informing members of St. Jude Hospital activities and ALSAC fundraising programs. Covers regional news. *Price:* Included in membership dues. • *Partners in Hope,* quarterly. Tabloid providing human interest stories and news of St. Jude Hospital activities. *Price:* Available to donors only. **Formerly:** (1972) Aiding Leukemia Stricken American Children.

★3157★ Ambulatory Pediatric Association
(APA)
6728 Old McLean Village Dr.
Mc Lean, VA 22101
Phone: (703)556-9222
Marge Degnon, Exec.Sec.

Founded: 1960. **Members:** 1,200. **Regional Groups:** 10. **Description:** Health care providers interested in the care of children in ambulatory care facilities, particularly directors of outpatient departments in private, university, and other teaching hospitals and those engaged in public health work or private practice. Aims to improve methods of care of children. Studies methods of research and the teaching of outpatient care. Conducts collaborative research; compiles statistics; presents annual scientific program. **Publications:** *Ambulatory Pediatric Association--*

Membership Directory, biennial. Membership Directory. *Price:* Included in membership dues. • *Ambulatory Pediatric Association-- Newsletter,* 3/year. Newsletter. Includes book reviews, calendar of events, listing of employment opportunities, research reports, and statistics. *Price:* Included in membership dues. Also publishes abstracts of scientific papers. **Formerly:** (1967) Association for Ambulatory Pediatric Services.

★3158★ American Academy of Child and
Adolescent Psychiatry (AACAP)
3615 Wisconsin Ave. NW
Washington, DC 20016
Phone: (202)966-7300
Free: 800-333-7636
Fax: (202)966-2891
Virginia Q. Anthony, Exec.Dir.

Founded: 1953. **Members:** 5,000. **Regional Groups:** 48. **Description:** Professional society of degreed physicians who have completed an additional five years of residency in child and adolescent psychiatry. Seeks to stimulate and advance medical contributions to the knowledge and treatment of psychiatric illnesses of children and adolescents. **Publications:** *AACAP News,* bimonthly. Newsletter. Includes listing of employment opportunities, research updates, and statistics. *Price:* Included in membership dues. • Bulletin, periodic. • Catalog. • *Journal of the AACAP,* bimonthly. Journal. • Manuals. • Membership Directory, periodic. **Formerly:** (1986) American Academy of Child Psychiatry.

★3159★ American Academy of Pediatric
Dentistry (AAPD)
211 E. Chicago Ave., Ste. 1036
Chicago, IL 60611
Phone: (312)337-2169
Dr. John A. Bogert, Exec.Dir.

Founded: 1947. **Members:** 3,700. **Regional Groups:** 45. **Description:** Professional society of dentists whose practice is limited to children; teachers and researchers in pediatric dentistry. Seeks to advance the specialty of pediatric dentistry through practice, education, and research. Sponsors graduate student pediatric dentistry award program. **Publications:** *American Academy of Pediatric Dentistry--Membership Roster,* annual. Membership Directory. • *American Academy of Pediatric Dentistry--Newsletter,* bimonthly. Newsletter. Includes employment listings, meetings calendar, research updates, and obituaries. *Price:* Included in membership dues. • Pamphlets. • *Pediatric Dentistry,* bimonthly. Journal. Includes employment listings and conference proceedings. *Price:* Included in membership dues; $50/year for nonmembers; $65/ year for institutions. **Formerly:** (1984) American Academy of Pedodontics.

★3160★ American Academy of Pediatrics
(AAP)
141 Northwest Point Blvd.
PO Box 927
Elk Grove Village, IL 60009-0927
Phone: (708)228-5005
Fax: (708)228-5097
Joe M. Sanders, M.D., Exec.Dir.

Founded: 1930. **Members:** 47,000. **State Groups:** 66. **Description:** Professional medical society of pediatricians and pediatric subspecialists. Operates small member library of books and journals on pediatric medicine, office practice, and child health care policy. Maintains 42 committees, councils, and tasks forces including: Accident and Poison Prevention; Early Childhood, Adoption and Dependent Care; Infectious Diseases. Operates 41 sections. Sponsors Pediatrics Review and Education Program (PREP), a self-assessment, continuing education program for practicing pediatricians. **Publications:** *AAP News*, monthly. Newspaper. Covers the social, economic, and professional aspects of pediatric care. Includes association news and chapter news. *Price:* Included in membership dues; $30/year for nonmembers. • *Fellowship List*, annual. • *Pediatrics*, monthly. Journal. Includes employment listings. *Price:* $90/year for individuals; $150/year for institutions; $55/year for students. • *Pediatrics in Review*, monthly. Journal. Contains review articles and abstracts. Includes continuing education calendar. *Price:* $100/year for members; $130/year for nonmembers and institutions. Also publishes reports, guides, and handbooks.

★ 3161 ★ **American Association for Pediatric Ophthalmology and Strabismus**
PO Box 193832
San Francisco, CA 94119
Phone: (415)561-8505
Fax: (415)561-8575
Sue A. Brown, M.D., Admin.

Founded: 1974. **Members:** 570. **Description:** Ophthalmologists who limit their practice largely to children. Encourages quality eye care for children by establishing high ethical standards of practice, supporting educational training programs for pediatric ophthalmologists, and promoting basic research in children's eye diseases. Conducts research programs. **Publications:** Journal, bimonthly. • Membership Directory, annual. **Formerly:** (1978) American Association of Pediatric Ophthalmology.

★ 3162 ★ **American Association of Psychiatric Services for Children (AAPSC)**
1200-C Scottsville Rd., Ste. 225
Rochester, NY 14624
Phone: (716)235-6910
Free: 800-777-6910
Fax: (716)235-0654
Dr. Sydney Koret, Exec.Dir.

Founded: 1948. **Members:** 165. **Description:** Fosters prevention and treatment of mental and emotional disorders of the child, adolescent, and family; furthers the development and application of clinical knowledge; researches and supports projects dealing with child and adolescent mental health; offers a national focus for the clinical point of view; acts as an information clearinghouse; provides accreditation services. Maintains speakers bureau and roster of available staff positions. Sponsors educational programs; compiles statistics. **Publications:** *AAPSC Membership Directory*, annual. Membership Directory. *Price:* Free. • *AAPSC Newsletter*, bimonthly. Newsletter. Includes calendar of events, employment listings, notices of personnel transitions, legislative and regulatory review, and current trends. *Price:* Included in

membership dues. • *Child Psychiatry and Human Development*, quarterly. Journal. Reports on the developing child and adolescent; includes research information. *Price:* Included in membership dues; $39/year for nonmember individuals; $94/year for institutions. **Formerly:** (1970) American Association of Psychiatric Clinics for Children.

★ 3163 ★ **American Board of Pediatric Dentistry (ABPD)**
1193 Woodgate Dr.
Carmel, IN 46033
Phone: (317)573-0877
Fax: (317)846-7235
James R. Roche, D.D.S., Exec.Sec.-Treas.

Founded: 1940. **Members:** 940. **Description:** Certification board whose purpose is to investigate the qualifications of, administer examinations to, and certify as diplomates, dentists specializing in the care of children. Sponsored by American Academy of Pediatric Dentistry. **Formerly:** (1986) American Board of Pedodontics.

★ 3164 ★ **American Board of Pediatrics (ABP)**
111 Silver Cedar Ct.
Chapel Hill, NC 27514
Phone: (919)929-0461
Fax: (919)929-9255
James A. Stockman, M.D., Pres.

Founded: 1933. **Members:** 250. **Description:** Certification board to establish qualifications, conduct examinations, and certify as diplomates those whom the board finds qualified as specialists in pediatrics. **Publications:** *American Board of Pediatrics--Booklet of Information*, annual. Booklet. Outlines requirements for admission to certifying examinations; includes details of examinations. *Price:* Free. • *American Board of Pediatrics--Informal Newsletter to Members*, periodic. Newsletter. • *American Board of Pediatrics--Newsletter for Diplomates*, annual. Newsletter. *Price:* Free. • *Newsletter to Pediatric Training Program Directors*. Newsletter. *Price:* Free.

★ 3165 ★ **American College of Foot and Ankle Pediatrics (ACFAP)**
8th & Race St.
Philadelphia, PA 19107
Phone: (215)625-5361
Fax: (215)629-0199
Philip J. Bresnahan, DPM, Pres.

Founded: 1977. **Members:** 200. **Description:** Podiatric physicians and surgeons, general physicians and surgeons, psychologists, and physical therapists. Seeks to bring together all professionals interested in children's foot health. Goals are to: disseminate information; consider all forms of therapy of value in foot and ankle pediatrics; bring to all those interested the most advanced and valuable forms of therapy through publications, seminars, and research sessions; establish teaching courses on foot and ankle pediatrics so that more podiatric students will consider specializing in the field. Encourages individual research projects; maintains speakers' bureau. **Publications:** *ACP Abstracts*, bimonthly. Newsletter. • Newsletter, annual. **Formerly:** (1993) American College of Podopediatrics.

★ 3166 ★ **American College of Osteopathic Pediatricians (ACOP)**
5301 Wisconsin Ave.
Washington, DC 20015
Phone: (202)686-1700
Theresa E. Goeke, Exec.Dir.

Founded: 1940. **Members:** 350. **Description:** Osteopathic physicians who have received or are receiving advanced training in pediatrics and who are specializing in pediatric practice. **Publications:** *American College of Osteopathic Pediatricians--Newsletter*, quarterly. Newsletter. Reports on new regulations and sources of information in the field of osteopathic pediatrics. Includes calendar of events and research updates. *Price:* $10/year. • Membership Directory, annual.

★ 3167 ★ **American Foundation for Maternal and Child Health (AFMCH)**
439 E. 51st St., 4th Fl.
New York, NY 10022
Phone: (212)759-5510
Doris Haire, Pres.

Founded: 1972. **Description:** Serves as a clearinghouse for interdisciplinary research on maternal and child health; focuses on the perinatal or birth period and its effect on infant development. Sponsors medical research designed to improve application of technology in maternal and child health; conducts educational programs; compiles statistics. Operates extensive reference library.

American Osteopathic Board of Pediatrics (AOBP)
See: Entry 9985

★ 3168 ★ **American Pediatric Gastroesophageal Reflux Association (APGERA)**
c/o Sharon Tiano
23 Acton St.
Watertown, MA 02172
Phone: (617)926-3586
Sharon Tiano, Pres.

Founded: 1987. **Members:** 250. **Description:** Parents of children who suffer from chronic gastroesophageal reflux (GER) and other gastrointestinal motility disorders; interested health care professionals. (GER produces symptoms including regurgitation, crankiness, respiratory problems, and poor weight gain in young children.) Provides encouragement, support, and medical information to members. Promotes research, interest, and awareness of GER among health professionals and the public. Collects information on GER research and medical management, and the family life of GER patients. Maintains professional advisory board comprising health care professionals specializing in diagnosis and treatment of the disorder. Maintains central registry of GER patients in the U.S. **Publications:** *A Guide for Parents of Children with Chronic Gastroesophageal Reflux and Gastrointestinal Motility Disorders*. • *APGERA Newsletter*, quarterly. Newsletter.

★3169★ **American Pediatric Society (APS)**
PO Box 675
Elk Grove Village, IL 60009-0675
Phone: (708)427-1205
Fax: (708)427-1305
Dr. Norman I. Sigel, Sec.-Treas.

Founded: 1888. **Members:** 1,400. **Description:** Professional academic society of M.D. educators and researchers interested in the study of children and their diseases, prevention of illness, and promotion of health in childhood. Maintains archives. **Publications:** *Pediatric Research - Program Issue*, annual. • *Program and Abstracts of Annual Meeting*.

★3170★ **American Pseudo-Obstruction and Hirschsprung's Disease Society (APHS)**
PO Box 772
Medford, MA 02155
Phone: (617)395-4255
Fax: (617)396-6868
Andrea M. Anastas, Pres.

Founded: 1988. **Members:** 1,500. **Description:** Parents, health care professionals, and other interested individuals. Provides support services for families such as the Family Assistance Program; conducts educational programs. **Publications:** *GI Track Video*. Video. *Price:* $49.95. • Newsletter, quarterly. • Pamphlets. Also publishes fact sheets on Intestinal Pseudo-obstruction, Hirschsprung's Disease and Gastroesophageal Reflux.

★3171★ **American Society for Adolescent Psychiatry (ASAP)**
4330 East West Hwy., Ste. 1117
Bethesda, MD 20814
Phone: (301)718-6502
Free: 800-899-6338
Fax: (301)656-0989
Ann Loew, Exec.Dir.

Founded: 1967. **Members:** 1,500. **Regional Groups:** 20. **Description:** Qualified psychiatrists concerned with the behavior of adolescents. Provides for the exchange of psychiatric knowledge; encourages the development of adequate standards and training facilities; stimulates research in the psychopathology and treatment of adolescents. Consults with national organizations interested in the welfare of youth and adolescence. **Publications:** *Adolescent Psychiatry*, annual. Journal. Up to date articles and case studies on adolescent psychiatry. *Price:*. Included in membership dues. • *American Society for Adolescent Psychiatry--Newsletter*, quarterly. Newsletter. Includes society news, calendar of events, and research updates. *Price:* Included in membership dues; $10/year for nonmembers. • *ASAP Membership Directory*, biennial. Membership Directory. • *Journal of Youth and Adolescence*, bimonthly. Journal.

★3172★ **American Society of Dentistry for Children (ASDC)**
875 N. Michigan Ave., Ste. 4040
Chicago, IL 60611-1901
Phone: (312)943-1244
Fax: (312)943-5341
Carol Teuscher, Asst.Exec.Dir.

Founded: 1927. **Members:** 7,000. **State Groups:** 50. **Description:** General practitioners and specialists interested in dentistry for children. Conducts specialized education and research programs. **Publications:** *Dental Recap*, bimonthly. Newsletter. Contains news about children's dental health concerns. Includes scientific references and governmental activities related to children's health. *Price:* Included in membership dues. • *Directory of the Membership of the American Society of Dentistry for Children*, annual. Membership Directory. • *Journal of Dentistry for Children*, bimonthly. Journal.

★3173★ **American Society of Pediatric Hematology / Oncology (ASPHO)**
c/o John N. Lukens
5700 Old Orchard Rd., 1st Fl.
Skokie, IL 60077-1057
Phone: (708)965-2776
Fax: (708)966-9418
John N. Lukens, M.D., Pres.

Founded: 1981. **Members:** 650. **Description:** Active members are: physicians who have served residencies in pediatrics and fellowships in pediatric hematology/oncology; specialists in allied disciplines including surgery, pathology, radiology, pedodontics, and psychiatry; physicians trained in hematology or oncology of adults who are interested in the treatment of blood diseases and cancer in children; individuals holding doctoral degrees who are involved in research relevant to the field. Affiliated members are: nurses and physician assistants working with children with cancer, sickle cell disease, thalassemia, hemophilia, and other hematological disorders; psychologists, social workers, research scientists, and others interested in comprehensive care or research in the field. Purpose is to promote the knowledge, understanding, and management of disorders of the blood and of cancer in children. Seeks improvements in the total care of children with these diseases through the fostering of education and all relevant clinical and basic research. Provides a forum for the exchange of ideas on issues in the field. Cooperates with other societies concerned with the field. **Publications:** *American Journal of Pediatric Hematology/Oncology*, quarterly. Journal. • *Directory of Members*, annual. Membership Directory. • *ph/o Forum*, bimonthly. Newsletter.

★3174★ **American Society for Pediatric Neurosurgery (ASPN)**
c/o M.L. Walker, Sec.
100 N. Medical Dr.
Salt Lake City, UT 84113
Phone: (801)588-3400
Fax: (801)588-3409
M. L. Walker, Pres.

Founded: 1978. **Members:** 63. **Description:** Pediatric neurosurgeons dedicated to the advancement and development of their specialty. Represents the interests of pediatric neurosurgery as they relate to government, the public, universities, and professional societies. Supports basic and clinical research in pediatric neurosurgery. Provides leadership in undergraduate, graduate, and continuing education in the field of pediatric neurosurgery. **Publications:** *Pediatric Neurosurgery*, monthly. Journal. Contains scientific papers.

★3175★ **American Sudden Infant Death Syndrome Institute (ASIDSI)**
6065 Roswell Rd., Ste. 876
Atlanta, GA 30328
Phone: (404)843-1030
Free: 800-232-SIDS
Fax: (404)843-0577
Dr. Alfred Steinschneider, Pres.

Founded: 1983. **Regional Groups:** 1. **Description:** Participants include health care professionals, researchers, and laypeople concerned about sudden infant death syndrome (SIDS); families who have lost babies to SIDS. Works to identify the cause and cure of SIDS. Promotes infant health through research, clinical services, education, and support for SIDS families. Operates Friends Against SIDS groups, comprising primarily parents who have suffered a SIDS loss; conducts research on siblings of SIDS babies; sponsors research programs seeking the cause and cure of SIDS. Conducts seminars for health care professionals and laypeople; maintains speakers' bureau. **Publications:** Brochures. • Newsletter, quarterly. Also publishes research results. **Also Known As:** American SIDS Institute.

★3176★ **Association of British Paediatric Nurses**
PO Box 14
Ashton-upon-Lyne, Lancs. L5 9WW, England
Phone: 1893 927742
Tony Harrison, Gen.Sec.

Members: 2,000. **Description:** Raises public awareness on the profession of pediatric nursing in England. Actively promotes the amelioration of standards required for nursing care of children. Facilitates partnership care with families as well as the recognition of the fundamental role of parents or carers of sick children. Provides information and advice on issues related to childhood illnesses. Supports innovation and constructive change in nursing practice and child care. Provides a forum for members to exchange information and experiences related to pediatric nursing. **Publications:** Newsletter, 3/year.

★3177★ **Association for the Care of Children's Health (ACCH)**
7910 Woodmont Ave., Ste. 300
Bethesda, MD 20814
Phone: (301)654-6549
Fax: (301)986-4553
William Sciarillo, Sc.D., Exec.Dir.

Founded: 1965. **Members:** 4,300. **Local Groups:** 25. **Description:** Pediatric child life/activity specialists, nurses, pediatricians, parents, child psychiatrists, psychologists, social workers, designers and architects, and others, all of whom share an interest in the emotional, psychological, or social needs of children in pediatric settings. Purposes are to seek better understanding of the psychosocial needs of children in health settings, and promote sound programs of comprehensive care which will support these children and their families; to provide a common forum for those who are concerned with children and their families in such settings; to foster high standards of training and competence in all professions working within the pediatric setting; to focus the attention of all health workers and the community at large on comprehensive pediatric care; to cooperate with other organizations and agencies having related purposes; to stimulate and support research related to these purposes. Sponsors annual CHILDREN AND HOSPITALS WEEK. Conducts special project and research grants program. **Publications:** *ACCH Advocate*, semiannual. Magazine. Promotes family-centered, psychosocial care. • *ACCH News*, quarterly. Newsletter. Contains news on association and national activities and events. • *Children's Health Care*, quarterly. Journal. Contains research of theoretical, programmatic, clinical, training, and professional practice issues of psychosocial care of children and families. • *Resource Catalog.* Catalog. Contains over 100 titles available on request. **Formerly:** Association for the Care of Children in Hospitals.

★3178★ **Association of Child and Adolescent Psychiatric Nurses (ACAPN)**
1211 Locust St.
Philadelphia, PA 19107
Phone: (215)545-2843
Free: 800-826-2950
Fax: (215)545-8107
Carol Dashiff, Pres.

Founded: 1971. **Members:** 450. **Description:** Nurses and others interested in child and adolescent psychiatry. Works to promote mental health of infants, children, adolescents, and their families through clinical practice, public policy, and research. **Publications:** *ACAPN News*, 3/year. Newsletter. *Price:* Included in membership dues. • *Journal of Child and Adolescent Psychiatric Nursing*, quarterly. Journal. *Price:* Included in membership dues. **Formerly:** (1992) Advocates for Child Psychiatric Nursing.

★3179★ **Association for Child Psychoanalysis (ACP)**
c/o Rachel May
PO Box 366
Great Falls, VA 22066
Phone: (703)759-6698
Fax: (703)759-6783
Rachel May, Exec.Sec.

Founded: 1965. **Members:** 500. **Description:** Child psychoanalysts united to provide a forum for discussion and dissemination of information in their field. Conducts national and international scientific meetings. **Publications:** *Abstracts*, triennial. • *Association for Child Psychoanalysis--Newsletter*, semiannual. Newsletter. Covers child analysis methods, child psychoanalysis training, and the treatment and education of children throughout the world. *Price:* Included in membership dues. • *Membership Roster*, biennial. **Formerly:** (1971) American Association for Child Psychoanalysis.

★3180★ **Association for Child Psychology and Psychiatry (ACPP)**
70 Borough High St.
London SE1 1XF, England
Phone: 171 4037458
Fax: 171 4037081
Carol Garnier, Admin. Officer

Founded: 1956. **Members:** 2,400. **National Groups:** 14. **Languages:** English. **Description:** Professionals working in the field of child mental health. Encourages dissemination of scientific research and information. **Publications:** *Journal of Child Psychology and Psychiatry*, 8/year. Journal.

★3181★ **Association of Child Psychotherapists (ACP)**
Burgh House
New End Sq.
London NW3 1LT, England
Phone: 171 7948881
Fax: 171 4331874
Dr. Jill Hodges, Chair

Founded: 1939. **Description:** Safeguards the interests of psychotherapists and fosters the exchange of information on the treatments of psychological disturbances of behavior, thinking, and feeling. Provides a forum for discussion. **Publications:** *Journal of Child Psychotherapy*, semiannual. Journal.

★3182★ **Association for Children with Russell-Silver Syndrome (ACRSS)**
22 Hoyt St.
Madison, NJ 07940
Phone: (201)377-4531
Fax: (201)822-2715
Jodi Zwain, Pres.

Founded: 1989. **Members:** 150. **Regional Groups:** 4. **Description:** Individuals with Russell-Silver Syndrome (RSS) and their families; medical and health care professionals. RSS is a form of asymmetrical dwarfism or short stature characterized by short and incurved fifth fingers, downturning of the mouth, triangular shape of face, syndactyly of toes, and delayed motor development. Seeks to educate and offer support and guidance to families with an RSS member. Acts as a clearinghouse on information related to RSS; fosters research into the etiology and treatment of RSS. Maintains library. **Publications:** Newsletter, quarterly. Contains medical information, high calorie recipes, biographies of RSS children, and book reviews. *Price:* Included in membership dues.

★3183★ **Association of Children's Prosthetic-Orthotic Clinics (ACPOC)**
6300 N. River Rd., No. 727
Rosemont, IL 60018
Phone: (708)698-1694
Fax: (708)823-0536
David Lyttle, M.D., Pres.

Founded: 1980. **Members:** 450. **Description:** Prosthetic-orthotic clinics for children. Promotes the exchange of information concerning children's prosthetic-orthotic devices. Fosters cooperative research development and evaluative efforts among member clinics. Seeks to improve care in member clinics. **Publications:** *Journal of the Association of Children's Prosthetic-Orthotic Clinics*, quarterly. Journal. *Price:* $35/two-year subscription in U.S.; $40 in Canada and Mexico; $45 overseas.

★3184★ **Association of Maternal and Child Health Programs (AMCHP)**
1350 Connecticut Ave. NW, Ste. 803
Washington, DC 20036
Phone: (202)775-0436
Fax: (202)775-0061
Catherine Hess, Exec.Dir.

Founded: 1944. **Members:** 300. **Description:** Individuals responsible for or involved in the administration of state and territorial maternal and child health programs and programs for children with special health care needs. Seeks to: inform public and private sector decision makers of the health care needs of mothers and children; develop and recommend maternal and child health policies and programs; develop coalitions with other interested organizations. Promotes exchange of ideas and experiences among members; studies and reports on the health of and services for mothers and children; develops models and standards for and provides technical assistance to maternal and child health programs. **Publications:** *AMCHP Updates*, bimonthly. Newsletter. *Price:* Included in membership dues. • *Building on the Basics: Four Approaches to Enhancing MCH Service Delivery.* • *Caring for Mothers and Children: A Report of a Survey of 1987 State MCH Program Activities.* • *Dedicated to Care for Children: A Report on States Use of OBRA 1986 Earmarked Title V Funds.* • *Magazines.* • *MCH Related Federal Programs: Legal Handbooks for Program Planners and Medicaid.* • *Proceedings.* • *Reports.* • *Title V in Review: Two Decades of Analysis of Selected Aspects of the Title V Program.* • *Toward the Future of Title V: A Report on Site Visits to Ten State Programs.* Also publishes cost-based reimbursement studies and health care reform studies. **Formerly:** Association of State and Territorial Maternal and Child Health and Crippled Children's Directors.

★3185★ **Association of Medical School Pediatric Department Chairmen (AMSPDC)**
c/o Jean Bartholomew
111 Silver Cedar Ct.
Chapel Hill, NC 27514-1651
Phone: (919)942-1993
Russell Chesney, M.D., Sec.-Treas.

Founded: 1961. **Members:** 147. **Description:** Chairmen of the department of pediatrics of each accredited medical school in the United States and Canada. Fosters education and research in the field of child health and human development. Is cooperating with other national pediatric groups to consider problems of pediatric education, research, and care. **Publications:** *AMSPDC Membership List*, annual.

Association of Paediatric Anaesthetists of Great Britain and Ireland (APA)
See: Entry 2356

★3186★ **Association of Pediatric Oncology Nurses (APON)**
5700 Old Orchard Rd.
Skokie, IL 60077
Phone: (708)966-3723
Fax: (708)966-9418
Richard Muir, Exec.Dir.

Founded: 1973. **Members:** 2,000. **Regional Groups:** 32. **Description:** Scientific and educational association seeking to establish lines of communication among nurses caring for children with cancer; encourages updating of literature and development of standards of care for children with cancer. Plans regional workshops. **Publications:** *APON Newsletter*, quarterly. •

Journal of Pediatric Oncology Nursing, quarterly. • *Nursing Care of the Child With Cancer.*

★3187★ Association of Pediatric Oncology Social Workers (APOSW)
c/o Lynda Walker
All Childrens Hospital
St. Petersburg, FL 33701
Phone: (813)360-1319
Lynda Walker, Pres.

Founded: 1977. **Members:** 200. **Description:** Social workers involved with pediatric cancer patients in medical settings nationwide. Purposes are to: advance the practice, enhance knowledge, and develop policy and programs of pediatric oncology social work; foster quality and effectiveness of the social work practice of pediatric oncology; promote solidarity among social workers; provide community and professional education; formulate and record local and federal legislation related to pediatric oncology. **Publications:** Brochure. • Newsletter, quarterly.

★3188★ Association of Pediatric Societies of the Southeast Asian Region (APSSEAR)
Medical Center Manila
PO Box EA 100
Manila, Philippines
Phone: 2 507874
Fax: 2 7216569
Prof. Perla D. Santos Ocampo, Sec.Gen.

Founded: 1974. **Members:** 20. **Languages:** English. **Description:** Pediatrics societies in Asian countries and the Pacific region. Works to disseminate information for the benefit of children and child health in the Southeast Asian region and surrounding countries. Encourages research. Participates in the fellowship program sponsored by the Australian College of Pediatrics. **Publications:** Bulletin, quarterly. • *State of Asian Children.* Report.

★3189★ Association for Research of Childhood Cancer (AROCC)
PO Box 251
Buffalo, NY 14225-0251
Phone: (716)681-4433
Ann O'Donnell, Exec. Officer

Founded: 1970. **Members:** 1,000. **Regional Groups:** 2. **Description:** Parents who have lost children to various pediatric cancers; persons supporting cancer research. Seeks to fund the expansion and continuation of research in pediatric cancer centers and to provide seed money for pilot projects in cancer research. Offers support to parents of children with cancer. Bestows research and clinical investigation grants; offers research and medical student fellowships. **Publications:** *AROCC--Newsletter*, quarterly. Newsletter. Contains book reviews; donations list; memorial list. *Price:* Included in membership dues. • *Parent/Child Handbook.*

★3190★ Association of SIDS Program Professionals (ASPP)
Massachusetts Center for SIDS
Boston City Hospital
818 Harrison Ave.
Boston, MA 02118
Phone: (617)534-7437
Fax: (617)534-5555
Mary McClain, Pres.

Founded: 1987. **Members:** 110. **Description:** Health and human services professionals who provide support services to those affected by Sudden Infant Death Syndrome (SIDS). Represents SIDS information and counseling services at the national, state, and international levels. Acts as an advocate for continued developmental and expansion of SIDS and bereavement services. Organizes activities which promote professional growth, develops practice standards and links together practitioners working with SIDS families. Supports research. **Publications:** *SIDs and Sleeping Position: Counseling Implications*, annual. Newsletter. • *Standards of Service.*

★3191★ Association of Teachers of Maternal and Child Health (ATMCH)
Johns Hopkins University
School of Public Health
624 N. Broadway
Baltimore, MD 21205
Phone: (301)955-3384
Fax: (301)955-2303
Bernard Guyer, MD

Founded: 1968. **Members:** 200. **Description:** Faculty and research staff in maternal and child health. Promotes the teaching and research of maternal and child health programs in public health schools and professional schools in the U.S. and abroad. Participates in the development and support of policy initiatives related to the field. **Publications:** *ATMCH News*, semiannual. Newsletter. *Price:* Free.

★3192★ Bahrain Pediatric Association (BPA)
PO Box 26640
Manama, Bahrain
Phone: 640841
Khalil Rasromani, Sec.

Founded: 1985. **Members:** 32. **Languages:** Arabic, English. **Description:** Pediatricians promoting research and public education aimed at improving pediatric sevices in Bahrain. Organizes biennial symposium; compiles statistics. **Publications:** *Bahrain Medical Bulletin*, quarterly.

Blind Children's Fund (BCF)
See: Entry 13422

★3193★ Brass Ring Society (BRS)
551 E. Semoran Blvd., No. E-5
Fern Park, FL 32730
Phone: (407)339-6188
Free: 800-666-9474
Fax: (407)339-6369
Ray Esposito, Pres.

Founded: 1983. **Members:** 1,000. **Local Groups:** 3. **Description:** Individuals who contribute their time, efforts, ideas, compassion, and monetary support toward programs for children with life-threatening illnesses including fulfilling the dreams of terminally ill children. The society estimates that each year approximately 13,000 children are stricken with a terminal illness and countless others are chronically ill. Encourages major hotel chains, airlines, and other services to offer assistance in granting the wishes of these children. **Publications:** *The Carousel.* Newsletter. Describes "dream fulfillment" and other society programs for terminally ill children. Includes chapter, donor and staff and new member news. *Price:* Included in membership dues.

★3194★ British Association of Paediatric Surgeons (BAPS)
Nicolson St.
Edinburgh EH8 9DW, Scotland
Phone: 131 6683975
Fax: 131 6671905
Mr. D. Burge, Hon.Sec.

Founded: 1953. **Members:** 700. **Languages:** English. **Description:** Pedriatric surgeons, consultants, and trainees. Works to improve the techniques of study, practice, and research in pediatric surgery; fosters professional relations among pediatric surgeons. Sponsors training program. **Publications:** *Journal of Pediatric Surgery*, periodic.

★3195★ Canadian Paediatric Society (CPS)
(Societe Canadienne de Pediatrie — SCP)
Children's Hospital of Eastern Ontario
401 Smyth Rd.
Ottawa, ON, Canada K1H 8L1
Phone: (613)737-2728
Fax: (613)737-2794
Danielle Solimka, Coord.

Founded: 1922. **Members:** 1,954. **Languages:** English, French. **Description:** Pediatricians in 18 countries. Promotes the advancement of scientific knowledge pertaining to infancy, childhood, and adolescence. Represents members' interests to public, government, and other professional groups. Acts as information and resource center. Offers primary and consultative care for children. Bestows awards. **Publications:** *Canada Immunization Guide*, periodic. Book. • *Membership List*, annual. • *News Bulletin*, bimonthly. Bulletin. • *Pediatrics in Canada.* Book. • Reports. • *Statements*, periodic. Paper. • *Well Beings.* Book. **Formerly:** (1951) Canadian Society for the Study of Diseases of Children.

★3196★ Candlelighters Childhood Cancer Foundation (CCCF)
7910 Woodmont Ave., Ste. 460
Bethesda, MD 20814-3015
Phone: (301)657-8401
Free: 800-366-2223
Fax: (301)718-2686
James R. Kitterman, Exec.Dir.

Founded: 1970. **Members:** 40,000. **National Groups:** 350. **Local Groups:** 1. **Description:** Family members of children or adolescents with cancer, survivors of childhood cancer, and professionals who work with them. Educates, supports, serves, and advocates for families and individuals touched by childhood cancer, empowering them to meet the challenges they face.

Coordinates a network of more than 400 peer support groups and contacts for parents of children/adolescents with cancer, and a survivors network. Offers literature and searches through the Information Clearinghouse. Operates CCCF Ombudsman Program, which assists with health insurance problems, second opinions, and employment issues. Conducts lobbying. Local groups offer meetings at which parents share information and emotional support and hear speakers. Many chapters offer parent-to-parent visitation, transportation, blood or wig banks, speakers' bureaus, meetings for young people, and bereavement groups. Named for the Chinese proverb, "It is better to light one candle than to curse the darkness." **Publications:** *Bone Marrow Transplant Guide.* Handbook. *Price:* $7.50. • *CCCF Bibliography and Resource Guide*, annual. Bibliography. Annotated reviews of books, articles, pamphlets, and videos. *Price:* $5 in U.S.; $8 in Canada and Mexico; $12 all other countries. • *CCCF Quarterly Newsletter*, quarterly. Newsletter. Articles, poetry, and reviews pertaining to living with and treating childhood cancer. *Price:* Free to family and health/education professionals. • *CCCF Youth Newsletter*, quarterly. Newsletter. Contains articles, poetry, and art by and for young cancer patients, survivors, and their siblings. *Price:* Free for young people with cancer, siblings. • *Educating the Child with Cancer.* Handbook. • *Parent-to-Parent Visitation Manual.* Manual. • *The Phoenix*, quarterly, For adult survivors of childhood cancer. Newsletter. *Price:* Free with membership in survivor program. • *Progress Reports*, periodic. Contains research updates. *Price:* Free. • *Spanish Bibliography*, periodic. Bibliography. *Price:* Free. Also publishes basic family library, publications list, camp list, and wish fulfillment organizations list. **Formerly:** (1984) Candlelighters Foundation.

★ 3197 ★ **Carnegie Council on Adolescent Development (CCAD)**
2400 N St. NW, 6th Fl.
Washington, DC 20037
Phone: (202)429-7979
Fax: (202)775-0134
Ruby Takanishi, Exec.Dir.

Founded: 1986. **Description:** A program of the Carnegie Corporation of New York. Works to "place the challenges of the adolescent years higher on the nation's agenda." Provides information to the general public on the risks and opportunities of the adolescent years; generates support for measures that facilitate the critical transition into adulthood. **Publications:** *A Matter of Time: Risk and Opportunity in the Nonschool Hours.* Book. • *Carnegie Council on Adolescent Development Working Papers*, periodic. Papers. • *Fateful Choices: Healthy Youth for the 21st Century.* Book. • Papers. • *Preventing Abuse of Drugs, Alcohol, and Tobacco by Adolescents.* • *Risk Taking in Adolescence: A Decision-Making Perspective.* • *Turning Points: Preparing American Youth for the 21st Century.* Book.

★ 3198 ★ **Child Health Foundation (ICHF)**
Century Plz., No. 325
10630 Little Patuxat Pky.
Columbia, MD 21044
Phone: (301)596-4514
Fax: (410)992-5641
Charlene B. Dale, Exec.VP

Founded: 1986. **Members:** 3,000. **Description:** Addresses significant health issues of children and families, primarily in developing countries and medically underserved populations in the U.S. Focuses on diarrheal diseases, related social and medical problems of malnutrition, and poverty. Develops and encourages use of simple, low-cost technologies. Conducts health programs in research training in oral rehydration therapies, nutrition, breastfeeding and other lowcost approaches to better health. Operates programs to strengthen research capabilities of institutions in developing countries to enable them to develop and perform research on diseases most prevalent in their own countries. Conducts educational training programs and workshops for: volunteers in disease prevention and simple treatments effective in rural and urban areas. Conducts charitable activities; maintains speakers' bureau. **Publications:** Annual Report. • *Cereal-Based Oral Rehydration Therapy Symposium Proceedings.* • *Food-based Oral Rehydration Therapy Report.* • *International Child Health Foundation Newsletter*, quarterly. Newsletter. Includes research summaries and foundation information. • *Proper Nutrition and Hygiene.* • *Training Manual for Treatment and Prevention of Childhood Diarrhea with Oral Rehydration Therapy.* **Formerly:** International Child Health Foundation; (1994) International Child Health Foundation.

★ 3199 ★ **Child Life Council (CLC)**
7910 Woodmont Ave., Ste. 310
Bethesda, MD 20814
Phone: (301)654-1343
Fax: (301)654-4964
Kathleen McCue, Contact

Founded: 1982. **Members:** 1,400. **Description:** Professional organization representing child life personnel, patient activities specialists, and students in the field. Promotes psychological well-being and optimum development of children, adolescents, and their families in health care settings. Works to minimize the stress and anxiety of illness and hospitalization. Addresses professional issues such as program standards, competencies, and core curriculum. Provides resources and conducts research and educational programs. Offers a Job Bank Service listing employment openings. **Publications:** *Child Life Council Bulletin*, quarterly. Bulletin. • *Child Life Council Directory*, periodic. Directory. • *Official Documents of the Child Life Council.* • *Program Review Guidelines.* **Formerly:** (1975) Child Life Specialist Committee; (1979) Child Life Activity Study Section; (1982) Child Life Task Force.

★ 3200 ★ **Child Neurology Society (CNS)**
475 Cleveland Ave. N., Ste. 220
St. Paul, MN 55104-5051
Phone: (612)641-1584
Fax: (612)641-1634
Mary Currey, Exec. Officer

Founded: 1971. **Members:** 1,000. **Description:** Neurologists certified by the American Board of Psychiatry and Neurology and specializing in child neurology; individuals eligible for the certifying examination and those who have made significant contributions to the field of child neurology; individuals enrolled in approved child neurology training programs. To advance child neurology by establishing a scientific forum for professionals in the field; to define areas of pediatric neurological practices and to make known these procedures among professionals and medical students. Promotes interest in the field of child neurology among medical students. Advertises positions available in pediatric neurology. **Publications:** *Annals of Neurology*, monthly. Journal. • Booklets.

★ 3201 ★ **Child Nutrition Forum (CNF)**
1875 Connecticut Ave. NW, Ste. 540
Washington, DC 20009
Phone: (202)986-2200
Fax: (202)986-2525
Edward M. Cooney, Coord.

Founded: 1981. **Members:** 230. **Description:** Organizations involved in agriculture, civil rights, education, and nutrition advocacy; consumer and religious groups, unions, and elected officials. Purpose is to serve as liaison among diverse organizations that support effective and adequately funded federal food programs for children. Compiles information concerning developments in national child nutrition policies. Maintains speakers' bureau. **Publications:** *Cost Saving Measures in School Lunch.* • *Report on the Federal Budget Process*, annual. **Formerly:** (1981) Child Nutrition Coalition.

Children and Adults With Attention Deficit Disorder (CHADD)
See: Entry 8201

Children of Alcoholics Foundation (COAF)
See: Entry 12016

★ 3202 ★ **Children in Hospitals (CIH)**
300 Longwood Ave.
Boston, MA 02115
Phone: (617)355-6000
Fax: (617)355-7429
Barbara K. Popper, Founder

Founded: 1971. **Members:** 200. **Description:** Parents, educators, and health care professionals who seek to minimize the trauma involved in a child's hospitalization by supporting and educating parents and medical personnel regarding the need for children to have parents present whenever possible. Encourages hospitals to adopt flexible visiting policies and to provide live-in accommodations for parents with hospitalized children. Advises parents to plan for a child's hospitalization by "shopping" for a sympathetic doctor and a hospital that allows frequent parent-child contact, and by preparing themselves and the child for what will occur during hospitalization. Is also concerned with aspects of family hospitalization, including maternity care and adult care relative to family contact. **Publications:** Brochure. • *CIH Consumer Directory of Hospitals*, semiannual. Directory. • *CIH Newsletter*, quarterly. Newsletter. Provides suggestions for parents regarding child health care; includes reports on CIH activities and reviews of current literature. *Price:* Included in membership dues; $10/year for nonmembers.

★ 3203 ★   Children's Aid International (CAI)
PO Box 83220
San Diego, CA 92138-3220
Phone: (619)694-0095
Free: 800-842-2810
Fax: (619)694-0188
Dr. T. J. Grosser, CEO & Pres.

Founded: 1977. **Description:** Nondenominational charitable program that provides nutritional, medical, and educational assistance to needy children in Southeast Asia, Africa, Latin America, Eastern Europe, and U.S. Provides resources to meet health needs, including nutrition supplements ("Nutri-Paks"), medicine, and the services of physicians, nurses, nutritionists, and paramedics. Operates primary health care clinics in Nairobi, Kenya, and Malaysia. Participates in foreign grant-matching programs; operates mobile nutrition, blood collection, and distribution vans; establishes and operates "health posts" to examine and care for malnourished children and mothers. Conducts "feed and teach programs," which train mothers in nutrition and in identifying, cultivating, and preparing nutritious foods available from local sources. Educates community members in preventive health care, proper sanitation, and growing nutritious foods. CAI is funded through contributions and the operation of, a child sponsorship program in Indonesia, Thailand, Guatemala, and Kenya in which individuals financially support and correspond with a needy child. Provides the opportunity for individuals or groups to donate gift "Nutri-Paks," Medical Gift-Paks, equipment, and training materials. Sponsors projects to provide a training ground for medical students in treatment of malnourished, ill, and destitute children. Operates speakers' bureau. **Publications:** *Focus on Children,* 2-3/year. Newsletter. Includes member news and information on programs. *Price:* Free.

★ 3204 ★   Children's Blood Foundation (CBF)
333 E. 38th, 8th Fl.
New York, NY 10016
Phone: (212)297-4336
Fax: (212)297-4340
Jules Rodman, Exec.Dir.

Founded: 1952. **Regional Groups:** 1. **Description:** Seeks to combat diseases of the blood in children, such as leukemia, hemophilia, thalassemia (Cooley's anemia), childhood cancers, sickle cell, and other anemias and diseases of the immune system, including transfusion-related AIDS. Supports a total patient care center in the New York Hospital-Cornell Medical Center, which includes diagnostic and treatment clinics, progressive research laboratories, and intensive training of physicians in the specialty of pediatric hematology/oncology. Also sponsors specialized social events.

★ 3205 ★   Children's Defense Fund (CDF)
25 E St. NW
Washington, DC 20001
Phone: (202)628-8787
Free: 800-CDF-1200
Fax: (202)662-3530
Marian Wright Edelman, Pres.

Founded: 1973. **State Groups:** 3. **Local Groups:** 4. **Description:** Provides systematic, long-range advocacy on behalf of the nation's children and teenagers. Engages in research, public education, monitoring of federal agencies, litigation, legislative drafting and testimony, assistance to state and local groups, and community organizing in areas of child welfare, child health, adolescent pregnancy prevention, child care and development, family services, and child mental health. Works with individuals and groups to change policies and practices resulting in neglect or maltreatment of millions of children. Advocates: access to existing programs and services; creation of new programs and services where necessary; enforcement of civil rights laws; program accountability; strong parent and community role in decision-making; adequate funding for essential programs for children. Compiles statistics. **Publications:** Books. • *CDF Reports,* monthly. Newsletter. Provides articles on issues relating to children and adolescents. Topics include child care, health, education, teen pregnancy prevention. *Price:* $29.95/year. • Handbooks. • *The Health of America's Children: Maternal and Child Health Data Book.* Book. • *Publications,* periodic. • *The State of America's Children,* annual. Examines the status of America's children, youths, and families. Emphasizes ways to improve child care welfare, and more. Also publishes posters on issues affecting children. **Formerly:** (1978) Children's Defense Fund of the Washington Research Project.

★ 3206 ★   Children's Healthcare is a Legal Duty (CHILD)
PO Box 2604
Sioux City, IA 51106
Phone: (712)948-3500
Fax: (712)948-3500
Dr. Rita Swan, Pres.

Founded: 1983. **Members:** 300. **Description:** Physicians, lawyers, and concerned individuals. Purpose is to promote the legal rights of children in obtaining medical care. Opposes: religion-based denial of medical care to children; child discipline through physical abuse that they feel is sanctioned by religious beliefs; the exemption of religious day care centers from state licensing because they are religious bodies. Collects and disseminates information regarding state laws and court cases that handle the legal rights of children to receive medical care regardless of religious convictions; disseminates information on child abuse and neglect related to religion. Provides speaking services. Offers support group for victims of religious-based medical care denial. **Publications:** *Child, Inc. Newsletter,* quarterly. Newsletter. *Price:* Included in membership dues; $25/year for nonmembers. • *The Law's Response When Religious Beliefs Against Medical Care Impact on Children.* Monograph. *Price:* $10. **Also Known As:** CHILD, Inc..

★ 3207 ★   Children's Health and Fitness Fund (CHeaFF)
PO Box 2882
Reston, VA 22090
Phone: (703)715-8536
Fax: (703)715-8537
Carl Grant, III, Exec.Dir.

Founded: 1991. **Description:** Educates the public on the rights and needs of children to have healthy, physically fit, and more productive lives. Believes in providing early, continuous, and consistent health and fitness training to children. Develops and produces television programming to promote children's health and fitness. Develops and distributes educational materials including interactive computer courseware, public service advertising campaigns, and instructional videotapes. Offers a school visitation program and participatory events for children.

★ 3208 ★   Children's Health Fund
317 E. 64th St.
New York, NY 10021
Phone: (212)535-9400
Fax: (212)535-7488
Irwin Redlener, M.D., Pres.

Founded: 1987. **Description:** Supports pediatric programs for chldren who are homeless, poor, or have no other access to medical care. Maintains Children's Health Projects in urban and rural areas throughout the United States. Provides mobile medical units in order to bring health care to deserving children.

★ 3209 ★   Children's Hospice International (CHI)
700 Princess St., Lower Level
Alexandria, VA 22314
Phone: (703)684-0330
Free: 800-24-CHILD
Fax: (703)684-0226
Ann Armstrong Dailey, Founding Dir.

Founded: 1983. **Members:** 600. **Description:** Physicians, nurses, teachers, social workers, clergy, psychologists, art and music occupational therapists, volunteers, and students who work or are interested in hospice programs. Objectives are to: promote hospice support through pediatric care facilities; encourage the inclusion of children in existing and developing hospices and home care programs; include hospice perspectives in all areas of pediatric care and education. Supports health care agencies that engage in the treatment of terminally ill children and their families. Disseminates information concerning support groups and research, education, and training programs. Children's hospice care involves an interdisciplinary team of physicians, social workers, nurses, clergy, therapists, teachers and trained volunteers; parents act as primary care-givers. Plans to develop clearinghouse and resource center. **Publications:** *Approaching Grief.* Pamphlet. • Audiotapes. • *Children's Hospice/Home Care.* Manual. • *Children's Hospice International--Newsletter,* quarterly. Newsletter. Contains calendar of events and list of resources. *Price:* Included in membership dues; $20/year for nonmembers. • *Home Care for Seriously Ill Children: A Manual for Parents.* Manual. • *Palliative Pain and Symptom Management for Children* and Adolescents. • *The Psychological Aspects of Pain and Symptom Management.* • Videos.

★3210★ Children's Wish Foundation International (CWFI)
7840 Roswell Rd., Ste. 301
Atlanta, GA 30358
Phone: (404)393-9474
Free: 800-323-WISH
Fax: (404)393-0683
Linda Dozoretz, Exec.Dir.

Founded: 1978. **Description:** Seeks to fulfill the wishes of terminally ill children under 18 years old. Maintains speakers' bureau; compiles statistics. Provides children's services throughout North America and Europe. **Publications:** Brochures. • Newsletter, bimonthly. **Formerly:** Children's Wish Foundation.

China Expert Consultancy Committee on Maternity
See: Entry 9642

Chinese Association for Birth Planning and Childhood Health Improvement Sciences
See: Entry 11209

★3211★ Chinese Taipei Pediatric Association (CTPA)
11 Ching-Tao W. Rd., 4F-4
Taipei 10022, Taiwan
Phone: 2 3314917
Fax: 2 3142184
Prof. Kue-Hsiung Hsieh, Pres.

Founded: 1960. **Members:** 2,200. **Languages:** Chinese, English. **Description:** Pediatricians and others working in the field of pediatric medicine in 6 countries. Promotes the health and welfare of infants, children, and adolescents. Encourages research and teaching in the field; sponsors educational and scientific programs. Facilitates information exchange. **Publications:** *Acta Paediatrica Sinica,* bimonthly. Journal. Medical Journal. • *Members' Directory,* triennial. • *Supplement,* semiannual. for the purpose of continuing medical education. **Formerly:** (1989) Pediatric Association of Republic of China.

Coeliac Society of the United Kingdom (CSUK)
See: Entry 5214

★3212★ Colombian Pedriatric Society (CPS)
(Sociedad Colombiana de Pediatria — SCP)
Hospital Militar Central
Entrepiso 1
Bogota, Colombia
Phone: 1 2883985
Fax: 923 673614
Dr. Gabriel Lamos, Pres.

Founded: 1917. **Members:** 845. **Local Groups:** 21. **Languages:** English, Spanish. **Description:** Health care professionals specializing in pediatric and adolescent medicine. Facilitates exchange of information among members; establishes unified guidelines for pediatric diagnosis and treatment. Conducts national immunization programs. **Publications:** *Acta Pediatrica,* quarterly. • *Pediatria,* 3/year. • *Revista Colombiana de Pediatria y Puericultura,* quarterly. Also publishes national listings of pediatricians and pediatric subspecialists.

★3213★ Confederation of European Specialists in Pediatrics (CESP)
20, ave. de la Couronne
B-1050 Brussels, Belgium
Phone: 2 6495164
Fax: 2 6403730
J.C. Schaack, M.D., Sec.Gen.

Founded: 1959. **Members:** 34. **National Groups:** 12. **Languages:** English, French. **Description:** Representatives of professional associations of member nations of the European Union and SEFTA countries. Purpose is to coordinate the practice of and training in pediatric medicine within the EEC. **Publications:** *Report of Annual Meeting.*

★3214★ Council for Children with Behavioral Disorders (CCBD)
c/o Council for Exceptional Children
1920 Association Dr.
Reston, VA 22091-1589
Phone: (703)620-3660
Fax: (703)264-9494
Dr. Cynthia Warger, Pres.

Founded: 1962. **Members:** 8,500. **Regional Groups:** 10. **State Groups:** 52. **Description:** A division of The Council for Exceptional Children. Works to promote and facilitate the education and welfare of children and youth with behavioral and emotional disturbances, and to promote professional growth and research as a means to better understand the problems of these children. Acts with CEC to improve educational programs for all exceptional children. **Publications:** *Behavioral Disorders,* quarterly. Journal. Includes book reviews. *Price:* Included in membership dues; $20/year for nonmember individuals; $50/year for institutions. • *Beyond Behavior,* 3/year. *Price:* $20 for individual; $35 for institution. • *CBBD Newsletter,* quarterly. Newsletter. Provides information on division activities. Includes convention and conference announcements. *Price:* Included in membership dues. • *Monographs,* annual. Monographs.

★3215★ Council for Exceptional Children (CEC)
1920 Association Dr.
Reston, VA 22091-1589
Phone: (703)620-3660
Fax: (703)264-9494
Nancy D. Safer, Exec.Dir.

Founded: 1922. **Members:** 54,000. **Local Groups:** 970. **Description:** Administrators, teachers, parents, and others who work with and on behalf of children with disabilities and/or who are gifted. Seeks to improve the educational outcomes for individuals with exceptionalities - children, youth, and young adults with disabilities and/or who are gifted. Advocates for appropriate government policies; provides information to the media. Operates the ERIC Clearinghouse on Disabilities and Gifted Education, the National Clearinghouse for Professions in Special Education, and the National Training Program for Gifted Education. Supports professional development by operating several federally funded projects including the Continuing Education Program on Attention Deficit Disorder and the National Institute on Comprehensive Systems of Personnel Development. **Publications:** Audiotapes. • Books. • *Exceptional Child Edu-*

cation Resources, quarterly. Journal. Includes abstracts of book, nonprint media, and journal literature. • *Exceptional Children,* bimonthly. Journal. Covers all facets of special education. *Price:* Included in membership dues; $52/year for nonmembers. • Films. • *Teaching Exceptional Children,* quarterly. Magazine. Includes classroom-oriented information about instructional methods, materials, and techniques for students of all ages with special needs. *Price:* Included in membership dues; $35/year for nonmembers. • Videos. Also publishes search reprints, other materials relevant to teaching exceptional children, and microfilms.

★3216★ Council for Exceptional Children (DCDT)
Division on Career Development and Transition
c/o The Council for Exceptional Children
1920 Association Dr.
Reston, VA 22091-1589
Phone: (703)620-3660
Fax: (703)264-9494
Jeanne Repetto, Pres.

Founded: 1979. **Members:** 2,000. **State Groups:** 35. **Description:** A division of The Council for Exceptional Children. Professionals and paraprofessionals involved in career development and transition of exceptional children, youth, and adults; students training in the field. Promotes professional growth, research, legislation, and information dissemination; encourages interaction among persons and organizations involved in the career development of exceptional individuals. **Publications:** *Career Development for Exceptional Individuals,* semiannual. Journal. Covers current research and practice in career development and transition issues for exceptional individuals. *Price:* Included in membership dues; $20/year for nonmembers. • *DCDT Network,* 3/year. Newsletter. *Price:* Included in membership dues. **Formerly:** (1993) Division on Career Development of the Council for Exceptional Children.

★3217★ Council for Exceptional Children (DEC)
Division for Early Childhood
Council for Exceptional Children
1920 Association Dr.
Reston, VA 22091
Phone: (703)620-3660
Fax: (703)264-9494
Deborah Ziegler, Pres.

Founded: 1973. **Members:** 7,000. **State Groups:** 45. **Description:** A division of The Council for Exceptional Children. Teachers, program administrators, students, parents, persons involved in health-related fields, and individuals interested in the development and education of handicapped infants and preschool children. Objectives are: to promote education for young children and infants with special needs; to initiate programs that cooperatively involve parents in their children's education; to stimulate communication and joint activity among early childhood organizations; to encourage professional development; to disseminate research findings and information addressing issues of early childhood. Believes that the provision of services to handicapped children from birth through the age of five must be made a priority in today's society. Encourages a national initiative to establish plans for systematic coordination between the social, educational, and health agencies currently serving handicapped children through the age of five. **Publications:** *Division for Early Childhood--Communicator*, quarterly. Newsletter. Provides information on working with handicapped children; covers current trends and practices; includes book reviews and calender of events. *Price:* Included in membership dues. • *Journal of Early Intervention*, quarterly. Journal. Provides information on current research and practice for individuals who work with disabled children. Includes book reviews. *Price:* Included in membership dues; $50/year for nonmembers.

★ 3218 ★ Council for Exceptional Children (DVH)
Division for Visual Handicaps
c/o Council for Exceptional Children
1920 Association Dr.
Reston, VA 22091-1589
Phone: (703)620-3660
Fax: (703)264-9494
Dr. Jane Erin, Pres.

Founded: 1954. **Members:** 1,000. **Description:** A division of the Council for Exceptional Children. Teachers, college faculty members, administrators and supervisors, and others concerned with the education and welfare of children and youth with visual impairments. **Publications:** *DVH Quarterly*, quarterly. Newsletter. Covers current developments in education of children & youth with visual impairments, and political action updates. Available in Braille and on tape. *Price:* Included in membership dues. **Formerly:** (1976) Council for the Education of the Partially Seeing; (1992) Division for the Visually Handicapped.

★ 3219 ★ Cyclic Vomiting Syndrome Association (CVSA)
13180 Caroline Ct.
Elm Grove, WI 53122

Founded: 1993. **Description:** Individuals suffering from Cyclic Vomiting Syndrome (CVS), their families, and interested medical professionals. CVS is a rare disorder that usually affects children ages 3-7, and is characterized by recurrent, prolonged attacks of unexplained nausea and vomiting. Promotes medical research on CVS, and seeks to raise public awareness about CVS. Encourages support and information exchange among members. Acts as an information clearinghouse. **Publications:** Newsletter, semiannual. *Price:* Available to members only.

★ 3220 ★ Dominican Society of Pediatrics (SDP)
(Sociedad Dominica de Pediatria)
Clinica Infantil Dr. Robert Reid Cabral
Centro de Los Heroes
Santo Domingo, Dominican Republic
Phone: (809)533-3222
Fax: (809)535-1052
Dr. Rodolfo Nunez-Musa, Pres.

Founded: 1947. **Members:** 850. **National Groups:** 1. **Regional Groups:** 3. **State Groups:** 10. **Description:** Pediatric physicians in the Do-

minican Republic. Sponsors educational programs. **Publications:** *Archivo Dominicanos de Pediatria*, 3/year. Journal. • Bulletin, monthly. • *Committee Papers*. Reports.

★ 3221 ★ Dream Factory (DF)
315 Guthrie Green
Louisville, KY 40202
Phone: (502)584-3928
Free: 800-456-7556
Denis P. Heavrin, Nat.Exec.Dir.

Founded: 1980. **Members:** 1,000. **Local Groups:** 41. **Description:** Volunteers devoted to granting the dreams of chronically or critically ill children. Seeks to: bring smiles to the faces of seriously ill children; promote a better family atmosphere during a prolonged illness; involve the community in granting wishes to children; raise funds necessary to provide dreams. Has honored requests for photographs of celebrities, trips to Disney World, a visit to Buckingham Palace, and for the building of a home. Sponsors annual summer camps. Maintains speakers' bureau. **Publications:** Newsletter, quarterly.

Dysautonomia Foundation (DF)
See: Entry 8208

European Association for Studies on Nutrition and Child Development (ADE)
(Association Europeenne pour l'Etude de l'Alimentation et du Developpement de l'Enfant — ADE)
See: Entry 9455

★ 3222 ★ European Society of Child and Adolescent Psychiatry (ESCAP)
(Societe Europeene de Psychiatrie de l'Enfant et de l'Adolescent — SEPEA)
Academisch Ziekenhuis Utrecht
Kinder en Juegdpsychiatrie
Postbus 85500
NL-3508 GA Utrecht, Netherlands
Phone: 30 506362
Prof. H. van Engeland, Pres.

Founded: 1954. **Members:** 18. **Languages:** English, French, German. **Description:** National societies. **Publications:** *European Child and Adolescent Psychiatry*, quarterly. Journal.

★ 3223 ★ European Society for Paediatric Endocrinology (ESPE)
Universitats-Kinderklinik
Department of Paediatrics
Schwanenweg 20
24105 Kiel, Germany
Phone: 431 5971926
Fax: 431 5971675
Prof. Wolfgang G. Sippell

Founded: 1961. **Members:** 345. **Languages:** English. **Description:** Pediatricians, medical practitioners, and scientific staff in 28 countries involved in research and clinical practice of pediatric endocrinology. Promotes discussion and collaboration in the field. Operates summer school for pediatric endocrinologists in training. **Publications:** *Hormone Research*, monthly. • *Membership Directory*, annual. • *Program of Annual Meeting*, annual.

★ 3224 ★ European Society for Paediatric Haematology and Immunology (ESPHI)
(Europese Vereniging voor Pediatrische Hematologie en Immunologie — EVPHI)
Universitats Kinderklinik
Dept. of Pediatrics
Robert-Koch-Strasse 40
37075 Gottingen, Germany
Phone: 551 392970
G. Prindull, M.D., Exec. Officer

Founded: 1970. **Members:** 190. **Languages:** English. **Description:** Researchers in pediatric hematology and immunology. Works to advance research; promotes the exchange of ideas among scientists and young researchers in the field.

★ 3225 ★ European Society for Paediatric Nephrology (ESPN)
Hospital des Enfants Malades
149, rue de Sevres
F-75730 Paris Cedex 15, France
Phone: 1 42738991
Fax: 1 42738451
Prof. Patrick Niaudet, M.D., Contact

Founded: 1967. **Members:** 280. **Languages:** English. **Description:** Pediatricians and medical scientists in 26 countries involved in pediatric nephrology. Promotes knowledge of and research on childhood renal disease. Coordinates international studies and disseminates information on pediatric nephrology. **Publications:** *Abstract of Communications*, annual. • *News Letter*, semiannual.

European Society of Paediatric Radiology (ESPR)
See: Entry 11113

European Union of Paediatric Surgical Associations (EUPSA)
See: Entry 12271

★ 3226 ★ Famous Fone Friends (FFF)
9101 Sawyer St.
Los Angeles, CA 90035
Phone: (310)204-5683
Fax: (310)204-5683
Linda Stone-Elster, Exec. Officer

Founded: 1986. **Members:** 100. **Regional Groups:** 1. **Description:** Seeks to raise the spirits of sick, hospitalized, and homebound children. A sick child's doctor or nurse contacts FFF, which in turn arranges for a well-known actor, athlete, or other celebrity to call the child for a friendly chat. Conducts annual Holiday Calling Day. (Because all participants in the FFF are volunteers, requests for specific stars are not recommended.) **Publications:** *Famous Friend News*, biennial. Includes news updates and membership and entertainer listings. • *FFF Memo*, 3/year.

Federation for Children with Special Needs (FCSN)
See: Entry 4485

★ 3227 ★ FORMULA
PO Box 39051
Washington, DC 20016
Phone: (703)527-7171
Carol Laskin, Exec. Officer

Founded: 1980. **Description:** To ensure the safety and nutritional completeness of all infant formulas. Gathers data from parents whose children have suffered learning disabilities, gross motor dysfunction, seizures, and other symptoms as a result of having been fed Neo-Mull-Soy or Cho-Free, infant formulas manufactured without chloride by the Syntex Corporation. Serves as an information center and communication link for concerned parents. Seeks to ensure that affected children receive proper medical attention and that the federal government acts to prevent similar incidents. Has successfully worked toward the passage of the Infant Formula Act, which sets nutrient standards for all infant formula and requires routine testing by manufacturers to see that each formula meets those standards.

★ 3228 ★ Foundation for Exceptional Children (FEC)
1920 Association Dr.
Reston, VA 22091
Phone: (703)620-1054
Ken Collins, Exec.Dir.

Founded: 1971. **Members:** 1,000. **Description:** Institutions, agencies, educators, parents, and persons concerned with the education and personal welfare of gifted or disabled children. Established to further the educational, vocational, social, and personal needs of the handicapped child or youth and the neglected educational needs of the gifted. Seeks funding from public memberships, foundations, and corporate and government grants. Conducts special programs and awards scholarships and grants for innovative educational projects. Bestows awards; operates charitable program and children's services. **Publications:** *Foundation for Exceptional Children--Focus*, 3/year. Newsletter. Provides information on the foundation's programs, committees, financial support, and board of directors. *Price:* Included in membership dues.

★ 3229 ★ French-Language Infant Pneumology and Phthisiology Group (FLIPPG)
(Groupe de Pneumologie et Phtisiologie Infantile de Langue Francaise)
Centre Hospitalier Interdepartmental Albert Calmette
1, rue de la Grange
F-91330 Yerres, France
Phone: 69 480947
Dr. J.P. Bouveret, Exec. Officer

Founded: 1972. **Members:** 100. **Languages:** French. **Description:** Pediatricians and lung specialists dedicated to the study of infant lung diseases, including phthisiology (the study of pulmonary tuberculosis), and pneumology (the study of the lung).

★ 3230 ★ French Society of Pediatric Surgery (FSPS)
(Societe Francaise de Chirurgie Pediatrique — SFCP)
Hopital Charles Nicolle
F-76000 Rouen, France
Phone: 35 088161
Fax: 35 088424
Prof. Paul Mitrofanoff, Sec.Gen.

Founded: 1959. **Members:** 250. **Languages:** French. Does not correspond in English. **Description:** Pediatric surgeons concerned with advancing pediatrics in France. **Publications:** *European Journal of Pediatric Surgery*, bimonthly. Journal. **Formerly:** Societe Francaise de Chirurgie Infantile.

★ 3231 ★ Friends of Karen (FK)
PO Box 190
Purdys, NY 10578
Phone: (914)277-4547
Free: 800-637-2774
Fax: (914)277-4967
John G. Murphy, Ph.D., Exec.Dir.

Founded: 1978. **Description:** Provides advocacy and financial and emotional support to children with life-threatening illnesses and to their families. Identifies and coordinates resources and provides direct assistance when needed. Has assisted over 800 families in the New York metropolitan area. Encourages the development of similar programs nationally and advises others on how to establish funding. (Karen MacInnes was the first child to be helped by Sheila Petersen, founder of the organization.) **Publications:** *A Special Way to Care*. Book. Advises how to help families with children diagnosed with life-threatening illnesses. *Price:* $15. • Newsletter.

★ 3232 ★ Give Kids the World (GKTW)
210 S. Bass Rd.
Kissimmee, FL 34746
Phone: (407)396-1114
Fax: (407)396-1207
Julia H. Wylam, Exec.VP

Founded: 1986. **Description:** Individuals who work to provide a six-day cost-free vacation for terminally ill children and their families at Walt Disney World Resort and other entertainment centers in the central Florida area (including Epcot Center, Magic Kingdom, Sea World, Wet 'N Wild, and King Henry's Feast). Operates resort. Aims to "make today count for children who have few tomorrows." Compiles statistics. Works with groups including Dream Factory, Make-A-Wish Foundation of America, and Operation Liftoff. **Publications:** Brochure. • *Give Kids The World*, quarterly. Newsletter.

★ 3233 ★ Gurson Foundation for Child Health (GFCH)
(Gurson Cocuk Sagligi Vakfi — GCSV)
Cocuk Sagligi Hastanesi
Univ. of Istanbul
Istanbul, Turkey
Phone: 1 2636441
Fax: 1 5240949
Dr. Nermin Gurson, Pres.

Founded: 1980. **Members:** 150. **Languages:** English, Turkish. **Description:** Operates in conjunction with the Institute of Child Health at Istanbul University. Supports the Pediatric Neurology Unit of the University Pediatric Hospital and a maternal-child health center near Istanbul. Conducts training workshops for health care workers. Plans to establish a day-care center for handicapped children. **Publications:** *The 1st 365 Days of Life*. Booklet.

★ 3234 ★ Healing the Children (HTC)
PO Box 9065
Spokane, WA 99209
Phone: (509)327-4281
Fax: (509)327-4284
Carol Borneman, Nat.Exec.Sec.

Founded: 1979. **Regional Groups:** 13. **Description:** Referral agency seeking to enable underprivileged children worldwide to receive medical care in the U.S. that is unavailable in their native countries. Acts as liaison for patients in making agreements with hospitals and arrangements with foreign governments in obtaining necessary visas; raises funds to provide air fare. Recruits foster families to care for the children in the community where they receive medical care. Compiles statistics. **Publications:** Brochure. • Newsletter, bimonthly. **Formerly:** (1989) Heal the Children.

★ 3235 ★ Healthy Mothers, Healthy Babies (HMHB)
409 12th St. SW, Rm. 309
Washington, DC 20024
Phone: (202)863-2458
Fax: (202)484-5107
Lori Cooper, Exec.Dir.

Founded: 1981. **Members:** 104. **State Groups:** 50. **Local Groups:** 50. **Description:** Coalition of national and state organizations concerned with maternal and child health. Serves as a network through which members share ideas and information regarding issues such as prenatal care, nutrition for pregnant women, and infant mortality. **Publications:** *Healthy Mothers, Healthy Babies Newsletter*, quarterly. Newsletter. *Price:* Free.

★ 3236 ★ Holt International Children's Services (HICS)
PO Box 2880
Eugene, OR 97402
Phone: (503)687-2202
Fax: (503)683-6175
John L. Williams, Exec.Dir.

Founded: 1956. **Description:** To deinstitutionalize children in developing countries by rehabilitating biological families, encouraging adoption within the developing country, and arranging inter-country adoption when in the best interest of the child. Offers assistance to children in Korea, India, the Philippines, Thailand, Cambodia, Vietnam, Hong Kong, China, Russia, Romania, and Latin America, as well as the U.S. Provides funds for food, clothing, housing, and medical care until an adoptive home can be found. Maintains Special Friends programs to provide funds for maintenance and medical care for handicapped children. Offers nutrition education, foster homes, well-baby clinics, physical, occupational, and speech therapy, and special care and education for the retarded. All services are supported through donations, sponsorships, and adoption fees. **Publications:** *Holt International Children's Services Annual Report.* Annual Report. • *Holt International Families!,* bimonthly. Magazine. For Holt supporters and families who have adopted children from foreign countries. Includes list of children ready for adoption, letter, and photos. *Price:* Free with a suggested 20 annual donation. **Formerly:** (1978) Holt Adoption Program and Holt Children's Services.

★ **3237** ★   **Human Growth Foundation (HGF)**
7777 Leesburg Pike
Falls Church, VA 22043
Phone: (703)883-1773
Free: 800-451-6434
Fax: (703)883-1776
Fran Price, Exec.Dir.

Founded: 1965. **Members:** 1,000. **National Groups:** 42. **Description:** Families of children with physical growth problems and interested persons united to help medical science better understand the process of growth. Distributes money for basic and clinical growth research. Disseminates informative literature and presents educational programs to families and physicians. **Publications:** *Fourth Friday,* monthly. Newsletter. • *Growth Series.* Brochure. **Formerly:** (1971) Human Growth.

★ **3238** ★   **International Academy for Child Brain Development (IACBD)**
8801 Stenton Ave.
Philadelphia, PA 19118
Phone: (215)233-2050
Fax: (215)233-3940
Neil Harvey, Ph.D., Sec.

Founded: 1985. **Description:** Professionals from a variety of disciplines including physicians, psychologists, and anthropologists, who are interested in the physical and psychological processes involved in child brain development. Seeks to gain recognition for the study of child brain development as a discipline in itself and establish criteria for the certification of child brain developmentalists. Provides a forum for presentation of scholarly works in the field; offers courses in child brain development; conducts field research and prepares reports of results. **Publications:** *The Journal for Child Brain Development,* periodic. Journal.

★ **3239** ★   **International Academy of Pediatric Transdisciplinary Education (IAPTE)**
90 Hay Ln.
London NW9 0LG, England
Dr. S. Lingham, Contact

Founded: 1972. **Members:** 300. **Languages:** English. **Description:** Pediatricians, nurses, psychologists, social workers, educators, and others involved in child care. Facilitates interdisciplinary cooperation in child health care. Interests include child health care in developing countries. Sponsors child health seminars. **Publications:** *World Pediatrics and Child Care,* quarterly.

★ **3240** ★   **International Association for Child and Adolescent Psychiatry and Allied Professions (IACAPAP)**
Child Study Center
PO Box 207900
New Haven, CT 06520-7900
Phone: (203)785-5759
Fax: (203)785-7402
Donald J. Cohen, M.D., Pres.

Founded: 1948. **Members:** 50. **National Groups:** 50. **Description:** National societies; others in the field of child and adolescent psychiatry. Promotes collaboration among related professions including pediatrics, psychology, public health, social work, education, nursing, and others involved in research and practice in the field of child and adolescent psychiatry. **Publications:** *Child in His Family,* annual. • Newsletter, periodic. **Also Known As:** Association Internationale de Psychiatrie de l'Enfant et de l'Adolescent et des Professions Associees. **Formerly:** (1978) International Association for Child Psychiatry and Allied Professions.

International Association for Maternal and Neonatal Health (IAMENEH)
See: Entry 9659

★ **3241** ★   **International Association of Paediatric Dentistry (IAPD)**
Dept. of Child Dental Health
London Hospital Medical College Dental
  School
Turner St.
London E1 2AD, England
Phone: 171 3777000
Fax: 171 3777058
Dr. M.P. Hector, Hon.Sec./Treas.

Founded: 1969. **Members:** 700. **Languages:** English, French. **Description:** Dentists, dental and medical libraries, bookshops, and research institutions in 36 countries. Encourages research and foster progress in the field of children's dental health. Provides a forum for the exchange of information concerning children's dentistry worldwide. Organizes international symposia and scientific meetings. **Publications:** *International Journal of Paediatric Dentistry.,* quarterly. Journal. • *Newsletter,* semiannual. Newsletter.

★ **3242** ★   **International Child Care (U.S.A.) (ICCUSA)**
Box 2645
Toledo, OH 43606
Phone: (419)472-7470
Free: 800-722-4453
Fax: (419)472-7470
Rev. Allan F. Waterson, Contact

Founded: 1965. **Description:** Nondenominational, church- and privately-funded organization that seeks to: create a better life for children in Haiti through nutritional care, education, and medical aid; help the peoples of developing countries become self-sufficient and assume responsibility for their own programs. Conducts Crusade Against Tuberculosis, a TB prevention and vaccination program for children and young adults up to the age of 20; also provides primary health care for all Haitians. Works in rural clinics and missions to train government-certified TB agents in order to allow native people to diag-

nose and treat TB and provide preventive health care education such as training in basic sanitation and hygiene. Sponsors program whereby TB drugs are dispensed at cost to Haitian clinics and hospitals. Trains local leaders in the Dominican Republic in community-based health promotion programs. Maintains Grace Children's Hospital in Port-au-Prince, Haiti. Operates speakers' bureau. **Publications:** Brochure. • *Grace,* quarterly. Newsletter. **Formerly:** (1978) Child Care Foundation.

★ **3243** ★   **International Federation of Infantile and Juvenile Gynecology (IFIJG)**
(Federation Internationale de Gynecologie Infantile et Juvenile — FIGIJ)
9 Kanazi St.
GR-106 71 Athens, Greece
Phone: 1 7770850
Fax: 1 3620484
George Creatsas, Gen.Sec.

Founded: 1972. **Members:** 500. **Languages:** English, French, German. **Description:** Gynecologists and pediatricians in 43 countries. Promotes the diagnosis and treatment of gynecological problems during childhood and adolescence. Maintains the FIGO Joint Committee for the Study of Gynecological Problems in Childhood and Adolescence. **Publications:** *Gynecologie,* periodic. • *Pediatric and Adolescent Gynecology,* periodic.

★ **3244** ★   **International Pediatric Association (IPA)**
(Association Internationale de Pediatrie — AIP)
Chateau de Longchamp
Bois de Boulogne
F-75016 Paris, France
Phone: 1 45271590
Fax: 1 45257367
Ihsan Dogramaci, M.D., Exec.Dir.

Founded: 1912. **Members:** 110. **Regional Groups:** 4. **Languages:** English, French, Spanish. **Description:** National pediatric societies in 107 countries. Objectives are to: disseminate information for the benefit of children; promote child health worldwide; encourage friendship among pediatricians. Bestows awards. Conducts workshops, symposia, seminars, and discussions. **Publications:** *Congress Proceedings,* triennial. • *Directory,* triennial. Directory. • *International Child Health,* quarterly. Journal.

★ **3245** ★   **International Pediatric Nephrology (IPNA)**
c/o Ira Greifer, M.D.
Hospital of the Albert Einstein College of Med.
1825 Eastchester Rd.
Bronx, NY 10461
Phone: (718)904-2857
Fax: (212)409-1048
Ira Greifer, M.D., Sec.Gen.

Founded: 1973. **Members:** 1,514. **Regional Groups:** 4. **Description:** Specialists in children's kidney disease. Purpose is to promote communication and disseminate information among pediatric nephrologists. Maintains facilities. **Publications:** *Pediatric Nephrology,* bimonthly. Journal. *Price:* Included with membership dues. • *Proceedings,* triennial. Book.

★3246★ International Rett Syndrome Association (IRSA)
9121 Piscataway Rd., No. 2B
Clinton, MD 20735
Phone: (301)856-3334
Free: 800-818-RETT
Fax: (301)856-3336
Kathy Hunter, Pres.

Founded: 1985. **Members:** 2,000. **State Groups:** 20. **Description:** Parents of children with Rett Syndrome; interested professionals and supporters. (A child afflicted with Rett Syndrome, which strikes only females, seems normal until 7 to 18 months of age, when autistic-like withdrawal sets in; though this symptom eases in time, higher brain functions continue to deteriorate, leading to severe retardation. The child also loses purposeful use of her hands, wringing them in a constant "hand-washing" movement in front of the face or chest. The syndrome is named for Dr. Andreas Rett, of Vienna, Austria, who described it in 1966. Research has not yet revealed a cause, but since the syndrome affects only girls, it is likely that it has a genetic origin in some defect of the X chromosome.) Provides support to parents; encourages research; collects and disseminates information. Assists in identifying syndrome victims; conducts activities aimed at the prevention, treatment, and eventual eradication of Rett Syndrome. **Publications:** *Educational and Therapeutic Intervention in Rett Syndrome.* Journal. • *International Rett Syndrome Association-Newsletter,* quarterly. Newsletter. *Price:* Included in membership dues. • *Orthopedic Problems in Rett Syndrome.* • *The Parent Idea Book.* • *Rett Sydrome: A Physician's Approach.* Video. • *Rett Syndrome: A Closer Look.* Video. • *Rett Syndrome: A Conversation with Families.* Video. • *Rett Syndrome: A Therapeutic Approach.* Video. • *Understanding Rett Syndrome.* • *What is Rett Syndrome.* **Formerly:** (1985) International Rett's Syndrome Association.

★3247★ International Society for Adolescent Psychiatry
610 Timber Ln.
Nashville, TN 37215
Mary Staples, Exec.Sec.

Founded: 1985. **Members:** 900. **Description:** Psychiatrists, psychologists, psychoanalysts, social workers, sociologists, pediatricians, educators, and health care professionals involved in the treatment of adolescents. Seeks to advance treatment of psychiatric illnesses of adolescents. Maintains research and educational programs. **Publications:** *International Annals of Adolescent Psychiatry,* triennial. Monograph. *Price:* Included in membership dues. • Newsletter, 3/year. *Price:* Included in membership dues.

★3248★ International Society for Pediatric Neurosurgery (ISPN)
c/o Shizuo Oi, MD
Department of Neurological Surgery
Kobe University School of Medicine
7-5-1 Kusunoki - Cho, Chuo-Ku
Kobe 650, Japan
Fax: 81783822691
M. L. Walker, Sec.

Founded: 1972. **Members:** 160. **Description:** Physicians specializing in pediatric neurosur-

gery. Objective is to contribute to the advancement of the specialty. Activities include the study of the most recent advancements in the field. **Publications:** *Child's Nervous System,* bimonthly. Journal.

★3249★ International Society of Pediatric Oncology (SIOP)
(Societe Internationale d'Oncologie Pediatrique — SIOP)
Bruistensingel 360
PO Box 3283
NL-5203 DG Hertogenbosch, Netherlands
Phone: 73 429285
Fax: 73 414766
Prof. Alan W. Craft, Sec.

Founded: 1969. **Members:** 680. **Languages:** English. **Description:** Pediatric oncologists, pediatric surgeons involved in oncology, pathologists, radiotherapists, researchers, and others interested in malignant tumors in children. Purpose is to promote research, treatment, and clinical review of cancerous growths in children. Facilitates collaboration and exchange of information among members and others in the field. Organizes and participates in controlled therapeutic trials. **Publications:** Brochure, periodic. • *Medical and Pediatric Oncology,* monthly. Journal. • Newsletter, semiannual.

★3250★ International Society of Tropical Pediatrics (ISTP)
Medical Center Manila, Ste. 326
1122 Gen. Luna St.
Ermita, Metro Manila, Philippines
Phone: 2 507874
Fax: 2 7216569
Prof. Perla D. Santos Ocampo, Sec.Gen.

Founded: 1986. **Members:** 100. **Languages:** English. **Description:** Promotes pediatrics in tropical and sub-tropical regions. Encourages pediatricians to familiarize themselves with diseases unique to these climates. Conducts seminars and workshops.

★3251★ Juvenile Diabetes Foundation International (JDFI)
432 Park Ave. S
New York, NY 10016-8013
Phone: (212)889-7575
Free: 800-JDF-CURE
Fax: (212)725-7259
Javier Broch, Public Info.Mgr.

Founded: 1970. **Local Groups:** 114. **Description:** Juvenile diabetics and their families. Objectives are: to solicit funds for diabetes research; to provide counseling and support services to juvenile diabetics and their families; to educate the public. Programs include: workshops that provide a forum for scientific discussion; efforts to stimulate government research funding. Holds seminars, discussion groups, and parent counseling. Conducts specialized education programs. **Publications:** *Countdown,* quarterly. Magazine. Covers diabetes treatment and research. *Price:* $25/year. Also publishes pamphlets and brochures for diabetics, families, medical personnel, and teachers; produces videotapes. **Formerly:** (1983) Juvenile Diabetes Foundation.

★3252★ Juvenile Diabetes Foundation in Israel (JDFI)
(Haagudah LeSukereth Neurim Beyisrael)
5 Jabotinsky St.
63479 Tel Aviv, Israel
Phone: 3 5462717
Fax: 3 5463830
Tamar Rafael, Contact

Founded: 1981. **Members:** 1,850. **Languages:** English, Hebrew. **Description:** Strives to improve the situation of children and young adults with diabetes in Israel. Conducts fundraising activities and research programs. **Publications:** *Ad-Kan,* semiannual. • *Update,* semiannual.

★3253★ Keren-Or, Inc. (K-OI)
350 7th Ave., Rm. 200
New York, NY 10001
Phone: (212)279-4070
Fax: (212)279-4043
Marden D. Paru, Exec. VP

Founded: 1956. **Description:** Maintains the Keren-Or Center for Multi-Handicapped Blind Children in Jerusalem for rehabilitation and training which houses more than 60 children and young adults. Funds acquired through public contributions (75%) and Israeli government funding (25%). **Publications:** *InSights,* quarterly. Newsletter. **Formerly:** (1987) Jerusalem Institutions for the Blind.

★3254★ Madagascar Pediatrics Society (MPS)
(Societe Malgache de Pediatrie — SOMAPED)
Service de Pediatrie A
Hopital Befelatanana
BP 14, bis
Antananarivo, Madagascar
Phone: 2 22384
Prof. Marcel Razanamparany, Pres.

Founded: 1987. **Members:** 30. **Languages:** English, French, Malagasy. **Description:** Physicians, midwives, and childcare specialists in Madagascar. Strives to reduce child mortality by advancing child healthcare. Fosters the development of continuing education in pediatrics and related fields. Investigates issues affecting pediatrics; informs government authorities of concerns. Promotes the exchange and dissemination of scientific information.

★3255★ Make-A-Wish Foundation of America (MAWFA)
100 W. Clarendon Ave., Ste. 2200
Phoenix, AZ 85013-3518
Phone: (602)279-9474
Free: 800-722-WISH
Fax: (602)275-0855
Stephen E. Torkelsen, DSW, Exec.Dir.

Founded: 1980. **Regional Groups:** 80. **Description:** Grants wishes to children with terminal or life-threatening illnesses, thereby providing these children and their families with special memories and a welcome respite from the daily stress of their situation. Considers the wish of any child with a terminal or life-threatening illness up to the age of 18. Many of the wishes are for trips to Disney World or Disneyland; however, the foundation has also accomplished the following: made one child a fireman, and another a lawyer with a degree; provided an AirEvac plane for a boy who wanted to die at home; sent a teenager to the Super Bowl; brought a girl from the Midwest to Phoenix, AZ in the winter because she missed the sunshine; sent birthday greetings to a boy who wanted nothing more. All expenses are covered by the foundation.

★ 3256 ★ Malaysian Paediatric Association (MPA)
(Persatuan Pediatric Malaysia — PPM)
PO Box 10153
59100 Kuala Lumpur, Malaysia
Fax: 603 2913446
Ms. Geraldine, Exec.Sec.

Founded: 1976. **Members:** 430. **Languages:** English. **Description:** Medical practitioners. Promotes the study of pediatrics in Malaysia. Conducts community-based children's health programs; sponsors research. Holds informational lectures and seminars. **Publications:** *Malaysian Journal of Child Health*, semiannual. Journal. • *Malaysian Pediatric Association Newsletter*, periodic. Newsletter.

★ 3257 ★ Maternal and Child Health Association of the Philippines (MCHAP)
NFP Bldg.
107 E. Rodriguez Sr. Blvd.
Quezon City, Metro Manila 1102, Philippines
Phone: 2 7121474
Carmelita B. Cuyugan, M.D., Pres.

Founded: 1972. **Members:** 513. **Regional Groups:** 2. **Local Groups:** 4. **Languages:** English. **Description:** Physicians, nurses, midwives, and other professionals interested in promoting maternal and child health in the Philippines. Fosters increased awareness of the health and medical care needs of mothers and children. Encourages up-to-date methods of research and data collection and evaluation. Seeks the integration of maternal and child health topics into all levels of medical education curricula. Sponsors conferences, seminars, and symposia. Offers children's services. Maintains speakers' bureau. Bestows awards. **Publications:** Newsletter, semiannual.

Maternity Action Alliance
See: Entry 9671

Maternity Alliance (MA)
See: Entry 9673

★ 3258 ★ Medical Network for Missing Children (MNMC)
67 Pleasant Ridge Rd.
Harrison, NY 10528
Phone: (914)967-6854
Fax: (914)337-4006
Peter S. Liebert, M.D., Dir.

Founded: 1984. **Description:** Purpose is to help identify missing children by medically identifiable characteristics such as dental patterns or scars. Conducts educational program to alert healthcare professionals to the problem of missing children. Provides medical-dental questionnaire to health care professionals and parents of missing children and offers medical profiles of known missing children to healthcare professionals. Plans to establish a computerized database of medical and dental records of missing children. **Publications:** *Safety Advice for Parents and Children*.

★ 3259 ★ Meres et Enfants d'Haiti (MEH)
Angle de Rues St. Honore et Monseigneur Guilloux
Port-au-Prince, Haiti
Phone: 1 222760
Prof. Jean Ronald Cornely, Pres.

Founded: 1987. **Members:** 71. **Languages:** English, French. **Description:** Obstetricians, gynecologists, pediatricians, nurses, and medical and nursing students in Haiti. Strives to improve maternal and child health. Encourages advancements in the fields of obstetrics, gynecology, and pediatrics. Promotes research on human reproduction and women's and child health. Organizes courses and programs aimed at improving maternal and child health; communicates with directors of educational institutions. Operates family planning program; offers consulting services. Sponsors seminars and training programs. **Publications:** *Bulletin*, periodic. Bulletin. • *MCI Bulletin*, quarterly. Bulletin.

★ 3260 ★ Moroccan Paediatric Society (MPS)
(Societe Marocaine de Pediatrie — SMP)
Hopital d'Enfants
CHU Ibnou-Sina
Rabat, Morocco
Phone: 7 670921
Fax: 7 670922
Dr. M.T. Lahrech

Founded: 1965. **Members:** 300. **Regional Groups:** 5. **Languages:** French. Does not correspond in English. **Description:** Pediatricians and other doctors specializing in child health. Encourages contact and information exchange among members. **Publications:** *Lettre du Pediatre*, monthly.

★ 3261 ★ MSUD Family Support Group (MSUDFSG)
1045 Piketown Rd.
Harrisburg, PA 17112
Phone: (717)445-5961
Dawn Marie Hahn, Contact

Founded: 1982. **Description:** Those affected by Maple Syrup Urine Disease (MSUD) and their families; health care professionals. (Maple Syrup Urine Disease usually occurs in infancy and is characterized by a strong odor of the urine, loss of sucking reflex, general listlessness, episodes of rigidity, and high-pitched crying. If undiagnosed, the condition can progress to seizures, coma and death. Symptoms sometimes do not occur for several months.) Gathers and distributes information on MSUD. Seeks to strengthen the liaison between families and health care professionals. Encourages increased research and newborn screening for MSUD. Sponsors education programs. **Publications:** Brochure. • Newsletter, 3/year. *Price:* $10. Also publishes information packet. **Formerly:** Families with Maple Syrup Urine Disease.

★ 3262 ★ National Association of Children's Hospitals and Related Institutions (NACHRI)
401 Wythe St.
Alexandria, VA 22314
Phone: (703)684-1355
Fax: (703)684-1589
Lawrence A. McAndrews, Pres. & CEO

Founded: 1968. **Members:** 135. **Description:** Children's hospitals and related institutions whose programs are clinical (as opposed to social or custodial). Purposes are: to promote the quality of child health care through the dissemination of information and the promotion of research and education programs related to such care; to participate in related charitable, scientific, and educational endeavors. Conducts surveys and research; disseminates information; maintains computerized services. Compiles statistics. **Publications:** *Guide to Children's Hospitals*, annual. • Magazine, quarterly.

National Association for Maternal and Child Welfare
See: Entry 1403

National Association of Pediatric Nurse Associates and Practitioners (NAPNAP)
See: Entry 9107

★ 3263 ★ National Association of Private Schools for Exceptional Children (NAPSEC)
1522 K St. NW, Ste. 1032
Washington, DC 20005
Phone: (202)408-3338
Fax: (202)408-3340
Sherry L. Kolbe, Exec.Dir.

Founded: 1971. **Members:** 210. **State Groups:** 12. **Description:** Represents 200 schools and serves as the national voice in Washington for its membership of educators regarding policies that affect children and youth with disabilities. Promotes excellence in educational opportunities for children with disabilities by enhancing the role of private special education as a vital component of the nation's educational system. Strives to educate the public about the services provided and needed to educate the students in member schools. **Publications:** *NAPSEC Membership Directory*, biennial. Directory. • *NAPSEC News*, quarterly. Newsletter. Reports association positions and statements and news of members. *Price:* Included in membership dues. • *National Issues Service*, monthly. Legislative update.

★ 3264 ★ National Association of Psychiatric Treatment Centers for Children (NAPTCC)
2000 L St. NW, Ste. 200
Washington, DC 20036
Phone: (202)955-3828
Fax: (202)362-5145
Joy Midman, Exec.Dir.

Founded: 1983. **Members:** 80. **Description:** Accredited residential centers for emotionally and mentally disturbed children. Promotes exellence in the care, delivery, accountability, and cost effectiveness of psychiatric services for children. Works to improve the business conditions in the industry. Supports and promotes standards, advocacy, educational programs, marketing, and research designed to ensure quality psychiatric care for children. Conducts lobbying activities and educational programs. **Publications:** Brochures. • *The Emerging Role of Psychiatric Treatment Centers.* • *Member Facilities,* annual. Directory. • *News from NAP-TCC,* quarterly. Newsletter. **Formerly:** (1982) CHAMPUS Coalition.

★ 3265 ★ **National Center for Education in Maternal and Child Health (NCEMCH)**
2000 15th St. N, Ste. 701
Arlington, VA 22201-2617
Phone: (703)524-7802
Fax: (703)524-9335
Dr. Rochelle Mayer, Dir.

Founded: 1982. **Description:** Provides information services to professionals and the public on maternal and child health. Collects and disseminates information on available materials, programs, and research. Offers summer internships for graduate students in public health schools. Develops, publishes, and disseminates more than 50 publications annually, including resource guides on selected topics, conference proceedings, directories, newsletters, and publications catalog. Advertising is not accepted. **Formerly:** (1982) National Clearinghouse for Human Genetic Diseases.

National Center for Youth with Disabilities (NCYD)
See: Entry 4522

★ 3266 ★ **National Children's Eye Care Foundation (NCECF)**
PO Box 795069
Dallas, TX 75379-5069
Phone: (214)407-0404
Fax: (214)407-0616
Suzanne C. Beauchamp, Exec.Dir.

Founded: 1970. **Description:** Purposes are to promote and advance the medical care of children's eyes and to decrease the incidence, prevalence, and severity of children's visual disorders. Sponsors public information campaign targeted toward parents, teachers, and children, stressing early detection and treatment. Sponsors Vision 2020: The Amblyopia Program, aimed at eliminating preventable blindness and vision loss from amblyopia. **Publications:** Annual Report. • Brochures. **Formerly:** (1982) Children's Eye Care Foundation.

★ 3267 ★ **National Consortium for Child Mental Health Services (NCCMHS)**
601 13th St. NW, Ste. 400 North
Washington, DC 20005
Phone: (202)347-8600
Fax: (202)393-6137
Virginia Q. Anthony, Exec.Dir.

Founded: 1971. **Members:** 5,000. **Description:** National psychiatric, psychologic, educational, social welfare, medical, parent and teacher, and consumer organizations. To serve as a forum for exchange of information on child mental health services and to bring concerns regarding child mental health services to appropriate local, state, and federal agencies.

★ 3268 ★ **National Council of Guilds for Infant Survival (NCGIS)**
8178 Nadine River Cir.
Fountain Valley, CA 92708
Free: 800-247-4370
Chris Elliot, Pres.

Founded: 1964. **Members:** 200. **State Groups:** 20. **Local Groups:** 25. **Description:** Families who have lost a child through a sudden, unexplained death; concerned individuals and organizations. The council carries out activities directed toward seeking a solution to the mystery of sudden, unexplained deaths of thousands of apparently healthy infants each year in the United States. The phenomenon, termed SIDS or sudden infant death syndrome, usually strikes infants aged two weeks to two years; fewer such deaths occur after age one, peaking during the one to six month age period. The council offers information and consolation to members of families who have lost a child to SIDS and who may blame themselves for the infant's death. The council also raises funds, supports and encourages medical research, and disseminates information on sudden infant death and in-home infant monitoring. Affiliates and regional representatives operate on an autonomous basis in 43 states. These guilds collectively form the Council for Infant Survival. Maintains speakers' bureau and small library. **Publications:** Newsletter, quarterly. Also publishes information brochure, research summaries, counseling letter, and affiliates roster. **Also Known As:** Council of Guilds for Infant Survival. **Formerly:** International Council for Infant Survival; International Guild for Infant Survival; (1968) Guild for Infant Survival.

★ 3269 ★ **National Maternal and Child Health Clearinghouse (NMCHC)**
8201 Greensboro Dr., Ste. 600
McLean, VA 22102-3810
Phone: (703)821-8955
Fax: (703)821-2098
Linda Cramer, Project Dir.

Founded: 1983. **Description:** Federal, state, and local agencies; voluntary organizations; health professionals; consumers. Collects, and disseminates information on maternal and child health, human genetics, nutrition, and pregnancy care, primarily from materials developed by the U.S. Department of Health and Human Services. **Publications:** Bibliographies. • Directories. • *Maternal and Child Health Publications Catalog,* annual. • Proceedings. • Videos.

National MPS Society
See: Entry 4863

★ 3270 ★ **National Organization of Circumcision Information Resource Centers (NOCIRC)**
PO Box 2512
San Anselmo, CA 94979
Phone: (415)488-9883
Fax: (415)488-9660
Marilyn Fayre Milos, R.N., Exec.Dir.

Founded: 1981. **Description:** Serves as an umbrella organization for circumcision information centers internationally; seeks to educate professionals and the public about routine male infant circumcision, a surgical procedure that is medically indicated only in North America, and the practice of female genital mutilation; hopes to end the practice of routine infant circumcision. Maintains mailing list of 20,000 hospitals, planned parenthood clinics, expectant parents, and individual professionals in fields related to health care. Conducts continuing education courses for registered nurses. Operates speakers' bureau. **Publications:** Booklets. • *Circumcision: Information, Misinformation, Disinformation.* Proceedings. Abstracts of the 2nd and 3rd International Symposia on Circumcision. • *Circumcision Why?.* Brochure. *Price:* Donation. • *Newborn Circumcision: An Enigma of Health.* • *NOCIRC Newsletter,* semiannual. Newsletter. Contains the latest medical and legal information on the issue of routine male infant circumcision and female genital mutilation internationally. *Price:* Available with donation of any amount. • Videos. **Formerly:** Informed Consent.

★ 3271 ★ **National Reye's Syndrome Foundation (NRSF)**
426 N. Lewis
PO Box 829
Bryan, OH 43506
Phone: (419)636-2679
Free: 800-233-7393
Fax: (419)636-3366
Sandi Nelson, Exec.Dir.

Founded: 1974. **Members:** 10,000. **State Groups:** 42. **Local Groups:** 148. **Description:** Families of children who have had Reye's Syndrome; doctors, scientists, nurses, and other health professionals and concerned individuals. (Reye's Syndrome is a disease affecting the liver and brain. Cause and cure unknown, its mortality rate is over 57 percent. Death may occur within a few hours after onset.) Aims to disseminate information to the public and the medical community and to raise and provide funds for research into the cause, treatment, cure, and prevention of the disease through research grants to individual scientists. Gives support and guidance to families experiencing Reye's Syndrome; assists federal and state agencies in obtaining data on Reye's cases; encourages governmental funding of research. Promotes service through a resource clearinghouse, financial aid programs, support groups, and referral services. Promotes awareness via lay-oriented literature, information services, professional training, lay/professional slide presentations, and emergency room posters. Sponsors National Reye's Syndrome Month in September. Compiles statistics; maintains speakers' bureau. **Publications:** *National Reye's Syndrome Foundation--In the News,* semiannual. Newsletter. *Price:* Included in membership dues.

★ 3272 ★ **National SIDS Resource Center (NSRC)**
8201 Greensboro Dr., Ste. 600
McLean, VA 22102
Phone: (703)821-8955
Fax: (703)821-2098
Olivia Coredrill, Project Dir.

Founded: 1980. **Description:** Funded by Maternal and Child Health Bureau, Health Resources and Services Administration, Public Health Service, and U.S. Department of Health and Human Services. Purpose is to provide health care professionals, community service workers, health educators, parents, and the public with information and educational materials on sudden infant death syndrome and related issues. Develops materials concerning SIDS, grief, apnea (a temporary stoppage of breathing), and apnea monitoring. Provides referrals to state SIDS programs and parent support groups. Distributes publications on SIDS and related topics. **Publications:** Bibliographies. • *National Sudden Infant Death Syndrome Resource Center Information Exchange*, periodic. Newsletter. Includes list of resources, calendar of events, and national, state and legislative news. • *What is SIDS?*. Also publishes fact sheets and educational publications. **Formerly:** (1991) National Sudden Infant Death Syndrome Clearinghouse.

National Tay-Sachs and Allied Diseases Association (NTSAD)
See: Entry 4865

★3273★   National Vaccine Information Center
512 Maple Ave. W, Ste. 206
Vienna, VA 22180
Phone: (703)938-DPT3
Free: 800-909-SHOT
Fax: (703)938-9768
Kathryn Williams, Contact

Founded: 1982. **Members:** 2,000. **Description:** Parents of children who have had reactions to or been injured by vaccines; individuals interested in working to reform the vaccine system. Disseminates information concerning vaccines, particularly the pertussis (whooping cough) portion of the DPT vaccine, to parents and doctors in order to assure safer administration of vaccines. Promotes the development of safer vaccines. Refers parents of vaccine-injured children to doctors, lawyers, and other parents for support services. Maintains speakers' bureau; compiles statistics. **Publications:** *The Compensation System and How It Works.* • *DPT News*, 2-4/year. • *Law Firm Directory.* Directory. • *Parent Information Packet*, periodic. *Price:* $5. **Also Known As:** Dissatisfied Parents Together.

★3274★   Newborn Rights Society (NRS)
2165 Coventryville Rd.
St. Peters, PA 19470-0048
Phone: (610)323-6061
Paul Zimmer, Contact

Founded: 1980. **Members:** 35. **Description:** Individuals interested in promoting the rights of newborn infants. Opposes "unnecessary medical procedures" such as circumcision of newborns. Disseminates information to physicians, childbirth educators, expectant parents, and activists. Compiles statistics; conducts children's services. Conducts research and educational programs; maintains speakers' bureau. **Publications:** Pamphlets. **Formerly:** INTACT of Pennsylvania.

★3275★   Non-Circumcision Educational Foundation (NCEF)
PO Box 5
Feasterville, PA 19053
Phone: (215)357-2792
James E. Peron, Exec.Dir.

Founded: 1973. **Members:** 11,000. **Description:** Parents, childbirth educators, nurse-midwives, nurses, doctors, and other interested individuals. Seeks to: stop routine infant circumcision; provide medical information regarding such surgery. Opposes what it calls the unnecessary surgery of baby boys, use of silver nitrate in eyes, and other medical treatments which violate the physical and emotional well-being of the newborn. Conducts research; offers services to parents, educators, and medical staff. Maintains extensive library on infant circumcision, childbirth, and infant and newborn care. Offers speakers' bureau; compiles statistics. Operates educational programs including seminars, lecture series, film and videotape educational services, workshops, and distribution of educational literature. **Publications:** *Educational Bulletin*, periodic. Bulletin. • Newsletter, semiannual.

★3276★   Non-Circumcision Information Center (NCIC)
PO Box 31
Waverley, MA 02179
Phone: (617)489-4530
Roger Saquet, Dir.

Founded: 1973. **Members:** 1. **Description:** Provides current, accurate, and complete information to the American public regarding the safety and necessity of circumcision; distributes information that discourages routine circumcision; assists in increasing the number of uncircumcised males from 40% to 95%.

★3277★   North American Society for Pediatric Gastroenterology and Nutrition (NASPGN)
c/o John T. Boyle, M.D.
Rainbow Babies and Children's Hospital
2074 Abington Rd.
Cleveland, OH 44106
Phone: (216)844-1767
Fax: (216)844-3757
John T. Boyle, M.D., Contact

Founded: 1970. **Members:** 350. **Description:** Physicians interested and specializing in gastro-intestinal, hepatobiliary, and nutritional disorders affecting children and adolescents. Provides the public with information on gastrointestinal disorders. Works to improve the quality and quantity of teaching, research, and patient care. Conducts research and educational programs. **Publications:** *NASPGN Membership Directory*, annual. Membership Directory. • *Newsletter of the NASPGN*, 4-6/year. Newsletter. **Formerly:** (1988) North American Society for Pediatric Gastroenterology.

Norwegian Association for Children and Adults with Minimal Brain Dysfunction (MBD-foreningen)
See: Entry 4300

★3278★   Papua New Guinea Paediatric Society (PNGPS)
Medical Faculty
PO Box 5623
Boroko, Papua New Guinea
Phone: 248461
Fax: 254935
J. Vince, Sec.

Founded: 1974. **Members:** 30. **Languages:** English. **Description:** Formulates practices and procedures in pediatric medicine in Papua New Guinea; advises the government on health policy; facilitates information exchange in the field; advises on undergraduate and postgraduate curricula in regards to child health. **Publications:** *Standard Treatment for Common Illnesses of Children in Papua New Guinea*, periodic. Handbook. Contains information on the management of commonly present pediatric problems.

★3279★   Peaceful Beginnings (PB)
13020 Homestead Ct.
Anchorage, AK 99516
Phone: (907)345-4813
Rosemary Romberg, Pres.

Founded: 1985. **Description:** Distributes information opposing routine infant circumcision. Presents data stating there are no valid medical reasons for circumcision of newborns and that the operation is severely traumatic and painful. Promotes other aspects of childbirth education including: positive birth options, breastfeeding, coping during the first trimester of pregnancy, perinatal loss, and postpartum adjustment. Has conducted a survey on circumcision rates in the U.S. **Publications:** Booklets. Also publishes information sheets and makes slides available.

★3280★   Pediatric AIDS Foundation
1311 Colorado Ave.
Santa Monica, CA 90404
Phone: (310)395-9051
Fax: (310)395-5149

Founded: 1988. **Description:** Confronts medical problems unique to children infected with HIV/AIDS, and focuses on finding medical answers that will bring hope. Identifies and funds critically needed pediatric AIDS research worldwide. Provides funds to hospitals around the country which serve children with HIV/AIDS through an Emergency Assistance Program. Encourages students to enter the field of pediatric AIDS through a Student Intern Award Program. Develops and distributes national Parent Education Program for parents of elementary and pre-school age children.

★3281★   Pediatric Orthopaedic Society of North America (POSNA)
6300 N. River Rd., Ste. 727
Rosemont, IL 60018-4226
Phone: (708)698-1692
Fax: (708)823-0536
Sherie King, Mgr.

Founded: 1983. **Members:** 600. **Description:** Orthopedic surgeons. Purpose is to provide continuing education to members. Conducts tutorial programs. **Publications:** Bulletin, quarterly. • Membership Directory, annual.

★ 3282 ★ Pediatric Projects

PO Box 571555
Tarzana, CA 91357
Phone: 800-947-0947
Fax: (818)705-3660
Ms. Pat Azarnoff, Exec.Dir.

Founded: 1981. **Description:** Parents of ill, disabled, or hospitalized children. Strives to provide information to prepare children for surgery, support groups for parents, and toll-free phone consultation. Offers educational and research programs and children's services. **Publications:** Directory.Lists parent support groups; includes over 400 organizations. • *Pediatric Mental Health*, bimonthly. Newsletter. Designed for medical and mental health professionals, health agencies, schools, and parents.

★ 3283 ★ People Against Rape (PAR)

PO Box 5876
Naperville, IL 60567-5876
Phone: (708)717-0310
Free: 800-877-7252
Fax: (708)717-0391
Marie Howard-Lena, Pres.

Founded: 1976. **Description:** Seeks to help teens and children avoid becoming the victims of sexual assault and rape by providing instruction in the basic principles of self-defense. Promotes self-esteem and motivation in teens through educational programs, offers substance abuse prevention programs, and teacher/ parent training programs. Sponsors speakers' bureau; operates referral service. Also provides experts to appear on television talk shows regarding rape, self defense, assertiveness training, advice on parents on protecting children. **Publications:** Brochures. • *Defend: Preventing Date Rape and Other Sexual Assault*. Book. • *Hands Off, I'm Special*, semiannual. Educational packet for use in classroom; includes information on rape, sexual assault, and defense techniques. *Price:* $5. • *My Power Book*. Booklet. • Pamphlets. • *Sexual Assault: How to Defend Yourself*. Book. • Videos.

★ 3284 ★ The Remain Intact "ORGAN"ization (RIO)

RR 2, Box 86
Larchwood, IA 51241
Phone: (712)477-2256
Rev. Russell Zangger, Dir.

Founded: 1980. **Members:** 1,800. **Description:** Persons opposed to routine circumcision. Believes circumcision has adverse effects on males both physically and psychologically. Distributes literature, audiotapes, and videotapes citing its views on the procedure.

★ 3285 ★ Ryan White National Teen Education Program (RWNTEP)

c/o Athletes and Entertainers for Kids
381 Van Ness Ave., Ste. 1507
Torrance, CA 90501
Phone: (310)783-0575
Free: 800-933-KIDS
Fax: (310)783-0585
Elise Kim, Exec.Dir.

Founded: 1986. **State Groups:** 5. **Description:** Participants include individuals and corporations concerned about children with catastrophic illnesses, particularly AIDS. Seeks to bring hope to seriously ill children. Provides services to children and their families including: mother and child clinics; counseling and referral services; community outings; educational rallies. Operates an AIDS clinic, which provides research and care, and Kids 'n AIDS National Program, which holds AIDS education and awareness rallies and organizes study groups in junior and senior high schools. Conducts hospital and charitable programs; provides placement and children's services; maintains speakers' bureau; compiles statistics. Sponsored by Athletes and Entertainers for Kids. **Publications:** *Financial Report*, annual. Report. • Newsletter, quarterly.

Scandinavian Association of Paediatric Surgeons (SCAPS) (Nordisk Barnkirurgisk Forening — NBF)

See: Entry 12299

Shriners Hospitals for Crippled Children (SHCC)

See: Entry 6470

★ 3286 ★ SIDS Alliance (NSIDSF)

10500 Little Patuxent Pky., Ste. 420
Columbia, MD 21044
Phone: (410)964-8000
Free: 800-221-SIDS
Fax: (410)964-8009
Thomas L. Moran, Pres.

Founded: 1991. **Description:** Concerned citizens, health professionals, and parents who have lost a child to sudden infant death syndrome (SIDS), a condition commonly known as "crib death" that accounts for about 6000 to 7000 infant and child deaths annually in the United States. (Deaths of this type usually occur at night among apparently healthy infants generally under seven months of age; the common causes and methods of prevention have not been determined.) Serves as a central source of medical and scientific information about SIDS. Works to eliminate SIDS through research. Assists bereaved parents who have lost a child to SIDS; works with families and professionals in caring for infants at risk due to cardiac/ respiratory problems; supports research and seeks to make the public aware of SIDS and related issues.

★ 3287 ★ Singapore Paediatric Society (SPS)

Alumni Medical Centre
2 College Rd.
Singapore 0316, Singapore
Phone: 65 3214831
Dr. Wong Keng Yean, Pres.

Founded: 1952. **Members:** 550. **Languages:** English. **Description:** Seeks to advance pediatric medicine in Singapore. Advocates research in pediatrics and child health care; fosters exchange of information among medical practitioners. Offers educational and research programs. **Publications:** *Journal of the Singapore Paediatric Society*, semiannual. Journal. Contains medical articles.

★ 3288 ★ Slovak Society of Pediatrics

1 Children's Clinic
Limbova 1
SK-833 40 Bratislava, Slovakia
Phone: 7 374511
Fax: 7 376243
Marta Benedekova, M.D., Contact

Languages: English, Slovak. **Description:** Pediatricians and other health care professionals with an interest in child health. Promotes proper pediatric medical care; represents members' interests.

★ 3289 ★ Society for Adolescent Medicine (SAM)

19401 E. 40 Hwy., Ste. 120
Independence, MO 64055
Phone: (816)795-TEEN
John W. Kulig, M.D., Exec.Sec.-Treas.

Founded: 1968. **Members:** 1,250. **Regional Groups:** 19. **Description:** Physicians, psychologists, social workers, psychiatrists, nurses, and other health care professionals. Goals are: to improve the quality of health care for adolescents; to encourage the investigation of normal growth and development during adolescence and of those diseases that affect adolescents; to stimulate the creation of health services for adolescents; to increase communication among health care professionals who care for adolescents; to foster and improve the quality of training of those individuals providing health care to adolescents. Seeks to: offer opportunities for discussion of teaching, research, and other common problems, through which coordinated efforts can be made toward their solution; publish and disseminate information related to adolescent medicine; identify, investigate, and list opportunities for careers in adolescent medicine; help plan and coordinate professional educational programs in the health care of the adolescent. Conducts research programs. **Publications:** *Journal of Adolescent Health*, monthly. Journal. Peer-reviewed scientific journal of articles on study results of the anthropology, biochemistry, endocrinology, physiology and psychology. *Price:* Included in membership dues; $130/year for nonmembers; $260/year for institutions.

★ 3290 ★ Society for Behavioral Pediatrics (SBP)

c/o Noreen M. Spota
19 Station Ln.
Philadelphia, PA 19118
Phone: (215)248-9168
Noreen M. Spota, Admin.Dir.

Founded: 1983. **Members:** 500. **Description:** Pediatricians, child psychiatrists and psychologists, and other related health care professionals. Seeks to improve the health care of infants, children, and adolescents by promoting research and scholarly instruction in the area of developmental-behavioral pediatrics. **Publications:** *Journal of Developmental and Behavioral Pediatrics*, bimonthly. Journal. Includes original scientific articles, book and journal article reviews, commentaries, and letters to the editor. *Price:* Included in membership dues; $114/year for nonmembers.

★3291★ **Society for Ear, Nose, and Throat Advances in Children (SENTAC)**
Division of OTO/HNS
1 Hospital Dr., MA314
Columbia, MO 65212
Phone: (314)882-8173
Fax: (314)884-4205
David S. Parsons, M.D., Contact

Founded: 1973. **Members:** 350. **Description:** Otolaryngologists, pediatricians, audiologists, speech pathologists, and related professionals. Works to evaluate the science and practice of medicine, surgery, and rehabilitation as related to diseases and disorders of the ear, nose, and throat in infants and children; to improve quality of care; to promote and coordinate research; to foster scientific exchange and coordination among professionals from related disciplines. Sponsors lectures and symposia. Provides forum for interchange of information on practice and research. **Publications:** Brochure. • *Directory and Meeting Abstracts*, annual. Directory.

★3292★ **Society of Nursery Nursing Administrators (SNNA)**
40 Archdale Rd.
East Dulwich
London SE22 9HJ, England
Phone: 181 2996889
Fax: 181 29901097
Dr. R. A. Herbert-Blankson, Sec.

Founded: 1991. **Members:** 50. **Languages:** English. **Description:** Nursing administrators and nurses, nursery teachers, school nurses, nannies, and other workers and employers with an interest in the health and welfare of children from birth to five years of age. Seeks to establish professional standards and a uniform code of ethics within the field; works to enhance the professional standing of members. Gathers and disseminates information to inform legislative debate concerning child health issues. Conducts educational programs and maintains speakers' bureau. **Publications:** *Nursery Nursing Administrator*, quarterly. Newsletter.

★3293★ **Society for Pediatric Dermatology (SPD)**
c/o James E. Rasmussen, M.D.
University of Michigan Hospitals
1910 Taubman Health Care Center
Ann Arbor, MI 48109-0314
Phone: (312)880-4697
Fax: (312)880-3025
Amy S. Paller, M.D., Sec.-Treas.

Founded: 1975. **Members:** 450. **Description:** Pediatricians, dermatologists, pediatric or dermatologic house officers, manufacturers of children's skin products, and researchers in biomedicine with studies in pediatric dermatology. Conducts research programs. **Publications:** *Society for Pediatric Dermatology--Newsletter*, quarterly. Newsletter. Reviews current publications in the field of pediatric dermatology; includes reviews in the areas of allergy and immunology, genetics and syndromes. *Price:* Included in membership dues.

★3294★ **Society for Pediatric Psychology (SPP)**
c/o William A. Rae, Ph.D.
Scott & White Clinic
Department of Psychiatry
2401 S 31st St.
Temple, TX 76508
Phone: (817)774-2275
Fax: (817)724-1747
William Rae, Ph.D., Pres.

Founded: 1968. **Members:** 980. **Description:** A section of the American Psychological Association (see separate entry). Psychologists working in children's hospitals, developmental clinics, and pediatric and medical group practices. Fosters the development of theory, research, training, and professional practice in pediatric psychology and the application of psychology to medical and psychological problems of children, youths, and their families. Supports legislation benefiting children's health and welfare. Sponsors colloquia and symposia; provides speakers. **Publications:** *Journal of Pediatric Psychology*, quarterly. Journal. Includes research reports, literature and book reviews, case studies, graphs, tables, charts, and society meeting minutes. *Price:* Included in membership dues; $50 for nonmembers. • *Progress Notes, Newsletter of the Society for Pediatric Psychology*, 3/year. Newsletter. Contains research articles on pediatric psychology. Includes abstracts of published literature, society news, and lists of employment opportunities. *Price:* Included in membership dues.

★3295★ **Society for Pediatric Radiology (SPR)**
2021 Spring Rd., Ste. 600
Oak Brook, IL 60521
Phone: (708)571-2197
Fax: (708)571-7837
Jennifer Boylan, Contact

Founded: 1958. **Members:** 800. **Description:** Physicians working in the field of pediatric radiology. Seeks to advance knowledge in pediatric imaging and improve medical care of infants and children. **Publications:** Membership Directory, annual.

★3296★ **Society for Pediatric Research (SPR)**
141 Northwest Point Blvd.
PO Box 675
Elk Grove Village, IL 60009-0675
Phone: (708)427-1205
Fax: (708)427-1305
Debbie Anagnostelis, Exec.Dir.

Founded: 1929. **Members:** 2,000. **Description:** Physicians and scientists under age 46 who are engaged in research in diseases of infancy and childhood; those over age 46 are senior members. **Publications:** *Pediatric Research*, monthly. Journal. Includes calendar of events, obituaries, and annual directory. *Price:* $75/year. **Formerly:** (1932) Eastern Society for Pediatric Research.

★3297★ **Society for Pediatric Urology (SPU)**
Children's Hospital & Medical Center
PO Box 5371
Seattle, WA 98105
Phone: (206)527-3950
Fax: (206)527-3966
Dr. Michael Mitchell, Sec.-Treas.

Founded: 1941. **Members:** 300. **Local Groups:** 45. **Description:** Medical doctors who are specialists in urology (relating to the genitourinary tract in health and disease) and who have a special interest in the field of childhood urological problems. Seeks to encourage the study, improve the practice, elevate the standards, and further the advancement of pediatric urology. Conducts educational programs. **Publications:** Audiotapes. • Books. • *Dialogues in Pediatric Urology*, monthly. Magazine. *Price:* $32. • Pamphlets. • *Pedictric Urology*, monthly. Newsletter. *Price:* Included in membership dues. • Videos.

Society of Professors of Child and Adolescent Psychiatry (SPCAP)
See: Entry 7516

Society for Protection of Motherhood and Childhood
See: Entry 9698

★3298★ **South African Association of Paediatric Surgeons (SAAPS) (Suid-Afrikaanse Vereniging van Kinderchirurge — SAVK)**
Dept. of Paediatric Surgery
Red Cross War Memorial Children's Hospital
Rondebosch 7700, Republic of South Africa
Phone: 21 6585339
Fax: 21 6891287
Prof. A.J.W. Millar, Hon.Sec.-Treas.

Founded: 1975. **Members:** 50. **Languages:** Afrikaans, English. **Description:** Pediatric surgeons in South Africa. Promotes research, training, and clinical services in pediatric surgery. Grants postgraduate fellowships. Conducts educational programs. Compiles statistics; bestows awards.

★3299★ **A Special Wish Foundation (ASWF)**
c/o Ramona Fickle
2244 S. Hamilton Rd., Ste. 202
Columbus, OH 43232
Phone: (614)575-9474
Free: 800-486-9474
Fax: (614)575-1866
Ramona Fickle, Exec.Dir.

Founded: 1982. **Members:** 350. **National Groups:** 21. **State Groups:** 15. **Local Groups:** 11. **Description:** Physicians, nurses, social workers, psychologists, attorneys, and businesspeople. Works to grant wishes of children and adolescents under 20 years of age who are afflicted with a life-threatening disorder. Recent wishes granted by the foundation include sending patients to Disney World and other trips and arranging for patients to meet celebrities. Offers in-service programs for hospital staffs. Operates speakers' bureau. **Publications:** Brochures.

★ 3300 ★ Starlight Foundation (SF)
12233 W. Olympic Blvd.
Los Angeles, CA 90064
Phone: (310)207-5558
Free: 800-274-7827
Fax: (310)207-2554
Holly Rasey, COO

Founded: 1982. **Members:** 2,500. **Description:** Individuals who work to help fulfill the wishes of critically, chronically, and terminally ill children. Attempts to arrange and finance children's wishes such as special trips, presents, or meeting a favorite celebrity. Provides entertainment programs in pediatric hospitals.

Stop Teen-Age Addiction to Tobacco (STAT)
See: Entry 11739

★ 3301 ★ Sunshine Foundation (SF)
2001 Bridge St.
Philadelphia, PA 19124
Phone: (215)535-1413
Free: 800-767-1976
Fax: (215)535-8397
Bill Sample, Pres.

Founded: 1976. **Description:** Works to fulfill the wishes of chronically or terminally ill children, many of whom suffer from kidney disease, leukemia, or cancer. Raises funds to send children and their families on vacations together (on advice of the children's doctors); arranges other events (attendance at wrestling matches or plays, meetings with celebrities) to make sick or dying children happy. Since its inception, the foundation has granted more than 19,800 requests.

★ 3302 ★ Task Force for Child Survival and Development (TFCSD)
The Carter Presidential Center
1 Copenhill Ave.
Atlanta, GA 30307
Phone: (404)872-4122
Fax: (404)872-9661
William H. Foege, M.D., Exec.Dir.

Founded: 1984. **Members:** 5. **Description:** Sponsored by United Nations Children's Fund, United Nations Development Programme, World Health Organization, Rockefeller Foundation, and the World Bank. Seeks to further efforts to immunize children worldwide against vaccine-preventable diseases (measles, polio, diphtheria, tuberculosis, neonatal tetanus, and whooping cough). Assists in the implementation of immunization programs; conducts research. Plans to implement programs dealing with dietary deficiency-related disorders. Coordinates activities between sponsoring organizations. **Publications:** *Child Survival - World Development*, bimonthly. Newsletter.

★ 3303 ★ Toxoplasmosis Trust (TTT)
61-71 Collier St.
London N1 9BE, England
Phone: 171 7130663
Fax: 171 7130611
Christine Asbury

Founded: 1989. **Members:** 5,000. **Languages:** English. **Description:** Health professionals, individuals affected by toxoplasmosis, and others.

Strives to foster public awareness of toxoplasmosis, a serious congenital or acquired disease that affects the central nervous system of infants. Provides support for those suffering from toxoplasmosis. Maintains an up-to-date information and advising center; promotes the testing of women for toxoplasmosis during pregnancy; supports medical research. **Publications:** *The Toxoplasmosis Trust Trust Update*, periodic. Magazine.

★ 3304 ★ Union of Middle Eastern and Mediterranean Pediatric Societies (UMEMPS)
(Union des Societes de Pediatrie du Moyen-Orient et de la Mediterranee — USPMOM)
Milioni 6
GR-106 73 Athens, Greece
Phone: 1 3615168
Fax: 1 6444260
Prof. T. Thomaidis, Sec.Gen.

Founded: 1966. **Members:** 22. **Regional Groups:** 1. **Languages:** English, French. **Description:** National societies of pediatricians and pediatric surgeons. **Publications:** *Newsletter*, annual. Bulletin.

★ 3305 ★ United Nations Children's Fund (UNICEF)
3 United Nations Plz.
New York, NY 10017
Phone: (212)326-7000
Fax: (212)888-7465
Richard Jolly, Exec.Dir.

Founded: 1946. **National Groups:** 37. **Description:** Semi-autonomous U.N. agency working for sustainable human development to ensure the survival, protection, and development of children. Cooperates with governments in the developing world to develop and implement low-cost community-based programs in social service, health, nutrition, education, water and sanitation, environment, and women in development. Works for universal ratification and implementation of the Convention on the Rights of the Child and achievement of the objectives and the goals of the 1990 World Summit for Children. Provides universal immunization against six childhood diseases-- diphtheria, measles, poliomyelitis, whooping cough, tetanus, and tuberculosis. Promotes the use of oral rehydration therapy to treat diarrheal dehydration, which is one of the leading causes of death in children in developing countries. Works to eliminate poliomyelitis in selected countries and regions, neonatal tetanus, Vitamin A deficiency, iodine deficiency disorders, and guinea worn diseases. In cooperation with the World Health Organization, has launched a "baby-friendly hospital initiative" to advance breastfeeding. Provides training for health workers and traditional birth attendants; furnishes technical supplies and equipment for health centers. Advocates with and helps governments in strengthening basic education for all, particularly in increasing schooling opportunities for girls. Supports efforts to improve the status of women by enhancing educational and vocational opportunities and supporting small-scale income generating projects and credit schemes to increase the earning power of women. Assists Urban

Basic Services programs to address the health and sanitation needs of the urban poor and supports local safe water supply projects. Seeks to help children in especially difficult circumstances, including children in armed conflicts. Provides relief and rehabilitation assistance in response to the needs of children and women affected by emergencies. Works with 37 national committees, mostly in industrialized countries, providing fund-raising and advocacy support. More than 190 non-governmental organizations (NGOs) maintain consultative relationships with the organization. **Publications:** *Facts and Figures*, annual. Brochure. Lists facts and statistical data on children and women. *Price:* Free. • *First Call for Children*, quarterly. Newsletter. • *The Progress of Nations*, annual. Report. • *State of the World's Children*, annual. Offered in 20 other national languages. • *UNICEF Annual Report*. Annual Report. Summarizes UNICEF policies and programs. • *UNICEF at a Glance*. **Formerly:** United Nations International Children's Emergency Fund.

★ 3306 ★ World Association for Infant Mental Health (WAIMH)
Michigan State University
Kellogg Center/1 CYF, Ste. 1
East Lansing, MI 48824-1022
Phone: (517)432-3793
Fax: (517)432-3694
Hiram E. Fitzgerald, Exec.Dir.

Founded: 1992. **Members:** 650. **Description:** Child development specialists, child psychiatrists, child psychoanalysts, infant care workers, linguists, nurses, obstetricians, pediatricians, psychologists, and social workers. Works to further research and understanding of mental development and disorders in children from conception through age 3. Promotes studies on the conditions affecting the mental health of infants, their parents, and other caregivers; explores mental development during infancy and its subsequent effects on psychopathological development. Advocates international multidisciplinary discussions of research and intervention in infant psychiatry within the framework of the total life cycle. Facilitates communication and exchange of information and theories; fosters discussion of questions, problems, and issues in infant mental health. **Publications:** *Infant Mental Health Journal*, quarterly. Journal. *Price:* $25 for members; $35 for members outside the U.S.; $52.50 for nonmembers; $62.50 for nonmembers outside the U.S. • Newsletter, quarterly.

★ 3307 ★ Zambia Paediatrics Association
PO Box 50001
Ridgeway
Lusaka, Zambia

Languages: English. **Description:** Pediatricians. Promotes improved delivery of children's health services in Zambia. Works to enhance members' professional standing; represents members' interests. Gathers and disseminates information.

★3308★ Zero to Three / NCCIP
2000 14th St. N, Ste. 380
Arlington, VA 22201
Phone: (703)528-4300
Free: 800-899-4301
Fax: (703)528-6848
Carol Berman, Ph.D., Co-Dir.

Founded: 1977. **Description:** Professionals and researchers in the health care industry, policymakers, and parents working to improve the healthy physical, cognitive and social development of infants, toddlers, and their families. Members share their expertise about infants, toddlers, and their families. Sponsors training and technical assistance activities. **Publications:** *Clinical Infant Reports.* Reports. Book series. • *Public Policy Pamphlets*, 1-3/year. Pamphlets. • *Zero to Three*, 6/year. Bulletin. Includes research and practice reports, book and video reviews, calendar of events, funding source information, and lists of training opportunities. *Price:* $37/year; $69/2 years; $99/3 years; $20 auxiliary subscriptions. **Formerly:** (1992) National Center for Clinical Infant Programs.

Research Centers

American Academy of Pediatrics
Department of Research
See: Entry 5606

★3309★ American Sudden Infant Death
   Syndrome Institute
6065 Roswell Rd., Ste. 876
Atlanta, GA 30328
Phone: (404)843-1030
Free: 800-232-SIDS
Fax: (404)843-0577
Dr. Alfred Steinschneider, Pres.

Research Activities and Fields: Sudden Infant Death Syndrome (SIDS), commonly known as crib death, including the search for abnormalities in SIDS victims, study of normal and abnormal infant control mechanisms, pregnancy-related factors, identification of infants at risk, effectiveness of preventive measures, effect of SIDS on families, and effect of preventive measures on families. **Publications:** *Towards an Understanding of SIDS.*

Autism Research Institute
See: Entry 7540

Barbara Davis Center for Childhood
   Diabetes
See: Entry 4879

★3310★ Baylor College of Medicine
General Clinical Research Center—Children
6621 Fannin, MC1-3360
Houston, TX 77030
Phone: (713)770-1353
Fax: (713)770-1393
Dr. Dennis M. Bier, Prog.Dir.

Research Activities and Fields: Cardiology, endocrinology, gastroenterology, genetics, infectious diseases, pulmonary system, pharmacology, immunology, hematology, rheumatology, and renal disease, including studies on ventricular dysrhythmias, hypopituitarism, bile acid metabolism, argininemia, HIV, and renal tubular acidosis.

★3311★ Baylor College of Medicine
Meyer Center for Developmental Pediatrics
Texas Children's Hospital-Clinical Care Center
6621 Fannin St.
Houston, TX 77030
Phone: (713)770-3400
Fax: (713)770-3399
Frank R. Brown, M.D., Dir.

Research Activities and Fields: Developmentally disabled, developmental pediatrics, learning disabilities, low-birth-weight infants, maternal medications, cytomegalo inclusion virus, congenital rubella syndrome, neonatal intracranial hemorrhage, and outcome prematurity. **Formerly:** Child Development Clinics.

★3312★ Baylor University
Child Health Research Center
College of Medicine, Dept. of Pediatrics
One Baylor Plaza
Houston, TX 77030
Phone: (713)770-1380
Fax: (713)770-2799
Dr. Thomas N. Hansen, M.D., Dir.

Research Activities and Fields: Pediatrics, focusing on the areas of molecular genetics, cell biology, and developmental biology. **E-mail Address:** thansen@neomailbcm.pedi.bcin.tmc.edu.

★3313★ Brown University
Child Study Center
Box 1836
Providence, RI 02912
Phone: (401)421-8241
Fax: (401)331-2768
Thomas F. Anders, M.D., Dir.

Research Activities and Fields: Child development and behavior, including studies on learning behavior of newborn and older children, developmental psychopathology, risk-taking behavior in children and adolescents, capacities of infants of all ages, and effectiveness of behavior modification interventions. Coordinates and sponsors research relating to normal child development and behavior at the University, administers the University's continuing studies in the national collaborative study of cerebral palsy, mental retardation, and other sensory and neurological disorders in children, and sponsors perceptual and learning studies at other institutions. Also studies risk taking and effects of behavioral misadventure on development. **Publications:** *Advances in Infancy Research.*

★3314★ Bryn Mawr College
Child Study Institute
Wyndon Ave., Roberts Rd.
Bryn Mawr, PA 19010
Phone: (610)527-5090
Fax: (610)527-5780
Prof. Leslie Rescorla, Contact

Research Activities and Fields: Delayed language development in children, nature and effectiveness of school admissions assessment techniques, and child reading disabilities.

★3315★ C.M. Hincks Institute
Hincks Treatment Centre
114 Maitland St.
Toronto, ON, Canada M4Y 1E1
Phone: (416)924-1164
Fax: (416)924-9808
Freda E. Martin, M.D., Dir.

Research Activities and Fields: Mental health research and training facility for child psychiatrists, psychologists, social workers, and childcare professionals. **Publications:** Research Department Activities.

★3316★ Camille Cosby Ambulatory Care
   Center
Judge Baker Children's Center
295 Longwood Ave.
Boston, MA 02115
Phone: (617)232-8390
Fax: (617)232-8399
Dr. Gloria Johnson-Powell, Dir.

Research Activities and Fields: Mental health of children and their families, focusing on minorities and urban poor. Activities include studies on the effects on children of severe mental illness in parents, resilient youth in high risk situations, development of boys with sex chromosome abnormalities, relationship between psychosocial and biological aspects of anorexia nervosa, and pscyological effects on children of the threat of nuclear war. Develops prevention intervention strategies for families with parental affective disorders.

★3317★ Center for Children with Chronic
   Illness and Disability
Univ. of Minnesota
Harvard St. at E. River Rd.
Box 721 UMHC
Minneapolis, MN 55455
Phone: (612)625-5177
Fax: (612)624-5920
Dr. Joan Patterson, Dir. of Research

Research Activities and Fields: Psychological and social development of children with chronic illness and disability. Activities include child and family assessments, survey research, and developing a data management system for studies conducted at collaborating sites. **E-mail Address:** jasu@maroon.tc.umn.edu.

★3318★ Chapin Hall Center for Children
Univ. of Chicago
1155 E. 60th St.
Chicago, IL 60637-2745
Phone: (312)753-5900
Fax: (312)753-5940
Harold A. Richman, Exec.Dir.

Research Activities and Fields: Child welfare and children's policy. Activities focus on monitoring the condition of children, improving delivery of children's services, and enhancing social support for the health development of children. Research projects include the areas of child abuse and neglect, child proverty, foster care, family preservation, child mental health, adolescent parenthood, juvenile delinquency, and community support for children. **Publications:** Discussion Papers.

★3319★ Child Development Center
120 W. 57th St.
New York, NY 10019
Phone: (212)582-9100
Fax: (212)245-2096
Alice Kross Frankel, M.D., Dir.

Research Activities and Fields: Therapeutic and educational techniques for emotionally disturbed, language-impaired, and central nervous system-impaired children. Developing criteria for assessment and monitoring. Conducting a ten-year demographic and current status, review of therapeutic nursery school graduates; also conducting onsite group treatment of preschool children in daycare centers. Research activities are pursued as part of a group of clinical programs offered for children ages six and under.

★3320★ Child Health Research Center
Children's Hospital
Dept. of Med.
300 Longwood Ave.
Boston, MA 02115
Phone: (617)735-7681
Fax: (617)738-7066
Dr. David Nathan, Dir.

Research Activities and Fields: Child health, particularly developmental biology. **E-mail Address:** bernfield@a1.tch.harvard.edu.

★3321★ Child Health Research Center
Primary Children's Medical Ctr.
100 N. Medical Dr.
Salt Lake City, UT 84113
Phone: (801)581-5000
Fax: (801)588-2380
Dr. Michael Dean, Dir.

Research Activities and Fields: Developmental biology, focusing on metabolic pathways and their regulation, genetic disease, and fetal and neonatal adaptations.

★3322★ Child Welfare League of America Research and Evaluation Staff
440 1st St. NW, Ste. 310
Washington, DC 20001
Phone: (202)942-0294
Fax: (202)638-4004
Patrick A. Curtis, Ph.D., Dir. of Research

Research Activities and Fields: Policy and practice issues related to child welfare such as family preservation, child abuse and neglect, adoption, foster care, teenage pregnancy, child rearing by young parents and protectors, chemical dependency, runaway youth, and management and administration of child welfare services. **Publications:** *CWLA 1993 Salary Study.* **Formerly:** Child Welfare League of America--Research Department.

Children's Cancer Research Institute
See: Entry 6020

Children's Center for Cancer and Blood Disorders
See: Entry 6021

★3323★ Children's Clinical Research Center
New York Hospital—Cornell Medical Center
525 E. 68th St., Rm. N236
New York, NY 10021
Phone: (212)746-3453
Fax: (212)746-8821
Joseph M. Gertner, Dir.

Research Activities and Fields: Steroidogenesis, hypertension, growth disorders, bone mineral metabolism, thalassemia, psychosocial failure-to-thrive, renal disorders, and pediatric AIDS. The Center's six beds, specialized equipment, and staff provide a multidisciplinary, controlled research environment separate from facilities serving the Medical College. Designated as a teaching unit within the University. **Publications:** *Research Reporter* (monthly). **Formerly:** Pediatric Clinical Research Center.

Children's Heart Institute of Texas
See: Entry 2887

★3324★ Children's Hospital Clinical Studies Center
700 Children's Dr.
Columbus, OH 43205
Phone: (614)722-4425
Fax: (614)722-4565
William B. Zipf, M.D., Dir.

Research Activities and Fields: Childhood illnesses, pharmacology, metabolic and infectious diseases, drug metabolism in children, and endocrine disorders of children.

★3325★ Children's Hospital Oakland Research Institute
747 52nd St.
Oakland, CA 94609
Phone: (510)428-3502
Fax: (510)428-3608
Dr. Bertram Lubin, Dir. of Medical Research

Research Activities and Fields: Biomedical research, including cellular immunology and the development of antigenicity, lipid metabolism, and the structure and function of cellular and model membranes, with emphasis on signal transduction, the molecular components involved in metabolic pathways, hypertension, vascular disease, hematology, platelet aggregation, thrombosis, gestation, experimental surgery, and nutrition as these are related to pediatric problems. Special areas of research include problems in sickle cell disease, cystic fibrosis, cancer gene markers, platelet disorders, and GI function in neonates.

★3326★ Children's Hospital Research Center
3020 Children's Way, MC 5074
San Diego, CA 92123
Phone: (619)576-5934
Fax: (619)467-0376
Sylvia McKinney, Contact

Research Activities and Fields: Causes and prevention of childhood diseases, including studies in diagnostic techniques and methods, neurosciences, autism, language development, sudden infant death syndrome, and industrial technology.

★3327★ Children's Hospital Research Foundation
700 Children's Dr.
Columbus, OH 43205
Phone: (614)722-4561
Fax: (614)722-4565
Thomas Hansen, Contact

Research Activities and Fields: Neonatology, pediatrics, children's cancer chemotherapy, cancer immunology, molecular retrovirology, gastroenterology, genetics, infectious diseases, nutrition, pathology, surgery, virology, metabolic disorders, Reye's Syndrome, cystic fibrosis, rheumatology, pulmonology, pharmacology/toxicology, cardiology, and clinical problems of infancy and childhood. **Publications:** Annual Report.

★3328★ Children's Hospital Research Foundation
3333 Burnet Ave.
Cincinnati, OH 45229-3039
Phone: (513)559-4588
Fax: (513)559-8453
Thomas F. Boat, M.D., Dir.

Research Activities and Fields: Molecular and cell biology, biochemistry, physiology, microbiology, pathology, and clinical investigations of infancy and childhood, and animal models of childhood illnesses. Research activities are carried out in the divisions of adolescent medicine, allergy/immunology, general pediatrics, basic science, cardiology, clinical pharmacology, critical care medicine, emergency medicine, endocrinology, gastroenterology, hematology-oncology, human genetics, infectious disease, inflammatory mechanisms, molecular cardiovascular biology, neonatology, nephrology, neurology, pathology, child psychiatry, pulmonary biology, pulmonary medicine, radiology, rheumatology, and surgery. The veterinary services division provides care and maintenance of laboratory animals.

Children's Psychopharmacology Unit
See: Entry 7553

★3329★ Children's Research Institute
111 Michigan Ave., NW
Washington, DC 20010
Phone: (202)884-4007
Gordon Avery, Ph.D., M.D., CEO

Research Activities and Fields: Pediatric research on the prevention, management, and treatment of childhood diseases. Studies focus on tumor cell biology, brain research, molecular virology and genetics, AIDS and other infectious diseases, cardiovasular disease, pharmacy, and nursing care. Operates six laboratory centers specializing in specific areas of research: Virology, Immunology, and Infectious Disease; Cancer and Transplantation Biology; Molecular Mechanisms of Disease Research; Neurosciences Research; and Health Services and Clinical Research.

★3330★ Clinical Research Center
Children's Hospital Medical Center
300 Longwood Ave.
Boston, MA 02115
Phone: (617)735-7201
Dr. Fred S. Rosen, Project Dir.

Research Activities and Fields: Protocols in bone marrow transplantation, immunodeficiencies, pediatric endocrinology, bone and mineral metabolism, pediatric hematology, neuroimmunology, oncology, and pediatric gastroenterology. Investigates drug therapy use for bone marrow transplant patients and examines the psychological effects of providing nursing care in isolation (a bacteria-free environment for bone marrow transplant patients). **Publications:** *Grand Rounds* (irregularly).

★3331★ Columbia University
Center for Clinical Research—Pediatric
  Unit
Columbia-Presbyterian Medical Center
Vanderbilt, 3rd Fl., Rm. 301
622 W. 168th St.
New York, NY 10032
Phone: (212)305-6638
Dr. Canfield, Dir.

Research Activities and Fields: Infant nutrition and total parenteral nutrition, hemolytic anemias, perinatology, muscular dystrophy, genetic disorders of metabolism, and pulmonary hypertension.

★3332★ Columbia University
National Center for Children in Poverty
154 Haven Ave.
Manhattan, NY 10032
Phone: (212)927-8793
Fax: (212)927-9162
Judith E. Jones, Dir.

Research Activities and Fields: Interdisciplinary research, policy analysis, and program evaluation focused on poor children under six and their families. Specific areas include child and family health, early childhood care and education, and efforts to integrate services for low-income families. **Publications:** *Urban Poverty Database Inventory.* **E-mail Address:** cj01@cunixf.columbia.edu.

Cornell University
Laboratory of Pediatric Critical Care
See: Entry 10430

★3333★ Duke University
Pediatric Cardiac Catheterization
  Laboratory
Pediatric Office
Medical Center
PO Box 3090
Durham, NC 27710
Phone: (919)681-2916
Fax: (919)681-5903
Dr. Martin P. O'Laughlin, M.D., Dir.

Research Activities and Fields: Pediatric cardiology, including development of a fetal cardiac ultrasound equipment to detect heart problems as early as 16 weeks into pregnancy.

★3334★ Duke University
Pediatric Oncology Consortium
Box 2916
Durham, NC 27710
Phone: (919)684-3401
Fax: (919)681-7950
Dr. Michael Frank, M.D., Dir.

Research Activities and Fields: Conducts clinical trials of new cancer therapies for children.

Special interests include neuro-oncology and bone marrow transplantation.

★3335★ Florida State University
Center for Prevention and Early
  Intervention
1118B Thomasville Rd.
Tallahassee, FL 32303
Phone: (904)644-6166
Fax: (904)644-0492
Dr. Mimi A. Graham, Dir.

Research Activities and Fields: Child growth and development, particularly the first five years; maternal and child health and early childhood issues on a state and national basis. Seeks to build families, prevent disabilities and other handicapping conditions, and minimize environmental and biological risks to young children. Also interested in violence prevention.

★3336★ General Clinical Research Center
  at Children's Hospital of Philadelphia
34th & Civic Center Blvd.
Philadelphia, PA 19104
Phone: (215)590-2017
Fax: (215)590-3044
Stuart Starr, M.D., Program Dir.

Research Activities and Fields: Biomedicine, allergy and immunology, cardiology, diabetes endocrinology, gastroenterology, gene therapy, genetics, hematology, infectious disease, metabolism, neonatology, neurology, nutrition, and oncology.

★3337★ General Clinical Research Center
  at Children's Hospital of Pittsburgh
3705 5th Ave.
Pittsburgh, PA 15213
Phone: (412)692-5573
Fax: (412)692-6783
Peter A. Lee, M.D., Dir.

Research Activities and Fields: Biomedicine, allergy and immunology, endocrinology, hematology and oncology, infectious disease, metabolism, nutrition, otolaryngology, pulmonology, pharmacology, transplantation surgery, gastroenterology, and diabetes mellitus.

★3338★ Howard University
Child Development Center
C.B. Powell Bldg.
525 Bryant St. NW
Washington, DC 20059
Phone: (202)806-6973
Fax: (202)806-7940
Merceline M. Dahl-Regis, M.D., Dir.

Research Activities and Fields: Child development and handicapping conditions of childhood, including interdisciplinary studies in pediatrics, neurology, genetics, psychology, speech pathology, and infant development.

Indiana University
Herman B. Wells Center for Pediatric
  Research
See: Entry 6051

★3339★ Indiana University-Purdue
  University at Indianapolis
Riley Child Psychiatry Clinic
702 Barnhill Dr., Rm. 3701
Indianapolis, IN 46202-5200
Phone: (317)274-8162
Fax: (317)278-0609
Susanne Blix, M.D., Dir.

Research Activities and Fields: Child psychiatry, including studies of the correlation between parental psychotherapy and child symptoms, treatment recommendations and outcome, language and learning disabilities, psychiatric effects of craniofacial anomalies, nursing staff and their relationship to severely ill children, psychophysiology and emotional factors affecting diabetes, outcome studies of psychiatric inpatient adolescents, adolescent self-concept, treatment of feeding disorder children, studies of children with psychiatric sequelae from sexual or physical abuse and how that abuse may relate to Dopamine Beta Hydroxylase, studies of the efficacy of using group therapy in the treatment of adolescent victims of sexual abuse, and hypnosis as an adjunct treatment. **Formerly:** Riley Child Guidance Clinic (1985).

Information Sciences Research Institute
See: Entry 7014

Institute for Families and Children
See: Entry 7570

Institutes for Achievement of Human
  Potential
See: Entry 8377

★3340★ Johns Hopkins University
Child Health Research Center
Ross 1125
720 Rutland Ave.
Baltimore, MD 21205
Phone: (410)955-3886
Fax: (410)955-8208
Dr. George Dover, Dir.

Research Activities and Fields: Applies molecular biology techniques to the diagnosis, treatment, and prevention of genetic and acquired disorders in children. Activities focus on developing techniques to analyze genes and gene products, especially those required for normal development. **E-mail Address:** gdover@welchlink.welch.jbu.edu.

★3341★ Johns Hopkins University
Pediatric Clinical Research Unit
CMSC, 6th Fl.
600 N. Wolfe St.
Baltimore, MD 21287-3923
Phone: (410)955-5884
Fax: (410)955-0229
Dr. Hugh Sampson, Program Dir.

Research Activities and Fields: Basic and clinical studies of medical problems of childhood.

Kennedy Krieger Institute
See: Entry 12735

Louisiana State University
Genetics Section of Pediatrics
See: Entry 5338

★ 3342 ★ McGill University
Montreal Children's Hospital Research Institute
2300 Tupper St.
Montreal, PQ, Canada H3H 1P3
Phone: (514)934-4300
Fax: (514)934-4331
Roy Gravel, Dir.

Research Activities and Fields: Basic, clinical, and epidemiologic research into various disorders affecting infants and children, including diabetes, cystic fibrosis, abnormal growth, learning disabilities, hyperactivity, and genetic diseases.

Medical University of South Carolina
Vince Moseley Center for Children with Developmental Disabilities
See: Entry 4579

★ 3343 ★ Miami Children's Hospital Research Institute
6125 SW 31st St.
Miami, FL 33155
Phone: (305)663-8522
Fax: (305)663-2461
Reuben Matalon, M.D., Dir.

Research Activities and Fields: Genetic diseases in children with emphasis on mucopolysaccharidoses, amino acid diseases, phenylketonuria (PKU), biopterin, organic acid diseases, and lysosmal storage diseases.

Mid-Missouri Mental Health Center
See: Entry 7584

Oregon Health Sciences University
Elks' Children's Eye Clinic
See: Entry 13623

Oregon Health Sciences University
Pediatric Metabolic Laboratory
See: Entry 5344

Pediatric Cancer Research Laboratory
See: Entry 6100

Pediatric Oncology Group
See: Entry 6101

Pediatric Pulmonary Unit
See: Entry 11612

★ 3344 ★ Pediatric Research Institute
Cardinal Glennon Children's Hospital
3662 Park Ave.
St. Louis, MO 63110
Phone: (314)577-5623
Fax: (314)577-5398
Dr. Mary J.C. Hendrix, Dir.

Research Activities and Fields: Neuronal growth and differentiation, surfactant production in lung development, interuterine growth retardation, regulation of gene expression in liver and muscle cells, oncogene expression, the role of the osteoblast in bone homeostatis, tumor cell invasion and metastasis. **Publications:** *PRI Investigator Newsletter*.

★ 3345 ★ Pediatric Rheumatoid Clinic
Duke Medical Center
Box 3212
Durham, NC 27710
Phone: (919)684-6575
Fax: (919)684-6616
Dr. Deborah Kredich, Contact

Research Activities and Fields: Clinical and laboratory pediatric rheumatology and immunology. **Formerly:** Arthritis Pediatric Research Center.

Portland State University
Research and Training Center on Family Support and Children's Mental Health
See: Entry 7593

★ 3346 ★ Reiss-Davis Child Study Center
3200 Motor Ave.
Los Angeles, CA 90034
Phone: (310)204-1666
Fax: (310)838-4637
Leonore W. Freehling, Libn.

Research Activities and Fields: Child psychology, child psychiatry, child development, psychiatric social work, educational psychology, child analysis, and psychoanalysis. **Publications:** *Acquisitions List* (quarterly).

★ 3347 ★ Research Unit on Children's Psychosocial Maladjustment
750 Gouin E.
C.P. 6128, succursale A
Montreal, PQ, Canada H2C 1A6
Phone: (514)385-2525
Fax: (514)385-5739
Prof. Richard E. Tremblay, Dir.

Research Activities and Fields: Child development, families, school adjustment, delinquency, aggression, substance abuse, socialization, and peers, focusing on longitudinal studies and experiments.

Rutgers University
Douglass Developmental Disabilities Center
See: Entry 7596

S.E. Child Safety Institute of the Childrens Hospital of Alabama
See: Entry 10456

★ 3348 ★ St. Jude Children's Research Hospital
332 N. Lauderdale
PO Box 318
Memphis, TN 38101
Phone: (901)522-0301
Fax: (901)525-2720
Arthur W. Nienhuis, M.D., Dir.

Research Activities and Fields: Pediatric studies in hematology, oncology, infectious diseases, neurology, cardiopulmonary diseases, diagnostic imaging, pharmacokinetics, psychology, and pathology; biomedical studies in biochemistry, immunology, pharmacology, virology and molecular biology, tumor cell biology, experimental oncology, genetics, and biostatistics. **Publications:** Biannual Scientific Report; Annual Report; *St. Jude Rounds* (quarterly newsletter for pediatricians). **E-mail Address:** dulle.@mbcf.stjude.org.

Shriners Hospital for Crippled Children
Metabolic Research Unit
See: Entry 7930

★ 3349 ★ Sleep Disorders Center for Children
Children's Medical Center of Dallas
1935 Motor St.
Dallas, TX 75235
Phone: (214)920-2793
Dr. John Herman, Dir.

Research Activities and Fields: Studies infants with respiratory problems, children with obstructive sleep apnea, and excessive daytime sleepiness (narcolepsy). Conducts studies of vigilance and related visual evoked potentials.

Sonia Shankman Orthogenic School
See: Entry 7601

★ 3350 ★ State University of New York Health Science Center at Brooklyn
Child Behavior Research Unit
450 Clarkson Ave., Box 1195
Brooklyn, NY 11203
Phone: (718)245-2326
Oliver J. David, M.D., Dir.

Research Activities and Fields: 1) Parent-child interactions, particularly communication patterns in families and their relationship to psychopathology. 2) Effects of lead on behavioral and academic problems of children, psychopharmacology, and deleading hyperactive children and evaluating the effect on the hyperactivity. Data are derived for studies on the incidence of sub-toxic lead levels in children with hyperkinesis, learning disabilities, and mental retardation and studies on the efficacy of chelation therapy in the treatment of these disorders.

★ 3351 ★ State University of New York Health Science Center at Brooklyn
Child Psychiatry Research Program
451 Clarkson Ave., Box 32
J Bldg.
Brooklyn, NY 11203
Phone: (718)270-1430
Fax: (718)778-5397
Adolf Christ, Dir.

Research Activities and Fields: Behavioral and physiological investigation of development and pathology. Projects include observations of mother-child interaction during infancy and later stages, the objective study of children with behavior disorders, autism, minimal brain damage, and mental retardation. Focuses on psychological, physiological, and neurological phenomena.

★ 3352 ★ State University of New York Health Science Center at Brooklyn
Infant and Child Behavior Laboratory
450 Clarkson Ave., Box 1203
Brooklyn, NY 11203
Phone: (718)270-2598
Fax: (718)270-3910
Dr. Joan Hittelman, Dir.

Research Activities and Fields: Infant development, including evaluation of various methods of eye protection in jaundiced newborn infants undergoing phototherapy with respect to behavioral, physiological, and biochemical parameters; studies of the contribution of the neonate's sex to the parent-child interaction, particularly with respect to neonatal eye contact and maternal attitudes toward the baby; and follow-up of high risk infants (infants born weighing less than 1000 grams and infants exposed to the HIV virus).

★3353★ Temple University
Motor Development Laboratory
Pearson Hall
Philadelphia, PA 19122
Phone: (215)204-1960
Fax: (215)204-4662
Dr. Marcella V. Ridenour, Dir.

Research Activities and Fields: Motor development of infants and young children, including studies on safety of toys, juvenile furniture, cribs, strollers, walkers, high chairs, tricycles and wheeled toys, and playgrounds. Performs biomechanics analysis of infants and young children and evaluations of toys and play equipment through the use of motion pictures.

Texas Scottish Rite Hospital for Children
Research Department
See: Entry 8433

U.S. Department of Agriculture
Agricultural Research Service
Children's Nutrition Research Center
See: Entry 9536

U.S. Department of Defense
Armed Forces Institute of Pathology
Center for Advanced Pathology
Pediatric Pathology Department
See: Entry 10161

U.S. Department of Health and Human Services
Centers for Disease Control and Prevention
International Health Program Office
See: Entry 10991

U.S. Department of Health and Human Services
National Cancer Institute
Division of Cancer Treatment
Pediatric Branch
See: Entry 6162

★3354★ U.S. Department of Health and Human Services
National Institute of Child Health and Human Development
NIH Bldg. 31, Rm. 2A03
9000 Rockville Pike
Bethesda, MD 20892
Phone: (301)496-3454
Fax: (301)402-1104
Dr. Duane Alexander, Director

Research Activities and Fields: NICHD conducts and supports basic and clinical research in the biomedical, behavioral, and social sciences relating to child and maternal health; medical rehabilitation; and in the population sciences, such as reproductive biology and the development and evaluation of contraceptives. The Institute's major research components in-

clude: the Center for Population Research, the Center for Medical Rehabilitation Research, and the Center for Research for Mothers and Children, which are extramural programs supporting research through grants and contracts; the Division of Intramural Research, which conducts research in NICHD's Bethesda, MD, laboratories; the Division of Epidemiology, Statistics, and Prevention Research; and the Division of Scientific Review. Areas of research emphasis in both the extramural and intramural programs include: high risk pregnancy, congenital abnormalities, maternal and pediatric AIDS, sudden infant death syndrome, childhood origins of adult disease, mental retardation, learning disorders (especially developmental dyslexia), fertility regulation and contraceptive safety, fertility and infertility, population dynamics, and medical rehabilitation. Mechanisms of research support include both grants and contracts. (Most support is given in the form of various types of grants, but contracts are awarded to both nonprofit and commercial organizations for research specifically solicited by the Institute.)

U.S. Department of Health and Human Services
National Institute of Child Health and Human Development
Center for Research for Mothers and Children
See: Entry 9712

U.S. Department of Health and Human Services
National Institute of Child Health and Human Development
Intramural Research Program
Human Genetics Branch
See: Entry 5360

U.S. Department of Health and Human Services
National Institute of Mental Health
Clinical Research Division
Child and Adolescent Disorders Research Branch
See: Entry 7620

U.S. Department of Health and Human Services
National Institute of Mental Health
Developmental Psychology Laboratory
See: Entry 7625

U.S. Department of Health and Human Services
National Institute of Mental Health
Intramural Research Programs Division (Clinical Research)
Child Psychiatry Branch
See: Entry 7636

★3355★ University of Alabama
Brewer-Porch Children's Center
Box 870156
University, AL 35487-0156
Phone: (205)348-7236
Dr. Robert D. Lyman, Exec.Dir.

Research Activities and Fields: Behaviorally disordered children and juvenile rehabilitation, including studies on token reinforcement strate-

gies in a classroom for emotionally disturbed children, contingency management and its effect on disruptive behavior, academic rate of progress and achievement test scores, and development of innovative programs to meet special needs of adolescents experiencing marked adjustment problems whose difficulties have led to contact with legal authorities. Concerned with perfecting motivational and therapeutic techniques with groups of behaviorally disordered children. Also concerned with selection and training of child care staff. Provides residential treatment for behaviorally disturbed children. Conducts joint studies with personnel in departments of psychology, special education, social work, and medicine at the University. **Formerly:** Center for Emotionally Disturbed Children.

University of Alabama at Birmingham
Civitan International Research Center/
Alabama UAP
See: Entry 4586

★3356★ University of California, San Diego
Center for Child and Family Studies
Dept. of Pediatrics
La Jolla, CA 92093-0927
Phone: (619)552-7660
Fax: (619)552-7670
Dr. Philip R. Nader, M.D., Dir.

Research Activities and Fields: Health behavior, epidemiology and survey research, and intervention evaluation, including the role of individual and family behavior in disease prevention and illness management. **E-mail Address:** pnader@ucsd.edu.

★3357★ University of California, San Francisco
Pediatric Clinical Research Center
Dept. of Pediatrics
Moffit Hospital, Rm. 601
San Francisco, CA 94143
Phone: (415)476-2171
Fax: (415)476-3466
Diane W. Wara, M.D., Dir.

Research Activities and Fields: Behavioral sciences, biochemistry, endocrinology, gastroenterology, genetics, hematology, immunology, nephrology, oncology, nutrition, pharmacology, and radiation therapy, and HIV. **E-mail Address:** wara@gcrc.ucsf.edu. **Formerly:** General Clinical Research Center--Children.

★3358★ University of Chicago
La Rabida Research and Policy Center for the Study of Children and Families with Special Health Care Needs
Woodlawn Social Services Bldg.
950 E. 61st St.
Chicago, IL 60637
Phone: (312)324-8262
Fax: (312)324-3571
Nancy A. Carlson, Ph.D., Exec.Dir.

Research Activities and Fields: Economic, psychological, sociological, educational, cultural, and medical effects of childhood chronic illness and disability on families and society. Areas of research include pediatric HIV/AIDS, cross-cultural themes, patterns of health care financing, effective foster care for medically complex children, community-based service systems, and the nature of family constellations, including the tracking of child development in varying family and institutional contexts, and intervention studies. **Publications:** Offers technical assistance and consulting. **E-mail Address:** nc12@midway.uchicago.edu.

★3359★ University of Colorado
General Clinical Research Center—
    Pediatric
Health Sciences Center
4200 E. 9th Ave.
Box C225
Denver, CO 80262
Phone: (303)837-2957
Fax: (303)837-2729
K. Michael Hambidge, M.D., Program Dir.

Research Activities and Fields: Developmental behavior, diabetes mellitus, gastroenterology, genetics, hematology, immunology, infectious disease, metabolism, neonatology, neurology, nephrology, nutrition, and pulmonary physiology.

University of Colorado
John F. Kennedy Center for Developmental
    Disabilities
See: Entry 4326

University of Connecticut
Division of Child and Family Studies
See: Entry 4587

★3360★ University of Florida
Institute for Child Health Policy
5700 SW 34th St., Ste. 323
Gainesville, FL 32608
Phone: (904)392-5904
Fax: (904)392-8822
Steve A. Freedman, Ph.D., Dir.

Research Activities and Fields: Child health policy and family and child health care delivery issues, including development of an equitable and comprehensive child health policy model for states; development of case management programs for children with special health care needs; development of health care financing strategies, including school enrollment-based health insurance; and comprehensive program development and health services research and evaluation. **Publications:** *SSI Liaison Newsletter; Think! A Forum for Ideas on Child Health Policy* (newsletter); *Developmental Screening and Family-Centered Care Module; SSInsights; Special Children, Special Care: SSI Handbook; Florida Children's Medical Services Five Year Plan; Maternal and Child Health Thesaurus.* **E-mail Address:** ichp@qm.server.ufl.edu.

University of Illinois at Chicago
Center for Handicapped Children
See: Entry 4588

University of Illinois at Chicago
Center for Health Services Research
See: Entry 9718

★3361★ University of Iowa
Child Health Research Center
Dept. of Pediatrics
Iowa City, IA 52242
Phone: (319)356-0469
Fax: (319)356-4855
Dr. Frank H. Morriss, Jr., Dir.

Research Activities and Fields: Pediatrics, particularly developmental molecular biology. Activities emphasize the identification and localization of genes on the human genome, investigations of the mechanisms used by specific genes to regulate the synthesis and timing of gene products, and a study on the effects of gene products on the structure and function of developing tissues.

University of Kansas
Bureau of Child Research
See: Entry 4329

University of Kentucky
Children's Cancer Study Group
See: Entry 6225

University of Louisville
Child Evaluation Center
See: Entry 4592

★3362★ University of Louisville
Keller Child Psychiatry Research Center
608 S. Jackson
Louisville, KY 40292
Phone: (502)852-5326
Laura J. Reed, Dir.

Research Activities and Fields: Normal and pathological psychosocial processes in children and their families, including comparison of psychotherapy and behavior therapy with phobic children, development of diagnostic instruments for assessment of childhood psychopathology, and study of age changes in Alpha rhythm associated with simple and complex learning tasks as measured by electroencephalographs. **Formerly:** Child Psychiatry Research Center.

★3363★ University of Maryland
Sudden Infant Death Syndrome Institute
22 S. Greene St., Rm. H5W67
Baltimore, MD 21201
Phone: (410)328-6523
Fax: (410)328-0645

Research Activities and Fields: Sudden Infant Death Syndrome (SIDS), including efforts to detect abnormalities present before or at death, correlation of data from clinical evaluation of infants at risk (especially those suffering from apnea or cyanosis), development of animal models to test hypotheses about the etiology of SIDS, examination of tissues from infants who have died from SIDS and other illnesses, animal studies to determine the relationship of specific tissue abnormalities to cause of death, and the psychological effect of infant death on family members.

University of Massachusetts Boston
Center for the Study of Social
    Development and Education
See: Entry 4594

★3364★ University of Miami
Mailman Center for Child Development
D-820
PO Box 016820
Miami, FL 33101
Phone: (305)547-6123
Fax: (305)547-5978
Mary Theresa Urbano, Ph.D., Assoc.Dir.

Research Activities and Fields: Handicapping conditions in children, genetic disorders, sensory disorders, and child behavior and development, including prevention and intervention strategies. **Publications:** Annual Report. **E-mail Address:** turano@admin.med.miami.edu.

University of Michigan
Pediatric Surgery Research Laboratories
See: Entry 12325

★3365★ University of Michigan
University Center for the Child and Family
1007 E. Huron St.
Ann Arbor, MI 48104-1690
Phone: (313)764-9466
Fax: (313)747-1051
Dr. A. Barbakin, Dir.

Research Activities and Fields: Infant, child, and family mental health; normal socioemotional development; effectiveness of treatment of children with conduct and mood disorders; prevention programming in schools and neighborhoods; and stress and coping in African American and Latino youth. **E-mail Address:** gbsu@um.cc.umich.edu.

University of Montreal
Sainte-Justine Hospital Research Centre
See: Entry 11297

★3366★ University of Nebraska at Omaha
Meyer Rehabilitation Institute
600 S. 42nd St.
Omaha, NE 68198-5450
Phone: (402)559-5233
Fax: (402)559-5737
Dr. Bruce Buehler, Dir.

Research Activities and Fields: Problems and needs of children and adults (medical, genetic, or behavioral), including interdisciplinary studies on congenital disorders, dentistry, infant development, language and cognitive disorders, behavioral disorders, and sensory/motor development. Subject populations include families receiving service at the Institute, infants, preschoolers, adolescents, and adults with developmental disabilities. **Publications:** Annual Report. **E-mail Address:** mleibowl@unmc.edu. **Formerly:** Meyer Children's Rehabilitation Institute.

★3367★ University of North Carolina at
    Chapel Hill
Child Development Institute
CB 8000
214 S. Bldg., 005A
Chapel Hill, NC 27599-8000
Phone: (919)962-1091
Fax: (919)962-2437
Dr. H. Garland Hershey, Dir.

Research Activities and Fields: Institute consists of interacting research centers conducting interdisciplinary research on children and families, especially those at risk for developmental disorders. The Frank Porter Graham Child Development Center (FPG) studies social, psychological, educational, and health aspects of child development. FPG conducts a demonstration family and child care program involving infants and preschool children with and without disabilities. The Brain Development and Research Center (BDRC) emphasizes neurobiological and genetic aspects of development focusing on both preclinical and clinical research. The North Carolina Mental Retardation Research Center (NC/MRRC) provides research support services for FPG and BDRC.

★3368★ University of North Carolina at Chapel Hill
Frank Porter Graham Child Development Center
105 Smith Level Rd.
CB 8180
Chapel Hill, NC 27599-8180
Phone: (919)966-1703
Fax: (919)966-7532
Don Bailey, Ph.D., Dir.

Research Activities and Fields: Prevention and treatment of developmental and learning disabilities; longitudinal study of children with disabilities and their families; conceptualization of adaptive behavior and social cognition in context; health and psychosocial development of children experiencing alternative forms of daycare; strategies to systematically evaluate the quality of home and educational environments across the life span; and contributing factors to child abuse and neglect. Conducts a research utilization program with involves research development and demonstration, outreach, social policy analysis, and information dissemination. **Publications:** Status Report on Programs and Projects (annually).

★3369★ University of Northern Iowa
Center for the Study of Adolescence
115 Sabin Hall
Cedar Falls, IA 50614-0401
Phone: (319)273-5910
Fax: (319)273-2222
Dr. William Downs, Dir.

Research Activities and Fields: Adolescence, including childhood and adolescent maltreatment, delinquincy, substance abuse, adolescent pregnancy, and depression, grief, and suicide. **E-mail Address:** in%"downs@cobra.uni.edu".

University of Quebec at Montreal
Laboratory of Research in Human and Social Ecology
See: Entry 11001

★3370★ University of Rochester
Strong Children's Research Center
Medical Center
Box 777
601 Elmwood Ave.
Rochester, NY 14642
Phone: (716)275-8447
Fax: (716)271-7512
Dr. Richard Insel, Dir.

Research Activities and Fields: Pediatrics. **Publications:** Newsletter (quarterly). **E-mail**

Address:
scrc@bphvax.biophysics.rochester.edu.

University of South Florida
Research and Training Center for Children's Mental Health
See: Entry 7689

University of Tennessee
Center of Excellence in Pediatric Pharmacokinetics and Therapeutics
See: Entry 10485

★3371★ University of Texas Medical Branch at Galveston
Child Health Research Center
300 Univ. Blvd.
Dept. of Pediatrics
Rte. C-51
Galveston, TX 77550
Phone: (409)772-1594
Fax: (409)772-4599
Dr. Pearay Ogra, Dir.

Research Activities and Fields: Pediatrics. Activities focus on applying research in developmental immunology to improving health and combatting diseases of children.

University of Virginia
Kluge Children's Rehabilitation Center and Research Institute
See: Entry 4598

University of Washington
Child Development and Mental Retardation Center
See: Entry 4338

University of Wisconsin—Madison
Children's Cancer Study Group
See: Entry 6259

★3372★ Vanderbilt University
Center for the Study of At-Risk Populations and Public Assistance Policy
1207 18th Ave. S.
Nashville, TN 37212
Phone: (615)322-8505
Fax: (615)322-8081
Davis S. Cordray, Dir.

Research Activities and Fields: Public policies affecting at-risk populations, including research on the effectiveness of interventions for homeless persons with alcohol and other drug problems, job training for the disadvantaged, the effects of teenage employment on young men, consequences of living in poor neighborhoods, and growing up in a welfare dependent household. **Formerly:** Center for the Study of Families, Children and Elderly.

Vanderbilt University
John F. Kennedy Center for Research on Human Development
See: Entry 4339

★3373★ W.M. Krogman Center for Research in Child Growth and Development
4019 Erving St.
Philadelphia, PA 19104-6003
Phone: (215)898-1470
Dr. Solomon H. Katz, Dir.

Research Activities and Fields: Obesity, nutrition, and other health and mental disorders, epidemiology of high blood pressure in adolescents, neuropsychological development, developmental disorders, hypertension, and subclinical lead intoxication and other trace element studies in children. Also establishes norms of physical growth and development of Philadelphia and international children from birth to 17 years of age, including norms for head, face, and jaws (cephalometric and roentgenographic cephalometric), body (height, weight, somatometric size, and proportion of trunk and limbs), and maturation levels (via X-ray films and hand and knee), applied to clinical problems in medicine and dentistry. **Formerly:** Philadelphia Center for Research in Child Growth and Development.

Washington University
William Greenleaf Eliot Division of Child Psychiatry
See: Entry 7701

Wayne State University
Fetal Alcohol Research Center
See: Entry 9722

★3374★ Yale University
Child Health Research Center
Dept. of Pediatrics
333 Cedar St.
New Haven, CT 06510
Phone: (203)785-4638
Fax: (203)785-7194
Dr. Joseph Warshaw, Chmn.

Research Activities and Fields: Cellular and molecular biological studies of normal development and the ability of the fetus and child to adapt to environmental or genetic influences.

★3375★ Yale University
Child Study Center
PO Box 3333
New Haven, CT 06510
Phone: (203)785-5759
Fax: (203)785-7402
Dr. Donald J. Cohen, Dir.

Research Activities and Fields: Child development and behavior, including multidisciplinary studies of various aspects of child development from the newborn period into adolescence, emphasizing serious neuropsychiatric disorders: autism, Tourette's syndrome, mental retardation, and deficit disorders; early child development; model school intervention programs; legal aspects of child development; divorce, child custody, and child abuse; molecular genetics, including study of homeobox genes, neuronal differentiation and migration, Fragile X, developmental neurochemistry, infant attention and habituation; and social policy. **E-mail Address:** cohendj@maspo2.mas.yale.edu.

★ 3376 ★ Yale University
Children's Clinical Research Center
School of Medicine
Dept. of Pediatrics, 3091 L.M.P.
PO Box 20-8064
New Haven, CT 06510-8064
Phone: (203)785-4648
Fax: (203)785-7194
William V. Tamborlane, Jr., M.D., Program Dir.
Research Activities and Fields: Pediatric problems, including metabolic, hematologic, neurologic, cardiovascular disease, and social and psychological aspects of patient care.

★ 3377 ★ Yeshiva University
Preventive Intervention Research Center
  for Child Health
1300 Morris Park Ave.
Bronx, NY 10461
Phone: (718)918-4390
Fax: (212)918-4388
Ruth E.K. Stein, M.D., Dir.
Research Activities and Fields: Children with serious ongoing health problems (infancy through adolescence) and their families. Activities include evaluating preventive interventions for mothers of low birth weight infants, children with physical health conditions during school transition, and job training of adolescents. Also studies the social support of minority mothers of chronically ill younsters, epidemiology and consequences of serious ongoing health conditions, psychological and social adaptation of adolescents with epilepsy, risk behavior in adolescence, and fathers of children with serious illness.

State Government Agencies

Maternal & Child Health

★ 3378 ★ Alabama Department of Public
  Health
Family Health Services Bureau
434 Monroe St.
Montgomery, AL 36130
Phone: (334)242-5661
Fax: (334)269-4865

★ 3379 ★ Alaska Department of Health and
  Social Services
Public Health Division
Maternal and Child Family Health Section
1231 Gambell St.
Anchorage, AK 99501-4627
Phone: (907)274-7626
Fax: (907)586-1877

★ 3380 ★ Arizona Department of Health
  Services
Family Health and Community Services
  Division
Women and Children's Health Office
1740 W. Adams Ave.
Phoenix, AZ 85007
Phone: (602)542-1870
Fax: (602)542-1265

★ 3381 ★ Arkansas Department of Health
Public Health Programs Bureau
Maternal and Child Health Division
PO Box 3278
Little Rock, AR 72203-3278
Phone: (501)661-2243
Fax: (501)671-1450

★ 3382 ★ California Health and Welfare
  Agency
Health Services Department
Maternal and Child Health Branch
714 P St., Rm. 1253
Sacramento, CA 95814
Phone: (916)657-1347
Fax: (916)657-3069

★ 3383 ★ Colorado Public and Environment
  Depratment
Health Office
Family and Community Health Services
  Division
4300 Cherry Creek Dr. S.
Denver, CO 80222-1530
Phone: (303)692-2310
Fax: (303)692-0095

★ 3384 ★ Connecticut Department of
  Public Health
Community Health Bureau
Child Adolescent Health Division
150 Washington St.
Hartford, CT 06106
Phone: (203)566-7024
Fax: (203)566-6055

★ 3385 ★ Delaware Department of Health
  and Social Services
Public Health Division
Women's and Infants' Health Service
Jesse Cooper Bldg.
PO Box 637
Dover, DE 19903
Phone: (302)739-3111
Fax: (302)739-6659

★ 3386 ★ District of Columbia Department
  of Human Services
Public Health Commission
Maternal and Child Health Services Office
1660 G St. NW
Washington, DC 20001
Phone: (202)727-0393
Fax: (202)727-0379

★ 3387 ★ Florida Department of Health and
  Rehabilitative Services
Family Health Services Office
1317 Winewood Blvd.
Tallahassee, FL 32399-0700
Phone: (904)487-1321
Fax: (904)922-2993

★ 3388 ★ Georgia Department of Medical
  Assistance
Maternal and Child Health Division
2 Peachtree St. NW
Atlanta, GA 30303
Phone: (404)651-5785
Fax: (404)651-6880

★ 3389 ★ Hawaii Department of Health
Health Resources Administration
Family Health Services Division
Maternal and Child Health Branch
3652 Kilauea Ave.
Honolulu, HI 96816
Phone: (808)733-9024
Fax: (808)586-4444

★ 3390 ★ Idaho Department of Health and
  Welfare
Health Division
Maternal and Child Health Bureau
PO Box 83720
Boise, ID 83720-0036
Phone: (208)334-5967
Fax: (208)334-6558

★ 3391 ★ Illinois Department of Public
  Health
Community Health Office
Family Health Division
535 W. Jefferson St.
Springfield, IL 62761
Phone: (217)782-2736
Fax: (217)782-3987

★ 3392 ★ Indiana Department of Health
Maternal and Child Health Services
  Division
2 N. Meridian
Indianapolis, IN 46204
Phone: (317)233-1262

★ 3393 ★ Iowa Department of Public
  Health
Family and Community Health Division
Maternal and Child Health Section
Lucas State Office Bldg.
321 E. 12th St.
Des Moines, IA 50319
Phone: (515)281-4911
Fax: (515)281-4958

★ 3394 ★ Kansas Department of Health
  and Environment
Health Division
Family Health Bureau
900 SW Jackson St., Ste. 620
Topeka, KS 66612
Phone: (913)296-1300
Fax: (913)296-1231

★ 3395 ★ Kentucky Human Resources
  Cabinet
Health Services Department
Maternal and Child Health Services
  Division
275 E. Main St.
Frankfort, KY 40621
Phone: (502)564-4830
Fax: (502)564-6533

★ 3396 ★ Louisiana Department of Health
  and Hospitals
Public Health Office
Health Services Programs
Maternal and Child Health Section
325 Loyola Ave., Rm. 612
PO Box 60630
New Orleans, LA 70160
Phone: (504)568-5073
Fax: (504)568-8162

★3397★ **Maine Department of Human Services**
Health Bureau
Maternal and Child Health Division
State House Sta. 11
Augusta, ME 04333
Phone: (207)287-3311
Fax: (207)287-3005

★3398★ **Maryland Department of Health and Mental Hygiene**
Public Health Services Office
Local and Family Health Administration
201 W. Preston St., 5th Fl.
Baltimore, MD 21201
Phone: (410)225-5300
Fax: (410)225-6489

★3399★ **Massachusetts Executive Office of Health and Human Services**
Public Health Department
Family Health Services Division
150 Tremont St.
Boston, MA 02111
Phone: (617)727-3372
Fax: (617)727-2559

★3400★ **Michigan Department of Public Health**
Child and Family Services Bureau
3423 N. Logan
PO Box 30195
Lansing, MI 48909
Phone: (517)335-8955
Fax: (517)335-9476

★3401★ **Minnesota Department of Health**
Family Health Division
717 Delaware St. SE
Box 9441
Minneapolis, MN 55440
Phone: (612)623-5166
Fax: (612)623-5794

★3402★ **Mississippi Department of Health**
Health Services Bureau
WIC Services
PO Box 1700
Jackson, MS 39215-1700
Phone: (601)960-7829
Fax: (601)354-6104

★3403★ **Missouri Department of Health**
Maternal, Child and Family Health Division
PO Box 570
Jefferson City, MO 65102
Phone: (314)751-6174
Fax: (314)751-6010

★3404★ **Montana Department of Health and Environmental Sciences**
Health Services Division
Family, Maternal and Child Health Bureau
Cogswell Bldg., Rm. C108
Helena, MT 59620
Phone: (406)444-4740

★3405★ **Nebraska Department of Health**
Health Promotion and Disease Prevention Bureau
Maternal and Child Health Division
301 Centennial Mall S.
PO Box 95007
Lincoln, NE 68509
Phone: (402)471-2907
Fax: (402)471-0383

★3406★ **Nevada Department of Human Resources**
Health Division
Family Health Service
505 E. King St., Rm. 201
Carson City, NV 89710
Phone: (702)687-4885
Fax: (702)687-4733

★3407★ **New Hampshire Department of Health and Human Services**
Public Health Services Division
Maternal and Child Health Bureau
6 Hazen Dr.
Concord, NH 03301
Phone: (603)271-4516
Fax: (603)271-3745

★3408★ **New Jersey Department of Health**
Family Health Services Division
Maternal and Child Health Services
50 E. State St., CN 364
Trenton, NJ 08625-0364
Phone: (609)292-5656
Fax: (609)292-3580

★3409★ **New Mexico Department of Health**
Public Health Division
Maternal and Child Health Bureau
1190 St. Francis Dr.
PO Box 26110
Santa Fe, NM 87502-6110
Phone: (505)827-2350
Fax: (505)827-2329

★3410★ **New York State Department of Health**
Community Health Center
Family Health Division
Corning Tower, Empire State Plaza
Albany, NY 12237
Phone: (518)473-7922

★3411★ **North Carolina Department of Environment, Health, and Natural Resources**
Health Director's Office
Maternal and Child Health Division
PO Box 27687
Raleigh, NC 27611
Phone: (919)715-4125
Fax: (919)715-3060

★3412★ **North Dakota Department of Health and Consolidated Laboratories**
Preventive Health Section
Maternal and Child Health Division
600 E. Boulevard
Bismarck, ND 58505
Phone: (701)328-2493
Fax: (701)328-4727

★3413★ **Ohio Department of Health**
Maternal and Child Health Division
Maternal and Child Health Bureau
246 N. High St.
Columbus, OH 43266-0588
Phone: (614)466-5332
Fax: (614)644-0085

★3414★ **Oklahoma Department of Health**
Maternal and Child Health Services
1000 NE 10th St.
PO Box 53551
Oklahoma City, OK 73152
Phone: (405)271-4476
Fax: (405)271-3431

★3415★ **Oregon Department of Human Resources**
Health Division
Child and Family Health Center
800 NE Oregon St.
Portland, OR 97232
Phone: (503)731-4016
Fax: (503)731-4083

★3416★ **Pennsylvania Department of Health**
Maternal and Child Health Bureau
Maternal and Child Health Division
PO Box 90
Harrisburg, PA 17108
Phone: (717)787-7440
Fax: (717)772-6939

★3417★ **Rhode Island Department of Health**
Family Health Office
3 Capitol Hill
Providence, RI 02908-5097
Phone: (401)277-2312
Fax: (401)277-1442

★3418★ **South Carolina Department of Health and Environmental Control**
Health Services Office
Maternal and Child Health Bureau
2600 Bull St.
Columbia, SC 29201
Phone: (803)734-4190
Fax: (803)737-3946

★3419★ **South Dakota Department of Health**
Maternal and Child Health Program
445 E. Capitol
Pierre, SD 57501-3185
Phone: (605)773-3737
Fax: (605)773-5683

★3420★ **Tennessee Department of Health**
Health Services Bureau
Maternal and Children's Health Section
312 8th Ave. N., 12th Fl.
Nashville, TN 37247-0101
Phone: (615)741-7353
Fax: (615)532-2286

★3421★ **Texas Department of Health**
Women and Children's Bureau
1100 W. 49th St.
Austin, TX 78756
Phone: (512)458-7700
Fax: (512)458-7477

★3422★ **Utah Department of Health**
Family Health Services Division
Maternal and Child Health Bureau
PO Box 144100
Salt Lake City, UT 84114-4100
Phone: (801)584-8237
Fax: (801)538-6510

★3423★ **Vermont Agency of Human**
    Services
Health Department
Maternal and Child Health Bureau
103 S. Main St.
Burlington, VT 05402
Phone: (802)863-7606
Fax: (802)863-7425

★3424★ **Virginia Office of Health and**
    Human Resources
Health Department
Women and Infants Health Division
1500 E. Main St.
PO Box 2448
Richmond, VA 23218
Phone: (804)786-7367
Fax: (804)786-4616

★3425★ **Washington Department of**
    Health
Community and Family Health Services
    Division
PO Box 47880
Olympia, WA 98504-7880
Phone: (360)753-7021
Fax: (360)586-7424

★3426★ **West Virginia Department of**
    Health and Human Resources
Public Health Bureau
Maternal and Child Health Office
State Capitol Complex, Bldg. 3, Rm. 519
Charleston, WV 25305-0501
Phone: (304)558-5388
Fax: (304)558-1035

★3427★ **Wisconsin Department of Health**
    and Social Services
Health Division
Public Health Bureau
Maternal and Child Health Section
144 E. Washington Ave., Rm. 167
Madison, WI 53703-3044
Phone: (608)267-0531
Fax: (608)267-3824

★3428★ **Wyoming Department of Health**
Public Health Division
Maternal and Child Health Services
Hathaway Bldg., 4th Fl.
Cheyenne, WY 82002-0710
Phone: (307)777-6186
Fax: (307)777-5402

Chapter 15
Chiropractic

Foundations & Other Funding Organizations

Other Funding Organizations

★3429★ Foundation for the Advancement of Chiropractic Tenets and Science
c/o Intl. Chiropractors Assn.
1110 N. Glebe Rd., Ste. 1000
Arlington, VA 22201
Phone: (703)528-5000
Fax: (703)528-5023

Description: Offers financial aid for education and research programs in colleges and independent institutions; supports chiropractic research program at University of Colorado.

★3430★ Foundation for Chiropractic Education and Research
1701 Clarendon Blvd.
Arlington, VA 22209
Phone: (703)276-7445
Fax: (703)276-8178
Steve Seater, CAE, Exec. Dir.

Description: Provides funding for scientific research and training relating to the practice of chiropractic. Offers research grants in clinical science, postdoctorate fellowship awards, and dissertation grants-in-aid in biomechanics and public health.

Medical & Allied Health Schools

Chiropractic

Listed below are programs and institutions accredited by The Council on Chiropractic Education, 7975 N. Hayden Rd., Ste. A-210, Scottsdale, AZ 85258, (602)443-8877. Information on chiropractic as a career is available from the American Chiropractic Association, 1701 Clarendon Blvd., Arlington, VA 22209, (703)276-8800.

California

★3431★ Cleveland Chiropractic College
590 N. Vermont Ave.
Los Angeles, CA 90004
Phone: (213)660-6166
Fax: (213)665-5387

★3432★ Life Chiropractic College, West
2005 Via Barrett
PO Box 367
San Lorenzo, CA 94580
Phone: (510)276-9013
Fax: (510)276-6798

★3433★ Los Angeles College of Chiropractic
PO Box 1166
Whittier, CA 90609-1166
Phone: (310)902-3330
Fax: (310)947-7863

★3434★ Palmer College of Chiropractic, West
90 East Tasman Dr.
San Jose, CA 95134
Phone: (408)944-6000
Fax: (408)944-6111

Connecticut

★3435★ University of Bridgeport College of Chiropractic
Bridgeport, CT 06601
Phone: (203)576-4278
Fax: (203)576-4483

Georgia

★3436★ Life College
1269 Barclay Circle
Marietta, GA 30060
Phone: (404)424-0554
Fax: (404)429-8359

Illinois

★3437★ National College of Chiropractic
200 E. Roosevelt Rd.
Lombard, IL 60148-4583
Phone: (708)629-2000
Fax: (708)268-6600

Iowa

★3438★ Palmer College of Chiropractic
1000 Brady St.
Davenport, IA 52803
Phone: (319)326-9600
Fax: (319)326-8409

Minnesota

★3439★ Northwestern College of Chiropractic
2501 W. 84th St.
Bloomington, MN 55431
Phone: (612)888-4777
Fax: (612)888-6713

Missouri

★3440★ Cleveland Chiropractic College
6401 Rockhill Rd.
Kansas City, MO 64131
Phone: (816)333-8230
Fax: (816)361-0272

★3441★ Logan College of Chiropractic
PO Box 1065
Chesterfield, MO 63006-1065
Phone: (314)227-2100
Fax: (314)227-3832

New York

★3442★ New York Chiropractic College
2360 State Rte. 89
PO Box 800
Seneca Falls, NY 13148-0800
Phone: (315)568-3000
Fax: (315)568-3015

Oregon

★3443★ Western States Chiropractic College
2900 NE 132nd Ave.
Portland, OR 97230
Phone: (503)256-3180
Fax: (503)251-5723

South Carolina

★3444★ Sherman College of Straight Chiropractic
PO Box 1452
Spartanburg, SC 29304
Phone: (803)578-8770
Fax: (803)599-7145

Texas

★3445★ Parker College of Chiropractic
2500 Walnut Hill Lane
Dallas, TX 75229
Phone: (214)438-6932
Fax: (214)357-3620

★3446★ Texas Chiropractic College
5912 Spencer Hwy.
Pasadena, TX 77505
Phone: (713)487-1170

National & International Organizations

★3447★ American Black Chiropractors Association (ABCA)
1918 E. Grand Blvd.
St. Louis, MO 63107
Phone: (314)531-0615
Dr. Bobby Westbrooks, Dir.

Founded: 1980. **Description:** Persons who have earned a recognized doctorate degree in chiropractic and students enrolled in a chiropractic college; associate members are institutions, organizations, and interested individuals. Objectives are to: educate the public, health care institutions, and health care providers about chiropractic and promote black chiropractic in the community; develop career orientation programs for high school and college students and sponsor scholarship funds; study history of chiropractic; sponsor publicity programs, public forums, counseling services, research, and establishment of free chiropractic clinics; provide for exchange of information, techniques, and reports of researchers and clinicians. Conducts research surveys and prepares educational programs and art icles on the history of blacks in chiropractic concerning aspects such as early Jim Crow chiropractic schools, discrimination in licensing and practice, and notable achievements of blacks in the profession. **Formerly:** (1981) Association of Black Chiropractors.

★3448★ American Chiropractic Association (ACA)
1701 Clarendon Blvd.
Arlington, VA 22209
Phone: (703)276-8800
Free: 800-986-4636
Fax: (703)243-2593
J. Ray Morgan, Exec.VP

Founded: 1930. **Members:** 20,000. **Description:** Enhances the philosophy, science, and art of chiropractic, and the professional welfare of individuals in the field. Promotes legislation de-fining chiropractic health care and improves the public's awareness and utilization of chiropractic. Conducts chiropractic survey and statistical study; maintains library. Sponsors Correct Posture Week in May and Spinal Health Month in October. Chiropractic colleges have student ACA groups. **Publications:** *ACA/Today*, monthly. Newsletter. Covers the issues facing the profession and the association. *Price:* Included in membership dues. • *American Chiropractic Association Membership Directory*, annual. Directory. • *Journal of Chiropractic*, monthly. Journal. Provides information on the progress of chiropractic procedures and research, and developments in other fields of interest to chiropractors. *Price:* Included in membership dues; $3/year for student members; $80/year for nonmembers; $150/year for international members. **Formerly:** (1963) National Chiropractic Association.

American Chiropractic Registry of Radiologic Technologists (ACRRT)
See: Entry 11086

American College of Chiropractic Orthopedists (ACCO)
See: Entry 9918

★3449★ Association of Chiropractic Colleges (ACC)
2005 Via Barrett
PO Box 367
San Lorenzo, CA 94580
Phone: (510)276-9013
Fax: (510)276-4893
Gerard W. Clum, D.C., Pres.

Founded: 1977. **Members:** 18. **Description:** Presidents of chiropractic colleges that are members of the Council on Chiropractic Education. Objective is to provide a cooperative base that assists members in the search for and promotion of the practices and concepts most effective in the academic and continuing education of doctors of chiropractic. Serves as a clearinghouse for information related to opportunities and advancement in research as they affect chiropractic education and health care. Seeks to enhance services to the consumer of chiropractic education and to the public. **Formerly:** (1985) Association of Chiropractic College Presidents.

★3450★ Chiropractic Association of South Africa (CASA)
(Chiropraktiese Vereniging van Suid-Afrika — CVSA)
121 Clarence Rd.
Morningside
Durban 4001, Republic of South Africa
Phone: 31 3094670
Fax: 31 3091480
Dr. R. Rethman, Sec.Gen.

Founded: 1970. **Members:** 131. **Regional Groups:** 4. **Languages:** Afrikaans, English. **Description:** Seeks to: heighten public awareness of the chiropractic system of therapy; improve medical insurance coverage of such treatment. Offers training curricula; conducts periodic seminars. **Publications:** *Clinician*, annual. Newsletter. • *Inter-Association Newsletter*, periodic. Newsletter.

★3451★ Council on Chiropractic Education (CCE)
7975 N. Hayden Rd., No. A-210
Scottsdale, AZ 85258-3246
Phone: (602)443-8877
Fax: (602)483-7333
Dr. Ralph G. Miller, Exec.VP

Founded: 1971. **Members:** 23. **Description:** Representatives of member colleges. Advocates high standards in chiropractic education; establishes criteria of institutional excellence for educating chiropractic physicians; acts as national accrediting agency for chiropractic colleges. Conducts workshops for college teams, consultants, and chiropractic college staffs. **Publications:** *CCE Board of Directors*, annual. • *Educational Standards for Chiropractic Colleges*, semiannual. • Newsletter, periodic. Also publishes pamphlets, news releases, and lists of institutions conforming to its standards and policies.

★3452★ Council on Chiropractic Orthopedics (CCO)
190 East 100 South
Provo, UT 84604
Phone: (801)373-2240
Fax: (801)373-5239
Phil L. Alken, D.C., Treas.

Founded: 1967. **Members:** 750. **Description:** Licensed doctors of chiropractic who have completed 300 hours of postgraduate courses in orthopedics (690); chiropractic physicians with an interest in orthopedics (60). Objectives are: to assist in the advancement of chiropractic as a science and healing art; to protect the welfare and interests of members; to encourage and maintain the highest standards of moral and ethical conduct; to romote research; to encourage the standardization of terminology; to disseminate information; to encourage the teaching of chiropractic orthopedics at all levels. Reviews and revises postgraduate courses in chiropractic. Fosters seminars and courses in personal, athletic, and industrial injuries; provides consulting. Maintains American Board Board of Chiropractic Orthopedists which serves as an examining body for certification. Certified orthopedists comprise the Academy of Chiropractic Orthopedists. A division of the American Chiropractic Association. **Publications:** Brochure. • Directory, annual. • *Orthopedic Briefs*, bimonthly.

★3453★ Council on Chiropractic Physiological Therapeutics (CCPT)
c/o Charles Brandstetter, D.C.
203 N. Holmes Ave.
Idaho Falls, ID 83401
Phone: (208)522-2591
Charles Brandstetter, D.C., Pres.

Founded: 1920. **Members:** 200. **Description:** Chiropractors who use physiotherapy in their practice and are dedicated to furthering the extended use of physiotherapy in the chiropractic field. Plans to provide a diplomate or certification program. **Publications:** *Physiotherapy Briefs*, periodic. **Formerly:** (1985) American Council on Chiropractic Physiotherapy.

★3454★ European Chiropractors' Union (ECU)
82 Waldegrave Rd.
Teddington
Middlesex, Greater London TW11 8LG, England
Phone: 181 9432424
Fax: 181 9776626
Anthony Metcalfe, D.C., Pres.

Founded: 1932. **Members:** 1,800. **National Groups:** 16. **Languages:** English. **Description:** National associations (16) representing 1800 chiropractors; interested others (25). Promotes the development of chiropractic medicine and colleges through legal, educational, and research activities; maintains standards for chiropractic education in Europe. Works to foster unity among European chiropractors' associations. Provides research funds. **Publications:** *European Chiropractors' Union Directory*, annual. Directory. • *European Journal of Chiropractic*, quarterly. Journal.

★3455★ Federation of Straight Chiropractors and Organizations (FSCO)
642 Broad St.
Clifton, NJ 07013
Phone: (201)777-1197
Free: 800-521-9856
Fax: (201)777-0739
Dr. Joseph Donofrio, Chm.

Founded: 1978. **Members:** 1,200. **State Groups:** 12. **Description:** Individuals and organizations in the chiropractic field. Promotes the practice of straight (traditional) chiropractic medicine. Conducts lobbying and educational programs. **Publications:** *FSCO Review*, quarterly. Newsletter. Reports on current news and professional information. **Formerly:** Federation of Straight Chiropractic Organizations.

★3456★ Flying Chiropractors Association (FCA)
7301 Hasbrook Ave.
Philadelphia, PA 19111-3003
Phone: (215)722-7200
Dr. W. J. Quinlan, Exec.Dir.

Founded: 1968. **Members:** 300. **Regional Groups:** 9. **Description:** Flying chiropractic physicians. Objectives are to: promote fellowship; seek designation as aviation medical examiners (doctors who examine pilots for their licensure); promote aviation safety. Conducts seminars. **Publications:** *D.C. Flyer*, quarterly.

★3457★ Foundation for the Advancement of Chiropractic Tenets and Science (FACTS)
c/o International Chiropractors Association
1110 N. Glebe Rd., Ste. 1000
Arlington, VA 22201
Phone: (703)528-5000
Fax: (703)528-5023
Ronald Hendrickson, Exec.Dir.

Founded: 1972. **Description:** Dedicated to the improvement of human health through understanding and development of new chiropractic information. Offers financial aid for education and research programs in colleges and independent institutions; supports chiropractic research program at University of Colorado in

Boulder. Has conducted extensive survey of the chiropractic profession for the federal government. Is approved by the National Institutes of Health of the U.S. Public Health Service. **Publications:** *Chiropractic Health Care*. **Formerly:** International Chiropractors Research Foundation.

★3458★ Foundation for Chiropractic Education and Research (FCER)
1701 Clarendon Blvd.
Arlington, VA 22209
Phone: (703)276-7445
Fax: (703)276-8178
Steve Seater, CAE, Exec.Dir.

Founded: 1944. **Members:** 6,000. **Description:** Chiropractors and laymen. Provides funding for scientific research and research training that will "enhance the knowledge and practice of chiropractic as a conservative approach to health care restoration, maintenance, and disease prevention." **Publications:** *Advance*, bimonthly. Newsletter. • *Foundation for Chiropractic Education and Research--Advance*, bimonthly. Newsletter. Foundation activities newsletter. *Price:* Included in membership dues. • *Spinal Manipulation*, quarterly. Journal. Reviews research concerning chiropractic and other forms of health care dealing with the spine. Includes abstracts and editorial summaries. *Price:* $42/year (inside the U.S.); $60/year (outside the U.S.). • *Staying Well Newsletter*, bimonthly. Newsletter. Promotes health and fitness. Includes research updates. *Price:* Included in membership dues. Also publishes pamphlets. **Formerly:** (1958) Chiropractic Research Foundation; (1967) Foundation for Accredited Chiropractic Education.

★3459★ International Chiropractors Association (ICA)
1110 N. Glebe Rd., Ste. 1000
Arlington, VA 22201
Phone: (703)528-5000
Fax: (703)528-5023
Ronald Hendrickson, VP

Founded: 1926. **Members:** 6,000. **Description:** Professional society of chiropractors, chiropractic educators, students, and laypersons. Sponsors professional development programs and practice management seminars. **Publications:** *Congressional Directory*, annual. Directory. • *ICA Today*, bimonthly. Newsletter. Covers membership and association activities; includes legislative information and research updates. *Price:* Included in membership dues. • *International Chiropractors Association Membership Directory*, annual. Directory. • *International Review of Chiropractic*, bimonthly. Also publishes materials on patient education. **Formerly:** (1941) Chiropractic Health Bureau.

★3460★ Precision Chiropractic Research Society (PCRS)
1412 Alta Mesa Way
Brea, CA 92621
Phone: (310)694-4181
Dr. A. C. Fulkerson, Pres.

Founded: 1976. **Members:** 200. **State Groups:** 5. **Description:** Doctors of chiropractic specializing in spinal stress. Conducts research into spinal problems and treatments. Is currently in-

vestigating the relationship between headaches and spinal adjustment. Documents research by x-raying the patient before treatments and then again after treatments to determine change (if any) of spinal position. Disseminates research findings through seminars and letters. **Also Known As:** Spinal Stress Research Society.

★3461★ Straight Chiropractic Academic Standards Association (SCASA)
PO Box 1452
Spartanburg, SC 29301
Phone: (803)578-8770
Dr. Leroy Moore, VP

Founded: 1977. **Description:** Chiropractic colleges. Develops and adopts standards for accreditation of straight chiropractic institutions. Evaluates programs that award the Doctor of Chiropractic degree. Assists in the formation and development of chiropractic institutions. **Publications:** *SCASA Annual Report*, annual. Report.

★3462★ Women's Auxiliary of the ICA (WAICA)
1110 N. Glebe Rd., Ste. 1000
Arlington, VA 22201
Phone: (703)528-5000
Fax: (703)528-5023
Joni Ressmeyer, Pres.

Founded: 1951. **Members:** 500. **Description:** Women chiropractors; wives, daughters, and mothers of chiropractors who are members of the International Chiropractors Association. Promotes and educates the public about chiropractice. Grants scholarships to chiropractic students. Supports charitable programs; bestows awards. **Publications:** *Membership Roster*, biennial. Membership Directory. • Newsletter, quarterly.

Research Centers

★3463★ Northwestern College of Chiropractic
Center for Clinical Studies
2501 W. 84th St.
Bloomington, MN 55431
Phone: (612)885-5444
Fax: (612)888-6713
Dr. Z. Zackman, D.C., Dir.

Research Activities and Fields: Chiropractic clinical research, including ambulatory health care.

★3464★ Precision Chiropractic Research Society
1412 Alta Mesa Way
Brea, CA 92621
Phone: (213)694-4181
Mr. A.C. Fulkerson, Pres.

Research Activities and Fields: Spinal problems and treatment, including an investigation of the relationship between the cure for headaches and spinal adjustment. Also studies Duchennne muscular dystrophy.

Chapter 16
Communicative Disorders

Federal Government Agencies

★3465★ U.S. Department of Health and Human Services
National Institute on Deafness and Other Communication Disorders
9000 Rockville Pike
Bethesda, MD 20892
Phone: (301)402-0900
Fax: (301)402-0500

Description: NIDCD conducts and supports research and training with respect to disorders of hearing and other communication processes, including diseases affecting hearing, balance, voice, speech, language, touch, taste, and smell through research performed in its own laboratories; a program of research grants, individual and institutional research training awards, career development awards, center grants, and contracts to public and private research institutions and organizations.

Foundations & Other Funding Organizations

Private Foundations

Margaret W. and Herbert Hoover, Jr. Foundation
See: Entry 377

Other Funding Organizations

★3466★ Alexander Graham Bell Association for the Deaf
3417 Volta Pl. NW
Washington, DC 20007-2778
Phone: (202)337-5220
Donna McCord Dickman, Ph.D., Exec. Dir.

Description: Provides educational scholarships for oral deaf students.

★3467★ American Hearing Research Foundation
55 E. Washington St., Ste. 2022
Chicago, IL 60602
Phone: (312)726-9670
Fax: (312)726-9685
William L. Lederer, Exec. Dir.

Description: Supports medical research and education concerning deafness and other hearing disorders.

★3468★ American Otological Society
Loyola University Medical School
2160 S. 1st Ave., Bldg. 105, No. 1870
Maywood, IL 60153
Phone: (708)216-4834
Fax: (708)216-4834
Dr. Gregory Matz, Sec.-Treas.

Description: Provides research grants to support research in otology and related disciplines; maintains research fund for advanced studies of otosclerosis.

★3469★ American Tinnitus Association
PO Box 5
Portland, OR 97207
Phone: (503)248-9985
Fax: (503)248-0024
Gloria E. Reich, Exec. Dir.

Description: Supports research relating to tinnitus and other defects or diseases of the ear.

★3470★ Deafness Research Foundation
9 E. 38th St., 7th Fl.
New York, NY 10016
Phone: (212)684-6556
Free: 800-535-3323
Fax: (212)779-2125
Monte H. Jacoby, Exec. Dir.

Description: Awards seed grants to support new research projects relating to hearing disorders and ear diseases; awards otological research fellowships for medical students.

★3471★ Hear Now
9745 E. Hampden Ave., No. 300
Denver, CO 80231
Phone: (303)758-4919
Free: 800-648-HEAR
Fax: (303)695-7789
Bernice Dinner, Ph.D., Pres.

Description: Provides finacial resources to hearing impaired persons wishing to acquire hearing-assistive devices such as hearing aids and cochlear implants. Seeks to increase public awareness of the need for available and affordable hearing-assistive technology.

★3472★ Voice Foundation
1721 Pine St.
Philadelphia, PA 19103
Phone: (215)735-7999
Fax: (215)735-9293
Richard A. Sharp, Exec. Dir.

Description: Sponsors research and education on the causes, prevention, and treatment of voice disorders.

National & International Organizations

★3473★ Academy of Aphasia (AA)
c/o Dr. Victoria A. Fromkin
UCLA
Department of Linguistics
Los Angeles, CA 90024
Phone: (310)206-3206
Dr. Victoria A. Fromkin, Chm.

Founded: 1962. **Members:** 189. **Description:** Neurologists, psychologists, linguists, speech pathologists, and others specializing in aphasia (impairment of language caused by focal brain damage). Seeks to encourage research and promote communication among the scientific disciplines that can contribute to the understanding of aphasia.

★3474★ Academy of Dispensing Audiologists (ADA)
3008 Millwood Ave.
Columbia, SC 29205
Phone: (803)252-5646
Fax: (803)765-0860
Carol H. Davis, Exec.Dir.

Founded: 1977. **Members:** 525. **Description:** Individuals with graduate degrees in audiology who dispense hearing aids as part of a rehabilitative practice. Fosters and supports professional dispensing of hearing aids by qualified audiologists; encourages audiology training programs to include pertinent aspects of hearing aid dispensing in their curriculums; conducts seminars on the business aspects of the hearing aid industry. **Publications:** *ADA Feedback*, quarterly. Newsletter. Includes book reviews and new members listing. *Price:* Free. • *ADA Membership Directory*, annual. Membership Directory. Arranged alphabetically and geographically. *Price:* Included in membership dues.

★3475★ **Academy of Rehabilitative Audiology (ARA)**
c/o Dr. Sharon Lesner
University of Akron
Dept. of Communication Disorders
Akron, OH 44325-3001
Phone: (216)920-6018
Fax: (216)920-6098
Frances J. Laven, Contact
Founded: 1966. **Members:** 400. **Description:** Individuals who hold graduate degrees in audiology, language, or speech pathology, education of the deaf, or allied fields, and who have at least two years of post-degree involvement in rehabilitative or educational programs for the hearing impaired. Provides a forum for exchange of ideas in audiology; fosters professional education, research, and interest in programs for hearing handicapped persons. Maintains speakers' bureau. **Publications:** *Journal of the Academy of Rehabilitative Audiology*, annual. Journal. *Price:* $25/year. • Membership Directory, annual. • *Monograph of Academy of Rehabilitative Audiology*, quinquennial. *Price:* $15.

★3476★ **Acoustic Neuroma Association (ANA)**
PO Box 12402
Atlanta, GA 30355
Phone: (404)237-8023
Fax: (404)237-2704
Linda Kees, Exec.Dir.
Founded: 1980. **Members:** 4,300. **Local Groups:** 36. **Description:** Persons who have had acoustic neuroma (a tumor growing in the inner ear) and others who have had tumors that affect the cranial nerves and adjacent neural tissue. Provides support and offers encouragement on overcoming effects of these tumors. Furnishes information on patient rehabilitation to physicians and health care personnel. Promotes research and public awareness regarding early diagnosis and treatment. Conducts seminars and research programs; compiles statistics. **Publications:** *A Glimpse of the Brain*. • *Acoustic Neuroma*. • *Acoustic Neuroma Notes*, quarterly. Newsletter. Newsletter covering advances in the treatment of acoustic neuroma. *Price:* Included in membership dues. • *Diagnosis Acoustic Neuroma: What Next?*. • *Eye Care after Acoustic Neuroma Surgery*. • *Facial Rehabilitation after Acoustic Neuroma Surgery*.

★3477★ **AFASIC - Overcoming Speech Impairments**
347 Central Markets
Smithfield
London EC1A 9NH, England
Phone: 171 2363632
Fax: 171 2368115
Norma Corkish, Dir.
Founded: 1968. **Members:** 2,300. **Local Groups:** 30. **Languages:** English. **Description:** Promotes the interests of young people with speech and/or language difficulties. Seeks to enhance understanding of speech and language disorders and improve educational and employment opportunities for young adults with such disorders. Encourages health authorities to improve and extend speech therapy services; fosters formation of open language and mobile speech therapy units. Offers advice and support for parents of individuals with speech and language disorders. Conducts research on children's language development. Organizes art/drama weekends, activity weeks, international symposia, national seminars, and workshops. Maintains speakers' bureau; compiles statistics. **Publications:** *Annual Review*. • *Newsletter*, 3/year, always January, May, and September. Newsletter.

★3478★ **Alexander Graham Bell Association for the Deaf (AGBAD)**
3417 Volta Pl. NW
Washington, DC 20007-2778
Phone: (202)337-5220
Donna McCord Dickman, Ph.D., Exec.Dir.
Founded: 1890. **Members:** 5,000. **State Groups:** 17. **Local Groups:** 110. **Description:** Teachers of the hearing impaired, speech-language pathologists and audiologists, physicians, parents of hearing impaired children, oral deaf adults, and others interested in the problems of the hearing impaired; affiliate members are organized groups of parents of deaf children and coordinators of state and provincial chapters. Works to: promote the teaching of speech, lipreading, and use of residual hearing to the deaf; encourage research on deafness; assist schools and agencies working for better educational facilities for deaf and oral hearing impaired children. Conducts workshops and educational programs. Compiles statistics. Maintains speakers' bureau. Serves as information center and maintains library on speech and hearing. Operates charitable program, biographical archives, museum, and placement service. **Publications:** *Alexander Graham Bell Association for the Deaf--Our Kids Magazine*, 2-3/year. Newsletter. For parents of hearing impaired children. *Price:* Included in membership dues. • *Children's Corner*. • *Newsounds*, 10/year. Membership activities newsletter. Includes chapter news and calendar of events. *Price:* Included in membership dues. • *OK Kids*. • *Volta Review*, bimonthly. Professional journal covering issues related to hearing impairment for teachers of the hearing impaired. *Price:* Included in membership dues; $35/year for institutions. Also publishes bibliographies, teachers' and clinicians' textbooks, lipreading books, and references; produces audiovisuals. **Formerly:** (1948) American Association to Promote the Teaching of Speech to the Deaf; (1953) Volta Speech Association for the Deaf.

★3479★ **All-Russian Federation of the Deaf (ARFD)**
(Vserossiiskoe Obshchestvo Glukhikh — VOG)
ulitsa 1905-goda 10A
123022 Moscow, Russia
Phone: 95 2556704
Fax: 95 2550417
Valeriy Aleksandrovi Koroblinov, Chm.
Founded: 1926. **Members:** 175,000. **Local Groups:** 71. **Languages:** Russian. **Description:** Protects the rights and interests of citizens with hearing problems. Promotes social rehabilitation and full participation in society. Coordinates the activities of governmental organizations providing for the deaf and hearing-impaired; conducts courses in sign language and computer use for hearing-impaired individuals. Operates 62 production associations, which make consumer and light industrial goods. **Publications:** *Beacon*, biweekly. Newspaper. • *V Yedinom Stroyu*, monthly. Newspaper. • *Wave*, monthly. **Formerly:** (1991) All-Union Society of the Deaf; (1993) All-Russian Society of the Deaf.

American Academy of Otolaryngic Allergy (AAOA)
See: Entry 2059

American Academy of Otolaryngology - Head and Neck Surgery (AAO-HNS)
See: Entry 12207

American Association of the Deaf-Blind (AADB)
See: Entry 13388

★3480★ **American Athletic Association for the Deaf (AAAD)**
3607 Washington Blvd., No. 4
Ogden, UT 84403-1737
Phone: (801)393-7916
Fax: (801)393-2263
Shirley H. Platt, Sec.-Treas.
Founded: 1945. **Members:** 25,000. **National Groups:** 20. **Regional Groups:** 8. **State Groups:** 50. **Local Groups:** 200. **Description:** Fosters athletic competition among the deaf and regulates uniform rules governing such competition; provides adequate competition for those members who are primarily interested in interclub athletics and a social outlet for deaf members and their friends. Sanctions and promotes state, regional, and national basketball tournaments, softball tournaments, and participation in activities of the Comite International des Sports des Sourds. Maintains hall of fame honoring outstanding players, leaders, and sportswriters. Compiles statistics. Sponsors a team to the World Games for Deaf. **Publications:** *AAAD Bulletin*, quarterly. Bulletin. • *Deaf Sports Review Magazine*, quarterly. Magazine.

★3481★ **American Auditory Society (AAS)**
512 E. Canterbury Ln.
Phoenix, AZ 85022
Phone: (602)789-0755
Fax: (602)942-1486
Wayne J. Staab, Ph.D., Sec.-Treas.
Founded: 1976. **Members:** 2,688. **Description:** Audiologists, otolaryngologists, scientists,

hearing aid industry professionals, and educators of hearing impaired people; individuals involved in industries serving hearing impaired people, including the amplification systems industry. Works to increase knowledge and understanding of: the ear, hearing, and balance; disorders of the ear, hearing, and balance; prevention of these disorders; habilitation and rehabilitation of individuals with hearing and balance dysfunction. **Publications:** *The Bulletin of the AAS*, 3/year. Newsletter. • *Ear and Hearing*, bimonthly. Journal. Includes periodic supplements. **Formerly:** (1982) American Audiology Society.

★3482★ **American Board of Otolaryngology (ABO)**
5615 Kirby Dr., Ste. 936
Houston, TX 77005
Phone: (713)528-6200
Dr. Robert W. Cantrell, Exec.VP

Founded: 1924. **Description:** Purposes are to: elevate standards of practice in otolaryngology (branch of medicine dealing with ear, nose, throat, head, and neck surgery); hold examinations and certify qualified otolaryngologists; advance the cause of the field. Conducts annual written and oral examinations. **Publications:** Newsletter, semiannual.

★3483★ **American Deaf Volleyball Association (ADVBA)**
7582 S. Rosemary Cir.
Englewood, CO 80112
Phone: (303)770-2708
Karen Boyd, Pres.

Founded: 1985. **Members:** 535. **Regional Groups:** 4. **Local Groups:** 86. **Description:** National amateur volleyball organizations, coaches, and players. Seeks to provide volleyball camps, development programs, training, and workshops for hearing impaired children and adults. Sponsors U.S. women's and men's volleyball teams in international sports competition. **Publications:** *ADVBA*, quarterly. *Price:* Included in membership dues.

★3484★ **American Deafness and Rehabilitation Association (ADARA)**
PO Box 251554
Little Rock, AR 72225
Phone: (501)868-8850
Fax: (501)868-8812
Deb Guthmann, Ph.D., Pres.

Founded: 1966. **Members:** 1,000. **State Groups:** 12. **Description:** Psychiatrists, mental health counselors, students, teachers, researchers, rehabilitation facility personnel, interpreters, speech therapists, social workers, doctors, and rehabilitation counselors who serve deaf and deaf-blind persons. Promotes the development and expansion of quality services to deaf and hard-of-hearing persons. Strives to bring about a better understanding of deaf, hard-of-hearing, and deaf-blind people as a whole by encouraging students, professionals, and laymen to develop more than a superficial understanding of the needs and problems of this group, especially the problems related to communication techniques needed to work effectively with deaf, hard-of-hearing, and deaf-blind persons in human services or a rehabilita-

tion setting. Encourages scientific research of the needs and problems engendered by deafness. Promotes and develops recruitment and training of professional workers with deaf, hard-of-hearing, and deaf-blind persons. Sponsors a professional publication for the promotion of inter- and intradisciplinary communication among professionals concerned with deaf adults and others interested in such activities. Cooperates with other organizations in promoting and encouraging legislation pertinent to the development of professional services and facilities for deaf, hard-of-hearing, and deaf-blind persons. **Publications:** *American Deafness and Rehabilitation Association Newsletter*, quarterly. Newsletter. Includes membership activities information, research reports, and list of employment opportunities. *Price:* Included in membership dues. • *Journal of American Deafness and Rehabilitation Association*, quarterly. Journal. Provides research findings and information on new ideas within the field. Includes reviews of current literature. *Price:* Included in membership dues; $46/year for nonmembers. • Monographs.

American Diopter and Decibel Society (ADDS)
See: Entry 13397

★3485★ **American Hearing Impaired Hockey Association (AHIHA)**
1143 W. Lake St.
Chicago, IL 60607
Phone: (312)226-5880
Fax: (312)829-2250
Stan Mikita, Pres.

Founded: 1973. **Members:** 80. **Description:** Hearing impaired boys and men, aged 5 to 26, who wish to play ice hockey. Seeks to develop members' skills and self-confidence, both as hockey players and as individuals, through participation in the annual Stan Mikita Hockey School for the Hearing Impaired. **Publications:** *Locker Room Briefs*. Newsletter.

★3486★ **American Hearing Research Foundation (AHRF)**
55 E. Washington St., Ste. 2022
Chicago, IL 60602
Phone: (312)726-9670
Fax: (312)726-9685
William L. Lederer, Exec.Dir.

Founded: 1956. **Members:** 1,585. **Local Groups:** 7. **Description:** Works to encourage and support medical research, education, and public information concerning deafness and other hearing disorders. Produces scientific exhibits and film exhibits for professional and public audiences. **Publications:** *American Hearing Research Foundation Newsletter*, 3/year. Newsletter. Reviews developments in hearing research and education. *Price:* Free. • *Hearing Health*. Brochure. • *Progress Report*, semiannual. Report. Also publishes research papers.

★3487★ **American Laryngological Association (ALA)**
c/o Gerald B. Healy, M.D.
Childern's Hospital
300 Longwood Ave.
Fasan 9
Boston, MA 02115
Phone: (617)355-6417
Fax: (617)735-8041
Gerald B. Healy, M.D., Sec.

Founded: 1879. **Members:** 190. **Description:** Professional medical society of otorhinolaryngologists (specialists in ear, nose, and throat diseases). Works to advance research in medicine and surgery, with emphasis on the upper aerodigestive tract. **Publications:** *Transactions*, annual.

★3488★ **American Laryngological, Rhinological and Otological Society (ALROS)**
10 S. Broadway, Ste. 1401
St. Louis, MO 63102
Phone: (314)621-6550
Fax: (314)621-6688
Daniel Henroid, Sr., Exec.Dir.

Founded: 1895. **Members:** 1,100. **Regional Groups:** 4. **Description:** Professional society of medical specialists dealing with the ear, nose, and throat. **Publications:** *American Laryngological, Rhinological and Otological Society-- Section Meetings Program*, annual. Proceedings. Covers annual meeting; includes membership list. *Price:* Included in membership dues. • *The Laryngoscope Journal*, monthly. **Also Known As:** Triological Society.

★3489★ **American Neurotology Society (ANS)**
950 York Rd., No. 102
Hinsdale, IL 60521-8608
Dr. Richard J. Wiet, Sec.-Treas.

Founded: 1965. **Members:** 401. **Description:** Physicians and audiologists interested in the diagnosis and treatment of hearing and balance disorders. Promotes education and research in the field of neurotology. **Publications:** Directory, annual. Published in conjunction with American Academy of Otolaryngology - Head and Neck Surgery. **Formerly:** (1965) ENG Study Group.

★3490★ **American Otological Society (AOS)**
Loyola University Medical School
2160 S. 1st Ave.
Bldg. 105, No. 1870
Maywood, IL 60153
Phone: (708)216-8526
Fax: (708)216-4834
Dr. Gregory Matz, Sec.-Treas.

Founded: 1868. **Members:** 220. **Description:** Otologists and contributors to the advancement of otology. Encourages study and research in otology (the science of the ear and its diseases). Objectives are to advance and promote medical and surgical otology, including the rehabilitation of the hearing impaired, and to encourage and promote research in otology and related disciplines. Maintains research fund for advanced studies of otosclerosis. **Publications:** *American Journal of Otology*. Journal.

★3491★ American Rhinologic Society (ARS)
c/o Frank Lucente
Long Island College Hospital
Otolaryngology Department
Brooklyn, NY 11201
Phone: (718)780-1281
Fax: (718)270-3924
Frank Lucente, M.D., Contact

Founded: 1954. **Members:** 604. **Description:** Physicians who are diplomates of the American Board of Otolaryngology, the American Board of Plastic Surgery, and other boards, and who have had additional training and interest in the study of medical and surgical rhinology. Works to advance knowledge of rhinology (branch of medicine that relates to the nose and its diseases) internationally through short, frequent teaching courses at universities in conjunction with their faculties. Conducts research in nasal physiology, rhinomanometry, and anatomy. **Publications:** *American Journal of Rhinology*, bimonthly. Journal. • Membership Directory, biennial. • Newsletter, 4-5/year.

★3492★ American Speech-Language-Hearing Association (ASHA)
10801 Rockville Pke.
Rockville, MD 20852
Phone: (301)897-5700
Free: 800-638-8255
Fax: (301)571-0457
Frederick T. Spahr, Ph.D., Exec.Dir.

Founded: 1925. **Members:** 78,000. **Description:** Professional association for speech-language pathologists and audiologists. Acts as an accrediting agency for college and university graduate school programs and clinic and hospital programs and as a certifying body for professionals providing speech, language, and hearing therapy to the public. Offers career information, listing of university training programs, and certification requirements. Conducts research on communication disorders and community needs. **Publications:** *American Journal of Audiology: A Journal of Clinical Practice*, 3/year. Journal. *Price:* Included in membership dues; $20/year for nonmembers. • *American Journal of Speech Language Pathology: A Journal of Clinical Practice*, periodic. Journal. *Price:* Included in membership dues; $20/year for nonmembers. • *Asha*, monthly. Journal. Contains information on the professional and administrative activities of speech-language pathologists, audiologists, and the association. *Price:* Included in membership dues; $90/year for nonmembers. • *ASHA Monographs*, periodic. Monographs. • *ASHA Reports*, periodic. Proceedings. On speech, language, and hearing. • *Guide to Graduate Education in Speech-Language Pathology and Audiology*, biennial. Directory. Lists accredited graduate programs. • *Journal of Speech and Hearing Research*, bimonthly. Journal. Covers the process and disorders of speech, language, and hearing. *Price:* Included in membership dues; $114/year for nonmembers. • *Language, Speech, and Hearing Services in Schools*, quarterly. Journal. *Price:* Included in membership dues; $36/year for nonmembers. **Formerly:** (1927) American Academy of Speech Correction; (1934) American Society for the Study of Disorders of Speech;

(1947) American Speech Correction Association; (1978) American Speech and Hearing Association.

★3493★ American Tinnitus Association (ATA)
PO Box 5
Portland, OR 97207
Phone: (503)248-9985
Fax: (503)248-0024
Gloria E. Reich, Exec.Dir.

Founded: 1971. **Members:** 150,000. **National Groups:** 115. **State Groups:** 1. **Description:** Physicians, audiologists, hearing aid dispensers, and individuals who suffer from tinnitus (noises in the head or ears). Disseminates information about tinnitus; provides regional referrals to patients seeking help; supports research into causes of tinnitus. Sponsors workshops on the testing, evaluating, and management of tinnitus patients and encourages and supports selfhelp groups for tinnitus patients. Compiles statistics. **Publications:** *Coping With the Stress of Tinnitus*. Brochure. • *Hyperacusis*. Brochure. • *Information About Tinnitus*. Brochure. • *Noise and its Effects on Hearing*. Brochure. • *Tinnitus Bibliography*. Bibliography. • *Tinnitus Family Information*. Brochure. • *Tinnitus Today*, quarterly. Newsletter. Includes book reviews, calendar of events, research updates, and statistics. *Price:* $25/year.

Assistance Dogs International (ADI)
See: Entry 13408

★3494★ Association of the Deaf in Israel (ADI)
(Agudat Hachershim Beisrael)
Helen Keller Center
31 Yad Lebanim Blvd.
PO Box 9001
61090 Tel Aviv, Israel
Phone: 3 303355
Fax: 3 396419
Chaim Apter, Dir.Gen.

Members: 2,200. **Languages:** English, Hebrew. **Description:** Works toward the cultural, social, and professional rehabilitation of the deaf in Israel. **Publications:** *Mabat Shelanu*, quarterly. Magazine.

★3495★ Association of Late-Deafened Adults (ALDA)
10310 Main St., No. 274
Fairfax, VA 22030-2410
Phone: (703)445-0860
Fax: (703)445-0860
Steve Laiew, Pres.

Founded: 1987. **Members:** 2,000. **Description:** People who have become deaf as adults. Provides information, support, and social opportunities through selfhelp groups, general membership meetings, and social events. Advocates for the needs of late-deafened people. Conducts and participates in surveys, workshops, and seminars on late-deafness. Maintains speakers' bureau and biographical archives. Conducts research programs; provides captioning at all meetings. Sponsors competitions and bestows awards; compiles statistics. **Publications:** *ALDA News*, bimonthly. Newsletter. Includes pen pal section. *Price:* Included in membership dues. • *Facing Deafness: Proceedings of ALDAcon III*. Monograph.

Association of Otolaryngology Administrators (AOA)
See: Entry 5562

★3496★ Association for Stammerers (AFS)
15 Old Ford Rd.
Bethnal Green
London E2 9PJ, England
Phone: 181 9831003
Fax: 181 9833591
Peter Cartwright, Contact

Founded: 1978. **Members:** 1,200. **Languages:** English. **Description:** Selfhelp organization aimed at assisting individuals with stammering speech patterns. Conducts free information and advice service for all stammerers and parents/teachers with stammering childern. Operates facilities and activities for members. **Publications:** *Annual Report*. • Pamphlets, periodic. Offers guidance to stutterers. • *Speaking Out*, quarterly.

★3497★ Better Hearing Australia (BHA)
PO Box 24
Waratah, NSW, Australia
Phone: 49 688050
Fax: 49 688050
Norman W. Collier, Exec.Dir.

Founded: 1940. **Members:** 3,000. **Local Groups:** 18. **Description:** Adults with acquired deafness. Works toward the rehabilitation of the deaf; represents the hearing impaired before government. Provides hearing education and rehabilitation activities. **Publications:** *Better Hearing*, quarterly.

★3498★ Better Hearing Institute (BHI)
Box 1840
Washington, DC 20013
Phone: (703)642-0580
Free: 800-EAR-WELL
Fax: (703)750-9302
Joseph J. Rizzo, Exec.Dir.

Founded: 1973. **Description:** Professionals and others dedicated to helping persons with impaired hearing. Purpose is to inform the public and the 28,000,000 Americans who have impaired hearing about the nature of hearing loss and the available medical, surgical, rehabilitative, and amplification help. Methods of communication used include television and radio public service announcements, films, speakers' bureaus, booklets, editorial publicity, and exhibits. Produces general information and education kits of communication tools. Promotes Better Hearing and Speech Month. Maintains telephone service that provides information on hearing loss and help to callers from anywhere in the United States and Canada. **Publications:** *Better Hearing News*, quarterly. *Price:* $10. • Pamphlets.

★3499★ British Association of the Hard of Hearing
Hearing Concern
7/11 Armstrong Rd.
London W3 7JL, England
Phone: 181 7431110
Fax: 181 7429043
Mr. Christopher Meyer Obe, Dir

Founded: 1947. **Members:** 6,000. **Regional Groups:** 180. **Languages:** English, Welsh. **Description:** Hearing impaired individuals and concerned persons in England. Addresses the problems of the hearing impaired community. **Publications:** *Hearing Concern*, quarterly. Magazine. • *Talkabout*. Magazine. Magazine of youth section. **Formerly:** (1993) British Association of the Hard of Hearing.

★3500★ Canadian Association of the Deaf (CAD)
205-2435 Holly Ln.
Ottawa, ON, Canada K1V 7P2
Phone: (613)526-4785
James D. Roots, Exec.Dir.

Founded: 1940. **Members:** 26. **Languages:** English, French. **Description:** Regional and local organizations for the deaf. Promotes interests of the deaf through advocacy; provides educational and support facilities. Maintains speakers' bureau; conducts research; compiles statistics; bestows awards.

Canadian Society of Otolaryngology - Head and Neck Surgery (CSO-HNS)
See: Entry 12263

★3501★ CAPCOM
6707 Old Dominion Dr., Ste 210
PO Box 149
Mc Lean, VA 22101-0149
Phone: (703)442-9788
Free: 800-241-2ADA
Fax: (703)760-9678
Richard F. Rosen, Ph.D., Exec.Dir.

Founded: 1982. **Description:** Board of directors (15) comprising hearing impaired or physically handicapped individuals and senior citizens. Conducts research on the special needs of the hearing impaired, including senior citizens. Presents workshops on law and the deaf and on promoting productive working relationships for the hearing impaired employees of agencies and corporations. Maintains speakers' bureau and file of publications from organizations serving the deaf. Serves as a center for interpreter referrals. **Publications:** *CAPCOM Reports*, semiannual. **Also Known As:** Capital Communications Service for the Hearing-Impaired.

★3502★ Children of Deaf Adults (CODA)
Box 30715
Santa Barbara, CA 93130
Phone: (805)682-0997
Millie Brother, Founder

Founded: 1983. **Description:** Hearing children of deaf parents who are interested in sharing experiences with others of similar backgrounds. Provides information to professional organizations, libraries, community agencies, researchers, and other interested persons. Acts upon is-

sues regarding deafness; provides support to deaf parent/hearing child families. Serves as clearinghouse for deaf parent/hearing children families. **Publications:** *CODA*, quarterly. Newsletter. For the adult hearing children of deaf parents. Reports on national and international meetings and resources. Includes association news. *Price:* Included in membership dues. • *Hearing Children/Deaf Parents*. Bibliography. • *Proceedings from Annual Conferences*. Proceedings.

★3503★ Cochlear Implant Club International (CICI)
PO Box 464
Buffalo, NY 14223-0464
Phone: (716)838-4662
Camille Jones, Pres. & CEO

Founded: 1981. **Members:** 1,050. **Local Groups:** 38. **Description:** Cochlear implant patients, candidates for cochlear implant, and their families and friends; health care professionals. Provides support services including advocacy for the hearing impaired. Promotes improved cochlear implant technology and research on hearing impairment. Serves as an information clearinghouse. Conducts educational programs and childrens' services; operates speakers' bureau. **Publications:** *Contact*, quarterly. Newsletter. Covers current research, legislation, insurance issues, association activities, and coping advice. *Price:* Included in membership dues.

★3504★ Commonwealth Society for the Deaf (CSD)
Dilke House
Malet St.
London WC1 7JA, England
Phone: 171 6315311
Christopher Holborow, Chm.

Founded: 1959. **Languages:** English. **Description:** Works for the deaf, especially children, in developing Commonwealth countries. In conjunction with governmental and voluntary organizations to provide electronic equipment to test hearing and to assist in the teaching of deaf children; encourages the use of body-worn hearing aids and the establishment of maintenance and repair services for such equipment. Arranges courses to train teachers in the education of the deaf; organizes visits by teams of specialists to work with colleagues in Third World countries. Conducts research into the prevention of deafness and compiles statistics on such research; has studied the incidence and causes of deafness in Gambia, Nigeria, and Botswana. Maintains contact with and disseminates information about schools, societies, and government councils for the deaf throughout the Commonwealth. **Publications:** Annual Report. • *Newsletter*, annual. Newsletter. • Reports, periodic.

★3505★ Compulsive Stutterers Anonymous (CSA)
PO Box 1406
Park Ridge, IL 60068
Phone: (815)895-9848

Founded: 1989. **Local Groups:** 6. **Description:** Men and women with the problem of compulsive stuttering. Uses an adaptation of the 12-step program used by Alcoholics Anonymous World Services. Encourages members to share

their experiences and maintain personal contact with others at meetings and on the telephone. Encourages members to combine a program of professional speech therapy with spiritual principles of recovery. Provides sponsors to encourage individual members in their recovery and in developing a speech plan with the goal of gaining greater freedom in speaking.

★3506★ Computer Users in Speech and Hearing (CUSH)
c/o William Seaton
PO Box 2160
Hudson, OH 44236
Phone: (216)689-3240
Michael Wynne, Exec. Officer

Founded: 1981. **Members:** 1,000. **Local Groups:** 2. **Description:** Professionals involved in communication sciences and communication disorders, companies that develop products for remediation and treatment of communication disorders, and individuals and family members who are experiencing communication disorders. **Publications:** Journal, semiannual.

★3507★ Conference of Educational Administrators Serving the Deaf (CEASD)
c/o Oscar Cohen
Lexington School for the Deaf
75th St. & 30th Ave.
Jackson Heights, NY 11370
Phone: (718)898-8800
Fax: (718)899-1621
Dr. Oscar Cohen, Pres.

Founded: 1868. **Members:** 355. **Description:** Executive heads of public, private, and denominational schools for the deaf in the U.S. and Canada. Coordinates research on the problems of deafness. Compiles statistics on pupils, teachers, and programs from schools for the deaf. **Publications:** *American Annals of the Deaf*, 5/year. • Newsletter, bimonthly. **Formerly:** Association of Superintendents and Principals of American Schools for the Deaf; (1980) Conference of Executives of American Schools for the Deaf.

★3508★ Convention of American Instructors of the Deaf (CAID)
c/o Carl Kirchner
TRIPOD, Burbank Unified S.D.
2901 N. Keystone St.
Burbank, CA 91504
Phone: (818)972-2080
Fax: (818)972-2090
Barbara Montan, Pres.

Founded: 1850. **Members:** 1,200. **Description:** Professional organization of teachers, administrators, and professionals in allied fields related to education of the deaf. Objectives are: to provide opportunities for a free interchange of views concerning methods and means of educating the deaf; to promote such education by the publication of reports, essays, and other information; to develop more effective methods of teaching hearing impaired children. Maintains speakers' bureau; offers placement services. **Publications:** *American Annals of the Deaf*, quarterly. Journal. Includes scholarly articles on deafness. *Price:* Included in membership dues; $77/year for nonmembers. • *Directory of Ser-*

vices for the Deaf in the U.S., annual. Directory. • News 'N' Notes, quarterly. Newsletter. Includes articles on education of the deaf and organization activities. Price: Free, for members only. • Proceedings. **Also Known As:** American Instructors of the Deaf.

★ 3509 ★ **Council for Better Hearing and Speech Month (CBHSM)**
10801 Rockville Pike
Rockville, MD 20852
Phone: (301)897-5700
Free: 800-EAR-WELL
Fax: (301)571-0457
Paige Wesley, Contact

Founded: 1979. **Members:** 28. **Description:** A consortium of major national, regional, and local nonprofit organizations involved in the hearing and speech fields. Purposes are to promote an intensified public information effort to alert Americans to problems in hearing and language, and to create an awareness regarding help available in overcoming these handicaps. Concentrates activities particularly during the month of May, celebrated since the early 1900s as Better Hearing and Speech Month. Selects annual celebrity spokesperson and poster child. Sponsors luncheons, parades, public ceremonies, and other entertainment and publicity events. Prepares public service announcements, with time and space often donated by the media; distributes television ads to leading networks throughout the U.S.; seeks to attract wire service coverage. Conducts competitions. **Publications:** Council for Better Hearing and Speech Month Resource Booklet. Brochure.

★ 3510 ★ **Council on Education of the Deaf (CED)**
800 Florida Ave. NE
Washington, DC 20002
Phone: (202)651-5020
Fax: (202)351-5708
Doin Hicks, Exec.Dir.

Founded: 1960. **Members:** 12. **Description:** Representatives from the Alexander Graham Bell Association for the Deaf, the Conference of Educational Administrators Serving the Deaf, the Convention of American Instructors of the Deaf, Association of College Educators; Deaf and Hard of Hearing, National Association of the Deaf and The American Society for Deaf Children. Seeks to improve educational opportunities for deaf and hearing impaired children through cooperation in publication practices, liaison with lay and peripheral groups, teacher certification, public information, and research. Provides certification programs for educators and professionals. Establishes, evaluates, and maintains certification standards for teacher education programs. **Publications:** Certification Standards Document. • Standards for Evaluation of Programs.

★ 3511 ★ **Council on Professional Standards in Speech-Language Pathology and Audiology**
American Speech-Language-Hearing Association
10801 Rockville Pike
Rockville, MD 20852
Phone: (301)897-5700
John Bernthal, Chair

Founded: 1959. **Members:** 11. **Description:** Defines standards for clinical certification and for the accreditation of graduate education programs, as well as for professional service programs. Monitors the interpretation and application of these standards to individuals, institutions, and organizations. Hears appeals regarding certification and accreditation. **Publications:** Annual Report, annual. **Formerly:** (1980) American Boards of Examiners in Speech Pathology and Audiology.

★ 3512 ★ **Cued Speech Center (CSC)**
PO Box 31345
Raleigh, NC 27622
Phone: (919)828-1218
Mary Elsie Daisey, Exec.Dir.

Founded: 1978. **Description:** Provides advocacy and support of Cued Speech use. Objective is to provide instruction, support services, and information pertaining to deafness and the application of Cued Speech. (Cued Speech is a communication system which utilizes hand shapes and placements to clarify lipreading and aid hearing-impaired persons in visually perceiving spoken language. It is used by families and professionals working with deaf and hard-of-hearing people. Speech pathologists also use it with hearing persons in teaching phonetics, phonics, the sounds of second languages, and in therapy for articulation and language disorders.) Provides classes and workshops in Cued Speech. Maintains speakers' bureau; provides counseling and support for hearing-impaired adults and the families of hearing impaired adults and children. Operates a state-wide preschool program for deaf and hard-of-hearing children from birth to five years of age. **Publications:** Cued Speech Center Annual Report. Annual Report. Price: $5. • Cued Speech Center Lines, semiannual. Magazine. Price: $15/year.

★ 3513 ★ **Deaf Advocacy Women's Network (DAWN)**
Te Aro
c/o PO Box
Wellington, New Zealand

Languages: English. **Description:** Hearing impaired individuals and their families, and other individuals with an interest in hearing impairments and the rights of people with hearing disabilities. Promotes improved availability of services for people with hearing impairments; works to increase public awareness of the needs of people with impaired hearing.

★ 3514 ★ **Deaf-REACH**
3521 12th St. NE
Washington, DC 20017
Phone: (202)832-6681
Fax: (202)832-8454
Rebecca A. Clark, CSW, Exec.Dir.

Founded: 1972. **Description:** Committed to maximizing the self-sufficiency of deaf people

needing special services by providing referral, education, advocacy, counseling, and housing. Seeks to establish residential homes and provide psychological, physical, spiritual, and social aid to deaf persons with mental and emotional problems. Operates Otis House and Kearny House, group homes for mentally ill deaf persons, designed to help meet the residents' emotional and social needs and teach them independent living skills. Administers the Community Housing for the Hearing Impaired Program which also provides a group home. Offers intake, referral, housing placement assistance, and personal counseling; provides day-programs for learni ng disabled and deaf adults. Works in community advocacy for the mentally ill hearing impaired. Conducts workshops. Activities are conducted primarily in the Washington, DC, area. **Publications:** Annual Report. Price: Free. • Brochure. • Newsletter, 3/year. **Formerly:** (1990) National Health Care Foundation for the Deaf.

★ 3515 ★ **Deafness Research Foundation (DRF)**
9 E. 38th St., 7th Fl.
New York, NY 10016
Phone: (212)684-6556
Free: 800-535-3323
Fax: (212)779-2125
Charles D. Kimpel, Pres.

Founded: 1958. **Members:** 2,400. **Description:** Participates in the National Temporal Bone and Balance Pathology Resource Registry Program of the National Institute on Deafness and Other Communication Disorders. Approximately 2400 physicians and other professionals in ear medicine and research and 52 medical societies underwrite the foundation's fundraising costs through membership in the Centurions of the Deafness Research Foundation; approximately 300 other interested individuals raise funds through membership in the Deafness Research Foundation Auxiliary. **Publications:** A Few Short Years Can Last a Lifetime. Brochure. Price: Free. • Booklets. • Brochures. • Deafness Research Foundation Annual Report. Annual Report. Includes named research grants. • The Gift of Hearing. Brochure. Price: Free. • Hearing Health: Have You Heard the Latest Facts?. Brochure. Price: Free. • Help Me...I Can't Hear You. Brochure. Price: Free. • Receiver, 3/year. Newsletter. Covers current developments in deafness research; includes foundation news. Price: Free.

★ 3516 ★ **Deafpride**
1350 Potomac Ave. SE
Washington, DC 20003
Phone: (202)675-6700
Fax: (202)547-0547
Ann Champ-Wilson, Exec.Dir.

Founded: 1972. **Members:** 300. **Description:** Individuals, organizations, and institutions interested in the rights of deaf persons. Promotes the human rights of deaf people and their families; brings together deaf and hearing persons and provides opportunities for them to develop their potentials as advocates, working for change with others; assists groups throughout the U.S. to organize and deal with issues in their communities. Committed to the support and development of a bilingual approach in the education and family life of deaf persons, using American Sign Language and English as two languages of equal dignity. Works with the whole family in the community, with emphasis on the needs of the prelingually, profoundly deaf and their families. Programs and activities include: Community Outreach; In-Service Training Workshops; Family Life; Bilingual Studies/Deaf Culture; Health Services Access; Project AIDS; Chemical Dependency Services; Information and Referral. Sponsors and designs conferences and workshops, and provides speakers and panelists for community programs throughout the U.S. **Publications:** Books. • *Deafpride Advocate Quarterly.* Newsletter. • *Deafpride Papers: Perspectives and Options.* • Pamphlets.

★ 3517 ★   **Dogs for the Deaf (DFD)**
10175 Wheeler Rd.
Central Point, OR 97502
Phone: (503)826-9220
Fax: (503)826-6696
Robin Dickson, Exec.Dir.

Founded: 1977. **Description:** Trains hearing dogs to alert deaf persons to certain sounds. Dogs are chosen from pet adoption shelters and assigned on the basis of a prioritized waiting list. They undergo four to five months of training during which they are taught to alert their masters to the sounds of alarm clocks, smoke alarms, doorbells, oven timers, crying babies, and telephones. Deaf or severely hearing impaired persons are eligible to be recipients if they are old enough to assume responsibility for the care of the dog. When assigned, a trainer and the dog travel to the recipient's home for a week to teach the dog and recipient to work together. Costs of dog selection, veterinary care, housing, training, and placement are covered; recipients make a donation only if able. Trains individuals to be certified audio canine trainers. Has appeared on local and national television programs to present the hearing ear dog training process and the results of dog placement. **Publications:** *Canine Listener*, quarterly. Provides information on the Hearing Ear Dog Program for the deaf; includes profiles of dogs and owners. *Price:* Free.

★ 3518 ★   **Dutch Deaf Association (SND)**
(Stichting Nederlandse Dovenraad)
Postbus 19
NL-3500 AA Utrecht, Netherlands
Phone: 30 316487
Fax: 30 316326
B.W. Elferink, Chm.

Languages: Dutch. **Description:** Umbrella organization of associations for the hearing impaired, including the Koninklijke Nederlandse Doven Sport Bond, Nederlandse Bond van Dovenverenigingen, Nederlandse Cristelijke Bond van Doven, Nederlandse Katholieke Dovenbond; Nederlandse Federatie van Organisaties van Ouders van Dove Kinderen , Stichting Christelijke Tehuizen voor Doven, and Stichting Dovernzorg. Encourages the emancipation and integration of the hearing impaired into society; provides assistance; disseminates information. Represents member organizations before government agencies and institutions; coordinates

contact between members; works with other organizations concerned with the welfare of the deaf.

★ 3519 ★   **Dutch Parents Organization of Hearing and Speech Impaired Children (FOSS)**
(Federaties van Ouders van Slechthorende- en Spraakgestoorde)
St. Jacobsstraat 14
Postbus 480
NL-3500 AL Utrecht, Netherlands
Phone: 30 340663
Fax: 30 343081
Mr. A. Verschoor, Contact

Founded: 1973. **Members:** 40. **Languages:** Dutch. **Description:** Institutions and organizations representing the parents of 4500 children in the Netherlands concerned with the welfare of hearing and speech impaired children. Works to insure the provision of quality education for the hearing and speech impaired; assists in diagnosis; provides moral support to the parents of hearing or speech impaired children; disseminates information. Sponsors competitions; maintains speakers' bureau. **Publications:** *FOSSTAAL.* Journal. • *Hearing and Speech Impaired Children.* • *What to Do When You Leave Elementary School?.* Brochure.

★ 3520 ★   **Ear Foundation (EF)**
2420 Castillo St., Ste. 100
Santa Barbara, CA 93105-4346
Phone: (805)569-1111
Fax: (805)563-2277
Joseph DiBartolomeo, M.D., Dir.

Founded: 1980. **Description:** Benefactors dedicated to advance medical knowledge concerning ear diseases and to encourage public understanding of such disorders. Offers professional and public education programs; operates speakers' bureau with lectures on ear diseases and related disorders such as tinnitus and vertigo/dizziness. Conducts research on the use of lasers to correct ear disease and hearing disorders. Sponsors seminars, symposia, and workshops. **Publications:** Brochures. • Monographs. • Newsletter, periodic. • Video. Describes ear surgery and the treatment of hearing loss.

★ 3521 ★   **European Association of Audiophonological Centres (EAAC)**
(Association Europeenne des Centres d'Audiophonologie — AECA)
5, ave. A. Wansart
B-1180 Brussels, Belgium
Phone: 2 3764269
Michel Courtoy, Pres.

Founded: 1970. **Members:** 70. **Languages:** English, French, Italian. **Description:** Ear, nose, and throat specialists, speech therapists, psychologists, hearing aid specialists, and dentists. Researches pediatric audiophonology.

★ 3522 ★   **European Rhinologic Society (ERS)**
University Utrecht
Department ORL
Postbus 85500
NL-3580 GA Utrecht, Netherlands
Phone: 30 509111
Fax: 30 541922
Dr. Adrian van Olphen, Sec.

Founded: 1963. **Members:** 500. **Languages:** English. **Description:** Rhinosurgeons and otolaryngologists in 42 countries. Offers education in rhinology; provides training in functional and aesthetic rhinosurgery. Holds courses; awards prizes. **Publications:** *Rhinology*, quarterly.

★ 3523 ★   **Finnish Association of the Deaf**
Postilokero 57
Ilkantie 4
SF-00400 Helsinki, Finland
Phone: 0 58031
Fax: 0 5803770
Raija Nieminen·

Description: Provides a network for the exchange of information on issues affecting the hearing impaired. Offers information on programs for the hearing impaired. Represents the interests of the hearing impaired in legislation development.

★ 3524 ★   **Foundation for Fluency (FFI)**
9242 Gross Point Rd., Ste. 305
Skokie, IL 60077
Phone: (708)677-8280
Herbert G. Goldberg, Pres.

Founded: 1977. **Description:** Organized to provide support grous to individuals who stutter. Sponsors support group meetings; provides speakers for support group conventions. Helps stutterers obtain the Edinburgh Masker, a device that prohibits the wearer from hearing his or her own voice, thereby instilling speaking confidence. Conducts selfhelp sessions; operates charitable program.

★ 3525 ★   **Hear Center (HEAR)**
301 E. Del Mar Blvd.
Pasadena, CA 91101
Phone: (818)796-2016
Fax: (818)796-2320
Josephine F. Wilson, Exec.Dir.

Founded: 1954. **Description:** Auditory and verbal program designed to help hearing impaired children, infants, and adults lead normal and productive lives. Seeks to develop auditory techniques to aid people who have communication problems due to deafness. Primary objectives include early identification of hearing loss in infants and children and early amplification. Operates a program involving: binaural hearing aids where appropriate; continuous exposure to sound; development of auditory perception; wide-range amplification; environmental stimulation. Provides services in: diagnosis and audiological evaluation; hearing aid evaluation and trial use; development of listening skills and articulation; speech therapy; parent counseling. **Publications:** *Conquering Childhood Deafness.* • *Effectiveness of Early Detection and Auditory Stimulation on the Speech and Language of Hearing Impaired Children.* • *HEAR Center Pro-*

ceedings, periodic. Proceedings. • *The Listener*, bimonthly. Newsletter. Covers topics of interest to the hearing and speech impaired community, as well as services and activities of the center. *Price:* Free. **Formerly:** (1975) Hearing Education Through Auditory Research Foundation.

★ 3526 ★ **Hearing Aided Young Adults (HAYA)**
7-11 Armstrong Rd.
London W3 7JL, England
Phone: 181 7431110
Fax: 181 7429043
Maria Butcher, Youth Coord.

Founded: 1947. **Members:** 140. **Regional Groups:** 7. **Languages:** English. **Description:** A section of Hearing Concern. Organizes social and educational programs for 18-30 year old hearing impaired individuals. Sponsors seminars to address the problems confronting the hearing impaired; makes available educational programs. Holds sporting events; conducts periodic young people's weekend; maintains a pen-pal club. **Publications:** *HAYA Now!*, quarterly. Newsletter. • *Talkabout*, quarterly. Magazine. **Formerly:** (1994) Young Hard of Hearing Adults.

★ 3527 ★ **Hearing Education and Awareness for Rockers (HEAR)**
PO Box 460847
San Francisco, CA 94146-0847
Phone: (415)773-9590
Kathy Peck, Exec.Dir.

Description: Musicians, music industry professionals, and music lovers. Seeks to prevent hearing loss by promoting public awareness regarding the nature of sound and other hearing issues. Promotes the use of hearing protection and enhancement devices, especially for members of the music community. Conducts educational programs; disseminates information. **Publications:** *HEAR Information Packet. Price:* $7.

Hearing Industries Association (HIA)
See: Entry 5856

Helen Keller National Center for Deaf-Blind Youths and Adults (HKNC)
See: Entry 13476

★ 3528 ★ **HIKE Fund**
10115 Cherryhill Pl.
Spring Hill, FL 34608-7116
Phone: (904)688-2579
Free: (904)688-2579
Charles E. Terrill, Sec.

Founded: 1985. **Members:** 9. **Description:** Supported by the International Order of Job's Daughters Works for complete equality and integration of the blind in society. Provides support and information services. Provides hearing devices for children (up to the age of 20) with financial need. **Also Known As:** Hearing Impaired Kids Endowment Fund.

★ 3529 ★ **House Ear Institute (HEI)**
2100 W. 3rd St., 5th Fl.
Los Angeles, CA 90057
Phone: (213)483-4431
Fax: (213)483-8789
James Boswell, CEO

Founded: 1946. **Description:** Develops conceptual and technically feasible approaches to resolving hearing and balance disorders through applied research. Conducts research on subjects including hearing aids, auditory implants, aging ear, brain mapping, nearoanatomy, infant hearing diagnosis, and acoustic tumor. Offers seminars and classes for senior residents and practicing physicians. Operates children's center to serve profoundly deaf children and their families. Maintains library of 2200 volumes on otology and various medical journals. Sponsors videotape seminars and conducts courses on the use of hearing devices and how to evaluate hearing disorders. Provides a support group for parents. Compiles statistics; offers children's services; maintains speakers' bureau, library, and museum. **Publications:** Annual Report. • *HEI Review*, quarterly. Newsletter. Covers institute activities, otological research updates, and news of interest to those with hearing disabilities. • Manuals. • Monographs. • Papers. **Formerly:** (1972) Los Angeles Foundation of Otology; (1981) Ear Research Institute.

International Association of Laryngectomees (IAL)
See: Entry 12683

★ 3530 ★ **International Association of Logopedics and Phoniatrics (IALP) (Association Internationale de Logopedie et Phoniatrie)**
Nilssons Berg 21
S-411 43 Goteborg, Sweden
Phone: 31 823165
Fax: 31 823415
Dr. Ewa Soderpalm, Exec. Officer

Founded: 1924. **Members:** 600. **Languages:** English, French, German. **Description:** Phoniatricians (voice disorder specialists), logopedists (speech-language defect therapists), and audiologists (hearing specialists) from 50 affiliated societies in 45 countries. Fosters and conducts scientific study of disorders in human communication. **Publications:** *Folia Phoniatrica et Logopedica*, bimonthly. Journal. • *IALP Directory*, biennial. Directory.

★ 3531 ★ **International Association of Physicians in Audiology (IAPA)**
Dept. of Audiology
Helsinki Univ.
SF-00290 Helsinki, Finland
Phone: 0 4713069
Fax: 0 4715037
Tapani Jauhiainen, M.D., Sec.Gen.

Founded: 1980. **Members:** 200. **Languages:** English. **Description:** Practitioners of medical audiology in 35 countries. Promotes the field of medical audiology and practitioners' interests worldwide. **Publications:** *Journal of Audiological Medicine*, 3/year. Journal.

★ 3532 ★ **International Committee of Sports for the Deaf (CISS) (Comite International des Sports des Sourds — CISS)**
Langaavej 41
DK-2650 Hvidovre, Denmark
Phone: 35361588
Fax: 35360155
Knud Sondergaard, Sec.Gen.-Treas.

Founded: 1924. **Members:** 60. **Languages:** English. **Description:** National athletic organizations for the deaf. Provides an international sports competition for the deaf patterned after the International Olympic Games. Promotes and develops physical education and the practice of sports among the deaf. Encourages friendly relations between countries with programs in silent sports and countries without programs for deaf athletes. Holds Summer World Games and Winter Games alternately at 2-year intervals for competitors with hearing loss of 55 decibels or more. The committee is recognized by the International Olympic Committee. **Publications:** *Bulletin*, quarterly. Bulletin. • *Handbook*, periodic.

★ 3533 ★ **International Federation of Hard of Hearing People (IFHOH)**
Radegunderstr. 10
A-8045 Graz, Austria
Phone: 316 671327
Fax: 316 681093
Dr. Andrea Lenger, Gen.Sec.

Founded: 1977. **Members:** 40. **Languages:** English. **Description:** National organizations for individuals with acquired deafness representing 24 countries. Objectives are to: improve the standards of technical and social provisions for the hearing impaired; increase the understanding of the problems and needs of the hard of hearing; stimulate research into hearing impairment and the development of facilities for the hearing impaired; improve communication between the hard of hearing and among organizations for the hearing impaired. Coordinates the work of member organizations. Cooperates with governments and organizations for the prevention and cure of hearing impairments. Collects research data, public relations materials, and technical aids. **Publications:** *Congress and Symposia Proceedings*. Proceedings. • *Congress Report*. Report. • *IFHOH Journal*, 3/year. Journal. • *Working for the Hard of Hearing Within the IFHOH*. Brochure. **Formerly:** International Federation of the Hard of Hearing.

★ 3534 ★ **International Federation of Hard of Hearing Young People (IFHOHYP)**
Flahackebacken 64
S-135 33 Tyreso, Sweden
Phone: 8 7421469
Fax: 8 7421469
Lena Wisen, Pres.

Founded: 1968. **Languages:** English, German. **Description:** National organizations; hearing impaired individuals under the age of 30 living in countries where no organizations for the hearing impaired exist. Encourages friendship between individuals of different nationalities. Objectives are to: increase understanding of the problems and needs of the hard of hearing; improve self-confidence of young hearing impaired people. Supervises annual summer camps. **Publications:** *IFHOHYP Annual Report*, annual. Annual Report. • *IFHOHYP Magazine*, quarterly. Magazine. • *IFHOHYP Newsletter*, quarterly. Newsletter. **Formerly:** (1994) International Committee of Hard of Hearing Young People.

★3535★ International Federation of Oto-Rhino-Laryngological Societies (IFOS) (Federation Internationale des Societes Oto-Rhino-Laryngologiques)
7-221 Eaton N
200 Elisabeth St.
Toronto, ON, Canada M5G 2C4
Phone: (416)340-4190
Fax: (416)340-4209
Dr. P.W. Albetti, Sec.Gen.

Founded: 1965. **Members:** 95. **National Groups:** 72. **Regional Groups:** 5. **Languages:** English, French, German, Japanese, Spanish. **Description:** National (83) and international otorhinolaryngological societies (12) in 72 countries. Promotes the advancement of otorhinolaryngology (ORL), the prevention and control of diseases and disorders of the ear, nose, and throat, and the training of otorhinolaryngologists. Participates, as an affiliate to the World Health Organization, in the Worldwide Prevention Action on Hearing Impairment. Encourages international cooperation between otorhinolaryngologists and members. Plans to establish a museum. Sponsors film and video competitions. **Publications:** Films, periodic. • *IFOS Newsletter*, 4/year. • *International ORL Directory*, periodic. • Reports, periodic. • Videos, periodic. • *Year Book*.

★3536★ International Foundation for Stutterers (IFS)
PO Box 462
Belle Mead, NJ 08502
Phone: (908)359-6469
Edward D. Riordan, Pres.

Founded: 1980. **Members:** 1,100. **Description:** Individuals who stutter, their families, speech therapists, and other interested persons. Goal is to provide for the treatment and cure of stuttering through speech therapy in conjunction with selfhelp groups. Believes it is imperative for stutterers to reinforce techniques learned through speech therapy in an atmosphere outside of clinics and with the support of other stutterers. Establishes, maintains, and encourages formation of regional selfhelp groups for individuals undergoing therapy. Aims to make the public aware of the availability of professional treatment for stutterers. Conducts research to examine the causes and treatments of stuttering and to provide findings to the public. Sponsors seminars for speech therapists. Maintains speakers' bureau. **Publications:** *Look Who's Talking*, quarterly. Newsletter. *Price:* $18/year.

★3537★ International Hearing Dog, Inc. (IHDI)
5901 E. 89th Ave.
Henderson, CO 80640
Phone: (303)287-EARS
Fax: (303)287-3425
Martha A. Foss, Pres.

Founded: 1979. **Description:** An independent organization formed to train and place dogs, free of cost, with the deaf. Hearing dogs are trained to alert the hearing impaired to important sounds that occur in the owners' environment, such as a door knock or bell, a baby crying, a smoke alarm, an alarm clock, a telephone, a security buzzer, and other sounds which might indicate danger. Presents public awareness demonstrations. **Publications:** *Paws for Silence*, 3/year. Newsletter. Reports on the group's current activities and includes stories about hearing dog recipients. *Price:* Free. **Formerly:** (1981) Hearing Dogs.

★3538★ International Hearing Society (IHS)
20361 Middlebelt Rd.
Livonia, MI 48152
Phone: (810)478-2610
Free: 800-521-5247
Fax: (810)478-4520
Robin Holm, Exec.Dir.

Founded: 1951. **Members:** 4,000. **Regional Groups:** 50. **Description:** Hearing aid specialists who test hearing for the selection, adaptation, fitting, adjusting, servicing, and sale of hearing aids. Members counsel the hearing impaired and instruct them in care and use of hearing aids. Activities include: administration of a qualification program for screening persons designated as Hearing Instrument Specialists; administration of a consumer information program; publication of information and research concerning hearing health care; establishment of standards of education, equipment, and techniques in the fitting of hearing aids; cooperation with other professional organizations engaged in hearing health care; cooperation and consultation with government officials and agencies in the development of policies and legislation. Accredits seminars and workshops for the education of hearing aid specialists. Maintains the National Institute for Hearing Instruments Studies as the educational arm of the society. **Publications:** Articles. • *Audecibel*, quarterly. Journal. Contains technical articles, business information, and news for hearing health professionals. Includes annual index, chapter news, and book reviews. *Price:* Free to members and hearing health professionals; $25/year for others. • Books. • Brochures. • *International Hearing Society--Confidential Report for Members Only*, bimonthly. Newsletter. Covering legislative and business issues. Includes information on educational opportunities and obituaries. *Price:* Included in membership dues. • *International Hearing Society--Directory of Members*, annual. Membership Directory. Arranged geographically and alphabetically. Includes supplemental directory of manufacturers, suppliers, hearing aid designers, and others. • Pamphlets. Also publishes bylaws and code of ethics. **Formerly:** (1966) Society of Hearing Aid Audiologists; (1990) National Hearing Aid Society.

★3539★ International Organization for the Education of the Hearing Impaired (IOEHI)
c/o Alexander Graham Bell Association for the Deaf
3417 Volta Pl. NW
Washington, DC 20007
Phone: (202)337-5220
Fax: (202)337-8311
Elizabeth Wilkes, Ph.D., Contact

Founded: 1967. **Members:** 450. **Description:** Professional educators of the hearing impaired; administrators. Promotes excellence in the education of hearing impaired children and adults. Develops quality oral communications programs; fosters the teaching of oral communications; encourages the scientific study of the educational and verbal communicative processes; facilitates the exchange of information among educators. Disseminates research findings; sponsors seminars. **Publications:** Membership Directory, periodic. **Formerly:** (1982) American Organization for the Education of the Hearing Impaired.

★3540★ International Society of Audiology (Sociedad Internacional de Audiologia)
Av Progreso 141A
18 Mexico City, DF, Mexico
Dr. P. Berruecos, Pres.

Description: Audiologists and other medical professionals concerned with human hearing and its disorders. **Publications:** *Journal of Auditory Communication*.

★3541★ Judaica Captioned Film Center (JCFC)
PO Box 21439
Baltimore, MD 21208-0439
Phone: (410)655-4750
Lois Lilienfeld-Weiner, Pres.

Founded: 1983. **Description:** Deaf, hearing impaired individuals, students of English as a second language and other users of captioned films. Locates, produces, and distributes captioned versions of films on Jewish subjects such as the Bible, archaeology, the Holocaust, and Israel. **Publications:** Newsletter, 1-4/year. *Price:* Free.

★3542★ Meniere's Network (MN)
Ear Foundation
2000 Church St.
Box 111
Nashville, TN 37236
Phone: (615)329-7807
Free: 800-545-HEAR
Fax: (615)329-7935
Dr. Eddie Thompson, Exec.Dir.

Founded: 1987. **Members:** 2,200. **Local Groups:** 42. **Description:** Persons suffering from Meniere's disease, an inner ear disorder of unknown cause which results in vertigo, tinnitus, and hearing fluctuation or loss. Seeks to develop a network of peer support groups to help integrate hearing- and balance-impaired people into mainstream society. Operates speakers' bureau and pen pals and "phone buddies" services; offers educational programs and materials. **Publications:** *A Dietary Guidebook for Me-*

niere's Disease. • An Introduction to Meniere's Disease. Booklet. • Meniere's Disease-Coping Skills. • Steady, quarterly. Newsletter. Provides medical information and lists selfhelp support groups, pen pals, and "phone buddies." Price: Included in membership dues.

★ 3543 ★ Model Secondary School for the Deaf (MSSD)
Gallaudet University
800 Florida Ave. NE
Washington, DC 20002
Phone: (202)651-5466
Fax: (202)651-5109
Vivian Rice, Interim Principal

Founded: 1969. Description: Authorized under Model Secondary School for the Deaf Act of 1966. An agreement between the Secretary of Health, Education, and Welfare and Gallaudet College provided for the establishment of the school. Operation was initiated in September 1969, with the intent to provide an exemplary program of instruction and construction of a facility which would exhibit excellence in both architecture and design and would include all innovative auditory and visual devices necessary for education of the deaf. The school's primary service area includes deaf residents of the District of Columbia, Maryland, Virginia, West Virginia, Delaware, and Pennsylvania. Students from all other states which do not have appropriate educational facilities may also be accepted as space is available. Additional criteria for admission, such as age level, degree of hearing loss, and previous educational attainment are included in the agreement. Publications: Brochures. • Family Newsletter. Newsletter. • LRC Update, monthly. Newsletter. Library newsletter. Price: Free. • Perspectives. Magazine. • Preview. Magazine. • SAERIE. Magazine. Features literary works by students.

★ 3544 ★ National Association of the Deaf (NAD)
814 Thayer Ave.
Silver Spring, MD 20910
Phone: (301)587-1788
Fax: (301)587-1791
Nancy J. Bloch, Exec.Dir.

Founded: 1880. Members: 22,000. State Groups: 51. Description: Adult deaf persons, parents of deaf children, professionals and students in the field of deafness, and interested individuals; organizations of and for deaf people. Protects the civil rights of people who are deaf and hard of hearing in the areas of employment, elimination of communication barriers, and full citizenship benefits and obligations; promotes legislation and programs that benefit deaf and hard of hearing people. Maintains a legal defense fund. Promotes legislation to benefit deaf and hard of hearing persons. Supports improved programs in vocational training, rehabilitative services, educational opportunities, and mental health services. Screens and evaluates films and recommends which films should be captioned for deaf and hard of hearing viewers. Cooperates with organizations representing other disabled persons on matters of common interest; assists cooperating state associations of deaf persons. Serves as a clearinghouse of information on deafness. Sponsors a Youth

Leadership Camp and a Junior NAD program. Publications: Deaf American, periodic. Journal. Contains articles on deafness-related topics. Price: Included in membership dues; $20/year for nonmembers. • NAD Broadcaster, 11/year. Tabloid for and about deaf and hearing impaired persons and their families. Covers political issues, sports, and activities of interest to the deaf. Price: Included in membership dues; $20/year for nonmembers. Also publishes catalog and textbooks on American Sign Language and other systems of manual communication.

★ 3545 ★ National Association of Hard of Hearing Young People (Horselskedadets Riksforbund — UH)
Postfack 5615
S-114 86 Stockholm, Sweden
Phone: 8 4535300
Fax: 8 203367
Mr. Bo Valbar, Mgr.Dir.

Founded: 1965. Members: 2,800. Local Groups: 30. Languages: English, Swedish. Description: Member group of National Swedish Association for the Hard of Hearing. Hearing disabled children and young people in Sweden between the ages of 7 and 25; families of hard-of-hearing young people. Assists members through a network of hearing centers and clinics throughout Sweden. Provides personal hearing aids and technical aids at home and in school. Offers counseling services (including home counseling services). Maintains an allowance for young people over the age of 16 and a care allowance for parents. Seeks to influence official policies in favor of the hard-of-hearing. Promotes exchange and discussions among members; disseminates information; organizes special teaching programs, camps, excursions, and lectures. Maintains 30 parent associations. Publications: AURIS, 6/year. • Klubbnytt, 4-6/year. • Rabalden, quarterly. Formerly: Horselframjandets Riksforbund Ungahonselskadade.

★ 3546 ★ National Association for Hearing and Speech Action (NAHSA)
10801 Rockville Pike
Rockville, MD 20852
Phone: (301)897-8682
Free: 800-638-8255
Fax: (301)571-0457
Russell L. Malone, Exec.Dir.

Founded: 1919. Description: Consumers of speech, language, and hearing services and their families. Provides educational and referral information on speech, language, and hearing disabilities. Publications: Pamphlets. On a wide range of communication disorders and development of speech, language, and hearing in children. Formerly: (1922) American Association for the Hard of Hearing; (1935) American Federation of Organizations for the Hard of Hearing; (1946) American Society for the Hard of Hearing; (1966) American Hearing Society; (1974) National Association of Hearing and Speech Agencies.

★ 3547 ★ National Black Association for Speech, Language and Hearing (NBASLH)
PO Box 50605
Washington, DC 20004-0605
Phone: (202)274-6161
Fax: (202)274-6350
M. Eugene Wiggins, Exec.Dir.

Founded: 1978. Members: 300. Description: Professionals and other individuals concerned with communicatively handicapped blacks. Strongly encourages the recruitment and training of black professionals to work with individuals suffering from speech, language, and hearing problems; maintains that conditions such as race, socioeconomic class, and cultural differences must be taken into account in order to understand and sensitively study the communicative process, and to treat communicative disorders. Supports related research; solicits, and provides, financial support for the training of black students in speech, hearing, and language fields. Disseminates information. Publications: Echo, semiannual. Magazine. Price: $7.

★ 3548 ★ National Captioning Institute (NCI)
1900 Gallows Rd., Ste. 3000
Vienna, VA 22182
Phone: (703)917-7600
Free: 800-533-WORD
Fax: (703)917-9878
Philip W. Bravin

Founded: 1979. Description: Purpose is to caption television programs for the deaf and hard-of-hearing on behalf of public and commercial television broadcasters, cablecasters, and the home video industry. Utilizes a "closed captioning" system that allows coded captions not visible on a normal television set to be decoded and made visible by the use of a special adapter which may be attached to a television set. At present, the PBS, NBC, ABC, and CBS networks, cable systems, advertisers, and syndicators are participating in the program with a total of over 800 captioned hours of television per week and over 6,000 captioned home videos.

★ 3549 ★ National Center for Law and Deafness (NCLD)
800 Florida Ave. NE
Washington, DC 20002
Phone: (202)651-5373
Fax: (202)651-5381
Sy DuBow, Legal Dir.

Founded: 1975. Description: Provides legal services and representation to deaf and hard of hearing individuals. Operates legal counseling and services clinic providing free legal aid to hearing impaired residents of Washington, DC; participates in state and federal administrative and legislative proceedings advocating the rights of the hearing impaired; sponsors legal education workshops for hearing impaired consumers; acts as a clearinghouse on legal issues. Publications: Legal Rights for Hearing-Impaired People. Book. Formerly: (1991) National Center for Law and the Deaf.

★3550★ **National Center for Stuttering (NCS)**
200 E. 33rd St.
New York, NY 10016
Phone: (212)532-1460
Free: 800-221-2483
Lorraine Schneider, Adm.Dir.

Founded: 1974. **Description:** Furnishes information to parents of children who stutter. Provides treatment for children and adults who stutter and training on the latest practices and theories for speech pathologists. **Publications:** *Annual Review of Published Literature.* • Newsletter, quarterly.

★3551★ **National Consumer Board for Stuttering (NCBS)**
c/o Sandra J. Wagner
PO Box 8791
Grand Rapids, MI 49518-8791
Sandra J. Wagner, Pres.

Founded: 1991. **Description:** Seeks to provide accurate information on stuttering by investigating media claims, programs, and research. Attempts to dissolve stereotypes of stutterers through education.

★3552★ **National Council for the Hard of Hearing**
PO Box 4528
Johne Evans Pl.
Harare, Zimbabwe
Phone: 4 721747
Fax: 4 721247
John Evans

Members: 50. **Description:** Works to raise public awareness of hearing impairments. Helps develop national policies on services available to the hearing-impaired. Esatblishes early detection procedures for children.

★3553★ **National Cued Speech Association (NCSA)**
PO Box 31345
Raleigh, NC 27622
Phone: (919)828-1218
Mary Elsie Daisey, Exec.Dir.

Founded: 1982. **Members:** 1,000. **Local Groups:** 13. **Description:** Hearing-impaired individuals, their friends, families, and professionals who work with the hearing-impaired using Cued Speech. (Cued Speech is a system designed by Orin Cornett to make spoken language visible using eight hand shapes and four placements of the hand, in combination with the natural mouth movements of speech.) Serves in an advocacy capacity; provides information and support to families and professionals who use Cued Speech. **Publications:** *Cued Speech Journal.* Journal. Covers various aspects of Cued Speech. *Price:* Included in membership dues; $10/year for nonmembers. • *NCSA Directory*, annual. Membership Directory. *Price:* Included in membership dues. • *On Cue*, quarterly. Newsletter. Contains calendar of events and regional reports. *Price:* Included in membership dues; $10/year for nonmembers.

★3554★ **National Deaf-Blind League (NDBL)**
18 Rainbow Ct.
Paston Ridings
Peterborough, Cambs. PE4 7UP, England
Phone: 1733 573511
Fax: 1733 325353
Jackie Scott, Chief Exec.

Founded: 1928. **Members:** 800. **Local Groups:** 10. **Languages:** English. **Description:** Deaf-blind persons. Helps alleviate the isolation felt by those with dual sensory loss. Negotiates with government to secure better services and facilities for individuals with visual and hearing impairments. Conducts public service programs. Offers advice and financial consultation and some housing assistance. Organizes conferences, seminars, and communication courses. **Publications:** Newspaper, biweekly. Available in Braille, Moon, and large print. • *The Rainbow*, quarterly. Available in large print, Braille, Moon, and cassette versions.

★3555★ **National Deaf Bowling Association (NDBA)**
9244 E. Mansfield Ave.
Denver, CO 80237
Free: 800-659-3656
Fax: (303)750-2115
Don Gene Warnick, Sec.-Treas.

Founded: 1964. **Members:** 300. **Regional Groups:** 5. **Local Groups:** 20. **Description:** Individuals, clubs, and organizations of hearing impaired bowlers. Conducts bowling tournaments including the World's Deaf Bowling Championship, National Deaf Team Doubles-Singles, National Deaf Seniors, and National Deaf Master Tournament. Maintains hall of fame; compiles statistics. **Publications:** *The Deaf Bowler*, quarterly. Newsletter. *Price:* Included in membership dues.

★3556★ **National Deaf Women's Bowling Association (NDWBA)**
c/o Kathy M. Darby
33 August Rd.
Simsbury, CT 06070
Phone: (203)651-8234
Kathy M. Darby, Sec.-Treas.

Founded: 1974. **Members:** 160. **Description:** Hearing impaired bowlers. Promotes fellowship and fair play among participants. **Publications:** *NDWBA Constitution and By Laws.*

★3557★ **National Education for Assistance Dog Services (NEADS)**
PO Box 213
West Boylston, MA 01583
Phone: (508)835-3304
Fax: (508)835-2526
Sheila O'Brien, Exec.Dir.

Founded: 1976. **Members:** 6,000. **Regional Groups:** 21. **State Groups:** 5. **Description:** Interested individuals, clubs, and organizations. Trains dogs to alert deaf or hearing impaired individuals to specific sounds of the environment; also trains dogs to help disabled individuals. After extensive screening, dogs are trained by a professional staff for three to five months, learning: basic obedience; how to respond to household and other sounds including alarm clocks, door bells, smoke alarms, telephone, babies' crying, kettle whistles, oven timer, car horns, and sirens; how to perform assistance tasks such as pulling wheelchairs, using light switches, and retrieving articles from the floor or high shelves. Maintains speakers' bureau. **Publications:** *Hearing Ear Dogs: A Sound Relationship.* Brochure. • *Help Make a Miracle--Participate in Our Puppy Program.* Brochure. • *New England Assistance Dog Program Newsletter*, quarterly. Newsletter. • *Service Dogs - Trained to Help the Physically Disabled.* Brochure. • *Sound Friendships - The Story of Willa and Her Hearing Ear Dog.* Book. • *Special Dogs for Special People.* Brochure. **Formerly:** New England Assistance Dog Service; (1989) Hearing Ear Dog Program; (1992) New England Assistance Dog Program.

★3558★ **National Hearing Conservation Association (NHCA)**
431 E. Locust, No. 202
Des Moines, IA 50309
Phone: (515)243-1558
Fax: (515)243-2049
Michele Johnson, Exec.Dir.

Founded: 1977. **Members:** 700. **Description:** Individuals holding advanced academic degrees in a discipline involving hearing and hearing loss; professional service organizations engaged in industrial hearing conservation programs; companies that manufacture or sell occupational noise or hearing loss products. Encourages education and standards development among members and industrial groups; monitors legislation and regulatory activities related to hearing conservation. **Publications:** *NHCA Membership Directory*, annual. Membership Directory. Arranged alphabetically, geographically, and by member category. Includes consumer guide. *Price:* Included in membership dues; $25 per issue. • *NHCA Professional Service Organization Directory*, annual. Directory. Lists members providing hearing conservation program professional services. Also lists company name, description, and equipment used by the company. *Price:* Free. • *Resources in Hearing Conservation*, annual. Compilation of references and films listed in previous "Spectrum" issues. *Price:* Included in membership dues; $20/issue. • *Spectrum*, quarterly. Newsletter. Provides information on technology, research, practice, and federal and state legal and regulatory activities. Includes book reviews. *Price:* Included in membership dues; $10/issue; $20 for supplements.

★3559★ **National Information Center on Deafness (NICD)**
Gallaudet University
800 Florida Ave. NE
Washington, DC 20002-3695
Phone: (202)651-5051
Fax: (202)651-5054
Loraine DiPietro, Dir.

Founded: 1980. **Description:** A resource center and information clearinghouse on all aspects of deafness and hearing loss. Makes referrals; identifies other resources for persons seeking information on deafness and hearing loss. **Publications:** *Resource List.* Directory.

★3560★ National Student Speech Language Hearing Association (NSSLHA)
10801 Rockville Pike
Rockville, MD 20852
Phone: (301)897-5700
Fax: (301)571-0457
Sr. Charleen Bloom, Ph.D., Chief Admin./Fin. Officer

Founded: 1972. **Members:** 17,000. **Local Groups:** 285. **Description:** Preprofessional organization for undergraduate and graduate students in speech-language pathology, speech and hearing sciences, and audiology. **Publications:** *Clinical Series*, biennial. • *NSSLHA Journal*, annual. Journal. *Price:* Included in membership dues; $9/year for nonmembers. **Formerly:** National Student Speech and Hearing Association.

★3561★ National Stuttering Project (NSP)
2151 Irving St., No. 208
San Francisco, CA 94122-1609
Free: 800-364-1677
Fax: (415)664-3721
John Ahlbach, Exec.Dir.

Founded: 1977. **Members:** 4,000. **Local Groups:** 75. **Description:** Selfhelp organization of people who stutter, parents of children who stutter, and speech pathologists. Seeks to provide a safe, supportive environment for stutterers and their families through chapter meetings, special programs, workshops, tape series, and selfhelp groups. Concentrates on issues such as improving self-image and assuming personal responsibility rather than focusing on speech fluency. Educates the public about stuttering and functions as a referral service for those seeking professional help. (Does not provide speech therapy or trained therapists.) Offers consulting in program development and technical assistance to school districts, speech clinics, hospitals, rehabilitation centers, and other agencies involved in speech services. Advises members on how to be wise consumers of speech and related therapies. Maintains speakers' bureau. **Publications:** Audiotapes. • Brochures. • *Letting Go*, monthly. • Pamphlets.

★3562★ National Temporal Bone Registry (NTBR)
Massachusetts Eye and Ear Infirmary
243 Charles St.
Boston, MA 02114
Phone: (617)573-3711
Free: 800-822-1321
Fax: (617)573-3838
Dr. Joseph B. Nadol, Jr., Contact

Founded: 1960. **Regional Groups:** 22. **Description:** Promotes research of hearing and balance disorders through the study of the temporal bone and related brain structures. Encourages individuals with hearing or balance disorders to bequeath their temporal bones to scientific research. Serves as a clearinghouse for information on temporal bone research. Develops strategies to conserve human temporal bone collections. Maintains a nationwide network to retrieve donated temporal bone and brain tissue. **Publications:** Brochures. • *The Registry*, semiannual. Newsletter. Includes information about donations to the bank. *Price:* Free. **Formerly:** (1992) National Temporal Bone Banks Program of The DRF.

★3563★ Nederlandse Federatie van Organisaties van Ouders van Dove Kinderen (FODOK)
Koningslaan 101
NL-3583 GS Utrecht, Netherlands
Phone: 30 523154
Els van der Zee, Contact

Members: 7. **Languages:** Dutch. **Description:** Organizations of parents of hearing impaired children. Addresses the concerns of parents with hearing impaired children; disseminates information.

★3564★ Nordic Council for the Deaf (NCD)
(Dovas Nordiske Rad — DNR)
Postilokero 57
SF-00401 Helsinki, Finland
Phone: 45 35365200
Fax: 45 35360155
Mrs. Lene Ravn, Pres.

Founded: 1907. **Members:** 14,000. **Languages:** English. **Description:** Individuals representing 5 National associations for the deaf from Denmark, Finland, Iceland, Norway, and Sweden. Works for cooperation in cultural, educational, and social matters. Seeks the establishment of special schools for the deaf, an improvement in the interpretation services, and the installment of public address systems which deaf will understand.

★3565★ Norwegian Association of the Deaf (NAD)
(Norges Doveforbund — NDF)
Postboks 6850
St. Olavs Plass
N-0130 Oslo, Norway
Phone: 22 111775
Fax: 22 111633
Svein Arne Peterson, Gen.Sec.

Founded: 1918. **Members:** 2,700. **Local Groups:** 35. **Languages:** English, Norwegian. **Description:** Hearing disabled, family, and friends in Norway. Offers support for the hearing disabled. Addresses concerns of members. **Publications:** *Doves Tidsskrift*, weekly. Magazine.

★3566★ Norwegian Association of Hard of Hearing People (NAHH)
(Horselshemmedes Landsforbund — HLF)
Postboks 5653
Briskeby
N-0209 Oslo 2, Norway
Phone: 2 2558205
Fax: 2 2551077
Knut M. Ellingsen, Sec.Gen.

Founded: 1947. **Members:** 15,000. **Local Groups:** 160. **Languages:** English, Norwegian. **Description:** Service organization working to improve living conditions for the hard of hearing. Offers technical aid and assistance on physical and practical problems related to hearing impairment. Addresses political issues; conducts educational programs for health personnel and the hard of hearing. Operates high school. **Publications:** *Din Horsel*, 9/year. Also publishes brochures.

★3567★ Norwegian Association of Stutterers (NAS)
(Norsk Interesse Forening for Stamme — NIFS)
Postboks 114
N-0308 Oslo 3, Norway
Phone: 2 235050
Fax: 2 235700
Bjorn Olav Olavssen, Contact

Founded: 1975. **Members:** 300. **Local Groups:** 5. **Languages:** English, Norwegian. **Description:** Individuals who stutter; families; institutions. Conducts group support therapy sessions. Sponsors research programs to advance services and therapy for members. Arranges information programs for the public and interested individuals. **Publications:** *Stamposten*, 3/year.

★3568★ Oral Hearing-Impaired Section (OHIS)
3417 Volta Pl. NW
Washington, DC 20007
Phone: (202)337-5220
Fax: (202)337-8314
Karen Karpf, Chairperson

Founded: 1964. **Members:** 345. **Local Groups:** 3. **Description:** Section of the Alexander Graham Bell Association for the Deaf. Deaf persons who use speech and lipreading. To encourage deaf young people and their families to use speech, lipreading, and residual hearing. Participates in regional, national, and international conferences on deafness. Appears on television and radio programs to demonstrate communications skills. Seeks to dispel outmoded conceptions about deafness. Supports: richer educational opportunities for the hearing impaired; workshops and outings for hearing impaired children and their families and teachers; scholarship funds for qualified hearing impaired students; improved methods for developing better speech, voice, lipreading, and auditory training techniques. **Publications:** *Alexander Graham Bell Association for the Deaf*. **Formerly:** (1988) Oral Deaf Adults Section.

★3569★ Orton Dyslexia Society (ODS)
Chester Bldg., Ste. 382
8600 LaSalle Rd.
Baltimore, MD 21286-2044
Phone: (410)296-0232
Free: 800-ABCD-123
Helen McFadden, Contact

Founded: 1949. **Members:** 9,000. **Regional Groups:** 44. **Description:** Professionals in the fields of neurology, pediatrics, psychiatry, education, social work, and psychology; parents; other persons interested in the study, treatment, and prevention of the problems of specific language disability, often called developmental dyslexia or simply dyslexia. Dyslexia is a condition in which individuals are unable to learn and use language skills in a manner consistent with their intellectual and social potential. Some authorities believe that 15 percent or more of American school children are in this group. Characteristics may include delayed or inadequate spoken language, difficulty in learning and remembering printed words, reversal of orientation of letters or sequence of letters in words, confusion about directions in space or time, and difficulty in finding the "right" word in speaking. Provides a focal point for activities and ideas generated in various fields as they relate to problems of language development and learning. The society is named for Dr. Samuel T. Orton, a pioneer in the field. Disseminates materials. Offers support groups. **Publications:** *Annals of Dyslexia*, annual. Journal. • *The Many Faces of Dyslexia*. Monograph. • *Perspectives on Dyslexia*, quarterly. Newsletter. Also issues reprints of papers. **Formerly:** (1981) Orton Society.

★3570★ Pan American Association of Oto-Rhino-Laryngology and Broncho-Esophagology (PAA ORL BE)
(Asociacion Panamericana de Otorrinolaringologia y Broncoesofagologia)
San Luis Potosi 44
06700 Mexico City, DF, Mexico
Phone: 5 5742527
Pedro Andrade Pradillo, M.D., Sec.Gen.

Founded: 1946. **Members:** 2,000. **National Groups:** 20. **Languages:** English, Portuguese, Spanish. **Description:** Otorhinolaryngologists (ear, nose, and throat specialists). Purpose is to advance the fields of otorhinolaryngology and broncho-esophagology (study of the esophagus and the tracheobronchial tree). Facilitates contact, cooperation, and exchange among American and Caribbean countries. Holds periodic seminars. **Publications:** *Newsletter*, periodic. Newsletter.

★3571★ Parents' Section of the Alexander Graham Bell Association for the Deaf (PS)
c/o Alexander Graham Bell Association for the Deaf
3417 Volta Pl. NW
Washington, DC 20007
Phone: (202)337-5220
Michael Hunter, Chairperson

Founded: 1958. **Members:** 8,000. **Local Groups:** 30. **Description:** Parents of hearing impaired children and individuals concerned with educational, social, pyschological, and vocational needs of hearing impaired children. Encourages and supports parent group action and programs on behalf of hearing impaired children; works for auditory/oral teaching of hearing impaired children. **Publications:** *Our Kids Magazine*, semiannual. Magazine. Also publishes material concerning the problems of deaf children. **Formerly:** (1989) International Parents' Organization.

★3572★ Phone-TTY
202 Lexington Ave.
Hackensack, NJ 07601
Phone: (201)489-7889
Fax: (201)489-7891
I. Lee Brody, Exec.Dir.

Founded: 1976. **Members:** 20. **Description:** Purpose is to develop and promote better communication for the deaf using an ordinary telephone and current technology. Installs computerized phone-teletype equipment in the homes of individuals who are deaf, enabling these individuals to communicate with local police, hospitals, answering services, and news services, as

well as members of the deaf community who have a PHONE-TTY in their homes. Researches, designs, manufactures, and distributes other communication devices for the deaf. Solicits grants and donations.

★3573★ Polish Deaf Union
(Polski Zwiazek Gluchych)
Podwale St. 23
PL-00-261 Warsaw, Poland
Phone: 22 310896
Fax: 22 357536
Kazimierz Diehl, Pres.

Description: Addresses the concerns of hearing impaired individuals and their families.

★3574★ Registry of Interpreters for the Deaf (RID)
8630 Fenton St., Ste. 324
Silver Spring, MD 20910
Phone: (301)608-0050
Fax: (301)608-0508
Clay Nettles, Admin.

Founded: 1964. **Members:** 5,000. **Regional Groups:** 5. **State Groups:** 54. **Description:** Professional interpreters and transliterators for the deaf. Maintains a registry of certified interpreters and transliterators; works to establish certification standards and offers a national certification test. Sponsors research and evaluation programs. Maintains 34 committees. Compiles statistics. **Publications:** *Registry of Interpreters for the Deaf--Proceedings of National Conventions*, biennial. Proceedings. *Price:* $11.95/copy. • *Views*, bimonthly. Also publishes texts and other materials on interpretation, transliteration, and translation. **Formerly:** National Registry of Professional Interpreters and Translators for the Deaf.

★3575★ Selective Mutism Foundation
c/o Sue Leszczyk
PO Box 450632
Sunrise, FL 33345
Phone: (305)748-7714
Fax: (305)748-7714
Sue Leszczyk, Dir.

Founded: 1991. **Members:** 2,000. **Description:** Individuals and families affected by selective mutism, an inherited anxiety disorder in which children with normal language skills or deficient language skills are unable to speak in school or other social situations. SM is often mistaken for normal shyness, and may go undetected for as long as two years. Promotes awareness and understanding of this condition. Encourages research and treatment. Maintains speakers' bureau. **Publications:** Brochure. • Newsletter, annual. *Price:* $15/year. **Formerly:** (1993) Foundation for Elective Mutism, Inc..

★3576★ Self Help for Hard of Hearing People (SHHH)
c/o Carla Beyer
7910 Woodmont Ave., Ste. 1200
Bethesda, MD 20814
Phone: (301)657-2248
Fax: (301)913-9413
Donna L. Sorkin, Exec.Dir.

Founded: 1979. **Members:** 13,000. **Local Groups:** 270. **Description:** Volunteer organiza-

tion of hard-of-hearing people and their relatives and friends; professionals working with hearing impaired persons. Educates members and the public about the nature, causes, and complications of hearing loss and instructs them in its detection, management, and possible prevention. Develops public and professional acceptance of the needs and values of hard-of-hearing people and encourages them to seek alternative communication skills. Sponsors workshop on coping strategies for people with hearing loss. Disseminates information on the Americans with Disability Act. Maintains library; compiles statistics; conducts educational programs. Operates Assistive Devices Demonstration Center. **Publications:** *A Good Investment: Meeting the Needs of Your Hard of Hearing Employees.* Video. • Brochures. • *Hospitality for Guests with Hearing Loss: A Guide for Hotel/Motel Compliance with the Americans with Disabilities Act.* • *Operation SHHH: Noise Abuse Prevention Posters.* • *Our Forgotten Children: Hard-of-Hearing Pupils in the Schools.* • Pamphlets. • *SHHH Journal*, bimonthly. Magazine. Contains articles by hearing health professionals and personal narratives by hearing impaired individuals. Contains information on resources. *Price:* $20 for individuals; $30 for hearing healthcare professionals; $50 for libraries; $50 for nonprofit organizations. • *SHHH News*, quarterly. Newsletter. • *Telephone Strategies: A Technical and Practical Guide for Hard of Hearing People.* • *Your Eyes Hear for You: A Self-help Course in Speechreading.* Book. Offers various publications on hearing loss, products, and related subjects. **Also Known As:** SHHH.

★3577★ Service Dog Center (SDC)
PO Box 1080
Renton, WA 98057-9906
Phone: (206)226-7357
Linda M. Hines, Exec.Dir.

Founded: 1989. **Description:** A joint program of the American Humane Association and the Delta Society. Provides a national service dog information and referral service, available at no charge to its users. Works to increase public awareness on service dogs and promotes the legal access rights of service dogs. **Publications:** *Alert*, quarterly. Newsletter. Reports on service dogs and issues of concern to those who work with, or are recipients of, service dogs. *Price:* $7.50/year; $10/year outside U.S. • *Legal Rights of Assistance Dogs.* Booklet. • *Service Dog Directory*, annual. Directory. Lists operational service dog training programs. *Price:* $3. • *Service Dog Packet.* Articles. *Price:* $21. **Formerly:** (1983) Hearing Dog Program; (1987) Hearing Dog Project; (1989) National Center for Hearing Dog Information; (1993) Hearing Dog Resource Center.

Society for Ear, Nose, and Throat Advances in Children (SENTAC)
See: Entry 3291

Society of Military Otolaryngologists - Head and Neck Surgeons (SMO-HNS)
See: Entry 7810

Society of Otorhinolaryngology and Head / Neck Nurses (SOHN)
See: Entry 9135

**Society of University Otolaryngologists -
Head and Neck Surgeons (SUO-HNS)**
See: Entry 12310

**★ 3578 ★ Society for the Welfare of the
Deaf**
c/o School for Deaf
Pope Hennessy St.
Beau Bassin, Mauritius
Phone: 4643834

Description: Promotes the rights and interests
of deaf people in Mauritius.

**★ 3579 ★ Speak Easy International
Foundation (SEIF)**
233 Concord Dr.
Paramus, NJ 07652
Phone: (201)262-0895
Antoinette Gathman, Exec.Dir.

Founded: 1977. **State Groups:** 8. **Local
Groups:** 1. **Description:** Support group and information source for individuals with a speech
dysfluency (stuttering). Seeks to instill confidence in stutterers and reinforce fluency in their
speech. Educates public, families, and friends
on the problems of speech dysfluent individuals.
Publications: *Speak Easy Newsletter*, quarterly. Newsletter. Contains activities of selfhelp
groups, research reports on stuttering; convention schedules. *Price:* $20/year.

**★ 3580 ★ Stuttering Foundation of America
(SFA)**
PO Box 11749
Memphis, TN 38111
Phone: (901)452-7343
Free: 800-992-9392
Fax: (901)452-3931
Jane Fraser, Pres.

Founded: 1947. **Description:** Provides comprehensive materials on stuttering to both the
public and professionals. Seeks to bring together speech pathologists concerned with the prevention and treatment of stuttering. Provides referrals to speech-language pathologists specializing in stuttering. **Publications:** *The Child Who
Stutters: To the Pediatrician.* • *Do You Stutter:
A Guide for Teens.* • *If Your Child Stutters: A
Guide for Parents.* • *Self Therapy for the Stutterer.* • *SFA Newsletter*, quarterly. Newsletter.
Contains SFA activities and information on stuttering. *Price:* Free. • *Stuttering and Your Child:
Questions and Answers.* • *To the Stutterer.*
Formerly: (1991) Speech Foundation of Ameri-
ca.

**★ 3581 ★ Telecommunications for the
Deaf, Inc. (TDI)**
8719 Colesville Rd., Ste. 300
Silver Spring, MD 20910
Phone: (301)589-3786
Fax: (301)589-3797
Alfred Sonnenstrahl, Exec.Dir.

Founded: 1968. **Members:** 45,000. **Description:** Hearing impaired individuals and their families, and organizations participating in telecommunications over regular telephone lines
through special equipment. Strives to constantly
improve technology and accessibility for all who
rely on visual telecommunications. Advocate for
standards and compatibility for all telecommuni-

cation devices. Promotes closed captioning on
television. Seeks to extend the installation of
text telephones (TTYs) in public buildings, rail-
roads, airlines, bus terminals, and other places
where they can be of service to the hearing impaired. Have closed captioned decoders and
the International TTY Logo available, for sale, to
the public. **Publications:** *GA-SK Newsletter*,
quarterly. Newsletter. • *National Directory of
TTY Numbers*, annual. Directory. • *Using Your
TTY/TDD.* **Formerly:** (1980) Teletypewriters for
the Deaf.

**★ 3582 ★ Tinnitus International Service
Association**
9600 Orange Ave.
Anaheim, CA 92804-3499
Phone: (714)956-3000
Fax: (714)772-5665
Ruby B. Velasquez, Planner

Founded: 1990. **Members:** 100. **Description:**
Educates the public of the problem of tinnitus
(ringing of the ears).

**★ 3583 ★ Trinidad and Tobago Association
in Aid of the Deaf (TTAID)**
13C Wrightson Rd.
Port of Spain, Trinidad and Tobago
Phone: (809)623-0613
Fax: (809)624-2303
Frances Serville, Exec. Officer

Founded: 1943. **Languages:** English. **Description:** Individuals working to improve educational, industrial, social, and economic conditions
for the deaf population of Trinidad and Tobago.
Operates a residential school for the deaf and
an educational unit for the mainstreaming of
deaf students. Assists in establishing and maintaining employment for deaf individuals. Maintains a center for early diagnosis and intervention of hearing impaired infants and children.
Operates a children's day school. Conducts
seminars, professional training programs, and
sign language courses. Conducts charitable and
research programs. Maintains telephone referral service. **Publications:** *Annual General Meeting Journal.* Also publishes papers.

**★ 3584 ★ United States Deaf Skiers
Association (USDSA)**
c/o Sandra McGee
130 Rosewood Pl.
Bridgeport, CT 06610
Phone: (203)372-7248
Sandra McGee, Sec.

Founded: 1968. **Members:** 350. **Regional
Groups:** 8. **Description:** Promotes recreational
and competitive skiing among the deaf and
hearing impaired in the U.S. Provides deaf skiers with benefits, activities, and opportunities
that will increase their enjoyment of the sport.
Encourages ski racing among the deaf and
sponsors national and regional races for deaf
skiers, including the U.S.A. National Deaf Alpine
and Nordic Ski Championships. Assists in the
selection, organization, and training of the United States Deaf Ski Teams for international competition such as the World Winter Games for the
Deaf. Presents awards; maintains hall of fame;
offers children's services. **Publications:** Newsletter, 3/year. Available to members only.

**Usher Syndrome Self-Help Network
(USSHN)**
See: Entry 5305

**★ 3585 ★ Vestibular Disorders Association
(VEDA)**
PO Box 4467
Portland, OR 97208-4467
Phone: (503)229-7705
Free: 800-837-8428
Fax: (503)229-8064
Jerry Underwood, Exec. Officer

Founded: 1983. **Members:** 4,700. **Local
Groups:** 90. **Description:** Individuals suffering
from vestibular disorders, their families and
friends, and health care professionals. (Vestibular disorders are characterized by persistent dizziness or vertigo which usually indicates a problem in the inner ear.) Provides support services
including information and referrals; encourages
public education about vestibular disorders and
their effects. Supports research and clinical activities that will enhance the quality of life for
those affected by vestibular disorders. **Publications:** Audiotapes. • *Balancing Act.* Booklet. •
Bibliographies. • *Off Balance.* Booklet. • *On the
Level*, quarterly. Newsletter. Includes coping
tips, health-related items, reviews, and association news. *Price:* Included in membership dues.
• Pamphlets. • Reports. • *Stories and Strategies: Coping with Vertibular Disorders.* Booklet.
• Videos. **Formerly:** (1989) Dizziness and Balance Disorders Association.

**★ 3586 ★ World Federation of the Deaf
(WFD)**
PO Box 65
SF-00401 Helsinki, Finland
Phone: 0 58031
Fax: 0 5803770
Liisa Kauppinen, Gen. Sec.

Founded: 1951. **Members:** 106. **Regional
Groups:** 4. **Languages:** English. **Description:**
National associations of the deaf that are legally
constituted and represent in the widest sense
the deaf in their country; all other national or international associations, societies, and bodies
for and of the deaf; health, educational, social,
and similar establishments that accept the aims
of the federation; professionals interested in
deafness and related subjects; persons performing special tasks connected with the aims
of the federation; parents and friends of the
deaf. Represents the worldwide deaf community in international forums such as the United Nations. Makes policy statements and recommendations. Coordinates research and other projects with the deaf community; conducts surveys. Has established a network of experts on
deafness and related issues. Promotes the use
of national sign language as the first language
of hearing-impaired people. **Publications:**
Booklets. • Brochures. • *Proceedings of International Congresses and Meetings.* Proceedings. • *WFD Manual on How to Establish and
Run an Organization of the Deaf.* Manual. • *The
WFD News*, quarterly. Journal. • *WFD Report
on the Status of Sign Language.* Report. • *WFD
Survey of Deaf People in the Developing World.*
Report.

★ 3587 ★ World Organisation of Jewish Deaf (WOJD)
Helen Keller Ctr.
PO Box 9001
61090 Tel Aviv, Israel
Phone: 3 303355
Fax: 3 396419
Chaim Apter, Sec.Gen.

Founded: 1973. **Members:** 500. **Languages:** English, Hebrew. **Description:** Jewish deaf and their spouses from 20 countries; organizations, experts, and other interested individuals of the Jewish faith. Objectives are to: further Jewish cultural development among the deaf; promote and defend the rights of Jewish deaf, organize and coordinate activities for the prevention of discrimination; promote a sense of unity and prevent assimilation among the Jewish deaf; encourage propagation of the Zionist ideal and support of Israel; develop contact between the deaf in Israel and Jewish deaf in the Diaspora; promote contact and understanding between Jewish and non-Jewish deaf; seek information and data on the current legal, personal, and social status of the Jewish deaf in different countries; organize, initiate, and maintain legal assistance for the needy; encourage activities in Jewish communal institutions such as homes for the aged, bar mitzvahs, and clubs. Conducts seminars promoting the Jewish religion among the deaf. Visit death camp in Auschwitz, Poland. Sponsors leadership courses, youth exchange of multinational Jewish people; offers children's services; sponsors competitions; bestows grants. **Publications:** *Demama Shelanu*, annual. Newsletter. Provides information from the Tel Aviv Branch. • Proceedings, quadrennial. Contains abstracts of the world congress. • *Review*, quarterly. • *Sign Language of the Deaf in Israel*, periodic. Directory. • *WOJD News*, periodic.

Research Centers

★ 3588 ★ Baylor College of Medicine Stuttering Center and Speech Motor Control Laboratory
College of Medicine
6501 Fannin, Ste. NB302
Houston, TX 77030
Phone: (713)798-7415
Fax: (713)798-3853
Dr. David Rosenfield, Dir.

Research Activities and Fields: Speech motor control system, including stuttering, voice problems, motor control, and digital signal and acoustic processing. **Publications:** *Neuro/Speech Newsletter*; Annual Report.

★ 3589 ★ Bill Wilkerson Center
1114 - 19th Ave. S.
Nashville, TN 37212
Phone: (615)320-5353
Fax: (615)343-7705
Dr. Fred H. Bess, Dir.

Research Activities and Fields: Hearing science, speech science, and language science, including psychoacoustics, speech perception and production, and child language acquisition

and development. Conducts clinical studies of communication disorders dealing with hearing, speech, and language in children and adults, and child language development and its assessment. **Publications:** Annual Report; Research Report.

★ 3590 ★ Boston University Center for the Study of Communication and Deafness
School of Education
605 Commonwealth Ave.
Boston, MA 02215
Phone: (617)353-3292
Fax: (617)353-3924
Dr. Robert J. Hoffmeister, Dir.

Research Activities and Fields: American sign language acquisition, educational considerations of signed systems, bilingual approaches to educating children, and attitudes toward the deaf and how they relate to discrimination in society and education. **E-mail Address:** rhofr@acs.bu.edu.

★ 3591 ★ Brooklyn College of City University of New York Carleton Washburne Early Childhood Center
2900 Bedford Ave.
Brooklyn, NY 11210-2889
Phone: (718)951-5431
Fax: (718)951-4861
Dr. Carol Korn-Bursztyn, Dir.

Research Activities and Fields: Behavior and social development of normal and atypical children between ages of three and seven years. Maintains a laboratory school of 36 children from diverse backgrounds, which serves as a study center for faculty members and students of the College for investigations of educative environment, coping patterns, behavioral patterns, and the relationship between theory and practice. Children with handicapping conditions are included in the general population.

★ 3592 ★ Brooklyn College of City University of New York Speech and Hearing Center
Boylan Hall, Rm. 4400
Brooklyn, NY 11210
Phone: (718)951-5186
Dr. Oliver Bloodstein, Dir.

Research Activities and Fields: Normal communications and communication disorders, including studies of speech, language, and hearing.

★ 3593 ★ Center for Communicative Development, Inc.
2550 Beverly Blvd., Ste. 200
Los Angeles, CA 90057
Phone: (213)483-0943
Fax: (213)483-0701
Dr. Virginia McKinney, Dir.

Research Activities and Fields: Communication development and evaluation of deaf adults, emphasizing reading, writing, sign language, fingerspelling, speech, speech reading, and auditory training as applied to language and vocabulary development, reading comprehension, basic math (how to tell time and count money),

independent living skills, social awareness, vocational and social responsibilities, notewriting to enhance deaf/hearing person communication, typing, constructive use of leisure time, and community mobility.

★ 3594 ★ Central Institute for the Deaf
818 S. Euclid Ave.
St. Louis, MO 63110
Phone: (314)652-3200
Fax: (314)531-0030
Donald W. Nielsen, Dir.

Research Activities and Fields: Auditory communication and its disorders, including studies of hearing function, auditory physiology, sensory neuroscience, auditory biophysics and biomechanics, effects of noise, and regeneration in the auditory nervous system. Also performs clinical studies of speech and linguistics, communication in infants, characteristics of deaf speech, evaluation of cochlear implants in children, and audiology. Also engineers, designs, and evaluates instruments to evaluate and/or assist the deaf and the hard-of-hearing, and develops multimedia network communication systems with special applications for the deaf community.

★ 3595 ★ City University of New York Center for Research in Speech and Hearing Sciences
33 W. 42nd St.
New York, NY 10036
Phone: (212)642-2352
Fax: (212)642-2379
Dr. Irving Hochberg, Dir.

Research Activities and Fields: Programmable digital hearing aids, nonauditory sensory aids, speech perception of hearing impaired, rehabilitation strategies for the deaf, rehabilitation of cochlear implant patients, acoustic analysis of speech, electrophysiology, neurolinguistics of bilingualism, aging and dementia, and child language disorders. **Publications:** Annual Report.

★ 3596 ★ Cleveland Hearing and Speech Center
11206 Euclid Ave.
Cleveland, OH 44106
Phone: (216)231-8787
Fax: (216)231-7141
Bernard P. Henri, Ph.D., Exec.Dir.

Research Activities and Fields: Speech, language, and hearing disorders, Alzheimer's Disease, and slow progressive aphasia. **Formerly:** Cleveland Association for the Hard of Hearing.

★ 3597 ★ Deafness Research Foundation
9 E. 38th St.
New York, NY 10016
Phone: (212)684-6556
Fax: (212)779-2125
Charles D. Kimpel, Pres.

Research Activities and Fields: Causes, treatment, and prevention of deafness and other serious ear disorders, including studies of implants, deafness in the young and the elderly, middle ear infections, Meniere's disease, tinnitus (ringing in the ears), excessive noise, hair cell regeneration, genetics, and otoacoustic emissions.

★ 3598 ★ Eaton-Peabody Laboratory of Auditory Physiology
Massachusetts Eye & Ear Infirmary
243 Charles St.
Boston, MA 02114
Phone: (617)573-3745
Fax: (617)720-4408
Nelson Y.S. Kiang, Ph.D., Dir.

Research Activities and Fields: Vertebrate auditory system and auditory information processing, including ear-brain interactions in normal and pathologic hearing, anatomical and physiological studies on the auditory nerve and cochlear nucleus of animals, and evoked-potential studies in humans.

★ 3599 ★ Florida State University Communication Science Laboratory
College of Communication
432 Diffenbaugh
Tallahassee, FL 32306-4021
Phone: (904)644-8748
Fax: (904)644-0611
Dr. John Mayo, Dean

Research Activities and Fields: Speech disorders. **Formerly:** Speech Research Laboratory.

★ 3600 ★ Gallaudet University Center for Assessment & Demographic Studies
800 Florida Ave. NE
Washington, DC 20002
Phone: (202)651-5575
Fax: (202)651-5746
Dr. Thomas E. Allen, Dir.

Research Activities and Fields: Demographics, assessment, and education as they relate to deafness and deaf people. Conducts the Annual Survey of Deaf and Hard of Hearing Children and Youth, which generates data on the characteristics of deaf and hard of hearing children, the factors that influence their achievement, and the schools they attend. Performs secondary analyses of National Center for Health Statistics databases as they pertain to adults with hearing loss and enumerates services and opportunities in postsecondary programs for deaf and hard of hearing students. Develops assessment instruments for use with deaf children. **E-mail Address:** teallen@gallux.gallaudet.edu. **Formerly:** Office of Demographic Studies.

★ 3601 ★ Gallaudet University Center for Auditory and Speech Sciences (CASS)
Mary Thornberry Bldg., B10
800 Florida Ave. NE
Washington, DC 20002
Phone: (202)651-5347
Fax: (202)651-5774
Sally G. Revoile, Dir.

Research Activities and Fields: Develops new hearing tests that use speech sounds instead of pure tones to measure hearing loss and develops new speech training devices. Also evaluates wearable tactile receivers that represent speech sounds on the skin of the hearing impaired person and develops speech signal processing (via computer) to enhance these signals for the hearing-impaired. **Formerly:** Sensory Communication Research Laboratory (1987).

★ 3602 ★ Gallaudet University Center for Studies in Education and Human Development
800 Florida Ave. NE
Washington, DC 20002
Phone: (202)651-5206
Fax: (202)651-5458
Dr. Donald F. Moores, Dir.

Research Activities and Fields: Education and development of deaf people, including studies in teaching, learning and cognition, child development, parent-child interaction, classroom communication, reading, writing, mental health, signed English for the deaf, and school placement. **Publications:** Annual Report. **Formerly:** Formed through the consolidation of the Teaching and Assessment Studies Group, Learning and Cognition Studies Group, Child Development Studies Group, and Signed English Research Program.

★ 3603 ★ Gallaudet University Gallaudet Research Institute
800 Florida Ave. NE
Washington, DC 20002
Phone: (202)651-5400
Free: 800-451-8834
Fax: (202)651-5296
Dr. Michael A. Karchmer, Dean

Research Activities and Fields: Multidisciplinary research on topics concerning deafness, hearing, and hearing-impaired and deaf people, including speech and hearing science, child development, genetic counseling, language and culture, technology assessment, public policy, health science, education, demographics, psychology, sociology, linguistics, cultural anthropology, mental health, and rehabilitation engineering. Projects are carried out under eight groups: Center for Studies in Education and Human Development, Center for Assessment and Demographic Studies, Center for Auditory and Speech Sciences, Technology Assessment Program, Genetic Services Center, and the Culture and Communication Studies Program. Shares resources with two demonstration schools on campus and collaborates with universities worldwide, including Canada, Australia, Uruguay, Israel, Denmark, and England. **Publications:** Research at Gallaudet (newsletter, three times yearly); A Tradition of Discovery (annual report). **E-mail Address:** makarchmer@gallua.gallaudet.edu. **Formerly:** Graduate Studies and Research.

★ 3604 ★ Haskins Laboratories
270 Crown St.
New Haven, CT 06511
Phone: (203)865-6163
Fax: (203)865-8963
Dr. Carol A. Fowler, Pres.

Research Activities and Fields: Speech production and perception by humans and computers, motor control, and reading. **Publications:** Status Report on Speech Research (quarterly). **E-mail Address:** haskins@haskins.yale.edu.

Head and Neck Center
See: Entry 6045

★ 3605 ★ Hollins Communications Research Institute
PO Box 9737
Roanoke, VA 24020-1737
Phone: (703)362-6528
Fax: (703)362-6663
Ronald L. Webster, Ph.D., Dir.

Research Activities and Fields: Basic features of stuttering, behaviorally-based stuttering therapy, and variables that modify speech fluency in people who stutter and fluent speakers.

★ 3606 ★ House Ear Institute
2100 W. 3rd St., 5th Fl.
Los Angeles, CA 90057
Phone: (213)483-4431
Fax: (213)483-8789
James D. Boswell, Ch.Exec.Off.

Research Activities and Fields: Cause, treatment, and prevention of hearing and balance disorders, including investigations on cochlear implants and auditory prostheses, electrophysiology, electron microscopy, anatomy, and psychoacoustics. **Publications:** The Review (three per year); Annual Report; Parent to Parent Resources Catalog. **Formerly:** Ear Research Institute (1981).

★ 3607 ★ Houston Ear Research Foundation
7737 Southwest Fwy., Ste. 630
Houston, TX 77074
Phone: (713)771-9966
Free: 800-843-0807
Fax: (713)771-0546
Jan Gilden, Exec.Dir.

Research Activities and Fields: Aims to improve health care and education for deaf and hearing-impaired children. Provides funds for follow-up testing for recipients of cochlear implants. **Publications:** Newsletter (semi-annual).

★ 3608 ★ International Center for Hearing and Speech Research
52 Lomb Memorial Dr.
PO Box 9887
Rochester, NY 14623
Phone: (716)475-6403
Fax: (716)475-6677
Dr. Robert Frisina, Sr., Dir.

Research Activities and Fields: Prevention, early detection, diagnosis, and treatment of people with hearing and speech impairments.

★ 3609 ★ Kent State University Speech and Hearing Clinic
Kent, OH 44242
Phone: (216)672-2672
Mary Eleise Jones, Ph.D., Contact

Research Activities and Fields: Speech pathology and audiology, including staff specialties in infant, children's, and adult languages, stuttering, phonology, aural rehabilitation, and hearing aids.

★ 3610 ★ The Lexington Center, Inc.
Research Division
30th Ave. & 75th St.
Jackson Heights, NY 11370
Phone: (718)899-8800
Fax: (718)899-3433
Matthew H. Bakke, Dir. of Research

Research Activities and Fields: Deaf and hard-of-hearing populations. Develops and tests hearing aids and other assistive devices, as well as auditory diagnostic instruments. **Publications:** Newletter; Special Reports. **E-mail Address:** mhb@cunyvms1.gc.cuny.edu. **Formerly:** T.R.E.E. Division.

★ 3611 ★ Louisiana State University
Kresge Hearing Research Laboratory of
**   the South**
2020 Gravier St., Ste. A
New Orleans, LA 70112
Phone: (504)568-4785
Fax: (504)568-4460
Dr. Charles I. Berlin, Dir.

Research Activities and Fields: Auditory research, pharmacology, anatomy, psychophysics, molecular genetics, and audiology, including studies on cochlear implants, auditory evoked potentials, ultra-high frequency hearing, effects of hearing impairments on brain structure, temporal order in hearing, auditory processing of frequency-varying signals, perceptual skills in learning-disabled children, speech perception, cochlear emissions, and the role of chemical elements in hearing. **Formerly:** Succeeded the Communication Sciences Laboratory.

★ 3612 ★ Loyola University Chicago
Parmly Hearing Institute
6525 N. Sheridan Rd.
Chicago, IL 60626
Phone: (312)508-2710
Fax: (312)508-2719
Dr. William A. Yost, Dir.

Research Activities and Fields: Psychophysics, physiology, and anatomy of audition and investigation of sensory/perceptual processes, including studies on relations among sense/organ action, anatomy and physiology of afferent nervous system, cerebral sensory mechanisms, psychophysical characteristics of auditory system, application of theory of signal detectability to psychophysics, and detection and recognition of auditory signals in noise. **Publications:** Parmly Hearing Institute Annual Report. **E-mail Address:** wyost@luc.edu. **Formerly:** Formerly associated with Illinois Institute of Technology and known as Parmly Institute for Auditory Research.

Medical University of South Carolina
Vince Moseley Center for Children with
**   Developmental Disabilities**
See: Entry 4579

★ 3613 ★ Michigan State University
Artificial Language Laboratory
405 Computer Center
East Lansing, MI 48823
Phone: (517)353-5399
Fax: (517)353-4766
Dr. John B. Eulenberg, Dir.

Research Activities and Fields: Computer processing of formal linguistic structures. Conducts basic studies of speech analysis and synthesis and neurolinguistics and applied research on computer-based systems for persons who are blind and for persons with cerebral palsy and head injury. Develops physical, cognitive, and linguistic assessment systems for matching individuals with communication enhancement technology; develops voice output communication aids; studies design factors which affect efficiency, articulateness, fluency, and expressiveness of augmented communication; and investigates the process of successful customization and modular manufacture of communication systems. Collaborates with industry in the areas of product development, evaluation, field testing, and market research. **Publications:** *Communication Outlook*, an international quarterly magazine focusing on the techniques and technology of augmentative communication. **E-mail Address:** john@all.cps.msu.edu.

★ 3614 ★ New York Foundation for
**   Otologic Research**
920 Park Ave.
New York, NY 10021
Phone: (212)988-3100
Dr. Alan Austin Scheer, Dir.

Research Activities and Fields: Unsolved hearing problems, including otosclerosis, nerve deafness, Menieres disease, and other associated problems of dizziness and head noises. Analyzes electrical patterns of sound conduction and studies conduction of sound through the skin and dental nerves.

★ 3615 ★ Ohio State University
Otological Research Laboratories
4331 Univ. Hospitals Clinic
456 W. 10th Ave.
Columbus, OH 43210
Phone: (614)293-8103
Fax: (614)293-5506
Dr. Thomas F. DeMaria, Act.Dir.

Research Activities and Fields: Clinical and basic research in otology, including animal models for otitis media, acoustic trauma, morphological studies on the inner ear, and immunologic investigations of the middle and inner ear. Also studies the development of animal models for studying middle ear infection using microbiological, immunologic, morphologic and molecular biological methods, temporal bone histopathology (human and animal), electron microscopy of auditory and vestibular systems, pathogenesis of otitis media, and sensory transduction mechanism. **E-mail Address:** demaria.2@osu.edu.

★ 3616 ★ Ohio University
School of Hearing and Speech Sciences
Lindley Hall, Rm. 201
Athens, OH 45701
Phone: (614)593-1407
Fax: (614)593-0287
Dr. Edwin Leach, Dir.

Research Activities and Fields: Audiology, speech pathology, and speech science, including studies on oral vibro-tactile sensation and perception, surface electromyography, language, esophageal speech perception, diagnostics, pediatric audiology, computer applications, and psychoacoustics. Conducts clinical programs in speech pathology, diagnostics, infant screening, and clinical audiology. **Publications:** *Journal for Computer Users in Speech and Hearing* (semiannually). **Formerly:** Speech/Hearing Center.

★ 3617 ★ Oregon Health Sciences
**   University**
Oregon Hearing Research Center
3515 SW Veterans Hospital Rd.
Portland, OR 97201-2997
Phone: (503)494-8032
Fax: (503)494-5656
Jack A. Vernon, Ph.D., Dir.

Research Activities and Fields: Hearing problems, including clinical studies of ototoxicity, vestibular physiology, noise damage, anatomy of the ear, tinnitus, and interactions between various insults to the ear, through a multiple attack utilizing electrophysiological measures, behavioral measures, histological evaluations, and human psychophysics. **Formerly:** Kresge Hearing Research Laboratory (1986).

★ 3618 ★ Rochester Institute of
**   Technology**
National Technical Institute for the Deaf
Lyndon Baines Johnson Bldg.
52 Lomb Memorial Dr.
Rochester, NY 14623-5604
Phone: (716)475-6400
Dr. Marc Marschark, Dir.

Research Activities and Fields: Provides technical and professional education and training for deaf students; prepares a professional work force to serve deaf people; and examines the social, educational, and economic accommodation of deaf people, also the language, social, and cognitive functioning of deaf students. Operates three research departments: educational research and development, communication research, and postsecondary career studies and institutional research. **Publications:** *NTID Focus* (three times per year); *Catalog of Educational Resources* (annually). **E-mail Address:** memrtl@ritvax.isc.rit.edu.

★ 3619 ★ Speech Simulation Research
**   Foundation**
PO Box 824
Nassawadox, VA 23413
Phone: (804)442-2755
Monte Penney, Dir.

Research Activities and Fields: Human communication development related to tactile speech reception for people who are deaf or hard of hearing.

★ 3620 ★ State University of New York at
**   Buffalo**
Hearing Research Laboratory
215 Parker Hall
Buffalo, NY 14214
Phone: (716)829-2001
Fax: (716)829-2980
Dr. Richard Salvi, Dir.

Research Activities and Fields: Hearing, including effects of noise, effects of ototoxic drugs, and basic auditory processes.

★3621★ State University of New York at Buffalo
Speech-Language and Hearing Clinic
130 Park Hall Rd.
Buffalo, NY 14260
Phone: (716)645-3410
Fax: (716)645-2216
Gary J. Rentschler, Ph.D., Dir.

Research Activities and Fields: Audiology, speech and hearing sciences, speech/language pathology, speech perception and acoustics, and augmentative communication. **Publications:** *Journal of Speech/Hearing Research*; *Journal of Speech and Hearing Disorders*. **Formerly:** Speech and Hearing Clinic.

★3622★ State University of New York College at Plattsburgh
Auditory Research Laboratory
107 Beaumont
Plattsburgh, NY 12901
Phone: (518)564-7701
Fax: (518)564-7827
Dr. Roger P. Hamernik, Dir.

Research Activities and Fields: Pathology of hearing associated with noise, drugs, congenital birth defects, and disease processes.

Syracuse University
Special Education Programs
See: Entry 12751

★3623★ Temple University
Section of Audiology and Auditory Research
3440 Kresge W. Bldg.
N. Broad St.
Philadelphia, PA 19140
Phone: (215)221-3661
William Hal Martin, Ph.D., Dir.

Research Activities and Fields: Psychological and physiological acoustics, clinical research in audiology, clinical and basic research in evoked potentials, auditory and vestibular functioning, and human and animal experimentation in otology. **Formerly:** Audiology Section (1979).

★3624★ Temple University
Speech and Hearing Science Laboratories
13th & Cecil B. Moore Ave.
Philadelphia, PA 19122
Phone: (215)204-7543
Fax: (215)204-5954
Dr. Aquiles Iglesias, Chair

Research Activities and Fields: Speech and hearing science, including investigation of clinical functions of speech pathology and therapy. Conducts research in normal speech, language, and hearing, as well as studies of disordered speech, fluency, voice, language, and hearing. **Formerly:** Speech and Hearing Center.

U.S. Department of Defense
Armed Forces Institute of Pathology
Otolaryngic and Endocrine Pathology Department
Otolaryngic Pathology Division
See: Entry 10175

★3625★ U.S. Department of Health and Human Services
National Institute on Deafness and Other Communication Disorders
NIH Bldg. 31, Rm. 3C02
9000 Rockville Pike
Bethesda, MD 20892
Phone: (301)402-0900
Fax: (301)402-1590
James B. Snow, Jr., M.D., Director

Research Activities and Fields: Conducts and supports biomedical and behavioral research and research training on normal processes and disorders of hearing, balance, smell, taste, voice, speech, and language, including hearing and deafness, hearing loss, hearing impairment, tinnitus, presbycusis, Waardenburg syndrome, Usher syndrome, dizziness, Meniere's disease, vestibular system, smell and taste disorders, voice disorders, spasmodic dysphonia, vocal cord paralysis, stuttering, speech disorders, language disorders, and aphasia.

★3626★ U.S. Department of Health and Human Services
National Institute on Deafness and Other Communication Disorders
Division of Communication and Sciences Disorders
Executive Plaza S., Rm. 400B
6120 Executive Blvd.
Rockville, MD 20892
Phone: (301)496-1804
Fax: (301)402-6251
Dr. Ralph Naunton, Director

Research Activities and Fields: Division administers grants, contracts, and national research service awards for extramural research on communicative disorders and research training. Principal areas of research interest are diagnosis, treatment, and prevention of hearing, chemosensory, language, and speech disorders, including: 1) the prevention and early diagnosis of hearing impairments that may result from exposure to noise or ototoxic drugs; 2) the causes and treatment of tinnitus; 3) the normal function of the central nervous system and the relationship of the taste, smell, and touch senses to the early detection of systemic disease; 4) disorders such as stuttering, misarticulation, delayed language development, and phonatory disorders; 5) treatment of dysarthria and aphasia following neurological disease, stroke, and trauma; and 6) the neurophysiology of speech and the coordination of articulators in disordered speech production.

★3627★ U.S. Department of Health and Human Services
National Institute on Deafness and Other Communication Disorders
Division of Intramural Research
Audiology Unit
NIH Bldg. 10
9000 Rockville Pike
Bethesda, MD 20892
Phone: (301)496-5368
Fax: (301)402-0409
Anita Pikus, Chief

Research Activities and Fields: Initiates units' own and collaborative protocols, emphasizing hearing and auditory function in various genetic,

immunologic, or acquired conditions, including type 2 neurofibromatosis, Waardenburg syndrome, inherited metabolic degenerative disorders, non-syndromic hereditary hearing loss, and von-Hippel Lindau disease.

★3628★ U.S. Department of Health and Human Services
National Institute on Deafness and Other Communication Disorders
Division of Intramural Research
Laboratory of Molecular Biology
NIH Bldg. 36
9000 Rockville Pike
Bethesda, MD 20892
Phone: (301)496-2583
Fax: (301)480-3242
Jorgen Fex, M.D., Ph.D., Chief

Research Activities and Fields: Conducts multidisciplinary studies on the mechanisms of hearing, including hereditary deafness in humans using mice with genetic ear deficiencies as models.

★3629★ U.S. Department of Health and Human Services
National Institute on Deafness and Other Communication Disorders
Division of Intramural Research
Voice and Speech Section
NIH Bldg. 10, Rm. 5D38
9000 Rockville Pike
Bethesda, MD 20892
Phone: (301)496-9365
Fax: (301)480-0803
Christy L. Ludlow, Ph.D., Chief

Research Activities and Fields: Speech and voice studies, including the neurophysiological and biomechanical bases of normal speech and voice production, pathophysiology of idiopathic speech and voice disorders such as spasmodic dysphonia and stuttering, and medical and surgical approaches to treatment of these disorders. Investigates sensorimotor regulation of the laryngeal musculature; motion and electromyographic analyses of laryngeal functioning during speech, respiration, and swallowing; magnetic and electrical stimulation of the central and peripheral laryngeal nervous system; and new treatment approaches including botulinum toxin, medication trials in patients with stuttering disorders, and phonosurgery for voice disorders.

★3630★ U.S. Department of Health and Human Services
National Institute on Deafness and Other Communication Disorders
Extramural Activities Division
6120 Executive Blvd.
Rockville, MD 20850
Phone: (301)496-8693
Fax: (301)402-0104
Earleen Elkins, Ph.D., Acting Director

Research Activities and Fields: Supports research on communication sciences and disorders.

★3631★ **University of Alabama**
Speech and Hearing Center
Department of Communicative Disorders
Box 870242
Tuscaloosa, AL 35487-0242
Phone: (205)348-7131
Dr. Eugene B. Cooper, Chm.

Research Activities and Fields: Communication disorders, including clinical studies associated with graduate training in speech-language pathology and audiology. **E-mail Address:** ecooper@ua/vm.ua.edu.

★3632★ **University of Alabama at Birmingham**
Biocommunication Research Laboratory
VH503
Birmingham, AL 35294-0019
Phone: (205)934-4814
Fax: (205)934-7420
James Emil Flege, Head

Research Activities and Fields: Physiology, aerodynamics, acoustics, and perception of speech. Activities focus on basic physiology and acoustic studies of normal and abnormal speech learning. Experimental populations include hearing impaired, foreign dialect, and oral surgical patients. Specific research includes studies of temporomandibular joint functions and disorders, second-language speech acquisition, deaf speech, and neurogenic communication disorders. **Publications:** *Biocommunication Research Reports* (periodically).

University of Alabama at Birmingham
Civitan International Research Center/
 Alabama UAP
See: Entry 4586

★3633★ **University of Arkansas at Little Rock**
Rehabilitation Research and Training Center for Persons Who Are Deaf or Hard of Hearing
4601 W. Markham
Little Rock, AR 72205
Phone: (501)686-9691
Fax: (501)686-9698
Dr. Douglas Watson, Dir.

Research Activities and Fields: Rehabilitation of individuals who are deaf and hard of hearing, focusing on improving career preparation, entry, retention, and advancement of these individuals in the workplace. **Formerly:** Research & Training Center on Deafness & Hearing Impairment.

★3634★ **University of California, San Francisco**
Center on Deafness
3333 California St., Ste. 10
San Francisco, CA 94143-1208
Phone: (415)476-4980
Fax: (415)476-7113
Asa De Matteo, Ph.D., Act.Dir.

Research Activities and Fields: Mental health rehabilitation of individuals with deafness, including developmental studies and educational interventions, mental health studies and clinical interventions, interpreter studies and training, and studies on the psychological effects of adult-onset hearing impairment and appropriate interventions. **Publications:** Brochure Series (summaries of research and clinical findings); Newsletter.

★3635★ **University of Chicago**
Temporal Bone Laboratory for Ear Research
5841 S. Maryland Ave., MC 1035
Chicago, IL 60637
Phone: (312)702-6686
Fax: (312)702-6809
Dr. Raul Hinojosa, Dir.

Research Activities and Fields: Pathological basis for impairment of hearing and deafness and animal research on auditory and vestibular systems. **Formerly:** Continuing program of former Midwestern Temporal Bone Bank Center.

★3636★ **University of Colorado at Boulder**
Communication Disorders Clinic
Communication Disorders & Speech Science Dept.
CB 409
Boulder, CO 80309
Phone: (303)492-5375
Fax: (303)492-2374
Susan M. Moore, Dir.

Research Activities and Fields: Evaluation and treatment of speech, language, learning, and hearing disorders. **Formerly:** Speech and Hearing Clinic.

★3637★ **University of Maine**
Conley Speech and Hearing Center
L-5 N. Stevans Hall
Orono, ME 04469
Phone: (207)486-7071
Fax: (207)581-1953
Dr. John M. Pettit, Coord.

Research Activities and Fields: Speech disorders of adults and children, including aphasia, voice disorders, acquisition of language by children, stuttering, articulation disorders, apraxia, and interpersonal skills in clinical processes.

★3638★ **University of Memphis**
Center for Research Initiatives and Strategies for the Communicatively Impaired (CRISCI)
807 Jefferson Ave.
Memphis, TN 38105
Phone: (901)678-5800
Fax: (901)525-1282
Maurice I. Mendel, Dir.

Research Activities and Fields: Speech and hearing, especially high technology applications to habilitation and rehabilitation of the communicatively impaired. Contributes to master's and doctoral programs in speech and hearing sciences. **Publications:** Reports.

★3639★ **University of Michigan**
Communicative Disorders Clinic
1111 E. Catherine St.
Ann Arbor, MI 48109-2054
Phone: (313)764-8440
Fax: (313)747-2489
Dr. Holly Craig, Dir.

Research Activities and Fields: Speech, language, and hearing disorders, including studies of clinical problems in child language development, aphasia, and stuttering. **Formerly:** Speech and Hearing Science Research Laboratories merged with Communicative Disorders Clinic, Shady Trails Camp.

★3640★ **University of Michigan**
Kresge Hearing Research Institute
1301 E. Ann St., Rm. 5032
Ann Arbor, MI 48109-0506
Phone: (313)764-8111
Fax: (313)764-0014
Josef M. Miller, Ph.D., Dir.

Research Activities and Fields: Auditory physiology and pathology, including studies on the reception, coding and processing of complex speech signals by the auditory system, transduction processes of the inner ear, cochlear blood flow and inner ear metabolism, development of cochlear prostheses and appropriate speech processor schemes, immune mediated hearing loss, the effects of age and environmental stress factors on hearing, biochemistry and motility of hair cells, afferent and efferent transmitters of the inner ear, psychophysics of hearing in normal individuals, and immunology and immune systems related to squamous cell carcinoma. **E-mail Address:** DONNA_REED@UMICHUM.BITNET.

★3641★ **University of Michigan**
Kresge Hearing Research Institute
Auditory Anatomy Laboratory
1301 E. Ann St.
Ann Arbor, MI 48109-0506
Phone: (313)763-0060
Fax: (313)764-0014
Dr. Richard Altschuler, Dir.

Research Activities and Fields: Structure of the damaged ear and damage to the auditory structures of the brain due to noise, drugs, or disease. Evaluates the risks of new otologic treatments, surgeries, and devices, including the cochlear prosthesis; identifies neurotransmitters in the cochlea and auditory brainstem; and examines auditory pathways. **Formerly:** Kresge Hearing Research Institute, Otopathology Laboratory.

★3642★ **University of Michigan**
Kresge Hearing Research Institute
Auditory Prosthesis Animal Psychophysics Laboratory
Box 0506
Ann Arbor, MI 48109
Phone: (313)763-2292
Fax: (313)764-0014
Dr. Bryan Pfingst, Dir.

Research Activities and Fields: Restoration of hearing in profoundly deaf persons. Studies the processing of speech in the brain and encoding of speech in the auditory system, and uses hearing tests with rhesus monkeys, humans, and other animals to design and develop bionic ear implants, also called cochlear prostheses.

★3643★ **University of Michigan**
Kresge Hearing Research Institute
Biochemistry Laboratory

1301 E. Ann St.
Ann Arbor, MI 48109-0506
Phone: (313)763-3572
Fax: (313)764-0014
Jochen Schacht, Dir.

Research Activities and Fields: Cellular and molecular mechanisms of hearing and deafness. Investigates the normal biochemical events that occur in cells of the inner ear when hearing and that are impaired in hearing disorders such as those induced by noise and certain drugs. Studies methods for ameliorating hearing loss.

★3644★ University of Michigan
Kresge Hearing Research Institute
Electrophysiology Laboratory
1301 E. Ann St.
Ann Arbor, MI 48109-0506
Phone: (313)763-8110
Fax: (313)764-0014
Dr. Alfred Nuttall, Dir.

Research Activities and Fields: Electrical responses to sound in the inner ear. Studies the response of individual receptor cells, or hair cells, of one ear while the other ear is acoustically or electrically stimulated. Also investigates the relationship between hearing loss and hair cell loss.

★3645★ University of Michigan
Kresge Hearing Research Institute
Microcirculation Laboratory
1301 E. Ann St.
Ann Arbor, MI 48109
Phone: (313)763-4116
Dr. Alfred Nuttall, Dir.

Research Activities and Fields: Studies blood flow in the cochlea using fluorescent red blood cells and conducts studies of the ear using a laser doppler.

★3646★ University of Michigan
Kresge Hearing Research Institute
Neuropharmacology Laboratory
1301 E. Ann St.
Ann Arbor, MI 48109-0506
Phone: (313)764-8111
Fax: (313)764-0014
Dr. Josef Miller, Dir.

Research Activities and Fields: Studies the chemical substances (transmitters), used in intercellular communication which mediate the transduction and encoding of sounds from the inner ear to the auditory structures of the brain. Also studies auditory physiology, psychophysics, molecular biology and genetics, clinical investigations of auditory function. **E-mail Address:** joe__miller@um.cc.umich.edu.

★3647★ University of Michigan
Kresge Hearing Research Institute
Neurophysiology and Biophysics
Laboratory
1301 E. Ann St.
Ann Arbor, MI 48109
Phone: (313)763-5417
Fax: (313)764-0014
Dr. Ben Clopton, Dir.

Research Activities and Fields: Studies the neural and electrical encoding of various auditory stimuli in the brain to determine how the brain aids in hearing. Projects include synthesis of artificial speech and other signals, computer analysis of electrically recorded neural signals, and histological preparations of sections.

★3648★ University of Montreal
Acoustics Group
Faculte de medecine
Ecole d'orthophonie et d'audiologie
C.P. 6128, Succursale A Centre-Ville
Montreal, PQ, Canada H3C 3J7
Phone: (514)343-7301
Fax: (514)343-5740
Prof. Raymond Hetu, Dir.

Research Activities and Fields: Noise and its effect on health and safety, effects of occupational hearing loss, occupational and psychosocial rehabilitation of individuals with hearing loss, audiological rehabilitation of individuals with acquired hearing loss, noise as a nuisance, cultural aspects of acquired hearing loss, and sound warning signal recognition in industrial rooms. **E-mail Address:** hetur@ere.umontreal.ca.

★3649★ University of Nebraska—Lincoln
Barkley Memorial Center
Barkley Center 301
Lincoln, NE 68583-0738
Phone: (402)472-2145
Fax: (402)472-7697
John Bernthal, Dir.

Research Activities and Fields: Communication deficiency and disorder research, including study of brain stem audiometry; fluency, motor speech disorders, phonological, acquisition of sign language, speech perception, language and learning disorders; behavioral and hearing impairment; auditory perception; augmentative and alternative communication; and use of paraprofessionals in special education. **E-mail Address:** bernthal@unlinfo.unl.edu.

★3650★ University of Nevada, Reno
Speech and Language Pathology and
Audiology Department
Redfield Bldg. 152
Reno, NV 89557
Phone: (702)784-4887
Fax: (702)784-4095
Dr. Stephen C. McFarlane, Chm.

Research Activities and Fields: Communication disorders, rehabilitation of children and adults who have speech, language, and hearing disorders, and prevention of such disorders. **Formerly:** Speech and Hearing Clinic.

★3651★ University of North Carolina at
Chapel Hill
Division of Speech and Hearing Sciences
Medical School, Wing D
CB 7190
Chapel Hill, NC 27599-7190
Phone: (919)966-1006
Fax: (919)966-3678
Dr. Jackson Roush, Dir.

Research Activities and Fields: Basic and clinical studies in speech and hearing as part of the overall training, research, and clinical services missions of the Division.

★3652★ University of Oklahoma
Keys Speech and Hearing Center
PO Box 26901
Oklahoma City, OK 73190
Phone: (405)271-4214
Fax: (405)271-3360
Dr. O. Ray Kling, Interim Dir.

Research Activities and Fields: Loudness and acoustic reflex, temporal integration and acoustic reflex, critical bands measured with pulsation pattern psychophysical technique, sensory scaling, absolute thresholds for frequency modulated signals, bone conduction vibrator calibration, bone conduction speech audiometry, intelligibility of distorted speech, respiration audiometry, electrocochleography, brain stem auditory-evoked responses, acoustic correlates of abnormal vocal quality, aerodynamics of voice production, phonemic and morphologic studies of language of the communicatively impaired, and assessment of receptive and expressive language abilities.

★3653★ University of Quebec at Montreal
Cognitive Neuroscience Laboratory
PB 8888, Sta. Centre-Ville
Montreal, PQ, Canada H3C 3P8
Phone: (514)987-4445
Fax: (514)987-8952
Henri Cohen, Ph.D., Dir.

Research Activities and Fields: Cognitive neuroscience, including movement disorders and cerebral bases of speech, language, attention, and memory. Also performs speech analysis and modeling localization of electroencephalogram (EEG) sources. **E-mail Address:** cohen.henri@ugam.ca.

★3654★ University of Texas at Dallas
Callier Center for Communication
Disorders
1966 Inwood Rd.
Dallas, TX 75235
Phone: (214)905-3000
Fax: (214)905-3022
Dr. Ross J. Roeser, Dir.

Research Activities and Fields: Behavioral, electrophysiological, and anatomical studies of audition; behavioral and electrophysiological studies of normal and disordered speech production and perception; evoked potential and brain mapping; the linguistic and cognitive abilities of persons with aphasia and other neurogenic speech and language impairments; language development of children with chronic otitis media; development and assessment of communicative abilities in children with multiple handicaps; vibrotactile aids; and aural rehabilitation.

★3655★ University of Texas
Southwestern Medical Center at Dallas
Communicative and Vestibular Disorder
Laboratory
Dept. of Otorhinolaryngology
5323 Harry Hines Blvd.
Dallas, TX 75235
Phone: (214)648-4757
Fax: (214)648-8263
Wende Yellin, Dir.

Research Activities and Fields: Dizziness, vertigo, gait and balance disorders and inner ear fluid disorders. **Formerly:** Audiovestibular Laboratory.

★3656★ University of Tulsa
Mary K. Chapman Center for
Communicative Disorders
600 S. College
Tulsa, OK 74104-3189
Phone: (918)631-2504
Fax: (918)631-2133
John M. Christensen, Ph.D., Dir.

Research Activities and Fields: Communication disorders, including laryngectomy and speech, and language and hearing problems. Also conducts hearing aid tests.

★3657★ University of Virginia
Communication Disorders Program
132 Emmet St.
PO Box 9022
Charlottesville, VA 22906-9022
Phone: (804)924-7107
Fax: (804)924-4621
Dr. Robert E. Novak, Dir.

Research Activities and Fields: Speech and language pathology, audiology, early detection in infant speech/language/hearing disorders, education of the deaf, and speech and hearing science, including computer applications to communications disorders treatment. Supervises doctoral research in these fields and sponsors meetings of interest to speech and language pathologists, audiologists, and educators of the hearing impaired. **E-mail Address:** ren3f@virginia.edu. **Formerly:** Speech and Hearing Center.

★3658★ University of Washington
Department of Speech and Hearing
Sciences
1417 NE 42nd St., JG-15
Seattle, WA 98195
Phone: (206)685-7400
Fax: (206)543-1093
Dr. Patricia K. Kuhl, Chair

Research Activities and Fields: Communication sciences and disorders, including both theoretical and clinical studies related to language, speech, and hearing. Projects concern early language development in children, auditory abilities in infants, speech perception in infants and primates, psychoacoustics, speech physiology, and voice production and disorders. **Publications:** Operates a speech and hearing clinic. **E-mail Address:** pkkuhl@u.washington.edu. **Formerly:** Outgrowth of former Program in Speech Pathology and Audiology.

★3659★ University of Wisconsin
Auditory Physiology Center
Dept. of Neurophysiology
MSC Rm. 275
1300 University Ave.
Madison, WI 53706-1532
Phone: (608)262-0818
Fax: (608)265-3500
Dr. John Brugge, Dir.

Research Activities and Fields: Auditory research at the systems, cellular, and molecular levels.

University of Wisconsin—Madison
Trace Research and Development Center
See: Entry 4600

★3660★ Yeshiva University
Institute of Communication Disorders
c/o Montefiore Medical Center
Dept. ENT, Gold Zone, Ste. 100
111 E. 210th St.
Bronx, NY 10467
Phone: (718)920-2991
Fax: (718)405-9014
Robert J. Ruben, M.D., Chm.

Research Activities and Fields: Studies include communicative disorders, including hearing, listening, voice, speech, and language studies; molecular developmental biology; molecular genetics; the synergy of culture and disease; morbidity; genetic studies; and genetics of communication disorders. **E-mail Address:** ruben@aecom.yu.edu.

Chapter 17
Death & Dying

Foundations & Other Funding Organizations

Private Foundations

Arthur Vining Davis Foundations
See: Entry 52

Eugene B. Casey Foundation
See: Entry 172

Perkins-Prothro Foundation
See: Entry 425

Corporate Foundations

First Maryland Foundation
See: Entry 6396

Fleet Bank of Upstate New York Foundation Trust
See: Entry 691

Medical & Allied Health Schools

Mortuary Science

The following colleges and programs in funeral service education and mortuary science are accredited by the American Board of Funeral Service Education, 13 Gurnet Rd., #316, PO Box 1305, Brunswick, ME 04011, (207) 798-5801.

Alabama

★3661★ **Bishop State Community College**
Department of Mortuary Science
351 N. Broad St.
Mobile, AL 36603-5898
Phone: (334)690-6872

★3662★ **Jefferson State Community College**
Funeral Service Education Program
2601 Carson Rd.
Birmingham, AL 35215
Phone: (205)856-7844
Fax: (205)853-0340

California

★3663★ **Cypress College**
Mortuary Science Department
9200 Valley View St.
Cypress, CA 90630
Phone: (714)826-1131
Fax: (714)826-7972

★3664★ **San Francisco College of Mortuary Science**
1598 Dolores St. at 29th
San Francisco, CA 94110
Phone: (415)824-1313
Fax: (415)824-1390

Connecticut

★3665★ **Briarwood College**
Department of Mortuary Science
2279 Mt. Vernon Rd.
Southington, CT 06489
Phone: (203)628-4751
Fax: (203)628-6444

District of Columbia

★3666★ **University of the District of Columbia**
Mortuary Science Department
Van Ness Campus
4200 Connecticut Ave. NW, MB4407
Washington, DC 20008
Phone: (202)274-5155

Florida

★3667★ **Lynn University**
Institute for Funeral Service Education
3601 N. Military Trail
Boca Raton, FL 33431-9990
Phone: (407)994-0770
Fax: (407)241-3552

★3668★ **Miami-Dade Community College**
W.L. Philbrick School of Funeral Sciences
11380 NW 27th Ave.
Miami, FL 33167
Phone: (305)237-1245
Fax: (305)237-1620

★3669★ **St. Petersburg Junior College**
Funeral Services Program
PO Box 13489
St. Petersburg, FL 33733-3489
Phone: (813)341-3781
Fax: (813)341-3770

Georgia

★3670★ **Gupton-Jones College of Funeral Service**
5141 Snapfinger Woods Dr.
Decatur, GA 30035-4022
Phone: (404)593-2257
Fax: (404)593-1891

Illinois

★3671★ **Malcolm X College**
Department of Mortuary Science
1900 W. Van Buren St.
Chicago, IL 60612
Phone: (312)850-7409
Fax: (312)942-2470

★3672★ **Southern Illinois University at Carbondale**
Mortuary Science and Funeral Service Program
Carbondale, IL 62901
Phone: (618)453-7214
Fax: (618)453-7286

★3673★ **Worsham College of Mortuary Science**
495 Northgate Pkwy.
Wheeling, IL 60090-2646
Phone: (708)808-8444
Fax: (708)808-8493

Indiana

★ 3674 ★ Mid-America College of Funeral Service
3111 Hamburg Pike
Jeffersonville, IN 47130
Phone: (812)288-8878
Fax: (812)288-5942

★ 3675 ★ Vincennes University
Funeral Service Education Program
N. 1st St.
Vincennes, IN 47591
Phone: (812)885-5469

Kansas

★ 3676 ★ Kansas City, Kansas Community College
Mortuary Science Department
7250 State Ave.
Kansas City, KS 66112
Phone: (913)596-9607
Fax: (913)596-9606

Louisiana

★ 3677 ★ Delgado Community College
Department of Funeral Service Education
City Park Campus
615 City Park Ave.
New Orleans, LA 70119-4399
Phone: (504)483-4014
Fax: (504)483-4577

Maryland

★ 3678 ★ Catonsville Community College
Mortuary Science Program
800 S. Rolling Rd.
Catonsville, MD 21228
Phone: (410)455-4162
Fax: (410)455-4411

Massachusetts

★ 3679 ★ Mount Ida College
New England Institute of Applied Arts and Sciences
Funeral Service Education Program
777 Dedham St.
Newton Centre, MA 02159
Phone: (617)928-4711
Fax: (617)928-4714

Michigan

★ 3680 ★ Wayne State University
Department of Mortuary Science
627 W. Alexandrine
Detroit, MI 48201
Phone: (313)577-2050
Fax: (313)577-4456

Minnesota

★ 3681 ★ University of Minnesota
Program of Mortuary Science
Box 740, UMHC
Harvard and E. River Rd.
Minneapolis, MN 55455
Phone: (612)624-6464
Fax: (612)624-8118

Mississippi

★ 3682 ★ East Mississippi Community College
Funeral Service Technology Program
Scooba, MS 39358
Phone: (601)476-8442
Fax: (601)476-5618

★ 3683 ★ Northwest Mississippi Community College
Funeral Service Technology Program
Desoto Center
Southaven, MS 38671
Phone: (601)342-1570
Fax: (601)342-5686

Missouri

★ 3684 ★ St. Louis Community College at Forest Park
Department of Funeral Service Education
5600 Oakland Ave.
St. Louis, MO 63110
Phone: (314)644-9327
Fax: (314)644-9752

New Jersey

★ 3685 ★ Mercer County Community College
Funeral Service Curriculum
1200 Old Trenton Rd.
PO Box B
Trenton, NJ 08690
Phone: (609)586-4800
Fax: (609)890-6338

New York

★ 3686 ★ American Academy McAllister Institute of Funeral Service, Inc.
450 W. 56th St.
New York, NY 10019
Phone: (212)757-1190
Fax: (212)765-5923

★ 3687 ★ Hudson Valley Community College
Mortuary Science Department
80 Vanderburgh Ave.
Troy, NY 12180
Phone: (518)270-7113
Fax: (518)270-7542

★ 3688 ★ Nassau Community College
Mortuary Science Department
Garden City, NY 11530
Phone: (516)572-7277

★ 3689 ★ Simmons Institute of Funeral Service
1828 South Ave.
Syracuse, NY 13207
Phone: (315)475-5142
Fax: (315)475-3817

★ 3690 ★ State University of New York College of Technology at Canton
Mortuary Science Program
Canton, NY 13617
Phone: (315)386-7407

North Carolina

★ 3691 ★ Fayetteville Technical Community College
Funeral Service Education Department
PO Box 35236
Fayetteville, NC 28303
Phone: (910)678-8301
Fax: (910)484-6600

Ohio

★ 3692 ★ Cincinnati College of Mortuary Science
Cohen Center
3860 Pacific Ave.
Cincinnati, OH 45207-1033
Phone: (513)745-3631
Fax: (513)745-1909

Oklahoma

★ 3693 ★ University of Central Oklahoma
Department of Funeral Service Education
Edmond, OK 73034-0186
Phone: (405)341-2980

Oregon

★ 3694 ★ Mt. Hood Community College
Department of Funeral Service Education
26000 SE Stark St.
Gresham, OR 97030
Phone: (503)667-7363
Fax: (503)667-7389

Pennsylvania

★ 3695 ★ Northhampton Community College
Department of Funeral Service Education
3835 Green Pond Rd.
Bethlehem, PA 18017
Phone: (215)861-5388
Fax: (215)861-4581

★ 3696 ★ Pittsburgh Institute of Mortuary Science
5808 Baum Blvd.
Pittsburgh, PA 15206
Phone: (412)362-8500
Fax: (412)362-1684

Tennessee

★3697★ **John A. Gupton College**
Funeral Service Education Program
1616 Church St.
Nashville, TN 37203
Phone: (615)327-3927
Fax: (615)321-4518

Texas

★3698★ **Commonwealth Institute of**
Funeral Service
415 Barren Springs
Houston, TX 77090
Phone: (713)873-0262
Fax: (713)873-5232

★3699★ **Dallas Institute of Funeral**
Service
3909 S. Buckner Blvd.
Dallas, TX 75227
Phone: (214)388-5466
Fax: (214)388-0316

★3700★ **San Antonio College**
Mortuary Science Program
1300 San Pedro Ave., NTC 212
San Antonio, TX 78212-4299
Phone: (210)733-2905
Fax: (210)733-2907

Virginia

★3701★ **John Tyler Community College**
Funeral Service Program
Chester, VA 23831
Phone: (804)796-4119
Fax: (804)796-4163

Wisconsin

★3702★ **Milwaukee Area Technical**
College
Funeral Service Department
West Campus
1200 S. 71st St.
West Allis, WI 53214
Phone: (414)456-5319
Fax: (414)456-5360

★3703★ **Milwaukee Area Technical**
College
Funeral Service Department
West Campus
1200 S. 71st St.
West Allis, WI 53214
Phone: (414)456-5319
Fax: (414)456-5360

National & International Organizations

★3704★ **Alcor Life Extension Foundation**
(ALEF)
7895 E. Acoma Dr., Ste. 110
Scottsdale, AZ 85260-6916
Phone: (602)922-9013
Free: 800-367-2228
Fax: (602)922-9027
Stephen W. Bridge, Pres.

Founded: 1972. **Members:** 540. **Regional Groups:** 13. **Description:** Individuals who have arranged to be cryonically suspended following their deaths. (Cryonics is the process of preserving clinically dead people at ultra-low temperatures in hopes of returning them to life and health when medicine has become more sophisticated.) Objective is to extend indefinitely the lives of members. Offers a comprehensive program of cryonic suspension services. Currently has 27 members in suspension; they are being maintained in liquid nitrogen. Conducts cryobiological research. Sponsors high school outreach programs on cryonics and aging research. Provides information on experimental life extension drugs and techniques. Maintains speakers' bureau. **Publications:** *Alcor Phoenix*, 8/year. Newsletter. *Price:* $20/year in the U.S.; $25/year in Canada and Mexico; $30/year in all other countries. • *Cryonics*, quarterly. Magazine. Covers cryonics, life extension, and immortality. *Price:* $15/year in the U.S.; $20/year in Canada and Mexico; $25/year overseas. • *Cryonics: Reaching for Tomorrow*, periodic. Booklet. *Price:* $8.95. **Also Known As:** Alcor Foundation.

★3705★ **American Board of Funeral**
Service Education (ABFSE)
PO Box 1305
Brunswick, ME 04011
Phone: (207)798-5801
Fax: (207)798-5988
Dr. Gordon S. Bigelow, Exec.Dir.

Founded: 1946. **Members:** 48. **Description:** Representatives from National Funeral Directors Association and Conference of Funeral Service Examining Boards of the United States; university and college program representatives and public members. Seeks to: formulate and enforce rules and regulations setting up standards concerning the schools and colleges teaching mortuary science; accredit schools and colleges of mortuary science. Sponsors the National Scholarship for Funeral Service program to provide capable young men and women studying in the field with financial assistance. Compiles statistics. **Publications:** *Accredited Colleges of Mortuary Science*, periodic. • *Directory of Accredited College Programs in Mortuary Science and Committees of the American Board of Funeral Service Education*, annual. Directory. Contains listings of member programs,officers, and committees of the Board. *Price:* Free. • *National Scholarships for Funeral Service*, periodic. **Formerly:** (1959) Joint Committee on Mortuary Education.

★3706★ **American Cryonics Society (ACS)**
PO Box 1509
Cupertino, CA 95015
Phone: (408)734-4200
Free: 800-523-2001
Fax: (408)734-4441
Jim Yount, Pres.

Founded: 1969. **Description:** Individuals interested in life extension through cryonics (the practice of freezing a clinically dead human in hopes of bringing the person back to life when resuscitation or reconstruction is possible). Promotes education and provides information about cryonic suspension, suspended animation, and low-temperature medicine. Enables individuals to arrange for their own cryonic suspension. Sponsors research into suspended animation, life extension sciences, and low temperature medicine. Conducts programs to freeze tissue samples from endangered species for possible future cloning. Maintains library; operates speakers' bureau; conducts charitable programs. **Publications:** *American Cryonics*, semiannual. Journal. • *American Cryonics News*, bimonthly. Newsletter. Covers cryonics and life extension. Includes calendar of events and research reports. *Price:* Included in membership dues; $35/year for nonmembers. • *The Immortalist*, monthly. Contains articles on cryonics, health, aging research, and science. **Formerly:** (1985) Bay Area Cryonics Society.

★3707★ **American Institute of Life**
Threatening Illness and Loss (FT)
630 W. 168th St.
New York, NY 10032
Phone: (212)928-2066
Maxine Lazarus, Admin.

Founded: 1967. **Members:** 400. **Description:** Health, theology, psychology, and social science professionals devoted to scientific and humanistic inquiries into death, loss, grief, and bereavement. Promotes improved psychosocial and medical care for critically ill and dying patients and assistance for their families. Stimulates and coordinates professional, educational, and research programs concerned with mortality and the management of grief. Maintains research programs, speakers' bureau, biographical archives, and library. **Publications:** *Advances in Thanatology*, quarterly. • *Archives of the Foundation of Thanatology*, quarterly. • *Loss, Grief, and Care*. • *National Directory*, periodic. Journal. • *Thanatology Abstracts*, annual. • *Thanatology News*, periodic. Also publishes books. **Formerly:** (1991) Foundation of Thanatology.

★3708★ **Association for Death Education**
and Counseling (ADEC)
638 Prospect Ave.
Hartford, CT 06105-4298
Phone: (203)232-4825
Fax: (203)232-0819
M. Suzanne C. Berry, Mng.Dir.

Founded: 1976. **Members:** 1,672. **Description:** Individuals and institutions interested in responsible and effective death education and counseling. Goals are: to upgrade the quality of death education and patient care in hospitals, residential care facilities, churches, schools, community organizations, and government facilities; to upgrade the quality of counseling in the areas of death, dying, and bereavement. Formulates and enforces codes of ethics and certifies death educators and counselors. Prepares and distributes educational materials; conducts workshops and conferences to improve the lifestyle of the dying and their survivors. **Publications:** *ADEC Directory*, annual. Directory. *Price:* Included in membership dues. • *Conference Proceedings*, annual. • Directory, annual. • *Forum Newsletter*, 6/year. Newsletter. Includes book reviews and calendar of events. *Price:* Included in membership dues. • *New Directions in Death Education and Counseling.* **Formerly:** (1986) Forum for Death Education and Counseling.

Association of SIDS Program Professionals (ASPP)
See: Entry 3190

★3709★ Center for the Rights of the Terminally Ill (CRTI)
PO Box 54246
Hurst, TX 76054-2064
Phone: (817)656-5143
Julie A. Grimstad, Exec.Dir.

Founded: 1986. **State Groups:** 3. **Description:** Provides information to patients, students, physicians, nurses, attorneys, pro-life organizations, and disability rights groups and other interested persons. Seeks to: secure for the elderly, the handicapped, and the sick and dying the right to competent, professional, compassionate, and ethical health care; oppose euthanasia, assisted suicide, and abortion; promote a climate of public opinion that recognizes the right of all people to be treated with respect and dignity regardless of age, disability, injury, disease, or illness. Engages in charitable, and literary activities and projects to improve and advance personal responsibility for human life and provide information to the public on euthanasia and related subjects. Develops materials and conducts educational programs designed to depict the humanity of all individuals and to raise awareness of the rights of the ill. Opposes "Living Will" legislation as unneccessary and dangerous; works to alert the public of the dangers of Living Will laws and other legislation which CRTI believes may adversely affect medical care and treatment. (A Living Will is a declaration or directive instructing a physician to withhold or discontinue medical treatment from the signer if that individual is terminally ill or irreversibly unconscious, and unable to make decisions.) Promotes a federal conscience clause law that would allow health care personnel to decline to perform any act of omission or commission that would cause or hasten the death of a patient. Offers information to patients and the public about patients rights. Operates speakers' bureau. **Publications:** *Can Cancer Pain Be Relieved?*. Booklet. • *CRTI Report*, quarterly. Newsletter. Includes commentaries and legislative and judicial updates. *Price:* $15/year. • *Hard Truth*. Pamphlets. • *Living Will Vs. Patient Self-Protection Document.* • *Living Wills: Unnecessary, Counterproductive, Dangerous.* • *Patient Self-Protection Document: An Advance Directive.* • *Suffering: A Key to the Meaning of Life.* Booklet.

★3710★ Choice in Dying—The National Council for the Right to Die (CID)
200 Varick St., 10th Fl.
New York, NY 10014-4810
Phone: (212)366-5540
Free: 800-989-WILL
Fax: (212)366-5337
Karen Orloff Kaplan, Sc.D, Exec.Dir.

Founded: 1991. **Members:** 160,000. **Description:** Seeks to serve the needs of dying patients and their families. Advocates for the right of patients to participate fully in decisions about their medical treatment at the end of their lives. Provides state-specific advance directive documents, including living wills and durable powers of attorney for health care, for directing end of life healthcare. (A living will allows individuals to state their wishes about medical treatment at the end of life; a durable power of attorney for healthcare is a legal document that allows individuals to appoint someone else to make medical decisions for them if they become incapacitated.) Will send one free, state-specific advance directive to individuals. Offers free public and professional education and counseling about the preparation and use of advance directives. Sponsors specialized education programs. Maintains speakers' bureau. **Publications:** *Advance Directive Protocols and the Patient Self-Determination Act.* Booklet. *Price:* $52. • *Advance Directives and Community Education.* *Price:* $25. • *Advance Directives and End-of-Life Decisions.* *Price:* $5.95/copy. • *Artificial Nutrition/Hydration.* *Price:* $5.95/copy. • Brochures. • *CHOICES: The Newsletter of Choice in Dying.* Newsletter. *Price:* $65. • *Dying at Home.* *Price:* $5.95/copy. • *Medical Treatments and Your Living Will.* *Price:* $5.95/copy. • Pamphlets. • *State Document with Guide Book.* *Price:* $5/copy. • Videos. • *You and Your Choices, Advance Directives.* *Price:* $5.95/copy.

★3711★ Conference of Funeral Service Examining Boards of the United States (CFSEB)
2404 Washington Blvd., Ste. 1000
Ogden, UT 84401
Phone: (801)392-7771
Fax: (801)392-7773
Charles W. Lindauist, Contact

Founded: 1929. **Members:** 130. **Description:** State licensing agencies (boards of health and departments of mortuary sciences) who govern the licensure of embalmers and funeral directors in the U.S. and in Ontario, Canada; membership includes executive secretaries and members of these boards. Accredited schools and colleges of mortuary science are associate members. Studies and recommends educational standards; examines and accredits embalming schools and colleges; cooperates in obtaining uniformity of rules and regulations governing state boards. Compiles and makes available to all member state boards and licensing agencies a standard examination to use in testing applicants. Participates in the American Board of Funeral Service Education to create maintain professional standards for schools and colleges. Maintains speakers' bureau and compiles statistics. **Publications:** Directory, annual. • *National Board Examination Brochure.* • *Proceedings of Convention*, annual.

Embalming Chemical Manufacturers Association (ECMA)
See: Entry 5842

★3712★ First Sunday (FS)
c/o Pope John XXIII Hospitality House
3977 2nd Ave.
Detroit, MI 48201
Phone: (313)832-4357
Fax: (313)965-4453
Rev. Russell Kohler, Advisor

Founded: 1974. **Members:** 200. **Description:** Couples who have experienced the death of a child and who wish to join with other couples as they make their individual and family adjustments. Seeks to help couples understand their many grief reactions through meetings with psychiatric social workers, clergy, and physicians. Couples actively share their experiences with each other and in seminars for clergy, health professionals, and police personnel-in-training. Holds liturgy for families on the first Sunday of each month. Sends artists to terminally ill children's homes, nursing homes, and the hematology/oncology waiting room at Children's Hospital of Michigan. Has developed summer arts day camp St. Patricks retreat in Irish Hills, MI. Funds hospitality home for chemotherapy ambulatory patients as well as for relatives of the critically ill. Offers transportation to six area hospitals for stranded chemotherapy and dialysis patients.

Foundation for Hospice and Homecare (FHH)
See: Entry 1299

★3713★ Hemlock Society U.S.A. (HSUSA)
PO Box 11830
Eugene, OR 97440-3900
Phone: (503)342-5748
Free: 800-247-7421
Fax: (503)345-2751
John A. Pridonoff, Ph.D., Exec. Officer

Founded: 1980. **Members:** 57,000. **Regional Groups:** 91. **Description:** Individuals supporting the option of active voluntary euthanasia for the advanced terminally ill. Promotes a climate of public opinion tolerant of the terminally ill individual's right to end his or her own life in a planned manner. Advocates changes in the law to allow voluntary physician aid in dying for the terminally ill. Does not encourage suicide for any primary reason other than terminal illness; approves suicide prevention work. Believes that the final decision to terminate one's life should be one's own. **Publications:** *Covers death and dying and physician aid in dying..* Books. • *Time Lines*, bimonthly. Newsletter. *Price:* Included in membership dues. Also publishes source materials. **Formerly:** (1993) Hemlock Society.

★3714★ Hospice Association of America (HAA)
519 C St. NE
Washington, DC 20002
Phone: (202)546-4759
Fax: (202)547-3540
Janet E. Neigh, Exec.Dir.

Founded: 1985. **Members:** 1,400. **Description:** Hospices, home health agencies, community cancer centers, and interested health care professionals. Promotes concept of hospice, a philosophy of health care which is expressed through the provision of a variety of medical and nonmedical services to terminally ill patients and their families. Provides nurses forum and hospice start-up programs. Offers hospice referral service and consultation service for medicare reimbursement problems. Maintains speakers' bureau. Compiles statistics. **Publications:** *Hospice Forum*, bimonthly. Newsletter. Provides information on research, regulatory issues, public policy, legislation, and state hospice programs. *Price:* Included in membership dues; $105/year for nonmembers.

★3715★ Hospice Education Institute (HEI)
190 Westbrook Rd.
Essex, CT 06426
Phone: (203)767-1620
Free: 800-331-1620
Fax: (203)767-2746
M. J. M. Galazka, Exec.Dir.

Founded: 1985. **Description:** Provides educational and informational services to health professionals and the public on subjects such as hospice and palliative care, death and dying, and bereavement counseling. Encourages educational exchange among hospice and palliative care professionals and volunteers. Offers advice and support to persons working to open local hospice programs. Organizes continuing education seminars on hospice care throughout the U.S. and abroad. **Publications:** Booklets. • *Notes on Symptom Control in Hospice and Palliative Care.* Book.

★3716★ International Anti-Euthanasia Task Force (IAETF)
PO Box 760
Steubenville, OH 43952
Phone: (614)282-3810
Fax: (614)282-0769
Rita Marker, Dir.

Founded: 1987. **Description:** A division of the Family Living Council. Participants include individuals from five continents concerned with disability rights, medicine, ethics, religion, law, education, and advocacy. Opposes "death-on-demand" and works to: provide information on euthanasia, suicide, assisted suicide, and related issues; resist attitudes, programs, and policies that the group feels threaten the lives and rights of those who are medically vulnerable, particularly elderly and disabled individuals. Promotes and defends the right of all persons to be treated with respect, dignity, and compassion. Maintains speakers' bureau, and film resources; provides speakers' training, news service, background information services for media, and information on advocacy and disability rights; conducts legislative and curriculum analyses. Informational packets and other publications on euthanasia-related issues.

★3717★ International Institute for the Study of Death (IISD)
PO Box 63-0026
Miami, FL 33163-0026
Phone: (305)936-1408
Arthur S. Berger, Dir.

Founded: 1985. **Members:** 85. **Description:** Investigative body of cross-cultural and interdisciplinary scholars and scientists interested in issues raised by death and dying. Seeks to nurture dialogue between academics in religion, nursing, medicine, philosophy, psychology, and parapsychology regarding the areas of death and dying. Hopes to develop new methods of thinking and investigation in the subjects of death and dying. Facilitates exchange of ideas with members. Plans to publish multilingual journal. **Formerly:** (1986) International Institute for the Study of Death and Immortality.

★3718★ Living / Dying Project (L/DP)
75 Digital Dr.
Novato, CA 94949
Phone: (415)884-2343
Fax: (415)884-2342
Dale Borglum, Dir.

Founded: 1977. **Description:** Seeks to "consciously and compassionately explore life through the mirror of the dying process." Provides national telephone and mail counseling services and outreach services to terminally ill patients. Provides training for health care professionals. Maintains speakers' bureau. **Publications:** Newsletter, periodic.

★3719★ National Funeral Directors Association (NFDA)
c/o Laura Glawe
11121 W. Oklahoma Ave.
Milwaukee, WI 53227-4096
Phone: (414)541-2500
Fax: (414)541-1909
Robert E. Harden, Exec.Dir.

Founded: 1882. **Members:** 15,000. **State Groups:** 50. **Description:** Federation of state funeral directors' associations. Founded by and associated with the Academy of Professional Funeral Service Practice (voluntary certification program). Maintains speakers' bureau and conducts professional education seminars and home study courses. Compiles statistics. **Publications:** Brochures. Contains statistical and consumer information. • *The Director*, monthly. Magazine. Contains articles regarding funeral service. Includes advertisers index, calendar of events, and book reviews. *Price:* Included in membership dues; $26/year for nonmembers. • *National Funeral Directors Association--Membership/Resource Guide*, annual. Directory. *Price:* Free to members and advertisers; $75/issue for others.

★3720★ National Funeral Directors and Morticians Association (NFDMA)
1800 E. Linwood Blvd.
Kansas City, MO 64109-2097
Phone: (816)921-1800
Fax: (816)924-2113
Lawrence A. Jones, Jr., Exec.Dir.

Founded: 1938. **Members:** 2,000. **State Groups:** 26. **Description:** State, district, and local funeral directing and embalming associations and their members. Promotes ethical practices; encourages just and uniform laws pertaining to funeral directing and embalming.

★3721★ National Hospice Organization (NHO)
1901 N. Moore St., Ste. 901
Arlington, VA 22209
Phone: (703)243-5900
Free: 800-658-8898
Fax: (703)525-5762
John J. Mahoney, Pres.

Founded: 1978. **Members:** 4,700. **Description:** Hospice organizations and individuals interested in the promotion of the hospice concept and program of care. (Hospice is a concept of caring for the terminally ill and their families which enables the patient to live as fully as possible, makes the entire family the unit of care, and centers the caring process in the home whenever appropriate. Inpatient facilities are available for those unable to be cared for at home.) Promotes standards of care in program planning and implementation; monitors health care legislation and regulation relevant to hospice care. Sponsors professional liaison and peer group networking. Collects data for the purpose of demonstrating definitive national trends in the hospice movement; encourages recognized medical and other health teaching institutions to provide instruction in hospice care of terminally ill patients and their families. Compiles statistics. Conducts educational and training programs in numerous aspects of hospice care for administrators and care-givers. Maintains nonlending library of hospice-related books. **Publications:** Annual Report, annual. Lists organizational activities and budget. • *Guide to the Nation's Hospices*, annual. • *The Hospice Journal*, quarterly. Journal. • *Hospice Magazine*, quarterly. Magazine. *Price:* Included in membership dues. • *NHO Newsline*, 20/year. Newsletter. Includes information on hospice careers and calendar of events. *Price:* Included in membership dues. Also publishes technical assistance materials, monographs, sample contracts, scriptographic informational booklets, and training manuals.

★3722★ National Institute for Jewish Hospice (NIJH)
8723 Alden Dr., Ste. 652
Los Angeles, CA 90048
Phone: (213)467-7423
Free: 800-446-4448
Fax: (619)322-3817
LeVana Lev, Exec.Dir.

Founded: 1985. **Members:** 43,320. **Description:** Individuals, business firms, and organizations concerned about terminally ill Jewish people. Serves as a resource center that seeks to help terminal patients and their families deal with their grief by providing information on traditional Jewish views on death, dying, and managing the loss of a loved one. Offers guidance and training to patients and interested hospice personnel, health care professionals, clergy, and family members who work with terminally ill Jewish people. Maintains speakers' bureau; conducts research programs. **Publications:** *At Bedside*. • *Caring for the Jewish Terminally Ill*. • *For Families of the Jewish Terminally Ill*. • *Hemlock Is Poison for Society*. • *How to Console*. • *Introduction to Jewish Hospice*. • *Jewish Hospice Times*, periodic. • *The Jewish Living Will*. • *The Jewish Orphaned Adult*. • *Realities* of the Dying. • Self-Healing and Hospice Care. • The Spiritual Component Cannot Be Ignored. • Strategies for Jewish Care. • The Undying Hope.

★ 3723 ★ St. Francis Center (SFC)
5135 McArthur Blvd. NW
Washington, DC 20016
Phone: (202)363-8500
Fax: (202)363-4989
Paul F. Tschudi, Exec.Dir.
Founded: 1975. **Members:** 1,000. **Description:** Nondenominational organization that provides information, individual and group counseling, and support to individuals of all ages, families, and organizations affected by life-threatening illness or death. Sponsors program which provides consultative, curriculum, and training resources for state, district, and school administrators, pyschologists, counselors, teachers, caregivers, partners, health care professionals, and parents; courses and programs for students in public and private schools; crisis intervention at the time of a death or other traumatic event which affects students and co-workers. Curriculum topics include personal loss experience, suicide, HIV/AIDS, children, communication, and grief and bereavement. Conducts educational workshops on death and dying for clergy, laypersons, students and professional caregivers. Maintains Friends Program where professionally trained volunteers provide emotional and practical support to individuals in homes and institutions who are coping with life-threatening illnesses or problems related to grief, separation, and loss. Offers resources for planning simple, dignified, and low-cost funerals as an alternative to costly and elaborate services. Maintains speakers' bureau. Makes available a list of educational materials including audiotapes, books, literature, and videotapes for educational purposes. **Publications:** *Centering*, quarterly. Newsletter. **Formerly:** (1978) Saint Francis Burial and Counseling Society.

Research Centers

★ 3724 ★ Center for Thanatology Research
391 Atlantic Ave.
Brooklyn, NY 11217
Phone: (718)858-3026
Roberta Halporn, Dir.
Research Activities and Fields: Aging, dying, death, bereavement, and gravestone studies.

★ 3725 ★ Hemlock Society U.S.A.
PO Box 11830
Eugene, OR 97440-4030
Free: 800-247-7421
John Pridonoff, Ph.D., Exec.Dir.
Research Activities and Fields: Voluntary euthanasia, including studies of religious viewpoints. Conducts public opinion polls. **Publications:** *Hemlock Newsletter*.

★ 3726 ★ National Foundation of Funeral Service
National Research and Information Center
2250 E. Devon Ave., Ste. 250
Des Plaines, IL 60018
Phone: (708)827-6337
Fax: (708)827-6342
Betty Murray, Contact
Research Activities and Fields: Death and funeral service, consumer assistance, and dispute handling. **Publications:** *NFFS News* (quarterly).

★ 3727 ★ University of Minnesota
Center for Death Education and Research
909 Social Science Bldg.
267 19th Ave. S.
Minneapolis, MN 55455
Phone: (612)624-1895
Dr. Robert Fulton, Dir.
Research Activities and Fields: Attitudes toward death and problems associated with death and dying and research on AIDS.

State Government Agencies

Funeral Service Examining Boards

★ 3728 ★ Alabama Board of Funeral Service
770 Washington Ave.
PO Box 309522
Montgomery, AL 36130
Phone: (205)242-4049

★ 3729 ★ Alaska Board of Mortuary Science
333 Willoughby Ave., 9th Fl.
PO Box 110806
Juneau, AK 99811-0806
Phone: (907)465-2541

★ 3730 ★ Arizona State Board of Funeral Directors and Embalmers
1645 W. Jefferson, Rm. 410
Phoenix, AZ 85007
Phone: (602)542-3095
Fax: (602)542-3093

★ 3731 ★ Arkansas State Board of Embalmers and Funeral Directors
PO Box 2673
Batesville, AR 72501
Phone: (501)698-2072
Fax: (501)698-1759

★ 3732 ★ California Board of Funeral Directors and Embalmers
2535 Capitol Oaks Dr., Ste. 300A
Sacramento, CA 95833
Phone: (916)263-3180

★ 3733 ★ Colorado Funeral Service Board
7853 E. Araphahoe Ct., No. 2100
Englewood, CO 80112
Phone: (303)694-4728
Fax: (303)694-4869

★ 3734 ★ Connecticut Board of Examiners of Embalmers and Funeral Directors
150 Washington St.
Hartford, CT 06106
Phone: (203)566-1039

★ 3735 ★ Delaware State Board of Funeral Services
Cannon Bldg., Ste. 203
PO Box 1401
Dover, DE 19903
Phone: (302)739-4522

★ 3736 ★ District of Columbia Board of Funeral Directors and Embalmers
Rm. 923
PO Box 37200
Washington, DC 20001
Phone: (202)727-7468

★ 3737 ★ Florida Board of Funeral Directors and Embalmers
1940 N. Monroe St., Ste. 60
Tallahassee, FL 32399-0750
Phone: (904)922-2918
Fax: (904)488-1830

★ 3738 ★ Georgia State Funeral Service Board
166 Pryor St. SW
Atlanta, GA 30303
Phone: (404)656-3933
Fax: (404)656-3903

★ 3739 ★ Hawaii Funeral Service Examining Board
591 Ala Moana Blvd., 1st Fl.
Honolulu, HI 96813
Phone: (808)586-8000
Fax: (808)586-4729

★ 3740 ★ Idaho State Board of Morticians
Statehouse
1109 Main St., Ste. 220
Boise, ID 83702
Phone: (208)334-3233

★ 3741 ★ Illinois Department of Professional Regulation
Funeral Directors and Embalmers Licensing and Discipline Boards
320 W. Washington St., 3rd Fl.
Springfield, IL 62786
Phone: (217)782-8556
Fax: (217)782-7645

★ 3742 ★ Indiana State Board of Funeral and Cemetery Services
302 W. Washington, Rm. E034
Indianapolis, IN 46204
Phone: (317)232-7209
Fax: (317)232-2312

★ 3743 ★ Iowa Board of Mortuary Science Examiners
Lucas State Office Bldg., 4th Fl.
321 E. 12th St.
Des Moines, IA 50319-0075
Phone: (515)281-4401
Fax: (515)281-4958

★3744★ Kansas State Board of Mortuary Arts
700 SW Jackson, Ste. 904
Topeka, KS 66603-3758
Phone: (913)296-3980
Fax: (913)296-0891

★3745★ Kentucky State Board of Embalmers and Funeral Directors
7025 W. Hwy. 22, Ste. 7
PO Box 324
Crestwood, KY 40014
Phone: (502)241-3918

★3746★ Louisiana State Board of Embalmers and Funeral Directors
PO Box 8757
Metairie, LA 70011
Phone: (504)838-5109
Fax: (504)838-5112

★3747★ Maine Board of Funeral Service
State House, Sta. 35
Augusta, ME 04333
Phone: (207)582-8723
Fax: (207)582-5415

★3748★ Maryland State Board of Morticians
4201 Patterson Ave.
Baltimore, MD 21215
Phone: (410)764-4792
Fax: (410)764-5987

★3749★ Massachusetts Board of Registration in Embalming and Funeral Service
Leverett Saltonstall Bldg., Rm. 1512
100 Cambridge St.
Boston, MA 02202
Phone: (617)727-7369
Fax: (617)727-2197

★3750★ Michigan Board of Examiners in Mortuary Science
611 W. Ottawa St.
PO Box 30018
Lansing, MI 48908
Phone: (517)373-3105

★3751★ Minnesota Mortuary Science Unit
121 E. 7th Pl.
PO Box 64975
St. Paul, MN 55164-0975
Phone: (612)282-3829
Fax: (612)282-3839

★3752★ Mississippi State Board of Funeral Service
1307 E. Fortification
Jackson, MS 39202
Phone: (601)354-6903
Fax: (601)352-7570

★3753★ Missouri State Board of Funeral Directors and Embalmers
3605 Missouri Blvd.
PO Box 423
Jefferson City, MO 65102
Phone: (314)751-0813
Fax: (314)751-1155

★3754★ Montana Board of Funeral Service
111 N. Jackson
PO Box 200513
Helena, MT 59620-0513
Phone: (406)444-5433

★3755★ Nebraska Board of Funeral Service
PO Box 95007
Lincoln, NE 68509-5007
Phone: (402)471-2115

★3756★ Nevada State Board of Funeral Directors, Embalmers, and Operators of Cemeterics and Crematoriums
14 Veterans Way
PO Box 1919
Fernley, NV 89408
Phone: (702)575-5165

★3757★ New Hampshire Board of Registration of Funeral Directors and Embalmers
Health & Welfare
6 Hazen Dr.
Concord, NH 03301-6527
Phone: (603)271-4648

★3758★ New Jersey State Board of Mortuary Science
124 Halsey St., 6th Fl.
PO Box 45009
Newark, NJ 07101
Phone: (201)504-6425
Fax: (201)648-3355

★3759★ New Mexico State Board of Thanatopractice
725 St. Michael's Dr.
PO Box 25101
Santa Fe, NM 87504
Phone: (505)827-7177

★3760★ New York Bureau of Funeral Directing
Corning Tower
Empire State Plaza
Albany, NY 12237-0681
Phone: (518)453-1989
Fax: (518)453-1973

★3761★ North Carolina Board of Mortuary Science
PO Box 27368
Raleigh, NC 27611-7365
Phone: (919)733-9380
Fax: (919)733-8271

★3762★ North Dakota State Board of Funeral Service
PO Box 633
Devils Lake, ND 58301
Phone: (701)662-2511

★3763★ Ohio Board of Embalmers and Funeral Directors
77 S. High St., 16th Fl.
Columbus, OH 43266-0313
Phone: (614)466-4252
Fax: (614)644-8112

★3764★ Oklahoma State Board of Embalmers and Funeral Directors
4545 N. Lincoln Blvd., Ste. 175
Oklahoma City, OK 73105
Phone: (405)525-0158
Fax: (405)557-1844

★3765★ Oregon State Mortuary and Cemetery Board
800 NE Oregon St., No. 21, Ste. 430
Portland, OR 97232
Phone: (503)731-4040
Fax: (503)731-4494

★3766★ Pennsylvania State Board of Funeral Directors
PO Box 2649
Harrisburg, PA 17105-2649
Phone: (717)783-1253
Fax: (717)787-7769

★3767★ Rhode Island Board of Examiners in Embalming and Funeral Directing
Dept. of Health, Rm. 104
3 Capitol Hill
Providence, RI 02908-5097
Phone: (401)277-2827

★3768★ South Carolina State Board of Funeral Service
3600 Forest Dr., Ste. 101
PO Box 11329-1329
Johnston, SC 29832-1329
Phone: (803)734-4238
Fax: (803)734-4236

★3769★ South Dakota State Board of Funeral Service
115 E. Sioux Ave.
PO Box 1115
Pierre, SD 57501-1115
Phone: (605)224-6281

★3770★ Tennessee Board of Funeral Directors and Embalmers
Volunteer Plaza, 2nd Fl.
500 James Robertson Pkwy.
Nashville, TN 37219
Phone: (615)741-2378
Fax: (615)741-6470

★3771★ Texas Funeral Service Commission
8100 Cameron Rd., Ste. 550
Austin, TX 78754
Phone: (512)834-9992
Fax: (512)834-1607

★3772★ Utah Funeral Service Board
160 East 300 South
PO Box 45805
Salt Lake City, UT 84145-0805
Phone: (801)530-6628

★3773★ Vermont Board of Funeral Service
Pavilion Office Bldg.
109 State St.
Montpelier, VT 05609-1106
Phone: (802)828-2390
Fax: (802)828-2496

★3774★ Virginia Board of Funeral
Directors and Embalmers
6606 W. Broad St., 4th Fl.
Richmond, VA 23230-1717
Phone: (804)662-9907
Fax: (804)662-9943

★3775★ Washington Funeral and
Cemetery Boards
PO Box 9012
Olympia, WA 98507-9012
Phone: (206)586-4905
Fax: (206)753-3747

★3776★ West Virginia Board of Funeral
Directors and Embalmers
179 Summers St., Ste. 305
Charleston, WV 25301
Phone: (304)558-0302
Fax: (304)558-0660

★3777★ Wisconsin Funeral Directors
Examining Board
1400 E. Washington Ave.
PO Box 8935
Madison, WI 53708-8935
Phone: (608)266-1630
Fax: (608)266-2264

★3778★ Wyoming State Board of
Embalming
Drawer A
Torrington, WY 82240
Phone: (307)532-2320
Fax: (307)532-7592

Chapter 18
Dentistry

Federal Government Agencies

★3779★ **U.S. Department of Health and Human Services**
National Institute of Dental Research
9000 Rockville Pike
Bethesda, MD 20892
Phone: (301)496-3571

Description: The Institute supports and conducts clinical and laboratory research directed toward the ultimate eradication of tooth decay and a broad array of oral-facial disorders.

Foundations & Other Funding Organizations

Private Foundations

Beazley Foundation/Frederick Foundation
See: Entry 62

Corporate Foundations

Wm. Jr. Wrigley Co. Foundation
See: Entry 911

Other Funding Organizations

★3780★ **American Academy of Implant Dentistry**
211 E. Chicago Ave., Ste. 750
Chicago, IL 60611
Phone: (312)335-1550
Fax: (312)335-9090
Joyce Sigmon, CAE, Central Off. Dir.

Description: Offers grants for clinical and/or laboratory research in the field of dental implantology.

★3781★ **American Association for Dental Research**
1111 14th St. NW, Ste. 1000
Washington, DC 20005
Phone: (202)898-1050
Fax: (202)789-1033
Dr. John J. Clarkson, Exec.Dir.

Description: Promotes the advancement of multidisciplinary research of the oral cavity, the adjacent structures, and their relation to the body as a whole. American Association for Dental Research (AADR) supports research fellows and trainees.

★3782★ **American Association of Oral and Maxillofacial Surgeons**
9700 W. Bryn Mawr
Rosemont, IL 60018-5701
Phone: (708)678-6200
Free: 800-822-6637
Fax: (708)678-6286
Bernard J. Degen, II, Exec. Dir.

Description: Offers annual research fellowship of $25,000, two research grants of $35,000 annually, one foundation fellowship of $23,000 for one year, one clinical surgery fellowship of $30,000, and up to five research awards annually of $1,000 each.

★3783★ **American Association of Women Dentists**
401 N. Michigan Ave.
Chicago, IL 60611-4267
Phone: (312)644-6610
Fax: (312)527-6640
Christine Norris, Exec. Dir.

Description: Bestows Colgate-Palmolive Award and scholarship award to women dental students.

★3784★ **American Dental Assistants Association**
203 N. LaSalle St., Ste. 1320
Chicago, IL 60601-1225
Phone: (312)541-1550
Fax: (312)541-1496
Lawrence H. Sepin, Exec. Dir.

Description: Supports dental assistant education by providing scholarships to qualified individuals.

★3785★ **American Dental Hygienists' Association**
444 N. Michigan Ave., Ste. 3400
Chicago, IL 60611
Phone: (312)440-8929
Free: 800-243-ADHA
Fax: (312)440-8929
Kathleen Bell, Exec. Dir.

Description: Administers various scholarship and research grant programs.

★3786★ **American Fund for Dental Health**
211 E. Chicago Ave., Ste. 820
Chicago, IL 60611
Phone: (312)787-6270
Free: 800-523-3438
Fax: (312)787-9114
Robert J. Klaus, Exec. Dir.

Description: Fund provides grants for research and dental health projects, and awards annual dental laboratory technology scholarships, dental minority scholarships, and dental teacher training fellowships, as well as biennial fellowships in dental administration.

Medical & Allied Health Schools

Dentistry

The following dental schools are accredited by the Commission on Dental Accreditation of the American Dental Association (ADA). For information on all dental programs, including advanced dental education, dental hygiene, dental assistant, and dental laboratory technician, contact the ADA at 211 E. Chicago Ave., Chicago, IL 60611, (312) 440-2500.

Alabama

★3787★ **University of Alabama at Birmingham**
School of Dentistry
1919 7th Ave. S.
Birmingham, AL 35294-0007
Phone: (205)934-4720
Fax: (205)934-9283

California

★ 3788 ★ Loma Linda University
School of Dentistry
Loma Linda, CA 92350-0001
Phone: (714)796-0141
Fax: (714)824-4211

★ 3789 ★ University of California, Los
Angeles
School of Dentistry
Center for the Health Sciences
Los Angeles, CA 90024-1668
Phone: (310)825-7354
Fax: (310)206-5539

★ 3790 ★ University of California, San
Francisco
School of Dentistry
513 Parnassus Ave., Room S-630
San Francisco, CA 94143-0430
Phone: (415)476-1323
Fax: (415)476-4226

★ 3791 ★ University of the Pacific
School of Dentistry
2155 Webster St.
San Francisco, CA 94115-2399
Phone: (415)929-6400
Fax: (415)929-6654

★ 3792 ★ University of Southern California
School of Dentistry
University Park, MC-0641
Los Angeles, CA 90089-0641
Phone: (213)740-2800
Fax: (213)740-3607

Colorado

★ 3793 ★ University of Colorado—Denver
School of Dentistry
4200 E. 9th Ave., Box C-284
Denver, CO 80262
Phone: (303)270-8773
Fax: (303)270-8299

Connecticut

★ 3794 ★ University of Connecticut
School of Dental Medicine
263 Farmington Ave.
Farmington, CT 06032
Phone: (203)679-2808
Fax: (203)679-1330

District of Columbia

★ 3795 ★ Howard University
College of Dentistry
600 W St. NW
Washington, DC 20059-3001
Phone: (202)806-0100
Fax: (202)806-0354

Florida

★ 3796 ★ University of Florida
College of Dentistry
J. Hillis Miller Health Center, Box J-405
Gainesville, FL 32610
Phone: (904)392-2946
Fax: (904)392-3070

Georgia

★ 3797 ★ Medical College of Georgia
School of Dentistry
Augusta, GA 30912
Phone: (706)721-0211
Fax: (706)721-6276

Illinois

★ 3798 ★ Northwestern University
Dental School
240 E. Huron Ave.
Chicago, IL 60611-2972
Phone: (312)908-5932
Fax: (312)908-0810

★ 3799 ★ Southern Illinois University at
Alton
School of Dental Medicine
2800 College Ave.
Alton, IL 62002
Phone: (618)474-7000
Fax: (618)474-7150

★ 3800 ★ University of Illinois at Chicago
College of Dentistry
801 S. Paulina St.
Chicago, IL 60612-4353
Phone: (312)996-1040
Fax: (312)996-1022

Indiana

★ 3801 ★ Indiana University
School of Dentistry
1121 W. Michigan St.
Indianapolis, IN 46202-5186
Phone: (317)274-7957
Fax: (317)274-2419

Iowa

★ 3802 ★ University of Iowa
College of Dentistry
Dental Bldg.
Iowa City, IA 52242-1010
Phone: (319)335-9650
Fax: (319)335-7155

Kentucky

★ 3803 ★ University of Kentucky
College of Dentistry
800 Rose St.
Lexington, KY 40536-0084
Phone: (606)233-5850
Fax: (606)258-1042

★ 3804 ★ University of Louisville
School of Dentistry
Health Sciences Center
501 S. Preston St.
Louisville, KY 40292-0001
Phone: (502)588-5293
Fax: (502)588-7163

Louisiana

★ 3805 ★ Louisiana State University
School of Dentistry
Bldg. 101
1100 Florida Ave.
New Orleans, LA 70119-2799
Phone: (504)947-9961
Fax: (504)942-8340

Maryland

★ 3806 ★ University of Maryland
Baltimore College of Dental Surgery
666 W. Baltimore St.
Baltimore, MD 21201
Phone: (410)328-7460
Fax: (410)328-3028

Massachusetts

★ 3807 ★ Boston University
Henry M. Goldman School of Graduate
Dentistry
100 E. Newton St.
Boston, MA 02118
Phone: (617)638-4700
Fax: (617)638-4490

★ 3808 ★ Harvard University
School of Dental Medicine
188 Longwood Ave.
Boston, MA 02115-5888
Phone: (617)432-1405
Fax: (617)432-4266

★ 3809 ★ Tufts University
School of Dental Medicine
1 Kneeland St.
Boston, MA 02111
Phone: (617)956-5000
Fax: (617)956-0309

Michigan

★ 3810 ★ University of Detroit Mercy
School of Dentistry
2985 E. Jefferson Ave.
Detroit, MI 48207-4282
Phone: (313)446-1800
Fax: (313)446-1839

★ 3811 ★ University of Michigan
School of Dentistry
1011 North University Ave.
Ann Arbor, MI 48109-1078
Phone: (313)763-6933
Fax: (313)747-4024

Minnesota

★3812★ **University of Minnesota**
School of Dentistry
15-209 Moos Tower
515 Delaware St. SE
Minneapolis, MN 55455-0348
Phone: (612)625-9982
Fax: (612)626-2654

Mississippi

★3813★ **University of Mississippi**
School of Dentistry
2500 N. State St.
Jackson, MS 39216-4505
Phone: (601)984-6000
Fax: (601)984-6014

Missouri

★3814★ **University of Missouri—Kansas City**
School of Dentistry
650 E. 25th St.
Kansas City, MO 64108-2795
Phone: (816)235-2100
Fax: (816)235-2157

Nebraska

★3815★ **Creighton University**
School of Dentistry
2500 California Plaza
Omaha, NE 68178
Phone: (402)280-5060
Fax: (402)280-5094

★3816★ **University of Nebraska—Lincoln**
College of Dentistry
40th and Holdrege Sts.
Lincoln, NE 68583-0740
Phone: (402)472-1344
Fax: (402)472-6681

New Jersey

★3817★ **University of Medicine and Dentistry of New Jersey**
New Jersey Dental School
110 Bergen St.
Newark, NJ 07103-2425
Phone: (201)456-4300
Fax: (201)456-3689

New York

★3818★ **Columbia University**
School of Dental and Oral Surgery
630 W. 168th St.
New York, NY 10032
Phone: (212)305-2500
Fax: (212)305-7134

★3819★ **New York University**
College of Dentistry
345 E. 24th St.
New York, NY 10010-4099
Phone: (212)998-9800
Fax: (212)995-4080

★3820★ **State University of New York at Buffalo**
School of Dental Medicine
Farber Hall
3435 Main St.
Buffalo, NY 14214
Phone: (716)829-2854
Fax: (716)829-2387

★3821★ **State University of New York at Stony Brook**
School of Dental Medicine
Rockland Hall
Stony Brook, NY 11794-8700
Phone: (516)632-8950
Fax: (516)632-7130

North Carolina

★3822★ **University of North Carolina at Chapel Hill**
School of Dentistry
104 Brauer Hall, 211-H
Chapel Hill, NC 27514
Phone: (919)966-1161
Fax: (919)966-4049

Ohio

★3823★ **Case Western Reserve University**
School of Dentistry
2123 Abington Rd.
Cleveland, OH 44106-4905
Phone: (216)368-3200
Fax: (216)368-3204

★3824★ **Ohio State University**
College of Dentistry
Postle Hall
305 W. 12th Ave.
Columbus, OH 43210-1241
Phone: (614)292-9755
Fax: (614)292-7619

Oklahoma

★3825★ **University of Oklahoma**
College of Dentistry
Health Sciences Center
PO Box 26901
Oklahoma City, OK 73190-3044
Phone: (405)271-6326
Fax: (405)271-3423

Oregon

★3826★ **Oregon Health Sciences University**
School of Dentistry
611 SW Campus Dr.
Portland, OR 97201-3097
Phone: (503)494-8801
Fax: (503)494-8801

Pennsylvania

★3827★ **Temple University**
School of Dentistry
3223 N. Broad St.
Philadelphia, PA 19140-5096
Phone: (215)221-2803
Fax: (215)221-2802

★3828★ **University of Pennsylvania**
School of Dental Medicine
4001 W. Spruce St.
Philadelphia, PA 19104-6003
Phone: (215)898-8961
Fax: (215)898-5243

★3829★ **University of Pittsburgh**
School of Dental Medicine
3501 Terrace St., C-333
Pittsburgh, PA 15261
Phone: (412)648-8900
Fax: (412)648-8219

Puerto Rico

★3830★ **University of Puerto Rico**
School of Dentistry
Medical Sciences Campus
PO Box 5067
San Juan, PR 00936-5067
Phone: (809)758-2525
Fax: (809)751-0990

South Carolina

★3831★ **Medical University of South Carolina**
College of Dental Medicine
171 Ashley Ave.
Charleston, SC 29425
Phone: (803)792-3811
Fax: (803)792-0390

Tennessee

★3832★ **Meharry Medical College**
School of Dentistry
1005 18th Ave. N.
Nashville, TN 37208-3599
Phone: (615)327-6489
Fax: (615)327-6213

★3833★ **University of Tennessee, Memphis**
College of Dentistry
875 Union Ave.
Memphis, TN 38163-2110
Phone: (901)528-6200
Fax: (901)528-7104

Texas

★3834★ **Baylor College of Dentistry**
3302 Gaston Ave.
Dallas, TX 75246-2098
Phone: (214)828-8100
Fax: (214)828-8496

★ 3835 ★ **University of Texas Health
Science Center at Houston
Dental Branch**
6516 John Freeman Ave.
Houston, TX 77030
Phone: (713)792-4021
Fax: (713)792-4189

★ 3836 ★ **University of Texas Health
Science Center at San Antonio
Dental School**
7703 Floyd Curl Dr.
San Antonio, TX 78284
Phone: (512)567-3160
Fax: (512)567-6721

Virginia

★ 3837 ★ **Virginia Commonwealth
University
Medical College of Virginia
School of Dentistry**
PO Box 566, MCV Station
Richmond, VA 23298-0566
Phone: (804)786-9183
Fax: (804)371-6072

Washington

★ 3838 ★ **University of Washington
School of Dentistry**
Health Sciences Bldg., SC-62
Seattle, WA 98195-9950
Phone: (206)543-5982
Fax: (206)685-3164

West Virginia

★ 3839 ★ **West Virginia University
School of Dentistry**
The Medical Center
Morgantown, WV 26506-9400
Phone: (304)293-2521
Fax: (304)293-2859

Wisconsin

★ 3840 ★ **Marquette University
School of Dentistry**
604 N. 16th St.
Milwaukee, WI 53233
Phone: (414)288-3586
Fax: (414)288-3586

National & International
Organizations

★ 3841 ★ **Academy of Dental Materials
(ADM)**
3302 Gaston Ave.
Dallas, TX 75246
Phone: (214)828-8278
Fax: (214)828-8458
Dr. Victoria Marker, Editor
Founded: 1940. **Members:** 300. **Description:**
Active members are licensed dentists, members

of academic institutions, industrial employees, and individuals active or interested in dental materials. Coordinates activities relating to the use of dental materials. **Publications:** *Dental Materials*, bimonthly. Journal. Covers scientific research. *Price:* Included in membership dues; $175 for nonmembers. • Directory, periodic. • *ODM Newsletter*, 3/year. Newsletter. • *Transactions of the Academy of Dental Materials*. **Formerly:** (1983) American Academy for Plastics Research in Dentistry.

★ 3842 ★ **Academy of Dentistry
International (ADI)**
5125 MacArthur Blvd. NW, Ste. 50
Washington, DC 20016-3315
Phone: (202)364-8349
Fax: (202)364-8349
Henry J. Sazima, D.D.S., Exec.Dir.
Founded: 1974. **Members:** 1,700. **National Groups:** 52. **Description:** Dentists; membership by invitation only. Works to further dentistry and the study of prevention of dental diseases worldwide. Disseminates and promotes the exchange of scientific information and fosters research. **Publications:** *International Communicator*, semiannual. Newsletter. *Price:* Included in membership dues. • *Roster of ADI*, periodic.

★ 3843 ★ **Academy of Dentistry for
Persons with Disabilities**
211 E. Chicago Ave., 17th Fl.
Chicago, IL 60611
Phone: (312)440-2661
Fax: (312)440-2824
John S. Rufkauskas, D.D.S., Exec.Dir.
Founded: 1952. **Members:** 500. **Description:** Dentists, dental hygienists, dental assistants, and allied professionals specializing in improving oral health of persons with special dental needs. Promotes dental education, research, legislation to improve oral health and sensitivity of parents, advocacy, and related professional groups. **Publications:** *Interface*, quarterly. Newsletter. • *Membership Referral Roster*, annual. • *Special Care in Dentistry*, bimonthly. **Formerly:** Academy of Dentistry for the Handicapped.

★ 3844 ★ **Academy of General Dentistry
(AGD)**
211 E. Chicago Ave., Ste. 1200
Chicago, IL 60611
Phone: (312)440-4300
Fax: (312)440-0559
Harold E. Donnell, Jr., Exec.Dir.
Founded: 1952. **Members:** 33,000. **Regional Groups:** 20. **State Groups:** 62. **Local Groups:** 35. **Description:** Dentists dedicated to promoting the continuing education and professional development of general practitioners. **Publications:** *AGD Impact*, 10/year. Newspaper. Covers issues, legislation, and trends that affect the practice and role of dentistry in the health care community. *Price:* Included in membership dues; $20 for nonmembers. • *Dentalnotes*, quarterly. Newsletter. Provides information on the latest dental issues and trends; intended for the national media and to be displayed in dentists' reception areas. *Price:* Free to national media; $6/year for all others. • *General Dentistry*, bimonthly. Journal. Provides research and

clinical reports for the continuing education of general dentists. Contains advertisers' index, book reviews, and quizzes. *Price:* Included in membership dues; $25/year for nonmembers. • Membership Directory, biennial.

★ 3845 ★ **Academy for Implants and
Transplants (AIT)**
PO Box 223
Springfield, VA 22150
Phone: (703)451-0001
Fax: (703)451-0004
Anthony J. Viscido, D.D.S., Sec.-Treas.
Founded: 1972. **Members:** 180. **Regional Groups:** 15. **Description:** Dentists united to: motivate and assist men and women in the general practice of dentistry in the field of implants and transplants; encourage and promote the art and science of implant and transplant dentistry; assist in research in this and allied fields. Conducts seminars; teaches implantology. **Publications:** *Implant Update*, quarterly. Newsletter. Discusses developments in the field of implant and transplant dentistry. *Price:* Included in membership dues. • Journal, periodic.

★ 3846 ★ **Academy of Laser Dentistry**
401 N. Michigan Ave.
Chicago, IL 60611
Phone: (312)644-6610
Fax: (312)321-6869
Nick Leever, Exec.Dir.
Founded: 1993. **Members:** 500. **Description:** Dentists, hygienists, dental teachers, and corporate laser dental vendors. Promotes clinical education, research, and development of standards and guidelines for the safe and ethical use of dental laser technology. Conducts educational programs. Provides certification. **Publications:** *Journal of Clinical, Laser, Medical, and Surgery*, bimonthly. Journal. • *Wavelengths*, quarterly. Newsletter.

★ 3847 ★ **Academy of Operative Dentistry
(AOD)**
643 Broadway
Menomonie, WI 54751
Phone: (715)235-7566
Dr. Greg Smith, Sec.
Founded: 1972. **Members:** 1,000. **Description:** Dentists and persons in allied industries. Seeks to ensure quality education in operative dentistry. **Publications:** *Membership Roster*, periodic. *Price:* $15. • *Operative Dentistry*, 4/year.

★ 3848 ★ **Academy of Oral Dynamics
(AOD)**
5950 Elmer Derr Rd.
Frederick, MD 21701
Phone: (301)473-9719
Joseph P. Skellchock, D.D.S., Sec.-Treas.
Founded: 1950. **Members:** 75. **Description:** Professional society of dentists. Promotes the study of oral dynamics, especially as it applies to the use of natural teeth in restoring and maintaining a healthy, functioning mouth; disseminates information gained through research. Conducts educational programs. **Formerly:** (1950) International Academy of Oral Dynamics.

★3849★ **Academy for Sports Dentistry (ASD)**
c/o Dr. William Olin
University of Iowa Hospitals
Iowa City, IA 52242
Phone: (319)356-2601
Fax: (319)356-4547
Dr. William Olin, Sec.-Treas.
Founded: 1983. **Members:** 300. **Description:** Dentists, dental students, physicians, athletic trainers, and others interested in the study and prevention of dental injuries incurred during sports participation. Purpose is to foster research, development, and education in all sciences related to sports dentistry and its relationship to the body as a whole. Encourages utilization of this knowledge in promoting better approaches to the prevention and treatment of athletic injuries and oral disease. Facilitates the exchange of ideas and experience among members. **Publications:** *ASD Newsletter*, 2-3/year. Newsletter. Provides information on the use of craniofacial protection such as helmets, mouthguards, and faceguards. *Price:* Included in membership dues.

★3850★ **Alliance of the American Dental Association (AADA)**
211 E. Chicago Ave., No. 918
Chicago, IL 60611
Phone: (312)440-2865
Fax: (312)440-2587
Margaret Henseler, Exec.Dir.
Founded: 1955. **Members:** 12,000. **National Groups:** 1. **State Groups:** 32. **Local Groups:** 160. **Description:** Spouses of dentists. Promotes public dental health and creates public awareness of dentistry. Conducts preventive dental health education programs and assists organized dentistry in encouraging state and national legislation that benefits the public and dentistry. Maintains legislative projects and leadership skill development. **Publications:** *Key Connection*, quarterly. Newsletter. • Manuals. **Formerly:** Auxiliary to the American Dental Association; (1982) Women's Auxiliary to the American Dental Association.

★3851★ **Alpha Omega International Dental Fraternity**
1314 Bedford Ave., Ste. 206
Baltimore, MD 21208
Phone: (410)602-3300
Free: 800-677-8468
Fax: (410)602-3394
Stephanie Black, Exec.Dir.
Founded: 1907. **Members:** 15,000. **Local Groups:** 125. **Description:** Professional fraternity - dentistry. Encourages fraternalism and monitors discrimination in dental schools. Maintains the Alpha Omega Foundation, which sends funds to dental schools in Israel and the U.S. Sponsors Project Renewal, which sends volunteer dentists to clinics throughout the world. Holds continuing education seminars. **Publications:** *Alpha Omega International Dental Fraternity--Leadership Newsletter*, quarterly. Newsletter. Provides information on dental education in the United States and Israel. *Price:* Included in membership dues. • *Alpha Omegan*, quarterly.

★3852★ **American Academy of Dental Electrosurgery (AADE)**
PO Box 374, Planetarium Sta.
New York, NY 10024
Phone: (212)595-1925
Maurice J. Oringer, D.D.S., Exec.Sec.
Founded: 1963. **Members:** 200. **Description:** Dentists who are qualified by special training to use electrosurgery therapeutically and research scientists who investigate the behavior of the therapeutic electrosurgical high frequency currents and their effects on the oral structures. Purposes are: to improve the clinical uses of electrosurgery in dentistry; to introduce instruction in dental electrosurgery at the undergraduate basic science and clinical level; to promote postgraduate training in electrosurgery; to promote research by qualified investigators; to improve electronic circuitry and clinical techniques. Conducts 2 scientific programs annually consisting of panel symposia, essays, clinical lectures, and table clinics. **Publications:** *Current Events*, quarterly. Newsletter. Covers academy activities and providing information about electrosurgery techniques, circuitry, and equipment. *Price:* Included in membership dues.

★3853★ **American Academy of Dental Group Practice (AADGP)**
5110 N. 40th St., Ste. 250
Phoenix, AZ 85018
Phone: (602)381-1185
Fax: (602)381-1093
Robert A. Hawkin, Ph.D., Exec.Dir.
Founded: 1973. **Members:** 1,575. **Regional Groups:** 3. **Description:** Active dentists and dental group practices. Purpose is to improve the level of dental service provided by members through exchanging and expanding of ideas and techniques for patient treatment and practice administration. Promotes group practice and research; accumulates and disseminates information; seeks to achieve the proper recognition for the aims and goals of group practice. Helps support an accreditation program as a system of voluntary peer review. **Publications:** *AADGP Contact*, quarterly. Newsletter. • Membership Directory, biennial.

★3854★ **American Academy of Dental Practice Administration (AADPA)**
c/o Kathleen Uebel
1063 Whippoorwill Ln.
Palatine, IL 60067
Phone: (708)934-4404
Kathleen Uebel, Exec.Dir.
Founded: 1958. **Members:** 250. **Description:** Professional society of dentists interested in efficient administration of dental practice. Offers educational programs. **Publications:** *American Academy of Dental Practice Administration--Communicator*, 3/year. Newsletter. • *American Academy of Dental Practice Administration--Roster*, annual. *Price:* For members only. • *Essay Tapes*, annual.

★3855★ **American Academy of Esthetic Dentistry (AAED)**
500 N. Michigan, Ste. 1920
Chicago, IL 60611
Phone: (312)464-2722
Free: 800-993-2626
Fax: (708)355-0474
Lanny L. Hardy, Exec.Dir.
Founded: 1975. **Members:** 100. **Description:** Dentists seeking to advance the art and science of esthetic dentistry (dentistry concerned with restorative procedures of natural teeth). **Publications:** *Esthetics*, semiannual. Newsletter. Presents information on the restoration of natural teeth. Includes calendar of events and research updates. *Price:* Included in membership dues. • *Journal of Esthetic Dentistry*. Journal.

★3856★ **American Academy of Fixed Prosthodontics (AAFP)**
PO Box 1409
Bodega Bay, CA 94923-1409
Phone: (707)875-3040
Fax: (707)875-2927
Dr. Robert S. Staffanou, Sec.
Founded: 1952. **Members:** 535. **Description:** Dentists. Provides 2-day professional continuing education course in the specialty of fixed prosthodontics. **Publications:** *American Academy of Fixed Prosthodontics Newsletter*, semiannual. Newsletter. *Price:* Included in membership dues. • *Journal of Prosthetic Dentistry*, monthly. Journal. • *Meeting Program/Directory*, annual. Directory. **Formerly:** (1991) American Academy of Crown and Bridge Prosthodontics.

★3857★ **American Academy of Gnathologic Orthopedics (AAGO)**
PO Box 548
Richmond, TX 77406-0548
Phone: (713)341-5250
L. M. Alderson, D.D.S., Exec.Dir.
Founded: 1970. **Members:** 700. **Regional Groups:** 9. **Description:** Dentists dealing with the prevention or correction of malocclusion and bony misformation of the jaw and face. Conducts activities in the fields of maxillofacial orthopedics/orthodontics and preventative and corrective orthodontics. **Publications:** *American Academy of Gnathologic Orthopedics--Journal*, quarterly. Journal. Includes scientific articles and case reports on orthodontic treatment. *Price:* $70 plus postage. • *American Academy of Gnathologic Orthopedics--Membership Roster*, annual. Membership Directory. *Price:* Included in membership dues. • Articles. On the Crozat Method.

★3858★ **American Academy of Gold Foil Operators (AAGFO)**
17922 Tallgrass Ct.
Noblesville, IN 46060
Phone: (317)867-3011
Fax: (317)867-3011
Dr. Ronald K. Harris, Sec.-Treas.
Founded: 1952. **Members:** 350. **Description:** Dentists who perform restorative procedures utilizing gold foil, cast gold, and the rubber dam. Formulates and applies new ideas for research on gold restorations and the rubber dam; encourages members of the dental profession and

research institutions in the armed forces, government, dental schools, and private enterprise to study gold restorations and rubber dam procedures. Presents chair demonstrations at dental schools. **Publications:** *Journal of Operative Dentistry*, bimonthly. Journal. • *Roster*, semiannual. Also prepares slides, charts, models, and written materials.

★ 3859 ★ American Academy of Head, Facial and Neck Pain and TMJ Orthopedics (AAHFNPTO)

520 W. Pipeline Rd.
Hurst, TX 76053
Phone: (817)545-2100
Free: 800-322-7651
Fax: (817)545-5076

Founded: 1985. **Members:** 200. **Description:** Dentists who treat head, facial, and neck pain. Functions as a referral service for patients suffering from head, facial, and neck pain worldwide. Maintains library of patient histories; plans to establish computerized medical procedures and insurance database. **Publications:** *Membership List*, periodic.

★ 3860 ★ American Academy of the History of Dentistry (AAHD)

c/o Aletha A. Kowitz
100 S. Vail Ave.
Arlington Heights, IL 60005-1866
Phone: (708)670-7561
Aletha A. Kowitz, Sec.-Treas.

Founded: 1951. **Members:** 600. **Description:** Seeks to stimulate interest, study, and research in the history of dentistry and promote the teaching of dental history. **Publications:** *Bulletin of the History of Dentistry*, 3/year. Bulletin. Includes articles on the history of dentistry, book reviews, and membership list. *Price:* $35/year.

★ 3861 ★ American Academy of Implant Dentistry (AAID)

211 E. Chicago Ave., Ste. 750
Chicago, IL 60611
Phone: (312)335-1550
Fax: (312)335-9090
J. Vincent Shuck, Exec.Dir.

Founded: 1952. **Members:** 2,500. **Regional Groups:** 4. **Description:** Dedicated to furthering scientific research and development in the field of implantology. **Publications:** *American Academy of Implant Dentistry*, annual. Directory. Arranged geographically and alphabetically. *Price:* Free to members. • *American Academy of Implant Dentistry*, bimonthly. Newsletter. Covers current activities in the field of implant dentistry, particularly the educational programs of the academy. *Price:* Included in membership dues. • *Journal of Oral Implantology*, quarterly. Journal. Contains original manuscripts, clinical presentations, research annotations, and educational reports pertinent to dental studies. *Price:* Included in membership dues; $75/year for nonmembers; $100/year for libraries, corporations, and institutes. **Formerly:** American Academy of Implant Dentures.

★ 3862 ★ American Academy of Implant Prosthodontics (AAIP)

5555 Peachtree-Dunwoody Rd. NE, Ste. 140
Atlanta, GA 30342
Phone: (404)847-9200
Free: 800-457-8171
Fax: (404)257-1201
Donna P. Vaughn, Exec.Dir.

Founded: 1980. **Members:** 300. **Description:** Experts in dental implantology; dental school professors. Encourages continuing education, advancement, and research in implant dentistry; believes that prosthodontics and implantology education and research should take place in academic institutions. Promotes the surgical insertion of dental transplants and the design and insertion of prosthodontic devices to replace missing teeth. Emphasizes research on the construction and maintenance of fixed and removable prostheses. Conducts continuing education courses in conjunction with dental schools. Maintains speakers' bureau and small library; bestows awards. **Publications:** *The Dental Implant - Clinical and Biological Response of Oral Tissues.* • *Implant Prosthodontics - Surgical and Prosthetic Techniques for Dental Implants.* • Membership Directory, periodic. • Newsletter, 3/year.

★ 3863 ★ American Academy of Maxillofacial Prosthetics (AAMP)

c/o Dr. Carl Andres
135 Bexhill Dr.
Carmel, IN 46032
Phone: (317)274-5628
Dr. Carl Andres, Exec.Sec.-Treas.

Founded: 1953. **Members:** 148. **Description:** Dentists specializing in maxillofacial prosthetics. **Publications:** *Journal of Prosthetic Dentistry*, monthly. Journal.

American Academy Oral and Maxillofacial Pathology (AAOMP)

See: Entry 10117

★ 3864 ★ American Academy of Oral and Maxillofacial Radiology (AAOMR)

PO Box 55722
Jackson, MS 39296
Phone: (601)984-6060
Fax: (601)984-6014
Dr. M. Kevin O Carroll, Exec.Sec.

Founded: 1949. **Members:** 500. **Description:** Dentists and other professionals who teach or specialize in oral and maxillofacial rediology. Serves as authoritative body on radiation hygiene and hazards for the American Dental Association . **Publications:** *AAOMR Newsletter*, quarterly. Newsletter. *Price:* Free. • *Oral and Maxillofacial Radiology Section of Oral Surgery, Oral Medicine, Oral Pathology, Oral Radiology, and Endodontics*, monthly. Journal. • *Roster of Membership*, annual. **Formerly:** (1968) American Academy of Oral Roentgenology; (1991) American Academy of Dental Radiology.

★ 3865 ★ American Academy of Oral Medicine (AAOM)

631 29th St. S
Arlington, VA 22202-2312
Phone: (703)684-6649
Fax: (703)684-2008
Ronald S. Brown, D.D.S., Sec.

Founded: 1946. **Members:** 800. **Regional Groups:** 4. **Description:** Dental educators, specialists, general dentists, and physicians interested in the study of diseases of the mouth. Promotes the study of the cause, prevention, and control of diseases of the teeth, their supporting structures, adnexa (accessory parts of the structures), and related subjects; fosters better scientific understanding between the fields of dentistry and medicine. Maintains speakers' bureau; offers continuing education lectures and seminars. **Publications:** *American Association of Stomatologists Newsletter*, quarterly. Newsletter. • *The Clinician's Guide to Treatment of Common Oral Conditions*, every 3-5 years. Monograph. *Price:* $11.95. • *The Clinician's Guide to Treatment of HIV-infected Patients.* • Monograph, periodic. *Price:* Included in membership dues; $30/year for nonmembers. • *Oral Surgery, Oral Medicine, Oral Pathology, Oral Radiology and Endodontics*. Journal.

★ 3866 ★ American Academy of Orofacial Pain (AAOP)

10 Joplin Ct.
Lafayette, CA 94549
Phone: (510)945-9298
Fax: (510)945-9299
Martha Boam, Exec.Dir.

Founded: 1975. **Members:** 220. **Description:** Medical and dental doctors seeking to further knowledge of craniofacial pain disorders. Maintains patient referral program. **Publications:** *Journal of Orofacial Pain*, quarterly. Journal. *Price:* $60/year. • *Temporomandibular Disorders: Guidelines for Classificiation, Assessment, and Management.* **Formerly:** (1979) American Academy of Craniomandibular Orthopedics; (1992) American Academy of Craniomandibular Disorders.

★ 3867 ★ American Academy of Orthodontics for the General Practitioner (AAOGP)

8634 W. Brown Deer Rd., No. 200
Milwaukee, WI 53224-2154
Phone: (414)354-6200
Jackie Hemmrich, Sec.

Founded: 1959. **Members:** 250. **Regional Groups:** 2. **State Groups:** 5. **Description:** Licensed dentists. Provides dentists in general practice with an organization through which they can augment their basic knowledge and training in orthodontics. Offers continuing education courses for dentists and auxiliary personnel; sponsors seminars. Provides facilities and audiovisual material for its affiliated study clubs. **Publications:** *American Academy of Orthodontics for the General Practitioner--Continuing Education*, annual. Brochure. Lists AAOGP-sponsored continuing education courses, seminars, and meetings for the coming year. *Price:* Free. • *International Journal of Orthodontics*, semiannual. Journal.

American Academy of Pediatric Dentistry (AAPD)
See: Entry 3159

★ 3868 ★ **American Academy of Periodontology (AAP)**
737 N. Michigan Ave., Ste. 800
Chicago, IL 60611-2615
Phone: (312)787-5518
Fax: (312)787-3670
Alice DeForest, Exec.Dir.

Founded: 1914. **Members:** 6,007. **Regional Groups:** 10. **Local Groups:** 53. **Description:** Professional society of dentists specializing in treatment of supporting and surrounding tissues of the teeth and their diseases. **Publications:** *Journal of Periodontology*, monthly. Journal. • Newsletter, 10/year. • *Roster of Members*, annual.

★ 3869 ★ **American Academy of Restorative Dentistry, D.D.S. (AARD)**
c/o Donald H. Downs
1235 Lake Plaza Dr.
Colorado Springs, CO 80906
Phone: (719)576-8840
Fax: (719)633-1060
Donald H. Downs, D.D.S., Sec.-Treas.

Founded: 1928. **Members:** 285. **Description:** Professional society of dentists practicing restorative dentistry, and educators interested in dentistry as it applies to treatment of the natural teeth to restore and maintain a healthy functioning mouth as part of a healthy body. **Publications:** *Journal of Prosthetic Dentistry*, periodic. Journal. • *Roster*, annual. **Formerly:** (1928) American Society of Dental Ceramics.

★ 3870 ★ **American Association of Dental Consultants (AADC)**
919 Deer Park Ave.
North Babylon, NY 11703
Phone: (516)587-5049
Alan M. Helerstein, D.D.S., Sec.-Treas.

Founded: 1977. **Members:** 325. **Description:** Dental insurance consultants and others concerned with dental insurance plans from administrative and design perspectives. Works to increase knowledge in the area of dental insurance plans, including the interrelationship between insurance carriers, the dental profession, and the insured. Operates certification program. **Publications:** *Beacon*, semiannual.

American Association of Dental Editors (AADE)
See: Entry 6966

★ 3871 ★ **American Association of Dental Examiners (AADE)**
211 E. Chicago Ave., Ste. 844
Chicago, IL 60611
Phone: (312)440-7464
Fax: (312)440-7494
Molly S. Nadler, Exec.Dir.

Founded: 1883. **Members:** 850. **Description:** Present and past members of state dental examining boards and board administrators. To assist member agencies with problems related to state dental board examinations and licensure, and enforcement of the state dental practice act. Conducts research; compiles statistics. **Publications:** *American Association of Dental Examiners Bulletin*, quarterly, 3-4/year. Newsletter. *Price:* Available to members and related organizations. • Proceedings, annual. **Formerly:** National Association of Dental Examiners.

★ 3872 ★ **American Association for Dental Research (AADR)**
1111 14th St. NW, Ste. 1000
Washington, DC 20005
Phone: (202)898-1050
Fax: (202)789-1033
John J. Clarkson, Ph.D., Exec.Dir.

Founded: 1972. **Members:** 5,000. **Regional Groups:** 40. **Description:** A division of the International Association for Dental Research (see separate entry). Dentists, researchers, dental schools, and dental products manufacturing companies. Seeks to promote better dental health and research activities. Presents current research information at annual meeting. Sponsors competitions; sponsors seminars. **Publications:** *Advances in Dental Research*, periodic. • *Dental Materials*. • *Dental Research Newsletter*, bimonthly. Newsletter. Association and professional newsletter for dental researchers. Includes calendar of events. *Price:* Included in membership dues. • *Journal of Dental Research*, 16/year. Journal. Provides information on all sciences relevant to dentistry and to the oral cavity and associated structures in health and disease. *Price:* $38/year for members; $16/year for student members; $270/year (within U.S.) and $280/year (foreign). • *Journal of Oral Implantology*, quarterly. Journal. • Membership Directory, periodic.

★ 3873 ★ **American Association of Dental Schools (AADS)**
1625 Massachusetts Ave. NW
Washington, DC 20036
Phone: (202)667-9433
Fax: (202)667-0642
Preston Littleton, Exec.Dir.

Founded: 1923. **Members:** 3,600. **Description:** Individuals interested in dental education; schools of dentistry, graduate dentistry, and dental auxiliary education in the U.S., Canada, and Puerto Rico; affiliated institutions of the federal government. To promote better teaching and education in dentistry and dental research and to facilitate exchange of ideas among dental educators. Sponsors meetings, conferences, and workshops; conducts surveys, studies, and special projects and publishes their results. Maintains 37 sections representing teaching and administrative areas of dentistry. **Publications:** *Admission Requirements of United States and Canadian Dental Schools*, annual. Catalog. Helps students decide on a career in dentistry, and explains how to go about it. *Price:* $25. • *Bulletin of Dental Education*, monthly. Bulletin. • *Directory of Dental Educators*, periodic. Directory. • *Directory of Institutional Members*, annual. Directory. • *Journal of Dental Education*, monthly. Journal. • Proceedings, annual.

★ 3874 ★ **American Association of Dental Victims (AADV)**
3316 E. 7th St.
Long Beach, CA 90804
Faye L. Willard, Founder

Founded: 1976. **Regional Groups:** 96. **State Groups:** 40. **Description:** Consumer-oriented movement composed of individuals who feel they have received improper, often harmful, treatment from dentists. Works to encourage the media to inform the public of issues that the association believes are not being addressed and to apply pressure on dentists and their supporters to improve conditions and the means of redress for dental patients. Compiles statistics; collects and files case histories of dental victims. **Publications:** Brochures. • Newsletter, 2-4/year.

★ 3875 ★ **American Association of Endodontists (AAE)**
211 E. Chicago Ave., Ste. 1100
Chicago, IL 60611
Phone: (312)266-7255
Fax: (312)266-9867
Irma S. Kudo, Exec.Dir.

Founded: 1943. **Members:** 4,200. **Description:** Endodontic specialists and other interested professionals. (Endodontics is a branch of dentistry that deals with the soft tissues inside the tooth.) Seeks to promote the exchange of ideas, to stimulate research, and to encourage the highest standard of quality care in the practice of endodontics. **Publications:** *Annotated Glossary*. • Brochures. • *Communique*, quarterly. Newsletter. • *Endodontics*, semiannual. Newsletter. • *Journal of Endodontics*, monthly. Journal. • *Membership Roster*, annual.

★ 3876 ★ **American Association of Hospital Dentists (AAHD)**
211 E. Chicago Ave., 17th Fl.
Chicago, IL 60611
Phone: (312)440-2661
Fax: (312)440-7494
John S. Rutkauskas, D.D.S., Exec.Dir.

Founded: 1927. **Members:** 900. **Description:** Directors and staff members of dental departments in hospitals. Promotes dental education programs in hospitals. Offers examinations. **Publications:** *InterFace*, quarterly. Newsletter. Reports on trends, legislation, policy changes, and issues that affect the practices of hospital dentists. Includes calendar of events. *Price:* Included in membership dues; $25/year for nonmembers. • *Special Care in Dentistry*, bimonthly. **Formerly:** American Association of Hospital Dental Chiefs.

★ 3877 ★ **American Association of Oral and Maxillofacial Surgeons (AAOMS)**
9700 W. Bryn Mawr
Rosemont, IL 60018-5701
Phone: (708)678-6200
Free: 800-822-6637
Fax: (708)678-6286
Barbara N. Moles, Exec.Dir.

Founded: 1918. **Members:** 6,100. **Regional Groups:** 9. **State Groups:** 53. **Description:** Dentists specializing in disease diagnosis and surgical, adjunctive, and esthetic treatment of diseases, injuries, and defects of the oral and maxillofacial region (jaw deformities, dental implants, infections, and oral cancer). **Publications:** *AAOMS Digest*, 6/year. Newsletter. Contains association news and events. • *AAOMS Directory*, annual. Directory. • *AAOMS Forum*, 4/year. • Annual Report. • *Journal of Oral Maxillofacial Surgery*, monthly. Journal. • *Office Anesthesia Evaluation Manual.* Manual. • *Report of Annual Meeting.* Report. • *Surgical Update*, 3/year. **Formerly:** (1944) American Society of Exodontists; (1977) American Society of Oral Surgeons.

★3878★ American Association of Orthodontists (AAO)
401 N. Lindbergh Blvd.
St. Louis, MO 63141-7816
Phone: (314)993-1700
Fax: (314)997-1745
Ronald S. Moen, Exec.Dir.

Founded: 1901. **Members:** 12,000. **Regional Groups:** 8. **State Groups:** 51. **Description:** Professional society of orthodontists. To advance the art and science of orthodontics through continuing education, encouragement of research, provision of information to the public, and cooperation with other health groups. Operates speakers' bureau; compiles statistics. Maintains museum. **Publications:** *AAO Bulletin*, bimonthly. Newsletter. Includes meetings schedules. *Price:* Included in membership dues. • *American Association of Orthodontists Membership Directory*, biennial. Membership Directory. *Price:* $35 for members; $65 for nonmembers. • *American Journal of Orthodontics and Dentofacial Orthopedics*, monthly. Journal. *Price:* Included in membership dues. • Pamphlets. Also publishes administration guide kits. **Formerly:** American Society of Orthodontists.

American Association of Public Health Dentistry (AAPHD)
See: Entry 10935

★3879★ American Association of Stomatologists (AAS)
c/o Dr. David A. Lederman
32 Cobblestone Way
Freehold, NJ 07728
Phone: (908)866-8822
Fax: (908)866-8830
Dr. David A. Lederman, Pres.

Founded: 1985. **Members:** 1,000. **Description:** Serves as a coordinating organization representing the American Academy of Oral Medicine and the Organization of Teachers of Oral Diagnosis, and their members. Acts as a voice for diagnostic and therapeutic disciplines in dentistry; seeks to establish oral diagnosis, radiology, and medicine as recognized specialty in dentistry; encourages excellence in the field to ensure excellence in patient care. **Publications:** *AAS News*, 3/year. Newsletter. **Formerly:** (1993) Academy of Oral Diagnosis, Radiology, and Medicine.

★3880★ American Association of Women Dentists (AAWD)
401 N. Michigan Ave.
Chicago, IL 60611-4267
Phone: (312)644-6610
Fax: (312)527-6640
Deene Alongi, Exec.Dir.

Founded: 1921. **Members:** 1,700. **Regional Groups:** 17. **Description:** Female dentists and dental students. Encourages young women to pursue an academic degree in dentistry and to advance the status of women already in the dental profession. **Publications:** *The Chronicle*, bimonthly. Newsletter. Includes book reviews, listings of employment opportunities, obituaries, research updates, and statistics. *Price:* Included in membership dues; $30/year for nonmembers. • Directory, annual. **Formerly:** (1978) Association of American Women Dentists.

★3881★ American Board of Dental Medicine and Surgery (ABDMS)
c/o Bartholomew A. Sinatra
522 Rossmore Dr.
Las Vegas, NV 89110-4123
Phone: (702)452-9538
Fax: (702)452-1031
Bartholomew A. Sinatra, M.D., Chm.

Founded: 1984. **Members:** 175. **Description:** Physicians specializing in dental medicine and surgery. Seeks to advance scientific knowledge and provide educational opportunities in the field. Conducts charitable activities.

American Board of Dental Public Health (ABDPH)
See: Entry 10937

★3882★ American Board of Endodontics (ABE)
211 E. Chicago Ave.
Chicago, IL 60611
Phone: (312)266-7310
Dr. Louis E. Rossman, Pres.

Description: Dentists who have successfully completed study and training in an advanced endodontics education program which is accredited by the Commission on Dental Accreditation of the American Dental Association. Administers examinations and certifies dentists who successfully complete the examinations. Primary objective is to protect the public by raising the standards of endodontic practice and requiring candidates for diplomate status to show strong evidence of specialized skills and knowledge in endodontics. **Publications:** *Membership Roster*, annual. Published in conjunction with American Association of Endodontists.

American Board of Oral and Maxillofacial Surgery (ABOMS)
See: Entry 12223

American Board of Oral Pathology (ABOP)
See: Entry 10120

★3883★ American Board of Orthodontics (ABO)
401 N. Lindbergh Blvd., Ste. 308
St. Louis, MO 63141
Phone: (314)432-6130
Fax: (314)432-8170
Dr. George D. Selfridge, Exec.Dir.

Founded: 1929. **Description:** Certification board to investigate the qualifications of, administer examinations to, and certify as diplomates dentists specializing in orthodontics (prevention and correction of irregularities and faulty positions of the teeth). Sponsored by the American Association of Orthodontists. **Publications:** *American Board of Orthodontics Directory*, annual. Directory. Lists diplomates. **Formerly:** (1938) American Board of Orthodontia.

American Board of Pediatric Dentistry (ABPD)
See: Entry 3163

★3884★ American Board of Periodontology (ABP)
Baltimore College of Dental Surgery
University of Maryland
666 W. Baltimore St.
Baltimore, MD 21201
Phone: (410)706-2432
Fax: (410)706-0074
Gerald M. Bowers, Sec.-Treas.

Founded: 1939. **Description:** Conducts examinations to determine the qualifications and competence of periodontists who voluntarily apply for certification as diplomates in the field of periodontology. Maintains registry of holders of diplomate certificates.

★3885★ American Board of Prosthodontics (ABP)
c/o Dr. William D. Culpepper
PO Box 8437
Atlanta, GA 30306
Phone: (706)876-2625
Fax: (404)872-8804
Dr. William D. Culpepper, Exec.Dir.

Description: Seeks to advance the science and art of prosthodontics by encouraging its study and improving its practice. Certifies dentists who specialize in the field of fixed, removable, and maxillofacial prosthodontics. Approved by the American Dental Association and the Council on Dental Education.

★3886★ American Central European Dental Institute (ACEDI)
60 Federal St.
Boston, MA 02110-2510
Phone: (617)423-6165
Fax: (617)426-0006
Dr. Arnold Watkin, Chm.

Founded: 1991. **Members:** 2. **Description:** Dentists and others serving in capacities related to the dental profession. Seeks to advance standards in the profession of dentistry. Conducts educational programs; maintains speakers' bureau. **Publications:** *ACEDI*, annual. Newsletter.

★3887★ American College of Dentists (ACD)
839-J Quince Orchard Blvd.
Gaithersburg, MD 20878
Phone: (301)977-3223
Fax: (301)977-3330
Dr. Sherry Keramidas, Exec.Dir.

Founded: 1920. **Members:** 6,500. **Regional Groups:** 8. **Local Groups:** 45. **Description:** Dentists and others serving in capacities related to the dental profession. Seeks to advance the standards of the profession of dentistry. Conducts educational and research programs. Maintains speakers' bureau and charitable programs. **Publications:** *American College of Dentists News and Views*, quarterly. Newsletter. *Price:* Included in membership dues. • *Journal of the American College of Dentists*, quarterly. Journal. Includes news and reserach reports. *Price:* Included in membership dues; $30/year for nonmembers.

American College of Oral and Maxillofacial Surgeons (ACOMS)
See: Entry 12232

★3888★ American College of Prosthodontists (ACP)
211 E Chicago Ave., Ste. 1000
Chicago, IL 60611-2616
Phone: (312)573-1260
Fax: (312)573-1257
Dr. David Schwab, Exec.Dir.

Founded: 1970. **Members:** 2,350. **Regional Groups:** 40. **Description:** Dentists specializing in prosthetics who are either board certified, board eligible, or under training in approved graduate or residency programs. Seeks to improve prosthodontic treatment for patients by encouraging educational activities designed to bring new ideas, techniques, and research into clinical practice. Sponsors annual prosthodontic research competition. **Publications:** *American College of Prosthodontists--Newsletter*, 4/year. Newsletter. Includes book reviews and calendar of events. *Price:* Included in membership dues. • Articles. • *Journal of Prosthodontics*, quarterly. Journal. Also publishes study guide.

★3889★ American Dental Assistants Association (ADAA)
203 N. LaSalle St., Ste. 1320
Chicago, IL 60601-1225
Phone: (312)541-1550
Fax: (312)541-1496
Lawrence H. Sepin, Exec.Dir.

Founded: 1923. **Members:** 16,000. **State Groups:** 50. **Local Groups:** 350. **Description:** Individuals employed as dental assistants in dental offices, clinics, hospitals, or institutions; instructors of dental assistants; dental students. Sponsors workshops and seminars; maintains governmental liaison. Offers group insurance; maintains scholarship trust fund. Dental Assisting National Board examines members who are candidates for title of Certified Dental Assistant. **Publications:** *The Dental Assistant*, 5/year. Journal. Features articles pertaining to dental assisting. *Price:* Included in membership dues. • *The Dental Assistant Update*, semiannual. Newsletter. *Price:* Included in membership dues; $30/year for nonmembers. Also publishes educational materials.

★3890★ American Dental Association (ADA)
211 E. Chicago Ave.
Chicago, IL 60611
Phone: (312)440-2500
Fax: (312)440-7494
John S. Zapp, D.D.S., Exec.Dir.

Founded: 1859. **Members:** 140,000. **State Groups:** 54. **Local Groups:** 492. **Description:** Professional society of dentists. Encourages the improvement of the health of the public and promotes the art and science of dentistry in matters of legislation and regulations. Inspects and accredits dental schools and schools for dental hygienists, assistants, and laboratory technicians. Conducts research programs at ADA Health Foundation Research Institute. Produces most of the dental health education material used in the U.S. Sponsors National Children's Dental Health Month. Compiles statistics on personnel, practice, and dental care needs and attitudes of patients with regard to dental health. Sponsors 12 councils. **Publications:** *American Dental Directory*, annual. Directory. Lists dentists in the United States; includes biographical information. *Price:* $110. • *Dental Teamwork*, bimonthly. *Price:* $28. • *Index to Dental Literature*, quarterly. Indexes worldwide literature on dentistry. *Price:* $175/Annual cumulation; $200/four quarters. • *Journal of the American Dental Association*, monthly. Journal. *Price:* $75 for nonmembers. • *News*, biweekly. *Price:* $35. **Formerly:** (1922) National Dental Association.

★3891★ American Dental Hygienists' Association (ADHA)
444 N. Michigan Ave., Ste. 3400
Chicago, IL 60611
Phone: (312)440-8929
Free: 800-243-ADHA
Fax: (312)440-8929
Kathleen Bell, Exec.Dir.

Founded: 1923. **Members:** 30,000. **Regional Groups:** 12. **State Groups:** 53. **Local Groups:** 360. **Description:** Professional organization of licensed dental hygienists possessing a degree or certificate in dental hygiene granted by an accredited school of dental hygiene. Administers Dental Hygiene Candidate Aptitude Testing Program and makes available scholarships, research grants, and continuing education programs. Maintains accrediting service through the American Dental Association's Commission on Dental Accreditation. Compiles statistics. **Publications:** *American Dental Hygienists' Association Access*, 10/year. Magazine. Covers current dental hygiene topics, regulatory and legislative developments, and association news. Includes membership profiles. *Price:* Included in membership dues; $18/year for nonmembers. • *Dental Hygiene*, 9/year. Journal. Includes association news, book reviews, abstracts, government news, and information on research and new products. *Price:* Included in membership dues; $40/year for nonmembers.

★3892★ American Dental Institute (DI)
2509 N. Campbell, No. 9
Tucson, AZ 85719
Phone: (602)882-9718
Soaring Bear, Pres.

Founded: 1980. **Description:** Conducts educational programs and research on nonsurgical dentistry and preventive health measures, stressing dental selfhelp and herbal treatments. Provides advisory services and information on research in progress. Operates speakers' bureau; compiles statistics. **Publications:** *Dental Self Help*. Book. **Formerly:** (1992) Dental Information.

★3893★ American Dental Interfraternity Council (ADIC)
c/o Alpha Omega Fraternity
1314 Bedford Ave., No. 206
Baltimore, MD 21208
Phone: (410)602-3300
Fax: (301)460-1777
Dr. Roger J. Spott, Exec. Sec.

Founded: 1923. **Members:** 4. **Description:** Federation of professional dental Greek letter societies. Promotes good public relations.

American Dental Society of Anesthesiology (ADSA)
See: Entry 2351

American Dental Trade Association (ADTA)
See: Entry 5821

★3894★ American Endodontic Society (AES)
1440 N. Harbor Blvd., Ste. 719
Fullerton, CA 92635
Phone: (714)870-5590
Dr. Ramon Werts, Exec.Dir.

Founded: 1969. **Members:** 10,000. **Description:** Dentists united to promote and provide educational and scientific information on simplified root canal therapy for the general practitioner. Conducts research programs. **Publications:** *American Endodontic Society Newsletter*, quarterly. Newsletter. Contains society news, member profiles, and instructional articles. • *Hotline*, periodic.

★3895★ American Equilibration Society (AES)
8726 N. Ferris Ave.
Morton Grove, IL 60053
Phone: (708)965-2888
Fax: (708)965-4888
Mr. Shel Marcus, Office Dir.

Founded: 1955. **Members:** 1,100. **Description:** Dentists, orthodontists, oral surgeons, and physicians interested in study and proficiency in the diagnosis and treatment of occlusal and temporomandibular joint disorders. Bestows Student Recognition Certificates annually to outstanding graduating students. **Publications:** *American Equilibration Society Newsletter*, 3/year. Newsletter. *Price:* Included in membership dues. • *Roster*, annual. • *TMJ Update*, bimonthly. *Price:* Included in membership dues.

★3896★ American Institute of Oral Biology (AIOB)
PO Box 7184
Loma Linda, CA 92354-7184
Phone: (909)824-4671
Fax: (909)824-4211
June J. Barrientos, Exec.Sec.

Founded: 1943. **Description:** Dental and medical health professionals united for continuing education. Conducts lectures. **Publications:** *AIOB Proceedings Manual*, annual. *Price:* $75.

★ 3897 ★ American Orthodontic Society (AOS)
11884 Greenville Ave., No. 112
Dallas, TX 75243-3537
Phone: (214)234-4000
Free: 800-448-1601
Fax: (214)234-4290
D. Glenn Whitten, Exec.Dir.

Founded: 1974. **Members:** 1,900. **Description:** General and pediatric dentists. Objectives are: to make orthodontic information readily available to any ethical dentist; to zealously protect the right of members to pursue orthodontic knowledge; to keep a watchful eye on third party services and government programs. Offers courses in orthodontic techniques. Conducts educational programs. **Publications:** *American Orthodontic Society Newsletter*, quarterly. Newsletter. Provides information on the society's seminars and conventions and news of interest to members. *Price:* Included in membership dues. • *American Orthodontic Society Technique Directory*, biennial. Membership Directory. Lists members by city and state; includes the type of orthodontic technique used by listee. *Price:* $150. • Brochures.

★ 3898 ★ American Prosthodontic Society (APS)
919 N. Michigan Ave., Ste. 460
Chicago, IL 60611
Phone: (312)944-7618
Fax: (312)664-3057
Howard J. Harvey, D.D.S., Exec.Dir.

Founded: 1928. **Members:** 1,300. **Description:** Dentists interested in the discipline of prosthodontics (the art and science of replacing missing teeth and supporting structures). **Publications:** *Journal of Prosthetic Dentistry*, monthly. Journal. Published in conjunction with 21 other prosthodonic organizations. *Price:* Included in membership dues.

American Society for Advancement of Anesthesia in Dentistry (ASAAD)
See: Entry 2352

★ 3899 ★ American Society for Dental Aesthetics (ASDA)
635 Madison Ave.
New York, NY 10022
Phone: (212)751-3263
Fax: (212)308-5182
Diana Okula, Exec. Officer

Founded: 1978. **Members:** 109. **Description:** Accredited dentists practicing aesthetic concepts in dentistry, including porcelain lamination (a technique where porcelain veneer is chemically fused to teeth to lengthen them, close spaces, or recontour the entire mouth). Dentists must have 5 years experience and submit 5 "before and after" photos of their work in aesthetic dentistry to qualify for membership. Promotes development, research, and teaching of aesthetic concepts in dentistry. Although centered in New York City, the group promotes expansion of aesthetic dentistry concepts in other states and abroad. Sponsors educational programs on tooth and crown repair, aesthetic fillings, orth-

odontics, periodontics, implantology, and other topics. **Publications:** Newsletter, semiannual.

American Society of Dentistry for Children (ASDC)
See: Entry 3172

American Society of Forensic Odontology (ASFO)
See: Entry 7170

American Society for Geriatric Dentistry (ASGD)
See: Entry 1888

★ 3900 ★ American Society of Master Dental Technologists (ASMDT)
PO Box 248
Oakland Gardens, NY 11364
Phone: (718)428-0075
Sue Heppenheimer, Exec.Sec.

Founded: 1976. **Members:** 125. **Description:** Dental lab technicians. Dedicated to the upgrading of dental technology. Seeks to provide educational resources such as texts, instructors, and guidance for technicians interested in becoming master dental technologists. Conducts associate and master level courses in conjunction with New York University School of Dentistry, Dept. of Continuing Education.

American Society of Maxillofacial Surgeons (ASMS)
See: Entry 12242

★ 3901 ★ American Student Dental Association (ASDA)
211 E. Chicago Ave., Ste. 840
Chicago, IL 60611
Phone: (312)440-2795
Fax: (312)440-2820
Karen S. Cervenka, CAE, Exec.Dir.

Founded: 1971. **Members:** 12,500. **Local Groups:** 54. **Description:** Predoctoral and postdoctoral dental students organized to improve the quality of dental education and to promote the accessibility of oral health care. Additional membership categories include predental, international and associate. Represents dental students before legislative bodies, organizations, and associations that affect dental students. Disseminates information to dental students. Sponsors advocacy program and Washington National Health Policy Externships, Chicago Administrative Externships and State Government Affairs Externship. **Publications:** *ASDA Handbook*, annual. Handbook. • *ASDA News*, monthly. • *Dentistry*, quarterly. Also publishes a series of guides to post-graduate programs in dentistry and reprints of National Board Examinations. **Formerly:** (1971) Student American Dental Association.

★ 3902 ★ Asian Pacific Dental Federation / Asian Pacific Regional Organization (APDF/APRO)
841 Mountbatten Rd.
Singapore 1543, Singapore
Phone: 3453125
Fax: 3442116
Dr. Oliver Hennedige, Sec.Gen.

Founded: 1955. **Members:** 17. **Languages:** English. **Description:** National dental associa-

tions in Australia, Bangladesh, Guam, Hong Kong, India, Indonesia, Japan, Malaysia, Myanmar, New Zealand, Pakistan, Philippines, Republic of Korea, Singapore, Sri Lanka, Taiwan, and Thailand. Works to improve dental and general health in the Asian Pacific region. Encourages education and research links between national dental associations. **Publications:** *APDF/APRO Technical Report*, periodic. • *Dentistry in the Asian Pacific Region*, periodic. **Also Known As:** Asian Pacific Regional Organisation of the International Dental Federation.

★ 3903 ★ Association of British Dental Surgery Assistants
DSA House
29 London St.
Fleetwood, Lancs. FY7 6JY, England
Lyn Ripley

Founded: 1940. **Members:** 2,500. **Description:** Represents the interests of dental surgery assistants in England. Promotes increased pay and improved status and working conditions. Supports educational programs and training and post-qualification courses. **Publications:** *British Dental Surgery Assistant*, quarterly. Newsletter.

★ 3904 ★ Association Dentaire Francaise (ADF)
92, ave. de Wagram
F-75017 Paris, France
Phone: 1 42278900
Fax: 1 47639028
Dr. P. Colombet, Sec.Gen.

Founded: 1970. **Members:** 33,000. **Languages:** French. **Description:** Federation of dental associations in France. Promotes and defends the dental profession; works for the evaluation and standardization of dental products.

★ 3905 ★ Association for Dental Education in Europe (ADEE)
Facultad de Odontologia
Universidad Computense
E-28040 Madrid, Spain
Phone: 1 3941905
Fax: 1 3941910
Prof. Mariano Sanz, Sec.Gen.

Founded: 1975. **Members:** 39. **Languages:** English. **Description:** Teachers of dentistry. Objectives are: to further dental education in Europe; to evaluate the goals and methods of dental education; to assess training programs for teachers; to promote ties among dentistry teachers. Holds lectures, seminars, and working discussion groups in conjunction with annual meeting. **Publications:** Proceedings, annual.

Association of State and Territorial Dental Directors (ASTDD)
See: Entry 5563

Association Suisse de l'Industrie et du Commerce Dentaires (ASICD)
See: Entry 5826

Associazione Italiana di Anestesia Odonto-Stomatologica (AINOS)
See: Entry 2358

★3906★ Australian Dental Association (ADA)
75 Lithgow St.
PO Box 520
St. Leonards, NSW 2065, Australia
Phone: 2 9064412
Fax: 2 9064676
Dr. Robert J.F. Butler, Contact

Founded: 1928. **Members:** 7,000. **State Groups:** 7. **Languages:** English. **Description:** Dentists, specialists, and dental students. Represents dentists' interests nationally and internationally. Seeks to improve the dental health of the community. Sponsors educational and research programs; cosponsors the Australian Dental Research Fund. **Publications:** *ADA News Bulletin*, 11/year. • *Australian Dental Journal*, bimonthly. • Directory, biennial. • *Facts and Figures - Australian Dentistry*, annual.

★3907★ Auxiliary to the National Dental Association (ANDA)
c/o Darlene Gay
8 NW 158th St.
Miami, FL 33169
Darlene Gay, Pres.

Founded: 1936. **Members:** 250. **Regional Groups:** 6. **Description:** Spouses and widows of dentists. Fosters professional, educational, ethical, and social measures that are conducive to the welfare of the dental profession; promotes and participates in health programs and projects; sponsors a student aid fund; encourages and correlates activities of local units throughout the country. Presents scholarships. Sponsors competitions; maintains charitable program. **Publications:** *ANDA Yearbook*. Directory. • *President's Newsletter*, periodic. Newsletter. **Formerly:** (1979) Ladies Auxiliary to the National Dental Association.

★3908★ Bangladesh Dental Society
GPO Box 4168
Dacca 1000, Bangladesh
Phone: 2 811154
Fax: 2 816374
Dr. Imtiaz Ahmed, Sec.

Founded: 1977. **Members:** 800. **Languages:** Bangla, English. **Description:** Dental surgeons. Promotes prevention, treatment, and reduction of oral and dental disease. Works to improve the standard of dental practice and to enhance the professional standing of members. Conducts charitable, educational, and children's programs. **Publications:** *Bangladesh Dental Journal*, quarterly. Journal.

★3909★ Barbados Dental Association (BDA)
PO Box 95
Bridgetown, Barbados

Founded: 1965. **Members:** 30. **Local Groups:** 1. **Languages:** English. **Description:** Promotes dentistry and the interests of dental professionals in Barbados; works to improve the dental and general health of the public. Conducts educational programs at schools. Offers competitions for school children to foster dental health awareness.

★3910★ Bermuda Dental Association (BDA)
PO Box 380
Hamilton 5, Bermuda

Members: 25. **Languages:** English. **Description:** Dentists in Bermuda. Promotes dentistry; represents members' interests. Sponsors study club.

★3911★ British Dental Association (BDA)
64 Wimpole St.
London W1M 8AL, England
Phone: 171 9350875
Fax: 171 4875232
Norman Whitehouse, CEO

Local Groups: 130. **Languages:** English. **Description:** Trade union for dental surgeons in the United Kingdom. Promotes dentistry and the provision of dental services to the public. Represents members' interests individually and collectively before the government. **Publications:** *BDA News*, bimonthly. Newsletter. • *British Dental Journal*, bimonthly. Journal.

British Dental Trade Association (BDTA)
See: Entry 5829

★3912★ Canadian Academy of Endodontics (CAE) (Academie Canadienne d'Endodontie — ACE)
10665 Jasper Ave., Ste. 1250
Edmonton, AB, Canada T5J 3S9
Phone: (403)425-8930
Fax: (403)420-1744
Dr. Carl Hawrish, Exec.Sec.

Founded: 1965. **Members:** 200. **Languages:** English, French. **Description:** Member dentists of the Canadian Dental Association or other Canadian national dental associations who have been graduated for at least 3 years or have earned recognition by graduate or postgraduate training, teaching, or research. Works to maintain and improve public health through the advancement of endodontics. Sponsors competitions and bestows awards; maintains speakers' bureau; compiles statistics. **Publications:** *Newsletter*, quarterly. Newsletter. • *Roster*, biennial.

★3913★ Canadian Dental Association (CDA)
1815 Alta Vista Dr.
Ottawa, ON, Canada K1G 3Y6
Phone: (613)523-1770
Fax: (613)523-7736
Mr. Jardine Neilson, Exec.Dir.

Founded: 1902. **Members:** 10,500. **Languages:** English, French. **Description:** Dentists. Works to: represent, protect, promote, and develop the interests of dentistry; contribute to the development of standards in dentistry and dental education, research, equipment, materials, and personnel; promote dialogue and cooperation with government bodies and consumers. Sponsors Dental Health Month and other dental awareness programs; conducts research programs. **Publications:** *Annual Review*. Journal. • *The Communique*, bimonthly. Newsletter. • *Journal of the Canadian Dental Association*, monthly. Journal.

Cayman Islands Medical and Dental Society
See: Entry 1229

★3914★ Christian Dental Society (CDS)
c/o Richard Haw, D.D.S.
PO Box 177
Sumner, IA 50674
Phone: (319)578-5232
Free: 800-CDS-SENT
Richard Haw, D.D.S., Sec.

Founded: 1962. **Members:** 550. **Description:** Encourages dentists of the American Dental Association (see separate entry) to donate their professional services to Christian schools, clinics, and hospitals. Members also supply materials and equipment to missions. Maintains speakers' bureau. **Publications:** *CDS News Update*, monthly. • *CDS Newsletter*, quarterly. Newsletter. **Formerly:** (1962) Presbyterian Missionary Committee.

★3915★ Clinical Dental Technicians Association
7 The Studios
The Row
New Ash Green, Kent DA3 8JL, England
Phone: 1474 879430
Fax: 1474 879430
Mr. C.J. Allen

Description: Dental technicians seeking legal status in the United Kingdom to train and qualify to make and fit dentures directly with the public under Act of Parliament. **Formerly:** Association for Denture Prosthesis.

★3916★ College of Diplomates of the American Board of Orthodontics (CDABO)
1323 Columbus Ave., Ste. 301
San Francisco, CA 94133
Phone: (415)776-4966
Fax: (415)441-5683
Philip Rollins, Exec.Dir.

Members: 1,726. **Description:** Members are diplomates of the American Board of Orthodontics who qualify by passing extra examinations. Promotes self-evaluation and ongoing professional improvement among orthodontists. Conducts seminars. **Publications:** *The Diplomate*, semiannual. Newsletter. *Price:* For members only.

★3917★ College International de Recherches Implantaires et Lariboisiere (CIRIL)
57, ave. de Bretagne
F-76100 Rouen, France
Phone: 35 730034
Fax: 35 032350
Dr. Manuel Chanavaz, Pres.

Founded: 1963. **Members:** 162. **Languages:** French. **Description:** Oral surgeons and clinicians in 14 countries involved in the teaching of and research in oral implantology (branch of medicine dealing with dental implants placed into or on top of the jaw bone). Encourages university and hospital consultations. Organizes symposia. **Publications:** *Implantologie Orale*, semiannual.

★3918★ Commonwealth Dental Association (CDA)

64 Wimpole St.
London W1M 8AL, England
Phone: 171 9350875
Fax: 171 4875232
K. Larkin, Sec.

Founded: 1991. **Members:** 44. **Languages:** English. **Description:** Local dental associations. Serves as a forum for discussion of matters of interest to members; works to coordinate members' activities. Promotes dental hygiene and oral health. Develops primary preventive dental strategies; conducts training programs for dental health workers; provides technical support to members in implementing programs. Holds educational courses. **Publications:** *CDA News*, semiannual. Newsletter.

★3919★ Craniofacial Biology Group of the International Association for Dental Research (CBG)

c/o Dr. G. H. Sperber
University of Alberta
Department of Oral Biology
Edmonton, AB, Canada T6G 2N8
Phone: (403)492-5194
Fax: (403)492-1624
Dr. G. H. Sperber, Sec.-Treas.

Founded: 1958. **Members:** 350. **Description:** Investigators and directors of research in craniofacial biology, including anthropologists, teratologists, pharmacologists, orthodontists, pedodontists, geneticists, cell biologists, anatomists, pediatricians, and neurologists. Facilitates study in the field; encourages contact between members; fosters presentations of scientific papers. **Publications:** *Craniofacial Biology Newsletter*, biennial. Newsletter. Contains announcements of meetings and awards. *Price:* Free to members. • Membership Directory, biennial. • Newsletter, semiannual. **Formerly:** (1971) International Society of Cranio-Facial Biology.

★3920★ Danish Dental Association (DDA) (Dansk Tandlaegeforening — DTF)

Amaliegade 17
Postboks 143
DK-1256 Copenhagen K, Denmark
Phone: 33157711
Fax: 33151637
Karsten Thuen, Dir.

Founded: 1873. **Members:** 5,957. **Regional Groups:** 11. **Languages:** Danish, English. **Description:** Danish dentists. Represents members' interests; promotes dental health care in Denmark. Offers postgraduate training. Maintains placement services; compiles statistics. **Publications:** *Tandlaegebladet*, 18/year. Journal. Provides scientific information.

Danish Dental Manufacturers (Dentalbranchforeningen Producentsektion)

See: Entry 5834

★3921★ Delta Dental Plans Association (DDPA)

211 E. Chicago Ave., Ste. 800
Chicago, IL 60611
Phone: (312)337-4707
Carl Zimmerman, Pres.

Founded: 1965. **Members:** 47. **Description:** Active state dental service corporations; inactive state dental service corporations; state dental societies; foreign dental service plans. Seeks to increase the availability of dental service to the public by assisting state dental societies in the formation of dental service corporations and by coordinating the activities of dental service corporations and helping them in the development of dental care programs for application to multistate and national accounts. A dental service corporation (or dental service plan) refers to a nonprofit corporation organized by the dental profession to provide prepaid dental care coverage to the public on a group basis. Maintains speakers' bureau; conducts specialized education programs; compiles statistics. Holds marketing, management, financial, and educational workshops, seminars, and conferences. **Publications:** *Delta Dictum*, quarterly. Newsletter. Covers legislative issues. • Membership Directory, annual. • Newsletter, bimonthly. • *Proceedings of Conferences*, annual. Also publishes educational and promotional literature. **Formerly:** National Association of Dental Service Plans.

★3922★ Delta Sigma Delta

W323 S3380 Hwy. E
Dousman, WI 53118
Phone: (414)968-2030
Fax: (414)968-5850
Dr. John H. Prey, Supreme Scribe

Founded: 1882. **Members:** 26,732. **Local Groups:** 38. **Description:** Professional fraternity - dentistry. Maintains museum; offers educational programs. **Publications:** *Alumni Directory*, quadrennial. Directory. • *Desmos*, quarterly. Magazine. Includes chapter news, scientific articles, and announcements. *Price:* Free to members.

DENIP

See: Entry 5835

★3923★ Dental Assisting National Board (DANB)

216 E. Ontario St.
Chicago, IL 60611
Phone: (312)642-3368
Richard D. Hengl, Exec.Dir.

Founded: 1948. **Description:** Certifying agency that administers examinations to dental assistants. **Formerly:** Certifying Board of the American Dental Assistants Association.

★3924★ Dental Association of South Africa (DASA)

Private Bag 1
Houghton 2041, Republic of South Africa
Phone: 11 6424687
Fax: 11 6425718
Dr. Helmut Heydt, Exec.Dir.

Founded: 1922. **Members:** 3,188. **Languages:** Afrikaans, English. **Description:** Practicing and retired dentists. Represents the dental profession in South Africa. Promotes research and investigation into dentistry and allied sciences. Sponsors National Dental Health Week in South Africa. **Publications:** *Journal of the Dental Association of South Africa*, monthly. Journal.

★3925★ Dental Association of Thailand (DAT)

71 Soi Prasarnmit
Sukumvit 23
Bangkok 10310, Thailand
Phone: 2 5141100
Fax: 2 5141100
Chavalit K. Opaswong, DDS, Sec.Gen.

Founded: 1947. **Members:** 2,600. **Languages:** English, Thai. **Description:** Licensed dentists. Promotes dental health and the advancement of the profession. **Publications:** *Dental Association of Thailand*, periodic. Journal. • *News Letter of the Dental Association of Thailand*, periodic.

★3926★ Dental Association of Trinidad and Tobago (DATT)

115 Abercromby St.
Port of Spain, Trinidad and Tobago
Dr. Joshua E. Scipo, Pres.

Founded: 1948. **Members:** 60. **Languages:** English. **Description:** Dentists in Trinidad and Tobago. Represents members' interests. Promotes dental health care through Dental Health Awareness Month. Sponsors educational programs.

★3927★ Dental Association of Zimbabwe

PO Box 3303
Harare, Zimbabwe
Phone: 4 733332
Fax: 4 733332
Dr. R. Sivertson, Contact

Members: 80. **Languages:** English. **Description:** Dentists and others working in the field of dentistry. Promotes dental health and the efficient practice of dentistry. Works to enhance the professional standing of members. **Publications:** Newsletter, periodic.

Dental Dealers of America (DDA)

See: Entry 5836

Dental Gold Institute (DGI)

See: Entry 5837

Dental Group Management Association (DGMA)

See: Entry 5573

★3928★ Dental Health International (DHI)

847 S. Milledge Ave.
Athens, GA 30605
Phone: (706)546-1715
Fax: (706)546-1715
Barry Simmons, D.D.S., Pres.

Founded: 1973. **Description:** Dentists, dental hygienists, dental technicians, and the International Association of Dental Students. Purposes are to promote dental health programs in developing countries; to provide general dental care using portable modular dental units in areas without electricity or water. Utilizes minimal fee structure to support projects; professionals in the field of dentistry donate their services for a period of 3 months. Volunteer dentists and dental technicians collect permanent non-obsolete dental equipment in their local areas and rendevous with the equipment in the host country and assist with the installation of it. Serves "pro-United States" countries.

Dental Manufacturers of America (DMA)
See: Entry 5838

★3929★ **Diving Dentists Society (DDS)**
1101 N. Calvert St.
Baltimore, MD 21202-3861
Phone: (410)837-5852
Fax: (410)752-0779
Leonore Chizever, Exec.Dir.

Founded: 1978. **Members:** 100. **Description:** North American dentists interested in scuba and other forms of diving. Researches and proposes solutions to the dental problems of scuba divers.

★3930★ **European Organization for Caries Research (ORCA)**
(Organisme Europeen de Recherche sur la Carie — ORCA)
Division of Oral Biology
Leeds Dental Institute
Clarendon Way
Leeds, W. Yorkshire LS2 9LU, England
Phone: 113 2336159
Fax: 113 2336158
Prof. Colin Robinson, Sec.Gen.

Founded: 1953. **Members:** 300. **Languages:** English. **Description:** Scientists and organizations in 24 countries engaged in research on dental caries. Promotes research on dental caries and evaluates research findings. Establishes contact among organizations and individuals involved in similar research. Bestows awards. **Publications:** *Caries Research*, bimonthly.

★3931★ **European Orthodontic Society (EOS)**
49 Hallam St., Flat 31
London W1N 5LL, England
Phone: 171 9352795
Fax: 171 9352795
Prof. J. P. Moss, Hon.Sec.

Founded: 1907. **Members:** 2,050. **Languages:** English. **Description:** Orthodontists in 64 countries promoting the science of orthodontics. **Publications:** *European Journal of Orthodontics*, bimonthly. Journal. **Formerly:** (1935) European Orthodontia Society.

★3932★ **European Regional Organization of the International Dental Federation (ERO)**
Postfach 41 01 68
50861 Cologne, Germany
Phone: 221 40010
Fax: 221 404035
Marion Bader, Sec.

Founded: 1955. **Members:** 28. **Languages:** English, French, German. **Description:** National dental associations belonging to the International Dental Federation. Works to establish common professional and health policies in European nations. Provides for the exchange of information; fosters cooperation among members. **Publications:** *ERO Circular Letter*, quarterly.

★3933★ **European Union of Dental Medicine Practitioners (UEPMD)**
(Union Europeenne des Practiciens en Medecine Dentaire — UEPMD)
Bilker Allee 64
40219 Dusseldorf, Germany
Phone: 211 308065
Fax: 211 3983627
Dr. Klaus Eicher, Sec.Gen.

Founded: 1974. **Members:** 1,000. **National Groups:** 6. **Languages:** English, French, German, Italian. **Description:** Western European dentists and dental associations. Objectives are to: defend the ethical and material interests and the autonomy of the dental profession in the European Communities; maintain high professional standards for the practice of dental medicine; foster solidarity and friendship among members; address organizational and professional issues in an effort to clearly define dentistry in the socioeconomic framework of the European Communities. Operates charitable program; offers assistance to students; organizes exchange programs. Cooperates with the Council of Europe.

★3934★ **European Union of Dentists**
(Europaische Union der Zahnarzte)
Dodelle 55
45239 Essen, Germany
Phone: 201 407987
Fax: 201 409542
Dr. Klaus Eicher, Contact

Founded: 1973. **Members:** 1,000. **Description:** Works to provide dental services to the socially and economically disadvantaged. Promotes solidarity and friendship among dentists of the EC.

Fachverband der Eisen- und Metallwarenindustrie Osterreichs
See: Entry 5847

★3935★ **FDI - World Dental Federation**
7 Carlisle St.
London W1V 5RG, England
Phone: 171 9357852
Fax: 171 4860183
Dr. P.A. Zillen, Exec.Dir.

Founded: 1900. **Members:** 375,000. **National Groups:** 97. **Regional Groups:** 5. **Languages:** English, French, German, Spanish. **Description:** Dentists from 85 countries. Represents the dental profession on a nongovernmental basis with the goal of advancing the profession. Seeks to improve dental and general health for all individuals. Studies problems of international concern; cooperates with other international health agencies; serves as an information resource center; promotes continuing education for members. Bestows prizes and awards. **Publications:** *Community Dental Health*, quarterly. Magazine. • *Dental Lexicon*. Book. • *The European Journal of Prosthodontics and Restorative Dentistry*, quarterly. Journal. • *FDI Basic Facts: Dentistry Around the World*. Book. • *FDI World*, bimonthly. Magazine. • *International Dental Journal*, bimonthly. Journal. • *Regulations for Dental Practice*. Book. **Formerly:** (1991) International Dental Federation.

Federacion Nacional de Empresas de Instrumentacion Cientifica, Medica, Tecnica y Dental (FENIN)
See: Entry 5848

Federation of the European Dental Industry
(Federation de l'Industrie Dentaire en Europe — FIDE)
See: Entry 5849

★3936★ **Federation of Orthodontic Associations (FOA)**
c/o Dr. Robert C. Webber
711 Giddings Ave.
Sheboygan Falls, WI 53085
Phone: (414)467-4070
Dr. David H. Watson, Exec.Dir.

Founded: 1969. **Description:** Orthodontically oriented dental associations united to increase members' knowledge of orthodontics on the postgraduate level. **Publications:** *International Journal of Orthodontics*, semiannual. Journal. Includes annual index, book reviews, and news from associations represented by the federation. *Price:* $20/year.

★3937★ **Federation of Prosthodontic Organizations (FPO)**
211 E. Chicago Ave., Ste. 948
Chicago, IL 60611
Phone: (312)642-7538
Fax: (312)642-9713
Peter C. Goulding, Exec.Dir.

Founded: 1965. **Members:** 16. **Description:** Organizations of dentists. To improve prosthodontic service rendered to the public and to improve communication among members and other organizations. (Prosthodontics is the branch of dentistry that specializes in use and implantation of artificial parts, including false teeth and bridges.) **Publications:** Directory, annual. • Newsletter, quarterly.

★3938★ **Federation of Special Care Organizations and Dentistry**
211 E. Chicago Ave., 17th Fl.
Chicago, IL 60611-9361
Phone: (312)440-2660
Fax: (312)440-7494
John S. Rutkauskas, DDS, Exec.Dir.

Founded: 1988. **Members:** 1,500. **Description:** Dentists and dental care providers. Seeks to improve the effectiveness of health care providers in providing quality patient care, especially for patients who for reasons of medical diagnosis, disabilities, or frailties prevalent in advanced age require special care and/or special settings for dental care. Conducts educational programs. **Publications:** *Special Care in Dentistry*, bimonthly. Journal.

★3939★ Finnish Dental Society (FDS)
(Suomen Hammaslaakariseura)
Rautatielaisenkatu 6
SF-00520 Helsinki 52, Finland
Phone: 0 15021
Fax: 0 143317
Prof. Keijo Paunio, Pres.

Founded: 1892. **Members:** 5,000. **Local Groups:** 24. **Languages:** English, Finnish, Swedish. **Description:** Dentists and dental students. Scientific society promoting dental research and its clinical applications. Encourages international cooperation in the dental health field. Conducts over 100 continuing education courses annually. Maintains 12 special interest sections. Offers research and travel grants; bestows awards. **Publications:** *Proceedings of the Finnish Dental Society*, quarterly. Also publishess *Course Calendar of the Finnish Dental Organisations*.

★3940★ Flying Dentists Association (FDA)
4700 Chamblee-Dunwoody Rd.
Dunwoody, GA 30338
Phone: (404)457-1351
Fax: (404)458-0890
Dr. Max J. Cohen, Exec.Sec.

Founded: 1960. **Members:** 500. **Regional Groups:** 4. **Description:** Members of the American Dental Association who have an active aircraft pilot's license. Many members make use of private air travel in conducting their dental practice. **Publications:** *Flight Watch*, monthly.

★3941★ German Dental Association
(Bundeszahnarziekammer)
Universitatsstr. 71-73
50931 Cologne, Germany
Phone: 221 40010
Fax: 221 404035
Dr. Detlef Schulze-Wilk, Contact

Founded: 1953. **Description:** Promotes the dental sciences in Germany. Promotes dental education and continuing education. Represents the interests of members to authorities, associations, and the public. **Formerly:** National Association of German Dentists; Bundesverband der Deutschen Zahnarzte.

★3942★ Group of Francophone Dentists'
Associations (GADEF)
(Groupement des Associations Dentaires
Francophones — GADEF)
22, ave. de Villiers
F-75017 Paris, France
Phone: 1 47660232
Dr. Jacques Charon, Hon.Pres.

Founded: 1971. **Members:** 26. **Languages:** French. Does not correspond in English. **Description:** National dental associations. Promotes use of the French language for international professional relations and works to advance dental science and public health. Maintains contacts in industrialized and developing countries. **Publications:** *Bulletin du GADEF*, semiannual. Bulletin. • *Directory*, quarterly. Directory.

★3943★ Holistic Dental Association (HDA)
c/o Dr. Paul Plowman
4801 Richmond Sq.
Oklahoma City, OK 73118
Phone: (405)840-5600
Fax: (405)843-0417
Dr. Paul Plowman, Pres.

Founded: 1980. **Members:** 200. **Description:** Dentists, chiropractors, dental hygienists, physical therapists, and medical doctors. Goals are: to provide a holistic approach to better dental care for patients; to expand techniques, medications, and philosophies that pertain to extractions, anesthetics, fillings, crowns, and orthodontics. Encourages use of homeopathic medications, acupuncture, cranial osteopathy, nutritional techniques, and physical therapy in treating patients in addition to conventional treatments. Classifies therapies; has developed a referral questionnaire for holistic practitioners. Sponsors training and educational seminars. **Publications:** *Luminary*, monthly. Newsletter. Includes calendar of events and research updates. *Price:* Included in membership dues. **Formerly:** Holistic Dental Association International.

★3944★ Hong Kong Dental Association
8/F Duke of Windsor Social Services Bldg.
15 Hennesey Rd.
Wanchai, Hong Kong
Phone: 5285327
Fax: 5290755
Dr. Chan Sai Kwing, Sec.

Founded: 1950. **Members:** 1,200. **Languages:** Chinese, English. **Description:** Dentists, orthodontists, and others with an interest in the provision of dental care in Hong Kong. Promotes the welfare of the dental profession; encourages continuing professional education of members. Represents members' interests before government agencies and the public. Conducts research to advance dental practice; disseminates information to encourage public dental health maintenance. Maintains liaison with other dental organizations worldwide. Operates speakers' bureau; sponsors competitions; compiles statistics. **Publications:** *Hong Kong Dental Association Yearbook*, annual. Yearbook. • Journal, periodic. • Newsletter, periodic.

★3945★ Icelandic Dental Association (TI)
(Tannlaeknafelag Islands — TFI)
Sidumuli 35
PO Box 8596
IS-128 Reykjavik, Iceland
Phone: 1 34646
Fax: 1 33562
Sigridur Dagbjartsdottir, Exec. Officer

Founded: 1927. **Members:** 274. **Local Groups:** 4. **Languages:** English, Swedish. **Description:** Professional association of active and retired dentists. Conducts charitable activities; provides emergency dental assistance. Bestows research grants; conducts educational programs. **Publications:** *Journal of Dentistry*, annual. Journal. • *Newsletter*, monthly. Newsletter.

INDENT
See: Entry 5857

★3946★ Independent Association of
German Dentists
(Freier Verband Deutscher Zahnarzte)
Mallwitzstr. 16
53177 Bonn, Germany
Phone: 228 85570
Fax: 228 347967
Dr. Ralph Gutmann, Contact

Members: 26,000. **Description:** Represents and promotes the professional interests of German dentists.

★3947★ Indian Dental Association (IDA)
20-A D B Rd.
R S Puram
Coimbatore 641 002, Tamil Nadu, India
Phone: 422 43684
Fax: 422 25800
Dr. V.M. Veerabahu, Hon.Gen.Sec.

Founded: 1945. **Members:** 8,000. **State Groups:** 22. **Local Groups:** 83. **Languages:** English. **Description:** Dental surgeons; dental students. Promotes the dental profession and educates the public concerning the contributions of dental professionals. Conducts competitions; bestows awards. Offers educational and public service programs; conducts research programs. **Publications:** Directory, annual. • *Journal of IDA*, monthly.

★3948★ Indian Dental Association (U.S.A.)
(IDA (USA))
146-02 89th Ave.
Jamaica, NY 11435
Phone: (718)523-8438
Narendre Patel, Pres.

Founded: 1983. **Members:** 345. **State Groups:** 2. **Description:** Dentists in the U.S. who are of Asian-Indian descent. Seeks to further the professional education of members. Conducts social events. **Publications:** *IDA Newsletter*, monthly. Newsletter.

★3949★ International Academy of
Gnathology—American Section (IAG)
4323 Palm Ave.
La Mesa, CA 91941
Phone: (619)462-9933
Fax: (619)462-0112
Dr. Charles G. Eller, Pres.

Founded: 1964. **Members:** 3,000. **Description:** Dentists and educators interested in the science of gnathology. (Gnathology is the science that treats the biology of chewing and the jaws and cheeks as related to the rest of the body.) Areas of concern include morphology, anatomy, psychology, physiology, pathology, and therapy of the mouth. **Publications:** *Journal of Gnathology*, annual. Journal.

★3950★ International Academy of
Myodontics (IAM)
c/o Harry N. Cooperman, D.D.S.
800 Airport Blvd.
Doylestown, PA 18901
Phone: (215)345-1149
Fax: (215)609-2588
Harry N. Cooperman, D.D.S., Pres.

Founded: 1970. **Members:** 1,100. **Regional Groups:** 2. **Description:** Dentists who specialize in the treatment of head and neck syndromes that cause dental or oral malfunction. Works with physicians and dentists in the field of myodontics, especially those working on the treatment of Cooperman-Muira Syndrome, also known as uvula-tongue malposture syndrome.

★3951★ International Academy of Myodontics, Asian Chapter (IAMA)
7-6-7, Ohjima
Kohto-Ku
Tokyo 136, Japan
Phone: 3 36819988
Fax: 3 36373093
Noboru Miura, D.D.S., Pres.

Founded: 1970. **Members:** 200. **Languages:** English, Japanese. **Description:** Dentists specializing in the treatment of head and neck syndromes that cause dental or oral malfunction. Encourages study in clinical diagnosis and treatment; promotes the use of holistic approaches to dentistry. Sponsors educational programs and speakers' bureau. **Publications:** *Myodontic News*, quarterly. • *Myodontic Theory*. • *Practical Myodontic Splints*.

★3952★ International Academy of Myodontics, Oceanic Chapter (IAM)
57 Darlinghurst Rd.
Potts Point
Sydney, NSW 2011, Australia
Phone: 2 3585563
Dr. Harry Rich, Pres.

Founded: 1985. **Members:** 6. **Languages:** English, German. **Description:** Practicing dental surgeons organized to study and apply theory and practical use of myodontic principles.

★3953★ International Academy of Oral Medicine and Toxicology (IAOMT)
PO Box 608531
Orlando, FL 32860-8531
Phone: (407)298-2450
Fax: (407)298-2450
Michael F. Ziff, D.D.S., Exec.Dir.

Founded: 1984. **Members:** 226. **National Groups:** 5. **Description:** Dentists, physicians, and medical scientists. Encourages, sponsors, and disseminates scientific research on the biocompatibility of materials used in dentistry. Offers educational programs; maintains speakers' bureau. **Publications:** *Bio-Probe Newsletter*, bimonthly. Newsletter. Review of scientific literature and legislative activities. *Price:* Included in membership dues. • *IN VIVO*, quarterly. Newsletter. *Price:* Included in membership dues. • Membership Directory. Indexed alphabetically and geographically.

★3954★ International Association for Dental Research (IADR)
1111 14th St. NW, Ste. 1000
Washington, DC 20005
Phone: (202)898-1050
Fax: (202)789-1033
John J. Clarkson, Ph.D., Exec.Dir.

Founded: 1920. **Members:** 9,500. **Description:** Individuals engaged or interested in advancing research in the various aspects of dental and related sciences. **Publications:** *Advances in Dental Research*, periodic. Journal. Covers developments in dental research and the chemistry, biology, and function of the oral cavity. Also includes conference proceedings. • *IADReports and Dental Research*, quarterly. Newsletter. Includes calender of events. *Price:* Included in membership dues. • *Journal of Dental Research*, monthly. Journal. Disseminates new information and knowledge on all sciences relevant to dentistry, the oral cavity, and associated structures in health and disease. • *Journal of Oral Implantology*, quarterly. Journal. • *Program and Abstracts*, annual. • *Special Care in Dentistry*, bimonthly.

★3955★ International Association of Dental Students (IADS) (Association Internationale des Etudiants Dentaires — AIED)
7 Carlisle St.
London W1V 5RG, England
Phone: 171 9357852
Fax: 171 4860183
Liz Stockell, Contact

Founded: 1951. **Members:** 60. **Languages:** English. **Description:** Dental schools in 40 countries. Promotes international contact among dental students; facilitates exchange of students between member countries; develops international programs. Sponsors educational and research programs. Conducts competitions. **Publications:** *IADS Exchange Guide*. • *Newsletter*, quarterly. Newsletter.

International Association of Dento-Maxillo-Facial Radiology (IADMFR)
See: Entry 11115

International Association of Equine Dental Technicians (IAEDT)
See: Entry 13084

International Association of Oral and Maxillofacial Surgeons (IAOMS)
See: Entry 12276

International Association of Oral Pathologists (IAOP)
See: Entry 10132

★3956★ International Association of Orthodontics (IAO)
1100 Lake St., No. 240
Oak Park, IL 60301
Phone: (708)445-0320
Free: 800-447-8770
Fax: (708)445-0321
Joanna Carey, Exec.Dir.

Founded: 1961. **Members:** 1,800. **Regional Groups:** 15. **Description:** Dentists. Promotes the study and dissemination of information on the cause, control, treatment, and prevention of malocclusion of the teeth; facilitates exchange of ideas and experiences, based on a biomechanical approach, between the various fields of dentistry related to orthodontics. **Publications:** *The Bandelette*, monthly. Newsletter. Provides information membership activities. *Price:* Included in membership dues; $15/year for nonmembers. • *International Association of Orthodontics--Directory of Members*, annual. Directory. *Price:* Included in membership dues; $15 for nonmembers. • *Journal of General Orthodontics*, quarterly. Journal. Contains clinical articles on orthodontics, self-assessment, troubleshooting, and new products. *Price:* $40/year. **Formerly:** International Academy of Orthodontics.

International Association of Paediatric Dentistry (IAPD)
See: Entry 3241

★3957★ International College of Dentists (ICD)
1 Metro Sq.
51 Monroe St., Ste. 1501
Rockville, MD 20850-2421
Phone: (301)251-8861
Fax: (301)738-9143
Richard G. Shaffer, D.D.S., Sec.Gen.

Founded: 1928. **Members:** 7,200. **Description:** Dentists who have made outstanding contributions to the profession. Acclaims meritorious service to dentistry; fosters growth and diffusion of dental information; upholds high standards in dental education and regulates the practice of dentistry. Supports the Dental Career Option Seminar for Students. Promotes continuing education through the International Clinicians Program. Operates charitable programs. **Publications:** *Globe*, annual. • *Key*, annual. Magazine. • *Keynotes*, semiannual. Newsletter. • *Roster*, periodic.

International College for Maxillo-Facial Surgery (ICMFS)
See: Entry 12277

★3958★ International Congress of Oral Implantologists (ICOI)
248 Lorraine Ave., 3rd Fl.
Upper Montclair, NJ 07043
Phone: (201)783-6300
Fax: (201)783-1175
R. Craig Johnson, Exec.Dir.

Founded: 1975. **Members:** 3,000. **Description:** Dentists and oral surgeons dedicated to the teaching of and research in oral implantology (branch of dentistry dealing with dental implants placed into or on top of the jaw bone). Offers fellowship and course certification programs. Compiles statistics and maintains registry of current research in the field. Sponsors classes, seminars, and workshops at universities, hospitals, and societies worldwide. Provides consultation and patient information/referral services. **Publications:** *ICOI News*, periodic. Newsletter. • *Implant Dentistry*, quarterly. Journal. Includes scientific manuscripts, new product reports, membership updates, and calendar of seminars. • Membership Directory, annual. **Formerly:** (1976) International College of Oral Implantologists.

★3959★ International Dental Health Foundation (IDHF)
11484 Washington Plz. W, Ste. 307
Reston, VA 22090
Phone: (703)471-8349
Patricia L. Cartwright, Exec.Dir.

Founded: 1981. **Members:** 450. **Description:** Dentists, dental hygienists, and other dental professionals. Advocates a method of treating periodontal disease that de-emphasizes cleaning and surgery and instead concentrates on eliminating the disease-causing bacteria. **Publications:** *Annotations*, bimonthly. Newsletter. *Price:* Included in membership dues. • Brochures.

International Federation of Dental Anesthesiology Societies (IFDAS)
See: Entry 2368

★3960★ **International Federation of Endodontic Associations**
c/o World Endodontic Congress
Ezequiel Montes 92
06030 Mexico City, DF, Mexico
Phone: 5 5660656
Dr. Jean-Marie Launchesse, Sec.-Treas.

Description: Promotes the practice and study of endodontics. Conducts research and educational programs.

★3961★ **International Group for Scientific Research in Stomatology and Odontology (GIRSO)**
(Groupement International pour la Recherche Scientifique en Stomatologie et Odontologie)
Hopital St.-Pierre
322, rue Haute
B-1000 Brussels, Belgium
Phone: 2 5556361
Fax: 2 5556345
Dr. Roland Rodembourg, Sec.

Founded: 1957. **Members:** 300. **Languages:** English, French, German, Italian. **Description:** Physicians and dentists doing basic research in stomatology (the science dealing with the treatment of the mouth and its diseases). Encourages exchange of material, documentation, and visits. **Publications:** *Bulletin*, quarterly. Bulletin.

★3962★ **International Institute of Dental Ergonomics and Technology (IIDET)**
(Institut International d'Ergonomie et Technology Dentaire — IIDET)
Loehrstrasse 1 39
56001 Koblenz, Germany
Phone: 261 34818
Fax: 261 34609
Dr. Karlheinz Kimmel, Exec. Officer

Founded: 1973. **Members:** 120. **Languages:** English, German. **Description:** Experts from 10 countries in dental equipment development, ergonomics, and infection control. **Publications:** Annual Report.

★3963★ **International Organization for Forensic Odonto-Stomatology (IOFOS)**
231 Bristol Rd.
Edgebaston
Birmingham, W. Midlands B5 7UB, England
Phone: 121 4401555
Fax: 121 4401555
Roy D. Simper, Pres.

Founded: 1973. **Members:** 800. **National Groups:** 23. **Languages:** English. **Description:** National professional societies active in the field of forensic odonto-stomatology. Promotes forensic dentistry worldwide. Fosters cooperation among members; collects and disseminates information and ideas on forensic dentistry. Compiles statistics. Supports educational and re-

search programs. **Publications:** *Forensic Odontology, Its Scope and History.* • *International Journal of Forensic Odonto-Homatology.* Journal. • *IOFOS Newsletter*, 3/year. Newsletter. • *The Journal of Forensic Odonto-Stomatology*, annual. **Formerly:** (1981) International Society of Forensic Odonto-Stomatology.

★3964★ **Missionary Dentists (MD)**
PO Box 7002
Seattle, WA 98133
Phone: (206)771-3241
Fax: (206)775-5155
Dr. Vaughn V. Chapman, Dir.

Founded: 1950. **Members:** 70. **Description:** Seeks to share the Gospel through the medium of dentistry. Provides dental services and conducts dental education programs in undeveloped or rural areas and cities overseas coupled with "the good news of the Gospel." Trains dentists, dental assistants, laboratory technicians, and hygenists for overseas service in their Overseas Training Seminar. **Publications:** *The Heartbeat*, quarterly. Newsletter. **Also Known As:** Worldwide Dental Health Service.

★3965★ **Myanmar Dental Association**
PO Box 1299
Yangon, Myanmar
Ba Mynit, Gen.Sec.

Founded: 1978. **Languages:** English, Thai. **Description:** Dental surgeons. Seeks to enhance the professional standing of members; promotes oral and dental health and hygiene. Conducts charitable and educational programs. **Publications:** Bulletin, periodic. • Journal, periodic. • Newsletter, periodic.

★3966★ **National Association of Dental Assistants (NADA)**
900 S. Washington St., No. G-13
Falls Church, VA 22046
Phone: (703)237-8616
Joseph Salta, Pres.

Founded: 1974. **Members:** 4,000. **Description:** Professional dental auxiliaries. Seeks to: bring added stature and purpose to the profession through continuing education; make available to dental assistants the special benefits normally limited to members of specialized professional and fraternal groups. Conducts seminars. **Publications:** *Communication in the Workplace.* • *Dental Assistant Salary Survey*, biennial. Survey. • *The Explorer*, monthly. Newsletter. Includes job exchange. *Price:* Included in membership dues; $15/year for nonmembers. • *Infection Control.* • *Mercury Poisoning.* • *Radiology.*

★3967★ **National Association of Dental Laboratories (NADL)**
555 E. Braddock Rd.
Alexandria, VA 22314-2106
Phone: (703)683-5263
Free: 800-950-1150
Fax: (703)549-4788
Robert W. Stanley, Exec.Dir.

Founded: 1951. **Members:** 2,900. **State Groups:** 48. **Description:** Federation of state associations representing 2900 commercial dental laboratories serving the dental profes-

sion. Develops criteria for ethical dental laboratories. Offers business and personal insurance programs, Hazardous Materials Training Program, and an infectious disease prevention training program. Compiles statistics; maintains speakers' bureau and museum; conducts educational and charitable programs. **Publications:** *Directory of Speakers and Lecturers*, periodic. Directory. • *Executive Information Series*, periodic. • *Fabrication Procedures*, periodic. • *Hazard Communication Manual*, periodic. • *Leadership Newsletter*, periodic. Newsletter. • *Managing for Profit.* Book. • *Trends and Techniques in the Contemporary Dental Laboratory*, 10/year. Magazine. *Price:* $40 for members; $50 for members outside U.S. • *Who's Who in the Dental Laboratory Industry*, annual. Directory. Also publishes standardized accounting system and makes available videotapes. **Formerly:** National Association of Certified Dental Laboratories.

★3968★ **National Association of Public Health Service Dentists**
(Bundesverband der Zahnarzte des Offentlichen Gesundheitsdienstes)
Unter der Rodebreite 26
37079 Gottingen, Germany
Phone: 551 61140
Fax: 551 61140
Dr. K.D. Rasch, Contact

Founded: 1954. **Description:** Safeguards the interests of public health service dentists and promotes their continuing education. Also promotes the prevention of oral diseases, especially in children. **Publications:** *Zahnaerztlichen Gesundheitsdienst*, quarterly, always last week of March, June, September, and December. Magazine.

★3969★ **National Association of Seventh-Day Adventist Dentists (NASDAD)**
c/o Karen Sutton
PO Box 101
Loma Linda, CA 92354
Phone: (714)824-4399
Karen Sutton, Exec.Dir.

Founded: 1944. **Members:** 600. **Regional Groups:** 11. **Publications:** *News*, quarterly. • *SDA Dentist*, annual.

★3970★ **National Board for Certification of Dental Laboratories (CDL)**
555 E. Braddock Rd.
Alexandria, VA 22314
Phone: (703)683-5263
Fax: (703)549-4788
Robert W. Stanley, Exec.Dir.

Founded: 1979. **Members:** 600. **Description:** Certified dental laboratories, including commercial, private, and dental or dental technology schools. Purpose is the certification and recognition of dental laboratories that demonstrate and document compliance with standards set by the industry for laboratory facilities, technical resources, safety, prevention of cross-contamination, and competence of personnel. **Publications:** *Certified Mail*, periodic. Newsletter. • Directory, semiannual.

★3971★ **National Board for Certification in Dental Technology (NBC)**
555 E. Braddock Rd.
Alexandria, VA 22314-2106
Phone: (703)683-5310
Fax: (703)549-4788
Sandra Stewart, Exec. Officer

Founded: 1958. **Description:** Dental technicians with formal education in dental technology and a minimum of three years' experience who have passed written and practical exams administered by the NBC. Provides continuing education to certificants and recognizes competent dental technicians. **Publications:** *Who's Who in the Dental Laboratory Industry*, annual. Published in conjunction with the National Association of Dental Laboratories.

★3972★ **National Dental Assistants Association (NDAA)**
c/o Robert Johns
5506 Connecticut Ave. NW, Ste. 24
Washington, DC 20015
Phone: (202)244-7555
Fax: (202)244-5992
Dr. Robert John, Exec.Dir.

Members: 500. **Description:** An auxiliary of the National Dental Association. Works to encourage education and certification among dental assistants. Conducts clinics and workshops to further the education of members. Bestows annual Humanitarian Award; offers scholarships. **Publications:** *NDAA Journal*, annual. Journal.

★3973★ **National Dental Association (NDA)**
5506 Connecticut Ave. NW, Ste. 24
Washington, DC 20015
Phone: (202)244-7555
Fax: (202)244-5992
Robert S. Johns, Exec.Dir.

Founded: 1913. **Members:** 5,000. **Regional Groups:** 6. **State Groups:** 15. **Local Groups:** 48. **Description:** Professional society for dentists. Aims to provide quality dental care to the unserved and underserved public and promote knowledge of the art and science of dentistry. Advocates the inclusion of dental care services in health care programs on local, state, and national levels. Fosters the integration of minority dental health care providers in the profession, and promotes dentistry as a viable career for minorities through support programs. Conducts research programs. Group is distinct from the former name of the American Dental Association. **Publications:** *Flossline*, quarterly. Contains educational news. *Price:* Included in membership dues. • Journal, quarterly. **Formerly:** (1932) Interstate Dental Association.

★3974★ **National Dental Hygienists' Association (NDHA)**
28315 Kalong Cir. W.
Southfield, MI 48034-5658
Phone: (810)358-0432
Dr. Barbara Purifoy-Seldon, Pres.

Founded: 1932. **Members:** 50. **State Groups:** 10. **Description:** Minority dental hygienists. To cultivate and promote the art and science of dental hygiene and to enhance the professional image of dental hygienists. Attempts to meet the needs of society through educational, political, and social activities while giving the minority dental hygienist a voice in shaping the profession. Encourages cooperation and mutual support among minority professionals. Seeks to increase opportunities for continuing education and employment in the field of dental hygiene. Works to improve individual and community dental health. Sponsors annual seminar, fundraising events, and scholarship programs; participates in career orientation programs; counsels and assists students applying for or enrolled in dental hygiene programs. Maintains liaison with American Dental Hygienists' Association. **Publications:** Newsletter, quarterly.

★3975★ **National Denturist Association (NDA)**
PO Box 40307
Portland, OR 97240-0307
Phone: (503)292-7994
Dr. James Davis, Exec.Dir.

Founded: 1975. **State Groups:** 22. **Description:** Denturists, dental laboratory technicians, and other dental professionals. Promotes recognition and authorization of the profession of denturitry. Conducts research regarding law pertaining to the dental profession and to the profession and practice of denturitry. Offers seminars to prepare denturists for certification. Compiles statistics. Provides political action counseling and organizing guidance. **Publications:** *NDA Denturist News*, quarterly. Newsletter. Contains educational and business management articles and political reports. Includes new product information and legal news. *Price:* Included in membership or free upon request.

National Foundation of Dentistry for the Handicapped (NFDH)
See: Entry 4526

★3976★ **National Medical and Dental Association (NMDA)**
9412 Academy Rd.
Philadelphia, PA 19114
Phone: (215)676-2242
Dorothy Czarnecki, M.D., Exec.Sec.

Founded: 1910. **Members:** 600. **Regional Groups:** 12. **State Groups:** 2. **Local Groups:** 2. **Description:** Physicians and dentists of Polish extraction. Offers continuing medical education conferences. Maintains speakers' bureau and hall of fame. **Publications:** Bulletin, annual.

★3977★ **New Zealand Dental Association (NZDA)**
PO Box 28084
Remeura
Auckland 5, New Zealand
Phone: 9 5242778
Fax: 9 5205256
Dr. L.J. Croxson, Exec.Dir.

Founded: 1905. **Members:** 1,500. **Local Groups:** 16. **Languages:** English. **Description:** Registered dental practitioners in New Zealand. Promotes improved dental health through the increased availability of dental and allied services. Collects and disseminates data on topics including AIDS, infection control, and oral health costs. Bestows awards. **Publications:** *Member-* *ship Booklet of the New Zealand Dental Association*, annual. Directory. • *New Zealand Dental Journal*, quarterly. Journal. • *NZDA News*, bimonthly. Newsletter.

★3978★ **New Zealand Dental Therapists Association**
115 Captain Scott Rd.
Titrangi
Auckland 7, New Zealand
Phone: 9 8174140
Andrea Jarrold, Contact

Founded: 1921. **Members:** 400. **Languages:** English. **Description:** Women dental therapists of New Zealand. Promotes the professional interests of members. Works to ensure the provision of dental services to children and adults in New Zealand. Establishes industry standards. **Publications:** *Dental Therapist Journal*, annual.

Nordic Society of Forensic Odonto-Stomatology (NSDS)
See: Entry 7190

North American Medical / Dental Association (NAMDA)
See: Entry 1443

★3979★ **Odontological Federation of Central America and Panama**
Avenida Olimpica 26-40
Apartado Postal 621
San Salvador, El Salvador
Gregorio Arevalo Molina

Description: Promotes the practice and study of odontology in Central America.

★3980★ **Omicron Kappa Upsilon**
Coll. of Dentistry
University of Nebraska
Lincoln, NE 68583-0740
Phone: (402)472-1339
Jan John, Sec.

Founded: 1914. **Members:** 17,500. **Description:** Honorary society of men and women in the field of dentistry. **Publications:** Bulletin, annual.

★3981★ **Organization of Teachers of Oral Diagnosis (OTOD)**
Indiana University
Department of Dental Diagnostic Sciences
1121 W. Michigan St., Rm. S-110
Indianapolis, IN 46202
Phone: (317)274-7474
H.W. Gilmer

Founded: 1963. **Members:** 200. **Description:** Teachers and university departments of oral diagnosis (oral medicine and oral pathology). Seeks to update techniques, materi al, and knowledge in oral diagnosis education. Sponsors seminars focusing on cur rent issues and breakthroughs in the field and provides speakers for dental soci eties and dental education organizations. Promotes the interests of dental educa tors. Cosponsors the American Board of Oral Medicine. **Publications:** Membership Directory, annual. • Newsletter, 3/year. • *Oral Surgery, Oral Medicine and Oral Pathology*, 3/year. • *Treatment Planning - Synopsis of 1981 Workshop*.

★3982★ Organizing Committee of the World Congress on Implantology and Biomaterials (CMIB)
(Comite d'Organisation du Congress Mondial d'Implantologie des Biomateriaux — CMIB)
57, ave. de Bretagne
F-76100 Rouen, France
Phone: 35 730034
Fax: 35 032350
Dr. Manuel Chanavaz, Pres.

Founded: 1987. **Members:** 300. **Languages:** English, French. **Description:** Medical doctors; dental surgeons; orthopedic, ophthalmic, and plastic implantologists; general anesthesiologists; researchers in 27 countries. Organizes a world congress, held every 2 years, on implantology, bio-materials, prosthetics, and dental occlusion. Congress is sponsored by the American Academy of Implant Dentistry, the College International de Recherches Implantaires de Lariboisiere, the European College of Research into Implantology and Biomaterials, the European Society of Biomaterials, the International Congress of Oral Implantologists, the Alabama Implant Study Group, the Deutsche Gesellschaft fur Zahnarztliche Implantologie, the French Ministry of Education and Scientific Research, and the French Ministry of Health.

★3983★ Orthodontic Education and Research Foundation (OERF)
3556 Caroline St.
St. Louis, MO 63104
Phone: (314)577-8189
Peter G. Sotiropoulos, Exec.Dir.

Founded: 1957. **Members:** 500. **Description:** Orthodontists. Promotes research; conducts continuing education programs, seminars, and clinical and professional training. **Publications:** *OERF Journal*, annual. Proceedings. Includes new members listing. *Price:* Included in membership dues. • *OERF Newsletter*, annual. Newsletter.

★3984★ Pancyprian Dental Association (PDA)
Princess Zina de Tyras Bldg.
PO Box 2063
Nicosia, Cyprus
Phone: 2 367401
Fax: 2 367016
Mrs. Pitsilli, Sec.

Founded: 1968. **Members:** 440. **Local Groups:** 4. **Languages:** English, Greek. **Description:** Dentists concerned with the dental health of the Cyprian populace. Conducts educational and public service programs. **Publications:** *Dental Tribune*, quarterly. Magazine. **Also Known As:** Cyprus Dental Association.

★3985★ Pierre Fauchard Academy (PFA)
c/o Dr. Richard Kozal
8021 W. 79th St.
Justice, IL 60458-1607
Phone: (708)594-5884
Free: 800-232-0099
Fax: (708)496-1066
Dr. Richard Kozal, Sec.-Treas.

Founded: 1936. **Members:** 5,000. **State Groups:** 50. **Description:** Dentists "of high standards and leadership" who are nominated to the academy by state or section chairmen. Objectives are to educate dentists by providing literature on developments and opinions in dentistry; promote continuing education for all members of the dental profession; facilitate the exchange of knowledge among dentists; foster contact between dentistry leaders and those who seek advice on scientific, technical, or economic subjects; encourage advancement of professional and scientific standards; further the improvement of oral health of the public through prevention, therapy, and restoration; emphasize professional responsibility to the public. Sponsors annual Memorial Lecture honoring a past leader of dentistry. The academy is named for Pierre Fauchard (1678-1761), a French dentist who pioneered modern dental practice and dental education. **Publications:** *Dental Abstracts*, quarterly. *Price:* $22/year. • *Dental World*, bimonthly. Newsletter. Includes member news, meeting announcements, abstracts, book reviews, and editorials. • *Leadership Manual of the PFA*. Manual. • *Legacy, The Dental Profession*. Book. • *The Life and Times of Pierre Fauchard*. Book. • Membership Directory, periodic.

★3986★ Portuguese Society of Stomatology and Dental Medicine (PSSDM)
(Sociedade Portugesa de Estomatologia Emedicina Dentaria — SPEMD)
Avda. Rainha D. Amelia, 36 r/c-dto.
P-1600 Lisbon, Portugal
Phone: 1 7593948
Fax: 1 7593948
Leite da Silva, Pres.

Founded: 1919. **Members:** 1,700. **Local Groups:** 3. **Languages:** English, Portuguese. **Description:** Stomatologists, dentists, and oral and maxillofacial surgeons in Portugal. Promotes research in all disciplines of oral medicine. Sponsors community dental hygiene programs. Establishes standards and qualifications for oral medicine specialists. Represents' members interests; operates legal defense fund for members. Monitors the manufacture of dental materials in Portugal. Promotes continuing education programs for members. **Publications:** *Revista Portuguese de Estomatologia e Cirurgia Maxilofacial*, quarterly. Journal. Journal of dentistry and maxillofacial surgery • *Stoma*, quarterly.

★3987★ Psi Omega
1030 Lincoln Ave.
Prospect Park, PA 19076
Phone: (215)532-2330
Dr. Edward M. Grosse, Exec.Dir.

Founded: 1892. **Members:** 30,000. **Regional Groups:** 35. **State Groups:** 36. **Description:** Professional fraternity - dentistry. **Publications:** *Frater*, quarterly.

★3988★ Scandinavian Endodontic Association (SEA)
Dept. of Endontics
Faculty of Odontology
Box 33070
S-400 33 Goteborg, Sweden
Phone: 31 674500
Dr. Claes Reit, Exec. Officer

Founded: 1981. **Members:** 150. **Languages:** Danish, Norwegian, Swedish. **Description:** Dentists specializing or interested in endodontics. (Endodontics is the branch of dentistry concerned with diseases of the pulp, the tissue found in the inner cavity of the tooth.)

★3989★ Sigma Phi Alpha
650 E. 25th St.
Kansas City, MO 64108
Phone: (816)235-2053
Fax: (816)235-2157
Lois Scott, Sec.-Treas.

Founded: 1958. **Members:** 5,380. **Local Groups:** 157. **Description:** Honorary society, dental hygiene. **Also Known As:** National Dental Hygiene Honor Society.

★3990★ Slovenian Dental Association (SDA)
Komenskega 4
SLO-61000 Ljubljana, Slovenia
Fax: 61 301955
Dr. M. Rode, Exec. Officer

Founded: 1945. **Members:** 350. **Description:** Dentists and others interested in promoting and maintaining good dental health. Conducts educational programs; makes available children's services. **Publications:** *Informator*. Bulletin.

Society of Medical-Dental Management Consultants (SMD)
See: Entry 5882

★3991★ Society for Occlusal Studies (SOS)
c/o Dr. Bernard Williams
1010 Carondelet Dr., No. 410
Kansas City, MO 64114
Phone: (816)941-0509
Fax: (816)941-4832
Dr. Bernard Williams, Pres.

Founded: 1964. **Members:** 800. **Local Groups:** 95. **Description:** Dentists and laboratory technicians who have completed the society's continuing education course in occlusion (bringing opposing surfaces of the teeth of the two jaws into contact). Promotes effective occlusal treatment. Conducts Principles of Occlusion Seminar, Advanced Restorative Seminar, laboratory technician program, and practice management program. **Publications:** *Roster*, annual. • *SOS Newsletter*, quarterly. Newsletter. Covers developments in the treatment and diagnosis of temporomandibular joint dysfunction and principles of occlusion instrumentation. *Price:* Included in membership dues.

★3992★ Stomatological Society of Greece
17 Kallirroes St.
GR-11743 Athens, Greece
Phone: 1 9214325
Fax: 1 9214204
R. Karapa-Damigos, Sec. Gen.

Founded: 1937. **Members:** 600. **Languages:** English, Greek. **Description:** Dentists. Promotes dentistry in Greece. Provides members with the latest technological information. **Publications:** *Stomatologia*, quarterly. Journal. Includes English summaries.

★3993★ Student National Dental Association (SNDA)
c/o Dr. Robert Knight
Howard University School of Dentistry
600 W. St. NW
Washington, DC 20059
Phone: (202)806-0301
Fax: (202)806-0354
Robert Knight, Pres.

Founded: 1972. **Members:** 9,000. **Regional Groups:** 10. **Local Groups:** 46. **Description:** A section of the National Dental Association. Minority dental students. Addresses the needs of minority dental students; strives to expose and eliminate discriminatory practices encountered by its members. Promotes increased minority enrollment in dental schools. Seeks to improve dental health care delivery to all disadvantaged people. Compiles statistics. **Publications:** *Convention Bulletin*, annual. Bulletin. • *Help Us to Build Your Dental Career*. Updated annually. • Membership Directory, annual. *Price:* Available to members only.

★3994★ Swedish Dental Association (SDA)
(Sveriges Tandlakarforbund — STF)
Nybrogatan 53
Box 5843
S-102 48 Stockholm, Sweden
Phone: 8 6661500
Fax: 8 6625842
Mr. Gunnar Luthman, Contact

Founded: 1908. **Members:** 11,900. **Languages:** English, Swedish. **Description:** Union of dentists in Sweden. Offers over 200 continuing dental education courses annually. **Publications:** *Swedish Dental Journal*, bimonthly. Journal. • *Tandlakartidningen*, 18/year. Journal.

Swedish Dental Trade Association
(Foreningen Svensk Dentalhandel — FSD)
See: Entry 5883

Syndicat des Industries Francaises pour l'Art Dentaire (SIFADENT)
See: Entry 5884

★3995★ Syrian Dental Association (SDA)
Jiser Al Abiad Raiss
Egypt St. Bldg. No. 52
PO Box 11104
Damascus, Syrian Arab Republic
Phone: 11 247204

Founded: 1952. **Members:** 5,920. **National Groups:** 14. **Languages:** Arabic, English, French. **Description:** Dentists in the Syrian Arab Republic. Represents members' interests. Promotes dental health care. Sponsors educational and research programs; provides children's services; bestows awards; compiles statistics. **Publications:** Journal, quarterly.

Union of American Physicians and Dentists (UAPD)
See: Entry 1524

Unione Nazionale Industrie Dentarie Italiane
See: Entry 5885

Verband der Deutschen Dental-Industrie
See: Entry 5886

★3996★ Women in Dentistry
609 Nelson House
Dolphin Sq.
London SW1V 3NZ, England
Phone: 121 4541443
Marion Press, Gen.Sec.

Founded: 1985. **Members:** 500. **Regional Groups:** 17. **Languages:** English. **Description:** Women dentists in the United Kingdom. Strives to assist women dentists in achieving professional goals through advice, practical support, and political representation. Cooperates with organizations in France, the United States, and Australia with similar aims. Disseminates information. **Publications:** *Women in Dentistry*, quarterly. Newsletter.

★3997★ Xi Psi Phi
c/o Dr. Keith W. Dickey
1623 Washington Ave., No. 300
Alton, IL 62002
Phone: (618)463-1889
Fax: (618)463-1881
Dr. Keith W. Dickey, Sec.-Treas.

Founded: 1889. **Members:** 19,000. **Local Groups:** 22. **Description:** Professional dental fraternity - dentistry. Maintains Hall of Fame. Conducts educational programs. **Publications:** *Quarterly*, quarterly. *Price:* $8.

Research Centers

American Society for the Advancement of Anesthesia in Dentistry
See: Entry 2377

★3998★ Case Western Reserve University Bolton-Brush Growth Study Center
Bolton Dental Bldg., 3rd Fl.
10900 Euclid Ave.
Cleveland, OH 44106-4905
Phone: (216)368-6715
Fax: (216)368-3204
B. Holly Broadbent, Jr., DDS, Dir.

Research Activities and Fields: Investigations into the growth and development of dentition, face and cranium, and roentgenographic studies of the epiphyses of the human body. Conducts an ongoing study of longitudinal cephalometric radiographs and dental casts. **E-mail Address:** mgh4@po.cwru.edu. **Formerly:** Bolton Study; Brush Inquiry.

★3999★ Craniofacial Center
1847 Old York Rd.
Abington, PA 19001
Phone: (215)657-7788
Fax: (215)657-5483
Dr. Neil Gottehrer, Dir.

Research Activities and Fields: Conducts clinical research on dental implants, including type of implant, longevity, and coatings used on implants.

★4000★ Eastman Dental Center
625 Elmwood Ave.
Rochester, NY 14620
Phone: (716)275-5001
Fax: (716)244-8772
Ronald J. Billings, D.D.S., Dir.

Research Activities and Fields: Clinical and basic scientific research on all aspects of oral disease, including dental caries, periodontal disease, craniofacial disorders, oral pain and health behavior. **Formerly:** Eastman Dental Dispensary (1964).

★4001★ Forsyth Dental Center
140 The Fenway
Boston, MA 02115
Phone: (617)262-5200
Fax: (617)262-4021
Dr. Ronald J. Gibbons, Dir.

Research Activities and Fields: Physical, biomedical, and clinical sciences pertinent to field of oral biology. Seeks to obtain a better understanding of normal and diseased structures of the oral cavity and its related parts, including microbiology, molecular genetics, immunology, biomineralization, biochemistry, pharmacology, bioengineering, clinical trials, cytokine biology, toxicology, periodontology, electron microscopy, food research, histochemistry, and cell biology. Seeks to control and prevent the three major oral diseases: dental caries, periodontal disease, and oral/facial deformities. **Formerly:** Forsyth Dental Infirmary for Children (1963).

★4002★ Immunology Laboratory
300 N. Ingalls Bldg., Rm. 1183 SE
Ann Arbor, MI 48109-0402
Phone: (313)747-3912
Dr. Dennis E. Lopatin, Research Scientist

Research Activities and Fields: Effects of the microbial flora on immune regulation and effector function. Performs enzyme immunoassays and tissue cultures and applies immunoadsorbant column methodology.

★4003★ Indiana University-Purdue University at Indianapolis
Oral Health Research Institute
415 Lansing St.
Indianapolis, IN 46202
Phone: (317)274-8822
Fax: (317)274-5425
Dr. George K. Stookey, Dir.

Research Activities and Fields: Studies of the etiology and prevention of dental caries and periodontal disease, and biocompatibility of dental materials. Investigates preventive measures concentrated on fluorides and antimicrobial agents, including a wide variety of in vitro test procedures, research on a number of animal models for determining safety and therapeutic potential, and human clinical investigations of safety and efficacy.

★4004★ New York University
David B. Kriser Dental Center
345 E. 24th St.
New York, NY 10010
Phone: (212)998-9794
Fax: (212)995-3529
Roy C. Johnson, Libn.

Research Activities and Fields: Dentistry, dental history, and allied health sciences. **Publications:** Newsletter (three times per year).

★ 4005 ★ **Ohio State University**
George C. Paffenbarger Dental Research
   Laboratory
College of Dentistry
Postle Hall
305 W. 12th Ave.
Columbus, OH 43210
Phone: (614)292-0880
Fax: (614)292-9422
Dr. S.F. Rosenstiel, Dir.

Research Activities and Fields: Dental biomaterials engineering. Currently studying dental polymers, maxillo-facial polymer synthesis, and optical properties of esthetic biomaterials. **E-mail Address:** rosenstiel.1@osu.edu.

★ 4006 ★ **Specialized Caries Research**
   Center
Forsyth Dental Center
140 The Fenway
Boston, MA 02115
Phone: (617)262-5200
Fax: (617)262-4021
Dr. Ron Gibbons, Dir.

Research Activities and Fields: Dental caries, especially decay on root surfaces.

★ 4007 ★ **State University of New York at**
   Buffalo
Periodontal Disease Research Center
Foster Hall
Buffalo, NY 14214
Phone: (716)829-2854
Fax: (716)829-2387
Dr. Robert J. Genco, Chm.

Research Activities and Fields: Laboratory, clinical, and epidemiological investigations of periodontal disease, particularly the etiology, pathogenesis, and management of this and other chronic bacterial infections; Specific areas of study include microbiology, host response mechanisms, clinical analysis, risk factors, and the development of genetic probes, novel antibiotics, and growth factors as they apply to periodontal diseases. **Publications:** *Contemporary Periodontics.* **Formerly:** Periodontal Disease Clinical Research Center.

U.S. Department of Defense
Armed Forces Institute of Pathology
Center for Advanced Pathology
Oral Pathology Department
See: Entry 10159

U.S. Department of Defense
Armed Forces Institute of Pathology
Oral Pathology Department
Forensic Dentistry Division
See: Entry 10173

U.S. Department of Defense
Naval Medical Research and Development
   Command
Naval Dental Research Institute
See: Entry 7839

★ 4008 ★ **U.S. Department of Health and**
   Human Services
National Institute of Dental Research
NIH Bldg. 31, Rm. 2C39
9000 Rockville Pike
Bethesda, MD 20892
Phone: (301)496-4261
Fax: (301)496-9988
Dr. Harald Loe, Director

Research Activities and Fields: Institute conducts and supports research relating to the normal development, maintenance, and aging of the oral and facial tissues, and the cause, prevention, and methods of diagnosis and treatment of oral diseases and conditions. Principal areas of research include dental caries; periodontal disease; congenital and acquired craniofacial malformations; orofacial pain and sensory-motor dysfunction; oral soft tissue diseases; AIDS; salivary glands and secretions; mineralized tissues and fluoride studies; pulp biology; nutrition research; behavioral studies; implants, replants, and transplants; and restorative dental materials. NIDR research components include the Epidemiology and Oral Disease Prevention Program, the Intramural Research Program, and Extramural Program. NIDR supports extramural research through grant and contract awards. The Institute also supports 22 research centers: five clinical core centers for oral biology, five specialized periodontal disease centers, two cariology centers, three centers for research on craniofacial anomalies, one for research on aging, three materials science centers, and three clinical core centers located at the Universities of Minnesota, Washington, and Iowa. The research centers for oral biology are located at the Universities of Alabama, Pennsylvania, and Washington, and the State University of New York--Buffalo and University of California, San Francisco. Their goals are to attract scientists from a broad range of disciplines to collaborate in studies related to oral health. The five specialized centers for clinical research on periodontal disease are located at Forsyth Dental Center in Boston, at the State University of New York--Buffalo, at Virginia Commonwealth University in Richmond, at the University of Florida, and at the University of Pennsylvania. The two caries centers are located at the University of Rochester and Forsyth Dental Clinic in Boston. The centers for research on craniofacial anomalies are at the Universities of Southern California, Iowa, and Pennyslvania. The center for research on aging is at the University of Florida, and the three materials science centers are at the Universities of Michigan and Florida and at the American Dental Association Health Foundation at the National Institute of Standards of Technology.

★ 4009 ★ **U.S. Department of Health and**
   Human Services
National Institute of Dental Research
Epidemiology and Oral Disease Prevention
   Program
Westwood Bldg.
5333 Westbard Ave., Rm. 528
Bethesda, MD 20892
Phone: (301)496-7239
Dr. L. Jackson Brown, Deputy Director

Research Activities and Fields: Program conducts descriptive and analytical epidemiologic

studies of the etiology, distribution, and trends in dental caries, periodontal diseases, and other oral diseases and disorders. Program's Disease Prevention and Health Promotion Branch manages activities involving health promotion research and application. Research is supported both through intramural projects and research and development contracts.

★ 4010 ★ **U.S. Department of Health and**
   Human Services
National Institute of Dental Research
Epidemiology and Oral Disease Prevention
   Program
Disease Prevention and Health Promotion
   Branch
Westwood Bldg., Rm. 538
Bethesda, MD 20892
Phone: (301)594-7615
Dr. Helen C. Gift, Chief Disease Prevention
   Section

Research Activities and Fields: Conducts clinical trials and epidemiological studies related to the prevention of dental caries.

★ 4011 ★ **U.S. Department of Health and**
   Human Services
National Institute of Dental Research
Epidemiology and Oral Disease Prevention
   Program
Epidemiology Branch
Westwood Bldg., Rm. 538
5333 Westbard Ave.
Bethesda, MD 20892
Phone: (301)594-7615

Research Activities and Fields: Epidemiology studies.

★ 4012 ★ **U.S. Department of Health and**
   Human Services
National Institute of Dental Research
Epidemiology and Oral Disease Prevention
   Program
Sampling, Statistics, and Data Management
Westwood Bldg., Rm. 525
Bethesda, MD 20892
Phone: (301)496-8192
Fax: (301)480-2092
Cecelia B. Snowden, Chief

Research Activities and Fields: Provides statistical and computer data management support for the Epidemiology and Oral Disease Prevention Program.

★ 4013 ★ **U.S. Department of Health and**
   Human Services
National Institute of Dental Research
Extramural Program
Westwood Bldg., Rm. 503
Bethesda, MD 20892
Phone: (301)594-7638
Fax: (301)594-7616
Lois K. Cohen, Director

Research Activities and Fields: NIDR's Extramural Program administers grant and contract funds for research and training research manpower. Support is provided for investigations ranging from basic laboratory studies on the causes of oral disorders to clinical trials of new therapies or means of disease prevention. Principal components are: the Caries and Restorative Materials Research Branch; Craniofacial Anomalies, Pain Control, and Behavioral Research Branch; Periodontal and Soft Tissue Diseases Research Branch; and the Scientific Review Branch.

★4014★ U.S. Department of Health and Human Services
National Institute of Dental Research
Extramural Program
Caries, Restorative Materials and Salivary
  Research Branch
5333 Westbard Ave., Rm. 509
Bethesda, MD 20892
Phone: (301)496-7884
Dr. Gerassimos G. Roussos, Ph.D., Chief

Research Activities and Fields: Branch seeks to develop information on the epidemiology, etiology, pathogenesis, prevention, treatment, and restoration of damage caused by dental diseases, including caries and disorders of the dental pulp and the effects of nutritional variations on oral health. Examples of research on caries include mechanisms of infection by oral bacteria, biochemistry of plaque, the salivary immune system, physicochemistry of the caries process, mechanisms of caries inhibition by fluoride, relationship of diet to caries, and public health aspects of caries prevention. The program also supports studies to improve knowledge of the development, structure, function, and diseases of the salivary glands and to determine the influence of salivary constituents on oral health. Restorative materials research includes studies that develop new and improved materials and techniques for the treatment of dental diseases and restoration of dental function. Areas of research include restorative filling materials, bonding agents, tooth surface sealants, adhesive coatings and cements, intraoral prostheses for replacement for missing teeth, materials and techniques for improved endodontic therapy, maxillofacial prosthetic materials and treatment instrumentation to improve dental care. Emphasizes research of biocompatibility of materials.

★4015★ U.S. Department of Health and Human Services
National Institute of Dental Research
Extramural Program
Craniofacial Anomalies Development and
  Disorders Program
Westwood Bldg., Rm. 509
Bethesda, MD 20892
Phone: (301)594-7641
Fax: (301)594-9720
Dr. Mohandas Bhat, Program Dir.

Research Activities and Fields: Branch supports studies of normal and abnormal craniofacial growth, development, and function, with emphasis on research pertaining to the etiology and treatment of craniofacial anomalies. Malocclusion as well as acquired disfigurement and dysfunction are also major areas of concern. Investigations supported include studies in treatment methods, developmental biology, wound healing, physiology of mastication, deglutition, speech, oral sensation, and perception. In the area of dental and oral-facial pain conditions, basic studies in trigeminal neurophysiology are included, in addition to clinical studies in dental anesthesiology, intravenous sedation, trigemi-

nal neuralgia, other facial pain syndromes, temporomandibular joint disorders, and bruxism. Also supported is research on oral-facial sensory and motor dysfunction. Behavioral research includes studies of social and behavioral factors influencing oral health, with emphasis on research related to oral health promotion and to factors involved in the adoption of preventive measures. Program also supports basic studies of bone biology and research on technological developments in areas that relate to improved diagnostic techniques and treatment modalities.

★4016★ U.S. Department of Health and Human Services
National Institute of Dental Research
Extramural Program
Periodontal and Soft Tissue Diseases
  Research Program
509 Westwood Bldg.
5333 Westbard Ave.
Bethesda, MD 20892
Phone: (301)594-7641
Dennis Mangan, Chief

Research Activities and Fields: Program supports research on the cause, nature, diagnosis, treatment, and prevention of periodontal diseases; and on oral ulcerative and viral diseases, oral cancer, and the effects of nutritional variations on oral health and on the development and function of craniofacial tissues. In studies of periodontal diseases, special attention is given to the identification and characterization of microorganisms that cause these diseases and to the host responses they evoke. Emphasis is on biochemical and immunologic mechanisms involved in inflammation and tissue destruction. Clinical and laboratory studies are coordinated in an effort to develop practical preventive measures suitable for the general public. In other studies, objectives are to obtain knowledge of: 1) the etiology, diagnosis, treatment, and prevention of oral soft tissue diseases and disorders; 2) the role of nutrition in growth, maintenance, function, and health of hard and soft tissues of the craniofacial complex; and 3) the development and function of normal and abnormal salivary glands and their secretions.

★4017★ U.S. Department of Health and Human Services
National Institute of Dental Research
Intramural Research Program
NIH Bldg. 30, Rm. 132
9000 Rockville Pike
Bethesda, MD 20892
Phone: (301)496-1483
Dr. Abner L. Notkins, Director

Research Activities and Fields: The Intramural Research Program conducts basic and clinical research directed toward increasing fundamental knowledge of oral diseases, including periodontal disease and related disorders, by using the latest techniques in molecular biology, immunology, and cell biology. Areas of interest include the biochemistry, structure, function, and development of bone, teeth, salivary glands, and connective tissues; the role of bacteria and viruses in oral disease; genetic disorders and tumors of the oral cavity; studies on the cause and treatment of acute and chronic pain; and the development of new and improved diag-

nostic methods. Program comprises branches for: Bone Research, Clinical Investigations and Patient Care, Diagnostic Systems, and Neurobiology and Anesthesiology. Program also involves research in laboratories for: Developmental Biology and Anomalies, Microbial Ecology, Microbiology and Immunology, Oral Biology and Physiology, and Oral Medicine.

★4018★ U.S. Department of Health and Human Services
National Institute of Dental Research
Intramural Research Program
Bone Research Branch
NIH Bldg. 30, Rm. 106
9000 Rockville Pike
Bethesda, MD 20892
Phone: (301)496-6255
Dr. Pam Robey, Chief

Research Activities and Fields: The Bone Research Branch studies the structure, development, biosynthesis, and regulation of bones, teeth, and cartilaginous tissues. Emphasis is on studies of acquired and heritable disorders of the skeleton. Fields of study include cell biology, molecular biology, protein and carbohydrate biochemistry, immunochemistry, and molecular biophysics.

★4019★ U.S. Department of Health and Human Services
National Institute of Dental Research
Intramural Research Program
Clinical Investigations and Patient Care
  Branch
NIH Bldg. 10, Rm. 1N113
9000 Rockville Pike
Bethesda, MD 20892
Phone: (301)496-1363
Fax: (301)402-1228
Dr. Bruce J. Baum, Chief

Research Activities and Fields: Branch conducts clinical research related to the diagnosis, prevention, and management of oral and dental diseases. Primary efforts are directed at understanding neurotransmitter receptor regulation of events involved in salivary secretion, such as water movement, ion fluxes, and protein synthesis and processing. Other studies focus on the complaint of xerostomia (dry mouth), establishing criteria for evaluating salivary gland status, and developing treatment procedures for hypofunctional glands. In addition, research is carried out on oral physiological effects of aging, including oral motor performance and oral sensory processes, and on the relationship between salivary gland function and oral opportunistic infections in AIDS. (Branch components include a Patient Care Section.)

★4020★ U.S. Department of Health and Human Services
National Institute of Dental Research
Intramural Research Program
Neurobiology and Anesthesiology Branch
NIH Bldg. 49, Rm. IA-04
9000 Rockville Pike
Bethesda, MD 20892
Phone: (301)496-6804
Fax: (301)402-0667
Dr. Ronald Dubner, Chief

Research Activities and Fields: The Neurobiology and Anesthesiology Branch studies oral-facial sensation, emphasizing mechanisms of pain and the development of new methods for controlling pain in humans. Branch sections utilize anatomical, physiological, behavioral, pharmacological, and psychophysical techniques to study neural function as it relates to the processing of sensory signals about the threat of tissue-damaging stimulation.

U.S. Department of Health and Human Services
National Institute of Dental Research
Intramural Research Program
Pain Research Clinic
See: Entry 8439

U.S. Department of Health and Human Services
National Institute of Dental Research
Laboratory of Cellular Development and Oncology
See: Entry 2640

U.S. Department of Health and Human Services
National Institute of Dental Research
Laboratory of Developmental Biology
See: Entry 2641

★ 4021 ★ U.S. Department of Health and Human Services
National Institute of Dental Research
Laboratory of Immunology
NIH Bldg. 30
9000 Rockville Pike
Bethesda, MD 20892
Phone: (301)496-4178
Dr. Stephan E. Mergenhagen, Chief

Research Activities and Fields: Conducts research on molecular basis of immunological mediated acute and chronic inflammatory diseases. More specifically, research is focused on the contributions of mononuclear leukocytes and cytokines to the regulation of connective tissue catabolism, tissue repair and inflammation, and to the development of chronic inflammatory diseases which include AIDS, rheumatoid arthritis, and chronic periodontitis. Research on the immediate hypersensitivity reaction utilizes molecular biological technologies to define receptors on basophils and mast cells for immunoglobulin E and explores the biochemical pathways that are involved in cell secretion.

★ 4022 ★ U.S. Department of Health and Human Services
National Institute of Dental Research
Laboratory of Microbial Ecology
NIH Bldg. 30, Rm. 316
9000 Rockville Pike
Bethesda, MD 20892
Phone: (301)496-2232

Research Activities and Fields: Microbial ecology.

★ 4023 ★ U.S. Department of Health and Human Services
National Institute of Dental Research
Laboratory of Oral Medicine

NIH Bldg. 30, Rm. 121
9000 Rockville Pike
Bethesda, MD 20892
Phone: (301)496-4535
Fax: (301)402-4163
Dr. Abner L. Notkins, Chief

Research Activities and Fields: TRA Studies on 1) treatment and pathogenesis of herpes simplex virus and the efficacy of vaccines to prevent latent infection; 2) development of transgenic mice to study the genes and proteins of HIV; 3) characterization of different components of the human immune B cell repertoire and, in particular, the properties of polyreactive antibodies; 4) isolation and characterization of novel genes from autoimmune diseases such as insulin-dependent diabetes mellitus; and 5) gene therapy.

University of Alabama at Birmingham
Regional Maxillofacial Prosthetics Treatment and Training Center
See: Entry 2475

★ 4024 ★ University of Alabama at Birmingham
Research Center in Oral Biology
BBRB 258
845 S. 19th St.
Birmingham, AL 35294-2170
Phone: (205)934-3470
Fax: (205)934-1426
Dr. Suzanne M. Michalek, Dir.

Research Activities and Fields: Oral biology, mucosal immunology, and connective tissue biochemistry. **E-mail Address:** medm013@uabdpo.uab.dpo.edu. **Formerly:** Replaces former Institute of Dental Research.

★ 4025 ★ University of California, Los Angeles
Dental Research Institute
Center for Health Sciences
Los Angeles, CA 90024-1762
Phone: (310)206-8045
Fax: (310)825-0921
Prof. Glenn Clark, D.D.S., Dir.

Research Activities and Fields: Immunology, immunogenetics, periodontal disease, oral cancer, virology, ultrastructure and cell biology, oral neurology/pain, craniofacial biology, and biomaterials. Also conducts clinical dental science studies. **Publications:** *UCLA Dental Research Annual Report.*

University of Florida
Claude D. Pepper Center for Research on Oral Health in Aging
See: Entry 1977

★ 4026 ★ University of Florida
Periodontal Disease Research Center
JHMHC, Box J-424
Gainesville, FL 32610
Phone: (904)392-4377
Fax: (904)392-2361
Dr. William B. Clark, Dir.

Research Activities and Fields: Microbial etiology of destructive periodontal diseases, antibiotic therapy in the treatment of periodontal diseases, mechanisms of bacterial attachment

to teeth, bacterial virulence factors in periodontal diseases, and immune response to bacterial antigens. Evaluates risk factors for periodontal disease. Studies statistical models for progression of periodontal disease. Specializes in clinical trials. **E-mail Address:** jbraddy@pdrc.ufl.edu. **Formerly:** Clinical Research Center for Periodontal Disease.

★ 4027 ★ University of Illinois at Chicago
Center for Molecular Biology of Oral Diseases
801 S. Paulina
M/C 860
Chicago, IL 60612
Phone: (312)996-6118
Fax: (312)413-1604
Dr. Donald A. Chambers, Dir.

Research Activities and Fields: Pathobiology of periodontal oral and allied diseases, host-microbial interactions, cutaneous and epithelial cell biology, inflammatory diseases, immunobiology, and mechanisms of osteogenesis and osteoporosis. **Formerly:** Center for Molecular Biology of Oral Diseases.

★ 4028 ★ University of Iowa
Center for Clinical Studies
College of Dentistry
Iowa City, IA 52242
Phone: (319)335-7414
Fax: (319)335-8895
Dr. James Wefel, Dir.

Research Activities and Fields: Oral health, including disease processes (caries, periodontal disease, and oral lesions), restorative materials, and preventive techniques and agents. **E-mail Address:** nellie-kremenak@uiowa.edu.

★ 4029 ★ University of Iowa
Dows Institute for Dental Research
Dental Science Bldg.
Iowa City, IA 52242
Phone: (319)335-7388
Dr. Christopher A. Squier, Assoc. Dean for Research

Research Activities and Fields: Normal and pathological development and ultrastructure of oral soft tissues, cariology, oral microbiology, craniofacial growth and development, and biomaterials. Center for clinical studies performs research and testing of new oral health materials, products, and treatment modalities in normal and special populations. Provides supportive environment for investigations contributing to the goal of achieving the maintenance of sound dental health through elimination of major oral diseases. **E-mail Address:** nellie-kremenak@uiowa.edu.

University of Maryland
Center for the Study of Human Performance in Dentistry
See: Entry 9855

★4030★ **University of Medicine and Dentistry of New Jersey**
Dental Research Center
110 Bergen St.
Newark, NJ 07103-2400
Phone: (201)982-7053
Fax: (201)982-2034
Dr. Richard Vogel, Dir.

Research Activities and Fields: Biochemistry and functional alimentary tract secretions, epidermal growth factor prostaglandins, biochemical pharmacology, mucus-drug interaction; synthesis, cotranslational, and posttranslational processing of mucus glycoproteins; sulfation; proteoglycans; and intergrins.

University of Michigan
Antiviral Laboratory
See: Entry 10478

★4031★ **University of Michigan**
Bacteriology Laboratory
3209 School of Dentistry
1101 N. University Ave.
Ann Arbor, MI 48109
Phone: (313)764-8386
Fax: (313)764-7406
Walter J. Loesche, Hd.

Research Activities and Fields: Oral bacteria and its role in human tooth decay and periodontal disease. Current studies focus on the development of diagnostic indicators of anaerobic infections in periodontal disease, the treatment of anaerobic infections, and the connection between good dental health, xerostomia, swallowing, and aspiration pneumonia in senior citizens.

★4032★ **University of Michigan**
Biochemistry Laboratory
4207 School of Dentistry
1101 N. University Ave.
Ann Arbor, MI 48109
Phone: (313)936-2600
Fax: (313)747-3896
Kauko K. Makinen, Hd.

Research Activities and Fields: Chemistry of proteolytic enzymes present in pathogenic microorganisms with special emphasis on enzymes produced by oral spirochetes; and alternative sweeteners such as xylitol and sorbitol.

★4033★ **University of Michigan**
Biomaterials Research Center
School of Dentistry
Dept. of Biologic & Materials Science
1011 N. Univ.
Ann Arbor, MI 48109-1078
Phone: (313)763-9339
Fax: (313)747-4024
Dr. William J. O'Brien, Dir.

Research Activities and Fields: Develops elastomers for dental prostheses and denture liners, polymerceramic composites for dental restorations, and advanced ceramics for crowns and bridges. Also establishes biocompatibility of dental materials. **Formerly:** Specialized Materials Science Research Center.

★4034★ **University of Michigan**
Clinical Research Laboratories
1390 School of Dentistry
1101 N. University Ave.
Ann Arbor, MI 48109
Phone: (313)763-9148
Robert O'Neal, Dir.

Research Activities and Fields: Etiology of periodontal diseases, focusing on preventive and surgical methods; determining risk factors to predict and treat periodontal disease; assessment of the effectiveness of specific factors and materials in the regeneration of tissues lost through disease; and assessment of implant materials for optimal osseous integration.

★4035★ **University of Michigan**
Electrodiagnostic and Electromyographic Laboratory
1011 N. Univ. St.
Ann Arbor, MI 48109
Phone: (313)763-3346
Fax: (313)663-7133
Dr. Sven E. Widmalm, Dir.

Research Activities and Fields: Etiology and treatment of functional disturbances of the masticatory system, including disturbances of the muscles and joints of mastication. **E-mail Address:** sew@umich.edu. **Formerly:** Stomatognathic Physiology Laboratory.

★4036★ **University of Michigan**
Epidemiology Laboratory
School of Dentistry
1101 N. University Ave.
Ann Arbor, MI 48109
Fred Burgett, Dir.

Research Activities and Fields: Dental disease etiology and its parameters, including assessment of periodontal diseases and dental caries in large populations.

University of Michigan
Experimental Pathology Laboratory
See: Entry 2491

★4037★ **University of Michigan**
Immunology Laboratory
1192 School of Dentistry
1101 N. University Ave.
Ann Arbor, MI 48109
Phone: (313)764-2425
Fax: (313)747-3912
Dennis E. Lopatin, Hd.

Research Activities and Fields: Aspects of the interactions between the oral microbial flora and the immune system. Studies address humoral immunity to specific oral microorganisms; cellular networks involved in the responses to different classes of antigens; oral factors in the elderly that put them at risk in the development of a variety of diseases and negative health consequences such as caries, periodontal disease, and aspiration pneumonia; and immunochemical reagents for the identification of specific microorganisms in dental plaque.

★4038★ **University of Michigan**
Prosthodontic Research Laboratory
1024 Kellogg
Ann Arbor, MI 48109
Phone: (313)763-5280
Brien R. Lang, Dir.

Research Activities and Fields: Measures wear of prosthodontic devices and conducts serial and longitudinal biopsies of bone.

University of Michigan
Stomatognathic Physiology Laboratory
See: Entry 8515

★4039★ **University of Minnesota**
Dental Research Institute
School of Dentistry
Minneapolis, MN 55455
Phone: (612)626-3349
Fax: (612)626-7017
Prof. Charles F. Schachtele, Ph.D., Dir.

Research Activities and Fields: Coordinates research and training proposals, pilot projects funding, space and equipment maintenance, and research faculty recruitment and development.

★4040★ **University of Missouri—Kansas City**
Dental Research Program
650 E. 25th St.
Kansas City, MO 64108
Phone: (816)235-2021
Fax: (816)235-2157
Karen B. Williams, Coord., Grants Admin.

Research Activities and Fields: Biochemistry, dental biomaterials, radiology, analgesics, and pathology, related to dentistry. Clinical programs include study of anomalies of oral region, hard and soft tissues, prosthodontics, occlusion, durapatite particles, prostaglandins and analgesic inflammation, orthodontics, pedodontics, oral diagnosis, periodontics, bone physiology, dental caries, and related pathoses. **Publications:** *Explorer* (quarterly).

★4041★ **University of North Carolina at Chapel Hill**
Dental Research Center
Rm. 101, CB 7455
Chapel Hill, NC 27599-7455
Phone: (919)966-1538
Fax: (919)966-3683
Dr. Roland Arnold, Dir.

Research Activities and Fields: Oral health problems organized into six primary areas: biomaterials research, growth mechanisms, hemostasis research, mechanisms of mineralization, neural mechanisms, and host-pathogen interaction in oral biology, involving both basic and clinical research. Studies problems in oral health related to growth, development, and function of craniofacial region.

★ 4042 ★ **University of Pennsylvania**
Periodontal Diseases Research Center
School of Dental Medicine
4010 Locust St.
Philadelphia, PA 19104-6002
Phone: (215)898-8903
Fax: (215)898-8380
Dr. N.S. Taichman, Dir.

Research Activities and Fields: Etiology and pathogenesis of periodontal diseases, including clinical and fundamental studies in microbiology, immunology, and leukocyte biology. Special focus on the etiology of localized juvenile periodontitus and on the pathobiology of Actinobacillus actinomycetemcomitans.

★ 4043 ★ **University of Pennsylvania**
Research Center in Oral Biology
4010 Locust St.
Philadelphia, PA 19104-6002
Phone: (215)898-8994
Fax: (215)573-2324
Dr. Joel Rosenbloom, Dir.

Research Activities and Fields: Oral health, including team studies on biochemistry of connective and hard tissues, analyses of structural and functional constituents of oral microbes, and immunobiology of oral tissues and investigation of plaque formation and effect on periodontal tissues. **Publications:** *COHR Newsletter.* **Formerly:** Center for Oral Health Research (COHR).

★ 4044 ★ **University of Pennsylvania**
W.D. Miller General Clinical Research
Center
School of Dental Medicine
4001 Spruce St.
Philadelphia, PA 19104
Phone: (215)898-4194
Fax: (215)573-2202
Vernon J. Brightman, Dir.

Research Activities and Fields: Dental bioengineering, toxicology, periodontal diseases, pharmacologic agents, soft tissue diseases (RAU, etc.), temporomandibular joint dysfunction, medical imaging, salivary function, oral hygiene, and taste and smell, including studies of oral pain, taste perception, salivary biochemistry, evaluation of oral hygiene products and devices, evaluation of dental therapeutics, and improvement of diagnostic systems. Provides a multidisciplinary controlled environment for conducting clinical trials and support for investigators in preparation and processing of grants.

★ 4045 ★ **University of Rochester**
Rochester Caries Research Center
Dept. of Dental Research
601 Elmwood Ave.
PO Box 611
Rochester, NY 14642-8611
Phone: (716)275-3441
Fax: (716)473-2679
Dr. William H. Bowen, Dir.

Research Activities and Fields: Saliva glucosyltransferase interactions on surfaces, polysaccharide metabolism by oral bacteria, base production in dental plaque, molecular biology of periodontal pathogens, regulation of mucous cell secretion, basic and applied microbial physi-

ology, interaction of infectious eukaryotic microorganisms with host defense systems, mechanisms and regulation of fluid and electrolyte secretion, genetic engineering of bacteria and regulation of bacterial gene expression, and biosynthesis, structure, and function of mucinglycoproteins. **Formerly:** Cariology Center.

★ 4046 ★ **University of Southern California**
Center for Craniofacial Molecular Biology
Sch. of Dentistry
2250 Alcazar
CSA 103
Los Angeles, CA 90033
Phone: (213)342-3170
Fax: (213)342-2981
Dr. Harold C. Slavkin, Dir.

Research Activities and Fields: Craniofacial molecular biology, including cleft palate, congenital malformations, myogenesis, and taste and biotechnologies. **E-mail Address:** slavkin@hsc.usc.edu.

University of Southern California
Laboratory for Developmental Biology
See: Entry 2686

★ 4047 ★ **University of Washington**
Research Center in Oral Biology
SM-42
Seattle, WA 98195
Phone: (206)543-5599
Fax: (206)685-8024
Dr. Roy C. Page, Dir.

Research Activities and Fields: Wound healing and tissue regeneration at the molecular and genetic levels and genetic regulation of cell growth and synthetic activities. **Publications:** Annual Report. **Formerly:** Center for Research in Oral Biology.

★ 4048 ★ **Virginia Commonwealth**
University
Clinical Research Center for Periodontal
Diseases
521 N. 11th St.
Richmond, VA 23298
Phone: (804)786-9185
Dr. Harvey A. Schenkein, Dir.

Research Activities and Fields: Periodontal diseases, including bacteriology, immunology, and genetics, to determine causative bacteria and the mechanism and role of host response in pathogenesis in order to devise improved preventive and therapeutic methods.

State Government Agencies

Dental Boards

★ 4049 ★ **Alabama State Board of Dental**
Examiners
2327 Pansy St., Ste. B
Huntsville, AL 35801
Phone: (205)533-4638
Fax: (205)533-4690

★ 4050 ★ **Alaska State Board of Dental**
Examiners
PO Box 110806
Juneau, AK 99811-0806
Phone: (907)465-2542
Fax: (907)465-2974

★ 4051 ★ **Arizona State Board of Dental**
Examiners
5060 N. 19th Ave., No. 406
Phoenix, AZ 85015
Phone: (602)255-3696
Fax: (602)255-3589

★ 4052 ★ **Arkansas State Board of Dental**
Examiners
101 E. Capitol, Ste. 111
Little Rock, AR 72201
Phone: (501)682-2085
Fax: (501)682-3543

★ 4053 ★ **California State Board of Dental**
Examiners
1432 Howe Ave., No. 85
Sacramento, CA 95825
Phone: (916)263-2292
Fax: (916)263-2140

★ 4054 ★ **Colorado State Board of Dental**
Examiners
1560 Broadway, Ste. 1310
Denver, CO 80202
Phone: (303)894-7758
Fax: (303)894-7764

★ 4055 ★ **Connecticut Dental Commission**
150 Washington St.
Hartford, CT 06106
Phone: (203)566-1606
Fax: (203)566-1464

★ 4056 ★ **Delaware State Board of Dental**
Examiners
Cannon Bldg., Ste. 203
PO Box 1401
Dover, DE 19903
Phone: (302)739-4522
Fax: (302)739-2711

★ 4057 ★ **District of Columbia Board of**
Dentistry
614 H St., NW, Rm. 923/OPLA
Washington, DC 20001
Phone: (202)727-7454
Fax: (202)727-8030

★ 4058 ★ **Florida Board of Dentistry**
1940 N. Monroe St.
Tallahassee, FL 32399-0765
Phone: (904)488-6015
Fax: (904)922-3040

★ 4059 ★ **Georgia Board of Dentistry**
166 Pryor St. SW
Atlanta, GA 30303
Phone: (404)656-3925
Fax: (404)651-9532

★ 4060 ★ **Hawaii State Board of Dental**
Examiners
PO Box 3469
Honolulu, HI 96801
Phone: (808)586-2702
Fax: (808)586-2689

★4061★ **Idaho State Board of Dentistry**
PO Box 83720
Boise, ID 83720-0021
Phone: (208)334-2369
Fax: (208)334-3247

★4062★ **Illinois State Board of Dentistry**
320 W. Washington Ave., 3rd Fl.
Springfield, IL 62786
Phone: (217)785-0872
Fax: (217)782-7645

★4063★ **Indiana State Board of Dental Examiners**
402 W. Washington, Rm. 041
Indianapolis, IN 46204
Phone: (317)232-1129
Fax: (317)233-4236

★4064★ **Iowa Board of Dental Examiners**
Executive Hills W.
1209 E. Court
Des Moines, IA 50319
Phone: (515)281-5157
Fax: (515)281-4609

★4065★ **Kansas Dental Board**
3601 SW 29th St., Ste. 134
Topeka, KS 66614-2062
Phone: (913)273-0780

★4066★ **Kentucky Board of Dentistry**
10101 Linn Station Rd., No. 420
Louisville, KY 40223
Phone: (502)423-0573
Fax: (502)423-1239

★4067★ **Louisiana State Board of Dentistry**
1515 Poydras St., No. 1850
New Orleans, LA 70112
Phone: (504)568-8574
Fax: (504)568-8598

★4068★ **Maine Board of Dental Examiners**
2 Banger St.
Statehouse Sta. 143
Augusta, ME 04333
Phone: (207)287-3333
Fax: (207)287-3333

★4069★ **Maryland State Board of Dental Examiners**
4201 Patterson Ave.
Baltimore, MD 21215-2299
Phone: (410)764-4730
Fax: (410)358-0128

★4070★ **Massachusetts Board of Registration in Dentistry**
100 Cambridge St., Rm. 1514
Boston, MA 02202
Phone: (617)727-9928
Fax: (617)727-2197

★4071★ **Michigan Board of Dentistry**
PO Box 30018
Lansing, MI 48909
Phone: (517)335-0918
Fax: (517)373-2179

★4072★ **Minnesota Board of Dentistry**
2700 University Ave. W., Ste. 70
St. Paul, MN 55114
Phone: (612)642-0579
Fax: (612)643-3021

★4073★ **Mississippi State Board of Dental Examiners**
580 Springridge Rd., Ste. C
PO Box 1960
Clinton, MS 39060
Phone: (601)924-9622
Fax: (601)924-9623

★4074★ **Missouri Dental Board**
PO Box 1367
Jefferson City, MO 65102
Phone: (314)751-0040
Fax: (314)751-8216

★4075★ **Montana Board of Dentistry**
111 N. Jackson
PO Box 200513
Helena, MT 59620-0513
Phone: (406)444-3745
Fax: (406)444-1667

★4076★ **Nebraska Board of Dental Examiners**
301 Centennial Mall S.
PO Box 95007
Lincoln, NE 68509-5007
Phone: (402)471-2115
Fax: (402)471-0383

★4077★ **Nevada State Board of Dental Examiners**
4535 W. Sahara Ave., No. 108
Las Vegas, NV 89102
Phone: (702)362-8993
Fax: (702)362-7121

★4078★ **New Hampshire Board of Dental Examiners**
2 Industrial Park Dr.
Concord, NH 03301-8520
Phone: (603)271-4561
Fax: (603)271-6702

★4079★ **New Jersey State Board of Dentistry**
124 Halsey St.
PO Box 45005
Newark, NJ 07101
Phone: (201)504-6405
Fax: (201)648-3481

★4080★ **New Mexico Board of Dentistry**
PO Box 8397
Santa Fe, NM 87504-8397
Phone: (505)827-7165
Fax: (505)827-7095

★4081★ **New York State Board of Dentistry**
Cultural Education Center, Rm. 3035
Albany, NY 12230
Phone: (518)474-3838
Fax: (518)473-6995

★4082★ **North Carolina State Board of Dental Examiners**
3716 National Dr., Ste. 221
PO Box 32270
Raleigh, NC 27622-2270
Phone: (919)781-4901
Fax: (919)571-8457

★4083★ **North Dakota Board of Dentistry**
PO Box 7246
Bismarck, ND 58507-7246
Phone: (701)223-1474
Fax: (701)224-0038

★4084★ **Ohio State Dental Board**
77 S. High St., 18th Fl.
Columbus, OH 43266-0306
Phone: (614)466-2580
Fax: (614)752-8995

★4085★ **Oklahoma Board of Governors of Registered Dentists**
6501 N. Broadway, No. 220
Oklahoma City, OK 73116
Phone: (405)848-1364
Fax: (405)848-3279

★4086★ **Oregon Board of Dentistry**
1515 SW 5th Ave., Ste. 400
Portland, OR 97201
Phone: (503)229-5520
Fax: (503)229-5120

★4087★ **Pennsylvania State Board of Dentistry**
PO Box 2649
Harrisburg, PA 17105
Phone: (717)783-7162
Fax: (717)783-4853

★4088★ **Puerto Rico Board of Dental Examiners**
Call Box 10200
San Juan, PR 00908
Phone: (809)725-8161
Fax: (809)725-7903

★4089★ **Rhode Island State Board of Examiners in Dentistry**
3 Capitol Hill , Rm. 404
Providence, RI 02908-5097
Phone: (401)277-2151
Fax: (401)277-1250

★4090★ **South Carolina State Board of Dentistry**
PO Box 11329
Columbia, SC 29211-1329
Phone: (803)734-4215
Fax: (803)734-4216

★4091★ **South Dakota State Board of Dentistry**
106 W. Capitol
PO Box 1037
Pierre, SD 57501
Phone: (605)224-1282
Fax: (605)224-7426

★4092★ **Tennessee Board of Dentistry**
283 Plus Park Blvd.
Nashville, TN 37247-1010
Phone: (615)367-6242
Fax: (615)367-6210

★4093★ **Texas State Board of Dental Examiners**
333 Guadalupe, Tower 3, No. 3800
Austin, TX 78701
Phone: (512)463-6400
Fax: (512)463-7452

★ 4094 ★ Utah Board of Dentists and Dental Hygienists
PO Box 45805
Salt Lake City, UT 84145-0805
Phone: (801)530-6767
Fax: (801)530-6511

★ 4095 ★ Vermont State Board of Dental Examiners
Secretary of State's Office
109 State St.
Montpelier, VT 05609-1106
Phone: (802)828-2390
Fax: (802)828-2496

★ 4096 ★ Virgin Islands Board of Dental Examiners
48 Sugar Estate
St. Thomas, VI 00802
Phone: (809)774-0117
Fax: (809)777-4001

★ 4097 ★ Virginia Board of Dentistry
6606 W. Broad St., 4th Fl.
Richmond, VA 23230-1717
Phone: (804)662-9906
Fax: (804)662-9943

★ 4098 ★ Washington Dental Health Care Boards
PO Box 47867
Olympia, WA 98504-7867
Phone: (206)753-2461
Fax: (206)664-9077

★ 4099 ★ West Virginia Board of Dental Examiners
PO Drawer 1459
Beckley, WV 25802-1459
Phone: (304)252-8266
Fax: (304)252-2779

★ 4100 ★ Wisconsin Dentistry Examining Board
1400 E. Washington Ave.
PO Box 8935
Madison, WI 53708
Phone: (608)266-0483
Fax: (608)267-0644

★ 4101 ★ Wyoming Board of Dental Examiners
PO Box 272
Kemmerer, WY 83101
Phone: (307)877-9649
Fax: (307)877-9649

Dental Health

★ 4102 ★ Alabama Department of Public Health
Dental Health Division
434 Monroe St.
Montgomery, AL 36130
Phone: (334)242-5767
Fax: (334)240-3167

★ 4103 ★ Alaska Department of Health and Social Services
Administrative Services Division
Dental Program
PO Box 110650
Juneau, AK 99811-0650
Phone: (907)465-3015
Fax: (907)465-2499

★ 4104 ★ Arizona Department of Health Services
Family Health and Community Services Division
Oral Health Office
1740 W. Adams
Phoenix, AZ 85007
Phone: (602)542-1866
Fax: (602)542-2936

★ 4105 ★ Arkansas Department of Health
Dental Health Office
4815 W. Markham St.
Little Rock, AR 72205
Phone: (501)661-2483
Fax: (501)661-2055

★ 4106 ★ California Health and Welfare Agency
Health Services Department
Chronic Disease and Injury Control Branch
Dental Program
601 N. 7th St., MS-725
PO Box 942732
Sacramento, CA 94234-7320
Phone: (916)327-6985
Fax: (916)324-7764

★ 4107 ★ Colorado Public and Environment Department
Family and Community Health Services Division
Oral Health Program
4300 Cherry Creek Dr., S.
Denver, CO 80222-1530
Phone: (303)692-2360
Fax: (303)782-5576

★ 4108 ★ Connecticut Department of Public Health
Community Health Bureau
Oral Health Program
150 Washington St.
Hartford, CT 06106
Phone: (203)566-3708
Fax: (203)566-8401

★ 4109 ★ Delaware Department of Health and Social Services
Public Health Division
Community Health Care Access Section
Dental Health Program
PO Box 637
Dover, DE 19903
Phone: (302)739-4768
Fax: (302)739-6617

★ 4110 ★ District of Columbia Department of Human Services
Public Health Commission
Ambulatory Health Care Administration Division
Dental Health Bureau
1900 Massachusetts Ave., SE
Anne Archibold Hall, Rm. 248
Washington, DC 20020
Phone: (202)727-5122
Fax: (202)727-9590

★ 4111 ★ Florida Department of Health and Rehabilitative Services
Family Health Services Office
Public Health Dental Program
1317 Winewood Blvd.
Tallahassee, FL 32301
Phone: (904)487-1845
Fax: (904)488-2341

★ 4112 ★ Georgia Department of Human Resources
Public Health Division
Oral Health Section
2 Peachtree St. NW, 6th Fl.
Atlanta, GA 30303
Phone: (404)657-2575
Fax: (404)657-6905

★ 4113 ★ Hawaii Department of Health
Health Resources Administration
Dental Health Division
1700 Lanakila Ave., Rm. 203
Honolulu, HI 96817
Phone: (808)832-5700
Fax: (808)832-5722

★ 4114 ★ Idaho Department of Health and Welfare
Health Division
Health Promotions Bureau
Oral Health Program
State House, 5th Fl.
PO Box 83720
Boise, ID 83720-0036
Phone: (208)334-5966
Fax: (208)334-6573

★ 4115 ★ Illinois Department of Public Health
Community Health Office
Dental Health Division
535 W. Jefferson St.
Springfield, IL 62761
Phone: (217)785-4899
Fax: (217)524-2491

★ 4116 ★ Indiana Department of Health
Oral Health Services Division
1330 W. Michigan St.
PO Box 1964
Indianapolis, IN 46206-1964
Phone: (317)383-6418
Fax: (317)633-6776

★ 4117 ★ Iowa Department of Public Health
Family and Community Health Division
Dental Health Bureau
Lucas State Office Bldg.
321 E. 12th St.
Des Moines, IA 50319-0075
Phone: (515)281-4916
Fax: (515)242-6384

★ 4118 ★ Kansas Department of Health and Environment
Health Division
Local and Rural Health Systems Bureau
Dental Program
109 SW, 9th St., Rm. 602
Topeka, KS 66612-1271
Phone: (913)296-6215
Fax: (913)296-4197

★4119★ Kentucky Human Resources Cabinet
Health Service Department
Maternal and Child Health Services Division
Dental Health Program
275 E. Main St.
Frankfort, KY 40621
Phone: (502)564-3246
Fax: (502)564-8389

★4120★ Louisiana Department of Health and Hospitals
Public Health Services Office
Maternal and Child Health Division
Dental Health Section
325 Loyola Ave.
New Orleans, LA 70112
Phone: (504)568-7706
Fax: (504)568-7703

★4121★ Maine Department of Human Services
Health Bureau
Dental Health Division
State House Station 11
Augusta, ME 04333
Phone: (207)287-2361
Fax: (207)287-4631

★4122★ Maryland Department of Health and Mental Hygiene
Local and Family Health Administration
Dental Program
201 W. Preston St.
Baltimore, MD 21201
Phone: (410)225-5300
Fax: (410)333-7106

★4123★ Massachusetts Executive Office of Health and Human Services
Public Health Department
Dental Health Division
150 Tremont St.
Boston, MA 02111
Phone: (617)727-0732
Fax: (617)723-2559

★4124★ Michigan Department of Public Health
Child and Family Services Bureau
Oral Health Program
3423 N. Martin Luther King Jr., Blvd.
PO Box 30195
Lansing, MI 48909-9222
Phone: (517)335-8909
Fax: (517)335-9222

★4125★ Minnesota Department of Health
Oral Health Section
717 Delaware St. SE
Minneapolis, MN 55440
Phone: (612)623-5441
Fax: (612)623-5775

★4126★ Mississippi Department of Health
Health Services Bureau
Dental Health Services
PO Box 1700
Jackson, MS 39215-1700
Phone: (601)960-7463
Fax: (601)354-6104

★4127★ Missouri Department of Health
Maternal, Child, and Family Health Division
Dental Health Bureau
1730 E. Elm
PO Box 570
Jefferson City, MO 65102
Phone: (314)751-6247
Fax: (314)526-2753

★4128★ Montana Department of Public Health and Human Services
Health Services Division
Preventive Health Services Bureau
Dental Program
1400 Broadway
Helena, MT 59620
Phone: (406)444-0276
Fax: (406)444-2920

★4129★ Nebraska Department of Health
Health Promotion and Disease Prevention
Dental Health Division
301 Centennial Mall S.
PO Box 95007
Lincoln, NE 68509-5007
Phone: (402)471-2822
Fax: (402)471-0383

★4130★ Nevada Department of Human Resources
Health Division
Dental Health Bureau
505 E. King St.
Carson City, NV 89710
Phone: (702)885-4475

★4131★ New Hampshire Department of Health and Human Services
Public Health Services Division
Dental Health Bureau
6 Hazen Dr.
Concord, NH 03301
Phone: (603)271-4726
Fax: (603)271-4779

★4132★ New Jersey Department of Health
Family Health Services Division
Special Child Health Services
Dental Program
Uptown Bldg., CN 364
120 S. Stockton St.
Trenton, NJ 08625
Phone: (609)292-1723
Fax: (609)292-9288

★4133★ New Mexico Department of Health
Public Health Division
Dental Health Program
1190 St. Francis Dr.
Santa Fe, NM 87502-6110
Phone: (505)827-2373
Fax: (505)827-2329

★4134★ New York State Department of Health
Dental Health Bureau
ESP Tower Bldg
194 Washington Ave.
Albany, NY 12237-0619
Phone: (518)474-1961
Fax: (518)474-8985

★4135★ North Carolina Department of Environment, Health, and Natural Resources
Health Director's Office
Dental Health Division
1815 B Capitol Blvd.
PO Box 27687
Raleigh, NC 27611
Phone: (919)715-4125
Fax: (919)715-3060

★4136★ North Dakota Department of Health and Consolidated Laboratories
Preventive Health Section
Maternal and Child Health Division
Dental Health Program
600 E. Boulevard Ave.
Bismarck, ND 58505-0200
Phone: (701)328-2356
Fax: (701)328-4727

★4137★ Ohio Department of Health
Maternal and Child Health
Dental Health Bureau
246 N. High St.
PO Box 118
Columbus, OH 43266-0118
Phone: (614)466-4180
Fax: (614)644-9850

★4138★ Oklahoma Department of Health
Dental Health Services
1000 NE 10th St.
PO Box 53551
Oklahoma City, OK 73152
Phone: (405)271-4476
Fax: (405)271-6199

★4139★ Oregon Department of Human Resources
Health Division
Dental Health Section
800 NE Oregon St., Ste. 825
Portland, OR 97232
Phone: (503)731-4098
Fax: (503)731-4083

★4140★ Pennsylvania Department of Health
Preventive Health Programs Bureau
Oral Health Program
PO Box 90
Harrisburg, PA 17108
Phone: (717)787-6214
Fax: (717)783-5498

★4141★ Puerto Rico Department of Health
Oral Health Division
Call Box 70184
San Juan, PR 00936
Phone: (809)765-0745
Fax: (809)765-5675

★4142★ Rhode Island Department of Health
Dental Health Division
Cannon Bldg., Rm. 303
75 Davis St.
Providence, RI 02908
Phone: (401)277-2588
Fax: (401)861-5751

★4143★ South Carolina Department of Health and Environmental Control
Women and Children's Services Division
Dental Health Program
29201 Calhoun St.
Columbia, SC 29211
Phone: (803)737-4061
Fax: (803)734-3255

★4144★ South Dakota Department of Health
Health and Medical Services Division
Dental Program
445 E. Capitol
Pierre, SD 57501
Phone: (605)773-3737
Fax: (605)773-5509

★4145★ Tennessee Department of Health
Oral Health Services Division
Tennessee Tower, 11th Fl.
312 8th Ave. N.
Nashville, TN 37247-5270
Phone: (615)741-7213
Fax: (615)741-1063

★4146★ Texas Department of Health
Dental Health Bureau
1100 W. 49th St.
Austin, TX 78756
Phone: (512)458-7323
Fax: (512)458-7249

★4147★ Utah Department of Health
Family Health Services Division
Dental Health Bureau
288 North 1460 West
Salt Lake City, UT 84114
Phone: (801)538-6179
Fax: (801)538-6510

★4148★ Vermont Agency of Human Services
Health Department
Dental Health Division
108 Cherry St.
PO Box 70
Burlington, VT 05402
Phone: (802)863-7341
Fax: (802)863-7425

★4149★ Virgin Islands Department of Health
Dental Health Services
St. Thomas Hospital
PO Box 21
St. Thomas, VI 00801
Phone: (809)776-8311
Fax: (809)776-9600

★4150★ Virginia Office of Health and Human Resources
Health Department
Dental Health Division
1500 E. Main St., Rm. 239
PO Box 2448
Richmond, VA 23218
Phone: (804)786-3556
Fax: (804)371-4004

★4151★ Washington Department of Health
Oral Health Services Program
PO Box 47880
Olympia, WA 98504-7880
Phone: (206)753-5423
Fax: (206)586-7868

★4152★ West Virginia Department of Health and Human Resources
Public Health Bureau
Maternal and Child Health Office
Dental Health Division
1411 Virginia St. E.
Charleston, WV 25301
Phone: (304)558-8850
Fax: (304)558-2183

★4153★ Wisconsin Department of Health and Social Services
Health Division
Public Health Bureau
Oral Health Program
1414 E. Washington Ave., Rm. 199
Madison, WI 53703-3044
Phone: (608)266-5152
Fax: (608)267-3824

★4154★ Wyoming Department of Health
Public Health Division
Dental Health Services
459 Hathaway Bldg.
Cheyenne, WY 82002
Phone: (307)777-7945
Fax: (307)777-5402

State & Regional Organizations

Dentistry

The following are constituent societies of the American Dental Association, 211 E. Chicago Ave., Chicago, IL 60611, (312) 440-2500.

Alabama

★4155★ Alabama Dental Association
836 Washington St.
Montgomery, AL 36104-3893
Phone: (205)265-1684
Fax: (205)262-6218

Alaska

★4156★ Alaska Dental Society
3400 Spenard Rd., Ste. 10
Anchorage, AK 99503-3783
Phone: (907)277-4675
Fax: (907)274-2960

Arizona

★4157★ Arizona State Dental Association
4131 N. 36th St.
Phoenix, AZ 85018-4761
Phone: (602)957-4777
Fax: (602)957-1342

Arkansas

★4158★ Arkansas State Dental Association
2501 Crestwood Dr., Ste. 205
North Little Rock, AR 72116
Phone: (501)771-7650
Fax: (501)771-1016

California

★4159★ California Dental Association
PO Box 13749
Sacramento, CA 95853-4749
Phone: (916)443-3382
Fax: (916)443-2943

Colorado

★4160★ Colorado Dental Association
3690 S. Yosemite, Ste. 100
Denver, CO 80237-1808
Phone: (303)740-6900
Fax: (303)740-7989

Connecticut

★4161★ Connecticut State Dental Association
62 Russ St.
Hartford, CT 06106-1589
Phone: (203)278-5550
Fax: (203)522-6587

Delaware

★4162★ Delaware State Dental Society
1925 Lovering Ave.
Wilmington, DE 19806-2147
Phone: (302)654-4335
Fax: (302)427-9412

District of Columbia

★4163★ District of Columbia Dental Society
502 C St. NE
Washington, DC 20002-5810
Phone: (202)547-7613
Fax: (202)546-1482

Florida

★4164★ Florida Dental Association
1111 E. Tennessee St., Ste. 102
Tallahassee, FL 32308-6913
Phone: (904)681-3629
Fax: (904)561-0504

Georgia

★4165★ Georgia Dental Association
2801 Buford Hwy. NE, Ste. T-60
Atlanta, GA 30329-2137
Phone: (404)636-7553
Fax: (404)633-3943

Hawaii

★4166★ Hawaii Dental Association
1000 Bishop St., Ste. 805
Honolulu, HI 96813-4281
Phone: (808)536-2135
Fax: (808)536-2137

Idaho

★4167★ Idaho State Dental Association
1220 W. Hays St.
Boise, ID 83702-5315
Phone: (208)343-7543
Fax: (208)343-0775

Illinois

★4168★ Illinois State Dental Society
PO Box 376
Springfield, IL 62705-0376
Phone: (217)525-1406
Fax: (217)525-8872

Indiana

★4169★ Indiana Dental Association
PO Box 2467
Indianapolis, IN 46206-2467
Phone: (317)634-2610
Fax: (317)634-2612

Iowa

★4170★ Iowa Dental Association
505 5th Ave., Ste. 333
Des Moines, IA 50309-2322
Phone: (515)282-7250
Fax: (515)282-7256

Kansas

★4171★ Kansas Dental Association
5200 SW Huntoon St.
Topeka, KS 66604-2398
Phone: (913)272-7360
Fax: (913)272-2301

Kentucky

★4172★ Kentucky Dental Association
1940 Princeton Dr.
Louisville, KY 40205-1873
Phone: (502)459-5373
Fax: (502)458-5915

Louisiana

★4173★ Louisiana Dental Association
320 3rd St., Ste. 201
Baton Rouge, LA 70801
Phone: (504)336-1692
Fax: (504)334-9215

Maine

★4174★ Maine Dental Association
PO Box 215
Manchester, ME 04351-0215
Phone: (207)622-7900
Fax: (207)622-6210

Maryland

★4175★ Maryland State Dental Association
6450 Dobbin Rd.
Columbia, MD 21045-5824
Phone: (410)964-2880
Fax: (410)964-0583

Massachusetts

★4176★ Massachusetts Dental Society
83 Speen St.
Natick, MA 01760-4125
Phone: (508)651-7511
Fax: (508)653-7115

Michigan

★4177★ Michigan Dental Association
230 N. Washington Sq., Ste. 208
Lansing, MI 48933-1392
Phone: (517)372-9070
Fax: (517)372-0008

Minnesota

★4178★ Minnesota Dental Association
2236 Marshall Ave.
St. Paul, MN 55104-5758
Phone: (612)646-7454
Fax: (612)646-8246

Mississippi

★4179★ Mississippi Dental Association
2630 Ridgewood Rd.
Jackson, MS 39216-4920
Phone: (601)982-0442
Fax: (601)366-3050

Missouri

★4180★ Missouri Dental Association
PO Box 1707
Jefferson City, MO 65102-1707
Phone: (314)634-3436
Fax: (314)635-0764

Montana

★4181★ Montana Dental Association
PO Box 1154
Helena, MT 59624-1154
Phone: (406)443-2061
Fax: (406)443-1546

Nebraska

★4182★ Nebraska Dental Association
3120 "O" St.
Lincoln, NE 68510-1599
Phone: (402)476-1704
Fax: (402)476-2641

Nevada

★4183★ Nevada Dental Association
6889 W. Charleston Blvd., Ste. B
Las Vegas, NV 89117
Phone: (702)255-4211
Fax: (702)255-3302

New Hampshire

★4184★ New Hampshire Dental Society
PO Box 2229
Concord, NH 03302-2229
Phone: (603)225-5961
Fax: (603)226-4880

New Jersey

★4185★ New Jersey Dental Association
1 Dental Plaza
North Brunswick, NJ 08902-4311
Phone: (908)821-9400
Fax: (908)821-1082

New Mexico

★4186★ New Mexico Dental Association
3736 Eubank Blvd., NE, Ste. 1A
Albuquerque, NM 87111-3556
Phone: (505)294-1368
Fax: (505)294-9958

New York

★4187★ Dental Society of the State of New York
7 Elk St.
Albany, NY 12207-1023
Phone: (518)465-0044
Fax: (518)427-0461

North Carolina

★4188★ North Carolina Dental Society
PO Box 12047
Raleigh, NC 27605-2047
Phone: (919)832-1222
Fax: (919)833-7666

North Dakota

★4189★ North Dakota Dental Association
PO Box 1332
Bismarck, ND 58502-1332
Phone: (701)223-8870
Fax: (701)223-0855

Ohio

★ 4190 ★ **Ohio Dental Association**
1370 Dublin Rd.
Columbus, OH 43215-1098
Phone: (614)486-2700
Fax: (614)486-0381

Oklahoma

★ 4191 ★ **Oklahoma Dental Association**
629 W. Interstate 44, Service Rd.
Oklahoma City, OK 73118-6832
Phone: (405)848-8873
Fax: (405)848-8875

Oregon

★ 4192 ★ **Oregon Dental Association**
17898 SW McEwan Rd.
Portland, OR 97224-7798
Phone: (503)620-3230
Fax: (503)620-4169

Pennsylvania

★ 4193 ★ **Pennsylvania Dental Association**
PO Box 3341
Harrisburg, PA 17105-3341
Phone: (717)234-5941
Fax: (717)232-7169

Puerto Rico

★ 4194 ★ **Colegio de Cirujanos Dentistas de Puerto Rico**
200 Avenida Dominik
Hato Rey, PR 00918-3507
Phone: (809)764-1969
Fax: (809)763-6335

Rhode Island

★ 4195 ★ **Rhode Island Dental Association**
200 Centerville Pl.
Warwick, RI 02886-0204
Phone: (401)732-6833
Fax: (401)732-9351

South Carolina

★ 4196 ★ **South Carolina Dental Association**
120 Stonemark Ln.
Columbia, SC 29210-3841
Phone: (803)750-2277
Fax: (803)750-1644

South Dakota

★ 4197 ★ **South Dakota Dental Association**
PO Box 1194
Pierre, SD 57501-1194
Phone: (605)224-9133
Fax: (605)224-9168

Tennessee

★ 4198 ★ **Tennessee Dental Association**
PO Box 120188
Nashville, TN 37212-0188
Phone: (615)383-8962
Fax: (615)383-0214

Texas

★ 4199 ★ **Texas Dental Association**
PO Box 3358
Austin, TX 78764-3358
Phone: (512)443-3675
Fax: (512)443-3031

Utah

★ 4200 ★ **Utah Dental Association**
1151 East 3900 South, Ste. B160
Salt Lake City, UT 84124-1216
Phone: (801)261-5315
Fax: (801)261-1235

Vermont

★ 4201 ★ **Vermont State Dental Society**
132 Church St.
Burlington, VT 05401-8401
Phone: (802)864-0115
Fax: (802)864-0116

Virgin Islands

★ 4202 ★ **Virgin Islands Dental Association**
PO Box 10422
Charlotte Amalie, VI 00801-3422
Phone: (809)775-9110
Fax: (809)779-8326

Virginia

★ 4203 ★ **Virginia Dental Association**
PO Box 6906
Richmond, VA 23230-0906
Phone: (804)358-4927
Fax: (804)353-7342

Washington

★ 4204 ★ **Washington State Dental Association**
2033 6th Ave., Ste. 333
Seattle, WA 98121-2514
Phone: (206)448-1914
Fax: (206)443-9266

West Virginia

★ 4205 ★ **West Virginia Dental Association**
1002 Kanawha Valley Bldg.
300 Capitol St.
Charleston, WV 25301-1794
Phone: (304)344-5246
Fax: (304)344-5316

Wisconsin

★ 4206 ★ **Wisconsin Dental Association**
111 E. Wisconsin Ave., Ste. 1300
Milwaukee, WI 53202-4811
Phone: (414)276-4520
Fax: (414)276-8431

Wyoming

★ 4207 ★ **Wyoming Dental Association**
330 S. Center St., Ste. 322
Casper, WY 82601-2875
Phone: (307)234-0777
Fax: (307)234-6040

Chapter 19
Dermatology

Federal Government Agencies

U.S. Department of Health and Human Services
National Institute of Arthritis and Musculoskeletal and Skin Diseases
See: Entry 7854

Foundations & Other Funding Organizations

Private Foundations

Carl J. Herzog Foundation
See: Entry 84

Corporate Foundations

Procter & Gamble Cosmetic & Fragrance Foundation
See: Entry 824

Other Funding Organizations

★4208★ **Dermatology Foundation**
1560 Sherman Ave., Ste. 302
Evanston, IL 60201-4802
Phone: (708)328-2256
Fax: (708)328-0509
Sandra Rahn Goldman, Exec. Dir.

Description: Raises funds for the control of skin diseases through research; supports basic and clinical investigations.

Dystrophic Epidermolysis Bullosa Research Association of America
See: Entry 5261

★4209★ **National Alopecia Areata Foundation**
PO Box 150760
San Rafael, CA 94915-0760
Phone: (415)456-4644
Fax: (415)456-4274
Vicki Kalabokes, Exec. Dir.

Description: Raises funds and awards grants for research on the cause and cure of alopecia areata.

★4210★ **National Psoriasis Foundation**
6600 SW 92nd, Ste. 300
Portland, OR 97223
Phone: (503)244-7404
Free: 800-723-9166
Fax: (503)245-0626
Gail M. Zimmerman, Exec. Dir.

Description: Supports research at various universities by offering predoctoral summer fellowships to medical and science students, and by awarding postdoctoral fellowships to physicians and scientists.

★4211★ **Psoriasis Research Association**
107 Vista del Grande
San Carlos, CA 94070
Phone: (415)593-1394
Diane Bradley Mullins, Founder & Exec. Sec.

Description: Supports clinical and basic research into the cause, cure, and treatment of psoriasis. Awards grants to Psoriasis Research Institute, Dermatology Foundation, and to individual researchers applying to the association for small grants.

Skin Cancer Foundation
See: Entry 5906

★4212★ **United Scleroderma Foundation**
PO Box 399
Watsonville, CA 95077-0399
Phone: (408)728-2202
Free: 800-722-HOPE
Fax: (408)728-3328
Diane Williams, Founder & Pres.

Description: Seeks to supplement and implement medical research on the cause, treatment, and cure of Scleroderma. Awards grants and summer fellowships for promising new studies aimed at the cause and cure for scleroderma and related collagen diseases.

National & International Organizations

★4213★ **American Academy of Dermatology (AAD)**
930 N. Meacham Rd.
Schaumburg, IL 60172-4965
Phone: (708)330-0230
Fax: (708)330-0050
Bradford W. Claxton, Exec.Dir.

Founded: 1938. **Members:** 11,200. **Description:** Professional society of medical doctors specializing in skin diseases. Conducts educational programs. Provides placement service; compiles statistics. **Publications:** *Dermatology World*, monthly. • *Dialogues in Dermatology*. Audiotapes. • *Directory of the American Academy of Dermatology*, biennial. Directory. • *Journal of the American Academy of Dermatology*, monthly. Journal. **Formerly:** American Academy of Dermatology and Syphilology.

American Academy of Veterinary Dermatology (AAVD)
See: Entry 13022

★4214★ **American Board of Dermatology (ABD)**
Henry Ford Hospital
1 Ford Pl.
Detroit, MI 48202-4350
Phone: (313)874-1088
Fax: (313)872-3221
Harry J. Hurley, M.D., Exec.Dir.

Founded: 1932. **Members:** 15. **Description:** Examining and certifying body. Seeks to assure provision of competent care for patients with cutaneous diseases, via capable board representation. Establishes requirements of postdoctoral training. Creates and conducts annual comprehensive examination to determine the competence of physicians who meet the requirements for examination by the board. Issues appropriate certificate to those who satisfactorily complete examination. Member of American Board of Medical Specialties. **Publications:** *Booklet of Information*, annual. Describes the states' requirements for certification. *Price:* Free.

American College of Veterinary Dermatology (ACVD)
See: Entry 13046

★4215★ American Dermatologic Society of Allergy and Immunology (ADSAI)
c/o Dr. R.S. Rogers, III
Mayo Clinic
Department of Dermatology
Rochester, MN 55905
Phone: (507)284-2555
Fax: (507)284-2072
Dr. R. S. Rogers, III, Sec.-Treas.

Founded: 1974. **Members:** 150. **Description:** Physicians with practice in dermatology, allergy, and immunology. Purpose is educational.

★4216★ American Dermatological Association (ADA)
Medical College of Georgia
Department of Dermatology
Augusta, GA 30912-2900
Phone: (706)721-6496
Fax: (706)721-3318
Donald C. Abele, M.D., Sec.

Founded: 1876. **Members:** 350. **Description:** Professional society of physicians specializing in dermatology. Promotes teaching, practice, and research in dermatology.

★4217★ American Hair Loss Council (AHLC)
401 N. Michigan Ave., 22nd Fl.
Chicago, IL 60611-4212
Free: 800-274-8717
Fax: (312)245-1080
Paul Dykstra, Exec.Dir.

Founded: 1985. **Members:** 420. **Description:** Dermatologists, plastic surgeons, cosmetologists, barbers, and interested others. Provides nonbiased information regarding treatments for hair loss in both men and women. Facilitates communication and information exchange between professionals in different areas of specialization. Conducts educational programs; offers children's services and placement service; compiles statistics. **Publications:** Brochures. • *Hair Loss Journal*, quarterly. Newsletter. Reports on hair loss and treatment. *Price:* $30/year.

American Osteopathic College of Dermatology (AOCD)
See: Entry 9988

American Society for Dermatologic Surgery (ASDS)
See: Entry 12238

★4218★ American Society of Dermatological Retailers (ASDR)
c/o Dr. Jeffrey Lauber
361 Hospital Rd., No. 428
Newport Beach, CA 92663-2511
Phone: (714)646-9098
Free: 800-469-3739
Fax: (714)645-9098
Dr. Jeffrey Lauber, M.D., Medical Dir.

Founded: 1989. **Members:** 10. **Regional Groups:** 1. **Description:** Board certified dermatologists. Promotes ethical and professional

marketing standards for skin care products. Conducts educational and research programs; sponsors competitions. Compiles statistics; maintains speakers' bureau, hall of fame, and museum. **Publications:** *Epex Quarterly*, quarterly. *Price:* Free. • *Health and Beauty*, periodic. • *Skin Saver*, annual. Newsletter. *Price:* Free.

American Society of Dermatopathology (ASD)
See: Entry 10124

American Society of Podiatric Dermatology (ASPD)
See: Entry 10765

★4219★ Argentinian Association of Dermatology (AAD)
(Asociacion Argentina de Dermatologia — AAD)
Mexico 1720
1100 Buenos Aires, Argentina
Phone: 1 3812737
Dr. Pedro H. Magnin, Chm.

Founded: 1907. **Members:** 910. **Local Groups:** 6. **Languages:** English, Spanish. **Description:** Dermatologists in Argentina. Bestows awards; provides educational programs. **Publications:** *Indice General*, periodic. • *Revista Argentina de Dermatologia*, quarterly. Includes summary in English. Also publishes books.

★4220★ Belgian Royal Society of Dermatology and Venereology (BSD)
(Societe Royale Belge de Dermatologie et de Venereologie — SRBDV)
9, ave. E. de Mot 14
B-1050 Brussels, Belgium
Phone: 2 6475399
Fax: 2 6419227
Dr. J. Delescluse, Sec.

Founded: 1901. **Members:** 500. **Languages:** Dutch, English, French. **Description:** Dermatologists and other scientists interested in dermatology. Conducts biennial postgraduate course. **Publications:** *Dermatologica*, 10/year.

★4221★ British Association of Dermatologists (BAD)
19 Fitzroy St.
London W1B 5HQ, England
Phone: 171 3830266
Fax: 171 3885263
Dr. R.A. Marsden, Contact

Founded: 1921. **Members:** 803. **National Groups:** 6. **Languages:** English. **Description:** Medical professionals united to further the knowledge and teaching of dermatology. Promotes the interests of members and their patients. Conducts medical and scientific research; disseminates information. **Publications:** *British Journal of Dermatology*, monthly. Journal. Also publishes results of research projects.

British Society for Dermatopathology (BSD)
See: Entry 10127

★4222★ Bulgarian Dermatological Society (BDS)
(Balgarsko Dermatologichno Drujestvo — BDD)
Georgi Sofiisky St. 1
BG-1431 Sofia, Bulgaria
Phone: 2 517342
Dr. N. Tsankov, Sec.

Founded: 1923. **Members:** 400. **Regional Groups:** 1. **Local Groups:** 7. **Languages:** Bulgarian, English, French. **Description:** Dermatologists and individuals interested in furthering the development of dermatology in Bulgaria. Coordinates efforts in combatting the spread of skin and venereal diseases. Furthers post-graduate education. Conducts educational and research programs. **Publications:** Books. • *Dermatologia i Venerologia Bulgaran*, quarterly. Journal. • Monographs.

★4223★ Canadian Dermatology Association (CDA)
Royal College Bldg.
774 Echo Dr., Ste. 521
Ottawa, ON, Canada K1S 5N8
Phone: (613)730-6262
Fax: (613)730-1116
Dr. David Gratton, Sec./Treas.

Members: 416. **Languages:** English, French. **Description:** Certified dermatologists and related professionals interested in the professional advancement of dermatology. Promotes continuing education programs. Conducts research on adverse dermatological reactions. Sponsors Cutaneous Adverse Reaction Program and annual SunAwareness Week. Coordinates charitable program. Provides public information on the dangers of sun exposure through pamphlets. **Publications:** *Canadian Dermatology Association Journal*, quarterly. • *Roster*, annual. Directory.

★4224★ Chilean Society of Dermatology and Venereology (CSDV)
(Sociedad Chilena de Dermatologia y Venereologia — SCDV)
Casilla 165
Providencia
Santiago, Chile
Phone: 2 3009108
Fax: 2 2322559
Dr. Ruben Guarda, Pres.

Founded: 1938. **Members:** 168. **Regional Groups:** 4. **Local Groups:** 8. **Languages:** Spanish. **Description:** Practicing dermatologists in Chile. Promotes the development of dermatology and venereology, especially the socio-medical aspects of dermatological and venereal diseases. Disseminates information in Chile and abroad. Offers continuing medical education in dermatology. **Publications:** *Dermatologia*, quarterly. Journal. • Papers.

★4225★ Colombian Society of Dermatology (CSD)
(Sociedad Colombiana de Dermatologia — SCD)
Apartado Aereo 90123
Bogota, Colombia
Phone: 1 2575568
Fax: 1 2182596
Dr. Maria Duran

Founded: 1947. **Members:** 300. **Languages:** Spanish. **Description:** Dermatologists interested in furthering the study and profession of dermatology in Colombia. Conducts research; disseminates information. **Publications:** *Revista de la Sociedad Colombiana de Dermatologia*, bimonthly. Journal.

★ 4226 ★   Czechoslovak
   Dermatovenerological Society (CDS)
   (Ceskoslovenska Dermatovenerologicka
      Spolecnost — CDS)
2, Department Dermatology
ulice Nemocnice 2
CS-128 08 Prague 2, Czech Republic
Phone: 2 290045
Prof. Frantisek Vosmik, M.D., Exec. Officer

Founded: 1922. **Members:** 650. **Regional Groups:** 2. **Local Groups:** 2. **Languages:** Czech, English, Slovak. **Description:** Dermatologists in Czechoslovakia. Promotes the study of dermatological diseases; encourages research and exchange of information. Operates postgraduate educational programs. **Publications:** *Ceskoslovenska Dermatologie*, bimonthly. • *Journal of Czechoslovak Dermatology*, bimonthly. Journal.

★ 4227 ★   Danish Dermatological Society
   (DDS)
(Dansk Dermatologisk Selskab — DDS)
Gentofte Hospital
Dept. of Dermatology K 1502
DK-2900 Hellerup, Denmark
Phone: 31651200
Fax: 31657137
Jytte Roed-Petersen, Pres.

Founded: 1899. **Members:** 291. **Languages:** Dutch, English. **Description:** Dermatologists in Denmark, Norway, and Sweden. Promotes advances in dermatology and venereology. Offers courses for members.

★ 4228 ★   Dermatological Society of
   Malaysia (DSM)
(Persatuan Dermatologi Malaysia — PDM)
Hospital Besar
50586 Kuala Lumpur, Malaysia
Phone: 3 2488110
Fax: 3 2448401
Dr. Kim Weng Chow, Hon.Sec.

Founded: 1975. **Members:** 55. **Languages:** English. **Description:** Dermatologists and other practitioners interested in dermatology. Promotes the research and development of dermatological medicine in Malaysia. Organizes scientific seminars. **Publications:** *Malaysian Journal of Dermatology*, annual. Journal.

★ 4229 ★   Dermatological Society of
   Singapore (DSS)
1 Mandalay Rd.
Singapore 1130, Singapore
Phone: 2534455
Fax: 2533255
Dr. Joyce Lim, Sec.

Founded: 1972. **Members:** 90. **Languages:** English. **Description:** Dermatologists in Singapore. Holds clinico-pathological sessions for dermatologists. Maintains research fund. **Publications:** *Proceedings of Dermatological Society of Singapore*, annual. Journal.

★ 4230 ★   Dermatology Foundation (DF)
1560 Sherman Ave., Ste. 302
Evanston, IL 60201-4802
Phone: (708)328-2256
Fax: (708)328-0509
Sandra Rahn Goldman, Exec.Dir.

Founded: 1964. **Members:** 3,300. **Description:** Members of national and regional dermatological societies; board-certified dermatologists. Raises funds for the control of skin diseases through research, improved education, and better patient care. Stimulates interest of graduate physicians in academic dermatology. Supports basic and clinical investigations. **Publications:** *Dermatology Focus*, quarterly. Newsletter. Covers membership activities. Includes research articles and lists recipients of foundation awards, fellowships, and grants. • *Progress in Dermatology*, quarterly. Bulletin. Bulletin containing research reports. *Price:* Included in membership dues. • *Stewardship Report.* Annual Report. *Price:* Free.

Dermatology Nurses' Association (DNA)
See: Entry 9084

★ 4231 ★   Dutch Association for
   Dermatology and Venereology (DADV)
(Nederlandse Vereniging voor
   Dermatologie en Venereologie — NVDV)
Postbus 8552
NL-3503 RN Utrecht, Netherlands
Phone: 30 474695
Fax: 30 474439
Ms. Auguste Glastra

Founded: 1896. **Members:** 500. **Description:** Physicians and interested individuals. Promotes the study of dermatology and venereal infection and treatment.

Dystrophic Epidermolysis Bullosa
   Research Association of America
   (DEBRA)
See: Entry 5277

★ 4232 ★   Eczema Association for Science
   and Education
1221 SW Yamhill, No. 303
Portland, OR 97205
Phone: (503)228-4430
Fax: (503)273-8778
Jerry Florence, Exec.Dir.

Founded: 1988. **Members:** 4,000. **Description:** Works to raise awareness of the inflammatory condition of the skin called eczema. Conducts research and educational programs on eczema. **Publications:** Brochures. • *EA ADvocate*, quarterly. Newsletter.

★ 4233 ★   Finnish Dermatological Society
   (FDS)
(Suomen Ihotautilaakariyhuistys Ry)
Dept. of Dermatology
Oulu University Hospital
SF-90220 Oulu, Finland
Phone: 81 3153504
Fax: 81 3153135
Arto Lahti, MD, Secretary

Founded: 1916. **Members:** 227. **Languages:** Finnish. Does not correspond in English. **Description:** Professional organization for derma-

tologists in Finland. Conducts educational programs. Bestows awards. **Publications:** *Skinfo*, 4-6/year. Newsletter.

★ 4234 ★   FIRST - Foundation for
   Ichthyosis and Related Skin Types
   (FIRST)
PO Box 20921
Raleigh, NC 27619
Phone: (919)782-5728
Free: 800-545-3286
Fax: (919)781-0679
Nicholas Gattuccio, Exec.Dir.

Founded: 1980. **Members:** 8,000. **Regional Groups:** 8. **Description:** Persons suffering from ichthyosis (a rare hereditary disease that causes the skin to be thick, dry, taut, and scaly) and related diseases; doctors, dermatologists, and others interested in the disease. Acts as a support group for persons with ichthyosis; puts families of sufferers in touch with one another. Provides education about technical, social, and psychological aspects of the disease. Conducts research programs; maintains speakers' bureau; compiles statistics. **Publications:** *A Handbook for Teachers of Children with Ichthyosis.* Handbook. Tool for parents to help make the transition to the school environment for children with ichthyosis. *Price:* $5. • Brochure. Brief summary of foundation. *Price:* Free. • *Free The Butterfly: A Handbook for Parents and Caregivers of Children with Ichthyosis.* Handbook. Covers care, medication, therapy, and nutrition for child with ichthyosis. *Price:* $5. • *Ichthyosis: An Overview. Price:* Free, for members only; $1 for nonmembers. • *Ichthyosis Focus*, quarterly. Magazine. Features medical news, tips for day-to-day coping, and correspondence column for members who would like to exchange letters. *Price:* Free for members only. • *Ichthyosis: The Genetics of Its Inheritance.* Booklet. Description of the genetic inheritance patterns for the different forms of ichthyosis. *Price:* Free, for members only; $1 for nonmembers. **Formerly:** (1986) National Ichthyosis Foundation.

★ 4235 ★   German Dermatological Society
   (GRS)
(Deutsche Dermatologische Gesellschaft —
   DDG)
Dept. of Dermatology
Univ. of Tubingen
Liebermeisterstr. 25
72076 Tuebingen, Germany
Phone: 7071 293473
Fax: 7071 295113
Dr. Gernot Rassner, Pres.

Founded: 1888. **Members:** 1,800. **Languages:** English, German. **Description:** Individuals united to promote dermatology. Conducts educational and research programs. **Publications:** *Der Hautarzt*, periodic.

★ 4236 ★   Hellenic Society of Dermatology
   and Venereology
University of Athens
A. Sygros Hospital
5 Ionos Dragoumi St. Kessariani
GR-161 21 Athens, Greece
Phone: 1 7212700
Fax: 1 7211122
Prof. J.D. Stratigos, M.D., Contact

Members: 600. **Languages:** English, Greek. **Description:** Offers awards; Conducts educational programs; Bestows awards; compiles statistics. Maintains museum. **Publications:** *Hellenic Dermato-Venereological Review*, quarterly.

★ 4237 ★   **History of Dermatology Society (HDS)**
1819 J.F. Kennedy Blvd., Ste. 465
Philadelphia, PA 19103
Phone: (215)563-8333
Fax: (215)563-3044
Lawrence C. Parish, M.D., Pres.

Founded: 1973. **Members:** 120. **Description:** Dermatologists interested in promoting the history of dermatology. **Publications:** *Program Guide*, annual.

★ 4238 ★   **Hong Kong Society of Dermatology and Venereology (HKSD)**
Sai Ying Pun Jockey Club Clinic, 3rd Fl.
Queen's Rd.
Hong Kong, Hong Kong
Phone: 8598233
Fax: 8582684
Dr. L.Y. Chong, Chm.

Founded: 1983. **Members:** 143. **Languages:** English. **Description:** Dermatologists and physicians in Hong Kong. Stimulates interest in dermatology; promotes exchange and cooperation among members; encourages discussions to address problems in the field. Inspires high standards of dermatological care. Fosters international contacts; disseminates information.

★ 4239 ★   **Hungarian Dermatological Society (HDS)**
(Magyar Dermatologiai Tarsulat — MDT)
Department of Dermatology
Szent-Gyorgyi Albert Medical University
Postafiok 480
H-6701 Szeged, Hungary
Phone: 61 2100310
Fax: 61 1340566
J. Matthew Balo-Banga, M.D., Ph.D., Exec. Officer

Founded: 1928. **Members:** 28. **Local Groups:** 3. **Languages:** English, Hungarian. **Description:** Promotes dermatological practice and research in 8 countries. Monitors progress in the field of dermatology. Participates in international forums. **Publications:** *Borgyogyaszati es Venerologiai Szemle*, bimonthly. Journal. Accepts English and German papers. Contains English abstracts. • *Progress of Dermatology and Venereology*. Yearbook.

★ 4240 ★   **Ibero-Latin American College of Dermatology (ILACD)**
(Colegio Ibero-Latino-Americano de Dermatologia — CILAD)
Pasaje 1, No. 137
Urbanizacion
La Esperanza
San Salvador, El Salvador
Phone: 260034
Fax: 261382
Dr. Sebastiao A.P. Sampaio, Contact

Founded: 1948. **Members:** 2,206. **Languages:** Portuguese, Spanish. **Description:** Iberian or Latin American doctors in 29 countries working in various fields related to dermatology including mycology (the study of fungi), venereology (the study of sexually transmitted diseases), the treatment of leprosy, dermatologic surgery, and criosurgery. Seeks to foster a working relationship between Ibero-Latin American specialists and those in other countries. **Publications:** *Boletin del CILAD*, quarterly. Bulletin. Contains information about the activities of the college. • *Ciladerma*, bimonthly. Magazine. • Directory, periodic. • *Medicina Cutanea Ibero-Latino-Americana*, bimonthly. • Monographs, periodic.

★ 4241 ★   **Institute of Trichologists (IT)**
228 Stockwell Rd.
London SW9 9SU, England
Phone: 171 7332056
Alan Samuel, Sec.

Founded: 1902. **Members:** 240. **Languages:** English. **Description:** Promotes study, research, and application in the treatment and care of human scalp and hair. Provides scientific training of individuals qualified to advise and offer treatment of hair and scalp disorders and serves as an examining body for students of trichology. Provides centers for clinical study. Maintains Scalp and Hair Hospital where students conduct clinical observations and gain practical experience. Bestows awards; sponsors charitable program; maintains speakers' bureau. **Publications:** *Membership Directory*, annual. Membership Directory. • *Monograph*, periodic. • Newsletter, 3/year. • *Update*, 3/year. Journal.

★ 4242 ★   **International Association of Trichologists (IAT)**
37320 22nd St.
Kalamazoo, MI 49009
Phone: (616)372-3224
David Salinger, Dir.

Founded: 1973. **Members:** 125. **Languages:** English. **Description:** Individuals licensed to practice or perform manipulative, electrical, light, or cosmetic therapy upon the scalp. Promotes the study, research, and legitimate practice of the treatment and care of the human hair and scalp. Prescribes and administers course of study of trichology. Conducts testing; grants certification; offers placement service. Has established code of ethics. **Publications:** *Guide to Hair Loss*. Book. • Newsletter, bimonthly. • *Simplified Hairdressing Science*.

★ 4243 ★   **International Federation of Psoriasis Associations (IFPA)**
(Federation Internationale des Associations de Psoriasis)
1, rue des Bois
F-95520 Osny, France
Phone: 1 30322917
Fax: 1 30759226
Mrs. Nichele Allaire, Contact

Founded: 1973. **Members:** 30. **Languages:** English. **Description:** National psoriasis organizations. Acts as advisory, consulting, and coordinating body for member groups implementing medical, social, and psychological research into psoriasis. Seeks to influence related social legislation and to collect all available information on psoriasis. Promotes public awareness of psoriasis and works to remove the social stigma associated with skin conditions. **Publications:** *IFPA Newsletter*, quarterly. Newsletter.

International Oculoplastic Society, Inc. (IOSI)
See: Entry 13492

International Society for Dermatologic Surgery (ISDS)
See: Entry 12281

★ 4244 ★   **International Society of Dermatology: Tropical, Geographic, and Ecologic (ISD)**
200 1st St. SW
Rochester, MN 55905
Phone: (507)284-3736
Fax: (507)284-2072
Dr. Degas Karlel, Pres.

Founded: 1957. **Members:** 3,000. **Description:** Dermatologists and general physicians. Promotes interest, education, and research in dermatology. **Publications:** Directory, biennial. • *International Journal of Dermatology*, monthly. Journal. **Formerly:** (1984) International Society of Tropical Dermatology.

★ 4245 ★   **International Society of Dermatology: Tropical, Geographic, and Ecological**
Aparatado Aereo 90123
Bogota, Colombia
Dr. Maria Mellida Duran de Rueda, Sec.Gen.

Description: Promotes the study of dermatology. Concerned with the education and tracking of skin diseases. **Publications:** *International Journal of Dermatology*, 10/year.

★ 4246 ★   **Israel Dermatological Society (IDS)**
Dept. of Dermatology
Beilinson Med. Center
49100 Petach Tikva, Israel
Phone: 3 9376650
Fax: 3 9229685
Prof. Miriam Sandbank, Sec.

Founded: 1927. **Members:** 215. **Local Groups:** 3. **Languages:** English, Hebrew. **Description:** Dermatologists and dermatopathologists. Organizes postgraduate educational programs; conducts research.

★ 4247 ★   **Mexican Academy of Dermatology (MAD)**
(Academia Mexicana de Dermatologia — AMD)
Eucken 15, 1st Fl.
Colonia Anzures
11590 Mexico City, DF, Mexico
Phone: 5 2110173
Fax: 5 2509161
Dr. Rocio Orozco, Contact

Founded: 1952. **Members:** 150. **Languages:** English, Spanish. **Description:** Provides continuing medical education programs to members. Offers support to dermatology residents. **Publications:** *Dermatologia-Revista Mexicana*, monthly.

★ 4248 ★ National Alopecia Areata Foundation (NAAF)
PO Box 150760
San Rafael, CA 94915-0760
Phone: (415)456-4644
Fax: (415)456-4274
Vicki Kalabokes, Exec.Dir.

Founded: 1981. **Members:** 5,000. **Regional Groups:** 1. **State Groups:** 42. **Local Groups:** 60. **Description:** Individuals concerned about alopecia areata, a disease causing partial scalp hair loss, total scalp hair loss (alopecia totalis), or total loss of body hair (alopecia universalis); cause and cure are unknown and the course of the disease is unpredictable. Objectives are to: develop public awareness of the disease; provide a support network; raise funds for research; keep patients medically informed with explanations about AA and the latest treatments. Maintains medical advisory board; operates information booth at meetings of the American Academy of Dermatology. **Publications:** Brochures. • *National Alopecia Areata Foundation Newsletter*, bimonthly. Newsletter. Covers treatment, research, and developments. Includes wig and cosmetic tips. *Price:* Included with donation of $30 or more. Also publishes medical description of AA.

National Arthritis and Musculoskeletal and Skin Diseases Information Clearinghouse (NAMSIC)
See: Entry 7891

★ 4249 ★ National Psoriasis Foundation (NPF)
6600 SW 92nd, Ste. 300
Portland, OR 97223
Phone: (503)244-7404
Free: 800-723-9166
Fax: (503)245-0626
Gail M. Zimmerman, Exec.Dir.

Founded: 1968. **Members:** 32,000. **Local Groups:** 20. **Description:** Individuals suffering from psoriasis, their families and friends; physicians, nurses, and representatives of pharmaceutical companies. Supports research at various university research centers. Facilitates communication among psoriasis victims through pen pal programs (for teenagers and adults), group sessions, and other activities. Testifies annually to Congress requesting additional funds for psoriasis research. Provides literature to schools and libraries; works with the media to disseminate information on psoriasis. Supplies members with samples of new antipsoriasis over-the-counter products. Makes physician referrals. Sponsors regional educational symposia. **Publications:** Brochures. Contains information on psoriasis, treatments, issues in psoriasis. • *National Psoriasis Foundation--Annual Report*. Annual Report. *Price:* Included in membership dues. • *National Psoriasis Foundation--Bulletin*, bimonthly. Newsletter. Covers psoriasis treatment and research. Includes doctor's question and answer column. *Price:* Included in membership dues. • *National Psoriasis Foundation--Pharmacy News*, periodic. *Price:* Included in membership dues. • Pamphlets.

★ 4250 ★ National Vitiligo Foundation (NVFI)
PO Box 6337
Tyler, TX 75711
Phone: (903)534-2925
Fax: (903)534-8075
Allen C. Locklin, Pres.

Founded: 1985. **Members:** 9,500. **Regional Groups:** 11. **Description:** Doctors and patients; contributors and supporters. Provides information and counseling to vitiligo patients and their families. (Vitiligo is a skin disease which destroys pigment cells causing smooth, white-colored patches of skin.) Seeks to increase awareness and concern for the vitiligo patient. Raises funds for scientific and clinical research on the cause, treatment, and cure of vitiligo. **Publications:** Brochures. • *Handbook for Patients*. • *Handbook for Physicians*. • *Handbook for Schools*. • *Vitiligo*, semiannual. Newsletter.

★ 4251 ★ Noah Worcester Dermatological Society (NWDS)
8780 Golf Rd.
Niles, IL 60714
Phone: (708)299-1044
Dr. Handler, Sec.-Treas.

Founded: 1958. **Members:** 170. **Description:** Dermatologists and allied medical scientists. Sponsors programs to exchange scientific information on diseases of the skin. Society is named for the author of the first American textbook of dermatology, published in 1845. Maintains Noah Worcester Library at the University of Cincinnati. Supports research in fledgling departments of dermatology and offers yearly support to Dermatology Foundation. **Publications:** *Membership Roster*, annual. Membership Directory.

★ 4252 ★ North American Clinical Dermatologic Society (NACDS)
c/o John W. White, Jr., M.D.
Mayo Clinic
4500 San Pablo Rd.
Jacksonville, FL 32224
Phone: (904)953-2219
John W. White, Jr., M, Sec.Gen.

Founded: 1959. **Members:** 180. **Description:** Clinical board-certified dermatologists practicing in the U.S. and Canada and leaders of dermatology throughout the world. Promotes the interchange of information and research. **Publications:** *Program*, annual.

★ 4253 ★ Norwegian Dermatological Society (NDS)
(Norsk Dermatologisk Selskap — NDS)
Rikshospitalet, Hudavd.
N-0027 Oslo 1, Norway
Phone: 2 868411
Fax: 2 868433
Dr. Tor Langeland, Contact

Founded: 1914. **Members:** 121. **Languages:** English, Norwegian. **Description:** Dermatologists and residents in dermatology. Promotes the advancement of dermatology in Norway; represents members' interests. Offers courses for pre- and postgraduates in dermatology.

★ 4254 ★ Pacific Dermatologic Association (PDA)
930 N. Meacham Rd.
Schaumburg, IL 60173-6016
Phone: (708)330-9830
Fax: (708)330-0050
Arnold W. Gurevitch, M.D., Pres.

Founded: 1948. **Members:** 1,200. **Regional Groups:** 1. **Description:** Dermatologists united to provide opportunities for exchange of information and advancement of knowledge of dermatology and syphilology among physicians within the Pacific Rim. Conducts specialized education programs; sponsors competitions. **Publications:** Membership Directory, triennial. • *Transactions*, annual.

★ 4255 ★ Psoriasis Research Association (PRA)
107 Vista del Grande
San Carlos, CA 94070
Phone: (415)593-1394
Diane Bradley Mullins, Founder & Exec.Sec.

Founded: 1952. **Description:** Supported by psoriasis patients, physicians, and others interested in research to find the cause and cure of psoriasis, a chronic skin disease characterized by red patches covered with white scales. Provides patient-volunteers across the U.S. for studies at University of California Medical School, San Francisco, and at the Psoriasis Research Institute. Maintains library of 1500 volumes on psoriasis and related subspecialties. Supports individual researchers applying for small grants from PRA. Has received grants from several pharmaceutical companies to compile medical statistics on psoriasis patients, including detailed epidemiologic data and names of patient-volunteers. Maintains speakers' bureau.

★ 4256 ★ Psoriasis Research Institute (PRI)
600 Town and Country Village
Palo Alto, CA 94301
Phone: (415)326-1848
Fax: (415)326-1262
Eugene M. Farber, M.D., Chrm. and CEO

Founded: 1979. **Description:** Creates projects for the study, diagnosis, treatment, and eventual cure of psoriasis. Collects and disseminates information about psoriasis in an effort to advance the science of dermatology. Maintains Psoriasis Medical Center, which offers advanced therapeutic programs and equipment to treat all aspects of the disease. Offers counseling and biofeedback stress control for patients. Compiles statistics; conducts epidemiological study of psoriasis patients. Sponsors monthly selfhelp workshop for psoriasis patients utilizing audiovisual presentations, written materials, and discussions. **Publications:** Pamphlets. • *Psoriasis Medical Center*. Brochure. • *Psoriasis Newsletter*, 3/year. Newsletter. Contains innovative concepts in the treatment of psoriasis. *Price:* Free. Also publishes research papers. **Formerly:** (1983) International Psoriasis Research Foundation.

Skin Cancer Foundation (SCF)
See: Entry 5986

★4257★ Society of Dermatology of Uruguay (SDU)
(Sociedad de Dermatologia del Uruguay — SDU)
Avenida 18 de Julio 1268, esq. 1105
11100 Montevideo, Uruguay
Phone: 2 915231
Dr. Jorge Sanguinetti, Pres.

Members: 120. **Local Groups:** 3. **Languages:** English, Spanish. **Description:** Dermatologists and others interested in dermatology. Encourages discussion on dermatology among members; facilitates international contact. Conducts postgraduate courses in dermatology; organizes dermatological research projects; holds monthly scientific meetings. Gathers and disseminates scientific information.

★4258★ Society for Investigative Dermatology (SID)
c/o David R. Bickers, M.D.
11001 Cedar Ave., Ste. 500A
Cleveland, OH 44106
Phone: (216)844-6859
Fax: (216)844-6810
Angela Welsh, Admin.Dir.

Founded: 1937. **Members:** 2,300. **Regional Groups:** 4. **Description:** Professional society promoting research in dermatology and allied subjects. **Publications:** *Journal of Investigative Dermatology*, monthly. Journal.

Society for Pediatric Dermatology (SPD)
See: Entry 3293

★4259★ Spanish Academy of Dermatology (SAD)
(Academia Espanola de Dermatologia — AED)
Ferraz 100
E-28008 Madrid, Spain
Phone: 1 5446284
Fax: 1 5494145
Jose M. Mascaro, Hon.Pres. & Sec.

Founded: 1909. **Members:** 1,085. **Regional Groups:** 8. **Local Groups:** 8. **Languages:** English, Spanish. **Description:** Promotes interaction between Spanish dermatologists and scientists outside of Spain. Cooperates with health and education authorities with regard to postgraduate certification. Provides research grants; conducts educational programs on allergies, pathology, surgery, pediatric dermatology, and sexually transmitted diseases. **Publications:** *Actas Dermosifiliograficas*, monthly. Journal.

★4260★ Swedish Society for Dermatology and Venereology
Dept. of Dermatology
University Hospital
S-581 85 Linkoping, Sweden
Phone: 13 222596
Fax: 13 222562
Thomas Andersson, Sec.

Languages: English. **Description:** Dermatologists in Sweden. Represents members' interests. **Formerly:** Swedish Dermatological Society.

Research Centers

★4261★ Acne Research Institute, Inc.
881 Dover, Ste. 100
New Port Beach, CA 92663
Phone: (714)722-1805
Sara Fulton, Dir.

Research Activities and Fields: Cause and treatment of acne.

★4262★ Baylor University
Baylor Hair Research and Treatment Center
3600 Gaston Ave., Ste. 1058
Dallas, TX 75246
Phone: (214)820-4247
Fax: (214)824-1900
David A. Whiting, M.D., Dir.

Research Activities and Fields: Hair-related problems, including hair loss, abnormal hair texture, scalp disease, hair overgrowth, and nail disorders. Activities include studies of methods to stimulate hair growth, studies of hair transplantation, and evaluation of transverse sections of the scalp.

★4263★ Fulton Skin Institute
1617 Westcliff Dr., Ste. 100
Newport Beach, CA 92660
Phone: (714)631-3376
Fax: (714)722-1284
Dr. James E. Fulton, Jr.

Research Activities and Fields: Cosmetic surgery, aggravating factors, and pathogenesis and treatment of acne.

★4264★ Laboratory of Dermatology Research
Memorial Sloan-Kettering Cancer Center
1275 York Ave.
New York, NY 10021
Phone: (212)639-2000
Fax: (212)717-3363
Bijan Safai, M.D., Head

Research Activities and Fields: Cutaneous biology, immunodermatology, and cutaneous oncology. Specific studies include identification of cell surface antigens and differentiation and kinetics of epidermal keratinocytes, identification and characterization of epidermal derived factors and their capability of exerting B- and T-cell inducing activities, investigation of the role of epidermal-derived factors in the development of cutaneous T-cell lymphoma, analysis of the growth factors involvement in Kaposi sarcoma, and analysis of the role of HTLV-1 as the cause of cutaneous T-cell lymphoma.

★4265★ Massachusetts General Hospital
Harvard Cutaneous Biology Research Center
Massachusetts General Hospital
MGH-East, Bldg. 149
Charlestown, MA 02129
Phone: (617)726-4425
Fax: (617)726-4027
Dr. John Parrish, Dir.

Research Activities and Fields: Dermatology, including 1) photobiology of skin, including pho-

---

toimmunology, photoaging, free radical biology and photoprotection; 2) pigment cell biology; 3) growth and differentiation of epidermis, hair and nails, and keratin biochemistry; 4) immunology, allergy, inflammation, and modifiers of host response; 5) physical properties of skin, including water content, percutaneous transport of chemicals, and optical properties; 6) physiology and pharmacology of the skin; and 7) biology of dermis and dermal-epidermal junction and their constituents. **E-mail Address:** cbrc.mgh.harvard.edu.

★4266★ Psoriasis Research Institute
600 Town & Country Village
Palo Alto, CA 94301
Phone: (415)326-1848
Eugene M. Farber, M.D., Pres.

Research Activities and Fields: Conducts research in the areas of biochemistry, virology, epidemiology, pharmacology, and pathology, with the goal of finding the cause of and a cure for psoriasis. **Publications:** *Psoriasis Newsletter* (quarterly). **Formerly:** International Psoriasis Research Institute.

★4267★ Rockefeller University
Laboratory for Investigative Dermatology
1230 York Ave.
New York, NY 10021-6399
Phone: (212)327-8091
Fax: (212)327-8232
Dr. James Krueger, Head

Research Activities and Fields: Mechanisms governing skin response to environmental influences, as modified by genetic factors and by age. Studies the ability of the skin to defend against or repair cellular damage (including potentially carcinogenic damage to DNA and to chromosomes) caused by environmental exposure, irradiation, atmospheric oxygen, toxic chemicals, and physical trauma. Conducts basic and clinical research on wound healing, psoriasis, and epidermolysis bullosa.

U.S. Department of Health and Human Services
National Cancer Institute
Division of Cancer Biology, Diagnosis, and Centers
Dermatology Branch
See: Entry 6132

U.S. Department of Health and Human Services
National Institute of Arthritis and Musculoskeletal and Skin Diseases
See: Entry 7936

★4268★ U.S. Department of Health and Human Services
National Institute of Arthritis and Musculoskeletal and Skin Diseases
Extramural Activities Program
Skin Diseases Branch
Westwood Bldg., Rm. 405
5333 Westbard Ave.
Bethesda, MD 20892
Phone: (301)496-7326
Fax: (301)480-7881
Alan N. Moshell, M.D., Director

Research Activities and Fields: Branch supports research on the structure, function, and

---

physiology of skin as well as on the causes and improved treatment of a wide variety of skin diseases, including psoriasis, lupus, eczema, vitiligo, bullous skin diseases, acne, and ichthyosis.

★ 4269 ★ University of California, San Francisco
Dermatology Drug Research Unit
515 Spruce
Box 1212
San Francisco, CA 94143
Phone: (415)476-4701
Fax: (415)502-4126
John Koo, M.D., Dir.

Research Activities and Fields: Conducts clinical testing of new or existing pharmacologic agents used in the treatment of skin disorders and develops protocols for drug testing. Areas of interest include phototherapy, psoriasis, and psychodermatology.

★ 4270 ★ University of Pennsylvania
Aging Skin Clinic
Ctr. for Human Appearance
Penn Tower Hotel, 10th Fl.
3400 Spruce St.
Philadelphia, PA 19104
Phone: (215)662-7093
Fax: (215)349-5895
Dr. Linton A. Whitaker, Chief of Plastic Surgery

Research Activities and Fields: Aging bone and skin, interface between bone and soft tissue, and bone structure of the human face as it relates to growth and aging. **Publications:** Annual Report.

Chapter 20
Developmental Disabilities

Foundations & Other Funding Organizations

Private Foundations

★4271★ Edith L. Trees Charitable Trust
c/o PNC Bank
Investment Management and Trust Division
One Oliver Plz., 29th Fl.
Pittsburgh, PA 15265-0970
Phone: (412)762-3808
Fax: (412)762-4160
James M. Ferguson, III, Contact

Foundation Philosophy: The Edith L. Trees Charitable Trust provides support to organizations that serve mentally retarded children. Generally, the trust focuses its efforts in three categories--social services, education, and civic causes. The trust's social service funding supports Associations for Retarded Citizens (ARCs), community service organizations, and community centers. The trust's contributions to education fund schools and special/gifted education, and its civic funds support philanthropic organizations. **Giving Priorities:** In 1993, the trust gave approximately 50% of its total giving to social service organizations, including a single $240,000 grant to ARC Allegheny County. About 23% of the trust's funding supported civic causes, primarily supporting the Verland Foundation with two grants totaling $285,000 for an endowment and debt retirement. Education received 18% of giving. Health care received 7% and the arts received 1% of funding. **Typical Health-Related Recipients:** Health Organizations, Mental Health, People with Disabilities. **Geographic Distribution:** Primarily in Pittsburgh, PA.

★4272★ Joseph P. Kennedy, Jr. Foundation
1325 G St., NW, Ste. 500
Washington, DC 20005-4709
Phone: (202)393-1250
Fax: (202)824-0200
Steven M. Eidelman, Executive Director

Foundation Philosophy: The foundation maintains two firm objectives: to seek the prevention

of mental retardation by identifying its causes and to improve the means by which society deals with its citizens with mental retardation. Recent grants have supported projects relating to access to medical care and the use of drugs by pregnant teens. Another major area of concern is teen pregnancy. Because a significant cause of mental retardation is prematurity and low birth weight among the newborn babies of adolescents, the foundation developed a values-based curriculum, "A Community of Caring," for use in programs for pregnant teens in clinics, hospitals, agencies, or schools. **Giving Priorities:** IN fiscal 1993, the foundation reported that 58% of its funding was given to social service organizations, with emphasis on services for people with disablties, family programs, and self-advocacy. Civic groups, specifically public policy issues regarding mental retardation, received 17%; health care, 12%; educational institutions, 8%; and the arts, 6%. **Typical Health-Related Recipients:** Children's Health/ Hospitals, Family Planning, Hospitals, Medical Education, Medical Research, People with Disabilities, Prenatal Health Issues. **Geographic Distribution:** No geographic restrictions.

Other Funding Organizations

★4273★ Association for Retarded Citizens
500 E. Border St., Ste. 300
Arlington, TX 76010
Phone: (817)261-6003
Fax: (817)277-3491
Alan Abeson, Ed.D., Exec. Dir.

Description: Awards grants for research dealing with mental retardation.

★4274★ National Down Syndrome Society
666 Broadway
New York, NY 10012
Phone: (212)460-9330
Free: 800-221-4602
Fax: (212)979-2873
Donna M. Rosenthal, Exec. Dir.

Description: Raises funds to support all areas of Down's Syndrome research.

★4275★ Order of Alhambra
4200 Leeds Ave.
Baltimore, MD 21229
Phone: (410)242-0660
Fax: (410)536-5729
Roger J. Reid, Supreme Cmdr.

Description: Awards scholarships to assist students in the field of special education who plan to work with the mentally retarded and handicapped. Operates Alhambra Institute for Mental Retardation Research, which provides grants for research on the causes of Down Syndrome.

National & International Organizations

★4276★ American Academy on Mental Retardation (AAMR)
c/o Jack A. Stark, Ph.D.
Creighton-Nebraska Univs.
Department of Psychiatry
2205 S. 10th St.
Omaha, NE 68108
Phone: (402)449-4783
Jack A. Stark, Ph.D., Contact

Founded: 1960. **Members:** 250. **Description:** Scientists actively engaged in research in any discipline relating to mental retardation; active membership is limited to scientists possessing a doctorate degree. Encourages and promotes investigative work in the clinical and experimental field of mental retardation; provides a forum for research workers in this field. Facilitates relations between various disciplines and stimulates cooperative research. Cooperates with national and international organizations and cosponsors colloquia, symposia, and other meetings. **Publications:** Newsletter, semiannual.

★4277★ American Association on Mental Retardation (AAMR)
444 N. Capitol St. NW, Ste. 846
Washington, DC 20001-1512
Phone: (202)387-1968
Free: 800-424-3688
Ms. M. Doreen Croser, Exec.Dir.

Founded: 1876. **Members:** 9,500. **Regional Groups:** 9. **Description:** Physicians, educators, administrators, social workers, psychologists, psychiatrists, students, and others interested in the general welfare of persons with mental retardation and the study of the cause, treatment, and prevention of mental retardation. Maintains 17 divisions and subdivisions. **Publications:** *American Journal of Mental Retardation*, bimonthly. Journal. • *Innovations: A Research to Practice Series*, 3/year. • Manual. Contains terminology and classification in mental retardation. • *Mental Retardation*, bimonthly. • Monograph. • *News and Notes*, quarterly. Also publishes testing materials. **Formerly:** (1906) Association of Medical Officers of American Institutions of Idiotic and Feebleminded Children; (1933) American Association for the Study of the Feebleminded; (1987) American Association on Mental Deficiency.

★ 4278 ★ American Network of Community Options and Resources (ANCOR)
4200 Evergreen Ln., Ste. 315
Annandale, VA 22003
Phone: (703)642-6614
Joni Fritz, Exec.Dir.

Founded: 1970. **Members:** 620. **Local Groups:** 10. **Description:** Agencies (620) which provide services and supports to persons with disabilities; others (60) interested in the field. Committed to enhancing the quality of life for persons with disabilities, with a direct concern for all living situations, and supports each individual's need to enchance his/her independence and chosen lifestyle. Works with others to develop a total array of options and resources necessary for the fulfillment of other human needs. Supports activities to develop standards and guidelines; conducts studies; offers placement assistance, workshops, and seminars. **Publications:** *ANCOR News and Notes*, monthly. • *Directory of Members*, annual. Membership Directory. *Price:* $25. • *Executives' Notebook*, monthly. • *Legislative Alert*, periodic. • *LINKS*, monthly. Newsletter. Provides information on current services for people with disabilities. Includes calendar of events, news of members, research news, and activities. *Price:* Included in membership dues. • *P's & Q's News*, quarterly. **Formerly:** (1987) National Association of Private Residential Facilities for the Mentally Retarded; (1993) National Association of Private Residential Resources.

★ 4279 ★ The ARC (ARC-U.S.)
500 E. Border St., Ste. 300
Arlington, TX 76010
Phone: (817)261-6003
Fax: (817)277-3491
Alan Abeson, Ed.D., Exec.Dir.

Founded: 1950. **Members:** 140,000. **State Groups:** 46. **Local Groups:** 1200. **Description:** Parents, professional workers, and others interested in individuals with mental retardation. Works on local, state, and national levels to promote services, research, public understanding, and legislation for mentally retarded persons and their families. **Publications:** *Advocates' Voice*. *Price:* $9/year. • *ARC Government Report*, semimonthly. Report. *Price:* $72/year. • *The Arc Now*, monthly. • *The Arc Today*, quarterly. *Price:* $15/year. **Also Known As:** Association for Retarded Citizens. **Formerly:** (1952)

National Association of Parents and Friends of Mentally Retarded Children; (1974) National Association for Retarded Children; (1980) National Association for Retarded Citizens; (1991) Association for Retarded Citizens of the United States.

★ 4280 ★ Association for Advancement of Blind and Retarded (AABR)
164-09 Hillside Ave.
Jamaica, NY 11432
Phone: (718)523-2222
Fax: (718)739-4750
Christopher Weldon, Exec.Dir.

Founded: 1955. **Description:** Community groups and individuals interested in multihandicapped blind and severely retarded adults. Operates: ten group residences providing intermediate care facilities for blind and retarded adults; two- to six-day treatment centers for blind, multihandicapped, and severely retarded adults; summer camp for blind and multihandicapped people. Provides information and referral services. **Formerly:** (1974) Association for Advancement of Blind Children.

★ 4281 ★ Association for Children with Retarded Mental Development (A/CRMD)
345 Hudson St.
New York, NY 10014
Phone: (212)741-0100
Free: 800-WOW-ACRM
Fax: (212)627-8318
Arthur Roza, Acting Exec.Dir.

Founded: 1951. **Members:** 400. **Description:** Professionals, parents, siblings, and others interested in mentally retarded and developmentally disabled children and adults. Membership centered in New York City area. Offers professionally supervised programs for mentally retarded and developmentally disabled young adults, including vocational rehabilitation centers, dual diagnosis programs, job placement, rehavilitation workshops, social centers, activities for daily living, day treatment, day training, supported work, and family support programs. Operates the Lubin Center for Independent Living, an apartment complex for gainfully employed adults capable of independent living. Also operates community residences, supportive apartments, and intermediate care facilities in the state of New York. Acts as an advocate for the mentally retarded and developmentally disabled in all phases of life in the city of New York. Sponsors conferences and training regarding mental retardation and developmental disability. Maintains speakers' bureau and job placement service. **Publications:** *Association for Children with Retarded Mental Development--On the Record: What's Happening in Our Agency*, quarterly. Newsletter. Informs A/CRMD members of developments in the human services field. Icludes information on recent research in the field. *Price:* $5/year. • Brochures. • Directory, annual. Also publishes agency profile. **Formerly:** (1964) Parents Association for Children with Retarded Mental Development.

★ 4282 ★ Association for the Help of Retarded Children
200 Park Ave. S., Ste. 1201
New York, NY 10003
Phone: (212)254-8203
Fax: (212)473-2225
Shirley Berenstein, Dir.

Founded: 1949. **Members:** 12,000. **Description:** Developmentally disabled children and adults; their families; interested individuals. Provides support services, training programs, clinics, schools, and residential facilities to the developmentally disabled. **Publications:** *The Chronicle*, monthly. Newsletter.

★ 4283 ★ Australian Society for the Study of Intellectual Disability (ASSID)
34 Wentwrithville
Kineswood, NSW 2750, Australia
Phone: 2 6859037
Fax: 2 6859023
Mr. Tim Green, Sec.

★ 4284 ★ AVKO Educational Research Foundation (AVKOEFR)
3084 W. Willard Rd.
Clio, MI 48420
Phone: (810)686-9283
Fax: (810)686-1101
Don McCabe, Research Dir.

Founded: 1974. **Members:** 500. **Description:** Teachers and individuals interested in helping others learn to read and spell and in developing reading training materials for individuals with dyslexia or other learning disabilities using a method involving audio, visual, kinesthetic, and oral (AVKO) techniques. Offers advice on the techniques of tutoring, classroom teaching, diagnosis, and remediation. Conducts research into the causes of reading, spelling, and writing disabilities. Publishes and disseminates information on research. Provides a reading and spelling center where children and adults with educational deficiencies can receive diagnostic attention and remediation. Sponsors adult community education courses to train adults in tutoring their spouses or children in reading and spelling skills. Maintains speakers' bureau; compiles statistics. **Publications:** *AVKO Educational Research Foundation--Newsletter*, quarterly. Newsletter. Covers techniques and materials for teaching reading and spelling to dyslexics and the learning disabled. *Price:* Included in membership dues. • *Helping Anyone Overcome Reading/Spelling Problems.* • *The Patterns of English Spelling.* • *Sequential Spelling.*

★ 4285 ★ Bethesda Lutheran Homes and Services
c/o Dr. A. L. Napolitano
700 Hoffman Dr.
Watertown, WI 53094
Phone: (414)261-3050
Free: 800-369-INFO
Dr. A. L. Napolitano, Exec.Dir.

Founded: 1904. **Members:** 5,000. **State Groups:** 10. **Description:** Bethesda's National Christian Resource Center provides information on resources, services, and agencies to parents, pastors, teachers, advocates, and mental retardation professionals to help them identify and respond to the physical, social, emotional, and spiritual needs of persons with mental retardation. Assists in training persons to care for individuals with mental retardation; sponsors cooperative education programs in nursing, social work, psychology, special education, Christian education, and public relations. Collects, catalogs, and houses religious materials and information on mental retardation. Conducts religious special education workshops on mental retardation and other disability related issues. Maintains speakers' bureau. **Publications:** *Behavior Treatment I and II.* Video. *Price:* $50 each. • *Breakthrough*, quarterly. Newsletter. Includes religious special education and disability ministry news, feature stories, and weekly Biblical curriculum guides. *Price:* Free. • *Developing a Response to Our Loving God.* Book. • *Eating Skills.* Video. Includes manual. • *Interacting With People Who Are Mentally Retarded.* Pamphlet. • *Leisure Skills Training.* Video. • *Opening the Door to Learning for People With Mental Retardation.* Video. • *Task Analysis.* • *Walking With Jesus: Daily Devotions for Group Homes.* Book. **Formerly:** (1992) Lutheran Liaison/National Christian Resource Center.

★4286★ Caribbean Association on Mental Retardation and Other Development Disabilities (CAMRODD)
Golden Ave.
PO Box 224
Kingston 7, Jamaica
Phone: (809)927-2054
Fax: (809)927-3038
Mrs. Aminta DaCosta Gomez, Pres.

Founded: 1970. **Members:** 25. **Languages:** Dutch, English, Spanish. **Description:** National voluntary associations in 25 Caribbean countries for mentally retarded persons. Sponsors workshops and training for leadership development. Bestows awards. **Publications:** *New Directions for the 21st Century.* • *20 Year Review.*

★4287★ Center for Family Support (CFS)
386 Park Ave. S.
New York, NY 10016
Phone: (212)481-1082
Alice Dick, Exec.Dir.

Founded: 1953. **Description:** Service agency devoted to the physical well-being and development of the retarded child and the sound mental health of the parents. Helps families with retarded children with all aspects of home care including counseling, referrals, home aide service, and consultation. Offers intervention for parents at the birth of a retarded child with in-home support, guidance, and infant stimulation. Emphasis is on working with entire families and keeping families together whenever possible; sponsors parents' groups. Pioneered training of nonprofessional women as Home Aides to provide supportive services in homes. **Formerly:** (1958) Parents With a Purpose; (1991) Retarded Infants Service.

Coffin-Lowry Syndrome Foundation
See: Entry 5273

Commission on Mental and Physical Disability Law (CMPDL)
See: Entry 4476

Commonwealth Association for Mental Handicap and Developmental Disabilities (CAMHDD)
See: Entry 4477

★4288★ Council for Exceptional Children (MRDD)
Division on Mental Retardation and Developmental Disabilities
c/o Dr. Tom Smith
Arkansas University Affiliated Facility
1120 Marshall St., Ste. 120
Little Rock, AR 72202
Dr. Dana M. Anderson, Exec.Sec.

Founded: 1963. **Members:** 8,120. **State Groups:** 24. **Description:** A division of the Council for Exceptional Children. Teachers and other professionals working with students with mental retardation and developmental disabilities. Goal is to advance education, general welfare, and research in the education of individuals with mental retardation and developmental disabilities. Promotes competency of teachers of students with mental retardation and developmental disabilities, public understanding, and legislation needed to accomplish goals. Conducts educational programs. Maintains speakers' bureau. Conducts educational programs. **Publications:** *Best Practices in Mild Mental Retardation.* Book. • *Education and Training in Mental Retardation and Developmental Disabilities*, quarterly. Journal. Covers education and welfare of people with mental retardation and developmental disabilities. Features educational product reviews. *Price:* Included in membership dues; $40/year for nonmembers; $55/year for institutions. • *Educational Programming for the Severely/Profoundly Handicapped.* Book. • *Mental Retardation - Topics of Today - Issues of Tomorrow.* Book. • *MR Express*, 3/year. Newsletter. Covers division activities. *Price:* Included in membership dues. • *Severe Mental Retardation.* Book. • *Social Skills for Home and Community.* Book. • *Transitions Issues and Directions.* Book. **Formerly:** (1993) Division on Mental Retardation of the Council for Execptional Children.

★4289★ Down's Syndrome Association (DSA)
155 Mitcham Rd.
London SW17 9PG, England
Phone: 181 6824001
Fax: 181 6824012
Anna Khan

Founded: 1970. **Members:** 5,000. **Languages:** English. **Description:** Works toward creating the conditions whereby individuals with Down's Syndrome can receive necessary medical, educational, social, and financial support to develop to their full potential. Organizes self-help groups in England, Northern Ireland, and Wales. Provides immediate assistance to new parents of children with Down's Syndrome through a 24-hour help line. Raises funds for research. **Publications:** Newsletter, quarterly. Contains information contributed by members and research updates.

★4290★ Hong Kong Association for the Mentally Handicapped (HKAMH)
Pinehill Village
Nam Hang, Tai Po
New Territories, Hong Kong
Phone: 6645107
Fax: 6614620
Nora Wong, Gen. Sec.

Founded: 1968. **Members:** 268. **Languages:** Cantonese, English. **Description:** Promotes improved quality of life for people with mental disabilities. Helps mentally disabled people become independent and productive members of the community through education and training programs. **Publications:** *Annual Report*, annual. **Formerly:** (1980) The Hong Kong Association for Mentally Handicapped Children and Young Persons, Ltd..

★4291★ International Association for the Scientific Study of Intellectual Disability (IASSID)
Association de Villepinte
27, rue Mauberge
F-75009 Paris, France
Phone: 1 48781431
Fax: 1 48741515
Dr. N. Ross, Pres.

Founded: 1964. **Languages:** English, French, Spanish. **Description:** National associations representing 15,000 scientists and clinicians in 40 countries working in the field of mental retardation. Encourages research in the field of mental retardation, including its causes, prevention, diagnosis, evaluation, therapy, and rehabilitation, management, education, and social habilitation. **Publications:** *JIDR - Journal of Intellectual Disability Research.* Journal. • Proceedings, quadrennial. **Formerly:** (1995) International Association for the Scientific Study of Mental Deficiency.

★4292★ JARC
28366 Franklin Rd.
Southfield, MI 48034
Phone: (810)352-5272
Fax: (810)352-5279
Joyce Keller, Exec.Dir.

Founded: 1969. **Description:** Jewish association providing residential care and support services to developmentally disabled adults. Operates 16 group homes that provide access to Jewish services, maintain kosher kitchens, and observe Jewish holidays. Although group primarily serves individuals in the Detroit, MI area, JARC has members nationwide. **Publications:** Brochure. • Newsletter, bimonthly. **Formerly:** (1975) Parents Association for Jewish Residential Care; (1980) Association for Jewish Retarded; (1989) Jewish Association for Retarded Citizens.

★4293★ Learning Disabilities Special Interest Group (LDSIG)
University of New Mexico
CAPS - Zimmerman Library
Albuquerque, NM 87131
Phone: (505)277-8291
Fax: (505)277-6019
Lorraine C. Peniston, Exec. Officer

Members: 75. **Description:** A Special interest group of the College Reading and Learning Association . Is concerned with the educational needs of college-level students with learning disabilities. Provides information to professionals and coordinates presentations on working with students having LD. **Publications:** *CRLA Learning Disabilities Special Interest Group: Newsletter*, quarterly. Newsletter. *Price:* Free. • *Learning Disability Newsbriefs*, quarterly. **Formerly:** (1991) Learning Disabled Student Sig.

★4294★ **Little City Foundation (LCF)**
1760 W. Algonquin Rd.
Palatine, IL 60067
Phone: (708)358-5510
Fax: (312)282-0423
Alan J. Dachman, Exec.Dir.

Founded: 1959. **Members:** 3,000. **Local Groups:** 19. **Description:** Residential community for up to 293 mentally retarded and emotionally disturbed children from six years of age and older. Engages in training, treatment, research, and rehabilitation. Curriculum includes: special education and training; an on-cottage training program working in the areas of self-help, self-care, and independent functioning; use of therapy, art therapy, recreational therapy, psychotherapy; prevocational and vocational training. Offers Project VITAL (Video Induced Training and Learning), which works to train the developmentally disabled as television technicians and television producers through the use of cable television facilities. Operates the Center for Research and Innovation in Mental Retardation, which provides research grants to academic behavioral scientists involved in improving care and training of developmentally disabled persons, a social rehabilitation program providing outpatient care for retarded in the Chicago, IL area, and on-campus facilities for 148 resident adults. Maintains job placement service. **Publications:** *Little City Network*, quarterly.

★4295★ **Mental Retardation Association of America (MRAA)**
211 East 300 South, Ste. 212
Salt Lake City, UT 84111
Phone: (801)328-1575
Dr. Ernest H. Dean, Pres.

Founded: 1974. **Description:** Purposes include: working for the improvement of the quality of life for the mentally retarded; promoting research aimed at preventing mental retardation in future generations; working for adequate national appropriations, supportive legislation, and implementation of statutes and regulations to benefit the mentally retarded; assisting federal government agencies serving the retarded to assure quality programming and new services; informing the public through educational programs as to the scope of the problem of mental retardation; providing referral services. Advocates alternative quality programs through support of both community-based and institutional services. Informs parents or legal guardians of the retarded of the right to a choice of quality services. Encourages the development of small family-like homes, constructed and furnished according to accepted community standards, on the campuses of our state institutions as well as in communities throughout the nation. Supports mentally retarded persons in their legal,

moral, and human rights of full citizenship as guaranteed by the Constitution of the U.S. Seeks recognition of the rights and responsibilities of parents and legal guardians.

National Association for Down Syndrome (NADS)
See: Entry 5287

★4296★ **National Association for Persons with Mental Handicap of Germany (Bundesvereinigung Lebenshilfe fur Geistig Behinderte)**
Raiffeisenstrasse 18
Postfach 70 11 63
35043 Marburg, Germany
Phone: 6421 4910
Fax: 6421 491167
Dr. Bernhard Conrads, Exec.Dir.

Founded: 1958. **Members:** 120,000. **State Groups:** 16. **Local Groups:** 540. **Languages:** English, French, German. **Description:** Mentally handicapped individuals and their families; doctors; psychologists; social workers. Seeks to: promote the rights of mentally handicapped persons; bring together families for mutual support; increase public awareness. Provides daycare facilities, sheltered workshops, hostels, and group homes. Offers educational and training courses, workshops, and seminars for parents and staff. Organizes leisure-time activities, parents counseling, children's services, and fundraising activities. Sponsors conferences and symposia on topics such as family affairs, educational problems, religion, and personnel training. **Publications:** *Geistige Behinderung*, quarterly. Journal. • *Grundsatzprogramm*, periodic. Book. • *Lebenshilfe Zeitung*, bimonthly. Newspaper. • *Pressedienst*, periodic. • *Verbandsdienste*, periodic. Newsletter. • *Workshop Handbook*. Manual. **Also Known As:** Lebenshilfe.

National Association of State Mental Retardation Program Directors
See: Entry 5591

★4297★ **National Council on Intellectual Disability (NCID)**
GPO Box 647
Canberra, ACT 2601, Australia
Phone: 6 2476022
Fax: 6 2470729
Margaret Verick, Exec. Officer

Founded: 1953. **Members:** 400. **Languages:** English. **Description:** Organizations in Australia representing 25,000 individuals involved in the study of or the provision of services to individuals with intellectual disabilities. Works to: ensure that the best services are provided to the intellectually disabled and their families; eliminate discrimination against and establish equality for the developmentally disabled. Acts as a liaison between member organizations and government authorities; lobbies public officials. Seeks the establishment of free public education in adapted environments when necessary, the provision of free health care, the establishment of freedom in the choice of an occupation, the granting of voting rights, and the equal participation by intellectually disabled in poli cy development and management of related service orga-

nizations. Monitors and proposes modifications to relevant legislation. Works for the establishment of regional authorities on intellectual disability which will monitor research on intellectual disability and services for the intellectually disabled. Sponsors training programs and seminars; offers courses. Maintains the Australian Institute on Intellectual Disability. **Publications:** *Interaction*, 5/year. Journal. • *Library Catalogue*, periodic. • Monographs, periodic. **Formerly:** (1957) Australian Council of Organizations for Subnormal Children; (1971) Australian Council for the Mentally Retarded; (1984) Australian Association for the Mentally Retarded; (1988) AAMR - National Association on Intellectual Disability.

National Down Syndrome Congress (NDSC)
See: Entry 5288

National Down Syndrome Society (NDSS)
See: Entry 5289

National Down's Syndrome Association (NDSA)
See: Entry 5290

National Fragile X Foundation (NFXF)
See: Entry 5293

★4298★ **National Society for Persons with Developmental Handicap (Landsforeningen Evnesvages Vel — LEV)**
Spaniensgade 15, 2
DK-2300 Copenhagen S, Denmark
Phone: 32840888
Fax: 32840077

Founded: 1952. **Members:** 10,000. **Local Groups:** 16. **Languages:** Danish, English, French, German. **Description:** Persons with developmental handicaps and their parents; professional staff. Seeks to establish equal rights and respect for people with developmental handicaps; encourages their integration into society. Represents individuals in negotiations with social, health, educational, and research institutions. Coordinates research and development programs. Provides instruction. **Publications:** *LEV*, monthly. Journal.

★4299★ **New Zealand Association for the Scientific Study of Mental Deficiency (NZASSMD)**
PO Box 8338
Havelock North
Hawke's Bay, New Zealand
Phone: 6 8774296
Fax: 6 8774296
Michael Ahrens, V.Pres.

Founded: 1980. **Languages:** English. **Description:** Promotes research on intellectual disability. Unites professionals working in the field and facilitates data exchange; disseminates information. Establishes standards for practice and ethics. Monitors relevant legislation. **Publications:** *Australia and New Zealand Journal of Developmental Disability*, periodic. • Magazine, periodic.

★4300★ **Norwegian Association for Children and Adults with Minimal Brain Dysfunction (MBD-foreningen)**
Alexandragarden
Arnstein Arnebergsv 30
N-1324 Lysaker, Norway
Phone: 67 583757
Fax: 67 583747
Brita Drabitzius, Sec.

Founded: 1979. **Members:** 2,000. **Local Groups:** 16. **Languages:** English, Norwegian. **Description:** Parents of children with Minimal Brain Dysfunction; health personnel. Acts as support group. **Publications:** *Artikkelsamling om MBD*. Book. • *Ett Oyeblikk.*

★4301★ **Organization for Swedish Speaking Mentally Retarded Persons in Finland (OSSMRPF) (Forbundet de Utvecklingsstordas Val — FDUV)**
Tologatan 27 A 15
SF-00260 Helsinki, Finland
Phone: 0 407070
Fax: 0 407748
Mikael Lindholm, Sec.Gen.

Founded: 1972. **Members:** 2,000. **Local Groups:** 11. **Languages:** Swedish. **Description:** Individuals working on behalf of Swedish-speaking mentally retarded people in Finland. Arranges holiday activities, training programs, and courses for mentally retarded individuals, parents, staff, and others. Develops experimental activities to improve quality of daily life. **Publications:** *Laka och Lara*, quarterly. Journal.

Parents of Children with Down Syndrome (PODS)
See: Entry 5300

★4302★ **People First International (PFI)**
PO Box 12642
Salem, OR 97309
Phone: (503)362-0336
Dennis Heath, Contact

Founded: 1974. **Description:** Seeks to provide mentally retarded and developmentally disabled persons with training in leadership skills and advocacy. Offers consultation. Helps new groups get started. **Publications:** Audiotapes. • *People First*. Film. • Videos. • *We Are People First*. Book.

★4303★ **Pilot Parents (PP)**
3610 Dodge St., Ste. 101
Omaha, NE 68131
Phone: (402)346-5220
Fax: (402)346-5253
Anne Adamson, Coord.

Founded: 1971. **Members:** 340. **Description:** Parents, professionals, and others concerned with providing emotional and peer support to new parents of children with special needs. Sponsors a parent-matching program which allows parents who have had sufficient experience and training in the care of their own children to share their knowledge and expertise with parents of children recently diagnosed as disabled. Provides information concerning developmental disabilities, medical services, and

supportive agencies within communities. Maintains speakers' bureau. Conducts educational programs. Although activities are conducted on a local level, program serves as a model for similar groups that are being organized throughout the U.S. **Publications:** *The Gazette*, 6/year. Newsletter.

★4304★ **Special Olympics International (SOI)**
1325 G St., NW, Ste. 500
Washington, DC 20005
Phone: (202)628-3630
Sargent Shriver, Bd.Chm.

Founded: 1968. **Members:** 1,200,000. **Regional Groups:** 8. **Description:** Created by the Joseph P. Kennedy, Jr. Foundation to promote physical fitness, sports training, and athletic competition for children and adults with mental retardation. Seeks to contribute to the physical, social, and psychological development of persons with mental retardation. Local, area, and chapter games are conducted in 140 countries. Participants range in age from 8 years to adult and compete in track and field, swimming, gymnastics, bowling, ice skating, basketball, and other sports. Disseminates information on organization of programs and participation of athletes. Maintains speakers' bureau; compiles statistics; sponsors research programs. **Publications:** *List of Chapter and National Directors*, annual. • *Program Memorandum*, monthly. Also publishes informational brochures, guides, instructional manual, and list of state programs. **Formerly:** (1987) Special Olympics.

Support Group for Monosomy 9P (9P)
See: Entry 5301

★4305★ **Voice of the Retarded (VOR)**
5005 Newport Dr., Ste. 108
Rolling Meadows, IL 60008
Phone: (708)253-6020
Fax: (708)253-6054
Polly Spare, Pres.

Founded: 1983. **Members:** 3,000. **State Groups:** 48. **Description:** Families and friends of mentally retarded individuals; mental health care professionals and providers. Advocates for the general welfare of mentally retarded individuals by: working to improve mental retardation care and services; monitoring related legislation; increasing public awareness of mental retardation issues; providing resources to individuals, guardians, and families. Promotes freedom of choice and residential alternatives for mentally retarded persons. Conducts research into cause, prevention, and treatment of mental retardation. **Publications:** *Office Bulletin*, biweekly. *Price:* Free, for members only. • *Voice of the Retarded*, quarterly. Newsletter.

★4306★ **Young Adult Institute and Workshop (YAI)**
460 W. 34th St.
New York, NY 10001
Phone: (212)563-7474
Fax: (212)268-1083
Joel M. Levy, Exec.Dir.

Founded: 1957. **Description:** A pioneer agency established to provide comprehensive programs that enable people with developmental

disabilities, mental retardation, learning disabilities, emotional disturbance, or brain damage to progress from a state of isolation and dependency to a more productive, self-sufficient, and integrated role in society. The institute is supported by tuition fees, government agencies, foundations, and private donations. Provides respite services to parents of mentally retarded and developmentally disabled people; conducts research; testifies at governmental hearings, appears on television and radio, sponsors professional conferences, and publishes material regarding the rights and needs of people with disabilities; produces and hosts weekly YAI Children with Special Needs and On Our Own television programs which provide counseling, training, referral, and other family support services; maintains speakers' bureau. Offers an alternative to institutionalization and focuses on the development of a series of supportive services to maintain individuals within the community; seeks to prevent institutionalization by providing services in local communities. Offers the opportunity for persons currently in institutions to move out into the community. Certain programs serve the multiply handicapped, including those who are deaf, blind, or have other physical disabilities. Provides early intervention, residential, employment, socialization, recreational, parent training, and clinical programs for people with various levels of retardation as well as a variety of family support services. Maintains day treatment programs in Manhattan, Brooklyn, and Nassau and West chester counties; ev ening adjustment centers in Manhattan and the Bronx; and community residential facilities throughout Brooklyn, the Bronx, Queens, Manhattan, Long Island, and Westchester County. Other programs include adjustment counseling, recreational activities, children's services, employment training and placement, remedial reading, money handling, budgeting, and sex education. **Publications:** *Model Programs and New Technologies for People With Disabilities.* **Formerly:** (1964) Young Adult Adjustment Center.

Zimbabwe Down Syndrome Association (ZDSA)
See: Entry 5307

Research Centers

★4307★ **American Association on Mental Retardation**
1719 Kalorama Rd. NW
Washington, DC 20009
Phone: (202)387-1968
Fax: (202)387-2193
M. Doreen Croser, Exec.Dir.

Research Activities and Fields: Mental retardation, including studies on programmatic aspects of service to persons with mental retardation in residential facilities and community-based settings. Prevention, behavioral, family support, employment, education and health are other areas of research and programmatic concern. **Publications:** *Adaptive Behavior Scales*; *American Journal on Mental Retardation* (bimonthly); *Mental Retardation* (bimonthly); *News & Notes* (bimonthly); Monographs.

★4308★ Baylor College of Medicine Mental Retardation Research Center
1 Baylor Plaza - 610E
Houston, TX 77030
Phone: (713)798-6523
Fax: (713)798-5073
Huda Y. Zoghbi, M.D., Dir.

Research Activities and Fields: Supports interdisciplinary research in mental retardation and its prevention. Topics include: Rett syndrome, epilepsy, Angelman and Prader-Willi syndrome, gene therapy, human X chromosome, cytomegalovirus infection, group b streptococci, hyperemia hemorrhage in newborns, chondrodysplasia punctata, and spinocerebral ataxia.

★4309★ Case Western Reserve University Mental Development Center
11130 Bellflower Rd.
Cleveland, OH 44106
Phone: (216)368-3540
Fax: (216)368-4891
Phillis J. Dukes, Ph.D., Dir.

Research Activities and Fields: Mental retardation and learning, including studies on cognitive development, parent-child interaction, parental attitudes toward mental retardation, early identification of mental retardation, dual diagnosis, development of teaching and in-service materials, and early assessment and diagnosis for "at risk" children of substance abusing parents. **Publications:** Technical Papers; Annual Reports.

Center on Children and the Law
See: Entry 7197

★4310★ Eunice Kennedy Shriver Center for Mental Retardation, Inc.
200 Trapelo Rd.
Waltham, MA 02254
Phone: (617)642-0001
Fax: (617)894-9968
Dr. Philip Reilly, Dir.

Research Activities and Fields: Interdisciplinary studies in mental retardation conducted through five research departments: Biomedical Sciences Department; Behavioral Sciences Department; Medical Genetics Department; Social Sciences, Ethics, and Law Department; and Developmental Neurobiology Department. **Publications:** Newsletter (quarterly).

★4311★ Harry A. Waisman Center
Univ. of Wisconsin—Madison
1500 Highland Ave.
Madison, WI 53705
Phone: (608)263-5940
Fax: (608)263-0529
Dr. Terrence R. Dolan, Dir.

Research Activities and Fields: Individuals with developmental disabilities, including noncompromised infants, children, and adults, as well as nonhuman subjects. Studies focus on genetics, molecular biology, neurochemistry, sensory and perceptual processes, neurophysiology, communication processes, development intervention processes, and biological, behavioral, and social processes across the lifespan. Divided into the following units: Molecular and Genetic Sciences Unit, Sensory and Motor Processes Unit, Communication Processes Unit, Social and Affective Processes Unit, Clinical Services Unit, and Applied Research and Technology Unit. **Publications:** *Waisman Center Interactions* (annually).

★4312★ Human Services Research Institute
2336 Massachusetts Ave.
Cambridge, MA 02140
Phone: (617)876-0426
Fax: (617)492-7401
Valerie J. Bradley, Pres.

Research Activities and Fields: Mental retardation, chronic mental illness, and developmental disabilities. Helps elected officials and public administrators manage and improve programs for mentally ill, mentally retarded, and handicapped persons. Participates in the formulation of federal program legislation, regulations, and guidelines, and in the development of state and local area mental health and mental retardation program plans. Conducts large- and small-scale evaluations at the federal, state, and local program levels. Conducts studies of the magnitude of mentally and physically disabled populations and subpopulations in order to assess their service needs. Studies the efficiency and cost/benefits of alternate services and providers. **E-mail Address:** hsri@hsri.org.

★4313★ Institute for Community Inclusion
Children's Hospital
300 Longwood Ave.
Boston, MA 02115
Phone: (617)735-6506
Fax: (617)735-7940
William E. Kiernan, Ph.D., Dir.

Research Activities and Fields: Etiology of mental retardation, the impact of AIDS among school age and adult populations, the history of inborn errors of metabolism, the development of employment opportunities for people with disabilities using natural supports, the development of supports for infants at risk, development of a managed care design for children with complex medical needs served in community settings, and clinical investigation of issues of autism and related behavior in community settings. **Publications:** *Institute Briefs.* **E-mail Address:** kiernanw@a1.tch.harvard.edu. **Formerly:** Institute is a consolidation of the Development Evaluation Center, the Training and Research Institute for People with Disabilities, and the Rehabilitation Research and Training Center for Promoting Employment.

Judge David L. Bazelon Center for Mental Health Law
See: Entry 7207

★4314★ Louisiana State University Human Development Center
School of Allied Health Professions
1100 Florida Ave., Bldg. 138
New Orleans, LA 70119-2799
Phone: (504)942-8200
Fax: (504)942-8305
Robert E. Crow, Ph.D., Dir.

Research Activities and Fields: Developmental disabilities, including educational technology, curriculum research, and integrated basic and applied behavioral interventions. Operates as a University Affiliated Program for interdisciplinary training, research, and dissemination.

★4315★ Mental Retardation Research and Human Development Center
300 Longwood Ave.
Boston, MA 02115
Phone: (617)735-7046
Joseph Volpe, M.D., Program Dir.

Research Activities and Fields: Causes of mental retardation, including multidisciplinary studies in genetics, neuroscience, behavioral science, and clinical application of results of such studies. **E-mail Address:** volpe__j@a1.tch.harvard.edu. **Formerly:** Child Development Research and Evaluation Center.

★4316★ Northwestern Woodhaven Center Evaluation and Research Group
2900 Southampton Rd.
Philadelphia, PA 19154
Phone: (215)671-5001
Fax: (215)671-7522
Dr. Michael Barton, Asst.V.Pres.

Research Activities and Fields: Treatment effectiveness, program evaluation, clinical treatment research (medications and behavior modification), and policy research in mental retardation at Woodhaven Center, a University-operated residential program for mentally retarded persons. **Publications:** Evaluation and Research Technical Report Series. **Formerly:** Woodhaven Center, Evaluation and Research Group.

★4317★ Ohio State University Nisonger Center for Mental Retardation and Developmental Disabilities
1581 Dodd Dr.
Columbus, OH 43210-1296
Phone: (614)292-8365
Fax: (614)292-3727
Steven Reiss, Ph.D., Dir.

Research Activities and Fields: Broad areas of study include developmental disabilities, psychometric assessment, rehabilitation engineering, psychopathology, psychopharmacology, adults and aging, and family studies. Special attention given to applied research related to mental retardation and development and implementation of training programs to prepare professional personnel to work with the developmentally disabled. Provides early childhood classes for developmentally disabled preschoolers and offers information services to clients, students, staff, and faculty. **Publications:** Newsletter (disseminated quarterly throughout Ohio). **Formerly:** Outgrowth of Mental Retardation Training Program, a joint project of Colleges of Social Work, Social and Behavioral Sciences, Education, and Medicine.

★4318★ Parsons Research Center
PO Box 738
Parsons, KS 67357
Phone: (316)421-6550

Research Activities and Fields: Experimental analysis of cognitive functions, including discrimination, classification, and representation skills among retarded persons; language and communication behavior, including sensory-motor, social, and symbolic behaviors of severely retarded persons; cognitive, social, and language skills among handicapped preschool children and infants; and analysis and treatment of self-injurious children and youth. **Publications:** *Parsons Research Center Reports*.

★4319★ **Temple University**
Institute on Disabilities
430 Ritter Hall Annex
Philadelphia, PA 19122
Phone: (215)204-1356
Dr. Diane Nelson Bryen, Dir.

Research Activities and Fields: Conducts research on those factors that contribute to the well-being and development of people with disabilities. Monitors the development and welfare of people in community residential, vocational, and other supportive programs. **Publications:** *Technical Reports*, newsletter (quarterly). **E-mail Address:** v211@vm.temple.edu.

★4320★ **U.S. Department of Health and**
Human Services
National Institute of Child Health and
Human Development
Center for Research for Mothers and
Children
Mental Retardation and Developmental
Disabilities Branch
Executive Plaza North
6130 Executive Blvd.
Bethesda, MD 20892
Phone: (301)496-1383
Fax: (301)402-2085
Felix dela Cruz, Chief

Research Activities and Fields: Branch supports research and research training concerned with prevention and/or amelioration of mental retardation and related developmental disabilities. Its activities involve the full range of research concerned with the etiology, pathophysiology, diagnosis, epidemiology, prevention, and amelioration of mental retardation, including biomedical research in mental retardation and behavioral and social science research in mental retardation. The Branch is also administratively responsible for Mental Retardation Research Centers (MRRCs) constructed for the purpose of research on mental retardation and related aspects of human development.

★4321★ **University Affiliated Cincinnati**
Center for Developmental Disorders
Pavilion Bldg.
3333 Burnet Ave.
Cincinnati, OH 45229-3039
Phone: (513)559-4626
Fax: (513)559-7361
Dr. Jack H. Rubinstein, Dir.

Research Activities and Fields: Prevention, early detection, and improved methods of therapy and management of developmental disabilities. Also studies genetics, learning disabilities, and birth defects.

★4322★ **University of Alberta**
Developmental Disabilities Centre
6-123 D Education North
Edmonton, AB, Canada T6G 2G5
Phone: (403)492-4505
Fax: (403)492-1318
Dr. R. Sobsey, Dir.

Research Activities and Fields: Psychological, social, educational, and biomedical studies on people with developmentally disabilities, including basic learning processes and behavior maladjustments, and violence against people with disabilities. Conducts demonstration programs and clinical research in education. **Publications:** *Developmental Disabilities Bulletin*. **E-mail Address:** henny__degroot@psych.educ.ualberta.ca. **Formerly:** Centre for the Study of Mental Retardation.

★4323★ **University of California, Los**
Angeles
Mental Retardation Research Center
760 Westwood Plaza
Los Angeles, CA 90024-1759
Phone: (310)825-5542
Fax: (310)206-5060
Dr. Nathaniel A. Buchwald, V.Ch.

Research Activities and Fields: Mental retardation and related aspects of human development, including interdisciplinary basic and clinical studies on problems in developmental biology, human genetics, neurobiochemistry, neurophysiology, and sociobehavioral categories. Collaborates with other institutes, schools, and departments at the University. **Publications:** Annual Report.

★4324★ **University of Chicago**
Joseph P. Kennedy, Jr. Mental Retardation
Research Center
Wyler Children's Hospital
5841 S. Maryland Ave.
MC 5058
Chicago, IL 60637
Phone: (312)702-6428
Fax: (312)702-9234
Dr. Nancy B. Schwartz, Dir.

Research Activities and Fields: Mental retardation, emphasizing membrane glycococonjugate structure and synthesis, lysosomes (inborn errors of metabolism), regulation of enzymatic action, protein chemistry, chemistry and metabolism of sphingolipids and other lipids and lipoprotein complexes, carbohydrate chemistry, biology of biochemistry of the extracellular matrix (normal development and inborn errors), collagen gene structure and expression, DNA sequence studies, DNA methylation and chromatin structure, recombinant DNA technology, cell-free translation and transcription in differentiating eukaryotic cells, regulation of gene expression and mRNA regulation during embryonic development, regulation of catecholamine neurotransmitter biosynthesis and secretion, signal transduction pathways in neuronal systems, opioid actions during embryogenesis and opioid signal transduction, muscarinic receptor signal transduction pathways in differentiating neurons, proteoglycan participation in CNS histomorphogenesis, glia phenotypes and the role of protein kinases, electron microscope visual-

ization of specific gene products in differentiating nervous system and cartilage (use of monoclonal antibodies), neurotransmitter receptor structure and function, mechanisms of synapse formation, neurobiology and neuropathology of dopaminergic pathways, regulation of myelination (oligodendrocyte neurobiology), isolation and tissue culture of specialized cells (oligodendrocytes, neurononal aggregates, neuroblastoma x neuron hybrids, chromaffin cells, and chondrocytes), neuroanatomical mapping, mitochondrial function and dysfunction, and neurological, genetic, biological, biochemical, and embryological studies. **E-mail Address:** nbs0@midway.uchicago.edu.

★4325★ **University of Colorado**
B.F. Stolinsky Research Laboratories
4200 E. 9th Ave., Box C233
Denver, CO 80262
Phone: (303)270-7301
Stephen I. Goodman, M.D., Dir.

Research Activities and Fields: Biochemical genetics and nutrition. The Laboratories are federally designated as a center for research in mental retardation or related aspects of human development.

★4326★ **University of Colorado**
John F. Kennedy Center for Developmental
Disabilities
4200 E. 9th Ave.
CB C234
Denver, CO 80262-0234
Phone: (303)270-8826
Fax: (303)270-6844
Cordelia Robinson, Ph.D., Dir.

Research Activities and Fields: Normal and a typical child growth and development, with emphasis on applied and clinical interdisciplinary studies on evaluation of care of infants, children, and adults with mental retardation or other developmental disabilities. Provides training of professionals and paraprofessionals from numerous disciplines in dealing with problems of the child and the family. Also offers development of community systems and supports systems to foster inclusion. **Publications:** Monographs. **E-mail Address:** cohrsm@essex.hsc.colorado.edu. **Formerly:** Rocky Mountain Child Development Center (1985); John F. Kennedy Child Development Center.

★4327★ **University of Georgia**
Georgia University Affiliated Program
Dawson Hall
Athens, GA 30602
Phone: (706)542-4827
Fax: (706)542-4815
Dr. Zolinda Stoneman, Dir.

Research Activities and Fields: Research, teaching, training, and public service in the field of developmentally disabled persons, especially pertaining to family relations and community services.

★4328★ University of Illinois at Chicago
Institute on Disability and Human
Development
1640 W. Roosevelt Rd.
Chicago, IL 60608
Phone: (312)413-1647
Fax: (312)413-1326
David Braddock, Ph.D., Dir.

Research Activities and Fields: Trends in the financing of developmental disabilities services, including state spending for mental retardation and developmental disabilities, and compensation, turnover, and personal administration in public and private residential programs for individuals with developmental disabilities. Also studies state agency and private provider initiatives in developing community services; factors affecting caregiving and placement decisions by minority families and families with aging caregivers; the changing demographics and emerging role of families; families' costs of caring for a disabled relative; and health promotion and disease prevention in adults with mental retardation.

★4329★ University of Kansas
Bureau of Child Research
1052 Dole Human Development Center
Lawrence, KS 66045
Phone: (913)864-4295
Fax: (913)864-5323
Stephen R. Schroeder, Dir.

Research Activities and Fields: Handicapped children in laboratory and community settings, international program of cooperation with member nations of the Organization of the American States, and national and international distribution of videotape and print media products. Emphasizes the development of methods and materials for the care and treatment of retarded children, handicapped children, and older persons with disabilities. **Publications:** *Research Register.* **E-mail Address:** bob@dole.lsi.ukans.edu.

★4330★ University of Kansas
Kansas Center for Research in Mental
Retardation
1052 Dole Human Development Center
Lawrence, KS 66045
Phone: (913)864-4295
Fax: (913)864-5323
Dr. Stephen R. Schroeder, Dir.

Research Activities and Fields: Prevention of developmental disabilities and rehabilitation of the developmentally disabled, including clinical studies with retarded children and children with other developmental disabilities, biomedical and psychobiological examination of physiology, and chemistry of retardation. Develops improved educational and training programs and studies fundamental aspects of speech and language development to aid children with severe articulation disorders. **E-mail Address:** schrfoede@kuhub.cc.ukans.edu. **Formerly:** Kansas Center for Mental Retardation and Human Development.

★4331★ University of Kansas
R.L. Smith Mental Retardation and Human
Development Research Center
Medical Center
39th & Rainbow Blvd.
Kansas City, KS 66103
Phone: (913)588-5970
Fax: (913)588-5677
Dr. Paul D. Cheney, Dir.

Research Activities and Fields: Fundamental problems of mental retardation and developmental disabilties, including molecular biology and physiology of pregnancy, neuroendocrinology, fetal development, impaired fetal and infant development, infant language, cognitive development, prenatal and postnatal risk factors, developmental neurobiology and neuroplasticity. Conducts animal models studies concerning pregnancy, early developmental processes, and neurobiological mechanisms involved in motor and sensory functions of the brain and neuropathology of AIDS.

★4332★ University of Kansas
Schiefelbusch Institute for Life Span
Studies
1052 Robert Dole Human Development Center
Lawrence, KS 66045
Phone: (913)864-4295
Fax: (913)864-5323
Stephen R. Schroeder, Dir.

Research Activities and Fields: Human growth and development throughout the lifespan, with emphasis on developmental disabilities and language development. Operates a three-setting center for research in mental retardation and related aspects of human development. **Publications:** *Research Register.* **E-mail Address:** schroede@kuhub.cc.ukans.edu.

★4333★ University of Maine
Center for Community Inclusion
5717 Corbett Hall
Orono, ME 04469-5703
Phone: (207)581-1084
Fax: (207)581-1231
Lucille Zeph, Contact

Research Activities and Fields: Developmental disabilities, focusing on improving the quality of life for persons with developmental disabilities and their families and policy development and analyses in Maine.

★4334★ University of Minnesota
Institute on Community Integration
102 Pattee Hall
150 Pillsbury Dr.
Minneapolis, MN 55455
Phone: (612)624-6300
Fax: (612)624-9344
Scott McConnell, Ph.D., Dir.

Research Activities and Fields: Developmental disabilities, focusing on intervention and systems training, policy issues, trends, and obstacles affecting persons with developmental disabilities. **Publications:** *Impact* (quarterly newsletter); *What's Working* (newsletter); Resource Guides. **E-mail Address:** smconnell@vx.cis.umn.edu.

★4335★ University of Missouri—Kansas
City
University Affiliated Program for
Developmental Disabilities
Institute for Human Development
2220 Holmes
Kansas City, MO 64108
Phone: (816)235-1755
Fax: (816)235-1762
Dr. Carl Calkins, Dir.

Research Activities and Fields: Effective methods for teaching children with both physical and developmental disabilities, impact of providing respite care on families' stress and well-being, enhancing person-environment fit with mentally retarded persons and their residential and program settings, and enhancing the quality of life and level of independence of elderly developmentally disabled persons. Research focuses on how to enhance the functioning of developmentally disabled persons with their families, and the service system that serves them. **E-mail Address:** cfcalkins@vax1.umkc.edu.

★4336★ University of North Carolina at
Chapel Hill
Brain and Development Research Center
CB 7250
Chapel Hill, NC 27599-7250
Phone: (919)966-2405
Fax: (919)966-1322
Kunihiko Suzuki, M.D., Dir.

Research Activities and Fields: Conducts basic and clinical research concerned with the prevention, diagnosis, and treatment of mental retardation and related aspects of human development utilizing a single disciplinary or interdisciplinary approach. Basic research is targeted at obtaining new knowledge of structure and function of the developing nervous system to be applied to other neurological and psychiatric illness. Studies include childhood autism, childhood hyperactivity with learning disabilities, genetic disorders associated with mental retardation, children whose nervous systems have been damaged by metallic environmental pollutants, and mentally retarded children whose aggressive stereotypic and self-injurious behavior requires that they be institutionalized. **Formerly:** Biological Sciences Research Center.

University of North Carolina at Charlotte
Social Science Working Group
See: Entry 7680

★4337★ University of Oregon
Center on Human Development
901 E. 18th Ave.
Eugene, OR 97403
Phone: (503)346-3591
Dr. Hill M. Walker, Dir.

Research Activities and Fields: Child development, training programs for severely retarded adults, and vocational potential of the mentally retarded. Operates a comprehensive program of research, training, and service through its related units: Western Regional Resource Center, Early Intervention Program, Parent and Child Education Programs, and the Specialized Training Program.

★4338★ **University of Washington**
Child Development and Mental Retardation
  Center
WJ-10
Seattle, WA 98195
Phone: (206)543-2832
Fax: (206)543-3417
Michael J. Guralnick, Ph.D., Dir.

Research Activities and Fields: Biomedical and behavioral research of human development, including studies in developmental biology, perinatal biology, neurological sciences, psychology, psychiatry, speech and hearing sciences, social work, nursing, and special education. **E-mail Address:** ceh@u.washington.edu.

★4339★ **Vanderbilt University**
John F. Kennedy Center for Research on
  Human Development
Peabody College, Box 40
Nashville, TN 37203
Phone: (615)322-8240
Fax: (615)322-8236
Travis Thompson, Ph.D., Dir.

Research Activities and Fields: Behavioral, biomedical, and educational aspects of mental retardation and other disabilities and child development, including cognitive strategies, social and communicative processes, neural development, neural plasticity, and behavioral pediatrics. Investigates cognitive modifiability, computer applications to facilitate thinking and learning, normal and abnormal nervous system maturation, perceptual and locomotor behavior, stereotyped and self-injurious behavior, language and social development, development of aggressive behavior, early education of mentally retarded and economically disadvantaged children, and child abuse, neglect, and nonorganic failure to thrive. **Formerly:** John F. Kennedy Center for Research on Education and Human Development.

★4340★ **Vocational and Rehabilitation**
  Research Institute
3304 33rd St. NW
Calgary, AB, Canada T2L 2A6
Phone: (403)284-1121
Fax: (403)289-6427
Gerrit Groeneweg, Ph.D., Exec.Dir.

Research Activities and Fields: Vocational, social, educational, home living, and leisure time training and rehabilitation of the developmentally handicapped, including demonstration and applied research projects in behavioral sciences, social work, education, and allied areas. Utilizes computer-assisted instruction and develops assessment scales and programming innovations for the developmentally handicapped. **Publications:** *Bridges News* magazine; *Journal of Practical Approaches to Developmental Handicap*; *Research Highlights*; *Research Reviews*; *Current Awareness Bulletin*; Annual General Report.

★4341★ **West Virginia University**
University Affiliated Center for
  Developmental Disabilities
Research Office Park
955 Hartman Run Rd.
Morgantown, WV 26505
Phone: (304)293-4692
Fax: (304)293-7294
Ashok Dey, Dir.

Research Activities and Fields: Developmental disabilities, mental retardation (all ages), nutrition, under nutrition, brain development, speech and language development, medical aspects of developmental disabilities, high-risk families, and program evaluation. Graduate research assistants come from various University disciplines to participate in applied research activities. **Publications:** Quarterly Report.

★4342★ **Yeshiva University**
Rose F. Kennedy Center for Research in
  Mental Retardation and Human
  Development
Albert Einstein College of Medicine
1410 Pelham Pkwy. S.
Bronx, NY 10461
Phone: (718)430-4228
Fax: (718)824-3058
Dr. John A. Kessler, Dir.

Research Activities and Fields: Mental retardation and other forms of aberrant human development, including biomedical, behavioral, educational, and social studies.

State Government Agencies

Developmental Disabilities

★4343★ **Alabama Department of Mental**
  Health and Mental Retardation
PO Box 3710
Montgomery, AL 36109-0710
Phone: (334)271-9208
Fax: (334)240-3195

★4344★ **Alaska Department of Health and**
  Social Services
Mental Health and Developmental
  Disabilities Division
PO Box 110620
Juneau, AK 99811-0620
Phone: (907)465-3370
Fax: (907)465-2668

★4345★ **Arizona Department of Economic**
  Security
Developmental Disabilities Division
PO Box 6123
Phoenix, AZ 85005
Phone: (602)542-6853
Fax: (602)542-5339

★4346★ **Arkansas Department of Human**
  Services
Developmental Disabilities Services
  Division
PO Box 1437
Little Rock, AR 72203
Phone: (501)682-8665
Fax: (501)686-6836

★4347★ **California Health and Welfare**
  Agency
Developmental Services Department
1600 9th St., 2nd Fl.
Sacramento, CA 95814
Phone: (916)654-1897
Fax: (916)654-2167

★4348★ **Colorado Department of Human**
  Services
Developmental Disabilities Division
3824 W. Princeton Cir.
Denver, CO 80236
Phone: (303)762-4560
Fax: (303)762-4300

★4349★ **Connecticut Department of**
  Mental Retardation
90 Pitkin St.
East Hartford, CT 06108
Phone: (203)528-7141
Fax: (203)566-3680

★4350★ **Delaware Department of Health**
  and Social Services
Mental Retardation Division
Jesse Cooper Bldg.
PO Box 637
Dover, DE 19903
Phone: (302)739-4452
Fax: (302)739-3839

★4351★ **District of Columbia Department**
  of Human Services
Social Services Commission
Mental Retardation and Developmental
  Disabilities Administration
609 H St. NE
Washington, DC 20002
Phone: (202)673-7657
Fax: (202)727-1687

★4352★ **Florida Department of Health and**
  Rehabilitative Services
Developmental Services Office
1317 Winewood Blvd.
Tallahassee, FL 32399-0700
Phone: (904)488-4257
Fax: (904)922-2993

★4353★ **Georgia Department of Human**
  Resources
Mental Health, Mental Retardation and
  Substance Abuse Division
2 Peachtree St. NW
Atlanta, GA 30303
Phone: (404)657-2252
Fax: (404)657-2256

★4354★ **Hawaii Department of Health**
Developmental Disabilities Council
919 Ala Moana Blvd, Rm. 113
Honolulu, HI 96813
Phone: (808)586-8100
Fax: (808)586-8129

★4355★ **Idaho Department of Health and**
  Welfare
Family and Community Services Division
Development Disabilities Bureau
PO Box 83720
Boise, ID 83720-0036
Phone: (208)334-5700
Fax: (208)334-6558

★ 4356 ★ Illinois Department of Mental Health and Developmental Disabilities
401 William G. Stratton Bldg.
Springfield, IL 62765
Phone: (217)782-2243
Fax: (217)524-0835

★ 4357 ★ Indiana Family and Social Services Administration
Disability, Aging and Rehabilitative Services Division
Developmental Disability Services Bureau
402 W. Washington, Rm. W341
Indianapolis, IN 46204
Phone: (317)232-7933
Fax: (317)233-4693

★ 4358 ★ Iowa Department of Human Services
Mental Health, Mental Retardation and Developmental Disabilities Division
Hoover State Office Bldg.
Des Moines, IA 50319
Phone: (515)281-5126
Fax: (515)281-4597

★ 4359 ★ Kansas Department of Social and Rehabilitation Services
Mental Health and Retardation Services Division
Docking State Office Bldg.
Topeka, KS 66612
Phone: (913)296-3773
Fax: (913)296-1158

★ 4360 ★ Kentucky Human Resources Cabinet
Mental Health and Mental Retardation Department
Mental Retardation Division
275 E. Main St.
Frankfort, KY 40621
Phone: (502)564-4527
Fax: (502)564-3844

★ 4361 ★ Louisiana Department of Health and Hospitals
Citizens with Developmental Disabilities Office
PO Box 2790
Baton Rouge, LA 70821
Phone: (504)342-0095
Fax: (504)342-3931

★ 4362 ★ Maine Department of Mental Health and Mental Retardation
Mental Retardation Division
State House Sta. 40
Augusta, ME 04333
Phone: (207)287-4242
Fax: (207)287-4268

★ 4363 ★ Maryland Department of Health and Mental Hygiene
Developmental Disabilities Administration
201 W. Preston St., 5th Fl.
Baltimore, MD 21201
Phone: (410)225-5600
Fax: (410)225-6489

★ 4364 ★ Massachusetts Executive Office of Health and Human Services
Mental Retardation Services Department
160 N. Washington St.
Boston, MA 02114
Phone: (617)727-5608
Fax: (617)727-9868

★ 4365 ★ Michigan Department of Mental Health
Developmental Disabilities Council
Lewis Cass Bldg., 6th Fl.
320 S. Walnut
Lansing, MI 48913
Phone: (517)334-6123
Fax: (517)335-3090

★ 4366 ★ Minnesota Department of Human Services
Social Services Administration
Developmental Disabilities Division
444 Lafayette Rd.
St. Paul, MN 55155
Phone: (612)296-9139
Fax: (612)297-1949

★ 4367 ★ Mississippi Department of Mental Health
Mental Retardation Bureau
1101 Robert E. Lee Bldg.
Jackson, MS 39201
Phone: (601)359-1288
Fax: (601)359-6295

★ 4368 ★ Missouri Department of Mental Health
Mental Retardation and Developmental Disability Division
1706 E. Elm St.
PO Box 687
Jefferson City, MO 65102
Phone: (314)751-4054
Fax: (314)751-8224

★ 4369 ★ Montana Department of Social and Rehabilitation Services
Developmental Disabilities Division
PO Box 4210
Helena, MT 59604-4210
Phone: (406)444-2995

★ 4370 ★ Nebraska Department of Public Institutions
Developmental Disabilities Division
PO Box 94728
Lincoln, NE 68509-4728
Phone: (402)471-2851
Fax: (402)479-5145

★ 4371 ★ Nevada Department of Human Resources
Mental Hygiene and Mental Retardation Division
505 E. King St., Rm. 603
Carson City, NV 89710
Phone: (702)687-5943
Fax: (702)687-4773

★ 4372 ★ New Hampshire Department of Health and Human Services
Mental Health Division
Community Developmental Services Bureau
105 Pleasant St.
Concord, NH 03301
Phone: (603)271-5013
Fax: (603)271-5058

★ 4373 ★ New Jersey Department of Human Services
Developmental Disabilities Division
Capitol Center, CN 726
Trenton, NJ 08625-0726
Phone: (609)292-7260
Fax: (609)292-3824

★ 4374 ★ New Mexico Department of Health
Developmental Disabilities Division
1190 St. Francis Dr.
PO Box 26110
Santa Fe, NM 87502-6110
Phone: (505)827-2589
Fax: (505)827-2595

★ 4375 ★ New York State Agency of Mental Retardation and Developmental Disabilities
44 Holland Ave.
Albany, NY 12229
Phone: (518)473-1997
Fax: (518)473-1271

★ 4376 ★ North Carolina Department of Human Resources
Mental Health, Developmental Disabilities and Substance Abuse Services Division
PO Box 29526
Raleigh, NC 27626-0526
Phone: (919)733-7011
Fax: (919)715-4645

★ 4377 ★ North Dakota Department of Human Services
Developmental Disabilities Division
600 E. Boulevard
State Capitol
Bismarck, ND 58505
Phone: (701)328-2768
Fax: (701)328-2359

★ 4378 ★ Ohio Department of Mental Retardation and Developmental Disabilities
30 E. Broad St., Rm. 1280
Columbus, OH 43266-0415
Phone: (614)466-5214
Fax: (614)644-5013

★ 4379 ★ Oklahoma Department of Human Services
Developmental Disability Services Division
PO Box 25352
Oklahoma City, OK 73125
Phone: (405)521-6267
Fax: (405)521-6458

★4380★ **Oregon Department of Human Resources**
Mental Health and Developmental Disabilities Services Division
Developmental Disabilities Services Office
2575 Bittern St. NE
Salem, OR 97310
Phone: (503)378-2429
Fax: (503)378-3796

★4381★ **Pennsylvania Department of Public Welfare**
Mental Retardation Office
Box 2675
Harrisburg, PA 17105
Phone: (717)787-3700
Fax: (717)772-2062

★4382★ **Rhode Island Department of Mental Health, Retardation and Hospitals**
Developmental Disabilities Division
600 New London Ave.
Cranston, RI 02920
Phone: (401)464-3234
Fax: (401)464-3204

★4383★ **South Carolina Department of Disabilities and Special Needs**
PO Box 4706
Columbia, SC 29240
Phone: (803)737-6444
Fax: (803)737-6323

★4384★ **South Dakota Department of Human Services**
Developmental Disabilities Division
E. Hwy. 344
Pierre, SD 57501
Phone: (605)773-4322
Fax: (605)773-5483

★4385★ **Tennessee Department of Mental Health and Mental Retardation**
Mental Retardation Services Division
706 Church St.
Nashville, TN 37243-0675
Phone: (615)532-6530
Fax: (615)532-6964

★4386★ **Texas Department of Mental Health and Mental Retardation**
Mental Retardation Division
PO Box 12668
Austin, TX 78711-2668
Phone: (512)206-4520
Fax: (512)206-4560

★4387★ **Utah Department of Human Services**
Services for People with Disabilities Division
PO Box 45500
Salt Lake City, UT 84145-0500
Phone: (801)538-3998
Fax: (801)538-4016

★4388★ **Vermont Agency of Human Services**
Mental Health Department
Mental Retardation Programs Division
103 S. Main St.
Waterbury, VT 05671-1601
Phone: (802)241-2636
Fax: (802)241-3052

★4389★ **Virginia Office of Health and Human Resources**
Mental Health, Retardation and Substance Abuse Services Department
Mental Retardation Division
PO Box 1797
Richmond, VA 23214
Phone: (804)786-1746
Fax: (804)371-6638

★4390★ **Washington Department of Social and Health Services**
Health and Rehabilitative Services Office
Developmental Disabilities Division
PO Box 45060
Olympia, WA 98504-5060
Phone: (360)753-3903
Fax: (360)586-5874

★4391★ **West Virginia Department of Health and Human Resources**
Human Resources Bureau
Developmental Disabilities Division
State Capitol Complex, Bldg. 6, Rm. 617
Charleston, WV 25305
Phone: (304)558-0627
Fax: (304)558-1008

★4392★ **Wisconsin Department of Health and Social Services**
Community Services Division
Developmental Disabilities Bureau
PO Box 7850
Madison, WI 53707-7850
Phone: (608)266-9329
Fax: (608)266-2579

★4393★ **Wyoming Department of Health**
Developmental Disabilities Division
117 Hathaway Bldg.
Cheyenne, WY 82002-0710
Phone: (307)777-7821
Fax: (307)777-7439

State & Regional Organizations

Mental Retardation

Listed below are state offices of The Arc (500 E. Border St., Ste. 300, Arlington, TX 76010, 817-261-6003), a national organization on mental retardation.

Alabama

★4394★ **Arc of Alabama**
444 S. Decatur
Montgomery, AL 36104
Phone: (205)262-7688

Alaska

★4395★ **Arc of Alaska**
2211-A Arca Dr.
Anchorage, AK 99508
Phone: (907)277-6677

Arizona

★4396★ **Arc of Arizona**
5610 S. Central
Phoenix, AZ 85040
Phone: (602)243-1787

Arkansas

★4397★ **Arc of Arkansas**
2000 Main St.
Little Rock, AR 72206-1597
Phone: (501)375-7770

California

★4398★ **Arc of California**
120 I St., 2nd Fl.
Sacramento, CA 95814
Phone: (916)552-6619

Colorado

★4399★ **ACL in Colorado**
4155 E. Jewell Ave., Ste. 916
Denver, CO 80222
Phone: (303)756-7234

Connecticut

★4400★ **Arc of Connecticut**
1030 New Britain Ave., Ste. 102B
West Hartford, CT 06110
Phone: (203)953-8335

Delaware

★4401★ **Arc of Delaware**
Tower Office Park
240 N. James St., Ste. B2
Wilmington, DE 19804
Phone: (302)966-9400

District of Columbia

★4402★ **District of Columbia Arc**
900 Varnum St. NE
Washington, DC 20017
Phone: (202)636-2950

Florida

★4403★ **Arc of Florida**
411 E. College Ave.
Tallahassee, FL 32301
Phone: (904)921-0460

Georgia

★4404★ **Arc of Georgia**
2860 E. Point St., No. 200
East Point, GA 30344
Phone: (404)761-3150

Hawaii

★ 4405 ★ Arc of Hawaii
3989 Diamond Head Rd.
Honolulu, HI 96816
Phone: (808)737-7995

Illinois

★ 4406 ★ Arc of Illinois
915 W. 175th St.
Homewood, IL 60430
Phone: (708)206-1930

Indiana

★ 4407 ★ Arc of Indiana
22 E. Washington, Ste. 210
Indianapolis, IN 46204
Phone: (317)632-4387

Iowa

★ 4408 ★ Arc of Iowa
715 E. Locust
Des Moines, IA 50309
Phone: (515)283-2358

Kansas

★ 4409 ★ Arc of Kansas
3601 SW 29th, Ste. 237
Topeka, KS 66614
Phone: (913)271-8783

Kentucky

★ 4410 ★ Arc of Kentucky
833 E. Main St.
Frankfort, KY 40601
Phone: (502)875-5225

Louisiana

★ 4411 ★ Arc of Louisiana
6554 Florida Blvd.
Baton Rouge, LA 70806
Phone: (504)927-0764

Maryland

★ 4412 ★ Arc of Maryland
6810 Deerpath Rd., Ste. 310
Baltimore, MD 21227
Phone: (410)379-0400

Massachusetts

★ 4413 ★ Arc of Massachusetts
217 South St.
Waltham, MA 02154
Phone: (617)891-6270

Michigan

★ 4414 ★ Arc of Michigan
333 S. Washington Sq., Ste. 200
Lansing, MI 48933
Phone: (517)487-5426

Minnesota

★ 4415 ★ Arc of Minnesota
3225 Lyndale Ave. S.
Minneapolis, MN 55408
Phone: (612)827-5641

Mississippi

★ 4416 ★ Arc of Mississippi
3111 N. State St.
Jackson, MS 39216
Phone: (601)362-4830

Montana

★ 4417 ★ Arc of Montana
400 Echo Rd.
Big Fork, MT 59911
Phone: (406)755-6588

Nebraska

★ 4418 ★ Arc of Nebraska
521 S. 14th, Ste. 211
Lincoln, NE 68508
Phone: (402)475-4407

New Hampshire

★ 4419 ★ Arc of New Hampshire
10 Ferry St.
Concord, NH 03301
Phone: (603)228-9092

New Jersey

★ 4420 ★ Arc of New Jersey
985 Livingston Ave.
North Brunswick, NJ 08902
Phone: (201)246-2525

New Mexico

★ 4421 ★ Arc of New Mexico
3500-G Comanche NE
Albuquerque, NM 87107
Phone: (505)883-4630

New York

★ 4422 ★ NYSARC
393 Delaware Ave.
Delmar, NY 12054
Phone: (518)439-8311

North Carolina

★ 4423 ★ Arc of North Carolina
16 Rowan St.
PO Box 20545
Raleigh, NC 27619
Phone: (919)782-4632

North Dakota

★ 4424 ★ Arc of North Dakota
418 E. Rosser Ave., Ste. 110
PO Box 2776
Bismarck, ND 58502-2776
Phone: (701)223-5349

Ohio

★ 4425 ★ Arc of Ohio
1335 Dublin Rd., Ste. 205C
Columbus, OH 43215
Phone: (614)487-4720

Oregon

★ 4426 ★ Arc of Oregon
1745 State St.
Salem, OR 97301
Phone: (503)581-2726

Pennsylvania

★ 4427 ★ Arc 0f Pennsylvania
Bldg. 2, Ste. 221
2001 N. Front St.
Harrisburg, PA 17102
Phone: (717)234-2621

Rhode Island

★ 4428 ★ Rhode Island Arc
99 Bald Hill Rd.
Cranston, RI 02920
Phone: (401)463-9191

South Carolina

★ 4429 ★ Arc of South Carolina
PO Box 61062
Columbia, SC 29260-1062
Phone: (803)894-5591

South Dakota

★ 4430 ★ Arc of South Dakota
PO Box 220
Pierre, SD 57501
Phone: (605)224-8211

Tennessee

★ 4431 ★ Arc of Tennessee
1805 Hayes St., Ste. 100
Nashville, TN 37203
Phone: (615)327-0294

Texas

★4432★ Arc of Texas
PO Box 5368
Austin, TX 78763
Phone: (512)454-6694

Utah

★4433★ Arc of Utah
455 East 400 South, Ste. 300
Salt Lake City, UT 84111
Phone: (801)364-5060

Virginia

★4434★ Arc of Virginia
6 N. 6th St.
Richmond, VA 23219
Phone: (804)649-8481

Washington

★4435★ Arc of Washington State
1703 E. State St.
Olympia, WA 98506
Phone: (206)357-5596

Wisconsin

★4436★ Arc of Wisconsin
121 S. Hancock
Madison, WI 53703
Phone: (608)251-9272

Wyoming

★4437★ Arc of Wyoming
PO Box 2161
Casper, WY 82602
Phone: (307)237-9110

Chapter 21
Disabilities

Federal Government Agencies

★4438★ Architectural and Transportation Barriers Compliance Board
1331 F St. NW, Ste. 1000
Washington, DC 20004-1111
Phone: (202)272-5434

Description: The Board was established to investigate and examine alternative approaches to the architectural, transportation, and attitudinal barriers confronting disabled persons; determine what measures are being taken by federal, state, and local governments and by other public and private agencies to elininate those barriers; and promote the use of the International Accessibility Symbol in all public facilities that meet the standards prescribed by the Administrator of the General Services Administration Board.

★4439★ National Council on Disability
1331 F St. NW
Washington, DC 20004-1107
Phone: (202)272-2004

Description: The Council reviews all laws, programs, and policies of the federal government that affect individuals with disabilities. The Council then makes recommendations to the President, Congress, and federal agencies on these issues. In addition, the Council is studying the availability of health insurance coverage for persons with disabilities and sponsors conferences for families caring for the disabled.

★4440★ President's Committee on Employment of People With Disabilities
1331 F St. NW
Washington, DC 20004-1107
Phone: (202)376-6200
Fax: (202)376-6219

Description: Seeks to identify and eliminate barriers standing in the way of full social and vocational opportunities for physically handicapped, mentally retarded, and mentally restored persons; promotes employment opportunities for the physically and mentally handicapped.

★4441★ U.S. Department of Education
Office of Special Education and
Rehabilitative Services
330 C St. SW
Washington, DC 20202
Phone: (202)205-5465

Description: The Assistant Secretary for Special Education and Rehabilitative Services is responsible for: 1) special education programs and services expressly designed to meet the needs and develop the full potential of handicapped children; and 2) comprehensive rehabilitation service programs specifically designed to reduce human dependency, to increase self-reliance and to fully utilize the productive capabilities of all handicapped persons. Programs include support of training for teachers and other professional personnel; grants for research; financial aid to help States initiate, expand, and improve their resources; and media services and captioned films for the hearing impaired.

★4442★ U.S. Department of Health and Human Services
Administration for Children and Families (ACF)
Administration on Developmental Disabilities (ADD)
200 Independence Ave. SW
Washington, DC 20201
Phone: (202)690-6590

Description: The Administration on Developmental Disabilities (ADD) assists states in increasing the provision of quality services to persons with developmental disabilities through the development and implementation of a comprehensive state plan which makes optimal use of all existing resources for the provision of treatment, services and habilitation in least restrictive environments, and protection of the rights of individuals with developmental disabilities. ADD administers formula grants program to address these goals and oversees project grants which provide administrative and operations support to interdisciplinary training programs for specialized personnel, clinical services, and research program services for the developmentally disabled; and administers grants for projects aimed at removing physical, mental, social, and environmental barriers encountered by developmentally disabled persons.

★4443★ U.S. Department of Veterans Affairs
Veterans Benefits Administration
Vocational Rehabilitation Service
810 Vermont Ave. NW
Washington, DC 20420
Phone: (202)273-7419

Description: The Vocational Rehabilitation Service administers programs for vocational rehabilitation of disabled veterans, readjustment educational benefits for veterans of post-Korean conflict service, and education assistance for spouses, surviving spouses, and children of veterans who are permanently and totally disabled or die from disability incurred or aggravated in active service in the Armed Forces, or are prisoners of war, or are missing in action. Special restorative training is also available to eligible children.

U.S. Library of Congress
National Library Service for the Blind and Physically Handicapped
See: Entry 6909

★4444★ U.S. Senate
Committee on Labor and Human Resources
Subcommittee on Disability Policy
SH-422 Dirksen Senate Office Bldg.
Washington, DC 20510
Phone: (202)224-7139

Foundations & Other Funding Organizations

Private Foundations

★4445★ Ann Jackson Family Foundation
PO Box 5580
Santa Barbara, CA 93150
Phone: (805)969-2258
Palmer G. Jackson, Chief Financial Officer

Foundation Philosophy: The Ann Jackson Family Foundation gives to charities and services which "foster religious, charitable, educational, and scientific purposes and to organizations which promote the prevention of cruelty to children and animals." **Giving Priorities:** In fiscal 1993, the Ann Jackson Family Foundation gave approximately 64% of its grants to civic and public affairs, including the highest grant of $656,000 to the El Adobe Corporation. Social service organizations, which primarily focused on youth and people with disabilities, received 14%. The arts were awarded 10%; education, 7%; and religious concerns, 3%. The remaining funds supported health care and international affairs. **Typical Health-Related Recipients:** Health Organizations, Heart, Hospitals, Medical Research, Multiple Sclerosis, People with Disabilities, Substance Abuse. **Geographic Distribution:** Focus on Santa Barbara, CA, and surrounding areas.

★ 4446 ★ **Conn Memorial Foundation**
5401 W Kennedy Blvd., Ste. 530
Tampa, FL 33609
Phone: (813)282-4922
Fax: (813)282-8542
Rosalie Hennessey, O.S.M., Director of Services

Foundation Philosophy: The Foundation's primary interests are children, youth, and family programs; education, human service, and emergency/disaster relief; and program capital support and agency expansion. **Giving Priorities:** In fiscal 1994, the foundation reported that it gave approximately 63% of its contributions to social services. Education received 31% of support; the arts, 4%; and other interests, 2%. **Typical Health-Related Recipients:** People with Disabilities, Substance Abuse. **Geographic Distribution:** Primarily Hillsborough and Pinellas counties, Florida.

★ 4447 ★ **Hugh I. Shott, Jr. Foundation**
c/o First Century Bank, NA
500 Federal St.
Bluefield, WV 24701
Phone: (304)325-8181
Richard W. Wilkinson, President

Foundation Philosophy: The Hugh I. Shott, Jr. Foundation supports education and civic affairs. Educational funding supports college foundations and public school districts. Civic affairs interests include municipalities, community development, and business. **Giving Priorities:** In 1993, the foundation gave approximately 60% of funding to educational institutions. The Salvation Army received about 10% of total contributions. The arts and humanities received about 8% of funding; civic concerns received about 8%; the environment, 8%; and social services, 6%. **Typical Health-Related Recipients:** People with Disabilities. **Geographic Distribution:** Focus on Bluefield County, WV.

★ 4448 ★ **J. Bulow Campbell Foundation**
1530 Trust Company Tower
25 Park Pl., NE
Atlanta, GA 30303
Phone: (404)658-9066
John W. Stephenson, Executive Director

Foundation Philosophy: The J. Bulow Campbell Foundation prefers to give grants to nongovernmental organizations "having a program of acknowledged or potential excellence and giving evidence or promise of regional leader-

ship." In considering grants for Presbyterian causes, the foundation follows Mr. Campbell's example "by identifying grant opportunities that are consistent with the purposes of the Southern Presbyterian Church." In considering grants to educational institutions, emphasis is placed on privately supported institutions noted for academic excellence, with priority given to "projects designed to improve the quality of intellectual performance, and the level of spiritual life." **Giving Priorities:** In 1994, the foundation reported that it gave approximately 30% of its contributions to education. Social services received about 30%. The arts received 20%, and religion received about 15%. Health care received the remaining 5% of funds. **Typical Health-Related Recipients:** People with Disabilities. **Geographic Distribution:** Georgia, primarily Atlanta; also limited giving in Alabama, Florida, North Carolina, South Carolina, and Tennessee.

JM Foundation
See: Entry 316

★ 4449 ★ **John Merck Fund**
11 Beacon St., Ste. 1230
Boston, MA 02108
Phone: (617)723-2932
Fax: (617)523-6029
Ruth Hennig, Administrator

Foundation Philosophy: The fund makes grants in the fields of developmental disabilities, to medical teaching hospitals for research in connection with developmental disabilities in children; the environment, to encourage preservation of productive farmland in Vermont and to address global problems relating to climate change, tropical deforestation, and loss of biodiversity; population policy, to support policy planning and implementation by governments and health care organizations; and international human rights and disarmament. **Giving Priorities:** In 1993, the foundation reported that 26% of funding supported its Population Policy program. Environmental efforts received 25%. The foundation's International Human Rights program was given 16% of funding; the Disarmament program, 15%; and the Developmental Disabilites program, 12%. The remaining 6% of funding supported special projects. **Typical Health-Related Recipients:** Adolescent Health Issues, Children's Health/Hospitals, Family Planning, Medical Education, Medical Research, People with Disabilities, Prenatal Health Issues. **Geographic Distribution:** Broad geographic distribution with some interest in Vermont.

Mary Ranken Jordan and Ettie A. Jordan Charitable Foundation
See: Entry 383

Rockefeller Family Fund
See: Entry 10905

St. Giles Foundation
See: Entry 3142

Wayne and Gladys Valley Foundation
See: Entry 538

Corporate Foundations

Advanced Micro Devices Charitable Foundation
See: Entry 6389

Woodward Governor Co. Charitable Trust
See: Entry 6420

Other Funding Organizations

★ 4450 ★ **American Amputee Foundation**
PO Box 250218, Hillcrest Sta.
Little Rock, AR 72225
Phone: (501)666-2523
Fax: (501)666-8369

Description: Offers programs that provide financial assistance for the purchase of prosthetic equipment, wheelchairs, crutches, braces, and modifications to the home. Provides low-interest loans for rehabilitation services and sponsors programs which offer aid for the purchase of the first limb for a qualified amputee.

Foundation for Exceptional Children
See: Entry 3150

★ 4451 ★ **Foundation for Science and Disability**
236 Grand St.
Morgantown, WV 26505-7509
Phone: (304)293-5201
Fax: (304)293-6363
E.C. Keller, Jr., Pres.

Description: Maintains a Student Grant Program for physically disabled students majoring in an area of science, mathematics, medicine, or engineering at a college, university, graduate, or professional school.

★ 4452 ★ **National Easter Seal Society Research Program**
230 W. Monroe
Chicago, IL 60606
Phone: (312)726-6200
Fax: (312)726-1494

Description: Administers grants-in-aid for applied research investigations concerned with the management and treatment of physical and associated disabilities.

National & International Organizations

Academy of Dentistry for Persons with Disabilities
See: Entry 3843

★ 4453 ★ **Accreditation Council on Services for People with Disabilities**
8100 Professional Pl., Ste. 204
Landover, MD 20785-2225
Phone: (301)459-3191
Fax: (301)577-0703
James F. Gardner, Ph.D., CEO

Founded: 1969. **Members:** 9. **Description:** Devoted to improving the quality of services available to people with disabilities. Works to develop, review, and revise valid standards for services provided to people with disabilities and to encourage their use. Assists organizations with quality improvement efforts. Assesses agency compliance with standards on request; awards accreditation. Sponsored by American Association on Mental Retardation, American Occupational Therapy Association, American Psychological Association, The Arc, Association for Behavior Analysis, Autism Society of America, Epilepsy Foundation of America, National Association of Private Residential Resources, and United Cerebal Palsy Associations. **Publications:** *Accreditation Update on Quality*, quarterly. Newsletter. • *An Effective Habilitation Planning Process.* • *Enhancing the Rights of People with Developmental Disabilities.* • *List of Accredited Agencies*, annual. Directory. • *The Manager's Guide to Managing Change.* • *Outcome Based Performance Measures*, biennial. • *Positive Behavior Intervention.* • *Standards for Services for People with Developmental Disabilities.* • *Standards Interpretation Guidelines.* **Formerly:** (1976) Accreditation Council for Facilities for the Mentally Retarded; (1986) Accreditation Council for Services for Mentally Retarded and Other Developmentally Disabled Persons; (1991) Accreditation Council on Services for People with Developmental Disabilities.

★4454★ Achilles Track Club (ATC)
1 Times Sq., 10th Fl.
New York, NY 10036
Phone: (212)354-0300
Fax: (212)354-3978
R. Traum, Pres.

Founded: 1982. **Members:** 3,400. **Local Groups:** 40. **Description:** Disabled runners; volunteer coaches. (Membership, though drawn primarily from New York City, also includes international members who are coached by mail.) Purpose is to encourage people with all types of disabilities to participate in running, and to improve the self-image of the disabled and demonstrate that they are energetic and capable people. Encourages the disabled to be aerobically fit and to run in competitions beside the able-bodied. Stresses that no previous athletic experience is necessary, just a desire to improve fitness with regular training. Conducts childrens' programs. Maintains speakers' bureau. Group is named for the mythical Greek hero whose disability was a vulnerable heel on an otherwise invincible body.

★4455★ Adventures in Movement for the Handicapped (AIM)
945 Danbury Rd.
Dayton, OH 45420
Phone: (513)294-4611
Free: 800-332-8210
Fax: (513)294-3783
Dr. Jo A. Geiger, Exec.Dir.

Founded: 1958. **Members:** 25,000. **Description:** Businesses, organizations, teachers, and other individuals interested in helping people with visual handicaps, hearing impairments, emotional or learning disabilities, and orthopedic or coordination problems to achieve their full potential. Has developed the AIM Method of

Specialized Movement Education, which consists of a series of rhythmical exercises involving gross and fine motor movements designed to improve muscle control and thereby enhance coordination and self-image. Program can be adapted to any type of handicap and all age groups. Sponsors AIM Water Program and fundraisers; has initiated research program concerning working with the blind/deaf child. Maintains speakers' bureau and hall of fame. Compiles statistics. **Publications:** *Adventurer*, quarterly. Newsletter. Includes organization news and calendar of events. *Price:* Free. • *Adventures in Movement*, semiannual. Newsletter. *Price:* Free. • *Adventures in Movement for the Handicapped Newsletter*, annual. Newsletter. *Price:* Free. • Books. • Brochure. **Formerly:** (1969) DANCE, Inc..

★4456★ American Academy of Disability Evaluating Physicians (AADEP)
2045 S. Arlington Hts., Ste. 104
Arlington Heights, IL 60005
Phone: (708)228-6095
Free: 800-456-6095
Fax: (708)228-6412
Sandra L. Yost, Exec.Dir.

Founded: 1987. **Members:** 1,300. **Description:** Seeks to provide graduate and continuing medical education programs to qualify doctors of medicine and doctors of osteopathy to meet the needs of the public in the practice of the medical science of disability evaluation as well as disability consultation. Works to develop educational programs and training programs in disability evaluation and disability consultation for health care professionals. Fosters and develops the medical science of disability evaluation. Sponsors research programs. Establishes standardards for physicians in the practice of disability evaluation and disability consultation. **Publications:** *Journal of Disability*, periodic. Journal. • Newsletter, periodic.

★4457★ American Academy of Orthotists and Prosthetists (AAOP)
1650 King St., Ste. 500
Alexandria, VA 22314
Phone: (703)836-7118
Fax: (703)836-0838
Dr. Ian R. Horen, Exec.Dir.

Founded: 1970. **Members:** 1,600. **Regional Groups:** 17. **Description:** Certified professional practitioners in orthotics and prosthetics. Dedicated to the advancement of the profession and the improvement of patient care. Conducts scientific seminars designed to increase professional competence of the individual practitioner. **Publications:** Handbooks. • *Journal of Prosthetics and Orthotics*, quarterly. Journal. In conjunction with the AOPA. Scientific, research articles on latest products, fitting techniques and patient care regimens. • Manuals. • *O&P Almanac*, monthly. Magazine. Features articles on healthcare reform, patient management, business and professional issues, insurance, law, government relations, and reimbursement. *Price:* Free for members. • *O&P Now*, monthly. Newsletter. Also publishes audiovisual equipment.

★4458★ American Amputee Foundation (AAF)
Box 250218, Hillcrest Sta.
Little Rock, AR 72225
Phone: (501)666-2523
Fax: (501)666-8369
Jack M. East, Exec.Dir.

Founded: 1975. **Members:** 2,000. **State Groups:** 13. **Local Groups:** 2. **Description:** Provides free peer counseling to new amputees and their families to aid them in their adjustment to the amputation of limbs. Also provides services on a limited basis to the spinal cord injured when no other agency is available. Other services include legal assistance, information and referral, rehabilitation, and technical and scientific information concerning prosthetics. Also offers programs that provide financial assistance for the purchase of prosthetic equipment, wheelchairs, crutches, braces, and modifications to the home; grants low-interest loans for rehabilitation services and sponsors give-a-limb programs offering, on a very limited basis, aid in buying the first limb for amputees who qualify. Sponsors programs on state-of-the-art prosthetics, coalition building, and selfhelp. **Publications:** *AAF Newsletter*, semiannual. Newsletter. *Price:* Included in membership dues. • Books. Provides information on self-help methods. • *National Resource Directory*, biennial. Directory.

★4459★ American Association of University Affiliated Programs for Persons With Developmental Disabilities (AAUAP)
c/o Encyclopedia of Associations
Gale Research Inc.
835 Penobscot Bldg.
Detroit, MI 48226-4094

Founded: 1968. **Members:** 52. **Description:** University-based or affiliated clinical service and interdisciplinary training centers for graduate students and others interested in the field of mental retardation and other developmental disabilities. Provides: coordination of federal funding for programs; technical assistance to Congress; information exchange among members; educational activities about programs. Compiles statistics. Computerized Services: Database of information from a member university affiliated programs; mailing list. **Publications:** *AAUAP Network News*, quarterly. Newsletter; includes training, research, and legislative updates, association news, calendar of events, and information on employment opportunities. *Price:* Included in membership dues. • *Resource Directory*, annual. • Also publishes *Developmental Handicaps: Prevention and Treatment* and *Prevention Update*. **Formerly:** (1975) Association of University Affiliated Facilities; (1983) American Association of University Affiliated Programs for the Developmentally Disabled.

★4460★ American Board for Certification in Orthotics and Prosthetics (ABC)
1650 King St., Ste. 500
Alexandria, VA 22314
Phone: (703)836-7114
Fax: (703)836-0838
Charles K. Unger, CAE, Assist.Exec.Dir.

Founded: 1948. **Members:** 3,600. **Description:** Certification board to establish qualifications, conduct examinations, and certify individuals (3000) and facilities (700) whom the board finds qualified to practice orthotics and prosthetics (the science of making and fitting artificial limbs and braces). **Publications:** *Registry of Board-Credentialed Orthotic and Prosthetic Professionals and Facilities*, annual. • *Role Delineation Report*. Report.

★4461★ **American Disability Association**
2121 8th Ave. N, Ste. 1623
Birmingham, AL 35203
Phone: (205)323-3030
Fax: (205)251-7417
William J. Freeman, Pres.

Founded: 1991. **Members:** 60,000. **Regional Groups:** 20. **State Groups:** 40. **Description:** Serves as a support group for individuals with disabilities. Provides exchange of information on disability issues. Makes available children's services, educational and research programs, and charitable services. **Publications:** *Journal of the American Disability Association*, monthly. Journal. *Price:* Free.

American Disabled for Attendant Program Today (ADAPT)
See: Entry 1883

American Orthotic and Prosthetic Association (AOPA)
See: Entry 5822

★4462★ **American Society of Handicapped Physicians (ASHP)**
105 Morris Dr.
Bastrop, LA 71220
Phone: (318)281-4436
Will Lambert, Dir.

Founded: 1981. **Members:** 1200. **Description:** Handicapped physicians and others concerned with the problems faced by handicapped physicians. Acts as a forum to address the needs of physically disabled physicians. Works against discrimination of the handicapped and serves as a support group and legal and career counselor. Disseminates information about resources for handicapped physicians. Plans to offer rehabilitation services. Bestows awards; maintains speakers' bureau and placement service; compiles statistics; offers specialized education. **Publications:** *American Society of Handicapped Physicians--SYNAPSE*, quarterly. Newsletter. Includes book reviews and research updates. *Price:* Free. • *Directory*, annual.

★4463★ **American Wheelchair Bowling Association (AWBA)**
3620 Tamarack Dr.
Redding, CA 96003
Phone: (916)243-2695
Fax: (916)244-6651
Walt Roy, Exec.Sec.-Treas.

Founded: 1962. **Members:** 600. **Regional Groups:** 12. **Description:** Male and female athletes with permanent disabilities who are confined to wheelchairs. To organize and promote wheelchair bowling and regulate rules. Provides information about wheelchair bowling. Conducts state and national wheelchair bowling tournaments. Maintains hall of fame and museum; compiles statistics. **Publications:** *The 11th Frame*, bimonthly. • *Wheelchair Bowling*. Book.

★4464★ **Amputee Shoe and Glove Exchange (ASGE)**
PO Box 27067
Houston, TX 77227
Dr. Richard E. Wainerdi, Dir.

Founded: 1959. **Members:** 175. **Description:** Free information exchange to facilitate swaps of unneeded shoes and gloves by amputees. Attempts to match amputees who need the opposite shoe or glove, who are about the same age, and who have reasonably similar tastes. All mailings of shoes or gloves are between the amputees matched. The exchange serves men, women, and children.

★4465★ **Amputees in Motion (AIM)**
PO Box 2703
Escondido, CA 92033
Phone: (619)454-9300

Founded: 1973. **Members:** 80. **Description:** Amputees and their families. Helps amputees of any age reestablish an active and satisfying life through visitation program and civic, social, and recreational participation. Attempts to prove that losing a limb doesn't mean losing the ability to participate in physical activities. Works with physicians, physical therapists, prosthetists, and others as part of the amputee rehabilitation team. Makes available sporting and social activities. **Publications:** *Amputees in Motion Newsletter*, 3/year. Newsletter. Includes membership meeting information. *Price:* Free.

★4466★ **Assistance Dogs of America (ADAI)**
8806 State Rte. 64
Swanton, OH 43558
Phone: (419)825-3622
Dino Brownson, Pres.

Founded: 1984. **Members:** 3,045. **Description:** Individuals, corporations, civic and fraternal organizations, and dog and kennel clubs. Provides specially trained dogs to persons with mobility impairments, multiple physical disabilities, or terminal illness for the purpose of increased independence. Maintains speakers' bureau. **Formerly:** (1989) Guide Dogs for the Handicapped, Inc..

Association of Children's Prosthetic-Orthotic Clinics (ACPOC)
See: Entry 3183

★4467★ **Association of Driver Educators for the Disabled (ADED)**
c/o Ricardo G. Cerna
PO Box 285
Edgerton, WI 53534
Phone: (608)884-8833
Fax: (608)884-4851
Ricardo G. Cerna, Contact

Founded: 1976. **Members:** 520. **Regional Groups:** 5. **Description:** Drivers' training instructors; suppliers of equipment used by handicapped drivers. Serves as a forum for exchange of ideas and information among members; gathers and disseminates information on drivers' education for the disabled. Promotes uniformity in the training and evaluation of disabled drivers. Conducts educational programs. **Publications:** *ADED Newsletter*, quarterly. Newsletter. • Bibliography. • *Membership Roster*.

★4468★ **Association on Higher Education and Disability (AHEAD)**
PO Box 21192
Columbus, OH 43221-0192
Phone: (614)488-4972
Fax: (614)488-1174
Jane E. Jarrow, Exec.Dir.

Founded: 1977. **Members:** 1,800. **Description:** Individuals interested in promoting the equal rights and opportunities of disabled postsecondary students, staff, faculty, and graduates. Provides an exchange of communication for those professionally involved with disabled students; collects, evaluates, and disseminates information; encourages and supports legislation for the benefit of disabled students. Conducts surveys on issues pertinent to college students with disabilities; offers resource referral system and employment exchange for positions in disability student services. Conducts research programs; compiles statistics. **Publications:** *ALERT*, bimonthly. Newsletter. • *Journal of Postsecondary Education & Disability*. Journal. • *Membership Directory*, annual. • *Proceedings of Abstracts of Annual Conferences on Disabled Students in Postsecondary Education*. Proceedings. **Also Known As:** AHEAD.

★4469★ **Association for Hispanic Handicapped of New Jersey (AHH)**
10 Jackson St.
Paterson, NJ 07501
Phone: (201)279-0212
Ligia Freine, Dir.

Founded: 1979. **Members:** 135. **Description:** Handicapped Hispanic children and their parents. Serves as advocate for the Hispanic handicapped. Aims to: develop a social network of Hispanic families for the exchange of information on services for the handicapped; increase parents' awareness of their rights and those of their children by overcoming language barriers. Promotes bilingual special education for the Hispanic handicapped; strives for optimum independence of handicapped Hispanic children. Conducts weekly Parent Teaching Parent Program that trains parents as advocates of their children in school and social settings. Offers placement services; compiles statistics; bestows awards. Operates primarily in New Jersey but accepts members from all states; encourages the formation of similar organizations. Offers vocational training.

Association of Maternal and Child Health Programs (AMCHP)
See: Entry 3184

Associazione la Nostra Famiglia (LNF)
See: Entry 12668

Canadian Rehabilitation Council for the Disabled (CRCD)
(Conseil Canadien pour la Readaptation des Handicapes — CCRH)
See: Entry 12671

★4470★ **Canine Companions for
Independence (CCI)**
PO Box 446
Santa Rosa, CA 95402
Phone: (707)528-0830
Free: 800-767-2275
Fax: (707)528-0146
Mr. Corey Hudson, Exec.Dir.

Founded: 1975. **National Groups:** 1. **Regional
Groups:** 5. **Description:** Provides to persons
with disibilities, specially-bred and trained dogs
enabling them to lead mor personally fulfilling
and socially productive lives. Believes that
human attendance care is drastically reduced
with the aid these dogs provide. Provides three
types of caines: Hearing Dogs trained to alert
the hearing-impaired to sounds such as the
doorbell, smoke alarm, or a baby's cry; Social
dogs used for children with disabilities, people
with developmental disabilities, or anywhere the
supervision of a third party is required; Service
Dogs trained to provide physical assistance,
such as retrieving dropped objects, operating el-
evator buttons and light switches, and pulling
wheelchairs. Works to expand services to aid
more persons with disabilities. Sponsors puppy
raising programs where puppies are placed and
raised in homes for 16 months; advanced training takes about 6-8 months to master over 50
required working commands. Conducts ongoing
research in canine breeding, training, and nutrition. Offers classes to train participants on how
to work with the dogs. Holds demonstrations.
Publications: Annual Report. • Brochures. •
Canine Companion Courier, quarterly. Newsletter. • Manuals.

★4471★ **Center on Human Policy (CHP)**
200 Huntington Hall, 2nd Fl.
Syracuse, NY 13244
Phone: (315)443-3851
Fax: (315)443-4338
Steven Taylor, Ph.D., Dir.

Founded: 1971. **Description:** Consumers and
students; parents of persons with disabilities;
human services administrators and staff members; professionals in psychology, special education, rehabilitation, sociology, law, social
work, and planning. Goal is to promote the integration of persons with severe disabilities into
the mainstream of society. Disseminates information to families, human services professionals, and others on laws, regulations, and programs affecting children and adults with disabilities, focusing on those with developmental disabilities. Provides speakers to professional
gatherings and parents' groups. Documents
outstanding community living and educational
programs and assists in creating exemplary services. Evaluates public policies to determine
their impact on people with disabilities. Participates in public forums, legislative hearings, national conventions, and other community events
involving issues relating to people with disabilities. Operates Research and Training Center on
Community Integration for people with developmental disabilities. Offers technical assistance,
consultation, and training on service system issues to local, regional, state, and national organizations and agencies. Conducts research related to community integration. Maintains the
Human Policy Press for the production of slide

presentations, posters, books, and other media.
Maintains the "Community Integration Reports"
series for dissemination of case reports, bibliographies, and pamphlets.

★4472★ **Cerebral Palsy International
Sports and Recreation Association (CP-
ISRA)**
Postbus 16
6666 Z.G.
NL-6813 GG Heteren, Netherlands
Phone: 8306 22593
Fax: 8306 22593
Elizabeth Dendy, Exec. Officer

Founded: 1978. **Members:** 60. **Languages:**
English. **Description:** Organizations in 60 countries interested in sports and recreation for the
cerebral palsied. Provides greater opportunities
for the cerebral palsied to participate in a wide
variety of sports and recreational activities. Assists members in developing sports and recreation programs through demonstrations,
courses, films, and seminars; provides means
for communication and dissemination of information among members. **Publications:** *Classification and Sport Rules Manual.* Manual. • *Classification Video.* Video. • *News,* semiannual.
Newsletter.

★4473★ **Cerebral Palsy Ireland (CPI)**
Sandymount Ave.
Dublin 4, Ireland
Phone: 1 2695355
Fax: 1 2694983
Dermot Ward, Chief Exec.

Founded: 1951. **Local Groups:** 20. **Languages:** English. **Description:** Works to provide therapy, training, and vocational education
programs for children and adults with cerebral
palsy.

★4474★ **Challenge International**
1204 Ina Ln.
Mc Lean, VA 22102
Phone: (703)821-3385
Fax: (703)790-1791
Mary Nemec Doremus, Pres. & Exec.Dir.

Founded: 1983. **Description:** A media awareness campaign designed to make disability a familiar and comfortable issue by closing the communication gap between the public and the disabled community. Purposes are to: serve the
disabled community by changing the way in
which Americans perceive disability and disabled individuals; promote positive images of
disabled persons in the media through newspaper articles, radio and television news reports,
television shows, motion pictures, and advertisements; educate the public about disability issues; serve as clearinghouse on the needs of
the disabled and the organizations that represent them; assist the media so that they report
realistically and positively on disability and disabled persons; encourage the acceptance of
people with disabilities, thus enabling them to
become more productive, contributing members
of society. Has established the National Media
Council on Disability. Other activities include:
providing internships for qualified disabled persons to pursue careers in media-related fields;
establishing a speakers' bureau; designing
school programs and educational materials. Is

forming a national network of education, information, and entertainment services for the disabled. Is planning to bestow awards for outstanding accomplishments by and for individuals with disabilities and produce a public service
announcement campaign on disability issues.
Formerly: (1985) National Challenge Committee of the Disabled; (1988) National Challenge
Committee on Disability.

★4475★ **Clearinghouse on Disability
Information (CDI)**
United States Department of Educ.
Office of Special Educ. and Rehabilitative
  Services
Switzer Bldg., Rm. 3132
Washington, DC 20202-2524
Phone: (202)205-8241
Fax: (202)205-9252

Founded: 1973. **Description:** Responds to inquiries on topics concerning federally-funded
programs serving disabled persons and federal
legislation affecting the disabled community.
Researches and documents information providers serving the handicapped. Makes resource
referrals. **Publications:** *A Summary of Existing
Legislation Affecting Persons with Disabilities.* •
OSERS, periodic. Magazine. Includes activities
and new developments in the information field.
• *Pocket Guide to Federal Help for Individuals
With Disabilities.* **Formerly:** (1989) Clearinghouse on the Handicapped.

Coalition on Sexuality and Disability (CSD)
See: Entry 11688

★4476★ **Commission on Mental and
Physical Disability Law (CMPDL)**
c/o American Bar Association
1800 M St. NW
Washington, DC 20036
Phone: (202)331-2240
Fax: (202)331-2220
John Parry, Dir.

Founded: 1976. **Description:** Gathers and disseminates information on court decisions, legislation, and administrative developments affecting people with mental and physical disabilities.
Topics covered include the ADA, court access,
civil commitment, institutional rights, rights in
the community, education of children with disabilities, discrimination against people with disabilities, and AIDS/HIV. Makes available legal
research tools including article reprints, and
conducts legal research in the field of disability
law. **Publications:** *The ADA and People with
Mental Illness.* • *ADA Manual.* Manual. • *AIDS/
HIV and Confidentiality.* • *AIDS/HIV and Confidentiality.* • Books. • *Court-Related Needs of
the Elderly and Persons With Disabilities.* •
Guardianship: An Agenda for Reform. • *Involuntary Civil Commitment: A Manual for Lawyers
and Judges.* Manual. • *Mental and Physical Disability Law Reporter,* bimonthly. • *Mental Disability Law Primer.* • Monograph. Provides information on AIDS. • *Right to Refuse Antipsychotic Medication.* • *Steps to Enhance Guardianship Monitoring.* • *Ten Year Index.* **Formerly:**
(1988) Mental Disability Legal Resource Center;
(1989) Mental and Physical Disability Legal Research Services and Databases; (1991) Commission on the Mentally Disabled.

★ 4477 ★ **Commonwealth Association for Mental Handicap and Developmental Disabilities (CAMHDD)**
36A Osberton Pl.
Sheffield, S. Yorkshire S11 8XL, England
Phone: 1114 2682695
Fax: 114 2678883
Dr. V.R. Pandurangi, Sec.Gen.

Founded: 1980. **Members:** 200. **National Groups:** 1. **Languages:** English. **Description:** Interested individuals and professionals in 30 countries employed in fields dealing with mental handicaps and developmental disability working to prevent mental retardation, especially in the developing countries. Promotes better health for the handicapped. Works to prevent mental handicaps through early detection of disabilities and to establish intervention programs in developing countries. Holds workshops and symposia; plans to organize a training course in developmental pediatrics. Sponsors children's services and charitable program; maintains speakers' bureau; compiles statistics. **Publications:** *CAMHDD Directory*, semiannual. Directory. • *Manual on Prevention of Handicap*. Book.

★ 4478 ★ **Congress of Organizations of the Physically Handicapped (COPH)**
16630 Beverly
Tinley Park, IL 60477-1904
Phone: (708)532-3566
Rose Wilson, Editor

Founded: 1958. **Description:** Organizations of physically handicapped persons. Assists member organizations with their programs and structure; serves as liaison to professional groups. Operates Technical Aid and Assistance to Disabled Centers. **Publications:** *COPH Bulletin*, quarterly. Bulletin. Tabloid. **Formerly:** (1980) National Congress of Organizations of the Physically Handicapped.

Council for Exceptional Children (CEC)
See: Entry 3215

Council for Exceptional Children (DEC) Division for Early Childhood
See: Entry 3217

★ 4479 ★ **Council for Exceptional Children (DPHD)**
Division for Physical and Health Disabilities
c/o Council for Exceptional Children
1920 Association Dr.
Reston, VA 22091-1589
Phone: (703)620-3660
Fax: (703)264-9494
Donna Kloppenburg, Pres.

Founded: 1960. **Members:** 2,200. **State Groups:** 7. **Description:** A division of the Council for Exceptional Children. Educators and others involved in supportive services to physically handicapped, multihandicapped, or health impaired children who are in classrooms, homebound, or hospitalized. Conducts educational programs. **Publications:** *DPHD Newsletter*, quarterly. Newsletter. Covers information regarding the education of individuals with physical disabilities and health impairments. *Price:* Included in membership dues. • *Physical Disabilities--Education and Related Services*, semiannual. Journal. Covers education and support

services for physically handicapped individuals; intended for teachers, administrators, and support personnel. *Price:* Included in membership dues. **Formerly:** (1968) Association of Educators for Homebound and Hospitalized Children; (1979) Division on Physically Handicapped, Homebound and Hospitalized; (1993) Division for Physically Handicapped.

★ 4480 ★ **Council for Learning Disabilities (CLD)**
PO Box 40303
Overland Park, KS 66204
Phone: (913)492-8755
Fax: (913)492-2546
Kirsten McBride, Exec.Sec.

Founded: 1967. **Members:** 4,500. **State Groups:** 18. **Description:** Professionals interested in the study of learning disabilities. Works to promote the education and general welfare of individuals having specific learning disabilities by: improving teacher preparation programs and local special education programs, and resolving important research issues. Sponsors educational sessions. **Publications:** *LD Forum*, quarterly. • *Learning Disability Quarterly*, quarterly. Journal. • Papers. • Video. **Formerly:** (1981) Division for Children with Learning Disabilities.

Council of State Administrators of Vocational Rehabilitation (CSAVR)
See: Entry 12675

★ 4481 ★ **Date-Able / HI**
35 Wisconsin Circle
Chevy Chase, MD 20815
Phone: (301)657-3283
Don E. Gibbons, Ph.D., Chmn.

Founded: 1982. **Members:** 1,500. **Description:** Purpose is to bring together persons with disabilities for love and friendship. Provides individual counseling and support network. **Publications:** *Hi Hopes*, semiannual. Newsletter. *Price:* Free. **Formerly:** (1994) Handicap Introductions.

Disability Insurance Training Council (DITC)
See: Entry 5726

★ 4482 ★ **Disability Rights Education and Defense Fund (DREDF)**
2212 6th St.
Berkeley, CA 94710
Phone: (510)644-2555
Fax: (510)841-8645
Linda Kilb, Mng.Dir.

Founded: 1979. **Description:** Dedicated to the principle that people with disabilities have the right to lead full and integrated lives, with the freedom of choice and dignity. Seeks to educate the public and policymakers in order to further the civil rights and liberties of the people with disabilities. Educational activities include: training state and local government officials, attorneys, and judges on disability rights compliance requirements such as the Americans with Disabilities Act; preparing materials pertaining to the right of children with disabilities to a free and appropriate public education. Houses the Disability Rights Clinical Legal Education Program

which educates law students about disability rights laws and represents people with disabilities who have experienced unlawful discrimination. Provides technical assistance. **Publications:** *Disability Rights News*, quarterly. • *Explanation of the Contents of the ADA*. Book. *Price:* $118. • Manuals.

★ 4483 ★ **Disabled American Veterans (DAV)**
PO Box 14301
Cincinnati, OH 45250-0301
Phone: (606)441-7300
Fax: (606)441-1416
Arthur H. Wilson, Nat. Adjutant

Founded: 1920. **Members:** 1,200,000. **Regional Groups:** 21. **State Groups:** 52. **Local Groups:** 2400. **Description:** Veterans with service-connected disabilities. Major activity is service to disabled veterans and their families. DAV employs 260 National Service Officers in Department of Veterans Affairs (VA) offices in 49 states and Puerto Rico to act as free-of-charge attorneys-in-fact, counseling and processing veterans' claims for compensation and benefits. Provides services in areas including disaster relief, employment, legislation, advocacy, and transportation. **Publications:** *DAV Magazine*, bimonthly. Magazine. Covers issues affecting disabled veterans and their families; includes association, department, chapter, and member news. *Price:* Included in membership dues; $15/year for nonmembers.

★ 4484 ★ **Disabled Womyn's Educational Project**
PO Box 8773
Madison, WI 53708-8773
Phone: (608)256-8883
Catherine Odette, Exec. Officer

Founded: 1988. **Description:** Lesbians with disabilities. Promotes members' interests. Supports legislation sensitive to members' needs. Maintains speakers' bureau. **Publications:** *Building Community Through Access*. • *Dykes, Disability, and Stuff*, quarterly. Newsletter. Available in the format of audiocassette, braille, DOS diskette, large print, modem transfer, audio tape. • *Dykes, Disability & Stuff*, quarterly. Newsletter. *Price:* $25/year. • *The Time for Access is Now*.

★ 4485 ★ **Federation for Children with Special Needs (FCSN)**
95 Berkley St., Ste. 104
Boston, MA 02116
Phone: (617)482-2915
Free: 800-331-0688
Fax: (617)695-2939
Martha Ziegler, Exec.Dir.

Founded: 1974. **Members:** 11. **Description:** Coalition of parents' organizations acting on behalf of children and adults with developmental disabilities. Provides information on special education laws and resources, and how to obtain related services. Operates Collaboration Among Parents and Health Professionals Project to increase and encourage parent involvement in the health care of children with disabilities or chronic illnesses. Other projects sponsored by FCSN are Parent Training and Information Project (PTI), which provides workshops in basic rights, parent consultations, and training, and an information service; and Technical Assistance for Parents Project, which provides assistance to parent training and information programs in the U.S. Coordinates National Network of Parents Center. Although membership is concentrated in the New England area, activities are conducted on a national level. **Publications:** *Coalition Quarterly*, 3/year. • *Newsline*, 5/year. Newsletter.

★ 4486 ★ **52 Association for the Handicapped**
1 Liberty Plz., Ste. 2922
New York, NY 10006
Phone: (212)346-5586
Fax: (212)346-5973
Allan D. Weinberg, Exec.Dir.

Founded: 1945. **Description:** Founded by a group of business and professional men who pledged "The Wounded Shall Never Be Forgotten." Provides 8000 amputee, paraplegic, and blind veterans and similarly handicapped civilians with Confidence Through Sports programs at its outdoor sports and recreation center in Ossining, NY. Conducts amputee and blind ski clinics at major ski areas in the U.S. during winter months. **Formerly:** (1969) 52 Association of the United States; (1985) 52 Association.

Foundation for Exceptional Children (FEC)
See: Entry 3228

★ 4487 ★ **Foundation for Science and Disability (FSD)**
236 Grand St.
Morgantown, WV 26505-7509
Phone: (304)293-5201
Fax: (304)293-6363
E. C. Keller, Jr., Treas.

Founded: 1978. **Members:** 265. **Description:** Disabled scientists and interested individuals. Offers consultation and advice concerning problems faced by handicapped persons in scientific fields. **Publications:** *The Abled Disabled in Science*. Book. • *Newsletter of FSD*, quarterly. Newsletter. *Price:* Available to members only. **Formerly:** (1993) Foundation for Science and the Handicapped.

★ 4488 ★ **Gazette International Networking Institute (GINI)**
5100 Oakland Ave., No. 206
St. Louis, MO 63110
Phone: (314)534-0475
Fax: (314)534-5070
Joan Headley, Dir.

Founded: 1958. **Members:** 12,500. **Description:** Polio and spinal cord injury survivors, ventilator users, other individuals with neuromuscular diseases, health care personnel, insurance agencies, government agencies, independent living centers, and interested others. Works to inform, encourage, dignify, and sustain people with disabilities. Seeks to create a communications network to provide information on issues related to disabilities. Serves as clearinghouse for information on polio, spinal cord injury, ventilators, neuromuscular diseases, and independent living. Sponsors seminars. Coordinates International Polio Network and International Ventilator Users Network. **Publications:** *Directory*

of Sources for Ventilation Face Masks. Directory. • *Handbook on the Late Effects of Poliomyelitis for Physicians and Survivors*. Handbook. • *IVUN News*, semiannual. Newsletter. Includes information for those interested in home mechanical ventilation. *Price:* $8 for individuals; $20 for institutions. • *Polio Network News*, quarterly. Contains information about the late effects of polio and topics related to disability. *Price:* $12 for individuals; $20 for institutions. • *Post Polio Directory*, annual. Directory. Lists self-identified clinics, health professionals, and support groups knowledgeable about the late effects of polio. *Price:* $3 for individuals; $6 for institutions. • *Proceedings of International Polio and Independent Living Conferences*, biennial. Proceedings. • *Rehabilitation Gazette*, semiannual. Journal. Written by persons with disabilities. *Price:* $8. • *Rehabilitation into Independent Living*. • *Ventilators and Muscular Dystrophy*. **Formerly:** (1983) Rehabilitation Gazette.

★ 4489 ★ **Goodwill Industries International (GII)**
9200 Wisconsin Ave.
Bethesda, MD 20814
Phone: (301)530-6500
Fax: (301)530-1516
David M. Cooney, Pres. & CEO

Founded: 1902. **Members:** 183. **Regional Groups:** 9. **State Groups:** 5. **Description:** Federation of Goodwill Industries organizations across North America and the world are concerned primarily with providing employment, training, evaluation, counseling, placement, job training, and other vocational rehabilitation services and opportunities for individual growth for people with disabilities and other special needs. Member Goodwill Industries organizations collect donated goods and sell them in Goodwill retail stores as a means of providing employment and generating income. Conducts seminars and training programs; compiles statistics. **Publications:** Annual Report. • Brochures. • *Corporate Brochure*, annual. Brochure. • *Forum*, 10/year. Magazine. • *Internal Membership Directory*, annual. Membership Directory. • Manuals. • Videos. Also publishes promotional materials. **Formerly:** (1910) Morgan Memorial and Cooperative Industries and Stores; (1946) National Association of Goodwill Industries; (1994) Goodwill Industries of America.

★ 4490 ★ **Handicap International (ERAC)**
14, ave. Berthelot
F-69361 Lyon Cedex 07, France
Phone: 7 8697979
Fax: 7 8697994
Jean-Noel Sersiron, Pres.

Founded: 1982. **Members:** 56,000. **Languages:** English, French, Portuguese, Spanish. **Description:** Works for the rehabilitation of physically disabled persons in Third World countries. Trains local technicians in appropriate technologies to create small prosthetics and physical rehabilitation units. Offers charitable programs. **Publications:** Books. Contains translations of text from other languages. • *L'Enfant Handicape et Village*. Book. • *Operations Handicap International*, quarterly. **Formerly:** Operation Handicap Internationale.

★ 4491 ★ **Handicapped Scuba Association (HSA)**
7172 W. Stanford Ave.
Littleton, CO 80123
Phone: (714)498-6128
Fax: (714)498-6128
Jim Gatacre, Program Dir.

Founded: 1975. **Members:** 2,000. **Regional Groups:** 19. **Description:** Individuals with handicaps and interested others. Purpose is to advance and promote scuba diving among the handicapped. Seeks to enhance the self-image of handicapped divers by emphasizing their abilities rather than their disabilities. Stresses importance of education and safety procedures in diving; maintains training agency for handicapped divers. Offers training and certification worldwide for scuba diving instructors in teaching the handicapped. Holds monthly diving excursion and lectures, and conducts four diving vacations per year. **Publications:** *Freedom in Depth*. Film. • *Getting Down Scuba News*, annual. *Price:* $20. • *Instructor Training Manual*. Manual. Also is producing a film about the association with the Cousteau Society (see separate entry).

★ 4492 ★ **HEATH**
1 Dupont Cir., Ste. 800
Washington, DC 20036-1193
Phone: (202)939-9320
Free: 800-544-3284
Fax: (202)833-4760
Rhona Hartman, Dir.

Founded: 1977. **Description:** A program of the American Council on Education, concerned with disability and education after high school. Assists colleges, universities, and other postsecondary programs in recruiting and retaining students with disabilities; acts as information clearinghouse through the HEATH Resource Center. Encourages input about experiences from administrators, educators, and students with disabilities. Offers workshops on working with disabled students. HEATH became inactive in 1983 but was reactivated in 1984. **Publications:** *How to Choose a College-Guide for the Student with a Disability*. Offers a step-by-step approach to the search and decision-making process. • *Information from HEATH*, 3/year. Newsletter. Provides information about new publications, highlights campus programs, and discusses new or pending legislation. • *Resource Directory*. Lists about 150 organizations which can be contacted for specific types of information. **Also Known As:** Project HEATH.

HEATH Resource Center (HRC)
See: Entry 6999

In Touch Networks (ITN)
See: Entry 7000

★ 4493 ★ **Independence Dogs, Inc. (IDI)**
146 State Line Rd.
Chadds Ford, PA 19317
Phone: (215)358-2723
Fax: (215)358-5314
Jean King, Founder & Pres.

Founded: 1984. **Members:** 50. **Description:** Volunteers working to increase the independence of the disabled through the use of trained service dogs. Trains and makes dogs available to the mobility disabled. Maintains speakers' bureau. **Publications:** *Clapper*, 3/year. Newsletter.

★ **4494** ★ **Indoor Sports Club (ISC)**
1145 Highland St.
Napoleon, OH 43545
Phone: (419)592-5756
Georgean Davis, Exec.Sec.

Founded: 1930. **Members:** 1,500. **Regional Groups:** 11. **Local Groups:** 84. **Description:** Social, benevolent, educational, and rehabilitative organization for physically disabled persons. To provide entertainment and amusement for disabled persons and shut-ins, seek aid for needy disabled persons, provide opportunities for active participation in civic affairs, and promote a better understanding and acceptance of the seriously disabled by the able-bodied. Local chapters are helped by units of the International Good Sports Club, whose able-bodied members provide transportation and other services to the disabled. **Publications:** *National Hookup*, biennial.

★ **4495** ★ **International Council on Disability (ICOD)**
25 E. 21st St., 4th fl.
New York, NY 10010
Phone: (212)420-1500
Fax: (212)505-0871
Abdullah Al-Ganim, Chairperson

Founded: 1953. **Members:** 68. **Description:** Nongovernmental organizations granted consultative status by the United Nations Economic and Social Council or in similar official relations with the International Labor Organization, United Nations Educational, Scientific and Cultural Organization, World Health Organization, or United Nations Children's Fund, and which have a direct interest in the welfare of the handicapped; other organizations having a direct interest in the handicapped may be granted associate membership. Assists the United Nations and specialized agencies, enlists their cooperation to develop a well coordinated program for the rehabilitation of the handicapped, serves as a permanent liaison body to develop cooperation between nongovernmental organizations interested in the handicapped and the U.N. and its specialized agencies, and develops cooperation among members. **Publications:** *Calendar of International Meetings*, annual. • *ICOD Compendium*, periodic. **Formerly:** (1968) Conference of World Organizations Interested in the Handicapped; (1986) Council of World Organizations Interested in the Handicapped.

★ **4496** ★ **International Federation of Disabled Workers and Civilian Handicapped (FIMITIC)**
(Federation Internationale des Mutiles, des Invalides du Travail et des Invalides Civils — FIMITIC)
Beethovenallee 56-58
53173 Bonn, Germany
Phone: 228 95640
Fax: 228 9564311
Marija Stiglic, Sec.Gen.

Founded: 1953. **Members:** 5000,000. **Languages:** English, French, German. **Descrip-**

tion: National organizations in 28 countries united to promote physical and vocational rehabilitation and full employment for the disabled. Seeks to foster international cooperation in the development of rehabilitation services; sponsors the International Day of the Disabled. Holds seminars. Acts as clearinghouse. Bestows awards. **Publications:** *Congress Reports*. • *Nouvelles*, quarterly. Bulletin.

International French-Speaking Association of Paraplegic Therapy Groups (AFIGAP) (Association Francophone Internationale des Groupes d'Animation de la Paraplegie — AFIGAP)
See: Entry 12686

★ **4497** ★ **International Mailbag Club (IMC)**
c/o Mrs. James T. Shepard
130 Center St.
Findlay, OH 45840
Phone: (419)422-2362
Mrs. James T. Shepard, Exec.Sec.

Founded: 1928. **Local Groups:** 5. **Description:** "To bring cheer and sunshine into lives of shut-in and handicapped persons through cards and letters." **Publications:** Newsletter, quarterly.

★ **4498** ★ **International Society for Prosthetics and Orthotics (ISPO)**
(Societe Internationale de Prothese et Orthese)
Borgervaenget 5
DK-2100 Copenhagen, Denmark
Phone: 31207260
Fax: 31181669
Prof. Mel Steel, Pres.

Founded: 1970. **Members:** 1,800. **National Groups:** 16. **Languages:** English. **Description:** Medical and paramedical professionals in 65 countries interested in prosthetics, orthotics, and other fields of rehabilitation engineering. Promotes improvements in the care of people with neuromuscular and skeletal impairments. Serves as nonpolitical coordinating and advisory organization on prosthetics, orthotics, rehabilitation engineering, and other matters related to the neuromuscular and skeletal system. Promotes and guides programs in research, development, and evaluation regarding prosthetics and orthotics. Fosters quality practice and develops standards for nomenclature, device design, techniques, processes, and patient care. Sponsors exhibits, conferences, regional and international courses, seminars, and symposia; suppo rts education and training in the field. **Publications:** *Directory of Officers and Members*, periodic. Directory. • *Prosthetics and Orthotics International*, 3/year. Also publishes *Directory of Films in Prosthetics and Orthotics*, *Standards for Lower-Limb Prostheses*, and proceedings of special meetings.

★ **4499** ★ **International Sports Organisation for the Disabled (ISOD)**
(Federation Internationale de Sport pour Handicapes)
353 Ontario St.
Newmarket, ON, Canada L3Y 2K2
Phone: (905)898-3661
Fax: (905)895-5527
Alan Dean, Contact

Founded: 1963. **Members:** 52. **Languages:** English, French, German, Spanish. **Description:** National federations in countries concerned with development of sports for the disabled. Encourages international cooperation among national organizations in the field of sports for the disabled; coordinates international activities of members. Sponsors training and education seminars and world championship Olympic games for the physically handicapped. **Publications:** *Circular*, semiannual. • *ISOD Handbook*, periodic.

★ **4500** ★ **International Stoke Mandeville Wheelchair Sports Federation (ISMWSF)**
Olympic Village
Barnard Crescent
Aylesbury, Bucks. HP21 9PP, England
Phone: 1296 436179
Fax: 1296 436484
Maura Strange, Sec.Gen.

Founded: 1952. **Members:** 80. **Description:** National organizations concerned with development of sport for paralyzed and other disabled individuals. Promotes sports activities and competitions to foster self-confidence in disabled individuals. **Publications:** Newsletter, 3/year. **Formerly:** (1991) International Stoke Mandeville Games Federation.

★ **4501** ★ **International Wheelchair Road Racers Club (IWRRC)**
c/o Joseph M. Dowling
30 Myano Ln., Box 3
Stamford, CT 06902
Phone: (203)967-2231
Joseph M. Dowling, Pres.

Founded: 1981. **Members:** 200. **Description:** Disabled persons, able-bodied persons, rehabilitation institutes, and major road race organizations interested in health and physical fitness for the disabled. Promotes wheelchair road racing in the U.S.; assists road race organizations in incorporating wheelchair divisions. Provides educational and technical assistance to race directors and road racers; maintains communications network concerning multi-sports for the disabled. Governs the sport of wheelchair road racing. **Publications:** Newsletter, semimonthly.

★ **4502** ★ **Job Accommodation Network (JAN)**
HRE/WVRRTC
West Virginia University
PO Box 6080
Morgantown, WV 26506
Phone: (304)293-7186
Free: 800-526-7234
Fax: (304)293-5407
Barbara T. Judy, Project Mgr.

Founded: 1984. **Description:** International information and referral service for employers, rehabilitation and social service counselors, and persons with disabilities. Offers information and counseling service to employers interested in learning how to hire, retain, or promote disabled persons. Compiles statistics.

★4503★ Just One Break (JOB)
373 Park Ave. S
New York, NY 10016
Phone: (212)725-2500
Fax: (212)213-6791
Mikki Lam, Exec.Dir.

Founded: 1949. **Description:** Employment service for people with disabilities. Works to place job-ready people with disabilities into competitive employment. Concentrates efforts in New York, New Jersey, and Connecticut, but advises companies nationwide. Offers placement services, employment counseling, skills evaluation, college recruitment, a summer intern program, and an annual jobs fair. Conducts on-site Americans with Disabilities Act accessibility studies and advisory assistance for human resources managers to help them ease the transition of people with disabilities into their workforce. **Publications:** Annual Report, annual. • *Informational Brochure.* Brochure.

★4504★ Learning Disabilities Association of America (LDA)
4156 Library Rd.
Pittsburgh, PA 15234
Phone: (412)341-1515
Fax: (412)344-0224
Jean Petersen, Exec.Dir.

Founded: 1964. **Members:** 60,000. **State Groups:** 50. **Local Groups:** 475. **Description:** Parents of children with learning disabilities; interested professionals. Works to "advance the education and general well-being of children with adequate intelligence who have learning disabilities arising from perceptual, conceptual, or subtle coordinative problems, sometimes accompanied by behavior difficulties." Disseminates information to the public; provides assistance to state and local groups. These affiliated groups carry out direct services to parents and children, including schools, camps, recreation programs, parent education, information services, and publication of books and pamphlets. Offers information and referral services. **Publications:** *LDA Newsbriefs*, bimonthly. Newsletter. *Price:* $13.50/year. • *Learning Disabilities*, semiannual. Journal. *Price:* $25/year. **Formerly:** Association for Children with Learning Disabilities; (1990) Association for Children and Adults with Learning Disabilities.

★4505★ Learning Disabilities Association of Canada (LDAC)
(Troubles d'Apprentissage - Association Canadienne)
323 Chapel St., Ste. 200
Ottawa, ON, Canada K1N 7Z2
Phone: (613)238-5721
Fax: (613)235-5391
Pauline Mantha, Exec.Dir.

Founded: 1963. **Members:** 10,000. **State Groups:** 12. **Local Groups:** 150. **Languages:** English, French. **Description:** Parents of children with learning disabilities and individuals with learning disabilities; educators and admin-

istrators, psychologists, language experts, lawyers, and health care professionals. Works to advance the education, social development, legal rights, and general well-being of individuals with learning disabilities. Encourages early recognition, diagnosis, and treatment of individuals with learning disabilities. Develops educational, social, recreational, and career-oriented programs and promotes legislation, research, and training of personnel in the field. Initiates programs to increase public awareness and understanding of learning disabilities. Acts as an advocate for individuals before government and other agencies; develops parent support services to maximize parental involvement. **Publications:** Handbooks, periodic. • *National*, quarterly. • Papers, periodic. **Formerly:** (1986) Canadian Association for Children and Adults with Learning Disabilities.

★4506★ Learning How (LH)
PO Box 35481
Charlotte, NC 28235
Phone: (704)376-4735
Fax: (704)376-4738
Cheryl Shore, Pres.

Founded: 1979. **Members:** 1,100. **Local Groups:** 19. **Description:** Disabled individuals interested in addressing the special needs of members. Strives to build self-esteem and confidence among disabled persons; encourages volunteer community involvement. Seeks to train the disabled for leadership positions and to serve as a support group for disabled persons. Works to prepare members for participation in the job market; acts as a referral service. Addresses legislative issues of concern to individuals with disabilities. Offers educational programs. Compiles statistics; maintains speakers' bureau. **Publications:** *Mentor Newsletter*, quarterly. Newsletter. Includes chapter news, information on member activities and resources, and legislative updates. *Price:* Included in membership dues; $5/year for nonmembers. **Formerly:** (1987) Handicapped Organized Women; (1988) HOW.

★4507★ Leonard Cheshire Foundation International
26-29 Maunsel St.
London SW1P 2QN, England
Phone: 171 8281822
Fax: 171 8280699
Rupert Ridge, Dir.

Founded: 1955. **Regional Groups:** 5. **Languages:** English, French, Spanish. **Description:** A humanitarian foundation created by the late Lord Cheshire and supported by autonomous associations and trusts involved in care for the disabled. Purpose is to provide optimal care and sustenance to disabled people. Operates 190 residential Cheshire Homes and rehabilitation and day care centers in 50 countries offering disabled people a home and an opportunity to attain self-confidence and independence. Sponsors staff training programs. Organizes biennial Creative Activity Contest for residents and offers prizes for literature, art, photography, and handicrafts. Engages in fundraising activities with a view toward expanding the network of Cheshire Homes. **Publications:** *Cheshire Smile*, quarterly. Magazine. • *The Leonard Cheshire Foundation*, periodic. Directory.

★4508★ Mainstream
3 Bethesda Metro Ctr., Ste. 830
Bethesda, MD 20814
Phone: (301)654-2400
Fax: (301)654-2403
Lawrence C. Pencak, Exec.Dir.

Founded: 1975. **Description:** Offers services and products to increase employment opportunities for people with disabilities. Assists companies and organizations in their efforts to "mainstream" people with disabilities into employment. Operates Mainstream Information Network, which includes a library of books, periodicals, and directories on disability issues. Also operates Project LINK (linking individuals with disabilities with competitive employment), which helps place job-ready disabled applicants in the Dallas, TX and Washington, DC areas. Provides in-house training; conducts workshops and seminars. **Publications:** *In the Mainstream*, bimonthly. Newsletter. Provides practical and legal information about placing disabled people into the workplace. *Price:* $60/year.

★4509★ Mobility International (MI)
228 Borough High St.
London SEI 1JX, England
Phone: 171 4035688
Fax: 171 3781292
Anthony Lumley, Sec.Gen.

Founded: 1974. **Members:** 100. **Languages:** English, French, German, Greek, Italian, Spanish. **Description:** Aim is to "give young people with disabilities opportunities to acquire the same skills and enjoy the same experiences as their non-handicapped peers." Provides information on travel exchange; establishes special international "participation projects" for disabled individuals from ages 18-30. Encourages the young disabled to explore new interests and to develop communication skills. Promotes strategies for integrating the disabled into mainstream life. Organizes summer camps and exchange programs. Conducts language courses and training courses for volunteer workers. **Publications:** Booklets. • *Mobility International News*, 3/year. • *Programme*, annual. • Videos.

★4510★ Mobility International U.S.A. (MIUSA)
PO Box 10767
Eugene, OR 97440
Phone: (503)343-1284
Fax: (503)343-6812
Susan Sygall, Exec.Dir.

Founded: 1981. **Members:** 500. **Description:** Disabled persons, organizations serving the disabled, exchange programs, and libraries. Advocates international, educational and recreational travel exchange programs that accommodate disabled persons. Organizes international exchange programs for the able-bodied and disabled. Provides information on exchange programs, book lists, referrals on homestays with foreign families, and placement in a variety of work-study programs for disabled youths and adults. Offers internships to undergraduate and graduate students. Conducts workshops, conferences, and seminars. **Publications:** *A New Manual for Integrating People with Disabilities into International Programs.* Manual. *Price:* $16 for members; $18 for nonmembers. • *A World* of Options for the 90s: A Guide to International Educational Exchange, Community Service, and Travel for Persons with Disabilities. Book. Price: $14 for members; $16 for nonmembers. • Crossing Borders. Contains U.S./Mexico exchange options. Price: $12 for members; $14 for nonmembers. • Emerging Leaders. Video. Available with or without captions. Price: $40 for members; $49 for nonmembers. • Equal Opportunities in International Educational Exchange: A Resource Guide. Price: $7.95 for members; $9.95 for nonmembers. • Global Perspectives on Disability: A Curriculum. Price: $40. • Home Is in the Heart: Recruiting and Accommodating Persons with Disabilities into the Homestay Experience. Video. Price: $40 for members; $49 for nonmembers. • The Impact of the Americans With Disabilities Act on the International Educational Exchange Field. Price: $2.50. • Looking Back, Looking Forward. Video. Available with or without captions. Price: $40 for members; $49 for nonmembers. • Mi Casa Es Su Casa. Video. Price: $40 for members; $49 for nonmembers. • Over the Rainbow, quarterly. Newsletter. Also available on audio cassette. Price: Included in membership dues; $10/year for nonmembers. • You Want to Go Where? A Guide to China for Travelers with Disabilities and Anyone Interested in Disability Issues. Price: $7.95 for members; $8.95 for nonmembers.

Multidisciplinary Institute for Neuropsychological Development (MIND)
See: Entry 8259

★ 4511 ★   National Amputation Foundation (NAF)
73 Church St.
Malverne, NY 11565
Phone: (516)887-3600
Fax: (516)887-3667
Sol Kaminsky, Exec.Sec.

Founded: 1919. **Members:** 5,200. **Description:** Veterans with service-connected amputation. Assists all amputees, including nonveterans, in employment, social, and mental rehabilitation. Provides services, including legal counsel, vocational guidance and placement, social activities, liaison with other groups, and psychological aid. Sponsors Amp-to-Amp program arranging for amputees who have returned to a normal life to visit new amputees. Maintains Prosthetic Centre for the manufacture and repair of prosthetic devices; provides training in the use of prosthetic devices. **Publications:** The Amp, bimonthly.

★ 4512 ★   National Amputee Golf Association (NAGA)
PO Box 1228
Amherst, NH 03031
Phone: (603)673-1135
Free: 800-633-6242
Fax: (603)672-7140
Bob Wilson, Exec.Dir.

Founded: 1955. **Members:** 3,700. **Regional Groups:** 3. **State Groups:** 6. **Description:** Individuals who have lost a hand, foot, or a combination thereof at a major joint. Purpose is to promote the mental and physical rehabilitation of amputees through the sport of golf. Conducts

first swing program for therapists. Organizes local, regional, national, and international tournaments. Compiles statistics. **Publications:** Amputee Golfer Magazine, annual. Magazine. Price: Included in membership dues; $5 to nonmembers in the U.S.; $7.50 to nonmembers outside the U.S. • Newsletter, semiannual, spring and fall. Price: Included in membership dues.

★ 4513 ★   National Association of Activity Professionals (NAAP)
1225 Eye St. NW, Ste. 300
Washington, DC 20005
Phone: (202)289-0722
Fax: (202)842-0621
Charles F. Price, Exec.Dir.

Founded: 1981. **Members:** 3,500. **Description:** Those who are or have been therapists, activity directors, and activity consultants in nursing homes, senior centers, retirement housing, or adult day care programs; other interested individuals. Purposes are to promote quality care and services for elderly and/or handicapped persons; to assist in the delivery of activity services; to foster research and the production of relevant literature; to upgrade educational programs. Sets standards and has established a certification process. Compiles statistics; maintains speakers' bureau, placement service, and resource review; sponsors National Activity Professional Day. Offers correspondence courses. **Publications:** NAAP News: News of the Activity Profession, monthly. Newsletter. Includes information on new members, upcoming events, and educational opportunities. Price: Included in membership dues.

★ 4514 ★   National Association for the Craniofacially Handicapped (FACES)
PO Box 11082
Chattanooga, TN 37401
Phone: (615)266-1632
Free: 800-332-2373
Fax: (615)267-3124
Lynne G. Mayfield, Contact

Founded: 1969. **Description:** Provides financial assistance for travel expenses to individuals with severe facial deformities resulting from congenital defects or accidents. Provides a resource file of available treatment centers, support groups, and general information concerning severe facial deformities. Is currently involved in an extensive fundraising campaign in order to increase awareness of the organization and to broaden its base of support. **Publications:** FACES, quarterly. Newsletter. Provides information and support for craniofacially handicapped persons. Includes updates on clients and medical updates. Price: Free. • FACES Brochure. Brochure. Provides information on the organization. **Formerly:** (1977) Debbie Fox Foundation for Treatment of Cranio-Facial Deformities; (1985) Debbie Fox Foundation.

★ 4515 ★   National Association of Developmental Disabilities Councils (NADDC)
1234 Massachusetts Ave. NW, Ste. 103
Washington, DC 20005
Phone: (202)347-1234
Fax: (202)347-4023
Susan Ames-Zierman, Contact

Founded: 1975. **Members:** 56. **Description:** State and territorial councils working to improve the lives of people with developmental disabilities. Promotes cooperation and communication among federal agencies, state governments, volunteer groups and other organizations, and individual state and territorial councils; educates and informs the public about the needs of persons with developmental disabilities. Works within the Washington, DC, community to represent the views of developmental disabilities councils; acts as information clearinghouse. Develops small groups of experts to consider issues of special concern. **Publications:** Highlights, monthly. Newsletter. Price: Available to members only. • Monographs. • Reports. **Formerly:** (1978) National Conference on Developmental Disabilities.

National Association for Independent Living (NAIL)
See: Entry 12693

★ 4516 ★   National Association of the Physically Handicapped (NAPH)
Bethesda Scarlet Oaks, No. GA4
440 Lafayette Ave.
Cincinnati, OH 45220-1000
Phone: (513)961-8040
Helen Lee Roudebush, Adm.Asst.

Founded: 1958. **Members:** 775. **National Groups:** 1. **State Groups:** 1. **Local Groups:** 19. **Description:** Physically handicapped persons; associate members are nonhandicapped. Seeks to advance the social, economic, and physical welfare of the physically handicapped. Promotes involvement of the physically handicapped in the planning and administration of all programs in their interest. Sponsors fundraising activities. **Publications:** Brochure. • NAPH National Newsletter, quarterly. Newsletter. Includes list of new members, president's page, chapter notes, new products section, editor's mailbox, and obituaries. Price: Included in membership dues; $12/year for nonmembers.

★ 4517 ★   National Association of Protection and Advocacy Systems (NAPAS)
900 2nd St. NE, Ste. 211
Washington, DC 20002
Phone: (202)408-9514
Fax: (202)408-9520
Curtis L. Decker, Exec.Dir.

Founded: 1978. **Members:** 96. **Regional Groups:** 5. **State Groups:** 56. **Description:** Executive directors and designees of state or territorial Developmental Disability, Mentally Ill Protection and Advocacy Systems, and Client Assistance Programs. Furthers the human, civil, and legal rights of persons with disabilities; advances the interests of protection and advocacy systems; facilitates coordination and mutual support among such systems and enhance their capacity to provide optimal services. Offers professional training; collects data. **Publications:** Manuals. • NAPAS Newsletter, periodic. Newsletter. • Reports. • State Protection and Advocacy Agencies, annual. Directory.

★4518★ **National Association of Special Needs State Administrators (NASNSA)**
c/o Sharon Full
Illinois State Board of Educ.
100 N. 1st St., No. C-421
Springfield, IL 62777
Phone: (217)782-4876
Fax: (217)782-9224
Sharon Full, Exec. Officer

Founded: 1983. **Members:** 60. **Description:** State administrators of vocational special needs programs. Provides information, technical assistance, leadership development, and legislative services. **Publications:** Newsletter, 3/year. Also publishes position papers.

★4519★ **National Association of State Directors of Special Education (NASDSE)**
1800 Diagonal Rd., Ste. 320
Alexandria, VA 22314
Phone: (703)519-3800
Fax: (703)519-3808
William Schipper, Exec.Dir.

Founded: 1938. **Members:** 2100. **Description:** Professional society of state directors; consultants, supervisors, and administrators who have statewide responsibilities for administering special education programs. Provides services to state agencies to facilitate their efforts to maximize educational opportunities for individuals with disabilities. Bestows awards. Computerized Services: Clearinghouse on Professions in Special Education. **Publications:** *Counterpoint*, quarterly. Newspaper. *Price::* $20. • *National Association of State Directors of Special Education--Liaison Bulletin*, periodic. Newsletter covering congressional action as well as that of the executive branch and other federal agencies, *Price::* $50/year. • Also produces audiovisual materials.

★4520★ **National Center for Disability Services (NCDS)**
201 I.U. Willets Rd.
Albertson, NY 11507
Phone: (516)747-5400
Fax: (516)747-5378
Dr. Edwin W. Martin, Jr., Pres.

Founded: 1952. **Description:** Serves as a center providing educational, vocational, rehabilitation, and research opportunities for persons with disabilities. Work is conducted through the following: Abilities Health and Rehabilitation Services, a New York state licensed diagnostic and treatment center which offers comprehensive outpatient programs in physical therapy, occupational therapy, speech therapy, and psychological services; Career and Employment Institute, which evaluates, trains, and counsels more than 600 adults with disabilities each year, with the goal of productive competitive employment; Henry Viscardi School, which conducts early childhood, elementary, and secondary programs, as well as adult and continuing education programs; Research and Training Institute, which conducts research on the education, employment, and career development of persons with disabilities, and holds seminars and workshops for rehabilitation services professionals. Maintains library and speakers' bureau; compiles statistics; offers placement service; conducts research and educational programs. **Formerly:** (1991) Human Resources Center.

★4521★ **National Center for Learning Disabilities (NCLD)**
381 Park Ave. S., Ste. 1420
New York, NY 10016
Phone: (212)545-7510
Fax: (212)545-9665
Shirley C. Cramer, Contact

Founded: 1977. **Members:** 4,000. **Description:** National voluntary organization promoting increased public awareness of learning disabilities. Makes available resources and provides referrals to volunteers, parents and professionals working with the learning disabled; develops and replicates programs for the learning disabled; NCLD also makes its services and publications available to U.S. citizens living overseas. Provides children's services. **Publications:** Newsletter, 3/year. • *Their World*, annual. Magazine. **Formerly:** (1989) Foundation for Children with Learning Disabilities.

★4522★ **National Center for Youth with Disabilities (NCYD)**
University of Minnesota
Division of General Pediatrics and Adolescent Health
Box 721
420 Delaware St. SE
Minneapolis, MN 55455
Phone: (612)626-2825
Free: 800-333-6293
Fax: (612)626-2134
Nancy A. Okinow, Exec.Dir.

Founded: 1986. **Description:** Encourages the use of strategies that enable adolescents and young adults with chronic illnesses or developmental disabilities to participate in community life to their fullest capacity. Promotes awareness of and responsiveness to the needs of youth with disabilities; fosters cooperation among agencies, professionals, parents, and youth. Provides technical assistance and consultation; offers educational programs. Maintains National Resource Library on Youth with Disabilities. **Publications:** *Connections*, periodic. Newsletter. Covers key issues facing youth with disabilities, current research, new programs, and training materials. *Price: Free.* • *CYDLINE Reviews*, periodic. Bibliography. Covers special topics. • *FYI Bulletins*, periodic. Covers statistical and demographic data on various aspects of the lives of youth with disabilities. *Price:* $1.50/copy. • *Teenagers at Risk: A National Perspective of State Level Services for Adolescents with Chronic Illness or Disability*. Report. Describes survey of public agencies and programs to understand the system of services available to adolescents with chronic illness or disabilities.

★4523★ **National Council on Independent Living (NCIL)**
2111 Wilson Blvd., Ste. 405
Arlington, VA 22201
Phone: (703)525-3406
Denise Figueroa, Pres.

Founded: 1982. **Members:** 380. **Local Groups:** 80. **Description:** Independent living centers, organizations that provide support to independent living centers, and individuals. (Independent living centers offer programs to assist disabled individuals, including help in locat-ing housing and finding appropriate personal care assistance, peer counseling, and independent living skills training.) Encourages the integration of people with disabilities into society; promotes independent lifestyles and decision-making for people with disabilities; works to strengthen independent living centers. Offers technical assistance and encourages cooperation among independent living centers. Seeks to develop leadership skills among people with disabilities; works to increase public awareness of the rights and needs of disabled individuals. Provides information and referral service; sponsors Peer Technical Assistance Network. Maintains speakers' bureau and placement service. **Publications:** *NCIL Newsletter*, quarterly. Newsletter. • *President's Bulletin*, monthly. Bulletin. **Formerly:** (1985) National Coalition of Independent Living Programs.

★4524★ **National Cristina Foundation (NCF)**
591 W. Putnam Ave.
Greenwich, CT 06830
Phone: (203)622-6000
Free: 800-274-7846
Fax: (203)622-6270
Dr. Yvette Marrin, Ph.D., Pres.

Founded: 1985. **Description:** Looks for donations of commercially obsolete computer equipment, software, and audio/visual equipment from the business community, the government sector, and the public; redistributes this technology to partner organizations that maintain programs for persons with special needs, such as the disabled, the disadvantaged, and students at risk of school failure. Conducts public awareness campaigns; accepts donations.

★4525★ **National Easter Seal Society (NESS)**
230 W. Monroe
Chicago, IL 60606
Phone: (312)726-6200
Fax: (312)726-1494
James E. Williams, Jr., Pres.

Founded: 1919. **Members:** 135. **Description:** Affiliated societies operating nearly 500 sites and serve one million children and adults with disabilities and their families. Seeks to establish and conduct programs that serve people with disabilities; works with other voluntary and governmental agencies to provide support services for the disabled; publishes and disseminates information. Sponsors activities involving advocacy, fundraising, public education, public relations, government relations, research, and resource development. Offers physical, occupational, and speech and language therapies, vocational evaluation and training, computer-assisted technological training, and camping and other recreational activities. Loans equipment. Maintains the National Easter Seal Society Research Program.

National Education for Assistance Dog Services (NEADS)
See: Entry 3557

★ 4526 ★ **National Foundation of Dentistry for the Handicapped (NFDH)**
1800 Glenarm Pl., Ste. 500
Denver, CO 80202
Phone: (303)298-9650
Fax: (303)573-0267
Larry Coffee, D.D.S., Exec.Dir.

Founded: 1974. **State Groups:** 12. **Description:** Promotes preventive dentistry for handicapped individuals in order to reduce dental disease. Sponsors Campaign of Concern which enlists the cooperation of members of the dental profession, special education personnel, disabled individuals and their parents, counselors, and civic organizations in helping developmentally disabled people enjoy good dental health. The campaign currently serves 35,000 people in seven states. Conducts preventive health education through in-service training for members of participating special education schools, sheltered workshops, day centers, and group/nursing homes; teaches handicapped individuals how to maintain their own oral hygiene and provide them with dental supplies; evaluate the oral health status of each participant; suggests dentists who will accept handicapped patients if such a referral is desired. Sponsors Donated Dental Services Programs, which match indigent, elderly, and handicapped individuals with volunteer dentists. Operates a portable dental treatment system for the homebound, nursing home residents, and the developmentally disabled that is currently in use in Denver, CO, Newark, NJ, and Chicago, IL; has assisted in developing similar programs in Detroit, MI and Houston, TX. **Publications:** Annual Report. • *Guidelines for Dental Programs in Institutions for Developmentally Disabled Persons.* • *Guidelines for Using Fluorides Among Handicapped Persons.* • *Special Smiles,* periodic. Also distributes audiovisual and written materials on dentistry for the handicapped.

★ 4527 ★ **National Foundation of Wheelchair Tennis (NFWT)**
940 Calle Amanecer, Ste. B
San Clemente, CA 92673
Phone: (714)361-6811
Fax: (714)361-6822
Bradley Parks, Pres.

Founded: 1980. **Members:** 1,000. **Description:** Individuals with an orthopedic disability that prevents participation in regular tennis. To organize, promote, and encourage enthusiasm for wheelchair tennis throughout the world. Conducts consultation programs for schools or parks and recreation administrators, tennis professionals, and physical or recreational therapists that include exhibitions, basic and advanced clinics, junior programs, and rehabilitative disability information. Maintains Junior Wheelchair Sports Camp program for disabled children seven to 18 years old. Holds National Wheelchair Tennis Championships annually; sponsors on-court demonstrations at annual National Coaches and Directors Conference. **Publications:** *Advanced Wheelchair Tennis.* Video. • Manual. • *National Tournament Program,* annual. • *Tennis in a Wheelchair.* Video. • *Two Bounce News,* bimonthly.

★ 4528 ★ **National Handicapped Sports (NHS)**
451 Hungerford Dr., Ste. 100
Rockville, MD 20850
Phone: (301)217-0960
Fax: (301)217-0968
Kirk M. Bauer, Exec.Dir.

Founded: 1967. **Members:** 20,000. **Regional Groups:** 7. **Local Groups:** 86. **Description:** Promotes sports and recreation opportunities for individuals with physical disabilities. Provides direct services to people with mobility impairments, including amputations, paraplegia, quadriplegia, spinal cord injuries, stroke, head injuries, cerebral palsy, polio, muscular dystrophy, multiple sclerosis, arthrogryposis, birth defects, neuromuscular disabilities, and visual impairments. Offers and sanctions recreational winter and summer programs, including learn-to-ski, learn-to-sail, and learn-to-race clinics, competitive alpine and nordic skiing, archery, basketball, cycling, lawnbowling, shooting, swimming, table tennis, track and field, volleyball, sailing, and weightlifting. Conducts special programs for children, women, and veterans with disabilities. Offers training and certification of adaptive fitness and adaptive ski instructors. Sponsors U.S. Disabled Ski Team, U.S. Amputee Summer Sports Team, and U.S. Disabled Sports Team. Maintains hall of fame. **Publications:** *Adaptive Ski Teaching Methods.* In two volumes. • *Aerobics for Amputees.* Video. • *Aerobics for Cerebral Palsy.* Video. • *Aerobics for Paraplegia.* Video. • *Aerobics for Quadriplegia.* Video. • *Disabled Children in Physical Education: Learning Through Movement.* Handbook. Overview of proper adapted physical education programs for disabled children. *Price:* $14.95. • *Fitness Programming and Physical Disabilities.* Manual. • *Manual for Adaptive Fitness Instructors.* Manual. • *Manual for Adaptive Ski Instructors.* Manual. • *Strengthen Flexibility Exercises for All Types of Disabilities.* Video. **Formerly:** (1972) National Amputee Skiers Association; (1977) National Inconvenienced Sportsmen's Association; (1989) National Handicapped Sports and Recreation Association.

★ 4529 ★ **National Information Center for Children and Youth with Disabilities (NICHCY)**
PO Box 1492
Washington, DC 20013
Phone: (202)884-8200
Free: 800-695-0285
Fax: (202)884-8441
Suzanne Ripley, Dir.

Founded: 1970. **Description:** Provides information to assist parents, educators, care-givers, advocates, and others in helping children and youth with disabilities participate as fully possible in school, at home, and in the community. Provides personal responses to specific questions, referrals to other organizations/sources of help, prepared information packets, and technical assistance to parent and professional groups. **Publications:** Booklets. • *Disability Fact Sheet,* annual. • *News Digest,* periodic. Newsletter. Addresses current issues affecting individuals concerned with handicapped children and youth with disabilities. *Price:* Free. • Papers. • *Parent Guide.* • *State Resource*

Sheet, annual. • *Transition Summary.* **Formerly:** National Information Center for the Handicapped; National Special Education Information Center; (1982) Parents Campaign for Handicapped Children and Youth; (1987) National Information Center for Handicapped Children and Youth; (1991) National Information Center for Children and Youth with Handicaps.

National Institute for Rehabilitation Engineering (NIRE)
See: Entry 2431

National Legal Center for the Medically Dependent and Disabled (NLCMDD)
See: Entry 7189

★ 4530 ★ **National Legislative Council for the Handicapped (NLCH)**
PO Box 262
Taylor, MI 48180
Gerald T. Harris, Chairperson

Founded: 1977. **Members:** 50. **State Groups:** 1. **Description:** Handicapped citizens, senior citizens, medical professionals, labor unions, and interested individuals. Objective is to endorse public officials who support sound legislation for a barrier-free environment, civil rights, acceptable living conditions, employment, education, and rehabilitation for the handicapped. Plans to develop an information center. Conducts research and advisement on local, state, and national elections. Maintains speakers' bureau; compiles statistics. **Publications:** *Directory for Handicapped and Senior Citizens,* annual. Directory. Lists state and national organizations, agencies, and travel and legal services for handicapped and senior citizens. *Price:* Available to anyone.

★ 4531 ★ **National Networker (NN)**
PO Box 32611
Phoenix, AZ 85064
Phone: (602)941-5112
Bill Butler, Ed.D., Editor

Founded: 1982. **Members:** 2,500. **Description:** Learning disabled adults; professionals and others interested in problems concerning LD. The term "learning disability" refers to a range of difficulties in acquiring, receiving, and storing information. Seeks to educate, compile statistics, and disseminate information about LD. Provides peer counseling network to assist members to develop themselves as leaders in this and other fields. **Publications:** *The National Networker,* quarterly. Newsletter. *Price:* $8. **Formerly:** (1992) National Network of Learning Disabled Adults.

★ 4532 ★ **National Ocean Access Project (NOAP)**
PO Box 10726
Rockville, MD 20849
Phone: (301)217-9843
Fax: (301)217-9843

Founded: 1986. **Members:** 500. **Local Groups:** 15. **Description:** Develops and promotes marine recreational opportunities for people with disabilities. Provides referral and technical assistance in fishing, kayaking, power boating, rowing, sailing, scuba diving, and water skiing. Offers Learn-to-Sail programs. Conducts model boat races. Maintains speakers' bureau. **Publications:** Brochure. • *Ocean Access*. Newsletter. Includes information on adapting boats and equipment. Contains calendar of events and chapter news.

★4533★ **National Odd Shoe Exchange (NOSE)**
7102 N. 35th Ave., Ste. 2
Phoenix, AZ 85051
Phone: (602)841-6691
Fax: (602)841-3349
Jeanne L. Sallman, Dir.

Founded: 1944. **Members:** 19,000. **Description:** Service organization to bring together persons with mutual shoe problems (foot amputees and persons having feet which differ physically due to disease, injury, or accident). The exchange supplies names of persons of similar ages and tastes in shoe styles who have extra shoes or who are seeking someone with whom to exchange mismated footwear. These persons then make their own arrangements for the disposal of shoes they now have and for purchase of future pairs. Also operates an odd glove exchange program. Maintains National Odd Shoe Foundation; operates National Odd Shoe Store with catalogs. Conducts medical surveys; compiles statistics. **Formerly:** (1972) National Odd Shoe Foundation; (1983) Ruth Rubin Feldman National Odd Shoe Exchange.

★4534★ **National Organization on Disability (NOD)**
910 16th St. NW, Ste. 600
Washington, DC 20006
Phone: (202)293-5960
Free: 800-248-2253
Fax: (202)293-7999
Alan A. Reich, Pres.

Founded: 1982. **State Groups:** 50. **Local Groups:** 4100. **Description:** Promotes the full participation of persons with mental and physical disabilities in all aspects of life; involves disabled and nondisabled persons and groups in voluntary working partnerships. Goals are to: improve the public's attitude toward disabled persons; promote greater educational and employment opportunities; improve access to buildings, polling places, and transportation; increase participation in recreational, social, religious, electoral, and cultural activities. Conducts seminars and workshops. Sponsors competitions and bestows awards. **Publications:** *NOD Report*, quarterly. Newsletter. • Also publishes brochures. **Formerly:** (1983) National Office on Disability. Supersedes: U.S. Council for the International Year of Disabled Persons (founded 1978).

★4535★ **National Orthotic and Prosthetic Research Institute (NOPRI)**
PO Box 491
Lenox Hill, NY 10021
Phone: (212)755-3366
Ralph Florio, Pres.

Founded: 1969. **Members:** 10. **Description:** Retired male and female nurses. Trains high school dropouts to work with aluminum by fabricating it into canes, crutches, and walkers, which are then distributed to needy persons free

of charge. Once they are accustomed to working with aluminum, trainees are placed with a company that produces aluminum products.

★4536★ **National Resource Center for Paraprofessionals in Education and Related Services (NRC)**
25 W. 43rd St., Rm. 620N
CASE
New York, NY 10036
Phone: (212)642-2948
Fax: (212)719-2488
Anna Lou Pickett, Dir.

Founded: 1979. **Description:** A resource center for administrators of state and local education agencies and community and four-year colleges and universities. Collects and disseminates information on the training and employment of paraprofessionals working with children and adults with special needs. Provides technical assistance and program evaluation services; conducts training courses for education administrators and policy makers. Maintains speakers' bureau; compiles statistics. **Publications:** *Employment and Training of Paraprofessional Personnel: A Technical Assistance Manual for Administrators and Staff Developers*. • *New Directions*, quarterly. Newsletter. Covers employment and personnel practices, supervision, and training of paraprofessionals who work in programs for individuals with special needs. *Price:* $10/year. • *Paraprofessional Bibliography: Training Materials and Resources for Paraprofessionals Working in Programs Serving People With Disabilities*. Also publishes training materials. **Formerly:** (1990) National Resource Center for Paraprofessionals in Special Education and Related Human Services; (1993) National Resource Center for Paraprofessionals in Education and Related Services.

National Therapeutic Recreation Society (NTRS)
See: Entry 12702

★4537★ **National Wheelchair Basketball Association (NWBA)**
University of Kentucky
110 Seaton Bldg.
Lexington, KY 40506-0219
Phone: (606)257-1623
Fax: (606)258-1090
Stan Labanowich, Ph.D., Commissioner

Founded: 1949. **Members:** 185. **Description:** Wheelchair basketball teams comprised of individuals with severe permanent physical disabilities of the lower extremities. Seeks to provide opportunities on a national basis for the physically disabled to participate in the sport of wheelchair basketball, with its adjunct psychological, social, and emotional benefits, and to maintain a high level of competition through continuing refinement and standardization of playing rules and officiating. Sponsors sectional and regional tournaments leading up to the National Wheelchair Basketball Tournament. Maintains hall of fame; compiles statistics; participates in charitable activities. **Publications:** Directory, annual. Conference officers, team representatives names & addresses. • *National Wheelchair Basketball Tournament Program*, annual. • Newsletter, 12/year. • *Rules and*

Case Book, annual. • *Standings and Statistics*, 10/year.

★4538★ **National Wheelchair Softball Association (NWSA)**
1616 Todd Ct.
Hastings, MN 55033
Phone: (612)437-1792
Jon Speake, Commissioner

Founded: 1976. **Members:** 24. **Description:** Teams that are active in wheelchair softball competitions. Acts as governing agency for the promotion, interpretation, standardization, and continued growth of wheelchair softball. Coordinates efforts of member teams and encourages formation of new teams; protects the interests of members and enforces existing rules and regulations established by member teams. Conducts seminars on wheelchair softball and wheelchair sports; sponsors tournaments. Maintains hall of fame and compiles statistics.

★4539★ **Networking Project for Young Adults with Disabilities (NPDWG)**
c/o YWCA of City of New York
610 Lexington Ave.
New York, NY 10022
Phone: (212)735-9767
Fax: (212)223-6438
Angela Perez, Dir.

Founded: 1984. **Description:** A project of the Young Women's Christian Association of New York City. Purpose is to increase the educational, social, and career aspirations of adolescents with disabilities by linking them to successful, disabled role models. Provides support groups; offers advocacy training, pre-employment skills development, and one-to-one mentoring. Organizes visits to the role model's workplace. Currently operates in the New York City area and is providing technical assistance to facilitate replication at several sites throughout the country. **Publications:** Books. • *Replication Manual*. Manual.

★4540★ **NISH**
2235 Cedar Ln.
Vienna, VA 22182-5200
Phone: (703)560-6800
Fax: (703)849-8916
Daniel W. McKinnon, Jr., Pres.

Founded: 1974. **Description:** Provides employment opportunities for people with severe disabilities under the Javits-Wagner O'Day Act. Promotes their placement into competitive industry. Conducts research and development to identify to the government commodities and services which are feasible for production and/or performance by work centers. (Work centers are nonprofit agencies that provide rehabilitative, training, and vocational services for persons with severe disabilities.) Provides training and technical assistance in the form of industrial engineering, production planning, quality control, inventory management, cost analysis, procurement, and contract administration. Acts as a liaison between work centers and the federal government. **Publications:** Annual Report. • Brochure. • *NISH News*, monthly. Newsletter. Reports on work centers employing persons with severe disabilities, and legislation and regulations affecting these centers. *Price:* Free to participants of the J-W O'Day Program. **Formerly:** (1991) National Industries for the Severely Handicapped.

★ **4541** ★ **Nordic Committee on Disability (Nordiska Namnden for Handikappfragor — NNH)**
Box 510
S-162 15 Vallingby, Sweden
Phone: 8 6201890
Fax: 8 7392400
Finn Petren, Dir.

Founded: 1980. **Members:** 5. **Languages:** Danish, English, Finnish, Norwegian, Swedish. **Description:** Initiates, organizes, and expedites cooperation among Nordic countries on efforts concerning disability and rehabilitation.

★ **4542** ★ **North American Riding for the Handicapped Association (NARHA)**
PO Box 33150
Denver, CO 80233
Phone: (303)452-1212
Free: 800-369-7433
Fax: (303)252-4610
William J. Scebbi, Exec.Dir.

Founded: 1969. **Members:** 3,000. **Regional Groups:** 11. **Local Groups:** 500. **Description:** Individuals and riding centers. Provides therapeutic riding for individuals with disabilities with good safety and proper care; offers appropriate training and certification for instructors working with the disabled. Requires accreditation for member centers. Provides educational programs. **Publications:** *NARHA Guide*, annual. Directory. *Price:* Included in membership dues. • *NARHA News*, bimonthly. *Price:* Included in membership; $20/year for nonmembers.

★ **4543** ★ **Norwegian Dyslexia Association (NDA) (Norsk Dysleksiforbund — NDF)**
Postboks 699
Sentrum
N-0106 Oslo 1, Norway
Phone: 22334275
Fax: 22429554
Mari Tangen, Sec.Gen.

Founded: 1976. **Members:** 4,700. **Local Groups:** 40. **Languages:** English, Norwegian. **Description:** Individuals with dyslexia and their parents; organizations. Acts as a support group. **Publications:** *Dyslektikeren*, bimonthly.

★ **4544** ★ **One-Arm Dove Hunt Association (OADH)**
Box 582
Olney, TX 76374
Phone: (817)564-2102
Fax: (817)564-3200
Jack R. Northrup, Co-Founder

Founded: 1972. **Members:** 250. **Description:** Hand or arm amputees who enjoy the sport of shotgun shooting; interested nonamputees. Works to help amputees accept their handicap and to provide fellowship and shooting competitions. Activities include dove hunts, One-Arm Tales, One-Arm Talent, and dove dinner. **Publications:** Newsletter, annual.

★ **4545** ★ **The One Shoe Crew, Inc. (TOSC)**
86 Clavela Ave.
Sacramento, CA 95828
Phone: (916)364-SHOE
Georgia M. Hehr, R.N., Dir.

Founded: 1986. **Members:** 2,500. **Description:** Service for adults or teens whose feet have stopped growing. Finds cost-sharing partners for people who wear only one shoe or those who wear shoes of two different sizes. (Clients include individuals with mismatched feet, amputees, people wearing a brace on one foot, and anyone with a one-sided foot problem who still wears one regular shoe.) Matches shoe size, width, needs, preferences, and approximate age of clients seeking partners. Over 50,000 new, unused shoes and over 3,000 pairs of mismated shoes (same shoe, different size) are available free to clients; shipping must be prepaid. Clients indicate the general shoe style they prefer and receive pictures of what is available in their size and width. **Publications:** Brochure. *Price:* Free. • *The One Shoe Crew News*, periodic. Newsletter. Includes practical tips and advice. *Price:* Free.

★ **4546** ★ **Operation Appreciation (OA)**
c/o Non-Commissioned Officers Association of the U.S.A.
225 N. Washington St.
Alexandria, VA 22314
Phone: (703)549-0311
Fax: (703)549-0245
Richard C. Schneider, Exec.Dir.

Founded: 1985. **Description:** Participants include veterans and citizens concerned with showing appreciation to disabled veterans. Helps hospitalized disabled veterans by raising funds by encouraging the public to send cards to boost their morale. Supports the veteran members of the two armed forces retirement homes (United States Soldier and Airman home in Washington D.C. and the Navel Home in Gulfport, MS). Assists lobbyists' efforts to increase disabled veterans' benefits. **Also Known As:** National Defense Foundation.

★ **4547** ★ **Paralyzed Veterans of America (PVA)**
801 18th St. NW
Washington, DC 20006
Phone: (202)872-1300
Fax: (202)785-4452
Gordon Mansfield, Exec.Dir.

Founded: 1947. **Members:** 15,000. **Regional Groups:** 32. **Description:** Veterans who have incurred an injury or disease affecting the spinal cord and causing paralysis. Through national service program, assists all veterans, dependents, and survivors in obtaining Department of Veterans Affairs benefits due them; works for federal benefits of various kinds. Sponsors wheelchair sporting events in basketball, swimming, bowling, archery, and track and field. Promotes legislation to create accessibility to establishments and facilities for individuals with a disability. Sponsors research, rehabilitation, and educational programs. Founded the Spinal Cord Research Foundation to fund spinal cord research projects and fellowships. Also founded the Education and Training Foundation to provide grants to improve the knowledge, abilities,

and skills of health professionals, spinal cord impaired patients, and their loved ones. **Publications:** Booklets. • *Paraplegia News*, monthly. Magazine. Reports on organization efforts to ensure better care for persons with spinal cord injuries and diseases. Contains chapter and veteran news. *Price:* $21/year. • *Sports-n-Spokes*, bimonthly. Magazine. Features articles on wheelchair sporting activities. Includes calender of events and new product reviews. *Price:* $18/year.

★ **4548** ★ **Paws With a Cause (PWC)**
1235 100th St. SE
Byron Center, MI 49315
Phone: (616)698-0688
Free: 800-253-PAWS
Fax: (616)698-2988
Antoinette Joni Sapp, CEO. & Pres.

Founded: 1979. **National Groups:** 26. **Regional Groups:** 2. **Description:** Trains and provides dogs to assist people with disabilities. Works to increase awareness of the need for service dogs and legal access rights. Conducts educational programs. **Publications:** *Dogs for Dignity*, quarterly. Newsletter.

★ **4549** ★ **People-to-People Committee on Disability (PPCOD)**
PO Box 18131
Washington, DC 20036
Phone: (301)774-7446
David L. Brigham, Chm.

Founded: 1956. **Members:** 250. **Description:** Individuals concerned about the circumstances of handicapped people throughout the world. Disseminates information; acts as consultant in promoting exchange activities; coordinates special assistance projects in developing countries. Compiles statistics. **Publications:** *Directory of Organizations Interested in the Handicapped*, biennial. Directory. • Newsletter, quarterly. Also publishes reports and surveys. **Formerly:** (1994) People-to-People Committee for the Handicapped.

★ **4550** ★ **People's Center for Housing Change (PCHC)**
PO Box 1151
Topanga, CA 90290
Phone: (213)455-1340
Fax: (213)455-3312
Stephen M. Kerpen, Exec. Officer

Founded: 1978. **Description:** Gathers and disseminates information and conducts research related to the accessibility of the handicapped to buildings and other sites. **Publications:** *Housing Adaptability Guidelines*.

PRIDE Foundation - Promote Real Independence for the Disabled and Elderly
See: Entry 12710

Rehabilitation Information Round Table (RIRT)
See: Entry 12712

Rehabilitation International (RI)
See: Entry 12713

★4551★ Research and Training Center on Independent Living (RTCIL)
University of Kansas
Rm. 4089 Dole
Lawrence, KS 66045
Phone: (913)864-4095
Fax: (913)864-5063
Dr. James Budde, Dir.

Founded: 1980. **Members:** 180. **Description:** U.S. independent living centers helping individuals with severe disabilities lead independent lives. Works to: identify attributes of successful self-help support groups; develop and test instruments to assess social support levels within self-help support groups; implement and evaluate intervention strategies for accurate and positive portrayals of people with disabilities by the media; deter unlawful parking in handicapped-designated parking spaces and enhance public awareness of issues related to disability and independent living; establish accreditation standards to evaluate ILC programs, services, and management. Has developed: Personal Attendant Care Management Training model in seven states to increase the ability of consumers to manage attendants an d reduce management problems and institutionalization; program to assist ILC consumers in identifying personal goals and initiating behavioral changes to attain them. Provides direct training and technical assistance to individuals, ILCs, state agencies, and consumers' groups; university courses, and presentations. **Publications:** *Catalogue of Publications*, annual. Lists publications available from the center; includes abstracts. • *Guidelines for Reporting and Writing About People with Disabilities*. • Manuals. • Monographs.

★4552★ Riding for the Disabled Association (RDA)
National Agricultural Centre
Ave. 'R'
Kenilworth, Warwickshire CV8 2LY, England
Phone: 1203 696510
Fax: 1203 696532
J.R. Moss, Dir.

Founded: 1969. **Members:** 39,000. **Regional Groups:** 18. **Local Groups:** 725. **Languages:** English. **Description:** Disabled individuals and supporters in the United Kingdom. Provides horseback riding opportunities for disabled people. Sponsors training sessions for helpers, instructors, and physiotherapists. Compiles statistics. **Publications:** Articles, periodic. • Books, periodic. • *List of Groups*, annual. Directory. • Pamphlets, periodic. • *RDA Handbook*, periodic. • *RDA News*, quarterly.

Shriners Hospitals for Crippled Children (SHCC)
See: Entry 6470

★4553★ Sibling Information Network
c/o A.J. Pappanikou Center
62 Washington St.
Middletown, CT 06457-2844
Phone: (203)344-7500
Fax: (203)644-2031
Lisa Glidden, Coord.

Founded: 1981. **Members:** 1,800. **Description:** Teachers, social workers, health care professionals, researchers, and families who have an interest in the welfare of siblings of children with disabilities and issues related to families of individuals with disabilities. Acts as clearinghouse for information and services regarding the siblings of persons with handicaps. **Publications:** *Sibling Information Network Newsletter*, quarterly. Newsletter. Contains manuscripts, announcements, and information for and about siblings of persons with disabilities.

★4554★ Siblings for Significant Change (SSC)
105 E. 22nd St., 7th Fl.
New York, NY 10010
Phone: (212)420-0776
Free: 800-841-8251
Fax: (212)420-0433
Gerri Zatlow, Dir.

Founded: 1982. **Members:** 75. **Description:** Siblings of disabled individuals; parents, educators, social workers, medical professionals, and researchers interested in siblings of disabled individuals. Provides peer support, legal assistance, and psychological counseling to siblings of the handicapped. Coordinates social activities for families with handicapped members and works on projects and audiovisual programs designed to increase national awareness of the difficulties faced by families of disabled individuals. Maintains speakers' bureau. Division of Special Citizens Futures Unlimited, a New York state organization that offers ongoing programs for autistic and autistic-like adults. **Publications:** *Directory of Sibling Related Services*. Directory. • Journal, semiannual. • Newsletter, periodic.

Sister Kenny Institute (SKI)
See: Entry 12718

★4555★ Ski for Light
1455 W. Lake St.
Minneapolis, MN 55408
Phone: (612)827-3232
Bud Keith, Pres.

Founded: 1975. **National Groups:** 1. **Regional Groups:** 35. **Description:** Dedicated to encouraging and assisting interested groups in conducting cross-country skiing programs and other health sports activities for visually impaired and other physically disabled people. Brings together disabled and nondisabled people from throughout the U.S., Canada, Norway, and other countries. The group is modeled after the Knight's Race (Ridderrennet) in Norway, which has been held annually since 1964 with international participation. Sponsors physically demanding health sports events throughout the year in North America including the Ski for Light International Program. Maintains speakers' bureau. **Publications:** *SFL Bulletin*, quarterly. Bulletin. Contains organizational news. *Price:* Free. **Formerly:** (1980) Ski for Light; (1983) HEALTHsports, Inc..

★4556★ Society for the Advancement of Travel for the Handicapped (SATH)
347 5th Ave., Ste. 610
New York, NY 10016
Phone: (212)447-7284
Fax: (212)725-8253
M.T.V. Shaw-Lawrence, Exec.Officer

Founded: 1976. **Members:** 1000. **Description:** Individuals and corporations interested in creating a forum for the exchange of ideas, information and resources to encourage and ease travel for handicapped persons. Goals are: to create awareness of the need and ability of handicapped persons to travel, and to have them accepted and welcomed; to serve as a resource center on travel facilities, data, and literature provided for the handicapped by tourist offices, carriers, hotels, destinations, and car rental agencies; to keep members informed on travel requirements and the variety and quality of special services available. Conducts seminars and lectures. Operates speaker's bureau; bestows awards. Maintains 300 volume library. Compiles statistics on the potential travel market of various handicapped groups and their locations. **Publications:** *SATH News*, quarterly. Newsletter containing information on travel and related matters of interest to all handicapped persons. *Price:* Included in membership dues. • Also publishes *U.S. Welcomes Handicapped Visitors*. • Information Sheets on travel-related matters.

★4557★ Society for Disability Studies
c/o David Pfeiffer
Suffolk University
Department of Public Management
Eight Ashburton Place
Boston, MA 02108-2770
Phone: (617)742-8280

Founded: 1986. **Members:** 300. **Description:** Social scientists and scholars studying the problems of disabled people in society. Strives to develop theoretical and practical knowledge about disability and promotes equal participation in society for individuals with disabilities. **Publications:** *Annual Proceedings*, annual.

★4558★ Society of Homes for the Handicapped (SHH)
Level 204, Shopping Block
Lai Yiu Estate
Kwai Chung, Hong Kong
Phone: 27454214
Fax: 7864097
Stephen Siu Yuen Chan, Exec.Dir.

Founded: 1977. **Members:** 190. **Languages:** English. **Description:** Works to integrate mentally and physically disabled individuals into Hong Kong society. Instructs family members on care for the disabled; operates residential homes and day care centers. Conducts courses for handicapped individuals; trains volunteers to work with the disabled. **Publications:** Annual Report, annual. • Brochures, periodic. • Journal, annual. • *SHH NEWS*, quarterly.

★4559★ Special Interest Group for Computers and the Physically Handicapped (SIGCAPH)
Association for Computing Machinery
1515 Broadway, 17th Fl.
New York, NY 10036
Phone: (212)869-7440
Fax: (212)302-5826
Diane Darron, CAE, Program Dir.

Founded: 1970. **Members:** 453. **Description:** A special interest group of the Association of Computing Machinery. Physically disabled computer professionals; persons involved in the application of computers to aid the disabled; persons involved in the training or employment of physically disabled computer professionals; others interested in aiding the disabled. To promote application of computer technology to aid the physically disabled; to educate the public about disabled computer professionals. Sponsors lectures and sessions at computer conferences on hiring and training disabled computer professionals. Compiles statistics. **Publications:** Newsletter, semiannual. **Also Known As:** SIGCAPH. **Formerly:** (1978) Special Interest Committee for Computers and the Physically Handicapped.

★ 4560 ★ **Special Recreation, Inc. (SRI)**
362 Koser Ave.
Iowa City, IA 52246
Phone: (319)337-7578
John A. Nesbitt, Ed.D., Pres.

Founded: 1978. **Description:** Disabled consumers, parents of the disabled, rehabilitation professionals, and volunteers. Promotes self-determination, equal opportunity, consumerism, and normalization in recreation and leisure for disabled individuals; works to advance the national and international policy and philosophy of special recreation; provides national information services on federal, state, and local laws, regulations, and public programs for special recreation. Conducts research and demonstrations; prepares and disseminates information; cooperates with and assists voluntary associations and public agencies in initiating, expanding, and improving special recreation programs and services and provides personnel training. Sponsors the International Center on Special Recreation that works to: collect and disseminate international information on special recreation services for disabled persons, special recreation programs, and personnel training; conduct, provide, and support international exchange of technical, professional, and general information on special recreation for the disabled; cooperate with both governmental and voluntary organizations on national and international levels. Maintains Pioneers in Special Recreation Hall of Fame. Offers career guidance and placement service. Maintains speakers' bureau; compiles statistics. **Publications:** Books. • Papers. • *Special Recreation AC Bold - A Catalog on Books on Leisure for the Disabled*, periodic. • *Special Recreation Access Library*, periodic. • *Special Recreation Compendium of 1500 Resources for Disabled People*, periodic. • *Special Recreation Digest*, periodic. • *Special Recreation Eric Guides*, periodic.

★ 4561 ★ **Support Dogs, Inc. (SD)**
3958 Union Rd.
St. Louis, MO 63125
Phone: (314)892-2554
Mitzi Kirkbride, Exec.Dir.

Founded: 1981. **Members:** 10,000. **Description:** Helps people with disabilities achieve greater independence and improve the quality of their lives by providing them with professionally trained dogs. Breeding program produces Golden Retrievers, Labradors, German Shepherds, and selected crossbreeds. Dogs are prematched and custom trained for each individual and assist their owners with tasks such as:

opening mall and house doors; pulling wheelchairs long distances and up ramps; loading wheelchairs into vehicles; retrieving a dropped or distant object; bringing the phone and operating an emergency assistance switch; rising to high counters to assist with business transactions. **Publications:** *Support Dog News*, quarterly. *Price:* Free. **Formerly:** (1992) Support Dogs for the Handicapped.

★ 4562 ★ **Swedish Organization for Disabled People (NAH) (Nordiska Handikappforbundet — NHF)**
Katrinebergsvaggen 6
S-117 43 Stockholm, Sweden
Phone: 8 189100
Fax: 8 6456541
Mrs. Birgitta Andersson, Pres.

Founded: 1946. **Members:** 5. **Languages:** Swedish. **Description:** National associations for the handicapped in Denmark, Finland, Iceland, Norway, and Sweden. Promotes the interests of handicapped individuals in Scandinavia. **Formerly:** Nordic Association for the Handicapped..

★ 4563 ★ **TASH: The Association for Persons With Severe Handicaps (TASH)**
11201 Greenwood Ave. N.
Seattle, WA 98133
Phone: (206)361-8870
Fax: (206)361-9208
Frank Laski, Acting Exec.Dir.

Founded: 1973. **Members:** 6,300. **Regional Groups:** 2. **State Groups:** 35. **Description:** Teachers, therapists, parents, administrators, university faculty, lawyers, and advocates involved in all areas of service to people with severe disabilities. Seeks to ensure an autonomous, dignified lifestyle for all people with severe disabilities; advocates quality education, from birth through adulthood, for disabled individuals. Disseminates updated information on solutions to problems, research findings, trends, and practices relevant to people with severe disabilities. Provides information and referral service. **Publications:** Books. • *Journal of the Association for Persons With Severe Handicaps*, quarterly. Journal. *Price:* Included in membership dues. • Papers. • *TASH Newsletter*, monthly. Newsletter. *Price:* Included in membership dues. **Formerly:** (1984) The Association for the Severely Handicapped.

★ 4564 ★ **Time Out to Enjoy (TOTE)**
c/o CDR
208 S. La Salle, No. 1330
Chicago, IL 60604
Phone: (312)444-9484
Fax: (312)444-1977

Founded: 1977. **Regional Groups:** 2. **Description:** Learning-disabled adults, persons associated with learning-disabled adults, and medical, educational, and social services professionals. (The group defines a learning-disabled adult as a person with normal to above-average intelligence with a deficit in one or more learning skills.) Purposes are to: educate the public about learning disabilities; provide support to and resources for learning-disabled adults. Collects and disseminates information on educational and employment services and programs;

provides referrals to learning-disabled adults with specific needs. Sponsors mutual support groups. Conducts in-services, workshops, and panels for teachers, social workers, psychologists, other professionals, and parents. Maintains speakers' bureau. Distributes taped interview with two learning-disabled adults.

★ 4565 ★ **Travel Industry and Disabled Exchange (TIDE)**
5435 Donna Ave.
Tarzana, CA 91356
Phone: (818)343-6339
Lou Nau, Pres.

Founded: 1986. **Members:** 1,000. **Description:** Travel industry personnel and disabled individuals united to enhance travel opportunities for the disabled. Surveys travel facilities for the disabled. **Publications:** *Tide's In*, quarterly. Newsletter. *Price:* Included in membership dues.

★ 4566 ★ **Very Special Arts (VSA)**
John F. Kennedy Center for the Performing Arts Educ. Office
Washington, DC 20566
Phone: (202)628-2800
Free: 800-933-VSA1
Fax: (202)737-0725
Eugene Maillard, CEO

Founded: 1974. **Regional Groups:** 52. **Description:** International coordinating agency for quality arts programs for individuals with disabilities from 55 countries. Purpose is to assure that individuals with disabilities have year-round opportunities to participate in educational programs demonstrating the value of the arts and to provide experiences to help them become active participants in mainstream society. Activities include: supporting quality arts in educational programs for persons with special needs; providing resources, information exchange, referrals, and workshops. Sponsors national, state, and local programs and festivals. Provides training and technical assistance for teachers, artists, and administrators in schools, museums, libraries, and recreation and art centers. Maintains databases; compiles statistics; sponsors competitions. Educational affiliate of the John F. Kennedy Center for the Performing Arts. **Publications:** *Very Special Arts*, 3/year. Newsletter. Also publishes manuals and guides and makes available videotapes. **Formerly:** (1985) National Committee, Arts for the Handicapped.

★ 4567 ★ **Wheelchair Motorcycle Association (WMA)**
101 Torrey St.
Brockton, MA 02401
Phone: (508)583-8614
Dr. Eli Factor, Pres.

Founded: 1975. **Members:** 1,000. **Description:** Handicapped persons confined to wheelchairs interested in rediscovering the outdoors; institutional and individual supporters. Researches, develops, and tests off-road vehicles for quadriplegics and other severely handicapped persons. Has produced an audiovisual program showing the use of cycles by the handicapped. Provides consultative and literature-searching services. Raises funds for research, rehabilitation, and education. **Publications:**

Climb for Independence, quarterly. Newsletter. *Price:* Included in membership dues.

★4568★ **Wheelchair Sports, USA (WSUSA)**
3595 E. Fountain Blvd., Ste. L-1
Colorado Springs, CO 80910
Phone: (719)574-1150
Fax: (719)574-9840
Patricia Long, Assoc. Exec.Dir.

Founded: 1958. **Members:** 4,000. **Regional Groups:** 12. **Description:** Men and women athletes with significant permanent neuromuscular-skeletal disability (spinal cord disorder, poliomyelitis, or amputation) who compete in various amateur sports events in wheelchairs. Members compete in regional events and in the annual National Wheelchair Games, which include competitions in track and field (including pentathlon), swimming, archery, shooting, table tennis, weightlifting, basketball, and rugby. Qualifying rounds are held in each region to select competitors for the national competition. Selection is made at the completion of the nationals to represent the U.S. team in annual international competition. Compiles statistics; maintains hall of fame and speakers' bureau. **Publications:** *Constitution and By-Laws*, biennial. • Newsletter, quarterly. *Price:* $10/year. Also publishes rule books. **Formerly:** (1994) National Wheelchair Athletic Association.

★4569★ **Wheelchair Tennis Players Association (WTPA)**
940 Calle Amanecer, Ste. B
San Clemente, CA 92673
Phone: (714)361-6811
Fax: (714)361-6822
Ron Hastings, Exec.Dir.

Founded: 1980. **Members:** 1,000. **Description:** Individuals with a physical disability that precludes participation in nonhandicapped tennis. Works to develop and improve the sport of wheelchair tennis and to promote fairness and uniformity in tournament play. Establishes competitive divisions and determines placement or ranking of players. Tournaments are sponsored by the National Foundation of Wheelchair Tennis. **Publications:** *Two Bounce News*, quarterly. Magazine. • *WTPA Newsletter*, monthly. Newsletter.

★4570★ **World Committee on Disability (WCD)**
910 16th St. NW, Ste. 600
Washington, DC 20006
Phone: (202)293-5960
Fax: (202)293-7999
Barbara M. Matos, Coord.

Founded: 1987. **Members:** 30. **Description:** Individuals promoting the full participation of the world's half billion people with disabilities by advocating U.N. leadership and action. Sends wheelchairs donated by Americans to needy individuals in Russia. **Publications:** *Spotlight*, periodic. Newsletter. **Formerly:** (1993) World Committee for the United Nations Decade of Disabled Persons.

★4571★ **World Community Projects (WCP)**
1755 Anaheim Ave., Ste. 9
Costa Mesa, CA 92627
Phone: (714)722-1122
Fax: (714)722-8381
Barbara Jean, Exec.Dir.

Founded: 1978. **Members:** 47. **Description:** Provides: disaster relief projects; relief camp management and personnel; medical supply acquisition; training materials for international projects that fit amputees with appliances and teach local people about prosthetics, orthotics, rehabilitation, and maintenance. Provides orphaned and displaced children's services and educational programs. Maintains speakers' bureau. Conducts research; sponsors charitable programs. Bestows annual World Community Project Award. **Publications:** *The Humanitarian*. Magazine. • *World Community Projects Newsletter*, quarterly. Newsletter. Includes methods and means, disaster relief and orthotic and prosthetic applications for developing nations relief programs. *Price:* Free. Also publishes books and prosthetic and orthotic educational materials for projects in developing countries.

★4572★ **World Institute on Disability (WID)**
510 16th St., Ste. 100
Oakland, CA 94612
Phone: (510)763-4100
Fax: (510)763-4109
Edward V. Roberts, Pres.

Founded: 1983. **Description:** Nonprofit organization run and staffed by disabled individuals with personal and professional knowledge of disability-related issues. Serves as a public policy institute seeking solutions to problems facing people of all ages who are disabled. Publications available upon request.

Research Centers

★4573★ **American International College Curtis Blake Center**
1000 State St.
Springfield, MA 01109
Phone: (413)737-7000
Fax: (413)737-2830
Dr. Brian Cleary, Dir.

Research Activities and Fields: Conducts research on learning disorders, including oral and written language, reading, arithmetic, and special education.

Boston University
Human Bioenergetics Laboratory
See: Entry 11958

★4574★ **Boston University**
Pike Institute on Law and Disability
765 Commonwealth Ave.
Boston, MA 02215
Phone: (617)353-2904
Henry A. Beyer, Dir.

Research Activities and Fields: Legal rights of individuals with mental and physical disabilities.

Publications: *Disability Advocates Bulletin*; also publishes information literature on disability discrimination. **E-mail Address:** hbeyer@bu.edu. **Formerly:** Pike Institute for the Handicapped (1993).

California State University, Sacramento
Assistive Device Center
See: Entry 2436

★4575★ **Center for Vulnerable Populations**
Brandeis Univ.
Heller Graduate School
415 South St.
Waltham, MA 02254-9110
Phone: (617)736-3921
Fax: (617)736-3905
Sara Bachman, Dir.

Research Activities and Fields: Health and human service policy issues related to adults with disabilities, especially those receiving public health benefits and services. Specific research includes impact of health care reform, the influence of various financing and service delivery mechanisms, the development of community-based systems of care, and the identification and analysis of national databases on people with disabilities. **Publications:** *Spotlight* (newsletter).

★4576★ **Dyslexia Research Institute**
4745 Centerville Rd.
Tallahassee, FL 32308-2899
Phone: (904)893-2216
Fax: (904)893-2440
Dr. Patricia K. Hardman, Ph.D., Dir.

Research Activities and Fields: Dyslexia and attention deficit disorders, including educational techniques, teacher training, diagnostic procedures, biochemistry, allergies, and links alcoholism and eye movement. **Publications:** *Hardman and Associates News and Views* (bimonthly).

Georgia Institute of Technology
Center for Rehabilitation Technology
See: Entry 12732

★4577★ **Howard University**
Research and Training Center for Access to Rehabilitation and Economic Opportunity
2900 Van Ness St., N.W.
Washington, DC 20008
Phone: (202)806-8727
Fax: (202)806-8148
Dr. Sylvia Walker, Dir.

Research Activities and Fields: Conducts surveys of ethnic and regional variations in the prevalence and distribution of disability among the economically disadvantaged; examines the extent to which cultural and other variables influence the utilization of rehabilitation services by individuals from low socioeconomic groups and minority persons with disabilities; and identifies factors which facilitate employment and career success among minority persons with disabilities. Other research projects include depression and suicide studies, impact of substance abuse on heath and socioeconomic status, predicting employment outcomes, and family coping strategies. **Publications:** Project Newsletters.

Human Services Research Institute
See: Entry 4312

★4578★ **Indiana University Bloomington Institute for the Study of Developmental Disabilities**
2853 E. 10th St.
Bloomington, IN 47408-2601
Phone: (812)855-6508
Fax: (812)855-9630
Dr. Henry J. Schroeder, Dir.

Research Activities and Fields: Applied research emphasizing community inclusion of all individuals with disabilities. Areas of research include family support services; the inclusion of persons with disabilities in school, work and recreational activities; the aging of the developmentally disabled population; and group decision support systems for planning and policy making. Institute seeks to improve services in the State of Indiana through the implementation of best educational practices for persons with disabilities, legislation, advocacy, educational psychology, adapted physical education, speech, language, hearing, therapeutic recreation, health, nursing, library science, and instructional systems technology. **Publications:** *Library Access*; *UAP Voice*; *IRCA Newsletter*; *Diversity Press*. **Formerly:** Mental Retardation Research Center; Developmental Training Center (1987).

★4579★ **Medical University of South Carolina**
Vince Moseley Center for Children with Developmental Disabilities
41 Bee St.
Charleston, SC 29403
Phone: (803)792-3190
Fax: (803)792-6799
Dr. Michelle Macias, Med.Dir.

Research Activities and Fields: Learning problems and communication disorders research, including attention deficit disorder, cognitive strengths and weaknesses, physical therapy, speech/language pathology, family dynamics, and self-esteem. **Formerly:** Vince Moseley Center for Handicapped Children.

★4580★ **National Center for Disability Services**
Research and Training Institute
201 I.U. Willets Rd.
Albertson, NY 11507
Phone: (516)747-5400
Fax: (516)747-5378
Dr. Craig Michaels, V.Pres.

Research Activities and Fields: Placement, vocational rehabilitation, special education, transition services, career development, and training of adults and children with disabilities, including studies on psychological and medical problems, engineering devices, adapted driver education, independent living, recreation and leisure, information services, industry-labor-rehabilitation cooperation, work readiness, training of rehabilitation counselors, adult and continuing education, and evaluation, training, and employment methods for people with disabilities. Identifies programs through PEER Regional Information Exchange. **Publications:** *PEER Newsletter*; *RTI Newsletter*; *Tech-*

Reaches Out Newsletter; *ADAPT (ADA) Newsletter*; Training Manuals and Curriculum.

★4581★ **National Easter Seal Society Research Program**
230 W. Monroe St., Ste. 1800
Chicago, IL 60606
Phone: (312)726-6200
Fax: (312)726-1494
Norman D. Grunewald, V.Pres.

Research Activities and Fields: Fosters and funds research on the delivery of services for people with disabilities, including the effectiveness of existing or new therapies, modalities, or other relevant services related to the rehabilitation of people with disabilities; the effectiveness of innovative service delivery models on the independence of people with disabilities; and the effectiveness of new technological devices on the independence of people with disabilities. **Publications:** *Communicator*; *Computer News*.

National Science Foundation
Directorate for Engineering
Division of Bioengineering and Environmental Systems
Bioengineering and Aiding Persons with Disabilities Program
See: Entry 2458

★4582★ **New York State Institute for Basic Research in Developmental Disabilities**
1050 Forest Hill Rd.
Staten Island, NY 10314-6399
Phone: (718)494-0600
Fax: (718)698-3803
Henry M. Wisniewski, M.D., Dir.

Research Activities and Fields: Molecular biology and developmental biochemistry of human development, developmental disabilities, and clinical, behavioral, and developmental psychology of mental retardation, including neuroimmunology, membrane biochemistry, lipid biochemistry, neurotransmitter physiology and pathology, inborn errors of metabolism, blood-brain barrier, and persistent, latent, and unconventional viruses. Focuses on the causes and prevention of developmental disabilities, aging and Alzheimer's disease, Down's syndrome, fragile X syndrome, autism, fetal alcohol syndrome, neurodegenerative diseases, pediatric AIDS and neuroinfectious diseases, environmental neurotoxicology (including alcohol, lead, aluminum, and cocaine), prevention (including vaccines, diagnostic tests, and early intervention), and treatment (including drug evaluation). **Publications:** *PRISM* (newsletter); *Prevention Connection* (newsletter); Annual Report. **E-mail Address:** petermnet@aol.com. **Formerly:** New York State Institute for Basic Research in Mental Retardation.

Northern Arizona University
American Indian Rehabilitation Research and Training Center
See: Entry 12740

★4583★ **Northern Arizona University Institute for Human Development**
NAU Box 5630
Flagstaff, AZ 86011
Phone: (602)523-4791
Fax: (602)523-9127
Dr. Richard W. Carroll, Dir.

Research Activities and Fields: Social sciences, with particular emphasis on disabled and handicapped persons from infancy through aged. Studies the social integration of preschool handicapped children, motor development in and the effects of therapy on the multiple handicapped, and child evaluations and parent conferencing with diverse cultural groups, particularly special interest problems of disabled Native Americans. Provides support services and coordinates campus research in the social sciences.

Packard Children's Hospital at Stanford Rehabilitation Engineering Center
See: Entry 12741

Prosthetics Research Study
See: Entry 2464

Rehabilitation Research and Development Center
See: Entry 7818

Research and Training Center for Positive Behavior Support
See: Entry 7594

★4584★ **Southern Illinois University at Carbondale**
Evaluation and Developmental Center
500-C Lewis Ln.
Carbondale, IL 62901
Phone: (618)453-2331
Fax: (618)453-6386
Dale Shelton, Dir.

Research Activities and Fields: The severely physically and emotionally disabled, including studies on effects of vocational evaluation, rehabilitation results, evaluation of assessment techniques, techniques in job placement, and independent living training. **Formerly:** Employment Training Center.

Southern Illinois University at Carbondale Rehabilitation Institute
See: Entry 12750

★4585★ **U.S. Department of Education National Institute on Disability and Rehabilitation Research**
400 Maryland Ave., S.W.
Washington, DC 20202-2705
Phone: (202)205-8134
Fax: (202)205-8515
William E. McLaughlin, Contact

Research Activities and Fields: NIDRR provides grants and contracts for the support of research and utilization of information to improve the lives of people of all ages with physical and mental handicaps, especially persons with severe disabilities. NIDRR conducts research on identifying and eliminating the causes and consequences of disability; maximizing the physical and emotional status of handicapped persons, their functional ability, self-sufficiency, self-development, and personal autonomy; preventing or minimizing personal and family, physical, mental, social, educational, vocational, and economic effects of disability; and reducing and eliminating physical, social, educational, vocational, and environmental barriers to permit access to service and assistance. **Publications:** *Rehab Briefs; ABLEDATA;* publications on disability statistics.

★4586★ **University of Alabama at Birmingham**
Civitan International Research Center/ Alabama UAP
PO Box 313, UAB Sta.
Birmingham, AL 35294
Phone: (205)934-8900
Fax: (205)975-6330
Dr. Craig Ramey, Codirector

Research Activities and Fields: Studies of stress in families with a handicapped child, parents' perception of temperament of handicapped and nonhandicapped infants, and developmentally disabled individuals and their families. Projects include studies of the memory function of children who are mentally retarded, the relationship between cognitive development and increasing auditory impairment of people with Down's syndrome, Head Start Program research, a Patient Outcomes Research Team, and the effects of therapeutic positioning on functional activities. **Formerly:** Chauncey Sparks Center for Developmental and Learning Disorders; Sparks Center (1991).

University of California, San Francisco
Brain-Behavior Research Center
See: Entry 8487

★4587★ **University of Connecticut**
Division of Child and Family Studies
School of Medicine, MC 6222
309 Farmington Ave.
Ste.A 200
Farmington, CT 06030
Phone: (203)679-4632
Fax: (203)679-4404
Mary Beth Bruder, Ph.D., Dir.

Research Activities and Fields: Developmental disabilities, physical handicaps, family adjustment, psychosocial developmental needs mainly for children who are disabled, and early intervention for Hispanic handicapped infants and their families. Establishes research and training programs in early intervention for children with disabilities and their families, trains early intervention researchers and personnel, and develops comprehensive and integrated service delivery systems that are family and community centered. **Publications:** PRTC Newsletter, PRTC Monographs; PRTC Workbooks. **Formerly:** Research and Training Center for Pediatric Rehabilitation; Pediatric Research and Training Center.

★4588★ **University of Illinois at Chicago**
Center for Handicapped Children
840 S. Wood St.
Chicago, IL 60612
Phone: (312)996-7202
Marylou Gorski, Coord. of Clinical Services

Research Activities and Fields: Neurologically handicapped children and those with inborn metabolic or endocrine disorders, including interdepartmental studies on growth and development, and maternal phenylketonuria (PKU). Clinical activities include developmental/ medical diagnostic assessments of children with developmental disabilities and operation of a genetic/metabolic clinic with a state PKU center.

University of Kansas
Bureau of Child Research
See: Entry 4329

★4589★ **University of Kansas**
Institute for Research in Learning Disabilities
3061 Dole Center
Lawrence, KS 66045
Phone: (913)864-4780
Fax: (913)864-4149
Donald D. Deshler, Dir.

Research Activities and Fields: Identification of learning disabilities in adolescents and young adults in school, employment, group homes, and juvenile justice and military institutions. Constructs interventions to lessen, remediate, or compensate for the effects of learning disabilities on the life performances of such individuals. **Publications:** *Strategram; Stratenotes;* and teachers manuals for learning strategies.

★4590★ **University of Kansas**
Research and Training Center on Independent Living
BCR-4088 Dole
Lawrence, KS 66045-2930
Phone: (913)864-4095
Fax: (913)864-5063
Dr. J. Buddy, Dir.

Research Activities and Fields: Development of products and procedures to promote independent living for the disabled community. Studies include development of service delivery systems, skill training methods, and techniques to improve human services and community support for people with disabilities. Additional interests include consumer involvement among disabled citizens, promotion of barrier-free access, teaching consumers how to train and manage personal attendants, assessment and training procedures for leaders of self-help groups, community-based information and referral systems, independent living center (ILC) program evaluations, guidelines for reporting and writing about disabled persons, and ILC fundraising techniques. **Publications:** *Independent Living Forum* (newsletter).

★4591★ **University of Kentucky**
Human Development Institute
114 Mideral Industries Bldg.
Lexington, KY 40506
Phone: (606)257-1714
Dr. M.C. Martinson, Dir.

Research Activities and Fields: People with handicaps or developmental disabilities, human development, developmental language, infant intervention, and interagency services. **Formerly:** Human Development Program (1986).

★4592★ **University of Louisville**
Child Evaluation Center
224 E. Broadway, Ste. 500
Louisville, KY 40202
Phone: (502)852-5331
Fax: (502)852-0955
Bernard Weisskopf, M.D., Dir.

Research Activities and Fields: Developmentally disabled and handicapped children in Kentucky. Clinical research is conducted in support of the following clinical, evaluative, and consultative service programs: diagnosis and evaluation, learning disorders, genetics and dysmorphology, genetics testing, education and counseling, genetics laboratory, community clinics and outreach, hyperactive child treatment, infant therapy, behavior modification, diagnostic teaching, pastoral counseling, and cytogenetics laboratory.

★4593★ **University of Maryland**
Institute for Study of Exceptional Children and Youth
College of Education
Dept. of Special Education
College Park, MD 20742
Phone: (301)405-6515
Fax: (301)314-9158
Dr. Philip J. Burke, Dir.

Research Activities and Fields: Policy studies, consumer involvement and evaluation, leadership development, and interdisciplinary studies as they relate to handicapped children, students with disabilities, and youth. Sample projects include leadership training program in policy, school restructuring, research concerning use of technology in special education, urban special education, and international disability policy.

★4594★ **University of Massachusetts Boston**
Center for the Study of Social Development and Education
100 Morissey Blvd.
Boston, MA 02125-3393
Phone: (617)287-7250
Fax: (617)287-7249
Gary N. Siperstein, Ph.D., Dir.

Research Activities and Fields: Children with disabilities, emphasizing social relationships, attitudes of children and adults toward individuals with disabilities, curriculum development in special education, and health care services for the disabled. **Formerly:** Center for the Study of Social Acceptance.

University of Miami
Mailman Center for Child Development
See: Entry 3364

★4595★ University of Mississippi
Research and Training Center for the Handicapped
304 Old Chemistry Bldg.
University, MS 38677
Phone: (601)232-5806
Dr. James W. Mann, Dir.

Research Activities and Fields: Physical and mental handicaps, including blindness, deafness, muteness, mental disease, and developmental disabilities. Conducts statewide surveys. **Publications:** Monographs; also publishes conference proceedings and reviews of literature on the handicapped.

★4596★ University of Montana
Montana University Affiliated Rural Institute on Disability
52 N. Corbin Hall
Missoula, MT 59812
Phone: (406)243-5467
Free: 800-732-0323
Fax: (406)243-2349
R. Timm Vogelsburg, Dir.

Research Activities and Fields: Human resources and technical services for rural Americans with disabilities. Studies encompass the areas of clinical psychology, rehabilitation psychology, rehabilitation counseling, physical therapy, occupational therapy, communication sciences and disorders, recreation therapy, special education, social work, guidance and counseling, physical medicine and rehabilitation (psychiatry), mechanical and rehabilitation engineering, business management, sociology, and interpersonal communication. **Publications:** *The Rural Exchange* (newsletter); Research Reports. **E-mail Address:** rtvogels@lewis.umt.edu. **Formerly:** Institute for Human Resources in rural America (1990).

University of Montana
Research and Training Center on Rural Rehabilitation
See: Entry 12761

★4597★ University of South Dakota
Interdisciplinary Center for Disabilities
414 E. Clark St.
Vermillion, SD 57069-2390
Phone: (605)677-5311
Free: 800-658-3080
Fax: (605)677-6274
Judy Struck, Act.Dir.

Research Activities and Fields: Children with special health care and related service needs. Works to enhance the lives of children and adults with disabilities and the lives of their families. Conducts assessments, evaluations, and impact studies for regional, state, and community-based services and training programs.

★4598★ University of Virginia
Kluge Children's Rehabilitation Center and Research Institute
2270 Ivy Rd.
Charlottesville, VA 22903
Phone: (804)924-5161
Fax: (804)982-1727
Sharon L. Hostler, M.D., Med.Dir.

Research Activities and Fields: Problems of physically disabled children and adolescents, including studies on their educational and psychosocial adjustment in school and community. Performs clinical and technical research and development in the area of augmentative communication. Conducts studies of children with cerebral palsy and meningomyelocele, examining attachment behaviors, tasks of adolescence, and adult development. **Publications:** Annual Review. **Formerly:** Children's Rehabilitation Center (1987).

★4599★ University of Waterloo
Centre for Habilitation Education and Research (CHER)
BMH, Rm. 3105
Waterloo, ON, Canada N2L 3GI
Phone: (519)885-1211
Fax: (519)746-6776
Dr. Eric Roy, Dir.

Research Activities and Fields: Integration of individuals with disabilities into the community. Studies focus on development of assistive devices, understanding problems in motor control, and examination of recreational programs and educational and employment opportunities.

★4600★ University of Wisconsin—Madison
Trace Research and Development Center
Waisman Center, S-151
1500 Highland Ave.
Madison, WI 53705
Phone: (608)262-6966
Fax: (608)262-8848
Gregg Vanderheiden, Ph.D, Dir.

Research Activities and Fields: Computer access by disabled individuals and augmentative communication and control for speech impaired individuals; research directed toward individuals with language and physical disabilities caused by stroke, head trauma, cerebral palsy, multiple sclerosis, muscular dystrophy, and other disorders. **Publications:** Annual Report; *Trace Resourcebook* series, describing communication aids, environmental controls, and software and hardware modifications that have been developed for individuals with disabilities. **Formerly:** Cerebral Palsy Communication Group.

★4601★ Utah State University
Center for Persons with Disabilities
UMC 68
Logan, UT 84322-6800
Phone: (801)750-1981
Fax: (801)750-2044
Dr. Marvin G. Fifield, Dir.

Research Activities and Fields: Developmental disabilities including biomedical research, the use of incidental teaching to promote social skills, and assistive technologies, including videodiscs. **Publications:** Annual Report; *Exceptional News*; Parent Newsletter. **Formerly:** Exceptional Child Center; Developmental Center for Handicapped Persons.

★4602★ Utah State University
Early Intervention Research Institute (EIRI)
Logan, UT 84322-6580
Phone: (801)797-1172
Fax: (801)797-2019
Dr. Richard Roberts, Codirector

Research Activities and Fields: Efficacy and cost-effectiveness of early intervention in education for children with disabilities, and cultural awareness and competency. Also synthesizes past research and conducts prospective studies. Collaborates in research with service agencies and other institutions. **Publications:** Comprehensive list available on request.

Vanderbilt University
John F. Kennedy Center for Research on Human Development
See: Entry 4339

★4603★ Western Michigan University
Enabling Technology Center
3509 Sangren
Kalamazoo, MI 49008-5194
Phone: (616)387-4382
Fax: (616)387-5703
Christine M. Bahr, Ph.D., Dir.

Research Activities and Fields: Research and development of enabling technology for individuals with disabilities. **E-mail Address:** etc@wmich.edu.

★4604★ World Institute on Disability (WID)
510 16th St.
Oakland, CA 94612
Phone: (510)763-4100
Fax: (510)763-4109
Edward V. Roberts, Pres.

Research Activities and Fields: Policy issues affecting the disabled community, including personal assistance services, AIDS and disability, telecommunications, general disability policy, independent living, studies of attendant services, attitudes toward people with disabilities, leadership development, independent living program effectiveness, health insurance needs, and quality of life issues. **E-mail Address:** sbrownz@delphi.com.

State & Regional Organizations

Disabilities

Listed below are intermediary affiliates of the National Easter Seal Society, 230 W. Monroe St., Ste. 1800, Chicago, IL 60606-4802, (312) 726-6200, (312) 726-4258 (TDD).

Alabama

★4605★ Alabama Easter Seal Society
2125 E. South Blvd.
PO Box 20320
Montgomery, AL 36120-0320
Phone: (205)288-8382
Fax: (205)281-8862

Alaska

★4606★ Easter Seal Society of Alaska
2525 Blueberry Rd., Ste. 106
Anchorage, AK 99503
Phone: (907)277-7325
Fax: (907)272-7325

Arizona

★4607★ **Easter Seal Society of Arizona**
903 N. 2nd St.
Phoenix, AZ 85004
Phone: (602)252-6061
Fax: (602)252-6065

Arkansas

★4608★ **Arkansas Easter Seal Society**
3920 Woodland Heights Rd.
Little Rock, AR 72212-2495
Phone: (501)227-3600
Fax: (501)227-3601

California

★4609★ **Central California Easter Seal Society**
2569 W. Shaw Ae., Ste. 104
Fresno, CA 93711
Phone: (209)252-5602
Fax: (209)252-5159

★4610★ **Easter Seal Society of the Bay Area**
2757 Telegraph Ave.
Oakland, CA 94612
Phone: (510)835-2702
Fax: (510)444-2470

★4611★ **Easter Seal Society of the Inland Counties**
241 E. 9th St.
San Bernardino, CA 92410
Phone: (908)888-4125
Fax: (908)884-5741

★4612★ **Easter Seal Society of Los Angeles and Orange Counties**
1801 E. Edinger Ave., Ste. 190
Santa Ana, CA 92705-4734
Phone: (714)834-1111
Fax: (714)834-1128

★4613★ **Easter Seal Society of the Monterey Bay Region**
9010 Soquel Dr., Ste. 1
Aptos, CA 95003
Phone: (408)684-2166
Fax: (408)684-1018

★4614★ **Easter Seal Society for the Redwood Coast**
555 Northgate Dr.
San Rafael, CA 94903
Phone: (415)472-3170
Fax: (415)472-3219

★4615★ **Easter Seal Society of San Diego County**
9370 Sky Park Ct., Ste. 190
San Diego, CA 92123
Phone: (619)541-0991
Fax: (619)541-7823

★4616★ **Easter Seal Society of Superior California**
3205 Hurley Way
PO Box 254868
Sacramento, CA 95864
Phone: (916)485-6711
Fax: (916)485-2653

★4617★ **Tri-Counties Easter Seal Society**
10730 Henderson Rd.
Ventura, CA 93004
Phone: (805)647-1141
Fax: (805)647-1148

Colorado

★4618★ **Colorado Easter Seal Society**
5755 W. Alameda Ave.
Lakewood, CO 80226
Phone: (303)233-1666
Fax: (303)233-1028

Connecticut

★4619★ **Easter Seal Society of Connecticut**
147 Jones St.
PO Box 100
Hebron, CT 06248-0100
Phone: (203)228-9438
Fax: (203)228-9670

Delaware

★4620★ **Easter Seal Society of Del-Mar**
Corporate Circle
New Castle, DE 19720
Phone: (302)324-4444
Fax: (302)324-4441

District of Columbia

★4621★ **District of Columbia Easter Seal Society for Disabled Children and Adults**
The Children's Center
2800 13th St. NW
Washington, DC 20009
Phone: (202)232-2342
Fax: (202)462-7379

Florida

★4622★ **Easter Seal Society of Broward County**
6951 W. Sunrise Blvd.
Plantation, FL 33313
Phone: (305)792-8772
Fax: (305)791-8275

★4623★ **Easter Seal Society of Dade County**
1475 NW 14th Ave.
Miami, FL 33125
Phone: (305)325-0470
Fax: (305)325-0578

★4624★ **Easter Seal Society of East Central Florida**
3661 S. Babcock St.
Melbourne, FL 32901-8221
Phone: (407)723-4474
Fax: (407)676-3843

★4625★ **Easter Seal Society of North Florida**
910 Myers Park Dr.
Tallahassee, FL 32301
Phone: (904)222-4465
Fax: (904)222-5909

★4626★ **Easter Seal Society of Southwest Florida**
350 Braden Ave.
Sarasota, FL 34243
Phone: (813)355-7637
Fax: (813)351-4997

★4627★ **Easter Seal Society of Volusia and Flagler Counties**
Ellen Black Easter Seal Center
1219 Dunn Ave.
PO Box 9117
Daytona Beach, FL 32115
Phone: (904)255-4568
Fax: (904)258-7677

★4628★ **Florida Easter Seal Society**
1010 Executive Center Dr., Ste. 231
Orlando, FL 32803
Phone: (407)896-7881
Fax: (407)896-8422

Georgia

★4629★ **Easter Seal Society of East Georgia**
1241 Reynolds St.
PO Box 2441
Augusta, GA 30903
Phone: (706)722-3175
Fax: (706)722-2688

★4630★ **Easter Seal Society of North Georgia**
3035 Druid Hills Rd.
Atlanta, GA 30329
Phone: (404)633-9609
Fax: (404)633-2740

★4631★ **Middle Georgia Easter Seal Society**
602 Kellam Rd.
PO Box 847
Dublin, GA 31040
Phone: (912)275-8850
Fax: (912)275-8852

★4632★ **Southwest Georgia Easter Seal Society**
1906 Palmyra Rd.
Albany, GA 31701
Phone: (912)439-7061
Fax: (912)439-0119

Hawaii

★4633★ **Easter Seal Society of Hawaii**
710 Green St.
Honolulu, HI 96813
Phone: (808)536-1015
Fax: (808)536-3765

Illinois

★4634★ Illinois Easter Seal Society
2715 S. 4th St.
PO Box 1767
Springfield, IL 62705
Phone: (217)525-0398
Fax: (217)525-0442

Indiana

★4635★ Central Indiana Easter Seal Society
Crossroads Rehabilitation Center
4740 Kingsway Dr.
Indianapolis, IN 46205
Phone: (317)466-1000
Fax: (317)466-2000

★4636★ Indiana Easter Seal Society
8425 Keystone Crossing, Ste. 190
Indianapolis, IN 46240
Phone: (317)254-8382
Fax: (317)254-8357

★4637★ Northeast Indiana Easter Seal Society
2826 S. Calhoun St.
Ft. Wayne, IN 46807
Phone: (219)744-6145
Fax: (219)744-0441

Iowa

★4638★ Easter Seal Society of Iowa
401 NE 66th Ave.
PO Box 4002, Highland Park Sta.
Des Moines, IA 50333
Phone: (515)289-1933
Fax: (515)289-1281

Kansas

★4639★ Goodwill Industries / Easter Seal Society of Kansas
3636 N. Oliver
PO Box 8169
Wichita, KS 67208
Phone: (316)744-9291
Fax: (316)744-1428

Kentucky

★4640★ Kentucky Easter Seal Society
233 E. Broadway
Louisville, KY 40202
Phone: (502)584-9781
Fax: (502)589-2409

Louisiana

★4641★ Easter Seal Society of Louisiana
PO Box 8425
Metairie, LA 70011
Phone: (504)455-5533
Fax: (504)455-5622

Maine

★4642★ Easter Seal Society of Maine
84 Front St.
PO Box 518
Bath, ME 04530
Phone: (207)443-3341
Fax: (207)443-1070

Massachusetts

★4643★ Massachusetts Easter Seal Society
Denholm Bldg.
484 Main St.
Worcester, MA 01608
Phone: (508)757-2756
Fax: (508)831-9768

Michigan

★4644★ Easter Seal Society of Michigan
4065 Saladin Dr. SE
Grand Rapids, MI 49546
Phone: (616)942-2081
Fax: (616)942-5932

★4645★ Easter Seal Society of Southeastern Michigan
1105 N. Telegraph Rd.
Waterford, MI 48328
Phone: (810)338-9626
Fax: (810)338-2936

Minnesota

★4646★ Goodwill Industries / Easter Seal Society of Minnesota
2543 Como Ave.
St. Paul, MN 55108
Phone: (612)646-2591
Fax: (612)649-0302

Mississippi

★4647★ Mississippi Easter Seal Society
3226 N. State
PO Box 4958
Jackson, MS 39296-4958
Phone: (601)982-7051
Fax: (601)982-1951

Missouri

★4648★ Missouri Easter Seal Society
5025 N. Northrup Ave., Ste. 110
St. Louis, MO 63110
Phone: (314)664-5025
Fax: (314)664-4838

Montana

★4649★ Northern Rocky Mountain Easter Seal Society
4400 Central Ave.
Great Falls, MT 59405-1695
Phone: (406)761-3680
Fax: (406)761-5110

Nebraska

★4650★ Easter Seal Society of Nebraska
Bell Air Plaza
12100 W. Center Rd., Ste. 820
Omaha, NE 68144
Phone: (402)330-6660
Fax: (402)330-0707

Nevada

★4651★ Nevada Easter Seal Society
1455 E. Tropicana, Ste. 660
Las Vegas, NV 89119
Phone: (702)739-7771
Fax: (702)739-6362

New Hampshire

★4652★ Easter Seal Society of New Hampshire
555 Auburn St.
Manchester, NH 03103
Phone: (603)623-8863
Fax: (603)625-1148

New Jersey

★4653★ Easter Seal Society of New Jersey
1 Kimberly Rd.
PO Box 1076
East Brunswick, NJ 08816-1076
Phone: (908)257-6662
Fax: (908)257-7373

New Mexico

★4654★ Easter Seal Society of New Mexico
2819 Richmond Dr. NE
Albuquerque, NM 87107
Phone: (505)888-3811
Fax: (505)883-1079

New York

★4655★ New York Easter Seal Society
845 Central Ave.
Albany, NY 12206
Phone: (518)438-8785
Fax: (518)489-4893

North Carolina

★4656★ Easter Seal Society of North Carolina
2315 Myron Dr.
Raleigh, NC 27607
Phone: (919)783-8898
Fax: (919)782-5486

North Dakota

★4657★ Easter Seal Society of North Dakota
211 Collins Ave.
PO Box 1206
Mandan, ND 58554
Phone: (701)663-6828
Fax: (701)663-6859

Ohio

★4658★ Easter Seal Society of Central Ohio
565 Children's Dr. W
PO Box 7166
Columbus, OH 43232-0462
Phone: (614)228-5523
Fax: (614)228-8249

★4659★ Easter Seal Society of Mahoning, Trumbull and Columbiana Counties
299 Edwards St.
Youngstown, OH 44502
Phone: (216)743-1168

★4660★ Easter Seal Society of Northeast Ohio
1929-A E. Royalton Rd.
Broadview Heights, OH 44147
Phone: (216)838-0990
Fax: (216)838-8440

★4661★ Easter Seal Society of Northwestern Ohio
1905 N. Ridge Rd.
Lorain, OH 44055
Phone: (216)277-7337
Fax: (216)277-7339

★4662★ Easter Seal Society of Southwestern Ohio
Easter Seal Center
231 Clark Rd.
Cincinnati, OH 45215-5590
Phone: (513)821-9890
Fax: (513)821-9895

★4663★ Easter Seal Society of West Central Ohio
320 N. Kenilworth Ave.
Lima, OH 45805
Phone: (419)222-7047
Fax: (419)222-9303

Oklahoma

★4664★ Oklahoma Easter Seal Society
2100 NW 63rd St.
Oklahoma City, OK 73116
Phone: (405)848-7603
Fax: (405)842-9704

Oregon

★4665★ Easter Seal Society of Oregon
5757 SW Macadam Ave.
Portland, OR 97201
Phone: (503)228-5108
Fax: (503)228-1352

Pennsylvania

★4666★ Easter Seal Society of Philadelphia, Bucks, Chester, Delaware and Montgomery Counties
3975 Conshohocken Ave.
Philadelphia, PA 19131-5848
Phone: (215)879-1000
Fax: (215)879-8424

★4667★ Pennsylvania Easter Seal Society
1500 Fulling Mill Rd.
Middletown, PA 17057-3116
Phone: (717)939-7801
Fax: (717)986-8324

Puerto Rico

★4668★ Easter Seal Society of Puerto Rico
GPO Box 325
San Juan, PR 00936-0325
Phone: (809)767-6710
Fax: (809)758-0950

Rhode Island

★4669★ Easter Seal Society of Rhode Island
667 Waterman Ave.
East Providence, RI 02914
Phone: (401)438-9500
Fax: (401)438-3760

South Carolina

★4670★ Life Abilities—Easter Seal Society of South Carolina
3020 Farrow Rd.
Columbia, SC 29203
Phone: (803)256-0735
Fax: (803)765-9765

South Dakota

★4671★ Easter Seal Society of South Dakota
1351 N. Harrison Ave.
Pierre, SD 57501-2373
Phone: (605)224-5879
Fax: (605)224-1033

Tennessee

★4672★ Easter Seal Society of Tennessee
1701 West End Ave., Ste. 300
Nashville, TN 37203
Phone: (615)251-0070
Fax: (615)251-0068

Texas

★4673★ Capital Area Easter Seal Society
919 W. 28 ½ St.
Austin, TX 78705
Phone: (512)478-2581
Fax: (512)476-1638

★4674★ Easter Seal Society for Children
Dallas Center
5701 Maple Ave.
Dallas, TX 75235
Phone: (214)358-5261
Fax: (214)357-6552

★4675★ Easter Seal Society for Children and Adults of Tarrant County
617 7th Ave.
Ft. Worth, TX 76104-2799
Phone: (817)336-8693
Fax: (817)332-5154

★4676★ Easter Seal Society of the Gulf Coast
10700 Northwest Fwy., Ste. 105
Houston, TX 77092
Phone: (713)957-2195
Fax: (713)957-0090

★4677★ Easter Seal Society of the Permian Basin
620 N. Alleghany
Odessa, TX 79761
Phone: (915)332-8244
Fax: (915)580-7428

★4678★ Easter Seal Society of the Rio Grande Valley
1217 Houston St.
PO Box 489
McAllen, TX 78505-0489
Phone: (210)631-9171
Fax: (210)631-9176

★4679★ Texarkana Easter Seal Society
1315 Walnut
PO Box 147
Texarkana, TX 75501
Phone: (903)794-2705
Fax: (903)793-1203

Utah

★4680★ Easter Seal Society of Utah
638 Wilmington Ave.
Salt Lake City, UT 84106
Phone: (801)486-3778
Fax: (801)531-0575

Virginia

★4681★ Easter Seal Society of Virginia
4841 Williamson Rd.
PO Box 5496
Roanoke, VA 24012
Phone: (703)362-1656
Fax: (703)563-8928

Washington

★4682★ Easter Seal Society of Washington
521 2nd Ave. W.
Seattle, WA 98119
Phone: (206)281-5700
Fax: (206)284-0938

Wisconsin

★ **4683 ★ Easter Seal Society of Wisconsin**
101 Nob Hill Rd., Ste. 301
Madison, WI 53713
Phone: (608)277-8288
Fax: (608)277-8333

Learning Disabilities

Listed below are state offices of the Learning Disabilities Association of America, 4156 Library Rd., Pittsburgh, PA 15234-1349, (412) 341-1515.

Alabama

★ **4684 ★ Learning Disabilities Association of Alabama**
PO Box 11588
Montgomery, AL 36111
Phone: (205)277-9151

Alaska

★ **4685 ★ Learning Disabilities Association of Alaska**
19400 Verdant Cir.
Eagle River, AK 99577
Phone: (907)694-7907

Arizona

★ **4686 ★ Learning Disabilities Association of Arizona**
PO Box 30606
Phoenix, AZ 85046
Phone: (602)495-1175
Fax: (602)495-1176

Arkansas

★ **4687 ★ Learning Disabilities Association of Arkansas**
PO Box 7316
Little Rock, AR 72217
Phone: (501)666-8777

California

★ **4688 ★ Learning Disabilities Association of California**
655 Lewelling Blvd., Ste. 355
San Leandro, CA 94579
Phone: (415)343-1411
Fax: (415)343-1854

Colorado

★ **4689 ★ Learning Disabilities Association of Colorado**
1045 Lincoln St., Ste. 106
Denver, CO 80203
Phone: (303)894-0992

Connecticut

★ **4690 ★ Learning Disabilities Association of Connecticut**
100 Constitution Plaza, Ste. 710
Hartford, CT 06103
Phone: (203)560-1711

District of Columbia

★ **4691 ★ Learning Disabilities Association of the District of Columbia**
PO Box 6350
Washington, DC 20015
Phone: (202)667-9140

Florida

★ **4692 ★ Learning Disabilities Association of Florida**
331 E. Henry St.
Punta Gorda, FL 33950
Phone: (813)637-8957

Georgia

★ **4693 ★ Learning Disabilities Association of Georgia**
PO Box 965505
Marietta, GA 30066
Phone: (404)514-8088

Hawaii

★ **4694 ★ Learning Disabilities Association of Hawaii**
200 N. Vineyard Blvd., Ste. 310
Honolulu, HI 96817
Phone: (808)536-9684
Fax: (808)537-6780

Idaho

★ **4695 ★ Learning Disabilities Association of Idaho**
12160 N. Forrest Rd.
Hayden, ID 83835
Phone: (208)762-3170

Illinois

★ **4696 ★ Learning Disabilities Association of Illinois**
10101 S. Roberts Rd., Ste. 205
Palos Hills, IL 60465
Phone: (708)430-7532

Indiana

★ **4697 ★ Learning Disabilities Association of Indiana**
PO Box 20584
Indianapolis, IN 46220
Phone: (317)898-5751

Iowa

★ **4698 ★ Learning Disabilities Association of Iowa**
PO Box 665
Indianola, IA 50125
Phone: (515)280-8558

Kansas

★ **4699 ★ Learning Disabilities Association of Kansas**
PO Box 4424
Topeka, KS 66604
Phone: (913)272-0033

Kentucky

★ **4700 ★ Learning Disabilities Association of Kentucky**
2210 Goldsmith Ln., No. 104
Louisville, KY 40218
Phone: (502)473-1256
Fax: (502)459-9287

Louisiana

★ **4701 ★ Learning Disabilities Association of Louisiana**
Teacher Ed. Ctr., Rm. 105-A
Northwestern State Univ.
Natchitoches, LA 71497
Phone: (318)357-5191
Fax: (318)357-6275

Maine

★ **4702 ★ Learning Disabilities Association of Maine**
2E Mechanic St.
PO Box 385
Gardiner, ME 04345
Phone: (207)582-2866
Fax: (207)437-2837

Maryland

★ **4703 ★ Learning Disabilities Association of Maryland**
76 Cranbrook Rd., Ste. 300
Cockeysville, MD 21030
Phone: (410)265-8188
Fax: (410)265-5739

Massachusetts

★ **4704 ★ Learning Disabilities Association of Massachusetts**
1275 Main St.
Waltham, MA 02154
Phone: (617)891-5009

Michigan

★4705★ **Learning Disabilities Association**
of Michigan
200 Museum Dr., Ste. 101
Lansing, MI 48933
Phone: (517)485-8160
Fax: (517)485-8462

Minnesota

★4706★ **Learning Disabilities Association**
of Minnesota
400 Selby Ave., Ste. D
St. Paul, MN 55102
Phone: (612)222-2696
Free: 800-488-4395

Mississippi

★4707★ **Learning Disabilities Association**
of Mississippi
PO Box 3691
Brookhaven, MS 39601
Phone: (601)833-6084
Fax: (601)835-0290

Missouri

★4708★ **Learning Disabilities Association**
of Missouri
1942 E. Meadowmere, No. 104
PO Box 3303
Springfield, MO 65808
Phone: (417)864-5110
Fax: (417)864-7290

Montana

★4709★ **Learning Disabilities Association**
of Montana
4026 Pine Cove Rd.
Billings, MT 59106
Phone: (406)656-7138

Nebraska

★4710★ **Learning Disabilities Association**
of Nebraska
PO Box 6464
Omaha, NE 68106
Phone: (402)571-7771
Fax: (402)572-8801

New Hampshire

★4711★ **Learning Disabilities Association**
of New Hampshire
PO Box 7118
Concord, NH 03301-7118
Phone: (603)228-0259
Free: 800-794-9700
Fax: (603)228-5278

New Jersey

★4712★ **Learning Disabilities Association**
of New Jersey
PO Box 187
Oceanport, NJ 07757
Phone: (908)571-1221

New Mexico

★4713★ **Learning Disabilities Association**
of New Mexico
6301 Menaul NE, Ste. 556
Albuquerque, NM 87110
Phone: (505)821-2545

New York

★4714★ **Learning Disabilities Association**
of New York
90 S. Swan St.
Albany, NY 12210
Phone: (518)436-4633

North Carolina

★4715★ **Learning Disabilities Association**
of North Carolina
Box 3542
Chapel Hill, NC 27515
Phone: (919)493-5362

North Dakota

★4716★ **Learning Disabilities Association**
of North Dakota
PO Box 2339
Bismarck, ND 58502
Phone: (701)247-2667

Ohio

★4717★ **Learning Disabilities Association**
of Ohio
1380 Pearl Rd., Ste. 203
Brunswick, OH 44212
Phone: (216)273-7388
Free: 800-543-7532
Fax: (216)225-0228

Oklahoma

★4718★ **Learning Disabilities Association**
of Oklahoma
Box 2315
Stillwater, OK 74076
Phone: (405)743-1366

Pennsylvania

★4719★ **Learning Disabilities Association**
of Pennsylvania
Toomey Bldg.
Eagle, Box 208
Uwchland, PA 19480
Phone: (610)458-8193

Puerto Rico

★4720★ **Learning Disabilities Association**
of Puerto Rico
76 Kings Ct., Apt. 701
Santurce, PR 00911
Phone: (809)728-5166

Rhode Island

★4721★ **Learning Disabilities Association**
of Rhode Island
PO Box 6685
Providence, RI 02940
Phone: (401)232-3822

South Carolina

★4722★ **Learning Disabilities Association**
of South Carolina
PO Box 12881
Charleston, SC 29422
Phone: (803)244-2579

Tennessee

★4723★ **Learning Disabilities Association**
of Tennessee
PO Box 381107
Germantown, TN 38183
Phone: (901)748-1323

Texas

★4724★ **Learning Disabilities Association**
of Texas
1011 W. 31st St.
Austin, TX 78705
Phone: (512)458-8234
Fax: (512)458-3826

Utah

★4725★ **Learning Disabilities Association**
of Utah
PO Box 112
Salt Lake City, UT 84110
Phone: (801)355-2881
Fax: (801)467-2148

Vermont

★4726★ **Learning Disabilities Association**
of Vermont
PO Box 1041
Manchester Center, VT 05255
Phone: (802)362-3127

Virginia

★4727★ **Learning Disabilities Association**
of Virginia
PO Box 573
Springfield, VA 22150
Phone: (703)451-5007

Washington

★ 4728 ★ **Learning Disabilities Association
of Washington**
7819 159th Pl., NE
Redmond, WA 98052
Phone: (206)882-0820
Free: 800-536-2343
Fax: (206)861-4642

West Virginia

★ 4729 ★ **Learning Disabilities Association
of West Virginia**
PO Box 602
Ansted, WV 25812
Phone: (304)658-4910

Wisconsin

★ 4730 ★ **Learning Disabilities Association
of Wisconsin**
15738 W. National Ave.
New Berlin, WI 53151
Phone: (414)821-0855

Chapter 22
Emergency Medicine

National & International Organizations

★4731★ AirLifeLine (ALL)
6133 Freeport Blvd.
Sacramento, CA 95822
Phone: (916)429-2500
Fax: (916)429-2166
Don Howton, Exec.Dir.

Founded: 1979. **Members:** 800. **Description:** Voluntary association of pilots who donate their time, skills, fuel, and aircraft to fly medical missions. Provides immediate transport for medical cargo such as whole blood, platelets, mother's milk, eye corneas, human organs for transplantation, and tissue samples or for financially needy patients who require specialized treatment at medical facilities far from their homes. **Publications:** *AirLifeLine--Newsletter*, quarterly. Newsletter. Includes Victory Roll, a list of volunteer pilots who have flown medical missions. *Price:* Free. • Membership Directory, annual. • *Skylines*, bimonthly. Newsletter. For volunteer pilots. Provides information on the program and on aviation in general.

★4732★ American Ambulance Association (AAA)
3800 Auburn Blvd., Ste. C
Sacramento, CA 95821
Phone: (916)483-3827
Fax: (916)482-5473
David Nevins, Exec.VP

Founded: 1977. **Members:** 640. **Description:** Private suppliers of ambulance service. Purposes are: to aid in developing private enterprise pre-hospital emergency medical treatment and medical transportation services as a viable cost-effective alternative to publicly-operated services; to promote improved patient care; to develop efficient medical transportation at a reasonable cost; to improve personnel and equipment standards; to work with organizations offering medical transportation; to encourage high standards of ethics and conduct. Acts as an information clearinghouse; informs members of developments in the industry. Offers advice on federal statutes and regulations related to the medical transportation industry, such as insurance and antitrust regulations. Holds four re-

gional seminars per year on topics such as training requirements, insurance systems, medicare reimbursement, and local, state, and federal legislation and regulations. Conducts quarterly emergency medical services management seminar. **Publications:** *Ambulance Industry: The Journal of the American Ambulance Association*, bimonthly. Includes book reviews and legislative reports. *Price:* Free to members; $25 for nonmembers. • *American Ambulance Association--Membership Directory*, annual. Membership Directory. *Price:* Available to members only. **Formerly:** (1978) Ambulance and Medical Service Association of America.

★4733★ American Board of Emergency Medicine (ABEM)
3000 Coolidge Rd.
East Lansing, MI 48823-6319
Phone: (517)332-4800
Fax: (517)332-2234
Benson S. Munger, Ph.D., Exec.Dir.

Founded: 1976. **Description:** Seeks to: improve the quality of emergency medical care; establish and maintain high standards of excellence in the specialty of emergency medicine; improve medical education and facilities for training emergency physicians; evaluate specialists in emergency medicine applying for certification and recertification; serve the public, physicians, hospitals, and medical schools by furnishing lists of those diplomats certified in emergency medicine. **Publications:** *ABEM Policies and Procedures*, annual. Booklet. • *ABEMemo*, semiannual. Newsletter. For diplomates and organizations associated with ABEM.

★4734★ American College of Emergency Physicians (ACEP)
PO Box 619911
Dallas, TX 75261-9911
Phone: (214)550-0911
Fax: (214)580-2816
Dr. Colin C. Rorrie, Jr., Exec.Dir.

Founded: 1968. **Members:** 17,100. **State Groups:** 53. **Description:** Physicians who devote a significant portion of their professional time to emergency medicine. Aim is to provide a unifying direction of purpose in the field, which is a new medical specialty. Encourages training of emergency physicians, with the aim of im-

proving emergency department care in hospitals; conducts continuing education programs for emergency physicians and other healthcare personnel. Provides information regarding the practice of emergency medicine. Compiles statistics. **Publications:** *ACEP News*, monthly. Newsletter. Discusses socioeconomic issues affecting emergency medicine. *Price:* Included in membership dues; $20/year for nonmembers. • *Annals of Emergency Medicine*, monthly. Journal. Covers emergency medicine and emergency health services. Includes abstracts of emergency medical literature, book reviews, and calendar of events. *Price:* Included in membership dues. • *Effective Emergency Department Management*. • *Foresight*, quarterly. Newsletter. Covers emergency medicine risk management. • *Physicians Evaluation and Education Review*. Also publishes a homestudy series, and reference manuals on diagnosis and procedure coding, quality assurance, independent contractor status, EMS medical direction, working with managed care plans, patient transfer, risk management, developing and negotiating contracts, and advanced pediatric life support.

American College of Osteopathic Emergency Physicians (ACOEP)
See: Entry 9974

American Osteopathic Board of Emergency Medicine (AOBEM)
See: Entry 9983

★4735★ American Trauma Society (ATS)
8903 Presidential Pky., Ste. 512
Upper Marlboro, MD 20772
Phone: (301)420-4189
Free: 800-556-7890
Fax: (301)420-0617
Harry Teter, Exec.Dir.

Founded: 1968. **Members:** 3,000. **State Groups:** 22. **Description:** Physicians, nurses, EMT personnel, other healthcare professionals, institutions, corporations, and interested individuals. Seeks to: prevent trauma situations; improve trauma care through professional and paraprofessional education; educate the public through campaigns and dissemination of information. **Publications:** *Promotional Media Resource Catalog*. Catalog. • *Traumagram News-*

letter, 4/year. Newsletter. Includes prevention activities, news on the annual meeting, and legislative and research updates. *Price:* Included in membership dues for institutions. • *Trauma-View Newsletter*. Newsletter. *Price:* Included in membership dues.

★4736★ The Angel Planes (TAP)
2700 Chandler Ave., No. A8
Las Vegas, NV 89120-4032
Phone: (702)261-0494
Fax: (702)261-0497
Ann Mishoulam, Pres.

Founded: 1985. **Members:** 500. **Description:** Pilots who fly blood to central blood banks before it deteriorates; make emergency flights to rural hospitals to deliver special types of blood; pick up blood from mobile blood drives so that the blood can be prepared for transfusion within six hours of its donation; transport critical care (but not trauma) patients; transport donated organs. Conducts children's programs. Conducts charitable programs. **Publications:** *Plane Talk*, quarterly. Newsletter. Includes safety and pilot news, flight updates, fundraising news. *Price:* Free.

★4737★ Association of Air Medical Services (AAMS)
35 S. Raymond Ave., Ste. 205
Pasadena, CA 91105
Phone: (818)793-1232
Fax: (818)793-1039
Nina Merrill, Exec.Dir.

Founded: 1980. **Members:** 300. **Description:** Air medical transport providers; manufacturers and distributors air medical transport equipment. Objective is to provide quality medical care during rapid air transport. Seeks to develop standards for aircraft configuration, minimum professional and educational requirements for personnel on board, medical and communications equipment, and operations. **Publications:** *Air Medical Journal*, monthly. Magazine. Published in conjunction with the National Flight Nurses Association, National Flight Paramedics Association, and National EMS Pilots Association. *Price:* Included in membership dues. • Membership Directory, annual. **Formerly:** (1988) American Society of Hospital-Based Emergency Air Medical Services.

★4738★ Doctors for Disaster Preparedness (DDP)
2509 N. Campbell
Box 272
Tucson, AZ 85719
Phone: (602)325-2680
Fax: (602)326-3529
Howard Maccabee, M.D., Pres.

Founded: 1982. **Members:** 200. **Description:** Doctors, health professionals, and medical students; interested individuals. Prepares physicians, health professionals and personnel, and the public for medical response in the case of natural or human-caused disaster. Seeks to prevent human suffering and death resulting from any catastrophe. Believes that "there is no disaster so great - including nuclear war - that the medical profession is not obliged to care for the survivors." Promotes accurate risk assessment. Supports civil defense measures; maintains no

position on specific military or foreign policy measures, weapons systems, or arms control. Sponsors lectures for health professionals, government leaders, and the public concerning disaster preparedness. Compiles statistics; maintains speakers' bureau. **Publications:** *Civil Defense Perspectives*, bimonthly. Newsletter. *Price:* Included in membership dues. • *Doctors for Disaster Preparedness Newsletter*, bimonthly. Newsletter. *Price:* Included in membership fees. • Reprints. Consists of literature related to disaster preparedness.

★4739★ Emergency Medicine Foundation (EMF)
PO Box 619911
Dallas, TX 75261
Phone: (214)550-0911
Fax: (214)580-2816
William R. Metcalf, Ph.D., Dir. of Policy Div.

Founded: 1972. **Description:** Board of trustees is composed of representatives of American College of Emergency Physicians, Emergency Medicine Residents' Association, Emergency Nurses Association, Society for Academic Emergency Medicine (see separate entries). To promote and provide improved education and research in the field of emergency medicine in order to improve the availability and quality of emergency medical treatment. Conducts research programs.

★4740★ Emergency Medicine Research Society (EMRS)
Windsor House
223 Princes Rd.
Hartshill
Stoke-on-Trent, Staffs, England
Phone: 1782 716503
Fax: 1782 747179
M.V. Prescott, Exec. Officer

Founded: 1984. **Languages:** English. **Description:** Clinicians and researchers. Forum for individuals interested in the scientific treatment of the acutely ill. **Publications:** *Archives of Emergency Medicine*, quarterly.

★4741★ Emergency Medicine Residents' Association (EMRA)
1125 Executive Cir.
Irving, TX 75038-2522
Phone: (214)550-0911
Free: 800-798-1822
Jennifer L. Baskin, DO, Contact

Founded: 1974. **Members:** 3,400. **Description:** Physicians enrolled in emergency medicine residency training programs; medical students. Purposes are to: provide a unified voice for emergency medicine residents; encourage high standards in training and continuing education for emergency physicians; study socioeconomic aspects of emergency medical care; promote education of patients and the public. Encourages research to improve emergency medicine; promotes community, state, and national representation for emergency medicine in organized and academic medicine; and advocates establishment of autonomous departments within all hospitals and medical staff structures providing full-time emergency coverage by emergency Physicians. Provides information about new specialty developments. Addresses

topics such as writing from research data and preparing to take certification examinations. Sponsors educational programs; maintains placement service. Compiles statistics on graduate residents. **Publications:** *EM Resident*, bimonthly. Newsletter. Focuses on issues such as residency electives, utilization of emergency department services, and educational opportunities. *Price:* Included in membership dues. • *Emergency Medicine in Focus: A Handbook for Medical Students and Prospective Residents*. Handbook. • *EMRA Job Catalog*, annual. Catalog. • *Outpatient Guide to Antibiotics*.

Emergency Nurses Association (ENA)
See: Entry 9086

★4742★ Emergency Service Association (Berufsverband fur den Rettungsdienst)
Cappenberger Str. 78
44534 Lunen, Germany
Phone: 2306 61080
Fax: 2306 61764
Christiane Schraitle, Contact

Founded: 1979. **Members:** 3,000. **Description:** Promotes the advancement of emergency medical services in Germany.

★4743★ International Society of Disaster Medicine (ISDM)
(Societe Internationale de Medecine de Catastrophe — SIMC)
Case Postale 133
Jussy
CH-1254 Geneva, Switzerland
Phone: 22 7591312
Fax: 22 7590550
Dr. Marcel R. Dubouloz, Gen.Sec.

Founded: 1975. **Members:** 500. **Regional Groups:** 8. **Languages:** Arabic, English, French, Spanish. **Description:** Physicians in 42 countries who promote study and advancement in the field of disaster medicine. Conducts symposia and research programs; organizes scientific commissions. **Publications:** *Education and Training in Disaster Medicine*. • Proceedings, quarterly.

★4744★ International Society of Emergency Medical Services (ISEMS)
4200 Park Meadow Dr.
PO Box 10810
Chantilly, VA 22021-0810
Phone: (703)222-3456
Fax: (703)968-5151
Dr. William R. Gemma, Pres.

Founded: 1982. **Members:** 32. **Languages:** English. **Description:** Emergency medical care leaders representing 32 countries. Purposes are: to improve access to and availability of emergency medical care; to upgrade emergency medical services; to increase public awareness of how to use these services; to promote quality training programs for EMS allied personnel; to provide technical assistance to participating members. Promotes universal recognition of EMS as an essential part of the community health care system. Plans to operate centers to improve EMS services worldwide.

★4745★ Joint Review Committee on Educational Programs for the EMT-Paramedic (JRCEMT-P)
1701 W. Euless Blvd., Ste. 300
Euless, TX 76040
Phone: (817)283-2836
Fax: (817)354-8519
Philip A. VonDerHeydt, Exec. Officer

Founded: 1979. Description: Cooperates with the Committee on Allied Health Education and Accreditation to accredit emergency medical technician-paramedic training programs across the U.S. Establishes national education standards and programs for the EMT-paramedic. Compiles statistics. Publications: Chairmans Newsletter, semiannual. Newsletter.

★4746★ National Association of Emergency Medical Service Physicians (NAEMSP)
230 McKee Pl., Ste. 500
Pittsburgh, PA 15213
Phone: (412)578-3222
Free: 800-228-3677
Fax: (412)578-3241
Kathleen Stage-Kern, Exec.Dir.

Founded: 1983. Members: 1,480. Description: Medical directors responsible for emergency medical services (EMS) programs throughout the United States; other physicians and nonphysicians dedicated to out-of-hospital emergency care. (Most physicians within this organization are medically-legally responsible for the provision of out-of-hospital emergency care.) Strives to foster excellence and provide medical leadership so that all individuals and communities receive quality out-of-hospital emergency medical services. Works to develop guidelines and strategies to reduce and prevent discomfort, disability, and death in the community; define roles, responsiblities, authority, and accountability of EMS physicians; promote communication and cooperation among EMS professionals; define the unique body of medical knowledge of prehospital and disaster medicine; promote cost-effective programs and interventions that optimize patient outcomes; advocate or initiate public policy for optimal emergency medical care; encourage and support quality EMS research. Provides forums for definition and debate of EMS issues. Encourages and promotes career development, career longevity, and professional well-being of EMS professionals. Defines and promotes ethical principles in the delivery of out-of-hospital emergency care. Publications: EMS Medical Directors' Handbook. Handbook. • NAEMSP Newsletter, bimonthly. Newsletter. • Prehospital and Disaster Medicine, quarterly. Journal. • Prehospital Systems and Medical Oversight. Book. • Quality Management in Prehospital Care. Book. Also Known As: National Association of EMS Physicians.

★4747★ National Association of Emergency Medical Technicians (NAEMT)
102 W. Leake St.
Clinton, MS 39056
Phone: (601)924-7744
Free: 800-34-NAEMT
Fax: (601)924-7325
Barbara Sanders, Exec.Dir.

Founded: 1975. Members: 5,000. State Groups: 25. Description: Nationally registered or state certified emergency medical technicians (EMTs) and EMT-paramedics. Promotes the professional status of EMTs and national acceptance of a uniform standard of recognition for their skills; encourages constant upgrading of these skills and EMT qualifications and educational requirements; engages in scientific research related to the care and transportation of the sick and injured; supports the establishment of emergency medical services systems. Sponsors insurance, credit card and member loan programs. Maintains placement services. Publications: NAEMT News, monthly. Price: $40/year.

★4748★ National Association of First Responders (AAFAR)
5334 Armadillo Ave.
Orange Beach, AL 36561
Phone: (205)981-3383
Henry Weir, Jr., Pres.

Founded: 1984. Members: 864. National Groups: 6. Regional Groups: 6. State Groups: 23. Local Groups: 12. Description: Emergency medical responders who have had 40 hours of training. (EMRs, or first responders, arrive on the scene of a medical emergency and administer assistance prior to the arrival of paramedics or emergency medical technicians.) Provides a forum for exchange of ideas and medical information among EMRs. Offers a national certification program for first responders and educational and research programs. Maintains placement services and speakers' bureau. Publications: National EMR Responder, monthly. Newsletter. Price: Included in membership dues. Formerly: (1989) American Association of First Responders.

National Association of State EMS Directors (NASEMSD)
See: Entry 5589

★4749★ National Council of State Emergency Medical Services Training Coordinators (NCSEMSTC)
c/o Council of State Governments
3560 Iron Works Pike
Lexington, KY 40578-1910
Phone: (606)244-8000
Fax: (606)244-8001
Sandra Cabot, Staff Dir.

Founded: 1977. Members: 159. Description: Individuals employed by state-level emergency medical services agencies who are responsible for coordination or supervision of EMS training programs. Promotes the responsible movement of emergency medical technicians (EMTs) throughout the nation through standardization of policies related, but not limited to, curriculum, certification, recertification, revocation, and reci-

procity; seeks to further develop the public recognition and trust of the emergency medical technician as a health care professional. Publications: Membership List, annual. Membership Directory.

★4750★ National Emergency Medicine Association (NEMA)
306 W. Joppa Rd.
Towson, MD 21204
Phone: (410)494-0300
Free: 800-332-6362
Howard A. Farrington, Pres.

Founded: 1982. Members: 5,000. Description: Seeks to prevent trauma and improve emergency medical care nationwide. Concerned with: promoting lifestyles that reduce the likelihood of trauma; educating the public on how to help a trauma victim before emergency personnel arrive; ensuring that trained emergency personnel have the necessary resources to effectively do their jobs; promoting effective treatment and care of trauma victims at hospitals and trauma centers; ensuring the availability of proper services and facilities to the recovering trauma victim. Provides The Heart of the Matter, an educational radio program, to more than 250 radio stations nationwide. Maintains speakers' bureau; offers grants; provides direct-mail program focusing on heart disease prevention. Publications: A Guide to the Emergency Room. • Heart of the Matter. • Heartlines, quarterly. Newsletter. • How to Survive Trauma.

★4751★ National Flight Paramedics Association (NFPA)
35 S. Raymond Ave., Ste. 205
Pasadena, CA 91105
Phone: (818)405-9851
Fax: (818)793-1039
Jeff Farkas, Pres.

Founded: 1986. Members: 700. State Groups: 1. Description: Flight paramedics. Promotes education, professionalism, and communication within the emergency medical service community. Maintains Foundation of Aeromedical Research. Operates speakers' bureau; compiles statistics. Publications: Air Medical Journal and AirMed, monthly. Journal. Price: Included in membership dues. • Flight Paramedic News, quarterly. Newsletter. Price: Included in membership dues.

National Heart Council (NHC)
See: Entry 2864

★4752★ National Registry of Emergency Medical Technicians (NREMT)
PO Box 29233
Columbus, OH 43229
Phone: (614)888-4484
William E. Brown, Jr., Exec.Dir.

Founded: 1970. Description: Promotes the improved delivery of emergency medical services by: assisting in the development and evaluation of educational programs to train emergency medical technicians; establishing qualifications for eligibility to apply for registration; preparing and conducting examinations designed to assure the competency of emergency medical technicians and paramedics; establishing a system for biennial registration; establishing procedures for revocation of certificates of registration for cause; maintaining a directory of registered emergency medical technicians. **Publications:** Newsletter, quarterly. **Formerly:** (1973) Registry of Emergency Medical Technicians - Ambulance.

★ 4753 ★ Professional Aeromedical Transport Association (PATA)
28000 A-11 Airport Rd.
Punta Gorda, FL 33982
Phone: (813)575-7710
Free: 800-541-7517
Fax: (813)639-3945
Dana W. Carr, Exec.Dir.

Founded: 1986. **Members:** 200. **Description:** Firms that provide air ambulance service, primarily by means of fixed-wing aircraft; suppliers to the industry; individuals interested in the field. Goals are to standardize operations and services, improve patient care, and educate members and the public. Provides a network for locating providers of professional aeromedical services. Conducts scientific programs. **Publications:** Newsletter, quarterly.

★ 4754 ★ Residency Review Committee for Emergency Medicine (RRCEM)
Accreditation Council for Graduate Med. Educ.
515 N. State St., Ste. 2000
Chicago, IL 60610
Phone: (312)464-5404
Fax: (312)464-4098
Founded: 1982. **Members:** 12. **Description:** Representatives from the American College of Emergency Physicians, the American Board of Emergency Medicine, Council on Medical Education of the American Medical Association, and the Emergency Medicine Residents' Association. Accredits residency training programs in emergency medicine. **Publications:** *Directory of Graduate Medical Education Programs*, annual. Directory.

★ 4755 ★ Saint John's Ambulance Association
1 Grosvenor Crescent
London SW1X 7EF, England
Phone: 171 2355231
Fax: 171 2350796
T.J.L. Gauvain

Founded: 1877. **Members:** 280,000. **Languages:** English. **Description:** International voluntary organization in 38 countries. Provides: first aid at public gatherings; community services for the aged and disabled in hospitals, nursing homes, and child welfare clinics; rescue missions in mountain and lake regions. Other services include Station John Ambulance Cadets, training youth in first aid and community care; the Station John Ambulance Aeromedical Services, offering medical transport to injured travelers abroad; the Station John Ambulance Air Wing, transporting organs, supplies, and surgeons for transplant operations. **Publications:** *Caring for the Sick*. Book. • *Essentials of First Aid*. Booklet. • *First Aid at Work*. Handbook. • *First Aid Manual*. Handbook. • *St. John World*, monthly. Newsletter.

★ 4756 ★ Shock Society
c/o Dr. Sherwood M. Reichard
Biotech Park, Ste. 9
1021 15th St.
Augusta, GA 30901
Phone: (706)721-2601
Fax: (706)721-3048
Dr. Sherwood M. Reichard, Exec.Dir.

Founded: 1978. **Members:** 500. **Description:** Physicians and scientists associated with universities; private, industrial, and government institutes; hospital clinics; and the pharmaceutical industry. Promotes research into and awareness of the health importance of shock and trauma; fosters the dissemination and application of information in these fields; provides a forum for the multidisciplinary integration of current and basic clinical knowledge and concepts in the study of shock and trauma. **Publications:** *Advances in Shock Research*. Book. • *Directory and Constitution*, annual. Directory. • *Shock*, monthly. Journal.

★ 4757 ★ Society for Academic Emergency Medicine (SAEM)
901 N. Washington Ave.
Lansing, MI 48906
Phone: (517)485-5484
Fax: (517)485-0801
Mary Ann Schropp, Exec.Dir.

Founded: 1975. **Members:** 3,000. **Description:** Physicians teaching emergency medicine, emergency medicine residents, and nonphysicians teaching emergency care. Purposes are: to educate teachers of emergency medicine and encourage its development as an academic discipline; to apply sound educational principles, thus improving the quality of teaching in the field; to promote research in educational methods and clinical procedures. Provides a forum for the exchange of ideas and information. Promotes improved emergency patient care through more direct involvement of teachers and consumers in the needs assessment, planning, and implementation of projects and programs. Sponsors educational workshops; conducts lectures. **Publications:** *Academic Emergency Medicine*, bimonthly. Journal. • *SAEM Newsletter*, monthly. Newsletter. Promotes research and education in emergency medicine. *Price:* Included in membership dues.

★ 4758 ★ Society of Critical Care Medicine (SCCM)
8101 E. Kaiser Blvd.
Anaheim Hills, CA 92808-2259
Phone: (714)282-6000
Fax: (714)282-6050
Norma Shoemaker, R.N., Exec.Dir.

Founded: 1970. **Members:** 8,000. **Description:** Physicians, nurses, scientists, technicians, respiratory technicians, and engineers involved in the field of critical care medicine. Purposes are: to improve care for acute life-threatening illnesses and injuries; to promote development of optimal care facilities; to guarantee high educational standards in critical care medicine. Has initiated self-assessment testing program in an effort to establish core curriculum and assist physicians in self-evaluation. Has established American College of Critical Care Medicine. **Publications:** *Concern*, quarterly. Magazine. •

Critical Care Medicine, monthly. Journal. • *Critical Care - State of the Art*. Textbook. • *Fellowship Description Handbook*. Handbook. • *New Horizons*, periodic. Monograph. • *Stat!*, bimonthly. Newsletter.

★ 4759 ★ Todos Santos Ambulance Fund (TSAF)
220 12th E.
Seattle, WA 98102
Phone: (206)323-2649
Roland Donisi, P.A., Exec. Officer

Founded: 1991. **Description:** Supports emergency medical services in Todos Santos, an indigenous village in the Guatemalan Highlands. Maintains speakers' bureau.

★ 4760 ★ World Federation of Societies of Intensive and Critical Care Medicine (WFSICCM)
(Federation Mondiale des Societes de Soins Intensifs et de Reanimation)
University Hospital
Intensive Care
CH-1211 Geneva, Switzerland
Phone: 22 3827452
Fax: 22 3827455
Prof. Malcolm Fisher, Pres.

Founded: 1974. **Members:** 42. **National Groups:** 42. **Languages:** English, French, Spanish. **Description:** Societies of physicians, nurses, and other professionals engaged in intensive and critical care medicine. (Intensive and critical care medicine is a branch of medicine dealing with patients in life-threatening pathophysiological conditions.) Seeks to promote high standards of patient care, training, equipment design, and safety measures. Provides advice; disseminates scientific and educational information; encourages research. Supports regional meetings. **Publications:** *Intensive and Critical Care Digest*, quarterly. Journal.

Research Centers

★ 4761 ★ Center for Emergency Medicine of Western Pennsylvania
230 McKee Pl., Ste. 500
Pittsburgh, PA 15213
Phone: (412)578-3204
Fax: (412)578-3241
Dr. Paul M. Paris, Dir.

Research Activities and Fields: Systems, therapy, and techniques involved in the delivery of emergency care, including monitoring and evaluation of field care, personnel training and performance, and patient outcome. Sample projects include study of resuscitation from cardiac arrest, endobronchial drug delivery, pediatric ventilation alternatives, surgical versus percutaneous cricothyrotomy, techniques used for the transport of the seriously ill or injured, and alternative methods of emergency airway management, including transillumination methods of intubation and translaryngeal jet ventilation.

★ 4762 ★ Institute of Critical Care Medicine
1695 N. Sunrise Way
Palm Springs, CA 92262
Phone: (619)323-6867
Fax: (619)323-6167
Dr. Max Harry Weil, M.D.,, Pres.

Research Activities and Fields: Critically ill patients, especially those in coronary care, intensive care, concentrated care, post anaesthesia recovery, and emergency services, suffering from heart attacks, accidents, post-surgical complications, overwhelming infections, blood loss, trauma, central nervous system injury, circulatory shock, burns, and shock from a variety of causes. Interdisciplinary studies focus on critical care medicine, automation of bedside equipment, computer application to bedside medicine, hospital environment, cardiopulmonary resuscitation, physiological instrumentation, and ethical studies of patient care. **Publications:** Newsletters. **E-mail Address:** weilm@aol.com. **Formerly:** Shock Research Unit at University of Southern California School of Medicine.

★ 4763 ★ Loyola University Chicago
Burn and Shock Trauma Institute
Loyola Medical Center
Bldg. 110, 4th Fl.
Maywood, IL 60153
Phone: (708)327-2400
Fax: (708)327-2813
Richard L. Gamelli, M.D., Dir.

Research Activities and Fields: Body responses to injury and post-injury sequelae of infection, metabolic change, alteration in host defense, and wound healing. Clinical research in care and management of injury victims, injury analysis and prevention, etiology, epidemiology, cost, rehabilitation, and outcome of trauma. **Publications:** *Loyola Shock Trauma Newsletter.*

★ 4764 ★ R.A. Cowley Shock Trauma
Center
Univ. of Maryland at Baltimore
22 S. Greene St.
Baltimore, MD 21201
Phone: (410)328-8976
Fax: (410)328-8925
John W. Ashworth, III, Contact

Research Activities and Fields: Shock and trauma, including traumatic injury, methods to prevent shock, and nutrition and shock. Activities include research and development of modifying equipment for shock and studies of field operation procedures with shock.

Trauma Foundation
See: Entry 10873

★ 4765 ★ University of Alaska Anchorage
Denali Medical Research
1200 Airport Hts., No. 320
Anchorage, AK 99508
Phone: (907)264-1471
Fax: (907)264-1570
Dr. Peter Hackett, M.D., Dir.

Research Activities and Fields: Prevention, diagnosis, and treatment of frostbite, mountain sickness, hypothermia, near drowning, and trauma subsequent to cold conditions. Studies means of rescue and transportation of victims of the above. Utilizes Mt. McKinley as a natural laboratory for studies related to cold injury and trauma. **Publications:** Has compiled an annotated bibliography of articles related to research topics and a guide to arctic and cold weather clothing, accessories, and recreational equipment. **Formerly:** Center for High Latitude Health Research Studies.

University of California, San Diego
Division of Pulmonary and Critical Care
Medicine
See: Entry 11620

★ 4766 ★ University of Pittsburgh
Safar Center for Resuscitation Research
3434 5th Ave.
Pittsburgh, PA 15260
Phone: (412)383-1900
Fax: (412)624-0943
Patrick M. Kochanek, M.D., Dir.

Research Activities and Fields: Traumatic brain injury and mechanisms of secondary injury, cardiopulmonary arrest and resuscitation, disaster medicine, and suspended animation. **Publications:** Annual Report. **E-mail Address:** kocha@smtp.anes.upmc.edu. **Formerly:** Resuscitation Research Center.

University of Wisconsin—Madison
Pulmonary and Critical Care Medicine
Section
See: Entry 11623

State Government Agencies

Emergency Medical Services

★ 4767 ★ Alabama Department of Public
Health
Health Care Standards Bureau
Emergency Medical Services Division
434 Monroe St.
Montgomery, AL 36130-1701
Phone: (334)613-5383
Fax: (334)240-3061

★ 4768 ★ Alaska Department of Health and
Social Services
Public Health Division
Emergency Medical Services Section
PO Box 110616
Juneau, AK 99811-0616
Phone: (907)465-3027
Fax: (907)465-4101

★ 4769 ★ Arizona Department of Health
Services
Emergency Medical Services Division
1651 E. Morten, Ste. 120
Phoenix, AZ 85020
Phone: (602)255-1170
Fax: (602)255-1134

★ 4770 ★ Arkansas Department of Health
Emergency Medical Services Division
4815 W. Markham St., Slot 38
Little Rock, AR 72205-3867
Phone: (501)661-2262
Fax: (501)280-4901

★ 4771 ★ California Health and Welfare
Agency
Emergency Medical Services Authority
1930 9th St., Ste. 100
Sacramento, CA 95814
Phone: (916)322-4336
Fax: (916)324-2875

★ 4772 ★ Colorado Public and Environment
Department
Health Office Emergency Medical Services
Division
4300 Cherry Creek Dr. S.
Denver, CO 80222
Phone: (303)692-2980
Fax: (303)782-0904

★ 4773 ★ Connecticut Department of
Public Health
Emergency Medical Services Office
150 Washington St.
Hartford, CT 06106
Phone: (203)566-7336
Fax: (203)566-7172

★ 4774 ★ Delaware Department of Health
and Social Services
Public Health Division
Emergency Medical Services Office
PO Box 637
Dover, DE 19903
Phone: (302)739-6637
Fax: (302)739-3008

★ 4775 ★ District of Columbia Department
of Human Services
Public Health Commission
Emergency Health and Medical Services
613 G. St. NW
Washington, DC 20001
Phone: (202)727-1622
Fax: (202)727-0379

★ 4776 ★ Florida Department of Health and
Rehabilitative Services
Health Program Office
Emergency Medical Services
1317 Winewood Blvd.
Tallahassee, FL 32399-0700
Phone: (904)488-9177
Fax: (904)487-2911

★ 4777 ★ Georgia Department of Human
Resources
Public Health Division
Emergency Medical Services
2 Peachtree St. SW, 7th Fl. Annex
Atlanta, GA 30303
Phone: (404)657-6700
Fax: (404)657-4255

★ 4778 ★ Hawaii Department of Health
Emergency Medical Services
3627 Kilauea Ave., Rm. 102
Honolulu, HI 96816
Phone: (808)733-9210
Fax: (808)733-8332

★4779★ Idaho Department of Health and
   Welfare
Health Division
Emergency Medical Services Bureau
3092 Elder St.
Boise, ID 83720
Phone: (208)334-4000
Fax: (208)334-4015

★4780★ Illinois Department of Public
   Health
Health Care Regulation Office
Emergency Medical Services Division
525 W. Jefferson
Springfield, IL 62761
Phone: (217)785-2080
Fax: (217)785-0253

★4781★ Indiana State Emergency
   Management Agency
Emergency Medical Services Commission
302 W. Washington, Rm. E208
Indianapolis, IN 46204-2258
Phone: (317)232-3983
Fax: (317)232-3895

★4782★ Iowa Department of Public
   Health
Emergency Medical Services
Lucas State Office Bldg.
Des Moines, IA 50319-0075
Phone: (515)281-3239
Fax: (515)281-4958

★4783★ Kansas Board of Emergency
   Medical Services
109 SW 6th Ave.
Topeka, KS 66603-3826
Phone: (913)296-7296
Fax: (913)296-6212

★4784★ Kentucky Human Resources
   Cabinet
Health Services Department
Emergency Medical Services Branch
275 E. Main St.
Frankfort, KY 40621
Phone: (502)564-8963
Fax: (502)564-6533

★4785★ Louisiana Department of Health
   and Hospitals
Public Health Services Office
Emergency Medical Services Bureau
PO Box 94215
Baton Rouge, LA 70804
Phone: (504)342-4881
Fax: (504)342-4876

★4786★ Maine Department of Public
   Safety
Emergency Medical Services
42 State House Station
36 Hospital St.
Augusta, ME 04333
Phone: (207)287-3953
Fax: (207)287-6251

★4787★ Maryland Institute for Emergency
   Medical Services Systems
636 W. Lombard St.
Baltimore, MD 21201-1528
Phone: (410)706-5074
Fax: (410)706-4768

★4788★ Massachusetts Executive Office
   of Health and Human Services
Public Health Department
Emergency Medical Services Division
150 Tremont St., 2nd Fl.
Boston, MA 02111
Phone: (617)727-8338
Fax: (617)727-3172

★4789★ Michigan Department of Public
   Health
Emergency Medical Services Division
3423 N. Logan
PO Box 30195
Lansing, MI 48909
Phone: (517)335-9502
Fax: (517)335-8582

★4790★ Minnesota Department of Health
Health Quality Assurance Bureau
Occupational and Systems Compliance
   Section
PO Box 64975
St. Paul, MN 55164-0975
Phone: (612)282-5627
Fax: (612)282-3839

★4791★ Mississippi Department of Health
Health Resources and Lab Services Bureau
Emergency Medical Services Division
PO Box 1700
Jackson, MS 39215-1700
Phone: (601)987-3880
Fax: (601)987-3993

★4792★ Missouri Department of Health
Health Resources Division
Emergency Medical Services Bureau
PO Box 570
Jefferson City, MO 65102
Phone: (314)751-6356
Fax: (314)526-4102

★4793★ Montana Department of Health
   and Environmental Sciences
Health Services Division
Emergency Medical Services Bureau
Cogswell Bldg.
Helena, MT 59620
Phone: (406)444-3895
Fax: (406)444-1814

★4794★ Nebraska Department of Health
Health Promotion and Disease Prevention
   Bureau
Emergency Medical Services Division
301 Centennial Mall S., 3rd Fl.
PO Box 95007
Lincoln, NE 68509-5007
Phone: (402)471-2158
Fax: (402)471-0383

★4795★ Nevada Department of Human
   Resources
Health Division
Emergency Medical Services Office
1550 E. College Pkwy., Ste. 158
Carson City, NV 89710
Phone: (702)687-3065
Fax: (702)687-6588

★4796★ New Hampshire Department of
   Health and Human Services
Public Health Services Division
Emergency Medical Services Bureau
6 Hazen Dr.
Concord, NH 03301-6527
Phone: (603)271-4569
Fax: (603)271-3745

★4797★ New Jersey Department of
   Health
Health Facilities Evaluation and Licensing
   Division
Emergency Medical Services
CN 367
Trenton, NJ 08625-0367
Phone: (609)588-7800
Fax: (609)588-7823

★4798★ New Mexico Department of
   Health
Public Health Division
Primary Care and Emergency Medical
   Services Bureau
PO Box 26110
Santa Fe, NM 87502-6110
Phone: (505)827-1400
Fax: (505)827-1410

★4799★ New York State Department of
   Health
Emergency Medical Services Program
1 Commerce Plaza, 1126
Albany, NY 12260
Phone: (518)474-2219
Fax: (518)486-6216

★4800★ North Carolina Department of
   Human Resources
Facility Services Division
Emergency Medical Services Office
701 Barbour Dr.
PO Box 29530
Raleigh, NC 27626-0530
Phone: (919)733-2285
Fax: (919)733-7021

★4801★ North Dakota Department of
   Health and Consolidated Laboratories
Health Resources Section
Emergency Health Services Division
600 E. Boulevard Ave.
Bismarck, ND 58505-0200
Phone: (701)328-2388
Fax: (701)328-4727

★4802★ Ohio Department of Public Safety
Emergency Medical Services
PO Box 7167
Columbus, OH 43266-0563
Phone: (614)466-9447
Fax: (614)466-0433

★4803★ Oklahoma Department of Health
Emergency Medical Services
1000 NE 10th St., Rm. 1104
PO Box 53551
Oklahoma City, OK 73152
Phone: (405)271-4027
Fax: (405)271-3442

★4804★ Oregon Department of Human Resources
Health Division
Emergency Medical Services and Systems
800 NE Oregon, Ste. 607
Portland, OR 97232
Phone: (503)731-4011
Fax: (503)731-4077

★4805★ Pennsylvania Department of Health
Emergency Medical Services Division
Health and Welfare Bldg., Rm. 1033
PO Box 90
Harrisburg, PA 17108
Phone: (717)787-8741
Fax: (717)772-0910

★4806★ Puerto Rico Department of Health
Emergency Medical System
Call Box 70184
San Juan, PR 00936
Phone: (809)766-1733
Fax: (809)765-5085

★4807★ Rhode Island Department of Health
Health Services Regulations Office
Emergency Medical Services Division
3 Capitol Hill, Rm. 404
Providence, RI 02908-5097
Phone: (401)277-2401
Fax: (401)277-6548

★4808★ South Carolina Department of Health and Environmental Control
Emergency Medical Services Division
2600 Bull St.
Columbia, SC 29201
Phone: (803)737-7204
Fax: (803)737-7212

★4809★ South Dakota Department of Health
Emergency Medical Services Program
445 E. Capitol
Pierre, SD 57501
Phone: (605)773-4779
Fax: (605)773-5683

★4810★ Tennessee Department of Health
Manpower and Facilities Bureau
Emergency Medical Services Division
287 Plus Park Blvd.
Nashville, TN 37247-0701
Phone: (615)367-6278
Fax: (615)367-6210

★4811★ Texas Department of Health
Emergency Medical Services Division
1100 W. 49th St.
Austin, TX 78756-3199
Phone: (512)834-6740
Fax: (512)834-6736

★4812★ Utah Department of Health
Health Systems Improvement Division
Emergency Medical Services Bureau
288 North 1460 West
PO Box 142852
Salt Lake City, UT 84114-2852
Phone: (801)538-6435
Fax: (801)538-6808

★4813★ Vermont Agency of Human Services
Health Department
Emergency Medical Services Division
108 Cherry St.
PO Box 70
Burlington, VT 05402
Phone: (802)863-7310
Fax: (802)863-7577

★4814★ Virgin Islands Department of Health
Emergency Medical Services
St. Thomas Hospital
charlotte Amalie
St. Thomas, VI 00802
Phone: (809)776-8311
Fax: (809)777-4001

★4815★ Virginia Office of Health Human Resources
Health Department
Emergency Medical Services Division
1538 E. Parham Rd.
Richmond, VA 23228
Phone: (804)371-3500
Fax: (804)371-3543

★4816★ Washington Department of Health
Emergency Medical Services and Trauma Systems
PO Box 47853
Olympia, WA 98504-7853
Phone: (360)705-6745
Fax: (360)705-6706

★4817★ West Virginia Department of Health and Human Resources
Public Health Bureau
Emergency Medical Services Division
1411 Virginia St. E., 2nd Fl.
Charleston, WV 25301
Phone: (304)558-3956
Fax: (304)558-1437

★4818★ Wisconsin Department of Health and Social Services
Health Division
Emergency Medical Services
PO Box 309
Madison, WI 53701-0309
Phone: (608)266-9781
Fax: (608)267-3696

★4819★ Wyoming Department of Health
Preventive Medicine Division
Emergency Medical Services Program
Hathaway Bldg., Rm. 527
Cheyenne, WY 82002
Phone: (307)777-7955
Fax: (307)777-5639

Chapter 23
Endocrinology & Metabolism

Federal Government Agencies

★4820★ U.S. Department of Health and Human Services
National Institute of Diabetes and Digestive and Kidney Diseases
9000 Rockville Pike
Bethesda, MD 20892
Phone: (301)496-5877

Description: The Institute conducts, fosters, and supports basic and clinical research into the causes, prevention, diagnosis, and treatment of the various metabolic and digestive diseases. It covers the broad areas of diabetes, blood, endocrine, and metabolic diseases; digestive diseases and nutrition; and kidney and urologic diseases.

Foundations & Other Funding Organizations

Private Foundations

Dale J. Bellamah Foundation
See: Entry 124

Nora Eccles Treadwell Foundation
See: Entry 2783

Robert G. Cabell III and Maude Morgan Cabell Foundation
See: Entry 452

Robert J. Kleberg, Jr. and Helen C. Kleberg Foundation
See: Entry 453

Willard T. C. Johnson Foundation
See: Entry 542

Corporate Foundations

Eli Lilly and Co. Foundation
See: Entry 672

Other Funding Organizations

★4821★ American Diabetes Association
National Center
1660 Duke St.
PO Box 25757
Alexandria, VA 22314
Phone: (703)549-1500
Free: 800-ADA-DISC
Fax: (703)836-7439
John H. Graham, IV, CEO

Description: Awards general, annual research grants; administers investigatorships; awards the annual Lions' SightFirst Retinopathy Research award; grants semi-annual funds for clinical or applied research in diabetic retinopathy.

★4822★ American Porphyria Foundation
PO Box 22712
Houston, TX 77227
Phone: (713)266-9617
Fax: (713)871-1788
Desiree H. Lyon, Exec. Dir.

Description: Provides financial support for researchers in porphyria.

★4823★ Human Growth Foundation
7777 Leesburg Pike
Falls Church, VA 22043
Phone: (703)883-1773
Free: 800-451-6434
Fax: (703)883-1776
Deborah S. Swansburg, Exec. Dir.

Description: Provides grants for basic and clinical research in physical growth.

★4824★ Juvenile Diabetes Foundation International
432 Park Ave. S
New York, NY 10016-8013
Phone: (212)889-7575
Free: 800-JDF-CURE
Fax: (212)725-7259
Ken Farber, Exec. Dir.

Description: Funds grants and postdoctoral fellowships for diabetes research and research training.

National Center for the Study of Wilson's Disease
See: Entry 5263

National Gaucher Foundation
See: Entry 5264

National & International Organizations

★4825★ Adrenal Metabolic Research Society of the Hypoglycemia Foundation (AMRSHF)
32 Sunrise Ter.
Clifton Park, NY 12065-2327
Phone: (518)272-7154
Marilyn H. Light, Pres. & Dir.

Founded: 1956. **Description:** Participants include 2000 physicians and paramedical investigators. Conducts scientific investigation and laboratory research to further the knowledge of metabolic anomalies involved in hypoglycemia (low blood sugar). Acts as liaison among physicians having special interest in this area. Conducts seminars and study groups for physicians and paramedical personnel. Distributes information nationally to the public. Maintains library of 2000 volumes on endocrinology. **Publications:** *Homeostasis Quarterly.* Newsletter. Focuses on health problems arising from hypoglycemia, adrenal cortex disorders, diabetes, and other deficiencies. *Price:* $10/year. Also publishes lay and technical booklets. **Formerly:** Hypoglycemia Foundation.

★4826★ Albinism World Alliance (AWA)
c/o National Organization for Albinism & Hypopigmentation
1500 Locust St., Ste. 2405
Philadelphia, PA 19102-4318
Phone: (215)545-2322
Free: 800-473-2310
Fax: (215)928-1772
Janice L. Knuth, Co-Chair

Founded: 1992. **Description:** Albinism support groups in 9 countries. (Albinism is an inherited metabolic disorder that results in reduced pigment in the hair, eyes, and/or skin of those it affects; people with albinism also have impaired eye function including decreased visual acuity, involuntary eye movements, and increased sensitivity to light.) Fosters communication among albinism support groups, and promotes development of albinism support groups worldwide. Disseminates information.

★ 4827 ★ American Association of Clinical Endocrinologists (AACE)
2589 Park St.
Jacksonville, FL 32204-4554
Phone: (904)384-9490
Fax: (904)384-8124
Robert J. Harvey, Exec.Dir.

Founded: 1991. **Members:** 2,280. **Description:** Clinical endocrinologists and endocrine surgeons. Seeks to create and maintain a society of qualified adult, pediatric, and reproductive endocrinologists for the coordination of their efforts in furthering the practice of clinical endocrinology. Studies the scientific, economic, social, and political aspects of medicine to maintain the highest standards of patient care and professional practice in endocrinology. Represents the interests of patients and endocrinologists in socio-economic and related matters with government agencies, the insurance industry, organized medicine, and health related organizations. **Publications:** *Endocrine Practice*, bimonthly. Journal. Features peer reviewed scientific articles on clinical endocrinology. • *The First Messenger*, bimonthly. Newsletter.

★ 4828 ★ American Association of Diabetes Educators (AADE)
444 N. Michigan Ave., Ste. 1240
Chicago, IL 60611-3901
Phone: (312)644-2233
Free: 800-338-DMED
Fax: (312)644-4411
James J. Balija, Exec.Dir.

Founded: 1974. **Members:** 9,000. **Local Groups:** 98. **Description:** Nurses, dietitians, social workers, physicians, pharmacists, podiatrists, and others involved in teaching diabetes management to diabetics. Purposes are: to provide educational opportunities for the professional growth and development of members; to promote the development of quality diabetes education for the diabetic consumer; to foster communication and cooperation among individuals and organizations involved in diabetes patient education. Maintains speakers' bureau. Offers continuing education programs for diabetes educators; holds certification program for qualified diabetes educators. **Publications:** *AADE News*, 9/year. Newsletter. Includes calendar of events, chapter news, employment listings, and organization information. *Price:* Included in membership dues. • *Core Curriculum for Diabetes Education.* • *Diabetes and Visual Impairment: An Educator's Resource Guide.* • *The Diabetes Educator*, bimonthly. Journal. Contains original articles from all disciplines regarding diabetes and diabetes patient education. Includes advertisers index and book reviews. *Price:* Included in membership dues; $45/year for non-members. • *Membership Directory*, annual. Also publishes position statements and various guidelines for diabetes education.

★ 4829 ★ American Diabetes Association (ADA)
National Center
PO Box 25757
1660 Duke St.
Alexandria, VA 22314
Phone: (703)549-1500
Free: 800-ADA-DISC
Fax: (703)836-7439
John H. Graham, IV, CEO

Founded: 1940. **Members:** 280,000. **State Groups:** 54. **Local Groups:** 800. **Description:** Physicians, laypersons, and health professionals interested in diabetes mellitus. Promotes the free exchange of information about diabetes mellitus by educating the public in the early recognition of the disease, the importance of medical supervision in its treatment, and the development of educational methods designed for people with diabetes. Seeks to find a preventive and cure for diabetes and improve the lives of all people affected by the condition. Administers investigatorships. Sponsors postgraduate course and diabetic summer camps. Compiles statistics. **Publications:** Books. • *Clinical Diabetes*, bimonthly. Newsletter. Provides current scientific information about diabetes and its treatment to the general physician without specialized training in diabetes. *Price:* $5/year. • *Diabetes*, monthly. Contains original research papers and review articles on the physiology and paraphysiology of diabetes mellitus and related disorders. *Price:* Included in membership dues (professional members); $100/year for non-members. • *Diabetes Care*, monthly. Journal. Covers applied research primarily directed toward improving the welfare of people with diabetes mellitus, and increasing understanding of the disease. *Price:* Included in membership dues (professional members); $75/year for non-members. • *Diabetes Forecast*, monthly. Magazine. Provides information about diabetes and related subjects such as exercise, diet, travel, personal development, and legislation. *Price:* Included in membership dues. • *Diabetes Reviews*, quarterly. Journal. Provides comprehensive reviews of clinical issues regarding diabetes. *Price:* $50/year for members; $60/year for nonmembers. • *Diabetes Spectrum: From Research to Practice*, bimonthly. Journal. *Price:* Included in membership dues; $30/year for non-members. • Videos. Publishes a catalog of publications available.

★ 4830 ★ American Porphyria Foundation (APF)
PO Box 22712
Houston, TX 77227
Phone: (713)266-9617
Fax: (713)871-1788
Desiree H. Lyon, Exec.Dir.

Founded: 1981. **Members:** 1,900. **Description:** Persons interested in advancing awareness and treatment of the porphyrias; affected patients. Porphyria is a class of seven rare (and usually inherited) metabolic disorders of varying severity affecting the nervous system or the skin. It is characterized by a deficiency of an enzyme used in making heme (a ring-shaped molecule called a porphyrin), which in turn is used in making hemoglobin. One of porphyria's recurrent though not requisite symptoms is purple-

red urine. The foundation's purposes are to: provide financial support for researchers in porphyria; improve the diagnosis and treatment of porphyria through educational programs; locate porphyria patients. Maintains a lending library of videotapes, papers, and pamphlets. **Publications:** *American Porphyria Foundation--Newsletter*, quarterly. Newsletter. *Price:* Included in membership dues. • Pamphlets. Also compiles list of physicians with experience in treating porphyria.

★ 4831 ★ American Prostate Society
1340 Charwood Rd., Ste. F
Hanover, MD 21076
Phone: (410)859-3735
Free: 800-678-1238
Fax: (410)850-0818
Claude Gerard, Chm.

Founded: 1991. **Members:** 42,000. **National Groups:** 1. **Local Groups:** 1. **Description:** Works to increase the public's awareness of prostate disease. Encourages men to get annual exams. Aids hospitals and other health care facilities that are dedicated exclusively to detection and treatment of prostate disease. Sponsors Prostate Awareness Week. Conducts speakers' bureau. Sponsors educational programs. **Publications:** Brochures, annual. • *Update*, quarterly. Newsletter. *Price:* Free.

★ 4832 ★ Association for Glycogen Storage Disease (AGSD)
PO Box 896
Durant, IA 52747
Phone: (319)785-6038
Fax: (319)785-6038
Hollie Swain, Pres.

Founded: 1979. **Members:** 400. **Description:** Individuals afflicted with glycogen storage disease; families of GSD sufferers; health care professionals. (GSD is a hereditary condition characterized by a lack of or deficiency in any of the enzymes used by the body to break down glycogen, resulting in hypoglycemia and related disorders, and requiring diet modifications and frequent or continual feeding, and in extreme cases resulting in death.) Acts as a forum for the discussion of GSD, its treatment, and the problems faced by parents raising children with GSD. Disseminates medical information; fosters communication between the families of GSD patients and health care professionals. Conducts fundraising drive. Aids members in obtaining equipment necessary for home care of GSD patients; provides referral services for individuals seeking GSD treatment facilities; will establish fellowship for students engaged in the study of GSD. **Publications:** Brochures. *Price:* Free. • *Parent Handbook. Price:* $5. • *The Ray*, quarterly. Newsletter. *Price:* Free.

Association of Neuro-Metabolic Disorders (ANMD)
See: Entry 5271

Billy Barty Foundation (BBF)
See: Entry 7869

Cystinosis Foundation (CF)
See: Entry 5276

★4833★ **Cytochrome C Oxidase Deficiency Parental Research and Support Foundation**
PO Box 156
Hartman, AR 72840-0156
Phone: (501)375-6193
Joyce Vaught, Contact

Founded: 1993. **Description:** Families and caregivers of children with Cytochrome C Oxidase Deficiency (COX). Cytochrome C Oxidase Deficiency is a rare genetic metabolic disorder with no known specific treatment. The Cytochrome is a respiratory enzyme that plays an important part in the oxidative process. Common symptoms could be seizures, tremors, poor muscle tone, failure to thrive, low body weight, slow growth, mental retardation, abnormalities of eye movement, vision problems, and sleep disorders. Works to unite parents, caregivers, and medical professionals of Cox Kids to facilitate increased and coordinated research and information sharing. Provides support programs. Also supports program for families dealing with any mitochondrial disease. **Publications:** Newsletter, 3/year. **Also Known As:** COX Foundation.

★4834★ **Daughters of Hirsutism Association of America (DOHA)**
203 N. LaSalle St., Ste. 2100
Chicago, IL 60601
Phone: (312)558-1365
Jennifer M. Smith, Contact

Founded: 1981. **Members:** 2,100. **State Groups:** 2. **Description:** Individuals with Hirsutism and their families and specialists in the treatment of Hirsutism. (Hirsutism is a hormonal imbalance causing excessive growth of facial and body hair in women.) Promotes understanding, support, and acceptance of Hirsute women and girls. Provides referral services for counseling, electrologists, endocrinology, dermatologists, and networking. Conducts research programs; maintains speakers' bureau; compiles statistics. **Publications:** Newsletter, quarterly.

★4835★ **Diabetes Research Institute Foundation (DRIF)**
3440 Hollywood Blvd., Ste. 100
Hollywood, FL 33021
Phone: (305)964-4040
Free: 800-321-3437
Fax: (305)964-7036
Robert A. Pearlman, Exec.VP

Founded: 1971. **Members:** 10,000. **Description:** Works to improve the quality of life for individuals with diabetes and to find a cure for diabetes. Acts as an information clearinghouse. Offers referral services. Fosters research on diabetes. Conducts educational programs; maintains speakers' bureau. Compiles statistics. **Publications:** *Focus*, 3/year. Newsletter. • *Pathways*, 3/year. Magazine. Includes updates on recent diabetes research.

★4836★ **Diabetic Association of Luxembourg (DAL) (Association Luxembourgeoise du Diabete — ALD)**
22, rue Goethe
BP 1316
Luxembourg, Luxembourg
Phone: 474545
Fax: 220836
Dr. Roger Wirion, Sec.

Founded: 1979. **Members:** 600. **Languages:** English, French, German. **Description:** Diabetics and health care providers. Aims to promote the medical, scientific, and social concerns of diabetics. Collaborates with doctors, related organizations, and interested individuals. Provides diabetes prevention information. Sponsors biennial diabetes education week. Participates in European programs for diabetic children. **Publications:** *Journal du Diabetique*, quarterly. Magazine.

★4837★ **Dr. John W. Tintera Memorial / Hypoglycemia Lay Group (HLG)**
149 Spindle Rd.
Hicksville, NY 11801
Phone: (516)731-3302
Elaine Arnstein, Pres. & Sec.

Founded: 1964. **Members:** 500. **Description:** Hypoglycemics; parents of minors with hypoglycemia. Hypoglycemia (more commonly known as low blood sugar) is an adrenal metabolic dysfunction that causes symptoms such as headaches, blurred vision, anxiety, allergies, depression, and addiction; it can be controlled by special dieting. Purposes are to disseminate information on hypoglycemia; encourage health professionals to become more interested in the study and treatment of the condition; report new medical findings. The group was named after John W. Tintera, M.D. (1911-69), who worked to educate the public and the medical profession about hypoglycemia. **Publications:** *Alcoholism and Low Blood Sugar*. Pamphlet. • *Dr. John W. Tintera Memorial/Hypoglycemia Lay Group--Newsletter*, quarterly. Newsletter. Provides health and diet information for hypoglycemics and lists new publications. *Price:* Included in membership dues. • *Glands*. Pamphlet. • *Glands and Alcohol*. Pamphlet. • *Glands and Allergies*. Pamphlet. • *Hayfever May Be Low Blood Sugar*. Pamphlet. • *How to Live With a Hypoglycemic*. Pamphlet. • *Hypoglycemia and Me*. Pamphlet. • *Neurosis or Hypoglycemia*. Pamphlet. • *Sugar, the Great Deceiver*. Pamphlet. • *Total Diet Program*. Pamphlet. **Formerly:** (1969) Health Frontiers.

★4838★ **Endocrine Society (ES)**
9650 Rockville Pike
Bethesda, MD 20814
Phone: (301)571-1800
Fax: (301)571-1869
Scott Hunt, Exec.Dir.

Founded: 1918. **Members:** 8,000. **Description:** Promotes excellence in research, education, and clinical practice in endocrinology and related disciplines. Maintains placement service. **Publications:** *Endocrine News*, bimonthly. Newsletter. Includes calendar of events and listing of honors and awards recipients; legislative issues and clinical practice column. *Price:* Included in membership dues. • *Endocrine Reviews*, bimonthly. Journal. Covers clinical and experimental endocrinology; readers are encouraged to suggest prospective authors and to submit their own manuscripts. *Price:* $45/year for members in U.S.; $105/year for nonmembers in U.S.; $170/year for institutions in U.S.; $80 for those in training in U.S. • *Endocrinology*, monthly. Journal. Covers current biomedical research for basic scientists. *Price:* $85/year for members in U.S.; $180/year for nonmembers in U.S.; $360/year for institutions in the U.S.; $115/year for those in training in U.S. • *Journal of Clinical Endocrinology and Metabolism*, monthly. Journal. Provides current information on the clinical applications of endocrine research for internists, pediatricians, and practicing obstetricians. *Price:* $70/year for members in U.S.; $155/year for nonmembers in U.S.; $260/year for institutions in U.S.; $100/year for those in training in U.S. • *Molecular Endocrinology*, monthly. Journal. Covers the molecular mechanisms of cellular regulation and hormone action. *Price:* $70/year for members in U.S.; $155/year for nonmembers in U.S.; $260/year for institutions in U.S.; $100/year for those in training in U.S.**Formerly:** Association for Study of Internal Secretions.

★4839★ **European Association for the Study of Diabetes (EASD) (Association Europeenne pour l'Etude du Diabete — AEED)**
Auf'm Hennekamp 32
40225 Dusseldorf, Germany
Phone: 211 316738
Fax: 211 3190987
Viktor Joergens, M.D., Exec.Dir.

Founded: 1964. **Members:** 4,200. **Languages:** English. **Description:** Individuals and firms in 55 countries. Promotes research into the disease of diabetes. Sponsors postgraduate education courses. **Publications:** *Diabetologia*, periodic. Journal. • *Membership List*, triennial.

European Diabetes Pregnancy Study Group (EDPSG)
See: Entry 9647

★4840★ **European Pineal Society (EPSG)**
Laboratoire de Zoologie
Universite Louis Pasteur
12, rue de l'Universite
F-67000 Strasbourg, France
Phone: 88 358509
Fax: 88 240461
Dr. P. Pevet, Pres.

Founded: 1977. **Members:** 255. **Languages:** English. **Description:** Scientists interested in the pineal gland. (The pineal gland is a cone-shaped organ, present in all vertebrates, that is situated in the brain.) Advances pineology by facilitating contacts among research teams. **Publications:** *EPSG Newsletter*, semiannual. Newsletter. • *Proceedings of Colloquium*, triennial.

European Society of Paediatric Radiology (ESPR)
See: Entry 11113

★ 4841 ★ European Study Group on Lysosomal Diseases (ESGLD)

Institute of Child Health, University of London
Division of Biochemistry and Genetics
30 Guilford St.
London WC1N 1EH, England
Phone: 171 2429789
Fax: 171 8310488
Dr. B. Winchester, Treas.

Founded: 1978. **Members:** 90. **Languages:** English. **Description:** Laboratories in 19 countries conducting research on lysosomal storage diseases. (Lysosomal storage diseases are hereditary disorders, resulting from defects in lysosomal enzymes or membrane components, characterized by accumulation of partially digested metabolites in tissues and excretion in urine.) Promotes research; encourages exchange of ideas and personnel among member laboratories. **Publications:** *Lysosome Newsletter*, biennial. Newsletter. • *Register of Laboratories*, biennial.

★ 4842 ★ European Thyroid Association (ETA)

(Association Europeenne Thyroide — AET)

Unite de Thyroide, Lab 4-767
Hopital Cantonal Universitaire
CH-1211 Geneva 4, Switzerland
Phone: 22 3729192
Fax: 22 3476486
Prof. Albert Burger, Sec.-Treas.

Founded: 1967. **Members:** 365. **Languages:** English, French. **Description:** Physicians and research scientists in 37 countries with an interest in the thyroid gland. Promotes research; works to improve knowledge of the thyroid gland and its diseases. Bestows awards. **Publications:** *Abstracts From Annual Meeting*.

★ 4843 ★ French Diabetes Association (FDA)

(Association Francaise des Diabetiques — AFD)

14, rue du Clos
F-75020 Paris, France
Phone: 1 40092425
Fax: 1 40092030
Mr. Levesque, Pres.

Founded: 1938. **Members:** 30,000. **Local Groups:** 122. **Languages:** English, French. **Description:** Individuals with diabetes in France. Works to inform, assist, and defend diabetics. Furthers public understanding of diabetes by disseminating information to the public and medical specialists. **Publications:** *Equilibre*, quarterly. Magazine. • *Medical and Informations au le Diabete*, periodic.

★ 4844 ★ HELP - Institute for Body Chemistry (HELP)

PO Box 1338
Bryn Mawr, PA 19010
Phone: (610)525-1225
Edward & Patricia Krimmel, Dirs.

Founded: 1979. **Members:** 2,500. **Description:** Health professionals and interested individuals. Promotes public awareness of body chemistry problems within the context of general health. Seeks to collect, verify, and distribute information related to body chemistry especially hypoglycemia (low blood sugar) and cholesteral management. Conducts seminars regarding nutrition, exercise, life style, and emotional stability. Develops support groups and encourages communication among members. **Publications:** *Advocate - Newsletter*. Newsletter. Includes information on body chemistry, nutrition, and related medical research. *Price:* Included in membership dues. • *Cholesterol Lowering and Controlling Handbook and Cookbook.* • *Low Blood Sugar Cookbook.* • *Low Blood Sugar Handbook.* • *Vital Health Foods and Composition of Foods.*

★ 4845 ★ Hemochromatosis Foundation (HF)

PO Box 8569
Albany, NY 12208
Phone: (518)489-0972
Fax: (518)489-0227
Margaret A. Krikker, M.D., Pres.

Founded: 1982. **Members:** 4,000. **Regional Groups:** 8. **State Groups:** 4. **Local Groups:** 2. **Description:** Physicians and other individuals concerned with hereditary hemochromatosis. (Hereditary hemochromatosis is a disorder of iron metabolism in which dietary iron absorption exceeds body needs. If not diagnosed and treated, the accumulating iron may result in one or more complications: liver enlargement, heart irregularities and failure, diabetes and other hormonal deficiencies, arthritis, and early death.) Seeks to increase public and professional awareness of hereditary hemochromatosis and of the hazards of supplemental iron. Encourages routine use of screening tests by physicians, conducts screening studies of apparently healthy blood donors. Assists public, patients, families, and physicians with HH diagnosis, treatment, and genetic counseling and in forming regional support networks. Sponsors periodic teaching day for physicians and patients and their families. Conducts research programs. Plans to establish a central registry of persons with the disorder. **Publications:** Booklets. • *Hemochromatosis Awareness: A Quarterly Update on Hereditary and Acquired Iron-Overload.* Newsletter. Includes calendar of events and information on available services. *Price:* Free. • Videos. **Formerly:** (1992) Hemochromatosis Research Foundation.

★ 4846 ★ Hypoglycemia Association

18008 New Hampshire Ave.
Box 165
Ashton, MD 20861-0165
Phone: (202)544-4044
Dorothy R. Schultz, Pres.

Founded: 1967. **Members:** 200. **State Groups:** 1. **Description:** Persons with hypoglycemia. (Hypoglycemia is a deficiency in the blood sugar that deprives the central nervous system of glucose needed to function normally.) Organized to promote interest in and knowledge about hypoglycemia. Believes that "a great many people who are overtired, anxious, depressed, incompetent, irritable, anti-social, and chronically ill could possibly be victims of hypoglycemia." Provides counseling, comfort, and moral support to persons with hypoglycemia through meetings and informational bulletins. **Publications:** *A Diet for Living with Hypoglycemia, Phase I and II.* Bulletin. Contains the dietary information included in the association's *Basic Packet.* *Price:* $3. • *Basic Packet.* Contains sample bulletin, dietary information, list of available literature, and eleven bulletins on coping with hypoglycemia and related issues. *Price:* $10 in U.S.; $12 in Canada (money orders only). • *Hypoglycemia Association*, 5/year. Bulletin. Contains announcements of meetings, tips from persons with hypoglycemia on coping with their illnesses, articles, and humor. • *Introductory Packet.* Contains list of available literature, flyer, sample bulletin, and current meeting information. *Price:* Send large self-addressed, stamped envelope. Also publishes bulletins on nutrition, glucose testing, allergies, biofeedback, hypoadrenocorticism, and other topics related to hypoglycemia.

★ 4847 ★ Indonesian Endocrinology Association (IEA)

(Perhimpunan Endocrinology Indonesia — PEI)

Jalan Diponegoro 71 RSCM
Jakarta, Indonesia
Phone: 21 3103729
Fax: 21 3907703
Prof.Dr. Supartondo, Chair

Founded: 1978. **Languages:** Indonesian. **Description:** Medical practitioners, research scientists, and other individuals involved in the clinical practice and study of endocrinology. Gathers and disseminates information; serves as a forum for exchange of ideas and information among members.

★ 4848 ★ International Diabetes Federation (IDF)

(Federation Internationale du Diabete — FID)

40, rue Washington
B-1050 Brussels, Belgium
Phone: 2 6474414
Fax: 2 6408565
H. Williams, Exec.Dir.

Founded: 1949. **Members:** 1,610. **National Groups:** 115. **Regional Groups:** 7. **Languages:** English, French. **Description:** National diabetes associations; diabetes sections of national academies; endocrinology, metabolic, and diabetes societies; diabetes supplies companies are supporting members; association represents over one million individuals through its national associations. Objectives are: to improve the quality of life in the global diabetic community; to promote the exchange of information; to improve standards of treatment; to develop educational methods designed to give patients a better understanding of their disease; to educate the public in the early recognition of the disease and the importance of its medically supervised treatment; to encourage medical, scientific, and socioeconomic research. Maintains liaison with the World Health Organization . Compiles statistics. Provides professional training courses through the IDF Educational Foundation. **Publications:** *Guidebook to Diabetes Magazines for the Lay Audience.* • *IDF Bulletin*, 3/year. Journal. • *IDF Directory*, triennial. • *IDF Newsletter*, quarterly. • *Triennial Report.* • *World Book of Diabetes in Practice.*

★4849★ **International Diabetic Athletes Association (IDAA)**
1931 E. Rovey Ave.
Phoenix, AZ 85016
Phone: (602)230-8155
Fax: (602)230-8155
Paula Harper, RN, Pres.

Founded: 1985. **Members:** 2,500. **Regional Groups:** 12. **Description:** Individuals with diabetes and healthcare professionals. Promotes the participation of individuals with diabetes in sports activities. Provides a network and support group for athletes with diabetes. Conducts educational programs to increase self care skills for individuals with diabetes and counseling skills for healthcare professionals. Offers blood sugar screenings; sponsors volunteer services and speakers' bureau. Conducts children's services. **Publications:** *Challenge*, quarterly. Newsletter. *Price:* Free for members.

★4850★ **International Society of Endocrinology (ISE)**
51-53 St. Bartholomew's Hospital
Bartholomew Close
London EC1A 7BE, England
Phone: 171 6064012
Fax: 171 7964676
Prof. Lesley H. Rees, Sec.Gen.

Founded: 1966. **Members:** 53. **Description:** Federation of national endocrinology societies with 15,000 individual members. Disseminates information on endocrinology and facilitates collaboration between national endocrinological societies and persons interested in the field. **Publications:** *Abstracts of Congresses*, annual. Newsletter. • *Symposia Abstracts*, periodic.

International Society on Metabolic Eye Disease (ISMED)
See: Entry 13501

★4851★ **International Study Group for Steroid Hormones (ISGSH)**
V Clinica Medica
Policlinico Umberto 1
Universita di Roma La Sapienza
I-00161 Rome, Italy
Phone: 6 4940568
Fax: 6 490530
Vincenzo Toscano, Sec.

Founded: 1961. **Members:** 350. **Languages:** English. **Description:** Researchers, physicians, and professors in medical specialties such as endocrinology, urology, oncology, and gynecology, whose main scientific activity concerns steroid hormones; pharmaceutical firms. Strives to encourage and advance steroid hormone studies and research. Promotes education and training in steroid assays. **Publications:** *Abstracts of the Meeting*, biennial. • *Research on Steroids*, biennial. Contains proceeding. • *Steroids*. Journal.

★4852★ **Iron Overload Diseases Association (IOD)**
433 Westwind Dr.
North Palm Beach, FL 33408
Phone: (407)840-8512
Fax: (407)842-9881
Roberta Crawford, Pres.

Founded: 1981. **Members:** 8,000. **Regional Groups:** 4. **Description:** Physicians and pa-

tients. Purposes are to: serve hemochromatosis patients and families; encourage research and public information; press for earlier diagnosis and more effective treatment. (Hemochromatosis is a genetic condition of iron overload in which excess iron damages organs and tissues, producing varying late-stage symptoms including liver cirrhosis, diabetes, heart failure, arthritis, and skin pigmentation, leading to death unless diagnosed early and treated adequately.) Specific plans are: to organize chapters and to develop a public relations plan, television interviews, and press releases; to sponsor screening programs and patient referral service; prepare diagnosis sheets for doctors and medical schools. Current emphasis is on alerting the public to the dangers of excess iron, since the disease is more prevalent than previously believed, and most susceptible individuals are unaware of the hazard. Authorities believe that five in 1000 carry both genes and that one in eight carries a single gene. Acts as a clearinghouse for doctors to call on for research materials and plans to establish a toll-free number for the public. Sponsors fundraising program. Is also in the process of setting up an index of laboratory research in progress. Conducts programs; compiles statistics; maintains speakers' bureau; conducts research programs. **Publications:** *Ironic Blood*, bimonthly. Newsletter. *Price:* Free. • *Overload: An Ironic Disease*. Booklet.

★4853★ **Joslin Diabetes Center (JDC)**
1 Joslin Pl.
Boston, MA 02215
Phone: (617)732-2400
Fax: (617)732-2562
Dr. Kenneth E. Quickel, Pres.

Founded: 1968. **Description:** Supported by persons interested in advancing knowledge and improving treatment of diabetes with the eventual goal of discovering a means of prevention and cure. Investigates new methods in the clinical treatment of diabetes; conducts research at its Elliott P. Joslin Research Laboratory. Supports two camps for diabetic children and maintains diabetes treatment unit to instruct diabetic patients in the proper management of their disease. Compiles statistics on grants for research on diabetes. Offers specialized education programs for health care professionals, including annual course for practicing physicians with the Harvard Medical School. **Publications:** *Joslin Magazine*, quarterly. Magazine. Provides information on diet, education, and research; also covers the activities of the center. *Price:* Included in membership dues. • Report, annual. Also publishes manual and other information resources. **Formerly:** (1981) Joslin Diabetes Foundation.

Juvenile Diabetes Foundation International (JDFI)
See: Entry 3251

Juvenile Diabetes Foundation in Israel (JDFI)
(Haagudah LeSukereth Neurim Beyisrael)
See: Entry 3252

★4854★ **Latin American Diabetes Association**
Apartado Postal 25
Curridabat
San Jose 2300, Costa Rica
Dr. Eric Mora Morales

Description: Promotes the study of diabetes. Works for the cure and prevention of diabetes.

Little People of America (LPA)
See: Entry 7886

★4855★ **Maltese Diabetes Association (MDA)**
(Ghaqda Kontra d-Dijabete — GKD)
PO Box 413
Valletta CMR 01, Malta
Phone: 235158
Tania Vassallo, Sec.

Founded: 1981. **Members:** 600. **Languages:** English. **Description:** Individuals with type I or type II diabetes and their families. Furthers awareness of the health problems associated with diabetes and encourages the study of causes and treatments. Works to safeguard the social and economic interests of diabetic individuals. Conducts lectures and discussions; distributes educational materials; disseminates information. **Publications:** *Id-Dijabete u Sahhtek*, quarterly. Magazine. • *What is Diabetes?*. Brochure.

★4856★ **National Adrenal Diseases Foundation (NADF)**
505 Northern Blvd., Ste. 200
Great Neck, NY 11021
Phone: (516)487-4992
Patti Gelman, Founder

Founded: 1985. **Members:** 500. **Description:** Individuals with adrenal diseases, especially Addison's disease, and their families; physicians. Seeks to provide a national selfhelp network for educational and emotional support for patients and their families. (Addison's disease is a severe or total deficiency of the hormones produced in the adrenal cortex, caused by a destruction of the adrenal cortex, usually by disease or trauma. The disease is controllable through medication, though patients must make provisions for Addisonian "crises," when regularly prescribed medications are insufficient.) **Publications:** *NADF News*, quarterly. Newsletter. Also publishes educational materials. **Formerly:** (1991) National Addison's Disease Foundation.

★4857★ **National Center for the Study of Wilson's Disease (NCSWD)**
432 W. 58th St., Ste. 614
New York, NY 10019
Phone: (212)523-8717
Fax: (212)523-8708
I. Herbert Scheinberg, M.D., Pres.

Founded: 1971. **Members:** 9. **Description:** Performs and supports research concerning hereditary diseases of metal metabolism, in particular Wilson's disease and Menkes' disease. Seeks to increase doctors' awareness of these diseases. (Wilson's disease, named for S.A.K. Wilson, who discovered the disease and published his findings in 1912, is caused by a genetic defect that permits excessive amounts of copper to accumulate in the liver and brain. The disease is fatal if untreated, but, if detected early enough, can be completely suppressed.) Encompasses research, diagnostic, and treatment center for Wilson's disease. Compiles statistics. **Publications:** Articles. • Brochure. **Formerly:** (1988) Foundation for the Study of Wilson's Disease.

★ 4858 ★ National Gaucher Foundation (NGF)

11140 Rockville Pike, No. 350
Rockville, MD 20852-3106
Phone: (301)816-1515
Fax: (301)816-1516
Ronda P. Buyers, Exec.Dir.

Founded: 1984. **Members:** 2,500. **Regional Groups:** 4. **Description:** Persons with Gaucher's Disease; interested medical professionals and individuals. Gaucher's Disease, one of the most common inherited metabolic disorders, is caused by an enzyme deficiency which renders the body unable to break down and dispose of complex lipids (fat-like substances). These lipids accumulate in the spleen, liver, and bone marrow, causing enlargement of the organs and intermittent pain of varying severity. (The disease is named for Phillippe C. E. Gaucher, a French physician who described it in 1882.) One in 12 Jews in the U.S. is a carrier and one in 450 has Gaucher's Disease. Sponsors direct funding of and support for research and clinical programs at medical centers in the U.S. and abroad to develop a cure and/or treatment for Gaucher's Disease. Seeks to help persons with the disorder by providing them the opportunity to share experiences and feelings on a confidential, personal basis. Disseminates technical and nontechnical information concerning the disease. Advocates increased screening for carriers and availability of prenatal diagnosis for families at risk. **Publications:** *Gaucher's Disease Registry Newsletter*, bimonthly. Newsletter. Includes index, reprints of recent literature, legislative reports, and medical questions and answers. *Price:* $45 for medical professionals; $35 for others.

★ 4859 ★ National Graves' Disease Foundation (NGDF)

320 Arlington Rd.
Jacksonville, FL 32211
Phone: (904)724-0770
Nancy H. Patterson, Ph.D., Exec.Dir.

Founded: 1990. **Members:** 800. **Description:** People with Graves' disease; families of those affected; physicians and other professionals. Facilitates establishments of support groups for members in all states. Fosters public awareness and education on the causes, effects, and treatment of Grave's disease, a result of hyperthyroidism (the excess production by the body of thyroxine and triiodothyronine) in which the thyroid gland may be slightly enlarged, and symptoms such as a rapid heartbeat, eye problems, weight loss, or fatigue may occur. Participates in research on Grave's disease. **Publications:** Bulletin, periodic. • Newsletter, quarterly.

★ 4860 ★ National Hormone and Pituitary Program (NHPP)

685 Lofstrand Dr.
Rockville, MD 20850
Phone: (301)309-3667
Fax: (301)340-9245
Dr. Philip Smith, Ph.D., Scientific Officer

Founded: 1963. **Description:** The agency collects human pituitary glands obtained through autopsies and extracts from them human growth hormone (hGH), human follicle stimulating hormone (hFSH), human luteinizing hormone (hLH), human adrenocorticotrophic hormone (ACTH), human thyroid stimulating hormone (hTSH), human prolactin, and beta-lipotropin. These and similar hormones of rat, ovine, bovine, porcine, and monkey origin are distributed to doctors in research centers for research in endocrinology. Promotes basic studies with all pituitary hormones and seeks to make these available to investigators. **Formerly:** (1983) National Pituitary Agency.

★ 4861 ★ National Hypoglycemia Association (NHA)

PO Box 120
Ridgewood, NJ 07451
Phone: (201)670-1189
Lenore L. Cohen, Founder & Dir.

Founded: 1982. **Description:** Hypoglycemics and health professionals who provide educational, informational, and support services to individuals with hypoglycemia and their families. (Hypoglycemia is a deficiency in the blood sugar level that deprives the central nervous system of glucose needed to function normally.) Maintains speakers' bureau; organizes support groups. Provides professional referrals, consultations, and evaluations for individuals with hypoglycemia and related conditions. **Publications:** Booklets. • *National Hypoglycemia Association--Newsletter*, bimonthly. Newsletter. Contains information on hypoglycemia for patients, families, doctors, and the public. Includes research reports and calendar of events. *Price:* Included in membership dues; $2/copy for non-members.

★ 4862 ★ National Lymphedema Network

2211 Post St., Ste. 404
San Francisco, CA 94115
Phone: 800-541-3259
Fax: (415)921-4284
Saskia R.J. Thiadens, R.N., Pres.

Founded: 1988. **Members:** 2,000. **State Groups:** 45. **Description:** Persons with lymphedema and their families. Disseminates information about lymphedema to patients and health care prefessionals. (Lymphedema is an accumulation of lymphatic fluid causing swelling in the arms and legs which increases risk of infection.) Provides counseling hotline; offers referral service to medical facilities. Helps locate and organize support groups. Compiles statistics. Sponsors research and educational programs. **Publications:** *NLN Newsletter*, quarterly. Newsletter.

★ 4863 ★ National MPS Society

17 Kraemer St.
Hicksville, NY 11801-4321
Phone: (516)931-6338
Fax: (516)822-2041
Marie Capobianco, Pres.

Founded: 1974. **Members:** 800. **Regional Groups:** 9. **Description:** Professionals and families devoted to educating the public and discovering and aiding families of MPS and ML children. Mucopolysaccharidoses (MPS) and mucolipidoses (ML) are extremely rare hereditary diseases caused by particular enzyme deficiencies and range in severity from strictly bone and joint involvement to massive complications in all organ systems. Helps to facilitate diagnosis and treatment through referrals to doctors and hospitals. Maintains parent referral service to direct families with newly diagnosed MPS and ML children to other members. **Publications:** *Courage*, quarterly. Newsletter. • *Ethan's Feeling Switch*. Book. *Price:* $5. • *Hunter*. Booklet. *Price:* $1. • *Hurler*. Booklet. *Price:* $1. • *Morciteaux-Lamy*. Booklet. *Price:* $1. • *Morquio*. Booklet. *Price:* $1. • *MPS Directory*, annual. Directory. • *San Filippo*. Booklet. *Price:* $1. **Formerly:** (1975) Parents for MPS; (1985) MPS Society.

★ 4864 ★ National Organization for Albinism and Hypopigmentation (NOAH)

1530 Locust St., No. 29
Philadelphia, PA 19102-4415
Phone: (215)545-2322
Free: 800-473-2310
Fax: (215)928-0634
Jennifer George, Co-Pres.

Founded: 1982. **Members:** 1,000. **Regional Groups:** 40. **State Groups:** 21. **Description:** Individuals with albinism and their familes; health care professionals; others interested in learning more about albinism. (Albinism is an inherited metabolic disorder that results in reduced pigment in the hair, eyes, and/or skin of those it affects; people with albinism also have impaired eye function including decreased visual acuity, involuntary eye movements, and increased sensitivity to light.) Seeks to educate teachers, health care professionals, and the public about albinism. Provides support to individuals with albinism and their families. Encourages research on the cause, results, and management of the disorder. **Publications:** *NOAH Information Bulletin*, periodic. Bulletin. • *NOAH News*, semiannual. • *The Student with Albinism in the Regular Classroomm*. Book.

★ 4865 ★ National Tay-Sachs and Allied Diseases Association (NTSAD)

2001 Beacon St.
Brookline, MA 02146
Phone: (617)277-4463
Fax: (617)277-0134
Debra Gutter, Dir.

Founded: 1956. **Members:** 5,000. **State Groups:** 7. **Description:** Supports educational, prevention, family service, and research programs concerning Tay-Sachs and allied degenerative lysosomal and neurological diseases occurring in infants, children, and adults. Provides educational literature on Tay-Sachs and allied diseases; serves as a referral agency for the layperson and professional on all aspects of

Tay-Sachs and related diseases; promotes mass screening programs and appropriate legislation locally and nationally; sponsors International Quality Control and Reference Sample Center for TSD laboratories. Offers support groups and services for parents of children with Tay-Sachs and related diseases. Compiles statistics; operates speakers' bureau. **Publications:** Booklets. *Price:* Free. • *National Tay-Sachs and Allied Diseases Association--Breakthrough,* semiannual. Newsletter. • Pamphlets. Also makes available sound/slide and video materials. **Formerly:** (1966) National Tay-Sachs Association.

★4866★ Norwegian Diabetes Association (NDF)
(Norges Diabetesforbund)
Postboks 6442
Etterstad
N-0605 Oslo, Norway
Phone: 22 654550
Fax: 22 630688
Bjornar Allgot, Sec.Gen.

Founded: 1948. **Members:** 24,000. **National Groups:** 5. **Regional Groups:** 19. **Local Groups:** 150. **Languages:** English. **Description:** Diabetics and their families; health personnel. Acts as support group. Disseminates information on availability of insulin, diabetes products, and health care. Lobbies the government to incorporate diabetes treatment into national health care plans and to provide free insulin, syringes, and urine and blood glucose strips. Provides research and medical services. Offers educational courses; conducts camps; maintains youth club. **Publications:** Booklets. • *Diabetikeren,* bimonthly. Magazine. Features educational material. Includes Annual medical supplement.

★4867★ Organic Acidemia Association (OAA)
c/o Carol Barton
2287 Cypress Ave.
San Pablo, CA 94806
Phone: (510)724-0297
Carol Barton, Exec.Dir.

Founded: 1982. **Members:** 300. **Description:** Dietitians, researchers, and geneticists; clinics; parents and relatives of children suffering from organic acidemia disorders. (Organic acidemia is a class of genetic metabolic disorders that lead to cellular enzyme deficiencies and require restricted diets.) Fosters communication among parents and professionals; acts as support group. **Publications:** *Organic Acidemia Association Newsletter,* 3/year. Newsletter.

★4868★ Oxalosis and Hyperoxaluria Foundation (OHF)
PO Box 1632
Kent, WA 98035
Phone: (206)631-0386
Free: 800-484-9698
Fax: (206)631-0386
Anne M. Dayton, Exec. Officer

Founded: 1989. **Description:** Individuals affected by oxalosis and hyperoxaluria; health care professionals. (Hyperoxaluria is a metabolic disease affecting the kidneys; calcium oxalate crystals or calcium oxalate kidney stones form,

causing kidney pain, urinary tract obstruction, and blood in the urine. Progressive kidney damage and eventual kidney failure can result. Oxalosis occurs when calcium crystals have deposited elsewhere in the body, often the eyes, bones, and joints. Onset of these disorders can occur at any time, but most often from infancy to mid-twenties. Treatment consists of dietary restrictions, medication, and vitamin supplements; dialysis and kidney transplant may eventually be required.) Provides support services and information regarding the conditions and their affects. Encourages research. Operates referral service. **Publications:** *In Touch,* 4/year. Newsletter. • *Understanding Hyperoxaluria and Oxalosis.* Brochure. Also publishes dietary guidelines.

★4869★ Parents of Galactosemic Children (PGC)
20981 Solano Way
Boca Raton, FL 33433-1621
Phone: (407)852-0266
Fax: (305)428-0830
Linda Manis, Contact

Founded: 1985. **Members:** 300. **Description:** Parents of children born with galactosemia. (Children with galactosemia are missing an enzyme in the liver that breaks galactose into gulcose, possibly causing jaundice, an enlarged liver, cataracts, kidney failure, and brain damage.) Seeks to errdicate galactosemia. Works to obtain financial support for galactosemia research professionals. Offers support, educational programs, and other information to galactosemic families and interested professionals.

★4870★ PKU Parents (PKU-P)
c/o Dale Hillard
8 Myrtle Ln.
San Anselmo, CA 94960
Phone: (415)457-4632
Dale Hillard, Pres.

Founded: 1977. **Members:** 200. **Description:** Parents and health care professionals who deal with patients of phenylketonuria (PKU), an inherited metabolic disease characterized by the inability to oxidize phenylalanine and by severe mental deficiency if untreated. However, mental retardation caused by PKU can be prevented by dietary treatment. Purposes are: to provide support and education for parents of children with PKU; to assist families with newly diagnosed PKU children in coping with initial shock; to provide a forum for the exchange of information and obtaining needed services and assistance. Conducts specialized education through telephone network and conferences. Maintains contacts with similar groups. **Publications:** Newsletter, quarterly.

Prader-Willi Syndrome Association U.S.A. (PWS)
See: Entry 2751

Sjogren's Syndrome Foundation (SSF)
See: Entry 7910

★4871★ Slovak Society of Diabetes
SK-975 17 Banska Bystrica, Slovakia
Phone: 88 712134
J. Hrnciar, M.D., Contact

Languages: English, Slovak. **Description:** Health care professionals with an interest in dia-

betes; people with diabetes and their families. Encourages advancement in the prevention and treatment of diabetes; fosters communication among members.

★4872★ Society for Mucopolysaccharide Diseases (MPS)
55 Hill Ave.
Amersham, Bucks. HP6 5BX, England
Phone: 1494 434156
Fax: 1494 434252
Christine Lavery, Founder & Hon.Dir.

Founded: 1982. **Members:** 700. **National Groups:** 12. **Regional Groups:** 12. **Languages:** English, French, German. **Description:** Acts as a support group for families of children in 20 countries afflicted with Mucopolysaccharide Diseases. (MPS diseases, known individually as Hurler, Scheie, Hunter, Sanfilippo, Morquio, Maroteaux-Lamy, and Sly, and associated diseases called mucolipidosis, Fucosidosis, and Sialic Acid Disease, are genetic diseases. Children born with MPS are unable to produce certain enzymes necessary for appropriate metabolism to take place; consequently complex sugars become stored in connective tissues, causing progressive damage, including physical and mental handicaps. In most cases, MPS patients die before reaching adulthood.) Encourages public awareness of MPS diseases and the international transmission of medical knowledge and techniques. Raises funds to further MPS research and arranges for MPS families to assist in research such as carrier testing and biochemical diagnosis. Accepts donations to provide vacations for MPS families. Sponsors research program on the natural history of MPS and the psychosocial problems of MPS children. **Publications:** *Conference Reports,* annual. Report. • Newsletter, quarterly. • Report, annual.

Society of Reproductive Endocrinologists (SRE)
See: Entry 11253

★4873★ Society for the Study of Inborn Errors of Metabolism (SSIEM)
Willink Biochemical Genetics Unit
Royal Manchester Children's Hospital
Pendlebury, Greater Manchester M27 4HA, England
Phone: 161 7944696
Fax: 161 7283898
Dr. John Walter, Sec.

Founded: 1962. **Members:** 698. **Languages:** English. **Description:** Biochemists, dietitians, pediatricians, pathologists, geneticists, and interested individuals in 41 countries. Purpose is to foster study of inherited metabolic disease diagnosis and treatment. Promotes exchange of ideas through meetings and publications. **Publications:** *Journal of Inherited Metabolic Diseases,* quarterly. Journal. • *Membership Handbook,* periodic. • Pamphlets. • Proceedings.

★ 4874 ★ South African Diabetes Association (SADA)
(Suid-Afrikaanse Diabetesberniging — SADV)
PO Box 3943
Cape Town 8000, Republic of South Africa
Phone: 21 4613715
Fax: 21 4622008
Josina W. Barnes, Exec.Dir.

Founded: 1969. **Members:** 6,000. **Local Groups:** 13. **Languages:** Afrikaans, English. **Description:** Individuals concerned with diabetes and associated diseases. Develops educational methods designed to give diabetics a better understanding and control of their disease. Promotes advancements in medical research and service to improve standards of treatment. Fosters exchange of information among members. Disseminates data on diabetes to increase public awareness of the disease; seeks to protect diabetics against discrimination due to their disease. Conducts research. Arranges social events and educational guidance for diabetics; organizes lectures. **Publications:** *Control*, quarterly. • *Sada News*, semiannual. Also publishes educational leaflets.

★ 4875 ★ Swedish Diabetic Association (SDA)
(Svenska Diabetesforbundet — SDF)
Box 1545
S-171 29 Solna, Sweden
Phone: 8 6298580
Fax: 8 982555
Anders Ericsson, Contact

Founded: 1943. **Members:** 34,500. **Regional Groups:** 14. **Local Groups:** 107. **Languages:** English, Swedish. **Description:** Provides support and information for diabetics in Sweden. Conducts educational and research programs. **Publications:** *Diabetes*, bimonthly.

★ 4876 ★ Thyroid Foundation of America
Massachusetts General Hospital
Ruth Sleeper Hall 350
Boston, MA 02114
Phone: (617)726-8500
Free: 800-832-8321
Fax: (617)726-4136
Dr. Lawrence C. Wood, Pres.

Founded: 1985. **Members:** 3,300. **State Groups:** 4. **Local Groups:** 1. **Description:** Individuals with thyroid conditions; health professionals. Provides education and support for thyroid patients and health professionals; promotes public awareness of thyroid problems. Sponsors fundraising to support thyroid research; conducts educational programs. Maintains speakers' bureau and placement services; compiles statistics. Operates referral service. **Publications:** *The Bridge*, quarterly. Newsletter. Reports on current research and chapter activities; includes book reviews. *Price:* Included in membership dues.

★ 4877 ★ Wilson's Disease Association (WDA)
PO Box 75324
Washington, DC 20013
Phone: (703)636-3003
Free: 800-399-0266
H. Ascher Sellner, Pres.

Founded: 1979. **Members:** 150. **Description:** Victims of Wilson's disease and related disorders of copper metabolism, such as Menkes' disease; relatives and friends of victims; physicians and other health care professionals. (Wilson's disease, named for S.A.K. Wilson, a pioneer in the study of the disease, is a genetic nervous disorder in which excessive amounts of copper collect in the liver, brain, and kidneys. Menkes' disease is the reverse of Wilson's disease, and is characterized by a defect in intestinal absorption of copper that leads to copper deficiency.) Purpose is to promote and sponsor research regarding the cause, treatment, cure, and prevention of Wilson's and related diseases. Stresses the importance of public awareness, early diagnosis, and treatment. Provides financial aid and moral support to needy individuals and organizations sharing the association's goals; serves as liaison among members and cooperating organizations. Collects and disseminates information to members and the public concerning developments, current research, and legislation in the field; acts as clearinghouse. **Publications:** Brochures. • *Wilson's Disease Association--Membership Directory*, annual. Membership Directory. *Price:* Included in membership dues. • *Wilson's Disease Association--Newsletter*, quarterly. Newsletter. Includes research reports, member profiles, and book reviews. *Price:* Free.

★ 4878 ★ Women's Caucus of the Endocrine Society (WE)
University of Maryland School of Medicine
Department of Physiology
655 W. Baltimore St.
Baltimore, MD 21201
Phone: (410)328-3851
Phyllis Wise, Sec.-Treas.

Founded: 1975. **Members:** 850. **Description:** To promote professional advancement of women and younger members of the Endocrine Society. Maintains biographical archives; compiles statistics; conducts seminars and workshops. **Publications:** *Letter to Membership*, periodic.

Research Centers

★ 4879 ★ Barbara Davis Center for Childhood Diabetes
4200 E. 9th Ave.
Box B140
Denver, CO 80262
Phone: (303)270-8796
Fax: (303)270-4124
Dr. H. Peter Chase, Clinical Dir.

Research Activities and Fields: Diabetes in children, including immunopathology, islet cell transplantation, and clinical trials of free radical scavengers in new onset type-I diabetes. Maintains clinical records of 2,000 diabetic children and young adults. **Publications:** Research Papers.

★ 4880 ★ Baylor College of Medicine Biochemical Genetics Laboratory
1 Baylor Plaza, Rm. T530
Houston, TX 77030
Phone: (713)798-4982
Fax: (713)798-6584
William E. O'Brien, PhD, Dir.

Research Activities and Fields: Diagnosing and monitoring patients with inborn errors of metabolism.

Baylor College of Medicine
Center for Experimental Therapeutics
See: Entry 10427

★ 4881 ★ Case Western Reserve University Center for Inherited Disorders of Energy Metabolism
2074 Abington Rd.
Cleveland, OH 44106
Phone: (216)844-1286
Fax: (216)844-3757
Dr. Douglas Kerr, Dir.

Research Activities and Fields: Defects of human energy metabolism, focusing on diagnosis and management. Emphasis is on disorders of pyruvate fatty acid oxidation, and mitochondrial function.

★ 4882 ★ Center for Endocrinology, Metabolism and Molecular Medicine
15-709 Tarry
303 Chicago Ave.
Chicago, IL 60611
Phone: (312)908-7970
Fax: (312)908-9032
Dr. Larry Jameson, Chief

Research Activities and Fields: Endocrinology, metabolism, and nutrition, including diabetes, growth hormones, obesity and hypertension, and catecholamines. **Formerly:** Center for Endocrinology Metabolism and Nutrition (1993).

★ 4883 ★ Clinical Research Center
Children's Hospital Research Foundation
Elland & Bethesda Aves.
Cincinnati, OH 45229
Phone: (513)559-4412
Fax: (513)559-7874
Dr. James Heubi, Dir.

Research Activities and Fields: Pediatrics, including studies of congenital and acquired diseases of the gastrointestinal tract, pancreas, and liver, cholestatic liver disease, hepatic storage diseases, and cystic fibrosis. Endocrinology program studies growth, diabetes mellitus, hypertension, child and adult bone disease (including rickets and osteoporosis), and insulin sensitivity. **E-mail Address:** heubi-je@ucbeh.san.uc.edu.

★ 4884 ★ Diabetes Research Center
Univ. of Virginia Diabetes Center
Health Sciences Center
Box 423
Charlottesville, VA 22908
Phone: (804)924-5246
Eugene J. Barrett, M.D., Dir.

Research Activities and Fields: Treatment, prevention, and cure of Type I and Type II diabetes mellitus, education and training of health care professionals and diabetics, and development of model care for diabetic patients. Conducts basic and clinical research with emphasis on hormone action and cyclic nucleotide metabolism. **Formerly:** Diabetes Research & Training Center (1987).

★4885★ **Diabetes Treatment and Research Center**
10 Emerson Place, Ste. 2
Boston, MA 02114
Phone: (617)726-1847
Fax: (617)726-1871
Dr. David Nathan, Dir.

Research Activities and Fields: Diabetes research, including a ten-year study of diabetics and studies of implantable pumps.

Dorothea Dix Hospital
Clinical Research Unit
See: Entry 1581

Endocrinology Research Laboratory
See: Entry 9706

★4886★ **Hauptman-Woodward Medical Research Institute, Inc.**
73 High St.
Buffalo, NY 14203-1196
Phone: (716)856-9600
Fax: (716)852-4846
Herbert A. Hauptman, Ph.D., Pres.

Research Activities and Fields: Hormone-related disorders, including studies in cancer, hypertension, heart disease, diabetes, arthritis, AIDS, and thyroid and digestive disorders. Research is carried out in three departments: Molecular Biophysics, Endocrine Biochemistry, and Electron Diffraction. Programs concentrate on molecular endocrinology and the quantitative study of the molecular structures and events that underlie endocrine processes, including structures of steroid hormones, thyroactive compounds, prostaglandins, antibiotics, ionophores, and phospholipids. Biosynthesis programs are centered on estrogens, androgens, progestins, adrenocortical hormones, cholesterol, and thyroid hormones at the molecular level. **Publications:** *Impact* (quarterly newsletter); Annual Report. **E-mail Address:** hauptman@hwi.buffalo.edu. **Formerly:** Medical Foundation of Buffalo, Inc. (1994).

★4887★ **Indiana University-Purdue University at Indianapolis**
Diabetes Research and Training Center
Regenstrief Health Center, 5th Fl.
1001 W. 10th St.
Indianapolis, IN 46202
Phone: (317)630-6374
Fax: (317)630-6962
Dr. Charles M. Clark, Jr., Dir.

Research Activities and Fields: Diabetes research, including basic and clinical studies in health education, clinical epidemiology, and molecular biology. **Publications:** Annual Report (distributed to the National Institutes of Health).

★4888★ **Indiana University-Purdue University at Indianapolis**
Endocrinology Research Laboratories
541 N. Clinical Dr.
Clinical Bldg. 459
Indianapolis, IN 46202-5111
Phone: (317)274-1339
Fax: (317)278-0658
Alain D. Baron, M.D., Dir.

Research Activities and Fields: Basic and clinical aspects of endocrinology and metabolism, including bone metabolism, alcohol metabolism, role of aldosterone and renin in hypertensive states, and insulin secretion and action. **E-mail Address:** alain@medicine.dmed.iupui.edu.

★4889★ **Institute for Metabolic Research**
3508 Market St., Ste. 420
Philadelphia, PA 19104
Phone: (215)222-1818
Fax: (215)222-5325
Margo P. Cohen, M.D.,, Dir.

Research Activities and Fields: Metabolic effects, diagnosis, and management of diabetes mellitus and other metabolic diseases. Studies include the biochemistry and metabolism of glomerular and retinal microvascular basement membranes; role of polyol pathway in complications of diabetes; red cell deformability and phospholipid metabolism in diabetes; structure/function effects of non-enzymatic glycosylation of proteins; measurement of glycohemoglobin and glycoalbumin in biologic samples by immunologic methods; identification and purification of islet cell antigens.

★4890★ **Johns Hopkins University**
Office of Psychohormonal Research
1235 E. Monument St., Ste. LL20
Baltimore, MD 21202
Phone: (410)955-3740
Dr. John Money, Dir.

Research Activities and Fields: Longitudinal psychohormonal research studies of patients with diverse endocrine, genital, and sexological syndromes, related to clinical psychoendocrinology, clinical sexology, gender identity/role (G-I/R), abuse-dwarfism (Kaspar Hauser syndrome), and Munchausen syndrome by proxy.

★4891★ **Joslin Diabetes Center**
1 Joslin Pl.
Boston, MA 02215
Phone: (617)732-2400
Fax: (617)732-2487
Kenneth E. Quickel, Jr., M.D., Pres.

Research Activities and Fields: Diabetes mellitus, including investigations on chemical composition of basement membrane, physiological control of glucose metabolism, neonatal and fetal growth and metabolism, cellular and molecular mechanisms of insulin action, vascular cell biology, ultrastructure of beta cell, pancreatic islets, muscle perfusion, experimental diabetes in animals, immunologic aspects of diabetes, diabetic eye disease, and epidemiology of diabetes. Conducts clinical studies of early stages of diabetic state, treatment, and prevention of diabetes and its complications, especially

of a vascular nature, with emphasis on diabetic retinopathy. **Publications:** Annual Report; *Joslin Magazine* (quarterly). **Formerly:** Diabetes Foundation (1968); Joslin Diabetes Foundation (1981).

★4892★ **Laval University**
Medical Research Centre
Diabetes Research Group
2705, boulevard Laurier
Ste. Foy, PQ, Canada G1V 4G2
Phone: (418)654-2741
Fax: (418)656-2247
Andre Nadeau, Dir.

Research Activities and Fields: The relationship between physical activity and diabetes, and the identification of factors responsible for the increased level of cardiac mortality in diabetes patients.

★4893★ **Laval University**
Medical Research Centre
Hormonal Bioregulation Research Group
2705, boulevard Laurier
Ste. Foy, PQ, Canada G1V 4G2
Phone: (418)654-2733
Fax: (418)654-2714
Roland R. Tremblay, Dir.

Research Activities and Fields: Function and physiology of muscle, muscle tissue, energy production by muscle, and physiology of fatigue. Physiologic effects of muscular carbonic anhydrase isoform inhibition, characterization and functional role of new kallikreins in human and dog prostrates. Influences of serine proteases in biology of reproduction.

★4894★ **Laval University**
Medical Research Centre
Molecular Endocrinology Research Group
2705, boulevard Laurier
Ste. Foy, PQ, Canada G1V 4G2
Phone: (418)654-2296
Fax: (418)654-2761
Fernand Labrie, Dir.

Research Activities and Fields: Prostate and other hormone-sensitive cancers, strategies for early screening for prostate cancer, mechanisms regulating C-19 steroid formation by adrenal glands, characterization of effects of steroid sex hormones, adrenal hormone effects on brain dopaminergic systems, molecular mechanisms responsible for the expression of genes in specific tissues and their extinction in others, cloning and characterization of enzymes implicated in steroidogenesis, hormonal control of growth factors, polyamine biosynthesis in human breast cancer, and regulation of the expression of enzymes involved in steroidogenesis in placenta and adrenal glands.

Laval University
Saint-Francois-d'Assise Hospital Research Centre
Reproductive Endocrinology Unit
See: Entry 11275

★ 4895 ★ Massachusetts General Hospital Reproductive Endocrine Unit
Bartlett Hall Extension-5
Boston, MA 02214
Phone: (617)726-8433
Fax: (617)726-5357
Alan Schneyer, Ph.D., Dir., R&D Lab

Research Activities and Fields: Reproductive endocrinology, focusing on local regulators of gonadal physiology and characterization and regulation of posttransitional processing of inhibin subunits using a variety of techniques, including protein purification and characterization and molecular biology.

Massachusetts Institute of Technology
Laboratory of Neuroendocrine Regulation
See: Entry 8391

★ 4896 ★ Medical Research Institute of Worcester, Inc.
70 Southbridge St., Unit 612
Worcester, MA 01608-2048
Phone: (508)755-3714
Eugenia Rosemberg, M.D., Research Dir.

Research Activities and Fields: Reproductive endocrinology, with special emphasis in pituitary gonadal relationships, including purification and biological and immunological characterization of human gonadotropins, development of techniques for immunoassay of protein and steroid hormones, characterization of normal ovarian and testicular function, characterization of specific types of male and female infertility, and use of pituitary hormones for treatment of specific cases of male and female infertility.

★ 4897 ★ New York Medical College Diabetes Research Center
Munger Pavilion
Valhalla, NY 10595
Phone: (914)285-7995
Fax: (914)993-4380
Dr. Merville Marshall, M.D., Dir.

Research Activities and Fields: Endocrinology, metabolism, diabetes mellitus, and glomerulosclerosis in mice with spontaneous diabetes, including research on the sequence of events leading to small blood vessel abnormalities in animals with spontaneous diabetes, the correlation between hormonal and biochemical derangement in diabetes and progression of structural changes in the kidney, the influence on renal microangiopathy of different genetic backgrounds, and the significant changes on some environmental factors, particularly diet.

Oregon Health Sciences University
Hormone Receptor Laboratory
See: Entry 6099

Oregon Health Sciences University
Vollum Institute for Advanced Biomedical Research
See: Entry 2602

★ 4898 ★ Princeton Bio Center
862 Rte. 518
Skillman, NJ 08558-9631
Phone: (609)924-8607
Fax: (609)924-9423

Research Activities and Fields: Use of naturally occurring substances in the treatment of metabolic disorders. Research encompasses the areas of neurology, psychiatry, brain biochemistry, pharmacology, nutrition and physiology of aging, schizophrenia, and trace element participation in all metabolic diseases. Engaged in the study of metabolic disorders, including: hypoglycemia; childhood hyperactivity; heavy metal poisoning due to mercury, cadmium, bismuth, lead, beryllium, and copper; epilepsy; senility; arthritis; food and inhalant allergies; and digestive disorders. **Formerly:** Brain Bio Center.

Rockefeller University
Laboratory of Biology of Addictive Diseases
See: Entry 12100

★ 4899 ★ Rockefeller University Laboratory of Human Behavior and Metabolism
1230 York Ave.
New York, NY 10021-6399
Phone: (212)327-8426
Fax: (212)327-7150
Prof. Jules Hirsch, M.D., Head

Research Activities and Fields: The biology of weight regulation ranging from changes in systematic energetics which result from weight changes to the molecular genetics of diabetes and obesity in rodents. **E-mail Address:** HIRSCH@ROCKVAX.BITNET.

Rockefeller University
Laboratory of Metabolism-Pharmacology
See: Entry 10453

Rockefeller University
Laboratory of Neuroendocrinology
See: Entry 8419

★ 4900 ★ Rush University Steroid Research Laboratory
1653 W. Congress Pkwy.
Chicago, IL 60612
Phone: (312)942-6165
Dr. Ludwig Kornel, Dir.

Research Activities and Fields: Concentrates on three areas of research: 1) role of mineralocorticoids and glucocorticoids in the molecular mechanism of hypertension; 2) role of insulin in the mechanism of essential hypertension; 3) autocrine regulation of intracellular cortisol concentrations by enzymes metabolizing cortisol. **Formerly:** Steroid Unit (1982).

Scripps Research Institute
Department of Neuropharmacology
See: Entry 8424

Sherbrooke University
Cellular Mechanisms of Action and Ontogenesis Research Group
See: Entry 2620

Shriners Hospital for Crippled Children
Metabolic Research Unit
See: Entry 7930

★ 4901 ★ Tulane University U.S.-Japan Biomedical Research Laboratories
Hebert Research Center
Belle Chasse, LA 70037
Phone: (504)394-7199
Fax: (504)394-7169
Akira Arimura, M.D., Dir.

Research Activities and Fields: Neuroendocrinology and neuroscience, particularly in the areas of neuropeptides and immune-neuroendocrine interactions. Studies include 1) physiology of hypothalamic neurohormones with emphasis on isolation and characterization of novel hypophysiotrophic hormones, and 2) role of cytokines in trophic brain function following injury. **Formerly:** Result of merger in 1985 with Laboratories for Molecular Neuroendocrinology & Diabetes.

U.S. Department of Defense
Armed Forces Institute of Pathology
Otolaryngic and Endocrine Pathology Department
Endocrine Pathology Division
See: Entry 10174

★ 4902 ★ U.S. Department of Energy Lawrence Berkeley Laboratory Cholesterol Research Center
3101 Telegraph Ave.
Berkeley, CA 94705
Phone: (510)486-4694
Fax: (510)486-4750
Ronald M. Krauss, M.D., Director

Research Activities and Fields: Center's research is concerned with the identification and characterization of genetic disorders of cholesterol and lipoprotein metabolism.

U.S. Department of Health and Human Services
National Cancer Institute
Division of Cancer Biology, Diagnosis, and Centers
Metabolism Branch
See: Entry 6135

U.S. Department of Health and Human Services
National Center for Chronic Disease Prevention and Health Promotion
Diabetes Translation Division
Epidemiology and Statistics Branch
See: Entry 10876

U.S. Department of Health and Human Services
National Heart, Lung, and Blood Institute
Division of Intramural Research
Molecular Disease Branch
See: Entry 2942

U.S. Department of Health and Human Services
National Heart, Lung, and Blood Institute
Laboratory of Kidney and Electrolyte Metabolism
See: Entry 2951

U.S. Department of Health and Human Services
National Institute on Alcohol Abuse and Alcoholism
Intramural Clinicaland Biological Research Division
Metabolism Laboratory
See: Entry 12112

★4903★ U.S. Department of Health and Human Services
National Institute of Child Health and Human Development
Center for Research for Mothers and Children
Endocrinology, Nutrition, and Growth Branch
Executive Plaza North, Rm. 637
6130 Executive Blvd.
Bethesda, MD 20892
Phone: (301)496-5593
Gilman Grave, Chief

Research Activities and Fields: Branch supports research and training on the interrelationships of nutrition and endocrinology with physical growth and mental development. This research involves a wide range of disciplines, including molecular biology, cell biology, biochemistry, metabolism, and genetics. Areas of support include: 1) developmental endocrinology and physical growth (e.g., studies on hormonal influence on growth and development, studies on growth factors, and studies on the development of the hypothalamic-pituitary axis in relation to the thyroid, adrenal glands, and gonads); 2) maternal-fetal nutrition, which involves the development of indicators of fetal nutritional status and well-being in order to assess the need for nutritional intervention during pregnancy; 3) infant nutrition (nutrient requirements of normal, premature, and growth-retarded infants; human milk, cow's milk, and synthetic formulas in relation to optimal infant development); 4) developmental gastroenterology (emphasizing the role of nutrients as effectors of gastrointestinal development); 5) cultural and behavioral aspects of nutrition; 6) nutritional status assessment; and 7) antecedents of adult disease to identify indicators during infancy and childhood of disease states that will be manifested later in life and to design various kinds of preventive therapy (emphasis is on childhood obesity and insulin resistance).

★4904★ U.S. Department of Health and Human Services
National Institute of Child Health and Human Development
Intramural Research Program
Developmental Endocrinology Branch
NIH Bldg. 10, Rm. 10N262
9000 Rockville Pike
Bethesda, MD 20892
Phone: (301)496-4686
Dr. Bruce Misula, Chief

Research Activities and Fields: Branch examines the endocrine concomitants of normal and abnormal human growth, development, and differentiation. Specific areas of study include: the mechanisms underlying the initiation of puberty; the regulatory physiology and biochemistry of the glycoprotein hormones; the roles of sex ste-

roid hormones, growth hormones, and other growth factors in bone growth; and the physiology and biochemistry of hypothalmic releasing hormones. In addition, clinical research on male and female reproductive disorders is conducted, and several syndromes of resistance to steroid hormone action are under investigation (both in patients and animal models). Principal Branch components are: Developmental Endocrinology Section, Medical Endocrinology Section, Reproductive Endocrinology Section, and Steroid Hormone Section.

★4905★ U.S. Department of Health and Human Services
National Institute of Child Health and Human Development
Intramural Research Program
Endocrinology and Reproduction Research Branch
NIH Bldg. 49, Rm. 6A36
9000 Rockville Pike
Bethesda, MD 20892
Phone: (301)496-2136
Dr. Kevin J. Catt, Chief

Research Activities and Fields: Branch focuses on studies of the mechanisms controlling hormone secretion and action, with particular reference to hypothalamic-pituitary hormones and their receptor-mediated responses in endocrine target cells. Principal Branch components are: the Adrenal Cell Biology Section, Hormonal Regulation Section, Metabolic Regulation Section, Molecular Endocrinology Section, and Molecular Structures and Protein Chemistry Section.

★4906★ U.S. Department of Health and Human Services
National Institute of Diabetes and Digestive and Kidney Diseases
NIH Bldg. 31
9000 Rockville Pike
Bethesda, MD 20892
Phone: (301)496-5877
Fax: (301)496-2830
Phillip Gorden, Director

Research Activities and Fields: NIDDK conducts and supports research on many of the most serious diseases affecting public health. The Institute supports clinical research on the diseases of internal medicine and related subspecialty fields as well as in many basic science disciplines. Institute's activities include both intramural programs, which are carried out in the Institute's laboratory and clinical facilities on the NIH campus in Bethesda, MD and Phoenix, AZ; and extramural programs, which are supported by NIDDK and carried out at universities, private and public research facilities, and hospital-based clinical research centers. The Institute's Intramural Research Division encompasses the broad spectrum of metabolic diseases such as diabetes and other inborn errors of metabolism, endocrine disorders, mineral metabolism, digestive diseases, renal disease, and hematology. Basic research includes studies in biochemistry; nutrition; pathology; histochemistry; chemistry; physical, chemical, and molecular biology; pharmacology; and toxicology. NIDDK extramural research is organized in four divisions: Diabetes, Endocrinology, and Metabolic Diseases; Diges-

tive Diseases and Nutrition; Kidney, Urologic, and Hematologic Diseases; and Extramural Activities. Mechanisms of NIDDK support for extramural programs include research and program project grants; center grants; conference grants; research, development, and demonstration contracts; resource awards and other support for research and development; scientific communication and evaluation awards; and manpower training awards.

★4907★ U.S. Department of Health and Human Services
National Institute of Diabetes and Digestive and Kidney Diseases
Clinical Nutrition Research Units Program
5333 Westbard Ave., Rm. 3A18B
Bethesda, MD 20892
Phone: (301)594-7573
Fax: (301)594-7504
Dr. Van S. Hubbard, Program Director

Research Activities and Fields: The Clinical Nutrition Research Units (CNRU) Program involves an integrated array of research, educational, and service activities focused on human nutrition in health and disease. Each unit serves as the focal point for an interdisciplinary approach to clinical nutrition research and for the stimulation of research in areas such as improved nutritional support of acutely and chronically ill persons, assessment of nutritional status, effects of disease states on nutrient needs, and effects of changes in nutritional status on disease. Funding for the CNRU program is provided through core center grants, which provide funds for: 1) core resources such as cell culture, immunoassay, biostatistics, or other central research service facilities; 2) pilot/feasibility projects, which support new investigators or investigators from other fields who wish to pursue new and innovative ideas to a point where they can compete for independent support; 3) program enrichment funds to provide for small conferences or symposia and special consultants for the center; and 4) a new investigator position. An existing base of high-quality nutrition-related research is a requirement for the establishment of a CNRU. Due to a restriction in the number of core center grants that can be made, investigator-initiated proposals are accepted only in response to a request for applications announced in the *NIH Guide for Grants and Contracts.*

★4908★ U.S. Department of Health and Human Services
National Institute of Diabetes and Digestive and Kidney Diseases
Division of Diabetes, Endocrinology, and Metabolic Diseases
NIH Bldg. 31, Rm. 9A16
9000 Rockville Pike
Bethesda, MD 20892
Phone: (301)496-7348
Fax: (301)496-2830

Research Activities and Fields: Division supports research and research training in: 1) diabetes mellitus (both insulin dependent and non-insulin dependent diabetes); 2) endocrinological diseases and disorders; and 3) metabolic diseases, including research on the etiology, pathogenesis, and treatment of acquired or inborn errors of metabolism. Support for basic and clinical biomedical research as well as epidemiologic and behavioral studies and clinical trials is provided through investigator-initiated research grants, new investigator awards, program project and center grants, and cooperative agreements. The Division also supports research fellowships, training grants, and a variety of career development awards as well as a limited number of resource and research and development contracts; and provides leadership in coordinating activities relating to diabetes and cystic fibrosis throughout the National Institutes of Health and various other federal agencies. Division's main branches are the Diabetes Programs Branch and the Endocrine and Metabolic Diseases Research Programs Branch.

U.S. Department of Health and Human Services
National Institute of Diabetes and Digestive and Kidney Diseases
Division of Diabetes, Endocrinology, and Metabolic Diseases
Cystic Fibrosis Research Program
See: Entry 5362

★4909★ U.S. Department of Health and Human Services
National Institute of Diabetes and Digestive and Kidney Diseases
Division of Diabetes, Endocrinology, and Metabolic Diseases
Diabetes Centers Program
5333 Westbard Ave., Rm. 622
Bethesda, MD 20892
Phone: (301)496-7418
Fax: (301)496-9721
Dr. Sanford A. Garfield, Program Director

Research Activities and Fields: The Diabetes Centers Program administers two types of center awards: 1) the Diabetes-Endocrinology Research Centers (DERC) and the Diabetes Research and Training Centers (DRTC). The DERC is exclusively oriented toward biomedical research goals, while the DRTCs include training and translation components in addition to biomedical research. An existing base of high-quality diabetes-related research is a primary requirement for establishment of either type of center. Through shared resources (core facilities), both types of center grants provide a mechanism for integrating, coordinating, and fostering the interdisciplinary cooperation of a group of established investigators conducting programs of active high quality research in diabetes and related endocrine and metabolic disorders.

★4910★ U.S. Department of Health and Human Services
National Institute of Diabetes and Digestive and Kidney Diseases
Division of Diabetes, Endocrinology, and Metabolic Diseases
Diabetes Clinical Trials Program
5333 Westbard Ave., Rm. 628
Bethesda, MD 20892
Phone: (301)594-7561
Carolyn W. Siebert, Program Director

Research Activities and Fields: The Clinical Trials Program supports a multicenter random-

ized clinical trial to assess the relationship between blood glucose control and the early vascular complications of insulin dependent diabetes mellitus. Participating in this study are 27 medical centers, a data coordinating center, and other supporting institutions that provide centralized technical and biochemical services. Two groups of expert consultants who are independent of the trial and external to the Institute continually review all operational aspects of the trial and provide policy advice to the Institute regarding the initiation of each subsequent phase of the trial.

★4911★ U.S. Department of Health and Human Services
National Institute of Diabetes and Digestive and Kidney Diseases
Division of Diabetes, Endocrinology, and Metabolic Diseases
Diabetes Research Program
5333 Westbard Ave., Rm. 622
Bethesda, MD 20892
Phone: (301)594-7565
Dr. Joan Harmon, Director

Research Activities and Fields: The Diabetes Research Program provides grant support for investigator-initiated studies covering a wide range of fundamental and clinical studies related to the etiology, pathogenesis, prevention, diagnosis, treatment, and cure of diabetes mellitus and its complications. Specific areas of research interest encompass the structure/function of the pancreatic hormones and related peptides and enzymes; carbohydrate, lipid, and protein metabolism; and nutritional interrelationships, including obesity. Other areas of research support include the genetic nature of diabetes and identification of specific markers that characterize individuals predisposed to diabetes; studies to assess immunologic, infectious, and environmental factors as they relate to diabetes; and studies related to nutrition, metabolic regulation, and hormone synthesis/secretion/action with respect to the pathobiology of diabetes mellitus and its sequelae. Program also provides support for studies related to pancreas and islet transportation, automated insulin delivery systems and glucose sensors, the psychosocial and behavioral aspects of diabetes, the epidemiology of diabetes, and diabetes-related conferences.

★4912★ U.S. Department of Health and Human Services
National Institute of Diabetes and Digestive and Kidney Diseases
Division of Diabetes, Endocrinology, and Metabolic Diseases
Endocrine and Metabolic Diseases Research Programs Branch
5333 Westbard Ave., Rm. 621
Bethesda, MD 20892
Phone: (301)594-7567
Fax: (301)594-9011
Dr. Judith Fradkin, Chief

Research Activities and Fields: Principal Branch components are: 1) Cystic Fibrosis Research Program; 2) Endocrinology Research Program; 3) Bone and Mineral Research Program; 4) Metabolism and Structural Biology Research Program; 5) Metabolic Diseases and

Gene Therapy Research Program; 6) Pituitary and Neuroendocrinology Research Program; and 7) Growth Factors Research Program.

★4913★ U.S. Department of Health and Human Services
National Institute of Diabetes and Digestive and Kidney Diseases
Division of Diabetes, Endocrinology, and Metabolic Diseases
Endocrinology Research Program
5333 Westbard Ave., Rm. 621
Bethesda, MD 20892
Phone: (301)594-7549
Fax: (301)594-9011
Dr. Ronald N. Margolis, Program Director

Research Activities and Fields: The Endocrinology Research Program supports (through research grants) investigator-initiated basic and clinical studies of normal and abnormal function of the pituitary, thyroid, parathyroid, adrenal, pineal, and thymus glands. Studies of the mode of action of hormones, their biosynthesis, secretion, and metabolism as well as their binding to protein carriers, subsequent release, and the kinetics of binding represent a major component of the Program. A substantial portion of the Program is devoted to structure/function studies of the hypothalamic releasing factors as they affect endocrine function as well as the physiology and pathophysiology of bone disease. In addition, studies of somatomedin and somatostatin and their effects on other hormones are supported, as is research on substances with hormone-like action such as prostaglandins and the brain peptides.

★4914★ U.S. Department of Health and Human Services
National Institute of Diabetes and Digestive and Kidney Diseases
Division of Diabetes, Endocrinology, and Metabolic Diseases
Metabolic Diseases and Gene Therapy Research Program
5333 Westbard Ave., Rm. 621
Bethesda, MD 20892
Phone: (301)594-7582
Fax: (301)594-9011
Catherine McKeon, Ph.D., Codirector

Research Activities and Fields: The primary objective of the Metabolic Diseases Research Program is to support investigator-initiated basic studies on fundamental metabolic processes of diseases within NIDDK. A major goal is support of basic and clinical metabolic studies on a significant number of inherited metabolic disorders. The Program supports research studies on: 1) synthesis and biosynthesis of metabolic substrates; 2) membrane structure and function, with special emphasis on transport phenomena, role of cations, and topology of cell surface; 3) enzyme and other protein structure and function relevant to understanding of intermediary metabolic processes and their regulation; 4) enzyme biosynthesis, with special emphasis on genetic control of synthesis; 5) normal and abnormal carbohydrate, fat, amino acid, urea, pyrimidine, and purine metabolism in vitro and in vivo (e.g., cell and tissue cultures, bacteria and animal models, and humans); and 6) basic and clinical aspects of etiology, pathogenesis, prevention, and treatment of inherited metabolic disorders, including the development of gene therapy as a method of treatment.

★4915★ U.S. Department of Health and Human Services
National Institute of Diabetes and Digestive and Kidney Diseases
Division of Diabetes, Endocrinology, and Metabolic Diseases
National Diabetes Data Group
5333 Westbard Ave., Rm. 620
Bethesda, MD 20892
Phone: (301)594-7559
Fax: (301)594-9011
Dr. Maureen I. Harris, Director

Research Activities and Fields: The National Diabetes Data Group (NDDG) serves as the major federal focus for the collection, analysis, and dissemination of data on diabetes and its complications. Drawing upon the expertise of the research, medical, and lay communities, the Data Group initiates efforts to: 1) define the data needed to address the scientific and public health issues in diabetes; 2) foster and coordinate the collection of these data from multiple sources; 3) promote the timely availability of reliable data to pertinent scientific, medical, and public organizations; 4) modify data reporting systems to identify and categorize more appropriately the medical and socio-economic impact of diabetes; and 5) promote the standardization of data collection and terminology in clinical and epidemiologic research. In addition, the NDDG staff works closely with members of the scientific community to stimulate development of new investigator-initiated research programs in diabetes epidemiology.

★4916★ U.S. Department of Health and Human Services
National Institute of Diabetes and Digestive and Kidney Diseases
Division of Diabetes, Endocrinology, and Metabolic Diseases
Research Career Development Program
5333 Westbard Ave., Rm. 621
Bethesda, MD 20892
Phone: (301)594-7549
Dr. Ron Margolis, Director

Research Activities and Fields: Program administers a variety of research training and career development awards that span the full range of research programs falling within the Division. Prospective applicants are encouraged to contact the Research Career Development Program office regarding any questions about eligibility or provisions of the awards and to obtain current instructions for preparing applications. The available awards include National Research Service Awards, Physician Scientist Award, Clinical Investigator Award, and Research Career Development Award.

★4917★ U.S. Department of Health and Human Services
National Institute of Diabetes and Digestive and Kidney Diseases
Division of Diabetes, Endocrinology, and Metabolic Diseases
Special Programs Branch
5333 Westbard Ave., Rm. 620
Bethesda, MD 20892
Phone: (301)594-7590
Dr. Teresa Radibaugh, Chief

Research Activities and Fields: The Special Programs Branch is responsible for all of the Division-related research career development and training awards. These include individual and institutional National Research Service Awards (NRSA), Physician Scientist Awards (PSA), Clinical Investigator Awards (CIA), and Research Career Development Awards (RCDA). Branch components include the National Diabetes Data Group, Research Career Development Program; and the National Diabetes Information Clearinghouse, which collects and distributes information concerning education, scientific materials, programs, and resources relevant to diabetes.

★4918★ U.S. Department of Health and Human Services
National Institute of Diabetes and Digestive and Kidney Diseases
Division of Digestive Diseases and Nutrition
Pancreas Program
5333 Westbard Ave., Rm. 3A17
Bethesda, MD 20892
Phone: (301)594-7858
Fax: (301)594-7504
Thomas F. Kresina, Ph.D., Director

Research Activities and Fields: Program supports research into the structure, function, and diseases (excluding cancer and cystic fibrosis) of the exocrine pancreas. Areas of research interest include: hormonal and neural regulation of electrolyte, fluid, and enzyme secretion; receptors for secretagogs; stimulus-secretion coupling mechanisms; gut-islet-acinar interrelations; organization and expression of pancreatic genes; protein synthesis and export; tissue injury, repair, and regeneration; physiology and pathology of trophic responses; neural innervention; transcapillary solute and fluid exchange; pancreatic tissue culture and storage, and preservation; imaging of the pancreas; pancreatic insufficiency; acute and chronic pancreatitis and relevant experimental models.

★4919★ U.S. Department of Health and Human Services
National Institute of Diabetes and Digestive and Kidney Diseases
Division of Intramural Research
NIH Bldg. 10
9000 Rockville Pike
Bethesda, MD 20892
Phone: (301)496-4128
Fax: (301)496-9943
Allen M. Spiegel, M.D., Director

Research Activities and Fields: The Institute's Intramural Research Division encompasses the broad spectrum of metabolic diseases such as diabetes, other inborn errors of metabolism, endocrine disorders, mineral metabolism, digestive diseases, nutrition, urology and renal disease, and hematology. Basic research includes studies in biochemistry; nutrition; pathology; histochemistry; chemistry; physical, chemical, and molecular biology; pharmacology; and toxicology. Division comprises branches for: Clinical Endocrinology; Clinical Hematology; Diabetes; Digestive Diseases; Genetics and Biochemistry; Mathematical Research; Metabolic Diseases; Molecular, Cellular, and Nutritional Endocrinology; and Pediatric Metabolism; the Phoenix Epidemiology and Clinical Research Branch; and numerous laboratories.

★4920★ U.S. Department of Health and Human Services
National Institute of Diabetes and Digestive and Kidney Diseases
Division of Intramural Research
Diabetes Branch
NIH Bldg. 10, 8S239
9000 Rockville Pike
Bethesda, MD 20892
Phone: (301)496-4658

Research Activities and Fields: The Diabetes Branch studies receptors for peptide hormones, especially insulin, insulin-like growth factors, and growth hormone. Current projects are focused on the role of receptors in disease states, receptor antibodies, and genetic disorders of glucose metabolism, isolation and characterization of receptor components, the role of receptors in hormone and drug action at the target cell, morphologic correlates of hormone binding to receptor (electron microscopy and immunocytochemistry), and receptors on circulating cells and cells in tissue culture. Other projects include insulin and insulin receptors in the central nervous system; the evolutionary origin of insulin, somatostatin, and other peptide messenger molecules; and their role in primitive (unicellular) organisms. The clinical service of the Diabetes Branch provides continuous access to patients with disorders of glucose metabolism and receptor-related disorders.

★4921★ U.S. Department of Health and Human Services
National Institute of Diabetes and Digestive and Kidney Diseases
Division of Intramural Research
Endocrinology Section
NIH Bldg. 10, Rm. 8N315
9000 Rockville Pike
Bethesda, MD 20892
Phone: (301)496-5761
Fax: (301)402-0387
Jacob Robbins, Chief

Research Activities and Fields: Activities focus on thyroid hormones and thyroid diseases, with an emphasis on thyroid cancer.

★4922★ U.S. Department of Health and Human Services
National Institute of Diabetes and Digestive and Kidney Diseases
Division of Intramural Research
Metabolic Diseases Branch
NIH Bldg. 10
9000 Rockville Pike
Bethesda, MD 20892
Phone: (301)496-5051
Dr. Allan Spiegel, Chief

Research Activities and Fields: The Metabolic Diseases Branch conducts clinical and laboratory research into the physiology and nature of metabolic diseases and disorders, with emphasis on the physiology, biochemistry, and mechanism of action of hormones controlling calcium metabolism. Investigations are directed at hormone-receptor interactions, regulation and characterization of adenylate cyclase, and cellular responses to hormones, particularly parathyroid hormone, calcitonin, and parathyroid related peptide. The clinical program involves studies of patients with disorders of mineral metabolism, including familial hyperparathyroid syndromes and patients with multiple endocrine neoplasia type I, hereditary resistance to parathyroid hormone or to calciferols. Patients with hyperparathyroidism are evaluated with arteriography, selective thyroid venous catheterization, and radioimmunoassays for parathyroid hormone and cyclic AMP in plasma and/or urine. Excised parathyroid tissue is used for in vitro studies gene characterization and on control of hormone secretion.

★ 4923 ★ U.S. Department of Health and Human Services
National Institute of Diabetes and Digestive and Kidney Diseases
Division of Intramural Research
Molecular, Cellular, and Nutritional Endocrinology Branch
NIH Bldg. 10, Rm. 8D14
9000 Rockville Pike
Bethesda, MD 20892
Phone: (301)496-1540
Fax: (301)496-1649
Dr. Bruce D. Weintraub, Chief

Research Activities and Fields: Activities are carried out in three areas: neuroendocrinology; experimental diabetes, metabolism, and nutrition; and growth and development. Research in neuroendocrinology includes basic and clinical investigations on the regulation of hypothalamic, pituitary, and placental polypeptide hormones. Studies in experimental diabetes, metabolism, and nutrition include investigation of the structure, function, and biosynthesis of integral membrane proteins involved in the hormonal regulation of carbohydrate and lipid metabolism; studies on the molecular and cellular basis of hormone action; and studies on the influence of altered metabolic and nutritional states on cellular function and its regulation by hormones. In the area of growth and development, Branch seeks to understand the mechanisms by which hormonal, nutritional, and cellular factors interact to regulate cell growth in different physiological states (e.g., fetal/embryonic development, post-natal growth, wound repair, neural cell growth, and maintenance), and how these controlled processes become deranged in pathological states involving excessive or inadequate cell growth (e.g., intrauterine growth retardation, dwarfism, neoplasia, atherosclerosis, diabetic retinopathy). The biosynthesis and action of polypeptide hormones/growth factors and their regulation is studied in appropriate model systems (e.g., cell cultures established from human subjects and animals) using state-of-the-art techniques of molecular and cell biology. Special emphasis is given to interactions between different cell types and their products, regulation of tissue responsiveness to growth factors, and alternative expression of growth factor genes resulting in novel peptides with biological functions not directly related to cell growth.

U.S. Department of Health and Human Services
National Institute of Diabetes and Digestive and Kidney Diseases
Division of Intramural Research
Phoenix Epidemiology and Clinical Research Branch
See: Entry 5191

★ 4924 ★ U.S. Department of Health and Human Services
National Institute of Diabetes and Digestive and Kidney Diseases
Laboratory of Analytical Chemistry
NIH Bldg. 8, Rm. B2A-17
9000 Rockville Pike
Bethesda, MD 20892
Phone: (301)496-6769
Edwin Becker, Acting Chief

Research Activities and Fields: The laboratory provides consultation and technical assistance to Institute scientists in the area of instrumental and chemical analysis, particularly related to experimental design and interpretation of spectra.

U.S. Department of Health and Human Services
National Institute of Diabetes and Digestive and Kidney Diseases
Laboratory of Biochemistry and Metabolism
See: Entry 2643

★ 4925 ★ U.S. Department of Health and Human Services
National Institute of Diabetes and Digestive and Kidney Diseases
Laboratory of Cell Biology and Genetics
NIH Bldg. 8, Rm. 403
9000 Rockville Pike
Bethesda, MD 20892
Phone: (301)496-3435
Dr. Harvey B. Pollard, Chief

Research Activities and Fields: Laboratory conducts basic studies and collaborative clinical studies relating to mechanisms regulating secretion of hormones and transmitters from endocrine nerve and endothelial cells. Other work includes analysis of endocytosis and phagocytosis by macrophages and macrophage cell lines and studies on the structure of nerve and other cell types by both light and electron microscopy; immunology and cytogenetics of autoimmunity; and the molecular biology of viral genomes.

U.S. Department of Health and Human Services
National Institute of Diabetes and Digestive and Kidney Diseases
Laboratory of Cellular and Developmental Biology
See: Entry 2645

U.S. Department of Health and Human Services
National Institute of Mental Health
Intramural Research Programs Division (Clinical Research)
Clinical Neuroendocrinology Branch
See: Entry 7637

★ 4926 ★ University of Alabama at Birmingham
Diabetes Research and Training Center
Dept. of Medicine
Division of Endocrinology & Metabolism
Univ. Sta.
Birmingham, AL 35294
Phone: (205)934-4116
Fax: (205)934-4389
Dr. Jeffrey E. Kudlow, Dir.

Research Activities and Fields: Diabetes, genetics, immunology, endocrinology, growth factors, hormones, insulin, molecular biology, and clinical pharmacology.

★ 4927 ★ University of Alabama at Birmingham
Laboratory of Exocrine Physiology
Univ. Sta.
Birmingham, AL 35294
Phone: (205)934-4588

Research Activities and Fields: Physiology of exocrine glands, focusing on clarifying mechanisms of regulation of glandular growth, development, and secretion, and principal mechanisms by which electrolytes are secreted. Collaborates with scientists in Thailand, Egypt, and Hungary.

★ 4928 ★ University of California, Irvine
UCI Diabetes Research Program
Dept. of Medicine
Med Sci I C264
Irvine, CA 92717
Phone: (714)824-7110
Fax: (714)824-2200
M. Arthur Charles, M.D., Head

Research Activities and Fields: Basic and clinical diabetes research, including studies in islet transplantation; diabetes remission, induction, and prevention studies; immunology of diabetes; programmable insulin delivery implant systems; aldose reductose inhibitors in humans; hypertension and oral hypoglycerric agent and insulin studies; and studies of growth factors for treatment of diabetic foot ulcers.

★ 4929 ★ University of California, San Francisco
Hormone Research Institute
San Francisco, CA 94143-0534
Phone: (415)476-2624
Fax: (415)731-3612
Regis B. Kelly, Dir.

Research Activities and Fields: Research comprises several investigators focusing on hormone receptors, gene regulation in endocrine tissue, mechanisms of regulated secretion, glutamic acid decarboxylase in juvenile diabetes, and the development of the endocrine pancreas. **Formerly:** Hormone Research Laboratory.

★ 4930 ★ University of California, San Francisco
Metabolic Research Unit
1141 Health Sciences W.
San Francisco, CA 94143-0540
Phone: (415)476-1364
Fax: (415)476-1660
Dr. John D. Baxter, Dir.

Research Activities and Fields: Investigations of metabolic and endocrine diseases, hormone action, hormone receptors, regulation of insulin release, and hormone genes, control of their expression, and their applications to medical problems such as diabetes and hypertension. Conducts a continuing program of basic and clinical research using biochemical, biophysical, physiological, and recombinant DNA methods. E-mail Address: baxter@metabolic.ucsf.edu.

★4931★ University of California, San Francisco
Reproductive Endocrinology Center
San Francisco, CA 94143
Phone: (415)476-4295
Fax: (415)476-1811
Dr. Robert B. Jaffe, Dir.

Research Activities and Fields: Hormonal regulation of reproductive events at the subcellular, cellular, tissular, and organismic levels. Research projects utilize a variety of species, including domestic and laboratory animals, subhuman primates, and humans. Conducts a multifaceted investigative and training program directed toward studies of the hypothalamic/pituitary/gonadal/target tissue axis and the endocrinologic physiology of pregnancy.

★4932★ University of Chicago
Diabetes Research and Training Center
5841 S. Maryland
Chicago, IL 60637
Phone: (312)702-6217
Fax: (312)702-9194
Dr. Kenneth Polonsky, M.D., Contact

Research Activities and Fields: Etiology and pathogenesis of diabetes mellitus and improvement of care of diabetic patients, including studies on isolation and properties of proinsulin, proglucagon and amylin, isolation and characterization of beta cell plasma membranes, regulation of insulin biosynthesis and secretion, hyperlipidemia in diabetes, tissue culture of islet cells and cell tumors, mechanism of enzymatic conversion of proinsulin to insulin, insulin binding, degradation and action, particularly involving glucose transporters in various cells, serum proinsulin and C-peptide levels in normal and diabetic subjects, including studies of insulin of secretion and metabolism. Encourages new endeavors and provides a framework and stimulus for additional collaborative research programs among investigators of different disciplines and backgrounds. Conducts studies into the genetic basis of diabetes and alterations in gene expression in diabetes. Works to define the role of ion channels in insulin secretion. Formerly: Diabetes-Endocrinology Research Center.

University of Illinois at Chicago
Center for Handicapped Children
See: Entry 4588

★4933★ University of Iowa
Diabetes and Endocrinology Research Center
3E19 VA Hospital
Iowa City, IA 52240
Phone: (319)338-0581
Fax: (319)339-7171
Robert S. Bar, M.D., Dir.

Research Activities and Fields: Mechanism of action of insulin and related hormones at the cellular level and eucaryotic gene regulation.

★4934★ University of Kansas
Pediatric Endocrine Department
3901 Rainbow Blvd.
Kansas City, KS 66160-7330
Phone: (913)588-6382
Fax: (913)588-6319
Wayne V. Moore, M.D., Chm.

Research Activities and Fields: Education, counseling, clinical treatment, and research to improve techniques and understanding of diabetic management and the causes of diabetes. Programs include studies of patient compliance, psychosocial and educational components of diabetic management, control as measured by the laboratory glycosylated (sugared) hemoglobin, biosynthetic human insulin, an artificial computerized pancreas, islet cell antibodies, diabetes and exercise, islet cell transplantation, self blood glucose monitoring, and human pancreatic polypeptides. Publications: Diabetes Newsletter. Formerly: Diabetes Educational and Clinical Research Center; Regional Diabetes Center.

★4935★ University of Maryland
Obesity and Diabetes Research Center
Sch. of Med.
10 S. Pine St.
Baltimore, MD 21201
Phone: (410)328-3168
Fax: (410)328-7540
Dr. Barbara Hansen, Dir.

Research Activities and Fields: Basic and applied research focusing on the mechanisms underlying the metabolic and endocrine disorders associated with obesity and diabetes. Also studies hypertriglyceridemia, low HDL-cholesterol, hypertension, nephropathy, neuropathy, and therapeutic agents for treatment of diabetes. E-mail Address: bchansen@aol.com.

★4936★ University of Massachusetts
Diabetes-Endocrinology Research Center
Medical School
Dept. of Biochemistry
55 Lake Ave. N.
Worcester, MA 01655
Phone: (508)856-3047
Fax: (508)856-6231
Thomas B. Miller, Jr., Ph.D., Dir.

Research Activities and Fields: Diabetes, including autoimmunity of diabetic rats (Biobreeding/Worcester variety), renin secretion of kidney, lipid metabolism, lipid and growth factor receptors, neurotensin calcium metabolism and bone disease steroid action, and steroid receptors. Publications: Annual Report; Highlights (both distributed to National Institutes of Health).

★4937★ University of Miami
Diabetes Research Institute
PO Box 016960
Miami, FL 33101
Phone: (305)547-6657
Fax: (305)548-4404
Daniel H. Mintz, M.D., Scientific Dir.

Research Activities and Fields: Etiology, pathogenesis, and treatment of diabetes mellitus, emphasizing the fundamental nature of diabetes, particularly the nature of the immunoregulatory defects that result in the destruction of the pancreatic beta cell as well as the transplantation of allogeneic and/or xenogeneic of pancreatic islets cells in insulin-deficient diabetic animals and humans. Clinical investigations include new intervention studies to prevent progression of latent insulin-dependent diabetes to clinical diseases, and studies of new insulin analogues and evaluation of procedures to quantitate high standards for care of patients with diabetes in community-based studies.

★4938★ University of Michigan
Diabetes Research and Training Center
3920 Taubman Center, Box 0354
1500 E. Medical Center Dr.
Ann Arbor, MI 48109-0354
Phone: (313)763-5256
Fax: (313)766-9240
Douglas A. Greene, M.D., Dir.

Research Activities and Fields: Diabetes, including studies on thematic foci of islet hormone secretion and action and complications of diabetes. Publications: MDRTC Newsletter.

★4939★ University of Michigan
Endocrine Laboratory
1500 E. Medical Center Dr.
L1221 Women's Hospital
Ann Arbor, MI 48109-0278
Phone: (313)764-8142
Fax: (313)936-8617
Dr. K.M.J. Menon, Dir.

Research Activities and Fields: Problems of endocrinology, especially as it pertains to female reproduction, and development of endocrine parameters for assessing welfare of mother and fetus. Formerly: Reuben Peterson Laboratory; Gyn-Endocrine Laboratory.

★4940★ University of Missouri—Columbia
Cosmopolitan International Diabetes Center
Columbia, MO 65212
Phone: (314)882-3818
Fax: (314)884-4609
Dr. George Griffing, Dir.

Research Activities and Fields: Hormonal control of lipolysis, glycosylated proteins, and the effect of diabetic control on vascular complications of diabetes.

★4941★ University of Pennsylvania
Diabetes Research Center
501 Medical Education Bldg.
36th & Hamilton Walk
Philadelphia, PA 19104-6015
Phone: (215)898-4365
Fax: (215)898-2178
Franz M. Matschinsky, M.D., Dir.

Research Activities and Fields: Diabetes. Conducts basic studies on both pancreatic islet cell function and insulin action; evaluates new methods to detect and measure early signs of diabetes affecting the nervous systems, the retina, the vascular system, the heart, and the kidney; performs controlled clinical trials of new diets, drugs, and insulin-administration techniques; defines the nature of genetic susceptibility to diabetes; studies factors that increase the risk of complications in diabetes; and re-evaluates the long-term benefits of kidney and pancreas transplants in diabetics. The Center is organized in two components: Core Basic Research Facilities, which supply investigators with special equipment and support, and the Clinical Center for Diabetes Research and Education, which provides the opportunity to perform controlled studies on volunteer ambulatory diabetic patients.

★4942★ **University of Pittsburgh**
Protein Research Laboratory
A1224 Scaife Hall
Pittsburgh, PA 15261
Phone: (412)648-9632
Fax: (412)648-2117
Dr. Frances M. Finn, Dir.

Research Activities and Fields: Endocrinology, including the application of avidin-biotin technology to the isolation of hormone receptors. Seeks to characterize functional domains of the insulin receptor and to identify, isolate, and characterize the receptors for the adreno-corticotrophic hormone ACTH and the hypertensive peptide angiotensin II.

★4943★ **University of Tennessee**
Division of Reproductive Endocrinology
956 Court Ave., Rm. D328
Memphis, TN 38163
Phone: (901)448-5859
Fax: (901)448-8782
Dr. Stephen Lincoln, Chief

Research Activities and Fields: Embryonic macromanipulation, pre-implantation diagnosis, menopausal studies, human genetic biology, ectopic pregnancies, and studies of endometriosis. **Formerly:** Division of Reproductive Medicine (1980).

University of Texas—Houston Health Science Center
Laboratory for Neuroendocrinology
See: Entry 8526

★4944★ **University of Virginia**
Center for Biological Timing
Gilmer Hall
Charlottesville, VA 22903
Phone: (804)982-5225
Fax: (804)982-5626
Dr. G.D. Block, Dir.

Research Activities and Fields: Problems of biological timing within the nervous and endocrine systems. Specific studies include cellular mechanisms within the neuroendocrine system, environmental control of reproductive cycles, neural basis of rhythmic motor behaviors, and circadian rhythmicity. **Formerly:** Biodynamics Institute.

★4945★ **University of Washington**
Diabetes Endocrinology Research Center
VA Medical Center, ZB-21
1660 S. Columbian Way
Seattle, WA 98108
Phone: (206)764-2688
Fax: (206)764-2693
Daniel Porte, Jr., M.D., Dir.

Research Activities and Fields: Diabetes mellitus and its complications. Provides biomedical

research facilities and services that are not readily available to individual investigators, including light and electron microscopy, recruitment of patient volunteers, radioimmunoassays, skin fibroblast and other culture assistance, and assistance in nonhuman studies. Provides a small amount of funds to new investigators in the field through a pilot and feasibility program.

University of Wisconsin—Madison
Endocrinology-Reproductive Physiology Program
See: Entry 9721

Vanderbilt University
Center for Fertility and Reproductive Research (C-FARR)
See: Entry 11300

Vanderbilt University
Clinical Nutrition Research Unit
See: Entry 9573

★4946★ **Vanderbilt University**
Diabetes Research and Training Center
Nashville, TN 37232-2230
Phone: (615)322-2197
Fax: (615)322-2198
Daryl K. Granner, M.D., Dir.

Research Activities and Fields: Strengthens and extends interdisciplinary diabetes research already under way in basic science and clinical departments at the University, including demonstration and education units for improving diabetes treatment.

Vanderbilt University
Energy Balance Laboratory
See: Entry 11996

★4947★ **Washington University**
Diabetes Research and Training Center
School of Medicine
660 S. Euclid Ave.
St. Louis, MO 63110
Phone: (314)454-6046
Fax: (314)454-6225
Julio V. Santiago, M.D., Dir.

Research Activities and Fields: Diabetes research, including the causes of diabetes, insulin action, growth factors, and diabetic complications. Promotes biomedical and psychosocial studies of diabetes mellitus by operating core facilities to support established investigators. Core facilities include the Clinical Research Facility, where a patient registry of 500 diabetic patients undergoes clinical evaluation and is available for clinical studies; Radioimmunoassay Facility, which provides assays of insulin and conducts hormone studies; Mass Spectrometry Facility, supporting analytic and metabolic studies requiring mass spectrometry techniques; Animal and Transgenic Core Facility; Morphology Facility; Training and Translation Facility with an Education Center specialized in training professionals for diabetic patient care; Molecular Biology Facility; and Human Pancreatic Islet Facility, which provides human islets for NIH-funded projects. **E-mail Address:** fair@kids.wustl.edu. **Formerly:** Diabetes and Endocrinology Research Center (1977).

★4948★ **Whittier Institute for Diabetes and Endocrinology**
9894 Genesee Ave.
La Jolla, CA 92037
Phone: (619)450-1280
Fax: (619)535-0894
Dr. John Engle, Exec.Dir.

Research Activities and Fields: Diabetes and endocrinology research, including islet transplantation, CNS and pituitary function, reproductive biology, growth factor biochemistry, and angiogenesis.

★4949★ **Yeshiva University**
Diabetes Research and Training Center
Albert Einstein College of Medicine
1300 Morris Park Ave.
Bronx, NY 10461
Phone: (718)430-4096
Fax: (718)828-6988
Norman Fleischer, M.D., Dir.

Research Activities and Fields: Cause and treatment of Type 1 diabetes, including gestational diabetes. Conducts behavioral, psychological, and social research related to treatment modalities and studies the application of microcomputer technology to diabetes; supports individual research and a multidisciplinary diabetes education team. **Publications:** *Professional Education in Diabetes.*

State & Regional Organizations

Diabetes

State affiliates of the American Diabetes Association are listed below. The national service center is located at 1660 Duke St., Alexandria, VA 22314, (703) 549-1500.

Alabama

★4950★ **American Diabetes Association**
Alabama Affiliate
200 Office Park Dr., Ste. 303
Birmingham, AL 35223
Phone: (205)870-5172
Free: 800-824-7891

Alaska

★4951★ **American Diabetes Association**
Alaska Affiliate
The Dimond Center
800 E. Dimond Blvd., Ste. 3-218
Anchorage, AK 99515
Phone: (907)344-4459

Arizona

★4952★ **American Diabetes Association**
Arizona Affiliate
2328 W. Royal Palm Rd., Ste. D
Phoenix, AZ 85021
Phone: (602)995-1515
Free: 800-992-5311

Arkansas

★ 4953 ★ American Diabetes Association
Arkansas Affiliate
11500 N. Rodney Parham, Ste. 19-20
Little Rock, AR 72212
Phone: (501)221-7444

California

★ 4954 ★ American Diabetes Association
California Affiliate
10445 Old Placerville Rd.
Sacramento, CA 95827
Phone: (916)369-0999
Free: 800-828-8293

Colorado

★ 4955 ★ American Diabetes Association
Colorado Affiliate
2450 S. Downing St.
Denver, CO 80210
Phone: (303)778-7556
Free: 800-782-2873

Connecticut

★ 4956 ★ American Diabetes Association
Connecticut Affiliate
300 Research Pkwy.
Meriden, CT 06450
Phone: (203)639-0385
Free: 800-842-6323

Delaware

★ 4957 ★ American Diabetes Association
Delaware Affiliate
110 S. French St., Ste. 200
Wilmington, DE 19801
Phone: (302)656-0030
Free: 800-734-5030

District of Columbia

★ 4958 ★ American Diabetes Association
Washington, DC Area Affiliate
1211 Connecticut Ave. NW, No. 501
Washington, DC 20036
Phone: (202)331-8303

Florida

★ 4959 ★ American Diabetes Association
Florida Affiliate
1101 N. Lake Destiny Rd., Ste. 415
Maitland, FL 32751
Phone: (407)660-1926
Free: 800-741-5698

Georgia

★ 4960 ★ American Diabetes Association
Georgia Affiliate
1 Corporate Sq., Ste. 127
Atlanta, GA 30329
Phone: (404)320-7100
Free: 800-241-4556

Hawaii

★ 4961 ★ American Diabetes Association
Hawaii Affiliate
Bldg. E, Rm. 204
310 Paoakalani Ave.
Honolulu, HI 96815
Phone: (808)924-7755

Idaho

★ 4962 ★ American Diabetes Association
Idaho Affiliate
1528 Vista Ave.
Boise, ID 83705
Phone: (208)342-2774

Illinois

★ 4963 ★ American Diabetes Association
Downstate Illinois Affiliate
2580 Federal Dr., Ste. 403
Decatur, IL 62526
Phone: (217)875-9011
Free: 800-445-1667

★ 4964 ★ American Diabetes Association
Northern Illinois Affiliate
6 N. Michigan Ave., Ste. 1202
Chicago, IL 60602
Phone: (312)346-1805
Free: 800-433-4966

Indiana

★ 4965 ★ American Diabetes Association
Indiana Affiliate
7363 E. 21st St.
Indianapolis, IN 46219
Phone: (317)352-9226
Free: 800-228-2897

Iowa

★ 4966 ★ American Diabetes Association
Iowa Affiliate
6200 Aurora Ave., Ste. 504W
Des Moines, IA 50322
Phone: (515)276-2237
Free: 800-678-4232

Kansas

★ 4967 ★ American Diabetes Association
Kansas Affiliate
3210 E. Douglas
Wichita, KS 67208
Phone: (316)684-6091
Free: 800-362-1355

Kentucky

★ 4968 ★ American Diabetes Association
Kentucky Affiliate
721 W. Main St., Ste. 102
Louisville, KY 40202
Phone: (502)589-3837
Free: 800-766-1698

Louisiana

★ 4969 ★ American Diabetes Association
Louisiana Affiliate
9420 Lindale Ave., Ste. B
Baton Rouge, LA 70815
Phone: (504)927-7732
Free: 800-960-7732

Maine

★ 4970 ★ American Diabetes Association
Maine Affiliate
PO Box 2208
Augusta, ME 04338
Phone: (207)623-2232
Free: 800-870-8000

Maryland

★ 4971 ★ American Diabetes Association
Maryland Affiliate
407 Central Ave.
Reisterstown, MD 21136
Phone: (410)526-2900
Free: 800-232-3662

Massachusetts

★ 4972 ★ American Diabetes Association
Massachusetts Affiliate
PO Box 968
Framingham, MA 01701
Phone: (508)879-1776
Free: 800-229-2559

Michigan

★ 4973 ★ American Diabetes Association
Michigan Affiliate
30600 Telegraph Rd., Ste. 2255
Bingham Farms, MI 48025
Phone: (810)433-3830
Free: 800-525-9292

Minnesota

★ 4974 ★ American Diabetes Association
Minnesota Affiliate
Florida West Bldg., Ste. 307
715 Florida Ave. S.
Minneapolis, MN 55426
Phone: (612)593-5333
Free: 800-232-4044

Mississippi

★ 4975 ★ **American Diabetes Association**
Mississippi Affiliate
16 Northtown Dr., Ste. 100
Jackson, MS 39211
Phone: (601)957-7878
Free: 800-232-8393

Missouri

★ 4976 ★ **American Diabetes Association**
Missouri Affiliate
PO Box 1013
Columbia, MO 65205
Phone: (314)443-8611
Free: 800-404-2873

Montana

★ 4977 ★ **American Diabetes Association**
Montana Affiliate
PO Box 2411
Great Falls, MT 59403
Phone: (406)761-0908
Free: 800-232-6668

Nebraska

★ 4978 ★ **American Diabetes Association**
Nebraska Affiliate
12838 Augusta Ave.
Omaha, NE 68144
Phone: (402)333-5556
Free: 800-852-0386

Nevada

★ 4979 ★ **American Diabetes Association**
Nevada Affiliate
2785 E. Desert Inn Rd., Ste. 140
Las Vegas, NV 89121
Phone: (702)369-9995
Free: 800-800-4232

New Hampshire

★ 4980 ★ **American Diabetes Association**
New Hampshire Affiliate
132 Middle St.
Manchester, NH 03101
Phone: (603)627-9579
Free: 800-477-9579

New Jersey

★ 4981 ★ **American Diabetes Association**
New Jersey Affiliate
Vantage Ct. N.
200 Cottontail Ln.
Somerset, NJ 08873
Phone: (908)469-7979
Free: 800-562-2063

New Mexico

★ 4982 ★ **American Diabetes Association**
New Mexico Affiliate
525 San Pedro NE, Ste. 101
Albuquerque, NM 87108
Phone: (505)266-5716
Free: 800-992-5142

New York

★ 4983 ★ **American Diabetes Association**
New York Downstate Affiliate
149 Madison Ave., 7th Fl.
New York, NY 10016
Phone: (212)725-4925
Free: 800-281-4925

★ 4984 ★ **American Diabetes Association**
New York Upstate Affiliate
1603 W. Genesee St.
Syracuse, NY 13204-1949
Phone: (315)488-9464
Free: 800-724-3060

North Carolina

★ 4985 ★ **American Diabetes Association**
North Carolina Affiliate
3109 Poplarwood Ct., Ste. 125
Raleigh, NC 27604-1043
Phone: (919)872-6006
Free: 800-682-9692

North Dakota

★ 4986 ★ **American Diabetes Association**
North Dakota Affiliate
PO Box 5234
Grand Forks, ND 58206-5234
Phone: (701)746-4426
Free: 800-666-6709

Ohio

★ 4987 ★ **American Diabetes Association**
Ohio Affiliate
937 N. High St.
Worthington, OH 43085
Phone: (614)436-1917
Free: 800-232-6366

Oklahoma

★ 4988 ★ **American Diabetes Association**
Oklahoma Affiliate
Warren Professional Bldg., Ste. 519
6465 S. Yale Ave.
Tulsa, OK 74136
Phone: (918)492-3839
Free: 800-259-6553

Oregon

★ 4989 ★ **American Diabetes Association**
Oregon Affiliate
6915 SW Macadam, Ste. 130
Portland, OR 97219
Phone: (503)245-2010
Free: 800-234-0849

Pennsylvania

★ 4990 ★ **American Diabetes Association**
Pennsylvania Affiliate
5020 Ritter Rd., Ste. 106
Mechanicsburg, PA 17055
Phone: (717)691-6170
Free: 800-351-5800

Rhode Island

★ 4991 ★ **American Diabetes Association**
Rhode Island Affiliate
107 Waterman Ave.
East Providence, RI 02914
Phone: (401)431-1900

South Carolina

★ 4992 ★ **American Diabetes Association**
South Carolina Affiliate
2711 Middleburg Dr., Ste. 311
Columbia, SC 29204
Phone: (803)799-4246
Free: 800-354-5292

South Dakota

★ 4993 ★ **American Diabetes Association**
South Dakota Affiliate
PO Box 659
Sioux Falls, SD 57101
Phone: (605)335-7670
Free: 800-658-4502

Tennessee

★ 4994 ★ **American Diabetes Association**
Tennessee Affiliate
4205 Hillsboro Rd., Ste. 200
Nashville, TN 37215
Phone: (615)298-3066
Free: 800-627-1152

Texas

★ 4995 ★ **American Diabetes Association**
Texas Affiliate
9430 Research, Echelon II, Ste. 300
Austin, TX 78759
Phone: (512)343-6981
Free: 800-252-8233

Utah

★4996★ **American Diabetes Association**
Utah Affiliate
340 East 400 South
Salt Lake City, UT 84111-2909
Phone: (801)363-3024
Free: 800-888-1734

Vermont

★4997★ **American Diabetes Association**
Vermont Affiliate
Maltex Bldg.
431 Pine St.
Burlington, VT 05401
Phone: (802)862-3882
Free: 800-639-2105

Virginia

★4998★ **American Diabetes Association**
Virginia Affiliate
1290 Seminole Trail, Ste. 2
Charlottesville, VA 22901
Phone: (804)974-9905
Free: 800-582-8323

Washington

★4999★ **American Diabetes Association**
Washington Affiliate
557 Roy St., Lower Level
Seattle, WA 98109
Phone: (206)282-4616
Free: 800-628-8808

West Virginia

★5000★ **American Diabetes Association**
West Virginia Affiliate
121-A Ohio Ave.
Dunbar, WV 25064
Phone: (304)768-2596
Free: 800-232-9824

Wisconsin

★5001★ **American Diabetes Association**
Wisconsin Affiliate
2949 N. Mayfair Rd., No. 306
Wauwatosa, WI 53222
Phone: (414)778-5500
Free: 800-776-7118

Wyoming

★5002★ **American Diabetes Association**
Wyoming Affiliate
Enterprise Center
400 E. 1st St., Ste. 205 C
Casper, WY 82601
Phone: (307)265-2725
Free: 800-877-0106

Chapter 24
Environmental Health & Medicine

Federal Government Agencies

★5003★ **Environmental Protection Agency (EPA)**
401 M St. SW
Washington, DC 20460
Phone: (202)260-4700

Description: The EPA functions to protect and enhance the environment in cooperation with state and local governments. Its mission is to control and abate pollution in the areas of air, water, solid waste, pesticides, radiation, and toxic substances.

★5004★ **U.S. Department of Energy**
Assistant Secretary for Environment, Safety, and Health
1000 Independence Ave. SW
Washington, DC 20585
Phone: (202)586-6151
Fax: (202)586-4059

Description: Purpose is to ensure that Department programs are in compliance with environmental safety and health regulations and that environmental and safety impacts of Department programs receive management review.

★5005★ **U.S. Department of Health and Human Services**
Agency for Toxic Substances and Disease Registry
1600 Clifton Rd. NE
Atlanta, GA 30333
Phone: (404)639-3291

Description: The Agency, in cooperation with states and other federal and local official agencies, collects, maintains, analyzes, and disseminates information relating to serious diseases, mortality, and human exposure to toxic or hazardous substances; establishes appropriate registries necessary for long-term followup or specific scientific studies; establishes and maintains a complete listing of areas closed to the public or otherwise restricted in use because of toxic substance contamination; assists, consults, and coordinates with private or public health care providers in the provision of medical care and testing of exposed individuals; assists

the Environmental Protection Agency in identifying hazardous waste substances to be regulated; develops scientific and technical procedures for evaluating public health risks from hazardous substance incidents and for developing recommendations to protect the public health; and provides medical, epidemiological, technical, and administrative advice and consultation to protect public health and worker safety and health in instances of exposure or potential exposure to hazardous substances, and arranges for program support to ensure adequate response to public health emergencies.

★5006★ **U.S. Department of Health and Human Services**
National Center for Environmental Health
1600 Clifton Rd. NE
Atlanta, GA 30333
Phone: (404)488-7000
Fax: (404)488-7015

Description: The Center administers national programs that promote a healthy environment and prevent premature death and avoidable illness and disability caused by non-infectious, non-occupational, environmental and related factors.

★5007★ **U.S. Department of Health and Human Services**
National Institute of Environmental Health Sciences
PO Box 12233
Research Triangle Park, NC 27709
Phone: (919)541-3201

Description: NIEHS conducts and supports fundamental research concerned with defining, measuring, and understanding the effects of chemical, biological, and physical factors in the environment on the health and well-being of man.

Medical & Allied Health Schools

Environmental Health

The following institutions offer undergraduate and graduate environmental health programs accredited by the National Environmental Health Science and Protection Accreditation Council, c/o National Environmental Health Association, 720 S. Colorado Blvd., S. Tower, Ste. 970, Denver, CO 80222, (303) 756-9090.

California

★5008★ **California State University, Fresno**
Health Science Department
Environmental Health Science Program
Fresno, CA 93740-0030
Phone: (209)278-4014

★5009★ **California State University, Northridge**
Department of Health Science
Environmental and Occupational Health Program
18111 Nordhoff St.
Northridge, CA 91330
Phone: (818)885-3100

Colorado

★5010★ **Colorado State University**
College of Environmental Health, Veterinary Medicine and Biomedical Sciences
Environmental Health Sciences Program
Ft. Collins, CO 80523
Phone: (303)491-5652

Georgia

★5011★ **University of Georgia**
College of Agriculture
Environmental Health Science Program
206 Dairy Science Bldg.
Athens, GA 30602
Phone: (404)542-2454

Idaho

★5012★ **Boise State University**
College of Health Sciences
Environmental Health Program
1910 University Dr.
Boise, ID 83725
Phone: (208)385-3999

Illinois

★5013★ **Illinois State University**
Department of Health Sciences
Environmental Health Program
Normal, IL 61761
Phone: (309)438-8329

Indiana

★5014★ **Indiana State University**
School of Health and Human Performance
Department of Health and Safety
Environmental Health Program
Rm. B-83
Terre Haute, IN 47809
Phone: (812)237-3079

Kentucky

★5015★ **Eastern Kentucky University**
Department of Environmental Health
Rowlette Bldg., Rm. 145
Richmond, KY 40475
Phone: (606)622-1939

Michigan

★5016★ **Ferris State University**
School of Allied Health
Industrial and Environmental Health
  Management Program
Big Rapids, MI 49307
Phone: (616)592-2000

Mississippi

★5017★ **Mississippi Valley State**
  University
Department of Natural Science and
  Environmental Health
PO Box 1240
Itta Bena, MS 38941
Phone: (601)254-9041

Montana

★5018★ **Montana State University**
Department of Microbiology
Environmental Health Option in
  Microbiology
Bozeman, MT 59717
Phone: (406)994-5658

North Carolina

★5019★ **East Carolina University**
School of Allied Health Sciences
Department of Environmental Health
Greenville, NC 27858
Phone: (919)757-6961

★5020★ **Western Carolina University**
School of Nursing and Health Sciences
Environmental Health Program
Moore Hall
Cullowhee, NC 28723
Phone: (704)227-7113

Ohio

★5021★ **Bowling Green State University**
College of Health and Human Services
Environmental Health Program
102 Health Center
Bowling Green, OH 43403-0280
Phone: (419)372-7774

★5022★ **Ohio University**
School of Health and Sport Sciences
Environmental Health Science Program
Grover Center
Athens, OH 45701-2979
Phone: (614)593-4656

★5023★ **Wright State University**
Department of Biological Sciences
Environmental Health Science Program
Dayton, OH 45435
Phone: (513)873-2655

Oklahoma

★5024★ **East Central University**
School of Mathematics and Sciences
Department of Environmental Science
Box N-4
Ada, OK 74820
Phone: (405)332-8000

Oregon

★5025★ **Oregon State University**
Rehabilitation Counseling Program
Wardlaw 252
Corvallis, OR 97331-6504
Phone: (503)754-3608

Tennessee

★5026★ **East Tennessee State University**
Department of Environmental Health
PO Box 22960A
Johnson City, TN 37614-0002
Phone: (615)929-4408

Virginia

★5027★ **Old Dominion University**
College of Health Sciences
School of Community Health
Environmental Health Program
Norfolk, VA 23508
Phone: (804)440-3611

Washington

★5028★ **University of Washington**
School of Public Health and Community
  Medicine
Department of Environmental Health
C-34
Seattle, WA 98195
Phone: (206)543-4252

Wisconsin

★5029★ **University of Wisconsin—Eau**
  Claire
Division of Allied Health Professions
Environmental and Public Health Program
Eau Claire, WI 54702-4004
Phone: (715)836-2628

National & International
Organizations

★5030★ **Alliance for Environmental**
  Education (AEE)
9309 Center St., No. 101
Manassas, VA 22110-5599
Phone: (703)330-5667
Fax: (703)253-5811
Steven C. Kussmann, Chm.

Founded: 1972. **Members:** 300. **Description:**
Organizations, corporations, and government
agencies that promote the science and art of
environmental education. Aims to advance all
phases of formal and nonformal environmental
education. Cooperates with state, federal, and
international agencies and private organizations. **Publications:** Annual Report. • *Center
Directory*, periodic. Directory. • Membership Directory. • *Network Exchange*, bimonthly. Newsletter. *Price:* $20.

★5031★ **American Academy of**
  Environmental Medicine (AAEM)
PO Box 16106
Denver, CO 80216
Phone: (303)622-9755
Fax: (303)622-4224
Matt Tidwell, Exec.Dir.

Founded: 1965. **Members:** 450. **Description:**
Physicians, and others interested in the clinical

aspect of environmental medicine. Promotes a better understanding of ecologic illness and stimulates methods of controlling ecologic illness. Promotes research in the field. Provides educational aids such as tapes and audiovisual presentations. **Publications:** *AAEM Directory*, annual. Directory. • *Archives of Clinical Ecology*, quarterly. Journal. • *Environmental Physician*, quarterly. Newsletter. **Formerly:** (1984) Society for Clinical Ecology.

★ 5032 ★ **American Academy of
Sanitarians (AAS)**
c/o James W. Pees
829 Brookside Dr.
Miami, OK 74354
Phone: (918)540-2025
James W. Pees, Exec.Sec.-Treas.

Founded: 1966. **Members:** 400. **Description:** Legally registered sanitarians who possess at least a master's degree in public health, environmental health sciences, or environmental management. Purpose is to improve the environmental health status of humanity through certification of those sanitarians who have helped or who are helping to achieve this long-range goal. **Publications:** Newsletter, semiannual. • *Register of Professional Sanitarians*, quinquennial. • *Roster of Diplomates*, annual. **Formerly:** American Intersociety Academy for Certification of Sanitarians.

★ 5033 ★ **American Board of
Environmental Medicine (ABEM)**
4510 W. 89th St., Ste. 110
Prairie Village, KS 66207-2282
Phone: (913)341-0765
Fax: (913)341-3625
Jill Ditz, Exec.Dir.

Founded: 1988. **Description:** An accrediting agency for medical doctors and osteopaths. Examines, evaluates, and certifies individuals in the field; evaluates training programs and hospital units, such as emergency care facilities, environmental control and biodetoxification units, and rehabilitation centers; makes recommendations to the medical and allied health science professions regarding standards for establishing, improving, and maintaining the adequacy of care in the discipline. Maintains biographical archives; compiles statistics. **Publications:** *Register of the American Board of Environmental Medicine*, annual. Directory.

★ 5034 ★ **American Institute of Biomedical
Climatology (AIBC)**
1023 Welsh Rd.
Philadelphia, PA 19115
Phone: (215)673-8368
Fax: (215)579-1494
Richmond Kent, Exec.Dir.

Founded: 1958. **Members:** 46. **Description:** Meteorologists, biologists, epidemiologists, physicians, atmospheric physicists, engineers, architects, physiologists, climatologists, and other professionals interested in investigating the influence of the natural environment on the health and diseases of man. Current areas of interest include: the greenhouse effect, acid rain, depletion of the ozone layer, indoor and outdoor air pollution, biological effects of electromagnetic fields and concentrated radon, and beneficial

and detrimental effects of climate and weather on health. **Publications:** *AIBC News Bulletin*, quarterly. Bibliography. *Price:* Included in membership dues. • Brochure. • *Membership List*, annual. • *News Bulletin*, quarterly. Bulletin. *Price:* Included in membership dues. **Formerly:** (1988) American Institute of Medical Climatology.

★ 5035 ★ **Association for the Electrically
Oversensitive**
Stubbanv. 2
N-7037 Trondheim, Norway
Per Husby, Contact

Languages: Norwegian. **Description:** Individuals suffering from electrical oversensitivity or electrical hypersensitivity in Norway (electrical oversensitivity and hypersensitivity are brought on from overexposure to electrical and magnetic fields emitted by appliances, particularly television sets and video display terminals). Supports afflicted individuals and works to stop the spread of these conditions; works to insure recognition of these maladies by insurance companies and government agencies; promotes research into the causes and cure of electrical over- and hypersensitivity. Organizes grass roots groups.

★ 5036 ★ **Association of University
Environmental Health Sciences Centers
(AUEHSC)**
Mt. Sinai School of Medicine
One Gustave L. Levey Place
New York, NY 10029
Phone: (212)241-6173
Fax: (212)996-0407
Dr. Philip Landrigan, Pres.

Founded: 1980. **Members:** 18. **Description:** University-based environmental health science centers supported by the National Institute of Environmental Health Sciences. Serves as a forum for exchange of information, collaboration, and cooperation among the centers.

★ 5037 ★ **Electrically and VDT Injured in
Denmark
(El-Og Billedskaermsskadede I Danmark)**
Lunden 1
Alum
DK-8900 Randers, Denmark
Aase Thomassen, Contact

Languages: Danish. **Description:** Individuals suffering from electrical oversensitivity or electrical hypersensitivity in Denmark (electrical oversensitivity and hypersensitivity are brought on from overexposure to electrical and magnetic fields emitted by appliances, particularly television sets and video display terminals). Supports afflicted individuals and works to stop the spread of these conditions; works to insure recognition of these maladies by insurance companies and government agencies; promotes research into the causes and cure of electrical over- and hypersensitivity. Organizes grass roots groups.

★ 5038 ★ **Epsilon Nu Eta**
PO Box 70682 A
Dept. of Environmental Health
East Tennessee State University
Johnson City, TN 37614
Phone: (615)929-5250
Phillip R. Scheuerman, Advisor/Dir.

Founded: 1978. **Members:** 130. **Description:** Honorary society - men and women, environmental health.

★ 5039 ★ **European Society of
Climatotherapy (ESC)
(Federation Europeenne de
Climatotherapie — FEC)**
2, Ave. Georges Pompidou
F-05100 Briancon, France
Phone: 92 211817
Fax: 92 204375
Dr. H. Razzouk, Pres.

Founded: 1987. **Members:** 300. **Languages:** English, French, German, Italian. **Description:** Associations, societies, biologists, botanists, climatologists, doctors, meteorologists, and other individuals interested in the correlation between climate and health. Promotes study of climatotherapy (practice of placing a person in a climate suitable to their disease) in Europe. Coordinates research on bioclimatology and climatotherapy materials. Standardizes measures and regulations. Disseminates information.

**Georgia Institute of Technology
Georgia Tech Research Institute (GTRI)**
See: Entry 2447

★ 5040 ★ **Human Ecology Action League
(HEAL)**
PO Box 49126
Atlanta, GA 30359
Phone: (404)248-1898
Fax: (404)248-0162
Muriel A. Dando, Pres.

Founded: 1977. **Members:** 7,000. **Local Groups:** 100. **Description:** Individuals and organizations interested in the study of human ecology and multiple chemical sensitivities, specifically how human health may be affected by synthetic and natural substances in the environment. Objectives are: to collect and disseminate information on human ecology and ecological illness to persons suffering from such illness, and to government agencies, scientists, and health care professionals; to raise public awareness about potential dangers from substances in the environment. **Publications:** Brochure. • *Hospitality Directory*, periodic. Directory. Lists environmentally safe lodgings in the United States for allergic and chemical-sensitive travelers; arranged by state. *Price:* $3.50/copy. • *Human Ecologist*, quarterly. Journal. Includes association news, book and video reviews, environmental health tips for children, and pesticide update. *Price:* Included in membership dues; $20/year for nonmembers. • *Multiple Chemical Sensitivities and the Americans with Disabilities Act: A Guide to Accommodation.* • *Selected Bibliography: Chemicals and Health.* Bibliography. • *Selected Bibliography: Perspectives on Pesticides and Human Health 1983-1993.* Bibliography. • *Service List/Back Issue Guide*, periodic.

★5041★ International Association of Medicine and Biology of Environment (IAMBE)
(Association Internationale de Medecine et de Biologie de l'Environnement — AIMBE)
115, rue de la Pompe
F-75116 Paris, France
Phone: 1 45534504
Fax: 1 45534175
Dr. Richard Abbou, Pres.

Languages: English, French, Spanish. **Description:** Individuals, associations, and firms in 72 countries concerned with ecological medicine and biology. Purpose is to study the adaptation of mankind to the environment and to study and treat sicknesses resulting from this adaptation. Examines natural cycles and balances; promotes research in ecological medicine and biology and corollary sciences; collects and disseminates information concerning the protection of mankind and the environment. Facilitates contacts with persons who deal professionally with problems related to the protection of humans and their surroundings. Organizes symposia and congresses; conducts courses and seminars.

★5042★ International Board of Environmental Medicine (IBEM)
Executive Office
4510 W. 89th St., Ste. 110
Prairie Village, KS 66207-2282
Phone: (913)341-0765
Fax: (913)341-3625
Jill Dietz, Exec.Dir.

Founded: 1988. **Members:** 98. **Description:** An accrediting agency for physicians, osteopaths, and persons working in related environmental professions. Examines licensed practitioners, facilities, and relevant training programs. Offers programs to evaluate qualifications of healthcare professionals, their training programs, and those facilities offering special types of treatment. Plans and supervises accrediting examinations. **Publications:** *Register of the International Board of Environmental Medicine*, annual. Directory. *Price:* $25.

★5043★ International Commission for Protection Against Environmental Mutagens and Carcinogens (ICPEMC)
c/o Dr. David Brusick
Hazelton Washington, Inc.
9200 Leesburg Tpke.
Vienna, VA 22182
Phone: (703)893-5400
Fax: (703)759-6947
Dr. David Brusick, Contact

Founded: 1977. **Members:** 45. **Description:** Scientists from academic and industrial institutes working in the areas of genetics, mutagenesis, cancer, the epidemiology of cancer, genetic toxicology, and related sciences. Works to identify and promote scientific principles and to determine guidelines and regulations for the purpose of preventing or minimizing the deleterious effects of chemicals on human genetic material. Plans to prepare critical evaluations that may serve as a basis for establishing priorities for further research or possible regulatory action. Seeks to identify substances and situations that may cause significant genotoxic damage to humans. **Publications:** *ICPEMC Membership Directory*, annual. • *ICPEMC News*, annual. • *Mutation Research*, periodic. Journal. Also publishes scientific reports and working papers.

★5044★ International Programme on Chemical Safety (IPCS)
(Programme International sur la Securite des Substances Chimiques — PISSC)
Avenue Appia
CH-1211 Geneva 27, Switzerland
Phone: 22 7913588
Fax: 22 794848
Dr. Michel Mercier, Dir.

Founded: 1980. **Members:** 33. **Languages:** English, French. **Description:** States belonging to the World Health Organization, the International Labour Organization, and the United Nations Environment Programme. Evaluates the health risks posed to humans and the environment by exposure to chemicals. Proposes methods and guidelines for measuring chemical exposure and for assessing health risks. Encourages the use and improvement of methods for laboratory testing and epidemiological studies. Provides guidelines on safe levels of chemical exposure through daily intake of food additives and pesticide and veterinary drug residues. Disseminates information regarding diagnosis and treatment of chemical poisoning; promotes international cooperation in dealing with chemical emergencies. Seeks to enhance the scientific basis for health risk assessment for determination of chemical hazards controls. Conducts training courses on subjects such as ecotoxicology, clinical toxicology, the detection of mutagenesis, and occupational hazards and human reproduction; coordinates international research programs; maintains expert advisory groups and offers advisory services for technical cooperation in regulation and control of chemicals. Organizes symposia and workshops on chemical safety. **Publications:** *Environmental Health Criteria Document*, 15/year. • *Health and Safety Guides*, 20/year. • *IPCS Newsletter*, 2-3/year. Newsletter. • *Poison Information Monographs*, periodic. • *Technical Document on Food Additives and on Pesticide Residues*, periodic. Also publishes monographs, research reports, guideline documents, and a glossary; makes available *International Chemical Safety Cards*.

★5045★ International Society for Environmental Toxicology and Cancer (ISETC)
PO Box 134
Park Forest, IL 60466
Phone: (708)758-3242
Fax: (708)758-3290
Dr. George Scherr, Exec. Officer

Founded: 1983. **Members:** 700. **Description:** Clinicians and researchers working in the fields of environmental toxicology and oncology. Promotes research and information exchange. Founded the World Institute of Ecology and Cancer jointly with the European Institute of Ecology and Cancer and the Panafrican Institute of Ecology and Cancer. **Publications:** *Journal of Environmental Pathology, Toxicology and Oncology*, bimonthly. Journal.

★5046★ International Society of Medical Hydrology and Climatology (ISMH)
(Societe Internationale d'Hydrologie et de Climatologie Medicale)
Institut fur Med. Baineologie und Klimatologie
Universitat Munich
Marchioninistrasse 17
81377 Munich, Germany
Phone: 89 70951
Fax: 89 70958829
Dr. Helmut G. Pratzel, Pres.

Founded: 1921. **Members:** 20,000. **National Groups:** 42. **Languages:** English, French, German, Italian. **Description:** National associations of medical hydrology; individuals interested in problems of medical hydrology and climatology. Disseminates information related to clinical and scientific research and teaching in this field; conducts research programs; bestows awards. Programs are carried out by individual national associations; reports results. **Publications:** *Archives of Health Resort Medicine*, quarterly. Bulletin. **Formerly:** (1978) International Society of Medical Hydrology.

★5047★ Latin American Association of Environmental Mutagens, Carcinogens, and Teratogens Societies (LAAEMCTS)
Instituto de Investigaciones Biomedicas
UNAM
Apartado Postal 70228
Mexico City, DF, Mexico
Dr. Cristina Cortinas de Nava, Pres.

Founded: 1980. **Languages:** English, Portuguese, Spanish. **Description:** Scientists and students in 11 countries. Promotes professional cooperation between Latin American scientists and researchers. Fosters study of common Latin American environmental problems related to the presence of mutagens, carcinogens, teratogens, or any toxic substance in the environment. Particular emphasis is given to genetic toxicology. Identifies potential problems in the field; determines training and information necessary for scientific research. Encourages information exchange and facilitates establishment of collaborative research projects. Organizes seminars, workshops, and educational courses on topics including health effects of environmental pollution, genetic monitoring, and environmental risks. **Publications:** *Boletin Alamcta*, periodic.

★5048★ Latin American Federation of Thermalism and Climatism (LAFTC)
(Federacion Latinoamericana de Termalismo — FLT)
Anchorena 1198
Apartado Postal 2
1425 Buenos Aires, Argentina
Phone: 1 9610825
Dr. Natalio Morduchowicz, Pres.

Founded: 1969. **Languages:** Spanish. **Description:** Scientists from varying disciplines interested in hydrothermalogy and climatology. Encourages research and therapeutic application of resources. Organizes professional training seminars and educational courses. Sponsors competitions; bestows awards. Maintains data base. **Publications:** *Boletines Latinoamericanos*, 3/year.

★5049★ National Alliance of Victims of Minamata Disease and Lawyers (NAVMDL)

Katshata Bldg., 4F/2-5
Kanda, Tsukasa-cho
Chiyoda-ku
Tokyo 101, Japan
Phone: 3 32933621
Fax: 3 32933627

Languages: Japanese. **Description:** People afflicted with minamata disease and the attorneys that represent them. (Minamata disease is a neurological disorder brought about by eating fish contaminated with high levels of mercury.) Represents members' interests before government agencies and the public.

★5050★ National Center for Environmental Health Strategies (NCEHS)

c/o Mary Lamielle
1100 Rural Ave.
Voorhees, NJ 08043
Phone: (609)429-5358
Mary Lamielle, Dir. & Pres.

Founded: 1986. **Members:** 2,000. **Description:** Persons with environmental illnesses, including those with chemical sensitivity disorders; medical, legal, and scientific professionals; government agencies; environmentalists; interested others. Promotes public awareness of health problems caused by chemical and environmental pollutants, focusing on chemical sensitivity disorders. Testifies before government agencies on behalf of persons with such health problems. Encourages the development and implementation of programs and policies aimed at assisting victims of pollutants and preventing future public health problems. Conducts educational programs and research. Gathers information and compiles statistics on indoor and outdoor pollutants, less-toxic products, pesticides, natural foods, and environmental disabilities, including alternative employment, workplace accommodations, social security disability and workmen's compensation, and housing. Maintains speakers' bureau. Provides advocacy and technical, referral, and children's services. Acts as a clearinghouse. Bestows awards. **Publications:** *Chemical Sensitivity: A Report to the New Jersey Department of Health.* • *The Delicate Balance*, quarterly. Newsletter. Covers issues related to indoor contaminants, outdoor toxins, legislative and policy updates, research summaries, information on consumer products. *Price:* Included in membership dues; $15/year for nonmembers. Also publishes reports, bibliographies, information packets, and books. **Formerly:** (1989) Environmental Health Association of New Jersey.

★5051★ National Coalition Against the Misuse of Pesticides (NCAMP)

701 E St. SE, Ste. 200
Washington, DC 20003
Phone: (202)543-5450
Fax: (202)543-4791
Jay Feldman, Exec.Dir.

Founded: 1981. **Members:** 1,400. **Description:** Individuals and consumer, environmental, farming, health, labor, and church organizations concerned with pesticide hazards and safety.

Seeks to advance national and international awareness of public health, environmental, and economic problems caused by pesticides; to protect individuals exposed to pesticides. Works to improve legislation, regulation, and enforcement affecting pesticide use and to stress a systematic approach emphasizing preventive public health measures to control pesticides from production through use and disposal. Promotes alternatives to pesticide use such as integrated pest management, which ensures reduced soil and water contamination and lower residues in food. Stresses that these alternatives will reduce environmental damage, ease economic burdens, and improve the general health of the public. Collects and disseminates information and monitors governmental activities. **Publications:** *ChemWatch Compendium.* Book. • *Legislative Alerts*, periodic. • *NCAMP Technical Report*, monthly. Report. • *Pest Control Without Toxic Chemicals.* Pamphlet. • *Pesticide Safety: Myths and Facts.* Pamphlet. • *Pesticides and You*, quarterly. Magazine. • *Pesticides and You Index*, annual. • *Publications List.* • *Safety at Home, A Guide to the Hazards of Lawn and Garden Pesticides.* Book. • *Unecessary Risks.* Book.

National Conference of Local Environmental Health Administrators (NCLEHA)
See: Entry 5594

★5052★ National Environmental Health Association (NEHA)

720 S. Colorado Blvd., Ste. 970, S. Tower
Denver, CO 80222
Phone: (303)756-9090
Fax: (303)691-9490
Nelson E. Fabian, Exec.Dir.

Founded: 1930. **Members:** 5,700. **State Groups:** 50. **Local Groups:** 3. **Description:** Professional society of persons engaged in environmental health and protection for governmental agencies, public health and environmental protection agencies, industry, colleges, and universities. Conducts national professional registration program and continuing education programs. Provides self-paced learning modules for field professionals. Offers placement service; compiles statistics. Maintains speakers' bureau. Plans to offer an electronic bulletin board service. **Publications:** *Directory of Local Health Departments*, annual. Directory. • *Journal of Environmental Health*, monthly. Journal. Contains peer-reviewed articles on environmental issues, news on association activities, and special columns Also includes annual index and listings. *Price:* Included in membership dues; $40/year for nonmembers. • Manuals. • *National Environmental Health Association-- Membership Directory*, annual. Membership Directory. • *NEHA Member Mailing List*, bimonthly. • Reports. **Formerly:** (1937) California Association of Sanitarians; (1970) National Association of Sanitarians.

★5053★ National Environmental Health Science and Protection Accreditation Council (EHAC)

c/o National Environmental Health Association
720 S. Colorado Blvd., Ste. 970
S. Tower
Denver, CO 80222
Phone: (303)756-9090
Dr. Gary Silverman, Chm.

Founded: 1969. **Regional Groups:** 23. **State Groups:** 4. **Description:** Purposes are: to establish a system for accreditation of environmental health curricula and related procedures; to accredit and carry out other responsibilities as may be essential to the accreditation of academic programs leading to baccalaureate and graduate degrees in environmental health. Assumes responsibility for all functions, related records, and correspondence pertaining to accreditation of environmental health curricula. Renders advice and counsel to institutions in the development of curricula and the conduct of educational programs in the environmental health sciences. Acts as clearinghouse for reports and information pertaining to the environmental health accreditation process and activities. **Formerly:** National Accreditation Council for Environmental Health Curricula; (1993) National Accreditation Council for Environmental Health Science and Protection.

National Foundation for the Chemically Hypersensitive (NFCH)
See: Entry 2083

★5054★ National Pesticide Telecommunication Network (NPTN)

Texas Tech University
Department of Preventive Medicine
Thompson Hall, Rm. S-129
Lubbock, TX 79430
Phone: 800-858-7378
Fax: (806)743-3094
Dr. Anthony Way, Exec. Officer

Founded: 1978. **Description:** Information clearinghouse for pesticides, toxicology and symptomatic reviews, health and environmental effects, safety, and cleanup and disposal. Assists the medical community with information on pesticides and poisoning. **Formerly:** National Pesticide Information Clearinghouse.

★5055★ NSF International (NSF)

3475 Plymouth Rd.
PO Box 130140
Ann Arbor, MI 48105
Phone: (313)769-8010
Fax: (313)769-0109
Dr. Denise Manqino, Pres. & CEO

Founded: 1944. **Members:** 2,000. **Description:** Representatives of the public health profession, business, and industry. Cooperates in research and educational programs and develops standards in the field of environmental sanitation and health. Services include: voluntary evaluation and listing of products and services that comply with NSF standards; voluntary evaluation and certification of goods and services that comply with Consensus Standards (other than NSF's) and government regulations relating to environmental quality and public health;

special projects, testing, and evaluation for industry, government, and foundations. **Publications:** *Class II Biohazard Cabinetry*, periodic. • *Drinking Water Additives*, periodic. • *Drinking Water Treatment Units and Related Products, Components, and Materials*, periodic. • *Food Service Equipment and Related Products, Components, and Materials*, periodic. • *Plastics Piping Components and Related Materials*, periodic. • *Reports*. • *Special Categories of Equipment, Products, and Services*, periodic. • *Standards and Criteria*, periodic. • *Swimming Pools, Spas, or Hot Tubs*, periodic. Also publishes educational material. **Formerly:** (1993) National Sanitation Foundation.

★5056★ Pesticide Action Network North America Regional Center (PANNA RC)
116 New Montgomery No. 810
San Francisco, CA 94105
Phone: (415)541-9140
Fax: (415)541-9253
Monica Moore, Regional Coord.

Founded: 1984. **Members:** 80. **Description:** North American regional center of Pesticide Action Network, a group of voluntary coalitions linking organizations and individuals involved with pesticide issues and sustainable agriculture worldwide. Serves as a networking tool for pesticide action groups. Promotes research on and implementation of alternatives to pesticide use in agriculture. Sponsors International Pesticides Referral and Information Service. **Publications:** Booklets. • *Demise of the Dirty Dozen Chart*. • *Dirty Dozen Fact Sheets*. • *FAO code: Missing Ingredients*. • *Global Pesticide Campaigner*, quarterly. Includes features on the pesticide industry, sustainable agriculture, and other related topics globally. *Price:* $25/year. • Manuals. **Formerly:** (1989) Pesticide Education and Action Project.

★5057★ Safety, Health, and Environmental Resource Center International (SHERCI)
Central Missouri State University
Homphreys Bldg., Ste. 202
Warrensburg, MO 64093
Phone: (816)543-4744
Fax: (816)543-4959
Dr. Robert L. Marshall, Pres.

Founded: 1986. **Members:** 68. **Regional Groups:** 68. **Description:** Cooperating organizations united to advance safety, health, and the environment worldwide. Acts as a clearinghouse for information on health, safety, and environmental issues. Maintains Safety and Health Hall of Fame International. Conducts educational and research programs; compiles statistics; maintains speakers' bureau; operates museum and placement service. **Publications:** *Annual Action Report*, annual. Report. • Brochure. • *Induction Ceremony Program*. • *SHERCI Newsletter*, monthly. Newsletter. *Price:* Free.

★5058★ Self-Help Association for the Electrically Sensitive (Selbhilfen fur Elektrosensible)
Oberbrunnerstrasse 1
81475 Munich 71, Germany
Languages: German. **Description:** Individuals suffering from electrical oversensitivity or elec-

trical hypersensitivity in Germany (electrical oversensitivity and hypersensitivity are brought on from overexposure to electrical and magnetic fields emitted by appliances, particularly television sets and video display terminals). Supports afflicted individuals and works to stop the spread of these conditions; works to insure recognition of these maladies by insurance companies and government agencies; promotes research into the causes and cure of electrical over- and hypersensitivity. Organizes grass roots groups.

★5059★ Society for Environmental Geochemistry and Health (SEGH)
c/o Dr. Paula Lutz
University of Missouri Rolla
Life Sciences Department
Rolla, MO 65401
Phone: (314)341-4831
Dr. Paula Lutz, Sec.-Treas.

Founded: 1971. **Members:** 350. **Description:** Organizations, scientists, and students committed to: furthering knowledge of the effects of the geochemical environment on the health and disease of plants and animals, including man; promoting scientific communication and exchange of views among members and nonmembers. **Publications:** *Environmental Geochemistry and Health*, quarterly. Journal. • *Interface*, quarterly. Newsletter.

★5060★ Society for Human Ecology (SHE)
College of the Atlantic
105 Eden St.
Bar Harbor, ME 04609
Phone: (207)288-5015
Fax: (207)288-4126
Melville P. Cote, Exec.Dir.

Founded: 1981. **Members:** 150. **Languages:** English. **Description:** Educators, health practitioners, scientists, and other professionals in 30 countries studying human ecology and its applications. Focuses attention on the consequences of human action on manufactured, natural, and social environments. Promotes interdisciplinary collaboration; facilitates the exchange of information; identifies problems and recommends solutions from an ecological perspective. Conducts workshops and symposia. Participates in human ecology consortium. Organization is distinct from the International Organization for Human Ecology, formerly known as the Society for Human Ecology. **Publications:** Brochure. • *Human Ecology: A Gathering of Perspectives*. Proceedings. Proceedings from SHE's First International Conference, held in 1985. • *Human Ecology and Decision Making: An International and Interdisciplinary Collaboration*. • *Human Ecology Bulletin*, semiannual. • *Human Ecology--Coming of Age: An International Overview*. Proceedings. Proceedings of the symposium organized at the International Congress of Ecology in 1990. • *Human Ecology: Crossing Boundaries*. Selected papers from the 6th conference of SHE. • *Human Ecology: Research and Applications*. Proceedings. Proceedings from SHE's Second International Conference, held in 1988. • *Human Ecology: Steps to the Future*. Proceedings. Proceedings from SHE's Third International Conference. • *Human Ecology: Strategies for

the Future*. Selected papers from the 4th conference of the SHE, held in 1990. • *International Directory of Human Ecologists*, periodic. Directory. Lists over 700 human ecologists worldwide, with descriptions of their work, research, and activities; includes addresses and phone numbers.

Society for Occupational and Environmental Health (SOEH)
See: Entry 9801

Society of Toxicologic Pathologists (STP)
See: Entry 10138

★5061★ Swedish Association for the Electrically and VDT Injured
Tornevalla Gamla Skola
S-590 62 Linghem, Sweden
Phone: 13 282788
Fax: 13 282599
Clas Tegenfeldt, Contact

Founded: 1987. **Members:** 1,800. **Languages:** English, Swedish. **Description:** Individuals suffering from electrical oversensitivity or electrical hypersensitivity in Sweden (electrical oversensitivity and hypersensitivity are brought on from overexposure to electrical and magnetic fields emitted by appliances, particularly television sets and video display terminals). Supports afflicted individuals and works to stop the spread of these conditions; works to insure recognition of these maladies by insurance companies and government agencies; promotes research into the causes and cure of electrical over- and hypersensitivity. Organizes grass roots groups. **Publications:** *Ljusglimten*, quarterly. Magazine.

Vietnam Veterans Agent Orange Victims (VVAOVI)
See: Entry 7814

★5062★ WHO Western Pacific Regional Environmental Health Centre
PO Box 12550
50782 Kuala Lumpur, Malaysia
Phone: 3 9480311
Fax: 3 9482349
Dr. P. Guo, Dir.

Founded: 1979. **Languages:** English. **Description:** Representatives of states belonging to the Western Pacific Region of the World Health Organization. Strives to promote: development of national environmental policies and planning; environmental health and resource education and training; exchange of environmental information as it relates to human health and well-being; identification and adaptation of appropriate technology in environmental health and engineering; collaboration among environmental institutions of member states; technological and administrative expertise in the environmental health care fields. Fosters the development of self-reliant institutions and capabilities, and supports the development of national policies and plans as well as information services for environmental health and related resource protection in member states. Key areas of concern include community water supply and sanitation, environmental health in rural and urban development and housing, chemical safety, control of environmental health hazards, and food safety.

Arranges seminars, training courses, and workshops on environmental health. **Publications:** *Activity Report*, annual. • Papers. With technical information. **Formerly:** (1994) WHO Western Pacific Regional Centre for the Promotion of Environmental Planning and Applied Studies; (1994) WHO Centre Regional du Pacifique Occidental pour la Promotion de la Planification et des Etudes Appliquees en Matiere d'Environnement.

World Association of Veterinary Food Hygienists (WAVFH) (Asociacion Mundial de Veterinarios Higienistas de los Alimentos — AMVHA)
See: Entry 13118

Research Centers

★5063★ Center for Bioenvironmental Research
1430 Tulane Ave., SL 3
New Orleans, LA 70112-2699
Phone: (504)588-6910
Fax: (504)588-6428
John McLachlan, Ph.D., Dir.

Research Activities and Fields: Research focuses on: 1) preventing and controlling environmental damage; 2) finding new ways to protect human health and ecosystems from harmful effects of environmental pollutants; 3) identifying damage and assessing risks of environmental pollutants; 4) developing technologies for managing toxic waste and restoring the environment; and 5) evaluating and analyzing scientific findings for use in the formation of public policy. Specific examples include: examining the causes of worker deaths in the Louisiana petrochemical industry; studying respiratory health of spray painters exposed to polyurethane paints containing isocyanate; using membrane filters to remove hazardous waste from water; developing strains of microbes and fungi to consume oil or kerosene spills; and using sulfate-reducing bacterium to treat wastewater. **Publications:** Annual Report.

★5064★ Center for Hazardous Materials Research
Univ. of Pittsburgh Applied Research Center
320 William Pitt Way
Pittsburgh, PA 15238
Phone: (412)826-5320
Free: 800-334-CHMR
Fax: (412)826-5552
Edgar Berkey, Ph.D., Pres.

Research Activities and Fields: Use and disposition of hazardous materials and waste, including treatment, processing, and disposal, health and environmental effects, and health and safety training for hazardous waste workers and emergency response personnel. Activities include international technology transfer and development of innovative environmental techniques.

★5065★ Center for Indoor Air Research
1099 Winterson Rd., Ste. 280
Linthicum, MD 21090
Phone: (410)684-3777
Fax: (410)684-3729
Max Eisenberg, Ph.D., Exec.Dir.

Research Activities and Fields: Sponsors, supports, and monitors individual investigators' research on the chemistry, physics, health consequences, or psychosocial factors of environmental tobacco smoke (ETS), chemical contaminants from organic and inorganic sources, and biological agents, including aeroallergens and aeropathogens. Research on all indoor air chemical contaminants emphasize investigating the effects of long-term steady exposures to low levels to determine overall adverse health effects, and evaluating methods to elucidate interactions of low-level complex exposures. Research on biological agents focuses on human diseases in the form of immunological disorders or respiratory infections. Activities emphasize standardizing indoor air sampling methods of moisture levels and environmental temperatures provided by heating and air conditioning systems and humidifiers to accurately study aeropathogens that induce allergenic responses, including bacteria, viruses, fungal spores, algae, arthropod fragments and dropping, and dander from animals and humans. Multidisciplinary studies focus on the role of individual, perceptual, occupational, and psychosocial factors in mediating the effects of indoor air quality on health and developing improved self-reporting measures and interview techniques to assess health problems and contributing factors affecting building occupants. Also develops experimental protocols for measuring emission rates of improved indoor sources such as presswood, carpet, and combustion sources. Research on engineering control strategies focus on the development and validation of protocols for the design of space and for systems control of indoor air quality.

★5066★ Center for Risk Management
Resources for the Future
1616 P St. NW
Washington, DC 20036
Phone: (202)328-5000
Fax: (202)939-3460
Dr. J. Clarence Davies, Dir.

Research Activities and Fields: Health and environmental risk management in modern society, focusing on air and water pollutants, toxic substances, and hazardous wastes. Studies include program evaluation, use of scientific information in regulation, public acceptance of regulatory programs, transportation of hazardous materials, environmental equity, evaluation of Superfund program and alternatives, and management of risks from non-ionizing electromagnetic fields. **Publications:** Working Paper Series.

★5067★ Clarkson University Hazardous Waste and Toxic Substance Research and Management Center
Rowley Laboratories
Box 5715
Potsdam, NY 13699-5715
Phone: (315)268-3853
Fax: (315)268-7636
Thomas L. Theis, Ph.D., Dir.

Research Activities and Fields: Hazardous waste management, including assessments of exposure, the environment, technology, and policy. Also studies toxicology, microbiology, biology, organic and inorganic chemistry, ecosystems, aquatic chemistry, groundwater and seepage, environmental health, transportation of waste, and air pollution. **E-mail Address:** adminyjb@clvm.clarkston.edu.

★5068★ Colorado State University Institute of Rural Environmental Health
College of Veterinary Medicine
Fort Collins, CO 80523
Phone: (303)491-5652
Fax: (303)491-7778
Dr. Roy M. Buchan, Dir.

Research Activities and Fields: Rural environmental health and safety, focusing on the health and well-being of agricultural workers in Colorado and the Rocky Mountain region. Studies applications of preventive medicine through chemical epidemiology, toxicology, occupational health and safety, comparative medicine, and zoonoses.

★5069★ Conte Institute for Environmental Health
The Berkshire Common
2 South St., Ste. 370
Pittsfield, MA 01201
Phone: (413)443-1740
Fax: (413)443-1740
Arthur D. Bloom, MD, Pres.

Research Activities and Fields: Environmental health, biological aspects of remediation, genetic studies of differences in individual variation in response to environmental agents, and environmental factors in neurodegenerative disorders. Operates the International Scientific Program in Environmental Health to set research priorities in Central and Eastern Europe. **Publications:** *Forum Newsletter*, *Environment in Practice* (quarterly newsletter); *Conte Institute Series*. **Formerly:** Environmental Health Institute (1991).

★5070★ Drexel University Environmental Studies Institute
Philadelphia, PA 19104
Phone: (215)895-2263
Dr. Bernard Hamel, Dir.

Research Activities and Fields: Water and wastewater treatment, environmental chemistry, environmental toxicology, environmental planning and management, air resources, environmental health, hazardous wastes, food toxicology and safety, and environmental assessment.

Emory University
Southeastern Clinical Occupational
   Medicine / Environmental Health
   Evaluation Center
See: Entry 9806

★5071★ **Environmental Health Service**
Rancho Los Amigos Medical Center, Inc.
Medical Science Bldg., Rm. 51
7601 E. Imperial Hwy.
Downey, CA 90242
Phone: (310)940-7561
Fax: (310)803-6883
Dr. Henry Gong, Jr., Chief

Research Activities and Fields: Air pollution, including effects of ozone on healthy subjects and patients with mild asthma; physiological and cellular responses to acute exposures to ozone, sulfur dioxide, nitrogen dioxide, carbon monoxide, and particulates; health effects of acid aerosols; pharmaceutical drugs; and development of field study programs, including in-home method for self-testing and lung function performance using research quality instrumentation and personal computers, and documentation of typical hourly and daily activity to assess potential effects of air pollution on those activities.

★5072★ **Environmental and Occupational**
   Health Sciences Institute (EOHSI)
681 Frelinghuysen Rd.
PO Box 1179
Piscataway, NJ 08855-1179
Phone: (908)932-0200
Fax: (908)932-0131
Mark G. Robson, Ph.D., Exec.Dir.

Research Activities and Fields: Toxicology, public education and risk communication, occupational health, exposure measurement and assessment, environmental health, and environmental policy. Studies the basic mechanisms by which environmental exposures harm the body, investigates methods for measuring and reducing exposure and improving health including clinical evaulation of individuals potentially affected adversely by environmental agents, and develops and analyzes ways to communicate information. **Publications:** *EOHSI News* (newsletter). **E-mail Address:** robson@zodiac.rutgers.edu.

★5073★ **Environmental Protection Agency**
Office of Research and Development
Office of Health and Environmental
   Assessment
Mail Code 8601
401 M St. SW
Washington, DC 20460
Phone: (202)260-7315
Fax: (202)260-0393
Dr. William H. Farland, Director

Research Activities and Fields: The Office provides the Environmental Protection Agency with a central capability for evaluating information on the potential health and environmental effects of toxic pollutants. Assessments are prepared on the risks to human health posed by the presence of toxic agents in water, air, and land. EPA uses this scientific and technical knowledge to implement its statutory responsibilities. Principal components of the Office are Environmental Criteria and Assessment Offices at Cin-

cinnati, OH, and Research Triangle Park, NC; Human Health Assessment Group; and Exposure Assessment Group in Washington, DC.

★5074★ **Environmental Protection Agency**
Office of Research and Development
Office of Health Research
Mail Code 8501
401 M St. SW
Washington, DC 20460
Phone: (202)260-5900
Fax: (202)260-0744
Ken Sexton, Director

Research Activities and Fields: Office is responsible for developing and evaluating toxicity test methods and for providing toxicity data to enable the Agency to accurately identify hazards and determine human risk from environmental exposure. Fields of interest include inhalation toxicology, genetic toxicology, neurotoxicology, developmental and reproductive toxicology, microbiology, epidemiology, biometry, and physical, biological, and chemical agents.

Florida State University
Center for Biomedical Toxicological
   Research and Hazardous Waste
   Management
See: Entry 10432

★5075★ **Harvard University**
Kresge Center for Environmental Health
665 Huntington Ave.
Boston, MA 02115
Phone: (617)432-1272
John B. Little, M.D., Dir.

Research Activities and Fields: Environmental health, including interdisciplinary studies on effects and control of air pollutants, occupational health and medicine, safeguards for nuclear power reactors, environmental and respiratory physiology, radiation biology, toxicology and air sampling, monitoring, and personnel protection. Serves as a focus for environmental health activities within the School. **Publications:** Report Series on contract work (semiannually).

Health Research, Inc.
See: Entry 10979

★5076★ **Inner-City Consortium, Inc.**
Gaither & Associates
3624 Market St., 1st Fl. E.
Philadelphia, PA 19104-2614
Phone: (215)386-6800
Fax: (215)386-3164
William S. Gaither, Pres.

Research Activities and Fields: Conducts sustainability education and research in an effort to encourage inner-city youth to pursue careers in energy-related scientific and technical areas and in environmental restoration and waste management.

★5077★ **International Institute of Concern**
   for Public Health
830 Bathurst St.
Toronto, ON, Canada M5R 3G1
Phone: (416)533-7351
Fax: (416)533-7879
Mary Turner, Research Coord.

Research Activities and Fields: Institute studies the health effects of pollution.

★5078★ **Kemper Research Foundation**
429 Mill St.
Milford, OH 45150-1027
Phone: (513)249-2489
Richard Kemper, Dir.

Research Activities and Fields: Building related illnesses, focusing on the effects of microorganisms on man and the environment, including heating, ventilating, and air conditioning equipment.

Laboratory of Radiobiology and
   Environmental Health
See: Entry 11073

★5079★ **Massachusetts Institute of**
   Technology
Center for Environmental Health Sciences
50 Ames St., Rm. E18-666
Cambridge, MA 02139
Phone: (617)253-6220
Fax: (617)258-5424
William G. Thilly, Sc.D., Dir.

Research Activities and Fields: Mutagens and carcinogens in fuel combustion, cooking processes, fungal contamination, and losses from hazardous waste sites. Studies include direct measurement of chemicals and genetic change in humans. Develops ways to assess the importance of individual chemicals in causing human cancer or genetic defects and to identify alternative methods and utilization strategies that could mitigate health hazards. **Publications:** Annual Report. **E-mail Address:** thilly@mt.edu. **Formerly:** Center for Health Effects of Fossil Fuel Utilization.

Michigan State University
Institute for Environmental Toxicology
See: Entry 10446

★5080★ **New York University**
Institute of Environmental Medicine
550 1st Ave.
New York, NY 10016
Phone: (212)263-5280
Fax: (914)351-2118
Max Costa, Ph.D., Dir.

Research Activities and Fields: Toxicology, chemical carcinogenesis, radiation carcinogenesis and dosimetry, respiratory disease and aerosol physiology, environmental pollution and ecology, epidemiology, and biostatistics and biomathematics, including studies on skin, bladder, and lung cancer from environmental sources, environmental hazards to which industrial and community populations are exposed, industrial and environmental health hazards and means for their control, and sources of human exposures to radiation. **Publications:** Annual Report. **E-mail Address:** costam@charlotte.med.nyu.edu. **Formerly:** Institute of Industrial Medicine.

★5081★ **New York University**
Laboratory of Microbial Ecology
752 Brown Bldg.
New York, NY 10003
Phone: (212)998-8268
Fax: (212)995-4015

Research Activities and Fields: Microbial ecology, soil and water microbiology, medical microbiology, environmental virology, clay mineralogy, immunology, and pollution, including studies on survival of genetically engineered microbes in natural environments and acid rain, heavy metals, and other pollutants.

★5082★ **North Carolina State University**
Center for Sound and Vibration
CB 7910
Raleigh, NC 27695
Phone: (919)737-3024
Fax: (919)737-7968
Dr. Robert T. Nagel, Dir.

Research Activities and Fields: Acoustics, vibration, and noise control, including studies on hearing conservation and noise control, human factors aspects of noise, sound intensity measurements in machinery noise in industry, aeroacoustics, active noise control, design of underwater acoustic transducers, wood working machinery noise reduction, computer simulation of noise emission from transportation systems, and sound and structural vibration analysis. Conducts studies and testing in association with other research, industrial, and governmental organizations on all aspects of noise and vibration, including noise survey and data analysis, computer-aided design, and finite-element analysis. **Formerly:** Center for Acoustical Studies.

Oregon Health Sciences University
Center for Research on Occupational and
Environmental Toxicology (CROET)
See: Entry 9816

★5083★ **Oregon State University**
Environmental Health Sciences Center
Agricultural and Life Sciences 1011
Corvallis, OR 97331-7302
Phone: (503)737-3608
Fax: (503)737-4371
Dr. Donald J. Reed, Dir.

Research Activities and Fields: Provides and stimulates coordinated multidisciplinary research to assess the impact of environmental chemicals on human health and to predict associated short- and long-term effects. Specific research draws upon capabilities of faculty, staff, and graduate students in chemistry, biochemistry, agricultural chemistry, biology, food science, fisheries and wildlife, veterinary medicine, pharmacology, toxicology, immunology, and statistics. Focal areas include toxicology of environmental chemicals and naturally occurring toxins, cellular and biochemical toxicology, carcinogenesis of environmental chemicals, mechanisms of toxicity, genetic toxicology, immunotoxicology, mass spectrometry, statistical studies, and analysis of enumerative data related to environmental health research. **E-mail Address:** bodiner@ccmail.orst.edu.

★5084★ **Queens College of City**
University of New York
Center for the Biology of Natural Systems
CBNS
Flushing, NY 11367
Phone: (718)670-4180
Fax: (718)670-4189
Dr. Barry Commoner, Dir.

Research Activities and Fields: Interdisciplinary investigations into problems generated by

development of modern production technologies, environmental degradation, and intensified use of energy and other resources, including problems of environmental health and health-related problems of the environment, problems related to municipal solid waste disposal and development of alternative methods of disposal, and an analysis of economic and resource impact of readjusting production in petrochemical industry.

★5085★ **Rutgers University**
Noise Technical Assistance Center
Cook College
Dept. of Environmental Science
PO Box 231
New Brunswick, NJ 08903
Phone: (908)932-8065
Fax: (908)932-8644
Eric M. Zwerling, Contact

Research Activities and Fields: Health effects of noise and community noise control. **Publications:** *Community Noise Control* (semiannually).

★5086★ **Southwest Research and**
Information Center
PO Box 4524
Albuquerque, NM 87106
Phone: (505)262-1862
Fax: (505)262-1864
Don Hancock, Information Coord.

Research Activities and Fields: The Center maintains ongoing projects that seek to protect the environment, improve the quality of life, and empower citizens and communities through research, public advocacy and consulting, and dissemination of information. Secondary and applied research in resource development, water quality, toxic chemicals, and nuclear waste handling, including studies of health effects of uranium, radioactive waste disposal, medical uses of radiation, coal development, instate electricity demand and rates, coal supply and demand, mine reclamation, water impacts, and relocation of Native Americans from mining areas. **Publications:** Workbook (quarterly).

Thomas Jefferson University
Environmental Medicine and Toxicology
Division
See: Entry 10461

★5087★ **Tufts University**
Center for Environmental Management
177 College Ave.
Medford, MA 02155
Phone: (617)627-3486
Fax: (617)627-3099
Dr. David M. Gute, Interim Dir.

Research Activities and Fields: Ecoefficiency and pollution prevention; motivation of environmentally sustainable actions; and anticipation of future impact, including health effects and technology. **Publications:** *CEM Report* (quarterly newsletter); Final Research Reports; Annual Report. **E-mail Address:** dgute@pearl.tufts.edu.

★5088★ **Tulane University**
Environmental Health Sciences Research
Laboratory
F. Edward Hebert Research Center
Belle Chasse, LA 70037
Phone: (504)394-2233
Jamal Y. Shamas, Lab Supv./Research
 Coord.

Research Activities and Fields: Air and water pollution abatement, water quality evaluation and control, environmental health management, bacterial and mammalian cell mutagenesis, vector control, toxicology, and occupational safety and health, including interdisciplinary studies of toxic effects of pesticides on the environment, biological and physical-chemical treatment of industrial waste, fumigation with air contaminants, environmental toxicology, industrial hygiene, and heavy metal, hazardous waste management, and related studies.

U.S. Department of Defense
Air Force Materiel Command
Occupational and Environmental Health
Directorate
Toxicology Division
See: Entry 2401

U.S. Department of Defense
Army Medical Research and Development
Command
Army Research Institute of Environmental
Medicine
See: Entry 7822

U.S. Department of Defense
Army Medical Research and Development
Command
Army Research Institute of Environmental
Medicine
Environmental Pathophysiology
Directorate
See: Entry 7823

U.S. Department of Defense
Army Medical Research and Development
Command
Army Research Institute of Environmental
Medicine
Environmental Physiology and Medicine
Directorate
See: Entry 7824

U.S. Department of Defense
Army Medical Research and Development
Command
Army Research Institute of Environmental
Medicine
Occupational Health and Performance
Directorate
See: Entry 7825

U.S. Department of Defense
Army Medical Research and Development
Command
Environmental Physiology and Medicine
Directorate
Altitude Physiology and Medicine Division
See: Entry 7826

U.S. Department of Defense
Naval Medical Research and Development
  Command
Naval Medical Research Institute
Diving Medicine Department
See: Entry 7848

★5089★ **U.S. Department of Energy**
Inhalation Toxicology Research Institute
PO Box 5890
Albuquerque, NM 87185
Phone: (505)845-1169
Fax: (505)845-1198
Dr. Joe L. Mauderly, President/Director

Research Activities and Fields: ITRI conducts basic and applied research on the toxicity of airborne materials encountered in the workplace, environment, and home. Materials of interest are toxic by virtue of their radiological, chemical, or physical properties. Multidisciplinary research is conducted on physical and chemical characteristics of airborne materials, their fate in the body when inhaled, and their health effects. Activities include research on fundamental respiratory tract biology and the mechanisms of respiratory tract disease.

★5090★ **U.S. Department of Energy**
Oak Ridge National Laboratory
Environmental, Life, and Social Sciences
  Directorate
Health Studies Section
PO Box 2008
Oak Ridge, TN 37831-6126
Phone: (615)576-2083
Fax: (615)576-2078

Research Activities and Fields: Section conducts research in four major areas related to the detection and analysis of possible human health impacts of technology implementation: 1) development of advanced instrumentation for measuring environmental concentrations of chemicals, in vivo concentrations of chemicals and/or their metabolites, and biochemical parameters that may reflect biological damage processes; 2) development and application of mathematical models for internal radiation dosimetry; 3) epidemiological, biostatistical, and assessment studies of exposed populations; and 4) development of advanced radiopharmaceuticals that are used for diagnosing diseases at medical cooperatives in the United States and Europe.

★5091★ **U.S. Department of Energy**
Office of Energy Research
Health Effects and Life Sciences Research
  Division
Mail Stop ER-72, (GTN)
Washington, DC 20874
Phone: (301)903-5468
Fax: (301)903-8521
David A. Smith, Director

Research Activities and Fields: Division supports (1) studies to develop experimental information from biological systems for estimating or predicting risks of carcinogenesis, mutagenesis, and delayed toxicological effects associated with low level human exposures to energy-related radiations and chemicals; (2) studies to define mechanisms involved in the induction of biological damage following exposure to low levels of energy-related agents; (3) studies to develop new technologies for detecting and quantifying latent health effects associated with such agents; (4) the development of structural biology user facilities at Department of Energy Laboratories and studies involving fundamental structural biology research primarily conducted at these facilities; and (5) studies to create and apply new technologies and resources for characterizing the molecular nature of the human genome.

★5092★ **U.S. Department of Energy**
Office of Energy Research
Office of Health and Environmental
  Research
Mail Stop ER-70, GTN
Washington, DC 20585
Phone: (301)353-3251
Fax: (301)353-5051
Dr. Robert Wood, Deputy Associate Director

Research Activities and Fields: Office is the health and environmental research arm of the Department of Energy. Its mission is to achieve understanding of the health and environmental effects associated with energy technologies and to develop and sustain basic and applied research programs in the biomedical and environmental sciences in which the Department has responsibilities or unique capabilities. Emphasis is on long-term research that is comprehensive and multidisciplinary in scope and quantitative and mechanistic in its approach to scientific questions. Office is also responsible for technology transfer to the academic and private sectors, and provides appropriate support to universities, and stimulates access to advanced multiuser research facilities at the national laboratories. Principal OHER divisions are the Health Effects and Life Science Research Division, Medical applications and Biophysical Research Division, and the Environmental Sciences Division. **Publications:** Research in Progress series (annually). **Additional Contact Information:** Office is located in Germantown, MD 20585.

★5093★ **U.S. Department of Energy**
Office of Health and Environmental
  Research
Medical Applications and Biophysical
  Research Division
Mail Stop ER-73
Washington, DC 20874
Phone: (301)903-3213
Fax: (301)903-5051
Dr. Robert W. Wood, Acting Director

Research Activities and Fields: Division is responsible for planning, implementing, and managing research in the physical sciences as related to health and environmental effects associated with the development of new or advanced energy technologies. Major areas of interest are physical and chemical characterization studies related to environmental radiation and complex chemical mixtures research; measurement science, health protection, and dosimetry research; instrumentation development for structural biology and human genome studies; radiological and chemical physics studies to determine radiation interaction mechanisms; and nuclear medicine and other medical applications of nuclear technology. **Additional Contact Information:** Division is located in Germantown, MD 20874.

★5094★ **U.S. Department of Health and**
  Human Services
Agency for Toxic Substances and Disease
  Registry
1600 Clifton Rd., N.E.
Mail Stop E-28
Atlanta, GA 30333
Phone: (404)639-0700
Fax: (404)639-0744
Barry L. Johnson, Ph.D., Assistant
  Administrator

Research Activities and Fields: Conducts and sponsors epidemiologic studies on human health effects related to hazardous substance exposure, emphasizing substance-specific research on priority hazardous substances. Comprises Division of Health Studies, Division of Toxicology, Division of Health Assessment and Consultation, and Division of Health Education. **Additional Contact Information:** Located at 37 Executive Park Dr., Atlanta, GA 30329.

★5095★ **U.S. Department of Health and**
  Human Services
Agency for Toxic Substances and Disease
  Registry
Division of Health Studies
1600 Clifton Rd., NE
Mail Stop E-31
Atlanta, GA 30333
Phone: (404)639-6200
Fax: (404)639-6220
Jeffrey A. Lybarger, M.D., M.S., Director

Research Activities and Fields: Epidemiology and other human health studies, evaluating the relationship between exposure to hazardous substances at waste sites and adverse health effects. Conducts health studies, surveillance programs, and registries. Subsidiary branches include Health Investigations Branch, Epidemiology and Surveillance Branch, and Exposure and Disease Registry Branch. Maintains National Exposure Registry and Emergency Event Surveillance System databases. **Additional Contact Information:** Located at 37 Executive Park Dr., Atlanta, GA 30329.

★5096★ **U.S. Department of Health and**
  Human Services
Agency for Toxic Substances and Disease
  Registry
Division of Toxicology
1600 Clifton Rd., NE
Mail Stop E-29
Atlanta, GA 30333
Phone: (404)639-6300
Fax: (404)639-6315
Dr. Christopher DeRosa, Director

Research Activities and Fields: Conducts substance-specific studies on priority hazardous substances. Sets priorities for research, initiates programs, and identifies data needs for publication of *Toxicological Profiles*. Comprises Quality Assurance Branch, Research Implementation Branch, and Toxicology Information Branch. **Publications:** *Toxicology Profiles*. **Additional Contact Information:** Located at 37 Executive Park Dr., Atlanta, GA 30329.

★5097★ U.S. Department of Health and Human Services
National Center for Environmental Health
4770 Buford Hwy.
Atlanta, GA 30341-3724
Phone: (404)488-4111
Stephen Thacker, Acting Director

Research Activities and Fields: Center administers national programs that promote a healthy environment and prevent premature death and avoidable illness and disability caused by non-infectious, non-occupational, environmental, and related factors. The Center is organized in divisions on Birth Defects and Developmental Disabilities; Environmental Hazards and Health Effects; Environmental Health Laboratory Sciences; and Injury Control.

★5098★ U.S. Department of Health and Human Services
National Center for Environmental Health
Environmental Hazards and Health Effects Division
4770 Buford Hwy., F-28
Atlanta, GA 30341-3724
Phone: (404)488-7300
Fax: (404)488-7310
Dr. Henry Falk, Director

Research Activities and Fields: Division primarily conducts field investigations related to environmental public health problems and their prevention. Specific areas of interest include toxic chemicals, natural environmental hazards, environmentally-induced disease, international environmental health, and indoor air pollution. **Additional Contact Information:** Division is located at the Koger Center, 2858 Woodcock Blvd., Atlanta, GA 30341.

★5099★ U.S. Department of Health and Human Services
National Center for Environmental Health
Environmental Hazards and Health Effects Division
Health Studies Branch
4770 Buford Hwy., F-46
Atlanta, GA 30341-3724
Phone: (404)488-7359
Thomas H. Sink, Chief

Research Activities and Fields: Branch conducts epidemiologic studies on environmental exposure and health effects. Also studies the epidemiology of natural disasters. This includes planning, implementing, and reporting epidemiologic research and providing technical assistance and assessment of risk from such environmental hazards as toxic chemicals, radiation, waste disposal, indoor air pollution, passive smoking, controlled substance analogs, and natural and man-made disasters.

★5100★ U.S. Department of Health and Human Services
National Center for Environmental Health
Environmental Health Laboratory Sciences Division
4770 Buford Hwy.
Atlanta, GA 30341-3724
Phone: (404)488-4152
Fax: (404)488-4151
Dr. Eric J. Sampson, Director

Research Activities and Fields: Division operates a complex program in laboratory research and service in the areas of chronic disease and toxicant exposure. Laboratory methods development accounts for most of the activities related to problem definition in chronic disease. These activities include developing laboratory methods in cardiovascular disease, cancer, genetic markers of certain chronic diseases, and biomedical indices of nutritional status. To improve problem definition in toxicant exposure, Division is developing new and improving existing laboratory methods for detecting and measuring: 1) body burdens of hazardous substances and their metabolites; and 2) early stages of organ damage (using biochemical markers for organ-specific dysfunction). Services, including advice, assistance, and information, are available to state and local public health authorities, federal agencies, international organizations, academic, international, and private laboratories, and professional organizations in support of laboratory science in the fields of environmental health and non-infectious chronic diseases. The Division also collaborates with other CDC organizations as appropriate. It consists of the Toxicology Branch, Clinical Biochemistry Branch, Nutritional Biochemistry Branch, Special Activities Branch, and Molecular Biology Branch.

★5101★ U.S. Department of Health and Human Services
National Institute of Environmental Health Sciences
PO Box 12233
Research Triangle Park, NC 27709
Phone: (919)541-3345
Dr. Kenneth Olden, Director

Research Activities and Fields: Institute conducts research in the environmental health sciences in the NIEHS laboratories at Research Triangle Park, NC, and supports research through its extramural programs. The Institute's Extramural Research and Training Division supports research within educational institutions, research institutes, and other public and private nonprofit organizations through individual grants, contracts, and Research Career Development Awards. Programs emphasize studies that provide information essential to an understanding of the way in which human health is adversely affected by environmental factors. Grant programs include support for Environmental Health Science Centers, Marine and Freshwater Biomedical Science Centers, and research manpower development programs, as well as the Superfund Basic Research Program, a university-based program of basic research supported by NIEHS as part of the 1986 Superfund Amendments and Reauthorization Act. This Program combines basic research in the fields of ecology, engineering, and hydrogeology into a core program of biomedical research to provide a broader and more detailed body of scientific information to be used in decision-making related to the management of hazardous substances. In addition to the Basic Research Program, the Institute supports a model worker training program for workers involved in hazardous waste cleanup and emergency response.

★5102★ U.S. Department of Health and Human Services
National Institute of Environmental Health Sciences
Biochemical Risk Analysis Laboratory
Mail Drop A3-02
PO Box 12233
Research Triangle Park, NC 27709
Phone: (919)541-4982
Fax: (919)541-3647
Dr. George Lucier, Director

Research Activities and Fields: Laboratory is primarily concerned with the development of laboratory procedures for quantifying exposures in terms of the biologically effective dose, and with the application of these procedures to human population monitoring and enhanced extrapolation of toxicologic outcomes across species.

★5103★ U.S. Department of Health and Human Services
National Institute of Environmental Health Sciences
Division of Extramural Research and Training
PO Box 12233
Research Triangle Park, NC 27709
Phone: (919)541-7723
Fax: (919)541-2843
Anne P. Sassaman, Ph.D., Director

Research Activities and Fields: The Extramural Research and Training Division supports basic and applied research on the consequences of the exposure of man and other biological systems to potentially toxic or harmful agents in the environment. Investigators at colleges, universities, and research foundations are supported through individual research grants, program project grants, and other support mechanisms. Research activities focus on the ways in which human health is adversely affected by chemical, physical, and other environmental factors. This involves: 1) characterization of environmental health hazards; 2) research on biological responses to environmental health hazards; 3) applied toxicological research and testing; 4) biometry and risk estimation; and 5) resource and manpower development. (Research and training may span one, several, or all program areas.) The extramural program also includes support for Environmental Health Sciences Centers and for Marine and Freshwater Biomedical Science Centers. Environmental Health Sciences Centers serve as national focal points and resources for research and manpower development in health problems related to air, water, and food pollution; occupational and industrial neighborhood health and safety; heavy metal toxicity; agricultural chemical hazards; and the relationships of environment to cancer, birth defects, behavioral anomalies, respiratory and cardiovascular diseases, and diseases of other organs. Marine and Freshwater Biomedical Science Centers provide core support to foster multidisciplinary research on marine and freshwater organisms in the study of mechanisms of toxicity of environmental agents and as models for human diseases and disorders resulting from exposure to environmental toxicants.

★5104★ U.S. Department of Health and Human Services
National Institute of Environmental Health Sciences
Division of Intramural Research
PO Box 12233, Bldg. 18-01
Research Triangle Park, NC 27709
Phone: (919)541-0262
Fax: (919)541-0669
Dr. Martin Rodbell, Chief

Research Activities and Fields: Programs of the Intramural Research Division include fundamental environmental research conducted at NIEHS laboratories, as well as evaluations of the NIEHS in-house research effort; establishment of priorities; allocation of funds, space, and personnel; and integration of ongoing and new research activities into the overall program structure. Division comprises the Comparative Medicine Branch, and laboratories of: Cellular and Molecular Pharmacology, Molecular Biophysics, Molecular Genetics, Molecular and Integrative Neurosciences, Pulmonary Pathobiology, and Reproductive and Developmental Toxicology.

★5105★ U.S. Department of Health and Human Services
National Institute of Environmental Health Sciences
Epidemiology Branch
Mail Drop A3-05
PO Box 12233
Research Triangle Park, NC 27709
Phone: (919)541-7703
Fax: (919)541-2511
Allen J. Wilcox, M.D., Ph.D., Branch Chief

Research Activities and Fields: The Epidemiology Branch initiates field studies of human disease (particularly chronic diseases) attributable to environmental pollutants; investigates the effects of environmental toxins on fetal and child development; and conducts basic and applied research in laboratory support methodology involved in the monitoring of human populations.

★5106★ U.S. Department of Health and Human Services
National Institute of Environmental Health Sciences
Laboratory of Cellular and Molecular Pharmacology
PO Box 12233
Research Triangle Park, NC 27709
Phone: (919)541-3332
Dr. J.W. Putney, Chief

Research Activities and Fields: Cellular and molecular pharmacology.

★5107★ U.S. Department of Health and Human Services
National Institute of Environmental Health Sciences
Laboratory of Molecular Biophysics
PO Box 12233
Research Triangle Park, NC 27709
Phone: (919)541-3196
Fax: (919)541-7880
Dr. Colin F. Chignell, Chief

Research Activities and Fields: Laboratory's goals are to develop, improve, and utilize spectroscopic methods to monitor the molecular interactions that occur between environmental agents and biological systems; develop, improve, and utilize analytical methodology for specified chemical agents; and conduct biochemical, physical, organic, and bio-organic studies of environmental agents and their conversion products, with emphasis on biomechanism elucidation.

★5108★ U.S. Department of Health and Human Services
National Institute of Environmental Health Sciences
Laboratory of Molecular Genetics
PO Box 12233
Research Triangle Park, NC 27709
Phone: (919)541-4690
Fax: (919)541-7593

Research Activities and Fields: Mutagenesis on a subcellular level and whole animal genetics. Focuses on the mechanisms of mutation, the nature of genes and how they function, and a greater understanding of mutation events and their impacts on reproduction and development in multicellular organisms.

★5109★ U.S. Department of Health and Human Services
National Institute of Environmental Health Sciences
Laboratory of Molecular and Integrative Neurosciences
PO Box 12233
Research Triangle Park, NC 27709
Phone: (919)541-2881
Fax: (919)541-4737
Andres Negrovilar, Chief

Research Activities and Fields: Molecular and integrative neurosciences.

★5110★ U.S. Department of Health and Human Services
National Institute of Environmental Health Sciences
Laboratory of Pulmonary Pathobiology
MD D2-01
Research Triangle Park, NC 27709
Phone: (919)541-3540
Fax: (919)541-4133
Dr. Paul Nettesheim, Chief

Research Activities and Fields: General research goals are to: 1) elucidate biochemical and molecular mechanisms of differentiation of airway epithelium; 2) elucidate the role of growth factors in regulation of growth of normal and neoplastically transformed airway cells; 3) explore pathogenetic mechanisms of inflammatory processes of the lung, particularly the cellular and biochemical basis of fibrogenesis; and 4) elucidate the mechanisms of regulation of surfactant biosynthesis.

★5111★ U.S. Department of Health and Human Services
National Institute of Environmental Health Sciences
Laboratory of Reproductive and Developmental Toxicology

PO Box 12233
Research Triangle Park, NC 27709
Phone: (919)541-3333
Fax: (919)541-0696
John A. McLachlan, Chief

Research Activities and Fields: Laboratory activities include research in reproductive and developmental biology/toxicology, including gamete biology, developmental endocrinology, pharmacology, germ cell differentiation, genital tract development, ontogeny of hormone response, and developmental regulation of gene expression.

★5112★ U.S. Department of Health and Human Services
National Institute of Environmental Health Sciences
Statistics and Biomathematics Branch
Mail Drop B3-02
PO Box 12233
Research Triangle Park, NC 27709
Phone: (919)541-7817
Fax: (919)541-7887
Dr. David Hoel, Director

Research Activities and Fields: The Statistics and Biomathematics Branch conducts a broad research effort ranging from statistical analysis to biomathematical modeling aimed at developing new or improved methods for quantitative risk estimation, particularly in the areas of carcinogenesis, mutagenesis, and reproduction. Branch's research program in statistical methodology involves design and analysis issues arising in laboratory experimentation, with special emphasis on toxicological screening assays.

Universities Associated for Research and Education in Pathology, Inc.
See: Entry 10180

★5113★ University of California at Berkeley
Environmental Engineering and Health Sciences Laboratory
Bldg. 112
1301 S. 46th
Richmond, CA 94804
Phone: (510)231-9521
Fax: (510)231-9500
Prof. Robert C. Spear, Dir.

Research Activities and Fields: Sanitary engineering, wastewater treatment, algology, limnology, reclamation and reuse, drinking water quality, occupational health, microbiology and chemistry of water and wastewater, and impact and abatement of hazardous waste such as organic solvents in groundwater. **Formerly:** Sanitary Engineering Research Laboratory (SERL) (1981); absorbed the Water Technology Center; Sanitary Engineering and Environmental Health Research Laboratory (1991).

University of California, Davis
Division of Occupational/Environmental Medicine and Epidemiology
See: Entry 9849

★5114★ **University of California, Davis**
Institute of Toxicology and Environmental
Health
Office of Research
Davis, CA 95616
Phone: (916)752-1340
Fax: (916)752-5300
Dr. James W. Overstreet, Dir.

Research Activities and Fields: Coordinates interdisciplinary research on biomedical and toxicological problems related to exposure to chemical, physical, and biological toxic agents or to ionizing radiation. Seeks to determine basic mechanisms of toxic effects and to predict human health hazards from continual exposure to realistic levels of toxic substances in the environment or in the workplace. **Formerly:** Radiobiology Laboratory (1979), Laboratory for Energy-Related Health Research, Institute for Environmental Health Research (1990).

★5115★ **University of California, Irvine**
Air Pollution Health Effects Laboratory
Dept. of Community & Environmental
  Medicine
Irvine, CA 92717-1825
Phone: (714)824-5860
Fax: (714)824-4763
Dr. Robert F. Phalen, Dir.

Research Activities and Fields: Lung development and defenses, particle deposition in the lungs, chronic inhalation exposure to oxidant fine particulate and acidic aerosol mixtures, inhalation exposure methodology, and environmental and occupational inhalation toxicology, emphasizing particle plus gas mixtures. Also develops and validates mathematical models of inhaled particle deposition.

★5116★ **University of Cincinnati**
Groundwater Research Center
College of Engineering
Mail Location 18
Cincinnati, OH 45221-0018
Phone: (513)556-2933
Fax: (513)556-2599
Dr. Constantine Papadakis, Dir.

Research Activities and Fields: Development of techniques for testing, calibration, and validation of software for modeling the transport and fate of groundwater contaminants; development of a knowledge base expert system for selection and application of appropriate models for predicting the fate of groundwater pollutants and analyzing remedial action alternatives; use of subsurface monitoring and mathematical modeling to study the processes of dispersion and absorption of solutes; study of physical processes governing the migration of contaminants in the saturated and partially-saturated soil zones; quantitative and qualitative health risk characterization involving biomedical and biomathematical analysis; exposure assessment of toxic substances involving source characterization transport, chemical transformations, and human intake; and analysis of the shifting chemical composition, toxicity, and migration patterns of complex mixtures. The Center is organized into a Groundwater Management Group, concerned with the migration and remediation of chemicals in groundwater, and a Groundwater Health Risk Assessment Group, concerned with

the health risks of groundwater contaminated with hazardous wastes. **E-mail Address:** mbeljn@uceng.uc.edu.

★5117★ **University of Colorado—Denver**
Center for Environmental Sciences (CES)
PO Box 173364
Denver, CO 80217-3364
Phone: (303)556-4277
Fax: (303)556-4822
Dr. Herman Sievering, Dir.

Research Activities and Fields: Coordinates interdisciplinary research for 20 faculty members in the sciences and social sciences. In the associated Analytical Laboratory, on-going research includes the effects of energy production on health and the environment, including studies on the relationship between coal burning and air and water pollution, and studies of biophysicochemical cycles, especially the exchange of pollutants at air/land and air/water interfaces. **Formerly:** Environmental Trace Substances Research Program (1979).

★5118★ **University of Connecticut**
Center for Environmental Health
3636 Horsebarn Rd.
Box U-39
Storrs, CT 06269-4039
Phone: (203)486-5067
Fax: (203)486-4375
Prof. Norman Klein, Dir.

Research Activities and Fields: Interdisciplinary studies of environmental health problems of concern to Connecticut, emphasizing carcinogenesis, pesticides, lead poisoning, epidemiology and biostatistics, genetic biomonitoring, and reproductive toxicology.

★5119★ **University of Florida**
Center for Environmental and Human
  Toxicology
Progress Center
1 Progress Blvd., Box 17
Alachua, FL 32615
Phone: (904)462-3281
Fax: (904)392-1529
Dr. D. D. Buss, Dir.

Research Activities and Fields: Environmental and human toxicology. **E-mail Address:** etox@gnv.ifas.ufl.edu. **Formerly:** Center for Environmental Toxicology.

★5120★ **University of Illinois at Urbana-**
  Champaign
Institute for Environmental Studies
1101 W. Peabody Dr.
Urbana, IL 61801
Phone: (217)333-4178
Fax: (217)333-8046
Dr. Roger A. Minear, Dir.

Research Activities and Fields: Identifies and investigates current environmental problems and develops methods of long-range planning for future environmental quality. Specific studies include interdisciplinary and multidisciplinary research in water resources, air pollution, environmental toxicology, environmental chemistry, environmental and resource economics, ecology, biostatistics and epidemiology, solid waste, environmental psychology, and social impact as-

sessment. Also conducts research on the environmental management approach to the study of mutagens/carcinogens, including detection, characterization, environmental transport, and risk assessment for human health. **E-mail Address:** madams@ux1.cso.uiuc.edu.

★5121★ **University of Iowa**
Center for Health Effects of Environmental
  Contamination (CHEEC)
100 Oakdale Campus No. N252 0H
Iowa City, IA 52242-5000
Phone: (319)335-4550
Fax: (319)335-4077
Pete Weyer, Contact

Research Activities and Fields: Fate and transport of toxic substances in the environment, radon and indoor air contaminants, non-point source chemical contamination of water supplies, and epidemiologic studies that relate the occurrence of diseases to contaminant exposure. **Publications:** Newsletter; Annual Report; Technical Report. **E-mail Address:** cheec@uiowa.edu.

★5122★ **University of Iowa**
Iowa Pesticide Hazard Assessment
  Program
Dept. of Preventive Medicine
100 Oakdale Campus, 124 AMRF
Iowa City, IA 52242-5000
Phone: (319)335-4423
Fax: (319)335-4225
Burton Kross, Dir.

Research Activities and Fields: Detection of pesticides in Iowa groundwater, including studies of pesticide metabolites, microtoxics, and hazardous waste analysis.

University of Iowa
State Hygienic Laboratory
See: Entry 10999

★5123★ **University of Miami**
Pesticide Residue, Toxic Waste and Basic
  Research Analytical Laboratory
Bldg. B
12500 SW 152 St.
Miami, FL 33177-1411
Phone: (305)232-8202
Fax: (305)232-7461
Jon B. Mann, Lab Mgr.

Research Activities and Fields: Pesticides, air pollutants, carcinogens, and chemicals, with emphasis on biological, agricultural, and environmental samples.

★5124★ **University of Michigan**
Institute of Environmental and Industrial
  Health
School of Public Health
109 S. Observatory
Ann Arbor, MI 48109
Phone: (313)764-3188
Fax: (313)764-9424
Khalil H. Mancy, Dir.

Research Activities and Fields: Environmental and industrial health and safety, including studies on water and air pollution; radiation protection; risk assessment; environmental toxicology and epidemiology; environmental monitoring and modeling; toxic contamination of the environment; molecular mechanisms of the effects of chemicals on biological systems; biomechanics; ergonomics; law and policy; ventilation control; occupational and preventive medicine; hazardous materials evaluation, control, and environmental impacts; and measurement, evaluation, and control of radiation in the workplace. **Formerly:** Institute of Industrial Health.

★5125★ University of Minnesota
Center for Environment and Health Policy
Box 807 UMHC
420 Delaware St., SE
Minneapolis, MN 55455
Phone: (612)626-0900
Fax: (612)626-0650

Research Activities and Fields: Center promotes the use of environmental, biological, and social science knowledge in the development of public policies relevant to environmental agents and their effects on the health of people. Center's focus is on applying existing scientific data to analyze environmental risks while considering economic, social, and political implications. Programmatic areas of the Center include risk analysis, risk communication, economic analysis, and legal/regulatory affairs.

University of Missouri—Columbia
Missouri Agricultural Experiment Station
See: Entry 9558

★5126★ University of North Carolina at Chapel Hill
Center for Environmental Medicine and Lung Biology
Medical Research Bldg. C.
CB 7310
Chapel Hill, NC 27599-7310
Phone: (919)962-0126
Fax: (919)966-9863
Philip A. Bromberg, M.D., Dir.

Research Activities and Fields: Environmental impacts on human health, including: 1) effects of inhaled agents on the respiratory system in diseased and healthy human subjects and on human cell lines; and 2) basic and clinical studies in environmental health sciences. **E-mail Address:** philipbromberg@unc.edu.

★5127★ University of Pennsylvania
Institute for Environmental Medicine
1 John Morgan Bldg.
36th St. & Hamilton Walk
Philadelphia, PA 19104-6068
Phone: (215)898-9100
Fax: (215)898-0868
Dr. Aron B. Fisher, Dir.

Research Activities and Fields: Conducts fundamental and applied interdisciplinary studies on cellular and molecular biology of lung function with special emphasis on the lung surfactant system, undersea physiology, physiological and toxic effects of oxygen, isobaric gas counterdiffusion, and hyperbaric oxygen therapy.

University of Quebec at Montreal
Centre for Study of Biological Interactions Between Environment and Health
See: Entry 9861

University of Utah
Rocky Mountain Center for Occupational and Environmental Health
See: Entry 9862

University of Wisconsin—Madison
Environmental Toxicology Center
See: Entry 10489

Wadsworth Center
See: Entry 11004

Wayne State University
Institute of Chemical Toxicology
See: Entry 10494

West Virginia University
Institute of Occupational and Environmental Health
See: Entry 9863

State Government Agencies

Environmental Health

★5128★ Alabama Department of Public Health
Environmental Services Bureau
434 Monroe St.
Montgomery, AL 36130
Phone: (205)613-5373
Fax: (205)240-3368

★5129★ Alaska Department of Environmental Conservation
Environmental Health Division
410 Willoughby Ave.
Juneau, AK 99811-1795
Phone: (907)465-5280
Fax: (907)465-5292

★5130★ Arizona Department of Environmental Quality
Disease Prevention Services Division
Risk Assessment and Environmental Investigation Office
3815 N. Black Canyon Hwy.
Phoenix, AZ 85015
Phone: (602)230-5857
Fax: (602)230-5959

★5131★ Arkansas Department of Health
Environmental Health Services Bureau
PO Box 3278
Little Rock, AR 72203-3278
Phone: (501)661-2574
Fax: (501)671-1450

★5132★ California Health and Welfare Agency
Health Services Department
Environmental Health and Occupational Disease Control Division
5801 Christie Ave., Ste. 600
Emeryville, CA 94608
Phone: (510)450-2400
Fax: (916)323-9869

★5133★ Colorado Public and Environment Department
Environment Office
4300 Cherry Creek Dr. S.
Denver, CO 80222-1530
Phone: (303)692-3000
Fax: (303)782-4969

★5134★ Connecticut Department of Public Health
Health Systems Regulation Bureau
Environmental Health Division
150 Washington St.
Hartford, CT 06106
Phone: (203)240-9200
Fax: (203)566-1710

★5135★ Delaware Department of Health and Social Services
Public Health Division
Health Systems Protection Branch
Jesse Cooper Bldg.
PO Box 637
Dover, DE 19903
Phone: (302)739-4731
Fax: (302)739-3008

★5136★ District of Columbia Department of Consumer and Regulatory Affairs
Business Regulation Administration
614 H St., NW
Washington, DC 20001
Phone: (202)727-7247
Fax: (202)927-7027

★5137★ Florida Department of Health and Rehabilitative Services
Health Program Office
Environmental Health Services Office
1317 Winewood Blvd.
Tallahassee, FL 32399-0700
Phone: (904)488-0004
Fax: (904)922-2993

★5138★ Georgia Department of Human Resources
Public Health Division
Environmental Health Section
47 Trinity Ave. SW
Atlanta, GA 30334-1202
Phone: (404)657-6534
Fax: (404)657-6533

★5139★ Hawaii Department of Health
Environmental Health Administration
1250 Punchbowl St.
Honolulu, HI 96813
Phone: (808)586-4424
Fax: (808)586-4444

★5140★ Idaho Department of Health and Welfare
Health Division
Environmental Health and Safety Bureau
PO Box 83720
Boise, ID 83720-0036
Phone: (208)334-5945
Fax: (208)334-6558

★5141★ **Illinois Department of Public Health**
Health Protection Office
Environmental Health Division
535 W. Jefferson St.
Springfield, IL 62761
Phone: (217)782-5830
Fax: (217)782-3987

★5142★ **Indiana Department of Health**
Consumer Health Services Division
1330 W. Michigan St.
PO Box 1964
Indianapolis, IN 46206-1964
Phone: (317)383-6403
Fax: (317)383-6779

★5143★ **Iowa Department of Public Health**
Health Protection Division
Environmental Health Bureau
Lucas State Office Bldg.
321 E. 12th St.
Des Moines, IA 50309
Phone: (515)281-3478
Fax: (515)242-6284

★5144★ **Kansas Department of Health and Environment**
Health Division
Environmental Health Services Bureau
900 SW Jackson, Ste. 620
Topeka, KS 66612-1290
Phone: (913)296-0189
Fax: (913)296-1231

★5145★ **Kentucky Human Resources Cabinet**
Health Services Department
Environmental Health and Community Safety Division
275 E. Main St.
Frankfort, KY 40621
Phone: (502)564-3722
Fax: (502)564-6533

★5146★ **Louisiana Department of Health and Hospitals**
Public Health Office
325 Loyola Ave.
PO Box 60630
New Orleans, LA 70160
Phone: (504)568-5181
Fax: (504)568-5119

★5147★ **Maine Department of Human Services**
Health Bureau
Disease Control Division
Environmental Health Unit
State House Station 11
Augusta, ME 04333
Phone: (207)287-3591
Fax: (207)287-3005

★5148★ **Maryland Department of the Environment**
Environmental Health Coordinator
2500 Broening Hwy.
Baltimore, MD 21224
Phone: (410)631-3851
Fax: (410)631-3888

★5149★ **Massachusetts Executive Office of Health and Human Services**
Public Health Department
Environmental Assessment Division
150 Tremont St.
Boston, MA 02111
Phone: (617)727-2660
Fax: (617)727-2559

★5150★ **Michigan Department of Public Health**
Environmental and Occupational Health Bureau
3423 N. Logan St.
PO Box 30195
Lansing, MI 48909
Phone: (517)335-9218
Fax: (517)335-9476

★5151★ **Minnesota Department of Health**
Health Protection Bureau
Environmental Health Division
717 Delaware St. SE
Box 9441
Minneapolis, MN 55440
Phone: (612)627-5033
Fax: (612)623-5794

★5152★ **Mississippi Department of Health**
Environmental Health Bureau
PO Box 1700
Jackson, MS 39215-1700
Phone: (601)960-7518
Fax: (601)960-7448

★5153★ **Missouri Department of Health**
Environmental Health and Epidemiology Division
PO Box 570
Jefferson City, MO 65102
Phone: (314)751-6080

★5154★ **Montana Department of Health and Environmental Sciences**
Health Services Division
Food and Consumer Safety Bureau
W.F. Cogswell Bldg.
1400 Broadway
PO Box 200901
Helena, MT 59620-0901
Phone: (406)444-2408
Fax: (406)444-2606

★5155★ **Nebraska Department of Health**
Environmental Health Bureau
301 Centennial Mall S.
PO Box 95007
Lincoln, NE 68509
Phone: (402)471-3979
Fax: (402)471-0383

★5156★ **Nevada Department of Human Resources**
Health Division
Health Protection Services Bureau
505 E. King St., Rm. 600
Carson City, NV 89710
Phone: (702)687-4750
Fax: (702)687-3859

★5157★ **New Hampshire Department of Health and Human Services**
Public Health Services Division
Environmental Health and Hazard Assessment Office
6 Hazen dr.
Concord, NH 03301
Phone: (603)271-4587
Fax: (603)271-3745

★5158★ **New Jersey Department of Health**
Epidemiology, Environmental, Occupational, and Health Services Division
Environmental Health Services Office
CN 369
Trenton, NJ 08625-0369
Phone: (609)984-6710
Fax: (609)588-7431

★5159★ **New Mexico Department of Environment**
1190 St. Francis Dr.
Santa Fe, NM 87503
Phone: (505)827-2855
Fax: (505)827-2836

★5160★ **New York State Department of Health**
Environmental Health Center
2 University Place
Albany, NY 12203-3313
Phone: (518)458-6400

★5161★ **North Carolina Department of Environment, Health, and Natural Resources**
Health Director's Office
Environmental Health Division
PO Box 27687
Raleigh, NC 27611
Phone: (919)715-4125
Fax: (919)715-3060

★5162★ **North Dakota Department of Health and Consolidated Laboratories**
Environmental Health Section
PO Box 5220
Bismarck, ND 58502-5520
Phone: (701)328-5150
Fax: (701)328-5200

★5163★ **Ohio Department of Health**
Environmental Health Services Division
246 N. High St.
Columbus, OH 43266-0588
Phone: (614)644-6811
Fax: (614)644-0085

★5164★ **Oklahoma Department of Health**
Environmental Health Services
1000 NE 10th St.
Oklahoma City, OK 73117-1299
Phone: (405)271-5217
Fax: (405)271-3458

★5165★ **Oregon Department of Human Resources**
Health Diivision
Environment and Health Systems Offic
PO Box 14450
Portland, OR 97214-0450
Phone: (503)731-4000
Fax: (503)731-4078

★ 5166 ★   **Pennsylvania Department of Health**
Environmental Health Division
PO Box 90
Harrisburg, PA 17108
Phone: (717)787-1708
Fax: (717)772-6959

★ 5167 ★   **Rhode Island Department of Health**
Environmental Health Services Office
3 Capitol Hill
Providence, RI 02908-5097
Phone: (401)277-3118
Fax: (401)277-6953

★ 5168 ★   **South Carolina Department of Health and Environmental Control**
Health Services Office
Environmental Health Bureau
2600 Bull St.
Columbia, SC 29201
Phone: (803)935-7945
Fax: (803)737-3946

★ 5169 ★   **South Dakota Department of Health**
Division of Public Health
Regulation and Quality Assurance Division
Foss Bldg.
523 E. Capitol
Pierre, SD 57501
Phone: (605)773-3364
Fax: (605)773-6667

★ 5170 ★   **Tennessee Department of Health**
Health Services Bureau
Environmental Epidemiologist
312 8th Ave., N., 12th Fl.
Nashville, TN 37247-0101
Phone: (615)741-5683
Fax: (615)532-2286

★ 5171 ★   **Texas Department of Health**
Environmental Health Bureau
1100 W. 49th St.
Austin, TX 78756
Phone: (512)834-6640
Fax: (512)458-7686

★ 5172 ★   **Utah Department of Health**
Community Health Services Division
Environmental Services Bureau
PO Box 142872
Salt Lake City, UT 84114-2872
Phone: (801)538-6856
Fax: (801)538-6036

★ 5173 ★   **Vermont Agency of Human Services**
Health Department
Environmental Health Division
PO Box 70
Burlington, VT 05402
Phone: (802)863-7220
Fax: (802)863-7425

★ 5174 ★   **Virginia Office of Health and Human Resources**
Health Department
Environmental Health Services Division

1500 E. Main St.
PO Box 2448
Richmond, VA 23218
Phone: (804)786-3559
Fax: (804)786-4616

★ 5175 ★   **Washington Department of Health**
Environmental Health Office
PO Box 47821
Olympia, WA 98504-7821
Phone: (360)586-5212
Fax: (360)586-7424

★ 5176 ★   **West Virginia Department of Health and Human Resources**
Public Health Bureau
Environmental Health Office
815 Quarrier St.
Charleston, WV 25301
Phone: (304)558-2981

★ 5177 ★   **Wisconsin Department of Health and Social Services**
Health Division
Environmental Health Bureau
1414 E. Washington
PO Box 309
Madison, WI 53702-0309
Phone: (608)266-2835
Fax: (608)267-2832

★ 5178 ★   **Wyoming Department of Health and Social Services**
Preventive Medicine Division
Environmental Health Program
117 Hathaway Bldg.
Cheyenne, WY 82002-0710
Phone: (307)777-7957
Fax: (307)777-5402

Chapter 25
Epidemiology

National & International Organizations

★5179★ American College of Epidemiology (ACE)
c/o Sally Vernon
University of Texas
School of Public Health
PO Box 20186
Houston, TX 77225
Phone: (713)792-4363
Fax: (713)792-4416
Dr. Sally Vernon, Sec.

Founded: 1979. **Members:** 850. **Description:** Medical professionals involved in the field of epidemiology. (Epidemiology is the study of the causes of human disease and the pattern of disease in human populations.) Promotes education in the practice of epidemiology and maintains professional standards in the field. Relates epidemiological issues to public policy. Plans to develop membership database. **Publications:** *Annals of Epidemiology*, quarterly. • Newsletter, quarterly.

★5180★ Association of French Language Epidemiologists (AFLE)
(Association des Epidemiologistes de Langue Francaise — ADELF)
INSERM U 88
Hopital Nationale de Saint Maurice
14, rue du Val d'Osne
F-94410 Saint Maurice, France
Phone: 1 45183859
Fax: 1 45183889
Dr. M. Goldberg, Pres.

Founded: 1976. **Members:** 700. **Languages:** French. **Description:** Epidemiologists, doctors, surgeons, veterinarians, biologists, medical and social science educators, and public health planners. Facilitates communication among epidemiologists. Develops and provides information on epidemiological methods. Promotes epidemiological research. Organizes annual scientific meetings. **Publications:** *ADELF-Info*, bimonthly. Newsletter.

★5181★ Council of State and Territorial Epidemiologists (CSTE)
20 Executive Park W., Suite. 2018
Atlanta, GA 30329
Phone: (404)982-0878
Fax: (404)982-0576
Mr. Willis Forrester, Contact

Founded: 1951. **Members:** 130. **Regional Groups:** 4. **Description:** State epidemiologists. Works to establish closer working relationships among members; consults with and advises appropriate disciplines in other health agencies; provides technical advice and assistance to the Association of State and Territorial Health Officials; works closely with Centers for Disease Control on epidemiology, surveillance, and prevention activities. **Publications:** *CSTE Update*, quarterly. • *Minutes to State and Territorial Epidemiologists*. **Formerly:** (1986) Conference of State and Territorial Epidemiologists.

★5182★ International Epidemiological Association (IEA)
KCSMD
Department of Public Health and Epidemiology
Bessemer Rd.
London SE5 9RJ, England
Phone: 171 346 3170
Fax: 171 737 3556
Kunio Aoki, Pres.

Founded: 1950. **Members:** 2,250. **Languages:** English. **Description:** Individuals interested in epidemiology (science dealing with incidence, distribution, and control of disease in populations). Studies methods and applications of disease control, clinical medicine, and health services. Conducts seminars and workshops. Encourages epidemiologic research. **Publications:** Books. • *Ditionary of Epidemiology*. • *International Journal of Epidemiology*, bimonthly. Journal. • Manuals. • Membership Directory, triennial. • Monographs.

★5183★ Organization for Co-Ordination and Co-Operation in the Control of Endemic Diseases (OCCGE)
(Organisation de Coordination et de Cooperation pour la Lutte Contre Grandes Endemies — OCCGE)
BP 153
Bobo-Dioulasso 1, Burkina Faso
Phone: 970101
Fax: 970099
Dr. Youssouf Kane, Exec. Officer

Founded: 1960. **Members:** 8. **Languages:** French. Does not correspond in English. **Description:** Doctors and scientists. Organizes, coordinates, supports, and evaluates programs aimed at controlling and eradicating major endemic and epidemic diseases within member states and in West Africa. Seeks achievements in applied medical research, investigations, missions, and operational actions in West Africa; promotes professional training of administrators; disseminates research information on epidemics and the methods and means of combatting them. Cooperates with the World Health Organization. Promotes educational program (EPIGEPS). Involved in Epidemioly and Management Formation Project. **Publications:** *Communique Bibliographique*, periodic. • *OCCGE Informations*, periodic.

★5184★ Society for Epidemiologic Research (SER)
c/o Joseph L. Lyon
Department of Family and Preventive Medicine
50 N. Medical Dr., 1C26
Salt Lake City, UT 84132
Phone: (801)581-7234
Fax: (801)581-2759
Dr. Joseph L. Lyon, Sec.-Treas.

Founded: 1967. **Members:** 2,600. **Description:** Epidemiologists, researchers, public health administrators, educators, mathematicians, statisticians, and others interested in epidemiologic research. To stimulate scientific interest in and promote the exchange of information about epidemiologic research. **Publications:** *American Journal of Epidemiology*, bimonthly. Journal. Includes research reports and reviews, computer programs for epidemiologists, and annual meeting abstracts. *Price:* $190/year. • *Society for Epidemiologic Re-*

search--*Membership Directory*, every 3-5 years. Membership Directory. • *Society for Epidemiologic Research--Newsletter*, semiannual. Newsletter.

★5185★ **Society of Hospital Epidemiologists of America**
875 Kings Hwy., Ste. 200
Woodbury, NJ 08096
Phone: (609)845-1720
Fax: (609)853-0411
Coley Lyons, Exec.Dir.

Founded: 1981. **Members:** 975. **Description:** Offers educational programs. **Publications:** *Infection Control and Hospital Epidemiology*, monthly. Journal.

Research Centers

Center for Epidemiologic Research
See: Entry 9802

Dana-Farber Cancer Institute
Division of Biostatistics
See: Entry 6028

★5186★ **Kaiser Permanente Medical Care Program**
Division of Research
3451 Piedmont Ave.
Oakland, CA 94611
Phone: (510)450-2129
Fax: (510)450-2073
Dr. Gary D. Friedman, Dir.

Research Activities and Fields: Medical epidemiology, biometrics and biostatistics, technology assessment, health services research, and health education research and evaluation. Supports clinical research in medical centers. **Formerly:** Permanente Medical Group, Inc., Department of Medical Methods Research.

★5187★ **Laval University**
Saint-Sacrement Hospital Research Centre
Epidemiology Research Group
1050, chemin Ste-Foy
Quebec, PQ, Canada G1S 4L8
Phone: (418)682-7390
Fax: (418)682-7949
Jean R. Joly, M.D., Dir.

Research Activities and Fields: Population health research, cancer, palliative care, maternal and child health, infectious diseases, environmental and work related diseases, biostatistics, and mathematical modelling. Research programs include clinical trials and cohort and case-control studies.

Pennsylvania State University
Center for Biostatistics and Epidemiology
See: Entry 7020

State University of New York at Buffalo
Center for Pharmacoepidemiology Research
See: Entry 10457

★5188★ **U.S. Department of Health and Human Services**
Centers for Disease Control and Prevention
Epidemiology Program Office
Bldg. 1, Rm. 5009
1600 Clifton Rd., N.E.
Atlanta, GA 30333
Phone: (404)639-3661
Fax: (404)639-3950
Stephen B. Thacker, M.D., M.S., Director

Research Activities and Fields: Office is responsible for public health surveillance, epidemiologic training and research, and consultation in statistical and epidemiologic methods.

★5189★ **U.S. Department of Health and Human Services**
Centers for Disease Control and Prevention
Epidemiology Program Office
Surveillance and Epidemiology Division
Mail Stop C08
1600 Clifton Rd., N.E.
Atlanta, GA 30333
Phone: (404)639-3411
Steven Teutsch, Asst. to the Director

Research Activities and Fields: Activities involve developing methods for assessing the effectiveness of prevention strategies.

U.S. Department of Health and Human Services
National Cancer Institute
Division of Cancer Etiology
Epidemiology and Biostatistics Program
See: Entry 6139

U.S. Department of Health and Human Services
National Cancer Institute
Epidemiology and Biostatistics Program
Biostatistics Branch
See: Entry 6167

U.S. Department of Health and Human Services
National Cancer Institute
Epidemiology and Biostatistics Program
Clinical Epidemiology Branch
See: Entry 6168

U.S. Department of Health and Human Services
National Cancer Institute
Epidemiology and Biostatistics Program
Environmental Epidemiology Branch
See: Entry 6169

U.S. Department of Health and Human Services
National Cancer Institute
Epidemiology and Biostatistics Program
Extramural Programs Branch
See: Entry 6170

U.S. Department of Health and Human Services
National Cancer Institute
Epidemiology and Biostatistics Program
Radiation Epidemiology Branch
See: Entry 6171

U.S. Department of Health and Human Services
National Center for Environmental Health
Birth Defects and Developmental Disabilities Division
See: Entry 2759

U.S. Department of Health and Human Services
National Center for Environmental Health
Environmental Hazards and Health Effects Division
Health Studies Branch
See: Entry 5099

U.S. Department of Health and Human Services
National Center for Prevention Services
Tuberculosis Elimination Division
Surveillance and Epidemiologic Investigations Branch
See: Entry 10880

U.S. Department of Health and Human Services
National Eye Institute
Biometry and Epidemiology Program
Epidemiology Branch
See: Entry 13631

U.S. Department of Health and Human Services
National Eye Institute
Division of Biometry and Epidemiology
See: Entry 13632

U.S. Department of Health and Human Services
National Heart, Lung, and Blood Institute
Division of Epidemiology and Clinical Applications
See: Entry 2930

U.S. Department of Health and Human Services
National Heart, Lung, and Blood Institute
Division of Epidemiology and Clinical Applications
Epidemiology and Biometry Program
See: Entry 2932

U.S. Department of Health and Human Services
National Institute on Aging
Epidemiology, Demography, and Biometry Program
See: Entry 1953

U.S. Department of Health and Human Services
National Institute on Alcohol Abuse and Alcoholism
Biometry and Epidemiology Division
See: Entry 12108

U.S. Department of Health and Human Services
National Institute of Allergy and Infectious Diseases
Division of Acquired Immunodeficiency Syndrome (AIDS)
Vaccine Trials and Epidemiology Branch
See: Entry 6822

U.S. Department of Health and Human Services
National Institute of Allergy and Infectious Diseases
Division of Microbiology and Infectious Diseases
Epidemiology and Biometry Branch
See: Entry 6828

★5190★ U.S. Department of Health and Human Services
National Institute of Child Health and Human Development
Epidemiology, Statistics and Prevention Research Division
6100 Executive Blvd, Rm. 7B05
Bethesda, MD 20892
Phone: (301)496-5064
Fax: (301)402-2084
Dr. Heinz W. Berendes, Director

Research Activities and Fields: Program provides the Institute with epidemiological and biostatistical research (including field studies) on factors associated with perinatal mortality and morbidity, disorders of reproduction, and disorders of human growth and development. Research is carried out by two branches: 1) the Biometry and Mathematical Statistics Branch provides statistical consultation and analysis for intramural and extramural investigators and conducts research in biometry and biostatistics; and 2) the Epidemiology Branch studies factors which favor or inhibit the occurrence of diseases and health problems; and 3) the Prevention Research Branch studies factors related to the development and explanation of health-related behaviors in mothers and children. Staff advises intramural and extramural scientists on trends in the incidence, frequency, and distribution of a variety of health problems.

U.S. Department of Health and Human Services
National Institute of Dental Research
Epidemiology and Oral Disease Prevention Program
See: Entry 4009

U.S. Department of Health and Human Services
National Institute of Dental Research
Epidemiology and Oral Disease Prevention Program
Epidemiology Branch
See: Entry 4011

U.S. Department of Health and Human Services
National Institute of Diabetes and Digestive and Kidney Diseases
Division of Digestive Diseases and Nutrition
Gastrointestinal Neuroendocrinology Program
See: Entry 5244

★5191★ U.S. Department of Health and Human Services
National Institute of Diabetes and Digestive and Kidney Diseases
Division of Intramural Research
Phoenix Epidemiology and Clinical Research Branch
1550 E. Indian School Rd.
Phoenix, AZ 85014
Phone: (602)263-1600
Fax: (602)263-1669
Dr. Peter H. Bennett, Chief

Research Activities and Fields: Branch conducts studies on the epidemiological and clinical aspects of diabetes, obesity, and arthritis in the Pima Indians of Arizona. This includes clinical studies on whole-body insulin resistance, nutrition-induced alterations in metabolism, lipid and lipoprotein metabolism, and dietary and exercise therapy in the treatment of diabetic patients. The laboratory research is centered on biochemistry and genetics of insulin-mediated glucose metabolism as well as a variety of studies supporting the clinical investigations. The Branch comprises sections on: 1) Clinical Diabetes and Nutrition; 2) Diabetes and Arthritis Epidemiology; and 3) Biostatistics and Data Management.

U.S. Department of Health and Human Services
National Institute on Drug Abuse
Epidemiology and Prevention Research Division
See: Entry 12129

U.S. Department of Health and Human Services
National Institute on Drug Abuse
Epidemiology and Prevention Research Division
Epidemiology Studies and Surveillance Branch
See: Entry 12130

U.S. Department of Health and Human Services
National Institute of Environmental Health Sciences
Epidemiology Branch
See: Entry 5105

U.S. Department of Health and Human Services
National Institute of Mental Health
Epidemiology and Services Research Division
Epidemiology and Psychopathology Research Branch
See: Entry 7629

U.S. Department of Health and Human Services
National Institute of Neurological Disorders and Stroke
Neuroepidemiology Branch
See: Entry 8469

U.S. Department of Health and Human Services
National Institute for Occupational Safety and Health
Surveillance, Hazard Evaluations, and Field Studies Division
See: Entry 9840

U.S. Department of Health and Human Services
National Institute for Occupational Safety and Health
Surveillance, Hazard Evaluations, and Field Studies Division
Industrywide Studies Branch
See: Entry 9842

★5192★ University of Cincinnati
Division of Epidemiology and Biostatistics
PO Box 670183
Cincinnati, OH 45267-0183
Phone: (513)558-5631
Fax: (513)558-1756
Dr. C.R. Buncher, Head

Research Activities and Fields: Epidemiologic and biostatistical research, especially in environmental, occupational, and medical fields.

University of Iowa
Center for Agricultural Disease and Injury Research, Education, and Prevention (CADIREP)
See: Entry 9852

University of Iowa
Center for Health Effects of Environmental Contamination (CHEEC)
See: Entry 5121

University of Michigan
Epidemiology Laboratory
See: Entry 4036

★5193★ University of Michigan
Tecumseh Community Health Study
School of Public Health
Dept. of Epidemiology
Ann Arbor, MI 48109-2029
Phone: (313)936-3892
Fax: (313)764-3192
Mary Fran Sowers, Ph.D., Chm.

Research Activities and Fields: Epidemiology of health and disease, including investigation of origins, nature, and interrelations of major chronic disorders, particularly cardiovascular diseases, diabetes, arthritis, chronic respiratory diseases, and cancer. Also studies biological, social, and physical variables of chronic disease, including environmental factors and stresses as observed in families, households, and other subgroups of the population. Focuses on interactions between constitutional/genetic factors and environmental influences. The Tecumseh Community Health Study, a continuing multidisciplinary, multifaceted investigation, has been underway since 1957 in a total community of 10,000 inhabitants, with the aim of identifying disease precursors and indices of susceptibility as early in life as possible, with a view to prevention. **Formerly:** Until 1976 organized under the Center for Research in Diseases of the Heart and Circulation and Related Disorders.

★5194★ University of Minnesota
Division of Epidemiology
School of Public Health
1300 S. 2nd St., Ste. 300
Minneapolis, MN 55454
Phone: (612)624-1818
Fax: (612)624-0315
Russell V. Luepker, M.D., Dir.

Research Activities and Fields: Chronic disease epidemiology, behavioral epidemiology, infectious disease, Epidemiology, human physiology, human nutrition, and community health education, designed to develop evidence on which rational public health policies can be based for prevention of major chronic diseases, including studies on diet, physical fitness, nutrition, smoking, lipid metabolism, and health behavior. **E-mail Address:** luepker@epivax.epi.umn.edu. **Formerly:** Laboratory of Physiological Hygiene (1983).

University of Montreal
Philippe Pinel Institute of Montreal
Research Centre
See: Entry 7677

★5195★ University of Pennsylvania
Center for Clinical Epidemiology and
Biostatistics
School of Medicine
221L/NEB
420 Service Dr.
Philadelphia, PA 19104-6095
Phone: (215)898-4623
Fax: (215)573-5315
Brian L. Strom, M.D., Dir.

Research Activities and Fields: Epidemiology of disease and risk factors of clinical importance, especially drug epidemiology, eye disease epidemiology, effects of aging, womens' health, renal disease, occupational disease, cancer, and neonatal health care delivery. **Formerly:** Clinical Epidemiology Unit.

★5196★ University of Pittsburgh
Nutrition Biochemistry Laboratory
Graduate School of Public Health
Dept. of Epidemiology
505 Parran Hall
Pittsburgh, PA 15261
Phone: (412)624-2020
Fax: (412)624-7397
Dr. Rhobert Evans, Dir.

Research Activities and Fields: Etiology and treatment of chronic diseases, including study of lipids, lipoproteins, osteoporsis, diabetes, hypertension, cancer, and aging.

★5197★ University of Southern California
International Twin Study
PM B-105
1420 San Pablo
Los Angeles, CA 90033
Phone: (213)342-1638
Fax: (213)342-1638
Dr. Thomas Mack, Dir.

Research Activities and Fields: Epidemiologic investigation of the etiology of various chronic diseases in twins, including cancers (breast, gastrointestinal tract, and melanoma), multiple sclerosis, diabetes, and other chronic diseases.

University of Texas—Houston Health
Science Center
Genetics Center
See: Entry 5383

Chapter 26
Gastroenterology

Federal Government Agencies

U.S. Department of Health and Human Services
National Institute of Diabetes and Digestive and Kidney Diseases
See: Entry 4820

Foundations & Other Funding Organizations

Other Funding Organizations

★5198★ American Liver Foundation
1425 Pompton Ave.
Cedar Grove, NJ 07009
Phone: (201)256-2550
Free: 800-223-0179
Fax: (201)256-3214
Thelma King Thiel, Pres.

Description: Bestows awards and fellowships to individuals for doctoral and postdoctoral liver disease research.

★5199★ Crohn's and Colitis Foundation of America
386 Park Ave. S
New York, NY 10016-7374
Phone: (212)685-3440
Free: 800-932-2423
Fax: (212)779-4098
Barbara Boyle

Description: Supports research to find the cause, treatment, and cure of ileitis and ulcerative colitis. Awards research grants and training fellowships.

★5200★ Cure Foundation
PO Box 84513
Los Angeles, CA 90073-0513
Phone: (213)296-6364

Description: Funds research and education on peptic ulcer disease; offers fellowships for post-

doctoral research. Supports the Center for Ulcer Research and Education, established for the study of peptic ulcer disease. Also finances a visiting scientist program for beginning and established scientists from around the world.

Cystic Fibrosis Foundation
See: Entry 5258

National & International Organizations

★5201★ American Association for the Study of Liver Diseases (AASLD)
6900 Grove Rd.
Thorofare, NJ 08086
Phone: (609)848-1000
Fax: (609)848-5274
Susan Nelson, Mgr.

Founded: 1950. **Members:** 1,700. **Description:** Physicians interested in liver disease and hepatic research. Objective is the exchange of scientific information, thereby contributing to the education of members and improving the quality of patient care. Conducts scientific meetings. **Publications:** *Hepatology*, monthly. Journal. • *Liver Transplantation and Surgery.* • Newsletter, semiannual.

American Board of Colon and Rectal Surgery (ABCRS)
See: Entry 12217

American Broncho-Esophagological Association (ABEA)
See: Entry 11589

★5202★ American Celiac Society / Dietary Support Coalition (ACS/DSC)
58 Musano Ct.
West Orange, NJ 07052
Phone: (201)325-8837
Annette Bentley, Exec. Officer

Founded: 1970. **Members:** 4,000. **Regional Groups:** 19. **Description:** Individuals interested in a gluten-free diet; physicians who diagnose and care for individuals with gluten-sensitive intestinal disease, dietitians, nutritionists, and

agencies that serve or have an interest in individuals with gluten-sensitive enteropathy, also known as celiac sprue. Provides information on how to follow a gluten-free diet; assists members in locating specialty foods that are gluten-free; encourages retailers to make gluten-free products available. Coordinates activities with other international celiac societies. Maintains speakers' bureau for patients and health care professionals. **Publications:** *Whoo's Report*, 3/year. Newsletter. **Formerly:** (1990) America Celiac Society.

★5203★ American College of Gastroenterology (ACG)
4900B S. 31st St.
Arlington, VA 22206-1656
Phone: (703)820-7400
Fax: (703)931-4520
Thomas F. Fise, Exec.Dir.

Founded: 1932. **Members:** 5,000. **Description:** Professional society of physicians and surgeons specializing in diseases and disorders of the gastrointestinal tract and accessory organs of digestion, including disorders due to nutrition. **Publications:** *American Journal of Gastroenterology*, monthly. Journal. **Formerly:** (1934) Society for the Advancement of Gastroenterology; (1954) National Gastroenterological Association.

★5204★ American Gastroenterological Association (AGA)
7910 Woodmont Ave., Ste. 914
Bethesda, MD 20814
Phone: (301)654-2055
Fax: (301)654-5920
Robert B. Greenberg, JD, Exec.VP

Founded: 1897. **Members:** 7,000. **Description:** Physicians of internal medicine certified in gastroenterology; radiologists, pathologists, surgeons, and physiologists with special interest and competency in gastroenterology. Studies normal and abnormal conditions of the digestive organs and problems connected with their metabolism; conducts scientific research; offers placement services. **Publications:** *AGA Membership Roster*, annual. • *AGA News*, monthly. *Price:* Included in membership dues. • *Directory of Researchers in Gastroenterology*, annual. Directory. • *Gastroenterology*, monthly. *Price:* $135 for individuals; $212 for institutions.

• *Gastrointestinal Diseases Today*, bimonthly. *Price:* Free for members.

★5205★ American Liver Foundation (ALF)
1425 Pompton Ave.
Cedar Grove, NJ 07009
Phone: (201)256-2550
Free: 800-223-0179
Fax: (201)256-3214
Alan P. Brownstein, Contact

Founded: 1976. **Members:** 24,000. **Regional Groups:** 23. **Description:** Health agency working to fund research, promote the understanding and prevention of liver diseases, and find cures for liver diseases. Disseminates public and patient information on liver diseases, liver functions, and preventive measures. Organizes support groups for liver disease patients and their families. Offers physician referral service. Sponsors postgraduate courses in liver disease diagnosis and management for physicians and other health professionals. Sponsors Meet the Researchers programs, which enables liver disease patients and concerned individuals to meet specialists and learn of recently developed information on treatment and research. Operates continuing organ donor awareness campaign in order to increase the number of organs available for transplant; monitors legislation (nationally and regionally) in areas affecting liver patients. Maintains speakers' bureau. Serves as trustee of funds raised to cover costs related to liver transplant surgery. Sponsors Corporate Wellness Program to provide information on liver disease for use in employee publications. Maintains Foundations for Decision Making, a substance abuse prevention program for use in schools. **Publications:** *American Liver Foundation--Annual Report. Price:* Free. • *American Liver Foundation--Progress*, 3/year. Newsletter. Covers foundation programs; reports on research, news of liver diseases. *Price:* Included in membership dues. • *Liver Update: Function and Disease*, 3/year. Newsletter. *Price:* Included in membership dues. Also publishes brochures, leaflets, and information sheets.

★5206★ American Motility Society (AMS)
c/o James Ryan
Department of Physiology
Temple University School of Medicine
Philadelphia, PA 19140
Phone: (215)708-6916
Fax: (215)221-4003
James Ryan, Ph.D., Treas.

Founded: 1980. **Members:** 220. **Description:** Professionals interested in the study of gastrointestinal (GI) motility. Promotes basic science and clinical research on the neural, humoral, and paracrine control of GI tract motility in health and disease.

★5207★ American Pancreatic Association (APA)
Surgical Service, No. 112
VA Hospital
16111 Plummer St.
Sepulveda, CA 91343
Phone: (818)895-9461
Fax: (818)895-9535
Howard A. Reber, M.D., Sec./Treas.

Founded: 1970. **Members:** 325. **Description:** Individuals interested in clinical and basic research related to diseases of the pancreas. To provide a forum for presentation of scientific research related to the pancreas. **Formerly:** (1975) American Pancreatic Study Group.

American Pediatric Gastroesophageal Reflux Association (APGERA)
See: Entry 3168

American Society of Abdominal Surgeons (ASAS)
See: Entry 12235

★5208★ American Society of Adults with Pseudo-Obstruction (ASAP)
19 Carroll Rd.
Woburn, MA 01801
Phone: (617)935-9776
Fax: (617)933-4151
Mary-Angela DeGrazia-DiTucci, Pres.-Exec.Dir.

Founded: 1991. **Members:** 200. **Description:** Adult and teenage sufferers of Chronic Intestinal Pseudo-Obstruction (CIP), their family members and friends, and interested physicians. Functions as an advocacy organization, support group, and information resource. Provides list of physicians at major medical centers who treat adults with CIP. Support groups are in the process of forming. **Publications:** *ASAP Forum.* Newsletter. Contains articles by physicians, personal accounts of patients, suggestions for everyday living, poetry, corporate spotlights, dialogue, and letters. • Booklets. • Videos. Also publishes information sheets concerning CIP, various aspects of living with the disease, and Social Security Disability Benefits.

★5209★ American Society for Gastrointestinal Endoscopy (ASGE)
13 Elm St.
Manchester, MA 01944
Phone: (508)526-8330
Fax: (508)526-4018
William T. Maloney, Exec.Dir.

Founded: 1941. **Members:** 5,000. **Description:** Gastroenterologists, internists, and surgeons who perform gastroscopic, esophagoscopic, coloscopic, and peritoneoscopic examinations. Works to further the knowledge of digestive disease by endoscopic methods (visual inspection of the intestinal tract). **Publications:** *Gastrointestinal Endoscopy*, bimonthly. Journal. Includes index, book reviews, case reports, and new materials and methods. *Price:* Included in membership dues; $50/year for nonmembers; $65/year for institutions. **Formerly:** American Gastroscopic Club; American Gastroscopic Society.

★5210★ Association of National, European and Mediterranean Societies of Gastroenterology (Association des Societes Nationales, Europeennes et Mediterraneennes de Gastroenterologie — ASNEMGE)
Guy's Hospital
Gastroenterology Unit
Guy's Tower, 18th Fl.
London SE1 9RT, England
Phone: 171 9554564
Fax: 171 9554230
Prof. R.H. Dowling

Founded: 1947. **Members:** 31. **Regional Groups:** 1. **Languages:** English, French, German. **Description:** A branch of the World Organization of Gastroenterology. National societies for gastroenterology in 32 European and Mediterranean countries. Promotes the exchange of scientific information in the field of gastroenterology. **Publications:** Proceedings, quadrennial.

★5211★ Bockus International Society of Gastroenterology (BISG)
9413 Bell Mountain Dr.
Austin, TX 78730
Phone: (512)794-0377
Fax: (512)794-9192
Dr. Thomas J. Humphries, M.D., Sec.Gen.

Founded: 1958. **Members:** 440. **Description:** Physicians in 22 countries specializing in gastroenterology (the study of the anatomy, physiology, and pathology of the stomach and intestines). Furthers scientific advances in gastroenterology worldwide. (The society is named for noted gastroenterologist H.L. Bockus of Philadelphia, PA.) **Publications:** Proceedings, biennial.

★5212★ Celiac Disease Foundation (CDF)
13251 Ventura Blvd., Ste. 3
Studio City, CA 91604-1838
Phone: (818)990-2354
Fax: (818)990-2379
Elaine Monarch, Exec.Dir.

Founded: 1990. **Description:** Persons with celiac disease and its related skin disorder, dermatitis herpetiformis; individuals interested in supporting the foundation. (Celiac disease is a digestive disease in which damage to the surface of the small intestine is caused by the ingestion of food products that contain gluten or similar proteins that are present in wheat, rye, oats, and barley. Symptoms of the disease include abdominal cramping, intestinal gas, bloating, diarrhea, anemia, fatigue, irritability, muscle cramps, and weight loss.) Provides services and support to persons with celiac disease and dermatitis herpetiformis and their families. Distributes information about the disease and the gluten free diet. Seeks to increase awareness among health care professionals, food and drug manufacturers, the food service industry, the media, and the public. Conducts educational, charitable, and research programs. Offers children's services and medical referrals. Maintains speakers' bureau. **Publications:** *Celiac Disease Foundation Newsletter*, quarterly. Newsletter. Includes information about the disease, treatment, nutrition, food and drug updates, support articles, and recipes. *Price:* Included in membership dues.

★5213★ Celiac Sprue Association—United States of America (CSA/USA)
PO Box 31700
Omaha, NE 68131-0700
Phone: (402)558-0600
Fax: (402)558-1347
Leon H. Rottmann, Exec.Dir.

Founded: 1979. **Members:** 5,562. **National Groups:** 1. **Regional Groups:** 6. **Local Groups:** 69. **Description:** Individuals with the conditions of celiac sprue and dermatitis herpetiformis; parents of celiac children. (Celiac sprue is a genetic disorder resulting in digestive malabsorption of the protein portion of wheat, rye, and other cereal grains, causing symptoms such as intestinal lesions, diarrhea, vomiting, weight loss, and abdominal discomfort; dermatitis herpetiformis is a gluten-related skin disorder. Successful treatment usually calls for removing all gluten-containing cereal grains and their derivatives from the diet.) Serves as a vehicle for the provision of mutual support groups and facilitates interaction with other organizations involved in digestive disorders. Encourages and supports research on celiac disease. Disseminates educational materials on gluten-free foods and research on results; exchanges information on maintaining a gluten-free diet. Consults with government and the food and drug industry about gluten-free products. Sponsors Celiac Sprue Month (October). **Publications:** Brochures. • *Cookbooks for Diets Free of Cereal Grains.* Books. • *Lifeline,* quarterly. Newsletter. • *On the Celiac Condition: A Handbook for Celiacs and Their Families.* Handbook. • Pamphlets. **Formerly:** (1986) Midwestern Celiac Sprue Association.

★5214★ Coeliac Society of the United Kingdom (CSUK)
Box 220
High Wycombe, Bucks. HP11 2HY, England
Phone: 1494 437278
Fax: 1494 474349
Jean Austin, Sec.

Members: 30,000. **Description:** Individuals and groups interested in celiac disease (a disease of the digestive system, frequently suffered by infants and young children). Provides member support. Promotes research programs. **Publications:** *List of Gluten-Free Manufactured Products,* annual. Directory. Directory of manufacturers and suppliers, including bakeries of products that do not contain gluten.

★5215★ Crohn's and Colitis Foundation of America (CCFA)
386 Park Ave. S
New York, NY 10016-7374
Phone: (212)685-3440
Free: 800-932-2423
Fax: (212)779-4098
Barbara Boyle, Exec.Dir.

Founded: 1967. **Members:** 18,000. **Local Groups:** 90. **Description:** Supports research to find the cause and cure of Crohn's Disease (ileitis) and ulcerative colitis; produces educational brochures and disseminates them to doctors, patients, and laypeople throughout the world. Maintains National Foundation for Ileitis and Colitis Speakers' Bureau, a program in which professional and amateur athletes and celebrities promote greater public awareness of inflammatory bowel diseases. Maintains speakers' bureau. **Publications:** *Crohn's Disease and Ulcerative Fact Book.* Book. • *Foundation Focus,* quarterly. Magazine. Contains personal accounts of persons living with colitis and ileitis. *Price:* Included in membership dues. • *The IBD Medical Record.* Book. • *IBD News,* quarterly. Newsletter. • *People Not Patients: A Source Book for Living with IBD.* Book. • *Treating IBD.* **Formerly:** (1969) Foundation for Ileitis and Colitis; (1992) National Foundation for Ileitis and Colitis.

★5216★ Cure Foundation
PO Box 84513
Los Angeles, CA 90073-0513
Phone: (213)296-6364

Founded: 1974. **Members:** 110. **Description:** To fund research and education on peptic ulcer disease and to disseminate knowledge to doctors, patients, and the public. Seeks fellowship funding for scientists and funds for purchase of research equipment. Provides support to the Center for Ulcer Research and Education which was established for the study of peptic ulcer disease. Finances visiting scientist program for beginning and established scientists from all parts of the world. Sponsors seminars and continuing medical education programs for physicians; also offers fellowships for postdoctoral research. **Publications:** *Proceedings from International Conferences,* 2-3/year. Also publishes book and brochures.

Cystic Fibrosis Foundation (CFF)
See: Entry 5275

★5217★ Digestive Disease National Coalition (DDNC)
711 2nd St. NE, Ste. 200
Washington, DC 20002
Phone: (202)544-7497
Fax: (202)546-7105
Dale P. Dirks, Washington Rep.

Founded: 1979. **Members:** 30. **Description:** Lay and professional medical organizations concerned with digestive diseases. Objectives are to: inform the public and the health care community about digestive diseases and related nutrition; seek federal funding for research, education, and training. Represents members' interests regarding federal and state legislation that affects digestive diseases research, health care, and education. **Formerly:** (1986) Coalition of Digestive Disease Organizations.

Gastrointestinal Pathology Society (GIPS)
See: Entry 10130

★5218★ Gluten Intolerance Group of North America (GIGNA)
PO Box 23053
Seattle, WA 98102-0353
Phone: (206)325-6980
Elaine I. Hartsook, Ph.D., Dir.

Founded: 1974. **Members:** 1,900. **State Groups:** 14. **Description:** Persons with gluten-sensitive enteropathy (celiac sprue) or dermatitis herpetiformis, family members, physicians, dietitians, and celiac sprue societies. (Gluten is a protein found in wheat, rye, oats, and barley. Gluten-sensitive enteropathy is an inherited disorder characterized by gluten-related destruction of the small intestine. Symptoms include diarrhea, weight loss, fatigue, and anemia.) Works to educate patients, health care personnel, and the public; to offer psychological support to celiac sprue patients and their families in dealing with the adjustment and nutritional limitations of the disease; to conduct research into the causes. Promotes practical application in specific food research, such as recipe development and information on gluten content of products. Offers children's services and group and individual counseling. **Publications:** Book. Instructions for a gluten-free diet. • *GIG Newsletter,* quarterly. Newsletter. Provides book reviews, product information, recipes, and research reports to help in monitoring the diets for persons with celiac sprue. *Price:* $25/year in U.S. • Videos. Also publishes cookbook and fact sheets. **Formerly:** (1985) Gluten Intolerance Group.

★5219★ Indonesian Society of Gastrointestinal Endoscopy (IEGA) (Perhimpunan Endoskopi Gastro-Intestinal Indonesia — PEGI)
c/o Bagian Penyakit Dalam RSCM
Jalan Diponegoro 71
Jakarta, Indonesia
Phone: 21 3153957
Fax: 21 3142454
Aziz Rani, M.D., Sec.

Founded: 1971. **Members:** 200. **Languages:** Indonesian. **Description:** Gastroenterologists and other health care professionals with an interest in endoscopy as a means of treating gastrointestinal disorders. Gathers and disseminates information on gastroenterology. **Publications:** *Indonesian Forum of Gastroentero-Hepatology,* quarterly.

★5220★ Inter-American Association of Gastroenterology (IAAG) (Asociacion Inter-Americana de Gastroenterologia — AIGE)
Apartado Postal 26 F
Guatemala City, Guatemala
Roberto Schneider, Pres.

Founded: 1948. **Languages:** English, Portuguese, Spanish. **Description:** Gastroenterologists from North, Central, and South American nations. Offers educational programs; plans to conduct research. **Publications:** Bulletin.

★5221★ International Association of Colon Therapy (ACTA)
c/o Connie Allred
11739 Washington Blvd.
Los Angeles, CA 90066
Phone: (310)572-6223
Fax: (310)572-6217
Connie Allred, Pres.

Founded: 1989. **Members:** 127. **Description:** Professional colon hygiene therapists and other health care practitioners. Works to unite the community of colon therapy professionals and increase visibility and recognition in the health care industry. Promotes the establishment of uniform guidelines and standards of practice and the establishment of accredited colon therapy schools. Conducts research and educational programs; plans to operate referral service. Maintains library. **Publications:** *ACTA Membership Directory*, periodic. Membership Directory. • *ACTA Newsletter*, quarterly. Newsletter. Provides organization updates, convention schedule, and continuing education course schedule. *Price:* Included in membership dues. • *ACTA Research Project on Colon Therapy*. **Formerly:** (1993) American Colon Therapy Association.

★5222★ **International Association for the Study of the Liver (IASL)**
(Association Internationale pour l'Etude du Foie)
Hepatic Hemodynamic Lab/1111J
West Haven, CT 06516
Phone: (203)932-5711
Fax: (203)937-3873
Roberto J. Groszmann, M.D., Sec.-Treas.

Founded: 1958. **Members:** 879. **Languages:** English. **Description:** Members of regional societies for the study of the liver representing 67 countries. Supports the training of experts in hepatology; encourages basic and clinical research on the liver and its diseases; acts to facilitate prevention, recognition, and treatment of diseases of the liver.

International Bronchoesophagological Society (IBES)
See: Entry 11597

International Cystic Fibrosis (Mucoviscidosis) Association (ICFMA)
See: Entry 5279

★5223★ **International Hepato-Pancreato-Biliary Association (IHPBA)**
c/o David L. Carr-Locke, M.D.
Brigham and Women's Hospital
Endoscopy Center
75 Francis St.
Boston, MA 02115
Phone: (617)732-7414
Fax: (617)732-7407
David L. Carr-Locke, M.D., Pres.

Founded: 1978. **Members:** 2,000. **Description:** Endoscopists, hepatologists, radiologists, and surgeons in 25 countries. Provides a forum for the presentation of papers concerning diagnostic and treatment modalities of lymphatic, pancreatic, and biliary disorders. Promotes exchange of ideas, reviews current standards of practice, and seeks to establish prospective controlled protocols in the field. Initiates research regarding factors involved in biliary, pancreatic, and liver diseases. **Formerly:** International Hepato-Biliary Pancreatic Association; (1988) International Biliary Association.

★5224★ **International Organization for Statistical Studies on Diseases of the Esophagus (OESO)**
(Organisation Internationale d'Etudes Statistiques pour les Maladies de l'Oesophage — OESO)
Hopital Beaujon
2 blvd. de Montparnasse
F-75015 Paris, France
Phone: 1 45669115
Fax: 1 45665072
Robert Giuli, M.D., Coordinator

Founded: 1979. **Languages:** English, French. **Description:** Thoracic and digestive surgeons,

ear, nose, and throat specialists, intensive care specialists, pathologists, nutritionists, endoscopists, radio- and chemotherapists, and others who diagnose and treat patients suffering from cancer and other diseases of the esophagus. Acts as a forum for specialists to meet, study, and discuss the epidemiology, histological classification, and treatments of esophageal diseases. Conducts research programs. **Publications:** *Program of the International Polydisciplinary Congress*, periodic. Also publishes books including *Cancer of the Esophagus*, *Primary Motility Disorders of the Esophagus*, and *The Esophageal Mucosa*.

★5225★ **International Society for Diseases of the Esophagus (ISDE)**
(Kokusai Shokudo Shikkan Kaigi)
Institute of Gastroentrology
Tokyo Women's Medical College
8-1, Kawada-cho
Shinjuku-ku
Tokyo 162, Japan
Phone: 3 33581435

Founded: 1979. **Members:** 660. **Languages:** English. **Description:** Physicians, researchers, and academicians in 44 countries. Purpose is to broaden scientific and medical understanding of diseases of the esophagus through the sharing of research information. Conducts scholastic meetings and symposia. **Publications:** *Disease of the Esophagus*, quarterly. Journal. • *ISDE News*, semiannual. Newsletter.

★5226★ **Latin American Association for the Study of the Liver (LAASL)**
Institute National de la Nurticion
San Fernando y Viaducto Tlalpan
22000 Mexico City, DF, Mexico
Phone: 5 5731200
Dr. Kershenobich, Exec. Officer

Founded: 1968. **Members:** 450. **Languages:** English, Spanish. **Description:** Clinicians, pathologists, pediatricians, and surgeons involved in research and the treatment of liver diseases. Promotes cooperation and closer contact between specialists. Sponsors young specialists in hepatology. **Publications:** *Boletin de la Sociedade Latinoamericana de Hepatologia*, periodic.

★5227★ **National Digestive Diseases Information Clearinghouse (NDDIC)**
2 Information Way
Bethesda, MD 20892-3570
Phone: (301)654-3810
Fax: (301)907-8906
Kathy Kranzfelder, Dir.

Founded: 1980. **Description:** Serves as a national resource to inform and educate physicians, health professionals, patients and their families, and the public on digestive health and disease. Provides services in the areas of: inquiry response and referral; publications development, review, and distribution; outreach and resource coordination. Maintains reference collection of fact sheets, informational brochures, and literature searches. **Publications:** *Age Page: Constipation*. • *Cirrhosis of the Liver*. • *Constipation*. • *Crohn's Disease*. • *Digestive Diseases Statistics*. • *Diverticulosis and Diverticulitis*. • *Facts and Fallacies About Digestive Diseases*. • *Gallstones*. • *Gas in the Digestive*

Tract. • *Gastroesophageal Reflux Disease (Hiatal Hernia and Heartburn)*. • *Harmful Effects of Medicines on the Adult Digestive System*. • *Hemorrhoids*. • *Irritable Bowel Syndrome*. • *Lactose Intolerance*. • *Pancreatitis*. • *Smoking and Your Digestive System*. • *Stomach and Duodenal Ulcers*. • *Ulcerative Colitis*. • *Your Digestive System and How it Works*. **Also Known As:** Digestive Diseases Clearinghouse. **Formerly:** (1985) National Digestive Diseases Education and Information Clearinghouse.

★5228★ **National Ulcer Foundation (NUF)**
675 Main St.
Melrose, MA 02176
Phone: (617)665-6210
Blaise F. Alfano, M.D., Exec.Sec.

Founded: 1968. **Description:** Conducts educational meetings; disseminates information concerning peptic ulcers to the public. **Publications:** Newsletter, periodic.

North American Society for Pediatric Gastroenterology and Nutrition (NASPGN)
See: Entry 3277

Norwegian Cystic Fibrosis Association (NCFA)
(Norsk Forening for Cystisk Fibrose — NFCF)
See: Entry 5296

★5229★ **Norwegian Ostomy Association (NORILCO)**
(Norsk Forening for Stomiopererte — NORILCO)
Postboks 5327
Majorstua
N-0304 Oslo 3, Norway
Phone: 22 461010
Fax: 22 606980
Karin Troennes, Gen.Sec.

Founded: 1971. **Members:** 6,000. **Local Groups:** 22. **Languages:** English, Norwegian. **Description:** Individuals representing the interests of ostomy patients. Promotes information exchange among members. Works to improve quality of health care before and after surgery. **Publications:** *NORILCO-NYTT*, bimonthly.

★5230★ **Society of American Gastrointestinal Endoscopic Surgeons (SAGES)**
2716 Ocean Park Blvd., Ste. 3000
Santa Monica, CA 90405
Phone: (310)314-2404
Fax: (310)314-2585
Barbara Saltzman, Exec.Dir.

Founded: 1980. **Members:** 1,500. **Description:** Surgeons who perform gastrointestinal endoscopy and laparascopy. Promotes the concepts of gastrointestinal endoscopy as an integral part of surgery and encourages academic, clinical, and research achievements in the field. Establishes standards of training and practice and guidelines for privileging. Provides a forum for the exchange of ideas on gastrointestinal endoscopy and related sciences. Conducts scientific studies. Offers Corporate Council membership which facilitates communication between the corporate sector and surgeons. **Publications:** *Clinical Guidelines.* • *Guidelines for Clinical Application - The Role of Laparoscopic Cholecystctomy.* • *Guidelines for Course Endorsement in Laparoscopic Surgery.* • *Guidelines for General Surgery Residency Education in Gastrointestinal Endoscopy.* • *Guidelines for Granting Privileges in G.I. Endoscopy and Laparoscopic Surgery.* • *Guidelines for Office Endoscopic Services.* • *Standards of Practice.*

★5231★ Society of Gastroenterology Nurses and Associates (SGNA)
1070 Sibley Tower
Rochester, NY 14604
Phone: (716)546-7241
Free: 800-245-SGNA
Fax: (716)546-5141
Margaret M. Crevey, Exec.Dir.

Founded: 1974. **Members:** 6,000. **Regional Groups:** 60. **Description:** To unite personnel engaged in the field of gastroenterology/ endoscopy in order to promote the highest professional standards for gastroenterology nurses and associates. Conducts national and regional educational courses and research programs. Cooperates with other professional associations, hospitals, universities, industries, technical societies, research organizations, and governmental agencies. **Publications:** *Gastroenterology Nursing*, bimonthly. Includes subject and author indexes, book reviews, new product information. *Price:* $52/year for individuals; $80/year for institutions; $25/year for students; $15/copy. • *Gastroenterology Nursing - A Core Curriculum.* • *Job Description Handbook.* • *Manual of Gastrointestinal Procedures.* • *Pediatric Supplement.* • *Pulmonary Supplement.* • *SGNA News*, bimonthly. Newsletter. Contains regional directory, regional news, and articles on research and finance. *Price:* Free to members. **Formerly:** (1989) Society of Gastrointestinal Assistants.

★5232★ United Ostomy Association (UOA)
36 Executive Park, Ste. 120
Irvine, CA 92714
Phone: (714)660-8624
Free: 800-826-0826
Fax: (714)660-9262
Darlene Smith, Exec.Dir.

Founded: 1962. **Members:** 40,000. **Regional Groups:** 12. **Local Groups:** 580. **Description:** Individuals who have lost the normal function of their bowel or bladder necessitating colostomy, ileostomy, ileal conduit, or ureterostomy surgery, known as ostomy. Aids in rehabilitation of these persons through mutual aid, moral support, and exchange of practical information in managing the stoma and its necessary prosthetic appliances; sponsors visiting program allowing patients to ask non-medical questions of individuals who have experienced a similar condition. Works to educate the public as to the nature of ostomy, with a view to ending job and insurance discrimination. Encourages research on management of ostomy and prosthetic equipment and appliances; also encourages study of the costs for rehabilitating ostomy patients. Prepares exhibits for medical conventions. Maintains speakers' bureau; compiles sta-

tistics. **Publications:** Annual Report, quarterly. • *Ostomy Quarterly.* Magazine. Contains information on ostomy management, human interest stories, organizational news, nutrition tips, and ostomy and alternate procedures. • *The Phoenix*, monthly. • *Services of the United Ostomy Association.* Brochure.

★5233★ World Organization of Gastroenterology (OMGE) (Organisation Mondiale de Gastroenterologie — OMGE)
Technischen Universitat Munchen
Medizinischen Klinik und Poliklinik
Ismaninger Strasse 22
81675 Munich, Germany
Phone: 89 41402250
Fax: 89 41402456
Prof. Meinhard Classen, Sec.Gen.

Founded: 1958. **Members:** 75. **Languages:** English, French, Spanish. **Description:** National gastroenterology societies. Promotes research in the field of gastroenterology (the study of the diseases and pathology of the stomach and intestines). Fosters exchange of information among members. Compiles statistics. **Publications:** *Directory*, quadrennial. Directory. • *Nomenclature of Digestive Diseases.* • *OMGE Bulletin*, quadrennial. Bulletin. • *OMGE Newsletter*, annual. Newsletter. • *OMGE Statutes*, quadrennial.

Research Centers

Case Western Reserve University
Cystic Fibrosis and Pediatric Pulmonary Center
See: Entry 5317

Cystic Fibrosis Center
See: Entry 5323

Cystic Fibrosis Center
See: Entry 5324

Cystic Fibrosis Foundation
See: Entry 5326

Cystic Fibrosis Research Center
See: Entry 5327

Emory University
Cystic Fibrosis Care, Teaching and Research Center
See: Entry 5329

Indiana University-Purdue University at Indianapolis
Cystic Fibrosis and Pediatric Pulmonary Clinic
See: Entry 5331

★5234★ Inflammatory Bowel Disease Research Center
1124 W. Carson St.
Torrance, CA 90502
Phone: (310)533-2475
Fax: (310)212-7837
Dr. Viktor Eysselin, Chief

Research Activities and Fields: Causes of and treatment for ulcerative colitis and Crohn's disease. Conducts related studies in molecular biology, cell biology, and immunology. Performs clinical trials.

★5235★ Medical College of Pennsylvania and Hahnemann University
Krancer Center for Inflammatory Bowel Disease Research
Broad & Vine Sts.
Philadelphia, PA 19102
Phone: (215)762-8101
Fax: (215)762-3417
Dr. Harris R. Clearfield, Dir.

Research Activities and Fields: Cause and treatment of ulcerative colitis and Crohn's disease.

Medical College of Wisconsin
Cystic Fibrosis Research Center
See: Entry 5340

★5236★ Stanford University
Gastroenterology Clinic
Medical Clinic, Rm. A160
300 Pasteur Dr.
Stanford, CA 94305-5309
Phone: (415)725-3360
Fax: (415)723-8305
Dr. Gabriel Garcia, Dir.

Research Activities and Fields: Gastroenterology, focusing on treatment of viral hepatitis. **E-mail Address:** ml.gxg@torsythe.stanford.edu.

State University of New York Health Science Center at Syracuse
Robert C. Schwartz Cystic Fibrosis Center
See: Entry 5353

★5237★ Temple University
Motility Laboratory/Gastroenterology
H5C Health Sciences Center Campus
School of Medicine
3400 N. Broad St.
Philadelphia, PA 19140
Phone: (215)707-2000
Fax: (215)707-2684
Dr. Robert Fisher, Dir.

Research Activities and Fields: Neurohumoral control of gastrointestinal motility, including mechanical properties and neuropeptide receptor characteristics of gastrointestinal tract smooth muscle and neurohormonal interactions in gastrointestinal motility; applied clinical research. **Formerly:** Institute of Gastroenterology (University of Pennsylvania).

U.S. Department of Defense
Armed Forces Institute of Pathology
Center for Advanced Pathology
Hepatic and Gastrointestinal Pathology Department
See: Entry 10154

U.S. Department of Health and Human Services
National Center for Infectious Diseases
Division of Viral and Rickettsial Diseases
Hepatitis Branch
See: Entry 6808

U.S. Department of Health and Human Services
National Center for Infectious Diseases
Division of Viral and Rickettsial Diseases
Respiratory and Enteric Virus Branch
See: Entry 6810

U.S. Department of Health and Human Services
National Institute of Diabetes and Digestive and Kidney Diseases
See: Entry 4906

U.S. Department of Health and Human Services
National Institute of Diabetes and Digestive and Kidney Diseases
Division of Diabetes, Endocrinology, and Metabolic Diseases
Cystic Fibrosis Research Program
See: Entry 5362

★5238★ U.S. Department of Health and Human Services
National Institute of Diabetes and Digestive and Kidney Diseases
Division of Digestive Diseases and Nutrition
NIH Bldg. 31, Rm. 9A23
9000 Rockville Pike
Bethesda, MD 20892
Phone: (301)496-1333
Fax: (301)496-2830
Jay H. Hoofnagle, Director

Research Activities and Fields: Division supports investigator-initiated research and research training in fundamental and clinical studies of the normal functions of the digestive tract (esophagus, stomach, intestines) and changes associated with diseases of the liver, gallbladder, biliary tract, and exocrine pancreas; and basic nutrition, nutritional requirements, trace minerals, dietary fiber, obesity, and clinical nutrition. Principal Division components include the Digestive Diseases Branch, Nutritional Sciences Branch, and Special Programs Branch.

★5239★ U.S. Department of Health and Human Services
National Institute of Diabetes and Digestive and Kidney Diseases
Division of Digestive Diseases and Nutrition
Clinical Trials Program
5333 Westbard Ave., Rm. 3A15B
Bethesda, MD 20892
Phone: (301)594-7592
Fax: (301)594-7504
Tommie Sue Tralka, Deputy Director

Research Activities and Fields: The Program administers multi- and single center clinical trials in digestive and nutritional diseases and disorders.

★5240★ U.S. Department of Health and Human Services
National Institute of Diabetes and Digestive and Kidney Diseases
Division of Digestive Diseases and Nutrition
Digestive Diseases Branch
5333 Westbard Ave.
Bethesda, MD 20892
Phone: (301)594-7571
Fax: (301)594-7504
Dr. Frank Hamilton, Program Director

Research Activities and Fields: Diabetes, digestive, and kidney diseases.

★5241★ U.S. Department of Health and Human Services
National Institute of Diabetes and Digestive and Kidney Diseases
Division of Digestive Diseases and Nutrition
Gastrointestinal Digestion Program
5333 Westbard Ave., Rm. 3A18A
Bethesda, MD 20892
Phone: (301)496-7121
Fax: (301)402-1278
Dr. Ken May, Program Director

Research Activities and Fields: Program supports research on the process of food digestion in the gastrointestinal tract (GIT). Other areas of research focus on the regulation of gene expression in the developing GIT; the structure and function of the gut mucosa; the cytoskeletal structure and contractility in brush border; the growth and differentiation of gastrointestinal cells in normal and disease states; intestinal transplantation, storage, and preservation; and gastrointestinal tissue injury, repair, and regeneration. Also supported are studies on gastrointestinal diseases such as maldigestion and malabsorption syndromes, celiac sprue, diarrhea, inflammatory bowel disease, gastric and duodenal ulcers, diseases of the salivary glands (excluding cystic fibrosis), and the effects of prostaglandins and other treatment modalities on the gastrointestinal tract and their possible role in the pathogenesis and treatment of digestive diseases.

★5242★ U.S. Department of Health and Human Services
National Institute of Diabetes and Digestive and Kidney Diseases
Division of Digestive Diseases and Nutrition
Gastrointestinal Immunology Program
5333 Westbard Ave., Rm. 3A18A
Bethesda, MD 20892
Phone: (301)594-7571
Fax: (301)594-7504
Dr. Frank A. Hamilton, Program Director

Research Activities and Fields: Research emphasis of this Program focuses on intestinal immunity and inflammation. Areas of interest include: ontogeny and differentiation of gut-associated lymphoid tissue; migratory pathways of intestinal lymphoid cells; humoral antibody responses; cell-mediated cytotoxic reactions and the role of cytotoxic effector cells in chronic intestinal inflammation; genetic control of the immune response at mucosal surfaces; immune response to enteric antigens in both intestinal

and extraintestinal sites; granulomatous inflammation; lymphokines and cellular immune regulation; leukotrienes/prostaglandin effects on intestinal immune responses; T-cell mediated intestinal tissue injury; the intestinal mast cell and its role in intestinal inflammation; approaches to optimal mucosal immunoprophylaxis, including viral, bacterial, and parasitic diseases; and diseases such as gluten sensitive, enteropathy, inflammatory bowel disease, and gastritis.

★5243★ U.S. Department of Health and Human Services
National Institute of Diabetes and Digestive and Kidney Diseases
Division of Digestive Diseases and Nutrition
Gastrointestinal Motility Program
5333 Westbard Ave., Rm. 3A16A
Bethesda, MD 20892
Phone: (301)594-7571
Fax: (301)594-7504
Dr. Frank A. Hamilton, Program Director

Research Activities and Fields: Investigators supported by this Program focus their research on the structure of gastrointestinal muscle, the biochemistry of contractile processes and mechanochemical energy conversion relations between metabolism and contractility in smooth muscle, extrinsic control of digestive tract motility, and the fluid mechanics of gastrointestinal flow. Other studies and areas of interest include the actions of drugs on gastrointestinal motility, intestinal obstruction, and diseases such as irritable bowel syndrome (functional digestive disorders), colonic diverticular disease, swallowing disorders, and gastroesophageal reflux.

★5244★ U.S. Department of Health and Human Services
National Institute of Diabetes and Digestive and Kidney Diseases
Division of Digestive Diseases and Nutrition
Gastrointestinal Neuroendocrinology Program
5333 Westbard Ave., Rm. 3A16A
Bethesda, MD 20892
Phone: (301)594-7571
Fax: (301)594-7504
Dr. Frank A. Hamilton, Program Director

Research Activities and Fields: The Gastrointestinal Neuroendocrinology Program supports both basic and clinical studies on normal and abnormal function of the enteric nervous system and the central nervous system elements that control the enteric nervous system. Neuroendocrine studies supported include: histochemistry and neurochemistry, electrical properties of enteric ganglion cells, chemical neurotransmission, neural control of effector function, and extrinsic nervous input. Emphasis is on gastrointestinal hormones and peptides. In addition, Program supports studies on disease conditions associated with excessive or deficient secretions of neuropeptides.

★5245★ U.S. Department of Health and Human Services
National Institute of Diabetes and Digestive and Kidney Diseases
Division of Digestive Diseases and Nutrition
Liver and Biliary Diseases Program
5333 Westbard Ave., Rm. 3A17
Bethesda, MD 20892
Phone: (301)594-7858
Fax: (301)594-7504
Thomas F. Kresina, Ph.D., Director

Research Activities and Fields: Program supports basic and clinical research into the normal function and the diseases of the liver and biliary tract. Areas of basic research include studies on: 1) factors initiating and maintaining hepatic regeneration; 2) factors leading to liver cell injury, fibrosis, and death; 3) basic and applied studies on liver transplantation, including techniques of preservation and storage; 4) metabolism of bile acids and bilirubin; 5) physiology of bile formation; 6) factors controlling cholesterol levels in bile; and 7) gallbladder and bile duct function. Areas of disease research include: cholesterol and pigment gallstones; inborn errors in bile acid metabolism; chronic hepatitis that evolves from autoimmune, viral, or alcoholic disease; and various liver diseases.

U.S. Department of Health and Human Services
National Institute of Diabetes and Digestive and Kidney Diseases
Division of Intramural Research
See: Entry 4919

★5246★ U.S. Department of Health and Human Services
National Institute of Diabetes and Digestive and Kidney Diseases
Division of Intramural Research
Digestive Diseases Branch
NIH Bldg. 10, Rm. 9C-103
9000 Rockville Pike
Bethesda, MD 20892
Phone: (301)496-4201
Fax: (301)402-0600
Dr. Robert T. Jensen, Chief

Research Activities and Fields: The Digestive Diseases Branch conducts clinical and laboratory research on diseases and disorders of the digestive tract, including the physiology, biochemistry, and etiology of diseases of the gastrointestinal tract and the liver, enzymes and metabolic pathways, disturbances in gastrointestinal tract function, and the effect of various treatments and therapies. Activities are carried out in sections for gastroenterology and liver diseases.

University of Alabama at Birmingham
Gregory Fleming James Cystic Fibrosis Research Center
See: Entry 5366

★5247★ University of California, Davis
Gastroenterology and Nutrition Center
Pediatric GI
UCD Medical Center
2516 Stocton Blvd.
Sacramento, CA 95817
Phone: (916)734-3750
Fax: (916)456-2236
Dr. Philip J. McDonald, Contact

Research Activities and Fields: Gastrointestinal motility and electrophysiology, nutritional support, and feeding problems in children.

★5248★ University of California, Los Angeles
Center for the Study of Inflammatory Bowel Disease
Harbor-UCLA Medical Center
1124 W. Carson St., N-21
Torrance, CA 90502
Phone: (310)222-2475
Fax: (310)212-7837
Viktor E. Eysselein, M.D., Ch.

Research Activities and Fields: Inflammatory bowel disease, particularly the origin, causes, and treatment of ulcerative colitis and Crohn's disease. Conducts related studies in molecular biology, cell biology, and immunology. Performs clinical trials of new drugs.

★5249★ University of California, Los Angeles
Center for Ulcer Research and Education (CURE)
VA W. L.A. Center
Bldg. 115, Rm. 203
Los Angeles, CA 90073
Phone: (310)312-9285
Fax: (310)824-6752
Dr. John H. Walsh, Dir.

Research Activities and Fields: Basic and clinical research related to peptic ulcer disease, including cause, checks and balances, relationship of stomach acid to ulcers, relationship of Helicobacter pylori infection to ulcers, stress-ulcer relationship, treatment, drug therapy, surgery, and prevention.

University of California, San Francisco
Liver Transplant Division
See: Entry 12889

★5250★ University of Chicago
Joseph B. Kirsner Center for the Study of Digestive Diseases
5841 S. Maryland Ave.
Chicago, IL 60637
Phone: (312)702-9790
Dr. Thomas Brasitus, Dir.

Research Activities and Fields: Gastroenterology, including colon cancer, inflammatory bowel disease, irritable bowel syndrome, disorders of the esophagus, and pancreatic cancer.

★5251★ University of Chicago
Liver Study Unit
5841 S. Maryland
MC 4076
Chicago, IL 60637
Phone: (312)702-6145
Fax: (312)702-2182
Dr. Alfred L. Baker, Dir.

Research Activities and Fields: Role of nutrition in avoiding or managing liver diseases and new therapeutic approaches for treatment of specific liver diseases. Provides comprehensive care for patients with liver diseases, including assessment of severity using noninvasion methods and management of chronic hepatitis patients.

University of Miami
Cystic Fibrosis Research Center
See: Entry 5373

★5252★ University of Michigan
Michigan Gastrointestinal Peptide Research Center
6520 MSRB I
1150 W. Medical Dr.
Ann Arbor, MI 48109-0682
Phone: (313)747-2942
Fax: (313)763-2535
Tadataka Yamada, M.D., Dir.

Research Activities and Fields: Gastroenterology, including chemistry and biology of gut hormones as they relate to the physiology and pathology of the digestive tract, liver cell differentiation, effect of nutrients on pancreatic endocrine and exocrine secretions, and neuroendocrine modulation of smooth muscle cell function and gut motility. **Formerly:** Gastroenterology Research Laboratory.

University of Minnesota
Cystic Fibrosis Center
See: Entry 5374

University of Missouri—Columbia
Cystic Fibrosis Research Center
See: Entry 5376

University of Nebraska at Omaha
Pediatric Pulmonary and Cystic Fibrosis Research Center
See: Entry 5378

University of Pittsburgh
Cystic Fibrosis Research Center
See: Entry 5380

★5253★ University of Southern California
Liver Research Unit
7601 E. Imperial Hwy.
Downey, CA 90242
Phone: (310)940-8961
Fax: (310)940-6628
Dr. Allan G. Redeker, Chf.

Research Activities and Fields: Liver diseases, including both clinical and basic biochemical and virologic studies of cirrhosis and viral hepatitis.

University of Utah
Intermountain Cystic Fibrosis Center
See: Entry 5385

★5254★ Virginia Commonwealth University
Liver Program Project
Box 980711
Richmond, VA 23298-0711
Phone: (804)828-5396
Fax: (804)828-4060
Dr. Z. Reno Vlahcevic, Project Dir.

Research Activities and Fields: Regulation of bile acid synthesis.

Washington University
Cystic Fibrosis Research Center
See: Entry 5391

West Virginia University
Cystic Fibrosis Center
See: Entry 5395

★5255★ Yale University
Yale Liver Center
Dept. of Med.
Internal Med.
PO Box 3333
New Haven, CT 06510
Phone: (203)785-4138
Dr. James Boyer, Dir.

Research Activities and Fields: Studies of liver structure, function, and disease; and molecular biology studies in expression of cloning of membrane transport proteins.

★5256★ Yeshiva University
Marion Bessin Liver Research Center
Albert Einstein College of Medicine
1300 Morris Park Ave.
Bronx, NY 10461
Phone: (718)430-2098
Fax: (718)918-0857
Dr. David A. Shafritz, Dir.

Research Activities and Fields: Mechanisms of liver cell injury and repair, gene regulation, membrane structure/function, cirrhosis, genetic diseases, heavy metal toxicity, cellular growth control, liver progenitor cells, somatic gene therapy, hepatitis virus infection, chronic liver diseases, and hepatic carcinogenesis.

Chapter 27
Genetics & Genetic Disorders

Federal Government Agencies

★5257★ U.S. Department of Health and Human Services
National Center for Human Genome Research
9000 Rockville Rd.
Bethesda, MD 20892
Phone: (301)496-0844

Description: The Center provides leadership for and formulates research goals and long-range plans, including the study of ethical, legal, and social implications of human genome research. It supports and administers research and research training programs and the systemic, targeted effort to create detailed maps of the genomes of organisms. It also maintains facilities that serve as a resource for the entire NIH intramural research community and collaborates with other NIH institutes and centers and external research institutions.

Foundations & Other Funding Organizations

Other Funding Organizations

Cooley's Anemia Foundation
See: Entry 5903

★5258★ Cystic Fibrosis Foundation
6931 Arlington Rd., No. 200
Bethesda, MD 20814
Phone: (301)951-4422
Free: 800-344-4823
Fax: (301)951-6378
Robert K. Dresing, Pres. & CEO

Description: Foundation awards grants and fellowships to support basic and clinical research and training pertinent to cystic fibrosis and related pulmonary and gastrointestinal childhood diseases.

★5259★ Dysautonomia Foundation
20 E. 46th St., 3rd Fl.
New York, NY 10017
Phone: (212)949-6644
Fax: (212)682-7625
Lenore F. Roseman, Exec. Dir.

Description: Funds research on the causes and cure of dysautonomia.

★5260★ Dystonia Medical Research Foundation
1 E. Wacker Dr., Ste. 2430
Chicago, IL 60601-2001
Phone: (312)755-0198
Fax: (312)803-0138
Nancy Harris, Svcs. Dir.

Description: Provides grants and fellowships for research directed to finding the causes of dystonia.

★5261★ Dystrophic Epidermolysis Bullosa Research Association of America
141 5th Ave., Ste. 7-S
New York, NY 10010
Phone: (212)995-2220
Miram Feder, Exec. Dir.

Description: Awards grants to support research into the cause, nature, and treatment of epidermolysis bullosa in all its forms. Works for federal funding for biomedical research of EB and related disorders.

★5262★ Hereditary Disease Foundation
1427 7th St., Ste. 2
Santa Monica, CA 90401
Phone: (310)458-4183
Fax: (310)458-3937
Nancy S. Wexler, Ph.D., Pres.

Description: Funds basic biomedical research on the causes, prevention, diagnosis, treatment, and cure of genetic disorders, particularly Huntington's Disease. Maintains grant programs to support scientific projects in major medical and basic science laboratories throughout the U.S. Also offers grants and postdoctoral fellowships.

Huntington's Disease Society of America
See: Entry 8131

Muscular Dystrophy Association
See: Entry 8132

★5263★ National Center for the Study of Wilson's Disease
432 W. 58th St., Ste. 614
New York, NY 10019
Phone: (212)523-8717
Fax: (212)523-8708
I. Herbert Scheinberg, M.D., Pres.

Description: Supports research concerning hereditary diseases of metal metabolism, in particular Wilson's disease and Menkes' disease; sponsors diagnostic and treatment center.

★5264★ National Gaucher Foundation
11140 Rockville Pike, No. 350
Rockville, MD 20852-3106
Phone: (301)816-1515
Fax: (301)816-1516
Karen A. Cohen, Exec. Dir.

Description: Sponsors funding of and support for research and clinical programs at medical centers in the U.S. and abroad to develop a cure and/or treatment for Gaucher's Disease.

National Hemophilia Foundation
See: Entry 5905

★5265★ National Marfan Foundation
382 Main St.
Port Washington, NY 11050
Phone: (516)883-8712
Free: 800-862-7326
Fax: (516)883-8712
Priscilla Ciccariello, Chp.

Description: Supports research into the causes and cures of Marfan syndrome.

★5266★ Osteogenesis Imperfecta Foundation
5005 W. Laurel Ave., Ste. 210
Tampa, FL 33607-3836
Phone: (813)282-1161
Fax: (813)287-8214
Vonnie H. Coleman, Exec. Dir.

Description: Awards the Michael Geisman Memorial Fellowship Awward for research and provides financial support to osteogenesis imperfecta research projects.

Tall Cedars of Lebanon of North America
See: Entry 8138

National & International Organizations

★5267★ Alliance of Genetic Support Groups (AGSG)

35 Wisconsin Cir., Ste. 440
Chevy Chase, MD 20815
Phone: (301)652-5553
Free: 800-336-4363
Fax: (301)654-0171
Joan O. Weiss, LCSW, Exec.Dir.

Founded: 1985. **Members:** 224. **Description:** Voluntary genetic organizations; professionals and other interested individuals. Promotes the health and well-being of individuals and families affected by genetic disorders. Provides a forum for the discussion of cross-disability similarities and the identification of available resources. Fosters a partnership among consumers and professionals to enhance education and service for and represent the needs of individuals affected by genetic disorders. Supports networking efforts of members with government agencies, professional groups, service providers, and organizations. Provides technical assistance to genetic support groups. Disseminates information to the public on available resources and referrals. Makes available traveling educational exhibit for member organizations. **Publications:** *Alliance Alert*, monthly. Newsletter. Includes announcements, calendar of events, and membership information. • *Alliance Health Insurance Resource Guide.* • *Alliance Resource Guide on Peer Support Training Programs.* • Brochures. • *Directory of Voluntary Genetic Organizations and Related Resources.* Directory. • *The Empty Pocket Syndrome: How to Get Funding.* Proceedings. • *Informed Consent: Participation in Genetic Research Studies.* • *Media Reporting in the Genetic Age.*

★5268★ American Board of Medical Genetics (ABMG)

9650 Rockville Pike
Bethesda, MD 20814-3998
Phone: (301)571-1825
Fax: (301)571-1825
Sharon Robinson, Admin.

Founded: 1979. **Members:** 2,100. **Description:** Individuals who have passed the board's examination. Certifies individuals for the delivery of medical genetics services; accredits medical genetics training programs. **Publications:** *American Board of Medical Genetics-- Membership Directory*, biennial. Membership Directory. Includes the ABMG, the Genetics Society of America, American Society of Human Genetics, American college of Medical Genetics, and the American Board of Genetic Counseling. *Price:* Included in membership dues; $50/copy for nonmembers.

★5269★ American Society of Human Genetics (ASHG)

9650 Rockville Pike
Bethesda, MD 20814-3998
Phone: (301)571-1825
Fax: (301)530-7079
Elaine Strass, Exec.Dir.

Founded: 1948. **Members:** 4,500. **Description:** Professional society of physicians, researchers, genetic counselors, and others interested in human genetics. **Publications:** *American Journal of Human Genetics*, monthly. Journal. • *Guide to Human Genetics Training Programs in North America.* • Membership Directory, biennial. • *Supplement to Journal*, annual. Journal.

Asociacion Distrofia Muscular
See: Entry 8182

Associacao Brasileira de Distrofia Muscular
See: Entry 8184

★5270★ Association for Children with Down Syndrome (ACDS)

2616 Martin Ave.
Bellmore, NY 11710
Phone: (516)221-4700
Fax: (516)221-4700
Fredda Stimell, Exec.Dir.

Founded: 1966. **Members:** 1,000. **Description:** Parents of children with Down Syndrome; health and educational professionals. Acts as resource and information center about Down Syndrome. Works to maintain contact with the medical and health related community and with parents of children with Down Syndrome; attempts to dispel myths about the capabilities of children with Down Syndrome through Learning is Necessary to Care, an outreach program. Provides referral services; sponsors conferences and workshops; conducts research; compiles statistics. Administers infant, toddler, and preschool programs in New York state and some sibling programs. Offers recreational and socialization programs and support groups for children over 5 years of age through adulthood. **Publications:** *ACDS Newsletter*, bimonthly. Newsletter. Features information on advocacy, law, reading materials, references and reviews, conferences, and association programs. • Bibliography. • Journal, annual. • *Special Kids Make Special Friends.* • Videos. **Formerly:** Association for Special Children.

Association for Glycogen Storage Disease (AGSD)
See: Entry 4832

★5271★ Association of Neuro-Metabolic Disorders (ANMD)

5223 Brookfield Ln.
Sylvania, OH 43560-1809
Phone: (419)885-1497
Cheryl C. Volk, Exec. Officer

Founded: 1980. **Members:** 100. **Description:** Individuals with neurometabolic disorders, their families and friends, and health care professionals. (Neurometabolic disorders are genetic diseases such as pheylketonuria, maple syrup urine disease, galactosemia, and biotinidase deficiency, which affect body chemistry and often result in brain damage. If detected early, symptoms can often be treated through dietary adjustment.) Provides information and support for those affected by a neurometabolic disorder, and works to enhance services available for infants, children, teens, and adults. Promotes public and personal awareness, deepened family understanding and participation in treatment programs, and improved professional health care intervention. Conducts educational programs; encourges research. Lobbies at the state and federal levels. Facilitates networking and acts in cooperation with similar organizations; provides peer counseling and support. **Publications:** *ANMD Newsletter*, 3/year. Newsletter. Includes dietary management strategies and recipes, educational material, and articles by parents and health care professionals. *Price:* $5/year. • *Membership Roster*, periodic. Includes contact information.

Ataxia Group
See: Entry 8192

Behavior Genetics Association (BGA)
See: Entry 7341

Billy Barty Foundation (BBF)
See: Entry 7869

Biruduma Muscular Dystrophy Association
See: Entry 8196

★5272★ Canadian Genetic Diseases Network

2125 East Mall, Rm. 348
Vancouver, BC, Canada V6T 1Z4
Phone: (604)822-7945
Dr. David Shindler, Mng.Dir.

Founded: 1990. **Members:** 37. **Regional Groups:** 13. **Languages:** English, French. **Description:** Canadian scientists and health care professionals engaged in medical genetic research. Works to develop and commercialize basic research in genetically related diseases including cancer, cystic fibrosis, myotonic dystrophy, and Huntington's disease. Forms partnerships with industry to develop basic research technologies; trains students in genetic research, with particular focus on the graduate and post-doctoral levels; conducts public education programs. Sponsors competitions. **Publications:** *The Scanner*, semiannual. Newsletter. Relates advances in genetically related disease research for members, related industries and government agencies.

Celiac Sprue Association—United States of America (CSA/USA)
See: Entry 5213

Charcot-Marie-Tooth Association (CMTA)
See: Entry 8198

Charcot-Marie-Tooth International (CMTI)
See: Entry 8199

★5273★ Coffin-Lowry Syndrome Foundation

PO Box 10033
Bainbridge Island, WA 98110
Phone: (206)842-1523
Mary Illa, Chair

Founded: 1991. **Description:** Serves as a clearinghouse for information on Coffin-Lowry Syndrome. (CLS is an inherited syndrome causing retardation, developmental delay, dysmorphic features, and skeletal anomelies.) Offers support services for families dealing with CLS. **Publications:** *CLSF News*, quarterly. Newsletter. *Price:* $75.

Cooley's Anemia Foundation (CAF)
See: Entry 5936

★5274★ **Corporation for Menke's Disease (CMD)**
5720 Buckfield Ct.
Fort Wayne, IN 46804
Phone: (219)436-0137
Jane Swiss, Secy.

Members: 86. **Description:** Families with children born with Menke's disease; medical professionals. (Menke's disease is a terminal genetic disorder, primarily found in males, in which the body is unable to process copper.) Supports research; promotes experimental treatments. **Publications:** Newsletter, annual.

★5275★ **Cystic Fibrosis Foundation (CFF)**
6931 Arlington Rd., No. 200
Bethesda, MD 20814
Phone: (301)951-4422
Free: 800-344-4823
Fax: (301)951-6378
Robert J. Beall, Ph.D., Pres. & CEO

Founded: 1955. **Local Groups:** 70. **Description:** Supports medical research, professional education, and care centers to benefit patients with cystic fibrosis (CF), an inherited fatal disease among children and young adults. With this disease a thick mucus clogs the lungs, creating breathing difficulties and high susceptibility to infection; the digestive system and other organs are also affected. More than 115 care centers affiliated with the foundation provide patient services. Medical programs provide support for a national network of multidisciplinary basic and clinical research grants. **Publications:** Annual Report, annual. • *Commitment*, semiannual. Also publishes consumer fact sheets.

★5276★ **Cystinosis Foundation (CF)**
1212 Broadway, No. 830
Oakland, CA 94612
Phone: (510)235-1052
Fax: (510)235-1052
Jean Hotz, Pres.

Founded: 1983. **Members:** 150. **Regional Groups:** 20. **Description:** Parents, relatives, and friends of cystinotic children; interested members of the medical community and the public. (Cystinosis is a genetic metabolic disease in which abnormal amounts of the amino acid cystine collect in the cells, leading to kidney failure.) Purposes are to increase public awareness about cystinosis; to act as a support group to parents of children with the disease; to raise funds for research. Compiles statistics. Maintains speakers' bureau. **Publications:** *Cystinosis Foundation Newsletter*, quarterly. Newsletter. • Directory, periodic. For parents of children with cysinosis. • *Facts About Cystinosis*. Brochure. • *National Directory of Information*, periodic. Directory. For physicians engaged in cystinosis research. **Formerly:** Alliance of Genetic Support Groups; (1986) Cystinosia Foundation of California.

★5277★ **Dystrophic Epidermolysis Bullosa Research Association of America (DEBRA)**
141 5th Ave., Ste. 7-S
New York, NY 10010
Phone: (212)995-2220
Miram Feder, Exec.Dir.

Founded: 1979. **Description:** People with Epidermolysis Bullosa and their families; other interested individuals. (Epidermolysis Bullosa represents a group of inherited disorders of the skin characterized by formation of blisters resulting from the most minimal trauma.) To raise funds to promote and support research into the cause, nature, and treatment of EB in all its forms; to relieve the physical and mental distress of victims by providing practical advice, guidance, support, and other assistance. Distributes educational material to the public and medical professionals. Works for federal funding for biomedical research of EB and related disorders. Offers children's services; conducts educational programs. **Publications:** Booklets. • *EB Currents*, semiannual. • *EB Reporter*, semiannual. Newsletter. Contains information on research, treatment, and legislation regarding EB. Includes regional news and pen pals section. *Price:* Included in membership dues. **Also Known As:** DEBRA of America.

Ehlers Danlos National Foundation (EDNF)
See: Entry 7872

European Study Group on Lysosomal Diseases (ESGLD)
See: Entry 4841

★5278★ **Fanconi's Anemia Research Fund (FARF)**
1902 Jefferson St., Ste. 2
Eugene, OR 97405
Phone: (503)687-4658
Fax: (503)687-0548
Linda DeSpain, Contact

Founded: 1989. **Members:** 300. **Description:** Families with children afflicted with Fanconi's anemia, a genetic disorder. Seeks to offer support to families, help them network, and keep them apprised of research relating to Fanconi's anemia; assists research on this disorder. Operates support group. Conducts fundraising for research through public awareness programs and special projects. **Publications:** *FA Family Directory*. Directory. • *FA Family Newsletter*, semiannual. Newsletter. • *Fanconi Anemia: A Handbook for Families and Their Physicians*. Handbook. **Formerly:** (1989) Fanconi's Anemia Support Group.

FIRST - Foundation for Ichthyosis and Related Skin Types (FIRST)
See: Entry 4234

The Foundation Fighting Blindness (RPFFB)
See: Entry 13456

Foundation for Nager and Miller Syndromes
See: Entry 2747

Friedreich's Ataxia Society of Ireland (FASI)
See: Entry 8222

F.S.H. Society
See: Entry 7879

Genetic Toxicology Association (GTA)
See: Entry 10410

Gluten Intolerance Group of North America (GIGNA)
See: Entry 5218

Hemochromatosis Foundation (HF)
See: Entry 4845

HHT Foundation International
See: Entry 2851

Huntington's Disease Association (HDA)
See: Entry 8227

Huntington's Disease Society of America (HDSA)
See: Entry 8228

Indian Muscular Dystrophy Association (IMDA)
See: Entry 8230

★5279★ **International Cystic Fibrosis (Mucoviscidosis) Association (ICFMA)**
323 Lippens Ave.
Montreal, PQ, Canada H2M 1H7
Phone: (514)381-0922
Fax: (514)381-8283
Michelle Roche, Sec.

Founded: 1964. **Members:** 51. **Description:** National medical/lay volunteer organizations concerned with cystic fibrosis. Works to: further the interests of persons with cystic fibrosis; improve medical care available to them and the psychological and social care available to them and their families. Stimulates, supports, and advances research in the nature, cause, prevention, treatment, alleviation, and care of cystic fibrosis. Coordinates information services and the interchange of knowledge of all phases of cystic fibrosis. **Publications:** *Directory of International Treatment Locations for Cystic Fibrosis Patients*, periodic.

★5280★ **International Federation of Teratology Societies (IFTS)**
c/o Dr. W.S. Webster
University of Sydney
Department of Anatomy
Sydney, NSW 2006, Australia
Phone: 0 6922498
Fax: 0 5522026
Dr. W. S. Webster, Sec.

Founded: 1982. **Members:** 2,600. **Description:** Individuals from the European Teratology Society, Teratology Society, Japanese Teratology Society, and Australian Teratology Society. Aims to foster international cooperation and a greater interest in and understanding of the global aspects of teratology. (Teratology is the study of congenital malformations and serious deviations from normal characteristics.) Provides for information exchange and collaboration with health and charitable agencies. Provides education to organizations and individuals interested in prevention and treatment of birth defects. Supports research in the area of teratology. Is in the process of establishing education programs.

★5281★ International Fibrodysplasia Ossificans Progressiva Association (IFOPA)
910 N. Jerico
Casselberry, FL 32707
Phone: (407)365-4194
Fax: (407)365-4194
Jeannie L. Peeper, Pres.

Founded: 1988. **Members:** 105. **Description:** Individuals affected by FOP, their families and friends, and health care professionals. (FOP, also known as fibrodysplasia ossificans progressiva, is a rare genetic disorder in which normal bone is produced in abnormal locations, causing joints to become rigid and immobile. Onset usually occurs during childhood and may eventuate in the complete immobilization of nearly every joint in the body. The cause is currently unknown.) Provides support services to those affected by FOP, including medical resources. Encourages and funds medical research into causes of FOP and other bone-related disorders; promotes public education regarding the disorder and its effects. Facilitates communication among those affected by FOP. **Publications:** *FOP Connection*, quarterly. Newsletter. Including articles on daily coping skills and new members. *Price:* Included in membership dues. **Also Known As:** International FOP Association.

International Joseph Diseases Foundation (IJDF)
See: Entry 8240

Iron Overload Diseases Association (IOD)
See: Entry 4852

★5282★ Joubert Syndrome Parents in Touch Network
12348 Summer Meadow Rd.
Rock, MI 49880
Phone: (906)359-4707
Mary Van Damme, Founder

Founded: 1992. **Description:** Support and information exchange group for families of people afflicted with Joubert's Syndrome, a genetically transmitted syndrome in which the cerebellar vermis, a section of the brain controlling balance and coordination, is partially or completely missing. Physical manifestations of JS include disturbances in breathing patterns, ataxia (unsteadiness), abnormal eye movements, hypotonia, and possible mental retardation. Promotes continuing education for medical professionals. **Publications:** *Joubert Syndrome Parents-In-Touch Networking List*, annual. • *Joubert Syndrome Parents-In-Touch Newsletter*, quarterly. Newsletter.

★5283★ Klinefelter Syndrome and Associates (KSA)
PO Box 119
Roseville, CA 95678-0119
Melissa Aylstock, Exec. Officer

Founded: 1989. **Members:** 2,000. **Regional Groups:** 3. **Description:** Individuals affected by Klinefelter Syndrome and their families. (Klinefelter syndrome is a genetic alteration, occurring only in males, identified by the presence of an extra "X" chromosome on the chromosome chain that determines gender.) Provides support services; facilitates networking and exchange of information. Conducts educational programs. **Publications:** Brochure. Contains information Klinefelter Syndrome. • Newsletter, periodic. **Also Known As:** KS and Associates.

Klippel-Trenaunay Support Group (KTSG)
See: Entry 7884

Latin American Association of Environmental Mutagens, Carcinogens, and Teratogens Societies (LAAEMCTS)
See: Entry 5047

★5284★ Laurence-Moon-Bardet-Biedl Syndrome Network (LMBBSN)
18 Strawberry Hill
Windsor, CT 06095
Phone: (203)688-7880
Linda Rickard, Contact

Founded: 1984. **Description:** Provides a network for individuals with Laurence-Moon-Bardet-Biedl syndrome, a genetic disorder. (Persons with LMBBS suffer from general developmental delay and exhibit symptoms of retinitis pigmentosa, a degenerative eye disease; hypogenitalism; polydactyly; obesity.) **Publications:** *LMBBS Network News*, periodic. Newsletter. Includes list of member families. **Also Known As:** Laurence-Moon-Biedl Syndrome Network; LMBS Network.

Little People of America (LPA)
See: Entry 7886

★5285★ Lowe's Syndrome Association (LSA)
222 Lincoln St.
West Lafayette, IN 47906
Phone: (317)743-3634
Kaye McSpadden, Sec.

Founded: 1983. **Members:** 300. **Description:** Parents, friends, and relatives of individuals with Lowe's syndrome; medical, educational, and social service professionals and agencies. Lowe's syndrome, also known as oculo-cerebro-renal (eye-brain-kidney) syndrome, is a genetic condition affecting males resulting in multiple handicaps. Symptoms include congenital cataracts, mental retardation, poor muscle tone, abnormal kidney function, and bone problems. Although there is no cure for the syndrome, some symptoms can be treated and controlled. Objectives are to: foster communication among families; provide medical and educational information; promote a better understanding of Lowe's syndrome; support and encourage research. **Publications:** *Living with Lowe's Syndrome*. • *On the Beam*, periodic. Membership newsletter for families affected by Lowe's syndrome. *Price:* Included in membership dues.

★5286★ Malignant Hyperthermia Association of the United States (MHAUS)
PO Box 1069
Sherburne, NY 13460-1069
Phone: (607)674-7901
Fax: (607)674-7910
Richard A. Hillman, Exec.Dir.

Founded: 1981. **Members:** 2,500. **Description:** Individuals susceptible to malignant hyperthermia (MH); anesthesiologists; other medical specialists, including dentists. (MH is a genetically transmitted, often fatal, muscular disorder triggered in susceptible individuals by certain anesthetic agents. It is characterized by rapid increases in metabolism, muscle rigidity, and body temperature, sometimes reaching 110 degrees and higher.) Objectives are to: help save lives by making information about MH available; discuss problems that confront families affected by MH; fund research on the causes, detection, and management of MH; disseminate research information. Provides information to MH patients and health care providers. **Publications:** *The Communicator*, 5/year. Newsletter. • *Directory of MH Biopsy Test Centers*. • *Emergency Treatment for MH*. • *Managing MH*. • *Preventing MH*. • *Testing for MH Susceptibility*. Pamphlet. • *Understanding Malignant Hyperthermia*. • *What is MH?*. Pamphlet. • *What is MHAUS?*. Pamphlet. Also publishes wallet cards.

★5287★ National Association for Down Syndrome (NADS)
PO Box 4542
Oak Brook, IL 60522-4542
Phone: (708)325-9112
Sheila Hebein, Exec.Dir.

Founded: 1961. **Members:** 1,700. **Description:** Primarily a local organization, serving the Chicago, IL, metropolitan area, composed of: parents of children and adults with Down syndrome; persons interested in their treatment and welfare. Seeks to bring about better understanding and acceptance of persons with Down Syndrome. Encourages medical and educational research on Down Syndrome; fosters the organization of community parent groups. Maintains speakers' bureau; conducts seminars and educational programs. **Publications:** *A Baby First*. Brochure. • Audiotapes. • Newsletter, bimonthly.

National Ataxia Foundation (NAF)
See: Entry 8267

National Center for the Study of Wilson's Disease (NCSWD)
See: Entry 4857

★5288★ National Down Syndrome Congress (NDSC)
1605 Chantilly Dr., Ste. 250
Atlanta, GA 30324
Phone: (404)633-1555
Free: 800-232-NDSC
Fax: (404)633-2817
Frank Murphy, Contact

Founded: 1973. **Members:** 5,000. **Local Groups:** 400. **Description:** Families of individuals with Down Syndrome; educators, health professionals, and other interested individuals. Works to promote the welfare of persons with Down Syndrome (DS), a chromosomal disorder which occurs in approximately one in every 800 to 1100 births and usually causes delays in physical and intellectual development; its exact cause is unknown. Promotes the belief that persons with DS have the right to a normal and dignified life, particularly in the areas of education, medical care, employment, and human services. Examines issues of social policy and conditions that limit the full growth and potential of children and adults with DS. Assists parents on possible solutions to the needs of the child with DS; coordinates efforts and activities of local parents' organizations. Acts as clearinghouse for information on DS. **Publications:** *Alpha Fetoprotein and Prenatal Screening.* Position statement. • Articles. • *Attanto-Axial Instability.* Position statement. • Bibliography. • *Depression in Persons with Down Syndrome.* Position statement. • *Doman-Delacato Treatment.* Position statement. • *Down Syndrome.* Booklet. • *Down Syndrome News*, 10/year. Newsletter. Provides information on the educational, research, and service programs of NDSC. Includes book and film reviews, calendar of events, and statistics. *Price:* $20/year. • Films. • Journals. • *Management of Challenging Behaviors.* Position statement. • *Mega Vitamin Therapy.* Position statement. • Pamphlets. • *Quality Education for Students with Down Syndrome.* Position statement. **Formerly:** (1983) Down's Syndrome Congress; (1984) National Down's Syndrome Congress.

★ **5289** ★ **National Down Syndrome Society (NDSS)**
666 Broadway
New York, NY 10012
Phone: (212)460-9330
Free: 800-221-4602
Fax: (212)979-2873
Elizabeth Goodwin, Pres.

Founded: 1979. **Description:** Devoted to research into the causes and treatment of Down Syndrome. Works to increase public awareness of Down Syndrome; raises funds to support all areas of Down Syndrome research. Sponsors educational programs. Provides information and referral for families and professionals; develops programs and services for families and individuals with Down Syndrome. **Publications:** Booklet. Designed for new parents of Down Syndrome children. • *Clinical Care Booklets.* • *Directory of Parent Support Groups and Early Intervention Programs*, periodic. Directory. • *Down Syndrome: Advances in Medical Care.* • *Down Syndrome Respite Manual.* Manual. • *Gifts of Love.* Video. • *NDSS Update*, quarterly. • *Opportunities to Grow.* Video. • *Opportunities to Grow.* Video. • Proceedings. • *Project Mainstream.* Monograph. • *Using Computers to Help Children With Down Syndrome.* Manual. Also publishes fact sheets.

★ **5290** ★ **National Down's Syndrome Association (NDSA)**
NDSA Inst. of Genetics
Hospital for Genetic Diseases
O.U. Begumpet
Hyderabad 500 016, Andhra Pradesh, India
Phone: 44 213681
P. Usha Rani, Sec.

Founded: 1987. **Members:** 250. **Languages:** English. **Description:** Interested individuals promoting the spread of knowledge about Down's Syndrome (a congenital condition resulting in moderate to severe mental deficiency). Stresses importance of improvement in quality of life for persons with Down's Syndrome. Furnishes the latest research available on the medical, psychosocial, and educational/vocational aspects of the disease; assists in the formation of selfhelp groups; provides training programs for children with the disease; works toward the establishment of special schools for Down's Syndrome children in India. Holds lectures and seminars. **Publications:** *Bulletin on Down's Syndrome*, semiannual. Bulletin. Also publishes public education material in Telugu, the local language of Andhra Pradesh, India.

★ **5291** ★ **National Foundation for Ectodermal Dysplasias (NFED)**
219 E. Main
Box 114
Mascoutah, IL 62258
Phone: (618)566-2020
Fax: (618)566-4718
Mary Kaye Richter, Exec.Dir.

Founded: 1981. **Members:** 1,000. **Description:** Families of ectodermal dysplasia patients and the medical community. (Ectodermal dysplasia is a genetic birth defect usually resulting in an abnormal development of the outer layer of cells in the embryo. The disorder may be characterized by absent or poorly functioning sweat glands, sparse hair follicles, abnormal hair texture, absence of hair and skin oils, disfigured finger and toe nails, hearing or sight deficiencies, mental retardation, abnormalities of the limbs, cleft palate, and urinary tract anomalies. With proper medical care, ED patients can live fairly normal lives.) Locates patients and provides them with support and information. Assists the medical community in acquiring the necessary information for treating an ED patient, locates treatment facilities and provides referral services. Makes funds available to qualifed applicants for dental and other necessary care. Conducts educational meetings and assists with research projects. Establishes regional centers for diagnosis and treatment of ED. Provides children's services; compiles statistics. **Publications:** Brochures. • *Dental Guide to the Ectodermal Dysplasia.* • *The Educator*, monthly. Newsletter. *Price:* $20/year. • *EENT Guide to Ectodermal Dysplasia.* • *Evan's New Teeth.* • *Family Guide to the Ectodermal Dysplasias.* • *National Foundation for Ectodermal Dysplasias--Participants Directory*, annual. Directory. *Price:* Included in membership dues. • Pamphlets. • *Skin Guide.*

★ **5292** ★ **National Foundation for Jewish Genetic Diseases (NFJGD)**
250 Park Ave., Ste. 1000
New York, NY 10177
Phone: (212)371-1030
George Crohn, Jr., Pres.

Founded: 1974. **Description:** Individuals concerned with the eradication of the seven known genetic diseases that affect children of predominantly Ashkenazi Jewish heritage. (These diseases include Gaucher's disease, Dystonia, Dysautonomia, Tay-Sachs, Bloom's Syndrome, Niemann-Pick, and Mucolipidosis IV.) Seeks to accomplish its goal by establishing carrier identification tests, providing genetic counseling which includes prenatal testing procedures, and conducting a nationwide education campaign to inform the public that these diseases exist and attack without warning. Supports basic medical research in the prevention and cure of these diseases. Acts as referral agency. Has sponsored symposia on chromosome breakage and neoplasia, Gaucher's disease, and cellular molecular biology of neuronal development. **Publications:** Books. • Brochures.

★ **5293** ★ **National Fragile X Foundation (NFXF)**
1441 York St., Ste. 303
Denver, CO 80206
Phone: (303)333-6155
Free: 800-688-8765
Fax: (303)333-4369
David Nommensen, Exec.Dir.

Founded: 1984. **State Groups:** 70. **Description:** Fragile X patients and their families; other individuals and institutions interested in the syndrome including health care professionals, special education teachers, genetics centers, hospitals, and libraries. (Fragile X syndrome is an X-linked genetic condition which causes varying degrees of mental retardation in affected males, and can cause mental retardation or psychological disorders in carrying females. FXS can be diagnosed by a DNA analysis test.) Seeks to increase awareness of the characteristics and treatment of FXS among members and the public. Works to stimulate research into the causes and treatment of the syndrome. Supports and provides assistance and advice to parents of children with FXS. Conducts research and educational programs. **Publications:** Audiotape. • Booklets. • Brochure. • *National Fragile X Foundation Newsletter*, bimonthly. Newsletter. *Price:* $36/year. • Videos. Also publishes family & professional information packets.

National Gaucher Foundation (NGF)
See: Entry 4858

National Hemophilia Foundation (NHF)
See: Entry 5977

National Marfan Foundation (NMF)
See: Entry 7892

National MPS Society
See: Entry 4863

National Organization for Albinism and Hypopigmentation (NOAH)
See: Entry 4864

★5294★ **National Society of Genetic Counselors (NSGC)**
c/o Bea Leopold
233 Canterbury Dr.
Wallingford, PA 19086
Phone: (610)872-7608
Fax: (610)872-1192
Bea Leopold, Exec.Dir.

Founded: 1979. **Members:** 1,200. **Regional Groups:** 6. **Description:** Genetic counselors with a master's or Ph.D. degree in human genetics, nursing, social work, or public health; physicians, dentists, and others with an interest in genetic counseling; students in master's degree program. Activities focus on the professional education of the genetic counselor and promotion of the field. Maintains speakers' bureau; compiles statistics. **Publications:** *Journal of Genetic Counseling*, quarterly. Journal. • *NSGC Membership Directory*, annual. Membership Directory. • *Perspectives in Genetic Counseling*, quarterly. Newsletter. Also publishes high school and college level career packets.

National Tay-Sachs and Allied Diseases Association (NTSAD)
See: Entry 4865

★5295★ **National Tuberous Sclerosis Association (NTSA)**
8000 Corporate Dr., Ste. 120
Landover, MD 20785
Phone: (301)459-9888
Free: 800-225-6872
Fax: (301)459-0394
Barbara K. Witten, Pres.

Founded: 1974. **Members:** 1,750. **Description:** Encourages and provides grants for research into the diagnosis, cause, management, and cure of tuberous sclerosis. (Tuberous sclerosis is a genetic disease characterized by one or more of the following: epileptic seizures, mental retardation, behavioral problems, tumors, or skin lesions.) Provides support to families affected by the disease through a nationwide network of volunteer area representatives and the distribution of informational packets. Conducts educational programs for medical and allied professionals. **Publications:** *Perspective Newsletter*, quarterly. Newsletter. Contains research articles, current resources for parents, legislative news, and parent question and answer column. *Price:* Available to members and professionals. • *Resource Newsletter*, semiannual. Newsletter. Also publishes brochures.

Neurofibromatosis, Inc. (NF)
See: Entry 8287

Norwegian Association for Huntington's Disease (NAHD)
(Landsforening for Huntingtons Sykdom — LHS)
See: Entry 8292

★5296★ **Norwegian Cystic Fibrosis Association (NCFA)**
(Norsk Forening for Cystisk Fibrose — NFCF)
Postboks 114
Kjelsas
N-0411 Oslo 4, Norway
Phone: 2 2235050
Reidun Jahnsen, Pres.

Founded: 1976. **Members:** 500. **National Groups:** 1. **Regional Groups:** 5. **Languages:** English, Norwegian. **Description:** Persons with cystic fibrosis and interested individuals. Promotes improvements in the methods of care for persons with cystic fibrosis. Disseminates information; coordinates clinical research. **Publications:** *Nordic Cystic Fibrosis Magazine*, quarterly. Magazine.

★5297★ **Norwegian LMBB's Syndrome Association (NLMBBSA)**
(Interesseforeningen fur LMBB i Norge)
Joh. Minsaas 18B
N-7053 Ronheim, Norway
Phone: 73572811
Knut Almaas, Contact

Founded: 1984. **Members:** 37. **Languages:** English. **Description:** Persons with Laurence-Moon-Bardet-Biedl syndrome and their families. (LMBB is a genetic disorder; symptoms include general developmental delay, retinitis pigmentosa, hypogenitalism, polydactyly, and obesity.) Offers assistance to children with LMBB, especially those newly diagnosed.

★5298★ **Norwegian Osteogenesis Imperfecta Foundation (NFOI)**
(Norsk Forening for Osteogenesis Imperfecta)
Postboks 114
Kjelsas
N-0411 Oslo, Norway
Phone: 2 348580
Fax: 2 342766
Lisbeth Myhre, Founder

Founded: 1979. **Members:** 560. **Languages:** English. **Description:** Persons with osteogenesis imperfecta; relatives. (Osteogenesis imperfecta is a hereditary disorder characterized by fragile bones, loose joints, short stature, poor teeth, and deafness.) Conducts educational programs for teachers. **Publications:** *OI-NYTT*, 5/year. • *OI-permen*, periodic. Includes medical and technical information. Also publishes brochures and pamphlets.

Organic Acidemia Association (OAA)
See: Entry 4867

★5299★ **Osteogenesis Imperfecta Foundation (OIF)**
5005 W. Laurel Ave., Ste. 210
Tampa, FL 33607-3836
Phone: (813)282-1161
Fax: (813)287-8214
Vonnie H. Coleman, Exec.Dir.

Founded: 1970. **Members:** 1,300. **State Groups:** 43. **Description:** Doctors, nurses, and other health professionals; patients; parents of children with osteogenesis imperfecta. (Osteogenesis imperfecta is a hereditary disorder

whose most common characteristics are fragility of bones, loose joints, excessive perspiration, poor teeth, deafness, short stature, and, frequently, blue sclera, or whites of the eyes.) Supports and encourages medical research regarding effective treatment for OI and the basic chemical defects in tissue which lead to OI. Aims to educate the public about osteogenesis imperfecta. Disseminates information to OI patients, their families, and medical professionals. Sponsors medical speakers. Compiles statistics. **Publications:** *Osteogenesis Imperfecta Foundation--Breakthrough*, quarterly. Newsletter. Contains medical reports, foundation news, and activities. *Price:* Free to members; $9/year for nonmembers. • Videos. Also publishes other medical and general literature.

★5300★ **Parents of Children with Down Syndrome (PODS)**
c/o The Arc of Montgomery County
11600 Nebel St.
Rockville, MD 20852
Phone: (301)984-5777
Fax: (301)816-2429

Founded: 1966. **Members:** 150. **Description:** Parents of children with Down Syndrome. Activities include formal and informal meetings; parent-to-parent counseling; contacting new parents of Down Syndrome children to offer support and information on community resources; providing information on doctors, hospitals, and professionals; promoting membership in The ARC. Maintains speakers' bureau. **Publications:** *Parents of Children with Down Syndrome*, monthly. Newsletter. • *PODS Monthly Newsletter*. Newsletter. Highlights legislation, education, recreation, medical information relating to Down Syndrome. *Price:* Free. **Formerly:** (1975) Mothers of Young Mongoloids; (1993) Parents of Down Syndrome Children.

PKU Parents (PKU-P)
See: Entry 4870

Society for Mucopolysaccharide Diseases (MPS)
See: Entry 4872

Society for the Study of Inborn Errors of Metabolism (SSIEM)
See: Entry 4873

★5301★ **Support Group for Monosomy 9P (9P)**
43304 Kipton Nickle Plate Rd.
La Grange, OH 44050
Phone: (216)775-4255
Jon Storr, Exec.Dir.

Founded: 1984. **Members:** 60. **Description:** Parents and caregivers of children that have Monosomy 9P. Offers support to families with children that suffer from Monosomy 9P. (Monosomy 9P is a rare chromosome disorder in which a piece of the 9th chromosome pair is broken off. It results in mental retardation, physical deformity, and triganocephaly of the forehead.) Acts as a clearinghouse for information on the disorder. Maintains a roster of families having a child with Monosomy 9P. **Publications:** Brochures.

★5302★ Support Organization for Trisomy 18/13 (SOFT 18/13)
c/o Barb VanHerreweghe
2982 S. Union St.
Rochester, NY 14624
Phone: (716)594-4621
Barb VanHerreweghe, Contact
Founded: 1979. **Members:** 2,100. **Local Groups:** 1. **Description:** Families, friends, and professionals involved with children born with Trisomy 18 or Trisomy 13. (Trisomy 18 and 13 are genetic disorders in which there are three no. 18 or no. 13 chromosomes rather than the usual two. The disorders are characterized by mental retardation, neurological problems, and respiratory and circulatory deficiencies, and occur in approximately 1000 births per year in the U.S.) Offers support, understanding, and encouragement to families of affected individuals. Provides the public with information on these conditions and birth defects in general. Makes available to families and professionals a file of medical information. Representatives participate in workshops, seminars, lectures, and group studies at universities and hospitals. Conducts surveys and compiles statistics about medical treatment and problems. Maintains speakers' bureau and placement service. **Publications:** Brochures. • *The SOFT Touch*, quarterly. Newsletter. Includes reader's forum and chapter news. *Price:* $20/year for families; $25/ year for professionals. • *Trisomy 18 - A Book for Families*. *Price:* $10.95. • *Trisomy 13 - A Guidebook for Families*. *Price:* $10.95.

★5303★ Treacher Collins Foundation (TCF)
PO Box 683
Norwich, VT 05055
Phone: (802)649-3050
Free: 800-823-2055
Hope Charkins, M.S.W., Exec.Dir.
Founded: 1988. **Description:** Families, individuals, and professionals interested in developing and sharing knowledge about Treacher Collins Syndrome and related disorders. (Treacher Collins Syndrome, also known as Franceschetti-Klein Syndrome, is a rare genetic condition involving underdevelopment of the structures of the head and face.) Promotes research to improve the quality of life of individuals affected by Treacher Collins Syndrome. Provides networking and support. Operates referral and resource listing service. **Publications:** *American Resource List*. • Newsletter, quarterly. *Price:* Donations accepted. • Pamphlet. • *Rare Does Not Mean Alone*. Video. Covers Treacher Collins syndrome and the services of the foundation. • *Terminology List*. • *Treacher Collins Syndrome - An Overview*. Booklet. Also publishes a networking list. **Formerly:** Treacher Collins Family Network.

★5304★ Turner's Syndrome Society of the U.S. (TSS)
c/o Lynn-Georgia Tesch
15500 Wayzata Blvd., No. 811
Wayzata, MN 55391
Phone: (612)475-9944
Free: 800-365-9944
Fax: (612)475-9949
Lynn-Georgia Tesch, Exec. Officer

Founded: 1987. **Members:** 3,500. **Local Groups:** 32. **Description:** Persons suffering from Turner's syndrome; families of persons with the disease; health care professionals. (TS is a genetic disorder affecting females causing short stature and cardiac, kidney, and spatial motor perception problems; TS can result in infertility and incomplete sexual maturation.) Seeks to increase public awareness of the medical and sociopsychological effects TS has on patients. Maintains speakers' bureau. **Publications:** Newsletter, quarterly. • *Turner's Syndrome: A Guide for Families*. • *Turner's Syndrome: A Guide for Physicians*.

Union of Muscular Dystrophy Societies of Croatia
See: Entry 8319

★5305★ Usher Syndrome Self-Help Network (USSHN)
c/o Foundation Fighting Blindness
1401 Mt. Royal Ave., 4th Fl.
Baltimore, MD 21217
Phone: (410)225-9400
Free: 800-683-5555
Fax: (410)225-3936
Description: A self-help network for individuals diagnosed with Usher Syndrome and their families and friends. (Usher Syndrome is a genetic disorder causing hearing loss at birth and eventual retinal degeneration.)

★5306★ VHL Family Alliance (VHLFA)
171 Clinton Rd.
Brookline, MA 02146
Phone: (617)232-5946
Free: 800-767-4VHL
Fax: (617)734-8233
Joyce Wilcox Graff, Co-Chair
Founded: 1993. **National Groups:** 4. **State Groups:** 17. **Description:** Patients affected by Von Hippel-Lindau Disease; their families; medical professionals; interested others. (Von Hippel-Lindau Disease is a genetic disorder involving abnormal growth and "knotting" of blood vessels in the retina, brain, or spinal cord areas. These knots can form or cause cancer-like tumors or cysts.) Promotes education of the medical community, patients, and the general public about the disease. Provides an international support network to families affected by VHL. Conducts research and educational programs; maintains speakers' bureau. **Publications:** Brochures. • *VHL Family Forum*, quarterly. Newsletter. Contains the latest information on VHL, research into the disease, and support network information. *Price:* Included in membership. • *VHL Patient Handbook*. Booklet. • *Your Family Health Tree*. Booklet. **Also Known As:** Von Hippel-Lindau Family Alliance.

Wilson's Disease Association (WDA)
See: Entry 4877

World Federation of Hemophilia (WFH) (Federation Mondiale de l'Hemophilie — FMH)
See: Entry 5994

World Hemophilia AIDS Center (WHAC)
See: Entry 6759

★5307★ Zimbabwe Down Syndrome Association (ZDSA)
240 Malvern Rd.
PO Box 24A
Waterfalls
Harare, Zimbabwe
Phone: 4 601023
Jackie Silva, Admin.Dir.
Founded: 1982. **Members:** 1,000. **Description:** Aims to provide those affected by Down's Syndrome with the necessary medical, educational, and financial support. Provides support to family and friends. **Publications:** Newsletter, bimonthly.

Research Centers

★5308★ Albany Medical College
Pediatric Pulmonary and Cystic Fibrosis Care, Research & Teaching Center
47 New Scotland Ave.
Albany, NY 12208
Phone: (518)262-6880
Fax: (518)262-6884
Glenna Winnie, M.D., Dir.
Research Activities and Fields: Cystic fibrosis, including immunological, viral, and bacterial studies of patients with the disease. Also performs studies on lung injury. **Formerly:** Cystic Fibrosis Care, Research and Teaching Center.

Armand-Frappier Institute
Immunology Research Center
See: Entry 2092

★5309★ Ball State University
Human Genetics and Bioethics Education Laboratory
2000 Univ. Ave.
Muncie, IN 47306
Phone: (317)285-8840
Fax: (317)285-1624
Dr. Jon R. Hendrix, Dir.
Research Activities and Fields: Human genetics and bioethics education designed to meet the unique needs of specific population groups. Conducts needs assessment surveys, tabulates and analyzes data, and designs, implements, and evaluates workshops for specific groups, including lawyers, medical doctors, classroom teachers, clergy, and prospective parents. Participates in statewide genetic disease program. **E-mail Address:** 01jrhendrix@leo.bsuvc.bsu.edu.

Baylor College of Medicine
Biochemical Genetics Laboratory
See: Entry 4880

★5310★ Baylor College of Medicine
Human Genome Center
1 Baylor Plaza
Houston, TX 77030
Phone: (713)798-5669
Fax: (713)798-5386
David L. Nelson, Ph.D., Dir.
Research Activities and Fields: Genes and their role in human diseases. Specific areas of

study include chromosomes 6, 15, 17, and X. **Publications:** *Baylor Genome Center News* (quarterly newsletter). **E-mail Address:** nelson@bcm.tmc.edu.

★5311★ **Baylor College of Medicine Institute for Molecular Genetics**
1 Baylor Plaza
Houston, TX 77030
Phone: (713)798-6522
Fax: (713)798-6521
Dr. Arthur L. Beauder, Dir.

Research Activities and Fields: Basic research in genetics includes determination of the molecular organization of the HPRT gene, gene replacement therapy, gene expression, structure of human chromosome, molecular studies of cystic fibrosis, gene mapping, glycerol kinase deficiency, cell protein synthesis, recombinant DNA techniques, teratology, dysmorphology, clinical cytogenetics, somatic gene transfer, human lipid storage diseases, molecular biology of immune development and human immunodeficiencies, DNA repair and replication, mechanisms of regulation and expression of liver specific genes, molecular genetics of heritable eye diseases, prenatal diagnosis of congenital malformations and in utero therapy of these lesions, and characterization of families of transgenic mice that show mutant phenotypes. Also coordinates research and patient services in the field of molecular genetics. **Formerly:** Robert J. Kleberg, Jr., Center for Human Genetics (1986).

★5312★ **Baylor College of Medicine Kleberg Cytogenetic Laboratory**
1 Baylor Plaza, Rm 15E
Houston, TX 77030
Phone: (713)798-4984
Fax: (713)798-3157
Lisa Shaffer, PhD, Dir.

Research Activities and Fields: High-resolution chromosome analysis and development of molecular diagnostic methods for cytogenetic disorders and chromosomal studies.

★5313★ **Baylor College of Medicine Kleberg DNA Diagnostic Laboratory**
Texas Medical Center
1 Baylor Plaza, Rm. T538
Houston, TX 77030
Phone: (713)798-6536
Fax: (713)798-6584
C. Sue Richards, PhD, Dir.

Research Activities and Fields: DNA-based testing for diagnosis, including carrier detection, prenatal diagnosis of more than 15 genetic diseases, densitometric detection of deletion and duplication mutations, estimations of carrier risk for cystic fibrosis, and rapid diagnosis of Duchenne muscular dystrophy with the multiplex amplication assay.

★5314★ **Boston University Center for Human Genetics**
80 E. Concord St.
Boston, MA 02118-2394
Phone: (617)638-7083
Fax: (617)638-7092
Aubrey Milunsky, D.Sc., Dir.

Research Activities and Fields: Routine and specialized chromosome studies, prenatal diagnosis of genetic disorders, molecular genetic (DNA) analysis for diagnosis and carrier detection, maternal serum triple screening, biochemical genetic studies, cancer cytogenetics, paternity testing with DNA analysis, and genetic counseling and birth defects evaluation.

★5315★ **California Institute of Biological Research**
11099 N. Torrey Pines Rd., Ste. 300
La Jolla, CA 92037
Phone: (619)535-5471
Fax: (619)535-5472
Dr. McCellion, Resident Dir.

Research Activities and Fields: Physical mapping of bacterial and human genomes, including tissue cultures, retrotransposons, transposons, and enzyme purification.

★5316★ **Case Western Reserve University Center for Human Genetics**
University of Hospitals of Cleveland
11001 Cedar Ave., Ste. 510
Cleveland, OH 44106
Phone: (216)844-3936
Fax: (216)844-7497
Huntington F. Willard, Ph.D.

Research Activities and Fields: Human genetics, clinical genetics, molecular genetics, and cytogenetics. **Formerly:** Genetics Center (1992).

Case Western Reserve University Center for Inherited Disorders of Energy Metabolism
See: Entry 4881

★5317★ **Case Western Reserve University Cystic Fibrosis and Pediatric Pulmonary Center**
2101 Adelbert Rd.
Cleveland, OH 44106
Phone: (216)844-3267
Fax: (216)844-5916
Dr. Pamela B. Davis, Dir.

Research Activities and Fields: Cystic fibrosis and pulmonary physiology in children, including basic and clinical studies on evolution and pathology of pulmonary lesion in cystic fibrosis, abnormal mucous secretions of patients with cystic fibrosis, developmental biology of the lung, pulmonary physiology, treatment of chronic obstructive pulmonary disease, intracellular signalling, electrolyte transport and membrane permeability of intestinal, sweat, and respiratory epithelial and individual cells and membrane biopotentials, gene therapy of pulmonary diseases, and inflammation in the cystic fibrosis lung. Asthma studies include basic cell biology of airways and studies of therapeutic regimens for safety and efficacy. Seeks to develop a comprehensive therapeutic regimen for cystic fibrosis. **Formerly:** Cystic Fibrosis Teaching, Research and Care Center; Cystic Fibrosis Teaching, Research and Care Institute.

★5318★ **Center for Human Genetics**
PO Box 770
Bar Harbor, ME 04609-0770
Phone: (207)288-5815
Melba Wilson, Dir.

Research Activities and Fields: Epidemiological and laboratory studies in human genetics, including studies on retinitis pigmentosa, hemochromatosis, hemophilia, Down's syndrome, and cystic fibrosis. **Publications:** Newsletter (three or four times per year). **Formerly:** Genetic Counseling Center.

★5319★ **Center for the Improvement of Human Functioning International, Inc. Research Division**
3100 N. Hillside
Wichita, KS 67219
Phone: (316)682-3100
Fax: (316)682-5052
Hugh Riordan, M.D., Dir.

Research Activities and Fields: Human genetic variability and its effects on body chemistry, health and disease, and diagnosis and treatment, especially cancer. Also investigates the measurement of naturally occurring infrared emission from the human body. **Formerly:** Olive W. Garvey Center for the Improvement of Human Functioning, Inc.

★5320★ **City of Hope Beckman Research Institute Department of Biochemical Genetics**
1450 E. Duarte Rd.
Duarte, CA 91010
Phone: (818)359-8111
Dr. Akira Yoshida, Department Dir.

Research Activities and Fields: Biochemical genetics, including phosphoglycerate kinase, glucose-6-phosphate dehydrogenase, blood groups, and alcohol metabolizing enzymes.

★5321★ **Columbia University Center for Reproductive Sciences**
630 W. 168th St.
New York, NY 10032
Phone: (212)305-4178
Fax: (212)305-3869
Georgiana M. Jagiello, M.D., Dir.

Research Activities and Fields: Genetics and early development. Gathers comprehensive information on the reproductive mechanisms that ultimately result in the production of mammalian germ cells. The Center includes the closely integrated Divisions of Genetics of Reproduction.

★5322★ **Columbia University Molecular Genetics Laboratory**
722 W. 168th St., Box 23
New York, NY 10032
Phone: (212)960-5640
Fax: (212)781-2661
Dr. Conrad Gilliam, Dir.

Research Activities and Fields: Human molecular genetics, including genetic and physical mapping of human chromosomes, and the mapping and characterization of human disease genes. **Formerly:** Molecular Research Laboratory.

★5323★ **Cystic Fibrosis Center**
Cedars-Sinai Medical Center, Rm. 4430
8700 Beverly Blvd.
Los Angeles, CA 90048
Phone: (310)855-6310
Fax: (310)657-1778
Dr. Benjamin M. Kagan, Dir.

Research Activities and Fields: Sputum in cystic fibrosis of the pancreas, including studies of nature of sputum and liquefaction, lysozyme content, L-forms of bacteria, and observations on new antimicrobial agents. **Publications:** *Current Pediatric Therapy* (biennially).

★ 5324 ★ **Cystic Fibrosis Center**
St. Christopher's Hospital for Children
Erie Ave. at Front St.
Philadelphia, PA 19134
Phone: (215)427-4801
Fax: (215)427-4805
Daniel Schidlow, M.D., Dir.

Research Activities and Fields: Cystic fibrosis and other chronic respiratory diseases, including cystic fibrosis of the pancreas in children, epidemiology of lung infections, airway injury in children, lung mechanics in infants, developmental respiratory physiology, and clinical trials for new therapies against cystic fibrosis. **Formerly:** Pediatric Pulmonary and Cystic Fibrosis Center; Cystic Fibrosis Research Center.

★ 5325 ★ **Cystic Fibrosis Center**
Pediatric Pulmonary Dept., UHN 56
3181 SW Sam Jackson Park Rd.
Portland, OR 97201
Phone: (503)494-8023
Fax: (503)494-6670
Michael A. Wall, M.D., Research Dir.

Research Activities and Fields: Cystic fibrosis, including laboratory and clinical studies of molecular abnormalities in cystic fibrosis and lyses of pulmonary mucus.

★ 5326 ★ **Cystic Fibrosis Foundation**
6931 Arlington Rd., Ste. 200
Bethesda, MD 20814
Phone: (301)951-4422
Fax: (301)951-6378
Robert Beall, Ph.D., Pres.

Research Activities and Fields: Conducts and supports research into the causes and treatment of cystic fibrosis. The Research Development Program involves a network of research centers supported by the Foundation; also supports many care centers thoughout the United States. **Publications:** Annual Report; *Commitment* (quarterly).

★ 5327 ★ **Cystic Fibrosis Research Center**
Northwestern Univ.
2300 Children's Plaza
Chicago, IL 60614
Phone: (312)880-4354
Dr. John D. Lloyd-Still, Dir.

Research Activities and Fields: Cystic fibrosis, pediatric pulmonary, and gastrointestinal diseases, including studies on screening techniques and clinical research procedures.

★ 5328 ★ **Duke University**
Cystic Fibrosis Research Center
PO Box 2994
Durham, NC 27710
Phone: (919)684-2289
Fax: (919)684-2292
Marc Majure, M.D., Dir.

Research Activities and Fields: Cystic fibrosis and related respiratory diseases of children.

★ 5329 ★ **Emory University**
Cystic Fibrosis Care, Teaching and Research Center
2040 Ridgewood NE
Atlanta, GA 30322
Phone: (404)727-5728
Dr. Daniel B. Caplan, Dir.

Research Activities and Fields: Cystic fibrosis and respiratory and gastrointestinal diseases of children.

★ 5330 ★ **Florida Institute of Technology**
Medical Genetics Laboratory
4340 W. New Haven Ave., Hwy. 192
West Melbourne, FL 32904
Phone: (407)768-8188
Fax: (407)723-1907
Dick Darlington, Gen.Mgr.

Research Activities and Fields: Human genetics, including genome organization and human mouth mapping using molecular and cytogenetics techniques.

Hereditary Cancer Institute
See: Entry 6046

★ 5331 ★ **Indiana University-Purdue University at Indianapolis**
Cystic Fibrosis and Pediatric Pulmonary Clinic
702 Barnhill Dr., Rm. 2750
Indianapolis, IN 46202-5225
Phone: (317)274-7208
Fax: (317)274-9773
Howard Eigen, M.D., Dir.

Research Activities and Fields: Cystic fibrosis and chronic lung diseases, including clinical studies of pediatric pulmonary, gastrointestinal, genetic problems, and lung inflammation. **Formerly:** Cystic Fibrosis Research Center.

★ 5332 ★ **Indiana University-Purdue University at Indianapolis**
Human Genetics Center
Sch. of Medicine
975 W. Walnut St., IB 130
Indianapolis, IN 46202-5251
Phone: (317)274-2241
Fax: (317)274-2387
Joe C. Christian, M.D., Chm.

Research Activities and Fields: Human population genetics, biochemical genetics, cytogenetics, molecular genetics, and clinical genetics. Past projects have included research on genetic counseling, carrier detection in genetic diseases, genetics of cleft lipand palate, twin studies, genetic linkage in Huntington's and Alzheimer's diseases, cloning of opioid receptor, genetics of aging, maternal influences in human families, protein glycosylation in diabetes mellitus, chromosomal abnormalities as causes of human diseases and defects, and familial factors associated with oral facial development.

★ 5333 ★ **International Center for Skeletal Dysplasia**
St. Joseph Hospital
7620 York Rd.
Towson, MD 21204
Phone: (410)337-1250
Fax: (410)337-1042
Dr. Steven Kopits, Dir.

Research Activities and Fields: Skeletal dysplasia, particularly dwarfism. Studies include metatropic dysplasia, a rare form of dwarfism identified in 1966.

★ 5334 ★ **Jackson Laboratory**
600 Main St.
Bar Harbor, ME 04609-1500
Phone: (207)288-3371
Fax: (207)288-5094
Kenneth Paigen, Ph.D., Dir.

Research Activities and Fields: Formal genetics, molecular genetics, developmental genetics, physiological genetics, immunology, cell biology, and biochemistry as related to cancer, diabetes, anemias, other human diseases, as well as normal growth and development. Annually produces 2,000,000 genetically standardized mutant and inbred mice strains for its own research staff and research workers throughout the world. **Publications:** Scientific Report; Annual Report; *Inside the Jackson Laboratory* (quarterly); *Animal Health & Genetic Quality Control Report* (quarterly); *Handbook of Genetically Standardized JAX Mice.* **E-mail Address:** library@aretha.jax.org. **Formerly:** Roscoe B. Jackson Memorial Laboratory.

Johns Hopkins University
Center for Hereditary Eye Diseases
See: Entry 13604

★ 5335 ★ **Johns Hopkins University**
Cystic Fibrosis Research Center
212 Wood Basic Science
725 N. Wolfe St.
Baltimore, MD 21205
Phone: (410)955-7166
Fax: (410)955-1609
Dr. William B. Guggino, Dir.

Research Activities and Fields: Cystic fibrosis and related fields, including epithelial cell transport, molecular genetics, respiratory cell biology, and biochemistry. **E-mail Address:** wguggin@wpo.bs.edu.

Johns Hopkins University
Welch Laboratory for Applied Bioinformatics
See: Entry 7016

★ 5336 ★ **Laval University**
Medical Research Centre
Ontogenesis and Molecular Genetics Research Group
2705, boulevard Laurier
Ste. Foy, PQ, Canada G1V 4G2
Phone: (418)654-2103
Fax: (418)654-2748
Jean H. Dussault, Dir.

Research Activities and Fields: Antidepressants and hypothalamic-pituitary-adrenocortical system; identification of genes associated with the phenotypes of bipolar illness and schizophrenia; molecular mechanisms controlling genetic expression; thyroid hormones and central nervous system development; molecular genetics of myotonic dystrophy; congenital malformations; implication of cytoskeletal and nucleoskeletal proteins in morphonogenetic and differentiation processes; molecular genetics of Charcot-Marie-Tooth disease; positional cloning and identification of the gene responsible for juvenile wide angle glaucoma; molecular mechanisms of dopaminergic receptor regulation; signal transduction; control of cell cycle; studies on the role of free radicals and antioxidant defenses in tumorigenesis and neurodegenerative pr ocesses; analysis of endocytitic processes of the EGF receptor; limb regeneration in the amphibian: Homeobox; position information and pattern formation.

★ 5337 ★ Laval University
**Molecular Microbiology and Protein
  Engineering Group**
Departemente de microbiologie
Faculte de medecine
Pav. Charles Marchand Blvd.
Quebec, PQ, Canada G1K 7P4
Phone: (418)656-3070
Fax: (418)656-7176
Roger C. Levesque, Dir.

Research Activities and Fields: Structure-function analysis of B-lactamases, dihydrofolate reductase and superoxide dismutase in pathogenic microorganisms. Studies also include molecular genetics, phylogeny, and evolution of multiresistant transposons, and sequencing pseudomonas genome. **E-mail Address:** rclevesq@rsus.ulaval.ca.

**Laval University
Saint-Francois-d'Assise Hospital Research
  Centre**
See: Entry 11274

★ 5338 ★ Louisiana State University
Genetics Section of Pediatrics
Medical Center
1501 Kings Hwy.
Shreveport, LA 71130
Phone: (318)674-6088
T.F. Thurmon, M.D., Dir.

Research Activities and Fields: Clinical applications of genetics, biochemical genetics, and cytogenetics. Studies include chromatographic diagnostic techniques, heredity of dysmorphic syndromes, and chromosome aberrations in cancer. **Formerly:** Birth Defects Center (1987).

★ 5339 ★ Medical College of Pennsylvania
  and Hahnemann University
**Hahnemann Cystic Fibrosis Research
  Center**
230 N. Broad St.
Philadelphia, PA 19102
Phone: (215)762-7766
Fax: (215)762-1601
Dr. Douglas S. Holsclaw, Jr., Dir.

Research Activities and Fields: Cystic fibrosis and pediatric pulmonary disease, including studies on tissue culture, gene identification, gene transfer and methods of evaluation of effect of treatment.

★ 5340 ★ Medical College of Wisconsin
Cystic Fibrosis Research Center
Milwaukee Children's Hospital
PO Box 1997
Milwaukee, WI 53201
Phone: (414)266-2372
Dr. M. L. Splaingard, Dir.

Research Activities and Fields: Cystic fibrosis, chest impedance measurements, and newborn screening studies. Provides patient care as a service to referring physicians and instruction for small groups of medical students from the College.

**Miami Children's Hospital Research
  Institute**
See: Entry 3343

★ 5341 ★ Molecular Diagnostics
  Laboratory
Cedars-Sinai Medical Center
110 George Burns Rd.
Davis, 2069
Los Angeles, CA 90048
Phone: (310)855-7627
Fax: (310)652-8010
Dr. Julie Korenburg, Contact

Research Activities and Fields: DNA isolation and diagnostics, including Southern blotting, libraryscreening, subcloning, probe growth, and preparation. **E-mail Address:** jkorenberg@mailgate.csmc.edu.

★ 5342 ★ Molecular Genetics / Oncology
  Laboratory
Pathology Dept., B120
The Children's Hospital
1056 E. 19th Ave.
Denver, CO 80218
Phone: (303)864-6440
Fax: (303)831-4112
Vincent Wilson, Ph.D., Dir.

Research Activities and Fields: Research and testing for genetic diseases, focusing on cancer. DNA diagnostics testing services include both major and minor breakpoint cluster region (BCR) rearrangments; pre-B cell ALL t(1;19) PCR analysis; Y DNA PCR and probe analysis; retinoblastoma gene deletion and linkage analysis; Wilms' tumor gene deletion analysis; and DNA and RNA isolation for special studies. Research efforts, both basic and applied, are focused on mechanisms of carcinogenesis, emphasizing the development of sensitive methods and techniques for the early (pre-clinical) detection of cancer; measuring biological (genetic) damage induced by human exposure to toxic agents; and determining genetic markers of diagnostic and prognostic value in the clinical care of cancer patients.

★ 5343 ★ New England Regional Genetics
  Group
PO Box 670
Mount Desert, ME 04660
Phone: (207)288-2704
Fax: (207)288-2705
Joseph Robinson, M.P.H., Coord.

Research Activities and Fields: Human genetic services planning and education, including continuing education in cytogenetics, studies of

prevalence of birth defects in New England, quality assurance for alpha-fetoprotein (AFP) testing, investigation of new markers for prenatal screening, study of heterozygosity for Tay-Sachs disease in Franco-Americans in New England, study of frequency of MCAD deficiency in SIDS cases, and development of genetic educational materials. **Publications:** Regional Newsletter; *Speakers' Bureau; The Genetic Resource.*

★ 5344 ★ Oregon Health Sciences
  University
Pediatric Metabolic Laboratory
Dept. of Molecular and Medical Genetics
3181 SW Sam Jackson Park Rd., L-473
Portland, OR 97201
Phone: (503)494-8392
Fax: (503)494-7645
Nancy Kennaway, Ph.D., Dir.

Research Activities and Fields: Inborn errors of metabolism and mitochondrial myopathies. **Formerly:** Molecular Diagnostic Laboratory.

**Oregon State University
Center for Gene Research and
  Biotechnology**
See: Entry 2725

★ 5345 ★ Pennsylvania State University
**Center for Developmental and Health
  Genetics**
101 Amy Gardner House
University Park, PA 16802
Phone: (814)865-1717
Fax: (814)865-4768
Robert Plomin, Dir.

Research Activities and Fields: Role of genetics in infant, child, and adolescent behavioral development, in aging, and in common drug and health problems. Also studies molecular, nutritional and immunological genetics. Uses human and animal model research projects to study personality, cognition, functional capacity, immune system functioning, and use and effects of alcohol and tobacco. **Formerly:** Institute for the Study of Human Development.

★ 5346 ★ Rockefeller University
**Laboratory of Biochemical Genetics and
  Metabolism**
1230 York Ave.
New York, NY 10021
Phone: (212)327-7700
Fax: (212)327-7165
Prof. Jan L. Breslow, M.D., Contact

Research Activities and Fields: Human genetic susceptibility to atherosclerosis, especially the molecular genetics and clincial significance of the apolipoproteins, a group of proteins that coat the lipoprotein particles and determine their metabolism.

★ 5347 ★ Saginaw Valley State University
Genetic Research Laboratory
2250 Pierce Rd.
University Center, MI 48710
Phone: (517)790-4358
Fax: (517)790-2717
Dr. Charles F. Pelzer, Head

Research Activities and Fields: Molecular genetics, emphasizing electrophoresis and Southern Blots of human DNA, isoelectric focusing of blood proteins in health and disease such as breast cancer, and biochemical genetics of red cell isozymes in the mouse. Performs restriction fragment length polymorphism (RFLP) analysis to help map human chromosone number 10 and Southern blotting to identify tumor suppressor genes. **E-mail Address:** lawrence@tardis.svsu.edu.

★5348★ **Sherbrooke University**
Molecular Biology Research Centre
Departement de Microbiologie
Faculte de Medecine
3001, 12e Ave. N.
Sherbrooke, PQ, Canada J1H 5N4
Phone: (819)564-5321
Fax: (819)564-5392
Joseph M. Weber, Dir.

Research Activities and Fields: Gene expression in vitro and in vivo, including the recombination of viral and cellular genes, alternative splicing of RNA, expression and function of transformation genes, and clinical applications of PCR. **E-mail Address:** j.weber@courrier.usherb.ca.

★5349★ **Southwest Biomedical Research**
Institute
6401 E. Thomas Rd.
Scottsdale, AZ 85251
Phone: (602)945-4363
Fax: (602)946-1005
Charles M. Atkinson, Pres.

Research Activities and Fields: Genetic diseases and chromosome disorders, cancer and cancer genetics, transplantation genetics, kidney and other transplants, immunogenetics, recombinant DNA diagnostics and research, birth defects, Jewish genetic diseases, prenatal education, and prenatal diagnosis. **Publications:** *Journal of Cancer Genetics and Cytogenetics.*

★5350★ **Southwest Foundation for**
Biomedical Research
Molecular Genetics Laboratory
Dept. of Genetics
PO Box 28147
San Antonio, TX 78228-0147
Phone: (210)674-1410
Fax: (210)670-3316
James E. Hixson, Ph.D., Dir.

Research Activities and Fields: Molecular genetics of heart disease in humans and nonhuman primates.

★5351★ **Stanford University**
Beckman Center for Molecular and Genetic
Medicine
School of Medicine
Dept. of Biochemistry
Stanford, CA 94305-5425
Phone: (415)723-7184
Fax: (415)725-4951
Dr. Paul Berg, Dir.

Research Activities and Fields: Molecular understanding of critical biological functions and how these are affected by disease, including study of genes related to human disease, development of new diagnostic tests for known and newly recognized diseases, and development of therapies based on gene or cell replacement models.

★5352★ **Stanford University**
Interdepartmental Medical Genetics
Program
Howard Hughes Med. Inst.
Beckman Ctr.
Stanford, CA 94305-5428
Phone: (415)725-8089
Fax: (415)725-8112
Dr. Uta Francke, Training Program Dir.

Research Activities and Fields: Molecular basis of heritable disorders, including polygenic and multi-factorial diseases, chromosome structure and function, and genome and gene mapping. Develops methods to manipulate and study large fragments of DNA and animal models and new treatment modalities of human genetic disease by homologous recombination. **E-mail Address:** mh.uta.@forsythe.stanford.edu.

★5353★ **State University of New York**
Health Science Center at Syracuse
Robert C. Schwartz Cystic Fibrosis Center
750 E. Adams, 5th Fl.-Pediatrics
Syracuse, NY 13210
Phone: (315)464-6323
Fax: (315)464-7564
Dr. Phillip T. Swender, Dir.

Research Activities and Fields: Cystic fibrosis, including clinical studies. Also conducts genetic studies into the cause of cystic fibrosis.

★5354★ **Texas A&M University**
Center for Genome Research
Alkek Institute of Biosciences and Technology
2121 W. Holcombe Blvd.
Houston, TX 77030-3303
Phone: (713)677-7651
Fax: (713)677-7689
Dr. Robert D. Wells, Dir.

Research Activities and Fields: Structure and biology of DNA in living cells and viruses and its role in the developmental expression of genetic information. Specific research areas include cancer and other human genetic diseases, maintenance and stability of chromosome ends, and the processing of information from DNA into functional messenger ribonucleic acid (RNA) for expression into proteins.

★5355★ **Texas A&M University**
W.M. Keck Center for Genome Informatics
Alkek Institute of Biosciences and Technology
2121 W. Holcombe Blvd.
Houston, TX 77030-3303
Phone: (713)677-7725
Fax: (713)677-7700
Dr. Leland Ellis, Dir.

Research Activities and Fields: Genome informatics and biocomputing, with emphasis on genomes of agricultural and biomedical interest.

★5356★ **Texas Southern University**
Biochemistry and Molecular Biology
Laboratory
3201 Wheeler Ave.
Houston, TX 77004
Phone: (713)527-7990
Dr. Marian Hillar, Head

Research Activities and Fields: Cell biology and genetics, emphasizing control of gene expression in normal cells and carcinogenesis, particularly isolation and purification of deprimerones (low molecular-weight peptides).

★5357★ **Tulane University**
Cystic Fibrosis Research Center and
Pediatric Pulmonary Disease Center
1430 Tulane Ave.
New Orleans, LA 70112
Phone: (504)588-5601
Fax: (504)588-5490
Dr. Robert C. Beckerman, Dir.

Research Activities and Fields: Cystic fibrosis, bronchopulmonary dysplasia, apnea, sleep disordered breathing, SIDS, and other acute and chronic pulmonary diseases, including basic and clinical studies on their causes and treatment, conducted in the three medical schools.

U.S. Department of Energy
Lawrence Berkeley Laboratory
Cholesterol Research Center
See: Entry 4902

U.S. Department of Health and Human
Services
National Cancer Institute
Laboratory of Genetics
See: Entry 6187

U.S. Department of Health and Human
Services
National Heart, Lung, and Blood Institute
Division of Intramural Research
Laboratory of Molecular Hematology
See: Entry 6205

U.S. Department of Health and Human
Services
National Institute of Allergy and Infectious
Diseases
Division of Allergy, Immunology, and
Transplantation
Genetics and Transplantation Branch
See: Entry 2128

U.S. Department of Health and Human
Services
National Institute of Allergy and Infectious
Diseases
Laboratory of Immunogenetics
See: Entry 2134

★5358★ **U.S. Department of Health and**
Human Services
National Institute of Child Health and
Human Development
Center for Research for Mothers and
Children
Developmental Biology, Genetics and
Teratology Branch
6100 Executive Blvd., Rm. 4B01
Bethesda, MD 20892
Phone: (301)496-5541
Fax: (301)402-2085
Dr. Delbert H. Dayton, Chief

Research Activities and Fields: Branch supports research in: 1) developmental genetics to elucidate the hereditary influences underlying developmental disorders and to understand the hereditary instructions for the developmental process (includes epidemiologic studies of families, twins, and populations, clinical studies of phenotype changes in relation to gene abnormalities and biochemical malfunctions as well as basic biologic approaches); 2) developmental biology to determine the mechanisms underlying human development as well as how specialized tissues and organs form from a series of divisions of a single fertilized egg; 3) developmental neurobiology to understand how the nervous system develops in its architectural complexity and how highly specific connections with other neurons or target organs occur; 4) teratology to assess adverse genetic and/or environmental influences on development and to clarify mechanisms by which developmental aberrations are produced (emphasis is on studies of structural defects (e.g. neural tube defects) and normal and abnormal limb developments); and 5) developmental immunology to understand maturation of the immune system and responses to neonatal infections.

★ 5359 ★ U.S. Department of Health and
  Human Services
National Institute of Child Health and
  Human Development
Human Genetics Branch
Drug Biotransformation Section
NIH Bldg. 10, 95242
9000 Rockville Pike
Bethesda, MD 20892
Phone: (301)496-8825
Dr. Ida S. Owens, Section Head

Research Activities and Fields: Studies focus on Phase II drug metabolism--i.e., conjugation reactions in which enzymes (UDP glucuronosyltransferases) use as substrates bilirubin and endogenous steroids or oxygenated drugs, carcinogens, and other environmental pollutants. Mechanisms of gene expression and enzyme induction are explored using immunochemical and recombinant DNA techniques, inbred strains of mice, and normal and mutant cells in culture. An additional goal is to understand the basis for human genetic diseases involving variants of the Phase II enzymes.

★ 5360 ★ U.S. Department of Health and
  Human Services
National Institute of Child Health and
  Human Development
Intramural Research Program
Human Genetics Branch
NIH Bldg. 10
9000 Rockville Pike
Bethesda, MD 20892
Phone: (301)496-6683
Fax: (301)402-0234
Dr. William A. Gahl, Chief

Research Activities and Fields: Branch conducts studies on the etiology, diagnosis, and treatment of genetic and developmental disorders of young people. Activities also encompass basic studies on eukaryotic gene expression utilizing recombinant DNA methodology. Research projects concern genetic disorders of lipid and carbohydrate metabolism, heritable disorders of bone and connective tissue, lysosomal storage diseases, and other inborn errors of metabolism. Principal Branch components are the: Biochemical Genetics Section, Cellular Differentiation Section, Developmental Genetics Section, Genetic Disorders of Drug Metabolism Section, Unit on Connective Tissued Disorders, and Unit on Heurogenetics.

★ 5361 ★ U.S. Department of Health and
  Human Services
National Institute of Child Health and
  Human Development
Laboratory of Molecular Genetics
NIH Bldg. 6
9000 Rockville Pike
Bethesda, MD 20892
Phone: (301)496-4448
Fax: (301)496-0243
Dr. Igor Dawid, Chief

Research Activities and Fields: Laboratory examines gene transmission, recombination, and regulation of genetic functions during development through studies in molecular and cellular biology. Model systems under investigation include bacterial and animal viruses, transformed animal cells, yeasts, and *Xenopus* embryos, and the fruit fly *Drosophila melanogaster*. Research is focused on cell interactions in development, the regulation of gene expression, mechanisms of protein/nucleic acid interactions, and the genetic regulation of animal development. Activities are carried out in the Laboratory's Developmental Biology Section, Microbial Genetics Section, Molecular Regulation Section, and Molecular Genetics of Lower Eukaryotes Section.

★ 5362 ★ U.S. Department of Health and
  Human Services
National Institute of Diabetes and
  Digestive and Kidney Diseases
**Division of Diabetes, Endocrinology, and
  Metabolic Diseases**
Cystic Fibrosis Research Program
5333 Westbard Ave., Rm. 607
Bethesda, MD 20892
Phone: (301)594-7567
Dr. Judith Fradkin, Director

Research Activities and Fields: The Cystic Fibrosis Research Program supports investigator-initiated research projects related to the etiology, pathogenesis, diagnosis, and treatment of cystic fibrosis. In addition, the Program supports a cystic fibrosis research center and small Business Innovation Research Grants. **Additional Contact Information:** Jeannie Wooford, Grants Assistant.

★ 5363 ★ U.S. Department of Health and
  Human Services
National Institute of Diabetes and
  Digestive and Kidney Diseases
**Division of Diabetes, Endocrinology, and
  Metabolic Diseases**
Diabetes Programs Branch
5333 Westbard Ave., Rm. 626
Bethesda, MD 20892
Phone: (301)594-7580
Fax: (301)496-9721
Dr. Judith Fradkin, Acting Chief

Research Activities and Fields: The major aims of NIDDK's Diabetes Programs are to define the disease fully in terms of its causes and many complications and to find improved methods for the diagnosis, treatment, cure, and prevention of both the disease and its chronic complications. The Program provides support for basic and clinical studies related to the etiology, pathogenesis, prevention, diagnosis, treatment, and cure of diabetes mellitus, as well as for investigations related to pancreas and islet transplantation, automated insulin delivery systems, and glucose sensors. Programs include the Diabetes Centers Program, Diabetes Clinical Trials Program, and the Diabetes Research Program.

★ 5364 ★ U.S. Department of Health and
  Human Services
National Institute of Diabetes and
  Digestive and Kidney Diseases
Division of Intramural Research
Genetics and Biochemistry Branch
NIH Bldg. 10, Rm. 9D15
9000 Rockville Pike
Bethesda, MD 20892
Phone: (301)496-2710
Fax: (301)496-9878
Dr. R. Daniel Camerini-Otero, Chief

Research Activities and Fields: Branch conducts studies in clinical, biochemical, developmental, and molecular genetics. The range of current projects covers a wide field, from the very basic (e.g., mechanisms of genetic recombination and gene conversion in mammalian cells, DNA-mediated gene transfer, the regulation of gene expression, the molecular biology of early development in *Xenopus laevis*, biosynthesis and transport of lysosomal proteins, the molecular mechanisms of endocytosis, and the biochemical and molecular bases of human genetic disorders) to the more applied (i.e., development of new diagnostic tests and carrier detection for a number of human genetic diseases and the development of new techniques for gene purification and transfer).

U.S. Department of Health and Human
  Services
National Institute of Diabetes and
  Digestive and Kidney Diseases
Laboratory of Chemical Biology
See: Entry 2646

U.S. Department of Health and Human
  Services
National Institute of Environmental Health
  Sciences
Laboratory of Molecular Genetics
See: Entry 5108

★ 5365 ★ U.S. Department of Health and
  Human Services
National Institute of General Medical
  Sciences
Genetics Program
5333 Westbard Ave.
Bethesda, MD 20892
Phone: (301)594-7773
Fax: (301)594-7727
Judith H. Greenberg, Ph.D., Director

Research Activities and Fields: Program supports genetics research to better understand the fundamental processes and mechanisms of inheritance. An objective of the program is the eventual prevention and improved treatment of genetic ills in man, including multifactoral diseases with a strong hereditary component, such as diabetes, atherosclerosis, hypertension, and schizophrenia. Research training support provided by the Genetics Program includes: 1) institutional predoctoral programs, which sponsor research training in the broad field of genetic principles and mechanisms; 2) individual post-doctoral awards, which support training for research that will lead to further understanding of genetic processes and of human genetic disorders; and 3) institutional postdoctoral programs (with emphasis on medical genetics), which provide advanced and special research training in genetics. Research is concerned with genetic information within cells and the ways in which that information is organized, transmitted, and expressed in health and disease. Research ranges from studies on nucleic acid chemistry to population and medical genetics. Topics include the physical and organic chemistry of nucleic acids; replication of DNA; mechanisms of mutagenesis; chromosome structure and mechanics; extrachromosomal inheritance; transcription, translation, and post-translational modification of macromolecules; developmental genetics; cytogenetics; and population genetics.

U.S. Department of Health and Human Services
National Institute of Mental Health
Intramural Research Programs Division (Clinical Research)
Clinical Neurogenetics Branch
See: Entry 7638

U.S. Department of Health and Human Services
National Institute of Neurological Disorders and Stroke
Developmental and Metabolic Neurology Branch
See: Entry 8445

U.S. Department of Health and Human Services
National Institute of Neurological Disorders and Stroke
Division of Convulsive, Developmental, and Neuromuscular Disorders
Developmental Neurology Branch
See: Entry 8447

★ 5366 ★ University of Alabama at Birmingham
Gregory Fleming James Cystic Fibrosis Research Center
1918 University Blvd.
BHSB 796
Birmingham, AL 35294-0005
Phone: (205)934-7210
Fax: (205)934-7593
Dr. Eric J. Sorscher, Dir.

Research Activities and Fields: Cystic fibrosis, including electrolyte transport and metabolism, mucin secretion and biochemistry, genetics, regulation of immune mechanisms, membrane traffic regulation, gene therapy, and pharmacologic therapy. **Formerly:** Cystic Fibrosis Research Center; FOB James Cystic Fibrosis Research Center (1986).

★ 5367 ★ University of Alabama at Birmingham
Laboratory of Medical Genetics
Univ. Sta.
Birmingham, AL 35294
Phone: (205)934-4983
Fax: (205)975-6389
Dr. Wayne H. Finley, Dir.

Research Activities and Fields: Medical genetics. Performs cell culture and cytogenetic studies of cells derived by means of culture from tissue biopsies, leukocytes, and bone marrow. Patients and their families are referred for evaluation, pedigree analysis, cytogenetic, biochemical, and/or molecular genetics studies, prenatal diagnosis, and genetic counseling. Specific research projects include delineation and classification of birth defects, clinical cytogenetics, detection of enzyme deficiencies, DNA probe analysis, drug effects on cell growth, chromosome polymorphisms, epidemiological aspects of genetic disease, effectiveness of genetic counseling, cancer cytogenetics, and chromosome microdissection and PCR analysis. **E-mail Address:** pedp050@uab.dpo.uab.edu.

★ 5368 ★ University of Arkansas at Little Rock
Arkansas Children's Hospital Cystic Fibrosis Center
800 Marshall
Little Rock, AR 72202-3591
Phone: (501)320-1018
Fax: (501)320-3930
Dr. Robert Warren, Dir.

Research Activities and Fields: Cystic fibrosis and related respiratory diseases of children, including aerosol deposition and pulmonary function testing in children. **Formerly:** Cystic Fibrosis Research Center.

★ 5369 ★ University of California, Irvine
Division of Human Genetics
UCI Medical Center
Dept. of Pediatrics
PO Box 14091
Orange, CA 92613-1491
Phone: (714)456-5791
Fax: (714)456-5330
Maureen Bocian, M.D., Chief

Research Activities and Fields: Molecular genetics of alcohol metabolizing enzymes and fetal alcohol syndrome, cancer cytogenetics and oncogenes, the effects of genetic counseling on family coping and adaptation, bioethics and law, gene mapping of tuberous sclerosis, syndrome identification, heterogeneity and variability in genetic syndromes, teratology, genetics of common disorders, dysmorphology, and genetic epidemiology. **Formerly:** Division of Developmental Disabilities and Clinical Genetics.

University of California, Los Angeles
Dental Research Institute
See: Entry 4025

University of California, San Diego
Pediatric Pulmonary and Cystic Fibrosis Center
See: Entry 11621

University of Colorado
B.F. Stolinsky Research Laboratories
See: Entry 4325

★ 5370 ★ University of Colorado
Cystic Fibrosis Center
4200 E. Ninth Ave., C-220
Denver, CO 80262
Phone: (303)270-7518
Frank J. Accurso, Dir.

Research Activities and Fields: Cystic fibrosis and related respiratory diseases of children. Conducts studies of airway inflammation. Screens and performs longitudinal follow-ups of newborns. Provides clinical facilities for treatment and care of children and young adults suffering from these diseases.

★ 5371 ★ University of Colorado at Boulder
Institute for Behavioral Genetics
CB 447
Boulder, CO 80309
Phone: (303)492-2839
Fax: (303)492-2342
Dr. Toni N. Smolen, Asst.Dir.

Research Activities and Fields: Application of behavioral genetics to pharmacogenetics, learning disabilities, cognitive development, and vulnerability to drug abuse. Specific interests include genetics of aging, reading disability, genetic and neurobiological correlates of animal behavior, human alcohol studies, and genetic factors in personality and cognitive development of twins and adopted children. **E-mail Address:** smolent@ibg.colorado.edu.

University of Iowa
Birth Defects and Genetic Disorders Unit
See: Entry 2762

★ 5372 ★ University of Louisville
Louisville Twin Study
Medical-Dental Research Bldg.
Health Sciences Center
Louisville, KY 40292
Phone: (502)852-1090
Fax: (502)852-1093
Dr. Adam P. Matheny, Jr., Dir.

Research Activities and Fields: Human behavior genetics, including a longitudinal study of twins and siblings from birth to early adulthood, assessment of temperament and mental development, biomedical studies of twins, and multivariate analyses of their cognitive, perceptual, and motor skills.

★ 5373 ★ University of Miami
Cystic Fibrosis Research Center
PO Box 016820
Miami, FL 33101
Phone: (305)547-6641
Fax: (305)547-6309
Dr. Robert M. McKey, Jr., Dir.

Research Activities and Fields: Cystic fibrosis, asthma, pulmonary manifestations of pediatric AIDS, and related respiratory and gastrointestinal diseases of children. Also studies pediatric exercise physiology.

University of Miami
Mailman Center for Child Development
See: Entry 3364

★5374★ **University of Minnesota**
Cystic Fibrosis Center
Univ. of Minnesota Hospital
420 Delaware St. SE
Minneapolis, MN 55455
Phone: (612)624-7175
Fax: (612)624-0696
Dr. Warren J. Warwick, Dir.

Research Activities and Fields: Pulmonary diseases and cystic fibrosis, including pediatric pulmonary diseases, pulmonary physiology, infant pulmonary function, biochemistry of cystic fibrosis, nutrition, liver disease, inflamation, psychosocial intervention, home monitoring, heart-lung and lung transplantation, sweat test, bioengineering, biophysics, and physical therapy. Activities include development of high frequency compression therapy. **Publications:** *CF Guidebook.* **E-mail Address:** warwil100@maroon.tc.umn.edu.

★5375★ **University of Minnesota**
Institute of Human Genetics
420 Delaware St. SE
Box 206 UMHC
Minneapolis, MN 55455-0392
Phone: (612)624-3110
Fax: (612)626-7031
Dr. Anthony J. Faras, Dir.

Research Activities and Fields: Human genetics and developmental biology, including biochemical, molecular, and clinical genetics, cytogenetics, metabolism, and genetic counseling. Current research involves tumor viruses; gene transfer; eukaryotic gene regulation; rearrangement and regulation of immunoglobulin genes; molecular genetics of the major histocompatibility complex; genetic defects of human pigment genes; and bone marrow transplantion. **Publications:** *MicroChem News.* **E-mail Address:** ihg@lenti.med.umn.edu.

★5376★ **University of Missouri—Columbia**
Cystic Fibrosis Research Center
Univ. of Missouri
Health Sciences Center
Columbia, MO 65212
Phone: (314)882-6119
Giulio J. Barbero, M.D., Dir.

Research Activities and Fields: Conducts studies in the following areas: intracellular control mechanisms of secretion as they relate to cystic fibrosis, secretory mechanisms for water and electroytes in exocrine glands, structure and function of pulmonary glycoproteins in cystic fibrosis and other chronic pulmonary diseases, and therapies for pulmonary disease in cystic fibrosis.

★5377★ **University of Nebraska Medical Center**
Hattie B. Munroe Center for Human Genetics
4420 Dewey St.
Omaha, NE 68131
Phone: (402)559-5070
Fax: (402)559-7248
Warren G. Sanger, Ph.D, Dir.

Research Activities and Fields: Research and treatment concentrating in cancer cytogenetics and prenatal diagnosis, including lymphoma, leukemia, and solid tumor research, chromosome changes in response to treatment, diagnostics of chromosome abnormalities, and treatment of prenatal genetic conditions associated with mental retardation and disability. **E-mail Address:** WGANGER@UNMCVM.

★5378★ **University of Nebraska at Omaha**
Pediatric Pulmonary and Cystic Fibrosis Research Center
600 S. 42 St.
PO Box 985190
Omaha, NE 68198-5190
Phone: (402)559-5537
Fax: (402)559-7062
Dr. John L. Colombo, Dir.

Research Activities and Fields: Cystic fibrosis, including optimal use of antibiotics and respiratory therapy modalities; optimal use of aerosolized drug therapy; pancreatic function; effects of chronic aspiration, particularly on airway hyperactivity and inflammation; and bronchoalveolar lavage cytology in acute and chronic pediatric diseases. **Formerly:** Cystic Fibrosis Research Center.

★5379★ **University of Oklahoma**
Pulmonary and Cystic Fibrosis Center
Children's Hospital of Oklahoma
University Hospital
PO Box 26307
Oklahoma City, OK 73126
Phone: (405)271-6390
Fax: (405)271-3017
Dr. Santiago Reyes de la Rocha, Dir.

Research Activities and Fields: Cystic fibrosis and related respiratory diseases of children.

University of Pennsylvania
Referral Center for Animal Models of Human Genetic Disease
See: Entry 13230

★5380★ **University of Pittsburgh**
Cystic Fibrosis Research Center
3705 5th Ave.
Pittsburgh, PA 15213
Phone: (412)692-5630
Fax: (412)692-6645
David M. Orenstein, M.D., Dir.

Research Activities and Fields: Cystic fibrosis and related diseases, including pediatric pulmonary and pediatric gastrointestinal diseases. Also studies pediatric exercise physiology, and lung cellular immunology.

★5381★ **University of Tennessee**
Molecular Resource Center
801 Molecular Science Bldg.
858 Madison Ave.
Memphis, TN 38163
Phone: (901)448-6176
Fax: (901)448-8462
Dr. Terrance Cooper

Research Activities and Fields: Function and regulation of genes. Conducts experiments with gene replication and with isolation and manipulation of genetic components, with applications to cancer. Studies include cloning, mapping, probing, and sequencing of genes. **Publications:** Annual Report. **E-mail Address:** tcooper@utmem.edu.

★5382★ **University of Texas—Houston Health Science Center**
Genetic Marker Laboratory
Genetic Center GSBS
PO Box 20334
Houston, TX 77225
Phone: (713)792-4585
Fax: (713)792-4615
Dr. Craig Hanis, Dir.

Research Activities and Fields: Investigates DNA polymorphisms to find genetic bases for diseases, with special emphasis on common chronic diseases such as diabetes and heart disease. Approaches include linkage and pedigree analysis, SSCP, automated typing, and sequencing.

★5383★ **University of Texas—Houston Health Science Center**
Genetics Center
PO Box 20334
Houston, TX 77225
Phone: (713)792-4680
Fax: (713)792-4615
Dr. William J. Schull, Dir.

Research Activities and Fields: Population genetics and genetic epidemiology to better understand the nature and extent of hereditary diseases and disabilities. Research involves the study of forces that contribute to changes in gene, genotype, and phenotype frequencies in the short- and long-term. Implementation of these interests has included study of diabetes, gallbladder disease, and cardiovascular disease among Mexican-Americans and familial aspects of cancer and related diseases in Texas; disease, disability, and high altitude adaptation among the Aymara Indians of Chile and Bolivia; radiation research in Japan; theoretical population studies; and studies of human isozymes. **Publications:** *Center for Demographic and Population Genetics Reports.* **Formerly:** Formed by merger of Medical Genetics Center and Center for Demographic and Population Genetics.

★5384★ **University of Texas**
Southwestern Medical Center at Dallas
Eugene McDermott Center for Human Growth and Development
6000 Harry Hines Blvd.
Dallas, TX 75235-8591
Phone: (214)648-1600
Fax: (214)648-1666
Dr. Glen A. Evans, Dir.

Research Activities and Fields: Physical mapping of human chromosomes and genomes of other complex organisms, technology development to support genome science, and engineering and computational development for DNA sequencing of the human genome. **Publications:** *The McDermott Center Bulletin* (quarterly newsletter). **E-mail Address:** gevans@swmed.edu. **Formerly:** San Diego Genome Center.

University of Utah
Cardiovascular Genetic Research Clinic
See: Entry 2980

★5385★ University of Utah
Intermountain Cystic Fibrosis Center
50 N. Medical Dr., Rm. 2A120 Som
Salt Lake City, UT 84132
Phone: (801)581-2410
Fax: (801)581-4920
Dennis W. Nielson, M.D., Pediatrics Center Dir.

Research Activities and Fields: Cystic fibrosis and pulmonary disease, including studies electrolyte metabolism in the lung, lung mechanics, clinical studies of new therapies, and antibiotic pharmacology.

★5386★ University of Utah
Perinatal Genetics Laboratory
Univ. of Utah Medical Center
Eccles Genetics Bldg.
Salt Lake City, UT 84112
Phone: (801)581-8334
Fax: (801)581-7199
Kenneth Ward, M.D., Dir.

Research Activities and Fields: Gene mapping, genetic diagnosis, preimplantation testing, pregnancy loss, birth defect genes, and preeclampsia genes. **E-mail Address:** ken@gene1.utah.edu. **Formerly:** Laboratory of Human Genetics.

★5387★ University of Vermont
Genetics Laboratory
Vermont Cancer Center
32 N. Prospect St.
Burlington, VT 05401-3498
Phone: (802)863-5716
Fax: (802)863-0381
Dr. Richard Albertini, Dir.

Research Activities and Fields: Genetic toxicology, including investigations of the mechanisms of mutation, development of tests for detecting the consequences of exposure to environmental toxicants which damage genes (genotoxicants), definition of human populations which are unusually susceptible to certain mutations, and correlation of the presence of indicators of genotoxicant exposure and/or genetic damage with subsequent health outcomes of monitored human populations.

★5388★ University of Washington
Cystic Fibrosis Research Center
4800 Sand Point Way NE
Seattle, WA 98105
Phone: (206)526-2024
Bonnie W. Ramsey, Assoc.Dir.

Research Activities and Fields: Cystic fibrosis, particularly cardiopulmonary and infectious disease-related pathophysiology, gene therapy, and evaluation of treatment of patients with cystic fibrosis and cardiorespiratory diseases, including clinically oriented research on lung mechanics, and sputum microbiology.

★5389★ University of Wisconsin—Madison
Laboratory of Genetics
445 Henry Mall
Madison, WI 53706
Phone: (608)262-3112
Fax: (608)262-2976
Prof. Carter Denniston, Chm.

Research Activities and Fields: Genetics, including molecular, human, nematode, population, microbial, behavioral, and plant genetics, cytogenetics, yeast genetics, somatic cells, immunogenetics, genetic engineering, and other areas ranging from theoretical genetics to agricultural and medical genetics.

★5390★ University of Wisconsin—Madison
Pediatric Pulmonary Center
Clinical Science Center
Univ. Hospitals
Madison, WI 53792-4108
Phone: (608)263-8555
Fax: (608)263-0440
Dr. Elaine H. Mischler, M.D., Dir.

Research Activities and Fields: Cystic fibrosis and other respiratory diseases of children. **Formerly:** Cystic Fibrosis/Pulmonary Center (1994); Cystic Fibrosis Center (1985).

★5391★ Washington University
Cystic Fibrosis Research Center
400 S. Kingshighway
St. Louis, MO 63110
Phone: (314)454-2694
Fax: (314)454-2515
Dr. George Mallory, Dir.

Research Activities and Fields: Cystic fibrosis and pulmonary diseases, plus nutrition and malabsorption in relation to cystic fibrosis and liver diseases and effects of mechanisms of inflammatory response in cystic fibrosis-related diseases. Conducts research on lung transplantation and nutrition in cystic fibrosis, as well as basic studies of immune mechanisms. Provides clinical material to departments of the University engaged in related research and offers educational programs for patients, parents, and professionals.

★5392★ Wayne State University
Center for Molecular Medicine and Genetics
540 E. Canfield
Detroit, MI 48201
Phone: (313)577-5323
Fax: (313)577-5218
Dr. Robert Rownd, Dir.

Research Activities and Fields: Research is focused on five general areas: 1) development and differentiation, including studies into meiotic differentiation, cell type-specific gene regulation, protein structure and function, and genome organization and stability; 2) cancer and metastasis, including mapping of cancer genes, induction of carcinogenesis, gene regulation in cancer, and mechanisms of metastasis; 3) human genetics and disease, comprising the genetic cause of Huntington's disease, arthritis and tissue remodeling, and diabetes and insulin action; 4) viral disease, including mother-fetus transmission of AIDS, and papilloma viruses in cervical cancer; and 5) gene therapeutics, including fetal gene therapy and gene therapy for lymphoma and leukemia. **E-mail Address:** cmmg@cmb.biosci.wayne.edu.

★5393★ Wayne State University
Cystic Fibrosis Care, Teaching and Resource Center
Children's Hospital of Michigan
3901 Beaubien
Detroit, MI 48201
Phone: (313)745-5541
Fax: (313)993-2948
Julie M.C. Hsu, M.D., Dir.

Research Activities and Fields: Cystic fibrosis and pediatric pulmonary diseases, including immunology of pediatric pulmonary diseases, inflammatory mediators in lung diseases, and interleukin-1 activity in pulmonary inflammation.

★5394★ Wayne State University
Cytogenetics Laboratory
Dept. of Pathology
9374 Scott Hall, Sch. of Medicine
540 E. Canfield
Detroit, MI 48201
Phone: (313)577-1208
Sandra R. Wolman, M.D., Dir.

Research Activities and Fields: Cytogenetics, including studies in the areas of neonatal development and endocrinology. Performs tests on amniotic fluids, CVS, bloods, bone marrows, and solid tissues.

★5395★ West Virginia University
Cystic Fibrosis Center
Dept. of Pediatrics
Health Sciences Center
PO Box 9214
Morgantown, WV 26506
Phone: (304)293-1216
Fax: (304)293-4341
Stephen C. Aronoff, M.D., Dir.

Research Activities and Fields: Efficacy of exercise programs in cystic fibrosis and attachment of pseudomonas to cells in cystic fibrosis.

★5396★ Yale University
Cystic Fibrosis Research Center
School of Medicine
333 Cedar St.
New Haven, CT 06510
Phone: (203)737-2176
Dr. Thomas F. Dolan, Jr., Dir.

Research Activities and Fields: Cystic fibrosis and related respiratory diseases of children, with special emphasis on control of respiration.

State & Regional Organizations

Cystic Fibrosis

Listed below are chapters of the Cystic Fibrosis Foundation, 6931 Arlington Rd., Bethesda, MD 20814, (301) 951-4422.

Alabama

★ 5397 ★ Cystic Fibrosis Foundation
Alabama Chapter
200 Century Park S., Ste. 202
Birmingham, AL 35226
Phone: (205)823-9113
Free: 800-523-2357
Fax: (205)823-8970

Arizona

★ 5398 ★ Cystic Fibrosis Foundation
Arizona Chapter
2345 E. Thomas Rd., Ste. 420
Phoenix, AZ 85016
Phone: (602)224-0068
Fax: (602)224-0432

Arkansas

★ 5399 ★ Cystic Fibrosis Foundation
Arkansas Chapter
7101 W. 12th St., Ste. 401
Little Rock, AR 72204
Phone: (501)664-1200
Fax: (501)663-6711

California

★ 5400 ★ Cystic Fibrosis Foundation
Northern California Chapter
417 Montgomery St., Ste. 404
San Francisco, CA 94104
Phone: (415)677-0155
Fax: (415)677-0156

★ 5401 ★ Cystic Fibrosis Foundation
Southern California Chapter
2320 5th Ave., Ste. A
San Diego, CA 92101
Phone: (619)234-5880
Fax: (619)234-4803

★ 5402 ★ Cystic Fibrosis Foundation
Southern California / Southern Nevada
   Chapter
2150 Towne Center Pl., Ste. 120
Anaheim, CA 92806
Phone: (714)938-1393
Fax: (714)938-1462

★ 5403 ★ Cystic Fibrosis Foundation
Southern California / Southern Nevada
   Chapter
Hacienda Heights Office
2440 S. Hacienda Blvd.
Hacienda Heights, CA 91745
Phone: (818)855-2896
Fax: (818)961-2404

★ 5404 ★ Cystic Fibrosis Foundation
Southern California / Southern Nevada
   Chapter
Los Angeles Office
1950 Sawtelle Blvd., Ste. 328
Los Angeles, CA 90025
Phone: (310)479-8585
Fax: (310)473-7307

Colorado

★ 5405 ★ Cystic Fibrosis Foundation
Colorado Chapter
1755 Blake St.
Denver, CO 80202
Phone: (303)296-6610
Fax: (303)296-6923

★ 5406 ★ Cystic Fibrosis Foundation
Colorado Chapter
Pikes Peak Office
118 N. Tejon St., Ste. 205H
Colorado Springs, CO 80903
Phone: (719)444-8966

Connecticut

★ 5407 ★ Cystic Fibrosis Foundation
Connecticut Chapter
630 Oakwood Ave., Ste. 317
West Hartford, CT 06110-1536
Phone: (203)953-0048
Fax: (203)953-1505

Delaware

★ 5408 ★ Cystic Fibrosis Foundation
Delaware Valley Chapter
1601 Market St., Ste. 2310
Philadelphia, PA 19103
Phone: (215)587-2800
Fax: (215)587-9530

District of Columbia

★ 5409 ★ Cystic Fibrosis Foundation
Metropolitan Washington, DC Chapter
6931 Arlington Rd., Ste. 200
Bethesda, MD 20814
Phone: (301)657-8444
Fax: (301)652-9571

Florida

★ 5410 ★ Cystic Fibrosis Foundation
Florida Chapter
2 Prospect Park Business Center
3443 NW 55th St., Bldg. 7
Ft. Lauderdale, FL 33309
Phone: (305)739-5006
Fax: (305)739-5009

★ 5411 ★ Cystic Fibrosis Foundation
Florida Chapter
Palm Beach Regional Office
319 Belvedere Rd., Ste. 7
West Palm Beach, FL 33405
Phone: (407)655-9577
Fax: (407)655-9750

★ 5412 ★ Cystic Fibrosis Foundation
Florida Chapter
Tampa Regional Office
1211 N. Westshore Blvd., Ste. 602
Tampa, FL 33607
Phone: (813)286-0266
Fax: (813)289-4472

Georgia

★ 5413 ★ Cystic Fibrosis Foundation
Georgia Chapter
2250 N. Druid Hills Rd., Ste. 275
Atlanta, GA 30329
Phone: (404)325-6973
Free: 800-476-4483
Fax: (404)325-7921

Hawaii

★ 5414 ★ Cystic Fibrosis Foundation
Southern California Chapter
2320 5th Ave., Ste. A
San Diego, CA 92101
Phone: (619)234-5880
Fax: (619)234-4803

Idaho

★ 5415 ★ Cystic Fibrosis Foundation
Oregon / Idaho / Montana Chapter
4445 SW Barbur Blvd., Ste. C-101
Portland, OR 97201
Phone: (503)226-3435
Free: 800-448-8404
Fax: (503)226-4165

Illinois

★ 5416 ★ Cystic Fibrosis Foundation
Greater Illinois Chapter
150 N. Michigan Ave., 4th Fl.
Chicago, IL 60601
Phone: (312)236-4491
Free: 800-824-5064
Fax: (312)236-2797

Indiana

★ 5417 ★ Cystic Fibrosis Foundation
Indiana Chapter
50 S. Meridian St., Ste. 301
Indianapolis, IN 46204
Phone: (317)631-4115
Free: 800-622-4826
Fax: (317)631-4410

Iowa

★ 5418 ★ Cystic Fibrosis Foundation
Iowa Chapter
2600 72nd St., Ste. M
Des Moines, IA 50322
Phone: (515)252-1530
Free: 800-798-5151
Fax: (515)252-7684

Kansas

★ 5419 ★ Cystic Fibrosis Foundation
Heart of America Chapter
5750 W. 9th St., Ste. 214
Overland Park, KS 66207
Phone: (913)648-2323
Fax: (913)648-2171

Kentucky

★5420★ Cystic Fibrosis Foundation
Kentucky / West Virginia Chapter
1941 Bishop Ln., Ste. 507
Louisville, KY 40218
Phone: (502)452-6353
Fax: (502)456-2936

Louisiana

★5421★ Cystic Fibrosis Foundation
Louisiana Chapter
4621 W. Napoleon Ave., Ste. 207
Metairie, LA 70001
Phone: (504)455-5194
Free: 800-257-4166
Fax: (504)889-2592

★5422★ Cystic Fibrosis Foundation
Louisiana Chapter
Baton Rouge Reginal Office
1200 S. Acadian Thruway, Ste. 214
Baton Rouge, LA 70806
Phone: (504)389-9993
Fax: (504)387-4573

Maine

★5423★ Cystic Fibrosis Foundation
Northern New England Chapter
136 Harvey Rd., Bldg. A
Londonderry, NH 03053
Phone: (603)669-8682
Free: 800-757-0203
Fax: (603)669-9729

Maryland

★5424★ Cystic Fibrosis Foundation
Maryland Chapter
10616 Beaver Dam Rd., Ste. S-1
Hunt Valley, MD 21030
Phone: (410)771-9000
Fax: (410)771-3208

Massachusetts

★5425★ Cystic Fibrosis Foundation
Massachusetts Chapter
220 N. Main St., Ste. 104
Natick, MA 01760
Phone: (508)655-6000
Free: 800-966-0444
Fax: (508)653-6942

Michigan

★5426★ Cystic Fibrosis Foundation
Greater Michigan Chapter—Eastern Region
2118 Marshall Ct.
Saginaw, MI 48602-3368
Phone: (517)790-2233
Free: 800-968-7169
Fax: (517)790-1050

★5427★ Cystic Fibrosis Foundation
Greater Michigan Chapter—Western Region
404 McKay Tower
146 Monroe Center St. NW
Grand Rapids, MI 49503
Phone: (616)451-4225
Free: 800-968-1050
Fax: (616)451-8615

★5428★ Cystic Fibrosis Foundation
Metro Detroit Chapter
1133 E. Maple Rd., Ste. 201
Troy, MI 48083-2853
Phone: (810)524-2873
Fax: (810)524-4755

★5429★ Cystic Fibrosis Foundation
Washtenaw County Chapter
1430 Kearney Rd.
Ann Arbor, MI 48104
Phone: (313)662-4635

Minnesota

★5430★ Cystic Fibrosis Foundation
Minnesota Chapter
Century Plaza
1111 3rd Ave. S., Ste. 370
Minneapolis, MN 55404
Phone: (612)338-0885
Fax: (612)338-1601

Mississippi

★5431★ Cystic Fibrosis Foundation
Mississippi Chapter
4800 McWillie Cir., Ste. B-6
Jackson, MS 39206
Phone: (601)981-3100
Fax: (601)981-0609

Missouri

★5432★ Cystic Fibrosis Foundation
Gateway Chapter
200 S. Hanley, Ste. 620
St. Louis, MO 63105
Phone: (314)721-2490
Fax: (314)721-2809

★5433★ Cystic Fibrosis Foundation
Heart of America Chapter
5750 W. 95th St., Ste. 214
Overland Park, KS 66207
Phone: (913)648-2323
Fax: (913)648-2171

Montana

★5434★ Cystic Fibrosis Foundation
Oregon / Idaho / Montana Chapter
4445 SW Barbur Blvd., Ste. C-101
Portland, OR 97201
Phone: (503)226-3435
Free: 800-448-8404
Fax: (503)226-4165

Nebraska

★5435★ Cystic Fibrosis Foundation
Nebraska Chapter
10838 Old Mill Rd., Ste. 6
Omaha, NE 68154
Phone: (402)330-6164
Fax: (402)330-8458

Nevada

★5436★ Cystic Fibrosis Foundation
Southern California / Southern Nevada Chapter
2150 Towne Center Pl., Ste. 120
Anaheim, CA 92806
Phone: (714)938-1393
Fax: (714)938-1462

New Hampshire

★5437★ Cystic Fibrosis Foundation
Northern New England Chapter
136 Harvey Rd., Bldg. A
Londonderry, NH 03053
Phone: (603)669-8682
Free: 800-757-0203
Fax: (603)669-9729

New Jersey

★5438★ Cystic Fibrosis Foundation
Greater New Jersey Chapter
119 Cherry Hill Rd.
Parsippany, NJ 07054
Phone: (201)331-1400
Fax: (201)331-1441

New Mexico

★5439★ Cystic Fibrosis Foundation
New Mexico Chapter
4004 Carlisle, NE, Ste. B
Albuquerque, NM 87107
Phone: (505)883-1455
Fax: (505)883-3998

New York

★5440★ Cystic Fibrosis Foundation
Central New York Chapter
6311 Fly Rd.
East Syracuse, NY 13057
Phone: (315)463-7965
Free: 800-962-6578
Fax: (315)463-8221

★5441★ Cystic Fibrosis Foundation
Greater New York Chapter
60 E. 42nd St., Ste. 1563
New York, NY 10165
Phone: (212)986-8783
Fax: (212)697-4282

★5442★ Cystic Fibrosis Foundation
Greater New York Chapter
Long Island Office
265 Post Ave., Ste. 115
Westbury, NY 11590-2237
Phone: (516)876-0580
Fax: (516)876-0585

★5443★ Cystic Fibrosis Foundation
Northeastern New York Chapter
50 Colvin Ave.
Albany, NY 12206
Phone: (518)489-2677
Fax: (518)489-2751

★5444★ Cystic Fibrosis Foundation
Rochester Chapter
307 Exchange Blvd.
Rochester, NY 14608
Phone: (716)546-5890
Fax: (716)546-3903

★5445★ Cystic Fibrosis Foundation
Western New York Chapter
4213 N. Buffalo Rd.
Orchard Park, NY 14127
Phone: (716)662-3710
Fax: (716)662-4080

North Carolina

★5446★ Cystic Fibrosis Foundation
Carolinas Chapter
3716 National Dr., Ste. 111
PO Box 31572
Raleigh, NC 27622
Phone: (919)782-5530
Free: 800-822-9941
Fax: (919)782-5831

North Dakota

★5447★ Cystic Fibrosis Foundation
6931 Arlington Rd.
Bethesda, MD 20814
Phone: (301)951-4422
Free: 800-344-4823
Fax: (301)951-6378

Ohio

★5448★ Cystic Fibrosis Foundation
Central Ohio Chapter
6555 Busch Blvd., Ste. 108
Columbus, OH 43229
Phone: (614)846-2440
Fax: (614)846-2472

★5449★ Cystic Fibrosis Foundation
Greater Cincinnati Chapter
2011 Madison Rd.
Cincinnati, OH 45208
Phone: (513)553-9300
Fax: (513)533-9301

★5450★ Cystic Fibrosis Foundation
Rainbow Chapter
5755 Granger Rd., Ste. 630
Independence, OH 44131
Phone: (216)485-8700
Fax: (216)485-8711

Oklahoma

★5451★ Cystic Fibrosis Foundation
Sooner Chapter
2642 E. 21st St., Stè. 100
Tulsa, OK 74114
Phone: (918)744-6354
Fax: (918)744-0806

Oregon

★5452★ Cystic Fibrosis Foundation
Oregon / Idaho / Montana Chapter
4445 SW Barbur Blvd., Ste. C-101
Portland, OR 97201
Phone: (503)226-3435
Free: 800-448-8404
Fax: (503)226-4165

Pennsylvania

★5453★ Cystic Fibrosis Foundation
Central Pennsylvania Chapter
55 S. Progress Ave.
Harrisburg, PA 17109
Phone: (717)617-4000
Fax: (717)617-4007

★5454★ Cystic Fibrosis Foundation
Delaware Valley Chapter
1601 Market St., Ste. 2310
Philadelphia, PA 19103
Phone: (215)587-2800
Fax: (215)587-9530

★5455★ Cystic Fibrosis Foundation
Northeastern Pennsylvania Chapter
1541 Alta Dr., Ste. 301
Whitehall, PA 18052-5632
Phone: (610)820-0206
Free: 800-552-2199
Fax: (610)820-9367

★5456★ Cystic Fibrosis Foundation
Western Pennsylvania Chapter
119 Federal St., Rm. 509
Pittsburgh, PA 15212
Phone: (412)321-4422
Fax: (412)321-9305

Rhode Island

★5457★ Cystic Fibrosis Foundation
Rhode Island Chapter
Office Commons 95
335 Centerville Rd., Bldg. 5
Warwick, RI 02886
Phone: (401)739-6900
Fax: (401)738-0054

South Carolina

★5458★ Cystic Fibrosis Foundation
Carolinas Chapter
3716 National Dr., Ste. 111
PO Box 31572
Raleigh, NC 27622
Phone: (919)782-5530
Free: 800-822-9941
Fax: (919)782-5831

South Dakota

★5459★ Cystic Fibrosis Foundation
6931 Arlington Rd.
Bethesda, MD 20814
Phone: (301)951-4422
Free: 800-344-4823
Fax: (301)951-6378

Tennessee

★5460★ Cystic Fibrosis Foundation
Tennessee Chapter
3814 Cleghorn Ave.
Nashville, TN 37215
Phone: (615)297-3582
Fax: (615)385-1032

Texas

★5461★ Cystic Fibrosis Foundation
Lone Star Chapter
901 NE Loop 410, Ste. 512
San Antonio, TX 78209
Phone: (210)829-7267
Fax: (210)829-4204

★5462★ Cystic Fibrosis Foundation
North-East Texas Chapter
2929 Carlisle, Ste. 230
Dallas, TX 75204-1058
Phone: (214)871-2222
Fax: (214)969-7439

★5463★ Cystic Fibrosis Foundation
Texas Gulf Coast Chapter
3730 Kirby Dr., Ste. 810
Houston, TX 77098
Phone: (713)523-9044
Fax: (713)523-9684

Utah

★5464★ Cystic Fibrosis Foundation
Southern California / Southern Nevada
** Chapter**
Utah Office
4848 S. Highland Dr., Ste. 653
Salt Lake City, UT 84117
Phone: (801)322-2226
Fax: (714)938-1462

Vermont

★5465★ Cystic Fibrosis Foundation
Northern New England Chapter
136 Harvey Rd., Bldg. A
Londonderry, NH 03053
Phone: (603)669-8682
Free: 800-757-0203
Fax: (603)669-9729

Virginia

★5466★ Cystic Fibrosis Foundation
Virginia Chapter
2720 Enterprise Pkwy., Ste. 107
Richmond, VA 23294
Phone: (804)527-1500
Fax: (804)527-0016

★5467★ **Cystic Fibrosis Foundation**
Virginia Chapter
Hampton Roads Office
1423 N. Great Neck Rd., Ste. 204
Virginia Beach, VA 23454
Phone: (804)481-1383
Free: 800-572-3213
Fax: (804)481-5919

Washington

★5468★ **Cystic Fibrosis Foundation**
Washington State Chapter
100 W. Harrison, North Tower, Ste. 510
Seattle, WA 98119
Phone: (206)282-4770
Free: 800-647-7774
Fax: (206)283-8359

West Virginia

★5469★ **Cystic Fibrosis Foundation**
Kentucky / West Virginia Chapter
1941 Bishop Ln., Ste. 507
Louisville, KY 40218
Phone: (502)452-6353
Fax: (502)456-2936

Wisconsin

★5470★ **Cystic Fibrosis Foundation**
Wisconsin Chapter
2421 N. Mayfair Rd., Ste. 320
Milwaukee, WI 53226
Phone: (414)778-4820
Free: 800-472-7720
Fax: (414)778-4824

Wyoming

★5471★ **Cystic Fibrosis Foundation**
Colorado Chapter
1755 Blake St.
Denver, CO 80202
Phone: (303)296-6610
Fax: (303)296-6923

Chapter 28
Health Care Administration

Medical & Allied Health Schools

Health Services Administration

The following master's level health services administration programs are accredited by the Accrediting Commission on Education for Health Services Administration. For further information on these programs, and for listings of undergraduate programs, contact the Association of University Programs in Health Administration, 1911 N. Ft. Meyer Dr., Ste. 503, Arlington, VA 22209, (703) 524-0511.

Alabama

★5472★ **University of Alabama at Birmingham**
School of Health Related Professions
Department of Health Services Administration
Master of Science in Health Administration Program
Susan Mott Webb Nutrition Sciences Bldg.
Birmingham, AL 35294-3361
Phone: (205)934-5661
Fax: (205)975-6608

Arizona

★5473★ **Arizona State University**
College of Business
School of Health Administration and Policy
Graduate Program in Health Services Adminstration
Tempe, AZ 85287-4506
Phone: (602)965-7778
Fax: (602)965-6654

Arkansas

★5474★ **University of Arkansas at Little Rock**
Department of Health Services Administration
Graduate Program in Health Services Administration
2801 South University Ave.
Little Rock, AR 72204-1099
Phone: (501)569-3293
Fax: (501)569-3039

California

★5475★ **San Diego State University**
Graduate School of Public Health
Graduate Program in Health Services Administration
San Diego, CA 92182-0405
Phone: (619)594-6317
Fax: (619)594-6112

★5476★ **University of California at Berkeley**
Graduate School of Business Administration
Graduate Program in Health Services Management
416 Wrren Hall
Berkeley, CA 94720
Phone: (510)642-4606
Fax: (510)643-6981

★5477★ **University of California, Los Angeles**
School of Public Health
Program in Health Services Management
Rm. 31-269 CHS
10833 Laconte Ave.
Los Angeles, CA 90024-1772
Phone: (310)825-2595
Fax: (310)825-8440

★5478★ **University of Southern California**
School of Public Administration
Health Services Administration Program
Von Kleinsmid Center 263
Los Angeles, CA 90089-0041
Phone: (213)740-0546
Fax: (213)740-0001

Colorado

★5479★ **University of Colorado—Denver**
Graduate School of Business Administration
Program in Health Administration
Campus Box 165
PO Box 173364
Denver, CO 80217-3364
Phone: (303)595-4007
Fax: (303)628-1299

★5480★ **University of Colorado—Denver / Western Network for Education in Health Administration**
Graduate School of Business Administration
Executive Program in Health Administration
PO Box 480006
Denver, CO 80248-0006
Phone: (303)623-1888
Fax: (303)623-6228

Connecticut

★5481★ **Yale University**
School of Medicine
Department of Epidemiology and Public Health
Program in Health Policy, Resources, and Administration
60 College St.
PO Box 208034
New Haven, CT 06520-8034
Phone: (203)785-2854
Fax: (203)785-6287

District of Columbia

★5482★ **George Washington University**
School of Business and Public Management
Department of Health Services Administration
Graduate Program in Health Services Management and Policy
600 21st St. NW
Washington, DC 20052
Phone: (202)994-6220
Fax: (202)994-4068

★5483★ Howard University
School of Business
Department of Health Administration
Graduate Program in Health Services
   Adminstration
2600 6th St. NW, Bldg. 4
Washington, DC 20059
Phone: (202)806-1584
Fax: (202)797-6393

Florida

★5484★ Florida International University
Department of Health Services
   Administration
Program in Health Services Administration
North Miami Campus
3000 NE 145th St.
North Miami, FL 33181-3600
Phone: (305)940-5895
Fax: (305)940-5980

★5485★ University of Florida
College of Health Related Professions
Graduate Program in Health and Hospital
   Administration
J. Hillis Miller Health Center
PO Box 100195
Gainesville, FL 32610-0195
Phone: (904)392-3578
Fax: (904)392-9402

★5486★ University of Miami
School of Business Administration
Health Administration Program
PO Box 248505
Coral Gables, FL 33124-6524
Phone: (305)284-5120
Fax: (305)284-6526

Georgia

★5487★ Georgia State University
College of Business Administration
Institute of Health Administration
Master of Health Administration Program
1060 Lawyer's Title Bldg., University Plaza
Atlanta, GA 30303-3083
Phone: (404)651-2637
Fax: (404)651-2804

Illinois

★5488★ Governors State University
College of Health Professions
Health Services Administration Program
University Park, IL 60466
Phone: (708)534-5000
Fax: (708)534-5459

★5489★ Northwestern University
J.L. Kellogg Graduate School of
   Management
Graduate Program in Health Services
   Management
Leverone Hall, Rm. 3-080
2001 Sheridan Rd.
Evanston, IL 60208-2007
Phone: (708)491-5540
Fax: (708)491-2683

★5490★ Rush University
College of Health Sciences
Graduate Program in Health Systems
   Management
Rm. 305, Kidston
Rush-Presbyterian / St. Luke's Medical Center
1653 W. Congress Parkway
Chicago, IL 60612
Phone: (312)942-5402
Fax: (312)942-8112

★5491★ University of Chicago
Graduate Program in Health Administration
   and Policy
Box 6011
969 E. 60th St.
Chicago, IL 60637
Phone: (312)702-7104
Fax: (312)702-7222

Indiana

★5492★ Indiana University
School of Public and Environmental Affairs
Graduate Program in Health Administration
801 W. Michigan St., Rm. BS-3025
Indianapolis, IN 46202-5152
Phone: (317)274-7189
Fax: (317)274-3753

Iowa

★5493★ University of Iowa
College of Medicine
Graduate Program in Hospital and Health
   Administration
2700 Steindler Bldg.
Iowa City, IA 52242
Phone: (319)335-9814
Fax: (319)335-8814

Kansas

★5494★ University of Kansas
Department of Health Services
   Administration
Health Services Administration Program
6050 Malott Hall
Lawrence, KS 66045-2503
Phone: (913)864-3212
Fax: (913)864-5089

Kentucky

★5495★ University of Kentucky
Martin School of Public Administration
Master of Health Administration Program
Medical Center Annex 2, Rm. 103
Lexington, KY 40536-0080
Phone: (606)233-6361
Fax: (606)257-2454

Louisiana

★5496★ Tulane University
School of Public Health and Tropical
   Medicine
Department of Health Systems
   Management
Master of Health Administration Program
1430 Tulane Ave.
New Orleans, LA 70112
Phone: (504)588-5428
Fax: (504)584-3653

Maryland

★5497★ Johns Hopkins University
School of Hygiene and Public Health
Department of Health Policy and
   Management
MHS Program in Health Finance and
   Management
Hampton House, 4th fl.
624 N. Broadway
Baltimore, MD 21205-1995
Phone: (410)955-5315
Fax: (410)955-6959

Massachusetts

★5498★ Boston University
School of Management
Health Care Management Program
685 Commonwealth Ave., Rm. 334
Boston, MA 02215
Phone: (617)353-2730
Fax: (617)353-5581

**★5499★ Clark University / University of
   Massachusetts Medical School**
Graduate School of Management
Master in Health Administration Program
Woodland Hall
950 Main St.
Worcester, MA 01610-1477
Phone: (508)793-7407
Fax: (508)793-8822

★5500★ Simmons College
Graduate Program in Health Care
   Administration
MCB, Rm. E-204
300 The Fenway
Boston, MA 02115
Phone: (617)521-2377
Fax: (617)521-8199

Michigan

★5501★ University of Michigan
School of Public Health
Department of Health Services
   Management and Policy
Graduate Program in Health Services
   Administration
1420 Washington Heights
Ann Arbor, MI 48109-2029
Phone: (313)763-9903
Fax: (313)764-4338

Minnesota

★5502★ University of Minnesota
School of Public Health
Program in Healthcare Administration
C-309 Mayo, Box 97
420 Delaware St. SE
Minneapolis, MN 55455-0381
Phone: (612)624-1110
Fax: (612)626-1186

Missouri

★5503★ St. Louis University
School of Public Health
Department of Health Administration
Graduate Program in Health Services
  Administration
3663 Lindell Blvd.
St. Louis, MO 63104
Phone: (314)658-8100
Fax: (314)658-8150

★5504★ University of Missouri—Columbia
Graduate Program in Health Services
  Management
324 Clark Hall
Columbia, MO 65211
Phone: (314)882-6178
Fax: (314)882-6158

★5505★ Washington University
School of Medicine
Health Administration Program
Campus Box 8084
4547 Clayton Ave.
St. Louis, MO 63110-1593
Phone: (314)362-4277
Fax: (314)362-3265

New Hampshire

★5506★ University of New Hampshire
School of Health and Human Services
Department of Health Management and
  Policy
Master of Health Administration Program
Hewitt Hall
4 Library Way
Durham, NH 03824
Phone: (603)862-2733
Fax: (603)862-3412

New York

★5507★ Bernard Baruch College / Mt.
  Sinai School of Medicine of City.
  University of New York
Graduate Program in Health Care
  Administration
17 Lexington Ave., Box 313
New York, NY 10010
Phone: (212)447-3600
Fax: (212)447-3364

★5508★ Cornell University
College of Human Ecology
Department of Human Services Studies
Sloan Program in Health Services
  Administration
N138 Martha Van Rensselaer Hall
Ithaca, NY 14853-4401
Phone: (607)255-7770
Fax: (607)255-1533

★5509★ New York University
Robert F. Wagner Graduate School of
  Public Service
Health Policy and Management Program
40 W. 4th St., Rm. 600
New York, NY 10012-1118
Phone: (212)998-7440
Fax: (212)995-4162

★5510★ Union College
Graduate Management Institute
Program in Health Systems Administration
Bailey Hall
Union Ave.
Schenectady, NY 12308-2311
Phone: (518)370-6238
Fax: (518)388-6686

North Carolina

★5511★ Duke University
Fuqua School of Businesss
Program in Health Services Management
PO Box 90120
Durham, NC 27708-0120
Phone: (919)660-7847
Fax: (919)681-6245

★5512★ University of North Carolina at
  Chapel Hill
School of Public Health
Department of Health Policy and
  Administration
Master's Program in Health Policy
  Administration
CB 7400 McGavran-Greenberg Hall
Chapel Hill, NC 27599-7400
Phone: (919)966-7350
Fax: (919)966-6961

Ohio

★5513★ Cleveland State University
James J. Nance College of Business
  Administration
Graduate Study in Health Care
  Administration
University Center, Rm. 503
2121 Euclid Avenue
Cleveland, OH 44115
Phone: (216)687-4711
Fax: (216)687-9366

★5514★ Ohio State University
Graduate Program in Hospital and Health
  Services Administration
1583 Perry St., Rm. 246
Columbus, OH 43210-1234
Phone: (614)292-9708
Fax: (614)292-3572

★5515★ Xavier University
Graduate Program in Health Services
  Administration
3800 Victory Pkwy.
Cincinnati, OH 45207
Phone: (513)745-3392
Fax: (513)745-1945

Pennsylvania

★5516★ Pennsylvania State University
College of Health and Human Development
Graduate Studies in Health Policy and
  Administration
115 Henderson Bldg.
University Park, PA 16802
Phone: (814)863-2900
Fax: (814)865-3282

★5517★ Temple University
School of Business and Management
Graduate Program in Health Administration
Speakman Hall (006-00)
Philadelphia, PA 19122
Phone: (215)204-8156
Fax: (215)204-3851

★5518★ University of Pennsylvania
The Wharton School
Graduate Program in Health Care
  Management
204 Colonial Penn Center
3641 Locust Wlak
Philadelphia, PA 19104-6218
Phone: (215)898-6861
Fax: (215)898-0229

★5519★ University of Pittsburgh
Graduate School of Business and Public
  Health
Health Administration Program
A-646 Crabtree Hall
130 DeSoto St.
Pittsburgh, PA 15261
Phone: (412)624-3123
Fax: (412)624-3146

★5520★ Widener University
School of Management
Graduate Program in Health and Medical
  Services Administration
Chester, PA 19013
Phone: (215)499-4384
Fax: (215)876-9751

Puerto Rico

★5521★ University of Puerto Rico
Graduate School of Public Health
Master in Health Services Administration
Medical Sciences Campus Bldg.
GPO Box 5067
San Juan, PR 00936
Phone: (809)758-2525
Fax: (809)759-6719

South Carolina

★5522★ Medical University of South Carolina
College of Health Professions
Department of Health Administration and Policy
Master of Health Administration Program
409 Harborview Tower, Ste. 408
Charleston, SC 29425
Phone: (803)792-2118
Fax: (803)792-3327

★5523★ University of South Carolina
School of Public Health
Department of Health Administration
Master of Health Administration Program
Columbia, SC 29208
Phone: (803)777-6096
Fax: (803)777-4783

Tennessee

★5524★ Meharry Medical College
Division of Community Health Sciences
Health Services Administration Program
Box 53-A
1005 D.B. Todd Jr. Blvd.
Nashville, TN 37208-9989
Phone: (615)327-6069
Fax: (615)327-6717

Texas

★5525★ Southwest Texas State University
School of Health Professions
Department of Health Administration
Graduate Program in Health Care Administration
San Marcos, TX 78666-4616
Phone: (512)245-3556
Fax: (512)245-8712

★5526★ Texas Tech University
College of Business Administration
Graduate Program in Health Organization Management
Lubbock, TX 79409-2101
Phone: (806)742-2134
Fax: (806)742-2099

★5527★ Trinity University
Graduate Program in Health Care Administration
715 Stadium Dr., Box 58
San Antonio, TX 78212
Phone: (210)736-8107
Fax: (210)736-8108

★5528★ U.S. Army / Baylor University
Graduate Program in Health Care Administration
Academy of Health Sciences, U.S. Army
Ft. Sam Houston, TX 78234-6100
Phone: (210)221-8874
Fax: (210)221-6901

★5529★ University of Houston—Clear Lake
School of Business and Public Administration
Healthcare Administration Program
Bayou Bldg.
2700 Bay Area Blvd.
Houston, TX 77058-1056
Phone: (713)283-3132
Fax: (713)283-3951

Virginia

★5530★ Virginia Commonwealth University
Medical College of Virginia
School of Allied Health Professions
Executive Program in Health Services Administration
Box 980203
Richmond, VA 23298-0203
Phone: (804)828-5212
Fax: (804)828-1894

★5531★ Virginia Commonwealth University
Medical College of Virginia
School of Allied Health Professions
Graduate Program in Health Services Administration
Box 980203
Richmond, VA 23298-0203
Phone: (804)828-5212
Fax: (804)828-1894

Washington

★5532★ University of Washington
School of Public Health and Community Medicine
Department of Health Services
Graduate Program in Health Services Administration
Seattle, WA 98195
Phone: (206)543-8778
Fax: (206)543-3964

Wisconsin

★5533★ University of Wisconsin—Madison
Schools of Medicine, Business, and Public Administration
Department of Preventive Medicine
Administrative Medicine Program
Bradley Memorial, 2nd Fl.
1300 University Ave.
Madison, WI 53706-1532
Phone: (608)262-8808
Fax: (608)263-4885

★5534★ University of Wisconsin—Madison
Schools of Medicine, Business and Public Administration
Department of Preventive Medicine
Programs in Health Management
Bradley Memorial, 2nd Fl.
1300 University Ave.
Madison, WI 53706-1532
Phone: (608)262-8808
Fax: (608)263-4885

National & International Organizations

★5535★ Accrediting Commission on Education for Health Services Administration (ACEHSA)
1911 N. Fort Myer Dr., Ste. 503
Arlington, VA 22209
Phone: (703)524-0511
Fax: (703)525-4791
Karen Kanefield, Interim Exec.Dir.

Founded: 1968. **Members:** 65. **Description:** Accredits graduate degree programs in health services administration, health planning, and health policy. Goal is the improvement of professional education. **Publications:** *Official List of Accredited Programs*, semiannual. *Price:* Free. **Formerly:** (1976) Accrediting Commission on Graduate Education for Hospital Administration.

★5536★ American Academy of Ambulatory Care Nursing (AAACN)
Box 56, N. Woodbury Rd.
Pitman, NJ 08071
Phone: (609)256-2350
Fax: (609)589-7463
Catherine A. Brown, MSN, RN, Exec.Dir.

Founded: 1978. **Members:** 1,000. **Local Groups:** 20. **Description:** Nurses with administrative/management responsibilities in ambulatory care. To improve the quality and efficiency of ambulatory care through continuing education programs. Program goals are to enhance the leadership and supervisory skills of nurse administrators, and improve members' abilities to influence organizational decisions. Conducts skill building workshops; provides educators to members' groups for in-service educational programs. **Publications:** *Ambulatory Care Nursing Administration and Practice Standards*, periodic. Reference manual. *Price:* $30 for members; $50 for nonmembers. • *American Academy of Ambulatory Nursing Administration Membership Directory*, annual. Directory. Arranged alphabetically and geographically. *Price:* Included in membership dues. • *Dermatology Nursing*. Journal. • *MedSurg Nursing*. Journal. • *Nursing Economics*, bimonthly. Journal. • *Pediatric Nursing*. Journal. • *Viewpoint*, bimonthly. Newsletter. Includes legislative updates and synopses of articles in current journals. *Price:* Included in membership dues. **Formerly:** American Academy of Ambulatory Nursing Administration.

★5537★ American Academy of Medical Administrators (AAMA)
30555 Southfield Rd., Ste. 150
Southfield, MI 48076-7747
Phone: (810)540-4310
Fax: (810)645-0590
Thomas R. O'Donovan, Ph.D., Pres.

Founded: 1957. **Members:** 3,800. **Regional Groups:** 7. **State Groups:** 50. **Description:** Individuals involved in medical administration at the executive- or middle-management levels. Promotes educational courses for the training of persons in medical administration. Conducts research. Offers placement service. **Publications:** *American Academy of Medical Adminis-*

trators--*Executive*, bimonthly. Newsletter. Covers membership activities. Includes triennial membership directory;also contains calendar of events, book reviews, and lists of new members. *Price:* Included in membership dues; $60/year for nonmembers. • *Journal of Cardiovascular Management*. Journal. • *Journal of Oncology Management*. Journal.

★5538★ **American Academy of Medical Administrators Research and Educational Foundation (AAMA)**
30555 Southfield Rd., Ste. 150
Southfield, MI 48076
Phone: (810)540-4310
Fax: (810)645-0590
Thomas R. O'Donovan, Ph.D., Pres.

Founded: 1957. **Members:** 3,800. **Regional Groups:** 7. **State Groups:** 50. **Description:** Individuals with health care backgrounds. Conducts research in the health care field and seminars geared toward professional development. Maintains placement services. **Publications:** *AAMA Executive*, bimonthly. Newsletter. Covers management topics, industry trends, current developments in health care administration, and association news. Includes book reviews. *Price:* Included in membership dues; $110/year for nonmembers.

★5539★ **American Academy of Podiatric Administration (AAPA)**
836 Farmington Ave., Ste. 105
West Hartford, CT 06119
Phone: (203)236-2564
Fax: (203)233-0251
Harvey Lederman, D.P.M., Pres.

Founded: 1961. **Members:** 200. **Description:** Doctors of podiatric medicine interested in practice administration. Works to standardize office management procedures to create more efficient podiatry practices; conducts research on the administration and function of podiatry offices; develops formalized procedures for obtaining and training podiatry office assistants. Disseminates pedal information and material on practice management. Investigates methods of delivering improved podiatric care to an increasing number of patients; seeks effective participation in the public health team. Maintains collection of newsletters and position papers; sponsors seminars and workshops. Compiles statistics. **Publications:** *AAPA Newsletter*, quarterly. Newsletter. • *Directory of Membership*, annual. Directory. **Formerly:** (1969) American Academy of Practice Management in Podiatry; (1970) American Academy of Podiatric Management.

★5540★ **American Association for Continuity of Care (AACC)**
11250 Roger Bacon Dr., Ste. 8
Reston, VA 22090-5202
Phone: (703)525-1191
Fax: (703)435-4390
Randall Price, Exec.Dir.

Founded: 1982. **Members:** 700. **Regional Groups:** 6. **Description:** Health care professionals involved in discharge planning, social work, hospital administration, home care, long-term care, home health agencies, and continuity of care. Studies and researches issues; proposes and supports legislation concerning Medicare changes and home health care. Maintains speakers' bureau. **Publications:** *ACCESS*, 4/year. Includes calendar of events, regional reports, member notes, and committee reports. *Price:* Included in membership dues. • *American Association for Continuity of Care--Membership Directory*, annual. Membership Directory. *Price:* Included in membership dues. • *IMPAACT*, bimonthly. Bulletin. *Price:* Included in membership dues.

★5541★ **American Association of Physician-Hospital Organizations (AAPHO)**
PO Box 4913
Glen Allen, VA 23058-4913
Phone: (804)747-5823
Fax: (804)747-5316
W. C. Williams, III, Pres.

Founded: 1993. **Members:** 500. **Description:** Physicians, hospital executives and board members, health plan executives, and other key entities and professionals employed by physician-hospital organizations. Seeks to provide advocacy for issues related to physician-hospital organizations through research, education, and communication. Conducts educational and research programs; maintains speakers' bureau. **Publications:** *Integrated Healthcare Delivery System*, quarterly. Newsletter.

★5542★ **American Association of Psychiatric Administrators (AAPA)**
c/o Dr. Dave Davis
1938 Peachtree Rd. NW, Ste. 505
Atlanta, GA 30304-1253
Phone: (404)355-2914
Fax: (404)355-2917
Dr. Dave Davis, Pres.

Founded: 1960. **Members:** 300. **State Groups:** 6. **Description:** Psychiatrists who occupy the position of chief administrative or clinical officer of a public or private neuropsychiatric hospital or clinic. Provides for the efficient consolidation and dissemination of information concerning the treatment, care, and rehabilitation of the mentally ill or handicapped; the effective application of training and research; and the development of the highest standards and qualifications for administrators of public neuropsychiatric hospitals. Conducts educational programs. Acts as a forum through which the common voice of the membership may be expressed and publicized. **Publications:** *Journal of American Association of Psychiatric Administrators*, periodic. Journal. • *List of Members*, biennial. Membership Directory. • Newsletter, quarterly. **Formerly:** (1975) Association of Medical Superintendents of Mental Hospitals.

★5543★ **American College of Addiction Treatment Administrators (ACATA)**
c/o Sam Muszynski
1 Massachusetts Ave., Ste. 860
Washington, DC 20001-1431
Phone: (202)371-6731
Fax: (202)682-0136
Sam Muszynski, Mng.Dir.

Founded: 1984. **Members:** 250. **Description:** Administrators of addiction treatment facilities. Promotes educational and professional standards in the field of addiction treatment administration. Encourages continuing education and training of members. Recognizes individuals who have provided outstanding service in the field. Seeks to educate members and the public on issues surrounding the administration of treatment programs. Sponsors workshops. **Publications:** *Update*, monthly. Newsletter.

★5544★ **American College of Cardiovascular Administrators (ACCA)**
30555 Southfield Rd., Ste, 150
Southfield, MI 48076
Phone: (810)540-4598
Fax: (810)645-0565
James C. Reinhardt, Pres.

Founded: 1986. **Members:** 1,200. **Regional Groups:** 7. **State Groups:** 50. **Description:** A chapter of the American Academy of Medical Administrators. Upper- and middle-level managers of health care professionals in the cardiovascular health care field; associate members are junior supervisors, salespersons, and individuals. Represents members within the medical industry; provides credentialing of cardiology administrators. Serves as a forum for the exchange of information. Conducts research; offers educational programs. **Publications:** *Journal of Cardiovacular Management*, bimonthly. Journal.

★5545★ **American College of Health Care Administrators (ACHCA)**
325 S. Patrick St.
Alexandria, VA 22314
Phone: (703)549-5822
Fax: (703)739-7901
Richard L. Thorpe, Exec. Officer

Founded: 1962. **Members:** 6,000. **Regional Groups:** 11. **State Groups:** 48. **Description:** Persons actively engaged in the administration of long-term care facilities, assisted-living facilities in medical administration, or activities designed to improve the quality of long-term administration. Certifies members' ability to meet and maintain a standard of competence in nursing home and long-term care administration. Works to elevate the standards in the field and to develop and promote a code of ethics and standards of education and training. Seeks to inform allied professions and the public that good administration of long-term care facilities calls for special formal academic training and experience. Encourages research in all aspects of geriatrics, the chronically ill, and administration. Maintains placement service. Conducts research and special education programs. **Publications:** *Journal of Long-Term Care Administration*, quarterly. Journal. *Price:* $70/year. • *Long-Term Care Administrator*, bimonthly. Newsletter. Includes information on legislation, research developments, and general administrator procedures. *Price:* $45/year. Also publishes educational materials. **Formerly:** American College of Nursing Home Administrators.

★ 5546 ★ American College of Healthcare Executives (ACHE)
1 N. Franklin, Ste. 1700
Chicago, IL 60606-3491
Phone: (312)424-2800
Fax: (312)424-0023
Thomas C. Dolan, Ph.D., Pres.

Founded: 1933. **Members:** 28,000. **Regional Groups:** 74. **State Groups:** 15. **Local Groups:** 126. **Description:** Professional society for hospital and health service executives. Works to: keep members abreast of current and future trends, issues, and developments; shape productive and effective organizational strategies and professional performance; increase the visibility and recognition of the health care management profession; act as advocate for health care management in legislative activities and with government agencies; develop cooperation among professional societies and other health care associations in dealing with current issues; strengthen and encourage the profession's code of ethics; maintain professional standards. Maintains database of personal and career data on its membership. Holds educational seminars and training programs on health care management. Offers student loans and personal loan program. Operates Healthcare Executives Career Resource Center. Maintains numerous committees and task forces; conducts research programs; compiles statistics. **Publications:** Directory, biennial. • *Frontiers of Health Services Management*, quarterly. Journal. Contains articles and commentaries from outstanding scholars and practitioners in the field. *Price:* $65/year. • *Health Services Research*, bimonthly. Journal. Provides information on new trends and the latest techniques of research and evaluation. *Price:* $60/year in U.S.; $70/year outside U.S. • *Healthcare Executive*, bimonthly. Magazine. Devoted to professional development issues in health care management. *Price:* $45/year in U.S.; $70/year outside U.S. • *Hospital and Health Services Administration*, quarterly. Journal. Focuses on hospital and health services administration. *Price:* $55/year (U.S.); $65/year (outside U.S.). Also publishes *Career Mart* (career listings), case studies, books, journals, manuals, and special studies; offers cassette tapes. **Formerly:** (1985) American College of Hospital Administrators.

★ 5547 ★ American College of Medical Practice Executives (ACMGA)
104 Inverness Ter. E.
Englewood, CO 80112-5306
Phone: (303)397-7869
Fax: (303)643-4427
Fred E. Graham, II, Ph, Sr.Assoc.Exec.Dir.

Founded: 1956. **Members:** 2,102. **Description:** Professional certification organization. Membership is drawn from Medical Group Management Association. Works to encourage medical group practice administrators to improve and maintain their proficiency and to provide appropriate recognition; to establish a program with uniform standards of admission, advancement, and certification in order to achieve the highest possible standards in the profession of medical group practice administration; to participate in the development of educational and research programs for the advancement of the

profession; to inform the medical profession and the public of the value of trained and experienced men and women in the management of the administrative affairs of all forms of group practice; to instill in its membership a constant awareness of the high ideals and traditions of the medical profession and medical group administration so that its members will conduct themselves in such a manner as to augment those ideals and traditions. Conducts educational programs such as Management Education Programs and Group Practice Governance Leadership Institute. **Publications:** *American College of Medical Practice Executives*, annual. Professional manuscripts submitted to the College for advancement credit since 1956; arranged by subject and author. *Price:* $10/copy to members; $16/copy to affiliates; $22/copy to nonmembers. • *College Review*, semiannual. Journal. Contains the best of the professional papers and case studies submitted by individuals seeking fellow status in the ACMGA. *Price:* Free to ACMGA affiliates; $30/year for nonmembers. • *Your Pathway to Excellence*. Brochure. Provides general information regarding ACMPE membership application. **Formerly:** (1976) American College of Clinic Managers; (1993) American College of Medical Group Administrators.

★ 5548 ★ American College of Mental Health Administration (ACMHA)
225 W. Swissvale Ave.
Pittsburgh, PA 15218-1632
Phone: (412)244-0670
Fax: (412)244-9916
Lawrence A. Heller, Ph.D., Exec.Dir.

Founded: 1980. **Members:** 200. **Description:** Mental health clinician administrators. **Publications:** *ACMHA Newsletter*, quarterly. Newsletter. Includes organization news and critical essays. *Price:* $12/year.

★ 5549 ★ American College of Physician Executives (ACPE)
4890 W. Kennedy Blvd., Ste. 200
Tampa, FL 33609
Phone: (813)287-2000
Free: 800-562-8088
Fax: (813)287-8993
Roger S. Schenke, Exec.VP

Founded: 1978. **Members:** 9,700. **Description:** Physicians whose primary professional responsibility is the management of health care organizations. Provides for continuing education and certification of the physician executive and the advancement and recognition of the physician executive and the profession. Offers specialized career planning, counseling, recruitment and placement services, and research and information data on physician managers. **Publications:** *American College of Physician Executives--Membership Directory*, annual. Membership Directory. *Price:* Included in membership dues. • *College Digest*, bimonthly. Newsletter. Includes employment opportunity and new member listings. *Price:* Included in membership dues. • *Fundamentals of Medical Management: A Guide for the Physician Executive*. Book. Includes discussion of organizational theory, effective communication, negotiating skills, conflict management, and organizational politics.

Price: $40 for members; $50 for nonmembers. • *Get the Job You Want and the Money You're Worth*. Monograph. Outlines a step-by-step strategy to planning a successful job pursuit, with advice on structuring your resume and setting up personal networking. *Price:* $15 for members; $25 for nonmembers. • *Health Care Quality Management for the 21st Century*. Book. Attempts to place the current health care delivery crisis into historical perspective. *Price:* $65 for members; $75 for nonmembers. • *International Health Care: A Bibliography*. Bibliography. Contains material on international health care systems such as up-to-date lists of citations from the literature. *Price:* $20 for members; $40 for nonmembers. • *Managing in an Academic Health Care Environment*. Book. Provides an overview of managing in this unique environment. *Price:* $40 for members; $50 for nonmembers. • *Medical Directors: What, Why, How*. Monograph. Covers the possible responsibilities for the position of Medical Director. *Price:* $15 for members; $20 for nonmembers. • *New Leadership in Health Care Managment--The Physician Executive*. Book. Outlines the knowledge base physician executives must master in order to effectively compete and succeed. *Price:* $35 for members; $49 for nonmembers. • *Physician Executive: Journal of Management*, monthly. Journal. Includes recurring columns on health economics and health law. *Price:* Included in membership dues.

★ 5550 ★ American Healthcare Radiology Administrators (AHRA)
PO Box 334
Sudbury, MA 01776
Phone: (508)443-7591
Teresa Cryan, Adm.Mgr.

Founded: 1973. **Members:** 3,500. **Regional Groups:** 5. **Description:** Radiology managers. Works to improve management of radiology departments in hospitals and other health care facilities; to provide a forum for publication of educational, scientific, and professional materials. Has established code of ethics for the profession. Provides liaison between related organizations such as radiology, health care and management groups, and government agencies. Compiles statistics; conducts specialized education programs. **Publications:** *Bibliography for the Radiology Administator*. • Membership Directory, annual. • *Radiology Management*, quarterly. **Formerly:** (1986) American Hospital Radiology Administrators.

★ 5551 ★ American Health Planning Association (AHPA)
1735 Eye St. NW, Ste. 501
Washington, DC 20006
Phone: (202)371-1515
Phyllis Kae, Contact

Founded: 1970. **Description:** State and local health planning agencies and affiliated organizations and individuals. Conducts research; disseminates information; serves as clearinghouse for health planning activities and concepts; sponsors programs of technical assistance; provides continuing education. **Publications:** *Directory of State and Local Health Planning Agencies*, annual. Directory. • *TODAY in Health Planning*, periodic. **Formerly:** Association of Areawide Health Planning Agencies; (1977) American Association for Comprehensive Health Planning.

★5552★ **American Organization of Nurse Executives (AONE)**
One N. Franklin, 34th Fl.
Chicago, IL 60606
Phone: (312)422-2800
Fax: (312)422-4503
Marjorie Beyers, RN, Exec.Dir.

Founded: 1967. **Members:** 6,000. **State Groups:** 69. **Description:** Provides leadership, professional development, advocacy, and research to advance nursing practice and patient care, promote nursing leadership and excellence, and shape healthcare public policy. Supports and enhances the management, leadership, educational, and professional development of nursing leaders. Offers placement service through Career Development and Referral Center. **Publications:** *AONE News*, quarterly. Newsletter. Independent look at issues facing nursing administrations and quality patient care. *Price:* Included in membership dues. • *AONE Updates*, 3/weeks. Newsletter. Bulleted update of information related to nursing administration. • Books. • Membership Directory, annual. *Price:* Included in membership dues. • Monographs. • Videos. **Formerly:** (1977) American Society for Hospital Nursing Service Administrators; (1984) American Society for Nursing Service Administrators.

★5553★ **American Society for Healthcare Human Resources Administration (ASHHRA)**
c/o American Hospital Association
1 N. Franklin
Chicago, IL 60606
Phone: (312)280-6722
Fax: (312)280-4152
Linda Brooks, Dir.

Founded: 1964. **Members:** 2,900. **Description:** Purposes are: to provide effective and continuous leadership in the field of health care human resources administration; to promote cooperation with hospitals and allied associations in matters pertaining to hospital human resources administration; to further the professional and educational development of members; to encourage and promote research; to encourage and assist local groups in chapter formation through regular programs and institutes on health care human resources issues. Offers placement service. **Publications:** *Directory of Health Care Human Resources Consultants*, annual. Directory. • *Hospitals,* bimonthly. • *Human Resources Administrator*, bimonthly. Newsletter. Reports on professional ethics and legislative activity. Includes calendar of events and chapter and member news. *Price:* Included in membership dues. • *Roster of Membership*, annual. Membership Directory.

★5554★ **American Society for Healthcare Risk Management (ASHRM)**
American Hospital Association
One N. Franklin
Chicago, IL 60606
Phone: (312)422-3980
Fax: (312)422-4580
Trudy Goldman, Exec.Dir.

Founded: 1980. **Members:** 2,800. **Description:** Employees actively involved in the risk management functions of hospitals or other health care providers; associate members are persons employed by non-health care providers. Purposes are to: promote professional development of hospital risk managers; provide educational resources and programs on hospital risk management; address risk management issues affecting the health care industry. **Publications:** *Journal of Healthcare Risk Management*, quarterly. Journal. Covers research, trends, and new developments in the field of healthcare risk management. Includes educational program calendar and legal update. *Price:* Included in membership dues.

★5555★ **American Society for Hospital Food Service Administrators (ASHFSA)**
c/o American Hospital Association
840 N. Lake Shore Dr.
Chicago, IL 60611
Phone: (312)280-6416
Kathleen Pontius, Dir.

Founded: 1967. **Members:** 1,800. **Local Groups:** 64. **Description:** Directors and assistant directors of food service departments in health care institutions. Members must be eligible for personal membership in the American Hospital Association. Promotes improved administration of food service departments through activities that foster continuing education and development of management skills by members. **Publications:** Newsletter, bimonthly. • *Summary of Chapter Activities*, annual. Also publishes food service reference works on administration, budgeting, cafeteria and financial management, and hospital food service system planning.

★5556★ **American Society of Ophthalmic Administrators (ASOA)**
4000 Legato Rd., No. 850
Fairfax, VA 22033
Phone: (703)591-2222
Free: 800-451-1339
Fax: (703)591-0614
Lucy Santiago, Exec.Admin.

Founded: 1986. **Members:** 1,700. **Description:** A division of the American Society of Cataract and Refractive Surgery . Persons involved with the administration of an ophthalmic office or clinic. Facilitates the exchange of ideas and information in order to improve management practices and working conditions. Offers placement services. **Publications:** *Administrative Ophthalmology*, quarterly. Magazine. *Price:* $45/year. • *Managed Care and Contracting*. Manual. *Price:* $150 for members; $225 for nonmembers. • *Ophthalmic Reimbursement Manual*. Manual. *Price:* $90 for members; $145 for nonmembers.

★5557★ **Association of Family Practice Residency Directors (AFPRD)**
8880 Ward Pky.
Kansas City, MO 64114-2756
Phone: (816)333-9700
Free: 800-274-2237
Fax: (816)333-9855
John W. Saultz, M.D., Pres.

Founded: 1990. **Members:** 382. **Description:** Directors of family practice residency programs. Promotes excellence in family practice graduate education. Provides representation for residency directors. Facilitates cooperation and communication among different branches of the family practice specialty. **Publications:** *Highlights*, 3/year. *Price:* Free.

★5558★ **Association of Healthcare Internal Auditors (AHIA)**
1101 Connecticut Ave. NW, Ste. 700
Washington, DC 20036
Phone: (202)429-5134
Fax: (202)223-4579
Dennis E. Smeage, Exec.Dir.

Founded: 1981. **Members:** 100. **Regional Groups:** 35. **Local Groups:** 6. **Description:** Health care internal auditors and other interested individuals. Promotes cost containment and increased productivity in health care institutions through internal auditing. Serves as a forum for the exchange of experience, ideas, and information among members; provides continuing professional education courses and informs members of developments in health care internal auditing. Offers employment clearinghouse services. **Publications:** *New Perspectives*, quarterly. Journal. Contains book reviews, audit findings, and local and regional group news. • *New Perspectives on Healthcare Internal Auditing*, annual. Membership Directory. **Formerly:** (1989) Healthcare Internal Audit Group.

★5559★ **Association of Health Facility Survey Agencies (AHFSA)**
Missouri Department of Health
Bureau of Hospital Licensing
1738 E. Elm
PO Box 570
Jefferson City, MO 65102
Phone: (314)751-6302
Fax: (314)526-3621
Darrell Hendrickson, Admin.

Founded: 1968. **Members:** 51. **Description:** Directors of state or territorial health facility licensure and certification programs; staff members of a state or territorial health facility licensure and certification agency; employees of the federal Health Care Financing Administration; interested individuals. (The term health facilities refers to health/medical institutions including hospitals, nursing homes, rehabilitation centers, reproductive health centers, independent clinical laboratories, hospices, and ambulatory surgical centers.) Purposes are to: exchange information among members and between members and the Association of State and Territorial Health Officials; constitute a "reservoir of expertise" to aid in the guidance of ASTHO; improve the quality of health facility licensure and certification programs; provide a forum for state and territorial issues at the national level. Has a representative on an ASTHO standing committee and liaises with the federal Department of Health and Human Services and the HCFA. Has developed new training programs with the HHS and testified before the U.S. Senate Special Committee on Aging on survey and certification procedures. Bestows annual Surveyor of the Year Award. **Publications:** *AHFSA Directory*, annual. Directory. • *Association of Health Facility Survey Agencies Newsletter*, semiannual. Newsletter. Reports on the quality of health facility licensure and certification programs and related issues. Includes calendar of events. *Price:* Included in membership dues. • Papers. **Formerly:** (1991) Association of Health Facility Licensure and Certification Directors.

★5560★ **Association of Managerial Hospital Doctors of Germany (Verband der Leitenden Krankenhausarzte Deutschlands)**
Tersteegenstr. 9
40474 Dusseldorf, Germany
Phone: 211 454990
Fax: 211 451834
Gerd Nordern, Contact

Founded: 1912. **Members:** 5,500. **Description:** Promotes the interests of physicians working in German hospitals.

★5561★ **Association of Mental Health Administrators (AMHA)**
60 Revere Dr., Ste. 500
Northbrook, IL 60062
Phone: (708)480-9626
Fax: (708)480-9282
Maria R. Helm, Exec.Dir.

Founded: 1959. **Members:** 1,100. **Description:** Administrators of services for the emotionally disturbed, mentally ill, mentally retarded, developmentally disabled, and those with problems of alcohol and substance abuse. Objectives are to: further the education of administrators; develop criteria for and certify the competence of administrators; promote adherence to a code of ethics. Aids in developing professional administrative skills and administration of services. Sponsors educational workshops. **Publications:** *AMHA Leader*, bimonthly. Newsletter. • *Journal of Mental Health Administration*, quarterly. Journal. Covers management practice, research, and policy issues in mental health field. **Formerly:** (1969) American Society of Mental Health Business Administrators.

★5562★ **Association of Otolaryngology Administrators (AOA)**
PO Box 3150
Iowa City, IA 52244-3150
Phone: (319)356-2371
Patrick R. Connolly, Ph.D., Exec.Sec.

Founded: 1983. **Members:** 600. **Regional Groups:** 8. **Description:** Persons employed in a managerial capacity for private or academic group medical practices specializing in otolaryngology (the study of the ear, nose, and throat). Seeks to: promote the concept of professional management in otolaryngology; provide a forum for interaction and exchange of information between otolaryngological managers; present educational programs. Maintains data exchange service for members researching specific topics. **Publications:** *Oto's Scope*, 3/year.

★5563★ **Association of State and Territorial Dental Directors (ASTDD)**
Minnesota Dept. of Health
717 Delaware St. SE
Minneapolis, MN 55440
Phone: (612)623-5441
Fax: (612)623-5775
Dr. Robert Isman, Sec.-Treas.

Members: 53. **Description:** Directors of state and territorial dental programs. Provides a forum for consideration of dental health administrative problems and policies on the state and territorial level; promotes constructive plans for better administrative procedures.

★5564★ **Association of State and Territorial Directors of Nursing (ASTDN)**
Ohio Department of Health
Bureau of Nursing
246 N. High St.
Columbus, OH 43266-0588
Phone: (614)466-2205
Joya Neff, R.N., Pres.

Members: 54. **Description:** Directors of nursing in the states and territories. Serves as a channel for sharing methods, techniques, and information to increase the effectiveness of public health nursing services; cooperates with other professional groups in public health and related fields. **Formerly:** (1966) Association of State and Territorial Directors of Public Health Nursing.

★5565★ **Association of State and Territorial Directors of Public Health Education (ASTDPHE)**
c/o Lydia Pendley
Health Promotion Bureau
New Mexico Department of Health
1190 St. Francis Dr.
PO Box 26110
Santa Fe, NM 87502-6110
Phone: (505)827-2380
Fax: (505)827-0021
Lydia Pendley, Pres.

Founded: 1946. **Members:** 76. **Description:** Directors of public health education in state and territorial departments of health and Indian health service areas. Seeks to improve the quality of public health education practice; promote information exchange and advocacy. Develops practice guidelines and supports collection and dissemination of data and information relevant to public health education. **Publications:** *Conference Call*, quarterly. Newsletter. • Proceedings, annual. • *Roster of Members*, quarterly. **Formerly:** (1989) Conference of State and Territorial Directors of Public Health Education.

★5566★ **Association of State and Territorial Health Officials (ASTHO)**
415 2nd St. NE, Ste. 200
Washington, DC 20002
Phone: (202)546-5400
Fax: (202)544-9349
Cheryl A. Beversdorf, Exec.VP

Founded: 1942. **Members:** 55. **Description:** Executive officers of state and territorial health departments. Represents state and territorial health officers on matters of federal health, legislation, and policies; aids public or private agencies dealing with human health, especially in interstate and federal relationships. **Publications:** *ASTHO Annual Report*, annual. Annual Report. *Price:* Free. • *Conference Proceedings*, annual. Proceedings. • Membership Directory, biennial. • Newsletter, periodic. • *State Public Health Agencies*, biennial. Directory. Lists state health departments. *Price:* $25. **Formerly:** (1975) Association of State and Territorial Health Officers.

★5567★ **Association of University Programs in Health Administration (AUPHA)**
1911 N. Fort Myer Dr., Ste. 503
Arlington, VA 22209
Phone: (703)524-5500
Eugene Schneller, Ph.D., Contact

Founded: 1948. **Members:** 1,200. **Description:** Universities offering graduate and undergraduate study in health services and hospital administration. To improve the quality of education in health services administration. Undertakes research and educational programs, such as studies of the criteria used for selection of students and curriculum patterns adopted by various universities. Conducts faculty institutes on topics relating to health administration. Compiles statistics. **Publications:** *AUPHA Exchange*, bimonthly. Newsletter. • *Health Services Administration Education*, biennial. Directory. • *Journal of Health Administration Education*, quarterly. Journal. **Formerly:** (1973) Association of University Programs in Hospital Administration.

★5568★ **Canadian College of Health Service Executives**
350 Sparks St., Ste. 402
Ottawa, ON, Canada K1R 7S2
Phone: (613)235-7218
Free: 800-363-9056
Fax: (613)235-5451
Jim Pealow, CMA, Contact

Founded: 1970. **Members:** 3,200. **Regional Groups:** 20. **Publications:** *Healthcare Management Forum*, quarterly, always March, June, September, and December. Journal. Articles on innovations in health services.

★5569★ **Center for Research in Ambulatory Health Care Administration (CRAHCA)**
104 Inverness Ter. E.
Englewood, CO 80112-5306
Phone: (303)397-7879
Fax: (303)643-4427
Frederick Wenzel, CEO

Founded: 1973. **Description:** Participants work with administrators of medical group practices in the U.S., Canada, Mexico, and Europe. Purpose is to promote efficient administration in medical group practices and thereby assist in upgrading the quality of medical care through innovative educational programs. Conducts educational programs and research on management systems, cost, and productivity. Compiles statistics. **Publications:** *Academic Practce Management Survey*, annual. Survey. • *Academic Practice Faculty Compensation and Production Survey*, annual. Survey. • *An Assessment Manual for Medical Groups*. Manual. • *Budgeting and Cost Management for Medical*

Groups. • *Cost Survey Report*, annual. Survey. Provides revenue and expense data on the operation of medical group practices by size, geographic location, and type of practice. • *Directions: Quality Assurance Manual for Physician Office Laboratories*. • *In-House Supervisory Training Program*. • *Membership Compensation Survey Report*, annual. Survey. Describes scope of compensation and fringe benefits for group practice administrators. • *Physican Compensation and Production Survey*, annual. Survey. • *Physician Compensation and Production Survey Report*, annual. Survey. • *Physician Recruitment and Retention: A Guide for Rural Medical Group Practice*. • *Telephone Nursing: The Manual*. Manual. • *Twelve Key Strategies to Improve Cash Flow in Medical Groups*.

★ 5570 ★ **College of Osteopathic**
  Healthcare Executives (COHE)
5301 Wisconsin Ave. NW, Ste. 630
Washington, DC 20015
Phone: (202)686-1700
Fax: (202)686-7615
David L. Kushner, Pres.

Founded: 1954. **Members:** 150. **Description:** Executives of osteopathic hospitals. To encourage development of hospital administration; to set criteria of competency; to assist in educational programs; to contribute to advancement of efficient hospital administration. **Publications:** Annual Report. • *COHE News Briefs*, periodic. Newsletter. Covers educational programs, evaluation systems, and new affiliates. Contains calendar of events and obituaries. *Price:* Included in membership dues. • *College of Osteopathic Healthcare Executives--Directory*, annual. Directory. *Price:* Included in membership dues. **Formerly:** (1986) American College of Osteopathic Hospital Administrators.

★ 5571 ★ **Committee for Nordic Hospital**
  Administrators Associations
Postboks 3042
Elisenberg
N-0207 Oslo, Norway
Phone: 2 445730
Fax: 2 449040
Thor Egeland, Gen.Sec.

Founded: 1974. **Members:** 1,800. **National Groups:** 4. **Languages:** Danish, English, Finnish, Icelandic, Norwegian, Swedish. **Description:** Hospital administrators in Denmark, Finland, Iceland, Norway, and Sweden. **Publications:** *Journal*, periodic. Journal.

★ 5572 ★ **Council of Administrators of**
  Special Education (CASE)
615 16th St. NW
Albuquerque, NM 87104
Phone: (505)243-7622
Fax: (505)247-4822
Dr. Jo Thomason, Exec.Dir.

Founded: 1951. **Members:** 4,900. **State Groups:** 41. **Description:** Current members of Council for Exceptional Children (see separate entry) who are administrators, directors, supervisors, and/or coordinators of programs, schools, or classes of special education for exceptional children; college faculty and graduate students whose major responsibility is the professional preparation of administrators of spe-

cial education; individuals interested in special education. Promotes professional leadership, provides opportunity for study of problems common to its members, and disseminates information that will develop improved services for exceptional children. Sponsors regional training institutes for special education administrator leadership skill development. Maintains speakers' bureau on topics concerning issues in administration of programs for exceptional, handicapped, and gifted children. **Publications:** *CASE in Point*, semiannual. Journal. Concerned with programs and developments affecting the special education field. *Price:* Included in membership dues. • *CASE Newsletter*, 5/year. Newsletter. Covers council activities and news. *Price:* Included in membership dues. • Monographs. Also publishes special education program management packets.

★ 5573 ★ **Dental Group Management**
  Association (DGMA)
c/o Ann Pakalski
North Point Dental Group
7040 N. Port Washington
Glendale, WI 53217
Phone: (414)224-1020
Lynn Shields, Exec. Officer

Founded: 1951. **Members:** 200. **Regional Groups:** 2. **Description:** Dental group business managers and others interested in group practice management. **Publications:** *DGMA Communicator*, bimonthly. Newsletter. Includes job listings and membership profiles. *Price:* Free. • Newsletter, semimonthly. Also publishes articles and books.

★ 5574 ★ **European Association of Hospital**
  Managers (EAHM)
  (Europaische Vereinigung der Krankenhaus
  Direkteren)
Centre Hospitalier Regional
1, place de l'Hopital
F-67091 Strasbourg Cedex, France
Phone: 88 161150
Fax: 88 161330
Claude-Guy Charlotte, Sec.Gen.

Founded: 1970. **Members:** 18. **Languages:** English, French, German. **Description:** National associations of hospital administrators. Promotes hospital organization and administration; conducts research on administration and publicizes findings; represents members before international organizations. **Formerly:** (1990) European Association of Hospital Administrators.

★ 5575 ★ **European Healthcare**
  Management Association (EHMA)
Vergemount Hall
Clonskeagh
Dublin 6, Ireland
Phone: 1 2839299
Fax: 1 2838653
Philip C. Berman, Dir.

Founded: 1966. **Members:** 180. **Languages:** English, French. **Description:** Policy makers, senior managers, personnel directors, academic institutions, and research organizations in the healthcare sector. Seeks to improve healthcare in Europe by raising standards of managerial performance in the health sector. Fosters cooperation between health service organizations

and institutions in the field of healthcare management education and training. Promotes the continuing education and development of healthcare managers. Offers advice and support to national governments in Europe; evaluates members' management development programs. **Publications:** *Conference Proceedings*, annual. Journal. • *Health Services Administration Education and Research*, annual. Directory. • *Management Development for Health Care: An International Perspective*. • *Management Education and Training in the Health Sector: A Perspective for Italy*. • Newsletter, bimonthly. **Formerly:** (1987) European Association of Programmes in Health Services Studies.

Federation of American Health Systems
  (FAHS)
See: Entry 6442

★ 5576 ★ **Foundation of American College**
  of Health Care Administrators (FACHCA)
325 S. Patrick St.
Alexandria, VA 22314
Phone: (703)549-5822
Fax: (703)739-7901
Richard L. Thorpe, Exec.VP

Founded: 1971. **Members:** 2,000. **Description:** Individuals dedicated to the improvement of the administration of long-term care facilities. Conducts professional training programs and research in administration; compiles statistics. **Publications:** *Foundation Focus in Long-term Care Administration*, quarterly. Newsletter. Includes research updates. *Price:* Included in membership dues. • *The Journal of Long-Term Care Administration*, quarterly. *Price:* $70/year. **Formerly:** (1983) Foundation of American College of Nursing Home Administrators.

★ 5577 ★ **The Healthcare Forum (THF)**
830 Market St., 8th Fl.
San Francisco, CA 94102
Phone: (415)421-8810
Fax: (415)421-8837
Kathryn E. Johnson, CEO & Pres.

Founded: 1927. **Members:** 1,000. **Description:** Individuals and organizational leaders worldwide. Provides education and applied research services. Works to create healthier communities through innovative leadership thinking, organizational learning and mastering change. **Publications:** *Healthcare Forum Journal*, bimonthly. Journal. *Price:* $45/year. • *VIS*. Also publishes executive summaries and compendia. **Formerly:** Association of Western Hospitals.

★ 5578 ★ **Health Care Material**
  Management Society (HCMMS)
306 Crestview Dr.
Grapevine, TX 76051-3569
Phone: (817)421-8517
Free: 800-543-5885
Fax: (817)421-8971
Richard D. Warmanen, Exec.Dir.

Founded: 1975. **Members:** 1,000. **Regional Groups:** 8. **Description:** Materials management personnel in health care and hospital fields. Purpose is to advance health care management. Provides forum for the exchange of professional and technical information and ideas among members. Develops and distributes educational materials; sponsors exhibitions, seminars, slide shows, and other educational activities. Administers certification program. Works to establish a foundation for the solicitation of research and development grants from health care oriented industries and to further develop audiovisual programs on topics such as hospital costs, distribution, logistics, life cycle costs, and recycling management of inventory. Operates referral service; maintains speakers' bureau. **Publications:** *The Material Difference*, monthly. Newsletter. Includes calender of events and articles. **Formerly:** (1982) Health Care Section of the International Material Management Society.

★5579★ **Hospital Directors Association of Germany**
(Verband der Krankenhausdirektoren Deutschlands)
Kaiserstr. 50
45468 Muhlheim, Germany
Phone: 208 3052755
Fax: 208 3052744
Gabriele Kirchner, Contact

Founded: 1903. **Members:** 3,559. **Description:** Directors of hospitals throughout Germany. Fosters exchange of information between members. Promotes continuing education for administrative executives and employees in hospital administration.

★5580★ **Hospital Research and Educational Trust (HRET)**
1 N. Franklin
Chicago, IL 60606
Phone: (312)422-2600
Deborah Bohr, VP

Founded: 1944. **Description:** Encourages and engages in educational, research, and demonstration activities to improve the management of hospital and health services. **Publications:** Books. • *Health Services Research*, bimonthly. • Manuals. • Monographs. **Formerly:** (1959) Educational Trust of the American Hospital Association.

★5581★ **Institute of Certified Professional Managers (ICPM)**
James Madison University
Harrisonburg, VA 22807
Phone: (703)568-3247
Free: 800-568-4120
Fax: (703)568-3587
Dr. Jackson E. Ramsey, Exec.Dir.

Founded: 1974. **Members:** 5,700. **Description:** Supervisors and managers meeting specific educational and experience prerequisites are qualified to take the certifying examination. Purposes are: to recognize management as a profession and acknowledge competence demonstrated in the managerial field; to provide opportunities for study in the supervisory and managerial field; to supply a critical, third party evaluation of managerial competence. Offers three preparatory courses for the examination including: personal skills focusing on leadership qualities; administrative skills to help the individual in becoming a well-rounded generalist; interpersonal skills that assist in motivating subordinates to maximum achievement. Compiles statistics. **Publications:** *Certified Letter*, quarterly. Newsletter.

Institute of Health Record Information and Management (IHRIM)
See: Entry 7001

★5582★ **Intergovernmental Health Policy Project (IHPP)**
2021 K St. NW, Ste. 800
Washington, DC 20006
Phone: (202)872-1445
Fax: (202)785-0114
Richard E. Merritt, Dir.

Founded: 1979. **Description:** Health policy researchers. Provides information on state health legislation and programs to state executive officials, legislators, legislative staff, and others. Serves as information clearinghouse; responds to specific information requests on state programs. Compiles statistics. Offers a customized legislative tracking service to customers. **Publications:** *Intergovernmental AIDS Report*, 10/year. Newsletter. • Monograph, annual. Summarizes state legislation relating to health care. • *Primary Care News*, bimonthly. Newsletter. • *State ADM Report*, 10/year. Newsletter. • *State Health Notes*, 24/year. Newsletter.

International Association of Healthcare Central Service Material Management (IAHCSM)
See: Entry 6449

★5583★ **Laboratory Animal Management Association Lab Animal Program (LAMA)**
c/o Fred Douglas
PO Box 1744
Silver Spring, MD 20915
Phone: (317)494-7592
Fax: (317)494-0781
Fred Douglas, Pres.

Founded: 1984. **Members:** 435. **Regional Groups:** 3. **Description:** Laboratory animal facility managers. Seeks to evaluate and update basic and advanced management techniques and to educate laboratory animal facility managers. Makes available resource material; coordinates exchange programs for management personnel. Offers consulting on management techniques. **Publications:** *LAMA Lines*, bimonthly. Includes branch news and a listing for employment opportunities. *Price:* Included in membership dues. • *Lama Review*, quarterly. Journal. • Membership Directory, annual. **Formerly:** Laboratory Animal Managers Association.

★5584★ **Medical Group Management Association (MGMA)**
104 Inverness Ter. E.
Englewood, CO 80112
Phone: (303)799-1111
Fax: (303)643-4427
Frederick Wenzel, Exec.Dir. & CEO

Founded: 1926. **Members:** 15,000. **Description:** Persons actively engaged in the business management of medical groups consisting of three or more physicians in medical practice with centralized business functions. Sponsors educational training programs. Provides placement and information services. Compiles statistics. **Publications:** *Administrators' Bookshelf*, annual. Bibliography. Lists new books in the health administration field. Includes directory of publishers and list of recommended journals.

Price: $12/copy for affiliates; $25/copy for nonmembers. • Booklets. • Brochures. • *Cost Survey Report*, annual. Report. Provides revenue and expense data on the operation of medical group practices by size, geographic location, and type of practice. *Price:* $65/copy for members; $210/copy for affiliates; $185/copy for nonmembers. • *Health Exchange*, quarterly. Newsletter. Contains general articles related to health and wellness. • *Medical Group Management Journal*, bimonthly. Journal. Covers group practice management topics including financial management and accounting, data processing, and purchasing and maintenance. *Price:* $42/year. • *Medical Group Management-- Management Update*, monthly. Reports on current legislative activities, practical management issues, and trends in the health care community. Includes association news. *Price:* Available to members only. • *Medical Group Management Washington Report*, monthly. Legislative and regulatory news service. *Price:* $30/year for members; $40/year for nonmembers. • *MGMA Directory*, annual. Membership Directory. Geographical and alphabetical listing of members; cross-referenced by services, personnel, facilities, and equipment. *Price:* Free to members and affiliates; $265/year for nonmembers. • *MGMA Membership Compensation Survey Report*, annual. Report. Shows compensation and fringe benefits for group practice administrators; includes analysis by CRAHCA. *Price:* Free to members; $100/year for nonmembers. **Formerly:** (1946) Association of Clinic Managers; (1963) National Association of Clinical Managers.

National Association of Boards of Examiners for Nursing Home Administrators (NAB)
See: Entry 9268

★5585★ **National Association of Directors of Nursing Administration in Long Term Care (NADONA/LTC)**
10999 Reed Hartman Hwy., Ste. 229
Cincinnati, OH 45242
Phone: (513)791-3679
Free: 800-222-0539
Fax: (513)791-3699
Joan C. Warden, R.N., Exec.Dir.

Founded: 1986. **Members:** 2,700. **Regional Groups:** 5. **State Groups:** 27. **Description:** Directors, assistant directors, and former directors of nursing in long term care. Goals are: to create and establish an acceptable ethical standard for practices in long term care nursing administration; to promote and encourage research in the profession; to develop and provide a consistent program of education and certification for the positions of director, associate director, and assistant director; to promote a positive image of the long term health care industry. Encourages members to share concerns and experiences; sponsors research programs. Advocates legislation pertaining to the practice of professional nursing. Maintains speakers' bureau. **Publications:** *Director*, quarterly. Journal. Includes research and clinical papers and news items. *Price:* Included in membership dues. • *Director II*, bimonthly.

★5586★ **National Association of Health Services Executives (NAHSE)**
10320 Little Patuxent Pky., Ste. 1106
Columbia, MD 21044
Phone: (202)628-3953
Fax: (301)588-0011
Ozzie Jenkins, Cmp.Dir.

Founded: 1968. **Members:** 500. **Regional Groups:** 16. **Local Groups:** 7. **Description:** Black health care executive managers, planners, educators, advocates, providers, organizers, researchers, and consumers participating in academic ventures, educational forums, seminars, workshops, systems design, legislation, and other activities. Conducts National Work-Study Program and sponsors educational programs. **Publications:** *NAHSE Notes*, quarterly. Newsletter. *Price:* Free.

★5587★ **National Association Medical Staff Services (NAMSS)**
PO Box 23350
Knoxville, TN 37933-1350
Phone: (615)531-3571
Fax: (615)531-9939
Margaret Nicholson, Exec. Officer

Founded: 1971. **Members:** 3,000. **Regional Groups:** 5. **State Groups:** 42. **Local Groups:** 32. **Description:** Individuals involved in the management and administration of medical staff services. Seeks to: enhance the knowledge and experience of medical staff services professionals; establish degree-level programs in the field; promote the certification of those involved in the profession. **Publications:** *Credentials Guidelines*, bimonthly. Journal. *Price:* $50. • *Job Classifications: Delineation of Clinical Privileges, Criteria, and Forms.* • *Medical Staff Leadership Orientation Manual.* • *NAMSS Membership Roster*, annual. Membership Directory. • *Overview*, bimonthly. Magazine. *Price:* Included in membership dues; $50/year for nonmembers.

National Association of Professional Geriatric Care Managers (NAPGCM)
See: Entry 1908

★5588★ **National Association of State Alcohol and Drug Abuse Directors (NASADAD)**
444 N. Capitol St. NW, Ste. 642
Washington, DC 20001
Phone: (202)783-6868
Fax: (202)783-2704
John S. Gustafson, Exec.Dir.

Founded: 1971. **Members:** 56. **Description:** Purposes are: to represent the interests of state alcohol and drug abuse directors and their agencies before Congress and federal agencies; to foster development of comprehensive alcohol and drug abuse programs on state resources/services, alcohol and drug issues related to AIDS, drunk driving, and criminal justice activities in each state. Operates Project for Addiction Counselor Training, AIDS Policy Project, Criminal Justice Programs, Methadone Treatment Quality Assurance System project, and the National Perinatal Addiction Prevention Resource and Technical Assistance Center. Serves as an information clearinghouse. Conducts seminars on current and emerging alcohol

and drug issues. **Publications:** *Directory of State Alcohol and Drug Abuse Directors*, monthly. Directory. • *National Prevention Network Newsletter*, 10/year. Newsletter. *Price:* $60. • *Public Policy Quarterly*, quarterly. Newsletter. Covers significant national and state development. *Price:* $80. • *Special Report. Price:* $80/year. • *State Alcohol and Drug Abuse Profile*, annual. Provides data on state fiscal resources, services to clients, drug trends, model products, and special needs. • *State Resource and Services Related to Alcohol and Drug Problems*, annual. • *Treatment Works.* **Formerly:** (1978) National Association of State Drug Abuse Program Coordinators.

★5589★ **National Association of State EMS Directors (NASEMSD)**
1947 Camino Vida Roble, Ste. 202
Carlsbad, CA 92008
Phone: (619)431-7054
Fax: (619)431-8135
Pam McMaster, Contact

Founded: 1981. **Members:** 56. **Regional Groups:** 4. **Description:** State emergency medical services directors united to: refine EMS activities; coordinate such activities between states; serve as a liaison with other national medical organizations. Compiles statistics. Conducts research programs. **Publications:** *EMS Offices, Structures, and Functions.* • *EMT Certification, Licensing, and Reciprocity Requirements.* • *NASEMSD Scanner*, quarterly. Newsletter. Includes information on state EMS programs. • *Training and Certification of EMS Personnel.* • *Trauma Center Designation Survey.* Survey.

★5590★ **National Association of State Mental Health Program Directors (NASMHPD)**
66 Canal Center Plz., Ste. 302
Alexandria, VA 22314
Phone: (703)739-9333
Fax: (703)548-9517
Dr. Robert W. Glover, Exec.Dir.

Founded: 1963. **Members:** 55. **Description:** State commissioners in charge of the state mental disability programs; associate members are assistant commissioners for children and youth, research, aged, legal services, forensic services, human resource development, and community programs. Promotes cooperation of state government agencies in delivery of services to mentally disabled persons; fosters the exchange of scientific and programmatic information in the administration of public mental health programs including mental illness treatment programs, community and hospital care of mentally ill, mentally retarded, alcoholic, and drug addicted persons. Monitors state and federal and congressional activities; gathers and analyzes information on organization, structure, funding, and programming of state government mental health programs. A cooperating agency of the National Governors' Association and the Council of State Governments. **Publications:** *Children and Youth Update*, periodic. Newsletter. • *Federal Agencies*, periodic. Newsletter. • *Legal Issues*, periodic. Newsletter. • *State Report*, periodic. Newsletter. • *Studies*, periodic. Newsletter. • *U.S. Congress*, periodic. Newsletter.

★5591★ **National Association of State Mental Retardation Program Directors**
113 Oronoco St.
Alexandria, VA 22314
Phone: (703)683-4202
Robert M. Gettings, Exec.Dir.

Founded: 1963. **Members:** 53. **Description:** State administrative personnel working with programs in the field of mental retardation. Monitors and reports on administrative, legislative, and judicial activities and other events affecting mental retardation programs. Provides technical assistance services. **Publications:** *Capitol Capsule*, monthly. Newsletter. Includes calendar of events, member news, and reports on association programs. *Price:* Included in membership dues; $35/year for nonmembers. • *Federal Funding Inquiry*, periodic. • *New Directions*, monthly. *Price:* $35. **Formerly:** (1977) National Association of Coordinators of State Programs for the Mentally Retarded.

★5592★ **National Association of State Public Health Veterinarians (NASPHV)**
Ohio Department of Health
PO Box 118
Columbus, OH 43266-0118
Phone: (614)466-0283
Fax: (614)644-7740
Kathy Smith, Sec.-Treas.

Founded: 1953. **Members:** 50. **Description:** Executive veterinary public health administrators in each state. Work to guide and develop veterinary public health programs in the states and on the national level. **Publications:** *Annual National Compendium of Animal Rabies Control*, annual. **Formerly:** (1968) Association of State Public Health Veterinarians; (1979) Association of State and Territorial Public Health Veterinarians; (1984) National Association of State and Territorial Public Health Veterinarians.

★5593★ **National Association of Supervisors and Administrators of Health Occupations Education (NASAHOE)**
c/o Jo Ann Wakelyn
Virginia Department of Education
PO Box 2120
Richmond, VA 23216-2060
Phone: (804)225-2893
Fax: (804)371-0249
Jo Ann Wakelyn, Pres.

Members: 35. **Description:** State administrators and local supervisors of health occupations education. Acts as resource sharing group, particularly in the area of curriculum development. Seeks to develop shared resources for recruitment. **Publications:** *NASAHOE News*, quarterly. Newsletter. **Formerly:** (1988) National Association for State Administrators of Health Occupations Education.

★5594★ **National Conference of Local Environmental Health Administrators (NCLEHA)**
1395 Blue Tent Ct.
Cool, CA 95614-2120
Phone: (916)823-1736
Richard Swenson, Exec. Officer

Founded: 1939. **Members:** 220. **Description:** Professional environmental health personnel engaged in or officially concerned with municipal (city, county, or district) environmental health administration or teaching of environmental health. Promotes improvement and greater use of science and practice of environmental health in community life. **Publications:** Newsletter, quarterly. **Formerly:** (1969) Conference of Municipal Public Health Engineers; (1981) Conference of Local Environmental Health Administrators.

★ 5595 ★ National Council for Prescription Drug Programs (NCPDP)
4201 N. 24th St., Ste. 365
Phoenix, AZ 85016
Phone: (602)957-9105
Fax: (602)955-0749
Lee Ann C. Stember, Pres.

Founded: 1977. **Members:** 1,050. **Description:** Companies, organizations, agencies, and individuals who have an active interest in third party prescription drug programs. Goal is to advance standardization of third party prescription drug programs. Is currently creating and maintaining a national pharmacy listing, a uniform claim form, and a standard tape format for third party programs. **Publications:** Telecommunications Standards Manual. Manual.

★ 5596 ★ National Council of State Human Service Administrators (NCSHSA)
810 1st St. NE, Ste. 500
Washington, DC 20002
Phone: (202)682-0100
Fax: (202)289-6555
Elaine Ryan, Chairperson

Founded: 1939. **Members:** 700. **Description:** Chief executives, managers, and staff aides of state public welfare agencies. Provides a forum for state public welfare administrators to discuss and develop positions on national policy issues affecting state welfare programs and to exchange information on state management practices and experiences. **Formerly:** (1984) National Council of State Public Welfare Administrators.

★ 5597 ★ National Council of State Pharmacy Association Executives (NCSPAE)
c/o Al Mebane
PO Box 151
Chapel Hill, NC 27514-0151
Free: 800-852-7343
Fax: (919)968-9430
Al Melbane, Sec.-Treas.

Founded: 1927. **Members:** 52. **Description:** Professional society of the executive officers of state pharmacy associations. **Formerly:** (1964) National Conference of State Pharmaceutical Association Secretaries; (1992) National Council of State Pharmaceutical Association.

National Network for Social Work Managers
See: Entry 11870

★ 5598 ★ National Renal Administrators Association (NRAA)
1555 Connecticut Ave. NW, Ste. 200
Washington, DC 20036
Phone: (202)462-9039
Fax: (202)462-9043
Keith Krueger, Exec.Dir.

Founded: 1977. **Members:** 475. **Description:** Administrative personnel involved with dialysis programs for patients suffering from kidney failure. Provides a vehicle for the development of educational and informational services for members. Maintains contact with health care facilities and government agencies. Operates placement service; compiles statistics; conducts political action committee. **Publications:** NRAA Journal, annual. Journal. Serves as an educational and informational resource for administrative personnel involved in the End Stage Renal Disease Program. *Price:* Free; $50 for nonmembers. • Presidents Letter, monthly. *Price:* Free to members; $10 nonmembers.

★ 5599 ★ Professional Association of Health Care Office Managers (PAHCOM)
461 E. 10 Mile Rd.
Pensacola, FL 32534
Phone: (904)474-9460
Free: 800-451-9311
Fax: (904)474-6352
Richard Blanchette, Contact

Founded: 1988. **Members:** 3,400. **Description:** Office managers of small group and individual medical practices. Operates certification program for health care office managers. **Publications:** Medical Office Management, bimonthly. Newsletter.

★ 5600 ★ Professional Standards Review Council of America (PSRCA)
200 Madison Ave., Ste. 1910
New York, NY 10016
Phone: (212)686-9147
Fax: (212)779-9307
Carol A. Wielk, Exec.Dir.

Founded: 1977. **Description:** Physicians, nurses, health care administrators, and consumers. Monitors the quality, appropriateness, and cost of health care given to patients in hospitals, ambulatory clinics, nursing facilities, and physicians' offices. **Publications:** Informational Health Care Bulletin, periodic.

★ 5601 ★ Radiology Business Management Association (RBMA)
2755 Bristol St., Ste. 110
Costa Mesa, CA 92626
Phone: (714)833-1651
Sharon Urch, Exec.Dir.

Founded: 1968. **Members:** 1,600. **Regional Groups:** 4. **State Groups:** 50. **Local Groups:** 10. **Description:** Business managers for radiology groups; vendors of equipment, services, or supplies. Purposes are to improve business administration of radiologists' practices to better serve patients and the medical profession; and to provide opportunities for professional development and recognition. Offers informal placement service. Maintains information services. **Publications:** Radiology Business Management Association--Bulletin, monthly. Newslet-

ter. Covers organizational topics, industry trends, and legislative developments affecting the private practice of radiology; includes annual index. *Price:* Included in membership dues; $100/year for nonmembers. • Radiology Business Management Association--Membership Directory, annual. Membership Directory. Includes list of industry vendors and suppliers. *Price:* Included in membership dues. **Formerly:** (1990) Radiologists Business Managers Association.

★ 5602 ★ Society of Medical Administrators (SMA)
c/o Dr. Ronald P. Kaufman
12901 Bruce B. Downs Blvd.
Box 2
University of South Florida
Tampa, FL 33612-4799
Phone: (813)974-2196
Maruin Dunn, Exec. VP

Founded: 1920. **Members:** 50. **Description:** Medical doctors in hospital or health care administration. Discusses issues concerning health care administration. **Publications:** Directory, annual. Also publishes minutes of the Annual Meeting. **Formerly:** (1951) Medical Superintendents Club.

Society of Medical-Dental Management Consultants (SMD)
See: Entry 5882

Society of Nursery Nursing Administrators (SNNA)
See: Entry 3292

★ 5603 ★ Society for Radiation Oncology Administrators (SROA)
2021 Spring Rd., Ste. 600
Oak Brook, IL 60521
Phone: (708)571-9065
Fax: (708)571-7837
Kimberly Pede, Exec.Sec.

Founded: 1984. **Members:** 540. **Description:** Individuals with managerial responsibilities in radiation oncology at the executive, divisional, or departmental level, and whose functions include personnel, budget, and development of operational procedures and guidelines for therapeutic radiology departments. Strives to improve the administration of the business and nonmedical management aspects of therapeutic radiology, to promote the field of therapeutic radiology administration, to provide a forum for communication among members, and to disseminate information among members. Maintains speakers' bureau; offers placement service. **Publications:** SROA Membership Directory, annual. Membership Directory. *Price:* Included in membership dues. • SROA Newsletter, quarterly. Newsletter. Includes calendar of events and employment listings. *Price:* Included in membership dues; $50 for nonmembers. **Formerly:** (1985) Radiation Oncology Administrators.

★5604★ **Society of State Directors of Health, Physical Education and Recreation (SSDHPER)**
9805 Hillridge Dr.
Kensington, MD 20895
Phone: (301)949-0709
Simon A. McNeely, Exec.Dir.

Founded: 1926. **Members:** 180. **Description:** State directors, supervisors, and coordinators of health, physical education, and recreation in state departments of education. Associate members include personnel in other state, federal, and nongovernmental agencies and organizations and interested individuals. To promote sound school programs of health, physical education, safety, recreation, and athletics. Conducts summer workshops on professional leadership. Presents Certificate of Honor annually, and Distinguished Service Certificate occasionally. **Publications:** Directory, annual. • Newsletter, periodic. Also publishes statement of basic beliefs. **Formerly:** Society of State Directors of Physical and Health Education.

★5605★ **United States Conference of Local Health Officers (USCLHO)**
1620 Eye St. NW
Washington, DC 20006
Phone: (202)293-7330
Fax: (202)293-2352
J. Thomas Cochran, Exec.Dir.

Founded: 1960. **Description:** Chief health officers, commissioners, directors, and other officials representing city, county, or city-county health departments. Promotes cooperation and exchange of ideas to assist in the improvement of local public health administration. Sponsors coordination of intergovernmental health agency efforts. **Publications:** *Local Health Department Directory*, periodic. Directory. • *Local Health Officers News*, bimonthly. Also publishes fact sheets on national policy and legislative developments. **Formerly:** (1983) United States Conference of City Health Officers.

Research Centers

★5606★ **American Academy of Pediatrics**
Department of Research
141 NW Point Blvd.
PO Box 927
Elk Grove Village, IL 60009-0927
Phone: (708)228-5005
Fax: (708)228-9651
Dr. Gretchen V. Fleming, Dir.

Research Activities and Fields: Organization, financing, and delivery of child health care, including studies on third-party payment programs, health care for low-income and high-risk children, office practices, the distribution of pediatricians, evaluations of pediatric programs, functional outcomes, and health manpower. **Publications:** *Working Papers Series.*

★5607★ **American Medical Association**
Center for Health Policy Research
515 N. State St.
Chicago, IL 60610
Phone: (312)464-5022
Fax: (312)464-5849
James F. Rodgers, Ph.D., Dir.

Research Activities and Fields: Research in health-related areas such as international health systems, physician payment, Medicare volume performance standards, health system reform, physician manpower, access to health care, medical practice costs, professional liability, and practice arrangements. **Publications:** *Socioeconomic Characteristics of Medical Practice* (annually); *Physician Marketplace Statistics* (annually).

★5608★ **Arizona State University**
School of Health Administration and Policy
Tempe, AZ 85287-4506
Phone: (602)965-7778
Fax: (602)965-6654
Frank G. Williams, Dir.

Research Activities and Fields: Health care delivery issues within U.S. with a special emphasis on Arizona, including program evaluation, health manpower studies, rural health, long-term care, assessment of industrial health promotion programs, compilation of data needed for decision making, development of new systems or new applications, AIDS in managed care systems, and other in-depth studies. Undertakes short-term research projects. Evaluates Arizona's health care program for the indigent. **E-mail Address:** icfgw@uvm.inre.asu.edu. **Formerly:** Center for Health Services Administration (1987).

★5609★ **Baylor College of Medicine**
Center for Ethics, Medicine, and Public Issues
Houston, TX 77030
Phone: (713)798-6290
Fax: (713)798-5678
Dr. Baruch Brody, Dir.

Research Activities and Fields: Priorities for health care services, methods of funding health care services, and social controls on health care service, including studies on ethics in clinical decision making and value issues in controlling the cost of medicine. **Publications:** News Bulletin (on bioethics, six times per year).

★5610★ **Boston University**
Center for Health and Advanced Policy Studies (CHAPS)
232 Bay State Rd.
Boston, MA 02215
Phone: (617)353-2770
Fax: (617)353-2385
Prof. John B. McKinlay, Dir.

Research Activities and Fields: Application of knowledge to the study of contemporary policy and program issues, including health and health services, aging, minority issues, criminal justice, community organization and development, intergroup relations, and education.

★5611★ **Brandeis University**
Institute for Health Policy
Heller Graduate School
415 South St.
Waltham, MA 02254-9110
Phone: (617)736-3900
Fax: (617)736-3928
Stanley S. Wallack, Ph.D., Dir.

Research Activities and Fields: Health services research and policy analysis, focusing on the design, development, implementation, and evaluation of innovative financing and delivery systems. Specific areas of research include establishing and implementing national health care expenditure limits, all-payer payment systems, an Alcohol and Drug Services Survey, the changing trends of substance abuse, financing and reimbursement of drug abuse treatment programs, and long-term care for the elderly, including home care services for the disabled elderly and cost effective models and standards for assisted living. Operates the Center for Substance Abuse Services Research, Center for Drug Abuse Policy Analysis, Center on Vulnerable Populations, and the National Resource Center. **Publications:** Newsletter (semiannually); Publication Catalogue; Annual Report; Background Reports; Program Analyses; Major Issue Papers. **Formerly:** Center for Health Policy Analysis and Research; Health Policy Center; Bigel Institute for Health Policy.

★5612★ **Brandeis University**
Policy Center on Aging
Heller Graduate School
Waltham, MA 02254
Phone: (617)736-3874
Fax: (617)736-3881
James J. Callahan, Jr., Ph.D., Dir.

Research Activities and Fields: Retirement income adequacy and policy, long term care and health service delivery, aging and mental health, supportive service in senior housing and resource allocation for the elderly. Generates, synthesizes, and disseminates knowledge on policy alternatives affecting the economic security of the aging; analyzes the economic, legal, administrative, and political consequences and feasibility of alternative policies; participates in the formulation and implementation of policy; and trains professionals for careers focused in the area of policy analysis. **E-mail Address:** callahan@birch.cc.brandies.edu.

★5613★ **Case Western Reserve University**
Health Systems Management Center
Weather Head School of Management
Cleveland, OH 44106-7235
Phone: (216)368-2143
Fax: (216)368-6861
J.B. Silvers, Ph.D., Dir.

Research Activities and Fields: Health systems management, including health care finance, clinical decision analysis, computer information systems in health care, the physician as manager, and quality and cost in health care. **Publications:** *HSMC Working Papers.*

★5614★ Center on the Organization and Financing of Care for the Severely Mentally Ill
Hampton House
624 N. Broadway
Baltimore, MD 21205
Phone: (410)955-6562
Fax: (410)955-0470
Donald M. Steinwachs, Ph.D., Dir.

Research Activities and Fields: Mental health care services, including cost effectiveness of alternative treatments, financial support, and alternative organizational and system methods.

★5615★ Center for Policy Studies
123 N. 3rd St., Ste. 814
Minneapolis, MN 55401
Phone: (612)929-6151
Walter McClure, Ph.D., Dir.

Research Activities and Fields: Improving health care and public education systems while reducing costs. Strategies are designed, field tested, and disseminated widely.

★5616★ Center for Research in Ambulatory Health Care Administration (CRAHCA)
104 Inverness Terr. E.
Englewood, CO 80112-5306
Phone: (303)799-1111
Fax: (303)643-4427
Dr. Barry Green, Assoc. Exec.Dir.

Research Activities and Fields: Medical group practice administration, including management technology and education. **Publications:** *Medical Group Management Journal* (bimonthly), published by MGMA; *CRAHCA Research News.*

★5617★ Center for the Study of Social Policy
1250 I St. NW, Ste. 503
Washington, DC 20005
Phone: (202)371-1565
Fax: (202)371-1472
Tom Joe, Dir.

Research Activities and Fields: Social policy, including studies or children and youth, income support, long-term care, health, disability and minorities. Focus on children and family services and policy.

★5618★ Centers for Health, Education and Social Systems Studies (CHESS)
Park Plaza
128 N. Craig St.
Pittsburgh, PA 15213-2713
Phone: (412)681-3000
Fax: (412)681-1471
Dr. Melvin H. Rudov, Pres.

Research Activities and Fields: Investigation, analysis, and evaluation of health care, education, industry, and other social systems. Operates computer service bureau for research projects. **Formerly:** Center for Health and Social Systems Research.

★5619★ Columbia University Center for the Study of Society and Medicine
College of Physicians & Surgeons
630 W. 168th St.
New York, NY 10032
Phone: (212)305-4184
Fax: (212)305-6416
Dr. David J. Rothman, Dir.

Research Activities and Fields: Conducts interdisciplinary research on issues that arise in clinical and research settings, including studies in bioethics and health policy. Projects include law; bioethics and medical decision making; social policy implications of single disease hospitals; trust, misconduct, and the integrity of biomedical research; outcome measures in clinical decision making; analyses of the social history of patienthood; organization and structure of the human genome project; clinical trials; and data sharing in biomedical research.

★5620★ Connecticut Hospital Research and Education Foundation, Inc.
110 Barnes Rd.
PO Box 90
Wallingford, CT 06492
Phone: (203)265-7611
Fax: (203)284-9318
Dennis May, Pres.

Research Activities and Fields: Hospital industry, including hospital administration, manpower development and training, quality of care, shared services and facilities, financial reimbursement, ancillary service utilization, and mental health planning. **E-mail Address:** lynch@chime.org.

★5621★ Creighton University Center for Health Policy and Ethics
2500 California Plaza
Omaha, NE 68178
Phone: (402)280-2017
Fax: (402)280-5735
Charles J. Dougherty, Ph.D., Dir.

Research Activities and Fields: Cross-cultural ethics, ethical issues involving the elderly and neonates, health care reform, legal ethics, medical economics, nursing ethics, pharmacy ethics, racial and ethnic health concerns, religious ethics, rural health policy, and women's issues. **Publications:** *FOCUS* (newsletter, twice per year). **E-mail Address:** charlied@creighton.edu.

★5622★ Dartmouth College Center for Evaluative Clincial Sciences
7251 Strasenburgh
Dartmouth Med. School
Hanover, NH 03755-3863
Phone: (603)650-1684
Fax: (603)650-1225
John E. Wennberg, M.D.,, Dir.

Research Activities and Fields: Evaluative clinical science and health care delivery, including medical care epidemiology, health policy, health behavior, competancy of medical procedures, quality of medical and surgical care, distribution of health care resources, medical interventions and consequences for patients, care at the end of life, distribution of health care resources across hospital market areas, geriatric health, and sociology of medical organizations.

★5623★ Duke University Center for Health Policy Research and Education
125 Old Chemistry Bldg.
Box 90253
Durham, NC 27706
Phone: (919)684-3023
Fax: (919)684-6246
David B. Matchar, M.D., Dir.

Research Activities and Fields: Quantitative analysis of clinical policies, decision analysis, Bayesian statistics, health economics, disease prevention, cancer and cancer detection, stroke prevention and management, and technology assessment, including evaluation of reimbursement policies for medical procedures, hospital and health care policies, and Health Maintenance Organization (HMO) medical policies. **E-mail Address:** match001@mc.duke.edu.

★5624★ Florida State University Institute for Health and Human Services Research
2035 E. Paul Dirac Dr.
Morgan Bldg., Ste. 236
Tallahassee, FL 32310-4086
Phone: (904)644-2710
Fax: (904)644-8331
Dr. McNeece, Dir.

Research Activities and Fields: Health and human services policies, community policing, the use of videotape in criminal courts, social work in the justice system, chemical dependency, and future issues in social work. **E-mail Address:** amcneece@garnet.fsu.edu.

★5625★ Harvard University Division of Health Policy Research and Education
25 Shattuck St., Parcel B, 1st Fl.
Boston, MA 02115
Phone: (617)432-1325
Fax: (617)432-0173
Dr. Joseph Newhouse, Dir.

Research Activities and Fields: Coordinates health policy resources throughout the University, including suggestion of new research initiatives, stimulation of educational activities, coordination of research and educational efforts, promotion of multidisciplinary analysis of complex health policy issues, and dissemination of health policy findings. **Publications:** Annual Report.

★5626★ Harvard University Malcolm Wiener Center for Social Policy
John F. Kennedy School of Government
79 JFK St.
Cambridge, MA 02138
Phone: (617)495-1461
Fax: (617)496-9053
Julie Wilson, Dir.

Research Activities and Fields: Multidisciplinary research on health policy, poverty and welfare, labor and education, and implementation and management of human services programs. Specific areas of research include the following: health policy organization and financing of health care, access to health care, mental health policy, poverty studies, the causes and severity of poverty among children, and the nature and causes of urban ghetto neighborhoods. **Formerly:** Center for Health Policy and Management (1987); Center for Health and Human Resources Policy (1989).

★ 5627 ★ Health Outcomes Institute

2001 Killebrew Dr., Ste. 122
Bloomington, MN 55425
Phone: (612)858-9188
Fax: (612)858-9189
Michael Huber, Exec.Dir.

Research Activities and Fields: Maintains the Outcomes Management System, which is a collection of several general and condition-specific measures of patient function, well-being, and clinical status to support the routine measurement of health outcomes through questionnaires completed by patients and providers. **Formerly:** InterStudy.

★ 5628 ★ Health Policy Advisory Center (Health/PAC)

237 Thompson St.
New York, NY 10003
New York, NY 10003
Phone: (212)614-1660
Fax: (212)614-1665
Joe Gordon, Exec. Editor

Research Activities and Fields: Analyzes health policies and services and advocates for high-quality, accessible health care for all. **Publications:** *Health/PAC Bulletin* (quarterly).

★ 5629 ★ Health Policy International

245 Nassau St.
Princeton, NJ 08540
Phone: (609)924-6086
Fax: (609)924-8087
Leroy L. Schwartz, M.D., Pres.

Research Activities and Fields: Issues in health policy, including generic and therapeutic substitution, health maintenance organizations (HMOs), medical malpractice, cost containment, the quality of health care, social problems, health care costs, and managed care.

★ 5630 ★ Hospital Research and Educational Trust

840 N. Lake Shore Dr.
Chicago, IL 60611
Phone: (312)280-6620
Fax: (312)280-6450
Dr. Mary Pittman, Pres.

Research Activities and Fields: Delivery and financing of health services, including the restructuring of health care delivery, public accountability, and hospital governance. **Publications:** *Health Services Research* (bimonthly).

★ 5631 ★ Johns Hopkins University Health Services Research and Development Center

624 N. Broadway
Baltimore, MD 21205
Phone: (410)955-6562
Fax: (410)955-0470
Dr. Donald M. Steinwachs, Dir.

Research Activities and Fields: Conducts health services research, including studies on the following: 1) determinants of health outcomes, 2) the impacts of alternative health care systems on cost and quality, 3) effective strategies for health promotion and disease prevention, and 4) methods of meeting the needs of high risk populations such as the poor, elderly, mentally ill, disabled, and children. Research is conducted using experimental (randomized controlled trials) or nonexperimental methods, and relies to varying degrees on primary data sources obtained through interviews and observation and secondary data sources obtained from management information systems, financial reports, and existing regional and national data sources and surveys.

★ 5632 ★ Kaiser Permanente Center for Health Research

3800 N. Kaiser Center Dr.
Portland, OR 97227-1098
Phone: (503)335-2400
Fax: (503)335-2424
Merwyn R. Greenlick, Ph.D., Dir.

Research Activities and Fields: Determinants of medical care utilization; organization, financing, costs and quality of medical care in an HMO; health behavior and intervention; physician practice patterns and outcomes; innovation demonstrations in health care organization and financing; epidemiology; effectiveness of alternative therapies and services; and biometry and research methods. Research programs include health services research, social and economic studies, and epidemiology and disease prevention, including behavior intervention and health promotion. **Publications:** *The Chronicle* (newsletter, three times per year); *Current Studies* (annual brochure); Annual Report.

★ 5633 ★ Medical University of South Carolina
Department of Health Administration and Policy
Applied Research Division

College of Health Professions
Charleston, SC 29425
Phone: (803)792-2118
Fax: (803)792-3327
James A. Johnson, Ph.D., Chair & Prof.

Research Activities and Fields: Health care management focusing on professionals and facilities, including AIDS in the workplace, health worker stress and burnout, organizational downsizing and its impact on personnel, decision making processes in HMOs, physician supply and demand, and service delivery and management. **Publications:** *Carolina Health Services Review.* **E-mail Address:** james__johnson@smtpgw.musc.edu.

★ 5634 ★ Meharry Medical College
Institute on Health Care for the Poor and Underserved

1005 D.B. Todd Blvd.
Nashville, TN 37208
Phone: (615)327-6279
Free: 800-669-1269
Fax: (615)327-6362
Dr. Amy Cato, Dir.

Research Activities and Fields: National and local health policies that affect the poor, including: cost of health care; federal, state, and local laws; service delivery and access thereto; bureaucratic regulations and procedures; and individual and group attitudes and behaviors. Specific topics of study include health care for the uninsured, Medicare and Medicaid reform, maternal and infant health care, economic viability of hospitals and their accessiblity by the poor, oral health care in underservedcommunities, AIDS and other debilitating diseases, and innovations in adolescentpregnancy prevention programs. **Publications:** *Journal of Health Care for the Poor and Underserved* (quarterly).

★ 5635 ★ Northwestern University
Center for Health Services and Policy Research

629 Noyes St.
Evanston, IL 60208-4170
Phone: (708)491-5643
Fax: (708)491-2202
Larry Manheim, Dir.

Research Activities and Fields: Health services research and policy analysis focusing on quality issues in health care delivery, gerontological health, organization behavior in health, competition in the delivery of health services, hospital decision making, hospital cost containment, physician and institutional reimbursement, care for veterans, managed care sector organization structure, and provision of services. **Publications:** *CHSPR Briefings*; Working Paper Series.

★ 5636 ★ Pennsylvania State University
Institute for Policy Research and Evaluation

N253 Burrowes Bldg.
University Park, PA 16802
Phone: (814)865-9561
Fax: (814)865-3098
Dr. Irwin Feller, Dir.

Research Activities and Fields: Principal fields of research are organized into two centers: Center for Health Policy Research, which conducts research on public policies relating to the organization, financing, and delivery of health services, and the design and assessment of substance abuse programs; Center for Public Policy Research, which conducts studies on the impacts of research and development on economic growth, the economic aspects of environmental pollution, the effects of government regulation, the diffusion of technology in the public sector, and the relationship between government and science. **Formerly:** Institute for Research on Human Resources (1978).

★ 5637 ★ Rockburn Institute

6581 Belmont Woods Rd.
Elkridge, MD 21227
Phone: (301)796-4554
Fax: (301)796-3173
Dale N. Schumacher, M.D., Pres.

Research Activities and Fields: Health care services and effective and efficient management of health care institutions.

★ 5638 ★   Rush University
Center for Health Management Studies
Rush-Presbyterian-St. Luke's Medical Ctr.
1653 Congress Pkwy.
Chicago, IL 60612
Phone: (312)942-5402
Fax: (312)942-4957
John E. Trufant, Dir.

Research Activities and Fields: Health care organizations, including studies in organization and administration, organizational behavior, research design and statistics, cost containment, health economics, health care financial management, quantitative methods and epidemiology, long-term care, and information systems. **Publications:** Annual Report; Working Paper Series (semiannually). **E-mail Address:** gglandon@hsm.rpslmc.edu.

★ 5639 ★   Temple University
Cochran Research Center
Speakman Hall, Rm. 12
Philadelphia, PA 19122
Phone: (215)204-5180
Fax: (215)204-5698
Paul Rappoport, Ph.D., Dir.

Research Activities and Fields: Health care financial management, labor and human resource studies, health care planning and evaluation, management information systems, computer and information sciences, robotics, data analysis, geographical information systems, economic forecasting, social economics, and strategic planning. **Publications:** *Journal of Economics and Business* (quarterly).

★ 5640 ★   Texas A&M University
Center for Health Systems & Technology
College of Medicine
Joe H. Reynolds Bldg.
College Station, TX 77843-1114
Phone: (409)845-9677
Robert Stone, M.D., Dir.

Research Activities and Fields: Effect of technology on health care organization and economics. Also studies independent living for the elderly. **Formerly:** Center for Health Care Technology.

★ 5641 ★   Tulane University
Center for International Resource Development
School of Public Health & Tropical Medicine
1501 Canal St., Ste. 1300
New Orleans, LA 70112
Phone: (504)584-1979
Fax: (504)584-3653
Dr. William Bertrand, Dir.

Research Activities and Fields: Research and evaluation of international health and administration. The Center conducts family planning projects in Africa and South and Central America, famine monitoring in Sahelian Africa, development of a school of public health in Kinshasa, Zaire, nutrition surveillance projects in Madagascar, health information systems projects in Niger and Kenya, family planning impact evaluations worldwide, and health and human resources analysis for Africa. **Formerly:** Institute for Health Services Research (1990); Center for International Health Development (1992).

★ 5642 ★   U.S. Department of Health and Human Services
Agency for Health Care Policy and Research
2101 E. Jefferson St., Rm. 300
Rockville, MD 20852
Phone: (301)594-6662
Fax: (301)594-2800
Dr. J. Jarrett Clinton, Administrator

Research Activities and Fields: AHCPR is the primary source of federal support for research on problems related to the quality and delivery of health services. Its programs evaluate the effectiveness of medical treatments and other health services, assess technologies, and improve access to new scientific and technical information for research users. Research is targeted to the needs of health care policymakers, including executive and legislative officials at federal, state, and local levels; those who operate hospitals and other health care institutions; and individuals who are responsible for health care expenditures. The AHCPR extramural research programs provide support for investigator-initiated projects in health services research conducted at universities; by nonprofit organizations and institutions such as hospitals; and by industry. Intramural (in-house) studies have immediate as well as long-term policy relevance.

★ 5643 ★   U.S. Department of Health and Human Services
Agency for Health Care Policy and Research
Center for General Health Services Extramural Research
Executive Office Center, Rm. 502
Rockville, MD 20852-4993
Phone: (301)594-1349
Fax: (301)594-2155
Dr. Norman W. Weissman, Director

Research Activities and Fields: Undertakes and supports research and evaluations with respect to: 1) the delivery of health care service in rural areas and frontier areas; and 2) the health of low-income groups, minority groups, and the elderly. Emphasizes the effectiveness, efficiency, and quality of health care services; the outcomes of health care services and procedures; clinical practice, including primary care and practice-oriented research; health care technologies, facilities, and equipment; health care costs, productivity, and market forces; health promotion and disease prevention; health statistics and epidemiology; and medical liability.

★ 5644 ★   U.S. Department of Health and Human Services
Agency for Health Care Policy and Research
Center of General Health Services Intramural Research
Executive Office Center
2101 E. Jefferson St., Ste. 500
Rockville, MD 20852
Phone: (301)594-1398
Dr. Donald E. Goldstone, Director

Research Activities and Fields: Emphasizes three major areas: 1) the Providers Studies Program examines how competition, reimbursement systems, and various types of regulation influence the use and cost of medical care; 2) National Medical Care Expenditures Study uses information from a large national survey to examine the ways in which Americans use and pay for health care services; 3) Long-Term Care Studies Program evaluates the impact of different reimbursement approaches on the admission practices and services of nursing homes, the feasibility of private, long-term care insurance, and the contribution of informal support systems for the elderly.

★ 5645 ★   U.S. Department of Health and Human Services
Agency for Health Care Policy and Research
Office of Health Technology Assessment
6000 Exec. Bldg., Ste. 309
Rockville, MD 20852
Phone: (301)594-4023
Fax: (301)594-4030
Dr. Thomas Holohan, Director

Research Activities and Fields: Office evaluates technologies and develops Public Health Service recommendations in response to requests from agencies administering federally financed health programs such as the Health Care Financing Administration and the Civilian Health and Medical Program of the Uniformed Services (CHAMPUS).

★ 5646 ★   University of California, San Francisco
Institute for Health Policy Studies
1388 Sutter St., 11th Fl.
San Francisco, CA 94109
Phone: (415)476-4921
Fax: (415)476-0705
Harold Luft, Actg.Dir.

Research Activities and Fields: Health policy and health services. **Formerly:** Health Policy Program (1981).

★ 5647 ★   University of Chicago
Center for Health Administration Studies
969 E. 60th St.
Chicago, IL 60637
Phone: (312)702-7104
Fax: (312)702-7222
Prof. Edward Lawlor, Dir.

Research Activities and Fields: Social and economic aspects of health care delivery, including six national surveys from 1953 to 1982 that emphasize access, use, and financing of health care services, two social survey evaluations of the Community Hospital-Group Practice Program and the Municipal Health Services Program of comprehensive primary care centers in inner-city neighborhoods, and various other studies on self care, HMO (Health Maintenance Organization) development, outcomes of medical care, and innovations in health care organizations. Currently collaborating with World Health Organization on a ten-county study of oral health status. Conducts the National Study of Internal Medicine which describes and analyzes trends and characteristics of residency program content and students from 1976 through 1991. **Publications:** Monographs; Working Paper Series. **E-mail Address:** chas@uchichago.edu. **Formerly:** Health Information Foundation.

★5648★ **University of Colorado—Denver**
Center for Health Ethics and Policy
1445 Market St., Ste. 220
Denver, CO 80202
Phone: (303)820-5635
Fax: (303)534-8774
Judy Hutchison, Proj.Dir.

Research Activities and Fields: Ethical and policy issues in health care, including health care for the medically indigent, cost of care, rural health care, medical malpractice costs, prenatal care, public health, euthanasia, and the role of public opinion in policy formation. **Publications:** *FrontLines.*

★5649★ **University of Florida**
Institute for Health Policy Research
JHMHC, Box 100177
Gainesville, FL 32610-0177
Phone: (904)392-2571
Fax: (904)392-3655
Prof. Michael K. Miller, Dir.

Research Activities and Fields: Policy research and evaluations of long-term care and aging, hospital cost controls, regulatory and administrative methods in the health sector, health economics and financing, maternal and child health, HIV/AIDS, and community epidemiology. **Formerly:** Center for Health Policy Research.

★5650★ **University of Iowa**
Center for Health Services Research
S-517 Westlawn
Iowa City, IA 52242
Phone: (319)335-8815
Fax: (319)335-8814
Dr. James E. Rohrer, Dir.

Research Activities and Fields: Delivery, organization, and financing of health care. Studies the health practices and needs of specific populations such as individuals in rural areas. Develops multidisciplinary research teams from the University's ten colleges and facilitates interaction between researchers, policy makers, and providers to address regional health care problems. **Publications:** Annual Activity Report. **Formerly:** Health Services Research Center (1982).

★5651★ **University of Kentucky**
Center for Rural Health
100 Airport Gardens Rd., Ste. 10
Hazard, KY 41701-9500
Phone: (606)439-3557
Fax: (606)436-8833
Wayne Myers, M.D., Dir.

Research Activities and Fields: Rural health in Kentucky, focusing on health manpower needs, health care delivery, health care policy, and health problems unique to rural populations. Specific areas of study include assessments of new health policy, legislation, and regulation and their impact on rural health delivery, health problems among rural low-income persons and rural population needs in the areas of mental health, substance abuse and prevention. Policy oriented studies include surveys of local attitudes and perceptions of health care, rural and small hospitals, longitudinal study on the impact of rural-based health professions education,

and health professionals distribution; and a survey of small businesses in Kentucky and their experiences with health insurance; a survey of physicians and midwives to determine the nature, scope, and future of obstetrical practice; and a household health survey of health needs, perceptions of health status and the health care system, and functional status of the elderly. **Publications:** *Rural Health Initiative* (newsletter).

★5652★ **University of Memphis**
Center for Health Services Research
427 Clement Hall
Department of Political Science
Memphis, TN 38152
Phone: (901)678-2794
Fax: (901)678-2983
Winsor C. Schmidt, L.M., Dir.

Research Activities and Fields: Health services research, including health administration, health utilization and access, health finance, health policy and law, guardianship, medical malpractice, mental health policy and law, health ethics, research methodology in health services research, and health decision making. Specific research activities focus on the differential economic impact of infectious diseases among children in various child care settings, physician and incident-specific characteristics that predict medical malpractice claims and lawsuits, and the impact of statutory criteria on civil commitment. **E-mail Address:** schmidt-ws@memstvxi.memst.edu.

★5653★ **University of Michigan**
Health Services Management and Policy
School of Public Health
1420 Washington Hts.
Ann Arbor, MI 48109-2029
Phone: (313)763-9903
Fax: (313)764-4338
John Wheeler, Chair

Research Activities and Fields: Health care economics; health insurance; hospital organization, operation, management, and performance; long-term care; health workforce; hospital financial management; multi-institutional systems; and operations research.

★5654★ **University of Minnesota**
Center for Biomedical Ethics
2221 University Ave, SE, Ste. 110
Minneapolis, MN 55414-3074
Phone: (612)625-9756
Fax: (612)626-9786
Dianne M. Bartels, R.N., M.D., Actg. Dir.

Research Activities and Fields: Biomedical ethics and ethical issues in health care and health policy, including the use of fetal tissue in medicine, human genetics and genetic counseling, ethical issues in long-term care, humane care of dying people, ethics and cost-containment, health care reform, and ethics of managed care. Sets up task forces on related issues. **Publications:** Newsletter (quarterly). **E-mail Address:** capla001@maroon.tc.umn.edu.

★5655★ **University of Minnesota**
Institute for Health Services Research
15-205 P.W.B., Box 729
420 Delaware St. SE
Minneapolis, MN 55455
Phone: (612)624-6151
Fax: (612)624-2196
Dr. John E. Kralewski, Dir.

Research Activities and Fields: Long-term care, health insurance, managed health care, patient care outcomes, rural health services, and health policy analysis. **Publications:** Research Brief (monthly); *Institute News* (three times per year). **Formerly:** Center for Health Services Research (1989); Division of Health Services Research and Policy (1992).

★5656★ **University of North Carolina at Chapel Hill**
Cecil G. Sheps Center for Health Services Research
725 Airport Rd.
CB 7590
Chapel Hill, NC 27599-7590
Phone: (919)966-5011
Fax: (919)966-5764
Gordon H. DeFriese, Ph.D., Dir.

Research Activities and Fields: Health care services, organization, and financing, including women's and children's health services; aging, disablement, and long-term care; mental health services; and international health. Evaluates primary health care services and role of primary health care sector in total health care system; seeks to improve the evaluation of health promotion and disease prevention programs, health services delivery in rural populations, and dental services delivery. **Publications:** *The Rural Gazette*; *NC Rap Line*; Reports; Working Papers. **E-mail Address:** gordon_defriese@schsr.unc.edu.

★5657★ **University of Pennsylvania**
Leonard Davis Institute of Health Economics
3641 Locust Walk
Philadelphia, PA 19104-6218
Phone: (215)898-5611
Fax: (215)898-0229
J. Sanford Schwartz, M.D., Exec.Dir.

Research Activities and Fields: Health economics; health care financing; systems design, organization, and management; evaluation of medical practices; and related policy issues that address the efficient allocation of health resources, the appropriate use of health services, the development of innovative health care delivery systems, and changing patient and provider behavior. Areas of concern include evaluation and optimization of clinical care and new technologies, access to health care, payment/reimbursement mechanisms and insurance, and institutional structure, management, and governance. **Publications:** *LDI Health Policy & Research Quarterly* (international newsletter); Occasional Issue Briefs; Brochures. **E-mail Address:** conway@wharton.upenn.edu.

★ 5658 ★ University of Pittsburgh
Health Policy Institute
Graduate School of Public Health
Pittsburgh, PA 15261
Phone: (412)624-6104
Fax: (412)624-7747
Dr. Beaufort B. Longest, Jr., Dir.

Research Activities and Fields: Policy issues related to cost, quality, and delivery of health care services.

★ 5659 ★ University of Southern Maine
Edmund S. Muskie Institute of Public
Affairs
96 Falmouth St.
Portland, ME 04103
Phone: (207)780-4430
Fax: (207)780-4417
Andrew F. Coburn, Ph.D., Assoc. Dir.

Research Activities and Fields: Health, rehabilitation and special education, aging, mental health, developmental disabilities, children, youth, and families, and alcoholism. Projects include program evaluations, policy/planning analysis and research, training systems, training and curriculum materials, policy forums, and communication technologies. **Formerly:** Human Services Development Institute.

★ 5660 ★ University of Texas—Houston
Health Science Center
Health Policy Institute
DCT 1707
PO Box 20036
Houston, TX 77225
Phone: (713)792-4975
Fax: (713)792-4986
M. David Low, M.D., Pres.

Research Activities and Fields: Health policy issues at the local, state, and national level, including cost, access, and quality of health care.

★ 5661 ★ University of Wisconsin—
Madison
Center for Health Systems Research and
Analysis
WARF Bldg., Rm. 1163
610 Walnut St.
Madison, WI 53705-2397
Phone: (608)263-4875
Fax: (608)263-4523
Dr. David R. Zimmerman, Dir.

Research Activities and Fields: Seeks to improve health policy, planning, and delivery through the use of systems engineering techniques and technology. Emphasizes the development of decision support systems, outcome measurement, health promotion, development and evaluation of patient management systems, and evaluation and improvement of health care and long term care, and hospital services throughout Wisconsin.

★ 5662 ★ University of Wisconsin—
Madison
Wisconsin International Center for Health
Services Studies
230 Bradley Bldg.
1300 University Ave.
Madison, WI 53706
Phone: (608)263-6998
Fax: (608)263-4885
Prof. Rockwell Shultz, Dir.

Research Activities and Fields: Health services management.

★ 5663 ★ West Virginia University
Office of Health Services Research
Health Sciences S.
PO Box 9145
Morgantown, WV 26506-9145
Phone: (304)293-2601
Fax: (304)293-6685
Cecil Pollard, Dir.

Research Activities and Fields: Health services research, manpower studies, resource allocation, demography, and computer technology support. **Publications:** Newsletter (quarterly).

State Government Agencies

Health Planning & Development

★ 5664 ★ Alabama Health Planning and
Development Agency
312 Montgomery St., 7th Fl.
Montgomery, AL 36104
Phone: (334)242-4108
Fax: (334)242-4113

★ 5665 ★ Arizona Department of Health
Services
Planning Office
1740 W. Adams St.
Phoenix, AZ 85007
Phone: (602)542-1216
Fax: (602)542-1062

★ 5666 ★ Arkansas Department of Health
Planning Bureau
PO Box 3278
Little Rock, AR 72203-3278
Phone: (501)661-2111
Fax: (501)671-1450

★ 5667 ★ California Health and Welfare
Agency
Statewide Health Planning and
Development Office
1600 9th St., Rm. 433
Sacramento, CA 95814
Phone: (916)654-1606
Fax: (916)653-1448

★ 5668 ★ Colorado Department of Human
Services
Health Care Policy and Financing Division
Health Plans and Medical Services
1575 Sherman St.
Denver, CO 80203-1714
Phone: (303)866-6092

★ 5669 ★ Connecticut Department of
Public Health
Health Surveillance and Planning Division
150 Washington St.
Hartford, CT 06106-1426
Phone: (203)566-1426
Fax: (203)566-3302

★ 5670 ★ Delaware Department of Health
and Social Services
Management Services Division
1901 N. DuPont Hwy.
New Castle, DE 19720
Phone: (302)577-4515
Fax: (302)577-4539

★ 5671 ★ District of Columbia Department
of Human Services
Health Systems Development Agency
613 G. St., NW, Ste. 309
Washington, DC 20001
Phone: (202)727-0744
Fax: (202)727-0379

★ 5672 ★ Florida Agency Health Care
Administration
2727 Mahan Dr.
Fort Knox Executive Center, Bldg. 3
Tallahassee, FL 32308
Phone: (904)487-2513

★ 5673 ★ Georgia State Health Planning
Agency
4 Executive Park Dr. NE, Ste. 2100
Atlanta, GA 30329
Phone: (404)679-4821
Fax: (404)679-4914

★ 5674 ★ Hawaii Department of Health
Health Planning and Development Agency
335 Merchant St., Rm. 412E
Honolulu, HI 96813
Phone: (808)587-0788
Fax: (808)587-0783

★ 5675 ★ Idaho Department of Health and
Welfare
Vital Statistics and Health Policy Center
PO Box 83720
Boise, ID 83720-0669
Phone: (208)334-0669
Fax: (208)334-6581

★ 5676 ★ Illinois Department of Public
Health
Epidemiology and Health Systems
Development Office
525 W. Jefferson St., 2nd Fl.
Springfield, IL 62761
Phone: (217)785-2040
Fax: (217)785-4308

★ 5677 ★ Indiana Department of Health
Health Planning Division
1330 W. Michigan St.
PO Box 1964
Indianapolis, IN 46206-1964
Phone: (317)383-6541
Fax: (317)383-6779

★5678★ **Iowa Department of Public Health**
Planning and Administration Division
Health Development Services Bureau
Lucas State Office Bldg.
321 E. 12th St.
Des Moines, IA 50319
Phone: (515)242-6385
Fax: (515)281-4958

★5679★ **Kansas Department of Health and Environment**
Health Division
900 SW Jackson, Rm. 663
Topeka, KS 66612-1290
Phone: (913)296-1086
Fax: (913)296-1231

★5680★ **Kentucky Human Resources Cabinet**
Health Planning and Certification Office
275 E. Main St.
Frankfort, KY 40621
Phone: (502)564-6620
Fax: (502)564-7573

★5681★ **Louisiana Department of Health and Hospitals**
Public Health Office
Health Resources Management Bureau
PO Box 1349
Baton Rouge, LA 70821
Phone: (504)342-1276
Fax: (504)342-5839

★5682★ **Maine Department of Human Services**
Health Planning Division
State House Station 11
Augusta, ME 04333
Phone: (207)624-5424
Fax: (207)287-3005

★5683★ **Maryland Department of Health and Mental Hygiene**
Health Resources Planning Commission
4201 Patterson Ave.
Baltimore, MD 21215
Phone: (301)764-3255

★5684★ **Massachusetts Executive Office of Health and Human Services**
Public Health Department
Policy and Planning Office
150 Tremont St.
Boston, MA 02111
Phone: (617)727-5567
Fax: (617)727-2559

★5685★ **Michigan Department of Public Health**
Policy, Planning, and Evaluation Office
3428 N. Logan St.
PO Box 30195
Lansing, MI 48909
Phone: (517)335-9476

★5686★ **Mississippi Department of Health**
Health Resources and Lab Services Bureau
Health Planning and Resource Development Division
PO Box 1700
Jackson, MS 39215-1700
Phone: (601)960-7874
Fax: (601)354-6123

★5687★ **Missouri Department of Health**
Director's Office
1738 E. Elm St.
PO Box 570
Jefferson City, MO 65101
Phone: (314)751-6001
Fax: (314)751-6041

★5688★ **Montana Department of Health and Environmental Sciences**
Health Services Division
Health Planning Bureau
Cogswell Bldg., Rm. C108
Helena, MT 59620
Phone: (406)444-3121

★5689★ **Nebraska Department of Health**
Systems Planning Evaluation Bureau
301 Centennial Mall S., 3rd Fl.
PO Box 95007
Lincoln, NE 68509
Phone: (402)471-2337

★5690★ **Nevada Department of Human Resources**
Health Division
Health Planning Bureau
505 E. King St., Rm. 201
Carson City, NV 89710
Phone: (702)687-4176

★5691★ **New Hampshire Department of Health and Human Services**
Public Health Services Division
Health Services Planning and Review Bureau
6 Hazen Dr.
Concord, NH 03301
Phone: (603)271-4712
Fax: (603)271-3745

★5692★ **New Jersey Department of Health**
Health Care Planning, Financing and Information Services Development Division
CN 360
Trenton, NJ 08625-0360
Phone: (609)292-8772
Fax: (609)292-3780

★5693★ **New Mexico Health Policy Commission**
435 St. Michael's Dr., Ste. 202A
Santa Fe, NM 87505
Phone: (505)827-7500
Fax: (505)827-7506

★5694★ **New York State Department of Health**
Administration Office
Planning, Policy, and Resource Group
Corning Tower
Empire State Plaza
Albany, NY 12237-0001
Phone: (518)473-7541
Fax: (518)474-5450

★5695★ **North Carolina Department of Human Resources**
Facility Services Division
State Medical Facilities Planning Section

Council Bldg.
701 Barbour Dr.
Raleigh, NC 27603
Phone: (919)733-4130

★5696★ **North Dakota Department of Health**
Administrative Services Section
Health Information Systems Division
600 E. Boulevard Ave.
Bismarck, ND 58505-0200
Phone: (701)328-2894

★5697★ **Ohio Department of Health**
Policy and Planning Office
Health Policy Unit
246 N. High St.
PO Box 118
Columbus, OH 43266-0118
Phone: (614)466-5308
Fax: (614)644-8526

★5698★ **Oklahoma Department of Health**
Health Promotion and Policy Analysis Office
1000 NE 10th St.
Oklahoma City, OK 73117-1299
Phone: (405)271-5161

★5699★ **Oregon Department of Human Resources**
Health Policy Office
800 NE Orgeon St. 23, Ste. 640
Portland, OR 97232-2162
Phone: (503)731-4091
Fax: (503)731-4056

★5700★ **Pennsylvania Department of Health**
Health Planning Bureau
Box 90
Harrisburg, PA 17108
Phone: (717)783-1078
Fax: (717)772-6959

★5701★ **South Carolina Health and Human Services Finance Commission**
Interagency Planning, Research and Coordination Bureau
1801 Main St., J10
PO Box 8206
Columbia, SC 29202-8206
Phone: (803)253-6177
Fax: (803)253-4173

★5702★ **South Dakota Department of Health**
Policy and External Affairs Office
445 E. Capitol Ave.
Pierre, SD 57501
Phone: (605)773-3361

★5703★ **Tennessee Department of Health**
TennCare
729 Church St.
Nashville, TN 37203
Phone: (615)741-0213

★5704★ **Texas Department of Health**
Health Data and Policy Analysis Bureau
1100 W. 49th St.
Austin, TX 78756
Phone: (512)458-7261

★5705★ Vermont Agency of Human Services
Social and Rehabilitation Services Department
Planning and Evaluation Division
103 S. Main St.
State Complex
Waterbury, VT 05671-2401
Phone: (802)241-2112

★5706★ Virginia Office of Health and Human Resources
Health Department
Health Policy Office
1500 E. Main St.
PO Box 2448
Richmond, VA 23218
Phone: (804)786-6970
Fax: (804)371-0116

★5707★ Washington Department of Social and Health Services
Planning, Research and Development Office
PO Box 45200
Olympia, WA 98504-5200
Phone: (360)586-9156
Fax: (360)586-5874

★5708★ Wisconsin Department of Health and Social Services
Health Division
Management and Policy Office
PO Box 7850
Madison, WI 53707-7850
Phone: (608)266-7384
Fax: (608)267-2832

Chapter 29
Health Care Financing

Federal Government Agencies

★5709★ Railroad Retirement Board
844 N. Rush St.
Chicago, IL 60611-2092
Phone: (312)751-4900
Fax: (312)751-7193
Description: The Railroad Retirement Board administers comprehensive retirement-survivor and unemployment-sickness benefit programs for the nation's railroad workers and their families under the Railroad Retirement and Railroad Unemployment Insurance Acts. In connection with the retirement program, the Board has administrative responsibilities under the Social Security Act for certain benefit payments and railroad workers' Medicare coverage.

★5710★ U.S. Department of Health and Human Services
Health Care Financing Administration (HCFA)
200 Independence Ave. SW
Washington, DC 20201
Phone: (202)690-6726
Fax: (202)690-6262
Description: The Health Care Financing Administration oversees the Medicare program, a federal health insurance program for persons over 65 years of age and certain disabled persons; the Medicaid program, which supplies grants to states to provide medical services to the needy; and related federal medical care quality control staffs.

★5711★ U.S. Department of Health and Human Services
Health Care Financing Administration
Bureau of Health Standards and Quality
6325 Security Blvd.
Baltimore, MD 21207
Phone: (301)966-6842
Description: Bureau is responsible for seeing that Medicare and Medicaid beneficiaries receive the most appropriate and highest quality care available, and that it is delivered in a cost-effective manner. HCFA's regional offices monitor the states' survey and certification procedures and standards enforcement.

★5712★ U.S. Department of Health and Human Services
Health Care Financing Administration
Bureau of Program Operations
6325 Security Blvd.
Baltimore, MD 21207
Phone: (301)965-8050
Description: Bureau manages contractual issues with Medicare intermediaries and carriers and with the state Medicaid agencies. It approves or disapproves state Medicaid plans and establishes performance standards for contractors. Within the Bureau, the Medicaid/Medicare Management Institute identifies management problems and provides advice and assistance to contractors and states to make improvements.

★5713★ U.S. Department of Health and Human Services
Health Care Financing Administration
Medicaid Bureau
East High Rise, Rm. 200
6325 Security Blvd.
Baltimore, MD 21207
Phone: (410)966-3870
Fax: (410)966-3252

★5714★ U.S. Department of Health and Human Services
Social Security Administration (SSA)
6401 Security Blvd.
Baltimore, MD 21235
Phone: (410)965-3120
Fax: (410)966-1463
Description: The Social Security Administration administers a national program of contributory social insurance whereby employees, employers, and the self-employed pay contributions which are pooled in special trust funds. When earnings stop or are reduced because the worker retires, dies, or becomes disabled, monthly cash benefits are paid to partially replace the earnings that the family has lost.

★5715★ U.S. House of Representatives
Committee on Ways and Means
Subcommittee on Health
1102 Longworth House Office Bldg.
Washington, DC 20515-6348
Phone: (202)225-3625

★5716★ U.S. Senate
Committee on Finance
Subcommittee on Medicaid and Health Care for Low-Income Families
SD-456 Dirksen Senate Office Bldg.
Washington, DC 20510
Phone: (202)224-8832
Fax: (202)224-1273

★5717★ U.S. Senate
Committee on Finance
Subcommittee on Medicare, Long-Term Care, and Health Insurance
SD-219 Dirksen Senate Office Bldg.
Washington, DC 20510-6200
Phone: (202)224-8832
Fax: (202)224-1273

Foundations & Other Funding Organizations

Private Foundations

★5718★ John A. Hartford Foundation
55 E 59th St.
New York, NY 10022-1178
Phone: (212)832-7788
Fax: (212)593-4913
Richard S. Sharpe, Program Director
Foundation Philosophy: The John A. Hartford Foundation has two programs: the Health Care Cost and Quality Program and the Aging and Health Program. The Health Care Cost and Quality Program focuses on the need to combine quality and cost-containment in American health care. The Aging and Health Program seeks to strengthen the capacity of the American health care. **Giving Priorities:** In 1993, the foundation reported that 100% of its giving went to health care including support for health policy research, development of biomedical technology, the delivery of comprehensive geriatric services, and medical education and research at colleges and universities. Percentage excludes foundation administered projects. **Typical Health-Related Recipients:** Clinics/Medical Centers, Geriatric Health, Health Funds, Health

Organizations, Health Policy/Cost Containment, Hospitals, Long-Term Care, Medical Education, Medical Rehabilitation, Medical Research, Medical Training, People with Disabilities, Research/Studies Institutes. **Geographic Distribution:** National.

National & International Organizations

★5719★ American Academy of Insurance Medicine (AAIM)
c/o Paul R. Bell, M.D.
2211 Congress St.
Portland, ME 04122
Phone: (207)770-2946

Founded: 1889. **Members:** 800. **Description:** Professional society of medical directors of life insurance companies. **Publications:** *Journal of Insurance Medicine*, quarterly. Journal. *Price:* Included in membership dues; $45/year for nonmembers. **Formerly:** (1992) Association of Life Insurance Medical Directors of America.

American Association of Dental Consultants (AADC)
See: Entry 3870

American Association of Managed Care Nurses (AAMCN)
See: Entry 9053

★5720★ American Association of Preferred Provider Organizations (AAPPO)
601 13th St. NW
Washington, DC 20005
Phone: (202)347-7600
Fax: (202)347-7601
Gordon B. Wheeler, Pres.&COO

Founded: 1983. **Members:** 1,300. **Regional Groups:** 11. **Description:** Health care executives, health care consultants, corporations, and preferred provider organizations (PPOs). (A PPO is a prenegotiated arrangement between purchasers and providers to furnish specified health care services to a group of employees/patients.) Provides educational and legislative support to organizations and individuals dedicated to the development and promotion of high-quality, cost-effective health care systems. Functions as a clearinghouse for information on PPOs, providing its membership with statistics and surveys on the industry and legislative action concerning PPOs. Conducts educational seminars and consulting services. **Publications:** *AAPPO Journal/PPO Perspectives*, bimonthly. Newsletter. Contains information on product innovations, systems, trends, and individuals in the managed care field. *Price:* Included in membership dues; $50/year for nonmembers. • Bibliography. Lists current reports, speeches, articles, and books on PPOs. • *Directory of Operational PPOs*, annual. Directory. Contains information on approximately 1000 PPO organizations and products. *Price:* Free to organizational members; $225 for individual members; $425 for nonmembers. • *Summary of PPO Legislation on a State Level*, annual. Provides information on state laws and regulations that govern the organization and operation of PPOs. *Price:* Free to organizational members; $50 for individual members; $100 for nonmembers.

★5721★ American Managed Care Pharmacy Association (AMCPA)
2300 9th St. S., Ste. 210
Arlington, VA 22204
Phone: (703)920-8480
Fax: (703)920-8491
Delbert D. Konnor, Exec.VP

Founded: 1975. **Members:** 15. **Description:** Preferred provider organizations that specialize in maintainence drug therapy in managed care environments and make available home-delivery pharmacy services. Promotes managed care prescription services as suppliers of medication to home-delivery pharmacy services. Seeks to assist health plan officers and consumers in obtaining maximum value from prescription services; inform consumers and health care organizations about members' efforts to improve prescription services through cost containment measures. Compiles statistics. **Publications:** Annual Report. • Booklet. • Directory. Also publishes speech resource references. **Formerly:** (1989) National Association of Mail Service Pharmacies.

★5722★ American Managed Care and Review Association (AMCRA)
1200 19th St. NW, No. 200
Washington, DC 20036-2437
Phone: (202)728-0506
Fax: (202)728-0609
Charles W. Stellar, Pres.

Founded: 1971. **Members:** 500. **Description:** Medical organizations from the managed health care industry, including health maintenance organizations (HMOs), preferred provider organizations (PPOs), independent practice/physician associations (IPAs), utilization review organizations (UROs), and physician hospital organizations (PHOs); represents over 250,000 practicing physicians and 25 million individuals with health insurance. Seeks to provide better medical care at a reasonable cost, and to render the most appropriate and economical setting for its delivery. Conducts educational sessions and seminars. Maintains American Managed Care and Review Association Foundation. Sponsors job placement service. **Publications:** *AMCRA's Managed Care Monitor*, bimonthly. Newsletter. Covers developments regarding the managed care industry. *Price:* Included in membership dues; $125/year for nonmembers. • *Managed Care Industry Overviews*, annual. Contains statistics, charts, and graphs profiling the managed care industry. *Price:* $50 for members $75 for nonmembers. • *Managed Health Care Directory*, annual. Directory. *Price:* $175 for members; $275 for nonmembers. **Formerly:** (1983) American Association of Foundations for Medical Care; (1989) American Medical Care and Review Association.

★5723★ Blue Cross and Blue Shield Association (BCBSA)
676 N. St. Clair St.
Chicago, IL 60611
Phone: (312)440-6000
Fax: (312)440-6609
Bernard R. Tresnowski, Pres.

Founded: 1982. **Description:** Local Blue Cross and Blue Shield Plans in the U.S., and other licensees in Europe, Japan, and Jamaica. To promote the betterment of public health and security; to secure the widest public acceptance of voluntary nonprofit, prepayment of health services; to provide services to Blue Cross and Blue Shield Plans and licensees. Contracts with federal government as administrative agency for federal health progams; sponsors and conducts programs on health care and prepayment issues. Also publishes reports and pamphlets.

★5724★ Combined Health Appeal of America (CHAA)
1745 Old Springhouse Ln., Ste. 413
Atlanta, GA 30338
Phone: (404)936-0362
Edward Godshall, Pres.

Founded: 1981. **Members:** 41. **Local Groups:** 18. **Description:** National voluntary health agencies. Conducts fundraising efforts to solicit funds from businesses through payroll deductions. Makes donations to member agencies. **Publications:** *CHA Newsletter*, quarterly. Newsletter. • Membership Directory, periodic. • *Partners in Health*, quarterly. **Formerly:** (1983) National Combined Health Appeal.

★5725★ Committee for National Health Insurance (CNHI)
1757 N St. NW
Washington, DC 20036
Phone: (202)223-9685
Fax: (202)293-3457
Denise E. Holmes, Dir.

Founded: 1969. **Members:** 100. **Description:** Persons from health care fields; government, labor, academic, business, economic, and citizen's organizations. Conducts research and education on the health care system in the U.S., its problems and the ways in which to bring about reform through enactment of a comprehensive national health insurance program. **Publications:** *Health Security News*, bimonthly. Newsletter. Also publishes information materials.

Delta Dental Plans Association (DDPA)
See: Entry 3921

★5726★ Disability Insurance Training Council (DITC)
1000 Connecticut Ave. NW, Ste. 810
Washington, DC 20036
Phone: (202)223-5533
Fax: (202)785-2274

Founded: 1951. **Members:** 11,000. **Regional Groups:** 6. **State Groups:** 33. **Local Groups:** 107. **Description:** Educational arm of the National Association of Health Underwriters . Provides institutional advanced disability income and health insurance research seminars as well as marketing and underwriting clinics. Maintains Health Insurance Training Council (HITC), Disability Training Insurance Council (DTIC), and Registered Health Underwriters (RHU). Seminars are sponsored by the NAHU and leading universities throughout the United States. Conducts research and educational programs. **Publications:** *Health Insurance Underwriter*, monthly. Magazine. Covers health legislation, products and services, and association news; includes column by "Dr. Disability." *Price:* $40/year.

★5727★ Group Health Association of America (GHAA)
1129 20th St. NW, Ste. 600
Washington, DC 20036
Phone: (202)778-3200
Fax: (202)331-7487
Karen Ignagni, Pres.

Founded: 1959. **Members:** 1,000. **Description:** Supports the Health Maintenance Organization industry. Lobbies; conducts research programs and workshops; compiles statistics. Maintains placement service. **Publications:** *Annual Industry Profile*, annual. Survey. Aggregated data on HMO premiums, benefits design, utilization, staffing, and demographics. *Price:* $150. • Audiotapes. • *HMO Directory*, annual. Directory. *Price:* $129. • *HMO Magazine*. Magazine. *Price:* $75/year. • *HMO Managers Letter*, biweekly. *Price:* $125/year. • Pamphlets. • *Proceedings of Annual Institute*. Proceedings. • Reports.

★5728★ Healthcare Financial Management Association (HFMA)
2 Westbrook Corporate Center, Ste. 700
Westchester, IL 60154
Phone: (708)531-9600
Fax: (708)531-0032
Richard L. Clarke, Pres.

Founded: 1946. **Members:** 33,000. **State Groups:** 70. **Description:** Financial management professionals employed by hospitals and long-term care facilities, public accounting and consulting firms, insurance companies, medical groups, managed care organizations, government agencies, and other organizations. Conducts educational seminars and two annual examinations, awarding rating of Fellow or Certified Manager of Patient Accounts to successful candidates. **Publications:** Books. • *Healthcare Financial Management*, monthly. Journal. Includes book reviews, product briefs, and employment listings. *Price:* $75/year. • *Notes from National*, monthly. Newsletter. *Price:* Included in membership dues. • *Patient Accounts*, monthly. Newsletter. Covers the financial operations of hospital business office and patient accounting functions, including preadmission information gathering. *Price:* $30/year for members; $65/year for nonmembers. • Videos. **Formerly:** (1968) American Association of Hospital Accountants; (1982) Hospital Financial Management Association.

★5729★ Healthcare Health Financing Study Group (HFSG)
1919 Pennsylvania Ave. NW, Ste. 800
Washington, DC 20006
Phone: (202)887-1400
Fax: (202)466-2198
Michael Colopy, Dir.

Founded: 1973. **Members:** 40. **Description:** Investment banking, law, consulting, and accounting firms involved in providing capital financing for health care institutions. Analyzes legislative and regulatory proposals from the standpoint of the health care financial community. Provides forum for exchange of information concerning health care financing. **Publications:** Bulletin, periodic. • Newsletter, monthly. **Formerly:** (1981) Hospital Financing Study Group.

★5730★ Health Insurance Association of America (HIAA)
1025 Connecticut Ave. NW, Ste. 1200
Washington, DC 20036
Phone: (202)223-7780
Willis D. Gradison, Jr., Pres.

Founded: 1956. **Members:** 250. **Description:** Represents commercial health insurers in the states and in Washington, DC. Works to create a positive image of the industry. Issues data on benefits and products, tracks legislation and regulations, and offers insurance education. Provides forum for industry leadership. **Publications:** *Research Bulletins*, periodic. Bulletins. • *Sourcebook of Health Insurance Data*, annual. Report. Covers the private health insurance business in the U.S. Includes charts, graphs, and tables. Also publishes consumer guides to health insurance products.

★5731★ Health Security Action Council (HSAC)
1757 N St. NW
Washington, DC 20036
Phone: (202)223-9685
Fax: (202)293-3457
Denise E. Holmes, Dir.

Founded: 1969. **Description:** Individuals and organizations united to increase grass roots support for national health insurance and progressive health plans through publicity and education. Conducts surveys on the effects of federal legislative actions on state and local health programs. Educational and informational materials.

★5732★ International Claim Association (ICA)
c/o State Mutual Life
440 Lincoln St.
Worcester, MA 01605-1959
Phone: (508)855-2718
James F. Adams, Chm.

Founded: 1909. **Members:** 465. **Description:** Claim executives and administrators representing companies writing life, health, or accident insurance. **Publications:** *Claim Administration: Principles and Practices.* • *The Claim Examiner.* • *Dentistry.* • *Dentistry and Dental Insurance Claims.* • *The Human Body - Its Function in Health and Disease.* • *International Claim Association--Newsletter*, periodic. Newsletter. • *International Claim Association--Proceedings*, annual. *Price:* $12. • *Life and Health Insurance Law.* • *Managing Claim Department Operations.*

★5733★ International Committee for Life Assurance Medicine (ICLAM) (Comite International de Medecine d'Assurances sur la Vie — CIMAV)
41, ave. Georges V
F-75008 Paris, France
Phone: 1 47208199
Fax: 1 47233881
Dr. Jacques Chouty, Gen.Sec.

Founded: 1899. **Members:** 55. **Languages:** English. **Description:** Medical doctors working in life insurance and reinsurance companies in 29 countries. Promotes fraternal benefit life insurance; facilitates contact and cooperation among members. Establishes societies of life assurance medicine in countries where they do not exist. **Publications:** *Annals of Life Assurance Medicine*, triennial.

★5734★ International Health Policy and Management Institute (IHPMI)
c/o Paul Detrick
Christian Health Services Dev. Corp.
10133 Dunn Rd., Ste. 400
St. Louis, MO 63136
Phone: (314)355-0095
Paul Detrick, Treas.

Founded: 1983. **Members:** 100. **Description:** Health policymakers, hospital presidents, physicians, business leaders, and educators. Dedicated to improving and expanding knowledge of health care economics and management systems. Goals are to: facilitate discussion for the exchange of health care techniques, strategies, and ideas at the theoretical and applied levels to improve the financing and delivery of health care; encourage research and understanding of health policy issues; examine and compare health care systems of industrialized and developing countries; promote the need to maintain access to quality health care while limiting costs within a free market framework. Conducts research and cross-cultural comparative studies on multihospital systems, government health regulations, health systems analysis and planning, health care finance and investment, alternative health care delivery systems, economics of aging, health care cost effectiveness within free market systems, and medical ethics. Disseminates research results; monitors and reports on events affecting health care; conducts demonstration projects. **Publications:** *International Perspectives*, quarterly. Newsletter. Contains excerpts from other publications. *Price:* Included in membership dues. Also publishes books, monographs, and proceedings. **Formerly:** (1991) International Health Economics and Management Institute.

★5735★ Life Insurers Conference (LIC)
The Pavilion
5770 Powers Ferry Rd. NW, Ste. 301
Atlanta, GA 30327
Phone: (404)933-9954
Fax: (404)933-9956
Bruce C. Dalzell, Pres.

Founded: 1910. **Members:** 110. **Description:** Home service insurance companies writing life, accident, and sickness insurance. **Publications:** *Home Service Insurance.* Brochure. • *Home Service Insurance, An Annotated Bibliography 1970-1990.* Brochure. • *Life Insurers*

Conference--Directory, periodic. Directory. Contains listing of member companies alphabetically and by state. Includes convention schedule. • *Pre-Need Funeral Insurance.* Brochure. **Formerly:** (1917) Southern Casualty and Surety Conference; (1925) Southern Industrial Insurers' Conference; (1948) Industrial Insurers' Conference.

★ 5736 ★ **Long Term Care Campaign (LTCC)**
P.O. Box 27394
Washington, DC 20038
Phone: (202)434-3740
Fax: (202)434-3708
James J. Eagan, Dir.

Founded: 1987. **Members:** 140. **Description:** Confederation of organizations promoting legislation to enact social insurance such as Social Security or Medicare that would provide for long-term health care. Conducts lobbying on state and national levels. Disseminates information. **Publications:** *Insiders Update on Long Term Care.* • Videos.

★ 5737 ★ **National Association of Disability Examiners (NADE)**
PO Box 4188
Frankfort, KY 40603
Phone: (502)875-8388
Fax: (502)825-8388
Marty Marshall, Pres.

Founded: 1963. **Members:** 2,373. **Regional Groups:** 7. **Local Groups:** 56. **Description:** Disability claims examiners, attorneys, and physicians involved in determining the eligibility of applicants for social security benefits based on disability. Purpose is to foster, promote, and participate in activities designed to improve the documentation of applications for disability insurance benefits and the evaluation of medical and/or vocational information obtained in connection with such applications. Provides for the exchange of technical information, ideas, and philosophies. **Publications:** Directory, annual. • *NADE Advocate,* bimonthly. Newsletter. Includes listings of newly-certified examiners. *Price:* Included in membership dues. • *Nationwide Report,* quarterly.

★ 5738 ★ **National Association of Health Underwriters (NAHU)**
1000 Connecticut Ave. NW, Ste. 810
Washington, DC 20036
Phone: (202)223-5533
Fax: (202)785-2274
Mark W. Lappen, Exec.VP

Founded: 1930. **Members:** 13,000. **State Groups:** 50. **Local Groups:** 162. **Description:** Insurance agencies and individuals engaged in the promotion, sale, and administration of disability income and health insurance. Sponsors advanced health insurance underwriting and research seminars at universities. Testifies before federal and state committees on pending health insurance legislation. Sponsors leading producers roundtable awards and health insurance quality awards for leading salesmen. Grants RHU certification to qualified Registered Disability Income and Health Insurance Underwriters. Is organizing a speakers' bureau and a political action committee. **Publications:** *Health Insur-*

ance Underwriter, monthly. Journal. *Price:* $40/year. **Formerly:** International Association of Accident and Health Underwriters; National Association of Accident and Health Underwriters; (1978) International Association of Health Underwriters.

★ 5739 ★ **National Association of Managed Care Physicians (NAMCP)**
4435 Waterfront Dr.
PO Box 4765
Glen Allen, VA 23058-4765
Phone: (804)527-1905
Free: 800-722-0376
Fax: (804)747-5316
Dr. W. C. Williams, III, Pres.

Founded: 1991. **Members:** 12,938. **Regional Groups:** 2. **State Groups:** 5. **Description:** Licensed physicians and allied health professionals working in managed health care programs; medical residents and students interested in managed health care; corporations or agencies providing services or goods to the industry; interested others. Purpose: to enhance the ability of practicing physicians to proactively participate within the managed health care arena through research, communication, and education. Provides a forum for members to communicate their concerns about the changing health care environment, integrate into managed health care delivery systems, and assure continuous improvement in the quality of health care services provided. Develops practice criteria, quality assurance measures, and appropriate utilization management criteria. Monitors regulatory and legislative issues and lobbies for legislation affecting managed care physicians. Offers educational programs; maintains speakers' bureau and placement services; conducts research programs; developing informational clearinghouse. **Publications:** *Managed Care Medicine,* bimonthly. Journal. *Price:* $95. • *NAMCP Guide to Managed Care.* Monograph.

★ 5740 ★ **National Committee to Preserve Social Security and Medicare (NCPSSM)**
2000 K St. NW, Ste. 800
Washington, DC 20006
Phone: (202)822-9459
Fax: (202)822-9612
Martha A. McSteen, Pres.

Founded: 1982. **Members:** 500,000. **Description:** Individuals concerned with and affected by social security and medicare programs. Researches and reviews: social security and medicare financing and benefits; medicare regulatory changes; nursing home reform; home health care alternatives; medical care cost containment. Seeks to educate the public through forums, speeches, correspondence, telephone communication, and distribution of educational materials. Conducts grass roots lobbying activities and maintains Washington, DC lobby staff; submits petitions to Congress. Maintains speakers' bureau. **Publications:** *Advance Directives -- Your Right to Decide.* Brochure. • *Buying Your Medigap Policy.* Brochure. • *Secure Retirement, the Newsmagazine for Mature Americans,* 8/year. Covers Social Security, Medicare, health care and other issues of interest to senior citizens. • *Supplemental Security Income.* Brochure. Also distributes monthly column *Under-*

standing Social Security to newspapers. **Formerly:** (1983) National Committee to Preserve Social Security.

★ 5741 ★ **National Committee for Quality Assurance (NCQA)**
1350 New York Ave. NW, Ste. 700
Washington, DC 20005
Phone: (202)628-5788
Fax: (202)628-0344
Margaret E. O'Kane, Pres.

Founded: 1979. **Description:** Board of 14 directors representing consumers, purchasers, and providers of managed health care. Promotes excellence in managed health care by ensuring that quality control programs comply with national standards. Accredits quality assurance programs in prepaid managed health care organizations. Develops and coordinates programs for assessing the quality of care and service in the managed health care industry. Conducts research; holds training and educational seminars; operates speakers' bureau.

★ 5742 ★ **National Health Care Anti-Fraud Association (NHCAA)**
1255 23rd St. NW, Ste. 850
Washington, DC 20037
Phone: (202)659-5955
Fax: (202)833-3636
William Mahon, Exec.Dir.

Founded: 1985. **Members:** 750. **Description:** Network of private insurance companies and public and private agencies that work against health insurance fraud and share information on claims. Maintains speakers' bureau. **Publications:** *NHCAA Network,* quarterly. Newsletter. Also plans to make available educational materials.

★ 5743 ★ **Physician Insurers Association of America (PIAA)**
1130 Connecticut Ave. NW, Ste. 800
Washington, DC 20036
Phone: (202)223-2223
Fax: (202)223-9090
Lawrence E. Smarr, Exec.Dir.

Founded: 1977. **Members:** 55. **Description:** Physician liability insurance companies, including domestic physician and dental liability insurers, international affiliates, and reinsurers. Seeks to further the best interests of member companies in areas related to physician liability insurance. Focuses on the availability and affordability of professional liability insurance and the effective delivery of quality healthcare. Conducts research and educational programs; monitors legislation. **Publications:** Membership Directory, annual. • *The Physician Insurer,* quarterly. Newsletter. Also publishes studies of major liability concerns in the insurance industry, including issues related to treatment of breast, lung, and colon cancer; medication errors; and laparoscopy procedures.

★ 5744 ★ **Physicians Forum (PF)**
1507 53rd St., Ste. 155
Chicago, IL 60615
Phone: (312)922-1968
Fax: (312)633-6442
Raymond Demers, M.D., Pres.

Founded: 1939. **Description:** Professional organization of physicians, particularly those holding salaried positions, who work for health care as a human right. Promotes development of a national health service with a single class of medical care for all, financed by a progressive income tax surcharge for health. **Publications:** *Physicians Forum Bulletin*, quarterly. Bulletin. Also publishes informational material on organization and delivery of medical care.

★5745★ **State Medicaid Directors Association (SMDA)**
810 1st St. NE, Ste. 500
Washington, DC 20002-4267
Phone: (202)682-0100
Fax: (202)289-6555
Lee Partridge, Dir.

Members: 54. **Description:** Directors and senior staff of state and territorial medical assistance programs. Promotes effective Medicaid policy and program administration; works with the federal government on issues through technical advisory groups; conducts forums on policy and technical issues.

★5746★ **Women Life Underwriters Confederation (WLUC)**
17 S. High St., Ste. 1200
Columbus, OH 43215
Phone: (614)224-4828
Free: 800-776-3008
Fax: (614)221-1989
Madeline Field, Managing Dir.

Founded: 1987. **Members:** 1,100. **Local Groups:** 36. **Description:** Life and health underwriters. Objectives are to: advance the life insurance field; inform women members of opportunities in the profession; develop educational opportunities; provide peer support and sales motivational techniques; act as a forum for exchange of sales ideas and industry news. Conducts seminars; encourages development of local chapters. Maintains speakers' bureau. **Publications:** Brochure. • *Roster*, annual. • *WLUC News*, bimonthly. Newsletter. *Price:* Included in membership dues.

Research Centers

★5747★ **Center for Health Economics Research**
300 5th Ave., 6th Fl.
Waltham, MA 02154
Phone: (617)487-0200
Fax: (617)487-0202
Dr. Janet B. Mitchell, Pres.

Research Activities and Fields: Health economics, including alternative ways of reimbursing capital under the Medicare prospective payment system, access to care, physician payment, hospital costs, black-white treatment differences, and cost-effectiveness of technology.

★5748★ **Cornell University Health Benefits Research Center**
52 Vanderbilt Ave., Rm. 1503
New York, NY 10017
Phone: (212)370-7820
Fax: (212)370-7308
Eugene G. McCarthy, M.D., Dir.

Research Activities and Fields: Health benefits, including a study on whether physicians offering a second opinion concurred with the original recommendation for elective surgery and a program to identify and direct patients to ambulatory surgical facilities. Arranges appointments between patients and approximately 28,000 board certified surgeons throughout the U.S.

★5749★ **Georgetown University Institute for Health Care Research and Policy**
2233 Wisconsin Ave. NW, Ste. 525
Washington, DC 20007
Phone: (202)687-0880
Fax: (202)687-5229
Jack Hadley, Codir.

Research Activities and Fields: Health care financing and public policy. **Formerly:** Center for Health Policy Studies (1994).

★5750★ **Harvard University Center for Cost-Effective Care**
Brigham & Women's Hospital
75 Francis St.
Boston, MA 02115
Phone: (617)732-5559
Barbara J. McNeil, M.D., Dir.

Research Activities and Fields: Seeks to develop mechanisms for delivering more cost-effective care in the teaching hospital setting, particularly through management control systems. **Publications:** Annual Report.

★5751★ **Health Research Institute**
1600 S. Main Plaza, Ste. 170
Walnut Creek, CA 94596
Phone: (510)676-2320
Fax: (510)676-2342
William E. Hembree, Dir.

Research Activities and Fields: Conducts applied research in health care financing and delivery, attitudinal studies, and feasibility studies on alternative funding arrangements such as self-insuring and in-house administration, alternative delivery systems, preferred provider organizations, incentive-based medical expense accounts, and prospective-based payment systems. Performs a biennial survey of 1,500 U.S. employers to determine the prevalence and effectiveness of health care cost containment efforts. **Publications:** Newsletters; *Health Resources Directory*.

★5752★ **Johns Hopkins University Center for Hospital Finance and Management**
624 N. Broadway, Rm. 300
Baltimore, MD 21205
Phone: (410)955-2300
Fax: (410)955-2301
Gerard Anderson, Ph.D., Dir.

Research Activities and Fields: Hospital finance and management, technology assess-

ment, reform of cost containment and payment, policies, clinical education, managed care, and medical effectiveness.

★5753★ **Michigan Health and Social Security Research Institute**
8000 E. Jefferson Ave.
Detroit, MI 48214-2699
Phone: (313)926-5321
Fax: (313)824-7220
Dr. William S. Hoffman, Dir.

Research Activities and Fields: Health, welfare, and social security problems of concern to workers and their families as well as government and voluntary agencies and the community, including organization, development, and utilization of social and health programs and benefits for workers and their families, effect of prepaid mental and dental health care, adjustment of survivors of recently deceased automobile workers, health and well-being of the advanced aged, utilization of nursing homes under Medicare and negotiated benefits, cancer mortality and epidemiology studies, and factors affecting decisions of Union members to retire early under various retirement options.

★5754★ **Pittsburgh Research Institute**
5th Ave. Pl., Ste. 1711
Pittsburgh, PA 15222
Phone: (412)255-7824
Fax: (412)255-7503
Wanda W. Young, Sc.D., Pres.

Research Activities and Fields: Health services research, particularly in health care delivery and financing systems, including hospital cost analyses/case mix measurement, case mix reporting to the health care industry, hospital and physician payment systems, hospital cost/product line analyses, quality assessment/utilization monitoring, clinical outcomes assessment, and information systems design. **E-mail Address:** wwy@pittvms.cis.pitt.edu. **Formerly:** Blue Cross of Western Pennsylvania-Research Department.

★5755★ **U.S. Department of Health and Human Services**
Health Care Financing Administration
Office of Demonstrations and Evaluations
Health Systems and Special Studies Division
2306 Oak Meadows Bldg.
6325 Security Blvd.
Baltimore, MD 21207
Phone: (410)966-6612
Fax: (410)966-6511
Sidney Trieger, Director

Research Activities and Fields: Division supports, monitors, and evaluates demonstration programs (through grants and contracts) involving the Medicare and Medicaid programs. Principal areas of research interest are Health Maintenance Organizations (HMOs), end-stage renal disease, preventive services, uninsured, state health reform, and Medicaid and Medicare reimbursement.

★5756★ U.S. Department of Health and Human Services
Health Care Financing Administration
Office of Demonstrations and Evaluations
Hospital Experimentation Division
2302 Oak Meadows Bldg.
6325 Security Blvd.
Baltimore, MD 21207
Phone: (410)966-6670
Michael Hupfer, Acting Director

Research Activities and Fields: Division's activities involve the design, testing, and evaluation of alternative health care payment systems for hospitals and other types of providers.

★5757★ U.S. Department of Health and Human Services
Health Care Financing Administration
Office of Demonstrations and Evaluations
Long-Term Care Experimentation Division
2424 Oak Meadows Bldg.
6325 Security Blvd.
Baltimore, MD 21207
Phone: (410)966-6505
Fax: (410)966-6551
Steven B. Clauser, Ph.D., Acting Director

Research Activities and Fields: Long-term care, provider payment, and Medicaid.

★5758★ U.S. Department of Health and Human Services
Health Care Financing Administration
Office of Research and Demonstrations
Oak Meadows Bldg.
6325 Security Blvd.
Baltimore, MD 21207
Phone: (301)966-6507
Fax: (301)966-6511
George Schieber, Acting Director

Research Activities and Fields: Office conducts intramural and extramural basic health research to support the Medicare and Medicaid programs as well as health care financing in general. Efforts include: 1) program evaluation; 2) health financing and delivery analysis; 3) program statistics and analysis; and 4) awards of research, demonstration, and evaluation grants and contracts. Purpose of the grants program is to provide funds for research and demonstration projects that will help resolve major health care financing policy and program issues, as well as to develop new methods for administration of Health Care Financing Administration (HCFA) programs. Grants are awarded for proposals which address specific areas of priority interest (solicited proposals), or for proposals which address general areas of interest outlined by HCFA (unsolicited proposals). Applications which do not fit into either the priority or general areas are returned. Applications may be made by nonprofit or public organizations and institutions, including state agencies responsible for administering the Medicaid program.

★5759★ U.S. Department of Health and Human Services
Health Care Financing Administration
Office of Research and Demonstrations
Beneficiary Studies Division
2504 Oak Meadows Bldg.
6325 Security Blvd.
Baltimore, MD 21207
Phone: (410)966-6687
Fax: (410)966-6511
Marian Gornick, Director

Research Activities and Fields: Division studies HCFA programs impact on beneficiaries, with emphasis on quality of care provided to HCFA beneficiaries; pricing for Health Maintenance Organizations; end stage renal disease; and epidemiology studies. **Publications:** *Health Care Financing Annual Review.*

★5760★ U.S. Department of Health and Human Services
Health Care Financing Administration
Office of Research and Demonstrations
Office of Demonstrations and Evaluations
2430 Oak Meadows Bldg.
6325 Security Blvd.
Baltimore, MD 21207
Phone: (410)966-6500
Fax: (410)966-6511
Mary S. Kenesson, Director

Research Activities and Fields: The Office funds, manages, and evaluates pilot programs that test new ways of delivering and financing Medicare and Medicaid services. Principal Office components include divisions of Health Systems and Special Studies, Hospital Experimentation, and Long-Term Care Experimentation.

★5761★ U.S. Department of Health and Human Services
Health Care Financing Administration
Office of Research and Demonstrations
Program Studies Division
2502 Oak Meadows Bldg.
6325 Security Blvd.
Baltimore, MD 21207
Phone: (410)966-7703
Carl Josephson, Director

Research Activities and Fields: Program studies.

★5762★ U.S. Department of Health and Human Services
Health Care Financing Administration
Office of Research and Demonstrations
Reimbursement and Economic Studies Division
2B14 Oak Meadows Bldg.
6325 Security Blvd.
Baltimore, MD 21207
Phone: (410)966-6588
Fax: (410)966-6511
William J. Sobaski, Director

Research Activities and Fields: Division investigates the impact of various methods of paying providers (hospitals, physicians) to determine impact on providers, beneficiaries, other providers, and other payers; prepares drafts of reports to Congress for the Secretary of Health and Human Services. Division is organized in branches for institutional and noninstitutional studies.

★5763★ U.S. Department of Health and Human Services
Office of Health Policy
Economic Analysis Division
U.S. Dept. of Health and Human Services
200 Independence Ave., S.W., Rm. 442E
Washington, DC 20201
Phone: (202)245-1870
Fax: (202)245-6518

Research Activities and Fields: Division conducts policy research and analyzes various health financing issues, including Medicaid, Medicare and employer-sponsored health insurance.

★5764★ University of Colorado
Center for Health Services Research
1355 S. Colorado Blvd., Ste. 706
Denver, CO 80222
Phone: (303)756-8350
Fax: (303)759-8196
Peter W. Shaughnessy, Ph.D., Dir.

Research Activities and Fields: Health services research and health policy research for federal and state governments, foundations, and related organizations, emphasizing general health policy topics and issues in long-term care quality, access, cost and cost effectiveness. Studies emphasize Medicare and Medicaid quality assurance and reimbursement for long-term care providers, including home health agencies, subacute care facilities, swing-bed hospitals, and traditional nursing homes. Studies focus on the collection and analysis of extensive primary and secondary cross-sectional and longitudinal data at the patient and facility levels. Contributes to federal and state policy deliberations on regulatory and reimbursement issues in long-term care, and to clinical practice and decision making (especially in quality assurance.)

University of Illinois at Chicago
Institute on Disability and Human Development
See: Entry 4328

University of Memphis
Center for Health Services Research
See: Entry 5652

★5765★ University of Minnesota
Health Care Financing Administration
Research Center
Institute of Health Services Research
420 Delaware St. SE, Box 729
Minneapolis, MN 55455-0381
Phone: (612)624-6151
Fax: (612)624-2196
John Kralewski, Dir.

Research Activities and Fields: Health care financial administration issues, including physician services volume and intensity, Medicare volume and intensity control effectiveness, diagnostic technical test pricing, inappropriate medication use in elderly Medicare beneficiaries, case management costs, hospital care outcome measures, psychoactive drug use among nursing home elderly, Medicare HMO premium alternatives, financing long term care, private sector drug utilization review assessment, Medicare hospital payment policies and the impact on nursing shortages, and laboratory industry technologies, productivity changes, and Medicare payments in different provider settings. **Publications:** Newsletter (three times per year). **E-mail Address:** krale001@maroon.tc.umn.edu.

★5766★ **University of Wisconsin—Madison**
Center for Advanced Study in Health Care Fiscal Management, Organization and Control
1155 Observatory Dr.
Madison, WI 53706
Phone: (608)262-4239
Fax: (608)263-0477
Prof. Mark Covaleski, Dir.

Research Activities and Fields: Cost containment, productivity, and management systems.

★5767★ **Vanderbilt University**
Health Policy Center
Box 1503, Sta. B
Nashville, TN 37235
Phone: (615)322-8530
Fax: (615)322-8535
Dr. Frank A. Sloan, Dir.

Research Activities and Fields: Health economics and policies.

State Government Agencies

Medicaid

★5768★ **Alabama Medicaid Agency**
PO Box 5624
Montgomery, AL 36103-5624
Phone: (334)242-5000
Fax: (334)242-5097

★5769★ **Alaska Department of Health and Social Services**
Public Health Division
Medicaid Services Unit
PO Box 110610
Juneau, AK 99811-0610
Phone: (907)465-2845
Fax: (907)586-1877

★5770★ **Arizona Health Care Cost Containment System**
Medicaid Program
801 E. Jefferson
Phoenix, AZ 85034
Phone: (602)417-4000

★5771★ **Arkansas Department of Human Services**
Medical Services Division
PO Box 1437, Slot 1100
Little Rock, AR 72203-1437
Phone: (501)682-8292
Fax: (501)682-1197

★5772★ **California Health and Welfare Agency**
Health Services Department
Medical Care Services
714 P St., No. 1253
Sacramento, CA 95814
Phone: (916)657-5173
Fax: (916)657-1156

★5773★ **Colorado Department of Human Services**
Health Care Policy and Financing Division
Medicaid Management Information System
1575 Sherman St.
Denver, CO 80203-1714
Phone: (303)866-5678
Fax: (303)866-4214

★5774★ **Connecticut Department of Social Services**
Health Care Financing Division
25 Sigourney St.
Hartford, CT 06106
Phone: (203)424-5053
Fax: (203)424-5129

★5775★ **Delaware Department of Health and Social Services**
Social Services Division
Medicaid Unit
1901 N. DuPont Hwy.
New Castle, DE 19720
Phone: (302)577-4900
Fax: (302)577-4510

★5776★ **District of Columbia Department of Human Services**
Social Services Commission
Income Maintenance Administration
Medicaid Unit
645 H St. NE
Washington, DC 20002
Phone: (202)724-5035
Fax: (202)727-1687

★5777★ **Florida Agency for Health Care Administration**
Medicaid Office
2728 Ft. Knox Blvd.
Tallahassee, FL 32308
Phone: (904)488-3560
Fax: (904)488-0043

★5778★ **Georgia Department of Medical Assistance**
2 Peachtree St. NW
Atlanta, GA 30303
Phone: (404)656-6359

★5779★ **Hawaii Department of Human Services**
Medical QUEST Division
PO Box 339
Honolulu, HI 96809-0339
Phone: (808)586-5390
Fax: (808)586-4890

★5780★ **Idaho Department of Health and Welfare**
Medicaid Division
PO Box 83720
Boise, ID 83720-0036
Phone: (208)334-5747
Fax: (208)334-6558

★5781★ **Illinois Department of Public Aid**
Medical Programs Division
100 S. Grand Ave. E., 3rd Fl.
Springfield, IL 62762
Phone: (217)782-1214
Fax: (217)785-5095

★5782★ **Indiana Family and Social Services Administration**
Medicaid Policy and Planning Office
402 W. Washington St., Rm. 341
Indianapolis, IN 46204
Phone: (317)233-4455
Fax: (317)233-4693

★5783★ **Iowa Department of Human Services**
Medical Services Division
Medicaid Program
Hoover State Office Bldg.
Des Moines, IA 50319
Phone: (515)281-8621
Fax: (515)281-7791

★5784★ **Kansas Department of Social and Rehabilitation Services**
Adult Medical Services Commission
915 SW Harrison
Topeka, KS 66612
Phone: (913)296-3981
Fax: (913)296-4813

★5785★ **Kentucky Human Resources Cabinet**
Medicaid Services Department
275 E. Main St.
Frankfort, KY 40621
Phone: (502)564-4321
Fax: (502)564-3232

★5786★ **Louisiana Department of Health and Hospitals**
Health Services Financing Bureau
PO Box 91030
Baton Rouge, LA 70821-9030
Phone: (504)342-5774
Fax: (504)342-0407

★5787★ **Maine Department of Human Services**
Medical Services Bureau
Policy and Program Division
Medicaid Program
State House Station 11
Augusta, ME 04333
Phone: (207)287-3799
Fax: (207)287-2675

★5788★ **Maryland Department of Health and Mental Hygiene**
Medical Care Policy Administration
Medical Care Finance and Compliance Division
201 W. Preston St., 2nd Fl.
Baltimore, MD 21201
Phone: (410)225-5204
Fax: (410)333-5260

★5789★ **Massachusetts Executive Office of Health and Human Services**
Medical Assistance Division
600 Washington St.
Boston, MA 02111
Phone: (617)348-8400
Fax: (617)348-8575

★5790★ Michigan Department of Social Services
Medical Services Administration
Medicaid Operations Bureau
400 S. Pine St.
PO Box 30043
Lansing, MI 48909
Phone: (517)335-5453
Fax: (517)335-5007

★5791★ Minnesota Department of Human Services
Health Care Administration
Health and Continuing Care Strategies Division
Health Care Purchasing Program
444 Lafayette Rd.
St. Paul, MN 55155-3853
Phone: (612)297-4113
Fax: (612)282-9922

★5792★ Mississippi Office of the Governor
Medicaid Division
PO Box 139
Jackson, MS 39215
Phone: (601)359-6050
Fax: (601)359-3741

★5793★ Missouri Department of Social Services
Medical Services Division
PO Box 6500
Jefferson City, MO 65102
Phone: (314)751-3425
Fax: (314)751-6564

★5794★ Montana Department of Social and Rehabilitation Services
Medicaid Services Division
PO Box 4210
Helena, MT 59604-4210
Phone: (406)444-4540

★5795★ Nebraska Department of Social Services
Medical Services Division
PO Box 95026
Lincoln, NE 68509
Phone: (402)471-9118
Fax: (402)471-9449

★5796★ Nevada Department of Human Resources
Welfare Division
Medicaid Program
2527 N. Carson St.
Carson City, NV 89710
Phone: (702)687-4354
Fax: (702)687-5080

★5797★ New Hampshire Department of Health and Human Services
Human Services Division
Medical Services Bureau
6 Hazen Dr.
Concord, NH 03301
Phone: (603)271-4353
Fax: (603)271-4727

★5798★ New Jersey Department of Human Services
Medical Assistance and Health Services Division
Medical Care Administration
CN 712
Trenton, NJ 08625-0712
Phone: (609)588-2611

★5799★ New Mexico Department of Human Services
Medical Assistance Division
PO Box 2348
Santa Fe, NM 87504-2348
Phone: (505)827-3100
Fax: (505)827-6286

★5800★ New York State Department of Social Services
Health and Long term Care Division
40 N. Pearl St.
Albany, NY 12243
Phone: (518)474-9132

★5801★ North Carolina Department of Human Resources
Medical Assistance Division
PO Box 29529
Raleigh, NC 27626-0529
Phone: (919)733-2060
Fax: (919)733-6608

★5802★ North Dakota Department of Human Services
Medical Services Division
600 E. Boulevard, 3rd Fl.
Bismarck, ND 58505
Phone: (701)328-2321
Fax: (701)328-2359

★5803★ Ohio Department of Human Services
Medicaid Bureau
30 E. Broad St., 32nd Fl.
Columbus, OH 43266-0423
Phone: (614)644-0140
Fax: (614)466-2815

★5804★ Oklahoma Health Care Authority
4545 N. Lincoln Blvd., Ste. 124
Oklahoma City, OK 73125
Phone: (405)530-3439
Fax: (405)530-3405

★5805★ Oregon Department of Human Resources
Medical Assistance Program Office
500 Summer St. NE
Salem, OR 97310-1013
Phone: (503)945-5772
Fax: (503)373-7689

★5806★ Pennsylvania Department of Public Welfare
Medical Assistance Office
PO Box 2675
Harrisburg, PA 17105
Phone: (717)787-1870
Fax: (717)772-2062

★5807★ Rhode Island Department of Human Services
Medical Services Division
600 New London Ave.
Cranston, RI 02920
Phone: (401)464-3575
Fax: (401)464-3350

★5808★ South Carolina Health and Human Services Department
Health Services Bureau
Medicaid Program
1801 Main St.
PO Box 8206
Columbia, SC 29202-8206
Phone: (803)253-6100
Fax: (803)253-4137

★5809★ South Dakota Department of Social Services
Program Management Division
Medical Services Office
700 Governors Dr.
Pierre, SD 57501
Phone: (605)773-3495
Fax: (605)773-4855

★5810★ Tennessee Department of Finance and Administration
Tenncare Division
729 Church St.
Nashville, TN 37247-6501
Phone: (615)741-0192
Fax: (615)741-0882

★5811★ Texas Department of Health
Health Care Financing Division
Managed Care Bureau
1100 W. 49th St.
Austin, TX 78756
Phone: (512)794-6838
Fax: (512)338-6945

★5812★ Utah Department of Health
Health Care Financing Division
Medicaid Policy and Planning Bureau
PO Box 142901
Salt Lake City, UT 84114-2901
Phone: (801)538-9925
Fax: (801)538-6478

★5813★ Vermont Agency of Human Services
Social Welfare Department
Medicaid Division
State Complex
103 S. Main St.
Waterbury, VT 05671-1201
Phone: (802)241-2880
Fax: (802)241-2830

★5814★ Virginia Office of Health and Human Resources
Social Services Department
Benefits Program Division
Medical Assistance Program
730 E. Broad St.
Richmond, VA 23219-1849
Phone: (804)692-1740
Fax: (804)692-1949

★5815★ **Washington Department of**
Social and Health Services
Medical Assistance Services
PO Box 45500
Olympia, WA 98504-5500
Phone: (360)753-1777
Fax: (360)586-5874

★5816★ **West Virginia Department of**
Health and Human Resources
Human Resources Bureau
Income Maintenance Office
State Capitol Complex
Bldg. 6, Rm. 617
Charleston, WV 25305
Phone: (304)558-8290
Fax: (304)558-1008

★5817★ **Wisconsin Department of Health**
and Social Services
Health Division
Health Care Financing Bureau
PO Box 7850
Madison, WI 53707-7850
Phone: (608)266-2522
Fax: (608)267-2832

★5818★ **Wyoming Department of Health**
Health Care Financing Division
Minimum Medical Program
117 Hathaway Bldg.
Cheyenne, WY 82002-0710
Phone: (307)777-7821
Fax: (307)777-7439

Chapter 30
Health Care Industry

Federal Government Agencies

★5819★ **Federal Trade Commission (FTC)**
Pennsylvania Ave. & 6th St. NW
Washington, DC 20580
Phone: (202)326-2222

Description: One of the principal functions of the FTC is to safeguard the public by preventing the dissemination of false or deceptive advertisements of consumer products in general; food, drug, cosmetics, and therapeutic devices in particular; as well as other unfair or deceptive practices.

U.S. Department of Health and Human Services
Food and Drug Administration
Center for Biologics Evaluation and Research
See: Entry 10898

U.S. Department of Health and Human Services
Food and Drug Administration
Center for Devices and Radiological Health
See: Entry 11058

U.S. Department of Health and Human Services
Food and Drug Administration
Center for Drug Evaluation and Research
See: Entry 10899

National & International Organizations

★5820★ **American Association of Healthcare Consultants (AAHC)**
11208 Waples Mill Rd., Ste. 109
Fairfax, VA 22030
Phone: (703)691-AAHC
Vaughan A. Smith, Pres.

Founded: 1949. **Members:** 250. **Description:** Professional association of individuals and firms

exclusively devoted to hospital and health care consultation. Serves as a resource for health care providers; offers continuing education to members. Provides information concerning the role of hospital/health consultants; functional fields of competence for AAHC consultants; selection of consultants and the association's code of professional ethics and standards for entering and maintaining AAHC membership. Maintains speakers' bureau. **Publications:** Membership Directory, annual. **Formerly:** (1984) American Association of Hospital Consultants.

★5821★ **American Dental Trade Association (ADTA)**
4222 King St. W.
Alexandria, VA 22302-1597
Phone: (703)379-7755
Fax: (703)931-9429
Nik M. Petrovic, CAE, Pres.

Founded: 1882. **Members:** 200. **Description:** Manufacturers and distributors of dental instruments, supplies, and equipment; dental laboratories. Membership represents 400 dental supply houses and 90% of the total volume of sales in the dental industry. Conducts sales and management training programs; develops systems to improve distributors' operating efficiency in such areas as inventory control, stocking of merchandise, and service department operations; compiles statistics and conducts periodic market surveys of the dental industry. Has produced Introduction to the Dental Industry, an employee training videotape. **Publications:** *Annual Operating Ratio for Distributors.* • *Dental Trade Newsletter*, bimonthly. Newsletter. • Membership Directory, annual. • *Monthly Report on Manufacturers' Sales.* • *Profile of Manufacturers' and Distributors' Salesmen.*

★5822★ **American Orthotic and Prosthetic Association (AOPA)**
1650 King St., Ste. 500
Alexandria, VA 22314
Phone: (703)836-7116
Fax: (703)836-0838
Dr. Ian R. Horen, Exec.Dir.

Founded: 1917. **Members:** 1,250. **Regional Groups:** 11. **Description:** Firms that manufacture and fit artificial limbs and braces. **Publications:** *AOPA Yearbook*, annual. Membership Di-

rectory. Includes product listings. • *Journal of Prosthetics and Orthotics*, quarterly. Journal. Contains articles detailing new products, fitting techniques, and patient management. *Price:* Included in membership dues; $60/year for U.S. nonmembers; $80/year for nonmembers outside the U.S. • *O&P Almanac*, monthly. Magazine. Provides up-to-date information on healthcare reform, government relations, reimbursement, patient management, and association activities. *Price:* $35 in the U.S.; $69 outside the U.S. • *O&P Now*, monthly. Newsletter. Contains information for members on association activities. • *Orthotics & Prosthetics Today*, semiannual. Newsletter. Provides information for patients. **Formerly:** (1937) Association of Limb Manufacturers of America; (1959) Orthopedic Appliance and Limb Manufacturers Association.

American Society of Dermatological Retailers (ASDR)
See: Entry 4218

★5823★ **Animal Health Institute (AHI)**
501 Wythe St.
PO Box 1417-D50
Alexandria, VA 22313-1480
Phone: (703)684-0011
Fax: (703)684-0125
Richard H. Ekfelt, Pres.

Founded: 1940. **Members:** 36. **Description:** Represents manufacturers of animal health products (vaccines, pharmaceuticals, and feed additives used in modern food production; and medicines for household pets). Works with government agencies and legislators; prepares position papers; compiles and disseminates information. Sponsors AHI Foundation. **Publications:** *AHI quarterly*, quarterly. Newsletter. Covers developments of significance to animal health, livestock, and veterinary industries. Includes legislative and regulatory updates and research. *Price:* Free. • Directory, annual. Provides information on membership activities. • *Net Sales Survey*, annual. Survey. • Report, annual. • *Resource Book*, annual. Book. Provides information on members, governmental agencies, and allied organizations. • Surveys. Provides information on research and development.

★ 5824 ★   Aspirin Foundation of America (AFA)
1330 Connecticut Ave. NW, No. 300
Washington, DC 20036
Phone: (202)659-0060
Fax: (202)659-1699
John J. Kneiss, Exec.Dir.

Founded: 1981. **Members:** 8. **Description:** Manufacturers, producers, distributors, and processors of aspirin and aspirin products. Works to facilitate and encourage an understanding of the potential health benefits of aspirin and to collect and disseminate that information. **Publications:** *Aspirin Advocate*, quarterly. • *Aspirin Foundation of America--Annual Report*. Annual Report.

★ 5825 ★   Association of Microbiological Diagnostic Manufacturers (AMDM)
555 13th St. NW, Ste. 7W-404
Washington, DC 20004
Phone: (202)637-6837
Fax: (202)637-5910
Debra L. Aleknavage, Admin.Asst.

Founded: 1976. **Members:** 75. **Description:** Medical device manufacturers, distributors, and users. Informs members of regulatory policies and government legislation affecting the microbiological diagnostic equipment manufacturing industry. Represents members at legislative hearings. **Publications:** Newsletter, biennial. **Formerly:** (1984) Association for Microbiological Media Manufacturers.

★ 5826 ★   Association Suisse de l'Industrie et du Commerce Dentaires (ASICD)
3, rue de la Mairie
CH-1211 Geneva 6, Switzerland
Phone: 22 7358760
Fax: 22 7863887
Dr. Ulrich Wanner, Sec.

Description: Companies manufacturing dental equipment and supplies. Establishes international standards and technical harmonization for dental equipment. Represents members' interests before government bodies, international agencies, and the public. Maintains liaison with organizations representing dentists, dental technicians, and dental supply dealers and distributors. Compiles statistics.

★ 5827 ★   Association of Tongue Depressors (ATD)
c/o Matthew Schorr
100 E. Maple St.
Teaneck, NJ 07666
Phone: (201)387-6969
Matthew Schorr, Contact

Founded: 1978. **Members:** 28. **Description:** Health care companies, researchers, and manufacturers of wooden tongue depressors. Objective is to strive for safe, sturdy, sterile sticks. **Publications:** *Wooden Stick*, monthly.

★ 5828 ★   Better Sleep Council (BSC)
333 Commerce St.
Alexandria, VA 22314
Phone: (703)683-8371
Fax: (703)683-4503
Andrea Herman, Dir.

Founded: 1978. **Members:** 750. **Description:** Bedding manufacturers, suppliers and retailers organized to increase public awareness of the importance of sleep to good health. **Publications:** *Good Night Guide*, bimonthly. Newsletter. • *Parent/Child Sleep Guide*. **Formerly:** (1987) Better Sleep Council (of the National Association of Bedding Manufacturers); (1993) Better Sleep Council (of the International Sleep Products Association).

★ 5829 ★   British Dental Trade Association (BDTA)
Merritt House
Hill Ave.
Amersham, Bucks. HP6 5BQ, England
Phone: 1494 431010
Fax: 1494 431360
Mr. Smith, Exec.Dir.

Languages: English. **Description:** Companies manufacturing dental equipment and supplies. Establishes international standards and technical harmonization for dental equipment. Represents members' interests before government bodies, international agencies, and the public. Maintains liaison with organizations representing dentists, dental technicians, and dental supply dealers and distributors. Compiles statistics.

★ 5830 ★   Chain Drug Marketing Association (CDMA)
c/o James Devine
104 Wilmot Rd., Ste. 550
Deerfield, IL 60015
Phone: (708)267-8800
Free: 800-935-2362
Fax: (708)267-9900
James Devine, Pres.

Founded: 1988. **Members:** 62. **Description:** Drug store chains located throughout the U.S., Puerto Rico, and Canada. Represents members in the market for merchandise; keeps them abreast of trends in relevant fields. **Publications:** *Notes to You*, weekly. Newsletter. Contains merchandise information for drug store owners. *Price:* Free, for members only. • *President's Update*, monthly. Newsletter. *Price:* Free. **Formerly:** Chain Drug Marketing Associates; (1992) Affiliated/Associated Drug Stores.

★ 5831 ★   China Proprietary Medicine Association
A38 Beilishilu
Beijing 100810, People's Republic of China
Phone: 1 8311986
Fax: 1 8315648
Gong-shan Huang, Sec.Gen.

Founded: 1989. **Members:** 78. **Description:** Promotes the use of proprietary medicines (packaged, over-the-counter drugs) in the People's Republic of China. Conducts research programs. Fosters communication with proprietary medicine groups in other countries. Disseminates information; offers consulting services.

★ 5832 ★   Contact Lens Society of America (CLSA)
11735 Bowman Green Dr.
Reston, VA 22090
Phone: (703)437-5100
Fax: (703)437-0727
Tina M. Schott, Exec.Dir.

Founded: 1955. **Members:** 1,000. **Description:** Contact lens fitters; manufacturers of products associated with contact lenses. Purposes are to share knowledge of contact lens technology and to foster the growth and ability of the contact lens technician throughout the world. Activities include: developing improvements in instrumentation, fitting procedures, and manufacturing processes; providing a national public relations medium through which information is disseminated to governmental agencies, legislative bodies, and other professional groups. Provides Home Study Course of Contact Lens Fitters. Operates speakers' bureau. **Publications:** *CLSA Roster*, annual. Directory. • *Eyewitness*, quarterly. Newsletter.

★ 5833 ★   Council on Family Health (CFH)
225 Park Ave. S., 17th Fl.
New York, NY 10003
Phone: (212)598-3617
William I. Bergman, Pres.

Founded: 1966. **Members:** 32. **Description:** Manufacturers of prescription and over-the-counter medications. Provides the public and interested organizations with information on proper usage of medications and other family health concerns, such as safety in the home. **Publications:** *How to Prevent Drug Interactions*. • *Medicines and You: A Guide for Older Americans*. Brochure. *Price:* Free. • *Nonprescription Medicines: A Consumer's Dictionary of Terms*. Brochure. • *Ten Guides to Proper Medicine Use*. Also produces television and radio public service announcements.

★ 5834 ★   Danish Dental Manufacturers (Dentalbranchforeningen Producentsektion)
Borsen
DK-1217 Copenhagen K, Denmark
Phone: 33950500
Fax: 33330464
Lars Bruhn Hansen, Sec.

Languages: Danish, English. **Description:** Companies manufacturing dental equipment and supplies. Establishes international standards and technical harmonization for dental equipment. Represents members' interests before government bodies, international agencies, and the public. Maintains liaison with organizations representing dentists, dental technicians, and dental supply dealers and distributors. Compiles statistics.

★ 5835 ★   DENIP
Leuvenstraat 29
B-1800 Vivoorde, Belgium
Phone: 2 2510509
Fax: 2 2524398
Mr. J. P. Ureel, Sec.

Languages: Dutch, French, German. **Description:** Companies manufacturing dental equipment and supplies. Establishes international standards and technical harmonization for dental equipment. Represents members' interests before government bodies, international agencies, and the public. Maintains liaison with organizations representing dentists, dental technicians, and dental supply dealers and distributors. Compiles statistics.

★5836★ Dental Dealers of America (DDA)
123 S. Broad St., Ste. 2531
Philadelphia, PA 19109-1025
Phone: (215)731-9975
Fax: (215)731-9984
Edward B. Shils, Exec.Dir.

Founded: 1943. **Members:** 70. **Description:** Wholesale dealers of dental instruments, equipment, and supplies. Conducts educational activities; works for better manufacturer and professional relations. Maintains information and employment services. **Publications:** Membership Directory, biennial.

★5837★ Dental Gold Institute (DGI)
PO Box 1
Butler, NJ 07405-0001
Phone: (201)838-2030
Ronald J. Leavesley, Exec.Dir.

Founded: 1981. **Members:** 15. **Regional Groups:** 3. **Description:** Suppliers of major precious metals to the dental profession. Provides dental professionals with information regarding current research and literature in the industry. Seeks to demonstrate to dentists, dental laboratory technicians, and patients the biological, economic, and technical superiority of gold as a dental restorative material. Works to counteract the economic effects brought about by increased use of base metals in dental work due to the sharp rise in the cost of gold. Encourages classification of alloys and the establishment of appropriate and standardized terminology. Fosters and sponsors continuing research in the field of dental alloys. Works toward improvements in dental technology and in the oral care industry. Compiles statistics.

★5838★ Dental Manufacturers of America (DMA)
Fidelity Bldg.
123 S. Broad St., Ste. 2531
Philadelphia, PA 19109-1025
Phone: (215)731-9975
Fax: (215)731-9984
Edward B. Shils, Exec.Dir.

Founded: 1932. **Members:** 204. **Description:** Manufacturing firms of dental equipment and supplies. Conducts industry workshops and disseminates information on foreign trade, exhibits and credit reports, and association insurance policy services. **Publications:** Membership Directory, annual.

★5839★ Disposable Hypodermic and Allied Equipment Manufacturers Association of Europe (DHAEMAE)
553 Finchley Rd.
Hampstead
London NW3 7BJ, England
Phone: 171 4312187
Fax: 171 7945271
Alan L. Berton, Sec.

Founded: 1980. **Members:** 11. **Languages:** English. **Description:** Manufacturers and distributors of single-use hypodermic syringes and needles and allied cannulae-related products in 8 countries. Monitors legislative directives and international requirements and specifications that affect the industry; offers recommendations to national, European, and international organi-

zations. Promotes ethical principles and good manufacturing practices. Gathers and disseminates scientific and technical information.

★5840★ Drug, Chemical and Allied Trades Association (DCAT)
2 Roosevelt Ave., Ste. 301
Syosset, NY 11791
Phone: (516)496-3317
Fax: (516)496-2231
Richard J. Lerman, Exec.Dir.

Founded: 1890. **Members:** 500. **Description:** Manufacturers of drugs, chemicals, and related products (packaging, cosmetics, essential oils); publications, advertising agencies, agents, brokers, and importers. **Publications:** *DCAT Digest*, monthly. Newsletter. Contains information on drug and chemical manufacturing, with emphasis on federal regulation. *Price:* Free, for members only. • Directory, annual. Provides information on membership activities. *Price:* Available to members only. **Formerly:** (1959) Drug, Chemical and Allied Trades Section of the New York Board of Trade.

★5841★ ECRI
c/o Ed Stevenson, Communications Dept.
5200 Butler Pke.
Plymouth Meeting, PA 19462
Phone: (610)825-6000
Fax: (610)834-1275
Joel J. Nobel, M.D., Pres.

Founded: 1955. **Members:** 2,500. **Description:** Seeks to significantly improve the safety, performance, reliability, and cost effectiveness of health care technology through objective investigation and testing, and publication of results. Provides technical consulting and accident investigation and educational programs. Functions as an information clearinghouse for health care technology assessment and hazards and deficiencies in medical devices; sponsors seminars. Conducts research; compiles statistics and operates speakers' bureau. **Publications:** *Health Devices*, monthly. • *Health Devices Alerts*, weekly. • *Health Devices Sourcebook*, annual. Directory. • *Health Technology Trends*, monthly. Newsletter. • *Healthcare Environmental Management*, monthly. • *Healthcare Product Comparison System*, monthly. • *Healthcare Technology Assessment Reports: Executive Briefings*, monthly. • *Hospital Hazardous Materials Management*, monthly. Newsletter. • *Hospital Risk Control*, monthly. • *Operating Room Risk Management*, bimonthly. • *Technology for Anesthesia*, periodic. Includes information on medical equipment and research updates. *Price:* $85/year. • *Technology for Cardiology*, monthly. Newsletter. Reports on ECRI comparative product evaluations; offers hazard reports on medical devices and device operation data. Includes research updates. *Price:* $85/year. • *Technology for Emergency Medicine*, monthly. Newsletter. Covers current problems in emergency medicine. Carries ECRI comparative product evaluations, issues analyses, and hazard reports on medical devices. *Price:* $85/year. • *Technology for Respiratory Therapy*, monthly. Newsletter. Evaluates medical devices and summarizes reported problems, hazards, and recalls. Includes research updates and health care technology abstracts. *Price:*

$85/year. **Formerly:** (1968) Graduate Pain Research Foundation; (1979) Emergency Care Research Institute.

★5842★ Embalming Chemical Manufacturers Association (ECMA)
1370 Honeyspot Extension
Stratford, CT 06497
Phone: (203)375-2984
Free: 800-243-6104
Fax: (203)378-9160
Richard Beck, Pres.

Founded: 1951. **Description:** Companies that manufacture embalming chemicals.

★5843★ Ethylene Oxide Industry Council (EOIC)
2501 M St. NW
Washington, DC 20037
Phone: (202)887-1198
Fax: (202)887-5427
Robert R. Romano, Ph.D., Contact

Founded: 1981. **Description:** Producers and users of ethylene oxide, which is used in the manufacture of consumer products such as antifreeze and polyester fibers and is widely used in the health care field as a sterilizing agent. Operates as special program of the Chemical Manufacturers Association. Works to develop scientific, technological, and economic data regarding the safe manufacture, use, and handling of ethylene oxide; provides government agencies and scientific organizations with representation of the industry's views and interests; acquaints the government and the public with responsible producer and user programs for control of occupational exposure.

★5844★ European Confederation of Medical Suppliers Associations (EUCOMED)
Aranas House
87, blvd. Louis Schmidt, bte. 3
B-1040 Brussels, Belgium
Phone: 2 7324320
Fax: 2 7325751

Founded: 1979. **Members:** 26. **Languages:** Dutch, English, French. **Description:** National (18) and international (8) organizations from 14 countries representing companies in the non-pharmaceutical health care field. Promotes and encourages ethical principles and practices among members. Works for the harmonization of standards and regulatory requirements applicable to non-pharmaceutical health care products in cooperation with governments and national and international authorities. Conducts workshops.

★5845★ European Federation of Associations of Health Product Manufacturers (EHPM)
(Europaische Vereinigung der Verbande der Reformwaren-Hersteller)
Schwedenpfad 2
61294 Bad Homburg, Germany
Phone: 6172 24064
Fax: 6172 21598
Wolfgang Reinsch, Gen.Sec.

Founded: 1975. **Members:** 23. **Languages:** English, French, German. **Description:** National health product manufacturers' associations in 23 countries. Purpose is to stimulate and coordinate the activities of member organizations. Objectives are: to establish and harmonize regulations concerning the manufacture of health products, particularly the labeling and advertising of and quality standards for health products; to address specific problems connected with health product manufacture and advertising; to encourage information exchange among members, particularly research findings and technical and sales data; to protect members' interests from competition outside the health product industry; to represent members' interests before governmental and European authorities; to maintain contacts with scholarly institutions in the fields of preventive medicine and other organizations with related interests. **Publications:** *EHPM Federation News*, monthly. Newsletter. Contains information on the economic and legal developments of the health product industry.

★ 5846 ★ European Proprietary Medicines Manufacturers' Association (AESGP) (Europaischer Fachverband der Arzneimittel-Hersteller)
7, ave. de Tervuren
B-1040 Brussels, Belgium
Phone: 2 7355130
Fax: 2 7355222
Dr. Hubertus Cranz, Dir.

Founded: 1964. **Members:** 22. **Languages:** English. **Description:** National European proprietary medicines associations. (Proprietary medicines are packaged, over-the-counter drugs.) Advocates self-medication, defined as the therapeutic use of drugs that are safe, effective, and available without prescription. Objectives are to: encourage the involvement of the pharmaceutical industry in European national health care systems; promote and maintain high standards of production, distribution, and advertising of proprietary drugs; ensure that the interests of the proprietary drug industry are recognized by institutions responsible for health legislation; enhance cooperation and the exchange of information among members, and with international professional, industrial, and governmental organizations; represent member associations in the World Federation of Proprietary Medicines' Manufacturers. Compiles statistics. **Publications:** *Annual Meeting Proceedings.* • *Developing Self-Medication in Central and Eastern Europe.* • *Self-Medication and the Pharmacist*, periodic. • *Summary of Product Characteristics for Non-Prescription Medicines in the EC.*

★ 5847 ★ Fachverband der Eisen- und Metallwarenindustrie Osterreichs
Wiedner Haupstrasse 63
PO Box 335
A-1045 Vienna, Austria
Phone: 1 50105
Fax: 1 5050928
Dr. Gunter Mock, Sec.

Languages: German. **Description:** Companies manufacturing dental equipment and supplies. Establishes international standards and technical harmonization for dental equipment. Represents members' interests before government bodies, international agencies, and the public. Maintains liaison with organizations represent-

ing dentists, dental technicians, and dental supply dealers and distributors. Compiles statistics.

★ 5848 ★ Federacion Nacional de Empresas de Instrumentacion Cientifica, Medica, Tecnica y Dental (FENIN)
Juan Bravo 10-3o planta
E-28006 Madrid, Spain
Phone: 1 5759800
Fax: 1 4353478
Ramon Perez Bordo, Sec.

Languages: Spanish. **Description:** Companies manufacturing dental equipment and supplies. Establishes international standards and technical harmonization for dental equipment. Represents members' interests before government bodies, international agencies, and the public. Maintains liaison with organizations representing dentists, dental technicians, and dental supply dealers and distributors. Compiles statistics.

★ 5849 ★ Federation of the European Dental Industry (Federation de l'Industrie Dentaire en Europe — FIDE)
Pipinstrasse 16
50667 Cologne, Germany
Phone: 221 9212120
Fax: 221 245013
Martina Kreuzer, Sec.

Founded: 1957. **Members:** 11. **Languages:** English. **Description:** National associations of companies engaged in the manufacture of dental instruments and supplies. Functions as a platform for coordination of development and works to harmonize international standards within the industry; represents members' interests before government and European Community agencies. Promotes environmental protection; conducts exhibitions; compiles statistics. **Also Known As:** Vereinigung der Europaischen Dental-Industrie.

★ 5850 ★ Generic Pharmaceutical Industry Association (GPIA)
1620 Eye St. NW, Ste. 800
Washington, DC 20006-4005
Phone: (202)833-9070
Fax: (202)833-9612
Lewis A. Engman, Pres.

Founded: 1981. **Members:** 43. **Description:** Manufacturers and distributors of generic medicines and providers of technical services and goods. Members are dedicated to providing quality pharmaceuticals to consumers at affordable prices. **Publications:** *List of Interchangeable Drugs.* • *Seven Quick Facts to Remember about Generic Drugs.*

★ 5851 ★ Health Care Compliance Packaging Council (HCPC)
1001 G St. NW, Ste. 500 W.
Washington, DC 20001
Phone: (202)434-4268
Fax: (202)434-4646
Peter G. Mayberry, Staff Dir.

Founded: 1991. **Members:** 25. **Description:** Promotes the use of "unit-dose blister packaging" as a way of insuring compliance with pharmaceutical regimens. Conducts speakers' bureau. Compiles statistics. Sponsors research

and educational programs. **Publications:** *Compliance News and Views*, 3/year, 3/year. Newsletter.

★ 5852 ★ Health Industry Business Communications Council (HIBCC)
5110 N. 40th St., Ste. 250
Phoenix, AZ 85018
Phone: (602)381-1091
Fax: (602)381-1093
Robert A. Hawkin, Ph.D., Pres.

Founded: 1984. **Members:** 1,000. **Description:** Individuals and companies in the health care industry. To improve the quality and economic efficiency of health care by instituting and overseeing a uniform system of computer bar coding (for identification of health care equipment) and by promoting the use of this and other automated technologies in the health care industry. Conducts workshops and seminars. **Publications:** *Health Industry Lines*, quarterly. Newsletter. *Price:* Included in membership dues. • *Proceedings from Unit Dose Focus Group*, periodic. Proceedings. • *Standards*, periodic. **Formerly:** (1987) Health Industry Bar Code Council.

★ 5853 ★ Health Industry Distributors Association (HIDA)
225 Reinekers Ln., No. 650
Alexandria, VA 22314-2875
Phone: (703)549-4432
Fax: (703)549-6495
S. Wayne Kag, Pres.

Founded: 1902. **Members:** 863. **Regional Groups:** 10. **Description:** Distributors of medical, laboratory, surgical, and home health care equipment and supplies to hospitals, physicians, nursing homes, and industrial medical departments. Conducts sales training, management seminars, and research through the HIDA Educational Foundation. Sponsors Louis H. Markle Foundation, charitable distribution organization which accepts surplus or outmoded instruments and equipment and donates them to foreign medical missions. **Publications:** Annual Report. • *HIDA Headlines*, biweekly. • *Home Health Care Catalog.* • *Manufacturers Directory*, annual. Directory. • *Membership Directory*, annual. • *Physicians Catalog.* **Formerly:** (1982) American Surgical Trade Association.

★ 5854 ★ Health Industry Manufacturers Association (HIMA)
1200 G St. NW, Ste. 4000
Washington, DC 20005
Phone: (202)783-8700
Fax: (202)783-8750
Alan H. Magazine, Pres.

Founded: 1974. **Members:** 334. **Description:** Represents domestic (including U.S. territories and possessions) manufacturers of medical devices, diagnostic products, and healthcare information systems. Develops programs and activities on economic, technical, medical, and scientific matters affecting the industry. Gathers and disseminates information concerning the United States and international developments in legislative, regulatory, scientific or standards-making areas. Conducts scientific and educational seminars and programs. **Publications:** *Health Industry Manufacturers Association--Directory*, annual. Directory. Covers issues facing the health industry. *Price:* Free, for members only. • Manuals, • *Primus*, monthly. *Price:* Free, for members only. • Proceedings. • Reports.

★ 5855 ★ **Health Industry Representatives Association (HIRA)**
5818 Reeds Rd.
Shawnee Mission, KS 66202
Phone: (913)262-4513
Fax: (913)262-0174
Frank Bistrom, CAE, Exec.Dir.

Founded: 1978. **Members:** 250. **Description:** Manufacturers' representatives who operate independent marketing firms under contract to manufacturers of noncompeting lines and manufacturers within the health care industry who market through independent marketing firms. Conducts special surveys at regular intervals for members. Provides panel discussions and special discounts for member firms on advertising and reference publications. **Publications:** *Health Industry Representatives Association--Association News*, monthly. Newsletter. • *Health Industry Representatives Association--Membership Directory*, annual. Membership Directory. *Price:* $100/year. • *Health Industry Representatives Association--Serial Publications*, monthly. **Formerly:** (1986) Health Associated Representatives.

★ 5856 ★ **Hearing Industries Association (HIA)**
515 King St., Ste. 420
Alexandria, VA 22314
Phone: (703)684-5744
Fax: (703)684-6048
Carole M. Rogin, Pres.

Founded: 1957. **Members:** 32. **Description:** Companies engaged in the manufacture and/or sale of electronic hearing aids, their component parts, and related products and services on a national basis. Cooperates in and contributes toward efforts to promote the number of hearing aid users; collects trade statistics; conducts market research activities, investigations, and experiments in connection with hearing and hearing aids. **Publications:** *The Marketing Edge*, quarterly. Newsletter. **Formerly:** (1977) Hearing Aid Industry Conference.

★ 5857 ★ **INDENT**
Postbus 190
NL-2700 AD Zoetermeer, Netherlands
Phone: 79 531353
Fax: 79 531365
Mr. J. W. van Pagee, Sec.

Languages: Dutch. **Description:** Companies manufacturing dental equipment and supplies. Establishes international standards and technical harmonization for dental equipment. Represents members' interests before government bodies, international agencies, and the public. Maintains liaison with organizations representing dentists, dental technicians, and dental supply dealers and distributors. Compiles statistics.

★ 5858 ★ **Independent Medical Distributors Association (IMDA)**
5818 Reeds Rd.
Shawnee Mission, KS 66202
Phone: (913)262-4510
Fax: (913)262-0174
Frank Bistrom, CAE, Exec.Dir.

Founded: 1978. **Members:** 100. **Description:** Independent distributors of high technology healthcare products. Objectives are to promote professionalism among distributors and improve business management skills. **Publications:** *Independent Medical Distributors Association Directory*, annual. Membership Directory. Lists members and their area of specialty in the industry. *Price:* $50. • *Independent Medical Distributors Association--Update*, monthly. Newsletter. Covers membership activities. *Price:* Available to members only.

★ 5859 ★ **Institute of Certified Professional Business Consultants (ICPBC)**
330 S. Wells St., Ste. 1422
Chicago, IL 60606
Phone: (312)360-0384
Free: 800-447-1684
Fax: (312)360-0388
Barbara Boden, Exec.Dir.

Founded: 1975. **Members:** 295. **Description:** Individuals providing business advisory services to physicians and dentists. Maintains code of ethics, rules of professional conduct, and certification program; administers examination and conducts review course. Membership by successful completion of certification examination only. **Publications:** *Institute of Certified Professional Business Consultants--Membership Directory*, annual. Membership Directory. • *Institute of Certified Professional Business Consultants--Newsletter*, quarterly. Newsletter. *Price:* Available to members only.

★ 5860 ★ **International Association of Biological Standardization (IABS) (Association Internationale de Standardisation Biologique — AISB)**
Case Postale 456
CH-1211 Geneva 4, Switzerland
Phone: 22 3469355
Fax: 22 3475610
Dr. C. Huygelen, Pres.

Founded: 1956. **Members:** 530. **Languages:** English, French. **Description:** Representatives of medical, veterinary, and scientific fields; pharmaceutical companies; state controllers; private and university research workers. Works to regulate the standardization of medical and veterinary biological products. Conducts symposia. **Publications:** *Journal of Biological Standardization*, quarterly. • Newsletter, semiannual.

★ 5861 ★ **International Health Evaluation Association (IHEA)**
90 W. Montgomery Ave., Ste. 340
Rockville, MD 20850
Phone: (301)762-6050
Fax: (301)762-7127
Harold A. Timken, Exec.VP & Sec.

Founded: 1971. **Members:** 300. **Regional Groups:** 3. **Description:** Users, suppliers, and manufacturers of computer-based health evaluation systems including clinics, hospitals, physicians, medical students, and research institutions. Is dedicated to the improvement of health care through: the advancement of computer-based health testing and evaluation techniques; the refinement of associated data-processing systems and biomedical devices; the development of a low-cost, high-quality health programs. Believes the technique of computer-based health evaluation can be used in the areas of testing industrial workers and others exposed to environmental hazards, mandatory tests conducted by governmental agencies, and pre-admission hospital testing. Sponsors seminars on clinical preventive medicine for the discussion of medical results, operational techniques, new applications, and cost-effectiveness data. Conducts research; compiles statistics; maintains library; operates speakers' bureau. **Publications:** Newsletter, quarterly. • *Proceedings of Annual Symposia*, quarterly. Proceedings. *Price:* Free. • *Regional Newsletter*, periodic. Newsletter.

★ 5862 ★ **Medical-Dental-Hospital Bureaus of America (MDHBA)**
1101 17th St. NW, Ste. 1200
Washington, DC 20036
Phone: (202)296-9200
Fax: (202)296-0023
Sanford J. Hill, Exec.Dir.

Founded: 1938. **Members:** 200. **Description:** Business bureaus providing physicians, dentists, hospitals, and clinics with management, bookkeeping, finance, tax, and collection services. Sponsors Certified Professional Bureau Executive (CPBE) certification program; holds training seminars. **Publications:** *Economics*, monthly. • *Newscope*, quarterly. **Formerly:** (1958) National Association of Medical Dental Bureaus.

★ 5863 ★ **NARD**
205 Daingerfield Rd.
Alexandria, VA 22314
Phone: (703)683-8200
Free: 800-544-7447
Fax: (703)683-3619
Charles M. West, Exec.VP

Founded: 1898. **Members:** 30,000. **State Groups:** 50. **Description:** Owners and managers of independent drugstores and pharmacists employed in retail drugstores offering pharmacy service. Provides support for undergraduate pharmacy education through National Association of Retail Druggists Foundation. **Publications:** *Almanac*, annual. • *Calendar*, annual. • *Journal*, monthly. • *NARD Journal*, monthly. Journal. Contains continuing education series, updates, and news from Washington. *Price:* Included in membership dues. • *NARD Newsletter*, semimonthly. Newsletter. Contains legislative information related to pharmaceutical field. *Price:* Included in membership dues; $50 for nonmembers; $70 for nonmembers (outside U.S.). **Formerly:** (1988) National Association of Retail Druggists.

★ 5864 ★ **National Association of Chain Drug Stores (NACDS)**
c/o Ronald L. Ziegler
413 N. Lee St.
PO Box 1417-D49
Alexandria, VA 22313
Phone: (703)549-3001
Fax: (703)836-4869
Ronald L. Ziegler, CEO & Pres.

Founded: 1933. **Members:** 1,255. **Description:** Chain drug members (155); associate members (1100) include manufacturers, suppliers, manufacturer's representatives, publishers, and advertising agencies. Interprets actions by government agencies in such areas as drugs, public health, federal trade, labor, and excise taxes. Sponsors meetings and pharmacy student recruitment program. Maintains library. Offers insurance and discount services to members. **Publications:** *Chain Pharmacists Newsletter*, periodic. Newsletter. • *Environmental Affairs Newsletter*, periodic. Newsletter. • *Federal Report*. • *NACDS Health Events Resource Guide*, annual. *Price:* Free. • *NACDS Industry Calendar*, annual. *Price:* Free. • *NACDS Membership Directory*, annual. Membership Directory. Lists chain drug stores, with separate geographical listings of company headquarters and all member stores. *Price:* Available to members only. • *NACDS Sourcebook*, annual. Directory. Lists related organizations, publications, state boards of pharmacy, industry associations, and pharmacy schools. *Price:* $50. • *National Association of Chain Drug Stores--Executive Newsletter*, biweekly. Newsletter. Covers government news and association programs, services, and activities. *Price:* Free to members; $100/year for nonmembers.

★ 5865 ★ **National Association for Healthcare Recruitment (NAHCR)**
PO Box 5769
Akron, OH 44372
Phone: (216)867-3088
Fax: (216)867-1630
Karen A. Hart, Exec.Dir.

Founded: 1975. **Members:** 2,142. **Regional Groups:** 57. **Local Groups:** 50. **Description:** Individuals employed directly by hospitals and other health care organizations which are involved in the practice of professional health care recruitment. Promotes sound principles of professional health care recruitment. Provides financial assistance to aid members in planning and implementing regional educational programs. Offers technical assistance and consultation services. Compiles statistics. **Publications:** *Annual Recruitment Survey*, annual. Survey. • *New Recruiter's Handbook*. Handbook. • *Recruitment Directions*, bimonthly. *Price:* $125/year. • *Who's Who in Recruitment Resources*, annual. **Formerly:** National Association of Nurse Recruiters; (1987) National Association of Healthcare Recruiters.

★ 5866 ★ **National Association of Manufacturing Opticians (NAMO)**
RR 2, Box 35Q
Rockwall, TX 75087-5100
Phone: (214)771-8848
Fax: (214)722-1619
William J. Flannery, III, Pres.

Founded: 1975. **Description:** Full-service optical laboratories. Promotes an economically viable ophthalmic industry. Encourages the creation of objective legislation and regulations. Initiated the development of the Optical Product Code Council and the use of bar coding within the industry. Works closely with the American National Standards Institute, American Optometric Association, Optical Laboratories Association, Optical Manufacturer's Association, and Opticians Association of America.

★ 5867 ★ **National Association for Medical Equipment Services (NAMES)**
625 Slaters Ln., Ste. 200
Alexandria, VA 22314-1171
Phone: (703)836-6263
Fax: (703)836-6730
Corrine Parver, Pres. & CEO

Founded: 1982. **Members:** 2,100. **Regional Groups:** 3. **State Groups:** 37. **Description:** Home medical equipment, oxygen suppliers and rehabilitation technology suppliers. To represent professionals in the home medical equipment service industry; to support legislation and regulations that are beneficial to the home health care industry and provide incentives for suppliers to continue to serve Medicare/Medicaid beneficiaries. Sponsors education programs; maintains speakers' bureau. Compiles statistics and does Congressional lobbying. **Publications:** *Associate Membership Directory*, annual. Membership Directory. Listing of associate members and product/services descriptions. • Brochures. • Manuals. • *Names Annual Report*, annual. *Price:* Free to members. • *Names News*, weekly. Covers industry news and developments in Congress and in regulatory agencies. *Price:* Free, for members only. • *Project Blueprint Report*, annual. *Price:* Free to members. Also publishes press releases. **Formerly:** (1994) National Association of Medical Equipment Suppliers.

★ 5868 ★ **National Association of Pharmaceutical Manufacturers (NAPM)**
320 Old Country Rd., Ste. 205
Garden City, NY 11530-1752
Phone: (516)741-3699
Fax: (516)741-3696
Robert S. Milanese, Pres.

Founded: 1954. **Members:** 65. **Description:** Pharmaceutical manufacturers and repackagers. Associate members are distributors of raw material, component, and service suppliers. Purpose is to consider problems arising from laws and regulations, and to establish rapport with federal and state agencies. Organized the Foundation for Pharmaceutical Research. Conducts technical and regulatory symposia and seminars. **Publications:** *NAPM News Bulletin*, monthly. Bulletin. Focuses on the legislative, regulatory, legal, and technical aspects of the pharmaceutical industry. Includes new product information. *Price:* Free. **Formerly:** Drug and Allied Products Guild.

★ 5869 ★ **National Association of Physician Recruiters (NAPR)**
PO Box 150127
Altamonte Springs, FL 32715-0127
Phone: (407)774-7880
Fax: (407)774-6440
Willard S. Kautter, CAE, Exec.VP

Founded: 1983. **Members:** 125. **Description:** Physician search firms (companies that recruit resident physicians or practicing physicians to fill positions nationwide). Promotes a positive public image of physician recruiting services. Seeks to establish accreditation standards for the field. Provides marketing services to the physician recruiting industry. Maintains library and speakers' bureau. Sponsors educational programs and seminars. Bestows awards; compiles statistics. **Publications:** Brochures. • *NAPR Business Report*, quarterly.

★ 5870 ★ **National Committee for Quality Health Care (NCQHC)**
1500 K St. NW, Ste. 360
Washington, DC 20005
Phone: (202)347-5731
Fax: (202)347-5836
Pamela G. Bailey, Pres.

Founded: 1978. **Members:** 151. **Description:** Coalition of health care professionals and organizations principally involved in the health care industry; includes hospitals, physicians, health maintenance organizations, nursing homes, manufacturers of health care equipment, investment bankers, architects, contractors, and accountants. Works to maintain and strengthen quality health care in the U.S. **Publications:** *An American Health Strategy: Ensuring the Availability of Quality Health Care*. • *Critical Condition: America's Health Care in Jeopardy*. • Pamphlets. • Papers. • *Quality Bulletin*, bimonthly. Bulletin. • *Quality Outlook*, bimonthly. **Formerly:** National Committee on Hospital Capital Expenditures.

★ 5871 ★ **National Drug Trade Conference (NDTC)**
c/o Gerald J. Mossinghoff
1100 15th St. NW
Washington, DC 20005
Phone: (202)835-3420
Fax: (202)855-3429
Gerald J. Mossinghoff, Pres.

Founded: 1913. **Members:** 10. **Description:** Federation of associations of manufacturers, wholesalers, and boards and colleges of pharmacy.

★ 5872 ★ **National Institute for Chemical Studies (NICS)**
2300 MacCorkle Ave. SE
Charleston, WV 25304
Phone: (304)346-6264
Fax: (304)346-6349
Paul L. Hill, Ph.D., Pres.

Founded: 1985. **Description:** Participants include representatives of the chemical industry, people living adjacent to chemical plants (plant neighbors), emergency responders, and other interested individuals. Serves as liaison between the chemical industry and the public. Maintains the Community Safety Assessment

Program, which brings representatives of the chemical industry and plant neighbors together to resolve issues. Conducts health and other relevant studies; issues reports. Though activities are currently centered in the Kanawha Valley of West Virginia, NICS plans to operate nationwide.

★5873★ **National Pharmaceutical Council (NPC)**
1894 Preston White Dr.
Reston, VA 22091
Phone: (703)620-6390
Fax: (703)476-0904
Mark R. Knowles, Pres.

Founded: 1953. **Members:** 29. **Description:** Pharmaceutical manufacturers producing high quality prescription medication and other pharmaceutical products. Generates research; compiles statistics; conducts specialized educational programs, and forums. **Publications:** Directory, annual. Also publishes educational materials.

★5874★ **National Wholesale Druggists' Association (NWDA)**
1821 Michael Faraday Dr., Ste. 400
Reston, VA 22090-5348
Phone: (703)787-0000
Fax: (703)787-6930
Ronald J. Streck, Pres. and CEO

Founded: 1876. **Members:** 456. **Description:** Wholesalers and manufacturers of drug, toiletry, and sundry products; advertising agencies; others interested in improving the flow of merchandise from manufacturer to consumer. Compiles statistics; sponsors research and specialized education programs; maintains video network. Offers speakers' bureau. **Publications:** *Fact Book*, annual. *Price:* $20 for members; $295 for nonmembers. • *Government Update*, monthly. • Membership Directory, annual. *Price:* $20 for members; $295 for nonmembers. • *NWDA Executive Newsletter*, monthly. Newsletter. Reports association activities and services, trends and changes in the wholesale drug industry. *Price:* Free to members. • *Operating Survey*, annual. *Price:* $30 for members; $295 for nonmembers. • Pamphlets. Covers operations, procedures, and sales. **Formerly:** (1881) Western Wholesale Druggists.

★5875★ **Nonprescription Drug Manufacturers Association (NDMA)**
1150 Connecticut Ave. NW
Washington, DC 20036
Phone: (202)429-9260
Fax: (202)223-6835
James D. Cope, Pres.

Founded: 1881. **Members:** 225. **Description:** Marketers (75) of nonprescription drugs, which are packaged, over-the-counter medicines; associate members (150) include suppliers, advertising agencies, and advertising media. Obtains and disseminates business, legislative, regulatory, and scientific information; conducts voluntary labeling review service to assist members in complying with laws and regulations. **Publications:** *Compilation of OTC Drug Regulations*, periodic. • Directory, annual. • *Executive Newsletter*, weekly. Newsletter. • *Legislative News Bulletin*, periodic. Bulletin. • Pamphlets. Subjects include self-medication and the safe use of over-the-counter medications. • *Proceedings of Research and Scientific Development Conference and Manufacturing Controls Seminar*. Proceedings. • *Scientific News Bulletin*, periodic. Bulletin. **Formerly:** (1989) The Proprietary Association.

★5876★ **Optical Industry Association (OMA)**
6055A Arlington Blvd.
Falls Church, VA 22044
Phone: (703)237-8433
Fax: (703)237-0643
Eugene Adams Keeney, Exec.VP

Founded: 1916. **Members:** 100. **Description:** Manufacturers, distributors, and importers of ophthalmic frames, lenses, cases, and optical machinery; suppliers of material and parts. **Formerly:** (1992) Optical Manufacturers Association.

★5877★ **Optical Laboratories Association (OLA)**
PO Box 2000
Merrifield, VA 22116-2000
Phone: (703)359-2830
Fax: (703)359-2834
Irby N. Hollans, Jr., Exec.Dir.

Founded: 1963. **Members:** 365. **Description:** Independent, wholesale ophthalmic laboratories and suppliers serving the ophthalmic field. **Publications:** *Clear Visions*, quarterly. Newsletter. *Price:* Free. **Formerly:** (1977) Optical Wholesalers Association.

★5878★ **Orthopedic Surgical Manufacturers Association (OSMA)**
c/o Charles Lawyer
359 Veterans Blvd.
Rutherford, NJ 07070
Phone: (201)507-7300
Fax: (201)507-7254
Charles Lawyer, Pres.

Founded: 1955. **Members:** 33. **Description:** Works to unite interested manufacturers of orthopedic surgical items in order to enhance the contributions made by the industry to orthopedic health. Fosters research and the dissemination of information relating to scientific and practical problems. Cooperates with professional health associations and government agencies. Promotes the development of high standards and ethics in all phases of the industry. Maintains task forces.

★5879★ **Parenteral Drug Association (PDA)**
7500 Old Georgetown Rd., Ste. 620
Bethesda, MD 20814
Phone: (301)986-0293
Fax: (301)986-0296
Edmund M. Fry, Exec. VP

Founded: 1946. **Members:** 5,500. **Regional Groups:** 9. **Description:** Individuals working in the research, development, or manufacture of parenteral (injectable) drugs and sterile products. Promotes the advance of parenteral science and technology in the interest of public health. Encourages the exchange of information and technical expertise. Conducts open forums for manufacturers, suppliers, users, regulatory agencies, and academia; sponsors research and educational programs; operates placement service and speakers' bureau. **Publications:** *Journal of Pharmaceutical Science and Technology*, bimonthly. Journal. Covers pharmaceutical science research, production, and development. *Price:* $70/year; $90/year (outside U.S.). • Membership Directory, annual. • *PDA Letter*, monthly. Newsletter. Covers governmental and industrial developments relating to pharmaceutical manufacturing and quality control. *Price:* Included in membership dues. Also publishes technical materials.

★5880★ **Pharmaceutical Manufacturers Association (PMA)**
1100 15th St. NW
Washington, DC 20005
Phone: (202)835-3400
Gerald J. Mossinghoff, Pres.

Founded: 1958. **Members:** 87. **Description:** Manufacturers of ethical pharmaceutical and biological products that are distributed under their own labels. Encourages high standards for quality control and good manufacturing practices; research toward development of new and better medical products; enactment of uniform and reasonable drug legislation for the protection of public health. Disseminates information on governmental regulations and policies, but does not maintain or supply information on specific products, prices, distribution, promotion, or sales policies of its individual members. Has established the Pharmaceutical Manufacturers Association Foundation to promote public health through scientific and medical research. **Publications:** Annual Report. • *Fact Book*, annual. • Newsletter, weekly. • *Trademarks Listed with the Pharmaceutical Manufacturers Association*, periodic. Includes monthly supplements. *Price:* $25/year.

★5881★ **Regulatory Affairs Professionals Society (RAPS)**
12300 Twinbrook Pky., Ste. 630
Rockville, MD 20852
Phone: (301)770-2920
Fax: (301)770-2924

Founded: 1976. **Members:** 5,600. **Description:** Professionals in the drug, medical device, biotechnology, diagnostic, cosmetic and food industries; lawyers, doctors, and consultants; others in the regulated health care field. Is dedicated to the advancement of the regulatory affairs profession in dealing with health care products. Seeks to identify and recognize regulatory affairs professionals and others in interacting disciplines. Facilitates communication between society and governmental regulatory agencies. Offers placement services. **Publications:** *RAPS*, annual. Membership Directory. • *RAPSnews*, monthly. • *Regulatory Affairs*, quarterly. Journal. *Price:* $120 in the U.S.; $145 outside the U.S.

★5882★ **Society of Medical-Dental Management Consultants (SMD)**
6215 Larson
Kansas City, MO 64133
Phone: 800-826-2264
Free: 800-826-2264
William H. Kidd, Exec.Sec.

Founded: 1968. Members: 135. State Groups: 43. Description: Professional medical and/or dental management consultants associated for educational and information sharing purposes. Objectives are to: advance the profession; share management techniques; improve individual skills; provide clients with competent and capable business management. Provides information on insurance and income tax. Conducts surveys; compiles statistics. Publications: Bulletin. • *Forms Manual.* Manual. • *Membership Roster*, annual. Membership Directory. • *SMD Statistics.* • *Society of Medical-Dental Management Consultants--Newsletter*, bimonthly. Newsletter. *Price:* Included in membership dues.

★5883★ Swedish Dental Trade Association
(Foreningen Svensk Dentalhandel — FSD)
Box 1416
S-111 84 Stockholm, Sweden
Phone: 8 240700
Fax: 8 218496
Lennart Uhlmann, Sec.

Languages: English, Swedish. Description: Companies manufacturing dental equipment and supplies. Establishes international standards and technical harmonization for dental equipment. Represents members' interests before government bodies, international agencies, and the public. Maintains liaison with organizations representing dentists, dental technicians, and dental supply dealers and distributors. Compiles statistics.

★5884★ Syndicat des Industries Francaises pour l'Art Dentaire
(SIFADENT)
8, rue Blanche
F-75009 Paris, France
Phone: 1 48741108
Fax: 1 42852032
Jean-Marc Loeser, Sec.

Languages: French. Description: Companies manufacturing dental equipment and supplies. Establishes international standards and technical harmonization for dental equipment. Represents members' interests before government bodies, international agencies, and the public. Maintains liaison with organizations representing dentists, dental technicians, and dental supply dealers and distributors. Compiles statistics.

★5885★ Unione Nazionale Industrie Dentarie Italiane
Via Tamburini 2
I-20123 Milan, Italy
Phone: 2 48008650
Fax: 2 461330
Dr. Arturo Chiurazzi, Sec.

Languages: Italian. Description: Companies manufacturing dental equipment and supplies. Establishes international standards and technical harmonization for dental equipment. Represents members' interests before government bodies, international agencies, and the public. Maintains liaison with organizations representing dentists, dental technicians, and dental supply dealers and distributors. Compiles statistics.

★5886★ Verband der Deutschen Dental-Industrie
Pipinstrasse 16
50667 Cologne, Germany
Phone: 221 9212120
Fax: 221 245013
Harald Russegger, Sec.

Languages: German. Description: Companies manufacturing dental equipment and supplies. Establishes international standards and technical harmonization for dental equipment. Represents members' interests before government bodies, international agencies, and the public. Maintains liaison with organizations representing dentists, dental technicians, and dental supply dealers and distributors. Compiles statistics.

★5887★ Woman's Organization of the National Association of Retail Druggists
(WONARD)
205 Daingerfield Rd.
Alexandria, VA 22314
Phone: (703)683-8200
Fax: (703)683-3619
Vivian Przondo, Contact

Founded: 1905. Members: 600. Regional Groups: 5. Description: Women and female relatives of men in the pharmaceutical business. Objective is to unite the families of persons interested in all aspects of the pharmaceutical profession. Promotes legislation for the betterment of the retail drug and pharmacy business. Conducts charitable program. Publications: *WONARD Newsletter*, quarterly. Newsletter. Reports on legislation, education, and association activities. *Price:* Free, for members only.

Research Centers

★5888★ Johns Hopkins University Drug and Device Development Center
Johns Hopkins Sch. of Med.
124 Adm. Bldg.
720 Rutland Ave.
Baltimore, MD 21205-2196
Phone: (410)955-1610
Fax: (410)614-1823
Scott L. Sherman, Asst. Dean

Research Activities and Fields: Coordinates evaluation and ensures cost effectiveness of new medical products at all stages of development. Also works to increase cooperative ventures between researchers at Hopkins Medical Institutions and biomedical companies and venture capitalists. Current projects include over 350 investigational drug studies and new device trials. Particular areas of study include anesthesia and critical care, biomedical engineering, cardiac surgery, cardiology, clinical immunology, clinical pharmacology, comparative medicine, dermatology, epidemiology, gastroenterology, infectious disease, medicine, nephrology, neurology, neuroscience, neurosurgery, pharmacology, psychiatry, pulmonary medicine, obstetrics and gynecology, ophthalmology, oncology, orthopedic surgery, otolaryngology-head and neck surgery, pathology, pediatrics, radiology, rehabilitation medicine, rheumatology, surgery, and urology.

U.S. Department of Health and Human Services
National Institute of Neurological Disorders and Stroke
Small Business Innovation Research Program
See: Entry 8471

Chapter 31
Hematology & Oncology

Federal Government Agencies

★ 5889 ★ **U.S. Department of Health and Human Services**
National Cancer Institute
9000 Rockville Pike
Bethesda, MD 20892
Phone: (301)496-5615

Description: NCI has developed a National Cancer Program to expand existing scientific knowledge on cancer cause and prevention, as well as on the diagnosis, treatment, and rehabilitation of cancer patients. Research activities, conducted in the Institute's laboratories or supported through grants or contracts, include many investigative approaches to cancer, including chemistry, biochemistry, biology, molecular biology, immunology, radiation, physics, experimental chemotherapy, epidemiology, biometry, radiotherapy, and pharmacology. Cancer research facilities are constructed with NCI support, and training is provided under university-based programs.

U.S. Department of Health and Human Services
National Heart, Lung, and Blood Institute
See: Entry 2781

Foundations & Other Funding Organizations

Private Foundations

★ 5890 ★ **Alexander and Margaret Stewart Trust u/w/o Mary E. Stewart**
c/o First Union National Bank of Washington
740 15th St., NW
Washington, DC 20005
Phone: (202)686-1552
Fax: (202)686-1553
Ruth C. Shaw, Vice President

Foundation Philosophy: Funds are granted to organizations involved in care and treatment of people afflicted with cancer, with particular emphasis placed on home care programs. The primary interest is direct patient care, and occasionally the trust may fund the purchase of equipment used in cancer diagnosis and treatment. The trust welcomes evidence that a requested program has ongoing community support and acceptance before funding is considered. It will consider start-up costs for a new program with the intention that the program will become self-sustaining. Programs aiding the economically deprived are favored. **Giving Priorities:** In 1993, the trust gave 97% of its funding to health care primarily to support cancer-related programs; the remaining 3% went to religious causes. **Typical Health-Related Recipients:** Cancer, Hospices, Hospitals, Long-Term Care, Nursing Services, Single-Disease Health Associations. **Geographic Distribution:** Primarily metropolitan Washington, DC, area.

★ 5891 ★ **Bruce McMillan, Jr. Foundation**
PO Box 9
Overton, TX 75684
Phone: (903)834-3148
Ralph Ward, Sr., President and Treasurer

Foundation Philosophy: The Bruce McMillan, Jr., Foundation supports the areas of education, agriculture, science, religion, and specialized health care. Health care support goes to cancer research, blood centers, and treatment centers. **Giving Priorities:** In fiscal 1994, the foundation gave 65% of its funds to higher education; most of these awards were given to universities in Texas. Religious organizations and churches received 20% of the contributions. Grants to health care accounted for 7% of the funding. Social service organizations received 6% of the funding, and civic organizations received the remaining funds. **Typical Health-Related Recipients:** Cancer, Family Planning, Health Organizations, Heart, Single-Disease Health Associations, Substance Abuse, Transplant Networks/Donor Banks. **Geographic Distribution:** Primarily in Texas, with emphasis on the Overton area.

Carl J. Herzog Foundation
See: Entry 84

Clara Blackford Smith and W. Aubrey Smith Charitable Foundation
See: Entry 102

E. L. Wiegand Foundation
See: Entry 150

Edward G. Schlieder Educational Foundation
See: Entry 158

Elmer and Mamdouha Bobst Foundation
See: Entry 169

★ 5892 ★ **Elsa U. Pardee Foundation**
Box 1866
Midland, MI 48641-1866
Phone: (517)832-3691
Lucille M. Dougherty, Staff Assistant

Foundation Philosophy: The purpose of the foundation is "to support research in the field of cancer, and to provide for others those advantages of knowledge and techniques still undiscovered in the treatment of cancer." Soon after the foundation's establishment, the trustees gave one-quarter of annual revenues to the treatment of cancer victims. The remaining three-quarters would go to cancer research projects and well-established institutes. Grants support hospitals, universities, and research institutes for projects to study control of, and cures for, cancer. **Giving Priorities:** In 1993, all of the foundation's funding was directed toward cancer research at various universities, hospitals, and medical research institutes throughout the country. A minimal grant was also awarded to the Council on Michigan Foundations. **Typical Health-Related Recipients:** Cancer, Hospitals, Medical Research, Transplant Networks/Donor Banks. **Geographic Distribution:** National; no geographic restrictions.

Evan and Marion Helfaer Foundation
See: Entry 6349

Fannie E. Rippel Foundation
See: Entry 178

Forest Foundation
See: Entry 188

Frances L. & Edwin L. Cummings Memorial Fund
See: Entry 195

Gordon / Rousmaniere / Roberts Fund
See: Entry 227

★5893★ Jane Coffin Childs Memorial Fund for Medical Research
c/o Yale University School of Medicine
PO Box 208000
New Haven, CT 06520-8000
Phone: (203)785-4612
Fax: (203)785-3301
Elizabeth M. Ford, Administrative Director

Foundation Philosophy: The fund traditionally has supported basic cancer research, rather than the investigation of the clinical aspects of the disease. Current funding is limited to postdoctoral fellowships for physicians and scientists. **Giving Priorities:** In fiscal 1993, all of the fund's contributions went to medical research. The majority of funding (68%) went to individuals conducting research at major universities. About 28% of donations went to research being conducted at health care institutes. About 2% went to the Travel Fund for Fellows for the Fund. The remaining 2% went to medical research overseas. **Typical Health-Related Recipients:** Cancer, Clinics/Medical Centers, Medical Education, Medical Research, Research/Studies Institutes. **Geographic Distribution:** National and international.

Joseph Alexander Foundation
See: Entry 329

Nathan Cummings Foundation
See: Entry 409

★5894★ Oliver S. and Jennie R. Donaldson Charitable Trust
c/o U.S. Trust of New York
114 W. 47th St.
New York, NY 10036
Phone: (212)852-3683
Anne L. Smith-Gainey, Assistant Vice President

Foundation Philosophy: The foundation makes grants across the major categories of support. Most of the grants are made in the areas of education, health, civic affairs, and social services. Funding for health care goes to support cancer treatment and research at a number of facilities, hospital, and health organizations. The foundation reports that cancer research is now a major funding interest. **Giving Priorities:** In 1993, the trust contributed 51% of its total giving to health care, including a single $156,500 grant to Cancer Research Institute, New York, NY. Social services and educational insitutions each received 12% of funds. International organizations received 8% of support; civic groups, 6%; the arts, 5%; environmental concerns, 3%; and religious organizations, 1%. **Typical Health-Related Recipients:** Cancer, Children's Health/Hospitals, Clinics/Medical Centers, Emergency/Ambulance Services, Health Organizations, Hospitals, Medical Research, People with Disabilities, Preventive Medicine/Wellness Organizations, Single-Disease Health Associations. **Geographic Distribution:** Eastern United States, with emphasis on Massachusetts.

★5895★ Samuel Freeman Charitable Trust
c/o U.S. Trust Company of New York
114 W 47th St.
New York, NY 10036-1532
Phone: (212)852-3683
Anne Smith-Ganey, Assistant Vice President

Foundation Philosophy: The Samuel Freeman Charitable Trust makes grants across the major categories of support. Major interests include municipalities, colleges, cancer research, museums, and social services. **Giving Priorities:** In 1993, the trust gave approximately 43% of its contributions to educational institutions, mainly colleges, universities, and private schools. Health concerns received 22% of giving; social service organizations, 13%; the arts, 11%; civic affairs, 7%; religion, 3%; and international affairs received the remaining funds. **Typical Health-Related Recipients:** AIDS/HIV, Cancer, Clinics/Medical Centers, Eyes/Blindness, Family Planning, People with Disabilities, Single-Disease Health Associations. **Geographic Distribution:** Mid-Atlantic United States.

Sidney J. Weinberg, Jr. Foundation
See: Entry 6380

Skirball Foundation
See: Entry 6381

Corporate Foundations

AMR / American Airlines Foundation
See: Entry 580

Avon Products Foundation
See: Entry 591

Beech Aircraft Foundation
See: Entry 6390

Benjamin Jacobson & Sons Foundation
See: Entry 604

Collins & Aikman Holdings Foundation
See: Entry 640

★5896★ EG & G Foundation
45 William St.
Wellesley, MA 02181
Phone: (617)237-5100
Kathleen M. Russo, Administrator

Giving Priorities: *Education:* 65% to 70% total contributions. *Social Services:* About 10%. *Health:* 5% to 10%. Two-thirds supports cancer research and treatment. One-third goes to hospitals. *Civic & Public Affairs:* 5% to 10%. *Arts & Humanities:* 5% to 10%. **Typical Health-Related Recipients:** Cancer, Hospitals, Medical Research, Preventive Medicine/Wellness Organizations, Single-Disease Health Associations, Substance Abuse. **Geographic Distribution:** Nationally.

Forbes Foundation
See: Entry 693

General American Charitable Foundation
See: Entry 699

IFF Foundation
See: Entry 732

J. T. Tai and Co. Foundation
See: Entry 740

Miles Inc. Foundation
See: Entry 779

Other Funding Organizations

★5897★ American Cancer Society
1599 Clifton Rd. NE
Atlanta, GA 30329
Phone: (404)320-3333
Free: 800-ACS-2345
Fax: (404)325-0230
John R. Seffrin, Ph.D., Exec. Dir.

Description: Offers a variety of grants and awards to support education and research in cancer prevention, diagnosis, detection, and treatment.

★5898★ Association for Research of Childhood Cancer
PO Box 251
Buffalo, NY 14225-0251
Phone: (716)681-4433
Charles Moll, Exec. Off.

Description: Provides funds for the expansion and continuation of research in pediatric cancer centers and seed money for pilot projects in cancer research. Bestows research and clinical investigation grants, and offers research and medical student fellowships.

★5899★ Cancer Research Foundation
135 S. La Salle, Ste. 1049
Chicago, IL 60603-4202
Phone: (312)630-0055
Fax: (312)630-0075
Sharon Swanson, Exec. Dir.

Description: Funds laboratory and clinical cancer research at Chicago universities and medical schools.

★5900★ Cancer Research Fund of the Damon Runyon-Walter Winchell Foundation
131 E. 36th St.
New York, NY 10016
Phone: (212)532-7000
Rebecca R. Kry, Exec. Dir.

Description: Supports cancer research efforts through fellowship grants to PhD.s and medical school graduates.

★5901★ Cancer Research Institute
681 5th Ave.
New York, NY 10022
Phone: (212)688-7515
Fax: (212)832-9376
Ursula J. Hahn, Grant Admin.

Description: Funds research aimed at furthering the development of immunological approachees to the diagnosis, treatment, and prevention of cancer. Offers postdoctoral fellowships to scientists who wish to receive training in cancer or general immunology. Supports immunological research in general, with emphasis to projects in tumor immunology.

★5902★ **Children's Leukemia Research Association**
585 Stewart Ave., Ste. 536
Garden City, NY 11530
Phone: (516)222-1944
Fax: (516)222-0457
Allan D. Weinberg, Exec. Dir.

Description: Provides financial aid to leukemia patients and their families, and sponsors grants for research into the causes and cure of leukemia.

★5903★ **Cooley's Anemia Foundation**
129-09 26th Ave.
Flushing, NY 11354
Phone: (718)321-2873
Free: 800-221-3571
Fax: (718)321-3340

Description: Makes grants-in-aid toward fellowships and innovative and promising research projects on Cooley's anemia and related disorders.

★5904★ **Leukemia Society of America**
600 3rd Ave.
New York, NY 10016
Phone: (212)573-8484
Free: 800-955-4LSA
Fax: (212)856-9686
Rudolf F. Badum, Acting Pres. & CEO

Description: Raises funds to combat leukemia and related cancers through research, patient service, and public and professional education. Awards scholarships and fellowships for research on leukemia and related diseases.

★5905★ **National Hemophilia Foundation**
110 Green St., Ste. 303
New York, NY 10012
Phone: (212)219-8180
Fax: (212)431-0906
Alan P. Brownstein, Exec. Dir.

Description: Sponsors postgraduate fellowship program for hemophilia-related research.

★5906★ **Skin Cancer Foundation**
245 5th Ave., Ste. 2402
New York, NY 10016
Phone: (212)725-5176
Fax: (212)725-5751
Perry Robins, Pres.

Description: Awards grants to individuals and institutions for skin cancer research.

National & International Organizations

★5907★ **Action Cancer**
1 Marlborough Park
Belfast, Antrim BT9 6HQ, Northern Ireland
Phone: 1232 661081
Fax: 1232 683931
Peter S. Quigley, MIPR, Contact

Founded: 1974. **Local Groups:** 40. **Description:** Works to heighten women's awareness of the importance of early cancer detection. Offers breast and cervical cancer screening services.

Provides counseling service for cancer patients, families, and friends. Maintains research lab. Disseminates information. **Publications:** *Action Cancer News*, semiannual. Magazine.

★5908★ **American Association for Cancer Education (AACE)**
c/o Robert M. Chamberlain
M.D. Anderson Cancer Center
Department of Epidemiology, 189
1515 Holcombe Blvd.
Houston, TX 77030
Phone: (713)792-3020
Fax: (713)792-0807
Dr. Robert M. Chamberlain, Ph.D., Contact

Founded: 1966. **Members:** 550. **Description:** Physicians, dentists, nurses, health educators, social workers, and occupational therapists; others interested in cancer education. Provides a forum for individuals concerned with the study and improvement of cancer education focusing on prevention, early detection, treatment, and rehabilitation. **Publications:** *Journal of Cancer Education*, quarterly. Journal. *Price:* $95 for members; $195 for institutions and libraries. • *Membership Directory*, annual.

★5909★ **American Association for Cancer Research (AACR)**
Public Ledger Bldg.
620 Chestnut St., Ste. 816
Philadelphia, PA 19106-3483
Phone: (215)440-9300
Fax: (215)440-9313
Margaret Foti, Exec.Dir.

Founded: 1907. **Members:** 8,000. **Local Groups:** 2. **Description:** Professional organization of research workers for presentation and discussion of new and significant observations and problems in cancer. Fosters research on cancer. **Publications:** *Cancer Research*, semimonthly. Journal. Contains reports in subfields of cancer research: biochemistry, biophysics, carcinogenesis, endocrinology, immunology, and molecular biology. *Price:* Included in membership; $390/year for nonmembers and institutions. • *Cell Growth and Differentiation*, monthly. Journal. Contains in vitro and in vivo studies of mechanisms underlying normal and abnormal cell behavior and cell growth control. *Price:* Included in membership dues; $90/year for nonmembers; $170/year for institutions. • Directory, annual. • Proceedings, annual. • *Supplement to Journal*, periodic. Journal.

American Board of Chelation Therapy (ABCT)
See: Entry 2160

★5910★ **American Cancer Society (ACS)**
1599 Clifton Rd. NE
Atlanta, GA 30329
Phone: (404)320-3333
Free: 800-ACS-2345
Fax: (404)325-0230
John R. Seffrin, Ph.D., Exec.VP

Founded: 1913. **Regional Groups:** 57. **Local Groups:** 3300. **Description:** Volunteers (2,500,000) supporting education and research in cancer prevention, diagnosis, detection, and treatment. Provides special services to cancer patients. Sponsors Reach to Recovery, CanSur-

mount, and I Can Cope. Conducts medical and educational programs. **Publications:** *American Cancer Society*. Annual Report. *Price:* Free. • *CA—A Cancer Journal for Clinicians*, bimonthly. Covers cancer treatment, prevention, and diagnosis. *Price:* Free for health professionals. • *Cancer*, semimonthly. Medical journal covering cancer prevention, research, diagnosis, and treatment. Includes proceedings supplements covering ACS conferences. *Price:* $75/year for individuals; $125/year for institutions. • *Cancer Facts and Figures*, annual. Report providing statistical information on the major sites of cancer including incidence, mortality and survival rates, and risk factors. *Price:* Free. • *Cancer News*, 3/year. Magazine for ACS volunteers and donors; includes news of society activities. *Price:* Free. • *Cancer Nursing News*, quarterly. Newsletter. Provides information on other publications, schedules of upcoming conferences and seminars, cancer nursing profiles, and ACS program updates. *Price:* Free. • *World Smoking and Health*, 3/year. Bulletin. For health professionals and general readers interested in the medical, social, economic, and political effects of tobacco smoking. *Price:* Free. **Formerly:** (1944) American Society for the Control Cancer.

★5911★ **American College of MOHS Micrographic Surgery and Cutaneous Oncology (ACMMSCO)**
PO Box 4014
Schaumburg, IL 60168-4014
Phone: (708)330-0230
Fax: (708)330-0050
Michael G. Thompson, M.D., Exec. Dir.

Founded: 1967. **Members:** 260. **Description:** Physicians, dermatologists, surgeons, plastic surgeons, and other specialists who have had a minimum of one year of training in chemosurgery at an approved institution. (Chemosurgery is used for the microscopically controlled excision of skin cancer.) Purposes are: to provide a means for accreditation of physicians who have become proficient in the method; to facilitate education and the exchange of ideas. **Formerly:** (1987) American College of Chemosurgery.

★5912★ **American Joint Committee on Cancer (AJCC)**
55 E. Erie St.
Chicago, IL 60611
Phone: (312)664-4050
Fax: (312)440-7144
David P. Winchester, Exec.Dir.

Founded: 1959. **Members:** 40. **Description:** Surgeons, physicians, radiologists, pathologists, American Cancer Society representatives, and National Cancer Institute representatives. Formulates and publishes systems of classification for cancer staging and end results reporting for the purpose of selecting the most effective treatment, determining prognosis, and continuing evaluation of cancer control measures. Promotes the use of developed systems of classification of cancer and evaluates systems of recording and reporting data. **Publications:** *Manual for Staging of Cancer*, every 3-4 years. Manual. **Formerly:** (1981) American Joint Committee for Cancer Staging and End Results Reporting.

★ 5913 ★ American Radium Society (ARS)
Office of the Secretariat
1101 Market St., 14th Fl.
Philadelphia, PA 19107
Phone: (215)574-3179
Fax: (215)928-0153
Suzanne Bohn, Adm.Dir.

Founded: 1916. **Members:** 850. **Description:** Professional society promoting the study of cancer in all its aspects, including the scientific study of the treatment of cancer patients. Encourages liaison among medical specialists and allied scientists concerned with cancer treatment. **Publications:** *American Radium Society- -Membership Directory*, annual. Directory. *Price:* Included in membership dues.

★ 5914 ★ American Society of Clinical Oncology (ASCO)
435 N. Michigan Ave., Ste. 1717
Chicago, IL 60611-4067
Phone: (312)644-0828
Fax: (312)644-8557
Robert B. Becker, Contact

Founded: 1964. **Members:** 9,200. **Description:** Experienced physicians and paramedical personnel who have a predominant interest in the diagnosis and total care of patients with neoplastic diseases. Conducts research and educational programs. **Publications:** *ASCO News*, quarterly. • Directory, annual. • *Journal of Clinical Oncology*, monthly. Journal. • Proceedings, annual.

★ 5915 ★ American Society of Hematology (ASH)
1101 Connecticut Ave. NW, 7th Fl.
Washington, DC 20036-4303
Phone: (202)857-1118
Fax: (202)857-1164
Michael L. Payne, Exec.Dir.

Founded: 1958. **Members:** 6,600. **Description:** Hematologists (specialists in the study of blood) and other persons holding doctorate degrees with an interest in the field. Promotes exchange of information and ideas related to blood and blood-forming tissues and investigation of hematologic problems. Offers educational programs. Maintains slide bank. **Publications:** *ASH Newsletter*, quarterly. Newsletter. • *Blood*, bimonthly. Journal. • *Meeting Program*, annual.

American Society of Pediatric Hematology / Oncology (ASPHO)
See: Entry 3173

American Society of Preventive Oncology (ASPO)
See: Entry 10841

American Society for Therapeutic Radiology and Oncology (ASTRO)
See: Entry 11099

**★ 5916 ★ Anti-Sickle Cell Anemia League (ASCAL)
(Ligue Anti-Anemie Falciforme — LAAF)**
181, rue Capois
BP 19006
Port-au-Prince, Haiti
Phone: 1 239553
Dr. Fleurival Jean

Founded: 1989. **Members:** 350. **Description:** Individuls in Haiti interested in fighting sickle cell disease. Offers counseling to patients and their relatives. Provides public education, newborn and mass screening. Conducts research.

★ 5917 ★ Aplastic Anemia Foundation of America (AAFA)
PO Box 22689
Baltimore, MD 21203
Phone: 800-747-2820
Fax: (410)955-0247
Marilyn Baker Kuipers, Exec.Dir.

Founded: 1984. **Description:** Serves as an information source for persons with aplastic anemia. (Aplastic anemia is an often fatal disease in which the bone marrow fails to produce new blood cells.) Provides free educational materials and medical information. Supports research. **Publications:** *Aplastic Anemia: A Primer*. • *Aplastic Anemia Foundation of America- -Newsletter*, quarterly. Newsletter. Provides information on aplastic anemia and foundation activities. *Price:* Free. • *Aplastic Anemia: The Answer Book*, periodic. Describes the course of the disease and current treatment options. Includes glossary of medical terms. *Price:* Free. • *Aplastic Anemia: The Other Blood Disease*, periodic. • *Communicating Patient and Family Needs to the Medical Care Team*. • *Families Coping with Hospital Life*, periodic.

★ 5918 ★ Asociacion Nacional Contra el Cancer (ANCEC)
C1-40 cerca del Edificio de los Casinos Nacionales
Panama, Panama
Phone: 254322
Fax: 255366

Languages: Spanish. **Description:** Works to educate Panamanian women on prevention and detect of breast cancer. Helps treat women with breast or uterine cancer. Informs women on prevention, self-testing, and importance of regular gynecological examinations. Maintains clinics offering mammograms and Pap smears.

★ 5919 ★ Association of American Cancer Institutes (AACI)
c/o Dr. Edwin A. Mirand
Elm & Carlton Sts.
Buffalo, NY 14263
Phone: (716)845-3028
Fax: (716)845-8178
Dr. Edwin A. Mirand, Sec.-Treas.

Founded: 1959. **Members:** 78. **Description:** Directors of cancer centers. Informs members of important legislative and program developments in the field. Promotes discussion among cancer center leadership throughout the world; fosters collaboration between members on research, education, and service programs; works to further educational and training opportunities

in related biomedical sciences; advises federal, state, and local governments, and private and civic organizations concerning cancer research and related health topics. **Publications:** *AACI Newsletter*, periodic. Newsletter. *Price:* Free. **Formerly:** (1968) Association of Cancer Institute Directors.

★ 5920 ★ Association of Community Cancer Centers (ACCC)
11600 Nebel St., Ste. 201
Rockville, MD 20852
Phone: (301)984-9496
Fax: (301)770-1949
Lee E. Mortenson, Exec.Dir.

Founded: 1974. **Members:** 828. **Description:** Institutions (480) and individuals (347) involved in the provision of community cancer care. Fosters communication among providers of community cancer care; seeks to improve the quality of care available to cancer patients in community settings; encourages clinical research utilizing the community as a setting. **Publications:** *Cancer DRGs: A Comparative Report on Key Cancer DRGs*, annual. Report. • *Community Cancer Programs in the U.S.*, annual. • *Compendia-Based Drug Bulletin*, quarterly. Bulletin. • *Oncology Issues: The Journal of Cancer Program Management*, bimonthly. Journal. Provides information on community cancer programs for association members, who are physicians, nurses, social workers, and other health professionals. *Price:* $40/year.

Association of Freestanding Radiation Oncology Centers (AFROC)
See: Entry 11100

★ 5921 ★ Association for International Cancer Research (AICR)
Technology Centre
North Haugh
St. Andrews, Fife KY16 9SR, Scotland
Phone: 1334 77910
Fax: 1334 78667
Dr. C. Thomson, Chm.

Founded: 1979. **Members:** 14. **Description:** Funds cancer research. Disseminates research results. **Publications:** *Progress*, 3/year.

Association of Oncology Social Work (AOSW)
See: Entry 11864

Association of Pediatric Oncology Nurses (APON)
See: Entry 3186

Association of Pediatric Oncology Social Workers (APOSW)
See: Entry 3187

Association for Research of Childhood Cancer (AROCC)
See: Entry 3189

★5922★ **Barbados Cancer Society (BCS)**
Lefferts Pl.
River Rd.
St. Michael, Barbados
Phone: (809)427-9005
Fax: (809)429-3227
Dr. Dorothy Cooke-Johnson, Contact
Founded: 1980. **Members:** 2,500. **Local Groups:** 1. **Languages:** English. **Description:** Doctors, nurses, social workers, and other concerned individuals. Researches cancer prevention methods and treatment strategies for cancer patients. Assists in coordinating efforts to reduce Barbadian mortality from cancer. Provides occupational therapy, transportation, and early detection services. Encourages efforts to educate the public in the problems, symptoms, and treatment of cancer; disseminates information. Aids in establishing and furthering cancer research activities. Sponsors researchers to attend international conferences and training sessions. Visits schools and distributes literature; offers financial assistance to children who have lost a parent to cancer. Maintains speakers' bureau. Works in cooperation with the American Cancer Society. **Publications:** *Newsletter*, 3/year. Newsletter.

★5923★ **Breast Cancer Action Aotearoa New Zealand**
19 Laurel St.
Mt. Albert
Auckland, New Zealand
Phone: 9 8460578
Languages: English. **Description:** Health care professionals, women with breast cancer, and other individuals with an interest in breast cancer and related health issues. Provides support and services to women with breast cancer; promotes research to develop more effective breast cancer treatments and to develop preventive strategies.

★5924★ **Breast Cancer Advisory Center (BCAC)**
PO Box 224
Kensington, MD 20895
Fax: (301)949-1132
Harvey D. Kushner, Exec.Dir.
Founded: 1975. **Description:** Medical service group for people, mostly women, with breast cancer. Provides information to patients and physicians concerning ongoing research. **Publications:** *If You've Thought About Breast Cancer.*

★5925★ **Breast Cancer Care**
15-19 Britten St.
London SW3 3TZ, England
Phone: 171 8678275
Andrea Whalley
Founded: 1973. **Languages:** English. **Description:** Doctors, scientists, and other interested individuals. Provides emotional and practical support to people who have had, or think they may have, breast cancer. Operates advice line. **Publications:** Newsletter, quarterly. • Pamphlets. Contains information on breast awareness, breast surgery, and cancer. **Formerly:** (1993) Breast Care and Masectomy Association.

★5926★ **Breast Cancer Support Service**
PO Box 7125
Wellington 5, New Zealand
Phone: 4 3898421
Fax: 4 3895994
Helen M. Hargreaves, Coordinator
Founded: 1975. **Members:** 200. **Regional Groups:** 35. **Languages:** English. **Description:** Works directly with breast cancer patients. Provides counselling and support. Disseminates information.

★5927★ **Breast Care and Mastectomy Support Service**
40 Eglantine Ave.
Belfast, Antrim BT9 6DX, Northern Ireland
Phone: 1232 663281
Fax: 1232 660081
Betty M.E. McCrum, Contact
Regional Groups: 10. **Description:** Promotes awareness of breast care and early detection of breast cancer. Supports the rehabilitation of women who have breast cancer or breast surgery. **Formerly:** Mastectomy Support/Advisory Service.

★5928★ **British Association for Cancer Research (BACR)**
Institute of Biology
20 Queensberry Pl.
London SW7 2DZ, England
Phone: 171 5818333
Fax: 171 8239409
Mrs. B.J. Cavilla, Exec.Sec.
Founded: 1960. **Members:** 1,300. **Languages:** English. **Description:** Laboratory and clinical cancer research workers. Conducts and promotes research into the prevention, causes, treatment, and cure of cancer.

★5929★ **Burger King Cancer Caring Center**
4117 Liberty Ave.
Pittsburgh, PA 15224
Phone: (412)622-1212
Fax: (412)622-1216
Rebecca Whitlinger, Exec.Dir.
Founded: 1981. **Members:** 1,000. **Description:** Cancer patients, professionals, and interested individuals. Helps patients cope with the psychological impact of cancer. Emphasizes the importance of the patient's attitude and emotions in the recovery process. Offers consulting services to help establish and maintain innovative programs such as selfhelp groups, patient/professional communication systems, and preparation of patient education materials for institutions and physicians' offices. Increases public awareness through television and radio appearances, and newspaper and magazine articles. Conducts lecture and workshop. **Publications:** *Live Well with Cancer*, monthly. Newsletter. Provides emotional support and resource information for cancer patients, family members, and the professional community; includes book reviews. *Price:* Included in membership dues. Also makes available a reading and resource list, and other cancer-related materials. **Formerly:** (1982) Lifeline Institute.

★5930★ **Cancer Care (CC)**
1180 Avenue of the Americas
New York, NY 10036
Phone: (212)221-3300
Fax: (212)719-0263
Diane Blum, Exec.Dir.
Founded: 1944. **Members:** 20,000. **Local Groups:** 38. **Description:** Promotes and aids the development of social services to patients and families of patients stricken by cancer, throughout the U.S. and worldwide. Offers professional social work counseling and guidance to help patients and families cope with the emotional and psychological consequences of cancer. Sponsors programs of professional consultation and education. Conducts social research on the impact of a catastrophic illness and on the alleviation of the emotional, economic, and social effects of cancer. Provides facts and guidelines on social services and related needs of the catastrophically ill through a public relations and public affairs program. Provides financial assistance to eligible families for certain home care, child care, transportation, and medical treatment costs. Testifies before government officials on national health insurance, Medicaid, Medicare, and multi-faceted problems of the aging. Holds symposia. **Publications:** Annual Report. *Price:* Free. • *Currents*, quarterly. Newsletter. Also publishes symposia proceedings, social research studies, professional papers, and brochures; distributes films and videotapes. **Formerly:** (1986) National Cancer Foundation; (1991) National Cancer Care Foundation.

★5931★ **Cancer Control Society (CCS)**
2043 N. Berendo St.
Los Angeles, CA 90027
Phone: (213)663-7801
Norman Fritz, Pres.
Founded: 1973. **Members:** 5,500. **Description:** Cancer patients, doctors, and interested individuals. Educates the public on the prevention and control of cancer and other diseases through nutrition, tests, and nontoxic alternative therapies, such as Laetrile, Gerson, Hoxsey, Koch, Enzymes, Wheat Grass, Immunology, Mega-Vitamins and Minerals, Detoxification and Nutrition, and DMSO and Chelation Therapy. Provides information through a 24-hour telephone hot line, direct mail, doctor and patient lists, speakers, films, cancer clinic tours, and Cancer Book House. **Publications:** *Cancer Book House List*, biennial. • *Cancer Control Journal*, periodic. Journal. Reports on one specific cancer-related topic in each issue. *Price:* Included in membership dues. • *Doctor and Clinic Directory*, 6/year. Directory. • *Patient Directory*, 6/year. Directory.

★5932★ **Cancer Federation, Inc. (CFI)**
21250 Box Springs Rd., No. 209
Moreno Valley, CA 92557
Phone: (909)682-7989
Fax: (714)682-0169
John Steinbacher, Exec.Dir.
Founded: 1977. **Members:** 1,500. **Description:** Physicians, scientists, nurses, and laymen (both cancer patients and nonpatients). Promotes research and education in the field of cancer immunology. Seeks to discover appro-

priate cancer therapies using natural biological modifiers. Funds research at major centers throughout the U.S., including the University of California (Riverside and Santa Barbara), University of Hawaii, and University of Pittsburgh, on biological modifiers, such as lymphokines; killer cells; Interleukin I and II; diet; and psychological aspects of cancer. Compiles statistics; conducts research and education in cancer therapy, including vaccines, and in psychological programming for patients. Offers counseling program for cancer patients and their families. Sponsors public medical conferences and in-service courses for nurses on the psychology of cancer, and research projects at many universities and hospitals in the field of immunology. Sponsors charitable program. **Publications:** Audiotapes. • Booklets. • Books. • *Challenge of the Cancer Federation*, quarterly. Newsletter. Provides general information on cancer research and treatments. Contains information on federation activities and book reviews. *Price:* Included in membership dues. • Monographs. • Videos.

Candlelighters Childhood Cancer Foundation (CCCF)
See: Entry 3196

Children's Blood Foundation (CBF)
See: Entry 3204

★5933★ **Children's Leukemia Research Association (NLA)**
585 Stewart Ave., Ste. 536
Garden City, NY 11530
Phone: (516)222-1944
Fax: (516)222-0457
Allan D. Weinberg, Exec.Dir.

Founded: 1965. **Description:** Promotes leukemia research and public awareness of the disease. Provides financial aid to leukemia patients and their families, based on need. Offers children's services; conducts referral service. **Formerly:** (1994) National Leukemia Association.

★5934★ **China Anticancer Association (CACA)**
Huan-Hu-Xi Rd.
Tiyuanbei
Tianjin 300060, People's Republic of China
Phone: 22 3359958
Fax: 22 3359984
Zhang Tian-ze, Pres.

Founded: 1985. **Members:** 20,000. **National Groups:** 1. **Regional Groups:** 3. **State Groups:** 26. **Local Groups:** 33. **Languages:** Chinese, English. **Description:** Physicians, researchers, and interested individuals in the People's Republic of China. Conducts research programs concentrating on the prevention of cancer. Sponsors research exchange with cancer experts in other countries. Maintains 23 academic commissions. Offers educational programs; disseminates information to the public about cancer prevention. Organizes academic conferences and symposia. **Publications:** *Cancer Research on Prevention and Treatment*, quarterly. Journal. • *Chinese Journal for Cancer Research*, quarterly. Journal. • *Chinese Journal of Clinical Oncology*, monthly. Journal. Includes English abstracts.

★5935★ **Cooleycare (MHC)**
Centro Trasfusionale e di Immunologia dei Trapianti
Ospedale Policlinico
Via Francesco Sforza 35
I-20122 Milan, Italy
Phone: 2 55034012
Fax: 2 5458129
Girolamo Sirchia, M.D., Dir.

Founded: 1984. **Members:** 36. **Languages:** English. **Description:** Hematologists and specialists from 7 countries dealing with thalassemia-related problems. (Thalassemia, also known as Cooley's Anemia, is a dysfunction of the red blood cells that occurs in individuals of Mediterranean descent.) Promotes the exchange of information on thalassemia; provides children's services. Offers professional training. **Publications:** *Meeting Proceedings*, biennial. Proceedings. • *Thalassemia Today*, periodic. Journal. • *Therapy of Thalassemia*, periodic. Journal.

★5936★ **Cooley's Anemia Foundation (CAF)**
129-09 26th Ave.
Flushing, NY 11354
Phone: (718)321-2873
Free: 800-221-3571
Fax: (718)321-3340
Peter Chieco, Nat.CAF Pres.

Founded: 1954. **Members:** 8,000. **Local Groups:** 15. **Description:** Parents of children afflicted with Cooley's anemia; doctors, technicians, nurses, and others interested in the treatment and eventual cure of the disease. (Cooley's anemia is an incurable blood disease requiring frequent blood transfusions to keep its victims alive; it is named after Dr. Thomas B. Cooley, a Detroit, MI, physician who first described it in 1925.) Distributes therapy materials including infusion pumps and batteries, at no charge, to victims of the disease. Presents awards for scientific and humanitarian achievement. Sponsors medical symposia to educate physicians and scientists about new drugs or therapies for Cooley's anemia or other thalassemias. Sponsors Thalassemia Action Group, a networking task force of young adult victims of thalassemia. Operates speakers' bureau. Conducts blood drives. **Publications:** *Lifeline*, quarterly. Newsletter. **Formerly:** (1977) Cooley's Anemia Blood and Research Foundation for Children.

★5937★ **Corporate Angel Network (CAN)**
Westchester County Airport, Bldg. 1
White Plains, NY 10604
Phone: (914)328-1313
Fax: 800-328-4226
Judith Haims, Admin.

Founded: 1981. **Members:** 550. **Description:** U.S. corporations that own aircraft and volunteer empty seats to cancer patients in need of transportation to or from recognized treatment centers. Patients must be able to board the aircraft unassisted, not require special equipment or services en route, and have proper medical authorization for the flight. CAN will transport one attendant or family member with the patient; patient must arrange his or her own ground transportation. **Publications:** Bulletin, quarterly.

★5938★ **European Association for Cancer Research (EACR)**
University of Nottingham
Cancer Research Laboratories
Nottingham, Notts. NG7 2RD, England
Phone: 1115 9515115
Fax: 115 9513418
Dr. M.R. Price, Sec.Gen.

Founded: 1968. **Members:** 1,500. **Languages:** English. **Description:** Persons who have worked actively in cancer research for at least 2 years and who have an academic degree or the equivalent; membership in 40 countries. Seeks to advance cancer research by facilitating communication among research workers, particularly by organizing meetings. Sponsors: EACR Italian Fellowship Program, providing financial support for researchers to spend from 3 months to 1 year in Italian research institutions; EACR Travel Fellowship Program, awarding travel expenses for member researchers to and from host institutions. **Publications:** *Directory of the EACR*, biennial. Directory. • *EACR Newsletter*, semiannual. Newsletter. • *European Journal of Cancer and Clinical Oncology*, monthly. Journal.

★5939★ **European Cancer Prevention Organization (ECP)**
1307, chaussee de Waterloo
B-1180 Brussels, Belgium
Phone: 2 3743488
Fax: 3759252
Dr. Attilio Giacosa, Scientific Coord.

Founded: 1983. **Members:** 120. **Languages:** English. **Description:** Scientists interested in cancer prevention research. Seeks to coordinate studies in cancer prevention and to inform the scientific community as well as the public. Conducts workshops. **Publications:** *ECP News*, quarterly. • *ECP Symposium Proceedings*, annual. • *European Journal of Cancer Prevention*, bimonthly. Journal.

★5940★ **European Group of Lymphology (EGL)**
(Groupement Europeen de Lymphologie — GEL)
Mansteen 87
B-1745 Opwijk, Belgium
Phone: 52 374258
Fax: 2 4774000
Dr. Yves Geysels, Sec.Gen.

Founded: 1980. **Members:** 180. **Languages:** English, French. **Description:** Lymphologists and other individuals in 12 countries interested in the lymphatic system. Promotes interaction between members; conducts research. **Publications:** *European Journal of Lymphology and Related Problems*, quarterly. Journal.

★5941★ **European Organization for Research and Treatment of Cancer (EORTC)**
(Organisation Europeenne pour la Recherche et le Traitement du Cancer)
83, ave. Mounier, bte. 11
B-1200 Brussels, Belgium
Phone: 2 7741630
Fax: 2 7712004
F. Meunier, M.D., Dir.

Founded: 1962. **Members:** 2,500. **Regional Groups:** 32. **Languages:** English. **Description:**

Doctors, pharmacologists, clinicians, statisticians, computer analysts, and others in 25 countries involved in the development of anticancer therapies. Aims to develop cancer research in Europe through the coordination of joint research projects by hospitals and laboratories. Maintains screening program of potential anticancer agents and clinical research groups formed to carry out trials with new therapeutic agents. Sponsors fellowship program that enables clinicians and researchers to study and work in other countries. Maintains EORTC New Drug Development Office to coordinate the development of new anticancer medications; operates EORTC Central Office and Data Center to facilitate the exchange of information among members. Cosponsors the European School of Oncology; conducts educational and research programs; makes available grants and fellowships. Compiles statistics. **Publications:** *EORTC Membership Directory*, annual. • *EORTC Organisation, Activities and Current Research*, annual. Directory. • *European Journal of Cancer*, monthly. **Formerly:** (1968) Groupe Europeen de Chimiotherapie Anticancereuse.

★5942★ European Society for Medical Oncology (ESMO)
36, voie Romaine
F-06054 Nice Cedex, France
Phone: 93 817133
Fax: 93 533512

Founded: 1975. **Members:** 520. **Languages:** English. **Description:** Medical oncologists; associate members are biologists, surgeons, radiotherapists, and other specialists. Sponsors and contributes to education in oncology. **Publications:** *Proceedings of Meeting*, annual.

European Society for Paediatric Haematology and Immunology (ESPHI) (Europese Vereniging voor Pediatrische Hematologie en Immunologie — EVPHI)
See: Entry 3224

★5943★ European Society for Therapeutic Radiology and Oncology (ESTRO)
Univ. Hospital St. Rafael
Dept. of Radiotherapy
Capucijnenvoer 33
B-3000 Louvain, Belgium
Phone: 16 336413
Fax: 16 336428
E. van der Schueren, Past-Pres.

Founded: 1980. **Members:** 1,700. **Languages:** English. **Description:** Individuals from 30 countries involved in the fields of radiotherapy and oncology. Works to improve standards of cancer treatment by promoting the exchange of information among radiation oncologists, radiophysicists, and radiobiologists and by communicating with clinical oncologists. Offers teaching courses, symposia, and seminars; bestows awards. **Publications:** *ESTRO Newsletter*, periodic. Newsletter. • *Journal of Radiotherapy and Oncology*, monthly. Journal.

★5944★ European Tumour Virus Group (ETVG)
Institut fur Hygiene
Fritz-Pregl-Strasse 3
A-6020 Innsbruck, Austria
Phone: 512 5073401
Fax: 512 5072870
Prof. Manfred Dierich, Exec.Sec.

Founded: 1960. **Members:** 400. **Languages:** English. **Description:** Professionals involved in tumor virus research. Promotes the exchange of information.

★5945★ Federation of Latin American Cancer Societies (Federacion Latinoamericana de Sociedades de Cancerologia)
Canonigos a Esperanza 43
Apartado 6702
Caracas 1010, Venezuela
Phone: 2 5619922
Dr. Ruben Merenfeld, Pres.

Description: Medical institutions in Latin America. Works to increase research and study into prevention and cures for cancer.

Foundation for Advancement in Cancer Therapy (FACT)
See: Entry 2194

★5946★ Friends of the Jose Carreras International Leukemia Foundation
Fred Hutchinson Cancer Research Ctr.
1124 Columbia St., Rm. M246
Seattle, WA 98104
Phone: (206)667-7108
Fax: (206)667-6498
Dorothy Thomas, Treas.

Founded: 1989. **Description:** Raises funds for research into the treatment and cure of leukemia and related blood disorders. Maintains research programs.

★5947★ Gynecologic Oncology Group (GOG)
1234 Market St., No. 1945
Philadelphia, PA 19107
Phone: (215)854-0770
Fax: (215)854-0716
John R. Kellner, Admin.Dir.

Founded: 1970. **Members:** 39. **Description:** Institutions and teaching hospitals conducting research in gynecological oncology. Sponsored by the American College of Obstetricians and Gynecologists.

★5948★ Histiocytosis Association of America
609 New York Rd.
Glassboro, NJ 08028
Phone: (609)881-4911
Free: 800-548-2758
Fax: (609)589-6614
Jeffrey M. Toughill, Pres.

Founded: 1985. **Members:** 2,500. **Description:** Patients, families, and friends of those suffering from histiocytic disorders; physicians, oncologists, and hematologists working in the field of histiocytosis research. (Histiocytosis is a rare disease that causes histiocytes, a type of white blood cell, to multiply and attack organs, body

systems, or bones.) Works to provide support for patients and their families and friends. Funds research on the cause and treatment of histiocytosis. Acts as a referral service. Maintains speakers' bureau. **Publications:** *The Facts about Langerhans Cell Histiocytosis*. Brochure. • *The Facts about Langerhans Cell Histiocytosis and Diabetes Insipidus*. Brochure. • Newsletter, quarterly. Reports on histiocytosis patients, their families, physicians, researchers, and other interested parties. *Price:* Free. • *Patient Directory*, periodic. Directory. **Formerly:** (1987) Histiocytosis-X Association of America.

IIT Research Institute
See: Entry 10436

★5949★ International Agency for Research on Cancer (IARC) (Centre International de Recherche sur le Cancer — IARC)
150, cours Albert Thomas
F-69372 Lyon Cedex 08, France
Phone: 7 2738485
Fax: 7 2738575
Dr. Paul Kleihues, Dir.

Founded: 1965. **Members:** 16. **Languages:** English, French. **Description:** Cancer research arm of the World Health Organization. Representatives of nations involved in international collaboration in cancer research. Generates and disseminates information on the causes and prevention of cancer; conducts research in the field of cancer epidemiology, biostatistics, and environmental carcinogenesis. Evaluates and examines populations with unusually high or low frequencies of cancer and identifies the role of environmental factors including cultural and dietary habits and chemicals. Assists governments in cancer control programs. Maintains laboratories and collaborates with scientists working in national laboratories. Organizes training courses; compiles statistics. **Publications:** *Biennial Report.* • *Directory of On-Going Research in Cancer Epidemiology*, biennial. Directory. • *IAR Cancer Disc*, annual. CD-ROM • Monographs, 3/year. • *Scientific Publications Series*, periodic. • *Technical Report Series*, periodic.

International Association of Cancer Registries (IACR) (Association Internationale des Registres du Cancer)
See: Entry 7003

★5950★ International Association of Cancer Victors and Friends (IACVF)
531 Main St., Ste. 1136
El Segundo, CA 90245-3060
Phone: (310)822-5032
Suzanne Landon, Exec.Dir.

Founded: 1963. **Members:** 4,000. **Regional Groups:** 13. **Description:** Encourages independent research on cancer therapies and disseminates information on "nontoxic" chemotherapies. Works directly with cancer patients providing one-on-one services. Offers educational programs on topics including carcinogens in air, food, and water and nutrition in relation to cancer. **Publications:** Audiotapes. • Books. • *Cancer Victors Journal*. Journal. Provides news on nontoxic cancer treatments and breakthroughs in cancer research; includes studies on carcinogenic conditions. *Price:* Included in membership dues. • Pamphlets. • Reprints. **Formerly:** (1985) International Association of Cancer Victims and Friends.

★ 5951 ★ **International Association for Comparative Research on Leukemia and Related Diseases (IACRLRD)**
300 W. 10th Ave., Ste. 1132
Columbus, OH 43210
Phone: (614)293-3067
Fax: (614)293-3305
Dr. David S. Yohn, Sec.Gen.

Founded: 1963. **Members:** 500. **Description:** Promotes cooperation and coordination of basic and clinical research on leukemia and related diseases. Emphasizes comparative aspects of different disciplines in order to develop new hypotheses and introduce comparable working methods. Sponsors educational programs. **Publications:** *Newsletter to Members*, annual. Newsletter. • *Symposium Proceedings*, annual. Proceedings. *Price:* Free for members only; $25/issue for nonmembers.

★ 5952 ★ **International Association for the Study of Lung Cancer (IASLC)**
The Finsen Institute/Rigshospitalet
Department of Oncology - 5074
Blegdamsvej 9
DK-2100 Copenhagen, Denmark
Phone: 31386633
Fax: 31356906
Heine H. Hansen, M.D., Exec. Dir.

Founded: 1974. **Members:** 1,050. **Languages:** English. **Description:** Oncologists promoting research and treatment of lung cancer. Collects and disseminates information; conducts periodic seminars and symposia. Compiles statistics. **Publications:** *IASLC Membership Directory*, annual. Directory. • *Lung Cancer*, bimonthly.

★ 5953 ★ **International Council for Standardization in Haematology (ICSH) (Conseil International de Standardisation en Hematologie)**
Haematology Department
Western Infirmary
Dumbarton Rd.
Glasgow G11 6NT, Scotland
Phone: 141 2112738
Fax: 141 3397327
Dr. R.M. Rowan, Exec.Sec.

Founded: 1963. **Languages:** English. **Description:** International, national, and regional hematological standardizing committees and test boards; national societies of hematology and clinical pathology; individuals; representatives of 48 countries. Purpose is to develop and promote standards for international comparability of results of hematological analysis related to specifications for biological and chemical reagents, reference preparations, methods and procedures, systems of nomenclature and classification, operating methods, equipment and test controls and calibrators, and other matters applicable to hematology. Initiates work in areas such as the study of platelet function, subtyping of leukemias, bone marrow culture techniques, and the measurement of survival of stored

blood. Provides a forum for communication among members and other organizations dedicated to improvements in hematology laboratory functions.

★ 5954 ★ **International Medical Sports Federation for Aid to Cancer Research (Federation Internationale du Sport Medical pour l'Aide a la Recherche Cancerologique — FISMARC)**
BP 444
F-34505 Beziers, France
Phone: 67 988484
Fax: 67 983685
Henry Devos, Gen.Sec.

Founded: 1970. **Members:** 25,000. **Languages:** French. **Description:** Supports medical and cancer research through the organization of social and recreational events for doctors, pharmacists, dentists, and veterinarians.

★ 5955 ★ **International Myeloma Foundation**
2120 Stanley Hills Dr.
Los Angeles, CA 90046
Free: 800-452-CURE
Fax: (213)656-1182
Susie Novis, Exec.Dir.

Founded: 1990. **Description:** Sponsors research in multiple myeloma, a blood cancer. **Publications:** *Myeloma Today*, quarterly. *Price:* $20 U.S. subscribers; $30 international subscribers.

★ 5956 ★ **International School for Cancer Care (Federation Mondiale pour les Soins du Cancer)**
Sir Michael Sobell House
Churchill House
Oxford, England
Phone: 1865 225891
Fax: 1865 741862

Founded: 1982. **Members:** 75. **Languages:** Arabic, English, French, Spanish. **Description:** Voluntary organizations, institutes, and individuals indirectly or directly involved in the care of cancer patients. Promotes developments in continuing cancer care, particularly pain control, and in the rehabilitation and resettlement of cancer patients throughout the world. (Continuing care refers to the continuing treatment of patients through surgery, radiation, and/or chemotherapy.) Endeavors to establish an international forum for the exchange of medical, nursing, scientific, and social welfare information. Encourages the study and discussion of possible solutions to the problems and needs of cancer patients and their families including bereavement and the special problems caused by cancer in specific age groups, particularly the very young. Advocates the establishment of day hospitals and hospices, general community care programs, pain clinics, research rehabilitation centers, and specialized oncology education and training courses for medical, nursing, and paramedical professionals. Seeks to stimulate improvements in facilities and services by offering workshops and full advisory assistance worldwide. Works to educate the public in matters of cancer care and to create an international network for information exchange. Organizes

conferences, congresses, courses, symposia, and other meetings. Compiles statistics. **Publications:** *Cancer Care: An International Survey.* Report.

★ 5957 ★ **International Society Against Breast Cancer (ISABC) (Societe Internationale pour la Lutte Contre le Cancer du Sein)**
26, rue de la Faisanderie
F-75116 Paris, France
Phone: 1 47047032
K.H. Hollmann, M.D., Pres.

Founded: 1973. **Members:** 150. **Languages:** English, French. **Description:** Medical doctors, scientists, computer specialists, and industry representatives in 15 countries concerned about breast cancer. Provides diagnostic assistance; coordinates research programs; organizes workshops and seminars. **Publications:** *New Frontiers in Mammary Pathology.*

★ 5958 ★ **International Society of Hematology (ISH)**
920 Hilton
200 1st St. SW
Rochester, MN 55905
Phone: (507)284-3937
Fax: (507)284-0043
Dr. Robert A. Kyle, Sec.Gen.

Founded: 1946. **Members:** 3,000. **Regional Groups:** 3. **Description:** Doctors of medicine and persons holding Ph.D. degrees who have completed at least 5 years in the practice or research of hematology (branch of medical science dealing with the blood, its formation, functions, and diseases). Works to promote hematology research and the advancement and recognition of hematology as a biological science. **Publications:** *Membership List*, biennial. • Newsletter, semiannual.

★ 5959 ★ **International Society of Hematology European African Division**
Hematology Laboratory Dept.
Hospital Clinic I Provincial
Calle Villarroel, 170
E-08036 Barcelona, Spain
Phone: 3 4548229
Fax: 3 4548229
Prof. J.IL. Vives-Corrons, MD, Sec.Gen.

Founded: 1946. **Members:** 1,300. **Languages:** English. **Description:** Scientists and physicians in 85 countries with at least 5 years experience in the field of hematology. Promotes the exchange of ideas and information relating to blood and blood forming tissues; provides an international forum for the dissemination of new information concerning hematological problems. Aims to standardize hematological methods and nomenclature on an international scale and to heighten awareness of clinical hematological problems among scientific investigators while recognizing hematology as a legitimate branch of the biological sciences. Sponsors educational programs. **Publications:** *ISH Constitutional Members*, biennial. • *ISH Newsletter*, semiannual. Newsletter.

★5960★ International Society of
      Lymphology (ISL)
University of Arizona
College of Medicine/Surgery
1501 N. Campbell Ave., No. 4406
Tucson, AZ 85724
Phone: (520)626-6118
Fax: (520)626-0822
Marlys H. Witte, M.D., Sec.Gen.

Founded: 1966. **Members:** 360. **National Groups:** 9. **Languages:** English. **Description:** Professionals active in the medical, biological, and technical sciences. Promotes the study of lymphology and seeks to advance and disseminate knowledge in the field. Activities include: stimulating and strengthening experimentation and clinical investigation in lymphology; establishing relations between researchers and clinicians in the different fields of lymphology; encouraging contact and exchange of ideas among members and national and international organizations. Organizes postgraduate courses. **Publications:** *Lymphology*, quarterly. Journal. • *Progress in Lymphology*, biennial. Proceedings.

International Society of Pediatric Oncology
   (SIOP)
(Societe Internationale d'Oncologie
   Pediatrique — SIOP)
See: Entry 3249

★5961★ International Society for
      Preventive Oncology (ISPO)
c/o Dr.Nieburgs
Department of Pathology
University of Massachusetts Medical Ctr.
55 Lake Ave. N
Box 20
Worcester, MA 01655
Phone: (212)534-4991
Fax: (508)856-1824
Herbert E. Nieburgs, M.D., Sec.

Founded: 1980. **Members:** 400. **Description:** Physicians and other professionals at the doctoral level; individuals with professional equivalence who are actively engaged in preventive oncology. Promotes the prevention of cancer through the identification and control of cancer causing factors; fosters secondary prevention through detection and treatment of cancer in its earliest, most curable stages. Sponsors basic research on cancer prevention and early detection and provides a forum for information exchange between scientists engaged in research and those working on preventive and clinical oncology. Conducts workshops. **Publications:** *Cancer Detection and Prevention*, 6/year. • *Proceedings of International Symposium on Immunobiology of Cancer and Allied Immune Dysfunctions*, biennial. • *Proceedings of the International Conference on Human Tumor Markers*, biennial. • *Proceedings of the International Symposium on Prevention and Detection of Cancer*, biennial.

★5962★ International Society on
      Thrombosis and Hemostasis (ISTH)
University of North Carolina Medical School
CB 7035
Chapel Hill, NC 27599-7035
Phone: (919)929-3807
Fax: (919)929-3935
Harold R. Roberts, M.D., Exec.Dir.

Founded: 1969. **Members:** 1,800. **Description:** Biomedical scientists in 50 countries interested in thrombosis (the presence of a clot in a blood vessel) and hemostasis (the arrest of bleeding). Engages in research and education concerning thrombosis, hemostasis, and blood clotting. Presents memorial lectures. **Publications:** *Thrombosis and Haemostasis*, monthly. Journal. Abstracts of congressional proceedings and lectures published as special issues of journal.

★5963★ International Union Against
      Cancer (UICC)
(Union Internationale Contre le Cancer)
3, rue du Conseil General
CH-1205 Geneva, Switzerland
Phone: 22 3201811
Fax: 22 3201810
A.J. Turnbull, Exec.Dir.

Founded: 1933. **Members:** 254. **Languages:** English. **Description:** Voluntary national organizations, private or public cancer research institutions, and ministries of health in 82 countries. Promotes a comprehensive international campaign against cancer. Directs activities in fields of prevention, research, and treatment; sponsors special projects in fields including cervical cancer, head and neck cancer, melanoma, and exchange of information on unproven methods in cancer treatment. Awards fellowships to oncology nurses and basic and clinical researchers. Conducts symposia, workshops, and training courses for researchers and physicians; makes available advisory visits by cancer experts. **Publications:** *International Calendar of Meetings on Cancer*, semiannual. • *International Journal of Cancer*, 18/year. Journal. • *UICC International Directory of Cancer Institutes and Organizations*, quadrennial. Directory. • *UICC News*, quarterly. Also publishes monographs, reports, publication lists, and new book announcements; produces cancer education packs and workshop guidelines.

★5964★ International Union of Phlebology
      (IUP)
(Union Internationale de Phlebologie)
106, ave. de Suffren
F-75015 Paris, France
Dr. Pierre Wallois, Sec.Gen.

Founded: 1955. **Members:** 16. **Description:** National societies of phlebology and departments dealing with the medicine of the veins. **Publications:** *Congress Proceedings*, triennial. • *Phlebologie*, periodic. Also publishes brochure.

★5965★ Israel Cancer Association (ICA)
(Haagudah Lemilchama Besartan Beyisrael)
7 Revivim St.
53485 Givatayem, Israel
Phone: 3 5717234
Fax: 3 5719578
Mrs. Miri Ziv, Dir.Gen.

Founded: 1952. **Local Groups:** 52. **Languages:** English, Hebrew. **Description:** Encourages and facilitates research on cancer prevention and early diagnosis. Supports cancer medical treatment services, and finances rehabilitation and social welfare programs for cancer patients. Provides educational programs. **Publications:** *Adcan*, semiannual. • *Bahamah*, periodic. Journal. Includes information on medical, psychosocial, and welfare aspects of cancer.

★5966★ Leukemia Society of America
      (LSA)
600 3rd Ave.
New York, NY 10016
Phone: (212)573-8484
Free: 800-955-4LSA
Fax: (212)856-9686
Dwayne Howell, Pres. & CEO

Founded: 1949. **Local Groups:** 57. **Description:** Raises funds to combat leukemia and related cancers through research, patient service, and public and professional education. Sponsors medical symposia; conducts research; provides financial aid for patients; sponsors support groups. **Publications:** Brochures. • Films. • *Leukemia Society of America--Newsline*, quarterly. Newsletter. Provides information on advances in the research into leukemia and other related diseases. Includes research updates. *Price:* Free. • Videos. **Formerly:** (1955) Robert Roesler de Villiers Foundation.

★5967★ Lisa Madonia Memorial Fund
      (LMMF)
c/o Board of Directors
943 N. East Ave.
Oak Park, IL 60302
Phone: (708)524-4879
Carlotta Madonia, Pres.

Founded: 1989. **Description:** Works to grant the wishes of cancer patients ages 18-25. **Publications:** Newsletter, annual.

★5968★ Make Today Count (MTC)
1235 E. Cherokee St.
Springfield, MO 65804-2203
Phone: (417)885-3324
Free: 800-432-2273
Connie Zimmerman, Exec.Dir.

Founded: 1974. **Members:** 5,000. **Local Groups:** 200. **Description:** Cancer patients and others with life-threatening illnesses, and their immediate families. Works to bring members and their neighbors together to discuss openly the false implications and the realities of life-threatening diseases. Takes a positive approach to the problems of serious illness in order to lessen the emotional trauma for all concerned. Assists professionals in communicating with and meeting the needs of seriously ill patients. Maintains speakers' bureau and referral service; plans educational programs, films, and tapes. **Publications:** *Chapter Directory*, annual. Directory. • *Make Today Count Newsletter*, bimonthly. Newsletter. Offers emotional support to people with cancer or other life-threatening illnesses, and to their family members, friends, and professionals. *Price:* $10/year. • *Make Today Count - Until Tomorrow Comes.*

★ **5969 ★ National Alliance of Breast Cancer Organizations (NABCO)**
9 E. 37th St., 10th Fl.
New York, NY 10016
Phone: (212)719-0154
Fax: (212)689-1213
Amy Langer, Exec.Dir.

Founded: 1986. **Members:** 300. **Description:** Breast centers; hospitals; government health offices; and support and research organizations providing information about breast cancer and breast diseases from early detection through continuing care. Serves as a resource for: organizations requiring information about breast cancer programs and organizations and medical advances; individuals seeking information about research, developments, and treatment options for breast cancer. Seeks to influence public and private health policy on issues pertaining to breast cancer, such as insurance reimbursement, health care legislation, and research funding priorities. Offers advice on how to propose and lobby for or against legislation regarding discrimination, informed consent, and third-party reimbursement. Disseminates educational materials and information on support groups, breast care centers, and hospital programs. **Publications:** *NABCO News*, quarterly. Newsletter. Monitors developments relating to breast cancer. *Price:* Included in membership dues. • *NABCO's Resource List*, annual. Contains information on materials and organizations that provide information about breast cancer. *Price:* Included in membership dues; $3/copy.

★ **5970 ★ National Biotherapy Study Group (NBSG)**
PO Box 680757
Franklin, TN 37068-0757
Phone: (615)791-6393
Fax: (615)791-4719
Rosalie A. Avent, Exec.Dir.

Founded: 1987. **Members:** 100. **Description:** Practicing oncologists, cancer management professionals, hospitals, and biopharmaceutical companies interested in using biologicals alone and with other agents in the treatment of all types of cancer. Promotes and sponsors research into biotherapy and other innovative cell biology technologies such as tumor-infiltrating lymphocytes, autologous vaccines and activated lymphocytes, pulsed LAK cells, and peripheral and bone marrow stem cells. Conducts cancer trials, and studies; provides networking opportunities. Publishes research results.

★ **5971 ★ National Cancer Center (NCC)**
88 Sunnyside Blvd.
Plainview, NY 11803
Phone: (516)349-0610
Fax: (516)349-0610
Regina English, Exec.Dir.

Founded: 1953. **Description:** Supports cancer research and educational programs. Concen-trates on cytology, immunology, detection, and prevention of cancer, and on invention and perfection of new methods and instruments for early diagnosis of cancer. **Formerly:** (1954) Eugene L. Garey Cancer Foundation; (1965) Cancer Cytology Foundation of America; (1986) National Cancer Cytology Center.

★ **5972 ★ National Cancer Institute of Canada (NCIC) (Institut National du Cancer du Canada — INCC)**
10 Alcorn Ave., Ste. 200
Toronto, ON, Canada M4V 3B1
Phone: (416)961-7223
Fax: (416)961-4189
Dr. J. David Beatty, Exec.Dir.

Founded: 1947. **Members:** 44. **Languages:** English, French. **Description:** Individuals united to promote cancer research. Offers financial support to Canadian universities and recognized institutions conducting cancer research. **Publications:** Annual Report, annual.

★ **5973 ★ National Cancer Registrars Association (NTRA)**
505 E. Hawley St.
Mundelein, IL 60060
Phone: (708)566-0833
Robert B. Willis, Exec.Dir.

Founded: 1974. **Members:** 1,700. **Description:** Persons involved in central, state, regional, and hospital-based tumor registries including physicians, hospital administrators, and health care planners who maintain ongoing records of the cancer patient's history, diagnosis, therapy, and outcome. Purposes are to: promote research and education in tumor registry administration and practice; improve service to cancer patients; establish standards of education and provide a standardized course of study for tumor registrars; raise the level of knowledge and performance of tumor registrars through continuing education; disseminate information regarding current activities, research, and trends in the cancer field; initiate and/or participate in programs to improve and standardize the compiling of tumor-related information; interact with professional and governmental organizations that use data derived from tumor registries. Has conducted national educational programs including: coding and tumor registry workshops; symposia on head and neck tumors, lymphatic and hematopoietic neoplasms, and non-Hodgkin's lymphoma; tumor registry training program and seminars. Sponsors registry management training program at the University of Pittsburgh School of Health Related Professions to instruct tumor registrars. Offers certification examinations for tumor registrars; provides continuing education program to help members maintain certification; offers educational assistance for new registrars. **Publications:** *Connection*, periodic. Newsletter. • *National Tumor Registrars Association--Membership Roster*, annual. *Price:* Included in membership dues. • *National Tumor Registrars Association--Proceedings/Annual Report*, annual. *Price:* Included in membership dues. • *National Tumor Registrars Association-- The Abstract*. Journal. Includes book reviews, state and local association news, and lists of employment opportunities. *Price:* Included in membership dues; $10/year for nonmembers. • Surveys. Contains information on compensation. Also publishes educational materials. **Formerly:** National Tumor Registrars Association.

★ **5974 ★ National Coalition for Cancer Research (NCCR)**
426 C St. NE
Washington, DC 20002
Phone: (202)544-1880
Fax: (202)543-2565
Terry Lierman, Exec.Dir.

Founded: 1984. **Members:** 19. **Description:** Cancer research and cancer care organizations and facilities. Works to educate the public and interested parties of the legislative and executive branches on the importance of cancer research and care. **Publications:** *Curing Cancer: Possible Mission*. • *National Coalition for Cancer Research Fact Sheet*. • *News Bulletin*, monthly. Bulletin.

★ **5975 ★ National Coalition for Cancer Survivorship (NCCS)**
1010 Wayne Ave., 5th Fl.
Silver Spring, MD 20910
Phone: (301)650-8868
Fax: (301)565-9670
Ellen Stovall, Exec.Dir.

Founded: 1986. **Members:** 2,500. **Description:** Institutions and organizations (400) and individuals (2100) concerned with survivorship and interested in supporting cancer survivors and their loved ones. (A survivor is anyone with a history of cancer.) Seeks to show that cancer survivors can continue leading productive and fulfilling lives. Facilitates communication among individuals involved with cancer survivorship and fosters peer support. Provides a forum for discussion of related issues and concerns. Promotes the interests of cancer survivors and advocates the reduction of cancer-based discrimination. Encourages study in survivorship. Collects and disseminates information and resources on supporting and helping survivors deal with life after cancer is diagnosed. Operates speakers' bureau. **Publications:** *A Bibliography on the Employment and Insurance Concerns of Cancer Survivors*. Bibliography. • Annual Report. • *Best Loved Books*. • *Charting the Journey: An Almanac of Resources for Cancer Survivors*. Book. • *NCCS Networker*, quarterly. Newsletter. Includes advocacy update and list of resources. • *Teamwork: The Cancer Patient's Guide to Talking With Your Doctor*.

★ **5976 ★ National Foundation for Cancer Research (NFCR)**
7315 Wisconsin Ave., Ste. 500W
Bethesda, MD 20814
Phone: (301)654-1250
Free: 800-321-2873
Fax: (301)654-5824
Franklin C. Salisbury, Pres.

Founded: 1974. **Description:** Purpose is to conduct basic scientific research and scientific investigation of the structure and function of normal and abnormal cells. This research is based on the belief that cancer is a disturbance of normal cellular function at the submolecular level. Funds 40 laboratories in the U.S. and 7 other countries. **Publications:** *National Cancer*

Bulletin, periodic. Newsletter. *Price:* Free to donors. Also publishes booklets and papers. **Formerly:** (1975) Bethesda National Foundation of Massachusetts.

★5977★ **National Hemophilia Foundation (NHF)**
110 Greene St., Ste. 303
New York, NY 10012
Phone: (212)219-8180
Fax: (212)431-0906

Founded: 1948. **Local Groups:** 48. **Description:** Voluntary health organization consisting of individuals with hemophilia, their families, medical and paramedical professionals, and other interested persons. (Hemophilia is a hereditary disease in which blood clotting is abnormally delayed.) Supports research through postgraduate fellowship program; disseminates literature for the public and medical and paramedical personnel. Conducts educational programs. Operates information center to provide research assistance, referrals, and comprehensive resources on hemophilia, HIV/AIDS, and related topics. Chapters help in blood recruitment drives and referral services for patients and sponsor summer camps for young people with hemophilia. Maintains library. **Publications:** *Directory of Hemophilia Treatment Centers*, periodic. Directory. • *HANDI Quarterly*. Newsletter. Covers research and current activities in the field. • *Hemophilia Newsnotes*, quarterly. Newsletter. Membership activities newsletter. Includes calendar of events and research updates. *Price:* Free to affiliated chapters and members of the med; $50/year for individuals. • *Nursing Network News*, quarterly. Covers hemophilia care and research. *Price:* Included in membership dues. • *Psychosocial News*, quarterly. Newsletter. Addresses the social attitudes and barriers facing individuals with hemophilia and offering advice for coping with these problems. *Price:* Included in membership dues. **Formerly:** (1956) Hemophilia Foundation.

★5978★ **National Immunotherapy Cancer Research Foundation**
PO Box 1027
Flemington, NJ 08822-1027
Phone: (908)806-4300
Robert A. Facchina, Chmn.

Founded: 1990. **Description:** Promotes the use of immune system stimulation including vaccines, biological response modifiers, and other immuno-augmentative treatments as a cure for cancer. Raises funds for immunotherapy and immunology research in the prevention and treatment of cancer.

National Marrow Donor Program (NMDP)
See: Entry 12874

National Oncology Nursing Society of South Africa (NONSSA)
(Nasionale Genootskap van Onkologiese Verpleging van Suid Afrika — NGOVSA)
See: Entry 9124

Oncology Nursing Society (ONS)
See: Entry 9132

★5979★ **Ovarian Cancer Prevention and Early Detection Foundation**
c/o Evan Shirley
841 Bishop St., Ste. 1615
Honolulu, HI 96813-3821
Ceil Sinnex, Exec.Dir.

Founded: 1991. **Description:** Strives to reduce the number of women who die from ovarian cancer each year. Conducts educational and charitable programs and scientific research. Maintains speakers' bureau. **Publications:** *Ovarian*, bimonthly. Newsletter. *Price:* $25 (donation).

★5980★ **Patient Advocates for Advanced Cancer Treatment (PAACT)**
1143 Parmelee NW
Grand Rapids, MI 49504-3844
Phone: (616)453-1477
Fax: (616)453-1846
Lloyd J. Ney, Sr., Exec. Officer

Founded: 1984. **Members:** 15,000. **Description:** Prostate cancer patients and physicians. Engages in advocacy activities. Provides educational materials to those with prostate cancer. Conducts protocol studies and research. **Publications:** *Cancer Communication*, quarterly. Newsletter. • *Onco-Logic*, quarterly. Newsletter. • *Prostate Cancer Report*, annual. Report.

★5981★ **People Against Cancer (PAC)**
c/o Frank D. Wiewel
PO Box 10
Otho, IA 50569-0010
Phone: (515)972-4444
Free: 800-NO-CANCER
Fax: (515)972-4415
Frank D. Wiewel, Contact

Founded: 1985. **Members:** 2,000. **Description:** Promotes research into alternative cancer therapy and prevention. Conducts educational, charitable, and research programs. Maintains a speakers' bureau. **Publications:** Bulletin. • Directory. • *Options*, bimonthly. Newsletter.

★5982★ **R. A. Bloch Cancer Foundation**
4410 Main
Kansas City, MO 64111
Phone: (816)932-8453
Fax: (816)753-8628
Steve Ford, Contact

Founded: 1980. **Description:** Sponsors the Cancer Hot Line, a support group that matches cancer patients with volunteers who have been cured, are in remission, or are being treated for the same type of cancer. Volunteers describe treatments they have received and offer information referrals to newly diagnosed cancer victims. Kansas City, MO, office refers inquirers desiring a second opinion to the Cancer Management Center, a multidisciplinary panel of doctors who pronounce such second opinions. A second opinion may have physical and psychological benefits; it can reassure the patient that he is receiving the best available treatment or, in some cases, suggest that additional or alternative treatments be considered. Maintains speakers' bureau in Kansas City, MO. Sponsors children's services and educational programs. Maintains cancer support center for cancer patients and their supporters. **Publications:** *Cancer. . .There's Hope*. Book. • *Cancer Hot Line News*,

quarterly. • *Fighting Cancer*. Book. • *Guide for Cancer Supporters*. Book. **Formerly:** (1989) Cancer Connection.

★5983★ **Radiation Therapy Oncology Group (RTOG)**
American College of Radiology
1101 Market St., 14th Fl.
Philadelphia, PA 19107
Phone: (215)574-3150
Fax: (215)928-0153
Nancy Smith, Admin.

Founded: 1971. **Members:** 180. **Description:** Clinical radiation therapy investigative centers united to conduct cooperative clinical trials and studies to improve the care of patients with cancer. Maintains 20 committees. **Publications:** *RTOG Report*. Reprint.

★5984★ **Sickle Cell Disease Association of America (SCDAA)**
200 Corporate Pointe, Ste. 495
Culver City, CA 90230-7633
Phone: (310)216-6363
Free: 800-421-8453
Fax: (310)215-3722
Lynda King Anderson, Contact

Founded: 1971. **Local Groups:** 86. **Description:** Community groups involved in sickle cell anemia programs throughout the U.S. (Sickle cell anemia is an inherited blood disease that primarily affects black people and is a major health problem within the black community.) Purposes are to: provide leadership on a national level in order to create awareness in all circles of the negative impact of sickle cell anemia on the health and economic, social, and educational well-being of the individual and his/her family and to create awareness of the requirements for resolution; prepare and distribute substantive educational materials; develop and promote implementation of service program standards that will be in the best interest of the affected population; provide ongoing technical assistance to interested groups; encourage adequate support for research. Resources include: counselor training; workshops and seminars; blood banks; screening and testing; tutorial services; camps for children with sickle cell disease; vocational rehabilitation. Operates Charles F. Whitten Sickle Cell Summer Research Apprenticeships, Roland J. Nyman Research Fund, and Rick Berry Fund. **Publications:** Brochures. • *HELP, A Guide to Sickle Cell Disease Programs and Services*, periodic. • Pamphlets. • *Sickle Cell Disease Association of America Newsletter*, quarterly. Newsletter. *Price:* Free. • *Sickle Cell Disease Association of America Viewpoint*, periodic. **Formerly:** National Association for Sickle Cell Disease.

★5985★ **Sickle Cell Disease Foundation of Greater New York (SCDFGNY)**
127 W. 127th St., Rm. 421
New York, NY 10027
Phone: (212)865-1500

Founded: 1972. **Members:** 500. **Regional Groups:** 5. **State Groups:** 5. **Local Groups:** 3. **Description:** Physicians and professionals in allied fields. A voluntary health agency formed to support and conduct research and educational programs aimed at control and, ultimately, eradication of sickle cell anemia. Activities thus far are conducted primarily in the New York City area, but the group also offers information and guidance to organizations in Europe, Africa, South America, Southeast Asia, London, England, and the Caribbean area. Assists in the establishment of local chapters that establish clinics for screening and genetic counseling; sponsors symposia, seminars, and public school programs; offers professional training for screening and counseling programs. Maintains a speakers' bureau; compiles statistics. Maintains extensive files on research being conducted, individuals and organizations working to overcome the disease, and advocacy services available to families and patients with the disease. Programs include: Outreach, an in-service hospital emergency program which informs hospital personnel of the implications of a crisis in a sickle cell anemia patient; a blood bank; referral services; counseling, social services assistance, and employment and aid services. **Publications:** Annual Report. • Brochure. • Newsletter, quarterly. *Price:* Free. • *SCR Newsletter. Price:* Free. Also makes available educational materials and film.

★ 5986 ★ **Skin Cancer Foundation (SCF)**
245 5th Ave., Ste. 2402
New York, NY 10016
Phone: (212)725-5176
Fax: (212)725-5751
Perry Robins, Pres.

Founded: 1977. **Description:** Sponsors medical symposia and public education programs on the prevention and early recognition of skin cancer. Grants its Seal of Recommendation to sunscreen products that meet the criteria and standards established by the SCF as effective aids in the prevention of sun-induced damage to the skin. **Publications:** Booklets. • *Melanoma Letter,* quarterly. Newsletter. Contains articles and commentary on advances in the prevention and treatment of skin cancer. *Price:* $25/year. • *Skin Cancer Foundation Journal,* annual. Journal. Contains short articles on the prevention, early detection, and treatment of skin cancer. Includes publications list. *Price:* $5/copy. • *Sun and Skin News,* quarterly. Newsletter. Provides practical advice on the prevention, treatment, and early detection of skin cancer. Includes research updates. *Price:* $25/year. Also publishes posters, charts, and sun protection guidelines. **Formerly:** (1978) National Skin Cancer Foundation.

★ 5987 ★ **Society of Gynecologic Oncologists (SGO)**
401 N. Michigan Ave.
Chicago, IL 60611
Phone: (312)644-6610
Fax: (312)321-6869
Rosemary Zuern, Exec.Dir.

Founded: 1969. **Members:** 630. **Description:** Purposes are to: improve the care of patients with gynecological cancer; encourage research in gynecologic oncology; advance knowledge in the field; upgrade standards of practice. Evaluates and seeks to address the trends in gynecologic oncology; assesses the future of the field.

★ 5988 ★ **Society for Hematopathology (SH)**
4576 Park Ave.
Memphis, TN 38117-4714
Phone: (901)685-2113
Elaine S. Jaffe, M.D., Pres.

Founded: 1981. **Members:** 400. **Description:** Physicians; doctors of science, osteopathy, veterinary medicine, and dental surgery. Promotes exchange of information and encourages clinical, morphologic, and functional investigation of the hematopoietic (pertaining to the formation of blood cells) and lymphoreticular (regarding reticuloendothelial cells of the lymph glands) systems. **Publications:** Newsletter.

Society for Radiation Oncology Administrators (SROA)
See: Entry 5603

★ 5989 ★ **Society of Surgical Oncology (SSO)**
c/o James R. Slawny
85 W. Algonquin Rd., Ste. 550
Arlington Heights, IL 60005
Phone: (708)427-1400
Fax: (708)427-1294
James R. Slawny, Exec.Dir.

Founded: 1940. **Members:** 1,350. **Description:** Physicians and scientists working in the field of cancer. **Publications:** *Annals of Surgical Oncology,* bimonthly. Journal. Includes proceedings of the society's annual scientific sessions. **Formerly:** (1974) James Ewing Society.

★ 5990 ★ **Susan G. Komen Breast Cancer Foundation (SGKF)**
5005 LBJ, Ste. 370
Dallas, TX 75244
Phone: (214)450-1777
Free: 800-IM-AWARE
Fax: (214)450-1710
Nancy Connell, Pres.

Founded: 1982. **Members:** 1,000. **Description:** Breast cancer patients, health care professionals, and other interested individuals. Works to: increase the recovery and survival rates of breast cancer patients; heighten public awareness of the risks of breast cancer and the need for early detection. Establishes breast screening and training in self-examination procedures; provides funding through grants for research and screening programs. Operates the Komen Alliance for Breast Disease Research, Education and Treatment, which conducts research into the genesis, progression, and treatment of the disease; sponsors educational programs. Bestows awards; sponsors competitions; maintains speakers' bureau. **Also Known As:** Susan G. Komen Foundation for the Advancement of Cancer Research. **Formerly:** (1989) Susan G. Komen Foundation.

★ 5991 ★ **Ulster Cancer Foundation (UCF)**
40-42 Eglantine Ave.
Belfast, Antrim BT9 6DX, Northern Ireland
Phone: 1232 663281
Fax: 1232 660081

Founded: 1970. **Languages:** English. **Description:** Encourages and facilitates research on cancer prevention and early diagnosis. Con-

ducts educational programs including clinics and training sessions for health care professionals; makes available children's services; sponsors competitions and bestows awards. Compiles statistics. **Publications:** *Cancer Education and Care in the Workplace.* • *Environmental Health Perspectives on Cancer.* • *Focus on Cancer in Schools.* • *Smoking Matters for Young People.*

Veterinary Cancer Society (VCS)
See: Entry 13112

★ 5992 ★ **WHO Melanoma Programme (WHO Gruppo Melanomi)**
Instituto Nazionale Tumori
Via Veneziana 1
I-20133 Milan, Italy
Phone: 2 2663992
Fax: 2 26680636
N. Cascinelli, M.D., Chm.

Founded: 1965. **Members:** 49. **Languages:** English. **Description:** A program of the World Health Organization. Medical centers, institutes, and hospitals in 25 countries. Encourages methods of early identification of melanoma. Provides doctors with current information and guidelines on clinical and differential diagnoses. Contributes to education of the public and of medical professionals. Proposes clinical trials of cancer-fighting procedures including lymph node dissection, pre-operative radiotherapy, chemotherapy, and procedures combining chemotherapy with surgery. **Also Known As:** WHO International Melanoma Group; WHO International Reference Centres for the Evaluation of Methods of Diagnosis and Treatment of Melanoma. **Formerly:** (1969) International Group for the Clinical Study of Melanoma; (1985) WHO Collaborating Centres for Evaluation of Methods of Diagnosis and Treatment of Melanoma.

★ 5993 ★ **Women's Nationwide Cancer Control Campaign (WNCCC)**
Suna House
128-130 Curtain Rd.
London EC2A 3AR, England
Phone: 171 7294688
Fax: 171 6130771
Miss Fran Godfrey, Information Off.

Founded: 1965. **Members:** 400. **National Groups:** 2. **Local Groups:** 1. **Description:** Women experienced in health care and counseling. Promotes education about cancer risks for women. Disseminates information on breast and cervical cancer. Operates confidential helpline. Sponsors mobile screening units. Maintains speakers' bureau; conducts research. **Publications:** *A Ray of Hope - Mammography and Breast Examination.* Video. • *An Abnormal Smear - What Does It Mean? (WHRRIC).* Brochure. • *Breast Awareness.* Pamphlet. • *Breast Awareness Poster.* • *Breast Screening by Mammography.* Pamphlet. • *Breast Self-Examination.* Video. • *Calling All Women - Smears and Breast Self-Examination.* Booklet. • *Cervical Cancer.* Pamphlet. • *Cervical Smear Poster.* • *Cervical Smear Test.* Pamphlet. • *Choice for Life.* Video. Covers the risk factors associated with cancer. • *Clinic Lists.* Lists of NHS and private clinics for almost every Health Authority and Board in the UK. • *Genital Warts*

Fact Sheet (WHRRIC). Brochure. • *Have You Been Recalled for a Repeat Smear Test?*. Pamphlet. • *Have You Been Referred to a Colposcopy Clinic?*. Pamphlet. • *Have Your Mother and Grandmother Had a Smear Test?*. Pamphlet. • *Health Care for the Older Woman*. Pamphlet. • *Helpline Poster*. • *Mammography Poster*. • *Positive Smear*. Book. Practical guide to the medical issues, i.e. what a positive smear can indicate and deals fully and directly with the emotional issues. • *Screening Helpline*. Pamphlet. • *Test in Time*. Video. • *What is the Wart Virus?*. Pamphlet. • *Why Won't You Have Your Cervical Smear Test?*. Pamphlet. **Formerly:** (1991) Women's National Cancer Control Campaign.

★5994★ World Federation of Hemophilia (WFH)
(Federation Mondiale de l'Hemophilie — FMH)
1310 Greene Ave., Ste. 500
Montreal, PQ, Canada H3Z 2B2
Phone: (514)933-7944
Fax: (514)933-8916
Brian O'Mahony, Pres.

Founded: 1963. **Members:** 76. **Regional Groups:** 3. **Description:** Representatives of national hemophilia committees or societies. Assists hemophiliacs and persons with related disorders. Aims to stimulate interest in the development and improvement of diagnosis, treatment, rehabilitation, education, and research in hemophilia; serves as a coordinating body to develop the collection, distribution and exchange of useful information and to make relevant investigations throughout the world; encourages the establishment and development of other hemophilia organizations; supervises the operation of international hemophiliac training centers; sponsors the Hemophilia Action Group; fosters the production and distribution of antihemophilic concentrates. Conducts children's services; compiles statistics. **Publications:** Bulletins, periodic. • *Congress Proceedings*, annual. • *Hemophilia World*, quarterly. Newsletter. • *Life Paths*, quarterly. Newsletter. • Monographs, periodic. • *Passport - Guide for Travellers with Hemophilia*, periodic.

World Hemophilia AIDS Center (WHAC)
See: Entry 6759

★5995★ Y-ME National Breast Cancer Organization (Y-ME)
c/o Sharon Green
212 W. Van Buren
Chicago, IL 60607
Phone: (312)986-8338
Free: 800-221-2141
Fax: (312)986-0020
Sharon Green, Exec.Dir.

Founded: 1978. **Members:** 4,600. **Description:** Purpose is to provide peer support and information to women who have or suspect they have breast cancer. Activities include presurgical counseling and referral service, inservice programs for health professionals, hot line volunteer training, and technical assistance. Administers the Deborah David Dewar Fund and the Billie Klein Memorial Fund. **Publications:** *For Single Women with Breast Cancer*. • *Guide-*

lines for Breast Cancer Support Groups. • *When the Woman You Love Has Breast Cancer*. • *Y-ME Hotline*, bimonthly. Newsletter. **Formerly:** (1989) Y-Me Breast Cancer Support; (1994) Y-Me National Organization for Breast Cancer Information and Support.

Research Centers

★5996★ Albany Medical College
Center for Cancer and Blood Disorders
A-52
Albany, NY 12208
Phone: (518)445-5297
Fax: (518)445-5555
Gregory R. Harper, Head

Research Activities and Fields: Cancer and blood disorders, focusing on medical oncology, hematology, radiotherapy, pathology, surgery, and bone marrow transplantation.

★5997★ AMC Cancer Research Center
1600 Pierce St.
Denver, CO 80214
Phone: (303)239-3372
Fax: (303)233-9562
Douglass C. Tormey, Ph.D., Dir.

Research Activities and Fields: Cancer prevention and control, focusing on early diagnosis, nutrition, chemoprevention, metabolic epidemiology, and intervention trials in human populations, particularly women and underserved populations. Promotes the application of knowledge to reduce cancer incidence and mortality rates. **E-mail Address:** tormey@jimmy.harvard.edu.

★5998★ American Health Foundation
1 Dana Rd.
Valhalla, NY 10595
Phone: (914)592-2600
Fax: (914)592-6317
Dr. Ernst L. Wynder, Pres.

Research Activities and Fields: Improves methods of prevention of cancer and other diseases, trains health professionals, and teaches the public how to reduce risk factors of disease. Conducts collaborative laboratory studies with hospitals in cellular and molecular biology, chemical and environmental carcinogenesis, cell genetics, and the nutritional aspects of disease. **Publications:** *Health Letter* (six per year, newsletter); *Preventive Medicine* (six per year).

★5999★ Arizona State University
Cancer Research Institute
Tempe, AZ 85287-2404
Phone: (602)965-3351
Dr. George R. Pettit, Dir.

Research Activities and Fields: Discovery of new cancer chemotherapeutic drugs for human treatment employing organic chemistry, biochemistry, and biology, including a unique program concerned with isolation, structural identification, and syntheses of naturally occurring anticancer agents from marine animals, plants, and microorganisms. **Formerly:** Cancer Research Laboratory.

Armand-Frappier Institute
Immunology Research Center
See: Entry 2092

★6000★ Armand Hammer Center for Cancer Biology
Salk Institute for Biological Studies
PO Box 85800
San Diego, CA 92186-5800
Phone: (619)453-4100
Fax: (619)457-4765
Dr. Walter Eckhart, Dir.

Research Activities and Fields: Participates as one of a group of selected nonclinical cancer centers in National Cancer Institute's nationwide program for coordinating multidisciplinary basic and clinical cancer research, improving methods of treatment, diagnosis, and prevention, training health professionals, and transferring cancer knowledge to surrounding communities, established under National Cancer Act of 1971. Areas of research include molecular biology, virology, cell biology, and developmental biology. Conducts basic research into mechanisms of cell regulation and growth control.

★6001★ Baton Rouge Regional Tumor Registry
4950 Essen Ln.
Baton Rouge, LA 70809
Phone: (504)767-0430
Fax: (504)766-7203
Lori McCallum, M.Ed., CTR Dir.

Research Activities and Fields: Provides a base of statistical information for cancer research in the Baton Rouge area and serves as a useful tool for physicians investigating the success rates of various forms of cancer treatment. Conducts specialized studies in conjunction with the American Cancer Society, National Cancer Institute, and the American College of Surgeons. **Publications:** Annual Report.

Baylor University
Bone Marrow Transplantation Research Center
See: Entry 12882

★6002★ Blood Center of Southeastern Wisconsin
Blood Research Institute
638 N. 18th St.
Milwaukee, WI 53233
Phone: (414)937-6318
Fax: (414)937-6284
Robert R. Montgomery, V.Pres. and Dir.

Research Activities and Fields: Blood-related research in the areas of platelets, hemostasis/thrombosis, immunogenetics, and transfusion medicine. Major activities include the collection and distribution of blood and blood products, basic research, clinical laboratory testing, and bone marrow donor recruitment. **Publications:** Annual Report.

★6003★ Boiron Research Foundation, Inc.
6 Campus Blvd.
Newtown Square, PA 19073
Phone: (215)532-8288
Thierry R. Montfort, V.Pres.

Research Activities and Fields: Sponsors university research in autohemic therapy and homeopathic medicine. **Publications:** *International al Journal of Immunotherapy.*

Bone Marrow Transplant Laboratory
See: Entry 12883

★6004★ Boston Sickle Cell Center
Boston City Hospital
818 Harrison Ave., FGH 2
Boston, MA 02118
Phone: (617)534-5727
Fax: (617)534-5739
Dr. Lillian E.C. McMahon, Dir.

Research Activities and Fields: Sickle cell trait and sickle cell anemia/disease, including molecular, cellular, tissue, and organ studies. Investigates glucose 6-phosphate dehydrogenase deficiency, coagulation and carbomylation of hemoglobin S, anti-sickling compounds, red cell membrane alterations, fetal jeopardy, fetal hemoglobin synthesis, cardiac manifestations, lung function, and infection. Conducts ultrastructural and clinical studies and seeks to translate basic and clinical research to improved health care at the community level. **Publications:** Educational Booklets.

★6005★ Boston University Cancer Research Center (CRC)
80 E. Concord St.
Boston, MA 02118
Phone: (617)638-4173
Fax: (617)638-4176
Douglas V. Faller, Dir.

Research Activities and Fields: Cancer, including cellular and molecular biology, receptors, carcinogenesis, immunology, toxicology, molecular genetics, nucleic acid damage and repair, mechanism of action of chemotherapeutic agents, and new approaches to cancer treatment. Affiliated hospitals provide a wide variety of specialized approaches to clinical management of cancer, including surgery, radiation therapy, chemotherapy, and immunotherapy. Patients entered on local, regional, and national treatment protocols. **Formerly:** Hubert H. Humphrey Cancer Research Center (1991).

★6006★ Brigham Young University Cancer Research Center
857 WIDB
Provo, UT 84602
Phone: (801)378-6207
Byron K. Murray, Ph.D., Dir.

Research Activities and Fields: Chemistry and biochemistry of nucleic acids and their derivatives as potential medicinal agents, including synthesis of antiviral and antitumor agents, detection of carcinogenic materials in the environment, isolation and study of antitumor agents from natural products, and study of the biochemical mechanism of action of various antitumor agents.

★6007★ Burzynski Research Institute
12000 Richmond Ave., Ste. 260
Houston, TX 77082-2431
Phone: (713)597-0111
Fax: (713)597-1166
Stanislaw R. Burzynski, M.D., Founder

Research Activities and Fields: Cancer therapy, including research and treatment with human antineoplastons, naturally occuring peptides and amino acid derivatives.

★6008★ Cancer Institute of Brooklyn
927 49th St.
Brooklyn, NY 11219
Phone: (718)972-5816
Fax: (718)972-8693
Annette Angelone, Exec.Dir.

Research Activities and Fields: Cancer, including diagnostic and treatment techniques, bone marrow transplants, biotherapeutics, immunotherapy, advanced hyperthermia, and intraoperative radiotherapy. **Publications:** Newsletters, brochures, and educational materials.

★6009★ Cancer and Leukemia Group B
444 Mt. Support Rd., Ste. 2
Lebanon, NH 03766
Phone: (603)650-6717
Fax: (603)650-6375
Ross McIntyre, M.D., Group Chm.

Research Activities and Fields: Cooperative group conducting therapeutic multi-modal, multi-institutional, randomized cancer clinical trials primarily in five disease areas: leukemia, lymphoma, breast, gastrointestinal, and respiratory. Aims to increase the number of cases brought under complete remission from cancer by increasing knowledge of the disease process and appropriate treatments. Affiliated with several pathology, immunology, and cytogenetic laboratories. **Formerly:** Acute Leukemia Group B.

★6010★ Cancer Prevention Research Institute
11 E. 22nd St., 8th Fl.
New York, NY 10010
Phone: (212)533-0555
Fax: (212)533-0798
Dr. Carlyler Miller, Dir.

Research Activities and Fields: Cancer prevention, with emphasis on DNA repair and biochemical research, including: laboratory studies, emphasizing biochemical studies of DNA enzymes to improve the accuracy and specificity of tests to determine individual cancer risk; case/control studies, emphasizing studies of cancer patients and healthy volunteers to verify the link between DNA biomarkers and cancer; and risk prediction and chemopreventive trials, emphasizing field tests of CPRI's measures of risk and of ways to reduce the risk of cancer. Projects include an assessment of the effectiveness of micronutrients in DNA repair.

★6011★ Cancer Research Center
3501 Berrywood Dr.
Columbia, MO 65201
Phone: (314)875-2255
Fax: (314)443-1202
Dr. Abraham Eisenstark, Dir.

Research Activities and Fields: Basic oncology and studies in immunology, microbiology, protein biochemistry, bioengineering, carcinogenesis, and cancer detection. Specific studies include biochemical markers for early detection of cancer cells, environmental carcinogenesis, and oxidative cellular damage. **Publications:** *The Mirror* (quarterly). **E-mail Address:** abe@biosci.mbp.missouri.edu.

★6012★ Cancer Research Center
Albert Einstein College of Medicine
1300 Morris Park Ave.
Bronx, NY 10461
Phone: (718)430-2302
Fax: (718)822-6538
Matthew D. Scharff, M.D., Dir.

Research Activities and Fields: Cancer, including studies on carcinogenesis and chemotherapeutic agents, regulation of growth and function in normal and cancer cells, cell structure and metabolism in normal and cancer cells, immuno-oncology, viral oncology, genetics, membrane synthesis, nucleic acid synthesis, gene expression in malignant cells, and cell function and regulation. Conducts clinical cancer studies.

★6013★ Cancer Therapy and Research Center
8122 Datapoint Dr., Ste. 700
San Antonio, TX 78229
Phone: (210)616-5864
Fax: (210)615-3664
Daniel D. Van Hoff, M.D., Contact

Research Activities and Fields: Causes and treatment of cancer, emphasizing the development of new anticancer agents. Maintains the Institute for Drug Development, a division that studies and tests drugs awaiting Food and Drug Administration approval. **Publications:** *Investigational New Drugs* (quarterly). **E-mail Address:** dan__von__hoff@mstp.idde.saci.org.

★6014★ Carson-Newman College Cancer Research Project
Jefferson City, TN 37760
Phone: (615)475-9061
Dr. Carl T. Bahner, Dir.

Research Activities and Fields: Synthesis of new compounds for testing against tumors in animals and the AIDS virus; photodynamic therapy; and drug delivery targeting.

★6015★ Center for Blood Research
800 Huntington Ave.
Boston, MA 02115
Phone: (617)731-6470
Fax: (617)278-3493
Fred S. Rosen, M.D., Pres.

Research Activities and Fields: Human blood, including multidisciplinary studies on heart disease, diabetes, cancer, AIDS, hemophilia, sickle cell anemia, mental illness, hepatitis, Rh factor in pregnancy, serum proteins, blood collection methods, preservation of formed elements, methods of plasma fractionation, and characterization of plasma components. **Formerly:** Until 1967 known as the Protein Foundation and subsequently as Blood Research Institute until its merger in 1972 with Blood Grouping Laboratory, formed in 1942.

Center for Molecular Medicine and Immunology / Garden State Cancer Center
See: Entry 2096

★6016★ Center for Radiation Therapy
5841 S. Maryland Ave.
MC 0085
Chicago, IL 60637
Phone: (312)702-6819
Fax: (312)702-5940
Ralph Weichselbaum, M.D., Dir.

Research Activities and Fields: Cancer and treatment, including studies in radiation oncology, radiation biology, chemotherapy, and oncology information systems.

★6017★ Center for Research in Thrombolysis
Brigham & Women's Hospital
75 Francis St.
Boston, MA 02115
Phone: (617)732-5771
Fax: (617)566-4092
Douglas Vaughan, M.D, Dir.

Research Activities and Fields: Biochemistry and molecular biology of the mammalian fibrinolytic system. Projects include isolating and cloning membrane receptors and constructing and characterizing mutant forms of fibrinolytic inhibitors.

★6018★ Charity Hospital Oncology Treatment Unit
Charity Hospital of New Orleans
Medical Center of Louisiana
1532 Tulane Ave.
New Orleans, LA 70140
Phone: (504)568-2427
James Wm. C. Holmes, Dir.

Research Activities and Fields: Cancer, including clinical studies in chemotherapy, immunotherapy, surgery, and hyperthermia. **Formerly:** Tulane Cancer Clinical Research Center.

★6019★ Chicago Medical School H.M. Bligh Cancer Research Laboratories
Veterans Administration Medical Center
3333 Green Bay Rd.
North Chicago, IL 60064
Phone: (708)578-3435
Fax: (708)578-3432
Prof. Georg F. Springer, M.D., Head

Research Activities and Fields: Human cancer research, especially breast and lung cancer. Research activities include early immuno-detection of carcinomas, and active use of T/Tn antigen vaccine to prevent recurrence of advanced breast carcinoma. **Formerly:** H.M. Bligh Cancer Biology Research Laboratory.

★6020★ Children's Cancer Research Institute
2130 Fillmore St. 235
San Francisco, CA 94115
Phone: (415)923-3535
Jordan R. Wilbur, M.D., Exec.Dir.

Research Activities and Fields: Cancer research and care for children with cancer. Through the clinical laboratory located at University of California, San Francisco, the Institute conducts pharmacokinetics research on anticancer drugs to improve their efficacy.

★6021★ Children's Center for Cancer and Blood Disorders
Univ. of South Carolina School of Medicine
Richland Memorial Hospital
7 Richland Medical Park, Ste. 203
Columbia, SC 29203
Phone: (803)434-3533
Fax: (803)434-3094
Dr. Robert S. Ettinger, Dir.

Research Activities and Fields: Causes, treatments, and prevention of childhood cancer. Current research covers retinoids as cancer differentiating agents and as chemopreventitives.

★6022★ City of Hope Cancer Research Center
1450 E. Duarte Rd.
Duarte, CA 91010
Phone: (818)357-9711
Fax: (818)930-5300
John S. Kovach, M.D., Dir.

Research Activities and Fields: Cancer, radiolabelled monoclonal antibodies, antisense RNA, ribozymes, molecular pharmacology, virology (AIDS), and marrow transplant for hematologic cancers. **Publications:** *City of Hope Annual Report, Cancer Center Report* (quarterly). **Formerly:** Specialized Center for Immunology Research (1981).

★6023★ Colorado Cancer Research Program
3955 E. Exposition, No. 104
Denver, CO 80209
Phone: (303)777-2663
Fax: (303)777-2642
Robert F. Berris, M.D., Exec.Dir.

Research Activities and Fields: Program conducts studies on cancer and oncology.

★6024★ Columbia University Columbia-Presbyterian Cancer Center
630 W. 168th St., Ste. PH 18-200
New York, NY 10032
Phone: (212)305-6921
Fax: (212)305-6889
I. Bernard Weinstein, M.D., Dir.

Research Activities and Fields: The Center is organized into four divisions: basic research; clinical research; cancer causation and prevention; and research education. Research areas include molecular tumor virology, oncogenes and molecular genetics, biophysics, cell biology, basic mechanisms of carcinogenesis, molecular epidemiology, biochemistry, endocrinology, and developmental biology. Cancer control research includes cancer epidemiology, sociomedical sciences, occupational health, and biostatistics and data management.

★6025★ Comprehensive Sickle Cell Center
Harlem Hospital
Sickle Cell Dept., Rm. 6146
506 Lenox Ave.
New York, NY 10037
Phone: (212)939-1701
Fax: (212)939-1692
Dr. Jeanne A. Smith, Dir.

Research Activities and Fields: Sickle cell disease, including studies of pathophysiological aspects, intellectual growth and development of children with sickle cell and allied diseases, biochemical factors involved in the clinical severity of the disease.

★6026★ Comprehensive Sickle Cell Center
Children's Hospital Medical Center
3333 Burnet Ave.
Cincinnati, OH 45229
Phone: (513)559-4200
Donald Rucknagel, M.D., Dir.

Research Activities and Fields: Sickle cell disease, including molecular, cellular, tissue, and organ studies. Conducts clinical trials and seeks to translate research to improved health care.

★6027★ Dana-Farber Cancer Institute
44 Binney St.
Boston, MA 02115
Phone: (617)632-3000
Dr. Christopher Walsh, Pres.

Research Activities and Fields: Medical oncology, cancer pharmacology, pediatric oncology, cell growth and regulation, cancer genetics, human retrovirology, tumor immunology and virology, immunogenetics, lymphocyte biology, biostatistics and epidemiology, molecular carcinogenesis, biochemical pharmacology, neoplastic disease mechanisms, structural molecular biology, membrane immunochemistry, cancer control, tumor virus genetics, immunopathology, gene regulation, eukaryotic transcription, molecular biology, molecular genetics, molecular immunology, molecular immunobiology, medicine, gynecologic oncology, oncodiagnostic radiology and nuclear medicine, radiotherapy, and surgical oncology. **Publications:** *Scientific Report* (biennially). **Formerly:** Children's Cancer Research Foundation (1947); Sidney Farber Cancer Institute (1976).

★6028★ Dana-Farber Cancer Institute Division of Biostatistics
44 Binney St.
Boston, MA 02115
Phone: (617)632-3012
Fax: (617)632-2444
Dr. Marvin Zelen, Chief

Research Activities and Fields: Organized into the laboratories of biostatistics and computing, which carry on a multifaceted program combining independent research, collaboration, and consulting in quantitative methods as they apply to cancer research. Project areas include methodological research in statistics, mathematical models in chronic disease epidemiology, statistical computing, and applied probability and database research. Conducts multi-institutional cancer clinical trials. **E-mail Address:** bio@jimmy.harvar.edu. **Formerly:** Division of Biostatistics and Epidemiology.

★6029★ Drew / Meharry / Morehouse Consortium Cancer Center
1005 D.B. Todd Blvd.
Nashville, TN 37208
Phone: (615)327-6315
Fax: (615)327-5844
Louis J. Bernard, M.D., Dir.

Research Activities and Fields: Cancer prevention and control, including epidemiological and behavioral research planning and implementation, and therapeutic clinical cancer trials. **E-mail Address:** BERNARD75.

★6030★ **Duke University**
Comprehensive Sickle Cell Center
Medical Center
Box 3934
Durham, NC 27710
Phone: (919)684-3724
Fax: (919)681-8477
Wendell F. Rosse, M.D., Dir.

Research Activities and Fields: Sickle cell disease, including molecular, cellular, tissue, and organ studies. Conducts clinical trials. Seeks to translate basic and clinical research to improved health care at the community level.

★6031★ **Duke University**
Duke Comprehensive Cancer Center
Medical Center
Box 3843, DUMC
Durham, NC 27710
Phone: (919)684-3377
Fax: (919)684-5653
Dr. Micheal Colvin, Dir.

Research Activities and Fields: Prevention, detection, diagnosis, and treatment of cancer, including multidisciplinary studies in cellular and molecular biology, chemical and environmental carcinogenesis, ultrastructure, cell genetics, virology, tumor immunology, epidemiology, and biostatistics. Conducts clinical investigations and cancer screening. **Publications:** Annual Progress Report; *Duke Cancer Report* (quarterly); *Digest* (biennially); Newsletters on Pediatric Brain Tumors, Melanoma, Recreation Therapy.

★6032★ **Duke University**
Southeastern Regional Trophoblastic
Disease Center
Medical Center
PO Box 3244
Durham, NC 27710
Phone: (919)684-2886
Fax: (919)684-6161
Dr. Charles B. Hammond, Dir.

Research Activities and Fields: Research related to assay techniques for human chorionic gonadotropin as a tumor marker, the natural history of trophoblastic tumors, and effective therapy for trophoblastic disease.

★6033★ **Eastern Cooperative Oncology**
Group (ECOG)
1600 Pierce St.
Denver, CO 80214
Phone: (303)239-3370
Fax: (303)233-9562
Dr. Tormey, Chm.

Research Activities and Fields: Multidisciplinary cancer trials, including treatment, biologic and basic research, and cancer control and prevention. **Publications:** Semi annual newsletter. **E-mail Address:** jimmy@harvard.edu.

★6034★ **Emory University**
Georgia Center for Cancer Statistics
1518 Clifton Rd. NE
Atlanta, GA 30322
Phone: (404)727-8700
Fax: (404)727-8737
Jonathan M. Liff, Ph.D., Dir.

Research Activities and Fields: Serves as a cancer registry for five counties of metropolitan Atlanta and ten rural counties in central Georgia. Seeks to 1) monitor the incidence of cancer in a geographically defined population, 2) identify groups with unusual risks of cancer, 3) monitor oncologic practices within the community, 4) assess the survival experience of cancer patients, and 5) provide a resource for epidemiological and biostatistical studies and training. Studies racial differences in cancer survival, cancers especially prevalent among blacks, passive exposure to cigarette smoke and risk of lung cancer, exposure to agent orange and risk of lymphoma and soft tissue sarcoma, risk factors for selected uterine malignancies, barriers to the early detection of cervical cancer, and viral infection and T-cell leukemias. **Publications:** Publishes cancer incidence, mortality, and survival data. **E-mail Address:** gerlach@fox.sph.emory.edu. **Formerly:** Atlanta Cancer Surveillance Center.

★6035★ **Emory University**
Winship Cancer Center
1327 Clifton Rd. NE
Atlanta, GA 30322
Phone: (404)248-5177
Fax: (404)248-5016
Dr. Howard Ozer, Dir.

Research Activities and Fields: A university-based cancer center coordinating multidisciplinary basic and clinical cancer research, improving methods of treatment, diagnosis, and prevention, training health professionals, and transferring cancer knowledge to surrounding communities. **Formerly:** Cancer Center.

★6036★ **Fitzpatrick Oncology Center**
Champlain Valley Physicians Hospital
75 Beekman St.
Plattsburgh, NY 12901
Phone: (518)561-2000

Research Activities and Fields: Oncological clinical research.

★6037★ **Foundation for Blood Research**
PO Box 190
Scarborough, ME 04070-0190
Phone: (207)883-4131
Fax: (207)883-1527
Robert F. Ritchie, M.D., Pres.

Research Activities and Fields: Applied research in health science education, epidemiology, genetics, immunology, oncology, perinatalogy, rheumatology, prenatal diagnosis, and cancer. Immunochemical analysis of human blood and other body fluids is performed and coupled with epidemiological data both for research on and for use in computer applications in disease diagnosis. Also performs clinical testing. **Publications:** *Genetics Digest* (newsletter, five times per year); *AFP Office Update* (quarterly newsletter); *Clinical Genetics Newsletter*

(quarterly); *RDL Newsletter* (quarterly); *Proceedings of Scarborough Meetings* (periodically).

★6038★ **Fox Chase Cancer Center**
7701 Burholme Ave.
Philadelphia, PA 19111
Phone: (215)728-6900
Fax: (215)728-2571
Robert C. Young, M.D., Pres.

Research Activities and Fields: Cancer, including oncogenes, tumor-suppressing genes, chemical carcinogens, immunology, virology, membrane biology, and molecular structure (basic science division); immunotherapy and other investigational therapies including interferons and specific monoclonal antibodies, tumor-cell resistance to therapeutic drugs and radiation, diagnostic imaging, and NMR spectroscopy (medical science division); identification of high cancer risk individuals, risk reduction and early detection, and impact of environmental and genetic factors (population science division). **Publications:** Scientific Report (annually); President's Report.

★6039★ **Fred Hutchinson Cancer**
Research Center
1124 Columbia St.
Seattle, WA 98104
Phone: (206)667-5000
Fax: (206)667-5216
Robert W. Day, M.D., Dir.

Research Activities and Fields: Cancer, including basic, clinical, and public health sciences. Research programs include basic science, molecular medicine, human immunogenetics, marrow transplantation, organ systems, pain and toxicity, pediatric oncology, transplantation biology, biostatistics, cancer biology, cancer prevention research, and epidemiology.

★6040★ **Frederick Cancer Research**
Center
PO Box B
Frederick, MD 21702-1201
Phone: (301)846-1000
Fax: (301)846-5866
Margaret Fanning, Contact

Research Activities and Fields: Cancer.

★6041★ **Georgetown University**
Vincent T. Lombardi Cancer Research
Center
3800 Reservoir Rd. NW, Podium Level
Washington, DC 20007
Phone: (202)687-2110
Fax: (202)687-6402
Marc Lippman, M.D., Dir.

Research Activities and Fields: Prevention, detection, diagnosis, and treatment of cancer, including clinical and basic science activities in all oncologic specialties (surgery, medicine, gynecology, pediatrics, radiology, pathology, urology, and immunology) and basic science studies in pharmacology, biochemistry, radiation biology, virology, molecular genetics, analytic chemistry, flow cytometry, and electron microscopy.

★6042★ Geraldine Brush Cancer Research Institute
Medical Research Institute
2330 Clay St.
San Francisco, CA 94115
Phone: (415)561-1728
Fax: (415)561-1390
Dr. Helene S. Smith, Dir.

Research Activities and Fields: Advanced molecular and cellular biology studies of human cancer. Special emphasis on breast cancer. **E-mail Address:** helene@copious.ucsf.edu.

★6043★ Goodwin Institute for Cancer Research
1850 NW 69th Ave.
Plantation, FL 33313
Phone: (305)587-9020
Fax: (305)587-6378
Claire Thuning-Roberson, Ph.D., Dir.

Research Activities and Fields: Fundamental investigations in biological sciences using specific pathogen-free animals to develop human tumor xenograft models and to determine association between viruses and cancer and to improve cancer therapy by drug synergism, immunotherapy and improved delivery of treatment modalities. Studies cover hybridoma technology and application, tumor therapy, immunohistochemistry, herpes simplex virus (mechanisms of latency and vaccine development), hemopoietic and tumor stem cell growth (promotion and inhibition), potentiation of chemotherapeutic responses by hyperthermia and DMSO, and tumor behavior in immunosuppressed animals. Research services include preclinical trials for anticancer agents, monoclonal antibody production in mouse ascites or in vitro and downstream processing. Mai ntains laboratories in biochemistry, virology, immunology, immunohistochemistry, molecular biology, instrument design, microbiology, cell culture, and photography. **Formerly:** Germfree Life Research Center (1972).

H.L. Snyder Memorial Research Foundation
See: Entry 2576

★6044★ H. Lee Moffitt Cancer Center and Research Institute
12902 Magnolia Dr.
Tampa, FL 33612
Phone: (813)972-4673
Fax: (813)972-8495
John C. Ruckdeschel, M.D., Dir./CEO

Research Activities and Fields: Basic, clinical, and cancer control programs in immunology, medical imaging, gastrointestinal tumors, bone marrow transplantation, breast cancer, thoracic oncology, and cancer prevention. Programs in developmental therapeutics, signal transduction, and molecular biology are under development. **Publications:** *Cancer Control* (quarterly); *Today's Tomorrows* (quarterly); *Lifetime Choices* (three per year).

Harvard Medical School
Laboratory of Viral Pathogenesis
See: Entry 2578

Harvard University
Laboratory for Cell and Molecular Biology
See: Entry 2579

★6045★ Head and Neck Center
2157 Main St.
Buffalo, NY 14214
Phone: (716)862-1830
Fax: (716)862-1839
Dr. John M. Lore, Jr., Dir.

Research Activities and Fields: Basic and clinical studies on head and neck cancer, especially in the areas of wound healing, bone regeneration, and biomaterials. **Formerly:** Center of Excellence in Otolaryncology.

Health Research, Inc.
See: Entry 10979

★6046★ Hereditary Cancer Institute
Creighton Univ.
School of Medicine
2500 California Plaza
Omaha, NE 68178
Phone: (402)280-2942
Fax: (402)280-1734
Henry T. Lynch, M.D., Pres.

Research Activities and Fields: Hereditary cancer, including studies of its incidence and patterns. Disseminates current genetic, diagnostic, and therapeutic information to patients. **Publications:** Newsletter. **Formerly:** Institute for Familial Cancer Management and Control, Inc.

★6047★ Hipple Cancer Research Center
4100 S. Kettering Blvd.
Dayton, OH 45439-2092
Phone: (513)293-8508
Fax: (513)293-7652
Dr. Martin J. Murphy, Jr., Pres./CEO

Research Activities and Fields: Cancer, primarily studies on hematopoietic growth factors, interferon mechanism of action, developing cloning technology, and the biology of metastasis. **Publications:** *Stem Cells.* **E-mail Address:** hipple@dialup.oar.net. **Formerly:** Bob Hipple Laboratory for Cancer Research (1985).

★6048★ Howard University
Cancer Center
2041 Georgia Ave.
Washington, DC 20060
Phone: (202)806-7697
Fax: (202)667-1686
Dr. Lucille Adams-Campbell, Actg.Dir.

Research Activities and Fields: Multidisciplinary genomic research of African-Americans. Basic research includes molecular biology of cancer, mechanisms of metastases, tumor immunology, pharmacology of antineoplastic drugs, clinical chemotherapeutic research, pilot studies for the treatment of various neoplasms, and radiotherapeutic research, including intraoperative radiation therapy, hyperthermia, and combined modality therapy. Epidemiological research includes nutrition, cancer treatment effectiveness and various studies on the medically underserved targeted participants. Purpose is to better understand the biomedical significance of genomic variability underlying susceptability and/or resistance to common, chronic debilitating diseases and disorders using breast cancer as a prototype. **Formerly:** Cancer Research Center.

★6049★ Howard University
Center for Sickle Cell Disease
2121 Georgia Ave. NW
Washington, DC 20059
Phone: (202)806-7930
Fax: (202)806-4517
Dr. Oswaldo Castro, Dir.

Research Activities and Fields: Sickle cell disease, including basic and clinical investigations of its nature, causes, effects, and potential control. Develops and implements high quality total care for victims of the disease. Develops and evaluates methods of prevention through screening for sickle and other abnormal hemoglobins and participates in the Mid-Atlantic Regional Genetic Counseling Program. **Publications:** Annual Report.

★6050★ Illinois Oncology Research Association
900 Main St., Ste. 780
Peoria, IL 61602
Phone: (309)672-5780
Fax: (309)672-4138
Robert Cooper, Dir.

Research Activities and Fields: Cancer treatment and control, including chemotherapy, immunotherapy, hormonal therapy, and radiation therapy.

★6051★ Indiana University
Herman B. Wells Center for Pediatric Research
School of Medicine
702 Barnhill Dr., Rm. 2600
Indianapolis, IN 46202
Phone: (317)274-8900
Fax: (317)274-8679
Dr. David Williams, Dir.

Research Activities and Fields: Hematology and oncology, cell biology of polarized cells (including the blood-brain barrier), protein sorting in eukaryotic cells, bone marrow transplantation, clinical oncology research, pediatric oncology, developmental biology of neuroblastoma, gene transfer into stem cells, tumor immunology, clinical aspects of childhood acute myelogenous leukemia, the role of protein phosphorylation in control of cell proliferation and differentiation, clinical aspects and molecular biology of neutrophil disorders, neurooncology, late effects of CNS therapy, clinical aspects of supportive care of oncology patients, therapy for neuroblastoma, clinical use of hemotopoietic growth factors, secondary leukemias, clinical aspects of hemostasis, molecular biology of myeloid-specific gene expression, cancer biogenesis using neuroblastoma as a model, and molecular biology of nuclear retinoic acid receptors in myeloid leukemia, neuroblastoma cells, endocrinology, neonatology, and pulmonary.

★6052★ Indiana University-Purdue University at Indianapolis
Laboratory for Experimental Oncology
Sch. of Medicine
702 Barnhill Dr.
Indianapolis, IN 46202-5200
Phone: (317)274-7921
Fax: (317)274-3939
Prof. George Weber, M.D., Dir.

Research Activities and Fields: Biochemical pharmacology and chemotherapy of experimental and clinical cancer. **Publications:** *Advances in Enzyme Regulation.*

★ 6053 ★   Institute for Cancer and Blood Diseases

Hahnemann Univ.
Broad & Vine Sts.
HU-MS412
Philadelphia, PA 19102
Phone: (215)762-8026
Fax: (215)762-8857
Isadore Brodsky, M.D., Dir.

Research Activities and Fields: Basic research program with possible clinical trials in the following areas: interferon, oncogenesis, differentiation, molecular biology, viral oncogenesis, immunology, cell biology, and cytogenesis. **Formerly:** Herbert L. Orlowitz Institute for Cancer and Blood Diseases (1983).

★ 6054 ★   Institute for Cancer and Blood Research

150 N. Robertson Blvd., 350N
Beverly Hills, CA 90211
Phone: (310)657-4706
Fax: (310)657-2185
Dr. Howard R. Bierman, Scientific Dir.

Research Activities and Fields: Biochemical regulation of cell growth and control of leukocyte maturation in leukemias, including clinical studies to isolate and purify substances that stimulate cell division and maintain normal maturation of neoplastic cells; ultrastructural immunolocalization of novel protein products in myeloid leukemias; prediagnostic detection of cancer, oncogenes, and products for antioncogenes; detailed computer analysis of predictive-oriented data acquired from healthy subjects and patients with neoplastic disease; investigation of tumor diathesis, including preclinical diagnosis of multiple primary neoplasms and studies of families to define increased susceptibility to develop neoplasms; and continuing studies of dermatoglyphics, predictive profiles, and other genetic markers as they relate to neoplasia.

★ 6055 ★   Institute for Cancer Research

Fox Chase Cancer Center
7701 Burholme Ave.
Philadelphia, PA 19111
Phone: (215)728-2490
Fax: (215)728-2778
Dr. Anna Marie Skalka, Dir.

Research Activities and Fields: Causes, nature, diagnosis, and treatment of cancer, including studies in cellular, molecular, and developmental biology, immunology, molecular oncology, structural biology, and virology. **Publications:** *Scientific Report* (annually).

Institute for Drug Development
See: Entry 10439

★ 6056 ★   Iowa Oncology Research Association

1223 Center St., Ste. 19
Des Moines, IA 50309-1014
Phone: (515)244-7586
Fax: (515)244-3037
Roscoe F. Morton, M.D., Prin. Investigator

Research Activities and Fields: Clinical cancer studies, including new chemotherapy agents and radiation therapy techniques. Participates in the NCI's Patterns of Care Study.

★ 6057 ★   J.L. and Helen Kellogg Cancer Care Center

Evanston Hospital
2650 Ridge Ave.
Evanston, IL 60201
Phone: (708)570-2108
Fax: (708)570-2918
Dr. J.D. Khandekar, Dir.

Research Activities and Fields: Treatment and diagnosis of cancer, including phase 1 and 2 studies, evaluation of new drug protocols, role of hyperthermia in the treatment of tumors, and brain tumor studies. Basic and clinical research also includes studies of breast, head and neck, lung, bladder, and pancreatic cancers, blood clotting and fibrinolytic mechanisms in tumor patients, thromboembolic problems in cancer patients, pituitary tumor surgery, immunology/virology, microbiology, hematology, clinical biochemistry, pharmacology, diagnosis by fine needle aspiration techniques, oncogens, medical oncology, and psychiatry. Also conducts studies in flow cytometry and magnetic resonance imaging and spectroscopy. **Formerly:** Evanston Cancer Care Center (1981).

★ 6058 ★   John P. Caufield Technology Extension Center for Investigational Cancer Treatment

1 Bruce St.
Newark, NJ 07103
Phone: (201)982-4600
Fax: (201)982-7047
David M. Goldenberg, Sc.D.,, Dir.

Research Activities and Fields: Develops and provides new and more effective technologies for the early detection, diagnosis, and treatment of cancer; facilitates the transfer of investigational, diagnostic and treatment methods to New Jersey practitioners and hospitals; provides minority populations with access to state-of-the-art cancer protocols and treatment within their own community. **Formerly:** Technology Extension Center for Investigational Cancer Therapy.

★ 6059 ★   Johns Hopkins University Oncology Center

600 N. Wolfe St.
Baltimore, MD 21287-8943
Phone: (410)955-8822
Fax: (410)955-6787
Martin D. Abeloff, M.D., Dir.

Research Activities and Fields: Cancer and related disorders, with bone marrow transplantation, cancer biology, medical oncology, pediatric oncology, pharmacology and experimental therapeutics, and radiological sciences. Activities emphasize the application of new knowledge to management of patients with cancer and prevention of neoplastic diseases and their complications, with major aim of the several complementary research programs of the Center being an increased understanding of human neoplasia and more effective clinical management.

Joint Center for Radiation Therapy
See: Entry 11145

★ 6060 ★   Kansas State University Center for Basic Cancer Research

Division of Biology
Ackert Hall
Manhattan, KS 66506
Phone: (913)532-6705
Fax: (913)532-6653
Dr. Terry C. Johnson, Dir.

Research Activities and Fields: Cancer autonomy and metastasis; tumor initiation, promotion, and progression; chemotherapeutic compounds; growth regulation, the immune system, and other cellular interactions; and oncogene expression. **Publications:** *Accepting a Challenge* (informational magazine); *A Day with Dr. Waddle* (children's workbook to introduce and explain cancer).

★ 6061 ★   Kentucky Cancer Program

Univ. of Kentucky
206 MRI/MCC
800 Rose St.
Lexington, KY 40536-0098
Phone: (606)233-6541
Fax: (606)258-1902
Gilbert H. Friedell, M.D., Codir.

Research Activities and Fields: Cancer control. Collects and disseminates information leading to improved prevention, diagnosis, and treatment of cancer. Serves communities throughout the Commonwealth through identified intermediaries, working through District Cancer Councils and community cancer coalitions. The KCP developed the computerized Kentucky Cancer Registry (KCR), to which Kentucky hospitals are legislatively mandated to report cancer incidence. Supports a community-based research component to evaluate cancer control efforts of joint interventions and information dissemination. **Publications:** *CHOICES; Pathfinder; KCR Cancer Incidence Report; Research Findings; Literacy Curriculum for Breast and Cervical Cancer; For Your Peace of Mind* (video). **Formerly:** McDowell Cancer Network (1990).

★ 6062 ★   La Jolla Cancer Research Foundation

10901 N. Torrey Pines Rd.
La Jolla, CA 92037
Phone: (619)455-6480
Fax: (619)455-0181
Erkki Ruoslahti, M.D., Pres./CEO

Research Activities and Fields: Oncodevelopmental biology, cell-matrix interactions, gene cloning, tumor markers, differentiation of teratocarcinoma, lymphocyte differentiation and neoplasia, basement membrane proteins, and oncotrophoblast gene expression. **Publications:** Annual Report.

★ 6063 ★   Laboratory of Signal Transduction

Memorial Sloan-Kettering Cancer Center
1275 York Ave.
Box 254
New York, NY 10021
Phone: (212)639-8573
Fax: (212)717-3053
Dr. Richard Kolesnick, Dir.

Research Activities and Fields: Signal transduction for cytokines and hormones, including tumor necrosis factor-alpha, interleukin-1, and activin.

★ 6064 ★ **Laboratory of Tumor Antigen Immunochemistry**
Memorial Sloan-Kettering Cancer Center
1275 York Ave.
New York, NY 10021
Phone: (212)639-2257
Fax: (212)717-3379
Dr. Kenneth D. Lloyd, Contact

Research Activities and Fields: Monoclonal antibodies and carbohydrate antigens. **Formerly:** Laboratory of Human Cancer Immunology.

Laval University
Medical Research Centre
Molecular Endocrinology Research Group
See: Entry 4894

★ 6065 ★ **Lincoln Cancer Center**
4600 Valley Rd., Ste. 336
Lincoln, NE 68510
Phone: (402)483-2827
Fax: (402)483-2882
Barb Morton, Dir.

Research Activities and Fields: Oncology, especially pathology and radiotherapy, and drug studies for pharmaceutical companies.

★ 6066 ★ **Mary Margaret Walther Program for Cancer Care Research**
School of Nursing, Indiana Univ.
1111 Middle Dr., Rm. 340
Indianapolis, IN 46202
Phone: (317)921-2040
Fax: (317)924-4688
Roberta Smith, Dir.

Research Activities and Fields: Medical, psychosocial, and spiritual aspects of cancer care from the time of diagnosis through the cure or terminal phase of the disease, emphasizing holistic needs of patient and family. Specific interests include continuity of care between the inpatient, outpatient, and home care components; management of pain; emotional support of both patients and families; and bereavement intervention. The Center is a network of health care and educational research facilities working together to improve the quality and effectiveness of care for cancer patients and their families. **E-mail Address:** rsmith@indyvax.edu.iupui.

★ 6067 ★ **Massachusetts Institute of Technology**
Center for Cancer Research
77 Massachusetts Ave.
E17-110
Cambridge, MA 02139-4307
Phone: (617)253-8511
Fax: (617)253-8728
Dr. Richard O. Hynes, Dir.

Research Activities and Fields: Cancer biology, emphasizing molecular biology, genetics, cell biology, developmental biology, and immunology. Specific areas of research include split genes and RNA splicing, cloning oncogenes and tumor suppressor genes from human tumors, T-cell receptors, integrin receptors and cell adhesion, mechanisms, used by tumor cells to evade chemotherapy, gene identification for myotonic dystrophy, Huntington's disease, and Wilm's tumor, the generation of various strains of mutant mice, biochemical mechanisms controlling RNA transcription and splicing, HIV gene studies, cytotoxic and helper T lymphocytes, lymphocyte antigen-specific receptors, molecular mechanisms of antigen presentation, cell surface proteins and cellular adhesion and migration, and cytoskeletal proteins and cell motility and shape.

★ 6068 ★ **Mayo Cancer Center**
200 1st St. SW
Rochester, MN 55905
Phone: (507)284-2065
Fax: (507)284-9349
John S. Kovach, M.D., Dir.

Research Activities and Fields: Broad-based cancer research program ranging from basic and clinical science to clinical studies on prevention, detection, diagnosis, and treatment of cancer. Participates as a comprehensive cancer center for conducting research, improving methods of treatment, diagnosis, and prevention, training health professionals, and transferring cancer knowledge to surrounding communities in National Cancer Institute's nationwide coordination program, established under National Cancer Act of 1971.

McGill University
Centre for the Study of Host Resistance
See: Entry 6776

★ 6069 ★ **Medical College of Georgia**
Sickle Cell Center
1435 Laney-Walker Blvd.
Augusta, GA 30912-2100
Phone: (706)721-3091
Fax: (706)721-6611
Dr. Abdulla H. Kutlar, Dir.

Research Activities and Fields: Hemoglobinopathy detection, identification, and characterization, including studies of factors determining severity of sickle cell anemia in adults and the young child, cardiac evaluation of children with sickle cell anemia, thalassemia in association with sickle cell syndromes, biochemical studies in sickle cell anemia and related disorders with special emphasis on heterogeneity of Hb F, immunological identification, DNA gene mapping of hemoglobin variants, nucleotide sequence, and thalassemia genes, and characterization of hemoglobin variants. **Publications:** *SPHERE* (six times per year); *Hemoglobin: International Journal for Hemoglobin Research* (six times per year). **Formerly:** Comprehensive Sickle Cell Center.

★ 6070 ★ **Medical College of Ohio**
Cancer Research Division
Dept. of Pathology
3000 Arlington Ave.
Toledo, OH 43699-0008
Phone: (419)381-4918
Fax: (419)381-3089
Dr. Herman A. J. Schut, Contact

Research Activities and Fields: Cancer, including chemical carcinogenesis, chemoprevention, molecular biology, toxicology, and tissue culture. Specific research includes oncogene activation and suppressor gene inactiva-tion in cancer, inhibition of cancer by dietary components, and regulation of tumor promotion.

★ 6071 ★ **Medical College of Pennsylvania and Hahnemann University**
Barry Ashbee Research Laboratories
230 N. Broad St.
Philadelphia, PA 19102
Phone: (215)448-8026
Fax: (215)762-8857
Dr. Isadore Brodsky, Dir.

Research Activities and Fields: Leukemia research.

★ 6072 ★ **Medical College of Wisconsin**
Cancer Center
8701 Watertown Plank Rd.
Milwaukee, WI 53226
Phone: (414)456-4410
Fax: (414)266-8905
Dr. J. Frank Wilson, Acting Dir.

Research Activities and Fields: Oncology, focusing on the genes involved in cancerous transformation, enhancing the immune system's attack on tumors, and developing effective cancer drugs. Specific areas of research include biology of hematopoietic cells, biological response modification, bone marrow transplantation and the influence of T-cell depletion, experimental chemotherapy, experimental radiation therapy, structural biology, assessments of cytokine and hormone actions, and evaluations of immune-effector cell function.

★ 6073 ★ **Meharry Medical College**
Comprehensive Sickle Cell Center
1005 D.B. Todd Blvd.
Nashville, TN 37208
Phone: (615)327-6763
Fax: (615)327-6008
Ernest A. Turner, M.D., Dir.

Research Activities and Fields: Basic, clinical, and psychosocial research in sickle cell disease and variants of the disease in the fields of biochemistry, biology, molecular biology, medicine, pediatric medicine, social science, and psychiatry. Specific research includes hearing loss and sickle cell anemia, hemoglobinopathies in Southeast Asians, complement activation in sickle cell anemia, recombinant human parvoviruses for gene therapy of hemoglobinopathies, vitamin E and sickle cell disease, and isolation and characterization of glycophorin. **E-mail Address:** sickle90@ccvax.mmc.edu.

★ 6074 ★ **Memorial Sloan-Kettering Cancer Center**
1275 York Ave.
New York, NY 10021
Phone: (212)639-2000
Fax: (212)794-5850
Dr. Paul A. Marks, Pres.

Research Activities and Fields: Molecular biology, cell biology and genetics, cellular biochemistry and biophysics, immunology, and molecular pharmacology and therapeutics. Aims to advance the understanding of the nature and fundamental causes of cancer and improve the means available for its prevention, diagnosis, and treatment. **Publications:** Report, *Memorial*

Sloan-Kettering Cancer Center Research and Educational Programs; Annual Report, Memorial Sloan-Kettering Cancer Center; *Center News* (newsletter).

★ 6075 ★ **Memorial Sloan-Kettering Cancer Center**
Laboratory of GI Tumor Biology
1275 York Ave.
Box 244
New York, NY 10021
Phone: (212)639-8379
Fax: (212)717-3053
Dr. Eileen A. Friedman, Contact

Research Activities and Fields: Signal transduction initiated by DAGs and FGF's through a common cellular tyrosine kinase substrate, focusing on pathway characterization and alteration during both enterocytic and goblet cell differentiation.

★ 6076 ★ **Mercy Cancer Institute**
Cancer Research Laboratory
Mercy Regional Oncology Ctr.
1400 Locust St.
Pittsburgh, PA 15219
Phone: (412)232-7185
Fax: (412)232-7794
Dr. Vicram Gupta, Medical Dir.

Research Activities and Fields: Molecular biology studies in the areas of akylating and multidrug resistance and the characterization of potentially new lung cancer genes.

★ 6077 ★ **Meyer L. Prentis Comprehensive Cancer Center of Metropolitan Detroit**
110 E. Warren
Detroit, MI 48201
Phone: (313)833-0710
Fax: (313)831-8714
Dr. Richard Sauter, Interim Dir.

Research Activities and Fields: Multidisciplinary cancer research, aimed toward improving methods of treatment, diagnosis, and prevention of cancer. **Publications:** *MCF Today* (quarterly newsletter); *Foundations* (newsletter).

★ 6078 ★ **Michigan Cancer Foundation**
110 E. Warren Ave.
Detroit, MI 48201
Phone: (313)833-0710
Fax: (313)831-8714
Joe Mikolajczyk, Dir., Marketing & PR

Research Activities and Fields: Breast cancer research, including cell and molecular biology, immunology, and biostatistics; MCF-7 (first human breast cancer cell line); tumor biology; molecular oncology; epidemiology; developmental therapeutics; and chemical carcinogenesis. **Publications:** *MCF Today* (quarterly). **Formerly:** Detroit Institute for Cancer Research.

★ 6079 ★ **Michigan State University**
Carcinogenesis Laboratory
Fee Hall
East Lansing, MI 48824
Phone: (517)353-7785
Fax: (517)353-9004
Veronica M. Maher, Ph.D., Professor

Research Activities and Fields: Carcinogenesis, including research in cellular and molecular

biology, mutagenesis, mammalian cell DNA repair, and homologous recombination. **Publications:** Newsletter (occasionally); Papers; Monographs. **E-mail Address:** 07349mah@msu.edu.

★ 6080 ★ **Midwest Cooperative Group**
Outreach Program
PO Box 119000
Kansas City, MO 64111-9000
Phone: (816)932-2085
Fax: (816)931-5531
Peggy Brinkman, Dir.

Research Activities and Fields: Oncological clinical trials.

Molecular Genetics / Oncology Laboratory
See: Entry 5342

★ 6081 ★ **Natalie Warren Bryant Cancer Center**
St. Francis Hospital
6161 S. Yale Ave.
Tulsa, OK 74145
Phone: (918)491-5800
Fax: (918)491-5837
Dr. Alan M. Keller, Prin. Investigator

Research Activities and Fields: Bone marrow transplants, medical oncology, radiotherapy, pathology, and surgery. Conducts clinical trials.

★ 6082 ★ **National Foundation for Cancer Research (NFCR)**
7315 Wisconsin Ave., Ste. 500 W.
Bethesda, MD 20814
Phone: (301)654-1250
Fax: (301)654-5824
Dr. Franklin C. Salisbury, Pres.

Research Activities and Fields: Contracts with major universities for basic science cancer research in the fields of biophysics, theoretical physics and chemistry, biochemistry, chemistry, and biological sciences. **Publications:** *NFCR Annual Report*; Annual Scientific Report.

★ 6083 ★ **New England Deaconess Hospital**
Laboratory of Cancer Biology
Harvard Medical School
Dept. of Surgery
50 Binney St.
Boston, MA 02115
Phone: (617)732-9875
Fax: (617)738-9188
Peter Thomas, Ph.D., Research Dir.

Research Activities and Fields: Human and animal cancer, including studies on biochemistry, cell and membrane biology, immunology, molecular biology, and virology of solid tumors. Develops and conducts clinical human studies on new diagnostic and therapeutic regimes for solid tumors. Collaborates with other laboratories and companies in basic and clinical solid tumor research. **Publications:** Annual Hospital Report.

★ 6084 ★ **New England Medical Center (GOG)**
Gynecologic Oncology Group
750 Washington St.
Box 232
Boston, MA 02111
Phone: (617)956-6058
Fax: (617)350-3258
Harrison G. Ball, M.D., Dir.

Research Activities and Fields: Treatment of gynecologic cancer. Evaluates surgical techniques, radiation therapy, and new chemotherapeutic agents. Emphasizes trophoblastic disease and cancers of the uterus, cervix, vulva, and ovaries.

★ 6085 ★ **New York Medical College**
Division of Neoplastic Diseases
Dept. of Medicine
Munger Pavillion, Rm. 250
Valhalla, NY 10595
Phone: (914)993-4000
Fax: (914)993-4420
Dr. Abraham Mittelman, Dir. of Clinical Investigations

Research Activities and Fields: Conducts research in neoplasia, biologic response modifiers, melanoma, and breast cancer.

★ 6086 ★ **New York Medical College**
Institute of Breast Diseases
Munger Pavilion, Rm. G-13
Valhalla, NY 10595
Phone: (914)285-8770
Fax: (914)285-1651
Reinhard E. Zachrau, M.D., Contact

Research Activities and Fields: Breast diseases, including skin window reactivity and second primary breast cancer.

★ 6087 ★ **New York University**
Kaplan Comprehensive Cancer Center
550 1st Ave.
New York, NY 10016
Phone: (212)263-5349
Fax: (212)263-8211
Vittorio Defendi, M.D., Dir.

Research Activities and Fields: Cancer research is carried out in designated program units of cancer epidemiology and prevention, cell interactions, clinical oncology, environmental carcinogenesis, genetic and molecular toxicology, growth regulation, molecular and tumor immunology, and molecular and viral oncology. **Publications:** *Kaplan Center Newsletter* (two times per year). **E-mail Address:** ira.goodman@mccm.med.nyu.edu. **Formerly:** Cancer Center (1983).

★ 6088 ★ **New York University**
Laboratory of Cancer and Radiobiological Research
754 Brown Bldg.
Washington Sq.
New York, NY 10003
Phone: (212)263-5349
Fax: (212)998-8200
Anna Goldfeder, D. SC., Dir.

Research Activities and Fields: Cancer and radiobiology, including basic studies on biological and structural properties of both normal and cancer cells and their relation to radiosensitivity and involvement of oncogenic viruses and chemical agents in neoplasia. Studies interactions of ionizing radiation, microwave-induced hyperthermia, and chemotherapy, including their effects on tumor regression in mice. Also researches detection of factors that may be involved in susceptibility or resistance to development of malignant neoplasms conducted on two inbred strains of mice, one of which is susceptible to development of malignant tumors and the other resistant, producing no malignant tumor spontaneously.

★6089★ Norris Cotton Cancer Center (NCCC)
Dartmouth-Hitchcock Medical Center
Lebanon, NH 03756
Phone: (603)650-4141
Fax: (603)650-4150
E. Robert Greenberg, M.D., Dir.

Research Activities and Fields: Clinical treatment trials, including bone marrow transplantation, intraoperative radiation therapy, hyperthermia, and monoclonal antibody treatment. Studies are conducted in the areas of tumor immunology, radiobiology, chemical carcinogenesis, cancer epidemiology, cytogenetics, tumor endocrinology, and molecular genetics. Participates as one of a group of regional clinical and nonclinical centers conducting multidisciplinary cancer research, improving methods of treatment, diagnosis, and prevention, training health professionals, and transferring cancer knowledge to surrounding communities. **Publications:** *NCCC Research Directory*; *NCCC Brochure*; *Pathfinder* (guide to local cancer resources).

★6090★ North Central Cancer Treatment Group
Operations Office
200 1st St. SW
Rochester, MN 55905
Phone: (507)284-8384
Fax: (507)284-1902
Dr. Michael J. O'Connell, Chm.

Research Activities and Fields: Cancer research and therapy, including surgery, medical oncology, therapeutic radiology, pathology, and cancer control. Seeks to transfer nationwide cancer research and therapy to patients at the community level. Group maintains a patient base of 5,000 and operates 50 separate research protocols.

★6091★ Northeast Louisiana University Cancer Research Center
700 Univ. Ave.
Monroe, LA 71209
Phone: (318)342-1819
Fax: (318)342-1824
Dr. Lawrence S. Baum, Dir.

Research Activities and Fields: Basic and applied cancer research, including epidemiology and causes of bladder, breast, prostate, myeloproliferative, and lympho-proliferative cancers.

★6092★ Northern California Cancer Center
32960 Alvarado-Niles Rd., Ste. 600
Union City, CA 94587
Phone: (510)429-2500
Fax: (510)429-2550
Dee W. West, Ph.D., Exec.Dir.

Research Activities and Fields: Conducts multidisciplinary studies in epidemiology and related fields. Also conducts cancer research and demonstration activities with communities in the Center's service area, focusing on the minority populations and the underserved. **Publications:** *Cancer Calendar* (quarterly); Estate Planning Brochure; Registry Newsletters; *Highlights* (cancer information for the public).

★6093★ Northwestern University John I. Brewer Trophoblastic Disease Center
Prentice Women's Hospital
333 E. Superior
Chicago, IL 60611
Phone: (312)503-5263
Fax: (312)908-2188
John R. Lurain, M.D., Dir.

Research Activities and Fields: Pathology, epidemiology, and experimental chemotherapy in patients with trophoblastic diseases; experimental protocols and new chemotherapeutic agents and combinations of agents; pathologic studies of choriocarcinoma and hydatidiform mole; and the effect of oral contraceptive use on the development of gestational trophoblastic diseases.

★6094★ Northwestern University Robert H. Lurie Cancer Center
Olson Pavilion 8250
303 E. Chicago Ave.
Chicago, IL 60611-3008
Phone: (312)908-5250
Fax: (312)908-1372
Steven T. Rosen, M.D., Dir.

Research Activities and Fields: The Center has six established programs. Basic science programs include 1) adhesion, motility, and angiogenesis; 2) differentiation and development; 3) hormone action and signal transduction; and 4) molecular oncogenesis. Clinical science research is conducted in the areas of 1) adult oncology and HIV-associated malignancies; and 2) pediatric oncology and cancer prevention and control research. Serves as a clinical cancer center in the National Cancer Institute's nationwide program coordinating multidisciplinary, basic, and clinical cancer research; improving methods of cancer treatment, diagnosis and prevention; training health care professionals; and transferring cancer knowledge to surrounding communities. The Center coordinates and integrates cancer research activities on Northwestern University's two campuses in Chicago and Evanston. **Publications:** *The Journal of the Robert H. Lurie Cancer Center of Northwestern University* (semiannually); *Lurie Cancer Center News and Calendar* (bimonthly); *Community Newsletter*. **E-mail Address:** str@nwu.edu.

★6095★ Ohio State University Comprehensive Cancer Center
300 W. 10th Ave.
Columbus, OH 43210
Phone: (614)293-3304
Fax: (614)293-3132
David E. Schuller, Dir.

Research Activities and Fields: Carcinogenesis, cancer chemoprevention, cancer control, immunology, developmental therapeutics, hormones and cancer, molecular biology, RNA oncogenic virus, neuro-oncology, head and neck oncology, urologic oncology, and pediatric oncology. Investigations also cover bone marrow transplantation, biochemistry and genetics, and pharmacology and toxicology. **Publications:** *Scientific Report* (biennially).

★6096★ Ohio State University Division of Hematology and Oncology
410 W. 10th Ave.
Columbus, OH 43210
Phone: (614)293-8729
Fax: (614)293-3112
Stanley P. Balcerzak, M.D., Dir.

Research Activities and Fields: Research, patient service, and training through a fellowship program on various aspects of hematology and oncology, including cancer immunology, white cell physiology, vasoactive intestinal polypeptide cross-reactive material, importance of complement in host defense against malignancy, the role of oxygen radicals in mononuclear effector cells and tumor cell targets, and clinical research in the development, implementation, and assessment of protocols in the treatment of leukemia, lymphoma, bone marrow transplantation, and solid tumors. The training program is designed to provide postdoctoral fellowship experience in the development and performance of clinical and laboratory research projects related to hematology and medical oncology.

★6097★ Ohio State University Lymphokine Research Laboratory
James Cancer Hospital and Research Institute
300 W. 10th Ave.
Columbus, OH 43210-1228
Phone: (614)293-3716
Dr. David Benjamin, Dir.

Research Activities and Fields: Molecular and cellular biology, focusing on B cell lymphokine secretion and receptor expression.

★6098★ Oklahoma Medical Research Foundation Immunology and Cancer Research Program
825 NE 13th St.
Oklahoma City, OK 73104
Phone: (405)271-6673
William G. Thurman, M.D., Pres.

Research Activities and Fields: Changes occurring in biochemical regulation of cell function during chemical carcinogenesis. Past research has dealt with the stages of rat liver cancer to develop a pathodiagnostic test for human liver cancer, including the role of the enzyme epoxide hydrolase in normal detoxification; the carcinogenic influence of acetyl aminofluorence (AAF) within liver cells; the role of promoters such as dietary fat in the carcinogenic process; movement of epoxide hydrolase from the endoplasmic reticulum into cell cytoplasm; and the development of preneoplastic nodules, tumor stage, and metastasis. **Formerly:** Cancer Research Laboratory.

★ 6099 ★ Oregon Health Sciences University
Hormone Receptor Laboratory
3181 SW Sam Jackson Park Rd., L471
Portland, OR 97201-3098
Phone: (503)494-7541
Fax: (503)494-5165
Edward Keenan, Dir.

Research Activities and Fields: Breast cancer, including tissue analyses to establish whether certain hormone receptor molecules are present in breast cancer cells and whether tumor cells are likely to depend on hormones for growth.

Palo Alto Institute of Molecular Medicine
See: Entry 2605

★ 6100 ★ Pediatric Cancer Research Laboratory
Children's Hospital of Orange County
455 S. Main St.
Orange, CA 92668
Phone: (714)532-8548
Fax: (714)532-8771
Dr. Mitchell Cairo, Dir.

Research Activities and Fields: Bone marrow transplantation, experimental hematopoiesis, molecular biology of hematopoietic growth factors, developmental neonatal hematopoiesis, and molecular oncology and lymphomas.

★ 6101 ★ Pediatric Oncology Group
Operations Office
645 N. Michigan Ave., Ste. 910
Chicago, IL 60611
Phone: (312)482-9944
Fax: (312)482-9460
Sue Giovanazzi-Bannon, Admin.

Research Activities and Fields: Investigations of childhood cancers. Provides a national cooperative mechanism to promote new treatment methods through comparison of patients who receive different treatments.

★ 6102 ★ Pittsburgh Cancer Institute
200 Meyran Ave.
Pittsburgh, PA 15213
Phone: (412)647-2072
Free: 800-537-4063
Fax: (412)621-9354
Dr. Ronald Herberman, Dir.

Research Activities and Fields: Develops interactive programs in basic and clinical cancer research; prevention, early detection, and treatment of cancer; and public and professional education. Basic research focuses on cellular, molecular, and biochemical interactions in cancer development. Clinical research examines the therapeutic effect of biological response modifiers in cancer treatment, the epidemiology of cancer and related diseases, and the effects of immunological and psychosocial factors on the natural history of cancer. **Publications:** *PCI Per-*

spectives (quarterly); *PCI Report* (bimonthly); *PCI Clinical News* (bimonthly). **Formerly:** University Health Center of Pittsburgh, Inc.

★ 6103 ★ Pohl Cancer Research Laboratory, Inc.
Georgia College C BX 082
Dept. of Chemistry & Physics
Milledgeville, GA 31061
Phone: (912)453-4565
Fax: (912)453-5271
Prof. Douglas G. Pohl, Dir.

Research Activities and Fields: Cancer research, including electroactive polymers, dielectrophoresis, biophysics, electric properties of cells, cellular response to electric fields, and cell growth and control. Applications of research include instrumentation, diagnostics, and cell fusion apparatus.

Princeton University
Department of Molecular Biology
See: Entry 2609

★ 6104 ★ Purdue University Cancer Center
Life Sciences Research Bldg.
1524 Hansen
West Lafayette, IN 47907-1524
Phone: (317)494-9129
Prof. William M. Baird, Dir.

Research Activities and Fields: Biochemical and molecular basis of tumorigenesis and malignant transformation, including multidisciplinary studies on molecular structure and drug development, experimental therapeutics and diagnostics, structural biology, cell growth and differentiation, veterinary comparative oncology, DNA sequencing, nuclear magnetic resonance, and carcinogenesis. **Publications:** Annual Summary Report; Newsletter (bimonthly).

Purdue University
William A. Hillenbrand Biomedical Engineering Center
See: Entry 2466

Radiation Oncology Research & Development Center
See: Entry 11154

Revici Foundation for Lipid Research
See: Entry 12747

★ 6105 ★ Rockefeller University Laboratory of Molecular Oncology
1230 York Ave.
New York, NY 10021-6399
Phone: (212)570-8803
Fax: (212)570-7974
Prof. Hidesaburo Hanafusa, Head

Research Activities and Fields: Mechanisms of carcinogenesis in virus-induced cancers. **Formerly:** Laboratory of Molecular Oncology.

★ 6106 ★ Roger Williams Cancer Center
Roger Williams Medical Center
825 Chalkstone Ave.
Providence, RI 02908
Phone: (401)456-2071
Fax: (401)456-2658
Mrs. Kennedy

Research Activities and Fields: Cancer research program with drug development, cancer biology, radiation biology, and clinical studies components. **Formerly:** Roger Williams Clinical Cancer Research Center.

★ 6107 ★ Roswell Park Cancer Institute
Elm & Carlton Sts.
Buffalo, NY 14263
Phone: (716)845-2300
Fax: (716)845-3545
Thomas B. Tomasi, M.D., Pres.

Research Activities and Fields: Molecular biology, biophysics, genetics, immunology, experimental therapeutics, and epidemiology of cancer, including the clinical application of recent findings in cancer research and the effectiveness of surgery, chemotherapy, and radiation in cancer therapy. Research program includes work in drug development, pharmacokinetics, crystallography, photodynamic therapy, and biological response modifiers. **Publications:** Annual Report.

Roswell Park Cancer Institute
Grace Cancer Drug Center
See: Entry 10454

★ 6108 ★ Rush Cancer Institute
Rush-Presbyterian-St. Luke's Medical Center
1725 W. Harrison St., Ste. 809
Chicago, IL 60612
Phone: (312)563-2190
Fax: (312)455-9635
Harvey D. Preisler, M.D., Dir.

Research Activities and Fields: Cancer, including biochemistry, immunology surveillance, virology, lymphomal leukemia, and psychosocial studies. Participates in the National Cancer Institute's nationwide program for coordinating multidisciplinary basic and clincial cancer research, improving methods of treatment, diagnosis, and prevention, training health professionals, and transferring cancer knowledge to surrounding communities. **Publications:** *Rush Center Institute Newsletter.* **Formerly:** Rush Cancer Center (1993).

★ 6109 ★ Rutgers University Laboratory for Cancer Research
Department of Chemical Biology and Pharmacognosy
College of Pharmacy
PO Box 789
Piscataway, NJ 08855-0789
Phone: (908)445-4940
Fax: (908)445-0687
Prof. Allan H. Conney, Dir.

Research Activities and Fields: Mechanisms of chemical carcinogenesis and mutagenesis; mechanisms of inhibition of carcinogenesis; factors influencing the metabolism and action of drugs, carcinogens, environmental chemicals and steroid hormones; regulation and biological significance of multiple cytochromes P-450; drug interactions; induced synthesis of microsomal enzymes.

St. Francis Hospital and Medical Center Department of Research
See: Entry 2616

St. Louis University Institute for Molecular Virology
See: Entry 2617

★6110★ Santa Barbara Breast Cancer Institute
116 Middle Rd., No. B
Santa Barbara, CA 93108-2460
Phone: (805)565-2244
Fax: (805)565-2246
Dr. Otto Sartorius, Pres./CEO

Research Activities and Fields: Breast cancer, including methods of detection and treatment.

★6111★ Saskatoon Cancer Centre Cancer Research Unit
20 Campus Dr.
Saskatoon, SK, Canada S7N 4H4
Phone: (306)655-2914
Fax: (306)655-2910
Dr. S.A. Carlsen, Dir.

Research Activities and Fields: Basic cancer research, including elucidation of the properties of signal transduction, oncogene expression, tumor metastasis, drug sensitivity, and genetic engineering of novel biological reagents for tumor diagnosis and therapy.

★6112★ Sherbrooke University Quebec Neuroblastoma Screening Research Group
3001, 12e Ave. Nord
Sherbrooke, PQ, Canada J1H 5N4
Phone: (819)564-5393
Fax: (819)564-5217
Bernard Lemieux, Dir.

Research Activities and Fields: Studies the clinical and biological aspects of screening infants for neuroblastoma in order to determine the effectiveness of screening and to better understand neuroblastoma biology.

★6113★ Stanford University Cancer Biology Research Laboratory
School of Medicine
CBRL
Stanford, CA 94305-5468
Phone: (415)723-7312
Fax: (415)723-7382
Dr. J. Martin Brown, Dir.

Research Activities and Fields: Human and murine cancer studies, including virologic, biologic, and immunologic characterization of several cell lines of human malignant lymphomas. Studies mechanisms and therapeutic potential of hyperthermia, and radiosensitizers and bioreductive cytotoxic agents in improving cancer cure rates.

★6114★ Stanford University Oncology Day Care Clinic
Stanford Medical Center, Rm. H0274
300 Pasteur Dr.
Stanford, CA 94305
Phone: (415)723-7621
Fax: (415)725-9113
Robert W. Carlson, M.D., Dir.

Research Activities and Fields: Lymphoma, Hodgkin's disease, breast cancer, genitourinary cancers, gynecological cancers, and new drug development.

★6115★ State University of New York Health Science Center at Brooklyn Sickle Cell Center
450 Clarkson Ave.
Box 120
Brooklyn, NY 11203
Phone: (718)270-1500
Fax: (718)270-4070
Dr. Peter Jillette, Program Dir.

Research Activities and Fields: Sickle cell disease, including studies on natural history of sickle cell disease, and genetic basis for variations in disease severity.

★6116★ Stehlin Foundation for Cancer Research
1315 Calhoun, Ste. 1818
Houston, TX 77002
Phone: (713)659-1336
Fax: (713)659-5084
John S. Stehlin, M.D., Scientific Dir.

Research Activities and Fields: Tissue culture of human cancers, transplantation of human cancers into athymic mice, experimental chemotherapy of human cancers growing in tissue culture or nude mice, investigation and development of new anticancer drugs, immunology of human cancers, effects of heat on human cancers, development and treatment of breast cancer, relationships between virus and human cancer, and rapid screening of anticancer drugs.

★6117★ Strang Cancer Prevention Center
428 E. 72nd St.
New York, NY 10021
Phone: (212)794-4900
Fax: (212)794-0749
Dr. Michael P. Osborne, Dir.

Research Activities and Fields: Prevention and cure of cancer through early detection. Conducts genetics research, epidemiology risk modelling, and cancer prevention trials. Also maintains the National High Risk Registry, a genetic research and counselling service for women with a family history of breast cancer. **Publications:** *Progressions* (newsletter); *Strang Cancer Genetics Newsletter* (newsletter).

★6118★ Syracuse Cancer Research Institute
600 E. Genesee St.
Syracuse, NY 13202
Phone: (315)472-6616
Joseph Gold, M.D., Dir.

Research Activities and Fields: Cachexia, or weight loss and debilitation as a result of cancer. Specifically studies the drug hydrazine sulfate, a chemical that acts to block the body's

chemical machinery which converts lactic acid, amino acids, and other carbon 2-5 molecules to glucose and thus depletes the normal body energy pools; and experimental combinations of chemotherapy with hydrazine sulfate and cytotoxic chemotherapeutic agents, hormones, and recombinant DNA products.

★6119★ Temple University Fels Institute for Cancer Research and Molecular Biology
School of Medicine
3420 N. Broad St., Rm. 700 MRB
Philadelphia, PA 19140
Phone: (215)707-4300
Fax: (215)707-4588
E. Premkumar Reddy, Dir.

Research Activities and Fields: Basic sciences, with emphasis on biochemical, molecular, and genetic aspects of cancer, including molecular biology, cell biology, and biochemistry. Performs cell culture media preparation and maintains a Biohazard Control and Safety Program and an Equipment Maintenance and Repair Program. **Publications:** Annual Report. **Formerly:** Fels Research Institute (1988).

★6120★ Texas A&M University Center for Cancer Biology
Alkek Institute of Biosciences and Technology
2121 W. Holcombe Blvd.
Houston, TX 77030-3303
Phone: (713)677-7522
Fax: (713)677-7512
Dr. Wallace L. McKeehan, Dir.

Research Activities and Fields: Cancer diagnosis and treatment, including cell and molecular biology, protein biochemistry, genetics, structure-function relationships and mechanisms of polypeptides (cytokines and growth factors) and the receptors that regulate cell growth and differentiation, dysfunction in normal cell growth, signal transduction at the cell membrane and intercellular and nuclear levels, and abnormal cell differentiation.

★6121★ Thomas Jefferson University Cardeza Foundation for Hematologic Research
1015 Walnut St.
Philadelphia, PA 19107
Phone: (215)955-7786
Fax: (215)955-2366
Sandor S. Shapiro, M.D., Dir.

Research Activities and Fields: Conducts basic and clinical hematologic research. Maintains a blood bank, hemophilia and sickle cell centers, and a photographic unit.

★6122★ Thompson Cancer Survival Center
1915 White Ave.
Knoxville, TN 37916
Phone: (615)541-1350
Fax: (615)541-1162
Timothy J. Panella, M.D., Dir.

Research Activities and Fields: Oncology, including phase I, II, and III trials of drug, radiation, or biology therapies and laser treatments. Center comprises the following research departments: 1) Clinical Trials; 2) Laser Photodynamic Therapy; and 3) Bone Marrow Transplant Laboratory.

★ 6123 ★ Tufts University
Baystate Medical Center
Springfield-Wesson Women's Unit
759 Chestnut St.
Springfield, MA 01199
Phone: (413)784-5252
Fax: (413)784-3613
Dr. Donald Higby, Dir.

Research Activities and Fields: Clinical research in hematology/oncology, including protocol studies in the treatment of cancers of the breast, gastrointestinal tract, lung, bladder, renal system, cervix and ovaries, and head and neck. Also studies treatment for Hodgkin's disease, leukemia, lymphomas, melanomas, and sarcomas.

U.S. Department of Defense
Armed Forces Institute of Pathology
Center for Advanced Pathology
Hematologic and Lymphatic Pathology
   Department
See: Entry 10153

U.S. Department of Defense
Armed Forces Radiobiology Research
   Institute
Experimental Hematology Department
See: Entry 11077

★ 6124 ★ U.S. Department of Energy
Lawrence Berkeley Laboratory
Life Science Division
University of California
1 Cyclotron Rd., 83-101
Berkeley, CA 94720
Phone: (510)486-4365
Fax: (510)486-5586
M.J. Bissell, Division Director

Research Activities and Fields: Cancer and DNA research.

★ 6125 ★ U.S. Department of Health and
   Human Services
National Cancer Institute
NIH Bldg. 31, Rm. 10A24
9000 Rockville Pike
Bethesda, MD 20892
Phone: (301)496-5583
Fax: (301)402-2594
Dr. Samuel Broder, Director

Research Activities and Fields: NCI has primary responsibility within the federal government for conducting and supporting cancer research. The Institute has developed a National Cancer Program to expand existing scientific knowledge on cancer cause and prevention as well as on the diagnosis, treatment, and rehabilitation of cancer patients. This program is carried out at NCI laboratories in Bethesda, MD; at the Frederick Cancer Research and Development Center in Frederick, MD; and through NCI support for programs conducted throughout the nation. NCI-awarded grants and contracts support cancer research in most of the nation's university medical centers and many other nonfederal institutions. In addition, a network of comprehensive cancer centers around the country engage in a wide range of cancer-related research and demonstration encompassing basic research, diagnosis, treatment, rehabilitation, and public and patient education. These centers

also educate and train professionals in various clinical and research specialties. Research activities conducted at NCI's laboratories or supported through grants and contracts include many investigative approaches to cancer, including research in chemistry, biochemistry, biology, molecular biology, immunology, radiation physics, experimental chemotherapy, epidemiology, biometry, radiotherapy, and pharmacology. Major components of NCI include: Cancer Biology, Diagnosis and Centers Division; Cancer Etiology Division; Cancer Prevention and Control Division; Cancer Treatment Division; and Extramural Activities Division.

★ 6126 ★ U.S. Department of Health and
   Human Services
National Cancer Institute
Chemical and Physical Carcinogenesis
   Program
Chemical and Physical Carcinogenesis
   Branch
Executive Plaza North, Ste. 700
6130 Executive Blvd.
Bethesda, MD 20892
Phone: (301)496-5471
Fax: (301)496-1040
Dr. David Longfellow, Chief

Research Activities and Fields: Branch plans, develops, directs, and manages a national extramural program of basic and applied research concerned with the occurrence and inhibition of cancer caused or promoted by chemical or physical agents, acting separately or together, or in combination with biological agents; and provides a broad spectrum of information, advice, and consultation to individual scientists and institutional science management officials relative to NIH and NCI funding and scientific review policies and procedures, preparation of grant applications, and choice of funding instruments. The Branch also: 1) provides NCI management with recommendations as to funding needs, priorities, and strategies for the support of relevant research areas consistent with the current state of development of individual research activities and the promise of new initiatives; 2) plans, develops, and manages research resources necessary for the conduct of the coordinated research program; and 3) plans, organizes, and conducts meetings and workshops to further program objectives and maintains contact with the relevant scientific community to identify and evaluate new research trends relating to its program responsibilities.

★ 6127 ★ U.S. Department of Health and
   Human Services
National Cancer Institute
Chemical and Physical Carcinogenesis
   Program
Radiation Effects Branch
Executive Plaza North, Rm. 530
9000 Rockville Pike
Bethesda, MD 20892
Phone: (301)496-9326
Fax: (301)496-1224
Bruce Wachholz, Chief

Research Activities and Fields: Mechanisms of radiation-induced mutagenesis and carcinogenesis, including supportive studies in radia-

tion chemistry, radiation physics, molecular biology, cytogenetics and cell transformation; studies of cancer among selected populations exposed to radionuclides intentionally or accidentally released into the environment.

★ 6128 ★ U.S. Department of Health and
   Human Services
National Cancer Institute
Division of Cancer Biology, Diagnosis, and
   Centers
NIH Bldg. 31
9000 Rockville Pike
Bethesda, MD 20892
Phone: (301)496-4345
Fax: (301)496-0775
Dr. Alan S. Rabson, Director

Research Activities and Fields: Division serves as the national focal point for programs to improve the detection and diagnosis of human cancers. It is broadly concerned with biochemical, genetic, physiologic, immunologic, and metabolic derangements that predispose organisms to neoplasia and that result from neoplasia. Within this area, a wide variety of research interests are pursued that involve basic questions of immunology, virology, molecular biology, and biochemistry of normal and pathologic states. Research activities are carried out through three main programs: Extramural Research Program, Intramural Research Program, and Centers, Training and Resources Program.

★ 6129 ★ U.S. Department of Health and
   Human Services
National Cancer Institute
Division of Cancer Biology, Diagnosis, and
   Centers
Cancer Centers Branch
6130 Executive Blvd., Rm. 502
Bethesda, MD 20892
Phone: (301)496-8531
Fax: (301)402-0181
Margaret E. Holmes, Ph.D., Chief

Research Activities and Fields: Branch supports multidisciplinary cancer research efforts, training, education, and detection; demonstrates advanced methods of cancer treatment and care. The Centers are engaged in basic, clinical, and cancer control research. Cancer Center Support Grant (CCSG) is intended to contribute stability and development and facilitate administrative and programmatic control of center activities. The CCSG provides funds for salaries of selected staff, operation of centrally shared resources and services, and administration of the center. CCSG may provide developmental funding for investigators who have not previously had funded grants and/or newly recruited investigators, interim research support for investigators of the center, new shared resources and pilot projects. A secondary funding mechanism is the Consortium Cancer Center Support Grant (CCCSG). The primary intent of this program is to stimulate and facilitate development of research in cancer control by encouraging the formation of an effective consortium among regional public health agencies such as city, county, or state health departments and other organizations with competence in disease control research, such as universities, cancer centers, centers for the study of the control of other diseases, health maintenance organizations, private foundations, and community based organizations. Program provides support for the development of a cancer control research program relevant to the populations in the region in which the consortium is formed. The grant supports planning and advisory committees, an administrative core, senior leadership, and shared resources and services. The grant provides developmental funds for recruitment of qualified researchers, interim research support for investigators of the Centers, and for new shared resources. The program currently supports 57 cancer centers located throughout the U.S. These are classified as: Basic (centers engaged only in laboratory research); Clinical (centers engaged only in clinical research); and Cancer Research Centers (centers engaged in both laboratory and clinical research).

★6130★ U.S. Department of Health and Human Services
National Cancer Institute
Division of Cancer Biology, Diagnosis, and Centers
Cancer Diagnosis Branch
Executive Plaza N., Rm. 513
Rockville, MD 20892
Phone: (301)496-1591
Fax: (301)402-1037
Dr. Sheila E. Taube, Chief

Research Activities and Fields: Branch emphasizes research on early detection, diagnosis (including staging, grading, and prognosis), and monitoring of changes during therapy or progression of disease. Projects in these areas are frequently concerned with improvement of existing techniques as well as the development of new tests and procedures. Supports research in the areas of immunodiagnosis, pathology/cytology, and biochemistry and genetics.

★6131★ U.S. Department of Health and Human Services
National Cancer Institute
Division of Cancer Biology, Diagnosis, and Centers
Cancer Immunology Branch
Executive Plaza N., Rm. 501
6130 Executive Blvd.
Rockville, MD 20892
Phone: (301)496-7815
Fax: (301)496-8656
John A. Sogn, Ph.D., Chief

Research Activities and Fields: Branch supports a broad spectrum of basic research in molecular immunology and cellular immunology, with special emphasis on understanding the role of the immune system in the development, growth, and spread of tumors as it relates to the problems of cause, prevention, treatment, and diagnosis of malignant diseases.

★6132★ U.S. Department of Health and Human Services
National Cancer Institute
Division of Cancer Biology, Diagnosis, and Centers
Dermatology Branch

NIH Bldg. 10, Rm. 12N238
9000 Rockville Pike
Bethesda, MD 20892
Phone: (301)496-2481
Dr. Stephen Katz, Chief

Research Activities and Fields: Branch studies the growth and differentiation of epithelium and lymphoreticular tissues in normal, hyperplastic, neoplastic, and inflammatory states; protein synthesis by epithelium, especially of tonofilaments, keratohaylin, and actin; immunologic determinants of tissue behavior in normal and neoplastic states; immunologic abnormalities in blistering diseases of the skin; physiology of lymphoreticular cells and lymphokine formation; and the biological activity of oncogenic viruses. Also studied are experimental allergic contact dermatitis; genodermatoses; biochemistry and keratinization; xeroderma pigmentosum, an inherited disease of sun sensitivity, and multiple cutaneous cancer with abnormal DNA repair; clinical, chemical, and ultrastructural effects of vitamin A on skin; the oncogenic potential of tumor viruses; and the development of therapy of epithelial cancers, skin lymphomas, and keratinizing diseases of the skin.

★6133★ U.S. Department of Health and Human Services
National Cancer Institute
Division of Cancer Biology, Diagnosis, and Centers
Extramural Research Program
6130 Executive Blvd., Ste. 500
Rockville, MD 20892
Phone: (301)496-8636
Fax: (301)496-8656
Faye C. Austin, Ph.D., Associate Director

Research Activities and Fields: Program provides coordination and support for research activities relating to basic tumor biology and immunology, and cancer detection and diagnosis. Principal components are the Cancer Biology Branch, Cancer Diagnosis Branch, and Cancer Immunology Branch. **Publications:** Annual Report.

★6134★ U.S. Department of Health and Human Services
National Cancer Institute
Division of Cancer Biology, Diagnosis, and Centers
Intramural Research Program
NIH Bldg. 31, Rm. 3A03
9000 Rockville Pike
Bethesda, MD 20892
Phone: (301)496-4345
Fax: (301)496-0775
Alan S. Rabson, M.D., Director

Research Activities and Fields: Program comprises branches for Dermatology, Immunology, and Metabolism and laboratories for studies in biochemistry, cell biology, cellular oncology, genetics, immunobiology, mathematical biology, molecular biology, pathology, and tumor immunology and biology.

★6135★ U.S. Department of Health and Human Services
National Cancer Institute
Division of Cancer Biology, Diagnosis, and Centers
Metabolism Branch
NIH Bldg. 10, Rm. 4N115
9000 Rockville Pike
Bethesda, MD 20892
Phone: (301)496-6653
Fax: (301)496-9956
Dr. Thomas A. Waldmann, Chief

Research Activities and Fields: Branch carries out clinical investigations aimed at: 1) performing molecular analyses of lymphocyte development and function, including purification of transactivating factors and the genes that encode them; 2) developing gene therapy for treatment of human disease; 3) developing applications to vaccine design for AIDS and cancer; 4) characterizing the multisubunit IL-2 receptor and developing its use as a target for immunotherapy using humanized monoclonal antibodies armed with toxins and alpha and beta emitting radionuclides; 5) studying the arrangement of immunoglobulin and T-cell antigen receptor genes in normal and neoplastic cells; and 6) evaluating biochemical events that accompany cell growth and the hormonal control of this growth as it related to the study of malignancies.

★6136★ U.S. Department of Health and Human Services
National Cancer Institute
Division of Cancer Biology, Diagnosis, and Centers Extramural Research Program
Cancer Biology Branch
6130 Executive Blvd., Rm. 505
Rockville, MD 20892
Phone: (301)496-7028
Fax: (301)402-1037
Colette S. Freeman, Ph.D., Chief

Research Activities and Fields: Branch supports a broad spectrum of basic biological research aimed at defining elements of the phenotype of the malignant cell through interdisciplinary approaches. Areas of emphasis include both positive and negative regulation of cell growth and differentiation, mechanisms involved in the process of metastasis, the influence of the extracellular environment on the tumor cell, and the molecular genetics of cancer cells.

★6137★ U.S. Department of Health and Human Services
National Cancer Institute
Division of Cancer Etiology
NIH Bldg. 3l, Rm. 11A03
9000 Rockville Pike
Bethesda, MD 20892
Phone: (301)496-6618
Dr. Richard Adamson, Director

Research Activities and Fields: Division plans and directs a program of laboratory, field, and epidemiologic research on the cause and natural history of cancer and means for preventing cancer, through direct in-house research and through research contracts; evaluates mechanisms of cancer induction by viruses and by environmental carcinogenic hazards; serves as the focal point for the federal government on the synthesis of clinical, epidemiological, and experimental data relating to the causes of cancer; and advises the Institute Director on basic research activities as they relate to cancer cause and prevention. Division is organized under programs for Biological Carcinogenesis, Chemical and Physical Carcinogenesis, and Epidemiology and Biostatistics.

★6138★ **U.S. Department of Health and Human Services**
National Cancer Institute
Division of Cancer Etiology
Biological Carcinogenesis Program
NIH Bldg. 41, Rm. A100
Bethesda, MD 20892
Phone: (301)496-4241
Edward Tabor, M.D., Associate Director

Research Activities and Fields: Program includes six intramural laboratories and one extramural branch devoted to the study of viral causes of cancer and the role of oncogenes in carcinogenesis. Research includes studies of human immunodeficiency virus (HIV); simian immunodeficiency virus (SIV); human T-cell lymphotropic virus type I (HTLV-I); papillomaviruses; and oncogenes. Program also includes a laboratory devoted to research on hepatocellular carcinoma and the hepatitis viruses.

★6139★ **U.S. Department of Health and Human Services**
National Cancer Institute
Division of Cancer Etiology
Epidemiology and Biostatistics Program
Executive Plaza North, Rm. 543
Bethesda, MD 20892
Phone: (301)496-1611
Fax: (301)402-3256
Dr. Joseph F. Fraumeni, Jr., Director

Research Activities and Fields: Program provides the focus for epidemiologic and biostatistical research within NCI into the causes of cancer. Activities involve: 1) conducting intramural and collaborative research into the environmental and host determinants of cancer; 2) analyzing the natural history of cancer and the efficacy of preventive measures; and 3) designing statistical methods for clinical and experimental investigations. Program comprises branches for Biostatistics, Clinical Epidemiology, Environmental Epidemiology, Extramural Programs, and Radiation Epidemiology.

★6140★ **U.S. Department of Health and Human Services**
National Cancer Institute
Division of Cancer Prevention and Control
NIH Bldg. 31, Rm. 10A52
9000 Rockville Pike
Bethesda, MD 20892-3100
Phone: (301)496-6616
Fax: (301)496-9931
Dr. Peter Greenwald, Director

Research Activities and Fields: Division is responsible for clinical trials and intervention research in cancer prevention and control. Emphasis is on: 1) prevention of cancer through clinical and laboratory nutrition and smoking cessation research programs; 2) cancer control science research, development, and training; and 3) establishment and fostering of communi-

ty oncology resources. Division comprises programs for Cancer Control Science, Cancer Prevention Research, Early Detection and Community Oncology, and Surveillance.

★6141★ **U.S. Department of Health and Human Services**
National Cancer Institute
Division of Cancer Prevention and Control
Cancer Control Science Program
9000 Rockville Pike
Bethesda, MD 20892
Phone: (301)496-8675
Thomas J. Glynn, Ph.D., Acting Director

Research Activities and Fields: The purpose of the Cancer Control Science Program is to: develop, support, and monitor applied research directed toward facilitating the widespread use of proven health promotion and other cancer prevention and management techniques by health professionals, patients and their families, populations at elevated risk, and the general public; monitor basic and clinical research activities in order to identify new interventions that will reduce cancer rates in populations and to facilitate research on their application; provide training opportunities for research and/or application of cancer prevention and management interventions; establish program priorities, allocate resources, and integrate the projects of the various participating branches; and provide programmatic and consultative support to other divisional, institute, governmental, and private sector organizations that facilitate the application of proven cancer control interventions in populations. Program comprises branches for Cancer Control Applications, Health Promotion Science, and Special Population Studies. (A fourth unit, the Cancer Training Branch, no longer exists.) **Additional Contact Information:** Program office is located at Executive Plaza North, Rm. 243, 6130 Executive Blvd., Rockville, MD 20852.

★6142★ **U.S. Department of Health and Human Services**
National Cancer Institute
Division of Cancer Prevention and Control
Cancer Prevention Research Program
9000 Rockville Pike
Bethesda, MD 20892
Phone: (301)496-8567
Fax: (301)402-0553
Dr. Winfred Malone, Acting Associate Director

Research Activities and Fields: Activities involve studies in: cancer detection to determine which techniques for early detection of cancer can reduce morbidity and mortality from cancer; chemoprevention research to determine whether selected micronutrients or synthetic compounds can be shown in human trials to reduce cancer incidence; and diet and cancer research to determine whether changes in the diet can be shown to reduce cancer incidence in human trials. Principal components are the Cancer Prevention Studies Branch, Chemoprevention Branch, Diet and Cancer Branch, and Nutrition and Cancer Research Laboratory (9000 Rockville Pike, Bethesda, MD 20892). **Additional Contact Information:** Program office is located at Executive Plaza North, Rm. 200, 6130 Executive Blvd., Rockville, MD 20852.

★6143★ **U.S. Department of Health and Human Services**
National Cancer Institute
Division of Cancer Prevention and Control
Cancer Prevention Studies Branch
Executive Plaza North, Rm. 211
9000 Rockville Pike
Bethesda, MD 20892-4200
Phone: (301)496-8559
Fax: (301)402-0553
Philip R. Taylor, M.D., Sc.D., Director

Research Activities and Fields: Overall objective of the Branch is to identify, develop, and test hypotheses relevant to cancer control. It conducts intramural research in the areas of diet, nutrition, and cancer; genetics and cancer; cancer chemoprevention; and other cancer prevention strategies aimed at lowering human cancer risk. Current focus is on nutrition, primarily through development of prevention trials. Research includes studies in cancer epidemiology, clinical nutrition, and genetic epidemiology; and development of cancer prevention trials and epidemiologic methods.

★6144★ **U.S. Department of Health and Human Services**
National Cancer Institute
Division of Cancer Prevention and Control
Chemoprevention Branch
Executive Plaza North, Rm. 201
Bethesda, MD 20892
Phone: (301)496-8566
Fax: (301)402-0553
Winfred F. Malone, Ph.D., Chief

Research Activities and Fields: Chemoprevention involves the study and development of selected micronutrients or other small molecular weight substances into the diet for the purposes of reducing cancer incidence. Research has focused on identifying or demonstrating (in animal models, epidemiological studies, and human clinical trials) natural or synthetic agents that can lower cancer incidence. Activities include 68 ongoing clinical trails nationally and internationally with 200,000 subjects. Also develops drugs.

★6145★ **U.S. Department of Health and Human Services**
National Cancer Institute
Division of Cancer Prevention and Control
Early Detection and Community Oncology Program
Executive Plaza North, Rm. 300
6130 Executive Blvd.
Rockville, MD 20892
Phone: (301)496-0265
Fax: (301)496-8667
Dr. Barnett S. Kramer, Associate Director

Research Activities and Fields: The Program supports research resources and activities of cancer centers and scientific investigations to improve cancer treatment, rehabilitation, and continuing care. EDCOP encourages collaboration and transfer of technology and information among cancer centers, community hospitals, physicians, and other health professionals; seeks ways to enhance the efforts of centers and community resources to advance cancer control; and stimulates integrated research, both basic and clinical, for specific cancers (breast, large bowel, pancreas, prostate, and urinary bladder). Support of Community programs generating basic and clinical data about cancer and accelerates transfer of knowledge to health professionals and to the general public. In the areas of treatment, continuing care, and rehabilitation, EDCOP supports comparative and demonstration research on effective techniques, procedures, and protocols that have specific applicability to physical, cosmetic, functional, social, and psychological problems related to cancer. Program comprises the Cancer Centers Branch, Community Oncology and Rehabilitation Branch, and Research Facilities Branch. Also conducts and supports research in screening technologies through population-based studies and in the Laboratory.

★6146★ U.S. Department of Health and Human Services
National Cancer Institute
Division of Cancer Prevention and Control
Health Education Section
9000 Rockville Pike
Bethesda, MD 20892
Phone: (301)496-8585
Fax: (301)496-8675
Dr. Suzanne G. Haynes, Chief

Research Activities and Fields: Section is responsible for the development, implementation, and evaluation of an extramural research program aimed at reducing risk factors for cancer and increasing early detection of cancer.

★6147★ U.S. Department of Health and Human Services
National Cancer Institute
Division of Cancer Prevention and Control
Special Population Studies Branch
9000 Rockville Pike
Bethesda, MD 20892
Phone: (301)496-8589
Fax: (301)496-8675
Dr. George A. Alexander, Chief

Research Activities and Fields: Cancer prevention and control in special populations.

★6148★ U.S. Department of Health and Human Services
National Cancer Institute
Division of Cancer Prevention and Control
Surveillance Program
9000 Rockville Pike
Bethesda, MD 20892
Phone: (301)496-8506
Fax: (301)496-8673
Dr. Brenda K. Edwards, Associate Director

Research Activities and Fields: Program activities include data collection, analysis, and evaluation to track and study the impact of cancer and monitor the effects of cancer prevention and control activities in research, prevention, screening, treatment, and rehabilitation. Program also provides application research support for a broad range of activities in the Cancer Prevention and Control Division. Principal areas of interest are incidence, survival, and mortality of cancer in the United States as monitored through the Surveillance, Epidemiology, and End Results (SEER) Program; health behavior and chemical practice patterns; economics of cancer; and cancer control resources alloca-

tions. Program comprises branches for Computer Systems, Career Statistics, and Applied Research. **Publications:** *Annual Cancer Statistics Review.* **Additional Contact Information:** Program is located at Executive Plaza North, Rm. 343, 6130 Executive Blvd., Rockville, MD 20852.

★6149★ U.S. Department of Health and Human Services
National Cancer Institute
Division of Cancer Treatment
NIH Bldg. 3I, 3A44
9000 Rockville Pike
Bethesda, MD 20892
Phone: (301)496-4291
Fax: (301)496-0826
Dr. Bruce A. Chabner, Director

Research Activities and Fields: Division plans, directs, and coordinates an integrated program of cancer treatment activities with the objective of curing or controlling cancer in man by utilizing combination modalities (including chemical, surgical, radiological, and certain immunological techniques); administers a total drug development program; and serves as the national focal point for information and data on cancer treatment studies. Major division components are: 1) the Biological Response Modifiers Program; 2) Cancer Therapy Evaluation Program; 3) Clinical Oncology Program; 4) Developmental Therapeutics Program; and 5) Radiation Research Program.

★6150★ U.S. Department of Health and Human Services
National Cancer Institute
Division of Cancer Treatment
Biological Resources Branch
Frederick Cancer Research and Development Center, Bldg. 426
Frederick, MD 21701
Phone: (301)698-1098
Fax: (301)698-5429
Dr. Stephen Creckmore, Chief

Research Activities and Fields: Branch is an extramural program that supports, through a balanced program of grants and contracts, preclinical and clinical biological response modifiers research in the biomedical community. The Branch monitors Phase I and early Phase II clinical studies that assess biological effects of biological response modifiers in cancer patients and correlate changes in the biological modifications with antitumor activity. In addition, Branch has established a preclinical screening program for the selection and preclinical assessment of the efficacy of biological response modifiers. A resource distribution system involving information acquisition and assessment as well as agent acquisition and testing has also been established.

★6151★ U.S. Department of Health and Human Services
National Cancer Institute
Division of Cancer Treatment
Biological Response Modifiers Program

Frederick Cancer Research and Development Center
Bldg. 576, Rm. 100
Frederick, MD 21702-1201
Phone: (301)846-1416
Fax: (301)846-5651
Dr. Dan Longo, Director

Research Activities and Fields: Comprehensive program with both extramural and intramural programs to investigate, develop, and bring to clinical trials biological therapeutic agents that may alter host responses or have direct effects on cancer growth and metastasis. The intramural research program focuses on basic research studies of the immunologic, biochemical, and molecular biological basis for the effects of biological response modifiers (BRMs) as well as on clinical investigations of promising BRMs. Current emphasis is on preclinical and clinical studies with cytokines (interferons, interleukins 1, 2 and colony-stimulating factors, and tumor cytotoxic factors), monoclonal antibodies to tumor-associated antigens, and cell-mediated immunity (particularly T cell, natural killer cells, and macrophages). The extramural research program is primarily concerned with the identification and characterization of BRMs that may be useful in the therapy of patients with cancer. Potentially useful agents are evaluated extensively in appropriate preclinical test systems. BRMs with potent immunomodulatory activity and antitumor activity in murine tumor models are evaluated further in phase I and II clinical trials to determine biological response modifying effects, therapeutic efficacy, and toxicity. Current clinical trials include studies with interferons, interleukin 2, and other cytokines, and monoclonal antibodies alone or conjugated with radioisotopes or toxins. The extramural program is supervised by the Biological Resources Branch; intramural components of BRMP are the Biochemical Physiology Laboratory, Clinical Research Branch, Experimental Immunology Laboratory, Molecular Immunoregulation Laboratory, Leukocyte Biology Laboratory, and Immune Cell Biology Laboratory.

★6152★ U.S. Department of Health and Human Services
National Cancer Institute
Division of Cancer Treatment
Biometric Research Branch
Executive Plaza North, Rm. 739
Bethesda, MD 20892
Phone: (301)496-4836
Fax: (301)402-0560
Dr. Richard Simon, Chief

Research Activities and Fields: Branch is the statistical component of the Cancer Treatment Division. It develops and evaluates clinical and biological data relating to cancer treatment.

★6153★ U.S. Department of Health and Human Services
National Cancer Institute
Division of Cancer Treatment
Cancer Therapy Evaluation Program
742 Executive Plaza North
Bethesda, MD 20892
Phone: (301)496-6138
Fax: (301)402-0084
Dr. Michael A. Friedman, Associate Director

Research Activities and Fields: The Cancer Therapy Evaluation Program (CTEP) is responsible for the administration and coordination of the majority of the extramural clinical trials supported by the Cancer Treatment Division. These programs include the activities of the clinical cooperative groups, the Phase I and Phase II drug development contractors, and the holders of investigator-initiated grants relating to cancer treatment. (Certain programs in developmental radiotherapy, such as high LET radiation, are administered in the Radiation Research Program; and the Phase I development of biologic response modifiers is handled by the Biological Response Modifiers Program.) Principal components of CTEP are: 1) the Biometric Research Branch, 2) Clinical Investigations Branch, 3) Investigational Drug Branch, and 4) the Regulatory Affairs Branch.

★ 6154 ★ **U.S. Department of Health and Human Services**
National Cancer Institute
Division of Cancer Treatment
Clinical Investigations Branch
Executive Plaza North, Rm. 741
Bethesda, MD 20892
Phone: (301)496-6056
Fax: (301)496-0557
Dr. Richard Ungerleider, Chief

Research Activities and Fields: Branch is responsible for the scientific administration of the national cooperative clinical trials groups, and portfolios of investigator-initiated (traditional and program project) grants in the medical oncology, pediatric oncology, and surgical oncology programs.

★ 6155 ★ **U.S. Department of Health and Human Services**
National Cancer Institute
Division of Cancer Treatment
Clinical Oncology Program
NIH Bldg. 10, Rm. 12N214
9000 Rockville Pike
Bethesda, MD 20892
Phone: (301)496-4251
Fax: (301)496-9962
Dr. Gregory A. Curt, Acting Associate Director

Research Activities and Fields: The Clinical Oncology Program is the intramural treatment-research arm of the National Cancer Institute. It comprises branches for: Clinical Pharmacology, Medicine, NCI-Navy Medical Oncology, Pediatrics, Radiation Oncology, and Surgery.

★ 6156 ★ **U.S. Department of Health and Human Services**
National Cancer Institute
Division of Cancer Treatment
Clinical Research Branch
Frederick Memorial Hospital
Frederick, MD 21701
Phone: (301)846-1520
Fax: (301)846-1436

Research Activities and Fields: Branch is responsible for the clinical testing of biological therapies, their integration with other modalities of cancer treatment, and the correlation of in vitro parameters of immune stimulation with in vivo antitumor effects.

★ 6157 ★ **U.S. Department of Health and Human Services**
National Cancer Institute
Division of Cancer Treatment
Developmental Therapeutics Program
Bethesda, MD 20892
Phone: (301)496-8720
Fax: (301)402-0831
Dr. Michael R. Grever, Associate Director

Research Activities and Fields: The Developmental Therapeutics Program has primary operational responsibility for all aspects of the preclinical discovery and development of anticancer and anti-HIV agents for the Cancer Treatment Division, particularly chemotherapy. It comprises both extramural and intramural elements. The extramural component includes nine branches: 1) Antiviral Evaluating Branch; 2) Biological Testing Branch; 3) Drug Synthesis and Chemistry Branch; 4) Grants and Contracts Operations Branch; 5) Information Technology Branch; 6) Natural Products Branch; 7) Pharmaceutical Resources Branch; 8) Pharmacology Branch; and 9) Toxicology Branch. The intramural program includes laboratories for Biological Chemistry, Drug Discovery Research and Development, Medicinal Chemistry, Molecular Pharmacology, and Pharmaceutical Chemistry. Program is responsible for all preclinical phases of development, including acquisition and synthesis of materials, screening, production of diverse products, pharmaceutical development, toxicology, and pharmacology.

★ 6158 ★ **U.S. Department of Health and Human Services**
National Cancer Institute
Division of Cancer Treatment
Diagnostic Imaging Research Branch
Executive Plaza North, Rm. 800
6130 Executive Blvd.
Rockville, MD 20892
Phone: (301)496-9531
Fax: (301)480-5785
Roger Powell, Program Director

Research Activities and Fields: Branch is responsible for both the stimulation of research in need-determined areas and the administration of grants, contracts, and cooperative agreements in support of development and evaluation of radiologic diagnostic imaging systems and related technology, including instrumentation and methodology to improve diagnosis of cancer and other diseases. This includes rapidly developing nonionizing modalities such as magnetic resonance imaging (MRI), diaphanography, and ultrasound as well as improvements in X-ray computed tomography (CT), digital radiography, positron emission tomography (PET), single photon emission computed tomography (SPECT), and other research in nuclear medicine and nuclide imaging such as the diagnostic applications of radio-labeled monoclonal antibodies.

★ 6159 ★ **U.S. Department of Health and Human Services**
National Cancer Institute
Division of Cancer Treatment
Investigational Drug Branch

Executive Plaza North, Rm. 715
Bethesda, MD 20892
Phone: (301)496-5223
Fax: (301)402-0428
David R. Parkinson, M.D., Chief

Research Activities and Fields: Develops new investigational drugs by sponsoring clinical trials to evaluate their pharmacology, toxicities, and efficacy. Activities focus on: 1) obtaining Investigational New Drug exemption (IND) authorization from the Food and Drug Administration; 2) managing and monitoring Phase I trials of new agents developed by the Division of Cancer Treatment ; 3) developing and implementing a plan for Phase II trials in specific tumor types and monitoring the results of these clinical trials; 4) developing and implementing, in collaboration with the Clinical Investigations Branch of CTEP, Phase III trials in selected areas of promising activity observed in Phase II; 5) meeting FDA regulatory requirements for all active INDs in collaboration with CTEP's Regulatory Affairs Branch; and 6) distributing investigational new drugs.

★ 6160 ★ **U.S. Department of Health and Human Services**
National Cancer Institute
Division of Cancer Treatment
Medicine Branch
NIH Bldg. 10, Rm. 12N226
9000 Rockville Pike
Bethesda, MD 20892
Phone: (301)496-4916
Dr. Richard Wittes, M.D., Chief

Research Activities and Fields: Branch is an adult medical oncology unit with clinical programs emphasizing the broad area of internal medicine as related to cancer. Clinical emphasis is given to the diagnosis, staging, and treatment of Hodgkin's disease, malignant lymphomas, breast cancer, ovarian carcinoma, sarcomas, melanoma, AIDS/Kaposi's Sarcoma, chronic leukemias, and testicular carcinoma. The research program focuses on the general areas of drug resistance and cytogenetics of neoplastic and hemopoietic cells, tumor immunology, and the biochemical pharmacology of antineoplastic agents. A collaborative effort with the Clinical Pharmacology Branch and other groups concerned with pharmacokinetics is maintained. In addition, an active research program is in progress in the fields of hormone receptors and the molecular biology of hormone action.

★ 6161 ★ **U.S. Department of Health and Human Services**
National Cancer Institute
Division of Cancer Treatment
NCI-Navy Medical Oncology Branch
Bldg. 8, Rm. 5101
Naval Hospital-Bethesda
Bethesda, MD 20889-5105
Phone: (301)496-0901
Fax: (301)496-0047
Dr. Carmen Allegra, Chief

Research Activities and Fields: Located across the street from the National Institutes of Health at the Naval Hospital in Bethesda, the NCI-Navy Medical Oncology Branch maintains close ties and collaboration with the NIH community. Major goals of the Branch are to develop new modes of detection, staging, and treatment of human cancers by integrating clinical and laboratory research with an emphasis on understanding the fundamental biology of human tumor cells and applying these lessons to the clinic. By combining the most recent techniques of cellular and molecular biology with innovative clinical treatment studies, entering patients into other NCI protocols, and providing clinical care to Department of Defense patients for the Naval Hospital, the Branch represents a unique resource to both the National Cancer Institute and the Naval Hospital. The Branch is concerned with the primary care and clinical investigation of patients with a variety of solid tumors and hematologic malignancies. A major effort involves the staging and treatment of carcinoma of the breast, lung, and gastrointestinal tract. Performs chemotherapeutic protocols. In addition, treatment protocols built around discoveries in the cell biology and molecular genetics laboratories are underway for mycosis fungoides (and other cutaneous T-cell lymphomas), Hodgkin's and non-Hodgkin's lymphoma, testicular carcinoma, and breast cancer.

★6162★ U.S. Department of Health and Human Services
National Cancer Institute
Division of Cancer Treatment
Pediatric Branch
NIH Bldg. 10, Rm. 13N240
9000 Rockville Pike
Bethesda, MD 20892
Phone: (301)496-4256
Fax: (301)402-0575
Dr. Philip Pizzo, Chief

Research Activities and Fields: Conducts clinical and laboratory research activities related to acute leukemias, non-Hodgkin's malignant lymphomas (especially Burkitt's lymphoma), soft-tissue sarcomas, osteogenic sarcoma, Ewing's sarcoma, neuroblastoma, and children with HIV infection. Children and adolescents are accepted for treatment. Three areas of clinical investigations are stressed: chemotherapy with new or established agents; and diagnostic and preventive techniques applicable to the infectious complications of the compromised host. Specific therapies in the neoplasms studied are designed to effect maximal reduction of the malignant cell population by chemical, surgical, and/or radiotherapeutic means, followed by experimental manipulation to prolong remission. The infectious disease program designs diagnostic and preventive maneuvers to reduce the significant morbidity and mortality of infectious complications in the compromised patient. In addition to clinical research, Branch has strong programs in: basic laboratory investigation, with emphasis on the cell and molecular biology of pediatric neoplasms (particularly neuroblastoma and sarcomas); clinical pharmacology and pharmacokinetics; tumor immunology; leukocyte physiology; and immunoregulation. The Branch also has a major program in the treatment of children with AIDS.

★6163★ U.S. Department of Health and Human Services
National Cancer Institute
Division of Cancer Treatment
Radiation Oncology Branch
NIH Bldg. 10, Rm. B3B69
9000 Rockville Pike
Bethesda, MD 20892
Phone: (301)496-5457
Fax: (301)480-5439
Dr. Paul Okunieff, Chief

Research Activities and Fields: Activities of the Radiation Oncology Branch include clinical investigation of cancer treatment using X-ray technology; and laboratory investigation of radiobiology of human tumor cell lines, mechanisms of action of various compounds and their effects on radiosensitization/radioprotection, and phototherapy and radioimmunoglobulin for prescriptions. Emphasis is on radiation sensitizing compounds, radioprotecting compounds, intraoperative irradiation, and atypical fractionation schemes. Areas of investigation include primary breast cancer, carcinoma of the bladder, small cell carcinoma of the lung, lymphoma, Hodgkin's disease, gliomas, mycosis fungoides, soft tissue sarcomas, and pediatric neoplasms.

★6164★ U.S. Department of Health and Human Services
National Cancer Institute
Division of Cancer Treatment
Radiation Research Program
Executive Plaza N., Rm. 800
6130 Executive Blvd.
Rockville, MD 20852
Phone: (301)496-6111
Eli Glatstein, M.D., Acting Associate Director

Research Activities and Fields: The mission of the Radiation Research Program is to plan, develop, administer, and evaluate research in the diagnosis, staging, treatment, and post-treatment evaluation of the cancer patient for whom radiation and related forms of energy are used. It is an extramural radiation research program which establishes program priorities, allocates resources, maintains project integration, evaluates program effectiveness, and represents the program area in the management and scientific decision-making processes of the National Cancer Institute. This requires the coordination of research program activities with related programs elsewhere at NCI and NIH, with other federal agencies, and with national and international research organizations. The Program's branches are Diagnostic Imaging Research and Radiotherapy Development.

★6165★ U.S. Department of Health and Human Services
National Cancer Institute
Division of Cancer Treatment
Radiotherapy Development Branch
Executive Plaza North, Ste. 803F
6130 Executive Blvd., Rm. 800
Rockville, MD 20852
Phone: (301)496-9360
Francis J. Mahoney, Ph.D., Acting Chief

Research Activities and Fields: Branch administers a program of basic and clinical research related to cancer treatment. The scientific disciplines represented are radiation oncolo-

gy, radiobiology, radiation chemistry, and radiation physics. Major areas of research in terms of funding are particle radiotherapy (photons, electrons, and particles), hyperthermia, radiation modifiers, radioimmunotherapy, radiobiology, expert systems, and radiation physics.

★6166★ U.S. Department of Health and Human Services
National Cancer Institute
Division of Cancer Treatment
Surgery Branch
NIH Bldg. 10, Rm. 2B42
9000 Rockville Pike
Bethesda, MD 20892
Phone: (301)496-4164
Dr. Steven Rosenberg, Chief

Research Activities and Fields: Branch is a surgical oncology unit emphasizing a combined modality approach to the treatment of solid tumors and a broad program of laboratory research in cancer. A wide variety of malignancies are studied, including melanomas, sarcomas, rectal cancer, breast carcinoma, pancreatic cancers, and head and neck cancers. The Branch investigates the use of adjuvant chemotherapy and immunotherapy and develops surgical techniques. Laboratory efforts of the Surgery Branch are closely related to its clinical activities and include programs in tumor immunology and surgical metabolism. Branch staff also serve as general surgeons to the entire National Institutes of Health and provide a variety of general surgical consultations not necessarily related to the field of cancer medicine.

★6167★ U.S. Department of Health and Human Services
National Cancer Institute
Epidemiology and Biostatistics Program
Biostatistics Branch
EPN-431
Bethesda, MD 20892
Phone: (301)496-4153
Fax: (301)402-0081
William J. Blot, Ph.D., Chief

Research Activities and Fields: Branch uses biometric and mathematical approaches to investigate the distribution, causes, and natural history of cancer. New statistical methods are developed for designing and analyzing epidemiologic, clinical, and experimental studies of cancer. Mathematical models are explored to clarify processes of cancer biology and carcinogenesis and improve methods of quantitative cancer risk assessment.

★6168★ U.S. Department of Health and Human Services
National Cancer Institute
Epidemiology and Biostatistics Program
Clinical Epidemiology Branch
EPN-400
Bethesda, MD 20892
Phone: (301)496-5785
Fax: (301)496-1854
Dr. Robert W. Miller, Chief

Research Activities and Fields: Activities of the Clinical Epidemiology Branch include: 1) development of new concepts about cancer etiology from bedside observations of cancer patients and from clinical studies of families and community and occupational groups and correlation of these results with laboratory findings; 2) studies of the late effects of childhood cancer and the therapy of childhood cancer; 3) operation of a clinic dealing with the genetics of human cancer to evaluate factors affecting risk of specific types of cancer such as neurofibromatosis; and 4) preparation of analytical reviews to define current status and future prospects for research in specific areas of clinical epidemiology.

★6169★ U.S. Department of Health and
     Human Services
National Cancer Institute
Epidemiology and Biostatistics Program
Environmental Epidemiology Branch
6130 Executive Bldg., Rm. 443
Rockville, MD 20892
Phone: (301)496-1691
Fax: (301)496-9146
Dr. Robert Hoover, Chief
Research Activities and Fields: Principal areas of research interest are: 1) epidemiologic studies of selected occupational groups to help identify chemical and physical carcinogens; 2) epidemiologic studies to evaluate the effects of exogenous hormones, immunosuppressive and cytotoxic agents, and other drugs suspected of being carcinogenic; 3) epidemiologic studies to clarify the role of dietary fat, fiber, micronutrients, food additives, and other nutritional factors in cancer etiology; 4) multidisciplinary studies utilizing laboratory measures to evaluate candidate viruses, dietary and metabolic factors, air and water pollutants, host susceptibility, and other risk factors in human cancer; 5) studies of cancer-prone families and other high risk groups to delineate mechanisms of genetic susceptibility and host-environmental interactions; and 6) demographic and geographic surveys of cancer mortality and incidence in the United States to generate etiologic hypotheses.

★6170★ U.S. Department of Health and
     Human Services
National Cancer Institute
Epidemiology and Biostatistics Program
Extramural Programs Branch
6130 Executive Blvd., Rm. 535
Bethesda, MD 20892
Phone: (301)496-9600
Dr. G. Iris Obrams, Chief
Research Activities and Fields: Plans, develops, directs and manages a national extramural program of basic and applied research in biometry, epidemiology, and related multidisciplinary activities; establishes program priorities and evaluates program effectiveness; provides a broad spectrum of information, advice, and consultation to individual scientists and institutional sciences management officials concerning National Institutes of Health and National Cancer Institute (NCI) funding and scientific review policies and procedures, preparation of grant applications, and choice of funding instruments; provides NCI management with recommendations as to funding needs, priorities and strategies for the support of relevant research areas consistent with the current state of development of individual research activities and the promise of new initiatives; plans, develops, and manages research resources necessary for the conduct

of the coordinated research program; and plans, organizes, and conducts meetings and workshops to further program objectives.

★6171★ U.S. Department of Health and
     Human Services
National Cancer Institute
Epidemiology and Biostatistics Program
Radiation Epidemiology Branch
9000 Rockville Pike
Bethesda, MD 20892
Phone: (301)496-6600
Fax: (301)402-0207
Dr. John D. Boice, Jr., Chief
Research Activities and Fields: Branch conducts studies to identify and quantify the risk of cancer in populations exposed to ionizing radiations, especially at low-dose levels. These include patient populations given diagnostic or therapeutic radiation alone or in combination with cytotoxic drugs and other forms of treatment. Current studies include Chernobyl workers, indoor radon, cellular telephone use, Li Fraumeni syndrome, and atomic bomb survivors and others.

★6172★ U.S. Department of Health and
     Human Services
National Cancer Institute
Frederick Cancer Research and
     Development Center
Frederick, MD 21702-1201
Phone: (301)846-1108
Fax: (301)846-1494
Cedric W. Long, General Manager/Project
  Officer
Research Activities and Fields: Cancer causes, biology, diagnosis, and treatment, and AIDS studies. The basic research program (operated by the biomedical research firm Advanced BioScience Laboratories, Inc.) and the NCI intramural research programs involve studies in macromolecular structure and function; mechanisms for inducing cancer using carcinogens; activation and expression of oncogenes; mechanisms, evolution, and control of transformation; in vitro and in vivo screening for cancer and AIDS therapeutic agents; regulation of host defense mechanisms; therapeutic use of immune effector mechanisms; phase I and II clinical trials of biological and chemotherapeutic agents; identification and regulation of AIDS virus genes and proteins; and genetics of cell differentiation and development. Support services are provided by the other four FCRDC contractors (see above). In addition, FCRDC provides research opportunities for researchers, pre- and postdoctoral fellows, professors on sabbatical from universities, clinicians, individuals sponsored by outside grants or fellowships, collaborative workers, student interns, and others in the scientific community to participate in research at the Center.

★6173★ U.S. Department of Health and
     Human Services
National Cancer Institute
International Cancer Research Data Bank

R.A. Bloch Bldg.
9030 Old Georgetown Rd.
Bethesda, MD 20892
Phone: (301)496-7403
Fax: (301)480-8105
Giselle Sarosy, M.D., Chief
Research Activities and Fields: Purpose of ICRDB is to collect, analyze, and disseminate all data useful in prevention, diagnosis, treatment and supportive care of cancer and, as feasible, to disseminate results of cancer research undertaken in any country for the use of anyone conducting cancer research in any country.

★6174★ U.S. Department of Health and
     Human Services
National Cancer Institute
Laboratory of Biochemical Physiology
Frederick Cancer Research and Development
Center
Bldg. 560, Rm. 31-71
Frederick, MD 21701
Phone: (301)846-5703
Fax: (301)846-6863
Dr. Hsiang-Fu Kung, Chief
Research Activities and Fields: Conducts research on the genetic and biochemical events related to the development and expression for the malignant phenotype; and develops strategies for therapeutic intervention in the malignant process based on these findings.

★6175★ U.S. Department of Health and
     Human Services
National Cancer Institute
Laboratory of Biochemistry
NIH Bldg. 37, Rm. 4E28
9000 Rockville Pike
Bethesda, MD 20892
Phone: (301)496-5957
Fax: (301)402-3095
Claude Klee, M.D., Director
Research Activities and Fields: Emphasis of the work in the Biochemistry Laboratory is on the relationship between structure and function in biological systems and on the regulation of cellular processes. The research involves prokaryotes and a range of eukaryote systems selected because of their potential for yielding important information on cellular structure, function, regulation, development, and differentiation. The study of regulation encompasses regulation of gene expression, regulation by interaction of macromolecules, and regulation of cells by hormones and ions. Work is carried out on both the molecular and cellular level. Techniques include those of biochemistry, physical chemistry, cell biology, and molecular genetics.

★6176★ U.S. Department of Health and
     Human Services
National Cancer Institute
Laboratory of Biological Chemistry
NIH Bldg. 37
9000 Rockville Pike
Bethesda, MD 20892
Phone: (301)496-4116
Fax: (301)496-5839
Dr. Richard Cysyk, Chief
Research Activities and Fields: Laboratory identifies (as targets for drug design) cellular re-

actions that are critical to the control of tumor cell proliferation or differentiation. Recent advances in cell biology are evaluated for possible targets, and agents are designed to interact with these targets and are evaluated for biochemical and antitumor effectiveness. An important aspect of this mission is to develop appropriate in vivo systems to evaluate the chemotherapeutic effectiveness of agents shown to be active in simpler in vitro model systems. Accordingly, the Laboratory is involved in identifying endogenous factors present in vivo that modify drug action and influence differential toxicity with the aim of manipulating these factors to enhance antitumor activity.

★6177★ U.S. Department of Health and
   Human Services
National Cancer Institute
Laboratory of Biology
NIH Bldg. 37, Rm. 2A19
9000 Rockville Pike
Bethesda, MD 20892
Phone: (301)496-6441
Fax: (301)496-3238
Dr. Joseph A. DiPaolo, Chief

Research Activities and Fields: Laboratory is primarily interested in the modulation of the transformation process that leads to malignancy. The primary objective is to determine the crucial molecular and physiological changes that occur in cells that have been treated with chemical viruses or physical agents as they transform from the normal to the neoplastic state. Laboratory uses biological preparations, cells from animals and humans, and a variety of intact mammals. Emphasis is on the study of oncogenes and DNA changes that are responsible for the activation of genes in neoplasia. The role of growth factors (particularly leukoregulin, a hormone which is noncytotoxic to normal cells and is capable of inhibiting the transformation process) is investigated in terms of its cell receptor and interaction with other physiological agents during carcinogenesis.

★6178★ U.S. Department of Health and
   Human Services
National Cancer Institute
Laboratory of Cell Biology
NIH Bldg. 37, Rm. 1B22
9000 Rockville Pike
Bethesda, MD 20892
Phone: (301)496-3363
Dr. Lloyd W. Law, Chief

Research Activities and Fields: Research efforts are directed toward various aspects of basic cell biology in relation to cancer immunology. Major emphasis is on characterization of tumor antigens biochemically and immunologically and the immune responses they evoke. Studies include antigens isolated from sarcomas, leukemias, and melanomas. As a corollary to this study, the biologic properties of alien histocompatibility antigens and variant antigens in neoplasms are also under study.

★6179★ U.S. Department of Health and
   Human Services
National Cancer Institute
Laboratory of Cellular Carcinogenesis and
   Tumor Promotion

NIH Bldg. 37
9000 Rockville Pike
Bethesda, MD 20892
Phone: (301)496-2162
Fax: (301)496-8709
Dr. Stuart Yuspa, Chief

Research Activities and Fields: Laboratory plans, develops, and implements a comprehensive research program to determine the molecular and biological changes that occur at the cellular and tissue level during the process of carcinogenesis. Objectives are to: 1) define normal regulatory mechanisms for cellular growth and differentiation; 2) determine the mechanism by which carcinogens alter normal regulation and the biological nature of these alterations; 3) investigate the mechanism by which tumor promoters enhance the expression of carcinogen-induced alterations; 4) identify cellular determinants for enhanced susceptibility or resistance to carcinogens and tumor promoters; and 5) elucidate the mechanism by which certain pharmacologic agents inhibit carcinogenesis.

★6180★ U.S. Department of Health and
   Human Services
National Cancer Institute
Laboratory of Cellular and Molecular
   Biology
NIH Bldg. 37, Rm. 1E24
9000 Rockville Pike
Bethesda, MD 20892
Phone: (301)496-9683
Fax: (301)496-8479
Dr. Stuart A. Aaronson, Chief

Research Activities and Fields: Laboratory conducts research to: 1) identify, isolate, and characterize the transforming genes of acute transforming retroviruses; 2) elucidate the molecular mechanisms of transformation by retroviruses and retroviral onc genes; 3) determine the role of cellular DNA analogs of retroviral transforming genes in naturally occurring malignancies of human and other species; 4) identify, isolate, and characterize transforming genes of human tumor cells; 5) elucidate the mechanisms by which replication-competent type C viruses cause leukemia; 6) search for new mammalian retroviruses and establish their origins and evolutionary relationships to known oncoviruses; 7) apply techniques developed in the investigation of naturally occurring and virus-induced cancers of animals to the search for viral etiology of human tumors; and 8) analyze the effect of environmental agents or specific mechanisms that control and promote transformation in mammalian cells.

★6181★ U.S. Department of Health and
   Human Services
National Cancer Institute
Laboratory of Cellular Oncology
NIH Bldg. 37, Rm. 1B26
9000 Rockville Pike
Bethesda, MD 20892
Phone: (301)496-9513
Fax: (301)480-5322
Dr. Douglas R. Lowy, Chief

Research Activities and Fields: Laboratory conducts research on the genetics and immunology of oncogenesis. Studies seek to identify

critical differences between normal and neoplastic cells. The purpose of these investigations is to acquire information that may ultimately lead to improved diagnosis, therapy, or prophylaxis of neoplastic diseases. Activities involve probing the mechanisms by which normal cells become neoplastic through studies of the effects of viral and cellular transforming genes (oncogenes) on tissue culture cells or experimental animals; and studying the alteration of tumor growth patterns by the immune system and by biological modifiers. Tumor virus systems utilized in the Laboratory include papillomaviruses, rodent and primate retroviruses, and acute transforming retroviruses. The structure and function of viral and cellular transforming genes has been the focus of many studies in the Laboratory. Current efforts seek to define the role of transforming genes in spontaneous tumors. A wide range of experimental techniques are employed in carrying out these studies, including gene cloning by recombinant DNA technology, DNA mediated gene transfer, morphological transformation of tissue culture cells, quantitative virological assays, fractionation of sub-cellular components, radioimmunoassays, molecular hybridization, and in vitro mutagenesis.

★6182★ U.S. Department of Health and
   Human Services
National Cancer Institute
Laboratory of Chemoprevention
NIH Bldg. 41, Rm. C629
9000 Rockville Pike
Bethesda, MD 20892
Phone: (301)496-5391
Michael Sporn, Chief

Research Activities and Fields: Chemoprevention studies.

★6183★ U.S. Department of Health and
   Human Services
National Cancer Institute
Laboratory of Comparative Carcinogenesis
Frederick Cancer Research and Development
   Center
Frederick, MD 21702-1201
Phone: (301)846-1241
Fax: (301)846-5946
Dr. Jerry M. Rice, Chief

Research Activities and Fields: The Laboratory plans, develops, and conducts a research program to compare effects of chemical carcinogens in rodents and nonhuman primates in order to identify differences between species that are important for interspecies extrapolations of the effects of chemical agents, including extrapolations to man, and that afford experimental approaches to the elucidation of mechanisms in chemical carcinogenesis. Research is oriented toward identification of susceptibility and resistance to chemical carcinogenesis and toward identification, description, and investigation of mechanisms for interspecies differences and for cell and organ specificity in chemical carcinogenesis. The Laboratory investigates the roles of perinatal age period and pregnancy in modifying susceptibility to chemical carcinogens; studies mechanisms of action of the carcinogenic metals, cadmium, and nickel; and utilizes synthetic nitric oxide carrier compounds

(NONOates) to investigate the biologic effects of this multifunctional bioregulatory compound.

★6184★ U.S. Department of Health and Human Services
National Cancer Institute
Laboratory of Experimental Carcinogenesis
NIH Bldg. 37, Rm. 3C28
9000 Rockville Pike
Bethesda, MD 20892
Phone: (301)496-1935
Fax: (301)496-0734
Dr. Snorri S. Thorgeirsson, Chief

Research Activities and Fields: Laboratory goals are to: elucidate mechanisms of malignant transformation in human and animal cells by chemical carcinogens; determine critical cellular and genetic factors involved in initiation, promotion, and progression of transformed cells; and apply the knowledge obtained from studying animal models toward effective prevention of cancer in man. Principal areas of research interest are: the use of transgenic mouse models in cancer research; molecular and cellular aspects of hepatic stem cells; multidrug resistant gene family; chemical carcinogenesis and mutagenesis; molecular biology; and protein chemistry.

★6185★ U.S. Department of Health and Human Services
National Cancer Institute
Laboratory of Experimental Immunology
Frederick Cancer Research and Development Center
Bldg. 560, Rm. 3193
Frederick, MD 21702-1201
Phone: (301)846-1323
Fax: (301)846-1673
John Ortaldo, Chief

Research Activities and Fields: The Laboratory: 1) conducts research on the cellular and humoral components of the immune response that may be involved in resistance to tumor growth; 2) studies growth factors and other biological response modifiers (BRMs) that may be involved in the regulation of tumor growth; 3) studies the mechanism of action of various biologicals at the cellular and molecular level; 4) develops new biologicals and BRMs and investigates the effects of selected BRMs on the host and on tumor growth; and 5) develops protocols for optimal biological response modification and evaluates the therapeutic efficacy of these substances in experimental animal tumor systems and cancer patients.

★6186★ U.S. Department of Health and Human Services
National Cancer Institute
Laboratory of Experimental Pathology
NIH Bldg. 41, Rm. C105
9000 Rockville Pike
Bethesda, MD 20892
Phone: (301)496-2818
Fax: (301)402-1829
Dr. Umberto Saffiotti, Chief

Research Activities and Fields: Laboratory focuses on the study of neoplastic transformation and its underlying mechanisms, with particular emphasis on epithelial target cells. It plans, develops, and implements research on the experimental pathology of carcinogenesis, and is especially concerned with the induction of neoplasia by chemical and physical factors in epithelial tissues. Activities include: development, characterization, and evaluation of experimental pathology models of human cancer, such as cancers of the respiratory tract, by in vivo and in vitro carcinogenesis methods; development and characterization of tissue culture systems for quantitative study of the effects of carcinogens alone or in combination; and research on mechanisms of carcinogenesis correlating different levels of biological organization, from human and animal whole organisms, organs, and tissue, to the cellular, subcellular, and molecular levels.

★6187★ U.S. Department of Health and Human Services
National Cancer Institute
Laboratory of Genetics
NIH Bldg. 37, Rm. 2B04
9000 Rockville Pike
Bethesda, MD 20892
Phone: (301)496-1734
Dr. Michael Potter, Chief

Research Activities and Fields: Research focuses on the role of genes that determine susceptibility and resistance to neoplastic development and special genes and their products that are associated with the neoplastic state (oncogenes, retroviral gene products, tumor associated antigens). Past activities have involved studies of the plasma cell tumor system in mice, and research continues on the organization of immunoglobulin genes and gene families and structure-function correlations with monoclonal antibodies. Areas of current research interest include: amino acid and DNA sequences, recombinant DNA technology, tissue culture, and hybridoma-monoclonal and antibody production.

★6188★ U.S. Department of Health and Human Services
National Cancer Institute
Laboratory of Human Carcinogenesis
NIH Bldg. 37, Rm. 2C01
9000 Rockville Pike
Bethesda, MD 20892
Phone: (301)496-2048
Curtis Harris, Chief

Research Activities and Fields: The Laboratory conducts investigations to assess mechanisms of carcinogenesis in epithelial cells from humans and experimental animals; experimental approaches in biological systems for the extrapolation of carcinogenesis data and mechanisms from experimental animals to the human situation; and host factors that determine differences in carcinogenic susceptibility among individuals. Research is carried out in three areas: 1) molecular and biochemical epidemiology; 2) carcinogen macromolecular interaction; and 3) in vitro carcinogenesis.

★6189★ U.S. Department of Health and Human Services
National Cancer Institute
Laboratory of Immunobiology

Frederick Cancer Research and Development Center
Fort Detrick
Frederick, MD 21702-1201
Phone: (301)846-1557
Dr. Berton Zbar, Chief

Research Activities and Fields: Laboratory conducts studies on the mechanisms of the effector arm of the immune system and cancer genetics. Its program comprises three interacting areas: the Office of the Chief, the Immunopathology Section, and the Cellular Immunity Section. Areas of research interest have included studies on cellular effectors of the immune system; the chemotaxis of leukocytes; the mechanisms of activation of macrophages to kill tumor cells; identification of genetic changes; human solid tumors; cloning of recessive oncogenes; and the suppression of malignant phenotype by gene replacement.

★6190★ U.S. Department of Health and Human Services
National Cancer Institute
Laboratory of Mathematical Biology
Frederick Cancer Research and Development Center
Bldg. 469, Rm. 151
Frederick, MD 21701
Phone: (301)846-5532
Fax: (301)846-5598
Dr. Jacob V. Maizel, Jr., Ph.D., Chief

Research Activities and Fields: Studies nucleic acid sequences, protein sequences, and macromolecular structure (including prediction of molecular structure) using methods of computation; kinetics of metabolic systems using computational and modeling methodology; applications of image analysis to micrographs and two-dimensional gels; theoretical immunology; and membrane biophysics and structure.

★6191★ U.S. Department of Health and Human Services
National Cancer Institute
Laboratory of Medicinal Chemistry
NIH Bldg. 37, Rm. 5B22
9000 Rockville Pike
Bethesda, MD 20892
Phone: (301)496-9257
Fax: (301)402-2275
John Briscoll, Chief

Research Activities and Fields: Laboratory conducts an integrated program for the rational discovery of antitumor agents; implements basic research on mechanisms of antitumor drug action and drug toxicity; incorporates knowledge of biochemical/molecular mechanisms into a drug synthesis program aimed at optimizing drug efficacy through enhancement of antitumor activity/selectivity and/or minimization of toxicity; and develops strategies for improving the clinical utility of new or existing anticancer drugs by overcoming tumor resistance and/or by protection of normal tissues against toxicity. Compounds with potential antitumor activity are synthesized and effects of such agents are assessed in experimental tumor systems in vitro and in vivo and on a variety of potential subcellular target sites (e.g., nucleic acids, nuclear proteins, microtubular protein, and enzyme systems). Analytical methodology for in vivo studies with new agents is developed, and where warranted, biological studies with these agents are extended to the preclinical and Phase I stages. A wide range of methodologies is currently in use.

★6192★ U.S. Department of Health and Human Services
National Cancer Institute
Laboratory of Molecular Biology
NIH Bldg. 37, Rm. 4E16
9000 Rockville Pike
Bethesda, MD 20892
Phone: (301)496-4797
Fax: (301)496-0260
Dr. Ira H. Pastan, Chief

Research Activities and Fields: Laboratory's interests involve the development of immunotoxins for treatment of human cancer. To accomplish this, *Pseudomonas* exotoxin is coupled to monoclonal antibodies that react with specific human cancers. The activity of these conjugates is assessed in cell culture and animal models. Toxicity studies are conducted with monkeys, and the first promising immunotoxins are being prepared for clinical testing. The mechanisms by which immunotoxins enter and kill cells is studied by biochemical, genetic, and cell biological approaches in order to devise ways to improve the therapeutic efficiency of these agents.

★6193★ U.S. Department of Health and Human Services
National Cancer Institute
Laboratory of Molecular Carcinogenesis
NIH Bldg. 37, Rm. 3E22
9000 Rockville Pike
Bethesda, MD 20892
Phone: (301)496-6849
Fax: (301)496-8419
Harry V. Gelboin, Ph.D., Chief

Research Activities and Fields: Laboratory's goal is to increase understanding of the cellular and biochemical events and mechanisms involved in carcinogenesis. Activities include: 1) examination of the unusual properties of cells from patients who may be predisposed to cancer because of hereditary disease and investigation of various mechanisms of DNA repair using DNA transfection and sequencing to define the genomic changes observed; 2) investigation of the genetics, multiplicity, and structure of the drug and carcinogen metabolizing enzyme systems; 3) studies using monoclonal antibodies to gain an understanding of individual differences and their relationship to drug and carcinogen sensitivity; 4) investigation of the mutation, recombination, and repair caused by carcinogen treatment using shuttle vectors that replicate in mammalian and bacterial cells; and 5) studies of the relationship between the structure and function in chromatin (using biochemical and immunological methods), including evaluation of the regulatory properties of the nonhistone proteins.

★6194★ U.S. Department of Health and Human Services
National Cancer Institute
Laboratory of Molecular Immunoregulation

Frederick Cancer Research and Development Center
Bldg. 560
Frederick, MD 21702-1201
Phone: (301)846-1551
Fax: (301)846-1673
Dr. Joost Oppenheim, Chief

Research Activities and Fields: Laboratory conducts research on the biochemical and molecular effects of biological response modifiers on host resistance to cancer. It investigates at a molecular level the inter- and intracellular processes that regulate host defense mechanisms, including isolation of proteins, RNA, and DNA that regulate production and activities of lymphokines, cytokines, and their receptors. It utilizes in vitro and in vivo models to study the modulation by lymphokines/cytokines of cellular functions that participate in host defense. In addition, Laboratory devises new tests for diagnosis of cancer and for better definition of the immune status and more critical evaluation of biological response modifiers (BRMs). It evaluates the effects of BRMs on immunoregulatory pathways and host defense mechanisms; and generates BRMs that modify host defense mechanisms.

★6195★ U.S. Department of Health and Human Services
National Cancer Institute
Laboratory of Molecular Oncology
Frederick Cancer Research and Development Center
Bldg. 469, Rm. 203
Frederick, MD 21702
Phone: (301)846-1576
Fax: (301)846-6164
Dr. James Lautenberger, Acting Chief

Research Activities and Fields: Laboratory conducts basic research on mechanisms of neoplastic processes in cells transformed by retroviruses, oncogenes, or chemical carcinogens. Comparisons are made to similar cellular processes in normal cells in order to study the nature of cellular changes occurring subsequent to malignant transformation.

★6196★ U.S. Department of Health and Human Services
National Cancer Institute
Laboratory of Molecular Pharmacology
NIH Bldg. 37, Rm. 5C25
9000 Rockville Pike
Bethesda, MD 20892
Phone: (301)496-2769
Fax: (301)496-5839
Dr. Kurt W. Kohn, Chief

Research Activities and Fields: Mechanisms of action of anticancer agents are studied in culture and subcellular systems, with particular attention to effects involving DNA and nuclear proteins. Investigations focus on the relation between drug-induced macromolecular damage (and its repair) and cell survival. Drugs are also used as probes of the structure and function of DNA and chromatin. Experimental approaches include cell culture, DNA macromolecular damage measurements, DNA sequence analysis, and nuclear protein fractionation techniques. Major areas of current interest are the effects of

anticancer drugs on topoisomerase enzymes and on cell cycle regulation.

★6197★ U.S. Department of Health and Human Services
National Cancer Institute
Laboratory of Molecular Virology
NIH Bldg. 41, Rm. A100
9000 Rockville Pike
Bethesda, MD 20892
Phone: (301)496-6201
Dr. Edward Tabor, Chief

Research Activities and Fields: Laboratory is concerned with the normal and abnormal regulation of gene expression. Studies employ methods from molecular biology, immunology, virology, and cell biology in an attempt to determine in specific cases what signals regulate gene expression. Current efforts involve both viral and eukaryotic genetic units. Research focuses on genes which are regulated at the level of transcription and which, in some cases, are responsive to induction by hormones or transacting proteins. Studies involve oncogenes and the mutations which are responsible for activation of these genes in neoplasia; and histocompatibility antigens and the roles of these genes in immune surveillance and tumor immunity.

★6198★ U.S. Department of Health and Human Services
National Cancer Institute
Laboratory of Pathology
NIH Bldg. 10, Rm. 2A33
9000 Rockville Pike
Bethesda, MD 20892
Phone: (301)496-3185
Fax: (301)402-0043
Dr. Lance Liotta, Chief

Research Activities and Fields: The Pathology Laboratory is responsible for surgical pathology and autopsy services at the Clinical Center of the NIH. Offers diagnostic electron microscopy studies and cytopathologic services, including exfoliative and fine needle aspiration; provides all types of histological services and staining procedures for National Cancer Institute scientists; and conducts research programs in various areas of experimental cancer research. It also provides a fully accredited residency program in anatomic pathology. Component sections of the Laboratory are: Biochemical Pathology Section, Cytopathology Section, Gene Regulation Section, Hematopathology Section, Surgical Pathology Section, Postmortem Section, Tumor Invasion and Metastases Section, Ultrastructural Pathology Section, Molecular Pathology Section, Extracellular Matrix Pathology Section, Molecular Immune Activation Section, and Women's Cancers Section.

★6199★ U.S. Department of Health and Human Services
National Cancer Institute
Laboratory of Tumor Cell Biology
NIH Bldg. 37
9000 Rockville Pike
Bethesda, MD 20892
Phone: (301)496-6007
Fax: (301)496-8394
Dr. Robert Gallo, Chief

Research Activities and Fields: Objectives of the Laboratory are to develop, implement, and analyze data obtained from studies of cellular proliferation, cell differentiation, and biochemical growth characteristics of normal and malignant mammalian cells both in vivo and in vitro, which will permit the optimal use of antitumor agents in the treatment of cancer and AIDS. Particular attention is given to human leukemias and lymphomas, acquired immunodeficiency syndrome (AIDS), Kaposi's sarcoma, antiviral agents, and vaccine development.

★6200★ U.S. Department of Health and Human Services
National Cancer Institute
Laboratory of Tumor Immunology and Biology
NIH Bldg. 10, Rm. 8B07
9000 Rockville Pike
Bethesda, MD 20892
Phone: (301)496-9573
Jeffrey Schlom, Ph.D., Chief

Research Activities and Fields: Laboratory conducts research to identify immunologic markers specific for or associated with various human neoplasms, with the ultimate aim of applying these toward the diagnosis, prognosis, and treatment of human cancer. Activities focus on: 1) the generation and characterization of monoclonal antibodies to tumor-associated determinants, with particular emphasis on the study of human carcinomas; 2) conjugation of monoclonal antibodies to isotopes or toxins to aid in the diagnosis, localization, and potential elimination of tumor cells; 3) studies on the association between specific murine and human genetic elements and tumorigenesis using techniques of gene cloning and molecular hybridization; and 4) development of immunoassays to aid in the characterization of human tumor cell populations and in the diagnosis or prognosis of certain human cancers.

★6201★ U.S. Department of Health and Human Services
National Cancer Institute
Laboratory of Tumor Virus Biology
NIH Bldg. 4l, Rm. C111
9000 Rockville Pike
Bethesda, MD 20892
Phone: (301)496-7608
Dr. Carl Baker, Acting Chief

Research Activities and Fields: Laboratory plans, develops, and implements a research program to elucidate mechanisms of carcinogenesis and malignant transformation in human and animal cells, particularly in instances where there is an association with tumor viruses; and conducts research to determine critical cellular and molecular factors involved in virus-associated transformation and carcinogenesis. Studies are designed to: 1) identify and characterize exogenous viruses associated with the initiation or progression of neoplasia in humans or animals as models for human neoplasia; 2) elucidate the mechanisms by which viruses associated with naturally occurring carcinomas may induce or initiate neoplasia; 3) characterize and define the biology and molecular biology of viruses associated with naturally occurring carcinomas; 4) identify and characterize factors involved in viral and cellular gene regulation pertinent to carcinogenesis; and 5) elucidate and de-

fine the cellular and molecular basis of transformation and carcinogenic progression.

★6202★ U.S. Department of Health and Human Services
National Cancer Institute
Laboratory of Viral Carcinogenesis
Frederick Cancer Research and Development Center
Frederick, MD 21702-1201
Phone: (301)846-1296
Fax: (301)846-1686
Stephen O'Brien, Ph.D., Chief

Research Activities and Fields: Laboratory conducts basic research to determine the genetic and cellular mechanism of neoplastic transformation in man and mammalian model systems. Studies are conducted on the specific cellular genes that participate in transformation from several distinct approaches. Interests include studies on: endogenous mammalian retroviruses and their role in gene regulation and neoplasia; the expression of transforming viruses, their included oncogenes, and their ancestral cellular homologs during development and carcinogenesis using recombinant DNA technologies and systems; molecular processes of chemical carcinogenesis using gene cloning, cell transfection, and cell biology procedures; somatic cell genetic approaches to neoplastic transformation and the cytogenetic consequences of transformation; and activities of hormone-like growth factors and tumor promoters to determine their regulation of transformation sensitivity genes and transforming genes and of the progressive stages of transformation of cells in vitro and in vivo.

U.S. Department of Health and Human Services
National Heart, Lung, and Blood Institute
See: Entry 2929

★6203★ U.S. Department of Health and Human Services
National Heart, Lung, and Blood Institute
Division of Blood Diseases and Resources
7550 Wisconsin Ave., Rm. 516
Bethesda, MD 20892
Phone: (301)496-4868
Fax: (301)402-1622
John C. Hoak, M.D., Director

Research Activities and Fields: Division plans and directs NHLBI's research grant, contract, and training programs to improve the diagnosis, prevention, and treatment of blood diseases and related disorders and to assure the efficient and safe use of an adequate supply of high-quality blood and blood products. Programs include fundamental and clinical research; professional development and training; and education, prevention, and control activities to assure orderly application of knowledge gained from research. Division supports research programs in: thrombosis and hemostasis; red blood cell disorders and erythropoiesis; sickle cell disease; and blood resources, including studies of platelets, leukocytes, erythrocytes, and plasma components and bone marrow transplantation. Division also participates in the U.S.-C.I.S. Health Exchange Program.

U.S. Department of Health and Human Services
National Heart, Lung, and Blood Institute
Division of Epidemiology and Clinical Applications
See: Entry 2930

U.S. Department of Health and Human Services
National Heart, Lung, and Blood Institute
Division of Epidemiology and Clinical Applications
Clinical Applications and Prevention Program
See: Entry 2931

U.S. Department of Health and Human Services
National Heart, Lung, and Blood Institute
Division of Epidemiology and Clinical Applications
Epidemiology and Biometry Program
See: Entry 2932

U.S. Department of Health and Human Services
National Heart, Lung, and Blood Institute
Division of Intramural Research
See: Entry 2939

★6204★ U.S. Department of Health and Human Services
National Heart, Lung, and Blood Institute
Division of Intramural Research
Hematology Branch
NIH Bldg. 10, Rm. 7C103
9000 Rockville Pike
Bethesda, MD 20892
Phone: (301)496-5093
Fax: (301)496-8396
Dr. Neal S. Young, Chief

Research Activities and Fields: Research activities of the Branch focus on normal and abnormal hematopoiesis. Clinical research is conducted on patients with bone marrow failure syndromes especially aplastic anemia, Fancon's anemia, and myelodysplasia; inherited anemias, including sickle cell anemia and thalassemia; and hematologic malignancies, including chronic myelogenous leukemia and multiple myeloma. The major areas of laboratory investigation are: 1) immune suppression of hematopoiesis; 2) viral interactions with bone marrow cells, especially of the human parvovirus; 3) gene transduction into hematopoietic stem cells; and 4) modulation of graft-versus-leukemia and graft-versus-host disease in allogeneic bone marrow transplantation. Techniques from cell biology, immunology, virology, and molecular biology are all employed in these efforts.

★6205★ U.S. Department of Health and Human Services
National Heart, Lung, and Blood Institute
Division of Intramural Research
Laboratory of Molecular Hematology

NIH Bldg. 10, Rm. 7D18
9000 Rockville Pike
Bethesda, MD 20892
Phone: (301)496-5844
Fax: (301)496-9985
Dr. W. French Anderson, Chief

Research Activities and Fields: Studies the mechanism and regulation of mammalian gene expression to develop the understanding and technology necessary to carry out human gene therapy. The types of diseases being targeted are genetic cancer, viral, and cardiovascular. Major areas of research include gene cloning and retroviral-mediated gene transfer, retroviral vector development and isolation and characterization of genes, development of primitive artificial organs by growing autologous cells on vascularizable implants in vivo, and cloning and expression of transacting factors involved in the regulation of gene expression, both at the transcriptional and translational level.

U.S. Department of Health and Human Services
National Heart, Lung, and Blood Institute
Laboratory of Biochemical Genetics
See: Entry 2944

U.S. Department of Health and Human Services
National Heart, Lung, and Blood Institute
Laboratory of Biochemistry
See: Entry 2945

U.S. Department of Health and Human Services
National Heart, Lung, and Blood Institute
Laboratory of Biophysical Chemistry
See: Entry 2946

U.S. Department of Health and Human Services
National Heart, Lung, and Blood Institute
Laboratory of Cell Biology
See: Entry 2948

U.S. Department of Health and Human Services
National Heart, Lung, and Blood Institute
Laboratory of Cellular Metabolism
See: Entry 2949

U.S. Department of Health and Human Services
National Heart, Lung, and Blood Institute
Laboratory of Chemical Pharmacology
See: Entry 2950

U.S. Department of Health and Human Services
National Institute of Diabetes and Digestive and Kidney Diseases
See: Entry 4906

U.S. Department of Health and Human Services
National Institute of Diabetes and Digestive and Kidney Diseases
Division of Intramural Research
See: Entry 4919

★ 6206 ★ U.S. Department of Health and Human Services
National Institute of Diabetes and Digestive and Kidney Diseases
Division of Intramural Research
Clinical Hematology Branch
NIH Bldg. 10, Rm. 4D51
9000 Rockville Pike
Bethesda, MD 20892
Phone: (301)496-4787
Fax: (301)402-4978
Dr. N. Raphael Shulman, Chief

Research Activities and Fields: Laboratory work concerns problems in the fields of immunohematology, platelet physiology and metabolism, and blood coagulation. Current interests include mechanisms of immune cellular injury involving drug-, allo-, and auto-antibodies, correlation of platelet metabolism and membrane reactions with function, and interrelationships between cellular and humoral factors in hemostasis. Clinical work involves patients with immunologic and hemorrhagic disorders relevant to laboratory studies.

U.S. Department of Health and Human Services
National Institute of Diabetes and Digestive and Kidney Diseases
Division of Kidney, Urologic, and Hematologic Diseases
See: Entry 12919

★ 6207 ★ U.S. Department of Health and Human Services
National Institute of Diabetes and Digestive and Kidney Diseases
Division of Kidney, Urologic, and Hematologic Diseases
Hematology Program
Westwood Building, Rm. 3A-05
Bethesda, MD 20892
Phone: (301)594-7541
Fax: (301)594-7501
David G. Badman, Ph.D., Program Director

Research Activities and Fields: Program provides support for basic, applied, and clinical research and training within a broad area related to blood, including: 1) hemoglobin structure and genetics; 2) anemias of chronic diseases such as chronic renal failure; 3) molecular and cellular role of erythropoietin; 4) blood cell production; 5) iron metabolism, transport, and storage; 6) iron overload and deficiency; 7) white blood cell metabolism and function; 8) development of new iron chelating compounds for clinical use and testing the toxicity of these compounds; and 9) hematologic aspects of AIDS, including bone marrow suppression.

★ 6208 ★ University of Alabama at Birmingham
Comprehensive Cancer Center
Univ. Sta.
Birmingham, AL 35294
Phone: (205)934-5077
Fax: (205)934-1608
Dr. Albert F. LoBuglio, Dir.

Research Activities and Fields: Oncology, involving medicine, dentistry, surgery, bone marrow transplantation, basic science, pathology, radiation oncology, obstetrics and gynecology,

virology, biophysics, molecular biology, epidemiology, and pediatrics. Programs concentrate on the molecular biology and molecular genetics of malignant tranformation, (including oncogene and retroviral mechanisms), nature of the transformed membrane, structure of its antigens and their biologic function, and role and interaction of T and B cells in protection against cancer. Also concerned with models for assessment of effect of surgery, immunotherapy and chemotherapy in intact animals, possessing models for myeloma and osteogenic sarcoma, and crystalline and solution biochem istry of anticancer agents. Conducts clinical activities, including investigations into biology and usefulness of certain tumor scanning agents, including monoclonal antibodies, magnetic resonance imaging, and use of new agents for treatment of a wide variety of human tumors. **Formerly:** Outgrowth of Cancer Research and Training Program established in 1970.

★ 6209 ★ University of Arizona
Arizona Cancer Center
1515 N. Campbell Ave.
Tucson, AZ 85724
Phone: (520)626-6044
Fax: (520)626-2284
Dr. Sydney E. Salmon, Dir.

Research Activities and Fields: Clinical and laboratory cancer studies, including tumor cell kinetics, clinical pharmacology and pharmacokinetics, new drug development, drug resistance mechanisms, human tumor cloning, markers of cellular activity in malignant tumors, cell and molecular biology, immunology, carcinogenesis, hyperthermia, medical imaging, cancer prevention and control, cytogenetics, pain management, stereotactic radiosurgery, bone marrow transplantation, gene therapy, epidemiology, and biostatistics. Clinical studies focus on histological tumor types, staging of disease, tumor kinetics, measurement of tumor burden, and new approaches to chemotherapy. New approaches to biological therapy include developing interleukins, interferons, colony stimulating factors, and tumor vaccines. Ongoing projects focus on developing new cytotoxic derivatives of anticancer drugs and pharmacokinetics in tumor systems. Conducts reversal of clinical drug resistance studies, clinical pharmacology of anticancer drugs research, and drug interaction evaluations. Performs clinical cancer research on patients with all types of tumors, with special competence in treating breast, ovarian, and prostate cancers; myeloma and melanoma; Hodgkin's disease; lymphoma, including mycosis fungoids; head and neck cancers; and brain tumors. **Publications:** Newsletter; Annual Report; Special Interest Periodicals; Scientific Report.

★ 6210 ★ University of Arkansas at Little Rock
Arkansas Cancer Research Center
Slot 623 UAMS
4301 W. Markham
Little Rock, AR 72205
Phone: (501)686-6000
Fax: (501)686-8165
Kent C. Westbrook, M.D., Med.Dir.

Research Activities and Fields: Cancer, including the biology of cancer, psychosocial and functional outcome issues, immunology and the effects of various agents on cancer, genetic control of cancer, how heat and radiation can control or impede cancerous growths, anti-cancer drugs, cancer in aging cells, and a chronobiological (body-cycle) approach to treating cancers. Specific research involves animal studies of genetically controlling the growth of malignancies, protection against the toxic nature of certain anti-tumor drugs, and changing enzyme profiles in the body through certain anti-cancer agents. Clinical research treatment plans are tested through the Southwest Oncology Group network.

★6211★ University of California at Berkeley
Cancer Research Laboratory
447 Life Sciences Addition
Berkeley, CA 94720
Phone: (510)642-4711
Fax: (510)642-5741
Dr. James P. Allison, Dir.

Research Activities and Fields: Biology of epithelial neoplasia, with special emphasis on mammary and hepatic cancers; molecular pathogenesis of leukemia; factors involved in transformation of normal cells to neoplastic cells; and mechanism of neoplasia. Also studies production of monoclonal antibodies to cell surface structures altered during neoplastic transformation. Formerly: Cancer Research Genetics Laboratory.

★6212★ University of California, Irvine
Cancer Research Institute
Dept. of Molecular Biology & Biochemistry
Irvine, CA 92717
Phone: (714)856-5886
Fax: (714)886-4023
Dr. Hung Fan, Dir.

Research Activities and Fields: Focuses on immunology, virology, and growth factors, emphasizing basic research in various aspects of cancer. Also conducts studies in other areas central to understanding regulation in eukaryotic cells.

University of California, Los Angeles
Bone Marrow Transplantation Program
See: Entry 12888

★6213★ University of California, Los Angeles
UCLA Jonsson Comprehensive Cancer Center
10-247 Factor Bldg.
10833 LeConte Ave.
Los Angeles, CA 90024
Phone: (310)825-5268
Fax: (310)206-5553
Dr. H. Rodney Withers, Interim Dir.

Research Activities and Fields: Cancer, including both basic and clinical studies in cell and molecular biology, chemical and viral carcinogenesis, tumor immunology, and genitourinary, gynecologic, head and neck, medical, neurosurgical, pediatric, radiation, and surgical oncology. Also conducts cancer control demonstrations and research projects. Publications: Advances (3 times yearly); UCLA Cancer Trials (quarterly); Scientific Report (annually).

★6214★ University of California, San Diego
Cancer Center
0658
La Jolla, CA 92093
Phone: (619)534-7600
Fax: (619)534-7628
Rose Guerrero, Assoc.Dir.

Research Activities and Fields: Cancer, including clinical trials, education and treatment, and studies in the areas of cancer genetics, cancer prevention and control, clinical investigation and developmental therapeutics, glycobiology, growth control, immunology, and molecular virology.

★6215★ University of California, San Francisco
Brain Tumor Research Center
Box 0520
San Francisco, CA 94143
Phone: (415)476-2905
Charles B. Wilson, M.D., Dir.

Research Activities and Fields: Studies cytotoxic therapies, radiation therapy, and chemotherapy; elucidates the difference between normal brain cells and brain tumor cells. E-mail Address: ddeen@ucsfvm.ucsf.edu.

★6216★ University of California, San Francisco
Cancer Research Institute
Box 0128
San Francisco, CA 94143-0128
Phone: (415)476-2201
Marc Shuman, M.D., Dir.

Research Activities and Fields: Clinical and basic studies of cancer and hematology, endocrinology, fundamental properties of cell membranes, role of interferon and cell-cell interactions in immune response to cancer, surface markers on leukemic cells, role of viruses in cancer, management of breast cancer, factors involved in control of cell proliferation and differentiation, use of liposomes to deliver drug and macromolecules into cells, mechanism of membrane fusion, molecular pharmacology of antineoplastic drugs, and interaction between the coagulation and fibrinolytic systems and cancer cells.

★6217★ University of California, San Francisco
Northern California Comprehensive Sickle Cell Center
San Francisco General Hospital
1001 Potrero Ave., Rm. 331, Bldg. 100
San Francisco, CA 94110
Phone: (415)206-5169
Fax: (415)206-3071
William C. Mentzer, M.D., Dir.

Research Activities and Fields: Sickle cell disease, including molecular, cellular, tissue, and organ studies. Conducts clinical trials. Seeks to translate research on sickle cell disease to improved health care at the community level. E-mail Address: in619oe@ucstvm.ucsf.edu. Formerly: Comprehensive Sickle Cell Center.

University of California, San Francisco
Radiation Oncology Research Laboratory
See: Entry 11164

★6218★ University of Chicago
Ben May Institute
5841 S. Maryland Ave.
MC 6027
Chicago, IL 60637
Phone: (312)702-6993
Fax: (312)702-6260
Frank W. Fitch, M.D., Dir.

Research Activities and Fields: Cancer and hormone-dependent tumors, including cancer of breast and prostate through studies in immunobiology, biochemistry, clinical medicine, experimental pathology, organic chemistry, and physiology on morphology and function of cells. Formerly: Ben May Laboratory for Cancer Research.

★6219★ University of Chicago
Cancer Research Center
5841 S. Maryland Ave.
Box MC1140
Chicago, IL 60637
Phone: (312)702-6180
Fax: (312)702-9311
Richard L. Schilsky, M.D., Dir.

Research Activities and Fields: Causes, prevention, and treatment of cancer, including investigations of gynecologic cancers, lung cancer, head and neck cancer, pediatric cancers, gastro-intestinal cancers, breast cancer, lymphoma, leukemia, autologous bone marrow transplantation. Conducts research in cancer biology, molecular genetics, tumor immunology, developmental therapeutics, clinical research, diagnostics using radiology and radionuclide imaging, radiotherapy, radiation physics, radiation biology, developmental biology, and biochemistry. Major program areas include: molecular biology of cell growth and differentiation, chromosomes and cancer, molecular genetics of human tumors, immunology and cancer, developmental therapeutics, clinical investigations. Developing programs include psychosocial oncology, cancer prevention, breast cancer and advanced medical imaging. Publications: Annual Report; UCCRC Newsletter.

University of Chicago
Franklin McLean Memorial Research Institute
See: Entry 11165

★6220★ University of Florida
Division of Medical Oncology/Hematology
JHMHC, Box 100277
Gainesville, FL 32610
Phone: (904)392-4611
Fax: (904)392-8530
Dr. Ward D. Noyes, Interim Dir.

Research Activities and Fields: Oncology, including medicine, radiotherapy, pathology, and surgery. Focuses on growth regulation of normal and malignant cells. E-mail Address: smtp:"smptnoyes.med@mhsl.sth.ufl.edu":noye.

University of Florida
Radiation Oncology Clinic
See: Entry 11167

★6221★ University of Hawaii
Cancer Research Center of Hawaii
1236 Lauhala St.
Honolulu, HI 96813
Phone: (808)586-3013
Fax: (808)586-3009
Brian F. Issell, M.D., Dir.

Research Activities and Fields: Cancer, with major emphasis in cancer epidemiology, focused on multidisciplinary cancer etiology studies that utilize Hawaii's unique ethnic population distribution for basic and demographic research; basic science, including environmental carcinogenesis, experimental therapeutics, and cell transformation and differentiation; and prevention and control; research, including clinical treatment trials, chemoprevention and other cancer control interventions. **Publications:** Scientific Report (biannually); Annual Reports; Newsletters.

★6222★ University of Illinois at Chicago
Cancer Center
College of Medicine
Clinical Sciences Bldg.
840 S. Wood St.
Chicago, IL 60612
Phone: (312)996-6666
Fax: (312)996-9365
Tapas K. Das Gupta, M.D., Dir.

Research Activities and Fields: Tumor biology, including molecular biology and molecular genetics, drug development, chemoprevention, drug resistance, genetic rearrangement, gene regulation, signal transduction, epidemiology prevention, and clinical research. Center specializes in the study of cancers of the head and neck region, breast, esophagus, stomach, small and large bowel, colon and rectum, liver and pancreas, skin, and soft body tissue.

★6223★ University of Iowa
Cancer Center
4555 JCP
Iowa City, IA 52242
Phone: (319)353-8620
Free: 800-237-1225
Fax: (319)353-8988
Robert B. Wallace, M.D., Dir.

Research Activities and Fields: Conducts 13 multidisciplinary clinical cancer programs involving: breast cancer; bone marrow transplantation and brain and spinal cord tumors; cancers of the eye; digestive system cancers; female reproductive tumors; head and neck tumors; leukemia and lymphoma; melanoma and sarcoma; supportive care and pain management; thoracic cancer; and urologic tumors, interdisciplinary diagnostic and therapeutic strategies, and modalities. Center oncologists participate in seven national cooperative study groups and engage in shared management programs with physicians referring patients to the University of Iowa Hospitals and Clinics.

★6224★ University of Kansas
Cancer Center
Medical Center
3901 Rainbow Blvd.
Kansas City, KS 66160-7312
Phone: (913)588-4700
Fax: (913)588-4701
Stephen W. Russell, D.V.M., Dir.

Research Activities and Fields: Cancer, including interdisciplinary studies on its prevention, detection, and diagnosis. Programs focus on hormonally regulated cancers, chemotherapy, radiation therapy, immunotherapy, surgical therapy, psychosocial rehabilitation of pediatric patients and families, drug development, cellular and molecular biology, chemical and environmental carcinogenesis, tumor immunology, epidemiology, and biostatistics. Also conducts clinical trial investigations.

★6225★ University of Kentucky
Children's Cancer Study Group
College of Medicine
Lexington, KY 40506
Phone: (606)233-6771
Fax: (606)258-5499
M.F. Greenwood, M.D., Dir.

Research Activities and Fields: Pediatric oncology, including clinical trials and bone marrow transplantation.

★6226★ University of Kentucky
Lucille Parker Markey Cancer Center
800 Rose St.
Lexington, KY 40536-0093
Phone: (606)257-4500
Fax: (606)323-2074
Kenneth A. Foon, M.D., Dir.

Research Activities and Fields: Cancer research, including tumor immunology, molecular genetics, membrane studies, and clinical trials. Core facilties include macromolecular structure, flow cytometry, electron microscopy, NMR spectroscopy, hybridoma production, and transgenic cell construction. **Publications:** Quarterly Newsletter; Annual Report. **E-mail Address:** lew@delos.kcr.uky.edu.

University of Kentucky
Radiation Therapy Oncology Center
See: Entry 11169

★6227★ University of Louisville
Henry Vogt Cancer Research Institute
James Graham Brown Cancer Center
529 S. Jackson St.
Louisville, KY 40292
Phone: (502)852-6905
Fax: (502)852-7799
Alfred Thompson, M.D., Actg.Dir.

Research Activities and Fields: Molecular hematology/oncology, marrow transplantation, horomone receptors, anticancer drug development, molecular carcinogenesis, methods of drug delivery, laser therapy, growth factors, and drug disposition (clinical pharmacy).

★6228★ University of Maryland at
Baltimore
University of Maryland Cancer Center
22 S. Greene St.
Baltimore, MD 21201
Phone: (410)328-5506
Fax: (410)328-2578
Ernest C. Borden, M.D., Dir.

Research Activities and Fields: Pharmacology, clinical pharmacology, infectious diseases, molecular biology, pathology, cytogenetics, immunology, electron microscopy, and drug and combined modality treatment of cancer patients, with emphasis on acute leukemia, breast cancer, sarcomas, lymphomas, lung cancer, and other solid tumors. Maintains programs in the following areas: 1) the chemotherapeutic approach to cancer therapy and the development of experimental protocols, 2) infectious disease relationship to cancer, 3) cell component therapy and cellular replacement, 4) critical care of cancer patients, 5) pharmacology and the use of cancer chemotherapeutic agents, 6) anti-cancer drug development, 7) combined modalities treatments, biological treatment, 8) cellular and molecular biology of cancer, 9) supportive care, and 10) pharmacokinetics and pharmacodynamics of antineoplastic agents. **E-mail   Address:**   eborden.umccol.umcc.ab.umd.edu.

★6229★ University of Miami
Sylvester Comprehensive Cancer Center
School of Medicine
PO Box 016960, (D72)
Miami, FL 33101
Phone: (305)548-4918
Fax: (305)548-4684
Dr. Azorides Morales, Dir.

Research Activities and Fields: Cancer, including clinical investigation related to treatment of cancer, especially solid tumors of adults; molecular and cell biology as related to causation and pathogenesis of cancer; epidemiological research as related to environmental etiology of cancer in Florida and its prevention; and cellular differentation, cell population kinetics, epidemiology of cancer, viral oncology, and immunology. Participates as one of 28 comprehensive cancer centers for conducting multidisciplinary research, improving methods of treatment, diagnosis, and prevention, training health professionals, and transferring cancer knowledge to surrounding communities in National Cancer Institute's nationwide coordination program for development of means to reduce incidence, morbidity, an d mortality of cancer as established under National Cancer Act of 1971. **E-mail   Address:**   asauerte@mednet.med.miami.edu. **Formerly:** Comprehensive Cancer Center for State of Florida merged with Papanicolau Cancer Research Institute and then known as Papanicolaou Comprehensive Cancer Center.

★6230★ University of Michigan
Coagulation Research Laboratory—Clinical
Univ. Hospital, Rm. 2F351
1500 E. Medical Center Dr.
Ann Arbor, MI 48109-0054
Phone: (313)936-5320
Fax: (313)936-6739
M. Darling, Dir.

Research Activities and Fields: Blood coagulation, focusing on clinical research and new developments. Provides continuing support of clinical services for coagulation unit of the University Hospital. **Formerly:** Blood Coagulation Research Laboratory.

★6231★ University of Michigan
Division of Hematology / Oncology
3119 Taubman Center
1500 E. Medical Center Dr.
Ann Arbor, MI 48109-0374
Phone: (313)764-8100
Fax: (313)936-7376
Dr. Robert F. Todd III, Div. Chief

Research Activities and Fields: Hematology, solid tumor, and neoplasia, including anemias, leukemia-lymphomas, immunohematologic disorders, coagulation defects and lipid-protein-coagulation interrelationships, and tumor cell growth and control. Biochemical, molecular biological, cytologic, immunologic, tissue culture, and isotopic techniques are employed to investigate factors concerned with regulation of cell growth and proliferation and variables that influence response to therapy. Research areas also include the genetic aspects of cancer, hematologic malignancies, and biological modifiers, as well as gene therapy. **Formerly:** Simpson Memorial Institute for Medical Research.

★6232★ University of Minnesota
Masonic Cancer Center
Division of Medical Oncology
Univ. Hospital & Clinic, Box 286
Harvard St. at E. River Rd.
Minneapolis, MN 55455
Phone: (612)624-7915
Fax: (612)625-8966
Gordon D. Ginder, Contact

Research Activities and Fields: Pediatric, surgical, medical, and radiation oncology in the areas of breast cancer, acute leukemia, lung cancer, lymphomas, testicular cancer, ovarian cancer, melanoma, and autologous marrow transplantation. Participates in cooperative group research, investigates local protocol, performs clinical analyses of malignancies. Conducts laboratory studies in signal transduction, gene regulation, biologic markers, cell differentiation, monoclonal antibodies, pharmacokinetics, cytogenetics, and molecular biology of normal and malignant cells. **Publications:** *Masonic Cancer Center News* (quarterly).

University of Missouri—Columbia
Radiation Oncology Program
See: Entry 11170

★6233★ University of Nebraska at Omaha
Eppley Institute for Research in Cancer and Allied Diseases
Medical Center
600 S. 42nd St.
Omaha, NE 68198-6805
Phone: (402)559-4238
Fax: (402)559-4651
Raymond Ruddon, M.D., Dir.

Research Activities and Fields: Mechanisms, causes, prevention, early diagnosis, and treatment of cancer, including programs in molecular and cellular biology and developmental therapeutics. **Publications:** *Cancer Research Update* (newsletter); Annual Report; Scientific Report; Graduate Brochure; *Eppley Facts.* **E-mail Address:** tjchappe@unmc.edu.

★6234★ University of Nevada, Reno
Allie M. Lee Cancer Research Laboratory
157 Howard Medical Sciences
Reno, NV 89557
Phone: (702)784-4107
Fax: (702)784-1419
Dr. Ronald S. Pardini, Dir.

Research Activities and Fields: Pharmacological investigations on effects of inhibition of mitochondrial electron and energy transfer pathways on tumor metabolism, including natural plant products, especially quinones and phenolic derivatives. Emphasizes oxidative stress and anti-oxidant enzymes. **E-mail Address:** ronp@unr.edu.

University of Nevada, Reno
Natural Products Lab
See: Entry 2680

★6235★ University of New Mexico
Cancer Research and Treatment Center
900 Camino de Salud NE
Albuquerque, NM 87131-5636
Phone: (505)277-2151
Fax: (505)277-2841
James A. Neidhart, M.D., Dir.

Research Activities and Fields: Clinical investigations in growth-factor-supplemented high dose chemotherapy, hyperthermia, and various national cooperative group trials; tumor immunology; non-invasive diagnostic technology and development of magnetic resonance imaging; cell surface marker studies in hematopoetic and solid tumors; HPV/cervical cancer; hepatitis virus replication; HTLV-I and II; and cancer in Hispanics and Native Americans. Studies also include biology of natural killer cells and molecular mechanisms of immunosuppression, gene expression, signal transduction, oncogenes, and immune regulation. **Formerly:** Cancer Center.

University of New Mexico
Center for Non-Invasive Diagnosis
See: Entry 11171

★6236★ University of New Mexico
New Mexico Tumor Registry
900 Camino de Salud NE
Albuquerque, NM 87131
Phone: (505)277-5541
Charles Key, M.D., Dir.

Research Activities and Fields: Cancer epidemiology, with emphasis on Hispanics and Amer-

ican Indians. Participates in the NCI's SEER (Surveillance Epidemiology and End Results) Program. **Publications:** *New Mexico Tumor Registry Newsletter* (semiannually).

★6237★ University of North Carolina at Chapel Hill
Center for Thrombosis and Hemostasis
Campus Box 7015
UNC-CH School of Medicine
Chapel Hill, NC 27599-7015
Phone: (919)966-3704
Fax: (919)966-6012
Harold R. Roberts, Dir.

Research Activities and Fields: Thrombosis and hemostasis; the genetics and molecular biology of blood coagulation, including recombinant factors VIII and VIIA and the rationale for treatment or prophylaxis of thrombosis and hemorrhage, including research on peptide growth factors, platelets, lipoprotein metabolism, von Willebrand factor, factor VIII, fibrinogen and fibrin assembly, fibronectin, protease inhibitors, heparin and antithrombins, endothelial cell culture, thrombin and prothrombin, and factor IX and its variants, factor X, acute phase reactants, actin filament system, and gene replacement therapy.

★6238★ University of North Carolina at Chapel Hill
UNC Lineberger Comprehensive Cancer Center
Lineberger
CB 7295
Chapel Hill, NC 27599-7295
Phone: (919)966-3036
Fax: (919)966-3015
Dr. Joseph S. Pagano, Dir.

Research Activities and Fields: Virology, cancer cell biology, immunology, molecular carcinogenesis, molecular therapeutics, epidemiology, clinical research, breast cancer, radiobiology and radiation oncology, bone marrow transplation, and cancer control/cancer prevention, including interdisciplinary studies. Participation is shared among the Schools of Medicine, Public Health, Dentistry, Pharmacy, and Nursing as well as the Department of Biology, Chemistry, and Computer Science at the University, Burroughs Wellcome Company, Glaxo, Inc., National Institute of Environmental Health Sciences, and U.S. Environmental Protection Agency. **Publications:** Newsletter; *Clinical Protocol Reference Book.* **Formerly:** Cancer Research Center (1990).

★6239★ University of Oklahoma
Thrombosis & Coagulation Laboratory
Oklahoma Memorial Hospital, Rm. EB 400
PO Box 26307
Oklahoma City, OK 73126
Phone: (405)271-7732
Fax: (405)271-3620
Philip C. Comp, M.D., Dir.

Research Activities and Fields: Thrombosis, fibrinolysis, and anticoagulation. Develops clinical assays for protein C and protein S.

★6240★ **University of Pennsylvania Cancer Center**
6 Penn Tower
3400 Spruce St.
Philadelphia, PA 19104-4283
Phone: (215)662-6334
Fax: (215)349-5326
John H. Glick, M.D., Dir.

Research Activities and Fields: Cancer biology, diagnosis, cause, prevention, treatment, control, and rehabilitation, including programs in immunobiology, tumor cell biology, gene structure and regulation, virology, clinical investigations, pediatric oncology, tumor metabolism, epidemiology, statistics, melanoma, psychosocial oncology, and cancer control.

★6241★ **University of Pennsylvania Comparative Leukemia Unit**
New Bolton Center
382 W. St. Rd.
Kennett Square, PA 19348
Phone: (610)444-5800
Fax: (610)444-4724
Jorge Ferrer, M.D., Dir.

Research Activities and Fields: Cancer research focusing primarily on the etiology and pathogenesis of bovine leukemia for the development of a new relevant animal model system for studies on the etiology, pathogenesis, and immunoprophylaxis of viral-induced leukemia in humans. Studies include bovine leukemia virus (BLV) and its relationship to other retroviruses, particularly human T-cell lymphotropic virus type one (HTLV-I) and acquired immune deficiency syndrome (AIDS) virus. Also studies vaccine development.

★6242★ **University of Pittsburgh National Surgical Adjuvant Breast and Bowel Project (NSABP)**
NSABP
Operations Ctr., Div. of Medical Affairs
230 McKee Pl., Ste. 402
Pittsburgh, PA 15213
Phone: (412)383-1400
Fax: (412)383-1388
Dr. Norman Wolmark, Chm.

Research Activities and Fields: Clinical research of breast and bowel cancer treatments and breast cancer prevention. Operates in cooperation with over 300 member institutions throughout the U.S., Canada, France, and Australia. **Publications:** Progress Reports (semiannually). **Formerly:** National Surgical Adjuvant Project for Breast and Bowel Cancers.

★6243★ **University of Puerto Rico Puerto Rico Cancer Center**
GPO Box 5067
San Juan, PR 00936
Phone: (809)758-2525
Fax: (809)751-6242
Dr. Reynold Lopez-Enriquez, Dir.

Research Activities and Fields: Cancer biology and carcinogenesis, solid-state carcinogenesis, bioactivation of precarcinogens, asbestos carcinogenesis, synthesis of antineoplastic agents, synthesis of radiosensitizers, tumor immunology, dietary factors in carcinogenesis, and radiation. Seeks cancer control through the Center's Cancer Tumor Registry, Detection Program, and public education. Cancer control research involves epidemiology, biostatistics, health management, and economics. **Publications:** Cancer in Puerto Rico (annually).

★6244★ **University of Rochester Cancer Center**
601 Elmwood Ave., Box 704
Rochester, NY 14642
Phone: (716)275-4911
Fax: (716)273-1042
Richard Borch, M.D., Dir.

Research Activities and Fields: Diagnosis and therapy of cancer, with particular emphasis on experimental therapeutics. Conducts laboratory research in biochemical genetics, radiation biology, immunology, endocrine biochemistry, and cancer pharmacology, utilizing animal tumor research, biomathematics/statistics, cell culture, nucleic acid sequencing, and ultrastructure facilities. Participant in five national cooperative groups. **Formerly:** Division of Oncology (1974).

★6245★ **University of Southern California Comprehensive Sickle Cell Center**
2025 Zonal Ave., Rm. 304
Los Angeles, CA 90033
Phone: (213)342-1259
Fax: (213)342-2644
Dr. Cage S. Johnson, Dir.

Research Activities and Fields: Sickle cell disease, including studies on molecular biology of red cells, fetal hemoglobin identification, and renal, cardiovascular, and endocrine functions.

★6246★ **University of Southern California Hematology Research Laboratory**
2025 Zonal Ave.
Los Angeles, CA 90033
Phone: (213)224-6412
Fax: (213)224-6687
Alexandra Levine, Head

Research Activities and Fields: Hemostasis, including studies on blood coagulation, platelets, etiology of thrombosis, chemical separation and characterization of blood clotting factors and antibodies to blood clotting factors, and hemoglobinopathies and megaloblastic anemias, including vitamin B-12, folate metabolism, and B-12 binding proteins. Maintains active research programs in immunology and in all types of hematologic malignancies, particularly non-Hodgkin's lymphomata, AIDS, and Kaposi's sarcoma.

★6247★ **University of Southern California Hematopathology Unit**
1200 N. State St., Rm 2422
Los Angeles, CA 90033
Phone: (213)226-7064
Fax: (213)226-7119
Dr. Bharat N. Nathwani, Chief

Research Activities and Fields: Investigates neoplasms of hematopoietic system, molecular biology, and polymerase chain reactions.

★6248★ **University of Southern California Medical Oncology Research Program**
1441 E. Lake
Los Angeles, CA 90033
Phone: (213)224-6677
Fax: (213)224-6687
Franco M. Muggia, M.D., Dir.

Research Activities and Fields: Medical oncology, chemotherapy, and immunotherapy of cancer. Conducts laboratory and clinical investigations into the biology and treatment of cancer, including studies on innovative treatments, new drugs and biological agents, locoregional therapy such as hyperthermia, and preclinical and clinical pharmacology. Major studies are also conducted in autologous bone marrow transplantation for solid tumors and in biological response modifiers, including interleukin-2 interferons, monoclonal antibodies, and melanoma vaccines. **E-mail Address:** muggia_f@norris.hsc.usc.edu.

★6249★ **University of Southern California Norris Comprehensive Cancer Center**
1441 Eastlake Ave.
PO Box 33800
Los Angeles, CA 90033-0800
Phone: (213)224-6503
Fax: (213)224-6593
Peter A. Jones, Ph.D., Dir.

Research Activities and Fields: Cancer, emphasizing multidisciplinary basic and clinical studies on cancer detection, prevention, cause, diagnosis, treatment, rehabilitation, and cancer education. Conducts interdisciplinary research in the following program areas: gene regulation; tumor biology; immunobiology, pathogenesis and therapy; developmental therapeutics; cancer etiology; and cancer prevention research and education. **Publications:** Cancer Center Report (quarterly). **Formerly:** Comprehensive Cancer Center (1988).

★6250★ **University of Tennessee Memphis Cancer Center**
N327 Van Vleet Bldg.
3 N. Dunlap St.
Memphis, TN 38163
Phone: (901)528-5150
Fax: (901)528-5033
Alvin M. Mauer, M.D., Dir.

Research Activities and Fields: Detection, evaluation, and treatment of cancer, specifically, clinical therapeutic research, cancer drug development, cell growth and regulation, and gene regulation and expression. **Publications:** Cancer Education Bulletin (Monthly). **E-mail Address:** amauer@utmem1.utmem.edu. **Formerly:** Comprehensive Cancer Center (1986).

★6251★ **University of Tennessee, Knoxville Experimental Oncology Laboratory**
PO Box 1071
Knoxville, TN 37901-1071
Phone: (615)974-8234
Fax: (615)974-5616
Dr. H.M. Schuller, Dir.

Research Activities and Fields: Oncology research, focusing on role of receptor mediated signal transduction pathways and their role in chemical carcinogenesis mechanisms.

★6252★ University of Tennessee, Knoxville
Human Immunology and Cancer Program (HICP)
1924 Alcoa Hwy.
Knoxville, TN 37920
Phone: (615)544-9165
Fax: (615)544-6865
Alan Solomon, M.D., Dir.

Research Activities and Fields: Multiple myeloma, AL amyloidosis, and monoclonal B cell-related neoplasms. Conducts basic and clinical investigatons related to the pathogenesis, diagnosis, and treatment of patients with B cell immunoproliferative diseases. **Publications:** Annual Report. **E-mail Address:** asolomon@wizard.hosp.utk.edu.

★6253★ University of Texas
University of Texas M.D. Anderson Cancer Center
Texas Medical Center
1515 Holcombe Blvd.
Houston, TX 77030
Phone: (713)792-2121
Fax: (713)790-9492
Frederick F. Becker, M.D., V.Pres. for Research

Research Activities and Fields: Chemotherapy, laser surgery, biologic response modifiers, imaging techniques, blood component utilization, fast neutron therapy, pharmacology, radiation physics, radiobiology, laser biology, cell biology, molecular pathology, veterinary medicine, tumor biology, virology, human genetics, molecular genetics immunology, biochemistry, molecular biology, invasion and metastasis, biomathematics and biostatistics, chemical carcinogenesis, epidemiology, behavioral science, and cancer prevention. Operates a diversified program of clinical and basic science research related to cancer designed to improve early detection, diagnostic techniques, therapy, rehabilitation, and cancer prevention. **Publications:** *Cancer Bulletin* (bimonthly); *OncoLog* (four times per year); Reports (biennially).

★6254★ University of Texas Medical Branch at Galveston
Cancer Center
106 Basic Science Bldg., F30
Galveston, TX 77550
Phone: (409)772-2981
Fax: (409)772-4865
Courtney M. Townsend, Jr., M.D., Interim Dir.

Research Activities and Fields: Cancer education, cancer prevention and control, and radiation, surgical, and medical oncology, including basic science investigation. Participates as one of a group of clinical and basic science centers for cancer research in nationwide program for development of means to reduce incidence, morbidity, and mortality of cancer established under National Cancer Act of 1971. Fosters intercampus, interdisciplinary cancer research and coordinates search for major foundation funds for equipment.

★6255★ University of Texas Southwestern Medical Center at Dallas
Sickle Cell Case Management Program
5323 Harry Hines Blvd.
Dallas, TX 75235
Phone: (214)648-3388
Fax: (214)648-8617
Dr. George Buchanan, Dir.

Research Activities and Fields: Researches morbidity and mortality of pediatric sickle cell patients.

★6256★ University of Utah
Rocky Mountain Cancer Data System
420 Chipeta Way, 120
Salt Lake City, UT 84108
Phone: (801)581-4307
Fax: (801)581-5704
Lawrence Derrick, Asst.Dir.

Research Activities and Fields: Conducts cancer research and provides data to participating hospitals and state registries.

★6257★ University of Vermont
Vermont Cancer Center
1 S. Prospect St.
Burlington, VT 05401-3498
Phone: (802)656-4414
Fax: (802)656-8788
Richard J. Albertini, M.D., Dir.

Research Activities and Fields: Cancer, including multidisciplinary programs in antineoplastic drug development, genetic toxicology, clinical research, cancer control research, immunobiology, DNA repair, and carcinogenesis. Conducts clinical studies in cancer chemotherapy, gynecologic oncology, surgical oncology, and radiotherapy. One of a group of NCI designated centers for conducting multidisciplinary cancer research and improving methods of treatment, diagnosis, and prevention. Trains health professionals and transfers cancer knowledge to surrounding communities as part of NCI's nationwide coordinated program to reduce incidence, morbidity, and mortality of cancer established under National Cancer Act of 1971. **Publications:** Newsletter (periodic). **Formerly:** Vermont Regional Cancer Center (1991).

★6258★ University of Wisconsin
Comprehensive Cancer Center
600 Highland Ave.
Madison, WI 53792
Phone: (608)263-8600
Fax: (608)263-8613
Paul P. Carbone, M.D., Dir.

Research Activities and Fields: Clinical and laboratory research in the biology of cancer, focused on human-oriented problems in etiology, prevention, and tumor localization and treatment. Conducts studies in breast, prostate, and bladder cancers, medical oncology, hyperthermia, immunobiology, radiobiology, experimental chemotherapy, hematologic oncology, pediatric oncology, radiation onocology, biostatistics, and medical physics. One of 27 regional comprehensive cancer centers conducting multidisciplinary research, improving methods of treatment, diagnosis, and prevention, training health professionals, and transferring cancer knowledge

to surrounding communities in the National Cancer Institute's nationwide coordination program established under the National Cancer Act of 1971. **Publications:** Annual Report. **Formerly:** Clinical Cancer Center (1991).

★6259★ University of Wisconsin— Madison
Children's Cancer Study Group
Dept. of Pediatrics
Div. of Hematology/Oncology, K4/430
600 Highland Ave.
Madison, WI 53792
Phone: (608)263-6200
Fax: (608)263-4226
Dr. Paul Gaynon, Prin. Investigator

Research Activities and Fields: Pediatric oncology, including trials of new treatment regimens.

★6260★ University of Wisconsin— Madison
Hematology Research Laboratory
Medical Sciences Center, Rm. 4459
1300 Univ. Ave.
Madison, WI 53706
Phone: (608)262-1576
Fax: (608)263-4969
Dr. Deane Mosher, Dir.

Research Activities and Fields: Biology and biochemistry. Conducts studies on cell cultures, particularly the plasma proteins, fibronectin, vitronectin, and the platelet protein thrombospondin. Characterizes proteins for biomedical applications.

★6261★ University of Wisconsin— Madison
McArdle Laboratory for Cancer Research
Madison, WI 53706
Phone: (608)262-2177
Fax: (608)262-2824
Dr. Norman Drinkwater, Dir.

Research Activities and Fields: Cellular, developmental, molecular, animal cell, and viral biology; and genetics, biochemistry, and immunology. Emphasizes mechanisms and controls of transcription, translation, and replication in cells and viruses; mechanisms of environmental, chemical, and viral carcinogenesis; and chemistry and metabolism of nucleic acids and proteins.

★6262★ Virginia Commonwealth University
Massey Cancer Center of the Medical College of Virginia
Box 980037, 401 College St.
Richmond, VA 23298-0037
Phone: (804)828-0450
Fax: (804)828-8453
I. David Goldman, M.D., Dir.

Research Activities and Fields: Molecular biology, immunobiology, developmental therapeutics, neurooncology, carcinogenesis, hematopoiesis, bone marrow transplantation, cancer prevention, and structural biology. Clinical studies include translational research and participation in national cooperative groups. Focuses on decision analysis methodologies for evaluation of cancer treatment outcomes and costs through a Health Sciences Research Program. **Publications:** *Advance* (semiannually); *In-Advance* (monthly). **E-mail Address:** seither@mcci.mcc.vcu.edu. **Formerly:** MCV/VCU Cancer Center (1983).

★6263★ Wake Forest University Comprehensive Cancer Center
Medical Center Blvd.
Winston-Salem, NC 27157-1082
Phone: (910)716-4464
Fax: (910)716-5687
Dr. Frank M. Torti, Dir.

Research Activities and Fields: Cause and therapy of cancer, in a multidisciplinary effort to determine cause of cancer and to develop more effective means of treating malignant disease. **Formerly:** Oncology Research Center.

★6264★ Walt Disney Memorial Cancer Institute
Cancer Research Division
12722 Research Pkwy.
Orlando, FL 32826
Phone: (407)380-9977
Fax: (407)380-9978
Leslie K. Aldrich, Contact

Research Activities and Fields: Cancer, including cell biology and cell regulation, molecular biology, structural biology and drug design, and hemostasis and thrombosis.

★6265★ Walther Cancer Institute, Inc.
3202 N. Meridian St.
Indianapolis, IN 46208
Phone: (317)921-2040
Fax: (317)924-4688
Joseph E. Walther, M.D., Pres. and CEO

Research Activities and Fields: Basic and clinical research on the treatment, prevention, and cure of cancer and studies on the care of cancer patients and families. **Publications:** Newsletter (quarterly); Annual Report. **Formerly:** Walther Medical Research Institute (1988).

★6266★ Walther Oncology Center
Indiana Univ. School of Medicine
Medical Research & Library Bldg., 501
975 W. Walnut St.
Indianapolis, IN 46202-5121
Phone: (317)274-7510
Fax: (317)274-7592
Hal E. Broxmeyer, Ph.D., Scientific Dir.

Research Activities and Fields: Blood cell and solid tumor studies, including regulation of the production of normal and cancer cells and umbilical cord blood transplantation, growth factors, suppressor molecules, receptors, gene regulation, oncogenes, differentiation, signal transduction, phosphorylation, cell division cycle genes, and protein tyrosine phosphatases.

Washington University
Hyperthermia Service
See: Entry 11625

Wayne State University
Center for Molecular Medicine and Genetics
See: Entry 5392

★6267★ Wayne State University Comprehensive Sickle Cell Center
Curricular Affairs Office
Scott Hall, Rm. 1206
540 E. Canfield
Detroit, MI 48201
Phone: (313)577-1546
Fax: (313)577-8777
Charles F. Whitten, M.D., Dir.

Research Activities and Fields: Sickle cell disease, including molecular, cellular, tissular, and organic studies. Seeks to apply sickle cell research to improved health care at the community level.

★6268★ West Virginia University Mary Babb Randolph Cancer Center
Health Sciences Center
PO Box 9300
Morgantown, WV 26506
Phone: (304)293-3528
Fax: (304)293-4667
Dr. Fred Butcher, Dir.

Research Activities and Fields: Clinical and scientific cancer research concentrating on residents of West Virginia.

Worcester Foundation for Experimental Biology
Cancer Center
See: Entry 2710

★6269★ Yale University Center for Molecular Medicine
School of Medicine
295 Congress Ave.
New Haven, CT 06536
Phone: (203)737-2263
Fax: (203)737-2267
Dr. Vincent Machesi, Dir.

Research Activities and Fields: Molecular oncology and medicine, focusing on multicellular oncology and organisms.

★6270★ Yale University Yale Comprehensive Cancer Center
333 Cedar St., Rm. 205, WWW
New Haven, CT 06520-8028
Phone: (203)785-4095
Fax: (203)785-4116
Dr. Vincent T. DeVita, Dir.

Research Activities and Fields: Basic research programs in cell biology, developmental therapeutics/chemotherapy, immunology, molecular oncology and development, molecular virology, as well as cancer control, prevention, and treatment of cancer patients at all stages of disease, including those with unusual and/or difficult cancer cases where multidisciplinary evaluation and/or treatment is available. Clinical science programs in dermatology, diagnostic radiology, medical oncology/hematology, gynecologic oncology, pediatric oncology, pathology, surgical oncology, and therapeutic radiology are also available. Conducts clinical trials in all forms of therapy. **Publications:** *Caring* (semiannual newsletter).

State & Regional Organizations

Cancer

Divisions of the American Cancer Society are listed below. The national office is located at 1599 Clifton Rd. NE, Atlanta, GA 30329, (404) 320-3333.

Alabama

★6271★ American Cancer Society Alabama Division
504 Brookwood Blvd.
Homewood, AL 35209
Phone: (205)879-2242
Fax: (205)870-7436

Alaska

★6272★ American Cancer Society Alaska Division
1057 W. Fireweed Ln., Ste. 204
Anchorage, AK 99503
Phone: (907)277-8696
Fax: (907)263-2073

Arizona

★6273★ American Cancer Society Arizona Division
2929 E. Thomas Rd.
Phoenix, AZ 85016
Phone: (602)224-0524
Fax: (602)381-3096

Arkansas

★6274★ American Cancer Society Arkansas Division
901 N. University
Little Rock, AR 72207
Phone: (501)664-3480
Fax: (501)666-0068

California

★6275★ American Cancer Society California Division
1710 Webster St.
Oakland, CA 94612
Phone: (510)893-7900
Fax: (510)835-8656

Colorado

★6276★ American Cancer Society Colorado Division
2255 S. Oneida
Denver, CO 80224
Phone: (303)758-2030
Fax: (303)758-7006

Connecticut

★6277★ American Cancer Society
Connecticut Division
Barnes Park S.
14 Village Ln.
Wallingford, CT 06492
Phone: (203)265-7161
Fax: (203)265-0281

Delaware

★6278★ American Cancer Society
Delaware Division
92 Read's Way, Ste. 205
New Castle, DE 19720
Phone: (302)324-4227
Fax: (302)324-4233

District of Columbia

★6279★ American Cancer Society
District of Columbia Division
1875 Connecticut Ave. NW, Ste. 730
Washington, DC 20009
Phone: (202)483-2600
Fax: (202)483-1174

Florida

★6280★ American Cancer Society
Florida Division
3709 W. Jetton Ave.
Tampa, FL 33629-5146
Phone: (813)253-0541
Fax: (813)254-5857

Georgia

★6281★ American Cancer Society
Georgia Division
Lenox Park
2200 Lake Blvd.
Atlanta, GA 30319
Phone: (404)816-7800
Fax: (404)816-9443

Hawaii

★6282★ American Cancer Society
Hawaii Pacific Division
Community Services Center Bldg.
200 N. Vineyard Blvd., Ste. 100-A
Honolulu, HI 96817
Phone: (808)531-1662
Fax: (808)526-9729

Idaho

★6283★ American Cancer Society
Idaho Division
2676 Vista Ave.
Boise, ID 83705
Phone: (208)343-4609
Fax: (208)343-9922

Illinois

★6284★ American Cancer Society
Illinois Division
77 E. Monroe St.
Chicago, IL 60603-5795
Phone: (312)641-6150
Fax: (312)641-6588

Indiana

★6285★ American Cancer Society
Indiana Division
8730 Commerce Park Pl.
Indianapolis, IN 46268
Phone: (317)872-4432
Fax: (317)879-4114

Iowa

★6286★ American Cancer Society
Iowa Division
8364 Hickman Rd., Ste. D
Des Moines, IA 50325-4300
Phone: (515)253-0147
Fax: (515)253-0806

Kansas

★6287★ American Cancer Society
Kansas Division
1315 SW Arrowhead Rd.
Topeka, KS 66604-4020
Phone: (913)273-4114
Fax: (913)273-1503

Kentucky

★6288★ American Cancer Society
Kentucky Division
701 W. Muhammad Ali Blvd.
Louisville, KY 40203-1909
Phone: (502)584-6782
Fax: (502)584-8946

Louisiana

★6289★ American Cancer Society
Louisiana Division
2200 Veterans Memorial Blvd., Ste. 214
Kenner, LA 70062
Phone: (504)469-0021
Fax: (504)469-0033

Maine

★6290★ American Cancer Society
Maine Division
52 Federal St.
Brunswick, ME 04011
Phone: (207)729-3339
Fax: (207)729-0635

Maryland

★6291★ American Cancer Society
Maryland Division
8219 Town Center Dr.
Baltimore, MD 21236-0026
Phone: (410)931-6850
Fax: (410)931-6875

Massachusetts

★6292★ American Cancer Society
Massachusetts Division
247 Commonwealth Ave.
Boston, MA 02116
Phone: (617)267-2650
Fax: (617)536-3163

Michigan

★6293★ American Cancer Society
Michigan Division
1205 E. Saginaw St.
Lansing, MI 48906
Phone: (517)371-2920
Fax: (517)371-2605

Minnesota

★6294★ American Cancer Society
Minnesota Division
3316 W. 66th St.
Minneapolis, MN 55435
Phone: (612)925-2772
Fax: (612)925-6333

Mississippi

★6295★ American Cancer Society
Mississippi Division
Lakeover Office Park
1380 Livingston Ln.
Jackson, MS 39213
Phone: (601)362-8874
Fax: (601)362-8876

Missouri

★6296★ American Cancer Society
Missouri Division
3322 American Ave.
Jefferson City, MO 65109
Phone: (314)893-4800
Fax: (314)893-2017

Montana

★6297★ American Cancer Society
Montana Division
17 N. 26th St.
Billings, MT 59101
Phone: (406)252-7111
Fax: (406)252-7112

Nebraska

★6298★ American Cancer Society
Nebraska Division
8502 W. Center Rd.
Omaha, NE 68124-5255
Phone: (402)393-5800
Fax: (402)393-7790

Nevada

★6299★ American Cancer Society
Nevada Division
1325 E. Harmon
Las Vegas, NV 89119
Phone: (702)798-6857
Fax: (702)798-0530

New Hampshire

★6300★ American Cancer Society
New Hampshire Division
Gail Singer Memorial Bldg., Ste. 501
360 State Rte. 101
Bedford, NH 03110-5032
Phone: (603)472-8899
Fax: (603)472-7093

New Jersey

★6301★ American Cancer Society
New Jersey Division
2600 US Hwy. 1
North Brunswick, NJ 08902-6001
Phone: (908)297-8000
Fax: (908)297-9043

New Mexico

★6302★ American Cancer Society
New Mexico Division
5800 Lomas Blvd. NE
Albuquerque, NM 87110
Phone: (505)260-2105
Fax: (505)266-9513

New York

★6303★ American Cancer Society
Long Island Division
75 Davids Dr.
Hauppauge, NY 11788
Phone: (516)436-7070
Fax: (516)436-5380

★6304★ American Cancer Society
New York City Division
19 W. 56th St.
New York, NY 10019
Phone: (212)586-8700
Fax: (212)237-3852

★6305★ American Cancer Society
New York State Division
6725 Lyons St.
East Syracuse, NY 13057
Phone: (315)437-7025
Fax: (315)437-0540

★6306★ American Cancer Society
Queens Division
112-25 Queens Blvd.
Forest Hills, NY 11375
Phone: (718)263-2224
Fax: (718)261-0758

★6307★ American Cancer Society
Westchester Division
30 Glenn St.
White Plains, NY 10603
Phone: (914)949-4800
Fax: (914)949-4279

North Carolina

★6308★ American Cancer Society
North Carolina Division
11 S. Boylan Ave., Ste. 221
Raleigh, NC 27603
Phone: (919)834-8463
Fax: (919)839-0551

North Dakota

★6309★ American Cancer Society
North Dakota Division
123 Roberts St.
Fargo, ND 58102
Phone: (701)232-1385
Fax: (701)232-1109

Ohio

★6310★ American Cancer Society
Ohio Division
5555 Frantz Rd.
Dublin, OH 43017
Phone: (614)889-9565
Fax: (614)889-6578

Oklahoma

★6311★ American Cancer Society
Oklahoma Division
4323 NW 63rd, St. 110
Oklahoma City, OK 73116
Phone: (405)843-9888
Fax: (405)848-0795

Oregon

★6312★ American Cancer Society
Oregon Division
0330 SW Curry St.
Portland, OR 97201
Phone: (503)295-6422
Fax: (503)228-1062

Pennsylvania

★6313★ American Cancer Society
Pennsylvania Division
Rte. 422 & Sipe Ave.
Hershey, PA 17033-0897
Phone: (717)533-6144
Fax: (717)534-1075

★6314★ American Cancer Society
Philadelphia Division
1626 Locust St.
Philadelphia, PA 19103
Phone: (215)985-5400
Fax: (215)985-5406

Puerto Rico

★6315★ American Cancer Society
Puerto Rico Division
Esquina Sargento Medina
Calle Alverio No. 577
Hato Rey, PR 00918
Phone: (809)764-2295
Fax: (809)764-0553

Rhode Island

★6316★ American Cancer Society
Rhode Island Division
400 Main St.
Pawtucket, RI 02860
Phone: (401)722-8480
Fax: (401)727-9449

South Carolina

★6317★ American Cancer Society
South Carolina Division
128 Stonemark Ln.
Columbia, SC 29210-3855
Phone: (803)750-1693
Fax: (803)750-4000

South Dakota

★6318★ American Cancer Society
South Dakota Division
4101 S. Carnegie Pl.
Sioux Falls, SD 57106-2322
Phone: (605)361-8277
Fax: (605)361-8537

Tennessee

★6319★ American Cancer Society
Tennessee Division
1315 8th Ave. S.
Nashville, TN 37203
Phone: (615)255-1227
Fax: (615)255-1230

Texas

★6320★ American Cancer Society
Texas Division
2433 Ridgepoint Dr.
Austin, TX 78754
Phone: (512)928-2262
Fax: (512)929-9243

Utah

★6321★ American Cancer Society
Utah Division
941 East 3300 South
Salt Lake City, UT 84106
Phone: (801)483-1500
Fax: (801)483-1558

Vermont

★6322★ American Cancer Society
Vermont Division
13 Loomis St.
Montpelier, VT 05602
Phone: (802)223-2348
Fax: (802)223-4818

Virginia

★6323★ American Cancer Society
Virginia Division
4240 Park Place Ct.
Glen Allen, VA 23060
Phone: (804)527-3700
Fax: (804)527-3797

Washington

★6324★ American Cancer Society
Washington Division
2120 1st Ave. N.
Seattle, WA 98109-1140
Phone: (206)283-1152
Fax: (206)285-3469

West Virginia

★6325★ American Cancer Society
West Virginia Division
2428 Kanawha Blvd. E.
Charleston, WV 25311
Phone: (304)344-3611
Fax: (304)343-6549

Wisconsin

★6326★ American Cancer Society
Wisconsin Division
N19 W24350 Riverwood Dr.
Waukesha, WI 53188
Phone: (414)523-5500
Fax: (414)523-5533

Wyoming

★6327★ American Cancer Society
Wyoming Division
4202 Ridge Rd.
Cheyenne, WY 82001
Phone: (307)638-3331
Fax: (307)638-1199

Chapter 32
Hospitals

Foundations & Other Funding Organizations

Private Foundations

A. C. Buehler Foundation
See: Entry 1869

★6328★ Abney Foundation
Peachtree Offices, Ste. D
1214 N Main St.
Anderson, SC 29621
Phone: (803)964-9201
Carl T. Edwards, Executive Director

Foundation Philosophy: The Abney Foundation primarily supports higher education in South Carolina. Interests include colleges, technical schools, and universities. The foundation also supports hospitals, hospices, homes, food distribution, and youth organizations. **Giving Priorities:** In 1993, the foundation reported that education received 80% of funding, primarily to colleges in South Carolina. Of the remainder, 10% went to religion, 5% went to social services, 4% went to other interests, and 1% was awarded to the arts. **Typical Health-Related Recipients:** Clinics/Medical Centers, Home-Care Services, Hospices, Hospitals. **Geographic Distribution:** Focus on South Carolina, principally to national organizations.

Alex Hillman Family Foundation
See: Entry 37

★6329★ Amelia Peabody Charitable Fund
201 Devonshire St.
Boston, MA 02110
Phone: (617)451-6178
JoAnne Borek, Executive Director

Foundation Philosophy: The purpose of the Amelia Peabody Charitable Fund is to assist local charitable and educational organizations, with emphasis on hospitals, cultural programs, secondary education institutions, and conservation groups. **Giving Priorities:** In 1992, the fund gave approximately 42% of its contributions to the arts. Educational institutions received 39% of funding, with another $1,000,000 grant going

to the Massachusetts Institute of Technology for a medical doctoral program. Health care received 7% of grants, with major support to children's hospitals. Social services and civic concerns each received 6% of contributions, and religious organizations, 1%. **Typical Health-Related Recipients:** Children's Health/Hospitals, Clinics/Medical Centers, Family Planning, Heart, Hospitals, Nursing Services, People with Disabilities, Single-Disease Health Associations. **Geographic Distribution:** Usually New England and largely greater Boston area.

Amelia Peabody Foundation
See: Entry 41

★6330★ American Foundation Corporation
720 National City Bank Bldg.
Cleveland, OH 44114
Phone: (216)241-6664
Maria G. Muth, Director of Contributions, Treasurer

Foundation Philosophy: The American Foundation Corporation makes most of its grants in the areas of civic affairs, education, the arts, and social services. Social service funding includes child welfare, youth organizations, and animal protection. The foundation also supports other recipient areas. **Giving Priorities:** In 1993, approximately 33% of funding went to civic affairs, including the highest grant of $214,033 to Holden Arboretum. Education and the arts each received 16% of support. About 12% of funds went to social services, and about 8% went to scientific organizations. Environmental concerns and health care each received 7%. The remaining funds went to religious affairs. **Typical Health-Related Recipients:** Children's Health/Hospitals, Clinics/Medical Centers, Hospitals, Long-Term Care, Mental Health, People with Disabilities. **Geographic Distribution:** National, with emphasis on Ohio.

Andersen Foundation
See: Entry 43

Arie and Ida Crown Memorial
See: Entry 49

★6331★ B. B. Owen Trust
PO Box 830068
Richardson, TX 75083
Phone: (214)783-7170
Monty J. Jackson, Trustee

Foundation Philosophy: The B. B. Owen Charitable Trust primarily contributes most of its grants to health care, specifically medical centers in Texas. Other areas of interest include food and clothing distribution, community centers, homes, religion, and civic affairs. **Giving Priorities:** In fiscal 1993, the foundation gave 96% of its funds to health services. Southwest Medical Foundation in Dallas, TX, received the highest grant of $911,660. The remaining 4% of funding supported religious organizations. **Typical Health-Related Recipients:** Clinics/Medical Centers, Hospitals, Medical Research. **Geographic Distribution:** Texas, focus on Dallas.

Beatrice P. Delany Charitable Trust
See: Entry 61

Benjamin and Mary Siddons Measey Foundation
See: Entry 66

★6332★ Benjamin and Roberta Russell Educational Foundation
PO Box 272
Alexander City, AL 35010
Phone: (205)329-4224
Fax: (205)329-5346
James D. Nabors, Secretary and Treasurer

Foundation Philosophy: The foundation's primary interest is education, with a focus on higher education. Support often goes to universities, community colleges, and private academies. The foundation also will contribute to hospitals, health relief agencies, single disease associations, and children's welfare organizations. **Giving Priorities:** In 1992, the foundation gave approximately 38% of its funds to educational institutions. Social services received about 33%, including the foundation's highest grant of $350,000 to Children's Harbor in Birmingham, AL. Health concerns received 21%, and the arts received the remaining funds. **Typical Health-Related Recipients:** Emergency/Ambulance Services, Hospitals, Kidney, Multiple Sclerosis, Single-Disease Health Associations. **Geo-**

graphic Distribution: Southeastern United States, with a focus on Alabama.

★ 6333 ★ Benson and Edith Ford Fund
100 Renaissance Ctr., 34th Fl.
Detroit, MI 48243
Phone: (313)259-7777
Pierre V. Heftler, Secretary

Foundation Philosophy: The foundation makes grants in the areas of youth organizations and child welfare, hospitals, civic affairs, the arts, and education. A wide variety of grants are given in each of these areas. **Giving Priorities:** In 1993, the foundation awarded approximately 37% of its total charitable giving to social services organizations, with major support for community centers and child welfare. Health care received about 26% of total giving, including a $100,000 grant to the Henry Ford Health System. Education received 17% of support, while 10% was given to arts organizations. Civic affairs received 7% of funds, and religion received 2%. The remaining funds, less than 1%, supported environmental affairs. **Typical Health-Related Recipients:** Children's Health/Hospitals, Family Planning, Health Organizations, Hospitals, People with Disabilities, Preventive Medicine/Wellness Organizations, Substance Abuse. **Geographic Distribution:** Michigan, with focus on Detroit.

Booth-Bricker Fund
See: Entry 73

Broyhill Family Foundation
See: Entry 77

★ 6334 ★ Buchanan Family Foundation
222 E Wisconsin Ave.
Lake Forest, IL 60045
Phone: (708)234-0235
Huntington Eldridge, Jr., Treasurer

Foundation Philosophy: The foundation generally supports hospitals and health organizations, cultural and environmental causes, and colleges and universities, all within the metropolitan Chicago, IL, area. **Giving Priorities:** In 1992, the foundation gave approximately 34% of its contributions to health care, including its two highest grants of $150,000 each for Northwestern Memorial Hospital and the Rush-Presbyterian-St. Luke's Medical Center, both located in Chicago, IL. Education received 19%. Civic organizations received 17%. The arts received 10%; social services, 9%; and science received 7%. Religion (2%) and international affairs (1%) received the remainder. **Typical Health-Related Recipients:** Children's Health/Hospitals, Clinics/Medical Centers, Emergency/Ambulance Services, Family Planning, Health Organizations, Hospitals, Medical Rehabilitation, Medical Research, Nursing Services, Single-Disease Health Associations. **Geographic Distribution:** Primarily Chicago, IL.

★ 6335 ★ Caleb C. and Julia W. Dula Educational and Charitable Foundation
c/o Chemical Bank
270 Park Ave., 21st Fl.
New York, NY 10017
Phone: (212)270-9066
Gale Fitch, Senior Trust Officer

Foundation Philosophy: The foundation primarily supports the arts and civic affairs. The

foundation also makes contributions to education, hospitals and nursing services, and social services. **Giving Priorities:** In 1993, the foundation awarded approximately 41% of its total contributions to the arts. Civic affairs received about 26%. Educational institutions received 11%. Environmental causes received 8%. Health concerns and social services each received 5%; religious organizations, 3%; and scientific interests received the remaining funds. **Typical Health-Related Recipients:** Cancer, Children's Health/Hospitals, Diabetes, Emergency/Ambulance Services, Health Organizations, Hospitals, Medical Education, Nursing Services, People with Disabilities, Single-Disease Health Associations. **Geographic Distribution:** Primarily New York and Missouri.

★ 6336 ★ Camp Younts Foundation
c/o Trust Company Bank
PO Box 4655
Atlanta, GA 30302
Phone: (404)588-7442
Ange Vaughan, Contact

Foundation Philosophy: The foundation typically supports small colleges, private academies, and military institutes. Another priority is civic affairs, specifically Southampton County, VA, and the Elms Foundation. Other areas of support include churches, homes, and child welfare organizations. **Giving Priorities:** In 1993, approximately 41% of funding went to higher education. Civic affairs received 23%; the arts, 13%; and religious causes, 12%, including the highest grant of $60,000 to the Franklin Baptist Church. Social services were awarded 7% of funding and health care received 4%. **Typical Health-Related Recipients:** Hospitals, Nursing Services, Single-Disease Health Associations. **Geographic Distribution:** Southeastern United States; focus on Virginia.

★ 6337 ★ Cannon Foundation
PO Box 548
Concord, NC 28026-0548
Phone: (704)786-8216
D. L. Gray, Executive Director

Foundation Philosophy: The foundation is dedicated to carrying out the donor's "commitment to the people of Cabarrus County and the state of North Carolina through his philanthropy in health, education, and religion." **Giving Priorities:** In fiscal 1993, the foundation reported that it gave approximately 36% to health care, and 28% to social services. Education received 27%; the arts, 5%; and religion, 4%. **Typical Health-Related Recipients:** Domestic Violence, Family Planning, Health Organizations, Hospitals, Nutrition, Substance Abuse. **Geographic Distribution:** Primarily North Carolina.

★ 6338 ★ Carl B. and Florence E. King Foundation
5956 Sherry Ln., Ste. 620
Dallas, TX 75225
Phone: (214)750-1884
Carl Yeckel, President

Foundation Philosophy: The King Foundation contributes to a variety of organizations, including support for youth activities, community centers, and relief for the needy. The foundation is also interested in funding the construction of

schools, hospitals, homes for the aged, and supporting the handicapped and the indigent. Educational institutes, medical research organizations, and other charitable or scientific associations also are supported. **Giving Priorities:** In 1992, the foundation contributed 35% of its total gifts to social services. Approximately 23% of support went to educational institutions. The arts received 20% of giving; civic groups, 11%; and health care, 7%. Religious groups and scientific institutions received the remainder. **Typical Health-Related Recipients:** Cancer, Children's Health/Hospitals, Clinics/Medical Centers, Health Funds, Health Organizations, Hospitals, Medical Education, Medical Research, Nursing Services, People with Disabilities. **Geographic Distribution:** Focus on the Dallas, TX, area.

Carrie Estelle Doheny Foundation
See: Entry 87

★ 6339 ★ Charles M. Bair Memorial Trust
c/o First Trust Company of Montana
PO Box 30678
Billings, MT 59115
Phone: (406)657-8134
Helen Hancock, Trust Administrator

Foundation Philosophy: The trust's priorities include hospitals and medical centers in Montana that were named in the original trust document. Christian Science churches and scholarships to graduates of Harlowton and White Sulpher Springs high schools and high schools in Meagher and Wheatland counties are also supported. **Giving Priorities:** In fiscal 1994, 97% of funding went to health care institutions. The remainder went to two First Churches of Christ Scientist. **Typical Health-Related Recipients:** Hospitals. **Geographic Distribution:** Limited to Montana.

★ 6340 ★ Clark Foundation
30 Wall St.
New York, NY 10005
Phone: (212)269-1833
Fax: (212)747-0087
Joseph H. Cruickshank, Secretary

Foundation Philosophy: The foundation continues to support the hospital and the museums in Cooperstown, NY. Funding is also given for educational, youth, employment, and social service organizations. **Giving Priorities:** In fiscal 1993, the foundation gave approximately 37% of funding to social services. Education received 21%. Civic causes received 19%, while health care received 11%. The remainder supported the arts (6%) and religious concerns (6%). **Typical Health-Related Recipients:** Cancer, Emergency/Ambulance Services, Family Planning, Health Funds, Hospitals, Kidney, Medical Education, Medical Training, Outpatient Health Care, People with Disabilities, Substance Abuse. **Geographic Distribution:** Primarily Cooperstown, NY, and New York City.

Coleman Foundation
See: Entry 110

★6341★ Constantin Foundation
3811 Turtle Creek Blvd.
L.B. 39
Dallas, TX 75219
Phone: (214)522-9300
Fax: (214)521-7025
Betty S. Hillin, Executive Director

Foundation Philosophy: Traditionally, most grants have been awarded to colleges, universities, and secondary schools. The remainder of funds have supported hospitals and medical centers, and social service organizations. **Giving Priorities:** In 1991, education benefited from approximately 46% of funding, with support for higher and private secondary educational institutions in Dallas. Social services received 37% of foundation giving, with an emphasis on youth services. Approximately 11% went to health-related concerns. Civic and public affairs received 3% of funding, the arts 3%, and science 1%. **Typical Health-Related Recipients:** Health Organizations, Hospitals. **Geographic Distribution:** Metropolitan Dallas, TX, only.

Dale J. Bellamah Foundation
See: Entry 124

Dan Murphy Foundation
See: Entry 125

Davenport-Hatch Foundation
See: Entry 130

★6342★ David, Helen, Marian Woodward Fund-Atlanta
c/o Wachovia Bank of Georgia
PO Box 4148
MC 705
Atlanta, GA 30302
Phone: (404)332-6677
Fax: (404)332-1389
Beverly Blake, Principal Manager

Foundation Philosophy: Health care topped the giving list of the fund with two children's hospitals in Atlanta receiving the two largest grants during fiscal 1991. The Henrietta Egleston Hospital for Children received $150,000 and the Scottish Rite Hospital for Crippled Children received $100,000. The fund gave more than $350,000 to health care. The fund evenly spread out its remaining contributions among several different groups primarily in the Atlanta area. Social services, education, religious organizations, civic groups, and the arts all received support from the fund. **Giving Priorities:** In fiscal 1991, the fund gave approximately 34% of its contributions to health care, 17% to social services, 16% to education, and 12% to religious organizations. Civic and public affairs received 11% of the fund's donations, and the arts received 10%. **Typical Health-Related Recipients:** Health Organizations, Hospitals, People with Disabilities, Public Health, Single-Disease Health Associations, Substance Abuse. **Geographic Distribution:** Georgia and neighboring states with an emphasis on Atlanta, GA.

★6343★ de Kay Foundation
c/o Chemical Bank
270 Park Ave., 21st Fl.
New York, NY 10017
Phone: (212)270-9077
John Boncada, Senior Trust Officer

Foundation Philosophy: The de Kay Foundation generally makes grants to a few organizations. One-third of contributions goes to St. Barnabas Hospital in New York. Another one-third of funds was split between the Federation for Protestant Welfare and the Community Service Society of New York. The remaining one-third funds the groups which enable elderly individuals (over age 65) in the Tri-State region to remain in their homes. Applications must be submitted through social service agencies. Individuals applying directly will be rejected. **Giving Priorities:** In fiscal 1993, the foundation gave 46% of its funding to St. Barnabas Hospital with a grant of $258,082. Religious organizations received 30% of support, and civic groups received 23%. **Typical Health-Related Recipients:** Hospitals. **Geographic Distribution:** New York, NY.

Dellora A. and Lester J. Norris Foundation
See: Entry 135

★6344★ DeRoy Testamentary Foundation
3274 Penobscot Bldg.
Detroit, MI 48226
Phone: (313)961-3814
Leonard H. Weiner, President

Foundation Philosophy: The Deroy Testamentary Foundation makes most of its grants in the areas of education, social services, the arts, and hospitals. The foundation also funds health foundations. **Giving Priorities:** In 1993, the foundation awarded 26% of its total giving to support health care, with major funding for Providence Hospital Foundation. About 24% of donations supported religious interests. Education received 21% of the support. Social service organizations were awarded 16% of distributed funds, with much of the support going to family and youth services. The arts received 10% of the funds, while civic affairs received 2%. The remaining 1% went to fund environmental concerns. **Typical Health-Related Recipients:** Cancer, Children's Health/Hospitals, Domestic Violence, Eyes/Blindness, Family Planning, Health Organizations, Hospices, Hospitals, Medical Education, Medical Rehabilitation, Medical Research, Mental Health, People with Disabilities, Trauma Treatment. **Geographic Distribution:** Focus on Michigan.

★6345★ Dr. C.C. and Mabel L. Criss Memorial Foundation
c/o Firstier Bank, N.A., Omaha
17th & Farnam Sts.
Omaha, NE 68102
Phone: (402)348-6391
Bob Timmons, Trust Officer

Foundation Philosophy: The foundation primarily supports organizations and institutions in Omaha, NE. Colleges and universities receive major contributions. Private secondary education is also a priority. Large grants usually support the construction and expansion of schools. Health care, research, and hospitals are sup-

ported. Local cultural associations and historical preservation organizations are of interest to the foundation. Community services also receive funding. **Giving Priorities:** In fiscal 1993, the foundation awarded approximately 84% of funding to educational institutions. Health care was given 10% of funding, primarily supporting hospitals. Local arts organizations received 5% and the remaining funds supported social services and community organizations. **Typical Health-Related Recipients:** Hospitals. **Geographic Distribution:** Nebraska, primarily in Omaha.

Dora Roberts Foundation
See: Entry 144

Dover Foundation
See: Entry 146

Duke Endowment
See: Entry 147

★6346★ E. J. Grassmann Trust
PO Box 4470
Warren, NJ 07059
Phone: (908)753-2440
Fax: (908)753-9384
William V. Engel, Executive Director and Trustee

Foundation Philosophy: Preferred organizations include local hospitals and health organizations; organizations engaged in ecological endeavors; educational institutions; and organizations that help the needy, particularly children. **Giving Priorities:** In 1993, the foundation awarded 35% of its giving to educational foundations and universities. Health organizations received 34% of funding, with hospitals and medical centers as the main beneficiaries. Environmental concerns received 8%, while both the arts and humanities and social services each received 6% of funding. Civic affairs received 5%, science received 4%, and religious organizations received 3%. **Typical Health-Related Recipients:** Children's Health/Hospitals, Clinics/Medical Centers, Health Organizations, Hospitals, Medical Education, Nursing Services, People with Disabilities. **Geographic Distribution:** Primarily New Jersey, particularly Union County; also middle Georgia.

★6347★ Eleanor and Edsel Ford Fund
100 Renaissance Ctr., Ste. 3400
Detroit, MI 48243
Phone: (313)259-7777
Pierre V. Heftler, Secretary

Foundation Philosophy: The fund makes grants to the arts, churches, hospitals, schools and educational organizations, and miscellaneous nonprofit groups. **Giving Priorities:** In 1993, the fund gave approximately 49% of its contributions to education. Health care received 23% of giving, in the form of a single grant for the Henry Ford Health System, Detroit, MI. The arts received 15%, including a grant of $145,000 for the Detroit Institute of Arts Founders Society. Science received the 9%, and religious institutions received 4%. **Typical Health-Related Recipients:** Health Organizations, Hospitals. **Geographic Distribution:** Primarily metropolitan Detroit, MI.

Ellen Browning Scripps Foundation
See: Entry 166

★6348★ English-Bonter-Mitchell Foundation
c/o Ft. Wayne National Bank Trust Dept.
900 Ft. Wayne Bank Bldg.
Ft. Wayne, IN 46802
Phone: (219)426-0555
Fax: (219)461-6214
Marlene Buesching, Trust Officer

Foundation Philosophy: The foundation's giving focuses on culture and youth programs. Support also is directed toward higher education, hospitals, churches and religious organizations, social services, and community development. **Giving Priorities:** In 1993, the foundation gave 28% of funding to educational institutions, including the foundation's highest grant of $220,000 to the Indiana University School of Medicine. The arts and humanities received approximately 26% of funds. Social services received 15% of total contributions; health groups, 14%; religious programs, 8%; civic concerns, 6%; environmental programs, 2%; and science groups, 1%. **Typical Health-Related Recipients:** Clinics/Medical Centers, Emergency/Ambulance Services, Health Funds, Health Organizations, Hospitals, Medical Education, Medical Rehabilitation, People with Disabilities, Single-Disease Health Associations, Substance Abuse. **Geographic Distribution:** Giving primarily in Ft. Wayne, IN.

★6349★ Evan and Marion Helfaer Foundation
735 N Water St.
Milwaukee, WI 53202-4188
Phone: (414)276-3600
Thomas L. Smallwood, Administrator

Foundation Philosophy: The foundation makes grants across the major categories of support. Educational funding favors universities, colleges, medical and engineering schools, and private high schools. Health service support goes to hospitals and cancer and blood centers. Funding for the arts includes performing arts, museums, and historic preservation. Social service interests include youth organizations, united funds, and community centers. The foundation will make grants to other recipient areas as well. **Giving Priorities:** In fiscal 1994, the foundation gave 27% of its funding to education. Health services also received 27% of the giving. Special foundation interests received 18% and the arts in Milwaukee received 14% of the funding. The foundation supported social services with 14% of its contributions. Support went to youth organizations, community centers, counseling centers, and homes. **Typical Health-Related Recipients:** Geriatric Health, Hospitals, Medical Education, Medical Research, Nursing Services, People with Disabilities, Single-Disease Health Associations. **Geographic Distribution:** Limited to Wisconsin, with a focus on Milwaukee.

Fletcher Jones Foundation
See: Entry 182

Fondren Foundation
See: Entry 186

Forest Lawn Foundation
See: Entry 189

Forrest C. Lattner Foundation
See: Entry 190

★6350★ Frank J. Lewis Foundation
PO Box 9726
Riviera Beach, FL 33419
Edward D. Lewis, President

Foundation Philosophy: The main goal of the organization is to preserve and extend the Roman Catholic faith. Support is given to Roman Catholic educational institutions, churches, social services, religious orders, and church-sponsored programs and hospitals. **Giving Priorities:** In 1993, the foundation gave approximately 59% of its contributions to religious organizations, including churches, dioceses, and organizations that seek to promote Roman Catholicism. Education received 21%, including support for colleges and religious education. Health care received 8%; social services, 6%; international affairs, 5%; and civic affairs, 1%. **Typical Health-Related Recipients:** Health Organizations, Hospitals, Medical Research, People with Disabilities, Substance Abuse. **Geographic Distribution:** National, some emphasis on the Midwest and Florida.

Frankel Foundation
See: Entry 201

Fred L. Emerson Foundation, Inc.
See: Entry 202

★6351★ Fritz B. Burns Foundation
4001 W Alemeda Ave., Ste. 203
Burbank, CA 91505
Phone: (818)840-8802
Fax: (818)849-0468
Joseph E. Rawlinson, President

Foundation Philosophy: The foundation offers "educational contributions with an emphasis on buildings, equipment, endowments, student scholarship and loan funds, and faculty fellowships." Hospitals, hospital equipment, and medical research also are supported. **Giving Priorities:** In fiscal 1993, education programs received approximately 59% of funding, including a $1,700,000 grant, the largest awarded, to Loyola-Marymount University. Health care programs received about 21% of total funding, mainly to hospitals and medical centers. Religious organizations were awarded 12% of donations, while social service programs received 7%. The remaining 1% of support was divided between the arts and civic affairs. **Typical Health-Related Recipients:** Children's Health/Hospitals, Clinics/Medical Centers, Emergency/Ambulance Services, Family Planning, Health Organizations, Hospitals, Medical Research, Nutrition, People with Disabilities, Single-Disease Health Associations. **Geographic Distribution:** Primarily metropolitan Los Angeles, CA.

Fullerton Foundation
See: Entry 207

George F. Baker Trust
See: Entry 213

★6352★ George Hoag Family Foundation
Century Plaza Towers, Ste. 4392
2029 Century Pk., E
Los Angeles, CA 90067
Phone: (310)785-0690
W. Dickerson Milliken, Secretary and Director

Foundation Philosophy: The foundation "primarily applies its resources to preserve and enrich the benefits to be derived by California residents, and principally those residing in Orange County, from improved and expanded medical services, opportunities for youth and other humanitarian or similar community projects." **Giving Priorities:** In 1993, the foundation gave approximately 75% of its contributions to health organizations, including the highest grant of $1,710,000 to the Hoag Hospital Foundation. Social services organizations received 8%; religious concerns, 7%; educational institutions, 5%; the arts, 4%; and civic affairs, 1%. **Typical Health-Related Recipients:** Cancer, Child Abuse, Children's Health/Hospitals, Clinics/Medical Centers, Domestic Violence, Emergency/Ambulance Services, Heart, Hospitals, Medical Research, People with Disabilities, Preventive Medicine/Wellness Organizations, Single-Disease Health Associations, Substance Abuse. **Geographic Distribution:** California, principally Orange County. **Formerly:** Hoag Foundation.

★6353★ Gladys Brooks Foundation
90 Broad St.
New York, NY 10004
Phone: (212)943-3217
Jessica L. Rutledge, Administrative Assistant

Foundation Philosophy: The foundation was created "to provide for the intellectual, moral, and physical welfare of the people of this country by establishing and supporting non-profit libraries, educational institutions, hospitals, and clinics." **Giving Priorities:** In 1992, the foundation awarded approximately 39% of its total contributions to educational institutions. Health care, primarily hospitals, received about 20% of funding. Social service organizations received 17%; the arts, 12%; and civic affairs, 10%. International organizations and religious groups received the remaining funds. **Typical Health-Related Recipients:** Children's Health/Hospitals, Hospitals, Medical Education, Medical Research, People with Disabilities, Single-Disease Health Associations. **Geographic Distribution:** Limited to Connecticut, Delaware, Maine, Massachusetts, New Hampshire, New Jersey, New York, Pennsylvania, Rhode Island, and Vermont.

Gladys and Roland Harriman Foundation
See: Entry 225

★6354★ Gore Family Memorial Foundation
4747 N Ocean Drive
Ste. 204
Ft. Lauderdale, FL 33308
Phone: (305)781-8634
Fax: (305)781-8638

Foundation Philosophy: The Gore Family Memorial Foundation supports a wide variety of charitable organizations. Most of the support is given to education. Health services is also a major priority. Most of the support goes to hospices, indigent care hospitals, and children's hospitals. A third major interest is social services in general. The foundation will also support civic affairs and Catholic organizations. **Giving Priorities:** In fiscal 1991, educational institutions received 38% of total funds. Health care concerns received 27%, including the highest grant of $50,000 to Holy Cross Hospital for Indigent Care. Social service organizations received 24%, with emphasis on the disabled. The remaining 11% went to religious organizations. Contributions analysis does not include $162,698 for graduate study scholarships to handicapped students and grants to individuals. **Typical Health-Related Recipients:** Hospices, Hospitals, People with Disabilities. **Geographic Distribution:** National, with a focus on Florida.

★6355★ **Grainger Foundation**
5500 W Howard St.
Skokie, IL 60077
Phone: (708)982-9000
Lee J. Flory, Vice President and Secretary

Foundation Philosophy: While the foundation's funding interests are broad, it places "emphasis on endowments, capital funds, and special program funds for higher education (colleges and universities), cultural and historical institutions (art, symphonies, and museums), hospitals, and human service organizations." **Giving Priorities:** In 1994, the foundation reported that it gave approximately 64% of its total contributions to higher education. Civic and public affairs received 11% of giving, with a focus on ecological issues. Approximately 10% of foundation funding went to social services, with support given to a wide range of organizations. Scientific, religious, and health organizations each received 4% of the foundation's support, and the remaining funds were allotted to the arts and international organizations. **Typical Health-Related Recipients:** Health Organizations, Hospitals, Medical Education, Medical Research, Substance Abuse. **Geographic Distribution:** Primarily the Chicago metropolitan area.

H. A. and Mary K. Chapman Charitable Trust
See: Entry 236

Hagedorn Fund
See: Entry 240

Harden Foundation
See: Entry 243

Harriett Ames Charitable Trust
See: Entry 246

★6356★ **Harvey and Bernice Jones Charitable Trust**
2323 First Commercial Bldg.
Little Rock, AR 72201
Phone: (501)374-5225
H. G. Frost, Jr., Director and Manager

Foundation Philosophy: The trust concentrates its grant program on education, medical services, and religious organizations in Arkansas. The trust concentrates on helping a few select organizations with ongoing support. The

trust's funds are committed through the next few years. **Giving Priorities:** In fiscal 1992, the trust gave approximately 48% of funding to educational institutions, 45% to health, and 8% to religious organizations. **Typical Health-Related Recipients:** Children's Health/Hospitals, Eyes/Blindness, Hospitals. **Geographic Distribution:** Arkansas.

Hawn Foundation
See: Entry 257

Helen Brach Foundation
See: Entry 260

Henry and Lucy Moses Fund
See: Entry 267

★6357★ **Hoover Foundation**
101 E Maple St.
North Canton, OH 44720
Phone: (216)499-9200
Fax: (216)497-5857
Lawrence R. Hoover, Chairman

Foundation Philosophy: The Hoover Foundation makes most of its grants in the areas of education, civic affairs, social services, and the arts. **Giving Priorities:** In 1993, the foundation gave approximately 27% of its contributions to hospitals and health agencies, including the highest grant of $500,000 to the North Canton Medical Foundation. The arts received 25% of funding and social service organizations received 23%. Educational institutions received 19%. The remaining funds supported civic affairs, religious organizations, and environmental concerns. **Typical Health-Related Recipients:** Family Planning, Health Funds, Health Organizations, Hospitals, Multiple Sclerosis, People with Disabilities, Respiratory, Substance Abuse. **Geographic Distribution:** Focus on Stark County, OH; some grants in Florida.

★6358★ **Howard Gilman Foundation**
111 W 50th St.
New York, NY 10020
Phone: (212)246-3300
Howard Gilman, President

Foundation Philosophy: The Howard Gilman Foundation's primary interest is supporting the arts. Interests include ballet, the symphony, opera, and museums. Civic affairs are a secondary interest. Support includes Israeli cultural foundations, international affairs, and the environment. **Giving Priorities:** In fiscal 1993, approximately 40% of funding went to health services including a $700,000 grant to the Cornell University Medical Center. The arts received 27%. Civic affairs received 15% and international organizations were awarded 8% of giving. Educational programs received 5%, environmental efforts, 2%, social services, 2%, and the remaining funds supported religious organizations. **Typical Health-Related Recipients:** AIDS/HIV, Clinics/Medical Centers, Health Organizations, Hospitals, Hospitals (University Affiliated), Single-Disease Health Associations. **Geographic Distribution:** Some national and international; focus on New York City, NY.

★6359★ **Hudson-Webber Foundation**
333 W Fort St., Ste. 1310
Detroit, MI 48226
Phone: (313)963-7777
Fax: (313)963-2818
Gilbert Hudson, President and Trustee

Foundation Philosophy: The Hudson-Webber Foundation concentrates its efforts and resources in five program areas: the Detroit Medical Center, economic development of southeastern Michigan (with emphasis on the creation of employment opportunities), Detroit physical revitalization, the arts, and crime abatement in Detroit. **Giving Priorities:** In 1993, civic and public affairs received approximately 28% of giving. Social service organizations received 21%. Educational institutions received 18% of funding and the arts received 16% of the contributions. Health-care organizations were awarded 12% of giving and religious organizations received approximately 4% of funds. **Typical Health-Related Recipients:** Cancer, Children's Health/Hospitals, Domestic Violence, Health Organizations, Hospitals, Public Health, Substance Abuse, Transplant Networks/Donor Banks. **Geographic Distribution:** Southeastern Michigan, primarily Wayne, Oakland, and Macomb counties; emphasis on Detroit.

★6360★ **Hugoton Foundation**
900 Park Ave.
New York, NY 10021
Phone: (212)734-5447
Joan K. Stout, President

Foundation Philosophy: The Hugoton Foundation makes most of its grants in the areas of health care and education. Funding for health care favors hospitals. Education support goes primarily to medical and nursing schools, colleges, and secondary education. The foundation also supports other recipient areas on a limited basis. **Giving Priorities:** In 1993, the foundation reported that health care organizations received 67% of total funding. Educational institutions received 19%. Religious organizations received 8%, and social services received 3%. The remaining funds went to the arts, civic groups, and environmental concerns. **Typical Health-Related Recipients:** Alzheimers Disease, Cancer, Children's Health/Hospitals, Clinics/Medical Centers, Emergency/Ambulance Services, Geriatric Health, Health Organizations, Heart, Hospitals, Medical Education, Medical Research, Mental Health, Nursing Services, People with Disabilities, Single-Disease Health Associations, Transplant Networks/Donor Banks. **Geographic Distribution:** Focus on New York, NY, and Miami, FL.

★6361★ **I. A. O'Shaughnessy Foundation**
W 1271 First Natl Bldg
St. Paul, MN 55101
Phone: (612)222-2323
John Bultena, Secretary/Treasurer

Foundation Philosophy: The foundation funds higher education, hospitals, youth organizations, community services, churches, the arts, and sciences. **Giving Priorities:** In 1991, the foundation gave approximately 47% of funding to educational institutions. The arts received 22% of giving, while social services received 13%. About 8% went to religious causes, 5% to health organizations, 5% to civic concerns, and the remainder to an international agency. **Typical Health-Related Recipients:** Alzheimers Disease, Domestic Violence, Heart, Hospices, Hospitals, Medical Rehabilitation, People with Disabilities, Prenatal Health Issues. **Geographic Distribution:** Emphasis on Minnesota, Kansas, Texas, and Illinois.

★ 6362 ★ Irene E. and George A. Davis Foundation
301 Chestnut St.
PO Box 504
East Longmeadow, MA 01028-0504
Phone: (413)525-3961
Ann T. Keiser, Manager, Financial Administration

Foundation Philosophy: The foundation focuses its grantmaking activities on the local Western Massachusetts community with an emphasis on higher education, religious organizations, and the fine arts. **Giving Priorities:** In 1993, the foundation gave approximately 39% of its contributions to educational institutions. Social service organizations received 30%, with major support for the United Way of Pioneer Valley, Springfield, MA. Health care, mainly hospitals and medical centers, received 17%. Religious causes and civic affairs each received 5% of the total grants. International organizations and the arts each received 2%. **Typical Health-Related Recipients:** Children's Health/Hospitals, Clinics/Medical Centers, Emergency/Ambulance Services, Hospitals, Nursing Services, People with Disabilities, Single-Disease Health Associations. **Geographic Distribution:** Limited to western Massachusetts.

★ 6363 ★ J. Aron Charitable Foundation
126 E 56th St., Ste. 2300
New York, NY 10022
Phone: (212)832-3405
Peter A. Aron, President, Executive Director

Foundation Philosophy: The foundation generally supports arts and cultural programs, educational institutions, hospitals and health organizations, and social service agencies. **Giving Priorities:** In 1993, the foundation contributed approximately 55% of its contributions to the arts. Education received 13% of giving, including four grants totaling $205,000 for Tulane University, New Orleans, LA. Health care organizations received 12%; social services, 7%; religious causes, 6%; enivronmental groups, 4%; international organizations, 2%; and the remaining funds went to civic and public affairs and scientific causes. **Typical Health-Related Recipients:** Clinics/Medical Centers, Emergency/Ambulance Services, Eyes/Blindness, Geriatric Health, Hospitals, Medical Research, Mental Health, Research/Studies Institutes, Single-Disease Health Associations, Substance Abuse. **Geographic Distribution:** Emphasis on the New York metropolitan area and New Orleans, LA.

J. E. and L. E. Mabee Foundation
See: Entry 295

J. M. McDonald Foundation
See: Entry 299

J. Willard Marriott Foundation
See: Entry 302

★ 6364 ★ Jacob and Valeria Langeloth Foundation
521 Fifth Ave.
Ste. 1612
New York, NY 10175-1699
Phone: (212)687-3760
William R. Cross, Jr., President and Director

Foundation Philosophy: The foundation's primary objective is to "make grants to organizations in the health field (mostly hospitals) which in turn use the funds to help patients pay their bills." **Giving Priorities:** In fiscal 1994, the foundation reported that it gave 100% of its contributions to health care, primarily hospitals, which in turn used the funds to help patients pay their bills. **Typical Health-Related Recipients:** Cancer, Clinics/Medical Centers, Health Organizations, Hospices, Hospitals, Hospitals (University Affiliated), Long-Term Care, Medical Rehabilitation, Nursing Services, People with Disabilities. **Geographic Distribution:** Only New York; primarily New York City metropolitan area and Westchester County.

★ 6365 ★ John L. Weinberg Foundation
c/o Goldman, Sachs & Co.
85 Broad St., 22nd Fl.
New York, NY 10004
Phone: (212)902-8555
Deborah Rogers, Secretary

Foundation Philosophy: The John L. Weinberg Foundation primarily supports hospitals and university-level education. Other areas of interest include civic affairs, the arts, and social services. **Giving Priorities:** In fiscal 1993, the foundation awarded approximately 32% of its total contributions to health care, including one of its two highest grants of $250,000 to the Presbyterian Hospital in New York, NY. Educational institutions also received about 32% of total funds, including the other highest grant of $250,000, which went to the Scripps College in Claremont, CA. Scientific interests, primarily the Carnegie Institution of Washington, received 25%. Religious groups received 5%; the arts, 2%; social services, 2%; and civic affairs received the remaining funds. **Typical Health-Related Recipients:** Emergency/Ambulance Services, Health Funds, Hospitals, Medical Research, Single-Disease Health Associations. **Geographic Distribution:** National, with an emphasis on New York, NY, and Greenwich, CT.

John M. Hopwood Charitable Trust
See: Entry 320

★ 6366 ★ John McShain Charities
540 N 17th St.
Philadelphia, PA 19130
Phone: (215)564-2322
Mary McShain, President

Foundation Philosophy: The foundation's purpose is to make donations primarily to education, as well as to benefit Roman Catholic churches, religious organizations, and welfare funds. The foundation has also supported music, community organizations, and hospitals. **Giving Priorities:** In fiscal 1994, the foundation gave approximately 68% of its total contributions to educational institutions. Religious organizations received about 20%. The arts received 6%; health concerns, 5%; and international organizations received the remaining funds. **Typical Health-Related Recipients:** Clinics/Medical Centers, Health Organizations, Hospitals, Long-Term Care. **Geographic Distribution:** Primarily Philadelphia area; some national grants.

John P. Murphy Foundation
See: Entry 323

★ 6367 ★ John R. McCune Charitable Trust
1104 Commonwealth Building
316 Fourth Ave.
Pittsburgh, PA 15222
Phone: (412)644-7796
Fax: (412)644-8059
Martha J. Perry, Managing Director

Foundation Philosophy: The trust primarily provides grants to health-care institutions, institutions of secondary and higher education, and social service agencies. **Giving Priorities:** In fiscal 1994, the trust gave approximately 39% to education. Health care received 32%, primarily to support hospitals and pediatric health. The trust's highest grant of $300,000 went to Mercy Health Center in Oaklahoma City, OK. Social services received 13%, including support for drug programs, helplines and youth organizations. The arts, civic affairs, and environmental groups each received 4%. The remaining funds supported international affairs, religious interests and science organizations. **Typical Health-Related Recipients:** Children's Health/Hospitals, Clinics/Medical Centers, Health Funds, Health Organizations, Hospitals, Medical Research, Mental Health, Multiple Sclerosis, People with Disabilities, Prenatal Health Issues, Public Health, Research/Studies Institutes, Single-Disease Health Associations, Substance Abuse. **Geographic Distribution:** Focus on western Pennsylvania.

★ 6368 ★ John Stauffer Charitable Trust
301 N Lake Ave., 10th Fl.
Pasadena, CA 91101
Phone: (818)793-9400
Fax: (818)793-5900
H. Jess Senecal, Trustee

Foundation Philosophy: The trust is limited to supporting colleges, universities, and hospitals. Support to hospitals goes toward acquiring land; erecting buildings and other facilities; and obtaining equipment, instruments, and furnishings. The trust prefers to give grants to institutions that maintain balanced operating budgets and avoid deficit financing. **Giving Priorities:** The trust reported that, in fiscal 1994, education received 80% of total funding. Interests in science received 20%. **Typical Health-Related Recipients:** Cancer, Children's Health/Hospitals, Clinics/Medical Centers, Family Planning, Health Organizations, Hospitals, Medical Rehabilitation, Outpatient Health Care, People with Disabilities, Substance Abuse. **Geographic Distribution:** Primarily California.

Josiah W. and Bessie H. Kline Foundation
See: Entry 333

★6369★ **Katherine Mabis McKenna Foundation**
PO Box 186
Latrobe, PA 15650
Phone: (412)537-6901
Linda Boxx, Secretary

Foundation Philosophy: The Katherine Mabis McKenna Foundation makes grants across the major categories of support. Grants are made primarily to charitable organizations in western Pennsylvania. **Giving Priorities:** In 1991, the foundation gave 36% of its funding to civic affairs. The foundation gave 20% of its funding to social services. Education received 17% of the funds, with a large contribution to the University of Pittsburgh. The foundation contributed 17% of its funding to the arts. The Westmoreland Symphony Orchestra received $50,000. A majority of health contributions, which accounted for 10% of the funds, went to the Latrobe Area Hospital. **Typical Health-Related Recipients:** Hospitals, Single-Disease Health Associations. **Geographic Distribution:** Limited to eastern Westmoreland County, PA.

Laffey-McHugh Foundation
See: Entry 349

★6370★ **Laura Moore Cunningham Foundation**
510 Main St.
Boise, ID 83702
Phone: (208)345-7852
Joan Davidson Carley, Secretary-Treasurer

Foundation Philosophy: The Laura Moore Cunningham Foundation is primarily interested in providing business scholarships through educational institutions located in Idaho. The foundation also contributes to several Idaho hospitals. In addition, the foundation awards various smaller grants to support social services, civic organizations, and the arts. **Giving Priorities:** In fiscal 1993, the foundation awarded 48% of total contributions to education. Social service organizations received about 18%, with grants supporting senior services, people with disabilities, youth organizations, shelters and homes, food/clothing distribution programs, and child welfare. Health concerns received 11%, with major support for hospitals. Civic affairs also received 11%, including the foundation's highest grant of $60,000 for the Peregrine Fund. The arts received 10%, with grants supporting the Boise Art Museum, the Boise Philharmonic Children's Program, and public broadcasting. Religious interests received the remaining funds. **Typical Health-Related Recipients:** Emergency/Ambulance Services, Hospitals, Medical Education, People with Disabilities, Single-Disease Health Associations. **Geographic Distribution:** Limited to Idaho.

★6371★ **Lester T. Sunderland Foundation**
PO Box 25900
Overland Park, KS 66204
Phone: (913)451-8900
James P. Sunderland, Chairman

Foundation Philosophy: The foundation primarily supports education, with emphasis on colleges and universities in the Midwest. Secondary interests include the arts, civic affairs, social services, religion, and hospitals. **Giving Priorities:** In 1994, the foundation reported that it contributed approximately 44% of its funding to education, with emphasis on higher education. The arts received 19% of the funding, including support to historical preservation and the performing arts. Contributions to civic affairs totaled 14% of the giving. The remainder went to social services, 11%; religion, 8%; and health care, 4%. **Typical Health-Related Recipients:** Hospitals. **Geographic Distribution:** Focus on Missouri and Nebraska.

Lon V. Smith Foundation
See: Entry 358

Longwood Foundation
See: Entry 359

Louise H. and David S. Ingalls Foundation
See: Entry 366

★6372★ **Lyndon C. Whitaker Charitable Foundation**
120 S Central St., Ste. 1122
Clayton, MO 63105
Phone: (314)726-5734
Betul A. Ozmat, Executive Director

Foundation Philosophy: The foundation supports a variety of charitable organizations, including social services, the arts, education, and health. Most of the contributions go to social service agencies for children's welfare and the disabled. Most of the funding for education favors universities. Other recipient areas also are supported regularly. **Giving Priorities:** In fiscal 1992, the foundation supported social services with 33% of its funding. Major support went to Grand Center, which received two grants totaling $125,000. Children's services also received major support. The arts received 25% of the contributions. Education received 24% of the giving. Health received 10%, with major support to the Salk Institute and the St. Louis Children's Hospital. The remainder went to civic affairs, 5%, and religion, 3%. **Typical Health-Related Recipients:** Hospices, Hospitals, Medical Education, Medical Research, People with Disabilities, Single-Disease Health Associations. **Geographic Distribution:** Focus on St. Louis, MO.

M. R. Bauer Foundation
See: Entry 371

Marion I. and Henry J. Knott Foundation
See: Entry 378

★6373★ **Marmot Foundation**
1004 Wilmington Trust Ctr.
Wilmington, DE 19801
Phone: (302)654-2477
Endsley P. Fairman, Secretary

Foundation Philosophy: The foundation's primary focus is social service organizations. Youth organizations are also a major priority. The trustees are also interested in education. Health services are considered a secondary interest, with most support going directly to hospitals. **Giving Priorities:** In 1993, approximately 23% of funding was awarded to social services. Health care also received 23%. Education received 22%. The arts received 14%; civic concerns, 8%; the environment, 5%; science, 3%; and religion, 2%. **Typical Health-Related Recipients:** Children's Health/Hospitals, Clinics/Medical Centers, Diabetes, Emergency/Ambulance Services, Eyes/Blindness, Family Planning, Heart, Hospitals, Medical Education, People with Disabilities, Research/Studies Institutes, Trauma Treatment. **Geographic Distribution:** Focus on Delaware and Florida.

★6374★ **Mary J. Hutchins Foundation**
110 William St.
New York, NY 10038
Richard J. Mirabella, Vice President

Foundation Philosophy: The Mary J. Hutchins Foundation primarily supports health care and social service organizations. Health support goes to general and specialty hospitals. Nursing is also supported. Social service support favors homes and shelters, charity and welfare organizations, and youth clubs. Civic affairs agencies are supported on a limted basis. The foundation also endeavors to provide aid to poor and needy adults regardless of age, race, and creed. **Giving Priorities:** In 1993, the foundation contributed 52% of its total support to health care, including a single $60,000 grant to North Shore University Hospital. Social service organizations received 29% of funding; religious welfare organizations, 11%; civic affairs, 4%; and environmental efforts, 3%. **Typical Health-Related Recipients:** Clinics/Medical Centers, Emergency/Ambulance Services, Eyes/Blindness, Family Planning, Hospices, Hospitals, Hospitals (University Affiliated), Medical Rehabilitation, Medical Research, Mental Health, Multiple Sclerosis, Nursing Services, People with Disabilities, Sexual Abuse, Single-Disease Health Associations. **Geographic Distribution:** Focus on the New York, NY, area.

McGregor Fund
See: Entry 394

★6375★ **Millbrook Tribute Garden**
PO Box AC
Millbrook, NY 12545
Phone: (914)677-3434
George T. Whalen, Jr., Trustee

Foundation Philosophy: The Millbrook Tribute Garden makes grants across the major categories of support. In social services, interests include children's homes, youth organizations, and recreation. Educational support favors Millbrook's private schools. Religious supports goes to individual churches. Support for civic affairs favors municipalities. Health and the arts also are supported. **Giving Priorities:** In fiscal 1993, educational institutions received 45% of total funding. Churches received 22%, with major support to the Grace Episcopal Church, Millbrook, NY. Health care received 15%; the arts, 6%; environmental efforts, 5%; social services, 4%; and civic affairs, 3%. **Typical Health-Related Recipients:** Hospitals. **Geographic Distribution:** Limited to Millbrook, NY.

Nicholas H. Noyes, Jr. Memorial Foundation
See: Entry 8540

★ 6376 ★ O'Donnell Foundation
100 Crescent Ct., No. 1660
Dallas, TX 75201
Phone: (214)855-8980
Carolyn Bacon, Chief Executive Director

Foundation Philosophy: The foundation's primary focus is on education, especially science and engineering. It also funds civic and public affairs organizations, medical centers, and the arts. **Giving Priorities:** In fiscal 1993, the foundation gave approximately 71% of funding to educational institutions, including the foundation's largest grant to the University of Texas Austin. Health concerns received 16% of funding; science, 12%; and arts and humanities, 1%. Civic causes rceivied less than 1%. **Typical Health-Related Recipients:** Clinics/Medical Centers, Medical Education. **Geographic Distribution:** Primarily Texas.

Offield Family Foundation
See: Entry 415

Overbrook Foundation
See: Entry 421

Pauline Allen Gill Foundation
See: Entry 423

Philip L. Van Every Foundation
See: Entry 430

★ 6377 ★ Pope Foundation
211 W 56th St., Ste. 5-E
New York, NY 10019
Phone: (212)765-4156
Fax: (212)765-4157
Anthony Pope, Vice President

Foundation Philosophy: The foundation reflects the personal philanthropic interests of the Pope family, especially their interest in Roman Catholic institutions and in organizations that study and record the experience of Italian immigrants in America. Many recipients are given funds annually. Other foundation interests include welfare funds, higher and secondary education, and hospitals. **Giving Priorities:** In 1993, the foundation gave approximately 50% of funding to health programs, including the foundation's highest grant of $187,500 to the New York University Medical Center. Religious institutions received approximately 19% of total contributions; educational institutions, 17%; civic concerns, 7%; the arts and humanities, 3%; social services, 2%; and international affairs, 2%. **Typical Health-Related Recipients:** Clinics/Medical Centers, Domestic Violence, Health Organizations, Hospitals, Long-Term Care, Medical Education, Medical Rehabilitation, Medical Research, Mental Health, Prenatal Health Issues, Single-Disease Health Associations. **Geographic Distribution:** Primarily metropolitan New York City; limited support elsewhere.

Prospect Hill Foundation
See: Entry 434

Raymond John Wean Foundation
See: Entry 440

★ 6378 ★ Reeves Foundation
PO Box 441
Dover, OH 44622-0441
Phone: (216)364-4660
Don A. Ulrich, Executive Director

Foundation Philosophy: Foundation interests include hospitals, historic preservation, municipalities, and educational projects. The foundation will also fund other recipient areas. **Giving Priorities:** In 1993, the foundation gave approximately 51% of its contributions to health care, including the largest grant of $250,000 to Union Hospital Association in Dover, OH. Social services and community centers received 24% of funding. The arts received 9%. Education was awarded 8%; religious organizations, 5%; and civic affairs received 3%. **Typical Health-Related Recipients:** Children's Health/Hospitals, Clinics/Medical Centers, Emergency/Ambulance Services, Hospices, Hospitals, People with Disabilities, Public Health. **Geographic Distribution:** Focus on Tuscarawas County, OH.

Robert R. Young Foundation
See: Entry 456

Rosamond Gifford Charitable Corporation
See: Entry 464

★ 6379 ★ Rowland Foundation
PO Box 13
Cambridge, MA 02238
Phone: (617)497-4634
Philip DuBois, Vice President

Foundation Philosophy: The foundation primarily funds "academic institutions, social welfare, hospitals, museums, conservation, historical associations, medical research, and the arts." **Giving Priorities:** In fiscal 1993, the foundation awarded approximately 43% of its total contributions to scientific interests, including its highest grant of $1,000,000 for the Rowland Institute for Science. Health concerns received about 18%; educational institutions, 14%; the arts, 13%; environmental causes, 6%; civic groups, 4%; and social service and religious organizations received the remaining funds. **Typical Health-Related Recipients:** Cancer, Children's Health/Hospitals, Eyes/Blindness, Family Planning, Health Organizations, Heart, Hospitals, Medical Education, Medical Rehabilitation, Medical Research, People with Disabilities, Single-Disease Health Associations. **Geographic Distribution:** Primarily New England.

Seymour H. Knox Foundation
See: Entry 485

★ 6380 ★ Sidney J. Weinberg, Jr. Foundation
c/o Goldman, Sachs & Co.
85 Broad St., Tax Department, 30th Fl.
New York, NY 10004
Phone: (212)902-1000
Sydney J. Weinberg, Jr., Trustee

Foundation Philosophy: The foundation makes most of its grants in the areas of health care, education, and civic affairs. Health care funding favors hospitals, cancer research, pediatrics, and single disease associations. Funding

in education emphasizes colleges, universities, and business education. Support for civic affairs goes to the Carnegie Institute in Washington, DC, and economic development. The foundation also will fund the arts, religion, and social services. **Giving Priorities:** In fiscal 1993, the foundation gave 31% of its funds to support health services. Presbyterian Hospital in New York received two grants totaling $275,000. Other recipients included a cancer center, a hospice, and a mental health center. Education received 30% of the contributions, with major support to Scripps College in the form of two grants totaling $265,000. Civic affairs received 30%, with a large contribution to the Carnegie Institute of Washington. The remainder went to religion, 5%; the arts, 2%; and social services, 2%. **Typical Health-Related Recipients:** Cancer, Children's Health/Hospitals, Emergency/Ambulance Services, Family Planning, Health Funds, Health Organizations, Hospices, Hospitals, Medical Research, Mental Health, Nursing Services, People with Disabilities, Single-Disease Health Associations, Substance Abuse. **Geographic Distribution:** Nationally, with a focus on New York, NY.

★ 6381 ★ Skirball Foundation
767 Fifth Ave., 43rd Fl.
New York, NY 10153
Phone: (212)832-8500
Fax: (212)593-6241
Morris H. Bergreen, President

Foundation Philosophy: The Skirball Foundation has had close ties with Hebrew Union College and the University of Southern California. In 1989, the Skirball Foundation pledged a gift of $500,000 for assisting in the construction and outfitting of a cancer pharmacology laboratory at USC's Kenneth Norris, Jr. Cancer Hospital and Research Institute. The Skirball Cancer Pharmacology Laboratory is part of a major addition to the Institute that opened in late 1991 on USC's Health Sciences Campus. The foundation is also a supporter of the arts and, in 1972, created the Skirball Museum at Hebrew Union College, one of the world's finest museums of Jewish culture. **Giving Priorities:** In 1992, the foundation awarded approximately 71% of its total contributions to educational institutions, including its highest grant of $5,000,000 to the New York University Skirball Institute of Biomolecular Medicine. The arts received about 9%; religious causes, 7%; international organizations, 5%; health concerns, 4%; social services, 3%; and civic affairs received the remaining funds. **Typical Health-Related Recipients:** Children's Health/Hospitals, Health Organizations, Hospitals, Medical Education, Medical Research, Single-Disease Health Associations. **Geographic Distribution:** Primarily Los Angeles, CA; New York, NY; and Cincinnati, OH.

South Texas Charitable Foundation
See: Entry 497

Starr Foundation
See: Entry 500

Steele-Reese Foundation
See: Entry 501

Temple Hoyne Buell Foundation
See: Entry 513

Thelma Doelger Charitable Trust
See: Entry 514

Theodore H. Barth Foundation
See: Entry 515

★ 6382 ★ Theresa and Edward O'Toole Foundation
Bank of New York, Trust Dept.
48 Wall St.
New York, NY 10286
Phone: (212)495-1177
Eskridge Culver, Trust Officer

Foundation Philosophy: The foundation is primarily interested in supporting Catholic churches and organizations. Some educational support goes to Catholic unions, universities, and schools. **Giving Priorities:** In fiscal 1993, the foundation gave approximately 60% of funding to religious organizations and churches. Two grants totaling $100,000 went to the Washington Theological Union in Silver Spring, MD. Health care institutions received 31%, with major support to St. Vincent's Hospital in New York. Educational institutions, primarily secondary schools and colleges and universities, received 7%, while civic and public affairs concerns received about 2% of funds. **Typical Health-Related Recipients:** Health Organizations, Hospitals, Long-Term Care. **Geographic Distribution:** Nationally, with a focus on New York and New Jersey.

Thomas and Agnes Carvel Foundation
See: Entry 516

Thomas Anthony Pappas Charitable Foundation
See: Entry 517

Thomas J. Emery Memorial
See: Entry 520

★ 6383 ★ Thomas M. and Irene B. Kirbo Charitable Trust
112 W Adams St., Ste. 1111
Jacksonville, FL 32202-3865
Phone: (904)354-7212
R. Murray Jenks, President and Trustee

Foundation Philosophy: The trust primarily supports education, health care, and religion. Educational funding favors smaller colleges in Florida and Georgia, and also nursing and law schools. Health care support focuses on hospitals. Religious support is primarily Christian-oriented. The trust also supports social services, civic affairs, and the arts. **Giving Priorities:** In fiscal 1990, 33% of funding supported educational institutions. Health care providers received 29%, including the two highest grants of $125,000 each to the Henrietta Egleston Hospital and the Scottish Rite Children's Hospital. Religious organizations received 17%; social service organizations, 13%; and the arts, 6%. Civic affairs received the remaining funds. **Typical Health-Related Recipients:** Hospitals, Medical Education, Nursing Services, People with Disabilities. **Geographic Distribution:** Georgia and Florida.

★ 6384 ★ Timken Foundation of Canton
236 Third St., S.W.
Canton, OH 44702
Phone: (216)455-5281
Don D. Dickes, Secretary-Treasurer

Foundation Philosophy: The foundation allocates major support for organizations that will benefit the citizens in Canton, OH, but also provides assistance to charitable organizations in the United States, Australia, France, South Africa, England, Germany, and Brazil where the Timken Company has manufacturing facilities. **Giving Priorities:** In fiscal 1994, the foundation reported that social services received 46% for youth and community programs. Education received 38% of giving, with emphasis on education funds and public education. Recreation received 8%; health care was awarded 6%; and the arts received 2%. **Typical Health-Related Recipients:** Emergency/Ambulance Services, Hospitals. **Geographic Distribution:** Broad geographic distribution, with emphasis on Canton, OH; some international giving.

★ 6385 ★ Vera Davis - W.D. Charities
5050 Edgewood Ct.
Jacksonville, FL 32254
Phone: (904)783-5490
H. J. Skelton, President, Director, Assistant Treasurer

Foundation Philosophy: The foundation gives most of its funding to the areas of health and education. Health services funding favors the Mayo Foundation and hospitals. Educational funding favors college funds and universities. Numerous smaller grants were given to social services, mostly to support youth organizations and child welfare. **Giving Priorities:** In 1993, the foundation gave approximately 52% of funding to health services, including the foundation's highest grant of $1,800,000 to the Mayo Foundation. Educational institutions received 29% of total contributions; religious institutions, 15%; international affairs, 2%; and social services, 2%. The remainder of funds went to civic concerns and the arts and humanities. **Typical Health-Related Recipients:** Cancer, Children's Health/Hospitals, Clinics/Medical Centers, Health Funds, Health Organizations, Hospitals, People with Disabilities, Public Health, Research/Studies Institutes, Speech & Hearing. **Geographic Distribution:** Southeastern states. **Formerly:** Vera Davis Parsons - W.D. Charities.

★ 6386 ★ Ware Foundation
147 Alhambra Circle, Ste. 215
Coral Gables, FL 33134
Phone: (305)443-8728
Rhoda C. Ware, Chairman

Foundation Philosophy: The foundation traditionally supports hospitals, health agencies, child welfare, and churches. **Giving Priorities:** In 1991, approximately 44% of the foundation's funds went to social services, which included donations to religious welfare organizations, family services, and the American Red Cross. Religious groups received 23%, while education received 21%. The remainder went to the arts, health, and civic concerns. **Typical Health-Related Recipients:** Hospices, Hospitals, Medical Education, Medical Research, Nursing Services, Substance Abuse. **Geographic Distribution:** National.

★ 6387 ★ Weezie Foundation
c/o Morgan Guaranty Trust Co. of New York
9 W 57th St.
New York, NY 10019
Phone: (212)826-7607
Robert Schwecherl, Secretary, Treasurer, and Trustee

Foundation Philosophy: The Weezie Foundation makes most of its grants in the areas of social services and education. Social service funding favors employment and job training and youth organizations. Funding for education goes to private schools and specialty colleges. The foundation also supports hospitals as a secondary interest. Other support areas are funded on a limited basis. **Giving Priorities:** In 1993, the foundation gave approximately 39% of total contributions to education. Social services received about 31% of giving, especially to programs serving youth. The arts received 12% of giving, in the form of one grant of $100,000 to the Nantucket Atheneum Building. Health concerns received 9% of funding. The remainder of funding went to civic, 7% and to religion, 1%. **Typical Health-Related Recipients:** Clinics/Medical Centers, Hospitals, Medical Education, Mental Health, People with Disabilities, Substance Abuse. **Geographic Distribution:** Focus on northeastern United States.

★ 6388 ★ Wilbur May Foundation
c/o Suellen Fulstone
Woodburn & Widge
One E. First St., Ste. 1600
Reno, NV 89505
Anita May Rosenstein, President

Foundation Philosophy: The foundation focuses its giving on programs for the young and hospitals. **Giving Priorities:** In fiscal 1992, approximately 51% of funding went to civic causes, with a major grant to Washoe County, while 24% went to social services, predominantly supporting youth-related groups. Health organizations received 17%, with educational institutions receiving 6%. The remainder went to the arts. **Typical Health-Related Recipients:** Health Organizations, Hospitals, Medical Rehabilitation, Medical Research, People with Disabilities, Single-Disease Health Associations. **Geographic Distribution:** Generally in Reno, NV, and Southern California, primarily the Los Angeles area.

William K. Warren Foundation
See: Entry 550

William T. Morris Foundation
See: Entry 556

Corporate Foundations

A.O. Smith Foundation
See: Entry 561

Abbott Laboratories Fund
See: Entry 562

★ 6389 ★ Advanced Micro Devices Charitable Foundation

One AMD Place
PO Box 3453, M/S 42
Sunnyvale, CA 94088-3453
Phone: (408)749-5373
Cheryl Conner, Corporate Contributions

Giving Priorities: *General Support Program:* Contributions are allocated to education, civic betterment, health and human services, and the United Way. Human services funding goes to the United Way, community service organizations, child welfare programs for the aged and the handicapped, community centers, counseling, delinquency and crime, prevention of substance abuse, emergency relief, employment, and food and clothing distribution. Areas of interest in the health category are hospitals and mental health. **Typical Health-Related Recipients:** Clinics/Medical Centers, Hospitals, People with Disabilities. **Geographic Distribution:** Near operating locations, primarily in California and Texas.

AMP Foundation
See: Entry 579

Armco Foundation
See: Entry 584

Armstrong Foundation
See: Entry 585

Baltimore Gas & Electric Foundation
See: Entry 593

Bancorp Hawaii Charitable Foundation
See: Entry 595

★ 6390 ★ Beech Aircraft Foundation

9709 E Central
Wichita, KS 67206
Phone: (316)676-8785
Robert B. Welton, Secretary-Treasurer

Giving Priorities: *Education:* 45% to 50% of total contributions. *Social Services:* 30% to 35% of funding. *Arts & Humanities:* 5% to 10% of total funding. *Civic & Public Affairs:* 5% to 10% of contributions. *Health:* 5% to 10% of giving. Primarily supported hospitals in Kansas. Funding also supported the Leukemia Society of America. *Science:* Less than 5% of total funding. **Typical Health-Related Recipients:** Cancer, Clinics/Medical Centers, Hospices, Hospitals, Medical Education, Medical Rehabilitation, People with Disabilities, Preventive Medicine/Wellness Organizations, Single-Disease Health Associations. **Geographic Distribution:** Primarily in communities with company facilities, with an emphasis on Kansas.

★ 6391 ★ Belk Foundation Trust

2801 W Tyvola Rd.
Charlotte, NC 28217-4500
Phone: (704)357-1000
Fax: (704)352-8052
Thomas M. Belk, Chairman, Board of Advisors

Giving Priorities: *Education:* 65% to 70% of contributions. *Social Services:* 10% to 15% of contributions. *Health:* 5% to 10%. Grants support building funds at North Carolina hospitals.

Civic & Public Affairs: 5% to 10%. *Arts & Humanities:* 5% to 10%. *Other:* Churches and religious organizations receive limited funding. **Typical Health-Related Recipients:** Family Planning, Hospitals, Medical Education, Substance Abuse. **Geographic Distribution:** Primarily North Carolina, South Carolina, and Georgia.

Bemis Company Foundation
See: Entry 603

BHP Petroleum Americas (HI) Foundation
See: Entry 607

★ 6392 ★ Brown Group Incorporated Charitable Trust

8300 Maryland Ave.
St. Louis, MO 63105
Phone: (314)854-4093
Fax: (314)854-4091
Mary Sylvia Siverts, Secretary, Board of Control

Giving Priorities: *Health & Human Services:* 40% to 45% of contributions, most going to united funds and youth organizations. Also supports recreation and athletics and community service organizations. Health interests include grants to hospitals and certain health organizations. *Arts & Humanities:* 25% to 30%. *Education:* 20% to 25% of contributions. *Civic & Community Activities:* 5% to 10%. **Typical Health-Related Recipients:** Hospitals. **Geographic Distribution:** Near major domestic operating locations, with emphasis on St. Louis, MO.

★ 6393 ★ BT Foundation

280 Park Ave.
19 West
New York, NY 10017
Phone: (212)454-3500
Fax: (212)454-2380
Page Chapman, III, President

Giving Priorities: *Community Development:* About 25%. *Matching Gifts:* About 25%. The program matches donations of up to $25,000 per employee. Recipients include arts and culture, community development, education, the environment, and hospitals. *Education:* About 10%. *Domestic Business Line Discretionary:* About 10%. *International Business Line Discretionary:* About 10%. *United Way:* About 5%. *Health & Hospitals:* About 10% of total annual contributions. Supports maintenance or improvement of hospitals and health programs. *General:* About 5%. Recipients programs for youth, social service agencies, and community services. *Arts & Culture:* About 5%. **Typical Health-Related Recipients:** Hospitals. **Geographic Distribution:** Primarily New York City; also in company operating locations in the United States and overseas.

Bucyrus-Erie Foundation
See: Entry 617

★ 6394 ★ Burlington Industries Foundation

PO Box 21207
Greensboro, NC 27420-1207
Phone: (919)379-2515
Fax: (919)379-2245
Park R. Davidson, Executive Director

Giving Priorities: *Education:* About 50 to 55% of total contributions. *Social Services:* About

15% to 20%. *Religion:* About 10% to 15%. *Hospitals & Health:* 5% to 10%. Supports local hospitals, generally preferring capital projects rather than operating expenses. Also supports local health care facilities in operating locations. Generally does not support other health-related organizations. *Civic & Public Affairs:* 5% to 10% of funding. *Arts & Humanities:* Less than 5% of total contributions. *International:* In 1993, the company gave $30,500 to US-based nonprofit organizations with an international focus. *Voluntarism:* Company does not have formal employee volunteer program, but it provides individual employees who volunteer for Junior Achievement. *Note:* About 3% of foundation's giving provides funds for employees in distress. **Typical Health-Related Recipients:** AIDS/HIV, Health Organizations, Hospitals, Multiple Sclerosis, Single-Disease Health Associations, Substance Abuse. **Geographic Distribution:** Primarily in North and South Carolina, Virginia, and near corporate operating locations.

Centerior Energy Foundation
See: Entry 627

Central Soya Foundation
See: Entry 629

Citizens Charitable Foundation
See: Entry 636

CLARCOR Foundation
See: Entry 637

Coltec Industries Charitable Foundation
See: Entry 641

★ 6395 ★ CP & L Foundation

PO Box 1551
Raleigh, NC 27602
Phone: (919)546-6309
Fax: (919)546-6615
Barbara K. Allen, Sec., Corp. Contributions Comm.

Giving Priorities: *Health & Welfare:* 35% to 40%, primarily to hospitals. Remaining funds support health organizations and single-disease health associations. Major recipients for welfare include North Carolina Division of Social Services and the United Way. *Education:* 30% to 35% of total annual contributions. *Civic & Public Affairs:* 10% to 15%. *Culture & Art:* 10% to 15%. *Other:* 5% to 10% to miscellaneous organizations not included in above categories. **Typical Health-Related Recipients:** Hospitals, Single-Disease Health Associations. **Geographic Distribution:** In areas served by the company.

Cranston Foundation
See: Entry 651

Crestar Foundation
See: Entry 652

Curtice-Burns / Pro-Fac Foundation
See: Entry 656

Demoulas Foundation
See: Entry 662

Duchossois Foundation
See: Entry 667

Eaton Charitable Fund
See: Entry 671

EG & G Foundation
See: Entry 5896

Fidelity Foundation
See: Entry 681

**First Interstate Bank of California
    Foundation**
See: Entry 684

★6396★ First Maryland Foundation
25 S Charles St.
Baltimore, MD 21201
Phone: (410)244-4907
Fax: (410)224-4459
Robert W. Schaefer, Secretary-Treasurer &
    Trustee

Giving Priorities: *Education:* 30% to 35% of contributions, *Social Services:* 25% to 30% of total grants. *Arts & Humanities:* About 15% of contributions. *Civic & Public Affairs:* 10% to 15% of funds. *Health:* 10% to 15% of contributions, with major support to hospitals and hospices. *Other:* Religious and scientific organizations each received less than 5%. **Typical Health-Related Recipients:** Hospices, Hospitals. **Geographic Distribution:** Emphasis on greater Baltimore; also gives near operating locations in Maryland.

**Fleet Bank of Upstate New York
    Foundation Trust**
See: Entry 691

★6397★ FMC Foundation
200 E Randolph Dr.
Chicago, IL 60601
Phone: (312)861-6105
Fax: (312)861-6105
Catherine Swigon, Executive Director

Giving Priorities: *Education:* 30% to 35% of total annual contributions. *Health & Human Services:* 30% to 35%. The majority of grants in this category went to United Ways. Foundation also funds hospitals and medical centers to ensure employees have access to stable, high-quality medical resources. Supports capital and major fund-raising campaigns. Emphasizes hospitals that engage in basic research, serve as teaching hospitals, and are affiliated with medical schools. Some support to human services in plant communities. *Community Improvement:* 15% to 20% annually. *Public Issues/Urban Affairs:* Generally 10% to 15%. **Typical Health-Related Recipients:** Emergency/Ambulance Services, Health Funds, Health Organizations, Health Policy/Cost Containment, Hospitals, Medical Rehabilitation. **Geographic Distribution:** Nationwide, with emphasis on operating locations.

**★6398★ Forest City Enterprises
    Charitable Foundation**
10800 Brookpark Rd.
Cleveland, OH 44130
Phone: (216)267-1200
Nathan Shafran, Vice Chairman

Giving Priorities: *Education:* 30% to 35% of annual total. *Health & Welfare:* 25% to 30% of annual giving, with major support to the United Way in Cleveland. Contributions also support religious welfare organizations. Majority of health support focuses on hospitals. Interests also include medical research and single-disease health associations. *Religion:* 15% to 20% of giving. *Civic:* 15% to 20%. *Culture & Arts:* 10% to 15% of total contributions. *Other:* Limited contributions go to international and scientific organizations. **Typical Health-Related Recipients:** AIDS/HIV, Cancer, Children's Health/Hospitals, Clinics/Medical Centers, Emergency/Ambulance Services, Health Organizations, Hospitals, Prenatal Health Issues, Sexual Abuse, Single-Disease Health Associations. **Geographic Distribution:** Near company locations, primarily the Cleveland and New York City areas.

Gallo Foundation
See: Entry 697

GEICO Philanthropic Foundation
See: Entry 698

★6399★ GenCorp Foundation
175 Ghent Rd.
Fairlawn, OH 44333
Phone: (216)869-4298
Fax: (216)869-4288
Joan Thompson, Director of Community
    Relations

Giving Priorities: *Education:* About 50% of funding. *Health:* About 30% of contributions. Supports the United Way. *Arts & Humanities:* About 10% of contributions. *Civic & Public Affairs:* About 10%. *Other:* Less than 5% of contributions to related business organizations. **Typical Health-Related Recipients:** Children's Health/Hospitals, Mental Health. **Geographic Distribution:** Near corporate operating locations.

General Mills Foundation
See: Entry 700

**Gillette Charitable & Educational
    Foundation**
See: Entry 704

★6400★ GTE Foundation
One Stamford Forum
Stamford, CT 06904
Phone: (203)965-3620
Fax: (203)965-2664
Maureen V. Gorman, Vice President

Giving Priorities: *Education:* 50% to 55% of total contributions. *Health & Human Services:* 20% to 25%. Supports societal issues such as the homeless and alcohol and drug abuse that affect the environment of corporate communities. Also supports United Way and hospitals. *Civic & Public Affairs:* 15% to 20%. *Arts & Hu-*

manities: About 5% to 10%. *Voluntarism:* Sponsors "Volunteer Initiatives Program" (VIP), which makes grants to organizations in which company employees volunteer. **Typical Health-Related Recipients:** Domestic Violence, Geriatric Health, Health Policy/Cost Containment, Hospitals, People with Disabilities, Substance Abuse. **Geographic Distribution:** Mainly in communities where company has business operations.

Handleman Charitable Foundation
See: Entry 717

Harsco Corp. Fund
See: Entry 722

★6401★ Herman O. West Foundation
PO Box 645
Lionville, PA 19341-0645
Phone: (610)594-2900
Fax: (610)594-3011
George R. Bennyhoff, Trustee

Giving Priorities: *Community Services:* About 50%. *Education:* About 30%. *Cultural:* About 15%. *Hospital & Health Care:* 5%. Focus on hospitals and health organizations. *Matching Gifts:* Operates an employee matching gift program to colleges, universities, private schools, and theological seminaries. *Scholarships:* Operates scholarship program for dependents of West Co. employees. Funds are distributed directly to college or university. Formal application form required. **Typical Health-Related Recipients:** Hospitals, Medical Research. **Geographic Distribution:** Headquarters and operating communities.

Heublein Foundation
See: Entry 726

Hubbard Foundation
See: Entry 729

**★6402★ IES Industries Charitable
    Foundation**
PO Box 351
Cedar Rapids, IA 52406
Phone: (319)398-4572
Fax: (319)398-4483
Robert J. Kucharski, Treasurer

Giving Priorities: *Social Services:* About 40% of total contributions. *Education:* 30% to 35% of giving. *Arts & Humanities:* 10% to 15% of funds. *Health:* About 10%. Primarily to hospitals. Also gives to single-disease health associations. *Civic & Public Affairs:* Less than 5%. **Typical Health-Related Recipients:** Hospitals, People with Disabilities, Single-Disease Health Associations. **Geographic Distribution:** Headquarters and service territory.

IFF Foundation
See: Entry 732

Interco Inc. Charitable Trust
See: Entry 735

★6403★ James M. Cox Foundation of Georgia
PO Box 105720
Atlanta, GA 30348
Phone: (404)843-7912
Fax: (404)843-7926
Leigh Ann Korns, Administrative Assistant

Giving Priorities: *Public Social Organizations*: 45% to 50% of total funding. *Universities & Schools*: 30% to 35%. *Hospitals*: 10% to 15%. Grants in this category also go to hospices and research facilities. *Performing Arts & Museums*: 5% to 10%. **Typical Health-Related Recipients:** Hospices, Hospitals. **Geographic Distribution:** In company operating locations, which are nationwide, with an emphasis on the Atlanta, GA, area.

Jochum-Moll Foundation
See: Entry 745

Kiewit Cos. Foundation
See: Entry 753

★6404★ Ladish Co. Foundation
5481 S Packard Ave.
Cudahy, WI 53110
Phone: (414)747-2900
Wayne Larson, Trustee

Giving Priorities: *Social Services*: 30% to 35% of total contributions. Interests include food distribution, child welfare, the disabled, and community service organization. *Education*: 25% to 30%. *Health*: 15% to 20%. Over half of support went to Trinity Memorial Hospital in Cudahy, WI. Other interests include hospitals and health care foundations in Milwaukee, WI, and organizations for blindness and disease prevention. *Religion*: 10% to 15%. *Other*: 5% to 10%. The foundation also supports public broadcasting, performing arts, public policy research, and housing. **Typical Health-Related Recipients:** Children's Health/Hospitals, Clinics/Medical Centers, Eyes/Blindness, Health Organizations, Hospitals, Medical Research, People with Disabilities, Single-Disease Health Associations. **Geographic Distribution:** Focus on Milwaukee and Cudahy, WI.

★6405★ Lincoln Electric Foundation Trust
22801 St. Clair Ave.
Cleveland, OH 44117
Phone: (216)481-8100
Ellis F. Smolik, Secretary

Giving Priorities: *Social Services*: About 30%. *Education*: 25% to 30% of total annual contributions. *Civic & Public Affairs*: 15% to 20%. *Health*: 10% to 15%. Generally assist area hospitals. Limited support to single-disease health organizations. *Arts & Humanities*: 5% to 10%. *Other*: Less than 5%. Funds international, religious welfare organizations, and scientific groups. **Typical Health-Related Recipients:** Cancer, Children's Health/Hospitals, Clinics/Medical Centers, Family Planning, Health Organizations, Hospitals, Long-Term Care, People with Disabilities, Respiratory, Single-Disease Health Associations, Substance Abuse. **Geographic Distribution:** Cleveland, OH, metropolitan area.

★6406★ Louisiana-Pacific Foundation
111 SW Fifth Ave.
Portland, OR 97204
Phone: (503)221-0800
Fax: (503)796-0170
Pamela A. Selis, Trustee

Giving Priorities: *Education*: 35% to 40% of contributions. *Arts & Humanities*: 15% to 20%. *Social Services*: 15% to 20% of contributions. *Civic & Public Affairs*: 15% to 20%. *Health*: 5% to 10%, most of which supports hospitals. *Other*: Under 5%. Limited support to science and religious organizations. **Typical Health-Related Recipients:** Children's Health/Hospitals, Emergency/Ambulance Services, Health Organizations, Heart, Hospices, Hospitals, People with Disabilities, Single-Disease Health Associations, Substance Abuse. **Geographic Distribution:** Primarily near headquarters and operating locations.

★6407★ Marshall and Ilsley Foundation
770 N Water St.
Milwaukee, WI 53202
Phone: (414)765-7835
Diana L. Sebion, Secretary

Giving Priorities: *Health*: 25% to 30%. Hospitals and health centers receive the largest portion of this. Other interests include medical research, single-disease health organizations, and nursing services. *Social Services*: About 20% of contributions, largely to youth organizations, united funds, and child welfare. Interests also include community services and centers, volunteer services, family services, and organizations concerned with the disabled. *Arts & Humanities*: 15% to 20%. *Civic & Public Affairs*: 10% to 15% of contributions. *Education*: 15% to 20%, largely to colleges and universities, and to scholarships and scholarship funds. **Typical Health-Related Recipients:** Cancer, Children's Health/Hospitals, Clinics/Medical Centers, Family Planning, Health Organizations, Hospitals, Medical Education, Medical Research, Medical Training, Mental Health, Nursing Services, People with Disabilities, Single-Disease Health Associations, Transplant Networks/Donor Banks, Trauma Treatment. **Geographic Distribution:** Wisconsin, with emphasis on Milwaukee.

★6408★ Material Service Foundation
222 N LaSalle St.
Chicago, IL 60601
Phone: (312)236-6300
Arnold I. Sobel, Vice President

Giving Priorities: *Social Services*: 45% to 50% of total funding. *Civic & Public Affairs*: 25% to 30%. *Education*: 10% to 15%. *Other*: The foundation also supported an arts center, hospitals, a scientific organization, and churches. **Typical Health-Related Recipients:** Hospitals, Medical Education. **Geographic Distribution:** Primarily in Illinois, with emphasis on Chicago.

★6409★ McDonnell Douglas Employee's Community Fund-West
3855 Lakewood Blvd.
Internal Mail Sta. 802-11
Long Beach, CA 90846
Phone: (310)593-2612
Fax: (310)982-2260
Beverly A. Hoskinson, Executive Director

Giving Priorities: *Human Services*: 40% to 45% of contributions. *Education*: 20% to 25%. *United Way*: 10% to 15% of contributions. *Community Enrichment*: 5% to 10%. *Youth*: 5% to 10%. *Health & Hospitals*: 5% to 10%. Support of hospitals directed largely to capital fund projects for building or, in some cases, major equipment purchases. Some consideration given to medical research and the initiation of new programs that provide community health maintenance and special services. **Typical Health-Related Recipients:** Health Organizations, Hospices, Hospitals, Medical Rehabilitation, Mental Health, People with Disabilities, Single-Disease Health Associations, Substance Abuse. **Geographic Distribution:** Nationally, primarily in those communities where McDonnell Douglas maintains corporate operations.

★6410★ McDonnell Douglas Foundation
PO Box 516
Mail Code 1001510
St. Louis, MO 63166
Phone: (314)232-8464
Fax: (314)232-7654
Antoinette Bailey, President

Giving Priorities: *Education*: About 50% of total annual contributions. *Health & Human Services*: 20% to 25% of contributions, with much of this going to united funds, hospitals, and youth organizations. *Business & Civic Affairs*: About 20%. *Arts & Culture*: About 5%. *International*: Less than 5%. **Typical Health-Related Recipients:** Children's Health/Hospitals, Hospitals, Substance Abuse. **Geographic Distribution:** Areas of corporate operations, including Alabama, Arizona, California, Colorado, Florida, Missouri, Ohio, Oklahoma, Texas, Utah, and Canada; also to national organizations.

★6411★ Menasha Corporation Foundation
PO Box 367
Neenah, WI 54957-0367
Phone: (414)751-1000
Fax: (414)751-1236
Steve Kromholz, President

Giving Priorities: *Education*: 45% to 50% of total contributions. *Health and Human Services*: 30% to 35% of giving. More than one-fourth of gifts go to United Way chapters. About one-tenth funds child welfare, including shelters, a children's hospital, and day care, and about one-tenth funds hospitals. *Arts & Humanities*: 5% to 10%. *Environment*: About 5%. *Special Interest/Other*: About 5% of funding. Supports economic development and safety. **Typical Health-Related Recipients:** Domestic Violence, Hospitals, Substance Abuse. **Geographic Distribution:** Focus on headquarters and operating locations.

Millipore Foundation
See: Entry 781

Mine Safety Appliances Co. Charitable Trust
See: Entry 782

Mobil Foundation
See: Entry 783

★6412★ Morgan Stanley Foundation
1251 Avenue of the Americas
39th Fl.
New York, NY 10020
Phone: (212)703-6610
Fax: (212)703-6503
Patricia Schaefer, Vice President

Giving Priorities: *Social Welfare:* 55% to 60% of annual giving. *Education:* About 20% of annual contributions. *Arts & Culture:* 10% to 15%. *Health:* 5% to 10%. Support goes to hospitals and other health-related services. *Other:* 5% to 10% goes to a variety of organizations disbursed through company branch offices. **Typical Health-Related Recipients:** Hospitals. **Geographic Distribution:** Primarily New York City; San Francisco, Los Angeles, and Chicago branches recommend some foundation contributions.

Nabisco Foundation Trust
See: Entry 787

National Starch & Chemical Foundation
See: Entry 791

Nationwide Insurance Enterprise Foundation
See: Entry 792

★6413★ New York Stock Exchange Foundation
11 Wall St., 6th Fl.
New York, NY 10005
Phone: (212)656-2060
James E. Buck, Secretary

Giving Priorities: *Social Services:* 50% to 55% of total funding. *Civic & Public Affairs:* 15% to 20%. *Education:* 10% to 15%. *Arts & Humanities:* 10% to 15%. *Health:* 5% to 10%. The New York Infirmary/Beekman Downtown Hospital and St. Vincent's Hospital and Medical Center each received $10,000. **Typical Health-Related Recipients:** Cancer, Hospitals, Medical Education, People with Disabilities. **Geographic Distribution:** Focus on New York City.

Olin Corp. Charitable Trust
See: Entry 803

OSG Foundation
See: Entry 805

★6414★ PACCAR Foundation
PO Box 1518
Bellevue, WA 98009
Phone: (206)455-7400
H. Dennis Sather, Vice President & General Manager

Giving Priorities: *Social Services:* About 50% of total contributions. *Arts & Humanities:* 10% to 15%. *Health:* 10% to 15%, entirely to hospitals, mainly specializing in pediatrics. *Civic & Public Affairs:* Less than 5%. *Other:* Scientific organi-

zations receive less than 1%. **Typical Health-Related Recipients:** Cancer, Children's Health/Hospitals, Clinics/Medical Centers, Emergency/Ambulance Services, Health Organizations, Hospitals, People with Disabilities, Substance Abuse. **Geographic Distribution:** Near headquarters and operating locations only.

Pittsburgh National Bank Foundation
See: Entry 818

Providence Journal Charitable Foundation
See: Entry 826

Revlon Foundation
See: Entry 835

★6415★ Robert I. Wishnick Foundation
375 Park Ave.
New York, NY 10152
Phone: (212)371-1844
William Wishnick, President, Director

Giving Priorities: *Arts & Humanities:* 30% to 35%. *Education:* About 25%. *Religion:* 15% to 20% of total funding. *Health:* 10% to 15%. Most of support went to the Mt. Sinai Annual Trustee Campaign. *Other:* The foundation also supports public affairs and social services. **Typical Health-Related Recipients:** Cancer, Clinics/Medical Centers, Emergency/Ambulance Services, Family Planning, Hospitals, Medical Education, People with Disabilities, Single-Disease Health Associations. **Geographic Distribution:** Operating communities. **Formerly:** Witco Foundation.

Ryder System Charitable Foundation
See: Entry 839

Stanley Works Foundation
See: Entry 860

★6416★ State Farm Cos. Foundation
One State Farm Plz.
Bloomington, IL 61710
Phone: (309)766-2161
Fax: (309)766-3700
Dave Polzin, Assistant Vice President

Giving Priorities: *Education:* 75% to 80% of contributions. *Arts & Humanities:* 15% to 20%. *Health:* 5% to 10% of contributions, more than half of which goes to the United Way. Remaining funds support youth organizations, other human service agencies, hospitals, and medical centers in regional office and corporate headquarters locations. *Civic & Public Affairs:* Less than 5%. Employees participate in activities on their own initiative. **Typical Health-Related Recipients:** Hospitals. **Geographic Distribution:** Near major offices.

Textron Charitable Trust
See: Entry 875

TRINOVA Foundation
See: Entry 883

TRW Foundation
See: Entry 884

Union Pacific Foundation
See: Entry 889

★6417★ United Airlines Foundation
PO Box 66100
Chicago, IL 60666
Phone: (708)952-5714
Fax: (708)952-4081
Eileen Younglove, Secretary & Contributions Manager

Giving Priorities: *Social Services:* 55% to 60% of total gifts. *Education:* 10% to 15% of contributions. *Health:* 10% to 15%. Supports hospitals in Chicago and related health organizations. *Science:* 5% to 10%. *Arts & Humanities:* About 5% of support. *Civic & Public Affairs:* About 5%. *Voluntarism:* Employees volunteer for Adopt-a-School program, Muscular Dystrophy Association, and United Way fund raising events. **Typical Health-Related Recipients:** Alzheimers Disease, Cancer, Children's Health/Hospitals, Heart, Hospitals, Single-Disease Health Associations. **Geographic Distribution:** Primarily in Washington, DC; Los Angeles and San Francisco, CA; Denver, CO; Honolulu, HI; Chicago, IL; and Seattle, WA.

★6418★ Universal Foods Foundation
433 E Michigan St.
Milwaukee, WI 53202
Phone: (414)347-3895
Fax: (414)347-3785
Carl L. Zaar, Secretary-Treasurer

Giving Priorities: *Health:* 50% to 55% of contributions. Primarily supports hospitals, but funding also goes to medical research. *Education:* 25% to 30% of total contributions. *Civic & Public Affairs:* 5% to 10% of total funds. *Arts & Humanities:* 5% to 10%. *Voluntarism:* Company sponsors a public TV Channel 10/36 Friends Annual Auction, a Friends Campaign with Boys and Girls Clubs, and a workplace giving campaign. **Typical Health-Related Recipients:** Hospitals, Medical Research, People with Disabilities. **Geographic Distribution:** In headquarters and operating communities.

★6419★ Upjohn Co. Foundation
7000 Portage Rd.
Kalamazoo, MI 49001
Phone: (616)323-7017
Fax: (616)323-4225
Vickie G. Heerlyn, Manager, Corporate Support Program

Giving Priorities: *General Support Program:* Supports educational institutions near major facilities, as well as those from which company recruits employees. Supports education and research programs related to the pharmaceuticals business. Health and welfare support is given through United Ways in company communities. Donates only to hospitals that are used frequently by Upjohn employees and their families for improvement of services. Also supports civic, cultural, and environmental groups in operating locations, and programs designed to increase opportunities for minorities and the disadvantaged. *Note:* In 1993, company donated $7,200,000 worth of products, including pharmaceutical products and seeds to relief programs through organizations such as World Vision Relief & Development, Feed the Children, and Catholic Medical Mision Board. **Typical Health-Related Recipients:** AIDS/HIV, Cancer, Emergency/Ambulance Services, Health Organizations, Hospitals, Medical Education, Medical Research, Mental Health, Nursing Services, People with Disabilities, Research/Studies Institutes, Substance Abuse, Transplant Networks/Donor Banks. **Geographic Distribution:** Almost entirely in major operating locations; about 55% of cash grants go to organizations in Kalamazoo, MI; product donations go only to Third World countries.

USX Foundation
See: Entry 894

Westvaco Foundation Trust
See: Entry 901

WICOR Foundation
See: Entry 905

Wisconsin Energy Corp. Foundation
See: Entry 908

★6420★ Woodward Governor Co. Charitable Trust
5001 N Second St.
Rockford, IL 61125
Phone: (815)877-7441
Mr. Harry Tallacksen, Contribution Committee Chairman

Giving Priorities: *Fund Raising & Support Organizations:* 45% to 50%. Contributions in this category support solely United Way organizations. *Social Welfare:* 15% to 20%. *Civic:* 15% to 20%. *Cultural & Educational:* 5% to 10% of contributions. *Health, Handicapped, & Disabled:* 5% to 10%. Most recipients are single-disease health organizations. Funds also support the handicapped, mental health groups, and some clinics. *Hospitals & Related Facilities:* 5% to 10%, to hospitals, clinics, nursing homes, and adult care facilities. **Typical Health-Related Recipients:** Emergency/Ambulance Services, Geriatric Health, Hospices, Hospitals, Medical Rehabilitation, Medical Research, Mental Health, People with Disabilities, Single-Disease Health Associations. **Geographic Distribution:** Primarily in areas where company operates.

★6421★ Zilkha Foundation
767 Fifth Avenue, Ste. 4605
New York, NY 10153
Phone: (212)758-7750
Fax: (212)758-7803
Ezra K. Zilkha, President

Giving Priorities: *Education:* 35% to 40% of total funding. *Civic & Public Affairs:* About 35%. *Arts & Humanities:* 10% to 15%. *Health:* About 10%, almost all of which went to the Hospital for Special Surgery. *Religion:* About 5%. **Typical Health-Related Recipients:** Hospitals, People with Disabilities. **Geographic Distribution:** Emphasis on New York, NY.

Other Funding Organizations

★6422★ American Women's Hospitals Service Committee of AMWA
801 N. Fairfax St., Ste. 400
Alexandria, VA 22314
Phone: (703)838-0500
Fax: (703)549-3864
Dr. Anne Barlow, Chwm.

Description: Supports medical and hospital services provided by women doctors and nurses for the care of the indigent sick and for the prevention of disease. Activities include giving financial aid to hospitals and clinics, family planning, home visits, and health education.

National & International Organizations

★6423★ American Association of Eye and Ear Hospitals (AAEEH)
1350 New York Ave. NW, No. 200
Washington, DC 20005
Phone: (202)347-1990
Fax: (202)628-2310
Robert Betz, Director

Founded: 1983. **Members:** 18. **Description:** Chief executive officers and administrators of eye and ear specialty hospitals. Seeks to advance, at the federal level, fair economic treatment for eye and ear specialty hospitals; to share business functions such as purchasing, planning, and information and data collection. Compiles statistics. **Publications:** *Bimonthly Update.*

American Association of Hospital Dentists (AAHD)
See: Entry 3876

American Association of Hospital Podiatrists (AAHP)
See: Entry 10756

American Association of Physician-Hospital Organizations (AAPHO)
See: Entry 5541

★6424★ American Committee for Shaare Zedek Hospital in Jerusalem (ACSZJ)
49 W. 45th St., Ste. 1100
New York, NY 10036
Phone: (212)354-8801
Free: 800-346-1592
Fax: (212)391-2674
Morris Talansky, Exec.VP

Founded: 1955. **Description:** Provides financial support to Shaare Zedek Hospital in Jerusalem, Israel. Fundraising activities include dinners, concerts, travel missions to Israel, and direct mail solicitations. Purchases medical equipment and supplies and finances new hospital departments. Maintains speakers' bureau. **Publications:** *Heartbeat,* quarterly.

★6425★ American Hospital Association (AHA)
1 N. Franklin, Ste. 27
Chicago, IL 60606
Phone: (312)422-3000
Fax: (312)422-4796
Richard J. Davidson, Ph.D., Pres.

Founded: 1898. **Members:** 54,500. **Description:** Individuals and health care institutions including hospitals, health care systems, and pre- and postacute health care delivery organizations. Is dedicated to promoting the welfare of the public through its leadership and assistance to its members in the provision of better health services for all people. Carries out research and education projects in such areas as health care administration, hospital economics, and community relations; represents hospitals in national legislation; offers programs for institutional effectiveness review, technology assessment, and hospital administrative services to hospitals; conducts educational programs furthering the in-service education of hospital personnel; collects and analyzes data; furnishes multimedia educational materials; maintains 44,000 volume health care administration library, and biographical archive. **Publications:** *AHANews,* weekly. • *Guide to the Health Care Field,* annual. • *Hospital Statistics,* annual. • *Hospitals and Health Networks,* biweekly. **Formerly:** (1906) Association of Hospital Superintendents of U.S. and Canada.

★6426★ American Osteopathic Healthcare Association (AOHA)
5301 Wisconsin Ave. NW, Ste. 630
Washington, DC 20015
Phone: (202)686-1700
Fax: (202)686-7615
David L. Kushner, Pres.

Founded: 1934. **Members:** 109. **Regional Groups:** 6. **Description:** Osteopathic hospitals. Holds educational institutes on health care management. Conducts research programs; compiles statistics. **Publications:** *AOHA Annual Directory.* Directory. Lists osteopathic hospitals; contains statistical data. *Price:* Included in membership dues. • *AOHA Newsletter,* monthly. Newsletter. *Price:* Included in membership dues. • *Directory of Postdoctoral Education,* annual. Directory. Lists osteopathic internship programs. *Price:* Included in membership dues. **Formerly:** (1993) American Osteopathic Hospital Association.

★6427★ American Society for Healthcare Central Service Personnel (ASHCSP)
c/o American Hospital Association
1 N. Franklin
Chicago, IL 60606
Phone: (312)422-3750
Fax: (312)422-4572
Jackie Croteau, Exec.Dir.

Founded: 1967. **Members:** 1,300. **Regional Groups:** 9. **Local Groups:** 48. **Description:** Objectives, programs, and activities of the society are educational. Maintains speakers' bureau; offers placement service; compiles statistics. **Publications:** *Healthcare Central Service,* bimonthly. Newsletter. *Price:* Available to members only. Also publishes technical materials and training manuals. **Formerly:** (1987) American Society for Hospital Central Service Personnel.

★6428★ American Society for Healthcare Education and Training of the American Hospital Association (ASHET)
840 N. Lake Shore Dr.
Chicago, IL 60611
Phone: (312)280-3556
Free: 800-621-6712
Beverly J. Rogers, Dir.

Founded: 1970. **Members:** 1,500. **State Groups:** 50. **Description:** Educators and trainers from hospitals and other healthcare institutions involved in staff development, and patient and community education. Purposes are: to foster professional development of members; to demonstrate the value of comprehensive education as a management strategy; to promote continuing education among all healthcare personnel; to develop coordination among organizations involved in the education of healthcare personnel; to formulate information and evaluation programs; to recommend action on national issues relating to healthcare education. Conducts educational programs. Sponsors competitions. **Publications:** *Healthcare Education Dateline*, 3/year. • *Hospitals*, biweekly. • *Journal of Healthcare Education and Training*, periodic. Journal. **Formerly:** (1973) American Society for Hospital Education and Training; (1981) American Society for Health Manpower Education and Training.

★6429★ American Society for Healthcare Engineering of the American Hospital Association (ASHE)
c/o Amer. Hospital Assn.
One N. Franklin, Ste. 2700
Chicago, IL 60606
Phone: (312)422-3800
Fax: (312)422-4571
Joseph J. Martori, Exec.Dir.

Founded: 1962. **Members:** 5,500. **Local Groups:** 75. **Description:** Hospital engineers, facilities managers, directors of buildings and grounds, assistant administrators, directors of maintenance, directors of clinical engineering, design and construction professionals, and safety officers. Works to: promote better patient care by encouraging and assisting members to develop their knowledge and increase their competence in the field of facilities management; cooperate with hospitals and allied associations in matters pertaining to facilities management; bring about closer cooperation among members; provide a medium for interchange of material relative to facilities management. Maintains library; conducts educational programs. Offers Actions for Professional Excellence Recognition Program (APEx). **Publications:** *American Society for Healthcare Engineering--Management and Compliance Series*, semiannual. Provides comprehensive coverage of a specific facilities management topic. *Price:* $75/volume for members; $98/volume for nonmembers. • *American Society for Healthcare Engineering--Technical Document Series*, monthly. Report. Covers a specific topic in clinical/biomedical engineering, facilities management engineering, or design and construction. • *American Society for Hospital Engineering--*

Yearbook. Membership Directory. Arranged alphabetically by name, hospital, and city and state; includes vendor directory. • *Health Facilities Management Magazine*, monthly. Journal. • *Publications Catalog*, semiannual. Lists books, films, tapes, documents, and publications available from the society. *Price:* Free. Also publishes books. **Formerly:** American Society for Hospital Engineering.

★6430★ American Society for Healthcare Environmental Services of the American Hospital Association (ASHES)
c/o Yvonne J. Cernick
840 N. Lake Shore Dr.
Chicago, IL 60611
Phone: (312)280-3365
Fax: (312)280-4152
Yvonne J. Cernick, Exec.Dir.

Founded: 1986. **Members:** 1,500. **Regional Groups:** 16. **Description:** Managers and directors of hospital environmental services, laundry and linen services, housekeeping departments, and long-term care units. Provides a forum for discussion among members of common problems including educational opportunities, professional development, and career advancement. Operates technical assistance center and placement services. Offers legal advocacy; maintains liaison between members and governmental and code-writing bodies. Bestows Accolades Awards, Phoenix Award, Years of Service Award, Professional Recognition of Achievement -- Actions for Professional Excellence Awards, and Scholarship Award. Compiles statistics; maintains library; conducts educational programs. **Publications:** *ASHES Members Directory*, annual. Membership Directory. • *ASHES Newsletter*, bimonthly. Newsletter. • *Professional Development Series*, periodic.

American Society for Healthcare Human Resources Administration (ASHHRA)
See: Entry 5553

★6431★ American Society for Health Care Marketing and Public Relations (ASHCMPR)
c/o Amer. Hospital Association
840 N. Lake Shore Dr.
Chicago, IL 60611
Phone: (312)422-3737
Fax: (312)422-4579
Lauren Barnett, Dir.

Founded: 1964. **Members:** 3,000. **Regional Groups:** 9. **Local Groups:** 57. **Description:** Persons in hospitals, hospital councils or associations, hospital-related schools, and health care organizations responsible for marketing and public relations. **Publications:** *Directory of Health Care Strategic Management and Communications Consultants*, annual. Directory. *Price:* Free to members; $40/copy for nonmembers. • *Membership Directory of the American Society for Health Care Marketing and Public Relations*, annual. Membership Directory. *Price:* Included in membership dues. • *MPR Exchange*, bimonthly. Tabloid; includes calendar of events. *Price:* Included in membership dues. **Formerly:** (1984) American Society for Hospital Public Relations; (1990) American Society for Hospital Marketing and Public Relations.

★6432★ American Society for Healthcare Materials Management (ASHMM)
c/o American Hospital Association
1 N. Franklin, 30th Fl.
Chicago, IL 60606
Phone: (312)422-3840
Fax: (312)422-3573
Shelly Johnson, Exec.Dir.

Founded: 1962. **Members:** 2,300. **Local Groups:** 45. **Description:** Individuals active in the field of purchasing, inventory and distribution, and materials management as performed in hospitals, related patient care institutions, or government and voluntary health organizations, and who are employed by an organization eligible for institutional membership in the American Hospital Association (see separate entry); associate members are individuals active in the areas of health care supply manufacturing, distributing, and consulting. Purposes are to: help members with their responsibilities; provide access to the latest ideas, methods, developments, information, and techniques in the field of hospital purchasing and materials management; establish associations with others in the profession; provide recognition in the profession through participation in policy-making; provide a link with the AHA. Conducts certification program in health care management. **Publications:** *American Society for Healthcare Materials Management--Conference Proceedings*, annual. Proceedings. Presents case studies. • *American Society for Healthcare Materials Management--Membership Roster*, annual. Membership Directory. *Price:* Included in membership dues. • *American Society for Helathcare Materials Management--Perspectives*, bimonthly. Newsletter. Contains case studies. *Price:* Included in membership dues. • *Collection of Fellowship Readings*, annual. Journal. Provides case studies on health care materials management. • *Healthcare Materials Management News*, bimonthly. Newsletter. Contains reviews of educational programs, current legal and legislative problems, new materials management techniques, and society news. *Price:* Included in membership dues. • *Resource Catalog*, annual. **Formerly:** (1976) American Society for Hospital Purchasing Agents; (1983) American Society for Hospital Purchasing and Materials Management; (1994) American Society for Hospital Materials Management.

American Society for Healthcare Risk Management (ASHRM)
See: Entry 5554

American Society for Hospital Food Service Administrators (ASHFSA)
See: Entry 5555

American Society of Hospital Pharmacists (ASHP)
See: Entry 10588

★ 6433 ★   American Women's Hospitals
Service Committee of AMWA (AWHS/
AMWA)
801 N. Fairfax St., Ste. 400
Alexandria, VA 22314
Phone: (703)838-0500
Fax: (703)549-3864
Dr. Anne Barlow, Chwm.

Founded: 1917. **Description:** Committee of
American Medical Women's Association. International philanthropic medical relief service that
supports medical and hospital services conducted by women doctors and nurses for the
care of the indigent sick and prevention of disease. Current activities, carried on in Bolivia,
Haiti, and the U.S., include family planning and
fostering health education through demonstrations, home visits, and giving financial aid to
hospitals and clinics. **Formerly:** (1959) American Women's Hospitals; (1982) American
Women's Hospitals Service.

★ 6434 ★   AMHS Institute
400 N. Capitol St. NW, Ste. 590
Washington, DC 20001
Phone: (202)393-0860
Fax: (202)393-0864
James L. Scott, Pres.

Founded: 1984. **Members:** 40. **Description:**
Nonprofit multi-hospital systems. Sponsors educational programs for corporate officers and
trustees of multi-hospital systems. Conducts research on multi-hospital systems and operations. Monitors, investigates, and develops policy positions on developments in the field. **Formerly:** Association AMHS Institute; (1988)
American Healthcare Institute.

Association of Air Medical Services
(AAMS)
See: Entry 4737

★ 6435 ★   Association for Healthcare
Philanthropy (AHP)
313 Park Ave., Ste. 400
Falls Church, VA 22046
Phone: (703)532-6243
Fax: (703)532-7170
Dr. William C. McGinly, Pres.

Founded: 1967. **Members:** 2,500. **Regional
Groups:** 13. **Description:** Persons employed by
healthcare organizations in the field of healthcare resource development and fundraising;
hospital administrators and trustees; hospitals;
interested individuals. Purposes are to create a
cohesive body of healthcare development executives in the U.S. and Canada; to advance the
interests and knowledge of healthcare fund development; to encourage and stimulate better
understanding of healthcare needs; to accomplish common goals through an exchange of
ideas and information. Conducts educational
programs. Holds regional seminars. Compiles
statistics; conducts research; sponsors competitions. Maintains library. **Publications:** *Association for Healthcare Philanthropy--Directory*, annual. Directory. Lists members and allied firms.
Includes calendar of events. *Price:* Included in
membership dues. • *Association for Healthcare
Philanthropy--Journal*, semiannual. Journal.
Price: Included in membership dues; $38/year
for nonmembers. • Newsletter, 8/year. • Re-

port on Giving. • *Salary and Benefits*. **Formerly:**
(1967) Developpartners; (1991) National Association for Hospital Development.

★ 6436 ★   Association of High Medicare
Hospitals (AHMH)
1620 Eye St. NW, Ste. 202
Washington, DC 20006
Phone: (202)785-9670
Bartlett S. Fleming, Pres.

Founded: 1988. **Members:** 36. **Description:**
Hospitals serving a high proportion of Medicare
patients (hospitals with Medicare utilization of
65% or more of total inpatient days). Works to
effect policy issues concerning hospitals and
communities. Acts as a clearinghouse for information relating to health policy issues such as
retirement communities. Lobbies government.
Publications: *Update on Activities*, weekly.
Newsletter.

★ 6437 ★   Association for Hospital Medical
Education (AHME)
1200 19th St. NW
Washington, DC 20036-2401
Phone: (202)857-1196
Fax: (202)223-4579
Michael S. Hamm, Exec.Dir.

Founded: 1954. **Members:** 700. **Description:**
Physician directors of medical education in hospitals and clinics and other health profession
educators. Conducts educational programs and
workshops for members and others in the area
of graduate and continuing medical education.
Publications: *AHME Congressional Record*. •
Membership Directory, annual. • Newsletter,
quarterly. **Formerly:** (1968) Association of Hospital Directors of Medical Education.

Association of Managerial Hospital Doctors
of Germany
(Verband der Leitenden Krankenhausarzte
Deutschlands)
See: Entry 5560

★ 6438 ★   Baptist Hospital Association
(BHA)
c/o Baptist Med. System
9601 Interstate 630
Little Rock, AR 72205
Phone: (501)227-2274
Bill Mason, Pres.

Founded: 1975. **Members:** 4. **Description:**
Baptists or Baptist-oriented hospitals. Purposes
are: to assist member hospitals in their growth,
development, and accreditation by exchange of
information, ideas, and experiences; to advance
the cause of Baptist hospital programs. **Publications:** *Advance*, 3/year. • *Consult*, monthly.
• *Hendrick '86*, monthly.

★ 6439 ★   Canadian Hospital Association
17 York St., Ste. 100
Ottawa, ON, Canada K1G 9J6
Phone: (613)241-8005
Fax: (613)241-5055
Carol Clemenhagen, Pres.

Founded: 1931. **Members:** 11. **State Groups:**
11. **Languages:** French. **Description:** Promotes a humane, effective, efficient health system of the highest quality. **Publications:** *Leadership in Health Services*, bimonthly. Journal.
Also Known As: Canadian Health Association.

Canadian Society of Hospital Pharmacists
(CSHP)
(Societe Canadienne des Pharmaciens
d'Hopitaux — SCPH)
See: Entry 10593

Children in Hospitals (CIH)
See: Entry 3202

★ 6440 ★   Commission on Professional and
Hospital Activities (CPHA)
2929 Plymouth Rd., Ste. 208
PO Box 304
Ann Arbor, MI 48106-0304
Phone: (313)995-9800
Fax: (313)973-2791
Dr. William Jessee, Pres. & CEO

Founded: 1953. **Description:** Medical information center dedicated to the improvement of
hospital and medical care. Serves as a national
repository for patient and health care data. Conducts research, consultation, and continuing education on hospital case mix, reimbursement,
and classification issues. Evaluates and markets selected health decision support and management computer software. Provides continuing education seminars in disease and procedure classification. Maintains Professional Activity Study, the basic component of a family of
computerized patient record information systems developed to display hospital medical
practices. Makes special comparative studies
on local, state, regional, national, and international levels from records of 300 million hospital-
izations. Conducts seminars, institutes, and regional workshops for individuals from participating and nonparticipating hospitals and other organizations. Sponsors workshops. Established
under grants from W. K. Kellogg Foundation,
Battle Creek, MI.

Committee for Nordic Hospital
Administrators Associations
See: Entry 5571

★ 6441 ★   Council of Teaching Hospitals
(COTH)
Association of American Medical Colleges
2450 N St. NW
Washington, DC 20037
Phone: (202)828-0490
Robert M. Dickler, VP

Founded: 1965. **Members:** 400. **Description:**
Teaching hospitals. Provides activities and programs relating to specific problems and opportunities in medical school-affiliated or university-
owned teaching hospitals. Distributes communications analyzing congressional activities, Executive Branch actions, court decisions affecting teaching hospitals, and teaching hospital
reimbursement regulations; disseminates special interest bibliographies, surveys of housestaff policies, comparative hospital financial
data, and other materials. Appoints study
groups and ad hoc advisory task forces. **Publications:** *COTH Report*, 8-10/year. Newsletter.
Reviews current federal and state legislation
and general activities of the association and its
affiliates. *Price:* $30/year. • *Survey of House
Staff Stipends, Benefits, and Funding*, annual.

European Association of Hospital Managers (EAHM)
(Europaische Vereinigung der Krankenhaus Direktoren)
See: Entry 5574

European Association of Hospital Pharmacists (EAHP)
See: Entry 10597

★6442★ Federation of American Health Systems (FAHS)
1405 N. Pierce, No. 311
Little Rock, AR 72217-8708
Phone: (501)661-9555
Fax: (501)663-4903
Michael D. Bromberg, Exec.Dir.

Founded: 1966. **Members:** 1,000. **Regional Groups:** 7. **Description:** Privately- or investor-owned (for-profit) hospitals. Compiles statistics on the investor-owned hospital industry. **Publications:** Annual Report. • *Directory of Investor-Owned Hospitals, Residential Treatment Facilities and Centers, Hospital Management Companies, and Health Systems,* annual. Directory. *Price:* $60 for members; $100 for nonmembers. • *Federation of American Health Systems Hotline,* biweekly. Newsletter. Monitors health legislation, regulatory and reimbursement matters and developments in the health care industry. *Price:* Included in membership dues; $150/year for nonmembers. • *Health Systems Review,* bimonthly. *Price:* $20/year for nonmembers. • *State-to-State Report,* periodic. Covers proposed legislation being considered by state governments. **Formerly:** (1985) Federation of American Hospitals.

★6443★ Floating Hospital (FH)
Pier 11 Wall at South St.
New York, NY 10005
Phone: (212)514-7440
Fax: (212)514-5645
Mary Bleiberg, Exec.Dir.

Founded: 1866. **Description:** Provides medical, dental and health education services. Programs occur within a 4-deck ship, docked in the East River at Wall Street. Provides health services to homeless children and their families, children in kinship foster care and their kinship families, and adolescents who engage in high risk behaviors. Programs take place dockside and while sailing around New York harbor. The ship is open during day and evening hours, six days each week. All programs integrate health education and nutrition, the keys of disease prevention, with comprehensive and continuous primary care. **Formerly:** (1980) St. John's Guild - The Floating Hospital.

★6444★ General Constituency Section for Small or Rural Hospitals (SSRH)
c/o American Hospital Association
840 N. Lake Shore Dr.
Chicago, IL 60611
Phone: (312)280-6395
John Supplitt, Dir.

Founded: 1976. **Members:** 3,500. **Description:** Section of the American Hospital Association. Community hospitals that have fewer than 100 acute care beds, are located outside a standard metropolitan statistical area, or admit 4000

or fewer patients per year. Seeks to: support small or rural hospitals through representation and advocacy before federal, legislative, and regulatory groups; participate in AHA policymaking; liaison with Joint Commission on Accreditation of Healthcare Organizations, American Medical Association, and other health organizations; monitor legislation and regulations. Conducts management strategy workshops and programs on issues of current interest to small or rural hospitals. **Publications:** *Update,* 3/year. Newsletter.

★6445★ German Hospital Association (GHA)
(Deutsche Krankenhausgesellschaft — DKG)
Tersteegenstrasse 9
40474 Dusseldorf, Germany
Phone: 211 454730
Fax: 211 4547361
Dr. Klaus Prussdof, Dir.

Founded: 1949. **Members:** 27. **Languages:** English. **Description:** Federal state hospital associations and welfare federations in Germany. Publicizes members' accomplishments in public health. Works to maintain and improve the performance of hospitals; fosters exchange of information among members. Serves as liaison between members and government and other organizations; makes recommendations to legislative bodies. **Publications:** *das Krankenhaus,* monthly. Magazine.

Healthcare Information and Management Systems Society (HIMSS)
See: Entry 6993

Hospital Directors Association of Germany (Verband der Krankenhausdirektoren Deutschlands)
See: Entry 5579

★6446★ Hungarian Hospital Association (HHF)
(Magyar Korhazszovetseg — MKSZ)
Furedi utca 9/c
H-1144 Budapest VIII, Hungary
Phone: 1 1635273
Fax: 1 1635273
Dr. Peter Lepes, Sec.Gen.

Founded: 1931. **Members:** 600. **Local Groups:** 14. **Languages:** English, German, Hungarian, Polish. **Description:** Doctors, nurses, and technical and administrative hospital personnel in Hungary. Disseminates research results and information based on the operation of hospitals and other health institutions. Fosters utilization of national and foreign medical achievements. Bestows awards. **Publications:** *A Korhaz,* quarterly. • Directory, quinquennial. Includes Dutch and English supplements.

★6447★ Independent Hospital Workers Union (IHWU)
PO Box 188
Alexandria, LA 71301
Phone: (318)448-1600
Irving Ward-Steinman, Ph.D., Gen. Counsel

Founded: 1980. **Description:** Independent. Represents hospital workers and protects their rights to fair salary and acceptable working conditions.

★6448★ Indian Hospital Association (IHA)
B-401, Sarita Vihar
New Delhi 110 044, Delhi, India
Phone: 11 6835648
Fax: 11 4620102
Dr. P. N. Ghei, Sec.Gen.

Founded: 1960. **Members:** 5,000. **Languages:** English. **Description:** Individuals and hospitals in India. Conducts research in primary health care, child survival, quality assurance, and maternal health and safety. Participates in international conferences; sponsors health care management seminars. Conducts annual essay competition. **Publications:** *Hospital Administration,* quarterly. Journal. • *Jubilee,* periodic. List of hospitals. • *Proceedings of the International Conference and Workshop.*

Institute for Hospital Clinical Nursing Education (IHCNE)
See: Entry 9093

★6449★ International Association of Healthcare Central Service Material Management (IAHCSM)
213 W. Institute Pl., Ste. 307
Chicago, IL 60610
Phone: (312)440-0078
Free: 800-962-8274
Betty Hanna, Exec.Dir.

Founded: 1958. **Members:** 9,000. **State Groups:** 31. **Description:** Professional personnel responsible for management and distribution of supplies from a central service materiel management department of a hospital. Works to improve the quality of central service materiel management departments in hospitals; share information and ideas; research hospital central service materiel management methods and practices; conduct and promote continuing education programs. Sponsors management correspondence courses and technician training courses through Purdue University in Indiana. Has established a certification program to recognize exceptional achievement. Maintains technician registry and placement service. Surveys salaries. Conducts research programs; compiles statistics. Maintains 23 committees. **Publications:** *Communique,* bimonthly. Also publishes technical management and training manuals. **Formerly:** (1969) National Association of Hospital Central Service Personnel; (1989) International Association of Hospital Central Service Management.

★6450★ International Association for Healthcare Security and Safety (IAHSS)
PO Box 637
Lombard, IL 60148
Phone: (708)953-0990
Fax: (708)957-1786
William Farnsworth, Pres.

Founded: 1968. **Members:** 1,700. **Regional Groups:** 15. **Local Groups:** 53. **Description:** Administrative and supervisory personnel in the field of hospital security and safety. To develop, promote, and coordinate better security/safety systems in medical care facilities. Offers placement services; conducts specialized education programs. **Publications:** *Healthcare Protection Management,* semiannual. Journal. • Membership Directory, annual. • Newsletter, quarterly.

Formerly: (1990) International Association for Hospital Security.

★6451★ **International Hospital Federation (IHF)**
c/o American Hospital Association
1 N. Franklin, 25th Fl.
Chicago, IL 60611
Phone: (312)422-3000
Jose Gonzalez, Contact

Founded: 1947. **Members:** 1,788. **Description:** Federation of national associations of public or private hospitals, ministries of health, and other organizations which cover hospitals at the national level; professional organizations and institutions connected with hospital service; members of hospital staffs, hospital management committees, and professions connected with hospital work; manufacturers and suppliers of hospital services in 90 countries. Assists members in visiting hospitals abroad; maintains information service and gives advice to members on hospital problems. **Publications:** *Membership List*, annual. • *Official Yearbook*. • *World Hospitals*, quarterly.

★6452★ **International Hospital Federation (IHF)**
(Federacion Internacional de Hospitales)
4 Abbots Pl.
London NW6 4NP, England
Phone: 171 3727181
Fax: 171 3287433
Dr. Errol Pickering, Dir.Gen.

Founded: 1929. **Members:** 1,694. **Regional Groups:** 1. **Languages:** English, French, Spanish. **Description:** Individuals (1117); organizations (388); professional firms (114); government representatives (75). Promotes improvement in the planning and management of hospitals and health services through study tours, information services, and research and development projects. Serves as an advocate for hospitals and related health service organizations in world health affairs. Sponsors regional conferences and courses for senior hospital and health services managers from developing countries. Compiles statistics. **Publications:** Books. • *Health Services International*, annual. Newsletter. • *Hospital Management International*, annual. • Reports, periodic. • *World Hospitals*, 3/year. Journal. Includes summaries in French and Spanish.

★6453★ **Korean Hospital Association (KHA)**
35-1 Mapo-dong
Mapo-gu
Seoul 121-050, Republic of Korea
Phone: 2 7187521
Fax: 2 7187522
Ho Uk Ha, Ph.D., V.Pres.

Founded: 1959. **Members:** 621. **Languages:** English, Korean. **Description:** Hospitals with 20 or more beds in the Republic of Korea. Aims to maintain high standards of hospital care and related health services. Advocates hospital and medical records standardization; promotes information exchange between hospitals; provides administrative assistance to member hospitals. Provides educational programs for hospital personnel. **Publications:** *Hospital Directory*, periodic. Directory. • Journal, monthly. • *Korean Hospital News*, semiweekly.

★6454★ **Latin American Hospital Federation (LAHF)**
(Federacion Latinoamericana de Hospitales — FLH)
Juarez 14 Casa 11
Tlacopac San Angel
01040 Mexico City, DF, Mexico
Phone: 5 5482650
Dr. Guillermo Fajardo Ortiz, Contact

Founded: 1976. **Members:** 10. **Languages:** Spanish. Does not correspond in English. **Description:** Hospital associations in 8 countries. Seeks to: improve medical care and meet Latin American health needs through region-specific programs. Maintains contact with directors and ministers of health and social security organizations. Conducts educational programs.

★6455★ **Lutheran Hospital Association of America (LHA)**
United Medical Center Trinity Medical Center
501 10th Ave.
Moline, IL 61265
Phone: (309)757-2611
Eric Crowell, Pres.

Members: 110. **Description:** Hospitals sponsored by a Lutheran church or bearing the title Lutheran. Offers periodic grants for the advancement of health care chaplaincy programs. **Publications:** *Lutheran Health Resources Directory*, periodic. Directory. • Newsletter, quarterly.

★6456★ **Lutheran Hospitals and Homes Society (LHHS)**
PO Box 6200
Fargo, ND 58106
Phone: (701)293-9053
Free: 800-843-5447
Fax: (701)277-7636
Steve Orr, Pres.

Founded: 1938. **Description:** Incorporated for the purpose of operating and maintaining hospitals, nursing homes, homes for the aged, and a hospital-school for disabled children. **Publications:** *Caring*, bimonthly. • *Institutional Directory*, semiannual. Directory. • *Sharing*, quarterly.

★6457★ **Membership Section for Health Care Systems (HCS)**
c/o Amer. Hospital Association
1 N. Franklin, Ste. 2700
Chicago, IL 60606
Phone: (312)280-6393
Free: 800-621-6712
Fax: (312)280-6252
Gene J. O'dell, Dir.

Founded: 1978. **Members:** 304. **Description:** A section of the American Hospital Association. Health care systems representing over 2900 hospitals. (A health care system is established when: a single hospital owns, leases, or contract manages nonhospital pre-acute and/or postacute health-related facilities; 2 or more hospitals are owned, leased, sponsored, or contract managed by a central organization.) Acts as a clearinghouse. Collects and analyzes data related to health care systems; maintains refer-

ence resources. Sponsors educational programs. **Publications:** *AHA Guide*, annual. • Bibliographies. • Books. • Monographs. **Formerly:** Center for Multi-Institutional Arrangements; (1988) Membership Section for Multihospital Systems.

National Association of Children's Hospitals and Related Institutions (NACHRI)
See: Entry 3262

★6458★ **National Association of Healthcare Access Management (NAHAM)**
1200 19th St. NW, Ste. 300
Washington, DC 20036
Phone: (202)857-1125
Fax: (202)223-4579
Carol A. Lively, Exec.Dir.

Founded: 1974. **Members:** 1,500. **Regional Groups:** 9. **Description:** Healthcare access managers united to improve patient care and community relations. Promotes professional recognition and provides educational resources for the healthcare patient access field. Serves as a central source of technical information on changes and trends in health care that affect patient access services. Advocates progressive changes in health care practices; provides information on admissions and registration procedures. **Publications:** *Connections*, bimonthly. Newsletter. Contains list of employment opportunities. *Price:* Included in membership dues; $75/year for nonmembers. • *The NAHAM Management Journal*, quarterly. Journal. Contains reports on trends affecting admissions, patient registration, and patient access; includes descriptions of techniques, systems, and services. *Price:* Included in membership dues; $90/year for nonmembers. • *National Association of Healthcare Access Management--Membership Directory*, annual. Membership Directory. **Formerly:** (1990) National Association of Hospital Admitting Managers.

★6459★ **National Association of Health Unit Coordinators (NAHUC)**
1821 University Ave., Ste. 162 S.
St. Paul, MN 55104
Phone: (612)641-8095
Florence Frye, Pres.&CEO

Founded: 1980. **Members:** 3,500. **Regional Groups:** 9. **Local Groups:** 74. **Description:** Coordinators of nonclinical nursing unit activities; educators, supervisors, students, and graduates in the field. Promotes the professional practice of unit coordinating. Has established standards of practice defining the role and responsibilities of health unit coordinators in the nonclinical area of health care and ensuring delivery of quality patient care. Works to establish certification guidelines for individual practitioners with a goal of national certification. Seeks recognition of the change in job title from clerk to that of coordinator, which the group believes better describes the nature of the position. Promotes continuing education and research; endeavors to develop accreditation of educational programs and standards of education for job entry. Provides vocational information to prospective students in the field; recruits students into the profession. Represents members' interests before allied health professionals, educational institutions, governmental bodies, and the community. Sponsors regional workshops, seminars, and other educational programs; compiles statistics. Maintains certification board and speakers' bureau; offers annual national certification exam. **Publications:** *Information Booklet.* Booklet. • *National Association of Health Unit Coordinators--Coordinator,* quarterly. Newsletter. *Price:* Included in membership dues; $10/year for nonmembers. • *National Association of Health Unit Coordinators-- Membership Directory,* annual. Membership Directory. *Price:* Included in membership dues. • *Question & Answer Brochures.* Brochures. **Formerly:** (1990) National Association of Health Unit Clerks-Coordinators.

★6460★ **National Association of Hospital Hospitality Houses (NAHHH)**
4013 W. Jackson St.
Muncie, IN 47304-3610
Phone: (317)288-3226
Free: 800-542-9730
Fax: (317)287-0321
Josephine Lee, Chm.

Founded: 1986. **Members:** 92. **Regional Groups:** 9. **Description:** Hospitals, hospital hospitality houses (HHH), charitable foundations, and interested individuals. (Hospital hospitality houses are temporary residential facilities for patients and their families.) Provides assistance to members and offers information and guidance to those who wish to establish an HHH. Conducts educational programs; operates resource center and speakers' bureau; compiles statistics. **Publications:** *House Notes,* bimonthly. Newsletter. *Price:* Available to members only. • *National Association of Hospitality Houses: Home Away From Home.* Brochure. Sent to members, and hospitals and healthcare agencies. • *National Referral Directory,* periodic. Directory. Lists member referral procedures, services, and donation requirements. *Price:* $75. • Newsletter, semiannual.

★6461★ **National Association of Psychiatric Health Systems (NAPHS)**
1319 F St. NW, Ste. 1000
Washington, DC 20004
Phone: (202)393-6700
Fax: (202)783-6041
Robert L. Trachtenberg, CAE, Exec.Dir.

Founded: 1933. **Members:** 292. **Description:** Represents and promotes the interests of healthcare systems that are committed to the delivery and financing of high-quality efficient, and clinically effective treatment and prevention programs for people with mental and substance abuse disorders. **Formerly:** (1993) National Association of Private Psychiatric Hospitals.

★6462★ **National Association of Public Hospitals (NAPH)**
1212 New York Ave. NW, Ste. 800
Washington, DC 20005
Phone: (202)408-0223
Fax: (202)408-0235
Larry S. Gage, Pres.

Founded: 1980. **Members:** 70. **Description:** Urban public hospitals. Promotes the develop-

ment of federal, state, and local legislative and policy agendas for members. **Publications:** Newsletter, periodic. • *Safety Net,* quarterly.

★6463★ **National Council of Community Hospitals (NCCH)**
1700 K St. NW, Ste. 906
Washington, DC 20006
Phone: (202)728-0830
Fax: (202)296-7689
John Horty, Pres.

Founded: 1974. **Members:** 126. **Description:** Community hospitals and hospital consultant groups (106) and individual health delivery representatives (20). Acts as lobbyist concerning legislation and federal issues affecting hospitals, physicians, and healthcare beneficiaries.

★6464★ **National Federation of Housestaff Organizations (NFHO)**
386 Park Ave. S, Rm. 1502
New York, NY 10016
Phone: (212)683-7475
Fax: (212)779-2413
Faidherbe Seus

Founded: 1984. **Members:** 11. **Description:** Federation of housestaff physicians unions. (Housestaff physicians are employed by the hospitals in which they practice, and are currently in speciality training.) Assists members in collective bargaining, lobbying state and local governments, and promoting unionization among housestaff physicians. Maintains speakers' bureau. **Publications:** *NFHO Newsletter,* quarterly. Newsletter.

★6465★ **National Hospital Association of the Netherlands (NHAN)**
(Nationale Ziekenhuisraad — NZR)
Postbus 9696
NL-3506 GR Utrecht, Netherlands
Phone: 30 739911
Fax: 30 739438
Mrs. M.F. Vos, PR Officer

Founded: 1971. **Members:** 780. **Languages:** Dutch, English, French, German. **Description:** General, specialized, and university hospitals (231); nursing homes (326); children's nursing homes (12); mental health care institutions (86); institutions for mentally retarded and disabled patients (127). Develops intramural health care in the Netherlands with respect for religious values. Contributes to and monitors national policies on residential health care; holds consultations with government and local authorities. Promotes discussion and information exchange among member organizations; represents members interests. Areas of concern include health care quality, financial and economic matters, conditions of employment for hospital workers, education, and planning and construction of new hospitals. Addresses ethical issues involved in health care. Represents employers in labor negotiations in the hospital sector. Operates National Hospital Institute of the Netherlands; organizes advisory committees. Disseminates information. **Publications:** *Directory,* periodic. Directory. • *Het Ziekenhuis,* biweekly. Also publishes reports (in Dutch).

★6466★ **National Hospital Institute of the Netherlands**
(Nationaal Ziekenhuisinstituut — NZI)
Postbus 9696
NL-3506 JR Utrecht, Netherlands
Phone: 30 739911
Mrs. W.H.C. Lensvelt, PR Officer

Founded: 1968. **Local Groups:** 11. **Languages:** Dutch, English, French, German. **Description:** Seeks to develop a "sound, humane, and financially feasible health service" in the Netherlands. Conducts scientific research; offers advisory services; maintains educational programs. Disseminates information to health institutions and health care services. **Publications:** *Annual Report.*

★6467★ **Private Hospitals Association of Malawi (PHAM)**
PO Box 30378
Lilongwe 3, Malawi

Description: National private Christian hospitals and health care associations. Provides a forum for discussion and exchange of information regarding health issues. Offers health information.

★6468★ **Section for Metropolitan Hospitals (SMH)**
c/o American Hospital Association
1 N. Franklin
Chicago, IL 60606
Phone: (312)422-3000
Fax: (312)280-6252
Robert P. Katzfey, Dir.

Founded: 1984. **Members:** 1,365. **Description:** Institutional members of the American Hospital Association that are located within a metropolitan statistical area and/or provide a significant proportion of Medicare, Medicaid, and uncompensated care; participate in undergraduate and/or graduate medical education programs and research; provide high volumes of ambulatory care; offer specialized services; and are involved in professional and paraprofessional education and training programs. Represents views of members to the AHA and assists in the development and implementation of policies and programs to promote recognition, support, and growth for its members within the health care field. Serves as clearinghouse for metropolitan hospital delivery, finance, governanc e, management, and organizational issues. Compiles statistics; maintains databases; conducts forums.

★6469★ **Section for Rehabilitation Hospitals and Programs (SRHP)**
c/o American Hospital Association
1 N. Franklin St.
Chicago, IL 60606
Phone: (312)422-3000
Susanne Sonik, Dir.

Founded: 1984. **Members:** 890. **Description:** Assists hospitals in helping persons with disabilities to reach their optimal level of functioning. Emphasizes comprehensive medical rehabilitation services. Monitors and attempts to influence national standards of medical rehabilitative care and pertinent federal legislation and regulations. Promotes public education on disability prevention and rehabilitation. Provides general information, case studies, and information on issues related to medical rehabilitation; compiles statistics and maintains database and speakers' bureau. Offers accreditation assistance for medical rehabilitation programs; provides professional consultation and technical assistance. Conducts research. **Publications:** *Director's Letter*, quarterly. *Price:* Included in membership dues. • *Guide to Choosing a Comprehensive Inpatient Medical Rehabilitation Facility.* • *Medical Rehabilitation Services in Health Care Institutions.* • *Outpatient Rehabilitation Services: A Guide to Planning and Management.* • *The Payment of Medical Rehabilitation Services: Current Mechanisms and Potential Models.* • *Quality Rehabilitation: Results-Oriented Patient Care.*

★ 6470 ★ **Shriners Hospitals for Crippled Children (SHCC)**
2900 Rocky Point Dr.
Tampa, FL 33607
Phone: (813)281-0300
Free: 800-237-5055
Fax: (813)281-8174
Lewis K. Molnar, Exec.VP

Founded: 1922. **Members:** 22. **Description:** 6SHCC operated orthopaedic hospitals (19) and burn hospitals (3) founded by and affiliated with the Imperial Council of the Ancient Arabic Order of the Nobles of the Mystic Shrine for North America . Provides no-cost orthopedic and burn care to children under 18 years of age. Maintains the Shriners Hospitals for Crippled Children Endowment Fund. Conducts research; compiles statistics. **Publications:** *Between Us*, 3/year. • Booklet. • Brochures. • *Imperial Council of the Ancient Arabic Order of the Nobles of the Mystic Shrine for North America.* • Pamphlets. Also publishes fact sheets.

★ 6471 ★ **Society for Healthcare Planning and Marketing of the American Hospital Association (SHPM)**
1 N. Franklin
Chicago, IL 60606
Phone: (312)442-3888
Linda Hill-Chinn, Acting Dir.

Founded: 1978. **Members:** 4,000. **Local Groups:** 25. **Description:** Employees of hospitals, allied hospital associations, multi-institutional systems, and any other direct provider of health care services; employees of consulting firms, health or hospital administration programs, government agencies, and national, state, or community health planning agencies; students in disciplines relevant to hospital planning. Goals are to address institutional and community strategic planning and marketing policies and issues; promote member development through academic and continuing education; foster professional interaction with other planning and marketing groups; provide a forum for the interchange of ideas among members. Is committed to the principle that planning and marketing are complementary approaches to direct the future course of a health care organization. Sponsors educational programs including Managed Care Forum, Physician Integration Forum, Strategy Forum. **Publications:** *Directory of Health Care Strategic Management and*

Communications Consultants, annual. Directory. • *Healthcare Planning and Marketing Newsletter*, monthly. Newsletter. *Price:* Included in membership dues. • *Managed Care Newsletter*, quarterly. Newsletter. • Membership Directory, annual. • *Physician Integration Newsletter*, quarterly. Newsletter. • Reports. Also publishes research studies and compendiums. **Formerly:** (1985) Society for Hospital Planning of the American Hospital Association; (1987) Society for Hospital Planning and Marketing of the American Hospital Association.

Society of Hospital Epidemiologists of America
See: Entry 5185

Society for Hospital Social Work Directors (SHSWD)
See: Entry 11872

★ 6472 ★ **Special Constituency Section for Aging and Long Term Care Services**
c/o American Hospital Association
840 N. Lake Shore Dr.
Chicago, IL 60611
Phone: (312)280-6372
Mary Jane Milano, Dir.

Founded: 1969. **Members:** 2,600. **Description:** Hospitals that are members of the American Hospital Association and have long-term care units or community-based long-term care and special services for the aging. Promotes recognition, growth, and support of aging and long-term care services developed by institutional membership within the AHA structure through representation, advocacy, technical assistance, and information. **Publications:** *Case Studies in Aging and Long-Term Care*, 3-4/year. *Price:* Included in membership dues. Also publishes monographs. **Formerly:** (1978) Assembly of Nursing Care and Related Institutions; (1982) Skilled Nursing and Related Long Term Care Services; (1984) Assembly of Skilled Nursing and Related Long Term Care Services; (1987) Special Constituency Section on Aging and Long Term Care.

★ 6473 ★ **Special Constituency Section for Psychiatric and Substance Abuse Services (SCSMHPS)**
c/o American Hospital Association
840 N. Lake Shore Dr.
Chicago, IL 60611
Phone: (312)280-6495

Founded: 1969. **Members:** 3,000. **Description:** Long- and short-term care institutional members of the American Hospital Association who provide psychiatric, substance abuse, mental retardation, and other mental health services. Assists the AHA in development and implementation of policies and programs to promote improvement of and advocacy for hospital-based mental health and psychiatric services. Sponsors annual educational program concentrating on administrative aspects of psychiatric services. Active in formulating and commenting on federal legislation and regulations relating to mental health and psychiatric services. **Formerly:** (1972) Psychiatric Hospital Section; (1984) Psychiatric Services Section; (1991) Special Constituency Section for Mental Health and Psychiatric Services.

★ 6474 ★ **Swiss Hospital Association (SHA) (Vereinigung Schweizerischer Krankenhaeuser — VESKA)**
Case 4202
Rain 32
CH-5001 Aarau, Switzerland
Phone: 64 241222
Fax: 64 223335

Founded: 1930. **Members:** 700. **Languages:** English, French, German. **Description:** Public and private hospitals, clinics, nursing homes, regional health care associations, government authorities, and corporations. Seeks to devise practical solutions to common problems faced by members. Serves as a liaison between health care authorities and facilities. Develops guidelines for compiling statistics. Provides counseling on insurance and recruitment matters. Operates publishing house and 2 continuing education centers. **Publications:** *List of Members*, periodic. • *Schweizer Spital*, monthly.

★ 6475 ★ **Volunteer Trustees of Not-for-Profit Hospitals**
818 18th St. NW, Ste. 900
Washington, DC 20006
Phone: (202)659-0338
Fax: (202)659-0116
Linda B. Miller, Pres.

Founded: 1980. **Members:** 150. **State Groups:** 45. **Description:** Representatives of 155 not-for-profit hospitals and their voluntary governing boards. Objectives are to: provide a trustee voice in policy-making and legislative activities; develop a communications network among trustees in order to provide the highest quality medical care at the lowest possible price; provide educational services to hospital governing boards; facilitate accurate portrayal of not-for-profit hospitals in the media and Congress. Areas of concern include: Medicare; controlling hospital costs; strategic planning for the not-for-profit hospital community. Compiles information on governing boards. Conducts roundtables.

Research Centers

Johns Hopkins University Center for Hospital Finance and Management
See: Entry 5752

Pittsburgh Research Institute
See: Entry 5754

U.S. Department of Health and Human Services National Center for Infectious Diseases Hospital Infections Program
See: Entry 6814

U.S. Department of Health and Human Services National Center for Infectious Diseases Hospital Infections Program Hospital Environment Laboratory Branch
See: Entry 6815

State Government Agencies

Hospital Licensure

★6476★ **Alabama Department of Public Health**
Health Care Standards Bureau
Licensure and Certification Division
671 S. Perry St.
Montgomery, AL 36130
Phone: (334)240-3500
Fax: (334)240-3147

★6477★ **Alaska Department of Health and Social Services**
Medical Assistance Division
Health Facilities Licensing and Certification Office
4730 Business Park Blvd., Ste. 18
Anchorage, AK 99503
Phone: (907)561-8081
Fax: (907)561-3011

★6478★ **Arizona Department of Health Services**
Health Care Licensure Office
1740 W. Adams
Phoenix, AZ 85007
Phone: (602)542-1025
Fax: (602)542-1062

★6479★ **Arkansas Department of Health**
Health Resources Bureau
Health Facility Services and Systems Division
PO Box 3278
Little Rock, AR 72203-3278
Phone: (501)661-2622
Fax: (501)671-1450

★6480★ **California Health and Welfare Agency**
Health Services Department
Licensing and Certification Division
1800 3rd St., Ste. 210
Sacramento, CA 95814
Phone: (916)445-2070

★6481★ **Colorado Public and Environment Department**
Health Office
Health Facilities Division
4300 Cherry Creek Dr. S
Denver, CO 80222-1530
Phone: (303)692-2800
Fax: (303)782-4883

★6482★ **Connecticut Department of Public Health**
Hospital and Medical Care Division
150 Washington St.
Hartford, CT 06106
Phone: (203)566-1073
Fax: (203)566-3302

★6483★ **Delaware Department of Health and Social Services**
Public Health Division
Health Facilities Licensing and Certification Office
3 Mill Rd., Ste. 308
Wilmington, DE 19806
Phone: (302)577-6666

★6484★ **District of Columbia Department of Consumer and Regulatory Affairs**
Service Facility Regulations Administration
Health Facility Division
614 H St. NW
Washington, DC 20001
Phone: (202)727-7190
Fax: (202)727-7780

★6485★ **Florida Department of Health and Rehabilitative Services**
Licensure and Certification Office
2727 Mahan Dr., Ste. 200
Tallahassee, FL 32308
Phone: (904)487-2527
Fax: (904)487-6240

★6486★ **Georgia Department of Human Resources**
Regulatory Services Office
Health Care Section
2 Peachtree St. NW, Ste. 19-204
Atlanta, GA 30303
Phone: (404)657-5430
Fax: (404)657-8934

★6487★ **Hawaii Department of Health**
Hospital and Medical Facilities Branch
1250 Punchbowl St.
PO Box 3378
Honolulu, HI 96801
Phone: (808)586-4080
Fax: (808)586-4745

★6488★ **Idaho Department of Health and Welfare**
Medicaid Division
Facility Standards Bureau
PO Box 83720
Boise, ID 83720-0036
Phone: (208)334-6630
Fax: (208)334-6558

★6489★ **Illinois Department of Public Health**
Health Care Regulation Office
Health Care Facilities and Programs Division
Hospital Licensing Section
535 W. Jefferson St.
Springfield, IL 62761
Phone: (217)782-7412
Fax: (217)782-3987

★6490★ **Indiana Department of Health**
Acute Care Division
1330 W. Michigan St.
PO Box 1964
Indianapolis, IN 46206-1964
Phone: (317)633-6481
Fax: (317)633-6779

★6491★ **Iowa Department of Inspections and Appeals**
Health Facilities Division
Lucas State Office Bldg.
Des Moines, IA 50319-0083
Phone: (515)281-4233
Fax: (515)281-7289

★6492★ **Kansas Department of Health and Environment**
Health Division
Adult and Child Care Facilities Bureau
Hospital Program
900 SW Jackson St., Ste. 1001
Topeka, KS 66612-1290
Phone: (913)296-1240
Fax: (913)296-1266

★6493★ **Kentucky Human Resources Cabinet**
Inspector General Office
Licensing and Regulation Division
275 E. Main St.
East Frankfort, KY 40621
Phone: (502)564-2800
Fax: (502)564-7573

★6494★ **Louisiana Department of Health and Hospitals**
Health Standards Section
Licensing and Certification Division
PO Box 629
Baton Rouge, LA 70821-0629
Phone: (504)342-0138
Fax: (504)342-9508

★6495★ **Maine Department of Human Services**
Medical Services Bureau
Licensing and Certification Division
State House Station 11
Augusta, ME 04333
Phone: (207)287-2606
Fax: (207)287-2675

★6496★ **Maryland Department of Health and Mental Hygiene**
Licensing and Certification Administration
4201 Patterson Ave.
Baltimore, MD 21215
Phone: (410)764-2750
Fax: (410)225-6489

★6497★ **Massachusetts Executive Office of Health and Human Services**
Public Health Department
Health Care Quality Division
150 Tremont St.
Boston, MA 02111
Phone: (617)727-1296
Fax: (617)727-2559

★6498★ **Michigan Department of Public Health**
Health Systems Bureau
Health Facilities, Licensing, and Certification
3423 N. Logan St.
PO Box 30195
Lansing, MI 48909
Phone: (517)335-8500
Fax: (517)335-9476

★6499★ Minnesota Department of Health
Health Quality Assurance Bureau
Facility and Provider Compliance Division
393 N. Dunlap St.
PO Box 64900
St. Paul, MN 55164-0900
Phone: (612)643-2100
Fax: (612)643-2593

★6500★ Mississippi Department of Health
Health Resources and Lab Sevices Bureau
Licensure and Certification Division
PO Box 1700
Jackson, MS 39215-1700
Phone: (601)987-3775
Fax: (601)354-6123

★6501★ Missouri Department of Health
Health Resources Division
Hospital Licensing and Certification Bureau
PO Box 570
Jefferson City, MO 65102
Phone: (314)751-6302
Fax: (314)526-3621

★6502★ Montana Department of Health
and Environmental Sciences
Health Facilities Division
Cogswell Bldg., Rm. C108
Helena, MT 59620
Phone: (406)444-2037

★6503★ Nebraska Department of Health
Environmental Health Bureau
Health Facilities Licensure Division
301 Centennial Mall S.
PO Box 95007
Lincoln, NE 68509
Phone: (402)471-2946
Fax: (402)471-0555

★6504★ Nevada Department of Human
Resources
Health Division
Licensure and Certification Bureau
505 E. King St., Rm. 201
Carson City, NV 89710
Phone: (702)687-4475
Fax: (702)687-5751

★6505★ New Hampshire Department of
Health and Human Services
Public Health Services Division
Health Facilities Administration Bureau
6 Hazen Dr.
Concord, NH 03301
Phone: (603)271-4592
Fax: (603)271-3745

★6506★ New Jersey Department of
Health
Health Facilities Evaluation and Licensing
Division
Licensing, Certification, and Standards
Ofice
CN 367
Trenton, NJ 08625-0367
Phone: (609)588-7726
Fax: (609)588-7823

★6507★ New Mexico Department of
Health
Public Health Division
Licensing and Certification Bureau
1190 St. Francis Dr.
PO Box 26110
Santa Fe, NM 87502-6110
Phone: (505)827-4200
Fax: (505)827-4222

★6508★ New York State Department of
Health
Health Systems Management Office
Hospital Services Bureau
Corning Tower, Empire State Plaza
Albany, NY 12237-0001
Phone: (518)474-5013
Fax: (518)474-2031

★6509★ North Carolina Department of
Human Resources
Facility Services Division
701 Barbour Dr.
PO Box 29530
Raleigh, NC 27626-0530
Phone: (919)733-2342

★6510★ North Dakota Department of
Health and Consolidated Laboratories
Health Resources Section
Health Facilities Division
600 E. Boulevard
Bismarck, ND 58505-0200
Phone: (701)328-2352
Fax: (701)328-4727

★6511★ Ohio Department of Health
Health Facilities Regulation Division
246 N. High St.
PO Box 118
Columbus, OH 43266-0118
Phone: (614)466-7857
Fax: (614)644-0085

★6512★ Oklahoma Department of Health
Medical Facilities Services
1000 NE 10th St.
PO Box 53551
Oklahoma City, OK 73152
Phone: (405)271-3960
Fax: (405)271-3431

★6513★ Oregon Department of Human
Resources
Health Division
Health Care Licensure and Certification
Section
PO Box 14450
Portland, OR 97214-0450
Phone: (503)731-4013
Fax: (503)731-4080

★6514★ Pennsylvania Department of
Health
Quality Assurance Bureau
Hospitals Division
Health and Welfare Bldg., Ste. 532
Harrisburg, PA 17120
Phone: (717)783-8980
Fax: (717)772-2163

★6515★ Rhode Island Department of
Health
Health Services Regulations Office
Facilities Regulations Division
3 Capitol Hill
Providence, RI 02908-5097
Phone: (401)277-2566
Fax: (401)273-4350

★6516★ South Carolina Department of
Health and Environmental Control
Health Regulation Division
Health Facilities Regulation Bureau
2600 Bull St.
Columbia, SC 29201
Phone: (803)737-7200
Fax: (803)737-7212

★6517★ South Dakota Department of
Health
Licensure and Certification Program
Sigurd Anderson Bldg.
445 E. Capitol
Pierre, SD 57501
Phone: (605)773-3364
Fax: (605)773-5904

★6518★ Tennessee Department of Health
Manpower and Facilities Bureau
Health Care Facilities Division
283 Plus Park Blvd.
Nashville, TN 37247-6303
Phone: (615)367-6303
Fax: (615)367-6397

★6519★ Texas Department of Health
Health Facility Licensure and Certification
Bureau
1100 W. 49th St.
Austin, TX 78756-3199
Phone: (512)834-6650
Fax: (512)458-7477

★6520★ Utah Department of Health
Health Systems Improvement Division
Facility Licensure Bureau
PO Box 142851
Salt Lake City, UT 84114-2851
Phone: (801)538-6107
Fax: (801)538-7053

★6521★ Vermont Agency of Human
Services
Health Department
Medical Care Regulation Division
PO Box 70
Burlington, VT 05402
Phone: (802)863-7272
Fax: (802)863-7425

★6522★ Virginia Office of Health and
Human Resources
Health Department
Health Facilities Regulation Office
PO Box 2448
Richmond, VA 23218
Phone: (804)367-2102
Fax: (804)786-4616

★6523★ **Washington Department of Health**
Facility and Services Licensing Division
Field Services Office
Acute Care and Construction Review Section
Target Plaza, Ste. 500
2725 Harrison Ave. NW
PO Box 47852
Olympia, WA 98504-7852
Phone: (206)360-6612
Fax: (206)360-6654

★6524★ **West Virginia Department of Health and Human Resources**
Public Health Bureau
Health Facility Licensure and Certification Office
State Capitol Complex, Bldg. 3
Charleston, WV 25305
Phone: (304)558-0050
Fax: (304)558-1130

★6525★ **Wisconsin Department of Health and Social Services**
Health Division
Quality Compliance Bureau
PO Box 7850
Madison, WI 53707-7850
Phone: (608)267-7185
Fax: (608)267-0352

★6526★ **Wyoming Department of Health**
Preventive Medicine Division
Facilities Licensure Section
Hathaway Bldg., 4th Fl.
Cheyenne, WY 82002
Phone: (307)777-7123
Fax: (307)777-5402

State & Regional Organizations

Hospitals

Listed below are state hospital associations that are allied with the American Hospital Association, 1 N. Franklin, Chicago, IL 60606, (312) 422-3000.

Alabama

★6527★ **Alabama Hospital Association**
500 N. East Blvd.
PO Box 210759
Montgomery, AL 36121-0759
Phone: (205)272-8781
Fax: (205)270-9527

Alaska

★6528★ **Alaska State Hospital and Nursing Home Association**
319 Seward St., Ste. 11
Juneau, AK 99801
Phone: (907)586-1790
Fax: (907)463-3573

Arizona

★6529★ **Arizona Hospital Association**
1501 W. Fountainhead Pkwy., Ste. 650
Tempe, AZ 85282
Phone: (602)968-1083
Fax: (602)967-2029

Arkansas

★6530★ **Arkansas Hospital Association**
419 Natural Resources Dr.
Little Rock, AR 72205-1539
Phone: (501)224-7878
Fax: (501)224-0519

California

★6531★ **California Association of Hospitals and Health Systems**
1201 K St., Ste. 800
PO Box 1100
Sacramento, CA 95812-1100
Phone: (916)443-7401
Fax: (916)552-7596

Colorado

★6532★ **Colorado Hospital Association**
2140 S. Holly St.
Denver, CO 80222-5607
Phone: (303)758-1630
Fax: (303)758-0047

Connecticut

★6533★ **Connecticut Hospital Association**
110 Barnes Rd.
PO Box 90
Wallingford, CT 06492-0090
Phone: (203)265-7611
Fax: (203)284-9318

Delaware

★6534★ **Association of Delaware Hospitals**
1280 S. Governors Ave.
Dover, DE 19901-4802
Phone: (302)674-2853
Fax: (302)734-2731

District of Columbia

★6535★ **District of Columbia Hospital Association**
1250 I St. NW, Ste. 700
Washington, DC 20005-3922
Phone: (202)682-1581
Fax: (202)371-8151

Florida

★6536★ **Florida Hospital Association**
307 Park Lake Circle
PO Box 531107
Orlando, FL 32853-1107
Phone: (407)841-6230
Fax: (407)422-5948

Georgia

★6537★ **Georgia Hospital Association**
1675 Terrell Mill Rd.
Marietta, GA 30067
Phone: (404)955-0324
Fax: (404)955-5801

Hawaii

★6538★ **Healthcare Association of Hawaii**
932 Ward Ave., Ste. 430
Honolulu, HI 96814-2126
Phone: (808)521-8961
Fax: (808)599-2879

Idaho

★6539★ **Idaho Hospital Association**
802 W. Bannock St., Ste. 500
PO Box 1278
Boise, ID 83701
Phone: (208)338-5100
Fax: (208)338-7800

Illinois

★6540★ **Illinois Hospital and Health Systems Association**
Center for Health Affairs
1151 E. Warrenville Rd.
PO Box 3015
Naperville, IL 60566-7015
Phone: (708)505-7777
Fax: (708)505-9457

Indiana

★6541★ **Indiana Hospital Association**
1 American Sq.
PO Box 82063
Indianapolis, IN 46282
Phone: (317)633-4870
Fax: (317)633-4875

Iowa

★6542★ **Iowa Hospital Association**
100 E. Grand Ave., Ste. 100
Des Moines, IA 50309
Phone: (515)288-1955
Fax: (515)283-9366

Kansas

★6543★ **Kansas Hospital Association**
1263 Topeka Ave.
PO Box 2308
Topeka, KS 66601
Phone: (913)233-7436
Fax: (913)233-6955

Kentucky

★6544★ **Kentucky Hospital Association**
1302 Clear Spring Trace
PO Box 24163
Louisville, KY 40224
Phone: (502)426-6220
Fax: (502)426-6226

Louisiana

★6545★ **Louisiana Hospital Association**
9521 Brookline Ave.
PO Box 80720
Baton Rouge, LA 70898-0720
Phone: (504)928-0026
Fax: (504)923-1004

Maine

★6546★ **Maine Hospital Association**
150 Capitol St.
Augusta, ME 04330
Phone: (207)622-4794
Fax: (207)622-3073

Maryland

★6547★ **Maryland Hospital Association**
1301 York Rd., Ste. 800
Lutherville, MD 21093-6087
Phone: (410)321-6200
Fax: (410)321-6268

Massachusetts

★6548★ **Massachusetts Hospital Association**
5 New England Executive Park
Burlington, MA 01803
Phone: (617)272-8000
Fax: (617)272-0466

Michigan

★6549★ **Michigan Health and Hospital Association**
6215 W. St. Joseph Hwy.
Lansing, MI 48917
Phone: (517)323-3443
Fax: (517)323-0946

Minnesota

★6550★ **Minnesota Hospital Association**
University Office Plaza, Ste. 425
2221 University Ave. SE
Minneapolis, MN 55414-3085
Phone: (612)331-5571
Fax: (612)331-1001

Mississippi

★6551★ **Mississippi Hospital Association**
6425 Lakeover Rd.
PO Box 16444
Jackson, MS 39236-6444
Phone: (601)982-3251
Fax: (601)982-2992

Missouri

★6552★ **Missouri Hospital Association**
4712 Country Club Dr.
PO Box 60
Jefferson City, MO 65102-0060
Phone: (314)893-3700
Fax: (314)893-2809

Montana

★6553★ **Montana Hospital Association**
1720 9th Ave.
PO Box 5119
Helena, MT 59604
Phone: (406)442-1911
Fax: (406)443-3894

Nebraska

★6554★ **Nebraska Association of Hospitals and Health Systems**
1640 L St., Ste. D
Lincoln, NE 68508-2509
Phone: (402)476-0141
Fax: (402)475-4091

Nevada

★6555★ **Nevada Hospital Association**
4600 Kietzke Ln., Ste. A-108
Reno, NV 89502
Phone: (702)827-0184
Fax: (702)827-0190

New Hampshire

★6556★ **New Hampshire Hospital Association**
125 Airport Rd.
Concord, NH 03301-5388
Phone: (603)225-0900
Fax: (603)225-4346

New Jersey

★6557★ **New Jersey Hospital Association**
Center for Health Affairs
746-760 Alexander Rd., CN-1
Princeton, NJ 08543-0001
Phone: (609)275-4000
Fax: (609)275-4100

New Mexico

★6558★ **New Mexico Hospital and Health Systems Association**
2121 Osuna Rd. NE
Albuquerque, NM 87113
Phone: (505)343-0010
Fax: (505)343-0012

New York

★6559★ **Healthcare Association of New York State**
74 N. Pearl St.
Albany, NY 12207
Phone: (518)431-7600
Fax: (518)431-7915

North Carolina

★6560★ **North Carolina Hospital Association**
PO Box 80428
Raleigh, NC 27623-0428
Phone: (919)677-2400
Fax: (919)677-4200

North Dakota

★6561★ **North Dakota Hospital Association**
1120 College Dr.
PO Box 7340
Bismarck, ND 58507-7340
Phone: (701)224-9732
Fax: (701)224-9529

Ohio

★6562★ **Ohio Hospital Association**
155 E. Broad St.
Columbus, OH 43215
Phone: (614)221-7614
Fax: (614)221-4771

Oklahoma

★6563★ **Oklahoma Hospital Association**
4000 Lincoln Blvd.
Oklahoma City, OK 73105
Phone: (405)427-9537
Fax: (405)424-4507

Oregon

★6564★ **Oregon Association of Hospitals and Health Systems**
4000 Kruse Way Pl., Bldg. 2, Ste. 100
Lake Oswego, OR 97035-2543
Phone: (503)636-2204
Fax: (503)636-8310

Pennsylvania

★6565★ **Hospital Association of Pennsylvania**
4750 Lindle Rd.
PO Box 8600
Harrisburg, PA 17105-8600
Phone: (717)564-9200
Fax: (717)561-5333

Puerto Rico

★ 6566 ★ Puerto Rico Hospital Association
Villa Nevarez Professional Center, Stes. 101-
  103
San Juan, PR 00927
Phone: (809)764-0290
Fax: (809)753-9748

Rhode Island

**★ 6567 ★ Hospital Association of Rhode
Island**
Weld Bldg., 2nd Fl.
345 Blackstone Blvd.
Providence, RI 02906
Phone: (401)453-8400
Fax: (401)453-8411

South Carolina

**★ 6568 ★ South Carolina Hospital
Association**
101 Medical Circle
PO Box 6009
West Columbia, SC 29171-6009
Phone: (803)796-3080
Fax: (803)796-2938

South Dakota

**★ 6569 ★ South Dakota Hospital
Association**
3708 Brooks Pl., Ste. 1
Sioux Falls, SD 57106
Phone: (605)361-2281
Fax: (605)361-5175

Tennessee

★ 6570 ★ Tennessee Hospital Association
500 Interstate Blvd. S.
Nashville, TN 37210
Phone: (615)256-8240
Fax: (615)242-4803

Texas

★ 6571 ★ Texas Hospital Association
6225 US Hwy. 290 E.
PO Box 15587
Austin, TX 78761-5587
Phone: (512)465-1000
Fax: (512)465-1090

Utah

**★ 6572 ★ Utah Association of Healthcare
Providers**
127 South 500 East, Ste. 625
Salt Lake City, UT 84102
Phone: (801)364-1515
Fax: (801)532-4806

Vermont

★ 6573 ★ Vermont Hospital Association
148 Main St.
Montpelier, VT 05602
Phone: (802)223-3461
Fax: (802)223-0364

Virginia

★ 6574 ★ Virginia Hospital Association
PO Box 31394
Richmond, VA 23294
Phone: (804)747-8600
Fax: (804)965-0475

Washington

**★ 6575 ★ Washington State Hospital
Association**
300 Elliott Ave. W., Ste. 300
Seattle, WA 98119-4118
Phone: (206)281-7211
Fax: (206)283-6122

West Virginia

**★ 6576 ★ West Virginia Hospital
Association**
600 D St., 2nd Level
South Charleston, WV 25303-3112
Phone: (304)744-9842
Fax: (304)744-9889

Wisconsin

★ 6577 ★ Wisconsin Hospital Association
5721 Odana Rd.
Madison, WI 53719-1289
Phone: (608)274-1820
Fax: (608)274-8554

Wyoming

★ 6578 ★ Wyoming Hospital Association
2005 Warren Ave.
PO Box 5539
Cheyenne, WY 82003
Phone: (307)632-9344
Fax: (307)632-9347

Chapter 33
Hypnosis

Foundations & Other Funding Organizations

Other Funding Organizations

★6579★ **Institute for Research in Hypnosis and Psychotherapy**
1991 Broadway, Apt. 18-B
New York, NY 10023
Phone: (212)874-5290
Fax: (914)238-1422
Dr. Milton V. Kline, Dir.

Description: Sponsors research in clinical and experimental hypnosis; offers research fellowships in clinical hypnotherapy.

National & International Organizations

★6580★ **Academy of Scientific Hypnotherapy (ASH)**
PO Box 12041
San Diego, CA 92112
Phone: (619)427-6225
Fax: (619)427-5650
William E. Kemery, Ph.D., Pres.

Founded: 1977. **Members:** 250. **Description:** Professionals in the healing arts who have been properly trained in hypnosis, and who are known to the academy to be ethical and of good professional reputation. The academy plans to fill the need for training programs, continuing education, and certification throughout the U.S. Maintains placement and referral service; compiles statistics. **Publications:** Bulletin, periodic. • *Hypnotherapy in Review*, periodic. Newsletter. Reports on medical and psychological research in hypnotherapy. Includes book reviews. *Price:* Included in membership dues. • Monograph, periodic. *Price:* Included in membership dues.

★6581★ **American Academy of Medical Hypnoanalysts (AAMH)**
25 W 550 Royce Rd.
Naperville, IL 60565
Phone: 800-344-9766
Free: 800-344-9766
Patricia J. Honiotes, Pres.

Founded: 1974. **Members:** 125. **Description:** Medical doctors, doctors of osteopathy, psychologists, social workers, and professional counselors. Provides training in and promotes the use of medical hypnoanalysis. (Medical hypnoanalysis employs an analytic approach to resolving emotional disorders that is applied while the subject is hypnotized.) Conducts 3-month residency training programs. **Publications:** *Medical Hypnoanalysis Journal*, quarterly. Journal. • Membership Directory, annual.

★6582★ **American Association of Professional Hypnotherapists (AAPH)**
PO Box 29
Boones Mill, VA 24065
Phone: (703)334-3035
William S. Brink, Exec.Dir.

Founded: 1980. **Members:** 1,550. **Description:** Hypnotherapists, marriage and family therapists, psychologists, clinical social workers, physicians, pastoral counselors, and others trained and experienced in hypnosis therapy. Promotes public awareness of hypnosis as applied to personal motivation and improvement, habit control, mental health services, and assisting the healing process. Acts as forum for the exchange of ideas and techniques; encourages a high level of professional ethics; promotes positive image of hypnotherapy. **Publications:** *Hypnotherapy Today*, quarterly. Newsletter. Covers techniques, new theories and innovations, case descriptions, and new uses of hypnotherapy. *Price:* Included in membership dues. • *National Register of Professional Hypnotherapists*, annual. Arranged by state and country. *Price:* Included in membership dues.

★6583★ **American Board of Psychological Hypnosis (ABPH)**
c/o Samuel M. Migdole
North Shore Counseling Center
23 Broadway
Beverly, MA 01915
Phone: (508)922-2280
Fax: (508)927-1758
Samuel M. Migdole, Ed.D., Sec.

Founded: 1959. **Description:** Awards specialty diplomas to qualified psychologists in experimental and clinical hypnosis. Purpose is to raise the standards of individuals conducting research in hypnosis and those using it in clinical practice by requiring specialized training and experience in the field as evidenced by advanced educational credentials in psychology, published research, written and oral examinations, and recommendations of colleagues. **Formerly:** American Board of Examiners in Psychological Hypnosis; American Board of Professional Psychology in Hypnosis.

★6584★ **American Council of Hypnotist Examiners (ACHE)**
1147 E. Broadway, Ste. 340
Glendale, CA 91205
Phone: (818)242-1159
Fax: (818)247-9379
Gil Boyne, Exec.Dir.

Founded: 1980. **Members:** 8,200. **National Groups:** 4. **Regional Groups:** 8. **State Groups:** 1. **Local Groups:** 1. **Description:** Educates, examines, and awards certification in the field of hypnotherapy. Maintains speakers' bureau. Sponsors educational programs. **Publications:** *American Hypnotherapy Report*, annual. Report. Contains news and information on the hypnotherapy profession. *Price:* Included in membership dues. • *Directory of Certified Members*, periodic. Membership Directory. • *International Hypnotherapy Report*, quarterly. Magazine. *Price:* Free to members. • Newsletter, periodic. *Price:* Free to members. **Also Known As:** Hypnotists Examining Council.

★ 6585 ★ American Guild of Hypnotherapists (AGH)
2200 Veterans Blvd., No. 108
Kenner, LA 70062-4005
Phone: (504)468-3223
Fax: (504)468-3213
Reg Sheldrick, Ph.D., Pres.

Founded: 1975. **Members:** 1,106. **Description:** Hypnotherapists and professional hypnotists; mental health, medical, dental, and chiropractic professionals who use hypnosis in their practices. Offers home study course in hypnosis/hypnotherapy. Is approved by many state licensing boards as a provider of continuing education credit. **Publications:** *Journal of Hypnotherapy*, quarterly. Journal. • Newsletter, periodic.

★ 6586 ★ American Hypnosis Association (AHA)
18607 Ventura Blvd., Ste. 310
Tarzana, CA 91356
Phone: (818)344-4464
Free: 800-9900-AHA
George Kappas, Pres.

Founded: 1972. **Members:** 500. **State Groups:** 2. **Description:** Professionals and paraprofessionals in hypnotherapy. Acts as a resource center for members. **Publications:** Newsletter, quarterly.

★ 6587 ★ American Society of Clinical Hypnosis (ASCH)
2200 E. Devon Ave., Ste. 291
Des Plaines, IL 60018-4534
Phone: (708)297-3317
Fax: (708)297-7309
William F. Hoffman, Jr., Exec.VP

Founded: 1957. **Members:** 4,000. **State Groups:** 15. **Local Groups:** 25. **Description:** Physicians, dentists, psychologists with doctoral degrees or masters degrees in social work, and nurses with master's degrees. Brings together professional people in medical, dental, and psychological fields using hypnosis; sets up standards of training; conducts teaching sessions and workshops at basic and advanced levels. Offers instruction on clinical hypnosis and various simple forms of psychotherapy and psychodynamics. Cooperates with all scientific disciplines with regard to use of hypnosis. Maintains speakers' bureau. **Publications:** *American Journal of Clinical Hypnosis*, quarterly. • *American Society of Clinical Hypnosis--Newsletter*, 5/year. Promotes the acceptance of hypnosis as a tool in clinical medicine and scientific research. Includes member news and calendar of events. *Price:* Included in membership dues. • Directory, annual.

★ 6588 ★ American Society of Clinical Hypnosis (ASCH-ERF)
Education and Research Foundation
2200 E. Devon Ave., Ste. 291
Des Plaines, IL 60018-4534
Phone: (708)297-3317
Fax: (708)297-7309
William F. Hoffman, Jr., Exec.Sec.

Founded: 1959. **Members:** 1,500. **Description:** Teaching and research arm of the American Society of Clinical Hypnosis. Physicians,

dentists, and psychologists. Underwrites workshops in the U.S. and Canada to train professionals in hypnosis and broaden their knowledge of psychotherapy. Basic section is designed to familiarize physicians, psychologists, and dentists with hypnosis and its applications to problems of the psychologically normal patient including preparation for childbirth, comfort in the dental chair, and other problems and complaints complicated by emotional conflicts, such as smoking and obesity. Advanced section deals with psychotherapeutic techniques that can be used in addition to hypnotherapy in treating patients. **Formerly:** (1962) Seminars on Hypnosis Foundation.

★ 6589 ★ Association to Advance Ethical Hypnosis (AAEH)
2675 Oakwood Dr.
Cuyahoga Falls, OH 44221
Phone: (216)923-8880
Fax: (216)923-8880
Nell R. Orndorf, Exec.Dir.

Founded: 1955. **Members:** 1,500. **National Groups:** 1. **State Groups:** 13. **Description:** Practitioners of all the healing arts; educators, police officers, attorneys, and lay technicians. To establish a code of ethics in the practice of hypnosis; to expose and discourage malpractice and the use and granting of nonacademic titles and degrees; to oppose the restriction of hypnosis to members of special professional groups. Conducts three-phase examination (written, oral, and practical) and certifies members as hypno-technicians. Maintains speakers' bureau; conducts research programs. **Publications:** *Suggestion*, quarterly. Bulletin. Contains membership profiles, chapter news, and list of AAEH-approved schools. *Price:* Included in membership dues.

★ 6590 ★ Association for Applied Hypnosis (AAH)
21B High Holme Rd.
Louth, Lincs. LN11 0EX, England
Phone: 1507 607336
P.D.R. Quinn, Dir.

Founded: 1980. **Members:** 650. **Languages:** English. **Description:** Hypnotherapists and trainees in England. Promotes excellence and education in the field of hypnotherapy. Provides instruction in psychotherapeutic techniques used in conjunction with hypnosis to resolve psychological problems. Serves as a forum for the exchange of ideas and the assessment of techniques, specific cases, research, and developments in hypnotherapy. Oversees the practices of members to ensure a high standard of public service; administrates professional negligence insurance for members and patients. Offers training course. Maintains registry of practitioners.

★ 6591 ★ Institute for Research in Hypnosis and Psychotherapy (IRHP)
1991 Broadway, Apt. 18B
New York, NY 10023
Phone: (212)874-5290
Fax: (914)238-1422
Dr. Milton V. Kline, Dir.

Founded: 1954. **Description:** Psychologists, psychiatrists, physicians, and social workers

trained in clinical hypnosis, hypnotherapy, and hypnoanalysis. Sponsors research in clinical and experimental hypnosis; offers postgraduate training in hypnosis and its applications; develops standards and procedures for advanced education in clinical and experimental hypnosis. Operates Morton Prince Centers, low-cost treatment centers for outpatients who cannot afford hypnotherapy or hypnoanalysis in private practice. Conducts consulting and educational training services. Compiles statistics; maintains databases and speakers' bureau. **Publications:** *Journal of Clinical Hypnotherapy and Hypnoanalysis*, quarterly. Journal. *Price:* $45. **Formerly:** (1982) Institute for Research in Hypnosis.

★ 6592 ★ International Center of Medical and Psychological Hypnosis (ICMPH) (Centro Internazionale di Ipnosi Medica e Psicologica)
Istituto di Indagini Psicologiche
Corso XXII Marzo 57
I-20129 Milan, Italy
Phone: 2 7388427
Fax: 2 7491051
Prof. Rolando Marchesan, Pres.

Founded: 1969. **Members:** 307. **Regional Groups:** 15. **Description:** Physicians, psychologists, and teachers of psychology and psychiatry at universities. Seeks to advance the knowledge of hypnosis and its applications. Organizes courses in psychosomatic medicine and medical and psychological hypnosis for physicians and psychologists. Conducts research on hypnosis, hypnoanesthesia, hypnotherapy, hypnotic eugenics, childbirth, and hypnotic contraception. Holds seminars and workshops. **Publications:** *Literature*, semiannual. Also publishes *Dictionary of Hypnopsychology and Handwriting Psychology*.

★ 6593 ★ International Society for Medical and Psychological Hypnosis, U.S.A . Office (ISMPH)
1991 Broadway, Apt. 18B
New York, NY 10023
Phone: (212)874-5290
Fax: (914)238-1422
Dr. Milton V. Kline, Dir.

Founded: 1982. **Members:** 4,000. **Description:** Health care professionals involved with medical and psychological hypnosis. Supports clinical research in hyponosis and research in psychotherapy strategies and tactics; offers advanced training and certification for hypnotherapists. Maintains speakers' bureau; compiles statistics. **Publications:** *Conference Proceedings*, annual. Proceedings. • *Journal of Clinical Hypnotherapy and Hypnoanalysis*, quarterly. Journal. Contains original research, membership news, book reviews, and conference reports. • Newsletter.

★ 6594 ★ International Society for Professional Hypnosis (ISPH)
PO Box 452
North Haven, CT 06473
Phone: (203)239-7046
Robert McGrath, M.A., Exec.Dir.

Founded: 1970. **Members:** 645. **Description:** Professional hypnotists and others involved or interested in the utilization of hypnosis. Provides referral service. Maintains speakers' bureau; compiles statistics. Sponsors educational programs. **Publications:** *Conference Tapes*, annual. • *International Journal of Professional Hypnosis*, semiannual. Journal. • *ISPH Newsletter*, quarterly. Newsletter.

★ 6595 ★   **Milton H. Erickson Foundation (MHEF)**
3606 N. 24th St.
Phoenix, AZ 85016
Phone: (602)956-6196
Fax: (602)956-0519
Jeffrey K. Zeig, Ph.D., Dir.

Founded: 1979. **Regional Groups:** 50. **Description:** Seeks to promote and advance the contributions made to health sciences by Milton H. Erickson, M.D. (1901-80), regarded as an authority on hypnotherapy and brief strategic therapy. (Erickson was a teacher of psychotherapy who relied primarily on "unconscious learning.") Dedicated to the training of health and mental health professionals. **Publications:** *A Teaching Seminar with Milton H. Erickson, M.D.*. Book. Transcript with commentary of a one-week teaching seminar. • *Ericksonian Methods: The Essence of the Story*. Book. • *Ericksonian Monographs*, up to 3/year. Monographs. Contains selected articles on Ericksonian hypnosis and psychotherapy, including technique, theory, and research topics. • *Newsletter*, 3/year. Contains articles and notices relating to Ericksonian approaches to psychotherapy and hypnosis. *Price:* Optional donation, available to professionals. • *The Process of Hypnotic Induction: A Training Videotape Featuring Inductions Conducted by Milton H. Erickson in 1964*. Video. Discusses the process and describes the microdynamics of Erickson's techniques. • *Symbolic Hypnotherapy*. Video. Presents information regarding the use of symbols in psychotherapy and hypnosis. • *What Is Psychotherapy?: Contemporary Perspectives*. Book. Contains edited commentaries of eminent clinicians.

★ 6596 ★   **National Association of Clergy Hypnotherapists (NACH)**
c/o Dr. William N. Curtis
501 Maynard Ave.
Florence, SC 29505
Phone: (803)662-9248
Dr. William N. Curtis, Founder & Dir.

Founded: 1984. **Members:** 150. **Description:** Ministers, priests, and rabbis who use hypnosis in their work. Promotes and encourages a positive attitude within the religious community and among the public on hypnosis and its application in the ministry. Focuses on removing misconceptions and combatting ignorance regarding hypnosis. Believes hypnosis can be used as a helpful modality in a holistic approach within the ministry. **Publications:** Newsletter, quarterly.

★ 6597 ★   **National Society of Hypnotherapists (NSH)**
c/o Dr. Kathie K. Wolfe
2175 NW 86th St., Ste. 6A
Des Moines, IA 50325
Phone: (515)270-2280
Dr. Kathie K. Wolfe, Exec.Dir.

Founded: 1983. **Members:** 600. **Description:** Doctors, lawyers, nurses, psychologists, and others interested in hypnosis. Promotes recognition of self-hypnosis as a mental aspect of healing. Acts as referral service for professional hypnotists and individuals seeking these services; maintains speakers' bureau. **Publications:** Newsletter, quarterly.

★ 6598 ★   **Society for Clinical and Experimental Hypnosis (SCEH)**
6728 Old McLean Village Dr.
McLean, VA 22101
Phone: (703)556-9222
Fax: (703)556-8729
George K. Degnon, Exec.Dir.

Founded: 1949. **Members:** 950. **Description:** United States constituent society of the International Society of Hypnosis. Professional society of physicians, dentists, doctoral level psychologists, and certain psychiatric social workers interested in research in hypnosis and its boundary areas as well as the therapeutic use of hypnosis in clinical practice. Encourages cooperation among professional and scientific disciplines in use of hypnosis; promotes educational standards; conducts introductory and advanced workshops and continuing education seminars in therapeutic hypnosis. Offers continuing education seminars in New York City and San Francisco, CA. **Publications:** *International Journal of Clinical and Experimental Hypnosis*, quarterly. Journal. Contains book reviews, statistics, and research and clinical reports. *Price:* Included in membership dues; $49/year for nonmembers. • *Membership Directory*, biennial. • *SCEH Newsletter*, quarterly. Newsletter. Contains research and clinical notes, society news, book reviews, and obituaries. *Price:* $8/year.

Research Centers

★ 6599 ★   **Institute for Research in Hypnosis and Psychotherapy**
Office of Director
1991 Broadway, 18B
New York, NY 10023
Phone: (212)874-5290
Fax: (914)238-1422
Milton V. Kline, Dir.

Research Activities and Fields: Hypnotic process, clinical hypnosis, and hypnotherapy in mental health, medicine, and psychology. Also involved in Employee Assistance Program research. Maintains preferred provider organizations for hypnotherapy. **Publications:** *Journal of Clinical Hypnotherapy and Hypnoanalysis*.

★ 6600 ★   **Life Sciences and Hypnotherapy Center**
Box 347
West Hempstead, NY 11552
Phone: (516)485-6726
Paul Zalasin, Dir.

Research Activities and Fields: Hypnotherapy for treatment of phobias, pain, and emotional suppression, focusing on recovery rates.

Chapter 34
Infectious Diseases

Federal Government Agencies

★6601★ **Executive Office of the President**
Domestic Policy Council
National Policy Director for AIDS
750 17th St. NW
Washington, DC 20503
Phone: (202)690-1090

★6602★ **U.S. Department of Health and**
Human Services
National Center for Infectious Diseases
1600 Clifton Rd. NE
Atlanta, GA 30333
Phone: (404)639-3401
Fax: (404)639-3039

Description: The Center for Infectious Diseases coordinates a national program to improve the identification, investigation, diagnosis, prevention, and control of infectious diseases. It maintains programs dealing with AIDS, hospital infections, sexually transmitted diseases, bacterial diseases, host factors, mycotic diseases, parasitic diseases, viral diseases, and vector-borne viral diseases.

U.S. Department of Health and Human
Services
National Institute of Allergy and Infectious
Diseases
See: Entry 2053

Foundations & Other Funding Organizations

Private Foundations

Aaron Diamond Foundation
See: Entry 24

★6603★ **Columbia Foundation**
One Lombard St., Ste. 305
San Francisco, CA 94111
Phone: (415)986-5179
Susan Clark Silk, Executive Director

Foundation Philosophy: The board of directors of the Columbia Foundation establishes program priorities based on changing conditions in society. Currently, the foundation focuses on projects that address important issues and that offer a promise of significant impact in these areas. The foundation has placed its priorities in several areas including the following: stopping the worldwide arms race; promoting international and cross-cultural understanding; protecting human rights; reversing the degradation of the environment; and enhancing urban life and culture. **Giving Priorities:** In fiscal 1994, the foundation gave approximately 44% of contributions to the arts and humanities. Environmental programs received about 17% of funding. Civic concerns received about 15% of funds. Religious institutions received about 11% of funding. International affairs and health concerns each received about 5% of total contributions. The remainder of funding went to educational institutions and social services. **Typical Health-Related Recipients:** AIDS/HIV, Domestic Violence, Health Funds, Hospices, Medical Research, Preventive Medicine/Wellness Organizations. **Geographic Distribution:** Primarily the San Francisco Bay Area.

Edna McConnell Clark Foundation
See: Entry 154

Eugene and Agnes E. Meyer Foundation
See: Entry 171

Florence V. Burden Foundation
See: Entry 184

Frances L. & Edwin L. Cummings Memorial
Fund
See: Entry 195

Ittleson Foundation
See: Entry 7229

J. M. Kaplan Fund
See: Entry 298

Joseph Alexander Foundation
See: Entry 329

★6604★ **Rockefeller Brothers Fund**
1290 Avenue of the Americas, Rm. 3450
New York, NY 10104
Phone: (212)373-4200
Fax: (212)315-0996
Benjamin R. Shute, Jr., Secretary and
Treasurer

Foundation Philosophy: The fund makes grants in five general areas: establishing global interdependence; promoting the health and vitality of the nonprofit sector, both nationally and internationally; strengthening the numbers and quality of teachers in public education in the United States and, in particular, to encourage minorities to enter the teaching profession; improving the quality of life in New York City; and improving the quality and accessibility of basic education for children and adults in South Africa. **Giving Priorities:** In 1993, the fund contributed about 40% of its total support to environmental organizations. Organizations concerned with international affairs received 25% of gifts and organizations concerned with the nonprofit sector received 23%. About 12% went to organizations supporting New York City, people with AIDS, and the fund's special concerns. **Typical Health-Related Recipients:** AIDS/HIV. **Geographic Distribution:** International, national, and New York City.

Corporate Foundations

★6605★ **Gap Foundation**
One Harrison St.
San Francisco, CA 94105
Phone: (415)291-2757
Fax: (415)495-2922
Molly White, Foundation Director

Giving Priorities: *Social Services:* 35% to 40% of total contributions. *Health:* 30% to 35%. Majority of contributions support AIDS services, including AIDS research, outpatient health care, and health associations. In fiscal 1990, a single $15,000 grant went to an AIDS task force. Also funds cancer research. *Education:* 25% to 30%. *Civic & Public Affairs:* About 20%. *Environment:* 15% to 20% of total contributions. *Arts & Hu-*

manities: 10% to 15%. *Voluntarism:* The Gap instituted a company-sponsored volunteer program called Gap Community Action Program (CAP) in its headquarters area. *Note:* Above percentages are for 1992. Percentages total more than 100% because the company reports charitable gifts cross into multiple giving categories, such as AIDS which falls into Health and Social Services. **Typical Health-Related Recipients:** Medical Research, Single-Disease Health Associations. **Geographic Distribution:** Headquarter counties of San Francisco and San Mateo, CA; with limited giving in New York, NY, Erlanger, KY, Baltimore, MD, and Ventura, CA.

General American Charitable Foundation
See: Entry 699

Gerber Cos. Foundation
See: Entry 3146

Levi Strauss Foundation
See: Entry 758

★ 6606 ★ Lotus Development Foundation
55 Cambridge Pkwy.
Cambridge, MA 02142
Phone: (617)693-1667
Fax: (617)693-1213
Michael Durney, Dir., Philanthropy &
   Community Affairs

Giving Priorities: *Education/Training/ Computer Literacy:* Between 30% and 35% of total annual giving. *Organizing & Advocacy:* Between 30% and 35%. *Social Services:* About 15%. Grants benefit pre- and postnatal care for at-risk mothers, teen leadership programs, and services for immigrants and refugees. *Multicultural & Antidiscrimination:* 10% to 15% of annual total. *Arts:* 5% to 10%. *Health:* About 5%. Sponsor of major funding-raising activity of AIDS Action Committee for Massachusetts. *International:* In 1993, company donated $600,000 to nonprofit organizations through foreign subsidiaries. **Typical Health-Related Recipients:** Health Organizations. **Geographic Distribution:** Only in Boston, Cambridge, or surrounding areas.

Miles Inc. Foundation
See: Entry 779

Principal Financial Group Foundation
See: Entry 823

Other Funding Organizations

**★ 6607 ★ American Foundation for AIDS
   Research**
733 3rd Ave., 12th Fl.
New York, NY 10017
Phone: (212)682-7440
Free: 800-39-AMEAR
Fax: (212)682-9812
Mervyn F. Silverman, M.D., Pres.

Description: Distributes grants and scholars awards to support research on the causes, early diagnosis, and treatment of Acquired Immune Deficiency Syndrome (AIDS), including pediatric AIDS.

★ 6608 ★ American Leprosy Missions
1 ALM Way
Greenville, SC 29601
Phone: (803)271-7040
Free: 800-543-3131
Fax: (803)271-7062
Thomas Ferran Frist, Pres.

Description: Sponsors research in the U.S., Brazil, India, and Ethiopia. Provides medical, rehabilitative, and social care for people with leprosy in approximately 30 countries.

**★ 6609 ★ American Society for
   Microbiology**
1325 Massachusetts Ave. NW
Washington, DC 20005
Phone: (202)737-3600
Michael I. Goldberg, Ph.D., Exec. Dir.

Description: Society awards undergraduate, graduate, and post-doctoral fellowships.

**★ 6610 ★ Design Industries Foundation for
   AIDS**
150 W. 26th Ave., Ste. 602
New York, NY 10001
Phone: (212)727-3100
Fax: (212)727-2574
John F. Hartman, Pres.

Description: Serves as a fundraising foundation. Supports: direct patient care and services; preventative, post-diagnostic and community education; housing, meals, emergency assistance and legal advocacy; treatment and community-based research.

**★ 6611 ★ Independent Citizens Research
   Foundation for the Study of
   Degenerative Diseases**
PO Box 97
Ardsley, NY 10502
Phone: (914)478-1862
Dorthea P. Seeber, Exec. Dir.

Description: Supports research on calibrated transcutaneous electric nerve stimulation and preventive medicine techniques.

**★ 6612 ★ National Foundation for
   Infectious Diseases**
4733 Bethesda Ave., Ste. 750
Bethesda, MD 20814
Phone: (301)656-0003
Fax: (301)907-0878
Richard J. Duma, M.D., Ph.D., Exec. Dir.

Description: Awards Young Investigator Matching Grant awards to support research on causes and cures of infectious diseases. Provides postdoctoral fellowships to assist physicians in becoming specialists in the field, and offers financial assistance for symposia and workshops related to infectious disease problems.

National & International
Organizations

★ 6613 ★ ACT UP
135 W. 29th St., 10th Fl.
New York, NY 10001
Phone: (212)564-2437
Fax: (212)594-5441
Walt Wilder, Workspace Mgr.

Founded: 1987. **Description:** Individuals "united in anger and committed to direct action to end the AIDS crisis." Seeks to increase public awareness and government involvement in the fight against AIDS. Conducts rallies and demonstrations aimed at public figures or institutions that the group feels should be doing more to combat AIDS. Lobbies for quicker availabiltiy of experimental AIDS drugs. **Publications:** *Act Up Americans.* Catalog. • *ACT UP Reports,* quarterly. Newsletter. • *AIDS, Act Up and Activism.* Handbook. • *Merchandise Catalog. Price:* Free upon request. • *Women and AIDS Handbook.* Handbook. **Also Known As:** AIDS Coalition to Unleash Power.

★ 6614 ★ African AIDS Project
898 N. Fair Oaks Ave., Ste. A
Pasadena, CA 91103
Phone: (818)795-7990
Fax: (818)795-7897

Languages: English. **Description:** Anglican congregations united to eradicate AIDS and ease the suffering of people with the disease in Africa. Promotes and supports AIDS research; makes available volunteer support and medical equipment and supplies to AIDS treatment and prevention programs; supports children orphaned by AIDS. Conducts field trips. **Publications:** *The Drum,* quarterly. Newsletter. Provides updates on association activities and the AIDS policies and programs of the Anglican church worldwide.

★ 6615 ★ AIDS Action Council (AAC)
1875 Connecticut Ave. NW, Ste. 700
Washington, DC 20009
Phone: (202)986-1300
Fax: (202)986-1345
Daniel T. Bross, Exec.Dir.

Founded: 1982. **Members:** 1,000. **Description:** Serves as a representative in Washington, DC, of more than 1000 community-based AIDS service organizations. Advocates, at the federal level, for more effective AIDS policy, legislation, and funding. Works collaboratively with AIDS Action Foundation, a national public policy research organization. **Publications:** *AIDS Action Alert,* periodic. Distributed to support campaigns for quick responses to federal initiatives. • *AIDS Action Briefing,* quarterly. Issue papers prepared by the AIDS Action Government Affairs Department reviewing major AIDS-related policy issues under consideration by Congress. • *AIDS Action Update,* every 6 weeks. Newsletter. *Price:* Available to members only. • *AIDS Care Is Health Care: An AIDS Action Guide to Health Care Reform.* Report. • *AIDS FactBook.* • *The Americans With Disabilities Act: What It Means for People Living With AIDS.* Brochure. Question and answer format. • *Blueprint for Reform-*

ing Federal AIDS Prevention Programs. • *Good Intentions: A Report on Federal HIV Prevention.* Report. Outlines the advances and shortcoming of efforts by the Centers for Disease Control and other federal agencies to prevent further HIV transmission. • *Public Policy Manual for Community-Based AIDS Service Providers.* Written to assist organizations serving people with HIV/AIDS in making their participation in the public policy arena more effective. • *Should HIV Testing Results Be Reportable?.* Monograph. Discusses the practice of reporting names of HIV-positive persons to public health services and notifying sex and needle-sharing partners.

★6616★ **AIDS Committee of Ottawa**
207 Queens St., 4th FL.
Ottawa, ON, Canada K1P 6E5
Phone: (613)238-5014
Fax: (613)238-3425

Languages: English.

★6617★ **AIDS Counseling Trust (ACT)**
PO Box 7225
Harare, Zimbabwe
Phone: 4 792340
Fax: 4 792340
Mrs. Elizabeth Matenga, Exec. Dir.

Members: 300. **Description:** Seeks to improve the quality of life for persons with AIDS. Conducts preventive education and outreach programs. **Publications:** Booklet. • Video. On HIV/AIDS.

★6618★ **AIDS Education and Research Trust (AVERT)**
11 Denne Parade
Horsham, W. Sussex RH12 1JD, England
Phone: 1403 210202
Fax: 1403 211001
Annabel Kanabus, Dir.

Founded: 1986. **Languages:** English. **Description:** Sponsors AIDS control programs in England. Seeks to improve the quality of life for persons with AIDS. Conducts research and educational programs. **Publications:** *AIDS: Working with Young People.* Book. • *Not Under My Roof: Families Talking about Sex & AIDS.* Book. • Pamphlets. • *Prisons, HIV and AIDS: Risks and Experiences in Custodial Care.* Book.

★6619★ **AIDS Helpline**
24 Mount Charles
Belfast, Antrim BT7 1NZ, Northern Ireland
Phone: 1232 249268
Fax: 1232 329845
Liz Law, Dir.

Description: Makes available women counselors to offer advice to women concerned about AIDS. Offers home support. Conducts preventative education and a outreach programs. Promotes fundraising.

★6620★ **AIDS Information Ministries**
6032 Jacksboro Hwy., Ste. 100
Lake Worth, TX 76135
Phone: (817)237-3146
Fax: (817)238-2048
Duane Crumb, Pres.

Founded: 1987. **Description:** Sponsors HIV/AIDS education programs in schools and

churches. Maintains speakers' bureau. **Publications:** *Developing Your Church AIDS Policy.* Book. • *Don't Let AIDS Catch You.* Brochure. HIV/AIDS education for teens. • *Guide to Positive HIV/AIDS Education.* Book. • *Staying Current*, bimonthly. *Price:* Free.

★6621★ **AIDS Information Support Centre**
PO Box 2493
Manzini, Swaziland
Phone: 52017

Description: Aims to insure reliable health in rural Swaziland. Educates health professionals to serve rural areas. **Also Known As:** Project Hope.

AIDS Prevention League (APPLE)
See: Entry 2151

★6622★ **AIDS Resource Foundation for Children (ARFC)**
St. Clare's Home for Children
182 Roseville Ave.
Newark, NJ 07107
Phone: (201)483-4250
Fax: (201)483-1998
Terrence P. Zealand, Exec.Dir.

Founded: 1985. **Description:** Operates homes for children with HIV, AIDS, or AIDS-Related Complex (ARC) who are well enough to be released from the hospital but are in need of foster care placement or respite care; provides support services to families coping with AIDS or related diseases. Operates foster parent recruitment, training, and support programs; collects and distributes toys and clothing. Sponsors summer camp for families. Conducts HIV training workshops, community outreach programs, and agency networking; maintains speakers' bureau. Provides referrals, bereavement counseling, and emergency assistance. Acts as a model program for transitional foster homes nationwide; although all homes are currently operating in the New Jersey area, any child with AIDS or a related disease is eligible for assistance. **Publications:** Newsletter, periodic. **Also Known As:** St. Clare's Home for Children.

★6623★ **AIDS Task Force for the American College Health Association**
c/o Dr. Richard P. Keeling
University Health Services
University of Wisconsin-Madison
1552 University Ave.
Madison, WI 53705
Dr. Richard P. Keeling, Chm.

Description: Alerts college students to the dangers of AIDS.

★6624★ **AIDS Unit**
Swiss Federation Office of Public Health
Division of Health Promotion
Hess-Str. 27e
CH-3097 Liebefeld, Switzerland
Phone: 31 9708811
Fax: 31 9708789

Languages: English, French, German, Italian.
Formerly: Bureau Central pour le SIDA.

★6625★ **Alliance for the Arts**
c/o Estate Project for Artists with AIDS
330 W. 40th St., Ste. 1701
New York, NY 10036
Phone: (212)947-6340
Fax: (212)947-6416
Randall Pourscheidt, Dir.

Founded: 1991. **Members:** 40,000. **Description:** Assists artists who are HIV-positive to plan for the preservation of their art. Maintains speakers' bureau; conducts educational programs. **Publications:** *Future Safe - Planning Handbook.* Book. • *The Report of the Estate Project.* Book.

★6626★ **American Academy of Microbiology (AAM)**
1325 Massachusetts Ave. NW
Washington, DC 20005
Phone: (202)737-3600
Fax: (202)942-9329
Carol A. Colgan, Contact

Founded: 1955. **Members:** 1000. **Description:** Professional arm of American Society for Microbiologists interested in microscopic and submicroscopic organisms. Encourages exchange of information among members. Conducts recognition program for microbiologists at the doctoral, masters, and baccalaureate levels. Organizes programs on professional aspects of microbiology. Bestows ASM awards and fellowships. Sponsors American Board of Medical Laboratory Immunology, American Board of Medical Microbiology, Certification Board of the National Registry of Microbiologists, and Committee on Postdoctoral Education Programs. **Publications:** *Directory of Fellows of the American Academy of Microbiology*, triennial. • Also publishes brochures.

★6627★ **American Academy of Tropical Medicine (AATM)**
16126 E. Warren
PO Box 24224
Detroit, MI 48224
Phone: (313)882-0641
Fax: (313)882-0641
Ben Allie, M.D., Pres.

Founded: 1984. **Members:** 2,600. **National Groups:** 10. **Regional Groups:** 10. **Description:** Physicians and allied health professionals interested in tropical medicine. Provides postgraduate continuing medical education; confers certificates and diplomas. Maintains speakers' bureau; provides placement service. Conducts research and compiles statistics. Conducts educational programs; offers children's services. **Publications:** *Journal of the American Academy of Tropical Medicine*, semiannual. Journal. Includes book reviews, employment opportunities, and information on new diagnostic equipment. *Price:* $125/year. • Monographs. • Newsletter, periodic. Also publishes case studies and plans to publish directory of physicians and hospitals in tropical countries.

★6628★ **American Board of Tropical Medicine (ABTM)**
PO Box 1794
Toledo, OH 43603
Fax: (313)882-5110
T. James, Assoc.Dir.

Founded: 1980. **Members:** 2,100. **State Groups:** 2. **Description:** Physicians including pediatricians, dermatologists, surgeons, professionals of public health and preventive medicine, and pathologists interested in tropical medicine. United to preserve the quality of care in tropical medicine. Investigates qualifications and determines the competency of candidates applying for membership and provides continuing medical education programs to specialists in tropical medicine. Issues certificate as evidence of meeting continuing medical education requirements. Compiles statistics. **Publications:** Newsletter, annual. Plans to publish *Directory of Specialists in Tropical Medicine.* **Also Known As:** American College of Tropical Medicine.

★ 6629 ★ **American Foundation for AIDS Research (AmFAR)**
733 Third Ave., 12th Fl.
New York, NY 10017
Phone: (212)682-7440
Free: 800-39-AMEAR
Fax: (212)682-9812
Mervyn F. Silverman, M.D., Pres.

Founded: 1985. **Description:** Raises funds to support research on AIDS. Research is currently focused on discovering the causes of the syndrome, developing early diagnosis, and determining successful treatment. Is currently organizing state and local fundraising and developing educational programs as a preventative to the spread of the disease. Maintains speakers' bureau; sponsors charitable program. **Publications:** *AIDS/HIV Treatment Directory,* quarterly. Directory. • *AmFar Report.* Reprint. • *Facts About AIDS.* Brochure.

★ 6630 ★ **American Foundation for the Prevention of Venereal Disease (AFPVD)**
799 Broadway, Ste. 638
New York, NY 10003
Phone: (212)759-2069
Mary O'Connell, Sec.

Founded: 1967. **Description:** Provides educational material to the public on the prevention of sexually transmitted diseases. Encourages every individual to assume responsibility for his or her own health; stresses the importance of responsible sexual relations and proper personal hygiene. Seeks to eliminate the feelings of guilt and shame that are associated with sexually transmitted diseases. **Publications:** *Sexually Transmitted Disease Prevention for Everyone,* annual. *Price:* $40/each hundred copies. **Formerly:** (1976) New York Alliance for the Eradication of Venereal Disease.

★ 6631 ★ **American Leprosy Missions (ALMI)**
1 ALM Way
Greenville, SC 29601
Phone: (803)271-7040
Free: 800-543-3131
Fax: (803)271-7062

Founded: 1906. **Description:** Provides medical, rehabilitative, and social care for people with leprosy, also known as Hansen's disease, in approximately 30 countries. Conducts specialized training for medical workers; supports medical and social rehabilitation; provides special literature on leprosy to medical personnel

abroad. Sponsors research in the U.S., Brazil, India, and Ethiopia. Provides personnel and resources to conduct training programs at National Hansen's Disease Center, Carville, LA, and to assist the national leprosy control programs of Brazil, Burma, Ethiopia, Mexico, the Philippines, and the People's Republic of China. Provides management assistance for the *International Journal of Leprosy.* Maintains hall of fame, museum of leprosy, and speakers' bureau. **Publications:** *Word and Deed,* quarterly. Newsletter. Includes ALM news. *Price:* Free.

★ 6632 ★ **American Social Health Association (ASHA)**
PO Box 13827
Research Triangle Park, NC 27709
Phone: (919)361-8400
Fax: (919)361-8425
Peggy Clarke, Exec.Dir.

Founded: 1914. **Description:** A national voluntary health agency dedicated to the prevention, control, and eventual elimination of the consequences of sexually transmitted diseases as a social health problem. Works to expand biomedical research, provide information and education programs, upgrade clinical care, and improve public policy. Provides leadership in public policy issues. Supplies public health agencies with patient education materials. Engages directly in biomedical research through its ASHA Research Fund. Operates Herpes Resource Center, a national program for those infected with the genital herpes virus, and HPV Support Program, a national program for those infected with the human papilloma virus. **Publications:** Brochures. • *Helper,* quarterly. Newsletter. Reports on the latest research on the herpes simplex virus; includes information on strategies for coping with the virus and on treatments. *Price:* Included in membership dues. • *HPV News,* quarterly. Includes latest research on HPV/genital warts and information on coping strategies. *Price:* Included in membership dues. • Manuals. • Pamphlets. Also publishes teachers' guides. **Formerly:** (1959) American Social Hygiene Association.

★ 6633 ★ **American Social Health Association (HRC)**
Herpes Resource Center
PO Box 13827
Research Triangle Park, NC 27709
Phone: (919)361-8488
Fax: (919)361-8425
Melissa Peacock, Prog.Coord.

Founded: 1979. **Local Groups:** 98. **Description:** Individuals with recurrent genital herpes infections; individuals interested in the dissemination of information about genital herpes. (Herpes is a sexually transmitted disease which is as yet incurable.) Works to give emotional support to individuals, and to provide current information about herpes. Maintains the National Herpes Hotline. Offers referrals to local support groups (HELP) throughout the U.S. and Canada for people living with herpes; HELP groups provide a safe, confidential environment in which to obtain accurate information about HSV and share experiences with other people concerned about herpes. Compiles statistics. **Publications:** *Herpes: Questions & Answers.* Pamphlet. • *Manag-*

ing Herpes: HOw to Live with a Chronic STD. Book. *Price:* $19.75. • *Telling Your Partner About Herpes.* Pamphlet. • *the helper,* quarterly. Journal. *Price:* $25. • *Understanding Herpes.* Booklet. • *When Your Partner Has Herpes.* Pamphlet.

★ 6634 ★ **American Social Health Association**
HPV Support Program
PO Box 13827
Research Triangle Park, NC 27709
Phone: (919)361-8485
Free: 800-227-8922
Fax: (919)361-8425
Melissa Peacock, Program Coord.

Founded: 1991. **Local Groups:** 6. **Description:** Disseminates information and educational materials about human papillomavirus (HPV). Offers assistance to local self-help/support groups and/or people living with HPV. **Publications:** *HPV News,* quarterly. *Price:* $25.

★ 6635 ★ **American Society for Microbiology (ASM)**
1325 Massachusetts Ave. NW
Washington, DC 20005
Phone: (202)737-3600
Michael I. Goldberg, Exec.Dir.

Founded: 1899. **Members:** 42,000. **Local Groups:** 36. **Description:** Scientific society of microbiologists. Promotes the advancement of scientific knowledge in order to improve education in microbiology. Encourages the highest professional and ethical standards, and the adoption of sound legislative and regulatory policies affecting the discipline of microbiology at all levels. Communicates microbiological scientific achievements to the public. Maintains numerous committees and 23 divisions, placement services and biographical archives; compiles statistics. **Publications:** *Abstracts of Annual Meetings.* • *Antimicrobial Agents and Chemotherapy,* monthly. *Price:* $49/year for members; $263/year for nonmembers. • *Applied and Environmental Microbiology,* monthly. *Price:* $50/year for members; $265/year for nonmembers. • *ASM Directory of Members,* every 2-3 years. *Price:* Available to members only. • *ASM News,* monthly. *Price:* Included in membership dues; $25/year for nonmembers. • *Clinical Microbiology Reviews,* quarterly. *Price:* $20/year for members; $121/year for nonmembers. • *Infection and Immunity,* monthly. *Price:* $51/year for members; $368/year for nonmembers. • *International Journal of Systematic Bacteriology,* quarterly. *Price:* $35/year for members; $158/year for nonmembers. • *Journal of Bacteriology,* semimonthly. *Price:* $79/year for members; $378/year for nonmembers. • *Journal of Clinical Microbiology,* monthly. *Price:* $49/year for members; $264/year for nonmembers. • *Journal of Virology,* monthly. *Price:* $81/year for members; $380/year for nonmembers. • *Microbiological Reviews,* quarterly. *Price:* $25/year for members; $120/year for nonmembers. • *Molecular and Cellular Biology,* monthly. *Price:* $80/year for members; $379/year for nonmembers. • Also publishes manuals, reprints, and books. **Formerly:** Society of American Bacteriologists.

★6636★ American Society of Tropical Medicine and Hygiene (ASTMH)
60 Revere Dr., Ste. 500
Northbrook, IL 60062
Phone: (708)480-9592
Fax: (708)480-9282
Joyce Paschall, Exec.Dir.

Founded: 1952. **Members:** 2,600. **Description:** Professional society of physicians and scientists interested in tropical medicine and hygiene, including the areas of arbovirology, entomology, medicine, nursing, and parasitology. **Publications:** *American Journal of Tropical Medicine and Hygiene*, monthly. Journal. • *Tropical Medicine and Hygiene News*, bimonthly.

★6637★ Americans for a Sound AIDS / HIV Policy (ASAP)
PO Box 17433
Washington, DC 20041
Phone: (703)471-7350
Fax: (703)471-8409
W. Shepherd Smith, Jr., Pres.

Founded: 1987. **Regional Groups:** 1. **State Groups:** 1. **Description:** Advisory board of doctors, public health professionals, legislators, educators, and clergy assisting in the formulation of a sound public policy on HIV/AIDS that will be understood and promoted by the public. Encourages the public to react compassionately toward persons affected, infected, or ill with HIV or AIDS. Advocates early diagnosis; promotes reducing transmission of the epidemic through public health intervention strategies such as confidential and voluntary partner notification. Supports development of treatments, diagnostics, vaccines, and an eventual cure for the disease. Promotes health care access for individuals infected with HIV and AIDS. Testifies before national, state, and local government agencies. Operates speakers' bureau. Sponsors charitable programs throught its Children's Assistance Fund. **Publications:** *AIDS/HIV News*, bimonthly. *Price:* $25/year. • Audiotapes. • Brochures. • *The Church's Response to the Challenge of AIDS/HIV*. Compiled in conjunction with MAP International. • *Guide to Federal Funding of HIV Disease*, periodic. • Videos. Also issues literature, conference transcripts, and testimonies. **Formerly:** (1993) Americans for a Sound AIDS Policy.

★6638★ Amis de Moulin a Poudre
Irene Bancilhon Blvd.
Cowin Beail, Mauritius
Phone: 41480

Description: Seeks to prevent leprosy and to develop advanced treatment methods. Fosters cooperation among similar organizations.

★6639★ Artists Confronting AIDS (ACA)
1616 Garden St.
Glendale, CA 91201-2614
Phone: (213)250-4487
James Carroll Pickett, Exec. Officer

Founded: 1985. **Description:** Individuals working to confront stereotypes and humanize AIDS through the creative and performing arts. **Publications:** *Purple Circuit Directory*, annual. Directory. Brochure listing gay and lesbian theaters and producers.

★6640★ Asian Parasite Control Organization (APCO)
c/o Japan Association of Parasite Control
1-2, Sadohara-cho
Ichigaya
Shinjuku-ku
Tokyo 162, Japan
Phone: 3 32681800
Fax: 3 32668767
Takaaki Hara, Sec.

Founded: 1974. **Members:** 12. **Languages:** English. **Description:** Family planning/parasite control projects of Bangladesh, China, Indonesia, Japan, Malaysia, Nepal, Philippines, Republic of Korea, Sri Lanka, Thailand, VietNam. Promotes and discusses parasite control in an effort to increase public awareness of a range of community health issues, in particular, family planning and primary health care. Provides technical support to parasite control integrated projects with a view to stimulating parasitological research. Bestows awards. **Publications:** *Collected Papers on the Control of Soil-Transmitted Helminthiases*. Book. • *Proceedings of Conference*, annual.

★6641★ Association of French-Language Leprologists (AFLL)
(Association des Leprologues de Langue Francaise)
Parc Montvert
9, rue des Flots Bleus 4C
F-13007 Marseille, France
Phone: 91 526435
Prof. Pierre Saint Andre, Sec.-Treas.

Founded: 1960. **Members:** 250. **Languages:** French. **Description:** Physicians in 25 countries involved in the treatment of leprosy. Promotes cooperation between French-speaking physicians in the field. **Publications:** *Acta Leprologica*, quarterly. Also publishes directory.

Association of Nurses in AIDS Care (ANAC)
See: Entry 9071

★6642★ Association for Practitioners in Infection Control (APIC)
1016 16th St. NW, 6th Fl.
Washington, DC 20036
Phone: (202)296-2742
Fax: (202)296-5645
Richard Dorman, CAE, Exec.Dir.

Founded: 1972. **Members:** 9,000. **Local Groups:** 100. **Description:** Physicians, microbiologists, nurses, epidemiologists, medical technicians, sanitarians, and pharmacists. Purpose is to improve patient care by improving the profession of infection control through the development of educational programs and standards. Promotes quality research and standardization of practices and procedures. Develops communications among members, and assesses and influences legislation related to the field. Conducts seminars at local level. **Publications:** *American Journal of Infection Control*, bimonthly. Journal. • Newsletter, quarterly.

★6643★ Australian National Council on AIDS (ANCA)
GPO Box 9848
Canberra, ACT 2601, Australia
Phone: 6 2897767
Fax: 6 2898098
Jenny Williams, Sec.

Founded: 1988. **Members:** 11. **Languages:** English. **Description:** Coordinates AIDS-related research in Australia. Advises government agencies. **Publications:** Bulletin, periodic.

★6644★ Body Positive
2095 Broadway, Ste. 306
New York, NY 10023
Phone: (212)721-1618
Fax: (212)787-9633
Frank Carbone, Contact

Founded: 1987. **Members:** 1,000. **Description:** Provides support services for people who are HIV-infected or have AIDS, and their families and friends. Organizes seminars on treatment issues and socials. Provides outreach programs and recreational services. **Publications:** *Body Positive*, monthly. Newsletter.

★6645★ Brazilian Interdisciplinary AIDS Association (ABIA)
Rua 7 de Setembro 48, Andar 12
20050-000 Rio de Janeiro, RJ, Brazil
Phone: 21 2212221
Fax: 21 2243414
Richard Parker, Coordinator

Founded: 1986. **Languages:** English, Portuguese, Spanish. **Description:** Advocates a multidisciplinary approach to issues raised by AIDS. Assesses AIDS-related government initiatives and works to develop adequate prevention, education, and information policies. Studies the social impact of AIDS in Brazil; compiles and disseminates updated information on HIV-infection prevention and control; critiques available information and works to lessen the spread of misinformation; provides consultancy and advisory services. Serves as a clearing house and resource center; maintains database in cooperation with the Brazilian Institute of Social and Economic Analyses . Conducts seminars on ethical, moral, and social aspects of the disease and educational and research programs. **Publications:** *ABIA Bulletin*, quarterly. Newsletter. • *Acao Anti AIDS*, bimonthly. Magazine. • *AIDS in Brazil*. Book. • *Directory*. • *Latin American Solidarity Bulletin*, quarterly. Newsletter. • *Life Before Death*. Book.

★6646★ Canadian AIDS Society (CAS)
100 Sparks St., Ste. 400
Ottawa, ON, Canada K1P 5B7
Phone: (613)563-4998

Languages: English. **Description:** Conducts research and educational programs.

★6647★ Canadian Public Health Association
AIDS Program
(Sante Canada par la Strategie Nationale sur la Sida)

400-1565 Carling Ave.
Ottawa, ON, Canada K1Z 8R1
Phone: (613)725-3769
Fax: (613)725-9826

Languages: English, French. **Description:** Works to prevent the spread of HIV and AIDS in Canada. Conducts public awareness campaigns on the dangers of unprotected sex and means to prevent communication of HIV; supports the human rights of people with HIV and AIDS; makes recommendations to health care professionals regarding the diagnosis and treatment of people with HIV and AIDS. **Publications:** *Canadian AIDS News*, monthly. Newsletter.

★6648★ **CAVDA-Citizens AIDS Project (CAP)**
PO Box 31915
Chicago, IL 60631-0915
Phone: (312)236-6339
Howard A. Mirsky, Dir.

Founded: 1986. **Members:** 125. **Description:** A project of the Citizens Alliance for VD Awareness. Physicians, pharmacists, nurses, health professionals, and interested others. Seeks to provide information and educational programs to professionals and the public in order to dispel myths associated with sexually transmitted diseases and Acquired Immune Deficiency Syndrome. Conducts research programs and disseminates information and surveys through media and group presentations. Compiles statistics; maintains speakers' bureau. **Publications:** Pamphlets. • *STD Spotlight*, quarterly. Newsletter. *Price:* $15/year.

★6649★ **CDC National AIDS Clearinghouse (NAC)**
PO Box 6003
Rockville, MD 20849-6003
Phone: 800-458-5231
Fax: (301)738-6616
Ruthann Bates, Project Dir.

Founded: 1987. **Description:** A service of the Centers for Disease Control. Collects, analyzes, and disseminates information on HIV/AIDS, primarily for health care professionals, educators, social service workers, attorneys, employers and human resource professionals, state HIV/AIDS programs, community organizations, and service associations. Responds to the information needs of health professionals. Offers referral service and AIDS Clinical Trials Information Service. **Publications:** Brochures. • *Materials Catalog*. Catalog. **Formerly:** (1991) National AIDS Information Clearinghouse; (1992) National AIDS Clearinghouse.

★6650★ **CFIDS Association of America**
PO Box 220398
Charlotte, NC 28222-0398
Phone: 800-442-3437
Fax: (704)365-9755
Kim Kenney, Exec. Officer

Founded: 1986. **Members:** 23,000. **Description:** Individuals with chronic fatigue and immune dysfunction syndrome (chronic viral illness associated with dysfunction of the immune system; formerly called chronic Epstein-Barr virus); doctors, nurses, and government offi-

cials. Advocates continued research into the cause and cure of the syndrome. Compiles statistics; sponsors support group. **Publications:** *The CFIDS Chronicle*, quarterly. Journal. Contains research and medical articles, advocacy efforts reports, and book and media reviews. *Price:* Included in membership dues. Also publishes patient guide and other educational materials. **Formerly:** (1994) CFIDS Association.

★6651★ **China Leprosy Association**
126 Gulou W St.
Xicheng District
Beijing 100009, People's Republic of China
Phone: 1 4033787
Da-Xun He, Sec.Gen.

Founded: 1985. **Members:** 5,761. **Description:** Individuals (5758) and organizations (3) in the People's Republic of China. Seeks to prevent leprosy; works to develop advanced treatment methods. Fosters exchange and cooperation with leprosy organizations in other countries. Conducts research and educational programs.

★6652★ **Chronic Fatigue Immune Dysfunction Syndrome Activation Network (CAN)**
PO Box 345
Larchmont, NY 10538
Phone: (212)627-5631
Fax: (914)636-6515
Ms. Jane Perlmutter, Contact

Founded: 1991. **Members:** 1,000. **Description:** Works to prompt government into action on research issues concerning Chronic Fatigue Immune Dysfunction Syndrome (CFIDS). (CFIDS is a disease that affects women more than men and causes flu-like symptoms such as aches, pains, and muscle weakness.) Promotes public awareness and knowledge of the disease. Provides information on CFIDS on local and national television and radio. Maintains political action committee to obtain government funding for further research. Compiles statistics. **Publications:** *CAN Bulletin*, monthly. Newsletter. *Price:* $12/year.

★6653★ **Cides-Centroamerica**
Apartado Postal 413
Guadalupe, Costa Rica

Description: Promotes the awareness of AIDS and documents the cases of HIV infection in Central America.

★6654★ **Citizens Alliance for VD Awareness (CAVDA)**
PO Box 31915
Chicago, IL 60631-0915
Phone: (312)236-6339
Howard A. Mirsky, Pres.

Founded: 1972. **Members:** 80. **Description:** Businessmen, corporations, social service agencies, public health agencies, physicians, nurses, and pharmacists. Provides information to the public, especially to high incidence groups, about symptoms, treatment, and prevention of sexually transmitted diseases, including AIDS (acquired immune deficiency syndrome). Seeks to increase commitment of health professionals and the public to venereal

disease and AIDS control. Conducts demonstrations, public service messages, and surveys. **Publications:** Pamphlets. • *STD Spotlight: Dedicated to Thought and Activity in STD Information-Education Programs*, quarterly. Newsletter. *Price:* $15/year. Also publishes fact sheets.

★6655★ **Comissao Nacional de Luta Contra a SIDA (CNLCS)**
Centro de Saude de Sete Rios
Largo Prof. Arnaldo Sampaio
P-1500 Lisbon, Portugal
Phone: 1 7270312
Fax: 1 7271224
Maria Odette Santos Ferreira, PhD, Natl. Coordinator

Founded: 1992. **Languages:** English, French, Spanish. **Description:** Works to prevent the spread of HIV and AIDS. Advises governmental and nongovernmental agencies. Conducts educational programs, compiles and disseminates information. **Publications:** Pamphlets. • *SIDA Informacao*, quarterly. Bulletin. Contains epidemiological data on AIDS in Portugal and Europe.

★6656★ **Comite Nationale de Lutte Contre le SIDA**
Direccion General de Servecios de Salud
9 Avenida 14-65, Zona 1
Guatemala City, Guatemala
Phone: 2 536071

★6657★ **Comite Nationale de Lutte Contre le SIDA**
Ministere de la Sante Publique
Quito, Ecuador
Phone: 2 521733

★6658★ **Comite Nationale de Lutte Contre le SIDA**
Ministere de la Sante Publique
Yaounde, Cameroon
Phone: 226719
Fax: 226719
Dr. Joseph Mbede, Contact

Founded: 1985. **Description:** Organizations and interested individuals in Cameroon. Coordinates AIDS treatment and education activities. Offers counseling; conducts research. **Publications:** *Felagsblao BK*, quarterly. Newsletter. • *Ny Menntamal*, quarterly. Journal.

★6659★ **Comite Nationale de Lutte Contre le SIDA**
Direction de l'Action Sanitaire et Sociale
13, rue Emile de Loth
MC-98000 Monaco, Monaco
Phone: 93 158310
Roger Passeron, Exec. Officer

★6660★ **Corporacion Chilena de Prevencion del SIDA (CChPS)**
Casilla 85, Correo 3
Santiago, Chile
Phone: 2 2225255
Fax: 2 2093816
Tim Frasca, Gen.Coord.

Founded: 1987. **Members:** 100. **Languages:** English, Spanish. **Description:** Promotes AIDS awareness, operating safe-sex eduational programs and distributing information on the facts of AIDS. Conducts AIDS and HIV testing and research programs. Offers counseling and referral to medical and social services. Maintains speakers' bureau. **Publications:** *Rapport Annuel*, annual. **Formerly:** Corporacion Chilena contra el SIDA; Comite Nationale de Lutte contre le SIDA.

★6661★ Damien Dutton Society for Leprosy Aid (DDSLA)
616 Bedford Ave.
Bellmore, NY 11710
Phone: (516)221-5829
Howard E. Crouch, Pres.

Founded: 1944. **Members:** 30,000. **Description:** Religious leaders and laypeople interested in aiding victims of Hansen's disease (leprosy). Provides relief, research, and recreation to victims of leprosy all over the world regardless of race, color, or creed. **Publications:** *Damien-Dutton Call*, quarterly. Newsletter. *Price:* Available to members only. • *Two Hearts - One Fire*. Book. **Formerly:** (1972) Damien-Dutton Society.

★6662★ Damien Foundation—Belgium (DFB)
(Fondation Damien)
263, Leopold II Laan
B-1080 Brussels, Belgium
Phone: 2 4225911
Fax: 2 4225900
Rigo Peeters, Gen.Sec.

Founded: 1964. **Members:** 3,000. **Languages:** Dutch, English, French. **Description:** Volunteers working to eradicate leprosy and tuberculosis. Promotes control of the disease through detection, treatment, training, and research. Supports field training as well as formal training in specialized institutions; maintains charitable programs. **Publications:** *Perspectives*, bimonthly.

★6663★ Damien Ministries (DM)
PO Box 10202
Washington, DC 20018
Phone: (202)387-2926
Fax: (202)332-7904
Howard J. McDonough, Exec.Dir.

Founded: 1987. **Description:** Roman Catholic faith community ministering to people with acquired immune deficiency syndrome (AIDS). Operates food bank and homes for men, women, and recovering substance abusers with AIDS. Cooperates with religious organizations working with people with AIDS. Sponsors spiritual retreats and visits to hospitals and prisons. Operations currently concentrated in Washington, DC. **Publications:** *DamienNews*, quarterly. Newsletter.

★6664★ Design Industries Foundation Fighting AIDS (DIFFA)
150 W. 26th St., Ste. 602
New York, NY 10001
Phone: (212)727-3100
Fax: (212)727-2574
Rosemary L. Kuropat, Exec.Dir.

Founded: 1984. **Local Groups:** 19. **Description:** Serves as a foundation bestowing grants to organizations providing direct patient care

and services; preventive, post-diagnostic, and community education; housing, meals, emergency assistance, and legal advocacy; treatment and community-based research. Seeks to educate firms, associations, and individuals through print materials, presentations, and referrals. **Publications:** *On-Line*, quarterly. Newsletter. **Formerly:** Design Industries Foundation for AIDS.

★6665★ Disinfected Mail Study Circle (DMSC)
25 Sinclair Grove
London NW11 9JH, England
Phone: 181 4559190
V. Denis Vandervelde, Chm.

Founded: 1974. **Members:** 170. **Languages:** English. **Description:** Postal historians, doctors, researchers, libraries, and research foundations in 25 countries. Studies the historic treatment of mail so as to prevent the spread of contagious diseases. The study circle is continuing the research work of the late Dr. K. F. Meyer and his associates, many of whom are members. The study has been extended to include health certificates and passports, antivaccination postal propaganda, and related subjects. Maintains speakers' bureau; conducts research programs. **Publications:** *Cumulative Indexes*. • *Pratique*, quarterly. Magazine. Contains Newsletter.

★6666★ European Society for Mycobacteriology (ESM)
Unite de la Tuberculose et de Mycobacteries
Institut Pasteur de la Guadeloupe
BP 484
97165 Pointe a Pitre Cedex, Guadeloupe
Phone: 893881
Fax: 893880
Dr. Nalin Rastogi, Sec.

Founded: 1980. **Members:** 300. **Languages:** English. **Description:** Individuals from 20 countries interested in mycobacteria. Seeks to further the understanding of mycobacteria and the diseases they cause. **Publications:** *ESM Manual for Diagnostic & Public Health Mycobacteriology*. • *ESM Newsletter*, annual. Newsletter.

★6667★ Exotic Pathology Society (EPS)
(Societe de Pathologie Exotique)
Institut Pasteur
25, rue du Docteur-Roux
F-75015 Paris, France
Phone: 1 45668869
Prof. Pierre Pene

Founded: 1908. **Members:** 915. **Languages:** French. **Description:** Doctors, bacteriologists, biologists, entomologists, epidemiologists, parasitologists, pharmacists, veterinarians, and virologists. Promotes the study of tropical diseases. Provides a forum for the presentation and discussion of research findings in the field. Offers quality control supervision for parasitologic examinations. **Publications:** *Annuaire*, quadrennial. Yearbook. • *Bulletin de la Societe de Pathologie Exotique*, bimonthly. Newsletter.

★6668★ Foundation for Microbiology (FFM)
c/o Byron H. Waksman
300 E. 54th St., Ste. 5K
New York, NY 10022
Phone: (212)759-8729
Fax: (212)263-8211
Byron H. Waksman, Pres.

Founded: 1951. **Members:** 11. **Description:** Encourages research in microbiology by: establishing lectureships; funding specialized courses in microbiology; aiding in the publishing of scientific works concerning microbiology; supporting innovative educational programs dealing with microbiological topics; and making use of contemporary communication techniques, as well as programs concerned with enhancing public awareness of science, including k-12 teaching programs that make use of microorganisms, and "all to the end that the science of microbiology shall progress in the service of mankind." **Publications:** Report, annual. • Report, quinquennial.

★6669★ Foundation of Pharmacists and Corporate America for AIDS Education (FPCA)
700 13th St. NW, Ste. 950
Washington, DC 20005
Phone: (202)434-4515
Fax: (202)434-4514
Nigel L. Gragg, R.Ph., Pres.

Founded: 1988. **Description:** Participants are pharmacists, pharmacy educators, and representatives of pharmacy trade, industry, and professional associations. Works to provide HIV/ AIDS education and prevention services to the public through pharmacists and pharmacies. Seeks to mobilize community pharmacists and pharmacies as promoters and educators for AIDS prevention, early intervention, risk assessment, and patient management of AIDS medication. Places special emphasis on programs that target minority communities. Develops continuing education programs. Is working to develop and implement a national pharmacy AIDS/HIV education and prevention program. on AIDS education in the pharmacy and outreach to the community; AIDS/HIV education for the public through pharmacy chains and independent pharmacies. **Publications:** *AIDS Education: A Guide for the Pharmacist*. • *AIDS & Pharmacy Update*.

★6670★ Gay Men's Health Crisis (GMHC)
129 W. 20th St.
New York, NY 10011
Phone: (212)807-6664
Fax: (212)337-3656
Jeff Richardson, Exec.Dir.

Founded: 1982. **Description:** Social service agency for the clinical treatment of AIDS. Provides support and therapy groups for persons with AIDS and their families. Offers Patient Recreation Services. Sends volunteer crisis counselors to work with persons with AIDS. Sponsors a buddy system in which helpers visit clients at home and assist with household tasks. Provides legal, financial, and health care advocacy services. Advocates for fair and effective AIDS policies on federal, state, and city levels. Compiles statistics; maintains speakers' bureau. Sponsors AIDS Prevention programs. Operates Drop-In Care Partners program. **Publications:** Annual Report, annual. • *GMHC News*, monthly. • *Medical Answers About AIDS*. Booklet. • *Treatment Issues*, 10/year. Newsletter. *Price:* Free. • *The Volunteer*, bimonthly. Newsletter. Updates medical, clinical, political, and referral information on AIDS. Includes calendar of events. *Price:* Free. • *When A Friend has AIDS*. Booklet. • *Women Need to Know About AIDS*. Booklet. Also offers audiovisual publications.

★6671★ **German-Speaking Mycological Society**
(Deutschsprachige Mykologische Gesellschaft)
Institut fur Medizinische Mykologie
Postfach 8 20
79008 Freiburg, Germany
Phone: 761 2032176
Fax: 761 2032187
Dr. Johannes Mueller, Pres.

Founded: 1961. **Members:** 360. **Languages:** German. **Description:** Physicians, microbiologists, technicians, and individuals in 16 countries interested in medical and veterinary mycology (the science of fungal diseases). Sponsors educational programs; conducts research.

★6672★ **Global Network of People Living with HIV / AIDS**
130 Harley St.
London W1N 1AH, England
Phone: 171 7281278
Pascal J. W. van den Noort, Exec.Dir.

Languages: English. **Description:** Individuals with AIDS, and people who test positive for HIV. Promotes self-empowerment for people with HIV and AIDS; facilitates communication among people with these diseases. Strives to ensure that people with HIV and AIDS are not discriminated against, and are able to access necessary medical care. Conducts educational programs to lessen public fears and dispel misconceptions about HIV and AIDS.

Group B Strep Association
See: Entry 9651

★6673★ **Haitian Coalition on AIDS (HCA)**
50 Court St., Ste. 605
Brooklyn, NY 11201
Phone: (718)855-0972
Fax: (718)852-5377
Henry Frank, Exec.Dir.

Founded: 1983. **Members:** 70. **Regional Groups:** 8. **State Groups:** 7. **Local Groups:** 6. **Description:** Community centers; professional groups of doctors, journalists, lawyers, nurses, social workers, and civil rights and media representatives. Purpose is to educate the public concerning what the coalition feels is the discriminatory classification of Haitians as an ethnonational group that runs a high risk of contracting AIDS. Seeks to heighten AIDS awareness within the Haitian community. Offers social services and placement for persons with AIDS; provides counseling to their families. Sponsors conferences and seminars at churches and universities. Compiles statistics; maintains speakers' bureau.

★6674★ **HIV / AIDS Program**
c/o United States Conference of Mayors
1620 Eye St. NW
Washington, DC 20006
Phone: (202)293-7330
Fax: (202)293-2352
Richard C. Johnson, Contact

Founded: 1983. **Description:** AIDS awareness program of the United States Conference of Mayors. Acts as a forum for information exchange among members; provides policy information to the media. Operates speakers' bureau and conducts educational programs. Lobbies for favorable legislation. **Publications:** *AIDS Information Exchange*, bimonthly. Newsletter. • *Local AIDS Policy*. • *Local AIDS Services: A National Directory*, periodic. Directory.

★6675★ **HIV Information Exchange and Support Group (HIVIES)**
610 Greenwood
Glenview, IL 60025
Phone: (708)724-3832

Founded: 1987. **Description:** Self-help support group for individuals who are HIV positive. Provides peer counseling based on an adaptation of the 12-step philosophy of Alcoholics Anonymous World Services. **Publications:** *HIVIES Manual*. Manual. *Price:* $15 in the United States; $20 outside the United States. **Also Known As:** HIVIES.

Ibero-Latin American College of Dermatology (ILACD)
(Colegio Ibero-Latino-Americano de Dermatologia — CILAD)
See: Entry 4240

★6676★ **Infectious Diseases Society of America (IDSA)**
1200 19th St. NW, Ste. 300
Washington, DC 20036-2401
Phone: (202)857-1139
Fax: (202)223-4579
Vincent T. Andriole, M.D., Pres.

Founded: 1963. **Members:** 4,500. **Description:** Physicians and microbiologists who have a career commitment to the field of infectious disease. Purpose is to foster research and training in the field. **Publications:** *Clinical Infectious Diseases*, monthly. • *Consult*, quarterly. Newsletter. *Price:* Available to members only. • *Journal of Infectious Diseases*, monthly. Journal. • *Membership Roster*, triennial. Membership Directory.

★6677★ **Infectious Diseases Society of Southern Africa (IDSSA)**
(Aansteeklike Siektesvereniging van Suider Afrika — ASVSA)
PO Box 1038
Johannesburg, Republic of South Africa
Phone: 11 7252865
Fax: 11 7252319
Prof. K.P. Klugman, Contact

Founded: 1983. **Members:** 150. **Languages:** English. **Description:** Health care professionals including doctors, medical researchers and technologists, and trade representatives in 4 countries. Stimulates interest among doctors in infectious disease; seeks to alleviate the current

shortage of infectious disease specialists in southern Africa. Compiles statistics. **Publications:** *Infectious Diseases Update*, 3/month. • *Southern African Journal of Epidemiology and Infection*, quarterly.

★6678★ **International AIDS Society (IAS)**
PO Box 5619
S-114 86 Stockholm, Sweden
Phone: 8 6121111
Fax: 8 6126292
Lars Olof Kallings, M.D., Sec.Gen.

Founded: 1988. **Members:** 5,700.

★6679★ **International Christian Leprosy Mission (ICLM)**
PO Box 23353
Portland, OR 97281-3353
Phone: (503)244-5935
Lauritz P. Pillers, Pres.

Founded: 1943. **Members:** 12. **Description:** Carries on evangelical missionary work and assists in physical treatment of people with leprosy and their children. **Publications:** *Global Missions*, quarterly.

★6680★ **International Federation of Anti-Leprosy Associations (ILEP)**
(Federation Internationale des Associations Contre la Lepre — ILEP)
234 Blythe Rd.
London W14 0HJ, England
Phone: 171 6026925
Fax: 171 3711621
Paul J. Sommerfeld, Gen.Sec.

Founded: 1966. **Members:** 20. **Languages:** English, French, German. **Description:** Leprosy relief associations. Members collect funds from general public and coordinates those funds for over 900 leprosy centers or projects in about 100 countries.

International Organization Against Trachoma (IOAT)
(Organisation Internationale pour la Lutte Contre le Trachome)
See: Entry 13495

★6681★ **International Polio Network (IPN)**
5100 Oakland Ave., No. 206
St. Louis, MO 63110-1406
Phone: (314)534-0475
Fax: (314)534-5070
Joan Headley, Dir.

Founded: 1985. **Members:** 6,500. **Description:** Individuals who have had polio; rehabilitation health professionals. Promotes networking and the exchange of information among the post-polio community; encourages research into the long-term effects of polio. **Publications:** *Handbook on the Late Effects of Poliomyelitis for Physicians and Survivors*. Handbook. • *Polio Network News*, quarterly. Newsletter. *Price:* $12. • *Post-Polio Directory*, annual. Directory. *Price:* $3. • Proceedings, biennial. • *Rehabilitation Gazette*. • *Ventilators and Muscular Dystrophy*.

★6682★ **International Society for AIDS Education (ISAE)**
University of South Carolina
School of Public Health
Columbia, SC 29208
Phone: (803)777-6217
Fax: (803)777-4783
Ruth C. Penney, Admin.

Founded: 1987. **Members:** 500. **Description:** AIDS researchers and health professionals. Promotes AIDS education, prevention, counseling, and research among universities, public health agencies, AIDS service organizations, and social science research institutes. Serves as information network for AIDS researchers and practioners. Conducts studies on ethical, social, and legal issues of AIDS education and counseling. Disseminates information to the public. **Publications:** *AIDS Education and Prevention -- An Interdisciplinary Journal*, bimonthly. Journal. Includes current information on AIDS education and prevention, research articles, critiques on existing programs, and book and film reviews. *Price:* $75 for institutions in U.S.; $95 for institutions outside of U.S.; $30 for individuals in U.S.; $50 for individuals outside of U.S. • Membership Directory, periodic.

★6683★ **International Union Against Venereal Diseases and Treponematoses (IUVDT)**
(Union Internationale Contre les Maladies Veneriennes et les Treponematoses)
General Infirmary at Leeds
Great George St.
Leeds, W. Yorkshire LS1 3EX, England
Phone: 113 2926762
Fax: 113 2926387
Dr. M.A. Waugh, Pres.

Founded: 1923. **Members:** 560. **Regional Groups:** 5. **Languages:** English, French. **Description:** Individuals and organizations in 54 countries concerned with the study of sexually transmitted and HIV related disease. Promotes research on the medical and sociological aspects of sexually transmitted and HIV related diseases; collects and disseminates information; compiles statistics. Works in conjunction with the World Health Organization and other United Nations bodies. **Publications:** *IUVDT Technical Bulletin*, annual. Bulletin. • *Membership List*, periodic. Directory.

★6684★ **International Union Against the Venereal Diseases and the Treponematoses, Regional Office for North America (IUVDT)**
c/o Lewis M. Drusin, M.D.
New York Hospital - Cornell Med. Center
525 E. 68th St.
New York, NY 10021
Phone: (212)746-1754
Fax: (212)746-8823
Lewis M. Drusin, M.D., Dir.

Founded: 1923. **Description:** U.S. office of the International Union Against Venereal Diseases and Treponematoses (see separate entry, *International Organizations*). Governmental and nongovernmental agencies and individuals working in the field of venereal disease control. Encourages campaigns, both medical and social, against venereal diseases and treponematoses. **Publications:** Proceedings, biennial.

★6685★ **International Union of Microbiological Societies (IUMS)**
(Union Internationale des Societes de Microbiologie)
IBMC
15, rue Descartes
F-67084 Strasbourg, France
Phone: 88 417022
Fax: 88 610680
Dr. Marc H. van Regenmortel, Sec.Gen.

Founded: 1930. **Members:** 106. **Description:** National microbiological societies in 62 countries representing 100,000 microbiologists united to maintain contact with microbiological societies throughout the world. Bestows awards. **Publications:** *Archives of Virology*, monthly. Journal. • *International Journal of Food Microbiology*, bimonthly. Journal. • *International Journal of Systematic Bacteriology*, quarterly. Journal. • *IUMS Directory*, quadrennial. Directory. • *Journal of Biological Standardization*, quarterly. Journal. • *World Journal of Microbiology and Biotechnology*, bimonthly. Journal.

★6686★ **IUMS Bacteriology Division (IUMSBD)**
National University of Singapore
Department of Microbiology
Faculty of Medicine
Lower Kent Ridge Rd.
Kent Ridge 0511, Singapore
Phone: 7723283
Fax: 7766872
Dr. Mah-Lee Ng, Sec.-Treas.

Founded: 1927. **Members:** 50,000. **Languages:** English. **Description:** A division of the International Union of Microbiological Societies. Scientists from private, educational, and governmental organizations in 60 countries. Purpose is to further the study of bacteriology and bacteriological research. Promotes high standards in the training of bacteriologists. Facilitates contact and cooperation among bacteriologists and microbiological societies worldwide. Conducts symposia.

★6687★ **Japan Association of Parasite Control (JAPC)**
(Nihon Kiseichu Yobokai)
Hoken Kaikan Bekkan
1-2, Sadohara-cho
Ichigaya
Shinjuku-ku
Tokyo 162, Japan
Phone: 3 32681800
Fax: 3 32668767
Chojiro Kunii, Contact

Founded: 1955. **Languages:** Japanese. **Description:** Conducts educational programs on parasite control for communities and schools in Japan. Sponsors research programs on parasite control in developing countries.

★6688★ **Kenya National AIDS Control Program**
PO Box 19361
Nairobi, Kenya
Phone: 2 729502
Fax: 2 729504

Formerly: National AIDS Committee.

★6689★ **Leonard Wood Memorial (American Leprosy Foundation) (LWM)**
11600 Nebel St., Ste. 210
Rockville, MD 20852
Phone: (301)984-1336
Fax: (301)770-0580
Gerald P. Walsh, Ph.D., Scientific Dir.

Founded: 1928. **Description:** Health and research foundation concerned with microbiological research of Hansen's Disease (leprosy). Conducts research programs in the U.S. and the Philippines. Supports clinical and basic laboratory research and epidemiological surveys. Sponsors exchange programs. Conducts collaborative studies with the Philippine Leprosy Mission, Culion Foundation, Colorado State University, Rockefeller University, the Delta Primate Center, American Leprosy Missions, International Sasakawa Memorial Health Foundation, Damien-Dutton Society, World Health Organization, UCLA School of Medicine, Ethiopia, India, Korea. **Publications:** Annual Report, annual. *Price:* Free. **Also Known As:** American Leprosy Foundation. **Formerly:** (1978) Leonard Wood Memorial for the Eradication of Leprosy.

★6690★ **LEPRA**
Fairfax House
Causton Rd.
Colchester, Essex CO1 1PU, England
Phone: 1206 562286
Fax: 1206 762151
Mr. Terry Vasey, Dir.

Founded: 1924. **Local Groups:** 2. **Languages:** English. **Description:** Objective is to eradicate leprosy throughout the world. Operates training programs for medical personnel. Supports research for the development of leprosy drugs and vaccines, and research projects of the World Health Organization. Concentrates efforts in Africa and Asia. Maintains special children's, eye, and hand remobilization funds. Investigates potential for treatment of leprosy in conjunction with that of other diseases. Sponsors competitions; bestows awards. **Publications:** *Leprosy Review*, quarterly. **Also Known As:** British Leprosy Relief Association.

★6691★ **LEPRA**
PO Box 496
Blantyre, Malawi

Description: Objective is to eradicate leprosy and assist persons afflicted with the disease. Operates training programs for medical personnel. Supports research for the development of leprosy drugs and vaccines and research projects for the World Health Organization (see separate entry). Investigates potential for treatment of leprosy in conjunction with that of other diseases.

★6692★ **Leprosy Mission - Southern Africa**
PO Box 1027
Manzini, Swaziland
Phone: 55310
Fax: 52211

Description: Represents the interests of leprosy patients throughout Southern Africa.

Lyme Disease Foundation (LDF)
See: Entry 7889

★6693★ Malawi Against Polio (MAP)
PO Box 30333
Blantyre, Malawi
Phone: 743403
Fax: 632928
S.A. Ndembe

Members: 112. **Description:** Engaged in the fight against polio. Works to rehabilitate those disabled by the disease. **Publications:** *Annual Report.* • *Financial Report.* • *MAP Feedback.* • Newsletter.

★6694★ Medical Mycological Society of the Americas (MMSA)
c/o Dr. W.G. Merz
Johns Hopkins Hospital
Department of Pathology (microbiology)
Meyer B1-193
Baltimore, MD 21287-7093
Phone: (410)955-5077
Fax: (410)955-0767
Dr. W. G. Merz, Sec.-Treas.

Founded: 1966. **Members:** 408. **Description:** Medical professionals interested in fungi and fungal diseases. Seeks to exchange professional information; promotes continuing education in medical mycology in association with American Society for Microbiology. **Publications:** Bulletin, quarterly. • Directory, periodic.

★6695★ Medical Society for the Study of Venereal Diseases (MSSVD)
Kings Healthcare
Department of Genito-Urinary Medicine
London SE5 9RS, England
Phone: 171 3263453
Fax: 171 3263458
Dr. T.J. McManus, Hon.Sec.

Founded: 1922. **Members:** 620. **Languages:** English. **Description:** Individuals from 40 countries interested in the study of sexually transmitted diseases, including AIDS. **Publications:** *Genito-Urinary Medicine*, bimonthly. Journal.

★6696★ Mobilization Against AIDS (MAA)
584-B Castro St.
San Francisco, CA 94114-1465
Phone: (415)863-4676
Free: 800-24-LOBBY
Mike Shriver, Exec.Dir.

Founded: 1984. **Members:** 2,000. **Local Groups:** 1. **Description:** Individuals supporting increased government expenditure on AIDS research, treatment, and social services. Purposes are to: lobby Congress, the Food and Drug Administration, and the National Institutes of Health to provide support and funding to AIDS organizations; mobilize people into public expressions of support for persons with AIDS; oppose civil rights attacks on persons with AIDS. Organizes annual International AIDS candlelight vigil, marches, and the Just Sign IT postcard campaign. Provides speakers on the civil rights ramifications of the AIDS crisis. **Publications:** *Action Alert*, quarterly. Newsletter. *Price:* Included in membership. • *International AIDS Candlelight Memorial and Mobilization.* Booklet. **Formerly:** (1987) Mobilization Against AIDS; (1992) National Mobilization Against AIDS.

★6697★ Names Project Foundation (NPF)
310 Townsend St.
San Francisco, CA 94107
Phone: (415)882-5500
Fax: (415)882-6200
Anthony Turney, Exec.Dir.

Founded: 1987. **Local Groups:** 36. **Description:** Promotes creation of a memorial quilt as an "appropriate, compassionate response" to the AIDS epidemic. Goals of the project are to provide a creative means of remembrance and healing; to illustrate the enormity of the AIDS epidemic; to increase public awareness of AIDS; to assist with HIV prevention education; and to raise funds for community-based AIDS service organizations. The 17 acre quilt currently contains 27,000 panels from each of the 50 states and 29 foreign countries bearing the names of persons who have died as a result of AIDS. Among materials sewn into the panels are stuffed animals, merit badges, records, feather boas, and a baseball jersey. **Publications:** Brochures. • Pamphlets. • *The Quilt: Stories From the NAMES Project.* Book. Also publishes fact sheets, flyers, and press releases. **Formerly:** Names Project.

★6698★ Namibia Network of AIDS Service Organisations
University of Namibia
PO Box 21779
Windhoek 9000, Namibia
Mrs. M. Mungunda

Description: Promotes AIDS awareness in Namibia, offering health education programs and assistance. Conducts research. Disseminates information.

★6699★ National Advisory Committee on AIDS (NACA)
Ministry of Health
Suva, Fiji
Phone: 306177
Fax: 306163
Dr. S.R. Govind, Contact

Founded: 1989. **Members:** 10. **Local Groups:** 3. **Description:** Monitors and evaluates HIV/AIDS-related policies and programs. Conducts research.

★6700★ National Advisory Committee on AIDS
Ministry of Health
Jemmotts Ln.
St. Michael, Barbados
Phone: (809)426-5080
Fax: (809)426-5570
Miss Eugene Campbell, Contact

Founded: 1987. **Members:** 10. **Languages:** English. **Description:** Conducts research and educational programs. Conducts surveys and compiles statistics. Sponsors poster contests; bestows awards. Maintains speakers' bureau; offers children's services. **Publications:** *Accidental Wounds in the Era of AIDS.* • *AIDS and the Hospitality Industry.* • *AIDS - For Youth and Children.* • *AIDS, What You Need to Know.* • *Blood Donors.* • *Caring for an Infected Person.* • *Have You Been in Contact?.* • *HIV Disease and AIDS.* Booklet. • *Living with HIV/AIDS.* • *The Test.* • *You Are Positive - What Now?.*

★6701★ National AIDS Committee
Dept. of Health
Hawkins House
Hawkins St.
Dublin 2, Ireland
Phone: 1 714711
Fax: 1 6711947
Dr. James Walsh, Coord.

★6702★ National AIDS Committee (NAC)
30-34 Half Way Tree Rd.
Kingston 5, Jamaica
Phone: (809)926-1818
Fax: (809)926-5674

Founded: 1988. **Members:** 62. **Languages:** English. **Description:** Organizes educational programs; maintains speakers' bureau.

★6703★ National AIDS Committee
Ministry of Health and Welfare
1-2-2, Kasumigaseki
Chiyoda-ku
Tokyo 100, Japan
Phone: 3 35913060
Fax: 3 35816251

Languages: Japanese.

★6704★ National AIDS Committee (Nationaler AIDS-Beirat — NAB)
Federal Ministry for Health
53108 Bonn, Germany
Phone: 228 9413200
Fax: 228 9414932
F.J. Bindert, Contact

Founded: 1987. **Members:** 35. **Languages:** German. Does not correspond in English. **Description:** Organizations and individuals interested in preventing the spread of HIV/AIDS. Counsels German government on AIDS related matters. **Publications:** *Voten des Nationalen AIDS-Beirates - 1987-1993.*

★6705★ National AIDS Committee
Direccion General de Salud
Apartado 10123
San Jose 1000, Costa Rica
Phone: 2230333

★6706★ National AIDS Committee
Ministry of Public Health
44 Houhai Beiyan
Beijing 100725, People's Republic of China
Phone: 1 4012871
Fax: 1 4012369

★6707★ National AIDS Committee
Ministry of Public Health and Social Service
Plaza del Estudiante
La Paz, Bolivia
Phone: 2 374350

★6708★ National AIDS Committee
Ministry of Health
PO Box 12
Manama, Bahrain
Phone: 252755
Fax: 251628
Dr. Mohmmed Khalil Al Haddad, Chief of Medical Staff

Founded: 1987. **Members:** 12. **Languages:** Arabic. **Description:** Provides educational programs; compiles statistics.

**★6709★ National AIDS Committee
(Osterreichisches AIDS Committee)**
Mariannengasse 14/11
A-1090 Vienna, Austria
Phone: 1 4052995
Fax: 1 4052995

Publications: *Spectrum STD & AIDS.*

★6710★ National AIDS Committee
Ministry of Health and Home Affairs
Cecil Charles Bldg.
Cross St. and Stapleton Ln.
St. Johns, Antigua-Barbuda
Felicity Aymer, Programme Mgr.

Languages: English. **Description:** Individuals in Antigua-Barbuda interested in fighting the spread of HIV/AIDS. Conducts public awareness and health programs.

★6711★ National AIDS Committee
Ministry of Health
PO Box 30205
Lusaka, Zambia
Phone: 1 221186
Fax: 1 223435
Dr. S. Nyaywa, Exec. Officer

Founded: 1987. **Members:** 30. **Regional Groups:** 9. **Languages:** English. **Description:** Provides guidance in the establishment of policy and the implementation of programs aimed at the prevention of AIDS in Zambia. Trains counselors; conducts workshops. Is developing a library of educational publications from the World Health Organization.

★6712★ National AIDS Committee
Ministry of Health
Mogadishu, Somalia

Description: Organizations and individuals interested in preventing the spread of HIV/AIDS in Somalia. Conducts educational programs.

★6713★ National AIDS Committee
Ministry of Public
PO Box 2993
Paramaribo, Suriname

Founded: 1987. **Members:** 9. **Languages:** Dutch, English. **Description:** Develops health policy in Suriname for controlling the spread of the HIV virus. Operates an AIDS hotline.

★6714★ National AIDS Committee
Dept. of Communicable Disease Control
Ministry of Public Health
275 Samsen Rd.
Bangkok 10200, Thailand
Phone: 2 2817500
Fax: 2 2828351
Paichit Pavabutr, M.D.

Founded: 1985. **Members:** 42. **Languages:** English, Thai. **Description:** Coordinates disease control programs for AIDS. Conducts. Compiles statistics. **Publications:** *AIDS Newsletter*, biweekly. Contains updates of activities, information, and statistics. • *Thai AIDS Journal*, quarterly. Contains research results and technical information. • *Thailand Medium Term Programme Review*. Also publishes brochures, leaflets, and posters.

★6715★ National AIDS Committee (NAC)
Eric Williams Medical Sciences Complex
Champs Fleurs
Porta Kabin 2
Port of Spain, Trinidad and Tobago
Phone: (809)645-2640
Fax: (809)638-8620
Dr. Glenda Maynard, Chairperson

Founded: 1987. **Members:** 25. **Languages:** English. **Description:** Identifies the policies that guide the National AIDS Programme of Trinidad and Tobago. Representatives from religious organizations, trade unions, and employers' organizations. Provides AIDS education for health care workers, schools, private organizations and the general public.

★6716★ National AIDS Committee
Ministry of Health
Chaussee Rd.
Castries, St. Lucia
Phone: (809)452-1732
Fax: (809)453-1080
Dr. Michele Ooms, Contact

Founded: 1990. **Members:** 13. **Languages:** English. **Description:** Sponsors educational and research programs. Compiles statistics; maintains speakers' bureau.

★6717★ National AIDS Committee
Ministry of Health
Kingstown, St. Vincent
Phone: (809)457-1745
Fax: (809)457-2152
Dr. H.R. Rampersand, Contact

Founded: 1985. **Description:** Organizations and individuals interested in preventing the spread of HIV/AIDS. Conducts educational programs.

★6718★ National AIDS Committee
Ministry of Public Health
Riyadh, Saudi Arabia

Publications: *Norsk Okonomisk Tidsskrift*, periodic. • *Sosial Okonomen*, monthly. Magazine.

**★6719★ National AIDS Committee
(Gezondheidsraad)**
Postbus 90517
NL-2509 LM The Hague, Netherlands
Phone: 70 3441800
Fax: 70 3837109
J.H. Jansen, Contact

★6720★ National AIDS Committee
Ministry of Health
PO Box 52
Victoria, Seychelles
Phone: 224400
Fax: 224792
Mrs. M. Pragassen, Contact

★6721★ National AIDS Committee
Ministry of Health
Complejo Civico Cmbte.
Camilo Ortega Saavedra
Managua, Nicaragua
Phone: 2 50039
Fax: 2 97483
Ernesto Salmeron, Minister

★6722★ National AIDS Committee
Director General of Health
Statens Helsetilsyn
Postboks 8128 Dep.
N-0032 Oslo 1, Norway
Phone: 22349090
Fax: 22349590
Anne Alvik, Dir.

Description: Coordinates AIDS research in Norway.

★6723★ National AIDS Committee
Secretary for Health
Lieja Numero 7, Col. Juarez
1er Piso
04360 Mexico City, DF, Mexico
Phone: 5 5549112
Fax: 5 5544202
Dr. Carlos del Rio Chiriboga, Pres.

Founded: 1986. **Languages:** English, Spanish. **Description:** Individual interested in preventing the spread of HIV/AIDS in Mexico. Offers public education programs on the transmission and effects of the disease. Campaigns to raise awareness and fund research. **Publications:** Booklet, periodic.

★6724★ National AIDS Committee
Ministry of Public Health
Tegucigalpa, DC, Honduras
Phone: 383270
Fax: 379422
Dr. Jorge Alberto Fernandez Vasquez, Contact

Founded: 1994. **Members:** 16. **National Groups:** 9. **Languages:** English.

**★6725★ National AIDS Control
    Programme**
Ministry of Health
PO Box 9083
Dar es Salaam, United Republic of Tanzania
Phone: 51 20261
Fax: 51 38281
Dr. K.M. Nyamuryekung'e, Contact

Founded: 1988. **Members:** 35. **Languages:** English, Swahili. **Publications:** *AIDS Newsletter*, quarterly. Newsletter.

**★6726★ National AIDS Control
    Programme**
Parirenyatwa Hospital
PO Box 8204
Causeway
Harare, Zimbabwe
Phone: 4 702446
Fax: 4 792981

Description: Works to strengthen AIDS programs and research nationwide by decentralizing them to provincial and district levels. Supports AIDS prevention campaigns and projects.

**★6727★ National AIDS Prevention and
    Control Program**
Dept. of Health
Rizal Ave.
Manila, Philippines
Phone: 2 7116693
Fax: 2 7417048
Dennis P. Maducdoc, Program Mgr.

Founded: 1988. **Languages:** English. **Description:** Provides AIDS information and education;

offers AIDS counseling training. Implements programs for the management and care of HIV-infected individuals and persons with AIDS. Conducts research; compiles statistics. Maintains speakers' bureau; operates children's services. **Publications:** *Monthly Update.* **Formerly:** (1994) National AIDS-STD Prevention and Control Program.

★ 6728 ★ **National AIDS Task Force**
Ministry of Health
Division of Health Services
Jalan Dungun, Bukit Damansara
50490 Kuala Lumpur, Malaysia
Phone: 3 2540088
Fax: 3 2561566
Dr. Sulajman Cate'Rus, Deputy Dir.

Founded: 1985. **Members:** 18. **Languages:** English, Malay.

★ 6729 ★ **National AIDS Trust**
Eileen House, 6th Fl.
80 Newington Causeway
London SE1 6EF, England
Phone: 171 9722845
Fax: 171 9722885
Dr. Les Rudd, Contact

Members: 15. **Languages:** English. **Description:** Individuals in England interested in preventing the spread of HIV/AIDS. Conducts educational programs. **Publications:** *AIDS Matters,* quarterly. Newsletter.

★ 6730 ★ **National Association of People With AIDS (NAPWA)**
1413 K St. NW
Washington, DC 20005
Phone: (202)898-0414
Fax: (202)898-0435
William J. Freeman, Exec.Dir.

Founded: 1987. **Members:** 400. **Local Groups:** 102. **Description:** Works to improve the lives of people with HIV/AIDS at home, in the community, and in the workplace. Serves as a national information resource and voice for the needs and concerns of all Americans affected by HIV. Committed to ensuring that people with HIV/AIDS understand their treatment options and have access to quality health care. Builds partnerships among people with HIV, service providers, business, government, philanthropy, and the media. Identifies the issues of critical importance to people with HIV infection and advocates for these needs at the national level. Provides technical assistance that enables community-based organizations and coalitions to build HIV-related services, management expertise, and networks. Maintains a network of speakers affected by HIV. Educates federal, state, and local governments, service organizations, and the media on policies and issues affecting people living with HIV/AIDS. **Publications:** *An Ounce of Prevention.* Informs family members and caregivers about the prevention of further HIV infection. • *Facts About AIDS.* Provides an introduction of HIV and related issues. • *HIV in America.* • *Living HIV,* quarterly. Provides information about lifestyle, healthcare, workplace and advocacy issues. • *Living with HIV.* Provides information on resources for treatment and offers prevention against further infection. • *Medical Alert,* bi-

monthly. Identifies new approaches to treating HIV/AIDS, explains what new drugs are being tested and how they work, and provides treatment strategies. *Price:* Free. • *When Someone You Know Has AIDS.* Strives to create a greater understanding about AIDS and people with AIDS among families, friends, and co-workers.

★ 6731 ★ **National Catholic AIDS Network (NCAN)**
PO Box 422984
San Francisco, CA 94142-2984
Phone: (707)874-3031
Fax: (707)874-1433
Fr. Rodney DeMartini, SM, Exec.Dir.

Founded: 1989. **Members:** 4,000. **Description:** Provides support and exchange of information among Roman Catholic HIV/AIDS service workers and pastoral ministers. Disseminates educational materials on HIV/AIDS. **Publications:** *Connections,* quarterly. Newsletter. *Price:* Free.

★ 6732 ★ **National Chronic Fatigue Syndrome and Fibromyalgia Association (NCFSFA)**
3521 Broadway, Ste. 222
Kansas City, MO 64111
Phone: (816)931-4777
Fax: (816)753-6706
Orvalene Prewitt, Pres.

Founded: 1985. **Members:** 35,000. **Regional Groups:** 2. **State Groups:** 20. **Local Groups:** 400. **Description:** Individuals suffering from chronic fatigue syndrome; health care professionals. (Chronic fatigue syndrome, also known as Chronic Epstein-Barr Virus syndrome, is characterized by persistent, recurring feelings of general weakness; other symptoms include low fever or chills, unexplained muscle pain, headaches, devastating fatigue, loss of concentration, confusion, forgetfulness, mild depression, and excessive sleep or insomnia.) Sponsors educational programs. Maintains speakers' bureau. **Publications:** *A Guide for Physicians When Considering a Diagnosis of Chronic Fatigue Syndrom in Children.* Brochure. • *A School's Guide for Students with CFS.* • Bibliography. • *CFS and School Success.* Brochure. • *CFS in the Workplace.* Brochure. • *CFS: Thief of Vitality.* Brochure. • *Coping Skills.* Brochure. • *Heart of America News,* quarterly. Newsletter. *Price:* $15/year; $25/year outside the U.S. • *How to be a Phone Contact Packet.* • *How to Start a Support Group Packet.* • *Neuro-Psychological Rehabilitation Techniques.* Brochure. • *Patient Information Packet.* • *Physician Information Packet.* • *Social Security Disability Benefits.* Brochure. • *Understanding the Emotions Surrounding CFS.* Brochure. • Video. Includes educational information. **Formerly:** National Chronic Epstein-Barr Virus Association; (1993) National Chronic Fatigue Syndrome Association.

★ 6733 ★ **National Committee for AIDS Prevention and Control**
Dept. of Health
15 Merchants St.
Valletta, Malta
Phone: 224071
Fax: 223050
Dr. R.G. Xerri, Chm.

Founded: 1986. **Members:** 10. **Languages:** English. **Description:** Makes recommendations for national AIDS policy formulation; advises chief medical officer in Malta.

★ 6734 ★ **National Council on AIDS**
AIDS Task Force
Dept. of Health
PO Box 5013
Wellington, New Zealand
Phone: 4 4962179
Fax: 4 4962342
Peggy Koopman-Boyden, Chm.

Founded: 1988. **Members:** 22. **Languages:** English. **Publications:** *Bulletin of CEA,* semiannual. Bulletin. • *Directory of Members,* periodic. Directory.

★ 6735 ★ **National Foundation for Infectious Diseases (NFID)**
4733 Bethesda Ave., Ste. 750
Bethesda, MD 20814
Phone: (301)656-0003
Fax: (301)907-0878
Richard J. Duma, M.D., Exec. Officer

Founded: 1973. **Members:** 17,000. **State Groups:** 3. **Description:** Receives, maintains, and disburses funds to: support research into the causes and cures of infectious diseases; assists in the education of both professionals and the public in infectious diseases. Conducts programs in prevention of infectious diseases. Offers financial assistance for symposia and workshops related to infectious disease problems. **Publications:** *Double Helix,* bimonthly. Newsletter. Reports on public welfare and support of research, education, and prevention of infectious disease. Monitors legislation. *Price:* Free. • *National Foundation for Infectious Diseases-- Annual Report.* Annual Report. • Proceedings. • *Recognition and Management of Nursing Home Infections.*

★ 6736 ★ **National Leadership Coalition on AIDS (NLCA)**
1730 M St. NW, No. 905
Washington, DC 20036
Phone: (202)429-0930
Fax: (202)872-1977
B. J. Stiles, Pres.

Founded: 1987. **Members:** 180. **Description:** Major corporations; labor, trade, and professional associations; civic, voluntary, religious, gay, and ethnic groups. Provides timely and pertinent information about AIDS to the business and labor community. Works with business and labor sectors on specific AIDS-related projects. Seeks to stimulate private sector involvement in, and suppport for, the fight against AIDS. **Publications:** Annual Report. *Price:* Free. • *Employee Attitudes About AIDS.* Survey. Findings from a national survey; explores working American's opinions about how employees with HIV/AIDS should be treated by colleagues. *Price:* One copy free to members; $25 for nonmembers. • *HIV/AID: A Guide for Employees.* Brochure. *Price:* $2 for members; $4 for nonmembers. • *HIV/AIDS in the Workplace.* Brochure. Provides basic questions and answers for employers on dealing with HIV/AIDS in the general workplace. *Price:* One copy free to members; $1.50 for non-members. • *HIV and AIDS: Understanding the Facts.* Brochure. Provides information about HIV/AIDS transmission and prevention, and working with HIV-infected colleagues. *Price:* One copy free to members; $1.50 for nonmembers. • *Managing Tuberculosis and HIV Infection in Today's General Workplace.* Provides guidance on dealing with questions and concerns aboaut TB, HIV infection, and AIDS in the workplace. *Price:* One copy free to members; $10 for nonmembers. • *Report to Members,* bimonthly. • *Sample Policies.* A compilation of personnel policies developed and currently in use addressing HIV/AIDS in the workplace. *Price:* One copy free to members; $15 for nonmembers. • *Small Business and AIDS.* Brochure. Contains general workplace HIV/AIDS guidelines for employers with 1-100 workers; addresses such issues as productivity, confidentiality, and privacy. *Price:* One copy free to members; $5 for nonmembers. • *Workplace Profiles Project.* Case studies of 13 HIC/AIDS workplace programs from business, labor, and private sector. *Price:* One copy free to members; $20 for nonmembers.

★6737★ **National Minority AIDS Council (NMAC)**
300 Eye St. NE, Ste. 400
Washington, DC 20002
Phone: (202)544-1076
Free: 800-544-0586
Fax: (202)544-0378
Paul A. Kawata, Exec.Dir.

Founded: 1986. **Members:** 480. **Regional Groups:** 2. **State Groups:** 20. **Local Groups:** 160. **Description:** Public health departments and AIDS service organizations. Serves as a clearinghouse of information on AIDS as it affects minority communities in the U.S. Facilitates discussion among national minority organizations about AIDS. Maintains Project Health, Education, and AIDS Leadership, which provides computer usage, strategic planning, financial management, and volunteer program development assistance to AIDS service organizations, and Project Volunteer Information, Technical Assistance, and Leadership, which provides technical assistance in volunteer program development and maintenance. Conducts training conferences. Offers educational and research programs; compiles statistics. Maintains speakers' bureau. **Publications:** *Computer Technical Assistance Manual.* • *Leadership Reprint Series,* quarterly. Includes information on strategies for addressing HIV/AIDS and scientific updates. • *Legislative Update,* bimonthly. • *NMAC HEALer,* bimonthly. Includes updates on projects, community needs, and statistics. • *NMAC Update,* bimonthly. Newsletter. Includes association information and coverage of HIV/AIDS issues. • *Technical Assistance Manual for Volunteer Program Development.* • *Technical Assistance Newsletter,* bimonthly. Newsletter.

★6738★ **National Resource Center on Women and AIDS (NRCWA)**
Center for Women Policy Studies
2000 P St. NW, Ste. 508
Washington, DC 20036
Phone: (202)872-1770
Fax: (202)296-8962
Leslie R. Wolfe, Pres.

Founded: 1987. **Description:** A project of the Center for Women Policy Studies. Provides information to advocates, educators, and policy-makers on issues involving women and AIDS. Focuses on AIDS among women of color and low-income women. Develops policy options through the National Collaboration for AIDS Policy for Women. Maintains speakers' bureau; provides assistance to other organizations working with women and/or AIDS. **Publications:** *Fighting for Our Lives: Women Confronting AIDS.* Video. • *Guide to Resources on Women and AIDS,* annual. Directory. Lists AIDS education programs and local, state, and national AIDS related organizations; includes summaries of federal legislation. • *Policy Papers,* periodic. Papers. Defines a particular issue, summarizes the current state of research and policy development, and makes policy and advocacy recommendations.

★6739★ **National STD / AIDS Control Programme**
Ministry of Health
AIDS Control Programme
PO Box 8
Entebbe, Uganda
Phone: 42 20297
Fax: 42 20608
Dr. Elizabeth Madraa, Pres.

Description: Individuals and organizations in Uganda. Seeks to prevent the spread of HIV/AIDS and sexually transmitted diseases.

★6740★ **Operation Venus (OV)**
1213 Clover St.
Philadelphia, PA 19107
Phone: (215)567-6969
Free: 800-462-4966
Fax: (215)567-6971
Susan Nelson, Ph.D., Dir.

Founded: 1971. **Description:** Volunteers who maintain a toll-free hotline service providing information and referral services concerning venereal diseases for Pennsylvania residents. Calls are handled anonymously, but written information can be sent on request. Maintains speakers' bureau; conducts educational programs in Philadelphia area schools. Organized in January, 1971, by Community Service Corps of Philadelphia, PA.

★6741★ **Organization for Co-Ordination in Control of Endemic Diseases in Central Africa (OCEAC)**
(Organisation de Coordination pour la Lutte Contre les Endemies en Afrique Centrale — OCEAC)
BP 288
Yaounde, Cameroon
Phone: 232232
Fax: 230061
Dr. Daniel Kouka-Bemba, Sec.Gen.

Founded: 1963. **Members:** 6. **Languages:** English, French, Spanish. **Description:** Central Af-

rican countries. Coordinates research programs that examine diseases common to central Africa including cholera, onchocerciasis, trypanosomiasis, schistomiasis, retroviruses, tuberculosis, malaria, and leprosy. Organizes working groups; compiles statistics. Operates Inter-States Higher School in Public Health. **Publications:** *Bulletin de Liaison et Documentation OCEAC,* quarterly. • *EPI-NOTES,* periodic.

Pediatric AIDS Foundation
See: Entry 3280

★6742★ **Polio Society (PS)**
PO Box 106273
Washington, DC 20016
Phone: (301)897-8180
Fax: (202)466-1911
Becky Evans, Contact

Founded: 1984. **Members:** 3,500. **Local Groups:** 3. **Description:** Polio survivors and health care professionals interested in the long-term health of patients who have had the disease. Gathers and disseminates information on post-polio syndrome. (PPS is a condition in which polio survivors suffer unaccustomed fatigue, joint and muscle pain, weakening or loss of muscle function, and respiratory problems.) Acts as liaison between members and medical facilities; maintains outreach program and referral service; sponsors support groups. Advocates on issues of disability and benefits. **Publications:** *Have You Had Polio?.* Booklet. • *Options,* quarterly. Newsletter. Also publishes information packets. **Formerly:** Post-Polio League for Information and Outreach.

★6743★ **Positively Women**
5 Sebastion St.
London EC1V 0HE, England
Phone: 171 4905501
Fax: 171 4901690
Stephanie Elsy, Dir.

Founded: 1987. **Languages:** English. **Description:** Provides counseling and support to women with the HIV virus or AIDs. Maintains a resource facility. **Publications:** Pamphlets, periodic.

★6744★ **Programa Nacional de Lucha Contra el SIDA**
Secretaria de Salud
Avda. 9 Julio 1925, Piso 8deg
1332 Buenos Aires, Argentina
Phone: 1 3837981
Fax: 1 3837981
Laura Astarloa, Dir.

Founded: 1991. **Members:** 6. **Description:** Organizations and individuals concerned with the prevention of AIDS in Argentina. Conducts educational and counseling programs. **Publications:** Newsletter, quarterly. Contains statistical information. **Formerly:** Comite Nacionale du Lutte Contre le SIDA.

★6745★ **Project Inform (PI)**
1965 Market St. Ste. 220
San Francisco, CA 94103
Phone: (415)558-8669
Free: 800-822-7422
Fax: (415)558-0684
Martin Delaney, Founding Dir.
Founded: 1985. **Members:** 60,000. **Description:** Information clearinghouse and hot line providing updated information on drug treatments for persons with AIDS or the Human Immunodeficiency Virus. Also provides information on organizations through which the drug treatments can be obtained. Works to speed up research process and focus on promising new treatments. Maintains speakers' bureau. **Publications:** *PI Perspective*, quarterly. Journal. Contains treatment information and focuses on advocacy issues. Also publishes information packet and fact sheets on treatments and standards of care.

★6746★ **Remdios AIDS Foundation**
1066 Remedios St.
Malate
Manila 1004, Philippines
Phone: 2 500924
Fax: 2 5223431
Pia Arboleda, Exec.Dir.
Founded: 1991. **Members:** 50. **Languages:** English, Tagalog. **Description:** Individuals seeking to prevent the spread of HIV and reduce the personal and social impact of AIDS. Works to: increase awareness of at-risk communities; improve access to medical care for people with HIV and AIDS; influence public policy regarding AIDS-related issues. Maintains training center for people wishing to work with people with HIV and AIDS; makes available counseling and other support services including HIV antibody testing. **Publications:** *Remedios Newsletter*, quarterly. Newsletter.

★6747★ **Romanian Anti-AIDS Association**
Str. Radu Cristian 6, Sector 2
Bucharest, Romania
Phone: 1 3112078
Fax: 1 3112068
Languages: Romanian. **Description:** Works to stop the spread of AIDS in Romania. Promotes an improved quality of life for people with AIDS; supports medical and pharmaceutical research programs.

★6748★ **Royal Society of Tropical Medicine and Hygiene (RSTMH)**
Manson House
26 Portland Pl.
London W1N 4EY, England
Phone: 171 5802127
Fax: 171 4361389
C.R. Guest, Contact
Founded: 1907. **Members:** 3,000. **Languages:** English. **Description:** Medical and veterinary practititioners, scientists, and interested others representing 88 countries. Promotes health and seeks to advance the study, control, and prevention of tropical diseases in humans and animals. Encourages information exchange and facilitates discussion. **Publications:** *Transactions of the Royal Society of Tropical Medicine and*

Hygiene, bimonthly. Journal. • *Yearbook of the Royal Society of Tropical Medicine and Hygiene*.

Ryan White National Teen Education Program (RWNTEP)
See: Entry 3285

★6749★ **San Francisco AIDS Foundation (SFAF)**
PO Box 426182
San Francisco, CA 94142-6182
Phone: (415)864-5855
Fax: (415)487-3097
Pat Christen, Exec.Dir.
Founded: 1982. **Description:** Regional organization whose goals are to educate the public on the prevention of AIDS and to make various social service programs accessible to people with AIDS. Provides community forums; develops and distributes educational materials. Provides assistance to people with AIDS in obtaining emergency housing, social security and veterans' benefits, medical and insurance benefits, and legal referral services. Works with legislators, corporations, public health coalitions, activists, and the media to advance public health policy and improve media coverage. Maintains speakers' bureau. **Publications:** *Advance*, monthly. Bulletin. Features current public education campaigns, public policy issues, foundation activities, and special events. *Price:* Free. • *AIDS Educator*, semiannual. Catalog. Lists educational material regarding AIDS. *Price:* Free. • Booklets. • Brochures. • *Bulletin of Experimental Treatments for AIDS*, quarterly. Bulletin. Covers AIDS-related diseases, research, care, treatment, and clinical trials. *Price:* $55 for individuals; $125 for institutions. • *Impetus*, quarterly. Newsletter. For donors and other supporters of the foundation. *Price:* Free to donors. • *Positive News*, 3/year. *Price:* Free. • Videos. Also distributes AIDS educational materials. **Formerly:** AIDS/Kaposi's Sarcoma Research and Education Foundation.

★6750★ **Shanti Project (SP)**
1546 Market St.
San Francisco, CA 94102-6007
Phone: (415)777-CARE
Fax: (415)777-5152
Gloria J. Sandoval, Exec.Dir.
Founded: 1975. **Regional Groups:** 1. **Description:** Volunteer counseling service offering ongoing support to individuals who face a diagnosis of acquired immune deficiency syndrome (AIDS) and their loved ones in the San Francisco, CA, area. Shanti is a Sanskrit word meaning "inner peace." Provides support groups, peer counseling, and practical assistance, including van service, to people with AIDS. Conducts psychosocial training programs for health care professionals, clergy, and laypeople. Serves as a model program for similar services nationwide. Maintains speakers' bureau. **Publications:** *Activities Program Update*, monthly. • *Eclipse*, quarterly. Newsletter. • *Heartspace*, monthly. Newsletter.

Society for Prevention of Infertility (SPI)
See: Entry 11252

★6751★ **Teens Teaching AIDS Prevention (TEENS TAP)**
3030 Walnut
Kansas City, MO 64108
Phone: (816)561-8784
Free: 800-234-8336
Fax: (816)531-7199
Gwena Scott-Johnson, Proj.Coord.
Founded: 1987. **Members:** 60. **Description:** Sponsored by the Good Samaritan Project. Provides teenagers with information on AIDS through peer counseling. Also provides information to interested adults. Maintains speakers' bureau for schools and youth groups. Provides companions for children and teens with AIDS and their families. Makes available training and technical guidance to groups interested in organizing teen peer education programs. **Publications:** Brochures. • Manuals.

★6752★ **Treatment Action Group (TAG)**
147 2nd Ave., Ste. 601
New York, NY 10003
Phone: (212)260-0300
Fax: (212)260-8561
Peter Staley, Founding Dir.
Founded: 1992. **Members:** 50. **Description:** Individuals who are HIV positive and individuals interested in AIDS treatment research. Promotes AIDS research. Conducts educational programs. **Publications:** *Tagline*, monthly. Newsletter. Features AIDS research and policy. *Price:* $30/year.

★6753★ **Tuvalu National AIDS Committee (TUNAC)**
PO Box 14
Funafuti, Tuvalu
Phone: 746
Description: Conducts HIV and AIDS awareness and educational activities.

★6754★ **Ugandan AIDS Project**
898 N. Fair Oaks Ave., Ste. A
Pasadena, CA 91103
Phone: (818)795-7990
Fax: (818)795-7897
Languages: English. **Description:** Anglican congregations united to eradicate AIDS and ease the suffering of people with the disease in Uganda. Promotes and supports AIDS research; makes available volunteer support and medical equipment and supplies to AIDS treatment and prevention programs; supports children orphaned by AIDS. Conducts field trips. Operates the Save Youth from AIDS Program and Ugandan AIDS Project Medical Initiative.

★6755★ **United Federation of CFS / CFIDS / CEBV Organizations**
114 Sand Ln. NW
Cedar Rapids, IA 52405-3114
Larry A. Sakin, Admin.
Founded: 1989. **Members:** 30. **Description:** Organizations representing over 50,000 patients with Chronic Fatigue Syndrome, Chronic Fatigue Immune Dysfunction Syndrome, or Chronic Epstein-Barr Virus Syndrome. Seeks to educate patients, their families, and the medical community about the debilitating effects of such illnesses. Provides referral service; maintains

speakers' bureau. **Publications:** Annual Report, annual. **Formerly:** (1993) United CFS/CFIDS/CEBV Federation.

★6756★ Women Organized to Respond to Life-Threatening Diseases (WORLD)
3948 Webster St.
Oakland, CA 94609
Phone: (510)658-6930
Fax: (510)601-9746
Rebecca Denison, Exec.Dir.

Founded: 1991. **Description:** An empowerment organization by and for women infected or affected by the HIV virus. Offers support and information to women who have AIDS and HIV. Acts as a clearinghouse for information about women and AIDS. **Publications:** *Mujer*, quarterly. • *WORLD*, monthly. Newsletter. **Also Known As:** WORLD.

★6757★ World Association on Sarcoidosis and Other Granulomatous Disorders (WASOG)
149 Harley St.
London W1N 1HG, England
Phone: 171 9354444
D. Geraint James, M.D.

Founded: 1958. **Members:** 300. **Languages:** English. **Description:** Physicians in 40 countries. Promotes and sponsors research and clinical activities on sarcoidosis concerning damage to the brain, eyes, heart, lungs, and skin. (Sarcoidosis is characterized by inflammation of the lungs, eyes, skin, and other tissue and results in immunological upset; its cause is unknown.) Maintains speakers' bureau and hall of fame. Organizes seminars and workshops. **Publications:** *Sarcoidosis*, semiannual. • *Transactions of the World Congress on Sarcoidosis*, biennial. **Formerly:** (1987) International Committee of Sarcoidosis.

World Association of Veterinary Microbiologists, Immunologists, and Specialists in Infectious Diseases (WAVMI)
(Association Mondiale des Veterinaires Microbiologistes, Immunologistes et Specialistes des Maladies Infectieuses — AMVMI)
See: Entry 13120

★6758★ World Federation for Culture Collections (WFCC)
Dept. of Microbiology
University of Queensland
St. Lucia
Brisbane, QLD 4067, Australia
Phone: 7 3773694
Fax: 7 3715896
Lindsay Sly, Pres.

Founded: 1970. **Members:** 200. **Description:** A federation of the International Union of Microbiological Societies and a multidisciplinary commission of the International Union of Biological Sciences . Microbiologists in 55 countries working in research, education, and industry. Encourages the study of procedures for the isolation, culture, characterization, conservation, and distribution of microorganisms. Works to establish an effective network of individuals and institutions possessing collections of microorganism

cultures and cell lines and to facilitate communication between collection owners and users. Seeks to: create a global network of information services charged with compiling and disseminating data on cultures; address practical questions such as the impact of postal regulations, quarantine rules, patent laws, and public health concerns on culture distribution. Conducts training courses in culture isolation, description, and conservation; offers individual training; sponsors periodic workshops. Operates speakers' bureau; bestows awards. **Publications:** *WFCC Newsletter*, biennial. Newsletter. • *World Directory of Collections of Microorganisms*, periodic. Directory. Also publishes *Living Resources for Biotechnology* and other resources.

★6759★ World Hemophilia AIDS Center (WHAC)
10 Congress St., Ste. 340
Pasadena, CA 91105
Phone: (818)577-4366
Fax: (818)796-2875
Dr. Shelby Dietrich, Admin.

Founded: 1983. **Description:** Established by the World Federation of Hemophilia, WHAC serves as an information clearinghouse and international surveillance center for acquired immune deficiency syndrome or potential cases of AIDS in hemophiliacs. Collects data on AIDS; conducts surveys to determine incidence of the syndrome. Plans to distribute information about AIDS to individuals and organizations. **Publications:** *Hemophilia World*, 3-4/year. Contains technical articles on AIDS and hemophilia and their treatment. *Price:* Free.

Research Centers

★6760★ Aaron Diamond Aids Research Center
455 1st Ave., 7th Fl.
New York, NY 10016
Phone: (212)725-0018
Fax: (212)725-1126
David D. Ho, M.D., Dir.

Research Activities and Fields: Pathogenesis of HIV-1 in vivo, maternal-fetal transmission of HIV-1, antibody responses to HIV and vaccine development, mechanism of HIV entry into CD4+ and CD4- cells, anti-HIV therapeutics and viral resistance, search for the causative agent of HIV-negative cases of immunodeficiency, cellular immune responses to HIV-1 in the pathogenesis of AIDS, cellular immune responses to HIV-1 in vaccine development, development of the scid mouse model for HIV studies, receptors for human retroviruses (HIV and HTLV), assembly of HIV virion, function of accessory genes of HIV, interaction of HIV envelope with the cellular receptor, mechanism of viral entry, and mapping of the functional determinants of HIV envelope glycoprotein.

★6761★ American Academy of Tropical Medicine and Surgery
16126 E. Warren
PO Box 24224
Detroit, MI 48224-0224
Phone: (313)882-0641
Fax: (313)882-5110
Dr. Ben Allie, Chm.

Research Activities and Fields: Tropical diseases, including diarrhea and ankle edema, and evaluation of disease spectrum. **Publications:** *Journal of the American Academy of Tropical Medicine and Surgery.*

★6762★ Baylor College of Medicine Acute Viral Respiratory Disease Unit
1 Baylor Plaza
Houston, TX 77030
Phone: (713)798-4474
Fax: (713)798-7375
Robert B. Couch, M.D., Dir.

Research Activities and Fields: Multidisciplinary studies of acute viral respiratory diseases in humans, including epidemiologic, virologic, and immunologic studies and vaccine and antiviral evaluations. **Publications:** *Acute Respiratory Disease Update* (bimonthly). **Formerly:** Influenza Research Center (1990).

★6763★ Biomedical Research Institute
12111 Parklawn Dr.
Rockville, MD 20852
Phone: (301)881-3300
Fax: (301)881-7640
Dr. James L. Leef, Dir.

Research Activities and Fields: Conducts research on malaria and schistosomiasis, prepares purified polysaccharides from bacteria for use in immunological studies, manages a low temperature repository, and performs large scale freeze-drying.

★6764★ California Collaborative Treatment Group
Univ. of California, San Diego
2760 5th Ave., Ste. 300
San Diego, CA 92103-6329
Phone: (619)543-8080
Fax: (619)298-0177
Jeanne Niosi, Administrative Analyst

Research Activities and Fields: Develops treatment protocols and drug therapies and recruits research volunteers for AIDS studies. Research focuses on opportunistic HIV infections such as cytomegalovirus, mycobacterium avium complex, cryptococcal meningitis, pneumocystis carinii pneumonia, Kaposi's sarcoma, neurosyphilis, and toxoplasmosis.

★6765★ City of Hope National Medical Center
National Cooperative Drug Discovery Group for the Treatment of AIDS
Virology & Infectious Diseases/Dept. of Pediatrics
1500 E. Duarte Rd.
Duarte, CA 91010
Phone: (818)359-8111
Fax: (818)301-8458
John A. Zaia, Prin. Investigator

Research Activities and Fields: Developmental therapeutics in the treatment of AIDS, including development and delivery of antiviral DNA and RNA; and pathogenesis and treatment of cytomegalovirus infection; and development of gene therapy for cancer and AIDS.

★ 6766 ★ Columbia University Developmental Disabilities Center
St. Lukes-Roosevelt Hospital Center
428 W. 59th St.
New York, NY 10019
Phone: (212)523-6280
Fax: (212)523-6487
Madeline Appell, Dir.

Research Activities and Fields: Rubella (German measles), including characterization of natural history of rubella and development of methods of management for children with congenital rubella. Develops and evaluates new laboratory techniques, vaccines, and sera for prevention and control of rubella. **Formerly:** Rubella Project.

★ 6767 ★ Comprehensive AIDS Center
Northwestern Univ. Med. School
680 N. Lake Shore Dr., Ste. 1106
Chicago, IL 60611
Phone: (312)908-7866
Fax: (312)908-5820
Dr. John Phair, Dir.

Research Activities and Fields: Acquired immune deficiency syndrome in adults, molecular virology of human immunodeficiency virus (HIV), and experimental therapy of HIV.

★ 6768 ★ Dana-Farber Cancer Institute National Cooperative Drug Discovery Group for the Treatment of AIDS
Dept. of Human Retrovirology
44 Binney St.
Boston, MA 02115
Phone: (617)632-3371
Fax: (617)632-3113
Dr. Joseph Sodroski, Prin. Investigator

Research Activities and Fields: Screening and drug design for HIV-1 and human t-cell lymphotropic virus type three (HTLV-III) therapeutics, and research on genetic therapy for AIDS treatment and HIV-1 integration.

Family Health International
See: Entry 11267

★ 6769 ★ Franciscan Shared Laboratory, Inc.
11020 W. Plank Ct., Ste. 100
Wauwatosa, WI 53226
Phone: (414)476-3400
Dr. W. Hollister, Med.Dir.

Research Activities and Fields: Diagnostic and molecular virology, coagulation, molecular biology, and medical informatics.

★ 6770 ★ George Washington University Center for Virology, Immunology and Infectious Disease Research
Children's National Medical Ctr.
111 Michigan Ave. NW
Washington, DC 20010
Phone: (202)884-3981
Fax: (202)884-3985
Dr. Christie A. Holland, Dir.

Research Activities and Fields: Virologic and immunologic problems relating to infectious diseases and vaccine development.

★ 6771 ★ George Washington University National Cooperative Drug Discovery Group for the Treatment of AIDS
Dept. of Pharmacology
2300 Eye St. NW
Washington, DC 20037-2313
Phone: (202)994-2706
Fax: (202)994-2870
Prof. Ti Li Loo, Research Professor of Pharmacology

Research Activities and Fields: Pharmacologic disposition of potential anti-AIDS agents. Also studies natural products and synthetic anti-AIDS agents.

★ 6772 ★ Human Immunodeficiency Virus Center for Clinical and Behavioral Studies
New York State Psychiatric Institute
722 W. 168th St.
New York, NY 10032
Phone: (212)960-2432
Fax: (212)740-1774
Anke A. Ehrhardt, Ph.D., Dir. and Prin. Invt.

Research Activities and Fields: Investigates high risk sexual behaviors leading to HIV infection among heterosexual adults (especially women), adolescents, and gay men. Studies include prevention among depressed adolescent girls and gay and lesbian adolescents, development of interventions aimed at heterosexual women and men, serodiscordant male couples, and homeless mentally ill men and women. Methods development and quality assurance proceed in the domains of psychosocial and qualitative assessment, psychosexual assessment, biostatistics, data management, and epidemiology. Conducts programs in community liaison, media-based interventions and education, and ethical, legal, and policy issues. **Publications:** Bibliography. **E-mail Address:** paw6@columbia.edu.

★ 6773 ★ James N. Gamble Institute of Medical Research
2141 Auburn Ave.
Cincinnati, OH 45219
Phone: (513)369-2582
Fax: (513)241-3899
Gilbert M. Schiff, M.D., Pres.

Research Activities and Fields: Virology and immunology, including studies on rubella and rubella vaccines, anti-influenza agents, basic virology of influenza, herpes virus latency, role of complement in sickle cell disease and burn wounds, and basic and clinical studies on rotaviruses, hepatitis, and human immunodeficiency virus. **Formerly:** Christ Hospital Institute of Medical Research (1984).

★ 6774 ★ Johns Hopkins University Center for Immunization Research
School of Hygiene & Public Health
Hampton House, 125
624 N. Broadway
Baltimore, MD 21205
Phone: (410)955-4376
Fax: (410)550-6898
Dr. Mary Lou Clements, Dir.

Research Activities and Fields: Influenza, parainfluenza, respiratory syncytial virus, AIDS, and rotavirus vaccines, hepatitis B, immunoglobulins, and antiviral drug efficacy studies. Uses volunteers 18 years of age or older for vaccine studies and children from the ages of 1 month to 48 months for pediatric vaccine studies.

Kuzell Institute for Arthritis and Infectious Diseases
See: Entry 7921

★ 6775 ★ Laval University Medical Research Centre Infection Research Group
2705, boulevard Laurier
Ste. Foy, PQ, Canada G1V 4G2
Phone: (418)654-2705
Fax: (418)654-2715
Michel G. Bergeron, Dir.

Research Activities and Fields: Group seeks to understand the molecular basis of action of antimicrobial agents and the mechanisms involved in the microbial resistance against these agents. Group also develops new transportation vehicles of antimicrobials in bacteria, parasites, and viruses; works on metabolic particularities of parasites; develops new diagnostic kits for quick detection of bacterial and viral infections; and works on new vaccines. Group also studies AIDS, treatments for HIV-infected patients, and the immunological, pharmacodynamic, and psychosocial factors controlling HIV infections.

★ 6776 ★ McGill University Centre for the Study of Host Resistance
Montreal General Hospital
1650 Cedar Ave., Rm. B.7118
Montreal, PQ, Canada H3G 1A4
Phone: (514)934-8038
Fax: (514)933-7146
Dr. Emil Skamene, Dir.

Research Activities and Fields: Genetic regulation of host susceptibility and resistance in diseases of adulthood, including cancer, tuberculosis, malaria, and other infectious diseases. **E-mail Address:** md88@musica.mcgill.ca.

★ 6777 ★ McGill University McGill AIDS Center
3755, chemin Cote Ste-Catherine
Institut Lady Davis, Bureau 318
Montreal, PQ, Canada H3T 1E2
Phone: (514)340-7536
Fax: (514)340-7537
Dr. Mark A. Wainberg, Dir.

Research Activities and Fields: Promotes research on all aspects of HIV/AIDS, the development of new drugs, treatments, and vaccines for HIV/AIDS, as well as the development of comprehensive cost-effective models of care and treatment for HIV infection and AIDS. Sponsors basic, clinical, epidemiological, preventive, and psychosocial studies of HIV/AIDS. Topics include residential drug abuse treatment models for AIDS prevention, immune response in AIDS, regulation of interferon gene expression, HIV-1 resistance to AZT and other drugs, Canadian women and HIV, HIV prevention through peer intervention among youth, assessment of social support for patients with HIV/AIDS, knowledge of HIV/AIDS among daycare workers and parents, and personal strivings and levels of self-determination in predicting adjustments in AIDS. **Publications:** Monthly Newsletter.

★6778★ **Meharry Medical College**
Center on Tropical Diseases
Div. of Biomedical Sciences
1005 D.B. Todd Blvd.
Nashville, TN 37208
Phone: (615)327-6193
Fax: (615)321-2999
Dr. George C. Hill, Dir.

Research Activities and Fields: Molecular, biochemical, and immunological aspects of tropical disease. Specific research includes studies on African trypanosomiasis, Chagas' disease, schistosomiasis, malaria, and leprosy. **Publications:** *Tropical Diseases Newsletter.* **E-mail Address:** HILLGC@VUCTRVAX (BIT-NET).

★6779★ **National Cooperative Drug**
Discovery Group for the Treatment of
AIDS
VA Medical Center
Medical Research 151E
1670 Clairmont Rd.
Decatur, GA 30033
Phone: (404)728-7711
Fax: (404)728-7726
Dr. Raymond F. Schinazi, Prin. Investigator

Research Activities and Fields: Developmental therapeutics in the treatment of AIDS, HIV, Hepatitis B virus, and Cryptosporidium.

★6780★ **Northwestern University**
Samuel Jefferson Sackett Research
Laboratory
303 E. Chicago Ave.
Chicago, IL 60611
Phone: (312)649-8196
Prof. John P. Phair, Dir.

Research Activities and Fields: Basic and clinical studies of cellular and humoral resistance to infection, viral central nervous system infections, pharmacology of antimicrobial agents, investigation of infectious diarrhea, and natural history of infectious diseases.

★6781★ **Ohio State University**
Infectious Diseases Research Laboratories
410 W. 10th Ave.
Columbus, OH 43210
Phone: (614)293-8732
Fax: (614)293-4556
Dr. Robert J. Fass, Dir.

Research Activities and Fields: Pathogenesis, prophylaxis, therapy, pathology, serology of infectious diseases (including Legionnaire's disease, herpes infections, acquired immune deficiency syndrome, and other opportunistic infec-

tions), and extensive in vitro and clinical evaluations of antimicrobial agents. **Formerly:** Infectious Disease Laboratories.

★6782★ **Oklahoma State University**
Center for Host-Arthropod-Pathogen
Studies
127 Noble Research Ctr.
Stillwater, OK 74078-0464
Phone: (405)744-5527
Fax: (405)744-6954
Dr. Stephen Wikel, Dir.

Research Activities and Fields: Blood-feeding anthropods, the diseases they transmit, and interactions with their hosts in the areas of biochemistry, immunology, microbiolgy, molecular biology, and physiology. **Formerly:** Center for Biotechnology Research.

★6783★ **Purdue University**
Center for AIDS Research
School of Pharmacy
Robert E. Heine Bldg.
West Lafayette, IN 47907
Phone: (317)494-5867
Fax: (317)494-6790
Stephen R. Byrn, Dir.

Research Activities and Fields: AIDS-therapy drug development.

Revici Foundation for Lipid Research
See: Entry 12747

★6784★ **Rockefeller University**
Laboratory of Bacteriology and
Immunology
1230 York Ave.
New York, NY 10021-6399
Phone: (212)327-8000
Fax: (212)327-7974
Emil C. Gotschlich, Head

Research Activities and Fields: Investigates the parastic mechanisms used by pathogenic bacteria, especially streptococci and neisseria. Also studies the derangements of the human immune system which lead to chronic diseases such as rheumatic fever and glomerulonephritis as a result of infection with streptococci.

★6785★ **Rockefeller University**
Laboratory of Cell Physiology and Virology
1230 York Ave.
New York, NY 10021-6399
Phone: (212)327-8353
Igor Tamm, Head

Research Activities and Fields: Identification and action of cellular regulatory molecules that act on the processes of cell proliferation, differentiation, motility, and death, including studies on cell growth factors and interleukin-6. Studies of the signal transduction mechanisms to understand cytokine networks. **Formerly:** Laboratory of Virology.

★6786★ **Rutgers University**
AIDS Research Group
Institute for Health
30 College Ave.
New Brunswick, NJ 08903
Phone: (908)932-8413
Fax: (908)932-6872
Stephen Crystal, Ph.D., Dir.

Research Activities and Fields: Social and behavioral research on AIDS, focusing on policy issues and applying social science methodology to the planning and evaluation of programs and policies designed to meet public health objectives. Specific areas of research include HIV health services, long-term care, social networks, mental health programs, the social context of health-related behavior in Hispanic and black subcultures, health cognition and health belief systems, legal aspects of serving endangered and high-risk populations, and cost of care and services utilization studies. **E-mail Address:** crystal@zodiac.rutgers.edu.

St. Louis University
Institute for Molecular Virology
See: Entry 2617

★6787★ **Seattle Biomedical Research**
Institute
4 Nickerson St.
Seattle, WA 98109-1651
Phone: (206)284-8846
Fax: (206)284-0313
Dr. Kenneth D. Stuart, Dir.

Research Activities and Fields: Parasitology, including immunology of host-parasite relationships, control of parasite gene expression, and development of means for preventing, diagnosing, and treating disease. Specific projects include molecular biology of parasites, immunology of protozoan parasites, organelle biogenesis of parasites, purine biosynthesis, mitochondrial genes of malarial parasites, immunology of antibody cells, and surface antigens of hematopoietic cells.

★6788★ **Sherbrooke University**
Actinomycete Biology Research Group
Department de biologie
Faculte des sciences
Sherbrooke, PQ, Canada J1K 2R1
Phone: (819)821-7070
Fax: (819)821-8049
Ryszard Brzezinski, Dir.

Research Activities and Fields: Molecular biology and genetic engineering of actinomycetes, gene cloning and characterization, development of new cloning vectors, and genetic regulation in bacteriophages of the genera

★6789★ **Spellman Center for HIV-Related**
Disease
St. Clare's Hospital and Health Center
415 W. 51st St.
New York, NY 10019
Phone: (212)459-8409
Fax: (212)459-8489
Dr. Victoria Sharp, Dir.

Research Activities and Fields: Clinical drug trials, including immune modulators, anti-retrovirals, prophylactic therapies for infections,

DDI, and granulocyte-macrophage colony-stimulating activity factors. **E-mail Address:** sharp.victoria@karloff.fstrf.org.

★ 6790 ★ **Stanford University**
Center for AIDS Research
Div. of Infectious Diseases
Rm. S-156
Stanford, CA 94305
Phone: (415)723-6231
Fax: (415)725-2395
Dr. Thomas Merigan, Dir.

Research Activities and Fields: Antiviral drug studies, including inhibitors of HIV, HBV, and herpes replication using in vitro and in vivo antiviral models.

★ 6791 ★ **State University of New York at**
Buffalo
National Cooperative Drug Discovery
Group for the Treatment of AIDS
Dept. of Biochemistry
304 Foster Hall
3435 Main St.
Buffalo, NY 14214
Phone: (716)829-3259
Fax: (716)831-3001
Dr. David M. Rekosh, Prin. Investigator

Research Activities and Fields: Structure and function of the human immunodeficiency virus (HIV) envelope and gag proteins; HIV gene regulation.

★ 6792 ★ **State University of New York**
Health Science Center at Stony Brook
SUNY Stony Brook AIDS Treatment and
Development Center
School of Medicine, Div. of Infectious
Diseases
T-15, 080
Stony Brook, NY 11794-8153
Phone: (516)444-1660
Fax: (516)444-7518
Dr. Roy T. Steigbigel, Dir.

Research Activities and Fields: Human immunodeficiency virus (HIV) research, focusing on pathogenesis, mechanism of replication, and development of inhibitors. **E-mail Address:** rsteigbigel@ccmail.sunysb.edu. **Formerly:** SUNY Stony Brook Drug Discovery Group.

U.S. Department of Defense
Armed Forces Institute of Pathology
Infectious and Parasitic Disease Pathology
Department
AIDS Pathology Division
See: Entry 10168

U.S. Department of Defense
Armed Forces Institute of Pathology
Infectious and Parasitic Disease Pathology
Department
Geographic Pathology Division
See: Entry 10169

U.S. Department of Defense
Army Medical Research and Development
Command
Army Medical Research Institute of
Infectious Diseases
See: Entry 7821

U.S. Department of Defense
Naval Medical Research and Development
Command
Naval Medical Research Institute
Infectious Diseases Department
See: Entry 7850

★ 6793 ★ **U.S. Department of Health and**
Human Services
Health Resources and Services
Administration
Gillis W. Long Hansen's Disease Center
Carville, LA 70721
Phone: (504)642-4740
Fax: (504)642-4728
Robert R. Jacobson, M.D., Ph. D., Director

Research Activities and Fields: Multidisciplinary center for the care and rehabilitation of patients with Hansen's disease (leprosy) and for basic and applied research related to all aspects of the disease. In addition, Center provides a training facility for professionals and paraprofessionals involved with the diagnosis and treatment of Hansen's disease, both within the United States and abroad. Areas of research interest include studies of the causative organism of leprosy and its effect on the body as well as research in methods of clinical treatment and rehabilitation; mycobacterioses other than tuberculosis; and other allied or related tropical and/or infectious diseases. Accomplishments have included the infection of an armadillo with the leprosy organism, the first experimental animal to be found naturally susceptible to the disseminated form of this disease, and earlier, the discovery of sulfone therapy, the first effective treatment for the disease.

★ 6794 ★ **U.S. Department of Health and**
Human Services
National Center for Infectious Diseases
1600 Clifton Rd., N.E.
Atlanta, GA 30333
Phone: (404)639-3401
James M Hughes, M.D., Director

Research Activities and Fields: The Center for Infectious Diseases coordinates a national program to improve the identification, investigation, diagnosis, prevention, and control of infectious diseases. Principal Center components include: 1) AIDS (Acquired Immunodeficiency Syndrome) Program; 2) Arctic Investigations Program; 3) Bacterial Diseases Division; 4) Hospital Infections Program; 5) Division of HIV/AIDS; 6) Mycotic Diseases Division; 7) Division of Parisitic Diseases; 8) Sexually Transmitted Diseases Laboratory Program; 9) Vector-Borne Diseases Division; and 10) Division of Viral and Rickettsial Diseases.

★ 6795 ★ **U.S. Department of Health and**
Human Services
National Center for Infectious Diseases
Arctic Investigations Program
225 Eagle St.
Anchorage, AK 99501
Phone: (907)271-4011
Fax: (907)271-4174
Dr. Robert Wainewright, Director

Research Activities and Fields: Mission of the Arctic Investigations Program is to improve the quality of life of people living in the arctic and subarctic through: 1) investigation of the causes of infectious diseases; 2) evaluation of methods for disease prevention and control; 3) dissemination of information; 4) provision of epidemiologic, statistical, and laboratory consultation and technical assistance; and 5) assistance in training of personnel to perform studies of conditions that impact health. Activities focus on studies of conditions which occur at high incidence, are unique to, or may be of potential benefit to populations in (and outside of) the arctic and subarctic. Emphasis is on acute infectious diseases, but investigations are also conducted on select chronic diseases which are sequelae of infectious diseases and/or in which an infectious disease is suspected to play a role. Specific areas of interest include: Hepatitis B, streptococcus pneumonia, Haemophilus influenzae b, botulism, Echinococcus multilocularis, and human papilloma virus.

★ 6796 ★ **U.S. Department of Health and**
Human Services
National Center for Infectious Diseases
Division of Bacterial and Mycotic Diseases
Childhood and Respiratory Diseases
Branch
Mail Stop D39
1600 Clifton Rd., NE
Atlanta, GA 30333
Phone: (404)639-2215
Fax: (404)639-3970
Dr. Mitch Cohen, Director

Research Activities and Fields: Branch conducts laboratory and epidemiologic investigations of organisms (except enteric and sexually transmitted diseases). Principal subjects of study are: H influenzae, type B; N. meningititis; Group A streptococcus; Group B streptococcus; Brazilian purpuric fever, sipneumoniae, legionella infections, Chlamydia and mycoplasma infections, and otitis media.

★ 6797 ★ **U.S. Department of Health and**
Human Services
National Center for Infectious Diseases
Division of HIV / AIDS
1600 Clifton Rd., N.E.
Mail Stop E49
Atlanta, GA 30333
Phone: (404)639-2076
Fax: (404)639-2029
Harold Jaffe, Director

Research Activities and Fields: Conducts epidemiologic and laboratory investigations, surveillance, and studies to determine risk factors, transmission patterns, prevalence/incidence of HIV/AIDS, and case reporting for acquired immunodeficiency syndrome. Program also develops and evaluates laboratory methods and procedures for the isolation and characterization of human immunodeficiency virus (HIV) and serodiagnosis and understanding of viral pathogenesis. Principal component units are: Office of the Director, Epidemiology Branch, Laboratory Investigations Branch, Statistics and Data Management Branch, HIV Seroepidemiology Branch, Field Services Branch, Technical Information Activity, International Activity, Surveillance Branch, Hematologic Diseases Branch, and Immunology Branch.

★6798★ U.S. Department of Health and Human Services
National Center for Infectious Diseases
Division of HIV / AIDS
Immunology Branch
1600 Clifton Rd., N.E., Rm. 1354
Atlanta, GA 30333
Phone: (404)639-3434
Fax: (404)639-2108
Dr. J. Steven McDougal, Chief

Research Activities and Fields: Principal areas of research interest are immunology and Acquired Immunodeficiency Syndrome (AIDS).

★6799★ U.S. Department of Health and Human Services
National Center for Infectious Diseases
Division of Parasitic Diseases
4770 Buford Hwy.
MS F22
Atlanta, GA 30341-3742
Phone: (404)639-3311
Fax: (404)488-4532
Dr. Thomas Navin, Director

Research Activities and Fields: Division conducts surveillance, field, and laboratory investigations of parasitic diseases to define disease etiology, mode of transmission, and populations at risk; and to develop effective methods for diagnosis, prevention, and control. Activities involve: 1) conducting research to develop, evaluate, and improve laboratory methodologies and therapeutic practices used for rapid diagnosis and treatment of parasitic diseases; 2) providing epidemic aid, consultation, and reference/diagnostic services upon request from state and local health departments, other federal agencies, and national and international health organizations; and 3) participating in intramural and extramural training in prevention and control of parasitic diseases. Principal areas of research interest are: biology, ecology, host-parasite relationships, and control of vectors of arthropod-borne parasitic diseases, including studies of pesticides for vector control; laboratory studies of selected parasitic infections, emphasizing in vivo and in vitro model systems for the study of host-parasite relationships, chemotherapy, and immunology; and development and evaluation of immunizing agents against malaria. Division comprises the Malaria Branch and Parasitic Diseases Branch. **Additional Contact Information:** Division is located at 4770 Buford Hwy., Chamblee, GA 30341.

★6800★ U.S. Department of Health and Human Services
National Center for Infectious Diseases
Division of Parasitic Diseases
Malaria Branch
1600 Clifton Rd., N.E.
Atlanta, GA 30333
Phone: (404)488-4046
Fax: (404)488-4427
Carlos C. Campbell, M.D., Director

Research Activities and Fields: The Malaria Branch conducts surveillance, investigations, and laboratory studies on malaria to define disease etiology, transmission dynamics, populations at risk, host-parasite relationships, effective chemotherapy, and appropriate immunologic techniques. Branch provides clinical advice and epidemiologic assistance on the prevention and control of malaria contracted in the United States and in malaria-endemic areas. Branch also serves as a World Health Organization (WHO) Collaborating Center for Host Parasite Relations in malaria. Activities involve promoting rapid and effective therapy and prevention of malaria infections in the United States and epidemic countries by compiling and disseminating information on diagnostic procedures, geographic variations, malaria incidence, drug sensitivity, and therapeutic and preventive strategies. Emphasis is on monitoring the risk of toxic side effects of antimalarial drugs used for prophylaxis in order to better understand the risks and benefits of chemoprophylaxis. **Additional Contact Information:** Branch is located in Bldg. 23, 4770 Buford Hwy., Chamblee, GA 30341.

★6801★ U.S. Department of Health and Human Services
National Center for Infectious Diseases
Division of Parasitic Diseases
Parasitic Diseases Branch
1600 Clifton Rd., N.E.
Atlanta, GA 30333
Phone: (404)488-4050
Fax: (404)488-4108
Victor C.W. Tsang, Ph.D., Chief

Research Activities and Fields: Branch conducts surveillance, outbreak investigations, epidemiologic studies, and laboratory studies on parasitic diseases to define etiology, transmission dynamics, populations at risk, host-parasite relationships, chemotherapy, immunology, and molecular biology. Branch provides laboratory, clinical, and epidemiologic assistance in the prevention and control of parasitic diseases; conducts a reference diagnostic service for parasitic diseases; and assists commercial firms in the development of quality reagents. **Additional Contact Information:** Branch is located in Bldg. 23, 4770 Buford Hwy., Chamblee, GA 30341.

★6802★ U.S. Department of Health and Human Services
National Center for Infectious Diseases
Division of Vector-Borne Infectious Diseases
PO Box 2087
Fort Collins, CO 80522-2087
Phone: (303)221-6428
Fax: (303)221-6476
Dr. Duane J. Gubler, Sc.D., Director

Research Activities and Fields: Primary mission of the Division is to: 1) provide state, federal, and international agencies with consultation, laboratory services, and epidemic aid in the area of arthropod-borne infections; 2) develop and apply new techniques for the study and control of arthropod-borne diseases; and 3) train technical and professional personnel in field and laboratory methods. Principal areas of research are arthropod-borne viral diseases, lyme disease, plague, and tularemia.

★6803★ U.S. Department of Health and Human Services
National Center for Infectious Diseases
Division of Vector-Borne Infectious Diseases
Arbovirus Diseases Branch
PO Box 2087
Fort Collins, CO 80522-2087
Phone: (303)221-6459
Fax: (303)221-6476
D. Bruce Francy, Ph.D., Chief

Research Activities and Fields: Branch conducts research on the epidemiology of mosquito and tick-borne viral diseases. Provides consultation and on-site investigations for local, state, national, and international health agencies during arthropod-borne viral disease outbreaks. Conducts a national surveillance of arboviral diseases.

★6804★ U.S. Department of Health and Human Services
National Center for Infectious Diseases
Division of Vector-Borne Infectious Diseases
Dengue Branch
2 Calle Casia
San Juan, PR 00921-3200
Phone: (809)766-5181
Fax: (809)766-6596
Gary G. Clark, Chief

Research Activities and Fields: Primary mission is the study of dengue (a viral disease spread by mosquitoes). Research includes investigation of vectors, reservoirs of disease, viruses that cause disease, and methods for surveillance prevention and control.

★6805★ U.S. Department of Health and Human Services
National Center for Infectious Diseases
Division of Vector-Borne Infectious Diseases
Plague Section
PO Box 2087
Fort Collins, CO 80522-2087
Phone: (303)221-6450
Fax: (303)221-6476
Dr. Kenneth Gage, Chief

Research Activities and Fields: Section conducts basic research on the diagnosis, therapy, epidemiology, and control of bubonic plague; maintains a surveillance system in collaboration with state and federal health agencies to detect fluctuations of infection in animal populations; and serves as a WHO Reference Center for plague diagnosis and control.

★6806★ U.S. Department of Health and Human Services
National Center for Infectious Diseases
Division of Viral and Rickettsial Diseases
1600 Clifton Rd., N.E.
Atlanta, GA 30333
Phone: (404)639-3574
Fax: (404)639-3163
Brian W. J. Mahy, Director

Research Activities and Fields: Division's mission is to conduct laboratory and epidemiologic investigations of viral and rickettsial diseases of national and international importance. The Division addresses significant disease problems by the integrated application of modern virologic and epidemiologic methodologies--from molecular biologic methodologies (including nucleic acid and protein biochemistry) to immunologic and pathophysiologic methodologies to epidemiologic and statistical methodologies. Division comprises the Biometrics Activity, Epidemiology Activity, Hepatitis Branch, Influenza Branch, Respiratory and Enteric Virus Branch, Retrovirus Diseases Branch, Special Pathogens Branch, Viral Exanthems and Herpesvirus Branch, and Viral and Rickettsial Zoonoses Branch.

★6807★ U.S. Department of Health and Human Services
National Center for Infectious Diseases
Division of Viral and Rickettsial Diseases
Biometrics Unit
1600 Clifton Rd., N.E.
Mail Stop A31
Atlanta, GA 30333
Phone: (404)639-3986
Howard Geary, Supervisory Mathematical Statistician

Research Activities and Fields: Unit is responsible for development of statistical and epidemiologic research methodology and conducts research in issues of data analysis, interpretation, and presentation.

★6808★ U.S. Department of Health and Human Services
National Center for Infectious Diseases
Division of Viral and Rickettsial Diseases
Hepatitis Branch
1600 Clifton Rd., N.E.
Atlanta, GA 30333
Phone: (404)639-2339
Fax: (404)639-1563
Harold S. Margolis, M.D., Chief

Research Activities and Fields: Conducts laboratory and epidemiologic investigations of hepatitis A, B, C, D, and E. Works to implement hepatitis B immunization programs nationally and internationally.

★6809★ U.S. Department of Health and Human Services
National Center for Infectious Diseases
Division of Viral and Rickettsial Diseases
Influenza Branch
1600 Clifton Rd., N.E.
Atlanta, GA 30333
Phone: (404)639-3591
Fax: (404)639-2334
Nancy Cox, Chief

Research Activities and Fields: Branch is the focal point within CDC for studies pertaining to influenza viruses, their variation and occurrence in populations, and their control.

★6810★ U.S. Department of Health and Human Services
National Center for Infectious Diseases
Division of Viral and Rickettsial Diseases
Respiratory and Enteric Virus Branch

1600 Clifton Rd., N.E.
Atlanta, GA 30333
Phone: (404)639-3596
Fax: (404)639-1307
Larry Anderson, Chief

Research Activities and Fields: Branch's laboratories are concerned with such respiratory viruses as adenoviruses and respiratory syncytial virus, polio and other enteroviruses, and viruses causing gastroenteritis.

★6811★ U.S. Department of Health and Human Services
National Center for Infectious Diseases
Division of Viral and Rickettsial Diseases
Retrovirus Diseases Branch
1600 Clifton Rd., N.E.
Atlanta, GA 30333
Phone: (404)639-1024
Fax: (404)639-1174
Thomas M. Folks, Ph.D., Chief

Research Activities and Fields: Retrovirus diseases and retroviral etiologies of chronic diseases.

★6812★ U.S. Department of Health and Human Services
National Center for Infectious Diseases
Division of Viral and Rickettsial Diseases
Viral Exanthems and Herpesvirus Branch
1600 Clifton Rd., N.E.
Atlanta, GA 30333
Phone: (404)639-1338
Fax: (404)639-3163
Dr. William Reeves, Chief

Research Activities and Fields: Branch's laboratories are responsible for studies of herpesviruses, poxviruses, rubella and measles viruses, and papillomaviruses as the cause of exanthematous, congenital, perinatal diseases, and cancer. Branch is responsible for the CDC's Chronic Fatigue Syndrome Research Program.

★6813★ U.S. Department of Health and Human Services
National Center for Infectious Diseases
Division of Viral and Rickettsial Diseases
Viral and Rickettsial Zoonoses Branch
Epidemiology Section
1600 Clifton Rd., N.E.
Atlanta, GA 30333
Phone: (404)639-1075
Fax: (404)639-1087
Dr. James Olson, Chief

Research Activities and Fields: Branch's laboratories are concerned with rickettsial agents (such as those of Rocky Mountain spotted fever and Q fever); and with rabies virus.

★6814★ U.S. Department of Health and Human Services
National Center for Infectious Diseases
Hospital Infections Program
Bldg. 1, Rm. 5065 (C10)
1600 Clifton Rd. NE
Mail Stop C-12
Atlanta, GA 30333
Phone: (404)639-3171
Fax: (404)639-0079
Dr. James Hughes, Director

Research Activities and Fields: Activities of the Hospital Infections Program include surveil-

lance, investigations, and laboratory and field studies of hospital-associated infections. The Program serves as the focal point within the Center for Infectious Diseases for the issuance of recommendations and guidelines on prevention and control of hospital infections. The Program involves research on methods for preventing and controlling hospital infections and for rapid diagnosis of disease and identification of unusual sources of infection; and research to identify methods for antimicrobial susceptibility testing of groups of microorganisms and to determine the role of drug-resistant microorganisms in hospital infections. Program also provides epidemic aid and epidemiological consultation, upon request from state health departments, to institutions and public health organizations regarding the identification and control of nosocomial infections, provides basic diagnostic services in support of field investigations and cooperates with other components of CID for more definitive diagnosis of nosocomial infections and identification of etiologic agents, provides antimicrobial susceptibility consultation and services to other components of CID, provides intramural and extramural technical expertise and assistance in professional training activities; and serves as designated national and international reference centers for certain nosocomial infections. Components of the Hospital Infections Program are: the Anaerobic Bacteria Branch, Antimicrobic Investigations Branch, Epidemiology Branch, Nosocomial Infections Laboratory Branch, and Statistics and Information Systems Branch.

★6815★ U.S. Department of Health and Human Services
National Center for Infectious Diseases
Hospital Infections Program
Hospital Environment Laboratory Branch
1600 Clifton Rd. N.E.
Mail Stop A-07
Atlanta, GA 30333
Phone: (404)639-1167
Fax: (404)639-3838
Martin S. Favero, Chief

Research Activities and Fields: Branch conducts studies on environmental microbiology, disinfection and sterilization, AIDS, hospital acquired infection, dialysis associated diseases, and endotoxemia and control.

U.S. Department of Health and Human Services
National Institute of Allergy and Infectious Diseases
See: Entry 2123

★6816★ U.S. Department of Health and Human Services
National Institute of Allergy and Infectious Diseases
Division of Acquired Immunodeficiency Syndrome (AIDS)
6003 Executive Blvd.
Rockville, MD 20852
Phone: (301)496-8000
Fax: (301)402-1505
Dr. Daniel Hoth, Director

Research Activities and Fields: NIAID's Division of AIDS is responsible for ensuring that scientific investigations of infection with the human immunodeficiency virus (HIV) are focused on the most critical biomedical research issues engendered by the AIDS epidemic. The Division does this by managing research grants and contracts, and other extramural activities supported by the Institute.

★6817★ U.S. Department of Health and Human Services
National Institute of Allergy and Infectious Diseases
Division of Acquired Immunodeficiency Syndrome (AIDS)
Basic Research and Development Program
Solar Bldg., Rm. 2C07
9000 Rockville Pike
Bethesda, MD 20892
Phone: (301)496-0638
Fax: (301)480-5703
Polly Sager, Acting Associate Director

Research Activities and Fields: Branch supports research on the preclinical development of therapies having potential for the treatment of HIV infections. Studies are aimed at identifying and developing strategies for treatment (including optimal approaches to therapy and novel methods of drug delivery) and evaluating the efficacy of therapeutic agents in cell and animal model systems. Multidisciplinary, multiinstitutional National Cooperative Drug Discovery Groups have been established to facilitate the design, synthesis, and preclinical evaluation of treatment strategies for AIDS.

★6818★ U.S. Department of Health and Human Services
National Institute of Allergy and Infectious Diseases
Division of Acquired Immunodeficiency Syndrome (AIDS)
Biostatistics Research Branch
6003 Executive Blvd., Rm. 2B27
Bethesda, MD 20892
Phone: (301)496-0694
Fax: (301)480-5703
Dr. Mary Soulkes, Chief

Research Activities and Fields: Sponsors and conducts biostatistical research relating to AIDS.

★6819★ U.S. Department of Health and Human Services
National Institute of Allergy and Infectious Diseases
Division of Acquired Immunodeficiency Syndrome (AIDS)
Pathogenesis Branch
6003 Executive Blvd., Rm. 2B33
Bethesda, MD 20892
Phone: (301)496-8378
Fax: (301)480-5703
Dr. Gregory Milman, Chief

Research Activities and Fields: Supports basic research directed toward understanding the complex pathogenesis of the AIDS virus in the areas of biology, biochemistry, molecular biology, immunology of human immunodeficiency virus (HIV) and related retroviruses. Manages the AIDS Research and Reference Reagent Program, one of three World Health Organization AIDS reagent centers that provides scien-

tists with access to essential reagents for AIDS research.

★6820★ U.S. Department of Health and Human Services
National Institute of Allergy and Infectious Diseases
Division of Acquired Immunodeficiency Syndrome (AIDS)
Treatment Research Operations Program
6003 Executive Blvd., Rm. 2A07
Rockville, MD 20892
Phone: (301)496-8210
Fax: (301)402-3684
Dr. William Duncan, Associate Director

Research Activities and Fields: Program is responsible for the support of research on the clinical development and evaluation of potentially effective therapies for HIV infection and related opportunistic infections. It is currently supporting 57 AIDS Clinical Trials Units (ACTUs) located at medical centers around the country. The ACTUs cooperate in the development of research protocols and conduct clinical trials of experimental therapies. Evaluation of potential therapies by the ACTUs provides information neeeded to move experimental therapeutic agents into more widespread use.

★6821★ U.S. Department of Health and Human Services
National Institute of Allergy and Infectious Diseases
Division of Acquired Immunodeficiency Syndrome (AIDS)
Vaccine Research and Development Branch
6003 Executive Blvd., Rm. 2B-01
Bethesda, MD 20892
Phone: (301)496-8200
Fax: (301)480-5703

Research Activities and Fields: Branch supports and coordinates the development and testing of vaccines to prevent HIV infection. Animal model systems are under development to test candidate vaccines. In addition, the Branch supports research resource activities to provide antisera, polypeptides, monoclonal antibodies, and viral pools to investigators engaged in research to develop an AIDS vaccine. The establishment of National Cooperative Vaccine Development Groups fosters collaboration among academic research institutions, industry, and government by pooling scientific talents and resources in vaccine development. Support and management of clinical trials of candidate HIV vaccines are supported by the Branch, and the trials are conducted in the NIAID AIDS Vaccine Evaluation Units.

★6822★ U.S. Department of Health and Human Services
National Institute of Allergy and Infectious Diseases
Division of Acquired Immunodeficiency Syndrome (AIDS)
Vaccine Trials and Epidemiology Branch
6003 Executive Blvd., Rm. 2A42
Rockville, MD 20852
Phone: (301)496-6177
Fax: (301)402-1506
Dr. Sten Vermund, Chief

Research Activities and Fields: Supports research on the epidemiology of AIDS. A Multicenter AIDS Cohort Study (MACS) has been initiated at four centers to follow the natural history and epidemiology of HIV infection. Data from the MACS have yielded valuable information about the transmission of HIV infection and the role of certain cofactors in the pathogenesis of AIDS. Patients are being solicited nationally for Women and Infants Transmission Study and Heterosexual HIV Transmission Study. Established a grant program for the preparation for AIDS vaccine evaluation to link U.S. institutions to research units at overseas sites and develop research centers of excellence in geographic areas with major health problems due to HIV infection. Also studies women's natural history (Women's Interagency HIV Study) and U.S.-based vaccine preparedness studies. **Publications:** Publishes Annual Branch Report.

U.S. Department of Health and Human Services
National Institute of Allergy and Infectious Diseases
Division of Extramural Activities
See: Entry 2129

U.S. Department of Health and Human Services
National Institute of Allergy and Infectious Diseases
Division of Intramural Research
See: Entry 2130

U.S. Department of Health and Human Services
National Institute of Allergy and Infectious Diseases
Division of Intramural Research
Laboratory of Molecular Structure
See: Entry 2131

★6823★ U.S. Department of Health and Human Services
National Institute of Allergy and Infectious Diseases
Division of Intramural Research
Rocky Mountain Operations Branch
903 S. 4th St.
Hamilton, MT 59840
Phone: (406)363-9200
Fax: (406)363-9204
Dr. Robert K. Bergman, Chief

Research Activities and Fields: Components of the Rocky Mountain Laboratories include: 1) the Microbial Structure and Function Laboratory; 2) Vectors and Pathogens Laboratory; 3) the Persistent Viral Diseases Laboratory; and 4) Intracellular Parasites Laboratory.

★6824★ U.S. Department of Health and Human Services
National Institute of Allergy and Infectious Diseases
Division of Microbiology and Infectious Diseases
Solar Bldg., Rm. 3A18
9000 Rockville Pike
Bethesda, MD 20892
Phone: (301)496-1884
Dr. John R. La Montagne, Director

Research Activities and Fields: Supports basic and clinical research activities associated with infectious diseases. These include studies relating to: 1) basic biology and immunology of microorganisms (bacterial, viral, and parasitic); 2) disturbances in immune mechanisms of hospitalized or immunocompromised patients; 3) hospital environment, including studies on viral transmission mechanisms and epidemiologic investigations; 4) development and testing of new vaccines; 5) development of better diagnostic tests; and 6) control and prevention of diseases. Support for multidisciplinary research projects in the United States includes support for an influenza center and research units for the study of sexually transmitted diseases, tropical diseases, and fungal infections. The program also supports multidisciplinary projects in developing countries. Principal components are the Antiviral Research Branch, Bateriology and Virology Branch, Enteric Diseases Branch, Epidemiology and Biometry Branch, Molecular Microbiology Branch, Parasitology and Tropical Diseases Branch, Respiratory Diseases Branch, and Sexually Transmitted Diseases Branch.

★ 6825 ★ U.S. Department of Health and Human Services
National Institute of Allergy and Infectious Diseases
Division of Microbiology and Infectious Diseases
Antiviral Research Branch
Solar Bldg.
6003 Executive Blvd., Rm. 3A22
Rockville, MD 20892
Phone: (301)496-8285
Fax: (301)402-1456
Dr. Catherine Laughlin, Chief

Research Activities and Fields: Supports grant and contract research in the design and evaluation of therapies for viral infections other than AIDS.

★ 6826 ★ U.S. Department of Health and Human Services
National Institute of Allergy and Infectious Diseases
Division of Microbiology and Infectious Diseases
Bacteriology and Mycology Branch
6003 Executive Blvd., Rm. 3A04
Bethesda, MD 20852
Phone: (301)496-7728
Fax: (301)402-0804
Dr. Robert L. Quackenbush, Chief

Research Activities and Fields: Branch supports research on a wide variety of problems involved directly or indirectly with diseases of man caused by bacteria and fungi, including: 1) investigations on the biology and physiology of bacteria and fungi, their morphology, antigenic structure and composition, and toxins and endotoxins; and 2) studies on pathogenesis, immunopathology, host defense mechanisms, diagnostic procedures, therapeutic measures, animal models, and the epidemiology of disease. Specific disease program areas include: medical mycology, turberculosis, and leprosy; hospital-associated infections; and streptococcal diseases and sequelae; and vector-borne bacterial diseases including Lyme disease. Other diseases and problem areas, such as Legionnaires' disease, listeriosis, mycoplasma infections, bru-

cellosis, and anaerobic infections, are also investigated.

★ 6827 ★ U.S. Department of Health and Human Services
National Institute of Allergy and Infectious Diseases
Division of Microbiology and Infectious Diseases
Enteric Diseases Branch
Control Data Bldg., Rm 3A05
Bethesda, MD 20892
Phone: (301)496-7051
Fax: (301)496-8030
Dr. Leslye Johnson, Chief

Research Activities and Fields: Research areas include bacterial and viral enteric diseases, viral hepatitis, hepatitis antiviral drug development, hepatitis C, helicobacter pylori, and mucosal immunity.

★ 6828 ★ U.S. Department of Health and Human Services
National Institute of Allergy and Infectious Diseases
Division of Microbiology and Infectious Diseases
Epidemiology and Biometry Branch
Solar Bldg., Rm. 3A24
Rockville, MD 20892
Phone: (301)496-7065
Fax: (301)402-0659
Dr. Richard Kaslow, Chief

Research Activities and Fields: Epidemiology of infectious and immune diseases. Performs clinical trials.

★ 6829 ★ U.S. Department of Health and Human Services
National Institute of Allergy and Infectious Diseases
Division of Microbiology and Infectious Diseases
Parasitology and Tropical Diseases Branch
Bethesda, MD 20892
Phone: (301)496-2544
Fax: (301)402-0804
Dr. Stephanie James, Chief

Research Activities and Fields: Supports research projects on host-parasite and vector-parasite relationships, with the ultimate goal of controlling parasitic diseases through such procedures as chemoprophylaxis, immunoprophylaxis, chemotherapy, and vector control. Research projects involve parasitology and medical entomology and use a broad spectrum of multidisciplinary approaches, including immunology, molecular biology, and biochemistry. Emphasis is directed toward studies on the infectious diseases of developing countries, through special programs on tropical disease research. As a means of stimulating research on schistosomiasis and filariasis, NIAID also supports two contracts to provide investigators with animals and vectors infected with various species of both these parasites.

★ 6830 ★ U.S. Department of Health and Human Services
National Institute of Allergy and Infectious Diseases
Division of Microbiology and Infectious Diseases
Respiratory Diseases Branch
Solar Bldg.
6003 Executive Blvd.
Rockville, MD 20892
Phone: (301)496-5305
Fax: (301)496-8030
Dr. Carole Heilman, Chief

Research Activities and Fields: Acute respiratory disease. Maintains programs in influenza, bacterial viral respiratory disease, bacterial vaccines, tuberculosis, pertussis, and pneumonia.

★ 6831 ★ U.S. Department of Health and Human Services
National Institute of Allergy and Infectious Diseases
Division of Microbiology and Infectious Diseases
Sexually Transmitted Diseases Branch
9000 Rockville Pike
Bethesda, MD 20892
Phone: (301)402-0443
Fax: (301)402-1456
Dr. Penelope Hitchcock, Chief

Research Activities and Fields: Sexually transmitted research encompasses basic, epidemiologic, clinical, and behavioral approaches.

U.S. Department of Health and Human Services
National Institute of Allergy and Infectious Diseases
Laboratory of Clinical Investigation
See: Entry 2133

U.S. Department of Health and Human Services
National Institute of Allergy and Infectious Diseases
Laboratory of Immunopathology
See: Entry 2137

★ 6832 ★ U.S. Department of Health and Human Services
National Institute of Allergy and Infectious Diseases
Laboratory of Infectious Diseases
NIH Bldg. 7, Rm. 100
9000 Rockville Pike
Bethesda, MD 20892
Phone: (301)496-2024
Robert M. Chanock, M.D., Chief

Research Activities and Fields: Defines the cause and epidemiology of medically important viral diseases and develops means for their control. Activities range from identification and antigenic characterization of viruses that cause acute disease of the respiratory and gastrointestinal tracts and liver to basic molecular studies of viral structure, function, and genome organization. Molecular biologic techniques are used to elucidate pathogenesis of disease as well as to develop purified subunit antigens and attenuated viral mutants for use in prevention of respiratory, gastrointestinal, and hepatic viral diseases.

★ 6833 ★ U.S. Department of Health and Human Services
National Institute of Allergy and Infectious Diseases
Laboratory of Microbial Structure and Function
Rocky Mountain Laboratories
903 S. 4th St.
Hamilton, MT 59840
Phone: (406)363-3211
Fax: (406)363-6406
John Swanson, Chief

Research Activities and Fields: Laboratory's efforts focus on defining structural and functional elements of pathogenic bacterial surface components involved in pathogenesis and/or virulence of selected organisms or in genesis of host immunological responses to infections by these agents. Studies involve *Neissera gonorrhoeae*, *Borellia burgdorferi*, and others; both protein and nonprotein components of these gram-negative organism outer membrane are prime study candidates as mediators of interactions between bacterium and host and as likely vaccine components. Chemical characteristics, immunochemical properties, and genetic control of selected surface proponents are investigated to delineate their relationship to infectious disease phenomena of these bacteria.

★ 6834 ★ U.S. Department of Health and Human Services
National Institute of Allergy and Infectious Diseases
Laboratory of Molecular Microbiology
NIH Bldg. 4, Rm. 315
9000 Rockville Pike
Bethesda, MD 20892
Phone: (301)496-4012
Fax: (301)402-0226
Dr. Malcolm A. Martin, Chief

Research Activities and Fields: The Laboratory uses molecular biological techniques to study microorganisms and their capacity to produce disease in vertebrate hosts. Of prime importance in this effort is the biochemical characterization of viral and bacterial genomes and the detailed analyses of gene products regulating expression or giving rise to mature structural proteins. A principal area of investigation has been the human immunodeficiency virus (HIV), with classical virological procedures used for the detection, quantitation, and biological characterization of HIV isolates of diverse origin. Biochemical and molecular biological techniques such as nucleic acid hybridization, gene cloning, DNA sequencing, in vitro mutagenesis, and transfection are used in combination with procedures such as immunoprecipitation or protein purification to study individual viral genes or potentially infectious proviral DNAs in order to assess structure/function relationships. Programs involving murine retroviruses concentrate on those portions of the viral genome that encode proteins that initiate and/or maintain the transformed state. The roles of host cellular determinants that augment or diminish disease/oncogenesis are also investigated.

★ 6835 ★ U.S. Department of Health and Human Services
National Institute of Allergy and Infectious Diseases
Laboratory of Parasitic Diseases
NIH Bldg. 4, Rm. 126
9000 Rockville Pike
Bethesda, MD 20892
Phone: (301)496-2486
Fax: (301)402-2201
Franklin A. Neva, M.D., Chief

Research Activities and Fields: Laboratory conducts both basic and applied studies of parasitic diseases of humans. A variety of protozoan (malaria, trypanosomes, giardia, leishmania) and helminth (schistosomes, filaria, and strongyloides) parasites are used for experimental work. Emphasis is on the immunologic response, molecular basis of parasite biology, and mechanisms of disease. A unit of clinical studies on patients is included.

★ 6836 ★ U.S. Department of Health and Human Services
National Institute of Allergy and Infectious Diseases
Laboratory of Persistent Viral Diseases
Rocky Mountain Laboratories
903 S. 4th St.
Hamilton, MT 59840
Phone: (406)363-9400
Fax: (406)363-9204
Bruce Chesebro, M.D., Chief

Research Activities and Fields: Laboratory conducts studies of virus-host interaction, with the primary aim of elucidating mechanisms involved in establishment, maintenance, and elimination of persistent viral infections. Particular emphasis is placed on persistent viral infections involving cells of the hemopoietic and lymphoid systems and the central nervous system. The role of persistent infection in the development of autoimmune or immune complex disease is also studied. Models examined include human AIDS retrovirus, murine, avian and equine retroviruses, rabies virus, Aleutian disease virus of mink, and the scrapie agent.

★ 6837 ★ U.S. Department of Health and Human Services
National Institute of Allergy and Infectious Diseases
Laboratory of Vectors and Pathogens
Rocky Mountain Laboratories
903 S. 4th St.
Hamilton, MT 59840
Phone: (406)363-9228
Fax: (406)363-9204
Dr. Claude F. Garon, Chief

Research Activities and Fields: Basic biology, biochemistry, immunology, electron microscopy, arthropod vector biology, and molecular biology concentrating on molecular cloning and pathogenesis. Study emphasis also includes characterizing features of the host-pathogen interaction and identifying and exploiting specific microbial bioproducts for improved diagnostics and/or vaccines.

★ 6838 ★ U.S. Department of Health and Human Services
National Institute of Allergy and Infectious Diseases
Laboratory of Viral Diseases
NIH Bldg. 4, Rm. 229A
9000 Rockville Pike
Bethesda, MD 20892
Phone: (301)496-9869
Fax: (301)480-1147
Dr. Bernard Moss, Chief

Research Activities and Fields: Laboratory conducts basic research on the genetic organization, expression, replication, assembly, and pathogenicity of viruses. Live recombinant viruses are genetically engineered for use as immunological tools and as vaccines against a variety of infectious agents. Current research topics include: regulation of gene expression in vitro and in vivo; mechanisms of DNA replication in vitro and in vivo; structure and function of RNA and DNA polymerases; genetic engineering of recombinant viruses as live vaccines; antiviral agents; determinants of virus virulence; host resistance genes; viral growth factors; and targets of humoral and cell-mediated immunity.

U.S. Department of Health and Human Services
National Institute on Drug Abuse
Basic Research Division
Clinical Medicine Branch
See: Entry 12124

U.S. Department of Health and Human Services
National Institute of Neurological Disorders and Stroke
Molecular Medicine and Neurological Science Laboratory
See: Entry 8468

University of Alabama at Birmingham
Ob/Gyn Infectious Disease Research Laboratory
See: Entry 9715

★ 6839 ★ University of California, Davis
AIDS Virus Diagnostic Laboratory
Dept. of Medical Pathology
Comparative Oncology
Old Davis Rd.
Davis, CA 95616
Phone: (916)752-8242
Fax: (916)752-4816
James R. Carlson, Ph.D., Dir.

Research Activities and Fields: Human immunodeficiency virus (HIV) serology, HIV production and purification, bioassays of HIV inactivation, comparative retrovirology, and vaccine development.

★ 6840 ★ University of California, Los Angeles
UCLA Center for Clinical AIDS Research and Education / AIDS Clinical Trials Unit
10833 Le Conte Ave., Rm. BH-412 CHS
Los Angeles, CA 90024-1793
Phone: (310)206-6414
Fax: (310)206-3311
Ronald T. Mitsuyasu, M.D., Dir.

Research Activities and Fields: Coordinates clinical research trials on AIDS and HIV-related disease. **Publications:** *Perspectives Newsletter*; *AIDS Reference Guide for Medical Professionals.* **E-mail Address:** rmitsuya@medicine.medsch.ucla.edu. **Formerly:** UCLA AIDS Clinical Research Center/AIDS Clinical Trials Unit.

★6841★ **University of California, San Francisco**
AIDS Clinical Research Center
Dept. of Stomatology
Rm. S-612, Box 0422
San Francisco, CA 94143
Phone: (415)476-5415
Fax: (415)476-4204
John S. Greenspan, Dir.

Research Activities and Fields: AIDS and Kaposi's sarcoma, including epidemiological studies and tissue and serum virological and immunological investigations. The Clinical Center integrates five support programs: Clinical Trials Coordinating Unit, which manages protocol development, data collection and analysis, and statistical consultation; Laboratory Support for specific trials that require specimen storage, immunological monitoring, or special viral diagnostic procedures; Community Consortium, a network of Bay Area physicians who treat AIDS patients and who enter patients in controlled clinical studies; Clinical Specialties that treat AIDS patients (Pediatrics, Neurology, Oral Medicine, Dermatology, Infectious Disease, Pulmonary, Gastroenterology, Oncology, and Behavioral Med icine); and Administration, which governs the Center, plans and projects budgets, manages project review and awards, and conducts educational programs.

University of California, San Francisco
Center for AIDS Prevention Studies (CAPS)
See: Entry 10884

★6842★ **University of California, San Francisco**
George Williams Hooper Foundation
San Francisco, CA 94143-0552
Phone: (415)476-5157
Fax: (415)476-6185
Dr. J. Michael Bishop, Dir.

Research Activities and Fields: Tumor virology, genetics and physiology of prokaryotic organisms, immunology, and the pathogenesis of infectious diseases.

★6843★ **University of Chicago**
Committee on Virology
Marjorie B. Kovler Viral Oncology Laboratories
910 E. 58th St.
Chicago, IL 60637
Phone: (312)702-1898
Fax: (312)702-3791
Prof. Bernard Roizman, Chm.

Research Activities and Fields: Molecular biology of herpes simplex virus, emphasizing the functional organization of the viral DNA genome, the regulation of transcription and post-transcriptional processing of viral DNA, and the elucidation of the function of virus specified proteins. Specific approaches involve site-specific mutations and deletions within the genome and translocation of specific genes from their normal position to the other sites within the genome.

★6844★ **University of Colorado**
Laboratory for Biochemical Parasitology
Division of Infectious Diseases
4200 E. 9th Ave.
Box B168
Denver, CO 80262
Phone: (303)270-7233
Fax: (303)270-8681
Randolph L. Berens, Dir.

Research Activities and Fields: Parasitic protozoans focusing on the purine metabolism of these organisms with the intention of developing chemotherapeutic agents for the diseases caused by these parasites.

★6845★ **University of Florida**
Malaria Genome Project
Biotech. Prog.
Gainesville, FL 32611
Phone: (904)392-8408
Fax: (904)392-8598
Dr. Sheldon M. Schuster, Dir.

Research Activities and Fields: Genome sequencing of the malaria parasite.

★6846★ **University of Maryland**
Division of Infectious Diseases
Medical School Teaching Facility
10 S. Pine St., Rm. 9-00
Baltimore, MD 21201
Phone: (410)706-7560
Fax: (410)706-8700
John W. Warren, M.D., Head

Research Activities and Fields: Infections in the elderly, including infection from urinary catheterization, epidemiology of nursing home patients, tests of antimicrobial agents, and pharmacokinetics and microbiology using animal models and clinical techniques.

University of Medicine and Dentistry of New Jersey
Lyme Disease Center
See: Entry 7952

★6847★ **University of Miami**
Center for Tropical and Parasitic Diseases
Medical School, Bldg. A
12500 SW 152nd St.
Miami, FL 33177
Phone: (305)232-5992
Fax: (305)232-8796
Dr. Arba Ager, Dir.

Research Activities and Fields: All aspects of malaria, including malaria drug testing in rodents. Also conducts nutritional and chemotherapy research.

★6848★ **University of Michigan**
National Cooperative Drug Discovery Group for the Treatment of AIDS
School of Denistry
Dept. of Biologic & Materials Sciences
1011 N. Univ.
Ann Arbor, MI 48109
Phone: (313)763-5481
Fax: (313)764-7406
John C. Drach, Ph.D., Coord.

Research Activities and Fields: Design and synthesis of drugs to fight acquired immune deficiency syndrome (AIDS). Research includes virologic and toxicity testing and biochemical and immunological analysis.

★6849★ **University of Pennsylvania**
Department of Molecular and Cellular Engineering
Wistar Institute, Rm. 204
3601 Spruce St.
Philadelphia, PA 19104
Phone: (215)898-1979
Fax: (215)898-6588
Dr. James Wilson, Dept.Ch.

Research Activities and Fields: Biology of infectious diseases, including respiratory infection, immunochemistry of pneumococcus and streptococcus, and epidemiology. **Formerly:** John Herr Musser Department of Research Medicine.

★6850★ **University of Rochester**
Department of Microbiology and Immunology
601 Elmwood Ave., Box 672
Rochester, NY 14642
Phone: (716)275-3402
Fax: (716)473-9573
Dr. Barbara Iglewski, Chair

Research Activities and Fields: Medical microbiology, genetics, molecular biology, parasitology, virology, immunology, and microbial physiology.

University of South Carolina
International Center for Public Health Research
See: Entry 11002

★6851★ **University of Southern California**
Hastings Foundation Infectious Disease Research Laboratories
LAC-USC Medical Center
Gen. Research Lab. Bldg., Rm. 264
1801 E. Marengo
Los Angeles, CA 90033
Phone: (213)226-3825
Fax: (213)226-2775
Dr. Paul Holtom, Dir.

Research Activities and Fields: Infectious diseases, bacteriology, and miscellaneous antibiotic trials.

★6852★ **University of Texas Health Science Center at San Antonio**
South Texas Vaccine Development Center
Dept. of Microbiology
7703 Floyd Curl Dr.
San Antonio, TX 78284-7758
Phone: (210)567-3938
Fax: (210)567-6612
Dr. Alan Barbour, Dir.

Research Activities and Fields: Basic and applied research related to infectious diseases. Studies focus on tick-transmitted Lyme disease, mycoplasma infections, syphilis, and leishmania, a skin or systemic infection usually resulting from a bite of a sandfly infected with leishmania, a protozoan flagellate. Also investigates diagnostics related to infectious diseases. **E-mail Address:** alan@taliesin.uthscsa.edu.

★ 6853 ★ University of Texas—Houston Health Science Center
Center for Infectious Diseases
Medical School
6431 Fannin St., 1729 JFB
Houston, TX 77030
Phone: (713)794-4254
Fax: (713)792-4937
Charles Ericsson, M.D., Interim Codir.

Research Activities and Fields: Intestinal immunity, intestinal protozology, and biochemical aspects of nutrition. Also conducts research on the enteric aspects of HIV infection among patients in Africa.

★ 6854 ★ University of Texas Medical Branch at Galveston
Clinical Microbiology Laboratories
Dept. of Pathology
Galveston, TX 77555-0609
Phone: (409)772-2856
Fax: (409)772-2500
David H. Walker, M.D., Chm. of Pathology

Research Activities and Fields: Clinical microbiology, pathobiology, immunobiology of infectious diseases, and pathogenic microorganisms. **E-mail Address:** dwalker@beach.utmb.edu.

★ 6855 ★ University of Texas Medical Branch at Galveston
National Cooperative Drug Discovery Group for the Treatment of AIDS
Dept. of Microbiology
Rt. J-19
Galveston, TX 77550
Phone: (409)772-4495
Dr. Miles W. Cloyd, Prin. Investigator

Research Activities and Fields: Mechanisms of human immunodeficiency virus (HIV) cytotoxicity and methods to counteract, including analysis of cell membrane perturbation, phospholipid synthesis depression, heterogeneity of HIV cell-associated antigens, and virus type specificities of human antibody response.

University of Wisconsin—Madison
Respiratory Virus Research Laboratory
See: Entry 11624

Wayne State University
Center for Molecular Medicine and Genetics
See: Entry 5392

★ 6856 ★ Yale University
Yale Arbovirus Research Unit
60 College St.
Box 208034
New Haven, CT 06520-8034
Phone: (203)785-2901
Fax: (203)785-4782
Dr. Robert E. Shope, Dir.

Research Activities and Fields: Epidemiology of arboviruses, rabies, and leishmania, including characterization and identification of agents and studies of their pathogenicity, immune reactions, morphology, morphogenesis, biochemistry, and epidemiology and relationships to vectors. **Formerly:** Rockefeller Foundation Virus Laboratories.

State Government Agencies

AIDS

★ 6857 ★ Alabama Department of Public Health
Disease Control Bureau
HIV / AIDS Division
434 Monroe St.
Montgomery, AL 36130-1701
Phone: (334)613-5364
Fax: (334)288-5021

★ 6858 ★ Alaska Department of Health and Social Services
Public Health Division
Epidemiology Section
PO Box 240249
Anchorage, AK 99524-0249
Phone: (907)561-4406
Fax: (907)586-1877

★ 6859 ★ Arizona Department of Health Services
Disease Prevention Services Division
HIV and AIDS Office
3815 N. Black Canyon Hwy.
Phoenix, AZ 85015
Phone: (602)230-5843
Fax: (602)230-5959

★ 6860 ★ Arkansas Department of Health
AIDS / STD Administrative Office
4815 W. Markham
Little Rock, AR 72205-3867
Phone: (501)661-2135
Fax: (501)671-1450

★ 6861 ★ California Health and Welfare Agency
Health Services Department
AIDS Office
714 P St., Rm. 1253
Sacramento, CA 95814
Phone: (916)445-0553
Fax: (916)657-1156

★ 6862 ★ Colorado Public Health and Environment Department
Health Office
Disease Control and Environmental Epidemiology Division
STD / AIDS Section
4300 Cherry Creek Dr., S.
Denver, CO 80222-1530
Phone: (303)692-2700
Fax: (303)782-0904

★ 6863 ★ Connecticut Department Public Health
AIDS Section
150 Washington St.
Hartford, CT 06106
Phone: (203)240-9122
Fax: (203)566-3302

★ 6864 ★ Delaware Department of Health and Social Services
Public Health Division
Communicable Disease Control Branch
HIV / Sexually Transmitted Disease Program
Jesse Cooper Bldg.
PO Box 637
Dover, DE 19903
Phone: (302)739-4744
Fax: (302)739-6659

★ 6865 ★ Florida Department of Health and Rehabilitative Services
Health Program Office
Disease Control and AIDS Prevention Office
1317 Winewood Blvd.
Tallahassee, FL 32399-0700
Phone: (904)921-2220
Fax: (904)922-2993

★ 6866 ★ Georgia Department of Human Resources
Public Health Division
Epidemiology Office
2 Peachtree St. NW
Atlanta, GA 30303
Phone: (404)657-2588
Fax: (404)657-2715

★ 6867 ★ Hawaii Department of Health
Health Resources Adminstration
STD / AIDS Prevention Services Bureau
1250 Punchbowl St.
Honolulu, HI 96813
Phone: (808)733-9010
Fax: (808)586-4444

★ 6868 ★ Idaho Department of Health and Welfare
Clinical and Preventive Services Bureau
STD / AIDS Program
450 W. State St.
PO Box 83720
Boise, ID 83720-0036
Phone: (208)334-6526

★ 6869 ★ Illinois Department of Public Health
Infectious Diseases Division
AIDS Activities Section
525 W. Jefferson St., 1st Fl.
Springfield, IL 62761
Phone: (217)524-5983
Fax: (217)524-6090

★ 6870 ★ Indiana Department of Health
HIV / STD Program
1330 W Michigan St.
PO Box 1964
Indianapolis, IN 46206-1964
Phone: (317)383-6851
Fax: (317)383-6779

★ 6871 ★ Iowa Department of Public Health
Health Protection Division
AIDS Section
Lucas State Office Bldg.
321 E. 12th St.
Des Moines, IA 50319
Phone: (515)281-4938
Fax: (515)281-4958

★6872★ **Kansas Department of Health and Environment**
Health Division
Disease Control Bureau
AIDS Section
900 SW Jackson, Ste. 620
Topeka, KS 66612-1290
Phone: (913)296-6173
Fax: (913)296-1231

★6873★ **Kentucky Human Resources Cabinet**
Health Services Department
Epidemiology and Disease Control Division
AIDS Education Program
275 E. Main St.
Frankfort, KY 40621
Phone: (502)564-6539
Fax: (502)564-6533

★6874★ **Louisiana Department of Health and Hospitals**
Communicable Disease Control Division
Health Protection and Promotion Bureau
AIDS Unit
PO Box 629
Baton Rouge, LA 70821-0629
Phone: (504)342-1799
Fax: (504)342-9508

★6875★ **Maine Department of Human Services**
Health Bureau
Disease Control Division
State House Station 11
Augusta, ME 04333
Phone: (207)287-3591
Fax: (207)287-3005

★6876★ **Maryland Department of Health and Mental Hygiene**
Public Health Services Office
AIDS Administration
201 W. Preston St., 5th Fl.
Baltimore, MD 21201
Phone: (410)225-6743
Fax: (410)225-6489

★6877★ **Massachusetts Executive Office of Health and Human Services**
Public Health Department
AIDS Office
150 Tremont St.
Boston, MA 02111
Phone: (617)727-0368
Fax: (617)727-2559

★6878★ **Michigan Department of Public Health**
Infectious Disease Control Bureau
HIV / AIDS Prevention and Intervention Section
3423 N. Logan
PO Box 30195
Lansing, MI 48909
Phone: (517)335-8063
Fax: (517)335-9476

★6879★ **Minnesota Department of Health**
AIDS / STD Prevention Services
717 Delaware St. SE
PO Box 9441
Minneapolis, MN 55440-9441
Phone: (612)623-5698
Fax: (612)623-5794

★6880★ **Mississippi Department of Health**
Preventive Health Bureau
Disease Control Office
AIDS Program
PO Box 1700
Jackson, MS 39215-1700
Phone: (601)960-7723
Fax: (601)960-7909

★6881★ **Missouri Department of Health**
Environmental Health and Epidemiology Division
STD / HIV Prevention Bureau
PO Box 570
Jefferson City, MO 65102
Phone: (314)751-6141
Fax: (314)751-6010

★6882★ **Montana Department of Health and Environmental Sciences**
Health Services Division
Preventive Health Services Bureau
AIDS Program
Cogswell Bldg., Rm. C108
PO Box 20091
Helena, MT 59620-0901
Phone: (406)444-2454

★6883★ **Nebraska Department of Health**
Health Promotion and Disease Prevention Bureau
Communicable Disease Section
HIV / AIDS Program
PO Box 95007
Lincoln, NE 68509
Phone: (402)471-2937
Fax: (402)471-6426

★6884★ **Nevada Department of Human Resources**
Health Division
Communicable Disease Section
505 E. King St., Rm. 201
Carson City, NV 89710
Phone: (702)687-4800

★6885★ **New Hampshire Department of Health and Human Services**
Public Health Services Division
STD / HIV Program
6 Hazen Dr.
Concord, NH 03301
Phone: (603)271-4576
Fax: (603)271-3745

★6886★ **New Jersey Department of Health**
Epidemiology, Environmental, Occupational, and Health Services Division
Communicable Disease Control Services Office
Sexually Transmitted Disease Program
CN 369
Trenton, NJ 08625-0369
Phone: (609)588-7526
Fax: (609)588-7431

★6887★ **New Mexico Department of Health**
Public Health Division
HIV / AIDS Bureau
525 Camino De Los Marquez
Santa Fe, NM 87501
Phone: (505)476-8456
Fax: (505)827-2329

★6888★ **New York State Department of Health**
AIDS Institute
Empire State Plaza
Corning Tower, Rm. 349
Albany, NY 12237-0001
Phone: (518)473-7542

★6889★ **North Carolina Department of Environment, Health, and Natural Resources**
Health Promotion Division
AIDS Care Branch
PO Box 27687
Raleigh, NC 27611-7687
Phone: (919)715-3118
Fax: (919)715-3144

★6890★ **North Dakota Department of Health**
Preventive Health Section
Disease Control Division
AIDS Program
600 E. Boulevard, 2nd Fl.
Bismarck, ND 58505-0200
Phone: (701)328-2378
Fax: (701)328-1412

★6891★ **Ohio Department of Health**
Preventive Medicine Division
AIDS Bureau
246 N. High St.
Columbus, OH 43266-0588
Phone: (614)466-0295
Fax: (614)644-0085

★6892★ **Oklahoma Department of Health**
HIV and STD Services
1000 NE 10th St.
PO Box 53551
Oklahoma City, OK 73152
Phone: (405)271-4276
Fax: (405)271-3431

★6893★ **Oregon Department of Human Resources**
Health Division
Sexually Transmitted Diseases Program
PO Box 14450
Portland, OR 97214-0450
Phone: (503)731-4000
Fax: (503)731-4078

★6894★ **Pennsylvania Department of Health**
HIV and AIDS Bureau
Box 90
Harrisburg, PA 17108
Phone: (717)783-0479
Fax: (717)772-6959

★6895★ **Rhode Island Department of Health**
Family Health Office
Disease Control Division
AIDS / STD Program
3 Capitol Hill, Rm. 105
Providence, RI 02908-5097
Phone: (401)277-2320
Fax: (401)272-3771

★6896★ **South Carolina Department of Health and Environmental Control**
Health Services Office
Preventive Health Services Bureau
STD / HIV Division
2600 Bull St.
Columbia, SC 29201
Phone: (803)737-4110
Fax: (803)737-3979

★6897★ **South Dakota Department of Health**
AIDS Specialist
445 E. Capital
Pierre, SD 57501-3185
Phone: (605)773-3364
Fax: (605)773-5683

★6898★ **Tennessee Department of Health**
AIDS Program
312 8th Ave., 9th Fl.
Nashville, TN 37247-0101
Phone: (615)741-7247
Fax: (615)741-2491

★6899★ **Texas Department of Health**
HIV / STD Prevention Bureau
1100 W. 49th St.
Austin, TX 78756
Phone: (512)458-7463
Fax: (512)458-9368

★6900★ **Utah Department of Health**
Community Health Services Division
HIV and AIDS Bureau
PO Box 142867
Salt Lake City, UT 84114-2867
Phone: (801)538-6129
Fax: (801)538-6036

★6901★ **Vermont Agency of Human Services**
Health Department
STD Program
PO Box 70
Burlington, VT 05402
Phone: (802)863-7245
Fax: (802)863-7425

★6902★ **Virginia Office of Health and Human Resources**
Health Department
Communicable Disease Control Division
STD / AIDS Bureau
1500 E. Main St.
PO Box 2448
Richmond, VA 23218
Phone: (804)786-6267
Fax: (804)786-4616

★6903★ **Washington Department of Health**
Community and Family Health Division
HIV / AIDS Office
PO Box 47844
Olympia, WA 98504-7844
Phone: (360)586-8334
Fax: (360)586-5525

★6904★ **West Virginia Department of Health and Human Resources**
Public Health Bureau
HIV / AIDS Program
State Capitol Complex, Bldg. 3, Rm. 518
Charleston, WV 23505-0501
Phone: (304)558-2950
Fax: (304)558-1035

★6905★ **Wisconsin Department of Health and Social Services**
Health Division
Public Health Bureau
AIDS / HIV Program
PO Box 7850
Madison, WI 53703-7850
Phone: (608)266-9853
Fax: (608)267-2832

★6906★ **Wyoming Department of Health**
Preventive Medicine Division
AIDS Prevention Program
Hathaway Bldg., 4th Fl.
Cheyenne, WY 82002-0710
Phone: (307)777-6004
Fax: (307)777-5402

Chapter 35
Information & Communications

Federal Government Agencies

★6907★ U.S. Department of Health and Human Services
National Center for Health Statistics
6525 Belcrest Rd.
Hyattsville, MD 20782
Phone: (301)436-7016

Description: The NCHS mission is to collect, analyze, and disseminate national health statistics; conduct research in survey and statistical methodology; provide specialized training programs and technical assistance; and coordinate cooperative programs with state, national, and international organizations. NCHS maintains data systems that produce data in the following areas: extent of illness and disability in the population; distribution and normative standards for physiological and nutritional measurements; national vital statistics, including births, deaths, marriages, and divorces; hospital, nursing home, and ambulatory care utilization; health expenditures; family formation, growth, and dissolution; and other major health topics.

★6908★ U.S. Department of Health and Human Services
National Institutes of Health
National Library of Medicine
9000 Rockville Pike
Bethesda, MD 20892
Phone: (301)496-6221

Description: The National Library of Medicine serves as the nation's chief medical information source. It is the world's largest research library in a single scientific and professional field. NLM is authorized to provide medical library services and on-line bibliographic searching capabilities, such as MEDLINE, TOXLINE, and others, to public and private agencies, and to organizations, institutions, and individuals. It is responsible for the development and management of a biomedical communications network and operates a computer-based toxicology information system for the scientific community, industry, and other federal agencies. In addition, the Library acquires and distributes audiovisual instructional material, and develops prototype audiovisual communication programs for the health educational community. Through grants and contracts, the Library administers programs of assistance to the nation's medical libraries that include support of a regional medical library network, research in the field of medical library science, establishment and improvement of the basic library resources, and supporting biomedical scientific publications of a nonprofit nature.

★6909★ U.S. Library of Congress
National Library Service for the Blind and Physically Handicapped
1291 Taylor St., NW
Washington, DC 20542
Phone: (202)707-5100

Description: Talking and braille books and magazines are distributed through 150 regional and subregional libraries to blind and physically handicapped residents of the U.S. and its territories.

Medical & Allied Health Schools

Medical Illustration

Schools listed below offer master's degree programs that are accredited by the Association of Medical Illustrators, 1819 Peachtree St. NE, Ste. 712, Atlanta, GA 30309, (404) 350-7900, in conjunction with the Commission on Accreditation of Allied Health Education Programs, 515 N. State St., Ste. 7530, Chicago, IL 60610, (312)464-4636

Georgia

★6910★ Medical College of Georgia
School of Allied Health Sciences / School of Graduate Studies
Graduate Program in Medical Illustration
Augusta, GA 30912-0300
Phone: (706)721-3266
Fax: (706)721-7855

Illinois

★6911★ University of Illinois at Chicago
College of Associated Health Professions
Department of Biomedical Visualization
Medical Illustrator Program
1919 W. Taylor St., Rm. 213 M/C-527
Chicago, IL 60612
Phone: (312)996-7337
Fax: (312)996-8342

Maryland

★6912★ Johns Hopkins University
School of Medicine
Department of Art as Applied to Medicine
Medical Illustrator Program
1830 E. Monument St., Ste. 7000
Baltimore, MD 21205
Phone: (410)955-3213
Fax: (410)955-1085

Michigan

★6913★ University of Michigan
M.F.A. Program in Medical and Biological Illustration
Northern Brewery, Ste. 102B
1327 Jones Dr.
Ann Arbor, MI 48105-1899
Phone: (313)998-6270
Fax: (313)998-6273

Texas

★6914★ University of Texas
Southwestern Medical Center at Dallas
Department of Biomedical Communications—Exchange Park
Biomedical Illustration Program
5323 Harry Hines Blvd.
Dallas, TX 75235-8881
Phone: (214)904-2364
Fax: (214)904-2522

Health Information Administration

The following baccalaureate, postbaccalaureate, and master's degree programs in health information (medical record) administration have been accredited by the Commission on Accrediatation of Allied Health Education Programs of the American Medical Association (515 N. State St., Ste. 7530, Chicago, IL 60610, 312-464-4623) in collaboration with the Council on Accreditation of the American Health Information Management Association, 919 N. Michigan Ave., Ste. 1400, Chicago, IL 60611-1683, (312) 787-2672. Contact either of these organizations for a listing of accredited academic programs for health information (medical record) technicians.

Alabama

★6915★ **University of Alabama at Birmingham**
Health Information Management Division
1675 University Blvd., Rm. 644
Birmingham, AL 35294-3361
Phone: (205)934-3509

Arkansas

★6916★ **Arkansas Tech University**
Health Information Administration Program
105 Wilson Hall
Russellville, AR 72801-2222
Phone: (501)968-0441

California

★6917★ **Loma Linda University**
Health Information Administration Program
1905 Nichol Hall
Loma Linda, CA 92350
Phone: (909)824-4976

Colorado

★6918★ **Regis College**
Health Information Administration Program
3333 Regis Blvd.
Denver, CO 80221-1099
Phone: (303)458-4157

Florida

★6919★ **Florida A&M University**
Health Information Management Division
Ware-Rhaney Bldg., Rm. 223D
Tallahassee, FL 32307
Phone: (904)599-3822

★6920★ **Florida International University**
Health Information Management Program
ACII, Rm. 388
North Miami, FL 33181
Phone: (305)940-5631

★6921★ **University of Central Florida**
Health Information Management Program
PO Box 25000
Orlando, FL 32816
Phone: (407)823-2359

Georgia

★6922★ **Clark Atlanta University**
Health Information Administration Program
James P. Brawley Dr. at Fair St. SW
Atlanta, GA 30314
Phone: (404)880-8115

★6923★ **Medical College of Georgia**
School of Allied Health Sciences
Department of Health Information Management
AL-122
Augusta, GA 30912-0400
Phone: (404)721-3436

Illinois

★6924★ **Chicago State University**
Health Information Administration Program
9501 S. King Dr., BHS 610
Chicago, IL 60628-1598
Phone: (312)995-2552

★6925★ **Illinois State University**
Department of Health Sciences
Health Information Administration Program
103 Moulton Hall
Normal, IL 61761
Phone: (309)438-8329

★6926★ **University of Illinois at Chicago**
College of Associated Health Professions
Department of Health Information Management
1919 W. Taylor, Rm. 811
Chicago, IL 60612
Phone: (312)996-3530

Indiana

★6927★ **Indiana University**
School of Medicine
Health Information Administration Program
1140 W. Michigan St., CF 326
Indianapolis, IN 46202-5119
Phone: (317)274-7317

Kansas

★6928★ **University of Kansas**
School of Allied Health
Department of Health Information Management
KU Hospital G-124 Blvd.
39th and Rainbow Blvd.
Kansas City, KS 66160-7607
Phone: (913)588-2423

Kentucky

★6929★ **Eastern Kentucky University**
Department of Health Information
Dizney 117
Richmond, KY 40475-3135
Phone: (606)622-1915

Louisiana

★6930★ **Louisiana Tech University**
Department of Health Information Management
PO Box 3171
Ruston, LA 71272
Phone: (318)257-2854

★6931★ **University of Southwestern Louisiana**
Department of Health Information Management
PO Box 41007, USL Station
Lafayette, LA 70504
Phone: (318)482-6629

Massachusetts

★6932★ **Northeastern University**
Health Information Administration Program
266 Ryder Hall
360 Huntington
Boston, MA 02115
Phone: (617)373-2525

Michigan

★6933★ **Ferris State University**
Health Information Administration Program
200 Ferris Dr.
VFS 402
Big Rapids, MI 49307
Phone: (616)592-2313

Minnesota

★6934★ **College of St. Scholastica**
Department of Health Information Administration
1200 Kenwood Ave.
Duluth, MN 55811
Phone: (218)723-6011

Mississippi

★6935★ **University of Mississippi**
School of Health Related Professions
Department of Health Information Management
2500 N. State St.
Jackson, MS 39216-4505
Phone: (601)984-6305

Missouri

★6936★ St. Louis University
School of Allied Health Professions
Department of Health Information
  Management
3525 Caroline, Rm. 510
St. Louis, MO 63104
Phone: (314)577-8516

★6937★ Stephens College
Health Information Management Program
Campus Box 2083
Columbia, MO 65215
Phone: (314)876-7283

Montana

★6938★ Carroll College
Health Information Management Program
Faculty Box 90
Helena, MT 59625
Phone: (406)442-3450

Nebraska

★6939★ College of St. Mary
Health Information Management Program
1901 S. 72nd St.
Omaha, NE 68124
Phone: (402)399-2400

New Jersey

★6940★ Kean College of New Jersey
Health Information Administration Program
Morris Ave., T206
Union, NJ 07083
Phone: (908)527-3010

New York

★6941★ Ithaca College
Health Information Administration Program
933 Danby Rd.
Ithaca, NY 14850
Phone: (607)274-3355

★6942★ Long Island University
Health Information Administration Program
C.W. Post Campus
Life Science Bldg., Rm. 257
Brookville, NY 11548
Phone: (516)299-2485

★6943★ State University of New York
  Health Science Center at Brooklyn
College of Health Related Professions
Health Information Administration Program
450 Clarkson Ave., Box 105
Brooklyn, NY 11203
Phone: (718)270-7770

★6944★ State University of New York
  Institute of Technology at Utica / Rome
Health Information Administration Program
PO Box 3050
Utica, NY 13504-3050
Phone: (315)792-7391

★6945★ Touro College
Health Information Administration Program
Box 126
525 E. 68th St.
New York, NY 10021
Phone: (212)746-4390

North Carolina

★6946★ East Carolina University
School of Allied Health Sciences
Department of Health Information
  Management
Greenville, NC 27858
Phone: (919)757-4444

★6947★ Western Carolina University
Health Information Management Program
139 Moore Hall
Cullowhee, NC 28723
Phone: (704)227-7113

Ohio

★6948★ Ohio State University
School of Allied Medical Professions
Medical Record Administration Division
1583 Perry St.
Columbus, OH 43210
Phone: (614)292-0567

Oklahoma

★6949★ East Central University
Department of Health Information
  Management
Ada, OK 74820
Phone: (405)332-8000

★6950★ Southwestern Oklahoma State
  University
Health Information Administration Program
100 Campus Dr.
Weatherford, OK 73096
Phone: (405)774-3287

Pennsylvania

★6951★ Gwynedd Mercy College
Health Information Administration Program
Sumneytown Pike
Gwynedd Valley, PA 19437
Phone: (215)646-7300

★6952★ Temple University
College of Allied Health Professions
Department of Health Information
  Management
3307 N. Broad St.
Philadelphia, PA 19140
Phone: (215)707-4811

★6953★ University of Pittsburgh
School of Health Related Professions
Department of Health Records
  Administration
308 Pennsylvania Hall
Pittsburgh, PA 15261
Phone: (412)624-8910

★6954★ York College of Pennsylvania
Health Record Administration Program
Country Club Rd.
York, PA 17403-3426
Phone: (717)846-7788

Puerto Rico

★6955★ University of Puerto Rico
College of Health Related Professions
Health Information Administration Program
Medical Science Campus
PO Box 5067
San Juan, PR 00936
Phone: (809)758-2525

South Carolina

★6956★ Medical University of South
  Carolina
College of Health Related Professions
Department of Health Information
  Administration
171 Ashley Ave.
Charleston, SC 29425
Phone: (803)792-4491

South Dakota

★6957★ Dakota State University
Health Information Administration Program
C.B. Kennedy Center, 151
Madison, SD 57042-1799
Phone: (605)256-5137

Tennessee

★6958★ Tennessee State University
Department of Medical Record
  Administration
Box 654
3500 John A. Merritt Blvd.
Nashville, TN 37209-1561
Phone: (615)320-3702

★6959★ University of Tennessee,
  Memphis
College of Allied Health Sciences
Department of Health Information
  Management
822 Beale St., 300
Memphis, TN 38163
Phone: (901)528-6486

Texas

★6960★ Southwest Texas State
  University
Health Information Management Program
San Marcos, TX 78666
Phone: (512)245-8242

★6961★ Texas Southern University
College of Pharmacy and Health Sciences
Health Information Administration Program
Nabritt Science Bldg.
3100 Cleburne
Houston, TX 77004
Phone: (713)527-7265

★6962★ **University of Texas Medical Branch at Galveston**
School of Allied Health Sciences
Department of Health Information Management
Galveston, TX 77550-1028
Phone: (409)772-3051

Virginia

★6963★ **Norfolk State University**
School of Health Related Professions and Natural Sciences
Health Information Administration Program
2401 Corprew Ave.
Norfolk, VA 23504
Phone: (804)683-8209

Washington

★6964★ **University of Washington**
Health Information Administration Program
Mail Stop JD-02
1107 NE 45th, Ste. 335
Seattle, WA 98105
Phone: (206)543-8810

Wisconsin

★6965★ **University of Wisconsin—Milwaukee**
School of Allied Health Professions
Health Information Administration Program
PO Box 413
Milwaukee, WI 53201
Phone: (414)229-5615

National & International Organizations

★6966★ **American Association of Dental Editors (AADE)**
1100 Lake St., No. 240
Oak Park, IL 60301
Phone: (708)445-0322
Fax: (708)445-0321
Joanna Carey, Exec.Dir.

Founded: 1931. **Members:** 325. **Description:** Seeks to promote and advance dental journalism. **Publications:** *Editors' Journal*, annual. Journal. Covers new developments in dental journalism. Includes membership directory. *Price:* Included in membership dues; $25/year for nonmembers. • *Editors' Newsletter*, 3/year. Newsletter. *Price:* Included in membership dues; $25/year for nonmembers.

★6967★ **American Association for Medical Transcription (AAMT)**
PO Box 576187
Modesto, CA 95357-6187
Phone: (209)551-0883
Free: 800-982-2182
Fax: (209)551-9317
Claudia Tessier, Exec.Dir.

Founded: 1978. **Members:** 9,500. **State Groups:** 26. **Local Groups:** 175. **Description:**

Medical transcriptionists, their supervisors, teachers and students of medical transcription, owners and managers of medical transcription services, and other interested health personnel. Purpose is to provide information about the profession of medical transcription and to provide continuing education for medical transcriptionists. (Medical transcriptionists translate patients' records of medical care and treatment from oral dictation to printed form.) Advocates professional recognition of medical transcriptionists in county, state, and national medical societies and in health care facilities nationwide. Sponsors voluntary certification/credentialing program. Offers updates on developments in medicine and curricula, and on new transcription methods and equipment; sponsors and encourages research in the field. Establishes guidelines for education of medical transcriptionists. Fosters positive relations among medical transcriptionists, the public, members of allied health services, and the legislature. **Publications:** *The AAMT Book of Style for Medical Transcription*. Book. • *BIS Source*, quarterly. Newsletter. • *Cert Alert*, quarterly. Newsletter. • *Journal of the American Association for Medical Transcription*, bimonthly. Journal. Offers guidance in quality assurance for medical transcription, medican and nonmedical educational articles, word lists, and technology updates. *Price:* Included in membership dues; $150/year for nonmembers; $30/issue. • *The Leading Edge*, bimonthly. Newsletter. • *Model Curriculum for Medical Transcription*. • *Model Job Description: Medical Transcriptionist*. Also publishes medical transcription modules and medical transcipion video programs.

★6968★ **American Health Information Management Association (AMRA)**
919 N. Michigan Ave., Ste. 1400
Chicago, IL 60611-1683
Phone: (312)787-2672
Fax: (312)787-9793
Linda Kloss, Exec.Dir.

Founded: 1928. **Members:** 31,000. **State Groups:** 52. **Description:** Registered record administrators; accredited record technicians with expertise in health information management, biostatistics, classification systems, and systems analysis. Sponsors Independent Study Program in Medical Record Technology. Conducts annual qualification examinations to credential medical record personnel as Registered Record Administrators (RRA) and Accredited Record Technicians (ART). Maintains Foundation of Record Education Resource Center. Provides resume referral service; maintains speakers' bureau. **Publications:** *American Medical Record Association--Membership Roster*, semiannual. Membership Directory. • *From the Couch: Official Newsletter of the Mental Health Record Section of the American Medical Record Association*, quarterly. Newsletter. *Price:* Included in membership dues. • *The Gavel: AMRA State Presidents' Newsletter*, quarterly. Newsletter. *Price:* Included in membership dues. • *Journal of AMRA: America's Health Information Leaders*, monthly. Journal. Contains articles on the theory, practice, and current issues in health inf ormation management. Includes book reviews and calendar of events. *Price:* Included in membership dues; $45/year

for nonmembers. • *Medical Record Educator*, quarterly. Newsletter. Provides association and academic news; includes reading list. *Price:* $15/year. • *QA Section Connection*, bimonthly. Newsletter. Provides educational information on the management and methodology of health care quality assurance programs. Includes annual subject index. *Price:* Included in membership dues. • *Spectrum*, quarterly. Newsletter. *Price:* Included in membership dues. Also publishes guides, workbooks, and other materials on medical record management and related subjects. **Formerly:** American Association of Medical Record Librarians; (1938) Association of Record Librarians of North America; (1993) American Medical Records Association.

★6969★ **American Medical Informatics Association (AMIA)**
4915 St. Elmo Ave., Ste. 302
Bethesda, MD 20814
Phone: (301)657-1291
Fax: (301)657-1296
Gail Mutnik, Exec.Dir.

Founded: 1990. **Members:** 3,200. **Description:** Medical personnel, physicians, physical scientists, engineers, data processors, researchers, educators, hospital administrators, nurses, medical record administrators, and computer professionals. Objectives are: to apply advanced systems and information technologies to scientific, literary, and educational activities; to promote excellence in health care; to promote patient care, teaching, research, and health administration. **Publications:** *Abstract Book*, annual. Book. Contains abstracts of sessions of the association's Spring Congress. *Price:* $50 plus shipping and handling. • *Journal of the American Medical Informatics Association*, bimonthly. Journal. • *Proceedings of Symposium on Computer Applications in Medical Care*. Proceedings.

★6970★ **American Medical Writers Association (AMWA)**
9650 Rockville Pike
Bethesda, MD 20814-3998
Phone: (301)493-0003
Fax: (301)493-6384
Lillian Sablack, Exec.Dir.

Founded: 1940. **Members:** 3,900. **Regional Groups:** 17. **Description:** Medical writers, editors, audiovisualists, public relations and pharmaceutical personnel, publishers, and others concerned with communication in medicine and allied sciences. **Publications:** *American Medical Writers Association--Freelance Directory*, biennial. Directory. Lists AMWA members available for work on a freelance basis. *Price:* Included in membership dues; $35/copy to nonmembers. • *American Medical Writers Association Journal*, quarterly. Journal. Includes calendar of events, book reviews, obituaries, and member news. *Price:* Included in membership dues; $35/year for nonmembers. • *American Medical Writers Association--Membership Directory*, annual. Membership Directory. Arranged alphabetically, by chapter, and by primary section affiliation. *Price:* Included in membership dues; $35/copy for nonmembers. • *Biomedical Communication: Selected AMWA Workshops*. Book. Includes 24 manuscripts of AMWA's workshop program, written by the workshop leaders. *Price:* $24 for members; $30 for nonmembers. **Formerly:** (1948) Mississippi Valley Medical Editors' Association.

★ 6971 ★ American Podiatric Medical Writers Association (APMWA)
PO Box 50
New York, NY 10044
Phone: (212)355-5216
Fax: (212)486-7706
Dr. Barry H. Block, Exec.Dir.

Founded: 1985. **Members:** 100. **Description:** Podiatric medical writers. Promotes the improvement of writing on podiatric topics. **Publications:** *American Podiatric Medical Writers Association--Membership Directory*, annual. Membership Directory. *Price:* Free. • *American Podiatric Medical Writers Association--Newsletter*, bimonthly. Newsletter. Lists new members. *Price:* Free with self-addressed stamped envelope.

★ 6972 ★ American Printing House for the Blind (APH)
1839 Frankfort Ave.
PO Box 6085
Louisville, KY 40206-0085
Phone: (502)895-2405
Free: 800-223-1839
Fax: (502)895-1509
Tuck Tinsley, III, Pres.

Founded: 1858. **Description:** Promotes the publication of literature in all media (braille, large type, recorded computer disc) for the blind and the manufacture of educational aids for special use by visually impaired students, such as preschool and vocational materials and talking educational software. Sponsors educational research program offering workshops and seminars involving APH products. Conducts art contest. Developing museum of artifacts from the education field. **Publications:** Annual Report. *Price:* Free. • *APH Slate*, semiannual. Newsletter. Provides information on new products for the visually impaired; also includes organization news and activities. *Price:* Free. • Magazines. Published in braille, large type, and recorded formats. • *Micro Materials Update*, semiannual. Newsletter. Covers microcomputer products designed for blind persons. *Price:* Free.

★ 6973 ★ Archivists and Librarians in the Health Sciences (ALHHS)
c/o Barbara Smith Irwin
University of Medicine and Dentistry of New Jersey
University Libraries
30 12th Ave.
Newark, NJ 07103-2754
Phone: (201)982-6293
Fax: (201)982-7474
Barbara Smith Irwin, Pres.

Founded: 1975. **Members:** 150. **Description:** Medical librarians and archivists with rare book collections, archives, and artifacts related to the history of the health sciences; societies, booksellers, retired librarians, and other interested people. Fosters rare book librarianship within the history of the health sciences field. Promotes continuing education programs. **Publications:** Membership Directory, biennial. • *The*

Watermark, quarterly. **Formerly:** (1992) Association of Librarians in the History of the Health Sciences.

★ 6974 ★ The Arlin J. Brown Information Center (TAJBIC)
PO Box 251
Fort Belvoir, VA 22060
Phone: (703)752-9511
Arlin J. Brown, Dir. & Pres.

Founded: 1963. **Members:** 215. **Description:** Cancer patients, holistic health practitioners, and other interested individuals. Works to educate the public about nontoxic, holistic therapies for cancer and other diseases via advertising and printed material. Offers phone consultation. **Publications:** *Comprehensive Cancer Therapy*. Monograph. • *Health Victory Bulletin*, monthly. Bulletin. Includes updates on alternative cancer treatments and other holistic health information. *Price:* $25. • *March of Truth on Cancer*.

★ 6975 ★ Association of Academic Health Sciences Library Directors (AAHSLD)
2033 6th Ave., No. 804
Seattle, WA 98121
Phone: (206)441-6020
Lynn Kasner Morgan, Pres.

Founded: 1978. **Members:** 136. **Description:** Academic medical and allied health science school libraries, represented by their directors. Promotes academic health sciences libraries in the U.S. and worldwide in cooperation with educational institutions and associations, government agencies, and other nonprofit organizations; seeks to improve the operation of academic health sciences libraries for the benefit of patrons and administrators. Serves as a forum for discussion of common concerns among members; sponsors research. Compiles annual statistics on medical school libraries in the U.S. and Canada. **Publications:** *AAHSLD Membership Directory*, annual. Membership Directory. • Annual Report. • *Association of Academic Health Sciences Library Directors News*. • *Statistics*, annual.

★ 6976 ★ Association of Biomedical Communication Directors (ABCD)
c/o Richard A. McNeely
Biomedical Communications
University of Arizona
Tucson, AZ 85724
Phone: (602)626-7343
Fax: (602)626-2145
Richard A. McNeely, Sec.

Founded: 1972. **Members:** 87. **Description:** Individuals with common managerial concerns in health science communications, such as persons with direct administrative responsibility for operations of a biomedical communications facility in a school or academic health science center. Provides a forum for the sharing and dissemination of information, materials, and ideas. Promotes research and education in administrative practices with regard to health sciences communications. Works to develop information materials such as surveys and profiles helpful in the management of biomedical communications. **Publications:** *Exchange*, quarterly. • *Journal of Biocommunication*, quarterly. Journal. • *Membership Roster*, annual. • *Report of*

Annual Survey of The Directors of Biomedical Communications.

★ 6977 ★ Association of Medical Illustrators (AMI)
1819 Peachtree St. NE, Ste. 620
Atlanta, GA 30309
Phone: (404)350-7900
Fax: (404)351-3348
William H. Just, CMP, Exec.Dir.

Founded: 1945. **Members:** 1,000. **Description:** Medical illustrators and individuals engaged in related pursuits. Promotes the study and encourages the advancement of medical illustration and allied fields of visual education. Works to advance medical education and to promote understanding and cooperation with medical and related professions. Offers placement services. Maintains speakers' bureau; accredits six postgraduate medical illustration programs. Offers continuing education program; provides professional certification; conducts research; compiles statistics. **Publications:** Directory, annual. • *Journal of Biocommunication*, quarterly. Journal. • *Medical Illustration Source Book*, annual. • Newsletter, bimonthly.

★ 6978 ★ Association of Mental Health Librarians (AMHL)
c/o Lenore W. Freehling
Research Library
Reiss-Davis Child Study Center
3200 Motor Ave.
Los Angeles, CA 90034
Phone: (213)204-1666
Lenore W. Freehling, Pres.

Founded: 1964. **Members:** 140. **Description:** Librarians with interest in the field of mental health. Provides a forum for the introduction of new audiovisual and printed materials in the field of mental health; acts as a communication network among mental health library professionals. Disseminates educational information on library management and acquisition methods; makes available research grants. **Publications:** *Directory of Mental Health Libraries and Information Centers*, periodic. Directory. • *President's Letter*, annual. Includes bibliography. **Formerly:** (1980) Society of Mental Health Librarians.

★ 6979 ★ Association for Vital Records and Health Statistics (AVRHS)
c/o Michael R. Lavoie
Vital Records and Health Statistics
47 Trinity Ave. SW, Rm. 217-H
Atlanta, GA 30334
Phone: (404)656-9298
Fax: (404)651-9427
Michael R. Lavoie, Pres.

Founded: 1933. **Members:** 300. **Description:** Officials of state and local health agencies responsible for registration, tabulation, and analysis of births, deaths, fetal deaths, marriages, divorces, and other health statistics. **Publications:** Journal, bimonthly. **Formerly:** (1958) American Association of Registration Executives; (1980) American Association for Vital Records and Public Health Statistics.

★ 6980 ★ **Benjamin Franklin Literary and Medical Society (BFLMS)**
PO Box 567
Indianapolis, IN 46206
Phone: (317)636-8881
Fax: (317)634-1791
Cory SerVaas, M.D., Pres. & CEO

Founded: 1976. **Members:** 2300,000. **Description:** Individuals, industries, and businesses united to support research and promote sciences, literature, and the arts in order to achieve greater public understanding of science and the humanities. Major emphasis is on the dissemination of health, preventive medicine, and nutrition information to the health community and the public. Advocates a preventive approach to health care including proper nutrition, daily exercise, and good health habits. Offers training in cardiopulmonary resuscitation and other lifesaving skills; conducts health education programs. Sponsors the Children's Better Health Institute, which publishes material designed to educate children of preschool through elementary school levels on health, nutrition, safety, and exercise, and provides parents with medical information concerning infants and children. Operates Medical Education and Research Foundation, which disseminates medical information in lay terms, covering concepts and developments in preventive medicine, safety procedures and techniques, health dangers, proper dietary habits, and reports on new and developing treatments and medications for cancer patients and techniques used for early detection of cancer. Sponsors the Saturday Evening Post Society which conducts national health surveys; publicizes advances in science, medicine, nutrition, and preventive medicine; funds research projects; and encourages commercial manufacturers to produce innovative health equipment. Is named for Benjamin Franklin (1706-90), who founded the Pennsylvania Gazette in 1728, which eventually became the Saturday Evening Post. (The society purchased this magazine from the Curtis Publishing Company in 1982.) Franklin was also a strong supporter of the arts and sciences. **Publications:** *Child Life*, 8/year. Magazine. Promotes reading and good health habits in children between the ages of seven and nine. Includes "Ask the Doctor" column, poems, and short stories. *Price:* $14.95/year. • *Children's Digest*, 8/year. Magazine. Promotes reading and good health habits in children between the ages of eight and ten. Includes book reviews. *Price:* $14.95/year. • *Children's Playmate Magazine*, 8/year. Magazine. Promotes reading and good health habits for children between the ages of five and seven. Includes book reviews. *Price:* $14.95/year. • *Humpty Dumpty*, 8/year. Magazine. Promotes reading and good health habits for children between the ages of four and six. *Price:* $14.95/year. • *Jack and Jill*, 8/year. Magazine. Promotes reading and good health habits for children between the ages of six and eight. *Price:* $14.95/year. • *Mecidal Update Newsletter*, monthly. Newsletter. Includes foundation news and research updates. *Price:* $12/year. • *Saturday Evening Post*, bimonthly. • *Turtle Magazine for Preschool Kids*, 8/year. Magazine. Promotes reading and good health, safety, and nutrition habits for children between the ages of two and five. Includes book reviews. *Price:* $14.95/year.

★ 6981 ★ **Biological Photographic Association (BPA)**
1819 Peachtree Rd. NE, Ste. 620
Atlanta, GA 30309-1849
Phone: (404)351-6300
Fax: (404)351-3348
Thomas P. Hurtgen, Exec.Dir.

Founded: 1931. **Members:** 920. **Local Groups:** 29. **Description:** Photographers, technicians, doctors, scientists, educators, and others concerned with photography in the health sciences and related fields. Seeks to advance the techniques of biophotography and biomedical communications through meetings, seminars, and workshops. Has established Board of Registry to offer qualifying examinations for Registered Biological Photographer. **Publications:** *BPA News*, quarterly. Newsletter. Includes list of employment opportunities and annual directory. *Price:* Included in membership dues. • *Journal of Biological Photography*, quarterly. Journal. Provides information on practical applications of the techniques and equipment used by biological photographers and other communications specialists. *Price:* Included in membership dues; $65/year for nonmembers (U.S., Canada, and Mexico); $75/year (overseas).

★ 6982 ★ **Biomedical Informatics Association (BIA)**
Uruguay 252, 2nd Fl. D
1015 Buenos Aires, Argentina
Phone: 1 405755
Fax: 1 4763950

Languages: Spanish. **Description:** An interest group of SADIO Argentina. Computer scientists and information technology professionals engaged in the development and operation of medical information systems. Promotes study, research, and advancement in the field; encourages continuing professional development of members.

★ 6983 ★ **Brain Information Service (BIS)**
BRI Publications Office
43-367 CHS/UCLA School of Medicine
Los Angeles, CA 90024-1746
Phone: (310)825-3417
Fax: (310)206-3499
Dr. Michael H. Chase, Dir.

Founded: 1964. **Description:** A cooperative effort of the UCLA Brain Research Institute and the Biomedical Library. Purpose is to provide rapid, accurate, and complete information in the basic brain sciences to aid investigators and teachers in the field. Subject area of the service includes alcohol and sleep research; it does not cover the literature of diagnosis and treatment of neurological diseases. **Publications:** *Alcohol, Drugs and Driving*, quarterly. Journal. Provides original research reports, review articles, and abstracts of other papers on the impairment of driving skills from alcohol and/or drugs. *Price:* Free. • *Bibliography of Recent Literature in Sleep Research*, quarterly. • *Brain Information Service--Sleep Research*, annual. Compilation of abstracts of sleep research papers presented at the annual meeting of the Association of Professional Sleep Societies. *Price:* $85/copy.

★ 6984 ★ **Canadian Health Libraries Association (CHLA)**
(Association des Bibliotheques de la Sante du Canada — ABSC)
3332 Yonge St.
PO Box 94038
Toronto, ON, Canada M4N 3R1
Phone: (416)485-0377
Fax: (416)485-0377
Dorothy Davey

Founded: 1976. **Members:** 450. **Regional Groups:** 16. **Languages:** English, French. **Description:** Individuals and institutions seeking to improve health and health care by promoting access to information. Represents health library interests on issues involving governmental and private agencies. Provides continuing education program and placement service. **Publications:** *Bibliotheca Medica Canadiana*, quarterly. Journal. • *Membership Directory*, annual. Directory. • Papers, periodic.

★ 6985 ★ **Canadian Organization for Advancement of Computers in Health (COACH)**
10458 Mayfield Rd., Ste. 216
Edmonton, AB, Canada T5P 4P4
Phone: (403)489-4553
Fax: (403)489-3290
Steven A. Huesing, Exec.Dir.

Founded: 1975. **Members:** 750. **Languages:** English. **Description:** Health care and information systems professionals. Promotes education and the exchange of ideas in the field of medical information systems. **Publications:** *Healthcare Computing and Communications Canada*, quarterly. Magazine. Healthcare information and calendar of events.

★ 6986 ★ **Center for Communication Programs (CCP)**
John Hopkins University
111 Market Pl., Ste. 310
Baltimore, MD 21202
Phone: (410)659-6300
Fax: (410)659-6266
Phyllis Tilson Piotrow, Ph.D., Dir.

Founded: 1988. **Description:** Promotes and develops public awareness of family planning, AIDS prevention, and maternal and child health primarily in developing countries. Seeks to increase knowledge of health education through research and technology; implement health communication in worldwide settings; develop innovative mass media programs, interpersonal communication, national campaigns, and training workshops; apply new concepts and technology in evaluating health communication projects. Administers Population Communication Services (founded in 1982), providing technical and financial assistance for information, education, and communication projects to promote family planning and health in developing countries, and Population Information Program (founded in 1972), which maintains the largest computerized bibliographic population data base. **Publications:** Papers, periodic. • *PCS Packet Series*. • *POPLINE Users' Guide*. • *Population Reports*, quarterly. *Price:* Free in developing countries. • *Users' Guide to POPLINE Keywords*. **Formerly:** (1988) Population Information Program.

Committees of Correspondence (COC)
See: Entry 12021

★6987★ **Council for Biomedical Communications Associations**
c/o Stewart White
University of Michigan
Biomedical Communications
1327 Jones Dr., Ste. 104
Ann Arbor, MI 48105
Phone: (313)998-6140
Fax: (313)998-6150
Stewart White, Coord.

Founded: 1970. **Members:** 5. **Description:** Works to explore areas of mutual concern in the health sciences communications field. Provides job placement services. **Publications:** Membership Directory, annual. **Formerly:** (1984) Federation of Biocommunications Societies.

★6988★ **Council on Health Information and Education (CHIE)**
2272 Colorado Blvd., No. 1228
Los Angeles, CA 90041
D. Andre, Dir.

Founded: 1978. **Description:** Promotes health and fitness of Americans through the dissemination of information on health care, nutrition, and exercise. Warns against fads in health and nutrition; conducts research on health and exercise products; reviews books on health, fitness, nutrition, sexuality, and sports. **Publications:** Pamphlets.

Council for Sex Information and Education (CSIE)
See: Entry 11690

★6989★ **Drug Information Association (DIA)**
PO Box 3113
Maple Glen, PA 19002
Phone: (215)628-2288
Fax: (215)641-1229
Erich F. Lukas, Jr., Exec.Dir.

Founded: 1965. **Members:** 6,000. **Description:** Persons who handle drug information in government, industry, the medical and pharmaceutical professions, and allied fields. Seeks to provide mutual instruction on the technology of drug information processing in all areas, including collecting, selecting, abstracting, indexing, coding, vocabulary building, terminology standardizing, computerizing data storage and retrieval, tabulating, correlating, computing, evaluating, writing, editing, reporting, and publishing. Conducts workshops, symposia, and seminars. **Publications:** *Drug Information Association--Membership Directory*, annual. Directory. *Price:* Included in membership dues; $25/copy for nonmembers. • *Drug Information Journal*, quarterly. Journal. *Price:* Included in membership dues.

★6990★ **European Association for Health Information and Libraries (EAHIL)**
60, rue de la Concorde
B-1050 Brussels, Belgium
Phone: 2 5118063
Fax: 2 5141172
Tony McSean, Pres.

Founded: 1987. **Members:** 450. **Languages:** English, French. **Description:** Individuals, institutions, and collectives in 28 countries. Seeks to promote the interests of health libraries worldwide; disseminates information to members. **Publications:** *EAHIL Medical Libraries in Europe, A Directory*, periodic. Directory. • *Newsletter to European Health Librarians*, quarterly. Newsletter.

★6991★ **European Federation for Medical Informatics (MIE)**
Bournemouth House
Christchurch Rd.
Bournemouth, Dorset BH1 3LG, England
Phone: 1202 504318
Fax: 1202 504326
John Bryant, Pres.

Founded: 1976. **Members:** 3,000. **Languages:** English. **Description:** A division of the International Medical Informatics Association. Members are medical informatics societies from 18 countries. Promotes research, development, and teaching of medical informatics. **Publications:** *Medical Informatics*, monthly. • *Methods of Information in Medicine*, monthly.

European Pharmacopoeia Commission (Commission Europeenne de Pharmacopee)
See: Entry 10598

Federation of Behavioral, Psychological and Cognitive Sciences (FBPCS)
See: Entry 7375

Gazette International Networking Institute (GINI)
See: Entry 4488

★6992★ **Health Academy (HA)**
c/o Public Relations Society of America
33 Irving Pl.
New York, NY 10003-2376
Phone: (212)995-2230
Fax: (212)995-0757
Ray Gaulke, COO

Founded: 1989. **Members:** 700. **Description:** A professional section of the Public Relations Society of America. Senior public relations professionals working in hospitals, multi-hospital systems, medical and dental organizations, insurance companies and Health Maintenance Organizations, foundations, rehabilitation facilities, pharmaceutical firms, government health care units, or health education and research organizations; public relations consultants working in the health care industry. Seeks to enhance the quality and stature of health care public relations. Conducts professional development seminars. **Publications:** *By-laws and Membership Directory*, annual. Directory. *Price:* Included in membership dues. • *Health Academy News*, quarterly. Newsletter. • Monographs.

★6993★ **Healthcare Information and Management Systems Society (HIMSS)**
230 E. Ohio St., Ste. 600
Chicago, IL 60611
Phone: (312)664-4467
Fax: (312)664-6143
John A. Page, Exec.Dir.

Founded: 1961. **Members:** 4,600. **Regional Groups:** 40. **Description:** Persons who, by education and/or appropriate experience, are professionally qualified to engage in the analysis, design, and operation of health care information systems, management engineering, telecommunications, and clinical professions. Provides leadership in health care for the management of systems, information, and change, while striving for high quality, efficient and effective patient care through analysis and technology implementation. Maintains speakers' bureau. Offers placement service. **Publications:** Audiotapes. • Audiotapes. • Catalog. Lists publications, including available case studies and technical papers. • *Healthcare Information and Management Systems Society--Membership Directory*, annual. Membership Directory. *Price:* Included in membership dues. • *Healthcare Information Management*, quarterly. Journal. Technical journal. *Price:* Included in membership dues. • *HIMSS News*, monthly. Newsletter. *Price:* Included in membership dues. • Proceedings. • Videos. **Formerly:** (1987) Hospital Management Systems Society.

★6994★ **Health Education Resource Organization (HERO)**
101 W. Read St., Ste. 825
Baltimore, MD 21201
Phone: (410)685-1180
Fax: (410)752-3353

Founded: 1983. **Description:** Provides client care services and preventive education regarding AIDS to Maryland residents; disseminates information on AIDS prevention and treatment to interested individuals nationwide. Provides social service and mental health counseling, support groups, legal aid, emergency funding, referrals, and case management. **Publications:** *Hero News*, monthly. Newsletter. Also produces a wide range of educational materials on AIDS prevention. **Also Known As:** HERO.

★6995★ **Health and Education Resources (HER)**
4733 Bethesda Ave., Ste. 700
Bethesda, MD 20814
Phone: (301)656-3178
Fax: (301)656-3179
Dallas Johnson, Pres.

Founded: 1969. **Description:** Develops audiovisual instruction materials for medical laboratory personnel. **Publications:** *Listen, Look and Learn*, periodic. Audiovisual instructional materials comprised of text, slides, and cassettes.

★6996★ **Health Media Education (HME)**
1207 De Haro St.
San Francisco, CA 94107
Phone: (415)282-9318
Ruth Davidow, Dir.

Founded: 1974. **Members:** 150. **Description:** Produces and distributes materials that provide consumers and health personnel with information needed to plan and implement community health programs. Services include: rental and sale of films; free exhibitions; discussions, and classes.

★ 6997 ★ Health Sciences Communications Association (HESCA)
c/o Eastern Brothers Service
1 Wedgewood Dr.
Jewett City, CT 06351
Phone: (203)376-5915
Fax: (203)376-6621

Founded: 1959. **Members:** 400. **Regional Groups:** 9. **Description:** Media managers, graphic artists, biomedical librarians, producers, faculty members of health science and veterinary medicine schools, health professional organizations, and industry representatives. Acts as a clearinghouse for information used by professionals engaged in health science communications. Coordinates Media Festivals Program which recognizes outstanding media productions in the health sciences. Offers placement service. **Publications:** Brochures. • *Feedback*, 5/year. Provides members with information on the field of biocommunications and on work of colleagues. Includes employment listings and regional news. *Price:* Included in membership dues; $30/year for nonmembers. • *Health Sciences Communications Association--Who's Who*, annual. Membership Directory. *Price:* Included in membership dues. • *HESCA Learning Resources Center Catalog*, annual. Catalog. • *Journal of Biocommunication*, quarterly. Journal. Includes abstracts of biocommunication literature, gallery of medical art, and video and other media reviews. *Price:* Included in membership dues; $25 for nonmembers; $28 for institutions; $20 for students. • Monographs. • *Patient Education Sourcebook*. Also publishes indexes; distributes audiovisual materials. **Formerly:** (1972) Council on Medical Television.

★ 6998 ★ Health Sciences Consortium (HSC)
201 Silver Cedar Ct.
Chapel Hill, NC 27514
Phone: (919)942-8731
Fax: (919)942-3689
Frank B. Penta, Ed.D., Exec.Dir.

Founded: 1971. **Members:** 1,000. **Description:** Cooperative of health science institutions dedicated to publishing effective instructional materials at a low cost. Distributes audiovisual and computer-based instructional programs. Conducts on-site faculty development workshops and seminars. **Publications:** *Consortium News*, quarterly. Newsletter. *Price:* Free. • *Medical, Nursing, Dental, Computer-Assisted Instruction, and Allied Health Catalogs*, periodic. Also publishes health education materials.

★ 6999 ★ HEATH Resource Center (HRC)
1 Dupont Cir., Ste. 800
Washington, DC 20036-1193
Phone: (202)939-9320
Free: 800-544-3284
Fax: (202)833-4760
Rhona Hartman, Dir.

Founded: 1977. **Description:** A program of the American Council on Education. Postsecondary administrators, teachers, and counselors; state and federal education and rehabilitation officials; journalists; librarians. To aid in the postsecondary education of people who are disabled. Provides information on educational support services, procedures, policies, adaptations,

campus opportunities, vocational technical schools, adult education programs, and independent living centers. **Publications:** *Fact Sheet*, 5/year. • *Information*, 3/year. Newsletter. • *Resource Directory*, semiannual. Directory. Also publishes topical informational materials.

★ 7000 ★ In Touch Networks (ITN)
15 W. 65th St.
New York, NY 10023
Phone: (212)769-6270
Free: 800-456-3166
Fax: (212)769-6266
Bruce E. Massis, Gen.Mgr. & VP

Founded: 1974. **Description:** Volunteer service that allows blind or physically impaired people to listen to readings of articles from more than 100 newspapers and magazines via closed-circuit radio. Broadcasts nationally accessible on Galaxy 4 and Satcom C4 satellites. **Publications:** *Program Guide*, annual. Also available on audiotape.

★ 7001 ★ Institute of Health Record Information and Management (IHRIM)
Winwick Hospital
Warrington, Cheshire WA2 8RR, England
Phone: 11925 639772
Brian Lund, Bus.Mgr.

Founded: 1948. **Members:** 1,000. **Regional Groups:** 19. **Languages:** English. **Description:** Individuals in health record information and management. Works to: develop and improve techniques of administrative management and records services; conduct examinations as a means of maintaining levels of quality professionalism; protect the integrity of the profession. Awards certificates and diplomas indicative of professional status. Sponsors lectures and discussions; facilitates information exchange. **Publications:** *The IHRIM Journal*, quarterly. Journal. **Formerly:** (1994) Association of Health Care Information & Medical Records Officers.

★ 7002 ★ International Anatomical Nomenclature Committee (IANC)
Department of Anatomy
UMDS
Guy's Campus
London Bridge SE1 9RT, England
Phone: 171 9555000
Fax: 171 9554915
Murray Brookes, Hon.Sec.

Founded: 1950. **Members:** 3,900. **Languages:** English. **Description:** Anatomists, cytologists, embryologists, zoologists, and anthropologists. Works to establish and standardize structural and developmental terminology in the science fields. **Publications:** *Nomina Anatomica*, quinquennial. Book. • *Nomina Cytologica*, quinquennial. Book. • *Nomina Embryologica*, quinquennial. Book.

★ 7003 ★ International Association of Cancer Registries (IACR) (Association Internationale des Registres du Cancer)
150, cours Albert Thomas
F-69372 Lyon Cedex 08, France
Phone: 72 738485
Fax: 72 738575
Dr. D.M. Parkin, Deputy Sec.

Founded: 1966. **Members:** 384. **Languages:** English. **Description:** Population-based cancer registries in 100 countries. Encourages the development and application of cancer registration and morbidity techniques to studies of defined populations. Endeavors to increase global awareness of the importance of producing accurate and comparable morbidity and mortality data which can be used to generate etiological hypotheses for cancer and as a basis for epidemiological studies, health planning, and other aspects of cancer control. **Publications:** *Cancer Incidence in Five Continents*. • *International Association of Cancer Registries' Newsletter*, biennial. Newsletter.

★ 7004 ★ International Medical Informatics Association (IMIA)
16, place Longemalle
CH-1204 Geneva, Switzerland
Phone: 22 3102649
Dr. Marion J. Ball

Founded: 1978. **Members:** 43. **Regional Groups:** 3. **Languages:** English. **Description:** National organizations in the field of medical information processing. Objective is the international exchange of knowledge concerning health care and biomedical research through medical informatics. Sponsors conferences.

★ 7005 ★ International Society for Clinical Biostatistics (ISCB)
CIBA
CH-4002 Basel, Switzerland
Phone: 61 6967485
Fax: 61 6968477
Dr. Stephen Senn, Contact

Founded: 1978. **Members:** 550. **Languages:** English. **Description:** Statisticians and physicians from 25 countries. Facilitates the exchange of information, experience, and ideas among clinicians, statisticians, and members of related disciplines including epidemiologists, clinical chemists, and pharmacologists. Organizes training courses. **Publications:** *Newsletter*, periodic. Newsletter. • *Statistics in Medicine*, annual.

Intersociety Committee on Pathology Information (ICPI)
See: Entry 10136

★ 7006 ★ Japan Medical Library Association (JMLA) (Nippon Igaku Toshokan Kyokai)
Gakkai Center Bldg. 5 F
2-4-16, Yayoi
Bunkyo-ku
Tokyo 113, Japan
Phone: 3 38151942
Fax: 3 38151608
Takano Masao, Dir. of P.R.

Founded: 1927. **Members:** 105. **Local Groups:** 8. **Languages:** English, Japanese. **De-**

scription: Medical libraries. Promotes progress in medicine through improved medical library services. Conducts research in library administration and information systems management. Facilitates domestic and international interlibrary loans. Provides document supply service for medical institutions, health care professionals, and medical researchers. Conducts research presentations. Bestows awards and distributes funds for research projects. **Publications:** *JMLA Kaiho*, periodic. Newsletter. • *JMLA Kameikan Tokei*, annual. Contains statistics. • *JMLA Kameikan'in Meibo*, periodic. Directory. Includes membership information. • *Medical Library*, quarterly. • *Union Catalog of Foreign Medical Books*. Directory. • *Union List of Medical Periodicals*, periodic. Directory.

★7007★ **Medical Library Association (MLA)**
6 N. Michigan Ave., Ste. 300
Chicago, IL 60602
Phone: (312)419-9094
Fax: (312)419-8950
Carla J. Funk, Contact

Founded: 1898. **Members:** 5,000. **Regional Groups:** 14. **Description:** Librarians and others engaged in professional library or bibliographical work in medical and allied scientific libraries. Purposes are to foster medical and allied scientific libraries, to promote the educational and professional growth of health science librarians, and to exchange medical literature among members. Offers continuing education courses, certification and recertification programs, and placement service. Compiles statistics. **Publications:** *Bulletin of the Medical Library Association*, quarterly. Journal. Contains articles on technical, administrative, and biomedical information research. Includes book reviews and obituaries. Also includes index. *Price:* Included in membership dues; $136/year for nonmembers inside North America; $174/year for nonmembers outside North America. • *Challenge to Action: Planning and Evaluation Guide for Academic Health Sciences Libraries*. Monograph. • *Directory of the Medical Library Association*, annual. Directory. *Price:* Included in membership dues; $150/year for nonmembers. • *Drug Information: A Guide to Current Resources*. Monograph. • *Educational Services in Special Libraries*. Monograph. • *Handbook of Medical Library Practice*. Monograph. Three volumes. • *Hospital Library Management*. Monograph. • *Introduction to Reference Sources in the Health Sciences*. Monograph. • *Medline: A Basic Guide to Searching*. Monograph. • *MLA News*, 10/year. Includes calendar of events, member news, legislative news, media and software news, and obituaries. *Price:* Included in membership dues; $48.50 for nonmembers in U.S., Canada, and Mexico; $61.50/year for nonmembers outside North America. • *Salary Survey*, triennial. Survey. Also publishes other administrative publications.

★7008★ **Medical Records Institute (MRI)**
PO Box 289
Newton, MA 02160
Phone: (617)964-3923
Fax: (617)964-3926
C. Peter Waegemann, Exec.Dir.

Founded: 1979. **Description:** Conducts research and education in the fields of medical documentation and computerization of patient information. Maintains committees and network groups. Compiles statistics. **Publications:** *Handbook of Optical Memory Systems*. Handbook. Monthly updates available. *Price:* $100.50. • Proceedings. • *Toward An Electronic Patient Record*, 10/year. *Price:* $145. **Formerly:** (1988) Institute for Medical Record Economics.

★7009★ **National Association of Health Data Organizations (NAHDO)**
254-B N. Washington St.
Falls Church, VA 22046
Phone: (703)532-3282
Fax: (703)532-3593
Mark H. Epstein, Exec.Dir.

Founded: 1986. **Members:** 200. **Description:** Members include state and federal health data organizations, employee benefits consultants, professional review organizations, data analysis firms, software vendors, and health services consultants, health care researchers, third-party payers, hospital associations, managed care organizations. Seeks to improve health care through the collection, dissemination, and application of health care data. Promotes public availability of and access to health data; supports use of health care data to guide formulation of health policy, purchasing, and establishment of needed health services. Encourages uniformity and accuracy in data collection to support the development of a national health care database. Sponsors technical seminars and programs. Conducts surveys and comparative studies; maintains speakers' bureau. **Publications:** *Ambulatory Health Care Data Collection: A Survey of State Health Data*. Reprint. • Annual Report. • Conference Proceedings. Audiotapes. • *Developing a Uniform Approach for Collecting Ambulatory Health Care Data*. Report. • *Fostering Uniformity for Health Care Data Gathering*. Reprint. • *NAHDO News*, bimonthly. Newsletter. *Price:* $60/year. • *State Health Data Resource Manual: Hospital Discharge Data Systems*. Manual.

National Cancer Registrars Association (NTRA)
See: Entry 5973

National Council on Patient Information and Education (NCPIE)
See: Entry 10612

National Families in Action (NFIA)
See: Entry 12061

National Institute of Electromedical Information (NIEI)
See: Entry 2430

Operation Venus (OV)
See: Entry 6740

R. A. Bloch Cancer Foundation
See: Entry 5982

Recording for the Blind (RFB)
See: Entry 13558

★7010★ **Self-Help Center**
Division of MHAI
150 N. Wacker Dr., Ste. 900
Chicago, IL 60606
Phone: (312)368-9070
Fax: (312)368-0283

Founded: 1974. **Description:** Serves as a clearinghouse for the collection and dissemination of information on all types of selfhelp groups. Organizes mutual consultancy workshops bringing laymen and professionals together with selfhelp group representatives. Conducts educational training programs and research on the emergence, functioning, and effectiveness of selfhelp groups. **Publications:** *Directory of Self-Help/Mutual Aid Groups in Illinois*, semiannual. Directory. Also publishes brochures, pamphlets, workbooks, and articles on selfhelp/mutual aid. **Formerly:** (1981) Self-Help Development Institute.

★7011★ **Substance Abuse Librarians and Information Specialists (SALIS)**
PO Box 9513
Berkeley, CA 94709-0513
Phone: (510)642-5208
Fax: (510)642-7175
Sharon Crockett, Chair

Founded: 1978. **Members:** 180. **Description:** Individuals and organizations interested in the collection, organization, dissemination, exchange, and retrieval of materials concerning substance abuse, including alcohol, tobacco, and other drugs. Provides professional development and exchange of information and concerns about access to and dissemination of information on substance abuse. Offers information on films, books, articles, pamphlets, reports, government publications, libraries, clearinghouses, and information centers. **Publications:** *SALIS Directory*, 3/year. Directory. Lists 197 substance abuse libraries, clearinghouses, and resource and information centers. *Price:* Included in membership dues; $35/copy for nonmembers. • *SALIS News*, quarterly. Newsletter. For substance abuse librarians and information specialists. *Price:* Included in membership dues; $25/year for nonmembers.

Taping for the Blind (TFTB)
See: Entry 13566

★7012★ **Tel-Med, Inc.**
PO Box 1768
Colton, CA 92324
Phone: (909)825-6034
Fax: (909)825-6455
Kenneth Steele, Pres.

Founded: 1971. **Members:** 200. **Description:** Hospitals, medical societies, universities, medical centers, public libraries, and other organizations offering the Tel-Med program. Tel-Med is a library of three to five minute tape-recorded health messages created to be played over the telephone for public use, free of charge. Provides tapes to communities; local libraries are established where individuals from the community can call to listen to tapes. Operates as an information service intended to educate and assist in recognizing early signs of illness and is not designed to diagnose or treat medical problems. Tape scripts are written by medical professionals and examined by a team of physicians; tapes are reviewed at least annually. Offers services and information on a wide range of medical subjects including alcoholism, arthritis, bee stings, cancer, diabetes, drug abuse, influenza, medical costs, mental health, nutrition, parenting, sex education, smoking, vasectomies, and vaginitis. **Publications:** Annual Report, annual. • Brochures. • *Tel-Med Newsletter*, quarterly. Newsletter. Also publishes tape listings and literature on implementation of the Tel-Med program.

Research Centers

Consumer Product Safety Commission National Injury Information Clearinghouse
See: Entry 10978

★7013★ **Harvard University**
Statistical Data and Analysis Center
Dept. of Biostatistics
677 Huntington Ave.
Boston, MA 02115
Phone: (617)432-2815
Fax: (617)432-2832
Stephen W. Lagakos, Dir.

Research Activities and Fields: Tests drugs and conducts research for institutions belonging to AIDS Clinical Trials Group.

★7014★ **Information Sciences Research Institute**
Maternal and Child Health Studies Project
8375 Leesburg Pike, Ste. 439
Vienna, VA 22182
Phone: (703)255-1408
Margaret W. Pratt, Contact

Research Activities and Fields: Center focuses on infant, child, and maternal mortality.

★7015★ **Johns Hopkins University**
Center for Communication Programs
111 Market Pl., Ste. 310
Baltimore, MD 21202-4024
Phone: (410)659-6300
Fax: (410)659-6266
Phyllis T. Piotrow, Ph.D., Dir.

Research Activities and Fields: Health communications in the areas of family planning, maternal and child health, and AIDS prevention. Develops mass media programs and national campaigns, and evaluates health communication projects. Uses behavioral, attitudinal, and other social science research and techniques to enhance and document the impact of mass media and interpersonal communication on family planning and related health behavior. Oversees the Population Communication Services project which conducts audience research, and provides technical and financial assistance for information, education, and communication projects to promote family planning and health in developing countries. **Publications:** *Population Reports* (five times per year).

★7016★ **Johns Hopkins University**
Welch Laboratory for Applied Bioinformatics
2024 E. Monument St., Ste. 1-200
Baltimore, MD 21205
Phone: (410)955-9637
Fax: (410)614-3200
David T. Kingsbury, Ph.D., Dir.

Research Activities and Fields: Database and software development in human genetics. Works extensively with the Genome Data Base (GDB). **Publications:** Annual Report.

★7017★ **Maryland Medical Research Institute**
600 Wyndhurst Ave.
Baltimore, MD 21210
Phone: (410)435-4200
Fax: (410)323-8622
Dr. Genell L. Knatterud, Pres.

Research Activities and Fields: Data gathering, analysis, and design for large-scale clinical trials and epidemiological studies in medical areas such as heart disease, cancer, blood disease, septicemia, AIDS, surgical treatment in retinal diseases, laser therapy, and the effects of diet on health status. **Publications:** *Controlled Clinical Trials* (quarterly).

★7018★ **Massachusetts Health Data Consortium**
400-1 Totten Pond Rd.
Waltham, MA 02154
Phone: (617)890-6040
Fax: (617)890-5460
Elliot M. Stone, Exec.Dir.

Research Activities and Fields: Health services research, including studies of hospitals, patient and physician databases, and discharged patients since 1978.

★7019★ **Oregon Health Sciences University**
Biomedical Information Communication Center
3181 SW Sam Jackson Park Rd.
Portland, OR 97201-3098
Phone: (503)494-4502
Fax: (503)494-4551
Dr. Lesley M. Hallick, Dir.

Research Activities and Fields: Health informatics. BICC comprises four divisions: Health Informatics, Information Services, Information Technology, and Educational Communications. Focused areas of study include: outcomes research, end-user computing in medicine, information retrieval, medical decision making and decision analysis, artificial intelligence and machine learning, image analysis, and patient decision making.

★7020★ **Pennsylvania State University**
Center for Biostatistics and Epidemiology
Milton S. Hershey Medical Center
Dept. of Biostatistics
PO Box 850
Hershey, PA 17033
Phone: (717)531-7178
Fax: (717)531-5779
Dr. Richard Landis, Dir.

Research Activities and Fields: Biostatistics and epidemiology. Current research project

studies effects of sex hormones on adolescent behavior.

★7021★ **Rockefeller University**
Laboratory of History of Medicine and Science
1230 York Ave.
New York, NY 10021-6399
Phone: (212)327-8616
Fax: (212)327-8996
Paul F. Cranefield, Head

Research Activities and Fields: History of electrophysiology, neurophysiology, and biophysics in the 19th century, and the relation between these fields and the early development of psychoanalysis, including studies on Carl Ludwig, Hermann von Helmholtz, Emil du Bois-Reymond, Francois Magendie, Charles Bell, and Joseph Breuer. Also conducts research on the history of the medical and social aspects of mental retardation. Current studies include the outbreak of East Coast Fever (Theilerosis) in the cattle of Southern Africa in 1901, with special reference to governmental and scientific response to the problem in Rhodesia, South Africa, and London.

★7022★ **Societal Institute of the Mathematical Sciences (SIMS)**
97 Parish Rd. S.
New Canaan, CT 06840
Phone: (203)966-1008
Fax: (203)972-6069
Donald L. Thomsen, Jr., Pres.

Research Activities and Fields: Conducts and coordinates studies relating to the application of mathematics and statistics to societal problems. Projects include development of statistical methods for monitoring air pollution, emphasizing acid rain deposits and their effects on human health, and determination of surface and subsurface toxic pollutants. Also develops and evaluates statistical methods for drug use and AIDS research. **Publications:** Technical Report Series (available free of charge); Working Paper Series; Conference Proceedings.

★7023★ **Southern Methodist University**
Center for Statistical Consulting and Research
Dept. of Statistical Science
Dallas, TX 75275-0332
Phone: (214)768-2441
Fax: (214)768-4035
Dr. William H. Frawley, Dir.

Research Activities and Fields: Theory and application of mathematical statistics on problems in engineering and medical, physical, natural, and social sciences, including design of experiments, studies on regression theory, and development of statistical models. **E-mail Address:** h9ar1001@vm.cis.smu.edu. **Formerly:** Statistical Research Laboratory.

★7024★ **Stanford University**
Institute for Communication Research
Dept. of Communication
Stanford, CA 94305
Phone: (415)723-3696
Fax: (415)725-2472
Byron Reeves, Dir.

Research Activities and Fields: Research activities are conducted within various areas of communication processes and effects. These include health communication, which covers community studies in health communication, communication campaigns to prevent heart disease, and a diet assessment project; communication and children, comprised of studies on the relationship of reading and television and children's comprehension of and response to various kinds of televised messages; communication technologies, including studies on instructional television for continuing education, the computer as a communication medium, social and economic impacts of new technologies, and the information society; media and politics, including a study of communication factors in political socialization; and psychological processing of media. **Publications:** Annual Report, listing published writings connected with the Institute.

★7025★ U.S. Department of Defense
Armed Forces Institute of Pathology
Center for Medical Illustration
Washington, DC 20306-6000
Phone: (202)576-2856
Billy C. Arnwine, Director

Research Activities and Fields: Mission of the Center is to: collect, publish, and exhibit illustrations of wounds, injuries, and diseases of medico-military importance; produce illustrations, lantern slides, transparencies, exhibits, and visual media; operate facilities for producing such materials; and provide for the loan of all types of medical illustrations. In support of this mission, research is conducted on medical illustration and all phases of medical photography.

★7026★ U.S. Department of Defense
Armed Forces Institute of Pathology
National Museum of Health and Medicine
6825 16th St., NW
Washington, DC 20306-6000
Phone: (202)576-0401
Fax: (202)576-3573
Dr. Marc S. Micozzi, Director

Research Activities and Fields: The mission of the Museum is to: 1) locate, collect, conserve, preserve, display, and make available selected medical, dental, and veterinary materials, artifacts, and data through exhibits, research, publication, and programs; 2) provide advice in museum technology for study, research, and presentations; 3) conduct research in museum techniques for the medical profession; 4) provide instruction and materials in support of pathology; and 5) provide scientific and historical orientations, briefings, and education to the general public. Museum comprises the Anatomical and Pathological Collections Division, Historical Collections Division, Museum Programs Office, Office of the Museum Registrar, and Otis Historical Archives.

U.S. Department of Health and Human Services
National Cancer Institute
Division of Cancer Treatment
Biometric Research Branch
See: Entry 6152

U.S. Department of Health and Human Services
National Cancer Institute
Epidemiology and Biostatistics Program
Biostatistics Branch
See: Entry 6167

U.S. Department of Health and Human Services
National Cancer Institute
Epidemiology and Biostatistics Program
Extramural Programs Branch
See: Entry 6170

U.S. Department of Health and Human Services
National Cancer Institute
International Cancer Research Data Bank
See: Entry 6173

★7027★ U.S. Department of Health and Human Services
National Center for Health Statistics
6525 Belcrest Rd.
Hyattsville, MD 20782
Phone: (301)436-8500
Manning Feinleib, Director

Research Activities and Fields: The NCHS mission is to collect, analyze, and disseminate national health statistics; conduct research in survey and statistical methodology; provide specialized training programs and technical assistance; and coordinate cooperative programs with state, national, and international organizations. NCHS maintains data systems that produce data in the following areas: extent of illness and disability in the population; distribution and normative standards for physiological and nutritional measurements; national vital statistics, including births, deaths, marriages, and divorces; hospital, nursing home, and ambulatory care utilization; health expenditures; family formation, growth, and dissolution; and other major health topics. Principal components include the Office of Analysis and Epidemiology, Office of Research and Methodology, and Office of Vital and Health Statistics Systems (Health Care Statistics Division, Health Examination Statistics Division, Health Interview Statistics Division, and Vital Statistics Division).

U.S. Department of Health and Human Services
National Institute on Alcohol Abuse and Alcoholism
Biometry and Epidemiology Division
See: Entry 12108

U.S. Department of Health and Human Services
National Institute of Child Health and Human Development
Epidemiology, Statistics and Prevention Research Division
See: Entry 5190

★7028★ U.S. Department of Health and Human Services
National Institute of Diabetes and Digestive and Kidney Diseases
Division of Intramural Research
Mathematical Research Branch

NIH Bldg. 31, Rm. 4B54
9000 Rockville Pike
Bethesda, MD 20892
Phone: (301)496-4325
Fax: (301)402-0535
Dr. John M. Rinzel, Chief

Research Activities and Fields: Branch conducts research on the mathematical and theoretical aspects of biological problems and the development of analytical and numerical methodology underlying such an approach. The research programs are designed to provide a formal basis and theoretical apparatus for the rational analysis and quantitative interpretation of biological phenomena. Research is organized around biological subject-matter areas rather than around subdisciplines of mathematics. Primary areas of research include neuroscience, physiology, cell biology, and endocrinology.

U.S. Department of Health and Human Services
National Institute on Drug Abuse
Epidemiology and Prevention Research Division
See: Entry 12129

U.S. Department of Health and Human Services
National Institute of Environmental Health Sciences
Statistics and Biomathematics Branch
See: Entry 5112

U.S. Department of Health and Human Services
National Institute of Mental Health
Division of State and Community Systems Development
Survey and Analysis Branch
See: Entry 7626

U.S. Department of Health and Human Services
National Institute of Mental Health
Epidemiologic and Services Research Division
See: Entry 7627

U.S. Department of Health and Human Services
National Institute of Mental Health
Epidemiology and Services Research Division
Services Research Branch
See: Entry 7631

U.S. Department of Health and Human Services
National Institute of Neurological Disorders and Stroke
Biometry and Field Studies Branch
See: Entry 8442

★7029★ U.S. Department of Health and Human Services
National Institutes of Health
Lister Hill National Center for Biomedical Communications

NIH Bldg. 38A
8600 Rockville Pike
Bethesda, MD 20894
Phone: (301)496-4441
Fax: (301)402-0118
Dr. Daniel R. Masys, Director

Research Activities and Fields: Information and computer science, biomedical imaging, and biomedical communications. This research supports the basic mission of the National Library of Medicine (NLM) as well as NLM services to the health sciences research, education, and clinical care communities, access to health data, medical informatics, and the use of new technologies in health science education. Research in medical informatics includes projects in expert systems, intelligent database systems, natural language systems, and machine learning. Research in biomedical imaging includes projects in electronic image processing, which include the capture, storage, processing, online retrieval, transmission and display of both biomedical documents (mainly journals) and medical images. Research in technology applications to health science education includes projects in computer and multimedia technologies, and supports their application in health professions education. Activities include development of new technologies and liaison to health professions schools and professional societies for field testing and other collaboration. Principal components are the: Audiovisual Program Development Branch, Communications Engineering Branch, Computer Science Branch, Educatioinal Technology Branch, and Information Technology Branch. Principal components are the: Audiovisual Program Development Branch, Communications Engineering Branch, Computer Science Branch, Educational Technology Branch, and Information Technology Branch.

★ 7030 ★ U.S. Department of Health and Human Services
National Institutes of Health
Lister Hill National Center for Biomedical Communications
Audiovisual Program Development Branch
NIH Bldg. 38A, Rm. B2N35
8600 Rockville Pike
Bethesda, MD 20894
Phone: (301)496-5721
James Main, Chief

Research Activities and Fields: Branch plans and develops prototype demonstration instructional products in collaboration with other Center branches; provides instructional design and multimedia technological services for the development of instructional materials; conducts research on the utilization of improvements in media production techniques; and provides professional and technical multimedia expertise for all Center projects.

★ 7031 ★ U.S. Department of Health and Human Services
National Institutes of Health
Lister Hill National Center for Biomedical Communications
Communications Engineering Branch

NIH Bldg. 38A
8600 Rockville Pike
Bethesda, MD 20894
Phone: (301)496-4496
Fax: (202)402-0341
Dr. George Thoma, Chief

Research Activities and Fields: Branch conducts and sponsors research and development in digital image processing, signal processing, and communication systems and techniques. It provides technical consultation and explores applications that offer the potential for improving biomedical information transfer and storage. It designs, demonstrates, and evaluates prototype systems for various modes of image processing and transmission, and supervises the engineering and technical operation of biomedical communications networks. Prototype systems have been developed for document capture, document image storage on digital optical disk media, automated document image delivery high-resolution document image retrieval and display, and digital imagery for biomedicine (both multiple gray levels and color). These prototype systems serve as testbeds to study issues related to the mission of the National Library of Medicine, such as digital X-ray archiving document preservation, document delivery, and patron access to the biomedical literature.

★ 7032 ★ U.S. Department of Health and Human Services
National Institutes of Health
Lister Hill National Center for Biomedical Communications
Computer Science Branch
National Library of Medicine
8600 Rockville Pike
Bethesda, MD 20894
Phone: (301)496-9300
Dr. Lawrence Kingsland III, Chief

Research Activities and Fields: Branch performs basic and applied research, including development of prototype systems and comprehensive models, in the areas of knowledge representation and reasoning, indexing vocabularies, natural language understanding, artificial intelligence, expert systems, machine learning, information storage and retrieval, data manipulation, and human factors engineering. This involves development and use of clinical database systems, knowledge-based systems, and literature-based systems. Branch also identifies salient features of extramurally developed information systems for determining complementary research areas and conducting experiments of mutual interest with other researchers; develops human performance models for intelligent medical information systems and studies techniques for man-machine interactive systems and man-machine dialogs; and initiates and sponsors research and development of decision-making models for use in health care delivery.

★ 7033 ★ U.S. Department of Health and Human Services
National Institutes of Health
Lister Hill National Center for Biomedical Communications
Educational Technology Branch

NIH Bldg. 38A
8600 Rockville Pike
Bethesda, MD 20894
Phone: (301)496-6280
Fax: (301)480-3035
Dr. Alexa McCray, Acting Chief

Research Activities and Fields: Branch conducts research and development in educational technology, including computer, audiovisual, and multimedia methods of supporting health professions education and information transfer. It identifies and demonstrates educational technologies and technology applications that meet identified needs in health science instruction; evaluates the effectiveness of educational and information technologies; carries out educational research to identify and define technology applications; and investigates educational applications of computer systems, programs, authoring languages, and collateral technologies. Branch also operates the Learning Center for Interactive Technology, which serves as the focus for using, investigating, and displaying new and effective applications of developing educational technologies to faculties and staff of health sciences educational institutions and other visitors. In addition, Branch assists health profession educators and others in improving the use of educational technologies in health sciences education through training, demonstration, and consultation activities.

★ 7034 ★ U.S. Department of Health and Human Services
National Institutes of Health
Lister Hill National Center for Biomedical Communications
Information Technology Branch
NIH Bldg. 38A
8600 Rockville Pike
Bethesda, MD 20894
Phone: (301)496-1936
Fax: (301)480-6183
Charles Goldstein, Chief

Research Activities and Fields: Branch conducts research and development, provides technical consultation and direction, identifies user needs, and conducts evaluations related to exploring the application of computer-based systems to the processing and transfer of health sciences information. It plans, designs, develops, and evaluates prototype systems for the processing, storage, and retrieval of biomedical information, with emphasis on full-text and factual databases and provides a laboratory for the demonstration and evaluation of these systems. Branch also consults and collaborates with other Center and Library of Medicine divisions to facilitate application of basic and applied information science to information transfer projects. In addition, Branch performs modifications and enhancements to operating systems,software tools, programming languages, and research computer networks as they impact these activities.

★ 7035 ★ U.S. Department of Health and Human Services
National Institutes of Health
National Library of Medicine
Extramural Programs Division

Bldg. 38A
8600 Rockville Pike
Bethesda, MD 20894
Phone: (301)496-4621
Fax: (301)402-0421
Dr. Milton Corn, Acting Associate Director

Research Activities and Fields: Division administers the National Library of Medicine's program of grants for support of fundamental and applied work in the organization, representation, utilization, and dissemination of health knowledge, with special interest in medical informatics and biotechnology information. Grants are generally awarded in three main categories: Research, Development, and Demonstration awards are investigator-initiated projects that address problems of health information access, retrieval, and utilization. Projects may investigate fundamental research problems, may undertake development of theoretical findings into practical applications, or may demonstrate the value of new technologies in operating situations. First Independent Research Support and Transition (FIRST) Awards are small project awards to young investigators. Eligibility is limited to those who have received the doctorate within five years but have not yet served as principal investigator on a research grant or contract. Research Career Development Awards are available to young scientists with three or more years of postdoctoral experience. These awards enable the scientist to devote full time to research.

University of Alabama at Birmingham
National Spinal Cord Injury Statistical
  Center
See: Entry 8474

★7036★ **University of Arizona**
Program in Applied Mathematics
Math Bldg. 89
Tucson, AZ 85721
Phone: (520)621-4664
Fax: (520)621-8322
Prof. Michael Tabor, Head

Research Activities and Fields: Application of mathematics to problems in biological sciences, engineering, geosciences, medicine, optics, and physics. **E-mail Address:** applmath@ccit.arizona.edu.

★7037★ **University of California at**
  Berkeley
Statistical Laboratory
367 Evans Hall
Berkeley, CA 94720
Phone: (510)642-2450
Fax: (510)642-7892
Dr. Leo Breiman, Dir.

Research Activities and Fields: Theory of statistics and its application to probabilistic and statistical problems in astronomy, biology, communications, econometrics, engineering, experimentation, medicine, meteorology, operations research, physics, probability theory, and public health, including studies in cosmology, population dynamics, competition of species, theory of diagnostic tests, bioassay, apparent associations between diseases, carcinogenesis, sequential analysis, decision making, nonparametric inference, and game theory. **Publications:** Publications in Statistics (irregularly).

University of Cincinnati
Division of Epidemiology and Biostatistics
See: Entry 5192

★7038★ **University of Minnesota**
Coordinating Centers for Biometric
  Research
Division of Biostatistics
2221 Univ. Ave. SE, Ste. 200
Minneapolis, MN 55414-3080
Phone: (612)626-8887
Fax: (612)626-0660
Tom Louis, Div.Hd.

Research Activities and Fields: Colon cancer, AIDS, chronic obstructive pulmonary disease, coronary heart disease, otitis media (ear infection), and hypertension. Research activities include developing new statistical methodology; collaborating on applied projects that influence clinical, public health, and public policy; and applied and methodological research.

University of Missouri—Kansas City
Drug Information Service
See: Entry 10638

★7039★ **University of Vermont**
Medical Biostatistics/Biometry Facility
27 Hills Science Bldg.
Burlington, VT 05405
Phone: (802)656-2526
Fax: (802)656-0632
Taka Ashikaga, Ph.D., Dir.

Research Activities and Fields: Survey research of health behaviors; epidemiologic surveys for respiratory disease, cancer, and lower back pain; clinical trials; and evaluative research in the areas of public education, school health education, patient education, and health professional education. Also performs psychiatric patient follow-up studies, cancer mortality studies, studies on genetic-based disease factors, and studies of impact of acid rain on forest ecosystems. Conducts surveys of public opinion, mass media patterns, marketing practices, and health status.

State Government Agencies

Vital Statistics

★7040★ **Alabama Department of Public**
  Health
Health Statistics Center
Vital Records Division
PO Box 5625
Montgomery, AL 36103-5625
Phone: (334)613-5426
Fax: (334)613-5408

★7041★ **Alaska Department of Health and**
  Social Services
Public Health Division
Vital Statistics Section
PO Box 110610
Juneau, AK 99811-0610
Phone: (907)465-3090
Fax: (907)586-1877

★7042★ **Arizona Department of Health**
  Services
Vital Records Office
1740 W. Adams
Phoenix, AZ 85007
Phone: (602)255-3260
Fax: (602)542-1062

★7043★ **Arkansas Department of Health**
Health Resources Bureau
Vital Records Division
PO Box 3278
Little Rock, AR 72203-3278
Phone: (501)661-2371
Fax: (501)671-1450

★7044★ **California Health and Welfare**
  Agency
Health Services Department
Vital Records Branch
304 S St.
Sacramento, CA 95814
Phone: (916)322-1356
Fax: 800-858-5553

★7045★ **Colorado Public and Environment**
  Department
Administration and Support Office
Health Statistics and Vital Records Division
4300 Cherry Creek Dr. S.
Denver, CO 80222-1530
Phone: (303)692-2200
Fax: (303)782-0095

★7046★ **Connecticut Department of**
  Public Health
Vital Records Division
150 Washington St.
Hartford, CT 06106
Phone: (203)566-6545
Fax: (203)566-3302

★7047★ **Delaware Department of Health**
  and Social Services
Public Health Division
Office of Vital Statistics
Jesse Cooper Bldg.
PO Box 637
Dover, DE 19903
Phone: (302)739-4721
Fax: (302)739-6659

★7048★ **District of Columbia Department**
  of Human Services
Research and Statistics Division
Vital Records Branch
PO Box 54047
Washington, DC 20032
Phone: (202)727-0682
Fax: (202)279-6014

★7049★ **Florida Department of Health and**
  Rehabilitative Services
Vital Statistics Office
1317 Winewood Blvd.
Tallahassee, FL 32399-0700
Phone: (904)359-6970
Fax: (904)922-2993

★ 7050 ★   Georgia Department of Human
Resources
Public Health Division
Vital Statistics Office
2 Peachtree St., NW
Atlanta, GA 30303
Phone: (404)656-4750
Fax: (404)657-2715

★ 7051 ★   Hawaii Department of Health
Health Status Monitoring Office
Vital Records Section
1250 Punchbowl St.
Honolulu, HI 96813
Phone: (808)586-4539

★ 7052 ★   Idaho Department of Health and
Welfare
Health Division
Vital Statistics Center
PO Box 83720
Boise, ID 83720-0036
Phone: (208)334-5976
Fax: (208)334-6558

★ 7053 ★   Illinois Department of Public
Health
Finance and Administration Office
Vital Records Division
535 W. Jefferson St.
Springfield, IL 62761
Phone: (217)782-3987

★ 7054 ★   Indiana Department of Health
Public Health Statistics Division
1330 W. Michigan St.
PO Box 1964
Indianapolis, IN 46206-1964
Phone: (317)383-6512
Fax: (317)633-6779

★ 7055 ★   Iowa Department of Public
Health
Planning and Administration Division
Vital Records Bureau
Lucas State Office Bldg.
321 E. 12th St.
Des Moines, IA 50319
Phone: (515)242-6332
Fax: (515)281-4958

★ 7056 ★   Kansas Department of Health
and Environment
Health and Environment Statistics Division
Vital Statistics Office
900 SW Jackson, Ste. 620
Topeka, KS 66612-1290
Phone: (913)296-1417
Fax: (913)296-1231

★ 7057 ★   Kentucky Human Resources
Cabinet
Health Services Department
Vital Statistics Division
275 E. Main St.
Frankfort, KY 40621
Phone: (502)564-8956
Fax: (502)564-6533

★ 7058 ★   Louisiana Department of Health
and Hospitals
Health Information Division
Vital Statistics Section
PO Box 3214
Baton Rouge, LA 70821
Phone: (504)342-8094
Fax: (504)342-8098

★ 7059 ★   Maine Department of Human
Services
Research and Vital Statistics Division
State House Sta. 11
Augusta, ME 04333
Phone: (207)287-3181
Fax: (207)287-3005

★ 7060 ★   Maryland Department of Health
and Mental Hygiene
Policy and Health Statistics Division
201 W. Preston St., 5th Fl.
Baltimore, MD 21201
Phone: (410)225-5806
Fax: (410)225-6489

★ 7061 ★   Massachusetts Executive Office
of Health and Human Services
Public Health Department
Vital Records and Statistics Division
150 Tremont St.
Boston, MA 02111
Phone: (617)727-0036
Fax: (617)727-2559

★ 7062 ★   Michigan Department of Public
Health
State Registrar and Health Statistics
Center
3423 N. Logan St.
PO Box 30195
Lansing, MI 48909
Phone: (517)335-8676
Fax: (517)335-9476

★ 7063 ★   Minnesota Department of Health
Health Delivery Systems Bureau
Vital Records Section
717 Delaware St. SE
PO Box 9441
Minneapolis, MN 55440
Phone: (612)623-5121
Fax: (612)623-5794

★ 7064 ★   Mississippi Department of Health
Information Resources Bureau
Vital Statistics Division
PO Box 1700
Jackson, MS 39215-1700
Phone: (601)987-4983
Fax: (601)987-4982

★ 7065 ★   Missouri Department of Health
Health Resources Division
Vital Records Bureau
PO Box 570
Jefferson City, MO 65102
Phone: (314)751-6383

★ 7066 ★   Montana Department of Health
and Environmental Sciences
Health Services Division
Vital Records and Statistics Bureau
Cogswell Bldg., Rm. C108
Helena, MT 59620
Phone: (406)444-2614

★ 7067 ★   Nebraska Department of Health
Vital Records Office
State Office Bldg., 3rd Fl.
14th and M St.
Lincoln, NE 68509
Phone: (402)471-2871
Fax: (402)471-0383

★ 7068 ★   Nevada Department of Human
Resources
Health Division
Vital Records Bureau
505 E. King St., Rm. 201
Carson City, NV 89710
Phone: (702)687-4480

★ 7069 ★   New Hampshire Department of
Health and Human Services
Public Health Services Division
Vital Records and Health Statistics Bureau
6 Hazen Dr.
Concord, NH 03301
Phone: (603)271-4514
Fax: (603)271-3745

★ 7070 ★   New Jersey Department of
Health
Health Care Planning, Financing, and
Information Services Development
Division
Health Statistics Center
CN 360
Trenton, NJ 08625-0360
Phone: (609)984-6702
Fax: (609)292-3780

★ 7071 ★   New Mexico Department of
Health
Public Health Division
Vital Statistics Section
1190 St. Francis Dr.
PO 26110
Santa Fe, NM 87502-6110
Phone: (505)827-2342
Fax: (505)827-2329

★ 7072 ★   New York State Department of
Health
Vital Statistics Section
Corning Tower, Empire State Plaza
Albany, NY 12237-0001
Phone: (518)474-3069

★ 7073 ★   North Carolina Department of
Environment, Health, and Natural
Resources
Health Director's Office
Vital Records Section
PO Box 27687
Raleigh, NC 27611
Phone: (919)715-4125
Fax: (919)715-3060

★ 7074 ★   North Dakota Department of
Health and Consolidated Laboratories
Administrative Services Section
Vital Records Division
600 E. Boulevard Ave.
Bismarck, ND 58505-0200
Phone: (701)328-2360
Fax: (701)328-4727

★7075★ **Ohio Department of Health**
Vital Statistics Bureau
246 N. High St.
Columbus, OH 43266-0588
Phone: (614)466-2533
Fax: (614)644-0085

★7076★ **Oklahoma Department of Health**
Vital Records Division
1000 NE 10th St.
PO Box 53551
Oklahoma City, OK 73152
Phone: (405)271-4040
Fax: (405)271-3431

★7077★ **Oregon Department of Human**
  Resources
Health Division
Vital Statistics Section
PO Box 14450
Portland, OR 97214-0450
Phone: (503)731-4000
Fax: (503)731-4078

★7078★ **Pennsylvania Department of**
  Health
Vital Records Division
PO Box 1528
New Castle, PA 16103
Phone: (412)656-3111

★7079★ **Rhode Island Department of**
  Health
Vital Record Division
3 Capitol Hill
Providence, RI 02908-5097
Phone: (401)277-2812
Fax: (401)277-6548

★7080★ **South Carolina Department of**
  Health and Environmental Control
Vital Records and Public Health Statistics
  Office
2600 Bull St.
Columbia, SC 29201
Phone: (803)734-4810
Fax: (803)734-4620

★7081★ **South Dakota Department of**
  Health
Vital Records Program
445 E. Capitol
Pierre, SD 57501-3185
Phone: (605)773-4961
Fax: (605)773-5683

★7082★ **Tennessee Department of Health**
Administrative Services Bureau
Health Statistics Division
Vital Records Section
312 8th Ave., 9th Fl.
Nashville, TN 37247-0101
Phone: (615)532-2679
Fax: (615)741-2491

★7083★ **Texas Department of Health**
Vital Statistics Bureau
1100 W. 49th St.
Austin, TX 78756
Phone: (512)458-7692
Fax: (512)458-1477

★7084★ **Utah Department of Health**
Health Statistics and Vital Records Bureau
PO Box 142802
Salt Lake City, UT 84114-2802
Phone: (801)538-6360
Fax: (801)538-6694

★7085★ **Vermont Agency of Human**
  Services
Health Department
Public Health, Analysis and Policy Division
Vital Records Unit
PO Box 70
Burlington, VT 05402
Phone: (802)863-7300
Fax: (802)863-7425

★7086★ **Virginia Office of Health and**
  Human Resources
Health Department
Vital Records and Health Statistics Office
1500 E. Main St.
PO Box 2448
Richmond, VA 23218
Phone: (804)786-6201
Fax: (804)786-4616

★7087★ **Washington Department of**
  Health
Health Statistics Center
PO Box 45010
Olympia, WA 98504-5010
Phone: (360)753-5936

★7088★ **West Virginia Department of**
  Health and Human Resources
Public Health Bureau
Epidemiology and Health Promotion Office
Health Statistics Division
State Capital Complex, Bldg. 3, Rm. 518
Charleston, WV 25305-0501
Phone: (304)558-9100
Fax: (304)558-1035

★7089★ **Wisconsin Department of Health**
  and Social Services
Health Division
Vital Statistics Office
PO Box 7850
Madison, WI 53707-7850
Phone: (608)266-0330
Fax: (608)267-2832

★7090★ **Wyoming Department of Health**
Preventive Medicine Division
Vital Records Section
Hathaway Bldg., 4th Fl.
Cheyenne, WY 82002-6004
Phone: (307)777-6004
Fax: (307)777-5402

Chapter 36
Laboratory Medicine

Medical & Allied Health Schools

Blood Bank Technology

Facilities listed below offer Specialist in Blood Bank (SBB) education programs accredited by the American Association of Blood Banks (8101 Glenbrook Rd., Bethesda, MD 20814-2749, 301-907-6977) in collaboration with the Commission on Accreditation of Allied Health Education Programs of the American Medical Association, 515 N. State St., Ste. 7530, Chicago, IL 60610, (312) 464-4623.

Alabama

★7091★ **University of Alabama at Birmingham / American Red Cross Blood Services, Alabama Region**
Specialist in Blood Bank Technology Program
SHRP Bldg., Rm. 381
1714 9th Ave. S.
Birmingham, AL 35294-1270
Phone: (205)934-5987

California

★7092★ **Sacramento Medical Foundation Blood Bank**
Specialist in Blood Bank Technology Program
1625 Stockton Blvd.
Sacramento, CA 95816-7089
Phone: (916)456-1500

District of Columbia

★7093★ **Walter Reed Army Medical Center**
Blood Bank Fellowship Program
Bldg. 2, Rm. 2B90
6825 16th St. NW
Washington, DC 20307-5001
Phone: (202)782-6210

Florida

★7094★ **Central Florida Blood Bank, Inc.**
Specialist in Blood Bank Technology Program
32 W. Gore St.
Orlando, FL 32806
Phone: (407)849-6100

★7095★ **Florida Blood Services**
Transfusion Medicine Academic Center
Specialist in Blood Bank Technology Program
445 31st St. N.
St. Petersburg, FL 33713
Phone: (813)327-0168

Georgia

★7096★ **American Red Cross Blood Services, Atlanta Region**
Specialist in Blood Bank Technology Program
1925 Monroe Dr. NE
Atlanta, GA 30324
Phone: (404)881-0668

Illinois

★7097★ **University of Illinois at Chicago / LifeSource**
Department of Medical Laboratory Sciences
Specialist in Blood Bank Technology Program
808 S. Wood St.
Rm. 690
Chicago, IL 60612-7307
Phone: (312)996-7767

Louisiana

★7098★ **Alton Ochsner Medical Foundation**
Specialist in Blood Bank Technology Program
1516 Jefferson Hwy.
New Orleans, LA 70121
Phone: (504)842-3530

★7099★ **Charity Hospital Medical Center of Louisiana**
Blood Bank Technology Program
1532 Tulane Ave.
New Orleans, LA 70112-2860
Phone: (504)568-2466

Maryland

★7100★ **Johns Hopkins Hospital**
Specialist in Blood Bank Technology Program
Carnegie Bldg., No. 667
600 N. Wolfe St.
Baltimore, MD 21287-6667
Phone: (410)955-6580

★7101★ **U.S. Department of Health and Human Services**
National Institutes of Health
Clinical Center Blood Bank
Specialist in Blood Bank Technology Program
Bldg. 10-A, Rm. 1C-711
9000 Rockville Pike
Bethesda, MD 20892-1184
Phone: (301)496-8335

Massachusetts

★7102★ **Deaconess Hospital**
Specialist in Blood Bank Technology Program
1 Deaconess Rd.
Boston, MA 02215
Phone: (617)632-0433

Minnesota

★7103★ **Memorial Blood Center of Minneapolis**
Specialist in Blood Bank Technology Program
2304 Park Ave. S.
Minneapolis, MN 55404
Phone: (612)871-3300

Missouri

★7104★ **Barnes Hospital**
School of Blood Banking
1 Barnes Hospital Plaza
St. Louis, MO 63110
Phone: (314)362-1478

Ohio

★7105★ **American Red Cross Blood**
Services, Northern Ohio Region
Specialist in Blood Bank Technology
Program
3747 Euclid Ave.
Cleveland, OH 44115-2501
Phone: (216)431-3052

★7106★ **Hoxworth Blood Center**
Specialist in Blood Bank Technology
Program
3130 Highland Ave.
PO Box 67005
Cincinnati, OH 45267-0055
Phone: (513)558-1271

★7107★ **Ohio State University Hospitals /**
American Red Cross Blood Services,
Central Ohio Region
Specialist in Blood Bank Technology
Program
995 E. Broad St.
Columbus, OH 43205
Phone: (614)253-7981

Texas

★7108★ **Gulf Coast School of Blood Bank**
Technology
1400 La Concha Lane
Houston, TX 77054-1802
Phone: (713)791-6201

★7109★ **University of Texas Health**
Science Center at San Antonio
University Health System Blood Bank
Specialist in Blood Bank Technology
Program
4502 Medical Dr.
San Antonio, TX 78229-4493
Phone: (210)616-2807

★7110★ **University of Texas Medical**
Branch at Galveston
Specialist in Blood Bank Technology
Program
301 University Blvd.
Galveston, TX 77555-0717
Phone: (409)772-4866

★7111★ **University of Texas**
Southwestern Medical Center at Dallas
Department of Medical Laboratory
Sciences
Specialist in Blood Bank Technology
Program
5323 Harry Hines Blvd.
Dallas, TX 75235-8878
Phone: (214)648-1780

Wisconsin

★7112★ **Blood Center of Southeastern**
Wisconsin
638 N. 18th St.
PO Box 2178
Milwaukee, WI 53201-2178
Phone: (414)933-5000

National & International Organizations

★7113★ **Accrediting Bureau of Health**
Education Schools (ABHES)
Oak Manor Office
29089 U.S. 20 W.
Elkhart, IN 46514
Phone: (219)293-0124
Fax: (219)295-8564
Mary Lou Reed, Exec.Sec.

Founded: 1964. **Members:** 161. **Description:**
Serves as a nationally recognized accrediting
agency of health education institutions and
schools conducting medical laboratory technician and medical assistant education programs.
Establishes criteria and standards for the administration and operation of health education
institutions. Seeks to enhance the profession
through the improvement of schools, courses,
and the competence of graduates. Schools
must apply voluntarily for accreditation; once
accredited, they must report to the bureau annually and be reexamined at least every 6 years.
Has accredited 15 programs for medical laboratory technicians, 124 medical assistants, and 80
institutions of allied health. **Publications:**
ABHES News, periodic. Newsletter. Includes
calendar of events and lists personnel promotions and appointments. • *Accrediting Bureau
of Health Education Schools--Directory of Accredited Schools and Programs*, periodic. Directory. Lists health education institutions and programs accredited by the commissioners of of
the ABHES. **Formerly:** Accrediting Bureau of
Medical Laboratory Schools.

★7114★ **American Association of**
Bioanalysts (AAB)
818 Olive St., Ste. 918
St. Louis, MO 63101-1598
Phone: (314)241-1445
Fax: (314)241-1449
Mark S. Birenbaum, Admin.

Founded: 1956. **Members:** 1,000. **Descrip-**
tion: Professional organization of directors,
owners, managers, and supervisors of bioanalytical clinical laboratories devoting their efforts to
clinical laboratory procedure and testing. Sponsors Proficiency Testing Service open to individuals engaged in the clinical laboratory field. Provides specialized education and representation
before federal and state legislatures and regulatory agencies. **Publications:** *AAB Bulletin*, bimonthly. Bulletin. • *AAB Update*, periodic.

★7115★ **American Association of Blood**
Banks (AABB)
8101 Glenbrook Rd.
Bethesda, MD 20814
Phone: (301)907-6977
Fax: (301)907-6895
Karen Lipton, JD, CEO

Founded: 1947. **Members:** 11,500. **Descrip-**
tion: Community and hospital blood centers and
transfusion and transplantation services, physicians, nurses, technologists, administrators,
blood donor recruiters, scientists, and individuals involved in related activities. Encourages the
voluntary donation of blood and other tissues
and organs through education, public information, and research. Operates the National Blood
Exchange; inspects and accredits blood banks
and parentage testing laboratories; sponsors
the National Blood Foundation; maintains a rare
donor file and reference laboratory system.
Maintains over 40 scientific, technical, and administrative committees and three councils.
Publications: *AABB News Briefs*, 11/year.
Newsletter. Includes calendar of events, employment listings, and government affairs update. *Price:* Included in membership dues. •
American Association of Blood Banks--
Membership Directory, biennial. Directory. Lists
institutional and individual members in alphabetical and geographic order. *Price:* Included in
membership dues; $50 for nonmembers. •
Blood Bank Week. Newsletter. Covers scientific, legislative, and regulatory events affecting
blood banking and transfusion medicine. *Price:*
$98/year for members; $128/year for nonmembers. • Books. • *Directory of Community Blood*
Centers, biennial. Directory. *Price:* $25 for par-
ticipating members; $50 for nonmembers. •
Monographs. • *Standards for Blood Banks and*
Transfusion Services, every 18 months. *Price:*
$20 for members; $35 for nonmembers. • *Tech-*
nical Manual, triennial. Manual. *Price:* $48 for
members; $60 for nonmembers; $45 for students. • *Transfusion*, monthly. Journal. Presents scientific, technical, and administrative papers relating to the field of blood banking. Includes advertisers index and convention abstract. *Price:* Included in membership dues;
$135/year for nonmember individuals; $195/
year for institutions.

★7116★ **American Association for Clinical**
Chemistry (AACC)
2101 L St. NW, Ste. 202
Washington, DC 20037-1526
Phone: (202)857-0717
Free: 800-892-1400
Fax: (202)887-5093
Richard Flaherty, Exec.VP

Founded: 1948. **Members:** 10,000. **Local**
Groups: 22. **Description:** Clinical laboratory
scientists and others engaged in the practice of
clinical chemistry in independent laboratories,
hospitals, and allied institutions. Maintains Endowment Fund for Research in Clinical Chemistry. Maintains employment service. Sponsors:
therapeutic drug monitoring and endocrinology
programs; continuing education programs; quality control programs. Compiles statistics; sponsors speakers' bureau. **Publications:** Annual
Report, annual. • Books. • *Clinical Chemistry*
Journal, monthly. Journal. • *Clinical Chemistry*

News, monthly. • *Clinical Chemistry Reference Edition*, monthly. • Membership Directory, annual. **Formerly:** (1976) American Association of Clinical Chemists.

American Association of Veterinary Laboratory Diagnosticians (AAVLD)
See: Entry 13037

★7117★ **American Blood Resources Association (ABRA)**
PO Box 669
Annapolis, MD 21404-0669
Phone: (410)263-8296
Fax: (410)263-2298
James P. Reilly, Exec.Dir.

Founded: 1972. **Members:** 100. **Description:** Operators of blood plasma centers and U.S. plasma fractionators. Represents the interests of plasma collection centers and promotes plasma as an important part of the blood industry. Has developed code of ethics. Conducts specialized education program; compiles statistics; maintains speakers' bureau. **Publications:** *Journal of the ABRA*, quarterly. Journal. Focuses on the business, operation, regulation, and scientific needs of the commercial blood and plasma collection industry. Includes industry news. *Price:* Included in membership dues; $75/year for nonmembers.

★7118★ **American Clinical Laboratory Association (ACLA)**
1919 Pennsylvania Ave. NW, Ste. 800
Washington, DC 20006
Phone: (202)887-1400
Fax: (202)466-2198
Hope S. Foster, Gen. Counsel

Founded: 1971. **Description:** Corporations, partnerships, or individuals owning or controlling one or more independent clinical laboratory facilities operating for a profit and licensed under the Clinical Laboratories Improvement Act of 1967 or the Clinical Laboratories Improvement Amendment of 1988, or accredited by the Medicare program. Purposes are: to promote the development of uniformly high quality laboratory testing; to eliminate the present inequalities in the standards applied to different segments of the clinical laboratory market; to discourage the enactment of restrictive legislative or regulatory policies that may impede the free flow of commerce or operate to the detriment of the public. Examines federal and state health care and laboratory regulatory and legislative proposals and submi ts comments and opinions to the appropriate agencies or legislative bodies.

★7119★ **American Federation for Clinical Research (AFCR)**
6900 Grove Rd.
Thorofare, NJ 08086
Phone: (609)848-7072
Fax: (609)853-5991
Pat McFadden, Contact

Founded: 1940. **Members:** 12,500. **Regional Groups:** 4. **Local Groups:** 19. **Description:** Provides a forum for young clinical scientists (under 43); promotes and encourages original research in clinical and laboratory medicine. Offers specialized education program; maintains

information services on membership status, files, and National Abstracting Processing. Annual scientific program presents sections on: Cardiovascular; Dermatology; Endocrinology; Gastroenterology; Genetics; Hematology; Immunology and Connective Tissue; Infectious Disease; Metabolism; Neoplastic Disease; Patient Care; Pulmonary; Renal and Electrolytes. **Publications:** *AFCR Newsletter*, quarterly. Newsletter. • *Clinical Research Journal*, quarterly. Journal.

★7120★ **American Medical Technologists (AMT)**
710 Higgins Rd.
Park Ridge, IL 60068
Phone: (708)823-5169
Free: 800-275-1268
Fax: (708)823-0458
Gerard P. Boe, Ph.D., Exec.Dir.

Founded: 1939. **Members:** 21,000. **State Groups:** 38. **Description:** National professional registry of medical laboratory technologists, technicians, medical assistants, dental assistants, and phlebotomists. Maintains job information service. Sponsors AMT Institute for Education, which has developed continuing education programs. **Publications:** *AMT Events and Continuing Education Supplement*, 8/year. Journal. Includes book reviews and legislative updates. *Price:* Included in membership dues; $35/year for nonmembers in the U.S.; $45/year for foreign nonmembers.

★7121★ **American Society for Apheresis (ASFA)**
3900 E. Timrod
Tucson, AZ 85711
Phone: (602)327-8584
Phillip Gutt, Contact

Founded: 1981. **Members:** 800. **Description:** Physicians, nurses, technologists, scientists, and other allied health professionals active in the field of apheresis, the separation and removal of components from blood. Aims to: promote training and research in apheresis therapy for patients; improve the care and management of apheresis donors; encourage the use of apheresis technology; assist in forming standards and regulations in the field of apheresis. Provides opportunity for the exchange of experiences and opinions through discussions, presentations, and publications; offers consulting on problems in the practice of apheresis. Conducts studies and courses. Plans to establish a central registry of apheresis information. **Publications:** *ASFA Newsletter*, periodic. Newsletter. • *Journal of Clinical Apheresis*, quarterly. Journal. *Price:* $124/year.

★7122★ **American Society for Clinical Laboratory Science (ASMT)**
7910 Woodmont Ave., Ste. 1301
Bethesda, MD 20814
Phone: (301)657-2768
Fax: (301)657-2909
Dr. Ian R. Horen, CAE, Exec.Dir.

Founded: 1932. **Members:** 20,000. **Description:** Primarily clinical laboratory personnel who have an associate or baccalaureate degree and clinical training and specialists who hold at least a master's degree in one of the major fields of

clinical laboratory science such as bacteriology, mycology, or biochemistry; also includes technicians, specialists, and educators with limited certificates and students enrolled in approved programs of clinical laboratory studies and military medical technology schools. Promotes and maintains high standards in clinical laboratory methods and research and advances standards of education and training of personnel. Conducts educational program of seminars and workshops. Sponsors award competition to encourage the writing of scientific papers. Approves programs of continuing education and maintains records on participation in continuing education programs for members. Maintains speakers' bureau. **Publications:** *ASCLS Today*, monthly. Newsletter. *Price:* Included in membership dues. • Books. • Brochures. • *Clinical Laboratory Science*, bimonthly. Journal. *Price:* Included in membership dues; $40 for individuals; $60 for corporations. • Manuals. • Videos. **Formerly:** American Society of Medical Technologists; (1936) American Society of Clinical Laboratory Technicians; (1993) American Society for Medical Technology.

★7123★ **American Society of Clinical Pathologists (ASCP)**
2100 W. Harrison
Chicago, IL 60612
Phone: (312)738-1336
Free: 800-621-4142
Fax: (312)738-1619
Robert C. Rock, M.D., Sr.VP

Founded: 1922. **Members:** 65,974. **Description:** Works to promote public health and safety by the appropriate application of pathology and laboratory medicine. Provides educational, scientific, and charitable services. **Publications:** *American Journal of Clinical Pathology*, monthly. Journal. • *ASCP News*, monthly. Newsletter. • *Laboratory Medicine*, monthly. • Membership Directory, biennial. • *Pathology Patterns*, semiannual.

★7124★ **American Society of Cytopathology (ASC)**
400 W. 9th St., Ste. 201
Wilmington, DE 19801
Phone: (302)429-8802
Fax: (302)429-8807
Y. S. Erozan, M.D., Sec.-Treas.

Founded: 1951. **Members:** 3,500. **Description:** Cytologists, pathologists, and clinicians with M.D.s; nonmedical professional personnel (Ph.D.s); associate members are cytotechnologists. (Cytology is the biological study of the formation, structure, and function of cells.) Seeks to make the cytological method of early cancer detection universally available to potential victims. Promotes establishment of additional educational and training facilities; encourages implementaion of research programs; inspects and accredits cytology laboratories; assists in preparation of national registry examination for cytotechnologists. Reviews cytotechnology training programs for accreditation. **Publications:** *Acta Cytologica*, bimonthly. Journal. • *The ASC Bulletin*, bimonthly. Bulletin. • *Consider a Career in Cytotechnology*. Brochure. • *Cytopathology Review Course Syllabus*. **Formerly:** Inter-Society Cytology Council.

★7125★ **American Society for Cytotechnology (ASCT)**
920 Paverstone Dr., No. D
Raleigh, NC 27615
Phone: (919)848-9911
Fax: (919)848-9853
Margaret A. Bundy, Exec.Dir.
Founded: 1979. **Members:** 1,500. **Description:** Cytotechnologists (technologists trained in the identification of cells and cellular abnormalities such as cancer), students of cytotechnology, and medical doctors in the field of cytopathology. Seeks to: enhance the role of the cytotechnologist in the health care system; stimulate communication and cooperation among cytotechnologists and other health professionals; inform members of current legislative and legal issues pertaining to the profession of cytotechnology and other related professions; support and promote educational opportunities. Urges participation in educational programs available through the American Society of Cytology. **Publications:** *ASCT News*, monthly. Newsletter. Covers educational, legislative, and other developments affecting the profession. Includes book reviews, calendar of events and employment listings.

★7126★ **Association of Clinical Scientists**
PO Box 1292
Farmington, CT 06034
Phone: (203)679-2154
Fax: (203)674-1700
Dr. F. William Sunderman, Jr., Sec.-Treas.
Founded: 1949. **Members:** 666. **Description:** Professional society of physicians and scientists working in various fields of laboratory medicine. Seeks to promote education and research in clinical science by practical methods; maintain and improve the accuracy of measurements in clinical laboratories and promote uniformity in clinical laboratory procedures; encourage cooperation between physicians and nonphysicians concerned with the application of scientific methods to medical practice. **Publications:** *Annals of Clinical and Laboratory Science*, bimonthly. Journal. *Price:* Included in membership dues. • *Clinical Science Trumpet*, bimonthly. Newsletter. • Membership Directory, annual. **Formerly:** (1956) Clinical Science Club.

★7127★ **Association of Medical Laboratory Technologists of Zimbabwe**
PO Box 8220
Causeway
Harare, Zimbabwe
Languages: English. **Description:** Medical and laboratory technologists. Seeks to maintain high standards in the practice of medical laboratory technology, and to insure effective and economical laboratory services. Promotes continuing professional education of members.

★7128★ **Canadian Society of Laboratory Technologists (CSLT)**
(Societe Canadienne des Technologistes de Laboratoire — SCTL)
PO Box 2830 LCD 1
Hamilton, ON, Canada L8N 3N8
Phone: (905)528-8642
Fax: (905)528-4968
E. Valerie Booth, Exec.Dir.

Founded: 1937. **Members:** 21,800. **Languages:** English, French. **Description:** Laboratory technologists in 20 countries. Seeks to maintain high standards of medical laboratory technology to insure effective and economical laboratory services. Promotes the interests of medical laboratory technologists. Emphasizes the importance of continuing education; sponsors courses. Communicates with government authorities concerning issues affecting members. Offers insurance program to members. Organizes national medical laboratory week annually. Bestows awards. **Publications:** *Annual Roster*. • Bulletin, monthly. • *Canadian Journal of Medical Technology*, quarterly. • *Catalogs of Continuing Education*. • *Guidelines for Laboratory Safety*. Manual.

★7129★ **Clinical Laboratory Management Association (CLMA)**
9 Old Lincoln Hwy., Ste. 201
Malvern, PA 19355
Phone: (610)647-8970
Fax: (610)889-9731
Paul Pomerantz, Exec.VP

Founded: 1971. **Members:** 7,000. **Local Groups:** 86. **Description:** Individuals holding managerial or supervisory positions with clinical laboratories; persons engaged in eduation of such individuals; manufacturers or distributors of equipment or services to clinical laboratories. Objectives are: to enhance management skills and promote more efficient and productive department operations; to further exchange of professional knowledge, new technology, and colleague experience; to encourage cooperation among those engaged in management or supervisory functions. Activities include: workshops, seminars, and expositions; dissemination of information about legislation and other topics. **Publications:** *Clinical Laboratory Management Association--Membership Directory*, annual. Directory. Arranged alphabetically and geographically. *Price:* Included in membership dues; $250/year for nonmembers. • *Clinical Laboratory Management Review*, bimonthly. Journal. Covers concepts and techniques of management and issues and trends in health care that affect the clinical laboratory. *Price:* Included in membership dues; $55/year for nonmembers; $80/year for institutions. • *CLMA Management Briefs*, monthly. Newsletter. Contains articles on time management, employee performance appraisals, selecting a laboratory, information system and communication skills. *Price:* Included in membership dues. • *Conference Proceedings*, periodic. **Formerly:** (1976) American Association of Clinical Laboratory Supervisors and Administrators.

★7130★ **Clinical Ligand Assay Society (CLAS)**
3139 S. Wayne Rd.
Wayne, MI 48184
Phone: (313)722-6290
Fax: (313)722-7006
Daisy S. McCann, Ph.D., Exec.Dir.

Founded: 1976. **Members:** 1,000. **Regional Groups:** 12. **Description:** Clinical laboratory directors and doctors, hospital technologists, private laboratories, industry, and other individuals interested in ligand assays. (Ligand assay is a

quantitative clinical laboratory technique for a specific area of diagnostic testing which measures proteins, peptides, or haptens and deals with methods such as radioimmunoassay, florescenceimmunoassay, and receptor assay.) Objectives are to establish and promote high standards in the science and application of ligand assay technology by encouraging research, educating practitioners, and fostering communication and cooperation among individuals in laboratories, medicine, academia, and industry. Sponsors job placement service. **Publications:** Directory, periodic. • *Journal of Clinical Immunoassay*, quarterly. Journal. Contains reviews and articles on clinical ligand assay techniques. Includes bibliography of recent articles and manufacturers' directory. *Price:* Included in membership dues. • *Journal of Clinical Ligand Associations*, periodic. Journal. Also publishes syllabi for annual meeting. **Formerly:** (1981) Clincial Radioassay Society.

★7131★ **College of American Pathologists (CAP)**
325 Waukegan Rd.
Northfield, IL 60093-2750
Phone: (708)446-8800
Free: 800-323-4040
Fax: (708)446-8807
Lee VanBremen, Ph.D.,,, Exec.VP

Founded: 1947. **Members:** 14,000. **Description:** Physicians practicing the specialty of pathology (diagnosis, treatment, observation, and understanding of the progress of disease or medical condition) obtained by morphologic, microscopic, chemical, microbiologic, serologic, or any other type of laboratory examination made on the patient. Fosters improvement of education, research, and medical laboratory service to physicians, hospitals, and the public. Provides job placement information for members. Conducts laboratory accreditation program and laboratory proficiency testing surveys. Maintains spokepersons network; provides free health information to the public; compiles statistics; sponsors educational programs. **Publications:** *Archives of Pathology and Laboratory Medicine*, monthly. Journal. *Price:* Free to members. • *CAP TODAY*, monthly. Newspaper. Includes scientific abstracts. *Price:* Included in membership dues; $24/year for nonmembers; $65/year for nonmembers (outside North America); $65/year for nonmembers (outside Mexico). • *College of American Pathologists--Directory*, annual. Directory. *Price:* Included in membership dues. • *College of American Pathologists--Job Placement Bulletin*, bimonthly. Bulletin. Updating service providing job listings. *Price:* Included in membership dues. Also publishes other materials of interest to pathologists and the public.

★7132★ **Council of Community Blood Centers (CCBC)**
725 15th St. NW, Ste. 700
Washington, DC 20005
Phone: (202)393-5725
Fax: (202)393-1282
James L. MacPherson, Exec.Dir.

Founded: 1962. **Members:** 63. **Description:** Independent, nonprofit, federally licensed blood centers serving defined geographic areas. Purpose is to ensure an optimal supply of blood,

blood components, and blood derivatives and the development of a comprehensive range of the highest quality blood services to meet the needs of the American people. Compiles data and statistics; conducts research concerning organizational, administrative, fiscal, and operational phases of blood banking; establishes liaison and conducts cooperative activities of all kinds with national, regional, and local associations, groups, and organizations having a relationship of any kind to the drawing, processing, storing, or distribution of blood. **Publications:** *CCBC Newsletter*, weekly. Newsletter. Includes calendar of events and list of employment opportunities. *Price:* Free to members; $192/year for nonmembers (U.S. and Canada); $240/year for nonmembers (outside the U.S. and Canada). • Membership Directory, semiannual. **Formerly:** (1971) Community Blood Bank Council.

★ 7133 ★ **Credentialing Commission (CC)**
818 Olive St., Ste. 918
St. Louis, MO 63101-1598
Phone: (314)241-1445
Fax: (314)241-1449
Mark S. Birenbaum, Ph.D., Admin.

Founded: 1962. **Description:** Autonomous certifying agency for general supervison, medical technologists, laboratory technicians, and physician office laboratory technicians. Maintains Continuing Education for Professional Advancement (CEPA) program to approve and record continuing education unit credits. **Formerly:** Accrediting Commission.

★ 7134 ★ **European Bank of Frozen Blood of Rare Groups (EBFBRG)**
(Banque Europeenne de Sange Congele de Groupes Rares)
Plesmanlaan 125
NL-1066 AD Amsterdam, Netherlands
Phone: 20 5123377
Fax: 20 5123474
Mrs. M.A.M. Overbeeke, Exec. Officer

Founded: 1969. **Members:** 54. **Languages:** English, French. **Description:** Individuals representing national blood banks and research centers.

★ 7135 ★ **European Committee for Clinical Laboratory Standardization (ECCLS)**
School of Postgraduate Medical Education
University of Warwick
Coventry, W. Midlands CV4 7AL, England
Phone: 1203 523523
Fax: 1203 524311
Prof. Keith Shinton, Sec.

Founded: 1979. **Members:** 10. **National Groups:** 10. **Languages:** English. **Description:** Academic, scientific, and professional societies concerned with clinical laboratory sciences such as clinical chemistry, haematology, microbiology, and general pathology; governmental and intergovernmental organizations and agencies involved in health services; industrial firms supplying materials to clinical laboratories. Devises and maintains standards of laboratory performance that ensure optimal medical and veterinary care. Provides a forum for exchange of information and for discussion, approval, and evaluation of laboratory standards; develops standards for other organizations on a consulta-

tive or contractual basis; advises government and government-related groups on the adoption and implementation of laboratory standards. Encourages the formation of national and regional committees for clinical laboratory standards. **Publications:** Journal, periodic. • Newsletter, periodic. • *Standards*, periodic. **Formerly:** (1992) European Committee for Clinical Laboratory Standards.

★ 7136 ★ **International Academy of Cytology (IAC)**
Dept. of Obstetrics and Gynecology
University of Freiburg
Hugstetterstrasse 55
79106 Freiburg, Germany
Phone: 761 2703012
Fax: 761 2703122
Manuel Hilgarth, Sec.

Founded: 1957. **Members:** 1,900. **Languages:** English, French, German, Japanese, Spanish. **Description:** Doctors of medicine concerned with research in clinical cytology (the scientific study of the structure, organization, and function of cells, particularly for cancer diagnosis); cytotechnologists actively engaged in the practice of cytodiagnosis and research. Encourages cooperation among persons engaged in the practice of clinical cytology; facilitates international exchange of information on specialized problems in this field; standardizes terminology; stimulates development of all phases of clinical cytology and encourages research. **Publications:** *Acta Cytologica*, bimonthly. • *Analytic and Quantitative Cytology and Histology*, bimonthly. • Newsletter, periodic.

★ 7137 ★ **International Association of Medical Laboratory Technologists (IAMLT)**
(Association Internationale des Technologistes de Laboratoire Medical)
Adolf Fredriks Kyrkogata 11
S-111 37 Stockholm, Sweden
Phone: 8 103031
Fax: 8 109061
Margareta Haag, Exec.Dir.

Founded: 1954. **Members:** 38. **National Groups:** 38. **Regional Groups:** 1. **Languages:** English, French, German. **Description:** Member of the World Health Organization. National societies united to provide a means of communication among medical laboratory technologists in 38 countries. Promotes the continued education of health laboratory workers; plans curriculum for courses in health laboratory technology and management. Advises governments and governmental agencies on these matters and on validation of examinations leading to qualifications in medical laboratory subjects. Maintains travel and training fund. **Publications:** *Curriculum for a Course in Health Safety*. Journal. • *International Directory of Medical Laboratory Science Education*, periodic. Directory. Details medical lab education in 26 countires. • *MedTecinternational*, semiannual. Journal. Covers information for medical laboratory technologists.

★ 7138 ★ **International Board of Cytopathology (IBC)**
Hugstetterstrasse 55
Universitaets-Frauenklinik
79106 Freiburg, Germany
Phone: 761 2703012
Fax: 761 2703122
Manuel Hilgarth, Sec.

Description: A committee of the International Academy Cytology.

★ 7139 ★ **International Federation of Blood Donor Organizations (IFBDO)**
(Federazione Internazionale delle Organizzazioni dei Donatori di Sangue)
30, rue du Boichot
F-39100 Dole, France
Phone: 84 723494
Pierre Pelletier, Sec.

Founded: 1955. **Members:** 43. **Languages:** English, French, Spanish. **Description:** National voluntary blood donor associations united to promote voluntary blood giving. Considers problems of common interest such as voluntary donations from which all political and religious considerations are excluded, and medical progress of blood transfusions. Seeks laws related to voluntary blood giving and governmental action prohibiting blood commerce. Exchanges information; acts as liaison with the European Council, League of Red Cross and Red Crescent Societies, United Nations Educational, Scientific and Cultural Organization, and World Health Organization. Provides specialized education. **Publications:** *FIODS Revue*, quarterly.

★ 7140 ★ **International Federation of Clinical Chemistry (IFCC)**
(Federation Internationale de Chimie Clinique)
Dept. of Clinical Biochemistry
Rambam Medical Center
31096 Haifa, Israel
Phone: 4 528628
Fax: 4 542409
Prof. Oren Zinder, Sec.

Founded: 1952. **Members:** 55. **Languages:** English, French. **Description:** National societies of clinical chemistry representing 25,000 individuals. Purposes are to advance the science and practice of clinical chemistry and to enhance its service to health and medicine. Authorizes and sponsors international congresses of clinical chemistry; encourages joint participation of members in related congresses. Conducts studies, reviews, and reports on clinical chemistry problems of international concern. Offers advice, consultation, and recommendations on clinical chemistry problems. Provides the basis for closer liaison and the free exchange of professional information and data among clinical chemists worldwide. Promotes international cooperation and coordination of clinical chemistry in matters of research, reference methods and materials, uniform regulations and statutes, and related subjects. Assists in the improvement of professional standards and codes of ethics wherever possible. Contributes in other ways wherever feasible to the improvement of clinical chemistry and its services to humanity. Maintains expert committees for investigation into such subjects as instrumentation, theory of reference values, nomenclature and principles of quality control, assessment of nutritional status, assessment of drugs of abuse, assessment of molecular biological techniques, proteins, immunoassay, enzymes, quantities, and units. Organizes training courses and regional seminars; sponsors IFCC travelling lectureship. **Publications:** Directory, periodic. • *Journal of the International Federation of Clinical Chemistry*, bimonthly. Journal. • *Recommendations on Clinical Chemistry*, periodic. Report. • *Report*, annual. **Formerly:** International Association of Clinical BioChemists.

★7141★ **International Society of Blood Transfusion (ISBT)**
(Societe Internationale de Transfusion Sanguine — SITS)
6, rue A. Cabanel
F-75739 Paris Cedex, France
M. Garretta, Sec.Gen.

Founded: 1937. **Members:** 1,950. **National Groups:** 105. **Languages:** English, French. **Description:** Members of national blood bank societies in 105 countries. Works toward solving the scientific, technical, social, and ethical problems related to the transfusion of blood. Encourages closer relations among individuals dealing with such problems; standardizes methods and equipment. Facilitates the exchange of information among members. **Publications:** *Transfusion Today*, quarterly. • *Vox Sanguinis*, quarterly. Also publishes congress proceedings and technical guides.

★7142★ **International Society for Clinical Enzymology (ISCE)**
New York State Dept. of Health
Wadsworth Center
PO Box 509
Albany, NY 12201-0509
Phone: (518)474-1166
Fax: (518)473-7130
Robert Rej, Ph.D., Sec.

Founded: 1976. **Members:** 450. **Description:** Scientists from 41 countries. Unites persons interested in the field. Works to attract young scientists and clinicians to the field of clinical enzymology. Sponsors courses. **Publications:** Newsletter, quarterly. • *Proceedings of ISCE Scientific Meetings*, annual.

★7143★ **International Society for Clinical Laboratory Technology (ISCLT)**
818 Olive St., Ste. 918
St. Louis, MO 63101-1598
Phone: (314)241-1445
Fax: (314)241-1449
Mark S. Birenbaum, PhD, Admin.

Founded: 1962. **Members:** 6,000. **State Groups:** 12. **Description:** Clinical laboratory supervisors, technologists and technicians; physician's office laboratory technicians. Conducts educational programs; maintains placement service; offers specialized education. **Publications:** *ISCLT Alert*, periodic. Features condensed reports of important news and legislative developments. • *ISCLT Newsletter*, bimonthly. Newsletter. **Formerly:** International Society of Clinical Laboratory Technologists.

★7144★ **National Accrediting Agency for Clinical Laboratory Sciences (NAACLS)**
8410 W. Bryn Mawr Ave., Ste. 670
Chicago, IL 60631
Phone: (312)714-8880
Fax: (312)714-8886
Olive M. Kimball, Exec.Dir.

Founded: 1973. **Members:** 695. **Description:** Independently accredits hospitals, colleges, and universities in four allied health professions - medical technologist, medical laboratory technician, histotechnologist, and pathologists assistant. Establishes standards for quality educational programs; determines if hospitals and colleges are maintaining standards through self-study and on-site visits. Provides workshops for program officials on self-study and accreditation. **Publications:** *Guide to Accreditation*. • *NAACLS News*, quarterly. Newsletter. Includes news related to allied health professions and listing of position vacancies. *Price:* Free to members and accredited program officials; $15/year for nonmembers. • *NAACLS Program Approval Guide*. • *National Accrediting Agency for Clinical Laboratory Sciences--Annual Report*. Annual Report. • *National Accrediting Agency for Clinical Laboratory Sciences--Essentials*. **Formerly:** (1973) Board of Schools of the ASCP.

★7145★ **National Blood Transfusion Service**
PO Box A101
Avondale
Harare, Zimbabwe
Phone: 4 707801
Fax: 4 707820
D.M. Connolly, Gen.Mgr.

Founded: 1986. **Description:** Promotes the availability of blood supplies for tranfusions in Zimbabwe. Disseminates information. **Publications:** *Annual Report*. • Booklet. AIDS awareness and giving blood.

★7146★ **National Certification Agency for Medical Lab Personnel (NCA)**
7910 Woodmont Ave., Ste. 1301
Bethesda, MD 20814
Phone: (301)654-1622
Fax: (301)657-2909
Kathleen M. Greenberg, Exec.Dir.

Founded: 1977. **Members:** 65,000. **Description:** Persons who direct, educate, supervise, or practice in clinical laboratory science. To assure the public and employers of the competence of clinical laboratory personnel; to provide a mechanism for individuals demonstrating competency in the field to achieve career mobility. Develops and administers competency-based examinations for certification of clinical laboratory personnel; provides for periodic recertification by examination or through documentation of continuing education. Compiles statistics.

★7147★ **National Phlebotomy Association (NPA)**
5615 Landover Rd.
Hyattsville, MD 20784
Phone: (301)699-3846
Fax: (301)699-5766
Diane Crawford, CEO

Founded: 1978. **Members:** 10,000. **Description:** Purposes are: to offer educational pro-

grams for phlebotomists; to accredit phlebotomy programs; to give national certification examinations in phlebotomy at the request of approved program. (Phlebotomy is the collection of a blood specimen for analysis in the treatment of disease.) Conducts regional workshops and educational programs. Compiles statistics. **Publications:** *National Phlebotomy Association Certified Phlebotomists Registry*, periodic. • *Self Study Modules in Phlebotomy*. • *The Tourniquet*, annual. Newsletter. Includes list of employment opportunities, research reports, and profiles of members. *Price:* Free.

★7148★ **National Rare Blood Club (NRBC)**
Associated Health Foundation
99 Madison Ave.
New York, NY 10016
Phone: (212)889-8245
Edward Birnbaum, Pres.

Founded: 1978. **Members:** 16,000. **Description:** Persons ages 18-65 with rare blood types who are physically able to donate blood. Operates as a voluntary community service with no fees or dues involved.

★7149★ **National Registry in Clinical Chemistry (NRCC)**
1155 16th St. NW
Washington, DC 20036
Phone: (202)745-1698
Fax: (202)872-4615
Gilbert E. Smith, PhD, Exec.Dir.

Founded: 1967. **Members:** 700. **Description:** Certifying agency to evaluate the credentials of clinical chemistry practitioners; issues certificates to those who are qualified. Provides annual evaluation of clinical laboratory specialists in the chemical field who voluntarily present their credentials to the registry. **Publications:** Directory, annual.

★7150★ **National Society for Histotechnology (NSH)**
4201 Northview Dr., Ste. 502
Bowie, MD 20716-1073
Phone: (301)262-6221
Fax: (301)262-9188
Roberta Mosedale, Exec.Sec.

Founded: 1973. **Members:** 4,800. **State Groups:** 42. **Description:** Histology laboratory technicians, pathologists, laboratory equipment manufacturers' representatives, and interested individuals. Encourages the professional growth and advancement of histoprofessionals and promotes the exchange of ideas and knowledge significant to histotechnology. Assists in the establishment and mutual understanding of related societies. Provides continuing education training courses. Investigates health hazards in the laboratory; ensures the safety of the laboratory; and participates in formulating federal laboratory regulations. Conducts placement service. **Publications:** Annual Report. • Booklets. Pertains to careers. • Films. • *Journal of Histotechnology*, quarterly. Journal. Topics include anatomy, pathology, enzyme histochemistry, special stains, immunohistochemistry, cytology, and electron microscopy. *Price:* Included in membership dues; $50/year for nonmembers; $60/year for nonmembers outside U.S. • *NSH in Action*, quarterly. Newsletter. Also publishes training aids.

★7151★ **NCCLS—The Clinical Laboratory Standards Organization (CLSO)**
771 E. Lancaster Ave.
Villanova, PA 19085
Phone: (610)525-2435
John V. Bergen, Ph.D., Exec.Dir.

Founded: 1968. **Members:** 2,000. **Description:** Government agencies, professional societies, clinical laboratories, and industrial firms with interests in clinical laboratory testing. Purposes are to promote the development of national and international standards for clinical laboratory testing and to provide a consensus mechanism for defining and resolving problems that influence the quality and cost of laboratory work performed. Maintains 100 subcommittees. **Publications:** *Member/Volunteer Handbook and Directory*, annual. Directory. Information on NCCLS programs, projects, committees, members, volunteers, staff, bylaws, and administrative procedures. *Price:* Included in membership dues. • *NCCLS Update*, bimonthly. Newsletter. Includes new member information and meeting calendar. *Price:* Free. • Reports. • Videos. Also publishes standards and guidelines and documents. **Formerly:** (1994) National Committee for Clinical Laboratory Standards.

★7152★ **Pan American Federation for Voluntary Bloodgiving**
(Federacion Panamericana pro Donacion Voluntaria de Sangre)
Apartado Postal 5830
Caracas, Venezuela
Jaime Gonzalez Angel, Exec.Pres.

Description: Promotes voluntary bloodgiving throughout the Americas. Collects and diffuses blood for hospitals and clinics throughout the region.

★7153★ **Society of Medical Laboratory Technologists of South Africa (SMLTSA)**
(Vereniging van Geneeskundige Laboratorium Tegnoloe van Suid-Afrika — VGLTSA)
PO Box 6014
Roggebaai
Cape Town 8012, Republic of South Africa
Phone: 21 4194857
Fax: 21 212566
Ms. S. Juling, Admin.Sec.

Founded: 1951. **Members:** 1,700. **Local Groups:** 15. **Languages:** Afrikaans, English. **Description:** Medical technologists, students, and interested persons organized to promote the medical technology profession. Works to: establish standards of practice; influence public policy; provide a forum for the exchange of ideas. Acts as an advisory and consulting body. Represents the profession before certifying, educational, employment, and registering authorities. Sponsors activities that advance scientific knowledge and encourage original work. **Publications:** *Constitution of the Society of Medical Laboratory Technologists of South Africa*. Book. • *Medical Technology*, semiannual. Journal. • *Medical Technology News*, periodic. Newspaper. • Newsletter.

★7154★ **Standing Representative Committee for Medical Laboratory Technology in the EEC (SRCMLT)**
Institute of Biomedical Science
12 Coldbath Sq.
London EC1R 5HL, England
Phone: 171 6368192
Fax: 171 4364946
Alan Potter, Contact

Founded: 1973. **Members:** 10. **Languages:** English. **Description:** Professional organizations representing medical laboratory technologists in the European Community. Offers advice to the European Commission in matters concerning the medical laboratory technological profession.

Research Centers

★7155★ **Jerome H. Holland Laboratory**
American Red Cross
15601 Crabbs Branch Way
Rockville, MD 20855
Phone: (301)738-0600
Fax: (301)738-0794
Leon W. Hoyer, M.D., Dir.

Research Activities and Fields: Blood cells, blood proteins, cytokines, receptors, blood services technology, organ transplantation, epidemiology of transfusion-transmitted diseases, plasma derivatives, adhesion factors, angiogenesis, inflammation, virology, and homeobox genes. Conducts basic and applied research and development for the Biomedical Services Division of the American Red Cross. **Publications:** *R&D Annual Report*. **Formerly:** American Red Cross National Headquarters Lab (1987).

★7156★ **Lindsley F. Kimball Research Institute**
New York Blood Center, Inc.
310 E. 67th St.
New York, NY 10021
Phone: (212)570-3000
Fax: (212)570-3195
John W. Adamson, M.D., Pres.

Research Activities and Fields: Immunogenetics and immunohematology, epidemiology and virology of AIDS and hepatitis viruses, molecular and cell biology of red blood cells and developing erythroid cells, platelet interactions with coagulation proteins, human genetics, and hematopoietic growth factors. Performs studies of plasma proteins and seeks to develop new plasma derivatives for therapeutic use.

U.S. Department of Health and Human Services
National Cancer Institute
Laboratory of Pathology
See: Entry 6198

★7157★ **University of Michigan Electron Microscope Laboratory**
School of Public Health
Ann Arbor, MI 48109-2029
Phone: (313)763-2161
Fax: (313)763-5955
Dr. Robert H. Gray, Dir.

Research Activities and Fields: Electron microscopy, specimen preparation for all types of electron microscopy, and ultrastructural studies in pathology, toxicology, virology, and related fields. Laboratory specializes in quantitative microscopy. **E-mail Address:** rh-gray@sph.umich.edu.

★7158★ **University of Wisconsin—Madison**
Division of Laboratory Medicine
Clinical Science Center, Rm. B4/249
600 Highland Ave.
Madison, WI 53792
Phone: (608)263-7507
Fax: (608)263-1568
Dr. Russell H. Tomar, Dir.

Research Activities and Fields: Clinical laboratory instrument design, comparisons, and applications, new test development and application, new techniques for quality control, and assistance in laboratory computer system design. Conducts basic investigations into the pathogenesis of AIDS and gene control. **Publications:** Laboratory Information Document; *In Focus*. **E-mail Address:** rh.tomar@hosp.wisc.edu. **Formerly:** Clinical Research Laboratories.

Chapter 37
Law & Medicine

National & International Organizations

★7159★ **American Academy of Hospital Attorneys (AAHA)**
American Hospital Association
840 N. Lake Shore Dr.
Chicago, IL 60611
Phone: (312)422-3700
Marietta Gaden, Dir.

Founded: 1968. **Members:** 3,200. **State Groups:** 8. **Description:** Attorneys who represent or are employees of hospitals or other health organizations. Works to disseminate information on health care law and legislation; keep members abreast of court decisions in the health care field; conduct legal seminars and institutes. Maintains a collection of leading decisions in health law, model agreements, and memoranda. **Publications:** *Academy Newsletter*, monthly. Newsletter. • *Membership Roster*, annual. **Formerly:** (1971) Society of Hospital Attorneys; (1984) American Society of Hospital Attorneys.

★7160★ **American Academy of Medical-Legal Analysis (AAMLA)**
522 Rossmore Dr.
Las Vegas, NV 89110
Phone: (702)452-9538
Fax: (702)452-1031
Bartholomew A. Sinatra, M.D., Chm.

Founded: 1981. **Members:** 500. **Description:** Physicians and attorneys certified as diplomates by the American Board of Medical-Legal Analysis in Medicine and Surgery (see separate entry); medical administrators; paramedical personnel. Disseminates information about the relationship between the medical and legal sciences; promotes research; improves patient care. Maintains speakers' bureau; compiles statistics. **Publications:** *Neurological-Orthopedic Journal*, quarterly. Journal.

★7161★ **American Academy of Psychiatry and the Law (AAPL)**
101 E. Read, Ste. 323
Baltimore, MD 21201
Phone: (203)242-5450
Free: 800-331-1389
Jacquelyn T. Coleman, M.D., Exec.Dir.

Founded: 1969. **Members:** 1,430. **Regional Groups:** 7. **Description:** Psychiatrists who are members in good standing of the American Psychiatric Association or the American Academy of Child and Adolescent Psychiatry. Seeks to exchange ideas and experience in those areas where psychiatry and the law overlap; develop standards of practice in the relationship of psychiatry to the law and encourage the development of training programs for psychiatrists seeking skill and knowledge in this area; stimulate and encourage research in the field; improve relationships between psychiatrists and other professionals in the field; inform the public of problems in the area of psychiatry and the law and the potential contributions from psychiatry. **Publications:** *Bulletin of the American Academy of Psychiatry and the Law*, quarterly. Bulletin. • Membership Directory, annual. • Newsletter, 3/year.

★7162★ **American Association of Legal Nurse Consultants (AALNC)**
5700 Old Orchard Rd.
Skokie, IL 60077-1057
Phone: (708)966-0212
Fax: (708)966-9418
Joan Magnusson, Pres.

Founded: 1989. **Members:** 1,350. **State Groups:** 30. **Description:** Promotes the professional advancement of registered nurses consulting with the legal arena by providing a forum for education and exchange of information. Conducts annual eduational program. **Publications:** *The Journal of Legal Nurse Consulting*, quarterly. Journal. Includes educational and legislative updates, and networking information. *Price:* Free to members. **Formerly:** San Diego Association of Medical Legal Nurse Consultants; (1989) National Association of Medical Legal Nurse Consultants.

★7163★ **American Association of Medico-Legal Consultants (AAMC)**
The Barclay
Rittenhouse Sq., Ste. 11D
Philadelphia, PA 19103
Phone: (215)545-6363
Fax: (215)545-2163
Evelyn M. Goldstein, Pres. & Exec.Dir.

Founded: 1972. **Members:** 1,200. **Description:** National medical malpractice screening panel. Members are physicians (1000) and physician-attorneys (200) united for medical malpractice screening, peer review, medical and hospital risk management, and medical audits. Holds seminars for physicians and attorneys in the field of medical-legal problems. Maintains library.

★7164★ **The American Association of Nurse Attorneys (TAANA)**
720 Light St.
Baltimore, MD 21230-3816
Phone: (410)752-3318
Fax: (410)752-8295
Carol T. Shaner, CAE, Exec.Dir.

Founded: 1982. **Members:** 600. **Local Groups:** 17. **Description:** Nurse attorneys, nurses in law school, and attorneys in nursing school. Aims to better nurse attorneys and inform the public on matters of nursing, health care, and law. Goals are to facilitate communication and information sharing between professional groups; to establish an employment network; to assist new and potential nurse attorneys; to develop the profession; to promote the image of nurse attorneys as experts and consultants in nursing and law. Maintains educational foundation. **Publications:** *Demonstrating Financial Responsibility in Nursing Practice*. • *Guidelines for the Selection of Counsel for the State Nurses Association*. • *Inside TAANA*, quarterly. Newsletter. Contains reports from committees and chapters, legislative information, and member notes. *Price:* Included in membership dues. • *Making the Transition: From Nursing to the Law*. • Membership Directory, annual. • *Model Curriculum for Legal Content in Nursing Education*. • *On Becoming A Nurse Attorney*.

★7165★ American Board of Forensic Anthropology (ABFA)
c/o Marcella H. Sorg
Sorg Associates
91 Mill St.
PO Box 70
Orono, ME 04473-0070
Phone: (207)866-7865
Fax: (207)866-5786
Marcella H. Sorg, Ph.D., Pres.

Founded: 1977. **Members:** 39. **Description:** Board for certification of physical anthropologists who wish to become forensic anthropologists. (Forensic anthropology refers to application of the science of physical anthropology in assistance of law enforcement agencies; forensic anthropologists identify and glean information from human remains.) Promotes improvement in the practice of forensic anthropology and encourages adherence to high standards in the field. Conducts written and practical examinations for prospective forensic anthropologists; awards certificates of qualification. Compiles statistics. **Publications:** *Diplomates, American Board of Forensic Anthropology Directory*, annual. Directory. Contains listings of current diplomates in forensic anthropology.

★7166★ American Board of Medical-Legal Analysis in Medicine and Surgery (ABMLAMS)
522 Rossmore Dr.
Las Vegas, NV 89110-4123
Phone: (702)452-9538
Fax: (702)452-1031
Bartholomew A. Sinatra, M.D., Chm.

Founded: 1981. **Members:** 400. **Description:** Physicians and attorneys who are candidates in the field of medical-legal analysis, which deals with forensic and jurisprudential aspects of medicine and surgery. Seeks to improve patient care and to further the science of medical-legal analysis. Maintains speakers' bureau. Compiles statistics.

★7167★ American College of Forensic Psychiatry
PO Box 5870
Balboa Island, CA 92662
Phone: (714)831-0236
Fax: (714)675-1107
Ed Miller, Contact

Founded: 1981. **Members:** 350. **Description:** Individuals who work in psychiatry and law. Serves as a professional association and educational provider. Offers referral services. **Publications:** *American Journal of Forensic Psychiatry*, quarterly. Journal. *Price:* $55/year.

★7168★ American College of Legal Medicine (ACLM)
611 E. Wells St.
Milwaukee, WI 53202
Phone: (414)276-1881
Free: 800-433-9137
Fax: (414)276-3349
David Baumann

Founded: 1960. **Members:** 1,500. **Description:** Persons who hold degrees in medicine and law. Promotes and advances the field of legal medicine or medical jurisprudence; arranges for meetings with medical, legal, and professional groups and legislative, judicial, and enforcement bodies interested in any province where law and medicine are contiguous; fosters and encourages centers for study and research in the field of legal medicine and publishes materials pertaining to legal medicine. **Publications:** *American College of Legal Medicine--Newsletter*, periodic. Newsletter. *Price:* Included in membership dues. • *College of Legal Medicine Membership Directory*, annual. Membership Directory. *Price:* Included in membership dues; $50/copy for nonmembers. • *Journal of Legal Medicine*, periodic. Journal. Offers discussion of topics of interest in legal medicine, health law, food and drug law, and medicolegal research and education. *Price:* Included in membership dues; $105/year for nonmembers. • *Legal Medicine Perspectives*, quarterly. • *Medical Legal Lessons*, bimonthly. Offers information of current medicolegal interest as well as news and information about upcoming programs.

★7169★ American Psychology-Law Society (AP-LS)
c/o Dr. Tom Grisso
University of Massachusetts Medical Center
Department of Psychology
55 Lake Ave. N.
Worcester, MA 01655-0329
Phone: (508)856-3625
Dr. Tom Grisso, Pres.

Founded: 1968. **Members:** 1,700. **Description:** A division of American Psychological Association. Objectives are: to promote exchanges between the disciplines of psychology and law in regard to teaching, research, administration of justice, jurisprudence, and other matters at the psychology-law interface; to foster research relevant to legal problems using psychological knowledge and methods and to advance psychological research using the legal setting and related legal research techniques; to promote education of lawyers at all levels regarding psychology, and of psychologists at all levels regarding the law; to encourage legislation and social policies consistent with current states of psychological knowledge; to promote the effective use of psychologists in the legal processes. **Publications:** *AP-LS Newsletter*, quarterly. Newsletter. Covers association activities; lists opportunities in psychology and law. *Price:* Included in membership dues. • *Journal of Law and Human Behavior*, quarterly. Journal. Contains scholarly research on psychology-law topics including jury decision-making, eyewitness identification, expert witnesses, and mental health. *Price:* Included in membership dues. • *Monograph Series*, periodic.

★7170★ American Society of Forensic Odontology (ASFO)
c/o Dr. E. Steven Smith
Northwestern University Dental School
240 E. Huron
Chicago, IL 60611
Dr. E. Steven Smith, Sec.

Founded: 1966. **Members:** 450. **Regional Groups:** 1. **Description:** Individuals interested in furthering the field of forensic dentistry. Conducts research and specialized education programs. Maintains library. **Publications:** *Field Workbook in Forensic Odontology*. • Membership Directory, annual. • Newsletter, quarterly.

★7171★ American Society of Law, Medicine and Ethics (ASLME)
765 Commonwealth Ave., 16th Fl.
Boston, MA 02215
Phone: (617)262-4990
Fax: (617)437-7596
Benjamin Moulton, Exec.Dir.

Founded: 1972. **Members:** 4,500. **Description:** Physicians, attorneys, health care management executives, nurses, insurance company personnel, members of the judiciary, and others interested in medicolegal relations, health law, and ethics. Purpose is to provide opportunities for continuing education through publications, conferences, and information clearinghouse. Maintains speakers' bureau. **Publications:** *American Journal of Law and Medicine*, quarterly. Journal. Law review containing annotations of recent court decisions, book releases, and student case and note section. *Price:* $90/year for individuals; $170/year for institutions. • *ASLME Briefings*, periodic. Newsletter. Includes conference calendar. • *Journal of Law, Medicine and Ethics*, quarterly. Journal. Reports on medically-related legal and social issues such as surrogate motherhood, AIDS, and euthanasia. Includes reviews of recent publications. *Price:* $90/year for individuals; $170/year for institutions. • *Legal and Ethical Aspects of Health Care for the Elderly*. Book. • *Legal and Ethical Aspects of Treating Critically and Terminally Ill Patients*. Book. • *Refusing Treatment in Mental Health Institutions*. Book. **Formerly:** (1973) Massachusetts Society of Law and Medicine; (1993) American Society of Law and Medicine.

★7172★ American Society of Legal and Industrial Medicine (AALIM)
15 E. 26th St.
New York, NY 10010
Phone: (212)447-5804
Dr. Jay Rosenblum, Pres.

Founded: 1946. **Members:** 200. **Description:** Physicians who meet certain qualifications established by the academy and are concerned with industrial medicine. To advance the study of industrial medicine and workmen's disability compensation; to develop medical criteria for the determination of causal relationship between injury, disease, and disability. **Publications:** *Compensation Medicine Newsletter*, periodic. Newsletter. **Formerly:** (1985) American Academy of Compensation Medicine; (1991) American Academy of Legal and Industrial Medicine.

★7173★ American Society for Pharmacy Law (ASPL)
c/o Donald A. Dee
PO Box 2184
Vienna, VA 22183
Phone: (703)281-0107
Fax: (703)281-2897
Donald A. Dee, Exec.VP

Founded: 1974. **Members:** 1,000. **Description:** Pharmacists, lawyers, and students. Purposes are to: further legal knowledge; communicate accurate legal information to pharmacists; foster knowledge and education pertaining to the rights and duties of pharmacists; distribute information of interest to members; provide a forum for exchange of information pertaining to pharmacy law. **Publications:** *ASPL Membership Directory*, annual. Membership Directory. • *RX Ipsa Loquitur*, monthly.

★**7174**★ **Asbestos Litigation Group (ALG)**
c/o Ness, Motley, Loadholt, Richardson, and
 Poole
PO Box 1137
Charleston, SC 29402
Phone: (803)577-6747
Fax: (803)577-7513
Ronald Motley, Pres.

Founded: 1979. **Members:** 150. **Description:** Lawyers representing litigants in asbestos-related disease cases throughout the U.S.

Children's Healthcare is a Legal Duty
 (CHILD)
See: Entry 3206

★**7175**★ **European Association of Centres**
 of Medical Ethics (EACME)
Kapucijnenvoer 35
B-3000 Leuven, Belgium
Phone: 76 336951
Fax: 76 336952

Founded: 1985. **Members:** 46. **Description:** Medical ethics centers. Promotes critical public and professional concern regarding ethical issues encountered in the practice of medicine. Gathers and disseminates information; conducts research and makes research tools available to members; coordinates collaborative research efforts among members. Encourages continuing ethical education for health care professionals. **Publications:** *EACME News*, periodic. Bulletin.

★**7176**★ **Hastings Center (HC)**
255 Elm Rd.
Briarcliff Manor, NY 10510
Phone: (914)762-8500
Fax: (914)762-2124
Daniel Callahan, Pres.

Founded: 1969. **Members:** 11,500. **Description:** Individuals concerned with medical and professional ethics including physicians, nurses, lawyers, administrators, public policymakers, and other academic and health care professionals. Conducts research on issues relevant to ethics. Offers consulting services. Provides in-house and international educational opportunities including student intern, visiting scholar, and international fellowship programs. Operates speakers' bureau. **Publications:** Books. • *Hastings Center Report*, bimonthly. • *IRB: A Review of Human Subjects Research*, bimonthly. • Monographs. • Reports. **Formerly:** (1987) Institute of Society, Ethics, and the Life Sciences.

★**7177**★ **Health, Ethics and Liberties**
 (Sante Ethique et Libertes — SEL)
95, blvd. Pinel
F-69677 Bron Cedex, France
Dr. Nicole Lery, Contact

Founded: 1976. **Members:** 140. **Languages:** English, French. **Description:** Health care professionals, ethicists, attorneys, and others with an interest in the ethical and legal ramifications of modern medical care. Seeks to identify emerging medical ethical questions; promotes study and research in the field. Functions as an expert consulting group in matters such as assisted suicide, organ donation, and the rights of the unborn; works to ensure the continuing ethical training of members. Creates and participates in medical ethics education programs. **Publications:** *Salagnon*, periodic. Newsletter.

★**7178**★ **International Academy of Legal**
 Medicine and Social Medicine
 (Academie Internationale de Medecine
 Legal et de Medecine Sociale)
49A, ave. Nicolai
BP 8
B-4802 Verviers, Belgium
Phone: 87 229821
Fax: 87 229821
Elizabeth Francson, Sec./Treas.

Founded: 1938. **Members:** 450. **Languages:** English, French. **Description:** Forensic pathologists, jurists, and individuals in 40 countries interested in the development of legal and social medicine. Promotes international scientific cooperation in legal medicine including the fields of criminology, industrial medicine, legal psychiatry, medical ethics, social medicine, and toxicology. Maintains liaison with the World Health Organization. **Publications:** *Acta Medicinae Legalis et Socialis*, annual. Contains proceedings of congresses and meetings. • Newsletter, 3/year.

★**7179**★ **International Association of**
 Coroners and Medical Examiners
 (IACME)
5401 N. Knoxville Ave., Ste. B-1
Peoria, IL 61614
Phone: (309)689-0200
Fax: (309)689-0260
Herbert H. Buzbee, Exec.Sec.-Treas.

Founded: 1938. **Members:** 335. **Description:** Educational seminar involving all aspects of death investigation such as pathology, autopsy, crime scene investigation, mass disasters and anthropology. Offers continuing medical education credit. **Publications:** *RECAP*, quarterly. Newsletter. *Price:* Included in membership dues.

★**7180**★ **International Center for Medicine**
 and Law (ICML)
170 Forest Green
Staten Island, NY 10312
Phone: (212)747-1755
A. Berkowitz, Exec.Dir.

Founded: 1982. **Description:** Promotes continuing education in medicine and law, especially in Israel, Europe, and the Orient. Engages in technical research; works with governments and medical organizations. Publishes conference programs.

International Organization for Forensic
 Odonto-Stomatology (IOFOS)
See: Entry 3963

★**7181**★ **International Reference**
 Organization in Forensic Medicine and
 Sciences (INFORM)
PO Box 16286
Panama City, FL 32406-6286
Phone: (316)685-7612
Dr. William G. Eckert, Dir.

Founded: 1966. **Members:** 1,200. **Languages:** English. **Description:** Practitioners of forensic sciences, pathologists, psychiatrists, toxicologists, lawyers, anthropologists, dentists, police criminalists, writers, and professors of legal medicine in 90 countries. Seeks to develop a channel of communication between workers dealing with medical, legal, and law enforcement problems and experts who can help in solving these problems. Sponsors projects on literature compilation; maintains library and forensic toxicology archives of historical information on the development of forensic toxicology, forensic serology, international crimes, and problems of the past century; serves as the archives of the American Academy of Forensic Sciences. Sponsors courses for lawyers on medicine and science. Has established the Milton Helpern Institute of Forensic Medicine (see separate entry, Vol. 1). **Publications:** *Conference Proceeding*, semiannual. Proceedings. • *Criminalist's Sourcebook*, annual. • *International Bibliography of Forensic Sciences*, annual. Bibliography. • Monograph, quarterly. Deals with special subjects in forensic medicine. • Newsletter, quarterly. Also offers an audiovisual lecture series.

★**7182**★ **Milton Helpern Institute of**
 Forensic Medicine (MHIFM)
520 1st Ave.
New York, NY 10016
Phone: (212)447-2318
Fax: (212)447-2094
Dr. Charles S. Hirsch, Chief Med.Exam.

Founded: 1968. **Members:** 405. **Description:** Operated by New York University and the city of New York to strengthen teaching and research in forensic medicine and forensic pathology. Trains postgraduate students; sponsors symposia, seminars, lectures, and courses; conducts research projects and undertakes investigations and related studies of sudden, suspicious, and violent deaths. Maintains Milton Helpern Library of Legal Medicine. **Publications:** *The International Microform Journal of Legal Medicine and Forensic Sciences*, quarterly. Journal. **Formerly:** (1978) Institute of Forensic Medicine.

National Alliance of Victims of Minamata
 Disease and Lawyers (NAVMDL)
See: Entry 5049

★**7183**★ **National Association of Disability**
 Evaluating Professionals (NADEP)
PO Box 35407
Richmond, VA 23235-0407
Phone: (804)378-8809
Virgil Robert May, III, Dir.

Founded: 1984. **Members:** 1,000. **Description:** Lawyers, doctors, psychologists, employers, and others interested or involved in disability claims process, evaluation, and case management. Provides a forum for the exchange of information. Serves as a training center which prepares health professionals to qualify for the Certified Disability Examiner credential offered by the Commission on Disability Examiner Certification. **Publications:** *Disability Evaluation and Rehabilitation Review*, quarterly. Newsletter. *Price:* Included in membership. **Formerly:** (1991) International Health Consultants.

★7184★ **National Association of Medical Examiners (NAME)**
1402 S. Grand Blvd.
St. Louis, MO 63104
Phone: (314)577-8298
Fax: (314)268-5124
Denise Randazzo, Exec.Sec.

Founded: 1966. **Members:** 786. **Description:** Medical examiners, pathologists, and other licensed physicians who have responsibilities in connection with the official investigation of sudden, suspicious, and violent deaths. Attempts to establish greater understanding and support for the medical examiner system among the public, government officials, and the medical and legal professions. Has established standards for inspection and accreditation of a modern medico-legal investigative system. **Publications:** *American Journal of Forensic Medicine and Pathology*, quarterly. Journal.

★7185★ **National Committee for Medical Research Ethics (NEM)**
Gaustadalleen 21
N-0371 Oslo 3, Norway
Phone: 22958780
Fax: 22698471
Dr. Jan Helge Solbakk, Exec. Officer

Founded: 1990. **Members:** 12. **Languages:** English, Norwegian. **Description:** Health care professionals, attorneys, ethicists, and others with an interest in ethical aspects of medical research. Promotes increased awareness of ethical issues within the medical research industry; conducts continuing professional education and public education programs. **Publications:** *NEM-Nytt*, quarterly. Newsletter.

★7186★ **National Council Against Health Fraud (NCAHF)**
PO Box 1276
Loma Linda, CA 92354
Phone: (909)824-4690
Free: 800-821-6671
Fax: (909)824-4838
Dr. William Jarvis, Pres.

Founded: 1977. **Members:** 1,200. **Regional Groups:** 13. **State Groups:** 12. **Local Groups:** 1. **Description:** Health professionals, researchers, legal professionals, and other interested individuals. Seeks to educate the public on fraud and quackery in health care; offers advice to consumers; provides witnesses for health fraud trials; assists law enforcement officials with health fraud cases. Administers the National Council Against Health Fraud Resource Center in Kansas City, MO. Maintains a collection of ''quack medical devices.'' Sponsors speakers' bureau, museum, and research programs. Offers aid to victims in the form of legal screening free of charge. **Publications:** *Available Resource Materials*, annual. Booklet. Lists available materials by category. *Price:* Free. • *Join in Combatting Health Fraud, Misinformation,*

and Quackery. Brochure. • *National Council Against Health Fraud Newsletter*, bimonthly. Newsletter. *Price:* Included in membership dues; $15/year for nonmembers; $18/year for libraries. • *NCAHF Bulletin Board*, bimonthly. Bulletin. *Price:* Available to members only. • *Position Paper on Acupuncture*. • *Position Paper on Chiropractic*. • *Position Paper on Homeopathy*. Paper. • *Recommended Anti-Quackery Publications List*. • Reports. **Formerly:** California Council Against Health Fraud.

★7187★ **National Health Law Program (NHeLP)**
2639 S. La Cienega Blvd.
Los Angeles, CA 90034
Phone: (310)204-6010
Fax: (310)204-0891
Laurence M. Lavin, Dir.

Founded: 1969. **Members:** 8. **Description:** Attorneys, health specialists, and other interested persons. Provides assistance to legal services program attorneys and their clients in matters involving health problems of the poor. Offers information, referral, and consultation on litigation strategy. Prepares materials for and conducts training sessions for and with field program attorneys and paralegals. Coordinates testimony for particular hearings. **Publications:** *Health Advocate*, quarterly. Also publishes law review articles and health advocates guides on issues such as medicaid access to emergency health care.

★7188★ **National Health Lawyers Association (NHLA)**
1120 Connecticut Ave. NW, Ste. 950
Washington, DC 20036
Phone: (202)833-1100
Fax: (202)833-1105
Marilou King, Exec.Dir.

Founded: 1971. **Members:** 7,000. **Description:** Private, corporate, institutional, and governmental lawyers, and health professionals. Seeks to establish a forum for nonpartisan objective treatment of issues in the field of health law and to disseminate differing points of view. Conducts research; sponsors educational programs for lawyers, their clients, and other professional and technical personnel in the health field. Maintains small library of information pertaining to health and legal issues. **Publications:** *Federal Health Monitor*, monthly. • *Health Law Digest*, monthly. • *Health Lawyers News Report*, monthly. Also publishes reports on health-related legal cases and occasional supplements to newsletter.

★7189★ **National Legal Center for the Medically Dependent and Disabled (NLCMDD)**
50 S. Meridian St., Ste. 605
Indianapolis, IN 46204
Phone: (317)632-6245
Fax: (317)632-6542
James Bopp, Jr., Pres.

Founded: 1984. **Description:** Service organization working to defend the legal rights of indigent older and disabled persons so that such people can obtain proper medical care. Provides lawyer referral services. Operates speakers' bureau. Provides analysis of pertinent legis-

lation on request of legislators. **Publications:** *Issues in Law and Medicine*, quarterly. Journal. Contains articles examining the legal and medical issues related to the right of disabled persons to receive beneficial medical care. *Price:* $49/year. • *Medical Treatment Rights of Children with Disabilities*. Manual. • Pamphlets. • Reprints.

★7190★ **Nordic Society of Forensic Odonto-Stomatology (NSDS)**
Department of Forensic Medicine
Frederik V's rei
DK-2100 Copenhagen 0, Denmark
Phone: 35 326160
Fax: 35 326150
Jan Jakobsen, Contact

Founded: 1961. **Members:** 400. **National Groups:** 5. **Languages:** Danish, English, Finnish, Icelandic, Norwegian, Swedish. **Description:** Private dental practitioners and university department faculty. Acts as liaison among Scandinavian national societies. Sponsors dental sections at the triennial meeting of the Scandinavian Society of Forensic Medicine. Conducts symposia. **Publications:** Newsletter, quarterly. **Formerly:** Scandinavian Society of Forensic Odonto-Stomatology.

★7191★ **Park Ridge Center (PRC)**
211 E. Ontario, Ste. 800
Chicago, IL 60611-3215
Phone: (312)266-2222
Fax: (312)266-6086
Laurence O'Connell, Pres. & CEO

Founded: 1985. **Members:** 2,000. **Description:** Physicians and other health care professionals, theologians, ethicists, clergy, and pastoral counselors. Interreligious, multidisciplinary institute for the study of health, faith, and ethics. Seeks to fill what the center perceives as a worldwide need for the study of religious aspects of human well-being, especially as they relate to prevention and treatment of disease, interpretation of illness and health, and similar concerns. Serves as an international forum for exchange and debate among experts in health care, religion, law, and ethics; acts as a resource for information on religion and bioethics. Conducts research. **Publications:** *Caring and Curing*. • *Healing and Restoring*. • *Health and Medicine in the Faith Traditions*. Monographs. • *Healthy People 2000--A Role for America's Religious Communities*. • *Second Opinion*, quarterly. Journal. *Price:* $45/year.

★7192★ **Scandinavian Society of Forensic Medicine (SSFM)
(Nordisk Rattsmedicinsk Forening)**
Inst. of Forensic Medicine
Rikhospitalet
N-0027 Oslo, Norway
Phone: 22868676
Fax: 22209583
Prof. B. Olaisen, Pres.

Founded: 1961. **Languages:** Danish, English, Norwegian, Swedish. **Description:** Experts on forensic medicine from 7 northern European countries. Promotes cooperation among members; mediates exchange of scientific and practical experiences. **Publications:** *Conference Proceedings*, triennial.

★7193★ **Society of Medical Jurisprudence (SMJ)**
PO Box 20678, Cherokee Sta.
New York, NY 10021-0073
Phone: (212)734-0564
Fax: (212)861-8796
Michael K. Bartalos, Pres.
Founded: 1883. **Members:** 300. **Description:** Lawyers, physicians, surgeons, health professionals, chemists, and law and medical school professors. Promotes the investigation, study, and advancement of medical jurisprudence and high standards of medical expert testimony. Sponsors individual lectures and serial presentations of medicolegal interest. **Publications:** Directory. • Newsletter, 9/year. Contains legislative and regulatory information. Also plans to publish essays on current issues of medicolegal interest. **Formerly:** (1883) Medico-Legal Society; (1891) Society of Medical Jurisprudence and State Medicine.

Research Centers

★7194★ **Case Western Reserve University Center for Biomedical Ethics**
School of Medicine
10900 Euclid Ave.
Cleveland, OH 44106-4976
Phone: (216)368-6196
Fax: (216)368-8713
Thomas Murray, Ph.D., Dir.
Research Activities and Fields: Bioethics, including human genetics, decisions to end life, aging, and reproductive alternatives. **Publications:** *CenterViews* (newsletter, three per year). **E-mail Address:** thm2@po.cwru.edu.

★7195★ **Case Western Reserve University Law-Medicine Center**
School of Law
Gund Hall
11075 E. Blvd.
Cleveland, OH 44106
Phone: (216)368-3983
Maxwell J. Mehlman, Dir.
Research Activities and Fields: Health care law and policy. Also seeks to improve administration of civil and criminal justice by application of scientific methods and utilization of medicine in the legal process. **Publications:** *Health Matrix: The Journal of Law-Medicine.*

★7196★ **Center for Bioethics**
Clinical Research Institute of Montreal
110 Pine Ave. W.
Montreal, PQ, Canada H2W 1R7
Phone: (514)987-5615
Fax: (514)987-5695
Dr. David J. Roy, Dir.
Research Activities and Fields: Bioethics and the integration of biomedical science and medical practice into a broader pattern of methodological, social, legal, and philosophical reflection. Projects include studies on abortion, euthanasia, right to die, compulsory sterilization, in vitro fertilization and embryo transfer, genetic screening and counseling, eugenics, recombinant DNA, human experimentation, policies regarding seriously defective newborns, sperm banking and artificial insemination, ethics committees, ethics of research, allocation of health care resources, palliative care, health care priorities, and two studies on AIDS commissioned by the government of the province of Quebec. **Publications:** *Journal of Palliative Care* (quarterly, Canadian-based international publication); Proceedings; Monographs.

★7197★ **Center on Children and the Law**
American Bar Assoc.
1800 M St., NW
Washington, DC 20036
Phone: (202)331-2250
Fax: (202)331-2225
Sally Inada, Contact
Research Activities and Fields: Child abuse and neglect, foster care, adoption, parental kidnapping of children, child support, grandparents' rights, developmentally disabled children's rights, and child exploitation. **Publications:** *ABA Juvenile and Child Welfare Law Reporter* (monthly); *Children's Legal Rights Journal* (quarterly).

Creighton University Center for Health Policy and Ethics
See: Entry 5621

★7198★ **Florida State University Center for Employment Relations and Law**
College of Law
Tallahassee, FL 32306
Phone: (904)644-4287
Fax: (904)644-5487
William F. McHugh, Dir.
Research Activities and Fields: Public and private sector labor relations/collective bargaining, Occupational Safety and Health Administration (OSHA), affirmative action, workmen's compensation, discrimination, AIDS in the workplace, and other aspects of employment relations. The Center's goal is to achieve a coordinated and neutral approach to improve the effectiveness of private practitioners and public officials at both state and local governmental levels in the field of employment relations and law.

★7199★ **Forensic Sciences Foundation, Inc.**
PO Box 669
Colorado Springs, CO 80901-0669
Phone: (719)636-1100
Fax: (719)636-1993
Anne H. Warren, Exec.Dir.
Research Activities and Fields: Technical and managerial aspects of forensic science, including drug abuse reporting systems and medicolegal investigation of death.

★7200★ **George Washington University Intergovernmental Health Policy Project**
2021 K St. NW, Ste. 800
Washington, DC 20006
Phone: (202)872-1445
Fax: (202)785-0114
Richard E. Merritt, Dir.
Research Activities and Fields: Health laws and programs of the states, including research in such areas as alternatives to institutional care, state health care reform, managing and funding health care programs, preventive health services for children, state Medicaid programs, state comprehensive and catastrophic health insurance programs, Medicaid cost containment, state health promotion and disease prevention initiatives, AIDS, and private health insurance benefits for alcoholism, drug abuse, and mental illness. **Publications:** *State Health Notes* (24 per year); *State Health Reports on Mental Health, Alcoholism & Drug Abuse* (10 per year); and *Primary Care News.*

★7201★ **Georgetown University Center for Bioethics Asian / International Bioethics Program**
Kennedy Institute of Ethics
Washington, DC 20057
Phone: (202)687-6747
Fax: (202)687-8089
Prof. Robert Veatch, Dir.
Research Activities and Fields: Cross-cultural bioethical issues focusing on Asian and international aspects of gene manipulation, death and dying, medical and nursing care, patients' attitudes, holistic medicine, and the environment, including public policy on human and animal experimentation. **Publications:** Conference Proceedings.

★7202★ **Georgetown University Kennedy Institute of Ethics**
Washington, DC 20057
Phone: (202)687-6774
Fax: (202)687-8089
Dr. Robert M. Veatch, Dir.
Research Activities and Fields: Social and ethical issues in biomedical sciences, such as resource allocation in health care, human experimentation, genetic engineering, euthanasia, death and dying, reproductive technologies, physician-patient relations, in vitro fertilization, abortion, and organ transplantation. Also researches other fields of applied ethics--international relations, government, law, journalism, business, and technology policy. **Publications:** *Bibliography of Bioethics* (annually); *Bioethics Thesaurus* (annually); *Searching BIOETHICSLINE; Kennedy Institute of Ethics Journal; Encyclopedia of Bioethics* (Free Press/Macmillan); *New Titles in Bioethics* (quarterly current awareness service); *Scope Notes; International Directory of Bioethics Organizations.* **Formerly:** Joseph and Rose Kennedy Institute for the Study of Human Reproduction and Bioethics.

★7203★ **Graduate Theological Union Center for Ethics and Social Policy**
2400 Ridge Rd.
Berkeley, CA 94709
Phone: (510)848-1674
Fax: (510)848-0626
Barry Stenger, Dir.
Research Activities and Fields: Ethical issues related to business, communities, public policy, the environment, and health care. **Publications:** Working Papers; *Ethics & Policy* (quarterly newsletter). **E-mail Address:** cesp@aol.com.

★7204★ HUC-UC Center for the Study of Ethics and Contemporary Moral Problems
3101 Clifton Ave.
Cincinnati, OH 45220-2488
Phone: (513)221-1875
Fax: (513)221-1842
Dr. Barry S. Kogan, Dir.

Research Activities and Fields: Ethical issues, including Bioethics (allocation of healthcare, birth and death, abortion, fetal tissue experimentation, euthanasia, and AIDS); Business Ethics (social responsibilities of the corporation and the community); The Ethics of War and Peace (Just War Theory, Holy Wars); and Pluralism (immigration, distribution of power, economics, affirmative action, conscience and the constituency in public life, and education). **Publications:** *A Time to be Born and A Time to Die: The Ethics of Choice; The Corporation and the Community: Mutual Antagonism and Mutual Responsibility.*

★7205★ Institute for Jewish Medical Ethics
645 14th Ave.
San Francisco, CA 94118
Phone: (415)752-7333
Fax: (415)752-5851
Rabbi Lipner, Pres.

Research Activities and Fields: Jewish principles of medical ethics, including Jewish law and human and animal experimentation, physician compassion for the patient, artificial insemination, in-vitro fertilization, surrogate motherhood and abortion, allocation of health care resources, organ transplantation (with emphasis on kidney and developments in Israel), and the right to die.

★7206★ Institute on Mental Disability and the Law
National Center for State Courts
300 Newport Ave.
Williamsburg, VA 23187-8798
Phone: (804)253-2000
Fax: (804)220-0449
Dr. Pamela Casey, Dir.

Research Activities and Fields: Mental health and justice systems interactions, including the guilty-but-mentally-ill verdict with implications for states considering it, inquiry into the verdict of guilty by reason of insanity, field studies on nonrestrictive treatments for the mentally ill compatible with adequate care and the safety of the community, development of a model process for forensic mental health screening and evaluation, establishment of national guidelines for involuntary civil commitment proceedings, research on cost containment for mental health evaluation and treatment mandated by courts, mental health malpractice, and court decisions to provide or withhold life-sustaining medical treatment. **Publications:** *Perspectives on Mental Disability and the Law.*

★7207★ Judge David L. Bazelon Center for Mental Health Law
1101 15th St. NW, Ste. 1212
Washington, DC 20005
Phone: (202)467-5730
Fax: (202)223-0409

Research Activities and Fields: Center focuses on mental and developmental disabilities law.

★7208★ Loyola University Chicago Institute for Health Law
Sch. of Law
One East Pearson St., Rm. 512
Chicago, IL 60611
Phone: (312)915-7174
Fax: (312)915-7201
John Blum, Dir.

Research Activities and Fields: Comparative health law and policy. **Publications:** *Annals of Health Law.*

★7209★ Medical College of Wisconsin Center for the Study of Bioethics
8701 Watertown Plank Rd.
Milwaukee, WI 53226
Phone: (414)456-8498
Fax: (414)266-8654
Robyn Shapiro, Dir.

Research Activities and Fields: Ethics studies, with special emphasis on AIDS, abortion, drug testing, euthanasia, fetal rights, genetics, technology assessment and allocation of resources, and multicultural approaches to bioethics. **E-mail Address:** molson@post.its.mcw.edu.

★7210★ Medical University of South Carolina
Crime Victims Research and Treatment Center (CVC)
Dept. of Psychiatry & Behavioral Sciences
171 Ashley Ave.
Charleston, SC 29425-0742
Phone: (803)792-2945
Fax: (803)792-3388
Dr. Dean Kilpatrick, Dir.

Research Activities and Fields: Psychological effects of criminal victimization, including effects of rape on married, cohabitating, and dating relationships; psychological impact of the criminal justice system on victims; characteristics of incest victims and their families; characteristics of criminal offenders; and trauma effects due to auto, industrial, or fire-related incidents, as well as natural disasters and other traumatic events.

★7211★ Odyssey Institute Corp. of Connecticut
5 Hedley Farms Rd.
Westport, CT 06880
Phone: (203)255-4198
Dr. Judianne Densen-Gerber, Chair

Research Activities and Fields: Reproductive rights, especially the legal and ethical issues raised by recent technological advancements. Areas of interest include surrogate parenting, artificial insemination, payment for genetic material, and speculative advances in medicine such as male pregnancy and the use of animal uteri for maturation of human fetuses. Focuses on child abuse and neglect, including sociological autopsies and institutional interventions prior to the deaths of abused children. **Publications:** *Odyssey Journal.*

★7212★ Park Ridge Center for the Study of Health, Faith and Ethics
211 E. Ontario, Ste. 800
Chicago, IL 60611
Phone: (312)266-2222
Fax: (312)266-6086
Laurence O'Connell, Pres.

Research Activities and Fields: Explores the relationships among health, faith, and ethics, including the religious dimensions of health and ethics. Also studies the role of religious beliefs in the search for health and contributes to ethical reflection on a wide range of health related issues. Collaborates with representatives from diverse cultures, religious communities, health care fields, and academic disciplines. Projects include euthanasia and assisted suicide; aging; population, consumption, and the environment; congregations as healing communities; and a book series on health, medicine, and the faith traditions. **Publications:** *Second Opinion; Centerline* (newsletter); Special Reports; Members' Updates.

★7213★ Pope John XXIII Medical-Moral Research and Education Center
186 Forbes Rd.
Braintree, MA 02184-2626
Phone: (617)848-6965
Fax: (617)849-1309
Rev. Russell E. Smith, S.T.D. Pres.

Research Activities and Fields: Medical and ethical issues facing the health care field as a result of unparalled developments in medical science and technology. Issues are studied according to Catholic teachings and Judeo-Christian virtues. **Publications:** *Ethics and Medics* (monthly newsletter).

★7214★ St. Louis University
Center for Health Care Ethics
Health Sciences Center
1402 S. Grand Blvd.
St. Louis, MO 63104
Phone: (314)577-8195
Fax: (314)268-5150
Fr. Kevin O'Rourke, Dir.

Research Activities and Fields: Issues in health care ethics, including the influence of physicians in decision making by the parents of newborn babies and the influence of for-profit hospital corporations on the cost of quality health care. Other interests include ethical considerations of the dying patient, defective newborns, genetic engineering, use of life-extending technology, sexual abuse of children, organ transplantation, health care financing, and informed consent. **Publications:** *Health Care Ethics in USA* (quarterly newsletter); Videotape Series.

★7215★ Santa Clara University
Center for Applied Ethics
Santa Clara, CA 95053
Phone: (408)554-5319
Fax: (408)554-2373
Thomas Shanks, S.J., Dir.

Research Activities and Fields: Conducts, coordinates, and supports interdisciplinary research in applied ethics in the areas of business, medicine, law, journalism, counseling, psychology, and social policy. Seeks to increase the understanding of the role of ethics in private and public decision-making processes. **Publications:** *Issues in Ethics* (newsletter).

★7216★ **Stanford University**
Center for Biomedical Ethics
701 Welch Rd., Ste. 222
Palo Alto, CA 94304
Phone: (415)723-5760
Fax: (415)725-6131
Ernle W.D. Young, Ph.D., Codir.

Research Activities and Fields: Conducts research and teaching in scientific and biomedical ethics. Main objectives are: 1) to apply ethical reasoning to actual moral problems in the practice of medicine and science; 2) to contribute to the national and international discussion of biomedical and scientific issues through research, with a focus on empirical bioethics studies; 3) to convene scholars, professionals, and policymakers to debate and propose policy solutions regarding biomedical and scientific ethical issues; and 4) to serve as a scholarly resource for the University and the community.

U.S. Department of Defense
Armed Forces Institute of Pathology
Center for Advanced Pathology
Legal Medicine, Quality Assurance, and Risk Management Department
See: Entry 10156

U.S. Department of Defense
Armed Forces Institute of Pathology
Center for Advanced Pathology
Oral Pathology Department
See: Entry 10159

U.S. Department of Defense
Armed Forces Institute of Pathology
Office of the Armed Forces Medical Examiner
Forensic and Aerospace Pathology Division
See: Entry 10171

U.S. Department of Defense
Armed Forces Institute of Pathology
Office of the Armed Forces Medical Examiner
Toxicology Division
See: Entry 10172

U.S. Department of Defense
Armed Forces Institute of Pathology
Oral Pathology Department
Forensic Dentistry Division
See: Entry 10173

★7217★ **University of British Columbia**
Center for Applied Ethics
227-6356 Agricultural Rd.
Vancouver, BC, Canada V6T 1Z2
Phone: (604)822-5139
Fax: (604)822-8627
Dr. Michael McDonald, Dir.

Research Activities and Fields: Business and professional ethics, accounting ethics, biomedical ethics, environmental ethics, and ethics in science and technology. Projects include computer modelling of moral agency. **Publications:** Working Paper Series. **E-mail Address:** centre@ethics.ubc.ca.

★7218★ **University of California, Los Angeles**
Program in Psychiatry, Law, and Human Sexuality
UCLA Neuropsychiatric Institute
760 Westwood Plaza
Los Angeles, CA 90024
Phone: (310)206-8716
Prof. Richard Green, M.D., Dir.

Research Activities and Fields: Interface between psychiatry, law, and human sexuality, including studies of sexual privacy laws. **Publications:** *Archives of Sexual Behavior* (bimonthly, published in conjunction with Plenum Publishing).

★7219★ **University of Chicago**
Center for Clinical Medical Ethics
Dept. of Medicine
5841 S. Maryland Ave.
MC 6098
Chicago, IL 60637
Phone: (312)702-1453
Fax: (312)702-0090
Mark Siegler, M.D., Dir.

Research Activities and Fields: Clinical medical ethics, bioethics, technology assessment, and medical outcomes research.

★7220★ **University of Colorado at Boulder**
Center for Values and Social Policy
CB 232
Boulder, CO 80309-0232
Phone: (303)492-6364
Fax: (303)492-8386
Prof. N. Ann Davis, Contact

Research Activities and Fields: Values and social policy, particularly biomedical ethics, environmental policy, and science and technology policy. Promotes interaction among philosophers, academics, and decision makers in business and government. **Publications:** *From the Center* (quarterly newsletter); Working Papers. **E-mail Address:** vspctr@spot.colorado.edu.

★7221★ **University of North Texas Health Science Center at Fort Worth**
Institute of Forensic Medicine
3500 Camp Bowie Blvd.
Ft. Worth, TX 76107-2699
Phone: (817)735-2429
Fax: (817)735-2424
Steven L. Putthoff, D.O., Dir.

Research Activities and Fields: Sudden death due to cardiovascular disease, sudden infant death syndrome, gunshot wounds, blunt and sharp force injuries, and forensic aspects of mass disasters.

★7222★ **University of Pittsburgh**
Center for Medical Ethics
Eureka Bldg., Ste. 110
3400 Forbes Ave.
Pittsburgh, PA 15213
Phone: (412)624-3465
Fax: (412)681-1261
Dr. Alan Meisel, J.D., Dir.

Research Activities and Fields: Theoretical and clinical analysis of the complex ethical issues surrounding the health care process from a multidisciplinary perspective. Research areas include ethical issues surrounding the recruitment of patients to cancer chemotherapy clinical trials, effectiveness of required request laws and policies for organ and tissue donation, quality of nursing care provided to patients with AIDS, doctor-patient communication regarding advance directives, doctor-family communication in an intensive care unit, coercion in management of psychiatric patients, and comparison of ethical issues in engineering with medical ethics issues. **E-mail Address:** dunn@med.pitt.edu.

Chapter 38
Mental Health & Mental Disorders

Federal Government Agencies

★7223★ U.S. Department of Health and Human Services
National Institute of Mental Health
5600 Fishers Lane
Rockville, MD 20857
Phone: (301)443-3673
Fax: (301)443-0008

Description: The Institute provides leadership for a national program to increase knowledge and advance effective strategies to deal with problems and issues in the promotion of mental health, and the prevention and treatment of mental illness.

Foundations & Other Funding Organizations

Private Foundations

Annie E. Casey Foundation
See: Entry 3133

Arcana Foundation
See: Entry 48

★7224★ Blowitz-Ridgeway Foundation
2700 River Rd., Ste. 211
Des Plaines, IL 60018
Phone: (708)298-2378
Robert N. Di Leonardi, Administrator

Foundation Philosophy: One of the primary funding areas of the foundation is "the support of non-profit agencies which provide medical, psychiatric and psychological care to the economically disadvantaged children and adolescents." Additional interests include child welfare, homes, family services, and youth organizations. **Giving Priorities:** In fiscal 1993, health organizations received approximately 51% of funding, principally supporting medical research efforts and health care for the elderly, indigent,

and those with AIDS/HIV. Social service organizations received 48% of giving, with emphasis on the disabled, youth activities, and family services. **Typical Health-Related Recipients:** AIDS/HIV, Cancer, Children's Health/Hospitals, Clinics/Medical Centers, Family Planning, Health Organizations, Home-Care Services, Hospices, Hospitals, Long-Term Care, Medical Rehabilitation, Medical Research, Mental Health, People with Disabilities, Single-Disease Health Associations. **Geographic Distribution:** Focus on Illinois.

Blumenthal Foundation
See: Entry 70

Dale J. Bellamah Foundation
See: Entry 124

Davenport-Hatch Foundation
See: Entry 130

★7225★ Essel Foundation
c/o Lieber Co.
2500 Westchester Ave.
Purchase, NY 10577
Phone: (914)694-2020
Constance E. Lieber, President

Foundation Philosophy: The Essel Foundation is primarily interested in supporting mental illness research. Regular contributions are made to support depression and schizophrenia treatment and research. Higher education is an additional area of interest. **Giving Priorities:** In fiscal 1993, approximately 75% of funding went to the National Alliance for Research on Schizophrenia and the Depressions with the highest grant of $1,300,000. Institutes of Higher education received about 15% of total contributions and religious interests received about 9% of funding. Civic causes and the arts received the remainder of funds. **Typical Health-Related Recipients:** Medical Research, Mental Health, Single-Disease Health Associations. **Geographic Distribution:** Focus on New York, NY.

Eugene B. Casey Foundation
See: Entry 172

Forrest C. Lattner Foundation
See: Entry 190

★7226★ Freed Foundation
3050 K St., NW, Ste. 335
Washington, DC 20007
Phone: (202)337-5487
Lorraine Barnhart, Executive Director

Foundation Philosophy: The Freed Foundation makes most of its grants in the areas of education, the arts, and social services. In social services, interests include the disabled, community services, food distribution, counseling, animal protection, domestic violence, and mental health programs for emotionally disturbed children, anxiety and addictive disorders, and depression. A variety of other recipient areas also are supported. **Giving Priorities:** In fiscal 1994, the foundation gave approximately 28% of its contributions to health organizations. Social service organizations received 26% of contributions; the arts and humanities, 21%; civic organizations, 14%; education, 7%; science, 2%; religious concerns, 1%. Environmental causes received the remaining funds. **Typical Health-Related Recipients:** AIDS/HIV, Child Abuse, Clinics/Medical Centers, Domestic Violence, Emergency/Ambulance Services, Family Planning, Hospitals, Medical Education, Mental Health, Nutrition, People with Disabilities, Sexual Abuse, Substance Abuse. **Geographic Distribution:** Focus on the Mid-Atlantic States.

★7227★ Greentree Foundation
110 W 51st St., Rm. 4600
New York, NY 10020
Phone: (212)603-8230
Kathryn Ritchie, Executive Secretary

Foundation Philosophy: The Greentree Foundation makes grants across the major categories of support. The foundation's primary giving interests include higher education, private secondary education, neighborhood counseling services, the arts, and civic affairs. The foundation also considers all other areas of support. **Giving Priorities:** In 1993, the foundation awarded approximately 29% of its total contributions to educational institutions, including its highest grant of $30,000 to the Manhattan Country School in New York, NY. Social service organizations received about 26%; civic affairs, 16%; scientific research, 10%; the arts, 7%; health concerns, 5%; environmental projects, 3%; religious causes, 3%; and international organizations received the remaining funds. **Typi-**

cal Health-Related Recipients: Mental Health, Research/Studies Institutes. **Geographic Distribution:** Focus on the New York, NY, metropolitan area.

★ 7228 ★ Hill Crest Foundation
310 N 19th St.
Bessemer, AL 35020
Phone: (205)425-5800
Fax: (205)428-0188
Jack G. Paden, Chairman

Foundation Philosophy: The Hill Crest Foundation is primarily engaged in making grants to programs in the field of mental health. In addition to the primary area of support, the officers have decided to support a wide variety of organizations in several fields including the arts, civic and public affairs, education, health care, religion, and social services. **Giving Priorities:** In fiscal 1992, the foundation gave approximately 54% of its contributions to educational institutions. Social services received 29% of funding; and the arts, 8%. Health care received 7% of grants; religious organizations, 2%; and civic concerns, 1%. **Typical Health-Related Recipients:** Diabetes, Eyes/Blindness, Health Organizations, Hospitals, Mental Health, Nutrition, People with Disabilities, Single-Disease Health Associations, Substance Abuse. **Geographic Distribution:** Limited to Alabama.

★ 7229 ★ Ittleson Foundation
645 Madison Ave., 16th Fl.
New York, NY 10022
Phone: (212)838-5010
Anthony C. Wood, Executive Director

Foundation Philosophy: The foundation is currently interested in programs which address issues associated with AIDS, mental health, the environment, and criminal justice. The foundation promotes the well-being of mankind through support for mental health, psychiatric research, and behavioral science research. Since 1932, mental health has been the primary focus. The foundation is especially interested in innovative projects that address underserved populations, such as the elderly, poor, and minorities. The foundation encourages projects that link formal professional competence to informal networks of support in order to make services available. It is also interested in projects that address the consequences of AIDS on the mental health of people with the disease, their families and caregivers. **Giving Priorities:** In 1993, the foundation gave approximately 42% of its charitable contributions in support of education, including a $400,000 grant to expand the environmental studies program at Brown University. Health care organizations received about 23% of the foundation's giving, while civic affairs organizations received 13%. Environmental affairs received 8% of the support, while the arts received 6%. Social services organizations received about 5% of the distributed funds, and international affairs received 3%. The remaining amount, less than 1%, supported religious affairs. **Typical Health-Related Recipients:** AIDS/HIV, Cancer, Children's Health/Hospitals, Geriatric Health, Health Organizations, Hospitals, Mental Health, People with Disabilities, Public Health, Research/Studies Institutes, Single-Disease Health Associations. **Geographic Distribution:** National.

★ 7230 ★ John D. and Catherine T. MacArthur Foundation
c/o Office of Grant Management, Research, and Information
140 S. Dearborn St., Ste. 1100
Chicago, IL 60603
Phone: (312)726-8000
Fax: (312)917-0334

Foundation Philosophy: The Foundation makes grants through Foundation-wide initiatives and through eight programs: The Community Initiatives Program; The General Program, which undertakes special initiatives and supports projects that promote diversity in the media; The Health Program, which is devoted primarily to research on mental health and human development, and on the biology of parasitic diseases; The MacArthur Fellows Program, which awards fellowships to exceptionally creative individuals; The Program on Peace and International Cooperation; The Population Program, which addresses complex issues related to population, reproductive rights, and women's reproductive health; and The World Environment and Resources Program. **Giving Priorities:** In 1993, the foundation gave approximately 24% of its total contributions to environmental concerns. Civic affairs received about 23% of giving. International organizations received 21%; health concerns, 13%; educational institutions and programs, 9%; the arts, 4%; and religious causes, scientific interests, and social services each received 2% of the remaining funds. **Typical Health-Related Recipients:** Family Planning, Geriatric Health, Health Organizations, Medical Education, Medical Research, Mental Health, Preventive Medicine/Wellness Organizations. **Geographic Distribution:** International and national: education reform grants primarily in Chicago, IL, and cultural grants primarily in Chicago, IL, and Palm Beach County, FL.

Marion I. and Henry J. Knott Foundation
See: Entry 378

Nathan Cummings Foundation
See: Entry 409

Ordean Foundation
See: Entry 418

Rollin M. Gerstacker Foundation
See: Entry 462

★ 7231 ★ Staunton Farm Foundation
Center City Tower, Ste. 240
650 Smithfield St.
Pittsburgh, PA 15222
Phone: (412)281-8020
Fax: (412)232-3115
Patricia MacDonald, Administrative Assistant

Foundation Philosophy: The foundation focuses on programs designed to address the needs of those suffering from neuroses and other mental disorders. A primary interest is taken in projects which represent new and different approaches for organizations which provide patient care. The foundation supports work in the fields of health, education, and social services. All organizations that are funded by Staunton Farm deal with mental health prob-

lems and the welfare of the emotionally handicapped, and are located in Southwestern Pennsylvania. The foundation reports that it is emphasizing organizations addressing the needs of children with mental illness. **Giving Priorities:** In 1993, the foundation reports that 100% of its contributions funded social and human services in the field of mental health. **Typical Health-Related Recipients:** AIDS/HIV, Children's Health/Hospitals, Domestic Violence, Health Funds, Health Organizations, Hospitals, Medical Education, Medical Rehabilitation, Mental Health, Sexual Abuse, Substance Abuse. **Geographic Distribution:** Southwestern Pennsylvania.

Swalm Foundation
See: Entry 510

★ 7232 ★ van Ameringen Foundation
509 Madison Ave.
New York, NY 10022
Phone: (212)758-6221
Henry P. van Ameringen, President and Chief Executive Officer

Foundation Philosophy: The foundation's primary interest is furthering "prevention, education, and direct care in the mental health field with an emphasis on those individuals and populations having a disadvantaged background and deprived opportunities." Priority interest areas include preventive and early-intervention strategies, particularly those which work in tandem with educational programs; programs to link existing resources for a client, particularly the mixing of public and private efforts; programs which increase the accessibility of the poor to mental health services; and programs which include a self-help model. **Giving Priorities:** In 1993, the foundation awarded 60% of its total contributions to health care, particularly programs involved with mental health issues. About 28% of funds went to social service organizations. The arts received 8% of gifts, and education received 3%. **Typical Health-Related Recipients:** AIDS/HIV, Cancer, Children's Health/Hospitals, Clinics/Medical Centers, Domestic Violence, Geriatric Health, Hospitals, Mental Health, People with Disabilities, Preventive Medicine/Wellness Organizations, Substance Abuse. **Geographic Distribution:** Northeastern United States.

★ 7233 ★ Wasie Foundation
First Bank Pl., Ste. 4700
601 Second Ave. S
Minneapolis, MN 55402-4319
Phone: (612)332-3883
Fax: (612)332-2440
Gregg D. Sjoquist, President and Executive Director

Foundation Philosophy: The foundation has shifted its giving priority. In the past, the foundation emphasized the needs of children in the Minneapolis-St. Paul metropolitan area. In 1993, the foundation reports its major priporty to center around two issues: education of American citizens of Polish ancestry and issues related to schizophrenia. **Giving Priorities:** In 1994, the foundation reported that it gave approximately 89% of funding to colleges and universities in Minnesota. Religious interests received 11%, in the form of one grant to the St. Therese Home in Minnesota. Civic concerns received less than 1%. **Typical Health-Related Recipients:** Mental Health. **Geographic Distribution:** No geographic restrictions.

William T. Grant Foundation
See: Entry 3145

Corporate Foundations

Advanced Micro Devices Charitable Foundation
See: Entry 6389

Alabama Power Foundation
See: Entry 566

Eli Lilly and Co. Foundation
See: Entry 672

GenCorp Foundation
See: Entry 6399

H & R Block Foundation
See: Entry 718

Millipore Foundation
See: Entry 781

Nationwide Insurance Enterprise Foundation
See: Entry 792

Vulcan Materials Co. Foundation
See: Entry 896

Woodward Governor Co. Charitable Trust
See: Entry 6420

Other Funding Organizations

★7234★ **National Alliance for Research on Schizophrenia and Depression**
60 Cutter Mill Rd., Ste. 200
Great Neck, NY 11021
Phone: (516)829-0091
Fax: (516)487-6930
Constance E. Lieber, Pres.

Description: Raises funds for research on schizophrenia, depression, and other mental illnesses. Awards grants for scientific research.

★7235★ **National Mental Health Association**
1021 Prince St.
Alexandria, VA 22314-2971
Phone: (703)684-7722
Free: 800-969-NMHA
Fax: (703)684-5968
John Horner, Pres.

Description: Raises funds to support expanded research into the causes and cures of mental illness.

★7236★ **Supreme Council, Ancient Accepted Scottish Rite of Free-Masonry**
33 Marrett Rd.
PO Box 519
Lexington, MA 02173
Phone: (617)862-4410
Fax: (617)863-1833
Winthrop L. Hall, Exec. Sec.

Description: Sponsors extensive research program on schizophrenia.

Medical & Allied Health Schools

Psychoanalysis

The psychoanalytic training institutes listed below are accredited by the National Association for the Advancement of Psychoanalysis and the American Board for Accreditation in Psychoanalysis Inc., 80 8th Ave., Ste. 1501, New York, NY 10011, (212) 741-0515.

California

★7237★ **C.G. Jung Institute of Los Angeles**
10349 W. Pico Blvd.
Los Angeles, CA 90064
Phone: (310)556-1193
Fax: (310)556-2290

★7238★ **California Graduate Institute Department of Psychoanalysis**
1100 Glendon Ave., Ste. 1119
Los Angeles, CA 90024
Phone: (310)208-4240
Fax: (310)208-0684

Colorado

★7239★ **Colorado Center for Modern Psychoanalytic Studies**
2240 Linden Ave.
Boulder, CO 80304
Phone: (303)447-0994

Illinois

★7240★ **C.G. Jung Institute of Chicago**
1567 Maple Ave.
Evanston, IL 60201
Phone: (708)475-4848
Fax: (708)475-4970

New Jersey

★7241★ **New Jersey Institute for Training in Psychoanalysis**
800 Catalpa Ave.
Teaneck, NJ 07666
Phone: (201)836-1065
Fax: (201)836-3902

★7242★ **Psychoanalytic Center of Northern New Jersey**
769 Northfield Ave., No LL2
West Orange, NJ 07052
Phone: (201)736-7600
Fax: (201)669-5855

New York

★7243★ **Alfred Adler Institute**
1780 Broadway, Ste. 502
New York, NY 10019
Phone: (212)974-0431

★7244★ **C.G. Jung Institute of New York**
28 E. 39th St.
New York, NY 10016
Phone: (212)986-5458
Fax: (212)867-0920

★7245★ **Institute for Expressive Analysis**
27 West 96 St., 1A
New York, NY 10025
Phone: (212)362-5085
Fax: (212)864-5383

★7246★ **Institute for Modern Psychoanalysis**
112 W. 87th St.
New York, NY 10024
Phone: (212)496-9043
Fax: (212)877-6217

★7247★ **Mid-Manhattan Institute for Psychoanalysis and Group Therapy**
25 5th Ave., Ste. 1B
New York, NY 10003
Phone: (212)505-7837

★7248★ **Psychoanalytic Psychotherapy Study Center**
31 W. 11th St., 6A
New York, NY 10011
Phone: (212)633-9162
Fax: (212)727-9424

★7249★ **Rockland Institute for Psychotherapy**
339 N. Main St., Ste. 9B
New City, NY 10956
Phone: (914)634-4226

★7250★ **Training Institute of the National Psychological Association for Psychoanalysis**
150 W. 13th St.
New York, NY 10011
Phone: (212)924-7440
Fax: (212)989-7543

★7251★ **Training and Research Institute for Self Psychology**
15 W. 96 St.
New York, NY 10025
Phone: (212)663-3508

★7252★ **Washington Square Institute for Psychotherapy and Mental Health**
41 E. 11th St.
New York, NY 10003
Phone: (212)477-2600
Fax: (212)477-2040

★ 7253 ★ **Westchester Institute for Training in Psychoanalysis and Psychotherapy**
2 Sarles St.
PO Box 89
Mt. Kisco, NY 10549
Phone: (914)666-0163

Pennsylvania

★ 7254 ★ **Institute for Psychoanalytic Psychotherapy**
26 Summit Grove Ave., Ste. 217
Bryn Mawr, PA 19010
Phone: (215)963-0346

★ 7255 ★ **Philadelphia School of Psychoanalysis**
313 S. 16 St.
Philadelphia, PA 19103
Phone: (215)732-8244
Fax: (215)732-8454

National & International Organizations

★ 7256 ★ **AboutFace (AF)**
99 Crowns Ln., 3rd Fl.
Toronto, ON, Canada M5R 3P4
Free: 800-665-3223
Fax: (416)944-2488
Elisabeth Bednar, Exec.Dir.

Founded: 1985. **Members:** 6,000. **Languages:** French, Portuguese, Spanish. **Description:** Individuals with facial disfigurements resulting from birth defects, surgery, or accidents; family members and physicians. Dedicated to helping with the social and emotional problems suffered by people with facial disfigurements. Serves as a network for mutual support and information exchange on coping skills and resources for recovery. Offers continuing education program to medical, nursing, and allied health professionals concerned with the lifelong needs of people with facial disfigurements. Provides phone consultation services. **Publications:** *Apert, Crouzon, and Other Craniosynostosis Syndromes.* Booklet. • Brochures, periodic. • *Newsletter*, bimonthly. Newsletter. • *Resource for Recovery List*, annual. • *We All Have Different Faces.*

★ 7257 ★ **Academy of Behaviorial Medicine Research (ABMR)**
Pittsburgh Cancer Institute
University of Pittsburgh Medical Center
3600 Forbes Ave., Ste. 405
Pittsburgh, PA 15213
Phone: (412)624-4800
Fax: (412)624-1936
Andrew Baum, Ph.D., Treas.

Founded: 1979. **Members:** 275. **Description:** Individuals actively involved in research in more than one aspect of biobehavioral science, and who have been published in refereed journals relevant to the field. Seeks to foster the integration of research in biomedical and behavioral science; identify current and future areas of research in the field; provide a multidisciplinary forum for review of research findings and assessment of applicability of such findings to prevention, diagnosis, and treatment of and rehabilitation from illness; serve as a technical and educational resource for academic, governmental, and public bodies. Promotes research and professional standards within the field. Assists in developing guidelines for research training in behavioral medicine. **Publications:** *AMBR Membership Directory*, periodic. Directory. • *Experimental Foundations of Behavioral Medicine*, annual. • *Perspectives on Behavioral Medicine*, annual.

★ 7258 ★ **Academy of Psychosomatic Medicine (APM)**
5824 N. Magnolia
Chicago, IL 60660
Phone: (312)784-2025
Evelyne A. Hallberg, Exec.Dir.

Founded: 1954. **Members:** 1,000. **Description:** Interdisciplinary organization of health care professionals dedicated to the concept of total health care of the physical and emotional needs of the patient. Objectives are: to advance scientific knowledge and the practice of medicine relating to the interaction of mind, body, and environment through study and research; to cooperate with other workers in these and related disciplines; to provide a forum for the presentation and discussion of these problems; to publish the results of research; to facilitate total and comprehensive care. **Publications:** *Academy of Psychosomatic Medicine--Directory*, annual. Directory. • *Psychosomatics*, bimonthly. Journal. Includes book reviews and calendar of events. *Price:* Included in membership dues; $99/year for nonmembers.

★ 7259 ★ **Ackerman Institute for Family Therapy (AIFT)**
149 E. 78th St.
New York, NY 10021
Phone: (212)879-4900
Fax: (212)744-0206
Dr. Peter Steinglass, Dir.

Founded: 1960. **Description:** Licensed clinic devoted to the emotional health of the family. Serves as: a training and research institute for the study of family relationships, family change, and family healing; a diagnostic, treatment, and educational center for the problems of family living. Examines values as they pertain to problems of mental health. Believes that: the individual and his or her family are indivisible in the struggle of life; the emotional life of the family is the unit of treatment, not the one member labeled as "sick"; to help one distressed person, it is necessary to mobilize the healing powers of the whole family. Sponsors the Chronic Illness Project, a study of the families of the chronically ill, which has in turn produced projects on hemophilia, catastrophic illness, school/families, and AIDS/ARC, projects on depression, infertility, gay and lesbian, and learning disabilities. Programs include family clinics, professional education, and research. Sponsors lecturers for universities, clinics, social agencies, and community centers; provides training films. Maintains speakers' bureau. **Formerly:** (1971) Family Institute; (1977) Nathan W. Ackerman Family Institute.

★ 7260 ★ **Agoraphobics Anonymous (AA)**
PO Box 43082
Upper Montclair, NJ 07043
Phone: (201)783-0007
Patricia Steffens, Dir.

Founded: 1974. **Members:** 3,000. **State Groups:** 27. **Local Groups:** 15. **Description:** Individuals suffering from severe anxiety. Offers support through educational programs. Maintains speakers' bureau. **Publications:** *The Connection*, quarterly. Newsletter. *Price:* $25.

★ 7261 ★ **Agoraphobics In Motion (AIM)**
1729 Crooks
Royal Oak, MI 48067
Phone: (810)547-0400
Mary Ann Gogoleski, Exec. Officer

Founded: 1983. **Members:** 500. **State Groups:** 11. **Local Groups:** 12. **Description:** Individuals suffering from agoraphobia and any anxiety disorder. (Agoraphobia is the fear of being above or in open or public places where escape is not possible). Offers support and the opportunity to share concerns and experiences. Maintains speakers' bureau. **Publications:** *AIM*. Video. • *AIM Workbook*. Book. *Price:* $15. • Audiotapes. Covers seminars. • *Expect a Miracle*. Book. • *Jogging Your Spiritual Consciousness*. Pamphlet. • Manual. Provides information on starting a group. • Newsletter, bimonthly.

★ 7262 ★ **Alfred Adler Institute (AAI)**
1780 Broadway
New York, NY 10019
Phone: (212)974-0431
Leo Rattner, Ph.D., Exec.Dir.

Founded: 1950. **Description:** Offers training in psychotherapy and counseling to psychiatrists, psychologists, social workers, teachers, clergymen, and other related professional persons. Conducts three-year program to provide an understanding of the dynamics of personality and interpersonal relationships and to teach therapeutic methods and techniques. Presents the theory of Individual Psychology as formulated by the Austrian psychiatrist Alfred Adler (1870-1937). Maintains the Alfred Adler Consultation Center. **Publications:** Bulletin, annual. • *Journal of Individual Psychology*, quarterly. Journal. • Newsletter, quarterly. **Formerly:** Alfred Adler Institute for Individual Psychology.

★ 7263 ★ **Alliance for the Mentally Ill**
200 N. Glebe Rd., Ste. 1001
Arlington, VA 22203-3754
Phone: (703)524-7600
Fax: (703)524-9094
Silyl Shalo, PR Assoc.

Founded: 1979. **Members:** 14,000. **Description:** Mentally ill persons and their families. Works to inform the public about mental illness and enhance the lives of people who are mentally ill. Conducts research and educational programs. **Publications:** *Decade of the Brain Research*, quarterly. • *Innovations in Research*, quarterly. Journal. • *National Alliance for the Mentally Ill*, monthly.

★7264★ AMEND
777 Grant St., Ste. 600
Denver, CO 80203
Phone: (303)832-6363
Fax: (303)832-6364
Robert C. Gallup, Exec.Dir.

Founded: 1979. **Members:** 65. **Regional Groups:** 6. **Description:** Provides psychotherapy for abusive men, advocacy for women, violence prevention programs in the schools, and educational programs on violence and its prevention. Sponsors training programs. Operates 5 county offices and 2 satellite offices. Maintains speakers' bureau. **Publications:** *A Slap In The Face Is No Solution.* Brochure. • *AMEND: Breaking the Cycle Philosophy and Curriculum for Treating Batterers.* Book. • *Battering: An AMEND Manual for Helpers.* Book. **Also Known As:** Abusive Men Exploring New Directions. **Formerly:** (1992) AMEND Network.

American Academy of Child and Adolescent Psychiatry (AACAP)
See: Entry 3158

★7265★ American Academy of Clinical Psychiatrists (AACP)
PO Box 3212
San Diego, CA 92163
Phone: (619)298-0538
Alicia A. Munoz, Exec.Dir.

Founded: 1975. **Members:** 600. **Description:** Practicing board-eligible or board-certified psychiatrists. Promotes the scientific practice of psychiatric medicine. Conducts educational and teaching research. **Publications:** *Annals of Clinical Psychiatry*, quarterly. *Price:* Included in membership dues. • *Clinical Psychiatry Quarterly*, quarterly. Newsletter. *Price:* Included in membership dues.

★7266★ American Academy of Crisis Interveners (AACI)
c/o Edward S. Rosenbluh, Ph.D.
215 Breckinridge Ln., Ste. 102
Louisville, KY 40207
Phone: (502)896-0200
Edward S. Rosenbluh, Ph.D., Pres.

Founded: 1977. **Members:** 200. **Description:** Professionals from the fields of mental health, law enforcement, education, religion, and medicine whose work causes them to deal with behavioral and psychological crises and emergencies. Provides a forum for professionals from many disciplines to interact, increase their knowledge and skill levels, and share research and educational ideas with others. Sponsors training institutes. Maintains speakers' bureau; provides instructors in all areas of crisis intervention. **Publications:** *Crisis Counseling: Emotional First Aid.* Manual.

★7267★ American Academy of Psychoanalysis (AAP)
47 E. 19th St., 6th Fl.
New York, NY 10003-1323
Phone: (212)475-7980
Fax: (212)475-8101
Vivian Mendelsohn, Exec.Dir.

Founded: 1956. **Members:** 750. **Description:** Psychoanalysts are fellows of the academy; associates are psychiatrists, scientists, or educators; candidates. Seeks to develop communication among psychoanalysts and persons in other disciplines in science and the humanities; provides a forum for inquiry into the phenomena of individual motivation and social behavior; encourages and supports research in psychoanalysis; fosters acceptance of psychoanalysis. Sponsors seminars and symposia. **Publications:** *Academy Forum*, quarterly. Magazine. Contains articles on psychoanalysis and related topics and book reviews. *Price:* $20. • *Journal of the American Academy of Psychoanalysis*, quarterly. Journal. • *Roster of the American Academy of Psychoanalysis*, triennial. **Formerly:** (1966) Academy of Psychoanalysis.

★7268★ American Academy of Psychotherapists (AAP)
PO Box 607
Decatur, GA 30031
Phone: (404)299-6336
Fax: (404)299-0206
Nancy Hunt, Adm.Dir.

Founded: 1955. **Members:** 725. **Regional Groups:** 4. **Description:** Professional society of psychologists, psychiatrists, clergy, and social workers engaged in the practice of psychotherapy. Provides meeting ground for psychotherapists of differing backgrounds and orientations. Facilitates cross-discipline thinking, planning, and research in psychotherapy. Sponsors workshops. **Publications:** *AAP Newsletter*, monthly. Newsletter. • Directory, biennial. • *VOICES*, quarterly. Journal. *Price:* $30/year.

★7269★ American Anorexia / Bulimia Association (AA/BA)
425 E. 61st St.
New York, NY 10021
Phone: (212)891-8686
Fax: (212)891-8613
Randi Wirth, Ph.D., Exec.Dir.

Founded: 1978. **Members:** 2,000. **State Groups:** 4. **Description:** Anorectics, families of anorectics, psychiatric social workers, nurses, psychiatrists, physicians, and individuals interested in the problems of anorexia nervosa and bulimia. (Anorexia nervosa is a serious illness of deliberate self-starvation with profound psychiatric and physical components. Symptoms are excessive weight loss, cessation of menstruation in women, distorted body image, bingeing, continual constipation, and eventual muscle wasting. Bulimia is characterized by recurrent episodes of binge eating, followed by self-induced vomiting or purging by laxatives and diuretics. Symptoms are inconspicuous binge eating, menstrual irregularities, frequent significant weight fluctuations, and fear of inability to stop eating voluntarily.) Acts as an information and referral service. Organizes selfhelp groups. Maintains speakers' bureau; offers outreach services. **Publications:** *American Anorexia/ Bulimia Association--Newsletter*, quarterly. Newsletter. Provides information on eating disorders; includes articles on selfhelp groups, current research, and recent conferences. *Price:* Included in membership dues; $50 contribution. **Formerly:** (1980) Anorexia Nervosa Aid Society; (1983) American Anorexia Nervosa Association.

★7270★ American Art Therapy Association (AATA)
1202 Allanson Rd.
Mundelein, IL 60060
Phone: (708)949-6064
Fax: (708)566-4580
Edward J. Stygar, Jr., Exec.Dir.

Founded: 1969. **Members:** 4,300. **Local Groups:** 30. **Description:** Art therapists, students, and individuals in related fields. Supports the progressive development of therapeutic uses of art, the advancement of research, and improvements in the standards of practice. Has established specific professional criteria for training art therapists. Facilitates the exchange of information and experience. Compiles statistics. **Publications:** *American Art Therapy Association--Newsletter*, quarterly. Newsletter. Provides information on related organizations and available resources; includes calendar of events, legislative news, and member news. *Price:* Included in membership dues; $16/year for nonmembers. • *Art Therapy*, quarterly. Journal. Includes referred articles and illustrations, news and summaries of national conferences, books reviews, media, and commentaries. *Price:* Included in membership dues; $40/year for nonmembers; $57/year for institutions; $64/year for nonmembers outside the U.S.. • *Proceedings of Annual Conference.* Proceedings.

★7271★ American Association of Behavioral Therapists (BT)
PO Box 1737
Ormond Beach, FL 32175
Phone: (904)248-0508
Dan J. Allen, Ph.D., Contact

Founded: 1987. **Members:** 1,156. **Description:** Professionals from the fields of mental health counseling, marriage/family counseling, biofeedback therapy, hypnotherapy, medicine, psychology, pastoral counseling, alcohol/drug counseling, and others disciplined and experienced in the use of the behavioral sciences. Promotes the profession and role of the behavioral therapist. Encourages the sharing of ideas and information among the various disciplines of behavioral therapists. Reports on skill improvements, member articles, new research, business improvements, and skills to help market a successful practice. Maintains national registry of members for referrals. **Publications:** *National Directory of Behavioral Therapists*, annual. Directory. • *Special Reports.* • *The Therapist Report*, quarterly. Newsletter. Provides information on therapy techniques, career opportunities, research, and skills updates. *Price:* Included in membership dues.

★7272★ American Association of Chairmen of Departments of Psychiatry (AACDP)
c/o Frederick G. Guggenheim
University of Arkansas Medical Sciences Center
Department of Psychiatry
4301 W. Markham, Mail Slot No. 554
Little Rock, AR 72205
Phone: (501)686-5480
Fax: (501)686-8154
Frederick G. Guggenheim, M.D., Sec.-Treas.

Founded: 1967. **Members:** 136. **Description:** Chairmen of departments of psychiatry in colleges of medicine. Purposes are: to promote medical education, research, and patient care, particularly as these concern psychiatry; to promote the growth and continuing development of psychiatry; to provide a forum for discussion and exchange of ideas among the chairmen of departments of psychiatry in medical schools; to provide appropriate liaison between chairmen and individuals and organizations whose activities bear on the objectives of the association. Membership list.

★7273★ **American Association of**
Children's Residential Centers (AACRC)
1021 Prince St.
Alexandria, VA 22314
Phone: (703)838-7522
Fax: (703)684-5968
Claudia C. Waller, Exec.Dir.

Founded: 1956. **Members:** 325. **Description:** Multidisciplinary mental health professionals involved in treatment services for emotionally disturbed children; agencies meeting quality standards of residential care. Promotes high standards and advances the concepts and methods of residential treatment; encourages public and government understanding of basic concepts and practices in residential treatment. Represents children and families before standard-setting and rate-setting bodies; participates in programs of education, training, and research in the field of residential treatment, and offers children's services and continuing education credit programs. Maintains speakers' bureau and placement service. **Publications:** *American Association of Children's Residential Centers--Directory of Organizational Members*, annual. Membership Directory. Includes costs, location, staffing patterns, treatment philosophy, and accreditations. *Price:* $20/year. • *Contributions to Residential Treatment*, annual. Proceedings. Contains papers presented at AACRC annual meeting. Topics include research, protocols, treatment, and quality assurance. *Price:* Included in membership dues; $20. • *Journal of Residential Treatment for Children and Youth*, quarterly. Journal. Includes book reviews, children's writings, poetry, research summaries, and scientific papers. *Price:* Included in membership dues. • *Residential Treatment Newsletter*, bimonthly. Newsletter. Reports on residential issues relating to children's mental health. Covers research, treatment, government programs, and AACRC news. *Price:* Included in membership dues.

★7274★ **American Association of**
Community Psychiatrists (AACP)
PO Box 1990
Clackamas, OR 97015
Phone: (503)698-3544
Michael Silver, M.D., Pres.

Founded: 1984. **Members:** 350. **Regional Groups:** 7. **Description:** Psychiatrists and psychiatry residents practicing in community mental health centers (CMHCs) or similar programs that provide care to populations of the mentally ill regardless of their ability to pay. Works to address issues faced by psychiatrists who practice within CMHCs, with the goal of ensuring quality patient care. Purposes are to: increase the number of psychiatrists who choose careers in com-

munity mental health; clarify and solve mutual problems regarding community mental health psychiatric practice; inform and educate the public about the community psychiatrist's role in treating the mentally ill; encourage research and training in psychiatry in the community mental health setting; establish liaison with similar professional associations and foster local and regional groups interested in public community psychiatry. Works to deal with issues such as professional burnout, the function of the psychiatrist within CMHCs, assuring relevant continuing medical education, and improving care in CMHCs. Proposes and promotes standards and guidelines of psychiatric practice and staffing in CMHCs; fosters a multidisciplinary approach to CMHC psychiatric care employing nurses, psychiatrists, psychologists, and social workers. Operates work groups in areas such as residency and fellowship training, standards of care, psychiatric leadership in community settings, and CMHCs and the homeless. Disseminates information on legislative activities, local and regional programs, treatment methods, and other matters relating to community psychiatry. **Publications:** *AACP Membership Directory*, annual. Membership Directory. • *Community Psychiatrist*, quarterly. Newsletter.

★7275★ **American Association of**
Directors of Psychiatric Residency
Training (AADPRT)
c/o David Goldberg, M.D.
The Institute of Living
400 Washington St.
Hartford, CT 06106
Phone: (203)241-6856
Fax: (203)241-8045
David Goldberg, M.D., Exec.Sec.

Founded: 1973. **Members:** 428. **Publications:** *Academic Psychiatry*, quarterly. • Newsletter, quarterly.

American Association for Geriatric
Psychiatry (AAGP)
See: Entry 1881

★7276★ **American Association for**
Marriage and Family Therapy (AAMFT)
1100 17th St. NW, 10th Fl.
Washington, DC 20036
Phone: (202)452-0109
Fax: (202)223-2329
Michael Bowers, Exec.Dir.

Founded: 1942. **Members:** 22,000. **Regional Groups:** 53. **Description:** Professional society of marriage and family therapists. Assumes a major role in maintaining and extending the highest standards of excellence in this field. Has 76 accredited training centers throughout the U.S. Individuals serve as international affiliates in 13 foreign countries. Sponsors educational and research programs. **Publications:** *Annual Conference Monographs*. • *Family Therapy Glossary*. • *Family Therapy News*, bimonthly. Includes research news, interviews, reports on legislative and organization acivities, and activities calendar. *Price:* Included in membership dues; $25/year for nonmembers; $40/year for institutions. • *Journal of Marital and Family Therapy*, quarterly. Journal. Also includes articles on clinical practice, research, theory, and

training. Includes book reviews. *Price:* Included in membership dues; $45/year for nonmembers; $75/year for institutions. • *Register of Marriage and Family Therapy Providers*, semiannual. Also publishes other brochures and books; produces series of professional training videos. **Formerly:** (1970) American Association of Marriage Counselors; (1978) American Association of Marriage and Family Counselors.

★7277★ **American Association of Mental**
Health Professionals in Corrections
(AAMHPC)
c/o John S. Zil, M.D., J.D.
PO Box 163359
Sacramento, CA 95816-9359
Phone: (707)864-0910
Fax: (707)864-0910
John S. Zil, M.D., Pres.

Founded: 1940. **Members:** 2,000. **Description:** Psychiatrists, psychologists, social workers, nurses, and other mental health professionals; individuals working in correctional settings. Fosters the progress of behavioral sciences related to corrections. Goals are: to improve the treatment, rehabilitation, and care of the mentally ill, mentally retarded, and emotionally disturbed; to promote research and professional education in psychiatry and allied fields in corrections; to advance standards of correctional services and facilities; to foster cooperation between individuals concerned with the medical, psychological, social, and legal aspects of corrections; to share knowledge with other medical practitioners, scientists, and the public. Conducts scientific meetings to contribute to the advancement of the therapeutic community in all its institutional settings, including correctional institutions, hospitals, churches, schools, industry, and the family. **Publications:** *Corrective and Social Psychiatry*, quarterly. Journal. Includes book reviews, calendar of events, and research reports. *Price:* Included in membership dues; $35/year for nonmembers. • Papers. **Formerly:** (1978) Medical Correctional Society of the American Correctional Association.

★7278★ **American Association for Music**
Therapy (AAMT)
PO Box 80012
Valley Forge, PA 19484
Phone: (610)265-4006
Fax: (610)265-1011
Katie H. Opher, Exec.Dir.

Founded: 1971. **Members:** 650. **Description:** Certified music therapists, students in music therapy, colleges and universities offering music therapy programs, and individuals interested in the field. Promotes the exchange of information; certifies music therapists; approves music therapy training programs; offers placement services. **Publications:** *Music Therapy*, annual. Journal. Covers clinical and empirical research and theoretical and philosophical issues impacting the music therapy community. *Price:* $20/year, plus postage, for individuals; $30/year, plus postage, for institutions. • *Music Therapy International Report*, annual. Newsletter. Reports on the status of music therapy in more than 20 countries and the activities of international music therapy organizations. *Price:* $10.50/year, plus postage, for individuals;

$10.50/year, plus postage, for institutions. • *Tuning In*, quarterly. Newsletter. Includes updates on legislative developments, notices of conferences and upcoming events, book reviews, and musical resources column. *Price:* $19/year, plus postage. **Formerly:** (1976) Urban Federation for Music Therapists.

★7279★ American Association for Partial Hospitalization (AAPH)
901 N. Washington St., Ste 600
Alexandria, VA 22314
Phone: (703)836-2274
Fax: (703)836-0083
Mark A. Knight, MSW, Exec. Officer

Founded: 1965. **Members:** 1,100. **Regional Groups:** 26. **Description:** Individuals interested in the development and improvement of partial hospitalization within the continuum of psychiatric treatment. To support, encourage, and stimulate the expansion of partial hospitalization services. Sponsors educational discussions on partial hospitalization, including clinical research and administrative issues. Provides consultation services to stimulate and support the study, evaluation, and implementation of partial hospitalization services. Collaborates with other groups in establishing standards of operation and performance in the field. Monitors local and national legislative activity directly related to partial hospitalization. **Publications:** *AAPH Membership Directory*, annual. Membership Directory. • *Bibliography*, triennial. • *Bibliography of Child and Adolescent Partial Hospitalization.* • *Inside AAPH*, bimonthly. Newsletter. • *Insurance and Partial Hospitalization.* • *Internation Journal for Partial Hospitalization*, quarterly. Journal. • *Standards and Guidelines for Child and Adolescent Partial Hospitalization.* • *Standards and Guidelines for Partial Hospitalization.* **Formerly:** (1975) Partial Hospitalization Study Group; (1979) Federation of Partial Hospitalization Study Groups.

American Association of Psychiatric Administrators (AAPA)
See: Entry 5542

American Association of Psychiatric Services for Children (AAPSC)
See: Entry 3162

★7280★ American Association of Psychiatric Technicians (AAPT)
2030 E. Broadway Blvd., Ste. 218
PO Box 13912
Mail Code EA
Tucson, AZ 85732
Phone: (602)623-0522
Fax: (602)748-0458
George Blake, Dir. & Pres.

Founded: 1991. **Members:** 2,153. **Regional Groups:** 10. **Description:** Psychiatric technicians, behavioral health technicians, mental health workers, counselors, social workers, psychiatric nurses, psychologists, and other individuals and companies interested in mental health. Promotes professionalism in mental health industry. Encourages further education of mental health workers and provides national certification of mental health workers. Works with colleges, schools, and mental health facilities to

develop education and training. Awards accreditation to mental health worker training programs. Promotes the last Wednesday in January as "Nationally Certified Psychiatric Technicians Day," and the first full week in September as "Mental Health Workers Week." Conducts educational programs; offers placement information; compiles statistics. **Publications:** *AAPT Conference Report*, annual. Report. • *AAPT News*, quarterly. Newsletter. *Price:* Included with membership; $2/copy. • *AAPT's Outline of Knowledge for Psychiatric Techniques (Learning Objectives).* *Price:* $29.50. • Books. • Brochures. • *Code of Ethics and Pledge.* • *Correspondence Course for Psychiatric Technicians.* • *Journal of the American Association of Psychiatric Technicians*, annual. Journal. *Price:* Included in membership dues; $5/copy. • Monographs. • Reports. • *Textbook for Psychiatric Technicians.* **Also Known As:** Mental Health Workers Association.

★7281★ American Association of Psychiatrists from India (AAP)
c/o Velandy Manohar, M.D.
28 Crescent St.
Middletown, CT 06457
Phone: (203)344-6155
Fax: (203)344-3460
Velandy Manohar, M.D., Sec.

Members: 400. **Regional Groups:** 3. **State Groups:** 3. **Description:** Psychiatrists and other mental health professionals of Asian-Indian descent in the U.S. Seeks to further the education and training of members and to enhance their interest in the mental health field. Bestows awards annually. **Publications:** *AAP Newsletter*, quarterly. Newsletter. **Formerly:** (1990) American Association of Psychiatrists.

★7282★ American Association for Social Psychiatry (AASP)
2021 K St. NW, Ste. 206
Washington, DC 20006
Phone: (202)785-9328
Fax: (202)785-9328
Eliot Sorel, Pres.

Founded: 1971. **Members:** 500. **Description:** Professionals and trainees devoted to the study, prevention, and treatment of mental illness, behavioral disorders, and human vicissitude. Studies the nature, prevention, and treatment of behavioral disorders; promotes the physical and cultural well-being of mankind; disseminates the knowledge and practice of social psychiatry to other sciences and to the public. Sponsors colloquia on timely topics of social psychiatry interest. Evaluates mental health care in transcultural psychiatry by visiting divisions in Europe, South America, and Asia. A division of World Association for Social Psychiatry. **Publications:** *American Journal of Social Psychiatry*, quarterly. Journal. • Newsletter, quarterly.

★7283★ American Association of Spinal Cord Injury Psychologists and Social Workers (AASCIPSW)
75-20 Astoria Blvd.
Jackson Heights, NY 11370
Phone: (718)803-3782
Fax: (718)803-0414
Vivian Beyda, Contact

Founded: 1986. **Members:** 530. **Description:** Psychologists and social workers who treat patients with spinal cord injuries; others interested in the spinal injury field. Promotes improved psychological care of spinal cord injury patients; develops and enhances related education and research programs. Focuses on topics such as sexuality and spinal cord injury, alcohol and drug dependent spinal cord injury patients, adjusting to spinal cord injuries, and planning for care in the community. Sponsors research grant program. **Publications:** *SCI Psychosocial Process*, quarterly. *Price:* Included in membership dues. Also publishes suggested reading list and practice guidelines.

★7284★ American Association of Suicidology (AAS)
2459 S. Ash
Denver, CO 80222
Phone: (303)692-0985
Fax: (303)756-3299
Julie Perlman, Exec.Dir.

Founded: 1968. **Members:** 1,100. **Regional Groups:** 5. **Description:** Psychologists, psychiatrists, social workers, nurses, health educators, physicians, directors of suicide prevention centers, clergy, and others from various disciplines and fields of experience who share a common interest in the advancement of studies of suicide prevention and life-threatening behavior. Seeks to recognize and encourage suicidology (the study of suicide, suicide prevention, and related phenomena of self-destruction). Advances education, disseminates information through programs and publications, and cooperates with other organizations in suicidology. **Publications:** *AAS Membership Roster*, periodic. Arranged by state and region. *Price:* $5/copy. • *American Association of Suicidology--Newslink*, quarterly. Newsletter. Includes association news and calendar of events. *Price:* Included in membership dues. • *Crisis Center Directory*, periodic. Directory. Lists approximately 600 suicide prevention and crisis intervention agencies in the United States. *Price:* $15/copy. • *Directory of Survivors of Suicide Support Group*, periodic. Directory. *Price:* $7. • *Proceedings of Annual Meeting.* *Price:* $20. • *Suicide and Life-Threatening Behavior*, quarterly. Journal. *Price:* Available to members only. • *Surviving Suicide*, quarterly. Newsletter. *Price:* $20/year.

★7285★ American Association for Therapeutic Humor (AATH)
222 S. Merimac, Ste. 303
St. Louis, MO 63105
Phone: (314)863-6232
Sue Wells, Exec.Dir.

Founded: 1987. **Members:** 500. **Description:** Health care providers, clergy, and educators; other interested individuals. Promotes the use of humor as a therapeutic technique; disseminates public information about laughter and humor; offers networking service to further understanding of therapeutic humor; conducts research programs that incorporate therapeutic uses of humor. Maintains speakers' bureau. **Publications:** Bibliographies. • *Laugh It Up*, quarterly. Newsletter. • *Laugh It Update*, bimonthly. Monograph. Also makes available tapes.

★ 7286 ★ American Board of Bionic
Rehabilitative Psychology (ABBRP)
c/o Bartholomew A. Sinatra, M.D.
522 Rossmore Dr.
Las Vegas, NV 89110-4123
Phone: (702)452-9538
Fax: (702)452-1031
Bartholomew A. Sinatra, M.D., Chm.

Founded: 1983. **Members:** 475. **Description:**
Physicians specializing in bionic rehabilitative
psychology. Seeks to advance scientific knowledge and provide educational opportunities in
the field. Conducts charitable activities.

★ 7287 ★ American Board of Examiners of
Psychodrama, Sociometry, and Group
Psychotherapy (ABEPSGP)
PO Box 15572
Washington, DC 20003
Phone: (202)483-0514
Dale Richard Buchanan, Exec.Dir.

Founded: 1975. **Members:** 350. **Description:**
Certifying body for professionals in the fields of
group psychotherapy, psychodrama, and sociometry. (Psychodrama was developed by Dr.
Jacob L. Moreno, 1889-1974, and is used to afford catharsis and social relearning. Sociometry
studies interpersonal relationships in groups of
people.) Works to establish and maintain national professional standards. Administers annual exam which includes on-site observation.
Compiles statistics. **Publications:** *Board News*,
semiannual. *Price:* Available to members only.
• Directory, annual. *Price:* Free. Also publishes
standards for psychodramatists.

★ 7288 ★ American Board of Medical
Psychotherapists (ABMP)
Physicians' Park B
300 25th Ave. N., Ste. 11
Nashville, TN 37203
Phone: (615)327-2984
Fax: (615)327-9235
Alex Harvey, M.D., Exec. Officer

Founded: 1982. **Members:** 2,349. **Description:** Psychiatrists, psychologists, social workers, and psychiatric nurses working in public or
private facilities. Promotes high standards of
professional practice of medical psychotherapy.
(Medical psychotherapy is the treatment of psychiatric and/or medical disorders from a mental
health perspective.) Offers certification review
and continuing education programs. Compiles
statistics. **Publications:** *Advances in Medical
Psychotherapy*, annual. Journal. Scholarly articles of interest to mental health practitioners.
Price: $36/volume. • *Medical Psychotherapist*,
semiannual. Newsletter. Includes listing of
board certification recipients. *Price:* $20/year. •
National Directory of Medical Psychotherapists,
annual. Directory. Includes geographic index.
Price: $32/copy.

★ 7289 ★ American Board of Professional
Psychology (ABPP)
2100 E. Broadway, Ste. 313
Columbia, MO 65201
Phone: (314)875-1267
Free: 800-255-7792
Fax: (314)443-1199
Nicholas Palo, Exec.Dir.

Founded: 1947. **Members:** 3,950. **National
Groups:** 9. **Description:** Certification board

which conducts oral examinations and awards
diplomas to advanced specialists in 9 professional specialties: behavioral psychology, clinical psychology, industrial and organizational
psychology, forensic psychology, counseling
psychology, clinical neuropsychology, family
psychology, health psychology, and school psychology. Candidates must have three years of
qualifying experience in psychological practice.
Publications: *American Board of Professional
Psychology--Diplomate*, semiannual. Newsletter. *Price:* Included in membership dues. • *Directory of Diplomates*, biennial. Directory. •
Manual for Oral Examinations, annual. • *Policies and Procedures*, annual. **Formerly:** (1968)
American Board of Examiners in Professional
Psychology.

★ 7290 ★ American Board of Psychiatry
and Neurology (ABPN)
500 Lake Cook Rd., Ste. 335
Deerfield, IL 60015
Phone: (708)945-7900
Fax: (708)945-1146
Stephen C. Scheiber, M.D., Exec.VP

Founded: 1934. **Description:** Physicians with
specialized training in psychiatry, neurology,
child neurology, child adolescent psychiatry,
clinical neurophysiology, and geriatric psychiatry. Determines eligibility requirements, administers examinations, and certifies physicians.

American College of Forensic Psychiatry
See: Entry 7167

American College of Mental Health
Administration (ACMHA)
See: Entry 5548

American College of Neuropsychiatrists
(ACN)
See: Entry 9973

American College of
Neuropsychopharmacology (ACNP)
See: Entry 10395

★ 7291 ★ American College of
Psychiatrists (ACP)
PO Box 365
Greenbelt, MD 20768
Phone: (301)345-3534
Fax: (301)474-0219
Alice Conde, Exec.Dir.

Founded: 1963. **Members:** 800. **Description:**
Established to honor men and women who have
made a significant contribution to psychiatry.
Members, in turn, invite into fellowship and
membership younger psychiatrists whose
scholarly work and demonstrated clinical excellence indicate that they show promise of becoming leaders in the field. **Publications:** Handbook. • Membership Directory, periodic. •
Newsletter, periodic.

★ 7292 ★ American College of
Psychoanalysts (ACPA)
520 Breck Ct.
Benicia, CA 94510-1372
Phone: (510)339-3723
Angela Clark, Exec.Sec.

Founded: 1969. **Members:** 200. **Description:**
Physician psychoanalysts. Honorary, scientific,

and professional organization. Goal is to contribute to the development of psychoanalysis.
Provides professional leadership and supports
high standards in the practice of psychoanalysis. Offers a scientific forum for theoretical
points of view and encourages the understanding, acceptance, and constructive utilization of
sound analytic concepts by an informed public.
Offers specialized education program. **Publications:** Bulletin, biennial.

★ 7293 ★ American Counseling Association
(ACA)
5999 Stevenson Ave.
Alexandria, VA 22304-3300
Phone: (703)823-9800
Free: 800-347-6647
Fax: (703)823-0252
John Jaco, Exec.Dir.

Founded: 1952. **Members:** 60,000. **State
Groups:** 53. **Description:** Counseling professionals in elementary and secondary schools,
higher education, community agencies and organizations, rehabilitation programs, government, industry, business, private practice, career counseling, and mental health counseling.
Provides placement service for members; conducts professional development institutes and
provides liability insurance. Maintains Counseling and Human Development Foundation to
fund counseling projects. **Publications:** *Career
Development Quarterly*. Includes career trends
and reviews of current assessment instruments.
Price: Included in membership dues; $20/year
for nonmembers. • *Counseling and Values*, 3/
year. Focuses on the role of values and religion
in counseling and psychology. *Price:* Included in
membership dues; $12/year for nonmembers. •
Counseling Today, monthly. Includes ethical
and legal issues, new products, book reviews,
association events, and continuing education.
Price: Included in membership dues; $30/year
for nonmembers. • *Counselor Education and
Supervision*, quarterly. *Price:* Included in membership dues; $12/year for nonmembers. • *Ele-
mentary School Guidance and Counseling*,
quarterly. *Price:* Included in membership dues;
$30/year for nonmembers. • *The Journal for
Specialists in Group Work*, quarterly. Journal.
Price: Included in membership dues; $12/year
for nonmembers. • *Journal of Addictions and
Offender Counseling*, semiannual. Journal.
Price: Included in membership dues; $6/year. •
Journal of Counseling and Development, bimonthly. Journal. *Price:* Included in membership
dues; $40/year for nonmembers. • *Journal of
Employment Counseling*, quarterly. Journal.
Price: Included in membership dues; $11/year
for nonmembers. • *The Journal of Humanistic
Education and Development*, quarterly. Journal.
Price: Included in membership dues; $12/year
for nonmembers. • *Journal of Multicultural
Counseling and Development*, quarterly. Journal. *Price:* Included in membership dues; $10/
year for nonmembers. • *Measurement and
Evaluation in Counseling and Development*,
quarterly. *Price:* Included in membership dues;
$23/year for nonmembers. • *Rehabilitation
Counseling Bulletin*, quarterly. Bulletin. *Price:* Included in membership dues; $18/year for non-
members. • *The School Counselor*, 5/year.
Price: Included in membership dues; $37.50/
year for nonmembers. **Formerly:** (1983) Ameri-

can Personnel and Guidance Association; (1992) American Association for Counseling and Development.

★7294★ **American Dance Therapy Association (ADTA)**
2000 Century Plz., Ste. 108
Columbia, MD 21044
Phone: (410)997-4040
Fax: (410)997-4048
Susan Kleinman, ADTR, Pres.

Founded: 1966. **Members:** 1,200. **Description:** Individuals professionally practicing dance therapy, students interested in becoming dance therapists, university departments with dance therapy programs, and individuals in related therapeutic fields. Purpose is to establish and maintain high standards of professional education and competence in dance therapy. Acts as information center; develops guidelines for educational programs and for approval of programs; maintains registry of qualified dance therapists. Maintains Marian Chace Memorial Fund to be used for educational, literary, or scientific projects related to dance in the field of mental health. **Publications:** *American Journal of Dance Therapy*, semiannual. Journal. • *Conference Proceedings*. Proceedings. • *Dance Therapy Bibliography*. Bibliography. • *Membership Directory*, annual. • Monographs. • Newsletter, quarterly.

★7295★ **American Foundation for Psychoanalysis and Psychoanalysis in Groups (AFPPG)**
c/o Louis E. DeRosis, M.D.
108 E. 96th St., No. 3E
New York, NY 10128-6218
Phone: (212)348-3500
Louis E. DeRosis, M.D., Exec. Officer

Founded: 1961. **Members:** 48. **Description:** Psychiatrists. Raises funds to foster research and education in the field of psychoanalytic medicine. Holds symposia; provides lecture service; produces educational motion pictures on therapy; offers patient placement service and referral service for psychoanalytic therapy.

★7296★ **American Group Psychotherapy Association (AGPA)**
25 E. 21st St., 6th Fl.
New York, NY 10010
Phone: (212)477-2677
Fax: (212)979-6627
Marsha Block, Exec. Officer

Founded: 1942. **Members:** 4,500. **Regional Groups:** 40. **Description:** Psychiatrists, psychologists, social workers, psychiatric nurses, and other mental health professionals who meet specific educational and professional requirements. Sponsors educational and research programs. Operates speakers' bureau and historical archives. **Publications:** *American Group Psychotherapy Association--Newsletter*, quarterly. Newsletter. Includes calendar of events and research updates. *Price:* Included in membership dues. • *Brief History of the Association 1943-1968*. • *Clinical Outcome Results*. • *Consumer's Guide to Group Psychotherapy*. • *Guidelines for Training of Group Psychotherapists*. • *International Journal of Group Psychotherapy*, quarterly. Journal. • *Membership Di-*

rectory, biennial. **Formerly:** (1957) American Group Therapy Association.

★7297★ **American Institute of Stress (AIS)**
124 Park Ave.
Yonkers, NY 10703
Phone: (914)963-1200
Free: 800-24-RELAX
Fax: (914)965-6267
Paul J. Rosch, M.D., Pres. & Chm.

Founded: 1979. **Description:** Physicians, health professionals, scholars, and others from varied disciplines constitute board of trustees. Explores the personal and social consequences of stress. Compiles research data on topics such as: relationships between emotional factors and cardiovascular disease; stress and the immune system with specific emphasis on cancer; stress reduction programs for industry; occupational stress (for example, that of law enforcement officers or air traffic controllers); executive stress ("burn out"); and pharmacological and holistic methods of stress reduction. Seeks a definition of health that recognizes the need for harmony between the individual and the physical and social environments as well as the effects of positive emotions such as creativity, faith, and humor on health. Evaluates ongoing research efforts and stress management programs in the U.S. and abroad. Disseminates information to individuals, institutions, and organizations. Serves as a network for rapid communication among individuals in different disciplines. Sponsors consulting services. **Publications:** *Newsletter of the American Institute of Stress*, monthly. Newsletter. *Price:* $35 in U.S. $45 outside U.S.. • *Readings in Oncology*. Book. Also publishes papers and speeches and issues reprints on stress.

★7298★ **American Mental Health Counselors Association (AMHCA)**
c/o American Counseling Association
5999 Stevenson Ave.
Alexandria, VA 22304-3300
Phone: (703)823-9800
Free: 800-326-2642
Fax: (703)751-1696
Mary Lyn Pike, Exec.Dir.

Founded: 1976. **Members:** 12,013. **Regional Groups:** 4. **State Groups:** 44. **Description:** A division of the American Counseling Association. Professional counselors employed in mental health services; students. Aims to: deliver quality mental health services to children, youth, adults, families, and organizations; improve the availability and quality of counseling services through licensure and certification, political and legislative action, training standards, and consumer advocacy. Supports specialty and special interest networks. Fosters communication among members. **Publications:** *Advocate*, 10/year. Newsletter. Contains current information on the mental health profession. *Price:* Included in membership dues. • *Journal of Mental Health Counseling*, quarterly. Journal.

★7299★ **American Mental Health Foundation (AMHF)**
1049 5th Ave.
New York, NY 10028-0505
Phone: (212)737-9027
Dr. Valentine W. Zetlin, Pres.

Founded: 1924. **Description:** Dedicated to extensive and intensive research in the theories and techniques of treatment of emotional illness, and to the implementation of reforms in the mental health system. Efforts have resulted in development of better and less expensive treatment methods. Findings are disseminated in English and other major languages. Is currently engaged in a long-term research project to determine which approaches anticipate future trends or hold hope for improvements in prevention, treatment, and mental health policy.

★7300★ **American Orthopsychiatric Association (ORTHO)**
330 7th Ave., 18th Fl.
New York, NY 10001-3010
Phone: (212)564-5930
Fax: (212)564-6180
Ernest Herman, Exec.Dir.

Founded: 1923. **Members:** 75,000. **Description:** Psychiatrists, psychologists, social workers, and educators; psychiatric nurses and lawyers; others in related fields, including anthropology, sociology, and economics. Seeks to unite and provide a common meeting ground for those engaged in the study and treatment of problems of human behavior. Fosters research and disseminates information concerning scientific work in the field of mental health. **Publications:** *American Journal of Orthopsychiatry*, quarterly. Journal. Covers therapeutic work with children and adults, community mental health, studies in interpersonal relations, and other related topics. *Price:* Included in membership dues; $45/year for nonmember individuals; $65/year for institutions. • *American Orthopsychiatric Association--Readings: A Journal of Reviews and Commentary in Mental Health*, quarterly. Journal. *Price:* Included in membership dues; $25/year for nonmember individuals; $35/year for institutions. • Books. • Catalog. • Monographs.

★7301★ **American Psychiatric Association (APA)**
1400 K St. NW
Washington, DC 20005
Phone: (202)682-6000
Fax: (202)682-6114
Melvin Sabshin, M.D., Med.Dir.

Founded: 1844. **Members:** 38,500. **Regional Groups:** 77. **Description:** Psychiatrists. Seeks to further the study of the nature, treatment, and prevention of mental disorders. Assists in formulating programs to meet mental health needs; compiles and disseminates facts and figures about psychiatry; furthers psychiatric education and research. **Publications:** *American Journal of Psychiatry*, monthly. Journal. Includes book reviews. *Price:* Included in membership dues; $56/year for nonmembers; $28/year for students; $85/year or institutions. • Books. • *Hospital and Community Psychiatry*, monthly. Journal. Covers the delivery of mental health services in organized settings. Includes book reviews and research reports. *Price:* $35/year for members; $18.50/year for students; $44/year for institutions. • Membership Directory, biennial. • Pamphlets. • *Psychiatric News*, semimonthly. **Formerly:** (1892) Association of Medical Superintendents of American Institutions for Insane; (1921) American Medico Psychological Association.

American Psychiatric Nurses Association (APNA)
See: Entry 9065

★ 7302 ★ **American Psychoanalytic Association (APsaA)**
309 E. 49th St.
New York, NY 10017
Phone: (212)752-0450
Fax: (212)593-0571
Dr. Doris L. Eder, Contact

Founded: 1911. **Members:** 3,025. **Local Groups:** 42. **Description:** Psychoanalysts who have graduated from or are currently attending an accredited institute. Seeks to establish and maintain standards for the training of psychoanalysts and for the practice of psychoanalysis; fosters the integration of psychoanalysis with other branches of medicine; encourages research. Conducts educational programs. **Publications:** *American Psychoanalyst Newsletter*, quarterly. Newsletter. • *Journal of the American Psychoanalytic Association*, quarterly. Journal. • *Roster*, biennial. • *Title Key Word and Author Index to Psychoanalytic Journals*. Also publishes material on psychoanalytic education and research.

★ 7303 ★ **American Psychological Association (APA)**
750 1st St. NE
Washington, DC 20002-4242
Phone: (202)336-5500
Raymond D. Fowler, PhD, CEO

Founded: 1892. **Members:** 124,000. **State Groups:** 57. **Description:** Scientific and professional society of psychologists. Students participate as affiliates. Works to advance psychology as a science, a profession, and as a means of promoting human welfare.

★ 7304 ★ **American Psychological Association (DAEEP)**
Division of Applied Experimental and Engineering Psychologists
c/o Jefferson Koonce
University of Illinois - Willard Airport
Institute of Aviation
Savoy, IL 61874
Phone: (217)244-8601
Fax: (217)244-8761
Dr. Ben Morgan, Pres.

Founded: 1957. **Members:** 600. **Description:** A division of the American Psychological Association (see separate entry). Individuals whose principal fields of study, research, or work are within the area of general engineering psychology. Promotes research on psychological factors in the design and use of environments and systems within which human beings work and live. **Publications:** *Applied Experimental and Engineering Psychology PsycSCAN*, quarterly. • Newsletter, quarterly. **Formerly:** (1982) Society of Engineering Psychologists.

★ 7305 ★ **American Psychological Association (Div. 43)**
Division of Family Psychology
3900 E. Camelback, No. 200
Phoenix, AZ 85018
Phone: (602)912-5300
Fax: (602)952-8230
Ronald F. Levant, Ph.D., Pres.

Founded: 1984. **Members:** 2,000. **Description:** A division of the American Psychological Association (see separate entry). Psychologists interested in research, teaching, prevention, treatment, evaluation, and public interest initiatives in family psychology. seeks to promote human welfare through the development, dissemination, and application of knowledge about the dynamics, structure, and functioning of the family. Conducts research and specialized education programs. Maintains speakers' bureau. **Publications:** *The Family Psychologist*, quarterly. Bulletin.

★ 7306 ★ **American Psychological Association**
Division of Psychotherapy
3900 E. Camelback Rd., Ste. 200
Phoenix, AZ 85018
Phone: (602)912-5329
Fax: (602)957-5387

Founded: 1964. **Members:** 7,700. **Description:** A division of the American Psychological Association. Psychologists and psychotherapists interested in exchanging scientific and technical information about psychotherapy. Conducts continuing education workshops. **Publications:** *Psychotherapy Bulletin*, quarterly. Bulletin. • *Psychotherapy Journal*, quarterly. Journal.

American Psychology-Law Society (AP-LS)
See: Entry 7169

★ 7307 ★ **American Psychopathological Association (APPA)**
Department of Psychiarty
Washington University Medical School
4940 Children's Place
St. Louis, MO 63110
Phone: (314)362-7005
Fax: (314)362-5594
Dr. Robert Cloninger, Sec.

Founded: 1912. **Members:** 500. **Description:** Physicians and scientists interested in the field of psychopathology. To investigate scientific problems of abnormal psychology including: study of phenomena arising from abnormal mental processes; study of organic pathological conditions directly connected with abnormal mental processes; study of means which may remove or modify social or individual factors operating in the production of mental disease; study of relationship between psychopathological and social or cultural problems. **Publications:** *Comprehensive Psychiatry*, quarterly. Journal. • *Proceedings of Annual Meeting*.

★ 7308 ★ **American Psychosomatic Society (APS)**
6728 Old McLean Village Dr.
Mc Lean, VA 22101
Phone: (703)556-9222
George K. Degnon, Exec.Dir.

Founded: 1943. **Members:** 750. **Description:** Specialists from all medical disciplines; social scientists and psychologists. A scientific society for presentation and review of research and clinical practice in psychosomatic medicine. Conducts educational programs; maintains speakers' bureau. **Publications:** *APS Newsletter*, semiannual. Newsletter. • *Psychosomatic Medicine*, 6/year. Journal. **Formerly:** (1948) American Society for Research in Psychosomatic Problems.

American Society for Adolescent Psychiatry (ASAP)
See: Entry 3171

★ 7309 ★ **American Society of Group Psychotherapy and Psychodrama (ASGPP)**
6728 Old McLean Village Dr.
Mc Lean, VA 22101
Phone: (703)556-9222
Fax: (703)556-8729
George K. Degnon, Exec.Dir.

Founded: 1942. **Members:** 800. **Local Groups:** 6. **Description:** Social workers, psychologists, psychiatrists, clergy members, nurses, and others interested in group psychotherapy, psychodrama, and sociometry. Conducts educational programs; compiles statistics. **Publications:** *Journal of Group Psychotherapy, Psychodrama and Sociometry*, quarterly. Journal. • *Psychodrama Network News*, quarterly. Newsletter.

★ 7310 ★ **American Society of Psychoanalytic Physicians (ASPP)**
4804 Jasmine Dr.
Rockville, MD 20853
Phone: (301)929-1470
Fax: (301)929-1491
Janice S. Wright, Exec.Dir.

Founded: 1985. **Members:** 300. **Description:** Physicians, psychiatrists, and psychoanalysts united to: foster a wider understanding and utilization of psychoanalytic concepts; provide an opportunity to study psychoanalytic theory from all schools of thought; encourage clinical and didactic research; promote social and professional fraternalism among members in the field and maintain good relationships with other professional groups. Offers lectures on therapy that combines psychoanalytic orientation with other disciplines. **Publications:** *The Bulletin*, semiannual. Bulletin. *Price:* Included in membership dues.

★ 7311 ★ **American Society of Psychopathology of Expression (ASPE)**
c/o Dr. Irene Jakab
74 Lawton St.
Brookline, MA 02146
Phone: (617)738-9821
Dr. Irene Jakab, Pres.

Founded: 1964. **Members:** 137. **Description:** Psychiatrists, psychologists, art therapists, sociologists, art critics, artists, social workers, linguists, educators, criminologists, writers, and historians. At least two-thirds of the members must be physicians. Fosters collaboration among specialists in the United States who are interested in the problems of expression and in the artistic activities connected with psychiatric, sociological, and psychological research. Disseminates information about research and clinical applications in the field of psychopathology of expression. Sponsors consultations, seminars, and lectures on art therapy. **Publications:** *American Society of Psychopathology of Expression--Newsletter*, semiannual. Newsletter. Includes obituaries. *Price:* Included in membership dues. • *Art Media as a Vehicle of Communication*. Price: $33. • *The Personality of the Therapist*. • Proceedings, annual. • *Psychiatry and Art*, periodic. • *The Role of the Imagination in the Healing Process*. • *Stress Management Through Art*. Price: $18.

★**7312★ ANAD - National Association of Anorexia Nervosa and Associated Disorders**
Box 7
Highland Park, IL 60035
Phone: (708)831-3438
Fax: (708)433-4632
Vivian Meehan, Exec.Dir.

Founded: 1976. **Description:** Anorexics and bulimics, their families, health professionals, and others intere sted in the problems of anorexia nervosa and bulimia. Maintains chapters in 45 states, Canada, South Africa, Ghana, France, Italy, Puerto Rico, Switzerland, Colombia, Spain and Germany. Aims to: seek a better understanding of, prevent, and cure anorexia nervosa and associated eating disorders; educate the public and health professionals on illnesses relating to eating disorders and methods of treatment. Encourages and promotes research on the cause of eating disorders, methods of prevention, types of treatment and their effectiveness, and basic facts about victims. Acts as a resource center, compiling and providing information about eating disorders. Serves as an advocacy agency for those concerned with eating disorders. Works to end insurance discrimination against sufferers of eating disorders. Fights against the production, marketing, and distribution of dangerous diet aids and the use of misleading advertisements. Encourages and cosponsors local and regional meetings. Maintains speakers' bureau; provides children's services; compiles statistics. Conducts referral service, surveys, education, and early detection programs. Organizes selfhelp groups. **Publications:** *Working Together*, quarterly. Newsletter. *Price:* Included in membership dues. **Formerly:** (1980) Anorexia Nervosa and Associated Disorders.

★**7313★ Anorexia Nervosa and Related Eating Disorders (ANRED)**
PO Box 5102
Eugene, OR 97405
Phone: (503)344-1144
Dr. J. Bradley Rubel, Pres.

Founded: 1979. **Members:** 20,000. **Description:** Anorectics and bulimics; families and friends of anorectics and bulimics; medical and mental health professionals, school personnel, pastors, and community youth workers involved with anorectics and bulimics. Collects and disseminates information on anorexia nervosa, bulimia, and other eating disorders; provides support groups, medical referrals, and counseling

for anorectics, bulimics, and their families. Conducts workshops, seminars, conferences, and training programs to help professionals identify, understand, and treat eating disorders. Conducts educational presentations for schools, clubs, civic organizations, churches, and counseling agencies. **Publications:** *ANRED Alert*, monthly. Newsletter. Covers causes, symptoms, selfhelp, treatment, and diagnosis of eating disorders. *Price:* Included in membership dues. • Brochures. • Pamphlets. Also publishes resource material.

★**7314★ Anxiety Disorders Association of America (ADAA)**
6000 Executive Blvd.
Rockville, MD 20852
Phone: (301)231-9350
Fax: (301)231-7392
Klaver Kamp, Exec.Dir.

Founded: 1980. **Members:** 3,000. **Description:** Health professionals involved in the research and treatment of anxiety disorders, including phobias, panic disorders, and obsessive/compulsive disorders; families of those suffering from an anxiety disorder; interested others. Purpose is to aid sufferers of such conditions and their families through educational and informational services and to facilitate research, progress in treatment, and public and professional education. Does not recommend any one approach to treatment, but believes numerous treatments need to be developed and made available and encourages individuals seeking treatment to learn about treatment options. Fosters local selfhelp groups; operates information clearinghouse. Works to remove the stigma of anxiety disorders. **Publications:** *AADA Reporter*, quarterly. Newsletter. Covers scientific developments, association activities, and educational programs. *Price:* $25/year. • Audiotapes. Conference programs. • Booklets. • *Help Yourself: A Guide to Organizing a Phobia Self-Help Group*. • *National Directory*, annual. Directory. • Pamphlets. On anxiety disoders. Also publishes a pamphlet series on anxiety disorders, and booklets; makes available audiotapes of conference programs. **Formerly:** (1990) Phobia Society of America.

★**7315★ ARCEPs**
Str. Locot. Paulescu 25
Bucharest, Romania
Phone: 1 6225817

Languages: Romanian. **Description:** Psychologists and others with an interest in developing fundamental and applicative research in psychotechnics. Conducts educational programs; gathers and disseminates information.

★**7316★ Association for Advancement of Behavior Therapy (AABT)**
305 7th Ave., Ste. 16A
New York, NY 10001
Phone: (212)647-1890
Fax: (212)647-1865
Mary Jane Eimer, CAE, Exec.Dir.

Founded: 1966. **Members:** 4,300. **Local Groups:** 11. **Description:** Psychologists primarily; approximately 25% of membership is made up of psychiatrists, social workers, dentists, nurses, students, and other professionals inter-

ested in the issues, problems, and development of the field of behavior therapy and cognitive behavioral therapy, with specific emphasis on research and clinical applications. Sponsors training program and lectures for professionals; maintains speakers' bureau; handles referrals for the public to locate behavior therapists in the area; arranges for communication between behavior therapists interested in specific problems or information. AABT affiliates hold training meetings, workshops, seminars, case demonstrations, and discussion groups. **Publications:** *Association for Advancement of Behavior Therapy--Membership Directory*, semiannual. Membership Directory. Contains alphabetical, and geographic listings; includes degree, license, specialties, diplomates, and boards. *Price:* Included in membership dues; $25 for nonmembers. • *AV Directory*, periodic. Directory. • *The Behavior Therapist*, 10/year. Newsletter. Reports on behavior therapy and cognitive behavior therapy, particularly uses in medical, psychological, educational, and business settings. *Price:* Included in membership dues; $30/year for nonmembers. • *Behavior Therapy*, quarterly. Journal. Contains emperically based research reports on psychological disorders, assessment, and treatment. *Price:* $65/year for individuals; $130/year for institutions. • *Cognitive and Behavioral Practice*, semiannual. Journal. Clinical methods, techniques, and applications for practicing psychologists, social workers, psychiatric nurses, and others. *Price:* $65/for individuals; $75/for institutions. • *Directory of Graduate Training in Behavior Therapy and Experimental-Clinical Psychology*, biennial. Lists over 300 psychology, special education, and counseling programs that offer training in behavior therapy. *Price:* $20 for members; $25 for non-members. • *Directory of Psychology Internships: Programs Offering Behavioral Training*, periodic. Contains information on admission requirements, application deadlines, and program structure; statistics. *Price:* $20 for members; $25 for nonmembers. Also publishes fact sheets to educate lay audiences about a variety of psychological disorders, including panic attacks, obsessive-compulsive disorder, post-traumatic stress syndrome, depression, eating disorders, and more. **Formerly:** (1968) Association for Advancement of the Behavioral Therapies.

★**7317★ Association for Advancement of Psychoanalysis (of the Karen Horney Psychoanalytic Institute and Center) (AAP)**
329 E. 62nd St.
New York, NY 10021
Phone: (212)838-8044
Barbara E. Bell, MD, Pres.

Founded: 1941. **Members:** 80. **Description:** Certified psychoanalysts interested in encouraging training in psychoanalysis and disseminating psychoanalytic principles to the medical-psychiatric profession and the general community. Conducts scientific meetings. Maintains a consultation and referral service, placement service, and speakers' bureau. Supports research programs; sponsors public educational lectures; maintains library of 4000 volumes. **Publications:** *The American Journal of Psychoanalysis*, quarterly. Journal. Includes book reviews. *Price:* $24 for individuals; $50 for libraries and institutions. • Newsletter, semiannual.

★7318★ Association for Advancement of Psychology (AAP)
PO Box 38129
Colorado Springs, CO 80937
Phone: (719)520-0688
Free: 800-869-6595
Fax: (719)520-0375
Rogers H. Wright, Ph.D., Exec. Officer

Founded: 1974. **Members:** 6,000. **Description:** Members of the American Psychological Association or other national psychological associations, students of psychology, and organizations with a primarily psychological focus. Purposes are to advance psychology and represent the interests of all psychologists (professional, social, and scientific) in the public policy arena. Maintains Psychologists For Legislative Action Now, a political action and education committee. **Publications:** *Association for Advancement of Psychology--Advance*, quarterly. Newsletter. Includes calendar of events and research updates. *Price:* Included in membership dues.

★7319★ Association for the Advancement of Psychotherapy (AAP)
c/o T. Byram Karasu, M.D.
Albert Einstein College of Medicine
Belfer Education Center, Rm. 402
1300 Morris Park Ave.
Bronx, NY 10461-1602
Phone: (718)430-2290
Free: 800-524-4723
T. Byram Karasu, M.D., Editor-in-Chief

Founded: 1939. **Members:** 400. **Description:** Medical doctors who are psychiatrists or in psychiatric training. Works to create a forum where all concepts of psychotherapeutic thought can be aired for the advancement of psychotherapy in practice, research, and training. **Publications:** *American Journal of Psychotherapy*, quarterly. Journal. Includes book reviews and reviews of overseas literature. *Price:* $56 for individuals; $81 for institutions; $62 for individuals in Canada; $87 for institutions in Canada.

★7320★ Association for Applied Poetry (AAP)
60 N. Main St.
Johnstown, OH 43031
Phone: (614)967-6060
Jennifer Welch Bosveld, Exec. Officer

Founded: 1984. **Description:** Poets, teachers, therapists, social workers, creative artists, librarians, and interested individuals. Promotes the application of poetry and creative writing to human services, healing, and self-awareness and self-actualization. Conducts support groups and tutorials. Operates Pudding House Bed and Breakfast retreat. Maintains speakers' bureau. Conducts educational programs. **Publications:** *Pudding Magazine: The International Journal of Applied Poetry*, periodic. Journal. *Price:* Included with membership. • *Topics for Getting in Touch: A Poetry Therapy Sourcebook*. Also publishes articles, chapbooks, and educational materials.

★7321★ Association for Applied Psychoanalysis (AAP)
116 Village Walk Dr.
Royal Palm Beach, FL 33411
Phone: (407)793-0686
Dr. William D. Katz, Exec.Dir.

Founded: 1952. **Members:** 300. **Description:** Practicing psychoanalysts and research psychoanalysts; psychoanalysts in training are associate members. Members must have undergone at least 300 hours of personal psychoanalysis. Seeks to facilitate and promote training and research in applied psychoanalysis, promote interdisciplinary cooperation, and raise professional standards. Encourages research. Sponsors specialized education program. **Publications:** *American Imago*, quarterly. • Directory, annual. • Newsletter, semiannual.

★7322★ Association for the Behavioral Sciences and Medical Education (ABSAME)
6728 Old McLean Village Dr.
Mc Lean, VA 22101
Phone: (703)556-9222
Carol Ann Kiner, Exec.Dir.

Founded: 1970. **Members:** 117. **Description:** A member society of the Council of Academic Societies of the Association of American Medical Colleges. Physicians and behavioral scientists committed to developing and advancing the teaching of behavioral science. Seeks to improve the effectiveness, efficiency, and quality of health care through the application of social and behavioral science knowledge. Aids the continuing education of teachers, clinicians, researchers, and administrators in the behavioral sciences. Conducts educational programs. **Publications:** *ABSAME Newsletter*, 6/year. Newsletter. *Price:* Included in membership dues. • *Basic Curriculum Content for the Behavioral Sciences in Preclinical Medical Education*, periodic. *Price:* $5. • Brochure. • *Membership List*, annual.

★7323★ Association for Birth Psychology (ABP)
444 E. 82nd St.
New York, NY 10028
Phone: (212)988-6617
Leslie Feher, Exec.Dir.

Founded: 1978. **Members:** 352. **Description:** Obstetricians, pediatricians, midwives, nurses, psychotherapists, psychologists, counselors, social workers, sociologists, and others interested in birth psychology, a developing discipline concerned with the experience of birth and the correlation between the birth process and personality development. Seeks to promote communication among professionals in the field; encourage commentary, research, and theory from different points of view; establish birth psychology as an autonomous science of human behavior; develop guidelines and give direction to the field. **Publications:** *Birth Psychology Bulletin*, semiannual. Journal. Covers conception to the first year of life. Includes book reviews, research reports, calendar of events, and case reports. *Price:* Included in membership dues; $9/year for nonmembers. • Books.

★7324★ Association of Black Psychologists (ABPsi)
PO Box 55999
Washington, DC 20040-5999
Phone: (202)722-0808
Fax: (202)722-5941

Founded: 1968. **Members:** 1,400. **Regional Groups:** 4. **State Groups:** 29. **Local Groups:** 34. **Description:** Professional psychologists and others in associated disciplines. Aims to: enhance the psychological well-being of black people in America; define mental health in consonance with newly established psychological concepts and standards; develop policies for local, state, and national decision-making that have impact on the mental health of the black community; support established black sister organizations and aid in the development of new, independent black institutions to enhance the psychological, educational, cultural, and economic situation. Offers training and information on AIDS. Conducts seminars, workshops, and research. **Publications:** *Association of Black Psychologists Publications Manual*. Manual. • *Journal of Black Psychology*, semiannual. Journal. Provides research results. Includes book reviews. *Price:* $30/year for individuals; $50/year for institutions. • *Monographs From the Journal of Black Psychology*, biennial. Monographs. • *Proceedings of Annual Convention*. Proceedings. • *Psych Discourse*, monthly. Journal. Includes calendar of events and research updates. *Price:* Included in membership dues; $95/year for nonmembers. • *Resource Manual for Black Psychology Students*. Manual. • *Sourcebook on the Teaching of Black Psychology*. Also publishes brochures, bulletins, and research projects; distributes videotapes on issues in black psychology.

Association of Child and Adolescent Psychiatric Nurses (ACAPN)
See: Entry 3178

Association for Child Psychoanalysis (ACP)
See: Entry 3179

Association for Child Psychology and Psychiatry (ACPP)
See: Entry 3180

Association of Child Psychotherapists (ACP)
See: Entry 3181

★7325★ Association of Gay and Lesbian Psychiatrists (AGLP)
24 Olmstead St.
Jamaica Plain, MA 02130
Phone: (617)522-1267
Marshall Forstein, M.D., Pres.

Founded: 1975. **Members:** 500. **Description:** Gay, lesbian, and bisexual members of the American Psychiatric Association and other psychiatrists throughout North America. Objectives are to: provide support and encouragement for gay and lesbian psychiatrists; serve as a vehicle for the promotion of social and legal equality for all gay people; further the understanding of members, colleagues, and the public in matters relating to homosexuality; promote improved mental health services for gays and lesbians; encourage research in areas related to homosexuality. Provides, by mail, referrals to private gay-sympathetic therapists. Conducts seminars and exhibits; maintains speakers' bureau; presents papers and panels. **Publications:** *Newsletter of the Association of Gay and Lesbian Psychiatrists*, quarterly. Newsletter. Includes book reviews, calendar of events, and obituaries. *Price:* Included in membership dues; $10/year for nonmembers. **Formerly:** (1979) Gay, Lesbian, and Bisexual Caucus of the American Psychiatric Association; (1980) Gay Caucus of Members of the American Psychiatric Association; (1985) Caucus of Gay, Lesbian, and Bisexual Members of the American Psychiatric Association.

★7326★ Association for Group Psychoanalysis and Process (AGPP)
c/o Dr. Milton M. Berger
501 E. 79th St.
New York, NY 10021
Phone: (212)288-2297
Dr. Milton M. Berger, Pres.

Founded: 1957. **Members:** 25. **Description:** Psychiatrists, psychologists, sociologists, and psychiatric social workers; has international membership. Programs include training, research, seminars, and consultative services for members. Maintains collection of 50 books, 75 videotapes, and 10,000 articles on group psychoanalysis and related topics.

★7327★ Association for Humanistic Psychology (AHP)
1772 Vallejo
San Francisco, CA 94123
Phone: (415)346-7929
Fax: (415)346-7993
Georgia Berland, Exec. Dir

Founded: 1962. **Members:** 3,000. **Regional Groups:** 1. **State Groups:** 1. **Local Groups:** 1. **Description:** Psychologists, social workers, clergy, educators, psychiatrists, and others engaged in humanistic practice. Functions as a worldwide network for the development of human sciences in ways that recognize distinctive human qualities and work toward fulfilling the innate capacities of people, both as individuals and in society. Seeks to link, sustain, and stimulate people who have a humanistic vision of the person, and show how this vision can be realized. **Publications:** *AHP Perspective*, bimonthly. Newsletter. Covers growth therapies, holistic education, interdisciplinary humanistic practices, and social concerns. Includes calendar of events. *Price:* Included in membership dues. • *Journal of Humanistic Psychology*, quarterly. Journal. **Formerly:** (1989) American Association for Humanistic Psychology.

★7328★ Association of Humanistic Psychology Practitioners (AHPP)
14 Mornington Grove
London E3 4NS, England
Phone: 181 9831492
Ian Doucet, Admin.

Founded: 1980. **Members:** 200. **Languages:** English. **Description:** Provides accreditation of humanistic psychotherapists as member organization of the U.K. Council for Psychotherapy; makes available referral services; conducts

training and professional development programs. Disseminates information to members.;

★7329★ Association Internationale de Psychologie du Travail de Langue Francaise (AIPTLF)
Departement de Psychologie
Universite de Rouen
rue Lavoisier
F-76821 Mont St. Aignan Cedex, France
Phone: 35 146115
Fax: 35 146104
Prof. Claude Lemoine, Pres.

Founded: 1980. **Members:** 1,000. **National Groups:** 1. **Languages:** French. Does not correspond in English. **Description:** Doctors, personnel directors, industrial psychologists, and sociologists in 30 countries. Promotes the French language within the field of industrial psychology. Seeks to keep members informed and to aid in the perfection of their work. Facilitates the exchange of current research and information among members. **Publications:** *Actes de Congres*, biennial. • *Psychologie du Travail et des Organisations*. Journal. **Formerly:** French-Language Association of Work Psychology; Association de Psychologie du Travail de Langue Francaise.

Association of Mental Health Administrators (AMHA)
See: Entry 5561

★7330★ Association of Mental Health Clergy (AMHC)
c/o George E. Doebler
12320 River Oaks Pt.
Knoxville, TN 37922
Phone: (615)544-9704
Fax: (615)544-8889
George E. Doebler, Exec.Dir.

Founded: 1948. **Members:** 450. **Regional Groups:** 6. **Description:** Clergy of all faiths (including pastors, priests, sisters, and rabbis) who minister to the religious needs of the mentally and emotionally troubled. Establishes standards for clergy in psychiatric and mental health facilities. Sponsors professional certification programs; compiles statistics; maintains biographical archives. **Publications:** *Cura Animarum*, annual. • *Journal of Pastoral Care*, quarterly. Journal. • Membership Directory, biennial. • Newsletter, 3/year. **Formerly:** (1963) Association of Mental Hospital Chaplains; (1974) Association of Mental Health Chaplains.

Association of Mental Health Librarians (AMHL)
See: Entry 6978

★7331★ Association for Psychoanalytic Medicine (APM)
4560 Delafield Ave.
New York, NY 10471
Phone: (718)548-6088
Fax: (718)548-8302
Dr. Stephan Levitan, Pres.

Founded: 1945. **Members:** 241. **Description:** Organization of physicians who are psychoanalysts. Provides forum on psychoanalytic developments for membership and community. Con-

ducts postgraduate seminars. Sponsors speakers for community or medical groups. Is conducting research on psychoanalytic involvement in social issues. **Publications:** *Between Analyst and Patient*. Book. • *Bulletin*, every 9 months. • *The Psychology of Men*. Book. • *Roster*, biennial. **Formerly:** (1946) Association for Psychoanalytic and Psychosomatic Medicine.

★7332★ Association for Psychological Type (APT)
9140 Ward Pky.
Kansas City, MO 64114
Phone: (816)444-3500
Fax: (816)444-0330
Barbara Olson, Exec. Officer

Founded: 1979. **Members:** 4,800. **Regional Groups:** 7. **State Groups:** 20. **Local Groups:** 40. **Description:** Individuals concerned with organizational development, religious communities, management, education, and counseling, and who are interested in psychological type, the Myers-Briggs Type Indicator, and the works of Carl G. Jung (1875-1961), Swiss psychologist and founder of analytical psychology. Purpose is to bring together and share ideas related to the uses of MBTI and the application of psychological type theory in any area; promotes research, development, and education in the field. (MBTI is a questionnaire developed by Isabel Briggs Myers and her mother, Katharine C. Briggs, to identify Jungian psychological types. Jung believed that seemingly random variations in behavior are actually consistent and orderly if one understands different methods by which people process information.) Sponsors seminars and training sessions on the use of psychological type; conducts MBTI Training Program. Maintains Isabel Briggs Myers Memorial Fund to financially assist those doing research on the constructive uses of people's differences in psychological type. **Publications:** *Association for Psychological Type--Membership Directory*, annual. Membership Directory. Arranged by name, ZIP code, and psychological-type interest. *Price:* Included in membership dues. • *Bulletin of Psychological Type*, quarterly. Bulletin. Includes member activities, regional and chapter news. *Price:* Included in membership dues. • *Journal of Psychological Type*, semiannual. Journal. *Price:* Included in membership dues.

★7333★ Association des Psychologues de l'Ocean Indien (APsyOI)
24, rue des Tec-Tecs
Plateau Caillou
97460 Saint-Paul, Reunion
Phone: 229476
Philippe Reigniere, Pres.

Founded: 1983. **Members:** 50. **Languages:** French. **Description:** Clinical psychologists in Indian Ocean countries. Promotes information exchange between psychologists. Works for improved continuing education programs. **Publications:** *Parages*, quarterly. Directory.

★7334★ Association of Psychology Postdoctoral and Internship Centers (APPIC)
733 15th St. NW, Ste. 717
Washington, DC 20005
Phone: (202)347-0022
Fax: (202)347-8480
Connie Hercey, Exec. Officer

Founded: 1968. **Members:** 550. **Description:** Veterans Administration hospitals, medical centers, state hospitals, university counseling centers, and other facilities that provide internship and postdoctoral programs in professional psychology. Promotes activities that assist in the development of professional psychology training programs. Serves as a clearinghouse to provide college students with internship placement assistance at member facilities. Conducts workshops and seminars on training procedures in professional psychology. **Publications:** *APPIC Newsletter*, semiannual. Newsletter. • Directory, annual. **Formerly:** (1991) Association of Psychology Internship Centers.

★7335★ Association for Research in Nervous and Mental Disease (ARNMD)
1 Gustave Levy Pl.
Box 1052
New York, NY 10029
Phone: (212)348-8133
Fax: (212)831-1816
Ivan Bodis-Wollner, M.D., Sec.-Treas.

Founded: 1920. **Members:** 950. **Description:** Individuals engaged in the practice or research of neurology, neurosurgery, or psychiatry who are members of neurologic or psychiatric societies. **Publications:** *Proceedings*, annual. **Formerly:** (1922) Neuropsychiatric Research Society.

★7336★ Association for the Study of Dreams (ASD)
PO Box 1600
Vienna, VA 22183
Phone: (703)242-8888
Rita Dwyer, Exec. Officer

Founded: 1984. **Members:** 600. **Description:** Medical professionals, sociologists, counselors, educators, researchers, students, and others whose disciplines are involved in the study of dreams and dreaming. Provides an international interdisciplinary forum for the promotion and public dissemination of information regarding research into the physiological and therapeutic aspects of dreams and their interpretation. **Publications:** *ASD Newsletter*, quarterly. Newsletter. Contains research reports, clinical reports, interviews, case studies, and book reviews. *Price:* Included in membership dues. • Audiotapes. Contains conference lectures. • *Dreaming*, quarterly. Journal. Contains scholarly articles on every aspect of dreams and dreaming. Includes book reviews.

★7337★ Association for Women in Psychology (AWP)
c/o Rosemary H. Rosales
3491 N. Arizona Ave., No. 9
Chandler, AZ 85225
Rosemary Rosales, Contact

Founded: 1969. **Members:** 1,500. **Description:** Seeks to: end the role that the association feels psychology has had in perpetuating unscientific and unquestioned assumptions about the "natures" of women and men; encourage unbiased psychological research on sex and gender in order to establish facts and expose myths; encourage research and theory directed toward alternative sex-role socialization, child rearing practices, life-styles, and language use; educate and sensitize the science and psychology professions as well as the public to the psychological, social, political, and economic rights of women; combat the oppression of women of color; encourage research on issues of concern to women of color; achieve equality of opportunity for women and men within the profession and science of psychology. Conducts business and professional sessions at meetings of regional psychology associations. Maintains hall of fame and speakers' bureau. Monitors sexism in APA. **Publications:** *AWP Membership Directory*, biennial. Membership Directory. • Newsletter, quarterly. **Formerly:** (1970) Association for Women Psychologists.

★7338★ Autism Network International (ANI)
PO Box 448
Syracuse, NY 13210-0448
Jim Sinclair, Coord.

Founded: 1992. **Members:** 100. **Description:** Autistic-run self-help and advocacy organization for autistic individuals. Seeks to provide a forum for autistic people to share information and tips for coping and problem-solving; advocates for appropriate services and civil rights for all autistic people at all levels of functioning. Provides information and referrals for parents and teachers of autistic people; sponsors group lobbying and educational campaigns. Serves as a support group. **Publications:** *Our Voice*, quarterly. *Price:* Included in membership dues. • *Pen Pal List*. Directory. Lists people interested in correspondence. *Price:* Available to members only.

★7339★ Autism Services Center (NAH)
Prichard Bldg.
605 9th St.
PO Box 507
Huntington, WV 25710
Phone: (304)525-8014
Fax: (304)525-8026
Ruth C. Sullivan, Ph.D., Dir.

Founded: 1979. **Description:** Service agency for individuals with autism and other developmental disabilities, and their families. (Autism is a disorder of communication and behavior which often manifests itself in social isolation, severe language deficiency, and compulsive insistence on routine and ritual in daily activities.) Assists families and agencies attempting to meet the unique needs of individuals with autism and other developmental disabilities; makes available technical assistance in designing programs. Provides supervised apartments, group homes, respite services, independent living services, and job-coached employment. Conducts workshops and consulting in autism; makes available case management and advocacy services for a four county area in West Virginia (Labell, Mason, Lincoln, and Wayne). Disseminates information regarding autism and its treatment. **Formerly:** (1993) National Autism Hotline.

★7340★ Autism Society of America (ASA)
7910 Woodmont Ave., Ste. 650
Bethesda, MD 20814
Phone: (301)657-0881
Free: 800-3-AUTISM
Fax: (301)657-0869
Veronica Zysk, Admin.Dir.

Founded: 1965. **Members:** 15,000. **Local Groups:** 200. **Description:** Parents, teachers, psychologists, speech therapists, pediatricians, neurologists, and others interested in the welfare of children with severe disorders of communication and behavior. Informs the public of the symptoms and problems of children and adults with autism; promotes better understanding of the condition in general; aids physicians in making earlier and more accurate diagnoses. Committed to the alleviation of this disorder through support of research, public and professional education, and development of habilitative services. Sponsors two mail-order book stores with over 100 titles on autism. **Publications:** *Advocate*, bimonthly. Newsletter. Promotes better understanding of autism by informing the public of the symptoms and problems of autistic children and adults; includes book reviews. *Price:* Included in membership dues. • Audiotapes. Covers conference. • Booklets. • Handbooks. • Pamphlets. • Proceedings, annual. • Reprints. **Formerly:** (1981) National Society for Autistic Children; (1987) NSAC, The National Society for Children and Adults with Autism.

★7341★ Behavior Genetics Association (BGA)
c/o George Vogler, Ph.D.
Div. of Biostatistics, Box 8067
Washington University School of Medicine
660 S. Euclid
St. Louis, MO 63110
Phone: (314)362-3642
Fax: (314)362-2693
George Vogler, Ph.D., Sec.

Founded: 1971. **Members:** 400. **Description:** Individuals engaged in teaching or research in some area of behavior genetics. Purposes are: to promote the scientific study of the interrelationship of genetic mechanisms and human and animal behavior through sponsorship of scientific meetings, publications, and communications among and by members; to encourage and aid the education and training of research workers in the field of behavior genetics; to aid in public dissemination and interpretation of information concerning the interrelationship of genetics and behavior and its implications for health, human development, and education. **Publications:** *Behavior Genetics*, bimonthly. Journal. Includes research reports. *Price:* Included in membership dues; $240/year for nonmembers in the U.S.; $267/year for nonmembers outside the U.S.

★7342★ Behavioral Pharmacology Society (BPS)
c/o Larry D. Byrd, Ph.D.
Emory University
Div. of Behavioral Biology
Yerkes Regional Primate Res. Center
Atlanta, GA 30322
Phone: (404)727-7730
Fax: (404)727-1266
Larry D. Byrd, Ph.D., CEO

Founded: 1957. **Members:** 200. **Description:** Professional psychologists and pharmacologists interested in behavioral pharmacology and psychopharmacology or the connection between drugs and behavior.

★7343★ **Black Mental Health Alliance (BMHA)**
2901 Druid Park Dr., Ste. 207
Baltimore, MD 21215
Phone: (410)523-6670
Fax: (410)225-7188
Jan Desper Maybin, Exec.Dir.
Founded: 1984. **Members:** 200. **Regional Groups:** 1. **State Groups:** 1. **Local Groups:** 1. **Description:** Seeks to increase clinicians, clergy, educators, and social service professionals awareness of African-Americans mental health needs and concerns on issues including stress, violence, racism, susbstance abuse, and parenting. Provides consultation, public information, and resource referrals. Conducts a public awareness campaign; educates the community about available resources; develops programs that benefit African-American children and families. Offers training to human service workers, teachers, police officers, and other service providers who work with culturally diverse populations. Maintains speakers' bureau. Provides the Family Outreach Support Group designed to provide mental health services to African American family members of mentally ill person. The support group provides emotional support, education and interaction for family members experiencing the stresses of caring for and/or living with a mentally ill relative. Provides a resource referral service; maintains an extensive list of African American mental health professionals who are sensitive to and appreciate cultural differences. **Publications:** *African-American Mental Health Care Provider Directory*. Directory. • *Visions*, quarterly. Newsletter. Contains updates, information, employment opportunities, community service information, and calendar. *Price:* Included in membership dues.

★7344★ **Black Psychiatrists of America (BPA)**
c/o Dr. Isaac Slaughter
2730 Adeline St.
Oakland, CA 94607
Phone: (510)465-1800
Fax: (510)465-1508
Dr. Isaac Slaughter, Exec.Off.
Founded: 1968. **Members:** 1,600. **Regional Groups:** 4. **Description:** Black psychiatrists, either in practice or training, united to promote black behavioral science and foster high quality psychiatric care for blacks and minority group members. Sponsors public information service. Maintains speakers' bureau and biographical archives; compiles statistics; conducts educational programs. Offers placement service. **Publications:** *BPA Newsletter*, bimonthly. Newsletter. *Price:* Free to members. • *BPA Quarterly*, quarterly. Journal. *Price:* Free to members.

★7345★ **The Bridge**
248 W. 108th St.
New York, NY 10025
Phone: (212)663-3000
Fax: (212)663-3181
Murray Itzkowitz, Exec.Dir.
Founded: 1954. **Members:** 350. **Description:** A mental health and rehabilitation center for chronic mentally disabled adults suffering serious emotional difficulties and homeless mentally disabled adults. Provides community residence housing, daily programs, evening and weekend programs, and vocational training and placement.

British Association for Psychopharmacology (BAP)
See: Entry 10401

★7346★ **British Psychoanalytical Society (BP-AS)**
63 New Cavendish St.
London W1M 7RD, England
Phone: 171 5804952
Mrs. J. Temperley, Hon.Sec.
Members: 400. **Languages:** English. **Description:** Psychoanalysts in England. Offers instructional programs. Promotes members' interests. **Publications:** *International Journal of Psycho-Analysis*, bimonthly.

★7347★ **British Psychological Society (BPS)**
St. Andrews House
48 Princess Rd. E
Leicester LE1 7DR, England
Phone: 116 2549568
Fax: 116 2470787
Dr. C.V. Newman, Exec.Sec.
Founded: 1901. **Members:** 20,140. **Local Groups:** 5. **Languages:** English. **Description:** Academic, research, and clinical psychologists. Promotes the advancement of psychological study and works to ensure high standards of professional education and conduct. Offers courses. Bestows awards. **Publications:** *British Journal of Clinical Psychology*, periodic. Journal. • *British Journal of Developmental Psychology*, periodic. Journal. • *British Journal of Mathematical and Statistical Psychology*, periodic. Journal. • *British Journal of Medical Psychology*, periodic. Journal. • *British Journal of Occupational Psychology*, periodic. Journal. • *British Journal of Psychology*, periodic. Journal. • *British Journal of Social Psychology*, periodic. Journal. • *The Psychologist*, monthly. Bulletin.

Burger King Cancer Caring Center
See: Entry 5929

★7348★ **C. G. Jung Foundation for Analytical Psychology**
28 E. 39th St.
New York, NY 10016
Phone: (212)697-6430
Fax: (212)953-3989
Janet M. Careswell, Exec.Dir.
Founded: 1963. **Members:** 2,500. **Description:** Analysts who follow the precepts of Carl G. Jung (1875-1961), Swiss psychologist; persons interested in analytical psychology. Provides information on analytical psychology. Sponsors public films. Subsidizes C. G. Jung Training Center which conducts training classes for professionally qualified persons who wish to become Jungian analysts. Operates book service which provides publications on analytical psychology and related topics, and lectures on audiocassettes. **Publications:** Annual Report. • *Quadrant*, semiannual.

★7349★ **Canadian Association for Music Therapy (CAMT) (Association de Musicotherapie du Canada — AMC)**
Wilfrid Laurier University
Waterloo, ON, Canada N2L 3C5
Phone: (519)884-1970
Fax: (519)884-8853
Johanne Brodeur, Ph.D., MTA, Pres.
Founded: 1974. **Members:** 250. **Regional Groups:** 3. **Local Groups:** 1. **Languages:** English, French. **Description:** Promotes the use and development of music for health and well-being in prevention and treatment with all age groups. Establishes, maintains, and improves standards of treatment and service in music therapy; encourages and develops research. Acts as a forum for the exchange of ideas, advice, guidance, and professional experience. Represents the interests of music therapists in matters relating to governmental legislation, jobs, and salary scales. Offers professional accreditation to music therapists. **Publications:** *CAMT Newsletter*, 3/year. Newsletter. News on professional issues concerning music therapists. • *Canadian Journal of Music Therapy*, annual. Journal. • *Conference Proceedings*, published from 1979-1992. • *Membership Directory*, annual. • *Music Therapy: A Health Care Profession*. Brochure.

★7350★ **Canadian Mental Health Association (Association Canadienne pour la Sante Mentale)**
2160 Yonge St.
Toronto, ON, Canada M4S 2Z3
Phone: (416)484-7750
Fax: (416)484-4617
Sue Muckleston, Contact
Founded: 1918. **Local Groups:** 135. **Languages:** English, French. **Description:** Mental health professionals and other individuals with an interest in community mental health. Works to enable individuals, groups, and communities to increase control over and enhance their mental health. Serves as a social advocate to encourage public action to strengthen community mental health services; conducts lobbying activities. Promotes mental health research; organizes and operates grass roots programs to help people whose mental health is at risk make use of the services available to them. Sponsors educational programs. **Publications:** Newsletter, periodic. • Pamphlets.

★7351★ Canadian Psychiatric Association (CPA)

(Association des Psychiatres du Canada — APC)

200-237 Argyle
Ottawa, ON, Canada K2P 1B8
Phone: (613)234-2815
Fax: (613)234-9857
B. Alex Saunders, Exec. Officer

Founded: 1951. **Members:** 2,300. **Languages:** English, French. **Description:** Works to improve mental health and psychiatric care delivery systems in Canada. Fosters high standards among Canadian psychiatrists; promotes continuing education of members; encourages and participates in educational programs for patient care providers; promotes research into psychiatric disorders; represents members before government bodies and licensing bureaus, universities, and related organizations. **Publications:** *Canadian Journal of Psychiatry*, 10/year. Journal. • *CPA Bulletin*, bimonthly. • *Journal of Psychiatry and Neuroscience*, 5/year. • *Membership Directory*, annual. • *Opportunities*, annual. Contains recruitment and research opportunities in Canada psychiatry.

★7352★ Center for Applications of Psychological Type (CAPT)

2815 NW 13th St., Ste. 401
Gainesville, FL 32609-2861
Phone: (904)375-0160
Free: 800-777-2278
Fax: (904)378-0503
Mary H. McCaulley, Ph.D., Pres.

Founded: 1975. **Description:** Works to disseminate information on Isabel Briggs Myers' works and encourage practical applications of Carl G. Jung's (1875-1961) theory of psychological types; seeks to foster understanding and constructive use of personality differences. Primary focus is on the theory of psychological types utilizing the Myers-Briggs Type Indicator (for young people and adults, created by Myers and her mother, Katharine Briggs) and the Murphy-Meisgeier Type Indicator For Children to identify Jungian types. (Jung's theory states that seemingly random variations in behavior are actually consistent and orderly if one understands differences in the ways people process information and make decisions.) Conducts introductory and advanced training through workshops, consultation, and other training sessions for psychologists in the areas of counseling, education, religion, organizations, and research; offers continuing education courses. Sponsors research and offers research consultation; provides computer scoring of MBTI forms to professionally qualified users. Provides consultation on the applications of the MBTI and on-site development of MBTI skills of qualified personnel. Operates the Isabel Briggs Myers Memorial Library containing MBTI- and Jungian-related material. Distributes teaching aids, question booklets, answer sheets, scoring keys, and computer software for MBTI analyses. Sponsors exhibits on professional conferences. Works closely with Association for Psychological Type. **Publications:** *Atlas of Type Tables*. • *Bibliography of the MBTI*, semiannual. Bibliography. • Books. • Reports. Also publishes papers, training exercises, and other materials.

★7353★ Center for Professional Well-Being (CWBHP)

21 W. Colony Pl., Ste. 150
Durham, NC 27705
Phone: (919)489-9167
Free: 800-473-5880
Fax: (919)489-9778
John-Henry Pfifferling, Ph.D., Pres.

Founded: 1979. **Members:** 800. **Description:** Society serving health and other professional associations. Promotes the well-being of health professionals and their families through: preventive education on manifestations of disabilities; increased awareness about the stresses inherent in the system of providing health services; efforts to improve and maintain effectiveness. Provides information on treatment centers. Conducts research and supports efforts to study the incidence and causes of professional impairment, with prevention as a goal. Maintains speakers' bureau; provides individual consulting and counseling. Offers workshops on The Joy of Medicine, Physician Burnout, and Preventive Malpractice Strategies; sponsors retreats, seminars, and lectures. **Publications:** *Being Well: Bulletin of the Society for Professional Well-Being*, quarterly. Bulletin. *Price:* Included in membership dues; $55. • Booklets. • Monographs. • Videos. **Formerly:** (1993) Center for the Well-Being of Health Professionals.

★7354★ Center for the Study of Psychiatry

4628 Chestnut St.
Bethesda, MD 20814
Fax: (301)652-5924
Peter D. Breggin, M.D., Dir.

Founded: 1971. **Description:** Fosters prevention and treatment of mental and emotional disorders. Promotes alternatives to administering psychiatric drugs to children. **Publications:** Report, periodic. Information on psychiatric reform issues.

★7355★ Chinese Psychological Society

Beishatan
Deshengmenwai
Beijing 100012, People's Republic of China
Phone: 1 4919664
Zhong-xian Lin, Sec.Gen.

Founded: 1921. **Members:** 3,000. **Description:** Psychologists, psychiatrists, and interested individuals in the People's Republic of China. Promotes the study of psychology. Organizes major research projects; sponsors educational programs. Fosters academic exchange among members; offers consulting services. **Publications:** *Journal of Psychology*, periodic. Journal.

★7356★ Christian Association for Psychological Studies (CAPS)

c/o Dr. Randolph K. Sanders
PO Box 310400
New Braunfels, TX 78131-0400
Phone: (210)629-2277
Fax: (210)629-2342
Dr. Randolph K. Sanders, Exec.Dir.

Founded: 1956. **Members:** 2,400. **Regional Groups:** 7. **Local Groups:** 65. **Description:** Psychologists, marriage and family therapists, social workers, educators, physicians, nurses, ministers, researchers, pastoral counselors, and rehabilitation workers and others professionally engaged in the fields of psychology, counseling, psychiatry, pastoring, and related areas. Association is based upon a genuine commitment to superior clinical, pastoral, and scientific enterprise in the theoretical and applied social sciences and theology, assuming persons in helping professions will be guided to professional and personal growth and a greater contribution to others in this way. Aims to help members cooperatively as Christians to explore the fields of psychology, pastoring, and psychotherapy for a better insight into perso nality and interpersonal relations and to articulate and promote the lordship of Christ in these scientific disciplines. **Publications:** *Christian Monograph Series*, periodic. Monograph. • *EnCAPSulate Newsletter*, semiannual. Newsletter. Includes information on membership activities and schedule of events. *Price:* Free. • *International Directory of the Christian Association for Psychological Studies*, biennial. Membership Directory. Arranged geographically, with separate listings for libraries. *Price:* $10. • *Journal of Psychology and Christianity*, quarterly. Journal. Contains articles on clinical and theoretical topics. Includes book reviews and professional employment opportunities. *Price:* Included in membership dues; $40/year for nonmembers; $50/year for libraries.

Collegium Internationale Activitatis Nervosae Superioris (CIANS)
See: Entry 8203

Collegium Internationale Neuro-Psychopharmacologicum (CINP)
See: Entry 8204

★7357★ Committee for Truth in Psychiatry (CTIP)

PO Box 1214
New York, NY 10003
Phone: (212)473-4786
Linda Andre, Director

Founded: 1984. **Members:** 500. **Description:** Former psychiatric patients who have had electroconvulsive therapy (ECT), working to bring about truthfully informed consent to shock treatment. According to the committee, shock treatment causes inevitable memory damage and also damages the brain, temporarily relaxing the nervous system. Works to retain ECT's current FDA classification as a high-risk procedure. Has submitted a proposal to the Food and Drug Administration regarding a statement of information about ECT that would be given to patients before they give consent for treatment. Seeks endorsements for the CTIP statement. Also has petitioned the FDA for an animal and human CAT scan study of ECT. **Publications:** *A Synopsis of the Conflict Over ECT at the FDA*. Pamphlet. *Price:* Free. • *FDA's Regulatory Proceedings Concerning ECT*. Pamphlet. *Price:* Free. • *Shockwaves*, quarterly. Newsletter. *Price:* $10/year for survivors and supporters; $5/year for low-income subscribers; $25/year for professionals, agencies, institutions.

★7358★ Common Boundary, Inc. (CBI)
5272 River Rd.
Bethesda, MD 20816
Phone: (301)652-9495
Fax: (301)652-0579
Charles H. Simpkinson, Ph.D., Publisher

Founded: 1980. **Members:** 35,000. **Description:** An educational organization of mental health professionals and others concerned with the relationship between spirituality and psychotherapy. **Publications:** *Common Boundary: Between Spirituality and Psychotherapy*, bimonthly. Magazine. Contains interviews, book and journal reviews, networking bulletin, articles, and calendar of events. *Price:* $22/year. • *Common Boundary Educational Guide to Graduate Education and Training Programs in Spirituality and Psychotherapy.* **Formerly:** (1980) Network of Kindred Spirits.

★7359★ Community Dreamsharing Network (CDN)
PO Box 8032
Hicksville, NY 11802
Phone: (516)735-1969
Fax: (516)731-2395
Harold Roger Ellis, Ph.D., Contact

Founded: 1982. **Members:** 500. **Local Groups:** 200. **Description:** Groups of individuals interested in discussing and understanding their dreams. Works to organize local dreamsharing groups and encourages networking between these groups. Refers qualified dreamsharing activity helpers to schools and groups. Trains elementary and high school teachers in using the dreams of students. Sponsors training sessions in dream interpretation methods; conducts research. Maintains speakers' bureau and placement service. Is preparing a database of dreamsharing groups. Regional or state meetings of local groups on a spontaneous basis. **Publications:** *Dream Switchboard*, quarterly. Newsletter. Includes networking notices. *Price:* $15/year. **Formerly:** (1970) Center for Dream Drama; (1982) New York/New Jersey Dreamsharing Network; (1988) Dreamsharing Grassroots Network.

★7360★ Community Guidance Service (CGS)
133 E. 73rd St.
New York, NY 10021
Phone: (212)988-4800
Barbara Esteves, Adm.Dir.

Founded: 1953. **Description:** Service agency providing low-cost personal guidance services at private offices throughout the New York City area. Staff includes psychiatrists, psychologists, and social workers. Operates in cooperation with and under the same board of directors as American Institute for Psychotherapy and Psychoanalysis, to offer advanced level training in psychotherapy and psychoanalysis to social workers, psychologists, and physicians. **Formerly:** Group for Community Guidance Centers.

★7361★ Congress of Romance Language Psychoanalysts (CPLF) (Congres des Psychanalystes de Langue Francaise — CPLF)
187, rue St.-Jacques
F-75005 Paris, France
Phone: 1 43296670
Dr. Pierre Luquet, Exec. Officer

Members: 400. **Languages:** French. **Description:** Psychoanalysts and students of the International Psycho-Analytical Association . Sponsors research work groups, plenary sessions, and meetings.

Council on Accreditation of Services for Families and Children (COA)
See: Entry 11865

★7362★ Council on Anxiety Disorders (CAD)
PO Box 17011
Winston-Salem, NC 27116
Phone: (910)722-7760
Sarah U. Vaughan, Dir.

Founded: 1988. **Local Groups:** 2. **Description:** Works to educate the public about anxiety disorders. Advocates appropriate treatment; liases between victims of anxiety disorders and treatment professionals; provides consultative services to local health care professionals and clinics. Provides assistance and consultation in establishing support groups; operates support group information phone line. Sponsors seminars for health care professionals and victims of panic disorder, post-traumatic stress disorder, and obsessive-compulsive disorder. Maintains library of periodicals and clippings related to anxiety disorders. **Publications:** Audiotapes. • Brochures. • *QUEST*, quarterly. Newsletter. Includes research information on anxiety disorders; research reports, and personal stories. *Price:* Included in membership dues. • Videos.

Council for Children with Behavioral Disorders (CCBD)
See: Entry 3214

★7363★ Council for the National Register of Health Service Providers in Psychology (CNRHSPP)
1120 G St. NW, Ste. 330
Washington, DC 20005
Phone: (202)783-7663
Fax: (202)347-0550
Judy E. Hall, Ph.D., Contact

Founded: 1974. **Description:** Psychologists who are licensed or certified by a state/provincial board of examiners of psychology and who have met council criteria as health service providers in psychology. **Publications:** *Designated Doctoral Programs in Psychology.* • *Legal Updates.* • *National Register of Health Service Providers in Psychology*, annual. • *Psychologist's Legal Handbook.* Handbook. • *Register Report*, quarterly. Newsletter. Includes current issues in practice.

Deaf-REACH
See: Entry 3514

★7364★ Debtors Anonymous (DA)
PO Box 400, Grand Central Sta.
New York, NY 10163-0400
Phone: (212)642-8220
Mary M., Contact

Founded: 1976. **Description:** Fellowship of men and women who share their experience, strength, and hope with each other that they may solve their commom problem of compulsive debting. Adapted the Twelve Steps and Twelve Traditions of Alcoholics Anonymous World Services for compulsive debtors. Establishes and coordinates selfhelp support groups for people seeking to live without incurring unsecured debt. Helps members develop workable plans for long-term financial and life-style goals. **Publications:** *Communicating with Creditors.* • *Debt Payment.* • *Debtors Anonymous.* • *Pressure Groups and Pressure Meetings.* • *Using the Telephone.* • *Ways and Means*, quarterly. Newsletter.

★7365★ Depression and Related Affective Disorders Association (DRADA)
Johns Hopkins Hospital Meyer 3-181
600 N. Wolfe St.
Baltimore, MD 21287-7381
Phone: (410)955-4647
Fax: (410)614-3241
Paul Hoagberg, Exec.Dir.

Founded: 1986. **Members:** 800. **Description:** Individuals with affective disorders, their families and friends, and mental health professionals. (Affective disorders include depressive illnesses and manic-depression.) Provides support services including referrals, educational programs, networking, and consultation. Encourages and facilitates the formation of local support groups for those with affective disorders; provides training for support group leaders. Conducts research and educational programs; maintains speakers' bureau. **Publications:** *A Patients Perspective: Dick Cavett.* Video. • *A Patients Perspective: Mike Wallace.* Video. • Books. • *Carrie's Story.* Video. • *Depressive Illness: What You Need to Know.* Video. • *Downtime: A Workplace Guide to Understanding Clinical Depression.* Video. • *Health Care Insurance and Psychiatric Illness.* • *Manual for Affective Disorder Support Groups.* Manual. • Pamphlets. • *Selected Readings on Mood Disorders.* • *Smooth Sailing*, quarterly. Newsletter. *Price:* Included in membership dues; $15 for nonmembers. • Videos. • *What You Need to Know About Psychiatric Medications.*

★7366★ Depressives Anonymous: Recovery From Depression (DARFD)
329 E. 62nd St.
New York, NY 10021
Phone: (212)689-2600
Dr. Helen DeRosis, Founder

Founded: 1977. **Members:** 3,000. **Description:** Individuals suffering from depression or anxiety. A selfhelp organization patterned after Alcoholics Anonymous that helps people deal with their anxiety or depression through weekly meeting and sharing of experiences. Conducts research; offers classes. **Publications:** Newsletter, 3-4/year. Also publishes brochures and pamphlets.

Dual Disorders Anonymous
See: Entry 12025

★ 7367 ★ Eating Disorders Association (EDA)
Sackville Pl.
44-48 Magdalen St.
Norwich, Norfolk NR3 1JE, England
Phone: 1603 621414
Fax: 1603 664915
Joanna Vincent, Dir.

Founded: 1989. **Members:** 3,700. **Local Groups:** 47. **Languages:** English. **Description:** Individuals suffering from anorexia and bulimia nervosa, their families, and friends. Offers support and counseling to members. Seeks to enhance awareness of these illnesses. Communicates with related organizations and individuals in the medical and counseling professions. Disseminates information. Organizes regional support days. **Publications:** *Eating Disorders Review*, 3/year. • *Signpost*, bimonthly. Newsletter.

★ 7368 ★ Emerge: Counseling and Education to Stop Male Violence
2380 Massachusetts Ave., Ste. 101
Cambridge, MA 02141
Phone: (617)422-1550
Fax: (617)547-9879
David Adams, Program Dir.

Founded: 1977. **Members:** 20. **Local Groups:** 1. **Description:** Counseling agencies in the Boston, MA, area dedicated to assisting men in the prevention of domestic violence. National activities include: technical assistance and training programs for human service and law enforcement professionals on counseling techniques; information and telephone referral service. Seeks to serve as model for the establishment of similar groups. Conducts research and training workshops on the abuse of women. **Publications:** Articles. Covers domestic violence. • Newsletter, annual. • *To Have and To Hold*. Film. Examines, from a male perspective, the problem of spouse abuse. **Formerly:** (1993) Emerge: A Men's Counseling Service on Domestic Violence.

★ 7369 ★ Emotions Anonymous (EA)
PO Box 4245
St. Paul, MN 55104-0245
Phone: (612)647-9712
Fax: (612)647-1593
Karen Crawford, Dir.

Founded: 1971. **Regional Groups:** 19. **Local Groups:** 1366. **Description:** "Fellowship of men and women who share their experience, strength and hope with each other, that they may solve their common problem and help others recover from emotional illness." Uses the Twelve Steps of Alcoholics Anonymous World Services, adapted to emotional problems. Disseminates literature and information; provides telephone referrals to local chapters. **Publications:** Booklets. • *Carrying the EA Message Magazine*, monthly. Magazine. Provides information on EA members and their recovery through EA. *Price:* $8/year; $.95/issue. • *Emotions Anonymous*. Book. • *Emotions Anonymous World Directory*, semiannual. Directory. • Pamphlets. • *Services Bulletin*, quarterly. Bulletin. • *Today*. Book.

★ 7370 ★ Employee Assistance Society of North America (EASNA)
2728 Phillips
Berkley, MI 48072
Phone: (810)545-3888
Fax: (810)545-5528
Joanne Sanborn, Admin.Dir.

Founded: 1984. **Members:** 800. **Description:** Individuals in the field of employee assistance, including psychiatrists, psychologists, and managers. Facilitates communication among members; provides resource information; serves as a network for employee assistance programs nationwide. Conducts research. **Publications:** *Accreditation Handbook and Employee Assistance Standards. Price:* $18. • *Employee Assistance Quarterly.* Journal. *Price:* Included in membership dues; $35/year. • *Employee Assistance Society of North America*, semiannual. Membership Directory. *Price:* Included in membership dues; $35. • *Employee Assistance Society of North America--The Source*, quarterly. Newsletter. *Price:* Included in membership dues.

European Association for Aviation Psychology (EAAP)
(Europaische Gesellschaft fur Luftfahrt Psychologie — EAAP)
See: Entry 2384

★ 7371 ★ European Association of Experimental Social Psychology (EAESP)
(Association Europeenne de Psychologie Sociale)
University of Oxford
Department of Experimental Psychology
South Parks Rd.
Oxford OX1 3UD, England
Dr. Nicholas P. Engler, Sec.

Founded: 1964. **Members:** 650. **Languages:** English, French. **Description:** Individuals in 28 countries working in the field of experimental and theoretical social psychology. Promotes theoretical and experimental social psychology and arranges for the exchange of information among members and related associations worldwide. Conducts summer schools for young researchers. **Publications:** *European Bulletin of Social Psychology*, 3/year. Newsletter. • *European Journal of Social Psychology*, bimonthly. Journal. • *European Monographs*, periodic.

★ 7372 ★ European Psycho-Analytical Federation (EPF)
(Federation Europeenne de Psychanalyse — FEP)
Michael Balint Institut
Finkenau 19
22081 Hamburg, Germany
Phone: 40 291884050
Fax: 40 291883847
Alex Holder, Contact

Founded: 1966. **Members:** 4,000. **Languages:** English, French, German. **Description:** Psychoanalysts from 19 countries belonging to European psychoanalytical societies. Seeks to further psychoanalysis as a comprehensive theory of personality and therapeutic method based on the teachings of Sigmund Freud (1856-1939), Austrian neurologist and founder of psychoanalysis. Works to maintain and improve standards of education and scientific inquiry and to foster theoretical research. Disseminates information on theoretical and practical aspects of psychoanalysis. Stimulates communication among psychoanalysts; provides a forum for discussion of psychoanalytic and related topics. Encourages the integration of psychoanalysis and other disciplines. Organizes seminars and symposia. **Publications:** *Bulletin*, semiannual. • *Psychoanalytic Training in Europe: 10 Years of Discussion.* • *Pulsion de Mort.*

European Society of Child and Adolescent Psychiatry (ESCAP)
(Societe Europeenne de Psychiatrie de l'Enfant et de l'Adolescent — SEPEA)
See: Entry 3222

★ 7373 ★ European Society of Handwriting Psychology (ESHP)
(Europaische Gesellschaft fur Schriftpsychologie und Schriftexpertise — EGS)
Klebestrasse 6
Postfach 88
CH-8041 Zurich, Switzerland
Phone: 1 4816218
Fax: 1 4816288
Rudolf Kanzig

Founded: 1972. **Members:** 1,000. **National Groups:** 12. **Languages:** English, French, German. **Description:** Psychologists, psychiatrists, physicians, personnel consultants, criminal investigators, and university professors. **Publications:** *EGS-ESHP Bulletin*, semiannual.

★ 7374 ★ Family Therapy Section of the National Council on Family Relations (FTSNCFR)
3989 Central Ave. NE, No. 550
Minneapolis, MN 55421
Phone: (612)781-9331
Fax: (612)781-9348

Founded: 1955. **Description:** A section of the National Council on Family Relations. Practicing family therapists and family therapy supervisors, educators, and researchers. Seeks to improve the practice of family therapy through the development of theory, research, and training. Promotes communication between family therapy researchers and clinicians; functions as a network for family therapy research projects; conducts educational programs. **Formerly:** (1991) National Council on Family Relations Family Therapy Section.

★ 7375 ★ Federation of Behavioral, Psychological and Cognitive Sciences (FBPCS)
c/o David H. Johnson, Ph.D.
750 1st NE, Ste. 5004
Washington, DC 20002-4242
Phone: (202)336-5920
Fax: (202)336-5953
David H. Johnson, Ph.D., Exec.Dir.

Founded: 1980. **Members:** 18. **Description:** Scientific societies representing 90,000 research scientists. Promotes research in behavioral, psychological, and cognitive sciences and their physiological bases and applications in health, education, and human development. Facilitates the exchange of information and interaction among governmental agencies and scientific organizations. Serves as a source of information and expertise on behavioral, psychological, and cognitive sciences. Works with other scientific societies in the fields of social science, psychology, education, and the neurosciences. Encourages legislation and policies that provide training and research in these areas; represents interests of members before Congress. Conducts scientific seminars to demonstrate the utility of science in add ressing public policy problems. Sponsors Forum on Research Management as a channel for increasing communication among university scientists and government officials. **Publications:** Annual Report. • *Federation News*, monthly. Newsletter. • *Science and Public Policy Seminar Transcripts*, periodic.

★7376★ **Finnish Association for Mental Health (FAMH)**
(Suomen Mielenterveysseura-Foreningen for Mental Halsa i Finland)
Lauttasaarentie 28-30
SF-00200 Helsinki, Finland
Phone: 0 615516
Fax: 0 6924065
Ms. Pirkko Lahti, Exec.Dir.

Founded: 1897. **Local Groups:** 40. **Languages:** English, Finnish, German, Swedish. **Description:** Voluntary organization for professional and lay people. Promotes mental health through programs of prevention. Introduces new procedures in voluntary and statutory mental health work. Provides support and crisis services; offers vocational training programs. Maintains 10 crisis centers. **Publications:** Books. • Journals. • *Mielenterveys*, bimonthly. Includes mental health information. • Newsletter, annual. • *Perheterapia*, quarterly. Provides family therapy information.

★7377★ **Finnish Society of Analytical Trilogy (FSAT)**
(Suomen Analyyttinen Trilogia Yhdistys — SATY)
Apollonkatu 17
SF-00100 Helsinki, Finland
Phone: 0 499921
Fax: 0 447897
P. Simula, Pres.

Founded: 1985. **Members:** 200. **Languages:** English, Finnish, Portuguese, Swedish. **Description:** Promotes the application of analytical trilogy to all professions. (Analytical trilogy, or integral psychoanalysis, is based on the beliefs of Sigmund Freud, Socrates, and other theorists of psychology and religion. The trilogy represents feeling, thought, and action, and in a broader sense, theology, philosophy, and science.) Offers psychoanalytic treatment and care for psychosomatic illness. Sponsors a socioeconomic development project in which workers own and live in group trilogical residences. **Publications:** *Integraalinen Psykoanalyysi Lehti*, semiannual. Magazine. • *Trilogy Newspaper*, bimonthly. Published in conjunction with ISAT.

★7378★ **Foundation for Depression and Manic Depression (FDMD)**
24 E. 81st St., Ste. 2B
New York, NY 10028
Phone: (212)772-3400
Fax: (212)288-0809
Ronald R. Fieve, M.D., Pres.

Founded: 1975. **Description:** Engaged in research and treatment of mood disorders including depression, manic depression, panic and anxiety states, and stress. Offers a major psychotherapy program including behavioral and cognitive psychotherapy as well as psychodynamic psychotherapy to patients who do not wish or need medication. Also offers clinical training for professionals in treatment and diagnosis of mood disorders. Sponsors clinical drug trial program for patients who do not respond to medications currently on the market, and a cocaine and substance abuse program. Provides an on-site psycho-diagnostic laboratory. **Publications:** Newsletter, periodic. Also publishes educational brochures.

★7379★ **French-Language Association of Scientific Psychology**
(Association de Psychologie Scientifique de Langue Francaise — APSLF)
Universite de Provence
29, ave. R. Shuman
F-13621 Aix-en-Provence, France
Phone: 42 481566
Fax: 42 481722
Prof. C. Bastien, Contact

Founded: 1952. **Members:** 600. **Languages:** French. **Description:** Individuals who have university degrees or who are professionally active in the field of scientific psychology, and who use the French language as their means of professional communication. Encourages communication among psychologists of French-speaking communities mainly through symposia. **Publications:** *Symposia Proceedings*, biennial.

French-Speaking Neuropsychological Society (FSNS)
(Societe de Neuropsychologie de Langue Francaise)
See: Entry 8221

★7380★ **German Academy for Psychoanalysis (GAP)**
(Deutsche Akademie fur Psychoanalyse — DAP)
Goethestrasse 54
80336 Munich, Germany
Phone: 89 539674
Fax: 89 5328837
Dipl. Psych Maria Ammon, Pres.

Founded: 1969. **Members:** 80. **Languages:** English, German. **Description:** Psychoanalysts, psychiatrists, and psychotherapists in Germany. Promotes training and research in psychoanalysis and psychotherapy within the framework of "dynamic psychiatry" as developed by the group's former president, Gunter Ammon. Conducts seminars. **Publications:** *Dynamic Psychiatry*, bimonthly. Journal. Also publishes *Handbook of Dynamic Psychiatry*.

★7381★ **German Association of Suicide Prevention (GASP)**
(Deutsche Gesellschaft fur Suizidpraevention — DGS)
Psychiatrisches Landeskrankenhaus Weissenau
Geschaeftsstelle
88214 Ravensburg, Germany
Phone: 51 7601394
Fax: 51 7601413
Dr. M. Wolfendorf, Exec. Officer

Founded: 1972. **Members:** 400. **Languages:** English, German. **Description:** Psychiatrists, psychologists, social workers, and nonprofessionals in Germany and Eastern Europe united to prevent suicide. Bestows awards. **Publications:** *Suizidprophylaxe*, quarterly. Journal. Includes English summaries.

★7382★ **GP Psychotherapy Association**
3 Gardenvale Rd.
Toronto, ON, Canada M8Z 4B8
Phone: (416)239-4644
Fax: (416)239-7428
Dr. Dianne McGibbon, Contact

Founded: 1984. **Members:** 1,300. **Description:** Psychiatrists and psychotherapists in Canada. Promotes the interests of individuals working in the psychotherapeutic medical field. Seeks to improve the psychological well being of Canadians. Informs members on professional topics. Grants educational credits to training seminars in both Class I and Class II. **Publications:** *GP Psychotherapist*, bimonthly. Contains letters, articles, book reviews, announcements of educational events, and classified ads. **Formerly:** (1984) Psychotherapy Network.

★7383★ **Group for the Advancement of Psychiatry (GAP)**
PO Box 28218
Dallas, TX 75228
Phone: (214)613-3044
Fax: (214)613-5532
Frances Roton, Contact

Founded: 1946. **Members:** 300. **Description:** Independent group of psychiatrists organized in working committees interested in applying the principles of psychiatry toward the study of human relations. Works closely with specialists in many other disciplines. Investigates such subjects as school desegregation, use of nuclear energy, religion, psychiatry in the armed forces, mental retardation, cross-cultural communication, medical uses of hypnosis, and the college experience. Maintains 24 committees. **Publications:** Reports.

★7384★ **Hong Kong Psychological Society**
Department of Psychology
University of Hong Kong
Pokfulam Rd.
Hong Kong, Hong Kong
Phone: 8592376
Fax: 8583518

Languages: Chinese, English. **Description:** Psychologists, psychiatrists, and others with an interest in psychology in Hong Kong. Promotes advancement in the study and practice of psychology; works to ensure high standards of ethical and professional conduct in the field.

★ 7385 ★ Humor Project

110 Spring St.
Saratoga Springs, NY 12866
Phone: (518)587-8770
Fax: (518)587-8771
Dr. Joel Goodman, Pres.

Founded: 1977. **Members:** 125,000. **Description:** Health care professionals, educators, counselors, therapists, business executives, and others interested in developing their sense of humor. Believes humor can be used as a constructive tool, personally and professionally. Provides speeches, training, grants, and programs on how to improve and apply one's sense of humor. Operates HUMOResources mail order information service. Develops, collects, and disseminates information. Offers graduate courses; operates Exhibit on American Humor; maintains speakers' bureau. Is developing projects that focus on the medical applications of humor and on the role of humor in parenting and families. Serves as clearinghouse. **Publications:** *Directory of People Doing Research on Humor*, periodic. Directory. • *Fun-Liners TidBits*. Software. • *Funny Business*. Book. • *Humor and Creativity Conference Six-Packs*. Audiotape. • *Humor: The Jest Machine*. Book. • *Laughing Matters*, quarterly. Journal. Examines the serious implications and applications of humor. Includes interviews with famous humorists and comedians. *Price:* $16/year in U.S. and Canada; $30/year outside North America. • *Playfair: Everybody's Guide to Noncompetitive Play*. Book. • *Some Days You're the Pigeon . . . Some Days You're the Statue*. Book. • *Taking Your Job Seriously and Yourself Lightly*. Book.

★ 7386 ★ Indonesian Psychology Association (IPA)

(Ikatan Sarjana Psikologi Indonesia — ISPI)
c/o Fakultas Psikologi UI - Komplek UI
Depok 16424
Jakarta, Indonesia
Phone: 21 7270005
Fax: 21 7270009
Dr. Mambu, V. Chairperson

Languages: Indonesian. **Description:** Professional psychologists. Works to advance the study and practice of psychology, and to ensure delivery of quality psychological services in Indonesia. Conducts research and educational programs. **Publications:** *Jurnal Psikologi Dan Masyarakat*. Journal. Abstract in English. • *Jurnal Psikologi Indonesia*, annual. Journal. Abstract in English.

★ 7387 ★ The Information Exchange (TIE)

20 Squadron Blvd., Ste. 400
New City, NY 10956
Phone: (914)634-0050
Fax: (914)634-1690
Bert Pepper, M.D., Exec.Dir.

Founded: 1983. **Description:** Promotes research and treatment for young adults with serious ongoing mental/emotional disorders. (Defines young adult patients as persons 18-35 years old who have a psychiatric disorder, are socially disabled, and have needed mental health services for at least two years. The psychiatric disorder may be a major mental illness or personality disorder, or a mixture of emotional problems with substance abuse or other disabili-

ties.) Goals are to gather information about young adults and about new research and effective program initiatives for them; to disseminate information to professionals and the public; to create an awareness of the needs of young adults and their families. Sponsors and encourages research on young adults and development of effective programs; provides consultation and teaching about the patients and on effective ways of meeting their needs. Conducts presentations for professional and community groups. **Publications:** Bulletin, quarterly. • *Tie-Lines*, quarterly. Newsletter. Includes conference calendar and articles about MICA clients and ongoing problems. *Price:* Included in membership dues. **Formerly:** (1994) The Information Exchange on Young Adult Chronic Patients.

★ 7388 ★ Institute for the Advancement of Human Behavior (IAHB)

4370 Alpine Rd., Ste. 108
Portola Valley, CA 94028
Phone: (415)851-8411
Fax: (415)851-0406
G. W. Piaget, Pres.

Founded: 1977. **Description:** Continuing educational organization for health care professionals. Provides training opportunities in behavioral topics such as: the psychology of health care; human sexuality; brief therapy, PTSD, couples therapy, maintaining long-term health behaviors, and the role of imagery in health care. **Publications:** Audiotapes, periodic. **Also Known As:** Institute for Behavioral Healthcare.

★ 7389 ★ Institute for Control Theory, Reality Therapy, and Quality Management (IRT)

7301 Med. Center Dr., Ste. 104
Canoga Park, CA 91307
Phone: (818)888-0688
Free: 800-899-0688
Fax: (818)888-3023
William Glasser, M.D., Pres.

Founded: 1967. **Regional Groups:** 9. **Description:** Board-certified psychiatrists, psychologists, social workers, and consultants in a variety of related fields. Teaches Reality Therapy, Control Theory, and Quality Management concepts to those who wish to use the knowledge in various working environments. (Reality Therapy is a method of working with individuals and groups emphasizing the responsibility of the individual for his or her own behavior; Control Theory explains how and why we behave, that all behavior is purposeful, and that we are internally motivated; Quality Management emphasizes lead versus boss management to create quality work places.) **Publications:** *Journal of Control Theory, Reality Therapy, and Quality Management*, semiannual. Journal. • Newsletter, 3/year. **Formerly:** Institute for Reality Therapy.

★ 7390 ★ Institute for the Development of Emotional and Life Skills (IDEALS)

4400 East- West Hwy., Ste. 28
Bethesda, MD 20814
Phone: (301)986-1479
Fax: (301)699-8835
Dr. William Nordling, Exec.Dir.

Founded: 1972. **Members:** 12. **Description:** Goals include developing and researching ef-

fective programs for improving emotional and interpersonal skills and providing high-quality training and supervision for mental health professionals, managers, workers, and the public. Conducts training programs for professionals in the areas of mental health, health care, human services, education, and business; sponsors training programs for laypeople in the areas of improving interpersonal relations, problem solving, and effective functioning in family and in business settings. Offers programs for workers and managers in communication, goal planning, motivation, negotiation, stress and time management, personnel management, and supervision. **Publications:** *A Scriptural Guide to a Fulfilling Marriage*. • Bibliography. Contains training programs, research articles, books and films. • *Parenting: A Skills Training Manual*. • *Relationship Skills Manual*.

★ 7391 ★ Institute for Expressive Analysis (IEA)

c/o Dr. Arthur Robbins
325 West End Ave., 12B
New York, NY 10023
Phone: (212)362-5085
Dr. Arthur Robbins, Dir.

Founded: 1976. **Members:** 64. **Local Groups:** 1. **Description:** Practicing art, dance, and music therapists, social workers, art teachers, and psychotherapists trained in expressive analysis (a psychotherapy that strives to develop the left and right brain activities to achieve body-mind integration and the mobilization of creative energies). Sponsors lectures and workshops for the public and professionals. Provides advanced courses leading to certification as associate, fellow, or full member of the institute. Maintains educational and counseling center. **Publications:** Journal, annual. **Formerly:** Center for Expressive Analysis; Center for Expressive Psychotherapy.

★ 7392 ★ Institute on Hospital and Community Psychiatry (IHCP)

1400 K St. NW
Washington, DC 20005
Phone: (202)682-6174
Fax: (202)682-6348
Sandra M. Hass-Yamhure, Coord.

Founded: 1949. **Description:** Annual forum sponsored by the American Psychiatric Association (see separate entry). Open to employees of all psychiatric and related health and educational facilities. Includes lectures by experts in the field and workshops and accredited courses on problems, programs, and trends. Offers onsite Job Bank, which lists opportunities for mental health professionals. Organizes scientific exhibits. **Publications:** *Hospital and Community Psychiatry*, monthly. • *Institute Syllabus*.

Institute for Labor and Mental Health (ILMH)

See: Entry 9796

★7393★ Institute for Rational-Emotive Therapy (IRET)
45 E. 65th St.
New York, NY 10021
Phone: (212)535-0822
Fax: (212)249-3582
Janet L. Wolfe, Ph.D., Exec.Dir.

Founded: 1968. **Description:** Provides professional training; moderate-cost treatment services, including individual and group psychotherapy, marriage and family counseling, and crisis intervention; consultative services for mental health professionals, corporations, and community agencies; research programs in applied psychology. Operates speakers' bureau. Rational emotive behavior therapy, the institute's chief treatment approach, is a psychological theory and technique devised in 1955 based on the assumption that human beings become disturbed through acquiring irrational thoughts, beliefs, philosophies, or attitudes. REBT asserts that people can be taught to change their negative and disturbed feelings and behaviors by consciously correcting the false beliefs and inaccurate perceptions that underlie and accompany these feelings. **Formerly:** (1978) Institute for Advanced Study in Rational Psychotherapy.

★7394★ Institute for Victims of Trauma (IVT)
6801 Market Square Dr.
McLean, VA 22101
Phone: (703)847-8456
Fax: (703)847-0470
Leila F. Dane, Ph.D., Exec.Dir.

Founded: 1987. **Description:** Professionals specializing in post-traumatic stress, crisis intervention, and the study of terrorism. A nonpolitical group assisting direct victims of terrorism, accidents, and natural and man-made disasters, as well as victims' families, friends, and associates. Committed to respond forcefully, effectively, and quickly to the increasing incidence of stress disorders resulting from the experiences of victims. Protects and promotes victims' health, welfare, and human rights. Provides professional and paraprofessional training in crisis intervention, emergency services, diagnosis and treatment, and counseling; offers services and assistance to organizations whose activities may be susceptible to incidents involving terrorism. Acts as a liaison with governmental and nongovernmental organizations and institutions; operates referral service and speakers' bureau. Offers graduate and undergraduate level internships. Conducts research. **Publications:** Proceedings. **Formerly:** (1989) Institute for Victims of Terrorism.

★7395★ International Academy of Behavioral Medicine, Counseling and Psychotherapy (IABMCP)
6750 Hillcrest Plz., Ste. 304
Dallas, TX 75230
Phone: (214)458-8334
Fax: (214)490-5228
George Mount, Exec.Sec.

Founded: 1988. **Members:** 1,100. **Description:** Psychologists, psychiatrists, physicians, social workers, health care specialists, educators, and others in the field of behavioral medicine. Provides liaison between members and other health professionals and disciplines; educates the public and health professionals about the benefits of behavioral medicine; assists in developmental training guidelines for behavioral medicine practice; develops guidelines for implementation of behavioral medicine for the American Psychological Association and other organizations. Disseminates behavioral/biomedical information; sponsors continuing education program. **Publications:** American Academy of Behavioral Medicine--Newsletter, quarterly. Newsletter. Price: Included in membership dues. • Journal, 1-3/year. • Membership Roster, annual.

★7396★ International Academy of Eclectic Psychotherapists (IAEP)
Apartado Postal 51-042
45080 Guadalajara, Mexico
Phone: 3 6342799
Fax: 3 6342799
Emmanuel O. Olukotun, Pres.

Founded: 1983. **Members:** 600. **National Groups:** 4. **Languages:** English, Spanish. **Description:** Psychologists, physicians, and psychotherapists from 12 countries seeking to improve the psychological well-being of all people. Maintains that this can be achieved by creating an environment conducive to dialogue among psychotherapists of diverse orientation. Sponsors professional training workshops and seminars; educational and research programs. Bestows fellowship. **Publications:** Conference Proceedings, 4-5/year. • Journal of Integrative and Eclectic Psychotherapy. • Newsletter, 4-5/year.

★7397★ International Association of Applied Psychology (IAAP) (Association Internationale de Psychologie Appliquee — AIPA)
Monash University
Department of Administrative Studies
Clayton, VIC 3168, Australia
Prof. M. Knowles, Contact

Founded: 1920. **Members:** 3,000. **Languages:** English, French. **Description:** Specialists in applied psychology from 90 countries. Seeks to establish contact between persons who engage in scientific work in various fields of applied psychology; studies ways to contribute to scientific and social development in these fields. Organizes parallel research and experiments in different countries. **Publications:** Applied Psychology: An International Review, quarterly. • Newsletter, semiannual. Newsletter.

International Association for Child and Adolescent Psychiatry and Allied Professions (IACAPAP)
See: Entry 3240

★7398★ International Association of Counselors and Therapists (IACT)
10915 Benita Beach Rd., Ste. 2142
Bonita Springs, FL 33923
Phone: (813)498-9710
Steven A. LaVelle, Pres.

Founded: 1990. **Members:** 7,000. **Description:** Mental health professionals, medical professionals, social workers, clergy, philosophers, educators, hypnotherapists, counselors, and individuals interested in the helping professions. Promotes enhanced professional image and prestige for hypnotherapists. Provides a forum for exchange of information and ideas among practitioners of traditional and nontraditional therapies and methodologies; fosters unity among "grassroots" practitioners and those with advanced academic credentials. Facilitates the development of new therapy programs. Conducts educational, research, and charitable programs. Awards credits for continuing education. Maintains speakers' bureau and library; operates referral and placement services; compiles statistics. Assists in the development of local chapters. **Publications:** Unlimited Human!, quarterly. Magazine. Includes health and wellness articles.

★7399★ International Association of Eating Disorders Professionals (IAEDP)
123 NW 13th St., No. 206
Boca Raton, FL 33432
Phone: (407)338-6494
Fax: (407)338-9913
Shirley Klein, Exec.Dir.

Founded: 1985. **Members:** 800. **Description:** Eating disorders counselors, specialists, and associates. Establishes and develops curricula; operates and implements a system for certifying eating disorders specialists and associates; provides public education and information on eating disorders. Offers professional consulting and assistance to the medical community, hospitals, courts, law enforcement agencies, schools, churches, and social welfare agencies. Facilitates networking among members; makes available employment opportunity information. Sponsors workshops; maintains speakers' bureau and annual symposia. **Publications:** Bulletin, monthly. Contains association news and activities and certification update. • Clinical Quorum. Price: Included in membership dues. Also publishes certification manual and curriculum for higher education.

★7400★ International Association of Group Psychotherapy (IAGP)
Wheelwrights Cottage
Wheelers Ln.
Brockham RH3 7LA, England
Phone: 1737 843446
Fax: 1737 843634
Dr. J. Stuart Whiteley, Sec.

Founded: 1954. **Members:** 550. **Description:** Physicians, psychologists, social workers, nurses, and clergy in 32 countries interested in group psychotherapy. Seeks to further communication and education between professionals in the practice and study of group psychotherapy. **Publications:** Directory, triennial. • Newsletter, semiannual.

★7401★ International Association of Individual Psychology (IAIP)
Markstr. 15
99867 Gotha, Germany
Phone: 3621 29691
Fax: 3621 29691
Horst Groner, Sec.Gen.

Founded: 1954. **Members:** 29. **Languages:** English, French, German. **Description:** Societies, associations, and institutes of Adlerian or individual psychology. Seeks to expand and deepen the scientific and practical aspects of Alfred Adler's (1870-1937) theory of individual psychology. Fosters cooperation and information exchange among members. **Publications:** *Directory and Constitution*, triennial. Directory. • *Individual Psychology Newsletter*, quarterly. Newsletter.

★ 7402 ★ **International Association of Psychosocial Rehabilitation Services (IAPSRS)**
10025 Governor Warfield Pky., Ste. 301
Columbia, MD 21044-3357
Phone: (410)730-7190
Fax: (410)730-5965
Ruth A. Hughes, Ph.D., Exec.Dir.
Founded: 1976. **Members:** 1,600. **Regional Groups:** 2. **State Groups:** 21. **Description:** Individuals (1000) and organizations (600) serving adults with a psychiatric disability. Promotes the advancement of the role, scope, and quality of service designed to facilitate the readjustment into the community of the psychiatrically disabled. Provides a forum for the exchange of ideas, experiences, and contributions to the field. Offers technical assistance to organizational members; sponsors regional training conferences. **Publications:** *National Directory: Organizations Providing Psychosocial Rehabilitation and Related Community Support Services in the U.S.*, periodic. Directory. • *PSR Connection*, quarterly. Newsletter. Updates members on association activities, legislation and regulation affecting membership, and policy developments in psychosocial rehabilitation. *Price:* Included in membership dues. • *Psychosocial Rehabilitation Journal*, quarterly. Journal. Includes calendar of events and research reports. *Price:* Included in membership dues. Also publishes legislative bulletins, documents, and professional information.

★ 7403 ★ **International Association for Suicide Prevention (IASP)**
Institut fur Medical Psychologie
Severingasse 9
A-1090 Vienna, Austria
Phone: 1 4083568
Fax: 1 408356812
Dr. Gernot Sonneck, Gen.Sec.
Founded: 1960. **Members:** 300. **National Groups:** 9. **Languages:** English. **Description:** Individuals and societies in 50 countries regularly engaged in suicide research and/or prevention activities. Societies may become members only when 2 members of their staff are regular members of IASP. Aims to provide a common platform for individuals and agencies of various disciplines and professions. Encourages the exchange of acquired experience, literature, and information about suicide. Disseminates information on suicide prevention to professional and public resources; arranges for specialized training of persons in suicide prevention; promotes and carries out cooperative research programs. **Publications:** *Crisis*, quarterly. Journal. • *IASP Newsletter*, periodic. • *Membership Directory*, biennial.

★ 7404 ★ **International Balint Federation (IBF)**
(Federation Internationale Balint)
42, rue des Bollandistes
B-1040 Brussels, Belgium
Phone: 2 7346436
Dr. R. Van Laethem, Sec.
Founded: 1975. **Languages:** English, French. **Description:** Groups and corresponding members in 34 countries. Promotes group training and practice according to the principles of Michael Balint (1896-1970), psychiatrist and author. Studies the patient-physician relationship on a psychosocial level and encourages improved psychological training and research in practice.

★ 7405 ★ **International Committee Against Mental Illness (ICAMI)**
PO Box 1921, Grand Central Sta.
New York, NY 10163
Phone: (914)357-8797
Fax: (914)359-7029
Dr. Robert Cancro, Pres.
Founded: 1958. **Languages:** English. **Description:** Fosters psychosocial rehabilitation and mental health research, services, and information systems. Provides technical assistance to professional rehabilitation organizations in expanding or installing computer information systems in psychiatry and in planning workshops, symposia, and conferences. Organizes international consortium of voluntary agencies and rehabilitation groups. Conducts research; operates speakers' bureau. Has worked on projects in Colombia, Indonesia, Iran, Israel, Kuwait, Liberia, Nepal, Pakistan, and Yugoslavia. The committee is a direct outgrowth of a pioneering psychiatric treatment project in Haiti that is now operated by the Haitian government.

★ 7406 ★ **International Committee on Social Psychological Research in Developing Countries (ICSPRDC)**
96, rue Pierre Demours
F-75017 Paris, France
Phone: 1 42278026
Fax: 1 42674187
Dr. Charles Pidoux, Chm.
Founded: 1966. **Languages:** English. **Description:** Serves as a medium for information exchange among scientists, scientific bodies, institutes, and universities actively researching social psychology in developing countries. Compiles statistics. **Publications:** *Newsletter*, annual. Newsletter.

★ 7407 ★ **International Council of Psychologists (ICP)**
SW Texas State University
Psych Department
San Marcos, TX 78666-4601
Patricia J. Fontes, Ph.D., Sec.Gen.
Founded: 1942. **Members:** 1,700. **Description:** Psychologists and individuals professionally active in fields allied to psychology. Seeks to advance psychology and further the application of its scientific findings. Conducts continuing education workshops and educational programs. **Publications:** Directory, biennial. • *International Psychologist*, quarterly. Newsletter.

Includes book reviews, calendar of events, and information on members. *Price:* Included in membership dues; $24/year for nonmembers. **Formerly:** (1959) International Council of Women Psychologists.

★ 7408 ★ **International Federation of Psychoanalytic Societies (IFPS)**
Lansitie 9
SF-02160 Espoo, Finland
Phone: 0 426425
Fax: 0 424614
Marja Lindquist, Sec.Gen.
Founded: 1962. **Members:** 18. **Languages:** English. **Description:** Psychoanalytic societies in 11 countries. Promotes interest in psychoanalytic theory; encourages information exchange and discussion; fosters practice of psychoanalytic theory. Bestows awards. **Publications:** *International Federation of Psychoanalytic Societies--Membership Directory*, periodic. Directory. • *Papers*, periodic.

★ 7409 ★ **International Federation of the Psychological-Medical Organizations (IFPMO)**
(Federation Internationale des Organismes de Psychologie Medicale — FIOPM)
Division Autonom de Medicine Psychosocial
Medicale BH 07
CH-1011 Lausanne, Switzerland
Phone: 21 3144051
Fax: 21 3144056
Patrice Guex, Ph.D., Chair
Founded: 1975. **Members:** 30. **Languages:** English, French, German. **Description:** Objectives are to establish a bulletin dealing with problems in medical psychology and to compile a list of related world congresses. **Publications:** *IFPMO Bulletin*, annual. Bulletin.

★ 7410 ★ **International Federation for Psychotherapy (IFP)**
Murtenstrasse 21
CH-3010 Bern, Switzerland
Fax: 33 431195
Prof. Edgar Heim, Pres.
Founded: 1946. **Members:** 4,000. **Languages:** English, French, German, Spanish. **Description:** Professional psychotherapists in 40 countries united to further research and teaching of psychotherapy through practical and theoretical cooperation among medical psychotherapists. Holds regional symposia. **Publications:** *Membership List and Newsletter*, periodic. • *Psychotherapy and Psychosomatics*, monthly. • *Scientific Papers*. **Formerly:** (1992) International Federation of Medical Psycho-theatrerapy.

★ 7411 ★ **International League of Societies for Persons With Mental Handicap (ILSMH)**
248, ave. Louise
BP 17
B-1050 Brussels, Belgium
Phone: 2 6476180
Fax: 2 6472969
Klaus Lachwitz, Sec.Gen.
Founded: 1960. **Members:** 149. **Regional Groups:** 6. **Languages:** English, French, German, Spanish. **Description:** Full members (62)

are national organizations that are exclusively concerned with the mentally disabled and support a range of services and programs; affiliated members (87) are national organizations with interests other than the mentally disabled. Strives to advance the interests of the mentally handicapped by securing, from all possible sources, remedial, residential, educational training, employment, and welfare services and to create a common bond of understanding among parents and families of the mentally disabled. Promotes international cooperation among organizations representing the mentally disabled. Seeks the integration of the mentally disabled into society and improved public attitudes towards persons with mental disabilities. **Publications:** Newsletter, periodic. Also publishes booklets, position papers, proceedings of congresses, monographs, and reports of symposia and conferences. **Formerly:** (1962) European League of Societies for the Mentally Handicapped; (1981) International League of Societies for the Mentally Handicapped.

★7412★ **International Network for Mutual Help Centers (INMHC)**
c/o Lori Dessau
2 Mt. Royal Ave.
Hamilton, ON, Canada L8P 4H6
Phone: (416)529-3480
Lori Dessau, Chairperson

Founded: 1985. **Members:** 50. **Description:** Representatives of 50 selfhelp clearinghouses in the U.S. and Canada. Seeks to: promote and support mutual help by increasing awareness, utilization, and development of selfhelp groups; share resources, and facilitate communications among selfhelp clearinghouses; encourage other activities that enhance clearinghouse operations.

★7413★ **International Organization of Psychophysiology (IOP)**
(Organisation Internationale de Psychophysiologie — IOP)
PO Box 1614, Sta. H
Montreal, PQ, Canada H3G 2N5
Phone: (514)284-9404
Fax: (514)284-1707
Dr. Constantine A. Mangina, Pres.

Founded: 1982. **National Groups:** 45. **Languages:** Arabic, Chinese, English, French, Russian, Spanish. **Description:** Scientists who hold a Ph.D., M.D., or equivalent degree and who specialize in psychophysiology or one of the neurosciences. (Psychophysiology is the study of the physiology of the psychic functions through the brain-body-behavior interrelationships of the living organism in conjunction with the environment.) Undertakes and promote psychophysiological research, teaching, and applications worldwide. Seeks to develop guidelines for the improvement of the human psychophysiological condition throughout the world. Disseminates information on subjects including aggression and defense, evolution and development of behavior, information processing, interhemispneric relations, learning and memory, motivation and emotion, and psychophysiological disorders. Collaborates with the United Nations and its specialized agencies with the aim of reinforcing international scientific coopera-

tion in psychophysiology and related fields for the good of the human race. Maintains International Centre of Psychophysiology, providing research, practice, and training opportunities for qualified graduates; assists participants in becoming contemporary psychophysiologists. **Publications:** *International Journal of Psychophysiology*, quarterly. Journal. • *IOP Newsletter*, quarterly. Newsletter.

★7414★ **International Phototherapy Association (IPA)**
c/o Judy Weiser
Photo Therapy Centre
1107 Homer St., Ste. 304
Vancouver, BC, Canada V6B 2Y1
Phone: (604)689-9709
Fax: (604)689-9709
Judy Weiser, Chairperson

Founded: 1981. **Members:** 225. **Description:** Art therapists, psychologists, social workers, psychiatric nurses, other human service professionals (150), and students (75) dedicated to furthering the scientific development and use of still photographs, films, and videotapes in human service interventions which include mental health and social welfare services. Seeks to: develop phototherapy practice into an effective therapy and human service intervention based upon sound scientific research and practice; train and supervise students and professionals in behavioral and psychological phototherapy. Supports existing phototherapy research. **Publications:** Directory, annual. • Magazine, 2-3/year. • *Phototherapy Techniques: Exploring the Secrets of Personal Snapshots and Family Albums*. Book.

★7415★ **International Psychoanalytical Association Trust (IPA)**
(Association Psychanalytique Internationale)
Broomhills
Woodside Ln.
London N12 8UD, England
Phone: 181 4468324
Fax: 181 4454729
Valerie Tufnell, Adm.Dir.

Founded: 1910. **Members:** 8,500. **National Groups:** 39. **Languages:** English, French, German, Spanish. **Description:** Organizations in 30 countries involved in psychoanalysis. Encourages communication among members and promotes high educational standards. Organizes training programs. **Publications:** *Bulletin*, annual. Bulletin. • *Information Booklet*, periodic. Booklet. • Monographs, annual. • *Newsletter*, semiannual. Newsletter. • *Roster*, annual.

International Psychogeriatric Association (IPA)
See: Entry 1903

★7416★ **International REST Investigators Society (IRIS)**
c/o Thomas H. Fine
Department of Psychiatry - Health Center
Med. College of Ohio
PO Box 10008
Toledo, OH 43699
Phone: (419)381-5695
Fax: (419)381-3031
Thomas H. Fine, Pres.

Founded: 1983. **Description:** Scientists and individuals interested in exploring the psychophysiological effects of floating. Serves as an information exchange for researchers, therapists, and individuals interested in restricted environmental stimulation techniques (REST). (Restricted environmental stimulation techniques include methods of producing a relaxed environment to create changes in consciousness and behavior such as floatation or isolation tanks.) Clinically, REST is being used in conjunction with relaxation training, biofeedback, psychotherapy, and a variety of stress-related disorders. Organizes meetings where members and other interested individuals can communicate current interests, exchange ideas and suggestions, and form collaborative research groups. **Publications:** Bulletin, 3/year. • *REST and Self-Regulation Conference Proceedings*, periodic. Also publishes bibliography.

★7417★ **International Rorschach Society (IRS)**
(Societe Rorschach Internationale)
Langgastrasse 76
CH-3000 Bern 9, Switzerland
Phone: 31 3004500
Fax: 31 3004590
Hans Huber Verlag, Contact

Founded: 1948. **Members:** 1,700. **Languages:** English, French, Italian, Spanish. **Description:** Societies (12) and individuals (76). Develops international contacts between Rorschach specialists and other interested individuals; promotes theoretical and practical knowledge of Rorschach and other projective techniques. (Rorschach test, named after Hermann Rorschach, a Swiss psychiatrist, is a test in which personality characteristics are made accessible to analysis by the subject's interpretation of the nature and meaning of a series of standard inkblot patterns.) Organizes regional and international meetings. Conducts research. **Publications:** *Bulletin of the International Rorschach Society*, annual. Bulletin. • *Rorschachiana*, triennial. Yearbook. Includes congress proceedings.

International Society for Adolescent Psychiatry
See: Entry 3247

★7418★ **International Society of Analytical Trilogy (ISAT)**
(Sociedade Internacional de Trilogia Analitica)
Avenida Reboucas 3819
05401 Sao Paulo, SP, Brazil
Phone: 11 2103616
Claudia B.S. Pacheo

Founded: 1970. **Members:** 762. **National Groups:** 9. **Regional Groups:** 6. **Languages:**

English, French, German, Portuguese, Spanish. **Description:** Accredited psychoanalysts having scientific training in Brazil, England, Finland, Portugal, and Sweden; individuals with a medical, human, or social science degree who are currently studying analytical trilogy; students working with accredited analysts. Promotes analytical trilogy, a form of psychoanalysis that uses dialogue to cure mental as well as physical illness through a technique called interiorization. (Also known as integral psychoanalysis, analytical trilogy was founded by Prof. Norberto R. Keppe as a continuation of the psychoanalytical discoveries of Sigmund Freud and his colleagues.) Conducts research and therapy for treatment of emotional and psychosomatic problems and encourages study of humanistic culture in all its forms including social, philosophical, religious, educational, and artistic. Promotes scientific investigation of psychoanalysis, philosophy, and theology. Fosters training in the integral psychoanalytical and trilogical fields. Activities include: group and individual analysis for treating neurosis, psychosis, and organic illness without drugs; children's services; radio and television programs; introductory courses for the public. Operates publishing company, bookshop, and cultural center. Is currently organizing a collection of case studies including written declarations, X-rays, medical examination data, and documented results obtained through the use of analytical trilogy. **Publications:** Bulletin, monthly. • *Integral Psychoanalysis Magazine*, semiannual. Magazine. • *Trilogy*, quarterly. Also publishes booklets and books. **Formerly:** (1982) Society of Integral Psychoanalysis.

★7419★ International Society of Art and Psychopathology (ISAP)
(Societe Internationale de Psychopathologie de l'Expression)
Centre Hospitalier de Ste.-Anne
Clinique de la Faculte
Centre d'Etude de l'Expression
100, rue de la Sante
F-75674 Paris Cedex 14, France
Phone: 1 45895521
Prof. Robert Volmat, Pres.

Founded: 1959. **Members:** 600. **Languages:** English, French, German. **Description:** Physicians and specialists including aestheticians, critics, artists, writers, art historians, psychologists, sociologists, and criminologists. Brings together specialists interested in the problems of expression and artistic activities in connection with psychiatric, sociological, and psychological research, as well as in the use of methods applied in fields other than that of mental and neurological illness. Organizes international discussion panels and symposia.

★7420★ International Society for Comparative Psychology (ISCP)
c/o Dr. Ethel Tobach
American Museum of Natural History
Central Park West at 79th St.
New York, NY 10024-5192
Phone: (212)769-5487
Fax: (212)769-5233
Dr. Ethel Tobach, Sec.

Founded: 1983. **Members:** 150. **Languages:** English. **Description:** Psychologists, biologists, anthropologists, and neuroscientists who work in or are interested in comparative psychology. Aims to: promote the international development of comparative psychology; establish worldwide communication among comparative psychologists; encourage the study of the development and evolution of behavior. **Publications:** *Advances in Comparative Psychology*, semiannual. • *International Journal of Comparative Psychology*, quarterly. Journal. • *ISCP Newsletter*, bimonthly. Newsletter.

★7421★ International Society for Developmental Psychobiology (ISDP)
c/o Dr. Christina Williams
Barnard Coll., Columbia Univ.
Department of Psychology
3009 Broadway
New York, NY 10027
Phone: (212)854-2329
Dr. Christina Williams, Sec.

Founded: 1967. **Members:** 335. **Description:** Research scientists in the field of developmental psychobiology; biology and psychology students. Promotes research in the field of developmental psychobiology, the study of the brain and behavior throughout the life span and in relation to other biological processes. Stimulates communication and interaction among scientists in the field. Provides the editorship for the journal, *Development Psychobiology*. Bestows awards. Compiles statistics. **Publications:** *Developmental Psychobiology*, bimonthly. Journal. Addresses the anatomical, physiological, biochemical, hormonal, pharmacological, genetic, and evolutionary aspects of behavioral development. *Price:* Included in membership dues. • Membership Directory, every 1-2 years. • Newsletter, 2-3/year.

★7422★ International Society for Mental Imagery Techniques (ISMIT)
(Societa Internazionale per le Techniche d'Imagerie Mentale)
12, rue St.-Julien-le-Pauvre
F-75005 Paris, France
Phone: 1 46345156
Andre Virel, President

Founded: 1966. **Members:** 80. **Description:** Fosters inquiry and interaction among researchers and practitioners of mental imagery techniques in psychotherapy. Conducts research on mental imagery psychotherapy; disseminates research results. Organizes seminars on psychotherapeutic practice. **Publications:** *Decentration*, periodic. • *Espace d'un Instant*, periodic. • *Mental Imagery*. • *Vocabulary of Psychotherapies*.

★7423★ International Society for Music in Medicine (ISMM)
(Internationale Gesellschaft fur Musik in der Medizin)
Paulmannshoher Str. 17
58515 Ludenscheid, Germany
Phone: 2351 9452260
Fax: 2351 94517
Dr. Ralph Spintge, Exec.Sec.

Founded: 1982. **Members:** 70. **Languages:** English. **Description:** Medical doctors, scientists, and music therapists. Initiates and coordinates interdisciplinary research into the psycho-

logical basis for and applications of music in medicine. **Publications:** *International Journal of Arts Medicine*, quarterly. Journal. • *Music Medicine, Vol. I, 1993*. Book. • *Music Medicine, Vol. 2, 1995*. Book.

★7424★ International Society of Political Psychology (ISPP)
c/o George E. Marcus
Williams College
304 Stetson Hall
Williamstown, MA 01267
Phone: (413)597-2538
Fax: (413)597-4200
Prof. George E. Marcus, Exec.Dir.

Founded: 1978. **Members:** 1,200. **Description:** Psychologists, psychiatrists, psychoanalysts, political scientists, historians, sociologists, economists, anthropologists, media representatives, and government officials. Promotes understanding and scientific interest in the relationship between psychological, political, social, and economic processes. Seeks to facilitate communication among members and to increase the quality and application of work in political psychology. Examines relationships between psychological and political events. Areas of interest include: political violence and terrorism; socialization and the media; human rights conflict resolution; bureaucracy negotiation and mediation; totalitarianism. Sponsors the Summer Institute in Political Psychology in conjunction with Ohio State University. Conducts panel discussions. **Publications:** *ISPPNews*, semiannual. Newsletter. Contains information on activities and news of the organization; includes availability of fellowships, grants, and visiting scholar programs. *Price:* Free for members. • Membership Directory, biennial. • *Political Psychology*, quarterly. Journal. Covers classics in political psychology, interdisciplinary foundations of political psychology, and issues in professional development.

★7425★ International Society of Psychology of Handwriting (ISPH)
(Societa Internazionale di Psicologia della Scrittura — SIPS)
Istituto di Indagini Psicologiche
Corso XXII Marzo 57
I-20129 Milan, Italy
Phone: 2 70126489
Fax: 2 7491051
Prof. Rolando Marchesan, Gen.Dir.

Founded: 1961. **Members:** 192. **Regional Groups:** 12. **Description:** Physicians, psychologists, psychiatrists, teachers, and others. Promotes study and research in the psychology of handwriting. Has prepared documentaries on the subject for classroom and public instruction. Offers children's services. **Publications:** *Albo dei Docenti e Specialisti dell'UIM*, triennial. Also publishes directory and catalog of publications.

International Society of Sports Psychology (ISSP)
See: Entry 11947

★7426★ International Society for the Study of Dissociation (ISSD)
5700 Old Orchard Rd., 1st Fl.
Skokie, IL 60077-1024
Phone: (708)966-4322
Fax: (708)966-9418
Jeffrey W. Engle, Exec.Dir.

Founded: 1982. **Members:** 3,100. **Description:** Mental health professionals; students. Promotes a greater understanding of the field of dissociation. Conducts research into the diagnosis and treatment of multiple personalities and dissociation. Sponsors educational programs. Maintains speakers' bureau. **Publications:** *Dissociation*, quarterly. Journal. • Membership Directory, annual. • Newsletter, bimonthly. • *Standards of Practice Guidelines*. *Price:* Included in membership dues; $5/additional copy for members; $10 for nonmembers. **Formerly:** International Society for the Study of Multiple Personalities and Dissociation.

★7427★ International Society for Traumatic Stress Studies (ISTSS)
60 Revere Dr., Ste. 500
Northbrook, IL 60062
Phone: (708)480-9080
Fax: (708)480-9282
Joyce Paschall, Exec. Officer

Founded: 1985. **Members:** 1,700. **Description:** Professionals who treat individuals suffering from traumatic stress. (Traumatic stress is a medical term applied to persons who experience severe mental or emotional reactions to extraordinary stressful situations such as war, crime, natural disasters, and high-stress occupations.) Conducts research in the treatment of these cases; disseminates information. Holds seminars. Bestows awards. **Publications:** *Journal of Traumatic Stress*, quarterly. Journal. Reports on the latest findings and innovations in the study and treatment of those affected by traumatic stress. *Price:* Included in membership dues; $29.50/year for nonmembers; $34.50/year for nonmembers (outside U.S.). • *Society for Traumatic Stress Studies Membership List*, periodic. *Price:* $150 for members and nonprofit organizations; $350 for nonmembers. • *Traumatic Stresspoints*, quarterly. Membership Directory. Contains book reviews. *Price:* Included in membership dues. **Formerly:** Society for Traumatic Stress Studies.

★7428★ International Stress Management Association (ISMA)
c/o Dr. F.J. McGuigan
U.S. International University
Institute Stress-Management
10455 Pomerado Rd.
San Diego, CA 92131
Phone: (619)693-4698
Fax: (619)693-4669
Dr. F. J. McGuigan, Exec.Dir.

Founded: 1973. **Members:** 1,000. **National Groups:** 8. **Description:** Members in 10 countries united to disseminate scientific and technological information on tension control and to incorporate systematic relaxation in everyday life. Fields of application include dentistry, education, medicine, psychology, physical therapy, speech pathology, human communications, nursing, and occupational therapy. **Publica-** tions: *Convention Proceedings*, annual. Proceedings. • *International Journal of Stress Management*, quarterly. Journal. • Newsletter, quarterly. **Formerly:** (1980) American Association for the Advancement of Tension Control; (1992) International Stress and Tension Control Association.

★7429★ International Transactional Analysis Association (ITAA)
1772 Vallejo St.
San Francisco, CA 94123-5009
Phone: (415)885-5992
Fax: (415)885-5998
Susan Sevilla, Exec.Dir.

Founded: 1958. **Members:** 7,000. **Description:** Educational corporation of persons in medical and behavioral sciences, including psychiatrists, psychologists, social workers, nurses, educators, marriage and family counselors, clergy, and organizational consultants. Maintains standards of practice and teaching of transactional analysis, which involves group therapy, social dynamics, and personality theory based on analysis of the "transactions" or interactions between persons. (The book, *Games People Play*, covers basic transactional analysis theory; its author, Dr. Eric Berne, was ITAA founder.) **Publications:** *Geographical List of Certified Members*, annual. • *ITAA Membership Directory*, annual. Membership Directory. • *Script*, 9/year. Newsletter. • *Transactional Analysis Journal*, quarterly. Journal. **Formerly:** (1961) San Francisco Social Psychiatry Seminar.

★7430★ International Union of Psychological Science (IUPsyS)
Dept. of Psychology
University of Leuven
B-3000 Louvain, Belgium
Phone: 16 285964
Fax: 16 286099
Prof. Kurt Pawlik, Sec.Gen.

Founded: 1951. **Members:** 51. **Languages:** English, French. **Description:** National psychological societies and commitees united for: the development of psychological science through exchange of ideas and scientific information; the exchange of scholars and students; the organization of international congresses of psychology; publication and documentation; cooperation with related scientific groups interested in the development of psychology as a discipline and a profession. Conducts educational programs and international research network project. **Publications:** *Congress Proceedings*, quadrennial. • *International Directory of Psychologists*, every 5-6 years. Directory. • *International Journal of Psychology*, bimonthly. Journal. • Monograph, periodic.

★7431★ International Union of Societies for the Aid of Mental Health (IUSAMH) (Union Internationale des Societes d'Aide a la Sante Mentale)
39, rue Charles Monselet
F-33000 Bordeaux, France
Phone: 56 816005
Dr. Michel Demangeat, Pres.

Founded: 1977. **Members:** 329. **Regional Groups:** 30. **Languages:** French. **Description:** National societies and committees in 42 coun- tries united to provide assistance and mutual aid for the mentally ill. Objectives are to: facilitate the exchange of information and research for the protection of the mentally handicapped; support the training of personnel dedicated to this task; organize international and regional conferences. Conducts meetings and workshops with doctors and health teams. **Publications:** *Practice of Psychology of Social Life and Mental Hygiene*, quarterly.

★7432★ Jean Piaget Society: Society for the Study of Knowledge and Development (JPSSSKD)
Human Development
Larsen 703
Harvard GS Education
Cambridge, MA 02138
Phone: (617)495-3614
Fax: (617)495-3626
Terry Brown, Pres.

Founded: 1970. **Members:** 500. **Description:** Scholars, teachers, and researchers interested in exploring the nature of the developmental construction of human knowledge. Purpose is to further research on knowledge and development, especially in relation to the work of Jean Piaget (1896-1980), a Swiss developmentalist noted for his work in child psychology, the study of human development, and the origin and growth of human knowledge. Conducts small meetings and programs. **Publications:** *Genetic Epistemologist*, quarterly. Newsletter. Covers the nature of human knowledge. *Price:* Included in membership dues. • *Jean Piaget Symposium Series*, annual. *Price:* Included in membership dues; $70 for nonmembers. **Formerly:** (1989) Jean Piaget Society.

★7433★ Karen Horney Clinic (KHC)
329 E. 62nd St.
New York, NY 10021
Phone: (212)838-4333
Fax: (212)838-7158
Henry A. Paul, M.D., Dir.

Founded: 1955. **Description:** To promote the psychoanalytic and psychotherapeutic treatment of individuals and groups focusing on the special problems of children, adolescents, victims of violent crimes, adult survivors of childhood sexual abuse, and persons with psychoneurotic and emotional problems. Named for Karen Horney (1885-1952), German/American psychoanalyst and author of several books on neurosis, psychoanalysis, and related topics. Conducts children's services. **Publications:** *American Journal of Psychoanalysis*, quarterly. Journal. • *Association for the Advancement of Psychoanalysis*, periodic. **Formerly:** (1979) Karen Horney Psychoanalytic Clinic.

★7434★ Korean Academy of Psychotherapists (KAP)
178-23 Song-buk dong
Song-buk-ku
Seoul 136-020, Republic of Korea
Phone: 2 7620273
Fax: 2 7659776
Dr. Rhee Dongshick, Hon.Pres.

Founded: 1974. **Members:** 100. **Local Groups:** 1. **Languages:** English, Korean. **Description:** Psychiatrists and psychologists united to study and integrate the principles of psychoanalysis and psychotherapy with those of Eastern Tao. (Eastern Tao is based on Taoist, Confucian, and Buddhist philosophies.) Operates training program. Conducts research; maintains speakers' bureau; compiles statistics. **Publications:** *Eastern Tao and Western Psychotherapy.* • *KAP Membership Directory*, annual. Directory. • *KAP Newsletter*, monthly. Newsletter. • *Psychotherapy*, semiannual. Includes abstract in English. • *Psychotherapy Protocol*, monthly. Plans to publish case books.

★ 7435 ★ **Latin American Association for Social Psychology (LAASP)**
(Asociacion Latinoamericana de Psicologia Social — ALPS)
Escuella de Psicologia
Pontificia University Catolica de Chile
Casilla 114D
Santiago, Chile
Phone: 2 519012
Julio F. Villegas, Sec.Gen.

Founded: 1974. **Members:** 256. **National Groups:** 15. **Regional Groups:** 5. **Languages:** Portuguese, Spanish. **Description:** Social psychologists and those working in related fields in 11 countries. Promotes the development of social psychology in Latin America through scientific investigation and academic exchange programs. Maintains data base. **Publications:** *Directorio de ALAPSO*, triennial. • *Latinamerican Social Psychology Review*, biennial. • *Revisita de la Asociacion Latinoamericana de Psicologia Social*, semiannual.

★ 7436 ★ **Latin American Psychiatric Association**
(Asociacion Latinoamericana de Psiquiatria)
Bulnes 1937
5 Piso of B
1425 Buenos Aires, Argentina
Description: Promotes interest in psychiatry throughout Latin America. Fosters communication among psychiatrists to exchange new advancements in the practice of psychiatry.

★ 7437 ★ **Latin American Transactional Analysis Association**
(Asociacion Latinoamericana de Analisis Transaccional)
Esquiel Montes No. 19
Col Revolucion
06030 Mexico City, DF, Mexico
Phone: 5 922884
Octavio Rivas, Pres.
Description: Concetrates on the study of transactional analysis as it relates to special fields such as labor, education, and family. Disseminates information and research results. Promotes training and education in transactional analysis among students of psychiatry. **Publications:** *Cancia.*

★ 7438 ★ **Life Line International (LLI)**
34 Middle St.
West End
Brisbane, QLD 4101, Australia
Phone: 7 8441767
Fax: 7 2529536
Dr. Charles Noller, Contact

Founded: 1966. **Members:** 225. **Languages:** English. **Description:** Christian crisis intervention telephone centers in 10 countries. Organizes and maintains Christian crisis intervention and listening centers; establishes and maintains standards for volunteer training, organization, and recruitment. Works to ensure an effective operation. Distributes educational/inspirational printed materials, films, filmstrips, and books. **Publications:** *Directory of Centers and Services*, annual. Directory. • *Newsletter*, semiannual. Newsletter.

★ 7439 ★ **Love-N-Addiction (LNA)**
PO Box 759
Willimantic, CT 06226
Phone: (203)423-2344
Carolyn C. Meister, Founder

Founded: 1986. **Description:** Selfhelp support groups; individual members are women who exhibit emotionally addictive and self-destructive behavior in relationships. Focuses on relationships that jeopardize the women's emotional and physical well-being. Members seek recovery through the sharing of knowledge and personal experiences. Offers consultations; maintains speakers' bureau. **Publications:** *Self-Help Group Starter Packet*. *Price:* $10.

★ 7440 ★ **Mauritius Mental Health Association**
E.S.N. School
Stanley
Rose Hill, Mauritius
Phone: 4641157

Description: Promotes mental health and encourages a better understanding of mental health disorders. Seeks to eliminate the stigma associated with mental illness; disseminates information.

★ 7441 ★ **Mental After Care Association (MACA)**
25 Bedford Sq.
London WC1B 3HW, England
Phone: 171 4366194
Fax: 171 6371980
Bruce Garner, Dir.

Founded: 1879. **Members:** 100. **Languages:** English. **Description:** Provides residential care and other community-based services for people with mental health needs and their carers. Services include: supported accommodation; community support; day care; social clubs; employment training; court liaison for offenders with mental health needs. **Publications:** *Annual Report*. • Pamphlets, periodic.

★ 7442 ★ **Mental Health Materials Center (MHMC)**
PO Box 304
Bronxville, NY 10708
Phone: (914)337-6596
Alex Sareyan, Pres.

Founded: 1953. **Members:** 10. **Description:** Professional workers in the field of mental health and health education. Seeks to stimulate the development of wider and more effective channels of communication between health educators and the public. Provides consulting services to nonprofit organizations on the imple-

mentation of their publishing operations in areas related to mental health and health. Develops new publishing and audiovisual properties. **Publications:** Booklets. • Books. • Pamphlets. • *Study on Suicide Training Manual - Trainee's Edition*. Manual. • *Study on Suicide Training Manual - Trainer's Edition*. Manual. • *Survival Manual for Medical Students*. Manual.

★ 7443 ★ **Mental Health Policy Resource Center**
1730 Rhode Island Ave. NW, Ste. 308
Washington, DC 20036
Phone: (202)775-8826
Fax: (202)659-7613
Leslie Scallet, Contact

Founded: 1987. **Description:** Promotes informed policy making on mental health issues at the state and national level. Disseminates information and research findings to public, state mental health departments, mental health organizations, and graduate schools. Enables policy makers to exchange information and ideas on mental health issues. Current research and information is focused on policy issues such as aging and cultural diversity, social and individual responsibility, social welfare, and economic productivity. **Publications:** *ANALYSIS: Beyond Moral Hazard in Financing Outpatient Mental Health Services*. Report. *Price:* $5. • *ANALYSIS: Critiquing the Empirical Evidence: Does Involuntary Outpatient Commitment Work?*. Report. *Price:* $25. • *ANALYSIS: Implications of Employment Complaints Filed by People with Mental Disabilities*. Report. *Price:* $25. • *ANALYSIS: Mental Health for Children: Can We Get There from Here?*. Report. *Price:* $15. • *BRIEF: Using Research: A Guide for the Policy Process*. Pamphlet. *Price:* Free; $12/10. • Catalog, periodic. Lists publications made available by organization. • *Choices in Case Management: Current Knowledge and Practice for Mental Health Programs*. Report. Contains annotated bibliography and typology. *Price:* $15. • *Into the Briarpatch: Mental Health in State and National Healthcare Reform*. Report. *Price:* $9. • *Medicaid Plans and Mental Health: 1992 Profiles of State Options and Limitations*. Report. *Price:* $36. • *National Healthcare Reform: A Comparison Twelve Major Legislative Initiatives and Their Implications for Mental Health Coverage*. Report. *Price:* $15. • *Policy in Perspective*, bimonthly. Newsletter. *Price:* $35/year. • *PROFILE: Journey to Passage: Establishing a Community-Based Stats Mental Health System*. Book. *Price:* $20. • *Proposals in the 103rd Congress Calling for Inclusion of Mental Healthcare Reform*. Report. *Price:* $6. • *The Psychological Needs of Refugees and Displaced Persons: A Primary Preventive Approach*. Article. *Price:* $6.

★ 7444 ★ **Mental Illness Foundation**
420 Lexington Ave., No. 2104
New York, NY 10170-0002
Phone: (212)629-0755
Fax: (212)629-3117
Anne Carrey-Cattes, Dir.

Founded: 1983. **Description:** Works to inform people about mental illness. **Publications:** Directory.Lists mental illnesses and provides information on how to contact related associations. • *Mental Illness Foundation*, quarterly. Newsletter.

★7445★ **Mental Research Institute (MRI)**
555 Middlefield Rd.
Palo Alto, CA 94301
Phone: (415)321-3055
Fax: (415)321-3785
Judith E. Foddrill, Admin.

Founded: 1959. **Description:** Psychiatrists, psychologists, and other professionals skilled in the disciplines related to the behavioral sciences. Conducts research, training, and service programs in the field of human behavior, with special emphasis on the family as a social unit. Research programs are primarily funded by government and foundation grants. Offers year-long courses, monthly residency programs, and short- and long-term workshops on family therapy, brief therapy, communication, and related subjects. Operates family-oriented and brief therapy-oriented sliding scale fee clinic, which also serves as a training and research base. Maintains speakers' bureau and library of 1500 books and periodicals dealing with human interaction, family and individual therapy, psychology, psychiatry, anthropology, and behavioral sciences. **Publications:** *MRI Training Brochure*, periodic. Provides information on MRI training programs. *Price:* Free.

★7446★ **M.I.N.D.**
Granta House
15-19 Broadway
Stratford
London E1S 4BQ, England
Phone: 181 5192122
Fax: 181 5221725
Judi Clements, Dir.

Founded: 1948. **Members:** 2,000. **Regional Groups:** 7. **Local Groups:** 240. **Languages:** English. **Description:** Promotes mental health and encourages a better understanding of mental health disorders. Assists in the treatment and rehabilitation of mental health patients and seeks to eliminate the stigma associated with mental illness. Conducts research; disseminates information. Offers legal referral services. Sponsors charitable program. Maintains information service; operates speakers' bureau. Conducts training and educational courses and seminars. **Publications:** *Annual Report.* • *OpenMIND*, bimonthly. Magazine. • *Publications from MIND*, periodic. Catalog. **Also Known As:** National Association for Mental Health.

★7447★ **Montgomery Medical and Psychological Institute (MMPI)**
PO Box 33311
Decatur, GA 30033
Phone: (404)603-9426
Lynn Montgomery, Dir.

Founded: 1983. **Members:** 400. **Regional Groups:** 3. **Description:** Professionals and other individuals interested in the proper diagnosis and the counseling and treatment of gender dysphoric individuals. Creates and maintains support groups; seeks to educate the public about gender dysphoric persons, particularly transsexuals. Offers counseling and referral services; compiles statistics; provides training for professional counselors. Maintains speakers' bureau. **Publications:** *Insight*, quarterly. Magazine. *Price:* $22/year for nonmembers. Transi-

tion to completion by Jerry and Lynn Montgomery. **Formerly:** (1987) Montgomery Foundation for Gender Dysphoric Association.

Multidisciplinary Institute for Neuropsychological Development (MIND)
See: Entry 8259

★7448★ **Music Therapy Association of Rio de Janeiro (AMT-RJ) (Associacio de Musicoterapia do Rio de Janeiro)**
Avenida Graca Aranha 57, Andar 12
20030-002 Rio de Janeiro, RJ, Brazil
Phone: 21 2405481
Fax: 21 2406131
Ronaldo Milleco

Founded: 1968. **Members:** 290. **Languages:** English, Portuguese, Spanish. **Description:** Promotes the use of music therapy and works to unite music therapists in Brazil. Offers educational and public service programs. **Publications:** *Boletim da Associacao de Musicoterapia do Rio de Janeiro*, periodic. Also publishes scientific papers and bulletins.

National Academy of Neuropsychology (NAN)
See: Entry 8265

★7449★ **National Alliance for the Mentally Ill (NAMI)**
2101 Wilson Blvd., Ste. 302
Arlington, VA 22201
Phone: (703)524-7600
Fax: (703)524-9094
Laurie M. Flynn, Exec.Dir.

Founded: 1979. **Members:** 130,000. **State Groups:** 50. **Local Groups:** 1000. **Description:** Alliance of selfhelp/advocacy groups concerned with severe and chronic mentally ill individuals. Objectives are to provide emotional support and practical guidance to families, and to educate and inform the public about mental illness. Conducts consumer advocacy activities at the local, state, and national levels to enact legislation and to promote funding for institutional and community-based settings for the seriously mentally ill. Monitors and assures quality treatment, rehabilitation, and support services. Promotes research in the neurosciences and clinical sciences. Many affiliates maintain libraries. National office coordinates and disseminates information and resource materials and maintains liaison with legislative agencies and other mental health organizations. Offers referrals to local groups. Operates speakers' bureau. **Publications:** Brochures. • Handbooks. • *Media Watch Kit.* • *NAMI Advocate*, bimonthly. Newsletter. *Price:* Included in membership dues. • Newsletters.

★7450★ **National Association for the Advancement of Psychoanalysis and the American Board for Accreditation in Psychoanalysis (NAAPABAP)**
80 8th Ave., Ste. 1501
New York, NY 10011-1501
Phone: (212)741-0515
Fax: (212)741-0515
Margery Quackenbush, Admin.

Founded: 1972. **Members:** 1,670. **Description:** Psychoanalytic training institutes and indi-

vidual psychoanalysts from a variety of schools of psychoanalytic thought united for the advancement of psychoanalysis as a profession. Establishes standards for psychoanalytic training and works to improve its quality by evaluating and accrediting psychoanalytic training institutes which may train medical doctors, psychologists, social workers, counselors, and others. Sets standards for certification of individual psychoanalysts; registers those who have met its training standards. **Publications:** *Handbook on Accreditation*, periodic. • *NAAP News*, quarterly. Covers institute, committee, and membership activities. Includes legislative news, calendar of events, and obituaries. *Price:* Included in membership dues; $10/year for nonmembers. • *National Registry of Psychoanalysts*, biennial. Directory. Lists qualified psychoanalysts and candidates-in-training. Includes listing of deceased members, list of member institutes, and geographic index. *Price:* $15/copy.

★7451★ **National Association for Drama Therapy (NADT)**
2022 Cutter Dr.
League City, TX 77573-6916
Phone: (713)538-1689
Fax: (713)538-1689
Pam Dunne, Pres.

Founded: 1979. **Members:** 325. **Regional Groups:** 2. **Description:** Drama therapists (those trained in the therapeutic applications of creative drama and theatre) and others interested in the field of drama therapy, including those in the psychotherapy, rehabilitation, and education professions. (The association defines drama therapy as the intentional use of drama and theatrical processes to achieve the therapeutic goals of symptom relief, emotional and physical integration, and personal growth. It is used with individuals, groups, and families to maintain health and to treat emotional disorders, learning difficulties, geriatric problems, and social maladjustments.) Purposes are to: develop criteria and standards of training for drama therapists; maintain a system of registration and peer review; encourage research and development of professional training opportunities in drama therapy; represent the interests of members to legislative and regulatory agencies regarding the inclusion of drama therapy in mental health and education bills, state job lines, and insurance policies. Sponsors educational events; maintains speakers' bureau. **Publications:** Bibliography. • *Dramascope*, semiannual. Newsletter. Includes book reviews, calendar of events, employment listings, descriptions of treatment programs and methods, and commentaries and reports. *Price:* Included in membership dues. • *Membership List/Registry*, annual. • Monographs. • *Proceedings of Annual Conference*, annual. Proceedings. • Survey. Also publishes information on workshops and courses in drama therapy.

★7452★ **National Association for Music Therapy (NAMT)**
8455 Colesville Rd., Ste. 930
Silver Spring, MD 20910
Phone: (301)589-3300
Fax: (301)589-5175
Dr. Andrea Farbman, Exec.Dir.

Founded: 1950. **Members:** 3,800. **Regional Groups:** 8. **Description:** Music therapists, physicians, psychologists, administrators, and educators concerned with music in therapy. Seeks to perfect techniques of music programming which effectively aid treatment. Aims to establish qualifications and standards of training for music therapists. Maintains placement services. **Publications:** *Journal of Music Therapy*, quarterly. Journal. *Price:* Included in membership dues. • *Music Therapy Clinical Training Facilities Handbook*, biennial. Handbook. Lists approved facilities and programs offering music therapy internships. *Price:* $90/copy. • *Music Therapy Perspectives*, semiannual. *Price:* Included in membership dues. • *NAMT Notes*, bimonthly. Newsletter. *Price:* Included in membership dues. • *National Association for Music Therapy--Membership Sourcebook*, annual. Membership Directory. Contains statistical information and association documents. *Price:* Included in membership dues; $30/year for nonmembers.

★7453★ **National Association for Poetry Therapy (NAPT)**
c/o Alicia Seeger
Box 551
Port Washington, NY 11050
Phone: (516)944-9791
Fax: (516)944-5818
Sherry Reiter, Pres.

Founded: 1981. **Members:** 303. **Regional Groups:** 16. **Description:** Psychiatrists, psychologists, social workers, teachers, nurses, librarians, occupational therapists, paraprofessionals, ministers, counselors, recreation and rehabilitation specialists, and poets and professors of English and psychology. Objective is to promulgate the principles and techniques of poetry therapy for healing and personal growth. (Poetry therapy is used with patients in a variety of mental states ranging from "normal neurosis" to acute psychosis, as well as the physically handicapped and the learning disabled. Methods of using poetry for therapy vary and include reading poems and encouraging clients to write their own poetry. The general purpose is to lead the person into talking or writing about himself or herself and bringing out emotions not previously shown or discussed). Sponsors two degrees in the field of poetry therapy: Certified Poetry Therapist (CPT) and Registered Poetry Therapist (RPT). **Publications:** *Journal of Poetry Therapy*, quarterly. Magazine. *Price:* Included in membership dues. • *NAPT Museletter*, 3/year. Includes training and conference information. *Price:* Included in membership dues; $10/year for nonmembers. • *Trainee's and Trainer's Guide. Price:* $11.50. **Formerly:** World Poetry Therapy Association; (1981) Association for Poetry Therapy.

National Association of Psychiatric Health Systems (NAPHS)
See: Entry 6461

National Association of Psychiatric Treatment Centers for Children (NAPTCC)
See: Entry 3264

★7454★ **National Association for Rural Mental Health (NARMH)**
PO Box 570
Wood River, IL 62095
Phone: (618)251-0589
Dennis Mohatt, Ph.D., Pres.

Founded: 1977. **Members:** 350. **Description:** Mental health practitioners and administrators and others dedicated to improving mental health services in rural areas. Promotes effective rural mental health services. Promotes the use of services by rural community dwellers. **Publications:** *Party-Line*, bimonthly. Newsletter. • *Rural Community Mental Health Newsletter*, quarterly. Newsletter.

★7455★ **National Association of School Psychologists (NASP)**
8455 Colesville Rd., Ste. 1000
Silver Spring, MD 20910
Phone: (301)608-0500
Fax: (301)608-2514
Susan Gorin, Exec.Dir.

Founded: 1969. **Members:** 17,100. **Regional Groups:** 5. **State Groups:** 51. **Description:** School psychologists. Serves the mental health and educational needs of all children and youth. Encourages and provides opportunities for professional growth of individual members. Informs the public on the services and practice of school psychology, and advances the standards of the profession. Operates national school psychologist certification system. Sponsors children's services. **Publications:** Catalog. Lists publications. • *Communique Newspaper*, 8/year. Newspaper. • Monographs. • Reports. • *School Psychology Review*, quarterly. Journal.

National Association of State Mental Retardation Program Directors
See: Entry 5591

★7456★ **National Autistic Society (NAS)**
276 Willesden Ln.
London NW2 5RB, England
Phone: 181 4511114
Fax: 181 4515865
Geraldine Peacock, CEO

Founded: 1962. **Members:** 3,500. **Local Groups:** 64. **Languages:** English. **Description:** Parents of people with autism; professionals; caregivers. Provides information, advice, and support for parents, caregivers, and professionals. Promotes public understanding of autism. Supports and develops a range of educational and support services. Encourages research; organizes courses and conferences for parents and practitioners; offers diagnostic and assessment services; provides training. Operates schools and adult centers. **Publications:** *Communication*, 3/year. Journal. • *Connection*, 3/year. Newsletter.

★7457★ **National Benevolent Association of the Christian Church (Disciples of Christ) (NBA, The)**
c/o Ron Hollon
11780 Borman Dr., Ste. 200
St. Louis, MO 63146-4157
Phone: (314)993-9000
Fax: (314)993-9018
Richard R. Lance, Pres.

Founded: 1887. **Description:** Division of Social and Health Services of the Christian Church (Disciples of Christ). Cares for older adults, children, youth, families, children and adults with mental retardation , and individuals who are chronically mentally ill. Services are provided through over 80 facilities or programs in 27 states offering residential living and independent retirement living, nursing care, treatment centers for children who are emotionally disturbed, crisis intervention centers for children, foster care and adoption, single parent training programs, sheltered workshops, group homes for persons who are chronically mentally ill, and day-care centers. Maintains liaison with interfaith and professional organizations concerned with children, older adults, and mentally retarded individuals. **Publications:** Brochures. • *Family Talk*, semiannual. Journal. • Monographs. • Newsletter, monthly. • Videos.

★7458★ **National Center for American Indian and Alaska Native Mental Health Research (NCAIANMHR)**
University of Colorado Health Sciences Center
Psychiatry Department
University N. Pavilion A011-13
4455 E. 12th Ave.
Denver, CO 80220
Phone: (303)372-3232
Fax: (303)372-3579
Spero M. Manson, Ph.D., Dir.

Founded: 1987. **Description:** Faculty, staff, and research associates in the mental health field. Conducts and supports research on management, prevention, and investigation of mental illness among Native Americans and Alaska Natives. Assists organizations in conducting and implementing mental health research. Disseminates information and statistics to public. **Publications:** *Behavioral Health Issues Among American Indians and Alaska Natives: Explorations on the Frontiers of the Biobehavioral Sciences*. Monograph. *Price:* $20. • *Calling From the Rim: Suicidal Behavior Among American Indian and Alaska Native Adolescents*. Monograph. *Price:* $20. • *Journal of the National Center for American Indian and Alaska Native Mental Health Research*, quarterly. Journal. Includes empirical research, case studies, unpublished dissertations, and articles on behavioral and social health sciences. *Price:* $35/year. • *Mental Health Programs for American Indians: Their Logic, Structure and Function*. Monograph. *Price:* $20. • *New Directions in Prevention Among American Indian and Alaska Native Communities*. Monograph. *Price:* $14.95. • *The People Who Give More: Health and Mental Health Among the Contemporary Puyallup Indian Tribal Community*. Monograph. *Price:* $20.

★7459★ **National Coalition of Arts Therapy Associations (NCATA)**
c/o ADTA
2000 Century Plz., Ste. 108
Columbia, MD 21044
Phone: (410)997-4040
Fax: (410)997-1608
Linda Gantt, Chairperson

Founded: 1979. **Members:** 8,000. **Description:** Creative arts therapists. Promotes therapeutic and rehabilitative uses of the arts in medicine, mental health, special education, and forensic and social services; coordinates member associations' activities and efforts in meeting common objectives while supporting and advancing each group's discipline. Works to: represent members' interests in legislative activities; define joint positions on public policy issues; facilitate communication among members; initiate educational and research programs. Compiles statistics.

★7460★ National Community Mental
Healthcare Council (NCMHC)
12300 Twinbrook Pky., No. 320
Rockville, MD 20852
Phone: (301)984-6200
Charles G. Ray, CEO

Founded: 1969. Members: 900. State Groups: 38. Description: Community mental health centers, state provider organizations, agencies, and interested individuals. Purpose is to improve the quality and accessibility of mental health services. Develops state and national legislative policy issues; works for full mental health care coverage by insurance companies and federal programs. Conducts workshops relating to significant issues and changes in community mental health; creates task forces to deal with specific problems; offers insurance programs to members at special rates. Offers technical assistance and consulting services; makes available publications and resource materials. Compiles statistics. Publications: Community Mental Health Journal, quarterly. Journal. Covers mental health theory, practice, and research. • Community Mental Health Salary Survey, periodic. Survey. Arranged by geographic region and type of service area. Price: $49/copy for members; $69/copy for nonmembers. • Monographs. • National Council News, 11/year. Newsletter. Includes legislative updates, program features, news, calendar of events, book reviews, lists of audiovisual resources and employment opportunities. Price: $25/year. • National Registry of Community Mental Health Services, periodic. Directory. Lists community mental health agencies, directors, and services. Formerly: (1970) National Council of Comprehensive Community Mental Health Centers; (1993) National Council of Community Mental Health Centers.

National Consortium for Child Mental
Health Services (NCCMHS)
See: Entry 3267

★7461★ National Depressive and Manic
Depressive Association (NDMDA)
730 N. Franklin, Ste. 501
Chicago, IL 60610
Phone: (312)642-0049
Free: 800-82-NDMDA
Fax: (312)642-7243
Susan Dime-Meenan, Exec.Dir.

Founded: 1978. Members: 35,000. Local Groups: 275. Description: Purposes are to: provide support to patients and their families and friends; help patients receive the most qualified treatment from doctors and other professionals; promote research into the causes and treatment of depressive and manic-depressive illness; remove the stigma associated with de-

pression and manic depression by educating the public on the biochemical nature of these illnesses. Local groups conduct confidential rap sessions and meetings for patients, and sponsor patient forums and lectures by health professionals. Compiles statistics; maintains speakers' bureau. Publications: Audiotapes. • Books. • NDMDA Newsletter, quarterly. Newsletter. Includes book reviews and calendar of events. • Pamphlets. • Videos. Formerly: (1985) Manic Depressive and Depressive Association.

★7462★ National Eating Disorder
Information Centre
College Wing, 1-211
200 Elizabeth St.
Toronto, ON, Canada M5G 2C4
Phone: (416)340-4156
Fax: (416)340-3430
Merryl Bear, Coord.

Founded: 1985. Languages: English. Description: Individuals interested in problems associated with people who suffer from eating disorders. Provides information and resources on causes, symptoms of, and therapeutic and health care treatments for eating disorders and the preoccupation with food and weight. Aims to raise awareness on eating disorders through conducting lectures and workshops. Publications: Bulletin, 5/year. Provides information and resources on range of topics related to food and weight preoccupation.

★7463★ National Eating Disorders
Organization (NEDO)
445 E. Granville Rd.
Worthington, OH 43085
Phone: (614)436-1112
Fax: (614)785-7471
Laura Hill, Ph.D., Dir.

Founded: 1977. Members: 1,500. Description: Persons suffering from anorexia nervosa, bulimia, binge eating, and related eating disorders; families of victims; educators, doctors, and mental health professionals. Provides community education programs and selfhelp groups for victims and their families; compiles state-by-state listing of doctors, hospitals, and clinics treating the disorders; offers information and referral services. Works with medical and mental health professionals to call attention to anorexia nervosa, bulimia, and binge eating so that problems can be discussed and causes and treatments explored. Provides parents, educators, family physicians, and clergy with information that will aid in the early recognition, diagnosis, and treatment of eating disorders. Maintains speakers' bureau. Publications: A 5 Day Lesson Plan on Eating Disorders: Grades 7-12. • NEDO Newsletter, quarterly. Newsletter. Includes book reviews. Price: Included in membership dues. • Skin Deep. Video. Covers eating disorder prevention. Also makes available information packets on eating disorders. Formerly: National Anorexic Aid Society; (1979) Anorexic Aid Society.

★7464★ National Federation for Biblio-
Poetry Therapy (NFBPT)
c/o Deborah S. Langosch
225 Lincoln Pl., No. 2F
Brooklyn, NY 11217
Phone: (718)636-0754
Deborah S. Langosch, Exec.Dir.

Founded: 1983. Members: 17. Description: Individuals, organizations, and institutions engaged in the training of biblio/poetry therapists or the practice of biblio/poetry therapy as a profession. (Biblio/poetry therapy uses literature or poetry to help patients "respond to an emotional impact which can then be integrated in self-awareness and self-understanding.") Seeks to establish advanced standards for board certification of biblio/poetry therapists. Plans to conduct research and educational programs.

★7465★ National Foundation for
Depressive Illness (NAFDI)
PO Box 2257
New York, NY 10116
Phone: (212)268-4260
Free: 800-248-4344
Fax: (212)268-4434
Peter Ross, Exec.Dir.

Founded: 1983. Description: Provides public and professional education and information on recent medical advances in affective mood disorders. Conducts seminars on affective disorders, pharmaceutical development, and disease-related loss of productivity. Maintains speakers' bureau. Provides support group and referral services to appropriate doctors. Publications: Brochures. • NAFDI News, quarterly. Newsletter. • Now We Can Treat the Illness Called Depression.

★7466★ National Guild of Catholic
Psychiatrists (NGCP)
Taylor Manor Hopital
4100 College Ave.
Ellicott City, MD 21041-0396
Phone: (410)465-3322
Fax: (410)461-7075
Dr. Taylor, Pres.

Founded: 1949. Members: 75. Description: Purposes are: to unite psychiatrists and other mental health professionals who share a belief in the spiritual dimension of human experience; to promote mutual respect for and to affirm the unique knowledge and skills of all members of the mental health professions; to establish a forum to further the integration of psychiatry and religion through the exchange of clinical experience and knowledge; to stimulate research on problems relating to psychiatry and religion. Conducts scientific program annually. Publications: Bulletin of the National Guild of Catholic Psychiatrists, annual. Bulletin. Includes book reviews and list of members. Price: Included in membership dues. Formerly: Guild of Catholic Psychiatrists.

★ 7467 ★ National Mental Health Association (NMHA)
1021 Prince St.
Alexandria, VA 22314-2971
Phone: (703)684-7722
Free: 800-969-NMHA
Fax: (703)684-5968
Ann Utley, Pres.

Founded: 1909. **State Groups:** 450. **Description:** Consumer advocacy organization devoted to fighting mental illnesses and promoting mental health. Advocates funding for research to discover new and better ways to treat and prevent mental illness; supports community mental health center program; engages in visitations to hospitals, nursing homes, board and care homes, and centers to assess adequacy of care; works with mental hospitals, government agencies, and private organizations for the rehabilitation of recovered patients; serves as central national source for educational materials on mental illness and mental health; conducts public education on mental illnesses and the need for public action through newspapers, magazines, radio, and television. **Publications:** *NMHA Focus*, 4/year. Tabloid; includes association news, calendar of events, legislative news, mental health/health trends and research news. • Pamphlets. • Reports. **Formerly:** National Association for Mental Health; (1980) Mental Health Association.

★ 7468 ★ National Mental Health Consumer Self-Help Clearinghouse (NMHCSHC)
311 S. Juniper St., Rm. 1000
Philadelphia, PA 19107
Phone: (215)735-6082
Free: 800-553-4539
Fax: (215)735-0275
Jerry Antner, Program Dir.

Founded: 1985. **Description:** Serves mental health consumers/ex-patients and consumer/ex-patient self-help groups. Provides technical assistance in the development of self-help projects. Offers informational referrals, written material, and consulting services. **Publications:** Manuals. • Newsletter, quarterly. • Pamphlets.

★ 7469 ★ National Organization for Seasonal Affective Disorder (NOSAD)
PO Box 40133
Washington, DC 20016
Nella Leppo, Pres.

Founded: 1988. **Members:** 550. **Regional Groups:** 4. **Description:** Individuals suffering from Seasonal Affective Disorder (SAD), their families and friends, and health care professionals; interested others. Provides a forum for exchange of information, advice, and support. (SAD is a cyclical illness characterized by episodes of depression in the fall and winter, alternating with nondepressed or elevated moods in the spring and summer. Symptoms are linked to the amount of sunlight available over the course of the seasons. Approximately 4 times as many women as men suffer from SAD.) **Publications:** Newsletter, quarterly. Reports on current research and findings, focusing on light and antidepression drug therapy issues. *Price:* Available to members only. Also issues information packet.

★ 7470 ★ National Psychological Association for Psychoanalysis (NPAP)
150 W. 13th St.
New York, NY 10011
Phone: (212)924-7440
Fax: (212)989-7543
Linda Korb, Exec. Officer

Founded: 1946. **Members:** 351. **Description:** Professional society for practicing psychoanalysts. Conducts training program leading to certification in psychoanalysis. Offers information and private referral service for the public. Operates speakers' bureau. **Publications:** *National Psychological Association for Psychoanalysis--Bulletin*, annual. Bulletin. *Price:* Free. • *National Psychological Association for Psychoanalysis--News and Reviews*, quarterly. *Price:* Included in membership dues. • *Psychoanalytic Review*, bimonthly. Journal. Includes book reviews.

★ 7471 ★ National Remotivation Therapy Organization (NRTO)
1901 N. DuPont Hwy.
New Castle, DE 19720
Phone: (302)577-4360
Fax: (302)577-4359
Hugh McElroy, Pres. & CEO

Founded: 1971. **Members:** 386. **State Groups:** 5. **Description:** Certified remotivation therapists organized to provide a forum for the discussion of ideas and information related to the field. (Remotivation therapy involves the use of small group sessions to stimulate and revitalize individuals who have experienced a decline in interest in their surroundings, themselves, and other people. Patients usually suffer from severe depression, Alzheimer's disease, mental illness, or mental retardation.) Conducts discussions of methods that allow patients an opportunity for verbal expression, renewal of listening skills, and resocialization. **Publications:** *NRTO Newsletter*, quarterly. Newsletter. *Price:* $20/year. • *Remotivation Therapy Information*. Brochure. • *Remotivator*, quarterly. Newsletter. **Also Known As:** National Remotivation Technique Organization.

★ 7472 ★ National Resource Center on Homelessness and Mental Illness (NRCHMI)
Policy Research Associates
262 Delaware Ave.
Delmar, NY 12054
Phone: (518)439-7415
Free: 800-444-7415
Fax: (518)439-7612
Deborah L. Dennis, Dir.

Founded: 1988. **Description:** Serves as a center for information and technical assistance on the housing and service needs of the mentally ill homeless. Compiles annotated bibliographies. **Publications:** *Access*, quarterly. Newsletter. Features articles on service delivery, housing, research and prgram evaluation, staff training, and federal, state, and local initiatives. *Price:* Free.

★ 7473 ★ National Runaway Switchboard (NRS)
3080 N. Lincoln Ave.
Chicago, IL 60657
Phone: 800-621-4000
Fax: (312)929-5150
Lora Thomas, Exec.Dir.

Founded: 1974. **Description:** A 24-hour, toll-free national switchboard for runaways, families of runaways, and other troubled youth. Provides names, addresses, and phone numbers of centers for shelter and other social services across the country, including counseling centers, referral lines, drug treatment facilities, and family planning services. Offers to relay messages between young people and their families if desired; can also set up conferences calls between youths and parents or agencies. The caller's confidentiality is maintained. Maintains speakers' bureau. Funded in part by the Family and Youth Services Bureau of the U.S. Department of Health and Human Services. **Publications:** Brochure. • *FrontLine*, quarterly. Newsletter. Contains statistical data and reports on activities.

★ 7474 ★ National Self-Help Clearinghouse (NSHC)
25 W. 43rd St., Rm. 620
New York, NY 10036-7406
Phone: (212)354-8525
Fax: (212)642-1956
Frank Riessman, Dir.

Founded: 1976. **Description:** Clearinghouse on selfhelp groups; provides referral services. Conducts research and training activities. Maintains speakers' bureau. **Publications:** Books. • Brochures. • Manuals. • Reports. *Self-Help Reporter*, quarterly. Newsletter.

★ 7475 ★ Neurotics Anonymous International Liaison (NAIL)
11140 Bainbridge Dr.
Little Rock, AR 72212
Phone: (501)221-2809
Grover Boydston, Chm.

Founded: 1964. **Members:** 10,000. **Description:** Individuals suffering or recovering from an emotional illness who use the techniques of Neurotics Anonymous to aid and maintain their recovery. Organization has adapted the Twelve Steps of Alcoholics Anonymous and applies them to the problems of mentally and emotionally disturbed (neurotic) individuals. Members exchange and discuss experiences and recovery stories. **Publications:** Books. • *Journal of Mental Health*, quarterly. Journal. • Pamphlets. Also publishes instruction sheets.

★ 7476 ★ New Zealand Psychological Society (NZPsS)
PO Box 4092
Wellington, New Zealand
Phone: 4 8015414
Fax: 4 3828763
Olive Webb, Pres.

Founded: 1967. **Members:** 500. **Local Groups:** 8. **Languages:** English. **Description:** Psychologists and interested individuals. Promotes psychology as a science. Represents interests of professional psychologists. **Publica-**

tions: AGM Agenda, annual. • *Annual General Meeting Agenda*, annual. Booklet. • *Connections*, monthly. Newsletter. • *New Zealand Journal of Psychology*, semiannual. Journal. Two issues per volume. • *NZPSS Bulletin*, quarterly. Bulletin. • *The Practise of Psychology & the Law: A Handbook*. Handbook.

★7477★ **North American Society of Adlerian Psychology (NASAP)**
65 E. Wacker Pl., No. 400
Chicago, IL 60601
Phone: (312)629-8801
Neva L. Hefner, Exec.Dir.

Founded: 1951. **Members:** 1,200. **Description:** Psychiatrists, psychologists, educators, social workers, clergymen, and others interested in promoting the knowledge, training, and teaching of individual psychology, developed by the Austrian psychiatrist Alfred Adler (1870-1937). Encourages development of professional workers and groups in individual psychology; establishes standards for professional activities of members. Conducts research in child behavior and psychology, counseling, psychotherapy, group therapy, and treatment of the mentally ill. Sponsors training institutes and summer school program. Promotes establishment of family education associations and parent study groups. **Publications:** *Alfred Adler: As We Remember Him*. Book. • *An Adlerian Resource Book*. • *Individual Psychology: Journal of Adlerian Theory, Research and Practice*, quarterly. Journal. • *Membership List*, biennial. • *North American Society of Adlerian Psychology--Newsletter*, monthly. Newsletter. Includes calendar of events. *Price:* Included in membership dues; $10/year for nonmembers. **Formerly:** (1977) American Society of Alderian Psychology.

★7478★ **Norwegian National Society for Autistic People (NNSAP)**
(Landsforeningen for Autister)
Postboks 118, Kjelsaas
N-0411 Oslo 4, Norway
Phone: 22 180923
Fax: 22 235700
Ase Garder, Sec.

Founded: 1965. **Members:** 1,200. **Local Groups:** 18. **Languages:** English, Norwegian. **Description:** Parents of autistic children; supporters; institutions. Acts as support group for families of autistics. **Publications:** *Autisme i dag*, semiannual. • *Autisme i dag Meldeblad*, quarterly.

★7479★ **O-Anon General Service Office (OGSO)**
PO Box 748
San Pedro, CA 90733
Phone: (310)547-1570
Jack Rudder

Founded: 1985. **Regional Groups:** 40. **Description:** Families and friends of compulsive overeaters. Provides support groups that offer opportunities for the sharing of experiences and viewpoints. Purposes are to: offer comfort, hope, and friendship to families and friends of compulsive overeaters; learn to grow spiritually by working with the Twelve Steps, patterned after Alcoholics Anonymous World Services; give understanding and encouragement to the

compulsive overeater. Works in cooperation with Overeaters Anonymous. **Publications:** Newsletter, 3-4/year. **Also Known As:** O-Anon.

★7480★ **Obsessive-Compulsive Anonymous (OCA)**
PO Box 215
New Hyde Park, NY 11040
Phone: (516)741-4901
Fax: (212)768-4679
Roy C., Contact

Founded: 1988. **Members:** 1,000. **Regional Groups:** 45. **Description:** Individuals suffering from obsessive-compulsive disorders. (OCD is characterized by recurrent unpleasant thoughts and/or repetitive, irrational mannerisms the sufferer feels compelled to perform.) Follows the 12-step method originated by Alcoholics Anonymous World Services to assist members in their recovery. **Publications:** *Obsessive Compulsive Anonymous*. Book. • *Obsessive Compulsive Disorder: A Survival Guide for Family and Friends*.

★7481★ **Obsessive Compulsive Foundation (OCF)**
PO Box 70
Milford, CT 06460-0070
Phone: (203)878-5669
Fax: (203)874-2826
James W. Broatch, Exec.Dir.

Founded: 1986. **Members:** 8,000. **State Groups:** 5. **Description:** Individuals with obsessive-compulsive disorders and their families and friends; professionals involved in the treatment of OCD. (OCD is often chronic and characterized by recurrent unpleasant thoughts and/or repetitive behaviors which the person feels driven to perform. Individuals with OCD realize their obsessions and compulsions are irrational or excessive, yet find they have no control over them. Individuals with OCD often become demoralized, depressed, and anxious.) Seeks to control and find a cure for OCD while improving the welfare of its individuals with OCD. Disseminates information on OCD and possible new therapies. Offers educational programs for professionals and the public. Assists with fundraising and forming local support groups; fosters communication between members. Conducts research into causes and treatments. **Publications:** Brochure. • *Kidscope*, semiannual. Newsletter. For children and teens with OCD. • *OCD Newsletter*, bimonthly. Newsletter. Also produces educational materials. **Also Known As:** OC Foundation. **Formerly:** (1988) Obsessive Compulsive Disorder Foundation.

★7482★ **Overeaters Anonymous (OA)**
6075 Zenith Ct. NE
Rio Rancho, NM 87124-6424
Phone: (505)891-2664
Fax: (505)891-4320
Jorge N. Sever, Exec.Dir.

Founded: 1960. **National Groups:** 47. **Local Groups:** 10300. **Description:** Individuals who have a desire to stop eating compulsively. A twelve-step self-help fellowship patterned after that of Alcoholics Anonymous. **Publications:** *A Step Ahead*, quarterly. Newsletter. *Price:* Free to groups and intergroups. • Audiotapes. • Books. • *Lifeline*, monthly. Magazine. *Price:*

$12.99/year. • Pamphlets. • Videos. Also publishes posters, wallet cards, and recovery medallions.

★7483★ **Pedagogical Psychotherapists Association**
(Berufsverband Padagogischer Psychotherapeuten)
Schubbendenweg 4
52249 Eschweiler, Germany
Phone: 2403 4726
Fax: 2403 20447
Dagmar Lumma, PPT, Contact

Founded: 1986. **Members:** 250. **Description:** Represents the interests of pedagogical psychotherapists. Provides a forum for the exchange of information. Secures professional standards; links different training institutes. **Publications:** *Halbjehrbuch*, semiannual. Yearbook.

★7484★ **Postgraduate Center for Mental Health (PCMH)**
124 E. 28th St.
New York, NY 10016
Phone: (212)689-7700
Fax: (212)576-4198
Richard Hlavacek, Pres. & CEO

Founded: 1945. **Description:** Provides: therapy for individuals, groups, couples, and families; training; psychiatric day and evening care program; community services and public educational programs. Conducts research. Maintains: social rehabilitation clinic; child/adolescent and family clinic; adult clinic; employee support service; group residence for the mentally ill preparing for independent living. Training opportunities include: Adult Fellowship, Advanced Training for Social Workers, Child and Adolescent Counseling, Family Therapy, Group Therapy, Pastoral Counseling, Psychology Internship, and Social Work Internship. Offers mental health and organizational consultation to industry and government agencies. **Publications:** *Dynamic Psychotherapy*, semiannual. Journal. Includes book reviews and author and title indexes. *Price:* $18/year; $38/year for institutions. • *Pathways*, semiannual. Newsletter. **Formerly:** Institute for Research in Psychotherapy; (1962) Postgraduate Center for Psychotherapy.

★7485★ **Postpartum Support, International (PSI)**
927 N. Kellogg Ave.
Santa Barbara, CA 93111
Phone: (805)967-7636
Fax: (805)967-0608
Jane Honikman, Exec.Dir.

Founded: 1987. **Members:** 200. **Description:** Promotes public awareness about the mental health issues of childbearing. Encourages research and the formation of support groups; addresses legal and insurance coverage issues. Provides educational programs. Maintains speakers' bureau. **Publications:** *Postpartum Equilibria*, quarterly. *Price:* Included in membership. • *PSI News*, quarterly. Contains association, research, and membership news.

★7486★ Project Overcome (PO)
PO Box 385226
Minneapolis, MN 55438-5226
Phone: (612)820-0464
Margaret Correll, Exec.Dir.

Founded: 1977. **Members:** 10. **State Groups:** 1. **Local Groups:** 1. **Description:** Recovered and recovering mental health patients. Works to eliminate the stigma attached to mental illness. Sponsors speakers' bureau of former mental health patients. Conducts advocacy services, seminars, support groups, lectures, and training events; offers professional consultation on the mental health system. **Publications:** *Mental Health and Wellness Curriculum*. Booklets. Booklets deal with emotional issues such as anger, and abuse, depression, stress, relationships, and family. *Price:* $25/set, plus shipping and handling. • *Project Overcome*. Brochure. • *Voices*, quarterly. Newsletter.

★7487★ Psi Chi, The National Honor Society in Psychology
407 E. 5th St., Ste. B
Chattanooga, TN 37403
Phone: (615)756-2044
Fax: (615)265-1529
Kay Wilson, Exec. Officer

Founded: 1929. **Members:** 260,000. **Regional Groups:** 6. **State Groups:** 842. **Description:** Honor society - men and women, psychology. **Publications:** *Handbook*, annual. • *Psi Chi Newsletter*, quarterly. Newsletter. *Price:* Included in membership dues.

★7488★ Psychiatrists Against Psychiatric Abuse (PAPA)
250 College St.
Toronto, ON, Canada M5T 1R8
Dr. F. Cashman, Sec.

Founded: 1977. **Members:** 15. **Languages:** English. **Description:** Psychiatrists united to prevent the abuse of psychiatry for political purposes.

★7489★ Psychohistory Forum (PF)
627 Dakota Trl.
Franklin Lakes, NJ 07417
Phone: (201)891-6866
Fax: (201)848-0454
Paul H. Elovitz, Ph.D., Dir.

Founded: 1983. **Members:** 100. **Description:** Psychologists, psychiatrists, psychotherapists, social workers, historians, psychohistorians, and laypeople having a scholarly interest in the integration of depth psychology and history (Psychohistory is the study of psychobiography, group process, the mechanisms of defense, the history of childhood, creativity, dreams, and the difference between stated intention and actual behavior). Seeks to further psychohistory through the exchange of information. Conducts bimonthly workshops on topics related to psychohistory and training seminars on dream analysis, innovation, teaching, and methodology. Aids individuals in psychohistorical research. Holds lecture series. **Publications:** *Clio's Psyche*, quarterly. Newsletter. *Price:* Included in membership dues; $18 for nonmembers in the U.S.; $22 for nonmembers outside the U.S. • *The Emotions of War*. Monograph. • *Immigrant Psychology*. Monograph. • *Varieties of Immigrant Experience: Personal Narrative and Psychological Analysis*. Monograph.

★7490★ Psychology of Religion
c/o Siang-Yang Tan
Fuller Theological Seminary
180 N. Oakland Ave.
Pasadena, CA 91101-1792
Dr. Margaret Gorman, Sec.

Founded: 1948. **Members:** 1,175. **Description:** A division of the American Psychological Association. Seeks to encourage and accelerate research, theory, and practice in the psychology of religion and related areas. Facilitates the dissemination of data on religious and allied issues and on the integration of these data with current psychological research, theory, and practice. **Publications:** *Psychology of Religion--Newsletter*, quarterly. Newsletter. Contains articles, interviews, book reviews, and announcements focusing on psychology and religion. *Price:* Free to members; $5/year to nonmembers. **Formerly:** (1971) American Catholic Psychological Association; (1993) Psychologists Interested in Religious Issues.

★7491★ Psychology Society (PS)
100 Beekman St.
New York, NY 10038-1810
Phone: (212)285-1872
Dr. Pierre C. Haber, Exec.Dir.

Founded: 1960. **Members:** 3,300. **National Groups:** 5. **Regional Groups:** 4. **Description:** Professional membership is limited to psychologists who have a doctorate and are certified/licensed as such in the state where they practice. Associate membership is intended for teachers and researchers as well as persons who will attain professional status shortly. Seeks to further the use of psychology in therapy, family and social problems, behavior modification, and treatment of drug abusers and prisoners. Encourages the use of psychology in the solution of social and political conflicts. Has established a referral service for laypeople and operates an information bureau to answer inquiries of authors, media, and students. Sponsors biennial overseas trip to enable members and their spouses to observe other programs and institutions. Collaborates with other associations. Evaluates programs in the use of psychology. Recommends legislation; maintains placement service for members and recent graduates. **Publications:** Papers. • *PS Newsletter*, monthly. Newsletter. Includes book reviews, calendar of events, and research updates. *Price:* Included in membership dues. • *PS Quarterly*. Journal. *Price:* Included in membership dues. • *Psychology Society--Membership List*, biennial. Membership Directory.

★7492★ Psychometric Society (PS)
c/o Dr. Terry Ackerman
260C Education Bldg.
1310 S. 6th St.
Champaign, IL 61820-6990
Phone: (217)244-3361
Fax: (217)244-7620
Dr. Terry Ackerman, Sec.

Founded: 1935. **Members:** 2,200. **Description:** Persons interested in development of quantitative models for psychological phenomena and quantitative methodology in the social and behavioral sciences. **Publications:** *Psychometrika*, quarterly. Journal. Covers statistical models of psychological phenomena. Includes book and software reviews. *Price:* $35 for members; $70 for organizations and nonmembers.

★7493★ Psychonomic Society (PS)
c/o Dr. Randi C. Martin
Rice University
Psychology Department
6100 S. Main St.
Houston, TX 77005
Phone: (713)527-8101
Fax: (713)258-5221
Dr. Randi C. Martin, Contact

Founded: 1959. **Members:** 2,400. **Description:** Persons qualified to conduct and supervise scientific research in psychology or allied sciences; members must hold a Ph.D. degree or its equivalent and must have published significant research other than the doctoral dissertation. Promotes the communication of scientific research in psychology and allied sciences. **Publications:** *Animal Learning and Behavior*, quarterly. Journal. Covers animal learning, motivation, emotion, and behavior, including classical and operant conditioning, sensory effects, and imprinting. *Price:* $36/year for individuals; $78/year for institutions. • *Behavior Research Methods, Instruments, and Computers*, quarterly. Journal. Contains articles in the areas of methods, techniques, and instrumentation of research in experimental psychology. *Price:* $46/year for individuals; $99/year for institutions. • *Memory and Cognition*, bimonthly. Journal. Covers human memory and learning, conceptual processes, thinking, decision making, and skilled performance. *Price:* $50/year for individuals; $107/year for institutions. • *Perception and Psychophysics*, monthly. Journal. Provides articles on sensory processes, perception, and psychophysics, including reports of experimental investigations. *Price:* $68/year for individuals; $149/year for institutions. • *Program of the Annual Meeting of the Psychonomic Society*. Schedule and abstracts. *Price:* Included in membership dues; $7/copy to nonmembers in North America; $8.50/copy to nonmembers outside North America. • *Psychobiology*, quarterly. Journal. Encompasses all of the allied fields of the neurosciences relating directly to behavior; includes experimental, review, and theoretical papers. *Price:* $36/year for individuals; $73/year for institutions. • *Psychonomic Bulletin and Review*, bimonthly. Journal. Contains short reports and full length review articles covering all areas of experimental psychology. *Price:* $42/year for individuals; $89/year for institutions.

★7494★ Rabbinic Center for Research and Counseling (RCRC)
128 E. Dudley Ave.
Westfield, NJ 07090
Phone: (908)233-0419
Fax: (908)233-2288
Rabbi Irwin H. Fishbein, Dir.

Founded: 1970. **Description:** Individuals interested in the marriage relationship and marriage counseling with special emphasis on interfaith marriage. Purpose is to provide courses, workshops and counseling for intermarried couples, and to establish and operate outpatient clinics for treatment of emotional and mental disabilities by the application of both psychotherapeutic knowledge and religious guidance. Conducts research; maintains list of rabbis who officiate at interfaith marriages; distributes literature.

★ 7495 ★ Radical Caucus in Psychiatry (RCP)
c/o Carl Cohen, M.D.
SUNY Downstate Med. Center
Box 1203
450 Clarkson Ave.
Brooklyn, NY 11203
Phone: (718)270-2907
Fax: (718)287-0337
Carl Cohen, M.D., Coord.

Founded: 1969. **Members:** 75. **Description:** Members of the American Psychiatric Association and individuals interested in mental health issues who take a politically progressive stand in psychiatry. Objective is to examine the socioeconomic and sociopolitical aspects of mental health issues from a left-oriented perspective. Areas of study have included a critical analysis of biological psychiatry, patient rights, and psychiatric treatment of mental patients in Latin America. Presents research findings to professionals and laypersons. Maintains speakers' bureau. **Publications:** Newsletter, annual.

★ 7496 ★ Radix Institute (RI)
6300 Ridglea Pl., No. 1212
Fort Worth, TX 76116-5738
William H. Thrash, Dir.

Founded: 1960. **Members:** 96. **Description:** Educational and scientific organization dedicated to studying the creative process in nature as described by Wilhelm Reich. Reich, a psychoanalyst who began his work with Sigmund Freud, discovered and described the existence of the "muscular armor," or how blocked emotion is held in the chronic patterns of tension in the body. His second major discovery was the concept of "orgone energy," the tangible life force also known as the Radix, the source of both energy and feeling. The Radix flow is experienced as feeling or emotion and is expressed in spontaneous movements of the body. Offers classes, workshops, and individual sessions in "Education in Feeling." Conducts teacher training and programs for professionals and research on the nature of the Radix. **Publications:** Calendar of Events, biennial. • List of Radix Teachers Worldwide, quarterly. • Radix Journal, quarterly. Journal. Also publishes books. **Formerly:** Interscience Research Institute.

★ 7497 ★ Radix Teachers Association (RTA)
5310 Harvest Hill Rd., No. 240; LB. 165
Dallas, TX 75230-5805
Phone: (214)661-1746
Stephen Atkinson, Pres.

Founded: 1981. **Members:** 77. **Description:** Licensed Radix practitioners certified by the Radix Institute; trainees of the institute; other psychotherapy professionals. Promotes the profession and the professional development of Radix instructors; upholds professional and ethical stan-

dards in the field. **Publications:** Journal of Radix Teachers Association, quarterly. Journal. • Membership Directory, annual.

★ 7498 ★ Reclamation, Inc.
2502 Waterford
San Antonio, TX 78217
Phone: (210)833-4946
Don H. Culwell, Dir.

Founded: 1974. **Members:** 200. **Local Groups:** 1. **Description:** Former mental health patients; interested others. Seeks to eliminate the stigma of mental illness and reclaim members' "human dignity." Serves as a unified voice for mental health patients in consumer, social, and political affairs. Helps members to live outside a hospital setting by providing assistance in the areas of resocialization, employment, and housing. Monitors media coverage; encourages "positive" presentations of mental health patients and increased coverage of mental health community service projects and events. Acts as a political force in the field. Maintains speakers' bureau. **Publications:** Positive Visibility, quarterly. Newsletter. Price: $5/year.

★ 7499 ★ Recovery
802 N. Dearborn St.
Chicago, IL 60610
Phone: (312)337-5661
Fax: (312)337-5756
Shirley Sachs, Exec.Dir.

Founded: 1937. **Members:** 10,000. **Local Groups:** 800. **Description:** Community mental health organization offering a self-help method developed by the neuropsychiatrist Dr. Abraham A. Low at the Psychiatric Institute of the University of Illinois Medical School. (The Recovery method is a system of techniques for controlling tempermental behavior and changing attitudes toward nervous symptoms and fears.) **Publications:** Directory of Group Meeting Information, annual. Price: $2. • Recovery Reporter, bimonthly. Newsletter. Price: Included in membership dues. • Recovery, Inc. Reports. Newsletter. • Recovery, The Association of Nervous and Former Mental Patients--Directory, annual. Directory. Lists the location and time of group meetings in the United States, Canada, and abroad. Price: $3/copy. Available to members only. **Also Known As:** Recovery, Inc., The Association of Nervous and Former Mental Patients.

★ 7500 ★ Richmond Fellowship International (RFI)
109 Strawberry Vale
Twickenham
Middlesex, Greater London TW1 4SJ, England
Phone: 181 7449585
Fax: 181 8910500
Elly Jansen, CEO

Founded: 1981. **Members:** 18. **National Groups:** 25. **Regional Groups:** 1. **Languages:** English, French, German, Spanish. **Description:** Promotes the establishment and operation of halfway houses and day centers for former psychiatric patients and recovering drug addicts. Organizes mental health training programs for social workers, psychologists, psychotherapists, and psychiatric nurses. Offers placement services. **Publications:** Annual Report. • Newsletter, periodic.

Rukariro Rehabilitation Organisation
See: Entry 12717

★ 7501 ★ Runaway Hotline (RH)
Governor's Office
PO Box 12428
Austin, TX 78711
Phone: (512)463-1980
Free: 800-231-6946
Jill Gardner, Dir.

Founded: 1973. **Description:** Maintains 24-hour, toll-free national hot line for runaways. Serves as a means for runaways to contact their parents or relatives to let them know that they are safe and well without the risk of having their location revealed. No attempt is made to discover the location of the caller and no information is given to relatives other than that which the caller wishes. Also maintains referral service for callers in need of shelter, counseling, medical help, legal assistance, transportation, or related services. Compiles statistics. **Publications:** Brochures. **Formerly:** (1979) Operation: Peace of Mind.

★ 7502 ★ SAFE - Self Abuse Finally Ends
c/o Karen Conterio
PO Box 267810
Chicago, IL 60626
Phone: (312)722-3113
Free: 800-DONT-CUT
Karen Conterio, Contact

Founded: 1984. **Local Groups:** 1. **Description:** Professional group assisting self-injurious individuals in the treatment of their addictive behavior patterns. Maintains speakers' bureau; compiles statistics. **Formerly:** (1987) Self-Mutilators Support Group.

★ 7503 ★ Samaritans
500 Commonwealth Ave.
Kenmore Sq.
Boston, MA 02215
Phone: (617)247-0220
Margaret R. O'Neil, Exec.Dir.

Founded: 1974. **Members:** 100. **Regional Groups:** 7. **Description:** People who volunteer their time to befriend the suicidal, the despairing, and the lonely. Provides daily walk-in service for suicidal and depressed people. Has founded "Lifeline," a suicide intervention program, in Boston, MA area jails using a team of trained inmates to spot and befriend potential suicides in jail. Holds over 100 talks annually for professionals and laypeople on suicide prevention. Provides information on suicide and suicide prevention. Maintains speakers' bureau. Not a religious organization and not related to the group of the same name located in La Jolla, CA. **Publications:** Drinking and the Teenager. • Elderly Suicide. Booklet. • The Suicidal Student: A Guide for Educators. Booklet. • Teen Suicide Information and Guidelines for Parents. Booklet.

★ 7504 ★ Schizophrenics Anonymous (SA)
1209 California Rd.
Eastchester, NY 10709
Phone: (914)337-2252
Elizabeth A. Plante, Dir.

Founded: 1967. **Local Groups:** 5. **Description:** Self-help organization sponsored by American Schizophrenia Association. Groups are comprised of diagnosed schizophrenics who meet to share experiences, strengths, and hopes in an effort to help each other cope with common problems and recover from the disease; rehabilitation program follows the 12 principles of Alcoholics Anonymous World Services. Discussion topics include: symptoms and how to deal with them; the need to be responsible even though one is ill; overcoming guilt related to the illness. Each of the local groups attempts to recruit a volunteer mental health consultant from the area. The volunteer aids in program development and group discussion. **Publications:** Newsletter, semiannual. Provides health information. *Price:* $20. Also distributes guidelines for establishing SA groups.

★ 7505 ★ **SEASONS: Suicide Bereavement**
c/o Tina Larsen
PO Box 187
Park City, UT 84060
Phone: (801)649-8327
Tina Larson, Contact

Founded: 1981. **State Groups:** 5. **Local Groups:** 1. **Description:** A support group of families and individuals united to bring together survivors of suicide victims so they may help each other develop a healthy understanding of their loss and grief, and work toward recovery. Objective is to provide selfhelp programs for the survivors of a suicide victim by putting them in contact with others who are dealing or have dealt with similar situations and emotions. Provides a place to discuss difficult issues; opportunities to benefit from others' experiences in coping with a suicide; information and referrals. Sponsors lectures, training seminars, and media presentations. Conducts children's services.

★ 7506 ★ **Social Psychiatry Research Institute (SPRI)**
150 E. 69th St., Ste. 2H
New York, NY 10021
Phone: (212)628-4800
Fax: (212)249-8546
Ari Kiev, MD, JD, Pres.

Founded: 1970. **Description:** To promote, support, and conduct, in and outside the U.S., research in the fields of mental health and psychiatry; to assemble data and findings for mental health and psychiatry. Is presently conducting double-blind psychopharmacological studies of antidepressant and antianxiety medications with volunteers. Has supported several suicide prevention and drug abuse projects. Sponsors Life Strategy Workshops for mental health professionals and lay organizations. Has developed a 15-week home-study program on panic and agoraphobia.

★ 7507 ★ **Social / Vocational Rehabilitation Clinic (SVRC)**
c/o Post-Graduate Center West
344 W. 36th St.
New York, NY 10018
Phone: (212)971-3200
Fax: (212)560-6794
Steala Hughus, Prog.Dir.

Founded: 1959. **Description:** Clinic employing a comprehensive therapeutic clinical program for psychiatric outpatients. Aims at reducing

hospital admissions and creating a therapeutic and social experience resulting in independent living, improved interpersonal relationships, and productivity in the work field. Offers a program of "therapeutic groups of creative, recreational, experiential, and work activities." Provides individual counseling, activity and therapy, and medication therapy; offers placement service; operates case management services. Sponsors vocational activities, family therapy, internship program, and community outreach activities. Functions as a psychotherapeutic service of the Postgraduate Center for Mental Health. **Formerly:** The Living Room; (1975) Social Rehabilitation Clinic; (1977) Psychiatric Day and Evening Clinic; (1988) Social Rehabilitation Clinic.

★ 7508 ★ **Society for the Advancement of the Field Theory (SAFT)**
c/o Martin McGurrin
903 N. 29th St.
Philadelphia, PA 19130
Phone: (215)232-8088
Martin McGurrin, Pres.

Founded: 1985. **Description:** Educators, psychologists, social workers, political scientists, and anthropologists. Promotes the field theory, a concept developed by Kurt Lewin (1890-1947), social psychologist. The field theory explains behavior by describing changes in one's situation, or field. The group focuses on a portion of the field theory referred to as life space, which attempts to schematically represent human motivation. **Also Known As:** Lewin Society.

★ 7509 ★ **Society for the Advancement of Social Psychology (SASP)**
c/o Francis C. Dane
Department of Psychology
Mercer University
Macon, GA 31207
Phone: (912)752-2972
Fax: (912)752-2956
Dr. Francis C. Dane, Sec.

Founded: 1974. **Members:** 400. **Regional Groups:** 4. **Description:** Social psychologists and students in social psychology. Advances social psychology as a profession by facilitating communication among social psychologists and improving dissemination and utilization of social psychological knowledge. Hosts social hours. **Publications:** *Contemporary Social Psychology*, quarterly. Journal. Includes research news. *Price:* $20/year. • Membership Directory, periodic.

★ 7510 ★ **Society of Behavioral Medicine (SBM)**
103 S. Adams St.
Rockville, MD 20850
Phone: (301)251-2790
Fax: (301)279-6749
Judith C. Woodward, Exec.Dir.

Founded: 1978. **Members:** 3,000. **Description:** Behavioral and biomedical researchers and clinicians studying health promotion and disease prevention, with primary focus on the interactions between health and behavior. Seeks to function as a forum for the exchange of ideas and information between health care providers and basic scientists and medical researchers.

Gathers and disseminates information to members and the public; conducts educational programs for health care professionals; works to integrate behavioral and biomedical research. **Publications:** *Annals of Behavioral Medicine*, quarterly. Journal. Features comprehensive area reviews of topics affecting biobehavioral research and practice; also contains abstracts of recent articles in the field. • *Annual Meeting Proceedings*. Proceedings. Supplement to *Annals of Behavioral Medicine* • *Education and Training Directory*. Directory. • Membership Directory, biennial. • *SBM Outlook*, quarterly. Newsletter.

Society for Behavioral Pediatrics (SBP)
See: Entry 3290

★ 7511 ★ **Society of Biological Psychiatry (SBP)**
Department of Psychiatry and Pharmacology
Mayo Clinic of Jacksonville
4500 San Pablo Rd.
Jacksonville, FL 32224
Phone: (904)953-2842
Fax: (904)953-7117
Elliott Richelson, M.D., Contact

Founded: 1945. **Members:** 950. **Description:** International professional society of psychiatrists, neurologists, neurosurgeons, pharmacologists, neuropharmacologists, physiologists, psychologists, and physicians in related biological studies. Studies the neuronal basis of human behavior and the biological basis of psychiatry. Compiles statistics. **Publications:** *Biological Psychiatry*, bimonthly. • *Membership Roster*, annual. Membership Directory.

★ 7512 ★ **Society of Experimental Psychologists (SEP)**
c/o Dr. Byron A. Campbell
Princeton University
Department of Psychology
Princeton, NJ 08544-1010
Phone: (609)258-0906
Fax: (609)258-1113
Dr. Byron A. Campbell, Sec.-Treas.

Founded: 1929. **Members:** 180. **Description:** Experimental psychologists of U.S. and Canada. Bestows annual Howard Crosby Warren Medal. **Publications:** Annual Report.

★ 7513 ★ **Society for the Exploration of Psychotherapy Integration (SEPI)**
134 Wooleys Ln.
Great Neck, NY 11023
Phone: (516)877-4803
Fax: (516)877-4805
Dr. George Stricker, Treas.

Founded: 1984. **Members:** 750. **Regional Groups:** 15. **Description:** Mental health professionals interested in the integration of theories and methods of psychotherapy. Encourages communication among members. Promotes collaborative work among psychotherapists who adhere to different theories and methods. **Publications:** Directory, annual. • *Journal of Psychotherapy Integration*, quarterly. Journal. Contains professional articles and book reviews. • *SEPI Newsletter*, quarterly. Newsletter.

★7514★ Society of Multivariate Experimental Psychology (SMEP)
c/o Dr. Jack McArdle
University of Virginia
Department of Psychology
102 Gilmer Hall
Charlottesville, VA 22903
Phone: (804)924-3374
Dr. Jack McArdle, Sec.-Treas.

Founded: 1960. **Members:** 65. **Description:** Psychologists interested in the branch of experimental psychology that centers on multivariate designs and associated special forms of analysis. Promotes substantive research and scientific discovery to develop mathematical/statistical models leading to their evaluation and integration into the development of psychological theory. **Publications:** *Multivariate Behavioral Research*, quarterly.

Society for Pediatric Psychology (SPP)
See: Entry 3294

★7515★ Society for Personality Assessment (SPA)
750 First St., NE
Washington, DC 20002
Phone: (202)336-6192
Fax: (202)336-5812

Founded: 1938. **Members:** 3,000. **Description:** Psychologists, behavioral scientists, anthropologists, and psychiatrists. Promotes the study, research, development, and application of personality assessment. **Publications:** *Journal of Personality Assessment*, quarterly. Journal. Includes book reviews, case reports, and annual directory. *Price:* Included in membership dues; $40/year for nonmembers; $80/year for institutions. • *SPA Exhange*, semiannual. Newsletter. **Formerly:** (1938) Rorschach Research Exchange; (1958) Society for Projective Techniques and Rorschach Institute; (1970) Society for Projective Techniques and Personality Assessment.

★7516★ Society of Professors of Child and Adolescent Psychiatry (SPCAP)
3615 Wisconsin Ave. NW
Washington, DC 20016-3007
Phone: (202)966-7300
Jean DeJarnette, Adm.Asst.

Founded: 1969. **Members:** 160. **Description:** Selected representatives from university psychiatric departments who meet annually to discuss issues in child and adolescent psychiatry. **Publications:** *SPCAP Directory*, annual. Directory. **Formerly:** (1987) Society of Professors of Child Psychiatry.

Society for the Psychological Study of Lesbian and Gay Issues (SPSLGI)
See: Entry 11714

★7517★ Society for the Psychological Study of Social Issues (SPSSI)
PO Box 1248
Ann Arbor, MI 48106-1248
Phone: (313)662-9130
Fax: (313)662-5607
Sandy West, Adm. Officer

Founded: 1936. **Members:** 3,000. **Description:** Psychologists, sociologists, anthropologists, psychiatrists, political scientists, and social workers. Works to: obtain and disseminate to the public scientific knowledge about social change and other social processes; promote psychological research on significant theoretical and practical questions of social life; encourage application of findings to problems of society. **Publications:** *Journal of Social Issues*, quarterly. Journal. • Newsletter, 3/year.

★7518★ Society for Psychophysiological Research (SPR)
c/o Robert J. Gatchel
University of Texas Southwestern Med. Center
Psychology Department
5323 Harry Hines Blvd.
Dallas, TX 75235-9044
Phone: (214)648-3111
Robert J. Gatchel, Sec.

Founded: 1960. **Members:** 906. **Description:** Research group comprising representatives from psychology, psychiatry, physiology, medicine, and biomedical engineering concerned with the interrelationship between behavioral and biological processes. Conducts research including the evaluation of biofeedback in the treatment of disease states. Maintains historical archives. Conducts workshops. **Publications:** *Psychophysiology*, bimonthly.

★7519★ Society for Psychosomatic Research (SPR)
Springfield Hospital
61 Glenburnie Rd.
London SW17 7DJ, England
Phone: 181 6729911
Fax: 181 7677608
Dr. Barry Matthews, Sec.

Founded: 1955. **Members:** 130. **Languages:** English. **Description:** Physicians, psychiatrists, psychologists, and other professionals interested in psychosomatic medicine. Seeks to encourage research in the field. Bestows awards; sponsors competitions, monthly discussions, and lectures.

★7520★ Society for Stress and Anxiety Research (STAR)
Psychometrics Unit
Univ. of Bergen
Sydnesplass 13
N-5007 Bergen, Norway
Phone: 55212469
Fax: 55231977
Dr. Tom Backer Johnsen, Sec.

Founded: 1980. **Members:** 300. **Languages:** English. **Description:** Psychologists from 22 countries studying the phenomenon of test anxiety. Conducts research on anxiety, with particular emphasis on test anxiety and related problems; encourages cooperation among members; promotes understanding among scholars with similar research interests. **Publications:** *Advances in Test Anxiety Research*, biennial. • *Newsletter*, semiannual. Newsletter. • *Yearbook*. **Formerly:** Society for Test Anxiety Research.

Special Constituency Section for Psychiatric and Substance Abuse Services (SCSMHPS)
See: Entry 6473

★7521★ Special Interest Group on Phobias and Related Anxiety Disorders (SIGPRAD)
c/o Carol Lindemann, Ph.D.
245 E. 87th St.
New York, NY 10028
Phone: (212)860-5560
Fax: (212)744-5751
Carol Lindemann, Ph.D., Chair

Founded: 1982. **Members:** 50. **Description:** Psychologists, psychiatrists, social workers, and other individuals interested in treatment of anxiety disorders. Objectives are to increase knowledge and expertise and facilitate communication regarding research and treatment of phobias and related anxiety disorders. Conducts programs at professional meetings.

★7522★ Standing Liaison Committee of Physiotherapists within the EC (SLCP) (Comite Permanent de Liaison des Kinesitherapeutes de la CE — CPLK)
24 High St.
Henley-in-Arden, W. Midlands B95 5AN, England
Phone: 1564 792751
Fax: 1564 795008
Julia Botteley, Gen.Sec.

Founded: 1979. **Members:** 12. **Languages:** English, French. **Description:** Associations of physiotherapists in European Economic Community countries. Coordinates professional standards and regulations affecting physiotherapists in member countries; promotes liaison with organizations having similar interests. **Publications:** *Physiotherapy Education in the European Community*. Book.

★7523★ Stop Abuse by Counselors (STOP ABC)
PO Box 68292
Seattle, WA 98168
Phone: (206)243-2723
Fax: (206)243-2723
Shirley Siegel, Coord.

Founded: 1981. **Members:** 2,500. **Description:** Consumer advocacy organization working to prevent abuse and exploitation of individuals by mental health practitioners. Assists and maintains a supportive network for persons who believe they have been victimized by mental health practitioners or unethical counseling practices. Fosters community awareness through the media, workshops, educational forums, and presentations. Participates in research into unethical counseling practices; works to determine the extent of unethical conduct and to identify types of abuse. Sponsors education on potential problems in counseling relationships and ways to select a counselor. Encourages victims to complain to licensing boards and employers or to initiate civil and criminal legal action when appropriate; develops and lobbies for remedial legislation. Urges organizations and individual mental health practitioners to develop or improve ethical practice standards. Maintains referral list of attorneys. Maintains speakers' bureau. **Publications:** *What to Do When Psychotherapy Goes Wrong*. Book. *Price:* $11.95. Also makes available how-to kits for organizing a consumer advocacy group, lists of attorneys, and catalog of clippings held by STOP ABC.

★ 7524 ★ Suicide Information and Education Centre (SIEC)
1615 10th Ave. SW, Ste. 201
Calgary, AB, Canada T3C 0J7
Phone: (403)245-3900
Fax: (403)245-0299
Karen Kiddey, Library Coord.

Founded: 1982. **Languages:** English. **Description:** Information center whose users include researchers, educators, students, health care professionals, social service agencies, librarians, and the general public. Obtains and provides access to a comprehensive collection of English language documents on suicide and suicidal behaviors. Provides information to teachers and guidance counselors on specific topics such as adolescent suicide and bereavement. Compiles statistics. **Publications:** *Current Awareness Bulletin*, quarterly. Bulletin. • *Selected Readings on Elderly Suicide*. • *SIEC Thesaurus of Subject Terms*, periodic. • *Youth Suicide Audio Visual Catalog*. Also publishes information on suicide attempts.

★ 7525 ★ Swaziland National Association of Mental Health
Office No. IB, 2nd Fl.
Liahaga House
Manzini, Swaziland
Phone: 52889
Fax: 55300
Dr. T.M. Malepe

Members: 200. **Description:** Works to improve the welfare of mental health patients. Supports research on the causes of and cure for mental illness. Raises public awareness about the facts of mental health; disseminates information. **Publications:** *Alcoholic Family and the Waiting Syndrome*. Book. • *Mental Health and the Gifted Child*. Book. • *Organised Violence*. Book. • *Rape and Its Psychological Traumas*. Book. • *Rape and the Law*. Book. • *Single Parented Children's Problems*. Book.

★ 7526 ★ Swedish Society of Analytical Trilogy (SSAT)
(Svenska Sallskapet for Analytisk Trilogi — SSAT)
Stockholmsvagen 22
S-122 32 Enskede, Sweden
Phone: 8 395187
Suely Keppe Simula, Pres.

Founded: 1986. **Members:** 80. **Languages:** English, Finnish, Portuguese, Swedish. **Description:** Promotes the application of analytical trilogy to all professions. (Analytical trilogy, or integral psychoanalysis, was developed by Dr. Norberto Keppe. The trilogy represents feeling, thought, and action.) Analytical trilogy is a method of psychoanalytic treatment and care for psychosomatic illness. Sponsors a socioeconomic development project in which workers own their workplaces and live in group trilogical residences. **Publications:** *Integral Psychoanalysis*, annual. Magazine.

★ 7527 ★ Well Spouse Foundation (WSF)
PO Box 801
New York, NY 10023
Phone: (212)724-7209
Free: 800-838-0879
Fax: (212)724-5209
Patricia Still, Exec.Dir.

Founded: 1988. **Members:** 2,600. **Local Groups:** 70. **Description:** Husbands, wives, and partners of chronically ill patients. An emotional support network functioning to raise public consciousness about and advocate for the caregivers and families of the chronically ill. Establishes local support groups and supplies information and materials. Compiles statistics; conducts educational programs. **Publications:** *Mainstay*, bimonthly. Newsletter. Contains membership news and information, advocacy issues, and helpful hints. *Price:* Included in membership dues. **Formerly:** National Well Spouse Foundation.

★ 7528 ★ Women in Transition (WIT)
21 S. 12th St., 6th Fl.
Philadelphia, PA 19107
Phone: (215)564-5301
Fax: (215)564-5723
Roberta L. Hacker, Exec.Dir.

Founded: 1971. **Description:** Offers support groups for abused women and women recovering from substance abuse problems. Provides outreach, assessment, and referrals to women with drug and/or alcohol addiction; makes available individual, and family counseling. Trains facilitators for selfhelp support groups. Offers consultation and training to mental health and social service agency personnel. Maintains speakers' bureau. **Publications:** Annual Report. • *Child Support: How You Can Obtain and Enforce Support Orders*. • *Facilitator's Guide to Working with Separated and Divorced Women*. • *Stepping Out to Work: A Facilitator's Guide*. • *Volunteer Newsletter*, periodic. Newsletter.

★ 7529 ★ World Association for Dynamic Psychiatry (WADP)
Dynamic-Psychiatric Clinic
Geiselgasteigstrasse 203
Menterschwaige
81545 Munich, Germany
Phone: 89 644015
Fax: 89 646922
Maria Ammon, Contact

Founded: 1980. **Members:** 500. **National Groups:** 22. **Languages:** English, German. **Description:** Disseminates the theory and practice of dynamic psychiatry developed at Gunter Ammon's Berlin School of Dynamic Psychiatry. Fosters and creates opportunities for dynamic psychiatry study in universities and other institutions. Promotes continuous advanced training in dynamic psychiatry for better patient care and improvement of public health. Conducts research into disease prevention, therapeutic method efficiency, and education standards; disseminates results. **Publications:** *Dynamische Psychiatrie/Dynamic Psychiatry*, bimonthly. • *WADP*, semiannual. Newsletter.

World Association for Infant Mental Health (WAIMH)
See: Entry 3306

★ 7530 ★ World Association for Psychosocial Rehabilitation, U.S. Branch (WAPR)
c/o Dr. Zedulon Taintor
Manhattan Psychiatric Center
Wards Island
New York, NY 10035
Phone: (212)369-0500
Dr. Zedulon Taintor, Pres.

Founded: 1987. **Members:** 500. **Description:** Professionals in the mental health field concerned with research, study, and training in psychosocial rehabilitation. (Psychosocial rehabilitation assists individuals whose primary problems or pathologies are related to psychiatric dysfunctions that limit their social, personal, or occupational functioning.) Conducts research and educational programs; maintains speakers' bureau and placement services. **Publications:** *Bulletin WAPR*, periodic. Bulletin. *Price:* Free, for members only. • *International Journal of Mental Health*, quarterly. Journal. *Price:* $50 to members. • Newsletter, periodic.

★ 7531 ★ World Association for Social Psychiatry (WASP)
656 Romero Cannon Rd.
Santa Barbara, CA 93108
Phone: (805)969-1376
Fax: (805)969-1376
John L. Carleton, M.D., Honorary Pres.

Founded: 1964. **Members:** 3,000. **Regional Groups:** 26. **Description:** Professionals, contributors, and interested individuals active in allied fields of social psychiatry including anthropology, social work, nursing, or occupational therapy. Objectives are to: study the nature of man and his surrounding culture; research methods to prevent and treat internal changes and behavioral disorders; advance the physical, social, and philosophic well-being of mankind. Fosters collaboration among members and distributes theoretical and practical information. Conducts workshops and demonstrations of rehabilitation centers. **Publications:** *French Journal of Social Psychiatry*, quarterly. Journal. • *International Journal of Social Psychiatry*, quarterly. Journal. **Formerly:** (1978) International Association for Social Psychiatry.

★ 7532 ★ World Federation for Mental Health (WFMH)
1021 Prince St.
Alexandria, VA 22314
Phone: (703)838-7543
Fax: (703)684-5968
Eugene B. Brody, M.D., Sec.Gen.

Founded: 1948. **Members:** 2,800. **Description:** Associations and individuals dedicated to achieving the highest level of public mental health. Objectives include charitable, scientific, literary, and educational activities in the field of mental health. Organizes training programs. **Publications:** Newsletter, 5/year. **Formerly:** (1948) International Committee for Mental Hygiene.

World Federation of the Societies of Biological Psychiatry (WFSBP)
See: Entry 2548

★7533★ World Psychiatric Association (WPA)
(Weltverband fur Psychiatrie)
Clinica Lopez Ibor
Avenida Nueva Zelanda 44
E-28035 Madrid, Spain
Phone: 1 3737361
Fax: 1 3162749
Pelice Ileh Mak, Pres.

Founded: 1961. **Members:** 465. **Regional Groups:** 7. **Languages:** English, French, German, Spanish. **Description:** Psychiatric societies and individuals in 90 countries. Objectives are: to promote international cooperation in the field of psychiatry; to advance inquiry into the etiology, pathology, and treatment of mental illness; to strengthen relations among psychiatrists working in various fields. Encourages the exchange of information concerning the medical problems of mental diseases; sponsors educational and research programs. Comprises 27 sections representing different specialties in psychiatry. **Publications:** *Communique*, quarterly. Magazine. • *WPA Bulletin*, quarterly. Bulletin.

★7534★ Youth Suicide Prevention (YSP)
11 Parkman Way
Needham, MA 02192-2863
Phone: (617)738-0700
Fax: (617)566-1423
Pamela Cantor, Ph.D., Exec.Dir.

Founded: 1984. **State Groups:** 49. **Description:** Volunteer network of concerned parents, professionals, and government officials. Works to: increase public awareness of youth suicide; publicize the warning signals preceding suicide attempts; establish a national information and referral system; acquire, organize, and disseminate current information to parents, educators, and professionals; assist in the development of youth suicide prevention programs in local communities, schools, and mental health centers. Encourages federal involvement in studying youth suicide and implementing youth suicide prevention programs. Sponsors interdisciplinary professional conferences. Maintains speakers' bureau; compiles statistics. **Publications:** *Young People in Crisis: How You Can Help.* **Formerly:** (1992) National Committee on Youth Suicide Prevention.

★7535★ Zimbabwe National Association for Mental Health
PO Box A 196
Avondale
Harare, Zimbabwe
Phone: 4 792946
Mrs. L. Tsomondo, Information Officer

Members: 150. **Description:** Works to educate and rehabilitate the mentally ill. Informs the public about mental health issues. **Publications:** Newsletter, quarterly. • Video. Pamphlets and handbooks on mental health.

Research Centers

★7536★ Ackerman Institute for Family Therapy
149 E. 78th St.
New York, NY 10021
Phone: (212)879-4900
Fax: (212)744-0206
Peter Steinglass, M.D., Exec.Dir.

Research Activities and Fields: Cancer and other chronic illnesses, catastrophic illness, AIDS/AIDS-Related Complex (ARC), school problems, women's issues, family violence, stressful life events, family life cycle issues, family factors in psychiatric disorders, alcoholism, and drug abuse. Also studies family factors in psychiatric disorders. **E-mail Address:** PSTEINGL@LIFE.JSC.NASA.GOV (Lifenet).

★7537★ American Institute for Biosocial Research, Inc.
PO Box 1174
Tacoma, WA 98401-1174
Phone: (206)922-0448
Fax: (206)922-0479
Rebecca Paulson, Contact

Research Activities and Fields: Behavioral science, including eating disorders, abnormal behavior, learning disabilities, and behavior disorders; mental illness; psychology; sociology; and criminology.

★7538★ American Institute of Stress
124 Park Ave.
Yonkers, NY 10703
Phone: (914)963-1200
Fax: (914)965-6267
Paul J. Rosch, M.D., Pres.

Research Activities and Fields: Personal and social effects of stress, including stress and cancer, stress and hypertension, stress-related sudden death, job stress, stress and women, technostress, statistics on stress-related subjects, workers' compensation for stress claims, stress and heart attacks, and gastrointestinal and skin disorders. **Publications:** Newsletter (monthly).

★7539★ Aurora Mental Health Research Institute
14301 E. Hampden Ave.
Aurora, CO 80014
Phone: (303)693-9500
Fax: (303)680-0104
Dr. Randy C. Stith, Dir. of Research

Research Activities and Fields: Community-based mental health services and the support systems they require. Provides technical assistance to private and public agencies with special emphasis on person-machine issues relating to microcomputer and mainframe computers.

★7540★ Autism Research Institute
4182 Adams Ave.
San Diego, CA 92116
Phone: (619)281-7165
Fax: (619)563-6840
Dr. Bernard Rimland, Dir.

Research Activities and Fields: Causes and treatment of severe behavior disorders in children, particularly autism. Conducts computerized analyses of its diagnostic reports on individual children with severe behavior disorders, and studies the relationship between nutrition and learning and behavior disorders. Serves as an international clearinghouse of information on autism, disseminating information to parents, researchers, hospitals, schools, and professional practitioners. **Publications:** *Autism Research Review International* (quarterly). **Formerly:** Institute for Child Behavior Research (1990).

★7541★ Bellefaire
22001 Fairmount Blvd.
Cleveland, OH 44118
Phone: (216)932-2800
Fax: (216)932-6704
Dr. Adam G. Jacob, Dir. of Research

Research Activities and Fields: Evaluates programs serving children, particularly residential treatment for emotionally disturbed adolescents. Areas of interest include child and family description, child diagnosis and assessment issues, child progress in treatment, and child functioning after discharge. Studies include the Odessey Project, an outcome study of residential treatment and foster care placement; and outcome studies on client satisfaction on managed care.

★7542★ Boston University
Center for Psychiatric Rehabilitation
Sargent College
730 Commonwealth Ave.
Boston, MA 02215
Phone: (617)353-3549
Fax: (617)353-7700
Kathy Norman, Contact

Research Activities and Fields: Personnel, programmatic, and systems issues in the delivery of services to persons with psychiatric disabilities, including the model case management approaches, consumer-controlled methodology for evaluation of user-run programs, impact of setting self-determined rehabilitation goals, and the characteristics and the outcomes of young adults with severe psychiatric disabilities. **Formerly:** Center for Rehabilitation Research and Training in Mental Health (1986).

Boston University
Laboratory of Neuropsychology
See: Entry 8336

C.M. Hincks Institute
See: Entry 3315

★7543★ Calgary WHO Centre for Research and Training in Mental Health
Dept. of Psychiatry
Calgary General Hosp.
841 Centre Ave. E.
Calgary, AB, Canada T2E 0A1
Phone: (403)268-9202
Fax: (403)268-9201
Dr. J. Arboleda-Florez, Dir.

Research Activities and Fields: Interdisciplinary studies in forensic psychiatry, psychiatric epidemiology, psychopharmacology, and occupational therapy and rehabilitation. **E-mail Address:** arboledj@acs.ucalgary.ca.

Camille Cosby Ambulatory Care Center
See: Entry 3316

★7544★ Canadian Center for Torture Victims
25 Merton
Toronto, ON, Canada M4S 1A2
Phone: (416)480-0489
Fax: (416)480-1984
Dr. Mulugera Abai, Exec.Dir.

Research Activities and Fields: Treatment of victims of political violence and torture from around the world, with emphasis on survivor therapy and post-traumatic stress syndrome. **Publications:** *CCVT Newsletter.* **Formerly:** Canadian Center for the Investigation and Prevention of Torture.

★7545★ Carrier Foundation
Division of Research
PO Box 147
Belle Mead, NJ 08502
Phone: (908)281-1394
Fax: (908)874-4439
Helen M. Pettinati, Ph.D., Dir.

Research Activities and Fields: Psychiatric research and clinical studies of psychopathology, including research on adolescents, substance abuse, aging, memory and attention disorders, depression, electroconvulsive therapy, and psychopharmacology. Conducts follow-up and evaluation studies. **Publications:** *Carrier Foundation Letter* (monthly).

Center for Addiction and Behavioral Health Research
See: Entry 12090

★7546★ Center for Advanced Study in Behavioral Sciences
202 Junipero Serra Blvd.
Stanford, CA 94305
Phone: (415)321-2052
Fax: (415)321-1192
Dr. Philip E. Converse, Dir.

Research Activities and Fields: Behavioral sciences, humanities, and biomedicine, including psychology, anthropology, sociology, political science, history, economics, philosophy, psychiatry, literature, law, education, linguistics, and certain areas of statistics, with 46-48 fellows accommodated each year. Fellows pursue individual research and writing programs or participate in formal and informal collaborative activities. **Publications:** Monographs; Annual Report; Bibliography of Ralph W. Tyler Collection.

★7547★ Center for Family Learning
28 Rye Ridge Plaza
Rye Brook, NY 10573
Phone: (914)253-9190
Fax: (914)253-9192
Philip J. Guerin, Jr., M.D., Dir.

Research Activities and Fields: Family, including studies in the areas of children and adolescents, marriage, divorce, parent-child relations, behavior problems, depression and anxiety, substance abuse, and critical and chronic illness.

★7548★ Center for Modern Psychoanalytic Studies
16 W. 10th St.
New York, NY 10011
Phone: (212)260-7050
Fax: (212)260-7052
Dr. Phyllis W. Meadow, Dean

Research Activities and Fields: Psychoanalytic research, focusing on single-case phenomena surrounding the theory and technique of modern psychoanalysis. **Publications:** *Modern Psychoanalysis* (semiannual journal). **Formerly:** Manhattan Center for Advanced Psychoanalytic Studies (1976).

Center on the Organization and Financing of Care for the Severely Mentally Ill
See: Entry 5614

★7549★ Center for Psychoanalytic Study
618 S. Michigan
Chicago, IL 60605
Phone: (312)337-8000
Fax: (708)446-6886
Gertrude Pollitt, Exec.Dir.

Research Activities and Fields: Psychoanalytic theory, including psychotherapy. Examines treatments of neurosis and narcissism, borderline disorders, schizophrenic disorders, sexual dysfunction, eating disorders, substance abuse, depression, and antisocial behaviors. **Publications:** Newsletter.

★7550★ Center for the Research and Treatment of Anorexia Nervosa
10921 Wilshire Blvd., Ste. 702
Los Angeles, CA 90024
Phone: (213)824-5881
Dr. Burt Crausman, Ph.D., Dir.

Research Activities and Fields: Anorexia nervosa and other eating disorders, including research into their causes, detection, and treatment.

★7551★ Center for the Study of Anorexia and Bulimia
1 W. 91st St.
New York, NY 10024
Phone: (212)595-3449
Fax: (212)595-9301
Jane B. Supino, Exec.Dir.

Research Activities and Fields: Clinical and empirical studies on the prevalence, demography, etiology, and treatment of anorexia and bulimia, and compulsive eating. **Publications:** Pamphlets and curriculum guides.

★7552★ Chestnut Lodge Research Institute
500 W. Montgomery Ave.
Rockville, MD 20850
Phone: (301)424-8300
Fax: (301)309-0915
Wayne S. Fenton, M.D., Dir.

Research Activities and Fields: Psychopharmacology, schizophrenia, mental health services, hospital care, and forms of treatment course and outcome of major mental disorders.

★7553★ Children's Psychopharmacology Unit
New York University Medical Center
Psychiatry Dept.
550 1st Ave.
New York, NY 10016
Phone: (212)263-6206
Fax: (212)263-8135
Dr. Magda Campbell, Dir.

Research Activities and Fields: Children and psychopharmacology, psychopharmacology in autism, and aggression.

★7554★ Clark University
Heinz Werner Institute for Developmental Analysis
950 Main St.
Worcester, MA 01610
Phone: (508)793-7278
Fax: (508)793-7289
Dr. Seymour Wapner, Exec. Committee Chair

Research Activities and Fields: Behavior from viewpoint of psychological development, including studies on normal and abnormal development of behavior, covering periods of infancy, adolescence, adulthood, and old age. Through a holistic program, also studies microgenesis, pathology, as well as political, economic, religious, technological, aesthetic, and legal conditions affecting psychological development. **Publications:** Heinz Werner Institute Monograph Series. **E-mail Address:** swapner@vax.clarku.edu. **Formerly:** Originally known as Institute of Human Development, then Heinz Werner Institute of Developmental Psychology (1986).

★7555★ Columbia University
Center for Psychoanalytic Training and Research
722 W. 168th St.
New York, NY 10032
Phone: (212)927-5000
Roger A. MacKinnon, Dir.

Research Activities and Fields: Theory and practice of psychoanalysis, including projects in psychosomatic illness, gender identity, body image disorders, anorexia nervosa, male and female sexuality, infant development, dreams, character organization, ego strength, esthetics, creativity, fantasy, psychobiography, literature, and the influence of culture on personality.

★7556★ Dave Garroway Laboratory for the Study of Depression
111 N. 49th St.
Pennsylvania Hospital
Philadelphia, PA 19139
Phone: (215)471-2584
Fax: (215)471-2893
Alan M. Gruenberg, M.D., Dir.

Research Activities and Fields: Longitudinal studies of depression, including recurring depression, anxiety, and personality disorders in individuals with major depression. Examines predictors of recurrence, objective and subjective measures of symptom severity, and patient vulnerability. Applies multiperspective approach, including biological, behavioral, social, interpersonal, psychoanalytical, and cognitive aspects of depression. **Publications:** *Archives of General Psychiatry; American Journal of Psychiatry; Psychiatry Research.*

★ 7557 ★ DePaul University
DePaul Community Health Center
2219 N. Kenmore Ave.
Chicago, IL 60614
Phone: (312)362-8292
Della Corirossi, L.C.S., Dir.

Research Activities and Fields: Brief psychotherapy and group psychotherapy. **Formerly:** Mental Health Clinic; Mental Health Community Center.

★ 7558 ★ Duke University
Anxiety and Traumatic Stress Program
Medical Center
Box 3812
Durham, NC 27710
Phone: (919)684-2880
Fax: (919)684-8866
Dr. Jonathan Davidson, Program Dir.

Research Activities and Fields: Activities focus on diagnosis and treatment of anxiety disorders, including panic disorder, agoraphobia, social phobias, Post-Traumatic Stress Disorder (PTSD), obsessive-compulsive disorder (OCD), and generalized anxiety. **Formerly:** Anxiety Disorders Program.

★ 7559 ★ Duke University
Behavioral Medicine Research Center
Duke Medical Center
PO Box 3926
Durham, NC 27710
Phone: (919)684-3863
Fax: (919)681-8960
Dr. Redford Williams, Dir.

Research Activities and Fields: Behavior, including emotional stress and personality factors as they affect physical diseases with emphasis on coronary disease and cancer. Uses epidemiological and experimental approaches.

★ 7560 ★ Eastern Washington University
Behavioral Medicine Laboratory
Mail Stop 94
526 5th St.
Cheney, WA 99004-2431
Phone: (509)359-7041
Fax: (509)359-6927
William A. Greene, Ph.D., Dir.

Research Activities and Fields: Psychophysiology and behavioral medicine, including physiological profiles of Type A personality, hypochondriasis, and fitness and stress control. **E-mail Address:** wgreene@ewuvms.edu. **Formerly:** Psychophysiology and Stress Laboratory (1987); Laboratory of Applied Physiology (1989).

★ 7561 ★ Eating Disorders Research & Treatment Program
Michael Reese Hospital & Medical Center
2929 S. Ellis Ave.
Chicago, IL 60616
Phone: (312)791-3800
Fax: (312)791-8060
Robert Jespersen, Dir. of Biological Psychiatry

Research Activities and Fields: Eating disorders, particularly anorexia nervosa and bulimia nervosa, and major affective disorders, particularly depression. Conducts studies on prognostic factors, epidemiology, personality dimensions, neuroendocrine regulation, energy expenditure, family interaction patterns, and genetic factors.

★ 7562 ★ Fairleigh Dickinson University
Psychological Research Center
131 Temple Ave.
Hackensack, NJ 07601
Phone: (201)692-2645
Dr. Charles Schaefer, Dir.

Research Activities and Fields: Problems of a psychological nature in children and adolescents, including depression, stress management, neuropsychological research and evaluation, and problem-solving skills. Conducts institutional research, including studies on a crying baby clinic, play therapy, sleep disorders, and hyperactivity.

★ 7563 ★ Family Institute
618 Library Pl.
Evanston, IL 60201
Phone: (708)733-4300
Fax: (708)733-0390
Petra A. Garrison

Research Activities and Fields: Adoption issues, death and mourning, anorexia, schizophrenia, dysfunctional families, ethnic issues, and family, marital, divorce, step-family, and adolescent therapy.

★ 7564 ★ Fordham University
Hispanic Research Center
Thebaud Hall
Bronx, NY 10458
Phone: (718)579-2629
Fax: (718)365-1591
Orlando Rodriguez, Dir.

Research Activities and Fields: Policy-oriented research focusing on mental health of Hispanic populations in United States and Puerto Rico, including emergence of mental health problems, utilization of mental health services, assessment of mental health, and therapeutic modalities and post-treatment rehabilitation tailored to Hispanic population. **E-mail Address:** rodrigul@murray.fordham.edu.

★ 7565 ★ Foundation for Behavioral Research
600 S. Lincoln St.
Augusta, MI 49012
Phone: (616)731-5775
Ronald R. Hutchinson, Ph.D., Dir.

Research Activities and Fields: Investigates principles of behavior, environmental causes of emotion, psychopharmacology, and early childhood education.

★ 7566 ★ Hofstra University
Psychological Evaluation and Research Center
Community Services Center
Hempstead, NY 11550
Phone: (516)463-5660
Fax: (516)565-0084
Joseph R. Scardapane, Ph.D., Dir.

Research Activities and Fields: Collection and analysis of data in the fields of psychology and mental health with a view toward refining services in educational, behavioral, personality, or adjustment problems. Services provided include psychological evaluation, intellectual evaluation, and treatment and remediation programs, which include anxiety management training, behavioral/educational counseling, behavior therapy, rational emotive psychotherapy, family and marriage counseling, and counseling for abused adults. Services are also offered in Spanish.

★ 7567 ★ Human Factor Programs Ltd.
18062 Irvine Blvd. Ste. 200
Tustin, CA 92680-3328
Phone: (714)505-0873
Dr. Victor Huckell, Dir.

Research Activities and Fields: Integration of psychological, social, physiological, and organizational factors in human behavior. **Publications:** *Bulletin of Human Factor Programs* and Monographs.

Human Services Research Institute
See: Entry 4312

★ 7568 ★ Illinois State Psychiatric Institute
1601 West Tayaor
Chicago, IL 60612
Phone: (312)433-8300
Fax: (312)433-8474
Dr. Morris, Dir.

Research Activities and Fields: Psychological and biological factors associated with schizophrenia and major depression and mania, drug trials, brain imaging (PET, MRI, EEG, and ERP), genetic vulnerability, neurotransmitter receptor studies, and information processing studies. Prior to assignment to a research protocol, patients may undergo a drug-free washout period lasting from 3 to 14 days. New research initiatives in dual diagnosis (mental illness and substance abuse) and in delivery of services for the mentally ill.

Indiana University
Neuropsychology Research Section
See: Entry 8374

★ 7569 ★ Indiana University-Purdue
    University at Indianapolis
Institute of Psychiatric Research
Sch. of Medicine
Dept. of Psychiatry
791 Union Dr.
Indianapolis, IN 46202-4887
Phone: (317)274-8382
Fax: (317)274-4394
John I. Nurnberger, Jr., M.D., Dir.

Research Activities and Fields: Basic and applied clinical research dealing with psychiatric disorders in the fields of neurochemistry, neuropharmacology, behavioral and clinical neurobiology, and molecular genetics, including investigations of neurotransmitters and metabolites in the central nervous system and in bodily fluids of laboratory animals and psychiatric patients.

Indiana University-Purdue University at Indianapolis
Riley Child Psychiatry Clinic
See: Entry 3339

★7570★ **Institute for Families and Children**
200 Church St.
New York, NY 10013
Phone: (212)233-5051
Fax: (212)233-5183
Douglas O'Dell, Exec.Dir.

Research Activities and Fields: Mental health of children, focusing on treatment and service issues regarding children and families. **Formerly:** Institute for Child Mental Health (1991).

★7571★ **Institute for Labor & Mental Health**
3137 Telegraph Ave.
Oakland, CA 94609
Phone: (510)528-9116
Fax: (510)528-2810
Abby Ginsberg, Assoc.Dir.

Research Activities and Fields: Working class people and mental health, including social support as a buffer to stress. Also conducts stress questionnaire surveys.

Institute on Mental Disability and the Law
See: Entry 7206

★7572★ **Institute for Psychoanalysis**
Chicago Institute
180 N. Michigan Ave.
Chicago, IL 60601
Phone: (312)726-6300
Fax: (312)726-6761
Dr. Thomas Pappadis, Dir.

Research Activities and Fields: Psychoanalysis, psychosomatic medicine, psychiatry, and related behavioral sciences. Topics of interest include parent loss, mourning, and creativity. **Publications:** *Annual of Pychoanalysis*; *Classics in Psychoanalysis*; *Emotions and Behavior Monographs*.

★7573★ **Institute for Psychosomatic and Psychiatric Research and Training**
Michael Reese Hospital & Medical Center
2929 S. Ellis Ave.
Chicago, IL 60616
Phone: (312)791-3877
Fax: (312)567-6251
Dr. Harry J. Soloway, Chief of Services

Research Activities and Fields: Mental health and mental illness, its etiology, treatment, and prevention, including psychiatry, psychophysiology, clinical psychology, and neurophysiology. Studies ego functions, schizophrenia, the modal adolescent, normal and disturbed adolescents, family dynamics, and comparison of scales of manifest anxiety. Conducts biological and clinical investigations of eating disorders, affective disorder in children and adolescence, patterns of self-image in normal, delinquent, and disturbed adolescents, and the psychosomatic aspects of juvenile diabetes.

★7574★ **Institute for Rational-Emotive Therapy**
45 E. 65th St.
New York, NY 10021
Phone: (212)535-0822
Fax: (212)249-3582
Dr. Albert Ellis, Pres.

Research Activities and Fields: Rational-emotive therapy and cognitive behavior therapy.

Publications: *Journal of Rational-Emotive and Cognitive-Behavior Therapy* (quarterly). **Formerly:** Institute for Rational Living (1981); Institute for Advanced Study in Rational Psychotherapy (1982).

★7575★ **Institutes for Behavior Resources, Inc.**
Francis Scott Key Medical Center
Triad Technology Ctr., Ste. 2200
333 Cassell Dr.
Baltimore, MD 21224
Phone: (410)550-3546
Fax: (410)550-3545
Joseph V. Brady, Ph.D., Pres.

Research Activities and Fields: Behavioral science, including basic studies on human behavior with extensions to controlled alterations of behavior in clinical, social, and educational settings. Conducts applied studies in drug abuse, human performance, law and behavior, and social problems and evaluates educational, training, and management systems.

★7576★ **International Association for Psychiatric Research**
Box 457
St. James, NY 11780
Phone: (516)444-2990
Fax: (516)862-8604
Dr. Max Fink, Exec.Dir.

Research Activities and Fields: Psychiatric investigation, including clinical studies on effects of drugs and seizures on human behavior. Supports ongoing studies at different laboratories, usually on a collaborative basis between institutions and Association personnel. **Publications:** *Convulsive Therapy* (quarterly scientific journal).

★7577★ **Iowa State University of Science and Technology**
Center for Family Research in Rural Mental Health
2625 N. Loop Dr., Ste. 500
Ames, IA 50010-8296
Phone: (515)294-4518
Fax: (515)294-3613
Rand Conger, Dir.

Research Activities and Fields: Investigates physical and emotional consequences associated with rapid socioeconomic changes in rural areas, particularly factors that promote tobacco, alcohol, and illicit drug use; and identifies new procedures for effectively delivering illness-prevention and self-help programs to rural people. Developing a coordinated research program on farm safety, focusing on livestock confinement operations, machinery use, grain handling, and chemicals in cooperation with the Department of Agricultural Engineering. Projects include studying economic strain, social support, and rural single-parent families; examining how economic stress affects rural adolescents' decisions to experiment with potentially dangerous behaviors, including substance abuse, smoking, and sex; investigating methods to help distinguish environmental influences from genetic influences in mental and behavioral disorders; and evaluating the effectiveness of family and community drug abuse prevention. **Publications:** Annual Report.

Judge David L. Bazelon Center for Mental Health Law
See: Entry 7207

★7578★ **Laval University**
Medical Research Centre
Mental Health Research Group
2725, boulevard Chemin
Ste. Foy, PQ, Canada G1V 4G5
Phone: (418)656-4790
Fax: (418)654-2166
Hughes Cormier, Dir.

Research Activities and Fields: Schizophrenic and affective disorders, evaluation of community support and psychiatric rehabilitation programs, and a clinical trial of self-help programs for schizophrenic patients.

★7579★ **Laval University**
Robert-Giffard Research Centre
2601, chemin de la Canardiere
Beauport, PQ, Canada G1J 2G3
Phone: (418)663-5741
Fax: (418)663-9540
Michel Maziade, Dir.

Research Activities and Fields: Mental disorders, including Alzheimer's disease, bipolar disorders, and autism. Center searches for diagnostics and treatments for neurological and psychiatric disorders, and works to identify susceptible genes by identifying and characterizing a linkage marker. Specific program includes the mapping and characterization of major genes that result in schizophrenia and mental depression.

★7580★ **Maryland Psychiatric Research Center**
Box 21247
Catonsville, MD 21228
Dr. William T. Carpenter, Jr., Dir.

Research Activities and Fields: Etiology and treatment of chronic schizophrenia and other major affective disorders, including assessment of therapeutic efficacy of treatment, design of safer approaches to antipsychotic and other drug treatments, definition of subgroups of patients to permit clinicians to match patients and treatments, design and implementation of experimental treatments, and assessment of the impact of family on the course of illness. Neuroscience program studies brain mechanisms involved in the causes, manifestations, and treatment of mental illness. Provides clinical and diagnostic services and education for families and patients.

★7581★ **Medical College of Pennsylvania and Hahnemann University**
Eastern Pennsylvania Psychiatric Institute
3200 Henry Ave.
Philadelphia, PA 19129
Phone: (215)842-4000
Fax: (215)843-7384
Charlotte C. Yoder, Asst.V.P.

Research Activities and Fields: Neurosciences, mental health, and pharmacology, including basic, clinical, and applied studies on etiology and treatment modalities in mental disability, mental health of normal children, and prevention of mental disorders. Provides residency training programs and training for psychologists, social service workers, student nurses, and occupational therapists at both undergraduate and graduate levels.

**Medical University of South Carolina
Crime Victims Research and Treatment
  Center (CVC)**
See: Entry 7210

**★7582★ Menninger Clinic
Department of Research**
Box 829
Topeka, KS 66601
Phone: (913)273-7500
Fax: (913)273-8625
Dr. Herbert E. Spohn, Dir.

Research Activities and Fields: Mental health and illness from an interdisciplinary perspective, presently focused on three major content areas: behavior genetics, experimental psychopathology of schizophrenia, and treatment outcome research. **Publications:** Monographs; *Bulletin of the Menninger Clinic* (bimonthly).

**★7583★ Mental Health Clinical Research
  Center for Schizophrenia and Psychiatric
  Rehabilitation**
VA Medical Center-Brentwood (B117)
Wilshire & Sawtelle Blvds.
Los Angeles, CA 90073
Phone: (310)794-2638
Fax: (310)824-3173
Dr. Robert P. Liberman, Dir.

Research Activities and Fields: Clinical research to improve understanding of the etiology and course of schizophrenia and treatment methods for intervention and rehabilitation of individuals diagnosed with schizophrenic disorders. Research is conducted in core laboratories, units, and projects united by a common vulnerability/stress conception of schizophrenia and guided by a multilevel study of environmental, psychological, and biological variables. Focuses on rehabilitation of mental patients to enable them to return to the mainstream of everyday life, determination of factors related to the vulnerability of individuals to psychosis, determination of factors related to relapse and recovery in schizophrenia, studies of social skills training, and antipsychotic drug treatment. **Publications:** Technical Manuals; Videos; Materials Catalogs. **E-mail Address:** idh9rpl@mvs.oac.ucla.edu. **Formerly:** Mental Health Clinical Research Center for the Study of Schizophrenia.

**★7584★ Mid-Missouri Mental Health
  Center**
3 Hospital Dr.
Columbia, MO 65201
Phone: (314)449-2511
Mark Stansberry, Supt.

Research Activities and Fields: Children's services, including biochemistry and epidemiology of childhood hyperkinesis and depression, violence in the family and forensic implications, and chronic mental illness. **Publications:** *Journal of Operational Psychiatry* (semiannually).

**★7585★ Mount Sinai School of Medicine
of City University of New York
Schizophrenic Biologic Research Center**
VA Medical Center
Psychiatry Service, 116A
130 W. Kingsbridge Rd.
Bronx, NY 10468
Phone: (718)579-1633
Fax: (212)933-2121
Michael Davidson, M.D., Dir.

Research Activities and Fields: Investigates the etiology of schizophrenia, particularly genetic factors. Conducts studies of potential diagnostic tools, markers of vulnerability in individuals at risk, neuropathology, drug therapies, and animal models useful for identifying new treatments.

**Multidisciplinary Institute for
  Neuropsychological Development, Inc.**
See: Entry 8400

**★7586★ Nathan S. Kline Institute for
  Psychiatric Research**
Orangeburg, NY 10962
Phone: (914)365-2000
Fax: (914)359-7029
Robert Cancro, M.D., Dir.

Research Activities and Fields: Mental illness, including multidisciplinary studies on its etiology, epidemiology, treatment, and control; computer sciences, emphasizing clinical and administrative services; and biochemical, genetic, physiological, neurochemical, and psychopharmacological research. Collaborates in research with investigators from other institutions and many countries. Consists of nine divisions: information sciences, statistical sciences and epidemiology, molecular biology, clinical research, analytical psychopharmacology, neurochemistry, child psychiatry, neurophysiology, and research support. **Publications:** Annual Report (jointly with Office of Mental Health); Newsletter. **Formerly:** Research Facility of the Rockland State Hospital; Rockland Research Center for Mental Illness; Rockland Research Institute.

**★7587★ New York Institute for Medical
  Research, Inc.**
150 White Plains Rd.
Tarrytown, NY 10591
Phone: (914)631-8998
Fax: (914)631-8816
Aileen Kunitz, Exec. Adm.

Research Activities and Fields: Behavioral, psychophysiological, and psychopharmacological research. Topics of interest include depression in young and elderly patients, dementia, anxiety neurosis, behavior and sleep disorders, and phase I studies on healthy volunteers. The Institute provides evaluation and treatment of selected psychiatric outpatients, such as psychiatric assessments, experimental psychological testing, physical and neurological examinations, clinical and diagnostic EEG, computer analyzed resting and sleep EEG, ECG, and clinical chemistry, including hormonal evaluations. **Publications:** Newsletter (irregularly). **Formerly:** New York Institute for Research into Contemporary Medicine, Inc. Center for Analytical Research (1980);

**★7588★ New York State Psychiatric
  Institute**
722 W. 168th St.
New York, NY 10032
Phone: (212)960-2200
Fax: (212)795-5886
Dr. John Oldham, Dir.

Research Activities and Fields: Psychiatry and neurosciences, including basic and clinical studies in biochemistry, psychoneuropharmacology, neuroendocrinology, neurotoxicology, psychosocial sciences, research and clinical psychology, genetics, nosology, psychophysiology, developmental psychobiology, sociology, epidemiology, communication sciences and psychoanalysis. **Publications:** Annual Report.

**★7589★ New York University
Mental Health Clinical Research Center**
Millhauser Laboratories
NYU School of Medicine
560 1st Ave., HN 323
New York, NY 10016
Phone: (212)263-5717
Fax: (212)263-7513
Dr. Arnold Friedhoff, Dir.

Research Activities and Fields: Psychiatry.

**★7590★ North Charles Mental Health
  Research and Training Foundation**
N. Charles, Inc.
Mental Health & Addiction Services
130 Bishop Allen Dr.
Cambridge, MA 02139
Phone: (617)864-0941
Fax: (617)876-9760
Dr. Gary Houle, Exec.Dir.

Research Activities and Fields: Mental health and addictions/substance abuse, including behavioral studies and evaluations of substance abuse trends and treatments.

**★7591★ Ohio State University
Laboratory of Psychobiology**
Townsend Hall, Rm. 48
1885 Neil Ave.
Columbus, OH 43210
Phone: (614)292-6512
Fax: (614)292-4537
Dr. Gary G. Berntson, Senior Member of
  Faculty

Research Activities and Fields: Psychobiology and comparative psychology, including studies on recovery of function after brain damage, psychopharmacology, psychophysiology, developmental processes, and animal cognition. **E-mail Address:** berntson.@osu.edu. **Formerly:** Laboratory of Comparative and Physiological Psychology.

★7592★ Oregon Research Institute
1899 Williamette St.
Eugene, OR 97401
Phone: (503)484-2123
Fax: (503)484-1108
Sarah Hampson, Science Coord.

Research Activities and Fields: Behavioral sciences, including studies in smoking prevention and cessation, compliance with diabetic regimens, children's social skills, computer-assisted video instruction, personality, sociometric assessment, health promotion in the workplace, drug abuse prevention, depression and family interaction, special education technology, behavioral gerontology, adolescent depression, and occupational training of handicapped persons. Provides behavioral research and consultation services to other public and private agencies in fields of education, health, and rehabilitation.

★ 7593 ★ **Portland State University**
Research and Training Center on Family
Support and Children's Mental Health
PO Box 751
Portland, OR 97207-0751
Phone: (503)725-4040
Free: 800-628-1696
Fax: (503)725-4180
Barbara J. Friesen, Ph.D., Dir.

Research Activities and Fields: Methods to improve services to families with children having serious mental, emotional, or behavioral disorders. Areas of interest include family support strategies, services to minority families, professional school curricula, and interorganizational collaboration. Conducts studies on parent organizations, family/professional collaboration, family coping strategies and the use of community resources, culturally appropriate service models, family involvement in the development and evaluation of community based services, and family empowerment in securing services through analysis of policies affecting children with emotional disabilities. **Publications:** *Focal Point* (newsletter, three per year); also publishes training materials and a directory of parent organizations in the U.S. **Formerly:** Research and Training Center to Improve Services for Seriously Emotionally Handicapped Children and their Families.

Reiss-Davis Child Study Center
See: Entry 3346

★ 7594 ★ **Research and Training Center for**
Positive Behavior Support
Dept. of Child & Family Studies
Florida Mental Health Institute
13301 Bruce B. Downs Blvd.
Tampa, FL 33612-3899
Phone: (813)974-4612
Fax: (813)974-4406
Glen Dunlap, Ph.D., Site Dir.

Research Activities and Fields: Behavior problems of people with severe disabilities, including assessment, nonaversive behavioral programming, promoting the generalization and maintenance of behavior gains, and implementing the nonaversive technology in school and community settings. **Publications:** Newsletter. **Formerly:** Research and Training Center for Community Referenced Behavior Management.

Research Unit on Children's Psychosocial
Maladjustment
See: Entry 3347

Rockefeller University
Laboratory of Human Behavior and
Metabolism
See: Entry 4899

★ 7595 ★ **Rutgers University**
Center for Research on the Organization
and Financing of Care for the Severely
Mentally Ill
30 College Ave.
New Brunswick, NJ 08903-5070
Phone: (908)932-8415
Fax: (908)932-6872
David Mechanic, Ph.D., Dir.

Research Activities and Fields: Research on mental health services and policy in the state. Research agenda includes aging caretakers of the mentally ill; barriers to hospital discharge; demographic change, mental illness, and state funding decisions; economic consequences of mental illness; facilitating appropriate housing for the severely mentally ill; insurance coverage for young mentally ill adults; improving general medical care for the severely mentally ill; impact of mental health services in HMOs; mental health aspects of the AIDS epidemic; psychiatric care in general hospitals; relationships between the general medical and the specialty psychiatric sectors; relationships between minority families and the public mental health system; resource use since the introduction o f psychiatric DRGs in New Jersey; service elements and the quality of functioning among the chronically mentally ill; study of post-World War II mental health policy; and using capitation to improve mental health services.

★ 7596 ★ **Rutgers University**
Douglass Developmental Disabilities
Center
Gibbons Campus-Douglass College
PO Box 270
New Brunswick, NJ 08903
Phone: (908)932-9137
Fax: (908)932-8011
Jan S. Handleman, Dir.

Research Activities and Fields: Behavioral treatment of autistic behavior, including investigation of behavioral techniques for teaching language to young nonverbal children. **Formerly:** Child Behavioral Research Center.

★ 7597 ★ **St. Louis University**
Center for the Applied Behavioral Sciences
(CABS)
221 N. Grand Blvd.
St. Louis, MO 63103
Phone: (314)658-2273
Fax: (314)658-3874
Dr. Thomas J. Kramer, Dir.

Research Activities and Fields: Program evaluation, organizational behavior, health psychology, and consumer research. CABS is associated with the Department of Psychology where faculty members are pursing research programs in psychology and law, work teams, health psychology, work values, depression and its physiological correlates, and issues related to the prevention of nuclear war.

★ 7598 ★ **St. Louis University**
David P. Wohl, Sr. Memorial Institute
1221 S. Grand Blvd.
St. Louis, MO 63104
Phone: (314)577-8720
Fax: (314)664-7248
George T. Grossberg, M.D., Chm.

Research Activities and Fields: Adult and child psychiatry, geriatric psychiatry, psychopharmacology, anthropology, psychology, and behavioral medicine, including psychophysiologic reactions in pyschotherapeutic relationships, personality profiles in a general hospital population, emotional response to cardiovascular surgery, emotional responses of children to chronic illness, factors influencing career choice in medicine, and impact of direct entry into psychiatric training on residents and their training programs.

★ 7599 ★ **Seattle Institute for**
Psychoanalysis
4020 E. Madison St., Ste. 230
Seattle, WA 98112
Phone: (206)328-5315
Fax: (206)328-5315
Roger C. Eddy, M.D., Contact

Research Activities and Fields: Psychoanalysis and allied health sciences.

★ 7600 ★ **Social Psychiatry Research**
Institute
150 E. 69th St.
New York, NY 10021
Phone: (212)249-6829
Fax: (212)249-8546
Ari Kiev, M.D., Pres.

Research Activities and Fields: Mental health and psychiatry, including psychopharmacological studies of antidepressant, anti-anxiety, Alzheimer's medications, and transcultural psychiatry. Conducts clinical drug trials. Assembles data for the mental health and psychiatric professions.

★ 7601 ★ **Sonia Shankman Orthogenic**
School
Univ. of Chicago
1365 E. 60th St.
Chicago, IL 60637
Phone: (312)702-1203
Fax: (312)702-1304
Bertram Cohler, Ph.D., Dir.

Research Activities and Fields: Emotional disorders of childhood and adolescence and their etiology and treatment, education of severely disturbed children, milieu therapy, changes in I.Q., and psychoanalytically oriented milieu therapy. Provides treatment for children and adolescents.

★ 7602 ★ **Stanford University**
Laboratory of Developmental
Psychobiology
Primate Facility 7-930T
Dept. of Psychiatry
Stanford, CA 94305
Phone: (415)725-5937
Fax: (415)725-5936
Dr. Seymour Levine, Dir.

Research Activities and Fields: Long-term consequences of postnatal stress using monkeys as models; and maternal regulation of infant physiology and behavior using rats as models.

★7603★ Stanford University
Stanford Behavior Medicine Laboratory
Sch. of Medicine
101 Quarry Rd.
Stanford, CA 94305-5542
Phone: (415)723-5868
Fax: (415)723-9807
Dr. W. Stewart Agras, Dir.

Research Activities and Fields: Anxiety and eating disorders, focusing on clinical outcomes and basic psychological factors that influence these disorders.

State University of New York Health Science Center at Brooklyn
Child Behavior Research Unit
See: Entry 3350

State University of New York Health Science Center at Brooklyn
Child Psychiatry Research Program
See: Entry 3351

★7604★ State University of New York Health Science Center at Brooklyn
Neurodynamic Laboratory
Dept. of Psychiatry
450 Clarkson Ave., Box 1203
Brooklyn, NY 11203
Phone: (718)270-2911
Fax: (718)270-4081
Henri Begleiter, Dir.

Research Activities and Fields: Use of evoked brain potentials to assess central nervous system changes due to alcoholism, drug addiction, and schizophrenia. Also studies the effects of various psychotropic drugs on animals. **E-mail Address:** hb@sv2.neurodyn.hscbklyn.edu. **Formerly:** Evoked Potential Laboratory.

★7605★ State University of New York Health Science Center at Brooklyn
Psychophysiological Laboratory
Dept. of Psychiatry
450 Clarkson Ave., Box 32
Brooklyn, NY 11203
Phone: (718)270-2307
Alvin S. Bernstein, Dir.

Research Activities and Fields: Monitors and records heart rate, skin resistance, skin potential, respiration, peripheral blood flow, EEG, and eyeblink response. Applies the orienting response construct to the processes of attention, stimulus-input, and stimulus-processing in response to stimuli of varying intensity, complexity, duration, significance, and modality. Conducts clinical research in psychopathology as related to adult schizophrenia, adult depression, and child psychoses.

★7606★ State University of New York Health Science Center at Brooklyn
Psychosomatic Research Program
450 Clarkson Ave.
Box 1203
Brooklyn, NY 11203
Phone: (718)270-2311
Fax: (718)778-5397
Dr. R. Vizwanatan, Dir.

Research Activities and Fields: Clinical research, including the following psychosomatic studies: psychological observance of patients with terminal renal disease before and after their acceptance for kidney transplantation or for maintenance (home) hemodialysis; exploration of the affective state of patients with sickle cell anemia before the onset of sickle cell crises; and psychoendrocrinological study of patients in treatment in the Psychiatric Crisis Clinic through the use of dexamethasone suppression.

★7607★ State University of New York Health Science Center at Brooklyn
Research Unit on Communicative Processes
450 Clarkson Ave.
Box 88
Brooklyn, NY 11203
Phone: (718)270-3078
Fax: (718)270-3017
Dr. Norbert Freedman, Dir.

Research Activities and Fields: Communicative issues in psychiatric treatment, including doctor-patient interaction, the clinical interview, the psychotherapeutic interview, and the psychoanalytic interview. Objective studies of communicative behavior are also conducted through analysis of language, kinesics, and cognitive processes.

★7608★ State University of New York at Stony Brook
Institute for Mental Health Research
Dept. of Psychiatry & Behavioral Science
Stony Brook, NY 11794
Phone: (516)444-2990
Fax: (516)444-7534
Mark J. Sedler, M.D., Actg.Chm.

Research Activities and Fields: Seeks to determine neurobiological factors in mental illnesses that can be used to aid in the development of improved treatments. Conducts basic neurobiological research and applied clinical studies. Areas of interest include psychopharmacology, molecular neurobiology, child psychopathology, behavioral biology, and behavioral medicine. **Formerly:** Replaces former Long Island Research Institute.

★7609★ Texas A&M University
Inquiry Group on Applied Psychometrics and Clinical Assessment
Dept. of Educational Psychology
College Station, TX 77843-4225
Phone: (409)845-1884
Fax: (409)845-6129
Dr. Cecil R. Reynolds, Cochairman

Research Activities and Fields: Develops applications of psychometrics to problems of clinical assessment and psychoeducational diagnosis.

★7610★ Texas A&M University
Laboratory for the Study of Social Deviance
Dept. of Sociology
College Station, TX 77843-4351
Phone: (409)845-2411
Fax: (409)862-4057
Howard B. Kaplan, Ph.D., Dir.

Research Activities and Fields: Conducts longitudinal surveys of development throughout the life course with special reference to the antecedents, concomitants, and consequences of deviant behavior, substance abuse, and health-related phenomena (including AIDS). **Formerly:** Continuation of former Sociological Research Laboratory, Baylor College of Medicine.

★7611★ Texas Christian University
Institute of Behavioral Research
Fort Worth, TX 76129
Phone: (817)921-7226
Fax: (817)921-7290
Dr. D. Dwayne Simpson, Dir.

Research Activities and Fields: Management and evaluation research for social and health service programs in community agencies and private industry. Program focuses on longitudinal studies of social behavior and deviancy, assessment of prevention and health promotion strategies, and epidemiology of substance abuse and other socially deviant or destructive behaviors.

★7612★ Timberlawn Psychiatric Research Foundation
2750 Grove Hill Rd.
PO Box 270789
Dallas, TX 75227
Phone: (214)388-0451
Fax: (214)381-1377
John T. Gossett, Ph.D., Dir.

Research Activities and Fields: Mental health, including studies in family development, healthy families, and program evaluation.

U.S. Department of Defense
Armed Forces Radiobiology Research Institute
Behavioral Sciences Department
See: Entry 11076

U.S. Department of Defense
Army Medical Research and Development Command
Walter Reed Army Institute of Research
Neuropsychiatry Division
See: Entry 7833

U.S. Department of Health and Human Services
National Institute on Aging
Laboratory of Behavioral Sciences
See: Entry 1956

U.S. Department of Health and Human Services
National Institute on Aging
Laboratory of Personality and Cognition
See: Entry 1963

★7613★ U.S. Department of Health and Human Services
National Institute of Child Health and Human Development
Center for Research for Mothers and Children
Human Learning and Behavior Branch

Executive Plaza North, Rm. 633
6130 Executive Blvd.
Bethesda, MD 20892
Phone: (301)496-6591
Fax: (301)496-0962
Dr. Norman A. Krasnegor, Chief

Research Activities and Fields: Branch supports research on processes and mechanisms of behavioral development from infancy to maturity. Program has five major areas of interest: 1) behavioral pediatrics, which focuses on the role of behavior in the promotion of health, life style factors that relate to disease, and studies of the adaptation of the child and its family to acute and chronic illness, hospitalization, pain, and stress; 2) developmental behavioral biology, with support for studies in behavioral endocrinology, behavioral genetics, and the neurobiological correlates of behavioral development as well as psychomotor and sensory development and comparative animal studies of learning and social development; 3) learning and cognitive development, with support for research to elucidate the development of learning, learning disabilities, perception, and memory during the period between birth and adulthood (of particular interest are experimental studies of learning during the perinatal period of development); 4) communications research to enlarge understanding of the normal acquisition and development of speech, language, and reading ability as well as those factors that interfere with the normal development of these capacities; and 5) social and affective development from birth to adulthood, with particular interest in development during infancy and adolescence (emphasis is on studies of intrafamilial relationships, emotional development, personality development, including the concept of self and competence, and prosocial behaviors such as affiliation, nurturance, and sharing).

★7614★ **U.S. Department of Health and Human Services**
National Institute of Child Health and Human Development
Laboratory of Comparative Ethology
NIH Bldg. 31, B2-B15
9000 Rockville Pike
Bethesda, MD 20892
Phone: (301)496-6832
Fax: (301)496-2766
Dr. Stephen J. Suomi, Chief

Research Activities and Fields: Laboratory focuses on the development of behavior in humans as well as primates and other animal models. Interactions of genetic and environmental factors are explored using the comparative mammalian approach in order to determine the origins and evolution of various behavioral phenotypes. Experimental results in animals are correlated with results of longitudinal studies in human infants and families. In addition, hypotheses concerning behavior and communication ("languages") in animal models are correlated with results obtained by physiological and molecular neuroscience techniques. Monkeys bred to yield specific behaviors under stress (e.g., laid back or uptight) are used extensively. Activities are carried out in the Brain, Behavior, and Communication Section, Child and Family Research Section, Comparative Behavioral Genetics Sec-

tion, and Social and Emotional Development Section.

★7615★ **U.S. Department of Health and Human Services**
National Institute of Diabetes and Digestive and Kidney Diseases
Division of Digestive Diseases and Nutrition
Obesity, Eating Disorders, and Energy Regulation Program
5333 Westbard Ave., Rm. 3A18B
Bethesda, MD 20892
Phone: (301)594-7573
Fax: (301)594-7504
Dr. Van S. Hubbard, Program Director

Research Activities and Fields: Program emphasizes research on the biomedical and behavioral aspects of obesity, anorexia nervosa, bulimia, and other eating disorders. Goals are to establish a clear understanding of the etiology, prevention, and treatment of these multifaceted conditions. Studies focus on the physiological, metabolic, psychological, and genetic factors that affect food choices, food intake, eating behavior, appetite, and satiety; the effects of taste, smell, and gastric and humoral (including neurotransmitters) response in association with dietary intake and subsequent behavior; the physiologic and metabolic consequences of weight loss or weight gain; the effect of mild exercise on appetite and weight control; and individual variabilities in energy utilization and thermogenesis. The program also encourages investigations on the dietary determinants of the growth and control of adipocyte size and number; the responsiveness of the adipocyte to various metabolic and pharmacologic stimuli; the prevention of obesity and other eating disorders; improved methods of assessing body composition; examination of health risk factors associated with specific degrees of obesity or body composition; and determining the effect of exercise on body composition. Program also supports an obesity research core center, which serves as resource for scientists studying various aspects of obesity.

U.S. Department of Health and Human Services
National Institute on Drug Abuse
Addiction Research Center
Etiology Research Branch
See: Entry 12117

★7616★ **U.S. Department of Health and Human Services**
National Institute of Mental Health
5600 Fishers Ln., Rm. 7-99
Rockville, MD 20857
Phone: (301)443-3673
Frederick K. Goodwin, M.D., Director

Research Activities and Fields: Plans, conducts, fosters, and supports research, research training, and services on the brain, mental illness, and mental health, particularly the causes, prevention, diagnosis, and treatment of mental illnesses. Principal components are: the Divisions of Neuroscience and Behavioral Science, Clinical and Treatment Research, Epidemiology and Services Research, Extramural Activities, and Intramural Research Programs; Offices of

Prevention, Equal Employment Opportunity, Rural Mental Health Research, Legislative Analysis and Coordination, Scientific Information, Resource Management, and Science Policy and Program Planning; Office for Special Populations; and Office on AIDS. Operates the Neuropsychiatric Research Hospital on the St. Elizabeth's Hospital campus in Washington, D.C.

★7617★ **U.S. Department of Health and Human Services**
National Institute of Mental Health
Biochemical Genetics Laboratory
2700 Martin Luther King Ave., S.E.
Washington, DC 20032
Phone: (202)373-6081
Fax: (202)373-6248
Carl R. Merril, M.D., Chief

Research Activities and Fields: Affects of aging on the central nervous system; and molecular neurobiology, focusing on proteins and nucleic acids in normal and disease states.

★7618★ **U.S. Department of Health and Human Services**
National Institute of Mental Health
Cell Biology Laboratory
NIH Bldg. 31, Rm. 3A-17
9000 Rockville Pike
Bethesda, MD 20892
Phone: (301)496-9444
Michael J. Brownstein, M.D., Ph.D., Chief

Research Activities and Fields: Areas of interest include light and electron microscope-level neuroanatomy, chronobiology, developmental neurobiology, biosynthesis of biologically active molecules, isolation of novel peptide hormones, and regulation of intracellular processes by chemical messenger. Laboratory has a section on biochemical pharmacology.

★7619★ **U.S. Department of Health and Human Services**
National Institute of Mental Health
Cerebral Metabolism Laboratory
NIH Bldg. 36, Rm. 1A-05
9000 Rockville Pike
Bethesda, MD 20892
Phone: (301)496-1371
Fax: (301)480-1668
Louis Sokoloff, M.D., Chief

Research Activities and Fields: Laboratory conducts research in neurochemistry and neurophysiology using biochemical methods for measuring local cerebral glucose utilization, local cerebral blood flow, and local cerebral protein synthesis in vivo. Laboratory comprises sections on clinical brain imaging and developmental neurochemistry.

★7620★ **U.S. Department of Health and Human Services**
National Institute of Mental Health
Clinical Research Division
Child and Adolescent Disorders Research Branch
5600 Fishers Ln., Rm. 18C-17
Rockville, MD 20857
Phone: (301)443-5944
Fax: (301)443-6000
Peter S. Jensen, M.D., Chief

Research Activities and Fields: Child and adolescent disorders, including attention deficit disorder, depression, conduct disorders, and autism. Also investigates suicide among children and adolescents. Focuses on classification, assessment, etiology, genetics, clinical course, outcome, and pharmacologic, somatic, and psychosocial treatment and rehabilitation of disorders affecting children and adolescents.

★7621★ U.S. Department of Health and Human Services
National Institute of Mental Health
Clinical Research Division
Mental Disorders of the Aging Research Branch
5600 Fishers Ln., Rm. 18-105
Rockville, MD 20857
Phone: (301)443-1185
Fax: (301)594-6784
Dr. Barry Lebowitz, Chief

Research Activities and Fields: The Branch supports those studies that have a primary focus on the mental health and illness implications of the aging process and old age. This includes studies on: 1) causes, treatment, and prevention of Alzheimer's disease, senile dementia, and related disorders, with emphasis on differential diagnosis, test of memory-enhancing agents, and issues of coexisting illness and excess ability; 2) causes, treatment, and prevention of depression in older persons (including investigations of the relationship of depression to dementing disorders, suicide, alcoholism, medical disease, and other behavioral disorders); 3) causes, treatment, and prevention of behavioral disturbance and dysfunction, with special reference to agitation, assaultive/aggressive behavior, confusion, disorientation, and other behavioral problems; 4) development and refinement of pharmacologic and psychosocial treatments, with special attention to efficacy, safety, side-effects, mechanisms of action, and drug/drug interaction; 5) behavioral medicine and the interface of physical illness and mental disorders in later life; 6) chronically mentally ill elderly, with special attention to treatment and management of schizophrenia and to psychosocial and behavioral approaches to quality of life; 7) design and refinement of methods for treatment intervention, clinical trials, and service delivery models for the elderly; 8) mental illness in nursing homes; 9) effects of families, support systems, and self-help groups on the care of older persons with significant mental disorders; 10) family stress and the care of Alzheimer's disease victims; and 11) prevention of pathology among elderly at risk for mental illness. Support is provided through a wide range of mechanisms, including the Geriatric Mental Health Academic Award; Scientist Development Awards; National Research Service Awards, including individual fellowships and institutional awards at predoctoral or postdoctoral levels; and Clinical/Faculty Scholars support. In addition, the Clinical Research Centers on Psychopathology of the Elderly Program provides support to a limited number of centers situated in clinical treatment settings with demonstrable interest in the study of mental health and aging.

★7622★ U.S. Department of Health and Human Services
National Institute of Mental Health
Clinical Research Division
Mood, Anxiety, and Personality Disorders Research Branch
5600 Fishers Ln., Rm. 10C16
Rockville, MD 20857
Phone: (301)443-4524
Fax: (301)443-6000
Jack D. Maser, Ph.D., Chief

Research Activities and Fields: Supports research on anxiety, somatoform, and certain personality disorders. This includes research on the nature, etiology, diagnosis, classification, course, and treatment of these disorders. Research may be biological, behavioral, psychological, social, cultural and/or methodological; or in vitro and in vivo clinical and laboratory investigations with both animals and humans, if the focus of the research is on etiology, treatment development, or assessment of the affective, anxiety, or related disorders. Branch also accepts studies of pharmacologic agents used to test etiologic hypotheses specific to these disorders in human and infrahuman species.

★7623★ U.S. Department of Health and Human Services
National Institute of Mental Health
Clinical Research Division
Schizophrenia Research Branch
5600 Fishers Ln., Rm. 10C06
Rockville, MD 20857
Phone: (301)443-3524
Fax: (301)443-4045
David Shore, Acting Chief

Research Activities and Fields: The Schizophrenia Research Branch plans, supports, and conducts programs of research, research training, and resource development in the classification, assessment, etiology, genetics, clinical course, outcome, and pharmacologic, somatic, and psychosocial treatment and rehabilitation of schizophrenia and related disorders. **Publications:** *Schizophrenia Bulletin.*

★7624★ U.S. Department of Health and Human Services
National Institute of Mental Health
Clinical Science Laboratory
NIH Bldg. 10, Rm. 3D41
9000 Rockville Pike
Bethesda, MD 20892
Phone: (301)496-2757
Fax: (301)402-0188
Dennis L. Murphy, M.D., Chief

Research Activities and Fields: Laboratory conducts medical research related to mental health. Principal components include the Analytical Biochemistry Section, Pharmacology Section, Geriatric Psychiatry Section, Histopharmacology Section, and Clinical Neuropharmacology Section.

★7625★ U.S. Department of Health and Human Services
National Institute of Mental Health
Developmental Psychology Laboratory
NIH Bldg. 15K
9000 Rockville Pike
Bethesda, MD 20892
Phone: (301)496-1091
Marian Radke-Yarrow, Ph.D., Chief

Research Activities and Fields: Emotional and social development of children, with emphasis on development under risk conditions such as parental psychopathology, parental child abuse, and adolescent changes. Recent projects have included the following; 1) longitudinal study of rearing processes in families of mentally healthy and depressed parents and a longitudinal study of the psychosocial development of the children in these families; 2) investigation of the psychobiological effects of child sexual abuse; 3) studies of the psychophysiology of multiple personality disorders; 4) study of early conduct disorders; and 5) study of healthy and deviant empathic processes. Laboratory comprises the Affective Development Section and Child Behavior Disorders Section.

★7626★ U.S. Department of Health and Human Services
National Institute of Mental Health
Division of State and Community Systems Development
Survey and Analysis Branch
5600 Fishers Ln.
Rockwell II, No. 501
Rockville, MD 20857
Phone: (301)443-3343
Fax: (301)443-7926
Ronald W. Mansderscheid, Chief

Research Activities and Fields: Operates a national reporting program to obtain, analyze, and disseminate statistics on the major characteristics of the nation's mental health service systems, their resources, staffing, utilization patterns, costs, and financing; develops methodology for statistical data collection and demography; and conducts ecological and demographic studies on the need and demand for mental health services. In addition, Branch provides consultation to state and local mental health agencies on statistical methodology, mental health information systems, and the use of data.

★7627★ U.S. Department of Health and Human Services
National Institute of Mental Health
Epidemiologic and Services Research Division
5600 Fishers Ln., Rm. 18C-26
Rockville, MD 20857
Phone: (301)443-3683
Fax: (301)443-6000
Darrel A. Regier, Director

Research Activities and Fields: The Division directs, plans, supports, and conducts programs of research, research training, and resource development on: service delivery and health economics at the clinical, institutional, and systems levels; the understanding, treatment, and prevention of antisocial and violent behavior and their effects, including law and mental health interaction; and the prevention, control, and treatment of rape, other sexual assault, and their effects. The Division consists of: the Child and Family Support Branch, Services Research

Branch, Statistical Research Branch, and Systems Development and Community Support Branch.

★ 7628 ★ **U.S. Department of Health and Human Services**
National Institute of Mental Health
Epidemiology and Services Research Division
Basic Prevention and Behavioral Medicine Research Branch
5600 Fishers Ln., Rm. 11C-06
Rockville, MD 20857
Phone: (301)443-4337
Fax: (301)443-4822
Leonard Mitnick, Ph.D., Chief

Research Activities and Fields: Branch plans and supports programs of research, research training, and resource development on the basic behavioral, biological, genetic, and social factors and psychological processes that impact on physical health and the maintenance of emotional well being. The Branch includes three program areas: Prevention and Behavior Change, Population and Risk, and Behavioral Medicine.

★ 7629 ★ **U.S. Department of Health and Human Services**
National Institute of Mental Health
Epidemiology and Services Research Division
Epidemiology and Psychopathology Research Branch
5600 Fishers Ln., Rm. 10C09
Rockville, MD 20857
Phone: (301)443-3774
Fax: (301)443-4045
Charles T. Kaelber, M.D., Acting Chief

Research Activities and Fields: Branch provides support for research and research training in: 1) assessing mental health/mental illness status of populations in terms of incidence and prevalence; 2) describing the natural history of disorders and identifying illness syndromes in the community as well as in clinical patient populations; 3) developing new epidemiologic, statistical, demographic, and other quantitatively oriented methodologies for assessing the mental illness/health of a population; 4) conducting epidemiologic studies to identify etiologic factors of mental health/mental disorder in different groups in terms of inheritance, experience, behavior, biologic factors, and environment in community or patient populations; 5) conducting case-control studies to test the efficacy of some positive action of intervention; and 6) conducting clinical research in the classification, assessment, etiology, genetics, clinical course, outcome, and treatment of general psychopathology and other mental outcome and treatment of general psychopathology and other mental disorders. Support is provided through research grants, conference grants, small grants, specifically announced cooperative agreements, and institutional research training grants, as well as Research Scientist Development, Research Scientist, Clinical Scientist, and Physician Scientist Awards, and pre- and post-doctoral individual fellowships. Branch comprises the Development and Application of Epidemiology Methods Section, Development and Testing of Epidemiology Hypotheses Section,

Experimental Epidemiology and Evaluation Section, and General Psychopathology Section.

★ 7630 ★ **U.S. Department of Health and Human Services**
National Institute of Mental Health
Epidemiology and Services Research Division
Prevention Research Branch
5600 Fishers Ln., Rm. 10-85
Rockville, MD 20857
Phone: (301)443-4140
Fax: (301)443-4045
Eve K. Moscicki, Sc.D., M.P.H., Chief

Research Activities and Fields: Branch serves as a focal point of the National Institute of Mental Health for activities pertaining to research and research training on the prevention of mental disorders and behavioral dysfunctions and the promotion of mental health. Activities focus on preventing socio-emotional problems among infants and young children at risk; preventing conduct and other behavioral disorders in school-aged children; preventing anxiety and depressive disorders in children and adults; promoting mental health through the enhancement of protective factors, including coping mechanisms; preventing suicide and suicidality in preclinical populations; and preventing affective and anxiety disorders in HIV-infected individuals, people at high-risk for infection, their families, caretakers, and loved ones.

★ 7631 ★ **U.S. Department of Health and Human Services**
National Institute of Mental Health
Epidemiology and Services Research Division
Services Research Branch
5600 Fishers Ln., Rm. 18C-14
Rockville, MD 20857
Phone: (301)443-3364
Thomas L. Lalley, Chief

Research Activities and Fields: Branch plans, supports, and conducts programs of research, research training, and resource development on services delivery and health economics at the clinical, institutional, and systems levels in specialty mental health and health settings; and evaluates interventions to improve diagnosis and clinical practice.

★ 7632 ★ **U.S. Department of Health and Human Services**
National Institute of Mental Health
Epidemiology and Services Research Division
Violence and Traumatic Stress Research Branch
5600 Fishers Ln., Parklawn 100-26
Rockville, MD 20857
Phone: (301)443-3728
Susan D. Solomon, Ph.D., Contact

Research Activities and Fields: Branch is the focal point in the National Institute of Mental Health for research on antisocial behavior, individual violent behavior, rape and sexual assault, and law and mental health interactions. The objectives of the program are to improve understanding of mental health issues and needs in these areas and to assist in the development of improved strategies for evaluation, prevention,

management, and treatment. The scope of the Branch's program encompasses biological science, behavioral science, psychosocial science, and empirical legal studies. Generally, a portion of the Branch's available funds is also used to support important investigator-initiated projects that do not fall within designated priority areas but are relevant to NIMH and Branch missions. The Branch does *not* support research that is not clearly relevant to mental health concerns or research that more appropriately falls within the mission of other federal programs.

★ 7633 ★ **U.S. Department of Health and Human Services**
National Institute of Mental Health
General and Comparative Biochemistry Laboratory
NIH Bldg. 36, Rm. 3D06
9000 Rockville Pike
Bethesda, MD 20892
Phone: (301)496-3241
Fax: (301)402-4747
Giulio L. Cantoni, M.D., Chief

Research Activities and Fields: Research studies are concerned with the mechanisms and pathways of biological methylation, alkaloid biosynthesis, peptides, cellular differentiation, and gene expression in eukaryotes. Focus is on the enzymatic mechanisms in methyl transfer reactions, mechanism of drug addiction, muscle differentiation in cell culture, and genetic engineering.

★ 7634 ★ **U.S. Department of Health and Human Services**
National Institute of Mental Health
Intramural Research Programs Division
NIH Bldg. 10, Rm. 4N-224
9000 Rockville Pike
Bethesda, MD 20892
Phone: (301)496-3501
Fax: (301)480-8348
Michael J. Brownstein, M.D., Ph.D., Director

Research Activities and Fields: Division plans and administers a comprehensive, long-term intramural research program of clinical and behavioral, biological, and special research dealing with the causes, diagnosis, treatment, and prevention of mental disorders and the biological and psychosocial factors that determine human behavior and development; provides a focus for national attention in the area of mental health research; and provides technical support through development and maintenance of electronic and mechanical instrumentation and equipment.

★ 7635 ★ **U.S. Department of Health and Human Services**
National Institute of Mental Health
Intramural Research Programs Division (Clinical Research)
Biological Psychiatry Branch
NIH Bldg. 10, Rm. 3N-212
9000 Rockville Pike
Bethesda, MD 20892
Phone: (301)496-4805
Fax: (301)402-0052
Dr. Robert Post, Chief

Research Activities and Fields: Branch conducts a broad program of research, training, and treatment of clinical psychiatric problems, including manic-depressive and schizo-affective illness, panic-anxiety disorders, menstrually related mood disorders, and suicide. The Branch's goal is to develop programs to investigate psychologic, biochemical, and neuroanatomic contributions to the study of manic-depressive illness, anxiety disorders, and related symptoms. Focus is on psychobiology, involving studies in psychiatry, psychology, neurology, genetics, pharmacology, and biochemistry. Specific research interests are the biochemistry of neurotransmission and the action of mood stabilizers, brain imaging of affective illness, and the models of sensitization and kindling. Branch comprises Anxiety and Affective Disorders Section, Behavioral Biology Unit, Behavioral Endocrinology Section, Molecular Neurobiology Section, Behavioral Pharmacology Unit, Neurochemistry Unit, and Psychobiology Section.

★7636★ U.S. Department of Health and Human Services
National Institute of Mental Health
Intramural Research Programs Division
(Clinical Research)
Child Psychiatry Branch
NIH Bldg. 10, Rm. 6N-240
9000 Rockville Pike
Bethesda, MD 20892
Phone: (301)496-6080
Fax: (301)402-0246
Judith L. Rapoport, M.D., Chief

Research Activities and Fields: Branch conducts clinical research on the biological aspects of child psychiatry, including learning disabilities, autism, childhood schizophrenia, obsessive compulsive disorder, and hyperactivity. Areas of interest include pediatric psychopharmacology and brain imaging in child psychiatry.

★7637★ U.S. Department of Health and Human Services
National Institute of Mental Health
Intramural Research Programs Division
(Clinical Research)
Clinical Neuroendocrinology Branch
NIH Bldg. 10, Rm. 3S-231
9000 Rockville Pike
Bethesda, MD 20892
Phone: (301)496-6884
Philip W. Gold, M.D., Chief

Research Activities and Fields: Branch coordinates and conducts research on the physiological organization of neuroendocrine systems and on the relevance of alterations in neuroendocrine function to the pathophysiology and etiology of major psychiatric disorders.

★7638★ U.S. Department of Health and Human Services
National Institute of Mental Health
Intramural Research Programs Division
(Clinical Research)
Clinical Neurogenetics Branch
NIH Bldg. 10, Rm. 3N-218
9000 Rockville Pike
Bethesda, MD 20892
Phone: (301)496-3465
Fax: (301)402-0859
Elliot S. Gershon, M.D., Chief

Research Activities and Fields: Branch conducts clinical and basic biologic and pharmacologic studies relating to the genetics of manic-depressive illness and schizophrenia.

★7639★ U.S. Department of Health and Human Services
National Institute of Mental Health
Intramural Research Programs Division
(Clinical Research)
Clinical Psychobiology Branch
NIH Bldg. 10, Rm. 4S-239
9000 Rockville Pike
Bethesda, MD 20892
Phone: (301)496-2141
Fax: (301)496-5439
Thomas A. Wehr, M.D., Chief

Research Activities and Fields: Branch conducts clinical psychiatric and psychobiological research. Research interest includes sleep physiology and biological rhythms, seasonal affective disorder (SAD) and light treatment.

★7640★ U.S. Department of Health and Human Services
National Institute of Mental Health
Intramural Research Programs Division
(Clinical Research)
Experimental Therapeutics Branch
NIH Bldg. 10, Rm. 4N-212
9000 Rockville Pike
Bethesda, MD 20892
Phone: (301)496-4303
David Pickar, M.D., Chief of Experimental Therapy

Research Activities and Fields: Branch conducts a multidisciplinary program in basic and clinical neuroscience and attempts to integrate data on the biochemistry and pharmacology of the central nervous system with an understanding of the pathogenesis and treatment of major psychiatric diseases. Branch comprises the Clinical and Pharmacology Section, Clinical Studies Section, Molecular Neurogenetics Section, and Molecular Pharmacology Section.

★7641★ U.S. Department of Health and Human Services
National Institute of Mental Health
Intramural Research Programs Division
(Research at St. Elizabeth's Hospital)
Clinical Brain Disorders Branch
2700 Martin Luther King Ave., S.E.
Washington, DC 20032
Phone: (202)373-6225
Fax: (202)373-6214
Daniel R. Weinberger, M.D., Chief

Research Activities and Fields: Branch conducts clinical research at the National Institutes of Health campus at St. Elizabeth's Hospital on neuropsychiatric disorders, with emphasis on schizophrenia, dementias, movement disorders, and suicide. Principal fields of research interest are pharmacology and neuropsychology, neuroimaging, and neuropathology. Branch comprises Clinical Studies Section and Neuropathology Section.

★7642★ U.S. Department of Health and Human Services
National Institute of Mental Health
Intramural Research Programs Division
(Research at St. Elizabeth's Hospital)
Neuropsychiatry Branch
2700 Martin Luther King Ave., S.E.
Washington, DC 20032
Phone: (202)373-6233
Fax: (202)373-6248
Richard J. Wyatt, M.D., Chief

Research Activities and Fields: Biomedical and clinical studies, focusing on biochemistry of schizophrenia, aging, regeneration, pharmacology, neuropsychiatry, drug abuse and tardive dyskinesia. Activities are carried out in the Aging Section, Clinical Neuropsychiatry Section, Molecular Neuropsychiatry Section, and Preclinical Neuroscience Section.

★7643★ U.S. Department of Health and Human Services
National Institute of Mental Health
Molecular Biology Laboratory
NIH Bldg. 36, Rm. 1B-08
9000 Rockville Pike
Bethesda, MD 20892
Phone: (301)496-6945
David M. Neville, M.D., Chief

Research Activities and Fields: Laboratory comprises sections on biophysical chemistry, molecular genetics, and regulatory proteins.

★7644★ U.S. Department of Health and Human Services
National Institute of Mental Health
Neurochemistry Laboratory
NIH Bldg. 36, Rm. 3D-30
9000 Rockville Pike
Bethesda, MD 20892
Phone: (301)496-3579
Fax: (301)480-9284
Seymour Kaufman, Ph.D., Chief

Research Activities and Fields: Laboratory conducts research into fundamental physical and chemical mechanisms of the nervous system as they relate to mental health. Subjects of recent interest include research in phenylketonuria and regulation of neurotransmitter biosynthesis.

★7645★ U.S. Department of Health and Human Services
National Institute of Mental Health
Neurophysiology Laboratory
NIHAC Bldg. 112, Rm. 205
Poolesville, MD 20837
Phone: (301)496-1201
Steven P. Wise, Ph.D., Chief

Research Activities and Fields: Neurophysiology.

★7646★ U.S. Department of Health and Human Services
National Institute of Mental Health
Neuropsychology Laboratory

NIH Bldg. 9, Rm. 1B80
9000 Rockville Pike
Bethesda, MD 20892
Phone: (301)496-5625
Fax: (301)402-0046
Mortimer Mishkin, Ph.D., Chief

Research Activities and Fields: Laboratory plans and conducts basic research on the relationships between neural structures and behavior in nonhuman primates using a multidisciplinary approach to study cognitive functions such as perception, attention, memory, and emotion in Old World monkeys.

★ 7647 ★ **U.S. Department of Health and Human Services**
National Institute of Mental Health
Neuroscience and Behavioral Science Division
5600 Fishers Ln., Rm. 11-103
Rockville, MD 20857
Phone: (301)443-3563
Fax: (301)443-4822
Stephen H. Koslow, Director

Research Activities and Fields: Division directs, plans, and supports programs of research, research training, and resource development in the neurosciences and the behavioral and psychobiological sciences; reviews and assesses the performance of such programs; and collaborates with other federal agencies and with outside organizations. The Division consists of the Behavioral and Integrative Neuroscience Research Branch, Behavioral and Cognitive and Social Science Research Branch, and Molecular and Cellular Neuroscience Research Branch.

★ 7648 ★ **U.S. Department of Health and Human Services**
National Institute of Mental Health
Neuroscience and Behavioral Science Division
Behavioral, Cognitive, and Social Science Research Branch
5600 Fishers Ln.
Rockville, MD 20857
Phone: (301)443-3942
Rodney Cocking, Acting Chief

Research Activities and Fields: Branch plans, supports, and conducts programs of research, research training, and resource development in the behavioral sciences to increase understanding of psychological, psychosocial, emotional, and cognitive factors influencing behavior.

★ 7649 ★ **U.S. Department of Health and Human Services**
National Institute of Mental Health
Neuroscience and Behavioral Science Division
Behavioral and Integrative Neuroscience Research Branch
5600 Fishers Ln., 11-102
Rockville, MD 20857
Phone: (301)443-1576
Fax: (301)443-4822
Richard Nakamura, Ph.D., Chief

Research Activities and Fields: Mission of the Branch is to support research on the brain mechanisms underlying behavior in functional organisms or through theoretical models, with a view to understanding how behavior develops, how it is maintained, and how it is regulated. Branch comprises four programs: 1) Cognitive Neuroscience, including the higher mental activities of thinking, perceiving, feeling, understanding, reasoning, communicating, and remembering; 2) Systems Neuroscience, including functional neural systems, homeostasis, social and survival behaviors, aggression, sexual and reproductive behavior, motivation and reward systems, sleep, and stress; 3) Theoretical and Computational Neuroscience, including models of neural mechanisms; and 4) Behavioral Pharmacology, including mechanisms of drug effects on cognition and behavior.

★ 7650 ★ **U.S. Department of Health and Human Services**
National Institute of Mental Health
Neuroscience and Behavioral Science Division
Molecular and Cellular Neuroscience Research Branch
5600 Fishers Ln.
Rockville, MD 20857
Phone: (301)443-1504
Dr. Stephen Zalcman, Chief

Research Activities and Fields: Branch supports research related to behavior and brain function in order to develop knowledge of basic biological/molecular mechanisms underlying mental disorders and to understand the basic processes involved in the action of psychoactive drugs. Activities involve biobehavioral research, neurobiological research, and psychopharmacological research, which includes support for clinical and preclinical studies on the physiological sites and mechanisms of actions of psychoactive drugs. Branch comprises the Biobehavior Section, Biology Section, and Psychopharmacology Section. **Publications:** *Neuroscience of Mental Health* and a report on the status and potential of neuroscience research for mental health illness.

★ 7651 ★ **U.S. Department of Health and Human Services**
National Institute of Mental Health
Psychology and Psychopathology Laboratory
NIH Bldg. 10, Rm. 4C110
9000 Rockville Pike
Bethesda, MD 20892
Phone: (301)496-2551
Fax: (301)402-0921
Allan F. Mirsky, Ph.D., Chief

Research Activities and Fields: Laboratory conducts basic and clinical research on genetic and neurobehavioral factors in psychopathology; and on normal cognition, emphasizing the pathology of attention.

★ 7652 ★ **U.S. Department of Health and Human Services**
National Institute of Mental Health
Socio-Environmental Studies Laboratory

Federal Bldg., Rm. B1A-14
7550 Wisconsin Ave.
Bethesda, MD 20892
Phone: (301)496-3383
Fax: (301)402-0621
Carmi Schooler, Ph.D., Acting Chief

Research Activities and Fields: Laboratory conducts research concerning social structure and personality, and cognition, including studies on basic cognitive and interpersonal processes in normal and schizophrenic individuals throughout the life span.

U.S. Department of Health and Human Services
National Institute for Occupational Safety and Health
Biomedical and Behavioral Science Division
Applied Psychology and Ergonomics Branch
See: Entry 9828

University of Alabama
Brewer-Porch Children's Center
See: Entry 3355

★ 7653 ★ **University of Alabama**
Psychology Clinic
Box 870356
Tuscaloosa, AL 35487-0356
Phone: (205)348-5000
Fax: (205)348-8648
Dr. Jean Spruill, Dir.

Research Activities and Fields: Mental health areas, including clinical studies relating to behavior problems. Serves as a mental health center providing services in group and individual psychotherapy, personality evaluations, intellectual evaluations, psychosocial evaluations, behavior modification, marriage and family counseling, consultation, training, and research.

★ 7654 ★ **University at Albany, State University of New York**
Center for Stress and Anxiety Disorders
1535 Western Ave.
Albany, NY 12203
Phone: (518)456-4143
Fax: (518)456-4146
Prof. Edward B. Blanchard, Codir.

Research Activities and Fields: Combines knowledge from psychology and medicine to explore the etiology, maintaining factors, assessment, and treatment of headache, hypertension, phobia, panic disorders, generalized anxiety disorders, and other stress and anxiety disorders.

★ 7655 ★ **University of California, Los Angeles**
Center for Research on Aging Project
Harbor-UCLA Medical Center
Dept. of Psychiatry, D-5 Annex
1000 W. Carson St.
Torrance, CA 90509
Phone: (310)222-3137
Fax: (310)328-5546
Ira Lesser, M.D., Dir.

Research Activities and Fields: Neuroanatomic and neurophysiologic aspects of psychotic states of the elderly and ethnic differences in psychopharmacology in psychiatric patients. Conducts clinical evaluations of elderly psychiatric patients with neuroimaging techniques and performs comparisons of clinical course and blood levels of psychotropic drugs in Asian and Caucasian schizophrenic and depressed patients. **Formerly:** Center for the Study and Care of the Treatment-Resistant Psychiatric Patient.

★ 7656 ★ **University of California, Los Angeles**
Neuropsychiatric Institute
760 Westwood Plaza
Los Angeles, CA 90024
Phone: (310)206-7125
Fax: (310)825-3942
Dr. Gary L. Tischler, Dir.

Research Activities and Fields: Clinical and basic studies in psychiatry, neurology, mental retardation, developmental disabilities, and behavioral sciences, including anthropology, biochemistry, neurophysiology, psychology, social and preventive psychiatry, psychopharmacology, sociology, personality differences, and psychosomatic problems.

★ 7657 ★ **University of California, Los Angeles**
Program on Psychosocial Adaptation and the Future
Neuropsychiatric Institute
760 Westwood Plaza
Los Angeles, CA 90024-1759
Phone: (310)825-0463
Roderic Gorney, M.D., Dir.

Research Activities and Fields: Studies psychosocial and cultural determinants of behavior, including impact of television on adults and the clinical role of the sense of the future in mental illness.

★ 7658 ★ **University of California, Los Angeles**
Research Center on the Psychobiology of Ethnicity
1124 W. Carson St.
B-4 S.
Torrance, CA 90502
Phone: (310)222-4266
Keh-Ming Lin, Dir.

Research Activities and Fields: Role of ethnicity (including culture) and biological variables in the mental health of ethnic minority populations. Conducts studies using pharmacokinetic, pharmacodynamic, and pharmacogenetic research techniques to examine ethnic and individual differences in responses to psychotropic drugs. **E-mail Address:** linkeh@harbor2.humc.edu.

University of California, San Francisco
Brain-Behavior Research Center
See: Entry 8487

★ 7659 ★ **University of California, San Francisco**
Center for Social and Behavioral Sciences
1350 7th Ave., Rm. 237
San Francisco, CA 94143-0848
Phone: (415)476-7285
Fax: (415)476-7739
Frank A. Johnson, M.D., Dir.

Research Activities and Fields: Sponsors pre- and postdoctoral research and training activities in the areas of stress and illness, cognitive factors in health behavior, mental health and aging, adult development, gerontology, Alzheimer's Disease, and AIDS.

★ 7660 ★ **University of California, San Francisco**
Center for Study of Trauma
Dept. of Psychiatry
401 Parnassus
San Francisco, CA 94143-0984
Phone: (415)388-0665
Fax: (415)388-4913
Chris Hatcher, Ph.D., Dir.

Research Activities and Fields: Trauma effects, stress, family dynamics and processes, violent behavior, and victimology. Projects focus on the families of children abducted by strangers or parents, disaster trauma, hostage/captivity behavior and post-traumatic adjustment, impact of medical devices/toxic exposure, and the violent, threatening individual and his or her family.

★ 7661 ★ **University of California, San Francisco**
Langley Porter Psychiatric Institute
401 Parnassus Ave.
San Francisco, CA 94143
Phone: (415)476-7000
Craig Van Dyke, M.D., Dir.

Research Activities and Fields: Conducts clinical studies of psychiatric disorders and psychotherapy and basic research studies in psychopharmacology, neurobiology, cellular and molecular biology, behavioral biology, and social sciences.

★ 7662 ★ **University of Cincinnati**
Central Psychiatric Clinic
Research and Evaluation Division
Univ. Hospital
3259 Elland Ave.
Cincinnati, OH 45267-0539
Phone: (513)558-5944
Fax: (513)558-3880
Mary C. Grace, Dir. of Research

Research Activities and Fields: Evaluates the Clinic's treatment programs for psychiatric problems of both adults and children, including evaluation of psychotropic medication and prediction of psychotherapy outcome. **Publications:** Semiannual Report.

★ 7663 ★ **University of Colorado**
National Center for American Indian and Alaska Native Mental Health Research
Dept. of Psychiatry
Univ. North Pavilion
4455 E. 12th Ave., A011-13
Denver, CO 80220
Phone: (303)372-3232
Fax: (303)372-3579
Dr. Spero Manson, Dir.

Research Activities and Fields: Center formulates, designs, conducts, and reports studies within four areas of inquiry: 1) determining and improving the performance characteristics of self-report measures of serious psychological dysfunction and diagnostic interviews for assessing alcohol, drug, and mental (ADM) disorders; 2) establishing the prevalence and incidence of ADM disorders and related risk factors through descriptive and experimental epidemiological investigations; 3) developing and evaluating methods for detecting and managing ADM disorders presented in human service settings; and 4) examining the effectiveness of interventions for preventing ADM disorders and promoting well-being. Ongoing studies include the American Indian Vietnam Veterans Project, which studies post-traumatic stress disorder and other psychological problems of Vietnam war veterans in readjusting to civilian life; Flower of Two Soils Reinterview Project, which studies emotional disorders in Native American adolescents; the Health Survey of Indian Boarding Students, which seeks to establish the prevalence and incidence of symptoms of depression, anxiety, suicidal behavior, and substance abuse, and to clarify relative contributions of stressful life events, coping strategies, social support, mastery, and self-esteem; the Foundations of Indian Teens Project, which develops more reliable and valid measures of psychopathology among Indian adolescents, with special emphasis on trauma; and the Voices of Indian Teens Project, a survey that includes psychometrically sound constructs, including substance abuse, substance dependence, depression, anxiety, academic achievement, delinquent behavior, social support, peer values and pressure, ethnic identity, stressful life events, drinking patterns and contexts, community values, and attitudes toward alcohol. **Publications:** *American Indian and Alaska Native Mental Health Research* (journal, three times annually); Annual Monograph. **E-mail Address:** spero@polaris.hsc.colorado.edu.

University of Florida
Center for Ambulatory Studies
See: Entry 2484

★ 7664 ★ **University of Georgia**
Center for Research on Deviance and Behavioral Health
Institute for Behavioral Research
102 Barrow Hall
Athens, GA 30602
Phone: (706)542-6090
Fax: (706)542-6064
Dr. Paul Roman, Dir.

Research Activities and Fields: Deviant behavior and mental health issues, including the organization of service delivery, employee assistance programs, alcohol abuse, alcoholism, drug use and addiction, and childhood disorders. **Publications:** *Journal of Employee Assistance Research.*

★ 7665 ★ University of Houston
Social Psychology/Behavioral Medicine
    Research and Graduate Training Group
Dept. of Psychology
Houston, TX 77204-5341
Phone: (713)743-8555
Fax: (713)743-8580
Richard I. Evans, Ph.D., Dir.

Research Activities and Fields: Health-related behaviors from a social-psychological perspective. Conceives, develops, and evaluates theory-based strategies aimed at impacting health-related behaviors, particularly among adolescents. Topics include prevention and control of cardiovascular disease and cancer, tobacco and other substance abuse prevention programs for adolescents, prevention of HIV/AIDS in adolescents, and other health promotion programs.

★ 7666 ★ University of Iowa
Affective Disorders Research Unit
Dept. of Psychiatry
500 Newton Rd.
Iowa City, IA 52242-1000
Phone: (319)353-4434
Fax: (319)353-3003
Dr. William H. Corgell, Head

Research Activities and Fields: Affective disorders, including clinical symptoms and genetics. Evaluates and follows approximately 200 patients suffering from affective disorders, 600 of their first-degree relatives, and 120 control subjects. **Formerly:** Collaborative Study of Depression.

★ 7667 ★ University of Iowa
Mental Health-Clinical Research Center
Univ. of Iowa Hospitals & Clinics
200 Hawkins Dr.
Iowa City, IA 52242
Phone: (319)356-1553
Fax: (319)356-2587
Dr. Nancy C. Andreasen, Dir.

Research Activities and Fields: Schizophrenia and other cognitive disorders, utilizing brain imaging modalities and neuropsychological testing to explore cognitive and neural deficits in schizophrenia. Also conducts family and genetic studies in schizophrenia, longitudinal follow-up studies, treatment-response studies, and drug trials. **Formerly:** Absorbed the activities of Schizophrenia and Cognitive Disorders Research Unit.

★ 7668 ★ University of Kentucky
Behavioral Physiology Laboratory
Dept. of Behavioral Science
College of Medicine Office Bldg.
Lexington, KY 40536-0086
Phone: (606)257-5254
Fax: (606)323-5350
James A. McCubbin, Ph.D., Dir.

Research Activities and Fields: Basic and clinical psychophysiology, including cardiovascular risk, ambulatory blood pressure monitor-

ing, psychoneuroendocrinology, blood biochemistry, psychopharmacology, stress-testing, human performance, and experimental behavioral therapeutics.

University of Louisville
Keller Child Psychiatry Research Center
See: Entry 3362

University of Louisville
Louisville Twin Study
See: Entry 5372

★ 7669 ★ University of Maryland
Institute of Psychiatry and Human
    Behavior
645 W. Redwood St.
Baltimore, MD 21201
Phone: (410)328-6735
Fax: (410)328-3693
John Talbott, M.D., Dir.

Research Activities and Fields: Psychiatry, neurophysiology and behavioral sciences, including alcoholism and drug abuse, psycholinguistics, violent behavior, human development, interpersonal relations, and psychotic disorders. Focuses on chronic mental illness, mental health care financing, and organization of mental health services. **Formerly:** Psychiatric Institute; Treatment Assessment Research Unit.

★ 7670 ★ University of Maryland
Neuroscience Center for Research in
    Schizophrenia
Maryland Psychiatric Research Center
PO Box 21247
Baltimore, MD 21228
Phone: (410)455-7101
Fax: (410)788-3837
Dr. William Carpenter, Dir.

Research Activities and Fields: Theoretical and technical neuroscience research, focusing on schizophrenia studies and human brain imaging.

★ 7671 ★ University of Michigan
Center for Self-Help Research and
    Knowledge Dissemination
School of Social Work
505 E. Huron St., Ste. 306
Ann Arbor, MI 48104-1567
Phone: (313)763-5930
Dr. Thomas J. Powell, Dir.

Research Activities and Fields: Autonomous and authentic self-help programs for persons with serious mental illness. Specific areas of study focus on how self-help and professional service providers can coordinate services for people with serious mental illness, how self-help groups can improve their programs, how persons with serious mental illness can gain access to non-mental health specialized self-help groups such as Alcoholics Anonymous, and how the public mental health system can be more organizationally supportive of consumer-run, self-help based programs.

★ 7672 ★ University of Michigan
Department of Psychiatry
1500 E. Medical Center Dr.
Ann Arbor, MI 48109-0704
Phone: (313)763-9629
Fax: (313)936-9761
John F. Greden, M.D., Chm.

Research Activities and Fields: Psychiatric diseases and their treatment, including studies on alcoholism, anorexia nervosa, anxiety and panic disorders, autism, behavior disorders, depression, eating disorders, electroconvulsive therapy, epilepsy, evoked responses of the brain, neuropeptides, obsessive-compulsive disorder, schizophrenia, Huntington's chorea, infant psychiatry, psychoactive drugs, psychotherapy, sleep disorders, social factors in emotional illness, suicide, traffic fatalities, and training of psychiatrists, psychologists, and social workers. **Formerly:** State Psychiatric Hospital; Neuropsychiatric Institute; Psychiatric Center.

★ 7673 ★ University of Michigan
Mental Health Research Institute
205 Zina Pitcher Pl.
Ann Arbor, MI 48109-0720
Phone: (313)764-4235
Dr. Bernard W. Agranoff, Dir.

Research Activities and Fields: Biological and behavioral studies relevant to normal and pathological human behavior and treatment of mental illness. Conducts studies on basic biological mechanisms relevant to normal and pathological behavior. **Publications:** *MHRI Annual Report.*

★ 7674 ★ University of Minnesota
Department of Psychiatry
Mayo Memorial Bldg., Box 393
420 Delaware St. SE
Minneapolis, MN 55455
Phone: (612)626-3853
Fax: (612)625-2989
Dr. Paula J. Clayton, Dir.

Research Activities and Fields: Psychiatry, psychology, and psychopharmacology, including various aspects of behavior and mental illness. **Formerly:** Psychiatry Research Laboratory.

★ 7675 ★ University of Missouri—Columbia
Missouri Institute of Mental Health
5247 Fyler Ave.
St. Louis, MO 63139-1494
Phone: (314)644-8851
Fax: (314)644-8834
Danny Wedding, Ph.D., Dir.

Research Activities and Fields: Mental health policy and ethics, mental health information systems, computer applications for the assessment and treatment of the mentally retarded and mentally ill, outcomes assessments, and mental health program evaluation research. **E-mail Address:** mimhdw@mizzou1.missouri.edu. **Formerly:** Missouri Institute of Psychiatry.

University of Montreal
Fernand Sequin Research Centre
See: Entry 10481

★7676★ **University of Montreal**
Mental Disorders and Crime Research
  Group
Departement de Psychologie
C.P. 6128, Succursale A
Montreal, PQ, Canada H3C 3J7
Phone: (514)343-7875
Fax: (514)494-4406
Prof. Sheilagh Hodgins, Ph.D., Dir.

Research Activities and Fields: Epidemiological and clinical studies of mental disorders and crime, including violent persons with major mental disorders, children with conduct disorders, adolescent homicide offenders, and parents who have killed their children.

★7677★ **University of Montreal**
Philippe Pinel Institute of Montreal
  Research Centre
10905 Henri-Bourassa Blvd. E.
Montreal, PQ, Canada H1C 1H1
Phone: (514)648-8461
Fax: (514)648-9586
Maurice Ohayon, M.D., Dir.

Research Activities and Fields: Epidemiology and mental health, including validation of new assessment and evaluation instruments. Also studies forensic psychiatry. **Publications:** *Effervescence.*

★7678★ **University of Montreal**
Psychology Department
Case Postale 6128, Sta. A
Montreal, PQ, Canada H3C 3J7
Phone: (514)343-6503
Fax: (514)343-2285
Dr. Franco Lepore, Head

Research Activities and Fields: Research in all major fields of basic and applied psychology, including developmental, social, physiological, cognitive, clinical, counseling, industrial/organizational, legal, and educational psychology; also studies artificial intelligence, motivation, perception, delinquency, neuropsychology, and couples and family psychology. **Publications:** Monographs. **E-mail Address:** leporefl@ere.umontreal.ca. **Formerly:** Institut de psychologie.

★7679★ **University of Montreal**
Riviere-des-Prairies Hospital Research
  Centre
7070, boulevard Perras
Montreal, PQ, Canada H1E 1A4
Phone: (514)323-7260
Fax: (514)323-4163
Jean-Jacques Breton, Dir.

Research Activities and Fields: Validation of measures for evaluating the mental health problems in children and adolescents. **E-mail Address:** fortinsy@ere.umontreal.ca.

★7680★ **University of North Carolina at**
  Charlotte
Social Science Working Group
Dept. of Psychology
4042 Colvard
Charlotte, NC 28223
Phone: (704)547-4758
James R. Cook, Ph.D., Chair

Research Activities and Fields: Multidisciplinary social science research, including development and evaluation of training materials for family caregivers of mentally ill, developmently disabled, and disabled aged. **Publications:** Works with local groups on program and proposal development.

★7681★ **University of Pennsylvania**
Center for Cognitive Therapy
School of Medicine
The Science Center, Rm. 754
3600 Market St.
Philadelphia, PA 19104-2648
Phone: (215)898-4100
Aaron T. Beck, M.D., Dir.

Research Activities and Fields: Psychiatric outpatient clinic, engaged in developing different assessment instruments to measure constructs of cognitive theory, extending the cognitive approach to anxiety and other psychiatric disorders, assessing and predicting suicidal risks, studying outpatient populations, and assessing different training models for cognitive therapists. **Publications:** *Center for Cognitive Therapy News* (newsletter).

★7682★ **University of Pennsylvania**
Depression Research Unit
University City Science Center
3600 Market St., 8th Fl.
Philadelphia, PA 19104-2649
Phone: (215)662-3462
Fax: (215)662-6443
Jay D. Amsterdam, M.D., Dir.

Research Activities and Fields: Clinical and preclinical research in affective disorders. Research areas include psychopharmacology, particularly development of new antidepressant drugs; clinical neuroendocrinology; and the biochemical causes of major depression.

★7683★ **University of Pennsylvania**
Private Practice Research Group
University Science Center
3600 Market St., Ste. 872
Philadelphia, PA 19104-2649
Phone: (215)898-4301
Fax: (215)898-0509
Dr. Karl Rickels, Dir.

Research Activities and Fields: Effects of new drugs on anxiety and depression.

University of Pennsylvania
Psychopharmacology Research Unit
See: Entry 10482

University of Pennsylvania
Weight and Eating Disorders Program
See: Entry 1717

★7684★ **University of Pittsburgh**
Western Psychiatric Institute and Clinic of
  Presbyterian University Hospital
Univ. of Pittsburgh Medical Center
Dept. of Psychiatry, School of Medicine
3811 O'Hara St.
Pittsburgh, PA 15213
Phone: (412)624-0682
Fax: (412)624-0714
Thomas Detre, M.D., Dir.

Research Activities and Fields: Advancement of basic and clinical knowledge in psychological, biological, environmental, and social interactions related to mental health and psychiatric care. Conducts research on psychiatric disorders, including depression, schizophrenia, anorexia nervosa, Alzheimer's disease, autism, anxiety, obsessive-compulsive disorders, and borderline disorders. Clinical services are organized around comprehensive treatment modules in the following areas: adolescent and young adult disorders, affective disorders, psychogeriatrics, schizophrenia, and children's services. Clinical laboratory investigations include studies in clinical pharmacology, neuroendocrinology, psychophysiology, neuropharmacology, neurophysics, molecular neurobiology and genetics, and EEG sleep. Also researches health habits and precursors of medical disease states such as hypertension, diabetes, obesity, effects of drug abuse, and epidemiology of psychiatric disorders.

★7685★ **University of Rochester**
Center for Community Study
575 Mt. Hope Ave.
Rochester, NY 14627
Phone: (716)275-2547
Dr. Emory L. Cowen, Dir.

Research Activities and Fields: Mental health problems, including studies on early detection and prevention of school maladjustment, stressful life events and school maladjustment, training and utilization of paraprofessionals in mental health roles, and young children's school adaptation problems. Prevention studies are based on analysis of the social environment of primary grade classrooms, training interpersonal skills and competencies in young children, and forestalling negative outcomes of stressful life events, including the study of resilience among young profoundly stressed urban children.

★7686★ **University of South Carolina at**
  Columbia
Center for the Study of Suicide
228 Callcott Bldg.
Columbia, SC 29208
Phone: (803)777-6870
Fax: (803)777-5251
Dr. Ronald Maris, Dir.

Research Activities and Fields: Legal, psychological, medical, and epidemiological aspects of suicide; Prozac and suicide; and the assessment and prediction of suicide. **Publications:** *Suicide and Life Threatening Behavior* (official journal of the American Association of Suicidology). **Formerly:** Center for the Study of Suicide and Life Threatening Behavior.

★7687★ **University of South Dakota**
Social Science Research Institute
Vermillion, SD 57069
Phone: (605)677-5401
Prof. Harlowe Hatle, Jr., Dir.

Research Activities and Fields: Research includes studies on organizations, economic and social development, criminology, juvenile delinquency, child abuse, aged population, communications, social work and welfare, court administration, prison education, alcoholism, medical and educational problems on American Indian reservations, and follow-up on juvenile offenders. Conducts anthropological studies, including site preservation. **Formerly:** Social Research Center; Social Behavior Research Institute (1991).

★ **7688** ★   **University of South Florida**
Florida Mental Health Institute
13301 Bruce B. Downs Blvd.
Tampa, FL 33612-3899
Phone: (813)974-4533
Fax: (813)974-4406
Max C. Dertke, Ph.D., Dean

Research Activities and Fields: Mental health care, including aging and mental health, child and family studies, community mental health, and mental health law and policy. **Publications:** *Mind Matters* (newsletter); *Mental Health Reviews*; *Update* (newsletter of the Research and Training Center for Children's Mental Health). Houses the *Journal of Mental Health Administration* (a peer-reviewed quarterly journal); and *Life Span* (newsletter). **E-mail Address:** probinso@hal.fmhi.usf.edu.

★ **7689** ★   **University of South Florida**
Research and Training Center for
  Children's Mental Health
Florida Mental Health Institute
13301 Bruce B. Downs Blvd.
Tampa, FL 33612-3899
Phone: (813)974-4661
Fax: (813)974-4406
Robert M. Friedman, Ph.D., Exec.Dir.

Research Activities and Fields: Children and adolescents with emotional disturbances, focusing on characteristics and development; factors associated with successful transition to adulthood; the relationship between functional abilities and successful employment, residential, educational, and social outcomes; identification and evaluation of model programs to assist transition from school to work; efficacy and cost-effectiveness of alternatives to residential treatment; and financing options, incentives, and disincentives for community and home-treatment. **Publications:** *UPDATE* (newsletter).

★ **7690** ★   **University of Tennessee,**
  Knoxville
Psychological Clinic
227 Austin-Peay Bldg.
Knoxville, TN 37996-0090
Phone: (615)974-2161
Fax: (615)974-3330
Dr. Leonard Handler, Dir.

Research Activities and Fields: Diagnostic testing, with emphasis on psychotherapy and psychological testing, and research conducted by graduate students under the supervision of the Clinic Director, Department Head, and the University's Committee on Research Participation.

★ **7691** ★   **University of Texas**
Hogg Foundation for Mental Health
Austin, TX 78713-7998
Phone: (512)471-5041
Fax: (512)471-9608
Dr. Charles M. Bonjean, Exec.Dir.

Research Activities and Fields: Mental health, including evaluative research of community programs and studies on education, school-based services for children and their families, children at risk, care of the mentally ill, and aging. Major research programs conducted through grants-in-aid to other organizations in Texas. **Publications:** Annual Report; Publications List. **E-mail Address:** bonjean@mail.utexas.edu. **Formerly:** Hogg Foundation for Mental Hygiene (1956).

★ **7692** ★   **University of Texas—Houston**
  Health Science Center
Mental Sciences Institute
1300 Moursund Ave.
Houston, TX 77030
Phone: (713)792-5531
Fax: (713)792-8478
Dr. Robert Guynn, Dir.

Research Activities and Fields: Biochemical and behavioral aspects of psychiatric diseases, particularly physiopathology and pharmacology of alcohol and drug addiction, and affective and anxiety disorders. Performs basic and clinical studies in neuroendocrinology, metabolism, behavioral science, disorders, mental retardation, neurochemistry, psychophysiology, biochemistry, crime and delinquency, and gerontology. **E-mail Address:** rguynn.utmsnwm@msi66.msi.uth.tmc.edu. **Formerly:** Houston State Psychiatric Institute (1967); Texas Research Institute of Mental Science.

★ **7693** ★   **University of Texas**
  Southwestern Medical Center at Dallas
Mental Health Clinical Research Center
St. Paul Professional Bldg. I, Ste. 600
5959 Harry Hines Blvd.
Dallas, TX 75235-9101
Phone: (214)648-8300
Fax: (214)648-4278
Dr. A. John Rush, Dir.

Research Activities and Fields: Major depression, bipolar, and dysthymic disorders. Conducts studies in treatment, pathobiology, prognosis, and mechanisms of depression.

★ **7694** ★   **University of Washington**
Addictive Behaviors Research Center
Dept. of Psychology
NI-25
Seattle, WA 98195
Phone: (206)685-1200
Fax: (206)685-1310
Dr. G. Alan Marlatt, Dir.

Research Activities and Fields: Addictive behaviors research, including alcohol abuse prevention, smoking, relapse prevention, harm reduction, and skills training.

University of Wisconsin—Madison
Harlow Primate Laboratory
See: Entry 13238

University of Wisconsin—Madison
Neuropsychology Laboratory
See: Entry 8533

★ **7695** ★   **University of Wisconsin—**
  Madison
Wisconsin Psychiatric Research Institute
600 Highland Ave.
Madison, WI 53792
Phone: (608)263-6079
Fax: (608)263-9340
Ned H. Kalin, M.D., Dir.

Research Activities and Fields: Biological and social aspects of mental health.

★ **7696** ★   **Van Ameringen Center for**
  Education and Research
Fountain House, Inc.
425 W. 47th St.
New York, NY 10036
Phone: (212)582-0340
Fax: (212)397-1649
Cathaleene Masias, Ph.D., Rsch.Dir.

Research Activities and Fields: Conducts basic research on the rehabilitation, symptomatology, and stigma of serious mental illness with a focus on member self-determination in recovery. Evaluates the effectiveness of clubhouse model programs of psychiatric rehabilitation in facilitating post-hospital community adjustment and evaluates the effectiveness of transitional employment and other employment models. **Publications:** *Fountain House Annual*.

★ **7697** ★   **Vanderbilt University**
Center for Psychotherapy Research
Nashville, TN 37240
Phone: (615)322-0058
Hans H. Strupp, Ph.D., Dir.

Research Activities and Fields: Time-limited dynamic psychotherapy. **Formerly:** Center for Short-Term Psychotherapy Research.

★ **7698** ★   **Veterans Affairs Medical Center**
NIMH Mental Health Clinical Research
  Center
MC 116A
3801 Miranda Ave.
Palo Alto, CA 94304
Phone: (415)852-3456
Fax: (415)493-4901
Adolf Pfefferbaum, M.D., Dir.

Research Activities and Fields: Mental illness, focusing on clinical, physiological, and neuropsychological factors, with special emphasis on neuroimaging studies of brain structure and function. Areas include schizophrenia and neurological disorders with psychotic symptoms.

★ **7699** ★   **Virginia Commonwealth**
  University
Center for Psychological Services and
  Development
PO Box 842018
Richmond, VA 23284-2018
Phone: (804)828-8069
Dr. Julie Williams, Dir.

Research Activities and Fields: Outcome studies of psychological intervention for individuals in a variety of problem areas, including dysthymia, personality disorders, and dysfunctional interpersonal style. Also examines computerized psychological assessment as a predictor of outcome. **Publications:** Annual Report. **Formerly:** Known as Psychological Services Center until merger with Midlife Counseling Center (1983).

★7700★ Washington Institute for Mental Illness Research and Training
Eastern Branch
PO Box A
Medical Lake, WA 99022-0045
Phone: (509)299-4501
Fax: (509)299-4664
Dennis G. Dyck, Ph.D., Dir.

Research Activities and Fields: Mental health clinical and services research for persons with severe and persistent mental illness; family and patient psychoeducation and support; and immune function and mental illness. **E-mail Address:** wimirt@wsuvm1.csc.wsu.edu. **Formerly:** Mental Illness Research and Education Institute.

★7701★ Washington University
William Greenleaf Eliot Division of Child Psychiatry
4940 Children's Place
St. Louis, MO 63110
Phone: (314)454-2303
Fax: (314)454-2330
Dr. Richard Mattison, Dir.

Research Activities and Fields: Conducts studies of pharmacotherapy and genetics of childhood depression, children of alcoholics, prevention of conduct disorders, neuroimaging of childhood affective disorders, and outcome of childhood sexual abuse. **Formerly:** Harry Edison Child Development Research Center.

★7702★ Wellesley College
Stone Center for Developmental Services and Studies
Wellesley, MA 02181-8268
Phone: (617)283-2838
Fax: (617)283-3646

Research Activities and Fields: Psychological development and studies of psychological problems in women and children. Current studies focus on the elimination of developmental problems in high risk populations, cross-cultural application of preventive medicine, social skills programs for school children, depression in mothers of young children, substance abuse prevention for young adult women, and social compentency in elementary schools. **Publications:** *Work in Progress*; *Stone Center Working Papers Series* (59 papers and books available).

★7703★ Yale University
Center for Biocognitive Studies
Yale Psychiatric Institute
184 Liberty St.
New Haven, CT 06519
Phone: (203)785-7200
Fax: (203)785-7855
Dr. Thomas McGlashan, Med.Dir.

Research Activities and Fields: Study of the cognitive, linguistic, psychophysiological, and neuropsychological bases of psychopathology.

★7704★ Yale University
Ribicoff Research Facilities of the Connecticut Mental Health Center
34 Park St.
New Haven, CT 06511
Phone: (203)789-7220
Fax: (203)562-7079
Dr. Eric J. Nestler, Dir.

Research Activities and Fields: Preclinical and clinical studies of the neurobiological basis of severe mental disorders, including depression, anxiety, schizophrenia, and drug addiction. Conducts basic research programs in molecular, biochemical, neurophysiological, neuropharmacological, and behavioral fields. **Publications:** *Yale Psychiatry*.

★7705★ Yale University
Yale Behavioral Medicine Clinic
Yale School of Medicine
333 Cedar St.
New Haven, CT 06510
Phone: (203)785-2112
Hoyle Leigh, M.D., Dir.

Research Activities and Fields: Research application of the patient evaluation grid; using biofeedback, hypnosis, and psychotherapy, the Clinic evaluates and treats patients with medical/behavioral problems, including agoraphobia, depression, and stress-related disorders.

★7706★ Yeshiva University
Sound View-Throgs Neck Community Mental Health Center
2527 Glebe Ave.
Bronx, NY 10461
Phone: (718)904-4400
Fax: (718)931-7307
Dr. Jack F. Wilder, Dir.

Research Activities and Fields: Mental health, mental illness, and recovery from mental illness.

★7707★ York University
Psychotherapy Research Centre
Behavioral Science Bldg., Rm. 410
4700 Keele St.
North York, ON, Canada M3J 1P3
Phone: (416)736-5364
Fax: (416)736-5814
Dr. Les Greenberg, Ph.D., Dir.

Research Activities and Fields: Process of psychotherapy and the outcomes, including affective and meaning construction processes and the treatment of depression.

State Government Agencies

Mental Health

★7708★ Alabama Department of Mental Health and Mental Retardation
PO Box 3710
Montgomery, AL 36109-0710
Phone: (334)271-9208
Fax: (334)240-3195

★7709★ Alaska Department of Health and Social Services
Mental Health and Developmental Disabilities Division
PO Box 110620
Juneau, AK 99811-0620
Phone: (907)465-3370
Fax: (907)465-2668

★7710★ Arizona Department of Health Services
Behavioral Health Services Division
2122 E. Highland
Phoenix, AZ 85016
Phone: (602)381-8999
Fax: (602)553-9143

★7711★ Arkansas Department of Human Services
Mental Health Services Division
PO Box 1437
Little Rock, AR 72203
Phone: (501)686-9165
Fax: (501)686-6836

★7712★ California Health and Welfare Agency
Mental Health Department
1600 9th St., Rm. 151
Sacramento, CA 95814
Phone: (916)654-2309
Fax: (916)654-3198

★7713★ Colorado Department of Human Services
Mental Health Division
3520 W. Oxford Ave.
Denver, CO 80236
Phone: (303)762-4088

★7714★ Connecticut Department of Mental Health
90 Washington St.
Hartford, CT 06106
Phone: (203)566-3650
Fax: (203)566-6195

★7715★ Delaware Department of Health and Social Services
Alcoholism, Drug Abuse, and Mental Health Division
1901 N. Dupont Hwy.
New Castle, DE 19720
Phone: (302)577-4461
Fax: (302)577-4510

★7716★ District of Columbia Department of Human Services
Mental Health Commission
PO Box 54047
Washington, DC 20032
Phone: (202)373-7166
Fax: (202)673-6484

★7717★ Florida Department of Health and Rehabilitative Services
Human Services Program Office
Alcohol, Drug Abuse and Mental Health Office
1317 Winewood Blvd.
Tallahassee, FL 32399-0700
Phone: (904)488-8304
Fax: (904)922-2993

★7718★ **Georgia Department of Human Resources**
Mental Health, Mental Retardation and Substance Abuse Division
2 Peachtree St. NW
Atlanta, GA 30303
Phone: (404)657-2252
Fax: (404)657-2256

★7719★ **Hawaii Department of Health**
Behavioral Health Administration
1250 Punchbowl St.
Honolulu, HI 96813
Phone: (808)586-4434
Fax: (808)586-4444

★7720★ **Idaho Department of Health and Welfare**
Family and Community Services Division
Mental Health Bureau
PO Box 83720
Boise, ID 83720-0036
Phone: (208)334-5700
Fax: (208)334-6558

★7721★ **Illinois Department of Mental Health and Developmental Disabilities**
401 William G. Stratton Bldg.
Springfield, IL 62765
Phone: (217)782-2243
Fax: (217)524-0835

★7722★ **Indiana Family and Social Services Administration**
Mental Health Division
402 W. Washington, Rm. W341
Indianapolis, IN 46204
Phone: (317)233-7845
Fax: (317)233-4693

★7723★ **Iowa Department of Human Services**
Mental Health, Mental Retardation and Developmental Disabilities Division
Hoover State Office Bldg.
Des Moines, IA 50319
Phone: (515)281-5126
Fax: (515)281-4597

★7724★ **Kansas Department of Social and Rehabilitation Services**
Mental Health and Retardation Services Division
Docking State Office Bldg.
Topeka, KS 66612
Phone: (913)296-3773
Fax: (913)296-1158

★7725★ **Kentucky Human Resources Cabinet**
Mental Health and Mental Retardation Department
Mental Health Division
275 E. Main St.
Frankfort, KY 40621
Phone: (502)564-4448
Fax: (502)564-3844

★7726★ **Louisiana Department of Health and Hospitals**
Mental Health Office
PO Box 2790
Baton Rouge, LA 70821
Phone: (504)342-0095
Fax: (504)342-3931

★7727★ **Maine Department of Mental Health and Mental Retardation**
Mental Health Division
State House, Sta. 40
Augusta, ME 04333
Phone: (207)287-7230
Fax: (207)287-4268

★7728★ **Maryland Department of Health and Mental Hygiene**
Mental Hygiene Administration
201 W. Preston St., 5th Fl.
Baltimore, MD 21201
Phone: (410)225-6611
Fax: (410)225-6489

★7729★ **Massachusetts Executive Office of Health and Human Services**
Mental Health Department
25 Staniford St.
Boston, MA 02114
Phone: (617)727-5600
Fax: (617)727-5500

★7730★ **Michigan Department of Mental Health**
Lewis Cass Bldg., 6th Fl.
320 S. Walnut
Lansing, MI 48913
Phone: (517)373-3500
Fax: (517)335-3090

★7731★ **Minnesota Department of Human Services**
Community Mental Health Administration
444 Lafayette Rd.
St. Paul, MN 55155
Phone: (612)296-2710
Fax: (612)297-1539

★7732★ **Mississippi Department of Mental Health**
1101 Robert E. Lee Bldg.
Jackson, MS 39201
Phone: (601)359-1288
Fax: (601)359-6295

★7733★ **Missouri Department of Mental Health**
Mental Health Administration Office
1706 E. Elm St.
PO Box 687
Jefferson City, MO 65102
Phone: (314)751-4055
Fax: (314)751-8224

★7734★ **Montana Department of Health and Environmental Sciences**
Mental Health Division
Cogswell Bldg.
PO Box 200901
Helena, MT 59620-0901
Phone: (406)444-3969

★7735★ **Nebraska Department of Public Institutions**
Community Mental Health Division
PO Box 94728
Lincoln, NE 68509-4728
Phone: (402)471-2851
Fax: (402)479-5145

★7736★ **Nevada Department of Human Resources**
Mental Hygiene and Mental Retardation Division
505 E. King St., Rm. 603
Carson City, NV 89710
Phone: (702)687-5943
Fax: (702)687-4773

★7737★ **New Hampshire Department of Health and Human Services**
Mental Health Division
105 Pleasant St.
Concord, NH 03301
Phone: (603)271-5007
Fax: (603)271-5058

★7738★ **New Jersey Department of Human Services**
Mental Health Services Division
Capitol Center, CN 727
Princeton, NJ 08625-0727
Phone: (609)777-0702
Fax: (609)292-3824

★7739★ **New Mexico Department of Health**
Mental Health Division
1190 St. Francis Dr.
PO Box 26110
Santa Fe, NM 87502-6110
Phone: (505)827-2650
Fax: (505)827-2695

★7740★ **New York State Office of Mental Health**
44 Holland Ave.
Albany, NY 12229
Phone: (518)474-4403
Fax: (518)474-2149

★7741★ **North Carolina Department of Human Resources**
Mental Health, Developmental Disabilities and Substance Abuse Services Division
PO Box 29526
Raleigh, NC 27626-0526
Phone: (919)733-7011
Fax: (919)715-4645

★7742★ **North Dakota Department of Human Services**
Mental Health Division
600 E. Boulevard Ave.
Bismarck, ND 58505
Phone: (701)328-2766
Fax: (701)328-2359

★7743★ **Ohio Department of Mental Health**
30 E. Broad St., 8th Fl.
Columbus, OH 43215
Phone: (614)466-2337
Fax: (614)752-9453

★7744★ **Oklahoma Department of Mental Health**
PO Box 53277
Oklahoma City, OK 73152-3277
Phone: (405)522-3908
Fax: (405)522-3650

★7745★ **Oregon Department of Human Resources**
Mental Health and Developmental Disabilities Services Division
Mental Health Services Office
2575 Bittern St. NE
Salem, OR 97310
Phone: (503)945-9499
Fax: (503)378-3796

★7746★ **Pennsylvania Department of Public Welfare**
Mental Health Office
Box 2675
Harrisburg, PA 17105
Phone: (717)787-6443
Fax: (717)772-2062

★7747★ **Rhode Island Department of Mental Health, Retardation and Hospitals**
Mental Health and Management Services Division
600 New London Ave.
Cranston, RI 02920
Phone: (401)464-2338
Fax: (401)464-3204

★7748★ **South Carolina Department of Mental Health**
PO Box 485
Columbia, SC 29202
Phone: (803)734-7780
Fax: (803)734-7879

★7749★ **South Dakota Department of Human Services**
Mental Health Division
E. Hwy. 344
Pierre, SD 57501
Phone: (605)773-4354
Fax: (605)773-5483

★7750★ **Tennessee Department of Mental Health and Mental Retardation**
Mental Health Services Division
706 Church St.
Nashville, TN 37243-0675
Phone: (615)532-6767
Fax: (615)532-6514

★7751★ **Texas Department of Mental Health and Mental Retardation**
Mental Health Division
PO Box 12668
Austin, TX 78711-2668
Phone: (512)206-4510
Fax: (512)206-4560

★7752★ **Utah Department of Human Services**
Mental Health Division
PO Box 45500
Salt Lake City, UT 84145-0500
Phone: (801)538-4270
Fax: (801)538-4016

★7753★ **Vermont Agency of Human Services**
Mental Health Department
Mental Health Division
103 S. Main St.
Waterbury, VT 05671-1601
Phone: (802)241-2604
Fax: (802)241-3052

★7754★ **Virginia Office of Health and Human Resources**
Mental Health, Retardation and Substance Abuse Services Department
Mental Health Division
PO Box 1797
Richmond, VA 23214
Phone: (804)786-2991
Fax: (804)371-6638

★7755★ **Washington Department of Social and Health Services**
Health and Rehabilitative Services Office
Mental Health Division
PO Box 45060
Olympia, WA 98504-5060
Phone: (360)753-4420
Fax: (360)586-5874

★7756★ **West Virginia Department of Health and Human Resources**
Human Resources Bureau
Mental Health and Community Rehabilitative Services Division
State Capitol Complex, Bldg. 6, Rm. 617
Charleston, WV 25305
Phone: (304)588-0627
Fax: (304)558-1008

★7757★ **Wisconsin Department of Health and Social Services**
Community Services Division
Community Mental Health Bureau
PO Box 7850
Madison, WI 53707-7850
Phone: (608)266-3249
Fax: (608)266-2579

★7758★ **Wyoming Department of Health**
Behavioral Health Division
Mental Health Program
446 Hathaway Bldg.
Cheyenne, WY 82002-0710
Phone: (307)777-7094
Fax: (307)777-5580

State & Regional Organizations

Associations listed below are state affiliates of the National Mental Health Association, 1021 Prince St., Alexandria, VA 22314-2971, (703) 684-7722. Contact the national association for information on states not listed.

Alaska

★7759★ **Alaska Mental Health Association**
4050 Lake Otis Pkwy., Ste. 202
Anchorage, AK 99508
Phone: (907)563-0880
Fax: (907)563-0881

California

★7760★ **Mental Health Association in California**
1100 11th St., Ste. 305
Sacramento, CA 95814-7321
Phone: (916)557-1167
Fax: (916)447-2350

Delaware

★7761★ **Mental Health Association in Delaware**
1813 N. Franklin St.
Wilmington, DE 19802-3893
Phone: (302)656-8308
Fax: (302)656-0747

Georgia

★7762★ **Mental Health Association of Georgia**
620 Peachtree St. NE, Ste. 300R
Atlanta, GA 30308
Phone: (404)875-7081
Fax: (404)607-8782

Hawaii

★7763★ **Mental Health Association in Hawaii**
200 N. Vineyard Blvd., No. 300
Honolulu, HI 96817
Phone: (808)521-1846
Fax: (808)533-6995

Illinois

★7764★ **Mental Health Association in Illinois**
150 N. Wacker, Ste. 900
Chicago, IL 60606
Phone: (312)368-9070
Fax: (312)368-0283

Indiana

★7765★ **Mental Health Association in Indiana**
55 Monument Cir., Ste. 700
Indianapolis, IN 46204
Phone: (317)638-3501
Fax: (317)638-3540

Kentucky

★7766★ **Mental Health Association of Kentucky**
120 Sears Ave., Ste. 213
Louisville, KY 40207
Phone: (502)893-0460
Fax: (502)894-0635

Louisiana

★ 7767 ★ **Mental Health Association in Louisiana**
200 Government St., Ste. 140
Baton Rouge, LA 70802
Phone: (504)343-1921
Fax: (504)343-6362

Maryland

★ 7768 ★ **Mental Health Association of Maryland**
711 W. 40th St., Ste. 428
Baltimore, MD 21211
Phone: (410)235-1178
Fax: (410)235-1180

Michigan

★ 7769 ★ **Mental Health Association in Michigan**
15920 W. 12 Mile Rd.
Southfield, MI 48076
Phone: (810)557-6777
Fax: (810)557-5995

Montana

★ 7770 ★ **Mental Health Association of Montana**
555 Fuller Ave.
Helena, MT 59601
Phone: (406)442-4276

New Jersey

★ 7771 ★ **Mental Health Association in New Jersey**
60 S. Fullerton Ave., Rm. 105
Montclair, NJ 07042
Phone: (201)744-2500
Fax: (201)744-1026

New York

★ 7772 ★ **Mental Health Association in New York State**
169 Central Ave.
Albany, NY 12206
Phone: (518)434-0439
Fax: (518)427-8676

North Carolina

★ 7773 ★ **Mental Health Association in North Carolina**
3820 Bland Rd.
Raleigh, NC 27609
Phone: (919)981-0740
Fax: (919)954-7238

North Dakota

★ 7774 ★ **Mental Health Association of North Dakota**
200 W. Bowen
PO Box 160
Bismarck, ND 58502-0160
Phone: (701)255-3692
Fax: (701)255-2411

Ohio

★ 7775 ★ **Mental Health Association in Ohio**
3300 Refugee Rd.
Columbus, OH 43232
Phone: (614)239-6204
Fax: (614)239-6206

Rhode Island

★ 7776 ★ **Mental Health Association of Rhode Island**
500 Prospect St.
Pawtucket, RI 02860
Phone: (401)726-2285
Fax: (401)727-2810

South Carolina

★ 7777 ★ **Mental Health Association in South Carolina**
1823 Gadsden St.
Columbia, SC 29201
Phone: (803)779-5363
Fax: (803)779-0017

Texas

★ 7778 ★ **Mental Health Association in Texas**
8401 Shoal Creek Blvd.
Austin, TX 78757-7597
Phone: (512)454-3706
Fax: (512)454-3725

Utah

★ 7779 ★ **Mental Health Association in Utah**
255 East 400 South, Ste. 150
Salt Lake City, UT 84111
Phone: (801)531-8996
Fax: (801)328-1243

Virginia

★ 7780 ★ **Mental Health Association of Virginia**
201 W. Broad St., Ste. 503
Richmond, VA 23220
Phone: (804)782-2225
Fax: (804)782-6939

West Virginia

★ 7781 ★ **Mental Health Association in West Virginia**
1 United Way Sq.
Charleston, WV 25301-1098
Phone: (304)340-3512

Chapter 39
Military Medicine

Federal Government Agencies

★7782★ U.S. Department of Defense
Department of the Air Force
Air Force Material Command
Human Systems Center (HSD)
Attn: HSD/PA
Brooks Air Force Base, TX 78235-5000
Phone: (210)536-3652
Fax: (210)536-3224

Description: Center has functions involving research, development, and acquisition; education; and occupational and environmental health. Within these mission areas, HSC conducts biotechnology research and development, medical evaluations and consultation, and personnel/training research and development. Center also provides support to field organizations in occupational, radiological, and environmental health programs.

★7783★ U.S. Department of Defense
Department of the Air Force
Vice Chief of Staff of the Air Force
Air Force Surgeon General
Bolling Air Force Base, Bldg. 5681
Washington, DC 20332
Phone: (202)767-4343
Fax: (202)767-6208

Description: The Surgeon General is part of the Special Staff, independent of the basic staff structure, providing advisory and support services to both the Chief of Staff and the Air Staff. Operating components are: 1) Assistant Surgeon General for Dental Services, 2) Biomedical Sciences Corps, 3) Congressional and Public Affairs, 4) Health Care Studies and Evaluations, 5) Medical Programs and Resources, 6) Medical Support, and 7) Nursing Services.

★7784★ U.S. Department of Defense
Department of the Army
Army Health Services Command
Ft. Sam Houston, TX 78234
Phone: (512)221-6313

Description: Performs health services for the Army within the U.S. and, as directed, for other governmental agencies and activities. Com-

mands the Army hospital system within the U.S. Is also responsible for the conduct of medical professional education for Army personnel, and the development of medical doctrine, concepts, organizations, material requirements, and systems in support of the Army.

★7785★ U.S. Department of Defense
Department of the Army
Army Surgeon General
Army Medical Research and Material
Command
Bldg. 521
Fort Detrick, MD 21701-6012
Phone: (301)619-7613

Description: The U.S. Army Medical Research and Development Command manages a worldwide research program aimed at solving medical problems of military importance. The program, which is designed to maintain or restore the health of the individual soldier, involves: assessment, prevention, diagnosis, and treatment of infectious diseases that would hamper military operations; disease vector surveillance; combat casualty care and rapid return to duty of injured soldiers; studies on health hazards of military materiel; studies on factors limiting soldier effectiveness; management of maxillofacial injury; assessment and prevention of oral diseases; and research in dental materials. Command headquarters determines the mission and concepts of its nine major research and development laboratories: 1) Letterman Army Institute of Research; 2) Aeromedical Research Laboratory; 3) Institute of Dental Research; 4) Institute of Surgical Research; 5) Biomedical Research and Development Laboratory; 6) Medical Research Institute of Chemical Defense; 7) Medical Research Institute of Infectious Diseases; 8) Research Institute of Environmental Medicine; and 9) Walter Reed Army Institute of Research. (See separate descriptions, Chapter 17, Federal Government Research Agencies, Facilities, and Programs.)

★7786★ U.S. Department of Defense
Department of the Army
Chief of Staff of the Army
Army Surgeon General

5109 Leesburg Pike
Skyline Pl., No. 6
Falls Church, VA 22041
Phone: (703)681-3000
Fax: (703)681-3243

Description: The office of the Surgeon General manages health services for the Army and, as directed, for other services, agencies, and organizations. Other responsibilities include health standards for Army personnel; health professional education and training; career management for missioned and warrant officer personnel of the Army Medical Department; medical research, material development and test and evaluation; policies concerning health aspects of Army environmental programs and prevention of diseases; and planning, programming, and budgeting for Army-wide health services. Major components of the Office of the Surgeon General include: 1) Dental Services/Dental Corps; 2) Veterinary Services/Veterinary Corps; 3) Army Medical Specialist Corps; 4) Army Nurse Corps; and 5) the Health Facility Planning Agency.

★7787★ U.S. Department of Defense
Department of the Navy
Chief of Naval Operations
Bureau of Medicine and Surgery
23rd & E Sts. NW
Washington, DC 20372
Phone: (202)653-1144
Fax: (202)653-0428

Description: The Bureau directs the provision of medical and dental services for Navy and Marine Corps personnel and other persons authorized by law.

★7788★ U.S. Department of Defense
Department of the Navy
Marine Corps
Office of Health Services
Arlington Annex
Columbia Pike and Southgate Rd.
Arlington, VA 22204
Phone: (703)614-4478

★7789★ U.S. Department of Defense
Department of the Navy
Naval Medical Research and Development
Command

8901 Wisconsin Ave.
Bethesda, MD 20889-5607
Phone: (301)295-0283

Description: Command is responsible for the management of the Navy's medical research, development, test, and evaluation programs concerned with the health, safety, and performance of Navy and Marine Corps personnel. Principal areas of research interest are: submarine and diving medicine, aviation medicine, human performance, fleet health care, infectious diseases, fleet occupational health, oral and dental health, and electromagnetic radiation. Major components of the Command are the Naval Medical Research Institute, Naval Submarine Medical Research Laboratory, Naval Aerospace Medical Research Laboratory, Naval Biodynamics Laboratory, Naval Health Research Center, and Naval Dental Research Institute. (For descriptions of components, see Chapter 17, Federal Government Research Agencies, Facilities, and Programs.)

★ 7790 ★ **U.S. Department of Defense**
Office of Assistant Secretary of Defense
for Health Affairs
The Pentagon
Washington, DC 20301
Phone: (703)697-2111
Fax: (703)614-3537

Description: Office is responsible for Department of Defense health matters, including preventive medicine; medical readiness; health care delivery; drug and alcohol abuse prevention; and procurement, development, and retention of medical personnel.

★ 7791 ★ **U.S. Department of Defense**
Office of Assistant Secretary of Defense
for Health Affairs
Office of Civilian Health and Medical
Program of the Uniformed Services
(OCHAMPUS)
Aurora, CO 80045-6900
Phone: (303)361-1313

Description: OCHAMPUS was established under the policy guidance and operational direction of the Assistant Secretary of Defense (Health Affairs) to administer a civilian health and medical care program for retirees and for the spouses and dependent children of active duty, retired, and deceased service members. Spouses and dependent children of totally disabled veterans are included as well. The Office also administers a program for payment of emergency medical/dental services provided to active duty service members by civilian medical personnel.

★ 7792 ★ **U.S. Department of Defense**
Office of Assistant Secretary of Defense
for Health Affairs (USUHS)
Uniformed Services University of the
Health Sciences
4301 Jones Bridge Rd.
Bethesda, MD 20814-4799
Phone: (301)295-3013
Fax: (301)295-3542

Description: The Uniformed Services University of the Health Sciences was established to educate career-oriented medical officers for the military services. In addition to the F. Edward Hebert School of Medicine, the University offers graduate programs in the basic sciences to both civilian and military applicants, and provides continuing medical education for the military services at the Bethesda campus and at military bases around the world.

★ 7793 ★ **U.S. Department of Veterans**
Affairs
Veterans Health Administration
810 Vermont Ave. NW
Washington, DC 20420
Phone: (202)273-5781

Description: The Veterans Health Administration (formerly Health Services and Research Administration) provides hospital, nursing home and domiciliary care, and outpatient medical and dental care to eligible veterans of military service in the Armed Forces. It operates medical centers, domiciliaries, clinics, and nursing home units in the U.S., the Commonwealth of Puerto Rico, and the Republic of the Philippines, and provides for similar care under VA auspices in non-VA hospitals and community nursing homes, and for visits by veterans to non-VA physicians and dentists for outpatient treatment. Under the Civilian Health and Medical Program, dependents of certain veterans are provided with medical care supplied by non-VA institutions and physicians. The Administration conducts both individual medical and health-care delivery research projects and multi-hospital research programs. It assists in the education of physicians and dentists, and with training of many other health care professionals through affiliations with educational institutions and organizations.

★ 7794 ★ **U.S. House of Representatives**
Committee on Veterans' Affairs
Subcommittee on Hospitals and Health
Care
333 Cannon House Office Bldg.
Washington, DC 20515-6335
Phone: (202)225-9154
Fax: (202)226-4536

★ 7795 ★ **U.S. Senate**
Committee on Veterans' Affairs
SR-414 Russell Senate Office Bldg.
Washington, DC 20510-6375
Phone: (202)224-9126

National & International Organizations

★ 7796 ★ **Air National Guard Optometric**
Society (ANGOS)
c/o Major Lyman Nordan
5517 Afton Dr.
Birmingham, AL 35242
Phone: (205)991-8663
Major Lyman Nordan, Pres.

Founded: 1975. **Members:** 50. **Description:** Civilian military reserve optometrists serving with the U.S. Air National Guard. Purposes are: to enhance and improve military eye care; to provide assistance in establishing occupational safety programs concerning vision; to promote cooperation among civilian and military optometrists; to conduct military visual research programs. Sponsors annual educational programs including reports of research and statistical projects. **Publications:** *Air National Guard Optometric Society--Newsletter*, 3/year. Newsletter. *Price:* Included in membership dues.

★ 7797 ★ **Association of Military Surgeons**
of the U.S. (AMSUS)
9320 Old Georgetown Rd.
Bethesda, MD 20814
Phone: (301)897-8800
Fax: (301)530-5446
Lt.Gen. Max Bralliar, Exec.Dir.

Founded: 1891. **Members:** 12,000. **Local Groups:** 10. **Description:** Physicians, dentists, veterinarians, nurses, pharmacists, dietitians, therapists, and others of commissioned rank or equivalent in the Army, Navy, Air Force, Public Health Service, and Veterans Administration; Reserve and National Guard officers are also eligible for membership. Advances all phases of federal medicine and allied sciences related to federal health services. Provides group insurance. **Publications:** *AMSUS Newsletter*, quarterly. Newsletter. • *Military Medicine*, monthly.

★ 7798 ★ **Help Hospitalized Veterans (HHV)**
2065 Kurtz St.
San Diego, CA 92110-2092
Phone: (619)291-5846
Fax: (619)291-3842
Roger Chapin, Founder/Pres.

Founded: 1971. **Description:** Seeks to improve the welfare and morale of hospitalized veterans and aid in their mental and physical rehabilitation. Sends arts and crafts materials in kit form to occupational therapy, recreation, and voluntary departments and wards of U.S. Veterans Hospitals and U.S. Armed Service Military Hospitals throughout the country; acts as a supplement to the hospitals' own programs. Conducts appeals by mail for donations and includes the name and address of the donor on a return card in each kit. Provides free literature and donation envelopes.

★ 7799 ★ **Hospitalized Veterans Writing**
Project (HVWP)
5920 Nall, Rm. 105
Mission, KS 66202
Phone: (913)432-1214
Sharon Smith, Pres.

Founded: 1946. **Description:** Individuals and organizations united to encourage hospitalized U.S. veterans to write for pleasure and rehabilitation during their hospital stay. Maintains speakers' bureau and slide program with commentary. Conducts writing sessions in hospitals. **Publications:** *HVWP in Action*, semiannual. Newsletter. Includes new developments and a list of financial contributors. *Price:* Free to contributors and VA Medical Centers. • *Veterans' Voices*, 3/year. Magazine. Contains prose, poetry, artwork, and cartoons submitted by hospitalized veterans. *Price:* $8/year for hospitalized veterans and outpatients; $15/year for others.

★ 7800 ★ International Committee of Military Medicine (ICMM)
(Comite International de Medecine Militaire — CIMM)
79, rue St.-Laurent
B-4000 Liege, Belgium
Phone: 41 222183
Fax: 41 222150
Dr. M. Cools, Sec.Gen.

Founded: 1921. **Members:** 91. **Description:** Medical representatives of the military forces of nations worldwide. Works to encourage and maintain professional cooperation among those in various countries whose mission is to care for the sick and wounded of the armed forces. Aims to improve such care by standardization of related disciplines and techniques, complete documentation and dissemination of military-medical information, and development of an international medical law. Conducts courses. **Publications:** *International Review of the Armed Forces Medical Services*, quarterly. **Formerly:** (1990) International Committee of Military Medicine and Pharmacy.

★ 7801 ★ International Office of Documentation on Military Medicine (IODMM)
(Office International de Documentation de Medecine Militaire — OIDMM)
79, rue St.-Laurent
B-4000 Liege, Belgium
Phone: 41 222183
Fax: 41 222150
Dr. M. Cools, Editor-in-Chief

Founded: 1930. **Members:** 91. **Languages:** English, French. **Description:** Directors general of armed forces medical services throughout the world. Purpose is to compile and update documentation on all matters concerning the military medical corps. Organizes international study sessions and advanced courses for junior medical officers. **Publications:** *International Review of the Armed Forces Medical Services*, quarterly.

★ 7802 ★ National Association of Air National Guard Health Technicians (NAANGHT)
6032 Chetwind Dr.
Cicero, NY 13039
Phone: (315)458-2251
Timothy C. Sager, Exec.Dir.

Founded: 1974. **Members:** 350. **Description:** Aims to provide more effective medical services in Federal Air National Guard health facilities through interchange of ideas and dissemination of information. Provides liaison with professional groups and educational and governmental institutions. **Publications:** *Health Technician Newsletter*, quarterly. Newsletter.

National Association of Atomic Veterans (NAAV)
See: Entry 11064

★ 7803 ★ National Association of State Veterans Homes (NASVH)
PO Box 409
Norfolk, NE 68702
Phone: (402)370-3177
Duane Hodge, Sec.-Treas.

Founded: 1953. **Members:** 68. **State Groups:** 78. **Description:** State supported veterans homes. Seeks to: maintain high standards of domiciliary, nursing home, and hospital care for veterans and eligible family members; provide a clearinghouse for techniques and expertise in veteran care and in the management of these institutions; represent the veterans' needs before Congress and the Veterans Administration. Encourages continued federal financial support for building state facilities and for providing care for veterans currently living in state homes. Works to sustain current veterans' benefits. Assists other states in establishing homes. Compiles statistics. **Publications:** *LINK*, quarterly. • *National Association of State Veterans Homes Directory*, annual. Directory.

★ 7804 ★ National Association of VA Physicians and Dentists (NAVAPD)
1341 G St. NW, Ste. 1100
Washington, DC 20005
Phone: (202)626-8588
Fax: (202)223-8323
Samuel V. Spagnolo, M.D., Pres.

Founded: 1975. **Members:** 2,000. **Description:** Physicians at Veterans Administration hospitals. Purpose is to strengthen and improve the quality of care and conditions at VA hospitals. Works to assure that veterans receive quality care. **Publications:** *NAVAPD News*, bimonthly. Newsletter. *Price:* Included in membership.

Nurses Organization of Veterans Affairs (NOVA)
See: Entry 9131

★ 7805 ★ Retired Army Nurse Corps Association (RANCA)
PO Box 39235, Serna Sta.
San Antonio, TX 78218-1235
Phone: (210)650-3534
Col. Marian Barbieri, Pres.

Founded: 1977. **Members:** 2,400. **Description:** Army Nurse Corps officers retired from either active or reserve duty; associate members are officers with 16 or more years of service still serving on active duty and former members of the Army Nurse Corps who were honorably discharged. Provides educational and social opportunities for members; disseminates information to the public. Seeks to preserve history of the U.S. Army Nurse Corps. **Publications:** *Connection*, quarterly. Newsletter.

★ 7806 ★ Societe Scientifique du Service Medical Militaire (SSSMM)
(Wetenschappelijke Vereniging van de Militaire Medische Dienst — WVMMD)
KSMD
G. De Crayerstraat 2
B-9000 Ghent, Belgium
Phone: 91 241901
Dr. P. DuBois, Exec. Officer

Founded: 1978. **Members:** 407. **Languages:** Dutch, English, French. **Description:** Belgian military officers in the medical corps united to investigate scientific issues relevant to both medicine and the army. Promotes professionalism and vocational education. Bestows awards. **Publications:** *Annales Medicinae Militaris Belgicae*, periodic.

★ 7807 ★ Society of Air Force Physicians (SAFP)
HQ AFMOA/SGPC
Bolling Air Force Base
170 Luke Ave., Ste. 400
Washington, DC 20332-5113
Phone: (202)767-1814
Fax: (202)404-7366
Dr. M. Benge, Contact

Founded: 1958. **Members:** 300. **Description:** Air Force internists, family practitioners, and specialists in emergency medicine, dermatology, allergy/immunology, and neurology. Objectives are to foster advancement of the art and science of medicine in the Air Force; encourage clinical and laboratory investigation; disseminate information.

★ 7808 ★ Society of Medical Consultants to the Armed Forces (SMCAF)
Box 2700
Kensington, MD 20891-2700
Phone: (301)295-3903
Anne Hufman, Exec.Dir.

Founded: 1945. **Members:** 1,000. **Description:** Professional society of physicians and surgeons who have been in active military service and who have acted as consultants to the Surgeons General of the Army, Navy, or Air Force. To preserve and encourage the association of civilian consultants and military medical personnel and to assist in the development and maintenance of the highest standards of medical practice in the Armed Forces. **Publications:** Newsletter, 3/year. • *Roster*, every 2-3 years. **Formerly:** Society of U.S. Medical Consultants in World War II.

★ 7809 ★ Society of Military Orthopaedic Surgeons (SMOS)
447 N. Lake St.
Grayslake, IL 60030
Phone: (708)223-9135
Ellen Yolich, Contanct

Founded: 1958. **Members:** 600. **Description:** Orthopedic surgeons who have served in the active or reserve military. Objectives are to: stimulate scholarly contribution by military medical residents; act as clearinghouse; provide opportunities for consultation with and contributions of surgeons who are retired from the military; further the continuing education of orthopedic surgeons and residents. Presents scientific papers at annual meeting.

★ 7810 ★ Society of Military Otolaryngologists - Head and Neck Surgeons (SMO-HNS)
c/o Josephine Kast
1902 Mossy Creek Dr.
San Antonio, TX 78245
Phone: (210)674-5188
Josephine Kast, Corr.Sec.

Founded: 1952. **Members:** 320. **Description:** Otolaryngologists, head and neck surgeons of the U.S. Army, Air Force, and Navy, and former active duty members. Purposes are to further the social and professional contacts of military otolaryngologists and to advance the science and art of the field. **Formerly:** (1952) Society of Military Otolaryngologists.

★7811★ Society of United States Air Force Flight Surgeons
PO Box 35387
Brooks AFB, TX 78235
Phone: (210)536-2844
LTC George Johnson, USAF, Contact

Founded: 1960. **Members:** 15,000. **Description:** Flight surgeons who are members of the Aerospace Medical Association and who are currently serving on active duty with or have retired from the United States Air Force, or are serving in the Air Force Reserve or Air National Guard. Fosters advancement of aerospace medicine throughout the Air Force and encourages the clinical, laboratory, flight line, and in-flight investigation of medical problems in Air Force flying, missile, and space operations. **Publications:** *Aircraft Mishap Investigation Handbook*. Handbook. • *Flight Surgeon's Checklist*. Book. • *Flightlines*, quarterly. Newsletter. *Price:* Included in membership dues; $15/year for nonmembers.

★7812★ Uniformed Services Academy of Family Physicians (USAFP)
11512 Allecingie Pky.
Richmond, VA 23235
Phone: (804)794-2106
Fax: (804)379-1386
Carolyn Yowell, CAE, Exec.Dir.

Founded: 1973. **Members:** 2,000. **Description:** Family physicians, teachers of family medicine, medical students, and residents in the armed services, public health service, or Indian health service. Sponsors continuing education program. Sponsors educational programs. **Publications:** *Uniformed Services Academy of Family Physicians--Newsletter*, quarterly. Newsletter. Includes calendar of events and membership lists. *Price:* Included in membership dues.

★7813★ Veterans Bedside Network (VBN)
252 7th Ave., 15T
New York, NY 10001-7305
Phone: (212)620-0748
Fax: (212)620-0842
Douglas Lutz, Admin.

Founded: 1948. **Members:** 700. **Description:** Professional actors, writers, producers, musicians, engineers, and others in radio and television who serve as weekly volunteers in Veterans Administration hospitals. Objectives are to provide recreation-therapy programs for hospitalized veterans and to help them produce and perform in their own radio and television programs for broadcast over closed circuit networks in the hospitals. The taped all-patient shows feature professional network scripts and music provided by VBN. More than 100 hospitals across the country participate in the "Script Kit" project. Conducts show tours in hospitals; escorts patients to entertainment and sports events. Serves as media consultant to the Veterans Administration. **Publications:** Newsletter, periodic. **Also Known As:** Veterans Hospital Radio and Television Guild.

★7814★ Vietnam Veterans Agent Orange Victims (VVAOVI)
PO Box 2465
Darien, CT 06820-0465
Phone: (203)656-0003
Free: 800-228-5940
Fax: (203)656-1957
James Sparrow, Exec.Dir.

Founded: 1977. **Members:** 7,229. **State Groups:** 8. **Description:** Vietnam veterans and their families who have suffered or are suffering from the effects of Agent Orange (Dioxin) poisoning. (Agent Orange is a herbicide that was used in Vietnam from 1962 to 1972, and over 9.2 million pounds per year have been sprayed in the United States.) Provides referral services; offers legal, medical, and V.A. counseling. Monitors local and state herbicide use and alternatives to herbicide brush management; lobbies the government. Attempts to alleviate the suffering of those adversely affected by Dioxin. Conducts research; educates the public on herbicides; sponsors seminars in prisons for incarcerated Vietnam veterans; compiles statistics on the effects of Dioxin. Maintains speakers' bureau and small library of books and over 300 medical surveys and studies. **Publications:** *Historical Perspective*. • Newsletter, periodic. • *Testicular Guide - What Vietnam Vets Should Know About Testicular Cancer*. **Formerly:** (1983) Agent Orange Victims International.

★7815★ Vietnam Veterans Institute (VVI)
John Deere Bldg.
PO Box 386
Timonium, MD 21093
Phone: (410)637-5584
J. Eldon Yates, Chm.

Founded: 1981. **Regional Groups:** 3. **Description:** American veterans of the Indochina theatre of operations during the Vietnam War, journalists, and non-U.S. Vietnam veterans who served with the allied forces. To explore employment and business opportunities for Vietnam War veterans; to study problems evolving from Vietnam service; to promote a positive public image of Vietnam veterans. Provides data to Congress, government agencies, veterans service organizations, private industry, and presidential commissions. Conducts lectures, seminars, and studies. Maintains speakers' bureau. Conducts lecture programs. **Publications:** *VVI Journal*, periodic. Journal. Covers current issues and legislation concerning veterans. *Price:* $30/year. Also publishes research papers and monographs. **Formerly:** Vietnam Veterans Institute for Research and Advocacy.

★7816★ VietNow National (VN)
1835 Broadway
Rockford, IL 61104
Phone: (815)227-5100
Free: 800-837-8669
Fax: (815)227-5127
Rich Sanders, Pres.

Founded: 1980. **Members:** 3,000. **State Groups:** 1. **Local Groups:** 37. **Description:** Vietnam era (1957-75) veterans; interested civilians and other veterans are associate members. Purpose is to provide a forum through which veterans can help other veterans with problems such as drug abuse, delayed stress syndrome, unemployment, and health problems related to Agent Orange exposure. Attempts to educate the public about those missing in action and prisoners of war in southeast Asia who have still not been accounted for. Conducts educational and charitable programs; maintains speakers' bureau and 15 standing committees. **Publications:** *VietNow Magazine*, bimonthly. Magazine. *Price:* $9.95/year. **Formerly:** Firebase 5; (1980) Vietnam Veterans Club; (1992) VietNow.

Research Centers

★7817★ Henry M. Jackson Foundation for the Advancement of Military Medicine
1401 Rockville Pike, Ste. 600
Rockville, MD 20852
Phone: (301)424-0800
Fax: (301)424-5771
John W. Lowe, Pres.

Research Activities and Fields: Infectious diseases, immunology, wound healing, sepsis, shock and traumatic injury, telemedicine, prostate cancer, cardiovascular disease, addiction medicine, pediatrics and preventive medicine, HIV research, emergency medical training, diagnostic radiology, head injury, and occupational health. Coordinates clinical trials sponsored by private industry. **Publications:** Annual Report.

★7818★ Rehabilitation Research and Development Center
Edward Hines, Jr. V.A. Hospital
PO Box 20
Hines, IL 60141
Phone: (708)216-2240
William R. Best, M.D., Actg.Dir.

Research Activities and Fields: Restoration, supplementation, and amelioration of mobility for disabled veterans. Activities are carried out through the Musculoskeletal Disorders Research Program, Rehabilitative Neurosciences Research Program, and Applied Exercise Science and Health Promotion Program. The Musculoskeletal Disorders Research Program focuses on disorders of the spine and degenerative joint disease, including studies and treatment for musculoskeletal disorders. The Rehabilitative Neurosciences Research Program targets the improvement or restoration of motor control of persons with spinal cord injuries. Studies focus on neural regeneration, neuromuscular electrical stimulation, and treatment for micturition dysfunction. The Applied Exercise Science and Health Promotion Program centers on the health and fitness of persons with mobility limitations. Studies include research on assessing and maintaining the cardiovascular fitness of people with mobility limitations. Other programs of the Center include the Technology Development Program, which acts as a technology transfer organization, and the University Affiliates Program, which joins researchers with similar projects in collaborative efforts, offers visiting scholar positions, and sponsors student design projects.

U.S. Department of Defense
Armed Forces Institute of Pathology
Center for Advanced Pathology
Neuropathology Department
See: Entry 10157

U.S. Department of Defense
Armed Forces Institute of Pathology
Infectious and Parasitic Disease Pathology
Department
Geographic Pathology Division
See: Entry 10169

U.S. Department of Defense
Armed Forces Radiobiology Research
Institute
See: Entry 11075

★ 7819 ★ **U.S. Department of Defense**
Army Medical Research and Development
Command
Army Institute of Surgical Research
Fort Sam Houston
San Antonio, TX 78234-5012
Phone: (512)221-2720
Fax: (512)227-8502
Basil A. Pruitt, Jr., M.D., Commander/Director

Research Activities and Fields: Institute's program of research involves: 1) investigation of problems of mechanical and thermal injuries; 2) care of patients with such injuries; 3) education and training of physicians and ancillary medical personnel in the principles of management of injured patients; and 4) investigative studies at both the basic and clinical levels. Principal subject of research (basic and applied) is burn care, including studies in fluid resuscitation, host resistance, metabolic response, nutrition, leukocyte dysfunction, thyroid hormone kinetics, wound care, surgical infection, inhalation injury, surgical critical care, skin substitutes, and mechanical trauma. **Publications:** USAISR Annual Reports, USAISR Anniversary Symposia.

★ 7820 ★ **U.S. Department of Defense**
Army Medical Research and Development
Command
Army Medical Research Institute of
Chemical Defense
Attn: SGRD-UV-RC
Aberdeen Proving Ground, MD 21010-5425
Phone: (410)671-3948
Fax: (410)676-7045
Col. Charles G. Hurst, Commander

Research Activities and Fields: USAMRICD conducts research, development, test, and evaluation in medical defense of chemical warfare (CW). This includes basic research on mechanisms of action of CW agents and antidotes to establish a database from which to devise improved methods for the prevention, resuscitation, treatment, and management of chemical casualties; and assistance in the integration of products into the logistical system, doctrine development, and training of medical and nonmedical personnel in the management and prevention of chemical casualties. Basic research is conducted on neuronal, physiologic, and pharmacologic mechanisms of chemical warfare agents and pretreatment and treatment compounds. Applied research is directed toward the development of biomedical models;

standardization of methods and procedures; pretreatment and treatment drug screening; biomedical data acquisition; analysis, prediction, and information transfer; toxicological and behavioral effects of sublethal doses of CW agents; tolerance to chronic CW agent exposure; toxicological effects of chemotherapeutics; safety and efficacy of pretreatment compounds; sensory effects of CW agents; vesicant treatment technology; soldier and patient decontamination technology; skin protection technology; skin toxicology; and management and treatment of mass chemical casualties. Research efforts are supplemented by a complementary research and development contract program and by collaboration with USAMRDC sister institutes, other government laboratories, universities, and research efforts with allied countries. Activities are conducted in five divisions: 1) Drug Assessment Division, 2) Pathophysiology Division, 3) Pharmacology Division, 4) Veterinary Medicine and Laboratory Resources Division, and 5) Chemical Casualty Care Division.

★ 7821 ★ **U.S. Department of Defense**
Army Medical Research and Development
Command
Army Medical Research Institute of
Infectious Diseases
Fort Detrick
Frederick, MD 21701
Phone: (301)663-2833
Fax: (301)663-2893
Col. Ronald G. Williams, Commander

Research Activities and Fields: Research is conducted on the pathogenesis, prophylaxis, and therapy of high-hazard, infectious diseases and toxins that could pose a biological warfare threat or harm U.S. Armed Forces deployed to areas where the diseases are endemic. Studies are designed to elucidate the mechanisms of action of disease agents and to identify means of preventing or countering the disease process through vaccines and immunotherapeutic or chemotherapeutic procedures. Derivative benefits to the public are vaccines and countermeasures that have been and are used to quell disease outbreaks worldwide.

★ 7822 ★ **U.S. Department of Defense**
Army Medical Research and Development
Command
Army Research Institute of Environmental
Medicine
42 Kansas St.
Natick, MA 01760-5007
Phone: (508)651-4811
Col. J.T. Krueger, Commander

Research Activities and Fields: USARIEM's activities involve: 1) conducting research to determine the effects of temperature, altitude, work, chemical defense, and military nutrition on the soldier's life processes, performance, and health; 2) defining the complex interaction of environmental stress, the body's defenses, and the techniques, equipment, and procedures best calculated to protect the soldier and make the soldier operationally effective; 3) assessing decrements to soldier performance caused by the synergy of environmental extremes and protective measures against chemical agents; and

4) conducting research in the physiology and health effects of Army physical fitness training. In coordination with the U.S. Army Natick Research, Development, and Engineering Center, Institute conducts nutrition research for the Department of Defense Food and Nutrition Research, Development, Testing, and Engineering Program to develop feeding strategies for operational rations and supplements to minimize decrements in the soldier's performance under sustained combat conditions. USARIEM also assists the Natick center in the development of personal clothing and equipment by assessing the physiological impact of these items under all climatic conditions. In addition, Institute acts as a liaison with other federal agencies to develop the research technology base to discharge the Army Surgeon General's responsibilities as DOD executive agent for nutrition. USARIEM also provides technical advice and consultant services to Army commanders, installations, and activities in support of the Army Preventive Medicine Program and, on request, to other federal agencies.

★ 7823 ★ **U.S. Department of Defense**
Army Medical Research and Development
Command
Army Research Institute of Environmental
Medicine
Environmental Pathophysiology
Directorate
Natick, MA 01760-5007
Phone: (508)651-5153
Fax: (508)651-4869
R.W. Hubbard, Director

Research Activities and Fields: Research focuses on the prevention, diagnosis, and treatment of common illnesses related to the environmental conditions of heat, cold, and high terrestrial altitude. Conducts both human and animal studies to identify the factors that may predispose an individual to environmental injury. Directorate's programs include studies in physiology, biochemistry, and cellular pathology.

★ 7824 ★ **U.S. Department of Defense**
Army Medical Research and Development
Command
Army Research Institute of Environmental
Medicine
Environmental Physiology and Medicine
Directorate
Natick, MA 01760-5007
Phone: (508)651-4832
Fax: (508)651-5298
Dr. Kent B. Pandolf, Director

Research Activities and Fields: Directorate conducts a research program on the illnesses, injuries, and physiological performance effects associated with exposure to the environmental extremes of heat, cold, and high altitude.

★ 7825 ★ **U.S. Department of Defense**
Army Medical Research and Development
Command
Army Research Institute of Environmental
Medicine
Occupational Health and Performance
Directorate

Natick, MA 01760-5007
Phone: (508)651-4800
J.A. Vogel, Director

Research Activities and Fields: Division conducts research to determine the interactive effects of environment, nutrition, and the physiologic and psychologic demands of military operations on soldier health and performance. Objectives focus on the identification and quantification of military operational stressors, characterization of dose-response or energy-injury manifestation, development of attenuation or prevention measures, and development of predictive health and performance models. Research activities include: 1) a program on epidemiologic field survey methods and models of environmental operational factors affecting soldier health and performance, designed to identify and relate environmental/operational stressors to soldier health and performance and develop predictive epidemiologic models for field validation; 2) studies on the impact of the environment and sustained operations on military performance, which use military tasks involving specified psychomotor and cognitive skills in laboratory/field experiments to determine task components most influenced by environmental stressors; and 3) assessment of the interactive effects of chemical defense factors and environmental stressors with animal/human performance models in order to evaluate independent and synergistic effects of environmental stressors and chemical defense factors (e.g., agents, antidotes, pretreatments) on performance parameters, determine dose-response relationships, develop attenuation/preventive measures of performance decrements, and develop and validate predictive models.

★ 7826 ★ **U.S. Department of Defense**
Army Medical Research and Development
    Command
Environmental Physiology and Medicine
    Directorate
Altitude Physiology and Medicine Division
Natick, MA 01760-5007
Phone: (508)651-4852
Fax: (508)651-5298
Dr. A. Cymerman, Chief

Research Activities and Fields: Division conducts field and laboratory research on problems encountered by military personnel exposed to high terrestrial elevations. It investigates and develops new approaches to improve military effectiveness based on scientific knowledge in physiology, biochemistry, pharmacology, and nutrition. Particular emphasis is placed on the etiology, prophylaxis, amelioration, and recovery of altitude-induced illnesses such as acute mountain sickness, high altitude pulmonary and cerebral edema, and related physical and mental functional deficits and disabilities.

★ 7827 ★ **U.S. Department of Defense**
Army Medical Research and Development
    Command
Occupational Health and Performance
    Directorate
Military Nutrition Division

Natick, MA 01760-5007
Phone: (508)651-4874
Fax: (508)651-5298
Col. E. Wayne Askew, Chief

Research Activities and Fields: Division conducts nutrition research, development, testing, evaluation, and engineering support to the Department of Defense Food and Nutrition Research, Development, Test, and Evaluation and Engineering Program; and provides technical assistance to the Surgeon General of the Army on biomedical aspects of nutrition and performance.

★ 7828 ★ **U.S. Department of Defense**
Army Medical Research and Development
    Command
Walter Reed Army Institute of Research
Washington, DC 20307-5100
Phone: (202)576-3551
Fax: (202)576-3114
Col. A.J. Salvado, Dir.

Research Activities and Fields: Conducts basic and applied biomedical research necessary to army combat effectiveness. Topics include: 1) biologically-active substances (bacteria, viruses, biological and chemical threat agents, and toxic environmental contaminants); 2) trauma and high-energy (wound infections, traumatic organ failure, and high-power microwaves); and 3) stress and performance (combat psychiatric casualties, and sustained operations).

★ 7829 ★ **U.S. Department of Defense**
Army Medical Research and Development
    Command
Walter Reed Army Institute of Research
Biochemistry Division
Washington, DC 20307-5100
Phone: (202)576-3001
Fax: (202)576-1304

Research Activities and Fields: Division: 1) conducts basic and applied biochemical research at all levels of biological organization; and 2) designs, develops, and conducts programs that support the separation, reconstitution, characterization, quantitation, and physiological interaction of all chemical entities (micro- and macromolecules) within the biological environment. Divisional components include departments of Applied Biochemistry, Biological Chemistry, and Membrane Biochemistry.

★ 7830 ★ **U.S. Department of Defense**
Army Medical Research and Development
    Command
Walter Reed Army Institute of Research
Communicable Diseases and Immunology
    Division
Washington, DC 20307-5100
Phone: (202)576-3756
Fax: (202)576-0748
Jerald C. Sadoff, Director

Research Activities and Fields: Division's mission is to: 1) conduct research on the ecology, etiology, pathogenesis, diagnosis, prevention, and therapy of selected diseases of military importance and develop, validate, and apply methods of disease control through the use of immunizing agents (including studies of modification

induced in the host by exposure to disease agents); 2) develop methods of production (including actual emergency manufacture) and methods of assaying the biologicals required by the Armed Forces; and 3) provide reference and consultative services on the diagnosis, epidemiology, control, and chemotherapy of infectious diseases of military importance. Divisional components include departments of Bacterial Diseases, Bacterial Immunology, Biologics Research, Cellular Immunity, Enteric Infections, Entomology, Immunology, and Virus Diseases.

★ 7831 ★ **U.S. Department of Defense**
Army Medical Research and Development
    Command
Walter Reed Army Institute of Research
Experimental Therapeutics Division
Washington, DC 20307-5100
Phone: (202)427-5438
Col. Brian Schuster, Director

Research Activities and Fields: Division's mission is to conduct basic and applied research leading to new prophylactic or therapeutic drugs or drug regimens for diseases of military importance. Current programs involve development of drugs against parasitic diseases and development of antidotes for chemical warfare agents. Divisional components include departments of Biology, Medicinal Chemistry, Parasitology, and Pharmacology.

★ 7832 ★ **U.S. Department of Defense**
Army Medical Research and Development
    Command
Walter Reed Army Institute of Research
Medicine Division
Washington, DC 20307-5100
Phone: (202)576-2300
Fax: (202)576-0703
Col. Robert C. Smallridge, Director

Research Activities and Fields: Division's mission is to resolve military medical problems that fall within the general domain of the disciplines of internal medicine through study, laboratory experiments, and consultation. Divisional components include departments of Clinical Physiology, Gastroenterology, Hematology, Medical Research Fellowship, Nephrology, and Respiratory Research.

★ 7833 ★ **U.S. Department of Defense**
Army Medical Research and Development
    Command
Walter Reed Army Institute of Research
Neuropsychiatry Division
Washington, DC 20307
Phone: (202)576-3006
Fax: (202)576-3114
Col. Steven R. Hursh, Director

Research Activities and Fields: Division's mission is to formulate, plan, coordinate, initiate, and conduct a research and training program in pertinent aspects of military neuropsychiatry, with special emphasis on mechanisms of behavior under stress and those variances that are likely to result in neuropsychiatric disorders in military environments. Divisional components include departments of Human Behavioral Biology, Medical Neurosciences, Microwave Research, and Military Psychiatry.

★7834★ U.S. Department of Defense
Army Medical Research and Development
Command
Walter Reed Army Institute of Research
Pathology Division
Washington, DC 20307-5100
Phone: (202)576-2677
Fax: (202)576-3114
Col. Anthony J. Johnson, Director

Research Activities and Fields: Division conducts research on the structural and functional alterations encountered in diseases of military importance, both human and veterinary; studies the mechanism of lesion induction and repair in these conditions; and investigates the entire spectrum of the organism's response to diverse natural or experimental injuries and stimuli, from the manifest pathology of its organs to the underlying altered physiology of its cells. Division also studies the interrelation of morphologic, functional, and biochemical alterations in the pathologic conditions under investigation in order to develop new and improved methods of prevention and treatment in these and related conditions. Other functions of the Division are to: 1) provide the morphologic anatomical parameter for research performed at the Institute, collaborate in research projects initiated by other divisions, and provide services and consultations in experimental pathology; and 2) acquire knowledge of the molecular pathobiology, develop effective vaccines and therapeutics for prophylaxis and treatment, and develop rapid detection means for staphylococcal enterotoxins; and 3) conduct ultrastructural studies involving independent and collaborative studies on subcellular basis of diseases of military importance. In addition, Division serves as the Institute's central electron microscope facility; operates the Institute's central tissue processing laboratory; and trains personnel in specialized techniques. Divisional components include departments of Comparative Pathology, Experimental Pathology, Molecular Pathology, and Ultrastructural Pathology.

★7835★ U.S. Department of Defense
Army Medical Research and Development
Command
Walter Reed Army Institute of Research
Preventive Medicine Division
Washington, DC 20307-5100
Phone: (202)576-3517
Lt. Col. John F. Rundage, Director

Research Activities and Fields: Division plans, conducts, and coordinates graduate education programs in the field of military preventive medicine; assists in the production of technical information concerned with this specialty; and designs and conducts epidemiologic studies. Division also provides epidemiologic consultation services. Components of this Division are departments of Advanced Preventive Medicine Studies, Epidemiology, and Field Studies.

★7836★ U.S. Department of Defense
Army Medical Research and Development
Command
Walter Reed Army Institute of Research
Surgery Division

Washington, DC 20307-5100
Phone: (202)576-3796
Col. William Wiesmann, Director

Research Activities and Fields: Division conducts fundamental and clinical research relevant to the military medical problems of combat injury, shock, wounding, and resuscitation (singly or in combination) in order to establish optimal prophylactic and therapeutic care of severely injured patients. Division also develops adjuncts for the diagnosis and management of blast-induced injury to the lung and/or gastrointestinal tract; and develops and provides laboratory models for biomedical assessment of medical material systems. Divisional components include departments of Cardiovascular Physiology, Experimental Surgery, and Surgical Gastroenterology.

★7837★ U.S. Department of Defense
Army Medical Research and Development
Command
Walter Reed Army Institute of Research
Veterinary Medicine Division
Washington, DC 20910
Phone: (301)427-5280
Dale G. Martin, LTC, VC, Director

Research Activities and Fields: Division: 1) advises and provides consultative service to the field on matters pertaining to Veterinary medicine; 2) provides centralized animal resource support to military medical research institutes within or near Washington, DC; 3) conducts basic and applied research on diseases of animals employed in medical research; 4) conducts comprehensive diagnostic surveillance of government-owned animals used in conjunction with direct service activities of medical research programs; 5) provides all experimental animals and related support resources to WRAIR, including development of methods for improvement and standardization of laboratory animals; and 6) conducts specialized training in laboratory animal medicine. Divisional components include departments of Animal Resources, Instruction, and Animal Medicine.

★7838★ U.S. Department of Defense
Naval Medical Research and Development
Command
Naval Biodynamics Laboratory
PO Box 29407
New Orleans, LA 70189
Phone: (504)257-3917
Fax: (504)257-5456
Cmdr. R.W. Rondin

Research Activities and Fields: Laboratory conducts biomedical research on the effects of mechanical forces (motion and impact) encountered in ships and aircraft on naval personnel in order to establish human tolerance limits for these forces and to develop preventive and therapeutic methods to protect personnel from the deleterious effects of such forces. Specific objectives are to: 1) determine the kinematic, dynamic, physiological, and performance effects of mechanical forces (acceleration and impact) on Navy and Marine Corps personnel; 2) determine mechanisms underlying the biomedical effects of mechanical forces; 3) develop human tolerance limits and standards for expo-

sure to mechanical forces; 4) develop and evaluate methods for prevention and treatment of deleterious effects of mechanical forces; 5) determine specifications for subsequent development of manikins that replicate human response to impact acceleration; 6) develop error, statistical, mechanical, and psychological models to classify, assess, and predict injury potential; and 7) investigate, develop, and test methods for enhancing human performance in operational shipboard and airborne environments.

★7839★ U.S. Department of Defense
Naval Medical Research and Development
Command
Naval Dental Research Institute
Bldg. 1-H
Great Lakes, IL 60088-5259
Phone: (312)688-4678
Fax: (708)688-4279
Capt. J.C. Cecil, III, Commanding Officer

Research Activities and Fields: Institute is a research laboratory for studies of: 1) oral diseases of Navy and Marine Corps personnel; 2) rapid diagnostic treatment methods for control of dental diseases; and 3) automated oral epidemiology information systems.

★7840★ U.S. Department of Defense
Naval Medical Research and Development
Command
Naval Health Research Center
PO Box 85122
San Diego, CA 92186-5122
Phone: (619)553-8400
Fax: (619)553-9389
Capt. Thomas N. Jones, MC, USN,
Commanding Officer

Research Activities and Fields: NHRC conducts research on the medical, physiological, and psychological aspects of the health and performance of Naval Service personnel. Center was reorganized in 1990-91.

★7841★ U.S. Department of Defense
Naval Medical Research and Development
Command
Naval Health Research Center
Department of Health Sciences and
Epidemiology
Bldg. 636
PO Box 85122
San Diego, CA 92186-5122
Phone: (619)553-6884
Fax: (619)553-6891
Dr. Frank C. Garland

Research Activities and Fields: Department conducts epidemiologic research and health promotion evaluation to: identify environmental hazards in the workplace and aboard ship; assess the impact of potentially harmful agents or conditions on health and performance; determine causal factors in illness and accident risks; and develop cost-effective intervention strategies to prevent or control such health risks. Epidemiology Division studies morbidity, disability, and mortality in relation to demographic, occupational, environmental, psychological, and service history variables and conducts long-term prospective studies of health risks in career naval personnel, including the impact of chronic disease on performance and retention. Division also determines incidence, course, and outcome of HIV infection, psychiatric and substance abuse disorders and devises improved diagnostic and prognostic guidelines for effective patient management. Other areas of interest include development of a Navy-wide medical surveillance program for acute and chronic conditions related to occupational and environmental exposures; and epidemiological studies to determine the etiology, course, and outcome of occupationally related diseases and injuries in naval service. In addition, the Division designs and maintains files of medical and service history information for all naval personnel as a basis for epidemiological studies of morbidity and mortality in naval populations.

★ 7842 ★ **U.S. Department of Defense**
Naval Medical Research and Development
  Command
Naval Health Research Center
Health Services Research Department
Bldg. 346
PO Box 85122
San Diego, CA 92186-5122
Fax: (619)553-9389

Research Activities and Fields: Department applies psychological theories, principles, and methods to research in the promotion and maintenance of health; the identification of etiologic and diagnostic correlates of health, illness, HIV and related dysfunction; and the analysis and improvement of the naval health care system and Navy health policy formation. In addition to studies of correlates of illness in selected naval populations, the Department conducts research on naval health care facilities to examine the organizational factors associated with effective, high quality health care delivery in shipboard and shore-based environments. Programs range from evaluation research in all aspects of the Health and Physical Readiness Program through work in health care delivery afloat and cost containment ashore. Activities include evaluations of the programs of physical conditioning, "The Healthy Back," cholesterol screening, smoking intervention and cessation, and case management procedures in containing the high costs incurred by occupational injury and illness. Also, research is conducted in determining incidence rates of hypertension, back injuries, cerebrovascular and cardiovascular disease as well as developing guidelines for the training of shipboard independent duty hospital corpsman.

★ 7843 ★ **U.S. Department of Defense**
Naval Medical Research and Development
  Command
Naval Health Research Center
Operational Performance Department
Bldg. 346
PO Box 85122
San Diego, CA 92186-5122
Phone: (619)553-0291
Dr. Paul Naitoh, Head

Research Activities and Fields: Department investigates the unique demands placed upon Navy and Marine Corps personnel by their operational environments. Emphasis is on psychological, physiological, and environmental stresses as they relate to human performance and im-

pact on biochemical homeostasis. This involves identification of the physical, mental, and emotional requirements for successful performance during sustained military operations and the development of supportive programs for augmentation, restoration, and maintenance of physical fitness and health. Special emphasis is on the implications of sex differences and aging for military job performance. Recent activities have involved neurometric and selective attention research, including studies on: effects of low level white lighting on performance (as compared to red ambient illumination); sleep management (sleep logistics) for personnel who must achieve mission objectives in a sustained operation; effects of sleep deprivation and moderate intermittent exercise on maximal aerobic capacity; and the relationship of endogenous effective radiated power (ERP) components to cognitive processes in workers performing complex cognitive tasks (e.g., sonar operators, aviators, and air traffic controllers).

★ 7844 ★ **U.S. Department of Defense**
Naval Medical Research and Development
  Command
Naval Health Research Center
Physiological Performance and Operational
  Department
PO Box 85122
San Diego, CA 92186-5122
Phone: (619)553-8400

Research Activities and Fields: Applied psychology.

★ 7845 ★ **U.S. Department of Defense**
Naval Medical Research and Development
  Command
Naval Health Research Center
Sleep Optimization Research Laboratory
Code 50
PO Box 85122
San Diego, CA 92186-5122
Phone: (619)532-6114
Fax: (619)553-9389
Dr. Paul Naitoh, Director

Research Activities and Fields: Department conducts research on the physiological, behavioral, and performance aspects of physical and emotional fitness among Navy and Marine Corps service personnel. Research investigates both exogenous and endogenous factors that affect human performance, health, and military effectiveness. Its goal is to quantify the physiological and performance effects of occupational/environmental conditions, pharmacological agents, and certain clinical entities that may impair health and performance in operational settings. Areas of investigation include, but are not limited to, the behavioral effects of environmental toxins; the psychophysiological aspects of typical work environments; the effects of pharmacological agents (both therapeutic and non-medicinal drugs) on performance; and the effects of disorders of arousal and sleep on personnel effectiveness. Specific areas of research interest have included: an international jet lag study coordinated by NASA to provide information on the degree of sleep loss that occurs on multiple layover, multitime zone flights, and its effects on human performance; and a study on the effects of caffeine on daytime performance

in support of an experimental evaluation of stimulants for possible operational use.

★ 7846 ★ **U.S. Department of Defense**
Naval Medical Research and Development
  Command
Naval Medical Research Institute
National Naval Medical Center
8901 Wisconsin Ave., Bldg. 17
Bethesda, MD 20814-5055
Phone: (202)295-0021
Capt. Robert G. Walter, Commanding Officer

Research Activities and Fields: As the Navy's largest biomedical research facility, NMRI's mission is to conduct basic and applied research and development concerned with the health, safety, and efficiency of naval personnel. Specific functions of the Institute are to: 1) provide basic and applied research competence in infectious disease, diving and hyperbaric medicine, casualty care, environmental stress, and human factors; 2) maintain a program of basic biomedical research in areas of military importance; 3) provide a scientific potential for the application of new biomedical knowledge to operational problems and requirements; 4) provide a source of scientific advisors and consultants readily available to the operational commands; 5) provide biomedical research capabilities to support field laboratories, naval hospitals, and other naval activities; and 6) provide support (in agreement with NMRI's mission) to other federal agencies. Research activities are conducted in departments for: casualty care research, diving medicine, environmental medicine, infectious diseases, and transplantation research.

★ 7847 ★ **U.S. Department of Defense**
Naval Medical Research and Development
  Command
Naval Medical Research Institute
Casualty Care Research Department
National Naval Medical Center
8901 Wisconsin Ave.
Bethesda, MD 20889-5607
Phone: (301)295-1817
Dr. Adam E. McKee, Director

Research Activities and Fields: Department's program is concerned with enhancing combat medical support technology in the areas of shock, early wound healing, and the repair of tissues and organs. Department conducts surgical, metabolic, and dental research and provides pathology support services. Current research is focused on studies of biochemical and cellular events that often accompany military casualties. Studies are aimed at the prevention of hemorrhagic and septic shock, the development of artificial blood substitutes, and the appropriate use of drugs and anesthesia in shock and trauma. Dental research is carried out to develop more effective combat medical support technology for the prevention and early treatment of oral and maxillofacial infections and injuries that result in the loss of hard and soft tissues.

★ 7848 ★ **U.S. Department of Defense**
Naval Medical Research and Development
  Command
Naval Medical Research Institute
Diving Medicine Department

National Capital Region
8901 Wisconsin Ave.
Bethesda, MD 20889-5607
Phone: (301)295-5914

Research Activities and Fields: Department conducts research in hyperbaric medicine (diving medicine), including research in the areas of decompression sickness and air embolism, anesthesia and drugs in hyperbaric environments, oxygen therapy, toxic contaminants and microbiological pathogens, long-term effects of occupational exposure to diving, and the development of appropriate medical controls for health hazards. Department also studies biological changes that may occur in hyperbaric situations, including effects on the central nervous system and changes in respiratory and cardiovascular function, the development of methods to allay oxygen poisoning, and a better understanding of the basic principles underlying decompression. In addition, design criteria are developed for the equipment and procedures used in diving and hyperbaric operations; and improved decompression schedules and the mathematical modeling of inert gas are studied.

★7849★ U.S. Department of Defense
Naval Medical Research and Development
  Command
Naval Medical Research Institute
Immune Cell Biology Program
Bethesda, MD 20814-5055
Phone: (202)295-1837
Fax: (202)295-2720

Research Activities and Fields: Department conducts research in the procurement, cryopreservation, and storage of viable and nonviable tissue for use in the treatment of combat casualties (including research to improve and refine the development of necessary technologies to procure, preserve, and transplant tissue). Special emphasis is placed on research related to the bone marrow stem-cell, including efforts to identify those cells capable of totally replacing hemopoietic capability in casualities exposed to radiation or chemical agents that destroy bone marrow. Factors that affect growth and differentiation of bone marrow stem-cells and methodologies to provide care for hemopoietic casualities at the forward medical unit level are studied. In addition, Department studies the basic biochemical mechanisms and events concerned with cell growth and differentiation to determine how these processes might influence the acceptance or rejection of transplanted tissues. Other factors that influence tissue acceptance or rejection are also studied (including the characterization of cells involved in organ rejection and graft-versus-host disease) and ways to identify and inactivate such cells are pursued.

★7850★ U.S. Department of Defense
Naval Medical Research and Development
  Command
Naval Medical Research Institute
Infectious Diseases Department
National Naval Medical Center
12300 Washington Ave.
Rockville, MD 20855-5055
Phone: (301)295-2079
Dr. Stephen L. Hoffman, Head

Research Activities and Fields: Research is focused on immunology, molecular genetics, biochemistry, microbiology, and parasitology as they relate to such infectious diseases as malaria, rickettsial disease, and bacterial diarrheal disease. Department studies host-bacterial and host-parasitic interactions as well as host immune mechanisms with the continuing goal of providing immunity to these diseases through vaccine development. Department also seeks other methods to improve prophylaxis and treatment of infectious diseases and has conducted studies involving the development of protective immunity, various topical or oral preparations that might be used to prevent infections, methods for rapid early diagnosis, and ways to accurately predict exposure risks in areas of strategic military importance.

★7851★ U.S. Department of Defense
Naval Medical Research and Development
  Command
Naval Medical Research Institute
  Detachment (Toxicology)
ATTN: NMRI/TD, Bldg. 433
2612 5th St.
Wright-Patterson AFB, OH 45433-7903
Phone: (513)255-6058
Fax: (513)476-7094
Capt. David A. Macys, MSC, USN, Officer-in-
  Charge

Research Activities and Fields: Detachment functions as a research laboratory for studies in toxicology, with specific interest in the protection of Navy personnel from potentially hazardous materials. Activities involve: 1) characterizing toxicological effects of materials and their mechanism of action; 2) performing hazard evaluations and risk assessments; and 3) establishing permissible exposure limits for operational uses. Fields of research include biochemistry, physiology, behavioral psychology, toxicology, industrial hygiene, and pharmacology. Detachment also manages a program in inhalation and general toxicology conducted under Air Force contract by personnel of ManTech Environmental Technology, Inc. working in the Toxic Hazards Research Unit, Toxicology Division, Armstrong Laboratory (AL/OET).

★7852★ U.S. Department of Defense
Naval Medical Research and Development
  Command
Naval Submarine Medical Research
  Laboratory
Naval Submarine Base, New London
Box 900
Groton, CT 06349-5900
Phone: (203)449-3263
Fax: (203)449-4809
Capt. Paul K. Weathersby, Commanding
  Officer

Research Activities and Fields: NSMRL is the Navy's principal in-house biomedical research center for studies in submarine and diving medicine and sonar. Specific interests include aural and visual perception of sonar signals, digital signal processing, submarine environments, hearing conservation, effects of stress on performance, physical/mental fitness, diver decompression procedures, and biomedical support/submarine systems. Laboratory comprises

the following Departments: Visual Sciences, Biomedical Sciences, Bioengineering and Submarine Systems. **Publications:** *Command History* (annually); Annual Progress Summary; transfer reports; cumulative bibliography of research reports.

★7853★ U.S. Department of Veterans
  Affairs
Veterans Health Administration
Office of Research and Development
810 Vermont Ave. NW
Washington, DC 20420
Phone: (202)535-7160
Fax: (202)535-7159

Research Activities and Fields: Office provides funding for intramural research performed by individual investigators at VA medical centers throughout the United States. These investigators are staff at the medical centers (physicians, basic scientists, nurses, dentists, psychologists, etc.) who apply for research funds from the Central Office of Research and Development through the medical centers' research and development committees.

Chapter 40
Musculoskeletal & Connective Tissue Disorders

Federal Government Agencies

★7854★ **U.S. Department of Health and Human Services**
National Institute of Arthritis and Musculoskeletal and Skin Diseases
9000 Rockville Pike
Bethesda, MD 20892
Phone: (301)496-4353

Description: The Institute conducts and supports fundamental research in the major disease categories of arthritis and musculoskeletal and skin diseases through research performed in its own laboratories and clinics, epidemiologic studies, research contracts and grants, and cooperative agreements to scientific institutions and to individuals. It also supports training of manpower in fundamental sciences and clinical disciplines and conducts educational activities, including the collection and dissemination of health educational materials on these diseases.

Foundations & Other Funding Organizations

Private Foundations

Nora Eccles Treadwell Foundation
See: Entry 2783

RGK Foundation
See: Entry 442

Corporate Foundations

Dickson Foundation
See: Entry 664

Other Funding Organizations

★7855★ **American Lupus Society**
260 Maple Ct., No. 123
Ventura, CA 93003
Phone: (310)542-8891
Free: 800-331-1802
Dr. William H. Kraus, Contact

Description: Distributes funds for research on the cause and treatment of lupus erythematosus.

★7856★ **Arthritis Foundation**
1314 Spring St. NW
Atlanta, GA 30309
Phone: (404)872-7100
Free: 800-283-7800
Fax: (404)872-0457
Don L. Riggin, CAE, Pres.

Description: Foundation grants and awards support allied health professional traineeships, fellowships, and research projects.

Dystonia Medical Research Foundation
See: Entry 5260

★7857★ **Lupus Foundation of America**
4 Research Pl., Ste. 180
Rockville, MD 20850-3226
Phone: (301)670-9292
Free: 800-558-0121
Fax: (301)670-9486
John M. Huler, Exec. Dir.

Description: Awards fellowships and grants for research in the causes and cures of lupus.

★7858★ **National Osteoporosis Foundation**
1150 17th St. NW, Ste. 500
Washington, DC 20037
Phone: (202)223-2226
Fax: (202)223-2237
Sandra C. Raymond, Exec. Dir.

Description: Supports basic biomedical, epidemiological, clinical, behavioral, and social research and research training. Sponsors Research Grant Award program.

Osteogenesis Imperfecta Foundation
See: Entry 5266

National & International Organizations

★7859★ **American Auto Immune Related Diseases Association**
Michigan National Bank Bldg.
15475 Gratiot
Detroit, MI 48205
Phone: (313)371-8600
Free: 800-598-4668
Fax: (313)371-9310
Virginia Ladd, Exec.Dir.

Founded: 1991. **Description:** Promotes national focus and collaborative efforts among state and national volunteer health groups on autoimmunity, the major cause of serious chronic diseases. Offers research and educational programs; maintains speakers' bureau. **Publications:** *InFocus*, quarterly. Newsletter. *Price:* $24/year.

★7860★ **American Behcet's Association (ABA)**
PO Box 54063
Minneapolis, MN 55454-0063
Phone: (612)338-3288
Free: 800-7BEHCETS
Fax: (612)338-4655
Susan Sternfels, Pres.

Founded: 1986. **Description:** Gathers statistics on people with Behcet's syndrome; educates the public and medical community about the disease. (Behcet's syndrome is characterized by painful oral ulcers which often resolve spontaneously, but recur at unpredictable intervals. Other symptons include recurring genital lesions, skin lesions, blurred vision, pain and redness of the eyes, and nervous system abnormalities. The disease is most common among young adults, and methods of treatment are varied and controversial.) Conducts educational programs; maintains speakers' bureau. **Publications:** *American Behcet's Association Newsletter*, quarterly. Newsletter. *Price:* $15. • *Behcet's Disease and Your Eyes*. Brochure. • *Behcet's Disease and Your Nervous System*. Brochure. • *Behcet's Disease: What You Should Know*. Brochure. • *Only Hope*. Brochure.

★ 7861 ★ American College of Rheumatology (ACR)
60 Executive Park S, Ste. 150
Atlanta, GA 30329
Phone: (404)633-3777
Fax: (404)633-1870
Mark Andrejeski, Exec.VP

Founded: 1934. **Members:** 6,500. **Regional Groups:** 4. **Description:** Rheumatologists and rheumatology health professionals. Provides unified leadership in research, education, and the care of people with rheumatic diseases. **Publications:** *ACR Membership Directory*, annual. Membership Directory. *Price:* $10/copy for members; $35/copy for nonmembers. • *ACR Scientific Program*, annual. • *Arthritis and Rheumatism*, monthly. Journal. Covers research and trends in the treatment and investigation in the field. Includes book reviews, calendar of events, and employment opportunities. *Price:* $90/year for individuals; $115/year for institutions; $45/year for students. Agency subscription rates are; $103.50/year for institutions. • *Arthritis Care and Research*, quarterly. Journal. For health professionals interested in the rheumatic diseases. *Price:* $115 institutions; $60 individuals. • *Dictionary of Rheumatic Diseases*. Book. • *Handbook of Rehabilitative Rheumatology*. Handbook. **Formerly:** (1989) American Rheumatism Association.

★ 7862 ★ American Juvenile Arthritis Organization (AJAO)
1314 Spring St. NW
Atlanta, GA 30309
Phone: (404)872-7100
Fax: (404)872-0457
Patricia Harrington, Contact

Founded: 1980. **Members:** 1,100. **Description:** Parents, health care professionals, and others interested in the problems of juvenile arthritis. Serves as advocate for the needs of those affected by juvenile arthritis. A council of the Arthritis Foundation. **Publications:** *AJAO Newsletter*, quarterly. Newsletter. Covers AJAO activities, current research, legislative topics, and chapter news. *Price:* Included in membership dues. • *Arthritis in Children*. Brochure. • Booklet. Provides information on pediatric rheumatology services. • *Educational Rights for Children with Arthritis: A Manual for Parents*. Manual. • *Juvenile Dermatomyositis, When Your Studnet Has Arthritis*. Brochure. • *Thinking About Tomorrow: A Career Guide for Teenagers with Arthritis*. Brochure.

★ 7863 ★ The American Lupus Society (TALS)
260 Maple Ct., No. 123
Ventura, CA 93003
Phone: (310)542-8891
Free: 800-331-1802
Dr. Charlean Wakefield, Admin.

Founded: 1973. **Description:** Works to increase knowledge and public awareness of lupus erythematosus, a noncontagious disease which may affect the skin alone or may manifest itself as a chronic, systemic, and inflammatory disease of the connective tissues. Assists lupus patients and their families, through chapters and patient support groups, to cope with the daily problems associated with lupus. Collects and distributes funds for research. Works to bring lupus to the attention of the public by encouraging the publication of articles on the disease by syndicated medical writers, national magazines, and newspapers, and by obtaining radio and television coverage. Has successfully worked for the establishment of an annual National Lupus Month. Chapters hold patient meetings and occasional medical seminars. **Publications:** *The American Lupus Society--Lupus Today*, quarterly. Newsletter. Reports current research both directly and indirectly related to lupus. *Price:* Free. • Booklet. For children. • *Lupus Erythematosus*. Pamphlet. Also publishes other informational materials in Braille and Spanish.

★ 7864 ★ American Society for Bone and Mineral Research (ASBMR)
1200 19th St., NW, Ste. 300
Washington, DC 20036
Phone: (202)857-1161
Fax: (202)223-4579
William E. Kelley, Exec.Dir.

Founded: 1977. **Members:** 2,300. **Description:** Physicians, dentists, veterinarians, and other doctors interested in research and bone and mineral diseases. Has established guidelines to aid in preventing osteoporosis, a bone thinning disease. Maintains speakers' bureau. Provides placement service. **Publications:** *Journal of Bone and Mineral Research*, monthly. Journal. • *Membership Directory*, annual. • *Primer on the Metabolic Bone Diseases and Disorders of Mineral Metabolism*.

★ 7865 ★ Arthritis Care (AC)
18 Stephenson Way
London NW1 2HD, England
Phone: 171 9161500
Fax: 171 9161505
Richard Gutch, CEO

Founded: 1948. **Members:** 67,000. **Local Groups:** 628. **Languages:** English. **Description:** Individuals with arthritis and concerned others. Seeks to: increase awareness of the problems associated with rheumatic diseases; disseminate information; establish a nationwide network of branches; improve welfare facilities; provide information, advice and practical aid. Maintains hotels, a residential home for severely disabled persons, and self catering units. Provides home-visiting service. Advises on nonmedical enquiries. Assists needy members. **Publications:** *Arthritis News*, quarterly. Magazine. • *Benefits for Beginners*, semiannual. Booklet. **Formerly:** British Rheumatism and Arthritis Association.

★ 7866 ★ Arthritis Foundation (AF)
1314 Spring St. NW
Atlanta, GA 30309
Phone: (404)872-7100
Free: 800-283-7800
Fax: (404)872-0457
Don L. Riggin, CAE, Pres.

Founded: 1948. **Members:** 700,000. **Local Groups:** 71. **Description:** Seeks to: discover the cause and improve the methods for the treatment and prevention of arthritis and other rheumatic diseases; increase the number of scientists investigating rheumatic diseases; provide training in rheumatic diseases for more doctors; extend knowledge of arthritis and other rheumatic diseases to the lay public, emphasizing the socioeconomic as well as medical aspects of these diseases. **Publications:** *Arthritis Today*, bimonthly. Magazine. Includes research reports and selfhelp tips from readers. *Price:* Included in membership dues. • *Bulletin on the Rheumatic Diseases*, bimonthly. Bulletin. Contains articles on developments in research and management of rheumatic diseases; geared for the nonrheumatologist. *Price:* Free. • *Index of Rheumatology*, annual. **Formerly:** Arthritis and Rheumatism Foundation.

★ 7867 ★ Arthritis Health Professions Association (AHPA)
1314 Spring St. NW
60 Executive Park S., Ste. 150
Atlanta, GA 30329
Phone: (404)633-3777
Fax: (404)633-1870
Don L. Riggin, Exec.Dir.

Founded: 1965. **Members:** 2,000. **Regional Groups:** 4. **Local Groups:** 13. **Description:** Nurses, occupational and physical therapists, social workers, psychologists, vocational counselors, physicians, pharmacists, and other health professionals concerned with the practice, education, and research of rheumatic diseases. Seeks to establish a scientific base of knowledge to improve the quality and provision of health services to individuals with rheumatic diseases. Disseminates information regarding the study and treatment of rheumatic diseases. Develops and implements medical and scientific programs in the field of rheumatology. A section of the Arthritis Foundation. **Publications:** *Arthritis Care and Research*, quarterly. • *Arthritis Today*, quarterly. • *Bulletin on the Rheumatic Diseases*, 12/year. Bulletin. • *Guide to Independent Living for People With Arthritis*. • *Membership Directory*, periodic. • *Newsletter*, periodic. Includes research updates. *Price:* Included in membership dues. • *Outcome Standards for Rheumatology Nursing Practice*. • *Primer on the Rheumatic Diseases*.

★ 7868 ★ Association of Muscle Disorders
Hatboyu cad. No. 12
Yesilkoy
Istanbul, Turkey
Phone: 212 5730975
Fax: 212 6630168
Prof. Coskum Osdemir, Contact

Founded: 1978. **Members:** 600. **Languages:** English. **Description:** Promotes study and research of neurological muscle diseases. Works as a support group for individuals suffering with muscle disorders. Conducts educational programs. **Publications:** *Hope and Life*, quarterly. Journal.

Avenues—National Support Group for Arthrogryposis Multiplex Congenita
See: Entry 2742

★ 7869 ★ Billy Barty Foundation (BBF)
929 W. Olive Ave., Ste. C
Burbank, CA 91506
Phone: (818)953-5410
Patricia P. Techaira, Admin.Dir.

Founded: 1975. **Description:** Provides medical, educational, vocational, social, and psychological support for people less than 4'10" tall. Advises on issues concerning adoption, public education on dwarfism, and legal aid. Assists individuals in living independently by supplying information on adapting automobiles and homes for use by little people and providing information on clothing and shoe stores offering small sizes. Promotes Billy Barty Collection of furniture designed for use by little people. Sponsors sports teams and annual golf tournament in California; offers placement and children's services; maintains speakers' bureau. Conducts charitable program; compiles statistics. **Publications:** *My Child is a Dwarf.* • Newsletter, quarterly. • Pamphlets. **Also Known As:** Billy Barty Foundation for Little People.

★7870★ **British Society for Rheumatology (BSR)**
3 St. Andrew's Pl.
Regent's Park
London NW1 4LB, England
Phone: 171 2243739
Fax: 171 2240156
Kate Baillie, Exec.Sec.

Founded: 1984. **Members:** 1,350. **Languages:** English. **Description:** Clinicians and scientists working in the field of rheumatic diseases. Promotes education, research, and improved clinical practices in the treatment and prevention of rheumatic diseases. Disseminates information; organizes educational courses and scientific meetings. **Publications:** *British Journal of Rheumatology*, monthly. Journal. • *Constitution and List of Members*, annual. • *Guidelines on Audit.* • *Information for Purchasers and Providers of Rheumatology Services.*

★7871★ **Canadian Association of Friedreich's Ataxia (ACAF)**
(Association Canadienne de l'Ataxie de Friedreich — ACAF)
5620, rue C.A. Jobin
Montreal, PQ, Canada H1P 1H8
Phone: (514)321-8684
Fax: (514)321-2957
Claude St. Jean, Pres.

Founded: 1972. **Members:** 1,500. **Local Groups:** 2. **Languages:** English, French. **Description:** Individuals with Friedreich's Ataxia (a muscular disorder which results in an inability to coordinate voluntary muscular movements). Encourages exchange between families of ataxic persons. Raises funds for medical research; offers social services to victims; recruits volunteer support. Facilitates contact with medical specialists and disseminates information about the disease. **Publications:** *Eldorado*, quarterly. Newsletter.

★7872★ **Ehlers Danlos National Foundation (EDNF)**
PO Box 1212
Southgate, MI 48195
Phone: (313)282-0180
Fax: (313)282-2793
Nancy A. Rogowski, Exec.Dir.

Founded: 1985. **Members:** 1,500. **Description:** Individuals who suffer from Ehlers Danlos Syndrome (EDS); medical professionals involved in the treatment of EDS. (Ehlers Danlos Syndrome, which is named after dermatologists Edward L. Ehlers (1863-1937) and Henri A. Danlos (1844-1912), is a inheritable connective tissue disorder characterized by fragile skin, hypermobile joints, and poor wound healing.) Provides networking among members for communication and support. Maintains mail-order library of materials pertaining to the disorder. Plans to compile statistics regarding the symptoms of EDS. **Publications:** Brochures. • *Loose Connections*, quarterly. Newsletter. Includes bibliography of EDS articles and book reviews. *Price:* Included in membership dues. • Pamphlets.

★7873★ **European League Against Rheumatism (EULAR)**
(Ligue Europeenne Contre le Rhumatisme)
Witikonerstrasse 15
CH-8032 Zurich, Switzerland
Phone: 1 3839690
Fax: 1 3839810
Fred K. Wyss, Exec.Sec.

Founded: 1947. **Members:** 10,000. **Regional Groups:** 4. **Languages:** English, French, German, Russian. **Description:** Members of social and scientific organizations and pharmaceutical firms in 31 countries. Maintains small collection of rheumatology journals. **Publications:** *EULAR Manual*, quadrennial. • *Rheumatology in Europe*, quarterly. Bulletin.

★7874★ **European Society of Osteoarthrology (ESOA)**
(Europaische Gesellschaft fur Osteoarthrologie)
Department of Reumatology
Academic Hospital
St. Radbond
NL-6525 Nijmegen, Netherlands
Phone: 80 616540
Fax: 80 541433
Prof. N. Limo, Contact

Founded: 1967. **Languages:** English, German, Russian. **Description:** Clinical, laboratory, theoretical, and professional medical and nonmedical researchers; national societies and working groups. Serves as an international link to promote knowledge and stimulate the study of bone and cartilage structure, function, and metabolism in health and disease. Studies emphasize articular bone and cartilage in normal and pathological joints and spine, and disorders of the skeleton and calcium metabolism accompanied by rheumatic and orthopedic symptoms. **Publications:** *Symposium Proceedings*, annual.

★7875★ **Evans Syndrome Research and Support Group**
5630 Devon St.
Port Orange, FL 32127
Phone: (904)760-3031
Fax: (904)761-6008
Lou Addington

Founded: 1992. **Description:** Provides mutual support and ongoing research for parents and concerned friends and caregivers of children with Evans Syndrome. (Evans Syndrome is a rare auto immune disease.) Facilitates networking and exchange of information. Distributes literature. Developing a group of interested physicians in immunology, genetics, and hematology/oncology. Works to formulate questions for caregivers/patients to ask their doctors.

Families of S.M.A. (FSMA)
See: Entry 8218

★7876★ **Fibromyalgia Association of Central Ohio (FACO)**
PO Box 21988
Columbus, OH 43221-0988
Phone: (614)457-4222
Fax: (614)457-2729
Mary Anne Saathoff, R.N., Pres.

Founded: 1986. **Members:** 3,000. **Regional Groups:** 25. **Local Groups:** 6. **Description:** Individuals with fibromyalgia, their families and friends, health care professionals. (Fibromyalgia is a chronic condition of severe muscle aching and severe fatigue, along with a sleep disorder. Pain can be sharp and stabbing and appears in muscles, tendons, and ligaments. Treatments are often ineffective; the condition can be functionally disabling.) Serves as an international informational clearinghouse on fibromyalgia. Promotes research, conducts charitable programs, operates speakers' bureau. Provides printed material and audiovisual resources to fibromyalgia patients, hospitals, and health care professionals. **Publications:** *Fibromyalgia Syndrome.* Booklet. Provides an overview of fibromyalgia. *Price:* $4. • *FMS Ohio Newsletter*, quarterly. Newsletter. *Price:* $15 contribution. **Formerly:** (1990) Central Ohio Fibrositis Association.

★7877★ **Foundation for Hand Research (FHR)**
310 E. 30th St.
New York, NY 10016
Phone: (212)685-3834
Fax: (212)545-1646
Dr. Robert Beasley, Dir.

Founded: 1977. **Description:** Promotes research and educational programs to improve care of upper extremity disorders. Sponsors educational programs and seminars. Grants clinical fellowships to develop special skills in care of the hand. Provides visiting professorships. Collaborates with bioengineers in the development of prosthetic hand devices, joint replacements, and other technical devices.

★7878★ **Foundation for Hand Research and Education**
8501 Harcourt Rd.
PO Box 80434
Indianapolis, IN 46280-0434
Phone: (317)471-4313
Free: 800-888-HAND
Fax: (317)875-8638
Jane T. Walker, Pres.

Founded: 1988. **Description:** Promotes the advancement of hand surgery and research. Aims to improve the quality of life of persons with injuries or disorders of the hands and upper extremities. Conducts educational programs. **Publications:** *Indiana Hand Center Newsletter*, quarterly. Newsletter. *Price:* $100/year. **Formerly:** Indiana Foundation for Hand Surgical Research.

★ 7879 ★ F.S.H. Society
3 Westwood Rd.
Lexington, MA 02173
Phone: (617)860-0501
Daniel Paul Perez, Pres.
Founded: 1992. **Members:** 150. **Description:** Individuals, families, and medical and business professionals interested in Facioscapulohumeral Muscular Dystrophy. (FSHD is an inheritable disease that causes a progressive loss of skeletal muscle with weakness of facial, scapular, and upper arm muscles.) Promotes research, solicits contributions and grants, and disperses information on FSHD. Offers support groups. **Publications:** *F.S.H. Watch*, semiannual.

★ 7880 ★ International Federation of
    Scoliosis Associations (IFOSA)
9908 Cape Scott Ct.
Raleigh, NC 27614
Phone: (919)846-2204
Fax: (919)846-6782
Howard M. Shulman, Chair
Founded: 1985. **Members:** 10. **National Groups:** 10. **Description:** Federation of patient and patient-oriented associations interested in scoliosis and other spinal disorders. Represents the interests of scoliosis patients and their families. (Scoliosis is a lateral or sideward curvature of the spine that may lead to deformity if left untreated.) Provides for the exchange of information, ideas, and publications among scoliosis associations worldwide. Maintains professional advisory board. (Does not provide services to individuals.)

International Fibrodysplasia Ossificans
Progressiva Association (IFOPA)
See: Entry 5281

★ 7881 ★ International League Against
    Rheumatism (ILAR)
c/o Charles M. Plotz, M.D.
SUNY Downstate Med. Center
450 Clarkson Ave.
Brooklyn, NY 11203
Phone: (718)270-1662
Fax: (718)270-1831
Charles M. Plotz, M.D., Treas.
Founded: 1927. **Members:** 12,000. **National Groups:** 63. **Regional Groups:** 3. **Description:** Physicians interested in rheumatism. Promotes research and education in rheumatic disease. Facilitates communication among members and with United Nations Educational, Scientific and Cultural Organization and World Health Organization. **Publications:** *Handbook*, quadrennial. Also publishes proceedings.

International Skeletal Society (ISS)
See: Entry 11118

★ 7882 ★ Israeli Arthritis Foundation (IAF)
192A Arlozorov Str.
64923 Tel Aviv, Israel
Phone: 3 6962760
Fax: 3 6962759
Dr. Michael Ehrenfeld, Exec. Officer
Founded: 1986. **Members:** 2,500. **Local Groups:** 10. **Languages:** Hebrew. **Description:** Seeks to aid individuals suffering from arthritis

in Israel. Offers physiotherapy services; provides counseling. Conducts educational programs. Offers children's services. Compiles statistics; disseminates information. Maintains speakers' bureau; coordinates social activities. **Publications:** *Inbar*, 2-3/year. Journal. Includes articles written by physicians. • Pamphlet, monthly. **Formerly:** (1992) Israeli League Against Rheumatism.

★ 7883 ★ Jaw Joints Allied Musculo-
    Skeletal Disorders Fo undation (JJAMD)
Forsyth's Research Institute
140 The Fenway
Boston, MA 02115
Phone: (617)266-2550
Fax: (617)262-4021
Renee Glass, Co-Pres.
Founded: 1982. **Description:** Promotes public awareness of temporomandibular joint disorder (TMJ) and related musculoskeletal disorders. Provides information on prevention, treatment, and responsible diagnosis. Conducts research and educational programs; monitors legislative activities. Provides advocacy, networking, assistance with insurance providers, and support group activities.

★ 7884 ★ Klippel-Trenaunay Support Group
    (KTSG)
4610 Wooddale Ave.
Minneapolis, MN 55424
Phone: (612)925-2596
Judy Vessey, Coord.
Founded: 1986. **Members:** 250. **Description:** Support group for individuals affected by Klippel-Trenaunay Syndrome and their families. (Klippel-Trenaunay Syndrome is a congenital malformation of the extremities and is characterized by birth marks the color of port wine, excessive growth of the soft tissue and bone, and varicose veins. The cause is presently unknown but believed to be either genetic or the result of an intrauterine insult occuring between the third and sixth week of gestation.) Acts as a clearinghouse of information and correspondence between members. **Publications:** *K-T Newsletter*, quarterly. **Also Known As:** K-T Support Group.

★ 7885 ★ L. E. Support Club (LESC)
8039 Nova Ct.
North Charleston, SC 29420
Phone: (803)764-1769
Harriet B. Mesic, Dir. & Editor
Founded: 1984. **Members:** 2,500. **Description:** Individuals suffering from lupus erythematosus and other autoimmune diseases; friends and families of patients. Offers emotional support and selfhelp education to lupus patients through newsletters and personal correspondence; provides information on nutrition and medication. Contributes funds to lupus research. **Publications:** *LE Beacon*, bimonthly. Newsletter. Contains research and treatment updates. *Price:* Included in membership dues.

★ 7886 ★ Little People of America (LPA)
7238 Piedmont Dr.
Dallas, TX 75227-9324
Phone: (214)388-9576
Free: 800-24-DWARF
Mary Carten, Contact

Founded: 1957. **Members:** 5,100. **Regional Groups:** 13. **State Groups:** 53. **Local Groups:** 50. **Description:** Adults of the proportionate or disproportionate dwarf types and others 4'10" or under; teens, young adults, and children. Provides fellowship, interchange of ideas, moral support, and solutions to unique problems of "little people"; promotes good faith, fair dealings, better relations, and understanding of their small size by other members and average-size people. Aids in exchange of information on medical treatment, employment, clothes, shoes, and education; sponsors sports and social activities. Conducts discussions with parents of dwarf children; works to bring together little couples interested in adoption and adoption agencies that have children of this type available. Cooperates with medical institutions; maintains medical advisory board. Organizes speakers' bureau. Endorses Dwarf Athletic Association and competitions. Conducts charitable programs. Motto of LPA is "Think Big." **Publications:** *Adoptions*. Brochure. • *LPA*. Brochure. • *LPA Today*, quarterly. Newsletter. Includes medical information, book reviews, personal stories, and meeting calendar. *Price:* Included in membership dues. • *My Child is a Dwarf*. Booklet.

★ 7887 ★ Lupus Foundation of America
    (LFA)
4 Research Pl., Ste. 180
Rockville, MD 20850-3226
Phone: (301)670-9292
Free: 800-558-0121
Fax: (301)670-9486
John M. Huber, Exec.Dir.
Founded: 1977. **Members:** 47,000. **Regional Groups:** 4. **Local Groups:** 100. **Description:** Nonprofit voluntary health foundation serving people with lupus erythematosus and their families. Objectives are to: provide patient education, services, and human support to members; educate the medical community and the public about the disease in order to obtain earlier diagnoses and better treatment for lupus patients; increase research into the cause and cure of lupus. **Publications:** *Lupus Erythematosus: A Handbook for Physicians, Patients, and Their Families*. Handbook. • *Lupus News*, 3/year. Newsletter. Covers foundation activities, volunteer work, research, and medical management of lupus erythematosus. Includes book reviews and statistics. *Price:* Included in membership dues. • Monographs. • Pamphlets. • *Understanding Lupus*.

★ 7888 ★ Lupus Network (LN)
230 Ranch Dr.
Bridgeport, CT 06606
Phone: (203)372-5795
Linda J. Rosinsky, Pres.
Founded: 1985. **Description:** Educators, medical professionals, and individuals suffering from systemic lupus erythematosus. (Systemic lupus erythematosus is a chronic inflammatory disease of the connective tissue that affects the skin, joints, kidneys, nervous system, and mucous membranes.) Seeks to foster better understanding of the disease among patients, educators, and professionals through the distribution of educational materials. **Publications:** Bro-

chures. • *Heliogram*, quarterly. Newsletter. Includes book reviews, personal anecdotes, a coping column, special reports, and medical literature abstracts. *Price:* Included in membership dues. • Pamphlets. • Reprints.

★7889★ **Lyme Disease Foundation (LDF)**
1 Financial Plaza, 18th Fl.
Hartford, CT 06103
Phone: (203)525-2000
Free: 800-886-LYME
Fax: (203)525-TICK
Karen Vanderhoof-Forschner, Chm. & Pres.

Founded: 1988. **Local Groups:** 200. **Description:** Seeks to educate medical professionals and the public about Lyme Borreliosis (Lyme disease), which is spread to humans by ticks with symptoms including rashes, joint swelling and pain, fever, severe headaches, and heart arrhythmia. Provides treatment protocols, diagnostic guidelines, and photographic case histories. Assists in the formation of support groups; offers referral service; maintains speakers' bureau. Sponsors medical seminars; provides videotape and slide programs; conducts research. Maintains registry of infected pregnant women and congenital cases. Works in cooperation with Congress, Centers for Disease Control, and National Institutes of Health. **Publications:** *Journal of Spirochetal and Tick Bourne Disease*, quarterly. *Price:* $75/year. • *Lymelight*, quarterly. Newsletter. *Price:* $30/year. • *Monthly Update. Price:* $50/year. • Pamphlets. **Formerly:** (1992) Lyme Borreliosis Foundation.

★7890★ **Muskelsvindfonden**
Vestervang 41
DK-8000 Arhus, Denmark
Phone: 86139777
Jette Moller

Description: Promotes the research of muscular diseases affecting individuals in Denmark. Fosters communication amog members. Offers supportive services to patients and their families.

★7891★ **National Arthritis and Musculoskeletal and Skin Diseases Information Clearinghouse (NAMSIC)**
9000 Rockville Pike
PO Box AMS
Bethesda, MD 20892-2903
Phone: (301)495-4484
Fax: (301)587-4352
CONVERSION 930122 National Arthritis and Musculoskeletal and Skin, Dise, ases Information Clearinghouse

Description: Collects, publishes, and disseminates professional and public educational materials for persons concerned with arthritis and musculoskeletal and skin diseases. **Publications:** *Arthritis, Rheumatic Diseases, and Related Disorders*, annual. Annual Report. Highlights advances in research on rheumatoid arthritis, ostearthritis, lupus, Lyme disease, scleroderma, and other connective tissue diseases. • Articles. • Bibliographies. • Catalogs. • Reports. • *Spanish Language Materials for Patients: a Bibliography on Arthritis, Musculoskeletal and Skin Diseases*. Bibliography.

★7892★ **National Marfan Foundation (NMF)**
382 Main St.
Port Washington, NY 11050
Phone: (516)883-8712
Free: 800-862-7326
Fax: (516)883-8712
Priscilla Ciccariello, Chairperson

Founded: 1981. **Members:** 11,000. **State Groups:** 15. **Local Groups:** 20. **Description:** Persons affected with the Marfan syndrome; families of affected persons; genetic counselors; cardiologists, ophthalmologists, orthopedists, and other medical professionals. (Marfan syndrome is a heritable disorder of the connective tissue affecting the skeleton, lungs, eyes, heart, and blood vessels.) Objectives are to: disseminate accurate and timely information on Marfan syndrome; act as support network and provide a means for patients and relatives to share experiences; improve medical care. Supports and fosters research. **Publications:** *Connective Issues*, quarterly. Newsletter. Includes research reports, chapter news, and legislative reports. *Price:* Included in membership dues. • *Do You Know Marfan*. Video. • *How John Was Unique*. Book. • *Marfan Syndrome*. Pamphlet. • *The Marfan Syndrome: A Booklet for Teachers.* Booklet. • *The Marfan Syndrome: A Booklet for Teenagers.* Booklet. • *The Marfan Syndrome: Physical Activity Guidelines for Physical Educators, Coaches, and Physicians.*

★7893★ **National Osteoporosis Foundation (NOF)**
1150 17th St. NW, Ste. 500
Washington, DC 20037
Phone: (202)223-2226
Fax: (202)223-2237
Sandra C. Raymond, Exec.Dir.

Founded: 1984. **Members:** 10,000. **Description:** A voluntary health organization dedicated to reducing the widespread prevalence of osteoporosis. (Osteoporosis is an excessive loss of bone tissue which often results in fractures of the hip, spine, and wrist.) Seeks to: increase public awareness and knowledge about osteoporosis; provide information about osteoporosis to sufferers and their families; educate physicians and allied health professionals; advocate for increased governmental support for research on osteoporosis; support basic biomedical, epidemiological, clinical, behavioral, and social research and research training. Sponsors Research Grant Award program; conducts public and professional education programs. Maintains speakers' bureau and library; sponsors charitable and research programs. **Publications:** *Boning Up on Osteoporosis: A Guide to Prevention and Treatment.* • *Journal of Bone and Mineral Research*, periodic. Journal. • *National Osteoporosis Foundation--Annual Report.* Annual Report. Summarizes the foundation's programs and activities; includes financial report. *Price:* Free. • *Osteoporosis: A Woman's Guide.* • *Osteoporosis International*, periodic. • *Osteoporosis Report*, quarterly. Newsletter. Includes current medical journal references and listing of consumer publications and recent articles related to the subject of osteoporosis. *Price:* Included in membership dues. • *Physician's Resource Manual on Osteo-*

porosis: A Decision-Making Guide, periodic. Covers the biology of bone, pathogenesis of fracture, and the prevention and treatment of osteoporosis. *Price:* Included in membership dues. • *Prevention Week Kit.* **Formerly:** (1985) The Osteoporosis Foundation.

★7894★ **National Scoliosis Foundation (NSF)**
72 Mt. Auburn St.
Watertown, MA 02172
Phone: (617)926-0397
Fax: (617)926-0398
Marie Donoghue, Admin.

Founded: 1976. **State Groups:** 3. **Description:** Supporters are businesses, organizations, and individuals concerned with the early detection and prevention of progressing scoliosis, kyphosis, and structural lordosis. Purposes are to promote programs and activities leading to the elimination of the crippling effects of scoliosis and to educate the public about all abnormal spinal curvatures. Assists local groups in identifying available medical resources and personnel to help conduct volunteer screening programs; encourages legislation requiring scoliosis screening for each student in the 5th through 10th grades throughout the U.S. Maintains resource center for individuals or schools seeking information on abnormal spinal curvatures; provides information on how to promote and assist in spinal screening programs; sponsors multimedia educational exhibits and programs for adults and children. Maintains speakers' bureau. **Publications:** Booklets. • Brochures. • Manuals. • *Spinal Connection*, biennial. Membership activities newsletter. *Price:* Free. Also publishes resource lists and produces school audiovisual materials.

National Sjogren's Syndrome Association (NSSA)
See: Entry 2084

★7895★ **National Support Group for Myositis**
PO Box 890
Cooperstown, NY 13326
Free: 800-230-0441
Tina Kline, Pres.

Founded: 1986. **Members:** 300. **Description:** Myositis patients and their families. (Myositis is a muscular pain or discomfort caused by an infection or other unknown causes.) Provides information on myositis treatment and research to members. Encourages communication and mutual support between members by distributing member mailing list. Maintains medical advisory board. **Publications:** *Newsletter for Myositis*, quarterly. Newsletter.

★7896★ **National Support Group for PM/DM (NSGD)**
21744 Silver Meadow Ln.
Parker, CO 80134-7217
Phone: (607)547-5446
Fax: (607)547-5970
Tina Kline, Exec. Officer

Founded: 1989. **Members:** 100. **Description:** Support group for individuals diagnosed with dermatomyositis and their families and friends. (Dermatomyositis is a chronic degenerative muscle disease; onset is usually characterized by general fatigue, joint and muscle pain, and progressive weakness.) Encourages and facilitates exchange of information among members. **Publications:** Newsletter, quarterly. Reports on current research and includes tips on coping with the disease. *Price:* Free. **Formerly:** (1992) National Support Group for Dermatiomyositis.

★ **7897 ★ Norwegian Fibrositis Patients' Association (NFP)**
(Norges Fibromialge Forbund — NFF)
Oksen Oesten 4
N-1324 Lysaker 6, Norway
Phone: 67583067
Fax: 67583158
Liv Andreassen, Chm.

Founded: 1985. **Members:** 8,500. **Local Groups:** 65. **Languages:** English, Norwegian. **Description:** Persons in Norway suffering from fibrositis or fibromyalgia (rheumatic disorders involving fibrous tissues). Funds research into the cause and cure of fibrositis or fibromyalgia. Promotes understanding of the disease; disseminates information. Conducts educational programs. **Publications:** *Fibrositt*, quarterly. Magazine. **Formerly:** Norsk Fibrositt Forbund.

★ **7898 ★ Ollier's Disease Self-Help Group**
PO Box 52616
Shaw AFB, SC 29152-1521
Phone: (803)775-1757
Bonnie Schmid, Pres.

Founded: 1987. **Members:** 25. **Description:** Self-help group for persons with Ollier's disease. (Ollier's disease is a rare, nongenetic bone disorder.) Aims to find as many patients as possible to support research program objectives.

Osteogenesis Imperfecta Foundation (OIF)
See: Entry 5299

★ **7899 ★ Osteoporosis Society of Canada**
(Societe de l'Osteoporose du Canada)
33 Laird Dr.
Toronto, ON, Canada M4G 3S9
Phone: (416)696-2817
Free: 800-463-6842
Kathryn D. Robins, Exec.Dir.

Founded: 1982. **Members:** 14,000. **Languages:** English, French. **Description:** Individuals and organizations interested in the prevention, diagnosis, and treatment of osteoporosis. Supports research programs that seek to improve the quality of life for women with osteoporosis. Promotes education about osteoporosis among professional health practitioners. Disseminates informational materials to women with osteoporosis, physicians, and the public. Offers audio visual programs; participates in public forums.

★ **7900 ★ Paget Foundation for Paget's Disease of Bone and Related Disorders (PFPDBRD)**
200 Varick St., Ste. 1004
New York, NY 10014-4810
Phone: (212)229-1582
Free: 800-23-PAGET
Fax: (212)229-1502
Charlene Waldman, Exec.Dir.

Founded: 1978. **Members:** 30,000. **Description:** Patients and their families and friends; physicians; paramedical professionals interested in improving health care of persons suffering from Paget's disease, a chronic disorder which may result in enlarged, deformed, and fragile bones in one or more regions of the skeleton and primary hyperparathyroidism (PHPT). Conducts educational programs for patients, health care professionals, and the public; provides patient assistance and research advocacy; maintains referral service for patients seeking physicians who specialize in treating Paget's disease and PHPT. **Publications:** *A Patient's Guide to Paget's Disease of Bone.* Brochures. • Bibliography. • *Paget's Disease of Bone: Clinical Assessment, Present and Future Therapy.* • Reprints. • *Update*, 3/year. Newsletter. *Price:* Free. **Formerly:** (1992) Paget's Disease Foundation.

★ **7901 ★ Pan American League Against Rheumatism (PANLAR)**
Toronto Hospital Arthritis Centre
1-215-FP TWD
399 Bathurst St.
Toronto, ON, Canada M5T 2S8
Phone: (416)369-5866
Fax: (416)368-9348
Dr. Duncan A. Gordon, Pres.

Founded: 1942. **Members:** 5,500. **Description:** Physicians and other professionals devoted to the prevention and treatment of rheumatic diseases. Seeks to educate health professionals. Conducts biomedical and epidemiological research. Offers assistance in the coordination of national, professional, and social agencies. Makes available professional publications.

★ **7902 ★ Roger Wyburn-Mason and Jack M. Blount Foundation for the Eradication of Rheumatoid Disease (RDF)**
5106 Old Harding Rd.
Franklin, TN 37064
Phone: (615)646-1030
Fax: (615)646-1030
Perry A. Chapdelaine, Exec.Dir. & Sec.

Founded: 1982. **Members:** 10,000. **Description:** Seeks to eradicate rheumatoid disease. Promotes professional university research and supplies free information to physicians and disease victims on Dr. Roger Wyburn-Mason's treatment protocol as modified by other physicians. (Such treatment includes oral medications, intraneural injections, and dietary control and, according to the foundation, has been successful in 80% of patients treated.) Conducts educational programs for the public and physicians; sponsors medical seminars; provides physician referrals and speakers' bureau. Emphasizes complementary, alternative, and holistic treatments especially for forms of arthritides. **Publications:** *The Art of Getting Well.* Book. In-

cludes recommended primary treatments plus important complementary treatments. *Price:* $25. • Books. • *The Causation of Rheumatoid Disease and Many Human Cancers -- A New Concept in Medicine. Price:* $4.50. • *Dedication, Love and Humor.* • *Fight Back Against Arthritis.* Book. Includes variety of traditional and untraditional treatments and practical information that arthritics should know. *Price:* $15. • *Historical Documents in Search of the Cure for Rheumatoid Disease.* • *Intraneural Injections for Rheumatoid Arthritis and Osteoarthritis and The Control of Pain in Arthritis of the Knee.* Explains a new concept on treating the pain of arthritis. *Price:* $9.95. • *Prevention, Treatment and Cure of Arthritis.* Contains alternative/complementary/holistic treatments, defined in simple yet scientific language. *Price:* $25. • *Rheumatoid Diseases Cured At Last.* Covers the original "amoebae theory." *Price:* $15. **Also Known As:** Rheumatoid Disease Foundation; Arthritis Fund.

★ **7903 ★ Scleroderma Federation (SF)**
Peabody Office Bldg.
1 Newbury St.
Peabody, MA 01960
Phone: (508)535-6600
Free: 800-422-1113
Fax: (508)535-6696
Peter Meyer, Pres.

Founded: 1983. **Members:** 15,000. **State Groups:** 21. **Description:** Scleroderma organizations. Promotes medical research to find a cure for scleroderma, a chronic systemic disease affecting all organs resulting from uncontrolled growth of connective tissue. Seeks to foster an understanding of the disease through media and outreach programs; raises funds. Provides patients with educational materials and referrals to local organizations and medical specialists. Offers encouragement and consultation services towards the formation and development of local support groups. Acts as a clearinghouse for information about scleroderma research, drugs, and therapies. Conducts accredited programs for professionals. Maintains speakers' bureau; compiles statistics. **Publications:** *About Localized Scleroderma.* Brochure. • *About Scleroderma.* Brochure. • *The Beacon*, quarterly. *Price:* Included in membership. • *Helpful Hints for Living with Scleroderma.* • *Understanding and Managing Scleroderma.* Booklet. **Formerly:** (1984) International Scleroderma Federation.

★ **7904 ★ Scleroderma International Foundation (SIF)**
704 Gardner Center Rd.
New Castle, PA 16101
Phone: (412)652-3109
Mrs. Arkie Barlet, Pres.

Founded: 1971. **Members:** 4,500. **Description:** Membership in 11 countries includes: individuals with scleroderma; family and friends of patients; doctors and nurses. (Scleroderma is a chronic condition resulting in the hardening of the skin, and in some cases, the connective tissue, arterial linings, and digestive tract.) Provides a supportive network for individuals with the disease. Supports research into the cause, cure, and control of scleroderma and strives to educate patients, physicians, and the public. **Publications:** *From Isolation to Communication. . .An Anthology of Scleroderma Patient's Experiences.* • Pamphlet. • *Scleroderma International Foundation--The Connector*, quarterly. Newsletter. Includes calendar of events. **Formerly:** (1978) National Scleroderma Club.

★7905★ **Scleroderma Research Foundation (SRF)**
Box 200
Columbus, NJ 08022
Phone: (609)261-2200
Free: 800-637-4005
Fax: 800-723-6700
Emanuel A. Coronis, Jr., Chm.

Founded: 1978. **Members:** 1,500. **Regional Groups:** 1. **Description:** Interested individuals and those who have had firsthand experience with scleroderma. Seeks to: supplement and implement medical research on the cause, treatment, and cure of scleroderma; develop a national network of support centers for patients and their families; inform the medical community and public about scleroderma symptoms to promote early diagnosis and treatment; encourage and gather donations, bequests, and memorials. Holds meetings featuring speakers on various aspects of the disease. Makes available a slide/sound program. **Publications:** *Advance*, quarterly. Newsletter. *Price:* Included in membership dues. • *Advance Research and Treatment: Informative Articles Pertaining to Scleroderma*, quarterly. *Price:* Included in membership dues. • *Learning to Cope.* • *Scleroderma.* • *What Is It.*

★7906★ **Scleroderma Support Group (SSG)**
8852 Enloe Ave.
Garden Grove, CA 92644
Phone: (714)892-5297
Fax: (714)893-2427
Clara K. Ihlbrock, Pres.

Founded: 1989. **Members:** 1,000. **State Groups:** 2. **Description:** Scleroderma patients and interested individuals. Serves as a support group for patients; provides information; raises funds for research; holds medical meetings and rap sessions.

★7907★ **Scoliosis Association (SA)**
PO Box 811705
Boca Raton, FL 33481-1705
Phone: (407)994-4435
Free: 800-800-0669
Fax: (407)368-8518
Janice T. Sacks, Pres.

Founded: 1976. **Members:** 5,000. **Local Groups:** 52. **Description:** Individuals or families involved or interested in scoliosis (lateral or sidewards curvature of the spine). Educates the public about scoliosis and other spinal deviations. Encourages and sponsors spinal screening programs in schools throughout the U.S. and Canada. Sponsors the formation of scoliosis chapters throughout the country which serve as support groups for the scoliosis patient and his or her family. Aids the patient in attaining a positive social and emotional adjustment during treatment of scoliosis. Maintains collection of videotapes; plans to compile statistics; works

with researchers in scoliosis. Raises funds for scoliosis research. Has sponsored scoliosis update seminar and film festival with several hospitals and schools nationwide. **Publications:** *Backtalk*, periodic. Newsletter. Contains research and chapter news, article reprints, book reviews, and listings of publications. *Price:* $15 for members; $30 for individuals outside the U.S.; $40 for institutions. • Bibliography. Lists books, articles, pamphlets, and papers on scoliosis. *Price:* $6 for part one; $3 for part two; $8 for parts one and two. • Brochure. • *Scoliosis, An Adult Perspective*. Video. *Price:* $19.95. Also issues posters.

★7908★ **Scoliosis Association (SAUK)**
380-384 Harrow Rd.
London W9 2HU, England
Phone: 171 2895652
Ailie Harrison, Gen.Sec.

Founded: 1981. **Members:** 2,000. **Local Groups:** 17. **Languages:** English. **Description:** Individuals affected by scoliosis; their parents and families. Seeks to increase knowledge and understanding of scoliosis (a lateral curvature of the spine) and emphasize the importance of early detection. Encourages contact between members; disseminates information to members and the public. **Publications:** *Newsletter*, 3/year. Newsletter. • *Scoliosis: An Information Booklet*. Booklet.

★7909★ **Scoliosis Research Society (SRSO)**
6300 N. River Rd., Ste. 727
Rosemont, IL 60018-4226
Phone: (708)698-1627
Fax: (708)823-0536
Tressa Goulding, Exec.Dir.

Founded: 1966. **Members:** 540. **Description:** Orthopedic surgeons and physicians. Furthers research and education in spinal deformities, particularly scoliosis, a twisting of the spine to one side. Most cases are of unknown cause, though scoliosis can result from a birth defect, polio, or spinal injury and usually develops in children during the growth spurt between ages ten and 15. Early detection followed with use of a brace and exercise can halt the curvature and prevent deformity.

★7910★ **Sjogren's Syndrome Foundation (SSF)**
333 N. Broadway, Ste. 2000
Jericho, NY 11753
Phone: (516)933-6365
Fax: (516)933-6368
Jean S. Kahan, Pres.

Founded: 1983. **Members:** 6,250. **Description:** Individuals who have Sjogren's Syndrome, xerostomia (dry mouth), or keratoconjunctivitis sicca (dry eyes); specialists, internists, immunologists, rheumatologists, otolaryngologists, opthalmologists, gynecologists, gastroenterologists, pulmonologists, dermatologists, neurologists, urologists, pharmaceutical companies, and dentists. (Sjogren's Syndrome is a disorder marked by dryness of all mucous membranes, resulting from deficient secretion of the glands, particularly the lacrimal and salivary glands, those of the upper respiratory tract, the sweat glands, and the vaginal area. Approximately

50% of Sjogren's Syndrome patients also have rheumatoid arthritis, lupus, or scleroderma.) Objectives are to increase public awareness and medical knowledge about Sjogren's Syndrome, educate patients and their families, and allow patients to share information on coping with the syndrome. Supports research. Sponsors support groups with meetings in which doctors speak on aspects of the syndrome. Provides patients with opportunities to participate in clinical investigative programs related to the treatment of the disorder. Compiles statistics. **Publications:** Articles. • Brochure. • *Moisture Seekers Newsletter*, monthly. Newsletter. Covers information on new products, treatments, and developments, status of research, and discussion by specialists. *Price:* Included in membership dues. • *Sjogren's Syndrome Handbook: An Authoritative Guide for Patients.* **Formerly:** (1985) Moisture Seekers.

★7911★ **Spondylitis Association of America (SAA)**
PO Box 5872
Sherman Oaks, CA 91413
Phone: (818)981-1616
Free: 800-777-8189
Jane Bruckel, Exec.Dir.

Founded: 1983. **Members:** 2,800. **Description:** Individuals affected by Ankylosing Spondylitis, psoriatic arthritis, and Reiter's Syndrome; and their families and friends; health care professionals; scientific researchers. (Ankylosing Spondylitis is a condition most often affecting those between 17-40 years of age and characterized by pain or stiffness in the lower back, shoulders, hips, knees, or heels. Although the cause and cure are not known, the condition may be contained through a program of anti-inflammatory drugs, posture awareness, and regular, therapeutic exercise; it is believed to be a hereditary condition.) Disseminates information; promotes public awareness and research; conducts educational programs. **Publications:** Audiotapes. • *Guidebook for Patients.* • *Juvenile AS.* Booklet. • *Spondylitis Plus*, quarterly. Newsletter. Includes information on treatment, research, and coping with the condition. *Price:* Included in membership dues. • *Straight Talk on Spondylitis.* Book. • Videos. **Formerly:** (1993) Ankylosing Spondylitis Association.

★7912★ **United Scleroderma Foundation (USF)**
PO Box 399
Watsonville, CA 95077-0399
Phone: (408)728-2202
Free: 800-722-HOPE
Fax: (408)728-3328
Nancy Wemp, Exec.Dir.

Founded: 1975. **Members:** 8,000. **Regional Groups:** 48. **Description:** Scleroderma patients, members of their families, physicians, nurses, allied health professionals, and others interested in scleroderma. Scleroderma is thought to result from a narrowing of blood vessels which leads to fibrosis or hardening of the skin (localized) and, in some cases, internal organs (systemic). There are thought to be hundreds of thousands of cases. 80% of victims are women between the ages of 25 and 55. Establishes and maintains support networks. Encourages medical research to find the cause and cure for scleroderma and related collagen diseases. **Publications:** Brochures. *Price:* $.25/ each. • Handbook. *Price:* $2.50. • Newsletter, quarterly. • *Sceleroderma Digests.* • *United Scleroderma Foundation--Handbook.* Handbook. **Formerly:** (1977) Monterey Bay Scleroderma Foundation.

Research Centers

★7913★ Benign Essential Blepharospasm Research Foundation (BEBRF)
Baptist Hospital Doctors Bldg.
3155 Stagg Dr., Ste. 110
PO Box 12468
Beaumont, TX 77726-2468
Phone: (409)832-0788
Fax: (409)832-0890
Mary Lou Thompson, Pres.

Research Activities and Fields: Benign Essential Blepharospasm/Meige (BEB/M) Syndrome and related disorders and infirmities of the facial musculature. BEB/M is an involuntary, uncontrollable spastic contraction of the eyelids and other facial musculature. **Publications:** Newsletter.

★7914★ Boston University
Arthritis Center
Conte Bldg., 5th Fl.
71 E. Newton St.
Boston, MA 02118
Phone: (617)638-4310
Fax: (617)638-5226
Dr. Alan S. Cohen, Dir.

Research Activities and Fields: Biophysical, biochemical, immunologic, and clinical aspects of scleroderma amyloidosis, experimental lupus, rheumatoid arthritis, infectious arthritis, and nonarticular rheumatic diseases, particularly fibromyalgia. Also conducts health services research in rheumatology and performs epidemiological studies. **Publications:** Annual *Amyloid Newsletter*; to date about 10 books on arthritis and rheumatic diseases referral center for patients with amyloid disease (including hereditary amyloid, secondary amyloid, primary amyloid, and amyloid of chronic hemodialysis) and scleroderma.

★7915★ Brigham and Women's Hospital
Robert B. Brigham Multipurpose Arthritis and Musculoskeletal Diseases Center
75 Francis St.
Boston, MA 02115
Phone: (617)732-5356
Fax: (617)732-5505
Dr. Matthew H. Liang, Dir.

Research Activities and Fields: Rheumatic disease, including technology assessment, policy studies, the relationship between clinical practice, outcome, and efficiency, and psychological, social, and economic factors. Also studies clinimetrics and epidemiology of rheumatic disease, Lyme disease, Carpal Tunnel Syndrome, spinal stenosis, doctor-patient communication, and SLE risk factors. **Formerly:** Brigham and Women's Hospital, Robert B. Brigham Multipurpose Arthritis Center (MAC).

Bucknell University
Immunobiology Research Laboratory
See: Entry 2095

★7916★ Case Western Reserve University
Northeast Ohio Multipurpose Arthritis Center
Univ. Hospitals of Cleveland
11100 Euclid Ave.
Cleveland, OH 44106
Phone: (216)844-3168
Fax: (216)844-5172
Dr. Roland W. Moskowitz, Dir.

Research Activities and Fields: Basic and clinical research into the causes, diagnosis, and treatment of arthritis, including biochemistry and pathophysiology of joints in osteoarthritis, models of degenerative joint disease and inflammatory arthritis, immunologic disorders such as systemic lupus erythematosus and rheumatoid arthritis, disorders of the spine, genetic control of arthritis disorders, and juvenile arthritis. Orthopedic studies include bioengineering, joint replacement, transplant surgery, and bone metabolism. Also investigates community health systems, including self care needs of the elderly, legal needs of patients with chronic illness such as rheumatoid arthritis, and patients' perceived needs for community services.

★7917★ Case Western Reserve University
Skeletal Research Center
Dept. of Biology
2080 Adelbert Rd.
Cleveland, OH 44106-7080
Phone: (216)368-3562
Fax: (216)368-4077
Arnold I. Caplan, Ph.D., Dir.

Research Activities and Fields: Engineering analysis and clinical aspects of skeletal tissue, including cartilage, bones, tendons, and ligaments.

★7918★ Center for Basic Research in Digestive Diseases
Guggenheim 17
Mayo Clinic
Rochester, MN 55905
Phone: (507)284-1000
Dr. N. F. LaRusso, Dir.

Research Activities and Fields: Cell biology, focusing on molecular and biochemical mechanisms of secretion in digestive tissues. **E-mail Address:** larusso.nicholas@mayo.edu.

★7919★ Harrington Arthritis Research Center
1800 E. Van Buren St.
Phoenix, AZ 85006
Phone: (602)254-0377
Fax: (602)253-4817

Research Activities and Fields: Arthritis, including research and education on assistive devices, and joint repair. **Publications:** *Harrington Annual Report.* **E-mail Address:** harcbone@enet.net.

Hospital for Special Surgery
Research Division
See: Entry 9941

★7920★ Indiana University-Purdue University at Indianapolis
Multipurpose Arthritis and Musculoskeletal Diseases Center
541 Clinical Dr., Rm. 492
Indianapolis, IN 46202-5103
Phone: (317)274-4225
Dr. Kenneth D. Brandt, Dir.

Research Activities and Fields: Basic and clinical research related to rheumatic diseases. Activities are structured in two major areas: a Biomedical Component and an Epidemiology, Education, and Health Services Research Component. **Publications:** Newsletter (three times per year). **Formerly:** Specialized Center of Research in Osteoarthritis; Multipurpose Arthritis Center and Specialized Center of Research.

★7921★ Kuzell Institute for Arthritis and Infectious Diseases
California Pacific Medical Center
2200 Webster St., R305
San Francisco, CA 94115
Phone: (415)561-1734
Fax: (415)441-8548
Lowell S. Young, M.D., Dir.

Research Activities and Fields: Basic and applied research in arthritis and related diseases and infectious diseases. In the area of arthritis, the Institute conducts fundamental investigations on the biology, biochemistry, and pharmacology of tissues and cellular inflammatory reactions, and studies of autoimmune diseases, including systematic lupus erthymatosus (SLE), the biology of neutrophils, replacement of joints, and pharmacology of steroidal and nonsteroidal anti-inflammatory agents. Infectious disease research emphasizes host defense against opportunistic pathogens and includes development of monoclonal antibodies against virulence factors of gram negative bacteria, evaluation of new antimicrobial agents, and the pathogenesis and treatment of atypical mycobacterial infections, particularly as they occur in AIDS. **Formerly:** Kuzell Institute for Arthritis Research.

Laval University
Medical Research Centre
Inflammation, Immunology, and Rheumatology Research Group
See: Entry 2107

★7922★ Medical College of Pennsylvania and Hahnemann University
Orthopedic and Arthritis Center
221 N. Broad St.
Philadelphia, PA 19107
Phone: (215)762-8500
Fax: (215)762-3442
Dr. Arnold T. Berman, Dir.

Research Activities and Fields: Arthritis.

★7923★ Medical University of South Carolina
Arthritis Clinical and Research Center
171 Ashley Ave.
Charleston, SC 29425
Phone: (803)792-2000
Fax: (803)792-7121
E. Carwile LeRoy, M.D., Dir.

Research Activities and Fields: Molecular mechanisms of connective tissue diseases, microvascular investigations, alterations in gene expression in fibroblasts, adhesion and nonadhesion molecular interactions in cell behavior, rheumatic disorders, immunologic investigations in rheumatic disease (such as the function of T-cell subsets), cell culture, and other clinical investigations, especially in Raynaud's, scleroderma, and undifferentiated connective tissue syndromes (UCTS). Research is undertaken in an effort to investigate the underlying mechanisms and the nature of rheumatic and connective tissue diseases, to expand education and training opportunities in t he management of musculoskeletal diseases, and to develop patient care and community programs which increase the awareness of arthritis and improve access to quality rheumatologic care. **Formerly:** Multipurpose Arthritis Center (MAC).

★ 7924 ★ **Multipurpose Arthritis and Musculoskeletal Diseases Center**
Univ. of California, San Diego
Dept. of Medicine
9500 Gilman Dr.
La Jolla, CA 92093-0664
Phone: (619)534-5393
Fax: (619)534-5475
Dr. Dennis Carson, Codirector

Research Activities and Fields: Causes and treatment of arthritis. **Formerly:** Scripps Clinic and Research Foundation, Multipurpose Arthritis Center.

★ 7925 ★ **New York Society for the Relief of the Ruptured and Crippled**
Hospital for Special Surgery
535 East 70th Street
New York, NY 10021
Phone: (212)606-1480
Fax: (212)717-1192
Adele L. Boskey, Ph.D, Dir.Rsch.

Research Activities and Fields: Musculoskeletal and immunology research (clinical and basic science) including : biomechanics and biomaterials (bone mechanics, joint kinematics, polyethylene, prosthesis design and retrieval analysis, soft tissue mechanics); bone and cartilage biology (calcification mechanisms, regulation of bone remodeling, cell and molecular biology, osteogenesis imperfecta, osteoporosis, osteoarthritis); soft tissue biology (ligament and tendon repair and regeneration, cell and molecular biology, basis of laser therapy); autoimmunity and inflammation (molecular basis of lupus and other autoimmune disorders, markers of inflammatory diseases, rheumatoid arthritis, B- and T- cell function, Fc-receptors); clinical research and outcome studies. **Publications:** *The Hospital for Special Surgery Horizon.*

New York University
Rusk Institute of Rehabilitation Medicine
See: Entry 12739

★ 7926 ★ **Northwestern University**
Multipurpose Arthritis and Musculoskeletal Diseases Center
303 E. Chicago Ave.
Chicago, IL 60611
Phone: (312)503-8197
Fax: (312)503-0994
Dr. Richard M. Pope, Dir.

Research Activities and Fields: Conducts biomedical, educational, and health services research in the musculoskeletal diseases. **Formerly:** Multipurpose Arthritis Center (1990).

★ 7927 ★ **Oklahoma Medical Research Foundation**
Arthritis / Immunology Research Program
825 NE 13th St.
Oklahoma City, OK 73104
Phone: (405)271-7766
Fax: (405)271-4110
Morris Reichlin, M.D., Chief

Research Activities and Fields: Molecular aspects of systemic autoimmunity.

★ 7928 ★ **Pain Institute**
22401 Foster-Winter Dr.
Southfield, MI 48075
Phone: (810)827-7790
Fax: (810)423-1482
Dr. Claude Oster, CEO

Research Activities and Fields: Epidemiology of musculoskeletal pain, especially its neurochemical and metabolic and biochemical causes. Examines stress and other psychiatric components of pain, tests experimental groups for certain metabolic disorders such as porphyria and hypoglycemia, and conducts longitudinal studies for occupational hazards. After recognizing an individual's pain, the Institute seeks treatment of both its mental and physical causes through a team system utilizing specialists in pain management, physical medicine and rehabilitation, orthopedics, nursing, internal medicine, Rheumatology, neurology, neurosurgery, anesthesiology, psychiatry, and psychology, as necessary. **Formerly:** Pain Research and Control Institute (1991); Institute for Pain Management (1992).

Palo Alto Institute of Molecular Medicine
See: Entry 2605

Pediatric Rheumatoid Clinic
See: Entry 3345

★ 7929 ★ **Regional Bone Center**
Helen Hayes Hospital
Rte. 9W
West Haverstraw, NY 10993
Phone: (914)947-3000
Fax: (914)947-2485
David W. Dempster, Ph.D., Dir.

Research Activities and Fields: Bone and calcium metabolism, including pathophysiology of bone and clinical research on the pathogenesis and treatment of diseases such as osteoporosis, primary hyperparathyroidism, and Paget's disease. Conducts calciotropic hormone assays, bone biopsies and histomorphometry, and bone mass measurements.

★ 7930 ★ **Shriners Hospital for Crippled Children**
Metabolic Research Unit
2001 S. Lindbergh Blvd.
St. Louis, MO 63131
Phone: (314)432-3600
Fax: (314)432-2930
Michael P. Whyte, M.D., Dir.

Research Activities and Fields: Metabolic bone diseases and skeletal dysplasias in chil-

dren, including evaluation of potential medical therapies and analysis of inheritance factors.

★ 7931 ★ **Shriners Hospitals for Crippled Children**
Research Unit
3101 SW Sam Jackson Park Rd.
Portland, OR 97201
Phone: (503)221-1537
Fax: (503)221-3451
Dr. Michael Sussman, M.D., Chief of Staff

Research Activities and Fields: Connective tissues.

★ 7932 ★ **Stanford University**
Stanford Arthritis Center
701 Welch Rd., Ste. 3301
Palo Alto, CA 94304
Phone: (415)723-7331
Dr. Halsted Holman, Dir.

Research Activities and Fields: Arthritis, including epidemiology, health policy, community education, measurement of patient outcomes, comparison of health care systems, and testing of novel treatments resulting from recent biomedical advances.

★ 7933 ★ **Terri Gotthelf Lupus Research Institute**
10 New England Way
Warwick, RI 02886-6904
Phone: (203)852-0120
Free: 800-82-LUPUS
Fax: (203)852-9720
Scott Morris, Contact

Research Activities and Fields: Supports, coordinates, and conducts clinical and experimental research into the cause, treatment, and cure of lupus. Projects include support of new generation drug development for treatment of lupus and related inflammatory diseases.

★ 7934 ★ **Thomas Jefferson University**
Lupus Study Center
111 S. 11th St.
Philadelphia, PA 19107
Phone: (215)955-1410
Fax: (215)923-7883
Raphael J. DeHoratius, M.D., Dir.

Research Activities and Fields: Systemic lupus erthematosus and autoimmune diseases, including reproductive immunology.

★ 7935 ★ **Thomas Jefferson University**
Scleroderma and Arthritis Research Center
233 S 10th St.
Philadelphia, PA 19107
Phone: (215)955-5042
Fax: (215)923-4649
Dr. Sergio A. Jimenez, Dir.

Research Activities and Fields: Molecular biology and biochemistry of the connective tissue, pathogenesis of scleroderma and other fibrotic diseases, biological functions of the immune system in health and disease, molecular biology of articular cartilage matrix and heritable diseases of articular cartilage, and identification of gene mutations in animal models of disease. **Formerly:** Arthritis Clinical Research Center.

Tufts University
Medical Rehabilitation Research & Training
  Center in Childhood Trauma
See: Entry 12754

★7936★ U.S. Department of Health and
  Human Services
National Institute of Arthritis and
  Musculoskeletal and Skin Diseases
NIH Bldg. 31, Rm. 4C32
9000 Rockville Pike
Bethesda, MD 20892
Phone: (301)496-4353
Fax: (301)480-6069
Lawrence E. Shulman, M.D., Ph.D., Director

Research Activities and Fields: Institute conducts and supports basic and clinical research on a large number of diverse diseases, including rheumatoid arthritis, osteoarthritis, systemic lupus erythematosus, muscle diseases, osteoporosis, Paget's disease, back disorders, osteogenesis imperfecta, psoriasis, acne, ichthyosis, epidermolysis bullosa, and vitiligo. The Institute's Intramural Research Program conducts basic research studies in immunology, biophysics, biochemistry, molecular biology, structural biology, pathology and histochemistry, and pharmacology. Through its Arthritis and Rheumatism Branch, the Institute leads basic and clinical research and treatment programs in lupus erythematosus, rheumatoid arthritis, and other connective tissue diseases. The Institute's Extramural Activities Program is organized in five branches: Rheumatic Diseases Branch, Musculoskeletal Diseases Branch, Bone Biology and Bone Diseases Branch, Muscle Biology Branch, and Skin Diseases Branch. Other extramural programs include the Centers Program. The Institute supports basic and clinical research through investigator-initiated research grants, research center grants, individual and institutional research training awards, career development awards, and contracts to public and private research institutions and organizations.

★7937★ U.S. Department of Health and
  Human Services
National Institute of Arthritis and
  Musculoskeletal and Skin Diseases
Extramural Activities Program
Centers Program
5333 Westbard Ave., Rm. 403
Bethesda, MD 20892
Phone: (301)496-7495
Fax: (301)496-7881
Julia B. Freeman, Ph.D., Director

Research Activities and Fields: NIAMS sponsors Multipurpose Arthritis and Musculoskeletal Diseases centers across the U.S. Activities at these centers include basic and clinical research in the causes of arthritis; developmental and feasibility studies; education research; epidemiologic research and health services research. NIAMS also sponsors Specialized Centers of Research (SCORs) in rheumatoid arthritis, osteoarthritis, and osteoporosis; and Skin Diseases Research Centers.

★7938★ U.S. Department of Health and
  Human Services
National Institute of Arthritis and
  Musculoskeletal and Skin Diseases
Extramural Activities Program
Muscle Biology Program
Westwood Bldg., Rm. 403
Bethesda, MD 20892
Phone: (301)594-9959
Richard W. Lymn, Ph.D., Director

Research Activities and Fields: Skeletal muscle development and function in normal disease conditions, including studies on the structure and function of muscle, development and regeneration of muscle, normal and abnormal muscle metabolism, and selected diseases and disorders of skeletal muscle.

★7939★ U.S. Department of Health and
  Human Services
National Institute of Arthritis and
  Musculoskeletal and Skin Diseases
Extramural Activities Program
Musculoskeletal Diseases Branch
Westwood Bldg., Rm. 407
5333 Westbard Ave.
Bethesda, MD 20892
Phone: (301)594-9951
Fax: (301)594-9376
Stephen L. Gordon, Ph.D., Director

Research Activities and Fields: Branch supports research projects directed toward an understanding of the structure, function, formation, metabolism, and biomechanics of bones, joints, and skeletal support structures. Research activity focuses on: 1) osteoporosis and other metabolic diseases; 2) joint replacement methods and materials; 3) developmental disorders, including scoliosis, bone immunology, and transplantation; 4) inherited connective tissue disorders; 5) back disorders; and 6) exercise pathophysiology.

★7940★ U.S. Department of Health and
  Human Services
National Institute of Arthritis and
  Musculoskeletal and Skin Diseases
Extramural Activities Program
Rheumatic Diseases Branch
5333 Westbard Ave.
Westwood Bldg., Rm. 405
Bethesda, MD 20892
Phone: (301)496-7326
Fax: (301)480-7881
L.M. Petrucelli, Director

Research Activities and Fields: Branch supports basic investigations involving studies in immunology, inflammation, infectious agents, genetic factors, purine metabolism, and the structure and function of the components of connective tissues. Areas of interest include rheumatoid arthritis, osteoarthritis, arthritis in children, systemic lupus erythematosus, spondylitis, other diffuse connective tissue disorders, gout and pseudogout, and the epidemiology of rheumatic disease.

★7941★ U.S. Department of Health and
  Human Services
National Institute of Arthritis and
  Musculoskeletal and Skin Diseases
Intramural Research Program
Arthritis and Rheumatism Branch
NIH Bldg. 10, Rm. 9N228
9000 Rockville Pike
Bethesda, MD 20892
Phone: (301)496-2612
Fax: (301)402-0012
Dr. Henry Metzger, Chief

Research Activities and Fields: Branch conducts laboratory and clinical research on arthritis, connective tissue diseases, and related areas, including immunology. Activities involve: 1) disease-related studies on the etiology, pathology, and therapy of connective tissue disorders, with special emphasis on systemic lupus erythematosus, polymyositis, and rheumatoid arthritis (both human disease and animal models of these diseases are studied); and 2) fundamental studies on immune regulation, with special emphasis on autoimmunity and mechanisms of immune responses at the cellular and molecular level.

★7942★ U.S. Department of Health and
  Human Services
National Institute of Arthritis and
  Musculoskeletal and Skin Diseases
Laboratory of Physical Biology
NIH Bldg. 6, Rm. 114
9000 Rockville Pike
Bethesda, MD 20892
Phone: (301)496-5415
Fax: (301)402-0009
Richard J. Podolsky, Ph.D., Chief

Research Activities and Fields: Laboratory carries out a broad range of studies on the mechanism of muscle contraction in intact cells and simplified preparations using time-resolved X-ray diffraction in conjunction with mechanochemical techniques. Electron microscopy is used with a wide variety of perparations, and digital image processing techniques are used to enhance resolution. Research also includes studies on enzyme organization in unicellular organisms, metamorphosis in insects, human red cell sickling, and biological rhythms and entrainment.

★7943★ University of Alabama at
  Birmingham
Division of Clinical Immunology and
  Rheumatology
Tinsley Harrison Tower, 429A
Birmingham, AL 35294-0006
Phone: (205)934-4703
Fax: (205)975-6859
Eugene Bell, Act.Dir.

Research Activities and Fields: Rheumatic diseases and clinical immunology, including clinical studies on antibody structures and function, glycopeptide chemistry, chemistry and physiology of complement, biochemical and biophysical properties of immunoglobulins, physical chemistry of complex polysaccharides, pathology of trace metals, and pathophysiology of bone calcification. Conducts laboratory investigations in macromolecular physical chemistry, protein structure, polysaccharide chemistry, and immunology. **Publications:** *Arthritis Today* (newsletter, biennially). **E-mail Address:** rheu007@uabdpo.dpo.uab.edu. **Formerly:** Division of Rheumatology.

★7944★ **University of Alabama at Birmingham**
Multipurpose Arthritis and Musculoskeletal Diseases Center (MAMDC)
Tinsley Harrison Tower, 429A
Birmingham, AL 35294-0006
Phone: (205)934-5306
Fax: (205)934-1564
Dr. William J. Koopman, Dir.

Research Activities and Fields: Arthritis and related rheumatic disorders, including investigations into cause, diagnosis, control, and treatment of arthritis and complications resulting from arthritis and related musculoskeletal disorders. **Publications:** *Arthritis Today* (newsletter, biennially). **E-mail Address:** rheu007@uabdpo.dpo.uab.edu. **Formerly:** Multipurpose Arthritis Center (1992).

University of California, Davis
Allergy-Clinical Immunology Program
See: Entry 2140

★7945★ **University of California, Los Angeles**
Bone Research Laboratory
1000 Veteran Ave., Rm. A3-34
Los Angeles, CA 90024-1790
Phone: (310)825-6521
Dr. Marshall R. Urist, Dir.

Research Activities and Fields: Bone morphogenesis in health and disease, including fundamental and clinical studies in bone biochemistry and physiology. The UCLA group discovered the inductive response of adult connective tissue cells to bone morphogenetic protein.

★7946★ **University of California, San Francisco**
Rosalind Russell Medical Research Center for Arthritis
350 Parnassus Ave., Ste. 600
San Francisco, CA 94117
Phone: (415)476-1141
Fax: (415)476-3526
Ephraim P. Engleman, M.D., Dir.

Research Activities and Fields: Arthritis and its probable causes, focusing on on immunology, immunogenetics, and inflammation. Examines health services and policy and educational approaches and methods for arthritis patients and health professionals.

★7947★ **University of Chicago**
Gwen Knapp Center for Lupus and Immunology Research
5841 S. Maryland Ave.
MC 1089
Chicago, IL 60637
Phone: (312)702-6755
Fax: (312)702-3701
Dr. Frank Firch, Contact

Research Activities and Fields: Immunological and molecular biological research on the cause and treatment of systemic lupus erythematosus.

★7948★ **University of Cincinnati**
Rheumatic Diseases Research Center for the Tri-State Area
231 Bethesda Ave., ML 563
Cincinnati, OH 45267
Phone: (513)558-4701
Fax: (513)558-3799
Evelyn V. Hess, M.D., Dir.

Research Activities and Fields: Rheumatic diseases, including immunobiology of cartilage and bone, abnormalities in systemic lupus erythematosus, immunogenetics of connective tissue disease, mechanisms of tolerance and immunomodulation, and AIDS/HIV and autoimmune disease. **Formerly:** Arthritis Foundation/Clinical Research Center for the Tri-State Area.

★7949★ **University of Connecticut**
Exercise Research Laboratory
Osteoporosis Ctr.
263 Farmington Ave.
Farmington, CT 06030-6145
Phone: (203)679-3855
Fax: (203)679-1312
Gail Dalsky, Ph.D., Dir.

Research Activities and Fields: Studies the effects of hormone treatment, exercise, and calcium on osteoporosis in women.

★7950★ **University of Connecticut**
Multipurpose Arthritis Center
School of Medicine
Division of Rheumatic Diseases
Farmington, CT 06030
Phone: (203)679-2160
Fax: (203)679-1287
Dr. Naomi Rothfield, Dir.

Research Activities and Fields: Rheumatic disease, role of endothelial cells in inflammation and immune response, blood coagulation and gout in rheumatic disease, fibroblasts in immune process, NT cell specificity, antinuclear antibodies, and cell biology. The Center conducts community research on coping with rheumatic disease, disability, and mathematical models of systemic lupus erythematosus; studies computer-based education for patients; and develops and evaluates arthritis curriculum for urban, low-income minority individuals.

★7951★ **University of Connecticut**
Osteoporosis Center
208 Farm Hollow, Ste. C
309 Farmington Ave.
Farmington, CT 06030
Phone: (203)679-3855
Fax: (203)679-1258
Lawrence G. Raisz, M.D., Dir.

Research Activities and Fields: Clinical and basic research on osteoporosis, including effects of exercise and diet on bone health. **Publications:** *Osteoporosis Newsletter*.

★7952★ **University of Medicine and Dentistry of New Jersey**
Lyme Disease Center
Medical Education Bldg.
1 Robert Wood Johnson's Pl.
New Brunswick, NJ 08901
Phone: (908)235-7702
Fax: (908)235-7238
Leonard H. Sigal, M.D., Dir.

Research Activities and Fields: Lyme disease, including epidemiology and clinical manifestations, immunopathogenesis, and the molecular biology of neurologic manifestations.

★7953★ **University of Michigan**
Laboratories for Connective Tissue Research
3310 School of Dentistry
1101 N. University Ave.
Ann Arbor, MI 48109
Phone: (313)763-3388
Fax: (313)763-5503
Martha Somerman, Dir.

Research Activities and Fields: Connective tissue formation and repair, focusing on identifying and characterizing proteins and their function during connective tissue development and wound healing, and aging understanding the role of the immune system in regulation of bone remodeling, and identifying proteins produced by lymphoid cells and their effects on bone metabolism; researches role of osteoblasts in regularity hemopoietic stem cells. **E-mail Address:** somerman@um.cc.umich.edu.

★7954★ **University of Michigan**
Multipurpose Arthritis Center
3918 Taubman Center
Ann Arbor, MI 48109-0358
Phone: (313)936-9539
Fax: (313)763-1253
David A. Fox, M.D., Dir.

Research Activities and Fields: Arthritis pilot projects include studies on ligand recognition by anti-DNA autoantibodies, function and regulation of BLC-2 proto-oncogene in T cell development, crystallographic analysis of the tyrosine phosphatase domains from a CD45-related receptor, and peptide inhibition of T cell adhesion to endothelium and extracellular matrix. Collaborates with Education, Community, and Health Services Research Division on the following research projects: 1) problem-based ambulatory care training for primary care house officers; 2) musculoskeletal work injury: epidemiology and disability; 3) bone mass, body composition, and predicting osteoarthritis; 4) musculoskeletal and physical functioning in older adults; and 5) work injury and disability, with focus on gender, health care, and outcomes. Core areas include biostatistics, flow cytometry, h y bridoma, molecular biology, protein and carbohydrate structure, transgenic animals, biomechanics, and imaging processing. **Publications:** *MAC Mainline* (monthly newsletter).

University of Michigan
Orthopaedic Research Laboratories
See: Entry 9948

★ 7955 ★ University of Michigan Rackham Arthritis Research Unit

Univ. of Michigan Medical Center
3918 Taubman Center
Ann Arbor, MI 48109-0358
Phone: (313)936-5566
Fax: (313)763-1253
David A. Fox, M.D., Dir.

Research Activities and Fields: Fundamental concepts of arthritis, including clinical, biochemical, and immunological aspects of various rheumatic diseases, and evaluation of therapeutic agents and surgical procedures. Studies metabolic and physiologic aspects of connective tissue, infectious agents as related to etiology and pathogenesis of connective tissues disease, biochemistry of hyperuricemia and gout, patients with other rheumatic disorders, molecular analysis of genetic bases for specific rheumatic diseases, and development of approaches to gene therapy. **Publications:** *Rackham Arthritis Research Unit Alumni and Friends Newsletter* (semiannually). **E-mail Address:** buckr@umich.edu.

★ 7956 ★ University of Michigan Specialized Center of Research in Rheumatoid Arthritis

200 Zina Pitcher Pl.
Kresge I R4550
Ann Arbor, MI 48109-0531
Phone: (313)763-0308
Fax: (313)763-8974
Dr. Joseph Holoshitz, Dir.

Research Activities and Fields: Rheumatoid arthritis, including studies in cellular and molecular biology and immunology. **E-mail Address:** jpickett@uv1.im.med.umich.edu.

★ 7957 ★ University of Missouri—Columbia Arthritis Center

MA427 Health Sciences Center
1 Hospital Dr.
Columbia, MO 65212
Phone: (314)882-8738
Fax: (314)884-3996
Gordon C. Sharp, M.D., Dir.

Research Activities and Fields: Arthritis, including rheumatic disease rehabilitation, small nuclear ribonucleoprotein characterization and reactivity, depression and arthritis, genetic associations with autoantibodies in Mixed Connective Tissue Disease (MCTD) and SLE, arthritis pain, personalized exercise programs via computer for elderly pediatric rheumatology, murine models of autoimmune disease, continuing rheumatology education for non-arthritis specialist health care providers, use of state agencies for arthritis education, use of a computerized educational videodisc to teach medical students, residents, and allied health professionals about arthritis, depression, coping strategies and stress management in rheumatoid arthritis, conditioning exercise in combination with medication for fibromyalgia, and osteoporosis in women with rheumatoid arthritis. **Publications:** *Arthritis NewsBreak* (semi-annual newsletter). **E-mail Address:** susan@imed.missouri.edu.

★ 7958 ★ University of North Carolina at Chapel Hill Thurston Arthritis Research Center

CB 7280, Rm. 3310
Thurston Bldg.
Chapel Hill, NC 27599-7280
Phone: (919)966-4191
Fax: (919)966-1739
John B. Winfield, M.D., Dir.

Research Activities and Fields: Arthritis and autoimmune disease. Laboratory research focuses on immunogenetics, immunoregulation, molecular biology, animal models, and complement studies. Non-laboratory research emphasizes social, behavioral, epidemiology, health services research, and educational aspects of chronic arthritis. **Formerly:** Multipurpose Arthritis Center.

★ 7959 ★ University of North Texas Health Science Center at Fort Worth Center for Osteoporosis Prevention and Treatment (COPT)

3500 Camp Bowie Blvd.
Ft. Worth, TX 76107-2699
Phone: (817)735-2661
Fax: (817)735-5441
Prof. Bernard Rubin, D.O., Contact

Research Activities and Fields: Treatment and prevention of postmenopausal osteoporosis, treatment of steroid-induced osteoporosis, and epidemiology of osteoporosis among various ethnic groups.

University of Pennsylvania Aging Skin Clinic
See: Entry 4270

★ 7960 ★ University of Puerto Rico Arthritis Research Unit

Medical Research Unit
PO Box 365067
San Juan, PR 00936-5067
Phone: (809)764-6839
Fax: (809)764-6839
Dr. Esther N. Gonzalez-Pares, Dir.

Research Activities and Fields: Immunologic studies of collagen diseases, mainly systemic lupus erythematosus.

University of Southern California Division of Rheumatology and Immunology
See: Entry 2146

★ 7961 ★ University of Texas Southwestern Medical Center at Dallas Harold C. Simmons Arthritis Research Center

5323 Harry Hines Blvd.
Dallas, TX 75235-8884
Phone: (214)648-9110
Fax: (214)648-7995
Peter E. Lipsky, M.D., Dir.

Research Activities and Fields: Conducts basic research on inflammatory arthritis. Acts as a resource facility for ankylosing spondylitis-related research.

★ 7962 ★ University of Vermont McClure Musculoskeletal Research Center

Dept. of Orthopaedic and Rehabilitation
Stafford Hall, 4th Fl.
Burlington, VT 05405-0084
Phone: (802)656-2250
Fax: (802)656-4247
Bruce D. Beynnon, Ph.D., Dir.

Research Activities and Fields: Occupational and sports injuries and nontraumatic and congenital disorders, including how musculoskeletal structures are injured and how they heal. Research focuses on lower back pain, including studies of lifting, posture, seating, vehicle vibration, exercise, and different low back pain treatments; sports medicine, including knee, shoulder, and ankle injuries; scoliosis, including the etiology of idiopathic scoliosis and growth asymmetry research; and joint replacement studies.

State & Regional Organizations

Arthritis

Listed below are chapters of the Arthritis Foundation, 1314 Spring St. NW, Atlanta, GA 30309, (404) 872-7100.

Alabama

★ 7963 ★ Arthritis Foundation Alabama Chapter

200 Vestavia Pkwy., Ste. 3050
Birmingham, AL 35216
Phone: (205)979-5700

Arizona

★ 7964 ★ Arthritis Foundation Central Arizona Chapter

777 E. Missouri Ave., Ste. 119
Phoenix, AZ 85014
Phone: (602)264-7679

★ 7965 ★ Arthritis Foundation Southern Arizona Chapter

6464 E. Grant Rd.
Tucson, AZ 85715
Phone: (602)290-9090

Arkansas

★ 7966 ★ Arthritis Foundation Arkansas Chapter

6213 Lee Ave.
Little Rock, AR 72205
Phone: (501)664-7242

California

★7967★ Arthritis Foundation
Northeastern California Chapter
3040 Explorer Dr., Ste. 1
Sacramento, CA 95827
Phone: (916)368-5599

★7968★ Arthritis Foundation
Northern California Chapter
203 Willow St., Ste. 201
San Francisco, CA 94109
Phone: (415)673-6882

★7969★ Arthritis Foundation
San Diego Chapter
9089 Clairmont Mesa Blvd., Ste. 300
San Diego, CA 92123
Phone: (619)492-1090

★7970★ Arthritis Foundation
Southern California Chapter
4311 Wilshire Blvd., Ste. 530
Los Angeles, CA 90010
Phone: (213)954-5750

Colorado

★7971★ Arthritis Foundation
Rocky Mountain Chapter
2280 S. Albion St.
Denver, CO 80222
Phone: (303)756-8622

Connecticut

★7972★ Arthritis Foundation
Connecticut Chapter
35 Cold Spring, Bldg. 400
Rocky Hill, CT 06067
Phone: (203)563-1177

Delaware

★7973★ Arthritis Foundation
Delaware Chapter
222 Philadelphia Pike, Ste. 1
Wilmington, DE 19809
Phone: (302)764-8254

District of Columbia

★7974★ Arthritis Foundation
Metro Washington, DC Chapter
4455 Connecticut Ave., NW, Ste. 300
Washington, DC 20008-2302
Phone: (202)537-6800

Florida

★7975★ Arthritis Foundation
Florida Chapter
5211 Manatee Ave. W.
Bradenton, FL 34209
Phone: (813)795-3010

Georgia

★7976★ Arthritis Foundation
Georgia Chapter
550 Pharr Rd., Ste. 550
Atlanta, GA 30305-3432
Phone: (404)237-8771

Hawaii

★7977★ Arthritis Foundation
Hawaii Chapter
Honfed Bank Bldg., Penthouse
45-1144 Kamehameha Hwy.
Kaneohe, HI 96744
Phone: (808)235-3636

Illinois

★7978★ Arthritis Foundation
Greater Chicago Chapter
111 E. Wacker Dr., Ste. 1928
Chicago, IL 60601
Phone: (312)616-3470

★7979★ Arthritis Foundation
Greater Illinois Chapter
2621 N. Knoxville
Peoria, IL 61604
Phone: (309)682-6600

Indiana

★7980★ Arthritis Foundation
Indiana Chapter
8646 Guion Rd.
Indianapolis, IN 46268-3011
Phone: (317)879-0321

Iowa

★7981★ Arthritis Foundation
Iowa Chapter
2600 72nd, Ste. D
Des Moines, IA 50322
Phone: (515)278-0636

Kansas

★7982★ Arthritis Foundation
Kansas Chapter
1602 E. Waterman
Wichita, KS 67211
Phone: (316)263-0116

Kentucky

★7983★ Arthritis Foundation
Kentucky Chapter
410 W. Chestnut St., Ste. 750
Louisville, KY 40202-2325
Phone: (502)585-1866

Louisiana

★7984★ Arthritis Foundation
Louisiana Chapter
3955 Government St., Ste. 7
Baton Rouge, LA 70806-5755
Phone: (504)387-6932

Maine

★7985★ Arthritis Foundation
Maine Chapter
930 Brighton Ave.
Portland, ME 04102
Phone: (207)773-0595

Maryland

★7986★ Arthritis Foundation
Maryland Chapter
1777 Reisterstown Rd., Ste. 175
Baltimore, MD 21208
Phone: (410)602-0160

Massachusetts

★7987★ Arthritis Foundation
Massachusetts Chapter
450 Chatham Center
29 Crafts St.
Newton, MA 02160-5829
Phone: (617)244-1800

Michigan

★7988★ Arthritis Foundation
Michigan Chapter
23999 Northwestern Hwy., Ste. 210
Southfield, MI 48075
Phone: (810)350-3030

Minnesota

★7989★ Arthritis Foundation
Minnesota Chapter
1730 Clifton Pl., Ste. A1
Minneapolis, MN 55403
Phone: (612)874-1201

Mississippi

★7990★ Arthritis Foundation
Mississippi Chapter
350 North Mart Plaza
PO Box 9185
Jackson, MS 39286-9185
Phone: (601)362-6283

Missouri

★7991★ Arthritis Foundation
Eastern Missouri Chapter
8390 Delmar Blvd.
St. Louis, MO 63124-2100
Phone: (314)991-9333

★7992★ Arthritis Foundation
Western Missouri / Greater Kansas City
    Chapter
1100 Pennsylvania Ave., Ste. 400
Kansas City, MO 64105
Phone: (816)842-0335

Nebraska

★7993★ Arthritis Foundation
Nebraska Chapter
7101 Newport Ave., Ste. 304
Omaha, NE 68152
Phone: (402)572-3040

Nevada

★7994★ Arthritis Foundation
Nevada Chapter
3850 W. Desert Inn Rd., Ste. 108
Las Vegas, NV 89102
Phone: (702)367-1626

New Hampshire

★7995★ Arthritis Foundation
New Hampshire Chapter
2 1/2 Beacon St., Ste. 10
Concord, NH 03301
Phone: (603)224-9322

New Jersey

★7996★ Arthritis Foundation
New Jersey Chapter
200 Middlesex Tpke.
Iselin, NJ 08830
Phone: (908)283-4300

New Mexico

★7997★ Arthritis Foundation
New Mexico Chapter
124 Alvarado SE
PO Box 8022
Albuquerque, NM 87108
Phone: (505)265-1545

New York

★7998★ Arthritis Foundation
Central New York Chapter
The Pickard Bldg., Ste. 123
5858 E. Molloy Rd.
Syracuse, NY 13211
Phone: (315)455-8553

★7999★ Arthritis Foundation
Genesee Valley Chapter
1 Mt. Hope Ave.
Rochester, NY 14620-1088
Phone: (716)423-9490

★8000★ Arthritis Foundation
Long Island Chapter
501 Walt Whitman Rd.
Melville, NY 11747
Phone: (516)427-8272

★8001★ Arthritis Foundation
New York Chapter
67 Irving Pl.
New York, NY 10003
Phone: (212)477-8310

★8002★ Arthritis Foundation
Northeastern New York Chapter
1717 Central Ave., Ste. 105
Albany, NY 12205
Phone: (518)456-1203

★8003★ Arthritis Foundation
Western New York Chapter
2440 Sheridan Dr., Ste. 201
Tonawanda, NY 14150
Phone: (716)837-8600

North Carolina

★8004★ Arthritis Foundation
Carolinas Chapter
Woodlawn Green Office Pky., Bldg. 7, Ste.
 217
Charlotte, NC 28217
Phone: (704)529-5166

North Dakota

★8005★ Arthritis Foundation
Dakota Chapter
115 Roberts St.
Fargo, ND 58102
Phone: (701)237-3310

Ohio

★8006★ Arthritis Foundation
Central Ohio Chapter
1460 W. Lane Ave.
Columbus, OH 43221
Phone: (614)488-0777

★8007★ Arthritis Foundation
Northeastern Ohio Chapter
23811 Chagrin Blvd.
Chagrin Plaza East, Ste. 210
Cleveland, OH 44122
Phone: (216)831-7000

★8008★ Arthritis Foundation
Northwestern Ohio Chapter
309 N. Reynolds Rd.
Toledo, OH 43615
Phone: (419)537-0888

★8009★ Arthritis Foundation
Southwestern Ohio Chapter
7811 Laurel Ave.
Cincinnati, OH 45243
Phone: (513)271-4545

Oklahoma

★8010★ Arthritis Foundation
Eastern Oklahoma Chapter
4520 S. Harvard, Ste. 100
Tulsa, OK 74135
Phone: (918)743-4526

★8011★ Arthritis Foundation
Oklahoma Chapter
2915 Classen Blvd., Ste. 325
Oklahoma City, OK 73106
Phone: (405)521-0066

Oregon

★8012★ Arthritis Foundation
Oregon Chapter
4412 SW Barbur Blvd., Ste. 220
Portland, OR 97201
Phone: (503)222-7246

Pennsylvania

★8013★ Arthritis Foundation
Central Pennsylvania Chapter
17 S. 19th St.
PO Box 668
Camp Hill, PA 17011
Phone: (717)763-0900

★8014★ Arthritis Foundation
Eastern Pennsylvania Chapter
Architects Bldg., Ste. 1905-15
117 S. 17th St.
Philadelphia, PA 19103
Phone: (215)665-9200

★8015★ Arthritis Foundation
Western Pennsylvania Chapter
Warner Centre, 5th Fl.
332 5th Ave.
Pittsburgh, PA 15222
Phone: (412)566-1645

Rhode Island

★8016★ Arthritis Foundation
Rhode Island Chapter
37 N. Blossom St.
East Providence, RI 02914-1300
Phone: (401)434-5792

South Carolina

★8017★ Arthritis Foundation
Carolinas Chapter
Woodlawn Green Office Pky., Bldg. 7, Ste.
 217
Charlotte, NC 28217
Phone: (704)529-5166

Tennessee

★8018★ Arthritis Foundation
Tennessee Chapter
1719 West End Ave., Ste. 303 W.
Nashville, TN 37203
Phone: (615)320-7626

Texas

★8019★ Arthritis Foundation
North Texas Chapter
2824 Swiss Ave.
Dallas, TX 75204
Phone: (214)826-4361

★8020★ Arthritis Foundation
Northwest Texas Chapter
3145 McCart Ave.
Ft. Worth, TX 76110
Phone: (817)926-7733

★8021★ Arthritis Foundation
South Central Texas Chapter
4118 McCullough, Ste. 18
San Antonio, TX 78212
Phone: (210)829-7573

★8022★ Arthritis Foundation
Texas Gulf Coast Chapter
7447 Harwin Dr., Ste. 118
Houston, TX 77036
Phone: (713)785-2360

Utah

★8023★ Arthritis Foundation
Utah Chapter
1733 South 1100 East
Salt Lake City, UT 84105
Phone: (801)486-4993

Vermont

★8024★ Arthritis Foundation
Vermont and Northern New York Chapter
257 S. Union St.
PO Box 422
Burlington, VT 05402
Phone: (802)864-4988

Virginia

★8025★ Arthritis Foundation
Virginia Chapter
3806 Cutshaw Ave., Ste. 200
Richmond, VA 23230
Phone: (804)359-1706

Washington

★8026★ Arthritis Foundation
Washington State Chapter
100 S. King, Ste. 300
Seattle, WA 98104-2864
Phone: (206)622-1378

Wisconsin

★8027★ Arthritis Foundation
Wisconsin Chapter
8556 W. National Ave.
West Allis, WI 53227
Phone: (414)321-3933

Lupus Erythematosus

The following are constituent chapters of the Lupus Foundation of America, 4 Research Pl., Ste. 180, Rockville, MD, 20850-3226, (301) 670-9292; (800)558-0121.

Alabama

★8028★ Lupus Foundation of America
Birmingham Chapter
4 Office Park Circle, Ste. 302
Birmingham, AL 35223
Phone: (205)870-0504

★8029★ Lupus Foundation of America
Montgomery Chapter
PO Box 11507
Montgomery, AL 36111
Phone: (334)288-3032

Alaska

★8030★ Lupus Foundation of America
Alaska Chapter
PO Box 211336
Anchorage, AK 99521-1336
Phone: (907)338-6332

Arizona

★8031★ Lupus Foundation of America
Greater Arizona Chapter
2001 W. Camelback Rd., Ste. 135
Phoenix, AZ 85015-4908
Phone: (602)242-2213

★8032★ Lupus Foundation of America
Southern Arizona Chapter
3113 E. 1st St., Ste. C
Tucson, AZ 85716
Phone: (602)327-9922

Arkansas

★8033★ Lupus Foundation of America
Arkansas Chapter
220 Mockingbird
Hot Springs, AR 71913
Phone: (501)525-9380
Free: 800-294-8878

California

★8034★ Lupus Foundation of America
Bay Area Chapter
2635 N. 1st St., Ste. 206
San Jose, CA 95134
Phone: (408)954-8600
Free: 800-523-3363

★8035★ Lupus Foundation of America
Southern California Chapter
17985 Sky Park Cir., Ste. J
Irvine, CA 92714
Phone: (714)833-2121
Free: 800-426-6026

Colorado

★8036★ Lupus Foundation of America
Colorado Chapter
1420 Ogden St., 2nd Fl.
Denver, CO 80218
Phone: (303)832-2131
Free: 800-858-1292

Connecticut

★8037★ Lupus Foundation of America
Connecticut Chapter
45 S. Main St., Rm. 208
West Hartford, CT 06107-2402
Phone: (203)521-9151

Delaware

★8038★ Lupus Foundation of America
Delaware Chapter
PO Box 6391
Wilmington, DE 19804
Phone: (302)999-8686

District of Columbia

★8039★ Lupus Foundation of America
Greater Washington, DC Chapter
515 A Braddock Rd., 2C
Alexandria, VA 22314
Phone: (703)684-2925

Florida

★8040★ Lupus Foundation of America
Florida Chapter
4406 Urban Ct.
Orlando, FL 32810
Phone: (407)295-8500

★8041★ Lupus Foundation of America
Northeast Florida Chapter
PO Box 10486
Jacksonville, FL 32247-0486
Phone: (904)645-8398
Free: 800-853-8398

★8042★ Lupus Foundation of America
Northwest Florida Chapter
PO Box 17841
Pensacola, FL 32522-7841
Phone: (904)444-7070
Free: 800-458-8211

★8043★ Lupus Foundation of America
Southeast Florida Chapter
6501 N. Federal Hwy., Ste. 5
Boca Raton, FL 33487
Phone: (407)241-5424
Free: 800-339-0586

★8044★ Lupus Foundation of America
Suncoast Chapter
PO Box 7485
Seminole, FL 34645
Phone: (813)391-3000
Free: 800-684-9276

**★ 8045 ★ Lupus Foundation of America
Tampa Area Chapter**
Dibbs Plaza
4119-20A Gunn Hwy.
Tampa, FL 33624
Phone: (813)960-3992
Free: 800-330-3992

Georgia

**★ 8046 ★ Lupus Foundation of America
Columbus Chapter**
233 12th St., Ste. 819
Columbus, GA 31901
Phone: (706)571-8950

**★ 8047 ★ Lupus Foundation of America
Greater Atlanta Chapter**
340 Interstate North Parkway, NW, Ste. 455
Atlanta, GA 30339-2203
Phone: (404)952-3891
Free: 800-800-4532

Hawaii

**★ 8048 ★ Lupus Foundation of America
Hawaii Chapter**
1200 College Walk, Ste. 114
Honolulu, HI 96817
Phone: (808)538-1522

Idaho

**★ 8049 ★ Lupus Foundation of America
Idaho Chapter**
4696 Overland Rd., Ste. 512
Boise, ID 83705
Phone: (208)343-4907

Illinois

**★ 8050 ★ Lupus Foundation of America
Danville Chapter**
322 E. 13th St.
Danville, IL 61832
Phone: (217)446-7672

**★ 8051 ★ Lupus Foundation of America
Illinois Chapter**
PO Box 42812-0812
Chicago, IL 60642
Phone: (312)779-3181
Free: 800-258-7872

Indiana

**★ 8052 ★ Lupus Foundation of America
Indiana Chapter**
2701 E. Southport Rd.
Indianapolis, IN 46227
Phone: (317)783-6033

**★ 8053 ★ Lupus Foundation of America
Northeast Indiana Chapter**
5401 Keystone Dr., Ste. 202
Ft. Wayne, IN 46825
Phone: (219)482-8205

**★ 8054 ★ Lupus Foundation of America
Northwest Indiana Chapter**
3819 W. 40th Ave.
Gary, IN 46408
Phone: (219)365-9943

Iowa

**★ 8055 ★ Lupus Foundation of America
Iowa Chapter**
12714 Kennedy Rd.
Dubuque, IA 52002-1044
Phone: (319)557-9324

Kansas

**★ 8056 ★ Lupus Foundation of America
Wichita Chapter**
PO Box 16094
Wichita, KS 67216
Phone: (316)262-6180

Kentucky

**★ 8057 ★ Lupus Foundation of America
Kentuckiana Chapter**
1850 Bluegrass Ave.
Louisville, KY 40215
Phone: (502)366-9681
Free: 800-277-9681

Louisiana

**★ 8058 ★ Lupus Foundation of America
Cenla Chapter**
PO Box 12565
Alexandria, LA 71315-2565
Phone: (318)473-0125

**★ 8059 ★ Lupus Foundation of America
Louisiana Chapter**
7732 Goodwood Blvd., Ste. B
Baton Rouge, LA 70806
Phone: (504)927-8052

**★ 8060 ★ Lupus Foundation of America
Northeast Louisiana Chapter**
102 Susan Dr.
West Monroe, LA 71291
Phone: (318)396-1333

**★ 8061 ★ Lupus Foundation of America
Shreveport Chapter**
6321 W. Canal Blvd.
Shreveport, LA 71108
Phone: (318)631-6531

Maine

**★ 8062 ★ Lupus Foundation of America
Maine Chapter**
PO Box 8168
Portland, ME 04104
Phone: (207)878-8104

Maryland

**★ 8063 ★ Lupus Foundation of America
Maryland Chapter**
7400 York Rd., 3rd Fl.
Baltimore, MD 21204
Phone: (410)337-9000
Free: 800-777-0934

Massachusetts

**★ 8064 ★ Lupus Foundation of America
Massachusetts Chapter**
425 Watertown St.
Newton, MA 02158
Phone: (617)332-9014

Michigan

**★ 8065 ★ Lupus Foundation of America
Michigan Chapter**
26202 Harper Ave.
St. Clair Shores, MI 48081
Phone: (810)775-8310

Minnesota

**★ 8066 ★ Lupus Foundation of America
Minnesota Chapter**
International Market Sq.
275 Market St., C-17
Minneapolis, MN 55405
Phone: (612)375-1131
Free: 800-645-1131

Mississippi

**★ 8067 ★ Lupus Foundation of America
Mississippi Chapter**
PO Box 24292
Jackson, MS 39225-4292
Phone: (601)366-5655

Missouri

**★ 8068 ★ Lupus Foundation of America
Kansas City Chapter**
10804 Fremont
Kansas City, MO 64134
Phone: (816)765-3887

**★ 8069 ★ Lupus Foundation of America
Missouri Chapter**
8420 Delmar Blvd., No. LL1
St. Louis, MO 63124
Phone: (314)432-0008

**★ 8070 ★ Lupus Foundation of America
Ozarks Chapter**
3150 W. Marty
Springfield, MO 65807
Phone: (417)887-1560

Montana

★8071★ Lupus Foundation of America
Montana Chapter
29 1/2 Alderson
Billings, MT 59102
Phone: (406)254-2082

Nebraska

★8072★ Lupus Foundation of America
Omaha Chapter
Community Health Plaza
7101 Newport Ave., Ste. 310
Omaha, NE 68152
Phone: (402)572-3150

★8073★ Lupus Foundation of America
Western Nebraska Chapter
HCR 72, Box 58
Sutherland, NE 69165
Phone: (308)764-2474

Nevada

★8074★ Lupus Foundation of America
Las Vegas Chapter
1555 E. Flamingo, Ste. 439
Las Vegas, NV 89119
Phone: (702)369-0474

★8075★ Lupus Foundation of America
Northern Nevada Chapter
1755 Vassar St.
Reno, NV 89502
Phone: (702)323-2444

New Hampshire

★8076★ Lupus Foundation of America
New Hampshire Chapter
PO Box 444
Nashua, NH 03061-0444
Phone: (603)424-5668

New Jersey

★8077★ Lupus Foundation of America
New Jersey Chapter
287 Market St.
PO Box 320
Elmwood Park, NJ 07407
Phone: (201)791-7868

★8078★ Lupus Foundation of America
South Jersey Chapter
Starrett Bldg.
6 White Horse Pike, No. 1-C
Haddon Heights, NJ 08035
Phone: (609)546-8555

New Mexico

★8079★ Lupus Foundation of America
New Mexico Chapter
PO Box 35891
Albuquerque, NM 87176-5891
Phone: (505)881-9081

New York

★8080★ Lupus Foundation of America
Bronx Chapter
PO Box 1117
Bronx, NY 10462
Phone: (718)822-6542

★8081★ Lupus Foundation of America
Central New York Chapter
Maria Regina Center, Bldg. 8
1118 Court St.
Syracuse, NY 13208
Phone: (315)472-6011

★8082★ Lupus Foundation of America
Genesee Valley Chapter
PO Box 14068
Rochester, NY 14614
Phone: (716)266-3340

★8083★ Lupus Foundation of America
Long Island/Queens Chapter
1602 N. Bellmore Ave.
North Bellmore, NY 11710-5566
Phone: (516)783-3370
Free: 800-850-9000

★8084★ Lupus Foundation of America
Marguerite Curri Chapter
PO Box 853
Utica, NY 13503
Phone: (315)732-4291

★8085★ Lupus Foundation of America
New York Southern Tier Chapter
19 Chenango St., Ste. 410
Binghamton, NY 13901
Phone: (607)772-6522
Free: 800-675-4546

★8086★ Lupus Foundation of America
Northeastern New York Chapter
132 State St.
Albany, NY 12207
Phone: (518)465-3603

★8087★ Lupus Foundation of America
Rockland/Orange County Chapter
14 Kingston Dr.
Spring Valley, NY 10977
Phone: (914)354-0372

★8088★ Lupus Foundation of America
Westchester Chapter
130 Elmcrest
Fishkill, NY 12524
Phone: (914)948-1032

★8089★ Lupus Foundation of America
Western New York Chapter
205 Yorkshire Rd.
Tonawanda, NY 14150
Phone: (716)835-7161

★8090★ SLE Foundation
149 Madison Ave.
New York, NY 10016
Phone: (212)685-4118

North Carolina

★8091★ Lupus Foundation of America
Charlotte Chapter
101 Colville Rd.
Charlotte, NC 28207
Phone: (704)375-8787

★8092★ Lupus Foundation of America
Raleigh Chapter
PO Box 10171
Raleigh, NC 27605
Phone: (919)772-8564

★8093★ Lupus Foundation of America
Winston-Triad Chapter
2841 Foxwood Ln.
Winston Salem, NC 27103
Phone: (910)768-1493

Ohio

★8094★ Lupus Foundation of America
Akron Area Chapter
942 N. Main St., Ste. 23
Akron, OH 44310
Phone: (216)235-1717

★8095★ Lupus Foundation of America
Columbus, Marcy Zitron Chapter
6161 Busch Blvd., Ste. 76
Columbus, OH 43229
Phone: (614)846-9249

★8096★ Lupus Foundation of America
Greater Cleveland Chapter
20524 1/2 Southgate Park
Maple Heights, OH 44137
Phone: (216)531-6563

★8097★ Lupus Foundation of America
Northwest Ohio Lupus Chapter
1615 Washington Ave.
Findlay, OH 45840
Phone: (419)423-9313

Oklahoma

★8098★ Lupus Foundation of America
Oklahoma Chapter
3131 N. MacArthur, Ste. 140-D
Oklahoma City, OK 73122
Phone: (405)495-8787

Pennsylvania

★8099★ Lupus Foundation of America
Delaware Valley Chapter
44 W. Lancaster Ave.
Ardmore, PA 19003
Phone: (215)649-9202

★8100★ Lupus Foundation of America
Northeast Pennsylvania Chapter
822 Ash Ave.
Scranton, PA 18510
Phone: (717)342-6146

★8101★ Lupus Foundation of America
Northwestern Pennsylvania Chapter
PO Box 885
Erie, PA 16512-0885
Phone: (814)866-0226

★8102★ Lupus Foundation of America
Philadelphia Chapter
5415 Claridge St.
Philadelphia, PA 19124
Phone: (215)743-7171

★8103★ Lupus Foundation of America
Western Pennsylvania Chapter
1323 Forbes Ave., Ste. 200
Pittsburgh, PA 15219
Phone: (412)261-5886
Free: 800-800-5776

Rhode Island

★8104★ Lupus Foundation of America
Rhode Island Chapter
8 Fallon Ave.
Providence, RI 02908
Phone: (401)421-7227

South Carolina

★8105★ Lupus Foundation of America
South Carolina Chapter
PO Box 7511
Columbia, SC 29202
Phone: (803)794-1000

Tennessee

★8106★ Lupus Foundation of America
East Tennessee Chapter
5612 Kingston Pike, Ste. 5
Knoxville, TN 37919
Phone: (615)584-5215

★8107★ Lupus Foundation of America
Memphis Area Chapter
3181 Poplar Ave., Ste. 100
Memphis, TN 38111
Phone: (901)458-5302

★8108★ Lupus Foundation of America
Nashville Area Chapter
2200 21st Ave., Ste. 253
Nashville, TN 37212-4929
Phone: (615)298-2273
Free: 800-595-8787

Texas

★8109★ Lupus Foundation of America
El Paso Chapter
PO Box 4965
El Paso, TX 79914-4965
Phone: (915)751-6941

★8110★ Lupus Foundation of America
Lubbock Area Chapter
1717 Avenue K, Ste. 127
Lubbock, TX 79401
Phone: (806)744-6666
Free: 800-580-5878

★8111★ Lupus Foundation of America
North Texas Chapter
2997 LBJ Freeway, Ste. 108-N
Dallas, TX 75234
Phone: (214)484-0503
Free: 800-262-4944

★8112★ Lupus Foundation of America
South Central Texas Chapter
McCullough Medical Center
4118 McCullough Ave., Ste. 19
San Antonio, TX 78212-1968
Phone: (210)824-1344
Free: 800-809-3953

★8113★ Lupus Foundation of America
Texas Gulf Coast Chapter
3100 Timmons Ln., Ste. 410
Houston, TX 77027
Phone: (713)623-8267
Free: 800-458-7870

Utah

★8114★ Lupus Foundation of America
Utah Chapter
4036 South 2700 East
Salt Lake City, UT 84124
Phone: (801)277-1767
Free: 800-657-6398

Vermont

★8115★ Lupus Foundation of America
Vermont Chapter
PO Box 115
Waterbury, VT 05676
Phone: (802)244-5988

Virginia

★8116★ Lupus Foundation of America
Central Virginia Chapter
PO Box 25418
Richmond, VA 23260-5418
Phone: (804)270-1626

★8117★ Lupus Foundation of America
Eastern Virginia Chapter
Pembroke One
281 Independence Blvd., Ste. 442
Virginia Beach, VA 23462
Phone: (804)490-2793

West Virginia

★8118★ Lupus Foundation of America
Kanawha Valley Chapter
PO Box 8274
South Charleston, WV 25303
Phone: (304)529-2600

Wisconsin

★8119★ Lupus Foundation of America
Wisconsin Chapter
1568 S. 24th St.
Milwaukee, WI 53204-2505
Phone: (414)643-8522

Chapter 41
Neurology

Federal Government Agencies

★8120★ **U.S. Department of Health and Human Services**
National Institute of Neurological Disorders and Stroke
9000 Rockville Pike
Bethesda, MD 20892
Phone: (301)496-9746

Description: Formerly the National Institute of Neurological and Communicative Disorders and Stroke. NINDS conducts and supports fundamental and applied research on human neurological disorders, such as Parkinson's disease, epilepsy, multiple sclerosis, muscular dystrophy, head and spinal cord injuries, and stroke. It also conducts and supports research on the development and function of the normal brain and nervous system in order to better understand normal processes relating to disease states.

Foundations & Other Funding Organizations

Private Foundations

★8121★ **Edna Sproull Williams Foundation**
PO Box 40129
Jacksonville, FL 32203
Phone: (904)356-5881
Charles J. Williams, III, Trustee

Foundation Philosophy: The Edna Sproull Williams Foundation supports a wide range of charitable organizations. All areas of giving are represented by the foundation, including community centers, family health, college funds, the Christian religion, civic affairs, alzheimer research, and others. **Giving Priorities:** In 1991, the foundation gave 33% of its funding to social services. Other interests included homes, family services, and united funds. Education received 20% of the funds. Religion received 19%, with emphasis on specific ministries. The remainder went to civic affairs, 10%; the arts, 9%; health,

8%; and international, 1%. **Typical Health-Related Recipients:** Health Funds, Single-Disease Health Associations. **Geographic Distribution:** Focus on Florida.

★8122★ **Esther A. and Joseph Klingenstein Fund**
787 Seventh Ave., 6th Fl.
New York, NY 10019-6016
Phone: (212)492-6181
Fax: (212)492-7007
John Klingenstein, President and Treasurer

Foundation Philosophy: The fund's major interests are in basic research in neuroscience related to epilepsy and in independent secondary education. Grants also are made in other areas including health, animal research, church/state separation, public/social policy, communications and media, population/family planning, environment, and minority affairs. **Giving Priorities:** In fiscal 1993, the fund gave approximately 66% of funding to educational institutions, primarily to colleges and universities for the Klingenstein fellows program. This also included the foundation's highest grant of $434,297 to Columbia University Teachers College. About 13% of funds went to science institutions. Health care received 7%; social service groups, 6%; religious groups, 4%; and civic causes, 4%. **Typical Health-Related Recipients:** Clinics/Medical Centers, Family Planning, Hospitals, Hospitals (University Affiliated), Medical Education, Medical Research, People with Disabilities, Preventive Medicine/Wellness Organizations, Research/Studies Institutes. **Geographic Distribution:** National; no geographical restrictions.

GAR Foundation
See: Entry 209

Oxford Foundation
See: Entry 422

Valley Foundation
See: Entry 526

Other Funding Organizations

★8123★ **Alzheimer's Association**
919 N. Michigan Ave., Ste. 1000
Chicago, IL 60611
Phone: (312)335-8700
Free: 800-272-3900
Fax: (312)335-1110
Edward Truschke, Pres.

Description: Association administers a research grant program to initiate new investigations into the causes, treatment, and cure of Alzheimer's disease.

★8124★ **American Association of Neurological Surgeons**
22 S. Washington St., Ste. 100
Park Ridge, IL 60068
Phone: (708)692-9500
Fax: (708)692-2589
Carl H. Hauber, Exec. Dir.

Description: Provides funding to foster research in the neurosciences.

★8125★ **American Brain Tumor Association**
2720 River Rd., Ste. 146
Des Plaines, IL 60018
Phone: (708)827-9910
Free: 800-886-2282
Fax: (708)827-9918
Naomi Berkowitz, Exec. Dir.

Description: Association raises funds for brain tumor research fellowships.

★8126★ **American Paralysis Association**
500 Morris Ave.
Springfield, NJ 07081
Phone: (201)379-2690
Free: 800-225-0292
Fax: (201)912-9433
Michael A. Calhoun, Pres.

Description: Raises funds to support research into central nervous system regeneration. Makes grants to research laboratories and to individuals for postgraduate study; presents awards to physicians and scientists conducting research on the spinal cord and central nervous system.

★8127★ **American Parkinson Disease Association**
60 Bay St., Ste 401
Staten Island, NY 10301
Phone: (718)981-8001
Free: 800-223-APDA
Fax: (718)981-4399
Mario Esposito, Pres.

Description: Works to find the cure and to alleviate the suffering of victims by subsidizing information and referral services and providing funds for research.

★8128★ **Amyotrophic Lateral Sclerosis Association**
21021 Ventura Blvd., Ste. 321
Woodland Hills, CA 91364
Phone: (818)340-7500
Free: 800-782-4747
Fax: (818)340-2060
Joseph M. Aguayo, Pres. & CEO

Description: Funds amyotrophic lateral sclerosis-specific research at major medical institutions throughout the U.S. and worldwide.

★8129★ **Brain Research Foundation**
208 S. La Salle St., Ste. 1426
Chicago, IL 60604
Phone: (312)782-4311
Fax: (312)782-6437

Description: Provides support for research projects, new equipment, and scientific education is neurology, psychiatry, neurobiology, neurosurgery, and pharmacology/physiology at the Brain Research Institute at the University of Chicago.

★8130★ **Epilepsy Foundation of America**
4351 Garden City Dr.
Landover, MD 20785
Phone: (301)459-3700
Free: 800-EFA-1000
Fax: (301)577-2684
William McLin, Exec. VP

Description: Awards grants and fellowships to support programs of research and training relating to epilepsy, including prevention, psychosocial needs, and improved methods of treatment.

★8131★ **Huntington's Disease Society of America**
140 W. 22nd St., 6th Fl.
New York, NY 10011-2420
Phone: (212)242-1968
Free: 800-345-4372
Fax: (212)243-2443
Steve Bajardi, Exec. Dir.

Description: Awards grants and fellowships to support basic and clinical research relating to the causes and cure of Huntington's Disease.

★8132★ **Muscular Dystrophy Association**
3300 E. Sunrise Dr.
Tucson, AZ 85718
Phone: (602)529-2000
Fax: (602)529-5300
Robert Ross, Exec. Dir.

Description: Supports international programs of more than 400 research awards and major neuromuscular disease research/clinical centers. Offers postdoctoral fellowships to researchers.

★8133★ **Myasthenia Gravis Foundation**
53 W. Jackson Blvd., Ste. 660
Chicago, IL 60604
Phone: (312)427-6252
Free: 800-541-5454
Fax: (312)427-8437
Anna El-Qudsi, Exec. Dir.

Description: Raises funds for research and for professional and public education programs. Offers Henry R. Viets Medical Student Fellowships, the Kermit E. Osserman/Blanche R. McClure Postdoctoral Research Grants, and a Nurse's Fellowship.

★8134★ **National Multiple Sclerosis Society**
733 3rd Ave.
New York, NY 10017
Phone: (212)986-3240
Free: 800-FIGHT-MS
Fax: (212)986-7981
Gen. Michael Dugan, Pres. & CEO

Description: Supports research into the cause, treatment, and care of multiple sclerosis.

★8135★ **National Parkinson Foundation**
1501 NW 9th Ave.
Miami, FL 33136
Phone: (305)547-6666
Fax: (305)548-4403
Nathan Slewett, Chp.

Description: Supports basic and clinical research for Parkinsonism and related neurological disorders.

★8136★ **Neurodevelopmental Treatment Association**
401 N. Michigan Ave.
Chicago, IL 60611-4267
Phone: (312)321-5151
Free: 800-869-9295
Fax: (312)321-5158
Carol Kinsey, Exec. Sec.

Description: Bestows Research Grant Award in neurodevelopmental treatment.

★8137★ **Parkinson's Disease Foundation**
William Black Medical Research Bldg.
Columbia Presbyterian Medical Center
650 W. 168th St.
New York, NY 10032
Phone: (212)923-4700
Free: 800-457-6676
Fax: (212)923-4778
Lewis P. Rowland, M.D., Pres.

Description: Raises funds for support of scientific research into causes, prevention, and cure of Parkinson's disease. Awards postdoctoral fellowships at Columbia College of Physicians and Surgeons, and other institutions; sponsors summer fellowship program for predoctoral students.

★8138★ **Tall Cedars of Lebanon of North America**
2609 N. Front St.
Harrisburg, PA 17110
Phone: (717)232-5991
Fax: (717)232-5997
Russell L. Ziegler, Supreme Scribe

Description: Supports muscular dystrophy research.

★8139★ **Tourette Syndrome Association**
42-40 Bell Blvd.
Bayside, NY 11361
Phone: (718)224-2999
Free: 800-237-0717
Fax: (718)279-9596
Steven M. Friedlander, Exec. Off.

Description: Awards grants and post-doctoral fellowships to support basic and clinical research on the nature and causes of Tourette syndrome.

★8140★ **United Cerebral Palsy Research and Educational Foundation**
1522 K St. NW, Ste. 1112
Washington, DC 20005
Phone: (202)842-1266
Free: 800-USA-5UCP
Fax: (202)842-3519
Leon Sternfeld, M.D., Med. Dir.

Description: Provides research grants to prevent cerebral palsy and to improve the treatment, management, and functioning of persons with cerebral palsy. Offers clinical fellowships for medical and dental specialists.

★8141★ **United Parkinson Foundation**
833 W. Washington Blvd.
Chicago, IL 60607
Phone: (312)733-1893
Judy Rosner, Exec. Dir.

Description: Awards grants to established scientists to study the cause and cure of Parkinson's disease and related disorders.

National & International Organizations

★8142★ **ALS Association**
78 Masikap Extension
Central District
Quezon City, Metro Manila 1100, Philippines
Phone: 2 9228274
Fax: 2 9229199
Joel Abad Pelayo

Description: Promotes interest in amyotrophic lateral sclerosis or ALS (also called Lou Gehrig's disease) research among medical and scientific communities and the public in the Philippines. Works as a support group for ALS sufferers and their families. Disseminates information about the disease.

★8143★ **ALS Association**
Lateral Amiotrofica
Callao 66, 1er. Piso
1022 Buenos Aires, Argentina
Enrique G. St. John

Description: Works as a support group for amyotrophic lateral sclerosis (ALS) sufferers and their families. Facilitates contacts with medical specialists; disseminates information about the disease.

★8144★ ALS Forbes Norris Research Center (ALSNRF)
c/o California Pacific Medical Center
3698 California St., Rm. 545
San Francisco, CA 94118
Phone: (415)750-2398
Fax: (415)750-5022
Robert G. Miller, M.D., Contact

Founded: 1981. **Local Groups:** 3. **Description:** Serves as clearinghouse for laboratory and clinical research into neuromuscular diseases, primarily Amyotrophic Lateral Sclerosis (Lou Gehrig's Disease). ALS is a paralytic and usually fatal disease of the motor neurons, nerves which innervate the muscles to allow movement. Although patients maintain their full intellectual capacities, they gradually lose their ability to move, talk, and breathe. Conducts monthly support group for ALS patients and families in the San Francisco Bay area. Sponsors the ALS Research Center at the California Pacific Medical Center in San Francisco, CA and maintains an extensive bank of ALS patient information. Offers educational programs and a speakers' bureau. **Publications:** *Forbes Norris Research Center--Support Group Newsletter*, monthly. Newsletter. *Price:* Free. • Newsletter, semiannual. **Formerly:** (1994) ALS and Neuromuscular Research Foundation.

★8145★ ALS - Motor Neurone Disease Research Institute
PO Box 635
Gordon, NSW 2072, Australia
Phone: 2 4987960
Fax: 2 4987960
Dr. Dawn Thew

Description: Promotes interest in motor neurone disease (MND) and amyotrophic lateral sclerosis (ALS) research among medical and scientific communities and the public in Australia. Offers support services to MND sufferers and their families. Disseminates information about the disease.

★8146★ ALS Society of Canada
220 - 6 Adelaide St. E
Toronto, ON, Canada M5C 1H6
Phone: (416)362-0269
Fax: (416)362-0414
Jan Rodman, Contact

Founded: 1977. **Description:** Individuals interested in amyotropic lateral sclerosis or ALS (also known as Lou Gehrig's Disease). Works to: heighten public awareness and understanding of the disease; encourage research among medical and scientific communities.

★8147★ ALS Society of Tunisia
Institut de Neurologie
1007 La Rabta, Tunisia
Prof. M. Ben Hamida

Description: Promotes interest in amyotrophic lateral sclerosis or ALS (also called Lou Gehrig's disease) research among medical and scientific communities and the public in Tunisia. Offers support services to ALS sufferers and their families. Disseminates information about the disease.

★8148★ ALS of South Africa
c/o Dr. A.H. Borowitz
42 Victoria St.
Oaklands
Johannesburg 2192, Republic of South Africa
Dr. A.H. Borowitz

Description: Individuals interested in amyotropic lateral sclerosis or ALS (also known as Lou Gehrig's Disease). Works to: heighten public awareness and understanding of the disease; encourage research among medical and scientific communities.

★8149★ Alzheimer's Association
919 N. Michigan Ave., Ste. 1000
Chicago, IL 60611
Phone: (312)335-8700
Free: 800-272-3900
Fax: (312)335-1110
Edward Truschke, Pres.

Founded: 1980. **Members:** 35,000. **Local Groups:** 218. **Description:** Family members of sufferers of Alzheimer's disease. Combats Alzheimer's disease and related disorders. (Alzheimer's disease is a progressive, degenerative brain disease in which changes occur in the central nervous system and outer region of the brain causing memory loss and other changes in thought, personality, and behavior. It is the fourth leading cause of death in adults in the U.S.) Promotes research to find the cause, treatment, and cure for the disease; provides educational programs for the public, media, and health care and medical professionals; represents the continuing care needs of the affected population before government and social service agencies. Seeks to destroy the myth that what were once called "senile behaviors" are a natural part of aging. Works to develop family support systems for relatives of victims of the disease. Sponsors educational forums; operates speakers' bureau. Compiles statistics. **Publications:** *Alzheimer's Association Newsletter*, quarterly. Newsletter. Covers stories and developments of interest to patients with Alzheimer's disease and related disorders, and their families and friends. *Price:* Free. • Brochures. • Catalog. Also publishes a variety of fact sheets, video kits, and patient care publications. **Formerly:** (1989) Alzheimer's Disease and Related Disorders Association.

★8150★ Alzheimer's Disease International (ADI)
12 S. Michigan Ave.
Chicago, IL 60603
Phone: (312)335-5777
Fax: (312)335-1122
Rachel Billington, Sec.Gen.

Founded: 1984. **Members:** 33. **National Groups:** 33. **Description:** Health professionals, scientists, caregivers, families of individuals with Alzheimer's disease, and others concerned with discovering the cause, treatment, and cure of Alzheimer's disease and providing support to families affected by the disease. (Alzheimer's disease is a degenerative brain disease in which changes occur in the central nervous system and outer region of the brain causing memory loss and other changes in thought, personality, and behavior.) **Publications:** *Careers Manual*. • *Global Perspective*, 2-4/year. Newsletter. *Price:* Free. • *How to Operate A Self-Help Group*.

★8151★ American Academy for Cerebral Palsy and Developmental Medicine (AACPDM)
6300 N. River Rd., Ste. 727
Rosemont, IL 60018
Phone: (708)698-1635
Fax: (708)823-0536
Arlene Napolilli, Exec.Dir.

Founded: 1947. **Members:** 1,800. **Description:** Professional organization of physicians, diplomates of specialty boards, Ph.D.s, and allied health care individuals concerned with diagnosis, care, treatment, and research of cerebral palsy and developmental disorders and with acceptance of the handicaps caused by these conditions. **Publications:** *AACPDM News*, biennial. Newsletter. Includes academy news. *Price:* Included in membership dues. • *Journal of Developmental Medicine and Child Neurology*, monthly. • *Membership Roster*, annual. **Formerly:** (1976) American Academy for Cerebral Palsy.

★8152★ American Academy of Clinical Neurophysiology
5700 Old Orchard Rd., 1st Fl.
Skokie, IL 60077-1057
Phone: (708)966-6910
Fax: (708)966-9418
Anne M. Cordes, Contact

Founded: 1985. **Members:** 800. **Description:** Clinical neurophysiologists. Fosters an understanding of the function of the nervous system among health professionals, scientists, and the public by serving as a forum for interaction and the communication of new developments. Offers educational programs.

American Academy of Neurological and Orthopaedic Surgeons (FAANaOS)
See: Entry 12204

American Academy of Neurological Surgery
See: Entry 12205

★8153★ American Academy of Neurology (AAN)
2221 University Ave. SE, Ste. 335
Minneapolis, MN 55414
Phone: (612)623-8115
Fax: (612)623-3504
Jan W. Kolehmainen, Exec.Dir.

Founded: 1948. **Members:** 12,800. **Description:** Professional society of medical doctors specializing in brain and nervous system diseases. Maintains placement service. Sponsors research and educational programs. Compiles statistics. **Publications:** *AAN Governmental Report*, quarterly. Newsletter. Includes news on database. • *AANews*, monthly. Newsletter. General information. • *American Academy of Neurology Membership Directory*, annual. Membership Directory. • *The Dendrite*, bimonthly. Placement publication. • *ICD-9-CM for Neurologists*. Booklet. To aid users of ICD-9 diagnostic codes. • *Medical Specialty of Neurology*. Brochure. Discusses neurology as a career. • *Neurologist*. Brochure. For patients. • *Neurology*, monthly. Journal. Includes research reports. • *Patient Information Guide for Neurology*. Handbook for patients to find educational information about disorders.

★ 8154 ★ American Academy of Pain Medicine (AAPM)
5700 Old Orchard Rd., 1st Fl.
Skokie, IL 60077-1057
Phone: (708)966-9510
Fax: (708)966-9418
Jeffrey W. Engle, Exec.Dir.

Founded: 1983. **Members:** 613. **Description:** Anesthesiologists, internists, neurologists, neurosurgeons, orthopedic surgeons, physiatrists, and psychiatrists. Promotes a socioeconomic and political climate conducive to the effective and efficient practice of pain medicine. Ensures quality medical care by physicians specializing in pain medicine. Participates in networking and liaison activities with other organizations dealing in pain medicine. Conducts educational programs. Holds a seat in the American Medical Association House of Delegates. **Publications:** *AAPM Membership Directory.* Membership Directory. Lists primary care and specialty physicians with an interest in pain medicine. • *AAPM Newsletter,* quarterly. Newsletter. Covers news about the academy and its members. • *Clinical Journal of Pain,* quarterly. Journal. Contains clinical articles, research information, articles concerning socioeconomic issues, and news. *Price:* Included in membership dues. • *Directory of Pain Management Facilities.* Directory. **Formerly:** American Academy of Algology.

★ 8155 ★ American Academy of Somnology (AAS)
PO Box 29124
Las Vegas, NV 89126
Phone: (702)594-5746
Fax: (702)456-9255
David L. Hopper, Ph.D., Founder & Pres.

Founded: 1986. **Members:** 75. **Description:** Clinicians, researchers, and students in the field of somnology; interested individuals. Promotes advancement of somnology as a health care specialty. (Somnology is the study of sleep and sleep disorders.) Advocates standardization of university programs in somnology and a multidisciplinary approach to the study and treatment of sleep disorders; conducts continuing education program. Sponsors American Board of Somnology to evaluate qualifications of applicants, administer examinations, and confer diplomate status on qualified individuals. Provides a forum for somnology clinicians and researchers to present findings and exchange ideas. Maintains speakers' bureau. **Publications:** *AAS Membership Directory,* annual. Membership Directory. • *Certification Handbook,* periodic. • *Journal of Somnology,* annual. Journal. • *The Somnologist,* quarterly. Also publishes constitution, ethical standards, and bylaws.

American Association of Neurological Surgeons (AANS)
See: Entry 12212

American Association of Neuropathologists (AANP)
See: Entry 10118

American Association of Neuroscience Nurses (AANN)
See: Entry 9054

American Association of Spinal Cord Injury Psychologists and Social Workers (AASCIPSW)
See: Entry 7283

★ 8156 ★ American Association for the Study of Headache (AASH)
875 Kings Hwy., Ste. 200
Woodbury, NJ 08096
Phone: (609)845-0322
Fax: (609)384-5811
Robert K. Talley, Exec.Dir.

Founded: 1959. **Members:** 950. **Description:** Physicians, dentists, and related scientists interested in the study of headaches. Brings together practitioners in different fields of medicine to discuss ideas and beliefs about headache and head pain. Provides an opportunity for the presentation and discussion of basic research, clinical investigation, and reports from clinical practice. **Publications:** *Headache: The Journal of Head and Face Pain,* 10/year. Journal. Presents papers concerning basic research and clinical studies. Includes book reviews. *Price:* Included in membership dues; $40/year for medical students, interns, and residents; $95/year for U.S. nonmembers; $110/year for nonmembers outside U.S.

American Board of Neurological and Orthopaedic Medicine and Surgery (ABNOMS)
See: Entry 12221

American Board of Neurological Surgery (ABNS)
See: Entry 12222

American Board of Neuroscience Nursing (ABNN)
See: Entry 9058

American Board of Psychiatry and Neurology (ABPN)
See: Entry 7290

★ 8157 ★ American Board of Registration of EEG and EP Technologists (ABRET)
PO Box 11434
Norfolk, VA 23517
Phone: (804)627-5503
Patricia Smith, Exec.Sec.

Founded: 1961. **Description:** Determines the competency of electroencephalography technologists through administration of written and oral examinations. **Formerly:** (1992) American Board of Registration of EEG Technologists.

★ 8158 ★ American Board of Sleep Medicine
1610 14th St. NW, Ste. 302
Rochester, MN 55901-0246
Phone: (507)287-9819
Fax: (507)287-6008
Judith Morton, Exam.Coord.

Founded: 1991. **Description:** Works to encourage the study and elevate the standards of sleep medicine. Offers certification in sleep medicine to licensed physicians and individuals with Ph.D.s in health related fields. **Publications:** Brochure. Contains information for applicants.

American Board of Thoracic Neurological Orthopaedic Medicine and Surgery (ABTNOMS)
See: Entry 12229

★ 8159 ★ American Brain Tumor Association (ABTA)
2720 River Rd., Ste. 146
Des Plaines, IL 60018
Phone: (708)827-9910
Free: 800-886-2282
Fax: (708)827-9918
Naomi Berkowitz, Exec.Dir.

Founded: 1973. **Description:** Medical professionals, patients, and family members interested in brain tumors and their treatment options. Purpose is to raise funds for brain tumor research, disseminate patient education information on brain tumors and brain tumor research, and increase public awareness. Offers referral service and Connections, a pen pal program. **Publications:** *A Brain Tumor-Sharing Hope.* • *A Primer of Brain Tumors.* Booklet. • *A Primer of Brain Tumors.* • *About Ependymoma.* • *About Glioblastoma Multiforme and Anaplastic Astrocytoma.* • *About Medulloblastoma/PNET.* • *About Meningioma.* • *About Metastatic Tumors to the Brain and Spine.* • *About Oligodendroglioma and Mixed Glioma.* • *About Pituitary Tumors.* • *Alex's Journey: The Story of a Child with a Brain Tumor.* • *Booklets.* • *Brochures.* • *Chemotherapy of Brain Tumors.* • *Coping with a Brain Tumor: Part 1; From Diagnosis to Treatment.* Booklet. • *Coping with a Brain Tumor: Part 2; During and After Treatment.* Booklet. • *Dictionary for Brain Tumor Patients.* Booklet. • *Immunotherapy of Brain Tumors.* • *Message Line,* 3/year. Newsletter. • *Organizing a Support Group.* Pamphlet. • Pamphlets. • *Radiation Therapy of Brain Tumors: Part 1; A Basic Guide.* • *Radiation Therapy of Brain Tumors: Part 2; Background and Research Guide.* • *Shunts.* • *Using a Medical Library.* • *When Your Child is Ready to Return to School.* Booklet. Also publishes lists of support groups by state and lists of physicians who offer investigational treatments for brain tumors in adults and children. **Formerly:** (1992) Association for Brain Tumor Research.

★ 8160 ★ American Chronic Pain Association (ACPA)
PO Box 850
Rocklin, CA 95677
Phone: (916)632-0922
Fax: (916)632-3208
Penney Cowan, Exec.Dir.

Founded: 1980. **Description:** Individuals suffering from chronic pain; health care professionals. Mutual support organization that works to help individuals suffering from chronic pain (pain lasting more than six months) learn positive ways to deal with pain and become involved in their own recovery. Fosters the managing of pain through methods such as exercise, assertiveness, self-awareness, and relaxation techniques. Consults with health care facilities in developing and upgrading pain management units; disseminates guidelines for selecting pain management facilities. (The organization stresses that it provides no medical advice or treatment.) Operates speakers' bureau; conducts charitable program. **Publications:** *ACPA Chronicle*, quarterly. Newsletter. • *ACPA Leaders Manual*, periodic. Directory. Features how-tos for ACPA goup development and ongoing resources. • *ACPA Leader's Newsletter*, quarterly. Newsletter. • *ACPA Member's Manual*, periodic. • *Staying Well: Advanced Pain Management for Members Workbook*. Handbook.

American College of Neuropsychiatrists (ACN)
See: Entry 9973

★8161★ American College of Pain Medicine (ACPM)
5700 Old Orchard Rd.
Skokie, IL 60077-1057
Phone: (708)966-0459
Fax: (708)966-9418

Description: Develops and administers practice-related examinations in the field of pain medicine. Awards certification to physicians successfully completing the examination and credentialing process.

★8162★ American Council for Headache Education
875 Kings Hwy., Ste. 200
Woodbury, NJ 08096
Phone: (609)384-8760
Free: 800-255-ACHE
Fax: (609)384-5811
Linda McGillicuddy, Exec.Dir.

Founded: 1989. **Description:** Individuals suffering from headaches; physicians. Seeks to conduct public education, scientific research, and advocacy for headache sufferers. Conducts research, educational, and charitable programs. **Publications:** Brochure. • *Headache*. Newsletter.

★8163★ American Electroencephalographic Society (AEEGS)
1 Regency Dr.
PO Box 30
Bloomfield, CT 06002
Phone: (203)243-3977
Jacquelyn T. Coleman, Exec.Dir.

Founded: 1946. **Members:** 1,320. **Description:** Professional society of electroencephalographers and neurophysiologists. Offers clinical course annually.

★8164★ American Epilepsy Society (AES)
638 Prospect Ave.
Hartford, CT 06105-4298
Phone: (203)232-4825
Fax: (203)232-0819
Suzanne C. Berry, Exec.Dir.

Founded: 1946. **Members:** 1,700. **Description:** Physicians and researchers engaged in practice and research in epilepsy or closely related fields such as electroencephalography. Fosters treatment of epilepsy in its biological, clinical, and social phases; promotes better care and treatment of persons subject to seizures. **Publications:** *Epilepsia*, bimonthly. Published in conjunction with the International League Against Epilepsy. **Formerly:** (1959) American League Against Epilepsy.

★8165★ American Medical Electroencephalographic Association (AMEEGA)
850 Elm Grove Rd.
Elm Grove, WI 53122
Phone: (414)797-7800
Fax: (414)782-8788
Robert H. Herzog, Exec.Dir.

Founded: 1964. **Members:** 700. **Description:** Works to advance clinical electroencephalography and to promote the development of clinical and technical training programs. **Publications:** *Clinical EEG*, quarterly.

★8166★ American Narcolepsy Association (ANA)
1255 Post St.
E.F. Towers, Ste. 404
San Francisco, CA 94109
Mary Lee Keane, Pres.

Founded: 1975. **Members:** 4,000. **Description:** Individuals suffering from narcolepsy, sleep apnea, or both; physicians and researchers; other interested individuals. (Narcolepsy is a physical disorder characterized by irresistible daytime sleep attacks and drowsiness, automatic behavior, cataplexy, sleep paralysis, hypnagogic hallucinations, and disrupted nighttime sleep. Sleep apnea refers to a condition in which a person repeatedly suffers temporary suspension of breathing during each night's sleep, resulting in excessive daytime sleepiness.) Purposes are to: help improve the quality of life of those who have narcolepsy through public education and information programs; stimulate, support, and conduct research on the detection, prevention, improved treatment, and ultimate cure for these illne sses; reduce average time between onset of symptoms and initial medical diagnosis; assist afflicted individuals with personal, community, and business problems arising from their illness; secure awareness and understanding of the syndrome and its treatment within the medical profession. Conducts programs of mutual support and selfhelp for afflicted persons; operates grant program for narcolepsy research. **Publications:** *Eye Opener*, quarterly. Newsletter. Covers association activities; includes practical information for people with narcolepsy. *Price:* Included in membership dues.

★8167★ American Neurological Association (ANA)
2221 University Ave. SE, Ste. 350
Minneapolis, MN 55414
Phone: (612)378-3290
Carol Hamel, Assoc.Mgr.

Founded: 1875. **Members:** 960. **Description:** Physicians and scientists interested in the form, functioning, and disorders of the nervous system. Conducts research programs. **Publications:** *Annals of Neurology*, monthly. Journal. Includes book reviews. *Price:* Included in membership dues; $68/year for nonmembers; $84/year for institutions; $52.50/year for students.

★8168★ American Pain Society (APS)
5700 Old Orchard Rd., 1st Fl.
Skokie, IL 60077-1024
Phone: (708)966-5595
Fax: (708)966-9418
Richard G. Muir, Exec.Dir.

Founded: 1977. **Members:** 2,850. **Regional Groups:** 6. **Description:** Physicians, dentists, psychologists, nurses, and other health professionals interested in the study and treatment of pain. Purposes are to: promote control, management, and understanding of pain through scientific meetings and research activities; develop standards for training and ethical management of pain patients. Conducts scientific conferences. **Publications:** *APS Bulletin*, quarterly. Newsletter. • *APS Journal*, quarterly. Journal. • *Pain Facilities Directory*, annual. Directory. • *Principles of Analgesic Use in the Treatment of Acute Pain and Cancer Pain*, periodic.

★8169★ American Paralysis Association (APA)
500 Morris Ave.
Springfield, NJ 07081
Phone: (201)379-2690
Free: 800-225-0292
Fax: (201)912-9433
Mitch Stoller, Pres.

Founded: 1979. **Members:** 10,000. **Regional Groups:** 1. **Local Groups:** 10. **Description:** Supporters are spinal cord-injured persons, their families, and other interested individuals. Purpose is to encourage and support research aimed at finding a cure for paralysis caused by spinal cord injury, head injury, or stroke. Compiles statistics on spinal cord injuries. Operates research seminars. Sponsors neuroscientific seminars and symposia. **Publications:** *American Paralysis Association Progress in Research*, quarterly. Newsletter. *Price:* Included in membership dues. • *Annual Review*. • *APA Alert*, bimonthly. Bulletin. • *Progress in Research*, 2-3/year. • *Walking Tomorrow*, semiannual. Newsletter. **Formerly:** (1981) Kent Waldrep International Spinal Cord Research Foundation.

★8170★ American Paraplegia Society (APS)
75-20 Astoria Blvd.
Jackson Heights, NY 11370-1177
Phone: (718)803-3782
Fax: (718)803-0414
Dr. Vivian Bejda, Exec.Admin.

Founded: 1954. **Members:** 350. **Description:** Physicians and researchers in the spinal cord injury field. Purpose is to advance and foster improved health care of spinal cord injury patients, and develop and promote education and research in the neuroscience fields. Sponsors seminars; maintains library. Conducts annual educational program. **Publications:** *Journal of American Paraplegia Society*, quarterly. Journal.

★8171★ American Parkinson Disease Association (APDA)

60 Bay St., Ste. 401
Staten Island, NY 10301
Phone: (718)981-8001
Free: 800-223-APDA
Fax: (718)981-4399
Mario Esposito, Pres.

Founded: 1961. **Members:** 2,000. **Regional Groups:** 90. **Local Groups:** 400. **Description:** Works to find the cure for Parkinson's disease and to alleviate the suffering of its victims by subsidizing information and referral centers and providing funds for research. Offers counseling services to patients and their families. Maintains 51 information and referral centers. Conducts symposia. **Publications:** *American Parkinson Disease Association--Newsletter*, quarterly. Newsletter. Includes association and research news, and calendar of events. *Price:* Free. • Annual Report. • *Be Active! A Suggested Exercise Program for People with Parkinson's Disease*. Booklet. • *Be Independent to Help the Patient with Parkinson's Disease in the Activities of Daily Living*. Booklet. • *Coping With Parkinson's Disease*. Booklet. • *Let's Communicate: Speech Problems and Swallowing Problems in Parkinson's Disease*. Booklet. • *Parkinson's Disease Handbook*. Booklet. Also publishes educational supplements.

★8172★ American Sleep Apnea Association (ASAA)

PO Box 66
Belmont, MA 02178
Phone: (202)232-1338
Fax: (617)489-4761
Frank T. Adams, Chair/Brd. of Dir.

Founded: 1990. **Members:** 6,500. **Local Groups:** 228. **Description:** Individuals affected by sleep apnea; health care professionals. Promotes public awareness of sleep apnea; encourages research on the causes and treatments of breathing abnormalities during sleep. Sponsors educational programs and support groups through the Awake Network. **Publications:** *Apnews*, quarterly. • *Awake Newsletter*, quarterly. Newsletter. Focuses on information for support group coordinators. • *What is Sleep Apnea?*. Brochure.

★8173★ American Sleep Disorders Association (ASDA)

1610 14th St. NW, Ste. 300
Rochester, MN 55901
Phone: (507)287-6006
Fax: (507)287-6008
Carolyn K. Hiller, Exec.Dir.

Founded: 1975. **Members:** 2,200. **Description:** Sleep disorders centers and individuals united to provide full diagnostic and treatment services and to improve the quality of care for patients with all types of sleep disorders. Fosters educational activities at medical schools and in continuing medical education programs; conducts site visits to assure minimum standards at member centers; trains and evaluates the competence of individuals who care for patients with sleep disorders. Conducts research programs, including a cooperative case study series on all patients seen by sleep disorders centers throughout the country. **Publications:** Monographs. • Newsletter, quarterly. • *SLEEP*, bimonthly. Journal. • *Update*, bimonthly. Also publishes a roster of centers. **Formerly:** American Association of Sleep Disorders Centers; (1987) Association of Sleep Disorders Centers.

★8174★ American Society for Clinical Evoked Potentials (ASCEP)

c/o Mrs. S. Moss
14 Soundview Ave., No. 51
White Plains, NY 10606
Phone: (914)761-4713
Mrs. S. Moss, Exec.Sec.

Founded: 1981. **Members:** 410. **Description:** Physicians in physical medicine and rehabilitation, neurology, neurosurgery, ophthalmology, and anesthesiology. Purpose is to study the central nervous system's transmissions and to teach electrodiagnostic reading of evoked potentials. (Evoked potential is the sum of the stimulus-evoked bioelectrical potentials from the peripheral nerve, retina, or cochlear mechanism, from the spinal cord or central conduction pathways, and from cortical and subcortical structures.) Teaches and encourages the practice of and research in the clinical application of evoked potentials for the betterment of patient care. Conducts seminars and workshops; maintains speakers' bureau. **Publications:** Membership Directory, periodic.

★8175★ American Society of Electroneurodiagnostic Technologists (ASET)

204 W. 7th St.
Carroll, IA 51401-2317
Phone: (712)792-2978
Fax: (712)792-6962
M. Fran Pedelty, Exec.Dir.

Founded: 1959. **Members:** 2,650. **Description:** Persons engaged mainly in clinical electroencephalographic technology, with some doing both clinical and research EEG and related neurodiagnostic procedures, such as Evoked Potential Responses and polysomnography. Objective is the advancement of electroneurodiagnostic technology and the development and maintenance of high standards of training and practice in this field. Conducts a scientific program and structured, short courses in various aspects of EEG technology and electroneurodiagnostics. Joint projects with the American Electroencephalographic Society Works for complete equality and integration of the blind in society. Provides support and information services. include the drawing up of job descriptions in EEG technology as guidelines for classification of personnel and working toward approved programs for training EEG technologists. Collaborates in videocassette/television productions. Provides employment exchange service. Is developing a library. **Publications:** *American Journal of EEG Technology*, quarterly. Journal. Covers EEG, evoked potentials, and related electroneurodiagnostics. Includes author, keyword, and subject index and book reviews. *Price:* Included in membership dues; $40/year for nonmembers in U.S.; $50/year for nonmembers outside U.S.; $60/year for institutions in U.S. • *ASET Newsletter*, quarterly. Newsletter. Includes calendar of events, local, state, and regional society news and workshop and seminar news. *Price:* Included in membership dues. • Monographs. • *Who's Who in Electroneurodiagnostics--Membership Directory*, annual. Membership Directory. Provides product listings for suppliers. Arranged alphabetically and geographically. *Price:* Included in membership dues. Also publishes study materials and guides. **Formerly:** (1985) American Society of Electroencephalographic Technologists.

★8176★ American Society for Neurochemistry (ASN)

200 University Blvd., No. 519
Galveston, TX 77555-0843
Phone: (409)772-2108
Fax: (409)762-9382
Dr. Bernard Haber, Contact

Founded: 1969. **Members:** 1,018. **State Groups:** 49. **Description:** Members are investigators in the field of neurochemistry and scientists who are qualified specialists in other disciplines and are interested in the activities of the society. Purposes are to advance and promote the science of neurochemistry and related neurosciences and to increase and enhance neurochemical knowledge; to facilitate the dissemination of information concerning neurochemical research; to encourage the research of individual neurochemists. Conducts roundtables; distributes research communications. Maintains placement service. **Publications:** *American Society for Neurochemistry--Membership Directory*, annual. Membership Directory. • *Basic Neurochemistry*. Book. • *Neurochemistry of Cholinergic Receptors*. Book. • Newsletter, semiannual. • *Transactions*, annual. Abstract volume.

American Society of Neuroimaging (ASN)

See: Entry 11096

American Society of Neuroradiology (ASNR)

See: Entry 11097

★8177★ American Society of Neurorehabilitation

2221 University Ave. SE, Ste. 360
Minneapolis, MN 55414-3076
Phone: (612)623-2405
Fax: (612)623-3500

Founded: 1990. **Members:** 642. **Description:** Neurologists, neurosurgeons, psychiatrists, pediatricians, and other medical professionals interested in disorders of the nervous system. Rehabilitates and monitors patients with neurological disabilities. Acts as an advocate for patients; liases with other neurological organizations. Promotes research. **Publications:** *Journal of Neurologic Rehabilitation*. Journal. • Newsletter, quarterly.

American Society for Pediatric Neurosurgery (ASPN)

See: Entry 3174

American Society for Stereotactic and Functional Neurosurgery (ASSFN)

See: Entry 12245

★8178★ American Spinal Injury Association (ASIA)
345 E. Superior, Rm. 1436
Chicago, IL 60611
Phone: (312)908-6207
Fax: (312)908-2208
Marianne G. Kaplan, Exec.Sec.

Founded: 1973. **Members:** 500. **Description:** Medical doctors and Allied Health Care professionals who have been trained in the care of spinal paralytic patients and who are either actively engaged in the field and acknowledged to be competent by their peers or who have made a significant contribution to the advancement of the basic sciences or one of the clinical fields of practice as they are applicable to the treatment of the spine. Purposes are to: develop knowledge and investigation of the causes, cure, and prevention of spinal injury and related trauma; pursue excellence in spinal injury patient care; promote and exchange ideas between professionals in the field; standardize medical terminology in spinal cord injury; coordinate and encourage basic research in the field; develop teaching and educational material; provide specialized training for physicians and allied health professional personnel in the lifelong management of of spinal injury including comprehensive rehabilitation, vocational and avocational pursuits, housing; foster education of the medical profession and laity in the prevention and proper management of spinal injury, including the necessity for specialized regional spinal injury centers, provision for educational and vocational training, removal of architectural barriers, and promotion of a society more sensitive to the physically inconvenienced individual, including adequate housing and transportation; establish criteria for centers and/or systems of total spinal injury management so as to provide optimal care of the spinal injured person. Conducts annual scientific sessions. Sponsors G. Heiner Sell Distinguished Lectureship. **Publications:** *ASIA Meeting Proceedings.* Proceedings. • *Bulletin,* semiannual. • *Facility Categorization.* • *Guidelines for Standards of Care: Spinal Cord Injury.* • *International Standards of Neurological Classification of Spinal Injuries.* • Reports. • *Task Force Report on Spinal Cord Administration.* Report.

★8179★ American Syringomyelia Alliance Project (ASAP)
PO Box 1586
Longview, TX 75606-1586
Phone: (903)236-7079
Free: 800-ASAP-282
Fax: (903)757-7456
Don White, Exec.Dir.

Founded: 1988. **Members:** 1,500. **Description:** Seeks to increase awareness of and promote research on syringomyelia, a rare spinal disorder. Conducts fundraising activities and children's services. **Publications:** *Syringomyelia Connections,* bimonthly. Newsletter. • *What Is Syringomyelia.* Brochure.

★8180★ Amyotrophic Lateral Sclerosis Association (ALSA)
21021 Ventura Blvd., Ste. 321
Woodland Hills, CA 91364
Phone: (818)340-7500
Free: 800-782-4747
Fax: (818)340-2060
Michael W. Havlicek, Exec.VP

Founded: 1985. **Members:** 250,000. **Regional Groups:** 135. **Description:** Patients; relatives and friends of patients; doctors, neurologists, physical therapists, nurses, and professional organizations dedicated to finding the cause, prevention, and cure for amyotrophic lateral sclerosis (ALS). Offers help and information to ALS patients and their families. Funds ALS-specific research at major medical institutions. Works with other agencies, including the government, to increase their involvement on a priority basis in ALS research. Conducts patient meetings. **Publications:** *Amyotrophic Lateral Sclerosis Association--Link,* quarterly. Newspaper. Includes book reviews and research and chapter news. *Price:* Free. Also publishes fact sheets and pamphlets on ALS and patient care. **Also Known As:** ALS Association.

**★8181★ Argentine Association for the Study of Pain (AASP)
(Asociacion Argentina para el Estudio del Dolor — AAED)**
Casilla de Correo 271, Sucursal 12
1412 Buenos Aires, Argentina
Fax: 1 3256488
Dr. Oreste Ceraso, Contact

Founded: 1975. **Members:** 230. **Languages:** English, Spanish. **Description:** Health professionals in Argentina. Conducts research and disseminates information on the mechanisms and treatment of pain; organizes courses and lectures; bestows awards. **Publications:** *Dolor,* bimonthly. Includes Annual directory.

Asian-Australasian Society of Neurological Surgeons (AASNS)
See: Entry 12250

★8182★ Asociacion Distrofia Muscular
Cordoba 5824
1414 Buenos Aires, Argentina
Phone: 1 7731714
Fax: 1 3256389
Dr. Alberto Dobrovsky

Description: Individuals in Argentina who work toward the dissemination of information and research concerning muscular dystrophy, a hereditary disease characterized by progressive deterioration of muscles.

★8183★ Asociatia Handicapatilor Neuromotori din Romania (AHNR)
Str. Sava Tekelija Nr. 2
29000 Arad, Romania
Phone: 966 15126
Ioana Monica Antoci

Description: Works to protect the rights of citizens suffering from motor neuron diseases (MND). Faciliates exchange of information and experience regarding the care of persons with this disease.

★8184★ Associacao Brasileira de Distrofia Muscular
Edificio da Biologia, Sala 348
Cidade Universitaria
Sao Paulo, SP, Brazil

Description: Promotes interest in muscular dystrophy research among medical and scientific communities and the public in Brazil. Disseminates information.

★8185★ Associacao Portuguesa de Miastenia Gravis e Doencas Neuromusculares (APMG-DNM)
Hospital de Santa Maria
P-1699 Lisbon, Portugal
Phone: 1 7976882
Fax: 1 7972855
Fernando Morgado, Contact

Founded: 1989. **Members:** 650. **Languages:** English. **Description:** Promotes interest in neuromuscular diseases research among medical and scientific communities and the public in Portugal. Disseminates information. **Publications:** *Boletim Informative,* quarterly. Journal.

★8186★ Associated Professional Sleep Societies (APSS)
1610 14th St. NW, Ste. 300
Rochester, MN 55901
Phone: (507)287-6006
Fax: (507)287-6008
Carolyn K. Hiller, Exec.Dir.

Founded: 1985. **Members:** 2. **Description:** Members are the Sleep Research Society and American Sleep Disorders Association. Works to facilitate sleep research and development of sleep disorder s medicine by encouraging cooperation and exchange of information among members . **Publications:** *SLEEP,* 8/year. Newsletter. *Price:* $129/year for individuals; $185/year for instituions; $159/year for foreign individuals; $220/year for foreign institutions. **Formerly:** Association of Professional Sleep Societies.

★8187★ Association for Chemoreception Sciences (AChemS)
c/o Panacea Associates
229 Westridge Dr.
Tallahassee, FL 32304
Phone: (904)576-5530
Fax: (215)898-2084
Dr. John Caprio, Chair

Founded: 1979. **Members:** 649. **Description:** Research scientists, experimental psychologists, and industrial researchers. Purpose is to study chemoreception (the physiological reception of chemical stimuli) by the senses of taste and smell. Conducts research on the differences in human and animal perception of chemical stimuli in taste and smell. Offers seminars, fellowships, and workshops. Maintains placement service. Bestows annual Best Student Presentation at conference. **Publications:** *AChemS Membership Directory,* annual. Membership Directory. • *Chemical Senses,* bimonthly. • Newsletter, periodic.

Association of Muscle Disorders
See: Entry 7868

★ 8188 ★ Association des Neurologues Liberaux de Langue Francaise (ANLLF)
39, blvd. du Roi
F-78000 Versailles, France
Phone: 1 39532064
Fax: 1 39519244
Dr. Hubert Dechy, Exec. Officer
Founded: 1987. **Members:** 413. **Regional Groups:** 6. **Local Groups:** 3. **Languages:** French. Does not correspond in English. **Description:** French-speaking clinical neurologists working in the private sector. Provides for information exchange and organizes post-university teaching adapted to meet the needs of members. Makes arrangements for follow-up treatment of patients who have relocated. **Publications:** *Neurologie Liberale*, quarterly.

Association of Neuro-Metabolic Disorders (ANMD)
See: Entry 5271

★ 8189 ★ Association of Polysomnographic Technologists (APT)
PO Box 14861
Lenexa, KS 66285-4861
Phone: (205)592-5656
Fax: (913)541-0156
Todd Eiken, Pres.
Founded: 1978. **Members:** 1,400. **Description:** Individuals who practice polysomnography in research or clinical settings. (Polysomnographic technology deals with the measurement and recording of multiple physiological activity, such as eye movement and heart rate, during sleep.) Seeks to establish standards for polysomnographic technology and provide education and training for people entering in the field. Acts as a forum for communication among members. **Publications:** *Journal of Polysomnographic Technology*, semiannual. Journal.

★ 8190 ★ Association pour la Recherche sur la Sclerose Laterale Amyotrophique (ARS)
Forum Saint-Eustache
1, rue Montmartre
F-75001 Paris, France
Phone: 1 23389983
Fax: 1 43383159
J. Claude Blanchard, Pres.
Founded: 1985. **Members:** 2,000. **National Groups:** 1. **Regional Groups:** 8. **State Groups:** 1. **Description:** Promotes interest in amyotropic lateral sclerosis or ALS (a rare progressive degenerative disease of the motor neurons, characterized by atrophy of the muscles of the hands, forearms, and legs spreading to involve most of the body; also called Lou Gehrig's Disease) research among medical and scientific communities and the public. Faciliates exchange of information with ALS patients, researchers, clinics, and discussion/support groups. **Publications:** Booklets. • Magazine, annual. • Newsletter, quarterly. • Reports.

Association for Repetitive Motion Syndromes (ARMS)
See: Entry 9792

Association for Research in Nervous and Mental Disease (ARNMD)
See: Entry 7335

★ 8191 ★ Associazione Sclerosis Lateral Amiotrofia
c/o Centro Medico di Riabilitazione
Via per Revislate
I-28010 Veruno, Italy
Phone: 322 830101
Fax: 322 830294
Description: Individuals interested in amyotropic lateral sclerosis or ALS (also known as Lou Gehrig's Disease). Works to: heighten public awareness and understanding of the disease; encourage research among medical and scientific communities.

★ 8192 ★ Ataxia Group
Copse Edge
Thursley Rd.
Elstead
Godalming, Surrey GU8 6DJ, England
Phone: 1252 702864
Fax: 1252 703715
Founded: 1965. **Members:** 2,700. **Languages:** English. **Description:** Fundraising organization supporting research into Friedreich's, Cerebellar, and other ataxias (hereditary spinal diseases which cause the loss of muscular coordination). Offers support services for ataxia sufferers and their families. **Publications:** Brochures, periodic. • *Fax*, quarterly. Magazine. • Videos, periodic.

Avenues—National Support Group for Arthrogryposis Multiplex Congenita
See: Entry 2742

★ 8193 ★ AVM Support Group
c/o Barry G. Milione
107 Bella Vista Way
San Francisco, CA 94127-1809
Phone: (415)334-8012
Barry Milione, Exec.Dir.
Founded: 1983. **Regional Groups:** 6. **Description:** Individuals who have or had an AVM (arteriovenous malformation) and experienced seizures, hemorrhaging inside the brain, or other neurological problems. AVM is a congenital vascular defect consisting of a tangled web of immaturely formed blood vessels in the brain, brainstem, or spinal cord. Seeks to remove the isolation that AVM patients feel by providing a forum in which members may share experiences, fears, and concerns. Collects and disseminates information on treatment and management of AVMs. Provides 24-hour telephone support line. Coordinates visits to hospital neurological units. **Publications:** *The Brainstormer*, quarterly. Newsletter. • Brochure.

★ 8194 ★ Batten's Disease Support and Research Association (BDSRA)
2600 Parsons Ave.
Columbus, OH 43207
Phone: (614)445-4161
Free: 800-448-4570
Fax: (614)445-4246
Lance W. Johnson, Pres.
Founded: 1987. **Members:** 300. **State Groups:** 9. **Description:** Families of children afflicted with Batten's Disease; health care professionals; interested others. (Batten's Disease, is a degenerative neurological disease affecting children, causing seizures, dementia, loss of motor skills, and blindness.) Represents the interest of individuals with Batten's; seeks to educate the public and professional community concerning the needs of Batten's Disease patients. Provides information and referral services. Conducts support group activities. Maintains registry. **Publications:** *Family Directory*, annual. Directory. *Price:* Free; available to member families only. • *Illuminator*, quarterly. Newsletter. Provides information on research, education, meetings, and other topics of interest. *Price:* Free.

★ 8195 ★ Benign Essential Blepharospasm Research Foundation (BEBRF)
PO Box 12468
Beaumont, TX 77726-2468
Phone: (409)832-0788
Fax: (409)832-0890
Mattie Loukoster, Contact
Founded: 1981. **Members:** 6,000. **Regional Groups:** 4. **State Groups:** 50. **Local Groups:** 170. **Description:** Victims of benign essential blepharospasm (BEB), a rare disorder of unknown cause characterized by an involuntary forcible closure of the eyelids. Purpose is to undertake, promote, and develop research into the cause and cure of BEB and related disorders and infirmities of the facial musculature, such as Meige's Syndrome (involving muscle spasms of the eyes, lower face, mouth, tongue, throat, and respiratory system). Seeks to foster public awareness of the disorder in order to guarantee detection at the onset of symptoms. Encourages continuity and cooperation among neurologists, neuro-ophthalmologists, ophthalmologists, plastic surgeons, psychologists, psychiatrists, and other medical professionals in rendering correct diagnoses, implementing effective treatment, improving surgical procedure, and discovering a cure. Organizes seminars, clinical studies, and other programs in continuing education; sponsors fundraising activities. Endeavors to locate sufferers of the disorder and to compile data in order to determine the incidence of BEB and to advise on available treatment. Carries out research activities in areas such as brain tissue collection and experimental treatments. **Publications:** *BEBRF Newsletter*, bimonthly. Newsletter. Includes research reports and statistics. *Price:* $15/year. • Films. • Journal. • *Medical Handbook*, annual. Contains articles by physicians and reprints of materials appearing in medical journals. *Price:* Free. • Pamphlets.

★ 8196 ★ Biruduma Muscular Dystrophy Association
PO Box 596
Mbarara, Uganda
Description: Individuals in Uganda who work toward the dissemination of information and research concerning muscular dystrophy, a hereditary disease characterized by progressive deterioration of muscles.

Brain Information Service (BIS)
See: Entry 6983

★8197★ Cajal Club (CC)
c/o Dr. David Whitlock
University of Colorado Health Sciences Center
Department of Cellular & Structural Biology,
  B-111
4200 E. 9th Ave.
Denver, CO 80262
Phone: (303)270-8201
Fax: (303)270-4729
Dr. David Whitlock, Apical Dendrite

Founded: 1947. **Members:** 450. **Description:** Neuroanatomists who meet for discussion and the presentation of papers on prospective research, technique, and history of neurology. (Club is named after Sr. Don Santiago Ramon y Cajal, a founder of and Nobel laureate for the science of neuroanatomy.) **Publications:** *History of Cajal Club*, quinquennial. • Proceedings, periodic.

Cerebral Palsy International Sports and
  Recreation Association (CP-ISRA)
See: Entry 4472

★8198★ Charcot-Marie-Tooth Association
  (CMTA)
c/o Crozer Mills Entpr. Center
601 Upland Ave.
Upland, PA 19015
Phone: (610)499-7486
Free: 800-606-CMTA
Fax: (610)499-7486
Karol B. Hitt, Pres.

Founded: 1983. **Members:** 6,400. **Regional Groups:** 32. **Description:** Charcot-Marie-Tooth patients and their families, medical professionals treating the disorder, and interested individuals. (Charcot-Marie-Tooth Disease, also known as peroneal muscular atrophy or hereditary motor sensory neuropathy, is a progressive neurological disorder beginning in childhood or adult life with weakness and muscle wasting in feet, legs, hands, and arms.) Works to inform and educate patients and their families, the medical community, and the public about medical treatment for CMT and research. Offers support groups for patients and their families; disseminates educational materials; encourages and funds research; sponsors lay and professional symposia. Makes available videotapes; maintains speakers' bureau. **Publications:** *A Physician's Guide to CMT Disorder*. Handbook. • *Charcot-Marie-Tooth Disorders*. Pamphlets. • *CMT Facts I*, periodic. Booklets. *Price:* $3. • *CMT-Facts II*, periodic. Booklets. *Price:* $5. • *CMTA Report*, quarterly. Newsletter. Containing articles on CMT topics, research news, patient profiles, and meeting and program announcements. *Price:* With membership. **Formerly:** (1990) National Foundation for Peroneal Muscular Atrophy.

★8199★ Charcot-Marie-Tooth
  International (CMTI)
1 Springbank Dr.
St. Catharines, ON, Canada L2S 2K1
Phone: (905)687-3670
Fax: (905)687-8753
Linda Crabtree, Exec.Dir. & Pres.

Founded: 1984. **Members:** 5,000. **Description:** Individuals in Canada, the U.S., Canada, France, Great Britain, Ireland, and New Zealand who work toward the dissemination of information and research concerning Charcot-Marie-Tooth Disease also known as Peroneal Muscular Atrophy and Hereditary Motor and Sensory Neuropathy. (CMT is marked by degeneration of motor and sensory nerves in the feet and hands.) Aims to: provide information to persons with CMT, the medical community, and the public; gather data and promote research; ensure the psychological well-being of people with CMT; establish an international network for information and counseling. Provides research funding. **Publications:** Booklets. Provide information on specific Charcot-Marie-Tooth problems. • *CMT Newsletter*, bimonthly. Newsletter. Also publishes booklets on specific CMT problems. **Also Known As:** Charcot-Marie-Tooth Disease/Peroral Muscular Antrophy International Association.

★8200★ Chemotherapy Foundation (CF)
183 Madison Ave., Rm. 403
New York, NY 10016
Phone: (212)213-9292
Fax: (212)689-5164
Shirley Cox, Exec.Dir.

Founded: 1968. **Members:** 4,000. **Description:** Objectives are to: stimulate and accelerate development of drug treatment for the control and cure of cancer through basic and clinical research; inform medical oncologists of latest innovative advances that improve survival and cure of cancer patients; educate patients and the public about the best treatment opportunities available. **Publications:** *Abstracts*. From professional education conferences. • *The Breast Cancer Epidemic in the United States - How 15,000 More Lives Can Be Saved Each Year*. Booklet. *Price:* Free. • *Chemotherapy - The Proven Way*. Booklet. *Price:* Free. • *Chemotherapy - Your Weapon Against Cancer*. Booklet. *Price:* Free. • *Major Research Achievements of the Chemotherapy Foundation Grant Programs*. • Newsletter, semiannual. Includes research reports and membership activities. • *What Every Woman and Her Doctor Could Discuss About Ovarian Cancer*. Booklet. *Price:* Free.

Child Neurology Society (CNS)
See: Entry 3200

★8201★ Children and Adults With
  Attention Deficit Disorder (CHADD)
499 NW 70th Ave., Ste. 109
Plantation, FL 33317
Phone: (305)587-3700
Fax: (305)587-4599
Joanne Evans, Pres.

Founded: 1987. **Members:** 29,000. **Local Groups:** 625. **Description:** Parents, adults, and professionals with an interest in attention-deficit disorders. (ADD is a neurologically-based disorder which affects an individual's behavior and learning. The disorder is characterized by deficits in attention span and impulse control, and is often accompanied by hyperactivity.) Goals are to: maintain a support group for parents of children with ADD; provide a forum for continuing education for parents and professionals about ADD; act as a resource for information about ADD; assure that the best educational op-

portunities are available to children with ADD so that their specific difficulties will be recognized and appropriately managed within educational settings. Operates speakers' bureau. **Publications:** *ATTENTION*, 2/year. Magazine. • Booklets. • Brochures. • *The Chadder Box*, 8/year. Newsletter. Also publishes fact sheets. **Formerly:** (1993) Children with Attention-Deficit Disorders.

★8202★ CMT International
1 Springbank Dr.
St. Catharines, ON, Canada L2S 2K1
Phone: (905)687-3630
Fax: (905)687-8753
Linda Crabtree, Exec.Dir.

Founded: 1984. **Members:** 4,700. **National Groups:** 1. **Description:** Individuals in Australia, Canada, New Zealand, the United Kingdom, and the United States who work toward the dissemination of information and research concerning Charcot-Marie-Tooth Disease. (CMT, also known as Peroneal Muscular Atrophy, is marked by degeneration of motor and sensory nerves in the feet and hands.) Aims to: provide information to sufferers of CMT, the medical community, and the public; gather data and promote research; ensure the psychological well-being of those with CMT; set up an international network for information and counseling. Bestows awards; provides research funding. **Publications:** *CMT Newsletter*, bimonthly. Newsletter. **Also Known As:** Charcot-Marie-Tooth Disease/Peroneal Muscular Atrophy International Association.

★8203★ Collegium Internationale
  Activitatis Nervosae Superioris (CIANS)
Piazza E. Duse 1
I-20122 Milan, Italy
Phone: 2 55792524
Fax: 2 55013070
Prof. Carlo Lorenzo Cazzullo, Exec. Officer

Members: 1,500. **Description:** Neurologists, psychiatrists, neurophysiologists, and psychologists. Promotes research of higher nervous system activity.

★8204★ Collegium Internationale Neuro-
  Psychopharmacologicum (CINP)
The Centre Bldg.
2014 Broadway, Ste. 320
Nashville, TN 37203
Phone: (615)322-2075
Fax: (615)343-0662
Oakley Ray, Ph.D., Counselor

Founded: 1957. **Members:** 1,000. **Description:** Individuals engaged in experimental and clinical neuropsychopharmacological research and teachers in this field. Purposes are to advance the experimental and clinical aspects of the neuropsychopharmacological sciences; facilitate international relations between branches of the neuropsychopharmacological disciplines; further the international exchange of information and promote personal relations; consider the medico-social problems of psychopharmacology. Supports research. **Publications:** Directory, periodic. • Proceedings. Covers symposia and congresses. • Reports. Also publishes abstracts.

★8205★ Coma Recovery Association (CRA)
377 Jerusalem Ave.
Hempstead, NY 11550
Phone: (516)486-2847
Fax: (516)486-3815
Florence Manginaro, Pres.

Founded: 1980. **Members:** 1,056. **State Groups:** 2. **Description:** Coma and head injury survivors and their families; medical professionals; interested persons. Goal is to provide support to and assist families of coma and head injury survivors. Provides information and referrals regarding treatment, rehabilitation, and socialization options. Represents the common needs of families and patients before legislative bodies. Offers legal consulting and Medicaid case management services. **Publications:** *Coma Recovery Association Newsletter*, quarterly. Newsletter. *Price:* Included in membership dues. • *Synaps*, annual. Journal. Contains articles on coma treatment.

Congress of Neurological Surgeons (CNS)
See: Entry 12266

★8206★ CounterStroke Fiji
355 Waimanu Rd.
PO Box 1432
Suva, Fiji
Phone: 305007
Chris Saumaiwai, Sec.

Members: 500. **Description:** Disseminates information about Stroke and Stroke prevention. Maintains a register of stroke patients. Operates rehabilitation programs, media awareness campaigns, and counseling service. Provides regional training programs.

★8207★ Danish ALS Society
Lojesouej
DK-3670 Vekso, Denmark

Description: Promotes interests in amyotrophic lateral sclerosis or ALS (also called Lou Gehrig's disease) research among medical and scientific communities and the public in Denmark. Offers support services to ALS sufferers and their families. Disseminates information about the disease.

★8208★ Dysautonomia Foundation (DF)
20 E. 46th St., 3rd Fl.
New York, NY 10017
Phone: (212)949-6644
Fax: (212)682-7625
Lenore F. Roseman, Exec.Dir.

Founded: 1954. **Members:** 5,000. **Description:** Parents, relatives, friends and benefactors of children afflicted with dysautonomia, a genetic disease of the autonomic nervous system. Purpose is to fund research in the causes and cure of the disease. **Publications:** *DYS/COURSE*, semiannual. Newsletter. Includes research updates. *Price:* Free. • *Dysautonomia Foundation--Journal*, annual. Journal. *Price:* Free, for members only. **Formerly:** (1969) Dysautonomia Association.

★8209★ Dystonia Medical Research Foundation
1 E. Wacker Dr., Ste. 2430
Chicago, IL 60601-2001
Phone: (312)755-0198
Fax: (312)803-0138
Valerie Flevitin, Contact

Founded: 1977. **Members:** 25,000. **State Groups:** 24. **Local Groups:** 4. **Description:** Dystonia patients and their families; medical personnel; health agencies; interested individuals. Promotes and funds research and encourages increased public awareness of dystonia, a neurologic muscular disorder causing muscles to jerk and contract into abnormal positions. Disseminates information concerning dystonia. Sponsors patient and family support groups. **Publications:** Brochures. • *Dystonia Dialogue*, quarterly. Includes foundation and chapter news and research updates. *Price:* Free.

★8210★ Epilepsy Concern Service Group (EC)
1282 Wynnewood Dr.
West Palm Beach, FL 33417
Phone: (407)683-0044
Fax: (407)881-5085
George L. McKay, Group Leader

Founded: 1975. **Description:** Persons with epilepsy and concerned friends and relatives. Starts and maintains selfhelp groups composed of caring people who are seeking help in dealing with epilepsy. Groups band together in self-governing, self-supporting area "councils" usually representing geographic areas. A council consists of one Friends (support) Group, one or more Epilepsy Groups (primary consumers), and one or more Love Groups (secondary consumers). Operates Long Distance Friends Program whereby individuals may communicate with a member by letter or tape. Provides group leader training; makes an Epilepsy Concern Starter Kit available to those wishing to organize a group in their community. **Publications:** *Concerns*, periodic. Newsletter. *Price:* Free. • *Dividends*, quarterly. Membership Directory. *Price:* Free. **Formerly:** (1986) Epilepsy Concern.

★8211★ Epilepsy Foundation of America (EFA)
4351 Garden City Dr.
Landover, MD 20785
Phone: (301)459-3700
Free: 800-EFA-1000
Fax: (301)577-2684
William McLin, Exec.VP

Founded: 1967. **Description:** National voluntary health agency which serves as the "focal point for the fight against epilepsy in the United States." Augmented by 85 affiliates in the U.S. committed to preventing and controlling epilepsy and improving the lives of those who have it. Provides federal government liaison. The foundation supports medical, social, rehabilitational, legal, employment, and information, education, and advocacy programs. Sponsors research in causes of epilepsy, prevention, psychosocial needs, and improved methods of treatment. Provides research and training grants and fellowships to students and professionals. Assistance and counseling for epilepsy patients and their families is provided through local organiza-

tions and a national information and referral service. Annual projects include National Epilepsy Month (November), School Alert (a national educational program for schools), selection of the Epilepsy Poster Child, and a continuing professional and public education and information program. Maintains a resource center. Provides members with access to mail order pharmacy program. Compiles statistics; maintains placement program. **Publications:** *Epilepsy Advances*, 8-10/year. Newsletter. Includes calendar of events. *Price:* Free. • *Epilepsy USA*, 8-10/year. Newsletter. Provides information on national legislation and administrative political decisions that affect the disabled, people with epilepsy, and others. Also publishes pamphlets and makes available audiovisual material and informational/educational pieces for diversified audiences.

★8212★ Epilepsy Support Foundation
No. 3 Crocket Rd.
PO Box 542
Borrowdale
Harare, Zimbabwe
Phone: 4 8874229
Fax: 4 303607
Jean McLean, Dir.

Founded: 1990. **Members:** 350. **Languages:** English, Shona. **Description:** Seeks to improve the quality of life for persons with epilepsy. Raises public awareness about epilepsy and its effects. Disseminates information. **Publications:** *Epilepsy Back Up*, monthly. Newsletter. Educational newsletter • *Epilepsy Back Up*, 3/year. Newsletter. Medical edition • Pamphlets, periodic. Contains information on epilepsy for patients, service providers, medical personnel, and various professionals.

★8213★ European Association of Neurosurgical Societies (EANS)
Universitatsklinikum Steglitz
Hindenburgdamm 30
10045 Berlin, Germany
L. Calliauw, Sec.

Languages: English. **Description:** European neurological societies in 22 countries. Sponsors annual training course. **Publications:** *Acta Neurochirurgica*, 3/month. • Directory, annual. • *EANS Bulletin*, semiannual. Bulletin.

★8214★ European Neuroscience Association (ENA)
Postbus 238
NL-1400 AE Bussum, Netherlands
Phone: 35 6947413
Fax: 35 6942640
Dr. Hugo Zwenk, Exec.Sec.

Founded: 1976. **Members:** 2,000. **Languages:** English. **Description:** Neuroanatomists, neurochemists, neurocytologists, neuroendocrinologists, neuropharmacologists, neurophysiologists, neuropsychologists, and behavioral scientists in 41 countries. Objectives are to: enhance comparative research in an effort to improve the understanding of the nervous system; promote the exchange of technical information and theoretical knowledge; establish high professional standards in the neurosciences. Seeks creation of a European platform for the neurosciences. **Publications:** *Abstracts of Meetings*, annual.

Book. • *ENA Membership Directory*, biennial. Directory. • *ENA Newsletter*, semiannual. Newsletter. • *European Journal of Neuroscience*, monthly. Journal.

★ 8215 ★ **European Society for Neurochemistry (ESN)**
Dept. of Neuro Chemistry Paul-Flechsig
Inst. for Brain Research
04100 Leipzig, Germany
Dr. Anthony J. Turner, Sec.

Founded: 1976. **Members:** 685. **Languages:** English. **Description:** Researchers in 33 countries working in neurochemistry, neurology, molecular neurobiology, molecular neuropharmacology, and psychiatry. Works toward a greater understanding of the biochemical foundations of nervous activity and insight into neural and mental diseases. Conducts seminars and workshops. **Publications:** *ESN Directory*, periodic. Directory. • *Newsletter*, periodic. Newsletter. • *Proceedings of Biennial General Meetings*.

★ 8216 ★ **European Society of Neuroradiology (ESNR)**
(Servizio di Neuroradiologia)
Via Francesco Sforza 35
I-20122 Milan, Italy
Phone: 2 55033811
Fax: 2 59901109
Prof. Marco Leonardi, M.D., Sec.Gen.

Founded: 1969. **Members:** 800. **Languages:** English. **Description:** Neuroradiologists and trainees in neuroradiology, neurosurgery, and neurology in 38 countries. Offers educational programs. **Publications:** Directory, periodic. • *Neuroradiology*, bimonthly.

★ 8217 ★ **Familiares y Amigos de Enfermos de la Neurona Motora (FYADENMAC)**
Maestro Rural Num. 74
Col. Un Hogar para Nostros
11330 Mexico City, DF, Mexico
Phone: 5 3411595

Description: Promotes interest in motor neurone disease (MND) research among medical and scientific communities and the public in Mexico. Offers support services to MND sufferers and their families. Disseminates information about the disease.

★ 8218 ★ **Families of S.M.A. (FSMA)**
PO Box 1465
Highland Park, IL 60035-7465
Phone: (708)432-5551
Free: 800-886-1762
Fax: (708)432-5551
Marilyn Naiditch, Sec.

Founded: 1985. **Members:** 1,600. **Regional Groups:** 1. **State Groups:** 3. **Description:** Individuals with spinal muscular atrophy; their families; medical professionals; and interested others. Promotes public awareness of spinal muscular atrophy (SMA), which includes infantile progressive SMA (Werdnig-Hoffman Disease), juvenile progressive SMA (Kugelberg-Welander Disease), and adult progressive SMA (Aran-Duchenne Type). Funds research. **Publications:** *Direction*, quarterly. Newsletter. Includes research updates and information network.

Price: $20/year for families in the U.S.; $25/year for professionals in the U.S.; $35/year outside the U.S. • *Living with SMA*. Video.

★ 8219 ★ **Finnish Society of Clinical Neurophysiology (FSCN)**
(Suomen Kliinisen Neurofysiologian Yhdistys — SKNY)
Division of Clinical Neurophysiology
University Hospital
SF-00290 Helsinki, Finland
Phone: 0 4713876
Fax: 0 4714088
Tapani Salmi, M.D., Sec.

Founded: 1972. **Members:** 95. **Languages:** English, Finnish, Swedish. **Description:** Physicians who specialize in clinical neurophysiology. Promotes research in new techniques and applications in the field. Disseminates current information. Encourages training and education of residents in clinical neurophysiology. Conducts Annual course and semiannual seminar. **Publications:** *Membership List*, periodic.

★ 8220 ★ **French-Language Society for Clinical Neurophysiology (FLSCN)**
(Societe de Neurophysiologie Clinique de Langue Francaise)
Hospital Station Vincent DePaul
82, ave. Denfert Rochereau
F-75014 Paris, France
Phone: 1 40488203
Fax: 1 40488371
Dr. Perrine Plouin, Sec.Gen.

Founded: 1948. **Members:** 550. **Languages:** English, French. **Description:** Medical specialists in electroencephalography, electromyography, and other functional explorations of the nervous system; researchers concerned with human and animal neurophysiology. Promotes clinical and experimental exploration of the nervous system. **Publications:** *Neurophysiologie Clinique*, bimonthly.

★ 8221 ★ **French-Speaking Neuropsychological Society (FSNS)**
(Societe de Neuropsychologie de Langue Francaise)
Groupe Hospitalier Pitie-Salpetriere
47/93, blvd. de l'Hopital
F-75051 Paris Cedex 13, France
Phone: 1 61498926
Fax: 1 61499524
A. Agniel, Sec.

Founded: 1977. **Members:** 450. **Languages:** French. **Description:** Individuals working in clinical or research neuropsychology in 12 countries. Promotes the study of behavior in connection with cerebral activity, clinical and experimental analysis, therapy, and understanding of socioprofessional implications. **Publications:** *Revue de Neuropsychologie*, quarterly. Journal.

★ 8222 ★ **Friedreich's Ataxia Society of Ireland (FASI)**
San Martino
Mart Ln.
Foxrock
Dublin 18, Ireland
Phone: 1 2894788
Clare Creedon, Pres.

Founded: 1980. **Members:** 382. **Languages:** English. **Description:** Individuals with Frie-

dreich's Ataxia (132); interested others (250). Provides assistance to those afflicted with Friedreich's Ataxia, a neurological disorder affecting muscular movement. Provides counseling. Encourages communication between members. Sponsors and conducts research on the disorder. **Publications:** *FASI Newsletter*, annual. Newsletter. General news and articles from and about member and society activities.

F.S.H. Society
See: Entry 7879

★ 8223 ★ **Fundacion Omega**
Carrera 30, No. 89-79
La Castellana
Bogota, Colombia
Phone: 1 2365004
Fax: 1 2183315
Ivan Dario Arteaga

Description: Provides supportive services and information to individuals striken with amyotrophic lateral sclerosis (ALS) or similar neurological-related diseases.

★ 8224 ★ **Guardians of Hydrocephalus Research Foundation (GHRF)**
2618 Avenue Z
Brooklyn, NY 11235-2023
Phone: (718)743-GHRF
Free: 800-458-8655
Fax: (718)743-1171
Katherine Soriano, Nat. VP

★ 8225 ★ **Guillain-Barre Syndrome Foundation International (GBSFI)**
PO Box 262
Wynnewood, PA 19096
Phone: (215)667-0131
Fax: (215)667-7036
Robert and Estelle Benson, Founders

Founded: 1980. **Members:** 15,000. **Regional Groups:** 130. **Description:** Individuals concerned with Guillain-Barre syndrome (Acute Idiopathic Polyneuritis), a rare, paralyzing, potentially catastrophic disorder of the peripheral nerves. Objectives are to: educate the public and medical community about the availability of support groups and maintain their awareness of the disorder; foster research on cause, prevention, and treatment; encourage financial support for research; develop nationwide support groups. Arranges for recovered or recovering patients to visit patients in acute care and rehabilitation hospitals; assists patients in dealing with disabilities should complete recovery not occur. Maintains steering committee of physicians, some of who have had the disorder. **Publications:** *Guillain-Barre Syndrome, an Overview for the Layperson*. **Formerly:** (1988) Guillian-Barre Syndrome Support Group; (1990) Guillian-Barre Syndrome Support Group International.

★ 8226 ★ **Head Injury Hotline (PP)**
c/o Constance Miller
PO Box 84151
Seattle, WA 98124
Phone: (206)329-1371
Fax: (206)623-4251
Constance Miller, Contact

Founded: 1986. **Description:** Disseminates head injury information and provides referrals to facilitate adjustment to life following head injury. Organizes seminars for professionals, head injury survivors, and their families. Maintains speakers' bureau. **Publications:** *From the Ashes: A Head Injury Self-Advocacy Guide*, periodic. Contains worksheets to assist in locating and assessing doctors and therapists; self-assessment inventories; glossary of commonly-used phrases. *Price:* $20/copy; $5 shipping and handling. **Formerly:** (1993) Phoenix Project.

★ 8227 ★ **Huntington's Disease Association (HDA)**
108 Battersea High St.
London SW11 3HP, England
Phone: 171 2237000
Fax: 171 2239489
Mark Payne

Founded: 1971. **Members:** 4,000. **Local Groups:** 40. **Languages:** English. **Description:** Individuals united to provide assistance, treatment, and information on the effects of Huntington's Disease, a hereditary nervous disorder causing terminal physical and mental disability. Services include: counseling program designed for families and involved professionals; network of regional advisers and local groups throughout the country; confidential telephone and correspondence service; financial assistance; aid to patients undergoing presymptomatic tests or brain tissue donations. Encourages research on the medical and social effects of Huntington's Disease; raises funds. **Publications:** *Facing Huntington's Disease*, periodic. Booklet. • Newsletter, semiannual. • Pamphlets, periodic. **Formerly:** (1991) Association to Combat Huntington's Disease.

★ 8228 ★ **Huntington's Disease Society of America (HDSA)**
140 W. 22nd St., 6th Fl.
New York, NY 10011-2420
Phone: (212)242-1968
Free: 800-345-4372
Fax: (212)243-2443
Stephen Bajardi, Exec.Dir.

Founded: 1986. **Members:** 45,000. **National Groups:** 31. **Local Groups:** 110. **Description:** Individuals and groups of volunteers concerned with Huntington's disease, an inherited and terminal neurological condition causing progressive brain and nerve deterioration. Goals are to: identify HD families; educate the public and professionals, with emphasis on increasing consumer awareness of HD; promote and support basic and clinical research into the causes and cure of HD; maintain patient services program, coordinated with various community services, to assist families in meeting the social, economic, and emotional problems resulting from HD. Is working to change the attitude of the working community toward the HD patient, enhance the HD patient's lifestyle, and promote better health care and treatment, both in the community and in facilities. Has launched nationwide campaign in support of federal and state legislation establishing clinics, genetic counseling and screening centers, and diagnostic and treatment centers for HD patients and those suffering from other chronic, debilitating diseases. Actively cooperates with researchers in ongoing studies; cosponsors and supports workshops and sym-

posia; provides grants to individual researchers; sponsors brain donor program. Crisis intervention and other support services are available. **Publications:** Booklets. • *Huntington's Disease Society of America--Marker*, 3/year. Newsletter. *Price:* Free. • Pamphlets.

★ 8229 ★ **Ibero-American Society for Neurochemistry**
Institute de Biologia Celular, Facultad e Medicina
University de Buenos Aires
Paraguay 2155-P2
Buenos Aires, Argentina

Description: Promotes study and research in the field of neurochemistry.

★ 8230 ★ **Indian Muscular Dystrophy Association (IMDA)**
21-136 Batchupet
Malchilipatnam 521 001, India
Phone: 8672 2817
R. Janardana Rao

Description: Individuals in India who work toward the dissemination of information and research concerning muscular dystrophy, a hereditary disease characterized by progressive deterioration of muscles.

★ 8231 ★ **Institutes for the Achievement of Human Potential (IAHP)**
8801 Stenton Ave.
Philadelphia, PA 19118
Phone: (215)233-2050
Glenn J. Doman, Chm.

Founded: 1955. **Description:** Promotes the achievement of full potential for all individuals. Maintains Children's Institute which conducts parent orientation and evaluation of brain-injured children with severe disabilities as well as apparently well children who are not realizing full potential. Conducts courses for parents interested in fostering the intellectual development and potential of their children. Sponsors the Institute for Clinical Investigation which promotes improved methods of helping brain-injured children reach a level of performance in accordance with their potential. Operates On-Campus International School and Off-Campus International School. **Publications:** Books. • *The In Report*, bimonthly.

International Academy for Child Brain Development (IACBD)
See: Entry 3238

★ 8232 ★ **International ALS / MND Research Foundation**
Tiradelza de Monteggio
CH-6998 Termine, Switzerland
Phone: 91 732231
Fax: 91 732232
W. Parlette, Contact

Founded: 1987. **Languages:** English, French, German. **Description:** Promotes international interest in amyotropic lateral sclerosis or ALS (a rare progressive degenerative disease of the motor neurons, characterized by atrophy of the muscles of the hands, forearms, and legs spreading to involve most of the body; also called Lou Gehrig's Disease) and other motor

neuron diseases (MND) research among medical and scientific communities and the public. Faciliates exchange of information with ALS and MND patients, researchers, clinics, and discussion/support groups.

★ 8233 ★ **International Association of Neuro-Linguistic Programming (IANLP)**
HCR Box 593-C
Payson, AZ 85541
Phone: (520)474-1552
Laura Shaw, Mgr.

Founded: 1983. **Members:** 1,300. **Regional Groups:** 9. **Description:** Certified neuro-linguistic programming practitioners and programmers (355); certified master programmers (393); certified NLP trainers (152); individuals with some training in NLP (400). (NLP is a discipline that examines the structure of human thought and response and is used in counseling, psychotherapy, and business applications.) Provides an international network for the exchange of ideas, materials, and services. Sets standards for the ethical use of NLP and for NLP training and certification. Encourages and supports research and development; fosters utilization of new technologies in NLP; seeks to integrate the skills and ideas of other disciplines with those of NLP. Promotes greater public understanding of NLP and its objectives. Sponsors NLP workshops. Cooperates with other professional organizations. **Publications:** *IANLP*, annual. Membership Directory. • *IANLP*, bimonthly. Newsletter. **Formerly:** (1991) International Association for Neuro-Linguistic Programming; (1993) International Association of Neuro-Linguistic Programming; (1995) North American Association of Neuro-Linguistic Programming.

★ 8234 ★ **International Association for the Study of Pain (IASP)**
909 NE 43rd St., Ste. 306
Seattle, WA 98105-6020
Phone: (206)547-6409
Fax: (206)547-1703
Louisa E. Jones, Exec. Officer

Founded: 1974. **Members:** 6,000. **Regional Groups:** 45. **Description:** Scientists, physicians, and other health professionals interested in pain research and therapy. Encourages research on pain mechanisms and syndromes; seeks to improve management of patients with acute and chronic pain. Promotes education and training in the field of pain; informs the public of results of current research. Fosters development of an international data bank, adoption of a uniform classification and definition regarding pain and pain syndromes, and creation of a uniform records system on information relating to pain mechanisms, syndromes, and management. Promotes the formation of national associations for the study and treatment of pain. **Publications:** *Classification of Chronic Pain*. Book. *Price:* $20. • *Congress Proceedings*, triennial. • *Core Curriculum for Professional Education in Pain*. • *Curriculum on Pain for Nursing Students*. • *Curriculum on Pain for Pharmacy Students*. • *Dental School Curriculum in Pain*. • *Guidelines for Desirable Characteristics of Pain Treatment Facilities*. • *IASP Newsletter*, bimonthly. Newsletter. Updates members on association activities; includes technical corner, calendar of events, available research grants and educational opportunities. • *International Association for the Study of Pain--Directory of Members*, annual. Membership Directory. Arranged alphabetically, geographically, and by specialty. *Price:* Included in membership dues; $25/copy for nonmembers. • *Management of Acute Pain: A Practical Guide.* • *Medical School Curriculum in Pain.* • *Pain*, monthly. Journal. Includes basic and clinical research and book reviews. *Price:* Included in membership dues. • *Pain Abstracts*, triennial. • *Standards for Physician Fellowship in Pain Management.*

★8235★ **International Brain Research Organization (IBRO)**
(Organisation Internationale de Recherche sur le Cerveau)
51, blvd. de Montmorency
F-75016 Paris, France
Phone: 1 46479292
Fax: 1 45206006
Dr. David Ottoson, Sec.Gen.

Founded: 1958. **Members:** 27,000. **Description:** Scientists working in neuroanatomy, neuroendocrinology, the behavioral sciences, neurocommunications and biophysics, brain pathology, and clinical and health-related sciences. Works to promote international cooperation in research on the nervous system. Sponsors fellowships, exchange of scientific workers, and traveling teams of instructors to supplement local teachings. Organizes international neuroscience symposia and workshops. **Publications:** *Directory of Members*, periodic. Directory. • *Neuroscience*, bimonthly. • *News*, 3/year. Also publishes symposia monograph series and handbook series.

★8236★ **International Bureau for Epilepsy (IBE)**
(Bureau International pour l'Epilepsie)
Postbus 21
NL-2100 AA Heemstede, Netherlands
Phone: 23 291019
Fax: 23 470119
Mrs. Liedewij Jepsen, Contact

Founded: 1961. **Members:** 42. **National Groups:** 40. **Languages:** English. **Description:** National organizations and individuals interested in the medical, social, and scientific aspects of epilepsy. Focuses on aspects of daily life with epilepsy. Facilitates exchange of information and experience regarding the care of persons with epilepsy. Provides material on how to organize and finance non-medical societies. Organizes training sessions. Works to build an international film library on epilepsy. **Publications:** *International Epilepsy News*, quarterly. Magazine.

★8237★ **International Cerebral Palsy Society (ICPS)**
19 St. Mary's Grove
London W4 3LL, England
Phone: 181 9955721
Fax: 181 9955721
Anita Loring, Sec.Gen.

Founded: 1969. **Members:** 317. **Languages:** English. **Description:** Professionals, parents, handicapped persons, and organizations in 60 countries. Seeks to stimulate research in cerebral palsy and promote related improvements and developments in early diagnosis, methods of treatment, and appropriate teaching and rehabilitation programs. Acts as the international coordinating organization for collection, distribution, and exchange of specialized information on cerebral palsy. Disseminates information about: architectural design for the handicapped; operation and equipment of a mobile visiting aid unit; aids and appliances; how to obtain entry visas for handicapped children emigrating with their families; medical matters; sex education; research on integration; publications for parents; alternative forms of physiotherapy; employment opportunities. Offers consulting services and referrals. **Publications:** *Bulletin*, 3/year. Bulletin.

★8238★ **International Federation of Clinical Neurophysiology (IFCN)**
c/o Dr. G. Caruso, M.D.
University of Naples
Sederico II
Via S. Pansini
I-80131 Milan, Italy
Fax: 81 5469861
Dr. G. Caruso, M.D., Sec.

Founded: 1949. **Members:** 46. **Description:** National electroencephalography and/or neurophysiology societies. Purposes are to: ensure that the highest possible standards are reached in all countries in the field of electroencephalography and clinical neurophysiology; encourage scientific research; promote effective international collaboration between learned societies, professional associations, institutions, and individuals contributing to progress in the field. **Publications:** *Electroencephalography and Clinical Neurophysiology*, monthly. Journal. • *EMG and Motor Control*, bimonthly. Journal. • *Evoked Potentials*, bimonthly. Journal. • *Handbook of EEG and Clinical Neurophysiology.* **Formerly:** (1990) International Federation of Societies for Electroencephalography and Clinical Neurophysiology.

★8239★ **International Federation of Multiple Sclerosis Societies (IFMSS)**
10 Heddon St.
London W1R 7LJ, England
Phone: 171 7349120
Fax: 171 2872587

Founded: 1967. **Members:** 34. **Languages:** English, French. **Description:** Promotes international interest in multiple sclerosis research among medical and scientific communities and the public. Goals are to help improve present treatments and treatment facilities, to search for new and better treatments worldwide, and to sponsor and participate in symposia. Facilitates exchange of information among members on all aspects of multiple sclerosis management including organizational and fundraising methods, patient services, professional and public information, and research. Sponsors annual medical advisory seminars. Compiles statistics. **Publications:** *Annual Report.* • *Federation Updates*, quarterly. • *Manual on MS.* • *Minimal Record of Disability.* • *MS Research in Progress.* • *MS Research Reports*, quarterly. Contains abstracts. • *MS Therapeutic Claims.*

★8240★ **International Joseph Diseases Foundation (IJDF)**
PO Box 2550
Livermore, CA 94551-2550
Phone: (510)371-1287
Fax: (510)371-1288
Rose Marie Silva, Exec.Dir.

Founded: 1977. **Description:** Geneticists, neurologists, patients and their families, and individuals interested in Joseph disease. (Joseph disease is a neurological genetic disorder of the motor system affecting all races and many ethnic groups, which is often misdiagnosed as multiple sclerosis, Parkinson's disease, or spinocerebellar degeneration.) Offers diagnostic services and treatment at free clinics. Provides genetic counseling to individuals concerned with inheriting the disorder or passing it on to future generations. Locates families throughout the world affected by the disease. Educates the medical profession and the public on Joseph disease in an effort to promote more accurate diagnosis and better treatment. Conducts research; maintains speakers' bureau. **Publications:** *IJDF Newsletter*, quarterly. Newsletter. Includes research developments.

★8241★ **International League Against Epilepsy (ILAE)**
c/o Dr. Peter Wolf
Klinik Mara I
Maraweg 21
33617 Bielefeld, Germany
Phone: 521 1444897
Fax: 521 1444637
Dr. Peter Wolf, Contact

Founded: 1909. **Members:** 46. **Description:** National organizations united to encourage scientific research on epilepsy, and to promote optimal treatment and rehabilitation of epileptic patients. Fosters development of and cooperation among associations with common interests. **Publications:** *Epilepsia*, bimonthly. Journal. Contains scientific papers and meeting abstracts for professional researchers in the field of epilepsy. Includes book reviews and research reports.

★8242★ **International Research Council of Neuromuscular Disorders (IRCND)**
1434 Pleasantville Rd.
Lancaster, OH 43130
Phone: (614)653-1098
James R. Grilliot, D.C., Exec.Dir.

Founded: 1982. **Members:** 82. **Description:** Health professionals interested in neuromuscular diseases of the human body. Purpose is to advance and disseminate information on the causes, effects, occurrence, cure, and prevention of neuromuscular disorders and associated topics related to the human spine. Coordinates and encourages basic research and the exchange of ideas and related materials between professionals in the field. Prepares teaching and educational materials. Compiles statistics for distribution; sponsors seminars and speakers' bureau. Is currently developing a library. **Publications:** *Information/Newsletter*, annual. Newsletter.

International Rett Syndrome Association (IRSA)
See: Entry 3246

★8243★ International Society for Developmental Neuroscience (ISDN)

c/o Bernard Haber, Ph.D.
University of Texas Medical Branch
200 University, No. 519
Galveston, TX 77550
Phone: (409)772-3667
Fax: (409)767-9382
Regino Perez-Polo, Ph.D., Sec.Gen.

Founded: 1978. **Members:** 850. **National Groups:** 25. **Description:** Independent researchers who have produced meritorious work in the field of developmental neuroscience; individuals who have made outstanding contributions to developmental neuroscience; doctoral students. Aims to advance research and knowledge concerning the development of the nervous system and to support the effective application of this information for the improvement of human health. **Publications:** *International Journal of Developmental Neuroscience*, bimonthly. Journal. *Price:* $90. • *ISDN Membership Directory*, biennial. Membership Directory. • *ISDN Newsletter*, semiannual. Newsletter.

★8244★ International Society for Neurochemistry (ISN) (Societe Internationale de Neurochimie)

University of Copenhagen
Protein Laboratory, Panum Institute
Blegdamsvej 3C, bld. 6.2
DK-2200 Copenhagen, Denmark
Phone: 31357900
Fax: 35360116
Prof. Elisabeth Bock, Sec.

Founded: 1965. **Members:** 1,530. **Languages:** English. **Description:** Scientists in 42 countries interested in promoting research in neurochemistry. Sponsors international travel of lecturers. Offers placement service; conducts charitable program. **Publications:** *Journal of Neurochemistry*, monthly. • *Membership Directory*, biennial. • Newsletter, semiannual.

International Society of Neuropathology (Societe Internationale de Neuropathologie)

See: Entry 10135

International Society for Pediatric Neurosurgery (ISPN)

See: Entry 3248

★8245★ International Tremor Foundation (ITF)

833 W. Washington Blvd.
Chicago, IL 60607
Phone: (312)733-1893
Judy Rosner, Exec.Dir.

Founded: 1988. **Members:** 25,000. **Regional Groups:** 3. **Description:** Individuals suffering from tremors, their families and friends and health care professionals. (Tremor is a common symptom of neurologic disease and may be due to trauma, tumor, stroke or degenerative disease. The hands and head are most often affected. Current treatment includes drug therapy and surgical intervention.) Promotes research and development of clinical care programs. Provides patient information and referrals. **Publications:** Newsletter, quarterly. Includes research reports and networking information. *Price:* Included in membership dues.

★8246★ Irish Motor Neurone Disease Association

Carmichael House
N. Brunswick St.
Dublin 7, Ireland
Phone: 1 8730422
Fax: 1 8735737
Eithne Frost, Contact

Founded: 1985. **Description:** Promotes interest in motor neurone disease (MND) research among medical and scientific communities and the public in Ireland. Offers support services to MND sufferers and their families. Disseminates information about the disease. **Publications:** *IMNDA Newsletter*, quarterly. Newsletter.

★8247★ IVH Parents (IVHP)

PO Box 56-1111
Miami, FL 33256-1111
Phone: (305)232-0381
Fax: (305)232-9890
Ronnie Londner, Dir.

Founded: 1984. **Members:** 400. **Description:** Parents of children with intraventricular hemorrhage; health care professionals. (Intraventricular hemorrhage is an intracerebral hemorrhage that can occur in an infant after premature or traumatic birth. Potential effects are hydrocephalus, cerebral palsy, sensory loss, seizures, mental retardation, and multiple handicaps.) Provides support services including information on development needs of IVH children. Conducts follow-ups; maintains speakers' bureau. Compiles statistics. **Publications:** *IVH Parents Newsletter*, periodic. Newsletter.

★8248★ Japan ALS Association

9-10-701, Shin-ogawa-Cho
Shinjuku
Tokyo 162, Japan
Phone: 3 32676942
Fax: 3 32676940
Yukio Matsuoka

Description: Individuals interested in amyotropic lateral sclerosis or ALS (also known as Lou Gehrig's Disease). Works to: heighten public awareness and understanding of the disease; encourage research among medical and scientific communities.

★8249★ Kontaktgruppen for ALS

Foreningen for Muskelsyke
Hardangervegen 314
N-5232 Helldal, Norway
Bjorg Hille Griman

Description: Promotes interest in amyotrophic lateral sclerosis or ALS (also called Lou Gehrig's disease) research among medical and scientific communities and the public in Norway. Offers support services to ALS sufferers and their families. Disseminates information about the disease.

★8250★ Ma Ayesha Memorial Center for Care and Control of Neuromuscular Diseases

SNPA-22 Block 7/8
Karachi, Pakistan
Shahida Abdullah

Description: Works to: encourage scientific and medical communities to research neuromuscular diseases; support patients and their families; heighten community awareness.

★8251★ Microneurography Society (MNS)

Cardiovascular Physiology
V.A. Med. Center
Richmond, VA 23249
Phone: (804)230-0001
Dwain L. Eckberg, M.D., Sec.

Founded: 1981. **Members:** 60. **Description:** Persons interested in research applications of microneurography in humans. (Microneurography involves insertion of a microelectrode, in this case a tungsten steel needle, into a nerve to record nerve activity.) Fosters interest in microneurography; identifies scientists involved with the technique. Conducts seminars. Plans to hold international symposium. **Publications:** Directory, annual.

Middle East Neurosurgical Society (Societe de Neurochirurgie du Moyen Orient)

See: Entry 12289

★8252★ Motor Neurone Disease and Amiotrofia Lateral Esclerosis in Uruguay (MNDALSU)

Av. Italia 3318
Montevideo, Uruguay
Phone: 2 471616
Fax: 2 475461
Dr. O. Vincent, Contact

Founded: 1991. **Members:** 3. **Languages:** English, French, Italian. **Description:** Promotes interest in motor neurone disease (MND) and amyotrophic lateral sclerosis (ALS) research among medical and scientific communities and the public in Uruguay. Offers support services to MND sufferers and their families. Disseminates information about the disease. **Publications:** *A Downstream Event in the Spinal Cord Slice: A Model of Early Excitotoxic Injury*. Report. • *Fisioterapia para las Enfermedades Neuromusculares*. Report. • *Mioterapia Oro Faringo Facial*. Report. **Formerly:** (1992) Asociacion de Enfermedades Motoneuronales y Esclerosis Lateral Amiotrofica del Uruguay (MON DELA).

★8253★ Motor Neurone Disease Association

PO Box 246
Northampton NN1 2PR, England
Phone: 1604 250505
Fax: 1604 24726
George Levvy, Contact

Description: Promotes interest in motor neurone disease (MND) research among medical and scientific communities and the public in the United Kingdom. Offers support services to MND sufferers and their families. Disseminates information about the disease.

★8254★ Motor Neurone Disease Association of Australia

PO Box 262
Caulfield South, VIC 3162, Australia
Phone: 3 5964761
Fax: 3 5968005
Mavis Gallienne

Description: Promotes interests in motor neurone disease (MND) research among medical and scientific communities and the public in Australia. Offers support services to MND sufferers and their families. Disseminates information about the disease.

★ 8255 ★ **Motor Neurone Disease Association of South Africa**
c/o PO Box 781880
Sandton
Transvaal 2146, Republic of South Africa
Phone: 11 7064883
Fax: 11 7064883
Diane Heron, Contact

Founded: 1991. **Regional Groups:** 3. **Description:** Promotes interests in motor neurone disease (MND) research among medical and scientific communities and the public in South Africa. Offers support services to MND sufferers and their families. Disseminates information about the disease.

★ 8256 ★ **Motor Neurone Disease Society in Iceland**
Bugdulaek 3
IS-105 Reykjavik, Iceland
Phone: 1 32005
Fax: 1 682633
Rafn Jonsson

Description: Promotes interests in motor neurone disease (MND) research among medical and scientific communities and the public in Iceland. Offers support services to MND sufferers and their families. Disseminates information about the disease.

★ 8257 ★ **Motor Neurone Disease Society of New Zealand**
PO Box 1613
Auckland, New Zealand
Phone: 9 3765405
Fax: 9 3602305
Susan Sweetman

Description: Promotes interest in motor neurone disease (MND) research among medical and scientific communities and the public in New Zealand. Offers support services to MND sufferers and their families. Disseminates information about the disease.

★ 8258 ★ **Motor Neurone Disease Support Group**
40 Kologarh Rd.
St. No. 5
Rajendra Nagar 248 001, Delhi, India
Phone: 135 23675
Nicky Bhagat

Description: Promotes interest in motor neurone disease (MND) research among medical and scientific communities and the public in India. Works as a support group for MND sufferers and their families. Disseminates information about the disease.

★ 8259 ★ **Multidisciplinary Institute for Neuropsychological Development (MIND)**
48 Garden St.
Cambridge, MA 02138
Phone: (617)547-9845
E. Christine Kris, Ph.D., Dir.

Founded: 1970. **Members:** 115. **Description:** Professionals from the fields of education, psychology, law, biomedical engineering, medicine, theology, and human services. Purposes are to: provide a forum for the cooperation of the arts, sciences, and technologies with the professions of law, medicine, and education in the study of

human development; promote the research, diagnosis, and remedy of learning and other disabilities; encourage the dissemination of knowledge in all fields of human perception, communication, and behavior. Maintains Diagnostic Learning and Tutorial Center to provide services for individuals with learning handicaps and developmental disabilities, including a Psychophysiological and EEG Research Laboratory. Provides field education placement internships in counseling and school psychology, developmental neuropsychology, and special diagnostic and remedial teaching. Offers children's services, placement and referral services, and rehabilitation services to the elderly and persons with brain and nervous system injuries; compiles statistics. Provides consultation services to clinics, governmental agencies, parent groups, and schools involved in handicapped affairs and education. Sponsors charitable program. Research results and papers presented at national and international meetings.

★ 8260 ★ **Multiple Sclerosis Foundation (MFS)**
6350 N. Andrews Ave.
Fort Lauderdale, FL 33309
Phone: (305)776-6805
Free: 800-441-7055
Fax: (305)938-8708
William Cody Garden, Exec.Dir.

Founded: 1986. **Description:** Provides funding toward research into the cause, prevention, treatment, and cure of multiple sclerosis. Disseminates information on research, referral, and support services, and health-care options. Works to improve the quality of life for individuals with MS. **Publications:** Brochures. • *MS Focus*, quarterly. Newsletter.

★ 8261 ★ **Multiple Sclerosis Society of Zimbabwe**
PO Box CY1177
Causeway
Harare, Zimbabwe
Phone: 4 728156
Fax: 4 794793

Founded: 1972. **Members:** 50. **National Groups:** 1. **State Groups:** 9. **Description:** Works to alleviate the suffering of persons with multiple sclerosis. Supports research to discover the cause of and cure for the disease. Offers financial assistance and counseling to individuals suffering from the disease. **Publications:** *Missive*, monthly. Newsletter.

★ 8262 ★ **Myasthenia Gravis Foundation (MG)**
53 W. Jackson Blvd., Ste. 660
Chicago, IL 60604
Phone: (312)427-6252
Free: 800-541-5454
Fax: (312)427-8437
Anna El-Qudsi, Exec.Dir.

Founded: 1952. **Members:** 30,000. **State Groups:** 50. **Local Groups:** 1. **Description:** Persons suffering from myasthenia gravis; their families, doctors, and nurses; others dedicated to the detection, treatment, and cure of MG. Raises funds for research and for professional and public education programs. Provides literature. Sponsors low-cost prescription service.

Lay and professional materials available upon request. **Publications:** Brochures. • Handbooks. For patients. • Manuals. For physicians and nurses. • Pamphlets.

★ 8263 ★ **Myoclonus Families United (MFU)**
1564 E. 34th St.
Brooklyn, NY 11234
Phone: (718)252-2133
Sharon Dobkin, Pres.

Founded: 1982. **Members:** 30. **Description:** Persons who have or are interested in myoclonus or other movement disorders. Seeks to educate the public and medical profession and to serve as a support group for the families of persons with myoclonus or other movement disorders. Maintains speakers' bureau; compiles statistics on the various types of myoclonus, their onsets, and duration of illness prior to correct diagnosis.

★ 8264 ★ **Narcolepsy Network**
c/o Niss Ryan
PO Box 1365, FDR Sta.
New York, NY 10150
Phone: (914)834-2855
Ms. Niss Ryan, Pres.

Founded: 1986. **Local Groups:** 60. **Description:** Individuals with narcolepsy, their friends and families, sleep professionals, and interested others. Seeks to improve the quality of life of individuals who have narcolepsy. Works to educate members and the general public about narcolepsy. Fosters communication among members. Offers referral service. Supports research; disseminates information. **Publications:** *Narcolepsy: A Guide to Understanding.* • *The Network*, quarterly. Newsletter.

★ 8265 ★ **National Academy of Neuropsychology (NAN)**
University of Colorado Health Sciences Center
University North Pavilion A-011-08
4455 E. 12th Ave., Ste. 129
Denver, CO 80220
Phone: (303)372-3123
Fax: (303)372-3569
C. Munro Cullum, Ph.D., Exec.Sec.

Founded: 1978. **Members:** 1,900. **Description:** Clinical neuropsychologists and others interested in brain-behavior relationships. Works to preserve and advance knowledge regarding the assessment and remediation of neuropsychological disorders. Promotes the development of neuropsychology as a science and profession; develops standards of practice and training guidelines for the field; fosters communication between members; represents the professional interests of members; serves as an information resource; facilitates the exchange of information among related organizations. Offers continuing education programs; conducts research. **Publications:** *Archives of Clinical Neuropsychology*, bimonthly. Journal. *Price:* Included in membership dues; $185/year for nonmember institutions. • *Bulletin of the National Academy of Neuropsychologists*, quarterly. Bulletin. *Price:* Included in membership dues. • Membership Directory, periodic.

National Alliance of Victims of Minamata Disease and Lawyers (NAVMDL)
See: Entry 5049

★ 8266 ★ National Association of Apnea Professionals (NAAP)
PO Box 4031
Waianae, HI 96792
Free: 800-392-2514
Amy Dill-Philips, R.N., Contact

Founded: 1987. **Members:** 325. **Description:** Physicians, nurses, respiratory therapists, social workers, polysomnographers (specialists in sleep studies), and manufacturers and suppliers of apnea monitoring equipment. Seeks to improve communication among apnea professionals and services provided for apnea patients and their families. (Apnea consists of interruptions in breathing of more than 15-20 seconds, usually during sleep.) Focuses on cases found in infants. Gathers scientific and clinical information about causes and treatments of apnea and related sleep disorders. Compiles statistics. **Publications:** *Handbook of Infant Apnea and Home Monitoring*. Handbook. • *NAAP*, quarterly. Newsletter. • *Proceedings of 1992 Summer Conference*. Proceedings.

★ 8267 ★ National Ataxia Foundation (NAF)
750 Twelve Oaks Center
15500 Wayzata Blvd.
Wayzata, MN 55391
Phone: (612)473-7666
Fax: (612)473-9289
Donna Gruetzmacher, Exec.Dir.

Founded: 1957. **Members:** 1,000. **Local Groups:** 32. **Description:** Membership is open to any individual who wishes to contribute to the eradication of ataxia (a genetic disease characterized by the degeneration of the nerves of the spinal cord and the cerebellum, causing a loss of coordination and disturbance in gait and related conditions such as peroneal muscular atrophy, hereditary spastic paraplegia, hereditary tremor, and ataxia telangiectasia. Ataxia may be inherited as a recessive or dominant trait and may strike persons from a very early age up to and even beyond 50 years of age. Ataxia is very similar to multiple sclerosis; however, multiple sclerosis is not inherited and has a different origin.) Objectives are: to make an early diagnosis of ataxia by locating all potential victims and encouraging them to have an examination; to educate the public and the helping professions about ataxia; to initiate basic research and coordinate efforts of worldwide research centers. Emphasis is on locating the genes responsible. Provides services and information to ataxia victims and their families. **Publications:** Brochures. • *Generations*, quarterly. Newsletter. Includes foundation news, calendar of events, and research updates. *Price:* Free to members and those who suffer from ataxia. • *Together. . .We Can*. Video. Also publishes *Together. . .We Can*. (video) and brochures.

★ 8268 ★ National Attention-Deficit Disorder Association (National ADDA)
PO Box 972
Mentor, OH 44061-0972
Free: 800-487-2282
Mary Jane Johnson, Pres.

Founded: 1989. **Description:** Support group for individuals with attention-deficit disorders (ADD); families of children with ADD; and local support groups which want national affiliation.

(ADD is a neurologically based disorder which affects an individual's behavior and learning. The disorder is characterized by deficits in attention span and impulse control, and is often accompanied by hyperactivity.) Seeks to: promote a greater public awareness of the multiple needs of individuals with ADD and their families; address their educational, psychological, and social needs; encourage more responsiveness with regard to ADD in the academic and health care communities. **Publications:** Catalog. Lists books, brochures, momographs, and other materials available for purchasing. • Monographs. • Newsletter. • Pamphlets. **Formerly:** (1992) Attention-Deficit Disorder Association.

★ 8269 ★ National Back Pain Association (NBPA)
16 Elmtree Rd.
Teddington, Greater London TW11 8ST, England
Phone: 181 9775474
Fax: 181 9435318
Mr. G.E. Thomas, Contact

Founded: 1968. **Members:** 3,200. **Local Groups:** 43. **Languages:** English. **Description:** Back pain sufferers, osteopaths, chiropractors, medical doctors, and safety and training officers in 12 countries. Sponsors research on the causes and treatment of back pain. Teaches individuals to use their bodies sensibly in order to prevent spinal damage. Promotes the formation of local branches. Keeps back pain sufferers informed on current developments in research, education, treatment and equipment. **Publications:** *Better Backs for Children*. Brochure. • *Guide to the Handling of Patients*. Third edition. • *Handling Careers Guide*. Manual. • *Lifting and Handling - An Ergonomic Approach*. Brochure. • *TalkBack*, quarterly.

★ 8270 ★ National Brain Injury Research Foundation (NBIRF)
5667 Stone Rd., No. 555
Centreville, VA 22030-1618
Free: 800-447-8445
Julien Dilks, Pres.

Founded: 1987. **Members:** 2,500. **Description:** Conducts research on brain injuries. Sponsors charitable and educational programs. Maintains library and speakers' bureau. Bestows awards. **Publications:** *JMA Bulletin*, semiannual. Bulletin. *Price:* Free to members. • *Journal of Head Injury*, quarterly. Journal. Includes articles on head injury survivors and neurological research; book reviews. *Price:* $20/year. Also publishes brochures.

★ 8271 ★ National Chronic Pain Outreach Association (NCPOA)
7979 Old Georgetown Rd., Ste. 100
Bethesda, MD 20814-2429
Phone: (301)652-4948
Fax: (301)907-0745

Founded: 1976. **Members:** 1,000. **Description:** Disseminates information about chronic pain and its management in an effort to lessen the suffering caused by chronic pain. Operates information clearinghouse for pain sufferers, family members, and health care professionals. Provides a Support Group Starter Kit to encourage the formation of local chronic pain support

groups. Provides referrals to NCPOA member health care providers and facilities; also provides referrals to chronic pain support groups. Maintains library. **Publications:** Audiotapes. • Booklets. • Brochures. • *Lifeline*, quarterly. Newsletter. Includes pain management information and book reviews. *Price:* Available to members only. • Pamphlets.

★ 8272 ★ National Coalition for Research in Neurological Disorders (NCR)
1250 24th St. NW, Ste. 600
Washington, DC 20037
Phone: (202)293-5453
Fax: (202)466-2888
Morgan Downey, Exec.Dir.

Founded: 1952. **Members:** 57. **Description:** Represents voluntary health agencies and professional societies concerned with obtaining funds for neurological research. Seeks to stimulate public information regarding the field of neurological disorders. Lobbies for increased funding for training and research in neurological disorders. **Publications:** *NCR News*, quarterly. **Formerly:** National Committee for Research in Neurological Disorders; (1988) National Committee for Research in Neruological and Communicative Disorders; (1989) National Coalition for Research in Neurological and Communicative Disorders.

★ 8273 ★ National Committee on the Treatment of Intractable Pain (NCTIP)
c/o Wayne Coy, Jr.
Cohn and Marks
1333 New Hampshire Ave. NW
Washington, DC 20036
Phone: (202)452-4836
Fax: (202)293-4827
Wayne Coy, Jr., Pres.

Founded: 1977. **Members:** 3,500. **Description:** Individuals promoting education and research into more effective methods of pain prevention and control with the coordinated help of professionals in the medical, legal, bioethical, psychological, and religious fields. Endorses the British hospice concept of care of the dying, which allows the dying person to remain among family, friends, community, and skilled professionals and provides constant, effective medical and psychological support for pain control. Advocates legalization of heroin for medical purposes. Plans to sponsor speakers' bureau. **Publications:** Monographs. • *Newsletter of the National Committee on the Treatment of Intractable Pain*, annual. Newsletter. Covers concern generated by the use of medication to relieve intractable pain caused by cancer, specifically the effort to legalize heroin. *Price:* Free. • Reports. **Formerly:** (1977) American Intractable Pain Foundation.

★ 8274 ★ National Foundation for Brain Research (NFBR)
1250 24th St. NW, Ste. 300
Washington, DC 20037
Phone: (202)293-5453
Fax: (202)466-2888
Lawrence S. Hoffheimer, M.D., Exec.Dir.

Description: Promotes the prevention and cure of disorders and diseases of the brain. Supports brain research. Collects, organizes, and disseminates information relating to the Decade of the Brain (the years 1990-2000, which were so designated by United States Congress and President George Bush to acknowledge the importance of neurological and mental research). Maintains the Decade of the Brain Coalition which strives to achieve by the end of the decade a large increase in federal funding for research on the brain. Seeks to increase public awareness of the importance of brain research through sponsoring educational symposia, the distribution of reports and pamphlets, and the organization of traveling museum exhibits. Provides educational programs for professionals. **Publications:** *Decade of the Brain News*, quarterly. Newsletter.

★ 8275 ★ **National Head Injury Foundation (NHIF)**
1776 Massachusetts Ave. NW, Ste. 100
Washington, DC 20036
Phone: (202)296-6443
Free: 800-444-6443
Fax: (202)296-8850
George Zitnay, Ph.D, Pres.& CEO

Founded: 1980. **Members:** 25,000. **State Groups:** 45. **Local Groups:** 400. **Description:** Individuals with traumatic brain injury and their families and friends; professionals working in head injury treatment and rehabilitation. Works to improve the quality of life for people with brain injury and their families, and to promote the prevention of brain injury through education, information provision, advocacy and support activities, and research. Serves as a national clearinghouse on brain injury and related issues; compiles statistics. **Publications:** *An Educator's Manual: What Educators Need to Know About Students with Head Injury*. Manual. • *Analysis, Understanding and Presentation of Cases involving TBI*. • Handbook. *Price:* $200. • *National Directory of Head Injury Rehabilitation Services*, annual. Directory. *Price:* $45. • *National Head Injury Foundation--Catalogue of Educational Materials*, annual. Catalog. Includes listings of books, articles, videotapes, audiocassette tapes, booklets, and other materials on head injury available through NHIF. *Price:* Free. • *TBI Challenge!*, quarterly. Newsletter. *Price:* Included in membership dues. • *Why Did It Happen on a School Day?*.

★ 8276 ★ **National Headache Foundation (NHF)**
5252 N. Western Ave.
Chicago, IL 60625
Phone: (312)878-7715
Free: 800-843-2256
Fax: (312)907-6278
Seymour Diamond, M.D., Exec.Dir.

Founded: 1970. **Members:** 20,000. **Description:** Disseminates information on headache causes and treatment, funds scientific studies, and promotes better public understanding of headache problems. Is establishing nationwide network of local support groups. **Publications:** *National Headache Foundation--Newsletter*, quarterly. Newsletter. Includes information headache causes and treatments, foundation news, book reviews, research reports, support group updates, and reader Q&A. *Price:* Included in membership dues. **Formerly:** (1986) National Migraine Foundation.

★ 8277 ★ **National Hydrocephalus Foundation (NHF)**
22427 S. River Rd.
Joliet, IL 60436
Phone: (815)467-6548
Linda Mazzetti, Treas.

Founded: 1979. **Members:** 500. **Description:** Persons with hydrocephalus, their families, and concerned individuals. (Hydrocephalus is the buildup of fluid in the brain cavities; if left untreated, the condition can lead to brain damage and death.) Goals are to: familiarize the public with hydrocephalus and eliminate stigma associated with the disease; define and help resolve specific problems that parents of children with hydrocephalus encounter; collect and disseminate information pertaining to hydrocephalus and inform parents of the educational rights of these children. Conducts symposia with physicians in the field of hydrocephalus aimed at informing parents. Compiles statistics. **Publications:** *An Introduction to Hydrocephalus*. Video. • Brochure. • *Hydrocephalus News and Notes*, quarterly. Newsletter. *Price:* Included in membership dues. • *Parents' Guide to Hydrocephalus*. • *Survey on Hydrocephalus*. Survey. Statistics on hydrocephalus types and related side affects. **Formerly:** (1984) Know Problems of Hydrocephalus.

★ 8278 ★ **National Multiple Sclerosis Society (NMSS)**
733 3rd Ave.
New York, NY 10017
Phone: (212)986-3240
Free: 800-FIGHT-MS
Fax: (212)986-7981
Gen. Michael Dugan, Pres. & CEO

Founded: 1946. **Members:** 470,000. **Description:** Stimulates, supports, and coordinates research into the cause, treatment, and cure of multiple sclerosis; provides services for persons with MS and related diseases and their families; aids in establishing MS clinics and therapy centers. Conducts Project Rembrandt, biennial competition for artists with MS. Maintains numerous committees including international and research and medical programs, and services. Maintains speakers' bureau; compiles statistics. **Publications:** *Inside MS*, 3/year. Magazine. Contains book reviews, research updates, legislative updates, and annual report. *Price:* Included in membership dues. **Formerly:** (1947) Association for Advancement of Research on Multiple Sclerosis.

★ 8279 ★ **National Organization for Apraxia and Dyspraxia**
32507 Cervin Cir.
Temecula, CA 92592
Phone: (909)695-9446
Fax: (909)695-9446
Vicci Hazelwood, CEO

Founded: 1994. **Description:** People having the neurological disorders Apraxia and Dyspraxia; researchers, students, physicians, speech pathologists, therapists, and interested others. Strives to create a complete database containing all available information and research on these disorders. Maintains national support group for people with the disorders and their families.

★ 8280 ★ **National Parkinson Foundation (NPF)**
1501 NW 9th Ave.
Miami, FL 33136
Phone: (305)547-6666
Fax: (305)548-4403
Nathan Slewett, Chairperson

Founded: 1957. **Description:** Doctors, nurses, scientists, pharmacologists, and therapists who research, diagnose, and treat Parkinsonism. Supports basic and clinical research for Parkinsonism and related neurological disorders and provides physical, speech, and occupational therapy. NPF is associated with the University of Miami School of Medicine, and supports the National Parkinson Institute, which provides diagnosis, treatment, care, and rehabilitation. Conducts educational programs. Distributes literature to medical libraries, nurses training schools, health clinics, physicians, and patients. Sponsors regional patient self-support groups where problems are discussed and experiences are exchanged under guidance of physicians, social workers, and psychologists. Maintains offices at 122 E. 42nd St., New York, NY 10017 and 4929 Wilshire Blvd., Los Angeles, CA 90010. **Publications:** *How to Start and Run a Support Group*. • *Membership List*, periodic. • *The Parkinson Handbook*. • *Parkinson Report*, quarterly. Newsletter. Contains research reports. *Price:* Included in membership dues; Available free of charge to others upon request. Also publishes other books and brochures.

★ 8281 ★ **National Sleep Foundation**
1367 Connecticut Ave. NW, Ste. 200
Washington, DC 20036
Phone: (202)785-2300
Fax: (202)785-2880
Allan I. Pack, M.D., Medical Dir.

Founded: 1990. **Description:** Works to improve the quality of life of people suffering from sleep disorders and to prevent accidents related to sleep disorders. (Sleep disorders include: insomnia, narcolepsy, sleep apnea syndrome, sudden infant death syndrome, stroke, epilepsy, and other disorders of sleep and daytime alertness.) Educates health care professionals and the public about the existance and treatment of sleep disorders. Promotes the development of patient services, community resources, and support groups for individuals affected by sleep disorders. Sponsors educational and research programs. **Publications:** Brochures.

★ 8282 ★ **National Spasmodic Dysphonia Association (NSDA)**
PO Box 1574
Birmingham, MI 48009-1574
Phone: (810)646-6885
Free: 800-714-6732
Fax: (810)645-9352
Lawrence F. Kolasa, Pres.

Founded: 1990. **Local Groups:** 75. **Description:** Individuals diagnosed with spasmodic dysphonia; doctors and scientists providing treatment and conducting research on the disease; interested others. Promotes public awareness of spasmodic dysphonia and the care, welfare, and rehabilitation of those with the disease. (Spasmodic dysphonia is a neurological movement disorder affecting muscular control of the vocal cords, often resulting in an abnormally raspy, breathy, or choppy speech pattern.) Makes information on the disease available to patients, their families, and the public. Encourages research to uncover the causes and treatments of spasmodic dysphonia; offers referral information on specialists administering the botulinum toxin (Botox) presently used in many cases to temporarily treat the disease. Assists in the formation of local support groups to assist patients. **Publications:** *NSDA Report*, quarterly. Newsletter.

★ 8283 ★ National Spasmodic Torticollis Association (NSTA)
PO Box 476
Elm Grove, WI 53122
Phone: (414)797-9912
Free: 800-HUR-TFUL
Fax: (414)797-9861
Howard Thiel, Executive Dir.

Founded: 1980. **Members:** 3,200. **Local Groups:** 48. **Description:** Persons afflicted with spasmodic torticollis (ST), a syndrome in which the muscles on one side of the neck contract and pull the head to the side, sometimes pushing the chin up or down. ST usually occurs in adults and can sometimes be treated successfully with medication and physical therapy. Educates the public on ST so that persons with early symptoms know to seek proper medical help from a neurologist or neurosurgeon. Provides forum for discussion among ST sufferers and their families in order to share information and experiences and diminish feelings of alienation and self-conciousness. **Publications:** *NSTA Newsletter*, quarterly. Newsletter. Includes medical advisor's column. *Price:* Included in membership dues. • *Physicians Referral Directory*, annual. Directory. Lists neurologists who treat spasmodic torticollis. *Price:* Free. • *What is NSTA?*. Also publishes fact sheet. **Formerly:** Project S.T..

★ 8284 ★ National Spinal Cord Injury Association (NSCIA)
545 Concord Ave., No. 29
Cambridge, MA 02138-1122
Phone: (617)441-8500
Free: 800-962-9629
Fax: (617)441-3449
Janna Jacobs, Exec.Dir.

Founded: 1948. **Members:** 9,000. **Local Groups:** 60. **Description:** Seeks to inform and educate the medical and allied professions, persons with spinal cord injury or disease, their families, and the public on spinal cord injury. Carries out activities in 3 major fields: support of research toward a cure for paralysis from spinal cord injury; public and professional prevention and education programs and services; assistance to individuals to reach their personal goals. Sponsors In Touch With Kids, a network for parents of children with spinal cord injury or disease. Conducts recreation, advocacy, support group, and peer counseling programs. Maintains placement service; offers information and referral service. **Publications:** *National Spinal Cord Injury Association Resource Directory: An Information Guide for Persons with Spinal Cord Injury and Other Physical Disabilities*, periodic. Directory. *Price:* Included in membership

dues; $20/year for nonmembers. • *NSCIA Directory*, annual. Directory. • *Options: Spinal Cord Injury and the Future*. • *Spinal Cord Injury Life*, quarterly. Journal. Provides news and articles concerning persons with spinal cord injuries caused by trauma or disease. Includes book reviews. *Price:* Included in membership dues; $30/year subscription. Also publishes fact sheets on research, sexuality and other topics. **Formerly:** National Spinal Cord Injury Foundation; (1979) National Paraplegia Foundation.

★ 8285 ★ National Stroke Association (NSA)
8480 E. Orchard Rd., Ste. 1000
Englewood, CO 80111
Phone: (303)771-1700
Free: 800-STR-OKES
Fax: (303)771-1886
James J. Lannon, Exec.Dir.

Founded: 1984. **Members:** 72,000. **State Groups:** 8. **Description:** Stroke survivors and their families; health care professionals and institutions; the lay community. Seeks to reduce the incidence and impact of stroke by promoting research, educating the public, and providing a network for stroke survivors and concerned persons. Serves as an information referral clearinghouse on stroke; makes available educational materials on stroke prevention, treatment, rehabilitation, resocialization, and research. Offers guidance in the development of stroke support groups and clubs. Maintains speakers' bureau and Stroke Information and Referral Center; compiles statistics. Conducts educational symposiums/meetings. **Publications:** Articles. • *Be Stroke Smart*, quarterly. Newsletter. *Price:* Free. • Booklets. • Brochures. • *Journal of Stroke and Cerebravascular Diseases*, quarterly. Journal. *Price:* $80/year for individual; $115/year for institution. • Pamphlet. • *The Road Ahead: A Stroke Recovery Guide*. Book. • *State Listing of Stroke Clubs*, periodic. Directory. • *Stroke: Clinical Updates*, bimonthly. Newsletter. professional newsletter with available slides. *Price:* Free.

National Tay-Sachs and Allied Diseases Association (NTSAD)
See: Entry 4865

★ 8286 ★ National Vascular Malformations Foundation
8320 Nightingale
Dearborn Heights, MI 48127
Phone: (313)274-1243
Mary P. Burris, Pres./Founder

Founded: 1990. **Members:** 300. **Description:** Vascular malformation patients and their families. (Vascular malformations are tumors or flat lesions made up of abnormally sized blood vessels and include such conditions as port wine stains, hemangiomas, arteriovenous malformations (AVMs), and Sturge-Weber Syndrome.) Provides support and information to patients and medical professionals. Collects information on vascular malformations, specialist doctors, and reference sources. Conducts fundraising for research activities; maintains speakers' bureau. **Publications:** Pamphlets.Information on doctors, support groups, treatments. *Price:* Free.

Neuro-developmental Treatment Association (NDTA)
See: Entry 12703

★ 8287 ★ Neurofibromatosis, Inc. (NF)
8855 Annapolis Rd., Ste. 110
Lanham, MD 20706-2924
Phone: (301)577-8984
Free: 800-942-6825
Fax: (301)577-0016
Michael Flamingo, Pres.

Founded: 1988. **Regional Groups:** 9. **Description:** Organizations providing support for individuals with neurofibromatosis (NF) and their families, physicians, and other health care providers. (NF is a genetic neurological disorder that can cause tumors to form on nerves and is linked to learning disabilities, hearing loss, vision impairment, epilepsy, and cancer.) Increases public awareness of NF through information dissemination; informs federal, state, and local legislators of the needs of NF families. Promotes, supports, and funds medical, clinical, educational, and sociological research that addresses the need to diagnose, treat, cure, and prevent NF. Identifies local NF support and peer counseling groups; offers referrals to medical resources and scientifically-evaluated research. Participates in networking of voluntary health organizations; operates pen pal service for deafened adults. **Publications:** Booklets. • *Neurofibromatosis Ink*, periodic. Newsletter. Includes research summaries, reports, chapter news, and symposia information.

★ 8288 ★ Neuromuscular Diseases Association of Romania
Institute of Neurology
C.P. 61-42
75622 Bucharest, Romania
Phone: 1 6756273
Dr. C. Vasilescu

Description: Promotes interest in neuromuscular diseases research among medical and scientific communities and the public in Romania. Disseminates information about the diseases.

Neurosurgical Society of America (NSA)
See: Entry 12292

★ 8289 ★ New Zealand Pain Society (NZPS)
Dept. of Anaesthesia
Waikato Hospital
Hamilton, New Zealand
Phone: 7 8398899
Fax: 7 8398799
Dr. Steve Jones, Sec.

Founded: 1983. **Members:** 238. **Languages:** English. **Description:** Health professionals and scientists interested in pain research and management. Works to improve the management of pain. Encourages research into pain mechanisms and pain syndromes; recommends the adoption of a uniform classification, nomenclature, and definition of pain and pain syndromes; advises national and regional agencies on standards relating to the use of drugs, appliances, and procedures in the therapy of pain; promotes education and training in pain management; facilitates information dissemination. Conducts lectures and workshops. Formerly a section of the Australasian Pain Society. **Publications:** *Di-*

rectory, annual. Directory. • *New Zealand Pain Society Newsletter*, 3/year. Newsletter.

★8290★ North American Spine Society (NASS)
6300 N. River Rd., 4th Fl.
Rosemont, IL 60018
Phone: (708)698-1630
Fax: (708)823-0536
Eric J. Muehlbauer, Exec.Dir.

Founded: 1985. **Members:** 1,100. **Description:** Educational organization of physicians, osteopaths, orthopedists, neurosurgeons, physiatrists, radiologists, and other professionals interested in the human spine. Works to improve the quality of scientific practice in spinal disorders; exchange ideas and disseminate scientific information about clinical techniques; investigate and propagate methods by which malfunction of the spine can be corrected. Makes inquiries into practice characteristics, language usage and terminology, and treatment methods. **Publications:** *NASS News*, quarterly. Newsletter. Contains news on association activities. • *Spine Journal*, monthly. Journal.

★8291★ Norway Multiple Sclerosis Society (NMSS)
(Multipel Sklerose Forbundet i Norge — MSFN)
Sorkedalsveien 3
N-0369 Oslo, Norway
Phone: 22 604960
Fax: 22 567695
Mrs. Gerd Hagen, Contact

Founded: 1961. **Members:** 5,000. **Regional Groups:** 45. **Languages:** English. **Description:** Promotes interest in multiple sclerosis research among medical and scientific communities and the public in Norway. Facilitates exchange of information among members. **Publications:** Books. • *MS-bladet*, 5/year. Magazine. • Pamphlets.

★8292★ Norwegian Association for Huntington's Disease (NAHD)
(Landsforening for Huntingtons Sykdom — LHS)
Damveien 23
N-0587 Oslo 5, Norway
Phone: 22222374
Tor Jenssen, Exec. Officer

Founded: 1980. **Members:** 350. **Local Groups:** 7. **Languages:** English, Norwegian. **Description:** Persons with Huntington's chorea and their families. Conducts seminars. **Publications:** *Tidsskrift for Huntingtons Sykdom*, quarterly. Magazine. Also publishes booklets and leaflets.

★8293★ Norwegian Epilepsy Association (NEA)
(Norsk Epilepsiforbund — NEF)
Kr. Augustsgate 19
N-0164 Oslo 1, Norway
Phone: 2 206021
Fax: 2 115976
Eva H. Johnson, Sec.

Founded: 1974. **Members:** 4,500. **Regional Groups:** 4. **Local Groups:** 85. **Languages:** English, Norwegian. **Description:** Disseminates information to individuals with epilepsy and their families, health care centers, hospitals, and schools. Collaborates with related groups. Bestows awards. **Publications:** *Epilepsy News*, quarterly. Also publishes brochures (in Norwegian).

★8294★ Norwegian Parkinson Association (NPA)
(Norges Parkinsonforbund — NPF)
Schweigaardsgt 34, F.1
N-0191 Oslo 1, Norway
Phone: 22 175861
Fax: 22 175862
Asbjorn Hanssen, Pres.

Founded: 1984. **Members:** 3,300. **National Groups:** 1. **Regional Groups:** 17. **Local Groups:** 13. **Languages:** English. **Description:** Parkinson patients and their relatives. Teaches patients about their disease and how to deal with the related problems. Represents members' interests in matters of social and health politics. Supports research efforts; conducts educational seminars. Offers lectures. **Publications:** *Ergoterapy*. Booklet. • *Hjemmeovelser*. Booklet. • *Hva er NPF?*. • *Informasjon om Fylkesforeninger*. • *Parkinsonposten Magazine*, quarterly. Newsletter. • *Parkinsons Sykdom*. Booklet.

★8295★ Pain Concern—U.K.
PO Box 318
Canterbury, Kent CT4 5DP, England
Phone: 1227 264677
Rosalie Everatt, Coordinator

Founded: 1988. **Local Groups:** 3. **Languages:** English. **Description:** Pain sufferers. Offers group support and counseling for people suffering from chronic pain. (Acute pain has an identifiable cause and can be treated; chronic pain also has a known cause, but it cannot be cured.) Seeks ways of enhancing the individual's ability to stimulate production of the body's natural pain killers (endorphins). Offers educational program to raise public awareness of pain sufferers. Conducts research. **Publications:** *Self Help Pain Management*, periodic. Magazine.

★8296★ Pan-African Association of Neurological Sciences (PAANS)
(Association Pan-Africaine des Sciences Neurologiques — PAANS)
PO Box 20413
Nairobi, Kenya
Phone: 2 722487
Fax: 2 725776
Prof. R. F. Ruberti, Exec. Officer

Founded: 1972. **Members:** 250. **Languages:** English, French. **Description:** African neurologists specializing in neurosurgery, neuroradiology, neuropathology, neurophysiology, neurobiochemistry, and other branches of neuroscience; non-African neurologists maintaining connections with Africa. Furthers neurological sciences and encourages the exchange of ideas and information among neurologists in Africa and worldwide. Strives to acquaint the public and interested laymen with current developments in neuroscience. Conducts epidemiological research. **Publications:** *African Journal of Neurological Sciences*, semiannual. Journal. Contains information on neurology, neurosur-gery, and neurosciencec. • *Pan African Association of Neurological Sciences Rules.*

★8297★ Parkinson Support Groups of America (PSGA)
11376 Cherry Hill Rd., No. 204
Beltsville, MD 20705
Phone: (301)937-1545
Ida M. Raitano, Pres.

Founded: 1981. **Members:** 150. **Description:** Selfhelp groups whose members are Parkinson's disease patients and their relatives and friends. To provide encouragement, companionship, physical therapy, and counseling; to offer programs and activities to aid Parkinsonians in sustaining and improving the quality of their lives and the lives of their families and friends. Seeks to define needs of support groups and their members; makes recommendations and supplies resources necessary for satisfying such needs; encourages research into the causes and treatment of Parkinson's disease. Works to educate Parkinsonians and the public on the importance of activity for Parkinsonians. Promotes state and national legislative and administrative efforts of benefit to Parkinsonians. Plans regional advisory groups, seminars, and symposia with health care professionals; sponsors speakers' bureau. Facilitates exchange of information among Parkinson's patients and health care professionals. Is in the process of establishing a library. Maintains ad hoc committees on Enactment of National Commission on Parkinson's Disease and Continuing and Expanding Training for Care Providers of Parkinson Patients. **Publications:** *PSGA Update*, bimonthly. Newsletter.

★8298★ Parkinson's Disease Foundation (PDF)
William Black Medical Research Bldg.
Columbia-Presbyterian Medical Center
650 W. 168th St.
New York, NY 10032
Phone: (212)923-4700
Free: 800-457-6676
Fax: (212)923-4778
Lewis P. Rowland, M.D., Pres.

Founded: 1957. **Members:** 85,000. **Local Groups:** 400. **Description:** Raises funds for support of scientific research into causes, prevention, and cure of Parkinson's disease. Supports its own laboratories for research in Parkinsonism. Prepares and distributes information on patient care and rehabilitation including list of clinics where treatment is available, and a list of patient selfhelp groups. Supports a brain bank to permit anatomical and chemical studies. Sponsors scientific symposia. Offers patient and family counseling and advocacy services. Conducts training programs. Maintains research advisory board. Sponsors summer fellowship program for predoctoral stu dents. **Publications:** Booklets. • Brochures. • *Exercises for the Parkinson Patient and Hints for Daily Living. Price:* $10. • *Health Care Manual for the Professional Team. Price:* $10. • *PDF Newsletter*, 3-4/year. Newsletter. Covers developments in Parkinson's disease research, hints for daily living, and advice to health care professionals. Includes case studies. *Price:* Free. • *Progress, Promise, and Hope: The Parkinson Patient at Home. Price:* $10.

★ 8299 ★ **Parkinson's Educational Program—U.S.A. (PEP/USA)**
3900 Birch St., No. 105
Newport Beach, CA 92660
Phone: (714)250-2975
Free: 800-344-7872
Fax: (714)250-8530
Charlotte Jayne, Exec.Dir.
Founded: 1982. **Local Groups:** 500. **Description:** Serves as a clearinghouse for information on Parkinson's disease, syndrome, and parkinsonism. Assists in establishing local support groups throughout the U.S. Maintains information exchange program in 32 countries. Seeks to inform and educate the public and professionals about parkinsonism. Supports research on the cause and cure of parkinsonism. Compiles statistics; maintains speakers' bureau. **Publications:** Audiotapes. Of speakers. • Booklets. • *PEP EXCHANGE: The Parkinson's Educational Program Newsletter by and for People with Parkinson's, Their Family and Friends*, monthly. Newsletter. Includes book reviews. *Price:* $25. • *Physicians Referral List*, monthly. • Videos. Also publishes list of Parkinson's support groups.

★ 8300 ★ **Reflex Sympathetic Dystrophy Association (RSDSA)**
PO Box 821
Haddonfield, NJ 08033
Phone: (609)795-8845
Fax: (609)795-8845
Nelson Hendler, MD, Chm.
Founded: 1984. **Members:** 2,300. **Local Groups:** 100. **Description:** People with Reflex Sympathetic Dystrophy Syndrome; health care professionals treating RSDS patients. (RSDS is a disorder of the autonomic nervous system whose onset is usually preceded by a minor trauma such as a muscle sprain; symptoms of RSDS include severe pain, loss of muscle motion and use, swelling, skin and nail changes, and softening of the bones in affected areas.) Promotes increased awareness of RSDS among health care professionals and the public; conducts media campaigns; maintains national network of physicians involved in RSDS treatment and research. Encourages and supports RSDS research; has a national data bank for the coordination of RSDS research and treatment information. Aids in the formation of support groups for people with RSDS; develops in-service programs and seminars for use at hospitals and educational institutions. Makes available referral services. Conducts educational programs; maintains speakers' bureau; compiles statistics. **Publications:** *Help Us to Stop the Pain*. Brochure. • Newsletter, quarterly. *Price:* Included in membership dues. • *RSDS Digest*, annual. Lists articles published in America and Canada and foreign articles from the previous year. *Price:* $6 for members; $12 for non-members. Also publishes fact sheets.

★ 8301 ★ **Romanian Society of Clinical Neurophysiology (RSCN) (Societatea Romana de Neurofiziologie Clinica)**
Neurological Clinic
Soseaua Berceni 10-12
Bucharest, Romania
Phone: 1 3214924
Fax: 1 3112787
Dr. Aurora Constantinovici, Pres.
Founded: 1952. **Members:** 40. **Local Groups:** 5. **Languages:** English, French. **Description:** Scientists, physicians, and professors united to develop the electrophysiologic investigation of neurological diseases. Conducts basic and clinical research. Organizes symposia, lectures, and EEG, EMG, and Evoked Potentials demonstrations. **Publications:** *Neurologia*, semiannual. Journal. • *Revue Roumaine de Physiologie*, periodic. • *Romanian Journal of Neurology and Psychiatry*, quarterly. Journal. • *Romanian Neurosurgery*. **Formerly:** (1993) Romanian Society of Clinical Neurophysiology.

★ 8302 ★ **Scandinavian Neurological Association (SNA) (Nordisk Neurologisk Forening — NNF)**
Department of Neurology
University of Helsinki
SF-00290 Helsinki, Finland
Phone: 0 4712261
Fax: 0 4714009
Prof. J. Palo, Pres.
Founded: 1922. **Members:** 5. **Languages:** Danish, English, Finnish, Icelandic, Norwegian, Swedish. **Description:** Scandinavian national societies representing 900 neurologists and other specialists with an interest in neuroscience. Promotes neurological research and cooperation among Scandinavian neurologists. Provides educational counseling. **Publications:** *Congress Abstracts*, biennial. Proceedings.

★ 8303 ★ **Scandinavian Neurosurgical Society (SNS) (Nordisk Neurokirurgisk Forening — NNF)**
Dept. of Neurosurgery
Universitetssjukhuset
S-901 85 Umea, Sweden
Phone: 90 101000
Fax: 90 122448
Dr. Joran Algert, Contact
Founded: 1945. **Members:** 160. **Languages:** English. **Description:** Scandinavian neurosurgeons and neurosurgical residents; practicing neurosurgeons outside of Scandinavia. Works to facilitate collaboration among Scandinavian neurosurgeons.

★ 8304 ★ **Scottish Motor Neurone Disease Association**
50 Parnie St.
Glasgow G1 5LS, Scotland
Phone: 141 5520507
Fax: 141 5526209
Anne Jarvis, Contact
Founded: 1981. **Members:** 600. **Regional Groups:** 14. **Description:** Promotes interest in motor neurone disease (MND) research among medical and scientific communities and the public in Scotland. Offers support services to MND sufferers and their families. Disseminates information about the disease. **Publications:** Newsletter, 3/year.

★ 8305 ★ **Sleep Research Society (SRS)**
c/o Wallace Mendelson
Cleveland Clinic S-83
Dept. of Neurology
9500 Euclid Ave.
Cleveland, OH 44195
Phone: (216)444-8275
Fax: (216)445-7471
Dr. Adrian Morrison, Pres.
Founded: 1961. **Members:** 600. **Description:** Physiologists, psychologists, and physicians with research interests in the study of sleep. Disseminates scientific papers on the physiological and psychological aspects of sleep. Facilitates communication among research workers in this field, but does not sponsor research investigations on its own. **Publications:** Books. • Catalogs. • *Sleep*, bimonthly. Journal. Includes book reviews and bibliography of recent literature. *Price:* Included in membership dues; $104/year for nonmembers; $138/year to institutions. • *Sleep Research Society--Sleep Research*, annual. Monograph. Series containing author and keyword-in-context index. *Price:* Included in membership dues. **Formerly:** (1983) Association for the Psychophysiological Study of Sleep.

★ 8306 ★ **Slovak Society of Clinical Neurophysiology**
Derer Hospital
Limbova 5
SK-833 05 Bratislava, Slovakia
Phone: 7 371141
Fax: 7 373708
Peter Kukumberg, M.D., Contact
Languages: English, Slovak. **Description:** Neurologists, neurosurgeons, and other health care professionals with an interest in neurophysiology. Promotes continued professional advancement of members; represents members' interests.

★ 8307 ★ **Slovak Society of Neurology**
Hospital Ruzinov
Ruzinovska 6
SK-826 06 Bratislava, Slovakia
Phone: 7 233248
Fax: 7 236433
Peter Spalek, M.D., Contact
Languages: English, Slovak. **Description:** Neurologists. Works to improve the treatment of neuromuscular diseases, and to advance the professional standing of members. Represents members' interests.

Society of Neurological Surgeons (SNS)
See: Entry 12306

★ 8308 ★ **Society for Neuroscience**
11 Dupont Cir. NW, Ste. 500
Washington, DC 20036
Phone: (202)462-6688
Nancy Beang, Exec.Dir.
Founded: 1969. **Members:** 23,000. **Local Groups:** 104. **Description:** Scientists engaged in research relating to the nervous system. Seeks to advance understanding of nervous

systems, including their relation to behavior, by bringing together scientists of various backgrounds and by facilitating research at all levels of biological organization. Maintains central source of information on interdisciplinary curricula and training programs in the neurosciences. Produces nontechnical reports on the results and implications of current research. **Publications:** *Abstracts Volume*, annual. Contains neuroscience-related abstracts written by members. *Price:* Included in membership dues; $34 for nonmembers. • *Brain Briefings*. Brochures. • *Brain Concepts*. Brochures. • *Brain Facts*. Booklet. A primer on the brain and nervous system. • *The Journal of Neuroscience*, monthly. Journal. • Membership Directory, annual. • *Neuroscience Newsletter*, bimonthly. Newsletter. *Price:* Included in membership dues; $50/year for nonmembers. • *Neuroscience Training Programs in North America*, biennial.

★8309★ Society of Neurosurgical Anesthesia and Critical Care (SNACC)
PO Box 1502
Midlothian, VA 23113-1502
Phone: (804)379-5513
Fax: (804)379-1386
Kimberly R. Roberts, CPA, Exec.Dir.

Founded: 1973. **Members:** 500. **Description:** Neurosurgeons and anesthesiologists interested in the care of patients with neurological disorders. Sponsors continuing medical education and research concerning the care of neurosurgical patients. **Publications:** *Annual Summary of Society Meeting Proceedings*, annual. Proceedings. • *Comprehensive Bibliography in Neuroanesthesia*, semiannual. Bibliography. • *Course Book*, annual. Book. • Newsletter, 3-4/year. • *Society Membership*, annual.

Society for Research into Hydrocephalus and Spina Bifida (SRHSB)
See: Entry 2754

★8310★ Spanish ALS Association (ADELA)
(Association Espanola de ELA)
Apartado Correos 40030
E-28080 Madrid, Spain
Phone: 1 3141010
Fax: 1 7336614
Nieves Rodriguez, Dir.

Description: Promotes interest in amyotrophic lateral sclerosis or ALS (also called Lou Gehrig's disease) research among medical and scientific communities and the public in Spain. Offers support services to ALS sufferers and their families. Disseminates information about the disease. **Publications:** *Adela Informa*, quarterly. Bulletin.

Spina Bifida Association of America (SBAA)
See: Entry 2755

★8311★ Spinal Cord Society (SCS)
Wendell Rd.
Fergus Falls, MN 56537
Phone: (218)739-5252
Fax: (218)739-5262
Dr. Charles E. Carson, Pres.

Founded: 1978. **Members:** 9,000. **Local Groups:** 170. **Description:** Spinal cord injury

victims and their friends and families; physicians, nurses, physical and rehabilitation therapists, and other medical professionals. Purposes are to promote research and increase public awareness concerning the potential for a cure of paralysis due to spinal cord injury. Focuses on the cure rather than rehabilitation for paralysis due to spinal injury. Promotes funding of reversal-oriented pure and applied medical research; encourages establishment of spinal injury centers in conjunction with existing hospitals and medical centers; maintains data bank of chronic spinal cord injury case histories, continuously monitored and upgraded for improving treatment, guiding research, and screening patients for referral to other physician s or to a spinal injury center. Through concentration on research, data, and treatment, seeks to provide a base of information, statistical analysis, and experience, with accelerated progress and minimal duplication of effort. Maintains medical center in Minneapolis, MN that applies state-of-art treatment to paralysis victims. **Publications:** *Spinal Cord Society Newsletter*, monthly. Newsletter. Includes convention news, letters, and information on services. *Price:* $30/year.

★8312★ Spinal Injuries Association (SIA)
Newpoint House
76 St. James's Ln.
London N1O 3DF, England
Phone: 181 4442121
Fax: 181 4443761
Stephen Bradshaw, Exec.Dir.

Founded: 1974. **Members:** 6,500. **Local Groups:** 10. **Languages:** English. **Description:** Selfhelp group operated by and for people with spinal cord injuries. Provides assistance through: an information service that answers member queries on all aspects of daily life following a spinal cord injury; a welfare service that sorts out problems and ongoing difficulties; a personal assistance service that arranges temporary or permanent help in the home; a personal injury claims service that gives legal support; a telephone counseling service. Has established holiday facilities that offer accessible accommodations. Conducts lobbying activities. **Publications:** Pamphlets. • *Politics of Disablement*. • *SIA Newsletter*, quarterly. Newsletter. • *So You're Paralysed*. • *Spinal Cord Injuries: Guidance for General Practitioners*. • *Your Rights to Housing and Support*.

★8313★ Stichting ALS Onderzoekfonds
Joos van Clevelaan 8
NL-3723 PG Bilthoven, Netherlands
Phone: 30 280346
Fax: 30 533665
Eric Trietsch, Contact

Founded: 1981. **Description:** Individuals interested in amyotropic lateral sclerosis or ALS (also known as Lou Gehrig's Disease). Works to: heighten public awareness and understanding of the disease; encourage research among medical and scientific communities. Sponsors researchers.

★8314★ Stroke Clubs, International (SCI)
805 12th St.
Galveston, TX 77550
Phone: (409)762-1022
Ellis Williamson, Pres.

Founded: 1968. **Members:** 45,000. **Description:** Active members are stroke victims; associate members are individuals interested in the problems of stroke victims. To unite stroke victims for the purpose of aiding each other; to instruct them and their families regarding the nature of stroke and the means for overcoming the resulting handicaps; to aid them in finding employment; and to give the stroke victim hope and encouragement. At monthly meetings, qualified speakers discuss the medical aspects of strokes and member stroke victims discuss their progress and problems. Maintains list of over 900 clubs throughout the U.S. **Publications:** *Stroke Club International Bulletin*, annual. Bulletin. Includes book and cassette recommendations. **Formerly:** (1973) The Stroke Club; (1978) Stroke Club of America.

★8315★ Sturge-Weber Foundation (SWF)
PO Box 418
Mount Freedom, NJ 07970-0418
Phone: (201)895-4445
Free: 800-627-5482
Fax: (201)895-4846
Karen L. Ball, Pres.

Founded: 1986. **Members:** 900. **Regional Groups:** 8. **Description:** Persons with Sturge-Weber syndrome and their families; concerned professionals and supporters. Serves as an information clearinghouse on Sturge-Weber syndrome, port-wine stains, and Klippel-Trenaunay Weber syndrome. (Sturge-Weber syndrome is a congenital neurological disorder characterized by facial port-wine stains, seizures, glaucoma, and loss of motor control, accompanied in rare cases by internal organ irregularities.) Disseminates information; offers support to afflicted persons. Maintains speakers' bureau; compiles statistics. Funds research. **Publications:** *Branching Out Newsletter*, quarterly. Newsletter. • Brochures.

★8316★ Tardive Dyskinesia / Tardive Dystonia National Association (TD/TDNA)
4244 University Way NE
PO Box 45732
Seattle, WA 98145-0732
Phone: (206)623-7297
S.K. Kjaer, Exec.Dir.

Founded: 1985. **Members:** 510. **Local Groups:** 5. **Description:** Tardive Dyskinesia and Tardive Dystonia patients and others disabled due to use of psychotropic and other prescription drugs; relatives of afflicted individuals and concerned citizens; legal and health care professionals. (Tardive Dyskinesia and Tardive Dystonia are neuromuscular disorders of the face, trunk, and extremities that occur primarily as a side effect of certain psychotropic and neuroleptic drugs.) Seeks to establish national legislation requiring that patients be warned of the potential side effects of prescription drug induced movement disorders, and that patients' informed consent be obtained before these drugs are administered. Works to increase public awareness of the disorders. Encourages research into alternative modalities and the prevention and cure of the dis orders. Provides guidance, support networks, referral services, and assistance for afflicted individuals and their families. Operates speakers' bureau; compiles statistics. Maintains library and biographical archives. **Publications:** *International Tardive Dyskinesia/Tardive Dystonia Newsletter*, semiannual. Newsletter. • *Living with TD/TD - Personal Perspectives*. • *Tardive Dyskinesia: Questions and Answers*.

★ 8317 ★ **Tourette Syndrome Association (TSA)**
42-40 Bell Blvd.
Bayside, NY 11361
Phone: (718)224-2999
Free: 800-237-0717
Fax: (718)279-9596

Founded: 1972. **Members:** 30,000. **Regional Groups:** 60. **Description:** People with Tourette Syndrome (TS) and their families and friends; physicians, nurses, teachers, psychologists, social workers, and other professionals; organizations such as mental health agencies. (TS is characterized by involuntary muscular movements and utterances of sounds or words, and is often undiagnosed or misdiagnosed.) Develops and disseminates educational materials to families, professionals, and agencies involved in health care, education, and governments. Schedules meetings and seminars for professionals and families to explore the latest information on TS. Stimulates support for research into the nature and causes of the disorder. Apprises members of rights, services, and benefits provided by the government and other organizations. Provides lists of doctors experienced in treating the disorder. Operates support groups and other services to help persons with TS and their families. Maintains sources for advocacy referral services in the areas of education, employment, and housing. **Publications:** *Leadership Bulletins*, 4/year. Bulletin. • *Medical Letter: Summary of the Recent Literature*, annual. • *Tourette Syndrome Association Newsletter*, quarterly. Newsletter. Includes book reviews. *Price:* Included in membership dues. **Formerly:** Gilles de la Tourette Syndrome Association.

Toxoplasmosis Trust (TTT)
See: Entry 3303

★ 8318 ★ **Trigeminal Neuralgia Association (TNA)**
PO Box 785
Barnegat Light, NJ 08006
Phone: (609)361-1014
Fax: (609)361-0982
Claire W. Patterson, Pres.

Founded: 1989. **State Groups:** 14. **Description:** Individuals with trigeminal neuralgia, a neurological disorder characterized by sudden attacks of pain along the distribution of one or more branches of the trigeminal nerve in the face and head. Works to increase public and professional awareness and understanding of the disorder . Provides a forum for discussion among individuals with trigeminal neuralgia in order to share information and experiences and offer support to patients and their families. Of-

fers physician referrals. Conducts educational programs. **Publications:** *TNAlert*, semiannual. Newsletter. *Price:* Free.

★ 8319 ★ **Union of Muscular Dystrophy Societies of Croatia**
Nova Ves 44
41000 Zagreb, Croatia
Phone: 41 271849
Marija Sostarko

Description: Works as a communication network for muscular dystrophy support and discussion groups. Encourages the medical and scientific communities to continue researching muscular dystrophy. Strives to heighten community awareness about the disease.

★ 8320 ★ **United Cerebral Palsy Associations (UCPA)**
1522 K St. NW, Ste. 1112
Washington, DC 20005
Phone: (202)842-1266
Free: 800-USA-5UCP
Fax: (202)842-3519
John D. Kemp, Exec.Dir.

Founded: 1948. **Members:** 155. **Description:** Voluntary national federation of state and local affiliates aiding persons with cerebral palsy and other disabilities, and their families. Goals are to prevent cerebral palsy, minimize its effects, and improve the quality of life for persons with cerebral palsy and other disabilities, and their families. Supports research and traineeships for medical and allied personnel; sponsors professional and public education in the prevention and management of cerebral palsy; cooperates with governmental and other agencies concerned with the welfare of persons with disabilities; acts as an advocate on the federal, state, and local levels for the civil rights of people with cerebral palsy and other disabilities, and their families. Establishes standards and promotes national accreditation of UCP affiliates; undertakes demonstration projects to establish models of exemplary community services for persons with cerebral palsy and other disabilities. Services provided by local and state affiliates include: medical, therapeutic, and social services for people with cerebral palsy and individuals with similar service needs; career development training; special education programs; recreational opportunities for children and adults; early intervention and assistive technology programs; family counseling services for parents of children with disabilities; personal assistance services; accessible and supported housing facilities where people with disabilities may live independently. **Publications:** *Family Support Bulletin*, quarterly. Bulletin. *Price:* Free. • *The Networker*, quarterly. *Price:* $12. • *Word from Washington*, bimonthly. Newsletter. Covers federal legislation, programs, and policy affecting persons with developmental disabilities. *Price:* $55/year; $25 for persons with disabilities or their families. **Formerly:** (1949) National Foundation for Cerebral Palsy.

★ 8321 ★ **United Leukodystrophy Foundation (ULF)**
2304 Highland Dr.
Sycamore, IL 60178
Phone: (815)895-3211
Free: 800-728-5483
Fax: (815)895-2432
Ron Brazeal, Exec.Dir.

Founded: 1982. **Members:** 3,000. **Description:** Leukodystrophy patients, their families, and medical care professionals. (Leukodystrophy refers to a group of disorders which affect the brain, spinal cord, and peripheral nerves by damaging the insulating sheath around nerve strands, interfering with the flow of electrical impulses.) Provides information on leukodystrophy to patients, their families, and the general public; assists in identifying sources of medical care, social services, and counseling; establishes and coordinates a communication network among affected families. Promotes and supports research into the causes, treatment, and prevention of white matter disorders. Coordinates cooperation between donor and government agencies, scientific programs, and the private sector. Conducts educational and research programs. **Publications:** *ULF News*, quarterly. Newsletter. *Price:* Included in membership dues.

★ 8322 ★ **United Parkinson Foundation (UPF)**
833 W. Washington Blvd.
Chicago, IL 60607
Phone: (312)733-1893
Judy Rosner, Exec.Dir.

Founded: 1963. **Members:** 38,000. **Description:** Patients, family members, medical personnel, and other interested persons. Assembles and publishes reliable information about symptoms, medication, and therapy helpful to sufferers of Parkinson's disease and related illnesses. Fosters and supports scientific research on the disease. Assists patients and their families with medical referrals, education, and other means. **Publications:** *One Step At a Time*. • *Patient Experience*. • *United Parkinson Foundation Newsletter*, quarterly. Newsletter. Includes research updates. *Price:* Included in membership dues. • *Your Questions Answered*. Also distributes exercise tape and book.

★ 8323 ★ **United States Cerebral Palsy Athletic Association (USCPAA)**
34518 Warren Rd., Ste. 264
Westland, MI 48185
Phone: (313)425-8961
Fax: (313)425-6510
Michael P. Mushett, Exec.Dir.

Founded: 1986. **Members:** 3,000. **Regional Groups:** 22. **State Groups:** 12. **Local Groups:** 100. **Description:** Athletes with cerebral palsy, athletic officials including coaches and administrators, health care professionals, and other interested individuals. Seeks to offer competitive athletic opportunities for athletes with cerebral palsy; provides support and training assistance to athletes with varying degrees of disability. Organizes multi-sport competitions at the local, regional, national, and international levels; maintains 8-level classification system to ensure that competition is based on the functional level of participants rather than their neurological capability. Selects athletes to represent the U.S. in the Paralympic Games and other international competitions. Provides referral service to assist members in obtaining support for local sports programs; develops fundraising programs. Operates Youth Sports Program, which provides guidelines and assistance to young people with special needs who wish to learn a sport. Conducts educational clinics and seminars. Bestows awards; compiles statistics; maintains speakers' bureau and library. Plans to make available to members liability insurance and reduced rates on special sports equipment. **Publications:** *Update*, quarterly. Newsletter. • *USC-PAA Classification and Rules Manual.*

★8324★ **Vereniging Spierziekten Nederland**
Lt. Gen. van Heutszlaan 6
NL-3743 JN Baarn, Netherlands
Phone: 2154 18400
Fax: 2154 21616

Description: Works as a support group for individuals suffering from neuromuscular diseases, among others amyotropic lateral sclerosis or ALS (also known as Lou Gehrig's Disease) in the Netherlands. Strives to: heighten public awareness and understanding of the diseases; encourage research among medical and scientific communities.

★8325★ **World Federation of Neurology (WFN)**
London Neurological Centre
110 Harley St.
London W1N 1AF, England
Phone: 171 9353546
Fax: 171 9354172
Dr. Clifford Rose, Sec.-Treas.

Founded: 1955. **Members:** 23,000. **National Groups:** 70. **Regional Groups:** 6. **Languages:** English. **Description:** Neurologists and neuroscientists dedicated to improving the care of neurological patients and to preventing diseases of the nervous system. Disseminates information in the field of neurology. Organizes research groups on disease topics; compiles statistics. Maintains speakers' bureau. Conducts educational and research programs. **Publications:** *Journal of Neurological Sciences*, bimonthly. • *World Neurology*, quarterly.

World Federation of Neurosurgical Societies (WFNS)
See: Entry 12316

World Society for Stereotactic and Functional Neurosurgery (WSSFN)
See: Entry 12317

Research Centers

★8326★ **Amyotrophic Lateral Sclerosis Clinical Research Center**
Univ. of Wisconsin Hospital & Clinics
J6/504 Clinical Science Center
600 Highland Ave.
Madison, WI 53792-5132
Phone: (608)263-9057
Fax: (608)263-0412
Benjamin Rix Brooks, M.D., Dir.

Research Activities and Fields: Amyotrophic lateral sclerosis (ALS), including bulbar function, exercise for ALS patients, and neurochemical, therapeutic, and epidemiological case control studies. Serves as operations center for Amyotrophic Lateral Sclerosis Ciliary Neurotrophic Factor Treatment Study Group. **E-mail Address:** brooks@vms.macc.wisc.edu.

★8327★ **Arthur M. Fishberg Research Center in Neurobiology**
Mt. Sinai Medical Center
1 Gustave Levy Pl.
New York, NY 10029
Phone: (212)241-7368
Fax: (212)996-9785
James L. Roberts, Ph.D., Codirector

Research Activities and Fields: Neurobiological systems in humans and mammals, emphasizing molecular and cellular biology approaches. Specific interests include the neuroendocrinology of stress and related disorders, the molecular biology of Alzheimer's disease, schitzophrenia, and other neurological/psychiatric diseases, and growth factors and growth factor receptor gene expression in the central nervous system.

★8328★ **Baltimore Headache Institute**
Foxleigh Bldg., Ste. 165
2330 W. Jopppa Rd.
Lutherville, MD 21093
Phone: (410)583-7171
Fax: (410)583-7171
Brian E. Mondell, M.D., Med.Dir.

Research Activities and Fields: Treatment of migraine, muscle contraction, and cluster headaches.

★8329★ **Barrow Neurological Institute**
350 W. Thomas Rd.
Phoenix, AZ 85013
Phone: (602)406-3196
Robert F. Spetzler, M.D., Dir.

Research Activities and Fields: Neurosciences.

★8330★ **Baylor College of Medicine Epilepsy Research Center**
1 Baylor Plaza
Houston, TX 77030
Phone: (713)790-3109
Fax: (713)793-1574
Dr. Peter Kellaway, Dir.

Research Activities and Fields: Epilepsy research (as related to human patients) in the following areas: clinical research on neurophysiological, pharmacological, and ontogenetic

aspects of epilepsy; design and application of computer-based systems to improve EEG detection, characterization, and quantification of the epileptic process in the brain; fundamental studies employing in-vitro brain slice technique to the elucidation of membrane and synaptic mechanisms in epileptogenesis and the mechanisms of action of anticonvulsant and convulsant agents; and developmental neurogenetics of epilepsy.

★8331★ **Baylor College of Medicine Jerry Lewis Neuromuscular Disease Research Center**
6501 Fannin
Houston, TX 77030
Phone: (713)798-4073
Stanley H. Appel, M.D., Codir.

Research Activities and Fields: Biochemistry, molecular genetics, and physiology of skeletal muscle and motor nerves, including biochemical, physiological, morphological, and genetic techniques to define and compare basic properties of skeletal muscle and neuromuscular disorders. Applies these approaches to animal models of human neuromuscular disease and to cultured muscle and nerve cells from normal and affected people.

★8332★ **Baylor College of Medicine Sleep Disorders and Research Center**
1 Baylor Plaza
Houston, TX 77030
Phone: (713)798-4886
Fax: (713)798-4099
Ismet Karacan, M.D., Dir.

Research Activities and Fields: Neuropsychopharmacology of sleep and sexual dysfunction in males.

★8333★ **Boston University Aphasia Research Center**
Dept. of Neurology
150 S. Huntington Ave.
Boston, MA 02130
Phone: (617)739-3487
Dr. Harold Goodglass, Dir.

Research Activities and Fields: Cognitive and language impairment following brain damage and closely related topics in psycholinguistics and cognition.

Boston University Design Laboratory
See: Entry 2435

★8334★ **Boston University Electrical Stimulation Laboratory**
Neuromuscular Research Center
44 Cummington St.
Boston, MA 02215
Phone: (617)353-9638
Prof. Roberto Merletti, Supvr.

Research Activities and Fields: Studies neuromuscular performance during voluntary and electrically elicited muscle contractions. Applications include the development of diagnostic procedures for motor system disorders, and the refinement of functional electrical stimulation to reduce accompanied muscle fatigue.

★ 8335 ★ Boston University Electrophysiology Laboratory

Neuromuscular Research Center
44 Cummington St.
Boston, MA 02215
Phone: (617)353-9757
Dr. Serge Roy, Supvr.

Research Activities and Fields: In vitro studies of isolated muscles of rats to compare muscle physiology/morphology to the electrical signals produced during muscle contraction. Aims to further the development of surface electromyography (EMG) as a means of assessing human muscle function and fatigue.

★ 8336 ★ Boston University Laboratory of Neuropsychology

Dept. of Behavioral Neuroscience
80 E. Concord St., M-9
Boston, MA 02118
Phone: (617)638-4803
Fax: (617)638-4806
Marlene Oscar Berman, Ph.D., Chief

Research Activities and Fields: Alcoholism, aphasia, apraxia, dementia, memory disorders, autism, schizophrenia, dyslexia, normal brain function and behavior, and psychopharmacology. Projects emphasize the relationship between brain structure and brain function, especially as related to human neurological disorders. **Publications:** *Bostonia Magazine* (quarterly); Research Reports (quarterly); *News & Notes* (monthly).

★ 8337 ★ Boston University Motion Analysis Laboratory

NeuroMuscular Research Center
44 Cummington St.
Boston, MA 02215
Phone: (617)353-9635
James J. Collins, Supvr.

Research Activities and Fields: Explores the full range of human movement, including dynamics and kinematics, with emphasis on the neural control and biomechanics of posture and locomotion.

★ 8338 ★ Boston University Motor Unit Laboratory

Neuromuscular Research Center
44 Cummington St.
Boston, MA 02215
Phone: (617)353-9634
Dr. Carlo J. De Luca, Supvr.

Research Activities and Fields: Investigates how the brain and spinal cord control the activation of muscle cells to produce muscle force. Seeks to examine muscle fiber discharge history in detail, to better understand the physiological rules that regulate muscle contractions, and to improve the ability of the neurologist to categorize and quantify neurological dysfunction.

★ 8339 ★ Boston University Muscle Fatigue Laboratory

Neuromuscular Reserch Center
44 Cummington Ave.
Boston, MA 02215
Phone: (617)353-9633
Serge Roy, Supvr.

Research Activities and Fields: Development and implementation of surface electromyo-graphic techniques to measure muscle fatigue, including the fatigue process of lower back muscles, measurement of forearm and hand fatigue related to the use of pressurized gloves, and investigation of physiological correlates of muscle fatigue using NMR spectroscopy combined with electromyography.

★ 8340 ★ Boston University Neuromuscular Research Center

44 Cummington St.
Boston, MA 02215
Phone: (617)353-9757
Fax: (617)353-5737
Dr. Carlo J. De Luca, Dir.

Research Activities and Fields: Motor control, including motor unit firing during sustained isometric contractions, synchronization evaluation, synchronization across muscles, and modeling of force production in the muscle; low back pain, including normative database study of back muscle function, EMG parameters of lumbar back muscles, development of test protocols related to the behavior of back muscles, and muscle performance in the back analysis system compared to lifting tasks; posture and movement, including computational posturography, visualizing the effects of filtering chaotic signals, a group-theoretic approach to rings of coupled biological oscillators, and integration of visual input into the aged postural control system; and muscle fatigue, including estimation of muscle fibers conduction velocity, multichannel surface EMG signals, and biochemical and myoelectric events during fatigue. The center is organized into the following components: Motor Unit Lab, Muscle Fatigue Lab, Electrical Stimulation Lab, Motion Analysis Lab, Design Lab, Motor Control Lab, and Electro-physiology Lab. **Publications:** Annual Activity Report. In addition, the faculty publishes numerous articles in various journals throughout the year.

★ 8341 ★ Brain Research Center

Children's Hospital National Medical Center
111 Michigan Ave. NW
Washington, DC 20010
Phone: (202)884-5000
Barbara Herman, Ph.D., Chief

Research Activities and Fields: Role of neuropeptides in pediatric psychiatry, neurology, and neurosurgery, including experiments with the drug naltrexone in the treatment of autism. Conducts animal research to investigate the role of neuropeptides in brain function and behavior.

★ 8342 ★ Brain Sciences Research Center

Veterans Adm. Med. Ctr., 11B
1 Veterans Dr.
Minneapolis, MN 55417
Phone: (612)725-2282
Fax: (612)725-2291
Apostolos P. Georgopoulos, M.D., Dir.

Research Activities and Fields: Brain physiology, cognitive psychology, and motor control. **E-mail Address:** omega@maroon.tc.umn.edu.

★ 8343 ★ Brain Tissue Resource Center

McLean Hospital
115 Mill St.
Belmont, MA 02178-9983
Phone: (617)855-2400
Fax: (617)855-3199
Edward D. Bird, Dir.

Research Activities and Fields: Neurochemistry of the human postmortem brain in Huntington's disease, Parkinson's disease, Alzheimer's disease, Tourette's syndrome, schizophrenia, and dystonia. Provides tissues to the neuroscience community for studies of neuropsychiatric disorders.

★ 8344 ★ Brigham and Women's Hospital Center for Neurologic Diseases

LMRC Bldg.
221 Longwood Ave.
Boston, MA 02115
Phone: (617)732-7601
Fax: (617)732-7787
Dr. Howard L. Weiner, Codirector

Research Activities and Fields: Human autoimmune diseases, including T-cell immunology, T-cell interactions and regulations by cytokines. Also studies immunoregulatory T-cell abnormalities in multiple sclerosis and other autoimmune diseases, and investigations of mechanisms of immunologic tolerance in humans.

★ 8345 ★ Brown University Center for Neural Sciences

Dept. of Neurosciences
PO Box 1953
Providence, RI 02912
Phone: (401)863-3548
Fax: (401)863-1074
Mary Ellen Flinn, Adm.Asst.

Research Activities and Fields: Brain and cerebral cortex, including models and mechanisms of learning, memory, and plasticity.

★ 8346 ★ Case Western Reserve University Applied Neural Control Laboratory

Charles B. Bolton Bldg., Rm. 3480
Cleveland, OH 44106-4912
Phone: (216)368-2960
Fax: (216)368-4872
J. Thomas Mortimer, Ph.D., Dir.

Research Activities and Fields: Development of technology based on the electrical excitability of nerve tissue for use in electrically controlling bodily organs or systems. Applications include restoration of paralyzed upper and lower extremities, restoration of diaphragm and bladder function, and stimulation of the central nervous system in epilepsy treatment.

★ 8347 ★ Center for Neurochemistry

Nathan S. Kline Institute for Psychiatric Research
Orangeburg, NY 10962
Phone: (914)365-6105
Fax: (914)365-6107
Laura Berlanga, Contact

Research Activities and Fields: Brain protein and peptide metabolism, chronic drug effects, properties of brain receptors, blood-brain barrier, and effects of addictive drugs. **E-mail Ad-**

dress: LAJTHA@NKI (BITNET). **Formerly:** New York State Research Institute for Neurochemistry & Drug Addiction.

★ 8348 ★ **Center for Neurodevelopmental Studies, Inc.**
8434 N. 39th Ave.
Phoenix, AZ 85051
Phone: (602)933-1400
Lorna Jean King, Dir. Emeritus

Research Activities and Fields: Effective treatment methods for autism and developmental disabilities and standardizing measures for evaluating adult sensory/motor functions (the Stepping Test, Vertical Writing Test, and Object Manipulation Speed Test). Collects data on specific responses of developmentally delayed children to various types of sensory stimulation. Evaluates the effectiveness of senory-integrative intervention for pre-school children at risk for learning disabilities. **Publications:** *Neurodevelopments* (quarterly newsletter).

★ 8349 ★ **Center for Neurologic Study**
11211 Sorrento Valley Rd., Ste. H
San Diego, CA 92121
Phone: (619)455-5463
Fax: (619)455-1713
Richard A. Smith, M.D., Dir.

Research Activities and Fields: Neuropharmacology and experimental treatment of neurologic diseases. **Publications:** *Handbook of Amyotrophic Lateral Sclerosis.*

Center for Senility Studies: Alzheimer's Disease Treatment Research
See: Entry 1929

★ 8350 ★ **Cerebral Blood Flow Laboratories (CBF Labs)**
Veterans Administration Medical Center 151A
Bldg. 110, Rm. 225
2002 Holcombe Blvd.
Houston, TX 77211
Phone: (713)795-5807
Fax: (713)794-7583
John S. Meyer, M.D., Dir.

Research Activities and Fields: Measurement of CT morphological changes and cerebral blood flow; cerebrovascular disorders; aging, Alzheimer's and ischemic vascular dementias and responses to medical, surgical, pharmacological, and behavioral treatment; prevention, diagnosis, and treatment of stroke and migraine; cerebral blood flow control and cerebral metabolism; neuropharmacology and physiology; aging; dementia; transient ischemic attacks; and risk factors for stroke. **Formerly:** Baylor Center for Cerebrovascular Research.

★ 8351 ★ **Chicago Institute of Neurosurgery and Neuroresearch**
428 W. Deming Pl.
Chicago, IL 60614
Phone: (312)883-8585
Fax: (312)935-2132
Joseph R. Moskal, Ph.D., Dir.

Research Activities and Fields: Molecular glycobiology of brain tumors, glycoryl transference molecular biology, and carbohydrate-growth factor receptor interactions.

★ 8352 ★ **City of Hope Beckman Research Institute**
Division of Neurosciences
1450 E. Duarte Rd.
Duarte, CA 91010
Phone: (818)357-9711
Fax: (818)301-8470
Dr. James E. Vaughn, Chair

Research Activities and Fields: The Division is composed of 12 research sections studying cell biology, cellular neurochemistry, cellular neurophysiology, developmental neurobiology, membrane biochemistry, molecular biology and genetics, neuroanatomy and ultrastructure, neurobiochemistry, neuroendocrinology, neuropharmacology, neurophysiology, and receptor physiology. Specific studies include the embryonic development of spinal cord neurons; identification, localization, and functions of neuroactive peptides; molecular and functional studies of transmembrane ion channels; the functional relationship between molecular chemical events and electrical excitability of neuronal elements; interactions between neurotransmitter receptor molecules of the membrane with synaptic proteins; developmental and molecular biological processes involved in the function of cholinergic neurons in normal and animal models of Alzheimer's disease; mechanisms of solute transport localized membranes and the effect of lipid components on operation of transport systems; developmental specificity of the formation of neuronal connections; and molecular genetic studies of Alzheimer's disease, schizophrenia, and manic depressive disorder. **E-mail Address:** jvaughn@coh.org.

★ 8353 ★ **College of Staten Island of City University of New York**
Center for Developmental Neuroscience and Developmental Disabilities
2800 Victory Blvd., 6S320
Staten Island, NY 10314
Phone: (718)982-3930
Fax: (718)982-3944
Dr. Yigal H. Ehrlich, Dir.

Research Activities and Fields: Developmental neurobiology and neurochemistry, and synaptic plasticity, focusing on the regulation and adaptation of neural function, utilizing brain slices neural cell lines, and CNS neurons grown in culture. **Formerly:** Center for Developmental Neuroscience.

★ 8354 ★ **Colorado State University**
Program in Neuronal Growth and Development
Dept. of Biochemistry
MRB, Rm. 235
Fort Collins, CO 80523
Phone: (303)491-0425
Fax: (303)491-0494
Dr. James R. Bamburg, Dir.

Research Activities and Fields: Cellular and molecular neurobiology. Examines basic components of the nervous system's development and repair, largely through studies of cultured neurons and animals, including rats, snails, salamanders, and land crabs. Also investigates how neurotransmitters provide regulatory control in the development of the nervous system, the development and function of taste receptor cells, the role of voltage-gated ion channels in development of nerve and muscle, and gene expression in early development of the nervous system. **E-mail Address:** jbamburg@vines.colostate.edu. **Formerly:** Neurosciences Program.

★ 8355 ★ **Columbia University**
Alzheimer's Disease Research Center
Dept. of Pathology
College of Physicians & Surgeons
630 W. 168th St.
New York, NY 10032
Phone: (212)305-6553
Fax: (212)305-4614
Michael L. Shelanski, M.D., Dir.

Research Activities and Fields: Alzheimer's disease and elderly care. Serves as a resource for tissue, cells, and DNA from Alzheimer's disease and control patients. Areas of research include epidemiology, cell biology, molecular biology, and care-giving. **Publications:** *Circles in Aging* (occasional). **E-mail Address:** ls35@columbia.edu.

★ 8356 ★ **Columbia University**
Clinical Research Center for Muscular Dystrophy
College of Physicians & Surgeons
Dept. of Neurology, 4-420
630 W. 168th St.
New York, NY 10032
Phone: (212)305-3533
Fax: (212)305-3986
Salvatore DiMauro, M.D., Codirector

Research Activities and Fields: Molecular genetics and hereditary neuromuscular diseases, particularly metabolic myopathies. Conducts autoimmune, biochemical, and morphological studies of ultrastructure, tissue enzymes, peripheral neuropathies, and myasthenia gravis.

★ 8357 ★ **Columbia University**
Dystonia Clinical Research Center
Neurological Institute
710 W. 168th St.
New York, NY 10032
Phone: (212)305-5779
Fax: (212)305-1304
Stanley Fahn, M.D., Dir.

Research Activities and Fields: Phenomenology, pharmacology, treatment, and genetics of dystonia. Research activities focus on dystonia molecular genetics and botulinum toxin to treat focal and segmental dystonia. **E-mail Address:** fahn@movdis.cis.columbia.edu.

★ 8358 ★ **Cornell University**
Aitken Neurosurgery Laboratory
1300 York Ave., Rm. LC 807
New York, NY 10021
Phone: (212)746-2396
Fax: (212)746-8038
Jam Ghajar, M.D., Dir.

Research Activities and Fields: Investigates the pathophysiology of traumatic brain injury, uses an in vitro human glial cell culture model of injury to study brain derived inflammatory mediators, and performs ventricular cerebrospinal fluid analysis in human patients. Established physiological model for post traumatic raised intracranial preserve analysis.

★ 8359 ★ Cornell University
Winifred Masterson Burke Medical
Research Institute
Dementia Research Service
785 Mamaroneck Ave.
White Plains, NY 10605
Phone: (914)948-0050
Fax: (914)946-1722
John P. Blass, M.D., Dir.

Research Activities and Fields: Clinical and basic studies in metabolic and nutritional aspects of degenerative diseases of the nervous system, especially Alzheimer's disease. **Formerly:** Burke Rehabilitation Center, Dementia Research Service.

★ 8360 ★ Dartmouth College
Sleep Disorders Center
Dartmouth Hitchcock Medical Center
1 Medical Center Dr.
Lebanon, NH 03756
Phone: (603)650-7534
Fax: (603)650-8208
Dr. Michael Sateia, Dir.

Research Activities and Fields: Overnight diagnostic studies for sleep disorders, sleep apnea due to obesity, and penile dysfunction.

★ 8361 ★ Duke University
Duke Center for the Advanced Study of
Epilepsy
401 Bryan Research Bldg.
Research Dr.
Box 3676
Durham, NC 27710
Phone: (919)684-4241
Fax: (919)684-8219
Dr. James O. McNamara, Dir.

Research Activities and Fields: Clinical and experimental approaches to limbic epilepsy. Current projects include studies of early gene expression in the kindling model of epilepsy, mechanisms of development of Ammon's horn sclerosis, microphysiology of limbic seizures, and role of excitatory amino acids and their receptors in limbic epilepsy.

★ 8362 ★ Duke University
Epilepsy Research Center
401 Bryan Research Bldg.
Box 3676
Durham, NC 27710
Phone: (919)684-4241
Fax: (919)684-8219
Dr. James McNamara, Dir.

Research Activities and Fields: Epilepsy, including its development following brain injury.

★ 8363 ★ Duke University
Preuss Laboratory for Brain Tumor
Research
Duke Medical Center
Research Dr.
PO Box 3156
Durham, NC 27710
Phone: (919)684-4187
Fax: (919)681-8337
Dr. Darell Bigner, Dir.

Research Activities and Fields: Brain tumors.

★ 8364 ★ Dystonia Medical Research
Foundation
1 E. Wacker Dr., Ste. 2430
Chicago, IL 60601-2098
Phone: (312)755-0198
Fax: (312)803-0138
Dr. Mahlon R. Dehong, Scientific Dir.

Research Activities and Fields: Causes and treatment of generalized dystonia, spasmodic torticollis, writer's cramp, blepharospasm, oromandibular dystonia, Meige's disease, and laryngeal dystonia. **Publications:** Newsletter (quarterly); Manuals.

★ 8365 ★ Emanuel Research Center
2801 N. Gantenbein Ave.
Portland, OR 97227
Phone: (503)280-3491
Fax: (503)280-4942
Dr. Lutz Kiesow, M.D., Chief of Research

Research Activities and Fields: Traumatic injuries, neurological damage, child abuse, effects of drug abuse, regulation and control of neonatal metabolism, neonatal nutrition, and temperature regulation. **Publications:** *Emanuel Research Letter*.

★ 8366 ★ Emory University
Sleep Research Laboratory
8 Executive Park W., Ste. 815
Atlanta, GA 30329
Phone: (404)315-8847
Fax: (404)853-4792
G. Vogel, Dir.

Research Activities and Fields: Neurophysiological studies of sleep.

★ 8367 ★ Epilepsy Foundation of America
4351 Garden City Dr.
Landover, MD 20785
Phone: (301)459-3700
Free: 800-332-1000
Fax: (301)577-2684
William M. McLin, Exec. V.Pres.

Research Activities and Fields: Supports research into the causes and treatment of epilepsy, pediatrics and epilepsy, and behavioral science applications. Also supports training of research and clinical fellows in epilepsy. **Publications:** Annual Report; *Epilepsy USA*. **E-mail Address:** EFANEL@CAPCON.NET.

★ 8368 ★ Florida Atlantic University
Center for Complex Systems
777 Glades Rd.
Boca Raton, FL 33431
Phone: (407)367-2230
Fax: (407)367-3634
J.A.S. Kelso, Contact

Research Activities and Fields: Multidisciplinary studies of complex biological systems, focusing on coordination between neural processes and their resultant behaviors. Contains three major laboratories: 1) Human Brain and Behavior Laboratory; 2) Laboratory of Experimental Mathematics; and 3) Neuroscience Research Laboratory, which includes neural growth and development, neurophysiology, and neuroanatomy. Houses National Training Program in Complex Systems and Brain Sciences for pre- and postdoctoral fellows.

★ 8369 ★ Georgetown University
Fidia-Georgetown Institute for the
Neurosciences
3900 Reservoir Rd., N.W.
Med-Dent Bldg., Rm. SE 402
Washington, DC 20007
Phone: (202)687-1296
Fax: (202)687-1782
Erminio Costa, M.D., Dir.

Research Activities and Fields: Multidisciplinary in vitro and in vivo studies of molecular mechanisms that regulate synaptic plasticity and interneuronal communication, including GABAergic and glutamateric signal transduction, neurotrophines and neurosteroids, glutamate excitotoxicity, and calcium homeostasis in neurons. **Publications:** *Neuroscience Facts*.

★ 8370 ★ Georgetown University
Sleep Disorders Center
3800 Reservoir Rd. NW
Washington, DC 20007
Phone: (202)784-3610
Fax: (202)784-2261
Dr. Samuel Potolicchio, Jr., Dir.

Research Activities and Fields: Treatment techniques for sleep apnea using nasal continuous positive airway pressure, evaluation of people with nocturnal hypoxia and possible correlates to memory impairment, sleep disturbances in geriatric populations, and psychiatric studies dealing with the presence of depression in people with schizophrenia. Other concentrations include monitoring of epilepsy patients and studies of sudden infant death syndrome.

★ 8371 ★ Harvard University
Laboratories for Molecular Neuroscience
McLean Hospital
115 Mill St.
Belmont, MA 02178
Phone: (617)855-2412
Fax: (617)855-2185
Dr. Ralph Nixon, Dir.

Research Activities and Fields: Molecular neuroscience and aging, including molecular neurobiology of proteases, signal transduction, neurodegenerative disease, protein/peptide analytical techniques, and molecular genetics.

★ 8372 ★ Huntington Medical Research
Institutes
734 Fairmount Ave.
Pasadena, CA 91105
Phone: (818)397-5436
Fax: (818)397-3330
William Opel, Exec.Dir.

Research Activities and Fields: Experimental neurology, electronic neural prosthetic device development, biology of vascular endothelium, cerebrovascular physiology and cardiovascular physiology, early stroke intervention, growth factors, prostate cancer, cell biology, and medical applications of magnetic resonance using protons, phosphorous, fluorine, and nitrogen. **Publications:** Newsletter (quarterly). **E-mail Address:** @hmr1.org.

★ 8373 ★ Huntington's Disease Center Without Walls
Massachusetts General Hospital
Molecular Neurogenetics Unit
13th St. Bldg. 149, Rm. 6214
Charlestown, MA 02129
Phone: (617)726-5724
Fax: (617)726-5735
Dr. James F. Gusella, Program Dir.

Research Activities and Fields: Huntington's Disease (HD), including protein abnormalities in the HD brain and their relationship to neuronal loss, neuropathological examination of autopsy brain sections, location and measurement of chemical messengers, neuropsychological tests evaluating deficits in memory and cognitive functioning, social and pyschological impact of HD on families, medications increasing levels of chemical messengers in the brain, DNA studies to determine the HD gene, and peptide localization in the nerve cells.

Illinois Institute of Technology
Pritzker Institute of Medical Engineering
See: Entry 2448

★ 8374 ★ Indiana University
Neuropsychology Research Section
702 Barnhill Dr., Rm. 3751
Indianapolis, IN 46202
Phone: (317)274-7327
Fax: (317)274-1337
Dr. Kathleen Fitzhugh-Bell, Dir.

Research Activities and Fields: Brain-behavior relationships and human neuropsychology, including studies of effects of various types of brain disorders on abilities of adults and children, neuropsychological effects of various treatment methods for diseases, and effects of various types of cerebral lesions.

★ 8375 ★ Indiana University Bloomington
Program in Neural Science
Psychology 361
Bloomington, IN 47405
Phone: (812)855-7756
Fax: (812)855-4520
Prof. George V. Rebec, Dir.

Research Activities and Fields: Neuroscience, including anatomical, biochemical, and physiological studies of nervous system functions, as it relates to behavioral processes. Specific research areas include neurochemical correlates of behavior, neuropharmacology, cellular bases of contingency-sensitive change in invertebrates, somatosensatory and sensorimotor function in brainstem and spinal cord, neural coding and cortical processing of complex movements, computational modeling of neural networks, neural development in retina and central visual targets, hormonal control of development in sexually dimorphic neural systems, and neural mechanisms of associative and nonassociative learning in mammals. **Formerly:** Center for the Neural Sciences.

Indiana University-Purdue University at Indianapolis
Institute of Psychiatric Research
See: Entry 7569

Institute for Rehabilitation and Research (TIRR)
See: Entry 12734

★ 8376 ★ Institute for Research in Behavioral Neuroscience
66 E. 79th St.
New York, NY 10021
Phone: (212)288-6010
Fax: (212)288-6024
Jason W. Brown, M.D., Pres.

Research Activities and Fields: Neuropsychology and aphasia. **Publications:** *IRBN Series in Neuropsychology.* **E-mail Address:** avscc@cunyvm.cuny.edu.

★ 8377 ★ Institutes for Achievement of Human Potential
8801 Stenton Ave.
Philadelphia, PA 19118
Phone: (215)233-2050
Fax: (215)233-3940
Janet Doman, Dir.

Research Activities and Fields: Methods of treating severely brain-injured children, including invest igations of effects of programs of sensory inputs individually designed according to each child's growth, as well as functional gains and effects of nutrition in enhancing children's response to therapeutic programs. Studies effects of applying similar environmental enrichment and neurological organization programs to non-disabled children of preschool age. **Publications:** *The Institute Report* (quarterly). **Formerly:** Rehabilitation Center of Philadelphia (1962).

★ 8378 ★ Jimmie Heuga Center
PO Box 5919
Avon, CO 81620-5919
Phone: (303)949-7172
Fax: (303)949-1308
Richard W. Hicks, Ph.D., Dir., Research and Education

Research Activities and Fields: Conducts and coordinates studies aimed at improving the quality of life for those with multiple sclerosis (MS) and other potentially debilitating neurological disorders. Focuses on the effects of goal-oriented exercise on the fitness of those with MS. Projects have included development of an exercise testing and prescription protocol.

★ 8379 ★ Johns Hopkins University
Alzheimer's Disease Research Center
509 Pathology Bldg.
600 Wolfe St.
Baltimore, MD 21205
Phone: (410)955-5632
Fax: (410)955-9777
Diane Martin, Dir.

Research Activities and Fields: Alzheimer's disease, including basic and applied studies of symptoms and psychiatric problems. **Publications:** *Family Guidelines Series.*

★ 8380 ★ Johns Hopkins University
Baltimore Huntington's Disease Project
Johns Hopkins Hospital
Ross Bldg. 618
720 Rutland Ave.
Baltimore, MD 21205
Phone: (410)955-2398
Fax: (410)614-0013
Dr. Christopher A. Ross, Contact

Research Activities and Fields: Basic and clinical research on Huntington's Disease (HD), a hereditary brain disorder and the gene which carries it. Research is conducted by faculty from Johns Hopkins Medical Institutions, Departments of Psychiatry, Neurology, Neuroradiology, Pharmacology, Neuroscience, Biostatistics, and Genetics. **Publications:** *A Physicians Guide to the Management of Huntington's Disease.*

★ 8381 ★ Johns Hopkins University
Blood-Brain Barrier Laboratory
Kennedy Kreger Institute
707 N. Broadway
Baltimore, MD 21205
Phone: (410)550-9483
Fax: (410)550-9524
Dr. Gary Goldstein, Dir.

Research Activities and Fields: Molecular aspects of brain microvessel differentiation, cell-cell signaling, second messengers, and transport systems. Investigates the effects of lead poisoning.

★ 8382 ★ Johns Hopkins University
Neuropathology Laboratory
558 Ross Research Bldg.
720 Rutland Ave.
Baltimore, MD 21205-2196
Phone: (410)955-5632
Fax: (410)955-9777
Dr. Donald L. Price, Dir.

Research Activities and Fields: Investigates molecular mechanisms of neurodegenerative diseases.

★ 8383 ★ Johns Hopkins University
Sleep Disorders Center
Johns Hopkins Bayview Medical Ctr.
Asthma & Allergy Center
5501 Hopkins Bayview Circle
Baltimore, MD 21224
Phone: (410)550-0571
Fax: (410)550-2612
Philip L. Smith, M.D., Dir.

Research Activities and Fields: Sleep-related disorders. Studies focus on disorders of daytime hypersomnolence, including narcolepsy, periodic leg movements, psychiatric illness, and sleep apnea; disorder-causing insomnia, psychiatric illness, shift work, and sleep apnea; and disruptive sleep patterns, loud snoring, nocturnal seizures, nocturnal terrors, and sleep walking. Also investigates male erectile impotence, using sleep recordings as a diagnostic tool.

★ **8384** ★ **Laboratory for Circadian and Sleep Disorders Medicine**
Brigham & Women's Hospital
221 Longwood Ave.
Boston, MA 02115
Phone: (617)732-4011
Fax: (617)732-4015
Dr. Charles A. Czeisler, Dir.

Research Activities and Fields: Sleep medicine, circadian aspects of individual personality, and sleep patterns of individuals.

Laval University
Robert-Giffard Research Centre
See: Entry 7579

★ **8385** ★ **Loma Linda University**
Sleep Disorders Center
Medical Services Center
VA Hospital
11201 Benton St.
Loma Linda, CA 92357
Phone: (909)422-3130
Fax: (909)422-3106
Dr. Ralph Downey, III, Dir.

Research Activities and Fields: Sleep disorders, including sleep apnea, insomnia, and narcolepsy.

★ **8386** ★ **Louisiana State University Medical Center**
Neuroscience Center of Excellence
2020 Gravier St., Ste. B
New Orleans, LA 70112
Phone: (504)568-6700
Fax: (504)568-5801
Dr. Nicolas G. Bazan, Dir.

Research Activities and Fields: Interdisciplinary unit studying clinical and basic neuroscience.

★ **8387** ★ **Loyola University Chicago**
Infant Research Project
2160 S. 1st Ave.
Maywood, IL 60153
Phone: (708)216-1067
Dr. Thomas Meyers, Dir.

Research Activities and Fields: Concerned with neurodevelopmental outcomes of premature infants with periventricular/intraventricular hemorrhages. Documents neurodevelopmental outcomes of infants at risk for handicapping conditions. Also documents the degree of hemorrhage with computer tomography and relates to standardized and innovative functional assessments.

★ **8388** ★ **Loyola University Chicago**
Neuroscience and Aging Institute
Bldg. No. 117, Rm. 29
2160 S. 1st Ave.
Maywood, IL 60153
Phone: (708)216-6755
Fax: (708)216-6823
Israel Hanin, Ph.D., Dir.

Research Activities and Fields: Neurodegenerative diseases such as Alzheimer's disease, neurodevelopment, neuropeptide receptor systems, neuroendocrinology, heuroimmunology, neurotoxicity, sensory neuroscience, and neurooncology. **Publications:** *Neurotransmitter Newsletter* (two to three times per year).

★ **8389** ★ **Massachusetts Alzheimer's Disease Research Center**
Massachusetts General Hospital
ACC, Ste. 830
15 Parkman St.
Boston, MA 02114
Phone: (617)726-1728
Fax: (617)726-7718
John H. Growdon, M.D., Dir.

Research Activities and Fields: Coordinates research on Alzheimer's disease, including memory loss, dementia, neuropathology, neuropsychology, neurochemistry, and investigational drug studies. Projects focus on biochemical studies on the abnormal proteins that accumulate in the brains of Alzheimer's patients, possible genetic markers or familial traits, anatomical and neurotransmitter abnormalities, and clinical studies of behavior and neuropharmacology.

★ **8390** ★ **Massachusetts Institute of Technology**
Center for Biological and Computational Learning
Dept. of Brain & Cognitive Sciences
45 Carleton St.
Cambridge, MA 02142
Phone: (617)253-5230
Tomaso Poggio, Ph.D., Codir.

Research Activities and Fields: Investigates mechanisms of biological information processing using artificial intelligence models of psychophysics, anatomy, and physiology. Studies focus on machine and human learning, vision, and language and motor control. **Formerly:** Center for Biological Information Processing.

★ **8391** ★ **Massachusetts Institute of Technology**
Laboratory of Neuroendocrine Regulation
Bldg. E25-604
Cambridge, MA 02139
Phone: (617)253-6731
Fax: (617)253-6882
Dr. Richard J. Wurtman, M.D., Dir.

Research Activities and Fields: Pineal gland and effects of drugs, nutrients, and hormones on brain neurotransmitters and behavior. Specific studies include utilization of choline for acetylcholine and membrane phosphatidylcholine synthesis in cultured neuroblastoma cells and in rat brain; neurotransmitter receptors and second messengers that modulate these two syntheses; interactions of precursor availability (tyrosine and tryptophan) and firing frequency in controlling neurotransmitter (catecholamines and serotonin) release from superfused rat brain slices; effects of tyrosine on catecholamine release from isolated retina; effects of supplemental tyrosine on capacity to withstand stress, sustain motor activity, and perform complex tasks; control of melatonin secretion in rats; mechanisms by which melatonin acts on neurons and induces sleep; aberrant patterns of melatonin secretion in aging and human diseases; effects of macronutrients (carbohydrates and proteins) on brain serotonin synthesis; involvement of serotoninergic neurons in appetite, mood, pain sensitivity, and various appetitive diseases; selective effects of serotoninergic drugs on nutrient selection; Alzheimer's dis-

ease; control of APP metabolism by neurotransmitters; and brain phospholipid synthesis.

★ **8392** ★ **Medical College of Georgia**
Alzheimer's Research Center for Clinical and Basic Research
Dept. of Pharmacology & Toxicology
Augusta, GA 30912-2300
Phone: (706)721-6355
Fax: (706)721-2347
Dr. Jerry J. Buccafusco, Coord.

Research Activities and Fields: Multidisciplinary research on all aspects of Alzheimer's disease, including new therapeutic approaches, diagnostic procedures, and basic studies of etiology.

★ **8393** ★ **Medical College of Pennsylvania and Hahnemann University**
Huntington's Disease Diagnostic and Referral Center
1427 Vine St., 1st Fl.
Philadelphia, PA 19102
Phone: (215)762-6890
Fax: (215)246-5043
Elliott L. Mancall, M.D., Medical Advisor

Research Activities and Fields: Huntington's disease (HD), a hereditary brain disorder, including neuropsychological and electrophysiological studies, psychological problems in HD families, cultured fibroblasts in HD, and miscellaneous chemical studies in HD. Acts as a focal point for the development and support of various regional research projects concerned with Huntington's disease and other genetically determined disorders of the nervous system.

★ **8394** ★ **Medical College of Pennsylvania and Hahnemann University**
Mid Atlantic Regional Epilepsy Center
3200 Henry Ave.
Philadelphia, PA 19129
Phone: (215)842-4500
Fax: (215)848-2035
Dr. Mercedes Jacobson, Dir.

Research Activities and Fields: Epileptic seizure detection, including seizure detection apparatus studies.

★ **8395** ★ **Medical College of Pennsylvania and Hahnemann University**
Neuroscience Program
3200 Henry Ave.
Philadelphia, PA 19129
Phone: (215)842-4600
Fax: (215)843-9082
Dr. Donald S. Faber, Chm.

Research Activities and Fields: Nervous system development, regeneration, and repair following injury; and the biology of contractile systems, including muscle and other cells.

★ **8396** ★ **Monell Chemical Senses Center**
3500 Market St.
Philadelphia, PA 19104-3308
Phone: (215)898-8878
Fax: (215)898-2084
Dr. Gary K. Beauchamp, Dir.

Research Activities and Fields: Multidisciplinary research on mechanisms and functions of the chemical senses (taste, smell) and chemesthesis, chemical irritation, including studies in the areas of biochemistry, biophysics, endocrinology, physiology, ethology, neurology, behavior, genetics, psychophysics, nutrition, organic chemistry, chemical ecology, and zoology. Research relates to solutions of problems in nutrition, environmental odors, reproduction, disease diagnosis, expansion of world food supply, and alternative means of vertebrate pest control. Projects focus on biochemistry of receptor mechanisms, sensory qualities of food, role of early diet in shaping food preferences, relationship between chemosensory function and nutritional and disease states, role of body volatiles in disease diagnosis, methods of altering salt preference, role of taste and smell in food utilization, effect of aging on taste and smell, information processing in taste and smell, diagnosis and treatment of taste and smell disorders, and genetic influence on production and detection of chemostimulants. **Publications:** *The Monell Connection* (newsletter).

★8397★ Monell-Jefferson Chemosensory Clinical Research Center
c/o Monell Chemical Senses Center
3500 Market St.
Philadelphia, PA 19104-3308
Phone: (215)955-6056
Beverly J. Cowart, Ph.D., Clinical Dir.

Research Activities and Fields: Clinical studies of smell and taste disorders using a multidisciplinary approach (psychophysical, biophysical, medical, and dental).

★8398★ Mount Sinai School of Medicine of City University of New York
Alzheimer's Disease Research Center
1 Gustave Levy Pl.
Box 1230
New York, NY 10029
Phone: (212)241-6623
Fax: (212)369-2344
Dr. Kenneth L. Davis, Chm., Dept. of Psychiatry

Research Activities and Fields: Etiology, diagnosis, and treatment of Alzheimer's disease and related dementias. Clinical studies include trials of new drugs and biological markers and longitudinal follow-up studies. An active autopsy network obtains brain material from Alzheimer patients.

★8399★ Mount Sinai School of Medicine of City University of New York
Clinical Center for Research in Parkinson's and Allied Disorders
5 E. 98th St.
Box 1139
New York, NY 10029
Phone: (212)241-6500
Fax: (212)534-3163
Dr. Melvin D. Yahr, Dir.

Research Activities and Fields: Research into the cause and cure of Parkinson's disease, Huntington's chorea, and dystonia.

★8400★ Multidisciplinary Institute for Neuropsychological Development, Inc.
48 Garden St.
Cambridge, MA 02138
Phone: (617)547-9845
Fax: (617)354-0012
Dr. E. Christine Kris, Pres. and Treasurer

Research Activities and Fields: Developmental learning and adjustment disabilities in children, adolescents, and young adults are profiled and analyzed to ascertain learning levels, styles, skill and information acquisition rates, and best working methods. Through its Psychophysiological and EEG Research Laboratory, the Institute monitors changes in the central and autonomic nervous systems, using EEG (electroencephalography) and other scanning and electro-diagnostic measurements of eye movement and cardiac functions, to determine the limits within which individuals can vary and yet function optimally. Research includes binocular-bi-dimensional eye movement and bi-hemispheric brainwave interaction-pattern studies of rest, arousal, vigilance, focusing, and attentive scanning during performance of perceptual and reading tasks in normal learners and dyslexics. Studies also include language acquisition, quantitative reasoning, and gross and fine movement integration proficiency. Statistical analyses of developmental profiles and subtest-clusters are carried out on old and new data. Research is applied to the development of diagnostic, therapeutic and remedial learning, and prescriptive teaching programs. Maintains a developmental neuropsychological compendium of case-outcome studies. **Publications:** *M.I.N.D. Monographs; M.I.N.D. Papers.*

★8401★ Neurological Institute
Columbia-Presbyterian Medical Center
New York, NY 10032-3784
Phone: (212)305-8551
Fax: (212)305-6978
Dr. Lewis P. Rowland, Dir. of Neurology Service

Research Activities and Fields: Neurology, neuropathology, neurophysiology, neurological surgery, dystonia, Parkinson's and Alzheimer's diseases, muscular dystrophy, amyotrophic lateral sclerosis (Lou Gehrig's disease), multiple sclerosis, and epilepsy, including basic and clinical studies on function and disease of the nervous system and treatment of nervous diseases and surgical conditions of brain and nervous system.

★8402★ Neurology Research Center
Helen Hayes Hospital
Rte. 9W
West Haverstraw, NY 10993-1195
Phone: (914)947-3000
Fax: (914)947-4521
Robert S. Sloviter, Ph.D., Research Dir.

Research Activities and Fields: Epilepsy, movement disorders, and neuroendocrinology. Degenerative neurological disorders such as Huntington's and Alzheimer's diseases are also investigated.

★8403★ Neuropsychiatric Research Institute
PO Box 1415
Fargo, ND 58107-1415
Phone: (701)239-1600
Fax: (701)239-1639
Dr. John Vennes, Pres.

Research Activities and Fields: Basic and clinical studies of the central nervous system, including intercommunication of brain cells and chemical reactions in the brain. Specific applications include studies of Alzheimer's disease, Parkinson's disease, Huntington's disease, and schizophrenia. **Formerly:** Outgrowth of the Neuropsychiatric Institute founded in 1955.

★8404★ Neurosciences Institute
3377 N. Torrey Pines Ct., Ste. 310
La Jolla, CA 92037
Phone: (619)554-3200
Fax: (619)554-9159
W. Einar Gall, Dir.

Research Activities and Fields: Promotes conceptual and theoretical progress in understanding the function of the nervous system at all levels, particularly higher functions of the brain (perception, memory, sensation) and their implications in understanding human behavior. A research program for resident Institute Fellows in theoretical neurobiology provides training in methods used to construct neural theories and develops theoretical models of neural systems that are biologically sound and experimentally testable at synaptic, cellular, and network levels. The Institute also conducts a research program in experimental neurobiology. The Institute provides opportunities for visiting scientists to interact in modes that would not ordinarily be possible in their home laboratories. Visiting in small groups or individually for periods from several days to several months, scientists design experiments, discuss research questions with experts in other fields, and share information about recent findings. **Publications:** Monographs Series; Edited Volumes. **E-mail Address:** wegall@msi.edu.

★8405★ New England Medical Center Electromyography Laboratory
Neurology Dept. EMG.
Box 314
Boston, MA 02111
Phone: (617)636-7580
Fax: (617)636-9124
Dr. William Brown, Dir.

Research Activities and Fields: Performs electrical studies of nerves and muscles to aid in the research and diagnosis of muscular dystrophy, amyotrophic lateral sclerosis, and other polyneuropathies.

★8406★ New York Medical College Medical Rehabilitation Research and Training Center for Multiple Sclerosis
St. Agnes Hospital
303 North St., Ste. 203
White Plains, NY 10605
Phone: (914)328-6410
Fax: (914)328-6408
Dr. Charles Smith, Dir.

Research Activities and Fields: Multiple sclerosis (MS), including quality of life, movement disorders, long term care; impact of parental MS on children, employment, assistive technology, bladder pathophysiology and management, evaluation of therapeutic trials for new drugs for MS, the role of immunological factors in MS, neurological impairments, the psychosocial aspects of MS, cost-effectiveness of alternative modes of care, immunological and biochemical markers of affective state, the quantitative assessment of tremor, cognitive remediation, and sexualtiy. **Publications:** *MS Quarterly Report*, published by Eastern Paralyzed Veterans Association; *Journal of Neurologic Rehabilitation* (quarterly). **E-mail Address:** nicklaroc@delphi.com.

New York State Psychiatric Institute
See: Entry 7588

★ 8407 ★ New York University
Center for Neural Science
4 Washington Pl., Rm. 809
New York, NY 10003
Phone: (212)998-7780
Fax: (212)995-4011
Prof. J. Anthony Movshon, Dir.

Research Activities and Fields: Neural science studies, ranging from molecular and cellular aspects to fully integrated systems and cognitive approaches. Specific research includes cell biological mechanisms underlying plasticity and stability of neurons; new sprout formation by adult mammalian neurons; drive and hedonic mechanisms in the brain and how they interact; use of image analysis procedures to study the functional anatomy of sensorimotor integration in the rat brain; neural processes that generate movements; genetic and molecular manipulations in the fruit fly to study the interplay between plasticity and programming in the nervous system; amino acid regulation of dopamine utilization under basal and stress conditions using a variety of techniques, including in vivo microdialysis; individual neurons in visual perception; magnetic fields accompanying the flow of currents within the brain's neurons; effects of developmental visual disorders on the structure and function of the visual system; problems of color vision using both psychophysical and electrophysical techniques; modeling of the human visual system; identification of the neural systems and cellular mechanisms used by the brain to assign emotional significance to sensory stimuli; the acquisition of color information, fusion of visual information from multiple sources, signal detection theory, and visual calibration; analysis of functional properties of neurons; and mathematical and computational models of complex behaviors.

★ 8408 ★ New York University
Jerry Lewis Neuromuscular Disease Center
Dept. of Rehabilitation Medicine
400 E. 34th St.
New York, NY 10016
Phone: (212)263-6350
Fax: (212)263-5499
Mathew Lee, M.D., Professor and Chm.

Research Activities and Fields: Diagnosis and clinical care of patients disabled by neuromuscular disease.

New York University
Medical Center Head Trauma Program
See: Entry 12737

★ 8409 ★ New York University
Millhauser Laboratories
550 1st Ave.
New York, NY 10016
Phone: (212)263-5717
Fax: (212)263-7513
Arnold J. Friedhoff, M.D., Dir.

Research Activities and Fields: Basic and clinical neurobiological approaches to adaptive mechanisms in brain, including molecular biology and neuropharmacology.

New York University
Rusk Institute of Rehabilitation Medicine
See: Entry 12739

★ 8410 ★ Northwestern University
Institute for Neuroscience
5-097 Ward Bldg.
Chicago, IL 60611

Research Activities and Fields: Sensory neurobiology and psychophysics, neuroendocrinology, biological rhythms, neural development and plasticity, electrophysiology and pharmacology of excitable membranes, and neuroimmunology and virology.

★ 8411 ★ Northwestern University
Spinal Cord Injury Center
250 E. Superior, Rm. 619
Chicago, IL 60611
Phone: (312)908-3425
Fax: (312)908-1819
Dr. Paul R. Meyer, Jr., Program Dir.

Research Activities and Fields: Research on health services for the spinal cord injured, including studies on cost-effectiveness of systematic care and the feasibility of expanding and improving community resources. Seeks to develop a multidisciplinary continuous system of comprehensive health services that meet the wide range of needs of persons severely disabled by a spinal cord injury: from point of injury requiring emergency treatment and evacuation, through acute care, rehabilitation, vocational and educational preparation, community job placement, and long-term follow-up. Seeks to decrease incidence, mortality, extent, and complications of spinal cord injury, while increasing functional capability, vocational, educational, and significant societal placement of the spinal cord injured. Also seeks to decrease duration and cost of acute and rehabilitation care. **Publications:** Progress Report (annually).

★ 8412 ★ Ohio State University
Neuroscience Program
4072 Graves Hall
333 W. 10th Ave.
Columbus, OH 43210
Phone: (614)292-4769
Fax: (614)292-1544
Dr. James S. King, Codirector

Research Activities and Fields: Spinal cord injury, brain tumors, Alzheimer's disease, head injury, neuromuscular disease, epilepsy, Parkinsonism, multiple sclerosis, stroke, neural devel-

opment, regeneration, plasticity, molecular neurobiology, tumor biology, myelin biology, neuroimmunology, and neural metabolism. **Formerly:** Neuroscience Research Laboratory.

★ 8413 ★ Ohio State University
Sleep Disorders Center
410 W. 10th
Rhodes Hall, Rm. S 1032
Columbus, OH 43210
Phone: (614)293-8260
Fax: (614)293-4506
Dr. Charles Pollak, Dir.

Research Activities and Fields: Diagnosis of impotence, applications of pharmaceutical agents in depression and other psychiatric disorders in adults, and disorders of sleep and arousal. Techniques include psychometric laboratory evaluation, monitoring sleep/awake disorders by all-night polysomnographic recordings, penile tumescence studies, multiple sleep latency studies, and electronic pupillometry. **Formerly:** Psychiatry and Sleep Disorders Center (1987).

★ 8414 ★ Ohio State University
Spinal Cord Injury Research Center
403 Hamilton Hall
1645 Neil Ave.
Columbus, OH 43210
Phone: (614)292-4953
Fax: (614)292-4888
Bradford T. Stokes, Ph.D., Dir., Prin. Investigator

Research Activities and Fields: Mechanical and histological parameters of cord injury, mechanisms of membrane injury, microenvironment of spinal cord tissues after impact injury, gangliosides metabolism in traumatized nerve, reorganization of sensory mechanisms after spinal lesions, effects of nerve on limb regeneration, and ontogeny and remodeling of spinal systems in the opossum. Examines sequelae of spinal cord injury in terms of cellular and molecular mechanisms of degeneration and regeneration, which are understood through study of the developing nervous system. Investigates the biochemical pathophysiology of degeneration and performs biochemical, physiologic, and anatomic analyses of regeneration and reorganization of nerve tissue subsequent to trauma. Utilizes recent techniques of fetal transplantation to effect anantomical repair of the injured spinal cord.

Oregon Health Sciences University
Vollum Institute for Advanced Biomedical
**   Research**
See: Entry 2602

Pain Institute
See: Entry 7928

★ 8415 ★ Princeton University
Cutaneous Communication Laboratory
Psychology Dept.
Green Hall
Princeton, NJ 08544-1010
Phone: (609)258-5277
Fax: (609)258-1113
Dr. Roger W. Cholewiak, Prin. Investigator

Research Activities and Fields: Sensory psychophysiology and experimental psychology, including experimental investigations in all phases of cutaneous sensitivity with special reference to utilization of data in communication systems, under conditions of sensory handicap, or when other sensory modalities are overloaded. Research includes studies of pattern recognition and discrimination with psychophysical procedures and scaling techniques, including multidimensional designs; more elementary dimensions of tactile experience; and the interrelations of various dimensions of touch. **Publications:** *Reports of Princeton Cutaneous Research Project* (semiannually). **E-mail Address:** pucclabs@pucc.princeton.edu.

★8416★ PVA/EPVA Center for Neuroscience and Regeneration Research of Yale University
VA Medical Center
Bldg. 34, 127A
West Haven, CT 06516
Phone: (203)937-3802
Fax: (203)937-3801
Stephen G. Waxman, M.D., Dir.

Research Activities and Fields: Basic mechanisms of central nervous system development, function, injury, and functional recovery. Concerns include molecular basis for neurological disorders, nerve cell growth and regeneration, pathophysiology of conduction in injured nerve fibers, regeneration of the central nervous system in mammalian species, and multiple sclerosis as a model for understanding how demyelinated nerve fibers regain their ability to effectively transmit electrical impulses. Areas of expertise of scientific staff include neurocytology, experimental neuropathology, immunology, developmental neuroscience, electrophysiology, biophysics, and molecular biology.

★8417★ R.S. Dow Neurological Sciences Institute
Good Samaritan Hospital & Medical Center
1120 NW 20th Ave.
Portland, OR 97209-1595
Phone: (503)229-7217
Fax: (503)229-7229
Neal H. Barmack, Ph.D., Chair

Research Activities and Fields: Research goal is to increase the knowledge and understanding of the structure and function of the nervous system, from the level of the molecule to the level of the brain and sensory organs. Examines the function of the nervous and sensory systems in the following five areas: 1) dizziness and balance disorders; 2) pain and other somatosensory disorders; 3) visual disorders; 4) neuronal development and regeneration; and 5) movement control disorders. **Publications:** Annual Report.

★8418★ Rockefeller University Laboratory of Motor Physiology
1230 York Ave.
New York, NY 10021-6399
Phone: (212)327-8592
Fax: (212)327-8343
Prof. Hiroshi Asanuma, Dir.

Research Activities and Fields: Neuronal mechanisms subserving cortical control of movements and the neural substrate that constitutes the basis of motor learning. **Formerly:** Laboratory of Neurophysiology.

★8419★ Rockefeller University Laboratory of Neuroendocrinology
1230 York Ave.
Box 139
New York, NY 10021-6399
Phone: (212)570-8624
Bruce S. McEwen, Head

Research Activities and Fields: Seeks to locate brain sites and understand the mechanisms by which hormones promote neural plasticity and thereby alter endocrine function, behavior, neurological states, and mood. Also studies the influence of gonadal and adrenal hormones on aging in the brain.

★8420★ Rocky Mountain Multiple Sclerosis Center
701 East Hampden, Ste. 430
Englewood, CO 80110
Phone: (303)788-4030
Fax: (303)788-5418
Jack S. Burks, M.D., Pres.

Research Activities and Fields: Basic and clinical research on the cause of and treatments for multiple sclerosis. Subjects include molecular virology, molecular biology, cellular immunology, disease pathogenesis, neurology, and psychiatry. Research activities include testing of drugs and therapies for effectiveness in treating multiple sclerosis. **Publications:** *INFORM* (quarterly newsletter).

★8421★ Rush Alzheimer's Disease Center
710 S. Paulina
8 North
Chicago, IL 60612
Phone: (312)942-4463
Fax: (312)942-4154
Jacob H. Fox, M.D., Dir.

Research Activities and Fields: Alzheimer's disease, including causes, treatment, and cure. Conducts clinical trials of new drug treatments and analyzes potential risk factors in the development of Alzheimer's disease.

★8422★ Rush University Multiple Sclerosis Center
1725 W. Harrison St., Ste. 309
Chicago, IL 60612
Phone: (312)942-8011
Fax: (312)942-2253
Floyd A. Davis, M.D., Dir.

Research Activities and Fields: Multiple sclerosis, including understanding of nerve impulse conduction in both normal and pathologic states and pathophysiology of conduction in multiple sclerosis and allied demyelinating conditions, improving conduction in diseased nerves by pharmacologic therapy, and development of a detailed molecular model of the organization of the ion-specific channels of the nerve membrane. Patient studies include programs in neuroactive drugs, thermolability phenomena, analysis of individual's psychological stresses and the resulting coping mechanisms, and the effect of disease on children of patients and the overall family unit.

★8423★ Rutgers University Center for Molecular and Behavioral Neuroscience
197 Univ. Ave.
Newark, NJ 07102
Phone: (201)648-1080
Fax: (201)648-1272
Dr. Paula Tallal, Codirector

Research Activities and Fields: Conducts molecular and behavioral neuroscience research for applications to behavioral dysfunctions in humans. Serves as a technology transfer unit between the University and the pharmaceutical industry.

★8424★ Scripps Research Institute Department of Neuropharmacology
10666 N. Torrey Pines Rd.
La Jolla, CA 92037
Phone: (619)554-9730
Fax: (619)554-8851
Dr. Floyd E. Bloom, Dir.

Research Activities and Fields: Mechanisms of cellular communication in the nervous and endocrine systems. Primary areas of research include: 1) the molecular identification of chemical messengers (neurotransmitters and hormones) and characterization of the structure and function of the cells that secrete them; 2) establishing the role of these substances in normal physiological regulation; 3) establishing the possible pathophysiological roles in clinical disorders of the brain and endocrine system; 4) employing molecular genetic methods to detect virus-selected pathologic mechanisms; 5) interactions between neurotransmitters, cytokines, neurons, glia, and brain macrophages in virus or neurodegenerative disorders; and 6) mechanisms of actions of addictive drugs. **E-mail Address:** fbloom@scripps.edu.

Sleep Disorders Center for Children
See: Entry 3349

★8425★ Sleep Disorders Center of Henry Ford Hospital
2921 W. Grand Blvd.
Detroit, MI 48202
Phone: (313)972-1800
Fax: (313)874-7158
Thomas Roth, Ph.D., Dir.

Research Activities and Fields: Basic and applied research in psychopharmacology of sleep, daytime sleepiness, and sleep disorders, including sleep-related apnea.

★8426★ Sleep Research Foundation
170 Morton St.
Boston, MA 02130
Phone: (617)522-9270
Dr. Ernest Hartmann, Dir.

Research Activities and Fields: Medical, biological, psychological, cultural, and social factors relating to sleep and sleep disorders, including studies on basic sleep mechanisms, sleep requirement, insomnia, sleeping medication, dreams, and nightmares.

★ 8427 ★ Solomon Park Research Institute
12815 NE 124th St., Ste. I
Kirkland, WA 98034-8313
Phone: (206)821-7005
Fax: (206)821-5508
Patric A. Clapshaw, Ph.D., Dir.

Research Activities and Fields: Amyotrophic lateral sclerosis (ALS), also known as Lou Gehrig's Disease, including androgenic determinants and viral causes.

★ 8428 ★ Southern California Neuropsychiatric Institute
6794 La Jolla Blvd.
La Jolla, CA 92037
Phone: (619)454-2102
Fax: (619)454-2104
Sydney Walker, III, M.D., Dir.

Research Activities and Fields: Sleep disorders, post-concussion syndrome, and hyperactivity. **Publications:** *Neuropsychiatric Bulletin* (quarterly).

★ 8429 ★ Stanford University Center for Research on Sleep and Circadian Rhythm
701 Welch Rd., Ste. 2226
Palo Alto, CA 94304
Phone: (415)723-8134
Fax: (415)725-7341
Dr. William Dement, Dir.

Research Activities and Fields: Sleep, including brain mechanisms which control transitions between sleep and wakefulness, transitions between sleep states, and the circadian timing between those various states.

★ 8430 ★ Stanford University Sleep Disorders Research Center
Stanford, CA 94305-4147
Phone: (415)723-8131
William C. Dement, Dir.

Research Activities and Fields: Mechanisms of sleep and wakefulness and sleep/wake functions and pathologies.

★ 8431 ★ Stanford University Stanford Pain Management Service
Medical Center
Anesthesia Dept.
Stanford, CA 94305
Phone: (415)723-6238
Fax: (415)725-8544
William Brose, M.D., Dir.

Research Activities and Fields: Clinical research into pain mechanisms, actions of analgesic substances, and pharmacokinetic and pharmacodynamic modeling. **E-mail Address:** ME.WGB. **Formerly:** Stanford Pain Clinic (1990).

State University of New York Health Science Center at Brooklyn Neurodynamic Laboratory
See: Entry 7604

★ 8432 ★ Syracuse University Institute for Sensory Research
Merrill Ln.
Syracuse, NY 13244-5290
Phone: (315)443-4164
Fax: (315)443-1184
Dr. Robert L. Smith, Dir.

Research Activities and Fields: Sensory processes (hearing, vision, and touch) using an interdisciplinary approach, including psychophysics, neurophysiology, neurochemistry, anatomy, cell biology, physiology, and biosimulation. Occasionally conducts applied research projects. **E-mail Address:** bob_smith@isr.syr.edu. **Formerly:** Bioacoustics Laboratory (1963); Laboratory of Sensory Communication (1974).

★ 8433 ★ Texas Scottish Rite Hospital for Children Research Department
2222 Welborn St.
Dallas, TX 75219
Phone: (214)559-7877
Richard H. Browne, Ph.D., Administrative Dir. of Research

Research Activities and Fields: Treatment of children with orthopedic and neuromuscular disorders. Primary areas of focus are bioengineering and orthopedic biomechanics, including Ilizarov fixators, spine mechanics, spinal implants design and evaluation, and physical properties of bone; and neurophysiology, including gait analysis and muscle strength assessment. Also conducts drug research, studies of innovative care, and application of new technology.

★ 8434 ★ Texas Tech University Tarbox Parkinson's Disease Institute
Health Science Center
3601 4th St., Rm. 4A105
Lubbock, TX 79430
Phone: (806)743-2391
Fax: (806)743-1866
Richard W. Homan, M.D., Dir.

Research Activities and Fields: Neurophysical and neuropharmacological studies of the central nervous system of vertebrates as they relate to Parkinson's disease and other neurological disorders.

★ 8435 ★ Thomas Jefferson University Neurosurgery Research Laboratories
1015 Chestnut St., 14th Fl.
Philadelphia, PA 19107
Phone: (215)955-6744
Fax: (215)923-8071
Dr. Jewell L. Osterholm, Dir.

Research Activities and Fields: Basic mechanisms involved in central nervous system trauma and stroke: cerebral and spinal cord blood flow, energetics, neurotransmitters, electrophysiology, amino acids, edema, and electrolytes. Provides clinical care and conducts clinical studies, primarily on subhuman primates.

Thomas Jefferson University Regional Spinal Cord Injury Center of Delaware Valley
See: Entry 12753

★ 8436 ★ Thomas Jefferson University Sleep Disorders Center
Jefferson Medical College
1015 Walnut St., 3rd Fl.
Philadelphia, PA 19107
Phone: (215)955-6175
Fax: (215)923-8219
Dr. Karl Doghramji, M.D., Dir.

Research Activities and Fields: Sleep/wake disorders or disorders which may have characteristic sleep markers. Also studies seasonal affective disorder, phototherapy for circadian rhythm disorders, and human sexuality, particularly erectile impotence. Research studies are developed in connection with clinical services and with subject groups recruited for special projects. **Formerly:** Center for the Study of Sleep.

Tulane University U.S.-Japan Biomedical Research Laboratories
See: Entry 4901

U.S. Department of Defense Armed Forces Institute of Pathology Center for Advanced Pathology Neuropathology Department
See: Entry 10157

U.S. Department of Health and Human Services National Institute on Aging Laboratory of Neurosciences
See: Entry 1962

U.S. Department of Health and Human Services National Institute on Aging Neuroscience and Neuropsychology of Aging Program
See: Entry 1964

U.S. Department of Health and Human Services National Institute on Alcohol Abuse and Alcoholism Basic Research Division Neurosciences and Behavioral Research Branch
See: Entry 12107

★ 8437 ★ U.S. Department of Health and Human Services National Institute of Child Health and Human Development Intramural Research Program Growth Factors Section
9000 Rockville Pike
Bethesda, MD 20892
Phone: (301)496-4751
Fax: (301)402-2079
Dr. Gordon Guroff, Head

Research Activities and Fields: Section studies the biochemical and physiological actions of nerve growth factor, a peptide required for the development of the sympathetic and sensory nervous systems. Reagents include the PC12 cell, a clone which differentiates in vitro into a sympathetic neuron in response to nerve growth factor. Phosphorylative events and changes in gene transcription which may underlie differentiation are studied to define the exact molecular mechanism by which such peptide factors act.

★8438★ U.S. Department of Health and Human Services
National Institute of Child Health and Human Development
Laboratory of Developmental Neurobiology
NIH Bldg. 36
9000 Rockville Pike
Bethesda, MD 20892
Phone: (301)496-1463
Fax: (301)496-9939
Dr. Phillip G. Nelson, Chief

Research Activities and Fields: Laboratory investigates neurobiologic mechanisms relevant to the development of the nervous system, with emphasis on studies at the cellular membrane and molecular levels. The basis for short- and long-term interaction between nerve cells is studied electrophysiologically, morphologically, and biochemically, using neurons growing in tissue culture. Combined molecular and morphological methods are used in the analysis of experiential modifications of brain function and gene expression, with particular emphasis on mechanisms of gene regulation during nervous system development. In addition, the pineal gland as a model of endocrine regulation and differentiation is studied, with emphasis on gene expression. Activities are carried out in the seven sections and units.

U.S. Department of Health and Human Services
National Institute of Dental Research
Intramural Research Program
Neurobiology and Anesthesiology Branch
See: Entry 4020

★8439★ U.S. Department of Health and Human Services
National Institute of Dental Research
Intramural Research Program
Pain Research Clinic
Bldg. 10, Rm. 3C403
9000 Rockville Pike
Bethesda, MD 20892
Phone: (301)496-5483
Fax: (301)402-0667
Dr. Ronald Dubner, Chief

Research Activities and Fields: The Pain Research Clinic collaborates with other units of the National Institutes of Health to conduct research on chronic pain problems of the face and oral cavity as well as reflex sympathetic dystrophy, cancer pain, diabetic neuropathy, and shingles. Multidisciplinary efforts involve studies in basic science, neurology, oncology, dentistry, pharmacology, and psychology to generate new understanding of pain mechanisms and pain control.

U.S. Department of Health and Human Services
National Institute of Diabetes and Digestive and Kidney Diseases
Division of Digestive Diseases and Nutrition
Gastrointestinal Neuroendocrinology Program
See: Entry 5244

★8440★ U.S. Department of Health and Human Services
National Institute of Diabetes and Digestive and Kidney Diseases
Laboratory of Neuroscience
NIH Bldg. 8
9000 Rockville Pike
Bethesda, MD 20892
Phone: (301)496-8100
Fax: (301)402-2872
Dr. Phil Skolnick, Chief

Research Activities and Fields: Neurosciences.

U.S. Department of Health and Human Services
National Institute on Drug Abuse
Addiction Research Center
Neuroscience Research Branch
See: Entry 12118

U.S. Department of Health and Human Services
National Institute on Drug Abuse
Basic Research Division
Neurosciences Research Branch
See: Entry 12125

U.S. Department of Health and Human Services
National Institute of Environmental Health Sciences
Laboratory of Molecular and Integrative Neurosciences
See: Entry 5109

U.S. Department of Health and Human Services
National Institute of Mental Health
Biochemical Genetics Laboratory
See: Entry 7617

U.S. Department of Health and Human Services
National Institute of Mental Health
Cerebral Metabolism Laboratory
See: Entry 7619

U.S. Department of Health and Human Services
National Institute of Mental Health
Intramural Research Programs Division (Clinical Research)
Clinical Neuroendocrinology Branch
See: Entry 7637

U.S. Department of Health and Human Services
National Institute of Mental Health
Intramural Research Programs Division (Clinical Research)
Experimental Therapeutics Branch
See: Entry 7640

U.S. Department of Health and Human Services
National Institute of Mental Health
Intramural Research Programs Division (Research at St. Elizabeth's Hospital)
Clinical Brain Disorders Branch
See: Entry 7641

U.S. Department of Health and Human Services
National Institute of Mental Health
Intramural Research Programs Division (Research at St. Elizabeth's Hospital)
Neuropsychiatry Branch
See: Entry 7642

U.S. Department of Health and Human Services
National Institute of Mental Health
Neurochemistry Laboratory
See: Entry 7644

U.S. Department of Health and Human Services
National Institute of Mental Health
Neurophysiology Laboratory
See: Entry 7645

U.S. Department of Health and Human Services
National Institute of Mental Health
Neuropsychology Laboratory
See: Entry 7646

U.S. Department of Health and Human Services
National Institute of Mental Health
Neuroscience and Behavioral Science Division
Molecular and Cellular Neuroscience Research Branch
See: Entry 7650

★8441★ U.S. Department of Health and Human Services
National Institute of Neurological Disorders and Stroke
NIH Bldg. 31
9000 Rockville Pike, Rm. 8A52
Bethesda, MD 20892
Phone: (301)496-9746
Fax: (301)496-0296
Patricia A. Grady, Ph.D., Acting Director

Research Activities and Fields: The mission of NINCDS is to conduct and support research and training on causes, prevention, diagnosis, and treatment of neurological disorders and stroke. The Institute conducts, fosters, and supports research and research training in neurological and muscle disorders through: intramural, collaborative, and field research in its own laboratories, branches, and clinics, and through contracts; research grants to scientific institutions and to individuals; individual and institutional research training awards to increase trained professional research manpower in neurological fields; and cooperation with various agencies in collecting and disseminating educational and informational material related to neurological disorders and stroke. The Institute is organized in four divisions that support research in specific areas through grants and contract administration: 1) Convulsive, Developmental, and Neuromuscular Disorders Division; 2) Demyelinating, Atrophic, and Dementing Disorders Division; 3) Fundamental Neurosciences Division; and 4) Stroke and Trauma Division. In addition, the Extramural Activities Division provides administrative support and coordination for the Institute's grants and contracts; and the

Intramural Division conducts basic and clinical research in-house in neurological disorders and relevant disciplines.

★ 8442 ★ U.S. Department of Health and Human Services
National Institute of Neurological Disorders and Stroke
Biometry and Field Studies Branch
7550 Wisconsin Ave., Rm. 7A12
Bethesda, MD 20892
Phone: (301)496-4106
Fax: (301)496-3444
Dr. Jonas H. Ellenberg, Chief

Research Activities and Fields: The NINDS Biometry and Field Studies Branch uses statistics and related disciplines to design, conduct, and analyze collaborative studies involving the etiology, natural history, prevention, treatment, incidence, and prevalence of neurological disorders. Branch also provides consultation in biostatistics, demography, and survey design to NINDS and other neuroscientists.

★ 8443 ★ U.S. Department of Health and Human Services
National Institute of Neurological Disorders and Stroke
Biophysics Section
NIH Bldg. 9, Rm. 1E124
9000 Rockville Pike
Bethesda, MD 20892
Phone: (301)496-3204
Fax: (301)480-0826
Dr. Gerald Eherenstein, Chief

Research Activities and Fields: Section studies the molecular and cellular mechanisms responsible for excitation, membrane potentials, the generation of the nerve impulse, and synaptic activity. Research includes the use of physical and chemical techniques, online and offline digital computers, and a variety of applied mathematical methods.

★ 8444 ★ U.S. Department of Health and Human Services
National Institute of Neurological Disorders and Stroke
Clinical Neuroscience Branch
NIH Bldg. 10, Rm. 5N214
9000 Rockville Pike
Bethesda, MD 20892
Phone: (301)496-4297
Fax: (301)496-4297
Irwin J. Kopin, Chief

Research Activities and Fields: Neurosciences.

★ 8445 ★ U.S. Department of Health and Human Services
National Institute of Neurological Disorders and Stroke
Developmental and Metabolic Neurology Branch
NIH Bldg. 10, Rm. 3D04
9000 Rockville Pike
Bethesda, MD 20892
Phone: (301)496-3285
Fax: (301)496-9480
Dr. Roscoe O. Brady, Chief

Research Activities and Fields: Branch conducts fundamental and clinical research on genetic disorders of metabolism, demyelinating disorders, biochemistry of cell membranes, and signal transduction mechanisms in normal and neoplastic tissues. Principal areas of interest are biochemistry, genetics, neurochemistry, neuroimmunology, molecular genetics, and adult and pediatric neurology.

★ 8446 ★ U.S. Department of Health and Human Services
National Institute of Neurological Disorders and Stroke
Division of Convulsive, Developmental, and Neuromuscular Disorders
Federal Bldg., Rm. 816
7550 Wisconsin Ave.
Bethesda, MD 20892
Phone: (301)496-6541
Fax: (301)402-0302
F.J. Brinley, Jr., Director

Research Activities and Fields: Areas of research supported by the Division include convulsive and paroxysmal disorders, neuromuscular disorders, the peripheral neuropathies, and pediatric neurological disorders. Division comprises branches for Developmental Neurology and Epilepsy.

★ 8447 ★ U.S. Department of Health and Human Services
National Institute of Neurological Disorders and Stroke
Division of Convulsive, Developmental, and Neuromuscular Disorders
Developmental Neurology Branch
7550 Wisconsin Ave.
Bethesda, MD 20892
Phone: (301)496-6701
Dr. Philip Sheridan, Chief

Research Activities and Fields: Branch initiates and supports basic and applied research in birth defects and genetic and developmental disorders, neuromuscular disorders, neonatal brain disorders, neural tube defects (spina bifida and related disorders), the neurophysiology of learning disorders, the phakomatoses (tuberous sclerosis, neurofibromatosis, and related disorders), and autism and related behavioral disorders; and supports centers of neurogenetic disorders of infants and children.

★ 8448 ★ U.S. Department of Health and Human Services
National Institute of Neurological Disorders and Stroke
Division of Convulsive, Developmental, and Neuromuscular Disorders
Epilepsy Branch
7550 Wisconsin Ave., Rm. 114
Bethesda, MD 20892
Phone: (301)496-1917
Fax: (301)496-9916
Dr. James J. Cereghino, Chief

Research Activities and Fields: Branch is responsible for the federal government's program in epilepsy research. Goals are to promote research into the basic mechanisms, etiologies, prevention, diagnosis, and treatment of epilepsies. Branch implements its program through grant- and contract-supported research programs, with emphasis on: 1) basic research (primarily grant-supported), identification of gap areas, and support of state-of-the-art monographs and international symposia; 2) development of anticonvulsant drugs in conjunction with the Antiepileptic Drug Development Program (ADD) conducted by the National Institute of Neurological Disorders and Stroke; and 3) the development of clinical research centers in epilepsy. The ADD Program comprises preclinical studies and clinical evaluations. Branch also supports comprehensive epilepsy programs for clinical and laboratory research in the diagnosis, treatment, prognosis, and prevention of epilepsy. These programs facilitate applied research and coordinate research and teaching with health care services.

★ 8449 ★ U.S. Department of Health and Human Services
National Institute of Neurological Disorders and Stroke
Division of Demyelinating, Atrophic, and Dementing Disorders
Federal Bldg., Rm. 810
7550 Wisconsin Ave.
Bethesda, MD 20892
Phone: (301)496-5679
Fax: (301)402-2060
Dr. Carl M. Leventhal, Director

Research Activities and Fields: The Division supports basic and clinical research relating to the understanding, diagnosis, treatment, and prevention of a broad scope of neurological disorders of adults and the aged. These diseases include Alzheimer's disease and other dementias, Parkinson's disease, Huntington's disease, and amyotrophic lateral sclerosis, as well as demyelinating disorders such as multiple sclerosis. In addition, research is funded on infectious diseases, including "slow" virus diseases, encephalitis, meningitis, and neurological aspects of AIDS. Biological research emphasizing neuroendocrinology and the neurological basis of pain is also supported. Research activities include studies of the physiology, biochemistry, pharmacology, anatomy, pathology, genetics, and epidemiology of these diseases and related conditions in humans and animal models.

★ 8450 ★ U.S. Department of Health and Human Services
National Institute of Neurological Disorders and Stroke
Division of Demyelinating, Atrophic, and Dementing Disorders
Huntington's Disease Research Roster
Department of Medical Genetics
Medical Research and Library Bldg.
Indiana University Medical Center
975 W Walnut St.
Indianapolis, IN 46202-5251
Phone: (317)274-2245
Fax: (317)274-2387
Dr. P. Michael Conneally, Principal Investigator

Research Activities and Fields: Purpose of the Roster program is to compile a registry of families with, or at risk for, Huntington's Disease (HD) that can be used as a resource for HD research. The Roster contains 113,055 records of individuals in 2340 families located in all 50 states as well as in other countries. **Publications:** *Huntington's Disease Research Roster.*

★ 8451 ★ U.S. Department of Health and Human Services
National Institute of Neurological Disorders and Stroke
Division of Fundamental Neurosciences
7550 Wisconsin Ave., Rm. 916
Bethesda, MD 20892
Phone: (301)496-5745
Eugene Streicher, Director

Research Activities and Fields: The Division supports (through grants, contracts, and awards) studies related to neurosciences. Research activity is highly diversified, involving: 1) studies of the neurophysiology of cognitive processes, including those which can be studied at the neuronal level; 2) investigation of somatic-autonomic mechanisms of neuronal interaction; 3) research on nerve impulse receptors, including isolation and purification of cholinergic receptors; 4) identification of specific opiate receptors (of relevance to the understanding of drug tolerance, habituation, and withdrawal as well as the problem of pain mechanisms); 5) studies of the plasticity of the central nervous system--its ability to drop or modify old connections, form new ones, and to reshape neural networks; and 6) development of neural prostheses for stroke, paraplegia, and deafness victims.

★ 8452 ★ U.S. Department of Health and Human Services
National Institute of Neurological Disorders and Stroke
Division of Fundamental Neurosciences
Neural Prosthesis Program
7550 Wisconsin Ave., Rm. 916
Bethesda, MD 20892
Phone: (301)496-5746
Fax: (301)402-1501
Dr. Frederick Terry Hambrecht, Head

Research Activities and Fields: Program supports research on the development of aids for the neurologically disabled based on direct interfaces with neural tissue. Principal areas of research interest are cochlear implants and cochlear nucleus implants for the deaf; visual prostheses for the blind and motor prostheses for the paralyzed. Research is carried out under contract and through grants at universities and commercial research laboratories.

★ 8453 ★ U.S. Department of Health and Human Services
National Institute of Neurological Disorders and Stroke
Division of Intramural Research
Bldg. 10, Rm. SN-314
9000 Rockville Pike
Bethesda, MD 20892
Phone: (301)496-4297
Fax: (301)402-0180
Irwin J. Kopin, Director

Research Activities and Fields: Division conducts basic and clinical research in the neurological sciences and relevant disciplines. Recent areas of interest have included drug therapies for debilitating neurological diseases such as Parkinsonism, new techniques to help scientists better understand how the brain and nervous system function, and major research advances in neurovirology, neurochemistry, and other fields. Current interests include central

nervous system disorders, such as Creutzfeldt-Jakob disease, that appear to be slow infections caused by transmissible virus-like agents; Inherited disorders of lipid metabolism, such as Gaucher's disease, Niemann-Pick disease, Fabry's disease, Krabbe's disease, and Tay-Sachs disease. Studies with the PET scanner, which have shown a relationship between glucose uptake and brain tumor growth, allow scientists to obtain axial transverse or coronal images of the brain. Intramural research is organized in two program areas: Basic Neurosciences and Clinical Neurosciences.

★ 8454 ★ U.S. Department of Health and Human Services
National Institute of Neurological Disorders and Stroke
Division of Intramural Research (Basic Neurosciences Program)
NIH Bldg. 36, Rm. 5A05
9000 Rockville Pike
Bethesda, MD 20892
Phone: (301)496-5468
Fax: (301)402-1566
Dr. Harold Gainer, Ph.D., Director

Research Activities and Fields: The Basic Neurosciences Program of the Institute's Division of Intramural Research comprises laboratories for: Adaptive Systems, Central Nervous System Studies, Experimental Neuropathology, Molecular Biology, Molecular and Cellular Neurobiology, Molecular Medicine and Neuroscience, Neural Control, Neurobiology, Neurochemistry, Neurophysiology, and Viral and Molecular Pathogenesis and sections for Neurogenetics and Synaptic Mechanisms.

★ 8455 ★ U.S. Department of Health and Human Services
National Institute of Neurological Disorders and Stroke
Division of Intramural Research (Clinical Neurosciences Program)
NIH Bldg. 10, Rm. 5N226
9000 Rockville Pike
Bethesda, MD 20892
Phone: (301)496-1561
Fax: (301)402-1007
Mark Hallett, M.D., Director

Research Activities and Fields: The Clinical Neurosciences Program of the Division of Intramural Research engages in research on problems important in Clinical Neurology and Neurosurgery. The Office of the Clinical Director provides clinical neurological services to investigators within the Institute and other NIH institutes. Activities include clinical neurophysiological laboratory investigations, neurology consultations, and neuropathology. Principal branches include Biometry and Field Studies, Clinical Neuroscience, Developmental and Metabolic Neurology, Epilepsy Research, Experimental Therapeutics, Medical Neurology, Neuroepidemiology, Neuroimmunology, Stroke, and Surgical Neurology.

★ 8456 ★ U.S. Department of Health and Human Services
National Institute of Neurological Disorders and Stroke
Division of Stroke and Trauma

7550 Wisconsin Ave.
Federal Bldg., 8A08
Bethesda, MD 20892
Phone: (301)496-2581
Fax: (301)480-1080
Dr. Michael Walker, Director

Research Activities and Fields: Division supports research and research training in stroke and central nervous system trauma, including support for basic, applied, and clinical research. This includes support for multidisciplinary cerebrovascular clinical research centers, a comprehensive stroke center program, spinal cord injury centers, a comprehensive CNS trauma center program, and head injury centers, as well as larger numbers of individual, investigator-initiated research grants. Program supports training of young investigators through formal institutional and individual training awards; support is also provided through new investigator research awards, research career development awards, and clinical teacher investigator development awards. In addition, Division administers grants to exploit the research opportunities presented by positron emission tomography (PET). Principal areas of research interest are: 1) cerebrovascular disease (including stroke and its consequences); 2) trauma to the brain, spinal cord, and peripheral nervous system; 3) central nervous system regeneration; 4) primary and metastatic tumors of the brain and/or spinal cord; 5) headache; 6) chronic pain; 7) positron emission tomography; and 8) manipulative therapy.

★ 8457 ★ U.S. Department of Health and Human Services
National Institute of Neurological Disorders and Stroke
Experimental Therapeutics Branch
NIH Bldg. 10, Rm. 5C103
9000 Rockville Pike
Bethesda, MD 20892
Phone: (301)496-7993
Fax: (301)496-6609
Dr. Thomas N. Chase, Chief

Research Activities and Fields: Develops improved pharmacotherapies for neurologic disease. The Branch operates a vertically integrated program of research, extending from basic molecular biology to clinical trials, focusing on neurodegenerative diseases such as Alzheimer's disease and Parkinson's disease. Current operating components: 1) the Molecular Pharmacology Section characterizes central transmitter receptors and information transduction processes; 2) the Genetic Pharmacology Unit investigates pharmaceutical approaches to the selective regulation of gene expression; 3) the Neurophysiology Pharmacology Section studies basal ganglia function in relation to transmitter system interactions; and 4) Clinical Pharmacology Section works clinically and in animal models to elucidate pathophysiologic mechanisms and evaluate novel pharmacologic interventions.

★ 8458 ★ U.S. Department of Health and Human Services
National Institute of Neurological Disorders and Stroke
Laboratory of Central Nervous System Studies
NIH Bldg. 36, Rm. 5B21
9000 Rockville Pike
Bethesda, MD 20892
Phone: (301)496-3281
Fax: (301)496-8275
Dr. D. Carleton Gajdusek, Chief

Research Activities and Fields: Focus is primarily on two main areas: 1) the medical surveillance of disease patterns in many primitive and isolated populations, with attention to child growth and development, behavior, and learning; and 2) the slow, latent, and temperate virus infections, particularly chronic degenerative neurologic diseases and their pathogenesis and mechanisms of virus persistence. Also studies configuration and change resulting in conversion of normal host precursors to infectious proteins in the transmissible amyloidoses of the brain. In addition, aging of the brain, Alzheimer's, Pick's, Parkinson's, and Huntington's diseases, multiple sclerosis, amyotrophic lateral sclerosis, chronic epilepsies, and other diseases are studied in microbiological, immunologic, genetic, and biochemical laboratories and clinics and in foci of high incidence throughout the world. Worldwide study of hemorrhagic fever with renal syndrome is conducted with isolation and molecular and virulence characterization of the hantavirus serotypes. HIV and HTLV I and II genetic variation, and involvement of the nervous system are studied worldwide.

★ 8459 ★ U.S. Department of Health and Human Services
National Institute of Neurological Disorders and Stroke
Laboratory of Experimental Neuropathology
NIH Bldg. 36, Rm. 4A29
9000 Rockville Pike
Bethesda, MD 20892
Phone: (301)496-4747
Fax: (301)402-1030
Dr. Henry Webster, Chief

Research Activities and Fields: Laboratory conducts research on the cellular organization of the developing and adult nervous system; and investigates cellular and subcellular abnormalities that cause or are associated with neurological diseases and experimental lesions in the nervous system. Laboratory develops and coordinates electron-microscopic, immunocytochemical, virological, immunological, and biochemical methods to explore: 1) cellular mechanisms of myelin formation, breakdown, and regeneration, especially those relevant to multiple sclerosis and other demyelinating diseases; and 2) toxins that induce disease or malfunction of the central and peripheral nervous systems, as well as mechanisms of neurotoxicity.

★ 8460 ★ U.S. Department of Health and Human Services
National Institute of Neurological Disorders and Stroke
Laboratory of Molecular Biology

NIH Bldg. 36, Rm. 3D02
9000 Rockville Pike
Bethesda, MD 20892
Phone: (301)496-6574
Fax: (301)496-4276
Dr. Ronald McKay, Acting Chief

Research Activities and Fields: Research in the Molecular Biology Laboratory has focused on investigation of the mechanism controlling the initiation and control of cell differentiation by physiological and genetic engineering methods and the synthesis and function of neuroreceptors. These studies contribute to the understanding of genetic and developmental disorders and have demonstrated how some of the disorders can be avoided by the careful use of drugs and proper nutrition during pregnancy.

★ 8461 ★ U.S. Department of Health and Human Services
National Institute of Neurological Disorders and Stroke
Laboratory of Molecular and Cellular Neurobiology
9000 Rockville Rd., Bldg. 49, Rm. 2A10
Bethesda, MD 20892
Phone: (301)496-6647
Fax: (301)496-8244
Dr. Richard Quarles, Contact

Research Activities and Fields: Molecular and cellular neurobiology, myelination, and cell surface receptors.

★ 8462 ★ U.S. Department of Health and Human Services
National Institute of Neurological Disorders and Stroke
Laboratory of Neural Control
NIH Bldg. 49, Rm. 3A50
9000 Rockville Pike
Bethesda, MD 20892
Phone: (301)496-4305
Fax: (301)402-4800
Dr. Robert Burke, Chief

Research Activities and Fields: Fundamental research is conducted on the properties of mammalian nerve cells and on the organization of the mammalian central nervous system, with particular reference to studies of the control of movement. Current experimental studies involve five main areas: 1) the neurobiology of spinal cord motorneurons and motor units; 2) the organization of interneuron circuits in the spinal cord; 3) the activity of motor cortex neurons; 4) the development of motor systems in the avian spinal cord; and 5) studies of peripheral nerve regeneration. Such studies utilize established as well as newly developed techniques for electrophysiologic recording from single neurons, but other methods, such as those of neuroanatomy or of muscle fiber histochemistry, are also used as appropriate. The laboratory has facilities for the development of specialized experimental equipment and novel electrode designs suitable for chronic implantation as well as for computer-oriented data analysis and model building.

★ 8463 ★ U.S. Department of Health and Human Services
National Institute of Neurological Disorders and Stroke
Laboratory of Neurobiology
NIH Bldg. 36, Rm. 2A21
9000 Rockville Pike
Bethesda, MD 20892
Phone: (301)496-1296
Fax: (301)480-1485
Dr. Thomas S. Reese, Chief

Research Activities and Fields: Laboratory conducts structural research on the organization of the nervous system. Specific areas of interest are: synaptic transmission, neural membranes, the intracellular sequestration of ions, the blood-brain barrier, and axonal transport. Structural tools used include electron microscopy, X-ray spectroscopy, immunocytochemistry, cryotechniques, and computer processed imaging of light microscopy and electron microscopic images.

★ 8464 ★ U.S. Department of Health and Human Services
National Institute of Neurological Disorders and Stroke
Laboratory of Neurochemistry
NIH Bldg. 36, Rm. 4D-20
9000 Rockville Pike
Bethesda, MD 20892
Phone: (301)496-1671
Fax: (301)496-1339
Dr. Harold Gainer, Chief

Research Activities and Fields: Laboratory conducts research on molecular events that underlie both the normal functioning of the developing and mature nervous system and the derangements that occur in neurological disease. Areas of study include: mechanisms of active ion transport, protein phosphorylation, neuronal development and regeneration, gene expression of neuropeptides and their receptors, and neuronal cytoskeletal proteins.

★ 8465 ★ U.S. Department of Health and Human Services
National Institute of Neurological Disorders and Stroke
Laboratory of Neurophysiology
NIH Bldg. 36, Rm. 2C-02
9000 Rockville Pike
Bethesda, MD 20892
Phone: (301)496-2414
Fax: (301)402-1565
Jeffery Barker, M.D., Chief

Research Activities and Fields: Laboratory conducts research in receptor biology, including studies in molecular biology, biochemistry, anatomy, and physiology. All of the Laboratory's projects involve multidisciplinary analysis of the physiological properties of vertebrate central neurons studied in vitro. A principal line of investigation is focused on the physiological properties of neurons cultured from different parts of the mammalian central nervous system. These studies are aimed at providing insight primarily into the question of what types of phenotypic properties are expressed by different central nervous system cells and, secondarily, into the related problem of how these properties differentiate the functions of one cell type from another. A long-term goal of the Laboratory is to develop a better understanding of the relationship between the activity of ion channels in neuronal membranes and the synthesis and secretion of specific transmitter substances. Another area of interest involves pharmacological experiments on the cellular mechanisms of actions of clinically important drugs like benzodiazepines, barbiturates, and convulsants using electrophysiological recording techniques (voltage-clamp and patch-clamp). **Publications:** Annual Report.

★8466★ **U.S. Department of Health and Human Services**
National Institute of Neurological Disorders and Stroke
Laboratory of Viral and Molecular Pathogenesis
NIH Bldg. 36, Rm. 5D04
9000 Rockville Pike
Bethesda, MD 20892
Phone: (301)496-9106
Dr. Monique Dubois-Dalcq, Chief

Research Activities and Fields: Laboratory investigates the molecular events that occur in the replication and expression of genetic materials in mammalian cells and their viruses. Genetic, biochemical, and recombinant DNA techniques are used to study gene replication and transcription. Post-transcriptional modification and translation of ribonucleic acids are also examined. The biological systems studied include: measles virus and vesicular stomatitis virus, two members of the negative strand RNA virus family, and glial cells of the central and peripheral nervous system, especially glial cell differentiation and development, with emphasis on the genes involved in myelin synthesis and maintenance.

★8467★ **U.S. Department of Health and Human Services**
National Institute of Neurological Disorders and Stroke
Medical Neurology Branch
NIH Bldg. 10, Rm. 5N226
9000 Rockville Pike
Bethesda, MD 20892
Phone: (301)496-1561
Fax: (301)402-1007
Mark Hallett, M.D., Chief

Research Activities and Fields: Laboratory investigates the basic and clinical aspects of a variety of neurologic disorders, including: pathophysiological mechanisms and treatment of movement disorders; pathophysiology of neuromuscular diseases; and cognitive neuropsychology.

★8468★ **U.S. Department of Health and Human Services**
National Institute of Neurological Disorders and Stroke
Molecular Medicine and Neurological Science Laboratory
NIH Bldg. 36, Rm. 5A23
9000 Rockville Pike
Bethesda, MD 20892
Phone: (301)496-5881
Dr. Eugene Major, Coordinator

Research Activities and Fields: Branch conducts medical research on infectious neurological diseases, including laboratory and clinical studies in: neurovirology; epidemiology; immunochemistry; electron microscopy; experimental pathology; and viral immunology.

★8469★ **U.S. Department of Health and Human Services**
National Institute of Neurological Disorders and Stroke
Neuroepidemiology Branch
Federal Bldg. 714
7550 Wisconsin Ave.
Bethesda, MD 20892
Phone: (301)496-1714
Fax: (301)496-2358
Karin B. Nelson, M.D., Acting Chief

Research Activities and Fields: Branch conducts national and international studies concerning the patterns of neurologic disorders in human populations. Both environmental and genetic factors in disease etiology are considered. Activities involve training in the utilization of neuroepidemiologic and neurogenetic techniques for the solution of practical problems in clinical neurology and neurosurgery. Although the Branch's program involves the application of epidemiologic methods to the study of any disorder of the nervous system, current research concentrates on retroviral diseases of the nervous system, epidemiology of dementia and other neurodegenerative disorders, pediatric neuroepidemiology and neurogenetics, racial, tropical, and geographical neuroepidemiology, cerebral palsy, torsion dystonias, epilepsy, and international variation in the occurrence of neurologic diseases.

★8470★ **U.S. Department of Health and Human Services**
National Institute of Neurological Disorders and Stroke
Neuroimmunology Branch
NIH Bldg. 10, Rm. 5B-16
9000 Rockville Pk.
Bethesda, MD 20892
Phone: (301)496-1801
Fax: (301)402-0373
Dr. Henry F. McFarland, Chief

Research Activities and Fields: Activities of the Neuroimmunology Branch include basic and clinical investigations related to multiple sclerosis (MS) and other possible immunological-based diseases. Studies focus on examining basic or fundamental immunological questions, including a study of experimental animal models and the cellular immune response to potential antigens in the nervous system. Research studies also examine the role of human retroviruses, including HTLV-I and HTLV-II in diseases of the nervous system. Clinical studies focus on examining the natural history of MS using magnetic resonance imaging and assessing new innovative therapies in MS.

★8471★ **U.S. Department of Health and Human Services**
National Institute of Neurological Disorders and Stroke
Small Business Innovation Research Program
7550 Wisconsin Ave.
Bethesda, MD 20892
Phone: (301)496-1968

Research Activities and Fields: The Small Business Innovation Research (SBIR) Program comprises awards for three phases of research: the objective of Phase I is to establish the technical merit and feasibility of proposed research efforts that may ultimately lead to commercial products or services; the objective of Phase II is to continue the research and development efforts initiated in Phase I that are likely to result in commercial products or services; and the objective of Phase III, where appropriate, is for the small business to pursue, with non-federal funds, the commercialization of the results of the research and development funded in Phases I and II. Recent areas of interest include: development of novel antiepileptic drugs; devices for automated seizure detection; research and development of magnetoencephalography (MEG); development of applications for evoked potentials; development of a portable EEG device; and development of instrumentation for monitoring autonomic nervous system (ANS) function.

★8472★ **U.S. Department of Health and Human Services**
National Institute of Neurological Disorders and Stroke
Surgical Neurology Branch
NIH Bldg. 10, Rm. 5037
9000 Rockville Pike
Bethesda, MD 20892
Phone: (301)496-5728
Fax: (301)402-0380
Dr. Edward H. Oldfield, Chief

Research Activities and Fields: Activities of the Surgical Neurology Branch involve studies of brain tumors, pituitary tumors, tissue implantation and central nervous system regeneration, and vascular disease of the central nervous system. Branch investigates and treats clinical problems of disordered neuronal and glial proliferation and differentiation. A major part of the program is devoted to the study of intracranial tumors, including pituitary tumors. Problems of both central and peripheral neuronal and glial regeneration are also under study. Clinical research in these areas is combined with basic techniques of cell biology, tissue culture, biochemistry, immunology, pharmacology, and light and electronmicroscopic histology to provide for an in-depth exploration and, ultimately, new approaches to these problems. Experimental neuropathology and neuroimmunology are emphasized in a program that includes clinical diagnostic neuropathology. Biochemistry, morphology, and immunochemistry of neoplasms are studied as means of improving detection and treatment and as clonal models of their nonneoplastic counterparts in nervous and lymphoid tissues. Studies are also carried out on cell-mediated immune mechanisms in human brain tumor patients. This work is complemented by studies in animal models on basic mechanisms of cell-mediated immune lysis of tumor cells.

★8473★ University of Alabama at Birmingham
Center for Neuroimmunology
Univ. Sta., Rm. 359
Birmingham, AL 35294
Phone: (205)934-2402
Fax: (205)975-6030
John Whitaker, M.D., Chm.

Research Activities and Fields: Multiple sclerosis, myasthenia gravis, glia, paraneoplastic syndromes, and idiotypes. **Formerly:** Multiple Sclerosis Research Center.

★8474★ University of Alabama at Birmingham
National Spinal Cord Injury Statistical Center
Spain Rehabilitation Center
1717 6th Ave. S.
Birmingham, AL 35233-7330
Phone: (205)934-3334
Samuel L. Stover, M.D., Dir.

Research Activities and Fields: Data collection, storage, and analyses of national spinal cord injury statistics, submitted by 13 federally sponsored Spinal Cord Injury Care Systems. **Publications:** *SCI: The Facts and Figures* (book available for a fee to the public); Annual Report; Semiannual Report; Newsletter.

★8475★ University of Alabama at Birmingham
Neurobiology Research Center
516 CIRC
Birmingham, AL 35294-0021
Phone: (205)934-0100
Fax: (205)934-6571
Prof. Michael J. Friedlander, Dir.

Research Activities and Fields: Basic biology of the brain, including studies of cellular and molecular biology, high resolution 3-dimensional imaging of nerve cells, neurophysiology, biochemistry, biophysics, computer simulation of the nervous system and individual nerve cells, and electrophysiology. Special interests include developmental neurobiology, synaptic transmission, signal transduction, control of coordinated movement, vision physiology, receptor and ion channel development, mechanisms of seizures, sensorimotor integration, neuroembryology, and pharmacological studies. Collaborates in research and training efforts with Civitan International Research Center on neurobiological models and mechanisms of mental retardation and developmental disorders. **Publications:** Annual Report. **E-mail Address:** mjf@nrcimg.nrc.uab.edu.

★8476★ University of Alabama at Birmingham
Pain Center
UAB Medical Center
2000 6th Ave. S., 3rd. Fl.
Birmingham, AL 35233
Phone: (205)801-8250
Fax: (205)801-8253
Dr. Judy McDanal, Med.Dir.

Research Activities and Fields: Chronic pain and the management of chronic pain from benign or malignant sources. Also conducts studies on the effectiveness of group outpatient therapy for pain patients and their families and prior physical and/or sexual trauma and its relation to pain. Multimodal therapeutic regimes include behavior therapy, nerve blocks, hypnotherapy, stimulation produced analgesia (transcutaneous electrical nerve stimulation, acupuncture, and deep brain stimulation), biofeedback, and neuroablation. Affiliated with numerous departments and research centers at the University, which allows for patients to be treated according to their specific needs.

★8477★ University of Alabama at Birmingham
Parkinson's Disease Center
Jefferson Tower, Rm. 1225
Birmingham, AL 35294
Phone: (205)934-9100
Fax: (205)934-0928
Paul Atchison, M.D., Dir.

Research Activities and Fields: Investigates Parkinson's disease, genetics, and basal ganglion, and conducts related drug studies.

★8478★ University of Arizona
Center for Complex Systems
Tucson, AZ 85721
Phone: (520)621-4190
Fax: (520)621-7449
Peter Carruthers, Dir.

Research Activities and Fields: Complex systems in neurobiology, physics, and other areas.

★8479★ University of Arizona
Sleep Disorders Center
College of Medicine
Univ. Medical Center, Rm. 7303
Tucson, AZ 85724
Phone: (520)626-6112
Fax: (520)626-6970
Stuart F. Quan, M.D., Dir.

Research Activities and Fields: Sleep disorders guided by studies in neurology, psychology, pulmonology, and pediatrics. Research efforts concentrate on sleep apnea, sudden infant death syndrome, nocturnal penile tumescence, male sexual dysfunction, seizure disorders, insomnia, narcolepsy, and restless leg syndrome. **E-mail Address:** squan@sneeze.respsci.arizona.edu.

★8480★ University of California, Davis
NIDRR Research & Training Center for Rehabilitation in Neuromuscular Diseases
School of Medicine
Dept. of Physical Medicine & Rehabilitation
TB 191
Davis, CA 95616
Phone: (916)752-2903
Fax: (916)752-3468
W.M. Fowler, Jr., M.D., RTC Dir.

Research Activities and Fields: Addresses the needs of individuals who are affected by chronically disabling neuromuscular diseases. Research is directed to physical performance and nutritional status; evaluation and treatment of swallowing disorders, dyspnea, respiratory control, and rehabilitation therapeutics; employment opportunities and vocational rehabilitation; the educational mainstreaming of children and young adults; and strategies to improve the quality of life and community integration.

★8481★ University of California, Irvine
Center for the Neurobiology of Learning and Memory
123 Bonney Ctr.
Irvine, CA 92717-3800
Phone: (714)824-5193
Fax: (714)824-8481
Dr. James L. McGaugh, Dir.

Research Activities and Fields: Neurobiology of learning and memory, including biochemical mechanisms, systems neurophysiology, modulation of memory, cognitive neuropsychology, and neural modeling. **Publications:** Annual Report; Conference Proceedings.

★8482★ University of California, Irvine
Memory Disorders Clinic
Dept. of Neurology
Med-Surg I, Rm. 154
Irvine, CA 92717-4290
Phone: (714)856-6088
Fax: (714)725-2132
Arnold Starr, M.D., Dir.

Research Activities and Fields: Multidisciplinary approach to diagnosis and treatment of memory disorders, including the development and testing of memory enhancement programs.

★8483★ University of California, Los Angeles
Brain Research Institute
Center for Health Sciences, Rm. 73364
Los Angeles, CA 90024-1761
Phone: (310)825-5061
Fax: (310)825-5061
Arnold B. Scheibel, Dir.

Research Activities and Fields: Brain and central nervous system, including interdisciplinary studies in developmental neurobiology, molecular neurobiology, neuroanatomy, neurobiophysics, neurochemistry, neurocytology, neuroendocrinology, neuroimaging, neuromuscular physiology, neuropathology, neuropharmacology, neurophysiology, behavior, neuroimmunology, and experimental epilepsy. Also conducts research on aging, Alzheimer's Disease, alcohol effects on the central nervous system, cellular neurobiology, neuroendocrinology, and neuromuscular plasticity. **E-mail Address:** eceder@bri.medsch.ocla.edu.

★8484★ University of California, Los Angeles
Jerry Lewis Neuromuscular Research Center
School of Medicine
Los Angeles, CA 90024
Phone: (310)825-3733
Fax: (310)206-5052
Dr. A.D. Grinnell, Dir.

Research Activities and Fields: Basic research into structure, function, and interaction of nerve and muscle, both in normal and diseased tissue. Studies concentrate on membrane biophysics, cell physiology, biochemistry, and their relation to neuromuscular disease.

University of California, Los Angeles
Neuropsychiatric Institute
See: Entry 7656

★8485★ **University of California, Los Angeles**
Reed Neurological Research Center
710 Westwood Plaza, Rm. 4-238
Los Angeles, CA 90024-1769
Phone: (310)206-2101
Fax: (310)206-5518
Dr. Arthur W. Toga, Co-Dir.

Research Activities and Fields: Neuroanatomy, neuroimaging, neurophysiology, and neurological diseases. **E-mail Address:** toga@loni.ucla.edu.

★8486★ **University of California, San Diego**
Alzheimer's Disease Research Center
9500 Gilman Dr.
La Jolla, CA 92093-0948
Phone: (619)622-5800
Fax: (619)622-1012
Dr. Leon Thal, Prin. Investigator

Research Activities and Fields: Conducts longitudinal research on the clinical and cognitive changes associated with Alzheimer's disease and other dementing illnesses by obtaining epidemiological data, medical histories, analysis of blood and sera, administration of batteries of neuropsychological tests, and neurological examinations of patients. Performs clinical drug trials, research on electrophysiology and neuroimaging studies, evaluations of the effects of caregiving stress on the caregivers, studies of memory and language dysfunction, and the possibility of a genetic or metabolic basis for Alzheimer's disease. Also conducts olfaction studies.

★8487★ **University of California, San Francisco**
Brain-Behavior Research Center
Sonoma Developmental Center
Eldridge, CA 95431
Phone: (707)938-4701
Fax: (707)938-1298
Dr. Harman V.S. Peeke, Dir.

Research Activities and Fields: Investigates developmental phenomena at the levels of behavior, electrophysiology, biochemistry, and endocrinology. Areas include the behavior of persons who are developmentally disabled. **Publications:** Annual Report.

University of California, San Francisco
Brain Tumor Research Center
See: Entry 6215

★8488★ **University of California, San Francisco**
CNS Injury and Edema Research Center
M 787
505 Parnassus
San Francisco, CA 94143-0112
Phone: (415)476-2987
Fax: (415)476-9650
Prof. Pak H. Chan, Contact

Research Activities and Fields: Basic and clinical research on brain edema and central nervous system injury; molecular biology of central nervous system. **Formerly:** Brain Edema Clinical Research Center.

★8489★ **University of California, San Francisco**
Keck Center for Integrative Neurosciences
Box 0444
San Francisco, CA 94143
Phone: (415)476-1062
Dr. Steve Lisberger, Dir.

Research Activities and Fields: Neurochemistry of pain modulatory systems in the brainstem and spinal cord, using in vivo microdialysis, cytochemistry and high pressure liquid chromotography.

★8490★ **University of California, San Francisco**
Laboratory for Neurotrauma
SFGH, Rm. 4M39
1001 Potrero Rd.
San Francisco, CA 94110
Phone: (415)476-3860
Fax: (415)476-5682
Lawrence H. Pitts, M.D., Contact

Research Activities and Fields: Models of traumatic brain injury, focal cerebral ischemia, and traumatic spinal cord and their treatment. Examines mechanisms of progressive cellular injury, in vivo and in vitro, and evaluates possible methods of cell protection.

★8491★ **University of California, Santa Barbara**
Neuroscience Research Institute
Santa Barbara, CA 93106
Phone: (805)893-3637
Fax: (805)893-2005
Dr. Steven K. Fisher, Dir.

Research Activities and Fields: Basic biology and medicine, pharmacology, psychology, chemistry, and electrical engineering. Research areas include the genetics, biochemistry, and structural organization of the developing nervous system; the ultrastructure, functi on (and malfunction) of the retina; the role of ion channels in neuronal function; the structural and enzymatic basis of vesicle function at axonal endings; the role of extracellular matrix in neurodevelopment; and the molecular biology of neurotrophins and their receptors. **Formerly:** Superseded an earlier Environmental Stress Laboratory; Institute of Environmental Stress.

★8492★ **University of Chicago**
Brain Research Institute
Dept. of Surgery, Box MC 3026
5841 S. Maryland
Chicago, IL 60637
Phone: (312)702-2123
Fax: (312)702-3518
Bryce Weir, M.D., Dir.

Research Activities and Fields: Alzheimer's disease, amyotrophic lateral sclerosis, myasthenia gravis, AIDS, sleep and sleep disorders, dyslexia, hyperkinesia, epilepsy and epileptoid disorders, mental retardation, mental illness, and brain and nervous system disorders such as multiple sclerosis, muscular dystrophy, cerebral palsy, encephalitis, Parkinson's disease, stroke, cerebral hemorrhage, aneurysm tumor, head injury, and intractable pain. Conducts basic research in neurophysiology, neuropharmacology, neuroanatomy, molecular biology, neuroimmunology, and virology.

★8493★ **University of Connecticut**
Center for Neurological Sciences
Univ. of Connecticut Health Ctr.
263 Farmington Ave.
Farmington, CT 06032
Phone: (203)679-4678
D. Kent Morest, M.D., Dir.

Research Activities and Fields: An interdisciplinary approach to understanding the normal functions and disorders of the nervous system. Programs encompass experimental approaches ranging from the molecular to the systems level including cellular, molecular, and developmental neurobiology, neuroanatomy, neurophysiology, neur ochemistry, neuroendocrinology, neuroimmunology, neuropharmacology, and neuropathology. Specific areas of interest include: biology of neurotransmission in the brain and in the autonomic nervous system; hormonal and transmitter receptors and their structure and function; structure and function of voltage sensitive ion channels; physical chemistry and physiology of neuropeptides; control of gene expression and membrane biogenesis in neurons and glia; gene expression, release, and physiological roles of endogenous opioids; electrophysiology of excitable tissue at the cellular and systems level; development of the heart and the autonomic nervous system; cell culture of neural tissue and neural crest development; stimulus coding, synaptic organization, and development of sensory systems; communicative sciences; structure and function of auditory and gustatory systems; mathematical modeling of neural systems; central nervous system trauma; biology of multiple sclerosis; regeneration and transplantation; biology of epilepsy; and neurobiology of Alzheimer's disease and neurodegenerative disorders. **E-mail Address:** nsinfo@neuron.uchc.edu.

★8494★ **University of Connecticut**
Connecticut Chemosensory Clinical Research Center
Health Center
Farmington, CT 06030
Phone: (203)674-2459
Fax: (203)674-2518
Dr. Marion E. Frank, Prin. Investigator

Research Activities and Fields: Taste and smell disorders of various etiologies, plus independent research projects studying chemosensory function.

★8495★ **University of Delaware**
Graduate Program in Neuroscience
Newark, DE 19716
Phone: (302)831-1191
Fax: (302)831-3645
Dr. David P.M. Northmore, Dir.

Research Activities and Fields: Neuroscience and behavior, including interdisciplinary studies of neural structure and function, sensory systems, inhibition and sleep, artificial (VLSI) neuronal sytems, psychophysics of animal vision, electrophysiology of taste, electrophysiology of vision, neural regeneration in lower vertebrates, motor systems, endocrine and immune system relations with CNS, neuropharmacology, circadian rhythms, and thermoregulation. **E-mail Address:** northmor@brahms.udel.edu. **Formerly:** Institute for Neuroscience (1989).

★ 8496 ★ University of Florida
Brain Institute
J.H.M. Health Science Ctr.
PO Box 100244
Gainesville, FL 32610-0244
Phone: (904)392-0490
Fax: (904)392-8347
William G. Luttge, Ph.D., Dir.

Research Activities and Fields: Peripheral Nerve Trauma Research Program, including biomaterials research, peripheral nerve regeneration, and mechanisms and control of pain associated with peripheral nerve trauma; Head Injury Research Program, including injury- and/or stroke-induced problems with memory, language, attention, emotion, motor skills, and epilepsy; molecular, cellular, and immunological mechanisms involved in nerve cell death and injury following stroke or closed head injury; Neurodegenerative Diseases Program, including molecular biologic studies of genetic bases of a variety of neurologic dysfunctions, including neurodegenerative movement disorders, cell biological studies on Batten's disease, and cell biological and MRI studies of laboratory animal models of multiple sclerosis. Additional studies include the underlying causes of Alzheimer's disease; the neurobiological consequences of alcohol and cocaine abuse in both adults and fetuses; and the molecular and cellular mechanisms and the behavioral and neurologic consequences of such viral-induced neurodegenerative diseases as AIDS, polio, and measles. **E-mail Address:** ufb@cortex.health.ufl.edu.

★ 8497 ★ University of Florida
Center for Neurobiological Sciences
Medical Sciences Bldg., Box J-244
Gainesville, FL 32610
Phone: (904)392-3383
Fax: (904)392-8347
Dr. Luttge, Dir.

Research Activities and Fields: Neurobiological sciences, including neuroanatomy, neurology, neuropsychology, neurophysiology, neurochemistry, neuropharmacology, and neuroendocrinology. Centralizes interdisciplinary communication and research training in neurobiological sciences and coordinates graduate student, postdoctoral, and faculty research in this area at the University.

★ 8498 ★ University of Florida
Center for the Neurobiology of Aging
Box 100 487
Hillis Miller Health Ctr.
Gainesville, FL 32610
Phone: (904)392-6394
Edwin M. Meyer, Ph.D., Codir.

Research Activities and Fields: Alzheimer's disease studies, including evaluation of gene expression in Alzheimer's patients and evaluation of complex behaviors, especially memory.

University of Illinois at Chicago
Center for Handicapped Children
See: Entry 4588

★ 8499 ★ University of Illinois at Chicago
Consultation Clinic for Epilepsy
912 S. Wood St., Rm. 156
Chicago, IL 60612
Phone: (312)996-7360
Fax: (312)996-4169
Dr. John R. Hughes, Dir.

Research Activities and Fields: Neurophysiology and neuropharmacology in the convulsive state, including studies on surgery for intractable psychomotor epilepsy, epidemiology of epilepsy, and side effects of various anticonvulsants. Also evaluates various new anticonvulsants.

★ 8500 ★ University of Illinois at Chicago
Electroencephalography Laboratory
Dept. of Neurology, M/C 722
1740 W. Taylor.
Chicago, IL 60612
Phone: (312)996-3865
Fax: (312)413-8540
Dr. John R. Hughes, Head

Research Activities and Fields: Psychophysiology, including studies on clinical correlates of electroencephalic abnormalities, epilepsy, and organic brain disease.

★ 8501 ★ University of Iowa
Alzheimer's Disease Research Center
College of Medicine
Dept. of Neurology
200 Hawkins Dr.
Iowa City, IA 52242
Phone: (319)356-2571
Fax: (319)356-4505
Antonio Damasio, Dir.

Research Activities and Fields: Alzheimer's disease and related conditions. Departments with participating specialists include anatomy, radiology, pathology, ophthalmology and psychology.

★ 8502 ★ University of Kansas
Center for Neurobiology and Immunology Research (CNIR)
Higuchi Biosciences Center
2099 Constant Ave.
Lawrence, KS 66047-2535
Phone: (913)864-5183
Fax: (913)749-7393
Dr. Elias K. Michaelis, M.D., Dir.

Research Activities and Fields: Neurobiology and immunology, focusing on the problems of chronic, neurodegenerative diseases and immunological disorders. Specific interests include the development of new analytical methods for monitoring nerve cell activity in the brain, exploratory research in the mechanisms of neurodegeneration and the development of new therapeutic strategies based on the use of proteins or oligonucleotides as drug treatments, studies of the regulation of antibody production by immune system cells and the development of new screening procedures for immunotherapeutic agents, designing of new peptide drugs for the control of immune rejection reactions, and new molecular biological tools for recombinant DNA research. **Publications:** Newsletters.

★ 8503 ★ University of Kansas
Neurobiology Research Laboratory
VA Medical Center
4801 Linwood Blvd.
Kansas City, MO 64128
Phone: (816)922-3375
Fax: (816)861-1110
Barry W. Festoff, M.D., Dir.

Research Activities and Fields: Development, plasticity, and diseases of the nervous system. Studies focus on synaptic formation and metabolism; roles of serine proteases and inhibitors (serpins); regulation of amyloid precursor protein processing in Alzheimer's disease; and biological markers in head injuries. **E-mail Address:** festoff.barry__w+@kansas-city.va.gov.

★ 8504 ★ University of Kentucky
Alzheimer's Disease Research Center
101 Sanders-Brown Bldg.
Lexington, KY 40536-0230
Phone: (606)323-6040
Fax: (606)323-2866
William R. Markesbery, M.D., Dir.

Research Activities and Fields: Alzheimer's disease, focusing on the cause, treatment, and eventual cure. **Publications:** *ADRC Update* (quarterly newsletter).

★ 8505 ★ University of Louisville
Center for Research in the Special Senses
Myers Hall
Louisville, KY 40292
Phone: (502)852-0340
Fax: (502)852-0865
Susan Barnet, Research Adm.

Research Activities and Fields: Sensory research, including deterioration through aging. Investigates the effects of chronic sinusitis, loss of balance, and diabetes on the senses. **E-mail Address:** SNBARNO1@ULKYUM (BITNET).

★ 8506 ★ University of Maryland
Center for the Study of Cerebrovascular Disease and Stroke
22 S. Green St.
Baltimore, MD 21201
Phone: (410)328-5080
Fax: (410)328-0697
Thomas R. Price, M.D., Prin. Investigator

Research Activities and Fields: Cerebrovascular disease, including stroke, computer modelling of stroke, use of artificial intelligence in stroke patient care, aphasia recovery in stroke patients, and development of prognostics for stroke patient care, criteria of diagnosis of embolic stroke, drug use/abuse as a cause of stroke, stroke in the young, and progressing ischemic stroke. Activities are carried out through the Stroke Epidemiology Unit, Systolic Hypertension in the Elderly Project, Cardiovascular Health Study. **Publications:** Newsletter (quarterly). **E-mail Address:** tprice@umab.umd.edu. **Formerly:** Clinical Stroke Research Center (1985) and Center for the Study of Cerebrovascular Disease and Stroke.

★8507★ University of Maryland
Multiple Sclerosis Clinical Center
Neurology Dept., N4W46
22 S. Greene St.
Baltimore, MD 21201
Phone: (410)328-5605
Fax: (410)328-5899
Kenneth P. Johnson, M.D., Chm.

Research Activities and Fields: Basic immunologic and virologic research in multiple sclerosis. Also conducts clinical trials of new treatment for multiple sclerosis.

★8508★ University of Memphis
Neuropsychology Laboratory
Psychology Dept.
Memphis, TN 38152
Phone: (901)678-2821
Fax: (901)678-2692
Dr. Charles J. Long, Dir.

Research Activities and Fields: Evaluation and development of assessment and treatment procedures for neurologically impaired patients. Specific studies focus on head trauma and chronic pain.

★8509★ University of Miami
Center for Neurological Diseases
1501 NW 9th Ave.
PO Box 016960
Miami, FL 33136
Phone: (305)547-6732
Fax: (305)548-4678
Noble David, M.D., Contact

Research Activities and Fields: Neuroscience, including physiological, neurochemical, anatomical, metabolic, neuropharmacological and vascular mechanisms that account for normal brain function, and the changes in these which underlie neurological diseases such as stroke, senile dementia, epilepsy, Parkinson's syndrome, Alzheimer's disease, multiple sclerosis, amyotrophic lateral sclerosis (ALS), and other neurological dysfunctions.

★8510★ University of Miami
Cerebral Vascular Disease Research
Center
Dept. of Neurology, (D4-5)
PO Box 016960
Miami, FL 33101
Phone: (305)547-6449
Fax: (305)547-5830
Dr. Myron D. Ginsberg, Head

Research Activities and Fields: Cerebrovascular physiology, brain metabolism, and pathophysiology of cerebral ischemia/hypoxia, focusing on animal models of focal and global ischemia.

★8511★ University of Miami
Miami Project to Cure Paralysis
1600 NW 10th Ave., (R-48)
Miami, FL 33136
Phone: (305)547-6226
Fax: (305)548-4427
Dr. Richard P. Bunge, M.D., Scientific Dir.

Research Activities and Fields: Basic, clinical, and rehabilitative studies of spinal cord injury (SCI), emphasizing characterization of SCI (magnetic resonance imaging, electron micros-

copy, experimental models, and electrophysiology); design of effective treatments (molecular neurobiology, cell therapy, and tissue transplantation); and maximization of function (electromyographic biofeedback, functional electrical stimulation, rehabilitative urology, and motor-evoked potentials). **Publications:** *The Project* (quarterly newsletter).

★8512★ University of Michigan
Michigan Alzheimer's Disease Research
Center
Dept. of Neurology
1914 Taubman Center
Ann Arbor, MI 48109-0316
Phone: (313)764-2190
Fax: (313)936-8967
Sid Gilman, M.D., Chair.

Research Activities and Fields: Alzheimer's disease and other neurodegenerative diseases associated with dementia, including Parkinson's disease, multiple system atrophy, progressive supranuclear palsy, and olivopontocerebellar atrophy. Studies involve positron emission tomography (PET) scanning of patients with neurological disorders, neuropathological studies of patients with neurodegenerative illnesses, animal models, and a statewide public opinion survey on Alzheimer's disease. **Publications:** *Bridges* (newsletter, three per year).

★8513★ University of Michigan
Neurobiology Laboratory
6223 School of Dentistry
1101 N. University Ave.
Ann Arbor, MI 48109-1078
Phone: (313)763-1080
Fax: (313)764-7406
Robert M. Bradley, Dir.

Research Activities and Fields: Sensory and motor circuits, taste sensation, and associated reflexes, including salivation. Specific areas of study include the sense of taste, focusing on the cellular factors that regulate functional differentiation of salt taste pathways; interrelations between afferent taste input and brainstem control of salivary gland reflexes; and regeneration of peripheral taste nerves through micro-electrode arrays to develop a system from chronic, in vivo study of regenerated sensory nerve fibers.

★8514★ University of Michigan
Neurosurgery Laboratory
Kresge Medical Research Bldg.
Ann Arbor, MI 48109
Phone: (313)764-1207
Dr. J.T. Hoff, Dir.

Research Activities and Fields: Cerebral ischemia, edema, structure and function of central nervous system and its ability to sustain trauma, vascular insufficiency, and brain tumor oncogenesis.

★8515★ University of Michigan
Stomatognathic Physiology Laboratory
3218 School of Dentistry
1101 N. University Ave.
Ann Arbor, MI 48109
Phone: (313)764-7149
Fax: (313)747-2110
Christian S. Stohler, Dir.

Research Activities and Fields: Central nervous system adaptations to pain, focusing on

the effect of muscle pain on motor function. Also investigates the significance of experimental pain models for various types of human pathology.

University of Montreal
Fernand Sequin Research Centre
See: Entry 10481

★8516★ University of Oregon
Institute of Neuroscience (ION)
Huestis Hall
Eugene, OR 97403
Phone: (503)686-4556
Fax: (503)686-4548
Dr. Monte Westerfield, Dir.

Research Activities and Fields: Interdisciplinary approaches to basic questions in neuroscience, with particular emphasis on behavior, neurochemistry, neurophysiology, developmental neurobiology, and sensory systems. The Institute is composed of faculty members from the Departments of Biology, Computer Science, Psychology, and Physical Education. **Publications:** Graduate Studies at the Institute of Neuroscience. **E-mail Address:** edwards@uoneuro.uoregon.edu.

★8517★ University of Ottawa
Neurosciences Research Institute
451 Smyth Rd.
Ottawa, ON, Canada K1H 8M5
Phone: (613)787-3750
Fax: (613)787-3760
Dr. Antoine Hakim, Dir.

Research Activities and Fields: Neuroprotection, neuronal regeneration and recovery, mechanisms of cell injury, stroke, and axotomy.

★8518★ University of Pennsylvania
Brain Behavior Laboratory
Dept. of Psychiatry
Gates Bldg., 10th Fl.
3500 Spruce St.
Philadelphia, PA 19104
Phone: (215)662-2826
Fax: (215)662-7903
Ruben Gur, Ph.D., Dir.

Research Activities and Fields: New techniques for measuring regional brain function in relationship to behavior including cerebral blood flow, and metabolism using positron emmission tomography (PET); anatomic measures using magnetic resonance imaging (MRI), and neuropsychological testing for studying brain behavior relationships. Populations studied include normals (average and talented), psychiatric (schizophrenic, major depression, anxiety disorders, and dementia), and neurologic (stroke or cerebrovascular disease, epilepsy and parkinsonism). **E-mail Address:** evr@bbl.psycha.upenn.edu.

★8519★ University of Pennsylvania
Cerebrovascular Research Center
Johnson Pavilion, Rm. 429
3610 St. Hamilton Walk
Philadelphia, PA 19104
Phone: (215)662-2632
Fax: (215)349-5629
Dr. Martin Reivich, Dir.

Research Activities and Fields: Cerebrovascular research with an emphasis on cerebral circulation and metabolism. Conducts PET, SPECT, MRI, neuropsychologic, and neurologic studies on various brain disorders, including acute stroke, brain tumor, epilepsy, dementia,Parkinson's disease,and schizophrenia. Studies include measurements of regional cerebral blood flow, glucose and oxygen metabolism, blood volume, and neuroreceptor number and affinity. Also conducts basic animal research, including development of blood flow agents for the brain, research on animal models of stroke, and studies on treatment modalities for acute stroke in animal models.

★ 8520 ★ University of Pennsylvania
David Mahoney Institute of Neurological Sciences
Stemmler Hall, Rm. 215
Philadelphia, PA 19104-6074
Phone: (215)898-8754
Fax: (215)573-2015
Dr. Robert L. Barchi, Dir.

Research Activities and Fields: Nervous system, including multidisciplinary basic studies in neuroanatomy, neurobiology, neurochemistry, neuroembryology, neurophysiology, neuropharmacology, physiological psychology, and computational neuroscience. Publications: Newsletter. Formerly: Institute of Neurological Sciences.

★ 8521 ★ University of Pennsylvania
Smell and Taste Center
5 Ravdin Bldg.
3400 Spruce St.
Philadelphia, PA 19104
Phone: (215)662-6580
Fax: (215)349-5566
Dr. Richard L. Doty, Dir.

Research Activities and Fields: Identifies and treats disorders of taste and smell. Develops clinical smell and taste tests, investigates nasal airflow parameters, examines gustatory glucose sensitivity in diabetes and depression, studies MRI-based measures of brain volume changes in olfactory disorders, studies neuroendocrine relations with chemosensory function, conducts behavioral and neurophysiological studies of olfactory and trigeminal function, and studies the pathophysiology of oral sensory abnormalities. Formerly: Clinical Smell and Taste Center.

★ 8522 ★ University of Pittsburgh
Center for Neuroscience
Biomedical Science Tower, W1656
Pittsburgh, PA 15261
Phone: (412)648-8322
Fax: (412)648-8376
Dr. Robert Y. Moore, Dir.

Research Activities and Fields: Neuroscience and neural diseases. E-mail Address: moore@bns.pitt.edu.

★ 8523 ★ University of Puerto Rico
Institute of Neurobiology
Medical Sciences Campus
Blvd. del Valle 201
Old San Juan, PR 00901
Phone: (809)721-4149
Fax: (809)725-3804
Richard K. Orkand, Ph.D., Dir.

Research Activities and Fields: Neurophysiology, neuroanatomy, neurochemistry, and neuropharmacology, primarily in relation to tropical marine invertebrates and lower vertebrates, including cell electrophysiology, and biochemical and immunological studies. E-mail Address: r_orkand@rcmaca.upr.clu.edu. Formerly: Laboratory of Neurobiology (1986).

University of Quebec at Montreal
Cognitive Neuroscience Laboratory
See: Entry 3653

★ 8524 ★ University of Tennessee at Memphis
Center for Neuroscience
855 Monroe Ave.
Memphis, TN 38163-2194
Phone: (901)448-5956
Fax: (901)448-7193
Dr. Stephen T. Kitai, Dir.

Research Activities and Fields: General neurosciences, including epilepsy studies; movement disorders (Parkinson's disease, Huntington's disease, and muscular dystrophy); vision studies (retinal disease and central visual pathways malfunction); developmental neurobiology (tissue culture and transplant in the basal ganglia, development of neural circuitry in the central visual system, neurological mutants and chimeras, development of cerebral and cerebellar cortical cytoarchitechtonics, and development of synapses in the retina); neuroendocrinology (control of brain neurotransmitters, temperature regulation in host defense response to infectious agents, and hormonal regulation of neuroeffector mechanisms); neurotransmitter action in the brain (biochemical analysis of neurotransmitters and hormone action, second messenger systems and effect of psychiatric medicine on these systems, and neuropeptide systems involved in pain and stress); and central nervous system control of the cardiovascular system (hypertension and temperature regulation); and sleep mechanisms. E-mail Address: cwilson@utmem1.utmem.edu. Formerly: Neuroscience Center of Excellence.

★ 8525 ★ University of Texas
Sleep Study Unit
Southwestern Medical Center
5323 Harry Hines Blvd.
Dallas, TX 75235-9070
Phone: (214)648-8758
Fax: (214)648-5444
Roseanne Armitage, Ph.D., Dir.

Research Activities and Fields: Sleep/wake studies, including insomnia, depression, narcolepsy, schizophrenia and normal sleep, as well as basic sleep neurophysiology. Publications: Biological Psychiatry; Sleep Psychiatry Research; Advances in Neuropsychopharmacology and Biological Psychiatry. E-mail Address: armitage@swmed.edu.

★ 8526 ★ University of Texas—Houston
Health Science Center
Laboratory for Neuroendocrinology
PO Box 20708
Houston, TX 77225
Phone: (713)792-8373
Fax: (713)792-3553
Dr. Ernst Knobil, Dir.

Research Activities and Fields: Neuroendocrinology and control of reproductive processes in nonhuman primates.

★ 8527 ★ University of Texas—Houston
Health Science Center
Sensory Sciences Center
6420 Lamar Fleming Ave.
Houston, TX 77030
Phone: (713)792-8650
Fax: (713)792-4513
Dr. Harry G. Sperling, Dir.

Research Activities and Fields: Basic research on behavioral, physiological, and biochemical aspects of sensory systems, the brain, and memory. E-mail Address: hsperling@gsbs.gs.uth.tmc.edu. Formerly: Department of Neural Sciences (1970).

★ 8528 ★ University of Texas
Southwestern Medical Center at Dallas
Alzheimer's Disease Center
Dept. of Psychiatry
5323 Harry Hines Blvd.
Dallas, TX 75235-8898
Phone: (214)648-3886
Fax: (214)648-2450
Dr. Jim Hom, Dir., Neuropsychology

Research Activities and Fields: Alzheimer's diseaese and aging in the brain, focusing on loss of cognitive functions and test measurements including IQ, problem solving, abstract thinking, pattern recognition, spatial and dexterity skills, attention and concentration, language function, and long- and short-term memory.

★ 8529 ★ University of Texas
Southwestern Medical Center at Dallas
Neuromuscular Treatment Center
Dept. of Neurology
5323 Harry Hines Blvd.
Dallas, TX 75235-8869
Phone: (214)648-9574
Fax: (214)648-7697
Wilson Bryan, M.D., Dir.

Research Activities and Fields: Basic and clinical studies of immune-mediated neuromuscular disorders, including myasthenia gravis, multiple sclerosis, polymyositis, and inflammatory polyneuropathy. Activities include clinical therapeutic trials.

University of Texas Southwestern Medical Center at Dallas
Neuroscience Program
See: Entry 2697

★ 8530 ★ University of Toronto
Centre for Research in Neurodegenerative Diseases
Tanz Neuroscience Bldg.
6 Queen's Park Crescent W.
Toronto, ON, Canada M5S 1A8
Phone: (416)978-7461
Dr. P. Carlen, Interim Dir.

Research Activities and Fields: Neurodegenerative diseases of the human brain, focusing on the causes of Alzheimer's disease, Amyotrophic Lateral Sclerosis, and other nerve cell defects, the development of effective treatment for patient care, and clinical trials. Specific areas of study include genetic mutation of chromosome 21, protein degeneration of synapses and synaptic vesicles, identification and characterization of the molecular development of the nervous systems, collaborative studies on the aluminum hypothesis for Alzheimer's disease, and the study of motor control and the mechanisms that result in nerve cell degeneration in both the brain and the spinal cord.

University of Vermont
Vermont Rehabilitation Engineering Center
   for Low Back Pain
See: Entry 12764

University of Virginia
Center for Biological Timing
See: Entry 4944

★ 8531 ★ University of Virginia
Neuromuscular Center
UVA Medical Center
Dept. of Neurology, Box 394
Charlottesville, VA 22908
Phone: (804)924-5304
Fax: (804)924-9068
Larry H. Phillips, II, M.D., Codirector

Research Activities and Fields: Electrophysiology of dystrophy skeletal muscle fibers, biochemical studies of the properties of normal and dystrophic cells in culture, structure and chromosome linkage of human muscle genes, genetic heterogeneity among the hereditary motor sensory neuropathies, long chain fatty acids in Olivo-Ponto-cerebellar atrophy, the axonal cytoskeleton following IDPN administration, biochemical differences in shrimp claw muscle protein, membrane enzymes involved in muscle regulation, safety margin of neuromuscular transmission in normal and diseased muscle, and the humoral hypothesis in the Eaton-Lambert syndrome. Also conducts clinical research in such neuromuscular diseases as myasthenia gravis, Eaton-Lambert syndrome, Charcot-Marie-tooth disease, and diabetic polyneuropathy.

★ 8532 ★ University of Wisconsin—
   Madison
Neuromuscular Disease Laboratory
H4/622 CSC
600 Highland Ave.
Madison, WI 53792
Phone: (608)263-9184
Fax: (608)263-0412
B. Lotz, M.D., Dir.

Research Activities and Fields: Muscle metabolism, morphology, and ultrastructure. Provides quantitative histochemical analysis of research tissue; processes human muscle tissue for diagnosis and research. Performs electrodiagnostic procedures relating to muscle or nerve dysfunciton. **E-mail Address:** lotz@neurology.wisc.edu.

★ 8533 ★ University of Wisconsin—
   Madison
Neuropsychology Laboratory
600 N. Highland Ave.
Madison, WI 53792-6180
Phone: (608)263-5430
Fax: (608)263-0412
Dr. Charles G. Matthews, Dir.

Research Activities and Fields: Clinical neuropsychology in neuropsychological correlates of epilepsy, cognitive and affective changes in aging, and differential diagnosis of dementia with a view toward cognitive and memory remediation.

Virginia Commonwealth University
Rehabilitation Research and Training
   Center on Severe Traumatic Brain Injury
See: Entry 12766

★ 8534 ★ Wake Forest University
Cerebrovascular Research Center
Bowman Gray School of Medicine
Dept. of Neurologyd.
Medical Center Blvd.
Winston-Salem, NC 27157-1068
Phone: (910)716-2338
Fax: (910)716-5477
Dr. James F. Toole, Dir.

Research Activities and Fields: Cerebrovascular research, including ultrasound, neurological diseases, coronary studies, biostatistics, transient ischemic attack (TIA), comparative medicine in atherosclerosis, neuropsychological evaluation, cerebral circulation, and anatomy/physiology. **Publications:** *Stroke Monitor* (quarterly newsletter).

★ 8535 ★ Wake Forest University
Comprehensive Epilepsy Program
Medical Center Blvd.
Winston-Salem, NC 27157-1023
Phone: (910)716-2321
Free: 800-642-0500
Fax: (910)716-9489
Dr. Kiffin Penry

Research Activities and Fields: Social and psychological aspects of epilepsy and clinical trials of anti-epileptic medication.

★ 8536 ★ Washington University
Alzheimer's Disease Research Center
School of Medicine
Campus Box 8111
660 S. Euclid Ave.
St. Louis, MO 63110
Phone: (314)362-2881
Fax: (314)362-4763
Leonard Berg, M.D., Dir.

Research Activities and Fields: Aging and dementia, neurobiology of aging and cognition, Alzheimer's disease and related disorders, and the impact of dementia on the family or caregiver and the community. Studies include clinical research, clinical drug trials, neuropathological (autopsy) studies, genetic and other medical studies of persons with dementia, and bench studies. **Publications:** *Horizons* (newsletter). **E-mail Address:** alzheimer-owner@wubios.wustl.edu.

★ 8537 ★ William T. Gossett Parkinson's
   Disease Center
Henry Ford Hospital
Dept. of Neurology
2799 W. Grand Blvd.
Detroit, MI 48202
Phone: (313)876-2585
Jay M. Gorell, M.D., Dir.

Research Activities and Fields: Parkinson's disease and its causes and treatments, including risk factors, cognitive and motor deficits, new medication trials, animal nerve cell investigations, and disordered brain chemistry measurements.

Yale University
Center for Biocognitive Studies
See: Entry 7703

Chapter 42
Nursing

Foundations & Other Funding Organizations

Private Foundations

Caleb C. and Julia W. Dula Educational and Charitable Foundation
See: Entry 6335

★8538★ Helene Fuld Health Trust
405 Lexington Ave., 26th Fl.
New York, NY 10174
Phone: (212)973-6859
Fax: (212)370-1348
Arlene J. Snyder, Grants Office Administrator

Foundation Philosophy: The trust is the largest foundation in the United States devoted solely to nursing education. Making grants to state-accredited nursing schools affiliated with accredited hospitals, the trust promotes health, education, and welfare of student nurses. **Giving Priorities:** In fiscal 1993, the trust gave 84% of funding to educational institutions, primarily funds that went to the purchase of medical equipment at various universities. Approximately 10% of total contributions went to health organizations, concentrating on buying equipment for hospitals and medical centers. The remaining 6% of funds went to international health organizations. **Typical Health-Related Recipients:** Clinics/Medical Centers, Health Organizations, Hospitals, Medical Education, Nursing Services. **Geographic Distribution:** National.

★8539★ Independence Foundation
2500 Philadelphia National Bank Bldg.
Philadelphia, PA 19107-3493
Phone: (215)563-8105
Fax: (215)563-6483
Theodore K. Warner, Jr., President

Foundation Philosophy: The foundation primarily supports nursing schools at colleges and universities located in the Philadelphia, PA area. The foundation also supports organizations that provide legal aid or other assistance to those living in poverty in the Philadelphia area. **Giving Priorities:** In 1993, the foundation gave approximately 73% of its contributions to education.

Health organizations received 11% of funding; civic and public affairs organizations, 10%; social services, 3%; the arts and humanities received 2%; and international concerns, 1%. Science and religious organizations received less than 1%. **Typical Health-Related Recipients:** Clinics/Medical Centers, Emergency/Ambulance Services, Family Planning, Health Organizations, Medical Education, Medical Rehabilitation, Medical Research, Nursing Services, Preventive Medicine/Wellness Organizations. **Geographic Distribution:** Restricted to Pennsylvania, with primary concentration in Philadelphia.

James M. Johnston Trust for Charitable and Educational Purposes
See: Entry 309

Lettie Pate Whitehead Foundation
See: Entry 353

Louis and Rachel Rudin Foundation
See: Entry 365

Mericos Foundation
See: Entry 400

★8540★ Nicholas H. Noyes, Jr. Memorial Foundation
7700-B W 38th St.
Indianapolis, IN 46254
Phone: (317)293-1157
James M. Cornelius, Treasurer

Foundation Philosophy: The foundation distributes its giving to a variety of interests. Educational funding favors secondary schools and private academies. Social service recipients include united funds, housing, work centers, and day care. Most of the support for the arts is centerd on the performing arts in Indianapolis. Health care favors nursing and hospitals. Other interests include zoos, conservation, and religion. **Giving Priorities:** In 1993, the arts received 33% of the foundation's grants. Social service organizations received 26%; education, 19%; health, 10%; civic and public affairs, 8%; the remaining 4% went to fund religious causes. **Typical Health-Related Recipients:** Cancer, Children's Health/Hospitals, Clinics/Medical Centers, Family Planning, Hospitals, Medical Rehabilitation, Medical Research, Nursing Ser-

vices, People with Disabilities, Single-Disease Health Associations, Substance Abuse. **Geographic Distribution:** Focus on Indianapolis, IN.

Other Funding Organizations

★8541★ American Nurses' Foundation
600 Maryland Ave. SW, Ste. 100W
Washington, DC 20024-2571
Phone: (202)651-7227
Fax: (202)651-7001
Barbara K. Redman, Ph.D., R.N., Contact

Description: Offers a Competitive Extramural Grants Program to support research conducted by registered nurses who are either beginning researchers or experienced researchers who are entering a new area of investigation, and sponsors Distinguished Scholar Program to conduct health policy research.

★8542★ National Student Nurses' Association
555 W. 57th St., No. 1327
New York, NY 10019
Phone: (212)581-2211
Fax: (212)581-2368
Robert V. Piemonte, Ed.D., R.N., Exec. Dir.

Description: Awards scholarships to student nurses.

★8543★ Nurses Educational Funds
555 W. 57th St., 13th Fl.
New York, NY 10019
Phone: (212)582-8820
Fax: (212)586-5462
Dr. Cynthia Sculo, Pres.

Description: Awards scholarships for registered nurses seeking the bachelor's, master's, or doctorate degree in nursing sciences. Also awards a scholarship to a registered nurse with high academic standing and potential for leadership and service to the nursing profession.

★8544★ Sigma Theta Tau International
550 W. North St.
Indianapolis, IN 46202
Phone: (317)634-8171
Fax: (317)634-8188
Nell J. Watts, Exec. Off.

Description: Provides grants to nurses for research at the graduate level.

Medical & Allied Health Schools

Nursing

The institutions listed below offer baccalaureate programs in nursing. For information on all types of educational programs, including master's, associate degree, diploma, and practical nursing, contact the National League for Nursing, 350 Hudson St., New York, NY 10014, (212) 989-9393.

Alabama

★8545★ **Auburn University**
School of Nursing
107 Miller Hall
Auburn, AL 36849-5505
Phone: (334)844-5665

★8546★ **Auburn University at Montgomery**
School of Nursing
7300 University Dr.
Montgomery, AL 36117-3596
Phone: (205)244-3343

★8547★ **Jacksonville State University**
Lurleen B. Wallace College of Nursing
700 Pelham Rd. N.
Jacksonville, AL 36265-9982
Phone: (205)782-5425

★8548★ **Samford University**
Ida V. Moffett School of Nursing
800 Lakeshore Dr.
Birmingham, AL 35229
Phone: (205)870-2872

★8549★ **Troy State University**
School of Nursing
Troy, AL 36082
Phone: (205)670-3428

★8550★ **Tuskegee University**
School of Nursing and Allied Health
Baccalaureate Nursing Program
Tuskegee Institute, AL 36088
Phone: (205)727-8115

★8551★ **University of Alabama**
Capstone College of Nursing
PO Box 870358
Tuscaloosa, AL 35487-0358
Phone: (205)348-6640

★8552★ **University of Alabama at Birmingham**
School of Nursing
1701 University Blvd.
Birmingham, AL 35294-1210
Phone: (205)934-5490

★8553★ **University of Alabama in Huntsville**
School of Nursing
Huntsville, AL 35899
Phone: (205)895-6742

★8554★ **University of Mobile**
School of Nursing
PO Box 13220
Mobile, AL 36663-0220
Phone: (334)675-5990

★8555★ **University of North Alabama**
School of Nursing
Stevens Hall
Florence, AL 35632-0001
Phone: (205)760-4311

★8556★ **University of South Alabama**
College of Nursing
USA Springhill Ave.
Mobile, AL 36688-0002
Phone: (334)434-3415

Alaska

★8557★ **University of Alaska Anchorage**
School of Nursing and Health Sciences
Baccalaureate Nursing Program
3211 Providence Dr.
Anchorage, AK 99516
Phone: (907)786-1854

Arizona

★8558★ **Arizona State University**
College of Nursing
Tempe, AZ 85287-2602
Phone: (602)965-2987

★8559★ **Grand Canyon University**
Samaritan College of Nursing
3300 W. Camelback Rd.
Phoenix, AZ 85012
Phone: (602)589-2431

★8560★ **Northern Arizona University**
Department of Nursing
PO Box 15035
Flagstaff, AZ 86001
Phone: (602)523-2671

★8561★ **University of Arizona**
College of Nursing
Tucson, AZ 85721
Phone: (602)626-6161

Arkansas

★8562★ **Arkansas State University**
College of Nursing and Health Professions
Department of Nursing
PO Box 69
State University, AR 72467-0069
Phone: (501)972-3074

★8563★ **Arkansas Tech University**
Department of Nursing
Dean Hall
Russellville, AR 72801
Phone: (501)968-0384

★8564★ **Harding University**
School of Nursing
PO Box 2265
Searcy, AR 72149-0001
Phone: (501)279-4476

★8565★ **Henderson State University**
Department of Nursing
Box 7803
1100 Henderson St.
Arkadelphia, AR 71999-0001
Phone: (501)230-5015

★8566★ **University of Arkansas**
School of Nursing
PO Box 3606
Monticello, AR 71655
Phone: (501)460-1069

★8567★ **University of Arkansas for Medical Sciences**
College of Nursing
4301 W. Markham, Slot 529
Little Rock, AR 72205
Phone: (501)686-5224

★8568★ **University of Arkansas at Pine Bluff**
Department of Nursing
Box 44
University Dr.
Pine Bluff, AR 71601
Phone: (501)543-8220

★8569★ **University of Central Arkansas**
Department of Nursing
201 S. Donaghey
Conway, AR 72035
Phone: (501)450-3119

California

★8570★ **Azusa Pacific University**
School of Nursing
901 E. Alosta Ave.
Azusa, CA 91702
Phone: (818)969-3434

★8571★ **Biola University**
Department of Baccalaureate Nursing
13800 Biola Ave.
La Mirada, CA 90639
Phone: (213)903-4850

★8572★ **California State University, Bakersfield**
Department of Nursing
9001 Stockdale Hwy.
Bakersfield, CA 93311-1099
Phone: (805)664-3102

★8573★ **California State University, Chico**
School of Nursing
Holt Hall, Rm. 369
Chico, CA 95929-2000
Phone: (916)898-5891

★8574★ **California State University, Fresno**
School of Health and Social Work
Department of Nursing
2345 E. San Ramon Ave.
Fresno, CA 93740-0025
Phone: (209)278-2041

★8575★ California State University, Hayward
Department of Nursing
25800 Carlos Bee Blvd.
Hayward, CA 94542-3086
Phone: (510)881-3481

★8576★ California State University, Long Beach
Department of Nursing
1250 Bellflower Blvd.
Long Beach, CA 90840
Phone: (310)985-4463

★8577★ California State University, Los Angeles
Department of Nursing
5151 State University Dr.
Los Angeles, CA 90032
Phone: (213)343-4700

★8578★ California State University, Sacramento
Division of Nursing
6000 J St.
Sacramento, CA 95819
Phone: (916)278-6525

★8579★ California State University, San Bernardino
School of Nursing
5500 University Pkwy.
San Bernardino, CA 92407
Phone: (909)880-5380

★8580★ Dominican College
School of Nursing
50 Acacia Ave.
San Rafael, CA 94901
Phone: (415)485-3295

★8581★ Humboldt State University
Department of Nursing
Arcata, CA 95521
Phone: (707)826-3215

★8582★ Loma Linda University
School of Nursing
11262 Campus St.
Loma Linda, CA 92350
Phone: (909)824-4360

★8583★ Mt. St. Mary's College
Department of Nursing
12001 Chalon Rd.
Los Angeles, CA 90049
Phone: (310)471-9521

★8584★ Point Loma Nazarene College
Department of Nursing
3900 Lomaland Dr.
San Diego, CA 92106
Phone: (619)221-2226

★8585★ Samuel Merritt College / St. Mary College
Intercollegiate Nursing Program
370 Hawthorne Ave.
Oakland, CA 94609-3108
Phone: (510)869-6576

★8586★ San Diego State University
School of Nursing
5300 Campanile Dr.
San Diego, CA 92182
Phone: (619)594-5357

★8587★ San Francisco State University
Department of Nursing
1600 Holloway Ave.
San Francisco, CA 94132
Phone: (415)338-1801

★8588★ San Jose State University
Department of Nursing
1 Washington Sq.
San Jose, CA 95192-0057
Phone: (408)924-3130

★8589★ San Jose State University
School of Nursing
One Washington Sq.
San Jose, CA 95192-0057
Phone: (408)924-3131

★8590★ University of California, Los Angeles
School of Nursing
Center for the Health Sciences
10833 Le Conte Ave.
Los Angeles, CA 90024
Phone: (310)825-5654

★8591★ University of California, San Francisco
School of Nursing
505 Parnassus Ave.
San Francisco, CA 94143-0604
Phone: (415)476-1435

★8592★ University of San Francisco
School of Nursing
2130 Fulton St.
San Francisco, CA 94117
Phone: (415)666-6681

★8593★ University of Southern California
Department of Nursing
Leavy Hall
302 W. 15th St.
Los Angeles, CA 90089
Phone: (213)743-2362

Colorado

★8594★ Beth El College of Nursing
2790 N. Academy Blvd.
Colorado Springs, CO 80917-5338
Phone: (719)475-5170

★8595★ Mesa State College
Department of Nursing and Allied Health
Baccalaureate Nursing Program
PO Box 2647
Grand Junction, CO 81502
Phone: (303)248-1398

★8596★ Regis University
School for Health Care Professions
Baccalaureate Nursing Program
3333 Regis Blvd.
W. 50th Ave. Lowell Blvd.
Denver, CO 80221-1099
Phone: (303)458-4168

★8597★ University of Colorado
School of Nursing
Health Sciences Center
4200 E. 9th Ave.
PO Box C 288
Denver, CO 80262
Phone: (303)270-7754

★8598★ University of Northern Colorado
School of Nursing
Greeley, CO 80639
Phone: (303)351-2293

★8599★ University of Southern Colorado
Department of Nursing
2200 Bonforte Blvd.
Pueblo, CO 81001
Phone: (719)549-2401

Connecticut

★8600★ Fairfield University
School of Nursing
N. Benson Rd.
Fairfield, CT 06430
Phone: (203)254-4150

★8601★ Quinnipiac College
School of Nursing
Mount Carmel Ave.
Hamden, CT 06518
Phone: (203)281-8686

★8602★ St. Joseph College
Division of Nursing
1678 Asylum Ave.
West Hartford, CT 06117
Phone: (203)232-4571

★8603★ Southern Connecticut State University
School of Nursing
Jennings Hall
501 Crescent St.
New Haven, CT 06515
Phone: (203)397-4614

★8604★ University of Connecticut
School of Nursing
231 Glenbrook Rd.
Storrs Mansfield, CT 06269
Phone: (203)486-4730

★8605★ Western Connecticut State University
Department of Nursing
181 White St.
Danbury, CT 06810
Phone: (203)797-4359

★8606★ Yale University
School of Nursing
25 Park St.
PO Box 9740
New Haven, CT 06536-0740
Phone: (203)785-2389

Delaware

★8607★ **Delaware State University**
Department of Nursing
1200 N. DuPont Hwy.
Dover, DE 19901
Phone: (302)739-4933

★8608★ **University of Delaware**
College of Nursing
Newark, DE 19716
Phone: (302)831-1253

District of Columbia

★8609★ **Catholic University of America**
School of Nursing
3800 Brookland Ave. NE
Washington, DC 20064
Phone: (202)319-5403

★8610★ **Georgetown University**
School of Nursing
3700 Reservoir Rd. NW
Washington, DC 20007
Phone: (202)687-4926

★8611★ **Howard University**
College of Nursing
2400 6th St. NW
Washington, DC 20059
Phone: (202)806-7459

★8612★ **University of the District of Columbia**
Division of Nursing Education
4200 Connecticut Ave. NW, Bldg. 44
Washington, DC 20008
Phone: (202)282-7388

Florida

★8613★ **Barry University**
School of Nursing
11300 2nd Ave. NE
Miami, FL 33161
Phone: (305)899-3800

★8614★ **Bethune-Cookman College**
School of Nursing
640 2nd Ave.
Daytona Beach, FL 32114
Phone: (904)255-1401

★8615★ **Florida A&M University**
School of Nursing
Box 136-FAMU
Tallahassee, FL 32307
Phone: (904)599-3017

★8616★ **Florida Atlantic University**
College of Nursing
500 NW 20th St.
PO Box 3091
Boca Raton, FL 33431
Phone: (407)367-3260

★8617★ **Florida International University**
School of Nursing
15100 St. Biscayne Blvd.
North Miami, FL 33181
Phone: (305)940-5915

★8618★ **Florida State University**
School of Nursing
202 S. Woodward St.
Tallahassee, FL 32306-3051
Phone: (904)644-3299

★8619★ **Jacksonville University**
School of Nursing
2800 University Blvd., N.
Jacksonville, FL 32211
Phone: (904)744-3950

★8620★ **Pensacola Christian College**
School of Nursing
Box 18000
Pensacola, FL 32523

★8621★ **University of Central Florida**
Department of Nursing
PO Box 162210
Orlando, FL 32816-2210
Phone: (407)823-2744

★8622★ **University of Florida**
College of Nursing
Box 100197
J. Hillis Miller Health Center
Gainesville, FL 32610
Phone: (904)392-3752

★8623★ **University of Miami**
School of Nursing
PO Box 016960 D2-5
Miami, FL 33101
Phone: (305)284-3666

★8624★ **University of North Florida**
College of Health
Department of Nursing
4567 St. Johns Bluff Rd. S.
Jacksonville, FL 32224
Phone: (904)646-2684

★8625★ **University of South Florida**
College of Nursing
12901 Bruce Downs Blvd., Box 22
Tampa, FL 33612
Phone: (813)974-2191

Georgia

★8626★ **Albany State College**
School of Nursing and Allied Health
Albany, GA 31705
Phone: (912)430-5106

★8627★ **Armstrong State College**
Department of Baccalaureate Nursing
Savannah, GA 31419-1997
Phone: (912)927-5302

★8628★ **Brenau University**
Nursing Department
1 Centennial Circle
University Nursing Department
Gainesville, GA 30501
Phone: (404)534-6261

★8629★ **Columbus College**
Department of Nursing
Algonquin Dr.
Columbus, GA 31907-2079
Phone: (404)568-2243

★8630★ **Emory University**
Nell Hodgson Woodruff School of Nursing
531 Asbury Circle
Atlanta, GA 30322
Phone: (404)727-7981

★8631★ **Georgia Baptist College of Nursing**
Box 411
300 Boulevard NE
Atlanta, GA 30312
Phone: (404)653-4795

★8632★ **Georgia College**
School of Nursing
PO Box 64
Milledgeville, GA 31061
Phone: (912)453-4004

★8633★ **Georgia Southern University**
Department of Nursing
Landrum Box 8158
Statesboro, GA 30460-8158
Phone: (912)681-5455

★8634★ **Georgia State University**
School of Nursing
PO Box 4019
Atlanta, GA 30302-4019
Phone: (404)651-3040

★8635★ **Kennesaw State College**
School of Nursing
PO Box 444
Marietta, GA 30061
Phone: (404)423-6061

★8636★ **Medical College of Georgia**
School of Nursing
Augusta, GA 30912-4200
Phone: (706)721-2725

★8637★ **Valdosta State College**
School of Nursing
Valdosta, GA 31601
Phone: (912)333-5959

Hawaii

★8638★ **Hawaii Pacific University**
School of Nursing
45-045 Kamehameha Hwy.
Kaneohe, HI 96744
Phone: (808)235-3641

★8639★ **University of Hawaii at Manoa**
School of Nursing
2528 The Mall
Honolulu, HI 96822
Phone: (808)956-8939

Idaho

★8640★ **Boise State University**
Department of Nursing
1910 University Dr.
Boise, ID 83725
Phone: (208)385-1768

★8641★ Idaho State University
Department of Nursing
PO Box 8101
Pocatello, ID 83209
Phone: (208)236-3085

Illinois

★8642★ Aurora University
School of Nursing and Health
347 S. Gladstone
Aurora, IL 60506
Phone: (708)844-5130

★8643★ Bradley University
Department of Nursing
Peoria, IL 61625
Phone: (309)677-2528

★8644★ Chicago State University
College of Nursing
95th St. at King Dr.
Chicago, IL 60628
Phone: (312)995-3987

★8645★ Concordia College
West Suburban College of Nursing
Erie at Austin
Oak Park, IL 60302
Phone: (708)383-6200

★8646★ Culver-Stockton / Blessing-
 Rieman College
School of Nursing
Box C3
Broadway at 11th St.
Quincy, IL 62301
Phone: (217)223-5811

★8647★ DePaul University
Department of Nursing
802 W. Belden
Chicago, IL 60614
Phone: (312)325-7280

★8648★ Elmhurst College
Deicke Center for Nursing Education
190 Prospect Ave.
Elmhurst, IL 60126-3296
Phone: (708)617-3503

★8649★ Illinois Wesleyan University
School of Nursing
210 E. University
PO Box 2900
Bloomington, IL 61702
Phone: (309)556-3959

★8650★ Lakeview College
School of Nursing
812 North Logan Ave.
Danville, IL 61832
Phone: (217)443-5238

★8651★ Lewis University
College of Nursing
Rte. 53
Romeoville, IL 60441
Phone: (815)838-0500

★8652★ Loyola University of Chicago
Marcella Niehoff School of Nursing
6525 N. Sheridan Rd.
Chicago, IL 60626
Phone: (312)508-3262

★8653★ MacMurray College
Nursing Department
447 E. College Ave.
Jacksonville, IL 62650
Phone: (217)479-7083

★8654★ Mennonite College of Nursing
804 N. East St.
Bloomington, IL 61701
Phone: (309)829-0715

★8655★ Millikin University
School of Nursing
1184 W. Main St.
Decatur, IL 62522
Phone: (217)424-6348

★8656★ North Park College
Division of Nursing
3255 W. Foster Ave.
Chicago, IL 60625
Phone: (312)583-2700

★8657★ Northern Illinois University
School of Nursing
1240 Normal Rd.
De Kalb, IL 60115
Phone: (815)753-1232

★8658★ Olivet Nazarene University
Division of Nursing
Kankakee, IL 60901
Phone: (815)939-5340

★8659★ Rockford College
School of Nursing
5050 East State St.
Rockford, IL 61108-2393
Phone: (815)226-4054

★8660★ Rush University
College of Nursing
1743 W. Harrison St.
Chicago, IL 60612
Phone: (312)942-2165

★8661★ St. Anthony College of Nursing
5658 East State St.
Rockford, IL 61108-2468
Phone: (815)395-5087

★8662★ St. Francis Medical Center
College of Nursing
511 NE Greenleaf St.
Peoria, IL 61603
Phone: (309)655-2086

★8663★ St. John's College-Department of
 Nursing
421 N. 9th St.
Springfield, IL 62702
Phone: (217)544-6464

★8664★ St. Joseph College of Nursing
290 N. Springfield Ave.
Joliet, IL 60435
Phone: (815)741-7123

★8665★ St. Xavier University
School of Nursing
3700 W. 103rd St.
Chicago, IL 60655
Phone: (312)298-3701

★8666★ Southern Illinois University at
 Edwardsville
School of Nursing
Bldg. 111, Rm. 2333
Edwardsville, IL 62026-1066
Phone: (618)692-3959

★8667★ Trinity Christian College
Department of Nursing
6601 W. College Dr.
Palos Heights, IL 60463
Phone: (708)597-3000

★8668★ University of Illinois at Chicago
College of Nursing
845 S. Damen Ave.
Chicago, IL 60612
Phone: (312)996-7805

Indiana

★8669★ Anderson University
School of Nursing
1100 E. 5th St.
Anderson, IN 46012
Phone: (317)641-4380

★8670★ Ball State University
School of Nursing
2000 University Ave.
Muncie, IN 47306
Phone: (317)285-5571

★8671★ Bethel College
Division of Nursing
1001 W. McKinley Ave.
Mishawaka, IN 46545
Phone: (219)259-8511

★8672★ DePauw University
School of Nursing
PO Box 1367
Indianapolis, IN 46206
Phone: (317)658-4692

★8673★ Goshen College
Department of Nursing
Goshen, IN 46526
Phone: (219)535-7000

★8674★ Indiana State University
School of Nursing
Terre Haute, IN 47809
Phone: (812)237-2317

★8675★ Indiana University
School of Nursing
1111 Middle Dr.
Indianapolis, IN 46202-5107
Phone: (317)274-1486

★8676★ Indiana University East
School of Nursing
2325 Chester Blvd.
Richmond, IN 47374
Phone: (317)973-8205

★ 8677 ★ Indiana University at Kokomo
School of Nursing
2300 S. Washington St.
PO Box 9003
Kokomo, IN 46904-9003
Phone: (317)455-9288

★ 8678 ★ Indiana University Northwest
School of Nursing
3400 Broadway
Gary, IN 46408
Phone: (219)890-6549

★ 8679 ★ Indiana University at South Bend
School of Nursing
1700 Mishawaka
PO Box 7111
South Bend, IN 46634
Phone: (219)237-4111

★ 8680 ★ Indiana University Southeast
School of Nursing
4201 Grant Line Rd.
New Albany, IN 47150
Phone: (812)845-2731

★ 8681 ★ Indiana Wesleyan University
Division of Nursing Education
4201 S. Washington St.
Marion, IN 46953
Phone: (317)677-2269

★ 8682 ★ Marian College
School of Nursing
3200 Cold Spring Rd.
Indianapolis, IN 46222
Phone: (317)929-0311

★ 8683 ★ Purdue University
School of Nursing
1336 Johnson Hall of Nursing
West Lafayette, IN 47907-1337
Phone: (317)494-4008

★ 8684 ★ St. Francis College
School of Nursing
2701 Spring St.
Fort Wayne, IN 46808
Phone: (219)434-3239

★ 8685 ★ St. Mary's College
Nursing Department
Havican Hall
Notre Dame, IN 46556
Phone: (219)284-4680

★ 8686 ★ University of Evansville
School of Nursing
1800 Lincoln Ave.
Evansville, IN 47722
Phone: (812)479-2343

★ 8687 ★ University of Indianapolis
School of Nursing
1400 E. Hanna Ave.
Indianapolis, IN 46227
Phone: (317)788-3206

★ 8688 ★ University of Southern Indiana
School of Nursing
600 Edgar St.
Evansville, IN 47710
Phone: (812)428-7256

★ 8689 ★ Valparaiso University
College of Nursing
Valparaiso, IN 46383
Phone: (219)464-5289

Iowa

★ 8690 ★ Allen College of Nursing
1825 Logan Ave.
Waterloo, IA 50703
Phone: (319)235-3649

★ 8691 ★ Briar Cliff College
Department of Nursing
3303 Rebecca St.
Sioux City, IA 51104
Phone: (712)279-5497

★ 8692 ★ Clarke College
Department of Nursing
1550 Clark Dr.
Dubuque, IA 52001
Phone: (319)588-6406

★ 8693 ★ Coe College
Department of Nursing Education
1220 1st Ave. NE
Cedar Rapids, IA 52402
Phone: (319)369-8120

★ 8694 ★ Grand View College
Division of Nursing
1200 Grandview Ave.
Des Moines, IA 50316
Phone: (515)263-2850

★ 8695 ★ Iowa Wesleyan College
Division of Nursing
601 N. Main
Mt. Pleasant, IA 52641
Phone: (319)385-6346

★ 8696 ★ Luther College
Department of Nursing
700 College Dr.
Decorah, IA 52101
Phone: (319)387-1057

★ 8697 ★ Morningside College
Department of Nursing Education
1501 Morningside Ave.
Sioux City, IA 51106
Phone: (712)274-5156

★ 8698 ★ Mt. Mercy College
Department of Nursing
1330 Elmhurst Dr. NE
Cedar Rapids, IA 52402
Phone: (319)363-8213

★ 8699 ★ Teikyo Marycrest University
Division of Nursing
1607 W. 12th St.
Davenport, IA 52804
Phone: (319)326-9279

★ 8700 ★ University of Iowa
College of Nursing
Iowa City, IA 52242
Phone: (319)335-7018

Kansas

★ 8701 ★ Bethel College
Department of Nursing
300 E. 27th St.
North Newton, KS 67117
Phone: (316)283-2500

★ 8702 ★ Ft. Hays State University
School of Nursing
Stroup Hall
600 Park St.
Hays, KS 67601
Phone: (913)628-4498

★ 8703 ★ Kansas Newman College
School of Nursing
3100 McCormish
Wichita, KS 67213
Phone: (316)942-4291

★ 8704 ★ Mid-America Nazarene College
Division of Nursing
2030 E. College Way
Olathe, KS 66062-1899
Phone: (913)782-3750

★ 8705 ★ Pittsburg State University
Department of Nursing
1700 S. Broadway
Pittsburg, KS 66762
Phone: (316)235-4431

★ 8706 ★ Southwestern College
Department of Nursing
100 N. College St.
Winfield, KS 67156
Phone: (316)221-4150

★ 8707 ★ University of Kansas
College of Health and Science
School of Nursing
3901 Rainbow Blvd.
Kansas City, KS 66160-7501
Phone: (913)588-1619

★ 8708 ★ Washburn University of Topeka
School of Nursing
1700 College St.
Topeka, KS 66621
Phone: (913)295-6525

★ 8709 ★ Wichita State University
School of Nursing
1845 Fairmont
Wichita, KS 67260-0041
Phone: (316)689-3610

Kentucky

★ 8710 ★ Bellarmine College
Lansing School of Nursing
2001 Newburg Rd.
Louisville, KY 40205-3305
Phone: (502)452-8216

★ 8711 ★ Berea College
Department of Nursing
2290 College Station
Berea, KY 40404
Phone: (606)986-9341

★8712★ **Eastern Kentucky University**
Department of Baccalaureate Nursing
Rowlett Bldg., Rm. 220
Richmond, KY 40475-0956
Phone: (606)622-1956

★8713★ **Morehead State University**
Department of Nursing and Allied Health
  Sciences
Baccalaureate Nursing Program
234 Reed Hall
Morehead, KY 40351
Phone: (606)783-2230

★8714★ **Murray State University**
Department of Nursing
Murray, KY 42071
Phone: (502)762-2196

★8715★ **Spalding University**
School of Nursing and Health Sciences
Baccalaureate Nursing Program
851 S. 4th St.
Louisville, KY 40203
Phone: (502)585-9911

★8716★ **Thomas More College**
Department of Nursing
2771 Turkeyfoot Rd.
Crestview Hills, KY 41017
Phone: (606)344-3412

★8717★ **University of Kentucky**
College of Nursing
760 Rose St., Rm. 315
Lexington, KY 40536-0232
Phone: (606)233-6533

★8718★ **University of Louisville**
School of Nursing
Health Sciences Center
Louisville, KY 40292
Phone: (502)588-5366

★8719★ **Western Kentucky University**
Department of Nursing
Bowling Green, KY 42101
Phone: (502)745-3391

Louisiana

★8720★ **Dillard University**
Division of Nursing
2601 Gentilly Blvd.
New Orleans, LA 70122
Phone: (504)283-8822

★8721★ **Dillard University**
School of Nursing
2601 Gentilly Blvd.
New Orleans, LA 70122
Phone: (504)283-8822

★8722★ **Grambling State University**
School of Nursing
Box 4272
Grambling, LA 71245
Phone: (318)274-2672

★8723★ **Louisiana College**
Department of Nursing
PO Box 556 CS
Pineville, LA 71359
Phone: (318)487-7127

★8724★ **Louisiana State University**
School of Nursing
1900 Gravier St.
New Orleans, LA 70112-2262
Phone: (504)568-4114

★8725★ **McNeese State University**
College of Nursing
Lake Charles, LA 70609
Phone: (318)475-5822

★8726★ **Nicholls State University**
Baccalaureate Nursing Program
PO Box 2143, College Sta.
Thibodaux, LA 70310
Phone: (504)448-4696

★8727★ **Northeast Louisiana University**
School of Nursing
700 University Ave.
Monroe, LA 71209-0460
Phone: (318)342-1644

★8728★ **Northwestern State University of**
  Louisiana
Division of Nursing
1800 Line Ave.
Shreveport, LA 71103
Phone: (318)677-3100

★8729★ **Our Lady of Holy Cross College**
Division of Nursing
4123 Woodland Dr.
New Orleans, LA 70131
Phone: (504)394-7744

★8730★ **Southeastern Louisiana**
  University
School of Nursing
Box 781, University Sta.
Hammond, LA 70402
Phone: (504)549-3772

★8731★ **Southern University and**
  Agricultural and Mechanical College
School of Nursing
PO Box 11794
Baton Rouge, LA 70813
Phone: (504)771-2151

★8732★ **University of Southwestern**
  Louisiana
College of Nursing
PO Box 43810
Lafayette, LA 70504
Phone: (318)482-5604

Maine

★8733★ **Husson College**
School of Nursing
Eastern Maine Medical Center
1 College Circle
Bangor, ME 04401
Phone: (207)941-7190

★8734★ **St. Joseph's College**
Department of Nursing
White Bridge Rd.
Windham, ME 04062
Phone: (207)892-6766

★8735★ **University of Maine**
School of Nursing
160 College Ave.
Orono, ME 04473
Phone: (207)581-2600

★8736★ **University of Maine at Ft. Kent**
Nursing Department
25 Pleasant St.
Ft. Kent, ME 04743
Phone: (207)834-3162

★8737★ **University of Southern Maine**
School of Nursing
96 Falmouth St.
Portland, ME 04103
Phone: (207)780-4133

★8738★ **Westbrook College**
Department of Nursing
Maine Medical Center
716 Stevens Ave.
Portland, ME 04103
Phone: (207)797-7261

Maryland

★8739★ **Columbia Union College**
Department of Nursing
7600 Flower Ave.
Takoma Park, MD 20912
Phone: (301)891-4144

★8740★ **Coppin State College**
Helene Fuld School of Nursing
2500 W. North Ave.
Baltimore, MD 21216
Phone: (410)383-5546

★8741★ **Johns Hopkins University**
School of Nursing
1830 E. Monument St., Rm. 215
Baltimore, MD 21205
Phone: (410)955-9840

★8742★ **Salisbury State College**
School of Nursing
Salisbury, MD 21801
Phone: (301)543-6402

★8743★ **Towson State University**
Department of Nursing
Towson, MD 21204
Phone: (410)830-2067

★8744★ **University of Maryland**
School of Nursing
655 W. Lombard St.
Baltimore, MD 21201
Phone: (410)706-6741

★8745★ **Villa Julie College / Union**
  Memorial Hospital
School of Nursing
Greenspring Valley Rd.
Stevenson, MD 21153
Phone: (410)554-2056

Massachusetts

★ 8746 ★ American International College
Divison of Nursing
1000 State St.
Springfield, MA 01109
Phone: (413)747-6361

★ 8747 ★ Boston College
School of Nursing
140 Commonwealth Ave.
Chestnut Hill, MA 02167
Phone: (617)552-4274

★ 8748 ★ Curry College
Division of Nursing Studies
1071 Blue Hill Ave.
Milton, MA 02186
Phone: (617)333-0500

★ 8749 ★ Elms College
Department of Nursing
291 Springfield St.
Chicopee, MA 01013
Phone: (413)594-2761

★ 8750 ★ Fitchburg State College
Department of Nursing
160 Pearl St.
Fitchburg, MA 01420
Phone: (508)345-2151

★ 8751 ★ Northeastern University
College of Nursing
360 Huntington Ave.
Boston, MA 02115
Phone: (617)437-3102

★ 8752 ★ Salem State College
School of Nursing
South Campus
352 Lafayette St.
Salem, MA 01970
Phone: (508)741-6649

★ 8753 ★ Simmons College
Department of Nursing
300 The Fenway
Boston, MA 02115
Phone: (617)738-2206

★ 8754 ★ University of Massachusetts
School of Nursing
Arnold House, Rm. 317
Amherst, MA 01003
Phone: (413)545-2703

★ 8755 ★ University of Massachusetts at
Boston
College of Nursing
100 Morrissey Blvd.
Boston, MA 02125-3393
Phone: (617)207-7500

★ 8756 ★ University of Massachusetts
Dartmouth
College of Nursing
Old Westport Rd.
North Dartmouth, MA 02747
Phone: (508)999-8586

★ 8757 ★ University of Massachusetts
Lowell
Department of Nursing
1 University Ave.
Lowell, MA 01854
Phone: (508)934-4466

★ 8758 ★ Worcester State University
Department of Nursing
486 Chandler St.
Worcester, MA 01602
Phone: (508)793-8129

Michigan

★ 8759 ★ Andrews University
Department of Nursing
Berrien Springs, MI 49104
Phone: (616)471-3311

★ 8760 ★ Eastern Michigan University
Department of Nursing
228 King Hall
Ypsilanti, MI 48197
Phone: (313)487-2310

★ 8761 ★ Grand Valley State University
Kirkhof School of Nursing
212 Henry Hall
Allendale, MI 49401
Phone: (616)895-3558

★ 8762 ★ Hope College / Calvin College
Hope-Calvin Department of Nursing
c/o Calvin College
3201 Burton SE
Grand Rapids, MI 49546
Phone: (616)957-7076

★ 8763 ★ Lake Superior State University
Department of Nursing
1000 College Dr.
Sault Sainte Marie, MI 49783
Phone: (906)635-2599

★ 8764 ★ Madonna University
College of Nursing
Baccalaureate Nursing Program
222 Magers Hall
Livonia, MI 48150
Phone: (313)591-8339

★ 8765 ★ Michigan State University
College of Nursing
A-230 Life Sciences Bldg.
East Lansing, MI 48824-1317
Phone: (517)353-4827

★ 8766 ★ Northern Michigan University
School of Nursing
222 Magers Hall
Marquette, MI 49855
Phone: (906)227-2830

★ 8767 ★ Oakland University
School of Nursing
444 O'Dowd Hall
Rochester, MI 48309
Phone: (810)370-4071

★ 8768 ★ Saginaw Valley State University
College of Nursing and Allied Health
Sciences
Baccalaureate Nursing Program
2250 Pierce Rd.
University Center, MI 48710
Phone: (517)790-4145

★ 8769 ★ University of Detroit Mercy
McAuley School of Nursing
8200 W. Outer Dr.
Detroit, MI 48219-3599
Phone: (313)592-6132

★ 8770 ★ University of Michigan
School of Nursing
400 N. Ingalls Bldg., Rm. 1320
Ann Arbor, MI 48109-0482
Phone: (313)764-7188

★ 8771 ★ Wayne State University
College of Nursing
5557 Cass Ave.
Detroit, MI 48202
Phone: (313)577-4070

Minnesota

★ 8772 ★ Bethel College
Department of Nursing
3900 Bethel Dr.
St. Paul, MN 55112
Phone: (612)638-6368

★ 8773 ★ College of St. Benedict
Department of Nursing
37 South College Dr.
St. Joseph, MN 56374-2099
Phone: (612)363-5404

★ 8774 ★ College of St. Catherine
Department of Nursing
2004 Randolph Ave.
St. Paul, MN 55105
Phone: (612)690-6583

★ 8775 ★ College of St. Scholastica
Department of Nursing
1200 Kenwood Ave.
Duluth, MN 55811-4199
Phone: (218)723-6025

★ 8776 ★ Mankato State University
School of Nursing
MSU 27
PO Box 8400
Mankato, MN 56002-8400
Phone: (507)389-2463

★ 8777 ★ Minnesota Intercollegiate Nursing
Consortium
Department of Nursing
St. Olaf College
1520 St. Olaf Ave.
Northfield, MN 55057-1098
Phone: (507)646-3265

★ 8778 ★ University of Minnesota
School of Nursing
308 Harvard St. SE, 6-101, Unit F
Minneapolis, MN 55455-0342
Phone: (612)624-4454

★8779★ Winona State University
College of Nursing and Health Sciences
Baccalaureate Nursing Program
Box 5838
325 Stark Hall
Winona, MN 55987
Phone: (507)457-5122

Mississippi

★8780★ Alcorn State University
Division of Nursing
PO Box 18399
Natchez, MS 39122
Phone: (601)442-3901

★8781★ Delta State University
School of Nursing
PO Box 3343
Cleveland, MS 38733
Phone: (601)846-4268

★8782★ Mississippi College
School of Nursing
Box 4225
Clinton, MS 39058
Phone: (601)925-3278

★8783★ Mississippi University for Women
Division of Nursing
Shattuck Hall
PO Box W910
Columbus, MS 39701
Phone: (601)329-7299

★8784★ University of Mississippi
School of Nursing
Medical Center
2500 N. State St.
Jackson, MS 39216
Phone: (601)984-6200

★8785★ University of Southern
  Mississippi
School of Nursing
PO Box 5095, Southern Sta.
Hattiesburg, MS 39406
Phone: (601)266-5445

★8786★ William Carey College
School of Nursing
498 Tuscan Ave.
Hattiesburg, MS 39401
Phone: (601)582-6147

Missouri

★8787★ Avila College
Department of Nursing
11901 Wornall Rd.
Kansas City, MO 64145
Phone: (816)942-8400

★8788★ Central Missouri State University
Department of Nursing
Warrensburg, MO 64093
Phone: (816)429-4775

★8789★ Deaconess College of Nursing
6150 Oakland Ave.
St. Louis, MO 63139-3297
Phone: (314)768-3038

★8790★ Graceland College
Division of Nursing
221 W. Lexington, Ste. 110
Independence, MO 64050
Phone: (816)833-0524

★8791★ Maryville University
Department of Nursing
13550 Conway Rd.
St. Louis, MO 63141
Phone: (314)576-9435

★8792★ Missouri Western State College
Department of Nursing
4525 Downs St.
St. Joseph, MO 64501
Phone: (816)271-4404

★8793★ Northeast Missouri State
  University
Baccalaureate Nursing Program
Kirk Bldg. 104
Kirksville, MO 63501
Phone: (816)785-4557

★8794★ Rockhurst College
Research College of Nursing
1100 Rockhurst Rd.
Kansas City, MO 64110-2508
Phone: (816)501-4547

★8795★ St. Louis University
School of Nursing
3525 Caroline St.
St. Louis, MO 63104
Phone: (314)577-8907

★8796★ St. Luke's College
School of Nursing
4426 Wornall Rd.
Kansas City, MO 64111
Phone: (816)932-2239

★8797★ Southeast Missouri State
  University
Department of Nursing
1 University Plaza
Cape Girardeau, MO 63701
Phone: (314)651-5961

★8798★ University of Missouri—Columbia
School of Nursing
5235 Nursing School Bldg.
Columbia, MO 65211
Phone: (314)882-0294

★8799★ William Jewell College
Department of Nursing
500 College Hill
Liberty, MO 64068
Phone: (816)781-7700

Montana

★8800★ Carroll College
Department of Nursing
1610 N. Benton Ave.
Helena, MT 59625
Phone: (406)447-4388

★8801★ Montana State University
College of Nursing
Bozeman, MT 59715
Phone: (406)994-2671

Nebraska

★8802★ Clarkson College
Department of Nursing
101 S. 42nd St.
Omaha, NE 68131-2739
Phone: (402)559-2288

★8803★ Creighton University
School of Nursing
2500 California Plaza
Omaha, NE 68178
Phone: (402)280-2006

★8804★ Midland Lutheran College
Division of Nursing
900 N. Clarkson
Fremont, NE 68025
Phone: (402)721-5480

★8805★ Nebraska Methodist College of
  Nursing and Allied Health
8501 W. Dodge Rd.
Omaha, NE 68114
Phone: (402)390-4981

★8806★ Union College
Division of Nursing
3800 S. 48th St.
Lincoln, NE 68506
Phone: (402)486-2524

★8807★ University of Nebraska at Omaha
College of Nursing
Medical Center
600 S. 42nd St.
Omaha, NE 68105
Phone: (402)559-6600

Nevada

★8808★ University of Nevada, Las Vegas
Department of Nursing
4505 Maryland Pkwy.
Las Vegas, NV 89154
Phone: (702)739-3360

★8809★ University of Nevada, Reno
Orvis School of Nursing
Mail Stop 134
Reno, NV 89557
Phone: (702)784-6841

New Hampshire

★8810★ Colby-Sawyer College
Department of Nursing
100 Maine St.
New London, NH 03257
Phone: (603)526-2010

★8811★ St. Anselm College
Department of Nursing
100 St. Anselm Dr., 1745
Manchester, NH 03102-1310
Phone: (603)641-7084

★8812★ University of New Hampshire
Department of Nursing
Hewitt Hall
Durham, NH 03824
Phone: (603)862-2260

New Jersey

★8813★ Bloomfield College
Division of Nursing
1 Park Place
Bloomfield, NJ 07003
Phone: (201)748-9000

★8814★ Bloomfield College
School of Nursing
467 Franklin Ave.
Bloomfield, NJ 07003
Phone: (201)748-9000

★8815★ Fairleigh Dickinson University
Department of Nursing
1000 River Rd.
Teaneck, NJ 07666
Phone: (201)692-2888

★8816★ Rutgers University
Camden College of Arts and Sciences
Department of Nursing
311 N. 5th St.
Camden, NJ 08102
Phone: (609)757-6226

★8817★ Rutgers University
College of Nursing
180 University Ave.
Newark, NJ 07102
Phone: (201)648-5142

★8818★ Seton Hall University
College of Nursing
400 S. Orange Ave.
South Orange, NJ 07079
Phone: (201)761-9015

★8819★ Trenton State College
School of Nursing
CN 4700
Hillwood Lakes
Trenton, NJ 08650
Phone: (609)771-2848

★8820★ William Paterson College of New Jersey
Department of Nursing
300 Pompton Rd.
Wayne, NJ 07470
Phone: (201)595-2286

New Mexico

★8821★ University of New Mexico
College of Nursing
PO Box 680
Albuquerque, NM 87131-1061
Phone: (505)277-4222

New York

★8822★ Adelphi University
School of Nursing
Box 516
Garden City, NY 11530
Phone: (516)877-3000

★8823★ City College of City University of New York
School of Nursing
Convent Ave. at 138th St.
New York, NY 10031
Phone: (212)690-4178

★8824★ College of Mt. St. Vincent
Department of Nursing
Riverdale, NY 10471
Phone: (718)405-3362

★8825★ College of New Rochelle
School of Nursing
New Rochelle, NY 10805
Phone: (914)654-5244

★8826★ Columbia University
School of Nursing
630 W. 168th St.
New York, NY 10032
Phone: (212)305-5756

★8827★ Dominican College of Blauvelt
Division of Nursing
10 Western Highway
Orangeburg, NY 10962
Phone: (914)359-9556

★8828★ D'Youville College
Division of Nursing
320 Porter Ave.
Buffalo, NY 14201
Phone: (716)881-7600

★8829★ Elmira College
Nursing Education Program
Elmira, NY 14901
Phone: (607)735-1724

★8830★ Hartwick College
Department of Nursing
Oneonta, NY 13820
Phone: (607)431-4780

★8831★ Herbert H. Lehman College of the City University of New York
Department of Nursing
250 Bedford Park Blvd., W.
Bronx, NY 10468-1589
Phone: (718)960-8213

★8832★ Hunter College of City University of New York
Hunter-Bellevue School of Nursing
425 E. 25th St.
New York, NY 10010
Phone: (212)481-7557

★8833★ Keuka College
Nursing Division
Keuka Park, NY 14478
Phone: (315)536-5273

★8834★ Long Island University
School of Health Professions
Division of Nursing
1 University Plaza
Brooklyn, NY 11201
Phone: (718)488-1512

★8835★ Molloy College
Department of Nursing
Rockville Centre, NY 11570
Phone: (516)678-5000

★8836★ Mt. St. Mary College
Division of Nursing
330 Powell Ave.
Newburgh, NY 12550
Phone: (914)561-0800

★8837★ New York University
Division of Nursing
50 W. 4th St.
New York, NY 10012
Phone: (212)998-5313

★8838★ Niagara University
College of Nursing
Niagara University, NY 14109
Phone: (716)286-8324

★8839★ Pace University
Lienhard School of Nursing
861 Bedford Rd.
Pleasantville, NY 10570
Phone: (914)773-3746

★8840★ Regents College
School of Nursing
1450 Western Ave.
Albany, NY 12203
Phone: (518)464-8500

★8841★ Roberts Wesleyan College
Division of Nursing
2301 Westside Dr.
Rochester, NY 14624
Phone: (716)594-6400

★8842★ Russell Sage College
Department of Nursing
Troy, NY 12180
Phone: (518)270-2231

★8843★ St. John Fisher College
Department of Nursing
3690 East Ave.
Rochester, NY 14618
Phone: (716)385-8064

★8844★ State University of New York at Binghamton
Decker School of Nursing
PO Box 6000
Binghamton, NY 13902-6000
Phone: (607)777-4713

★8845★ State University of New York at Buffalo
School of Nursing
1017 Kimball Tower
Buffalo, NY 14214
Phone: (716)831-2536

★ 8846 ★ State University of New York
  College at Brockport
Nursing Department
Brockport, NY 14420
Phone: (716)395-2355

★ 8847 ★ State University of New York
  College at Plattsburgh
Department of Nursing
Plattsburgh, NY 12901
Phone: (518)564-3124

★ 8848 ★ State University of New York
  Health Science Center at Brooklyn
College of Nursing
450 Clarkson Ave.
Brooklyn, NY 11203
Phone: (718)270-2446

★ 8849 ★ State University of New York at
  Stony Brook
School of Nursing
Health Sciences Center
Stony Brook, NY 11790
Phone: (516)444-3200

★ 8850 ★ Syracuse University
College of Nursing
426 Ostrom Ave.
Syracuse, NY 13244-3240
Phone: (315)443-2027

★ 8851 ★ Syracuse University
Utica College
Department of Nursing
1600 Burrstone Rd.
Utica, NY 13502
Phone: (315)792-3059

★ 8852 ★ University of Rochester
School of Nursing
Box SON
601 Elmwood Ave.
Rochester, NY 14620
Phone: (716)275-8894

★ 8853 ★ Wagner College
Nursing Department
631 Howard Ave.
Staten Island, NY 10301
Phone: (718)390-3436

North Carolina

★ 8854 ★ Barton College
Department of Nursing
College Sta.
Wilson, NC 27893
Phone: (919)399-6400

★ 8855 ★ East Carolina University
School of Nursing
Greenville, NC 27858
Phone: (919)757-6075

★ 8856 ★ Lenoir Rhyne College
Department of Nursing
PO Box 7292
Hickory, NC 28603
Phone: (704)328-7280

★ 8857 ★ North Carolina A&T State
  University
School of Nursing
Greensboro, NC 27411
Phone: (919)334-7751

★ 8858 ★ North Carolina Central University
Department of Nursing
PO Box 19798
Durham, NC 27707
Phone: (919)560-6322

★ 8859 ★ Queens College
Division of Nursing
1900 Selwyn Ave.
Charlotte, NC 28274
Phone: (704)337-2276

★ 8860 ★ University of North Carolina at
  Chapel Hill
School of Nursing
College Box 7460
Carrington Hall
Chapel Hill, NC 27599-7460
Phone: (919)966-4260

★ 8861 ★ University of North Carolina at
  Charlotte
College of Nursing
Charlotte, NC 28223
Phone: (704)547-4682

★ 8862 ★ University of North Carolina at
  Greensboro
School of Nursing
1000 Spring Garden St.
Greensboro, NC 27412-5001
Phone: (919)334-5010

★ 8863 ★ University of North Carolina at
  Wilmington
School of Nursing
601 S. College Rd.
Wilmington, NC 28403
Phone: (910)395-3784

★ 8864 ★ Western Carolina University
Department of Nursing
210 Moore Hall
Cullowhee, NC 28723
Phone: (704)227-7467

★ 8865 ★ Winston-Salem State University
Division of Nursing and Allied Health
Baccalaureate Nursing Program
PO Box 13326
Winston-Salem, NC 27110
Phone: (919)750-2660

North Dakota

★ 8866 ★ Jamestown College
Department of Nursing
Jamestown, ND 58401
Phone: (701)252-3467

★ 8867 ★ Medcenter One College of
  Nursing
512 N. 7th St.
Bismarck, ND 58501
Phone: (701)224-6270

★ 8868 ★ Minot State University
College of Nursing
Minot, ND 58701
Phone: (701)857-3101

★ 8869 ★ North Dakota State University
Tri-College University Nursing Consortium
136 Sudro Hall
Fargo, ND 58105
Phone: (701)231-7395

★ 8870 ★ University of Mary
Division of Nursing
7500 University Dr.
Bismarck, ND 58501
Phone: (701)255-7500

★ 8871 ★ University of North Dakota
College of Nursing
PO Box 8195, University Sta.
Grand Forks, ND 58201
Phone: (701)777-4173

Ohio

★ 8872 ★ Capital University
School of Nursing
2199 E. Main St.
Columbus, OH 43209
Phone: (614)236-6101

★ 8873 ★ Case Western Reserve University
Frances Payne Bolton School of Nursing
10900 Euclid Ave.
Cleveland, OH 44106
Phone: (216)368-2540

★ 8874 ★ Cedarville College
Department of Nursing
PO Box 601
Cedarville, OH 45314
Phone: (513)766-7700

★ 8875 ★ Cleveland State University
Department of Nursing
1860 E. 22nd St., RT915
Cleveland, OH 44115
Phone: (216)687-3598

★ 8876 ★ College of Mt. St. Joseph
Department of Nursing
5701 Delhi Rd.
Mt. St. Joseph, OH 45051
Phone: (513)244-4511

★ 8877 ★ Franciscan University of
  Steubenville
Department of Nursing
100 Franciscan Way
Steubenville, OH 43952
Phone: (614)283-6324

★ 8878 ★ Kent State University
School of Nursing
113 School of Nursing Bldg.
Kent, OH 44242
Phone: (216)672-7930

★ 8879 ★ Lourdes College
Department of Nursing
6832 Convent Blvd.
Sylvania, OH 43560-2898
Phone: (419)885-3211

★8880★ **Malone College**
Department of Nursing Education
515 25th St. NW
Canton, OH 44709-3877
Phone: (216)471-8166

★8881★ **Medical College of Ohio /**
Bowling Green State University /
University of Toledo
School of Nursing
PO Box 10008
Toledo, OH 43699
Phone: (419)381-5800

★8882★ **Mount Carmel College of Nursing**
127 S. Davis Ave.
Columbus, OH 43222-1504
Phone: (614)225-5032

★8883★ **Ohio State University**
College of Nursing
1585 Neil Ave.
Columbus, OH 43210
Phone: (614)292-4041

★8884★ **Ohio Wesleyan University**
Riverside School of Nursing
S. Sandusky
Delaware, OH 43015
Phone: (614)368-3865

★8885★ **Otterbein College**
Nursing Program
Westerville, OH 43081
Phone: (614)898-1483

★8886★ **University of Akron**
College of Nursing
209 Carroll St.
Akron, OH 44325-3701
Phone: (216)972-5103

★8887★ **University of Cincinnati**
College of Nursing and Health
3110 Vine St.
Cincinnati, OH 45219
Phone: (513)558-5070

★8888★ **Ursuline College**
Division of Nursing
2550 Lander Rd.
Pepper Pike, OH 44124
Phone: (216)646-4203

★8889★ **Wright State University**
College of Health and Human Services
School of Nursing
3640 Colonel Glenn Hwy.
Dayton, OH 45435
Phone: (513)873-3134

★8890★ **Youngstown State University**
College of Health and Human Services
School of Nursing
410 Wick Ave.
Youngstown, OH 44555
Phone: (216)742-3292

Oklahoma

★8891★ **East Central University**
Department of Nursing
1000 E. 14th St.
Ada, OK 74820
Phone: (405)332-8000

★8892★ **Langston University**
School of Nursing
302 Univ. Women Bldg.
Langston, OK 73050
Phone: (405)466-3411

★8893★ **Northwestern Oklahoma State**
University
School of Nursing
Alva, OK 73717
Phone: (405)327-1700

★8894★ **Oklahoma Baptist University**
School of Nursing
500 W. University
PO Box 61805
Shawnee, OK 74801
Phone: (405)275-2850

★8895★ **Oklahoma City University**
School of Nursing
Box 96B
2501 Blackwelder Ave.
Oklahoma City, OK 73106
Phone: (405)521-5901

★8896★ **Oral Roberts University**
Anna Vaughn School of Nursing
7777 S. Lewis Ave.
Tulsa, OK 74171
Phone: (918)495-6142

★8897★ **Southern Nazarene University**
School of Nursing
6729 NW 39th Expwy.
Bethany, OK 73008
Phone: (405)491-6365

★8898★ **Southwestern Oklahoma State**
University
Division of Nursing
100 Campus Dr.
Weatherford, OK 73096-3098
Phone: (405)774-3261

★8899★ **University of Central Oklahoma**
Department of Nursing
100 N. University Dr.
Edmond, OK 73034
Phone: (405)341-2980

★8900★ **University of Oklahoma**
College of Nursing
Health Sciences Center
PO Box 26901
Oklahoma City, OK 73190
Phone: (405)271-2125

★8901★ **University of Tulsa**
School of Nursing
600 S. College
Tulsa, OK 74104
Phone: (918)631-3116

Oregon

★8902★ **Linfield College**
Linfield-Good Samaritan School of Nursing
2255 NW Northrup R304
Portland, OR 97201
Phone: (503)229-8481

★8903★ **Oregon Health Sciences**
University
School of Nursing
3181 SW Sam Jackson Park Rd.
Portland, OR 97201
Phone: (503)494-7790

★8904★ **Oregon Institute of Technology**
School of Nursing
3201 Campus Dr.
Klamath Falls, OR 97601
Phone: (503)885-1360

★8905★ **Southern Oregon State College**
School of Nursing
1250 Siskiyou Blvd.
Ashland, OR 97520-5027
Phone: (503)552-6226

★8906★ **University of Portland**
School of Nursing
5000 N. Willamette Blvd.
Portland, OR 97203
Phone: (503)283-7147

★8907★ **Walla Walla School of Nursing**
10345 SE Market
Portland, OR 97216
Phone: (503)251-6115

Pennsylvania

★8908★ **Albright College**
Department of Nursing
1621 N. 13th St.
PO Box 15234
Reading, PA 19604
Phone: (215)921-2381

★8909★ **Allentown College of St. Francis**
de Sales
Department of Nursing and Health
Baccalaureate Nursing Program
2755 Station Ave.
Center Valley, PA 18034
Phone: (215)282-1100

★8910★ **Bloomsburg University of**
Pennsylvania
Department of Nursing
3109 McCormick
Bloomsburg, PA 17815
Phone: (717)389-4600

★8911★ **Carlow College**
Division of Nursing
3333 5th Ave.
Pittsburgh, PA 15213
Phone: (412)578-6059

★8912★ **Cedar Crest College**
Nursing Department
100 College Dr.
Allentown, PA 18104-6196
Phone: (215)437-4471

★ 8913 ★ College Misericordia
Nursing Program
301 Lake St.
Dallas, PA 18612
Phone: (717)675-2441

★ 8914 ★ Duquesne University
School of Nursing
600 Forbes Ave.
Pittsburgh, PA 15282
Phone: (412)434-6222

★ 8915 ★ East Stroudsburg University of
   Pennsylvania
Department of Nursing
200 Prospect St.
East Stroudsburg, PA 18301
Phone: (717)424-3474

★ 8916 ★ Edinboro University of
   Pennsylvania
Department of Nursing
Butterfield Hall
Edinboro, PA 16444
Phone: (814)732-2761

★ 8917 ★ Gannon University
Department of Nursing
University Square
Erie, PA 16541
Phone: (814)838-5520

★ 8918 ★ Holy Family College
Division of Nursing
Grant and Frankford Ave.
Philadelphia, PA 19114-2094
Phone: (215)637-3050

★ 8919 ★ Indiana University of
   Pennsylvania
Department of Nursing and Allied Health
   Professions
Baccalaureate Nursing Program
210 Johnson Hall
Indiana, PA 15705
Phone: (412)357-2230

★ 8920 ★ Lycoming College
Department of Nursing
700 College Pl.
Williamsport, PA 17701
Phone: (717)321-4224

★ 8921 ★ Mansfield University
School of Nursing
Home Economics Center
Mansfield, PA 16933
Phone: (717)622-4520

★ 8922 ★ Marywood College
Department of Nursing
2300 Adams Ave.
Scranton, PA 18509
Phone: (717)348-6275

★ 8923 ★ Messiah College
Department of Nursing
Grantham, PA 17027
Phone: (717)691-6029

★ 8924 ★ Neumann College
Division of Nursing and Health Sciences
Baccalaureate Nursing Program
Concord Rd.
Aston, PA 19014
Phone: (610)558-5616

★ 8925 ★ Pennsylvania State University
School of Nursing
201 Health and Human Development, E.
University Park, PA 16802
Phone: (814)863-0245

★ 8926 ★ St. Francis College
Department of Nursing
Loretto, PA 15940
Phone: (814)472-3184

★ 8927 ★ Temple University
College of Allied Health Professions
Department of Nursing
3307 N. Broad St.
Philadelphia, PA 19140
Phone: (215)221-4687

★ 8928 ★ Thiel College
Nursing Department
75 College Ave.
Greenville, PA 16125
Phone: (412)589-2053

★ 8929 ★ Thomas Jefferson University
College of Allied Health Sciences
Department of Nursing
130 S. 9th St., 12th Fl.
Philadelphia, PA 19107
Phone: (215)955-8390

★ 8930 ★ University of Pennsylvania
School of Nursing
Nursing Education Bldg.
420 Guardian Dr.
Philadelphia, PA 19104-6096
Phone: (215)898-4271

★ 8931 ★ University of Pittsburgh
School of Nursing
3500 Victoria St.
Pittsburgh, PA 15261
Phone: (412)624-2407

★ 8932 ★ University of Scranton
Department of Nursing
800 Linden St.
Scranton, PA 18510-4699
Phone: (717)941-7540

★ 8933 ★ Villanova University
College of Nursing
Villanova, PA 19085-1690
Phone: (610)519-4900

★ 8934 ★ Waynesburg College
Department of Nursing
51 West College St.
Waynesburg, PA 15370
Phone: (412)627-8191

★ 8935 ★ West Chester University of
   Pennsylvania
Department of Nursing
West Chester, PA 19383
Phone: (610)436-2219

★ 8936 ★ Widener University
School of Nursing
1 University Place
Chester, PA 19013-5792
Phone: (215)499-4210

★ 8937 ★ Wilkes College
Department of Nursing
217-219 S. Franklin St.
Wilkes Barre, PA 18766
Phone: (717)824-0733

★ 8938 ★ York College of Pennsylvania
Department of Nursing
Country Club Rd.
York, PA 17405-7199
Phone: (717)846-7788

Puerto Rico

★ 8939 ★ Antillian Adventista University
School of Nursing
PO Box 118
Mayaguez, PR 00681
Phone: (809)834-9595

★ 8940 ★ Caribbean University College
School of Nursing
Box 493
Bayamon, PR 00960
Phone: (809)780-0070

★ 8941 ★ Inter-American University of
   Puerto Rico
Carmen Torres de Tiburcio School of
   Nursing
Metropolitan Campus
PO Box 191293
San Juan, PR 00919
Phone: (809)758-8000

★ 8942 ★ Interamerican University of
   Puerto Rico
School of Nursing
Call Box 5100
San German, PR 00683
Phone: (809)264-1912

★ 8943 ★ Interamerican University of
   Puerto Rico
School of Nursing
PO Box U1
Arecibo, PR 00613
Phone: (809)878-5475

★ 8944 ★ Pontifical Catholic University of
   Puerto Rico
Department of Nursing
Avenue Las Americas, Sta. 6
Ponce, PR 00732
Phone: (809)841-2000

★ 8945 ★ Universidad Central De Bayamon
School of Nursing
Box 1725
Bayamon, PR 00960-1725

★ 8946 ★ Universidad Metropolitana
Department of Nursing
PO Box 21150
Rio Piedras, PR 00928
Phone: (809)766-1717

★ 8947 ★ University of Puerto Rico
School of Nursing
Medical Sciences Campus
PO Box 365067
San Juan, PR 00936-5067
Phone: (809)758-2525

★ 8948 ★ University of Puerto Rico /
Arecibo Technical College
School of Nursing
Call Box 4010
Arecibo, PR 00613-4010
Phone: (809)878-2830

★ 8949 ★ University of Puerto Rico-
Humacao
School of Nursing
Cuh Station
Humacao, PR 00791
Phone: (809)850-9346

★ 8950 ★ University of Puerto Rico,
Mayaguez
Nursing Department
PO Box 5000
Mayaguez, PR 00681
Phone: (809)265-3842

★ 8951 ★ University of the Sacred Heart
Nursing Program
Loiza St.
PO Box 12383
Santurce, PR 00914
Phone: (809)728-1515

Rhode Island

★ 8952 ★ Rhode Island College
Department of Nursing
600 Mt. Pleasant Ave.
Providence, RI 02908
Phone: (401)456-8234

★ 8953 ★ Salve Regina University
Department of Nursing
100 Ochre Point Ave.
Newport, RI 02840
Phone: (401)847-6650

★ 8954 ★ University of Rhode Island
College of Nursing
White Hall
Kingston, RI 02881
Phone: (401)792-2766

South Carolina

★ 8955 ★ Bob Jones University
School of Nursing
1700 Wade Hampton Blvd.
Greenville, SC 29614
Phone: (803)242-5100

★ 8956 ★ Clemson University
College of Nursing
309 Edwards Hall
Clemson, SC 29632
Phone: (803)656-5495

★ 8957 ★ Lander College
School of Nursing
320 Stanley Ave.
Greenwood, SC 29649
Phone: (803)229-8337

★ 8958 ★ Medical University of South
Carolina
College of Nursing
171 Ashley Ave.
Charleston, SC 29425
Phone: (803)792-8515

★ 8959 ★ South Carolina State College
School of Nursing
300 College St. NC
PO Box 7158
Orangeburg, SC 29117
Phone: (803)536-8193

★ 8960 ★ University of South Carolina at
Columbia
College of Nursing
Williams Brice Bldg.
Columbia, SC 29208
Phone: (803)777-7412

★ 8961 ★ University of South Carolina at
Spartanburg
Mary Black School of Nursing
800 University Way
Spartanburg, SC 29303
Phone: (803)599-2471

South Dakota

★ 8962 ★ Augustana College
Department of Nursing
29th St. and Summit Ave.
Sioux Falls, SD 57197
Phone: (605)336-4121

★ 8963 ★ Mt. Marty College
Nursing Program
1100 W. 8th St.
Yankton, SD 57078
Phone: (605)668-1594

★ 8964 ★ Presentation College
School of Nursing
1500 North Main St.
Aberdeen, SD 57401
Phone: (605)229-8473

★ 8965 ★ South Dakota State University
College of Nursing
Box 0213/2275
Brookings, SD 57007
Phone: (605)688-4106

Tennessee

★ 8966 ★ Austin Peay State University
School of Nursing
PO Box 4658
Clarksville, TN 37044
Phone: (615)648-7710

★ 8967 ★ Belmont University
School of Nursing
1900 Belmont Blvd.
Nashville, TN 37212
Phone: (615)385-6457

★ 8968 ★ Carson-Newman College
Department of Nursing
Jefferson City, TN 37760
Phone: (615)471-3425

★ 8969 ★ Cumberland University
School of Nursing
South Greenwood St.
Lebanon, TN 37087
Phone: (615)444-2567

★ 8970 ★ East Tennessee State University
College of Nursing
PO Box 70617
Johnson City, TN 37614-0617
Phone: (615)929-5880

★ 8971 ★ Memphis State University
School of Nursing
Memphis, TN 38152
Phone: (901)678-2020

★ 8972 ★ Middle Tennessee State
University
Department of Nursing
E.Main St., Box 81
Murfreesboro, TN 37132
Phone: (615)898-2446

★ 8973 ★ Tennessee State University
School of Nursing
3500 J.A. Merrit Blvd.
Nashville, TN 37209
Phone: (615)320-3768

★ 8974 ★ Tennessee Technological
University
School of Nursing
Cookeville, TN 38505
Phone: (615)372-3203

★ 8975 ★ Union University
School of Nursing
Jackson, TN 38305-9901
Phone: (901)668-1818

★ 8976 ★ University of Tennessee at
Chattanooga
School of Nursing
615 McCallie Ave.
Chattanooga, TN 37403
Phone: (615)755-4652

★ 8977 ★ University of Tennessee,
Knoxville
College of Nursing
1200 Volunteer Blvd.
Knoxville, TN 37996
Phone: (615)974-7604

★ 8978 ★ University of Tennessee,
Memphis
College of Nursing
877 Madison Ave.
Memphis, TN 38103
Phone: (901)528-6118

Texas

★ 8979 ★ Abilene Christian University
Abilene Intercollegiate School of Nursing
2149 Hickory St.
Abilene, TX 79601
Phone: (915)672-2441

★8980★ Baylor University
School of Nursing
3700 Worth St.
Dallas, TX 75246
Phone: (214)820-3361

★8981★ Corpus Christi State University
School of Nursing
6300 Ocean Dr.
Corpus Christi, TX 78412
Phone: (512)994-2648

★8982★ Dallas Baptist University
School of Nursing
3000 Mountain Creek Pkwy.
Dallas, TX 75211-9299
Phone: (214)333-5365

★8983★ East Texas Baptist University
1209 North Grove
Marshall, TX 75670
Phone: (903)935-7963

★8984★ Houston Baptist University
College of Nursing
7502 Fondren Rd.
Houston, TX 77074-3298
Phone: (713)995-3420

★8985★ Incarnate Word College
Division of Nursing
4301 Broadway
San Antonio, TX 78209
Phone: (210)829-6029

★8986★ Lamar University —Beaumont
Department of Nursing
PO Box 10081
Beaumont, TX 77710
Phone: (409)880-8868

★8987★ Midwestern State University
School of Nursing
3410 Taft Blvd.
Wichita Falls, TX 76308
Phone: (817)689-4595

★8988★ Prairie View A&M University
College of Nursing
6436 Fannin
Houston, TX 77030
Phone: (713)797-7000

★8989★ Stephen F. Austin State
University
Division of Nursing
PO Box 6156, SFA Sta.
Nacogdoches, TX 75962
Phone: (409)568-3604

★8990★ Texas Christian University
Harris College of Nursing
PO Box 32899, TCU sta.
Ft. Worth, TX 76129
Phone: (817)921-7497

★8991★ Texas Tech University
Health Sciences Center
School of Nursing
3601 4th St.
Lubbock, TX 79430
Phone: (806)743-2737

★8992★ Texas Woman's University
College of Nursing
PO Box 23026, TWU Sta.
Denton, TX 76204
Phone: (817)898-2403

★8993★ University of Mary Hardin-Baylor
Scott and White School of Nursing
UMH-B Station, Box 8015
Belton, TX 76513
Phone: (817)939-4662

★8994★ University of Texas at Arlington
School of Nursing
PO Box 19407
Arlington, TX 76019
Phone: (817)273-2776

★8995★ University of Texas at Austin
School of Nursing
1700 Red River
Austin, TX 78701-1499
Phone: (512)471-7311

★8996★ University of Texas at El Paso
College of Nursing and Health Sciences
Baccalaureate Nursing Program
1101 N. Campbell St.
El Paso, TX 79902
Phone: (915)747-7246

★8997★ University of Texas Health
Science Center at Houston
School of Nursing
1100 Holcombe Blvd.
Houston, TX 77030
Phone: (713)792-7873

★8998★ University of Texas Health
Science Center at San Antonio
School of Nursing
7703 Floyd Curl Dr.
San Antonio, TX 78284-7942
Phone: (210)567-2670

★8999★ University of Texas Medical
Branch at Galveston
School of Nursing
301 University Blvd.
Galveston, TX 77550
Phone: (409)772-6111

★9000★ University of Texas—Pan
American
Department of Nursing
1201 W. University Dr.
Edinburg, TX 78539
Phone: (210)381-3491

★9001★ University of Texas at Tyler
Division of Nursing
3900 University Blvd.
Tyler, TX 75799
Phone: (903)566-7201

★9002★ West Texas A&M University
Division of Nursing
313A Old Main
Canyon, TX 79016-0001
Phone: (806)656-2630

Utah

★9003★ Brigham Young University
College of Nursing
Provo, UT 84602
Phone: (801)378-7211

★9004★ University of Utah
College of Nursing
25 S. Medical Dr.
Salt Lake City, UT 84112
Phone: (801)581-3414

★9005★ Westminster College
St. Mark's Westminster School of Nursing
1840 South 1300 East
Salt Lake City, UT 84105
Phone: (801)488-4234

Vermont

★9006★ University of Vermont
School of Nursing
216 Rowell Bldg.
Burlington, VT 05405
Phone: (802)656-3830

Virgin Islands

★9007★ University of the Virgin Islands
Division of Nursing
Charlotte Amalie, St. Thomas, VI 00802-9999
Phone: (809)776-9200

Virginia

★9008★ Eastern Mennonite College
Nursing Department
1200 Park Rd.
Harrisonburg, VA 22801
Phone: (703)432-4186

★9009★ George Mason University
College of Nursing and Health
Baccalaureate Nursing Program
4400 University Dr.
Fairfax, VA 22030-4444
Phone: (703)993-1914

★9010★ Hampton University
School of Nursing
Hampton, VA 23668
Phone: (804)727-5251

★9011★ James Madison University
Department of Nursing
Main St.
Harrisonburg, VA 22807
Phone: (703)568-6314

★9012★ Liberty University
School of Nursing
Box 2000
Lynchburg, VA 24506
Phone: (804)582-2519

★9013★ Lynchburg College
Department of Nursing
1501 Lakeside Dr.
Lynchburg, VA 24501
Phone: (804)522-8324

★9014★ Norfolk State University
Department of Nursing
2401 Corprew Ave.
Norfolk, VA 23504
Phone: (804)683-9014

★9015★ Old Dominion University
School of Nursing
358 Technology Bldg.
Norfolk, VA 23529
Phone: (804)683-5245

★9016★ Radford University
School of Nursing
PO Box 6964
Radford, VA 24142
Phone: (703)831-5415

★9017★ University of Virginia
School of Nursing
McLeod Hall
Charlottesville, VA 22903
Phone: (804)924-0068

★9018★ Virginia Commonwealth
University
Medical College of Virginia
School of Nursing
PO Box 567
Richmond, VA 23204
Phone: (804)371-5171

Washington

★9019★ Eastern Washington University /
Washington State University / Whitworth
College
Intercollegiate Center for Nursing
Education
2917 W. Ft. George Wright Dr.
Spokane, WA 99204-5291
Phone: (509)324-7360

★9020★ Pacific Lutheran University
School of Nursing
Tacoma, WA 98447
Phone: (206)535-7677

★9021★ Seattle Pacific University
School of Health Sciences
Department of Nursing
3307 3rd Ave., W. at Nickerson
Seattle, WA 98119
Phone: (206)281-2233

★9022★ Seattle University
School of Nursing
900 Broadway
Seattle, WA 98122
Phone: (206)296-5660

★9023★ University of Washington
School of Nursing
Health Sciences Bldg.
Seattle, WA 98195
Phone: (206)543-8736

West Virginia

★9024★ Alderson-Broaddus College
Department of Nursing
Box 246
Philippi, WV 26416
Phone: (304)457-1700

★9025★ College of West Virginia
School of Nursing
609 S. Kanawha St.
Beckley, WV 25801
Phone: (304)253-7351

★9026★ Marshall University
School of Nursing
400 Hal Greer Blvd.
Huntington, WV 25701
Phone: (304)696-6759

★9027★ Shepherd College
School of Nursing
Shepherdstown, WV 25443
Phone: (304)876-2511

★9028★ University of Charleston
School of Nursing
2300 MacCorkle Ave. SE
Charleston, WV 25304
Phone: (304)357-4835

★9029★ West Liberty State College
School of Nursing
West Liberty, WV 26074
Phone: (304)336-8108

★9030★ West Virginia University
School of Nursing
PO Box 9600
Morgantown, WV 26506-9600
Phone: (304)293-4831

★9031★ West Virginia Wesleyan College
Department of Nursing
59 College Ave.
Buckhannon, WV 26201-2995
Phone: (304)473-8224

★9032★ Wheeling Jesuit College
Department of Nursing
316 Washington Ave.
Wheeling, WV 26003
Phone: (304)243-2359

Wisconsin

★9033★ Alverno College
Nursing Division
3401 S. 39th St.
PO Box 343922
Milwaukee, WI 53234-3922
Phone: (414)382-6281

★9034★ Bellin College of Nursing
929 Cass St.
PO Box 23400
Green Bay, WI 54305
Phone: (414)433-5803

★9035★ Cardinal Stritch College
Department of Nursing
6801 N. Yates Rd.
Milwaukee, WI 53217
Phone: (414)352-5400

★9036★ Columbia College of Nursing
2121 E. Newport Ave.
Milwaukee, WI 53211
Phone: (414)961-4121

★9037★ Concordia University Wisconsin
Nursing Division
12800 N. Lake Shore Dr.
Mequon, WI 53097
Phone: (414)243-4233

★9038★ Edgewood College
Nursing Department
805 Woodrow St.
Madison, WI 53711
Phone: (608)257-4861

★9039★ Marian College of Fond du Lac
Division of Nursing Studies
45 S. National Ave.
Fond du Lac, WI 54935
Phone: (414)923-7650

★9040★ Marquette University
College of Nursing
530 N 16th St.
Milwaukee, WI 53233
Phone: (414)288-3808

★9041★ University of Wisconsin—Eau
Claire
School of Nursing
105 Garfield Ave.
Box 4004
Eau Claire, WI 54702-4004
Phone: (715)836-5287

★9042★ University of Wisconsin—
Madison
School of Nursing
600 Highland Ave.
Madison, WI 53792-2455
Phone: (608)263-5166

★9043★ University of Wisconsin—
Milwaukee
School of Nursing
PO Box 413
Milwaukee, WI 53201
Phone: (414)229-5482

★9044★ University of Wisconsin—
Oshkosh
College of Nursing
800 Algoma Blvd.
Oshkosh, WI 54901
Phone: (414)424-1028

★9045★ Viterbo College
School of Nursing
815 S. 9th St.
La Crosse, WI 54601
Phone: (608)791-0420

Wyoming

★9046★ University of Wyoming School of Nursing
PO Box 3065
Laramie, WY 82071-3065
Phone: (307)766-4314

National & International Organizations

★9047★ Alpha Tau Delta (ATD)
5207 Mesada St.
Alta Loma, CA 91701
Phone: (714)980-3536
Fax: (909)980-3536
Robin E. Coppi, Pres.

Founded: 1921. **Members:** 6,000. **National Groups:** 1. **Regional Groups:** 2. **Description:** Professional fraternity - nursing. Seeks to further educational standards for the nursing profession. Maintains scholarship program for members only. **Publications:** Brochure. • *Cap'tions of Alpha Tau Delta*, semiannual. Newsletter. Contains reports, member and chapter news, and calendar of events. *Price:* Included in membership dues. • *President's Letter*, quarterly.

American Academy of Ambulatory Care Nursing (AAACN)
See: Entry 5536

★9048★ American Academy of Nurse Practitioners (AANP)
LBJ Bldg.
PO Box 12846, Capital Sta.
Austin, TX 78711
Phone: (512)442-4262
Fax: (512)442-6469
Zo DeMarchi, Exec.Sec.

Founded: 1985. **Members:** 3,600. **Regional Groups:** 11. **Description:** Groups (2000) and individuals (1600) promoting high standards of health care delivered by nurse practitioners. Acts as a forum to enhance the identity and continuity of nurse practitioners. Addresses national and state legislative issues that affect members; acts as a resource center on legislative activity. Supports continuing education programs. Encourages research in the field. Compiles statistics. **Publications:** *Academy Update*, monthly. Newsletter. • Brochures. • *Journal of the American Academy of Nurse Practitioners*, quarterly. Journal. Focuses on clinical practice, management, and education.

★9049★ American Assembly for Men in Nursing (AAMN)
PO Box 31753
Independence, OH 44131
Phone: (216)524-3504
Leland B. Cohen, Pres.

Founded: 1971. **State Groups:** 4. **Description:** Registered nurses. Works to: help eliminate prejudice in nursing; interest men in the nursing profession; provide opportunities for the discussion of common problems; encourage education and promote further professional growth; advise and assist in areas of professional inequity; help develop sensitivities to various social needs; promote the principles and practices of positive health care. Acts as a clearinghouse for information on men in nursing. Conducts educational programs. **Publications:** *Interaction*, quarterly. Newsletter. Contains statement of objectives and information on officers, events, and activities. *Price:* Included in membership dues. **Formerly:** (1982) National Male Nurse Association.

★9050★ American Association of Colleges of Nursing (AACN)
1 Dupont Cir. NW, Ste. 530
Washington, DC 20036
Phone: (202)463-6930
Fax: (202)785-8320
Dr. Geraldine Bednash, Exec.Dir.

Founded: 1969. **Members:** 461. **Description:** Institutions offering baccalaureate and/or graduate degrees in nursing. Seeks to advance the practice of professional nursing by improving the quality of baccalaureate and graduate programs, promoting research, and developing academic leaders. Works with other professional nursing organizations and organizations in other health professions to evaluate and improve health care. Conducts educational programs on doctoral nursing education, legal issues, student recruitment and retention strategies, and other topics; sponsors executive development series for new and aspiring deans of nursing. **Publications:** Annual Report. • *Data Base for Graduate Education in Nursing*. *Price:* $6. • *The Ecoomic Investment in Nursing Education*. *Price:* $5. • *Enrollment and Graduations in Baccalaureate and Graduate Programs in Nursing*, annual. Report. • *Essentials of College and University Education for Professional Nursing*. *Price:* $2.75 for members; $3.75 for nonmembers. • *Executive Development Series II: The Dean's Role in Organizational Assessment and Development*. *Price:* $26.95 for members; $36.95 for nonmembers. • *Faculty Salaries in Baccalaureate and Graduate Programs in Nursing*, annual. Report. • *Issue Bulletin*, 3/year. Bulletin. Examines issues in nursing education and research. • *Journal of Professional Nursing*, bimonthly. Journal. • *Meet the Press. . .and Succeed: A Handbook for Nurse Educators*. *Price:* $4.75 for members; $5.75 for nonmembers. • *Position Statement on Nursing Research*. *Price:* $3. • *Primary Health Care: Nurses Lead the Way--A Global Perspective*. *Price:* $16.95 for members; $19.95 for nonmembers. • *Salaries of Administrative Nursing Faculty in Baccalaureate and Graduate Programs in Nursing*, biennial. Report. • *Salaries of Deans in Baccalaureate and Graduate Programs in Nursing*, annual. Report. • *Special Report on Institutional Resources and Budgets in Baccalaureate and Graduate Programs in Nursing*, biennial. Report. • *Syllabus*, bimonthly. Newsletter.

★9051★ American Association of Critical-Care Nurses (AACN)
101 Columbia
Aliso Viejo, CA 92656
Phone: (714)362-2000
Free: 800-899-AACN
Fax: (714)362-2020
Sarah Sanford, CEO

Founded: 1969. **Members:** 78,000. **Local Groups:** 275. **Description:** Professional critical care nurses. Established to provide continuing education programs for nurses specializing in critical care and to develop standards of nursing care of critically ill patients. Conducts educational programs. Offers certification program for critical care nurses through AACN Certification Corporation. Seeks liaison with other professional nursing organizations and related health agencies. **Publications:** *AACN Clinical Issues*, quarterly. Journal. Contains peer-reviewed articles on clinically relevant topics. *Price:* $49.30/year for members; $58/year for nonmembers; $90/year for institutions. • *AACN Nursing Scan in Critical Care*, bimonthly. Newsletter. Includes nursing literature reviews. *Price:* $30/year for members; $40/year for nonmembers; $60/year for institutions. • *American Journal of Critical Care*, bimonthly. Journal. Covers original research in critical care. Contains directory of educational programs. *Price:* Included in membership dues; $45/year for nonmembers; $110 for institutions. • *Core Curriculum for Critical-Care Nursing*. • *Critical Care Nurse*, bimonthly. Clinical, peer-reviewed magazine focusing on critical care clinical practice. Contains listing of educational programs. *Price:* Included in membership dues; $27/year for nonmembers; $45/year for institutions. Also publishes standards for nursing care of the critically ill, outcome standards, reference and research materials, and critical care nursing texts. **Formerly:** (1970) American Association of Cardiovascular Nurses.

★9052★ American Association for the History of Nursing (AAHN)
PO Box 90803
Washington, DC 20090-0803
Phone: (202)543-2127
Fax: (202)543-0724
Dr. Rosemary T. McCarthy, Exec.Dir.

Founded: 1980. **Members:** 410. **Description:** Individuals interested in promoting the history of nursing. Conducts research and educational programs. **Publications:** *Bulletin of AAHN*, quarterly. Newsletter. Includes association news and research reports. *Price:* Included in membership dues. • *Nursing History Review*, annual. *Price:* Included in membership dues; $50 for libraries.

American Association of Legal Nurse Consultants (AALNC)
See: Entry 7162

★9053★ American Association of Managed Care Nurses (AAMCN)
PO Box 4975
Glen Allen, VA 23058-4975
Phone: (804)747-9698
Fax: (804)747-5316
W. C. Williams, III, Exec.Dir.

Founded: 1994. **Members:** 300. **Description:** Managed health care professionals, including registered nurses, licensed practical nurses, physicians assistants, and accredited records technicians. Seeks to enhance the abilities of members to meet the future needs of the managed health care profession through education, networking, and legislative lobbying. Conducts educational programs; maintains speakers' bureau. **Publications:** *Nurses' Notes*, quarterly. Newsletter. *Price:* Included in membership dues.

★9054★ **American Association of Neuroscience Nurses (AANN)**
224 N. Des Plaines, No. 601
Chicago, IL 60661
Phone: (312)993-0043
Fax: (312)993-0362
John F. Settich, Exec.Dir.
Founded: 1968. **Members:** 4,000. **Regional Groups:** 77. **Description:** Registered nurses engaged in or primarily interested in neurosurgical or neurological nursing. Objectives are to: foster interest, education, and high standards of practice in the field of neuroscience nursing; encourage continuing growth in the field; provide a medium for communication among neuroscience nurses in the U.S. and Canada. Has developed clinical and surgical core curriculum for neuroscience nursing practice. **Publications:** *American Association of Neuroscience Nurses Synapse*, bimonthly. Newsletter. Includes calendar of events, continuing education course listings, employment listings, and information on new members and publications. *Price:* Included in membership dues. • *Core Curriculum for Neuroscience Nursing*. • *Journal of Neuroscience Nursing*, bimonthly. Journal. Includes book reviews, pharmacology update, and research reports. *Price:* Included in membership dues; $39/year for nonmembers; $52/year for institutions.

American Association of Nurse Anesthetists (AANA)
See: Entry 2348

The American Association of Nurse Attorneys (TAANA)
See: Entry 7164

★9055★ **American Association of Occupational Health Nurses (AAOHN)**
50 Lenox Pointe
Atlanta, GA 30324
Phone: (404)262-1162
Fax: (404)262-1165
Ann Cox, CAE, Exec.Dir.
Founded: 1942. **Members:** 12,500. **Regional Groups:** 1. **State Groups:** 36. **Local Groups:** 144. **Description:** Registered professional nurses employed by business and industrial firms; nurse educators, nurse editors, nurse writers, and others interested in occupational health nursing. Promotes and sets standards for the profession. Provides and approves continuing education; maintains governmental affairs program; offers placement service. **Publications:** *AAOHN Journal*, monthly. Journal. • *AAOHN News*, monthly. Newsletter. **Formerly:** (1977) American Association of Industrial Nurses.

★9056★ **American Association of Office Nurses (AAON)**
109 Kinderkamack Rd.
Montvale, NJ 07645
Phone: (201)391-2600
Fax: (201)573-8543
Joyce Logan, Exec.Dir.
Founded: 1988. **Members:** 6,500. **Regional Groups:** 21. **Description:** Nurses working primarily in physicians' offices. Promotes improvement of the image of the office nurse. Encourages professional growth and development; facilitates exchange of information among members. Provides continuing education opportunities. Issues publications. **Publications:** *NEON*, quarterly. Newsletter.

★9057★ **American Association of Spinal Cord Injury Nurses (AASCIN)**
75-20 Astoria Blvd.
Jackson Heights, NY 11370
Phone: (718)803-3782
Fax: (718)803-0414
Dr. Vivian Beyda, Exec.Admin.
Founded: 1983. **Members:** 1,600. **Description:** Nurses who care for patients with spinal cord injuries; nurses interested in the field of spinal cord injury; persons who have provided extraordinary service to improve the quality of life for spinal cord injury patients. Purposes are to: promote and improve nursing care of spinal cord injury patients; develop and advance related education and research; recognize nurses whose careers are devoted to the problems of spinal cord injury; keep medical personnel informed of state-of-the-art techniques. Focuses on topics such as sexuality and spinal cord injury, care of respiratory dependent spinal cord injury patients, alcohol and drug dependent spinal cord injury patients, and planning for care in the community. Monitors and participates in legislative and regulatory activities affecting spinal cord injury and professional nursing practice. Conducts research and educational programs. **Publications:** *Education Guide for Spinal Cord Injury Nurses: A Manual for Teaching Patients, Families and Caregivers*. Manual. *Price:* $20. • *SCI Nursing*, quarterly. Journal. Contains articles on all facets on spinal cord injury patient care and association news. • *Spinal Cord Injury: Educational Guidelines for Professional Nursing Practice*. *Price:* $25. • *Standards of Spinal Cord Injury Practice*. Pamphlet. *Price:* $6.

★9058★ **American Board of Neuroscience Nursing (ABNN)**
224 N. Des Plaines, Ste. 601
Chicago, IL 60661
Phone: (312)993-0256
Founded: 1978. **Description:** Certifying body for registered nurses who have passed a written examination demonstrating achievement in neuroscience nursing. Objective is to promote excellence in the field by encouraging professional growth and individual study; granting neuroscience nursing certification; measuring knowledge and level of theory required for certification; establishing certification standards. Administers certifying examination. **Formerly:** (1984) Neurosurgical Nurses.

★9059★ **American Board for Occupational Health Nurses (ABOHN)**
10503 N. Cedarburg Rd.
Mequon, WI 53092-4403
Phone: (414)242-0704
Fax: (414)242-0486
Charlene C. Ossler, Ph.D., Exec.Dir.
Founded: 1972. **Members:** 7,100. **Description:** Occupational health nurses. Establishes standards and confers initial and ongoing certification in occupational health nursing. Conducts annual certification examination. **Publications:** *The COHN Report*, semiannual. Newsletter. • *Directory of Certified Occupational Health Nurses*, annual. Directory. Contains contact information for certified occupational health nurses. • *Scope and Standards of Certified OHN Practice*. • *Study Reference Guide*. Also publishes position papers on nursing.

American Board of Post Anesthesia Nursing Certification (ABPANC)
See: Entry 2350

American College of Nurse-Midwives (ACNM)
See: Entry 9625

American Holistic Nurses Association (AHNA)
See: Entry 2167

★9060★ **American Licensed Practical Nurses Association (ALPNA)**
1090 Vermont Ave. NW, Ste. 1200
Washington, DC 20005
Phone: (202)682-5800
Fax: (202)682-0168
Paul M. Tendler, Exec.Dir.
Founded: 1984. **Members:** 6,200. **Description:** Licensed practical nurses. Promotes the practical nursing profession; lobbies and maintains relations with the government on issues and legislation that may have an impact on LPNs. Conducts continuing education classes. Facilitates discussion of issues affecting the nursing and health professions. **Publications:** Pamphlets. Contain information on legislation and nursing standards. • Papers.

★9061★ **American Nephrology Nurses' Association (ANNA)**
Box 56, E. Holly Ave.
Pitman, NJ 08071
Phone: (609)256-2320
Fax: (609)589-7463
Karen E. Schardin, BSN, Contact
Founded: 1969. **Members:** 8,100. **Regional Groups:** 4. **Local Groups:** 100. **Description:** Registered nurses; physicians, dietitians, social workers, and technicians. Promotes continuing education of members at national, regional, and local levels. **Publications:** *Certification Review Course*. • *Certification Review Guide*. • *Clinical Ladder Program*. • *Core Curriculum for Nephrology Nursing*. • Journal, bimonthly. *Price:* $24/year. • *Professional Development Guide*. • *Quality Assurance Manual*. Manual. • *Standards of Clinical Practice in Nephrology Nursing*. • *Update*, bimonthly. **Formerly:** (1984) American Association of Nephrology Nurses and Technicians.

★9062★ American Nurses Association (ANA)
600 Maryland Ave. SW, Ste. 100 W.
Washington, DC 20024-2571
Phone: (202)651-7000
Fax: (202)651-7001
Virginia Trotter-Betts, J.D., Pres.
Founded: 1896. **Members:** 210,000. **State Groups:** 53. **Local Groups:** 860. **Description:** Member associations representing registered nurses. Sponsors American Nurses Foundation (for research), American Academy of Nursing (see separate entries), Center for Ethics and Human Rights, International Nursing Center, Ethnic/Racial Minority Fellowship Programs, and American Nurses Credentialing Center. Maintains hall of fame. **Publications:** *The American Nurse*, monthly, 10/year. Newspaper. Includes employment listings. *Price:* Included in membership dues; $20/year for nonmembers; $10/year for full-time nursing students. • Catalog, annual. • *Facts About Nursing*, semiannual. • *Proceedings of the House of Delegates*, periodic. Proceedings. Also publishes nursing standards and professional literature. **Formerly:** (1911) Nurses Associated Alumnae of United States and Canada.

★9063★ American Nurses in Business Association (ANBA)
PO Box 741384
Houston, TX 77274-1384
Phone: (713)771-5016
Fax: (713)771-6619
Sharon Mathis, Pres. & CEO
Founded: 1992. **Members:** 30. **State Groups:** 1. **Local Groups:** 2. **Description:** Nursing students, companies, self-employed nurses, registered nurses, and licensed vocational nurses. Serves as support group for nurses interested in seeking business opportunities. Provides business-related information. Sponsors speakers' bureau; offers placement service. **Publications:** Newsletter.

★9064★ American Nursing Care Foundation (ANCF)
PO Box 2734
Fort Riley, KS 66442-0734
Steve P. Gorsline, Exec.Dir.
Founded: 1982. **Members:** 210. **Description:** Professional organization of certified nursing assistants and nurses' aides. Represents the interests of members. Sponsors seminars. **Publications:** *Nursing Notes*, annual. Covers educational and professional and semiprofessional nursing information. Includes employment opportunity listings. *Price:* Included in membership; $1.25/copy to nonmembers. **Formerly:** (1993) American Nursing Care Foundation.

American Organization of Nurse Executives (AONE)
See: Entry 5552

★9065★ American Psychiatric Nurses Association (APNA)
c/o Carolyn Freeland
1200 19th St. NW, Ste. 300
Washington, DC 20036
Phone: (202)857-1133
Fax: (202)223-4579
Carolyn M. Freeland, Ph.D., Exec.Dir.
Founded: 1987. **Members:** 2,600. **Regional Groups:** 20. **Description:** Psychiatric nurses. Works to improve patient care by fostering clinical research and encouraging community involvement. Facilitates continuing education and professional development of members. Provides a forum for professional and social contact between members. **Publications:** *APNA News*, bimonthly. Newsletter. • *Journal of the American Psychiatric Nurses Association*, bimonthly. Journal.

American Radiological Nurses Association (ARNA)
See: Entry 11091

★9066★ American Society of Ophthalmic Registered Nurses (ASORN)
PO Box 193030
San Francisco, CA 94119
Phone: (415)561-8513
Fax: (415)561-8575
Sue Brown, Exec.Admin.
Founded: 1976. **Members:** 1,800. **Local Groups:** 25. **Description:** Registered nurses specializing in the field of ophthalmology. Promotes excellence in ophthalmic nursing for the best and safest care of patients with eye disorders or injuries. Facilitates continuing education through the study, discussion, and exchange of knowledge, experience, and ideas in the field. Represents members' interests before governmental agencies, hospitals, industries, research organizations, technical societies, universities, and other professional associations. Conducts educational programs. **Publications:** *Insight, The Journal of the American Society of Ophthalmic Registered Nurses*, quarterly. Journal. Covers trends in ophthalmology, standards of care, and legislative issues. Includes society news, calendar of events, and chapter news. *Price:* Included in membership dues; $35/year for nonmembers.

★9067★ American Society of Plastic and Reconstructive Surgical Nurses (ASPRSN)
E. Holly Ave.
Box 56
Pitman, NJ 08071
Phone: (609)256-2340
Fax: (609)589-7463
Ron Brady, Exec.Dir.
Founded: 1975. **Members:** 1,200. **Description:** Registered nurses, licensed practical nurses, and licensed vocational nurses working with plastic surgeons or interested in plastic and reconstructive nursing. Objectives are: to enhance leadership qualities of nurses in the field of plastic surgery; to increase the skills, knowledge, and understanding of personnel in plastic surgery nursing through continuing education; to study existing practices and new developments in the field; to encourage participation

and interest in professional organizations; to co-operate with others in the profession. **Publications:** *ASPRS News*, bimonthly. Newsletter. *Price:* Available to members only. • *ASPRSN Membership Directory*, annual. Membership Directory. • *Core Curriculum for Plastic and Reconstructive Surgical Nursing*. • *Plastic Surgical Nursing*, quarterly. Journal.

★9068★ American Society of Post Anesthesia Nurses (ASPAN)
6900 Grove Rd.
Thorofare, NJ 08086
Phone: (609)845-5557
Keven Dill, Dir.
Founded: 1980. **Members:** 8,500. **State Groups:** 42. **Description:** Postanesthesia nurses. Promotes upgrading of standards of postanesthesia patient care and the professional growth of licensed nurses involved in the care of patients in the immediate postanesthesia period. Provides forum for exchange of knowledge and ideas on patient care; facilitates cooperation among postanesthesia nurses and physicians and other medical personnel; encourages specialization and research in the field. Promotes public awareness and understanding of the care of postanesthesia patients. Conducts courses. **Publications:** *Breathline*, bimonthly. Newsletter. Includes calendar of events, member profiles, resource reviews, news of other related organizations, and listings of award recipients. *Price:* Included in membership dues. • *Journal of Postanesthesia Nursing*, bimonthly. Journal. Includes scientific/educational articles covering standards of care, ethical/legal issues, pharmacology, communication, and educational resources. *Price:* Included in membership dues; $48/year for nonmember individuals; $74/year for institutions.

★9069★ Anthroposophical Nurses Association of America
215 E. Main St.
Elkton, MD 21921
Phone: (410)392-3283
Catherine Barnes, Sec.
Founded: 1985. **Members:** 62. **Description:** Seeks to further the practice of anthroposophical nursing in the U.S. (Anthroposophy is a 20th century religious system centering on human development.) Encourages nurses to apply their knowledge of humankind to nursing practices. Promotes members' continued education. **Publications:** Newsletter, annual.

★9070★ Association of Black Nursing Faculty (ABNF)
5823 Queens Cove
Lisle, IL 60532
Phone: (708)969-3809
Fax: (708)969-3895
Sallie Tucker-Allen, Ph.D., Exec.Dir.
Founded: 1987. **Members:** 127. **State Groups:** 25. **Description:** Black nursing faculty teaching in nursing programs accredited by the National League for Nursing. Works to promote health-related issues and educational concerns of interest to the black community and ABNF. Serves as a forum for communication and the exchange of information among members; develops strategies for expressing concerns to

other individuals, institutions, and communities. Assists members in professional development; develops and sponsors continuing education activities; fosters networking and guidance in employment and recruitment activities. Promotes health-related issues of legislation, government programs, and community activities. Supports black consumer advocacy issues. Encourages research. Maintains speakers' bureau and hall of fame. Offers charitable program and placement services. Compiles statistics. Is establishing a computer-assisted job bank; plans to develop bibliographies related to research groups. **Publications:** *ABNF Journal*, bimonthly. Journal. Includes research reports and scholarly papers. *Price:* $125/year. • *ABNF Newsletter*, quarterly. Newsletter. Includes member profiles and activities, research abstracts, conference information, job opportunities, and fellowship information. *Price:* Included in membership dues; $25/year. • *Membership Directory of the ABNF*, annual. Membership Directory.

Association of British Paediatric Nurses
See: Entry 3176

Association of Child and Adolescent Psychiatric Nurses (ACAPN)
See: Entry 3178

★ 9071 ★ Association of Nurses in AIDS Care (ANAC)
704 Stony Hill Rd., Ste. 106
Yardley, PA 19067
Phone: (215)321-2371
Fax: (215)321-2370
Gwen Barnett, Contact

Founded: 1987. **Members:** 2,500. **State Groups:** 34. **Description:** Nurses and other health care professionals involved in caring for people who are HIV-infected or have AIDS. Functions as a network and provides leadership and educational services for members. Promotes public awareness of AIDS issues; advocates for HIV-infected individuals. Plans to develop a national standard for care of people with AIDS. **Publications:** *Journal of the Association of Nurses in AIDS Care*, quarterly. Journal. • Newsletter, 4-8/year. Also publishes position papers.

★ 9072 ★ Association of Nurses Endorsing Transplantation (ANET)
3270 Suntree Blvd., Ste. 206
Melbourne, FL 32940
Phone: (407)254-3050
Fax: (407)253-5826
Mary Gainey, RNC, Pres.

Founded: 1983. **Members:** 75. **Description:** Registered nurses, LVNs, LPNs, student nurses, chaplains, social workers, hospitals, health care facilities. Promotes organ and tissue donation for transplantation and research. **Publications:** *ANET Newsletter*, quarterly. Newsletter. • *Handbook*, annual. **Formerly:** (1989) Consortium of Registered Nurses for Eye Acquisition.

★ 9073 ★ Association of Operating Room Nurses (AORN)
2170 S. Parker Rd., Ste. 300
Denver, CO 80231
Phone: (303)755-6300
Free: 800-755-2676
Fax: (303)752-0299
Lola M. Fehr, R.N.,, Exec.Dir.

Founded: 1949. **Members:** 46,000. **Local Groups:** 390. **Description:** Professional perioperative (operating room) nurses. Provides education, representation, and standards for quality patient care. **Publications:** *AORN Journal*, monthly. Journal. Includes film and book reviews, educational opportunities, employment listings, and legislation. *Price:* Included in membership dues; $50/year for nonmembers. • *O.R. Product Directory*. Directory. *Price:* One complimentary copy to members; $45 for nonmembers. • *View into Products. Price:* Free to qualified subscribers; $24.

Association of Pediatric Oncology Nurses (APON)
See: Entry 3186

★ 9074 ★ Association of Rehabilitation Nurses (ARN)
5700 Old Orchard Rd., 1st Fl.
Skokie, IL 60077-1057
Phone: (708)966-3433
Fax: (708)966-9418
Dagny N. Engle, R.N.,, Exec.Dir.

Founded: 1974. **Members:** 10,000. **Local Groups:** 92. **Description:** Registered nurses concerned with or actively engaged in the practice of rehabilitation nursing; others interested in rehabilitation. Works to advance the quality of rehabilitation nursing practice through educational opportunities and to facilitate the exchange of ideas. Committees involve members in issues of organizational, local, and national importance and provide an avenue to effect change. Has formed the Rehabilitation Nursing Foundation to promote, develop, and engage in educational activities and scientific research in the rehabilitation field. **Publications:** *Application of Rehabilitation Concepts to Nursing Practice: Self-Study Program*. Audiotapes. • *ARN Newsletter*, 10/year. Newsletter. • *Membership Directory*, annual. • *Rehabilitation Nursing: Concepts and Practices - A Core Curriculum*. • *Rehabilitation Nursing Journal*, bimonthly. Journal. • *Rehabilitation Nursing Research*, quarterly. • *Rehabilitation Nursing: Scope of Practice*. • *Standards and Scope of Rehabilitation Practice*.

Association of State and Territorial Directors of Nursing (ASTDN)
See: Entry 5564

★ 9075 ★ Association of Women's Health, Obstetric, and Neonatal Nurses (AWHONN)
c/o Communications Department
700 14th St. NW, Ste. 600
Washington, DC 20005-2019
Phone: (202)662-1600
Fax: (202)737-0575
Gail Kincaide, Contact

Founded: 1969. **Members:** 28,000. **Regional Groups:** 10. **State Groups:** 62. **Description:** Members are registered nurses; associate members are allied health workers with an interest in obstetric, women's health, and neonatal (OGN) nursing. Promotes and establishes the highest standards of OGN nursing practice, education, and research; cooperates with all members of the health team; stimulates interest in OGN nursing. Sponsors educational meetings, audiovisual programs, and continuing education courses. **Publications:** *Journal of Obstetric, Gynecologic, and Neonatal Nursing*, bimonthly. Journal. Includes advertisers' index and annual subject and author index. Contains book reviews, case studies, and employment opportunity listings. *Price:* $26/year for individuals; $39/year for institutions; $18/year for students. • *NAACOG Newsletter*, monthly. Newsletter. Includes annual index, calendar of events, employment opportunity listings, and legislative news. *Price:* $5/copy for nonmembers. Also publishes manual of standards and OGN nursing practice resources. **Formerly:** Nurses Association of the American College of Obstetricians and Gynecologists; (1993) NAACOG: The Organization of Obstetric, Gynecologic, and Neonatal Nurses.

★ 9076 ★ Baromedical Nurses Association (BNA)
PO Box 2727
Palm Desert, CA 92261
Phone: (619)770-3676
Michael Hartsell, R.N., Pres.

Founded: 1985. **Members:** 160. **Regional Groups:** 6. **Description:** Registered nurses practicing baromedicine (hyperbaric medicine), involved in research related to baromedical nursing, completing basic orientation in baromedicine, or contributing to literature on baromedicine or baromedical nursing. Defines, develops, and promotes the status and standards of baromedical nursing. Facilitates professional activities and continuing education programs. Provides a forum for the exchange of ideas, information, and support; maintains speakers' bureau. Is developing a credentialing/certification program. **Publications:** *BNA Update*, quarterly. Newsletter. Includes research findings, safety and educational information, and upcoming events. *Price:* Free, for members only. • Membership Directory, periodic.

★ 9077 ★ Board of Nephrology Examiners—Nursing and Technology (BONENT)
PO Box 44085
Madison, WI 53719
Phone: (608)873-7454
Free: 800-9-BONENT
Fax: (608)873-1988
Leissa Cmar, Pres.

Founded: 1974. **Members:** 3,000. **Description:** Registered nurses, licensed practical nurses, licensed vocational nurses, and dialysis technicians. Provides nephrology nursing and technology certification examinations. Through certification, seeks to ensure: safe, competent practitioners in nephrology nursing and technology; excellence in the quality of care of the nephrology patient; the continued study and advance of the science of nursing and technological fields in nephrology. Compiles statistics.

Publications: *Bonent Directions*, periodic. Newsletter. *Price:* Included in membership dues.

★9078★ **Canadian Intravenous Nurses Association (CINA)**
4433 Sheppard Ave. E, Ste. 200
Agincourt, ON, Canada M1S 1V3
Phone: (416)292-0687
Fax: (416)292-1038
Pamela Smith, Exec. Officer

Founded: 1975. **Members:** 450. **Local Groups:** 6. **Languages:** English. **Description:** Registered nurses specializing in intravenous therapy or employed in supervisory, educational, or administrative positions related to intravenous therapy. Works to establish and promote standards of intravenous therapy. Offers educational programs designed to enhance patient care and safety. Facilitates discussion of intravenous therapy issues. **Publications:** *CINA Journal*, quarterly. Journal. • *CINA Mainliner*, quarterly. Newsletter.

★9079★ **Canadian Nurses Association (CNA)**
(Association des Infirmieres et Infirmiers du Canada — AIIC)
50 Driveway
Ottawa, ON, Canada K2P 1E2
Phone: (613)237-2133
Fax: (613)237-3520
Judith Oulton, Exec.Dir.

Founded: 1908. **Members:** 111,708. **Local Groups:** 11. **Languages:** English, French. **Description:** Represents the interests of Canadian nurses and works to influence and improve national health care policy. Promotes high standards of nursing education, research, and administration and strives to better the quality of nursing provided. Organizes certification exams; compiles statistics. **Publications:** *Canadian Nurse/Infirmiere Canadienne*, 11/year. Journal. • Monograph, periodic. • Pamphlets, periodic.

★9080★ **Chi Eta Phi Sorority**
3029 13th St. NW
Washington, DC 20009
Phone: (202)232-3858
Fax: (202)232-3460
Catherine W. Binns, R.N., Contact

Founded: 1932. **Members:** 5,000. **Description:** Professional sorority - registered and student nurses. Objectives are to: encourage continuing education; stimulate friendship among members; develop working relationships with other professional groups for the improvement and delivery of health care services. Sponsors leadership training seminars every two years and holds additional seminars at the local, regional, and national levels. Offers educational programs for entrance into nursing and allied health fields. Maintains health screening and consumer health education programs; volunteers assistance to senior citizens; sponsors recruitment and retention programs for minority students in nursing. Operates speakers' bureau on health education. **Publications:** *Chi Line*, semiannual. Newsletter. Includes membership activities. *Price:* Available to members only. • *The Directory*, biennial. Directory. • *Glowing Lamp - Journal of Chi Eta Phi Sorority*, annual.

Journal. *Price:* $15. • *History of Chi Eta Phi Sorority, Inc.* • *Mary Eliza Mahoney, America's First Black Professional Nurse.*

★9081★ **China Nursing Association**
42 Dongsi Xi Da St.
Beijing 100710, People's Republic of China
Phone: 1 5134368
Ying-hua Yang, Sec.Gen.

Founded: 1909. **Members:** 78,797. **Description:** Nurses and nursing attendants in the People's Republic of China. Promotes research and advanced technological developments in the nursing profession; represents members' interests. Conducts educational programs; bestows awards. **Publications:** *Chinese Journal of Nursing*, periodic.

★9082★ **Commission on Graduates of Foreign Nursing Schools (CGFNS)**
3600 Market St., Ste. 400
Philadelphia, PA 19104
Phone: (215)222-8454
Fax: (215)662-0425
Virginia M. Maroun, Exec.Dir.

Founded: 1977. **Description:** Established to help ensure safe nursing care for the American public while assisting nurses educated outside the United States in assesing their ability to become licensed, as well as to practice, in the U.S. Offers a certification program with credentials review and exam of nursing knowledge and English-language proficiency for registered nurses. Provides the CGFNS Credentials Evaluation Service which can evaluate any nurse's academic records in terms of U.S. comparability. Conducts studies and surveys; participates in policy discussions concerning international nursing education, licensure, and practice. **Publications:** *CGFNS Qualifying Exam: Practice English*. Booklet. Includes audiotape. • *Official Study Guide for the CGFNS Qualifying Examination*. Book. Includes study materials and practice exam.

★9083★ **Commonwealth Nurses Federation (CNF)**
Royal College of Nursing
20 Cavendish Sq.
London W1M 0AB, England
Phone: 171 4933539
Fax: 171 3551379
Patricia M. Larby, Exec.Sec.

Founded: 1973. **Members:** 50. **National Groups:** 50. **Regional Groups:** 6. **Languages:** English. **Description:** Organization of national nurses associations in Commonwealth countries. Strives to further the development of nursing and midwifery for the benefit of the community in Commonwealth nations; promotes the advancement of the profession. Encourages the use of facilities within the various regions of the Commonwealth for further education of nurses; promotes cooperation and coordinated activities among member associations. Seeks to create closer links among national nurses' associations within the Commonwealth as a means of providing mutual help and support. Offers assistance to governments and health agencies to facilitate the delivery of appropriate health services. Encourages the establishment of scholarships to enable nurses to undertake

advanced studies. Disseminates professional information, advice, and assistance. Supports regional and pan-Commonwealth educational nursing projects. Conducts seminars and research programs. **Publications:** *CNF Newsletter*, semiannual. Newsletter. • Directories, periodic. • Reports, periodic.

Council on Accreditation of Nurse Anesthesia Educational Programs / Schools
See: Entry 2360

Council on Certification of Nurse Anesthetists (CCNA)
See: Entry 2361

★9084★ **Dermatology Nurses' Association (DNA)**
Box 56, N. Woodbury Rd.
Pitman, NJ 08071
Phone: (609)582-1915
Catherine A. Brown, R.N., Exec.Dir.

Founded: 1982. **Members:** 1,600. **Description:** Addresses professional issues involving dermatology nurses; develops high standards of dermatologic nursing care; facilitates communication and interdisciplinary cooperation among members. Conducts educational meetings. **Publications:** *DNA Membership Directory*, annual. Directory. • Newsletter, bimonthly. • *Product Guide*, annual.

★9085★ **Drug and Alcohol Nursing Association (DANA)**
660 Lonely Cottage Dr.
Upper Black Eddy, PA 18972-9313
Phone: (610)847-5396
Judi A. Mellendick, Exec.Dir.

Founded: 1979. **Members:** 340. **Regional Groups:** 2. **Local Groups:** 7. **Description:** Registered nurses, licensed practical nurses, and other health professionals involved in the treatment, prevention, and control of drug and/or alcohol addictions. Purposes are to: promote and maintain the participation of the nursing profession in the treatment of addictions; uphold the highest standards of nursing education and practice; ensure that addicted patients and their families receive high quality nursing care. Provides a forum for discussion of issues and common concerns and the dissemination of current information in the drug and alcohol addictions fields. Represents drug and alcohol nursing to allied professional groups, governmental bodies, and the public; provides consulting in reference to professional nursing-related issues. Works with federal agencies to keep nurses involved in setting national policies and furthering education and research. Cooperates with other professional nurses' organizations and serves as a member of the Nursing Organization Liaison Forum, a component of the American Nurses' Association. Participates in regional and local seminars for nurses. **Publications:** *DANA Newsletter*, quarterly. Newsletter.

★ 9086 ★ Emergency Nurses Association (ENA)
216 Higgins Rd.
Park Ridge, IL 60068
Phone: (708)698-9400
Fax: (708)698-9406
H. Stephen Lieber, CAE, Exec.Dir.

Founded: 1970. **Members:** 23,000. **State Groups:** 51. **Local Groups:** 250. **Description:** Registered nurses, licensed practical nurses, and licensed vocational nurses; emergency medical technicians or nurses and members of allied health fields engaged or interested in emergency patient care. Objectives are: to promote emergency nursing and to establish standards in the field; to work with other health-related organizations toward the improvement of emergency care; to serve as a resource for emergency nursing education and research. Seeks to identify and address emergency nursing issues. Disseminates educational and research information in the field. Sponsors: Emergency Nursing Core Curriculum; Standards of Emergency Nursing Practice; Emergency Nursing Pediatric Course; Trauma Nursing Core Course. **Publications:** *CEN Review Manual.* • *Emergency Nursing Core Curriculum.* • *Emergency Nursing Scope of Practice.* • *Etcetera*, 9/year. Newsletter. • *International Journal of Trauma Nursing*, quarterly. Journal. • *Journal of Emergency Nursing*, bimonthly. Journal. • *Leadership and Clinical Monograph Series.* • *Standards of Emergency Nursing Practice.* • *Triage: Meeting the Challenge.* **Formerly:** (1974) National Emergency Department Nurses Association; (1984) Emergency Department Nurses Association.

★ 9087 ★ European Dialysis and Transplant Nurses Association / European Renal Care Association (EDTNA/ERCA)
6, chemin du Clos
CH-1212 Grand-Lancy, Switzerland
Phone: 22 7949955
Fax: 22 7949782
Sibylle Rupprecht, Exec.Dir.

Founded: 1972. **Members:** 3,900. **National Groups:** 2. **Languages:** Dutch, English, French, German, Italian, Spanish. **Description:** Nurses working in the field of nephrology, dialysis technicians, paramedical personnel, dietitians, social workers, and companies involved in renal disease research and treatment. Promotes research on renal disease to develop preventive methods and to improve patient care. Organizes educational programs. **Publications:** *Journal of the European Dialysis and Transplant Nurses Association/European Renal Care Association*, quarterly. Journal. Contains selected presentations made at the annual conference. • *Newsletter*, semiannual. Newsletter.

★ 9088 ★ Federation for Accessible Nursing Education and Licensure (FANEL)
PO Box 1418
Lewisburg, WV 24901
Phone: (304)645-4357
Fax: (304)645-4357
Twyla Wallace, Pres.

Founded: 1983. **Description:** Registered nurses, licensed practical nurses, educators, health organizations, schools, and hospital administrators seeking to maintain licensure through current educational programs for RNs and LPNs. **Publications:** Brochures. • Newsletter, biennial.

★ 9089 ★ Federation of Nurses and Health Professionals (FNHP)
555 New Jersey Ave. NW
Washington, DC 20001
Phone: (202)879-4491
Katherine Kany, Prof. Issues Coord.

Founded: 1978. **Members:** 50,000. **Description:** AFL-CIO. A division of the American Federation of Teachers. Collective bargaining organization of registered nurses, licensed practical nurses, and other professional and technical employees in the health field. Works to improve members' professional standards through promoting continuing education, advancing their economic status, and securing working conditions conducive to optimum performance and the most effective delivery of health care. Seeks to have an impact on legislation affecting national health insurance, cost containment, utilization of manpower resources, consumer health education, health personnel training funds, allocation of health research grants, and other national health issues. Maintains legal defense fund to provide assistance to members whose legal or contractual rights have been violated. **Publications:** Brochures. • *Healthwire*, 10/year. Newsletter. Includes book reviews. *Price:* Included in membership dues. • Pamphlets.

★ 9090 ★ Frontier Nursing Service (FNS)
100 Wendover Rd.
Wendover, KY 41775
Phone: (606)672-2317
Fax: (606)672-3022
Deanna Severance, Dir.

Founded: 1925. **Members:** 15. **Description:** Provides health care to persons in approximately 1000 square miles of eastern Kentucky using a 40-bed hospital, two primary care centers, three rural health clinics, and a home health agency. Operates Frontier School of Midwifery and Family Nursing. Provides social and ancillary services; conducts research on health services; compiles statistics; offers educational programs. Maintains a hall of fame and museum. Founded by Mary Breckinridge (1881-1965), FNS cares for more than 16,000 individuals per year and has delivered more than 23,000 babies since its founding. **Publications:** Brochure, annual. For Christmas appeal. • *Quarterly Bulletin.* Bulletin. *Price:* $5 for individuals; $10 for institutions.

★ 9091 ★ Health Visitors' Association (HVA)
50 Southwark St.
London SE1 1UN, England
Phone: 171 3787255
Fax: 171 4073521
Eileen Burke, Information Officer

Founded: 1896. **Members:** 16,000. **Local Groups:** 125. **Languages:** English. **Description:** Certified health visitors and managers of health visiting and community and school nursing services. Works to improve the status of health visitors and other community health workers. Conducts refresher courses. **Publications:** *Health Visitor*, monthly. Newsletter. • *HVA Current Awareness Bulletin*, quarterly. Bulletin.

★ 9092 ★ Hospice Nurses Association (HNA)
5512 Northumberland St.
Pittsburgh, PA 15217-1131
Phone: (412)687-3231
Fax: (412)687-9095
Madalon Amenta, Exec.Dir.

Founded: 1985. **Members:** 1,750. **Regional Groups:** 25. **Description:** Registered nurses involved in hospice care. Promotes high professional standards in hospice nursing. Conducts education and research programs. Has a certification process. **Publications:** *Fanfare*, quarterly. Newsletter. • Newsletter, quarterly.

★ 9093 ★ Institute for Hospital Clinical Nursing Education (IHCNE)
American Hospital Association
Center for Nursing
840 N. Lake Shore Dr.
Chicago, IL 60611
Phone: (312)280-6432
Fax: (312)280-5995
Marcia R. Hagopian, RN, Dir.

Founded: 1967. **Members:** 165. **Description:** Hospital schools of nursing. Provides support for issues common to hospital schools of nursing and promotes advancement of schools through educational programs and other activities. **Publications:** *Directory of Program Offerings and Curriculum Characteristics*, periodic. Directory. Provides curriculum descriptions of educational programs for directors, deans, administrators and chief executive officers. • *Institute Communique*, quarterly. Newsletter. Covers national and state legislation affecting hospital nursing schools. Reports on activities of national nursing organizations. *Price:* Included in membership dues. **Formerly:** (1991) Assembly of Hospital Schools of Nursing.

★ 9094 ★ International Committee of Catholic Nurses and Medico-Social Assistants (ICCN) (Comite International Catholique des Infirmieres et Assistantes Medico Sociales — CICIAMS)
43, sq. Vergote
B-1040 Brussels, Belgium
Phone: 2 7321050
Fax: 2 7348460
An Verlinde, Gen.Sec.

Founded: 1928. **Members:** 79. **Regional Groups:** 5. **Languages:** English, French, German. **Description:** Professional Catholic nursing associations, Catholic nursing and medico-social work schools, and other Catholic groups representing the nursing profession in 57 countries. Works to encourage the development of members and ensure their technical ability in accordance with Christian moral principles. Promotes development of the nursing profession in general; fosters health and social welfare measures consistent with Christian principles and scientific progress while respecting individual religious convictions. Provides assistance to nursing schools and associations in developing countries; facilitates exchange of statistics between hospital establishments and medico-social organizations. **Publications:** *CICIAMS News*, quarterly. **Formerly:** (1946) International Study Committee of Catholic Nursing Associations.

★9095★ International Council of Nurses (ICN)
(Conseil International des Infirmieres — CII)
3, place Jean-Marteau
CH-1201 Geneva, Switzerland
Phone: 22 7312960
Fax: 22 7381036
Constance Holleran, Exec.Dir.

Founded: 1899. **Members:** 112. **Languages:** English, French, Spanish. **Description:** National nurses' association. Provides a medium through which members can work together to promote the health of people and the care of the sick. Objectives are to: improve the standards and status of nursing; promote the development of strong national nurses' associations; serve as the authoritative voice for nurses and the nursing profession worldwide. **Publications:** Books, periodic. • Brochures, periodic. • *International Nursing Review*, bimonthly. Journal. Contains information on nursing and health issues.

★9096★ International Neural Network Society (INNS)
1250 24th St. NW, Ste. 300
Washington, DC 20037
Phone: (202)466-4667
Fax: (202)466-2888
Morgan Downey, Exec.Dir.

Founded: 1987. **Members:** 4,000. **Description:** Individuals interested in theoretical and computational understanding of the brain. Provides a forum for neurocomputing and theoretical approaches to neuroscience. Promotes research into behavioral processes and models of the brain. Encourages development of computing applications which use neural modeling concepts. **Publications:** *Above Threshold*, quarterly. Newsletter. Includes calendar of events and special interest group information. • *INNS Series on Neural Networks*. Published in conjunction with Lawrence Erlbaum Associates. • *Neural Networks*, monthly.

International Nurses Anonymous (INA)
See: Entry 12043

★9097★ International Nursing Foundation of Japan
(Kokusai Kango Kouryu Kyokai)
Medical Friend Bldg.
Kudan-kita 3-2-4
Chiyoda-ku
Tokyo 102, Japan
Phone: 3 32646667
Fax: 3 52753499

Description: Represents the interests of Japanese nurses. Promotes research and continuing education.

★9098★ International Transplant Nurses Society (ITNS)
Foster Plz., Bldg. S
651 Holiday Dr., Ste. 300
Pittsburgh, PA 15220-2740
Phone: (412)928-3667
Fax: (412)928-4951
Francine W. Rickenbach, CAE, Exec.Dir.

Founded: 1992. **Members:** 500. **Regional Groups:** 4. **Description:** Nurses, LVNs, LPNs, and others involved in patient care for organ transplantation. Works to encourage cooperation among all medical disciplines involved in transplantation, disseminate information, and establish certification for this nursing specialty. **Publications:** Newsletter, quarterly. *Price:* Included in membership dues.

★9099★ Intravenous Nurses Society (INS)
2 Brighton St.
Belmont, MA 02178
Phone: (617)489-5205
Fax: (617)489-0656
Mary Larkin, CEO

Founded: 1973. **Members:** 8,000. **Regional Groups:** 57. **Local Groups:** 57. **Description:** Registered nurses involved in intravenous (I.V.) therapy; licensed practical nurses and pharmacists. Works to promote the education of individuals practicing intravenous therapy. Conducts certification program for I.V. nurses and advanced studies program in intravenous nursing. Maintains speakers' bureau; compiles statistics. **Publications:** *CRNI News*, quarterly. Newsletter. Provides information and statistics on credentialing and certification. • *Intravenous Nurses Society Convention Program*, periodic. • *Intravenous Nurses Society Newsline*, bimonthly. Newsletter. Includes convention news, legislative network information, chapter agendas, and calendar of events. • *Journal of Intravenous Nursing*, bimonthly. Journal. Includes information on meetings, clinical manuscripts, products, and certification and recertification exams. *Price:* Included in membership dues; $35/year for nonmembers; $45/year for institutions; $20/year for students. Also publishes news releases and nursing standards.

★9100★ Japanese Nursing Association
(Nihon Kango Kyokai)
Jingu-mae 5-8-2
Shibuya-ku
Tokyo 150, Japan
Phone: 3 34008331
Fax: 3 34008767

Description: Promotes the status of nurses in Japan.

★9101★ National Alliance of Nurse Practitioners (NANP)
325 Pennsylvania Ave. SE
Washington, DC 20003-1100
Phone: (202)675-6350
Judith Dempster, Chairperson

Founded: 1985. **Members:** 30,000. **Regional Groups:** 10. **State Groups:** 4. **Description:** Nurse practitioners and other health care professionals. Seeks to emphasize the role of Nurse Practitioners in efficient and cost-effective health care services. Promotes continuing education for all health care professionals.

National Association of Directors of Nursing Administration in Long Term Care (NADONA/LTC)
See: Entry 5585

★9102★ National Association of Hispanic Nurses (NAHN)
1501 16st NW
Washington, DC 20036
Phone: (202)387-2477
Fax: (202)797-4353
Dr. Sara Torres, Pres.

Founded: 1976. **Members:** 1,000. **National Groups:** 1. **State Groups:** 10. **Local Groups:** 24. **Description:** Nurses on all educational levels, from all Hispanic subgroups; non-Hispanic nurses concerned about the health delivery needs of the Hispanic community; nursing students. Serves the nursing and health care delivery needs of the Hispanic community and the professional needs of Hispanic nurses. Provides a forum in which Hispanic nurses can analyze, research, and evaluate the health care needs of the Hispanic community. Disseminates findings of that research to local, state, and federal agencies so as to affect policy-making and resource allocation. Aims to ensure that Hispanic nurses have equal access to educational, professional, and economic opportunities. Identifies Hispanic nurses throughout the nation to determine the size of the work force available to provide culturally sensitive nursing care to Hispanics. **Publications:** *First National Hispanic Nurse Symposium Proceedings: Recruitment, Retention, Career Mobility - Strategy for Change*. Proceedings. • *Hispanic Nurse*, quarterly. *Price:* $15. **Formerly:** (1979) National Association of Spanish Speaking-Spanish Surnamed Nurses.

★9103★ National Association of Neonatal Nurses (NANN)
1304 Southpoint Blvd., Ste. 280
Petaluma, CA 94954
Phone: (707)762-5588
Fax: (707)762-0401
Charles Rait, Exec.Dir.

Founded: 1984. **Members:** 13,000. **Regional Groups:** 46. **Description:** Nurses currently working in neonatal intensive care units. Promotes professional development of members. Provides educational and networking opportunities. Disseminates legislative information. **Publications:** *Central Lines*, quarterly. Newsletter. • *Neonatal Network*, 8/year. Journal.

★9104★ National Association of Nurse Massage Therapists (NANMT)
PO Box 1268
Osprey, FL 34229
Phone: (813)966-6288
Fax: (813)918-0522
Barbara Harris, RN,LMT, Pres.

Founded: 1987. **Members:** 650. **Description:** Nurses and other healthcare professionals who practice massage therapy. Promotes the integration of massage and other therapeutic forms of bodywork into existing healthcare practice. Promotes Nurse Massage Therapists as specialists within the nursing profession. Seeks to establish standards of professional practice and criteria for national certification of Nurse Massage Therapists. Educates the medical community and the general public about bodywork therapies. Monitors legislation. **Publications:** *NANMT Membership Directory*, annual. Membership Directory. *Price:* Included in membership dues. • *Nurse's Touch*, quarterly. Newsletter. *Price:* Included in membership dues.

★**9105**★ **National Association of Nurse Practitioners in Reproductive Health (NANPRH)**
2401 Pennsylvania Ave. NW, Ste. 350
Washington, DC 20037
Phone: (202)466-4825
Fax: (202)466-3826
Susan Wysocki, Exec.Dir.

Founded: 1980. **Members:** 1,500. **Description:** Nurse practitioners involved in reproductive healthcare. Advocates quality reproductive healthcare services and reproductive freedom. Supports the rights of nurse practitioners to administer reproductive healthcare services to patients. Encourages nurses to participate in continuing education programs. Disseminates information. **Publications:** *NANPRH Newsletter*, 3/year. Newsletter. *Price:* Available to members only.

★**9106**★ **National Association of Orthopaedic Nurses (NAON)**
E. Holly Ave.
Box 56
Pitman, NJ 08071-0056
Phone: (609)256-2310
Fax: (609)589-7463
Pat Reichart, Exec.Sec.

Founded: 1980. **Members:** 8,300. **Local Groups:** 144. **Description:** Registered, licensed practical, or licensed vocational nurses involved or knowledgeable in orthopedic nursing. Enhances the personal and professional growth of orthopedic nurses through continuing education programs. Promotes research development and advances in orthopedic nursing; promotes an awareness of patients' rights. Stresses the concept of man's physical, psychological, social, emotional, and spiritual needs in the development of patient care plans. Maintains liaison with and serves as resource to hospitals, universities, industries, and government agencies. Operates special interest groups. Sponsors workshops; maintains speakers' bureau; offers research grants. Makes available audiovisual presentation. **Publications:** Bibliographies. • Monographs. • *News*, bimonthly. • *Orthopaedic Nursing*, bimonthly. Journal. • Proceedings.

★**9107**★ **National Association of Pediatric Nurse Associates and Practitioners (NAPNAP)**
1101 Kings Hwy. N., No. 206
Cherry Hill, NJ 08034
Phone: (609)667-1773
Fax: (609)667-7187
Mavis McGuire, Exec.Dir.

Founded: 1973. **Members:** 4,200. **State Groups:** 40. **Description:** Pediatric, school, and family nurse practitioners and interested persons. Seeks to improve the quality of infant, child, and adolescent health care by making health care services accessible and providing a

forum for continuing education of members. Facilitates and supports legislation designed to promote the role of pediatric nurse practitioners and associates; promotes salary ranges commensurate with practitioners' and associates' responsibilities; facilitates exchange of information between prospective employers and job seekers in the field. Participates in the implementation of certification and certification maintenance of practitioners and associates, in cooperation with the National Certification Board of Pediatric Nurse Practitioners and Nurses. Supports research programs; compiles statistics. **Publications:** Brochures. • *Journal of Pediatric Health Care*, bimonthly. Journal. Includes annual index, book reviews, legislative news, literature abstracts, multi-media reviews, and product news. *Price:* $21/year for individuals; $39.75/year for institutions; $16/year for students. • *Pediatric Nurse Practitioner*, bimonthly. Newsletter. Contains calendar of events and legislative news. *Price:* Free to members.

★**9108**★ **National Association of Physician Nurses (NAPN)**
900 S. Washington St., No. G-13
Falls Church, VA 22046
Phone: (703)237-8616
Susan Young, Dir.

Founded: 1973. **Members:** 3,000. **Description:** Physicians' nurses united to bring added stature and purpose to their profession and to create for themselves the benefits normally limited to members of specialized professional and fraternal groups. **Publications:** *The Nightingale*, monthly. Newsletter. *Price:* Included in membership dues; $15/year for nonmembers. • *Salary Survey Report*, biennial. Report. Also publishes special reports.

★**9109**★ **National Association for Practical Nurse Education and Service (NAPNES)**
1400 Spring St., Ste. 310
Silver Spring, MD 20910
Phone: (301)588-2491
Fax: (301)588-2839
John H. Word, Exec.Dir.

Founded: 1941. **Members:** 30,000. **State Groups:** 20. **Description:** Licensed practical/vocational nurses, registered nurses, physicians, hospital and nursing home administrators, and interested others. Provides consultation service to advise schools wishing to develop a practical/vocational nursing program on facilities, equipment, policies, curriculum, and staffing. Promotes recruitment of students through preparation and distribution of recruitment materials. Sponsors seminars for directors and instructors in schools of practical/vocational nursing and continuing education programs for LPNs/LVNs; approves continuing education programs and awards contact hours; holds national certification courses in pharmacology and gerontics. Maintains library of nursing and health publications. Compiles statistics. **Publications:** *Journal of Practical Nursing*, quarterly. Journal. Contains news of association activities, nursing law, and pending legislation affecting the nursing profession. *Price:* Included in membership dues; $15/year for nonmembers; $22/year for nonmembers outside the U.S. • *NAPNES Forum*, 8/year. Journal. Sup-

plement to the *Journal of Practical Nusing*. Also publishes brochures, pamphlets, and reprints.

★**9110**★ **National Association of Registered Nurses (NARN)**
11508 Allecingie Pky., Ste. C
Richmond, VA 23235
Phone: (804)794-6513
Fax: (804)379-7698
Francis R. deBondt, Ph.D., Admin.

Founded: 1979. **Members:** 250. **Description:** Nurses' associations. Seeks to offer nurses the opportunity to plan and create a financially sound future through financial management programs. Provides financial products, consultation, and services including Individual Retirement Accounts, full investment services, and group life insurance. Conducts educational programs. **Publications:** Brochures, periodic. • Newsletter, periodic.

★**9111**★ **National Association of School Nurses (NASN)**
Lamplighter Ln.
PO Box 1300
Scarborough, ME 04070
Phone: (207)883-2117
Fax: (207)883-2683
Beverly Farquhar, Exec.Dir.

Founded: 1969. **Members:** 8,000. **State Groups:** 47. **Description:** School nurses who conduct comprehensive school health programs in public and private schools. Objectives are: to provide national leadership in the promotion of health services for schoolchildren; to promote school health interests to the nursing and health community and the public; to monitor legislation pertaining to school nursing. Provides continuing education programs at the national level and assistance to states for program implementation. Operates the National Board for Certification of School Nurses and certifies school nurses. Has established workshops and grants for study of child and drug abuse, the female body, and skin care. **Publications:** *EPSDT Manual*. Manual. *Price:* $30 for members; Not available to nonmembers. • *Evaluating School Nursing Practice: A Guide for Administrators*. *Price:* $4.95 for members; $5.95 for nonmembers. • *Hearing Screening Guidelines for School Nurses*. *Price:* $6.50 for members; Not available to nonmembers. • *Journal of School Nursing*, quarterly. Magazine. Includes book reviews, obituaries, employment opportunities, and legislative updates. • *NASNewsletter*, quarterly. Newsletter. *Price:* Included in membership dues. • *School Nursing Practice: Roles and Standards*. *Price:* $15 for members; Not available to nonmembers. • *Vision Screening Guidelines for School Nurses*. *Price:* $6.50 for members; Not available to nonmembers. Offers various guides, brochures, manuals, and other publications. **Formerly:** (1977) Department of School Nurses/NEA.

★**9112**★ **National Association of Traveling Nurses (NATN)**
PO Box 417-120
Chicago, IL 60641-7120
Phone: (708)453-0080
Fax: (708)453-0083
L. David Stoller, Chm.

Founded: 1990. **Description:** Members of the medical profession. Provides travel information. Offers substantial discounts for members at major hotels, resorts, and car rental agencies. Provides members with complete list of approved travel industry suppliers, including travel agents, vendors, airlines, cruise ship companies, and hotels. **Publications:** *Journal of Traveling Nurses*, quarterly. Journal. *Price:* $2.95. • Newsletter.

★9113★ **National Black Nurses Association (NBNA)**
1511 K St. NW, Ste. 415
Washington, DC 20005
Phone: (202)393-6870
Fax: (202)347-3808
Patricia Tompkins, Exec.Dir.

Founded: 1971. **Members:** 5,000. **Description:** Registered nurses, licensed practical nurses, licensed vocational nurses, and student nurses. Functions as a professional support group and as an advocacy group for the black community and their health care. Recruits and assists blacks interested in pursuing nursing as a career. Presents scholarships to student nurses, including the Dr. Lauranne Sams and Ambi scholarships. Compiles statistics; maintains biographical archives and charitable program. **Publications:** Annual Report. • *Journal of Black Nurses Association*, semiannual. Journal. *Price:* Included in membership dues. • *National Black Nurses Association--Book of Reports*, annual. *Price:* Available to members only. • *National Black Nurses Association--Proceedings*, periodic. • *NBNA Newsletter*, quarterly. Newsletter. Includes calendar of events, research updates, scholarships, grants, and fellowships. *Price:* Included in membership dues.

★9114★ **National Certification Corporation for the Obstetric, Gynecologic and Neonatal Nursing Specialties (NCC)**
645 N. Michigan Ave., Ste. 900
Chicago, IL 60611
Phone: (312)951-0207
Free: 800-367-5613
Betty Burns, CAE, Exec.Dir.

Founded: 1975. **Members:** 40,000. **Description:** Promotes quality nursing care by encouraging nurses to demonstrate special knowledge by participating in a voluntary national certification program for obstetric/gynecologic nurse practitioners, inpatient obstetric nurses, neonatal intensive care nurses, neonatal nurse practitioners, low-risk neonatal nurses, reproductive endocrinology/infertility nurses, ambulatory women's health care nurses, high obstetric nurses, and maternal newborn nurses. **Publications:** Booklet. • Brochures. • *NCC News*, periodic. **Formerly:** (1991) NAACOG Certification Corporation.

★9115★ **National Consortium of Chemical Dependency Nurses (NCCDN)**
1720 Willow Creek Cir., Ste. 519
Eugene, OR 97402
Phone: (503)485-4421
Free: 800-87-NCCDN
Fax: (503)485-7372
Randy Bryson, Exec.Dir.

Founded: 1987. **Members:** 3,296. **Regional Groups:** 28. **Description:** Professional nurses specializing in chemical dependency treatment. Goals are: to increase the effectiveness of nursing services for chemical dependency; to establish a professional standard in chemical dependency nursing through a system of competency-based testing and programs of professional development and certification. Aims to increase public awareness of the need for chemical dependency treatment and nurses specializing in this field. Encourages the growth of knowledge, skills, and competency in chemical dependency nursing. Offers certification exam for nurses with 4000 hours experience in the previous 5 years and 30 hours of chemical dependency coursework; conducts educational programs. Maintains speakers' bureau. **Publications:** *CD Nurse Briefing*, quarterly. Newsletter. Covers issues of interest of NCCDN membership. *Price:* Available to members only. • Pamphlets.

★9116★ **National Council of Maori Nurses (Te Kaunihera O Nga Neehi Maori O Aotearoa)**
470 Wellington Rd.
Marton, New Zealand
Linda Thompson, Pres.

Local Groups: 6. **Languages:** English. **Description:** Nurses of Maori descent. Promotes continuing professional development and advancement of members; works to ensure accessibility of health care to Maori people; conducts educational and training programs.

★9117★ **National Council of State Boards of Nursing (NCSBN)**
676 N. St. Clair St., Ste. 550
Chicago, IL 60611
Phone: (312)787-6555
Fax: (312)787-6898
Dr. Genifer Bosma, Ph.D., Exec.Dir.

Founded: 1978. **Members:** 61. **Description:** State boards of nursing. Assists member boards in administering the National Council Licensure Examinations for Registered Nurses and Practical Nurses and works to insure relevancy of the exams to current nursing practice. Aids boards in the collection and analysis of information pertaining to the licensure and discipline of nurses. Provides consultative services, conducts research, develops model nursing legislation and administrative regulations, and sponsors educational programs. **Publications:** *National Council of State Boards of Nursing Issues*, bimonthly. Covers regulatory trends. Includes international nursing index and cumulative index to nursing and allied health literature. *Price:* Free. • *National Council of State Boards of Nursing Newsletter to the Member Boards*, biweekly. Newsletter. *Price:* Included in membership dues. • *State Nursing Legislation Quarterly*. Also publishes research results and monographs.

★9118★ **National Federation of Licensed Practical Nurses (NFLPN)**
1418 Aversboro Rd.
Garner, NC 27529-4547
Phone: (919)779-0046
Fax: (919)779-5642
Charlene Barbour, Admin.

Founded: 1949. **Members:** 5,000. **State Groups:** 22. **Description:** Federation of state associations of licensed practical and vocational nurses. Aims to: preserve and foster the ideal of comprehensive nursing care for the ill and aged; improve standards of practice; secure recognition and effective utilization of LPNs; further continued improvement in the education of LPNs. Acts as clearinghouse for information on practical nursing and cooperates with other groups concerned with better patient care. Maintains loan program. **Publications:** *Licensed Practical Nurse*, quarterly. Journal. Includes state and legislative news and list of new members. *Price:* Included in membership dues. • *LPN*, quarterly. Magazine.

★9119★ **National Federation for Specialty Nursing Organizations (NFSNO)**
E. Holly Ave., Box 56
Pitman, NJ 08071
Phone: (609)256-2333
Fax: (609)589-7463
Ron Brady, Exec.Dir.

Founded: 1972. **Members:** 42. **Description:** Nursing specialty organizations representing approximately 370,000 individuals. Provides a forum for the discussion of issues of mutual concern to members; attempts to gain more input in the establishment of nursing standards. Sponsors Nurse in Washington Internship. **Formerly:** (1981) Federation of Specialty Nursing Organizations and the American Nurses Association.

★9120★ **National Flight Nurses Association (NFNA)**
c/o Christine Dorsen
6900 Grove Rd.
Thorofare, NJ 08086
Phone: (609)384-6725
Fax: (609)848-5274
Jill Verbin, Exec.Dir.

Founded: 1981. **Members:** 1,700. **Regional Groups:** 10. **Description:** Flight nurses. Seeks to promote the quality of flight nursing by developing standards for the profession and exploring educational opportunities. Seeks optimum working conditions for members. Provides assistance to hospitals for developing air medical services programs. Maintains speakers' bureau. **Publications:** *Across the Board*, bimonthly. Newsletter. • *Journal of Air Medical Transport*, monthly. Journal. Also produces educational learning module.

★9121★ **National League for Nursing (NLN)**
350 Hudson St.
New York, NY 10014
Phone: (212)989-9393
Free: 800-669-1656
Fax: (212)989-9256
Dr. Patricia Moccia, CEO

Founded: 1952. **Members:** 19,800. **State Groups:** 46. **Description:** Individuals and leaders in nursing and other health professions, and community members interested in solving health care problems (18,000); agencies, nursing educational institutions, departments of nursing in hospitals and related facilities, and home and community health agencies (1800). Works to assess nursing needs, improve organized nursing services and nursing education, and foster collaboration between nursing and other health and community services. Provides tests used in selection of applicants to schools of nursing; also prepares tests for evaluating nursing student progress and nursing service tests. Nationally accredits nursing education programs and community health agencies. Collects and disseminates data on nursing services and nursing education. Conducts studies and demonstration projects on community planning for nursing and nursing service and education. **Publications:** Books. Covers health policy, administration, management, and education. • Manuals. • *NLN Newsletter*, periodic. Newsletter. • *Nurse Faculty Census*, biennial. • *Nursing and Health Care*, 10/year. Journal. Contains news, legislative updates, education, service analyses, and editorials. • *Nursing Data Review*, annual. • *Nursing Student Census*, annual. • *Public Policy Bulletin*, periodic. Bulletin. • Reports. • *State Approved Schools of Nursing - LPN*, annual. • *State Approved Schools of Nursing - RN*, annual. • Videos. Covers nursing theory, curriculum, home care, and recruitment. Also publishes memos to members, curriculum and evaluation guides, and career guidance materials.

★9122★ **National Nurses Association of Kenya (NNAK)**
PO Box 49422
Nairobi, Kenya
Phone: 2 229083
Tabitha A. Hezron, Contact

Founded: 1958. **Local Groups:** 19. **Languages:** English. **Description:** Nurses in Kenya. Goal is to ensure health for all by the year 2000. Promotes primary health care; facilitates exchange and cooperation between members; upholds ethics of the profession and encourages high standards. Represents members' interests before the government; provides help for members in times of difficulty; offers scholarships and operates trust fund. Operates foster child program. Works in conjunction with the National Council of Women in Kenya. Conducts workshops and seminars. **Publications:** *Kenya Nurses Newsletter*, quarterly. Newsletter. • *Kenya Nursing Journal*, semiannual. Journal.

★9123★ **National Nurses Society on Addictions (NNSA)**
4101 Lake Boone Trl., Ste. 201
Raleigh, NC 27607
Phone: (919)783-5871
Fax: (919)787-4916
Kim Bain, Exec.Dir.

Founded: 1975. **Members:** 1,200. **Regional Groups:** 10. **Description:** Promotes quality nursing care for persons addicted to alcohol and other drugs, and their families. Fosters continuing education and development of skills among nurses involved in the field; works to enhance

the professional image of addictions nurses. Participates in public policy and social issues related to alcohol or chemical abuse. Serves as liaison between members and professional groups with common goals. Represents members' interests before national organizations. Regional groups sponsor workshops. Provides certification program. **Publications:** Booklets. • *The Care of Clients with Addictions: Dimensions of Nursing Practice and Standards of Addictions*. Book. • *The Core Curriculum of Addictions Nursing*. Book. • Monographs. • *Nursing Care Planning with the Addicted Client*. Book. • *Nursing Practice with Selected Diagnoses and Criteria*. Book. • Papers. • *Perspectives on Addictions Nursing*, quarterly. Newsletter. Includes articles on clinical and research areas of addictions field. *Price:* $20/year for nonmembers. **Formerly:** (1983) National Nurses Society on Alcoholism.

★9124★ **National Oncology Nursing Society of South Africa (NONSSA) (Nasionale Genootskap van Onkologiese Verpleging van Suid Afrika — NGOVSA)**
PO Box 911-417
Rosslyn 0200, Republic of South Africa
Phone: 12 3293036
Fax: 12 3293048
Wilma Grobbelaar, Chair

Founded: 1984. **Members:** 800. **Local Groups:** 6. **Languages:** English. **Description:** Registered nurses interested in oncology. Establishes standards for quality cancer nursing in South Africa; promotes continuing education for nurses. Seeks to: expand cancer programs and cancer nursing at national and international levels; cooperate with related groups in research endeavors; increase public awareness. Sponsors symposia.

★9125★ **National Organization for Associate Degree Nursing (NOADN)**
11250 Roger Bacon Dr., Ste. 8
Reston, VA 22090-5202
Phone: (703)525-1191
Fax: (703)276-8196
Randall C. Price, Exec.Dir.

Founded: 1986. **Members:** 4,000. **State Groups:** 32. **Description:** Individuals interested in retaining current competency level examinations and endorsement of RN licensure from state to state for associate degree nursing graduates. Represents and advances the status of associate degree nursing education and practice. Provides networking among members to facilitate the exchange of legislative information and support. Offers clearinghouse for interpretation of legal issues and liability insurance. **Publications:** Brochures. • Newsletter, quarterly. Includes national and state association news, activities, and information. Also issues position papers. **Formerly:** (1991) National Organization for Advancement of Associate Degree Nursing.

★9126★ **National Organization of World War Nurses (NOWWN)**
569 S. Main St.
Red Lion, PA 17356
Phone: (717)244-9132
Ethel M. Redfield, Sec.-Treas.

Founded: 1921. **Members:** 400. **Description:** Nurses who served in World Wars I and II, the

Korean and Vietnam Wars, and Desert Storm. **Publications:** *National Organization of World War Nurses--Annual Report*. Annual Report. *Price:* Included in membership dues. • *National Organization of World War Nurses--Newsletter*, semiannual. Newsletter. Includes listing of new members. *Price:* Included in membership dues.

★9127★ **National Student Nurses' Association (NSNA)**
555 W. 57th St., Ste. 1327
New York, NY 10019
Phone: (212)581-2211
Fax: (212)581-2368
Robert V. Piemonte, Ed.D., Exec.Dir.

Founded: 1952. **Members:** 35,000. **State Groups:** 44. **Local Groups:** 650. **Description:** Students enrolled in state-approved schools for the preparation of registered nurses. Seeks to aid in the development of the individual nursing student and to urge students of nursing, as future health professionals, to be aware of and to contribute to improving the health care of all people. Encourages programs and activities in state groups concerning nursing, health, and the community. Provides assistance for state board review, as well as materials for preparation for state RN licensing examination. Cooperates with nursing organizations in recruitment of nurses and in professional, community, and civic programs. Sponsors essay writing contest for members. Sponsors Foundation of the National Student Nurses' Association in Honor of Frances Tompkins to award scholarships to student nurses. **Publications:** *Career Planning Guide*, annual. • *Convention News*. • *Dean's Notes*, 5/year. • *Imprint*, 5/year. • Manuals. • *NSNA News*, 5/year.

★9128★ **New Zealand Nurses Association (NZNA)**
PO Box 2128
Wellington, New Zealand
Phone: 4 3850847
Fax: 4 3829993
Ms. Gay Williams

Founded: 1909. **Members:** 23,000. **Description:** Nurses and nurses' aids. Represents and promotes nurses' interests and concerns on health issues through participation in health and social policy development. Conducts research on health issues. Offers health education programs. **Publications:** *New Zealand Nursing Journal*, 11/year. Journal.

★9129★ **North American Nursing Diagnosis Association (NANDA)**
1211 Locust St.
Philadelphia, PA 19107
Phone: (215)545-8105
Free: 800-647-9002
Fax: (215)545-8107
Joseph Braden, Exec.Dir.

Founded: 1972. **Members:** 1,000. **Regional Groups:** 7. **Description:** Registered nurses; individuals interested in nursing diagnosis. Purpose is to develop, refine, and promote a taxonomy of diagnostic terminology for use by professional nurses. **Publications:** *Conference Proceedings*, biennial. Proceedings. • *NANDA Nursing Diagnoses: Definitions and Classification 1992-1993*. Book. • *Nursing Diagnosis*

Journal, quarterly. Journal. *Price:* $42/year; $54/year for members outside the U.S.

★9130★ **Nurses' House**
350 Hudson St.
New York, NY 10014
Phone: (212)989-9393
Fax: (212)989-3710
Patricia B. Barry, Exec.Dir.

Founded: 1925. **Members:** 1,100. **Regional Groups:** 6. **Description:** Registered nurses and interested individuals united to assist registered nurses in financial and other crises. Provides short-term financial aid for shelter, food, and utilities until nurses obtain entitlements or jobs. Offers counseling and referrals. Encourages homebound or retired nurses through a volunteer corps. Participates in the American Nurses Association and the National League for Nursing conventions. **Publications:** *Appeal*, annual. Newsletter. • *The Dolphin*, semiannual. Newsletter. Also publishes promotional flyer.

★9131★ **Nurses Organization of Veterans Affairs (NOVA)**
1726 M St. NW, Ste. 1101
Washington, DC 20036
Phone: (202)296-0888
Fax: (202)833-1577
I. Regina Borkoski, Contact

Founded: 1980. **Members:** 2,295. **Regional Groups:** 99. **Description:** Voluntary, nonprofit professional society of Department of Veterans Affairs registered nurses. Objective is to provide VA nurses with the opportunity to preserve and improve quality care and professionalism through legislative influence. Conducts competitions, seminars, and educational programs. **Publications:** *News From NOVA*, quarterly. Newsletter. *Price:* $40/year for nonmembers. **Formerly:** (1989) Nurses Organization of the Veterans Administration.

★9132★ **Oncology Nursing Society (ONS)**
501 Holiday Dr.
Pittsburgh, PA 15220
Phone: (412)921-7373
Fax: (412)921-6565
Linda Johnson, Pres.

Founded: 1975. **Members:** 25,000. **Local Groups:** 179. **Description:** Registered nurses interested in oncology. Seeks to: promote high professional standards in oncology nursing; provide a network for the exchange of information, resources, and peer support; encourage nurses to specialize in oncology; promote and develop educational programs in oncology nursing extending through the graduate level; identify, encourage, and foster nursing research in improving the quality of patient care. Conducts instructional and abstract sessions. Compiles statistics. Maintains speakers' bureau. **Publications:** *Oncology Nursing Forum*, 10/year. Journal. Contains advertisers' index, calendar of events, information on new products, employment opportunity listings, chapter directory, and promotion news. *Price:* Included in membership dues; $16.25/year for nonmembers; $42/year for institutions. • *Oncology Nursing Society Membership Directory*, semiannual. Membership Directory. Arranged alphabetically and geographically. *Price:* Available to members only. • *Oncology*

Nursing Society Proceedings of Annual Congress. Proceedings. Includes abstracts of papers presented and indexes of authors and advertisers. *Price:* Included in membership dues; $6/year for nonmembers. • *ONS News*, monthly. Newsletter. Contains Washington, DC, news, calendar of events, employment opportunity listings, member news, and chapter news. *Price:* Included in membership dues. • *Standards of Cancer Nursing Practice Education*.

★9133★ **Respiratory Nursing Society (RNS)**
5700 Old Orchard Rd., 1st Fl.
Skokie, IL 60077-1057
Phone: (708)966-8673
Fax: (708)966-9418
Dagny Engle, Exec.Dir.

Founded: 1990. **Members:** 400. **Local Groups:** 2. **Description:** Nurses who care for clients with pulmonary dysfunction, and who are interested in the promotion of pulmonary health. Fosters the personal and professional development of respiratory nurses, and quality care of their clients. Provides educational opportunities and promotes research in the field. **Publications:** *Perspectives in Respiratory Nursing - Newsletter*, quarterly. Newsletter.

Retired Army Nurse Corps Association (RANCA)
See: Entry 7805

★9134★ **Sigma Theta Tau International (STTI)**
550 W. North St.
Indianapolis, IN 46202
Phone: (317)634-8171
Fax: (317)634-8188
Nancy Dickenson-Hazard, Exec. Officer

Founded: 1922. **Members:** 210,000. **Local Groups:** 346. **Description:** Honor society - nursing. **Publications:** *Directory of Nurse Researchers*, triennial. Directory. • *Image, Journal of Nursing Scholarship*, quarterly. Journal. Includes manuscripts, books reviews, and opinion pieces. *Price:* $16/year. • *Reflections*, quarterly. Newsletter. Includes President's message, executive update, chapter spotlight, recent doctorates, calender of events, and current nursing news. *Price:* $5/year. **Formerly:** (1985) Sigma Theta Tau.

Society of Nursery Nursing Administrators (SNNA)
See: Entry 3292

★9135★ **Society of Otorhinolaryngology and Head / Neck Nurses (SOHN)**
116 Canal St., Ste. A
New Smyrna Beach, FL 32168
Phone: (904)428-1695
Sandra Schwartz, R.N., Exec.Dir.

Founded: 1976. **Members:** 1,200. **Local Groups:** 15. **Description:** Registered nurses specializing in otorhinolaryngology (the study of the ear, nose, and throat) and the head and neck. Seeks to: promote awareness of professional techniques and new developments in the field; enhance professional standards; create a channel for the exchange of ideas, concerns,

and information; develop interaction with similar groups. Offers programs and seminars that have been approved for continuing education credits by the American Nurses' Association. **Publications:** *ORL-Head and Neck Nursing*, quarterly. Includes book reviews and current trends in nursing. *Price:* Included in membership dues; $30/year for nonmembers. • *Society of Otorhinolaryngology and Head-Neck Nurses-- Update*, quarterly. Newsletter. Includes employment opportunity listings. *Price:* Included in membership dues.

★9136★ **Society of Trauma Nurses (STN)**
1211 Locust St.
Philadelphia, PA 19107
Phone: (215)545-5687
Free: 800-237-6966
Fax: (215)545-8107
Eileen Whalan, Pres.

Founded: 1989. **Members:** 500. **Description:** Nurses involved in all facets of trauma care. Seeks to communicate trauma nursing information and recognize excellence and innovation in trauma nursing. Addresses legislative issues; assists in the development of standards. Facilitates research. **Publications:** *Journal of Trauma Nursing*, quarterly. Journal. *Price:* Included in membership dues; $42/year for nonmembers.

★9137★ **Society for Vascular Nursing (SVN)**
309 Winter St.
Norwood, MA 02062
Phone: (617)762-3630
Fax: (617)762-5582
Jeanne E. Doyle, R.N., Exec.Dir.

Founded: 1982. **Members:** 900. **Description:** Nurses and other health care professionals interested in providing comprehensive care for persons with vascular disease. Seeks to educate public about prevention of PVD. Provides educational programs; conducts research. Operates speakers' bureau. **Publications:** *Journal of Vascular Nursing*, quarterly. Journal. *Price:* Included in membership dues. • Newsletter. Also publishes patient educational materials. **Formerly:** (1992) Society for Peripheral Vascular Nursing.

★9138★ **Visiting Nurse Associations of America (VNAA)**
3801 E. Florida, Ste. 900
Denver, CO 80210-2545
Phone: (303)753-0218
Free: 800-426-2547
Fax: (303)753-0258
William G. Varnell, Contact

Founded: 1982. **Members:** 185. **Description:** Voluntary, nonprofit home health care agencies. Develops competitive strength among community-based nonprofit visiting nurse organizations; works to strengthen business resources and economic programs through contracting, marketing, and governmental affairs. Offers training programs and a placement service for those seeking employment with VNAS. **Publications:** *Housecalls*, periodic. Newsletter. For clinical staff of VNAA. • *Nursing Procedure Manual*. Manual. • *VNAA Spectrum*, monthly. *Price:* Free for members' CEOs. • *VNAA Voice*, quarterly. Newsletter. *Price:* Free for members. **Formerly:** (1985) American Affiliation of Visiting Nurses Associations and Services.

★9139★ **Western Samoa Registered Nurses Association**
PO Box 3480
WSNA Centre Motootua
Apia, Western Samoa
Phone: 24439
Faamanatu Nielsen, Pres.

Founded: 1952. **Members:** 250. **Description:** Practicing registered nurses. Conducts educational and training programs.

Wound, Ostomy and Continence Nurses Society: An Association of E.T. Nurses (WOCN)
See: Entry 12729

Research Centers

★9140★ **City of Hope National Medical Center**
Department of Nursing Research and Education
1500 E. Duarte Rd.
Duarte, CA 91010
Phone: (818)301-8346
Fax: (818)301-8941
Marcia Grant, R.N., Dir.

Research Activities and Fields: Clinical nursing, including nursing administration, nursing education, delivery of nursing services, nursing organization, and the relationship of patient problems to nursing. Research focuses on quality of life, pain and symptom management, improving nursing attitudes and skills in caring for patients and their families, and reducing complications and side effects of therapy and patient psychological distresses associated with therapeutic and diagnostic procedures.

★9141★ **Medical College of Georgia**
Center for Nursing Research
School of Nursing
Jennings Wing, EB-202
Augusta, GA 30912
Phone: (706)721-3162
Fax: (706)721-0655
Jeri W. Dunkin, Ph.D., Research Coord.

Research Activities and Fields: Cognitive functioning and control in institutionalized elderly; exercise and functional status in elderly; health risk, instruction, and lifestyle change; status of persons with AIDS; learning with computer-aided education (CAE) equipment, and computer-aided instruction (CAI); and cancer and rehabilitation nursing, rural health, self-esteem, and abuse and homeless issues. **Publications:** *Informer.* **E-mail Address:** jdunkin@uscn.cc.uga.edu.

★9142★ **U.S. Department of Health and Human Services**
National Center for Nursing Research
Division of Extramural Programs
Acute and Chronic Illness Branch

Westwood Bldg., Rm. 754
5333 Westbard Ave.
Bethesda, MD 20892
Phone: (301)594-7397
Fax: (301)594-7603
Dr. Mary Lucas, Chief

Research Activities and Fields: Research supported in this area deals with human responses to acute and chronic illness and disability. It is concerned with the biological, biomedical, behavioral, and environmental factors that contribute to the causes, prevalence, amelioration, and remediation of illness and disability. Examples include studies on adaptation and functioning in such chronic illnesses as arthritis, diabetes, hypertension, and renal disease; technological developments in rehabilitation therapies; adherence to therapeutic regimens; nursing interventions, including physical, behavioral, and educational interventions; biochemical factors and changes associated with acute and chronic illness and disability; and biomedical, behavioral, cognitive, and perceptual responses to illness or disability.

★9143★ **U.S. Department of Health and Human Services**
National Center for Nursing Research
Division of Extramural Programs
Health Promotion and Disease Prevention Branch
Westwood Bldg.
5333 Westbard Ave.
Bethesda, MD 20892
Phone: (301)496-0523
Dr. Sharlene M. Weiss, Chief

Research Activities and Fields: Research support is provided to decrease the vulnerability of individuals and families to illness or disability across the life span. Health promotion research addresses the general health of the population and is not directed at any particular illness or disability. Examples include studies that consider the nutritional requirements of the various developmental phases of life and studies on the relationship between the biomedical and behavioral dimensions of human health. Disease prevention research focuses on a particular illness or disability and ways to intercept the onset of the illness or disability. Examples include the identification of biomedical, behavioral, and environmental risk factors and the development or refinement of methods that enhance the abilities of at-risk individuals and their families to respond to potential health problems.

★9144★ **U.S. Department of Health and Human Services**
National Center for Nursing Research
Division of Extramural Programs
Nursing Systems Branch
Westwood Bldg., Rm. 738
5333 Westbard Ave.
Bethesda, MD 20892
Phone: (301)594-7493
Fax: (301)594-7603
Dr. Patricia Moritz, Chief

Research Activities and Fields: The primary focus of research is inquiry into the delivery of health care which includes the study of the structural, organizational, and economic context

of clinical practice and the processes of care delivery in relation to the assessment of clinical endpoints of appropriate care which encompass quality, efficacy, and effectiveness. Reflecting the NINR focus on patient care research, the Branch includes research on approaches to nursing management and patient care delivery. Branch also addresses such areas as models of clinical practice, assessment of clinical interventions and resulting outcomes, design and implementation of nursing information systems to facilitate clinical practice, and the impact of availability and allocation of nursing resources, including the multidisciplinary health care team, on the quality of care. Areas of study may also include special populations such as minorities and the disadvantaged, long-term care patients, and residents of rural areas.

★9145★ **U.S. Department of Health and Human Services**
National Institute of Nursing Research
NIH Bldg. 31, Rm. 5B-03
9000 Rockville Pike
Bethesda, MD 20892
Phone: (301)496-8230
Fax: (301)480-4969
Dr. Ada Sue Hinshaw, Director

Research Activities and Fields: The mission of NINR is to conduct and support basic and clinical nursing research, training, and other programs in patient care research and information dissemination. The research programs of the Institute address actual and potential health problems. These programs focus on health promotion and disease prevention, understanding and mitigating the effects of acute and chronic illnesses and disabilities, and the delivery of nursing services. Nursing research examines the biological, biomedical, and behavioral processes in health care and its environment. Its purpose is to accomplish both short- and long-term improvements in nursing practice, patient health, and recovery from illness.

★9146★ **U.S. Department of Health and Human Services**
National Institute for Nursing Research
Division of Extramural Programs
Westwood Bldg.
5333 Westbard Ave.
Bethesda, MD 20892
Phone: (301)594-7590
Fax: (301)594-7630
Dr. Teresa Radebaugh, Director

Research Activities and Fields: Division is responsible for program management of NINR research and research training activities. It coordinates the activities of the research programs as well as the research training and career development program and the NINR Nursing Science Review Committee. The research programs and activities are carried out in: Acute and Chronic Illness Branch, Health Promotion and Disease Prevention Branch, and the Nursing Systems Branch.

★9147★ **University of Akron**
Center for Nursing
Caroll St.
Akron, OH 44325
Phone: (216)972-6968
Maryhelen Kreidler, Ed.D., Dir.

Research Activities and Fields: Family health nursing practice, education, and research and the relationship between family influences and health behaviors. Offers health care services to individuals and families and provides a laboratory for faculty and students to build and test nursing theory.

★9148★ **University of Miami**
Institute for the Study of Culture and
   Nursing
School of Nursing
PO Box 248153
5801 Red Rd.
Coral Gables, FL 33124-3850
Phone: (305)284-5686
Fax: (305)547-3808
Dr. Georgie Labadie, Dir.

Research Activities and Fields: Clinical nursing, focusing on serving multicultural populations and managing multicultural organizations.

★9149★ **University of Texas at Arlington**
Center for Nursing Research
PO Box 19407
Arlington, TX 76019
Phone: (817)273-2776
Fax: (817)794-5006
Dr. Nancy Burns, Dir.

Research Activities and Fields: Health promotion and prevention of illness, hospice care, rural health care, nursing care outcomes, and economics of health care delivery. **E-mail Address:** bruns@uta.edu.

★9150★ **University of Texas at Austin**
Center for Health Care Research and
   Evaluation
1700 Red River St.
Austin, TX 78701-1499
Phone: (512)471-7311
Fax: (512)471-4910
Susan J. Grobe, Ph.D., FAAN Dir.

Research Activities and Fields: Community health nursing, nursing administration, program evaluation, nursing education, and basic research in human responses to actual and potential health problems. Offers research assistance to practicing nurses, faculty, and graduate students, including preparation of funding proposals, implementation of research methods, data entry and analysis, report writing, presentation, and publication of results. **Publications:** *Centerline* (semiannually, newsletter). **E-mail Address:** grobe@utxvm.cc.utexas.edu.

★9151★ **University of Wisconsin—**
   Milwaukee
Center for Nursing Research and
   Evaluation
1909 E. Hartford Ave.
PO Box 413
Milwaukee, WI 53201
Phone: (414)229-5647
Fax: (414)229-6474
Dr. Elizabeth Devine, Dir.

Research Activities and Fields: Assists students and faculty with research in the areas of nursing diagnosis, patient care and education, nursing intervention strategies, professionalism, client and family coping techniques, nursing administration, maternal/infant health, chronic disease, program evaluation, gerontology, mental health, public/community health, and women in nursing issues. **Publications:** *CNRE News* (quarterly in-house newsletter). **E-mail Address:** ecdevine@csd.uwm.edu.

State Government Agencies

Nursing Boards

★9152★ **Alabama Board of Nursing**
770 Washington Ave., Ste. 250
PO Box 303900
Montgomery, AL 36130-3900
Phone: (334)242-4060
Fax: (334)242-4360

★9153★ **Alaska Board of Nursing**
3601 C St., Ste. 722
Anchorage, AK 99503
Phone: (907)561-2878
Fax: (907)562-5781

★9154★ **Arizona State Board of Nursing**
1651 E. Morten Ave., Ste. 150
Phoenix, AZ 85020
Phone: (602)255-5092
Fax: (602)255-5130

★9155★ **Arkansas State Board of Nursing**
University Tower Bldg., Ste. 800
1123 S. University
Little Rock, AR 72204
Phone: (501)686-2700
Fax: (501)686-2714

★9156★ **California Board of Registered**
   Nursing
400 R St., Ste. 4030
PO Box 944210
Sacramento, CA 94244-2100
Phone: (916)322-3350
Fax: (916)327-4402

★9157★ **California Board of Vocational**
   Nurses and Psychiatric Technician
   examiners
2535 Capitol Oaks Dr., Ste. 205
Sacramento, CA 95833
Phone: (916)263-7800
Fax: (916)263-7859

★9158★ **Colorado Board of Nursing**
1560 Broadway, Ste. 670
Denver, CO 80202
Phone: (303)894-2430
Fax: (303)894-2821

★9159★ **Connecticut Board of Examiners**
   for Nursing
150 W. Washington St.
Hartford, CT 06106
Phone: (203)566-1041
Fax: (203)566-1464

★9160★ **Delaware Board of Nursing**
Margaret O'Neill Bldg.
PO Box 1401
Dover, DE 19903
Phone: (302)739-4522
Fax: (302)739-2711

★9161★ **District of Columbia Board of**
   Nursing
614 H St. NW
Washington, DC 20001
Phone: (202)727-7468
Fax: (202)727-7662

★9162★ **Florida Board of Nursing**
111 E. Coastline Dr., Ste. 516
Jacksonville, FL 32202
Phone: (904)359-6331
Fax: (904)359-6323

★9163★ **Georgia Board of Nursing**
166 Pryor St. SW
Atlanta, GA 30303
Phone: (404)656-3943
Fax: (404)651-9532

★9164★ **Georgia State Board of Licensed**
   Practical Nurses
166 Pryor St. SW
Atlanta, GA 30303
Phone: (404)656-3921
Fax: (404)651-9532

★9165★ **Guam Board of Nurse Examiners**
PO Box 2816
Agana, GU 96910
Phone: (671)734-7295
Fax: (671)734-2066

★9166★ **Hawaii Board of Nursing**
PO Box 3469
Honolulu, HI 96801
Phone: (808)586-2695
Fax: (808)586-2689

★9167★ **Idaho Board of Nursing**
PO Box 83720
Boise, ID 83720-0061
Phone: (208)334-3110
Fax: (208)334-3262

★9168★ **Illinois Department of**
   Professional Regulation
Board of Nursing
320 W. Washington St., 3rd Fl.
Springfield, IL 62786
Phone: (217)785-9465
Fax: (217)782-7645

★9169★ Indiana Health Professions Bureau
State Board of Nursing
402 W. Washington St., Rm. 041
Indianapolis, IN 46204
Phone: (317)232-2960
Fax: (317)233-4236

★9170★ Iowa Board of Nursing
State Capitol Complex
1223 E. Court Ave.
Des Moines, IA 50319
Phone: (515)281-3255
Fax: (515)281-4825

★9171★ Kansas State Board of Nursing
Landon State Office Bldg.
900 SW Jackson, Ste. 551-S
Topeka, KS 66612-1230
Phone: (913)296-4929
Fax: (913)296-3929

★9172★ Kentucky Board of Nursing
312 Wittington Parkway, Ste. 300
Louisville, KY 40222-5172
Phone: (502)329-7000
Fax: (502)329-7011

★9173★ Louisiana State Board of Nursing
912 Pere Marquette Bldg.
150 Baronne St.
New Orleans, LA 70112
Phone: (504)568-5464
Fax: (504)568-5467

★9174★ Louisiana State Board of Practical Nurse Examiners
3421 N. Causeway Blvd., Ste. 203
Metairie, LA 70002
Phone: (504)838-5791
Fax: (504)838-5279

★9175★ Maine State Board of Nursing
State House Station 158
Augusta, ME 04333-0158
Phone: (207)624-5275
Fax: (207)624-5290

★9176★ Maryland Board of Nursing
4140 Patterson Ave.
Baltimore, MD 21215-2299
Phone: (410)764-5124
Fax: (410)358-3530

★9177★ Massachusetts Board of Registration in Nursing
Leverett Saltonstall Bldg.
100 Cambridge St., Rm. 1519
Boston, MA 02202
Phone: (617)727-9962
Fax: (617)727-2197

★9178★ Michigan Board of Nursing
Ottawa Towers N.
611 W. Ottawa
Lansing, MI 48933
Phone: (517)373-1600
Fax: (517)373-2179

★9179★ Minnesota Board of Nursing
2700 University Ave. W., Ste. 108
St. Paul, MN 55114
Phone: (612)642-0567
Fax: (612)642-0574

★9180★ Mississippi Board of Nursing
239 N. Lamar St., Ste. 401
Jackson, MS 39201
Phone: (601)359-6170
Fax: (601)359-6185

★9181★ Missouri State Board of Nursing
3605 Missouri Blvd.
PO Box 656
Jefferson City, MO 65102
Phone: (314)751-0681
Fax: (314)751-0075

★9182★ Montana State Board of Nursing
111 N. Jackson
PO Box 200513
Helena, MT 59620-0513
Phone: (406)444-2071
Fax: (406)444-7759

★9183★ Nebraska Board of Nursing
301 Centennial Mall S.
PO Box 95007
Lincoln, NE 68509
Phone: (402)471-2115
Fax: (402)471-0383

★9184★ Nevada State Board of Nursing
4335 S. Industrial Rd., Ste. 430
PO Box 46886
Las Vegas, NV 89114
Phone: (702)739-1575
Fax: (702)739-0298

★9185★ New Hampshire Board of Nursing
Health & Welfare Bldg.
6 Hazen Dr.
Concord, NH 03301-6527
Phone: (603)271-2323
Fax: (603)271-6605

★9186★ New Jersey Board of Nursing
124 Halsey St., 6th Fl.
PO Box 45010
Newark, NJ 07101
Phone: (201)504-6493
Fax: (201)648-3481

★9187★ New Mexico Board of Nursing
4206 Louisiana Blvd. NE, Ste. A
Albuquerque, NM 87109
Phone: (505)841-8340
Fax: (505)841-8347

★9188★ New York State Board of Nursing
Cultural Education Center, Rm. 3023
Albany, NY 12230
Phone: (518)474-3843
Fax: (518)473-0578

★9189★ North Carolina Board of Nursing
3274 National Dr.
PO Box 2129
Raleigh, NC 27602
Phone: (919)782-3211
Fax: (919)781-9461

★9190★ North Dakota Board of Nursing
919 S. 7th St., Ste. 504
Bismarck, ND 58504-5881
Phone: (701)224-2974
Fax: (701)224-4614

★9191★ Ohio Board of Nursing
77 S. High St., 17th Fl.
Columbus, OH 43266-0316
Phone: (614)466-3947
Fax: (614)466-0388

★9192★ Oklahoma Board of Nursing
2915 N. Classen Blvd., Ste. 524
Oklahoma City, OK 73106
Phone: (405)525-2076
Fax: (405)521-6089

★9193★ Oregon State Board of Nursing
800 NE Oregon St., Ste. 465
PO Box 25
Portland, OR 97232
Phone: (503)731-4745
Fax: (503)731-4755

★9194★ Pennsylvania State Board of Nursing
124 Pine St.
PO Box 2649
Harrisburg, PA 17105-2649
Phone: (717)783-7142
Fax: (717)787-7769

★9195★ Puerto Rico Board of Nurse Examiners
Call Box 10200
Santurce, PR 00908
Phone: (809)725-8161
Fax: (809)725-7903

★9196★ Rhode Island Board of Nurse Registration and Nursing Education
Cannon Health Bldg., Rm. 104
3 Capitol Hill, Rm. 104
Providence, RI 02908-5097
Phone: (401)277-2827
Fax: (401)277-1272

★9197★ South Carolina State Board of Nursing
220 Executive Center Dr., Ste. 220
Columbia, SC 29210
Phone: (803)731-1648
Fax: (803)731-1647

★9198★ South Dakota Board of Nursing
3307 S. Lincoln Ave.
Sioux Falls, SD 57105-5224
Phone: (605)367-5940
Fax: (605)367-5945

★9199★ Tennessee State Board of Nursing
283 Plus Park Blvd.
Nashville, TN 37217-1010
Phone: (615)367-6232
Fax: (615)367-6397

★9200★ Texas Board of Nurse Examiners
9101 Burnet Rd.
PO Box 140466
Austin, TX 78714
Phone: (512)835-4880
Fax: (512)835-8684

★9201★ Texas Board of Vocational Nurse Examiners
9101 Burnet Rd., Ste. 105
Austin, TX 78758
Phone: (512)835-2071
Fax: (512)835-1367

★9202★ **Utah State Board of Nursing**
Heber M. Wells Bldg., 4th Fl.
160 East 300 South
PO Box 45805
Salt Lake City, UT 84145-0805
Phone: (801)530-6628
Fax: (801)530-6511

★9203★ **Vermont State Board of Nursing**
109 State St.
Montpelier, VT 05609-1106
Phone: (802)828-2396
Fax: (802)828-2853

★9204★ **Virgin Islands Board of Nurse Licensure**
Plot No. 3, Kongens Gade
PO Box 4247, Veterans Dr. Station
St. Thomas, VI 00803
Phone: (809)776-7397
Fax: (809)777-4003

★9205★ **Virginia Board of Nursing**
6606 W. Broad St., 4th Fl.
Richmond, VA 23230-1717
Phone: (804)662-9909
Fax: (804)662-9943

★9206★ **Washington State Board of Nursing Care Quality Assurance Commission**
PO Box 47864
Olympia, WA 98504-7864
Phone: (360)753-2686
Fax: (360)586-5935

★9207★ **West Virginia Board of Examiners for Practical Nurses**
101 Dee Dr.
Charleston, WV 25311-1688
Phone: (304)558-3572
Fax: (304)558-3666

★9208★ **West Virginia Board of Examiners for Registered Professional Nurses**
101 Dee Dr.
Charleston, WV 25311-1620
Phone: (304)558-3596
Fax: (304)558-3666

★9209★ **Wisconsin Board of Nursing**
1400 E. Washington Ave.
PO Box 8935
Madison, WI 53708-8935
Phone: (608)266-0257
Fax: (608)267-0644

★9210★ **Wyoming State Board of Nursing**
Barrett Bldg., 2nd Fl.
2301 Central Ave.
Cheyenne, WY 82002
Phone: (307)777-7601
Fax: (307)777-6005

State & Regional Organizations

Nursing

The following state organizations are affiliates of the American Nurses Association, 600 Maryland Ave. SW, Ste. 100 West, Washington DC 20024-2571, (202) 544-4444.

Alabama

★9211★ **Alabama State Nurses Association**
360 N. Hull St.
Montgomery, AL 36104-3658
Phone: (334)262-8321
Fax: (334)262-8578

Alaska

★9212★ **Alaska Nurses Association**
237 E. 3rd Ave.
Anchorage, AK 99501
Phone: (907)274-0827
Fax: (907)272-0292

Arizona

★9213★ **Arizona Nurses Association**
1850 E. Southern Ave., Ste. 1
Tempe, AZ 85282
Phone: (602)831-0404
Fax: (602)839-4780

Arkansas

★9214★ **Arkansas Nurses Association**
117 S. Cedar St.
Little Rock, AR 72205
Phone: (501)664-5853
Fax: (501)664-5859

California

★9215★ **California Nurses Association**
1145 Market St., Ste. 1100
San Francisco, CA 94103
Phone: (415)864-4141
Fax: (415)252-9083

Colorado

★9216★ **Colorado Nurses Association**
5453 E. Evans Pl.
Denver, CO 80222
Phone: (303)757-7483
Fax: (303)757-2679

Connecticut

★9217★ **Connecticut Nurses Association**
Meritech Business Park
377 Research Pkwy., Ste 2D
Meriden, CT 06450
Phone: (203)238-1207
Fax: (203)238-3437

Delaware

★9218★ **Delaware Nurses Association**
2634 Capitol Trail, Ste. A
Newark, DE 19711
Phone: (302)368-2333
Fax: (302)366-1775

District of Columbia

★9219★ **District of Columbia Nurses Association**
5100 Wisconsin Ave. NW, Ste. 306
Washington, DC 20016
Phone: (202)244-2705
Fax: (202)362-8285

Florida

★9220★ **Florida Nurses Association**
PO Box 536985
Orlando, FL 32853-6985
Phone: (407)896-3261
Fax: (407)896-9042

Georgia

★9221★ **Georgia Nurses Association**
1362 W. Peachtree St. NW
Atlanta, GA 30309
Phone: (404)876-4624
Fax: (404)876-4621

Guam

★9222★ **Guam Nurses Association**
PO Box CG
Agana, GU 96910
Phone: (671)477-6877
Fax: (671)472-1350

Hawaii

★9223★ **Hawaii Nurses Association**
677 Ala Moana Blvd., Ste. 301
Honolulu, HI 96813
Phone: (808)521-8361
Fax: (808)524-2760

Idaho

★9224★ **Idaho Nurses Association**
200 N. 4th St., Ste. 20
Boise, ID 83702-6001
Phone: (208)345-0500
Fax: (208)345-1163

Illinois

★9225★ **Illinois Nurses Association**
300 S. Wacker Dr., Ste. 2200
Chicago, IL 60606
Phone: (312)360-2300
Fax: (312)360-9380

Indiana

★9226★ **Indiana State Nurses Association**
2915 N. High School Rd.
Indianapolis, IN 46224
Phone: (317)299-4575
Fax: (317)297-3525

Iowa

★9227★ **Iowa Nurses Association**
1501 42nd St., Ste. 471
West Des Moines, IA 50266
Phone: (515)225-0495
Fax: (515)225-2201

Kansas

★9228★ **Kansas State Nurses Association**
700 SW Jackson, Ste. 601
Topeka, KS 66603
Phone: (913)233-8638
Fax: (913)233-5222

Kentucky

★9229★ **Kentucky Nurses Association**
1400 S. 1st St.
PO Box 2616
Louisville, KY 40201
Phone: (502)637-2546
Fax: (502)637-8236

Louisiana

★9230★ **Louisiana State Nurses Association**
712 Transcontinental Dr.
Metairie, LA 70001
Phone: (504)889-1030
Fax: (504)888-1158

Maine

★9231★ **Maine State Nurses Association**
PO Box 2240
Augusta, ME 04338-2240
Phone: (207)622-1057
Fax: (207)623-4072

Maryland

★9232★ **Maryland Nurses Association**
Airport Sq. 21, Ste. 255
849 International Dr.
Linthicum Heights, MD 21090
Phone: (410)859-3000
Fax: (410)859-3001

Massachusetts

★9233★ **Massachusetts Nurses Association**
340 Turnpike St.
Canton, MA 02021
Phone: (617)821-4625
Fax: (617)821-4445

Michigan

★9234★ **Michigan Nurses Association**
2310 Jolly Oak Rd.
Okemos, MI 48864-4599
Phone: (517)349-5640
Fax: (517)349-5818

Minnesota

★9235★ **Minnesota Nurses Association**
1295 Bandana Blvd. N., Ste. 140
St. Paul, MN 55108-5115
Phone: (612)646-4807
Free: 800-647-5301
Fax: (612)647-5301

Mississippi

★9236★ **Mississippi Nurses Association**
135 Bounds St., Ste. 100
Jackson, MS 39206
Phone: (601)982-9182
Fax: (601)982-9183

Missouri

★9237★ **Missouri Nurses Association**
1904 Bubba Ln.
PO Box 105228
Jefferson City, MO 65110
Phone: (314)636-4623
Fax: (314)636-9576

Montana

★9238★ **Montana Nurses Association**
104 Broadway, Ste. G-2
PO Box 5718
Helena, MT 59601
Phone: (406)442-6710
Fax: (406)442-6738

Nebraska

★9239★ **Nebraska Nurses Association**
1430 South St., Ste. 202
Lincoln, NE 68502-2446
Phone: (402)475-3859
Fax: (402)475-3961

Nevada

★9240★ **Nevada Nurses Association**
3660 Baker Ln., Ste. 104
Reno, NV 89509
Phone: (702)825-3555
Fax: (702)825-3555

New Hampshire

★9241★ **New Hampshire Nurses Association**
48 West St.
Concord, NH 03301
Phone: (603)225-3783
Fax: (603)228-6672

New Jersey

★9242★ **New Jersey State Nurses Association**
320 W. State St.
Trenton, NJ 08618
Phone: (609)392-4884
Fax: (609)396-2330

New Mexico

★9243★ **New Mexico Nurses Association**
909 Virginia NE, Ste. 101
Albuquerque, NM 87108
Phone: (505)268-7744
Fax: (505)268-7711

New York

★9244★ **New York State Nurses Association**
2113 Western Ave.
Guilderland, NY 12084
Phone: (518)456-5371
Fax: (518)456-0697

North Carolina

★9245★ **North Carolina Nurses Association**
103 Enterprise St.
Box 12025
Raleigh, NC 27605-2025
Phone: (919)821-4250
Fax: (919)829-5807

North Dakota

★9246★ **North Dakota Nurses Association**
212 N. 4th St.
Bismarck, ND 58501
Phone: (701)223-1385
Fax: (701)223-0575

Ohio

★9247★ **Ohio Nurses Association**
4000 E. Main St.
Columbus, OH 43213-2950
Phone: (614)237-5414
Fax: (614)237-6074

Oklahoma

★9248★ **Oklahoma Nurses Association**
6414 N. Santa Fe, Ste. A
Oklahoma City, OK 73116
Phone: (405)840-3476
Fax: (405)840-3013

Oregon

★9249★ **Oregon Nurses Association**
9600 SW Oak St., Ste. 550
Portland, OR 97223
Phone: (503)293-0011
Fax: (503)293-0013

Pennsylvania

★9250★ **Pennsylvania Nurses Association**
2578 Interstate Dr.
PO Box 68525
Harrisburg, PA 17106-8525
Phone: (717)657-1222
Fax: (717)657-3796

Rhode Island

★9251★ **Rhode Island State Nurses Association**
550 S. Water St., Unit 540B
Providence, RI 02903-4861
Phone: (401)421-9703
Fax: (401)421-6793

South Carolina

★9252★ **South Carolina Nurses Association**
1821 Gadsden St.
Columbia, SC 29201
Phone: (803)252-4781
Fax: (803)779-3870

South Dakota

★9253★ **South Dakota Nurses Association**
1505 S. Minnesota Ave., Ste. 3
Sioux Falls, SD 57105
Phone: (605)338-1401
Fax: (605)338-0516

Tennessee

★9254★ **Tennessee Nurses Association**
545 Mainstream Dr., Ste. 405
Nashville, TN 37228-1201
Phone: (615)254-0350
Fax: (615)254-0303

Texas

★9255★ **Texas Nurses Association**
7600 Burnet Rd., Ste. 440
Austin, TX 78757-1292
Phone: (512)452-0645
Fax: (512)452-0648

Utah

★9256★ **Utah Nurses Association**
455 East 400 South, No. 402
Salt Lake City, UT 84111
Phone: (801)322-3439
Fax: (801)322-3430

Vermont

★9257★ **Vermont State Nurses Association**
Box 26, Champlain Mill
1 Main St.
Winooski, VT 05404-2230
Phone: (802)655-7123
Fax: (802)655-7187

Virgin Islands

★9258★ **Virgin Islands State Nurses Association**
PO Box 583
Christiansted, VI 00821-0583
Phone: (809)773-2323

Virginia

★9259★ **Virginia Nurses Association**
7113 Three Chopt Rd., Ste. 204
Richmond, VA 23226
Phone: (804)282-1808
Fax: (804)282-4916

Washington

★9260★ **Washington State Nurses Association**
2505 2nd Ave., Ste. 500
Seattle, WA 98121
Phone: (206)443-9762
Fax: (206)728-2074

West Virginia

★9261★ **West Virginia Nurses Association**
PO Box 1946
Charleston, WV 25327
Phone: (304)342-1169
Fax: (304)345-1538

Wisconsin

★9262★ **Wisconsin Nurses Association**
6117 Monona Dr.
Madison, WI 53716
Phone: (608)221-0383
Fax: (608)221-2788

Wyoming

★9263★ **Wyoming Nurses Association**
Majestic Bldg., Rm. 305
1603 Capitol Ave.
Cheyenne, WY 82001
Phone: (307)635-3955
Fax: (307)635-2173

Chapter 43
Nursing Homes

National & International Organizations

American College of Health Care Administrators (ACHCA)
See: Entry 5545

American Disabled for Attendant Program Today (ADAPT)
See: Entry 1883

★9264★ **American Health Care** ✓
Association (AHCA)
1201 L St. NW
Washington, DC 20005
Phone: (202)842-4444
Fax: (202)842-3860
Dr. Paul R. Willging, Exec.VP

Founded: 1949. **Members:** 11,000. **State Groups:** 51. **Description:** Federation of state associations of long-term health care facilities. Promotes standards for professionals in long-term health care delivery and quality care for patients and residents in a safe environment. Focuses on issues of availability, quality, affordability, and fair payment. Operates as liaison with governmental agencies, Congress, and professional associations. Compiles statistics. **Publications:** *AHCA Notes*, monthly. Newsletter. Covers legislation and regulations. *Price:* Included in membership dues. • Manuals. • *Provider: For Long Term Care Professionals*, monthly. Magazine. Includes buyers' guide, news reports, advertisers' index, a listing of new products and services, and calendar of events. *Price:* Free to long-term health care professionals; $48/year for nonmembers and libraries. • *Thinking About a Nursing Home?*. • *Welcome to Our Nursing Home*. Also produces audiovisual aids. **Formerly:** (1975) American Nursing Home Association.

★9265★ **American Medical Directors Association (AMDA)**
10480 Little Patuxent Pky., Ste. 760
Columbia, MD 21044
Phone: (410)740-9743
Free: 800-876-AMDA
Fax: (410)740-4572
Lorraine Tarnove, Exec.Dir.

Founded: 1975. **Members:** 4,100. **Regional Groups:** 33. **Description:** Physicians providing care in long-term facilities such as nursing homes. Sponsors continuing medical education in geriatrics and medical administration. Promotes improved long term. **Publications:** *AMDA Reports*, quarterly. Newsletter. Includes calendar of events, reviews of articles, publications, and other resources. *Price:* Available to members only. • Audiotapes. Related to medical direction. • *Nursing Home Medicine: The Journal of the American Medical Directors Association*, 10/year. Journal. *Price:* Free for members; $2/single issue. • Videos. Related to long term care issues such as restraints, CPT coding, and advance directions.

American Society of Consultant Pharmacists (ASCP)
See: Entry 10587

★9266★ **Concerned Relatives of Nursing Home Patients (CRNHP)**
PO Box 18820
Cleveland Heights, OH 44118
Phone: (216)321-0403
Mary A. Mendelson, Dir.

Founded: 1976. **Members:** 1,500. **Description:** A program of the Nursing Home Advisory and Research Council. Volunteers, family members, friends, or guardians of nursing home patients. Seeks to achieve dignity and comfort for all nursing home patients whether they are private pay, Medicare, or Medicaid patients. Monitors quality of care in nursing homes and legislation affecting patients' lives. Disseminates information on nursing homes to consumers, legislators, and local and state agencies. Advises families and social service workers on nursing home placement, Medicaid, Medicare, and other areas of nursing home life. Acts as advocacy group for patients' rights; represents patients' interests before legislative bodies. Compiles statistics. **Publications:** *Insight*, bimonthly. • *Selecting a Nursing Home*.

★9267★ **Intercare**
PO Box 8561
Moscow, ID 83843
Phone: (509)229-3259
Fax: (509)229-3259
Theodore Carcich, Jr., Pres.

Founded: 1976. **Members:** 600. **Description:** Individuals involved or interested in the long-term health care of the chronically ill. Works to improve long-term health care; to encourage high standards of professional care and administration; to interact with professional groups, academic institutions, and governmental agencies; to provide opportunities for individual research; to discover solutions to the problems of the aged, chronically ill, and disabled; to establish a clearinghouse of research findings and resources. Maintains speakers' bureau. Provides quarterly educational program in various countries. **Publications:** *Intercare, International Directory*, annual. Directory. • Journal, quarterly.

Lutheran Hospitals and Homes Society (LHHS)
See: Entry 6456

★9268★ **National Association of Boards of Examiners for Nursing Home Administrators (NAB)**
808 17th St. NW, Ste. 200
Washington, DC 20006
Phone: (202)223-9750
Jerome A. Miller, Exec.Dir.

Founded: 1972. **Members:** 51. **Description:** State boards responsible for licensing nursing homes. Produces exam to test the competence of nursing home adminstrators; operates continuing education review service; disseminates information and educational materials on nursing home administration. **Publications:** *NAB Study Guide: How To Prepare For the Nursing Home Administrators Examination*. The second edition. *Price:* $59.95. • *State Roster of Licensing Boards*, annual. *Price:* $17.50/year for members; $22.50/year for nonmembers.

★9269★ **National Citizens Coalition for Nursing Home Reform (NCCNHR)**
1224 M St. NW, Ste. 301
Washington, DC 20005-5183
Phone: (202)393-2018
Fax: (202)393-4122
Elma Holder, Exec.Dir.

Founded: 1975. **Members:** 1,000. **Local Groups:** 250. **Description:** Local consumer/citizen action groups and individuals seeking nursing home and board and care reform. Seeks to provide a consumer voice at the national, state, and local levels in the development and implementation of the long-term care system.

Provides a platform through which groups can keep informed of current movements for change and can make their views known. Conducts seminars and training programs and utilizes a speakers' bureau consisting of advocates from around the country. Serves as a clearinghouse for information on nursing home and board care issues. Maintains speakers' bureau; conducts research and advocacy programs. **Publications:** *A Consumer Perspective on Quality Care: The Resident's Point of View.* • *Avoiding Physical Restraint Use: New Standard in Care.* Booklet. • *Citizens Guide to Reimbursement Issues.* • *Inappropriate Use of Physical and Chemical Restraints.* • *Quality Care Advocate,* bimonthly. Newsletter. • *The Rights of Nursing Home Residents.* **Also Known As:** Nursing Home Reform Coalition.

North American Association of Jewish Homes and Housing for the Aging (NAJHHA)
See: Entry 1916

★ 9270 ★ **Nursing Home Advisory and Research Council (NHARC)**
PO Box 18820
Cleveland Heights, OH 44118
Phone: (216)321-4499
Mary A. Mendelson, Exec.Dir.
Founded: 1976. **Members:** 1,500. **Description:** Relatives, friends, and guardians of nursing home patients. Provides education and research on nursing home patients. Works for legislation to improve the conditions of nursing homes. Sponsors Concerned Relatives of Nursing Home Patients. **Publications:** *Insight,* bimonthly. • *Patient's Bill of Rights.* • *Selecting a Nursing Home.*

★ 9271 ★ **Nursing Home Information Service (NHIS)**
c/o National Council of Senior Citizens
1331 F St. NW
Washington, DC 20004-1171
Phone: (202)347-8800
Fax: (202)624-9595
Lawrence T. Smedley, Exec. Dir.
Founded: 1975. **Description:** A project of the National Senior Citizens Research and Education Center. Provides information on nursing home standards and regulations, alternative community and health services, criteria for choosing a nursing home, and guidelines for obtaining "medigap" insurance (insurance covering medical expenses after Medicare's percentage is paid). Encourages consumer advocacy by persons desiring long-term care for themselves or for family or friends. Promotes compliance with the *Nursing Home Patients Bill of Rights*, a document listing some of the requirements for a federally certified nursing home. **Publications:** *Long-Term Care Directory: Metropolitan Washington Area.* Provides a how-to-guide for the preparation of similar directories, brochures, and other materials. • *News and Notes from NHIS,* 6/year.

Research Centers

★ 9272 ★ **Dallas Geriatric Research Institute**
2525 Centerville Rd.
Dallas, TX 75228-2693
Phone: (214)327-4503
Herbert Shore, Dir. of Research
Research Activities and Fields: Social and behavioral studies on long-term care and the frail elderly, particularly the multiple aspects of caring for nursing home residents with Alzheimer's disease and related disorders. Evaluates services provided by a geriatric nurse practitioner to well-elderly apartment residents. Projects have included periodic resident assessments and studies of job satisfaction, stress and burnout, and staff training.

★ 9273 ★ **Oxford Gerontology Center**
New York State Veterans' Home
Oxford, NY 13830
Phone: (607)843-6991
Fax: (607)843-6991
Raymond Vickers, M.D., Project Dir.
Research Activities and Fields: Studies health care needs of the elderly in long-term facilities and funds two to six related projects per year. Grantees restricted to members of nonprofit institutions within New York state. **Publications:** *Oxford Gerontology Center News* (newsletter).

★ 9274 ★ **Research Institute of the Hebrew Home of Greater Washington**
6121 Montrose Rd.
Rockville, MD 20852
Phone: (301)770-8449
Fax: (301)770-8455
Jiska Cohen-Mansfield, Dir.
Research Activities and Fields: Gerontology, aging, and issues concerning the elderly, focusing on nursing home residents, their families, and staff. Areas include: agitated behaviors among the elderly; stress in families caring for elderly relatives; staff stress; back injuries among staff caretakers; the preferences of nursing home residents regarding life-sustaining treatments; standardized assessment procedures of the physical and emotional states of nursing home residents; sleep patterns of nursing home residents; the use of physical restraints in the nursing home; and the use of psychotropic medication in the nursing home. **Publications:** Monograph Series. **E-mail Address:** mansfield@guvm.bitnet.

University of Arizona
Arizona Center on Aging
See: Entry 1970

State Government Agencies

Nursing Home Administrator Examining Boards

★ 9275 ★ **Alabama State Board of Examiners for Nursing Home Administrators**
4156 Carmichael Rd.
Montgomery, AL 36106
Phone: (205)271-6214
Fax: (205)244-6509

★ 9276 ★ **Alaska Board of Nursing Home Administrators**
PO Box 110806
Juneau, AK 99811-0806
Phone: (907)465-2541
Fax: (907)465-2974

★ 9277 ★ **Arizona Board of Examiners for Nursing Care Institution Administrators**
1645 W. Jefferson, Rm. 410
Phoenix, AZ 85007
Phone: (602)542-3095
Fax: (602)542-3093

★ 9278 ★ **Arkansas Department of Human Services**
Medical Services Division
Long Term Care Office
Nursing Home Certification and Licensure Section
PO Box 8059
Little Rock, AR 72203-8059
Phone: (501)682-8430
Fax: (501)682-6171

★ 9279 ★ **California Board of Examiners of Nursing Home Administrators**
1420 Howe Ave., Ste. 2
Sacramento, CA 95825
Phone: (916)263-2685
Fax: (916)263-2469

★ 9280 ★ **Colorado Board of Examiners of Nursing Home Administrators**
1560 Broadwawy, Ste. 1310
Denver, CO 80202
Phone: (303)894-7760
Fax: (303)894-7764

★ 9281 ★ **Connecticut Department of Public Health**
Nursing Home Administrator Licensure
150 Washington St.
Hartford, CT 06106-4068
Phone: (203)566-1039

★ 9282 ★ **Delaware State Board of Examiners of Nursing Home Administrators**
PO Box 1401
O'Neill Bldg.
Dover, DE 19903
Phone: (302)739-4522
Fax: (302)739-2711

★9283★ **District of Columbia Board of Nursing Home Administration**
614 H St. NW, Rm. 904
Washington, DC 20001
Phone: (202)727-9794
Fax: (202)373-5384

★9284★ **Florida Board of Nursing Home Administrators**
1940 N. Monroe St.
Tallahassee, FL 32399-0777
Phone: (904)488-7487
Fax: (904)922-2918

★9285★ **Georgia State Board of Examiners for Nursing Home Administrators**
166 Pryor St. SW
Atlanta, GA 30303
Phone: (404)656-3989
Fax: (404)651-9532

★9286★ **Hawaii Board of Examiners of Nursing Home Administrators**
1010 Richards St.
Honolulu, HI 96813
Phone: (808)586-2695
Fax: (808)586-2689

★9287★ **Idaho Bureau of Occupational Licenses**
Nursing Home Administrator Examining Board
1109 Main St., Ste. 220
Boise, ID 83702-5642
Phone: (208)334-3233
Fax: (208)334-3945

★9288★ **Illinois Department of Professional Regulation**
Nursing Home Administrators Licensing and Disciplinary Board
320 W. Washington St., 3rd Fl.
Springfield, IL 62786
Phone: (217)785-0872
Fax: (217)782-7645

★9289★ **Indiana Health Professions Bureau**
Board of Registration and Education for Health Facility Administrators
402 W. Washington, Rm. 041
Indianapolis, IN 46204
Phone: (317)233-4405
Fax: (317)233-4236

★9290★ **Iowa State Board of Examiners for Nursing Home Administrators**
Lucas State Office Bldg.
E. 12th & Grand
Des Moines, IA 50319-0075
Phone: (515)281-4401
Fax: (515)281-4958

★9291★ **Kansas Board of Adult Care Home Administrators**
Mill Bldg.
109 SW, 9th St., Ste. 400-B
Topeka, KS 66612
Phone: (913)296-0061
Fax: (913)296-1266

★9292★ **Kentucky Board of Licensure for Nursing Home Administrators**
PO Box 456
Frankfort, KY 40602
Phone: (502)564-3296
Fax: (502)564-4818

★9293★ **Louisiana State Board of Examiners for Nursing Home Administrators**
4560 North Blvd., Ste. 115A
Baton Rouge, LA 70806
Phone: (504)925-4132
Fax: (504)925-4583

★9294★ **Maine Nursing Home Administrator Licensing Board**
State House Station 35
Augusta, ME 04333
Phone: (207)582-8723
Fax: (207)582-5415

★9295★ **Maryland Board of Examiners for Nursing Home Administrators**
4201 Patterson Ave., Rm. 313
Baltimore, MD 21215-2299
Phone: (410)764-4750
Fax: (410)764-5987

★9296★ **Massachusetts Board of Registration for Nursing Home Administrators**
Leverett Saltonstall Bldg., No. 1516
100 Cambridge St.
Boston, MA 02202
Phone: (617)727-3069
Fax: (617)727-2197

★9297★ **Michigan Board of Nursing Home Administrators**
PO Box 30018
Lansing, MI 48909
Phone: (517)373-1699
Fax: (517)373-2795

★9298★ **Minnesota Board of Examiners for Nursing Home Administrators**
2700 University Ave., W.
St. Paul, MN 55114
Phone: (612)642-0595
Fax: (612)642-0393

★9299★ **Mississippi State Board of Nursing Home Administrators**
1400 Lakeover Rd., Ste. 120
Jackson, MS 39213
Phone: (601)359-6044
Fax: (601)359-6654

★9300★ **Missouri Board of Nursing Home Administrators**
615 Howerton Ct.
PO Box 1337
Jefferson City, MO 65102
Phone: (314)751-3511
Fax: (314)751-8687

★9301★ **Montana Board of Nursing Home Administrators**
Arcade Bldg.
111 N. Jackson
Helena, MT 59620-0513
Phone: (406)444-3728
Fax: (406)444-1667

★9302★ **Nebraska Board of Examiners of Nursing Home Administration**
301 Centennial Mall, S.
PO Box 95007
Lincoln, NE 68509
Phone: (402)471-2115
Fax: (402)471-0383

★9303★ **Nevada State Board of Examiners for Nursing Home Administrators**
PO Box 3226
Carson City, NV 89702
Phone: (702)871-0542
Fax: (702)382-4453

★9304★ **New Hampshire Board of Examiners of Nursing Home Administrators**
2 Industrial Park Dr.
Concord, NH 03301
Phone: (603)271-4728

★9305★ **New Jersey Nursing Home Administrators Licensing Board**
CN 367
Trenton, NJ 08625-0387
Phone: (609)588-7772
Fax: (609)588-7823

★9306★ **New Mexico Board of Nursing Home Administrators**
PO Box 25101
Santa Fe, NM 87501
Phone: (505)827-7170
Fax: (505)827-7095

★9307★ **New York Board of Examiners of Nursing Home Administrators**
260 Washington Ave. Ext., Ste. 102
Empire State Plaza
Albany, NY 12203-5499
Phone: (518)474-3042

★9308★ **North Carolina State Board of Examiners for Nursing Home Administrators**
3701 National Dr.
Raleigh, NC 27612
Phone: (919)571-4164
Fax: (919)571-4166

★9309★ **North Dakota Board of Examiners for Nursing Home Administrators**
120 W. Thayer Ave.
Bismarck, ND 58501
Phone: (701)222-4867
Fax: (701)233-0977

★9310★ **Ohio Board of Examiners for Nursing Home Administrators**
246 N. High St., 1st Fl.
Columbus, OH 43266-0118
Phone: (614)466-5114
Fax: (614)466-0271

★9311★ **Oklahoma State Board of Examiners for Nursing Home Administrators**
3033 N. Walnut, Ste. 100-E
Oklahoma City, OK 73105
Phone: (405)521-0991
Fax: (405)521-0982

★9312★ Oregon Board of Examiners of Nursing Home Administrators
800 NE Oregon, Ste. 407
Portland, OR 97232
Phone: (503)731-4046
Fax: (503)731-4207

★9313★ Pennsylvania State Board of Examiners of Nursing Home Administrators
PO Box 2649
Harrisburg, PA 17105-2649
Phone: (717)783-7155
Fax: (717)787-7769

★9314★ Rhode Island Board of Examiners for Nursing Home Administrators
104 Cannon Bldg.
3 Capitol Hill
Providence, RI 02908-5097
Phone: (401)277-2827
Fax: (401)277-2172

★9315★ South Carolina Board of Long Term Health Care Administrators
2221 Devine St., Ste. 414
Columbia, SC 29205
Phone: (803)734-9187

★9316★ South Dakota Board of Examiners for Nursing Home Administrators
804 Western Ave. N.
Sioux Falls, SD 57104-2098
Phone: (605)339-2071
Fax: (605)339-1354

★9317★ Tennessee Board of Examiners for Nursing Home Administrators
283 Plus Park Blvd.
Nashville, TN 37247-1010
Phone: (615)367-6280

★9318★ Texas Board of Nursing Facility Administrators
1100 W. 49th St.
Austin, TX 78756-3106
Phone: (512)834-6787

★9319★ Utah Board of Nursing Home Administrator Licensure
160 East 300 South
PO Box 45802
Salt Lake City, UT 84145
Phone: (801)530-6628
Fax: (801)530-6511

★9320★ Vermont Board of Examiners of Nursing Home Administrators
Office of the Secretary of State
109 State St.
Montpelier, VT 05609-1106
Phone: (802)828-2363
Fax: (802)828-2496

★9321★ Virginia Board of Nursing Home Administrators
6606 W. Broad St., 4th Fl.
Richmond, VA 23230-1717
Phone: (804)662-9111
Fax: (804)662-9943

★9322★ Washington Board for Nursing Home Administrators
1300 SE Quince
PO Box 47869
Olympia, WA 98504-7869
Phone: (206)586-6350
Fax: (206)586-7774

★9323★ West Virginia Nursing Home Administration Licensing Board
236 Capitol St.
Charleston, WV 25301
Phone: (304)558-1414
Fax: (304)558-0572

★9324★ Wisconsin Nursing Home Administrators Examining Board
PO Box 8935
Madison, WI 53708-8935
Phone: (608)266-3423
Fax: (608)267-0644

★9325★ Wyoming State Board of Nursing Home Administrators
2301 Central Ave., Rm. 349
Cheyenne, WY 82002
Phone: (307)777-6313
Fax: (307)777-6005

State & Regional Organizations

Health Care

The following are state affiliates of the American Health Care Association (1201 L St. NW, Washington, DC 20005-4014, 202-842-4444), a national organization representing long term health care facilities.

Alabama

★9326★ Alabama Nursing Home Association
4156 Carmichael Rd.
Montgomery, AL 36106
Phone: (205)271-6214
Fax: (205)244-6509

Alaska

★9327★ Alaska State Hospital and Nursing Home Association
319 Seward St.
Juneau, AK 99801
Phone: (907)586-1790
Fax: (907)463-3573

Arizona

★9328★ Arizona Health Care Association
1440 E. Missouri Ave., Ste. 215
Phoenix, AZ 85014-2461
Phone: (602)265-5331
Fax: (602)265-4401

Arkansas

★9329★ Arkansas Health Care Association
501 Woodlane Dr., Ste. 300
Little Rock, AR 72201
Phone: (501)374-4422
Fax: (501)374-1077

California

★9330★ California Association of Health Facilities
1251 Beacon Blvd.
West Sacramento, CA 95691
Phone: (916)371-4700
Fax: (916)372-5449

Colorado

★9331★ Colorado Health Care Association
225 E. 16th Ave., Ste. 1100
Denver, CO 80203
Phone: (303)861-8228
Fax: (303)839-8068

Connecticut

★9332★ Connecticut Association of Health Care Facilities
131 New London Tpke., Ste. 318
Glastonbury, CT 06033
Phone: (203)659-0391
Fax: (203)657-4962

Delaware

★9333★ Delaware Health Care Facilities Association
1013 Centre Rd., Ste. 101
Wilmington, DE 19805
Phone: (302)633-7880
Fax: (302)633-7863

District of Columbia

★9334★ District of Columbia Health Care Association
1233 20th St. NW, No. 800
Washington, DC 20036
Phone: (202)778-1220
Fax: (202)338-1479

Florida

★9335★ Florida Health Care Association
PO Box 1459
Tallahassee, FL 32302-1459
Phone: (904)224-3907
Fax: (904)681-2075

Georgia

★9336★ **Georgia Nursing Home Association**
3735 Memorial Dr.
Decatur, GA 30032
Phone: (404)284-8700
Fax: (404)286-0752

Hawaii

★9337★ **Health Care Association of Hawaii**
932 Ward Ave., Ste. 430
Honolulu, HI 96814
Phone: (808)521-8961
Fax: (808)599-2879

Idaho

★9338★ **Idaho Health Care Association**
PO Box 2623
Boise, ID 83701
Phone: (208)343-9735
Fax: (208)342-6891

Illinois

★9339★ **Illinois Health Care Association**
1029 S. 4th St.
Springfield, IL 62703
Phone: (217)528-6455
Fax: (217)528-0452

Indiana

★9340★ **Indiana Health Care Association**
1 N. Capitol, Ste. 1115
Indianapolis, IN 46204
Phone: (317)636-6406
Fax: (317)638-3749

Iowa

★9341★ **Iowa Health Care Association**
950 12th St.
Des Moines, IA 50309
Phone: (515)282-0666
Fax: (515)282-4011

Kansas

★9342★ **Kansas Health Care Association**
221 SW 33rd
Topeka, KS 66611
Phone: (913)267-6003
Fax: (913)267-0833

Kentucky

★9343★ **Kentucky Association of Health Care Facilities**
9403 Mill Brook Rd.
Louisville, KY 40223
Phone: (502)425-5000
Fax: (502)425-3431

Louisiana

★9344★ **Louisiana Nursing Home Association**
7921 Picardy Ave.
Baton Rouge, LA 70809
Phone: (504)769-3705
Fax: (504)769-3730

Maine

★9345★ **Maine Health Care Association**
303 State St.
Augusta, ME 04330
Phone: (207)623-1146
Fax: (207)623-4080

Maryland

★9346★ **Health Facilities Association of Maryland**
229 Hanover St.
Annapolis, MD 21401
Phone: (410)269-1390
Fax: (410)269-1393

Massachusetts

★9347★ **Massachusetts Federation of Nursing Homes**
990 Washington St., Ste. 207S
Dedham, MA 02026
Phone: (617)326-8967
Fax: (617)461-0623

Michigan

★9348★ **Health Care Association of Michigan**
PO Box 80050
Lansing, MI 48908
Phone: (517)627-1561
Fax: (517)627-3016

Minnesota

★9349★ **Care Providers of Minnesota**
2850 Metro Dr., Ste. 200
Minneapolis, MN 55425
Phone: (612)854-2844
Fax: (612)854-6214

Mississippi

★9350★ **Mississippi Health Care Association**
114 Marketridge Dr.
Jackson, MS 39213
Phone: (601)956-3472
Fax: (601)977-0273

Missouri

★9351★ **Missouri Health Care Association**
263 Metro Dr.
Jefferson City, MO 65109
Phone: (314)893-2060
Fax: (314)893-5248

Montana

★9352★ **Montana Health Care Association**
36 S. Last Chance Gulch, Ste. A
Helena, MT 59601
Phone: (406)443-2876
Fax: (406)443-4614

Nebraska

★9353★ **Nebraska Health Care Association**
421 S. 9th St., Ste. 137
Lincoln, NE 68508
Phone: (402)435-3551
Fax: (402)435-4829

Nevada

★9354★ **Nevada Health Care Association**
PO Box 3226
Carson City, NV 89702
Phone: (702)885-1006
Fax: (702)885-8681

New Hampshire

★9355★ **New Hampshire Health Care Association**
125 Airport Rd.
Concord, NH 03301
Phone: (603)225-0900
Fax: (603)225-4346

New Jersey

★9356★ **New Jersey Association of Health Care Facilities**
2131 Rte. 33
Trenton, NJ 08690
Phone: (609)890-8700
Fax: (609)584-1047

New Mexico

★9357★ **New Mexico Health Care Association**
6400 Uptown Blvd., Ste. 520W
Albuquerque, NM 87110
Phone: (505)880-1088
Fax: (505)880-1157

New York

★9358★ **New York State Health Facilities Association**
33 Elk St., No. 300
Albany, NY 12207
Phone: (518)462-4800
Fax: (518)426-4051

North Carolina

★9359★ North Carolina Health Care Facilities Association
5109 Bur Oak Cir.
Raleigh, NC 27612
Phone: (919)782-3827
Fax: (919)787-8418

North Dakota

★9360★ North Dakota Long Term Care Association
120 W. Thayer Ave.
Bismarck, ND 58501
Phone: (701)222-0660
Fax: (701)223-0977

Ohio

★9361★ Ohio Health Care Association
55 Green Meadows Dr. S.
Westerville, OH 43081
Phone: (614)436-4154
Fax: (614)436-0939

Oklahoma

★9362★ Oklahoma Health Care Association
5801 N. Broadway, Ste. 500
Oklahoma City, OK 73118
Phone: (405)848-8338
Fax: (405)848-7631

Oregon

★9363★ Oregon Health Care Association
15895 SW 72nd Ave., Ste. 250
Portland, OR 97224
Phone: (503)620-9300
Fax: (503)620-9393

Pennsylvania

★9364★ Pennsylvania Health Care Association
2401 Park Dr.
Harrisburg, PA 17110
Phone: (717)657-4902
Fax: (717)657-0459

Rhode Island

★9365★ Rhode Island Health Care Association
144 Bignall St.
Warwick, RI 02888
Phone: (401)785-9530
Fax: (401)785-0550

South Carolina

★9366★ South Carolina Health Care Association
170 Laurelhurst Dr.
Columbia, SC 29210
Phone: (803)772-7511
Fax: (803)772-7943

South Dakota

★9367★ South Dakota Health Care Association
804 N. Western Ave.
Sioux Falls, SD 57104-2098
Phone: (605)339-2071
Fax: (605)339-1354

Tennessee

★9368★ Tennessee Health Care Association
PO Box 100129
Nashville, TN 37224
Phone: (615)834-6520
Fax: (615)834-2502

Texas

★9369★ Texas Health Care Association
PO Box 4554
Austin, TX 78765
Phone: (512)458-1257
Fax: (512)467-9575

Utah

★9370★ Utah Health Care Association
4190 S. Highland Dr., Ste. 113
Salt Lake City, UT 84124
Phone: (801)272-4368
Fax: (801)272-4582

Vermont

★9371★ Vermont Health Care Association
2 Moonlight Terr.
Montpelier, VT 05602
Phone: (802)229-5700
Fax: (802)223-4826

Virginia

★9372★ Virginia Health Care Association
2112 W. Laburnum Ave., Ste. 206
Richmond, VA 23227
Phone: (804)353-9101
Fax: (804)353-3098

Washington

★9373★ Washington Health Care Association
2120 State Ave. NE, Ste. 102
Olympia, WA 98506
Phone: (206)352-3304
Fax: (206)754-2412

West Virginia

★9374★ West Virginia Health Care Association
8 Capitol St., Ste. 700
Charleston, WV 25301
Phone: (304)346-4575
Fax: (304)342-0519

Wisconsin

★9375★ Wisconsin Health Care Association
14 S. Carroll St., Ste. 200
Madison, WI 53703
Phone: (608)257-0125
Fax: (608)257-0025

Wyoming

★9376★ Wyoming Health Care Association
2020 Club House Rd.
Greeley, CO 80634
Phone: (303)330-7222
Fax: (303)339-4295

Chapter 44
Nutrition

Federal Government Agencies

★9377★ U.S. Department of Agriculture Agricultural Research Service (ARS)
14th St. and Independence Ave. SW
Washington, DC 20250
Phone: (202)720-3656
Fax: (202)720-5427

Description: The Agricultural Research Service conducts a national program of basic and applied agricultural research aimed at producing high-quality food and fiber. Seeks to improve and conserve the nation's soil, water, and air resources; solve problems in animal and plant protection and production; the processing, storage, and distribution of farm products; and human nutrition. Conducts programs in laboratories and in the field at 122 domestic and 8 foreign locations, frequently in cooperation with state agricultural experiment stations, other federal agencies, and private organizations.

★9378★ U.S. Department of Agriculture Center for Nutrition Policy and Promotion
1120 20th St. NW, Ste. 200
Washington, DC 20036
Phone: (202)418-2312
Fax: (202)208-2321

Description: The Center for Nutrition Policy and Promotion conducts applied research and analysis in nutrition knowledge and attitudes, dietary survey methodology, and dietary guidance and nutrition education techniques. CNPP uses research data to: 1. Further understanding of the factors that influence consumer food choices; 2. Provide dietary guidance in food selection and management; and 3. Develop materials and techniques to help increase nutrition knowledge and to improve food selection and management. CNPP maintains data on the nutrient content of the U.S. Food Supply, a continuous time series which began in 1909. CNPP also maintains and periodically updates the USDA Food Plans (upon which the Thrifty Food Plan is based) that is used to determine food stamp allotments. Within the USDA, CNPP coordinates the review and publication of the Dietary Guidelines for Americans and develops information to help Americans put the Guidelines into practice.

★9379★ U.S. Department of Agriculture Food and Consumer Service Special Nutrition Programs
3101 Park Center Dr.
Alexandria, VA 22302
Phone: (703)305-2052
Fax: (703)305-2420

Description: The Food and Consumer Service, operated in cooperation with states and local governments, administers programs to make food assistance available to people in need. Service administers Special Nutrition Programs designed to improve the nutrition of children, particularly those from low income families.

U.S. Department of Health and Human Services Food and Drug Administration Center for Food Safety and Applied Nutrition
See: Entry 10900

★9380★ U.S. House of Representatives Committee on Agriculture
1301 Longworth House Office Bldg.
Washington, DC 20515-6001
Phone: (202)225-2171
Fax: (202)225-0917

★9381★ U.S. Senate Committee on Agriculture, Nutrition, and Forestry Subcommittee on Research, Nutrition and General Legislation
SR-328A Russell Senate Office Bldg.
Washington, DC 20510-6000
Phone: (202)224-6901
Fax: (202)224-9278

Foundations & Other Funding Organizations

Corporate Foundations

Campbell Soup Foundation
See: Entry 619

Hershey Foods Corp. Fund
See: Entry 725

NutraSweet Co. Charitable Trust
See: Entry 800

Thomas J. Lipton Foundation
See: Entry 877

Other Funding Organizations

★9382★ American Dietetic Association Foundation
216 W. Jackson Blvd., Ste. 800
Chicago, IL 60606
Phone: (312)899-0040
Fax: (312)899-1979
Beverly Bajus, CEO/Exec. Dir.

Description: Conducts fund-raising to support specific reseach projects in the field of dietetics; awards a small number of fellowships for graduate study; administers a small number of grant programs for dietetic research.

★9383★ National Live Stock and Meat Board
444 N. Michigan Ave.
Chicago, IL 60611
Phone: (312)467-5520
John L. Huston, Pres.

Description: Awards grants for research on red meat in the diet and its relation to health.

Medical & Allied Health Schools

Dietetics

Listed below are coordinated dietetic programs accredited by the American Dietetic Association. These programs offer academic preparation and clinical experience at the bachelor and master's levels. The Association also accredits postbaccalaureate dietetic internships and pre-professional practice programs and approves didactic programs in dietetics, as well as dietetic technician programs. For information on these, as well as advanced degree programs in nutrition and related areas, contact the American Dietetic Association, 216 W. Jackson Blvd., Ste. 800, Chicago, IL 60606-6995, (312) 899-0040.

Alabama

★9384★ University of Alabama
Department of Human Nutrition and
** Hospitality**
Dietetics Program
PO Box 870158
Tuscaloosa, AL 35487-0158
Phone: (205)348-6157
Fax: (205)348-3789

California

★9385★ California State University, Los
** Angeles**
Department of Health and Nutritional
** Sciences**
Dietetics Program
5151 State University Dr.
Los Angeles, CA 90032-8161
Phone: (213)343-4630
Fax: (213)343-2670

★9386★ Charles R. Drew University of
** Medicine and Science**
College of Allied Health
Dietetics Program
1621 E. 120th St.
Los Angeles, CA 90059
Phone: (213)563-4811
Fax: (213)563-4923

★9387★ Loma Linda University
School of Allied Health Professions
Department of Nutrition and Dietetics
Loma Linda, CA 92350
Phone: (909)824-4593
Fax: (909)824-4701

Connecticut

★9388★ St. Joseph College
Department of Nutrition and Resource
** Management**
Dietetics Program
1678 Asylum Ave.
West Hartford, CT 06117
Phone: (203)232-4571
Fax: (203)233-5695

★9389★ University of Connecticut
School of Allied Health Professions
Dietetics Program
Koons Hall, Rm. 214
358 Mansfield Rd.
Storrs Mansfield, CT 06268-2101
Phone: (203)486-0016
Fax: (203)486-4191

Delaware

★9390★ University of Delaware
Department of Nutrition and Dietetics
332 Alison Hall
Newark, DE 19716
Phone: (302)831-2732
Fax: (302)831-4186

District of Columbia

★9391★ Howard University
College of Allied Health Sciences
Department of Nutritional Sciences
Dietetics Program
Annex 1, Rm. 343
6th and Bryant Sts. NW
Washington, DC 20059
Phone: (202)806-6238
Fax: (202)806-7918

Florida

★9392★ Florida International University
Department of Dietetics and Nutrition
Health Bldg., Rm. 201
University Park
Miami, FL 33199
Phone: (305)348-2878

Georgia

★9393★ Georgia State University
Department of Nutrition and Dietetics
Box 873, University Plaza
Atlanta, GA 30303-3083
Phone: (404)651-1108
Fax: (404)651-1235

Idaho

★9394★ University of Idaho
College of Agriculture
School of Family and Consumer Sciences
Dietetics Program
Moscow, ID 83844-3183
Phone: (208)885-6026
Fax: (208)885-5751

Illinois

★9395★ University of Illinois at Chicago
College of Associated Health Professions
Department of Nutrition and Medical
** Dietetics**
1919 W. Taylor St., Rm. 850
Chicago, IL 60612
Phone: (312)996-2083
Fax: (312)413-0319

Indiana

★9396★ Indiana State University
Home Economics Department
Dietetics Program
Terre Haute, IN 47809
Phone: (812)237-3309

★9397★ Purdue University
Department of Foods and Nutrition
Dietetics Program
1264 Stone Hall
West Lafayette, IN 47907-1264
Phone: (317)494-8232
Fax: (317)494-0674

Iowa

★9398★ Iowa State University
Department of Food Science and Human
** Nutrition**
Dietetics Program
1127 Human Nutritional Sciences Bldg., Hall Addition
Ames, IA 50011
Phone: (515)294-4436
Fax: (515)294-6193

Kansas

★9399★ Kansas State University
Department of Hotel, Restaurant,
** Institution Management and Dietetics**
Justin Hall, Rm. 103
Manhattan, KS 66506-1404
Phone: (913)532-5521
Fax: (913)532-5504

Kentucky

★9400★ University of Kentucky
Department of Nutrition and Food Science
Dietetics Program
218 Funkhouser
Lexington, KY 40506-0054
Phone: (606)257-1031
Fax: (606)257-3707

Massachusetts

★9401★ Framingham State College
Department of Home Economics
Dietetics Program
100 State St.
Framingham, MA 01701
Phone: (508)626-4754
Fax: (508)626-8132

Michigan

★9402★ Eastern Michigan University
Department of Human, Environmental and
** Consumer Resources**
Dietetics Program
Ypsilanti, MI 48197
Phone: (313)487-3389
Fax: (313)484-0575

★9403★ Wayne State University
Department of Nutrition and Food Science
Dietetics Program
3009 Science Hall
Detroit, MI 48202
Phone: (313)577-2920
Fax: (313)577-8616

Minnesota

★9404★ College of St. Benedict
Nutrition Department
Dietetics Program
37 S. College Ave.
St. Joseph, MN 56374
Phone: (612)363-5976
Fax: (612)363-5582

★9405★ University of Minnesota
Department of Food Science and Nutrition
Dietetics Program
1334 Eckles Ave.
St. Paul, MN 55108
Phone: (612)624-9278
Fax: (612)625-5272

Mississippi

★9406★ University of Southern Mississippi
College of Health and Human Sciences
Dietetics Program
PO Box 5035, Southern Sta.
Hattiesburg, MS 39406
Phone: (601)266-4679
Fax: (601)266-4680

Missouri

★9407★ University of Missouri—Columbia
Dietetic Education Program
318 Clark Hall
Columbia, MO 65211
Phone: (314)882-4136
Fax: (314)884-4885

New York

★9408★ D'Youville College
Dietetics Program
320 Porter Ave.
Buffalo, NY 14201-1084
Phone: (716)881-3200
Fax: (716)881-7790

★9409★ Rochester Institute of Technology
School of Food, Hotel, and Travel Management
Dietetics Program
1 Lomb Memorial Dr.
Rochester, NY 14623
Phone: (716)475-2357
Fax: (716)475-5099

★9410★ State University of New York at Buffalo
Nutrition, Hospitality, and Fashion Department
Dietetics Program
1300 Elmwood Ave.
Buffalo, NY 14222-1095
Phone: (716)878-5818

★9411★ Syracuse University
Department of Nutrition and Foodservice
Dietetics Program
034 Slocum Hall
Syracuse, NY 13244-1250
Phone: (315)443-4550
Fax: (315)443-2562

North Carolina

★9412★ University of North Carolina at Chapel Hill
Department of Nutrition
Dietetics Program
McGavran-Greenburg Hall, CB 7400
Chapel Hill, NC 27599-7400
Phone: (919)966-7214

North Dakota

★9413★ North Dakota State University
College of Human Development and Education
Department of Food and Nutrition
Dietetics Program
Fargo, ND 58105
Phone: (701)237-7480
Fax: (701)237-7174

★9414★ University of North Dakota
Department of Home Economics and Nutrition
Dietetics Program
Box 8237, University Sta.
Grand Forks, ND 58202
Phone: (701)777-3752
Fax: (701)777-3650

Ohio

★9415★ Ohio State University
School of Allied Medical Professions
Dietetics Program
1583 Perry St.
Columbus, OH 43210
Phone: (614)292-5424
Fax: (614)292-0210

★9416★ University of Akron
School of Home Economics and Family Ecology
Dietetics Program
215 Schrank Hall S.
Akron, OH 44325-6103
Phone: (216)972-6046
Fax: (216)972-4934

★9417★ Youngstown State University
Home Economics Department
Dietetics Program
410 Wick Ave.
Youngstown, OH 44555-0001
Phone: (216)742-1822
Fax: (216)652-3683

Oklahoma

★9418★ University of Oklahoma
College of Allied Health
Department of Nutritional Sciences
Dietetics Program
Health Sciences Center
801 NE 13th St., Rm. 465
PO Box 26901
Oklahoma City, OK 73190
Phone: (405)271-2113
Fax: (405)271-3120

Pennsylvania

★9419★ Edinboro University of Pennsylvania
Department of Biology and Health Services
Dietetics Program
Edinboro, PA 16444
Phone: (814)732-2447

★9420★ Gannon University
Villa Maria College of Health Sciences
Department of Science and Mathematics
Dietetics Program
University Square
Erie, PA 16541-0001
Phone: (814)871-5452
Fax: (814)871-5662

★9421★ Marywood College
Department of Human Ecology
Dietetics Program
2300 Adams Ave.
Scranton, PA 18509-1598
Phone: (717)348-6277
Fax: (717)348-1817

★9422★ Mercyhurst College
Department of Human Ecology
Dietetics Program
Glenwood Hills
Erie, PA 16546
Phone: (814)824-2462
Fax: (814)824-2438

★9423★ Seton Hill College
Department of Human Ecology
Dietetics Program
Greensburg, PA 15601
Phone: (412)834-2200
Fax: (412)838-4203

★9424★ University of Pittsburgh
School of Health and Rehabilitation Sciences
Dietetics Program
212 Pennsylvania Hall
Pittsburgh, PA 15261
Phone: (412)624-8927
Fax: (412)624-5019

Texas

★9425★ Texas Christian University
Department of Nutrition and Dietetics
PO Box 32869
Ft. Worth, TX 76129
Phone: (817)921-7309
Fax: (817)921-7704

★9426★ University of Texas at Austin
Department of Human Ecology
Dietetics Program
GEA 117
Austin, TX 78712
Phone: (512)471-4934
Fax: (512)471-5630

★9427★ University of Texas Health Science Center at Houston
School of Allied Health Sciences
Department of Nutrition and Dietetics

2440 C Doctors Center
7000 Fannin
Houston, TX 77030
Phone: (713)792-4466
Fax: (713)745-0772

★9428★ **University of Texas—Pan American**
Dietetics Program
NE 226
Edinburg, TX 78539-2999
Phone: (512)381-2294

★9429★ **University of Texas Southwestern Medical Center at Dallas**
Southwestern Allied Health Sciences School
Department of Clinical Nutrition
Dietetics Program
5323 Harry Hines Blvd.
Dallas, TX 75235-8877
Phone: (214)648-1520
Fax: (214)648-1505

Utah

★9430★ **Brigham Young University**
Food Science and Nutrition Department
Dietetics Program
2218 SFLC
Provo, UT 84602
Phone: (801)378-3912
Fax: (801)378-2800

★9431★ **University of Utah**
College of Health
Division of Foods and Nutrition
Dietetics Program
239N-HPR
Salt Lake City, UT 84112
Phone: (801)581-8240
Fax: (801)581-5580

★9432★ **Utah State University**
Department of Nutrition and Food Sciences
Dietetics Program
Logan, UT 84322-8700
Phone: (801)797-2105
Fax: (801)797-2379

Washington

★9433★ **Washington State University**
Dietetics Program
FSHN Bldg. 108
Pullman, WA 99164-6376
Phone: (509)335-1395
Fax: (509)335-4815

Wisconsin

★9434★ **Mt. Mary College**
Department of Dietetics
2900 N. Menomonee River Pkwy.
Milwaukee, WI 53222
Phone: (414)475-7433
Fax: (414)256-1205

★9435★ **University of Wisconsin— Madison**
Department of Nutritional Sciences
Dietetics Program
1415 Linden Dr.
Madison, WI 53706
Phone: (608)262-2727
Fax: (608)262-5860

★9436★ **Viterbo College**
Dietetics Program
815 S. 9th St.
La Crosse, WI 54601-4797
Phone: (608)791-0227
Fax: (608)791-0367

National & International Organizations

★9437★ **African-American Natural Foods Association (AANFA)**
c/o Cheryl A. Simms
7122 S. Jeffery
Chicago, IL 60649
Phone: (312)363-3939
Cheryl A. Simms, Pres.

Founded: 1990. **Description:** Natural and health food retailers, health practitioners, manufacturers, and distributors; interested individuals. Works to increase awareness of natural foods and the nutritional industry in minority communities. Sponsors seminars and workshops; offers children's services; bestows awards; maintains library and speakers' bureau. Plans to establish a natural food resource and information center.

American Academy of Veterinary Nutrition (AAVN)
See: Entry 13023

★9438★ **American Association of Nutritional Consultants (AANC)**
880 Canarios Court, Ste. 210
Chula Vista, CA 91910
Phone: (619)482-8533
Lenda Summerfield, Asst. Admin.

Founded: 1980. **Members:** 5,000. **Description:** Professional nutritional consultants. Seeks to: develop a certification board; create a forum for exchange of nutritional information; establish state chapters. Offers benefits such as car rental and laboratory discounts. **Publications:** Membership Directory, annual. • *Nutrition and Dietary Consultant*, monthly. Magazine. Focuses on innovation in the field of professional nutritional counseling, and vitamin, mineral, and food therapies. Includes nutrition digest. *Price:* Included in membership dues; $15.96/year for nonmembers.

★9439★ **American Board of Nutrition (ABN)**
University of Alabama at Birmingham
1675 University Blvd./WEBB 234
Birmingham, AL 35294
Phone: (205)975-8788
Fax: (205)934-7049
Treva McAboy, Contact

Founded: 1948. **Members:** 524. **Description:** Physicians qualified to treat nutritional and metabolic disorders; doctoral recipients working on problems of human nutrition and nutrient requirements. Establishes standards for qualification of persons as specialists in the field of clinical human nutrition; holds examinations and certifies those who meet its qualifications. **Publications:** *Directory of Diplomates in Human Nutrition and Clinical Nutrition*, biennial. Directory.

★9440★ **American College of Nutrition (ACN)**
301 E. 17th St.
New York, NY 10003
Phone: (212)777-1037
Fax: (212)777-1103
Stanley Wallach, M.D., Exec.Dir.

Founded: 1959. **Members:** 1,170. **Description:** Physicians, research scientists, nutritionists, dietitians, allied health personnel, and postbaccalaureate students and trainees in these fields. Provides education on clinical and experimental developments in the field of nutrition. Stimulates the exchange of information between nutrition scientists and physicians interested in applying research findings to the care of patients; encourages nutrition education in medical schools; provides for continuing education of physicians and other scientists on nutritional subjects. Sponsors postgraduate courses on nutritional problems. Advises physicians on nutrition developments of clinical importance. **Publications:** *Journal of the American College of Nutrition*, bimonthly. Journal. Contains peer-reviewed articles. *Price:* Included in membership dues; $70/year for U.S. nonmembers; $160/year for U.S. institutions; $100/year for nonmembers outside the U.S. • Newsletter, quarterly.

★9441★ **American Council of Applied Clinical Nutrition (ACACN)**
PO Box 509
Florissant, MO 63032
Phone: (314)921-3997
Fax: (314)921-8485
Clarence T. Smith, Ph.D., Pres.

Founded: 1974. **Members:** 500. **Description:** Clinical nutrition specialists. Offers structured academic course and certification; conducts research.

★9442★ **American Dietetic Association (ADA)**
216 W. Jackson Blvd., Ste. 800
Chicago, IL 60606
Phone: (312)899-0040
Fax: (312)899-1979
Beverly Bajus, COO

Founded: 1917. **Members:** 64,000. **State Groups:** 52. **Description:** Dietetic professionals, registered dietitians and dietetic technicians serving the public through promotion of optimal nutrition, health and well being. Seeks to shape the food choices and impact the nutritional status of the public in hospitals, colleges, universities, schools, day care centers, research, business and industry. Sets and approves standards of education and practice. Provides career guidance. **Publications:** *Journal of the American Dietetic Association*, monthly. Journal. Contains research and practice articles, association news, literature abstracts, and a list of new publications. *Price:* Included in membership dues; $98/year for nonmembers.

★9443★ American Institute of Nutrition (AIN)

9650 Rockville Pke.
Bethesda, MD 20814-3990
Phone: (301)530-7050
Fax: (301)571-1892
Richard G. Allison, Ph.D., Exec. Officer

Founded: 1928. **Members:** 3,100. **Description:** Professional society of nutrition research scientists from universities, government, and industry. **Publications:** *Journal of Nutrition*, monthly. Journal. Peer-reviewed research papers covering all aspects of experimental nutrition, critical reviews, biographies, and commentaries on controversial issues. *Price:* Included in membership dues; $90/year for nonmembers; $200/year for institutions; $25/ year for students. • *Nutrition Notes*, quarterly. Newsletter. Provides information about the Institute's activities as well as topical national and international issues in nutrition. *Price:* Included in membership dues; $30/year for nonmembers.

★9444★ American Society for Clinical Nutrition (ASCN)

9650 Rockville Pke.
Bethesda, MD 20814-3998
Phone: (301)530-7110
Fax: (301)571-1892
David Schnakenberg, Ph.D., Exec. Officer

Founded: 1959. **Members:** 1,400. **Description:** Physicians and scientists actively engaged in clinical nutrition research. Promotes teaching, research, and reporting of progress in clinical nutrition. Offers annual postgraduate course. **Publications:** *The American Journal of Clinical Nutrition*, monthly. Journal. Contains original research findings. Includes book reviews, commentaries, letters to the editor, and editorials. *Price:* $45/year for members; $90/year for nonmembers; $35/year for students; $135/year for institutions. Publishes supplements on irregular basis.

★9445★ American Society for Parenteral and Enteral Nutrition (ASPEN)

8630 Fenton Ste., No. 412
Silver Spring, MD 20910-3805
Phone: (301)587-6315
Fax: (301)587-2365
Barney Sellers, Exec.Dir.

Founded: 1975. **Members:** 7,700. **State Groups:** 47. **Description:** Physicians, dietitians, nurses, pharmacists, and members of the industry. Works to promote quality patient care, education, and research in the field of nutrition and metabolic support in all health care settings. Educates health care professionals. Conducts postgraduate courses and research programs; compiles statistics. **Publications:** *Journal of Parenteral and Enteral Nutrition*, bimonthly. Journal. Includes book reviews, case reports, and citations from world literature. *Price:* Included in membership dues; $45/year for students; $115 for institutions; $85 for individuals. • Manual. Covers product resources. • Monographs. • *Nutrition in Clinical Practice*, bimonthly. Journal. Contains abstracts of literature in the field from other publications, ASPEN news, case reports, legislative news, and a list of new products. *Price:* Included in membership dues; $25/ year for students; $70 for institutions; $40 for individuals. Also publishes course syllabi on a variety of clinical nutrition topics, self-assessment programs, and reference anthologies.

★9446★ Association of French-Speaking Dietitians (Association de Dieteticiens de Lange Francaise)

35, Allee Vivaldi
F-75012 Paris, France
Phone: 1 40020302

Members: 1,640. **Languages:** French. **Description:** Professional dietitians. Promotes advancement in the study and application of dietetics; advises government agencies and the public regarding a healthy diet. Conducts research and educational programs.

★9447★ Association of German Dietitians (AGD) (Verband Deutscher Diatassistenten — VDD)

Bismarckstrasse 96
Postfach 10 51 12
40042 Dusseldorf, Germany
Phone: 211 162175
Fax: 211 357389
Heidrun Blochwitz, Mgr.

Founded: 1957. **Members:** 4,500. **Languages:** English, German. **Description:** Nutritionists in Germany working to improve nutritional practices. Represents interests of members. Provides a forum for information exchange among dieticians, doctors, and other medical workers. Supports training of dietitians. Affiliated with the European Federation of the Associations of Dietitians. **Publications:** *Diet & Information*, bimonthly. Journal. • *Ernahrungs Umschau*, annual. Journal.

★9448★ Association of Vegetarian Dietitians and Nutrition Educators (VEGEDINE)

3835 State Rte. 414
Burdett, NY 14818
Phone: (607)546-7171

Founded: 1983. **Members:** 118. **Description:** Professional dietitians and nutritionists. Promotes a vegetarian lifestyle; represents members' interests. Sponsors correspondence course in vegetarian nutrition for the general public. Provides a speakers' bureau. **Publications:** *Course Book in Vegetarian Nutrition*. • *Directory of Vegetarian-Oriented Health Professionals*, periodic. Directory. *Price:* Free. • *The Most Noble Diet*. Book.

★9449★ British Dietetic Association (BDA)

Elizabeth House, 7th Fl.
22 Suffolk St.
Queensway
Birmingham, W. Midlands B1 1LS, England
Phone: 121 6435483
Fax: 121 6634399
J.C.J. Grigg, Admin.

Founded: 1936. **Members:** 2,800. **Local Groups:** 11. **Languages:** English. **Description:** Professional registered dietitians. Promotes advancement of the science and practice of dietetics and related subjects. Sponsors training and educational programs. Arranges meetings, refresher courses, and study conferences. Provides liaison between dietitians in the United Kingdom and other countries. **Publications:** *Adviser Magazine*, quarterly. • *Journal of Human Nutrition and Dietetics*, bimonthly. • *Members' Newsletter*, monthly. Newsletter.

Child Nutrition Forum (CNF)

See: Entry 3201

★9450★ Chinese Association for Promotion of Students' Nutrition

11 Boluocang
Xicheng District
Beijing 100035, People's Republic of China
Phone: 1 6011049
Cheng-bin Shi, Sec.Gen.

Founded: 1988. **Members:** 14. **Description:** Organizations of nutritionists, educators, and interested individuals in the People's Republic of China. Promotes the improvement of students' nutrition in China's educational system. Develops nutritional guidelines. Offers consulting services.

★9451★ Community Nutrition Institute (CNI)

2001 S St. NW, Ste. 530
Washington, DC 20009
Phone: (202)462-4700
Fax: (202)462-5241
Rodney E. Leonard, Exec.Dir.

Founded: 1970. **Description:** Citizen advocates specializing in food and nutrition issues including hunger, food quality and safety, nutrition research, food programs, education, and food labeling and marketing. Major goal is to secure a food system that provides access to a diet that sustains cultural and social values and maintains human health. Offers advocacy-training courses for federal, state, and community impact. Supports litigation on food policy issues. Assists federal agencies in analyzing and implementing food programs and research. Develops standards for food products and lobbies for USDA and FDA ratification. **Publications:** Booklets. • *Nutrition Week*, weekly. Newsletter. Includes association news, employment listings, research notes, and statistics. *Price:* $75/year. Also publishes training materials.

★9452★ Consultant Dietitians in Health Care Facilities (CDHCF)
216 W. Jackson Blvd., Ste. 800
Chicago, IL 60606
Phone: (312)899-0040
Free: 800-877-1600
Fax: (312)899-1758
Phyllis Nichols, Chm.

Founded: 1975. **Members:** 5,100. **State Groups:** 50. **Description:** A special interest group of the American Dietetic Association. Dietitians employed in extended care facilities, nursing homes, and a variety of food service operations. Disseminates information; assists in solving their problems in the field. Conducts workshops; offers networking opportunities for professionals. **Publications:** *The Consultant Dietitian*, quarterly. Newsletter. • *Dining Skills.* • *How to Consult Manual.* • *Video Tapes on Dysphagia and Chemical Hazards.* **Formerly:** Consultant Dieticians Special Interest Group.

★9453★ Dietary Managers Association (DMA)
1 Pierce Pl., No. 1220W
Itasca, IL 60143
Phone: (708)775-9200
Free: 800-323-1908
Fax: (708)775-9250
William S. St. John, Exec.Dir.

Founded: 1960. **Members:** 14,000. **State Groups:** 50. **Description:** Dietary managers united to maintain a high level of competency and quality in dietary departments through continuing education. Provides educational programs and placement service. **Publications:** *Diet Therapy for the Dietary Manager.* Book. *Price:* $47.50 for nonmembers. • *Dietary Manager*, bimonthly. Magazine. *Price:* $24/year. • *Managing Foodservice Operations.* Book. • *Professional Procurement Practices.* Book. **Formerly:** Hospital, Institution and Educational Food Service Society.

★9454★ Diplom Dietician Association Austria (DDAA)
(Verband der Diplomierten Diatassistentinen Osterreichs — VDDO)
Raaber-Bahn-Gasse 3/2/8
A-1100 Vienna, Austria
Phone: 1 6269984
Gertrud Fitzner, Contact

Founded: 1961. **Members:** 400. **Local Groups:** 8. **Languages:** English, German. **Description:** Dieticians and nutritionists. Cooperates with medical practitioners and related organizations to further advancement in the field. Offers advanced training and professional development courses; sponsors research programs. **Publications:** *Ernahrung Aktuell*, periodic. • *Interne Verbands Nachrichten*, periodic. • *Nutrition*, periodic.

★9455★ European Association for Studies on Nutrition and Child Development (ADE)
(Association Europeenne pour l'Etude de l'Alimentation et du Developpement de l'Enfant — ADE)
9, blvd. des Capucines
F-75002 Paris, France
Phone: 1 44736739
Fax: 1 44736739
Z.L. Ostrowski, M.D., Pres.

Founded: 1969. **Members:** 150. **Languages:** English, French. **Description:** Medical doctors, dieticians, nutritionists, biologists, statisticians, and others working in related fields. Conducts surveys and research in nutrition and early childhood development; holds training sessions. Provides children's services. **Publications:** *Abstracts*, periodic. • *Bulletin*, periodic. • *Proceedings*, periodic. Also publishes (in French) *Intellectual Development at the Very Beginning of Life, Nutritional Status of Children to 3 years in 4 European Countries*, and food tables.

★9456★ European Federation of the Associations of Dietitians (EFAD)
(Federation Europeenne des Associations de Dieteticiens — FEAD)
Boterstraat 1a
NL-5341 6H Oss, Netherlands
Phone: 4120 24543
Fax: 4120 37736
H.M. von Oosten, Sec.

Founded: 1978. **Members:** 20. **Languages:** English, French. **Description:** National association of dietitians. Furthers dietetics as a scientific discipline and a profession. Objectives are: to improve the nutritional practices of European populations; to advance education in dietetics; to harmonize professional qualification criteria. Evaluates opportunities in the field.

★9457★ Feingold Association of the United States (FAUS)
PO Box 6550
Alexandria, VA 22306
Phone: (703)768-FAUS
Free: 800-321-FAUS
Jane Hersey, Dir.

Founded: 1976. **Members:** 30,000. **Regional Groups:** 7. **Local Groups:** 30. **Description:** Individuals who believe that symptoms such as overactivity, anxiety, aggression, sleep disturbances, and learning disabilities are often alleviated by adherence to a program developed by Ben F. Feingold, M.D. which eliminates synthetic colors, synthetic flavors, and BHA, BHT, and TBHQ (preservatives) from the diet. Goals are: to support the dietary management schedule known as the Feingold Program; to gather and disseminate information on food supply and to support public availability of such information. **Publications:** Books. • *Dietary Management of Hyperactivity.* Audiotape. • *Impossible Kids? Possible Answers.* Video. • Pamphlet. • *Pure Facts*, 10/year. Newsletter. *Price:* Included in membership dues; $25/year for nonmembers.

★9458★ Finnish Dietetic Association (Association Suomen Dieteetikkoyhdists)
Mannerheimintie 144 A 2
SF-00270 Helsinki, Finland
Phone: 0 4771455
Fax: 0 4771733

Members: 3,167. **Languages:** Finnish. **Description:** Professional dietitians. Promotes advancement in the study and application of dietetics; advises government agencies and the public regarding a healthy diet. Conducts research and educational programs.

★9459★ Food and Nutrition Board (FNB)
Institute of Medicine
2101 Constitution Ave. NW
Washington, DC 20418
Phone: (202)334-1732
Allison A. Yates, Exec. Officer

Founded: 1940. **Members:** 17. **Description:** Division of National Academy of Sciences - Institute of Medicine. Evaluates and offers advice concerning the relationship between food consumption, nutritional status, and public health. **Publications:** *Activities Report*, periodic. Report. • Directory, annual. • Monographs. Covers nutrition, public health and food safety.

Gerson Institute (GI)
See: Entry 2197

★9460★ Greek Dietetic Association
Michalakopoulou 86 Str.
GR-11 528 Athens, Greece
Phone: 1 7783037
Fax: 1 7783037

Members: 180. **Languages:** Greek. **Description:** Professional dietitians. Promotes advancement in the study and application of dietetics; advises government agencies and the public regarding a healthy diet. Conducts research and educational programs. **Also Known As:** Hellenic Dietetic Association.

★9461★ Greek Society of Nutrition and Foods
Dept. of Nutrition and Biochemistry
Athens School of Public Health
Leoforos Alexandras 196
GR-115 28 Athens, Greece
Phone: 1 6461831
Fax: 1 6436536
Prof. Antonia Trichopoulou, Contact

Founded: 1981. **Members:** 93. **Languages:** Greek. **Description:** Physicians and nutritionists in Greece. Promotes education in nutrition. Conducts research; compiles statistics. Maintains speakers' bureau. Sponsors seminars. **Publications:** *Statitute*, periodic. Also publishes conference proceedings and pamphlets.

HELP - Institute for Body Chemistry (HELP)
See: Entry 4844

★9462★ Hungarian Society of Nutrition (HSN)
(Magyar Taplalkozastudomanyi Tarsasag — MTT)
Gyali ut. 3/a
H-1097 Budapest, Hungary
Phone: 1 2155393
Fax: 1 2151545
Prof. Dr. Gyorgy Biro, Pres.

Founded: 1966. **Members:** 430. **Languages:** Hungarian. **Description:** Promotes the study of general and clinical nutrition. Researches medical aspects of food production and consumption. Conducts periodic discussion groups on nutrition related issues and problems; offers postgraduate training courses. **Formerly:** Hungarian Society of Nutritional Sciences.

★9463★ Icelandic Dietetic Association
(Naeringarradgjafafelag Islands)
St. Josejsspitali Landaroti
IS-101 Reykjavik, Iceland
Phone: 1 604300
Fax: 1 625422
Mrs. A. E. Asgeirdottir, Contact

Members: 11. **Languages:** Icelandic. **Description:** Professional dietitians. Promotes advancement in the study and application of dietetics; advises government agencies and the public regarding a healthy diet. Conducts research and educational programs.

★9464★ Institute of Nutrition of Central America and Panama (INCAP)
(Instituto de Nutricion de Centro America y Panama — INCAP)
Carretera Roosevelt, Zona 11
Apartado Postal 1188
01901 Guatemala City, Guatemala
Phone: 2 723762
Fax: 2 736529
Dr. Hernan L. Delgado, Dir.

Founded: 1949. **Languages:** English, Spanish. **Description:** Representatives of Belize, Costa Rica, El Salvador, Guatemala, Honduras, Nicaragua, and Panama. Advises members on policies concerning nutrition in their countries. Encourages technical cooperation by coordinating available resources and promoting exchange of information and personnel in areas such as food and nutrition surveillance, maternal-infant nutrition, food aid programs, food and nutrition in school programs, improvement of basic grains, development of food resources, and nutritional fortification of foods. Conducts research in the areas of agricultural and food sciences, food technology, animal nutrition, and agro-industrial activities. Provides specialized training courses for professional, technical, and auxiliary personnel. Sponsors tutorial training programs for all levels in related fields; offers postgraduate courses in food and nutrition, health, and food sciences and technology. Conducts periodic conferences, seminars, and workshops. Compiles statistics. Administered by the Pan American Health Organization. **Publications:** Books. • *Informe Anual*, annual. • Papers, periodic.

★9465★ International Academy of Nutrition and Preventive Medicine (IANPM)
PO Box 18433
Asheville, NC 28814-0433
Phone: (704)258-3243
Carroll Thompson, Exec.Dir.

Founded: 1971. **Members:** 400. **Description:** Physicians, dentists, ophthalmologists, osteopaths, chiropractors, veterinarians, and scientists in fields related to nutrition, all holding an accredited degree. Members work in 12 countries to: stimulate and encourage research in the nutritional aspects of disease; promote science and study of nutrition and allied subjects in medical and dental schools, hospitals, colleges, and research institutions; provides referral service for people seeking nutrition/preventative health care providers. **Publications:** *International Academy of Nutrition and Preventive Medicine Membership Directory*, annual. Directory. *Price:* Included in membership dues; $10/copy for nonmembers. • *Journal of Applied Nutrition*, quarterly. Journal. *Price:* Included in membership dues; $75/year for nonmembers and institutions; $30/year for students; $100/year outside U.S. • *Your Health*, bimonthly. Newsletter. For laypeople. Includes information on nutrition and preventative medicine applied to a variety of health issues. *Price:* Included in membership dues.

International Life Sciences Institute—North America (ILSINA)
See: Entry 10412

International Nutritional Immunology Group (INIG)
See: Entry 2076

★9466★ International Union of Nutritional Sciences (IUNS)
(Union Internationale des Sciences de la Nutrition — UISN)
Dept. of Human Nutrition
Agricultural Univ.
Postbus 8129
NL-6700 EV Wageningen, Netherlands
Phone: 8370 82589
Fax: 8370 83342
Prof. Joseph Hautvast, Sec.Gen.

Founded: 1946. **Members:** 65. **Languages:** English. **Description:** National nutritional societies. Promotes international cooperation in the scientific study of nutrition and its applications. Encourages research and the exchange of scientific information. Cooperates with the Food and Agriculture Organization of the United Nations, the United Nations Educational, Scientific and Cultural Organization, and the World Health Organization. Maintains 24 committees. **Publications:** *Annual Report.* • *Directory*, quadrennial. Directory. • *Newsletter*, 1-2/year. Newsletter.

★9467★ International Vitamin A Consultative Group (IVACG)
c/o The Nutrition Foundation, Inc.
1126 16th St. NW
Washington, DC 20036
Phone: (202)659-9024
Fax: (202)659-3617
Laurie Lindsay Aomari, R.D., Program Mgr.

Founded: 1974. **Description:** Participants from 70 countries interested in international activities aimed at reducing the incidence of vitamin A deficiency in humans. Offers consultation and guidance to operating and donor agencies that are seeking to reduce vitamin A deficiencies. Prepares guidelines and recommendations for assessing the regional distribution and magnitude of vitamin A deficiency, developing intervention methods and strategies against the deficiency, evaluating the effectiveness of implemented programs, and conducting research needed to support the assessment of intervention. Maintains library; conducts task forces. **Publications:** *IUNS International Directory of Scientists and Administrators Involved in the Alleviation of Vitamin A Deficiency and Nutritional Blindness*, periodic. Directory. • *Xerophthalmia Bulletin*, 3/year. Bulletin. Also publishes monographs, guidelines, and books.

★9468★ Irish Nutrition and Dietetics Institute (INDI)
Terenure Enterprise Centre
Rathfarnham Rd.
Dublin 6W, Ireland
Phone: 1 4903237
Fax: 1 4903237
Kathryn Holly, Sec.

Founded: 1968. **Members:** 170. **Languages:** English. **Description:** Professional dieticians. Promotes growth in the number of dietary and nutrition-related positions in the Republic of Ireland. Represents the interests of members.

★9469★ Italian Association of Dietitians
Via Lucilio 29
I-00136 Rome, Italy
Phone: 6 3498033
Fax: 6 33250108
Mrs. Novella Dell'Orto, Pres.

Members: 700. **Languages:** Italian. **Description:** Professional dietitians. Promotes advancement in the study and application of dietetics; advises government agencies and the public regarding a healthy diet. Conducts research and educational programs.

★9470★ Kenya Food and Nutrition Action Network (KEFAN)
PO Box 47639
Wood Ave.
Nairobi, Kenya
Phone: 2 561766
Joyce B.K. Meme

Description: Fosters improved nutritional awareness in Kenya. Provides educational programs; disseminates information.

★9471★ Lean Line (LL)
151 New World Way
South Plainfield, NJ 07080
Phone: (908)757-7677
Free: 800-624-3108
Fax: (908)757-6622
Antonia Marotta, Pres.

Founded: 1968. **Description:** Promotes a weight-reducing program that utilizes nutritional, psychological, inspirational, and image-building techniques. Maintains speakers' bureau; conducts research and educational programs in the field. The program was developed and is supervised by Drs. Arnold Lazarus and Hans Fisher of Rutgers University. **Publications:** *Lean Line Newsletter*, periodic. Newsletter. • *One Month Lighter*.

★9472★ Luxembourg Dietetic Association (Association Nationales des Dieteticiens du Luxembourg)
Postbus 62
L-7201 Walferdange, Luxembourg

Members: 22. **Languages:** French, German. **Description:** Professional dietitians. Promotes advancement in the study and application of dietetics; advises government agencies and the public regarding a healthy diet. Conducts research and educational programs.

★9473★ National Alliance for Infusion Therapy (NAIT)
1001 Pennsylvania Ave. NW, Ste. 600 S
Washington, DC 20004-2582
Phone: (202)347-0066
Fax: (202)624-7222
Jana Sansbury, Contact

Founded: 1991. **Members:** 20. **Description:** National health care providers and manufacturers. Promotes the appropriate use of infusion therapies (parenteral or enteral administration of drugs or nutrients) at home or in other alternate-site settings. Seeks to raise awareness of infusion therapies through educational and research programs. Works to influence public policy and private payer advocacy of infusion therapy. Establishes and disseminates guidelines for quality patient care. **Publications:** *Infusion News*, bimonthly. Newsletter. *Price:* Free to members.

National Association of Nutrition and Aging Services Programs (NANASP)
See: Entry 1907

★9474★ Natural Food Associates (NFA)
PO Box 210
Atlanta, TX 75551
Phone: 800-594-2136
Bill Francis, Exec.Dir.

Founded: 1952. **Members:** 5,000. **State Groups:** 29. **Local Groups:** 100. **Description:** Professionals and consumers interested in organic farming, natural foods, and human health. Objectives are: to inform the public of the values of natural, chemical-free food grown in rich, fertile soil; to expose the dangers of chemical contamination of food, water, and land; to offer preventive measures to metabolic disease. Conducts demonstrations on garden preparation for growing fruits and vegetables organically; also conducts demonstrations on composting, proper pasture care and woodlands management, and meat production using organic methods. Operates a bookstore which offers books on organiculture, nutrition, and natural living. **Publications:** *Natural Food and Farming*, bimonthly. Magazine. • Reprints, periodic.

★9475★ Netherlands Dietetic Association (NVD) (Nederlandse Vereniging van Dietisten)
Postbus 341
NL-5340 AH Oss, Netherlands
Phone: 4120 24543
Fax: 4120 37736
Mrs. C. Jonkers, Pres.

Founded: 1941. **Members:** 2,300. **Description:** Strives to maintain high professional standards for dieticians working in the Netherlands. Represents members interests. Offers postgraduate training courses. **Publications:** Brochures. • *Dutch Journal for Dietitians*, periodic. Journal.

North American Society for Pediatric Gastroenterology and Nutrition (NASPGN)
See: Entry 3277

★9476★ Norwegian Dietetics Association (Norsk Forening for Ernaering og Dietetikk)
Postboks 9202
Vaterland
N-0134 Oslo, Norway
Phone: 2 173355

Members: 640. **Languages:** Norwegian. **Description:** Professional dietitians. Promotes advancement in the study and application of dietetics; advises government agencies and the public regarding a healthy diet. Conducts research and educational programs.

★9477★ Nutrition Education Association (INC.)
PO Box 20301
3647 Glen Haven
Houston, TX 77225
Phone: (713)665-2946
Ruth Yale Long, Ph.D., Pres.

Founded: 1977. **Description:** Health professionals and other interested individuals. Educates the public on the importance of good nutrition as a means of acquiring and maintaining good health, and encourages research in nutrition. Promotes communication among medical investigators, researchers, and practitioners concerned with nutrition. Offers 12-lesson home study course in the new nutrition, which emphasizes the importance of nutrition in the prevention and cure of disease. Sponsors new nutrition study groups. **Publications:** Books. • *Crackdown on Cancer with Good Nutrition*. Book. • *Home Study Course in the New Nutrition*. Book. • *Switchover! Cookbook*. Book.

★9478★ Nutrition Foundation of the Philippines (NFP)
107 E. Rodriguez, Sr. Blvd.
Quezon City, Metro Manila 1102, Philippines
Phone: 2 7121474
Fax: 2 7113980
Azucena B. Limbo, Dir.

Founded: 1959. **Members:** 350. **Languages:** English. **Description:** Nutritionists, educators, medical doctors, scientists, midwives, and food companies in the Philippines. Promotes public awareness and practice of sound nutritional principles. Conducts nutrition education campaigns primarily directed toward those most vulnerable to malnutrition. Trains individuals to participate in community nutrition programs and offers continuing educational opportunities for health care professionals. Provides technical assistance to public and private agencies working to improve nutrition in the Philippines, consulting services for program planning and implementation, and diet counseling programs. Undertakes nutrition research and aids institutions conducting studies in the field; offers reference service. Operates speakers' bureau and placement and children's services. **Publications:** *Bulletin of the NFP*, bimonthly. Newsletter. Current trends in foods, nutrition, and dietetics. • *Directory of Non-Governmental Organizations*. Directory. • *Low-Fat, Low-Cholesterol Cookbook*. Book.

★9479★ Nutrition for Optimal Health Association (NOHA)
PO Box 380
Winnetka, IL 60093
Phone: (708)786-5326
Donna Ichikawa, Pres.

Founded: 1972. **Members:** 500. **Description:** Physicians and others interested in making informed health decisions through better nutrition. Promotes good nutrition as a means of achieving and maintaining optimal health; advances and disseminates scientifically based information on the practical application of sound nutritional principles to daily living. Offers cooking classes and workshops; conducts nutrition education programs and seminars. Maintains speakers' bureau. **Publications:** *Audio and Video Tape List*, annual. Catalog. *Price:* $2. • *Audio and Video Tape List*, annual. Catalog. *Price:* $2. • *Enjoy Nutritious Variety*. • Membership Directory, annual. • *NOHA News: Is Good News*, quarterly. Newsletter. Includes association news and book reviews. *Price:* Included in membership dues; $8/year for nonmembers.

★9480★ Nutrition Society (NS)
10 Cambridge Ct.
210 Shepherds Bush Rd.
London W6 7NJ, England
Phone: 171 6020228
Fax: 171 6021756
Prof. A.J.F. Webster, Pres.

Founded: 1941. **Members:** 1,850. **Languages:** English. **Description:** Persons involved in nutrition research or in health maintenance organized to promote the scientific study of nutrition. Maintains special interest groups; disseminates information. **Publications:** *British Journal of Nutrition*, bimonthly. • *Gazette*, periodic. Magazine. • *Nutrition Research Reviews*. Report. •

Proceedings of the Nutrition Society, 3/year. Proceedings.

★9481★ **Oley Foundation for Home Parenteral and Enteral Nutrition**
Albany Medical Center
Hun Memorial, A-23
New Scotland Ave.
Albany, NY 12208
Phone: (518)262-5079
Free: 800-776-OLEY
Fax: (518)262-5528
Laura Ellis, Exec.Dir.

Founded: 1983. **Members:** 60. **Description:** Promotes optimal care for persons requiring infused nutrition at home. Seeks to enrich and enhance the lives of those requiring home nutrition support through an outreach system of patient volunteers. Conducts an annual research registry of patients in North America. **Publications:** Brochures. • *Lifeline Letter*, monthly. Newsletter. *Price:* Free to consumers and family; $35/year for others. • *North American Home Patient Annual Report*, annual. Annual Report.

Pakistan Voluntary Health and Nutrition Association (PVHNA)
See: Entry 10964

★9482★ **Portuguese Association of Dietitians**
(Associacao Portuguesa Dietistas)
Rua Carlos Mardel 5
P-1900 Lisbon, Portugal

Members: 111. **Languages:** Portuguese. **Description:** Professional dietitians. Promotes advancement in the study and application of dietetics; advises government agencies and the public regarding a healthy diet. Conducts research and educational programs.

★9483★ **Price-Pottenger Nutrition Foundation (PPNF)**
PO Box 2614
La Mesa, CA 91943
Phone: (619)574-7763
Fax: (619)574-1314
Mrs. Marion Patricia Connolly, Exec.Dir.

Founded: 1952. **Members:** 750. **Description:** Seeks to increase awareness of natural health, organic gardening, nutrition and ecology. Disseminates information to the medical and dental professions, as well as to the public, through publications, seminars, classes, study groups, and scientific exhibits. Stresses the benefits of chemically-untreated "whole" foods. Named in honor of Weston A. Price, DDS and Francis M. Pottenger, Jr., M.D., known for their work in nutrition research. **Publications:** *Membership Journal*, quarterly. Journal. *Price:* $25/yr; $50/yr for professional. **Formerly:** (1954) Santa Barbara Medical Research Foundation; (1965) Weston A. Price Memorial Foundation; (1973) Price-Pottenger Foundation.

★9484★ **Protein Foods and Nutrition Development Association of India (PFNDAI)**
Mahalaxmi Chambers
22 Bhulabhai Desai Rd.
Bombay 400 026, Maharashtra, India
Phone: 22 4928858
Fax: 22 4938998
Mr. H.S. Gurudas, Exec.Dir.

Founded: 1968. **Members:** 46. **Languages:** English. **Description:** Indian food industries. Collects, analyzes, and disseminates information on nutrition and food science and technology. Promotes balanced nutrition; identifies nutrient needs and food preferences through surveys; offers consultive services to national and international agencies for the development of low-cost nutritional supplements; offers project consultive services to the food industry. Assists government agencies in formulating food standards, regulations, and legislation; compiles statistics. Provides job placement assistance for food scientists. Conducts research; organizes seminars and workshops. Sponsors competitions; bestows awards. **Publications:** Papers. Contains research reports and proceedings. • *Pfndai Bulletin*, monthly. Bulletin. Contains news items connected with food science and nutrition. • Videos.

★9485★ **Research Organization on African Alimentation and Nutrition (ORAAN)**
(Organisme de Recherches sur l'Alimentation et la Nutrition Africaines — ORANA)
39, ave. Pasteur
BP 2089
Dakar, Senegal
Phone: 225892
Dr. A.M. Ndiaye, Dir.

Founded: 1956. **Members:** 20. **Languages:** English, French. **Description:** Conducts clinical and nutritional studies on food consumption in western Africa. Areas of interest include nutrition and infection, nutrition and crop cultivation, protein analysis, infant nutrition, nutritional anemias, and etiology of endemic goiters. **Publications:** *Catalogue des Publications*, quarterly. • *Diarrhee-Dialogue*, quarterly. • *ORT*, annual. • *Research Reports*, periodic. Also publishes *Titres et Travaux Scientifiques*. **Formerly:** Research Organization for Food and Nutrition in Africa.

★9486★ **Seventh-Day Adventist Dietetic Association (SDADA)**
Box 75
Loma Linda, CA 92354
Founded: 1956. **Members:** 475. **Regional Groups:** 10. **Description:** Seventh-Day Adventist registered dietitians; dietitians working in Seventh-Day Adventist institutions. Strives to motivate members to attain high professional standards and to actively promote Seventh-Day Adventist health principles. Provides resources and guidance concerning vegetarian lifestyles to dietitians. Disseminates nutrition information. **Publications:** *Diet Manual*. Vegetarian options. *Price:* $54.95. • *SDADA News*, quarterly. *Price:* Available to members only. • *Seventh-Day Adventist Dietetic Association Diet Manual*.

★9487★ **Society for Nutrition Education (SNE)**
2001 Killebrew Dr., Ste. 340
Minneapolis, MN 55425-1882
Phone: (612)854-0035
Fax: (612)854-7869
Darlene Lansing, Exec. Dir.

Founded: 1967. **Members:** 2,200. **Regional Groups:** 12. **Description:** Nutrition educators from the fields of dietetics, public health, home economics, medicine, industry, and education (elementary, secondary, college, university, and consumer affairs). Goal is to promote nutritional well-being for the public. **Publications:** *Journal of Nutrition Education*, bimonthly. Journal. For educators, practitioners, and researchers on nutrition education. Includes book reviews and employment opportunity listings. *Price:* Included in membership dues; $80/year for individuals; $120/year for institutions; $32/year for individuals in training. Also publishes journal supplements.

★9488★ **Spanish Dietetic Association (Asociacion Espanola de Dietistas/Nutricion)**
Calle Mallorca 273
E-08008 Barcelona, Spain
Members: 210. **Languages:** Spanish. **Description:** Professional dietitians. Promotes advancement in the study and application of dietetics; advises government agencies and the public regarding a healthy diet. Conducts research and educational programs.

★9489★ **Sup Sup Garden Club**
PO Box 324
Honiara, Solomon Islands
Phone: 21556
Founded: 1986. **Description:** Promotes improved nutrition through home gardening. Conducts workshops.

★9490★ **Survival Consciousness (CSC)**
Box 26762
Elkins Park, PA 19027-0762
Phone: (215)635-1022
Beatrice Wittels, Pres.

Founded: 1977. **Description:** An educational and scientific membership foundation dedicated to disseminating information about outer space and the possiblity of discovering a habitable planet in the event that Earth can no longer sustain life. **Publications:** *CSC Reports: Journal of Cooking for Survival Consciousness*, quarterly. Journal. Includes information on new members, book reviews, recipes, and member profiles. *Price:* Included in membership dues. • *Outer Space*. Video. **Formerly:** (1994) Cooking for Survival Consciousness.

★9491★ **Swedish Association of Dietitians (SAD)**
(Svensk Dietistforening — SD)
St. Eriksgatan 26
Box 12069
S-102 22 Stockholm, Sweden
Phone: 8 6520120
Fax: 8 6503493
Karin Hadell, Contact

Founded: 1921. **Members:** 1,800. **Local Groups:** 20. **Languages:** English. **Description:**

Professional dietitians. Promotes the study and practice of nutrition science in Sweden. **Publications:** *Dietisten*, 8/year. Journal.

★9492★ Swiss Dietetic Association (Schweizerischer Verband Diplomierter)
ErnahrungsbeaterInnen
Postfach 8241
CH-3001 Bern, Switzerland
Phone: 1 8810528
Members: 520. **Languages:** Greek. **Description:** Professional dietitians. Promotes advancement in the study and application of dietetics; advises government agencies and the public regarding a healthy diet. Conducts research and educational programs.

★9493★ Turkish Dietetic Association (Turkiye Diyetisyenler Dernegi)
Esat Cad. Hulya Sok 2/9
Kukesat
Ankara, Turkey
Members: 675. **Languages:** Turkish. **Description:** Professional dietitians. Promotes advancement in the study and application of dietetics; advises government agencies and the public regarding a healthy diet. Conducts research and educational programs.

★9494★ Vitamin E Research and Information Service (VERIS)
5325 S. 9th Ave.
La Grange, IL 60525-3602
Phone: (612)927-7104
Fax: (612)927-7104
Sharon Landvik, Exec. Officer
Description: Acts as an information clearinghouse on vitamin E for health care professionals, researchers, and nutrition and health communicators. **Publications:** *VERIS*, quarterly. Newsletter. Reports on current research. Also publishes research summaries.

Research Centers

★9495★ American Institute of Baking
1213 Bakers Way
Manhattan, KS 66502
Phone: (913)537-4750
Fax: (913)537-1493
Dr. William J. Hoover, Pres.
Research Activities and Fields: Nutrition, including effects of ingredients, processing, and baked products on physiological responses in animals and humans; and cereal science, particularly separation and functionality of wheat flour proteins subunits. Contract research projects include performance characteristics of new and improved ingredients for the baking industry and product and process development utilizing laboratory and pilot bakeries. **Publications:** Technical Bulletins (monthly).

Center for Endocrinology, Metabolism and Molecular Medicine
See: Entry 4882

★9496★ Center for Science in the Public Interest
1875 Connecticut Ave. NW, Ste. 300
Washington, DC 20009-5728
Phone: (202)332-9110
Fax: (202)265-4954
Dr. Michael F. Jacobson, Ph.D., Exec.Dir.
Research Activities and Fields: Food safety, diet, nutrition, food labeling, alcohol labeling, alcohol advertising, alcohol taxation, pesticides, agricultural reform, and children's nutrition. **Publications:** *Nutrition Action Health Letter* (ten times per year).

★9497★ Colorado State University Nutrition Institute
205 Gifford
Fort Collins, CO 80523
Phone: (303)491-6712
Fax: (303)491-7252
Peter J. Bechtel, Dir.
Research Activities and Fields: Nutrition, food consumption patterns, food compostion, product development, consumer food selection, and nutrition education.

Columbia University Center for Clinical Research—Pediatric Unit
See: Entry 3331

★9498★ Columbia University Institute of Human Nutrition
College of Physicians & Surgeons
HSC, 7th Fl.
701 W. 168th St.
New York, NY 10032
Phone: (212)305-6991
Fax: (212)305-6955
Richard J. Deckelbaum, M.D., Dir.
Research Activities and Fields: Atherosclerosis, lipoprotein-receptor-cell interaction; lipid emulsion metabolism; free fatty acids and cell lipid metabolism; basic retinoid and vitamin A physiology, biochemistry, and molecular biology; food and nutrition policy and law; intestinal ion transport mechanisms; enteric nervous system; human lipoprotein metabolism; lipolytic enzymes and endothelial cell biology; atherosclerosis; mineral metabolism and toxicology; carbohydrate and lipid metabolism, obesity, diabetes mellitus, food intake regulation; calcium metabolism; vascular cell biology; pathogenesis of thrombosis; regulation of intracellular cholesterol metabolism; endocytic pathways in macrophages; cholestryl ester transfer; protein structure/function and mutagenesis; regulation of gene expression; molecular nutrition; molecular mechanisms of carcinogenesis. **Formerly:** Institute of Nutrition Sciences (1970).

★9499★ Cooperative Core Laboratories and Clinical Nutrition Research Unit
Memorial Sloan-Kettering Cancer Center
Box 140
1275 York Ave.
New York, NY 10021
Phone: (212)639-8352
Fax: (212)639-5115
Dr. Richard S. Rivlin, Prin. Investigator
Research Activities and Fields: Promotes nutrition activities to 1) advance multidisciplinary

research, 2) upgrade teaching of nutrition for medical students, physicians, and other health professionals, and 3) improve the clinical care of patients at participating medical centers and in the general population.

★9500★ Cornell University Agricultural Experiment Station
245 Roberts Hall
Ithaca, NY 14853
Phone: (607)255-2554
Fax: (607)255-9499
Dr. W. Ronnie Coffman, Dir.
Research Activities and Fields: Agriculture, food, and human ecology, including agricultural economics, agricultural engineering, agronomy, animal and poultry science, biological sciences, plant pathology, horticulture, biochemistry, food sciences and human nutrition, entomology, natural resources, plant breeding, biometrics, rural sociology, communication, design and environmental analysis, human development and family studies, textiles and apparel, consumer economics, and public policy. **Publications:** *Cornell Focus*; Annual Report. **E-mail Address:** img5@cornell.edu.

★9501★ Cornell University Cornell International Institute for Food, Agriculture and Development
Ithaca, NY 14853-7801
Phone: (607)255-5453
Fax: (607)255-9984
Prof. Daniel Sisler, Contact
Research Activities and Fields: Rural proverty, malnutrition, population change, and environmental degradation in developing countries in Africa and Asia. Activities focus on agricultural technology and productivity, human nutritional needs, conservation of natural resources, and policy improvement and implementation. **Formerly:** International Institute for Food, Agriculture, and Development.

★9502★ Cornell University Program in International Nutrition
Ithaca, NY 14853
Phone: (607)255-8001
Fax: (607)255-7906
Dr. Jere D. Haas, Codir.
Research Activities and Fields: Nutritional and food problems of developing countries in Africa, Asia, Latin America, and the Caribbean. Programs concentrate on infant feeding practices, nutritional surveillance, relationship of high altitude and anemia, dietary methodologies and food consumption patterns and preferences, maternal and child nutrition, urinary schistosomiasis and its relation to child growth and anemia, nutrition and cancer in the People's Republic of China, ascaris infection and food intake, vitamin A deficiency, parasitic infections and nutrition, functional consequences of malnutrition in Guatemala, effects of macroeconomic adjustment policies on nutrition, and social/political factors that influence nutrition interventions and delivery of primary health care. **Publications:** *Cornell International Nutrition Monograph Series* (three per year). **E-mail Address:** jdh12@cornell.edu.

★9503★ **Fort Valley State College**
Agricultural Research Station
State College Dr.
PO Box 5744
Fort Valley, GA 31030-3298
Phone: (912)825-6344
Fax: (912)825-6376
Melvin Walker, Jr., Research Dir.

Research Activities and Fields: Agriculture, social science, psychology, chemistry, and human nutrition, involving six general programs covering areas of nutrition, chemical and biological nitrogen fixation, environmental protection, plant physiology, animal production, and rural development. **Publications:** *Research Bulletin* (annually). **Formerly:** Office of Research Coordinator.

★9504★ **International Life Sciences**
Institute Research Foundation
1126 16th St. NW
Washington, DC 20036
Phone: (202)659-0074
Fax: (202)659-3859
Dr. Alex Malaspina, Pres.

Research Activities and Fields: Comparative toxicology and nutrition, and nutritional effects on growth and development.

★9505★ **Iowa State University of Science**
and Technology
Center for Designing Foods to Improve
Nutrition
Dept. of Food Science and Human Nutrition
Human Nutritional Sciences Bldg.
Ames, IA 50011
Phone: (515)294-9363
Fax: (515)294-6193
Wayne R. Bidlack, Dir.

Research Activities and Fields: Food designing and nutrition, focusing on pork, soybean oils, modified starches, soy milk, vitamin A and B carotene, cholesterol reducers, sensory analysis, community nutrition, human nutrition, body composition, metabolic regulation, obesity, and the elderly.

★9506★ **Iowa State University of Science**
and Technology
Family and Consumer Sciences Research
Institute
126 MacKay Hall
Ames, IA 50011
Phone: (515)294-5982
Fax: (515)294-9449
Dr. Dianne C. Draper, Dir.

Research Activities and Fields: Home economics, including studies of child development, family relations, family economics, housing, consumer studies, management, food science and human nutrition, family and consumer science education, hotel, restaurant, and institution management, and textiles and clothing. **Publications:** *Research: Issues and Applications* (three per year). **E-mail Address:** dcdrapar@iastate.edu. **Formerly:** Home Economics Research Institute (1987).

★9507★ **King James Medical Laboratory /**
Omegatech
24700 Center Ridge Rd.
Westlake, OH 44145
Phone: (216)835-2150
Fax: (216)835-2177
Dr. Raymond J. Shamberger, Dir.

Research Activities and Fields: Nutrition and trace elements, including role of dietary thiamine, serum enzyme activities, synthesis and utilization of creatine, effect of zinc supplement, and sorption from the gut. **Formerly:** Preventive Medicine Research Center of Cleveland; formed by merger of King James Medical Laboratory and Omegatech in 1992.

★9508★ **Laval University**
Human Nutrition Research Group
Dept. of Human Nutrition
Quebec, PQ, Canada G1K 7P4
Phone: (418)656-3864
Fax: (418)656-5518
Helene Jacques, Dir.

Research Activities and Fields: Group assesses the impact of nutrient interactions on human health.

★9509★ **Laval University**
Joseph-Rheaume Laboratory
Pavillon Paul-Comtois
Quebec, PQ, Canada G1K 7P4
Phone: (418)656-2315
Fax: (418)656-5518
Laurent Savoie, Dir.

Research Activities and Fields: Nutrient bioavailability, the effect of food proteins on mineral bioavailability in vitro and in vivo, and kinetics and forms of amino acids at various levels of blood circulation.

★9510★ **Lincoln University**
Cooperative Research Program
Jefferson City, MO 65102-0029
Phone: (314)681-5174
Fax: (314)681-5546
Dr. Mary Wyatt, Dir.

Research Activities and Fields: Food and agricultural science studies, including human nutrition, animal physiology, crop science, natural resources, small-scale agriculture, rural economic development, and international agricultural development. **Publications:** Annual Report.

★9511★ **Medical College of Georgia**
Georgia Institute of Human Nutrition
Augusta, GA 30912
Phone: (706)721-4861
Fax: (706)721-4400
Terrence Kuske, M.D., Dir.

Research Activities and Fields: Investigates the role of nutrition in the etiology of diseases. The Institute encompasses regional programs in prevention and treatment of nutrition-related disorders in relation to the cardiovascular system, hypertension, neoplasia, mothers and infants, obesity and metabolism, alcoholism, and nutritional deficiencies.

★9512★ **Montana State University-**
Bozeman
Home Economics Research Program
Herrick Hall
Bozeman, MT 59717
Phone: (406)994-3244
Dr. Ellen Kreighbaum, Head

Research Activities and Fields: Foods and nutrition, textiles and clothing, family relations, child development, home economics education, marriage and family therapy, and nutrition and cancer.

★9513★ **National Center for Food and**
Agricultural Policy
1616 P St. NW
Washington, DC 20036
Phone: (202)328-5074
Fax: (202)939-3460
Dale E. Hathaway, Dir.

Research Activities and Fields: Examines interrelated public policy issues involving agriculture, food safety and health, natural resources, and the environment internationally.

★9514★ **National Institute of Nutrition**
265 Carling Ave., Ste. 302
Ottawa, ON, Canada K1S 2E1
Phone: (613)235-3355
Fax: (613)235-7032
Sheryl Conrad, Comm.Mgr.

Research Activities and Fields: Center focuses on nutrition, nutrition trends, dietary and fiber intake, and nutrition labeling. **Publications:** *Rapport* (quarterly); *NIN Review* (two per year).

★9515★ **New Mexico State University**
Agricultural Experiment Station
Box 30003, Dept. 3BF
Las Cruces, NM 88003
Phone: (505)646-3125
Fax: (505)646-5975
Dr. Gary Cunningham, Dir.

Research Activities and Fields: New Mexico and western U.S. agriculture, especially as it applies to livestock, crops, soils, and improvement of rural living. Conducts studies in agricultural economics, agricultural business, agronomy, animal, range, fish, and wildlife sciences, entomology, plant physiology, dairy science, home economics, food and nutrition, and horticulture. **Publications:** Bulletins; Project Reports; Annual Report. **E-mail Address:** garyc@nmsu.edu.

★9516★ **North Carolina State University**
North Carolina Agricultural Research
Service
Box 7643
Raleigh, NC 27695-7643
Phone: (919)515-2718
Fax: (919)515-7745
Johnny C. Wynne, Dir.

Research Activities and Fields: Biological sciences, agricultural economics, biological and agricultural engineering, animal science, crop science, home economics, horticulture, poultry science, rural sociology, soils, zoology, genetics, physiology, botany, entomology, food science, microbiology, veterinary science, nutrition, biochemistry, plant pathology, toxicology and statistics designed to aid in production and marketing of agricultural commodities and to broaden base of knowledge and understanding of plant and animal life and rural development. **Publications:** *Research Perspectives* (quarterly); *Tarheel Farm Economist* (monthly); *Tobacco Abstracts* (monthly). **E-mail Address:** jwynne@calsl.cals.ncsu.edu. **Formerly:** North Carolina Agricultural Experiment Station; absorbed former Center for Rural Resource Development.

★ 9517 ★ **North Dakota State University**
Food and Nutrition Research Laboratory
College of Human Development and
    Education
Fargo, ND 58105
Phone: (701)237-7474
Fax: (701)237-7174
Edna T. Holm, Dept.Chair

Research Activities and Fields: Food and nutrition research, including sensory evaluation of foods, sunflower seed products for human foods, food product development, dry edible beans, diabetes, fiber, and community intervention for dietary change. **Publications:** *North Dakota Farm Research* (bimonthly). **E-mail Address:** eholm@plains.nodak.edu.

★ 9518 ★ **Northeast Dairy Foods Research**
    Center
Cornell Univ.
Dept. of Food Sciences
Stocking Hall
Ithaca, NY 14853
Phone: (607)255-5482
Fax: (607)254-4868
Dr. David Barbano, Dir.

Research Activities and Fields: Dairy products, including studies on development, processing and engineering, quality and safety, dairy marketing and policy, chemistry and microbiology, nutritional attributes, and packaging technology. Develops standardized methods for analysis and testing of foods and ingredients. **Publications:** Annual Report.

★ 9519 ★ **Nutritional Effects Foundation**
c/o Winrock International
Rte. 3, Box 376
Morrilton, AR 72110
Phone: (501)727-5435
Fax: (501)727-5242

Research Activities and Fields: Goal is to provide healthier, leaner, and safer meat and other food products for consumers through research in meat and muscle biology, fatty acid, alterations related to animal feeding and forage, and human nutrition, including lipids and atherogenesis. Establishes standards and compliance systems for breeding, managing, and processing meat animals.

★ 9520 ★ **Ohio State University**
Human Nutrition Research Laboratory
1787 Neil Ave.
Columbus, OH 43210
Phone: (614)292-4485
Fax: (614)291-7536
Dr. Wayne A. Johnson, Dir.

Research Activities and Fields: The lipid, nitrogen, and energy status of humans. Performs selenium, zinc, calcium and vitamin studies.

Conducts research on dietary intake, nutrient needs, and natural antioxidants. Supports faculty, theses, and honors students' research.

★ 9521 ★ **Oregon Health Sciences**
    University
Institute for Nutrition and Cardiovascular
    Research
Division of Nephrology & Hypertension
3144 SW U.S. Veterans Hosp. Rd., PP 262
Portland, OR 97201
Phone: (503)494-8490
Fax: (503)494-5330
David A. McCarron, M.D., Co-head

Research Activities and Fields: Nutritional and metabolic factors that contribute to blood pressure regulation, particularly in the areas of calcium metabolism, cellular mechanisms, and the role of nutrition in cardiovascular physiology. **Formerly:** National Dairy Board Institute for Nutrition and Cardiovascular Research.

★ 9522 ★ **Oregon State University**
Department of Food Science and
    Technology
Corvallis, OR 97331-6602
Phone: (503)737-3131
Fax: (503)737-1877
Dr. Daniel F. Farkas, Head

Research Activities and Fields: Microbiology, enzymology, nutrition, and toxicology of food, food lipids, proteins and pigments, flavor chemistry and flavor evaluation, and food processing, food engineering, ultra high pressure preservation of foods, sensory studies, enology, and brewing.   **E-mail   Address:** farkasd@bcc.orst.edu.

★ 9523 ★ **Oregon State University**
Oregon Agricultural Experiment Station
Strand Hall 138
Corvallis, OR 97331-2201
Phone: (503)737-4251
Fax: (503)737-3178
Dr. Thayne R. Dutson, Dean and Dir.

Research Activities and Fields: Agriculture, forestry, animal science, fisheries, wildlife, and home economics. Conducts research designed to conserve and efficiently utilize Oregon's natural resources, including soil, water, fish, wildlife, forests, and ranges; to increase efficiency of agricultural, animal, and forest production; to improve processing, distribution, and marketing of plant and animal products; to test and develop new crops and new uses for old crops; and to advance human welfare through research on nutrition, food preparation, clothing, and textiles. **Publications:** *Oregon Agricultural Progress* (quarterly).

★ 9524 ★ **Rutgers University**
New Jersey Agricultural Experiment
    Station
Cook College
PO Box 231
New Brunswick, NJ 08903
Phone: (908)932-9447
Fax: (908)932-6769
Dr. Daryl B. Lund, Exec. Dean

Research Activities and Fields: Agricultural, biological, environmental, physical, and social

sciences, including studies in animal and plant sciences, soil science, biochemistry, biodiversity, microbiology, analytical chemistry, farm crops, food and nutrition, entomology, horticulture, agricultural engineering, aquaculture, natural resource and wildlife management, ecosystem policy, environmental science, agricultural and environmental economics, land use planning and management, community planning and development, advanced biotechnology, and advanced food technology. **E-mail Address:** dean@aesop.rutgers.edu.

★ 9525 ★ **St. Joseph's University**
Food Nutrition and Health Research
    Institute
Dept. of Food Marketing
5600 City Ave.
Philadelphia, PA 19131
Phone: (610)660-1607
Fax: (610)660-1604
Richard Kochersperger, Dir.

Research Activities and Fields: Conducts surveys on health and nutritional lifestyles. Seeks to develop products and marketing communications which encourage sound nutrition and promote good health.

★ 9526 ★ **Salt Institute**
700 N. Fairfax St., Ste. 600
Alexandria, VA 22314-2040
Phone: (703)549-4648
Fax: (703)548-2194
Richard L. Hanneman, Pres.

Research Activities and Fields: Engineering and chemical research, field studies, and laboratory investigations on all uses of salt, including winter road maintenance, road base construction, manufacturing and industry, water conditioning, human nutrition, and agricultural feeding. **Publications:** *Salt and Trace Minerals*; *Salt and Highway Deicing*; Newsletter. **Formerly:** Salt Producers' Association (1963).

★ 9527 ★ **Texas A&M University**
Center for Cellular and Molecular Nutrition
Alkek Institute of Biosciences and Technology
2121 W. Holcombe Blvd.
Houston, TX 77030-3303
Phone: (713)677-7522
Fax: (713)677-7512
Dr. Wallace L. McKeehan, Chair

Research Activities and Fields: Human and animal nutrition studies at the molecular and cellular levels, with emphasis on membrane biology, hormone/cytokine and receptor mechanisms, signal transduction, and gene regulation.

★ 9528 ★ **Texas A&M University**
Lipid Research Laboratory
Dept. of Biochemistry
College Station, TX 77843
Phone: (409)845-5616
Fax: (409)845-9274
Prof. Randall Wood, Dir.

Research Activities and Fields: Conducts basic and applied studies in nutrition, biochemistry, and analysis of fats, lipids, and related substances in plants, animals, and diseased tissue. Also conducts dietary fat studies on humans.

★9529★ **Texas A&M University**
Texas Agricultural Experiment Station
College Station, TX 77843-2147
Phone: (409)845-8484
Fax: (409)845-9938
Dr. Edward A. Hiler, V. Chancellor, Dir.

Research Activities and Fields: Animal and crop sciences, biochemistry, biotechnology, food technology, entomology, engineering, economics, nutrition and natural resources, sociology, and veterinary medicine. Also charged with administration and enforcement of feed, fertilizer, and foulbrood regulatory laws. **Publications:** Annual Report. **E-mail Address:** d__liccioni@tamu.edu.

★9530★ **Tuskegee University**
George Washington Carver Agricultural
   Experiment Station
Cambell Bldg. Rm. 100
School of Agric. and Home Econ.
Tuskegee, AL 36088
Phone: (205)727-8157
Fax: (205)727-8493
Dr. Walter A. Hill, Dean and Research Dir.

Research Activities and Fields: Animal science, including genetics, biotechnology, nutrition, animal health, livestock management, and reproductive physiology; human and community resource development; food science and human nutrition; water quality; waste management; and plant and soil science, including breeding and genetics, biotechnology, nitrogen fixation, physiology, nutrition, crop protection, crop production, carbon dioxide cycling, and plant pathology. Research activities emphasize nutrition and health, water quality, sweet potato, vegetables, small fruits, poultry, small farm research, and rural youth and community development. **Publications:** Annual Report; Newsletter; Journal. **Formerly:** Agricultural Experiment Station (1983).

★9531★ **U.S. Department of Agriculture**
Agricultural Research Service
Beltsville Human Nutrition Research Center
BARC—East
Bldg. 308, Rm. 223
Beltsville, MD 20705
Phone: (301)504-8157
Fax: (301)504-9381
Dr. Joseph Spencis, Director

Research Activities and Fields: Center is concerned with determining human requirements for energy, protein, carbohydrates, lipids, vitamins, and minerals; and with understanding the many interactions of these individual nutrients and their consequences for health. Activities include investigating the nutritional qualities of foods, including composition, biological interactions, and the availability of macronutrients and micronutrients. Center comprises the Family Economics Research Group and five laboratories: Carbohydrate Nutrition, Diet and Human Performance, Lipid Nutrition, Food Composition, and Vitamin and Mineral Nutrition.

★9532★ **U.S. Department of Agriculture**
Agricultural Research Service
Beltsville Human Nutrition Research Center
Carbohydrate Nutrition Laboratory
BARC—East
Bldg. 307, Rm. 315
Beltsville, MD 20705
Phone: (301)504-8396
Dr. O. Michaelis, Research Leader

Research Activities and Fields: Primary mission is to study the effect of dietary carbohydrates on metabolic risk factors associated with such diseases as heart disease and diabetes. Emphasis is on metabolic processes and the interactions between carbohydrates and other components of the diet. Population groups with different genetic predispositions are also studied to identify those individuals at particular risk.

★9533★ **U.S. Department of Agriculture**
Agricultural Research Service
Beltsville Human Nutrition Research Center
Diet and Human Performance
BARC—East
Bldg. 308, Rm. 214A
Beltsville, MD 20705
Phone: (301)504-8159
Fax: (301)504-9098
Joseph T. Judd, Research Leader

Research Activities and Fields: Determines human energy requirements as influenced by dietary factors and energy expenditures, and examines metabolic responses to protein and minerals in the diet and their interaction.

★9534★ **U.S. Department of Agriculture**
Agricultural Research Service
Beltsville Human Nutrition Research Center
Food Composition Laboratory
BARC—East
Bldg. 161, Rm. 102
Beltsville, MD 20705
Phone: (301)504-8356
Fax: (301)504-8314
G.R. Beecher, Research Leader

Research Activities and Fields: Laboratory develops new analytical methods and assay techniques for the analysis of components in foods associated with improved health. Emphasis is on sampling techniques to ensure that representative samples are selected from the U.S. food supply for testing. Food composition data are provided to the Department of Agriculture's Human Nutrition Information Service and other groups.

★9535★ **U.S. Department of Agriculture**
Agricultural Research Service
Beltsville Human Nutrition Research Center
Lipid Nutrition Laboratory
BARC—East
Bldg. 308, Rm. 126
Beltsville, MD 20705
Phone: (301)504-9014
Joseph Joseph T. Judd, Research Leader

Research Activities and Fields: Activities involve the use of human volunteers and experimental animal models to study the effects of dietary lipid and cholesterol on physiological parameters related to good health. Research focuses on the essential fatty acids and the bioavailability of vitamins involved in lipid metabolism.

★9536★ **U.S. Department of Agriculture**
Agricultural Research Service
Children's Nutrition Research Center
1100 Bates St.
Houston, TX 77030-2600
Phone: (713)798-7022
Fax: (713)798-7098
Dennis M. Bier, M.D., Director

Research Activities and Fields: Center conducts research to develop a scientific basis for standards of nutrient intake and assessments of nutritional status. Research activities are concerned with: 1) nutrient requirements in infants, children, and pregnant and lactating women; 2) relationships between nutrition and physical and mental development; and 3) the role of diet for optimum growth and development.

★9537★ **U.S. Department of Agriculture**
Agricultural Research Service
Grand Forks Human Nutrition Research
   Center
2420 Second Ave., North
PO Box 7166, University Station
Grand Forks, ND 58202
Phone: (701)795-8353
Fax: (701)795-8395
Dr. Forrest H. Nielsen, Director

Research Activities and Fields: Mineral elements in nutrition--the ways in which these elements sustain life, promote growth, and contribute to the health and well-being of humans. Research is performed on animal models, cell cultures, and human volunteers. Principal fields of study (as related to human requirements for trace elements) include absorption and bioavailability; bone and cardiovascular development, maintenance, and function; behavior and neuropsychological changes; body composition; energy expenditure; biochemical function; hormone regulation; and status assessment.

★9538★ **U.S. Department of Agriculture**
Agricultural Research Service
Human Nutrition Research Center on Aging
Tufts University
711 Washington St.
Boston, MA 02111
Phone: (617)556-3000
Fax: (617)556-3344
Jeffrey Blumberg, Ph.D., Dir.

Research Activities and Fields: Explores the relationship between nutrition and good health and determines nutritional and dietary requirements of the maturing and elderly population. Conducts cell and molecular biology, animal model, and human metabolic and field studies to better understand the processes of nutrient utilization and metabolism, to determine ways that diet in combination with genetic and environmental factors may promote health and vigor over the lifespan.

★9539★ **U.S. Department of Agriculture**
Agricultural Research Service
National Center for Agricultural Utilization
   Research
Food Quality and Safety Research Unit

1815 N. University St.
Peoria, IL 61604
Phone: (309)681-6555
Fax: (309)681-6686
Timothy L. Mounts, Research Leader

Research Activities and Fields: Research is directed toward providing an understanding of the basic processes that lead to deterioration of soybean and other vegetable oil quality and functionality during use as a major human food. Investigations concentrate on supercritical fluid investigations of vegetable oil processing and extraction technology and analysis, and pre-harvest and post-harvest events (genetic engineering, field damage, handling, transportation, and storage) which impact on such oil quality factors as processability, oxidative stability, flavor stability, and stability during cooking. Human metabolic studies are conducted to clarify the role of soybean and other oils in human nutrition and disease.

★9540★ U.S. Department of Agriculture Agricultural Research Service Western Human Nutrition Research Center
PO Box 29997
The Presidio
San Francisco, CA 94129
Phone: (415)556-9697
Fax: (415)556-1432
Dr. Judith R. Turnlund, Acting Dir.

Research Activities and Fields: Center's mission is to conduct research on human nutritional requirements, involving nutritional status, surveillance, intervention, and monitoring. Center serves to assist in establishing nutritional status and effectiveness of nutrition/food programs, such as nutritional requirements, nutritional status and evaluation methodology, intake methodology, coordination of survey nutrition status methodologies, and methodologies to assess the impact of nutritional intervention programs and field operations in nutrition status monitoring. Research activities are concerned with: 1) identifying the factors, forces, and trends resulting in malnutrition; 2) developing reliable, efficient, and inexpensive methods for defining nutritional status; 3) planning and conducting research on human nutritional requirements; and 4) developing nutritional criteria for design and evaluation of intervention programs. Activities are carried out in these units: Biochemistry Research, Bioenergetics Research, and Micronutrient Research.

★9541★ U.S. Department of Agriculture Agricultural Research Service Western Human Nutrition Research Center Biochemistry Research Unit
PO Box 29997
The Presidio
San Francisco, CA 94129
Phone: (415)556-0899
Fax: (415)556-1432
Dr. Gary Nelson, Acting Research Leader

Research Activities and Fields: Mission of the Unit is: to perform research that defines optimal human nutrient requirements for promoting and maintaining health, and to develop biochemical methods for assessing human nutritional status on a population basis. Within these two objectives, Unit focuses on the effect of diet on plas-

ma lipoproteins, blood pressure, and blood coagulation as functional measures of nutritional status.

★9542★ U.S. Department of Agriculture Agricultural Research Service Western Human Nutrition Research Center Bioenergetics Research Unit
PO Box 29997
The Presidio
San Francisco, CA 94129
Phone: (415)556-4381
Fax: (415)556-1432
Dr. Darshan Kelley n, Research Leader

Research Activities and Fields: Goal of Unit is to develop improved methods for measuring body composition and energy expenditure in order to: 1) apply these methods to evaluation of the nutritional status of target populations and research volunteers; and 2) conduct studies on the interactions among nutritional status, body composition, and performance parameters; and 3) conduct research to improve methodology to assess dietary intake of foods.

★9543★ U.S. Department of Agriculture Agricultural Research Service Western Human Nutrition Research Center Micronutrients Research Unit
PO Box 29997
The Presidio
San Francisco, CA 94129
Phone: (415)556-5662
Fax: (415)556-1432
Dr. Robert A. Jacob, Research Leader

Research Activities and Fields: Research projects include: 1) developing new or improving existing methods for the analysis of vitamins and minerals and measurement of human nutritional status; 2) evaluating effects of vitamins and minerals on behavior and the nervous system, and correlating those effects with biochemical and physiological changes; and 3) determining dietary requirements for those micronutrients and to describe factors affecting those requirements.

U.S. Department of Defense Army Medical Research and Development Command Occupational Health and Performance Directorate Military Nutrition Division
See: Entry 7827

U.S. Department of Health and Human Services Food and Drug Administration Center for Food Safety and Applied Nutrition
See: Entry 10996

U.S. Department of Health and Human Services National Eye Institute Office of International Program Activities
See: Entry 13644

U.S. Department of Health and Human Services National Institute of Child Health and Human Development Center for Research for Mothers and Children Endocrinology, Nutrition, and Growth Branch
See: Entry 4903

U.S. Department of Health and Human Services National Institute of Diabetes and Digestive and Kidney Diseases Division of Digestive Diseases and Nutrition
See: Entry 5238

★9544★ U.S. Department of Health and Human Services National Institute of Diabetes and Digestive and Kidney Diseases Division of Digestive Diseases and Nutrition Nutrient Metabolism Program
5333 Westbard Ave., Rm. 3A18A
Bethesda, MD 20892
Phone: (301)496-7823
Fax: (301)402-1278
Dr. Ken May, Program Director

Research Activities and Fields: Program supports basic and clinical studies related to the requirement, bioavailability, and metabolism of nutrients and other dietary components at the organ, cellular, and subcellular levels in normal and diseased states. Specific areas of research interest include: the physiological function and mechanism of action/interaction of nutrients within the body; the effects of environment, heredity, stress, drug use, toxicants, and physical activity on problems of nutrient imbalance and nutrient requirements in health and disease; and specific metabolic considerations relating to alternative forms of nutrient delivery and use, such as total parenteral nutrition. Program also supports research to improve methods of assessing nutritional status in health and disease.

U.S. Department of Health and Human Services National Institute of Diabetes and Digestive and Kidney Diseases Division of Intramural Research Molecular, Cellular, and Nutritional Endocrinology Branch
See: Entry 4923

★9545★ U.S. Department of Health and Human Services National Institute of Diabetes and Digestive and Kidney Diseases U.S.-Japan Malnutrition Panel
5333 Westbard Ave., Rm. 3A18B
Bethesda, MD 20892
Phone: (301)594-7573
Fax: (301)594-7504
Dr. Van S. Hubbard, Program Director

Research Activities and Fields: Panel's mission is to foster and support investigator-initiated research to help alleviate the serious problem of malnutrition. The increasing westernization of the Japanese diet and the increasing affluence among the Japanese people may play a role in the changes seen in nutritional status and incidence of nutritionally related diseases in that country. Thus, current topics of importance to both the U.S. and Japan focus on consequences of changing dietary patterns on health, development of disease, and disease prevention. Specific research areas addressing these topics include the nutritional significance of varying the polyunsaturated fatty acids in the diet, nutritional aspects of bone disease, endogenous mediators of nutritional metabolism, and improved methodologies applicable to nutritional assessment.

★9546★ **University of Alabama at Birmingham**
Department of Nutrition Sciences
Univ. Sta.
Birmingham, AL 35294
Phone: (205)934-6103
Fax: (205)934-7049
Dr. Roland Weinsier, Chm.

Research Activities and Fields: Human nutrition, including studies on folic acid and vitamin B-12 metabolism, iron metabolism and iron storage diseases, nutrition and cancer, intestinal absorption, purine, pteridine, riboflavin biosynthesis, and parenteral nutrition. **Formerly:** Outgrowth of research activities of Nutrition Division established in 1966 and from 1972 through 1977 known as Nutrition Program.

★9547★ **University of Arizona**
Arizona Agricultural Experiment Station
Tucson, AZ 85721
Phone: (520)621-3859
Fax: (520)621-7196
Dr. Colin Kaltenbach, Codir.

Research Activities and Fields: Plant and animal sciences, arid lands agriculture, plant and animal diseases and pests, soils, water utilization, agricultural biotechnology, agricultural engineering, human nutrition, food science, family and consumer science, agricultural economics, agricultural education, remote sensing, environmental studies, watershed management, range management, recreation resources, landscape design, wildlife ecology, and fisheries science. Special emphasis placed on research toward increasing quantity and effective use of water; new crops for semiarid areas; improving ability of plants, animals, and people to withstand hot, semiarid conditions; improving quality and marketing of agricultural products; and reducing arduous labor involved in agricultural production. **Publications:** *Arizona Land and People*; *Arid Lands Newsletter*; *Arizona Water Resources Newsletter* (all quarterly). **E-mail Address:** kltnbch@ag.arizona.edu.

★9548★ **University of California**
Cooperative Extension
21150 Box Springs Rd.
Moreno Valley, CA 92557-8708
Phone: (909)683-6491
Fax: (909)788-2615
Eunice T. Williamson, County Dir.

Research Activities and Fields: Agriculture and home economics, food safety, food preservation, consumer economics, and human nutrition. Provides assistance in the development

and dissemination of information about the public's supply of food and fiber and seeks to educate the public on the wide use of natural resources. **Publications:** Bimonthly newsletters are issued on the subjects of home economics, poultry, vegetable crops, and table and wine grapes. **E-mail Address:** ceriverside@ucdavis.edu. **Formerly:** Agricultural Extension (1975).

★9549★ **University of California, Davis**
Agricultural Experiment Station
234 Mrak Hall
Davis, CA 95616
Phone: (916)752-1605
Fax: (916)752-9049
Dr. Barbara O. Schneeman, Dean

Research Activities and Fields: Sustainable agricultural systems, environmental and resource sciences, and human health and wellbeing and related fields of plant and animal sciences, pest and disease management, applied ecology, resource conservation, human development, nutrition, and fiber and consumer sciences. **E-mail Address:** deancaes@agdean.ucdavis.edu.

★9550★ **University of California, Davis**
Clinical Nutrition Research Unit
Division of Clinical Nutrition
School of Medicine, TB-156
Davis, CA 95616
Phone: (916)752-6778
Fax: (916)752-3470
Charles Halsted, M.D., Dir.

Research Activities and Fields: Human nutrition in health and disease. Studies focus on the relationship of diet to disease, energy metabolism, and development.

University of California, Davis
Gastroenterology and Nutrition Center
See: Entry 5247

★9551★ **University of Chicago**
Clinical Nutrition Research Unit
5841 S. Maryland Ave., Box MC4080
Chicago, IL 60637
Phone: (312)702-6741
Fax: (312)702-2182
Michael D. Sitrin, M.D., Dir.

Research Activities and Fields: Human and clinical nutritional biology, particularly in relation to pregnancy, growth retardation, digestive and cardiovascular diseases, diabetes, and cancer. Conducts vitamin metabolism, lipoprotein, lipid, stable isotope, trace metal, and radioimmunoassay analyses.

University of Chicago
Liver Study Unit
See: Entry 5251

University of Colorado
B.F. Stolinsky Research Laboratories
See: Entry 4325

★9552★ **University of Florida**
Center for Nutritional Sciences
201 Food Science & Human Nutrition Bldg.
Gainesville, FL 32611
Phone: (904)392-2133
Fax: (904)392-1008
Dr. Robert J. Cousins, Dir.

Research Activities and Fields: Nutritional sciences, including bioavailability of vitamins and minerals, bioinstrumentation in nutrition research, dietary regulation of gene expression, neonatal and developmental nutrition, trace elements and defense mechanisms, mechanisms of nutrient absorption, neuroendocrine control of food intake, hormonal control of nutrient metabolism, metabolic studies with stable isotopes, animal models for total parenteral nutrition, nutritional status assessment in man and domestic animals, and nutritional anthropology.

★9553★ **University of Georgia**
Center for Food Safety & Quality Enhancement
Georgia Experiment Station
1109 Experiment St.
Griffin, GA 30223
Phone: (404)228-7284
Fax: (404)229-3216
Dr. Michael P. Doyle, Head

Research Activities and Fields: Food safety, food quality enhancement, and storage stability of food products, focusing on improving methods for eliminating, controlling, or detecting pathogenic microorganisms or their toxins and modifying chemical and physical properties of foods to meet consumer expectations. **Publications:** *At a Glance* (newsletter). **E-mail Address:** mdoyle@gaes.griffin.peachnet.edu.

★9554★ **University of Idaho**
Idaho Agricultural Experiment Station
Agricultural Science Bldg.
Moscow, ID 83843
Phone: (208)885-7173
Fax: (208)885-6654
Dr. Gary A. Lee, Dir.

Research Activities and Fields: Plant and animal production, plant and animal biotechnology, pest management, marketing, agricultural economics, agricultural engineering, utilization of farm products, farm equipment, food quality and safety, and nutrition. Projects conducted at the University by eight departments and throughout the state at seven research and extension centers. Offers special programs related to rural development and provides soil, crop, seed, pesticide and food testing services. Also supports work in statistics, nematology, climatology, analytical and animal health laboratories. Basic and applied research laboratories on the campus are supplemented by farms where livestock and field crop research is conducted. **Publications:** Bulletins; Progress Reports; Abstracts; Proceedings.

★9555★ **University of Illinois at Urbana-Champaign**
International Soybean Program (INTSOY)
169 Environmental and Agriculture Sciences Bldg.
1101 W. Peabody Dr.
Urbana, IL 61801
Phone: (217)333-6422
Fax: (217)333-5838
Dr. Wilmot Wijeratne, Contact

Research Activities and Fields: Seeks to improve human nutrition around the world through increased use of soybeans and other food legumes. Conducts applied research on the processing and utilization of soybeans (and other food legumes) into foods and animal feed. **Publications:** Research Series; *INTSOY Newsletter* (semiannual). **E-mail Address:** intsoy@vivc.edu.

★9556★ **University of Kentucky**
Cell Nutrition Group
Dept. of Nutrition and Food Science
219 Funkhouser Building
Lexington, KY 40506-0054
Phone: (606)257-6880
Fax: (606)257-3707
Dr. Bernhard Hennig, Contact

Research Activities and Fields: Tissue culture model systems in the study of nutrition and atherosclerosis with emphasis on the role of nutrients on biochemical mechanisms of vascular endothelial cell function, injury, and protection.

★9557★ **University of Maryland**
Nutrition Laboratory
Dept. of Human Ecology
Henson Center, Rm. 2101
Princess Anne, MD 21853
Phone: (410)651-6207
Dr. Shirley Hymon-Parker, Act.Chair

Research Activities and Fields: Nutrition and metabolism.

★9558★ **University of Missouri—Columbia**
Missouri Agricultural Experiment Station
2-44 Agriculture Bldg.
Columbia, MO 65211
Phone: (314)882-7488
Fax: (314)882-0388
Roger Mitchell, Dir.

Research Activities and Fields: Agricultural sciences, home economics, environmental science, pest management, veterinary medicine, forestry, agricultural economics, and rural sociology, including studies in biochemistry of plants and animals, fisheries and wildlife, environmental stress, marketing and consumers, rural health, safety, diffusion of information, soils, water pollution and toxicity by natural causes, meteorology and climatology, human nutrition, textiles, and family living. **Publications:** Research Bulletins; Special Reports; Circulars. **E-mail Address:** agroger@muccmail.missouri.edu.

★9559★ **University of Nevada, Reno**
Nevada Agricultural Experiment Station-221
Reno, NV 89557-0107
Phone: (702)784-6237
Fax: (702)784-6604
Dr. Bernard M. Jones, Dir.

Research Activities and Fields: Biochemistry, agricultural economics, environmental and resource sciences, human development, family studies, nutrition, and veterinary medicine. **Publications:** Reports.

★9560★ **University of Nevada, Reno**
Nutritional Education & Research Program
School of Medicine
Redfield Bldg., No. 153
Reno, NV 89557
Phone: (702)784-4474
Fax: (702)784-4468
Dr. Sachiko T. St. Jeor, Dir.

Research Activities and Fields: Clinical nutrition. **E-mail Address:** sach@unr.edu.

★9561★ **University of New Hampshire**
New Hampshire Agricultural Experiment Station
Durham, NH 03824
Phone: (603)862-1450
Fax: (603)862-1585
William T. Mautz, Interim Dir.

Research Activities and Fields: Agriculture, forestry, wildlife, biochemistry, botany, microbiology, zoology, and entomology, including plant and animal pathology, animal and human nutrition, poultry genetics, plant breeding, marine biology, soils, hydrology, resource economics, and marketing. **Publications:** Research Reports; Bulletins.

★9562★ **University of North Carolina**
Institute of Nutrition
Franklin Center, CB 7410
1829 E. Franklin St., Bldg 900 D
Chapel Hill, NC 27599-7410
Phone: (919)966-1094
Fax: (919)966-6762
Dr. John Longenecker, Dir.

Research Activities and Fields: Nutrition-related projects and nutrition/health assessment, including studies on nitrates and nitrites, lactose intolerance, and caffeine. **Publications:** *Institute of Nutrition News* (monthly); *Currents in Food, Nutrition and Health* (quarterly); Project Reports; Catalogue of Nutrition Research and Instruction, University of North Carolina.

★9563★ **University of Rhode Island**
Food Science and Nutrition Research Center
530 Liberty Ln.
West Kingston, RI 02892
Phone: (401)792-2466
Fax: (401)792-4017
R.W. Traxler, Chm.

Research Activities and Fields: Food science studies, including international nutrition and vitamin studies and yeast technology.

★9564★ **University of Texas—Houston**
Health Science Center
Human Nutrition Center
PO Box 20186
Houston, TX 77225
Phone: (713)792-4660
Fax: (713)792-5332
Dr. Milton Z. Nichaman, Dir.

Research Activities and Fields: Information resource center on community, national, and international health issues for individuals and institutions interested in food and nutrition and their effect on health. Research in nutritional epidemiology focusing on cardiovascular disease, cancer, and other chronic diseases.

★9565★ **University of Texas**
Southwestern Medical Center at Dallas
Center for Human Nutrition
5323 Harry Hines Blvd.
Dallas, TX 75235-9052
Phone: (214)648-3111
Fax: (214)648-4837
Dr. Scott M. Grundy, Dir.

Research Activities and Fields: Human nutrition. Investigates the preventive effects of vitamins C and E on atherosclerosis.

★9566★ **University of Washington**
Clinical Nutrition Research Unit
Dept. of Medicine
Division of Metabolism, RG-26
Seattle, WA 98195
Phone: (206)543-6166
Fax: (206)685-3781
Prof. Alan Chait, M.D., Prin. Investigator

Research Activities and Fields: Human nutrition in health and disease, including nutritional health maintenance, improved nutritional support of the acutely and chronically ill, assessment of nutritional status, effects of diseased states on nutritional needs, and effects of nutrition on disease states. Conducts research with human subjects and populations. Also basic and animal research.

★9567★ **University of Washington**
Nutrition Research Laboratory
305 Raitt Hall, DL-10
Seattle, WA 98195
Phone: (206)543-1730
Fax: (206)685-1696
Dr. Elaine R. Monsen, Dir.

Research Activities and Fields: Human nutrition and clinical nutrition. Conducts studies through its Clinical Research Unit and Clinical Nutrition Research Unit. **E-mail Address:** ermonsen@u.washington.edu.

★9568★ **University of Wisconsin—Madison**
Clinical Nutrition Center
430 Nutrition Science Bldg.
Madison, WI 53706
Phone: (608)262-1286
Fax: (608)262-5860
Dr. Richard Atkinson, Head

Research Activities and Fields: Clinical nutrition and obesity. **E-mail Address:** rla@admin.medicine.wisc.edu.

★9569★ University of Wisconsin—
    Madison
Food Research Institute
Dept. of Food Microbiology & Toxicology
1925 Willow Dr.
Madison, WI 53706
Phone: (608)263-7777
Fax: (608)263-1114
Michael W. Pariza, Dir.

Research Activities and Fields: Food microbiology and toxicology, with emphasis on practical problems of food producers and distributors, including studies on foodborne diseases; food safety, preservation, processing, handling, spoilage, quality, and allergens; mycotoxins; heat induced mutagens in food; and anticarcinogens in food. **Publications:** *Food Safety* (an annually annotated bibliography of the literature); FRI Annual Report (issued to supporting agencies); Newsletter (quarterly).

★9570★ University of Wisconsin—
    Madison
Wisconsin Agricultural Experiment Station
140 Agricultural Hall
Madison, WI 53706
Phone: (608)262-4930
Fax: (608)262-4556
Dr. Roger E. Wyse, Dir.

Research Activities and Fields: Food production, processing, and marketing and rural development, including land use, preservation and proper use of natural resources, and environmental concerns. Other projects focus on human nutrition, agronomy, bacteriology, biochemistry, dairy science, agricultural economics, agricultural engineering, agricultural journalism, continuing and vocational education, entomology, food science, food microbiology and toxicology, forestry, genetics, horticulture, landscape architecture, meat and animal science, nutritional science, plant pathology, poultry science, rural sociology, soils, veterinary science, and wildlife ecology.

★9571★ University of Wyoming
Wyoming Agricultural Experiment Station
Box 3354
Laramie, WY 82071
Phone: (307)766-3667
Fax: (307)766-3379
Dr. James J. Jacob, Assoc. Dir.

Research Activities and Fields: Agriculture, including agricultural engineering, agricultural economics, animal and plant science, veterinary science, home economics, human nutrition, microbiology, and molecular biology. **Publications:** Bulletins; Circulars. **E-mail Address:** jab@uwyo.edu.

★9572★ Utah State University
Utah Agricultural Experiment Station
Logan, UT 84322-4810
Phone: (801)750-2206
Fax: (801)750-3321
Dr. H. Paul Rasmussen, Dir.

Research Activities and Fields: Agricultural economics, agricultural engineering, agronomy, animal and plant sciences, bacteriology and public health, biotechnology, dairy sciences, forestry and horticulture, home economics, human nutrition, food science, irrigation and drainage, range management, rural sociology, soil science, veterinary science, ornamental horticulture, and alternative land use. **Publications:** Bulletins; Circulars; Utah Science (quarterly).

★9573★ Vanderbilt University
Clinical Nutrition Research Unit
S4322 Medical Center N.
21st and Garland Ave.
Nashville, TN 37232-2195
Phone: (615)322-7449
Fax: (615)343-8915
Dr. Fayez Ghishan, Dir.

Research Activities and Fields: Mechanisms of body weight and regulation, focusing on exercise and energy expenditure. Metabolism of amino acids, carbohydrates, lipids, minerals, and trace metals. Research also includes molecular nutrition.

★9574★ Vanderbilt University
Nutrition Center
D-4100, Medical Center N.
Nashville, TN 37232
Phone: (615)322-7363
Fax: (615)343-8915
Fayez K. Ghishan, M.D., Dir.

Research Activities and Fields: Facilities of the Nutrition Center are available to faculty of the Medical Center and investigators in clinical and basic science departments within the University for research which incorporates a nutrition component or relates to the nutritional state of research subjects. Research activities focus on four primary areas: metabolism of amino acids, and lipids, cell and molecular biology of epithelial function, nutrient needs during parenteral feeding, nutrition in disease and trauma, and energy expenditure.

★9575★ Virginia Polytechnic Institute and
    State University
Virginia Agricultural Experiment Station
Blacksburg, VA 24061-0402
Phone: (703)961-6336
Fax: (703)231-4163
R.Q. Cannell, Dir.

Research Activities and Fields: Agricultural and applied economics, biological systems crop and soil environmental sciences, engineering, horticulture, plant pathology, physiology and weed science, animal science, poultry science, dairy science, entomology, fisheries and wildlife, forestry, wood science and forest products, biochemistry, genetics, statistics, botany, zoology, veterinary medicine, horse nutrition, food science, anaerobic microbiology, water resources, and farm management. Conducts studies on agricultural production, sustainable agriculture, forestry, fisheries, aquaculture, seafood processing, biotechnology, artificial intelligence, computer-aided decision making, off-farm agricultural service, safety, integrated pest management, supply processing and marketing, housing, interior design, home management, human nutrition and foods, clothing and textiles, gerontology, and family and child development. **Publications:** Information Series; *Virginia Agricultural Experiment Station Bulletin*. **E-mail Address:** cannell@mail.vt.edu.

Chapter 45
Obstetrics & Gynecology

Foundations & Other Funding Organizations

Other Funding Organizations

★9576★ **American College of Obstetricians and Gynecologists**
409 12th St. SW
Washington, DC 20024
Phone: (202)638-5577
Warren H. Pearse, M.D., Exec. Dir.

Description: Awards Mead Johnson Fellowships to junior investigators for clinical research in obstetrics-gynecology, and Ortho Academic Training Fellowships to residents in obstetrics and gynecology.

★9577★ **Maternity Center Association**
48 E. 92nd St.
New York, NY 10128
Phone: (212)369-7300
Fax: (212)369-8747
Ruth W. Lubic, Gen. Dir.

Description: Sponsors research and administers a nurse-midwifery student assistance fund.

Medical & Allied Health Schools

Nurse-Midwifery

The following are certificate and graduate nurse-midwifery programs accredited by the Division of Accreditation of the American College of Nurse-Midwives, 818 Connecticut Ave. NW, Ste. 900, Washington, DC 20006, (202) 728-9860.

Alabama

★9578★ **University of Alabama at Birmingham**
School of Nursing
Graduate Program in Nurse-Midwifery
UAB Station
Birmingham, AL 35294-1210
Phone: (205)934-6648

California

★9579★ **Charles R. Drew University of Medicine and Science**
College of Allied Health Sciences
Nurse-Midwifery Certificate Education Program
1621 E. 120th St.
Los Angeles, CA 90059
Phone: (213)563-4951

★9580★ **Education Program Associates**
Midwifery Certificate Education Program
1 W. Campbell Ave.
Campbell, CA 95008
Phone: (408)374-3720

★9581★ **University of California, Irvine**
UCI Birthing Center
Nurse-Midwifery Education Program
300 W. Cerritos Ave., 7
Anaheim, CA 92805
Phone: (714)456-7209

★9582★ **University of California, Los Angeles**
School of Nursing
Graduate Nurse-Midwifery Education Program
10833 LeConte Ave.
Los Angeles, CA 90024
Phone: (310)825-7181

★9583★ **University of California, San Diego**
USCD School of Medicine
Department of Community and Family Medicine
Nurse-Midwifery Certificate Education Program
9500 Gilman Dr.
La Jolla, CA 92093-0809
Phone: (619)294-6179

★9584★ **University of California, San Francisco / San Francisco General Hospital**
Interdepartmental Nurse-Midwifery Certificate Education Program
San Francisco General Hospital, Ward 6D, Rm. 24
1001 Potrero Ave.
San Francisco, CA 94110
Phone: (415)206-5106

★9585★ **University of California, San Francisco / San Francisco General Hospital**
Interdepartmental Nurse-Midwifery Graduate Education Program
San Francisco General Hospital, Ward 6D, Rm. 24
1001 Potrero Ave.
San Francisco, CA 94110
Phone: (415)206-5106

★9586★ **University of California, San Francisco / University of California, San Diego**
UCSD School of Medicine
Department of Community and Family Medicine
Intercampus Nurse-Midwifery Graduate Education Program
9500 Gilman Dr.
La Jolla, CA 92093-0809
Phone: (619)294-6179

★9587★ **University of Southern California**
Nurse-Midwifery Certificate Education Program
Women's Hospital, Rm. 8K5
1240 N. Mission Rd.
Los Angeles, CA 90033
Phone: (213)226-3386

Colorado

★9588★ **University of Colorado**
School of Nursing
Graduate Program in Nurse-Midwifery
4200 E. 9th Ave.
PO Box C-288
Denver, CO 80262
Phone: (303)270-8654

Connecticut

★9589★ Yale University
School of Nursing
Nurse-Midwifery Graduate Program
25 Park St.
PO Box 9740
New Haven, CT 06536-0740
Phone: (203)737-2344

District of Columbia

★9590★ Georgetown University
School of Nursing
Graduate Program in Nurse-Midwifery
3700 Reservoir Rd. NW
Washington, DC 20007
Phone: (202)687-4772

Florida

★9591★ University of Florida
College of Nursing
Graduate Program in Nurse-Midwifery
Health Sciences Center, Jacksonville
653 W. 8th St., Bldg. 1, 2nd Fl.
Jacksonville, FL 32209-6561
Phone: (904)549-3245

★9592★ University of Miami
School of Nursing
Graduate Program in Nurse-Midwifery
5801 Red Rd.
PO Box 248153
Coral Gables, FL 33124-3850
Phone: (305)284-3666

Georgia

★9593★ Emory University
Nell Hodgson Woodruff School of Nursing
Graduate Program in Nurse-Midwifery
Atlanta, GA 30322
Phone: (404)727-6918

Illinois

★9594★ University of Illinois at Chicago
College of Nursing
Graduate Program in Nurse-Midwifery
845 S. Damen Ave.
Chicago, IL 60612
Phone: (312)996-7982

Kentucky

★9595★ Frontier School of Midwifery and
Family Nursing
Community-Based Nurse-Midwifery
Certificate Education Program
PO Box 528
Hyden, KY 41749
Phone: (606)672-2312

★9596★ University of Kentucky
College of Nursing
Graduate Program in Nurse-Midwifery
760 Rose St.
Lexington, KY 40536-6253
Phone: (606)323-6253

Massachusetts

★9597★ Baystate Medical Center
Nurse-Midwifery Certificate Education
Program
759 Chestnut St.
Springfield, MA 01199
Phone: (413)784-4448

★9598★ Boston University
School of Public Health
Nurse-Midwifery Graduate Education
Program
80 E. Concord St., Rm. A-207
Boston, MA 02118
Phone: (617)638-5012

Michigan

★9599★ University of Michigan
School of Nursing
Nurse-Midwifery Graduate Program
400 N. Ingalls, Rm. 3320
Ann Arbor, MI 48109
Phone: (313)763-3710

Minnesota

★9600★ University of Minnesota
School of Nursing
Graduate Program in Nurse-Midwifery
308 Harvard St. SE, 6-101, Unit F
Minneapolis, MN 55455
Phone: (612)624-6494

New Jersey

★9601★ University of Medicine and
Dentistry of New Jersey
School of Health Related Professions
Nurse-Midwifery Certificate Program
65 Bergen St.
Newark, NJ 07107-3001
Phone: (201)982-4249

New Mexico

★9602★ University of New Mexico
College of Nursing
Nurse-Midwifery Graduate Program
Albuquerque, NM 87131
Phone: (505)277-1184

New York

★9603★ Columbia University
School of Nursing
Graduate Program in Nurse-Midwifery
630 W. 168th St.
New York, NY 10032
Phone: (212)305-5756

★9604★ New York University
Nurse-Midwifery Education Program
429 Shimkin Hall
50 W. 4th St.
New York, NY 10012
Phone: (212)998-5895

★9605★ State University of New York
Health Science Center at Brooklyn
College of Health Related Professions
Nurse-Midwifery Certificate Program
450 Clarkson Ave.
Box 1227
Brooklyn, NY 11203
Phone: (718)270-7740

★9606★ University of Rochester
School of Nursing
Graduate Program in Nurse-Midwifery
Box SON
601 Elmwood Ave.
Rochester, NY 14642
Phone: (716)275-2375

North Carolina

★9607★ East Carolina University
School of Nursing
Nurse-Midwifery Graduate Program
Greenville, NC 27858
Phone: (919)328-4298

Ohio

★9608★ Case Western Reserve University
Frances Payne Bolton School of Nursing
Graduate Program in Nurse-Midwifery
10900 Euclid Ave.
Cleveland, OH 44106-4904
Phone: (216)368-3532

Oregon

★9609★ Oregon Health Sciences
University
School of Nursing
Graduate Program in Nurse-Midwifery
3181 SW Sam Jackson Park Rd.
Portland, OR 97201
Phone: (503)494-3822

Pennsylvania

★9610★ University of Pennsylvania
School of Nursing
Graduate Program in Nurse-Midwifery
Nursing Education Bldg.
420 Guardian Dr.
Philadelphia, PA 19104-6096
Phone: (215)898-4335

Rhode Island

★9611★ University of Rhode Island
College of Nursing
Nurse-Midwifery Graduate Program
White Hall
Kingston, RI 02881-0814
Phone: (401)792-2766

South Carolina

★9612★ **Medical University of South Carolina**
College of Nursing
Graduate Program in Nurse-Midwifery
171 Ashley Ave.
Charleston, SC 29425
Phone: (803)792-3077

Texas

★9613★ **Baylor College of Medicine**
Nurse-Midwifery Graduate Education Program
Smith Towers, Ste. 901
6550 Fannin St.
Houston, TX 77030
Phone: (713)798-7594

★9614★ **Parkland School of Nurse-Midwifery**
Nurse-Midwifery Certificate Program
Parkland Memorial Hospital, MS 6017A
5201 Harry Hines Blvd.
Dallas, TX 75235
Phone: (214)590-2580

★9615★ **University of Texas at El Paso / Texas Tech University**
Collaborative Nurse-Midwifery Graduate Program
Texas Tech University, HSC, OB/GYN Dept.
4800 Alberta Ave.
El Paso, TX 79905
Phone: (915)545-6490

★9616★ **University of Texas Medical Branch at Galveston**
School of Nursing
Graduate Program in Nurse-Midwifery
301 University
Galveston, TX 77555-1029
Phone: (409)772-1181

Utah

★9617★ **University of Utah**
College of Nursing
Graduate Program in Nurse-Midwifery
25 S. Medical Dr.
Salt Lake City, UT 84112
Phone: (801)581-8274

Washington

★9618★ **University of Washington**
School of Nursing
Department of Parent and Child Nursing
Nurse-Midwifery Program
T432 Health Sciences Bldg.
Seattle, WA 98195
Phone: (206)543-8241

Wisconsin

★9619★ **Marquette University**
College of Nursing
Graduate Nurse-Midwifery Program
530 N. 16th St.
Milwaukee, WI 53233
Phone: (414)288-3844

National & International Organizations

★9620★ **Amarant Trust (AT)**
80 Lambeth Rd.
London SE1 7PW, England
Phone: 171 4013855
Fax: 171 9281702
Debbie Catt, Contact

Languages: English. **Description:** Works to promote a better understanding of menopause through research and exchange of information. Seeks to educate women in Britain on the benefits of Hormone Replacement Therapy (HRT).

★9621★ **American Academy of Husband-Coached Childbirth (AAHCC)**
PO Box 5224
Sherman Oaks, CA 91413
Phone: (818)788-6662
Marjie Hathaway, Exec.Dir.

Founded: 1970. **Members:** 1,200. **Description:** Trains instructors in the Bradley method of natural childbirth. **Publications:** *Directory of Instructors*, 2-3/year. • *Fetal Advocate*, periodic.

★9622★ **American Association of Gynecological Laparoscopists (AAGL)**
13021 E. Florence Ave.
Santa Fe Springs, CA 90670
Phone: (310)946-8774
Free: 800-554-2245
Fax: (310)946-0073
Jordan M. Phillips, M.D., Bd.Chm.

Founded: 1972. **Members:** 7,200. **Description:** Physicians who specialize in obstetrics and gynecology and who are interested in gynecological endoscopic procedures. Purposes are to: teach; demonstrate; exchange ideas; distribute literature; stimulate interest in gynecological laparoscopy; maintain and improve medical standards in medical schools and hospitals regarding gynecological laparoscopy; maintain and improve the ethics, practice, and efficiency of the medical practice pertaining to obstetrics and laparoscopy. Conducts seminars and workshops. **Publications:** *Endoscopy in Gynecology*. • *Female Endoscopic Sterilization*. • *Gynecological Laparoscopy: Principles and Techniques*. • *The Journal of the American Association of Gynelogical Laparoscopists*, quarterly. Journal. *Price:* $100 individual; $125 institution. • *Microsurgery in Gynecology II*.

American Association of Pro Life Obstetricians and Gynecologists (AAPLOG)
See: Entry 11199

★9623★ **American Board of Obstetrics and Gynecology (ABOG)**
2915 Vine St.
Dallas, TX 75204-1069
Phone: (214)871-1619
Fax: (214)871-1943
Norman F. Gant, M.D., Exec.Dir.

Founded: 1927. **Members:** 15. **Description:** Certification board to establish qualifications, conduct examinations, and certify as diplomates those doctors whom the board finds qualified to specialize in obstetrics and gynecology. **Publications:** Bulletin, annual.

★9624★ **American College of Home Obstetrics (ACHO)**
PO Box 508
Oak Park, IL 60303
Phone: (708)383-1461
Gregory White, M.D., Pres.

Founded: 1978. **Members:** 40. **Description:** Physicians interested in cooperating with families who wish to give birth in the home. Objective is to accumulate and exchange data on home birth. Maintains speakers' bureau; compiles statistics. Plans to conduct research. **Publications:** Newsletter, periodic. Also publishes statement of purpose.

★9625★ **American College of Nurse-Midwives (ACNM)**
1522 K St. NW, Ste. 1000
Washington, DC 20005
Phone: (202)728-9860
Fax: (202)289-4395
Ronald E. Nitzsche, COO

Founded: 1955. **Members:** 3,000. **Regional Groups:** 6. **Local Groups:** 53. **Description:** Registered nurses certified to extend their practice into providing gynecological services and care of mothers and babies throughout the maternity cycle; members have completed an ACNM accredited program of study and clinical experience in midwifery and passed a national certification exam. Cooperates with allied groups to enable nurse-midwives to concentrate their efforts in the improvement of services for mothers and newborn babies. Seeks to identify areas of nurse-midwifery practices as they relate to the total service and educational aspects of maternal and newborn care. Studies and evaluates activities of nurse-midwives in order to establish qualifications; cooperates in planning and developing educational programs. conducts research and continuing education workshops. sponsors research. Compiles statistics. Maintains speakers' bureau and archives; offers placement service. **Publications:** *American College of Nurse-Midwives Membership Directory Supplement*, annual. Directory. *Price:* Included in membership dues. • *Directory of Nurse-Midwifery Practices*, annual. Directory. Computer listing of certified nurse-midwives by state. *Price:* Included in membership dues; $10 for nonmembers. • *Journal of Nurse-Midwifery*, bimonthly. Journal. Covers topics relevant to maternal and newborn health, obstetrics, well-woman gynecology, family planning, and midwifery education. *Price:* Included in membership dues; $48/year for nonmembers; $69/year for institutions. • *Quickening*, bimonthly. Newsletter. Includes activities, calendar of events, employment listings, and legislative updates. *Price:* Included in membership dues. Also publishes pamphlets and brochures. **Formerly:** (1969) American College of Nurse-Midwifery.

★ 9626 ★ **American College of Obstetricians and Gynecologists (ACOG)**
409 12th St. SW
Washington, DC 20024
Phone: (202)638-5577
Fax: (202)484-8107
Ralph Hale, M.D., Exec.Dir.

Founded: 1951. **Members:** 33,000. **Description:** Physicians specializing in childbirth and the diseases of women. Sponsors continuing professional development program. **Publications:** Booklets. • *Committee Opinions and Technical Bulletin*, periodic. Bulletin. Includes technical information. • *Directory of Fellows*, biennial. Directory. • Manuals. • Newsletter, monthly. • *Obstetrics and Gynecology*, monthly. **Formerly:** (1956) American Academy of Obstetrics and Gynecology.

American College of Osteopathic Obstetricians and Gynecologists (ACOOG)
See: Entry 9977

American Foundation for Maternal and Child Health (AFMCH)
See: Entry 3167

★ 9627 ★ **American Gynecological and Obstetrical Society (AGOS)**
c/o Paul B. Underwood, Jr.
UVA Health Science Center
Box 387
Charlottesville, VA 22908
Phone: (804)923-9937
Fax: (804)982-1840
Paul B. Underwood, Jr., Sec.

Founded: 1981. **Members:** 243. **Description:** Works to cultivate and promote knowledge concerning obstetrics and gynecology. **Publications:** *Transactions*, annual.

★ 9628 ★ **American Society of Breast Disease (SSBD)**
PO Box 140186
Dallas, TX 75214
Phone: (214)368-6836
Fax: (214)368-5719
Gerorg N. Peters, M.D., Pres.

Founded: 1976. **Members:** 400. **Description:** Physicians and nurses, primarily those engaged in the fields of obstetrics and gynecology, surgery, radiology, family practice, and medical and radiation oncology. Seeks to further the study of diseases of the breast and to inform physicians and other health care professionals of developments in the diagnosis and treatment of breast cancer and benign diseases of the breast. Serves as a forum for discussion among members. Encourages research pertaining to breast disease. **Publications:** *Breast Disease - An International Journal*, quarterly. Journal. • Newsletter, periodic. **Formerly:** (1994) Society for the Study of Breast Disease.

★ 9629 ★ **American Society for Colposcopy and Cervical Pathology (ASCCP)**
409 12th St. SW
Washington, DC 20024-2188
Phone: (202)863-2453
Free: 800-787-7227
Fax: (202)484-5107
Kathleen Poole, Admin.Dir.

Founded: 1964. **Members:** 2,500. **Description:** Obstetricians, gynecologists, family physicians, nurses, and other individuals interested in promoting the accurate and ethical application of colposcopy (the examination of the lower genital tract by means of a colposcope). Organizes and approves training programs in colposcopy. Conducts research and postgraduate courses. **Publications:** *ASCCP Videoguide to Colposcopy*. Video. 30-minute videotape on colposcopy, LGSIL, HGSIL, and cancer. *Price:* $20 in U.S.; $35 outside U.S.. • *Colposcopist*, quarterly. *Price:* $15/year. • *Home Study Program*, quarterly. *Price:* $40/year. • Membership Directory, biennial. **Formerly:** American Society for Colposcopy and Colpomicroscopy.

★ 9630 ★ **American Society for Psychoprophylaxis in Obstetrics (ASPO/LAMAZ)**
1200 19th St. NW, No. 300
Washington, DC 20036-2401
Phone: (202)857-1128
Free: 800-368-4404
Fax: (202)223-4579
Linda Harmon, Exec.Dir.

Founded: 1960. **Members:** 5,000. **Local Groups:** 25. **Description:** Physicians, nurses, nurse-midwives, certified teachers of psychoprophylatic (Lamaze) method of childbirth, other professionals, parents, and others interested in Lamaze childbirth preparation and family-centered maternity care. Disseminates information about the theory and practical application of psychoprophylaxis in obstetrics; administers teacher training courses and certifies qualified Lamaze teachers; provides educational lectures, public forums, films, and written materials; maintains national and local teacher and physician referral service. Also presents materials to prospective parents concerning the demands of childrearing. National office serves as information clearinghouse. **Publications:** *Genesis*, quarterly. Newsletter. Contains book and film reviews and calendar of events. *Price:* Included in membership dues. • *Journal of Perinatal Education*, quarterly. Journal. *Price:* Free for members; $39 for individual; $145 for institution.

★ 9631 ★ **Asociacion Ayuda a Madres de Minusvalidos**
Villa de Marin 47, 3 D
E-28029 Madrid, Spain
Phone: 1 3147785

Languages: Spanish. **Description:** Offers supportive services to pregnant women of low income. Provides information about prenatal care, child care, and maternal health.

Asociacion Nacional Contra el Cancer (ANCEC)
See: Entry 5918

★ 9632 ★ **Association for Childbirth at Home, International (ACHI)**
PO Box 430
Glendale, CA 91209
Phone: (818)545-7128
Fax: (818)409-1728
Tonya Brooks, Founder & Pres.

Founded: 1972. **Members:** 30,000. **Regional Groups:** 9. **State Groups:** 40. **Local Groups:** 120. **Description:** Parents, midwives, doctors, childbirth educators, other professionals, and interested individuals, all of whom support childbirth at home. Purposes are to bring accurate information and competent support to parents seeking home birth and safe hospital birth; to identify and implement correct obstetrical and pediatric practice. Offers parent education classes, leader training programs, international resource and referral service, and professional education seminars and programs; instructs parents, childbirth educators, midwives, and physicians in safe home birth and noninterventive alternative techniques. Conducts research; compiles statistics. Maintains speakers' bureau. **Publications:** *Birth Notes*, quarterly. Newsletter. *Price:* $25/year. • Brochures. • *Founders Letter*, 6/year. • *Giving Birth at Home*. Handbook. **Formerly:** Association for Childbirth at Home.

Association of Maternal and Child Health Programs (AMCHP)
See: Entry 3184

★ 9633 ★ **Association of Professors of Gynecology and Obstetrics (APGO)**
409 12th St. SW
Washington, DC 20024
Phone: (202)863-2507
Fax: (202)863-2514
Donna Wachter, Exec.Dir.

Founded: 1962. **Members:** 1,200. **Description:** Departments of obstetrics and gynecology in approved medical schools in the U.S. and Canada. Works to consider problems relating to the departments of obstetrics and gynecology; to advance and improve the study of gynecology and obstetrics; to provide a means of exchanging information relating to the programs of study, teaching methods, and research activities of such departments. Compiles statistics. **Publications:** *Academic Position Report*, quarterly. Report. • *Exploring Issues in Obstetric and Gynecologic Medicare Ethics*. • *Instructional Objectives for a Clinical Curriculum in Obstetrics and Gynecology*. • Membership Directory, annual. • Newsletter, quarterly.

★ 9634 ★ **Association of Radical Midwives (ARM)**
62 Greetby Hill
Ormskirk, Lancs. L39 2DT, England
Phone: 1695 572776
Fax: 1695 572776
Ishbel Kargar, Sec.

Founded: 1976. **Members:** 1,700. **Local Groups:** 50. **Languages:** English. **Description:** Midwives, mothers, health professionals, and interested individuals. Supports the interests of midwives. Provides supportive services and information to women experiencing difficulty in securing adequate and sympathetic maternity care. **Publications:** *Choices in Childbirth.* Booklet. • *Midwifery Matters,* quarterly. Magazine.

★9635★ **Association Rwandaise pour le Bien-Etre Familial (ARBEF)**
BP 1580
Kigali, Rwanda
Phone: 76127

Languages: French. **Description:** Promotes maternal and infant health through educational efforts. Encourages the practice of family planning in Rwanda.

Association of Women's Health, Obstetric, and Neonatal Nurses (AWHONN)
See: Entry 9075

Breast Cancer Care
See: Entry 5925

★9636★ **C/SEC**
22 Forest Rd.
Framingham, MA 01701
Phone: (508)877-8266
Norma Shulman, Dir.

Founded: 1972. **Members:** 2,000. **Description:** Childbirth groups, doctors, laypersons, and nurses. Established out of concern for the lack of resources available to couples who anticipate or have had a cesarean delivery. Goals are to: improve the cesarean childbirth experience and make the cesarean delivery a good and meaningful childbirth experience for each couple; provide information and promote education on cesarean prevention and vaginal birth after cesarean; change attitudes and policies that affect the cesarean childbirth experience. Offers support for cesarean couples through informal discussion meetings, telephone contact, and personal reply to letters. Provides information on many aspects of cesarean childbirth in order to make couples aware of exactly what the procedure entails and what options are available. Works with doctors, hospitals, childbirth educators, and others in the medical community to effect policy changes and to promote family-centered maternity care for cesarean couples. Conducts in-service programs for hospital staffs and has spoken at conventions and workshops on childbirth. Acronym C/SEC stands for Cesareans/Support, Education and Concern. **Publications:** *Frankly Speaking.* Book. Discussion of cesarean birth. *Price:* $4. • *Preventing Unnecessary Cesareans: A Guide to Labor Management and Detailed Bibliography.* Pamphlet. Outlines avoidable factors which may lead to preventable cesareans. *Price:* $2. **Formerly:** (1976) C/SEC (Cesarean Sections: Education and Concern).

★9637★ **Canadian Pelvic Inflammatory Disease Society**
PO Box 33804, Sta. D
Vancouver, BC, Canada V6J 4L6
Phone: (604)684-5704
Jill Weiss, Coord.

Founded: 1985. **Members:** 300. **Languages:** English, French. **Description:** Women with Pelvic Inflammatory Disease (PID), medical professionals, health care organizations, and interested individuals. (PID is an infection or inflamma-

tion of a women's pelvic organs which can result in scarring and adhesion of the pelvic organs, infertility, recurring or chronic infecion, ectopic pregnancy, chronic abdominal pain, disability, and death.) Provides information and support to women with PID and their families. Promotes public education and the prevention of PID; produces and distributes educational materials; supports research on prevention of PID. Maintains speakers' bureau. **Publications:** *Fact Sheet for Men about PID,* periodic. • *News Coverage of PID.* Video. • *Pelvic Inflammatory Disease (PID).* Booklet. • *PID True/False Public Education Questionnaire,* periodic. • *Royal Commission Briefs on PID,* periodic.

★9638★ **Center for Humane Options in Childbirth Experiences (CHOICE)**
3474 N. High St.
Columbus, OH 43214
Phone: (614)263-2229
Abby Kinne, Dir.

Founded: 1977. **Members:** 1,200. **Local Groups:** 1. **Description:** Medical professionals, paraprofessionals, and interested individuals. Purpose is to teach and encourage parents, parents-to-be, groups, and interested individuals working in family-oriented childbirth in hospital birth centers and out-of-hospital situations. Trains and certifies attendants to attend or coach births. Acts as consumer advocate for hospital births. Services include medical referrals, childbirth education classes, and supplementary prenatal care. Sponsors community educational programs; operates speakers' bureau; compiles statistics.

Center for Study of Multiple Birth (CSMB)
See: Entry 11208

★9639★ **Childbirth Education Foundation (CEF)**
PO Box 5
Richboro, PA 18954
Phone: (215)357-2792
James E. Peron, Founder & Exec.Dir.

Founded: 1972. **Members:** 18,000. **Description:** Physicians, nurses, childbirth educators, childbirth reform activists, concerned parents, and individuals dedicated to providing alternatives for a more meaningful childbirth experience, and to promoting reform in childbirth issues and in the treatment of the newborn. Promotes home births, birthing centers, certified nurse-midwife pregnancy management and delivery, family togetherness and infant bonding, "nonviolent birth" for mother and child, and breast-feeding. Distributes literature to libraries, parents, maternal care providers, and educators regarding childbirth, trends in childbirth, safe alternatives, the avoidance of "violence in birth," and the treatment of newborns and infants. Compiles statistics and conducts extensive research related to childbirth, newborn, and infant care; provides seminars and educational workshops for childbirth educators, Lamaze instructors, the La Leche League International, and right-to-life and birthright organizations. Provides referrals and film and videotape services to childbirth educators and maternal and child-care organizations. Maintains speakers' bureau and library. Sponsors charitable programs. **Pub-**

lications: *CEF Newsletter,* semiannual. Newsletter. • *Membership Directory,* periodic. Also publishes a bibliography and educational bulletins.

★9640★ **Childbirth Educators—New Zealand**
94 Rattray St.
Christchurch 4, New Zealand
Phone: 3 3488920
Wendy Maw, National Coord.

Founded: 1986. **Members:** 180. **National Groups:** 1. **Regional Groups:** 6. **Languages:** English. **Description:** Promotes education concerning the principles of natural childbirth; facilitates communication and cooperation among parents and medical professionals. Provides educational opportunities to parents and parents-to-be. **Publications:** *News & Views,* quarterly, always March, June, September, and December. Magazine.

★9641★ **Childbirth Without Pain Education Association (CWPEA)**
20134 Snowden
Detroit, MI 48235
Phone: (313)341-3816
Flora Hommel, Exec.Dir.

Founded: 1958. **Members:** 2,000. **Description:** Former and current students of the Lamaze-Pavlov (psychoprophylactic) method of painless childbirth; physicians, nurses, midwifes, and interested individuals. Sponsors classes and films for women with or without partners, nurses, midwifes and medical and lay groups about the method, which is based on conditioning reflexes to help prevent pain, thus allowing for natural, usually drug-free childbirth. Works to provide a method-trained registered nurse (monitrice) in attendance at the birth where possible. Collects data for further development of the method; surveys maternity services. Sponsors childbirth teacher and monitrice training and certification. Provides teen pregnancy programs. Offers referral service. **Publications:** *Childbirth Without Pain Education Association Memo,* bimonthly. Newsletter. Includes association news and book reviews. *Price:* Included in membership dues; $25/year for physicians; $10/year for nurses and nonmembers; $6/year for alumni. **Also Known As:** Lamaze Birth Without Pain Education Association.

★9642★ **China Expert Consultancy Committee on Maternity**
1 Xixhiku St.
Xicheng District
Beijing 100034, People's Republic of China
Phone: 1 3049020
Yan Renying, Chair

Founded: 1989. **Members:** 28. **Languages:** Chinese. **Description:** Professionals in maternity and child care. Seeks to improve the quality of health care for mothers and children. Offers consultancy service to maternity and child care facilities in China.

★9643★ Contacts-Informations-Femmes 40/60 (CIF 40/60)
Dreve des Weigelias 14
B-1170 Brussels, Belgium
Phone: 2 6736248
Mrs. Jo Poortmans, Contact

Founded: 1988. **Members:** 100. **Languages:** English, French. **Description:** Provides social, medical, and psychological assistance to menopausal and postmenopausal women. Conducts educational programs. **Publications:** *La Boussole*, quarterly. Newsletter.

★9644★ Council on Resident Education in Obstetrics and Gynecology (CREOG)
409 12th St. SW
Washington, DC 20024
Phone: (202)863-2554
Fax: (202)484-7480
DeAnne Nehra, Exec.Dir.

Founded: 1967. **Members:** 450. **Description:** A semiautonomous nonregulatory organization founded by the American College of Obstetricians and Gynecologists and comprised of national specialty organizations. Works to promote and maintain high standards of resident training in obstetrics and gynecology. Services include: consultative site visits to residency programs; clearinghouse for residency positions; conferences; a resident data bank; national in-training examination. **Publications:** *A Design for Resident Education in Obstetrics and Gynecology*. • *Basic Science Monographs in Obstetrics and Gynecology*, periodic. Monograph. Covers metabolism, genetics, maternal physiology, pharmacology, microbiology, and other aspects of reproductive health. *Price:* $10 for members; $15 for nonmembers. • *Council on Resident Education in Obstetrics and Gynecology--Council News*, 3/year. Newsletter. Contains membership activities and *CREOG Directory of Obstetric and Gynecologic Residency Programs* update. • *CREOG Directory of Obstetric and Gynecologic Residency Programs and Directors*, annual. Directory. Lists accredited residency programs in the U.S. and Canada. *Price:* $10. • *Educational Objectives for Residents in Obstetrics and Gynecology*.

DES Action Canada
See: Entry 11214

★9645★ DES Action, U.S.A.
1615 Broadway, Ste. 510
Oakland, CA 94612
Phone: (510)465-4011
Fax: (510)465-4815
Karen Fernandes, Pres.

Founded: 1977. **State Groups:** 30. **Description:** DES-exposed persons and others "working to try to ameliorate the problems caused by DES." DES (diethylstilbestrol) is a synthetic estrogen in use since 1940 and often prescribed for prevention of miscarriage, diabetes during pregnancy, difficulty in conceiving, staining during pregnancy, and cessation of premature labor. It has since been found that, in some cases, daughters born to women taking DES in the first five months of pregnancy have developed cervical and vaginal abnormalities, a very small percentage of which have resulted in cancer, and a greater number of DES daughters ex-

perience problems with pregnancies, including seven times the rate of tubal pregnancy and twice the rate of miscarriage. DES mothers have a higher risk of breast cancer. There have been some reports of urinary problems, genital abnormalities, and infertility among DES sons, although research has not been completed in this area. Goal is to reach DES-exposed persons and to stress to them the need for medical attention and monitoring; to educate professionals and the public; and to work for federal legislation. Worked for passage of the first DES legislation in the U.S., in New York State. Offers support, counseling, and doctor referral service. Maintains speakers' bureau. **Publications:** Bibliography. • *DES Action Voice: A Focus on Diethylstilbestrol Exposure*, quarterly. Newsletter. Includes medical question and answer column; book reviews; legislation and litigation news; conference reports. *Price:* $30/year. • *Fertility and Pregnancy Guide for DES Daughters and Sons*. • *Reproductive Outcomes in DES Daughters*. Also publishes fact sheets and doctor referral sheet. **Formerly:** (1986) DES Action, National.

★9646★ Endometriosis Association (EA)
8585 N. 76th Pl.
Milwaukee, WI 53223
Phone: (414)355-2200
Free: 800-992-3636
Fax: (414)355-6065
Mary Lou Ballweg, Exec.Dir.

Founded: 1980. **Description:** Women who have endometriosis and others interested in the condition. (Endometriosis is a disorder in which endometrial tissue, which lines the uterus, is also found in other locations in the body, usually the abdomen. Symptoms can include extremely painful menstruation, infertility, painful sexual intercourse, and heavy or irregular bleeding.) Disseminates information on the treatment, research, and attitudes concerning endometriosis. Offers selfhelp support and informational meetings for women with endometriosis and others. Conducts public education programs; maintains speakers' bureau; gathers data on individual experiences with endometriosis. **Publications:** *The Choice is Ours: New Surgeries for Endometriosis*. Video. • *Endometriosis Association Newsletter*, bimonthly. Newsletter. Includes news, tips, reviews, and research reports; also covers association and chapter news and activities. *Price:* Included in membership dues. • *Overcoming Endometriosis*. Book. • *What is Endometriosis*. Brochure. In 11 languages. • *You're Not Alone: Understanding Endometriosis*. Video.

★9647★ European Diabetes Pregnancy Study Group (EDPSG)
Auf'm Hennekamp 32
40225 Dusseldorf, Germany
Phone: 211 316738
Fax: 211 3190987

Founded: 1971. **Members:** 40. **Languages:** English. **Description:** A study group of the European Association for the Study of Diabetes. Members are diabetologists, obstetricians, pathologists, and pediatricians in 10 countries united to promote better understanding and more effective investigation of the problems of pregnancy and diabetes.

★9648★ Federation of French-Language Gynecologists and Obstetricians (Federation des Gynecologues et Obstetriciens de Langue Francaise — FGOLF)
Clinique Universitaire Baudelocque
123, blvd. de Port-Royal
F-75674 Paris Cedex 14, France
Phone: 1 42341143
Prof. E. Papiernik, Sec.Gen.

Founded: 1950. **Members:** 2,000. **Languages:** French. **Description:** French-speaking gynecologists and obstetricians. Purpose is to promote scientific study in the French language of all aspects of the biology of human reproduction. Conducts training sessions and travel and exchange programs; sponsors seminars. Maintains permanent committees to deal with special topics. **Publications:** *Journal de Gynecologie Obstetrique et Biologie de la Reproduction*, bimonthly. Journal.

★9649★ Federation of Scandinavian Societies of Obstetrics and Gynecology (Nordisk Forening for Obstetrikk og Gynekologi — NFOG)
Obst Gyn. Dept.
University Hospital
N-7006 Trondheim, Norway
Phone: 73 998000
Fax: 73 997602
Mette H. Moen, M.D., Sec.Gen.

Founded: 1933. **Members:** 3,212. **National Groups:** 5. **Languages:** Swedish. **Description:** Gynecologists and obstetricians from Nordic countries. Conducts educational programs; sponsors competitions and bestows awards. **Publications:** *Acta Obstetrica Gynecologicia Scandinavica*, 10/year. Journal. Includes supplements. • *Bulletin*, quarterly. Newsletter. **Formerly:** Scandinavian Association of Obstetrics and Gynecology; Nordisk Forening for Obstretik Och Gynekologi.

★9650★ Gabriela Commission on Women's Health and Reproductive Rights (GCWHRR)
PO Box 4386
Manila 2800, Philippines

Languages: English, Tagalog. **Description:** Designs and establishes community-based health services, focusing on the needs of women and children. Provides prenatal and postpartum care and obstetric and gynecological services; makes available discount medications; conducts pregnancy testing and other laboratory testing for specific ailments.

★9651★ Group B Strep Association
PO Box 16515
Chapel Hill, NC 27516
Phone: (919)932-5344
Fax: (919)932-5344
Gina Burns, Pres.

Founded: 1990. **Members:** 3,000. **State Groups:** 50. **Description:** Seeks to educate the public about Group B Strep (GBS) infections during pregnancy. Promotes screening of mothers and the development of a vaccine. Seeks to control the disease which is a leading cause of life-threatening infections in newborns. Acts as a support group; provides educational programs. **Publications:** *Update Newsletter*, semiannual. Newsletter. Also provides GBSA Public Education Packet.

Gynecologic Oncology Group (GOG)
See: Entry 5947

Healthy Mothers, Healthy Babies (HMHB)
See: Entry 3235

★9652★ **Home Birth Association**
PO Box 7093
Wellesley St.
Auckland, New Zealand

Languages: English. **Description:** Encourages natural childbirth methods. Disseminates information.

★9653★ **Human Lactation Center (HLC)**
666 Sturges Hwy.
Westport, CT 06880
Phone: (203)259-5995
Fax: (203)259-7667
Dana Raphael, Ph.D., Dir.

Founded: 1975. **Description:** Dedicated to international education and research on lactation (breastfeeding). Current activities include: research into the effects of lactation as a factor that inhibits fertility; consultation for national and international government, industry, and medical institutions on food policy, indigenous weaning foods, and infant and maternal nutrition and feeding practices; design and management of conferences to encourage dialogue among professionals; cooperative meetings with health and family planning groups; development of methodology for use by researchers in anthropology, nutrition, and public health in field work on childbirth, effect of early child abuse on birth and lactation, breastfeeding, breast milk and AIDS virus. Maintains museum of items related to infant feeding including nursing chairs, amulets, feeding bottles, animal skin milk carrying cases, and breastfeeding posters. **Publications:** *The Lactation Review*, periodic. • *Only Mothers Know: Infant Feeding Practices in Traditional Cultures.* • *The Tender Gift: Breastfeeding.*

★9654★ **Hysterectomy Educational Resources and Services Foundation (HERS)**
422 Bryn Mawr Ave.
Bala Cynwyd, PA 19004
Phone: (215)667-7757
Fax: (215)667-8096
Nora W. Coffey, Pres.

Founded: 1982. **Description:** Seeks to help women make informed decisions regarding hysterectomy. Provides educational materials concerning hysterectomy and alternative procedures. Functions as a referral service matching women who have had or will have a hysterectomy for one-to-one sharing of experiences and concerns. Offers referral list of doctors for second opinions. Also provides legal referrals. Maintains speakers' bureau. **Publications:** *HERS Annual Hysterectomy Conference Proceedings.* Proceedings. • *HERS Newsletter*, quarterly. Newsletter. Contains book reviews,

medical and scientific literature reviews, writer's chronicle of journal, and letters from readers. *Price:* $20/year. • Reprints. Also makes available reading list and copies of articles; distributes audio cassettes and other related materials. **Also Known As:** HERS Foundation.

★9655★ **Indonesian Society for Perinatology (PERINASIA)**
(Perkumpulan Perinatologi Indonesia — PERINASIA)
Jalan Tebet Utara IA/22
12820 Jakarta, Indonesia
Phone: 21 8281243
Fax: 21 8281243
Gulardi H. Wiknjosastro, M.D., Contact

Founded: 1981. **Members:** 300. **Local Groups:** 17. **Languages:** English, Indonesian. **Description:** Obstetricians, gynecologists, pediatricians, midwives, and interested others. Strives to reduce the perinatal mortality rate; works to improve prenatal, natal, and postnatal health care; seeks improved medical facilities. Holds workshops, congresses, seminars, and symposia on perinatal health care and related subjects. Advocates research in safe birth practices; promotes the use of preventive medicine in prenatal care. Encourages community participation in health care improvement programs. Offers technical assistance to government authorities. Cooperates with similar international organizations. Conducts surveys. Disseminates information. **Publications:** *Perinasia Bulletin*, quarterly. Bulletin. • Proceedings, periodic.

Infertility Awareness Association of Canada (IAAC)
(Association Canadienne de Sensibilisation a l'Infertilite)
See: Entry 11221

★9656★ **Informed Homebirth / Informed Birth and Parenting (IH/IBP)**
PO Box 3675
Ann Arbor, MI 48106
Phone: (313)662-6857
Rahima Baldwin, Pres.

Founded: 1977. **Members:** 1,000. **Description:** Expectant and new parents, childbirth educators, midwives, nurses, preschool and elementary school teachers, and others interested in safe childbirth alternatives. Seeks to provide information on alternatives in childbirth methods, parenting, and education. Sponsors Childbirth Educator Training Program leading to certification as Childbirth Educator; Childbirth Assistant Training emphasizing practical skills to help the birthing woman and the primary caregiver. Maintains mail order book/video service on alternative education. Conducts correspondence course to train childbirth educators. **Publications:** *Special Delivery*, quarterly. Journal. Contains articles on midwifery and birth, book reviews, calendar of events, and schedule of upcoming workshops. *Price:* Included in membership dues; $20/year for nonmembers. **Formerly:** (1981) Informed Homebirth.

Institute for Social Studies and Action (ISSA)
See: Entry 1328

★9657★ **Integral Health for Women (Salud Integral para la Mujer — SIPAM)**
Vista Hermosa 89
Col. Portales
C.P. 03300
Mexico City, DF, Mexico
Phone: 5 5398703
Fax: 5 5398703
Pilar Muriedas, Dir.

Founded: 1987. **Languages:** English, Spanish. **Description:** Individuals interested in improving the quality of life and health of women. Works to ensure access to health care, which the group views as a fundamental human right. Promotes the feminist movement; participates in the development and advancement of the concept of integral health for women; fights to ensure that women have a voice in the formulation of and implementation of public health policies. Gathers and disseminates information on the women's movement and women's health care issues. Conducts research and educational programs; makes available gynecological and psychological services. **Publications:** *La Trenza*, quarterly. Bulletin.

★9658★ **International Association— Hopecenter for the Defense of Women's and Children's Rights**
26 Sudakskaya, Apt. 69
334270 Alushta, Ukraine

Languages: English, Ukrainian. **Description:** Works to uphold the human rights of women and children in the Ukraine. Primary concerns include: risks to maternal and fetal health presented by nuclear contamination resulting from the Chernobyl accident; availability of contraception and effective obestetric and gynecologic care; education of Ukrainian women in matters relating to their own health.

★9659★ **International Association for Maternal and Neonatal Health (IAMENEH)**
16, chemin Grande Gorge
CH-1255 Veyrier, Switzerland
Phone: 22 7840658
Fax: 22 7840658
Mrs. Gerda M. Santschi, Exec.Sec.

Founded: 1977. **Members:** 4,500. **National Groups:** 34. **Languages:** English, French. **Description:** Medical professionals and individuals interested in improving maternal and neonatal care throughout the world, especially at the primary health care level. Objectives are to: promote and finance basic and applied research in the field of human reproduction and publish and distribute the findings; improve the standards of medical and paramedical care in the field of obstetrics and gynecology; foster and finance research programs on social problems related to maternal and perinatal health; propose curriculum on improving maternal and perinatal health to higher education institutions; disseminate scientific information concerning women, mothers, fetuses, newborns, and children. Supports projects to improve maternal and neonatal care in developing countries. **Publications:** *High Risk Mothers and Newborns - Detection, Management and Prevention.* Book. • *Maternal and Child Care in Developing Countries - Assessment, Promotion and Implementation.* Book. • *Maternal and Infant Mortality.* Book. • *MCI*

Newsletter, 3/year. Newsletter. • *Primary Maternal and Neonatal Health - A Global Concern*. Book. • *Proceedings of Congress*, triennial. • *Proceedings of Workshop*, annual. **Formerly:** (1994) Mother and Child International.

★ 9660 ★ International Association of Parents and Professionals for Safe Alternatives in Childbirth (NAPSAC)

Rte. 1, Box 646
Marble Hill, MO 63764-9725
Phone: (314)238-2010
Lee Stewart, Pres.

Founded: 1975. **Members:** 2,000. **National Groups:** 15. **Languages:** English. **Description:** Parents, midwives, physicians, nurses, health officials, social workers, and childbirth educators in 10 countries who are "dedicated to exploring, examining, implementing, and establishing family-centered childbirth programs which meet the needs of families as well as provide the safe aspects of medical science." Promotes education concerning the principles of natural childbirth; facilitates communication and cooperation among parents, medical professionals, and childbirth educators; assists in the establishment of maternity and childbearing centers. Provides educational opportunities to parents and parents-to-be, enabling them to assume more personal responsibility for pregnancy, childbirth, infant care, and child rearing. **Publications:** *Childbirth Activitists Handbook*. • *Five Standards for Safe Childbearing*. • *NAPSAC Directory of Alternative Birth Services and Consumer Guide*, biennial. Directory. Lists midwives, birth centers, noninterventive physicians, and educators for safe alternatives in childbirth. • *NAPSAC News*, quarterly. Newsletter. Includes association news, book reviews, and calendar of events. • *Safe Alternatives in Childbirth*. • *Transitions*. • *21st Century Obstetrics Now*. **Formerly:** (1979) National Association of Parents and Professionals for Safe Alternatives in Childbirth.

★ 9661 ★ International Cesarean Awareness Network (ICAN)

PO Box 276
Clarks Summit, PA 18411-0276
Esther Booth Zorn, Pres.

Founded: 1982. **Members:** 2,000. **Regional Groups:** 80. **Description:** Men and women concerned with the increasing rate of cesarean births. Objectives are: to promote vaginal births; to offer encouragement, information, and support for women wanting vaginal births after cesarean (VBAC); to assist in organizing and informing new parents and cesarean parents on preventing future cesareans by opposing unnecessary medical intervention during the birth process and by working to make hospital routines more responsive to women in labor. Offers teacher training and course materials. Sponsors childbirth education certification program, Birth Works, a birth education program that emphasizes a holistic approach. Provides support network to link women anticipating a VBAC and VBAC mothers, supportive physicians, midwives, and child birth educators. Compiles statistics. **Publications:** *Cesarean Facts*. • *The Clarion*, quarterly. Includes research and informational articles, book reviews and chapter

news. *Price:* Included in membership dues; One free copy for nonmembers. **Formerly:** (1992) Cesarean Prevention Movement.

★ 9662 ★ International Confederation of Midwives (ICM) (Confederation Internationale des Sages-Femmes — CISF)

10 Barley Mow Passage
Chiswick
London W4 4PH, England
Phone: 181 9946477
Fax: 181 9951332
Miss J. Walker, Sec.Gen.

Founded: 1919. **Members:** 67. **Regional Groups:** 4. **Languages:** English, French, Spanish. **Description:** National midwives' associations in 55 countries. Seeks to improve the standard of care provided to mothers, babies, and the family by promoting midwifery education and disseminating information about the art and science of midwifery. Conducts workshops and seminars on midwifery and safe motherhood. **Publications:** *A Birthday for Midwives - Seventy Five Years of International Collaboration*. Book. • *Congress Proceedings*, triennial. • *International Code of Ethics for Midwives, 1993*. Book. • *Introductory Brochure*. Brochure. • *Maternity Care in the World*. • *Newsletter*, 3/year. Newsletter. • *Planning for Action for Midwives*. • *Workshop Report*. Report.

★ 9663 ★ International Correspondence Society of Obstetricians and Gynecologists (ICSOG)

367 W. Main St.
PO Box 1130
Northborough, MA 01532
Phone: (508)393-1644
Fax: (508)393-1594
Dean M. Laux, Publisher

Founded: 1960. **Members:** 3,000. **Description:** Physicians concerned with obstetrics and gynecology and related surgery; medical schools and libraries; civilian and military hospitals; others with research interests. **Publications:** *The Collected Letters*, monthly. Newsletter.

★ 9664 ★ International Federation of Cervical Pathology and Colposcopy (IFCPC) (Federacion Internacional de Patologia Cervical y Colposcopia)

Dept. of Gynecology and Obstetrics
Saga Medical School
Nabeshima
Saga 849, Japan
Phone: 952 316511
Fax: 952 316543
Dr. H. Sugimori, Sec.Gen.

Founded: 1972. **Members:** 22. **Languages:** English, French, German, Spanish. **Description:** National societies encouraging basic and applied research and the dissemination of information concerning uterine cervical pathology and colposcopy.

★ 9665 ★ International Federation of Gynecology and Obstetrics (FIGO) (Federation Internationale de Gynecologie et d'Obstetrique — FIGO)

27 Sussex Pl.
Regent's Park
London NW1 4RG, England
Phone: 171 7232951
Fax: 171 7247725
Prof. D.V.I. Fairweather, Sec.Gen.

Founded: 1954. **Members:** 89. **Languages:** English, French, Spanish. **Description:** National societies of obstetrics and gynecology. Objectives are to: promote and assist in the development of scientific and research work relating to all facets of gynecology and obstetrics; improve the physical and mental health of women, mothers, and their children; provide an exchange of information and ideas; improve teaching standards; promote international cooperation among medical bodies. Acts as liaison with World Health Organization and other international organizations. Compiles statistics. **Publications:** *Annual Report*. Provides results of treatment in gynecological cancer. • *International Journal of Gynecology and Obstetrics*, monthly. Journal.

International Federation of Infantile and Juvenile Gynecology (IFIJG) (Federation Internationale de Gynecologie Infantile et Juvenile — FIGIJ)

See: Entry 3243

★ 9666 ★ International Lactation Consultant Association (ILCA)

201 Brown Ave.
Evanston, IL 60202-3601
Phone: (708)260-8874
Linda Kutner, Pres.

Founded: 1985. **Members:** 2,500. **Regional Groups:** 33. **Description:** Lactation consultants, institutions, and health professionals from 20 countries interested in breastfeeding and lactation. Works to: establish and maintain quality educational and practice standards and ethical principles for lactation consultants; initiate and conduct continuing education and research in the field; promote work concerning lactation/breastfeeding issues; increase public and health care worker awareness of lactation and breastfeeding. Facilitates communication among members. Bestows ILCA Outstanding Achievement in Human Lactation Award. **Publications:** *Annual Syllabus of Conference*. • *ILCA Membership Directory*, annual. Directory. • *Journal of Human Lactation*, quarterly. Journal. Contains research and scientific articles, book reviews, association news, and film reviews. *Price:* Included in membership dues. Also publishes journal supplements, recommendations, papers, and brochure.

★ 9667 ★ International Menopause Society

116, ave. de Broqueville
Bte. 9
B-1200 Brussels, Belgium
Phone: 2 7719598
Fax: 2 7624295
Monique Boulet, Exec. Dir.

Founded: 1978. **Members:** 650. **National Groups:** 15. **Languages:** English. **Description:**

Medical doctors, sociologists, psychologists, anthropologists, and others in 42 countries interested in basic research and clinical work in the field of menopause and climacteric. Objectives are to promote study of medical, sociological, and psychological aspects of the climacteric, or menopausal stage in men and women ages 40-60, and to advance international exchange of information and research plans. Studies subjects such as anatomy, gynecology, biochemistry, and psychology as they relate to the aging process; examines methods of management, preventive measures, and therapeutic problems related to aging. **Publications:** *Maturitas*, quarterly. Journal. • *Newsletter*, 3/year. Newsletter. • *Proceedings of International Congress*, triennial.

★9668★ International Perinatal Doppler Society
c/o Continuing Medical Education
University of Toronto
150 College St., Ste. 121
Toronto, ON, Canada M5S 1A8
Phone: (416)978-2719
Fax: (416)971-2200

Description: Obstetricians, pediatricians, gynecologists, and other individuals who are interested in fetal and maternal health. Promotes improvements and techniques in the standards of perinatal medicine. Works to inform the public on the aspects of perinatology.

★9669★ International Society for the Advancement of Humanistic Studies in Gynecology (ISFAHSIG)
7861 W. 38th Ave.
Wheat Ridge, CO 80033-6109
Phone: (303)756-6140
Bruce Richards, Contact

Founded: 1969. **Members:** 250. **Description:** Obstetricians, gynecologists, urologists, surgeons, radiologists, and opthalmologists; professionals who support humanistic studies in obstetrics and gynecology. Works to: promote and further education on the humanistic aspects of medicine; improve the quality of medical care. Contributes to the continuing education of health practitioners working for the betterment of human reproduction and the resolution of social, political, and economic problems in the field. Facilitates exchange of professional, philosophic, and scientific information among health professionals and experts on the nontechnical aspects of human relationships related to reproduction.

★9670★ La Leche League International (LLLI)
1400 Meacham
Schaumburg, IL 60173
Phone: (708)519-7730
Free: 800-LA-LECHE
Fax: (708)519-0035
Lee Ann Deal, Contact

Founded: 1956. **Members:** 40,000. **Local Groups:** 3000. **Description:** Helps mothers worldwide to breastfeed through mother-to-mother support, encouragement, information, and education and promotes a better understanding of breastfeeding as an important element in the healthy development of the baby and mother. Provides support through informal discussions and individualized phone counseling. Group maintains that breastfeeding infants will encourage closer family relationships. Has organized a professional advisory board and 550 breastfeeding resource centers in 48 countries. Supplies information through publications, telephone service, and correspondence. **Publications:** *Alumnae News*, quarterly. • Annual Report. • *Becoming a Father*. • Booklets. • *Breastfeeding Abstracts*, quarterly. Emphasizes clinical applications; includes book reviews. *Price:* $12.50/year. • *Breastfeeding Answer Book*. • *LaLeche League Directory*, annual. Directory. • *LaLeche League International Catalogue*, semiannual. Catalog. • *Leaven*, bimonthly. • *LLLI Personnel Directory*, annual. Directory. • *Mothering Multiples*. • *New Beginnings*, bimonthly. Journal. Includes articles about breastfeeding, parenting, family life, and nutrition, and book reviews. *Price:* Included in membership dues; $15 for nonmembers. • *Nightime Parenting*. • *Nighttime Parenting*. • *Of Cradles and Careers: A Guide to Reshaping Your Job to Include a Baby in Your Life*. • Pamphlets. • Reprints. • *Safe and Healthy: A Parents Guide to Children's Illnesses and Accidents*. • *Whole Foods for the Whole Family*. • *The Womanly Art of Breastfeeding*.

★9671★ Maternity Action Alliance
PO Box 884
Christchurch, New Zealand
Rhea Daellenbach, Contact

Languages: English. **Description:** Works to improve services for mothers, fathers, and babies, through the first year of life. Disseminates information on maternity benefits and rights. Campaigns for policies designed to meet the needs of users of healthcare services; provides a forum for discussion between users and service providers.

★9672★ Maternity Alliance (MA)
PO Box 314
Katoomba, NSW 2780, Australia
Phone: 47 822008
Fax: 47 825090
Ms. Hilda Bastian, Convenor

Founded: 1987. **Members:** 140. **Languages:** English. **Description:** Maternity consumer groups, interested consumers, and maternity professionals. Organizes consumer groups to ensure that women have an effective voice in issues relating to maternity care in Australia. Strives to improve the services offered to women during pregnancy, childbirth, and children's first years of life. **Publications:** *MA News*, semiannual. Journal.

★9673★ Maternity Alliance (MA)
15 Britannia St.
London WCIX 9JP, England
Phone: 171 8371265
Fax: 171 8379151
Christine Gowdridge, Contact

Founded: 1979. **Languages:** English. **Description:** Individuals and organizations concerned with rights and services for parents and babies. Campaigns for improvements in rights and services for mothers, fathers, and babies. Concerns include: improvement in health care before conception and the first year of life; financial support for low income families; protection of working mothers' rights; and availability of transportation and housing. Conducts research on child health services, homeless families, sugar content of baby foods, and parents with special needs. **Publications:** *Getting Fit for Pregnancy*. Bulletin. • *Maternity Action*, periodic. Bulletin. • *Money for Mothers and Babies*, periodic. Bulletin. • *Pregnant at Work*, annual. • *Thinking About a Baby - A Man's Guide to Pre-Pregnancy Health*, periodic.

★9674★ Maternity Center Association (MCA)
48 E. 92nd St.
New York, NY 10128
Phone: (212)369-7300
Fax: (212)369-8747
Ruth W. Lubic, Gen.Dir.

Founded: 1918. **Members:** 450. **Description:** Laypersons, physicians, nurses, nurse-midwives, childbirth educators, and public health workers interested in improvement of maternity care, maternal and infant health, and family life. Maintains Childbearing Center for healthy mothers and their families. Conducts well woman program and expectant parents and sibling preparation classes. Sponsors research; administers nurse-midwifery student assistance fund. Co-sponsors community-based Nurse-Midwifery Education Program. **Publications:** *The Birth Atlas*. • Booklets. • Books. • Pamphlets. • *Preparation for Childbearing*. • *Publications Catalog*, annual. Catalog. *Price:* Free. • *Special Delivery*, semiannual. Newsletter. Contains information on the activities of the organization. *Price:* Included in membership dues. • Videos. Also publishes teaching aids for health professionals, charts, and slides.

★9675★ Menopauze: Probleemopvang
University Hospital Sasthuisberg-St. Rafael
Dept. of Obstetrics and Gynecology
Capucienenvoer 33
B-3000 Louvain, Belgium
Phone: 16 332632
Prof. P. Nijs, Contact

Founded: 1968. **Members:** 8. **Languages:** Dutch, English, French. **Description:** Promotes the study of menopause. Supports theories of psychosomatic menopause. Conducts clinical training and teaching programs in psychosomatic gynecology. Offers marriage and family therapy sessions. Conducts sexological research.

★9676★ Midwest Parentcraft Center (MPC)
3921 N. Lincoln
Chicago, IL 60613
Phone: (312)725-7767
Margaret Gamper, R.N., Exec.Dir.

Founded: 1950. **Description:** Prenatal instructors, parents, and professionals involved in parenting and pregnancy. To instruct and educate expectant mothers and others in the Gamper Method of childbirth. (The Gamper Method, based on the teachings of several 19th century physicians and developed by Margaret Gamper in 1946, is designed to prepare the prospective mother for childbirth by instilling self-determination and confidence in her ability to work with the physiological changes of her body during pregnancy, labor, and delivery.) Conducts prenatal and grandparenting classes and workshops; operates in-service programs for hospitals and clinics; sponsors programs on topics such as grieving and history of birth procedures. Disseminates teaching aids including slides, films, records, and tapes. Grants childbirth educator certificates to qualified applicants who have taught Gamper Method classes under the supervision of an instructor. Operates charitable program and speakers' bureau; maintains library of 6000 volumes on childbirth, midwifery, marriage, sex, and childcare. The center's activities are currently concentrated in Ohio, Illinois, Indiana, Wisconsin, and Michigan. **Publications:** *Heir Raising News*, quarterly. • *Preparation for the Heir Minded.*

★ 9677 ★ **Midwives Alliance of North America (MANA)**
PO Box 175
Newton, KS 67114
Phone: (316)283-4543
Fax: (316)283-4543
Diane Barnes, Pres.

Founded: 1982. **Members:** 900. **Regional Groups:** 10. **Description:** Midwives, student/apprentice midwives, and persons supportive of midwifery. Seeks to expand communication and support among midwives. Works to promote basic competency in midwives; develops and encourages guidelines for their education. Offers legal, legislative, and political information and resource referrals; conducts networking on local, state, and regional bases; compiles statistics. **Publications:** Brochures. • *MANA News*, quarterly. Also publishes information packets.

★ 9678 ★ **Midwives Information and Resource Service (MIDIRS)**
9 Elmdale Rd.
Clifton
Bristol, Avon BS8 1SL, England
Phone: 117 9251791
Fax: 117 9251792
Joy Rodwell, Contact

Founded: 1983. **Languages:** English. **Description:** Provides information to health professionals on maternal health care. Acts as a clearinghouse, offering articles, books, and other information concerning midwifery. Conducts educational programs. **Publications:** *Directory of Maternity Organisations*, periodic. Directory. • *How To Find Out - Information Sources in Midwifery*, periodic. Bulletin. • *MIDIRS Midwifery Digest*, quarterly.

Miscarriage Association
See: Entry 11234

★ 9679 ★ **Museum of Menstruation**
PO Box 2398
Landover Hills Branch
Hyattsville, MD 20784-2398
Phone: (301)459-4450
Fax: (301)577-2913
Harry Finley, Founder & Dir.

Founded: 1994. **Description:** Seeks to educate the public on the cultural history of menstruation. Conducts research and statistical studies. Offers assistance to individuals conducting patent and advertising research. **Publications:** *CATAMENIA: Studies in the Cultural History of Menstrual Hygiene and Menstruation*, quarterly. *Price:* Free.

★ 9680 ★ **National Association of Childbearing Centers (NACC)**
3123 Gottschall Rd.
Perkiomenville, PA 18074
Phone: (215)234-8068
Fax: (215)234-8829
Kate Ernst, Dir.

Founded: 1983. **Members:** 525. **Regional Groups:** 6. **State Groups:** 1. **Description:** Birth centers; interested individuals and businesses that support the group's work. Acts as national information service on freestanding birth centers for state health departments, insurance companies, government agencies, consultants, hospitals, physicians, certified nurse-midwives, nurses, and families; promotes quality care in freestanding birth centers through state licensure and national standard-setting mechanisms, educational workshops, and support of professional education for midwives. Provides standards for certification of birth centers. Compiles statistics. **Publications:** *Birth Center Information Packet*. Articles. Covers growth and development, regulation, costs, reimbursement, research, and selected issues of NACC News. *Price:* $30. • *NACC Membership Directory*, annual. Membership Directory. *Price:* Included in membership dues. • *NACC News*, bimonthly. • *National Birth Center Study*. Reprint. *Price:* $1. • *Quality Assurance/Risk Management Manual*. Manual. Contains forms and instructions for implementing a quality assurance/risk management program in birth centers. *Price:* $75 for members; $110 for nonmembers. • *Sample Birth Center Policy and Procedure Manual*. Manual. Contains revised policies and procedures of Maternity Center Association's demonstration center, The Childbearing Center. Includes diskettes for customization. *Price:* $200. • *Standards for Freestanding Birth Centers*. *Price:* $15. • *"The Birth Center" Brochure*. Brochure. Contains information describing freestanding birth centers. Designed for public education and promotion of the concept of birth centers. *Price:* $1. • *"The Birth Center" Video*. Video. Designed to increase public awareness of the presence of birth centers. *Price:* $39.95.

★ 9681 ★ **National Association of Childbirth Assistants (NACA)**
205 Copco Ln.
San Jose, CA 95126
Free: 800-868-NACA
Claudia Lowe, Founder

Founded: 1985. **Members:** 500. **Description:** Professional organization of childbirth assistants. Provides information, resources, and referrals to childbearing families. Conducts national training workshops. Awards childbirth assistant certification. Compiles statistics; maintains speakers' bureau. **Publications:** *Becoming a Childbirth Assistant: The Lowe Method.* • *Childbirth Assistant Journal*, periodic. Journal. • *Inside NACA*, periodic. Newsletter. • *Professional Membership Directory*. Membership Directory. • *You and Me: Becoming a Family*, periodic. Newsletter.

National Association of Neonatal Nurses (NANN)
See: Entry 9103

National Association for Perinatal Addiction Research and Educati on (NAPARE)
See: Entry 12054

National Certification Corporation for the Obstetric, Gynecologic and Neonatal Nursing Specialties (NCC)
See: Entry 9114

★ 9682 ★ **National Council on Women's Health**
1300 York Ave.
Box 52
New York, NY 10021
Phone: (212)535-0031
Fax: (212)472-9871
Laura Scharf, Exec.Dir.

Founded: 1979. **Members:** 500. **Description:** Health professionals and interested individuals. Promotes the education of the public and policy makers on women's health issues. Provides medical information to assist women in making informed medical decisions. Maintains speakers' bureau. Conducts educational programs. **Publications:** Newsletter, quarterly.

★ 9683 ★ **National Perinatal Association (NPA)**
3500 E. Fletcher Ave., Ste. 209
Tampa, FL 33613
Phone: (813)971-1008
Fax: (813)971-9306
Julie A. Leachman, Exec.Dir.

Founded: 1976. **Members:** 1,500. **Regional Groups:** 1. **State Groups:** 23. **Description:** Organizations and individuals interested in perinatal health care. Purpose is to promote improved patient care, education, research, advocacy and delivery systems for perinatal health. **Publications:** *Journal of Perinatology*, bimonthly. Journal. Examines all facets of perinatology/neonatology from a variety of perspectives. *Price:* Included in membership dues; $50/year for nonmembers. • *National Perinatal Association Bulletin*, quarterly. Newsletter. Includes article reviews and legislative news. *Price:* Included in membership dues; $15/year for nonmembers. • *Proceedings*.

★ 9684 ★ **National Women's Coalition**
PO Box 4386
Manila 2800, Philippines

Languages: English, Tagalog. **Description:** Individuals interested in women's health issues, particularly maternal and neonatal mortality, in the Philippines. Promotes: improvement of reproductive health centers; integration of community education and reproductive information dissemination; centralization of women's health services to ease access; institutionalization of legal consulting services available to women.

★9685★ New Zealand College of Midwives
PO Box 21-106
906-908 Colombo St.
Christchurch, New Zealand
Phone: 3 3772732
Fax: 3 3772732
Karen Guilliland, Coord.

Founded: 1990. **Members:** 1,500. **Regional Groups:** 10. **Languages:** English. **Description:** Midwives, consumer groups, and interested individuals. Promotes midwifery services and education, and represents the interests of midwives to governmental bodies and the public. Prescribes and monitors standards for the practice and education of midwifery. Acts as a consultant for governmental agencies; engages in the negotiation of government funding for community and independent midwifery services. Offers courses jointly with colleges and universities. **Publications:** *New Zealand College of Midwives*, semiannual. Journal. • Newsletter, bimonthly.

★9686★ New Zealand Endometriosis Foundation
PO Box 1683
Palmerston North, New Zealand
Margaret McKenzie, Coord.

Founded: 1986. **Members:** 400. **Languages:** English. **Description:** Works to educate the public on the symptoms and treatments for endometriosis. Provides information kits and conducts lectures. Encourages women to seek proper treatment and emotional support. Fosters friendship among sufferers of endometriosis. Operates a 24-hour hotline. **Publications:** Newsletter, quarterly.

★9687★ North American Menopause Society (NAMS)
University Hospitals of Cleveland
Department of OB/GYN
11100 Uleed
Cleveland, OH 44106
Phone: (216)844-3334
Fax: (216)844-3348
Wulf H. Utian, M.D., Pres.

Founded: 1989. **Members:** 1,550. **Description:** Physicians, scientists, research and clinical personnel, and other health care professionals are active members; student or physicians serving residencies or fellowships are associate members. Promotes the study of the climacteric in men and women. Advances the exchange of research plans and experience between members. Offers educational programs. **Publications:** *Flashes*, quarterly. Newsletter. *Price:* Free. • *Menopause Management*.

★9688★ Organisation Gestosis - Society for the Study of Pathophysiology of Pregnancy (OG)
(Geburtshilfe und Gynakologie FMH)
Geburtshilfe und Gynakologie FMH
Gerbergasse 14
CH-4051 Basel, Switzerland
Phone: 61 2615555
Fax: 61 2615934
PD Ernest T. Rippmann, Sec.Gen.

Founded: 1969. **Members:** 4,500. **Regional Groups:** 11. **Languages:** English, German. **Description:** Obstetricians, gynecologists, neonatologists, nephrologists, epidemiologists, pathologists, geneticists, immunologists, physiologists, and health officials in 75 countries in the field of EPH-Gestosis. EPH-Gestosis is a term adopted by the society to describe a malady that may occur during pregnancy wherein a woman exhibits excessive accumulation of body water, protein in the urine, and/or abnormal elevation of blood pressure; EPH is derived from the terms for 3 conditions: edema, proteinuria, and hypertension; gestosis is derived from the word gestation and the suffix -osis which means disturbance. The condition is prevalent in socioeconomically depressed areas where poor hygiene and malnutrition aggravate the effects of inadequate prenatal care. The society reports that EPH-Gestosis occurs in 10% of world population births, is responsible for as much as 50% of perinatal/fetal death, and is the cause of up to 33% of maternal mortality. Objectives are to: disseminate information to medical and lay personnel and the public; foster research, preventive health care, and therapy; internationalize nomenclature, classification, and definitions in the field of EPH-Gestosis for diagnosis, therapy, and comparative techniques; standardize methods of investigation; serve as documentation center; foster exchange of scientists. Conducts discussion groups and study groups on topics such as edema, proteinuria, cytology, serum-protein, and hypertension. Suggests alterations of definitions of EPH-Gestosis as offered by International Classification of Diseases of the World Health Organization. Makes recommendations for the most modern and successful measures of prevention and treatment of EPH-Gestosis. Collects and publishes papers submitted by researchers worldwide. Sponsors symposia and workshops; conducts surveys. Operates Organisation Gestosis Press, a publishing house. **Publications:** *Congress Volume*, annual. • *Instruction Bulletin*, periodic. Bulletin. • *International Journal of Feto-Maternal Medicine*, periodic. Journal. • *La Malformazioni Uterine*. Book. • *OG News*, periodic. • Proceedings. **Also Known As:** Society for the Study of Pathophysiology of Pregnancy.

★9689★ Perinatal Society of New Zealand (PSNZ)
Wellington Hospital
Dept. of Obstetrics and Gynecology
Wellington, New Zealand
Phone: 4 3855943
Dr. P. Stone, Pres.

Founded: 1979. **Members:** 240. **Local Groups:** 12. **Languages:** English. **Description:** Pediatricians, obstetricians, neo-natal and obstetric nurses, and midwives in New Zealand. Aims to foster continued improvement in the standards of perinatal medicine and nursing. Works to increase public understanding of the activities in and the objectives of perinatology. Sponsors continuing education programs in perinatology. Promotes collaboration and open discussion among members. **Formerly:** (1990) New Zealand Perinatal Society.

Postpartum Support, International (PSI)
See: Entry 7485

Pregnancy Advisory Service
See: Entry 11248

★9690★ Professional Midwives Association of Germany
(Bund Freiberuflicher Hebammen Deutschlands eV)
Freiheitsstr. 11
41352 Korschenbroich, Germany
Phone: 2161 648577
Fax: 2161 648577
Gabriele Schippers, Contact

Founded: 1984. **Members:** 480. **Languages:** English, Spanish. **Description:** Midwives in Germany. Represents the interests of midwives. Informs and contributes to the health education of the population. Promotes continuing education for midwives in the interests of mother and child. **Publications:** *Hebammen Info*, quarterly. Newsletter.

★9691★ Read Natural Childbirth Foundation (RNCF)
PO Box 150956
San Rafael, CA 94915
Phone: (415)456-8462
Margaret B. Farley, Pres.

Founded: 1978. **Members:** 30. **State Groups:** 3. **Description:** Doctors, nurses, childbirth instructors, and parents. Promotes and teaches expectant parents the philosophies of natural childbirth pioneered by Grantly Dick-Read, a British doctor who began writing in 1932 about the then extremely controversial concept of natural childbirth and advocated relaxation as the key to comfortable labor. Techniques include abdominal and rib cage breathing and alleviation of fear, and thus pain, through knowledge. Acts as resource agency for the International Childbirth Education Association. Conducts charitable programs. Offers speakers' bureau. **Publications:** *A Time to Be Born*. Film. • Newsletter, periodic. • *Preparation for Childbirth: Handbook for Use in Exercise Classes for Expectant Parents*. Handbook.

★9692★ Royal College of Midwives
13-15 Mansfield St.
London W1M 0BE, England
Phone: 171 8725100
Fax: 171 8725101
Julia Allison, Gen.Sec.

Founded: 1881. **Members:** 34,500. **Languages:** English. **Description:** Promotes the practice of midwifery, and works to maintain high standards in the field. Provides educational programs to midwives in the areas of maternity, child care, and personal development. Represents worker rights of midwives to national legal and political authorities. Encourages and supports research. **Publications:** *Current Awareness Service*, quarterly. Bulletin. Contains a list of recent literature on midwifery. • *Delivery*. Newsletter. • *Midwives Chronicle*. Magazine.

★9693★ Safe Motherhood Initiative
Plot 196 Upper Mawanda Rd.
PO Box 1191
Kampala, Uganda
Phone: 41 530500
Fax: 41 230784
Dr. Josephine Kaselo, Contact

Founded: 1988. **Members:** 15. **National Groups:** 1. **Regional Groups:** 4. **State Groups:** 1. **Local Groups:** 387. **Languages:** English. **Description:** Seeks to improve women's health and to reduce the number of women who die from complications of pregnancy and childbirth. Promotes family planning activities; conducts educational programs on teenage sexuality, sexually transmitted diseases, AIDS, and parenting. **Publications:** *Africa Women and Health*, quarterly. Magazine.

★ 9694 ★ **Society for Gynecologic Investigation (SGI)**
409 12th St. SW
Washington, DC 20024
Phone: (202)863-2544
Fax: (202)544-0453
Ava Tayman, Dir.

Founded: 1953. **Members:** 650. **Description:** Present and former faculty members of institutions interested or engaged in fundamental gynecologic research. Purpose is to stimulate, encourage, assist, and conduct gynecologic research. **Publications:** *Gynecologic Investigation*, semiannual. Published as a section of the *American Journal of Obstetrics and Gynecology*.

Society of Gynecologic Oncologists (SGO)
See: Entry 5987

★ 9695 ★ **Society for Menstrual Cycle Research (SMCR)**
10559 N. 104th Pl.
Scottsdale, AZ 85258
Phone: (602)451-9731
Mary Anna Friederich, M.D., Sec.-Treas.

Founded: 1979. **Members:** 100. **Description:** Physicians, nurses, endocrinologists, geneticists, physiologists, psychologists, sociologists, researchers, educators, students, and others interested in the health needs of women as related to the menstrual cycle. Goals are: to identify research priorities, recommend research strategies, and promote interdisciplinary research on the menstrual cycle; to establish a communication network for facilitating interdisciplinary dialogue on menstrual cycle events; to disseminate information and promote discussion of issues among public groups. **Publications:** *Changing Perspectives on Menopause*. Book. • *Culture, Society and Menstruation*. Book. • *Membership Roster*, annual. Membership Directory. • *Menarche: The Transition from Girl to Woman*. Book. • *The Menstrual Cycle, Volume 1: A Synthesis of Interdisciplinary Research*. • *The Menstrual Cycle, Volume 2: Research and Implications for Women's Health*. • *Menstrual Health in Women's Lives*. • *Menstruation, Health, and Illness*. • *Mind-Body Rhythmicity, A Menstrual Cycle Prospective*. Book. • Newsletter, quarterly. • *Proceedings 8th Conference Society for Menstrual Cycle Research*. Proceedings.

★ 9696 ★ **Society for Obstetric Anesthesia and Perinatology (SOAP)**
1910 Byrd Ave., Ste. 100
PO Box 11086
Richmond, VA 23230-1086
Phone: (804)282-5051
Fax: (804)282-0090
John A. Hinckley, Exec.Sec.

Founded: 1969. **Members:** 785. **Description:** Physicians and scientists interested in perinatal health care. Purpose is to improve the health care of pregnant women and their unborn children. Conducts specialized education programs; compiles statistics. **Publications:** Newsletter, quarterly. *Price:* Included in membership dues.

★ 9697 ★ **Society of Perinatal Obstetricians (SPO)**
409 12th St. SW
Washington, DC 20024-2188
Phone: (202)863-2476
Fax: (202)554-0453
Pat Stahr, Exec.Dir.

Founded: 1977. **Members:** 1,450. **Description:** Obstetricians and gynecologists specializing in maternal-fetal medicine. Works to improve perinatal care through promotion and expansion of education in obstetrical perinatology. Provides a forum for exchange between members. **Publications:** *American Journal of Obstetrics and Gynecology*, periodic. Journal.

Society for Prevention of Infertility (SPI)
See: Entry 11252

★ 9698 ★ **Society for Protection of Motherhood and Childhood**
Krasnopolyanskaya str. 6-2, Apt. 363
127599 Moscow, Russia
Phone: 95 4862379
Olga Popova, Co-Chairwoman

Founded: 1989. **Members:** 11. **Description:** Promotes the quality of maternal and infant healthcare in Russia. Conducts charitable programs.

★ 9699 ★ **THAW Partnership**
627 Eagle Rock Ave., Ste. 309
West Orange, NJ 07052
Phone: (201)744-4482
Fax: (201)746-6302
Lisa Finan, Pres.

Languages: English. **Description:** Women opposed harmful social practices in traditional societies, including female circumcision and other forms of genital mutilation. Works to educate people living in traditional societies of the harmful health and psychological effects of these practices. **Also Known As:** The Health and Welfare of All Women Partnership.

★ 9700 ★ **Triplet Connection (TC)**
PO Box 99571
Stockton, CA 95209
Phone: (209)474-0885
Fax: (209)474-2233
Janet Bleyl, Pres.

Founded: 1983. **Members:** 10,000. **Description:** Parents and expectant parents of triplets or larger multiple births. Works to help families prepare and deal with high-risk multiple pregnancy and birth, and aftermath of such births. Acts as support group for members. Provides information on issues of relevance, including breastfeeding, medical sources, and clothing and equipment exchanges. Offers advice on prevention of premature birth. Reports on experiences of families of multiple births; networks families. Compiles statistics on multiple births, and makes data available to expectant parents and medical researchers. Maintains Tender Hearts, a group which offers support to mothers of multiple births who have lost one or more of their babies. Operates speakers' bureau. **Publications:** *The Triplet Connection--Newsletter*, quarterly. Newsletter. Reports on multiple pregnancy and the problems faced by the birth and care of these children. Includes medical updates. *Price:* $15/year.

★ 9701 ★ **Uganda Traditional Birth Attendants Association**
PO Box 31049
Kampala, Uganda

Languages: English. **Description:** Promotes education concerning natural childbirth. Conducts research and educational programs regarding midwifery.

★ 9702 ★ **Vulvar Pain Foundation**
PO Drawer 177
Graham, NC 27253
Phone: (910)226-0704
Fax: (910)226-8518
Joanne J. Yount, Exec.Dir.

Founded: 1992. **Members:** 2,200. **Description:** Women with vulvar pain; medical doctors, scientists, clinical psychologists, nurse practitioners, and other healthcare professionals interested in the treatment of vulvar pain. Seeks to provide women with vulvar pain information about their conditions and appropriate treatments. Educates patients, physicians, and the public about vulvar pain, its causes, diagnostic techniques, treatments, and current research. Provides physician referral service. Promotes research into the causes and treatments of vulvar pain. Develops support networks for women with vulvar pain. Maintains speakers' bureau. **Publications:** Brochure. Describes the purposes and activities of the foundation. • *The Vulvar Pain Newsletter*, quarterly. Newsletter.

Women's Health
See: Entry 1535

★ 9703 ★ **Women's Health Concern**
83 Earl's Court Rd.
London W8 6EF, England
Phone: 171 9383932
Fax: 171 37608
Joan Jenkins, Pres.

Founded: 1972. **Description:** Works to advance research aimed towards finding cures for and relief from gynecological and obstetrical disorders. Offers counseling services and information helplines. Disseminates informational booklets.

Women's Nationwide Cancer Control Campaign (WNCCC)
See: Entry 5993

Y-ME National Breast Cancer Organization
(Y-ME)
See: Entry 5995

Research Centers

★9704★ Baylor College of Medicine
Prenatal Diagnostic Center
1 Baylor Plaza
Houston, TX 77030
Phone: (713)798-7500
Fax: (713)798-3800
Robert J. Carpenter, Jr., M.D., Dir.

Research Activities and Fields: Prenatal diagnosis by ultrasonography, amniocentesis, and fetal blood sampling, chorionic villi sampling, longitudinal fetal growth, and pre/post-conceptual counseling. Conducts evaluation of intrauterine growth retardation in at-risk patients on prospective basis. **Publications:** Annual Report of Department of Obstetrics/Gynecology.

★9705★ Center for Study of Multiple Birth
333 E. Superior St., Ste. 476
Chicago, IL 60611
Phone: (312)266-9093
Fax: (312)908-8500
Donald M. Keith, Exec.Dir.

Research Activities and Fields: Multiple birth, twin gestation, twin pregnancy diagnosis, and twin care. Research is aimed at decreasing the high infant mortality rate involved in multiple births. **Publications:** Resource list on twin care and other topics of concern to multiple birth families. **Formerly:** Center for Study of Multiple Gestation.

★9706★ Endocrinology Research
Laboratory
Cabrini Medical Center
247 3rd Ave.
New York, NY 10010
Phone: (212)995-7081
Dr. Leonid Poretsky, Dir.

Research Activities and Fields: Effects of insulin and insulin-like growth factors on ovarian function. Focuses on expression and regulation of insulin receptors and type I IGF receptors in human ovarian cells. Studies serve to better understand ovarian dysfunction related to insulin resistance, diabetes mellitus, obesity, and polycystic ovary syndrome.

★9707★ Human Lactation Center, Ltd.
666 Sturges Hwy.
Westport, CT 06880
Phone: (203)259-5995
Fax: (203)259-7667
Dana Raphael, Ph.D., Dir.

Research Activities and Fields: Human lactation and maternal and infant feeding behavior. **Publications:** *The Lactation Review* (occasionally).

★9708★ Jeanette Kennelly Kroch Center
for Twin Studies
Northwestern Memorial Hospital
Prentice Pavilion
333 E. Superior St.
Chicago, IL 60611
Phone: (312)908-7519
Fax: (312)908-0367
Alan M. Peaceman, M.D., Dir.

Research Activities and Fields: Multiple births. Conducts ultrasound and genetic research for the early detection of identical or fraternal twins; longitudinal ultrasound studies to determine normal growth patterns in multiple-birth pregnancies; clinical studies of methods to prevent premature labor and delivery, which result in low-birthweight twins; and studies related to specific aspects of twin development, such as speech patterns.

★9709★ Joint Division of Newborn
Medicine
Creighton Univ. - Univ. of Nebraska
Medical Center
600 S. 42nd St.
Omaha, NE 68198-1205
Phone: (402)559-6750
Fax: (402)559-7341
M. Patricia Leuschen, Ph.D., Research Dir.

Research Activities and Fields: Cell and molecular basis of cerebral ischemia, ontogeny of C3 complement in human lung, ultrastructural morphometry telencephalic microvasculature in subependymal hemorrhage in premature infants using the beagle pup model, and physiologic and pharmacodynamic evaluation of infants on ECMO therapy. Conducts clinical trials of two types of high frequency ventilation. Participating in clinical trials of Infasurf, a fetal calf surfactant. **Formerly:** Neonatology Research Laboratory.

★9710★ Medical College of Pennsylvania
and Hahnemann University
Center for Women's Health
Presidential City, Monroe Pavillion
Cityline & Presidential Blvd.
Philadelphia, PA 19131
Phone: (215)581-6267
Fax: (215)878-2128
Marie Savard, Contact

Research Activities and Fields: Health of the mature woman, including osteoporosis, mammography, urinary incontinence, and menopause. **Formerly:** Center for the Mature Woman.

Melpomene Institute for Women's Health
Research
See: Entry 11970

New England Medical Center (GOG)
Gynecologic Oncology Group
See: Entry 6084

Northwestern University
John I. Brewer Trophoblastic Disease
Center
See: Entry 6093

★9711★ Perinatal Research Institute
231 Bethesda Ave.
Cincinnati, OH 45267-0541
Phone: (513)558-0543
Fax: (513)558-7770
Reginald C. Tsang, M.D., Exec.Dir.

Research Activities and Fields: Developmental perinatology, including molecular genetics and cell regulation; perinatal nutrition, metabolism, and endocrinology; fetal and neonatal physiology; and perinatal bioengineering and computer engineering. Long-term projects include studies of diabetes in pregnancy and intrauterine growth retardation. Developed Alcyon Patient Information System, a computer system that regulates temperatures in standard convectively heated incubators.

U.S. Department of Defense
Armed Forces Institute of Pathology
Center for Advanced Pathology
Gynecologic and Breast Pathology
Department
See: Entry 10152

U.S. Department of Health and Human
Services
National Institute of Child Health and
Human Development
See: Entry 3354

★9712★ U.S. Department of Health and
Human Services
National Institute of Child Health and
Human Development
Center for Research for Mothers and
Children
6100 Executive Blvd., Rm. 4B05K
Bethesda, MD 20892
Phone: (301)496-5097
Fax: (301)402-2085
Dr. Sumner Yaffe, Director

Research Activities and Fields: Center's mission is to support research and research training on the special health problems of mothers and children. Using all of the NIH research support mechanisms, the Center encompasses research in the biomedical and behavioral sciences, with special emphasis on pregnancy, perinatal biology, and human biological and behavioral development from conception through adolescence to maturity. Center maintains a close liaison with other NICHD units, other federal agencies, and private organizations concerned with relevant research. Center comprises branches for: 1) Endocrinology, Nutrition, and Growth; 2) Genetics and Teratology; 3) Human Learning and Behavior; 4) Mental Retardation and Developmental Disabilities; 5) Pregnancy and Perinatology; and 6) Pediatric, Adolescent and Maternal AIDS.

★9713★ U.S. Department of Health and
Human Services
National Institute of Child Health and
Human Development
Center for Research for Mothers and
Children
Perinatal Emphasis Research Centers
Program

Executive Plaza North, Rm. 643
6130 Executive Blvd.
Bethesda, MD 20892
Phone: (301)496-5575
Fax: (301)402-2085
Dr. Charlotte S. Catz, Branch Chief

Research Activities and Fields: Program promotes and supports multidisciplinary research efforts directed toward improving pregnancy outcomes and ensuring infant survival and well-being. Supported centers address issues in high-risk pregnancies (diabetes, hypertension), prevention of prematurity, fetal hypoxia, intra-uterine growth retardation, Sudden Infant Death Sydrome (SIDS), and sleep patterns. Centers are presently located at: 1) Brown University (Dr. William Oh, Principal Investigator); 2) Case Western Reserve University (Dr. Satish Kalhan, Principal Investigator); 3) University of Colorado (Dr. William W. Hay, Principal Investigator); 4) University of Cincinnati (Dr. Reginald Tsang, Principal Investigator); 5) Columbia University (Dr. Raymond Stark, Principal Investigator); 6) University of Texas (Dr. Paul MacDonald, Principal Investigator); 7) University of California, Los Angeles (Dr. Alan Jobe, Principal Investigator); and Stanford University (Dr. Horace Heller, Principal Investigator).

★9714★ U.S. Department of Health and Human Services
National Institute of Child Health and Human Development
Center for Research for Mothers and Children
Pregnancy and Perinatology Branch
6100 Executive Blvd., Rm. 4B03
Bethesda, MD 20892
Phone: (301)496-5575
Fax: (301)402-2085
Dr. Charlotte S. Catz, Chief

Research Activities and Fields: Objective of the Pregnancy and Perinatology Branch is to increase knowledge related to pregnancy and maternal health, embryonic development, fetal growth and maturation, labor and delivery, and infant well-being. Emphasis is on reducing infant mortality, ameliorating infant morbidity, and speeding the process by which new knowledge is transferred and incorporated into health care. Specific areas of interest are high-risk pregnancy, fetal pathophysiology, premature labor and birth, disorders of the newborn, and sudden infant death syndrome (SIDS).

★9715★ University of Alabama at Birmingham
Ob/Gyn Infectious Disease Research Laboratory
Dept. of Ob/Gyn
UAB Sta.
Birmingham, AL 35233-7333
Phone: (205)934-1191
Fax: (205)975-4375
William W. Andrews, Ph.D., Dir.

Research Activities and Fields: Infectious etiologies of preterm labor, fetal growth restriction, premature rupture of membranes, new antimicrobial therapies for postpartum endometritis, and the relationship between maternal infection and subsequent neonatal sepsis. **Formerly:** OB/GYN Bacteriology Research Laboratory.

★9716★ University of Arizona
Southwest Institute for Research on Women (SIROW)
102 Douglass Bldg.
Tucson, AZ 85721
Phone: (520)621-7338
Fax: (520)621-1533
Dr. Janice Monk, Exec.Dir.

Research Activities and Fields: Women in the Southwest, with emphasis on multicultural character of the region, educational issues, and impact of regional growth on women, particularly elderly women. Also studies women's health issues and women in public policy. **Publications:** *SIROW Newsletter* (two per year); SIROW Working Paper Series; Monographs.

★9717★ University of Chicago
Perinatal Center
Dept. of OB/GYN
5841 S. Maryland Ave., Box 446
MC 4076
Chicago, IL 60637
Phone: (312)702-6584
Fax: (312)702-5160
Prof. Atef H. Moawad, M.D., Chief of Obstetrics/Codir.

Research Activities and Fields: Fetal-maternal medicine, neonatology, and morbidity and mortality within perinatal medicine.

★9718★ University of Illinois at Chicago
Center for Health Services Research
M/C 922, Box 6998
Chicago, IL 60612
Phone: (312)996-7012
Fax: (312)413-7912
Dr. Robert J. Zalenski, Dir.

Research Activities and Fields: New health care tehnologies, medical informatics, health manpower, observation unit medicine in the hospital emergency room, and performance of preventive through tertiary healthcare delivery at the systems, program, and specific intervention levels. Studies focus on access, appropriateness, acceptibility, cost, safety, availability, effectiveness, benefits, and overall quality of healthcare. Specific topics include clinical decision-making, health information management, psychological and social sciences, and public health policy analysis. **Formerly:** Center for Study of Patient Care and Community Health (1981).

University of Michigan
Endocrine Laboratory
See: Entry 4939

University of Montreal
Sainte-Justine Hospital Research Centre
See: Entry 11297

★9719★ University of Southern California
Neonatology Research Units
1240 Mission Rd., Rm. L919
Los Angeles, CA 90033
Phone: (213)226-3408
Fax: (213)226-3440
Paul Y.K. Wu, M.D., Dir.

Research Activities and Fields: Clinical problems of the newborn and premature infant, in-

cluding studies on neonatal jaundice, phototherapy, nutrition and energy metabolism, body composition, renal function, pulmonary function and assisted ventilation, circulation, Sudden Infant Death Syndrome, biophysical monitoring of neonates, and follow-up of motor/mental performance of high risk infants. Operates in conjunction with the Hospital's newborn service, which delivers and cares for 18,000 infants yearly; investigation of research problems is integrated with clinical care of infants and training program for physicians.

★9720★ University of Western Ontario
Lawson Research Institute
St. Joseph's Health Centre
268 Grosvenor St.
London, ON, Canada N6A 4V2
Dr. John R.G. Challis, Scientific Dir.

Research Activities and Fields: Pregnancy and perinatology, including fetal endocrinology, fetal physiology, fetal neonatal growth, and fetal neonatal and infant health; endocrinology and metabolism, including diabetes and steroid metabolism; neurology and diagnostic imaging, including heart disease, cognitive neurology, development of new diagnostic imaging techniques and approaches, and magnetic resonance (MR) spectroscopy; cell biology, including hemostasis, thrombosis, and lung biology; gastroenterology and GI surgery; and clinical research. **Publications:** *Probe* (newsletter, nine per year).

★9721★ University of Wisconsin—Madison
Endocrinology-Reproductive Physiology Program
860 Animal Sciences Bldg.
1675 Observatory Dr.
Madison, WI 53706
Phone: (608)262-3222
Fax: (608)262-5436
Dr. Lewis G. Sheffield, Program Dir.

Research Activities and Fields: Reproductive biology, including ovarian function, examination of pregnancy, postpartum recovery period, regulation of testicular function as it relates to the gametogenic process, the effect of the female reproductive tract environment on the male gamete and its gametogenic process, the role of the sperm in fertilization and embryo loss, the neural, endocrinological, and related mechanisms of the sexual cycle, and cellular and molecular aspects of hormonal synthesis and action.

★9722★ Wayne State University
Fetal Alcohol Research Center
C.S. Mott Center
275 E. Hancock
Detroit, MI 48201
Phone: (313)577-1068
Fax: (313)577-8554
Dr. Ernest Abel, Dir.

Research Activities and Fields: Consequences of prenatal alcohol and drug exposure in animals and humans. Investigates methods for medical professionals to identify pregnancies at risk for alcohol-related birth defects. Seeks early identification of children exposed to prenatal alcohol.

★9723★ Women's Research Centre
2245 W. Broadway, Ste. 101
Vancouver, BC, Canada V6K 2E4
Phone: (604)734-0485
Fax: (604)734-0484
Jan Barnsley, Coord.
Research Activities and Fields: Women's issues, including wife assault, protection and housing for battered women, rape legislation, pornography, child sexual abuse, sexual discrimination, pay equity, and women in the work force. Develops research methodologies, disseminates information to Canadian women's organizations, and consults with women's groups regarding project and organizational development, and government and institutional responses to women's issues.

State Government Agencies

Maternal & Child Health

★9724★ Alabama Department of Public Health
Family Health Services Bureau
434 Monroe St.
Montgomery, AL 36130
Phone: (334)242-5661
Fax: (334)269-4865

★9725★ Alaska Department of Health and Social Services
Public Health Division
Maternal and Child Family Health Section
1231 Gambell St.
Anchorage, AK 99501-4627
Phone: (907)274-7626
Fax: (907)586-1877

★9726★ Arizona Department of Health Services
Family Health and Community Services Division
Women and Children's Health Office
1740 W. Adams Ave.
Phoenix, AZ 85007
Phone: (602)542-1870
Fax: (602)542-1265

★9727★ Arkansas Department of Health
Public Health Programs Bureau
Maternal and Child Health Division
PO Box 3278
Little Rock, AR 72203-3278
Phone: (501)661-2243
Fax: (501)671-1450

★9728★ California Health and Welfare Agency
Health Services Department
Maternal and Child Health Branch
714 P St., Rm. 1253
Sacramento, CA 95814
Phone: (916)657-1347
Fax: (916)657-3069

★9729★ Colorado Public and Environment Depratment
Health Office
Family and Community Health Services Division
4300 Cherry Creek Dr. S.
Denver, CO 80222-1530
Phone: (303)692-2310
Fax: (303)692-0095

★9730★ Connecticut Department of Public Health
Community Health Bureau
Child Adolescent Health Division
150 Washington St.
Hartford, CT 06106
Phone: (203)566-7024
Fax: (203)566-6055

★9731★ Delaware Department of Health and Social Services
Public Health Division
Women's and Infants' Health Service
Jesse Cooper Bldg.
PO Box 637
Dover, DE 19903
Phone: (302)739-3111
Fax: (302)739-6659

★9732★ District of Columbia Department of Human Services
Public Health Commission
Maternal and Child Health Services Office
1660 G St. NW
Washington, DC 20001
Phone: (202)727-0393
Fax: (202)727-0379

★9733★ Florida Department of Health and Rehabilitative Services
Family Health Services Office
1317 Winewood Blvd.
Tallahassee, FL 32399-0700
Phone: (904)487-1321
Fax: (904)922-2993

★9734★ Georgia Department of Medical Assistance
Maternal and Child Health Division
2 Peachtree St. NW
Atlanta, GA 30303
Phone: (404)651-5785
Fax: (404)651-6880

★9735★ Hawaii Department of Health
Health Resources Administration
Family Health Services Division
Maternal and Child Health Branch
3652 Kilauea Ave.
Honolulu, HI 96816
Phone: (808)733-9024
Fax: (808)586-4444

★9736★ Idaho Department of Health and Welfare
Health Division
Maternal and Child Health Bureau
PO Box 83720
Boise, ID 83720-0036
Phone: (208)334-5967
Fax: (208)334-6558

★9737★ Illinois Department of Public Health
Community Health Office
Family Health Division
535 W. Jefferson St.
Springfield, IL 62761
Phone: (217)782-2736
Fax: (217)782-3987

★9738★ Indiana Department of Health
Maternal and Child Health Services Division
2 N. Meridian
Indianapolis, IN 46204
Phone: (317)233-1262

★9739★ Iowa Department of Public Health
Family and Community Health Division
Maternal and Child Health Section
Lucas State Office Bldg.
321 E. 12th St.
Des Moines, IA 50319
Phone: (515)281-4911
Fax: (515)281-4958

★9740★ Kansas Department of Health and Environment
Health Division
Family Health Bureau
900 SW Jackson St., Ste. 620
Topeka, KS 66612
Phone: (913)296-1300
Fax: (913)296-1231

★9741★ Kentucky Human Resources Cabinet
Health Services Department
Maternal and Child Health Services Division
275 E. Main St.
Frankfort, KY 40621
Phone: (502)564-4830
Fax: (502)564-6533

★9742★ Louisiana Department of Health and Hospitals
Public Health Office
Health Services Programs
Maternal and Child Health Section
325 Loyola Ave., Rm. 612
PO Box 60630
New Orleans, LA 70160
Phone: (504)568-5073
Fax: (504)568-8162

★9743★ Maine Department of Human Services
Health Bureau
Maternal and Child Health Division
State House Sta. 11
Augusta, ME 04333
Phone: (207)287-3311
Fax: (207)287-3005

★9744★ Maryland Department of Health and Mental Hygiene
Public Health Services Office
Local and Family Health Administration
201 W. Preston St., 5th Fl.
Baltimore, MD 21201
Phone: (410)225-5300
Fax: (410)225-6489

★9745★ Massachusetts Executive Office of Health and Human Services
Public Health Department
Family Health Services Division
150 Tremont St.
Boston, MA 02111
Phone: (617)727-3372
Fax: (617)727-2559

★9746★ Michigan Department of Public Health
Child and Family Services Bureau
3423 N. Logan
PO Box 30195
Lansing, MI 48909
Phone: (517)335-8955
Fax: (517)335-9476

★9747★ Minnesota Department of Health
Family Health Division
717 Delaware St. SE
Box 9441
Minneapolis, MN 55440
Phone: (612)623-5166
Fax: (612)623-5794

★9748★ Mississippi Department of Health
Health Services Bureau
WIC Services
PO Box 1700
Jackson, MS 39215-1700
Phone: (601)960-7829
Fax: (601)354-6104

★9749★ Missouri Department of Health
Maternal, Child and Family Health Division
PO Box 570
Jefferson City, MO 65102
Phone: (314)751-6174
Fax: (314)751-6010

★9750★ Montana Department of Health and Environmental Sciences
Health Services Division
Family, Maternal and Child Health Bureau
Cogswell Bldg., Rm. C108
Helena, MT 59620
Phone: (406)444-4740

★9751★ Nebraska Department of Health
Health Promotion and Disease Prevention Bureau
Maternal and Child Health Division
301 Centennial Mall S.
PO Box 95007
Lincoln, NE 68509
Phone: (402)471-2907
Fax: (402)471-0383

★9752★ Nevada Department of Human Resources
Health Division
Family Health Service
505 E. King St., Rm. 201
Carson City, NV 89710
Phone: (702)687-4885
Fax: (702)687-4733

★9753★ New Hampshire Department of Health and Human Services
Public Health Services Division
Maternal and Child Health Bureau

6 Hazen Dr.
Concord, NH 03301
Phone: (603)271-4516
Fax: (603)271-3745

★9754★ New Jersey Department of Health
Family Health Services Division
Maternal and Child Health Services
50 E. State St., CN 364
Trenton, NJ 08625-0364
Phone: (609)292-5656
Fax: (609)292-3580

★9755★ New Mexico Department of Health
Public Health Division
Maternal and Child Health Bureau
1190 St. Francis Dr.
PO Box 26110
Santa Fe, NM 87502-6110
Phone: (505)827-2350
Fax: (505)827-2329

★9756★ New York State Department of Health
Community Health Center
Family Health Division
Corning Tower, Empire State Plaza
Albany, NY 12237
Phone: (518)473-7922

★9757★ North Carolina Department of Environment, Health, and Natural Resources
Health Director's Office
Maternal and Child Health Division
PO Box 27687
Raleigh, NC 27611
Phone: (919)715-4125
Fax: (919)715-3060

★9758★ North Dakota Department of Health and Consolidated Laboratories
Preventive Health Section
Maternal and Child Health Division
600 E. Boulevard
Bismarck, ND 58505
Phone: (701)328-2493
Fax: (701)328-4727

★9759★ Ohio Department of Health
Maternal and Child Health Division
Maternal and Child Health Bureau
246 N. High St.
Columbus, OH 43266-0588
Phone: (614)466-5332
Fax: (614)644-0085

★9760★ Oklahoma Department of Health
Maternal and Child Health Services
1000 NE 10th St.
PO Box 53551
Oklahoma City, OK 73152
Phone: (405)271-4476
Fax: (405)271-3431

★9761★ Oregon Department of Human Resources
Health Division
Child and Family Health Center
800 NE Oregon St.
Portland, OR 97232
Phone: (503)731-4016
Fax: (503)731-4083

★9762★ Pennsylvania Department of Health
Maternal and Child Health Bureau
Maternal and Child Health Division
PO Box 90
Harrisburg, PA 17108
Phone: (717)787-7440
Fax: (717)772-6939

★9763★ Rhode Island Department of Health
Family Health Office
3 Capitol Hill
Providence, RI 02908-5097
Phone: (401)277-2312
Fax: (401)277-1442

★9764★ South Carolina Department of Health and Environmental Control
Health Services Office
Maternal and Child Health Bureau
2600 Bull St.
Columbia, SC 29201
Phone: (803)734-4190
Fax: (803)737-3946

★9765★ South Dakota Department of Health
Maternal and Child Health Program
445 E. Capitol
Pierre, SD 57501-3185
Phone: (605)773-3737
Fax: (605)773-5683

★9766★ Tennessee Department of Health
Health Services Bureau
Maternal and Children's Health Section
312 8th Ave. N., 12th Fl.
Nashville, TN 37247-0101
Phone: (615)741-7353
Fax: (615)532-2286

★9767★ Texas Department of Health
Women and Children's Bureau
1100 W. 49th St.
Austin, TX 78756
Phone: (512)458-7700
Fax: (512)458-7477

★9768★ Utah Department of Health
Family Health Services Division
Maternal and Child Health Bureau
PO Box 144100
Salt Lake City, UT 84114-4100
Phone: (801)584-8237
Fax: (801)538-6510

★9769★ Vermont Agency of Human Services
Health Department
Maternal and Child Health Bureau
103 S. Main St.
Burlington, VT 05402
Phone: (802)863-7606
Fax: (802)863-7425

★9770★ Virginia Office of Health and Human Resources
Health Department
Women and Infants Health Division
1500 E. Main St.
PO Box 2448
Richmond, VA 23218
Phone: (804)786-7367
Fax: (804)786-4616

★9771★ Washington Department of Health
Community and Family Health Services Division
PO Box 47880
Olympia, WA 98504-7880
Phone: (360)753-7021
Fax: (360)586-7424

★9772★ West Virginia Department of Health and Human Resources
Public Health Bureau
Maternal and Child Health Office
State Capitol Complex, Bldg. 3, Rm. 519
Charleston, WV 25305-0501
Phone: (304)558-5388
Fax: (304)558-1035

★9773★ Wisconsin Department of Health and Social Services
Health Division
Public Health Bureau
Maternal and Child Health Section
144 E. Washington Ave., Rm. 167
Madison, WI 53703-3044
Phone: (608)267-0531
Fax: (608)267-3824

★9774★ Wyoming Department of Health
Public Health Division
Maternal and Child Health Services
Hathaway Bldg., 4th Fl.
Cheyenne, WY 82002-0710
Phone: (307)777-6186
Fax: (307)777-5402

Chapter 46
Occupational Health & Medicine

Federal Government Agencies

★9775★ Federal Mine Safety and Health Review Commission
1730 K St. NW
Washington, DC 20006
Phone: (202)653-5633

Description: The Commission, and its Office of Administrative Law Judges are charged with deciding cases brought pursuant to the Federal Mine Safety and Health Act of 1977 by the Mine Safety and Health Administration, mine operators, and miners or their representatives. These cases generally involve review of the Administration's enforcement actions including citations, mine closure orders, and proposals for civil penalties issued for violations of the act or the mandatory safety and health standards promulgated by the Secretary.

★9776★ Occupational Safety and Health Review Commission
1 Lafayette Centre
1120 20th St. NW
Washington, DC 20036-3419
Phone: (202)606-5398

Description: The Occupational Safety and Health Review Commission is charged with ruling on cases forwarded to it by the Department of Labor when disagreements arise over the results of safety and health inspections performed by the Department's Occupational Safety and Health Administration.

★9777★ Tennessee Valley Authority
Vice President of Human Resources
Occupational Health and Safety Division
400 W. Summitt Hill Dr.
Knoxville, TN 37902
Phone: (615)632-7870

★9778★ U.S. Department of Commerce
National Institute of Standards and Technology
Office of the Director of Administration
Occupational Health and Safety Division
Quince Orchard & Clopper Rds.
Gaithersburg, MD 20899
Phone: (301)975-5818

★9779★ U.S. Department of Health and Human Services
National Institute for Occupational Safety and Health
200 Independence Ave. SW
Washington, DC 20201
Phone: (202)401-6995
Fax: (202)260-4464

Description: NIOSH is the primary federal agency engaged in research to eliminate on-the-job hazards to health and safety. Institute is responsible for identifying occupational safety and health hazards, for determining methods to control them, and for recommending federal standards to limit the hazards. Institute is also responsible for administering the X-ray surveillance program for coal miners, and testing and certifying respirators and hazard measuring devices.

★9780★ U.S. Department of Labor
Bureau of Labor Statistics
Office of Compensation and Working Conditions
Office of Safety, Health, and Working Conditions
2 Massachusetts Ave. NE
Washington, DC 20210
Phone: (202)606-6304

Description: Office compiles occupational safety and health statistics; and makes grants to states and other local agencies to assist in the development and administration of programs dealing with occupational safety and health statistics. Office maintains the nationwide employer recordkeeping system on job-related injuries and illnesses, conducts the annual survey based on these records, analyzes the results, and compiles supplementary statistics from other sources. Office also implements the Supplementary Data System (SDS), by which states provide additional information on occupational accidents and exposures from workers' compensation records in order to give a more accurate definition of occupational safety and health problems, associated characteristics, and possible action indicators. In addit ion, Office examines selected types of work injuries in order to develop a detailed profile of characteristics associated with data from questionnaires completed by injured workers.

★9781★ U.S. Department of Labor
Mine Safety and Health Administration (MSHA)
4015 Wilson Blvd.
Arlington, VA 22203
Phone: (703)235-1385
Fax: (703)235-1563

Description: The Mine Safety and Health Administration develops and promulgates mandatory safety and health standards; ensures compliance with such standards; assesses civil penalties for violations; investigates accidents; cooperates with and provides assistance to the states in the development of effective state mine safety and health programs; improves and expands training programs in cooperation with the states and the mining industry; and in coordination with the Department of Health and Human Services and the Department of the Interior, contributes to the improvement and expansion of mine safety and health research and development. All of these activities are aimed at preventing and reducing mine accidents and occupational diseases in the mining industry.

★9782★ U.S. Department of Labor
Occupational Safety and Health Administation (OSHA)
200 Constitution Ave. NW
Washington, DC 20210
Phone: (202)219-8151

Description: The Occupational Safety and Health Administration develops and promulgates occupational safety and health standards; develops and issues regulations; conducts investigations and inspections to determine the status of compliance with safety and health standards and regulations; and issues citations and proposes penalties for non-compliance with safety and health standards and regulations.

National & International Organizations

★9783★ American Academy of Industrial Hygiene (AAIH)
4600 W. Saginaw, Ste. 101
Lansing, MI 48917
Phone: (517)321-5025
Fax: (517)321-4624
Lynn C. O'Donnell, CIH, Exec.Dir.

Founded: 1966. **Members:** 6,000. **Description:** Certified industrial hygiene professionals. Monitors the professional aspects of industrial hygienists who have passed board exams and have become certified members. **Publications:** *American Academy of Industrial Hygiene Newsletter*, quarterly. Newsletter. • *Roster of the American Academy of Industrial Hygiene*, annual. • *Roster of the American Board of Industrial Hygiene/American Academy of Industrial Hygiene*, annual.

American Association of Occupational Health Nurses (AAOHN)
See: Entry 9055

★9784★ American Board of Industrial Hygiene (ABIH)
4600 W. Saginaw, Ste. 101
Lansing, MI 48917-2737
Phone: (517)321-2638
Lynn C. O'Donnell, Exec.Dir.

Founded: 1960. **Members:** 18. **Description:** Certifies industrial hygienists and promotes high standards within the profession. Maintains a record of holders of certificates. **Publications:** *ABIH Examination Information.* • *American Academy of Industrial Hygiene Newsletter*, quarterly. Newsletter. • *Roster of the American Board of Industrial Hygiene*, annual.

★9785★ American Board of Industrial Medicine and Surgery (ABIMS)
c/o Bartholomew A. Sinatra
522 Rossmore Dr.
Las Vegas, NV 89110-4123
Phone: (702)452-9538
Fax: (702)452-1031
Bartholomew A. Sinatra, M.D., Chm.

Founded: 1984. **Members:** 300. **Description:** Physicians specializing in industrial medicine and surgery. Promotes scientific advancement and provides educational courses in the field. Conducts charitable activities.

American Board for Occupational Health Nurses (ABOHN)
See: Entry 9059

★9786★ American College of Occupational and Environmental Medicine (ACOEM)
55 W. Seegers Rd.
Arlington Heights, IL 60005
Phone: (708)228-6850
Fax: (708)228-1856
Donald L. Hoops, Ph.D., Exec. VP

Founded: 1916. **Members:** 6,000. **Regional Groups:** 31. **Description:** Physicians specializ-

ing in occupational and environmental medicine. Promotes maintenance and improvement of the health of workers; works to increase awareness of occupational medicine as a medical specialty. Sponsors educational programs; maintains placement service. **Publications:** *ACOEM Report*, monthly. Newsletter. Covers Occupational Safety and Health Administration rulings. *Price:* Included in membership dues. • *American College of Occupational and Environmental Medicine--Membership Directory*, annual. Membership Directory. Arranged alphabetically, geographically, and by affiliation. *Price:* Included in membership dues; $150/copy for nonmembers. • *Journal of Occupational Medicine*, monthly. Journal. Contains book reviews, calendar of events, and employment listings. **Formerly:** (1992) American College of Occupational Medicine.

★9787★ American Conference of Governmental Industrial Hygienists (ACGIH)
1330 Kemper Meadow Dr.
Cincinnati, OH 45240
Phone: (513)742-2020
Fax: (513)742-3355
Richard A. Strono, Contact

Founded: 1938. **Members:** 5,500. **Description:** Professional society of persons employed by official governmental units responsible for full-time programs of industrial hygiene, educators, and others conducting research in industrial hygiene. Devoted to the development of administrative and technical aspects of worker health protection. Functions mainly as a medium for the exchange of ideas and the promotion of standards and techniques in industrial health. Compiles statistics; conducts educational programs. **Publications:** *Applied Occupational and Environmental Hygiene*, monthly. Journal. Includes association news, book reviews, calendar of events, employment listings and information on new products and literature. *Price:* Included in membership dues; $85/year for nonmembers; $135 for institutions. • *Industrial Ventilation--A Manual of Recommended Practice.* • *Threshold Limit Values and Biological Exposure Indices.* • *Ventilation System Testing.* Also publishes over 100 other manuals, guides, and studies. **Formerly:** (1945) National Conference of Governmental Industrial Hygienists.

★9788★ American Industrial Health Council (AIHC)
2001 Pennsylvania Ave. NW, Ste. 760
Washington, DC 20006
Phone: (202)833-2131
Fax: (202)833-2201
Ms. Gaylen M. Camera, Exec.Dir.

Founded: 1977. **Members:** 50. **Description:** Advocates the importance of sound science in regulatory decision-making on chronic human health hazards. Promotes the sound use of scientific principles and procedures in the assessment and regulation of risks of chronic human health effects and directly related public policy issues. Does not act as an advocate for any product or substance. **Publications:** *American Industrial Health Council--Annual Report*, annual. Annual Report. Covers AIHC activities and committees. *Price:* Free. • *American Industrial*

Health Council--Journal. Journal. *Price:* Included in membership dues.

★9789★ American Industrial Hygiene Association (AIHA)
2700 Prosperity Ave., Ste. 250
Fairfax, VA 22031
Phone: (703)849-8888
Fax: (703)207-3561
O. Gordon Banks, Exec.Dir.

Founded: 1939. **Members:** 11,500. **Local Groups:** 90. **Description:** Professional society of industrial hygienists. Promotes the study and control of environmental factors affecting the health and well-being of workers. Sponsors continuing education courses in industrial hygiene, government affairs program, and public relations. Accredits laboratories. Maintains 40 technical committees and a foundation. Operates placement service. Conducts educational and research programs. **Publications:** *The AIHA Journal*, monthly. Journal. Includes peer-reviewed technical and scientific articles. *Price:* $110/year in U.S.. • Books. • Directory, annual. • Manuals. • *The Synergist*, monthly.

★9790★ Art Hazards Information Center (AHIC)
5 Beekman St., Ste. 820
New York, NY 10038
Phone: (212)227-6220
Fax: (212)233-3846
Angela Babin, M.S., Dir.

Founded: 1977. **Description:** A project of the Center for Safety in the Arts engaged in research and education on the health hazards found in the performing and visual arts, museums, and school arts programs. Answers written and telephone inquiries on art hazards and suggests suitable precautions. Provides referrals. Conducts courses. **Publications:** Articles. • Books. • Newsletter. *Price:* $24/year. • Pamphlets. Also publishes data sheets listing hazards and precautions.

Asbestos Litigation Group (ALG)
See: Entry 7174

★9791★ Asbestos Victims of America (AVA)
PO Box 559
Capitola, CA 95010
Phone: (408)476-3646
Fax: (408)476-3646
Heather R. Maurer, CEO

Founded: 1980. **Members:** 18,500. **Regional Groups:** 7. **State Groups:** 5. **Local Groups:** 4. **Description:** Individuals suffering from asbestos-related diseases, families and friends of asbestos victims, and those concerned about the hazards of asbestos. Has been endorsed by union members. Assists asbestos victims and their families in solving related medical, emotional, and financial problems; acts as information center and support network; seeks to prevent future asbestos diseases through increasing public awareness of the hazards of exposure. Provides: personal referrals to doctors and attorneys; contact with others in the same geographical area; information on consumer products, construction materials containing asbestos, and asbestos substitute materials; representation before high-level decision-making bodies. Sponsors research on asbestos disease, treatment, and exposure rates. Conducts asbestos medical screening programs. Holds public education meetings on the hazards of asbestos; sponsors surveys. Assists homeowners, workers, school groups, boards, and other agencies in identifying asbestos and in developing a solid, safe abatement program. Operates speakers' bureau; provides counseling services with focus on individuals with chronic or terminal asbestos-related diseases. **Publications:** *AVA Advisor*, semiannual. Bulletin. Includes information on asbestos topics, association and membership news, information on treatment and compensation, obituaries, and book reviews. *Price:* Included in membership dues; $15/year for nonmembers. • *AVA Resource Directory*, periodic. Directory. • Pamphlets, periodic.

Association for the Electrically Oversensitive
See: Entry 5035

★9792★ Association for Repetitive Motion Syndromes (ARMS)
PO Box 514
Santa Rosa, CA 95402
Phone: (707)571-0397
Stephanie M. Barnes, Exec.Dir.

Founded: 1990. **Regional Groups:** 1. **State Groups:** 1. **Description:** Individuals suffering from repetitive motion injuries; other interested individuals and organizations. Promotes the welfare of persons afflicted with carpal tunnel syndrome and those at risk of repetitive motion injuries. (Carpal tunnel syndrome is a condition caused by repeated finger-pounding or wrist-bending motions, usually related to an individual's occupation, and is characterized by numbness, tingling, or burning pain in the middle and index fingers and thumb; all fingers can be affected in severe cases.) Works to increase public awareness of repetitive motion injuries and prevention and treatment. Develops and implements occupational safety standards and educational programs. Compiles, analyzes, and disseminates data; conducts research programs; operates placement services and clearinghouse. **Publications:** *ARMS News*, quarterly. Newsletter.

Black Lung Association (BLA)
See: Entry 11592

★9793★ British Occupational Hygiene Society (BOHS)
Georgian House, Ste. 2
Great Northern Rd.
Derby DE1 1LT, England
Phone: 1332 298101
Fax: 1332 298099
Mrs. P.M. Blythe, Office Admin.

Founded: 1953. **Members:** 1,450. **Local Groups:** 7. **Languages:** English. **Description:** Individuals and students. Promotes public and professional awareness of occupational and environmental hygiene practices and standards. Encourages research. **Publications:** *Annals of Occupational Hygiene*, bimonthly. Journal. • *Directory*, annual. Directory. • *Occupational Hygiene Newsletter*, quarterly. Newsletter.

★9794★ Center for Safety in the Arts (CSA)
5 Beekman St.
New York, NY 10038
Phone: (212)227-6220
Fax: (212)233-3846
Michael McCann, Pres.

Founded: 1977. **Description:** Seeks to gather and disseminate information about health hazards encountered by artists, craftsmen, teachers, children, and others in the visual and performing arts, museums, and social arts programs. Provides on-site assessments of the health and safety features of facilites used by artists, craftsmen, and students; responds to inquiries concerning art-related health hazards. Operates the Art Hazards Information Center; conducts consultation program. **Publications:** *Art Hazards News*, 5/year. Newsletter. Provides information on safety in visual and performing arts. *Price:* $24/year inside the U.S.; $26/year in Canada; $27/year outside the U.S. and Canada. • *Art Safety: Hazards and Precautions*. Video. • *Art Safety Procedures!*. Manual. Provides information for art schools and art departments. • Articles. • *Artist Beware*. • Books. • *Lights! Camera! Safety!*. Manual. Provides information on health and safety for motion pictures and television production. • Pamphlets. Also publishes data sheets on specific hazards. **Formerly:** (1987) Center for Occupational Hazards.

★9795★ Council for Accreditation in Occupational Hearing Conservation (CAOHC)
611 E. Wells St.
Milwaukee, WI 53202
Phone: (414)276-5338
Fax: (414)276-3349
Sandra M. Koehler, Exec.Dir.

Founded: 1973. **Description:** Participants are professional associations in the industrial health field. To establish and maintain standards for the training of industrial audiometric technicians (persons certified to conduct pure tone air conduction hearing tests and related duties as part of an occupational hearing conservation program). Approves courses in occupational hearing conservation and certifies those who pass these courses. **Publications:** *Occupational Hearing Conservation Manual*. Manual. Contains information on the hearing conservationist's mission, training, and role; and federal and state regulations. *Price:* $50/each. • *The Update*, 3/year. Newsletter.

Electrically and VDT Injured in Denmark (El-Og Billedskaermsskadede I Danmark)
See: Entry 5037

★9796★ Institute for Labor and Mental Health (ILMH)
3137 Telegraph Ave.
Oakland, CA 94609
Phone: (510)653-6166
Dr. Richard Epstein, Dir.

Founded: 1977. **Members:** 50. **Description:** Purpose is to help working people with problems related to the workplace. Seeks to identify conditions at work that cause stress; believes that education and communication about common work problems are the first steps in dealing with

job stress. Assists unions in handling grievances and stress-related disabilities; provides counseling to union members and their families; offers legal and worker compensation assistance to working people. Provides consultation to government and businesses on ways to reduce stress. Develops ongoing stress programs; operates summer institute on occupational stress. **Publications:** Directory, periodic. • *Occupational Stress*, bimonthly. Newsletter. • *Occupational Stress: A Union Based Approach*. • *Occupational Stress: The Inside Story*. • *Surplus Powerlessness*. Book.

★9797★ International Association of Agricultural Medicine and Rural Health (IAAMRH)
(Association Internationale de Medecine Agricole et de Sante Rurale)
Saku Central Hospital
197, Usuda
Minamisaku-gun
Nagano 384-03, Japan
Phone: 267 823131
Fax: 267 829602
Toshikazu Wakatsuki, M.D., Sec.Gen.

Founded: 1961. **Members:** 450. **Languages:** English, French, German, Russian. **Description:** Physicians, nurses, paramedics, and other health care professionals in 40 countries. Studies problems of agricultural medicine and rural health around the world. Seeks means of averting the detrimental effects of certain agricultural and rural work conditions. **Publications:** *Agricultural Medicine and Rural Health*, semiannual. • *Journal*, quarterly.

International Ergophthalmological Society (Societas Ergophthalmologica Internationalis — SEI)
See: Entry 13484

★9798★ International Healthcare Safety Professional Certi fication Board (IHSPCB)
8009 Carita Ct.
Bethesda, MD 20817
Phone: (301)984-8969
Harold M. Gordon, Exec.Dir.

Description: Individuals working or consulting in hospitals or healthcare facilities who are responsible for the handling and control of hazardous materials. Areas of concern include: emergency and disaster planning; biological, chemical, and physical hazards; ventilation; fire prevention and protection; maintenance and engineering; personal protective equipment; sanitation; life safety code. Grants affiliate, associate, and executive level distinctions for the title of Certified Healthcare Safety Professional. Encourages exchange of ideas and technology to improve performance. Sponsors HSP Academy, which conducts professional development activities. **Publications:** Brochure. • *Directory of Certified Healthcare Safety Professionals*, annual. Directory.

★9799★ International Union of Railway Medical Services (Union Internationale des Services Medicaux des Chemins de Fer — UIMC)
85, rue de France
B-1070 Brussels, Belgium
Phone: 2 5252550
Fax: 2 5252501
N. Nordvik, Treas.

Founded: 1948. **Members:** 39. **Languages:** English, French, German. **Description:** Union of doctors in the railroad industry in 35 countries. Constituent members' principal activity is the transport of passengers and merchandise; associate members are affiliated with public transport enterprises. Promotes the progress of medicine as it pertains to the railroad industry and for the benefit of those who travel by train. **Publications:** Report, annual. • *Scientific Conference*, quadrennial. Proceedings.

Self-Help Association for the Electrically Sensitive (Selbhilfen fur Elektrosensible)
See: Entry 5058

★9800★ Sheet Metal Occupational Health Institute (SMOHI)
1750 New York Ave. NW, Ste. 350
Washington, DC 20006
Phone: (202)662-0885
Fax: (202)662-0895
Gary E. Briggs, Exec. Officer

Founded: 1986. **Description:** Joint labor management trust sponsored by the Sheet Metal Workers International Association and Sheet Metal and Air Conditioning Contractors National Association. Works to educate the sheet metal industry about hazardous materials; monitors and disseminates information about proposed state and federal occupational health regulations that will affect workers and the industry; fosters labor/management awareness of safety programs. Conducts medical screening.

★9801★ Society for Occupational and Environmental Health (SOEH)
6728 Old McLean Village Dr.
McLean, VA 22101
Phone: (703)556-9222
Marge Deqnon, Exec.Dir.

Founded: 1972. **Members:** 350. **Description:** Scientists, academicians, and industry and labor representatives. Seeks to improve the quality of both working and living places by operating as a neutral forum for conferences involving all aspects of occupational health. Focuses public attention on scientific, social, and regulatory problems; studies specific categories of hazards, methods for assessment of health effects, and diseases associated with particular jobs. Identifies hazards in the occupational and general environment and proposes actions to reduce their danger. **Publications:** *Archives of Environmental Health Journal. Price:* Included in membership dues. • *Society for Occupational and Environmental Health--Bulletin*, quarterly. Newsletter. *Price:* Free, for members only.

Swedish Association for the Electrically and VDT Injured
See: Entry 5061

White Lung Association (WLA)
See: Entry 11607

Research Centers

★9802★ Center for Epidemiologic Research
Oak Ridge Institute for Science and Education
210 Badger Rd.
PO Box 117
Oak Ridge, TN 37830-0117
Phone: (615)576-2866
Fax: (615)576-9557
Dr. Donna Cragle, Dir.

Research Activities and Fields: Occupational health and safety. **E-mail Address:** cragled@orau.gov.

★9803★ Center for Professional Well Being
Colony W. Professional Park
21 W. Colony Pl., Ste. 150
Durham, NC 27705
Phone: (919)489-9167
Fax: (919)490-5587
John-Henry Pfifferling, Ph.D., Dir.

Research Activities and Fields: Epidemiology of health/wellness/impairment among health professionals, including a study on stress syndromes among professionals. Seeks to prevent distress. **Publications:** Monograph Series; Newsletter. **Formerly:** Center for the Well-Being of Health Professionals.

★9804★ Center for Safety in the Arts
5 Beekman St., Ste. 820
New York, NY 10038
Phone: (212)227-6220

Research Activities and Fields: Serves as national clearinghouse for information on hazards in the arts, including visual and performing arts and museums. Conducts studies of hazards of arts, crafts, theaters, and materials and processes used in art conservation. Studies focus on hazards of specific materials and precautions such as ventilation and personal protection equipment. **Publications:** *Art Hazards News* (five per year). **E-mail Address:** csa@dmn.com. **Formerly:** Center for Occupational Hazards.

★9805★ Duke University Occupational Mental Health Programs
Box 2914
Durham, NC 27710
Phone: (919)286-1244
Fax: (919)286-1021
Craig Stenberg, Dir.

Research Activities and Fields: Occupational mental health, including managed mental health care, employee assistance programs, and mental health outcome research. **E-mail Address:** stenb001@mc.duke.edu. **Formerly:** Career Assessment and Development Laboratory.

★9806★ Emory University Southeastern Clinical Occupational Medicine / Environmental Health Evaluation Center
Division of Environmental & Occupational Health
c/o Emory School of Public Health
1599 Clifton St.
Atlanta, GA 30329
Phone: (404)727-3697
Fax: (404)727-8744
Howard Frumkin, M.D., Dir.

Research Activities and Fields: Occupational medicine, environmental health, neurotoxicology, agricultural safety and health, and occupational injuries. **E-mail Address:** frumiun@sph.emory.edu.

Environmental and Occupational Health Sciences Institute (EOHSI)
See: Entry 5072

Inhalation Toxicology Research Institute
See: Entry 10438

★9807★ Institute for Advanced Safety Studies
5950 W. Touhy Ave.
Niles, IL 60714
Phone: (708)647-1101
Fax: (708)647-2047
Leslie A. Savage, Exec.Dir.

Research Activities and Fields: Applied research and training in the areas of safety and health. Examines new technologies and develops effective standards, management tools, practices, and designs to improve safety and health in the workplace. Investigates the failure of current safety devices and practices and develops alternatives. Interests and areas of expertise include fires and explosions, aerospace engineering, vehicle engineering, construction and industrial machinery (includes agricultural and airport ground equipment), chemical processing, fuels and lubricants, electrical processes and electrocution, ergonomics, product liability and forensic engineering, product design, safeguarding systems, safety and accident investigation and reconstruction, and structural design and stress analysis.

★9808★ Institute for Injury Reduction
2191 Defense Hwy, Ste.222
Crofton, MD 21114
Phone: (301)261-0090
Fax: (301)261-3078
Linda A. Barley, Prog. Dir.

Research Activities and Fields: Product-related deaths and injuries, emphasizing automotive hazards. Conducts epidemiologic and policy research. **Publications:** *Journal of Product Injury Analyses* (semiannually); newsletter (quarterly).

★9809★ **Iowa Center for Agricultural Safety and Health (I-CASH)**
Institute of Agricultural Medicine
University of Iowa Oakdale Campus
Iowa City, IA 52242-5000
Phone: (319)335-4415
Fax: (319)335-4225
Kelley J. Donham, DVM, Dir.

Research Activities and Fields: Coordinates state's resources to improve the health and safety of Iowa's farm families, farm workers, and the agricultural community. Priority areas include provision of agricultural health and safety services, prevention of tractor injuries, prevention of injuries and illnesses in farm youth, prevention of illnesses among producers working in livestock confinement operations, and surveillance of farm injuries and illnesses. **E-mail Address:** kelly-donham@uiowa.edu.

★9810★ **Iowa State University of Science and Technology**
Occupational and Traffic Safety Education Research Laboratory
IED Bldg. II, Rm. 122
Ames, IA 50011
Phone: (515)294-5945
Dr. Jack Beno, Coord.

Research Activities and Fields: Primary research areas include driver behavior personality; motorcycles; accident frequency and causation; road design; farm, water, child, and occupational safety and health; fire hazards; teacher preparation and certification; and child restraints, including proper attachment of child safety seats. Special projects include random surveys in selected Iowa towns and cities of belt use of children under the age of six. **Publications:** *Traffic Quarterly*; *Educational Gerontology*; *Hawkeye Safety News*; *Journal of Marriage in the Family*. **Formerly:** Driving Research Laboratory (1963); Safety and Driver Education Laboratory; Safety Education and Research Laboratory (1979).

★9811★ **Johns Hopkins University**
Center for VDT and Health Research
School of Hygiene and Public Health
615 N. Wolfe St., Rm. 4028
Baltimore, MD 21205
Phone: (410)955-7820
Fax: (410)955-0792
Dr. Ronald H. Gray, Dir.

Research Activities and Fields: Health effects of video display terminal (VDT) use, focusing on methodologies for the measurement of electromagnetic field (EMF) exposures associated with VDTs, and the contribution of VDTs to total field exposures; the association between VDT use and reproductive health problems; the moderating influence of psychosocial stress on VDT use and reproductive health problems or risks of neoplasia; the measurement of physical stresses/forces associated with VDT use and the effects on cumulative trauma disorders (CTDs); and the biological effects of electromagnetic fields at the cellular or subcellular level.

★9812★ **Laval University**
Interdisciplinary Research Group on Work Organization and Occupational Health and Safety
Pavillon de l'Est
Quebec, PQ, Canada G1K 7P4
Phone: (418)656-7645
Fax: (418)656-7759
Michel Vezina, Dir.

Research Activities and Fields: Research focuses on the impact of organizational factors on health and safety. Topics include repetitive time-controlled work, workload, autonomy, social support, workplace management, and work-related chronic health problems.

★9813★ **National Farm Medicine Center**
1000 N. Oak Ave.
Marshfield, WI 54449-5790
Phone: (715)387-9298
Fax: (715)389-3131
Dean T. Stueland, M.D., Med.Dir.

Research Activities and Fields: Agriculture-related health problems, including injury, respiratory diseases, noise-induced hearing loss, and cancer. **Publications:** Annual Report. **E-mail Address:** stueland@dgabby.mfidline.edu.

★9814★ **National Safe Workplace Institute**
3008 Bishop Ridge
Monroe, NC 28110
Phone: (704)289-6061
Fax: (704)289-6766
Joseph A. Kinney, Exec.Dir.

Research Activities and Fields: Workplace safety and health, including workplace violence, behavioral emergencies, occupational stress, legal research, and corporate surveys. **Publications:** *The Workplace Violence and Behavior Letter* (monthly).

★9815★ **New York Center for Agricultural Medicine and Health**
Mary Imogene Bassett Hospital
1 Atwell Rd.
Cooperstown, NY 13326
Phone: (607)547-6023
Fax: (607)547-6087
John J. May, M.D., Dir.

Research Activities and Fields: Studies barn dusts, mites, health needs of agricultural workers in New York, dosimetry on farms, agricultural lung hazards, and farm machinery safety. **Publications:** *Respiratory Hazards in the Farm Environment*; *What You Should Know About Using Dust/Mist Masks on the Farm*; *Using Personal Protective Equipment on the Farm*; *How Safe Are Your Farm Tractors?*; *FARM SAFE: Focus on Agricultural Health* (videotape series).

Oak Ridge Institute for Science and Education (ORISE)
See: Entry 2597

★9816★ **Oregon Health Sciences University**
Center for Research on Occupational and Environmental Toxicology (CROET)
3181 SW Sam Jackson Park Rd., L606
Portland, OR 97201
Phone: (503)494-4273
Fax: (503)494-4278
Dr. Peter S. Spencer, Dir.

Research Activities and Fields: Studies the adverse effects of occupational and environmental chemicals on the human nervous system, exposure to neurotoxic chemicals for behavior, endocrine and neurological function, and the links between neurotoxic chemicals, and degenerative disorders of the nervous system, molecular and cellular mechanisms underlying the adverse effects of chemicals on the nervous system during development, in the adult and in the aged, chronic and delayed actions of chemical substances, the genetic basis for susceptibility to chemical attack, and the role of occupational and environmental chemical agents in triggering developmental defects, neuroendocrine dysfunction, various neurological and psychiatric conditions, and neurodegenerative disorders such as Parkinson and Alzheimer diseases, cancer developmental disorders, and genetic and immune-system dysfunction. Employs epidemiological and other field methods to research relationships between chemical exposures and neurodegenerative disorders such as amyotrophic lateral sclerosisand Parkinson's disease, assessing the validity and reliability of neurobehavioral (and other) screening batteries for the detection of early, reversible abnormalities in brain function. Employs epidemiological and other field methods to research relationships between chemical exposures and neurodegenerative disorders such as amyotrophic lateral sclerosis and Parkinson's disease, assessing the validity and reliability of neurobehavioral (and other) screening batteries for the detection of early, reversible abnormalities in brain function. **Formerly:** Outgrowth of the Institute of Neurotoxicology at Albert Einstein College of Medicine of Yeshiva University.

★9817★ **Pennsylvania State University**
Center for Worksite Health Enhancement
1 White Bldg.
University Park, PA 16802
Phone: (814)863-2237
Fax: (814)863-8586
Dr. Robin C. Rager, Dir.

Research Activities and Fields: Worksite health promotion and health management, including needs assessment, feasibility studies, program planning, marketing, program evaluation, and policy studies. **E-mail Address:** ryr@psuvm.psu.edu.

★9818★ **Productive Rehabilitation Institute of Dallas for Ergonomics (PRIDE)**
1540 Empire Central
Dallas, TX 75247
Phone: (214)630-8400
Fax: (214)630-5520
Pat Estes, Dir. of Support Svcs.

Research Activities and Fields: Ergonomics. Projects focus on utilizing physical exercise for rehabilitating chronic back problems. Patients use gym and spa equipment, participate in aerobics, and mimic job-related conditions such as crawling through pipes, moving equipment on assembly lines, driving four-wheelers, crawling around on building skeletons, and jumping up and onto a moving platform. **Publications:** *Functional Restoration* (quarterly).

★ 9819 ★ **Repetitive Motion Institute**
Santa Clara Valley Medical Center
2400 Moore Park, Ste. 400
San Jose, CA 95128
Phone: (408)885-5920
Fax: (408)885-4728
Linda Morse, M.D., Chief, Occupational Medicine

Research Activities and Fields: Injuries due to repetitive motion, especially job-related injuries, and treatment. **Publications:** *Women and Ergonomics.*

★ 9820 ★ **Texas A&M University**
Occupational Health & Safety Institute
Dept. of Nuclear Engineering
College Station, TX 77843-3133
Phone: (409)862-4409
Fax: (409)845-6443
Dr. James C. Rock, Dir.

Research Activities and Fields: Occupational health and safety, with a goal of safe use and disposal of essential hazardous materials and processes. Areas of study include industrial hygiene, health physics, safety engineering, aerosol science, occupational epidemiology, fire protection engineering, product safety engineering, occupational exposure assessment, industrial ventilation, indoor air quality, noise and vibration control, material substitution, electrofiltration, separation sciences, indoor bioaerosols, electrostatic separation for hazardous waste streams, and low toxicity product substitution. **E-mail Address:** j-rock@tamu.edu.

U.S. Department of Defense
Naval Medical Research and Development
Command
Naval Health Research Center
Department of Health Sciences and
Epidemiology
See: Entry 7841

★ 9821 ★ **U.S. Department of Energy**
Lawrence Berkeley Laboratory
Environment, Health and Safety Division
1 Cyclotron Rd.
Berkeley, CA 94720
Phone: (510)486-5551
Fax: (510)486-7488
D.C. McGraw, Division Director

Research Activities and Fields: Radiation as it relates to accelerator technology, advanced dosimeters, dispersion of radionuclides, waste management, site characterization, and occupational medical surveillance.

★ 9822 ★ **U.S. Department of Energy**
Lawrence Livermore National Laboratory
Hazards Control Department
Special Projects Division

PO Box 5505
Livermore, CA 94550
Phone: (415)422-5217
Fax: (415)422-5176
Jim Johnson, Division Leader

Research Activities and Fields: The Hazards Control Department is responsible for radiation safety, industrial hygiene, industrial safety, fire safety, and explosive safety at the Lawrence Livermore National Laboratory. Its Special Projects Division provides health and safety technology development support in these areas for the Laboratory's energy and defense programs and provides support directly to the Department of Energy and other federal agencies for development of solutions to health and safety related problems. Principal areas of research interest are fire science, radiation dosimetry, radiation spectrometry, aerosol physics, respiratory protection, protective clothing evaluation, health physics technology development, and industrial hygiene.

★ 9823 ★ **U.S. Department of Energy**
Los Alamos National Laboratory
Quality, Environment, Safety, and Health
Assurance Division
Mail Stop K491
PO Box 1663
Los Alamos, NM 87545
Phone: (505)667-4218
Fax: (505)665-3811
Dennis Erickson, Division Director

Research Activities and Fields: Division is primarily responsible for providing comprehensive occupational health and safety programs, and radiation protection programs. These activities are designed to protect workers, the public, and the environment. Division conducts applied research programs on: 1) worker protection (respirators, protective clothing); 2) occupational health (aerosols); 3) epidemiology of radiation workers; and 4) health physics (emergency response and radiation monitoring).

★ 9824 ★ **U.S. Department of Health and**
Human Services
National Institute for Occupational Safety
and Health
Centers for Disease Control and Prevention
Mail D-36
1600 Clifton Rd., N.E.
Atlanta, GA 30333
Phone: (404)639-3771
Richard A. Lemea, Ph. D., Acting Director

Research Activities and Fields: NIOSH is the primary federal agency engaged in research to eliminate on-the-job hazards to health and safety. Institute is responsible for identifying occupational safety and health hazards, for determining methods to control them, and for recommending federal standards to limit the hazards. Institute is also responsible for administering the x-ray surveillance program for coal miners and for testing and certifying respirators and hazard measuring devices. In addition to research done in laboratories, NIOSH conducts health hazard evaluations in all types of workplaces (including mines), assists other agencies to investigate potentially hazardous situations, and supports research and training programs through extramu-

ral grants. To focus research efforts and resources, the Institute has identified ten leading work-related diseases and injuries and has developed a proposed prevention strategy for each. The Institute is working with other groups, both local and national, to establish a comprehensive national surveillance system for occupational diseases and injuries. NIOSH recommendations are transmitted to the Department of Labor, which is responsible for setting and enforcing occupational standards. NIOSH laboratory research is conducted at the Robert A. Taft Laboratory and the Alice Hamilton Laboratory for Occupational Safety and Health in Cincinnati, OH, and at the Appalachian Laboratory for Occupational Safety and Health in Morgantown, WV.

★ 9825 ★ **U.S. Department of Health and**
Human Services
National Institute for Occupational Safety
and Health
Appalachian Laboratory for Occupational
Safety and Health
944 Chestnut Ridge Rd.
Morgantown, WV 26505-2888
Phone: (304)291-4126
Fax: (304)291-4937

Research Activities and Fields: Occupational safety and health, focusing on safe working environments, occupational-related respiratory diseases, cross-sectional prospective morbidity and mortality studies, and performance records of respirators and hazard measuring instruments. Maintains a national surveillance data system for the early detection and monitoring of occupational accidents and injuries, and NIOSHTIC database and microfiche collection. **Additional Contact Information:** Dr. Gregory Wagner, director, Division of Respiratory Disease Studies; Dr. Thomas R. Bender, director, Division of Safety Research.

★ 9826 ★ **U.S. Department of Health and**
Human Services
National Institute for Occupational Safety
and Health
Biomedical and Behavioral Science
Division
Robert A. Taft Laboratories
4676 Columbia Pkwy.
Cincinnati, OH 45226-1998
Phone: (513)533-8465
Fax: (513)533-8510
Janet C. Haartz, Ph.D., Director

Research Activities and Fields: Occupational health research in the areas of toxicology, occupational stress, and physical agents (noise and non-ionizing radiation). Laboratory and field investigations identify occupational hazards and methods to control and prevent them. Division components include the Applied Biology Branch, Applied Psychology and Ergonomics Branch, Experimental Toxicology Branch, and the Physical Agents Effects Branch.

★ 9827 ★ U.S. Department of Health and
Human Services
National Institute for Occupational Safety
and Health
Biomedical and Behavioral Science
Division
Applied Biology Branch
Robert A. Taft Laboratories
4676 Columbia Pkwy.
Cincinnati, OH 45226-1998
Phone: (513)533-8433
Fax: (513)533-8371
Lloyd Stettler, Ph.D., Chief

Research Activities and Fields: Biological
monitoring and immunochemistry/
immunotoxicology studies, inhalation toxicology, animal husbandry, and pathology.

★ 9828 ★ U.S. Department of Health and
Human Services
National Institute for Occupational Safety
and Health
Biomedical and Behavioral Science
Division
Applied Psychology and Ergonomics
Branch
Robert A. Taft Laboratories
4676 Columbia Pkwy.
Cincinnati, OH 45226-1998
Phone: (513)533-8291
Steve Savter, Chief

Research Activities and Fields: Activities of
the Applied Psychology and Ergonomics
Branch involve neurotoxicity and behavioral research.

★ 9829 ★ U.S. Department of Health and
Human Services
National Institute for Occupational Safety
and Health
Biomedical and Behavioral Science
Division
Experimental Toxicology Branch
Robert A. Taft Laboratories
Mail Stop C-23
4676 Columbia Pkwy.
Cincinnati, OH 45226-1998
Phone: (513)533-8392
Dr. Russell Savage, Chief

Research Activities and Fields: The Experimental Toxicology Branch conducts basic and
applied research (using multiple routes of exposure and multiple species of laboratory animals)
on the toxicity of industrial chemicals. Activities
involve investigations of carcinogenesis, mutagenesis, toxicity to the male and female reproductive systems, developmental toxicity, cardiovascular disease, pulmonary toxicology, derma-
totoxicology, and biological monitoring and metabolism of xenobiotics.

★ 9830 ★ U.S. Department of Health and
Human Services
National Institute for Occupational Safety
and Health
Biomedical and Behavioral Science
Division
Physical Agents Effects Branch

Robert A. Taft Laboratories
4676 Columbia Pkwy.
Cincinnati, OH 45226-1998
Phone: (513)533-8281
Fax: (513)533-8510
Greg Lotz, Chief

Research Activities and Fields: The Physical
Agents Effects Branch conducts investigative
research on the health effects of radiation,
noise, and vibration in the workplace.

★ 9831 ★ U.S. Department of Health and
Human Services
National Institute for Occupational Safety
and Health
Physical Sciences and Engineering Division
Robert A. Taft Laboratories
4676 Columbia Pkwy.
Cincinnati, OH 45226-1998
Phone: (513)841-4500
Fax: (513)841-4321
Laurence Doemeny, Acting Director

Research Activities and Fields: Division's activities involve: 1) developing and evaluating
performance criteria for environmental (industrial hygiene) monitoring equipment; 2) assessing
control technology for occupational health hazards; 3) conducting research and developing
equipment for control of occupational health
hazards; 4) conducting research and developing
sampling and analytical methods for occupational toxic substances; 5) providing analytical
chemistry support for the Institute's laboratory
and field research programs; and 6) providing
assistance to the industrial hygiene community
in operating a quality control reference program
for industrial hygiene laboratories. Division comprises branches for Engineering Control Technology, Measurements Research Support,
Methods Research, and Quality Assurance and
Statistics.

★ 9832 ★ U.S. Department of Health and
Human Services
National Institute for Occupational Safety
and Health
Physical Sciences and Engineering Division
Engineering Control Technology Branch
Robert A. Taft Laboratories
Mail Stop R-5
4676 Columbia Pkwy.
Cincinnati, OH 45226-1998
Phone: (513)841-4221
Dennis O'Brien, Chief

Research Activities and Fields: Branch's activities include: 1) planning and conducting
worksite and laboratory research to identify and
evaluate engineering control technology that
will prevent worker exposure to toxic substances and harmful physical agents; 2) promoting the transfer and widespread application of
effective preventive engineering control measures for safeguarding worker health; 3) providing engineering expertise in formulating effective and credible workplace standards; and 4)
providing technical consultation to other elements of the National Institute for Occupational
Safety and Health and the Department of Labor
in the application of new and improved techniques for hazard prevention and engineering
controls. Branch comprises sections for chemi-

cal industry, minerals, materials processing, and
general industry.

★ 9833 ★ U.S. Department of Health and
Human Services
National Institute for Occupational Safety
and Health
Physical Sciences and Engineering Division
Measurements Research Support Branch
Robert A. Taft Laboratories
4676 Columbia Pkwy.
Cincinnati, OH 45226-1998
Phone: (513)841-4263
Fax: (513)841-4500
Robert Larkin, Chief

Research Activities and Fields: Branch conducts research in sampling and analytical chemistry measurements for industrial hygiene field
investigations and other National Institute for
Occupational Safety and Health activities; and
provides field industrial hygiene measurement
support, including research, to develop new
sampling and analysis techniques. Branch comprises sections for measurement, development,
and support.

★ 9834 ★ U.S. Department of Health and
Human Services
National Institute for Occupational Safety
and Health
Physical Sciences and Engineering Division
Methods Research Branch
Robert A. Taft Laboratories
Mail Stop R-7
4676 Columbia Pkwy.
Cincinnati, OH 45226-1998
Phone: (513)841-4241
Fax: (513)841-4500
Mr. Martin Abell, Chief

Research Activities and Fields: Branch's activities include: 1) conducting research that develops, improves, and evaluates analytical
methods for the evaluation of levels of toxic materials, their products, and other significant hazards found in the workplace, physical environment, and in industrial and biologic materials; 2)
providing expert consultation for the development of occupational health criteria and standards on methods for microbiological and
chemical analytical procedures; 3) providing
special consultation to the National Institute for
Occupational Safety and Health and other government agencies; and 4) providing validated
NIOSH procedures for sampling and analytical
methods. Branch comprises one section for the
development and evaluation of field instruments
and two sections for labortory methods development.

★ 9835 ★ U.S. Department of Health and
Human Services
National Institute for Occupational Safety
and Health
Respiratory Disease Studies Division
Appalachian Lab. for Occupational Safety &
Health, Rm. 221
944 Chestnut Ridge Rd.
Morgantown, WV 26505-2888
Phone: (304)291-4474
Fax: (304)284-5467
Gregory Wagner, M.D., Director

Research Activities and Fields: The NIOSH
Respiratory Disease Studies Division: 1) con-

ducts clinical and epidemiological research on occupational respiratory disease; 2) provides medical, surveillance, and autopsy services; 3) conducts medical and environmental research; 4) conducts health hazard evaluations in mining industries; 5) designs and conducts research programs in agricultural and noncoal mining health; and 6) plans, coordinates, and conducts energy research relating to occupational safety and health, including research in the areas of synthetic fuel production and occupational hazards associated with solar and other new energy sources. Division comprises the Clinical Investigations Branch, Environmental Investigations Branch, Epidemiological Investigations Branch, Examination Processing Branch, and Laboratory Investigations Branch.

★ 9836 ★ **U.S. Department of Health and Human Services**
National Institute for Occupational Safety and Health
Respiratory Disease Studies Division
Clinical Investigations Branch
Appalachian Laboratory for Occupational Safety and Health
944 Chestnut Ridge Rd.
Morgantown, WV 26505-2888
Phone: (304)291-4755
Fax: (304)291-4067
John L. Hankinson, Ph.D., Chief

Research Activities and Fields: Branch conducts research on occupational lung diseases.

★ 9837 ★ **U.S. Department of Health and Human Services**
National Institute for Occupational Safety and Health
Respiratory Disease Studies Division
Environmental Investigations Branch
Appalachian Laboratory for Occupational Safety and Health
Mail Stop 117
944 Chestnut Ridge Rd.
Morgantown, WV 26505
Phone: (304)291-4304
Fax: (304)291-4067
Frank J. Hearl, Chief

Research Activities and Fields: Principal area of research interest is industrial hygiene, particularly as related to sampling and analytical methods, survey protocols, epidemiology, and surface physics. Conducts basic industrial hygiene research on agents causing or likely to cause respiratory diseases.

★ 9838 ★ **U.S. Department of Health and Human Services**
National Institute for Occupational Safety and Health
Robert A. Taft Laboratories
Humphrey Bldg., Rm. 715-H
200 Independence Ave. SW
Washington, DC 20201
Phone: (202)401-6997
Dr. Linda Rosenstock, Director

Research Activities and Fields: Effects of exposure to hazardous substances in the workplace and the psychological factors involved in occupational safety and health. Other studies include methods for analyzing and measuring toxic substances and determining worker exposure.

★ 9839 ★ **U.S. Department of Health and Human Services**
National Institute for Occupational Safety and Health
Safety Research Division
Appalachian Laboratory for Occup. Safety & Health
944 Chestnut Ridge Rd.
Morgantown, WV 26505-2888
Phone: (304)284-5700
Fax: (304)284-5876
Dr. Thomas R. Bender, Director

Research Activities and Fields: Division conducts research in the areas of: occupational traumatic injuries and deaths; musculoskeletal injuries; worker protection technology, particularly the study of respirator and chemical protective clothing characteristics and performance; related hazard sensing, measuring, and monitoring technologies; and physiological effects of work and protective ensemble use. The Division is mandated to investigate ways to reduce the incidence of occupational injuries and deaths and to administer the federal respirator testing and certification program. Areas of emphasis include the surveillance and investigation of traumatic occupational fatalities, particularly electrocutions, fatal falls, machine-related deaths, occupational motor vehicle crashes, homicides, and deaths occurring in confined spaces. Division research and outreach activities have focused on injuries and fatalities in agriculture and construction, two of the highest risk industries. The Division is organized to: 1) study methods of defining high-risk industry and occupational groups through surveillance and data analysis; 2) examine the impact of demographic trends in the workforce, changes in the composition of U.S. industry, and economic forces and fluctuations on the incidence of work-related injury and fatality; 3) identify factors that cause or influence workplace injuries; 4) identify preventive strategies; 5) evaluate preventive strategies; and 6) communicate findings to appropriate audiences. Through its varied activities, the Division promotes the control and containment of hazardous energy and materials by the use of effective preventive strategies and programs that incorporate task analyses, equipment and task design, engineering controls, safe work practices, prudent selection and use of personal protective equipment, and communication and training.

★ 9840 ★ **U.S. Department of Health and Human Services**
National Institute for Occupational Safety and Health
Surveillance, Hazard Evaluations, and Field Studies Division
Mail Stop R-12
Robert A. Taft Laboratories
4676 Columbia Pkwy.
Cincinnati, OH 45226-1998
Phone: (513)841-4428
Fax: (513)841-4540
Mr. Dave Sundin, Chief

Research Activities and Fields: Branch responds to general industry requests (excluding mining and milling activities) for assistance in potential health hazard situations, including requests from employers, employees, employee

representatives, other federal agencies, and state and local agencies. Branch evaluates whether or not chemical, biological, or physical agents are hazardous as used or found in the workplace and makes recommendations for control procedures; improved work practics, and medical screening to reduce exposure levels and subsequent health effects. Branch comprises sections for industrial hygiene and medical studies.

★ 9841 ★ **U.S. Department of Health and Human Services**
National Institute for Occupational Safety and Health
Surveillance, Hazard Evaluations, and Field Studies Division
Hazard Evaluations and Technical Assistance Branch
Robert A. Taft Laboratories
Mail Stop R-9
4676 Columbia Pkwy.
Cincinnati, OH 45226-1998
Phone: (513)841-4428
Fax: (513)841-4488
Mr. Dave Sundin, Chief

Research Activities and Fields: Branch responds to general industry requests (excluding mining and milling activities) for assistance in potential health hazard situations, including requests from employers, employees, employee representatives, other federal agencies, and state and local agencies. Branch evaluates whether or not chemical, biological, or physical agents are hazardous as used or found in the workplace and makes recommendations for control procedures, improved work practices, and medical screening to reduce exposure levels and subsequent health effects. Branch comprises sections for industrial hygiene and medical studies. **Additional Contact Information:** Located at 5555 Ridge Rd., Rm. 220, Cincinnati, OH 45213.

★ 9842 ★ **U.S. Department of Health and Human Services**
National Institute for Occupational Safety and Health
Surveillance, Hazard Evaluations, and Field Studies Division
Industrywide Studies Branch
Robert A. Taft Laboratories
4676 Columbia Pkwy.
Cincinnati, OH 45226-1998
Phone: (513)841-4203
Fax: (513)841-4486
Dr. Marilyn Fingerhut, Chief

Research Activities and Fields: Objective of the Branch is to conduct industrywide studies, through record studies and clinical/environmental studies, to: 1) identify occupational causes of disease in the working population and their offspring; 2) determine the incidence and prevalence of acute and chronic effects from work-related exposures to toxic and hazardous substances; and 3) provide information needed to develop standards to control occupational health hazards. Branch comprises sections for industrial hygiene and epidemiology.

★9843★ **U.S. Department of Health and Human Services**
National Institute for Occupational Safety and Health
Surveillance, Hazard Evaluations, and Field Studies Division
Surveillance Branch
Robert A. Taft Laboratories
4676 Columbia Pkwy.
Cincinnati, OH 45226-1998
Phone: (513)841-4303
Fax: (513)841-4540
Bill Halperin, Chief

Research Activities and Fields: Objective of the Surveillance Branch is to develop and maintain a surveillance system of the nation's work force and its environs and to make an early detection and continuous assessment of the magnitude and extent of job-related illnesses, exposures, and hazardous agents. Branch comprises sections for medical activity, hazards, and illness effects.

★9844★ **U.S. Department of the Interior**
Bureau of Mines
Denver Research Center
Denver Federal Center, Bldg. 20
Denver, CO 80225-0086
Phone: (303)236-0697
Fax: (303)236-0828
Edward Hollop, Research Director

Research Activities and Fields: Center conducts basic and applied studies on mine design, roof support, hazard detection and warning, ionizing radiation, and related mine health and safety, production, and environmental problems. **Publications:** Annual Research Report.

★9845★ **U.S. Department of the Interior**
Bureau of Mines
Pittsburgh Research Center
U.S. Bureau of Mines
Cochrans Mill Rd.
PO Box 18070
Pittsburgh, PA 15236-0070
Phone: (412)892-6601
Fax: (412)892-6614
John N. Murphy, Research Director

Research Activities and Fields: Mine health and safety, methods to improve mine productivity and enhance resource recovery, and control of environmental problems due to current and past mining operations. Principal areas of research interest are respirable dust, noise control, mine ventilation, mine fires, gas and dust explosions, ground control, industrial safety, explosives, postdisaster survival and rescue, alternative mining methods or techniques, acid mind drainage, control of fires in abandoned mines or mine refuse piles, subsidence engineering, safer lasting practices, electrical safety, computer-assisted technology, expert systems, methane control, ergonomic studies, wire rope, and biotechnology.

★9846★ **U.S. Department of the Interior**
Bureau of Mines
Twin Cities Research Center
Occupational Health Division

5629 Minnehaha Ave. S.
Minneapolis, MN 55417
Phone: (612)725-4750
Fax: (612)725-4526
Mr. Kelly C. Strebig, Research Supervisor

Research Activities and Fields: Division conducts laboratory and field studies directed toward minimizing diesel emissions and respirable dust generation and entrainment. Diesel research is conducted to reduce potential health and safety hazards associated with diesel exhaust exposure and promote safe diesel equipment operation. Goal is to reduce exposure of miners to diesel exhaust by developing and testing exhaust control devices in the laboratory and in the field. Dust research is conducted to reduce respirable dust hazards through development of an understanding of the fundamental characteristics of dust aerosols and how they are formed and dispersed during the mining process. Mechanical coal cutting studies are directed toward improving efficiency to minimize the generation of respirable dust and explosion hazards through the improvement of existing machines and the development of completely new cutting technology.

★9847★ **U.S. Department of Labor**
Bureau of Labor Statistics
Office of Compensation and Working Conditions
Office of Safety, Health, and Working Conditions
2 Massachusetts Ave. NE, Rm. 4130
Washington, DC 20212
Phone: (202)606-6304
Fax: (202)606-6310
William M. Eisenberg, Assistant Commissioner

Research Activities and Fields: Office compiles occupational safety and health statistics; and makes grants to states and other local agencies to assist in the development and administration of programs dealing with occupational safety and health statistics. Office conducts an annual survey of non-fatal job-related injuries and illnesses, analyzes the results, and compiles Fatality statistics from other sources. **Publications:** *Occupational Injuries and Illnesses in the United State s by Industry* (annually) and *Recordkeeping Guidelines for Occupational Injuries and Illnesses* (updated periodically).

★9848★ **University of California**
Center for Occupational and Environmental Health
School of Public Health
Berkeley, CA 94720
Phone: (510)642-0761
Fax: (510)642-5815
Dr. Robert C. Spear, Dir.

Research Activities and Fields: Occupational medicine, toxicology, industrial hygiene, epidemiology, and occupational health nursing. Specific research includes studies on the causes, diagnosis, and prevention of occupational injuries and illnesses. **Publications:** *Center for Occupational and Environmental Health Newsletter* (four per year). **Formerly:** Northern California Occupational Health Center.

★9849★ **University of California, Davis**
Division of Occupational/Environmental Medicine and Epidemiology
Davis, CA 95616
Phone: (916)752-3317
Fax: (916)752-5300
Dr. Marc B. Schenker, Division Chief

Research Activities and Fields: Epidemiology of occupational and environmental health problems, focusing on agricultural health problems, occupational cancer, reproductive hazards, and respiratory disease. Collaborates on studies of biologic markers of exposure. **E-mail Address:** postmaster@oem.ucdavis.edu. **Formerly:** Occupational and Environmental Health Unit; Division of Occupational and Environmental Medicine.

★9850★ **University of California, Irvine**
Environmental Simulation Laboratory
School of Social Ecology
Irvine, CA 92717
Phone: (714)824-7442
Fax: (714)824-2056
Daniel Stokols, Ph.D., Dean

Research Activities and Fields: Health and performance effects of conditions within simulated interior environments, especially office environments. Physical conditions considered include ambient lighting and color patterns, music and noise, spacial arrangements and physical density, and ergonomic furnishings. Social factors studied include processes of privacy management, interpersonal and group communication patterns, and human-computer interactions.

★9851★ **University of Florida**
Air Pollution Research Laboratory
408 Black Hall
Gainesville, FL 32611
Phone: (904)392-0845
Fax: (904)392-3076
Dr. Dale Lundgren, Dir.

Research Activities and Fields: Causes, effects, evaluation, and control of air pollution, and problems of occupational health. Research focuses on atmospheric and air pollution chemistry, photochemistry, chemical kinetics, and atmospheric aerosol mechanics and dynamics.

★9852★ **University of Iowa**
Center for Agricultural Disease and Injury Research, Education, and Prevention (CADIREP)
Inst. of Agricultural Med. & Occupational Health
Iowa City, IA 52242
Phone: (319)335-4415
Fax: (319)335-4225
Dr. James Merchant, Contact

Research Activities and Fields: Experimental exposures to grain dust, studies of airway disease in grain handlers, assessment of respiratory disease among dairy farmers, studies of agricultural chemical applicators, epidemiological assessment of farmers.

★9853★ University of Iowa
Institute of Agricultural Medicine and
**   Occupational Health**
Preventive Medicine & Environmental Health
   Dept.
AMRF, Oakdale Campus
Iowa City, IA 52242
Phone: (319)335-4415
Fax: (319)335-4225
James A. Merchant, M.D., Dir.

Research Activities and Fields: Occupational injury and disease research and prevention and environmental health among farmers, those living in rural areas, and general industry. Conducts multidisciplinary studies of health effects due to modern agricultural and industrial practices, particularly in the areas of agricultural medicine, occupational medicine, industrial hygiene, environmental health, and environmental chemistry. **E-mail Address:** james-merchant@uiowa.edu.

★9854★ University of Kentucky
Behavioral Research Aspects of Safety
**   and Health Working Group (BRASH)**
643 Maxwelton Ct.
Lexington, KY 40506-0350
Phone: (606)257-3796
Fax: (606)258-1046
Dr. Henry P. Cole, Dir.

Research Activities and Fields: Social-behavioral research related to occupational safety and health, especially in the mining and minerals extraction industry, agriculture, the construction industry and manufacturing. Studies include improvement of worker adherence to safe work practices, increased worker participation in preventive health measures, improvement of health and safety training, judgement and decision making involved in preventing and coping with workplace emergencies, and relationships between nutrition, smoking, work, chemical exposure, and health. Designs performance measures for occupational respiratory protection courses and similar programs for plant health and safety personnel, teaching judgement and decision making skills to new mine inspectors, and assisting rural women and youth to prevent farm accidents and injuries. **E-mail Address:** cpd167@ukcc.uky.edu.

★9855★ University of Maryland
Center for the Study of Human
**   Performance in Dentistry**
Baltimore College of Dental Surgery
Dental School
Baltimore, MD 21201
Phone: (410)706-7342
Fax: (410)706-3028
Michael M. Belenky, DDS, Dir.

Research Activities and Fields: Physical posture and ergonomic process for practicing dentistry, human-centered ergonomics for preclinical psychomotor education, and psychomotor skill applications to patient dental care. Studies optimal proprioceptive posture for peak performance, patient support, aseptic performance process, facility design, performance logic, performance simulation, psychomotor education, and the reduction/elimination of back, neck, and shoulder pain.

★9856★ University of Michigan
Center for Ergonomics
I.O.E. Bldg.
1205 Beal St.
Ann Arbor, MI 48109-2117
Phone: (313)763-2243
Fax: (313)764-3451
Dr. D.B. Chaffin, Dir.

Research Activities and Fields: Ergonomics and safety engineering, including studies on contemporary techniques and methods necessary to minimize occupational health and safety problems and maximize human-hardware performance capability. **E-mail Address:** randy.rabourn@um.cc.umich.edu. **Formerly:** Human Performance and Safety Engineering Laboratory.

★9857★ University of Michigan
Center for Occupational Rehabilitation and
**   Health**
Williamsburg Office Complex
400 E. Eisenhower Parkway, Ste. E
Ann Arbor, MI 48104
Phone: (313)998-7676
Fax: (313)998-9990
Lynette Rasussen, MS, OTR, Dir.

Research Activities and Fields: Evaluates and recommends efficient and safe work environments to enhance health and minimize injury. Other activities include assessing physical and cognitive functions relating to endurance, speed, and accuracy; identifying and addressing primary and secondary limitations; assessing and specifying home and work-site accessibility; providing case management services; and analyzing the work site to integrate the individual's physical, cognitive, and social abilities into the specific job setting.

University of Michigan
Institute of Environmental and Industrial
**   Health**
See: Entry 5124

★9858★ University of Michigan—Flint
Physical Therapy Laboratory for
**   Cumulative Trauma Disorders**
Rm. 140 LSA
Physical Therapy Dept.
School of Health Professions and Studies
Flint, MI 48502-2186
Phone: (810)762-3373
Fax: (810)766-6668
Lucinda Pfalzer, Ph.D., Contact

Research Activities and Fields: Cumulative Trauma Disorders (CTD's) in the workplace, particularly carpal tunnel syndrome. Also studies the biomechanical, lifestyle, psychosocial and economic factors involved in injury prevention in the work place. **Publications:** Instructional Video, Practice Video and Booklet. **E-mail Address:** pfalzer_l@lsa.flint.umich.edu.

★9859★ University of Montreal
Centre for Occupational Stress and Health
265, avenue du Mont-Royal Ouest
Montreal, PQ, Canada H2V 2S3
Phone: (514)845-4043
Fax: (514)343-5764
Dr. Shimon L. Dolan, Dir.

Research Activities and Fields: Diagnosis and intervention in the field of occupational stress, focusing on stress in police officers, social workers, hospital workers, executive personnel, and workers in other stressful occupations. **E-mail Address:** dolan@ere.umontreal.ca.

★9860★ University of Montreal
Occupational and Environmental
**   Toxicology Research Group**
Medecine du travail et d'hygiene du milieu
Faculte de medecine
C.P. 6128, succursale A
Montreal, PQ, Canada H3C 3J7
Phone: (514)343-7817
Fax: (514)343-2200
Michel Gerin, Dir.

Research Activities and Fields: Industrial hygiene and toxicology, focusing on evaluations of atmospheric concentrations of chemical contaminants in the workplace and biological monitoring of exposure. Specific areas of research include job exposure matrices, physiologically based toxicokinetics modeling of exposure to solvents, in vitro toxicity testing of neurotoxicants, biological monitoring of exposure to polycyclic aromatic hydrocarbons, and preparation of criteria documents for contaminants.

★9861★ University of Quebec at Montreal
Centre for Study of Biological Interactions
**   Between Environment and Health**
C.P. 8888, succursale A
Montreal, PQ, Canada H3C 3P8
Phone: (514)987-3915
Fax: (514)987-6183
Karen Messing, Dir.

Research Activities and Fields: Centre studies occupational health, ergonomics, and genotoxicology.

★9862★ University of Utah
Rocky Mountain Center for Occupational
**   and Environmental Health**
Bldg. 512
Salt Lake City, UT 84112
Phone: (801)581-8719
Fax: (801)581-7224
Royce Moser, Jr., M.D., Dir.

Research Activities and Fields: Occupational and environmental health and safety with emphasis on PM10 quantification, international studies, environmental epidemiology, asbestos-related health problems, musculoskeletal and other injury evaluation and prevention, and ergonomic aspects of the work environment. **E-mail Address:** rmoser@rmcoeh.utah.edu.

University of Vermont
McClure Musculoskeletal Research Center
See: Entry 7962

Wayne State University
Institute of Chemical Toxicology
See: Entry 10494

★9863★ West Virginia University
Institute of Occupational and
  Environmental Health
WVU School of Medicine
3313 HSC-S
Morgantown, WV 26506-9190
Phone: (304)293-3693
Fax: (304)293-2629
Alan M. Ducatman, M.D., Dir.
Research Activities and Fields: Occupational
and environmental health, including occupation-
al medicine and environmental toxicology. **For-
merly:** Institute of Occupational Health and
Safety.

Western Michigan University
Occupational Therapy Teaching Research
  Clinic
See: Entry 12768

★9864★ Work Environments Research
  Center
Univ. of California, Irvine
School of Social Ecology
Irvine, CA 92717
Phone: (714)856-5574
Fax: (714)725-2056
Daniel Stokols, Ph.D., Dir.
Research Activities and Fields: Effect of work
environment on employee performance and
health. Seeks improved environmental design
and development of public and corporate poli-
cies to enhance quality of work life, employee
health and productivity, and organizational ef-
fectiveness. **Publications:** Annual Report (dis-
tributed to members); Newsletter.

State Government Agencies

Occupational Health

★9865★ Alabama Department of Labor
Occupational Injury Statistics and Fatality
  Data Division
100 N. Union, Ste. 620
PO Box 303500
Montgomery, AL 36130-3500
Phone: (334)242-3460
Fax: (334)240-3417

★9866★ Alaska Department of Labor
Labor Standards and Safety Division
Occupational Safety and Health Section
PO Box 107022
Anchorage, AK 99510-7022
Phone: (907)269-4940
Fax: (907)465-3584

★9867★ Arizona Industrial Commission
Occupational Safety Division
PO Box 19070
Phoenix, AZ 85005-9070
Phone: (602)542-5795
Fax: (602)542-3104

★9868★ Arkansas Department of Labor
Safety Division
10421 W. Markham
Little Rock, AR 72205
Phone: (501)682-4500
Fax: (501)682-4532

★9869★ California Department of
  Industrial Relations
Occupational Safety and Health Division
455 Golden Gate Ave.
San Francisco, CA 94102
Phone: (415)703-4590
Fax: (415)703-3331

★9870★ Colorado Department of Labor
  and Employment
Risk Management Division
1515 Arapahoe St., Tower 2, Ste. 400
Denver, CO 80202-2117
Phone: (303)837-3801
Fax: (303)837-3956

★9871★ Connecticut Department of Labor
Occupational Safety and Health Division
200 Folly Brook Blvd.
Wethersfield, CT 06109
Phone: (203)566-4550
Fax: (203)566-1520

★9872★ Delaware Department of Labor
Industrial Affairs Division
Occupational Safety and Health
  Administration
4425 N. Market St.
Wilmington, DE 19802
Phone: (302)577-2877
Fax: (302)577-3750

★9873★ District of Columbia Department
  of Employment Services
Labor Standards Office
Occupational Safety and Health Office
950 Upshur St. NW
Washington, DC 20011
Phone: (202)576-6339

★9874★ Florida Department of Labor and
  Employment Security
Safety Division
Hartman Bldg.
2012 Capitol Circle SE
Tallahassee, FL 32399-2152
Phone: (904)488-3044
Fax: (904)488-8930

★9875★ Georgia Department of Labor
Occupational Safety and Health Division
223 Courtland St., NE
148 International Blvd.
Atlanta, GA 30303
Phone: (404)656-2966
Fax: (404)651-8477

★9876★ Hawaii Department of Labor and
  Industrial Relations
Occupational Safety and Health Branch
830 Punchbowl St., Rm. 423
Honolulu, HI 96813
Phone: (808)586-9116
Fax: (808)586-9104

★9877★ Idaho Department of Labor and
  Industrial Services
Safety Division
PO Box 83720
Boise, ID 83720-0048
Phone: (208)334-2327
Fax: (208)334-2683

★9878★ Illinois Department of Labor
Public Safety Division
1 W. Old State Capitol Plaza, Rm. 300
Chicago, IL 62701
Phone: (217)782-1488
Fax: (217)782-0596

★9879★ Indiana Department of Labor
Safety, Education and Training Bureau
402 W. Washington, Rm. W195
Indianapolis, IN 46204
Phone: (317)232-2687
Fax: (317)233-3790

★9880★ Iowa Department of Employment
  Services
Occupational Safety and Health Bureau
1000 E. Grand Ave.
Des Moines, IA 50319-0209
Phone: (515)281-3606
Fax: (515)242-5144

★9881★ Kansas Department of Human
  Resources
Labor-Management Relations and
  Employment Standards Division
Industrial Safety and Health Section
512 SW 6th St.
Topeka, KS 66603
Phone: (913)296-4386
Fax: (913)296-0179

★9882★ Kentucky Labor Cabinet
Occupational Safety and Health Review
  Commission
4 Mill Creek Rd.
Frankfort, KY 40601-9427
Phone: (502)573-6892
Fax: (502)573-4619

★9883★ Louisiana Department of Labor
Worker's Compensation Office
Health and Safety Division
PO Box 94094
Baton Rouge, LA 70804-7556
Phone: (504)342-7556
Fax: (504)342-3778

★9884★ Maine Department of Labor
Labor Standards Bureau
Safety Division
State House Station 45
Augusta, ME 04333-0045
Phone: (207)624-6460
Fax: (207)624-6449

★9885★ Maryland Department of
  Licensing and Regulation
Labor and Industry Division
Occupational Safety and Health Section
501 St. Paul Pl.
Baltimore, MD 21202
Phone: (410)333-4100

★9886★ Massachusetts Executive Office
  of Labor
Labor and Industries Department
OSHA Consultation Division
100 Cambridge St., Rm. 1107
Boston, MA 02202
Phone: (617)727-3492
Fax: (617)727-8022

★9887★ **Michigan Department of Public Health**
Environmental and Occupational Health Bureau
3423 N. Logan St.
PO Box 30195
Lansing, MI 48909
Phone: (517)335-9218
Fax: (517)335-9476

★9888★ **Minnesota Department of Labor and Industry**
Work Place Services Division
OSHA Consultation Unit
443 Lafayette Rd.
St. Paul, MN 55155
Phone: (612)296-5433
Fax: (612)282-5405

★9889★ **Mississippi Department of Health**
Environmental Health Bureau
Occupational Safety and Health Division
PO Box 1700
Jackson, MS 39215-1700
Phone: (601)960-7518
Fax: (601)960-7448

★9890★ **Missouri Department of Labor and Industrial Relations**
Labor Standards Division
On-site Safety and Health Consultation Program
3315 W. Truman Blvd.
PO Box 449
Jefferson City, MO 65102
Phone: (314)751-3403
Fax: (314)751-3721

★9891★ **Montana Department of Labor and Industry**
Employment Relations Division
Safety Bureau
PO Box 1728
Helena, MT 59624
Phone: (406)444-1605
Fax: (406)444-1419

★9892★ **Nebraska Department of Labor**
Safety Division
PO Box 94600
Lincoln, NE 68509
Phone: (402)471-2239
Fax: (402)471-2318

★9893★ **Nevada Department of Business and Industry**
Industrial Relations Division
Occupational Safety and Health Enforcement Section
1370 S. Curry St.
Carson City, NV 89710
Phone: (702)687-5240
Fax: (702)687-6150

★9894★ **New Hampshire Department of Labor**
Inspection Division
Safety Office
95 Pleasant St.
PO Box 2076
Concord, NH 03302
Phone: (603)271-3176
Fax: (603)271-2668

★9895★ **New Jersey Department of Health**
Epidemiology, Environmental, Occupational, and Health Services Division
Occupational Health Services Office
CN 369
Trenton, NJ 08625-0369
Phone: (609)984-1843
Fax: (609)588-7431

★9896★ **New Mexico Department Environment**
Environmental Protection Division
Occupational Health and Safety Bureau
PO Box 26110
Santa Fe, NM 87502
Phone: (505)827-2877
Fax: (505)827-2836

★9897★ **New York State Department of Labor**
Occupational Safety and Health Division
State Campus, Bldg. 12
Albany, NY 12240
Phone: (518)457-3518
Fax: (518)457-6908

★9898★ **North Carolina Department of Labor**
Occupational Safety and Health Review Board
217 W Jones St.
Raleigh, NC 27603
Phone: (919)733-3589
Fax: (919)733-3020

★9899★ **North Dakota Department of Loss Prevention**
Worker's Compensation Bureau
500 E. Front Ave.
Bismarck, ND 58504-5685
Phone: (701)328-3800
Fax: (701)328-3750

★9900★ **Ohio Department of Health**
Prevention Medicine Division
Occupational Health Bureau
246 N. High St.
Columbus, OH 43215
Phone: (614)466-4183
Fax: (614)644-0085

★9901★ **Oklahoma Department of Labor**
OSHA Consultation Division
4001 N. Lincoln Blvd.
Oklahoma City, OK 73105
Phone: (405)528-1500
Fax: (405)528-5751

★9902★ **Oregon Consumer and Business Services Department**
Occupational Safety and Health Division
350 Winter St., NE
Salem, OR 97310
Phone: (503)378-3272
Fax: (503)378-6444

★9903★ **Pennsylvania Department of Labor and Industry**
Occupational and Industrial Safety Bureau
Labor and Industry Bldg.
Harrisburg, PA 17120
Phone: (717)787-8665
Fax: (717)783-5225

★9904★ **Rhode Island Department of Labor**
Occupational Safety Division
610 Manton Ave.
Providence, RI 02907
Phone: (401)272-3510

★9905★ **South Carolina Department of Labor, Licensing, and Regulation**
Occupational Safety and Health Division
PO Box 11329
Columbia, SC 29211-1329
Phone: (803)734-9644
Fax: (803)734-9716

★9906★ **South Dakota Department of Health**
Systems Development and Regulation Division
445 E. Capitol
Pierre, SD 57501
Phone: (605)773-3364
Fax: (605)773-5904

★9907★ **Tennessee Department of Labor**
Occupational Safety and Health Division
710 James Robertson Pkwy., 2nd Fl.
Nashville, TN 37243-0655
Phone: (615)741-2793
Fax: (615)741-5078

★9908★ **Texas Department of Health**
Environmental Health Bureau
Occupational Health Division
1100 W. 49th St.
Austin, TX 78756
Phone: (512)834-6600
Fax: (512)834-6644

★9909★ **Utah Industrial Commission**
OSHA Division
160 East 300 South, 3rd Fl.
Salt Lake City, UT 84114-6610
Phone: (801)530-6901
Fax: (801)530-6804

★9910★ **Vermont Department of Labor and Industry**
Occupational Safety and Health Division
National Life Insurance Bldg.
Montpelier, VT 05620-3401
Phone: (802)828-2765
Fax: (802)828-2195

★9911★ **Virginia Department of Labor and Industry**
Occupational Health and Enforcement Division
Powers Taylor Bldg.
13 S. 13th St.
Richmond, VA 23219
Phone: (804)786-2391

★9912★ **Washington Department of Labor and Industries**
Consultation and Compliance Services Division
PO Box 44600
Olympia, WA 98504-4600
Phone: (360)902-5500
Fax: (360)902-5529

★9913★ **West Virginia Department of Health and Human Resources**
Public Health Bureau
Environmental Health Office
Radiation, Toxic, and Indoor Air Quality Division
815 Quarrier St., Ste. 418
Charleston, WV 25301-2616
Phone: (304)558-3526

★9914★ **Wisconsin Department of Industry, Labor and Human Relations**
Safety and Buildings Division
PO Box 7969
Madison, WI 53707
Phone: (608)266-1816
Fax: (608)266-1784

★9915★ **Wyoming Department of Employment**
Workers Safety and Compensation Division
122 W. 25th St.
Cheyenne, WY 82002-0700
Phone: (307)777-7441
Fax: (307)777-5805

Chapter 47
Orthopedics

National & International Organizations

★9916★ Academic Orthopaedic Society (AOS)
6300 N. River Rd., Ste. 727
Rosemont, IL 60018-4226
Phone: (708)698-1694
Fax: (708)823-0536
Nancy E. Franzon, Soc.Dir.

Founded: 1971. **Description:** Chairpersons and faculty members of orthopedic departments and divisions of medical schools; directors of orthopedic residency programs; fellowship directors. Provides forum for discussion of administrative and departmental problems concerning undergraduate and graduate orthopedics education in medical schools. Coordinates and plans activities requiring cooperation between orthopedic departments and residencies. Acts as liaison between orthopedic organizations and organizations interested in medical education. **Publications:** Directory, annual. • *Presidential Newsletter*, semiannual. Newsletter. **Formerly:** (1989) Association of Orthopaedic Chairmen; (1991) American Orthopaedic Society.

American Academy of Neurological and Orthopaedic Surgeons (FAANaOS)
See: Entry 12204

American Academy of Orthopaedic Surgeons (AAOS)
See: Entry 12206

★9917★ American Association of Orthopedic Medicine (AAOM)
315 Boulevard NE, Ste. 336
Atlanta, GA 30312
Phone: (404)577-5455
Free: 800-992-2063
Fax: (404)681-4401
Alan Lippitt, M.D., Sec.-Treas.

Founded: 1982. **Members:** 300. **Description:** Physicians and allied health professionals interested in the advancement of knowledge, diagnosis, and nonsurgical treatment of musculoskeletal and related disorders. Seeks to: ad-

vance the standards of practice and quality of service in the field of orthopedic medicine; unite the common interests and skills of medicine and osteopathy; serve as a forum of learning for all of the specialties that deal with pain and dysfunction in the neural, muscular, skeletal, and vascular systems. Encourages research and the dissemination of results. Provides training and continuing medical education in orthopedic medicine; conducts regional seminars every two to three months. **Publications:** *AAOM Membership Directory*, annual. Membership Directory. • *AAOM News*, quarterly. • *The Journal of Orthopaedic Medicine*, 3/year. Journal. Contains scientific papers and articles, editorials, and book reviews. *Price:* Included in membership dues.

American Board of Neurological and Orthopaedic Medicine and Surgery (ABNOMS)
See: Entry 12221

American Board of Orthopaedic Microneurosurgery (ABOM)
See: Entry 12224

American Board of Orthopaedic Surgery (ABOS)
See: Entry 12225

American Board of Podiatric Orthopedics and Primary Medicine (ABPOPPM)
See: Entry 10758

American Board of Thoracic Neurological Orthopaedic Medicine and Surgery (ABTNOMS)
See: Entry 12229

★9918★ American College of Chiropractic Orthopedists (ACCO)
c/o William P. Valusek, D.C.
1030 Broadway, Ste. 101
El Centro, CA 92243
Phone: (619)352-1452
Fax: (619)352-3966
Marcus Bernardi, D.C., Pres.

Founded: 1964. **Members:** 716. **Description:** Certified (337) and noncertified (379) chiropractic orthopedists; students enrolled in a postgraduate chiropractic orthopedic program (124). Seeks to establish and maintain optimal educa-

tional and clinical standards within the field of chiropractic orthopedics. Sponsors educational programs. **Publications:** Membership Directory, annual. • *Ortho-Briefs*, semiannual. Journal. *Price:* Available to members only. Also publishes orthopedic and neurologic tests.

American College of Foot and Ankle Orthopedics and Medicine (ACFAOM)
See: Entry 10760

★9919★ American Fracture Association (AFA)
2416 E. Washington, Ste. D-3
Bloomington, IL 61704
Phone: (309)663-6272
Barbara J. Dehority, Exec.Dir.

Founded: 1938. **Members:** 500. **Description:** Orthopedic, general, industrial, plastic, traumatic, and dental surgeons and physicians interested in the care and treatment of fractures. Seeks to further and create interest in the study of the various accepted types of bone fracture therapy. **Publications:** Directory, periodic. • *Orthopedic Transactions*, annual. **Formerly:** American Ambulatory Fracture Association.

★9920★ American-Israeli Orthopaedic Society
1218 W. Kilbourn Ave., Ste. 301
Milwaukee, WI 53233-1386
Phone: (414)276-6000
Alfred D. Grant, M.D., Pres.

Founded: 1990. **Members:** 75. **Description:** American orthopedists. Exchanges information and research on orthopedics to Israel Orthopaedic Association. Serves as a support group. Conducts exchange program and seminars in the United States and Israel. Conducts charitable programs; maintains speakers' bureau.

★9921★ American Orthopaedic Association (AOA)
6300 N. River Rd., Ste. 300
Rosemont, IL 60018-4263
Phone: (708)318-7330
Hildegard Weiler, Exec.Dir.

Founded: 1887. **Members:** 700. **Description:** Professional society of bone and joint surgeons. Seeks to further knowledge in the diagnosis and treatment of crippling diseases. **Publications:**

American Orthopedic Association--Newsletter, 3/year. Journal. • *Journal on Bone and Joint Surgery*, 8/year. Journal.

★ 9922 ★   **American Orthopaedic Foot and Ankle Society (AOFAS)**
701 16th Ave.
Seattle, WA 98122
Phone: (206)720-1070
Fax: (708)823-0536
Richard Cantrell, Exec.Dir.

Founded: 1969. **Members:** 685. **Description:** Members of American Academy of Orthopaedic Surgeons interested in research on, education in, and care of the foot and ankle. Sponsors continuing medical education courses. **Publications:** *A Guide to Children's Shoes.* • *The Adult Foot.* Pamphlet. • *The Child's Foot.* Pamphlet. • *The Diabetic Foot.* • *How to Select Sport Shoes.* • *In-Stride*, quarterly. Newsletter. *Price:* Included in membership dues. • *Journal of the Foot and Ankle*, bimonthly. Journal. *Price:* Included in membership dues; $55/year for nonmembers; $65/year for institutions; $11/copy. • *Ten Points of Shoe Fit.* **Formerly:** (1983) American Orthopaedic Foot Society.

★ 9923 ★   **American Orthopaedic Society for Sports Medicine (AOSSM)**
6300 N. River Rd., Ste. 200
Rosemont, IL 60018
Phone: (708)292-4900
Fax: (708)292-4905
Donald W. Rome, Exec.Sec.

Founded: 1972. **Members:** 1,000. **Description:** Orthopedic surgeons working in sports medicine; others in related fields involved in the care of athletes. Increases the knowledge and improves care of athletic injuries. Performs educational and research functions; disseminates information. **Publications:** *American Journal of Sports Medicine*, bimonthly. Journal. Reports on the diagnosis, treatment, prevention, and rehabilitation of sports-related injury and disease; also includes society news and book reviews. *Price:* $50/year for individuals; $60/year for institutions; $30/year students.

American Osteopathic Academy of Orthopedics (AOAO)
See: Entry 9979

American Shoulder and Elbow Surgeons (ASES)
See: Entry 12234

Arthroscopy Association of North America (AANA)
See: Entry 12249

★ 9924 ★   **Association of Bone and Joint Surgeons (ABJS)**
6300 N. River Rd., Ste. 727
Rosemont, IL 60018-4226
Phone: (708)698-1630
Fax: (708)823-0536
Arlene Napolilli, Soc.Dir.

Founded: 1947. **Members:** 185. **Description:** Orthopedic surgeons interested in clinical aspects of orthopedics and in training of leaders in the specialty. **Publications:** *Clinical Orthopedics and Related Research*, monthly. Journal.

★ 9925 ★   **Canadian Society of Orthopaedic Technologists (CSOT)**
(Societe Canadienne des Technologistes en Orthopedie — SCTO)
4433 Sheppard Ave. E, Ste. 200
Agincourt, ON, Canada M1S 1V3
Phone: (416)292-0687
Fax: (416)292-1038
Pamela Smith, Registar

Founded: 1972. **Members:** 325. **Languages:** English. **Description:** Individuals employed in the application of plaster casts and traction assemblies; associate members are persons working in related fields; industrial members are those engaged in the manufacture or sale of orthopedic equipment or supplies. Promotes and develops uniform training programs and examinations that contribute to the science of medicine. Facilitates cooperation between orthopedic technologists and the medical profession. **Publications:** *Body Cast*, quarterly. Journal. • *News Cast*, quarterly.

Clinical Orthopaedic Society (COS)
See: Entry 12265

★ 9926 ★   **Conservative Orthopedics International Association (COIA)**
1811 Monroe St.
Dearborn, MI 48124
Phone: (313)563-0360
Fax: (313)563-0360
Dr. Stephen R. Castor, Pres.

Founded: 1982. **Members:** 3,621. **Description:** Medical doctors, osteopaths, chiropractors, orthopedists, psychiatrists, and physical therapists. Promotes continuing education, research, and practice of conservative orthopedics. (Conservative orthopedics concentrates on nonoperative, nonradical, preventive and rehabilitive treatment of musculoskeletal disorders.) Seeks to advance the science and art of conservative orthopedics as they relate to the whole person. Operates charitable program; compiles statistics. Maintains speakers' bureau; offers educational and research programs. Sponsors hall of fame. **Publications:** *Conservative Orthopedics International Bulletin*, annual. Bulletin. • Membership Directory, periodic. • Newsletter, quarterly. • *Updates*, periodic.

Council on Chiropractic Orthopedics (CCO)
See: Entry 3452

★ 9927 ★   **International Arthroscopy Association (IAA)**
6300 N. River Rd., Ste. 727
Rosemont, IL 60018
Phone: (708)698-1632
Fax: (708)823-0536
Karen Jared, Society Mgr.

Founded: 1974. **Members:** 1,000. **Languages:** English. **Description:** Orthopedic surgeons. Purpose is to advance and promote arthroscopy, a diagnostic or surgical procedure in which a thin tool, an arthroscope, is inserted into a joint. The surgeon can either look directly into the arthroscope or observe the view projected on a screen, enabling the surgeon to diagnose a condition after making only one small incision through which to insert the arthroscope. When used in conjunction with other tools the arthros-

cope also allows certain surgical procedures to be performed within viewing range of the scope. Bestows biennial IAA/Linvatec scholarship. Sponsors educational seminars. **Publications:** *Arthroscopy - The Journal of Arthroscopic and Related Surgery*, periodic. Journal. • *IAA Membership Directory*, annual. Membership Directory. • *IAA Newsletter*, semiannual. Newsletter.

★ 9928 ★   **International Society of the Knee (ISK)**
6300 N. River Rd., Ste. 727
Rosemont, IL 60018-4226
Phone: (708)698-1632
Fax: (708)823-0536
Priscilla Wessell, Contact

Founded: 1978. **Members:** 300. **Languages:** English. **Description:** Orthopedic surgeons specializing in problems of the knee. **Publications:** *ISK Membership Directory*, annual. Membership Directory. • *ISK Newsletter*, semiannual. Newsletter.

★ 9929 ★   **International Society of Orthopaedic Surgery and Traumatology (Societe Internationale de Chirurgie Orthopedique et de Traumatologie — SICOT)**
40, rue Washington, bte. 9
B-1050 Brussels, Belgium
Phone: 2 6486823
Fax: 2 6498601
Mr. A.J. Hall, Sec.Gen.

Founded: 1929. **Members:** 3,000. **Languages:** English, French. **Description:** Orthopaedic surgeons in 70 countries united to contribute to the progress of science by conducting studies related to orthopedic surgery and traumatology. **Publications:** *International Orthopedics*, bimonthly. Journal. Includes Newsletter.

National Association of Orthopaedic Nurses (NAON)
See: Entry 9106

★ 9930 ★   **National Association of Orthopaedic Technologists (NAOT)**
3725 National Dr., Ste. 213
Raleigh, NC 27612
Phone: (919)787-0755
Fax: (919)781-3186
Sid Rubinstein, Pres.

Founded: 1982. **Members:** 1,100. **Regional Groups:** 4. **Local Groups:** 23. **Description:** Allied health assistants working with orthopedic patients. Promotes continued professional education of members and other orthopedic health care providers; administers certification examination. Seeks to enhance public understanding of orthopedics. Conducts seminars; compiles statistics. **Publications:** *OnLine: Advancements in Orthopaedic Technology*, bimonthly. Newsletter. Includes orthopaedic articles, meeting updates, and technology tips.

★ 9931 ★ National Board for Certification of Orthopaedic Technologists (NBCOT)
c/o Columbia Assessment Services
3725 National Dr., Ste. 213
Raleigh, NC 27615
Phone: (919)787-2721
Fax: (919)781-3186
Richard J. Woodbeck, Contact

Founded: 1983. **Description:** Determines educational standards for certification in orthopedics. Provides educational programs for recertification. Offers telephone referral service.

Orthopaedic Section, American Physical Therapy Association
See: Entry 12708

★ 9932 ★ Orthopaedics Overseas (OO)
PO Box 65157, Washington Sta.
Washington, DC 20035-5157
Phone: (202)296-0928
Fax: (202)296-8018
Nancy Kelly, Exec.Dir.

Founded: 1959. **Members:** 775. **Description:** Orthopedic surgeons interested in volunteering as consultants in developing countries. Trains physicians in developing countries in diagnostic, conservative, and operative management techniques. Addresses chronic and acute orthopedic problems and crippling diseases such as polio and arthritis. Operates programs in Bangladesh, Bhutan, Indonesia, Malawi, Pakistan, St. Lucia, Transkei, Uganda, Vietnam, and the People's Republic of China. Formerly a project of CARE, the group is a division of Health Volunteers Overseas. HVO also sponsors Anesthesia Overseas, Dentistry Overseas, General Surgery Overseas, Oral and Maxillofacial Surgery Overseas, and Pediatrics Overseas, Internal Medicine Overseas, Nurse Anesthesia Overseas, and Physical Therapy Overseas.

★ 9933 ★ Orthopedic Research Society (ORS)
6300 N. River Rd., Ste. 727
Rosemont, IL 60018-4238
Phone: (708)698-1625
Fax: (708)823-0536
Sheril King, Soc.Mgr.

Founded: 1954. **Members:** 1,600. **Description:** Orthopedic surgeons and other investigators who are elected as active members on the basis of previous scientific activity, continued participation in the field of research, and accomplishments in orthopedic surgery. Promotes orthopedic research and provides a meeting place for presentation and discussion of orthopedic research activities. **Publications:** *Journal of Orthopedic Research*, quarterly. Journal. • *Proceedings of Annual Meeting.* Proceedings.

Orthopedic Surgical Manufacturers Association (OSMA)
See: Entry 5878

Pediatric Orthopaedic Society of North America (POSNA)
See: Entry 3281

★ 9934 ★ Physicians Association for Orthopedics (Berufsverband der Arzte fur Orthopadie)
Am Lindenbaum 6-8
60433 Frankfurt, Germany
Phone: 69 520095
Fax: 69 532083
Dr. Georg Holfelder, Contact

Members: 5,200. **Description:** Orthopedic physicians in Germany. Promotes the practice of orthopedics.

★ 9935 ★ Ruth Jackson Orthopaedic Society (RJS)
c/o Carole Murphy
6300 North River Rd., Ste. 727
Rosemont, IL 60018
Phone: (708)698-1632
Fax: (708)823-0536
Priscilla Wessell, Contact

Founded: 1983. **Members:** 530. **Description:** Women orthopedic surgeons, residents, fellows, and medical students. Seeks to advance the science of orthopedic surgery and to provide support for women orthopedic surgeons. Named for practicing orthopedic surgeon Dr. Ruth Jackson (1902-94), the first woman certified by the American Board of Orthopedic Surgery and the first female member of the American Academy of Orthopedic Surgeons. Conducts educational programs; operates placement service and speakers' bureau. **Publications:** *Membership List*, periodic. *Price:* $125. • *Ruth Jackson Society Newsletter*, semiannual. Newsletter. Includes articles on international members and careers and personal life; also contains calendar of events. *Price:* Free. **Formerly:** (1991) Ruth Jackson Society.

★ 9936 ★ Scandinavian Orthopaedic Association (SOA)
Dept. of Arthopaedics
Arhus Hospital
DK-8000 Arhus, Denmark
Prof. Ian Goldie, Sec.Gen.

Founded: 1919. **Members:** 1,264. **Languages:** Danish, English, Norwegian, Swedish. **Description:** Orthopedic surgeons from Denmark, Finland, Iceland, Norway, and Sweden. Promotes research in orthopedic surgery. Organizes postgraduate courses. **Publications:** *Acta Orthopaedica Scandinavica*, bimonthly.

Society of Military Orthopaedic Surgeons (SMOS)
See: Entry 7809

★ 9937 ★ South African Orthopaedic Association (SAOA) (Suid-Afrikaanse Ortopediese Vereniging — SAOV)
PO Box 72524
Parkview 2122, Republic of South Africa
Phone: 31 4846213
Fax: 11 4846220
Lee van der Merwe, Admin.Sec.

Founded: 1942. **Members:** 700. **Languages:** Afrikaans, English. **Description:** Works to advance the science and art of orthopedic surgery and to protect the professional, financial, and educational interests of members. Provides or-thopedic services to neighboring regions without orthopedic facilities. Promotes research in the field. **Publications:** *Journal of Bone and Joint Surgery*, monthly. Journal. • *Membership Directory*, annual. Directory. • *SA Orthopaedic Bulletin*, quarterly. Bulletin.

★ 9938 ★ Turkish Association of Orthopaedics and Traumatology (TAOT) (Turk Ortopedi ve Travmatoloji Dernegi — TOTD)
I.U. Istanbul Tip Fakultesi
Ortopedi ve Travmatoloji
Anabilim Dali
Capa
TR-34390 Istanbul, Turkey
Phone: 212 5241053
Fax: 212 6352835
Prof. Dr. Fahri Seyhan, Contact

Founded: 1939. **Members:** 1,115. **Languages:** English, Turkish. **Description:** Medical professionals specializing in orthopedics and trauma care. Conducts seminars on orthopedic surgery. Offers postgraduate educational courses; conducts research. **Publications:** *Acta Orthopaedica et Traumatologica Turcica*, 5/year. Journal. Includes abstracts in English. • Books.

Veterinary Orthopaedic Society (VOS)
See: Entry 13113

★ 9939 ★ Western Pacific Orthopaedic Association (WPOA)
Queen Mary Hospital
Univ. Dept. Orthopaedic Surgery
Professional Block
Hong Kong, Hong Kong
Phone: 28554254
Fax: 28174392
Prof. John C.Y. Leong, Pres.

Founded: 1962. **Members:** 1,101. **Regional Groups:** 12. **Languages:** English. **Description:** Orthopedic surgeons in 12 Western Pacific countries. Facilitates the exchange of ideas and discuss new developments and methods relating to orthopedic surgery. Sponsors the Zimmer-WPOA Travelling Fellowship which enables young orthopedic surgeons to travel to academic training centers in the Western Pacific region. **Publications:** *Journal of Orthopaedic Surgery*, 3/year. Journal. • *Newsletter of the Western Pacific Orthopaedic Association*, quarterly.

Research Centers

★ 9940 ★ Center for Hip and Knee Surgery
Orthopaedic Research Foundation, Inc.
1199 Hadley Rd.
Mooresville, IN 46158
Phone: (317)831-2273
Fax: (317)831-9347
Marjorie J. Albohm, Dir.

Research Activities and Fields: Total joint replacement surgery, arthritis surgery, reconstructive joint surgery, sports medicine, physical therapy, and foot, ankle, and shoulder surgery.

Cincinnati Sports Medicine Research and Education Foundation
See: Entry 11962

★ 9941 ★ Hospital for Special Surgery Research Division
535 E. 70th St.
New York, NY 10021
Phone: (212)606-1480
Fax: (212)717-1192
Adele Boskey, Ph.D., Dir. of Research

Research Activities and Fields: Orthopedics and rheumatic diseases, including studies on bone, cartilage, connective tissues, immune system, and related areas of musculoskeletal disease. **Formerly:** Philip D. Wilson Research Foundation.

★ 9942 ★ Johns Hopkins University Orthopaedic Research Laboratories
Johns Hopkins Hospital
Ross Bldg., 2nd Fl.
720 Rutland Ave.
Baltimore, MD 21205
Phone: (410)955-5000
Fax: (410)550-6414
A.H. Reddi, Dir.

Research Activities and Fields: Bone morphogenetic proteins, tissue engineering, cartilage repair, nerve repair, biomechanics, and bioengineering.

★ 9943 ★ Orthopaedic Biomechanics Laboratory
Shriners Hospital for Crippled Children
1701 19th Ave.
San Francisco, CA 94122
Phone: (415)665-1100
Fax: (415)661-3615
Stephen R. Skinner, M.D., Clinical Dir.

Research Activities and Fields: Long-term studies of abnormalities in walking or hand function in children, including research on children with spastic cerebral palsy or myelomeningocele and evaluation of results of surgical and orthotic treatment of these children. **Formerly:** Gait Analysis Laboratory (1982).

★ 9944 ★ Orthopaedic Institute Department of Bioengineering
Hospital for Joint Diseases
301 E. 17th St., 15th Fl.
New York, NY 10003
Phone: (212)598-6567
Fax: (212)598-6096
Harold Alexander, Ph.D., Dir.

Research Activities and Fields: Prevention and treatment of musculoskeletal diseases, including basic studies of biological and synthetic biomaterials, biomechanics, kinematics, and mathematical modeling. **E-mail Address:** halexander@aol.com. **Formerly:** Biomechanics Laboratory (1986).

★ 9945 ★ Orthopaedic Research Institute
929 N. St. Francis
Wichita, KS 67214-3882
Phone: (316)268-8674
Dr. Francis Cooke, Dir.

Research Activities and Fields: Design, development, and testing of orthopaedic implants, materials, and instruments. Specific areas of research include artificial replacement joints, absorbable pins and rods for surgically stabilizing bone fractures, devices for the fusion of severely compromised knees, applying a metal foam to orthopaedic implants for tissue attachment, improving external frames for controlling grossly unstable fractures of the pelvis, and combining absorbable glass fibers and plastics for composite implants in the human body. **Publications:** *Orthopaedic Technology Brief* (occasionally).

★ 9946 ★ Orthopedic Engineering and Research Center
Helen Hayes Hospital
Rte. 9W
West Haverstraw, NY 10993
Phone: (914)947-3000
George V.B. Cochran, M.D., Dir.

Research Activities and Fields: Orthopedic biomechanics, focusing on biomechanics of bone healing, remodeling and internal fixation, electrophysiology of bone, gait analysis of disabled patients (locomotor and upper extremity function), and rehabilitation engineering, including devices to alleviate pressure sores in patients and rehabilitate spinal cord injuries. **Formerly:** Biomechanics Research Unit (1981).

★ 9947 ★ Pennsylvania State University Center for Locomotion Studies
Intramural Bldg., Rm. 10
University Park, PA 16802-2002
Phone: (814)865-1972
Fax: (814)863-4755
Peter R. Cavanagh, Ph.D., Dir.

Research Activities and Fields: Gait analysis and foot mechanics with particular emphasis on diabetic patients and the elderly. Conducts research on the nature and causes of locomotor pathologies, space flight-induced osteoporosis, foot pressure profiles, posture and balance, and effects of alcohol on gait and posture. **Publications:** *The Foot in Diabetes: A Bibliography.* **E-mail Address:** prc@ecl.psu.edu.

Polytechnical School of Montreal Research Group in Biomechanics and Biomaterials
See: Entry 2463

U.S. Department of Defense Armed Forces Institute of Pathology Center for Advanced Pathology Orthopedic Pathology Department
See: Entry 10160

★ 9948 ★ University of Michigan Orthopaedic Research Laboratories
400 N. Ingalls Bldg.
Ann Arbor, MI 48109-0486
Phone: (313)763-9674
Fax: (313)747-0003
Dr. S.A. Goldstein, Dir.

Research Activities and Fields: Applies principles of engineering to understand the musculoskeletal system, investigates orthopedic clinical problems, and develops prosthetic devices for treatment of arthritis. **Formerly:** Biomechanics, Trauma and Sports Medicine Laboratory (1991).

Wayne State University Bioengineering Center
See: Entry 2506

Chapter 48
Osteopathic Medicine

Foundations & Other Funding Organizations

Private Foundations

Gebbie Foundation
See: Entry 210

Other Funding Organizations

★9949★ **American Osteopathic Association**
142 E. Ontario St.
Chicago, IL 60611
Phone: (312)280-5800
Free: 800-621-1773
Fax: (312)280-3860

Description: Sponsors research activities at osteopathic colleges and hospitals; also awards student scholarships and loans annually.

★9950★ **Auxiliary to the American Osteopathic Association**
142 E. Ontario St.
Chicago, IL 60611
Phone: (312)266-5640
Fax: (312)280-3860
Bridget Price, Exec. Dir.

Description: Provides funds for scholarships for the training of osteopathic physicians and surgeons, and for research and other activities at osteopathic colleges. Awards scholarships annually to sophomores attending an accredited osteopathic college.

★9951★ **National Osteopathic Foundation**
c/o Mike Levin
American Osteopathic Association
5775 G. Peachtree-Dunwoody Rd., Ste. 500
Atlanta, GA 30342
Phone: (404)705-9999
Fax: (404)252-0774
Irine Lump, Exec. Dir.

Description: Raises and administers funds for osteopathic medical education, research, colleges, and hospitals.

Medical & Allied Health Schools

Osteopathic Medicine

The following schools of osteopathic medicine are accredited by the American Osteopathic Association, Bureau of Professional Education. Professional associations to contact for general information on osteopathic medical education are the American Osteopathic Association, 142 E. Ontario St., Chicago, IL 60611, (312) 280-5800 and the American Association of Colleges of Osteopathic Medicine, 6110 Executive Blvd., Ste. 405, Rockville, MD 20852, (301) 468-0990.

California

★9952★ **College of Osteopathic Medicine of the Pacific**
309 E. College Plaza
Pomona, CA 91766-1889
Phone: (909)623-6116

Florida

★9953★ **Nova Southeastern University Health Professions Division College of Osteopathic Medicine**
1750 NE 167th St.
North Miami Beach, FL 33162
Phone: (305)949-4000

Illinois

★9954★ **Midwestern University Chicago College of Osteopathic Medicine**
555 31st St.
Downers Grove, IL 60515-1235
Phone: (708)515-6060

Iowa

★9955★ **University of Osteopathic Medicine and Health Sciences College of Osteopathic Medicine and Surgery**
3200 Grand Ave.
Des Moines, IA 50312
Phone: (515)271-1400

Maine

★9956★ **University of New England College of Osteopathic Medicine**
11 Hills Beach Rd.
Biddeford, ME 04005
Phone: (207)283-0171

Michigan

★9957★ **Michigan State University College of Osteopathic Medicine**
E. Fee Hall
East Lansing, MI 48824
Phone: (517)355-9611

Missouri

★9958★ **Kirksville College of Osteopathic Medicine**
800 W. Jefferson St.
Kirksville, MO 63501
Phone: (816)626-2121

★9959★ **University of Health Sciences College of Osteopathic Medicine**
2105 Independence Blvd.
Kansas City, MO 64124
Phone: (816)283-2000

New Jersey

★9960★ **University of Medicine and Dentistry of New Jersey School of Osteopathic Medicine**
1 Medical Center Dr., Ste. 312
Stratford, NJ 08084
Phone: (609)566-6000

New York

**★9961★ New York Institute of
Technology**
New York College of Osteopathic Medicine
Academic Health Care Center
Old Westbury, NY 11568
Phone: (516)626-6900

Ohio

★9962★ Ohio University
College of Osteopathic Medicine
Grosvenor and Irvine Halls
Athens, OH 45701
Phone: (614)593-2500

Oklahoma

★9963★ Oklahoma State University
College of Osteopathic Medicine
1111 W. 17th St.
Tulsa, OK 74107
Phone: (918)582-1972

Pennsylvania

**★9964★ Lake Erie College of Osteopathic
Medicine**
1858 W. Grandview Blvd.
Erie, PA 16509
Phone: (814)866-6641

**★9965★ Philadelphia College of
Osteopathic Medicine**
4170 City Ave.
Philadelphia, PA 19131
Phone: (215)871-6100

Texas

**★9966★ University of North Texas Health
Science Center at Fort Worth**
Texas College of Osteopathic Medicine
3500 Camp Bowie Blvd.
Ft. Worth, TX 76107
Phone: (817)735-2000

West Virginia

**★9967★ West Virginia School of
Osteopathic Medicine**
400 N. Lee St.
Lewisburg, WV 24901
Phone: (304)645-6270

National & International Organizations

**★9968★ Academy of Osteopathic
Directors of Medical Education (AODME)**
2700 Martin Luther King Jr. Blvd.
Detroit, MI 48208
Phone: (313)361-8062
Robert Litchfield, Ph.D., Treas.

Founded: 1965. **Members:** 190. **Regional
Groups:** 9. **Description:** Medical directors and
directors of medical education of osteopathic
hospitals or colleges. Purposes are to: promote
housestaff training programs; review crucial issues in curriculum, supervision, and marketing;
update members on their roles and responsibilities in medical education and medical administration; co-manage clerk, intern, and residency
programs. Conducts normative surveys and
continuing medical education programs. **Publications:** *AODME Members*, annual. • *AODME
Newsletter*, quarterly. Newsletter. • *Manual for
Beginning Directors of Medical Education.* •
Monograph, semiannual.

**★9969★ American Academy of
Osteopathy (AAO)**
3500 DePauw Blvd., Ste. 1080
Indianapolis, IN 46268-1136
Phone: (317)879-1881
Fax: (317)879-0563
Stephen J. Noone, CAE, Exec.Dir.

Founded: 1937. **Members:** 3,500. **Regional
Groups:** 14. **Description:** Doctors of osteopathy. Seeks to develop and teach the science
and art of osteopathic manipulative treatment
and encourage greater proficiency in the use of
osteopathic structural diagnostic and therapeutic procedures. Conducts graduate courses and
seminars; offers structural consultation and
treatment service at meetings. Conducts research. **Publications:** *American Academy of
Osteopathy--Quarterly Journal*, quarterly. Journal. *Price:* $25/year. • Directory, annual. • Vid-
eos. • Yearbooks. **Formerly:** (1944) Osteopathic Manipulative Therapeutic and Clinical
Research Association; (1970) Academy of Applied Osteopathy.

**★9970★ American Association of
Colleges of Osteopathic Medicine
(AACOM)**
6110 Executive Blvd., No. 405
Rockville, MD 20852
Phone: (301)468-0990
Fax: (301)770-5738
Sherry R. Arnstein, Exec.Dir.

Founded: 1898. **Members:** 16. **Description:**
Osteopathic medical colleges. Operates centralized application service; monitors and works
with Congress and other government agencies
in the planning of health care programs. Gathers statistics on osteopathic medical students,
faculty, and diplomates. **Publications:** *AACOM
Organizational Guide*, annual. Directory including lists of members and administrative staff and
faculty at U.S. colleges of osteopathic medicine.
Price: $14/copy. • *American Association of Col-
leges of Osteopathic Medicine--Annual Statistical Report*. Covers activities of the colleges of

osteopathic medicine; provides information on
enrollment , student costs, and scholarships
and loans. *Price:* $13/copy. • *Debts and Career
Plans of Osteopathic Medical Students*, annual.
Report describing financial debt and career
plans of freshmen and seniors in osteopathic
colleges. Contains statistics on debts. *Price:*
$10/copy. • *Education of the Osteopathic Phy-
sician.* • *Osteopathic Medical Education.* • *Osteopathic Medical Education: A Handbook for
Minority Applicants.* **Formerly:** (1970) American
Association of Osteopathic Colleges.

**★9971★ American Association of
Osteopathic Examiners (AAOE)**
300 5th St. NE
Washington, DC 20002
Phone: (202)544-5060
Fax: (202)544-3525
Eliz Beckwith, Dir.

Founded: 1935. **Members:** 100. **Description:**
Private physicians; state medical boards. Works
for adequate osteopathic representation on all
physician licensing boards. Conducts examinations and offers certification of osteopathic physicians. **Publications:** Bulletin, semiannual.

**★9972★ American Association of
Osteopathic Specialists (AAOS)**
804 Main St., Ste. D
Forest Park, GA 30050
Phone: (404)363-8263
Free: 800-447-9397
Fax: (404)361-2285
Floyd C. Pennington, Ph.D, Exec.Dir.

Founded: 1952. **Members:** 700. **Description:**
Osteopathic and allopathic physicians. Formed
for the benevolent, scientific, and educational
purposes of improving the practice of the specialty disciplines. Promotes the study and education of specialty disciplines and high intellectual, moral, and ethical standards in specialty
practice. Encourages improved quality of osteopathic medical and surgical patient care. Maintains continuing education programs: American
Academy of Osteopathic Anesthesiologists;
American Academy of Osteopathic Dermatologists; American Academy of Osteopathic Emergency Physicians; American Academy of Osteopathic Family Practitioners; American Academy
of Osteopathic Internists; American Academy of
Osteopathic Neurologists and Psychiatrists;
American Academy of Osteopathic Obstetricians and Gynecologists; American Academy of
Plastic and Reconstructive Surgeons; American
Academy of Osteopathic Radiologists; American Academy of Osteopathic Orthopedic Surgeons. Provides certification programs in 26 different areas ofspecialization. Bestows degree
of Fellow. **Publications:** *AAOS Directory*, periodic. Directory. Provides alphabetical and geographical list of members. *Price:* Included in
membership dues. **Formerly:** (1984) American
Academy of Osteopathic Surgeons.

**★9973★ American College of
Neuropsychiatrists (ACN)**
28595 Orchard Lake Rd., Ste. 200
Farmington Hills, MI 48334
Phone: (810)553-9877
Fax: (810)553-5957
Louis E. Rentz, Exec.Dir.

Founded: 1937. Members: 420. Description: Psychiatrists, neurologists, physicians in training, and persons in interrelated professions. Promotes study and research in neurology and psychiatry in the osteopathic profession. Maintains specialized education programs. Publications: Directory, annual. • *Journal of the American College of Neuropsychiatrists*, semiannual. Journal. Reports information on medical developments, case studies, and analysis of political actions. Includes calendar of events and research updates. *Price:* Included in membership dues.

★9974★ American College of Osteopathic Emergency Physicians (ACOEP)
142 E. Ontario St., Ste. 218
Chicago, IL 60611-2818
Phone: (312)587-3709
Free: 800-521-3709
Fax: (312)587-3713
George J. Miller, III,DO, Pres.

Founded: 1975. Members: 910. Description: Provides and evaluates postdoctoral and continuing education for osteopathic emergency physicians; encourages and implements the training of emergency physicians; promotes the coordination of community emergency care facilities and personnel. Maintains American Osteopathic Board of Emergency Medicine. Sponsors Emergency Medicine CME Program for Accreditation. Serves as evaluating body for Osteopathic Emergency Medicine Residency Programs. Conducts research and educational programs. Maintains speakers' bureau. Publications: *ACOEP Newsletter*, quarterly. Newsletter. *Price:* Included in membership dues; $25/year for nonmembers. • *Student's Guide to AOA Approved Emergency Medicine Residency Programs*.

★9975★ American College of Osteopathic Family Physicians (ACFP)
330 E. Algonquin
Arlington Heights, IL 60005
Phone: (708)228-6090
Free: 800-323-0790
George Nyhart, Exec.Dir.

Founded: 1950. Members: 14,000. State Groups: 30. Description: Doctors of osteopathic medicine in family practice. To advance standards of family practice by encouraging and increasing educational opportunities; to promote general understanding of the scope of family physician and establish a department of family practice in hospitals. Maintains collection of medical tapes and cross references of available libraries owned by individual physicians; keeps complete records of members and their training. Publications: *ACFP Newsletter*, monthly. Newsletter. Includes calendar of events and member news. *Price:* Free. • *American College of Osteopathic Family Physicians Membership Directory*, annual. Membership Directory. Formerly: (1993) American College of General Practitioners in Osteopathic Medicine and Surgery.

★9976★ American College of Osteopathic Internists (ACOI)
300 5th St. NE
Washington, DC 20002
Phone: (202)546-0095
Free: 800-327-5183
Fax: (202)543-5584
Brian J. Donadio, D.O., Exec.Dir.

Founded: 1943. Members: 1,300. Description: Osteopathic doctors who limit their practice to internal medicine and various subspecialties and who intend, through postdoctoral education, to qualify as certified specialists in the field. Aims to provide educational programs and to improve educational standards in the field of osteopathic internal medicine. Sponsors competitions. Compiles statistics; offers placement service. Publications: Directory, annual. • Newsletter, monthly.

★9977★ American College of Osteopathic Obstetricians and Gynecologists (ACOOG)
900 Auburn Rd.
Pontiac, MI 48342-3365
Phone: (810)332-6360
Free: 800-875-6360
Fax: (810)332-4607
J. Polsinelli, D.O., Exec.Dir.

Founded: 1934. Members: 720. Description: Osteopathic physicians and surgeons specializing in obstetrics and gynecology. Conducts educational programs, and reviews osteopathic obstetric and gynecologic residency training programs. Holds annual postgraduate course. Publications: *ACOOG Newsletter*, quarterly. Newsletter. Includes legislative news, calendar of events, employment listings, and lists of residents completing training and newly certified physicians. *Price:* Free. • *American College of Osteopathic Obstetricians and Gynecologists Membership Directory*, annual. Membership Directory. *Price:* Included in membership dues.

American College of Osteopathic Pediatricians (ACOP)
See: Entry 3166

★9978★ American College of Osteopathic Surgeons (ACOS)
123 N. Henry St.
Alexandria, VA 22314-2903
Phone: (703)684-0416
Guy D. Beaumont, Jr., Exec.Dir.

Founded: 1927. Members: 1,350. Description: Professional society of physicians specializing in surgery and surgical specialties. Maintains placement service; conducts postgraduate courses in continuing surgical education. Publications: *ACOS News*, monthly. Newsletter. Covers association activities and legislative and regulatory issues affecting osteopathic surgeons. Includes calendar of events. *Price:* Included in membership dues. • *American College of Osteopathic Surgeons--Membership Directory and By-laws*, annual. Membership Directory. *Price:* Included in membership dues.

American Osteopathic Academy of Addictionology
See: Entry 12008

★9979★ American Osteopathic Academy of Orthopedics (AOAO)
2500 Hollywood Blvd., No. 212
Hollywood, FL 33020
Phone: (305)922-1110
Fax: (305)922-1189
Dr. Morton Morris, Exec.Dir.

Founded: 1941. Members: 450. Description: Professional society of osteopathic orthopedic surgeons. Publications: *American Osteopathic Academy of Orthopedics--Membership Roster*, annual. Membership Directory. Arranged alphabetically and geographically; also lists resident candidates and AOAO-approved residency programs. *Price:* Free. • *Orthopod*, semiannual. *Price:* Included in membership dues.

★9980★ American Osteopathic Academy of Sclerotherapy (AOAS)
107 Maple Ave.
Wilmington, DE 19809
Phone: (302)792-9280
Judy Wilbank, Exec.Sec.

Founded: 1954. Members: 145. Description: Dedicated to improving the practice of and disseminating knowledge about sclerotherapy. (The academy defines sclerotherapy as the stimulation of the formation of fibrous-connective tissues by the body, in a specific location, by the specific application of a sclerosing modality.) The most frequently used modality is the injection of certain medications, known as sclerosants. Primary studies involve the treatment of: unstable joints, venous abnormalities, and tendeno-osseous points of hyper-irritability. Supports research program; maintains speakers' bureau. Publications: Directory, periodic. • *Get the Point*, semiannual. Newsletter. Reports on the results of studies; evaluates differing sclerotherapeutic treatments. *Price:* Included in membership dues. Formerly: (1956) American Osteopathic Academy of Sclerotherapy; (1959) American Academy of Sclerotherapy.

★9981★ American Osteopathic Academy of Sports Medicine (AOASM)
7611 Elmwood Ave., Ste. 201
Middleton, WI 53562
Phone: (608)831-4400
Fax: (608)831-5122
Robin Brown, Exec.Dir.

Founded: 1975. Members: 750. Description: Members of the American Osteopathic Association and students enrolled in approved colleges of osteopathic medicine. Objectives are to promote education, development of high ethical standards, communication, and research in the field of sports medicine. Conducts study programs, lectures, forums, and seminars. Encourages publication of articles and dissertations in scientific and professional journals. Sponsors student academy organizations at osteopathic education institutions. Maintains speakers' bureau. Publications: *Journal of Osteopathic Sports Medicine*, annual. Journal. • Membership Directory, annual. • *Sport Medicine Today*, quarterly. Newsletter. Reviews research and educational programs in sports medicine. Contains calendar of events. *Price:* Included in membership dues.

★9982★ American Osteopathic Association (AOA)
142 E. Ontario St.
Chicago, IL 60611
Phone: (312)280-5800
Free: 800-621-1773
Fax: (312)280-3860
Robert E. Draba, Ph.D., Exec.Dir.

Founded: 1897. **Members:** 23,000. **State Groups:** 50. **Description:** Osteopathic physicians, surgeons, and graduates of approved colleges of osteopathic medicine. Associate members include teaching, research, administrative, and executive employees of approved colleges, hospitals, divisional societies, and affiliated organizations. Forms (with its affiliates) an officially recognized structure of the osteopathic profession. Promotes the public health, to encourage scientific research, and to maintain and improve high standards of medical education in osteopathic colleges. Inspects and accredits colleges and hospitals; conducts a specialty certification program; sponsors a national examining board satisfactory to state licensing agencies; maintains mandatory program of continuing medical education for members. Compiles statistics on location and type of practice of osteopathic physicians. Sponsors research activities through Bureau of Research in osteopathic colleges and hospitals. Maintains Physician Placement Service. Produces public service radio and television programs; maintains 2000 item library and biographical archives on osteopathic medicine and history. Offers speakers' bureau. **Publications:** *American Osteopathic Association Yearbook and Directory*. Directory. • Brochures. • *The D.O.*, monthly. • *Journal of AOA*, monthly. Journal.

★9983★ American Osteopathic Board of Emergency Medicine (AOBEM)
142 E. Ontario St., Ste. 217
Chicago, IL 60611
Phone: (312)335-1065
Free: 800-847-0057
Fax: (312)335-5489
A. Dale Chisum, D.O., Sec.

Founded: 1980. **Description:** Seeks to improve the quality of emergency medical care, to establish and maintain high standards of excellence in the specialty of emergency medicine, to improve medical education and facilities for training emergency physicians, to evaluate specialists in emergency medicine applying for certification and recertification, and to serve the public, physicians, hospitality, and medical schools by furnishing lists of medical schools by furnishing lists of those diplomates certified by the board. **Publications:** *American Osteopathic Association Yearbook and Directory of Osteopathic Physicians*. Directory.

★9984★ American Osteopathic Board of Family Physicians (AOBFP)
330 E. Algonquin Rd., Ste. 2
Arlington Heights, IL 60005
Phone: (708)640-8477
Free: 800-390-5801
Carol A. Thoma, Exec.Dir.

Founded: 1972. **Description:** Certifying board for osteopathic physicians. Prepares and administers semiannual certification examination

and annual recertification exam. **Formerly:** (1993) American Osteopathic Board of General Practice.

★9985★ American Osteopathic Board of Pediatrics (AOBP)
142 E. Ontario St., 8th Fl.
Chicago, IL 60611
Phone: (312)280-7434
Fax: (312)280-5887

Description: Certification board for osteopathic pediatricians. Standards are formulated by the American Osteopathic Association. Certification is conducted by annual examination.

★9986★ American Osteopathic College of Allergy and Immunology (AOCAI)
3030 N. Hayden, No. 26
Scottsdale, AZ 85251
Phone: (602)949-8898
William Higgins, Sec.-Treas.

Founded: 1975. **Members:** 70. **Description:** Osteopaths with an interest in allergies and immunology. Works to improve education in the field. **Publications:** Newsletter, annual.

★9987★ American Osteopathic College of Anesthesiologists (AOCA)
17201 E. US Hwy. 40, No. 204
Independence, MO 64055
Phone: (816)373-4700
Free: 800-842-AOCA
Fax: (816)373-1529
Bert M. Bez, D.O., Sec.-Treas.

Founded: 1952. **Members:** 500. **Description:** Members of American Osteopathic Association who are engaged in the practice of anesthesiology. **Publications:** Membership Directory, annual. • Newsletter, 3/year. **Formerly:** (1952) American Osteopathic Society of Anesthesiologists.

★9988★ American Osteopathic College of Dermatology (AOCD)
PO Box 7525
Kirksville, MO 63501-7525
Phone: (816)665-2184
Fax: (816)626-2714
Rebecca A. Mansfield, Exec.Dir.

Founded: 1955. **Members:** 130. **Description:** Members of the osteopathic profession certified or involved in dermatology. Conducts specialized education programs. **Publications:** Directory, annual. • Newsletter, quarterly.

★9989★ American Osteopathic College of Pathologists (AOCP)
c/o Joan Gross
12368 NW 13th Ct.
Pembroke Pines, FL 33026
Phone: (305)432-9640
Fax: (305)432-9640
Joan Gross, Exec.Dir.

Founded: 1954. **Members:** 180. **Description:** Osteopathic physicians who have completed residency training programs in pathology and clinical pathology; candidate members are in residency training in pathology. Establishes guidelines for training programs in pathology and clinical pathology for osteopathic physicians; maintains standards in residency training

programs. Offers placement service and midyear tutorial program. Maintains collection of slide study sets. **Publications:** *American Osteopathic College of Pathologists Directory*, annual. Directory. • *Nova*, monthly. Newsletter. Includes reports on employment opportunities and topics of interest. *Price:* Included in membership dues.

★9990★ American Osteopathic College of Preventive Medicine (AOCPM)
1900 The Exchange, Ste. 160
Atlanta, GA 30339-2022
Phone: (404)953-1083
Fax: (404)952-5651
Cathy M. Garris, Exec.Dir.

Founded: 1982. **Members:** 160. **Description:** Osteopathic doctors. Prepares and educates doctors of osteopathy who wish to specialize in aerospace medicine, occupational/environmental medicine, or public health preventive medicine. Seeks to foster an understanding of these fields of study among osteopathic doctors and the public. Provides consultant services to other physicians. Maintains speakers' bureau. Conducts studies. **Publications:** Directory, annual. • Newsletter, quarterly.

★9991★ American Osteopathic College of Proctology (AOCPr)
1020 Galloping Hill Rd.
Union, NJ 07083
Phone: (908)687-2062
Fax: (908)687-8169
Dr. Zolton Brody, Exec.Officer

Members: 155. **Description:** Osteopathic physicians and surgeons specializing in treatment of diseases of the anus, rectum, and colon.

★9992★ American Osteopathic College of Radiology (AOCR)
119 E. 2nd St.
Milan, MO 63556
Phone: (816)265-4011
Fax: (816)265-3494
Pamela A. Smith, Exec.Dir.

Founded: 1941. **Members:** 730. **Description:** Certified radiologists, residents-in-training, and others active in the field of radiology. **Publications:** Membership Directory, annual. • *Viewbox*, quarterly.

★9993★ American Osteopathic College of Rehabilitation Medicine (AOCRM)
9058 W. Church
Des Plaines, IL 60016
Phone: (708)699-0048
Fax: (708)296-1366
Julie Pickett, Sec.

Founded: 1954. **Members:** 125. **Description:** Osteopathic physicians with a strong interest in physical and rehabilitation medicine as a specialty. Active members are those certified in the specialty by the American Osteopathic Board of Rehabilitation Medicine of the American Osteopathic Association. To stimulate study, extend knowledge, and improve practice in rehabilitation medicine. Cosponsors training programs; sponsors competitive writing for predoctoral osteopathic medical students, interns, and residents. **Publications:** Directory, annual. • Newsletter, periodic. **Formerly:** (1955) American Osteopathic Academy of Physical Medicine and Rehabilitation; (1970) American Osteopathic College of Physical Medicine and Rehabilitation.

American Osteopathic Healthcare Association (AOHA)
See: Entry 6426

★ 9994 ★ Association of Osteopathic State Executive Directors (AOSED)
455 Capitol Mall, Ste. 225
Sacramento, CA 95814
Phone: (916)447-2004
Fax: (916)447-4828
Matt Weyuker, Exec.VP

Founded: 1918. **Members:** 112. **Description:** Divisional and affiliated societies of the American Osteopathic Association. Objectives are: to promote and improve associations and procedures among members; to examine and develop procedures and policies that will bring about an efficient unit of operation within the divisional societies; to disseminate information on the activities of members and foster and participate in the objects of the AOA. **Publications:** *Association of Osteopathic State Executive Directors--Newsletter*, quarterly. Newsletter. • *Directory of Osteopathic Publications*, biennial. Directory.

★ 9995 ★ Auxiliary to the American Osteopathic Association (AAOA)
142 E. Ontario St.
Chicago, IL 60611
Phone: (312)266-5640
Fax: (312)280-3860
Bridget Price, Exec.Dir.

Founded: 1940. **Members:** 5,000. **Description:** Immediate family members of osteopathic physicians; spouses of students of osteopathic medicine. Promotes public health education; provides funds for scholarships for the training of osteopathic physicians and surgeons, and for research and other activities at osteopathic colleges; encourages establishment and continuation of volunteer service organizations in non-profit osteopathic hospitals; participates in national and community health programs. Sponsors summer seminars. **Publications:** *AAOA Accent*, quarterly. Newsletter. Covers osteopathic medicine and related subjects such as safety projects, public health information, and osteopathic college scholarship awards. *Price:* Included in membership dues. • Annual Report. • *Newsbriefs*, bimonthly. • *Roster of Affiliates*, annual. Also publishes handbooks.

★ 9996 ★ British and European Osteopathic Association (BEOA)
6 Adelaide Rd.
Teddington
London TW11 0AY, England
Phone: 181 9778532
M.J. Johnson, Sec.

Founded: 1976. **Members:** 150. **Languages:** English. **Description:** Osteopaths united to promote osteopathy and to maintain high ethical, educational, and professional standards. Organizes courses; bestows awards. **Publications:** *BEOA Newsletter*, quarterly. Newsletter. • Brochures, periodic. • *Register of Members*, annual. Directory.

★ 9997 ★ Bureau of Professional Education of the American Osteopathic Association (BPEAOA)
c/o Douglas Ward, Ph.D.
American Osteopathic Association
142 E. Ontario St.
Chicago, IL 60611
Phone: (312)280-5800
Free: 800-621-1773
Fax: (312)280-3860
Douglas Ward, Ph.D., Contact

Description: Membership comprises American Osteopathic Associations representatives of the American Association of Colleges of Osteopathic Medicine (see separate entry), and public representatives. Approves policy regarding new and/or different intern and residency training programs in approved osteopathic hospitals. Serves as accrediting agency for colleges of osteopathic medicine.

College of Osteopathic Healthcare Executives (COHE)
See: Entry 5570

★ 9998 ★ Cranial Academy (CA)
3500 Depauw Blvd., No. 1080
Indianapolis, IN 46268
Phone: (317)879-0713
Fax: (317)879-0718
Patricia Crampton, Exec.Dir.

Founded: 1946. **Members:** 900. **Description:** A component society of the American Academy of Osteopathy. Osteopathic physicians interested in study and development of osteopathic cranial concepts and techniques of diagnosis and treatment in structural manipulation of the body; members have taken a Cranial Academy approved basic course in Osteopathy in the cranial field. Promotes research programs. **Publications:** *Clinical Cranial Osteopathy*. Book. *Price:* $45 for members; $50 for nonmembers. • *The Cranial Bowl*. Book. *Price:* $15. • *The Cranial Bowl*. Brochure. *Price:* $.90 for members; $1 for nonmembers. • *The Cranial Concept*. Brochure. *Price:* $27/100 for members; $30/100 for nonmembers. • *The Cranial Letter*, quarterly. Newsletter. Contains articles related to new developments in cranial osteopathy. *Price:* $60/year. • Directory, annual. *Price:* Included in membership dues. • *Journal of OCA 1948, 49, 54, 57, & 58*. *Price:* $18 for members; $20 for nonmembers. • *Osteopathy in the Cranial Field*. Book. *Price:* $67.50 for members; $75 for nonmembers. • *With Thinking Fingers*. Book. *Price:* $9 for members; $10 for nonmembers. **Formerly:** (1960) Osteopathic Cranial Association.

★ 9999 ★ European Liaison Committee for Osteopaths (ELCO)
(Comite de Liaison Europeen des Osteopathes — CLEO)
1, rue Hoche
F-93599 Pantin, France
Phone: 1 48459136
Fernand-Paul Berthenet, Sec.Gen.

Founded: 1978. **Members:** 4. **Languages:** French. **Description:** National associations in Belgium, England, France, and Greece. Seeks to protect the rights of osteopaths in the European Economic Community .

★ 10000 ★ International Federation of Manual Medicine (IFMM)
(Federation Internationale de Medicine Manuelle — FIMM)
Amtssygehus University Hospital
Department of Rheumatology
DK-8000 Arhus C, Denmark
Phone: 86126866
Fax: 86136961
Dr. Johannes Fossgreen, Sec.Gen.

Founded: 1968. **Members:** 13,000. **Languages:** English, French, German. **Description:** Medical and osteopathic doctors in 22 countries. Promotes cooperation and coordination of activities among medical bodies concerned with manual medicine. Encourages research in and recognition of manual medicine; fosters development of educational programs. **Publications:** *Manuelle Medicine*, quarterly. Includes English abstracts. Also publishes books.

★ 10001 ★ Iota Tau Sigma
PO Box 792
Kirksville, MO 63501
Phone: (816)665-7741
Fax: (816)665-0331
Wilson P. Bailey, Sec.-Treas.

Founded: 1902. **Description:** Professional fraternity - osteopathic medicine. **Publications:** *Gozzle Nipper*, semiannual.

★ 10002 ★ Lambda Omicron Gamma Medical Society
636 Argyle Rd.
Wynnewood, PA 19096
Phone: (610)649-8086
Dr. Jeffrey Brodsky, Pres.

Founded: 1924. **Members:** 1,200. **Description:** Professional fraternity - osteopathy. Maintains speakers' bureau. **Publications:** *LOG National Fraternity Yearbook*. Contains directory and member updates. *Price:* Included in membership dues. • *LOGNF Newsletter*, quarterly. *Price:* Included in membership dues. **Formerly:** (1993) Lambda Omicron Gamma.

★ 10003 ★ National Board of Osteopathic Medical Examiners (NBOME)
2700 River Rd., Ste. 407
Des Plaines, IL 60018
Phone: (708)635-9955
Fax: (708)635-6053
Joseph F. Smoley, Ph.D., Exec.Dir.

Founded: 1935. **Members:** 12. **Description:** Examining and evaluating board to investigate the qualifications of, and administer examinations and grant diplomate status to osteopathic physicians. **Publications:** *Information Bulletin*, annual. Bulletin. **Formerly:** (1986) National Board of Examiners for Osteopathic Physicians and Surgeons.

★ 10004 ★ National Osteopathic Foundation (NOF)
c/o Mike Levin
5775 G. Peachtree-Dunwoody Rd., Ste. 500
Atlanta, GA 30342
Phone: (404)705-9999
Fax: (404)252-0774
Mike Levin, Exec.Dir.

Founded: 1949. **Members:** 1,500. **Description:** Osteopathic physicians and laypersons interested in raising and administering funds for osteopathic medical education, research, colleges, and hospitals. Functions as philanthropic affiliate of the American Osteopathic Association; seeks to foster understanding of osteopathic theory and practice. **Formerly:** (1960) Osteopathic Foundation.

★ 10005 ★   **National Osteopathic Guild Association (NOGA)**
c/o Auxiliary to the American Osteopathic Association
142 E. Ontario St.
Chicago, IL 60611
Phone: (312)266-5640
Laverne Furlong, Pres.

Founded: 1955. **Members:** 1,800. **Description:** Guilds that provide volunteer services in osteopathic hospitals. **Publications:** Newsletter, quarterly.

★ 10006 ★   **National Osteopathic Women Physician's Association (NOWPA)**
West Virginia School of Osteopathic Medicine
400 N. Lee St.
Lewisburg, WV 24901
Phone: (304)645-6270
Fax: (304)645-4859
Marlene A. Wager, D.O., Exec. Officer

Founded: 1904. **Members:** 200. **Description:** Professional sorority - osteopathy. Gives Grant-in-Aid annually. **Publications:** The Alpha, annual. **Formerly:** (1988) Delta Omega.

★ 10007 ★   **Osteopathic College of Ophthalmology and Otorhinolaryngology (OCOO)**
Dayton District Academy of Osteopathic Medicine
405 Grand Ave.
Dayton, OH 45405
Phone: (513)226-3438
Fax: (513)461-2971
George Saul, Exec.Dir.

Founded: 1916. **Members:** 385. **Description:** Osteopathic physicians who have completed formal specialty training or are acquiring such training in ophthalmology, otorhinolaryngology, and orofacial plastic surgery, and those who are certified specialists in one or more of the above named areas. Develops application of osteopathic concepts in this specialty; determines minimum standards of education at undergraduate and postgraduate levels. Sponsors research programs. **Publications:** Osteopathic College of Ophthalmology and Otorhinolaryngology--News Letter, quarterly. Price: Included in membership dues. • Photo Roster, periodic. Also publishes collected papers.

★ 10008 ★   **Psi Sigma Alpha**
c/o Dr. Charles A. Knouse
85 S. May Ave.
Athens, OH 45701
Phone: (614)592-4124
Fax: (614)592-4505
Dr. Charles A. Knouse, Contact

Founded: 1924. **Members:** 1,110. **Description:** Honor society of men and women in the field of osteopathy. Presents annual award for service to osteopathy. **Publications:** The Skull, semiannual.

★ 10009 ★   **Sigma Sigma Phi**
2004 Woodnote
Garland, TX 75040
Phone: (214)272-7693
Deborah Brimelow, Exec. Officer

Founded: 1921. **Members:** 3,600. **Description:** Honorary fraternity - osteopathy. Objectives are: to further the science of osteopathic medicine and its practice; to improve scholastic standings of its students; to promote a closer relationship between students and college officials and faculties. Provides financial and supportive aid to chapters at osteopathic medical colleges.

★ 10010 ★   **Theta Psi**
c/o KCOM
800 W. Jefferson
Kirksville, MO 63501
Phone: (816)665-2844
Dr. Randall C. Barnes, Contact

Founded: 1903. **Members:** 650. **Description:** Professional fraternity - osteopathy. **Publications:** Signet, annual.

Research Centers

★ 10011 ★   **A.T. Still Osteopathic Library and Research Center**
American Osteopathic Assoc.
142 E. Ontario St.
Chicago, IL 60611
Phone: (312)280-5800
Sandra Williamson, Dir. of Pubs.

Research Activities and Fields: Center focuses on medicine and osteopathic medicine.

State Government Agencies

Osteopathic Medical Boards

★ 10012 ★   **Alabama State Board of Medical Examiners**
848 Washington Ave.
PO Box 946
Montgomery, AL 36101-0946
Phone: (334)242-4116
Fax: (334)242-4155

★ 10013 ★   **Alaska State Medical Board**
3601 C St., Ste. 722
Anchorage, AK 99503
Phone: (907)561-2878
Fax: (907)562-5781

★ 10014 ★   **Arizona Board of Osteopathic Examiners in Medicine and Surgery**
141 E. Palm Lane, Ste. 205
Phoenix, AZ 85004
Phone: (602)255-1747
Fax: (602)255-1756

★ 10015 ★   **Arkansas State Medical Board**
2100 Riverfront Dr., Ste. 200
Harrisburg, AR 72432
Phone: (501)296-1802
Fax: (501)296-1805

★ 10016 ★   **California Osteopathic Medical Board**
444 N. 3rd. St., Ste. A200
Sacramento, CA 95814
Phone: (916)322-4306
Fax: (916)327-6119

★ 10017 ★   **Colorado State Board of Medical Examiners**
1560 Broadway, Ste. 1550
Denver, CO 80202
Phone: (303)894-7719
Fax: (303)894-7885

★ 10018 ★   **Connecticut State Board of Medical Quality Assurance**
150 Washington St.
Hartford, CT 06106
Phone: (203)566-7398
Fax: (203)566-6606

★ 10019 ★   **Delaware Board of Medical Practice**
Cannon Bldg., Ste. 203
861 Silver Lake Blvd.
PO Box 1401
Dover, DE 19903
Phone: (302)739-4522
Fax: (302)739-2711

★ 10020 ★   **District of Columbia Board of Medicine**
605 G St. NW, Rm. 202
PO Box 37200
Washington, DC 20013-7200
Phone: (202)727-5365
Fax: (202)727-4087

★ 10021 ★   **Florida Board of Osteopathic Medicine**
Norhtwood Centre, No. 60
1940 N. Monroe St.
Tallahassee, FL 32399-0757
Phone: (904)922-6725
Fax: (904)921-6184

★ 10022 ★   **Georgia Composite State Board of Medical Examiners**
166 Pryor St. SW
Atlanta, GA 30303-3465
Phone: (404)656-3913
Fax: (404)656-9723

★ 10023 ★   **Guam Board of Medical Examiners**
PO Box 2816
Agana, GU 96910
Phone: (671)734-7296
Fax: (671)734-2066

★ 10024 ★   **Hawaii Board of Medical Examiners**
1010 Richards St.
PO Box 3469
Honolulu, HI 96801
Phone: (808)586-2708
Fax: (808)586-2689

★ 10025 ★   **Idaho State Board of Medicine**
280 N. 8th St., No. 202
PO Box 83720
Boise, ID 83720-0058
Phone: (208)334-2822
Fax: (208)334-2801

★ 10026 ★ Illinois Department of
Professional Regulation
Board of Osteopathic Medicine
320 W. Washington St.
Springfield, IL 62786
Phone: (217)785-0800
Fax: (217)524-2169

★ 10027 ★ Indiana Health Professions
Bureau
Board of Osteopathic Medicine
402 W. Washington, Rm. 041
Indianapolis, IN 46204
Phone: (317)232-2960
Fax: (317)233-4236

★ 10028 ★ Iowa State Board of Medical
Examiners
State Capitol Complex
Executive Hills West
1209 E. Court Ave.
Des Moines, IA 50319-0180
Phone: (515)281-5171
Fax: (515)242-5908

★ 10029 ★ Kansas State Board of Healing
Arts
235 SW Topeka Blvd.
Topeka, KS 66603
Phone: (913)296-7413
Fax: (913)296-0852

★ 10030 ★ Kentucky Board of Medical
Licensure
Hurstbourne Office Park
310 Whittington Pkwy., Ste. 1B
Louisville, KY 40222
Phone: (502)429-8046
Fax: (502)429-9923

★ 10031 ★ Louisiana State Board of
Medical Examiners
830 Union St., Ste. 100
New Orleans, LA 70112
Phone: (504)524-6763
Fax: (504)568-8893

★ 10032 ★ Maine Board of Osteopathic
Licensure
State House, Station 142
Augusta, ME 04333
Phone: (207)287-2480
Fax: (207)287-2480

★ 10033 ★ Maryland Board of Physician
Quality Assurance
4201 Patterson Ave., 3rd Fl.
PO Box 2571
Baltimore, MD 21215-0095
Phone: (410)764-4777
Fax: (410)764-2478

★ 10034 ★ Massachusetts Board of
Registration in Medicine
10 West St., 3rd. Fl.
Boston, MA 02111
Phone: (617)727-3086
Fax: (617)451-9568

★ 10035 ★ Michigan Board of Osteopathic
Medicine and Surgery
611 W. Ottawa St., 4th Fl.
PO Box 30018
Lansing, MI 48909
Phone: (517)373-6873
Fax: (517)373-2179

★ 10036 ★ Minnesota Board of Medical
Practice
2700 University Ave. W., Ste. 106
St. Paul, MN 55114-1080
Phone: (612)642-0538
Fax: (612)642-0393

★ 10037 ★ Mississippi State Board of
Medical Licensure
2688-D Insurance Center Dr.
Jackson, MS 39216
Phone: (601)354-6645
Fax: (601)987-4159

★ 10038 ★ Missouri State Board of
Registration for the Healing Arts
3605 Missouri Blvd.
PO Box 4
Jefferson City, MO 65102
Phone: (314)751-0098
Fax: (314)751-3166

★ 10039 ★ Montana Board of Medical
Examiners
111 N. Jackson
PO Box 200513
Helena, MT 59620-0513
Phone: (406)444-4284
Fax: (406)444-1667

★ 10040 ★ Nebraska State Board of
Examiners in Medicine and Surgery
301 Centennial Mall, S.
PO Box 95007
Lincoln, NE 68509-5007
Phone: (402)471-2115
Fax: (402)471-0383

★ 10041 ★ Nevada State Board of
Osteopathic Medicine
2950 E. Flamingo Rd., Ste. E-3
Las Vegas, NV 89121
Phone: (702)732-2147
Fax: (702)732-2079

★ 10042 ★ New Hampshire Board of
Registration in Medicine
Health and Welfare Bldg.
6 Hazen Dr.
Concord, NH 03301
Phone: (603)271-4501
Fax: (603)271-3745

★ 10043 ★ New Jersey State Board of
Medical Examiners
140 E. Front St., 2nd Fl.
Trenton, NJ 08608
Phone: (609)826-7100
Fax: (609)984-3930

★ 10044 ★ New Mexico Board of
Osteopathic Medical Examiners
725 St. Michaels Dr.
PO Box 25101
Santa Fe, NM 87504
Phone: (505)827-7171
Fax: (505)827-7095

★ 10045 ★ New York State Board for
Medicine
Cultural Education Center, Ste. 3023
Empire State Plaza
Albany, NY 12230
Phone: (518)474-3841
Fax: (518)473-0578

★ 10046 ★ North Carolina Board of Medical
Examiners
1203 Front St.
PO Box 20007
Raleigh, NC 27619
Phone: (919)828-1212
Fax: (919)828-1295

★ 10047 ★ North Dakota State Board of
Medical Examiners
City Center Plaza
418 E. Broadway, Ste. 12
Bismarck, ND 58501
Phone: (701)223-9485
Fax: (701)223-9756

★ 10048 ★ Ohio State Medical Board
77 S. High St., 17th Fl.
Columbus, OH 43266-0315
Phone: (614)466-3934
Fax: (614)728-5946

★ 10049 ★ Oklahoma Board of Osteopathic
Examiners
4848 N. Lincoln Blvd., Ste. 100
Oklahoma City, OK 73105-3321
Phone: (405)528-8625
Fax: (405)528-6102

★ 10050 ★ Oregon Board of Medical
Examiners
Crown Plaza, No. 620
1500 SW 1st Ave.
Portland, OR 97201-5826
Phone: (503)229-5770
Fax: (503)229-6543

★ 10051 ★ Pennsylvania State Board of
Osteopathic Medicine
PO Box 2649
Harrisburg, PA 17105-2649
Phone: (717)783-4858
Fax: (717)783-4853

★ 10052 ★ Puerto Rico Board of Medical
Examiners
Call Box 13969
San Juan, PR 00908
Phone: (809)782-8989
Fax: (809)782-8733

★ 10053 ★ Rhode Island Board of Medical
Licensure and Discipline
3 Capitol Hill, Rm. 205
Providence, RI 02908-5097
Phone: (401)277-3855
Fax: (401)277-2158

★ 10054 ★ South Carolina Board of Medical
Examiners
Salvda Bldg., Ste. 120
101 Executive Center Dr.
PO Box 212269
Columbia, SC 29221-2269
Phone: (803)731-1650
Fax: (803)731-1660

★ 10055 ★ South Dakota State Board of
Medical and Osteopathic Examiners
1323 S. Minnesota Ave.
Sioux Falls, SD 57105
Phone: (605)336-1965
Fax: (605)336-0270

★ 10056 ★ **Tennessee State Board of Osteopathic Examination**
283 Plus Park Blvd.
Nashville, TN 37247-1010
Phone: (615)367-6281
Fax: (615)361-6210

★ 10057 ★ **Texas State Board of Medical Examiners**
1812 Centre Creek, Ste. 300
PO Box 149134
Austin, TX 78714-9134
Phone: (512)834-7728
Fax: (512)834-4597

★ 10058 ★ **Utah Physicians Licensing Board**
Heber M. Wells Bldg., 4th Fl.
160 East 300 South
PO Box 45805
Salt Lake City, UT 84145-0805
Phone: (801)530-6628
Fax: (801)530-6511

★ 10059 ★ **Vermont Board of Medical Practice**
109 State St.
Montpelier, VT 05609-1101
Phone: (802)828-2363
Fax: (802)828-2496

★ 10060 ★ **Virgin Islands Board of Medical Examiners**
48 Sugar Estate
St. Thomas, VI 00802
Phone: (809)776-8311
Fax: (809)777-4001

★ 10061 ★ **Virginia Board of Medicine**
6606 W. Broad St., 4th Fl.
Richmond, VA 23230-1717
Phone: (804)662-9908
Fax: (804)662-9943

★ 10062 ★ **Washington Board of Osteopathic Medicine and Surgery**
1300 SE Quince St.
PO Box 47868
Olympia, WA 98504-7868
Phone: (206)586-8438
Fax: (206)753-0657

★ 10063 ★ **West Virginia Board of Osteopathy**
334 Penco Rd.
Weirton, WV 26062
Phone: (304)723-4638
Fax: (304)723-4638

★ 10064 ★ **Wisconsin Medical Examining Board**
1400 E. Washington Ave.
PO Box 8935
Madison, WI 53708
Phone: (608)266-2811
Fax: (608)267-0644

★ 10065 ★ **Wyoming Board of Medicine**
Barrett Bldg., Rm. 208
2301 Central Ave.
Cheyenne, WY 82002
Phone: (307)777-6463
Fax: (307)777-6478

State & Regional Organizations

Osteopathic Medicine

Listed below are state divisional societies of the American Osteopathic Association, 142 E. Ontario St., Chicago, IL 60611, (312) 280-5800.

Alabama

★ 10066 ★ **Alabama Osteopathic Medical Association**
PO Box 240248
Montgomery, AL 36124-0248
Phone: (334)272-1002
Fax: (334)272-1002

Alaska

★ 10067 ★ **Alaska Osteopathic Medical Association**
PO Box 870470
Wasilla, AK 99687
Phone: (907)376-2006

Arizona

★ 10068 ★ **Arizona Osteopathic Medical Association**
5057 E. Thomas Rd.
Phoenix, AZ 85018
Phone: (602)840-0460
Fax: (602)840-0480

Arkansas

★ 10069 ★ **Arkansas Osteopathic Medical Association**
412 Union Train Sta.
Little Rock, AR 72201
Phone: (501)374-8900

California

★ 10070 ★ **Osteopathic Physicians and Surgeons of California**
455 Capitol Mall, Ste. 230
Sacramento, CA 95814
Phone: (916)447-2004
Fax: (916)447-4828

Colorado

★ 10071 ★ **Colorado Society of Osteopathic Medicine**
50 S. Steele St., Ste. 770
Denver, CO 80209
Phone: (303)322-1752
Fax: (303)322-1956

Connecticut

★ 10072 ★ **Connecticut Osteopathic Medical Society**
225 Main St.
Manchester, CT 06040
Phone: (203)646-6969
Fax: (203)643-6112

Delaware

★ 10073 ★ **Delaware State Osteopathic Medical Society**
PO Box 845
Wilmington, DE 19899
Phone: (302)475-6881
Fax: (302)475-5160

District of Columbia

★ 10074 ★ **Osteopathic Association of the District of Columbia**
4001 N. 9th St., Ste. 216
Arlington, VA 22203
Phone: (703)522-8404
Fax: (703)522-2692

Florida

★ 10075 ★ **Florida Osteopathic Medical Association**
The Hull Bldg.
2007 Apalachee Pkwy.
Tallahassee, FL 32301
Phone: (904)878-7364
Fax: (904)942-7538

Georgia

★ 10076 ★ **Georgia Osteopathic Medical Association**
1900 The Exchange, Ste. 160
Atlanta, GA 30339
Phone: (404)953-0801

Hawaii

★ 10077 ★ **Hawaii Association of Osteopathic Physicians and Surgeons**
122 Oneawa St.
Kailua, HI 96734
Phone: (808)261-6105

Idaho

★ 10078 ★ **Idaho Osteopathic Medical Association**
522 W. Main St.
Grangeville, ID 83530
Phone: (208)983-1133

Illinois

★ 10079 ★ **Illinois Association of Osteopathic Physicians and Surgeons**
PO Box 1037
Ottawa, IL 61350
Phone: (815)434-5576
Fax: (815)434-2540

Indiana

★ 10080 ★ **Indiana Association of Osteopathic Physicians and Surgeons**
3520 Guion Rd., No. 202
Indianapolis, IN 46222
Phone: (317)926-3009
Fax: (317)926-3984

Iowa

★ 10081 ★ **Iowa Osteopathic Medical Association**
1113 Locust St., Ste. 2B
Des Moines, IA 50309
Phone: (515)283-0002
Fax: (515)283-0355

Kansas

★ 10082 ★ **Kansas Association of Osteopathic Medicine**
1260 SW Topeka Blvd.
Topeka, KS 66612
Phone: (913)234-5563
Fax: (913)234-5564

Kentucky

★ 10083 ★ **Kentucky Osteopathic Medical Association**
c/o Association Professionals
1501 Twilight Trail
Frankfort, KY 40601
Phone: (502)223-5322
Fax: (502)223-4937

Louisiana

★ 10084 ★ **Louisiana Association of Osteopathic Physicians**
6018 Colbert St.
New Orleans, LA 70124
Phone: (504)488-6743

Maine

★ 10085 ★ **Maine Osteopathic Association**
RR 2, Box 1920
Manchester, ME 04351
Phone: (207)623-1101
Fax: (207)623-4228

Maryland

★ 10086 ★ **Maryland Osteopathic Association**
Rtes. 32 & 144
West Friendship, MD 21794
Phone: (301)489-7272

Massachusetts

★ 10087 ★ **Massachusetts Osteopathic Society**
100 Concord St.
Framingham, MA 01701
Phone: (508)872-8900
Fax: (508)872-8998

Michigan

★ 10088 ★ **Michigan Association of Osteopathic Physicians and Surgeons**
33100 Freedom Rd.
Farmington, MI 48336
Phone: (810)476-2800
Free: 800-626-7736
Fax: (810)476-1834

Minnesota

★ 10089 ★ **Minnesota Osteopathic Medical Society**
2912 80th Circle N
Brooklyn Park, MN 55444
Phone: (612)560-3346

Mississippi

★ 10090 ★ **Mississippi Osteopathic Medical Association**
89 Jeff St.
Oxford, MS 38655
Phone: (601)234-6551
Fax: (601)234-0468

Missouri

★ 10091 ★ **Missouri Association of Osteopathic Physicians and Surgeons**
1423 Randy Ln.
PO Box 748
Jefferson City, MO 65102
Phone: (314)634-3415
Fax: (314)634-5635

Montana

★ 10092 ★ **Montana Osteopathic Association**
Montana Bldg., Ste. 401
Lewistown, MT 59457
Phone: (406)538-7721

Nebraska

★ 10093 ★ **Nebraska Association of Osteopathic Physicians and Surgeons**
Box 24744, W. Omaha Sta.
Omaha, NE 68124
Phone: (402)333-2744

Nevada

★ 10094 ★ **Nevada Osteopathic Medical Association**
2950 E. Flamingo Rd., Ste. E-4
Las Vegas, NV 89121
Phone: (702)731-0304
Fax: (702)732-2079

New Hampshire

★ 10095 ★ **New Hampshire Osteopathic Association**
PO Box 1624
Derry, NH 03038
Phone: (603)625-1254

New Jersey

★ 10096 ★ **New Jersey Association of Osteopathic Physicians and Surgeons**
1212 Stuyvesant Ave.
Trenton, NJ 08618
Phone: (609)396-0466

New Mexico

★ 10097 ★ **New Mexico Osteopathic Medical Association**
PO Box 90396
Albuquerque, NM 87199-0396
Phone: (505)828-1905
Fax: (505)821-1050

New York

★ 10098 ★ **New York State Osteopathic Medical Society**
87 S. Lake Ave.
Albany, NY 12203
Phone: (518)663-8812
Free: 800-841-4131
Fax: (518)663-8170

North Dakota

★ 10099 ★ **North Dakota Association of Osteopathic Physicians and Surgeons**
1714 S. 9th St.
Fargo, ND 58103

Ohio

★ 10100 ★ **Ohio Osteopathic Association**
53 W. 3rd Ave.
PO Box 8130
Columbus, OH 43201
Phone: (614)299-2107
Fax: (614)294-0457

Oklahoma

★ 10101 ★ **Oklahoma Osteopathic Association**
4848 N. Lincoln Blvd.
Oklahoma City, OK 73105-3321
Phone: (405)528-4848
Free: 800-522-8379
Fax: (405)528-6102

Oregon

★ 10102 ★ **Osteopathic Physicians and Surgeons of Oregon**
2121 SW Broadway
Portland, OR 97201
Phone: (503)244-7592
Fax: (503)244-8009

Pennsylvania

★ 10103 ★ **Pennsylvania Osteopathic Medical Association**
1330 Eisenhower Blvd.
Harrisburg, PA 17111
Phone: (717)939-9318
Free: 800-544-7662
Fax: (717)939-7255

Rhode Island

★ 10104 ★ **Rhode Island Society of Osteopathic Physicians and Surgeons**
Community Hospital of Rhode Island
1763 Broad St.
Cranston, RI 02905
Phone: (401)781-3940
Fax: (401)781-3940

South Carolina

★ 10105 ★ **South Carolina Osteopathic Medical Association**
401 N. 5th St.
Hartsville, SC 29550

South Dakota

★ 10106 ★ **South Dakota Osteopathic Association**
c/o MASSA-Berry Clinic
Sturgis, SD 57785
Phone: (605)347-3616
Fax: (605)347-4713

Tennessee

★ 10107 ★ **Tennessee Osteopathic Medical Association**
1900 The Exchange, Ste. 380
Atlanta, GA 30339
Phone: (404)955-5538
Fax: (404)952-5651

Texas

★ 10108 ★ **Texas Osteopathic Medical Association**
1 Financial Center, Ste. 100
IH35
Round Rock, TX 78664-2901
Phone: (512)388-9400
Free: 800-444-8662
Fax: (512)388-5957

Utah

★ 10109 ★ **Utah Osteopathic Medical Association**
70 East 1100 North
Richfield, UT 84701
Phone: (801)896-8254

Vermont

★ 10110 ★ **Vermont State Association of Osteopathic Physicians and Surgeons**
28 School St.
Montpelier, VT 05602
Phone: (802)229-9418
Free: 800-229-5619

Virginia

★ 10111 ★ **Virginia Osteopathic Medical Association**
11900 Hull St Rd.
Midlothian, VA 23112-2904
Phone: (804)288-6414

Washington

★ 10112 ★ **Washington Osteopathic Medical Association**
PO Box 16486
Seattle, WA 98116-0486
Phone: (206)937-5358
Fax: (206)933-6529

West Virginia

★ 10113 ★ **West Virginia Society of Osteopathic Medicine**
PO Box 5266
Charleston, WV 25361-0266
Phone: (304)345-9836
Fax: (304)345-9865

Wisconsin

★ 10114 ★ **Wisconsin Association of Osteopathic Physicians and Surgeons**
34615 Rd. E
Oconomowoc, WI 53066
Phone: (414)567-0520

Wyoming

★ 10115 ★ **Wyoming Association of Osteopathic Physicians and Surgeons**
625 Albany Ave.
Torrington, WY 82240
Phone: (307)532-2107
Fax: (307)532-5206

Chapter 49
Pathology

Federal Government Agencies

★10116★ U.S. Department of Defense Armed Forces Institute of Pathology (AFIP)
Washington, DC 20306-6000
Phone: (202)782-2111
Description: The threefold mission of the Institute is consultation, education, and research. Specifically, AFIP: 1) provides a consultation service for the diagnosis of pathologic tissue for the Department of Defense, other federal agencies, and civilian pathologists, and serves as chief reviewing authority on diagnosis of pathologic tissue for the Army, Navy, and Air Force; 2) conducts experimental, statistical, and morphological research and investigation in the broad field of pathology, including correlation with other medical specialties; and 3) provides education in pathology and related subjects to officers of the Armed Forces, and to federal and civilian medical personnel, and trains enlisted personnel of the Armed Forces in histopathology, its related techniques, and relevant medical photography, medical arts, and museum activities. In carrying out these responsibilities, the Institute manages and directs the Center for Advanced Pathology, the Center for Advanced Medical Education, the Center for Scientific Publications, the Department of Repository and Research Services, the Armed Forces Medical Museum, and the Center for Medical Illustration as cooperative enterprises in medical research and education between AFIP, Department of Defense, other federal agencies, and the civilian medical profession. (See Chapter 17 for further information on the Institute's research activities.)

National & International Organizations

★10117★ American Academy Oral and Maxillofacial Pathology (AAOMP)
c/o Leslie A. Davis
11 Tamarac Ave.
New City, NY 10956
Phone: (914)639-1166
Fax: (914)639-1168
Leslie A. Davis, Contact
Founded: 1946. **Members:** 800. **Description:** Professional society of oral pathologists. **Publications:** *Oral Surgery, Oral Medicine, Oral Pathology*, monthly. **Formerly:** (1994) American Academy Oral Pathology.

★10118★ American Association of Neuropathologists (AANP)
c/o Jeannette J. Townsend, M.D.
Department of Pathology
University of Utah School of Medicine
50 N. Medical Dr.
Salt Lake City, UT 84132
Phone: (801)581-2507
Fax: (801)585-3831
Jeannette J. Townsend, M.D., Sec.-Treas.
Founded: 1924. **Members:** 778. **Description:** Professional society of physicians specializing in neuropathology. Seeks to advance research and training in neuropathology. Offers placement service. **Publications:** *Journal of Neuropathology and Experimental Neurology*, bimonthly. Journal. • *Roster of Members*, annual. **Formerly:** (1932) Club of Neuropathologists.

★10119★ American Association of Pathologists' Assistants (AAPA)
183 Main St. E., No. 1200
Rochester, NY 14604-1617
Phone: (716)232-4030
Free: 800-532-2272
Fax: (716)232-1669
Leo J. Kelly, Admin.
Founded: 1972. **Members:** 337. **Description:** Pathologists' assistants and individuals qualified by academic and practical training to provide service in anatomic pathology under the direction of a qualified pathologist who is responsible for the performance of the assistant. Promotes the mutual association of trained pathologists' assistants and informs the public and the medical profession concerning the goals of this profession. Compiles statistics on salaries, geographic distribution, and duties of pathologists' assistants. Sponsors a continuing medical education program; offers placement services. **Publications:** *AAPA Newsletter*, quarterly. Newsletter. Includes employment and educational opportunity listings. *Price:* Included in membership dues. • Membership Directory, biennial.

★10120★ American Board of Oral Pathology (ABOP)
4830 W. Kennedy Blvd., Ste. 690
PO Box 25915
Tampa, FL 33622-5915
Phone: (813)286-2444
Fax: (813)289-5279
Clarita Wendrich, Exec.Sec.
Founded: 1948. **Members:** 260. **Description:** Works to encourage the study and promote and improve the practice of oral pathology; arrange, conduct, and control examinations to determine the competence of applicants; grant and issue certificates.

★10121★ American Board of Pathology (ABP)
PO Box 25915
Tampa, FL 33622
Phone: (813)286-2444
Fax: (813)289-5279
William H. Hartmann, M.D., Exec.VP
Founded: 1936. **Members:** 12. **Description:** Seeks to: encourage study of pathology; maintain profesional standards and advance practice in the field; maintain registry of certified pathologists; participate in the evaluation and review of graduate medical school pathology programs. Examines doctors of medicine or osteopathy who have had three to five years postgraduate training in laboratory medicine and pathology and certifies them as specialists in pathology. **Publications:** *The American Board of Pathology*, 2-3/year. Newsletter. • *Information Booklet*, annual. Booklet.

American College of Veterinary Pathologists (ACVP)
See: Entry 13049

American Osteopathic College of Pathologists (AOCP)
See: Entry 9989

★ 10122 ★ **American Pathology Foundation (APF)**
1202 Allanson Rd.
Mundelein, IL 60060
Phone: (708)949-6055
Fax: (708)566-4580
Edward J. Stygar, Jr., Exec.Dir.

Founded: 1959. **Members:** 500. **Description:** Board-certified pathologists. Objectives are: to promote the practice of pathology in private laboratories; to provide for exchange of information that will improve anatomic and clinical pathology; to cooperate in the development of the art and sciences of medicine and pathology. Compiles statistics. **Publications:** Directory, annual. • Newsletter, quarterly. **Formerly:** Private Practitioners of Pathology Foundation.

★ 10123 ★ **American Registry of Pathology (ARP)**
c/o Armed Forces Institute of Pathology
14th St. & Alaska Ave. NW
Washington, DC 20306-6000
Phone: (202)782-2143
Fax: (202)782-4567
Donald Westking, M.D., Exec.Dir.

Founded: 1976. **Description:** National medical professional societies. Engages in cooperative enterprises in medical research and education with the Armed Forces Institute of Pathology. Functions as a fiscal agent in the management of research grants and monies derived from tuition fees and contributions. Serves as a link between, and encourages cooperation among, the military and civilian medical, dental, and veterinary communities for the mutual benefit of military and civilian medicine. Provides personnel and other services in support of research on morphometry and the pathology of AIDS, leprosy, and diseases of the cardiovascular and other organ systems. Offers 38 continuing medical education courses annually. Bestows annual John Hill Brinton Award in recognition of outstanding young researcher, John Shaw Billings Lifetime Achievement Awart to senior AFIP staff member, and two Callender-Binford fellowships of $30,000 each in support of training and research.

American Society of Clinical Pathologists (ASCP)
See: Entry 7123

★ 10124 ★ **American Society of Dermatopathology (ASD)**
3601 4th St., Ste. 4A-118
Lubbock, TX 79430
Phone: (806)743-1106
Fax: (806)743-1106
Carol Daugherty, Contact

Founded: 1962. **Members:** 965. **Description:** Seeks to: improve the quality of dermatopathology (the study of abnormal skin conditions, especially the structural and functional changes produced by disease); aid in the dissemination of information; encourage continuing education and research. **Publications:** *Journal of Cutaneous Pathology*, bimonthly. Journal. • Membership Directory, annual.

★ 10125 ★ **American Society for Investigative Pathology (ASIP)**
9650 Rockville Pke.
Bethesda, MD 20814-3993
Phone: (301)530-7130
Fax: (301)571-1879
Frances A. Pitlick, Ph.D., Exec. Officer

Founded: 1976. **Members:** 2,300. **Description:** Experimental research pathologists who have made significant contributions to the knowledge of disease. **Publications:** *The American Journal of Pathology*, monthly. Journal. Research papers in experimental pathology. Covers cell injury and death, inflammatory reactions, disturbances in circulation, and neoplastic growth. *Price:* Included in membership dues; $165/year for nonmembers; $250/year for institutions; $90/year for students. • *ASIP Newsletter*, quarterly. Newsletter. Contains articles on public policy issues and research opportunities. Includes new members and personnel promotions and appointments. *Price:* Included in membership dues. • Membership Directory, annual. **Formerly:** (1992) American Association of Pathologists.

★ 10126 ★ **Association of Pathology Chairs (APC)**
c/o Dr. Frances A. Pitlick
9650 Rockville Pke.
Bethesda, MD 20814-3993
Phone: (301)571-1880
Fax: (301)571-1879
Frances A. Pitlick, Ph.D., Admin.

Founded: 1967. **Members:** 152. **Regional Groups:** 4. **Description:** Chairs of medical school departments of pathology. Acts as a communications center for exchange of information and for workshops on innovations for teaching and resident training, department administration, and relationships with governmental and other nonuniversity agencies. Compiles statistics. **Publications:** Newsletter, quarterly. *Price:* Available to members only. **Formerly:** (1970) American Association of Chairmen of Medical School Departments of Pathology; (1993) Association of Pathology Chairmen.

★ 10127 ★ **British Society for Dermatopathology (BSD)**
British Assn. of Dermatologists
3 St. Andrew's Pl.
London NW1 4LB, England
Phone: 171 9358576
Fax: 171 224 0321
Rino Cerio, Sec.

Founded: 1976. **Members:** 200. **Languages:** English. **Description:** Doctors and residents specializing in dermatopathology. Conducts research; disseminates information.

College of American Pathologists (CAP)
See: Entry 7131

★ 10128 ★ **European Society of Pathology (ESP)**
Department of Pathology, Medical Faculty
Hospital of Joao
P-4200 Porto, Portugal
Phone: 2 590591
Fax: 2 5503940
Dr. Manuel Sobrinho-Simoes

Founded: 1964. **Members:** 1,352. **Languages:** English, French, German, Italian, Russian, Spanish. **Description:** Pathologists and other medical doctors in 49 countries with an interest in pathology. Fosters communication among pathologists; promotes publication of works on pathology and the development of a European school of pathology. **Publications:** *European Pathology Newsletter*, periodic. • *Pathology Research and Practice*, periodic. Journal. • *Pathology Update*, periodic. Journal.

European Society of Veterinary Pathology (ESVP) (Europaische Gesellschaft fur Veterinarpathologie)
See: Entry 13072

★ 10129 ★ **Finnish Society for Dermatopathology (FSD) (Suomen Dermatopatologiyhdistys)**
Department of Dermatology
Meilahdentie 2
SF-00250 Helsinki, Finland
Phone: 0 4716363
Fax: 0 4716270
Arja-Leena Kariniemi, M.D., Exec. Officer

Founded: 1984. **Members:** 96. **Languages:** English, Finnish. **Description:** Medical doctors. Promotes the study of dermatopathology. **Formerly:** (1993) Danish Society for Dermatopathology.

★ 10130 ★ **Gastrointestinal Pathology Society (GIPS)**
c/o Cecilia Fenoglio-Priser, M.D.
University of Co. Inc.
231 Bethesda Ave.
Cincinnati, OH 45267-0529
Phone: (513)558-4500
Fax: (513)558-2289
Cecilia Fenoglio-Priser, M.D., Sec.-Treas.

Founded: 1979. **Members:** 145. **Description:** Medical doctors and Ph.D.s; others with an interest in gastrointestinal pathology. Disseminates information and works to increase knowledge about the pathology of the gastrointestinal tract; encourages the development of gastrointestinal pathology as a specialized field. Presents research and educational programs at the annual meetings of the American Gastroenterological Association, American Society of Clinical Pathologists, and United States and Canadian Academy of Pathology. **Publications:** *American Journal of Surgical Pathology*, monthly. Journal. Covers diagnostic and technical advances that provide practical and clinical solutions to surgical and pathologic problems. *Price:* $98/year for individuals; $119 for institutions. • *Gastrointestinal Pathology Society--Newsletter*, semiannual. Newsletter. Includes meeting minutes and membership list. *Price:* Included in membership dues. **Formerly:** (1987) Gastrointestinal Pathology Club.

★ 10131 ★ International Academy of Pathology (IAP)
Armed Forces Institute of Pathology
Center for Advanced Pathology
14th St. & Alaska Ave. NW
Washington, DC 20306-6000
Phone: (202)782-2550
Fax: (202)782-7166
Florabel G. Mullick, M.D., Sec.

Founded: 1906. **Members:** 8,300. **Regional Groups:** 32. **Languages:** English. **Description:** Professional society of pathologists and medical scientists. Aim is to improve methods of teaching pathology. Coordinates anatomical pathology, pathologic physiology, and comparative pathology; promotes research in pathology in medical schools, laboratories, hospitals, and medical museums. **Publications:** *International Pathology*, quarterly. Newsletter. **Formerly:** (1954) International Association of Medical Museums.

★ 10132 ★ International Association of Oral Pathologists (IAOP)
c/o Dr. Peter R. Morgan
Guy's Hospital Dental School, 28th Fl.
Guy's Tower
London SE1 9RT, England
Phone: 71 9554288
Fax: 71 4077361
Dr. Peter R. Morgan, Sec.-Treas.

Founded: 1976. **Members:** 380. **Description:** Dentists who have had postgraduate instruction in pathology. Seeks to advance the science of oral pathology; works to foster international cooperation in the field. **Publications:** *Journal of Oral Pathology and Medicine*, 10/year. Journal. • *Membership List*, periodic.

★ 10133 ★ International Council of Societies of Pathology (ICSP)
7001 Georgia St.
Chevy Chase, MD 20815
Phone: (202)576-2961
Fax: (202)576-3056
F. K. Mostofi, M.D., Sec.-Treas.

Founded: 1962. **Members:** 60. **Description:** National pathology societies. Distributes teaching sets and professional aids to pathology societies worldwide. Offers seminars and specialized education; conducts professional training and research programs.

International Federation of Cervical Pathology and Colposcopy (IFCPC) (Federacion Internacional de Patologia Cervical y Colposcopia)
See: Entry 9664

★ 10134 ★ International Society of Geographical Pathology (Societe Internationale de Pathologie Geographique — SIPG)
Vorstand
Pathologisches Institut
Waehringerguertel 18-20
A-1090 Vienna, Austria
Phone: 1 404003651
Prof. Werner Dutz, Contact

Languages: English, French, German. **Description:** Pathologists interested in geographi-

cal pathology. Promotes knowledge and understanding of diseases that occur more frequently in certain countries or environments than in others.

★ 10135 ★ International Society of Neuropathology (Societe Internationale de Neuropathologie)
Dept. of Histopathology
Addenbrooke's Hospital
Cambridge CB2 2QQ, England
Dr. Janice R. Anderson, Sec.Gen.

Founded: 1972. **Members:** 2,500. **Languages:** English. **Description:** Members of national societies of neuropathology in 30 countries. Works to foster the formation of national and regional societies of neuropathology and to promote cooperation among these societies. Maintains liaison with international organizations in various fields of neurological sciences. Encourages the exchange of information and persons engaged in neuropathology. Initiates research projects. **Publications:** *Brain Pathology*, quarterly. Journal. • *Membership Directory*, periodic. Directory.

★ 10136 ★ Intersociety Committee on Pathology Information (ICPI)
4733 Bethesda Ave., Ste. 700
Bethesda, MD 20814
Phone: (301)656-2944
Fax: (301)656-3179
Eileen M. Lavine, Info. Counsel

Founded: 1957. **Members:** 5. **Description:** One representative from each sponsoring society: American Society for Investigative Pathology; American Society of Clinical Pathologists; Association of Pathology Chairs; College of American Pathologists; U.S. & Canadian Academy of Pathology. Disseminates information about the medical practice and research achievements of pathology. Produces career information and supplies it to schools and students; assists writers and editors in preparing articles about pathology. **Publications:** *Directory of Pathology Residency and Postgraduate Fellowship Programs*. Directory. • *Directory of Pathology Training Programs: Anatomic, Clinical, Specialized*, annual. Directory. Lists pathology residency programs and fellowships for postgraduate training in the United States and Canada. *Price:* Free to members and medical schools/med. libraries; $25/copy for nonmembers; $5/copy for students and residents. • *Pathology as a Career in Medicine*. Brochure.

★ 10137 ★ Registry of Comparative Pathology (RCP)
c/o Armed Forces Institute of Pathology
Washington, DC 20306
Phone: (202)576-2452
Fax: (202)576-2164
Linda K. Johnson, D.V.M., Chief Pathologist

Founded: 1966. **Members:** 11. **Description:** Veterinary and medical pathologists; biomedical scientists in related fields; medical personnel. To collect, classify, and disseminate information on comparative pathology of animals to the biomedical community. Promotes communication in biomedical research by scientists interested in comparative pathology. Sponsors ex-

hibits, lectures, and symposia; offers annual continuing education course in comparative pathology. **Publications:** *Animal Models of Human Disease*, biennial. Handbook. *Price:* $275/set. • *Comparative Pathology Bulletin*, quarterly. Bulletin. • *Educational Opportunities in Comparative Pathology*, periodic. *Price:* Free. • *Resources of Biomedical and Zoological Specimens*, biennial. Directory. *Price:* Free. • *Symposia Proceedings*, periodic. • *Training Programs in Pathology and Clinical Pathology in North American Colleges and Schools of Veterinary Medicine*, periodic. *Price:* Free.

★ 10138 ★ Society of Toxicologic Pathologists (STP)
875 Kings Hwy., Ste. 200
Woodbury, NJ 08096-3172
Phone: (609)845-7220
Fax: (609)853-0411
Linda McGillicuddy, Dir.

Founded: 1971. **Members:** 650. **Regional Groups:** 5. **Description:** Toxicologic pathologists, veterinarians, and physicians interested in the advancement of pathology. Evaluates criteria and requirements applied to the interpretation of pathological changes produced by pharmacological, chemical, and environmental agents. Fosters training and recognition in environmental and pharmacological pathology. Conducts discussion groups. Sponsors a registry for Toxicologic Pathology. **Publications:** Newsletter, quarterly. *Price:* Available to members only. *Toxicologic Pathology*, bimonthly. Journal. *Price:* $175/year for individuals in the U.S.; $195/year for individuals outside the U.S.; $195/year for institutions in the U.S.; $215/year for institutions outside the U.S.

★ 10139 ★ United States and Canadian Academy of Pathology
3643 Walton Way Extension
Augusta, GA 30909
Phone: (706)733-7550
Fax: (706)733-8033
F. Stephen Vogel, Sec.-Treas.

Founded: 1906. **Members:** 6,500. **Description:** Works for the advancement of pathology teaching, practice, and research. Disseminates information to members. Sponsors educational programs to serve the needs of pathologists of various levels of experience. Presents Maude Abbott Lectureship to a recognized and respected person in contemporary pathology. **Publications:** *Directory of Members*, annual. Membership Directory. *Price:* Free to members. • *Laboratory Investigation*, monthly. Journal. Focuses on significant advances in research dealing with human and experimental diseases. *Price:* Free to members. • *Modern Pathology*, bimonthly. Journal. Concentrates on the practice of diagnostic human pathology. *Price:* Free to members. • *Monograph Series in Pathology*, annual. Monograph. Contains topics presented at the annual Long Course. • *Techniques in Pathology*, annual. Monographs. Based on some of the special courses presented at the annual Academy meeting.

★ 10140 ★ Universities Associated for Research and Education in Pathology (UAREP)
9650 Rockville Pike
Bethesda, MD 20814-3993
Phone: (301)571-1880
Fax: (301)571-1879
Frances A. Pitlick, Ph.D., Exec. Officer
Founded: 1964. **Members:** 25. **Description:** University pathology departments, including faculty members, residents, and research fellows. Provides core material in convenient form for updating and enriching teaching and researching of pathology, with special emphasis on toxicology and chemical carcinogens. Encourages biomedical projects; administers contracts. Has developed guidelines for the National Highway Safety Bureau for use in scientific investigations in accidents. Operates the Registry of Comparative Pathology which provides news of progress in the experimental study of disease from animal models. **Publications:** *Atlas of Tumor Pathology*. Book. • Monographs.

★ 10141 ★ World Association of Societies of Pathology—Anatomic and Clinical (WASP)
(Association Mondiale des Societes de Pathologie - Anatomique et Clinique)
Mitsui-Sugamo Bldg. 7F
Sugamo 2-11-1, Toshima-ku
Tokyo 170, Japan
Phone: 3 39188161
Fax: 3 39496168
Mikio Mori, M.D., Exec.Dir.
Founded: 1947. **Members:** 55. **Languages:** English. **Description:** National societies of anatomic and clinical pathology in 39 countries united to foster cooperation between members and improve standards in anatomic and clinical pathology. Maintains a variety of committees and educational programs. **Publications:** *Directory*, biennial. Directory. • *News Bulletin of the World Association of Societies of Pathology/Commission on World Standards*, quarterly. Bulletin. **Formerly:** (1969) International Society of Clinical Pathology.

Research Centers

★ 10142 ★ Case Western Reserve University
Institute of Pathology
2085 Adelbert Rd.
Cleveland, OH 44106
Phone: (216)368-5172
Fax: (216)844-8078
Dr. Michael E. Lamm, Dir.
Research Activities and Fields: Immunology, immunopathology, aging, cell biology, neurobiology, Alzheimer disease, oncology, and drug delivery.

★ 10143 ★ Institute for Clinical Science, Inc.
1833 Delancey Pl.
Philadelphia, PA 19103
Phone: (215)829-7068
Fax: (215)829-3094
F. William Sunderman, M.D., Pres. and Dir.
Research Activities and Fields: Anatomic and clinical pathology, including studies in metal carcinogenesis and toxicology. **Publications:** *Annals of Clinical and Laboratory Science*; also publishes a procedures manual for the Institute's Applied Seminars.

★ 10144 ★ Mallory Institute of Pathology Foundation
784 Massachusetts Ave.
Boston, MA 02118
Phone: (617)534-5314
Fax: (617)534-5315
Dr. Leonard S. Gottlieb, Dir.
Research Activities and Fields: Experimental medicine and pathology, with particular reference to cardiovascular diseases, gastrointestinal diseases, liver and kidney diseases, pulmonary diseases, hematopathology, nutritional pathology, immunopathology, environmental pathology, and oncology.

★ 10145 ★ U.S. Department of Defense Armed Forces Institute of Pathology
Cellular Pathology Department
Washington, DC 20306-6000
Phone: (202)576-2915
Fax: (202)576-2164
Timothy J. O'Leary, M.D., Ph.D., Chairman
Research Activities and Fields: The Cellular Pathology Department conducts research in forensic pathology, immunopathology, molecular biology, biochemistry, and quantitative analysis of cells and tissues. Methods used are quantitative cytochemistry, morphometry, image analysis, analytical electron microscopy, scanning calorimetry, infrared spectroscopy, flow cytometry, and immunoperoxidase and DNA hybridization techniques (including polymerase chain reaction). Department comprises the Cytopathology Division, Immunopathology Division, Molecular Pathology Division, and Quantitative Pathology Division.

★ 10146 ★ U.S. Department of Defense Armed Forces Institute of Pathology
Cellular Pathology Department
Cytopathology Division
Washington, DC 20306-6000
Phone: (202)576-2915
Fax: (202)576-2164
LTC Richard Marsella, M.D., Ph.D., Director
Research Activities and Fields: Laboratory's activities involve: 1) conducting basic and applied research programs in cellular pathology, including application of classical, immunohistochemical, electron microscopic, morphometric, and molecular biological techniques to the interpretation of exfoliative cytology and fine needle aspiration biopsy material; 2) providing intramural and extramural consultations in exfoliative cytology and fine needle aspiration biopsy interpretation; and 3) instructing pathologists and cytotechnologists in the interpretation of exfoliative cytology and fine needle aspiration biopsy specimens.

★ 10147 ★ U.S. Department of Defense Armed Forces Institute of Pathology
Cellular Pathology Department
Molecular Pathology Division
Washington, DC 20306-6000
Phone: (202)576-3401
Fax: (202)576-2164
Dr. Thomas Fanning, Director
Research Activities and Fields: Division's mission is to: 1) conduct research using molecular biologic methods to further the understanding of human disease; 2) develop and implement new methods for applying molecular biologic methods in diagnostic pathology; 3) provide intramural consultation on cases involving techniques, such as in situ hybridization, restriction fragment analysis, and gene-rearrangement studies; and 4) conduct courses on uses of molecular biology in diagnostic pathology.

★ 10148 ★ U.S. Department of Defense Armed Forces Institute of Pathology
Center for Advanced Pathology
Cardiovascular Pathology Department
Washington, DC 20306-6000
Phone: (202)576-2806
Fax: (202)576-2164
Renu Virmani, M.D., Director
Research Activities and Fields: Department designs, conducts, and publishes research studies on selected congenital and acquired heart lesions in patients and animal models and conducts cooperative studies with other federal agencies on various cardiovascular problems. Department also: 1) maintains a consultation service to the Armed Forces, other federal agencies, and civilian pathologists on cardiovascular diseases; 2) develops teaching aids and other educational materials; 3) instructs physicians in cardiovascular diseases and conducts training programs as part of the Army, Navy, and Air Force residency programs in cardiology and thoracic surgery.

★ 10149 ★ U.S. Department of Defense Armed Forces Institute of Pathology
Center for Advanced Pathology
Dermatopathology Department
Washington, DC 20306-6000
Phone: (202)576-2140
Fax: (202)576-2164
George P. Lupton, M.D., Chairman
Research Activities and Fields: Department's functions are to: 1) maintain a consultation service for diagnosis of pathologic tissue for the Department of Defense, other federal agencies, and civilian pathologists; 2) conduct experimental, statistical, and morphological research in the field of dermatopathology; 3) provide advanced instruction in the field of skin pathology to officers of the Armed Forces and other qualified personnel; 4) provide teaching sets and instruction in the fields of dermatopathology; and 5) conduct a one-year dermatopathology program for four military fellows (training is accredited by the Residency Review Committees for Dermatology and Pathology under the Accreditation Council for Graduate Medical Education).

★ 10150 ★ U.S. Department of Defense
Armed Forces Institute of Pathology
Center for Advanced Pathology
Environmental and Drug-Induced
   Pathology Department
Washington, DC 20306-6000
Phone: (202)576-2434
Fax: (202)576-2164
Nelson S. Irey, M.D., Chairman

Research Activities and Fields: Department's activities include research, education (presentation of training courses and preparation of educational materials), and consultation. Research efforts focus on groups or "clusters" of similar drug-site-process combination cases. Department also maintains statistical data on drugs and adverse drug reactions and serves as a collecting point for special groups of cases relating to industrial and environmental toxicity and carcinogenesis.

★ 10151 ★ U.S. Department of Defense
Armed Forces Institute of Pathology
Center for Advanced Pathology
Genitourinary Pathology Department
Washington, DC 20306-6000
Phone: (202)576-2961
Fax: (202)576-3056
F. Kash Mostofi, M.D., Contact

Research Activities and Fields: Department conducts research on human tissues from diseases of bladder, prostate, testes, penis, kidney, and scrotum; develops techniques for improvement of diagnostic criteria; conducts experimental studies to elucidate pathogenesis of various genitourinary diseases and develops individual and cooperative intramural and extramural research programs; develops the educational program of the Institute in the field of genitourinary pathology; and trains fellows sponsored by outside programs. Department is organized in two main divisions: 1) Medical Nephropathology Division; and 2) Urologic Pathology Division. (Activities of a third unit, the Urogenital Research Division, have been absorbed by the remaining divisions.)

★ 10152 ★ U.S. Department of Defense
Armed Forces Institute of Pathology
Center for Advanced Pathology
Gynecologic and Breast Pathology
   Department
Washington, DC 20306-6000
Phone: (202)576-2981
Fax: (202)576-2164
Henry J. Norris, Chairperson

Research Activities and Fields: Department conducts research in gynecologic, breast, and obstetric diseases and provides diagnostic consultative service on these diseases to the Armed Services, Veterans Administration, other federal agencies, and civilian pathologists and offers recommendations on proper treatment of disorders in these areas when requested. Department provides training in gynecologic and breast pathology, participates in educational and other training programs, and conducts a review course for candidates preparing for examination by the American Board of Obstetrics and Gynecology. Department also supervises the addition of selected examples of diseases to the Institute's Repository and Research Services Department.

★ 10153 ★ U.S. Department of Defense
Armed Forces Institute of Pathology
Center for Advanced Pathology
Hematologic and Lymphatic Pathology
   Department
6825 16 St. NW, Rm. 3025
Washington, DC 20306-6000
Phone: (202)576-2986
Fax: (202)576-2164
Susan L. Abbondanzo, M.D., Dir.

Research Activities and Fields: Department uses morphological methods (light and electron microscopy), histochemical methods (including enzymes and immunoperoidase techniques), and molecular biologic techniques (PCR and southern blotting) to make correlations between pathologic features and clinical prognosis on disease processes related to the blood and reticuloendothelial system (i.e., lymph nodes, spleen, and bone marrow).

★ 10154 ★ U.S. Department of Defense
Armed Forces Institute of Pathology
Center for Advanced Pathology
Hepatic and Gastrointestinal Pathology
   Department
Washington, DC 20306-6000
Phone: (202)576-2951
Fax: (202)576-4694
Dr. Kamal G. Ishak, Director

Research Activities and Fields: Department conducts clinicopathologic studies of diseases of the liver (including benign and malignant tumors, viral hepatitis, and drug-induced injury) and studies selected diseases of the liver by electron microscopy, both for diagnostic and research purposes. Conducts experimental, statistical, and morphological research in the field of gastrointestinal pathology. Department participates in the training of Gastroenterology Fellows and Residents assigned to the Department from Armed Forces hospitals and the Liver and Metabolic Unit of the Veterans Administration Hospital, Washington, DC. Department also participates in courses in hepatic and gastrointestinal pathology at national and international meetings, prepares training aids in hepatic and gastrointestinal pathology for the American Registry of Pathology, and provides diagnostic consultation to pathologists of the Armed Forces, Veterans Administration, Public Health Service, other federal agencies, and civilian medical centers.

★ 10155 ★ U.S. Department of Defense
Armed Forces Institute of Pathology
Center for Advanced Pathology
Infectious and Parasitic Disease Pathology
   Department
Rm. 40B3
Washington, DC 20306-6000
Phone: (202)576-2213
Dr. Wear, Director

Research Activities and Fields: Department is made up of three main Divisions: 1) AIDS Pathology Division; 2) Geographic Pathology Division; and 3) Microbiology Division.

★ 10156 ★ U.S. Department of Defense
Armed Forces Institute of Pathology
Center for Advanced Pathology
Legal Medicine, Quality Assurance, and
   Risk Management Department
Washington, DC 20306-6000
Phone: (301)427-5323
Fax: (301)427-5098
Frank T. Flannery, M.D., J.D., Chairman

Research Activities and Fields: Department participates in educational programs; provides liaison and consultation services; and conducts research projects relating to all aspects of legal medicine.

★ 10157 ★ U.S. Department of Defense
Armed Forces Institute of Pathology
Center for Advanced Pathology
Neuropathology Department
6825 16th St., N.W.
Bldg. 54, Rm. G051
Washington, DC 20306-6000
Phone: (202)576-2928

Research Activities and Fields: Department conducts independent and collaborative research, with particular emphasis on diseases of importance to military and Veterans Administration hospitals. It also provides consultation and support for research projects of other governmental and civilian agencies and provides training and education in neuropathology and its related research techniques for personnel from other government and civilian agencies. In addition, Department provides written and oral consultation on all cases of diseases of the central and peripheral nervous system that are referred to the Department from the Armed Services, Veterans Administration, Public Health Service, and other federal agencies as well as from civilian pathologists. Training is provided for pathologists and for residents in other specialties, and training manuals, teaching sets, and other educational materials are prepared by the Department. Division comprises the Neuromuscular Pathology Division and the Yakovlev Collection.

★ 10158 ★ U.S. Department of Defense
Armed Forces Institute of Pathology
Center for Advanced Pathology
Ophthalmic Pathology Department
Washington, DC 20306-6000
Fax: (202)576-2955
Col. Mclean, Director

Research Activities and Fields: Department conducts research based on case material on file in the Registry of Ophthalmic Pathology as well as research involving special histochemical, immunological, and electron microscopic techniques and specialized equipment. Department also provides consultative services to other pathologists and educational services, including the conduct of courses in ophthalmic pathology and administration of AFIP's graduate research training program in ophthalmic pathology. Complete gross and microscopic reports on enucleated eyeballs are prepared for contributors located in hospitals where facilities and trained personnel are not available for this specialized work.

★ 10159 ★ U.S. Department of Defense
Armed Forces Institute of Pathology
Center for Advanced Pathology
Oral Pathology Department
14th St. and Alaska Ave., N.W.
Washington, DC 20306-6000
Phone: (202)576-2679
Fax: (202)576-2164
Dr. Paul L. Auclair, Contact

Research Activities and Fields: Department is made up of two Divisions: 1) the Forensic Dentistry Division, and 2) the Oral Pathology Division. The Forensic Dentistry Division supports the Armed Forces medical examiner by performing dental identification of human remains. The Oral Pathology Division performs morphologic and basic research in special oral pathology; provides diagnostic and consultative services for those pathologic conditions affecting the hard/soft tissue structures of oral and perioral sites, including the major salvary glands; provides training in oral pathology; and participates in continuing education courses in oral pathology and forensic dentistry.

★ 10160 ★ U.S. Department of Defense
Armed Forces Institute of Pathology
Center for Advanced Pathology
Orthopedic Pathology Department
Washington, DC 20306-6000
Phone: (202)576-2932
Dr. Donald E. Sweet, Director

Research Activities and Fields: Department conducts research based primarily on consultative material and secondarily on experimental models. Purpose is to clarify and explain diseases and to illuminate the basic biology of the musculoskeletal system. Department also: 1) provides consultation and diagnosis of pathologic tissue for the Department of Defense, other federal agencies, and civilian pathologists; and 2) provides advanced instruction in orthopedic pathology, produces teaching sets and other materials for use in Department of Defense hospitals and in medical schools throughout the world, and provides advanced training in orthopedic pathology for surgery fellows and for Department of Defense and other federal pathologists.

★ 10161 ★ U.S. Department of Defense
Armed Forces Institute of Pathology
Center for Advanced Pathology
Pediatric Pathology Department
Washington, DC 20306-6000
Phone: (202)576-2947
Fax: (202)576-2164
Edwina J. Popek, D.O., Chairperson

Research Activities and Fields: Mission is to provide consultation, education, and research in the field of pediatric pathology. Current emphasis is on placental, perinatal and neonatal pathology. Department's activities focus on training of fellows and residents as well as visiting pathologists assigned to AFIP and on the preparation of educational materials in pediatric pathology.

★ 10162 ★ U.S. Department of Defense
Armed Forces Institute of Pathology
Center for Advanced Pathology
Pulmonary and Mediastinal Pathology
  Department
6825 16th., N.W.
Washington, DC 20306-6000
Phone: (202)576-2870
Fax: (202)576-5017
Michael Koss, M.D., Director

Research Activities and Fields: Department provides consultation services in pulmonary and mediastinal pathology, including special consultations to the Veterans Administration in cases involving veterans' appeals on claims of service-connected disabilities. Department trains Chest Service Residents and Fellows from the Veterans Administration Hospital in Washington, DC, the U.S. Naval Hospitals in Bethesda, MD, and Portsmouth, VA, and Georgetown University Hospital. Research functions include projects in anatomic pathology. Department also participates in preparation of microslide and lantern slide studies and teaching sets in pulmonary and mediastinal pathology.

★ 10163 ★ U.S. Department of Defense
Armed Forces Institute of Pathology
Center for Advanced Pathology
Radiologic Pathology Department
Washington, DC 20306-6000
Phone: (202)576-2973
Cmdr. James Buck, Contact

Research Activities and Fields: Radiologic-pathologic correlations and analysis of roentgen signs.

★ 10164 ★ U.S. Department of Defense
Armed Forces Institute of Pathology
Center for Advanced Pathology
Soft Tissue Pathology Department
6825 16th St., N.W.
Washington, DC 20306-6000
Phone: (202)576-2158
Dr. G. Meese, Director

Research Activities and Fields: Department conducts research on various aspects of diseases of soft tissues using both traditional methods as well as newer technologies such as immunohistochemistry and DNA flow cytometric analysis; provides training and educational services and materials; and furnishes diagnostic and consultative services in soft tissue pathology to the Armed Services, Veterans Administration, other federal agencies, and to civilian pathologists. Special consultation is furnished to the Veterans Administration in cases involving veterans' appeals on claims of service-connected disabilities. Department also serves as the World Health Organization's International Center for the Classification of Soft Tissue Tumors and as the pathology coordinator for the Southwest Oncology Group Intergroup Sarcoma Study.

★ 10165 ★ U.S. Department of Defense
Armed Forces Institute of Pathology
Environmental Pathology Department
Biochemistry Division

Washington, DC 20306-6000
Phone: (202)576-2855
Fax: (202)576-2164
William N. Fishbein, M.D., Ph.D., Chief

Research Activities and Fields: Division conducts basic and applied research in biochemistry, centering on: 1) the nature of enzymatic activity and the relation of enzyme modifiers to environmental disease; and 2) the mechanism of energy generation within the cell and its relation to various types of cellular pathology as produced by physical damage or physiological malfunction. Current research emphasis is on metabolic muscle disease as the basis for performance failures in recruits. New myopathies identified by the Division include myoadenylate deaminase deficiency and lactate transporter defect. Also studies urease of Helico (or Campylo) bacter pylori and its relation to peptic ulcer disease. Division also studies biochemical and genetic indicators of chromosomal damage from environmental agents to assist in presenting/treating further exposure. In addition, Division provides training for students and fellows and reviews manuscripts for accuracy with respect to biochemical and molecular biological aspects.

★ 10166 ★ U.S. Department of Defense
Armed Forces Institute of Pathology
Genitourinary Pathology Department
Medical Nephropathology Division
Washington, DC 20306-6000
Phone: (202)576-2891
Fax: (202)576-2164
Dr. Tatiana T. Antonovych, Chief

Research Activities and Fields: Division conducts research (on human material) on medical diseases of the kidney; prepares consultation reports in renal pathology, including electron and fluorescent microscopic processing, examination, and reporting; and provides education and training in nephropathology.

★ 10167 ★ U.S. Department of Defense
Armed Forces Institute of Pathology
Genitourinary Pathology Department
Urologic Pathology Division
Washington, DC 20306-6000
Phone: (202)576-2962
Fax: (202)576-2164
F.K. Mostofi, M.D., Dept. Chairman

Research Activities and Fields: Division's activities involve: 1) conducting research on human and experimental material collected in the files on diseases of the bladder, prostate, testes, penis, kidney, and scrotum; 2) developing new techniques or modifying existing ones for improvement of diagnostic criteria; 3) conducting, as indicated, experimental studies to elucidate pathogenesis of various genitourinary diseases; 4) working with other divisions and departments of the AFIP and other military, governmental, and non-governmental agencies in developing individual or cooperative intra- and extramural research programs; 5) conducting joint research, educational, and other programs with the World Health Organization, International Agency for Research in Cancer, International Union Against Cancer, Pan American Health Organization, International Council of Society of

Pathology, and other international health organizations; 6) preparing consultation reports for genitourinary pathology cases sent to the AFIP, including testicular, penile, bladder, and prostatic biopsies, surgical diseases of the kidney, and autopsy material; and 7) training residents and conducting courses in urology and pathology.

★ 10168 ★ U.S. Department of Defense
Armed Forces Institute of Pathology
Infectious and Parasitic Disease Pathology
    Department
AIDS Pathology Division
Washington, DC 20306-6000
Phone: (202)576-2825
Fax: (202)576-9160
Col. Peter Angritt, Director

Research Activities and Fields: Division: 1) studies all the pathologic changes in the human body resulting from exposure to active infection with the human immunodeficiency virus (HIV), from the very earliest changes to the end of the AIDS cycle; 2) coordinates and actively supports the study of HIV-related changes at other pathology branches within the AFIP; 3) cooperates with other federal or civilian institutions in the development of study programs of mutual interest, including the study and diagnosis of tissues received from these institutions; 4) maintains a Registry of AIDS Pathology, consisting of a database reflecting current and historical information and pertinent correlations concerning all opportunistic infections and their effects on HIV-infected patients; 5) maintains a consultation service for the Armed Forces, federal agencies, and civilian pathologists regarding the pathology of HIV infection and AIDS and provides internal consultation to other pathology branches as requested; and 6) supports the AFIP's educational diagnostic and research programs by providing appropriate lectures and courses as well as tangible resources whenever possible.
Publications: *AFIP Newsletter; AIDS Information.*

★ 10169 ★ U.S. Department of Defense
Armed Forces Institute of Pathology
Infectious and Parasitic Disease Pathology
    Department
Geographic Pathology Division
Washington, DC 20306-6000
Phone: (202)576-2182
Fax: (202)576-2164
Robert F. Karnei, Jr., Director

Research Activities and Fields: Division studies the problems of infectious and parasitic disease throughout the world, emphasizing: 1) those diseases and causal agents which are of military importance; 2) diseases in geographic areas of military importance; 3) zoonotic diseases; and 4) animal models for human parasitic diseases. Research programs developed and conducted by the Division focus on both geographic areas (rather than a particular disease) and particular diseases and agents (regardless of the geographic area). Basic and applied research projects are concerned with explaining variations in the patterns of disease in order to provide insight into the complex causes and effects of certain diseases. Division performs original research on the pathogenesis of various bacterial, protozoan, and helminthic diseases;

on tropical diseases of obscure or unknown causes; and on specific zoonotic diseases and animal models for parasitic diseases.

★ 10170 ★ U.S. Department of Defense
Armed Forces Institute of Pathology
Infectious and Parasitic Disease Pathology
    Department
Microbiology Division
Washington, DC 20306-6000
Phone: (202)576-2954
Fax: (202)576-2477
Lt. Col. Ted L. Hadfield, USAF, BSC, Director

Research Activities and Fields: Conducts basic microbiologic and immunological research on the pathogenesis of infectious diseases. Division also: 1) develops improved methods of cytologic (light and electron microscopic) and histochemical diagnosis of viral, bacterial, and mycotic diseases, and AIDS; 2) provides consultation services on these diseases; and 3) provides advanced instruction in bacteriology, mycology, and immunology to officers of the Armed Forces and other qualified personnel. Current research includes: histopathologic studies of Hansen's disease in vaccine trials and antibiotic therapy trials; classification and DNA sequencing of Cat-Scratch Bacillus and other unusual bacteria; development of skin test antigen for heishmania tropia; and development of a vaccine for bruccell melitensis.

★ 10171 ★ U.S. Department of Defense
Armed Forces Institute of Pathology
Office of the Armed Forces Medical
    Examiner
Forensic and Aerospace Pathology
    Division
14th St. and Alaska Ave., N.W.
Washington, DC 20306-6000
Phone: (202)576-3287

Research Activities and Fields: Division conducts research and provides consultation and education related to forensic and aerospace pathology. Research programs conducted by this Division are designed to study human performance under various conditions and optimize the man-machine-environment interface and involve both intramural and extramural projects in forensic sciences, particularly forensic pathology. Division also: 1) develops and maintains aircraft accident information systems in order to identify unsafe trends and aeromedical factors, focus research efforts, and render recommendations; 2) develops and maintains aviation pathology programs to promote survivability regarding aircraft accidents, provide vital information to the validation of medical standards in selection of aviation personnel, and assure the effectiveness of medical personnel; 3) provides assistance in the educational and research programs of the Uniformed Services University of the Health Sciences; 4) provides diagnostic and consultative services involving review of medicolegal cases of natural, homicidal, suicidal, accidental, and undetermined manners of death; 5) participates in medicolegal investigations, postmortem examinations, and exhumations; 6) recommends changes in military regulations and/or legislative action as may be required for recognition of environmental hazards in the military community; 7) provides on-site investiga-

tions of military and civilian aircraft accidents; 8) provides consultation reports to military safety centers and aircraft accident boards; and 9) participates in seminars on aeromedical factors. In addition, Division's Chief conducts the only residency in forensic pathology in the Armed Forces recognized by the American Board of Pathology and the Council on Medical Education of the American Medical Association.

★ 10172 ★ U.S. Department of Defense
Armed Forces Institute of Pathology
Office of the Armed Forces Medical
    Examiner
Toxicology Division
6825 16th St. N.W.
Bldg. 54
Washington, DC 20306-6000
Phone: (202)576-2910
Lt. Col. Michael Simth, Director

Research Activities and Fields: The Toxicology Division provides the U.S. military services with the only worldwide service in the toxicologic examination of body fluids and tissues from victims of fatal and nonfatal aircraft accidents. Analogous service is provided for civil aviation authorities in special cases. Complete toxicology support is also provided to the National Aeronautics and Space Administration on astronaut deaths. Toxicological analyses and consultations are provided on selected specimens submitted by the Forensic and Aerospace Pathology Division (also in the Forensic Sciences Department), by the Environmental and Drug-Induced Pathology Department, and by military medical laboratories requiring expert assistance. A mission-oriented toxicology service is conducted for the Veterans Administration, which includes a continuous program of research designed to: 1) improve the specificity, sensitivity, and scope of the toxicologic tests performed; and 2) test, develop, or adapt procedures for the isolation, identification, and quantification of newly developed therapeutic agents when present in biological specimens. Division also maintains the Department of Defense Drug Detection Proficiency Testing Program and performs toxicological analyses for all Army postmortem forensic pathology cases. Some educational services are also provided by this Division.

★ 10173 ★ U.S. Department of Defense
Armed Forces Institute of Pathology
Oral Pathology Department
Forensic Dentistry Division
Washington, DC 20306-6000
Phone: (202)576-2958

Research Activities and Fields: Division's activities involve: 1) performing research in forensic dental identification; 2) maintaining a registry of all dental identifications performed by this Division for medicolegal documentation; 3) providing diagnostic and consultative services in the dental identification of human remains to military and civilian authorities; 4) providing peer review, upon request, for dental identification made by other government agencies; 5) coordinating and providing lecture and laboratory exercise in forensic dentistry to military and civilian agencies upon request; and 6) assisting the Department in matters pertaining to the Tri-Service Committee on Identification of Military Casualties.

**★ 10174 ★ U.S. Department of Defense
Armed Forces Institute of Pathology
Otolaryngic and Endocrine Pathology
  Department
Endocrine Pathology Division**
Bldg. 54
Washington, DC 20306-6000
Phone: (202)576-2974
Fax: (202)576-2164

Research Activities and Fields: Conducts investigations into the pathology of endocrine organs, with special emphasis on clinicopathologic correlations. Division receives problem cases in surgical and postmortem pathology from all branches of the Armed Forces, from Veterans Administration facilities, and from civilian pathologists involving thyroid and parathyroid glands, adrenals, and the pancreas. Consultation services are provided intramurally at the Institute and for pathologists from the National Institutes of Health Naval Hospital (NMC-NCR), Walter Reed Army Medical Center, and the Malcolm Grow USAF Medical Center. Department also provides instruction for junior pathologists and residents and prepares educational materials.

**★ 10175 ★ U.S. Department of Defense
Armed Forces Institute of Pathology
Otolaryngic and Endocrine Pathology
  Department
Otolaryngic Pathology Division**
Washington, DC 20306-6000
Phone: (202)576-2366
Fax: (202)576-2164
Dennis K. Heffner, Chairman

Research Activities and Fields: Conducts histomorphologic and clinicopathologic research in the field of otorhinolaryngic pathology. Other activites include: 1) providing diagnostic consultation service on surgical and autopsy material of the otorhinolaryngic anatomic area submitted by Department of Defense, Public Health Service, Veterans Administration, and nongovernment medical facilities through the United States and foreign countries; 2) providing consultation for settlement of Veterans' Benefits Claims cases related to the otorhinolaryngic anatomic area; and 3) conducting a continuous year-round educational program in otorhinolaryngic pathology (available to pathologists and otorhinolaryngologists of the U.S. Military, Veterans Administration, Public Health Service, and qualified individuals of the civilian medical communities).

**★ 10176 ★ U.S. Department of Defense
Armed Forces Institute of Pathology
Scientific Laboratories Department
Altitude and Hyperbaric Physiology
  Division**
Washington, DC 20306-6000
Phone: (202)576-2868
Fax: (202)576-2164
Maj. Loraine H. Anderson, USAF, BSC, Chief

Research Activities and Fields: Division studies the effects of oxygen on biological systems at high and low atmospheric pressures. Experiments with cells in culture and small animals are planned and conducted utilizing specialized environmental boxes and pressure chambers. Specific studies include those on wound healing, immune function, oxygen toxici-

ty, decompression sickness, and various aspects of altitude hypoxia. Data from these investigations are used to support flight crews in the operational aerospace environment and to provide a basic science foundation for the applications of clinical hyperbaric oxygen therapy. Other activities include: providing research and consultative services to the Armed Forces, federal agencies, and civilian contributors on performance data in physiological pressure and component gas environments; coordinating maintenance and operation of AFIP hyperbaric and hypobaric research facilities; maintaining liaison and conducting cooperative studies with other federal institutions and private agencies, including the Undersea and Hyperbaric Medical Society, involved in clinical hyperbaric medicine research; supporting national and internatinal scientific societies through continuing seminars, lectures, and collaborative research in clinical hyperbaric oxygen therapy; and participating in the Joint Advisory Committee on Clinical Hyperbaric Medicine (JACCHM) and the Research Subcommittee of JACCHM.

**★ 10177 ★ U.S. Department of Defense
Armed Forces Institute of Pathology
Scientific Laboratory Department
Immunopathology Division**
Washington, DC 20306-6000
Phone: (202)576-2873
Dr. Mullick, Director

Research Activities and Fields: Division conducts independent and collaborative research studies in which immunological concepts and techniques are used to gain understanding of specific pathological conditions. Division also: 1) provides intramural consultation services on cases requiring immunopathological interpretation or in which immunohistochemical identification and localization of specific antigenic substances can aid in interpretation and diagnosis; and 2) participates in informal discussions with professional and technical personnel on conceptual and technical aspects of immunopathology.

**★ 10178 ★ U.S. Department of Defense
Armed Forces Institute of Pathology
Veterinary Pathology Department
Laboratory Animal Medicine Division**
6825 16th St., N.W.
Washington, DC 20306-6000
Phone: (202)576-2923
Dr. Patricia Fritz, Chief

Research Activities and Fields: Division provides veterinary support to research and educational projects that utilize laboratory animals in AFIP's biomedical research program. This includes procurement, quarantine, maintenance, and veterinary medical and surgical care of laboratory animals. Division also conducts and directs research studies to improve laboratory animal science; provides various education and consultation services; provides experimental surgery, clinical pathology laboratory, necropsy, and radiology services; coordinates AFIP's animal research program; provides professional and technical support to investigators; establishes standards for procurement of animals, animal support equipment, animal husbandry supplies, animal housing, and veterinary medi-

cal equipment as well as standards for human animal care and experimentation techniques; insures compliance of AFIP's animal facilities and practices with federal and military laws and regulations; monitors procedures involving laboratory animals; and determines the number and mix of animals allowed within areas of AFIP.

**★ 10179 ★ U.S. Department of Defense
Armed Forces Institute of Pathology
Veterinary Pathology Department
Veterinary Pathology Division**
6825 16th St., N.W.
Washington, DC 20306-6000
Phone: (202)576-2453
Lt. Col. Harris, Chairman

Research Activities and Fields: Division provides consultation, education, and research (extramural and intramural) on animal diseases. Special functions include a primary histopathology service provided worldwide for all necropsy and biopsy specimens from military working dogs; and a veterinary pathology residency program for military and federal veterinarians. Division maintains the Military Working Dog Registry; and provides a surgical and necropsy pathology service for the Department's Laboratory Animal Medicine Division.

**U.S. Department of Defense
Army Medical Research and Development
  Command
Walter Reed Army Institute of Research
Pathology Division**
See: Entry 7834

**U.S. Department of Health and Human
  Services
National Cancer Institute
Laboratory of Experimental
  Carcinogenesis**
See: Entry 6184

**U.S. Department of Health and Human
  Services
National Heart, Lung, and Blood Institute
Division of Intramural Research
Pathology Branch**
See: Entry 2943

**U.S. Department of Health and Human
  Services
National Institute of Allergy and Infectious
  Diseases
Laboratory of Immunology
Experimental Pathology Section**
See: Entry 2136

**U.S. Department of Health and Human
  Services
National Institute of Environmental Health
  Sciences
Laboratory of Pulmonary Pathobiology**
See: Entry 5110

★10180★ **Universities Associated for Research and Education in Pathology, Inc.**
9650 Rockville Pike
Bethesda, MD 20814-3993
Phone: (301)571-1880
Fax: (301)571-1879
Frances A. Pitlick, Ph.D., Exec. Officer

Research Activities and Fields: Administers and coordinates educational and research activities in human pathology, including studies on environmental factors in human diseases, environmental pathology, safety of food additives, health effects attributed to unregulated toxic waste disposal sites, accident and forensic pathology, and environmental health policies. Provides core material for pathology instruction to medical students and residents. Operates the Registry of Comparative Pathology. **Publications:** *Atlas of Tumor Pathology.*

★10181★ **University of Southern California**
Lung Disease, Cancer, Lymphocytes, Air Pollution, and General Pathobiology Unit
2011 Zonal Ave., HMR 201
Los Angeles, CA 90033
Phone: (213)342-1165
Fax: (213)342-3049
Dr. Russell P. Sherwin, Head

Research Activities and Fields: Environmental and oncologic pathology, lung disease, cancer, lymphocytes, macrophages, air toxicants, general pathobiology, histochemistry, histopathology, radioisotopes, tissue culture, and electron microscopy, including studies on pathogenesis of lung and breast cancer, pathogenesis and pathologic diagnosis of pulmonary emphysema, biologic effects of air pollution, and computer-assisted image analysis.

Chapter 50
Pharmacology & Toxicology

Federal Government Agencies

★10182★ U.S. Department of Health and Human Services
Food and Drug Administration
National Center for Toxicological Research
3900 N.C.T.R. Dr.
Jefferson, AR 72079-9502
Phone: (501)543-7000
Fax: (501)543-7576

Description: The National Center for Toxicological Research conducts research programs to study the biological effects of potentially toxic chemical substances found in the environment, emphasizing the determination of the health effects resulting from long-term, low-level exposure to chemical toxicants, and the basic biological processes for chemical toxicants in animal organisms; develops improved methodologies and test protocols for evaluating the safety of chemical toxicants and the data that will facilitate the extrapolation of toxicological data from laboratory animals to man; and develops Center programs as a natural resource under the National Toxicology Program.

Foundations & Other Funding Organizations

Private Foundations

Rockefeller Foundation
See: Entry 460

Other Funding Organizations

★10183★ American Society for Pharmacology and Experimental Therapeutics
9650 Rockville Pike
Bethesda, MD 20814-3995
Phone: (301)530-7060
Kay A. Croker, Exec. Off.

Description: Administers various awards to recognize outstanding research in, and contri-

butions to, the field of pharmacology and experimental therapeutics.

★10184★ Pharmaceutical Manufacturers Association
1100 15th St. NW
Washington, DC 20005
Phone: (202)835-3400
Gerald J. Mossinghoff, Pres.

Description: Established the Pharmaceutical Manufacturers Association Foundation to promote public health through scientific and medical research.

Medical & Allied Health Schools

Pharmacology

Listed below are schools of medicine, schools of osteopathic medicine, schools of pharmacy, and schools of veterinary medicine that offer graduate training programs in pharmacology. To obtain general information on these programs, including specialties offered, contact the American Society for Pharmacology and Experimental Therapeutics, 9650 Rockville Pike, Bethesda, MD 20814-3995, (301) 530-7060.

Alabama

★10185★ Auburn University
College of Veterinary Medicine
Department of Physiology and Pharmacology
Auburn, AL 36849
Phone: (205)844-4425

★10186★ Auburn University
School of Pharmacy
Department of Pharmacal Science
Division of Pharmacology and Toxicology
Auburn, AL 36849-5503
Phone: (205)844-4037

★10187★ Tuskegee University
School of Veterinary Medicine
Department of Physiology, Pharmacology and Toxicology
Tuskegee, AL 36088
Phone: (205)727-8472

★10188★ University of Alabama at Birmingham
School of Medicine
Pharmacology Department
Volker Hall
Box 600
Birmingham, AL 35294
Phone: (205)934-4578

★10189★ University of South Alabama
College of Medicine
Pharmacology Department
3130 Medical Sciences Bldg.
Mobile, AL 36688
Phone: (205)460-6497
Fax: (205)460-6798

Arizona

★10190★ University of Arizona
College of Medicine and College of Pharmacy
Department of Pharmacology
1501 N. Campbell Ave., Rm. 5103
Tucson, AZ 85724
Phone: (602)626-7218
Fax: (602)626-5183

Arkansas

★10191★ University of Arkansas at Little Rock
School of Medicine
Department of Pharmacology and Toxicology
4301 W. Markham St.
Little Rock, AR 72205
Phone: (501)686-5511

California

★ 10192 ★ **College of Osteopathic Medicine of the Pacific**
Department of Pharmacology
College Plaza
Pomona, CA 91766-1889
Phone: (909)623-6116

★ 10193 ★ **Loma Linda University**
School of Medicine
Department of Physiology and Pharmacology
Loma Linda, CA 92350
Phone: (909)824-4564

★ 10194 ★ **Stanford University**
School of Medicine
Department of Molecular Pharmacology
300 Pasteur Dr.
Stanford, CA 94305
Phone: (415)723-6834

★ 10195 ★ **University of California, Davis**
School of Medicine
Department of Medical Pharmacology and Toxicology
Davis, CA 95616
Phone: (916)752-3200

★ 10196 ★ **University of California, Davis**
School of Veterinary Medicine
Department of Veterinary Pharmacology and Toxicology
Davis, CA 95616
Phone: (916)752-1059

★ 10197 ★ **University of California, Irvine**
College of Medicine
Department of Pharmacology
Irvine, CA 92717
Phone: (714)856-6771

★ 10198 ★ **University of California, Los Angeles**
School of Medicine
Department of Molecular and Medical Pharmacology
UCLA Center for Health Sciences
Los Angeles, CA 90024
Phone: (310)825-6539

★ 10199 ★ **University of California, San Diego**
School of Medicine
Department of Pharmacology
M-036
La Jolla, CA 92093
Phone: (619)534-4028

★ 10200 ★ **University of California, San Francisco**
School of Medicine
Department of Pharmacology
San Francisco, CA 94143
Phone: (415)476-1951

★ 10201 ★ **University of California, San Francisco**
School of Pharmacy
Graduate Pharmacology Program
513 Parnassus Ave., Rm. S-926
San Francisco, CA 94143-0446
Phone: (415)476-1913 ·

★ 10202 ★ **University of the Pacific**
School of Pharmacy
Department of Physiology and Pharmacology
751 Brookside Rd.
Stockton, CA 95211-0197
Phone: (209)946-2487

★ 10203 ★ **University of Southern California**
School of Medicine
Department of Pharmacology and Nutrition
2025 Zonal Ave.
Los Angeles, CA 90033
Phone: (213)226-2251

★ 10204 ★ **University of Southern California**
School of Pharmacy
Department of Molecular Pharmacology and Toxiology
1985 Zonal Ave.
Los Angeles, CA 90033
Phone: (213)342-1551

Colorado

★ 10205 ★ **University of Colorado**
School of Pharmacy
Department of Pharmaceutical Sciences
Health Sciences Center
4200 E. 9th Ave., No. C-238
Denver, CO 80262
Phone: (303)270-5055

★ 10206 ★ **University of Colorado—Denver**
School of Medicine
Department of Pharmacology
Campus Box C236
4200 e. 9th Ave.
Denver, CO 80262
Phone: (303)270-8120

Connecticut

★ 10207 ★ **University of Connecticut**
School of Medicine
Department of Pharmacology
Farmington, CT 06030
Phone: (203)679-2210

★ 10208 ★ **University of Connecticut**
School of Pharmacy
Pharmacology and Toxicology Section
372 Fairfield Rd.
PO Box U-92
Storrs Mansfield, CT 06269-2029
Phone: (203)486-3051

★ 10209 ★ **Yale University**
School of Medicine
Department of Pharmacology
333 Cedar St.
New Haven, CT 06520
Phone: (203)785-4372

District of Columbia

★ 10210 ★ **George Washington University**
School of Medicine and Health Sciences
Department of Pharmacology
2300 I St. NW
Washington, DC 20037
Phone: (202)994-3541

★ 10211 ★ **Georgetown University**
School of Medicine
Department of Pharmacology
3900 Reservoir Rd. NW
Washington, DC 20007
Phone: (202)687-1064

★ 10212 ★ **Howard University**
College of Medicine
Department of Pharmacology
520 W St. NW
Washington, DC 20059
Phone: (202)806-6311
Fax: (202)806-4453

Florida

★ 10213 ★ **Florida A&M University**
College of Pharmacy and Pharmaceutical Sciences
Pharmacology and Toxicology Program
Tallahassee, FL 32307
Phone: (904)599-3593

★ 10214 ★ **Southeastern College of Osteopathic Medicine**
1750 NE 168th St.
North Miami Beach, FL 33162
Phone: (305)949-4000

★ 10215 ★ **University of Florida**
College of Medicine
Department of Pharmacology and Therapeutics
J. Hillis Miller Health Center
Box 100267
Gainesville, FL 32610
Phone: (904)392-3541

★ 10216 ★ **University of Florida**
College of Veterinary Medicine
Department of Physiological Sciences
Graduate Pharmacology Programs
J. Hillis Miller Health Center
PO Box 100144
Gainesville, FL 32610
Phone: (904)392-4700

★ 10217 ★ **University of Miami**
School of Medicine
Department of Molecular and Cellular Pharmacology
PO Box 016189
Miami, FL 33101
Phone: (305)547-5874

★ 10218 ★ **University of South Florida**
College of Medicine
Department of Pharmacology and Therapeutics
Box 9
12901 Bruce B. Downs Blvd.
Tampa, FL 33612
Phone: (813)974-2543

Georgia

★ 10219 ★ **Emory University**
School of Medicine
Interdepartmental Program in Physiological
and Pharmacological Sciences
Atlanta, GA 30322
Phone: (404)727-5747

★ 10220 ★ **Medical College of Georgia**
School of Medicine
Department of Pharmacology and
Toxicology
Augusta, GA 30912
Phone: (706)721-2345

★ 10221 ★ **Morehouse School of Medicine**
Department of Graduate Education in the
Biomedical Sciences
720 Westview Dr. SW
Atlanta, GA 30310-1495
Phone: (404)752-1720

★ 10222 ★ **University of Georgia**
College of Pharmacy
Department of Pharmacology and
Toxicology
Athens, GA 30602
Phone: (706)542-7410

★ 10223 ★ **University of Georgia**
College of Veterinary Medicine
Department of Physiology and
Pharmacology
Athens, GA 30602
Phone: (706)542-3014

Hawaii

★ 10224 ★ **University of Hawaii at Manoa**
John A. Burns School of Medicine
Department of Pharmacology
1960 East-West Rd.
Honolulu, HI 96822
Phone: (808)956-8936

Idaho

★ 10225 ★ **Idaho State University**
College of Pharmacy
Department of Pharmaceutical Sciences
Graduate Pharmacology Programs
Pocatello, ID 83209
Phone: (208)236-2682

Illinois

★ 10226 ★ **Chicago College of Osteopathic**
Medicine
Department of Pharmacology
555 31st Downer's Grove
Chicago, IL 60615
Phone: (708)515-6381

★ 10227 ★ **Finch University of Health**
Sciences / Chicago Medical School
Department of Pharmacology
3333 Green Bay Rd.
North Chicago, IL 60064
Phone: (708)578-3271

★ 10228 ★ **Loyola University of Chicago**
Stritch School of Medicine
Department of Pharmacology and
Experimental Therapeutics
2160 S. 1st Ave.
Maywood, IL 60153
Phone: (708)216-3261
Fax: (708)216-6596

★ 10229 ★ **Northwestern University**
Medical School
Department of Pharmacology
303 E. Chicago Ave.
Chicago, IL 60611
Phone: (312)503-8284

★ 10230 ★ **Southern Illinois University at**
Springfield
School of Medicine
Department of Pharmacology
PO Box 19230
Springfield, IL 62794-9230
Phone: (217)785-2191

★ 10231 ★ **University of Chicago**
Pritzker School of Medicine
Department of Pharmacological and
Physiological Sciences
947 E. 58th St.
Chicago, IL 60637
Phone: (312)702-9340

★ 10232 ★ **University of Illinois**
College of Medicine at Peoria
Department of Pharmacology
Box 1649
Peoria, IL 61656
Phone: (309)671-8525

★ 10233 ★ **University of Illinois**
College of Veterinary Medicine
Department of Veterinary Biosciences
Graduate Pharmacology Programs
2001 S. Lincoln
Urbana, IL 61801
Phone: (217)333-2506

★ 10234 ★ **University of Illinois at Chicago**
College of Medicine
Department of Pharmacology
835 S. Wolcott Ave.
M/C 868
Chicago, IL 60612
Phone: (312)996-7635

Indiana

★ 10235 ★ **Butler University**
College of Pharmacy
Graduate Pharmacology Program
4600 Sunset Ave.
Indianapolis, IN 46208
Phone: (317)283-9322

★ 10236 ★ **Indiana University**
School of Medicine
Medical Sciences Program
Graduate Pharmacology Programs
Myers Hall
Bloomington, IN 47405
Phone: (812)855-9066

★ 10237 ★ **Indiana University**
School of Medicine
Pharmacology and Toxicology Department
635 Barnhill Dr.
Indianapolis, IN 46202-5120
Phone: (317)274-7844

★ 10238 ★ **Purdue University**
School of Pharmacy and Pharmacal
Sciences
Pharmacology and Toxicology Department
West Lafayette, IN 47907
Phone: (317)494-1403

★ 10239 ★ **Purdue University**
School of Veterinary Medicine
Department of Veterinary Physiology and
Pharmacology
West Lafayette, IN 47907
Phone: (317)494-8633
Fax: (317)494-0781

Iowa

★ 10240 ★ **Iowa State University**
College of Veterinary Medicine
Department of Veterinary Physiology and
Pharmacology
Ames, IA 50011
Phone: (515)294-2440

★ 10241 ★ **University of Iowa**
College of Medicine
Department of Pharmacology
Iowa City, IA 52242
Phone: (319)335-7965

★ 10242 ★ **University of Osteopathic**
Medicine and Health Sciences
Department of Physiology and
Pharmacology
3200 Grand Ave.
Des Moines, IA 50312
Phone: (515)271-1433

Kansas

★ 10243 ★ **Kansas State University**
College of Veterinary Medicine
Department of Anatomy and Physiology
Graduate Veterinary Pharmacology
Programs
VMS 228
Manhattan, KS 66506
Phone: (913)532-5666

★ 10244 ★ **University of Kansas**
School of Medicine
Department of Pharmacology, Toxicology,
and Therapeutics
3901 Rainbow Blvd.
Kansas City, KS 66160
Phone: (913)588-7140

★ 10245 ★ **University of Kansas**
School of Pharmacy
Department of Pharmacology and
Toxicology
5064 Malott
Lawrence, KS 66045
Phone: (913)864-4001

Kentucky

★ **10246** ★ **University of Kentucky**
College of Medicine
Department of Pharmacology
MS-305, Albert B. Chandler Medical Center
Lexington, KY 40536
Phone: (606)323-6209

★ **10247** ★ **University of Kentucky**
Graduate Center for Toxicology
204 Funkhouser Bldg.
Lexington, KY 40506-0078
Phone: (606)257-3760
Fax: (606)323-1059

★ **10248** ★ **University of Louisville**
School of Medicine
Department of Pharmacology and
Toxicology
Louisville, KY 40292
Phone: (502)852-5141

Louisiana

★ **10249** ★ **Louisiana State University**
School of Medicine
Department of Pharmacology and
Experimental Therapeutics
1901 Perdido St.
New Orleans, LA 70112
Phone: (504)568-4740

★ **10250** ★ **Louisiana State University**
School of Medicine in Shreveport
Department of Pharmacology and
Therapeutics
PO Box 33932
Shreveport, LA 71130-3932
Phone: (318)674-7850

★ **10251** ★ **Louisiana State University**
School of Veterinary Medicine
Department of Veterinary Physiology,
Pharmacology, and Toxicology
S. Stadium Rd.
Baton Rouge, LA 70803
Phone: (504)346-3201

★ **10252** ★ **Northeast Louisiana University**
School of Pharmacy
College of Pharmacy and Health Science
Division of Pharmacology and Toxicology
Monroe, LA 71209
Phone: (318)342-1695

★ **10253** ★ **Tulane University**
School of Medicine
Department of Pharmacology
1430 Tulane Ave.
New Orleans, LA 70112
Phone: (504)588-5444

Maine

★ **10254** ★ **University of New England**
College of Osteopathic Medicine
Department of Pharmacology
11 Hills Beach Rd.
Biddeford, ME 04005
Phone: (207)283-0171

Maryland

★ **10255** ★ **Johns Hopkins University**
School of Medicine
Department of Pharmacology and
Molecular Sciences
725 N. Wolfe St.
Baltimore, MD 21205
Phone: (410)955-3985

★ **10256** ★ **Uniformed Services University**
of the Health Sciences
F. Edward Hebert School of Medicine
Pharmacology Department
4301 Jones Bridge Rd.
Bethesda, MD 20889-4799
Phone: (301)295-3223

★ **10257** ★ **University of Maryland**
School of Medicine
Department of Pharmacology and
Experimental Therapeutics
655 W. Baltimore St.
Baltimore, MD 21201
Phone: (410)328-7330

★ **10258** ★ **University of Maryland**
School of Pharmacy
Department of Pharmacology and
Toxicology
20 N. Pine St.
Baltimore, MD 21201
Phone: (410)706-7509

Massachusetts

★ **10259** ★ **Boston University**
School of Medicine
Department of Pharmacology and
Experimental Therapeutics
80 E. Concord St.
Boston, MA 02118
Phone: (617)638-4300

★ **10260** ★ **Harvard University**
School of Medicine
Department of Biological Chemistry and
Molecular Pharmacology
240 Longwood Ave.
Boston, MA 02115
Phone: (617)432-1984

★ **10261** ★ **Massachusetts College of**
Pharmacy and Allied Health Sciences
Department of Pharmacology
179 Longwood Ave.
Boston, MA 02115
Phone: (617)732-2940

★ **10262** ★ **Northeastern University**
Bouve College of Pharmacy and Health
Sciences
Pharmacology Program
312 Mugar Hall
360 Huntington Ave.
Boston, MA 02115
Phone: (617)373-3312

★ **10263** ★ **Tufts University**
School of Medicine
Department of Pharmacology and
Experimental Therapeutics
136 Harrison Ave.
Boston, MA 02111
Phone: (617)956-6863

★ **10264** ★ **University of Massachusetts**
Medical Center at Worcester
Department of Pharmacology
55 N. Lake Ave.
Worcester, MA 01605
Phone: (508)856-2151

Michigan

★ **10265** ★ **Michigan State University**
College of Osteopathic Medicine
E. Fee Hall
East Lansing, MI 48824
Phone: (517)355-9611

★ **10266** ★ **Michigan State University**
College of Veterinary Medicine
Department of Pharmacology and
Toxicology
B440 Life Sciences Bldg.
East Lansing, MI 48824
Phone: (517)353-7147

★ **10267** ★ **Michigan State University**
Colleges of Human, Osteopathic, and
Veterinary Medicine
Department of Pharmacology and
Toxicology
East Lansing, MI 48824
Phone: (517)353-7147

★ **10268** ★ **University of Michigan**
Medical School
Department of Pharmacology
M6322 Medical Science Bldg. 1
Ann Arbor, MI 48109
Phone: (313)764-8166

★ **10269** ★ **Wayne State University**
College of Pharmacy and Allied Health
Professions
Department of Pharmaceutical Sciences
Shapero Hall, Rm. 528
Detroit, MI 48202
Phone: (313)577-1737

★ **10270** ★ **Wayne State University**
School of Medicine
Department of Pharmacology
540 E. Canfield
Detroit, MI 48201
Phone: (313)577-1580

Minnesota

★ **10271** ★ **Mayo Medical School**
Department of Pharmacology
Rochester, MN 55905
Phone: (507)284-2699

★ 10272 ★ University of Minnesota
College of Veterinary Medicine
Department of Veterinary Biology and
     Veterinary Pathobiology
Graduate Pharmacology Programs
205 Veterinary Science
1971 Commonwealth Ave
St. Paul, MN 55108
Phone: (612)625-5255

★ 10273 ★ University of Minnesota
School of Medicine
Department of Pharmacology
3-249 Millard Hall
435 Delaware St., SE
Minneapolis, MN 55455
Phone: (612)625-9997

★ 10274 ★ University of Minnesota, Duluth
School of Medicine
Department of Pharmacology
Duluth, MN 55812
Phone: (218)726-8512

Mississippi

★ 10275 ★ University of Mississippi
School of Medicine
Department of Pharmacology and
     Toxicology
Jackson, MS 39216
Phone: (601)984-1600

★ 10276 ★ University of Mississippi
School of Pharmacy
Pharmacology Department
University, MS 38677
Phone: (601)232-7330

Missouri

★ 10277 ★ St. Louis University
School of Medicine
Department of Pharmacology
1402 S. Grand Blvd.
St. Louis, MO 63104
Phone: (314)577-8551

★ 10278 ★ University of Missouri—
     Columbia
School of Medicine
Department of Pharmacology
M-517B Medical Science Bldg.
Columbia, MO 65212
Phone: (314)882-7186

★ 10279 ★ University of Missouri—Kansas
     City
School of Pharmacy
Division of Pharmacology
M3-C15
2411 Holmes St.
Kansas City, MO 64108
Phone: (816)276-1792

★ 10280 ★ Washington University
School of Medicine
Department of Molecular Biology and
     Pharmacology
660 S. Euclid St.
St. Louis, MO 63110
Phone: (314)362-7243

Montana

★ 10281 ★ University of Montana
School of Pharmacy and Allied Health
     Sciences
Department of Pharmaceutical Sciences
Graduate Pharmacology Programs
PhP Bldg., Rm. 119
32 Campus Dr.
Missoula, MT 59812-1075
Phone: (406)243-4765
Fax: (406)243-4353

Nebraska

★ 10282 ★ Creighton University
School of Medicine
Department of Pharmacology
2500 California St.
Omaha, NE 68178
Phone: (402)280-2983

★ 10283 ★ University of Nebraska at
     Omaha
College of Medicine
Department of Pharmacology
600 S. 42nd St.
Omaha, NE 68198-6260
Phone: (402)599-4044

Nevada

★ 10284 ★ University of Nevada—Reno
School of Medicine
Department of Pharmacology
Reno, NV 89557
Phone: (702)784-6956

New Hampshire

★ 10285 ★ Dartmouth College
Medical School
Department of Pharmacology and
     Toxicology
Dartmouth Hitchcock Medical Center
1 Medical Center Dr.
Lebanon, NH 03756
Phone: (603)650-5000

New Jersey

★ 10286 ★ Rutgers University / Robert
     Wood Johnson Medical School
Graduate Program in Pharmacology
675 Hoes Lane
Piscataway, NJ 08854
Phone: (908)235-4590

★ 10287 ★ Rutgers University / Robert
     Wood Johnson Medical School
Rutgers College of Pharmacy
Graduate Program in Pharmacology
Box 789
Piscataway, NJ 08855-0789
Phone: (908)932-3720

★ 10288 ★ University of Medicine and
     Dentistry of New Jersey
New Jersey Medical School
Department of Pharmacology and
     Toxicology
185 S. Orange Ave.
Newark, NJ 07103
Phone: (201)982-4444

★ 10289 ★ University of Medicine and
     Dentistry of New Jersey
School of Osteopathic Medicine
401 Hadden Ave.
Camden, NJ 08103
Phone: (609)757-7700

New Mexico

★ 10290 ★ University of New Mexico
School of Medicine
Department of Pharmacology
Albuquerque, NM 87131
Phone: (505)277-4411

New York

★ 10291 ★ Albany Medical College
Department of Pharmacology and
     Toxicology
47 New Scotland Ave.
Albany, NY 12208
Phone: (518)262-5303

★ 10292 ★ City University of New York
School of Medicine
Department of Pharmacology
138th St. and Convent Ave.
New York, NY 10031
Phone: (212)650-7751

★ 10293 ★ Columbia University
College of Physicians and Surgeons
Department of Pharmacology
630 W. 168th St.
New York, NY 10032
Phone: (212)305-8778

★ 10294 ★ Cornell University
Medical College
Department of Pharmacology
1300 York Ave.
New York, NY 10021
Phone: (212)746-6250

★ 10295 ★ Cornell University
New York State College of Veterinary
     Medicine
Department of Pharmacology
Ithaca, NY 14853
Phone: (607)253-3650

★ 10296 ★ Mt. Sinai School of Medicine of
     City University of New York
Department of Pharmacology
5th Ave. and 100th St.
New York, NY 10029
Phone: (212)241-7014

★ 10297 ★ New York College of Osteopathic Medicine
Department of Pharmacology, Toxicology, and Experimental Therapeutics
Wheatley Rd.
PO Box 170
Old Westbury, NY 11568
Phone: (516)626-6928

★ 10298 ★ New York Medical College
Department of Pharmacology
Basic Science Bldg. & Munger Pavilion
Valhalla, NY 10595
Phone: (914)993-4115

★ 10299 ★ New York Medical College
School of Pharmacy
Department of Pharmacology
Basic Science Bldg. and Munger Pavilion
Valhalla, NY 10595
Phone: (914)993-4115

★ 10300 ★ New York University
School of Medicine
Department of Pharmacology
550 1st Ave.
New York, NY 10016
Phone: (212)340-7110

★ 10301 ★ St. John's University
College of Pharmacy and Allied Health Professions
Department of Pharmaceutical Sciences
8000 Utopia Pkwy.
Jamaica, NY 11432
Phone: (718)990-6678

★ 10302 ★ State University of New York at Buffalo
School of Medicine
Department of Pharmacology and Therapeutics
102 Farber Hall
Buffalo, NY 14214
Phone: (716)831-2800

★ 10303 ★ State University of New York at Buffalo
School of Pharmacy
Department of Biochemical Pharmacology
313 Hochstetter
Buffalo, NY 14260
Phone: (716)645-2860

★ 10304 ★ State University of New York Health Science Center at Brooklyn
College of Medicine
Department of Pharmacology
450 Clarkson Ave.
Brooklyn, NY 11203
Phone: (718)270-1338

★ 10305 ★ State University of New York Health Science Center at Syracuse
College of Medicine
Department of Pharmacology
766 Irving Ave.
Syracuse, NY 13210
Phone: (315)464-5138

★ 10306 ★ State University of New York at Stony Brook
School of Medicine
Department of Pharmacological Sciences
Health Science Center
Stony Brook, NY 11794
Phone: (516)444-3050

★ 10307 ★ University of Rochester
School of Medicine and Dentistry
Department of Pharmacology
Rochester, NY 14642
Phone: (716)275-1681
Fax: (716)244-9283

★ 10308 ★ Yeshiva University
Albert Einstein College of Medicine
Department of Molecular Pharmacology
1300 Morris Park Ave.
Bronx, NY 10461
Phone: (718)430-2911

North Carolina

★ 10309 ★ Duke University
School of Medicine
Department of Pharmacology
Duke University Medical Center
Durham, NC 27710
Phone: (919)684-5224

★ 10310 ★ East Carolina University
School of Medicine
Department of Pharmacology
Greenville, NC 27858
Phone: (919)816-2736

★ 10311 ★ University of North Carolina at Chapel Hill
School of Medicine
Department of Pharmacology
CB 7365 Faculty Lab Bldg.
Chapel Hill, NC 27599-7365
Phone: (919)966-1153

★ 10312 ★ Wake Forest University
Bowman Gray School of Medicine
Department of Physiology and Pharmacology
Medical Center Blvd.
Winston-Salem, NC 27157
Phone: (910)716-4698

North Dakota

★ 10313 ★ North Dakota State University
College of Pharmacy
Department of Pharmaceutical Science
Fargo, ND 58105
Phone: (701)231-7773

★ 10314 ★ University of North Dakota
School of Medicine
Department of Pharmacology and Toxicology
501 N. Columbia Rd.
Grand Forks, ND 58203
Phone: (701)777-4293

Ohio

★ 10315 ★ Case Western Reserve University
School of Medicine
Department of Pharmacology
2109 Adelbert Rd.
Cleveland, OH 44106
Phone: (216)368-3394

★ 10316 ★ Medical College of Ohio
Department of Pharmacology
CS 10008
Toledo, OH 43699
Phone: (419)381-4182

★ 10317 ★ Northeastern Ohio Universities
College of Medicine
Psychopharmacology Program
4209 SR 44
Rootstown, OH 44272
Phone: (216)325-2511

★ 10318 ★ Ohio State University
College of Medicine
Department of Pharmacology
333 W. 10th Ave.
Columbus, OH 43210
Phone: (614)292-8608

★ 10319 ★ Ohio State University
College of Pharmacy
Pharmacology Division
500 W. 12th Ave.
Columbus, OH 43210
Phone: (614)292-1614

★ 10320 ★ Ohio State University
College of Veterinary Medicine
Department of Veterinary Physiology and Pharmacology
1900 Coffey Rd.
Columbus, OH 43210-1092
Phone: (614)292-1391

★ 10321 ★ Ohio University
Department of Zoological and Biomedical Sciences
Irvine Hall
Athens, OH 45701
Phone: (614)593-2406

★ 10322 ★ University of Cincinnati
College of Medicine
Department of Environmental Health
Graduate Toxicology Programs
3223 Eden Ave.
Cincinnati, OH 45267
Phone: (513)558-1706

★ 10323 ★ University of Cincinnati
College of Medicine
Department of Pharmacology and Cell Biophysics
231 Bethesda Ave.
Cincinnati, OH 45267-0575
Phone: (513)558-2400

★ 10324 ★ University of Toledo
College of Pharmacy
Pharmacology Department
2801 W. Bancroft St.
Toledo, OH 43606
Phone: (419)537-2010

★ 10325 ★ **Wright State University**
School of Medicine
Department of Pharmacology and
**   Toxicology**
PO Box 927
Dayton, OH 45409
Phone: (513)873-2168

Oklahoma

★ 10326 ★ **Oklahoma State University**
College of Osteopathic Medicine
Department of Physiology and
**   Pharmacology**
1111 W. 17th St.
Tulsa, OK 74107
Phone: (918)582-1972

★ 10327 ★ **Oklahoma State University**
College of Veterinary Medicine
Department of Physiological Sciences
Graduate Pharmacology Programs
Stillwater, OK 74078
Phone: (405)744-6748

★ 10328 ★ **University of Oklahoma**
College of Medicine
Department of Pharmacology
Health Sciences Center
PO Box 26901
Oklahoma City, OK 73190
Phone: (405)271-2100

★ 10329 ★ **University of Oklahoma**
College of Pharmacy
Department of Pharmacodynamics and
**   Toxicology**
Health Sciences Center
1110 N. Stonewall Ave.
Oklahoma City, OK 73190
Phone: (405)271-6481

Oregon

★ 10330 ★ **Oregon Health Sciences**
**   University**
School of Medicine
Department of Pharmacology
3181 SW Sam Jackson Park Rd.
Portland, OR 97201-3098
Phone: (503)494-7805

★ 10331 ★ **Oregon State University**
College of Pharmacy
Department of Pharmacology
Corvallis, OR 97331
Phone: (503)737-5802

★ 10332 ★ **Oregon State University**
Mark O. Hatfield Marine Science Center
Graduate Pharmacology Programs
2030 Marine Science Dr.
Newport, OR 97365
Phone: (503)867-0211

★ 10333 ★ **Oregon State University**
School of Medicine
Mark O. Hatfield Marine Science Center
Newport, OR 97365
Phone: (503)867-0211

Pennsylvania

★ 10334 ★ **Duquesne University**
School of Pharmacy
Department of Pharmacology and
**   Toxicology**
Pittsburgh, PA 15282
Phone: (412)396-6361

★ 10335 ★ **Medical College of Pennsylvania**
**   and Hahnemann University**
School of Medicine
Department of Pharmacology
2900 Queen Lane
Philadelphia, PA 19129
Phone: (215)991-8202

★ 10336 ★ **Pennsylvania State University**
College of Medicine
Department of Pharmacology
Milton S. Hershey Medical Center
PO Box 850
Hershey, PA 17033
Phone: (717)531-8286

★ 10337 ★ **Philadelphia College of**
**   Osteopathic Medicine**
Department of Physiology and
**   Pharmacology**
4170 Cityline Ave.
Philadelphia, PA 19131
Phone: (215)871-2888

★ 10338 ★ **Philadelphia College of**
**   Pharmacy and Science**
Department of Pharmacology and
**   Toxicology**
43rd St. and Woodland Ave.
Philadelphia, PA 19104
Phone: (215)596-8830

★ 10339 ★ **Temple University**
School of Medicine
Department of Pharmacology
3420 N. Broad St.
Philadelphia, PA 19140
Phone: (215)707-3237

★ 10340 ★ **Temple University**
School of Pharmacy
Department of Pharmacology
3307 N. Broad St.
Philadelphia, PA 19140
Phone: (215)221-4976

★ 10341 ★ **Thomas Jefferson University**
Jefferson Medical College
Department of Pharmacology
1020 Locust St.
Philadelphia, PA 19107
Phone: (215)955-4634

★ 10342 ★ **University of Pennsylvania**
School of Medicine
Department of Pharmacology
36th and Hamilton Walk
Philadelphia, PA 19104-6084
Phone: (215)898-1790

★ 10343 ★ **University of Pittsburgh**
Graduate School of Public Health
Department of Environmental and
**   Occupational Health**
Toxicology Program
RIDC Park
260 Kappa Dr.
Pittsburgh, PA 15238
Phone: (412)967-6521

★ 10344 ★ **University of Pittsburgh**
School of Medicine
Department of Pharmacology
E. 1340 Biomedical Science Tower
Pittsburgh, PA 15261
Phone: (412)648-9321

Puerto Rico

★ 10345 ★ **Ponce School of Medicine**
Department of Pharmacology and
**   Toxicology**
University St.
PO Box 7004
Ponce, PR 00732-7004
Phone: (809)259-7085
Fax: (809)841-1045

★ 10346 ★ **Universidad Central Del Caribe**
School of Medicine
Department of Pharmacology
PO Box 935
Cayey, PR 00737
Phone: (809)738-7656

★ 10347 ★ **University of Puerto Rico**
School of Medicine
Department of Pharmacology
Medical Sciences Campus
GPO Box 365067
San Juan, PR 00936-5067
Phone: (809)766-4441

Rhode Island

★ 10348 ★ **Brown University**
Division of Biology and Medicine
Molecular and Biochemical Pharmacology
**   Section**
Providence, RI 02912
Phone: (401)863-1596

★ 10349 ★ **University of Rhode Island**
College of Pharmacy
Department of Pharmacology and
**   Toxicology**
Kingston, RI 02881
Phone: (401)792-2362

South Carolina

★ 10350 ★ **Medical University of South**
**   Carolina**
College of Medicine
Department of Pharmacology
171 Ashley Ave.
Charleston, SC 29425
Phone: (803)792-2471
Fax: (803)792-2475

★ 10351 ★ University of South Carolina
College of Pharmacy
Department of Basic Pharmaceutical
 Sciences
Division of Pharmacology
Columbia, SC 29208
Phone: (803)777-7824

★ 10352 ★ University of South Carolina
School of Medicine
Department of Pharmacology
VA Bldg. 1
Columbia, SC 29208
Phone: (803)733-3254

South Dakota

★ 10353 ★ University of South Dakota
School of Medicine
Department of Physiology and
 Pharmacology
Vermillion, SD 57069
Phone: (605)677-5479

Tennessee

★ 10354 ★ East Tennessee State University
James H. Quillen College of Medicine
Department of Pharmacology
PO Box 70577
Johnson City, TN 37614
Phone: (615)929-6207

★ 10355 ★ Meharry Medical College
School of Medicine
Department of Pharmacology
1005 18th Ave. N.
Nashville, TN 37208
Phone: (615)327-6510

★ 10356 ★ University of Tennessee,
 Knoxville
College of Veterinary Medicine
Department of Environmental Practice
Graduate Pharmacology Programs
Knoxville, TN 37901
Phone: (615)974-5576
Fax: (615)974-5640

★ 10357 ★ University of Tennessee,
 Memphis
College of Medicine
Department of Pharmacology
Health Science Center
874 Union Ave.
Memphis, TN 38163
Phone: (901)448-6000

★ 10358 ★ Vanderbilt University
School of Medicine
Department of Biochemistry
Center in Molecular Toxicology
T-1219 Medical Center, N.
Nashville, TN 37232
Phone: (615)322-2261

★ 10359 ★ Vanderbilt University
School of Medicine
Department of Pharmacology
Nashville, TN 37232
Phone: (615)322-2207

Texas

★ 10360 ★ Baylor College of Medicine
Department of Pharmacology
1 Baylor Plaza
Houston, TX 77030
Phone: (713)798-4457

★ 10361 ★ Texas A&M University
College of Medicine
Department of Medical Pharmacology and
 Toxicology
College Station, TX 77843
Phone: (409)845-2817

★ 10362 ★ Texas A&M University
College of Veterinary Medicine
Department of Veterinary Physiology and
 Pharmacology
College Station, TX 77843
Phone: (713)845-7261

★ 10363 ★ Texas Tech University
School of Medicine
Department of Pharmacology
Health Sciences Center
Lubbock, TX 79430
Phone: (806)743-2425
Fax: (806)743-2744

★ 10364 ★ University of Houston
College of Pharmacy
Department of Pharmacological and
 Pharmaceutical Sciences
523 SR-2
Houston, TX 77204-5515
Phone: (713)743-1213

★ 10365 ★ University of North Texas
 Health Science Center at Fort Worth
Graduate Program in Pharmacology
3500 Camp Bowie at Montgomery
Ft. Worth, TX 76107
Phone: (817)735-2064

★ 10366 ★ University of Texas at Austin
College of Pharmacy
Department of Pharmacology and
 Toxicology
Austin, TX 78712
Phone: (512)471-5158

★ 10367 ★ University of Texas Health
 Science Center at Houston
School of Medicine
Department of Pharmacology
PO Box 20708
Houston, TX 77225
Phone: (713)792-5550

★ 10368 ★ University of Texas Health
 Science Center at San Antonio
School of Medicine
Department of Pharmacology
7703 Floyd Curl Dr.
San Antonio, TX 78284-7764
Phone: (512)567-4200

★ 10369 ★ University of Texas Medical
 Branch at Galveston
Graduate School of Biochemical Sciences
Department of Pharmacology and
 Toxicology
Galveston, TX 77555-1031
Phone: (409)772-1561
Fax: (409)772-9642

★ 10370 ★ University of Texas
 Southwestern Medical Center at Dallas
Southwestern Medical School
Department of Pharmacology
5323 Harry Hines Blvd.
Dallas, TX 75235
Phone: (214)648-3619

Utah

★ 10371 ★ University of Utah
College of Pharmacy
Department of Pharmacology and
 Toxicology
112 Skaggs Hall
Salt Lake City, UT 84112
Phone: (801)581-6287

★ 10372 ★ University of Utah
School of Medicine
Department of Pharmacology and
 Toxicology
112 Skaggs Hall
Salt Lake City, UT 84112
Phone: (801)581-6287

★ 10373 ★ Utah State University
Interdepartmental Toxicology Program
Center for Environmental Toxicology
Logan, UT 84322
Phone: (801)750-1890

Vermont

★ 10374 ★ University of Vermont
College of Medicine
Department of Pharmacology
Burlington, VT 05401
Phone: (802)656-2500

Virginia

★ 10375 ★ Medical College of Hampton
 Roads
Eastern Virginia Medical School
Department of Pharmacology
PO Box 1980
Norfolk, VA 23501
Phone: (804)446-5630

★ 10376 ★ University of Virginia
School of Medicine
Department of Pharmacology
Box 448
Jordan Hall
Charlottesville, VA 22908
Phone: (804)924-5207

★10377★ Virginia Commonwealth University
Medical College of Virginia
School of Basic Health Sciences
Department of Pharmacology and Toxicology
Box 980613, MCV Station
Richmond, VA 23298-0613
Phone: (804)786-8431
Fax: (804)371-7519

★10378★ Virginia Polytechnic Institute and State University / University of Maryland
Virginia-Maryland Regional College of Veterinary Medicine
Department of Biomedical Sciences
Pharmacology and Toxicology Program
Blacksburg, VA 24061
Phone: (703)231-7666

Washington

★10379★ University of Washington
School of Medicine
Department of Pharmacology
SJ-30, E-401 Health Science Bldg.
Seattle, WA 98195
Phone: (206)543-1970
Fax: (206)685-3822

★10380★ Washington State University
College of Pharmacy
Graduate Program in Pharmacology and Toxicology
Pullman, WA 99164-6510
Phone: (509)335-8664

★10381★ Washington State University
College of Veterinary Medicine
Department of Veterinary and Comparative Anatomy, Pharmacology and Physiology
Pullman, WA 99164-6520
Phone: (509)335-7898

West Virginia

★10382★ Marshall University
School of Medicine
Department of Pharmacology
Huntington, WV 25755-9310
Phone: (304)696-7313

★10383★ West Virginia School of Osteopathic Medicine
Department of Pharmacology
400 N. Lee St.
Lewisburg, WV 24901
Phone: (304)645-6270

★10384★ West Virginia University
School of Medicine
Department of Pharmacology and Toxicology
West Virginia Medical Center
Morgantown, WV 26506
Phone: (304)293-4449

Wisconsin

★10385★ Medical College of Wisconsin
Department of Pharmacology and Toxicology
8701 Watertown Plank Rd.
Milwaukee, WI 53226
Phone: (414)257-8267

★10386★ University of Wisconsin—Madison
Medical School
Department of Pharmacology
1300 University Ave.
Madison, WI 53706
Phone: (608)262-1733

★10387★ University of Wisconsin—Madison
School of Pharmacy
Pharmacology Program
425 N. Charles St.
Madison, WI 53706
Phone: (608)262-1416

★10388★ University of Wisconsin—Madison
School of Veterinary Medicine
Department of Comparative Biosciences
Pharmacology Program
2015 Linden Dr. W.
Madison, WI 53706
Phone: (608)263-5878

National & International Organizations

Alliance to End Childhood Lead Poisoning
See: Entry 3155

★10389★ Alliance for the Prudent Use of Antibiotics (APUA)
PO Box 1372
Boston, MA 02117
Phone: (617)636-6765
Fax: (617)636-0458
Stuart B. Levy, M.D., Pres.

Founded: 1981. Members: 850. Description: International membership of physicians, scientists, and medical and public health personnel; other individuals supporting prudent use of antibiotics. (Believes that extensive use of antibiotics leads to development of resistant strains of pathogenic and common, nonpathogenic bacteria with resistance traits transferable from one bacterium to others. These resistant strains are no longer susceptible to antibiotics and therefore can undermine treatment of infectious bacterial diseases.) Advocates and defines "good usage" of antibiotics; informs and educates the public about the dangers of misusing and overusing antibiotics and other antimicrobial agents; provides data to individuals and organizations interested in preventing antibiotic misuse and overuse. Informs and educates medical and paramedical personnel worldwide about the defined and specific action of antibiotics and the necessity of controlling their dispensation and prescription. Supports research projects. Maintains speakers' bureau; plans to offer computerized services. Publications: *APUA Newsletter*, quarterly. Newsletter. Includes pharmacology reviews. *Price:* Included in membership dues.

★10390★ American Academy of Clinical Toxicology (AACT)
Pittsburgh Poison Center
3705 5th Ave.
Pittsburgh, PA 15213
Phone: (412)692-6669
Fax: (412)692-7497
Edward P. Krenzelak, Ph.D., Sec.-Treas.

Founded: 1968. Members: 450. Description: Physicians, veterinarians, pharmacists, research scientists, and analytical chemists. Objectives are to: unite medical scientists and facilitate the exchange of information; encourage the development of therapeutic methods and technology; establish a mechanism for the certification of medical scientists in clinical toxicology. Conducts professional training in poison information and emergency service personnel. Maintains placement services and speakers' bureau. Publications: *Clinical Toxicology*, bimonthly. Journal. Includes annual directory. *Price:* Included in membership dues.

American Academy of Veterinary and Comparative Toxicology (AAVCT)
See: Entry 13021

American Academy of Veterinary Pharmacology and Therapeutics (AAVPT)
See: Entry 13024

★10391★ American Association of Poison Control Centers (AAPCC)
3201 New Mexico Ave. NW, Ste. 310
Washington, DC 20016
Phone: (202)362-7217
Fax: (202)362-8377
Rose Ann Soloway, RN, Admin.

Founded: 1958. Members: 1,000. Description: Individuals and organizations engaged in operation of poison control centers. Aids in the procurement of information on the ingredients and potential acute toxicity of substances that may cause accidental poisonings and on the proper management of such poisonings. Has established standards for poison information and control centers. Conducts educational programs and prepares visual aids on prevention of accidental poisoning. Offers children's services; compiles statistics. Publications: Annual Report. • Membership Directory, annual.

★10392★ American Board of Medical Toxicology (ABMT)
c/o William Banner
St. Frances Hospital
PICU
6161 S. Yale
Tulsa, OK 74136
Phone: (918)494-5491
William Banner, Pres.

Founded: 1968. Members: 100. Description: Physicians with substantial interest, training, and experience in clinical toxicology who have passed the certifying toxicology examination. Purpose is to evaluate and certify physicians in medical toxicology. Administers certifying examinations to qualified licensed physicians during sessions at annual meetings. Formerly an arm of American Academy of Clinical Toxicology; became independent in 1980. **Publications:** *American Board of Medical Toxicology Journal*, annual. Journal. *Price:* Included in membership dues. • *Directory*, annual. • *Veterinary and Human Toxicology*, bimonthly. Journal. Includes research articles, scientific reviews, field observations in domestic and wild animals, and general news items and announcements. *Price:* Included in membership dues; $40/year for nonmembers. **Formerly:** American Board of Medical Toxicology of the American Academy of Clinical Toxicology.

★ 10393 ★ **American Board of Toxicology (ABT)**
PO Box 30054
Raleigh, NC 27622
Phone: (919)782-0036
Fax: (919)782-0036

Founded: 1979. **Description:** Certifies toxicologists. Administers annual certification and recertification exams. **Publications:** *Directory of Diplomates*, annual. Directory. Includes alphabetical listing of certified toxicologists. *Price:* $50. • Newsletter, annual.

American Board of Veterinary Toxicology (ABVT)
See: Entry 13043

★ 10394 ★ **American College of Clinical Pharmacology (ACCP)**
300 Oriskany Blvd.
Yorkville, NY 13495
Phone: (315)768-6117
Fax: (315)768-6119
Susan Ulrich, Exec.Dir.

Founded: 1969. **Members:** 1,000. **Regional Groups:** 2. **Local Groups:** 14. **Description:** Strives to be the premier professional society with the size, influence, and diversity of membership consistent with the breadth of the discipline of clinical pharmacology. Provides educational programs and forum for membership, health professionals, students, and the public. Assists in the development and dissemination of basic and clinical knowledge to improve rational drug use and patient outcomes. Supports and encourages the discovery and development efforts designed to provide improved therapeutic modalities. **Publications:** *ACCP Newsletter*, quarterly. Newsletter. *Price:* Free for members. • *American College of Clinical Pharmacology--Directory*, annual. Membership Directory. *Price:* Included in membership dues. • *Journal of Clinical Pharmacology*, monthly. Journal. *Price:* Included in membership dues; $95 for nonmembers in the U.S.; $135 for nonmembers outside the U.S.

★ 10395 ★ **American College of Neuropsychopharmacology (ACNP)**
320 Centre Bldg.
2014 Broadway
Nashville, TN 37203
Phone: (615)322-2075
Fax: (615)343-0662
Oakley Ray, Ph.D., Exec.Sec.

Founded: 1961. **Members:** 667. **Description:** Experienced investigators whose work is related to neuropsychopharmacology. Promotes and encourages the scientific study and application of neuropsychopharmacology. Conducts study groups and plenary sessions. **Publications:** *Mailings*, monthly. • *Neuropsychopharmacology*, quarterly. Journal. Focuses on clinical and basic science contributions to neuropharmacology. *Price:* Included in membership dues. • *Roster*, annual.

★ 10396 ★ **American College of Toxicology (ACT)**
9650 Rockville Pike
Bethesda, MD 20814
Phone: (301)571-1840
Fax: (301)571-1852
Carol C. Lemire, Exec.Dir.

Founded: 1977. **Members:** 750. **Description:** Individuals interested in toxicology and related disciplines such as analytical chemistry, biology, pathology, teratology, and immunology. Addresses toxicological issues. Disseminates information and provides a forum for discussion of approaches to problems in the field in order to advance toxicological science and better serve society during the annual meeting. **Publications:** *Acute Toxicity Data*, bimonthly. Describes experimental procedures; includes statistics. • *Journal of American College of Toxicology*, bimonthly. Journal. Contains peer-reviewed papers in toxicology. • *Membership Directory*, annual. *Price:* Included in membership dues.

★ 10397 ★ **American Society for Clinical Pharmacology and Therapeutics (ASCPT)**
1718 Gallagher Rd.
Norristown, PA 19401-2800
Phone: (610)825-3838
Fax: (610)834-8652
Elaine Galasso, Exec.Dir.

Founded: 1900. **Members:** 2,082. **Description:** Works to "promote and advance the science of human pharmacology and therapeutics and in so doing to maintain the highest standards of research, education, and exchange of scientific information." Provides a Medical Education Program of Continuing Education for practicing physicians. **Publications:** *Clinical Pharmacology and Therapeutics*, monthly. Journal. *Price:* Included in membership dues.

★ 10398 ★ **American Society of Pharmacognosy (ASP)**
c/o Dr. William J. Keller
School of Pharmacy
Northeast Louisiana University
Monroe, LA 71209
Phone: (318)342-1692
Fax: (318)342-1600
Dr. William J. Keller, Sec.

Founded: 1959. **Members:** 1,000. **Description:** Professional society of pharmacognosists (persons engaged in the study of drugs from a natural origin) and others interested in the plant sciences and natural products. **Publications:** *Journal of Natural Products*, monthly. Journal. • Newsletter, quarterly.

★ 10399 ★ **American Society for Pharmacology and Experimental Therapeutics (ASPET)**
9650 Rockville Pike
Bethesda, MD 20814-3995
Phone: (301)530-7060
Kay A. Croker, Exec. Officer

Founded: 1908. **Members:** 4,300. **Description:** Scientific society of investigators in pharmacology and toxicology interested in research and promotion of pharmacological knowledge and its use among scientists and the public. **Publications:** Brochures. • *Clinical Pharmacology and Therapeutics*, monthly. • *Drug Metabolism and Disposition*, bimonthly. • *Journal of Pharmacology and Experimental Therapeutics*, monthly. Journal. • *Molecular Pharmacology*, monthly. • *Pharmacological Reviews*, quarterly. • *Pharmacologist*, quarterly. Also distributes listings of schools of medicine and pharmacy.

★ 10400 ★ **Associates of Clinical Pharmacology (ACP)**
16923 Maplewild Ave. SW, Ste. A
Seattle, WA 98166-3165
Denise F. Olson, Exec.Dir.

Founded: 1977. **Members:** 4,100. **Description:** Individuals engaged in clinical pharmacology and other related research professions, including clinical monitors and research associates, nurses, pharmacists, pharmacologists, physicians, and regulatory professionals. Promotes professional growth in the field through the dissemination of information, the exchange of ideas, and the development of educational programs. Provides continuing education credits to pharmacy and nursing professionals through the American Council on Pharmaceutical Education and the American Nurses Association. **Publications:** *ACP Membership Directory*, annual. Membership Directory. *Price:*. Free, for members only. • *Journal of Clinical Research and Drug Development*, quarterly. Journal. Includes papers on medical, legal, and ethical issues, pharmacoepidemiological problems, drug devices, drug regulatory affairs involvement, education. *Price:* Included in membership dues. • *Monitor*, quarterly. Newsletter. Includes activities information and committee reports, industry news, calendar of events, regulatory affairs column, and study coordinator column. *Price:* Free, for members only.

Behavioral Pharmacology Society (BPS)
See: Entry 7342

★ 10401 ★ **British Association for Psychopharmacology (BAP)**
Baker Bldg. Flat
Engineering Dept.
Trumpington St.
Cambridge CB2 1PZ, England
Phone: 1223 358395
Fax: 1223 321268
Susan Chandler, Sec.

Founded: 1974. **Members:** 650. **Languages:** English. **Description:** Psychopharmacologists, psychiatrists, neuropharmacologists, psychologists, and neurochemists. Brings together scientists working in academic, clinical, and industrial applications of psychopharmacology. Arranges scientific meetings, study groups, and seminars; encourages basic research and pharmaceutical development. Offers professional guidance to the public on matters related to psychopharmacology. **Publications:** *Journal of Psychopharmacology*, bimonthly. Journal. • *Monographs*, periodic.

★ 10402 ★ **British Pharmacological Society**
The Medical College
Charterhouse Sq.
London EC1M 6BQ, England
Phone: 171 9826171
Fax: 171 9826173
Dr. J. Maclagan, Hon.Gen.Sec.

Founded: 1931. **Members:** 2,200. **Languages:** English. **Description:** Pharmacologists and clinical pharmacologists in academia and industry in 20 countries. Conducts educational symposia and lectures; makes available travel bursaries. **Publications:** *British Journal of Clinical Pharmacology*, monthly. Journal. • *British Journal of Pharmacology*, monthly. Journal.

Center for the Study of Pharmacy and Therapeutics for the Elderly (CSPTE)
See: Entry 1895

★ 10403 ★ **Central American Society of Pharmacology (CASP)**
(Sociedad Centro-Americana de Farmacologia — SCF)
Dept. of Pharmacology
Faculty of Medicine
Univ. of Panama
Panama, Panama
Phone: 643701
Fax: 635622
Emperatriz De Quintero

Founded: 1976. **Members:** 38. **Languages:** English, Spanish. **Description:** Pharmacologists in 6 Central American countries.

★ 10404 ★ **Chemical Industry Institute of Toxicology (CIIT)**
PO Box 12137
Research Triangle Park, NC 27709
Phone: (919)558-1200
Fax: (919)558-1300
Dr. Roger O. McClellan, CEO & Pres.

Founded: 1974. **Members:** 47. **Description:** Chemical and pharmaceutical companies. Aims to develop the scientific data required for evaluation of the potential health risks of chemicals, pharmaceuticals, and consumer products. Works to: understand human health risk from occupational or environmental exposures; improve species extrapolations used in product safety evaluations; update the existing toxicological testing and investigation of commodity chemicals; develop improved testing methods; train professional toxicologists; serve health and environmental needs of the public through research in toxicology. Maintains scientific advisory panel. Provides assistantships for graduate and postdoctoral toxicological training. Conducts workshops. **Publications:** *CIIT Activities*, monthly. Newsletter.

★ 10405 ★ **Chinese Pharmacological Society**
1 Xian Nong Tan St.
Beijing 100050, People's Republic of China
Phone: 1 3013366
Fax: 1 3017757
Prof. Zhi-Bin Lin, Sec.Gen.

Founded: 1985. **Members:** 3,303. **Languages:** English, Japanese. **Description:** Pharmacologists and interested individuals in the People's Republic of China. Promotes the study of pharmacology. Conducts research programs. Fosters exchange among members and pharmacologists in other countries. Provides consulting services. **Publications:** *China Journal of Pharmacology and Toxicology*, periodic. Journal. • *Chinese Pharmacological Bulletin*. Newsletter. • *Chinese Pharmacology and Clinical Application*, periodic. Journal. • *Pharmacologica Sinica*, periodic. Journal. • *Pharmacology and Clinics of Chinese Materia Medica*. Directory.

Collegium Internationale Neuro-Psychopharmacologicum (CINP)
See: Entry 8204

★ 10406 ★ **CURE Formaldehyde Poisoning Association (CURE)**
9255 Lynnwood Rd.
Waconia, MN 55387
Phone: (612)442-4665
Connie Smrecek, Exec. Officer

Founded: 1980. **Description:** Individuals, health professionals, and attorneys who share an interest in the toxic effects of formaldehyde. Seeks to educate health and legal professionals concerning problems caused by formaldehyde. Lobbies on matters relating to formaldehyde. Conducts seminars. CURE is an acronym for Citizens United to Reduce Emissions (of Formaldehyde Poisoning Association). **Publications:** *Environmental Guardian*, 4/year. **Formerly:** Save Us From Formaldehyde Environmental Repercussions; (1985) SUFFER.

★ 10407 ★ **European Association of Poisons Centres and Clinical Toxicologists (EAPCCT)**
(Association Europeenne des Centres Anti-Poisons et de Toxicologie Clinique)
National Posions Information Service
(Birmingham Centre)
City Hospital
Birmingham, W. Midlands B18 7QH, England
Phone: 121 5074123
Fax: 121 5075580
Dr. Allister Vale, Pres.

Founded: 1964. **Members:** 269. **Languages:** English. **Description:** Scientists working in clinical toxicology and related fields. Works to improve contacts between clinical toxicologists and poisons information specialists. Represents clinical toxicologists before international organizations including the World Health Organization and the Commission of European Communities. **Publications:** *Journal of Toxicology: Clinical Toxicology*, bimonthly. Journal. • *Newsletter*, quarterly. Newsletter. **Formerly:** (1990) European Association of Poison Control Centres.

★ 10408 ★ **European Federation of Medicinal Chemistry (EFMC)**
Facultie de Medicin et de Pharmacie de Rouen
Ave. de l'Universite
BP 97
F-76803 Sainte Etienne Cedex, France
Prof. Olivier Lafont, Contact

Founded: 1962. **Members:** 19. **Languages:** English. **Description:** National medicinal chemistry societies. Works to advance the science of medicinal chemistry by promoting cooperation among member societies.

★ 10409 ★ **EUROTOX**
DLO State Institute for Quality Control of Agricultural Prod
PO Box 230
NL-6700 AE Wageningen, Netherlands
Phone: 8370 75453
Fax: 8370 17717
Aalbert Baars, Ph.D., Sec.Gen.

Founded: 1962. **Members:** 5,000. **National Groups:** 22. **Languages:** English. **Description:** Industrial, university, and government toxicology researchers in 50 countries. Purpose is to encourage and advance research in the field of drug toxicity and in other areas of toxicology. Fosters exchange of information concerning problems in toxicology. Topics of interest have included the effects of drugs on the human fetus, toxicological methods and their reliability, toxicity problems of organs such as the liver and the nervous system, carcinogenesis, and sensitization. Sponsors working groups and training courses in toxicology. **Publications:** *EUROTOX*, 3/year. Newsletter. • *EUROTOX Membership Directory*, periodic. Directory. Contains names and addresses of members. • *Proceedings of the Annual Meeting*.

★ 10410 ★ **Genetic Toxicology Association (GTA)**
c/o Gary Blackburn
1111 General Sullivan Rd.
Washington Crossing, PA 18977
Maria Cifone, Ph.D., Chm.

Founded: 1977. **Members:** 250. **Description:** Academic, industrial, and governmental genetic toxicologists. (Genetic toxicology is the study of the mutagenic properties of substances; mutagenicity is the capacity to induce mutations.) Seeks to keep members abreast of recent developments in genetic toxicology. Sponsors tutorials on research findings. Conducts placement service.

★ 10411 ★   International Association of Radiopharmacology (IAR)
Faculty of Pharmacy and Pharmaceutical Sciences
University of Alberta
Edmonton, AB, Canada T6G 2N8
Phone: (403)492-5905
Fax: (403)492-8241
Leonard I. Wiebe, Ph.D., Contact

Founded: 1980. **Members:** 185. **Description:** Scientists who utilize radiotracers (radioactive tracers) in biology and medicine. Promotes information regarding radiotracers used for biological or medical purposes. Sponsors teaching programs at medical schools. **Publications:** *Symposium Proceedings*, biennial.

★ 10412 ★   International Life Sciences Institute—North America (ILSINA)
1126 16th St. NW, No. 300
Washington, DC 20036
Phone: (202)659-0074
Fax: (202)659-3859
George E. Hardy, Jr., Exec.Dir.

Founded: 1985. **Members:** 60. **Description:** Sponsored by companies within the food, pharmaceutical, chemical, toxicology, and related industries. Promotes basic research and education in the areas of nutrition toxicology through support of research, scientific symposia, workshops, and monographs. Fosters career development of outstanding young scientists. **Publications:** *Nutrition Reviews*, monthly. • *Present Knowledge in Nutrition*, quinquennial. Also publishes monographs, reprints, scientific reports, and educational materials. **Formerly:** (1991) International Life Sciences Institute - Nutrition Foundation.

★ 10413 ★   International Society of Chemotherapy (ISC)
(Societe Internationale de Chimiotherapie)
Bakt. Institute
Rikshospitalet
N-0027 Oslo, Norway
Prof. T. Bergan, Sec.Gen.

Founded: 1961. **Members:** 10,000. **National Groups:** 30. **Regional Groups:** 5. **Local Groups:** 3. **Languages:** English. **Description:** Societies or specialized groups within societies that are concerned with chemotherapy; scientists and clinicians working in chemotherapy. (Chemotherapy is the use of chemical agents in the treatment or control of infectious and neoplastic diseases and immunological disorder.) Promotes the development of chemotherapy through scientific and educational means. Encourages cooperation between members and scientists in related fields. Urges formation of new societies in countries where such groups do not exist. Promotes and/or sponsors formation of international working groups and training projects in the field of antimicrobial, antiparasitic, and antineoplastic chemotherapy; coordinates their activities. Appoints commissions for special activities; sponsors conferences, symposia, lectures, and workshops. **Publications:** *Congress Proceedings*, biennial. • *Newsletter*, biennial. Newsletter.

★ 10414 ★   International Society on Toxinology (IST)
c/o Dr. Dietrich Mebs
University of Frankfurt
Kennedyallee 104
W-60596 Frankfurt, Germany
Phone: 69 63017563
Fax: 69 63015882
Mr. Dietrich Mebs, Sec.

Founded: 1961. **Members:** 600. **Regional Groups:** 3. **Description:** Biochemists, pharmacologists, immunologists, herpetologists, physiologists, microbiologists, ichthyologists, physicians, and others studying animal, plant, and microbial toxins (poisons and venoms). Seeks to advance knowledge on the properties of toxins and antitoxins derived from plant and animal tissues. **Publications:** Membership Directory, periodic. • Newsletter, quarterly. • *Toxicon: An International Journal Devoted to the Exchange of Knowledge on the Poisons Derived from Animals, Plants, and Microorganisms*, monthly. Includes meeting announcements. *Price:* $99.50/year for members; $635.25/year for institutions.

★ 10415 ★   International Union of Pharmacology (IUPHAR)
Universite Catholique de Louvain
Laboratoire de Pharmacologie
54, ave. Hippocrate
B-1200 Brussels, Belgium
Phone: 2 7645410
Fax: 2 7647308
Prof. Theophile Godfraind, Sec.Gen.

Founded: 1966. **Members:** 50. **Languages:** English. **Description:** National and international societies in pharmacology and related disciplines representing approximately 20,000 individuals. Purpose is to promote cooperation between pharmacological societies and encourage free international exchange of ideas and research. Acts as a forum for participation between related scientific bodies. Works to standardize the use of drugs worldwide. **Publications:** *Congress Proceedings*, quadrennial. • *Directory of IUPHAR*, annual. • Newsletter, semiannual.

★ 10416 ★   Korean Society of Pharmacology (KSP)
Yonsei Univ.
Dept. of Pharmacology
Seoul 120-752, Republic of Korea
Phone: 2 3615210
Fax: 2 3131894
Dong Goo Kim, M.D., Ph.D., Sec.Gen.

Founded: 1947. **Members:** 318. **Languages:** Korean. Does not correspond in English. **Description:** Pharmacologists; interested others. Encourages growth in the industry through information exchange. Promotes advancement in the field through research and educational programs. Represents members' interests. **Publications:** *Korean Journal of Pharmacology*, 3/year. Journal. • *Pharmacology Experiments for Students*, periodic.

Latin American Association of Environmental Mutagens, Carcinogens, and Teratogens Societies (LAAEMCTS)
See: Entry 5047

★ 10417 ★   Medical Letter (ML)
1000 Main St.
New Rochelle, NY 10801
Phone: (914)235-0500
Fax: (914)576-3377
Mark Abramowicz, M.D., Editor

Founded: 1959. **Description:** Gathers and publishes information on the therapeutic and side effects of drugs for the benefit of physicians and other members of the health professions. Emphasis is on new drugs. **Publications:** *Drugs of Choice from the Medical Letter*. • *Handbook of Antimicrobial Therapy*. Handbook. • *Medical Letter Handbook of Adverse Drug Interactions*. Handbook. • *Medical Letter on Drugs and Therapeutics*, biweekly. Newsletter. Evaluates drugs for physicians. *Price:* $37.50/year. **Formerly:** Drug and Therapeutic Information.

★ 10418 ★   Mediterranean Society of Chemotherapy (MSC)
(Societe Mediterraneenne de Chimiotherapie — SMC)
Istituto di Microbiologia Medica
Via C. Pascal 36
I-20133 Milan, Italy
Phone: 2 2664595
Fax: 2 70638741
Prof. Zivojin Zagar, Gen.Sec.

Founded: 1976. **Members:** 850. **National Groups:** 12. **Languages:** English, French. **Description:** University professors of microbiology, oncology, pharmacology, and infectious diseases; pharmaceutical research laboratory staff. Promotes antimicrobial and anti-tumor chemotherapy. **Publications:** *Journal of Chemotherapy - the International Journal of MSC*, bimonthly. Journal.

National Pesticide Telecommunication Network (NPTN)
See: Entry 5054

★ 10419 ★   Pan-American Society for Chemotherapy of Tuberculosis (PASCT)
(Sociedad Panamericana de Quimioterapia de la Tuberculosis — SAQT)
Las Heras 2131
1127 Buenos Aires, Argentina

Founded: 1970. **Members:** 600. **Languages:** English, French, Spanish. **Description:** Organizes international, national, and regional meetings to discuss all subjects related to chemotherapy of tuberculosis.

★ 10420 ★   Society for Medicinal Plant Research
(Gesellschaft fur Arzneipflanzenforschung — GA)
Am Grundbach 5
97271 Kleinrinderfeld, Germany
Phone: 931 8002271
Fax: 931 8002275
Dr. B. Frank, Sec.

Founded: 1953. **Members:** 1,000. **Languages:** English, German. **Description:** Scientists in 70 countries who promote medicinal plant research. Organized to serve as an international focal point for such interests as pharmacognosy, pharmacology, phytochemistry, plant biochemistry and physiology, chemistry of natural products; plant cell culture and application of medicinal plants in medicine. Acts as liaison with governments, pharmacopoeia commissions, and international health organizations on matters pertaining to the medicinal plant field. Serves as forum for international exchange of information on the different aspects of medicinal plant research. **Publications:** *Newsletter*, semiannual. Newsletter. • *Planta Medica*, bimonthly. Journal. **Formerly:** (1970) German Society for Medicinal Plant Research.

Society of Toxicologic Pathologists (STP)
See: Entry 10138

★ 10421 ★ Society of Toxicology (SOT)
1767 Business Center Dr., Ste. 302
Reston, VA 22090-5332
Phone: (703)438-3115
Fax: (703)438-3113
Shawn Douglas Lopez, Exec.Dir.

Founded: 1961. **Members:** 3,400. **Regional Groups:** 16. **Description:** Persons who have conducted and published original investigations in some phase of toxicology and who have a continuing professional interest in this field. (Toxicology is the quantitative study of materials that may or may not adversely affect the health of humans, animals, and/or the environment.) Sponsors placement service. **Publications:** *Fundamental and Applied Toxicology*, 8/year. Technical journal of current research in the field of toxicology as it relates to pharmacology; includes book reviews. *Price:* Included in membership dues; $264/year for U.S. and Canadian nonmembers; $313/year for overseas nonmembers. • *Society of Toxicology--Membership Directory*, annual. Directory. Arranged by name, specialty, geographical location, and employer. Includes corporate member list and calendar of events. *Price:* Included in membership dues. • *Society of Toxicology--Newsletter*, 5/year. Newsletter. Membership activities newsletter. Includes calendar of events, chapter news, legislative news, obituaries, classified ads, and publications list. *Price:* Included in membership dues. • *Toxicology and Applied Pharmacology*, monthly. Technical journal on toxicology research. *Price:* Included in membership dues; $762/year for U.S. and Canadian nonmembers; $904/year for overseas nonmembers.

★ 10422 ★ South African Pharmacological Society (SAPS) (Suid Afrikaanse Farmakologie Vereniging — SAFV)
Dept. of Pharmacology
PO Box 225
Medunsa 0204, Republic of South Africa
Phone: 11 9292173
Fax: 12 582323
Dr. A.K. Aucamp, Sec.

Members: 265. **Languages:** Afrikaans, English. **Description:** Pharmacists; pharmacologists; physicians; chemical pathologists; psychiatrists; analytical chemists; statisticians. Promotes work in pharmacology and related fields.

Tardive Dyskinesia / Tardive Dystonia National Association (TD/TDNA)
See: Entry 8316

★ 10423 ★ Toxicological History Society (THiS)
5757 Hall St. SE
Grand Rapids, MI 49546-3845
Phone: (616)774-5329
John H. Trestrail, III, Sec.

Founded: 1990. **Members:** 60. **Description:** Individuals interested in the researching and documentation of the history of poisons, antidotes, and the impact of toxicology on events in world history. Maintains speakers' bureau; has compiled bibliography. **Publications:** *Mithridata*, semiannual. Newsletter. Available to members only.

★ 10424 ★ Toxicology Forum (TF)
1575 Eye St. NW, Ste. 800
Washington, DC 20005
Phone: (202)659-0030
Fax: (202)789-7668
Charlene D. Anderson, Admin.

Founded: 1975. **Members:** 127. **Description:** Corporations (68) and individuals (59) interested in toxicology and representing industry, government, universities, and laboratories throughout the world. Seeks to facilitate communication among scientific decision-makers. Aids in developing safety assessments and establishing regulations concerning toxicology. Areas of study and research reflect concerns of membership and the public, and have dealt with subjects such as epidemiology, biotechnology, genetics, carcinogens, saccharine, and caffeine. Maintains archives.

★ 10425 ★ World Federation of Associations of Clinical Toxicology Centers and Poison Control Centers (Federation Mondiale des Associations des Centres de Toxicologies Clinique et des Centres Anti-Poisons)
150, cours Albert-Thomas
F-69372 Lyon Cedex 2, France
Phone: 7 8541414
Fax: 7 2345567
Prof. Louis Roche, Gen.Sec.

Founded: 1975. **Members:** 37. **Languages:** English, French, Russian, Spanish. **Description:** National and international organizations dealing with toxicology, associations of poison control centers, and national poison control centers. Purposes are: to provide a focal point for members; to assist developing countries in toxicology education and training; to collect and disseminate information; to encourage primary prevention in terms of the control of products and their distribution, and consumer information and education. Maintains liaison with the World Health Organization. Compiles statistics. Organizes working groups. **Publications:** *Bulletin of the World Federation*, quarterly. Bulletin. • *Collection de Medecine Legale et Toxicologie Medicale*, periodic. • *Journal de Toxicologie Medicale*, bimonthly. Journal. • *Membership List*, periodic. Has also published *Catastrophes Toxiques* and other books. **Also Known As:** CTC World Federation.

Research Centers

★ 10426 ★ Aloe Research Foundation
4250 N. Beltline
Irving, TX 75038
Phone: (214)257-2563
Fax: (214)594-0654
Elizabeth Cooke, Contact

Research Activities and Fields: Aloe vera, UVB, skin damage and the skin immune system; establishment of standards for aloe; effect of aloe on the inhibition of chemical carcinogenesis; effect of aloe vera on denature stomatitis; bioactivities of aloe substances; effect of aloe on wound healing; aloe extracts as potential antisickling agents; differentiation function of aloe on human leukemia HL-60 cells; antioxidative activity and liposomal encapsulation of aloe extracts; stabilization and preservation of bioactive substances of aloe gel; experimental research of aloe on the effect of anti-senility; effects of aloe vera on biological aging and pathological processes; wound healing potential of aloe and antibacterial actions; and characterization and identification of bioactive components of aloe. **Publications:** *ALOE Today*.

Arizona Heart Institute
See: Entry 2881

★ 10427 ★ Baylor College of Medicine Center for Experimental Therapeutics
6550 Fannin St.
Houston, TX 77030
Phone: (713)798-7593
Fax: (713)798-6956
Kenneth Moise, M.D., Dir.

Research Activities and Fields: Metabolic problems, including clinical laboratory studies of drug metabolism and drug toxicity. Develops new analytical biochemical methods for study of human metabolic problems and conducts laboratory studies in gas chromatography, mass spectrometry, and computer technology. **Formerly:** Lipid Research Center; Institute for Lipid Research.

★ 10428 ★ Center for Imaging and Pharmaceutical Research
Massachusetts General Hospital East
Bldg. 149, 13th St.
Charlestown, MA 02129-2060
Phone: (617)726-7828
Fax: (617)726-7830
Dr. Gerald Wolf, Dir.

Research Activities and Fields: Use of modern imaging technology in drug development, including investigation of radiologic imaging approaches that more accurately measure local drug concentrations, drug activity, and drug-induced alterations in tissue perfusion and tissue metabolism. Specific activities include in vivo imaging to investigate the underlying mechanisms of disease progression; correlation of blood-brain barrier and neurochemical events with clinically relevant imaging parameters; designing and testing of novel computational techniques for measuring local spatial and temporal changes and the correlations between them on spatially aligned dynamic images; discovery and testing of new contrast aents; and validating noninvasive quantitative methods for visualizing dynamic in vivo functions using CT and MRI. **E-mail Address:** gerry@upr.mgh.harvard.edu.

★ **10429** ★ **Chemical Industry Institute of Toxicology**
6 Davis Dr.
PO Box 12137
Research Triangle Park, NC 27709
Phone: (919)558-1200
Fax: (919)558-1300
Roger O. McClellan, D.V.M., Pres.

Research Activities and Fields: Toxicity data obtained at various levels of biological organization in order to assess exposure-related human health risks. Specific research includes chemical carcinogenesis with investigations in DNA-reactive, mitogenic, cytotoxic, and receptor-mediated agents; risk assessment methodology and extrapolation modeling; respiratory/fiber toxicology; genetic toxicology; neurotoxicology; and reproductive/developmental toxicology. **Publications:** Newsletter, *CIIT Activities* (monthly); Annual Report.

Children's Psychopharmacology Unit
See: Entry 7553

★ **10430** ★ **Cornell University**
Laboratory of Pediatric Critical Care
515 E. 71st St., Rm. S613
New York, NY 10021
Phone: (212)746-3270
Daniel A. Notterman, M.D., Dir.

Research Activities and Fields: Adrenergic receptor pharmacology, including receptor-related events at the cellular and molecular levels, and molecular biology of acute lung injury. **E-mail Address:** danotte@mail.mtd.cornell.edu.

Dana-Farber Cancer Institute
National Cooperative Drug Discovery Group for the Treatment of AIDS
See: Entry 6768

★ **10431** ★ **Florida A&M University**
Center for Anti-Inflammatory Research
201 Dyson Pharmacy
Tallahassee, FL 32307
Phone: (904)559-3661
Fax: (904)599-3347
Henry J. Lee, Dir.

Research Activities and Fields: Anti-inflammatory steroids, including development of organic extraction procedures for pharmacokinetic studies.

★ **10432** ★ **Florida State University**
Center for Biomedical Toxicological Research and Hazardous Waste Management
Bellamy Bldg.
Tallahassee, FL 32306
Phone: (904)644-5524
Fax: (906)574-6704
Dr. Roy C. Herndon, Dir.

Research Activities and Fields: Provides an administrative and resource base from which faculty within the University can conduct re-search in the areas of biomedicine, environmental toxicology, health effects assessment, environmental assessment, risk analysis, and hazardous waste management. Other areas include occupational health concerns, ecological effects of aquatic pollutants, effects of toxic organic substances in the environment, and the effects of heavy metals and other inorganic pollutants on aquatic organisms. **E-mail Address:** buda94@chaerse.fsu.edu. **Formerly:** Center for Biomedical and Toxicological Research and Hazardous Waste Management.

George Washington University
National Cooperative Drug Discovery Group for the Treatment of AIDS
See: Entry 6771

★ **10433** ★ **Hawaii Heptachlor Research and Education Foundation**
1188 Bishop St., Ste. 2308
Honolulu, HI 96813
Phone: (808)531-2963
Fax: (808)531-3050
Dr. Willis Butler, Pres.

Research Activities and Fields: Sponsors and supports medical research and medical treatment programs, including research on the effects of pesticides and other toxic substances on humans, and methods and treatment of medical problems caused by exposure to such substances. Current research projects include a medical monitoring program, which will examine the health effects of chronic exposure of Oahu's residents to Heptachlor in dairy products. Other projects sponsored by the Foundation include Induction of Parkinsonian Syndrome by Heptachlor and a feasibility study on the long-term health effects in women of exposure to chlorinated hydrocarbon insecticides. **Publications:** *Heptachlor and Health* (newsletter); videotape providing an overview of heptachlor exposure on Oahu.

★ **10434** ★ **Hazardous Substance Management Research Center**
New Jersey Institute of Technology
Newark, NJ 07102
Phone: (201)596-3233
Fax: (201)802-1946
Dr. Richard S. Magee, Exec.Dir.

Research Activities and Fields: Hazardous and toxic substances, particularly in the processes of incineration, biological and chemical treatment, and physical treatment. Also interested in geotechnical site assessment and remedial action, health effects assessment, and public policy and education. **Publications:** Newsletter (quarterly). **E-mail Address:** magee@admin1.njit.edu. **Formerly:** Industry/University Cooperative Center for Research in Hazardous and Toxic Substances (1988).

★ **10435** ★ **Herb Research Foundation**
1007 Pearl St., Ste. 200
Boulder, CO 80302
Phone: (303)449-2265
Fax: (303)449-7849
Rob McCaleb, Pres.

Research Activities and Fields: Pharmacognosy, ethnobotany, and toxicology of medicinal plants. **Publications:** *HerbalGram*; Newsletter.

★ **10436** ★ **IIT Research Institute**
10 W. 35th St.
Chicago, IL 60616
Phone: (312)567-4000
Fax: (312)567-4087
John B. Scott, Pres.

Research Activities and Fields: Chemistry, electronics, toxicology, cancer research, hazards analysis, fire/safety research, electromagnetic effects, microwave and electro-optics, thermodynamics, railroad technology, petroleum and energy research, manufacturing productivity, life sciences, computer sciences, software engineering, medical electronics, air and water pollution, environmental quality, indoor air quality, and product and process development. **Publications:** *Manufacturing Competetiveness Frontiers* (monthly). **Formerly:** Armour Research Foundation.

Indiana University-Purdue University at Indianapolis
Laboratory for Experimental Oncology
See: Entry 6052

★ **10437** ★ **Indiana University-Purdue University at Indianapolis**
Pharmacology Research Laboratory
Sch. of Medicine
635 Barnhill Dr.
Indianapolis, IN 46202-5120
Phone: (317)274-7844
Fax: (317)274-7714
Dr. Henry R. Besch, Jr., Chm.

Research Activities and Fields: Cardiovascular pharmacology, molecular toxicology, drug metabolism, cyclic AMP, membrane biophysics, cancer chemotherapy and cardiac glycosides, and antiarrythmics, including studies on metabolism of transplanted tumors, structure activity relations of cardiac glycosides, and analyesics. **E-mail Address:** istp100@indyvax.edu.

★ **10438** ★ **Inhalation Toxicology Research Institute**
PO Box 5890
Albuquerque, NM 87185
Phone: (505)845-1169
Fax: (505)845-1193
Dr. Joe L. Mauderly, Pres. and Dir.

Research Activities and Fields: Inhalation toxicology of airborne particles, fibers, vapors, and gases encountered in the general environment or in occupational settings. Studies focus on the chemical and radioactive properties of materials. Research program includes basic and applied studies of aerosol generation and characterization, deposition and retention of inhaled materials, pathogenesis of respiratory diseases, and toxicokinetics of inhaled materials. Activities emphasize mechanisms of lung cancer and noncancerous lung disease. **Publications:** Annual Report; *ITRI Newsletter* (bimonthly). **E-mail Address:** mauderly@lucy.tli.org.

Institute for Clinical Science, Inc.
See: Entry 10143

★ 10439 ★ Institute for Drug Development
14960 Omnicron
San Antonio, TX 78245-3217
Phone: (210)677-3800
Fax: (210)677-0058
Daniel D. Von Hoff, M.D., Dir.

Research Activities and Fields: Anticancer drug development. Research activities in the Discovery Research Section include functions of extrachromosomal DNA fragments in tumor cells; tumor progression (oncogenesis); differentiation of human tumors; amplified oncogenes and drug resistance genes on extrachromosomal DNA fragments; chromosomal rearrangement and mechanism of repair of broken chromosomes in mammalian cells; mapping of human chromosome 3; mapping on the short arm of human chromosome 17; and transgenic mouse models for various types of cancer. Research areas in the Preclinical Research and Development Section include the interruption of oncogenic pathways involving specific subtypes of tubulin and topoisomerase I and II; measurement of telomerase activity; growth inhibitory activity of cancer cells from biopsy tissue; and cell cycle distribution in relation to drug-cell interactions, drug resistance, and programmed cell death. Clinical Investigations Section researches new drugs as they are first introduced into humans, and examines the pharmacokinetic profile of new drugs.

International Life Sciences Institute Research Foundation
See: Entry 9504

★ 10440 ★ Inter-University Centre for Toxicology
Departement de pharmacologie
Faculte de medecine
C.P. 6128, succursale A
Montreal, PQ, Canada H3C 3J7
Phone: (514)343-7722
Fax: (514)343-6120
Gabriel L. Plaa, Dir.

Research Activities and Fields: Biological detection of environmental contaminants in living organisms, characterization of harmful effects of potentially toxic chemicals, and development of diagnostic tests and methods for evaluating toxicity.

Johns Hopkins University Behavioral Pharmacology Research Unit
See: Entry 12095

★ 10441 ★ Laboratories for Developmental Therapeutics
St. Jude Children's Research Hosptial
332 N. Lauderdale
Memphis, TN 38101
Phone: (901)522-0456
Fax: (901)521-1688
Dr. Janet Houghton, Dir.

Research Activities and Fields: Human tumor xenografts, experimental chemotherapy, selectivity of drug action in in vivo, cytostasis and cytotoxicity, colon carcinoma and rhabdomyosarcoma, thymidylate synthase, molecular events controlling cell death, and relationships between genes involved in cell cycle control and sensitivity to chemotherapy.

Long Island University Pharmaceutical Study Center
See: Entry 10629

Massachusetts Institute of Technology Laboratory of Neuroendocrine Regulation
See: Entry 8391

★ 10442 ★ Medical Care and Research Foundation
1420 Ogden
Denver, CO 80218-1910
Phone: (303)831-0267
Frank B. McGlone, M.D., Exec.Dir.

Research Activities and Fields: Drug studies. **Publications:** *Court Visitor Training Manual*; *Providing New Directions, New Hope in Board and Care: Guidelines for Establishing and Operating Small Facilities.*

★ 10443 ★ Medical College of Pennsylvania and Hahnemann University Clinical Research Unit
Division of Clinical Pharmacology
3200 Henry Ave.
Philadelphia, PA 19129
Phone: (215)842-4575
Fax: (215)848-9560
Anthony J. Piraino, M.D., Division Chief

Research Activities and Fields: Pharmacology, including phase one and two clinical drug trials. Maintains a 15-bed clinical research unit.

★ 10444 ★ Medical College of Pennsylvania and Hahnemann University Laboratory of Human Pharmacology
Dept. of Pharmacology
School of Medicine
Broad & Vine Sts.
Philadelphia, PA 19102
Phone: (215)762-8237
Fax: (215)762-3722
Benjamin Calesnick, M.D., Dir.

Research Activities and Fields: Using such analytical methods as chromatography, colorimetry, and spectrometry, the Laboratory studies the metabolism, potentiation, and toxicity of drugs, including antibiotics, ataractics, pesticides, sedatives, solvents, stimulants, aerosols, fumes, and radioactive chemicals. Also examines the induction or inhibition of microsomal metabolizing systems, and pollutants.

★ 10445 ★ Medical University of South Carolina Interdisciplinary Program in Cell and Molecular Pharmacology and Experimental Therapeutics
171 Ashley Ave.
Charleston, SC 29425
Phone: (803)792-2471
Dr. Harry Margolius, Chm.

Research Activities and Fields: Basic and clinical research in pharmacology, toxicology, molecular genetics and structural biology, including structure-function studies of proteins for primary sequence, posttranslational modifications, and characterization of the binding site of ligands; investigations of molecular design; and studies on cellular and molecular processes that control systemic arterial pressure, especially arachidonate metabolism, neurotransmitters, drug disposition and drug toxicity. Conducts studies of excitation-contraction coupling, excitation-secretion coupling, and water transport and regulation in cells and membrane mechanisms by norepinephrine, arachidonic acid metabolites, kallikrein-kinins, atrial peptides, and antihypertensive drugs. Also conducts studies of isolated cells, cell fragments, and isolated membranes, as well as studies on anesthetized and conscious animals and volunteer patients with hypertension, shock, and other cardiovascular-renal abnormalities.

★ 10446 ★ Michigan State University Institute for Environmental Toxicology
C231 Holden Hall
East Lansing, MI 48824
Phone: (517)353-6469
Fax: (517)335-4603
Lawrence J. Fischer, Ph.D., Dir.

Research Activities and Fields: Analytical toxicology, behavioral toxicology, biochemical toxicology, botany and plant pathology, carcinogenesis, ecotoxicology, environmental law, fate of chemicals in the environment, food toxicology, genetic toxicology, human epidemiology, risk/benefit assessment and regulatory decision making, terrestrial toxicology, and hazardous waste management. **E-mail Address:** lfisher@msu.edu. **Formerly:** Center for Environmental Toxicology (1991).

★ 10447 ★ Mississippi State Chemical Laboratory
Mississippi State Univ.
PO Box CR
Mississippi State, MS 39762
Phone: (601)325-3324
Fax: (601)325-7807
Dr. Earl G. Alley, State Chemist

Research Activities and Fields: Chemistry, toxicology of pesticides, natural toxins, industrial chemicals and exposure of humans in work environments, and priority pollutants, including analytical studies on fertilizers, foods, animal feeds, paints, oils, varnishes, gasoline, and environmental distribution and degradation of pesticides. **Publications:** Research Progress Reports; Annual Report. **E-mail Address:** earl@u5000.mscl.msstate.edu.

Ohio State University Analytical Toxicology Laboratory
See: Entry 13154

★ 10448 ★ Ohio State University Clinical Pharmacology Division
College of Medicine
Graves Hall, Rm. 5084
333 W. 10th Ave.
Columbus, OH 43210-1239
Phone: (614)292-8600
Fax: (614)292-4253
Dr. Nicholas Gerber, Dir.

Research Activities and Fields: Clinical drug studies.

★ **10449** ★ **Oregon Health Sciences University**
DMSO Research Laboratory and Clinic
3181 SW Sam Jackson Park Rd., L225
Portland, OR 97201
Phone: (503)494-8474
Fax: (503)494-5738
Stanley W. Jacob, M.D., Head

Research Activities and Fields: Clinical and basic science studies of pharmacological properties of dimethyl sulfoxide (DMSO). Provides staff consultants in clinical and basic research relevant to pharmacological activity of dimethyl sulfoxide. Supervises DMSO clinic.

Oregon State University
Department of Food Science and Technology
See: Entry 9522

★ **10450** ★ **Oregon State University**
Marine / Freshwater Biomedical Sciences Center
Dept. of Food Science
Corvallis, OR 97331
Phone: (503)737-4193
Dr. George S. Bailey, Dir.

Research Activities and Fields: Food toxicology, carcinogenesis, and nutrition, especially studies on food-borne carcinogens and anti-carcinogens using rainbow trout. Also studies neurotoxicology and immunotoxicology in model fish systems. **Formerly:** Food Toxicology and Nutrition Laboratory.

Purdue University
Center for AIDS Research
See: Entry 6783

★ **10451** ★ **Reproductive Toxicology Center**
Columbia Hospital for Women
2440 M St. NW, Ste. 217
Washington, DC 20037-1404
Phone: (202)293-5137
Fax: (202)778-6199
Dr. Anthony Scialli, M.D., Dir.

Research Activities and Fields: Effects of the chemical and physical environment on human fertility, pregnancy, and development. **Publications:** *Reproductive Toxicology.*

★ **10452** ★ **Risk Science Research Center**
2801 S. Univ. Ave.
Little Rock, AR 72204-1085
Phone: (501)371-1980
Joyce Wroten, Dir.

Research Activities and Fields: Methods for assessing and verifying the risk of chemical agents to human health, including studies on reproductive and developmental problems. Also investigates chemical contamination of food.

★ **10453** ★ **Rockefeller University**
Laboratory of Metabolism-Pharmacology
1230 York Ave.
New York, NY 10021-6399
Phone: (212)327-8000
Attallah Kappas, Head

Research Activities and Fields: Regulation of heme biosynthesis and heme catabolism as affected by those genetic and environmental factors that have major influences on the oxidative metabolism of drugs, hormones, and environmental chemicals in liver and other tissues.

★ **10454** ★ **Roswell Park Cancer Institute**
Grace Cancer Drug Center
Elm & Carlton Sts.
Buffalo, NY 14263
Phone: (716)845-5860
Fax: (716)845-8857
Dr. Enrico Mihich, Dir.

Research Activities and Fields: Basic and developmental studies of new therapeutic means to control cancer, establishment of a strong program in clinical pharmacology in cooperation with clinical departments at the Institute, and further development of basic research and advance training in various areas of biochemical pharmacology related to cancer therapeutics. Emphasizes the study of chemotherapeutic agents and the evaluation of their selective toxicity against tumors.

★ **10455** ★ **Rutgers University**
Controlled Drug-Delivery Research Center
College of Pharmacy
41 Gordon Rd., Ste. D
Piscataway, NJ 08854
Phone: (908)445-6180
Fax: (908)445-6175
Prof. Yie W. Chien, Dir.

Research Activities and Fields: Transdermal controlled and enhanced drug delivery, noninvasive and modulated delivery of peptide/protein drugs, targeting drug delivery, and transmucosal controlled drug administration, as applied to the development of novel drug delivery systems. **Publications:** *Novel Drug Delivery Systems; Nasal Systemic Drug Delivery; Transdermal Controlled Systemic Medications.*

★ **10456** ★ **S.E. Child Safety Institute of the Childrens Hospital of Alabama**
1600 7th Ave. S.
Birmingham, AL 35233
Phone: (205)939-9720
Fax: (205)939-9245
Dr. Bill King, Dir.

Research Activities and Fields: Poisonings, including studies on prescription drug ingestions in preschool age children, research on adolescent parasuicides, and epidemiology of childhood trauma. Provides statewide poison control. **Publications:** *Poison Bulletin* (quarterly). **Formerly:** Poison Control Center of the Childrens Hospital of Alabama.

Southern Illinois University at Carbondale
Comparative Physiology Lab
See: Entry 2622

Spellman Center for HIV-Related Disease
See: Entry 6789

Stanford University
Center for AIDS Research
See: Entry 6790

Stanford University
Laboratory for Transplantation Immunology
See: Entry 12886

★ **10457** ★ **State University of New York at Buffalo**
Center for Pharmacoepidemiology Research
310 Cooke Hall
Buffalo, NY 14260
Phone: (716)636-2826
Thaddeus H. Grasela, Jr., Ph.d, Dir.

Research Activities and Fields: Maintains the Drug Surveillance Network, which monitors the incidence of specific drug-associated adverse events, identifies risk factors, detects previously unsuspected adverse effects of newly-approved drugs in patients, and assesses the relative efficacy of newly marked agents as compared to established therapies.

★ **10458** ★ **State University of New York at Buffalo**
Clinical Pharmacokinetics Laboratory
Millard Fillmore Hospital
3 Gates Circle
Buffalo, NY 14209
Phone: (716)887-4704
Fax: (716)887-4566
Dr. Jerome J. Schentag, Dir.

Research Activities and Fields: Pharmacokinetics and pharmacodynamics of drugs in volunteers and hospitalized patients. Major emphasis on geriatric patients, pharmacology, nutrition, metabolism, and infectious disease states. Other research activities include technology transfer using computer software in the critical care unit and influence of disease states on the pharmacokinetics and pharmacodynamics of drugs. **Publications:** Research Papers.

★ **10459** ★ **State University of New York at Buffalo**
Toxicology Research Center
102 Farber Hall
Buffalo, NY 14214-3000
Phone: (716)829-2125
Paul Kostyniak, Ph.D., Dir.

Research Activities and Fields: Toxicology-related research and services, including the development of tests to evaluate toxic effects of new or presently existing drugs and chemicals, experiment design and analysis, assay development, metabolite identification, development of in vitro models to evaluate toxicity and mechanism of action of chemicals, chemical compounds research, drug-receptor interactions, drug development, organic synthesis, and xenobiotic metabolism and deposition. Serves as a Certified Analytical Laboratory for U.S. Environmental Protection Agency (EPA) methodology.

★ **10460** ★ **Texas A&M University**
Institute of Ocular Pharmacology
College of Medicine
College Station, TX 77843
Phone: (409)845-2817
Fax: (409)845-0699
Dr. George C.Y. Chiou, Dir.

Research Activities and Fields: Ocular pharmacology (the use of drugs for treating eye disease), including glaucoma, ocular inflamation, retinal degeneration, myopia, and cataract treatment. **Publications:** *Journal of Ocular Pharmacology; Opthalmic Toxicology.*

★ 10461 ★ **Thomas Jefferson University**
Environmental Medicine and Toxicology
Division
Jefferson Medical College
1020 Locust St., Rm. 314-JAH
Philadelphia, PA 19107
Phone: (215)955-8381
Dr. Lance Simpson, Dir.

Research Activities and Fields: Mechanisms and actions of toxins at the cellular, subcellular, and molecular levels.

★ 10462 ★ **Toxicology Research Centre**
Univ. of Saskatchewan
Saskatoon, SK, Canada S7N 0W0
Phone: (306)966-7441
Fax: (306)931-1664
Dr. H.B. Schiefer, Dir.

Research Activities and Fields: Toxicology research and consultation as related to western Canada, including food and nutritional toxicology, water quality, ecotoxicology, biopesticide toxicology, and toxicology related to agriculture, buildings, petroleum, mining, and new industries. Develops and validates alternative toxicity assays. **Publications:** Pesticide and other Factsheets (in response to need).

U.S. Department of Agriculture
Agricultural Research Service
Food Animal Protection Research
Laboratory
See: Entry 13185

★ 10463 ★ **U.S. Department of Agriculture**
Agricultural Research Service
Richard B. Russell Agricultural Research
Center
Toxicology and Mycotoxin Research Unit
PO Box 5677
Athens, GA 30613
Phone: (404)546-3158
Fax: (404)546-3367
Dr. William P. Norred, Research Leader

Research Activities and Fields: Mission is to investigate the toxicological properties of mycotoxins and other naturally-occuring toxins in order to assess the potential hazards to human and animal health and to provide the means for reducing or eliminating toxins from food and feed. Properties of fungal metabolites are studied, with major emphasis on: 1) isolation, identification, and growth of suspect fungi from toxic foods, feeds, and forages; 2) development of chemical and biological tests to define the fungi toxins; 3) determination of the actions of the toxins on biological systems in order to determine mechanisms of toxicity; and 4) definition of control mechanisms that can be used to reduce or eliminate the hazards of fungal contamination of crops.

U.S. Department of Defense
Armed Forces Institute of Pathology
Center for Advanced Pathology
Environmental and Drug-Induced
Pathology Department
See: Entry 10150

U.S. Department of Defense
Armed Forces Institute of Pathology
Office of the Armed Forces Medical
Examiner
Toxicology Division
See: Entry 10172

U.S. Department of Defense
Army Medical Research and Development
Command
Walter Reed Army Institute of Research
Experimental Therapeutics Division
See: Entry 7831

U.S. Department of Defense
Naval Medical Research and Development
Command
Naval Medical Research Institute
Detachment (Toxicology)
See: Entry 7851

U.S. Department of Health and Human
Services
Food and Drug Administration
Center for Food Safety and Applied
Nutrition
See: Entry 10996

★ 10464 ★ **U.S. Department of Health and**
Human Services
Food and Drug Administration
National Center for Toxicological Research
NCTR Drive, Hwy. 365 N.
County Rd. 3
Jefferson, AR 72079
Phone: (501)543-7516
Fax: (501)543-7576
Dr. Arthur R. Norris, Acting Director

Research Activities and Fields: Conducts highly sophisticated research efforts to study the biological effects of potentially toxic chemicals, as well as the complex mechanisms that govern their toxicity. Collectively these programs seek to define risks to human health of exposure to toxicants in foods, animal and human drugs, cosmetics, medical devices, and biologics, and to improve the ability to predict the human risk factor imposed by toxic agents. Conducts studies aimed at understanding of dose-response relationships for evaluation of genetic aberrations, birth defects, cancer, and biochemical and metabolic alterations induced in animals, and their relevance to human health. Research programs include: applied and environmental microbiology, applied toxicology, neurotoxicology, nutritional modulation or risk and toxicity, quantitative risk assessment/extrapolation, solid toxicity, and transgenics.

U.S. Department of Health and Human
Services
National Cancer Institute
Division of Cancer Treatment
Developmental Therapeutics Program
See: Entry 6157

U.S. Department of Health and Human
Services
National Cancer Institute
Division of Cancer Treatment
Investigational Drug Branch
See: Entry 6159

U.S. Department of Health and Human
Services
National Cancer Institute
Laboratory of Biological Chemistry
See: Entry 6176

U.S. Department of Health and Human
Services
National Cancer Institute
Laboratory of Molecular Pharmacology
See: Entry 6196

U.S. Department of Health and Human
Services
National Heart, Lung, and Blood Institute
Laboratory of Chemical Pharmacology
See: Entry 2950

U.S. Department of Health and Human
Services
National Institute on Alcohol Abuse and
Alcoholism
Physiologic and Pharmacologic Studies
Laboratory
See: Entry 12113

U.S. Department of Health and Human
Services
National Institute of Diabetes and
Digestive and Kidney Diseases
Laboratory of Biochemical Pharmacology
See: Entry 2642

U.S. Department of Health and Human
Services
National Institute of Diabetes and
Digestive and Kidney Diseases
Laboratory of Bioorganic Chemistry
See: Entry 2644

U.S. Department of Health and Human
Services
National Institute on Drug Abuse
Addiction Research Center
Clinical Pharmacology Branch
See: Entry 12116

U.S. Department of Health and Human
Services
National Institute on Drug Abuse
Addiction Research Center
Preclinical Pharmacology Research
Laboratory
See: Entry 12119

U.S. Department of Health and Human
Services
National Institute on Drug Abuse
Basic Research Division
Behavioral Pharmacology Branch
See: Entry 12122

U.S. Department of Health and Human
Services
National Institute of Environmental Health
Sciences
Laboratory of Cellular and Molecular
Pharmacology
See: Entry 5106

U.S. Department of Health and Human Services
National Institute of Environmental Health Sciences
Laboratory of Reproductive and Developmental Toxicology
See: Entry 5111

★ 10465 ★ **U.S. Department of Health and Human Services**
National Institute of General Medical Sciences
Pharmacology and Biorelated Chemistry Program
5333 Westbard Ave., Rm. 919
Bethesda, MD 20892
Phone: (301)594-7808
Fax: (301)594-7728
Dr. Michael E. Rogers, Acting Director

Research Activities and Fields: PBC supports research and research training in the pharmacological sciences. Program's goal is to provide an improved understanding of the biological phenomena and related chemical and molecular processes involved in the actions of therapeutic drugs and their metabolites. Support for research is provided through the award of individual investigator-initiated research project grants and research center and program project grants. The center grants and the smaller program project grants consist of core groups of pharmacologists, anesthesiologists, chemists, and other basic scientists and clinicians involved in a multifaceted approach to a common problem. PBC supports the training of predoctoral students by institutional awards in the areas of pharmacological sciences and biotechnology; and the National Institute of General Medical Sciences provides postdoctoral support to physicians for research training in clinical pharmacology and anesthesiology at specific institutions. In addition to these formal institutional training programs, PBC supports postdoctoral fellows on individual fellowships in the areas of biochemistry, pharmacological sciences, anesthesiology, clinical pharmacology, and biotechnology (Lawton Chiles Fellowships in Biotechnology).

★ 10466 ★ **U.S. Department of Health and Human Services**
National Institute of General Medical Sciences
Pharmacology Research Associate Program
5333 Westbard Ave.
Bethesda, MD 20892
Phone: (301)496-7707
Fax: (301)402-0019
Christine K. Carrico, Ph.D., Director

Research Activities and Fields: Program is a small, highly selective intramural activity aimed at developing leaders in pharmacological research for key positions in academic, industrial, and government research laboratories. Each year 11 recently trained scientists are selected for a two-year period of postdoctoral research in laboratories of the National Institutes of Health and Alcohol, Drug Abuse, and Mental Health Administration. Associates conduct research under the direction of one or more than 120 senior scientists and may take coursework

in areas of their choice, such as applied mathematics, experimental statistics, medicinal chemistry, human biochemical genetics, and molecular biophysics. Since 1978, Program has specifically targeted several positions to clinical pharmacology (considered a shortage area). Applicants for such positions must have an M.D. degree, a minimum of one year of graduate medical training (internship or residency), and a demonstrated interest in a research career in clinical pharmacology.

U.S. Department of Health and Human Services
National Institute of Mental Health
Biochemical Genetics Laboratory
See: Entry 7617

U.S. Department of Health and Human Services
National Institute for Occupational Safety and Health
Biomedical and Behavioral Science Division
Experimental Toxicology Branch
See: Entry 9829

★ 10467 ★ **U.S. Department of Health and Human Services**
Public Health Service
National Toxicology Program
PO Box 12233
Research Triangle Park, NC 27709
Phone: (919)541-3991
Fax: (919)541-2260
Dr. Kenneth Olden, Director

Research Activities and Fields: Program's primary mission is to strengthen the science base in toxicology and coordinate research and testing activities on toxic chemicals. NTP's goals are to: 1) develop a reliable series of relatively inexpensive short-term tests and protocols useful for the public health regulation of toxic chemicals, including the development of test batteries to assess genetic, neurobehavioral, and immunological toxicities; 2) expand the toxicological profiles of chemicals tested; 3) increase the rate of testing of chemicals for such toxic effects as carcinogenicity, mutagenicity, and reproductive and developmental effects (NTP also examines the chemicals for neurobehavioral, immunological, and other toxic effects where appropriate) within funding limits; and 4) disseminate results of NTP's testing and methods development programs to government research and regulatory agencies, industry, labor, environmental groups, the scientific community, and the public. Chemicals chosen for testing are those that involve widespread or intense human exposure, or those for which existing data on toxic effects are inadequate. Some chemicals are selected for testing because study of them may tell more about how structurally related chemicals are likely to affect human health. Other criteria include: amount produced, significant physical and chemical properties, interest by regulatory and research agencies, and possible public health significance. The NTP testing strategy is to identify the major toxic effects of each chemical studied (genetic mutations; damage to critical organs such as the lungs, liver, and nervous system; birth defects; or cancer).

Chemicals are nominated for testing by a variety of sources, including representatives of the agencies on the NTP Executive Committee; government agencies not represented on the Committee; academic, industry, and labor groups; state and local governments; and individuals. Persons interested in proposing chemicals for testing should give the reasons for their nominations and, when known, include production and usage information, data on human exposures, results of toxicological studies, data on the chemical's reactions in the human body, information concerning the chemical's relationship to structurally similar chemicals about which there are data, and other pertinent information.

★ 10468 ★ **University of Arizona**
Arizona Poison and Drug Information Center
College of Pharmacy
Tucson, AZ 85721
Phone: (520)626-6016
Fax: (520)626-4063
Dr. Theodore G. Tong, Dir.

Research Activities and Fields: Toxicology and psychopharmacology, including studies of relative efficacy of certain antidotes in treatment of various poisonings. Conducts research in drug information, including patent information services, post-marketing surveillances, and adverse drug reactions. **Publications:** Newsletter (quarterly). **Formerly:** Arizona Poison Control Center (1979).

University of California, Davis
Institute of Toxicology and Environmental Health
See: Entry 5114

★ 10469 ★ **University of California, Los Angeles**
Institute for Toxicology
1985 Zonal Ave.
Los Angeles, CA 90033
Phone: (310)342-1414
Fax: (310)224-7473
Dr. Alex Sevanian, Dir.

Research Activities and Fields: Biomedicine, including toxicology, free-radical biology and chemistry, molecular biology of signal transduction, and atherosclerosis. **E-mail Address:** asevan@hsc.usc.edu.

University of California, San Francisco
Brain Tumor Research Center
See: Entry 6215

★ 10470 ★ **University of California, San Francisco**
Computer Graphics Laboratory
School of Pharmacy
Dept. of Pharmaceutical Chemistry
San Francisco, CA 94143-0446
Phone: (415)476-2299
Fax: (415)476-0688
Thomas Ferrin, Ph.D., Dir.

Research Activities and Fields: Computational approaches to the structure and function of large biological molecules using three-dimensional computer graphics as the principal mode of interaction. Activities include interactive visualization and manipulation of nucleic acids, proteins, and protein-ligand complexes using fast computers and numerical analysis techniques such as molecular mechanics. Also investigates new techniques such as genetic algorithms, neural networks, and specialized database systems that provide new software paradigms. Applications include drug design, protein engineering, biomaterials design and fabrication, and bioremediation. **E-mail Address:** tef@cgl.ucsf.edu.

University of California, San Francisco
Immunogenetics and Transplantation
Laboratory
See: Entry 2141

University of Florida
Center for Environmental and Human
Toxicology
See: Entry 5119

University of Georgia
College of Pharmacy
Department of Research and Graduate
Studies
See: Entry 10633

★ 10471 ★ University of Illinois at Chicago
Center for Pharmaceutical Biotechnology
College of Pharmacy
833 S. Wood St. - M/C 874
Chicago, IL 60612-7231
Phone: (312)996-0796
Fax: (312)413-8084
Dr. Michael E. Johnson, Int.Dir.

Research Activities and Fields: Structural and molecular biology focusing on pharmaceutical applications. **E-mail Address:** u40190@uicvm.uic.edu.

University of Kansas
Center for Biomedical Research
See: Entry 2673

★ 10472 ★ University of Kansas
Center for Drug Delivery Research
Dept. of Pharmaceutical Chemistry
3006 Malott Hall
Lawrence, KS 66045
Phone: (913)864-3755
Fax: (913)864-5389
Valentino Stella, Ph.D., Dir.

Research Activities and Fields: Basic and applied research on chemically-driven drug delivery systems; physiochemical and biological factors that affect delivery systems; and unstable and insoluble drugs such as anticancer agents, peptides, and proteins. **E-mail Address:** stella@smissman.hbc.ukans.edu.

★ 10473 ★ University of Kansas
Higuchi Biosciences Center (HBC)
2099 Constant Ave.
Lawrence, KS 66047-2535
Phone: (913)864-5183
Fax: (913)749-7393
Dr. Elias Michaelis, M.D., Dir.

Research Activities and Fields: Pharmaceutical chemistry, bioanalytical chemistry, drug de-

sign, drug delivery systems, neurological sciences, immunology, and related technology, focusing on the discovery, analysis, formulation, delivery, toxicology, and pharmacology of drugs. **Publications:** *News from HBC* (monthly newsletter).

★ 10474 ★ University of Kentucky
Graduate Center for Toxicology
204 Funkhouser Bldg.
Lexington, KY 40506-0054
Phone: (606)257-3760
Fax: (606)258-1059
Dr. D. Jones, Contact

Research Activities and Fields: Environmental toxicology, molecular mechanisms of toxicology, immunotoxicology, molecular biology and toxicology, risk assessment, and halogenated hydrocarbon toxicity. Also studies the molecular regulation of gene expression in a host-parasite system, including analysis of parasite regulation of hormone-sensitive host genes and the expression and mode of action of parasite regulatory mediators and these effects. **Publications:** Newsletter.

★ 10475 ★ University of Maryland
Center for the Study of Pharmacy and
Therapeutics for the Elderly
School of Pharmacy
20 N. Pine St.
Baltimore, MD 21201-1180
Phone: (410)706-3011
Fax: (401)706-4012
Prof. Madeline Feinberg, Dir.

Research Activities and Fields: Geriatrics and gerontology, emphasizing drug use in the elderly and the development of artificial intelligence programs in support of optimal drug use. Also responsible for three elder care programs, the Parke-Davis Center for the Education of the Elderly, the Elder-Health Program, and the Maryland Caregiver Program. **Publications:** *Eldercare News* (quarterly newsletter).

★ 10476 ★ University of Medicine and
Dentistry of New Jersey
Clinical Research Center
Johnson Med. School
One Robert Wood Johnson Place, CN19
New Brunswick, NJ 08903-0019
Phone: (908)418-8484
Fax: (908)418-8480
Dr. James R. Seibold, M.D., Dir.

Research Activities and Fields: Drug development, clinical pharmacology, anti-sense strategies in cancer and autoimmune diseases, cytokine pharmacology, and cell cycle regulatory proteins and their control.

★ 10477 ★ University of Miami
Marine and Freshwater Biomedical
Sciences Center
Rosenstiel School of Marine & Atmospheric Sciences
4600 Rickenbacker Cswy.
Miami, FL 33149-1098
Phone: (305)361-4738
Fax: (305)361-4001
Daniel G. Baden, Ph.D., Dir.

Research Activities and Fields: Neurotoxicology, potent marine metabolites present in

seafood, a description of a piscine model for human neurofibromatosis, environmental toxicants, fisheries models for hepatic metabolism, and development of sentinel species for xenobiotic evaluation. **E-mail Address:** dbaden@rsmas.miami.edu.

★ 10478 ★ University of Michigan
Antiviral Laboratory
4222 School of Dentistry
1101 N. University Ave.
Ann Arbor, MI 48109
Phone: (313)763-5481
John C. Drach, Hd.

Research Activities and Fields: Antiviral and antineoplastic drugs, including the discovery of new antiviral drugs, how such drugs act at the cellular and biochemical level, and how they are metabolized in uninfected and virus-infected cells. Areas of research include viruses, herpes, and AIDS. **E-mail Address:** jcdrach@umich.edu.

University of Michigan
National Cooperative Drug Discovery
Group for the Treatment of AIDS
See: Entry 6848

★ 10479 ★ University of Michigan
Upjohn Center for Clinical Pharmacology
3709 Upjohn Center
University Medical Center
Ann Arbor, MI 48109-0504
Phone: (313)764-9121
William D. Ensminger, M.D., Dir.

Research Activities and Fields: Clinical pharmacology.

University of Mississippi
Research Institute of Pharmaceutical
Sciences
See: Entry 10637

★ 10480 ★ University of Montreal
Experimental Inhalation Research Group
Medecine du travail et d'hygiene du milieu
Faculte de medecine
C.P 6128, succursale Centre-ville
Montreal, PQ, Canada H3C 3J7
Phone: (514)343-6147
Fax: (514)343-2200
Jules Brodeur, Dir.

Research Activities and Fields: Group studies mechanisms of toxic action, identification of biological markers of toxicity, and toxicological risk assessment of substances present as gas or vapors. **E-mail Address:** lapares@alize.ere.umontreal.ca.

★ 10481 ★ University of Montreal
Fernand Sequin Research Centre
Hopital Louis-H.-Lafontaine
7331, rue Hochelaga
Montreal, PQ, Canada H1N 3V2
Phone: (514)251-4015
Fax: (514)251-2617
Dr. Hugues Cormier, Dir.

Research Activities and Fields: Centre focuses on neurochemistry, including drug mechanisms of action; psychopharmacology, including pharmacodynamics and pharmacokinetics of psychoactive drugs; and psychosocial behavioral and clinical evaluations, including the development of psychotherapeutic methods, evaluation of programs, and societal problems.

University of Montreal
Occupational and Environmental
Toxicology Research Group
See: Entry 9860

University of Nevada, Reno
Allie M. Lee Cancer Research Laboratory
See: Entry 6234

University of Pennsylvania
Private Practice Research Group
See: Entry 7683

★ 10482 ★ University of Pennsylvania
Psychopharmacology Research Unit
3600 Market St., Ste. 872
Philadelphia, PA 19104-2649
Phone: (215)898-4301
Fax: (215)898-0509
Dr. Edward E. Schweizer, Dir.

Research Activities and Fields: Psychopharmacology, including short- and long-term clinical trials on the effects of antidepressive and antianxiety medications. **E-mail Address:** schweizer@al.mscf.upenn.edu.

★ 10483 ★ University of Southern
California
Institute for Toxicology
1985 Zonal Ave.
Los Angeles, CA 90033
Phone: (213)342-1414
Fax: (213)224-7473
Dr. M. Yasui, Dir.

Research Activities and Fields: DNA research, including mutations and toxicology. Also studies Southern blotting and radiolabeling.

★ 10484 ★ University of Southern
California
Laboratory of Applied Pharmacokinetics
USC School of Medicine
Clinical Science Center, Rm. 134-B
2250 Alcazar St.
Los Angeles, CA 90033
Phone: (213)342-1300
Fax: (213)342-1302
Roger W. Jelliffe, M.D., Prin. Investigator

Research Activities and Fields: Designing systems for pharmacokinetic studies and strategies for optimal therapeutic drug monitoring in patients and optimal adaptive control of drug dosage regimens for patients. Activities include development and testing of computer programs for simulation, parameter identification, and optimal adaptive control of drug dosage regimens and pharmacokinetic systems in clinical settings; investigation of process and measurement noise in the clinical therapeutic environment; development of software for making population pharmacokinetic models; software for stochastic adaptive control of drug dosage regimens; and develop ment of clinically reliable interfaces and intelligent automated apparatus for delivering complex drug regimens. **E-mail Address:** jelliffe@hsc.usc.edu.

University of Southwestern Louisiana
New Iberia Research Center
See: Entry 1723

★ 10485 ★ University of Tennessee
Center of Excellence in Pediatric
Pharmacokinetics and Therapeutics
Dept. of Clinical Pharmacy
26 S. Dunlap
Memphis, TN 38163
Phone: (901)528-6043
Fax: (901)528-6064
Dr. William E. Evans, Codirector

Research Activities and Fields: Drug therapy research in children. Seeks to promote and protect children's well-being by minimizing or eliminating pharmaceutical risks. Addresses the child's stage of physical development and rate of metabolism, in addition to body-weight and size, in determining effects of drugs.

★ 10486 ★ University of Tennessee
Drug Information Center
847 Monroe, Ste. 238
Memphis, TN 38163
Phone: (901)448-5555
Fax: (901)448-5419
Dr. Peter A. Chyka, Dir.

Research Activities and Fields: Therapeutic and pharmaceutical drugs. Provides therapeutic and pharmaceutic drug information to health care professionals.

University of Texas at Austin
Drug Dynamics Institute
See: Entry 10639

University of Texas Medical Branch at
Galveston
National Cooperative Drug Discovery
Group for the Treatment of AIDS
See: Entry 6855

★ 10487 ★ University of Utah
Center for Controlled Chemical Delivery
421 Wakara Way, Ste. 318
Salt Lake City, UT 84108
Phone: (801)581-6801
Fax: (801)581-7848
Dr. Sung Wan Kim, Dir.

Research Activities and Fields: Controlled drug delivery systems. Specific studies include the following: 1) hydrogel and polymer synthesis, including water-soluble, bioactive, and biodegradable polymers; 2) transdermal drug delivery, including skin immunoreaction and sensitization, irritation mechanism, drug interaction with stratum corneum membranes, physicochemical analysis of drug permeation mechanisms, and design of optimum delivery of matrix or rate-controlling membranes; 3) functional polymers for gastrointestinal drug delivery; 4) polymeric prodrugs and chemical modification of drugs for specific organ targeting or long-term delivery of therapeutic agents; and 5) delivery of peptides and protein drugs.

★ 10488 ★ University of Utah
Center for Human Toxicology
417 Wakara Way, Rm. 290
Salt Lake City, UT 84108
Phone: (801)581-5117
Fax: (801)581-5034
Douglas E. Rollins, M.D., Dir.

Research Activities and Fields: Clinical, forensic, and bioanalytical toxicology, including studies in clinical pharmacology and toxicology, drug metabolism, disposition, adverse interactions, alcohol/drugs and driving, proficiency testing, postmortem toxicology, data interpretation, and new chromatographic and mass spectrometry techniques in toxicology.

University of Vermont
Genetics Laboratory
See: Entry 5387

★ 10489 ★ University of Wisconsin—
Madison
Environmental Toxicology Center
B157 Steenbock Library
550 Babcock Dr.
Madison, WI 53706-1293
Phone: (608)263-4580
Prof. Colin R. Jefcoate, Dir.

Research Activities and Fields: Toxicology and problems related to presence of potentially hazardous synthetic and naturally occurring chemicals in the environment, e.g. heavy metals, chlorinated hydrocarbons, pesticides, mycotoxins, and food-borne toxins, including identification, quantification, and toxicologic studies of such chemicals. **Publications:** Newsletter (occasionality).

University of Wisconsin—Madison
Food Research Institute
See: Entry 9569

University of Wisconsin—Milwaukee
Marine and Freshwater Biomedical
Sciences Center
See: Entry 2700

★ 10490 ★ University of Wisconsin—
Milwaukee
Medicinal Chemistry Group
Dept. of Chemistry
PO Box 413
Milwaukee, WI 53201
Phone: (414)229-5856
Fax: (414)229-5530
Prof. James M. Cook, Dir.

Research Activities and Fields: Research on drugs, including studies of valium receptors in the brain; drugs that do not sedate patients, including anticonvulsive agents, sedative/hypnotic agents, and muscle relaxants; and antimalarial agents, barbituate antagonists, antagonists of alcohol/barbituate overdoses, and cardiovascular agents. Activities focus on synthesis of compounds to reduce drug addiction and control illness.

★10491★ Vanderbilt University
Center for Clinical Pharmacology
532 Medical Research Bldg.
Nashville, TN 37232-6602
Phone: (615)322-3304
Dr. Dan M. Roden, Dir.

Research Activities and Fields: Interdisciplinary research in drug actions, especially in humans. Specific research includes xenobiotic disposition, ion channel physiology and pharmacology, hypertension and the autonomic nervous system, and eicosanoid biology.

★10492★ Vanderbilt University
Center in Molecular Toxicology
21st Ave. S. & Garland
Nashville, TN 37232
Phone: (615)322-2261
Fax: (615)322-3141
Dr. F. Peter Guengerich, Dir.

Research Activities and Fields: Biochemical and chemical toxicology and carcinogenesis, including enzymatic oxidation, oxidative damage, DNA-adduct chemistry, mechanisms of mutagenesis, structural and regulatory biology, analytic method development, and molecular epidemiology and prevention. Special services include analytical chemistry and spectroscopy, cell culture, protein chemistry, and recombinant DNA techniques. **Publications:** Annual Report. **E-mail Address:** info@toxicology.mc.vanderbilt.edu. **Formerly:** Center in Environmental Toxicology (1984).

★10493★ Veterans Affairs Medical Center
(GRECC)
Geriatric Research, Education and Clinical center
GRECC, (182)
1601 Archer Rd.
Gainesville, FL 32608-1197
Phone: (904)374-6077
Fax: (904)374-6142
Dr. David Lowenthal, Dir.

Research Activities and Fields: Geropharmacology, including mechanisms of drug action, pharmacokinetics, therapeutic uses, drug abuse, polypharmacy and drug compliance as it applies to geriatric patients. Clinical research is conducted in the areas of exercise, cardiovascular function, and cognitive disorders in the elderly. Basic research is conducted in pharmacologic mechanisms of temperature regulation, febrile response to infections, and immunology. **E-mail Address:** dlowenthal@qm.server.ufl.edu.

★10494★ Wayne State University
Institute of Chemical Toxicology
2727 Second Ave., Rm. 4000
Detroit, MI 48201
Phone: (313)577-0100
Fax: (313)577-0082
Dr. Raymond F. Novak, Dir.

Research Activities and Fields: Chemical hazards of the environment and industrial workplace, including toxicology of air pollutants, solvents, and heavy metals. Also studies carcinogenesis, metabolic, and hematologic effects resulting from exposure to toxic agents; and molecular and cellular approaches to examine early events in toxicity. **E-mail Address:** RNOVAK@WAYNEST1.BITNET.

★10495★ West Virginia University
West Virginia Poison Center
3110 MacCorkle Ave. SE
Charleston, WV 25304
Phone: (304)347-1212
Fax: (304)348-9560
Elizabeth J. Scharman, Dir.

Research Activities and Fields: Demographics of poison victims and epidemiology of poisoning. Research is conducted in support of the Center's service program in poison prevention and management.

★10496★ World Life Research Institute
23000 Grand Terr. Rd.
Colton, CA 92324
Phone: (909)825-4773
Fax: (909)783-3477
Bruce W. Halstead, M.D., Dir.

Research Activities and Fields: Toxicology, medical research, poisonous and venomous marine animals, drugs from the sea, chronic degenerative diseases, marine biotoxicology, and ethnobotany and terrestrial phytochemistry in a search for new drugs from natural resources, especially organic chemical agents derived from plants or animals having application to therapeutic medicine and human nutrition. Maintains extensive foreign contacts in 6,000 regions of the world, particularly underdeveloped areas in Asia and Latin America, in search of new drugs.

Chapter 51
Pharmacy

Foundations & Other Funding Organizations

Other Funding Organizations

★ 10497 ★ **American Foundation for Pharmaceutical Education**
618 Somerset St.
PO Box 7126
North Plainfield, NJ 07060
Phone: (908)561-8077
Fax: (908)561-8169
Richard E. Faust, Ph.D., Pres.
Description: Makes disbursements for fellowships and the promotion of pharmaceutical education.

★ 10498 ★ **American Society of Hospital Pharmacists Research and Education Foundation**
7272 Wisconsin Ave.
Bethesda, MD 20814
Phone: (301)657-3000
Fax: (301)652-8278
Charles M. King, Jr., Exec. VP
Description: Awards grants to support research relating to institutional pharmacy practice, and offers fellowships in cancer immunotherapy, psychiatric, pediatric, geriatric, and clinical pharmacokinetics, critical care, and nutritional support.

Medical & Allied Health Schools

Pharmacy

The following colleges and schools of pharmacy offer baccalaureate and/or doctoral programs accredited by the American Council on Pharmaceutical Education, 311 W. Superior St., Ste. 512, Chicago, IL 60610, (312) 664-3575. For additional information on the colleges, and on pharmacy as a career, contact the American Association of Colleges of Pharmacy, 1426 Prince St., Alexandria, VA 22314, (703) 739-2330.

Alabama

★ 10499 ★ **Auburn University**
School of Pharmacy
Auburn, AL 36849-5501
Phone: (205)844-8351
Fax: (205)844-8353

★ 10500 ★ **Samford University**
School of Pharmacy
800 Lakeshore Dr.
Birmingham, AL 35229
Phone: (205)870-2820
Fax: (205)870-2759

Arizona

★ 10501 ★ **University of Arizona**
College of Pharmacy
Tucson, AZ 85721
Phone: (602)626-1427
Fax: (602)626-4063

Arkansas

★ 10502 ★ **University of Arkansas for Medical Sciences**
College of Pharmacy
4301 W. Markham St., Slot 522
Little Rock, AR 72205
Phone: (501)686-5557
Fax: (501)686-8315

California

★ 10503 ★ **University of California, San Francisco**
School of Pharmacy
San Francisco, CA 94143-0446
Phone: (415)476-1225
Fax: (415)476-0688

★ 10504 ★ **University of the Pacific**
School of Pharmacy
3601 Pacific Ave.
Stockton, CA 95211
Phone: (209)946-2561
Fax: (209)946-2410

★ 10505 ★ **University of Southern California**
School of Pharmacy
1985 Zonal Ave.
Los Angeles, CA 90033-1086
Phone: (213)342-1369
Fax: (213)342-1681

Colorado

★ 10506 ★ **University of Colorado—Denver**
School of Pharmacy
Health Sciences Center, C-238
4200 E. 9th Ave.
Denver, CO 80262
Phone: (303)270-5055
Fax: (303)270-6281

Connecticut

★ 10507 ★ **University of Connecticut**
School of Pharmacy
Box U-92, Rm. R-103
372 Fairfield Rd.
Storrs Mansfield, CT 06269-2092
Phone: (203)486-2129
Fax: (203)486-1553

District of Columbia

★ 10508 ★ **Howard University**
College of Pharmacy and Pharmacal Sciences
2300 4th St. NW
Washington, DC 20059
Phone: (202)806-6530
Fax: (202)806-4636

Florida

★ 10509 ★ **Florida A&M University**
College of Pharmacy and Pharmaceutical Sciences
Tallahassee, FL 32307
Phone: (904)599-3593
Fax: (904)599-3347

★ 10510 ★ Nova Southeastern University
Health Professions Division
College of Pharmacy
1750 NE 167th St.
North Miami Beach, FL 33162-3017
Phone: (305)949-4000
Fax: (305)957-1607

★ 10511 ★ University of Florida
College of Pharmacy
Box 100484
J. Hillis Miller Health Center
Gainesville, FL 32610
Phone: (904)392-9713
Fax: (904)392-3480

Georgia

★ 10512 ★ Mercer University
Southern School of Pharmacy
3001 Mercer University Dr.
Atlanta, GA 30341-4415
Phone: (404)986-3300
Fax: (404)986-3315

★ 10513 ★ University of Georgia
College of Pharmacy
Athens, GA 30602-2351
Phone: (706)542-1914
Fax: (706)542-5269

Idaho

★ 10514 ★ Idaho State University
College of Pharmacy
Pocatello, ID 83209
Phone: (208)236-2175
Fax: (208)236-4482

Illinois

★ 10515 ★ Midwestern University
Chicago College of Pharmacy
555 31st St.
Downers Grove, IL 60515
Phone: (708)971-6417
Fax: (708)971-6097

★ 10516 ★ University of Illinois at Chicago
College of Pharmacy
PO Box 6998
Chicago, IL 60680
Phone: (312)996-7240
Fax: (312)996-3272

Indiana

★ 10517 ★ Butler University
College of Pharmacy
46th and Sunset Ave.
Indianapolis, IN 46208
Phone: (317)283-9735
Fax: (317)921-6172

★ 10518 ★ Purdue University
School of Pharmacy and Pharmacal
  Sciences
West Lafayette, IN 47907
Phone: (317)494-1368
Fax: (317)494-7880

Iowa

★ 10519 ★ Drake University
College of Pharmacy and Health Sciences
Pharmacy Programs
25th Ave. & University Ave.
Des Moines, IA 50311
Phone: (515)271-2172
Fax: (515)271-4171

★ 10520 ★ University of Iowa
College of Pharmacy
Iowa City, IA 52242
Phone: (319)335-8794
Fax: (319)335-9418

Kansas

★ 10521 ★ University of Kansas
School of Pharmacy
Lawrence, KS 66045-2500
Phone: (913)864-3591
Fax: (913)864-5265

Kentucky

★ 10522 ★ University of Kentucky
College of Pharmacy
Lexington, KY 40536-0082
Phone: (606)257-2737
Fax: (606)257-2128

Louisiana

★ 10523 ★ Northeast Louisiana University
School of Pharmacy
Monroe, LA 71209
Phone: (318)342-1600
Fax: (318)342-1606

★ 10524 ★ Xavier University of Louisiana
College of Pharmacy
7325 Palmetto St.
New Orleans, LA 70125
Phone: (504)483-7424
Fax: (504)488-3108

Maryland

★ 10525 ★ University of Maryland at
  Baltimore
School of Pharmacy
20 N. Pine St.
Baltimore, MD 21201
Phone: (410)706-7650
Fax: (410)706-4012

Massachusetts

★ 10526 ★ Massachusetts College of
  Pharmacy and Allied Health Sciences
Pharmacy Programs
179 Longwood Ave.
Boston, MA 02115
Phone: (617)732-2800
Fax: (617)732-2801

★ 10527 ★ Northeastern University
Bouve College of Pharmacy and Health
  Sciences
Pharmacy Programs
360 Huntington Ave.
Boston, MA 02115
Phone: (617)373-3323
Fax: (617)373-3030

Michigan

★ 10528 ★ Ferris State University
College of Pharmacy
Big Rapids, MI 49307
Phone: (616)592-2254
Fax: (616)592-3829

★ 10529 ★ University of Michigan
College of Pharmacy
Ann Arbor, MI 48109-1065
Phone: (313)764-7144
Fax: (313)763-2022

★ 10530 ★ Wayne State University
College of Pharmacy and Allied Health
  Professions
Pharmacy Programs
105 Shapero Hall
Detroit, MI 48202
Phone: (313)577-1574
Fax: (313)577-5589

Minnesota

★ 10531 ★ University of Minnesota
College of Pharmacy
308 Harvard St. SE
Minneapolis, MN 55455-0343
Phone: (612)624-1900
Fax: (612)624-2974

Mississippi

★ 10532 ★ University of Mississippi
School of Pharmacy
University, MS 38677
Phone: (601)232-7265
Fax: (601)232-5118

Missouri

★ 10533 ★ St. Louis College of Pharmacy
4588 Parkview Pl.
St. Louis, MO 63110
Phone: (314)367-8700
Fax: (314)367-2784

★ 10534 ★ University of Missouri—Kansas
  City
School of Pharmacy
5005 Rockhill Rd.
Kansas City, MO 64110-2499
Phone: (816)235-1607

Montana

★ 10535 ★ **University of Montana**
School of Pharmacy and Allied Health
  Sciences
Pharmacy Program
Missoula, MT 59812
Phone: (406)243-4621
Fax: (406)243-4353

Nebraska

★ 10536 ★ **Creighton University**
School of Pharmacy and Allied Health
  Professions
2500 California Plaza
Omaha, NE 68178
Phone: (402)280-2950
Fax: (402)280-5738

★ 10537 ★ **University of Nebraska at**
  Omaha
College of Pharmacy
600 S. 42nd St.
Omaha, NE 68198-6000
Phone: (402)559-4333
Fax: (402)559-5060

New Jersey

★ 10538 ★ **Rutgers University**
College of Pharmacy
William Levine Hall, Busch Campus
PO Box 789
Piscataway, NJ 08855-0789
Phone: (908)445-2666
Fax: (908)445-5767

New Mexico

★ 10539 ★ **University of New Mexico**
College of Pharmacy
Albuquerque, NM 87131
Phone: (505)277-3241
Fax: (505)277-6749

New York

★ 10540 ★ **Long Island University**
Arnold and Marie Schwartz College of
  Pharmacy and Health Sciences
75 DeKalb Ave. at University Plaza
Brooklyn, NY 11201
Phone: (718)488-1004
Fax: (718)488-0628

★ 10541 ★ **St. John's University**
College of Pharmacy and Allied Health
  Professions
Pharmacy Programs
8000 Utopia Pkwy.
Jamaica, NY 11439
Phone: (718)990-6275
Fax: (718)990-1871

★ 10542 ★ **State University of New York at**
  Buffalo
School of Pharmacy
C-126 Cooke-Hochstetter Complex
Buffalo, NY 14260-1200
Phone: (716)645-2823
Fax: (716)645-3688

★ 10543 ★ **Union University**
Albany College of Pharmacy
106 New Scotland Ave.
Albany, NY 12208
Phone: (518)445-7200
Fax: (518)445-7202

North Carolina

★ 10544 ★ **Campbell University**
School of Pharmacy
Buies Creek, NC 27506
Phone: (919)893-1200
Fax: (919)893-1476

★ 10545 ★ **University of North Carolina at**
  Chapel Hill
School of Pharmacy
Beard Hall, CB No. 7360
Chapel Hill, NC 27599
Phone: (919)966-1121
Fax: (919)966-6919

North Dakota

★ 10546 ★ **North Dakota State University**
College of Pharmacy
PO Box 5055, State University Sta.
Fargo, ND 58105
Phone: (701)237-7456
Fax: (701)237-7606

Ohio

★ 10547 ★ **Ohio Northern University**
College of Pharmacy
Ada, OH 45810
Phone: (419)772-2275
Fax: (419)772-1917

★ 10548 ★ **Ohio State University**
College of Pharmacy
500 W. 12th Ave.
Columbus, OH 43210-1291
Phone: (614)292-2266
Fax: (614)292-2588

★ 10549 ★ **University of Cincinnati**
College of Pharmacy
PO Box 670004
Cincinnati, OH 45267-0004
Phone: (513)558-3326
Fax: (513)558-4372

★ 10550 ★ **University of Toledo**
College of Pharmacy
2801 W. Bancroft St.
Toledo, OH 43606
Phone: (419)537-4235
Fax: (419)537-4940

Oklahoma

★ 10551 ★ **Southwestern Oklahoma State**
  University
School of Pharmacy
Weatherford, OK 73096
Phone: (405)774-3105
Fax: (405)774-3795

★ 10552 ★ **University of Oklahoma**
College of Pharmacy
1110 N. Stonewall
PO Box 26901
Oklahoma City, OK 73190
Phone: (405)271-6484
Fax: (405)271-3830

Oregon

★ 10553 ★ **Oregon State University**
College of Pharmacy
Corvallis, OR 97331-3507
Phone: (503)737-3424
Fax: (503)737-3999

Pennsylvania

★ 10554 ★ **Duquesne University**
School of Pharmacy
Pittsburgh, PA 15282
Phone: (412)396-6377
Fax: (412)396-5130

★ 10555 ★ **Philadelphia College of**
  Pharmacy and Science
Pharmacy Programs
600 S. 43rd St.
Philadelphia, PA 19104
Phone: (215)596-8866
Fax: (215)596-8544

★ 10556 ★ **Temple University**
School of Pharmacy
3307 N. Broad St.
Philadelphia, PA 19140
Phone: (215)221-4990
Fax: (215)221-3678

★ 10557 ★ **University of Pittsburgh**
School of Pharmacy
1103 Salk Hall
3501 Terrace St.
Pittsburgh, PA 15261
Phone: (412)624-3270
Fax: (412)648-1086

Puerto Rico

★ 10558 ★ **University of Puerto Rico**
School of Pharmacy
Medical Sciences Campus
PO Box 365067
San Juan, PR 00936-5067
Phone: (809)751-5680
Fax: (809)751-5680

Rhode Island

★ 10559 ★ **University of Rhode Island**
College of Pharmacy
Kingston, RI 02881
Phone: (401)792-2761
Fax: (401)792-2181

South Carolina

★ 10560 ★ **Medical University of South Carolina**
College of Pharmacy
171 Ashley Ave.
Charleston, SC 29425
Phone: (803)792-8450
Fax: (803)792-9081

★ 10561 ★ **University of South Carolina**
College of Pharmacy
Columbia, SC 29208
Phone: (803)777-2149
Fax: (803)777-2775

South Dakota

★ 10562 ★ **South Dakota State University**
College of Pharmacy
Brookings, SD 57007
Phone: (605)688-6197
Fax: (605)688-6232

Tennessee

★ 10563 ★ **University of Tennessee, Memphis**
College of Pharmacy
847 Monroe Ave.
Memphis, TN 38163
Phone: (901)448-6036
Fax: (901)448-7053

Texas

★ 10564 ★ **Texas Southern University**
College of Pharmacy and Health Sciences
Pharmacy Programs
3100 Cleburne St.
Houston, TX 77004
Phone: (713)527-7561
Fax: (713)639-1091

★ 10565 ★ **University of Houston**
College of Pharmacy
4800 Calhoun Blvd.
Houston, TX 77204-5511
Phone: (713)743-1300
Fax: (713)743-1259

★ 10566 ★ **University of Texas at Austin**
College of Pharmacy
Austin, TX 78712
Phone: (512)471-1737
Fax: (512)471-8783

Utah

★ 10567 ★ **University of Utah**
College of Pharmacy
Salt Lake City, UT 84112
Phone: (801)581-3402
Fax: (801)581-3716

Virginia

★ 10568 ★ **Virginia Commonwealth University**
Medical College of Virginia
School of Pharmacy
MCV Box 980581
410 N. 12th St.
Richmond, VA 23298-0581
Phone: (804)828-3006
Fax: (804)786-7436

Washington

★ 10569 ★ **University of Washington**
School of Pharmacy
H364 Health Sciences Center, SC-69
Seattle, WA 98195
Phone: (206)543-2453
Fax: (206)543-3835

★ 10570 ★ **Washington State University**
College of Pharmacy
Pullman, WA 99164-6510
Phone: (509)335-4750
Fax: (509)335-0162

West Virginia

★ 10571 ★ **West Virginia University**
School of Pharmacy
Health Sciences Center
Morgantown, WV 26506-9500
Phone: (304)293-5212
Fax: (304)293-5483

Wisconsin

★ 10572 ★ **University of Wisconsin— Madison**
School of Pharmacy
425 N. Charter St.
Madison, WI 53706
Phone: (608)262-1414
Fax: (608)262-3397

Wyoming

★ 10573 ★ **University of Wyoming**
School of Pharmacy
Box 3375
Laramie, WY 82071-3375
Phone: (307)766-6120
Fax: (307)766-2953

National & International Organizations

★ 10574 ★ **Academy of Pharmaceutical Research and Science (APRS)**
c/o Naomi U. Kaminsky
American Pharmaceutical Association
2215 Constitution Ave. NW
Washington, DC 20037
Phone: (202)628-4410
Fax: (202)783-2351
Naomi U. Kaminsky, Scientific Affairs Program Mng.

Founded: 1965. **Members:** 3,000. **Local Groups:** 1. **Description:** A part of American Pharmaceutical Association. Pharmaceutical scientists from industry and academia. Objective is to serve the profession of pharmacy by developing knowledge and integrating the process of science into the profession. Sponsors national meetings to provide a forum for presentation and discussion of original laboratory research, controversial topics, and continuing communication. Provides consultation and advice to: pharmacists on scientific matters as they relate to policy; congressional committees on bills of interest to pharmaceutical scientists; governmental agencies. **Publications:** *Abstracts of Papers*, annual. • *Academy Reporter*, quarterly. Newsletter. Provides information on association activities and pharmaceutical sciences. Includes calendar of events and news of section update. *Price:* Included in membership dues; $25/year for nonmembers. • *Journal of Pharmaceutical Sciences*, monthly. Journal. • Manuals. • Monographs. • Proceedings. **Formerly:** (1987) Academy of Pharmaceutical Sciences.

★ 10575 ★ **Academy of Pharmacy Practice and Management (APPM)**
c/o Susan C. Winckler
American Pharmaceutical Association
2215 Constitution Ave. NW
Washington, DC 20037
Phone: (202)628-4410
Free: 800-237-APHA
Fax: (202)783-2351
Susan C. Winckler, Dir.

Founded: 1965. **Members:** 18,500. **Description:** Pharmacists concerned with rendering professional services directly to the public, without regard for status of employment or environment of practice. Purposes are to provide a forum and mechanism whereby pharmacists may meet to discuss and implement programs and activities relevant and helpful to the practitioner of pharmacy; to recommend programs and courses of action which should be undertaken or implemented by the profession; to coordinate academy efforts so as to be an asset to the progress of the profession. Provides and cosponsors continuing education meetings, seminars, and workshops; produces audiovisual materials. **Publications:** *Academy Reporter*, quarterly. Newsletter. *Price:* Included in membership dues; $25/year for nonmembers. **Formerly:** (1966) General Practice Section of APhA; (1975) Academy of General Practice of Pharmacy; (1987) Academy of Pharmacy Practice.

★ 10576 ★ **Academy of Students of Pharmacy (APhA-ASP)**
2215 Constitution Ave. NW
Washington, DC 20037
Phone: (202)628-4410
Fax: (202)783-2351
Jann B. Hinkle, Dir. Student Affairs

Founded: 1954. **Members:** 14,200. **Regional Groups:** 8. **Local Groups:** 76. **Description:** A program of the American Pharmaceutical Association. Professional society of pharmacy students. Keeps members informed of the affairs of the APhA and the profession. Provides a forum for the expression of student opinion on activities and policies. Seeks to strengthen the program whereby student members, upon graduation, become active members of the APhA. Encourages participation by pharmacy students in interdisciplinary projects that attempt to find solutions to social problems; works in community-oriented drug education programs; supports interdisciplinary clinical training for pharmacists. **Publications:** *Academy of Students of Pharmacy--Chapter Management*, monthly. Newsletter. For chapter presidents only. • *The Pharmacy Student*, quarterly. Magazine. *Price:* Included in membership dues; $25/year for nonmembers. **Formerly:** (1969) American Pharmaceutical Association Student Section; (1988) Student American Pharmaceutical Association.

★ 10577 ★ **Alpha Zeta Omega**
4422 Porpoise Dr.
Tampa, FL 33617
Bruce Strell, Dir.

Founded: 1919. **Members:** 11,000. **Description:** Professional fraternity - men and women, pharmacy. Sponsors scholarships, grants-in-aid, and visiting lectureships at colleges where a chapter of AZO is maintained. Raises funds for the ''City of Hope'' in Los Angeles, CA, the Arthritis Foundation, and the Hebrew University of Pharmacy in Israel. **Publications:** *The Azoan and The Azomedic.* • Newsletter, monthly.

★ 10578 ★ **American Association of Colleges of Pharmacy (AACP)**
1426 Prince St.
Alexandria, VA 22314
Phone: (703)739-2330
Fax: (703)836-8982
Carl E. Trinca, Ph.D., Exec.Dir.

Founded: 1900. **Members:** 2,300. **Description:** College of pharmacy programs accredited by American Council on Pharmaceutical Education; corporations and individuals. Compiles statistics. **Publications:** *AACP News*, monthly. Newsletter. Includes information on association activities, employment opportunities, and new members. *Price:* Included in membership dues; $100/year for nonmembers. • *American Association of Colleges of Pharmacy--Graduate Programs in the Pharmaceutical Sciences*, annual. Directory. Lists graduate programs in pharmacy; provides comparative analysis of pharmacy schools and admissions criteria for graduate programs. *Price:* $25/copy. • *American Journal of Pharmaceutical Education*, quarterly. Journal. Includes book reviews, listing of recent publications, and statistics. *Price:* Included in membership dues; $40/year for nonmembers in the U.S. and Canada; $65/year for nonmembers outside

the U.S. and Canada; $100/year for libraries. • *Pharmacy School Admission Requirements*, annual. Directory. Lists pharmacy schools arranged by state; provides comparative analysis of pharmacy schools and admissions criteria for professional programs. *Price:* $25/copy. • *Roster of Teaching Personnel in Colleges of Pharmacy*, annual. Includes calendar of events. *Price:* Included in membership dues; $100/copy for nonmembers. **Formerly:** (1925) American Conference of Pharmaceutical Faculties.

★ 10579 ★ **American Association of Pharmaceutical Scientists (AAPS)**
1650 King St.
Alexandria, VA 22314-2747
Phone: (703)548-3000
Fax: (703)684-7349
Lorraine L. Hurlburt, Exec.Dir.

Founded: 1986. **Members:** 7,000. **Regional Groups:** 4. **Description:** Pharmaceutical scientists. Provides a forum for exchange of scientific information; serves as a resource in forming public policies to regulate pharmaceutical sciences and related issues of public concern. Promotes pharmaceutical sciences and provides for recognition of individual achievement; works to foster career growth and the development of members. Offers placement service. **Publications:** *AAPS Newsletter*, monthly. Newsletter. *Price:* Included in membership dues. • *Journal of Pharmaceutical and Biomedical Analysis*, monthly. Journal. Features original research reports and authoritative reviews on pharmaceutical and biomedical analysis. *Price:* $70/year for members; $136/year for nonmembers. • *Journal of Pharmaceutical Marketing and Management*, quarterly. Journal. Focuses on the use of pharmaceuticals in health care, with particular emphasis on drug marketing and management. *Price:* $26.25 in U.S.; $36.75 outside U.S. • *Pharmaceutical Research*, monthly. Journal. Reports on applied and basic research in the pharmaceutical-biomedical sciences; includes research reports. *Price:* $50/year for members; $110/year for nonmembers.

★ 10580 ★ **American College of Apothecaries (ACA)**
205 Daingerfield Rd.
Alexandria, VA 22314
Phone: (703)684-8603
Fax: (703)683-3619
Dr. D. C. Huffman, Jr., Exec.VP

Founded: 1940. **Members:** 1,000. **Regional Groups:** 13. **State Groups:** 24. **Description:** Professional society of pharmacists owning and operating ethical prescription pharmacies, including hospital pharmacists, pharmacy students, and faculty of colleges of pharmacy. Primary objective is the translation, transformation, and dissemination of knowledge, research data, and recent developments in the pharmaceutical industry and public health. Sponsors Community Pharmacy Residency Program; offers continuing education courses. Conducts research programs; sponsors charitable program. Maintains museum; compiles statistics; operates speakers' bureau. **Publications:** *American College of Apothecaries--Directory*, annual. Membership Directory. *Price:* Included in membership dues. • *American College of Apothecaries--*

Newsletter, monthly. Newsletter. Includes book reviews. *Price:* Included in membership dues. • *American College of Apothecaries--Patron's Newsletter*, monthly. Newsletter. Provides tips on health and medications for patrons of member pharmacists. *Price:* Included in membership dues. • *American College of Apothecaries--Physician's Newsletter*, monthly. Newsletter. Provides health tips on the use of drugs and medications. *Price:* Included in membership dues. • *American College of Apothecaries--Secretary's Newsletter*, monthly. Newsletter. Covers membership activities and developments affecting the profession. *Price:* Included in membership dues. • Books. • Handbooks. • *Voice of the Pharmacist*, quarterly. Newsletter. Provides information on issues affecting pharmacy practice, including legislative developments. *Price:* Included in membership dues; $25/year for nonmembers. Also publishes by-laws.

★ 10581 ★ **American College of Clinical Pharmacy (ACCP)**
3101 Broadway, Ste. 380
Kansas City, MO 64111
Phone: (816)531-2177
Fax: (816)531-4990
Robert M. Elenbaas, Exec.Dir.

Founded: 1979. **Members:** 1,600. **Description:** Clinical pharmacists dedicated to: promoting rational use of drugs in society; advancing the practice of clinical pharmacy and interdisciplinary health care; assuring high quality clinical pharmacy by establishing and maintaining standards in education and training at advanced levels. Encourages research and recognizes excellence in clinical pharmacy. Offers educational programs, symposia, research forums, fellowship training, and college-funded grants through competitions. Maintains placement service. **Publications:** *ACCP Report*, monthly. Newsletter. *Price:* Free. • *American College of Clinical Pharmacy--Membership Directory*, annual. Directory. *Price:* Included in membership dues; $30/copy for nonmembers. • *Pharmacotherapy: The Journal of Human Pharmacology and Drug Therapy*, bimonthly. Journal. *Price:* Included in membership dues. • *Residency and Fellowship Programs Offered by ACCP Members*, annual. Directory of training programs in clinical pharmacy. *Price:* Free.

★ 10582 ★ **American Council on Pharmaceutical Education (ACPE)**
311 W. Superior St., Ste. 512
Chicago, IL 60610
Phone: (312)664-3575
Fax: (312)664-4652
Daniel A. Nona, Exec.Dir.

Founded: 1932. **Members:** 10. **Description:** Accrediting agency for the professional programs of colleges and schools of pharmacy and approval of providers of continuing pharmaceutical education. **Publications:** *Accredited Professional Programs of Colleges of Schools of Pharmacy*, annual. Directory. • *Approved Providers of Continuing Pharmaceutical Education.*

★ 10583 ★ American Foundation for Pharmaceutical Education (AFPE)

618 Somerset St.
PO Box 7126
North Plainfield, NJ 07060
Phone: (908)561-8077
Fax: (908)561-8169
Richard E. Faust, Ph.D., Pres.

Founded: 1942. **Members:** 40. **Description:** Established by pharmaceutical and drug trade associations to improve pharmaceutical education, colleges of pharmacy, and pharmacy student performance. Accepts and administers gifts, legacies, bequests, and funds and makes disbursements for fellowships and the promotion of pharmaceutical education. **Publications:** *Annual Progress Report*, annual. Report. Reports on contributions and programs. *Price:* Free.

★ 10584 ★ American Institute of the History of Pharmacy (AIHP)

Pharmacy Bldg.
425 N. Chater St.
Madison, WI 53706
Phone: (608)262-5378
Gregory J. Higby, Dir.

Founded: 1941. **Members:** 1,000. **Description:** Pharmacists, firms, and organizations interested in historical and social aspects of the pharmaceutical field. Maintains pharmaceutical Americana collection; conducts research programs. **Publications:** *AIHP Notes*, quarterly. Newsletter. *Price:* Included in membership dues. • *Pharmacy in History*, quarterly. Journal. Contains writings on the history of pharmaceutical practice, including drugs and therapeutics and related facets of the medical sciences. *Price:* Included in membership dues.

American Managed Care Pharmacy Association (AMCPA)

See: Entry 5721

★ 10585 ★ American Pharmaceutical Association (APhA)

2215 Constitution Ave. NW
Washington, DC 20037
Phone: (202)628-4410
Free: 800-237-APHA
Fax: (202)783-2351
Dr. John A. Gans, Exec.VP

Founded: 1852. **Members:** 44,000. **Description:** Professional society that includes pharmacists in all practice settings, educators, students, researchers, editors and publishers of pharmaceutical literature, pharmaceutical chemists and scientists, and food and drug officials. Promotes quality health care and comprehensive pharmaceutical care through the appropriate use of pharmacy services. Works to: represent the interests of the profession before governmental bodies; interpret and disseminate information on developments in health care; assure quality pharmacy services and patient care. Fosters professional education and training of pharmacists; supports Academy of Pharmaceutical Research and Science, Academy of Pharmacy Practice and Management, and Academy of Stu dents of Pharmacy. Maintains headquarters building in Washington, DC, called American Institute of Pharmacy, which houses library,

staff offices, and the APhA Foundation. **Publications:** *Academy Reporter*, quarterly. Newsletter. • *American Pharmacy*, monthly. Journal. *Price:* Included in membership dues; $50/year for nonmembers; $25/year for institutions. • Booklets. • *Handbook of Nonprescription Drugs*. Handbook. • *Handbook of Pharmaceutical Excipients*. Handbook. • *Journal of Pharmaceutical Sciences*, monthly. Journal. *Price:* Included in membership dues; $85/year for nonmembers; $278/year for institutions. • Manuals. • *Pediatric Dosage Handbook*. Handbook. • *The Pharmacy Student*, quarterly. Magazine. *Price:* Included in student membership dues; $25/year for nonmembers. • *Pharmacy Today*, biweekly. Newsletter. Reports on federal and state legislation and regulation of pharmaceutical products and dispensing pharmacists. Includes list of new products. *Price:* Included in membership dues; $50/year for nonmembers. Also issues kits on professional practice, history of pharmacy, and public relations.

★ 10586 ★ American Society for Automation in Pharmacy (ASAP)

c/o William A. Lockwood, Jr.
482 Norristown Rd., Ste. 112
Blue Bell, PA 19422
Phone: (610)825-7783
Fax: (610)825-7641
William A. Lockwood, Jr., Exec.Dir.

Founded: 1989. **Members:** 470. **Description:** Pharmaceutical software developers; pharmaceutical and insurance companies; related organizatios. Addresses issues related to computer use in the pharmaceutical industry. **Publications:** *Byteline*, quarterly.

★ 10587 ★ American Society of Consultant Pharmacists (ASCP)

1321 Duke St.
Alexandria, VA 22314-3563
Phone: (703)739-1300
Fax: (703)739-1321
R. Timothy Webster, Exec.Dir.

Founded: 1969. **Members:** 6,000. **Description:** Registered pharmacists and educators who are largely concerned with pharmaceutical procedures within nursing homes and related health facilities. Works to: improve consultant pharmacist services to nursing homes and other long-term care facilities; define professional standards and to promote the certification of the profession; exchange information; sponsor and encourage the development of educational facilities and courses for the advancement of the profession; promote wider public information efforts; represent the interests of the profession before legislative and administrative branches of government; sponsor group service programs; promote public health and welfare. Conducts surveys of long-term care pharmacy operations. Sponsors educational and research programs. Maintains information center, hall of fame, and speakers' bureau; operates placement service; compiles statistics. **Publications:** *Clinical Consult*, monthly. Newsletter. *Price:* Included in membership dues. • *The Consultant Pharmacist Journal*, monthly. *Price:* $45/year U.S.; $65/year outside U.S. • *UPDATE*, monthly. Newsletter. *Price:* Included in membership dues. Also publishes books and manuals.

★ 10588 ★ American Society of Hospital Pharmacists (ASHP)

7272 Wisconsin Ave.
Bethesda, MD 20814
Phone: (301)657-3000
Fax: (301)652-8278
Joseph A. Oddis, Exec.VP

Founded: 1942. **Members:** 30,000. **State Groups:** 50. **Description:** Professional society of pharmacists employed by hospitals, HMOs, clinics, and other health systems. Provides personnel placement service for members; sponsors professional and personal liability program. Conducts educational and exhibit programs. Has 30 practice interest areas, special sections for home care practitioners and clinical specialists, and research and education foundation. **Publications:** *AHFS Drug Information*, annual. *Price:* $115/year. • *American Journal of Hospital Pharmacy*, semimonthly. Journal. *Price:* Included in membership dues; $137/year for nonmembers (U.S.). • *ASHP Newsletter*, monthly. Newsletter. Covers developments in pharmacy and health care. Includes information on legislation and regulations and association news. *Price:* Included in membership dues. • Books. • *Drug Products Information File.* • *Handbook on Injectable Drugs*, biennial. • *International Pharmaceutical Abstracts*, semimonthly. *Price:* $100/year for members; $425/year for nonmembers (U.S.); $450/year for nonmembers (outside U.S.); $20 for single copy. • Videos. Also publishes user manuals and aids, and produces software, CD-ROMS, and training programs.

American Society for Pharmacy Law (ASPL)

See: Entry 7173

★ 10589 ★ Association of Democratic Pharmacists (Verein Demokratischer Pharmazeutinnen und Pharmazeuten)

Grindelalle 182
20144 Hamburg, Germany
Phone: 40 458768
Fax: 40 458768
Gudrun Hahn, Contact

Founded: 1989. **Members:** 160. **Description:** Promotes the interests of registered pharmacists in Germany. Concerned with issues focusing on environmental and public health policies. **Publications:** *VDPP-Rundbriet*, bimonthly. Journal.

★ 10590 ★ Association of Pharmacy Proprietors

Farmacia Divel
Bajos del Edificio Marichal, Apt. 1350
Tegucigalpa, Honduras
Phone: 374064
Fax: 382831
Dr. Lietzelar, Contact

Languages: Spanish. **Description:** Pharmacists and owners of pharmacies in Honduras. Represents members' economic interests. Gathers and disseminates industry information.

★ 10591 ★ **Auxiliary to the American Pharmaceutical Association**
305 W. Old Middle Creek Rd.
Prestonsburg, KY 41653
Phone: (606)886-0249
Peggy Gawronski, Pres.

Founded: 1936. **Members:** 400. **Description:** Individuals related to members in the American Pharmaceutical Association; others interested in pharmacy. Grants low-interest loans to pharmacy students annually. **Publications:** *APhA Auxiliary Newsletter*, semiannual. Newsletter. • *The Auxiliary Handbook*. **Formerly:** (1975) Women's Auxiliary of the American Pharmaceutical Association.

★ 10592 ★ **Canadian Pharmaceutical Association (CPhA)**
(Association Pharmaceutique Canadienne — APhC)
1785 Alta Vista Dr.
Ottawa, ON, Canada K1G 3Y6
Phone: (613)523-7877
Fax: (613)523-0445
Leroy Fevang, Exec. Officer

Founded: 1907. **Members:** 10,900. **Languages:** English, French. **Description:** Pharmacists in Canada. Works to improve the professional image of pharmacists and the quality of pharmacy services and health care in Canada. Monitors government health care policies and legislation; lobbies for the interests of pharmacists. Maintains liaison with government departments, pharmaceutical manufacturers, and health care organizations. Conducts education and research programs. Bestows awards. **Publications:** *A Summary of Prescription Drug Benefit Plans Sponsored by Canada Provincial Governments*, periodic. • *Activities Report*, annual. • *Canadian Pharmaceutical Journal*, monthly. • *Compendium of Pharmaceuticals and Specialties*, annual. • *Impact*, bimonthly. Newsletter. • Pamphlets, periodic. • *Pharmacy Directory*, annual. • *Self-Medication*, periodic.

★ 10593 ★ **Canadian Society of Hospital Pharmacists (CSHP)**
(Societe Canadienne des Pharmaciens d'Hopitaux — SCPH)
1145 Hunt Club Rd., Ste. 350
Ottawa, ON, Canada K1V 0Y3
Phone: (613)736-9733
Fax: (613)736-5660
Bill Leslie, Exec.Dir.

Founded: 1947. **Members:** 2,400. **State Groups:** 8. **Languages:** English, French. **Description:** Hospital pharmacists, graduate pharmacists, and students. Promotes safe and effective drug therapy in organized health care settings. Provides leadership to members in institutional pharmacy practice. Evaluates and accredits postgraduate training programs in hospital pharmacy through the Canadian Hospital Pharmacy Residency Board. Enhances the visibility of hospital pharmacy in the health care field through public relations activities and meetings with government and health care associations. Promotes programs of continuing education; operates the CSHP Research and Educational Foundation. Maintains committees and task forces to recommend development of areas of interest and need to members; promotes funding and research programs. **Publications:** *Canadian Journal of Hospital Pharmacy*, bimonthly. Journal. • *Employment Opportunities Bulletin*, biweekly. Bulletin. • *Pharmascope*, bimonthly. Newsletter.

China Association of Research and Development of Traditional Chinese Medicine and Pharmacy
See: Entry 2183

★ 10594 ★ **Chinese Pharmaceutical Association**
A38 N. Lishi Rd.
Beijing 100810, People's Republic of China
Phone: 1 8316576
Fax: 1 2016358
Hai-Jun Zhou, Sec.Gen.

Founded: 1907. **Members:** 44. **Description:** Pharmacists' organizations representing the interests of 450,000 pharmacists in the People's Republic of China. Promotes advanced pharmaceutical technologies. Organizes research projects concerned with traditional Chinese medicine, Western medicine, and pharmacological history. Conducts educational and training programs. Fosters cooperation and information exchange with pharmacists in other countries. **Publications:** *Journal of Chinese Pharmacology*, periodic. Journal. • *Pharmaceuticals*, periodic. • *Pharmacology*, periodic.

★ 10595 ★ **Christian Pharmacists Fellowship International (CPFI)**
PO Box 1667
Buies Creek, NC 27506
Phone: (910)814-2014
Fred M. Eckel, Exec.Dir.

Founded: 1984. **Members:** 1,200. **Regional Groups:** 3. **State Groups:** 3. **Local Groups:** 7. **Description:** To promote and maintain fellowship among Christian pharmacists. Establishes clubs and chapters at universities, colleges, schools, hospitals, and in communities; sponsors activities and retreats for Christian pharmacists and their families. Encourages active Christian witness and evangelism; teaches pharmacists how to share and present the Gospel of Jesus Christ in their practice; disseminates information among Christian pharmacists; identifies areas of service for pharmacists in missions worldwide and sponsors missionaries in the field. Provides and promotes Christian pharmacist-speakers. Conducts gatherings, such as prayer groups, with speakers at state and national pharmacy meetings. **Publications:** *Christian Pharmacists Fellowship International-- Newsletter*, quarterly. Newsletter. Reports on the activities of members and the fellowship, as well as Christian events in pharmacy. Includes book reviews and directory. *Price:* Free. • Membership Directory, biennial.

★ 10596 ★ **Commonwealth Pharmaceutical Association (CPA)**
1 Lambeth High St.
London SE1 7JN, England
Phone: 171 7359141
Fax: 171 7357629
Mr. Philip Green, Sec.

Founded: 1970. **Regional Groups:** 6. **Languages:** English. **Description:** Pharmaceutical organizations in 38 Commonwealth countries; pharmacists. Objectives are to: maintain the honor and traditions of the profession and promote high standards of conduct, practice, and education at all levels; encourage close links among members in the profession and facilitate personal contacts between pharmacists and students; disseminate information about the professional practice of pharmacy and the pharmaceutical sciences. **Publications:** *Newsletter*, quarterly. Newsletter.

★ 10597 ★ **European Association of Hospital Pharmacists (EAHP)**
Universitatsklinikum Steglitz Apotheke
Freie Universitat Berlin
Hindenburgdamm 30
12200 Berlin, Germany
Phone: 30 84450
Fax: 30 8347650
Mr. J. Kotwas, Pres.

Founded: 1972. **Members:** 9,000. **Languages:** English, French, German. **Description:** Individuals from 16 countries. Promotes and protects the interests of hospital pharmacists; disseminates information. **Publications:** *European Journal of Hospital Pharmacy*, periodic. Journal.

★ 10598 ★ **European Pharmacopoeia Commission**
(Commission Europeenne de Pharmacopee)
Coun. of Europe
BP 431 R6
F-67006 Strasbourg Cedex, France
Phone: 88 412000
Fax: 88 412771
Dr. P.J. Schorn, Tech.Sec.

Founded: 1964. **Members:** 19. **Languages:** English, French. **Description:** European countries. Works to develop a European pharmacopoeia (an officially sanctioned book describing drugs, chemicals, and medical preparations). Seeks to establish uniform control methods and standards of quality for medicines in member countries. **Publications:** *Pharmeuropa: European Pharmacopoeia Forum*, quarterly.

European Proprietary Medicines Manufacturers' Association (AESGP)
(Europaischer Fachverband der Arzneimittel-Hersteller)
See: Entry 5846

★ 10599 ★ **Foreign Pharmacy Graduate Examination Committee (FPGEC)**
c/o Carmen A. Catizone
National Association of Boards of Pharmacy
700 Busse Hwy.
Park Ridge, IL 60068
Phone: (708)698-6227
Fax: (708)698-0124
Carmen A. Catizone, Exec.Dir.

Founded: 1982. **Description:** A committee of the National Association of Boards of Pharmacy. Provides information to foreign pharmacy graduates regarding entry into the U.S. pharmacy profession and health care systems. Evaluates qualifications of foreign pharmacy graduates. Gathers and disseminates data on foreign graduates; maintains information on foreign pharmacy schools in order to produce an examination that measures academic competence with regard to U.S. pharmacy school standards. **Formerly:** (1988) Foreign Pharmacy Graduate Examination Commission.

Foundation of Pharmacists and Corporate America for AIDS Education (FPCA)
See: Entry 6669

Generic Pharmaceutical Industry Association (GPIA)
See: Entry 5850

★ 10600 ★ **German Druggists Association (Verband Deutscher Drogisten)**
Friedrich-Schmidt-Str. 53
50935 Cologne, Germany
Phone: 221 401038
Fax: 221 404436
Norbert Fecke, Contact

Description: Pharmacists in Germany. Promotes the professional and economic interests of members.

Health Care Compliance Packaging Council (HCPC)
See: Entry 5851

★ 10601 ★ **Hong Kong General Chamber of Pharmacy**
401 Winning House
10 Cochrane St.
Hong Kong, Hong Kong
Phone: 5439123

Languages: Chinese, English. **Description:** Pharmacies, pharmacists, and other individuals with an interest in the retail pharmaceutical trade in Hong Kong. Works to enhance the professional status of members; develops standards of practice; conducts educational programs.

International Committee of Homeopathic Pharmacists
(Comite International des Pharmaciens Homeopathiques — CIPH)
See: Entry 2212

★ 10602 ★ **International Federation of Associations of Pharmaceutical Physicians (IFAPP)**
43 Galgenstraat
B-3078 Everburg, Belgium
Phone: 2 7594531
Fax: 2 7599980
Dr. Herman F.J. Lahon, Contact

Founded: 1975. **Members:** 25. **Languages:** English. **Description:** National organizations representing 3000 physicians in 24 countries specializing in pharmaceutical medicine. Encourages contact among members.

★ 10603 ★ **International Federation of Catholic Pharmacists**
(Federation Internationale des Pharmaciens Catholiques — FIPC)
Bergstrasse 59
B-4700 Eupen, Belgium
Phone: 87 742054
Fax: 87 742054
Manfred Schunck, Sec.Gen.

Founded: 1950. **Members:** 20. **Languages:** English, French, German. **Description:** Nation-al associations of Catholic pharmacists. Seeks Christian solutions to all problems affecting the profession; promotes international understanding among members. Sponsors study commissions and regional study days. **Publications:** *Acta-FIPC*, biennial. • *Listing-FIPC*, biennial.

★ 10604 ★ **International Pharmaceutical Federation (IPF)**
(Federation Internationale Pharmaceutique — FIP)
Andries Bickerweg 5
NL-2517 JP The Hague, Netherlands
Phone: 70 3631925
Fax: 70 3633914
L.G. Felix-Faure, Deputy Gen.Sec.

Founded: 1912. **Members:** 4,000. **Languages:** English, French, German, Spanish. **Description:** Pharmaceutical organizations, pharmacists, and other interested organizations in 80 countries. Objectives are to: develop pharmacy at the international level in professional and scientific fields; extend the role of the pharmacist in the health care field; foster communication among members; act as a clearinghouse; collaborate with efforts to improve pharmaceutical structures in various countries; advocate and support measures to ensure distribution, dispensation, and proper use of medicines. Exchanges opinions on professional and ethical issues; develops research and study programs; fosters cooperation among pharmacists, teachers, research workers, and the practitioners in the field of drug information; improves methods for assembling, selecting, summarizing, indexing, storing, classifying, and analyzing clinical and social surveys. Subjects studied include biopharmaceutics, pharmacokinetics and drug metabolism, administrative and social pharmacy, pharmacognosy, and the history of pharmacy. Collaborates with World Health Organization **Publications:** *International Pharmacy Journal*, bimonthly. Journal. Includes summaries in German and Spanish. • *Scientific Congress Proceedings*, biennial. Also publishes abstracts.

★ 10605 ★ **International Pharmaceutical Students' Federation (IPSF)**
(Federation Internationale des Etudiants en Pharmacie)
Andries Bickerweg 5
NL-2517 JP The Hague, Netherlands
Phone: 70 3631925
Fax: 70 3633914
Ms. Naomi Smith, Sec. Gen.

Founded: 1949. **Members:** 250,000. **Languages:** English, French, German, Spanish. **Description:** National organizations of pharmacy students who represent 50% of all pharmacy students in their countries; national or local pharmacy student organizations; pharmacists who have been graduated at least 4 years; pharmacy students and graduates who have been graduated less than 4 years. Objectives are to study and promote interests of pharmacy students and encourage international cooperation. Sponsors student exchange program; maintains development fund; collects documentation and information on student issues. Organizes competitions and presents awards. Sponsors development fund for Third World countries and book appeal. **Publications:** *IPSF News and Views*, 4-6/year. Newsletter. • *IPSF News Bulletin*, 3-4/year. Bulletin. Also publishes reports on meetings and symposia papers.

★ 10606 ★ **Kappa Psi**
c/o Kappa Psi Central Office
University of Oklahoma HSC
College of Pharmacy
1110 N. Stonewall
Oklahoma City, OK 73190
Phone: (405)271-6942
Fax: (405)271-3830
Robert A. Magarian, Ph.D., Exec.Dir.

Founded: 1879. **Members:** 46,000. **Regional Groups:** 62. **State Groups:** 41. **Description:** Professional fraternity - pharmacy. **Publications:** *Constitution and By-Laws*. • Handbook. • *The History of Kappa Psi*. • *The Mask*, quarterly. • *Pledge Manual*.

★ 10607 ★ **Lambda Kappa Sigma (LKS)**
745 W. Sunset Rd., Ste. 3
Henderson, NV 89015
Phone: (517)356-8797
Fax: (517)356-6574
Michelle Berrier, Exec.Dir.

Founded: 1913. **Members:** 18,000. **Regional Groups:** 8. **Local Groups:** 60. **Description:** Professional fraternity - pharmacy. **Publications:** *Blue and Gold Triangle*, quarterly. • *Compounding Was More Fun*. • *Lambda Kappa Sigma Membership Directory*, every four to five years. Membership Directory. • *LinKS*, periodic. Newsletter. • *Prospectus*. • *Women in Pharmacy Leadership Directory*. Directory. *Price:* $25.

NARD
See: Entry 5863

★ 10608 ★ **National Association of Boards of Pharmacy (NABP)**
700 Busse Hwy.
Park Ridge, IL 60068
Phone: (708)698-6227
Fax: (708)698-0124
Carmen A. Catizone, Exec.Dir.

Founded: 1904. **Members:** 63. **Description:** Pharmacy boards of several states, District of Columbia, Puerto Rico, Virgin Islands, several Canadian provinces, and the states of Victoria, Australia, and New South Wales. Provides for inter-state reciprocity in pharmaceutic licensure based upon a uniform minimum standard of pharmaceutical education and uniform legislation; improves the standards of pharmaceutical education licensure and practice. Provides legislative information; sponsors uniform licensure examination; also provides information on accredited school and college requirements. Maintains pharmacy and drug law statistics. **Publications:** *NABP Newsletter*, 10/year. Newsletter. Reports on regulation and licensure in the pharmacy profession. Contains information on the NABP licensure exam. *Price:* $25/year. • *The NAB-PLEX Candidate's Review Guide*, annual. • Proceedings, annual. • *State Board Newsletter*, quarterly. Newsletter. Covers 35 states. • *Survey of Pharmacy Law*, annual. Survey. • Surveys. Also publishes periodically updated guides and examination manuals.

★ 10609 ★ National Association of German
Pharmacists
(Bundesverband Deutscher Apotheker)
Liederbacher Str. 97
65929 Frankfurt, Germany
Phone: 69 312464
Fax: 69 313335
Barbara Frank, Contact

Description: Pharmacists in Germany. Represents members' interests. Promotes the pharmaceutical industry.

★ 10610 ★ National Association of Women
Pharmacists (NAWP)
c/o Office Manager
Royal Pharmaceutical Society of Great Britain
1 Lambeth High St.
London SE1 7JN, England
Dr. Cherrie Temple

Founded: 1905. Members: 400. Regional
Groups: 5. Languages: English. Description:
Women pharmacists. Promotes the careers of
women in pharmacy and the role of women
pharmacists in public life. Encourages continuing education and career development for
women pharmacists. Maintains communication
with pharmacists who have left the Register of
the Royal Pharmaceutical Society of Great Britian (RPSGB) during a career break. Works with
other women's organizations. Conducts
courses and lectures. Publications: NAWP, 3/
year. Newsletter. • Women in Pharmacy Information Pack. Book.

★ 10611 ★ National Catholic Pharmacists
Guild of the United States (NCPG)
1012 Surrey Hills Dr.
St. Louis, MO 63117-1438
Phone: (314)645-0085
John Paul Winkelmann, Exec.Dir.& Co-Pres.

Founded: 1962. Members: 400. National
Groups: 1. Description: Catholic pharmacists,
pharmacy graduates, students, and pharmacy
technicians. Upholds the principles of the Catholic faith and all laws of church and country, especially those pertaining to the practice of pharmacy; assists ecclesiastical authorities in the
diffusion of Catholic pharmacy ethics; promotes
donations of funds and supplies to the needy;
opposes the sale of pornographic literature, especially that which is being sold in pharmacies;
fosters brotherhood and goodwill among all
pharmacists. Provides pharmaceuticals and
funds for people worldwide. Publications: Catholic Pharmacist, quarterly. Includes obituaries,
membership and professional news, new member listings, and book reports. Price: Included in
membership dues; $20/year for nonmembers.

★ 10612 ★ National Council on Patient
Information and Education (NCPIE)
666 11th St. NW, Ste. 810
Washington, DC 20001
Phone: (202)347-6711
Fax: (202)638-0773
William Ray Bullman, Exec.Dir.

Founded: 1982. Members: 389. Description:
Health care professional organizations, pharmaceutical manufacturing organizations, federal agencies, voluntary health agencies, and consumer groups. Increases the availability of infor-

mation and improves the dialogue between consumers and health care providers about
prescription medicines; increases professional
awareness of the need to give adequate information on prescription therapy; expands consumers' participation with health professionals
on matters of drug therapy. Communicates with
health care providers on the importance of giving consumers oral and written information on
prescription medicines and encourages consumers to ask questions about medicines and
explain factors that may affect their ability to follow prescriptions. Distributes public service announcements for television and radio and conducts print media campaigns. Sponsors the National Brown Bag Medicine Review Program.
Publications: A Consumer's Guide to Prescription Medicine. Brochure. • A Parents Guide to
Medicine Use By Children. Brochure. • Alcohol
and Medicines: Ask Before You Mix. Brochure.
• Get the Answers. Brochure. • Guidelines for
Improving Prescription Medicine Use Among
Children and Teenagers. Brochure. • Medicine: Before
You Take It, Talk About It. Brochure. • Medicines: What Every Woman Should Know. Brochure. • NCPIE News, quarterly. Newsletter. •
Talk About Prescriptions: Month Planning
Guide, annual. Newsletter.

National Council for Prescription Drug
Programs (NCPDP)
See: Entry 5595

National Council of State Pharmacy
Association Executives (NCSPAE)
See: Entry 5597

★ 10613 ★ National Pharmaceutical
Association (NPhA)
Howard University
College of Pharmacy and Pharmacal Sciences
P.O. Box 835332
Richardson, TX 75083
Phone: (214)806-6530
Fax: (214)235-4211
Dr. Billie McMiller, Pres.

Founded: 1947. Members: 325. Description:
State and local associations of professional minority pharmacists. To provide a means whereby members may "contribute to their common
improvement, share their experiences, and contribute to the public good." Publications: Journal of the NPhA, quarterly. Journal. Price: $20/
year for individuals (U.S.); $35/year for institutions (U.S.); $30/year for individuals (outside
U.S.); $45/year for institutions (outside U.S.).

★ 10614 ★ Panhellenic Association of
Pharmacists (PEF)
Korizi 6
Makrigianni
GR-117 43 Athens, Greece
Phone: 1 9227182
Fax: 1 9232964
Manolis Agelakas, Pres.

Founded: 1928. Members: 1,700. Languages:
English, German, Greek. Description: Pharmacists in Greece. Represents the interests of
pharmacists. Seeks to improve the level of pharmaceutical science. Sponsors seminars. Publications: Abstracts of PEF Seminars, Meetings,
and Conferences. • Pharmakeutika Chronika,
quarterly. Magazine. Features professional and
scientific articles.

★ 10615 ★ Pharmaceutical Association
PO Box 3794
Harare, Zimbabwe
Phone: 4 702431

Languages: English. Description: Pharmacists
and pharmacists' organizations in Zimbabwe.
Promotes advancement in pharmaceutical technologies. Organizes and conducts research
projects. Fosters communication and exchange
of information among members and between
members and their counterparts worldwide.

★ 10616 ★ Pharmaceutical Group of the
European Community
13, sq. Ambiorix
B-1040 Brussels, Belgium
Phone: 2 7367281
Fax: 2 7360206
Paul Baetens, Sec.Gen.

★ 10617 ★ Pharmaceutical Society of
Singapore (PSS)
Alumni Medical Centre
2 College Rd.
Singapore 0316, Singapore
Phone: 2211136
Fax: 2230969
Mr. Eng Tong Seng, Hon.Sec.

Founded: 1967. Members: 753. Languages:
English. Description: Seeks to maximize the
contribution of pharmacists to health care by enforcing a code of ethics, cooperating with other
organizations, and providing educational programs. Sponsors competitions and bestows
awards. Publications: Singapore Pharmaceutical Bulletin, quarterly. Bulletin. Formerly:
(1967) Malayan Pharmaceutical Association.

Pharmacists Against Drug Abuse (PADA)
See: Entry 12069

Pharmacists for Life International (PFLI)
See: Entry 11243

★ 10618 ★ Pharmacists in Ophthalmic
Practice (P1OP)
Wills Eye Hospital
900 Walnut Sts.
Philadelphia, PA 19107
Phone: (215)928-3002
Fax: (215)928-3002
Clement A. Weisbecker, Bd.Chm.

Founded: 1984. Members: 26. Description:
Pharmacists who serve as directors or chief
pharmacists of institutions that specialize in
ophthalmology or otolaryngology. Exchanges
information and determines standards relating
to ophthalmological pharmacy, pharmacology,
and formulations. Conducts research and compiles statistics on ophthalmic pharmacy, products, and medication. Publications: Directory of
Pharmacists in Ophthalmic Institutions, periodic.
Directory. • Newsletter, semiannual.

★ 10619 ★ Phi Delta Chi
PO Box 6565
Athens, GA 30604
Phone: (706)613-0100
Fax: (706)613-0200
L. Michael Posey, Exec.Dir.

Founded: 1883. Members: 37,000. Regional
Groups: 5. Description: Professional fraternity

- pharmacy. Compiles statistics. **Publications:** *The Communicator*, quarterly. • *Who's Who in Phi Delta Chi*, annual.

★ 10620 ★ **Rho Chi**
Duquesne University
School of Pharmacy
Mellon Hall of Science
Pittsburgh, PA 15282
Phone: (412)396-6361
Fax: (412)396-5130
J. Douglas Bricker, Contact

Founded: 1922. **Members:** 43,000. **Description:** Honor society - men and women, pharmacy. Presents annual Rho Chi Lecture. **Publications:** *History, Constitution and Bylaws*, annual. • Membership Directory, annual, every 10 years. Includes annual supplements. • Report, annual. **Formerly:** (1922) Aristolochite Society.

★ 10621 ★ **Royal Dutch Society for Advancement of Pharmacy (RDSAP) (Koninklijke Nederlandse Maatschappij ter Bevordering der Pharmacie — KNMP)**
Alexanderstrasse 11
NL-2514 JL The Hague, Netherlands
Phone: 70 3624111
Fax: 70 3106530
C.J. de Blaey, Dir.

Founded: 1843. **Members:** 3,500. **Languages:** English, French, German. **Description:** Works to advance the pharmacy profession in the Netherlands. **Publications:** *Informatorium Medicamentorum*, annual. • *Taxen*, monthly. Contains price lists.

★ 10622 ★ **Royal Institute of Public Health and Hygiene (RIPHH)**
28 Portland Pl.
London W1N 4DE, England
Phone: 171 5802731
Fax: 171 5806157
R.A. Smith, Exec.Officer

Founded: 1937. **Members:** 2,000. **Languages:** English. **Description:** Caterers, doctors, environmental health officers, food technologists, laboratory and mortuary technicians, microbiologists, nurses, and teachers promoting the advancement of domestic, industrial, and personal health and hygiene. Encourages the study of hygiene, preventive medicine, and public health. Bestows awards; offers courses; holds seminars. **Publications:** *Handbook of Mortuary Practice and Safety for Anatomical Pathology Technicians*. Handbook. • *Handbook of the Royal Institute*, annual. Handbook. • *Health and Hygiene*, quarterly. Book.

★ 10623 ★ **Royal Pharmaceutical Society of Great Britain (RPSGB)**
1 Lambeth High St.
London SE1 7JN, England
Phone: 171 7359141
Fax: 171 7357629
John Ferguson, Sec. and Registrar

Languages: English. **Description:** Pharmaceutical manufacturers, medical practitioners, and pharmacists. **Publications:** *The Extra Pharmacopeia*. Book. • *Martindale Online Newsletter*, periodic. Newsletter. • *Martindale Online User Guide*. Handbook. • *Martindale Thesaurus*. Book.

★ 10624 ★ **Society for Medicines Research (SMR)**
Institute of Biology
20 Queensberry Pl.
London SW7 2DZ, England
Phone: 171 5818333
Fax: 171 8239409
Mrs. B. J. Cavilla, Sec.

Founded: 1966. **Members:** 1,100. **Languages:** English. **Description:** Researchers at academic institutions and in the pharmaceutical industry; other concerned individuals. Promotes advancement in the field of drug education and research in order to provide the public with proper information on drug usage for relief of sickness. **Publications:** Newsletter, 3-4/year. • *Proceedings*, periodic. **Formerly:** (1994) Society for Drug Research.

★ 10625 ★ **United States Pharmacopeial Convention (USP)**
12601 Twinbrook Pky.
Rockville, MD 20852
Phone: (301)881-0666
Free: 800-227-8772
Fax: (301)816-8247
Jerome A. Halperin, Exec.Dir.

Founded: 1820. **Members:** 395. **Description:** Recognized authorities in medicine, pharmacy, and allied sciences. Revises and publishes legally recognized compendia of drug standards. Offers continuing pharmacy education. **Publications:** *About Your High Blood Pressure Medicines*, semiannual. • *About Your Medicines*, semiannual. • *National Formulary*, quinquennial. Includes semiannual supplement. • *Pharmacopeial Forum*, bimonthly. • *Proceedings of Quinquennial Meetings*. Proceedings. • *United States Pharmacopeia*, quinquennial. Includes semiannual supplement. • *USAN and USP Dictionary of Drug Names*, annual. • *USP DI Update*, monthly. • *USP DI, Volume I, Drug Information for Health Care Professional*, annual. Includes monthly supplement. • *USP DI, Volume II, Advice for the Patient*, annual. • *USP DI, Volume III, Approved Drug Products and Legal Requirements*, annual. • Videos. On diabetes.

Woman's Organization of the National Association of Retail Druggists (WONARD)
See: Entry 5887

Research Centers

★ 10626 ★ **American College of Apothecaries Research and Education Foundation**
205 Daingerfield Rd.
Alexandria, VA 22314
Phone: (703)684-8603
Fax: (703)683-3619
D.C. Huffman, Jr., Exec.Dir.

Research Activities and Fields: Three-fold objective of the Foundation is to promote public welfare through development of services in institutions providing health care, encourage and conduct research to improve health care and

education, and encourage health care practitioners to improve the quality and availability of their services.

★ 10627 ★ **American Institute of the History of Pharmacy**
Pharmacy Bldg.
425 N. Charter St.
Madison, WI 53706
Phone: (608)262-5378
Gregory Higby, Ph.D., Dir.

Research Activities and Fields: Historical aspects of pharmacy as a profession, a science, and an industry, and history of materia medica. Conducts and stimulates research and collects American pharmaceutical manuscript material, for which State Historical Society of Wisconsin serves as depository. Presents recognition awards and grants-in-aid for historical research. Maintains publication and historical markers programs. **Publications:** *Pharmacy in History* (quarterly); Papers; Pamphlets.

★ 10628 ★ **Center for the Study of Drug Development**
Tufts Univ.
192 South St., Ste. 550
Boston, MA 02111
Phone: (617)636-0070
Fax: (617)350-0070
Dr. Louis Lasagna, Dir.

Research Activities and Fields: Worldwide drug development and its trends, including study of the impact of drug regulation on pharmaceutical innovation, survey of pharmaceutical firms to determine origin, flow, and fate of new chemical entities (NCEs)in U.S., Great Britain, Switzerland, and Germany, evaluation of therapeutic significance of marketed drugs, and economic analysis of drug development costs. **Publications:** Newsletter (three times per year).

★ 10629 ★ **Long Island University Pharmaceutical Study Center**
Schwartz College of Pharmacy
One University Plaza
75 DeKalb Ave.
Brooklyn, NY 11201
Phone: (718)488-1234
Fax: (718)643-9687
Alisa Yalan, Media Dir.

Research Activities and Fields: Pharmacy, pharmacology, pharmacy administration, drug information, and hospital pharmacy.

U.S. Department of Health and Human Services
Food and Drug Administration
Center for Drug Evaluation and Research
See: Entry 10995

★ 10630 ★ **U.S. Department of Health and Human Services**
Food and Drug Administration
Office of Orphan Products Development
5600 Fishers Ln.
HF-35
Rockville, MD 20857
Phone: (301)443-4903
Fax: (301)443-4915
Marlene E. Haffner, M.D., M.P.H., Director

Research Activities and Fields: Function is to identify and facilitate the availability of orphan products. Orphan products are defined as drugs, biologics, medical devices, and foods for medical purposes which are indicated for a rare disease or condition (i.e., one affecting fewer than 200,00 people in the U.S.). Grants and contracts support clinical research intended to provide safety and efficacy data acceptable to the FDA which will either result in or substantially contribute to the approval of the products.

★ 10631 ★　University of Arizona
Center for Pharmaceutical Economics
College of Pharmacy
Tucson, AZ 85721
Phone: (520)626-4450
Fax: (520)626-2023
Stephen Joel Coons, Ph.D., Dir.

Research Activities and Fields: Assessment of outcomes associated with the use of pharmaceuticals, including quality of life assessment and pharmacoeconomic analysis (cost-effectiveness and cost-utility analysis). Also focuses on the development and assessment of disease intervention models and disease management programs.

★ 10632 ★　University of Florida
Center for Drug Discovery
College of Pharmacy
Box 100487
Gainesville, FL 32610
Phone: (904)392-8509
Fax: (904)392-9364
Dr. Jim Simpkins, Dir.

Research Activities and Fields: Alzheimer's drug research, including calcium in Alzheimer's disease, mechanisms of anabaseine and DMAB anabaseine as it enhances neuron viability, brain targeted delivery of TRH, brain enhanced delivery of neurotrophomodulators, estrogen therapy, and nicotine receptors. **Formerly:** Program for Drug Discovery.

★ 10633 ★　University of Georgia
College of Pharmacy
Department of Research and Graduate Studies
Athens, GA 30602
Phone: (706)542-5417
Dr. Matthew Perri, Coord.

Research Activities and Fields: Medicinal chemistry, pharmaceutics, pharmacology, toxicology, and pharmacy administration, including studies of synthetic antimalarials, antineoplastics, anti-AIDS compounds, microencapsulation of drugs, drug induced enzyme induction, dietary influences on drug metabolism, analytical chemistry, hypertension and anti-hypertension drug action, drug utilization studies, drug abuse, pharmacy manpower, marketing of drug products, and socioeconomics of pharmacy practice. **E-mail Address:** mah.merc.rx.uga.edu.

★ 10634 ★　University of Kentucky
Pharmaceutical Science and Technology Center
College of Pharmacy, Rm. 234
907 Rose St.
Lexington, KY 40536-0082
Phone: (606)323-5329
Fax: (606)323-1921
Dr. Thomas S. Foster, Dir.

Research Activities and Fields: Drug product development and evaluation. Provides industrial support through the development and preparation of clinical supplies of drug products under government regulations. **E-mail Address:** fostert@uklans.uky.edu.

★ 10635 ★　University of Maryland
Center on Drugs and Public Policy
School of Pharmacy
20 N. Pine St.
Baltimore, MD 21201-1180
Phone: (410)455-1218
Fax: (410)455-3978
David A. Knapp, Ph.D., Dir.

Research Activities and Fields: Drug utilization review, outpatient drug benefits under the OBRA 90, cost effective drug therapies, pharmaceutical care services, health outcomes related to drug therapy, pharmacoepidemiology, pharmacy manpower, the pharmaceutical industry, impact of changes in the organization and financing of health care services, and patient compliance with prescribed drug regimen.

★ 10636 ★　University of Mississippi
Pharmaceutical Marketing and Management Research Program
School of Pharmacy
Faser Hall
University, MS 38677
Phone: (601)232-5948
Dr. Mickey Smith, Dir.

Research Activities and Fields: Proprietary and inhouse marketing and management studies relating to pharmaceutical products, including formulary decision factors, vendor selection, reimbursement issues, and consumer preferences. Conducts mail surveys, mall intercept surveys, telephone interviews, focus groups, consumer reaction panels, cost-effectiveness studies, and surveys of professionals at national and state meetings.

★ 10637 ★　University of Mississippi
Research Institute of Pharmaceutical Sciences
School of Pharmacy
University, MS 38677
Phone: (601)232-7132
Fax: (601)232-5118
Dr. James D. McChesney, Dir.

Research Activities and Fields: Health services, concerned with rural health and gerontology; biological sciences, conducting toxicology studies and studies on the biological effects of drugs and drug abuse; and physical sciences, providing contractual analyses of specific chemical substances and conducting methodological research, drug discovery research, and studies on the chemistry and metabolism of drugs and drugs of abuse. **Publications:** *Pharmacy Report* (semiannually).

★ 10638 ★　University of Missouri—Kansas City
Drug Information Service
2411 Holmes; MG-200
Kansas City, MO 64108
Phone: (816)235-5490
Fax: (816)235-5491
Kevin G. Moores, Pharm., Dir.

Research Activities and Fields: Literature research and evaluation of clinical drug problems and questions from health professionals.

★ 10639 ★　University of Texas at Austin
Drug Dynamics Institute
College of Pharmacy
Austin, TX 78712-1074
Phone: (512)471-4841
Fax: (512)471-2746
Dr. Thomas G. Gerding, Dir.

Research Activities and Fields: Pharmaceutical research, development, and testing, including discovery of new medicinal agents, improvement of drug therapy, mechanisms of drug action, and re-evaluation of marketed products.

★ 10640 ★　University of Wisconsin—Madison
Sonderegger Research Center
School of Pharmacy
425 N. Charter St.
Madison, WI 53706
Phone: (608)263-9664
Betty Chewning, Ph.D., Dir.

Research Activities and Fields: Interdisciplinary health care research, including quality of health care in nursing homes, economic issues in delivery and reimbursement of pharmacy services, health care provider-patient communication, legal aspects of pharmacy practice, use of computerized education and decision-making programs for consumers, and impact of federal and state policy/regulation in pharmacy prescribing and practice. **Formerly:** Sonderegger Center for Research in Pharmacy Administration (1988).

State Government Agencies

Pharmacy Boards

★ 10641 ★　Alabama State Board of Pharmacy
1 Perimeter Park S., Ste. 425
Birmingham, AL 35243
Phone: (205)967-0130

★ 10642 ★　Alaska Board of Pharmacy
PO Box 110806
Juneau, AK 99811-0806
Phone: (907)465-2589

★ 10643 ★　Arizona State Board of Pharmacy
5060 N. 19th Ave., Ste. 101
Phoenix, AZ 85015
Phone: (602)255-5125

★ 10644 ★　Arkansas State Board of Pharmacy
101 E. Capitol, Ste. 218
Little Rock, AR 72201
Phone: (501)682-0190

★ 10645 ★　California State Board of Pharmacy
400 R St., Ste. 4070
Sacramento, CA 95814
Phone: (916)445-5014

★ 10646 ★ Colorado State Board of
Pharmacy
1560 Broadway, Ste. 1310
Denver, CO 80202-5146
Phone: (303)894-7750

★ 10647 ★ Connecticut Board of Pharmacy
State Office Bldg., Rm. G1-A
Hartford, CT 06106
Phone: (203)566-3290

★ 10648 ★ Delaware State Board of
Pharmacy
Jesse Cooper Bldg.
Federal & Water Sts.
Dover, DE 19901
Phone: (302)739-4708

★ 10649 ★ District of Columbia Board of
Pharmacy
614 H St. NW, Rm. 904
Washington, DC 20001
Phone: (202)727-7468

★ 10650 ★ Florida Board of Pharmacy
Northwood Center
1940 N. Monroe, Ste. 60
Tallahassee, FL 32399-0775
Phone: (904)488-7546

★ 10651 ★ Georgia State Board of
Pharmacy
166 Pryor St. SW
Atlanta, GA 30303
Phone: (404)656-3912

★ 10652 ★ Hawaii State Board of Pharmacy
PO Box 3469
Honolulu, HI 96801
Phone: (808)586-2698

★ 10653 ★ Idaho Board of Pharmacy
280 N. 8th St., Ste. 204
Boise, ID 83720
Phone: (208)334-2356

★ 10654 ★ Illinois Department of
Professional Regulation
Board of Pharmacy
320 W. Washington St., 3rd Fl.
Springfield, IL 62786
Phone: (217)782-8556

★ 10655 ★ Indiana Health Professions
Bureau
Board of Pharmacy
402 W. Washington St., Rm. 041
Indianapolis, IN 46204-2739
Phone: (317)232-1140

★ 10656 ★ Iowa Board of Pharmacy
Examiners
1209 E. Court
Executive Hills W.
Des Moines, IA 50319
Phone: (515)281-5944

★ 10657 ★ Kansas State Board of
Pharmacy
Landon State Office Bldg., Rm. 513
900 Jackson
Topeka, KS 66612
Phone: (913)296-4056

★ 10658 ★ Kentucky Board of Pharmacy
1228 U.S. 127 S.
Frankfort, KY 40601
Phone: (502)564-3833

★ 10659 ★ Louisiana Board of Pharmacy
5615 Corporate Blvd., Ste. 8-E
Baton Rouge, LA 70808
Phone: (504)925-6496

★ 10660 ★ Maine Board of Commissioners
of the Profession of Pharmacy
State House Sta. 35
Augusta, ME 04333
Phone: (207)582-8723

★ 10661 ★ Maryland Board of Pharmacy
4201 Patterson Ave.
Baltimore, MD 21215-2299
Phone: (410)764-4755

★ 10662 ★ Massachusetts Board of
Pharmacy
100 Cambridge St., Rm. 1514
Boston, MA 02202
Phone: (617)727-7390

★ 10663 ★ Michigan Board of Pharmacy
611 W. Ottawa, 4th Fl.
PO Box 30018
Lansing, MI 48909
Phone: (517)373-0620

★ 10664 ★ Minnesota Board of Pharmacy
2700 University Ave. W., No. 107
St. Paul, MN 55114-1079
Phone: (612)642-0541

★ 10665 ★ Mississippi State Board of
Pharmacy
PO Box 24507
Jackson, MS 39225-4507
Phone: (601)354-6750

★ 10666 ★ Missouri State Board of
Pharmacy
PO Box 625
Jefferson City, MO 65102
Phone: (314)751-0091

★ 10667 ★ Montana Board of Pharmacy
510 1st Ave. N., Ste. 100
Great Falls, MT 59401
Phone: (406)761-5131

★ 10668 ★ Nebraska Board of Examiners in
Pharmacy
PO Box 95007
Lincoln, NE 68509
Phone: (402)471-2115

★ 10669 ★ Nevada State Board of
Pharmacy
1201 Terminal Way, Ste. 122
Reno, NV 89502
Phone: (702)322-0691

★ 10670 ★ New Hampshire Board of
Pharmacy
57 Regional Dr.
Concord, NH 03301
Phone: (603)271-2350

★ 10671 ★ New Jersey State Board of
Pharmacy
PO Box 45013
Newark, NJ 07101
Phone: (201)504-6450

★ 10672 ★ New Mexico Board of Pharmacy
University Towers
1650 University Blvd. NE, Ste. 400-B
Albuquerque, NM 87102
Phone: (505)841-9102

★ 10673 ★ New York State Board of
Pharmacy
Cultural Education Center, Rm. 3035
Albany, NY 12230
Phone: (518)474-3848

★ 10674 ★ North Carolina Board of
Pharmacy
PO Box 459
Carrboro, NC 27510-0459
Phone: (919)942-4454

★ 10675 ★ North Dakota State Board of
Pharmacy
PO Box 1354
Bismarck, ND 58502-1354
Phone: (701)258-1535

★ 10676 ★ Ohio State Board of Pharmacy
77 S. High St., 17th Fl.
Columbus, OH 43266-0320
Phone: (614)466-4143

★ 10677 ★ Oklahoma State Board of
Pharmacy
4545 N. Lincoln, Ste. 112
Oklahoma City, OK 73105
Phone: (405)521-3815

★ 10678 ★ Oregon State Board of
Pharmacy
State Office Bldg., Ste. 425
800 NE Oregon St., No. 9
Portland, OR 97232
Phone: (503)731-4032

★ 10679 ★ Pennsylvania State Board of
Pharmacy
PO Box 2649
Harrisburg, PA 17105-2649
Phone: (717)783-7157

★ 10680 ★ Puerto Rico Division of
Examining Boards
Regulations and Certification of Health
Professionals Office
Board of Pharmacy
Call Box 10200
Santurce, PR 00908
Phone: (809)725-8161

★ 10681 ★ Rhode Island Board of
Pharmacy
3 Capitol Hill, Rm. 304
Providence, RI 02908-5097
Phone: (401)277-2837

★ 10682 ★ South Carolina Board of
Pharmacy
PO Box 11927
Columbia, SC 29211
Phone: (803)734-1010

★10683★ **South Dakota State Board of
Pharmacy**
PO Box 518
Pierre, SD 57501-0518
Phone: (605)224-2338

★10684★ **Tennessee Board of Pharmacy**
Volunteer Plaza, 2nd Fl.
500 James Robertson Pkwy.
Nashville, TN 37243-1149
Phone: (615)741-2718

★10685★ **Texas State Board of Pharmacy**
8505 Cross Park Dr., Ste. 110
Austin, TX 78754-4594
Phone: (512)832-0661

★10686★ **Utah Board of Pharmacy**
160 East 300 South
PO Box 45802
Salt Lake City, UT 84145
Phone: (801)530-6633

★10687★ **Vermont Board of Pharmacy**
109 State St.
Montpelier, VT 05609-1106
Phone: (802)828-2875

★10688★ **Virgin Islands Board of
Pharmacy**
St. Thomas Hospital
48 Sugar Estate
St. Thomas, VI 00801
Phone: (809)774-0117

★10689★ **Virginia Board of Pharmacy**
6606 W. Broad St., Ste. 400
Richmond, VA 23230-1717
Phone: (804)662-9911

★10690★ **Washington State Board of
Pharmacy**
1300 SE Quince St. SE
Box 47863
Olympia, WA 98504-7863
Phone: (206)753-6834

★10691★ **West Virginia Board of
Pharmacy**
236 Capitol St.
Charleston, WV 25301
Phone: (304)558-0558

★10692★ **Wisconsin Pharmacy Examining
Board**
1400 E. Washington
PO Box 8935
Madison, WI 53708
Phone: (608)266-2812

★10693★ **Wyoming State Board of
Pharmacy**
1720 S. Poplar St., Ste. 5
Casper, WY 82601
Phone: (307)234-0294

State & Regional Organizations

Pharmacy

*Listed below are state pharmacy associations.
The national organization is the National Council of State Pharmacy Association Executives,
c/o Al Melbane, Secy-Treas., PO Box 151,
Chapel Hill, NC 27514-0151, 800-852-7343.*

Alabama

★10694★ **Alabama Pharmacy Association**
1211 Carmichael Way
Montgomery, AL 36106-3672
Phone: (205)271-4222
Fax: (205)271-5423

Alaska

★10695★ **Alaska Pharmaceutical
Association**
Box 10-1185
Anchorage, AK 99510
Phone: (907)563-8880

Arizona

★10696★ **Arizona Pharmacy Association**
1845 E. Southern Ave.
Tempe, AZ 85282-5831
Phone: (602)838-3385
Fax: (602)838-3557

Arkansas

★10697★ **Arkansas Pharmacists
Association**
417 S. Victory
Little Rock, AR 72201
Phone: (501)372-5250
Fax: (501)372-0546

California

★10698★ **California Pharmacists
Association**
1112 I St., Ste. 300
Sacramento, CA 95814
Phone: (916)444-7811
Fax: (916)444-7929

Colorado

★10699★ **Colorado Pharmacists
Association**
7853 E. Arapahoe Ct., Ste. 1500
Englewood, CO 80112-1360
Phone: (303)843-0835
Fax: (303)843-0786

Connecticut

★10700★ **Connecticut Pharmacists
Association**
35 Cold Spring Rd., Ste. 125
Rocky Hill, CT 06067
Phone: (203)563-4619
Fax: (203)257-8241

Delaware

★10701★ **Delaware Pharmaceutical
Society**
1601 Milltown Rd., Ste. 8
Wilmington, DE 19808
Phone: (302)892-2880

District of Columbia

★10702★ **Washington, DC Pharmaceutical
Association**
6406 Georgia Ave. NW, Ste. 202
Washington, DC 20012
Phone: (202)829-1515

Florida

★10703★ **Florida Pharmacy Association**
610 N. Adams St.
Tallahassee, FL 32301
Phone: (904)222-2400
Fax: (904)561-6758

Georgia

★10704★ **Georgia Pharmacy Association**
PO Box 95527
Atlanta, GA 30347
Phone: (404)231-5074
Fax: (404)237-8435

Hawaii

★10705★ **Hawaii Pharmaceutical
Association**
2448 E. Manoa Rd.
Honolulu, HI 96807-1198
Phone: (808)247-0047

Idaho

★10706★ **Idaho State Pharmaceutical
Association**
1365 N. Orchard St., Ste. 316
Boise, ID 83706
Phone: (208)376-2273
Fax: (208)376-5814

Illinois

★10707★ **Illinois Pharmacists Association**
223 W. Jackson Blvd., Ste. 1000
Chicago, IL 60606-6906
Phone: (312)939-7300
Fax: (312)939-7220

Indiana

★ 10708 ★ Indiana Pharmacists Association
729 N. Pennsylvania St.
Indianapolis, IN 46204-1171
Phone: (317)634-4968
Fax: (317)632-1219

Iowa

★ 10709 ★ Iowa Pharmacists Association
8515 Douglas Ave., Ste. 16
Des Moines, IA 50322
Phone: (515)270-0713
Fax: (515)270-2979

Kansas

★ 10710 ★ Kansas Pharmacists Association
1308 W. 10th St.
Topeka, KS 66604
Phone: (913)232-0439
Fax: (913)232-3764

Kentucky

★ 10711 ★ Kentucky Pharmacists Association
1228 US Hwy. 127 S.
Frankfort, KY 40601-4330
Phone: (502)227-2303
Fax: (502)227-2258

Louisiana

★ 10712 ★ Louisiana Pharmacists Association
PO Box 14446
Baton Rouge, LA 70898
Phone: (504)926-2666
Fax: (504)926-1020

Maine

★ 10713 ★ Maine Pharmacy Association
PO Box 817
Bangor, ME 04402-0817
Phone: (207)947-0885
Fax: (207)947-1046

Maryland

★ 10714 ★ Maryland Pharmacists Association
650 W. Lombard St.
Baltimore, MD 21201
Phone: (410)727-0746
Fax: (410)727-2253

Massachusetts

★ 10715 ★ Massachusetts Pharmacists Association
5 Lexington St.
Waltham, MA 02154
Phone: (617)736-0101
Fax: (617)736-0080

Michigan

★ 10716 ★ Michigan Pharmacists Association
815 N. Washington Ave.
Lansing, MI 48906
Phone: (517)484-1466
Fax: (517)484-4893

Minnesota

★ 10717 ★ Minnesota Pharmacists Association
2550 University Ave. W., Ste. 320N
St. Paul, MN 55114
Phone: (612)644-3566
Fax: (612)644-3965

Mississippi

★ 10718 ★ Mississippi Pharmacists Association
341 Edgewood Terrace Dr.
Jackson, MS 39206-6299
Phone: (601)981-0416
Fax: (601)981-0451

Missouri

★ 10719 ★ Missouri Pharmacy Association
410 Madison St.
Jefferson City, MO 65101
Phone: (314)636-7522
Fax: (314)636-7485

Montana

★ 10720 ★ Montana State Pharmaceutical Association
PO Box 4718
Helena, MT 59604
Phone: (406)449-3843
Fax: (406)442-8018

Nebraska

★ 10721 ★ Nebraska Pharmacists Association
6221 S. 58th St., Ste. A
Lincoln, NE 68516
Phone: (402)420-1500
Fax: (402)420-1406

Nevada

★ 10722 ★ Nevada Pharmacists Association
3660 Baker Ln.
Reno, NV 89509
Phone: (702)826-3981
Fax: (702)825-0785

New Hampshire

★ 10723 ★ New Hampshire Pharmacists Association
2 Eagle Sq., Ste. 400
Concord, NH 03301-4956
Phone: (603)229-0292
Fax: (603)224-7769

New Jersey

★ 10724 ★ New Jersey Pharmacists Association
120 W. State St.
Trenton, NJ 08608-1102
Phone: (609)394-5596
Fax: (609)394-7806

New Mexico

★ 10725 ★ New Mexico Pharmaceutical Association
4800 Zuni SE
Albuquerque, NM 87108
Phone: (505)265-8720
Fax: (505)255-8476

New York

★ 10726 ★ Pharmaceutical Society of the State of New York
Pine West Plaza IV
Washington Ave. Ext.
Albany, NY 12205
Phone: (518)869-6595
Fax: (518)464-0618

North Carolina

★ 10727 ★ North Carolina Pharmaceutical Association
PO Box 151
Chapel Hill, NC 27514-0151
Phone: (919)967-2237
Fax: (919)968-9430

North Dakota

★ 10728 ★ North Dakota Pharmaceutical Association
PO Box 5008
Bismarck, ND 58502-5008
Phone: (701)258-4968
Fax: (701)258-9312

Ohio

★ 10729 ★ Ohio Pharmacists Association
6037 Frantz Rd., Ste. 106
Dublin, OH 43017
Phone: (614)798-0037
Fax: (614)798-0978

Oklahoma

★ 10730 ★ Oklahoma Pharmaceutical Association
Box 18731
Oklahoma City, OK 73154
Phone: (405)528-3338
Fax: (405)528-1417

Oregon

★ 10731 ★ Oregon State Pharmacists Association
1460 State St.
Salem, OR 97301
Phone: (503)585-4887
Fax: (503)378-9067

Pennsylvania

★ 10732 ★ Pennsylvania Pharmacists Association
508 N. 3rd St.
Harrisburg, PA 17101-1199
Phone: (717)234-6151
Fax: (717)236-1618

Puerto Rico

★ 10733 ★ Colegio de Farmaceuticos de Puerto Rico
PO Box 360206
San Juan, PR 00936
Phone: (809)753-7157
Fax: (809)759-9793

Rhode Island

★ 10734 ★ Rhode Island Pharmaceutical Association
500 Prospect St.
Pawtucket, RI 02860
Phone: (401)725-4141
Fax: (401)725-9960

South Carolina

★ 10735 ★ South Carolina Pharmacy Association
1405 Calhoun St.
Columbia, SC 29201
Phone: (803)254-1065
Fax: (803)254-9379

South Dakota

★ 10736 ★ South Dakota Pharmaceutical Association
Box 518
Pierre, SD 57501-0518
Phone: (605)224-2338
Fax: (605)224-1280

Tennessee

★ 10737 ★ Tennessee Pharmacists Association
226 Capitol Blvd., Ste. 810
Nashville, TN 37219-1893
Phone: (615)256-3023
Fax: (615)225-3528

Texas

★ 10738 ★ Texas Pharmacy Association
PO Box 14709
Austin, TX 78761-4709
Phone: (512)836-8350
Fax: (512)836-0308

Utah

★ 10739 ★ Utah Pharmaceutical Association
1062 East 21st St. South, Ste. 212
Salt Lake City, UT 84106
Phone: (801)484-9141
Fax: (801)484-8090

Vermont

★ 10740 ★ Vermont Pharmacists Association
PO Box 790
Richmond, VT 05477-0790
Phone: (802)434-3001
Fax: (802)434-4803

Virginia

★ 10741 ★ Virginia Pharmacists Association
3119 W. Clay St.
Richmond, VA 23230
Phone: (804)355-7941
Fax: (804)355-7991

Washington

★ 10742 ★ Washington State Pharmacists Association
1501 Taylor Ave. SW
Renton, WA 98055-3139
Phone: (206)228-7171
Fax: (206)277-3897

West Virginia

★ 10743 ★ West Virginia Pharmacists Association
300 Capitol St., Ste. 1002
Charleston, WV 25301
Phone: (304)344-5302
Fax: (304)344-5316

Wisconsin

★ 10744 ★ Wisconsin Pharmacists Association
202 Price Pl.
Madison, WI 53705
Phone: (608)238-5515
Fax: (608)238-5546

Wyoming

★ 10745 ★ Wyoming Pharmacists Association
PO Box 541
Powell, WY 82435
Phone: (307)754-4284

Chapter 52
Podiatry

Foundations & Other Funding Organizations

Other Funding Organizations

★10746★ **American Podiatric Medical Association**
9312 Old Georgetown Rd.
Bethesda, MD 20814
Phone: (301)571-9200
Fax: (301)530-2752
Frank J. Malouff, Exec. Dir.

Description: Seeks funding to support patient, provider, and student education in foothealth. Student education support is in the form of grants and scholarships to support study in podiatric medicine. Education funding offered through the fund for Podiatric Medical Education.

Medical & Allied Health Schools

Podiatry

The following colleges of podiatric medicine are accredited by the Council on Podiatric Medical Education. For further information, contact the council or the American Podiatric Medical Association at 9312 Old Georgetown Rd., Bethesda, MD 20814-1621, (301) 571-9200.

California

★10747★ **California College of Podiatric Medicine**
1210 Scott St.
San Francisco, CA 94115
Phone: (415)292-0407

Florida

★10748★ **Barry University School of Podiatric Medicine**
11300 NE 2nd Ave.
Miami Shores, FL 33161
Phone: (305)899-3000
Fax: (305)899-3104

Illinois

★10749★ **Dr. William M. Scholl College of Podiatric Medicine**
1001 N. Dearborn St.
Chicago, IL 60610
Phone: (312)280-2880
Free: 800-843-3059

Iowa

★10750★ **University of Osteopathic Medicine and Health Sciences College of Podiatric Medicine and Surgery**
3200 Grand Ave.
Des Moines, IA 50312
Phone: (515)271-1538

New York

★10751★ **New York College of Podiatric Medicine**
53 E. 124th St.
New York, NY 10035
Phone: (212)410-8023
Fax: (212)369-4608

Ohio

★10752★ **Ohio College of Podiatric Medicine**
10515 Carnegie Ave.
Cleveland, OH 44106
Phone: (216)231-3300

Pennsylvania

★10753★ **Pennsylvania College of Podiatric Medicine**
8th at Race St.
Philadelphia, PA 19107
Phone: (215)629-0300
Free: 800-220-FEET

National & International Organizations

★10754★ **Academy of Ambulatory Foot Surgery (AAFS)**
PO Box 2730, Ste. 263
Tuscaloosa, AL 35403
Phone: (205)758-3678
Fax: (205)758-3688
Dr. Stanford Rosen, Exec.Dir.

Founded: 1972. **Members:** 1,500. **Description:** Podiatric physicians who advocate performing foot surgery in their offices or on an outpatient basis, thereby keeping patients ambulatory and able to function normally, and lowering the patients' medical costs. Promotes the advancement of podiatric surgical procedures that can eliminate the necessity of hospital admission. Sponsors national and regional continuing medical education seminars and semiannual research program. Compiles statistics. **Publications:** *Action Letter*, bimonthly. Newsletter. • Directory, periodic. • *Journal of the Academy of Ambulatory Foot Surgery*, periodic. Journal.

American Academy of Podiatric Administration (AAPA)
See: Entry 5539

★10755★ **American Association of Colleges of Podiatric Medicine (AACPM)**
1350 Piccard Dr., Ste. 322
Rockville, MD 20850
Phone: (301)990-7400
Free: 800-922-9266
Fax: (301)990-2807
Anthony J. McNevin, CAE, Pres.

Founded: 1932. **Local Groups:** 7. **Description:** Professional organization of administrators, faculty, practitioners, students, and other individuals associated with podiatric medical education. Provides vocational guidance material for secondary schools and colleges. Conducts public affairs activities and legislative advocacy. Compiles statistics. **Publications:** Newsletter, 3/year. **Formerly:** American Association of Colleges of Chiropody; (1970) American Association of Colleges of Podiatry.

★ 10756 ★ **American Association of Hospital Podiatrists (AAHP)**
420 74th St.
Brooklyn, NY 11209
Phone: (718)836-1017
Dr. Louis J. Arancia, Exec.Dir.

Founded: 1950. **Members:** 800. **Description:** A general specialty group of the American Podiatric Medical Association. Podiatrists (trained and certified persons dealing in the care and diseases of the foot) who are affiliated with hospitals. Seeks to: elevate the standards of podiatry practices in hospitals and health institutions; standardize hospital podiatry procedures, charting, recording forms, and methods; promote understanding among personnel in podiatry, medicine, and allied health professions; aid podiatrists in attaining institutional affiliations; assist in the educational and teaching programs of health institutions and hospitals; foster the development of podiatric internships and residencies in hospitals and institutions. Compiles statistics. **Publications:** *The Hospital Podiatrist*, annual. • Newsletter, annual.

★ 10757 ★ **American Association of Podiatric Physicians and Surgeons (AAPPS)**
1328 Southern Ave. SE, Ste. 200
Washington, DC 20032
Phone: (202)562-2777
Fax: (703)264-7745
Richard S. Benjamin, DPM, Exec.Sec.

Founded: 1979. **Members:** 1,500. **State Groups:** 14. **Description:** Podiatrists. Seeks to represent members' interests and educate podiatrists and the public. Provides training and certification for podiatry and podiatric surgery. Offers accreditation to agencies providing podiatric services, education, or training; also provides podiatric peer review. Operates speakers' bureau and placement service; compiles statistics. **Publications:** *AAPPS Newsletter*, annual. Newsletter.

★ 10758 ★ **American Board of Podiatric Orthopedics and Primary Medicine (ABPOPPM)**
401 N. Michigan Ave.
Chicago, IL 60611-4267
Phone: (312)321-5139
Fax: (312)644-1815
Jeferey Knezovich, Dir.

Founded: 1975. **Members:** 1,781. **Description:** Podiatrists who have taken a competency exam prepared by the board. Offers certifying examinations in foot orthopedics for podiatrists; aims at improving public health by encouraging and elevating standards for practicing podiatric orthopedists. **Publications:** *Directory of Diplomates*, annual. Directory. • Newsletter, semiannual. **Formerly:** American Board of Podiatric Orthopedics.

★ 10759 ★ **American Board of Podiatric Surgery (ABPS)**
1601 Dolores St.
San Francisco, CA 94110-4906
Phone: (415)826-3200
Fax: (415)826-4640
John L. Bennett, Exec.Dir.

Founded: 1975. **Members:** 3,500. **Description:** Podiatrists certified as diplomates. Objectives are: to protect and improve public health by advancing the science of foot surgery and by encouraging the study and evaluation of standards of foot surgery; to act upon application for certification of legally licensed podiatrists to ascertain their competency in foot surgery; to grant certificates to candidates who have met all qualifications.

★ 10760 ★ **American College of Foot and Ankle Orthopedics and Medicine (ACFAOM)**
4603 Hwy. 95 S
PO Box 39
Cocolalla, ID 83813-0039
Phone: (208)683-3900
Fax: (208)683-3700
Judith A. Baerg, Exec.Dir.

Founded: 1949. **Members:** 1,300. **Description:** Professional society of podiatrists sanctioned as specialists to practice foot orthopedics (deformities and diseases of bones, joints, and muscles of the foot) and primary podiatric medicine. **Publications:** *ACFAOM News*, quarterly. Newsletter. *Price:* Included in membership dues; $5 for nonmembers. • *The Lower Extremity*, quarterly. Journal. Focuses on multi-specialty issues and concerns of physicians. *Price:* Included in membership dues; $75 for nonmembers; $105 for nonmembers outside U.S.; $110 for institutions. **Formerly:** (1993) American College of Foot Orthopedists.

American College of Foot and Ankle Pediatrics (ACFAP)
See: Entry 3165

American College of Foot and Ankle Surgeons (ACFAS)
See: Entry 12231

★ 10761 ★ **American College of Podiatric Radiologists (ACPR)**
169 Lincoln Rd., No. 308
Miami Beach, FL 33139
Phone: (305)531-9866
Irving H. Block, D.P.M., Sec.-Treas.

Founded: 1944. **Members:** 80. **Description:** Professional society of podiatrists interested in the use and interpretation of X-rays in treating ailments of the lower extremities. Sponsors postgraduate seminars on podiatric radiology; supports research. Makes available 1400 volume archives to members. Maintains speakers' bureau. **Publications:** Newsletter, 2-4/year. • *Post Convention Reports*, 1-2/year. **Formerly:** (1962) American College of Chiropodial Roentgenologists; (1974) American College of Foot Roentgenologists.

★ 10762 ★ **American Podiatric Medical Association (APMA)**
9312 Old Georgetown Rd.
Bethesda, MD 20814
Phone: (301)571-9200
Fax: (301)530-2752
Frank J. Malouff, Exec.Dir.

Founded: 1912. **Members:** 9,800. **State Groups:** 53. **Description:** Professional society of podiatrists. **Publications:** *APMA News*, monthly. Newspaper. Includes calendar of events, research updates, and statistics. *Price:* Included in membership dues; $50/year for nonmembers. • *Catalogue of Audiovisual, Informational and Educational Materials*, periodic. Catalog. • *Desk Reference of the APMA*, annual. • *Journal of the American Podiatric Medical Association*, monthly. Journal. *Price:* $75. Also publishes foot health literature. **Formerly:** (1958) National Association of Chiropodists; (1984) American Podiatry Association.

★ 10763 ★ **American Podiatric Medical Association Auxiliary (APMAA)**
c/o Peggy A. Gearhard
3344 N. Humboldt Ave.
Milwaukee, WI 53212-1762
Peggy A. Gearhard, Exec.Sec.

Founded: 1938. **Members:** 1,000. **State Groups:** 17. **Description:** Spouses and relatives of members of the American Podiatric Medical Association. Seeks to educate the public about proper foot health and foot care. Disseminates information; sponsors student loan program; produces educational film. **Publications:** Bulletin, quarterly. • *Life's Foundation. . .Your Baby's Feet*. Pamphlet. • Membership Directory, biennial. **Formerly:** Women's Auxiliary, American Podiatry Association; (1984) American Podiatry Association Auxiliary.

★ 10764 ★ **American Podiatric Medical Students Association (APMSA)**
9312 Old Georgetown Rd.
Bethesda, MD 20814
Phone: (301)493-9667
Betsy Herman, Exec. Officer

Members: 2,500. **Description:** Podiatric medical students enrolled at seven podiatric schools in the U.S. Purpose is to represent the interests of podiatric medical students in legislative, professional, and educational programs. Cosponsors seminars and writing contests. Compiles statistics. **Publications:** *First Step*, biennial. • *Graduation Handbook*. **Formerly:** American Podiatric Students Association.

American Podiatric Medical Writers Association (APMWA)
See: Entry 6971

★ 10765 ★ **American Society of Podiatric Dermatology (ASPD)**
c/o Dr. Steven Berlin
PO Box 7378
Baltimore, MD 21227-0378
Phone: (410)247-4770
Fax: (410)247-7329
Dr. Steven Berlin, Pres.

Founded: 1914. **Members:** 260. **Description:** Doctors of podiatric medicine with demonstrated expertise in foot dermatology (100); candidates for D.P.M. degrees in colleges of podiatric medicine (400). Fosters research in podiatric dermatology; supports college-affiliated study groups; conducts semiannual continuing education programs; sponsors student affiliates. Maintains speakers' bureau; conducts research programs; sponsors competitions. **Publications:** Monographs. • Newsletter, quarterly. Includes book reviews, information on new products, and obituaries. *Price:* Free. **Formerly:** (1973) American Board of Chiropodical Dermatology.

★ 10766 ★ **American Society of Podiatric Medical Assistants (ASPMA)**
2124 S. Austin Blvd.
Cicero, IL 60650
Phone: (708)863-6303
Fax: (708)863-5375
Sandra Lohrantz, Exec.Dir.

Founded: 1964. **Members:** 1,350. **Regional Groups:** 14. **Description:** Podiatric assistants. Purposes are to hold educational seminars and to administer certification examinations. **Publications:** Journal, quarterly.

★ 10767 ★ **American Society of Podiatric Medicine (ASPM)**
c/o Dr. Warren L. Simmonds
7331 Collins Ave.
Miami Beach, FL 33141
Phone: (305)866-9608
Dr. Warren L. Simmonds, Sec.

Founded: 1944. **Members:** 110. **Description:** Promotes research in podiatry; sponsors postgraduate courses and presents scientific programs at annual meeting. Focuses on aging and diabetes. Maintains collection of material presented by candidates for fellowship. Maintains speakers' bureau; conducts research programs. **Formerly:** American Academy of Chiropody.

★ 10768 ★ **Board of Certification in Pedorthics (BCP)**
9861 Broken Land Pky., Ste. 255
Columbia, MD 21046-1151
Phone: (410)381-5729
Fax: (410)381-1167
William Boettge, Pres.

Founded: 1958. **Description:** Certifies Pedorthists. (Pedorthists fit and provide prescription footwear to clients referred by physicians and assist in the design of pedorthic devices.) Sponsors certification program; seeks to maintain high standards of practice in pedorthics and facilitate continuing education of members. **Publications:** *Pedorthic Candidate's Handbook*, annual. • *Study Guide for Pedorthic Skills Examination.*

★ 10769 ★ **Central Association of Medical Chiropodists of Germany (Zentralverband der Medizinischen Fusspfleger Deutschlands)**
Johannisstr. 12
58452 Witten, Germany
Phone: 2302 83781
Fax: 2302 88537
Karl-Dieter Hoeper, Contact

Members: 2,500. **Description:** Promotes the professional interests of medical chiropodists in Germany. Disseminates information.

★ 10770 ★ **Conference of Podiatry Executives (COPE)**
5310 McKitrick Blvd.
Columbus, OH 43235
Phone: (614)457-6269
Fax: (614)457-3375
John Bailey, Contact

Founded: 1960. **Members:** 22. **Description:** Executive directors of state podiatry associations. Purposes are to facilitate communication among member associations and their executives and to promote the exchange of information. Coordinates individual efforts in areas of common concern to podiatry associations.

★ 10771 ★ **Council on Podiatric Medical Education (CPME)**
9312 Old Georgetown Rd.
Bethesda, MD 20814-1621
Phone: (301)571-9200
Fax: (301)530-2752
Jay Levrio, Dir.

Founded: 1918. **Members:** 11. **Description:** Accrediting agency for colleges of podiatric medicine, podiatric residency programs, podiatric assistant programs, and continuing education programs in podiatry. Conducts in-service training programs for members engaged in accrediting activities. **Publications:** *Council on Podiatric Medical Education--Annual Report.* Annual Report. • *Standards and Requirements for Accreditation.* Also publishes lists of accredited institutions and approved programs. **Formerly:** (1984) Council on Podiatry Education.

★ 10772 ★ **Federation of Podiatric Medical Boards (FPMB)**
1729 Glastonberry Rd.
Potomac, MD 20854
Phone: (301)424-1001
Will Buklad, Exec.Dir. & Editor

Founded: 1936. **Members:** 45. **State Groups:** 52. **Description:** State boards of podiatry examiners. Goals are to: serve as a repository for information relating to common problems among boards of podiatry examiners; promote competency examinations with national standards to be utilized by examining boards; monitor and catalog legislation pertaining to podiatry. Conducts business sessions and educational programs on topics concerning the licensure and regulation of health professions. Compiles statistics. Bestows awards. **Publications:** *Directory of State Licensing Boards of Podiatric Medicine*, biennial. Directory. • *Disciplinary Data Reports*, semiannual. • *Federation News*, quarterly. Bulletin. *Price:* Included in membership dues; $25/year for nonmembers. **Formerly:** (1985) Federation of Podiatry Boards; (1986) Federation of Podiatry Medical Boards.

★ 10773 ★ **International Society of Podiatric Laser Surgery (ISPLS)**
2945 Snake Hill Rd.
Doylestown, PA 18901-1750
Phone: (215)794-5180
Free: 800-231-9024
Fax: (215)794-5180
Mary E. Montgomery, Exec.Dir.

Founded: 1983. **Members:** 350. **Description:** Podiatric laser surgeons and other health pro-

fessionals. Fosters the advancement of laser technology in podiatry. Promotes the interests and professionalism of members. Disseminates information to the public regarding laser surgery. Sponsors research and educational programs on laser surgery. Offers patient referral service. Maintains speakers' bureau. **Publications:** Audiotapes. • *Laser Letter*, quarterly. Newsletter. *Price:* Free. • *What You Should Know About Laser Surgery.* Brochures. • *What You Should Know About Nails.* Brochure. • *What You Should Know About Warts.* Brochure. Also publishes textbook. **Formerly:** (1985) International Society of Podiatric Laser Surgery; (1988) International College of Podiatric Laser Surgery.

★ 10774 ★ **National Board of Podiatric Medical Examiners (NBPME)**
PO Box 6516
Princeton, NJ 08541-6516
Phone: (609)951-6335
Fax: (609)951-6240
Linda Skelton, Dir.

Founded: 1956. **Members:** 12. **Description:** Professional podiatrists. Purpose is to prepare and administer examinations for podiatry students seeking state licensure. Monitors test validity and reliability. **Publications:** Annual Report. • Bulletin, annual. • Membership Directory, annual. **Formerly:** (1985) National Board of Podiatry Examiners.

National College of Foot Surgeons (NCFS)
See: Entry 12290

★ 10775 ★ **National Podiatric Medical Association (NPMA)**
c/o Raymond E. Lee, D.P.M.
1706 E. 87th St.
Chicago, IL 60617
Phone: (312)374-1616
Fax: (312)374-5860
Raymond E. Lee, D.P.M., Contact

Founded: 1971. **Members:** 200. **Description:** Minority podiatrists, predominantly black. Promotes the science and art of podiatry. Seeks to: improve public health; raise the standards of the podiatric profession and education; stimulate a favorable relationship between all podiatrists; nurture growth and diffusion of podiatric information; stimulate public education concerning public health and features of podiatric medicine. Sponsors proposal of podiatric laws; works to eliminate religious and racial discrimination and segregation in American medical institutions. **Publications:** *Annual Seminar Ad Book.* • *National Podiatric Medical Association-- Newsletter*, annual. Newsletter. Includes calendar of events and news from student-affiliated associations. *Price:* Included in membership dues. **Formerly:** (1987) National Podiatry Association.

★ 10776 ★ **Student National Podiatric Medical Association (SNPMA)**
c/o Wilburn E. Thomas
1001 N. Dearborn
Mail Box 814
Chicago, IL 60610
Phone: (312)642-0248
Wilburn E. Thomas, Pres.

Founded: 1973. **Members:** 300. **Description:** Minorities in the podiatric medical field furthering podiatric medicine. Promotes minority equality in the podiatric colleges and profession. Conducts charitable and educational programs. Maintains speakers' bureau; compiles statistics. **Publications:** Newsletter, semiannual.

Research Centers

★ 10777 ★ **Pennsylvania College of Podiatric Medicine**
Center for the History of Foot Care and Footwear
8th St. & Race
Philadelphia, PA 19107
Phone: (215)625-5243
Barbara Williams, Dir.

Research Activities and Fields: History of podiatric medicine, anatomy and diseases of the foot, podiatry, chiropody as a profession, and ethnic footwear. **Publications:** *The ClioPedic Items* (irregular newsletter).

★ 10778 ★ **Pennsylvania College of Podiatric Medicine**
Gait Study Center
8th & Race Sts.
Philadelphia, PA 19107
Phone: (215)629-0300
Fax: (215)629-1622
Dr. Howard Hilstrom, Ph.D, Dir.

Research Activities and Fields: Performs posture and locomotion studies, focusing on the causes of abnormal gait conditions. Conducts basic and clinical research in biomechanics and biomedical engineering with special emphasis on the lower extremities. Areas of interest include the functional role of in-shoe orthoses and insoles; the percentage of spasticity and contractive in equinus patients, and the effectiveness of their treatment; the etiology of neuropathic ulcers in the diabetic foot; and optimization of foot and ankle surgeries and related fixation parameters.

State Government Agencies

Podiatry Boards

★ 10779 ★ **Alabama State Board of Podiatric Medicine**
13 Innisbrook Ln.
Shoal Creek, AL 35242
Phone: (205)995-9334

★ 10780 ★ **Alaska State Medical Board**
3601 C St., Ste. 722
PO Box 110806
Juneau, AK 99811
Phone: (907)561-2878

★ 10781 ★ **Arizona State Board of Podiatry Examiners**
1645 W. Jefferson, Rm. 410
Phoenix, AZ 85007
Phone: (602)542-3095

★ 10782 ★ **Arkansas State Podiatry Examining Board**
2001 Georgia Ave.
Little Rock, AR 72207-5014
Phone: (501)664-3668

★ 10783 ★ **California Board of Podiatric Medicine**
1420 Howe Ave., Ste. 8
Sacramento, CA 95825
Phone: (916)263-2651

★ 10784 ★ **Colorado Podiatry Board**
1560 Broadway, Ste. 1300
Denver, CO 80202
Phone: (303)894-7690

★ 10785 ★ **Connecticut Board of Podiatry Licensure**
150 Washington St.
Hartford, CT 06106
Phone: (203)566-1035

★ 10786 ★ **Delaware Board of Examiners in Podiatry**
O'Neill Bldg.
PO Box 1401
Dover, DE 19903
Phone: (302)739-4522

★ 10787 ★ **District of Columbia Board of Podiatry Examiners**
614 H St., NW, Rm. 904
Washington, DC 20001
Phone: (202)727-7454

★ 10788 ★ **Florida Board of Podiatric Medicine**
130 N. Monroe St.
Tallahassee, FL 32301
Phone: (904)487-1814

★ 10789 ★ **Georgia State Board of Podiatry**
166 Pryor St. SW
Atlanta, GA 30303
Phone: (404)656-3912

★ 10790 ★ **Hawaii Board of Podiatric Medicine**
PO Box 3469
Honolulu, HI 96801
Phone: (808)586-2708

★ 10791 ★ **Idaho State Board of Podiatry**
Owyhee Plaza
1109 Main Plaza S-220
Boise, ID 83705-5642
Phone: (208)334-3233

★ 10792 ★ **Illinois Department of Professional Regulation**
Podiatry Examining Committee
320 W. Washington St., 3rd Fl.
Springfield, IL 62786
Phone: (217)785-0800

★ 10793 ★ **Indiana Health Professions Bureau**
Committee of Podiatric Medicine
402 W. Washington, Rm. 041
Indianapolis, IN 46204
Phone: (317)233-4395

★ 10794 ★ **Iowa Board of Podiatric Medicine**
Lucas State Office Bldg., 4th Fl.
321 E. 12th St.
Des Moines, IA 50319-0075
Phone: (515)281-7074

★ 10795 ★ **Kansas Board of Healing Arts**
235 S. Topeka Blvd.
Topeka, KS 66603-3059
Phone: (913)296-7413

★ 10796 ★ **Kentucky Board of Podiatry**
110 N. Hubbard Ln.
Louisville, KY 40207
Phone: (502)425-1333

★ 10797 ★ **Louisiana Board of Medical Examiners**
830 Union St., Ste. 100
New Orleans, LA 70112-1499
Phone: (504)524-6763

★ 10798 ★ **Maine Board of Podiatric Examiners**
State House Sta. No. 35
Augusta, ME 04333
Phone: (207)582-8723

★ 10799 ★ **Maryland Board of Podiatric Medicine**
4201 Patterson Ave.
Baltimore, MD 21215-2299
Phone: (410)764-4785

★ 10800 ★ **Massachusetts Board of Examiners in Podiatry**
100 Cambridge St., Rm. 1514
Boston, MA 02202
Phone: (617)727-1817

★ 10801 ★ **Michigan Board of Podiatric Medicine and Surgery**
PO Box 30018
Lansing, MI 48909
Phone: (517)373-3596

★ 10802 ★ **Minnesota Board of Podiatric Medicine**
2700 University Ave. W.
St. Paul, MN 55114
Phone: (612)642-0401

★ 10803 ★ **Mississippi State Board of Medical Licensure**
2688-D Insurance Center Dr.
Jackson, MS 39216
Phone: (601)354-6645

★ 10804 ★ **Missouri State Board of Podiatry**
PO Box 423
Jefferson City, MO 65102
Phone: (314)751-0873

★ 10805 ★ Montana Professional and Occupational Licensing Bureau
Arcade Bldg.
111 N. Jackson St.
PO Box 200513
Helena, MT 59620-0513
Phone: (406)444-3737

★ 10806 ★ Nebraska Bureau of Examining Boards
301 Centennial Mall, S.
PO Box 95007
Lincoln, NE 68509-5007
Phone: (402)471-2115

★ 10807 ★ Nevada State Board of Podiatric Medicine
2413 South Eastern Ave., Ste. 142
Las Vegas, NV 89104
Phone: (702)733-7617

★ 10808 ★ New Hampshire Board of Registration in Podiatry
Health and Welfare Bldg.
2 Industrial Park Dr., Ste. 8
Concord, NH 03301-8321
Phone: (603)271-1203

★ 10809 ★ New Jersey Board of Medical Examiners
140 E. Front St., 2nd Fl.
Trenton, NJ 08608
Phone: (609)826-7100

★ 10810 ★ New Mexico Board of Podiatric Medicine
PO Box 25101
1599 St. Francis Dr.
Santa Fe, NM 87505
Phone: (505)827-7554

★ 10811 ★ New York State Board of Podiatry
Cultural Education Center, Rm. 3019
Albany, NY 12230
Phone: (518)474-6374

★ 10812 ★ North Carolina Board of Podiatry Examiners
1225 Haddington Dr.
PO Box 1088
Raleigh, NC 27602
Phone: (919)380-8522

★ 10813 ★ North Dakota Board of Registry in Podiatry
RD 1, Box 95
Jamestown, ND 58401
Phone: (701)252-1050

★ 10814 ★ Ohio State Medical Board
77 S. High St., 17th Fl.
Columbus, OH 43266-0315
Phone: (614)466-3934

★ 10815 ★ Oklahoma State Board of Podiatry
5104 N. Francis, Ste. C
PO Box 18256
Oklahoma City, OK 73154-0256
Phone: (405)848-2189

★ 10816 ★ Oregon Board of Medical Examiners
Crown Plaza, Ste. 620
1500 SW 1st Ave.
Portland, OR 97201-5826
Phone: (503)229-5770

★ 10817 ★ Pennsylvania State Board of Podiatry
PO Box 2649
Harrisburg, PA 17105-2649
Phone: (717)783-7134

★ 10818 ★ Puerto Rico Board of Podiatry Examiners
Call Box 10200
San Juan, PR 00908
Phone: (809)725-7904

★ 10819 ★ Rhode Island Podiatry Board
3 Capitol Hill, Rm. 104
Providence, RI 02908
Phone: (401)277-2827

★ 10820 ★ South Carolina Board of Podiatric Medicine
PO Box 11329
Columbia, SC 29211-1329
Phone: (803)734-9631

★ 10821 ★ South Dakota Board of Podiatry
808 S. Minnesota Ave.
Sioux Falls, SD 57104
Phone: (605)336-7753

★ 10822 ★ Tennessee State Board of Registration in Podiatry
283 Plus Park Blvd.
Nashville, TN 37219-5407
Phone: (615)367-6400

★ 10823 ★ Texas State Board of Podiatric Medicine
3420 Executive Center Dr., Ste. 305
Austin, TX 78731-1626
Phone: (512)794-0145

★ 10824 ★ Utah Podiatry Examining Board
PO Box 45805
Salt Lake City, UT 84145-0805
Phone: (801)355-5359

★ 10825 ★ Vermont State Board of Medical Practice
Secretary of State Office
109 State St.
Montpelier, VT 05609-1106
Phone: (802)828-2673

★ 10826 ★ Virginia Podiatry Licensing Committee
6606 W. Broad St., 4th Fl.
Richmond, VA 23230-1717
Phone: (804)662-9908

★ 10827 ★ Washington State Board of Podiatry
1300 Quince St.
PO Box 47868
Olympia, WA 98504-7868
Phone: (206)586-5962

★ 10828 ★ West Virginia State Board of Medicine
100 Dee Dr.
Charleston, WV 25311
Phone: (304)558-2921

★ 10829 ★ Wisconsin Podiatry Council
PO Box 8935
Madison, WI 53708
Phone: (608)266-2812

★ 10830 ★ Wyoming Board of Registration in Podiatry
Barrett Bldg., 3rd Fl.
2301 Central Ave.
PO Box 6019
Cheyenne, WY 82002
Phone: (307)777-6313

Chapter 53
Preventive Medicine

Federal Government Agencies

★10831★ U.S. Department of Health and Human Services
National Center for Chronic Disease Prevention and Health Promotion
1600 Clifton Rd. NE
Atlanta, GA 30333
Phone: (404)488-5401
Fax: (404)639-1552

Description: The National Center for Chronic Disease Prevention and Health Promotion is concerned with the prevention of chronic diseases such as cardiovascular disease, diabetes, and cancer. Translates research findings into community programs and healthier lifestyles. Supports programs to improve nutrition, reproductive health, and exercise, and to discourage destructive behaviors, such as alcohol abuse and smoking.

Foundations & Other Funding Organizations

Private Foundations

JM Foundation
See: Entry 316

Corporate Foundations

★10832★ Medtronic Foundation
7000 Central Ave., NE
Minneapolis, MN 55432
Phone: (612)574-3024
Fax: (612)574-3464
Penny Hunt, Dir., Community Affairs & Foundation

Giving Priorities: *Education:* 45% of annual giving. Goal is to increase the number of people in the science, medical, and technical fields and to encourage employees to support educational

institutions. Also sponsors employee matching gifts program. *Community Services:* 35% of contributions. *Health:* 15% of contributions, to programs that promote physical health and that are available to the general community. Foundation favors health promotion programs that encourage older people to maintain active, healthy lifestyles by offering accessible, affordable, health related information. Also supports health promotion or disease prevention efforts geared toward minorities and the economically disadvantaged. *Special Projects:* 5% of contributions. **Typical Health-Related Recipients:** Adolescent Health Issues, Cancer, Emergency/Ambulance Services, Geriatric Health, Health Organizations, Health Policy/Cost Containment, Public Health, Trauma Treatment. **Geographic Distribution:** In Minneapolis-St. Paul; also in nine Medtronic plant communities.

Pacific Mutual Charitable Foundation
See: Entry 808

★10833★ Weyerhaeuser Co. Foundation
CH1F 31
Tacoma, WA 98477
Phone: (206)924-3159
Elizabeth Crossman, Vice President

Giving Priorities: *Education:* About 35% of total contributions. *Health and Human Services:* 30% to 35% of toal contributions. Supports preventive health care services that show a reasonable promise of reducing costs. Grants for facilities are normally considered only in key Weyerhaeuser locales where no other services are available. No awards are made to national-level organizations. The foundation supports the United Way as the primary means for helping with critical human services. *Civic and Community Affairs:* 20% to 25%. *Arts & Humanities:* 5% to 10% of total contributions. **Typical Health-Related Recipients:** Hospices, Hospitals, Substance Abuse. **Geographic Distribution:** Nationally and in Canada, with emphasis on communities, particularly remote communities, in which company has significant numbers of employees.

National & International Organizations

★10834★ Aerobics and Fitness Foundation of America (AFFA)
15250 Ventura Blvd., Ste. 200
Sherman Oaks, CA 91403
Phone: (818)905-0040
Free: 800-BE FIT 86
Fax: (818)990-5468
Linda D. Pfeffer, R.N., Exec. Officer

Founded: 1983. **Description:** Established by the Aerobics and Fitness Association of America (see separate entry). To foster and sponsor research on and product evaluation of safe and effective aerobic exercise and fitness activities. Sponsors health-related charitable events. Maintains small collection of books, videos, and fitness flash cards. **Publications:** *American Fitness,* bimonthly. Magazine. Features exercise trends, research, interviews, products, travel, and nutrition. *Price:* Included in membership dues; $27/year for nonmembers.

★10835★ Aerobics International Research Society (AIRS)
12330 Preston Rd.
Dallas, TX 75230
Phone: (214)701-8001
Fax: (214)991-4626
Mark Donovan, Controller

Founded: 1977. **Members:** 361. **Description:** Physically active persons committed to improving health and fitness through aerobic exercising. Determines the role of exercising in health maintenance and disease prevention. Offers continuing education and children's services. Sponsors competitions.

★10836★ American Board of Preventive Medicine (ABPM)
9950 W. Lawrence Ave., Ste. 106
Schiller Park, IL 60176
Phone: (708)671-1750
Fax: (708)671-1751
Alice R. Ring, M.D., Exec. Dir.

Founded: 1948. **Members:** 6,800. **Description:** Determines requirements, administers examinations, and certifies physicians in the specialized fields of public health and general preventive medicine, aerospace medicine, and occupational medicine. **Publications:** *ABPM Booklet of Information.* Booklet. Covers board requirements. *Price:* Free. • *Study Guide.* **Formerly:** (1952) American Board of Preventive Medicine and Public Health.

★ 10837 ★ American College for
Advancement in Medicine (ACAM)
23121 Verdugo Dr., Ste. 204
Laguna Hills, CA 92653
Phone: (714)583-7666
Free: 800-854-2608
Fax: (714)455-9679
Edward A. Shaw, Ph.D., Exec. Officer

Founded: 1973. **Members:** 535. **Description:** Physicians organized for the promotion of preventive medicine throughout the world. Conducts research and educational programs in the fields of chelation therapy, nutritional medicine, and other preventive modalities. Maintains physician referrals. Offers specialized education program; compiles statistics. **Publications:** *ACAM Update,* monthly. Newsletter. Contains abstracts on issues and developments in preventive medicine. Includes book reviews and calendar of events. *Price:* Included in membership dues. • *Journal of Advancement in Medicine,* quarterly. Journal. Covers research and clinical applications pertaining to preventive and nutritional medicine. *Price:* Included in membership dues. • *Membership Directory,* annual. **Formerly:** (1987) American Academy of Medical Preventics.

★ 10838 ★ American College of Preventive
Medicine (ACPM)
1015 15th St. NW, Ste. 403
Washington, DC 20005
Phone: (202)789-0003
Fax: (202)289-8274
Hazel K. Keimowitz, Exec.Dir.

Founded: 1954. **Members:** 2,000. **Description:** Professional society of medical doctors specializing in preventive medicine, public health, aerospace medicine, and occupational medicine. Sponsors educational programs. **Publications:** *ACPM News,* quarterly. Newsletter. Reports on continuing medical education, legislative activities, and programs of the college. Includes calendar of events and research updates. *Price:* Included in membership dues; $25/year for nonmembers. • *American Journal of Preventive Medicine,* bimonthly. Journal. • *Careers in Preventative Medicine.* • *Directory of Residency Programs,* periodic. Directory. • *Katharine Boucot Sturgis Lectureship,* annual. • *Paying for Preventive Care: Moving the Debate Forward.*

★ 10839 ★ American Fitness Association
(AFA)
PO Box 401
Durango, CO 81302
Phone: (303)247-4109
Jean Rosenbaum, M.D., Dir.

Founded: 1981. **Members:** 3,000. **Description:** Conducts research and educational activities in the field of aerobic exercise; disseminates information on research findings, such as the effects of stress to muscles, joints, and tendons.

Monitors the aerobics industry; tests exercise products such as shoes, mats, and weights; conducts surveys on injury rates. Participates in a task force sponsored by the ASTM and the Sporting Goods Manufacturers Association to establish safety standards for aerobic shoes. Offers expert legal testimony on behalf of members should the need arise. Maintains speakers' bureau and small library. Unrelated to group of same name. **Publications:** *Aerobic Dance.* Book. • *Aerobics on the Easy Side.* Video. Demonstrates an exercise program for overweight individuals and those over the age of 45. • *American Fitness Association--Newsletter,* monthly. Newsletter. *Price:* Included in membership dues. • *Facial Fitness.* Video. • *Mindscapes Stress Reduction.* Video. • *No Fat Cooking Series.* Videos. **Formerly:** (1990) American Aerobics Association.

★ 10840 ★ American Health Foundation
(AHF)
320 E. 43rd St.
New York, NY 10017
Phone: (212)953-1900
Fax: (212)687-2339
Richard B. Klarberg, Exec.VP

Founded: 1969. **Description:** Devoted to promoting preventive medicine, emphasizing four major fields: research (nutrition, environmental carcinogenesis, molecular biology, experimental pathology, and epidemiology); clinical research and service for children (through screening and intervention); public health action (educating laymen and medical and government personnel in the principles of preventive medicine); health economics research (investigating direct and indirect costs of major diseases and comparing them with preventive approaches). Maintains Naylor Dana Institute for Disease Prevention and the Child Health Center in Valhalla, NY and The Mahoney Institute for Health Promotion Research in New York City. **Publications:** *Health Letter,* bimonthly. • *Preventive Medicine,* bimonthly. **Formerly:** (1968) Environmental Health Foundation.

American Osteopathic College of
Preventive Medicine (AOCPM)
See: Entry 9990

★ 10841 ★ American Society of Preventive
Oncology (ASPO)
c/o Dr. Richard R. Love
1300 University Ave., No. 7C
Madison, WI 53706
Phone: (608)263-6809
Fax: (608)263-4497
Dr. Richard R. Love, Exec. Officer

Founded: 1977. **Members:** 310. **Description:** Professionals in clinical, educational, or research disciplines concerned with the field of cancer prevention. Promotes the exchange of information and ideas relating to cancer prevention and the causes of human cancer, including environmental exposures and lifestyles; encourages research. Works to implement programs for the prevention and early detection of cancer. Evaluates programs intended to reduce cancer incidence, mortality, and morbidity. Encourages professional and public education regarding cancer prevention. Maintains communication

and liaison with other oncological societies. Provides expert advice to scientific, public health, and governmental organizations and agencies. **Publications:** *Cancer Epidemiology, Biomarkers, and Prevention,* bimonthly. Journal. *Price:* Included in membership dues.

★ 10842 ★ Association for the
Advancement of Automotive Medicine
(AAAM)
2340 Des Plaines Ave., Ste. 106
Des Plaines, IL 60018
Phone: (708)390-8927
Fax: (708)390-9962
Elaine Petrucelli, Exec.Dir.

Founded: 1957. **Members:** 650. **Description:** Physicians and other professionals concerned with motor vehicle safety, design, and road engineering. Works to reduce the number of injuries and fatalities on the nation's highways by encouraging research on the effects of diseases, disabilities, and environmental factors on driver capabilities. Supports laws and regulations to upgrade the standards for licensing drivers and research and development programs leading to improved bio-engineering of motor vehicles. Encourages the use of appropriate protective devices and disseminates new information in the field of traffic, vehicular, and pedestrian safety. Individual members conduct research programs. **Publications:** *Abreviated Injury Scale.* • *Accident Analysis and Prevention,* bimonthly. Journal. Features papers relating to accidental injury and damage including pre- and post-injury phases. *Price:* Included in membership dues; $65 for nonmembers. • *Bulletin,* bimonthly. • *Proceedings,* annual. **Formerly:** (1987) American Association for Automotive Medicine.

★ 10843 ★ Association of Teachers of
Preventive Medicine (ATPM)
c/o Barbara J. Calkins
1015 15th St. NW, Ste. 405
Washington, DC 20005
Phone: (202)682-1698
Barbara J. Calkins, Exec.Dir.

Founded: 1942. **Members:** 700. **Description:** Professional society of teachers in medical schools, research, and other phases of preventive medicine and public health. **Publications:** *American Journal of Preventive Medicine,* bimonthly. Journal. • *ATPM Membership Directory,* periodic. Membership Directory. • *Directory and Profile of Academic Units in Preventive Medicine,* periodic. Directory. • *Newsletter,* quarterly. **Formerly:** (1955) Conference of Professors of Preventive Medicine.

★ 10844 ★ Association for Worksite Health
Promotion (AWHP)
60 Revere Dr., Ste. 500
Northbrook, IL 60062-1577
Phone: (708)480-9574
Fax: (708)480-9282
Kevin Hacke, Exec.Dir.

Founded: 1974. **Members:** 2,500. **Regional Groups:** 11. **State Groups:** 50. **Local Groups:** 20. **Description:** Health and fitness professionals employed by major companies (some smaller companies and businesses are also represented) and conducting wellness fitness programs for employees; interested persons in personnel and sales to fitness facilities; health educators and other health professionals; students interested in the field. Supports and assists in the development of quality programs of health and fitness in business and industry. Seeks to create an awareness of the importance of physical, emotional, and mental health among employees. Stimulates active research and serves as a clearinghouse on employee health and fitness. Sponsors seminars and an educational committee that studies effectiveness of preparation, training programs, and certification. Conducts open discussions and workshops on health and nutrition. Compiles statistics. **Publications:** *Action*, bimonthly. Newsletter. Contains association news, book reviews, research summaries, worksite fitness internship programs information, and calendar of events. *Price:* Free, for members only. • *AWHP Membership Directory*. Membership Directory. Lists health educators, health/fitness professionals employed by major companies, and others involved in supporting worksite health/fitness programs. *Price:* Included in membership dues. • *AWHP's Worksite Health*, quarterly. Journal. *Price:* Included in membership dues; $70 for extra subscriptions; $70 for nonmembers. Also distributes proceedings of conferences on cassette tapes. **Formerly:** (1983) American Association of Fitness Directors in Business and Industry; (1993) Association for Fitness in Business.

★ 10845 ★ Canadian Injury Prevention Foundation
20 Queen St. W, Ste. 200
Toronto, ON, Canada M5H 3V7
Phone: (416)979-4012
Fax: (416)977-3538
Crystal Snelling, Contact

Languages: English, French. **Description:** Works to reduce the number of injuries in Canada. Sponsors campaigns to raise public awareness of preventable causes of injury in automobiles, the home, and the workplace.

Cancer Control Society (CCS)
See: Entry 5931

★ 10846 ★ Center for Dance Medicine (CDM)
41 E. 42nd St.
New York, NY 10017
Phone: (212)661-8401
Lynne Kemen, Adm.Dir.

Founded: 1978. **Description:** Educates dancers about their bodies and preventive medicine in order to help them avoid injuries. Activities are currently concentrated in New York City area.

**★ 10847 ★ Estonian Health Protection Association
(Eesti Tervikaitse Selts)**
Paldiski Mnt. 81
EE-0109 Tallinn, Estonia
Phone: 2 450451
Kalju Nestrik, Contact

Description: Promotes better health care for people living in Estonia.

★ 10848 ★ Exer-Safety Association (ESA)
120 University Park Dr., Ste. 280B
Winter Park, FL 32792
Phone: (407)677-9501
Sharon Foy, Dir.

Founded: 1980. **Members:** 10,000. **Local Groups:** 150. **Description:** Fitness instructors, personal trainers, health spas, YMCAs, community recreation departments, and hospital wellness programs. Purposes are: to improve the qualifications of exercise instructors; to train instructors to develop safe exercise routines that will help people avoid injury while exercising; to prepare instructors for national certification. Offers training in aerobics and exercise and on the physiological aspects of exercise. Conducts exercise safety and research programs. Sponsors charitable program; maintains speakers' bureau. Offers placement and children's services. **Publications:** *ESA Member Directory*, annual. Membership Directory. • *Exer-Safety News*, periodic. Newsletter. Provides exercise information based on current scientific research. Includes schedule of upcoming programs. *Price:* Included in membership dues. **Formerly:** (1985) International Exer-Safety Association.

★ 10849 ★ Fitness Motivation Institute of America Association (FMIAA)
5521 Scotts Valley Dr.
Scotts Valley, CA 95066
Phone: (408)439-9898
Free: 800-538-7790
Fax: (408)439-9504
Ronald E. Useldinger, Pres.

Founded: 1971. **Members:** 50. **Description:** Persons professionally involved with health and physical fitness. works to motivate, educate, activate, and evaluate individuals in the area of physical fitness. Program is based on four parameters: why the body needs exercise; what a fit body is; methods of getting fit; motivation to stay fit. Offers quarterly training session. **Publications:** *Fitfacts Journal*, quarterly. Journal. Provides new ideas on using Isorobics exercise programs. *Price:* $25/year. • *Fitness Motivation Institute of America Association--Newsletter*, bimonthly. Newsletter. Reports on the fitness industry. *Price:* Available to members only.

★ 10850 ★ IDEA: International Association of Fitness Professionals (IDEA)
6190 Cornerstone Ct. E., Ste. 204
San Diego, CA 92121
Phone: (619)535-8979
Free: 800-999-IDEA
Fax: (619)535-8234
Kathie Davis, Exec.Dir.

Founded: 1982. **Members:** 23,000. **Regional Groups:** 9. **State Groups:** 57. **Description:** Provides continuing education for fitness professionals including; aerobics instructors, personal trainers, and club/studio owners. Offers workshops for continuing education credits. **Publications:** Brochures. • *IDEA Fitness Manager*, 10/year. Newsletter. • *IDEA Personal Trainer*, 10/year. Magazine. Includes marketing client relationship and business information • *IDEA Today*, 10/year. Magazine. Includes articles on exercise science, teaching techniques, and business management. Also includes annual index to articles and calendar of events. *Price:*

Included in membership dues. • Pamphlets. • Videos. **Also Known As:** International Dance Exercise. **Formerly:** (1989) IDEA: International Dance Exercise Association; (1993) IDEA: The Association for Fitness Professionals.

★ 10851 ★ Injury Control Center (ICC)
Harvard Univ.
School of Public Health
718 Huntington Ave.
Boston, MA 02115
Phone: (617)432-2123
Fax: (617)432-0190
John D. Graham, Dir.

Founded: 1987. **Description:** Participants include universities, medical centers, doctors, and research associates. Supports scientific research and training to improve injury control, particularly prevention activities, acute care of trauma patients, and rehabilitation of the disabled. Focuses specifically on trauma occuring within the elderly population and the very young. Sponsors internships, educational programs, and doctoral and post-doctoral work. Presents testimony on relevant legislative issues. Disseminates information; maintains speakers' bureau. **Publications:** *Injury Update*, semiannual. Newsletter. Includes research results and articles on specific injuries. *Price:* Free.

★ 10852 ★ Institute for Aerobics Research (IAR)
12330 Preston Rd.
Dallas, TX 75230
Phone: (214)701-8001
Free: 800-635-7050
Fax: (214)991-4626
Mark Donovan, Controller

Founded: 1970. **Description:** Goals are to promote understanding of the relationship between living habits and health, to provide leadership in enhancing the physical and emotional well-being of individuals, and to promote participation in aerobics. Seeks to increase the quality and quantity of fitness programs within major institutions. Conducts innovative studies on health and living habits and methods of facilitating changes in living habits; promotes the awareness and skills needed to develop a positive life-style. Sponsors workshops and seminars; conducts weekly training course and certification testing of fitness leaders in education, government, human services, and corporate sectors. Operates speakers' bureau. Maintains 10,000 volume library.

International Academy of Nutrition and Preventive Medicine (IANPM)
See: Entry 9465

★ 10853 ★ International Council for Physical Activity and Fitness Research (ICPFR)
Faculty of Physical Education & Physiotherapy
Katholieke Universitet Leuven
Tervuursevest 101
B-3001 Heverlee, Belgium
Phone: 16 329083
Fax: 16 329197
Albrecht L. Claessens, Ph.D.

Founded: 1964. **Members:** 106. **National Groups:** 36. **Languages:** English. **Description:**

Medical doctors, physiologists, anthropologists, biochemists, physical educators, and psychologists in 30 countries who have done substantial research on physical fitness. Promotes international comparative studies on the effect of physical fitness upon the welfare of children, adults, and the aged. Works toward establishing standardized physical fitness assessment and measurement procedures. Operates speakers' bureau. Maintains advisory committees for the establishment of a sports research center and for the facilitation of scientific cooperation in the preparation, execution, and publication of comparative studies. **Publications:** *Fitness for the Aged, Disabled and Industrial Worker.* • *Fitness, Health, and Work Capacity: International Standards for Assessments.* • *Physical Fitness and the Ages of Man.* • *Physical Fitness Assessment: Principles, Practices and Application.* • *Physical Fitness Research XIV.* • *Proceedings*, biennial. Also publishes a guide and book of standards on health and fitness. **Formerly:** (1978) International Committee on Physical Fitness Research; (1992) International Council for Physical Fitness Research.

International Society for Preventive Oncology (ISPO)
See: Entry 5961

★ **10854** ★ **Lifegain Institute (LI)**
115 Dunder Rd.
Burlington, VT 05401
Phone: (802)862-8855
Fax: (802)862-6389
Judd Allen, Ph.D., Pres.

Founded: 1977. **Members:** 600. **Description:** People who work with health promotion programs in hospitals, corporations, colleges, and communities. Promotes healthy practices such as exercise, nutrition, safety, and the reduction or curtailment of smoking and alcohol consumption through health promotion programs that provide a supportive environment in which to change unhealthy practices. Maintains speakers' bureau. Compiles data on improvements in health practices nationwide. **Publications:** *American Journal of Health Promotion*, quarterly. Journal. • Articles. • *Lifegain: A Culture-Based Approach to Positive Health.* Book. • *Lifegain Healthy Communities System.* Also publishes support materials.

★ **10855** ★ **National Association of Governor's Councils on Physical Fitness and Sports**
201 S. Capitol Ave., Ste. 440
Indianapolis, IN 46225
Phone: (317)237-5630
Fax: (317)237-5632

Founded: 1979. **Members:** 38. **Regional Groups:** 4. **State Groups:** 38. **Description:** State governor's fitness councils. Works with state government to establish and maintain governor's councils on physical fitness and health. Provides technical assistance and information on fundraising. Offers strategies for promoting fitness at all levels of state and local government. **Publications:** *State by State*, monthly. Newsletter. *Price:* Available to members only.

★ **10856** ★ **National Wellness Association (NWA)**
1045 Clark St., Ste. 210
Stevens Point, WI 54481-2962
Phone: (715)342-2969
Fax: (715)342-2979
Linda R. Chapin, M.S., Exec.Dir.

Founded: 1985. **Members:** 2,400. **Description:** Membership division of the National Wellness Institute. Health and wellness promotion professionals from corporations, universities, hospitals, clinics, community organizations, consulting firms, government organizations, schools (K-12) and fitness clubs. Acts as clearinghouse for information on wellness and health promotion; refers inquiries to other information sources. **Publications:** *American Journal of Health Promotion*, bimonthly. Journal. *Price:* Included in professional membership. • *Health Issues Update*, quarterly. Newsletter. Covers national health developments, legislation, and policy. *Price:* Included in professional membership. • *Job Opportunities Bulletin*, monthly. Bulletin. • *National Wellness Institute Wellness Resource Directory*, annual. Directory. *Price:* Included in membership dues. • *NWA Membership Directory*, annual. Membership Directory. *Price:* Included in membership dues. • *Wellness Management*, quarterly. Newsletter. Covers recent developments; includes calendar of events; lists employment and educational opportunities and recent publications. *Price:* Included in membership dues.

★ **10857** ★ **National Wellness Institute**
1045 Clark St., Ste. 210
Stevens Point, WI 54481-2962
Phone: (715)342-2969
Fax: (715)342-2979
Linda R. Chapin, DDS, Exec.Dir.

Founded: 1977. **Description:** Purposes are to provide national leadership in the wellness movement; to assist professionals working in health and wellness promotion in all types of settings; and organizations with planning, development, implementation, and evaluation of wellness programs; and to assist in the development of high quality wellness products and services. Acts as clearinghouse on wellness information. Provides consultations; offers professional development conferences. Sponsors National Wellness Association. **Publications:** Brochures. • *Health Issues Update*, quarterly. Newsletter. *Price:* Included in membership dues. • *Lifestyle Assessment Questionnaire.* • *Testwell Assessment Series.* • *Wellness Management*, quarterly. Newsletter. *Price:* Included in membership dues. • *Wellness Resource Directory*. Directory.

★ **10858** ★ **Society of Prospective Medicine (SPM)**
4417 Anchor Mill Dr.
Omaha, NE 68123
Phone: (402)291-3297
Fax: (317)549-3670
Jan Foerster, Exec.Officer

Founded: 1972. **Members:** 250. **Description:** Physicians, allied health workers, scientists, and others committed to extending the useful life expectancy of persons by identifying actual and potential health hazards and by developing and implementing risk assessment techniques and risk reduction programs. Conducts research; compiles statistics. Develops education programs and supplies information concerning diseases that frequently cause death and disability. Maintains speakers' bureau. **Publications:** *An Ounce of Prevention--Newsletter*, quarterly. Newsletter. Reports on developments in health hazard appraisal. Includes calendar of events. *Price:* Included in membership dues; $20/year for nonmembers. • *Health Risk Appraisal Book.* Book. • *Proceedings of Annual Meeting.* Proceedings. *Price:* $35. • *SPM Handbook of Health Risk Appraisal.* Directory. *Price:* $35.

Swiss Institute for Public Health
See: Entry 10970

★ **10859** ★ **Wellness Associates (WA)**
21489 Orr Springs Rd.
Ukiah, CA 95482
Phone: (707)937-2331
John W. Travis, M.D., Dir.

Founded: 1975. **Description:** Provides high quality resource materials for lifestyle improvement integrating the major components of wellness: self-responsibility, stress management, nutrition, and physical awareness. Spreads wellness education to the fields of emotional and physical health. Recognizes spiritual growth and the search for meaning to be essential elements in the experience of wellness. Offers wellness publications and resources for helping professionals to assist them in realizing the principles of wellness in their own lives and to help their clients experience their own capacity for good health and well-being. Provides consultation for wellness centers, individuals, universities, agencies, hospitals, and government groups. **Publications:** *Global Wellness Inventory.* Book. *Price:* $15.95. • *Wellness for Helping Professionals.* Book. *Price:* $24.95. • *Wellness Index.* Book. *Price:* $2.95. • *Wellness Inventory.* Book. *Price:* $1.95. • *Wellness Resource Kit.* Book. *Price:* $87. • *Wellness: Small Changes You Can Use to Make a Big Difference.* Book. *Price:* $6.95. • *Wellness Workbook.* Book. *Price:* $14.95. **Formerly:** (1979) Wellness Resource Center.

★ **10860** ★ **A Wellness Center, Inc. (AWCI)**
145 W. 28th St., Rm. 9R
New York, NY 10001
Phone: (212)465-8062
Howard Morse

Founded: 1979. **Members:** 1,500. **Description:** Individuals concerned with wellness and preventive health care; firms, institutions, and organizations with wellness centers or employee assistance programs. Educates health practitioners and the public on methods of developing healthier lifestyles through the prevention and treatment of degenerative diseases and other health disorders. Provides professional training workshops in wellness counseling, an approach that integrates many scientific and medical disciplines, to assist members with problems related to weight control, stress, alcoholism, personal relationships, drug addiction, and other physical, mental, or social problems. Conducts individual and group counseling sessions and support groups for individuals suffering from arthritis, asthma, cancer, depression, diabetes, and hypertension. Provides speakers on topics such as wellness, lifestyle changes, longevity, diseases, and medical and alternative therapies. **Publications:** *Bibliographical Essay*, periodic. • *Directory of Members*, annual. Membership Directory. • *Life-Style for Wellness*, quarterly. Journal. Includes research reports, book reviews, and listings of employment opportunities. *Price:* $50/year. • *Mailing List*, periodic.

★ **10861 ★ Wellness and Health Activation Networks (WHAN)**
9802 Lindsay Lake Blaine
Great Falls, VA 22066-3819
Phone: (703)759-6256
Fax: (703)657-6542
Joseph T. Nocerino, Pres.

Founded: 1980. **Members:** 5,000. **Description:** Established to help individuals become "health activated." (The health activated person is described as one who more fully understands their role in maintaining good health and preventing illness.) Concentrates on programs designed to increase awareness of health rights and responsibilities. Teaches individuals how to promote wellness, handle common health problems, become more health self-reliant, and make more effective use of the health resources of the community. Activities include: Wellness, Yoga, and Health Activation Training Institutes; on-site program planning and development; technical assistance; grant proposal preparation and reviews. Serves as a clearinghouse for Wellness and Health Activation Program, which designs and acts as national distributor of trainer's course guides, planning guides, program texts, home health care equipment, and other health activation materials. Conducts semimonthly workshop.

Research Centers

★ **10862 ★ Academy Research Center**
1 Academy Dr.
Daphne, AL 36526-9552
Phone: (334)626-3303
Fax: (334)626-1149
Dr. Brian Bergemeer, Ph.D., Dean of
Academic Affairs & Research

Research Activities and Fields: Basic exercise physiology and preventive medicine for disease, emphasizing analysis of cardiovascular disease risk factor and life-style change intervention; biomechanical research in gait analysis, sports skills, and structural anomalies; sports medicine research in injury prevention, treatment, and diagnosis; and drug abuse in sports. **Publications:** Quarterly Newsletter. **Formerly:** United States Sports Academy, Preventive Medicine and Fitness Center; Preventive Medicine Clinic.

★ **10863 ★ American University National Center for Health Fitness**
Nebraska Hall, Lower Level
4400 Massachusetts Ave. NW
Washington, DC 20016-8037
Phone: (202)885-6275
Fax: (202)885-6288
Robert C. Karch, Dir.

Research Activities and Fields: Worksite health promotion programs, focusing on costs, benefits, and cost-effectiveness, and including international health promotion and special populations. Consulting activities include health promotion program design, implementation, and management. **Publications:** *Fitness News* (monthly newsletter); *Army Life* (monthly newsletter). **E-mail Address:** nchfm@american.edu.

★ **10864 ★ Cooper Institute for Aerobics Research**
12330 Preston Rd.
Dallas, TX 75230
Phone: (214)701-8001
Fax: (214)991-4626
Dr. Charles L. Sterling, Exec.Dir.

Research Activities and Fields: Cardiovascular disease, stress management, women's health, exercise physiology, health promotion, nutrition, youth fitness, hypertension, aging, and epidemiology. Using data from the affiliated Cooper Clinic, the Institute conducts the Aerobics Center Longitudinal Study, which monitors 25,000 subjects over their lifetime to study the effects of exercise and health habits on death and disability rates from chronic diseases.

★ **10865 ★ Harvard University Harvard Injury Control Center**
Harvard Sch. of Public Health
718 Huntington Ave.
Boston, MA 02115
Phone: (617)432-2123
Fax: (617)432-0190
John D. Graham, Ph.D., Dir.

Research Activities and Fields: Injury control, including prevention, acute care, and rehabilitation of trauma patients. Activities focus on three areas: trauma care systems; violence prevention; and traffic injury prevention. Trauma Care Systems Program projects are designed to inform the development of a trauma system in Massachusetts, particularly with regard to the emergency care needs of children; assess the reliability of trauma registry data; and evaluate the relative costs and quality of long-term care in institutional settings versus community settings. Violence Prevention Program works to establish incidence and prevalence rates of peer and intimate violence among adolescents; determine the correlates of unsafe gun storage and examine the use of guns for self protection; evaluate a school-based domestic violence prevention curriculum; assess the effects of policy changes on implementing emergency department protocols for response to battered women; and focus on the related problems of peer adolescent violence, intimate violence, and gun-related violence. Traffic Injury Prevention Program projects center on occupant crash protection and the prevention of drinking and driving, including strategic advertising plans to deter drunk driving, and assessing higher gaso-

line taxes and developing new car safety ratings as injury control interventions.

★ **10866 ★ Indiana University Bloomington Center for Health and Safety Studies**
Bloomington, IN 47405
Phone: (812)855-3627
Fax: (812)855-3936
Dr. James W. Crowe, Dir.

Research Activities and Fields: Health behavior, quantitative and qualitative evaluation of instructional materials, and human behavior and attitudes relating to safety and driver education, including studies on industrial safety, health and safety practices in industry and recreational settings, childhood accident prevention and injury control, nutrition, family life, and human development. **E-mail Address:** crowe@indiana.edu. **Formerly:** Center for Safety and Traffic Education (1979).

★ **10867 ★ Johns Hopkins University Center for Injury Research and Policy**
Dept. of Health Policy & Mgmt.
Sch. of Public Health
624 N. Broadway
Baltimore, MD 21205
Phone: (410)614-4026
Fax: (410)614-2797
Ellen J. Mackenzie, Ph.D., Dir.

Research Activities and Fields: Adolescent drowning and poisoning, alcohol related injuries, aviation safety, childhood injuries, fall injuries in nursing homes, financing trauma care and rehabilitation, homicide and suicide, injuries from firearms, injuries in developing countries, injury sequelae and rehabilitation, injury severity scoring, injury surveillance systems, mathematical models of response to impact, motor vehicle related injuries, occupational injuries, and elderly and highway safety. Develops injury interventions, evaluates legal interventions, examines preventive measures, and evaluates trauma care. **E-mail Address:** thenson@phnet.sph.jhu.edu. **Formerly:** Injury Prevention Center.

★ **10868 ★ Oakland University Meadowbrook Health Enhancement Institute**
Rochester, MI 48309-4401
Phone: (810)370-3198
Fax: (810)370-4522
Dr. Stransky, Dir.

Research Activities and Fields: Clinical research in exercise physiology and enhancing the health profile of residents in internal medicine. **Publications:** *Way of Life* (quarterly newsletter).

Prevention Research Center
See: Entry 12098

★ **10869 ★ Preventive Medicine Research Institute**
900 Bridgeway, Ste. 2
Sausalito, CA 94965
Phone: (415)332-2525
Fax: (415)332-5730
Dean Ornish, M.D., Pres.

Research Activities and Fields: Prevention and treatment of heart disease through modification of diet, exercise, and relaxation techniques such as yoga, meditation, and visualization.

★ 10870 ★ San Francisco Injury Center for Research and Prevention
San Francisco General Hospital
Bldg. 1, Rm. 400
San Francisco, CA 94110
Phone: (415)821-8209
Fax: (415)282-2563
Elizabeth McLoughlin, Sc.D., Dir.

Research Activities and Fields: Prevention of injury resulting from youth violence, domestic violence, head injuries, fatal fires, firearm, and alcohol-related injuries; acute care; rehabilitation, including personal assistant services and countering negative images of disability; epidemiology, including regionalization of trauma care, outcomes of trauma care, and economic impact of California's motorcycle helmet law; and engineering, focusing on increasing wheelchair stability. **E-mail Address:** emcl@itsa.ucsf.edu. **Formerly:** San Francisco Injury Prevention Center.

★ 10871 ★ Sid W. Richardson Institute for Preventive Medicine of the Methodist Hospital
6565 Fannin
Mail Sta. SM583
Houston, TX 77030
Phone: (713)790-6450
Fax: (713)793-1269
Clifford Dacso, M.D., Med.Dir.

Research Activities and Fields: Analyzes health insurance claims and employee absentee data to evaluate various preventive medicine programs, evaluates the effect of smoking cessation on the occurrence of chronic lung disease, compares different program approaches taken in cardiac rehabilitation (exercise versus comprehensive approaches), and studies depression in patients with heart disease and their spouses. **Publications:** *The Journal* (employee journal).

★ 10872 ★ Stanford Center for Research in Disease Prevention
Stanford Univ. School of Medicine
1000 Welch Rd.
Palo Alto, CA 94304-1885
Phone: (415)723-1000
Fax: (415)725-6906
John W. Farquhar, M.D., Dir.

Research Activities and Fields: Prevention and control of chronic disease, alcohol and drug abuse, adolescent pregancy, and injury and death. Stresses a public health or community approach to disease prevention and health promotion and seeks methods to improve the overall level of community health by favorably modifying the environmental and personal factors known to influence chronic disease incidence, including blood pressure, blood cholesterol, cigarette use, obesity, physical activity, and stress. **Publications:** Catalogue available for health promotion materials. **Formerly:** Stanford Heart Disease Prevention Program (1984).

Strang Cancer Prevention Center
See: Entry 6117

★ 10873 ★ Trauma Foundation
San Francisco General Hospital
Bldg. 1, Rm. 300
San Francisco, CA 94110
Phone: (415)821-8209
Fax: (415)282-2563
Andrew McGuire, Exec.Dir.

Research Activities and Fields: Injury control, public policy, and epidemiology, including epidemiology of traumatic injuries and health policy research on such issues as fire-safe cigarettes, air bags, handgun control, and alcohol policy. **Publications:** *Injury Prevention Network* (quarterly newsletter). **Formerly:** Trauma Center Foundation(1984).

U.S. Department of Defense
Army Medical Research and Development Command
Walter Reed Army Institute of Research
Preventive Medicine Division
See: Entry 7835

U.S. Department of Health and Human Services
National Cancer Institute
Division of Cancer Prevention and Control
See: Entry 6140

U.S. Department of Health and Human Services
National Cancer Institute
Division of Cancer Prevention and Control
Cancer Control Science Program
See: Entry 6141

U.S. Department of Health and Human Services
National Cancer Institute
Division of Cancer Prevention and Control
Cancer Prevention Research Program
See: Entry 6142

U.S. Department of Health and Human Services
National Cancer Institute
Division of Cancer Prevention and Control
Chemoprevention Branch
See: Entry 6144

U.S. Department of Health and Human Services
National Cancer Institute
Division of Cancer Prevention and Control
Early Detection and Community Oncology Program
See: Entry 6145

U.S. Department of Health and Human Services
National Cancer Institute
Division of Cancer Prevention and Control
Health Education Section
See: Entry 6146

U.S. Department of Health and Human Services
National Cancer Institute
Division of Cancer Prevention and Control
Special Population Studies Branch
See: Entry 6147

U.S. Department of Health and Human Services
National Cancer Institute
Division of Cancer Prevention and Control
Surveillance Program
See: Entry 6148

★ 10874 ★ U.S. Department of Health and Human Services
National Center for Chronic Disease Prevention and Health Promotion
Mail Stop K40
1600 Clifton Rd., N.E.
Atlanta, GA 30333
Phone: (404)488-5401
Fax: (404)488-5971
Jeffrey P. Koplan, M.D., Director

Research Activities and Fields: Activities of the National Center for Chronic Disease Prevention and Health Promotion are concerned with the prevention of chronic diseases such as cardiovascular disease, diabetes, and cancer. Translates research findings into community programs and healthier lifestyles. Supports programs to improve nutrition, reproductive health, and exercise, and to discourage destructive behaviors, such as alcohol abuse and smoking. NCCDPHP's seven major organization units are: Office on Smoking and Health, the Office of Surveillance and Analysis, the Division of Reproductive Health, the Division of Nutrition, the Division of Adolescent and School Health, the Division of Diabetes Translation, and the Division of Chronic Disease Control and Community Intervention.

★ 10875 ★ U.S. Department of Health and Human Services
National Center for Chronic Disease Prevention and Health Promotion
Chronic Disease Control and Community Intervention Division
1600 Clifton Rd., N.E.
Atlanta, GA 30333
Phone: (404)488-4251
Marjorie A. Speers, M.D., Director

Research Activities and Fields: Chronic diseases, including maternal and child health, breast and cervical cancer, diabetes, smoking, adolescents and school health, AIDS and women, and rerproductive health. **Publications:** Publishes Chronic Disease Notes and Reports.

★ 10876 ★ U.S. Department of Health and Human Services
National Center for Chronic Disease Prevention and Health Promotion
Diabetes Translation Division
Epidemiology and Statistics Branch
1600 Clifton Rd., N.E.
Atlanta, GA 30333
Phone: (404)639-3311
Virginia Bells, Chief

Research Activities and Fields: Performs epidemiologic research related to preventing diabetes and its complications. Conducts national surveys on the incidence of diabetes and its complications.

★ 10877 ★ **U.S. Department of Health and Human Services**
National Center for Chronic Disease Prevention and Health Promotion
Office of Surveillance and Analysis
Mail Stop K-30
1600 Clifton Rd., N.E.
Atlanta, GA 30333
Phone: (404)488-5269
Fax: (404)488-5974
Stephen B. Blount, M.D., Director

Research Activities and Fields: Conducts surveillance and epidemiologic studies of chronic disease morbidity, mortality, and behavioral risk factors; develops surveillance tools and provides assistance to state and local health departments, universities, and voluntary agencies; administers and reports to Congress on the Preventive Health and Health Services Block Grant; and studies health status of special populations, including women, minorities, and the elderly. **Publications:** *Behavioral Risk Factor Surveillance System Annual Report.*

★ 10878 ★ **U.S. Department of Health and Human Services**
National Center for Prevention Services
Immunization Division
Surveillance, Investigations, and Research Branch
1600 Clifton Rd., N.E.
Atlanta, GA 30333
Phone: (404)639-3311
Stephen C. Hadler, Chief

Research Activities and Fields: Branch collects and analyzes data on the incidence of diseases preventable by vaccination and conducts studies on the safety and efficacy of new or existing vaccines. **Additional Contact Information:** Branch is located at 1600 Tully Circle, Atlanta, GA, 30329.

★ 10879 ★ **U.S. Department of Health and Human Services**
National Center for Prevention Services
Sexually Transmitted Disease/HIV Prevention Division
Behavioral and Prevention Research Branch
Mail Stop E-44
1600 Clifton Rd., N.E.
Atlanta, GA 30333
Phone: (404)639-0829
Fax: (404)639-0868
William W. Darrow, Ph.D., Chief

Research Activities and Fields: Plans and conducts research projects on individual and group behavior patterns as they affect STD and HIV occurrence and transmission. Undertakes studies to evaluate new methods of prevention and intervention of HIV and STDs, and conducts surveys, studies, and methodological research on the prevalence of sexual and drug-using behavior with increased risks of STDs and HIV. Performs community-based intervention to prevent HIV/STD transmission among gay and bisexual males, injecting drug users, youth in high-risk situations, prostitutes, and sex partners of all these groups. Evaluates HIV counseling, and testing of methadone patients, patients in detox, and STD patient clinics. **Publications:** *MMWR.*

★ 10880 ★ **U.S. Department of Health and Human Services**
National Center for Prevention Services
Tuberculosis Elimination Division
Surveillance and Epidemiologic Investigations Branch
1600 Clifton Rd., N.E.
Atlanta, GA 30333
Phone: (404)639-8116
Fax: (404)639-8604
Ida Onorato, M.D., Chief

Research Activities and Fields: Branch conducts research on the epidemiology of tuberculosis, HIV virus, and drug-resistant tuberculosis.

U.S. Department of Health and Human Services
National Heart, Lung, and Blood Institute
Division of Epidemiology and Clinical Applications
Clinical Applications and Prevention Program
See: Entry 2931

★ 10881 ★ **University of Alabama at Birmingham**
Center for Health Risk Assessment and Disease Prevention
School of Public Health
Tidwell Hall, 201
Birmingham, AL 35294
Phone: (205)934-7132
Fax: (205)934-8665
Dr. Jeffrey M. Roseman, Dir.

Research Activities and Fields: Health risk assessment, disease prevention, and genetic risk assessment.

★ 10882 ★ **University of Alabama at Birmingham**
Injury Control Research Center
933 19th St. S., Ste. 403
CH-19
Birmingham, AL 35294-2041
Phone: (205)934-1448
Fax: (205)934-3749
Philip R. Fine, Ph.D., Dir.

Research Activities and Fields: Primary focus is on rehabilitation and occupationally-related injuries, especially burns, intra-articular fractures of the lower extremities, spinal cord injuries, and traumatic brain injuries. Center's main objectives are: 1) improve rehabilitation practices and processes to help persons with injuries achieve maximum rehabilitation potential; 2) stimulate local faculty development of prevention, acute-care, rehabilitation, epidemiology, and biomechanics research projects; 3) train health care workers and other practitioners, scientists, and students in the discipline of injury prevention and control; 4) provide technical assistance and disseminate information in support of the nation's injury control agenda; and 5) promote the explicit incorporation of injury prevention initiatives targeting high-risk populations. Center also conducts multidisciplinary research involving faculty from other areas of the University. **Publications:** Newsletter. **Formerly:** Injury Prevention Research Center (1991).

★ 10883 ★ **University of California, Los Angeles**
Southern California Injury Prevention Research Center
UCLA Sch. of Public Health
10833 Le Conte Ave.
Los Angeles, CA 90024-1772
Phone: (310)206-4115
Fax: (310)794-7989
Jess F. Kraus, Ph.D., Dir.

Research Activities and Fields: Intentional and unintentional injuries in the socioeconomically disadvantaged, underserved, and ethnically diverse populations in the Southern California region. Research projects include: work-related injuries in high-risk occupations; immigration and risk of motor vehicle crash; homicide of children; immediate rescusitation in children; firearm injuries and deaths; earthquake injury and preparedness; expanding methods in injury epidemiology; repetitive poisonings of children; alcohol and suicide; long-term consequences of spinal cord injuries; multiple organ failure from trauma; violence in contemporary American film; undetermined causes of death; evaluation of the 1992 California Helmet Law; workplace assaults; back supports in material handlers; marital violence; and youth violence . **E-mail Address:** ejc3inj.@mvs.oac.ucla.edu.

★ 10884 ★ **University of California, San Francisco**
Center for AIDS Prevention Studies (CAPS)
Prevention Sciences Group
74 New Montgomery St., Ste. 600
San Francisco, CA 94105
Phone: (415)597-9100
Fax: (415)597-9213
Thomas J. Coates, Ph.D., Dir.

Research Activities and Fields: Methods to change AIDS high risk behavior. Activities include developing and testing AIDS prevention strategies for at-risk populations, promoting multidisciplinary research on the prevention of HIV disease, funding pilot studies on minority issues in AIDS, and operating the CAPS International Visiting Scholars Program, which brings scholars from Africa, Asia, Eastern Europe, and Latin America to work with CAPS scientists in developing AIDS prevention research protocols. **Publications:** *CAPS Bibliography.* **E-mail Address:** tom__coates.psg@quickmal.ucsf.edu.

University of Houston
Social Psychology/Behavioral Medicine Research and Graduate Training Group
See: Entry 7665

★ 10885 ★ **University of Iowa**
Injury Prevention Research Center
College of Medicine
100 Oakdale Campus, No. 126 AMRF
Iowa City, IA 52242-5000
Phone: (319)335-4418
Fax: (319)335-4225
Dr. Craig Zwerling, Dir.

Research Activities and Fields: Prevention and control of rural injuries, including validation of an electronic emergency room log for injury surveillance and evaluation of acute rural injuries; evaluation of the public health implications of age- and illness-associated driving impairments; experimental studies to assess the biomechanical dynamics of tractor runover injuries; evaluation of a traumatic injury prevention program designed to reduce motor vehicle deaths and injuries in Iowa youth; evaluation of the efficacy of community-based interventions to prevent tractor-related injuries; and assessment of incidence, risk factors, and methods to prevent secondary injuries among farmers participating in a rural rehabilitation program. **E-mail Address:** john.lundell@uiowa.edu.

★ 10886 ★ **University of Louisville**
Health Promotion and Wellness Center
102 C. Carmichael
Louisville, KY 40292
Phone: (502)852-5711
Fax: (502)852-5711
Bryant A. Stamford, Ph.D., Dir.

Research Activities and Fields: Performs fitness analyses for county police departments, fire fighters, and commonwealth police. Also studies exercise routines.

University of Michigan—Flint
Physical Therapy Laboratory for Cumulative Trauma Disorders
See: Entry 9858

★ 10887 ★ **University of North Carolina at Chapel Hill**
Center for Health Promotion and Disease Prevention
255 Rosenau Hall
Campus Box 7400
Chapel Hill, NC 27599-7400
Phone: (919)966-6039
Fax: (919)966-6264
Dr. Alan W. Cross, Dir.

Research Activities and Fields: Health promotion and disease prevention at state, regional, and national levels, focusing on cardiovascular disease, cancer, injury, low birth weight prevention, public health and safety, child abuse and neglect, health of minority youth, injury prevention, and health promotion in the workplace.

★ 10888 ★ **University of North Carolina at Chapel Hill**
Injury Prevention Research Center
Chase Hall
Campus Box 7505
Chapel Hill, NC 27599-7400
Phone: (919)966-2251
Fax: (919)966-7955
Carol W. Runyan, Ph.D., Dir.

Research Activities and Fields: Studies the epidemiology, prevention, acute care, and rehabilitation aspects of injuries, including workplace injury, road safety, violence, childhood injury, and program development and evaluation. **Publications:** *IPRC News.* **E-mail Address:** unciprc@phvax.sph.unc.edu.

★ 10889 ★ **University of Southern California**
Institute for Health Promotion and Disease Prevention Research
1540 Alcazar St.
CHP 207
Los Angeles, CA 90033
Phone: (213)342-2600
Fax: (213)342-2601
C. Anderson Johnson, Ph.D., Dir.

Research Activities and Fields: Chronic disease prevention, behavioral epidemiology, patient compliance, HIV/AIDS, and tobacco, alcohol, and other and drug abuse. Activities focus on research in health promotion and disease prevention, with young people as the principal target. **Publications:** Technical Reports (ad hoc). Sponsors a weekly seminar on health behavior. **Formerly:** Health Behavior Research Institute (1986).

★ 10890 ★ **University of Texas—Houston Health Science Center**
Center for Health Promotion Research & Development
PO Box 20186
Houston, TX 77225
Phone: (713)792-8540
Fax: (713)794-1756
Dr. Guy S. Parcel, Dir.

Research Activities and Fields: Health promotion research and development, with emphasis on institutional settings (worksites, medical care facilities, schools, and communities). Studies include the interaction of educational, economic, and environmental influences on health promotion, testing interventions directed toward institutions and individuals, and the innovation, diffusion, and maintenance of health promotion programs. Conducts survey research for monitoring and surveillance of health knowledge, attitudes, opinion, and behavior; evaluates methods and strategies for health care adapted to select populations; provides technical assistance, consultation, and collaboration with agencies, industries, institutions, media, and universities throughout Texas; and helps develop educational materials. **E-mail Address:** sph0253@utsph.sph.uth.tmc.edu.

★ 10891 ★ **University of Vermont**
Office of Health Promotion Research
1 S. Prospect St.
Burlington, VT 05401
Phone: (802)656-4187
Fax: (802)656-8826
Roger H. Secker-Walker, M.D., Dir.

Research Activities and Fields: Health education, smoking prevention (primarily with youth and in schools), smoking cessation, particularly in primary care physician's offices and whole communities breast screening promotion, breast self-exam education, AIDS prevention, diabetes prevention, behavioral/lifestyle change, community-based projects, and projects utilizing mass media. The Office emphasizes interdisciplinary research. **Formerly:** Vermont Lung Center.

★ 10892 ★ **University of Washington**
Harborview Injury Prevention and Research Center
325 9th Ave., ZX-10
Seattle, WA 98104
Phone: (206)521-1530
Fax: (206)521-1562
Frederick P. Rivara, M.D., Dir.

Research Activities and Fields: Injury prevention and the causes and effects of injuries, including studies in epidemiology, health education, and psychology. **E-mail Address:** fpr@u.washington.edu.

Chapter 54
Public Health

Federal Government Agencies

★ 10893 ★ Consumer Product Safety Commission
4330 East West Hwy.
Bethesda, MD 20814
Phone: (301)504-0100

Description: The purpose of the Consumer Product Safety Commission is to protect the public against unreasonable risks of injury from consumer products; to assist consumers in evaluating the comparative safety of consumer products; to develop uniform safety standards for consumer products and minimize conflicting state and local regulations; and to promote research and investigation into the causes and prevention of product-related deaths, illnesses, and injuries. It also collects information on consumer product-related injuries and maintains a comprehensive Injury Information Clearinghouse.

★ 10894 ★ Nuclear Regulatory Commission (NRC)
11555 Rockville Pike
Rockville, MD 20852
Phone: (301)415-8200

Description: The Nuclear Regulatory Commission licenses and regulates the civilian uses of nuclear energy to protect public health and safety and the environment.

★ 10895 ★ U.S. Department of Agriculture
Food Safety and Inspection Service
14th & Independence Ave. SW
Washington, DC 20250
Phone: (202)720-7025

Description: The service is responsible for ensuring that meat and poultry products moving in interstate and foreign commerce for human consumption are safe, wholesome, and accurately labeled.

★ 10896 ★ U.S. Department of Health and Human Services
Centers for Disease Control and Prevention
1600 Clifton Rd. NE
Atlanta, GA 30333
Phone: (404)639-3291

Description: The Centers for Disease Control administers national programs for the prevention and control of communicable and vector-borne diseases and other preventable conditions. It develops and implements programs to deal with environmental health problems, including responding to environmental, chemical, and radiation emergencies. CDC directs and enforces foreign quarantine activities and regulations; provides consultation and assistance in upgrading the performance of public health and clinical laboratories; and participates in a nation-wide program of research, information, and education in the field of smoking and health. The CDC also provides consultation to other nations in the control of preventable diseases, and participates with national and international agencies in the eradication or control of communicable diseases and other preventable conditions. CDC's major operating components include: the Center for Environmental Health and Injury Control, Center for Chronic Disease Prevention and Health Promotion, Center for Infectious Diseases, Center for Prevention Services, National Center for Health Statistics, and the National Institute for Occupational Safety and Health (see separate entries).

★ 10897 ★ U.S. Department of Health and Human Services
Food and Drug Administration
5600 Fishers Ln.
Rockville, MD 20857
Phone: (301)443-2410

Description: The mission of the Food and Drug Administration is to protect the public health of the nation as it may be impaired by foods, drugs, biological products, cosmetics, medical devices, ionizing and nonionizing radiation-emitting products and substances, poisons, pesticides, and food additives. Its regulatory functions are geared to insure that foods are safe, pure, and wholesome; that drugs, medical devices, and biological products are safe and effective; that cosmetics are harmless; that all of the above are honestly and informatively packaged; and that exposure to potentially injurious radiation is minimized. The Administration's major operating components are: 1) the Center for Biologics Evaluation and Research, 2) the Center for Devices and Radiological Health, 3) the Center for Drug Evaluation and Research, 4) the Center for Food Safety and Applied Nutrition, 5) the Center for Veterinary Medicine, and 6) the National Center for Toxicological Research.

★ 10898 ★ U.S. Department of Health and Human Services
Food and Drug Administration
Center for Biologics Evaluation and Research
9000 Rockville Pike
Bethesda, MD 20892
Phone: (301)827-0548
Fax: (301)827-0440

Description: Center administers regulation of biological products under the biological product control provisions of the Public Health Service Act and applicable provision of the Federal Food, Drug, and Cosmetic Act. It provides dominant focus in the Administration for coordination of the AIDS program, works to develop an AIDS vaccine and AIDS diagnostic tests, and conducts other AIDS-related activities. It inspects manufacturers' facilities for compliance with standards, tests products submitted for release, established written and physical standards, and approves licensing of manufacturers to produce biological products. The Center plans and conducts research related to the development, manufacture, testing, and use of both new and old biological products and coordinates with the Center for Drug Evaluation and research regarding activities for biological drug products, including research, compliance, and product review and approval. The Center plans and conducts research on the preparation, preservation, and safety of blood and blood products, the methods of testing safety, purity, potency, and efficacy of such products for therapeutic use, and the immunological problems concerned with products, testing, and use of diagnostic reagents employed in grouping and typing blood.

U.S. Department of Health and Human Services
Food and Drug Administration
Center for Devices and Radiological Health
See: Entry 11058

★ 10899 ★ U.S. Department of Health and Human Services
Food and Drug Administration
Center for Drug Evaluation and Research
1451 Rockville Pike
Rockville, MD 20852
Phone: (301)594-6740

Description: Center develops FDA policy with regard to the safety, effectiveness, and labeling of all drugs for human use; reviews and evaluates new drug applications and notices of claimed investigational exemption of new drugs; develops and implements standards for the safety and effectiveness of all over-the-counter drugs; monitors the quality of marketed drugs through product testing, surveillance, and compliance programs; develops guidelines on current Good Manufacturing Practices for use by the drug industry; develops and disseminates information and educational material on drugs to the medical community and the public; conducts research and develops scientific standards on the composition, quality, safety, and efficacy of human drugs; collects and evaluates information on the effects and use trends of marketed drugs; monitors prescription drug advertising and promotional labeling to assure their accuracy and integrity; analyzes data on accidental poisonings; and disseminates toxicity and treatment information on medicines.

★ 10900 ★ U.S. Department of Health and Human Services
Food and Drug Administration
Center for Food Safety and Applied Nutrition
200 C St. SW
Washington, DC 20204
Phone: (202)205-4850

Description: The Center conducts research and develops standards on the composition, quality, nutrition, and safety of foods, food additives, colors, and cosmetics; conducts research designed to improve the detection, prevention, and control of contamination that may be responsible for illness or injury conveyed by foods, colors, and cosmetics; coordinates and evaluates FDA's surveillance and compliance programs relating to foods, color, and cosmetics; reviews industry petitions and develops regulations for food standards to permit the safe use of color additives and food additives; collects and interprets data on nutrition, food additives, and environmental factors affecting the total chemical result posed by food additives; and maintains a nutritional data bank.

★ 10901 ★ U.S. Department of Health and Human Services
Public Health Service (PHS)
200 Independence Ave. SW
Washington, DC 20201
Phone: (202)690-6867

Description: The mission of the Public Health Service is to promote the protection and advancement of the nation's physical and mental health. This is accomplished by coordinating with the states to set and implement national health policy and pursue effective intergovernmental relations; generating and upholding cooperative international health-related agreements, policies, and programs; conducting medical and biomedical research; sponsoring and administering programs for the development of health resources, prevention and control of diseases, and alcohol and drug abuse; providing resources and expertise to the states and other public and private institutions in the planning, direction, and delivery of physical and mental health care services; and enforcing laws to assure the safety and efficacy of drugs and protection against impure and unsafe foods, cosmetics, medical devices, and radiation-producing projects. In addition to the Office of the Assistant Secretary for Health, the Public Health Service includes the following major components: the Agency for Toxic Substances and Disease Registry; the Substance Abuse and Mental Health Services Administration; the Centers for Disease Control; the Food and Drug Administration; the Health Resources and Services Administration; the Indian Health Service; and the National Institutes of Health.

★ 10902 ★ U.S. Department of Health and Human Services
Public Health Service
Office of the Assistant Secretary for Health
200 Independence Ave. SW
Washington, DC 20201
Phone: (202)690-6867

Description: The Office consists of general and special staff offices that support the Assistant Secretary for Health in planning and directing the activities of the Public Health Service. Components include the Office of the Surgeon General, the Office of Disease Prevention and Health Promotion, the Office of Health Communications, the Office of Health Operations, the Office of Health Planning and Evaluation, the Office of Intergovernmental Affairs, and the Office of Population Affairs. Also under the administration of the Assistant Secretary for Health are the President's Council on Physical Fitness and Sports and a major operating center, the Agency for Health Care Policy and Research (see separate entry, Chapter 17, Federal Government Research Agencies, Facilities, and Programs).

Foundations & Other Funding Organizations

Private Foundations

★ 10903 ★ New World Foundation
100 E 85th St.
New York, NY 10028
Phone: (212)249-1023
Colin Greer, President

Foundation Philosophy: The five principal areas of giving (as defined by the foundation) are Equal Rights and Opportunities: those programs which promote participation of all groups in all aspects of American life; Education and Youth; Public Health: programs to raise public and personal health standards, including health needs of the disadvantaged, as well as environmental and occupational health and safety; Community Initiatives; and Avoidance of War. Giving Priorities: In fiscal 1993, the foundation contributed 60% of its total funding to civic groups. Environmental groups received 10% of the funds, and social services, religious organizations, and educational projects each received 8%. International affairs funding received the remaining 6% of funds. Typical Health-Related Recipients: Health Organizations, People with Disabilities. Geographic Distribution: National.

★ 10904 ★ Public Welfare Foundation
2600 Virginia Ave., NW, Ste. 505
Washington, DC 20037-1977
Phone: (202)965-1800
Fax: (202)625-1348
Larry Kressley, Executive Director

Foundation Philosophy: The Public Welfare Foundation provides support to organizations which serve low-income or disadvantaged people throughout the United States and the world. At the forefront of the foundation's work are direct services to people in need of the basic necessities of life: food, shelter, health, and the ability to live independently. Traditionally, the foundation has focused its efforts on six priority areas: the environment, criminal justice, health, population, disadvantaged youth, and disadvantaged elderly. The foundation reports that it has incorporated the issues of community violence and violence prevention into its disadvantaged youth, criminal justice, and health initiatives. Giving Priorities: In fiscal 1994, the foundation reported that community support received approximately 22% of total contributions, including funds for food and nutrition, civil and social justice, and homelessness and traditional housing. Health care received about 19% of funds. Environmental and population issues each received 18%. Criminal justice programs received 11%; disadvantaged youth, 9%; and disadvantaged elderly people received the remaining 3% of giving. Typical Health-Related Recipients: Adolescent Health Issues, AIDS/HIV, Children's Health/Hospitals, Clinics/Medical Centers, Domestic Violence, Family Planning, Geriatric Health, Health Organizations, Hospitals, Mental Health, People with Disabilities, Prenatal Health Issues, Public Health. Geographic Distribution: International and national.

★ 10905 ★ Rockefeller Family Fund
1290 Avenue of the Americas, Rm. 3450
New York, NY 10104
Phone: (212)373-4252
Fax: (212)315-0996
Donald K. Ross, Director

Foundation Philosophy: The Rockefeller Family Fund makes grants in five program areas: citizen education and participation; economic justice for women; the environment, emphasizing the reduction of military pollution, the conservation of natural resources and the protection of health as affected by the environment; institutional responsiveness; and self-sufficiency. Giving Priorities: In 1994, based on the fund's designated areas of interest, the environment received approximately 31% of funding; institutional responsiveness, another 31%; economic justice for women, about 21%; self-sufficiency, 8%; and citizen education and participation, roughly 8%. **Typical Health-Related Recipients:** Health Policy/Cost Containment, People with Disabilities, Public Health. **Geographic Distribution:** National (the fund does not generally consider projects which pertain to one city or state, unless the project could serve as a national model).

Medical & Allied Health Schools

Public Health

The following graduate schools of public health are members of the Association of Schools of Public Health, 1660 L St. NW, Ste. 204, Washington, DC 20036, (202) 296-1099 and are accredited by the Council on Education for Public Health, 1015 15th St. NW, Ste. 403, Wahington, DC 20005, (202) 789-1050.

Alabama

★ 10906 ★ **University of Alabama at Birmingham**
School of Public Health
720 S. 20th St.
Birmingham, AL 35294-0008
Phone: (205)934-7730
Fax: (205)934-7539

California

★ 10907 ★ **Loma Linda University**
School of Public Health
Loma Linda, CA 92350
Phone: (909)824-4578
Fax: (909)824-4087

★ 10908 ★ **San Diego State University**
Graduate School of Public Health
San Diego, CA 92182-0405
Phone: (619)594-6317
Fax: (619)594-6112

★ 10909 ★ **University of California at Berkeley**
School of Public Health
19 Earl Warren Hall
Berkeley, CA 94720
Phone: (510)642-2082
Fax: (510)643-5676

★ 10910 ★ **University of California, Los Angeles**
School of Public Health
Center for Health Sciences, Rm. 16-035
10833 Le Conte Ave.
Los Angeles, CA 90024-1772
Phone: (310)825-6381
Fax: (310)825-8440

Connecticut

★ 10911 ★ **Yale University**
School of Medicine
Department of Epidemiology and Public Health
60 College St.
PO Box 3333
New Haven, CT 06510
Phone: (203)785-2867
Fax: (203)785-7296

Florida

★ 10912 ★ **University of South Florida**
College of Public Health
MHH-104
13201 Bruce B. Downs Blvd.
Tampa, FL 33612-3805
Phone: (813)974-3623
Fax: (813)974-4718

Georgia

★ 10913 ★ **Emory University**
School of Public Health
1518 Clifton Rd. NE
Atlanta, GA 30329
Phone: (404)727-8720
Fax: (404)727-3996

Hawaii

★ 10914 ★ **University of Hawaii at Manoa**
School of Public Health
1960 East-West Rd.
Honolulu, HI 96822
Phone: (808)956-8066
Fax: (808)956-4585

Illinois

★ 10915 ★ **University of Illinois at Chicago**
School of Public Health
Health Sciences Center, Rm. 113
2121 W. Taylor St.
Chicago, IL 60612
Phone: (312)996-6620
Fax: (312)996-1374

Louisiana

★ 10916 ★ **Tulane University**
School of Public Health and Tropical Medicine
1430 Tulane Ave.
New Orleans, LA 70112
Phone: (504)588-5397
Fax: (504)588-5718

Maryland

★ 10917 ★ **Johns Hopkins University**
School of Hygiene and Public Health
615 N. Wolfe St.
Baltimore, MD 21205-2179
Phone: (410)955-3540
Fax: (410)955-0121

Massachusetts

★ 10918 ★ **Boston University**
School of Public Health
80 E. Concord St., Rm. A-407
Boston, MA 02118-2394
Phone: (617)638-4640
Fax: (617)638-5299

★ 10919 ★ **Harvard University**
School of Public Health
677 Huntington Ave.
Boston, MA 02115
Phone: (617)432-1025
Fax: (617)277-5320

★ 10920 ★ **University of Massachusetts**
School of Public Health
108 Arnold House
Amherst, MA 01003-0037
Phone: (413)545-1303
Fax: (413)545-1264

Michigan

★ 10921 ★ **University of Michigan**
School of Public Health
109 S. Observatory St.
Ann Arbor, MI 48109-2029
Phone: (313)763-5454
Fax: (313)763-5455

Minnesota

★ 10922 ★ **University of Minnesota**
School of Public Health
Mayo Memorial Bldg., A-304, Box 197
420 Delaware St. SE
Minneapolis, MN 55455-0381
Phone: (612)625-1179
Fax: (612)626-6931

Missouri

★ 10923 ★ **St. Louis University**
School of Public Health
O'Donnell Hall, Rm. 380
3663 Lindell Ave.
St. Louis, MO 63108
Phone: (314)977-8111
Fax: (314)977-8150

New York

★ 10924 ★ **Columbia University**
School of Public Health
617 W. 168th St.
New York, NY 10032
Phone: (212)305-3929
Fax: (212)305-1460

★ 10925 ★ **State University of New York at Albany**
School of Public Health
Executive Park S.
Albany, NY 12203-3727
Phone: (518)485-5500
Fax: (518)485-5565

North Carolina

★ 10926 ★ **University of North Carolina at Chapel Hill**
School of Public Health
Rosenau Hall, Campus Box 7400
S. Columbia St.
Chapel Hill, NC 27599-7400
Phone: (919)966-3215
Fax: (919)966-7678

Oklahoma

★ 10927 ★ **University of Oklahoma**
College of Public Health
Health Sciences Center
801 NE 13th St.
Oklahoma City, OK 73104-5072
Phone: (405)271-2232
Fax: (405)271-3039

Pennsylvania

★ 10928 ★ **University of Pittsburgh**
Graduate School of Public Health
111 Parran Hall
Pittsburgh, PA 15261
Phone: (412)624-3001
Fax: (412)624-3309

Puerto Rico

★ 10929 ★ **University of Puerto Rico**
School of Public Health
Medical Center - Main Bldg.
GPO Box 5067
San Juan, PR 00936
Phone: (809)758-2525
Fax: (809)759-6719

South Carolina

★ 10930 ★ **University of South Carolina**
School of Public Health
Sumter & Greene
Columbia, SC 29208
Phone: (803)777-5032
Fax: (803)777-4783

Texas

★ 10931 ★ **University of Texas Health Science Center at Houston**
School of Public Health
Reuel A. Stallones Bldg.
1200 Hermann Pressler
Houston, TX 77225
Phone: (713)792-4425
Fax: (713)791-1369

Washington

★ 10932 ★ **University of Washington**
School of Public Health and Community Medicine
1599 NE Pacific (SC-30)
Seattle, WA 98195
Phone: (206)543-1144
Fax: (206)543-3813

National & International Organizations

★ 10933 ★ **African Medical and Research Foundation (AMREF/Ugan)**
PO Box 10663
Kampala, Uganda
Phone: 41 250319
Fax: 41 244565
D. Shuey, Director

Founded: 1957. **Description:** Purpose is to improve the health of people living in Uganda. Focus is on public heath education, sanitation, medical auxilaries, preventive medicine, health care teams, and clinics.

★ 10934 ★ **American Association of Medical Milk Commissions (AAMMC)**
c/o Paul Fleiss, M.D.
1824 N. Hillhurst Ave.
Los Angeles, CA 90027
Phone: (213)664-1977
Fax: (213)664-0870
Paul Fleiss, M.D., Pres.

Founded: 1907. **Members:** 35. **Description:** Professional society of physician members of local Medical Milk Commissions, including veterinarians, sanitarians, and bacteriologists who supervise production of certified milk (milk from dairies conforming to official standards of sanitation). **Publications:** *Methods and Standards for the Production of Certified Milk*, annual.

★ 10935 ★ **American Association of Public Health Dentistry (AAPHD)**
10619 Jousting Ln.
Richmond, VA 23235
Phone: (804)272-8344
Fax: (804)272-0802
Rhys Jones, DDS, Pres.

Founded: 1937. **Members:** 650. **Description:** Professional society of dentists, dental hygienists, health educators, and others actively engaged in dental public health. Sponsors competitions. **Publications:** *American Association of Public Health Dentistry--Communique*, quarterly. Newsletter. *Price:* Included in membership dues; $10/year for nonmembers. • *Journal of Public Health Dentistry*, quarterly. Journal. Covers fluoridation, sealants, demographics, and utilization of dental services. Includes research reports and book reviews. *Price:* Included in membership dues; $85/year for nonmembers in U.S.; $90/year for nonmembers outside U.S.; $115/year airmail. **Formerly:** (1983) American Association of Public Health Dentists.

★ 10936 ★ **American Association of Public Health Physicians (AAPHP)**
c/o Armand Start, M.D.
Dept. of Family Practice
777 S. Mills St.
Madison, WI 53715
Phone: (608)263-1326
Fax: (608)263-5813
Armand Start, M.D., Contact

Founded: 1954. **Members:** 200. **Description:** Physicians actively engaged in public health. Promotes leadership in the field of public health;

speaks for its membership on proposed health legislation at various levels; supports coordination of public health responsibilities in a variety of agencies. Conducts or cosponsors educational seminars. **Publications:** *American Association of Public Health Physicians--Bulletin*, monthly. Newsletter. Includes abstracts of recent public health literature. *Price:* Included in membership dues. • *Membership Roster*, annual.

★ 10937 ★ **American Board of Dental Public Health (ABDPH)**
c/o Stanley Lotzkar, D.D.S.
1321 NW 47th Ter.
Gainesville, FL 32605
Phone: (904)378-6301
Stanley Lotzkar, D.D.S., Exec.Sec.

Founded: 1950. **Members:** 5. **Description:** Board whose purpose is to investigate the qualifications of, administer examinations to, and certify as diplomates, dentists specializing in dental public health. Sponsored by American Association of Public Health Dentistry. **Publications:** *ABDPH Membership Directory*, triennial. Directory. • Newsletter, annual.

★ 10938 ★ **American Council on Science and Health (ACSH)**
1995 Broadway, 2nd Fl.
New York, NY 10023-5860
Phone: (212)362-7044
Fax: (212)362-4919
Dr. Elizabeth M. Whelan, Pres.

Founded: 1978. **Members:** 5,000. **Description:** Provides consumers with scientifically balanced evaluations of food, chemicals, the environment, and human health. Council personnel participate in government regulatory proceedings, congressional hearings, radio and television programs, public debates and other forums, and write regularly for professional and scientific journals, popular magazines, and newspaper columns. Holds national press conferences; produces documentary films. Maintains speakers' bureau. **Publications:** Booklets, 8-10/year. Peer-reviewed, health and environmental reports for consumers. • *Directory of Scientific Advisors*, triennial. Directory. • *Financial Statement*, annual. • *Media Updates*, semiannual. • *News From ACSH*, semiannual. • Papers. • *Priorities: For Long Life and Good Health*, quarterly. Magazine. For consumers. *Price:* Included in membership dues. • Reports. On health risks and benefits associated with public health and environmental issues.

★ 10939 ★ **American Public Health Association (APHA)**
1015 15th St. NW
Washington, DC 20005
Phone: (202)789-5600
Fax: (202)789-5681
Fernando M. Trevino, Ph.D., Exec.Dir.

Founded: 1872. **Members:** 31,500. **Description:** Professional organization of physicians, nurses, educators, academicians, environmentalists, epidemiologists, new professionals, social workers, health administrators, optometrists, podiatrists, pharmacists, dentists, nutritionists, health planners, other community and mental health specialists, and interested consumers. Seeks to protect and promote personal, mental, and environmental health. Services include: promulgation of standards; establishment of uniform practices and procedures; development of the etiology of communicable diseases; research in public health; exploration of medical care programs and their relationships to public health. Sponsors job placement service. **Publications:** *American Journal of Public Health*, monthly. Journal. Includes news briefs and annual leadership directory. *Price:* Included in membership dues; $80/year for nonmembers. • *The Nation's Health*, 10/year. Reports on current and proposed legislation, regulations, and policy issues affecting public health; includes reports on current health issues. *Price:* Included in membership dues; $8/year for nonmembers. Also publishes books, manuals, and pamphlets; maintains publications service.

★ 10940 ★ **American Public Welfare Association (APWA)**
810 1st St. NE, Ste. 500
Washington, DC 20002-4267
Phone: (202)682-0100
Fax: (202)289-6555
A. Sidney Johnson, Exec.Dir.

Founded: 1930. **Members:** 4,000. **Description:** Public welfare agencies, their professional staff members, and others interested in public welfare. **Publications:** *APWA News*, quarterly. Newspaper. Covers membership activities. Includes calendar of events. *Price:* Free, for members only. • *Public Welfare*, quarterly. Journal. Contains articles, research reports, and book reviews. *Price:* $25/year. • *Public Welfare Directory*, annual. Directory. Describes public welfare programs and agencies in the United States and Canada. Lists contacts and phone numbers and programs offered. *Price:* $65/year for members; $70/year for nonmembers. • *This Week in Washington*, weekly. Newsletter. Summarizes congressional action on human service issues. *Price:* $85/year for members; $95/year for nonmembers. • *W-Memo*, monthly. Magazine. Analyzes congressional and federal agency action affecting human service programs. *Price:* $65/year for members; $75/year for nonmembers.

★ 10941 ★ **Asian Health Institute (AHI)**
987-30 Minamiyama
Komenogi, Nisshin-Cho
Aichi-gun
Aichi 470-01, Japan
Phone: 5617 31950
Yoshio Ikezumi, Gen.Sec.

Description: Promotes improved public health in southeast Asia. Conducts public educational campaigns to create indigenous leadership for public health initiatives in the region.

★ 10942 ★ **Association of Schools of Public Health (ASPH)**
1660 L St. NW, Ste. 204
Washington, DC 20036
Phone: (202)296-1099
Fax: (202)296-1252
Michael K. Gemmell, Exec.Dir.

Founded: 1941. **Members:** 26. **Description:** Accredited graduate schools of public health. Provides focus for the enhancement of academic public health programs. Serves as an informa-

tion center for governmental and private groups, and individuals whose concerns overlap those of higher education for public health. **Publications:** *Gerontology Programs and Curricula in U.S. Schools of Public Health*. • *Public Health Career Information*. • *Reach*.

★ 10943 ★ **Association of Schools of Public Health in the European Regional (ASPHER) (Association des Ecoles de Sante Publique de la Regional Europeenne)**
Nottingham Health Authority
Forest House
Berkeley Ave.
Nottingham NG5 1PG, England
Phone: 115 9691691
Maurice Beaver

Founded: 1966. **Members:** 65. **Languages:** English, French, German, Russian. **Description:** Schools of public health and other institutions offering graduate instruction in public health. Promotes the study and development of education in public health and health services. Conducts workshops and seminars. Organizes exchange of students and staff between member schools.

★ 10944 ★ **Association of State Drinking Water Administrators (ASDWA)**
1120 Connecticut Ave. NW, Ste. 1060
Washington, DC 20036-3902
Vanessa M. Leiby, Exec.Dir.

Founded: 1984. **Members:** 56. **Description:** Managers of state and territorial drinking water programs; state regulatory personnel. Works to meet communication and coordination needs of state drinking water program managers; facilitates the exchange of information and experience among state drinking water agents. Acts as a collective voice for the protection of public health through assurance of high quality drinking water; oversees the implementation of the Safe Drinking Water Act. Liaises with Congress and the Environmental Protection Agency. Holds training sessions. **Publications:** *ASDWA Update*, bimonthly. Newsletter. For state drinking water administrators, water industry personnel, and all others interested in the latest issues related to drinking water. *Price:* Included in membership dues; $40/year for nonmembers.

Association of State and Territorial Directors of Nursing (ASTDN)
See: Entry 5564

Association of State and Territorial Directors of Public Health Education (ASTDPHE)
See: Entry 5565

★ 10945 ★ **Brazilian Association for the Promotion of Appropriate Technology in Healthcare (Associacao Brasileira de Tecnologia Alternativa na Promocao da Saude — TAPS)**
Caixa Postal 20396
04041-990 Sao Paulo, SP, Brazil
Phone: 11 5720466
Fax: 11 5720465
Hildegard Bromberg Richter, Chm. of the Bd.

Founded: 1981. **Languages:** Portuguese. **Description:** Promotes public health and domestic

development in Brazil with emphasis on improving health care through acquisition of appropriate technology. Functional in the following areas: health and nutrition; identification, preparation, and supervision of projects; technical assistance; training and administration; publications. **Publications:** *ComTAPS*, quarterly. Newsletter. • *Onde nao ha medico*. Book. • *Voce sabe se alimentar?*. Book. **Also Known As:** Temas Atuais na Promocao da Saude.

★ 10946 ★ **Canadian Public Health Association**
1565 Carling Ave., Ste. 400
Ottawa, ON, Canada K1Z 8R1
Phone: (613)725-3769
Fax: (613)725-9826

Languages: English, French. **Description:** Works to mobilize national charitable and volunteer resources to address public health concerns worldwide. Conducts immunization, maternal and child health, and nutritional programs in at-risk areas.

★ 10947 ★ **Commissioned Officers Association of the United States Public Health Service (COA)**
1400 Eye St. NW, Ste. 725
Washington, DC 20005
Phone: (703)243-1301
Fax: (703)243-0151
William J. Lucca, Jr., Exec.Dir.

Founded: 1910. **Members:** 7,300. **Local Groups:** 44. **Description:** Commissioned officers of the U.S. Public Health Service; includes career active duty, retired, and inactive reserve officers who are physicians, dentists, scientists, engineers, pharmacists, nurses, and other types of professional personnel. Acts as a spokesman for the Commissioned Corps, as an information center for its members, and "as a sounding board where views and concerns of the Corps may be brought to the proper authorities for official action." **Publications:** *COA Bulletin*, monthly. Bulletin. • *Directory*, annual. • *Proceedings of Annual Meeting*. Proceedings.

★ 10948 ★ **Community Health Education (Educacion Comunitaria para la Salud — EDUCSA)**
Apartado Postal 3312
Bo. La Guadalupe
Vuelta del Codo
Edificio EDUCSA
Tegucigalpa, Honduras
Phone: 310968
Fax: 310318
Manuel A. Villamil, Pres.

Founded: 1983. **Languages:** English, Spanish. **Description:** Works to improve the health and nutrition of rural communities in Honduras. Conducts educational programs to develop indigenous infrastructure and expertise required to sustain public health awareness programs. Emphasizes health maintenance and the use of medicinal plants in the treatment of disease.

★ 10949 ★ **Council on Education for Public Health (CEPH)**
1015 15th St. NW
Washington, DC 20005
Phone: (202)789-1050
Patricia P. Evans, Exec.Dir.

Founded: 1974. **Description:** Participants are professional associations representing public health practice (American Public Health Association) and public health education (Association of Schools of Public Health). Seeks to strengthen educational programs in schools of public health and graduate public health programs through accreditation, consultation, research, and other appropriate services; and to encourage the development of experimental and innovative programs which will ensure educational quality. **Publications:** *Manuals for Accreditation of Graduate Schools of Public Health and Graduate Public Health Programs.* Manuals.

★ 10950 ★ **Delta Omega**
c/o Dr. Greg Alexander
University of Minnesota
School of Public Health
Minneapolis, MN 55455
Phone: (612)624-6669
Dr. Greg Alexander, Contact

Founded: 1924. **Members:** 4,000. **Regional Groups:** 18. **Local Groups:** 18. **Description:** Honorary society - men and women, public health. Promotes research and scholarly attainment; sponsors lectures.

★ 10951 ★ **Estonian Centre of Health Education**
(Eesti Tervisekasvatuse Keskus)
Ruutli St. 24
EE-0001 Tallinn, Estonia
Phone: 2 440801
Anu Kasmel, Dir.

Description: Conducts health education activities in Estonia to control disease.

★ 10952 ★ **European Public Health Alliance**
1, pl. du Luxembourg
B-1040 Brussels, Belgium
Phone: 2 5129360
Fax: 2 5126673
Andrews Hayes, Sec.

Founded: 1993. **Members:** 35. **Description:** Strives to improve public health care in Europe through policy monitoring and development. Works to heighten public awareness on current public health reforms. Communicates with other organizations with similar interests. **Publications:** Newsletter, monthly.

★ 10953 ★ **European Union of Social Medicine (UEMS)**
(Unione Europea di Medicina Sociale)
Via Sacchi 24
I-10128 Turin, Italy
Phone: 11 5627017
Fax: 11 5627341
Prof. Enrico Belli, Sec.Gen.

Founded: 1955. **Languages:** English, French, Italian. **Description:** European national societies of social medicine. Purpose is to study medico-social problems in European countries. Facilitates exchange of information on problems of public health. **Publications:** *Rivista Italiana di Medicina Sociale e Preventiva*, semiannual.

Food and Nutrition Board (FNB)
See: Entry 9459

★ 10954 ★ **General Association of Municipal Health and Technical Experts (GAMHTE)**
(Association Generale des Hygienistes et Techniciens Municipaux — AGHTM)
9, rue de Phalsbourg
F-75854 Paris Cedex 17, France
Phone: 1 53701350
Fax: 1 53701340
Alain Lasalmonie, Sec.Gen.

Founded: 1905. **Members:** 1,200. **Local Groups:** 5. **Languages:** French. **Description:** Engineers, engineering consultants, technicians, architects, scientists, administrators, and municipal and private services in 32 countries. Objectives are to: stimulate fundamental and applied research on urban and rural public hygiene; disseminate findings of such research; encourage the exchange of information and ideas among members. Areas of interest include city planning, energy management, traffic problems, and pollution prevention. Operates information service; organizes field tours. **Publications:** *Techniques Sciences-Methodes*, monthly. Also publishes monographs. **Formerly:** Association Generale des Ingenieurs, Architectes et Hygienistes Municipaux de France, Algerie, Tunisie, Belgique, Suisse et Luxembourg.

★ 10955 ★ **Health Education Foundation (HEF)**
2600 Virginia Ave. NW, Ste. 502
Washington, DC 20037
Phone: (202)338-3501
Fax: (202)342-8728
Morris E. Chafetz, M.D., Pres.

Founded: 1975. **Description:** Seeks to develop cost-effective health promotion programs for government, industry, and the business community; helps people make informed decisions about their physical and mental health; participates in research for analysis and development of standards and programs to meet public health needs. **Publications:** *Conference Proceedings*, periodic. Proceedings. • *Health Fact Tips*, semiannual. • *HEF News: Perspectives on Health, Behavior, and Lifestyle*, quarterly. Newsletter. *Price:* $15/year. • Monograph. • Pamphlets.

★ 10956 ★ **Lesbian and Gay Caucus of Public Health Workers (LGCPHW)**
2341 Hidalgo Ave.
Los Angeles, CA 90039
Phone: (213)664-9002
Donald Gabard, Ph.D., Contact

Founded: 1975. **Members:** 150. **Description:** A caucus of the American Public Health Association (see separate entry). Public health workers in the fields of administration, government, nursing, direct care, and teaching. Promotes dissemination of information on the health needs of lesbians and gay men. Serves as a support network for gay public health workers. The caucus believes homophobia interferes with the proper delivery of health care to gays and lesbians, restricts or eliminates their contributions as health workers, and causes physical and mental health problems. Holds scientific

sessions on gay and lesbian health issues at annual meeting. **Formerly:** (1990) Gay Public Health Workers Caucus.

★ 10957 ★ **MAP International - Kenya**
Studio House on Argwings Kodhek
Chaka Rd.
PO Box 21663
Nairobi, Kenya
Phone: 2 569513
Fax: 2 714422
Dr. Meredith Long, Dir.

Members: 10. **Description:** Provides training, consultancy, and health education services. Disseminates information about AIDS and other health issues. Provides a forum for the exchange of information. **Publications:** *A Pastoral Counselling Manual for AIDS*. Booklet. • *AIDS in Your Community*. Booklet. • *Community Balanced Development*. Booklet. • *Facts and Feelings About AIDS*. Booklet. • *Giving and Getting AIDS*. Booklet. • *Helpers for a Healing Community*. Booklet.

★ 10958 ★ **MAP International - Regional Office for Latin America**
(Map Internacional - Oficina Regional para America Latina)
Casilla 17-08-8184
Los Shyris 3517 y Tomas de Berlanga
Quito, Ecuador
Phone: 2 249476
Fax: 2 452373
Dr. Raul Ayala, Coordinator

Languages: Spanish. **Description:** Individuals, organizations, churches, and corporations with an interest in helping the needy. Provides training, consulting, and health education services. Disseminates information about AIDS and other health issues. Provides a forum for the exchange of public health information.

★ 10959 ★ **Medicine in the Public Interest (MIPI)**
192 South St., Ste. 500
Boston, MA 02111
Phone: (617)728-7977
Fax: (617)728-9135
Louis Lasagna, M.D., Pres.

Founded: 1973. **Description:** Professionals in medicine, law, and the social sciences. Promotes and funds research into medicine and related social, legal, and ethical issues; disseminates research findings and proposals. Encourages the development of long-range public health, welfare, and social planning at the federal, state, and local levels. Cooperates with governmental representatives in analyzing and developing legislation and programs designed to serve the public health and welfare. **Publications:** Reports.

★ 10960 ★ **Ministry of Concern for Public Health (MCPH)**
5495 Main St., Ste. 147
Buffalo, NY 14221-6701
Mary K. Bertell, Exec.Sec.

Founded: 1978. **Description:** A task force of Global Education Associates which provides scientific and informational services to individuals and groups who seek to understand, control, and, if possible, eliminate disease epidemics brought on by environmental pollution. Seeks: to prevent genetic damage and chronic degenerative diseases; to discover ways to lessen global security tensions and the threat of nuclear war; to promote understanding of pollution-health-environment systems and epidemic management through environment, host, or agent modification. Initiates research projects and programs; provides professional consultation on biostatistical, epidemiological, and public health-related projects; testifies and provides affida vits in legal suits. Maintains Citizen Health Register recording human health effects of a variety of environmental pollutants and occupational hazards. Operates Cluster Program to provide assistance to scientists. Provides assistance to government agencies, scientific research groups, citizens' organizations, and labor unions on problems of radioactive chemical exposure of the workplace or environment or other radiation exposure problems; arranges for blood tests, chromosome and urine analyses, and other biomedical tests for exposure to hazardous chemicals and radiation. Researches legal avenues for social change and strategies for strengthening international law in the areas of air and water pollution control, exporting of unsafe commodities, and damage to human health by degradation of the biosphere and gene pool. **Publications:** Books. • Brochures. • *Handbook for Estimating Health Effects from Exposure to Ionizing Radiation.* Handbook. • *International Perspectives in Public Health*, periodic. Journal. *Price:* $25 for 4 issues (U.S. and Canada); $30 for 4 issues (outside U.S. and Canada). • Papers.

★ 10961 ★ National Association of County and City Health Officials (NACCHO)
440 1st St. NW, Ste. 500
Washington, DC 20001
Phone: (202)783-5550
Fax: (202)783-1583
Nancy Rawding, Exec.Dir.

Founded: 1965. **Members:** 2,000. **Description:** County and city (local) health officials. Purposes are to stimulate and contribute to the improvement of local health programs and public health practices throughout the U.S.; disseminate information on local health programs and practices; participate in the formulation of the policies of the National Association of Counties (see separate entry). Is developing self-assessment instrument for use by local health officials. Operates Primary Care Project which helps to strengthen the link between local health departments and community health centers. Provides educational workshops for local health officials. **Publications:** Annual Report. • *Membership Monthly*, monthly. Information guide for members. *Price:* Included in membership dues. • *NACHO News*, bimonthly. *Price:* Included in membership dues. **Formerly:** National Association of County Health Officials; (1975) National Association of County Health Officers.

National Association of Public Health Service Dentists (Bundesverband der Zahnarzte des Offentlichen Gesundheitsdienstes)
See: Entry 3968

National Association of Public Hospitals (NAPH)
See: Entry 6462

National Association of State Public Health Veterinarians (NASPHV)
See: Entry 5592

National Council of State Human Service Administrators (NCSHSA)
See: Entry 5596

★ 10962 ★ National Latina Health Organization (NLHO)
PO Box 7567
Oakland, CA 94601
Phone: (510)534-1362
Fax: (510)534-1364
Luz Alvarez Martinez, Dir.

Founded: 1986. **Description:** Puerto Rican, Chicana, Mexican, Cuban, and South and Central American women. Works to increase awareness of health issues among Latin American women. Works to achieve bilingual access to quality health care and self-empowerment of Latinas through culturally sensitive educational programs, health advocacy, outreach, research, and the development of public policy. Cooperates with other organizations to defend reproductive choice, affordable birth control, sex education, prenatal care, and freedom from sterilization abuse. Offers technical training for community health facilitators. Organizes forums. **Publications:** Newsletter, periodic. Includes Latina health issues, legislation affecting Latinas, and calendar of events and activities on health and reproductive rights.

★ 10963 ★ National Pediculosis Association (NPA)
PO Box 149
Newton, MA 02161
Phone: (617)449-NITS
Fax: (617)449-8129
Deborah Z. Altschuler, Pres.

Founded: 1983. **Members:** 1,200. **Description:** Parents, physicians, school nurses, and individuals representing hospitals and county health departments. Works to eliminate the incidence, particularly among children, of pediculosis (head lice). Conducts public education campaign to make pediculosis control a public health priority; acts as consumer advocate to ensure the quality and safety of products for treating pediculosis; encourages scientific research to discover methods of treatment that minimize the use of pesticides, which may harm pregnant and nursing women as well as infants and children. Disseminates information on identifying, treating, and preventing pediculosis, with emphasis on finding and removing nits (louse eggs) in the hair. Provides consultations to schools, camps, and other organizations. Maintains speakers' bureau and creates exhibits for professional meetings and conferences. Offers in-service training and workshops for health professionals. Operates lending library of audiovisual aids; makes available other educational tools including posters and pamphlets. Sponsors National Pediculosis Prevention Month in September. Sponsors scientific advisory board of experts in such fields as entomology, derma-

tology, toxicology, pediatrics, parasitology, and pharmacology. Has testified before and works closely with the U.S. Food and Drug Administration. Bestows annual Drug Chain Leadership Award and Manufacturers Leadership Award. **Publications:** *Keep Your Wits Not Your Nits.* • *Latest Greatest Coloring Book About Lice.* • *Natalie and the Uninvited Guest Pest.* • *Progress*, periodic.

★ 10964 ★ Pakistan Voluntary Health and Nutrition Association (PVHNA)
PECHS
179/E, Block-2
Karachi 29, Pakistan
Phone: 21 446709
Fax: 21 437653
Begum Zeba Zubair, Chmn.

Founded: 1979. **Members:** 30. **Languages:** English, Urdu. **Description:** Seeks to improve public health in Pakistan. Promotes education in nutrition and family planning. Provides family planning organizations with training manuals. Conducts training programs in: water sanitation, child care, health care, and vocational education. Offers immunization services.

★ 10965 ★ Public Citizen Health Research Group (PCHRG)
2000 P St. NW, 7th Fl.
Washington, DC 20036
Phone: (202)833-3000
Fax: (202)463-8842
Sidney M. Wolfe, M.D., Dir.

Founded: 1971. **Description:** Works on issues of health care delivery, workplace safety and health, drug regulation, food additives, medical device safety, and environmental influences on health. Petitions or sues federal agencies on consumers' behalf, testifies before Congress on health matters, and monitors the enforcement of health and safety legislation. Publicizes important health findings; makes available to the public a broad spectrum of research and consumer action materials in the form of books and reports. **Publications:** *Health Letter*, monthly. Consumer newsletter reporting on health and health policy issues. *Price:* $18/year. • *Health Research Group List of Publications*, annual.

★ 10966 ★ Safe Water Coalition (SWC)
PO Box 1611
San Anselmo, CA 94979
Phone: (415)883-4834
Shirley Graves, Chm.

Founded: 1968. **Members:** 25. **Regional Groups:** 20. **Description:** Organizations, laypersons, and scientific professionals. Seeks to inform members and the public of the toxic effects of fluoride in public water systems and in dental hygiene products. Collects information pertaining to fluoride research; maintains collection of research reports and statistics. Provides and recommends speakers. Although membership is local, the coalition works on a national level through the regional groups. **Publications:** *National Fluoridation News*, quarterly. *Price:* $6/year.

★ 10967 ★ Singapore Medical Association (SMA)

Alumni Medical Centre
2 College Rd.
Singapore 0316, Singapore
Phone: 2231264
Fax: 2247827
Lynn Lee, Exec.Sec.

Founded: 1959. **Members:** 2,500. **Languages:** English. **Description:** Promotes medicine and allied sciences in Singapore. Works to increase public awareness of health care issues. Represents the medical profession before government and other organizations. Maintains standards of medical ethics and conduct. Provides a forum for social, cultural, and professional contact among members. Sponsors public health educational programs; offers CPR training; administers a training programme for health care assistants. **Publications:** Newsletter, monthly. • *Singapore Medical Journal*, bimonthly. Journal. Includes scientific papers.

Society for Nutrition Education (SNE)

See: Entry 9487

★ 10968 ★ Society of Public Health (SPH)

31 Battye Ave.
Huddersfield, W. Yorkshire HD4 5PW, England
Dr. P.A. Gardner, Hon.Sec.

Founded: 1856. **Members:** 1,400. **National Groups:** 12. **Languages:** English. **Description:** Medical and dental practitioners from 19 countries. Seeks to advance public health and integrated health services. Provides a forum for information exchange among specialists. Reviews existing methodologies and proposes new practices. Serves as an advisory body to governmental and other organizations. Assists in developing continuing professional training for specialists in public health and preventive medicine. Conducts research. **Publications:** *Communicable Disease Control.* • *Faculty Newsletter*, quarterly. Newsletter. • *Public Health*, bimonthly. Journal. Contains articles submitted on public health matters worldwide. • *Public Health Matters!.* • *Society Newsletter*, quarterly. Newsletter. • *Women's Health Issues - Are They Being Met?*. **Formerly:** (1856) Society of Medical Officers of Health; (1973) Society of Community Medicine.

★ 10969 ★ Society for Public Health Education (SOPHE)

2001 Addison St., Ste. 220
Berkeley, CA 94704
Phone: (510)644-9242
Fax: (510)845-4113
James P. Lovegren, Exec.Dir.

Founded: 1950. **Members:** 1,200. **Local Groups:** 18. **Description:** Professional workers in health education concerned with personal and community health problems. Seeks to promote, encourage, and contribute to the advancement of health of all people by encouraging study, improving health practices, and elevating standards of achievement in public health education. **Publications:** *Health Education Quarterly.* • Newsletter, quarterly. **Formerly:** Society of Public Health Educators.

★ 10970 ★ Swiss Institute for Public Health

Rue Bugnon 21A
CH-1005 Lausanne, Switzerland
Phone: 21 3132424

Languages: French, German, Italian. **Description:** Health care professionals and others interested in the Swiss health care system. Works to prevent disease through public education, fitness, and proper diet. Conducts research and educational programs to increase public awareness of disease prevention and health maintenance.

Uniformed Services Academy of Family Physicians (USAFP)

See: Entry 7812

United States Conference of Local Health Officers (USCLHO)

See: Entry 5605

★ 10971 ★ United States-Mexico Border Health Association (USMBHA)

6006 N. Mesa, Ste. 600
El Paso, TX 79912
Phone: (915)581-6645
Fax: (915)833-4768
Ignacio G. Gossett, M.D., Contact

Founded: 1943. **Members:** 2,300. **Description:** Physicians, public health administrators, nurses, sanitary engineers, veterinarians, scientists, laboratory workers, and other health officers from the 4 American and 6 Mexican states bordering the two countries. Seeks to make easier and more efficient the improvement of public health along both sides of the border; provides for exchange of experiences, discussion of mutual problems in human and animal diseases, and development of personal and professional contacts necessary for carrying out health projects. Sponsors seminars and workshops covering topics such as: food handling; rabies; tuberculosis; epidemiological principles; sexually transmitted diseases. Compiles statistics. **Publications:** *Border Health*, quarterly. Journal. Contains articles on U.S.-Mexico border health issues. *Price:* $3/issue. • *Epidemiological Bulletin*, bimonthly. Bulletin. • *Maternal Child Health Services Directory*, periodic. Directory. • *Report of Activities*, annual. • *U.S.-Mexico Border Health Association--News/Noticias*, quarterly. **Formerly:** (1975) United States-Mexico Border Public Health Association.

★ 10972 ★ World Federation of Public Health Associations (WFPHA)

c/o Amer. Public Health Assn.
1015 15th St. NW
Washington, DC 20005
Phone: (202)789-5696
Fax: (202)789-5681
Diane Kuntz, Exec.Sec.

Founded: 1967. **Members:** 45. **Description:** National public health associations united "to strengthen the public health professions and to improve community health throughout the world." Encourages formation of national public health associations. Organizes field projects; conducts special studies; offers lectures; compiles reports. **Publications:** *Reports of Triennial International Congresses*. Reports. • *WFPHA Report*, quarterly. Report.

Research Centers

★ 10973 ★ Ball State University Public Health Entomology Laboratory

2000 Univ. Ave.
Muncie, IN 47306
Phone: (317)285-1504
Dr. Robert R. Pinger, Dir.

Research Activities and Fields: Mosquitoes and mosquito-borne diseases, ticks and tick-borne diseases in Indiana, and other insects affecting human and animal health. Projects include a National Institutes of Health funded study on Lyme disease and a Rocky Mountain spotted fever tick testing program funded by the Indiana State Board of Health. Provides identification of insects of public health importance.

★ 10974 ★ California Public Health Foundation

2001 Addison St., Ste. 210
Berkeley, CA 94704-1103
Phone: (510)644-8200
Fax: (510)644-9319
Joseph M. Hafey, Exec.Dir.

Research Activities and Fields: Conducts research on a broad range of public health issues, including epidemiology, occupational health, toxic chemicals, genetics, diet and nutrition, and cancer prevention.

★ 10975 ★ Consumer Product Safety Commission Epidemiology Directorate

5401 Westbard Ave.
Bethesda, MD 20207
Phone: (301)504-0440
Fax: (301)504-0234
Dr. Robert Verhalen, Director

Research Activities and Fields: Directorate collects and analyzes epidemiological and statistical data relating to consumer product safety and performs human factors analyses. Principal components of the Directorate are: 1) Hazard Analysis Division; 2) Hazard and Injury Data Systems Division; 3) the National Injury Information Clearinghouse; and 4) Human Factors Division.

★ 10976 ★ Consumer Product Safety Commission Epidemiology Directorate Hazard Analysis Division

5401 Westbard Ave.
Bethesda, MD 20207
Phone: (301)492-6470
Robert E. Frye, Director

Research Activities and Fields: Division provides analyses of product-related injury data to the Commission and other organizations to guide and support remedial strategy development and decision-making. As a part of this function, Division analysts and statisticians participate in the selection and planning of projects; develop guidelines for investigations and surveys and monitor their progress; compile and analyze data and information available from established Commission projects, other health and safety-oriented organizations, and computer searches of medical, scientific, and technical literature databases; prepare issue-oriented data summaries, reports, and memoranda describing the frequency and severity of injuries and major hazard patterns related to specific types of products; participate in oral briefings of the Commission on the nature and scope of injuries to be addressed by each remedial option considered; participate in the identification of injury reductions related to past Commission actions; and identify emerging hazards through continuous monitoring of injury trends.

★ 10977 ★ Consumer Product Safety Commission
Health Sciences Directorate
5401 Westbard Ave.
Bethesda, MD 20207-0001
Phone: (301)504-0957
Fax: (301)504-0124
Dr. Andrew G. Ulsamer, Director

Research Activities and Fields: Directorate conducts studies to determine exposure to hazardous chemicals from consumer products. This includes investigation of: 1) children's products; 2) pollutant emissions (both chemical and biological) from structural materials, consumer products, and indoor combustion sources and their impact on indoor air quality; 3) bioavailability and potential for consumer exposure to carcinogenic commercial substances; and 4) acute toxicity of various household products to determine proper precautionary and first aid labeling. Directorate is also responsible for implementation of the Poison Prevention Packaging Act with respect to hazardous household substances, including drugs; and processing requests for exemption from regulations under this Act. Also studies design and effectiveness of child resistant packaging and supports work on physiological modeling and other injury behavior.

★ 10978 ★ Consumer Product Safety Commission
National Injury Information Clearinghouse
5401 Westbard Ave.
Bethesda, MD 20207
Phone: (301)504-0424
Joel I. Friedman, Director

Research Activities and Fields: Clearinghouse collects and disseminates injury data and information on the causes and prevention of death, injury, and illness associated with consumer products and maintains detailed investigative reports of such injuries. Also maintains access to automated databases with approximately two million incidents of injuries reported by a nationwide network of hospital emergency departments. Product-associated deaths extracted from death certificates also provide a major information resource. Other important resources of the Clearinghouse are: 1) the National Electronic Injury Surveillance System (NEISS), a national data collection system on injuries associated with consumer products; 2) accident investigations involving interviews with victims or witnesses; and 3) consumer complaints received by letters or telephone calls to the Commission citing injuries or potential injury situations, as well as other injury reports such as newspaper accounts of product-related incidents.

★ 10979 ★ Health Research, Inc.
66 Hackett Blvd.
Albany, NY 12209-1718
Phone: (518)431-1200
Fax: (518)431-1234
Michael Barth, Exec.Dir.

Research Activities and Fields: Public health and cancer, including basic and clinical research in cause and treatment of cancer and related malignancies; environmental studies to determine long-range health hazards of pesticides, industrial discharge, and radioactive and sewage wastes; and detection and prevention of infectious diseases, including AIDS and tuberculosis. Also studies rehabilitation, biology, immunology, hematology, virology, chemistry, toxicology, and environment. **E-mail Address:** EAM01@ALBNYDH2.BITNET.

★ 10980 ★ Iowa State University of Science and Technology
Food Safety Research Center
Dept. of Veterinary Medicine
Rm. 2134
Ames, IA 50011
Phone: (515)294-7630
Fax: (515)294-8500
George Beran, Dir.

Research Activities and Fields: Food safety, including virus stability in meats, decontamination of carcasses, serological tests for salmonella infection.

★ 10981 ★ Laval University
Medical Research Centre
Public Health Research Group
2705, boulevard Laurier
Ste. Foy, PQ, Canada G1V 4G2
Phone: (418)687-1090
Fax: (418)681-5635
Michel Vezina, Dir.

Research Activities and Fields: Operational research, including effectiveness of interventions of sexual behavior of seropositive individuals; psychological stress of homosexual AIDS patients; and studies on organochlorinated contaminants.

★ 10982 ★ Marshall University
Center for Rural Health Research
School of Medicine
Huntington, WV 25701
Phone: (304)696-7255
Fax: (304)696-7048
Robert Walker, M.D., Chm.

Research Activities and Fields: Rural health problems. Also guides predoctoral and postdoctoral research on rural health, rural geriatrics, and prevention in rural populations. **Formerly:** Department of Family and Community Health, Section of Rural Health Research.

★ 10983 ★ Portland State University
Center for Public Health Studies
PO Box 751
Portland, OR 97207
Phone: (503)725-3473
Fax: (503)725-4882
Dr. David A. Dunnette, Dir.

Research Activities and Fields: Public health, including studies of environmental and occupa-

tional disease, with emphasis on risk assessment and control. Cancer prevention research specializing in strategies for disseminating screening modalities.

★ 10984 ★ Public Citizen Health Research Group
2000 P St. NW, Ste. 700
Washington, DC 20036
Phone: (202)833-3000
Fax: (202)463-8842
Sidney M. Wolfe, M.D., Dir.

Research Activities and Fields: Health care delivery, workplace safety and health, drug regulation, food additives, medical device safety, and environmental influences on health. Conducts consumer advocacy and lobbying on health matters and monitors the enforcement of health and safety legislation. **Publications:** Health Letter (monthly); Health Research Group List of Publications (annually).

★ 10985 ★ Texas A&M University
Center for Urban and Public Health Entomology
Dept. of Entomology
College Station, TX 77843-2475
Phone: (409)845-5855
Fax: (409)845-5926
Dr. Roger Gold, Dir.

Research Activities and Fields: Urban and public health entomology, focusing on investigations of the parasites and predators of cockroaches.

★ 10986 ★ U.S. Department of Agriculture
Agricultural Research Service
Eastern Regional Research Center
Food Safety Research Unit
600 E. Mermaid Ln.
Philadelphia, PA 19118
Phone: (215)233-6582
Fax: (215)233-6559
Dr. Donald W. Thayer, Research Leader

Research Activities and Fields: Basic and applied chemical and biological research related to food safety. Unit's four objectives are to: 1) investigate the physical and chemical parameters that influence nitrosamine (NA) formation in foods, particularly cured meats and to develop means to reduce or eliminate the NAs from cured meats; 2) to develop methodologies capable of identifying meats and poultry that have been subjected to low-dose ionizing radiation; 3) to investigate the efficacy and safety of ionizing radiation treatments of fresh and processed meats and poultry to improve microbiological safety and shelf-life of the products while preserving the vitamin content; and 4) to devise analytical and immunological methods for the detection of drug residues and herbicides in animal tissues.

★ 10987 ★ U.S. Department of Agriculture
Agricultural Research Service
Eastern Regional Research Center
Microbial Food Safety Research Unit
600 E. Mermaid Ln.
Philadelphia, PA 19118
Phone: (215)233-6620
Fax: (215)233-6581
Dr. Robert L. Buchanan, Research Leader

Research Activities and Fields: Unit conducts basic and applied research on the microbiology of fresh and processed foods in order to develop methods for assuring a safe, wholesome food supply. The behavior and characteristics of microorganisms capable of causing diseases in humans are studied to facilitate methods for detecting and controlling the potential for disease transmission through the food supply. This includes two major approaches: 1) identifying the genetic and biochemical factors that allow the microorganisms to cause disease in humans; and 2) determining how food processing and handling practices can be modified to minimize safety concerns while maximizing food quality. An integral part of the research is identifying the ways in which changing technologies affect the safety of foods and identifying appropriate corrective measures that can be employed before process deficiencies result in public health problems.

★ 10988 ★ **U.S. Department of Agriculture**
Agricultural Research Service
Richard B. Russell Agricultural Research
  Center
Poultry Processing and Meat Quality and
  Safety Research Unit
PO Box 5677
Athens, GA 30613
Phone: (706)546-3152
Dr. Frank Green, Research Leader

Research Activities and Fields: Unit conducts research aimed at development of fundamental knowledge of the factors affecting poultry meat quality and microbiological safety for use in the development of new technologies. Objectives are to: 1) define and develop sensory (organoleptic) and physical/chemical standards for desirable qualities as a basis for development of quality assessment methods and devise the means to control flavor, texture, and juiciness of poultry meat by determining the fundamental physiological and biochemical mechanisms that regulate these quality parameters so that defects such as oxidative rancidity, warmed-over flavor, and toughness can be prevented; 2) explore the potential for development of known mixtures of bacteria that can be used to manipulate the gut ecosystem of young chickens so as to competitively exclude human pathogens (e.g., salmonellae and *Campylobacter*) and for development of highly specific antagonists of human pathogens, such as bacteriocins that can be used to prevent colonization of young chickens by these pathogens; and 3) develop innovative and improved processing systems to control external and internal microbiological contamination of raw processed poultry.

★ 10989 ★ **U.S. Department of Agriculture**
Western Regional Research Center
Food Safety Research Unit
800 Buchanan St.
Albany, CA 94706
Phone: (510)559-5615
Fax: (510)559-5777
Dr. Mendel Friedman, Lead Scientist

Research Activities and Fields: The Food Safety Research Unit's mission is to conduct research in chemistry, pharmacology, physiology, toxicology, and microbiology aimed at solving

public health problems related to the presence of toxicants, antinutrients, or pathogenic microorganisms in the food supply. Efforts focus on the naturally-occurring toxicants and antinutrients that are human dietary components derived from major agricultural commodities (e.g., grain and oilseed products, fruits and vegetables, meats and poultry, dairy products, or processed foods). Research on pathogenic microorganisms emphasizes health problems associated with contamination of fresh and lightly processed foods.

★ 10990 ★ **U.S. Department of Health and**
  Human Services
Centers for Disease Control and
  Prevention
1600 Clifton Rd., N.E.
Atlanta, GA 30333
Phone: (404)639-3291
Fax: (404)639-3889
David Satcher, M.D., Ph. D., Director

Research Activities and Fields: Federal agency responsible for protecting the public health of the nation by preventing unnecessary disease, disability, and premature death and promoting healthy lifestyles for all Americans. Specifically, CDC research focuses on the prevention of infectious diseases, chronic diseases, injury or disease associated with environmental, home, and workplace hazards, and controllable risk factors such as poor nutrition, smoking, lack of exercise, high blood pressure, stress, and drug misuse.

U.S. Department of Health and Human
Services
Centers for Disease Control and
Prevention
Epidemiology Program Office
See: Entry 5188

U.S. Department of Health and Human
Services
Centers for Disease Control and
Prevention
Epidemiology Program Office
Surveillance and Epidemiology Division
See: Entry 5189

★ 10991 ★ **U.S. Department of Health and**
  Human Services
Centers for Disease Control and
  Prevention
International Health Program Office
1600 Clifton Rd., N.E.
Atlanta, GA 30333
Phone: (404)639-3111
Fax: (404)639-2195
Joe H. Davis, M.D.,, Director

Research Activities and Fields: The International Health Program Office is involved in operational research in support of public health programs to reduce childhood morbidity and mortality in developing countries. Emphasis is on malaria, diarrheal disease, and diseases preventable by immunization. In addition, operational research activities are carried out on health information systems, surveillance, surveys, and health education. IHPO also supports small scale operational research projects by African researchers through the Combatting Child-

hood Communicable Diseases (CCCD) project, which is financed by the Agency for International Development.

★ 10992 ★ **U.S. Department of Health and**
  Human Services
Food and Drug Administration
Rm. 1471, HF-1
5600 Fishers Ln.
Rockville, MD 20857
Phone: (301)443-2410
Mr. David A. Kessler, Acting Commissioner

Research Activities and Fields: Activities of the Food and Drug Administration relate to protecting the public health of the nation as it may be impaired by foods, drugs, biological products, cosmetics, medical devices, ionizing and nonionizing radiation-emitting products and substances, poisons, pesticides, and food additives. FDA's functions are to ensure that: foods are safe, pure, and wholesome; drugs, medical devices, and biological products are safe and effective; cosmetics are harmless; that all of the above are honestly and informatively packaged; and that exposure to potentially injurious radiation is minimized. The principal components of FDA are: 1) the Center for Biologics Evaluation and Research; 2) Center for Devices and Radiological Health; 3) Center for Drug Evaluation and Research; 4) Center for Food Safety and Applied Nutrition; 5) Center for Veterinary Medicine; 6) the National Center for Toxicological Research; and 7) the Office of Regulatory Affairs. Research activities are also carried out in field laboratories and research centers located throughout the country.

★ 10993 ★ **U.S. Department of Health and**
  Human Services
Food and Drug Administration
Center for Biologics Evaluation and
  Research
1401 Rockville Pike
Rockville, MD 20852
Phone: (301)496-3556
Fax: (301)402-0763
Kathryn C. Zoon, Director

Research Activities and Fields: Ensures the safety, efficacy, potency, and purity of biological products intended for use in the treatment, prevention, or cure of human diseases. Reviews the safety and effectiveness of vaccines, blood products, diagnostic products, and other biological and biotechnology-derived human products. Supports active applied research programs and provides regulatory review of biological products. Investigates viral and bacterial vaccines, immunology, developmental biology, parasitic diseases, cytokines, growth factors, and AIDS and related diseases.

★ 10994 ★ **U.S. Department of Health and**
  Human Services
Food and Drug Administration
Center for Devices and Radiological Health
5600 Fishers Ln., HFZ-1
Rockville, MD 20857
Phone: (301)443-4690
Fax: (301)594-1320
D. Bruce Burlington, M.D., Director

Research Activities and Fields: Center develops and carries out a national program designed to control unnecessary exposures of humans to and assure the safe and efficacious use of ionizing and nonionizing radiation-emitting electronic products; and develops and carries out a national program to assure the safety, effectiveness, and proper labeling of medical devices for human use. **Additional Contact Information:** Center is located at 12720 Twinbrook Pkwy., Rockville, MD 20857.

★ 10995 ★ U.S. Department of Health and Human Services
Food and Drug Administration
Center for Drug Evaluation and Research
5600 Fishers Ln., HFD-1
Rockville, MD 20857
Phone: (301)443-2894
Gerald F. Meyer, Acting Director

Research Activities and Fields: Center develops FDA policy with regard to the safety, effectiveness, and labeling of all drugs for human use; reviews and evaluates new drug applications and notices of claimed investigational exemption of new drugs; develops and implements standards for the safety and effectiveness of all over-the-counter drugs; monitors the quality of marketed drugs through product testing, surveillance, and compliance programs; develops guidelines on current Good Manufacturing Practices for use by the drug industry; develops and disseminates information and educational material on drugs to the medical community and the public; conducts research and develops scientific standards on the composition, quality, safety, and efficacy of human drugs; collects and evaluates information on the effects and use trends of marketed drugs; monitors prescription drug advertising and promotional labeling to assure their accuracy and integrity; analyzes data on accidental poisonings; and disseminates toxicity and treatment information on medicines. Principal Center components are the Office of Compliance, Office of Drug Evaluation I, Office of Drug Evaluation II, Office of Drug Standards, Office of Epidemiology and Biostatistics, and Office of Research Resources.

★ 10996 ★ U.S. Department of Health and Human Services
Food and Drug Administration
Center for Food Safety and Applied Nutrition
200 C St., S.W.
Washington, DC 20204
Phone: (202)245-8850
Fax: (202)485-0325
Fred R. Shank, Acting Director

Research Activities and Fields: Principal goals of the Center's research program are to: 1) gather, analyze, and monitor published and unpublished information pertinent to the consumption, quality, and safety of foods and cosmetics; 2) determine the nutritional needs of various population groups and develop strategies to improve the nutritional status of those at risk; 3) isolate, purify, and identify potentially hazardous food and cosmetic constituents and adulterants, including biological, microbial, and chemical contaminants; 4) develop, validate, and apply quantitative methods of analysis for potentially hazardous constituents, adulterants,

and contaminants of foods and cosmetics, including environmental contaminants, animal drugs, and metabolites of microbial origin; 5) develop, improve, and validate biological tests for various forms of human toxicity, including chronic toxicity, fetal and neonatal toxicity, behavioral and immunotoxicity, and dermal and ocular toxicity; 6) apply toxicity tests and epidemiological studies to determine the adverse effects (hazards) of food constituents and contaminants and of cosmetics ingredients, singly or in combination; 7) improve the accuracy of methods used to assess potential risks to human health associated with the constituents and contaminants of foods and cosmetics; 8) develop practical control technologies necessary to detect or prevent hazards resulting from the storage or processing of foods or cosmetics; and 9) assess social, economic, and environmental determinants and impacts of Center actions. Research activities are primarily carried out in units of the Center's Office of Nutrition and Food Sciences, Office of Physical Sciences, and Office of Toxicological Sciences.

U.S. Department of Health and Human Services
Food and Drug Administration
National Center for Toxicological Research
See: Entry 10464

★ 10997 ★ University of Connecticut
Center for International Community Health Studies
Dept. of Community Medicine
Univ. Health Center
Farmington, CT 06030-6330
Phone: (203)679-1570
Fax: (203)679-1581
Stephen L. Schensul, Ph.D., Dir.

Research Activities and Fields: The health of underprivileged people in the U.S. and abroad, emphasizing international primary health care and community health, including international health policy, urban health in developing and developed countries, maternal and child health, health programs and problems in Peru, Sri Lanka, Kenya, Mauritius, and Connecticut, effects of economic development on health, and the role of the hospital in the developing world. Facilitates international health research for faculty and graduate students through consultation on grant proposals, networking with international contacts, advocating for researchers within international agencies, and establishing foreign research and educational placements. **Publications:** *Annual Training Program Catalogue*; *CICHS Connections* (newsletter for international training program alumni). **E-mail Address:** schensul@uconnvm.uconn.edu.

★ 10998 ★ University of Florida
Florida Medical Entomology Laboratory
Institute of Food & Agricultural Sciences
200 9th St. SE
Vero Beach, FL 32962
Phone: (407)778-7200
Fax: (407)778-7205
Dr. Richard H. Baker, Dir.

Research Activities and Fields: Biology and control of biting insects and other arthropods with emphasis on transmitters of disease and

pest annoyances. Studies the entomological aspects of public health, veterinary science, sanitation, mosquito control, drainage and irrigation design, and wetlands management. **E-mail Address:** fme@gnv.ifas.ufl.edu.

★ 10999 ★ University of Iowa
State Hygienic Laboratory
Oakdale Hall
Iowa City, IA 52242
Phone: (319)335-4500
Fax: (319)335-4600
Dr. W.J. Hausler, Jr., Dir.

Research Activities and Fields: Virolology, limnology, industrial hygiene, neonatal metabolic and prenatal diseases detection, microbiology, and organic, inorganic, and radiation chemistry. Conducts research and service in all areas relating to the environment and public health, including rapid diagnosis of disease agents by molecular methods and enzyme immunoassay, and monitoring immune status by flow cytometry. Studies the epidemiology of infectious diseases, food quality control, surface and/or groundwater contaminants, radioisotopes in groundwater, airborne contaminants and various contaminants in soil. The Laboratory develops and evaluates test methods for a wide variety of analyses and sample matrices, often to provide data as an aid to the decision and rule making process. **Publications:** Annual Report; *Lab Hotline* (monthly).

★ 11000 ★ University of Puerto Rico
School of Public Health Demography Program
Recinto de Ciencias Medicas
PO Box 365067
San Juan, PR 00936-5067
Phone: (809)758-2525
Fax: (809)759-6719
Dr. Ana Luisa Davila, Coord.

Research Activities and Fields: Demography, sociology, and gerontology. **Publications:** Monographs; *CIDE* (biennially). **E-mail Address:** an_davila@rcmac.upr.clu.edu.

★ 11001 ★ University of Quebec at Montreal
Laboratory of Research in Human and Social Ecology
CP 8888, Succ. Centre-Ville
Montreal, PQ, Canada H3C 3P8
Phone: (514)987-6190
Fax: (514)987-8408
Sylvie Jutras, Ph.D., Dir.

Research Activities and Fields: Social epidemiology, ecology of suicide among adolescents, parent/child relations, children's perceptual field of health, child abuse and neglect, and immigrants' and refugees' families. **Publications:** *Bulletin du LAREHS*.

★ 11002 ★ University of South Carolina
International Center for Public Health Research
Wedge Plantation
PO Box 699
McClellanville, SC 29458
Phone: (803)527-1371
Fax: (803)527-1372
Dr. Dwight C. Williams, Dir.

Research Activities and Fields: Chemical and biological control of mosquitoes, mosquito taxonomy, biting-fly, tick surveillance, and effects of pesticides on nontarget aquatic organisms. Specific studies include field and laboratory testing of microbial mosquito larvicides and insect growth regulators against target and nontarget organisms, studies of the bionomics and control of dengue vectors, and surveillance of ticks in South Carolina. **Publications:** *The Wedge Newsletter* (annually). **Formerly:** Center for Public Health Research.

★ 11003 ★ **University of Wisconsin—Madison**
State Laboratory of Hygiene
465 Henry Mall
Madison, WI 53706
Phone: (608)262-1293
Fax: (608)262-3257
Dr. R.H. Laessig, Dir.

Research Activities and Fields: Bacteriology, cancer cytology, cytogenetics, immunology, industrial hygiene, environmental health, pathology, clinical chemistry, toxicology, and virology, including respiratory and enterovirus infections, a survey of zoonosis in Wisconsin, especially California encephalitis virus, and chromosomal studies in congenital anomalies.

★ 11004 ★ **Wadsworth Center**
New York State Dept. of Health
PO Box 509
Albany, NY 12201-0509
Phone: (518)474-7592
Fax: (518)474-3439
Lawrence S. Sturman, M.D., Dir.

Research Activities and Fields: Protects and promotes the health of the citizens of the state of New York through laboratory investigations related to disease and environmental hazards of public health concern. Research programs are conducted through 21 major laboratories organized within four scientific divisions: the Division of Environmental Disease Prevention includes the Laboratory of Environmental Biology, Laboratory of Environmental Immunology, Laboratory of Human Toxicology and Molecular Epidemiology, Laboratory of Organic Analytical Chemistry, and Laboratory of Inorganic and Nuclear Chemistry; the Division of Genetic Disorders includes the Laboratory of Newborn Screening and Genetic Services, Laboratory of Clinical Genetics and Genetic Epidemiology, Laboratory of Human Molecular Genetics, Laboratory of Developmental Genetics, Laboratory of Reproductive and Metabolic Disorders, and Laboratory of Nervous Systems Disorders; the Division of Infectious Disease includes the Laboratory of Bacterial Disease, Laboratory of Infectious Disease Immunology, Laboratory of Mycobacterial, Fungal, and Parasitic Disease, Laboratory of Viral Disease, and Laboratory of Zoonotic Disease and Epidemiology; and the Division of Molecular Medicine includes the Laboratory of Structural Pathology, Laboratory of Cellular Regulation, Laboratory of Computational Biology and Molecular Imaging, Laboratory of Molecular Diagnostics, and Laboratory of Diagnostic Oncology. **E-mail Address:** information@wadsworth.ph.albany.edu.

State Government Agencies

Public Health

★ 11005 ★ **Alabama Department of Public Health**
434 Monroe St.
Montgomery, AL 36130-3017
Phone: (334)613-5200
Fax: (334)240-3387

★ 11006 ★ **Alaska Department of Health and Social Services**
Public Health Division
PO Box 110610
Juneau, AK 99811-0610
Phone: (907)465-3090
Fax: (907)586-1877

★ 11007 ★ **Arizona Department of Health Services**
1740 W. Adams
Phoenix, AZ 85007
Phone: (602)542-1025
Fax: (602)542-1062

★ 11008 ★ **Arkansas Department of Health**
PO Box 3278
Little Rock, AR 72203-3278
Phone: (501)661-2111
Fax: (501)671-1450

★ 11009 ★ **California Health and Welfare Agency**
Health Services Department
714 P St., No. 1253
Sacramento, CA 95814
Phone: (916)657-1425
Fax: (916)657-1156

★ 11010 ★ **Colorado Public and Environment Department**
Health Office
4300 Cherry Creek Dr., S
Denver, CO 80222-1530
Phone: (303)692-2100
Fax: (303)692-0095

★ 11011 ★ **Connecticut Department of Public Health**
150 Washington St.
Hartford, CT 06106
Phone: (203)566-2038
Fax: (203)566-3302

★ 11012 ★ **Delaware Department of Health and Social Services**
Public Health Division
Jesse Cooper Bldg.
PO Box 637
Dover, DE 19903
Phone: (302)739-4701
Fax: (302)739-6659

★ 11013 ★ **District of Columbia Department of Human Services**
Public Health Commission
1660 G St. NW
Washington, DC 20001
Phone: (202)727-0014
Fax: (202)727-0379

★ 11014 ★ **Florida Department of Health and Rehabilitative Services**
Health Program Office
1317 Winewood Blvd.
Tallahassee, FL 32399-0700
Phone: (904)487-2945
Fax: (904)922-2993

★ 11015 ★ **Georgia Department of Human Resources**
Public Health Division
2 Peachtree St. NW
Atlanta, GA 30303
Phone: (404)657-2700
Fax: (404)657-2715

★ 11016 ★ **Hawaii Department of Health**
1250 Punchbowl St.
Honolulu, HI 96813
Phone: (808)586-4410
Fax: (808)586-4444

★ 11017 ★ **Idaho Department of Health and Welfare**
Health Division
PO Box 83720
Boise, ID 83720-0036
Phone: (208)334-5945
Fax: (208)334-6558

★ 11018 ★ **Illinois Department of Public Health**
535 W. Jefferson St.
Springfield, IL 62761
Phone: (217)782-4977
Fax: (217)782-3987

★ 11019 ★ **Indiana Department of Health**
1330 W. Michigan St.
PO Box 1964
Indianapolis, IN 46206-1964
Phone: (317)383-6400
Fax: (317)383-6779

★ 11020 ★ **Iowa Department of Public Health**
Lucas State Office Bldg.
321 E. 12th St.
Des Moines, IA 50319
Phone: (515)281-5605
Fax: (515)281-4958

★ 11021 ★ **Kansas Department of Health and Environment**
Health Division
900 SW Jackson, Ste. 620
Topeka, KS 66612-1290
Phone: (913)296-1086
Fax: (913)296-1231

★ 11022 ★ **Kentucky Human Resources Cabinet**
Health Services Department
275 E. Main St.
Frankfort, KY 40621
Phone: (502)564-3970
Fax: (502)564-6533

★ 11023 ★ **Louisiana Department of Health and Hospitals**
Public Health Services Office
PO Box 3214
New Orleans, LA 70177
Phone: (504)342-8094
Fax: (504)342-8098

★11024★ **Maine Department of Human
Services**
Health Bureau
State House, Sta. 11
Augusta, ME 04333
Phone: (207)287-3201
Fax: (207)287-3005

★11025★ **Maryland Department of Health
and Mental Hygiene**
Public Health Services Office
201 W. Preston St., 5th Fl.
Baltimore, MD 21201
Phone: (410)225-6525
Fax: (410)225-6489

★11026★ **Massachusetts Executive Office
of Health and Human Services**
Public Health Department
150 Tremont St.
Boston, MA 02111
Phone: (617)727-0201
Fax: (617)727-2559

★11027★ **Michigan Department of Public
Health**
3423 N. Logan St.
PO Box 30195
Lansing, MI 48909
Phone: (517)335-8024
Fax: (517)335-9476

★11028★ **Minnesota Department of Health**
717 Delaware St. SE
PO Box 9441
Minneapolis, MN 55440
Phone: (612)623-5460
Fax: (612)623-5794

★11029★ **Mississippi Department of
Health**
PO Box 1700
Jackson, MS 39215-1700
Phone: (601)960-7634
Fax: (601)960-7948

★11030★ **Missouri Department of Health**
PO Box 570
Jefferson City, MO 65102
Phone: (314)751-6001
Fax: (314)751-6010

★11031★ **Montana Department of Health
and Environmental Sciences**
Health Services Division
Cogswell Bldg., Rm. C-108
PO Box 200901
Helena, MT 59620-0901
Phone: (406)444-4473

★11032★ **Nebraska Department of Health**
301 Centennial Mall S.
PO Box 95007
Lincoln, NE 68509
Phone: (402)471-2133
Fax: (402)471-0383

★11033★ **Nevada Department of Human
Resources**
Health Division
505 E. King St., Rm. 201
Carson City, NV 89710
Phone: (702)687-4740

★11034★ **New Hampshire Department of
Health and Human Services**
Public Health Services Division
6 Hazen Dr.
Concord, NH 03301
Phone: (603)271-4501
Fax: (603)271-3745

★11035★ **New Jersey Department of
Health**
John Fitch Plaza, CN 360
Trenton, NJ 08625-0360
Phone: (609)292-7837
Fax: (609)984-5474

★11036★ **New Mexico Department of
Health**
Public Health Division
1190 St. Francis Dr.
PO Box 26110
Santa Fe, NM 87502-6110
Phone: (505)827-2389
Fax: (505)827-2329

★11037★ **New York State Department of
Health**
Corning Tower
Empire State Plaza
Albany, NY 12237-0001
Phone: (518)474-2011
Fax: (518)474-5450

★11038★ **North Carolina Department of
Environment, Health, and Natural
Resources**
Health Director's Office
PO Box 27687
Raleigh, NC 27611
Phone: (919)715-4125
Fax: (919)715-3060

★11039★ **North Dakota Department of
Health and Consolidated Laboratories**
600 E. Boulevard Ave.
Bismarck, ND 58505
Phone: (701)328-2372
Fax: (701)328-4727

★11040★ **Ohio Department of Health**
246 N. High St.
Columbus, OH 43215
Phone: (614)466-2253
Fax: (614)644-0085

★11041★ **Oklahoma Department of Health**
1000 NE 10th St.
Oklahoma City, OK 73117-1299
Phone: (405)271-4200
Fax: (405)271-7339

★11042★ **Oregon Department of Human
Resources**
Health Division
PO Box 14450
Portland, OR 97214-0450
Phone: (503)731-4078

★11043★ **Pennsylvania Department of
Health**
Box 90
Harrisburg, PA 17108
Phone: (717)787-6436
Fax: (717)787-0191

★11044★ **Puerto Rico Department of
Health**
PO Box 70184
San Juan, PR 00936
Phone: (809)766-2210

★11045★ **Rhode Island Department of
Health**
3 Capitol Hill
Providence, RI 02908-5097
Phone: (401)277-2231
Fax: (401)277-6548

★11046★ **South Carolina Department of
Health and Environmental Control**
Health Services Office
2600 Bull St.
Columbia, SC 29201
Phone: (803)737-3900
Fax: (803)737-3946

★11047★ **South Dakota Department of
Health**
445 E. Capitol
Pierre, SD 57501-3185
Phone: (605)773-3361
Fax: (605)773-5683

★11048★ **Tennessee Department of
Health**
Health Services Bureau
312 8th Ave., N., 12th Fl.
Nashville, TN 37247-4501
Phone: (615)741-7305
Fax: (615)741-2491

★11049★ **Texas Department of Health**
1100 W. 49th St.
Austin, TX 78756-3199
Phone: (512)458-7375
Fax: (512)458-7477

★11050★ **Utah Department of Health**
PO Box 142802
Salt Lake City, UT 84114-2802
Phone: (801)538-6111
Fax: (801)538-6694

★11051★ **Vermont Agency of Human
Services**
Health Department
PO Box 70
Burlington, VT 05402
Phone: (802)863-7280
Fax: (802)863-7425

★11052★ **Virgin Islands Department of
Health**
Office of the Governor
Kogens Glade
St. Thomas, VI 00802
Phone: (809)776-8311

★11053★ **Virginia Office of Health and
Human Resources**
Health Department
1500 E. Main St.
PO Box 2448
Richmond, VA 23218
Phone: (804)786-3561
Fax: (804)786-4616

★ 11054 ★ Washington Department of Health
PO Box 47890
Olympia, WA 98504-7890
Phone: (360)753-5871
Fax: (360)586-7424

★ 11055 ★ West Virginia Department of Health and Human Resources
Public Health Bureau
State Capitol Complex, Bldg. 3, Rm. 518
Charleston, WV 25305-0501
Phone: (304)558-2971
Fax: (304)558-1035

★ 11056 ★ Wisconsin Department of Health and Social Services
Health Division
PO Box 7850
Madison, WI 53707-7850
Phone: (608)266-1511
Fax: (608)267-2832

★ 11057 ★ Wyoming Department of Health
Public Health Division
Hathaway Bldg., 4th Fl.
Cheyenne, WY 82002-0710
Phone: (307)777-6186
Fax: (307)777-5402

Chapter 55
Radiological Health

Federal Government Agencies

★ 11058 ★ **U.S. Department of Health and Human Services**
Food and Drug Administration
Center for Devices and Radiological Health
9200 Corporate Blvd.
Rockville, MD 20850
Phone: (301)443-4690
Fax: (301)594-1320

Description: The Center develops and carries out a national program designed to control unnecessary exposure of humans to, and assure the safe use of, potentially hazardous ionizing and non-ionizing radiation. It also develops policy and priorities relating to the safety, effectiveness, and labeling of medical devices for human use; conducts an electronic product radiation control program; develops, plans, and evaluates surveillance and compliance programs for medical devices and radiation exposure; plans, conducts, and supports research and testing relating to medical devices and to the health effects of radiation exposure; reviews and evaluates medical devices premarket approval applications, product development protocols, and exemption requests for investigational devices; develops, promulgates, and enforces performance standards for appropriate categories of medical devices and Good Manufacturing Practice (GMP) regulations for manufacturers; provides technical and other nonfinancial assistance to small manufacturers of medical devices; develops regulations, standards, and criteria and recommends changes in FDA legislative authority necessary to protect the public health; provides scientific and technical support to other components within FDA and other agencies on matters relating to radiological health and medical devices; and maintains appropriate liaison with other federal, state, and international agencies, with industry, and with consumer and professional organizations.

National & International Organizations

★ 11059 ★ **Chernobyl Union of the Republic of Kazakhstan**
Vinogradov St. 85-415
Alma-Ata, Kazakhstan
Phone: 327 2633900

Description: Offers rehabilitation, medical services, and care for those who participated in the liquidation of Chernobyl and victims of the accident. Provides support to the families of victims.

★ 11060 ★ **Children of Chernobyl**
Gefta St. 1
Odessa, Ukraine
Nina Kaptsova, Chm.

Description: Offers assistance to children and their families affected by the accident at Chernobyl.

★ 11061 ★ **Conference of Radiation Control Program Directors (CRCPD)**
205 Capital Ave.
Frankfort, KY 40601-2832
Phone: (502)227-4543
Fax: (502)227-7862
Charles M. Hardin, Exec.Dir.

Founded: 1968. **Members:** 746. **Description:** State and local radiological program directors; individuals from related federal protection agencies. Serves as a forum for the interchange of experience, concerns, developments, and recommendations among radiation control programs and related agencies. Encourages cooperation between enforcement programs and agencies at state and federal levels. Promotes radiological health and uniform radiation control laws and regulations; supports radiation control programs; provides assistance with members' technical work and development. Researches and recommends radiation control regulations at state levels in an effort to implement uniform regulations nationwide. Collects and disseminates information, statistics, and data. maintains speakers' bureau; conducts mammography training seminars. Maintains 30 committees. **Publications:** Brochures. • CRCPD Newsbrief, monthly. Reviews federal and state

legislation and regulation, conference membership, and executive board actions. *Price:* Free to membership; $25/year for nonmembers. • *Directory of Personnel Responsible for Radiological Health Programs*, annual. Directory. Lists federal, state, and local agencies associated with CRCPD dealing directly or indirectly with radiation control. *Price:* $30/copy. • *Directory of State Agencies Involved with the Transportation of Radioactive Material*, annual. Directory. *Price:* Free. • *National Conference on Radiation Control--Proceedings*, annual. Includes papers presented at the National Conference on Radiation Control. *Price:* Free to conference attendees; $35/copy for nonmembers. • *Patient Exposure Guides for Diagnostic X-Ray.* • *Profile of State and Local Radiation Control Programs in the U.S.*, annual. Report. Updates the status of state and local radiation control programs. *Price:* $35/copy. • Reports. • *Task Force Report on Bonding and Perpetual Care of Licensed Nuclear Activities.*

★ 11062 ★ **Health Physics Society (HPS)**
1313 Dolley Madison Blvd., Ste. 402
McLean, VA 22101-3926
Phone: (703)790-1745
Fax: (703)790-9063
Richard J. Burk, Jr., Exec.Sec.

Founded: 1956. **Members:** 6,890. **Local Groups:** 41. **Description:** Persons engaged in some form of activity in the field of health physics (the profession devoted to radiation protection). To improve public understanding of the problems and needs in radiation protection; to promote health physics as a profession. Maintains Elda E. Anderson Memorial Fund to be used for teachers, researchers, and others. Provides placement service at annual meeting. Cosponsors American Board of Health Physics for certification of health physicists. **Publications:** *Health Physics Journal*, monthly. Journal. • *Health Physics Society--Membership Handbook*, annual. • *Health Physics Society--Newsletter*, monthly. Newsletter.

International Association—Hopecenter for the Defense of Women's and Children's Rights
See: Entry 9658

★11063★ **International Radiation Protection Association (IRPA)**
Postbus 662
NL-5600 AR Eindhoven, Netherlands
Phone: 40 473355
Fax: 40 435020
Chris J. Huyskens, Exec. Officer

Founded: 1966. **Members:** 15,000. **National Groups:** 40. **Languages:** English. **Description:** Scientists in radiation protection fields united to provide an international forum for interaction and exchange of information among those involved in radiation protection activities. Seeks to protect human beings and the environment from the hazards of ionizing radiation. Works to promote the use of radiation and atomic energy for the good of humankind. **Publications:** Brochure, every 3-4 years. • *IRPA Bulletin*, quarterly. Bulletin.

★11064★ **National Association of Atomic Veterans (NAAV)**
PO Box 4424
Salem, MA 01970
Phone: (508)744-9396
Free: 800-955-1186
Dr. Oscar Rosen, Commander

Founded: 1979. **Members:** 4,000. **Description:** Veterans of U.S. nuclear weapons testing and Nagasaki/Hiroshima occupation forces who now have cancer or other diseases believed to be radiation-related; their widows and interested persons. Works to assure veterans and widows that such diseases are recognized as service-related illnesses and assist in obtaining proper medical attention, compensation, and other benefits through the Veterans Administration. Participates in related legislative activities. **Publications:** *Atomic Veterans Newsletter*, quarterly. Newsletter.

★11065★ **National Committee for Radiation Victims (NCRV)**
6935 Laurel Ave., Ste. 201
Takoma Park, MD 20912
Phone: (301)891-3990
Fax: (301)891-3992
E. Cooper Brown, Dir.

Founded: 1979. **Description:** To serve the needs and concerns of Americans affected by exposure to human-made ionizing radiation. Offers public service information on the effects of ionizing radiation; coordinates and encourages national action on radiation health and safety issues. Serves as a clearinghouse for information and materials on radiation exposure, existing radiation standards and practices, radiation victims' organizations, and legislation affecting radiation victims. Maintains speakers' bureau. **Formerly:** National Citizens Hearings for Radiation Victims.

★11066★ **Professional Board for Radiography (PBR)**
533 Vermenlen St.
Arcadia
PO Box 205
Pretoria 0083, Republic of South Africa
Phone: 12 3286680
Fax: 12 3285120
Mr. N.M. Prinsloo, Registrar

Founded: 1974. **Members:** 3,500. **Languages:** Afrikaans, English. **Description:** Works to maintain professional standards of education and conduct of radiographers; strives to prevent the admission of unqualified individuals into the radiography profession. Cooperates with the South African Medical and Dental Council in approving training courses in radiography. Investigates reports of unprofessional conduct. Represents members' interests before government authorities. Disseminates information; compiles statisics. **Publications:** *SAMDC Bulletin*, quarterly. Bulletin. • *Technical Journal*, periodic. Journal.

★11067★ **Radiation Effects Research Foundation (RERF)**
(Hoshasen Eikyo Kenkyu-sho)
5-2, Hijiyama Park
Minami-ku
Hiroshima 732, Japan
Phone: 82 2613131
Fax: 82 2637279
Dr. Itsuzo Shigematsu, Chm.

Founded: 1975. **Languages:** English, Japanese. **Description:** Works to determine the long-term health effects of exposure to atomic bomb radiation. Medical research programs include studies to: determine whether the life span and causes of death of exposed people in the cities of Hiroshima and Nagasaki differ from those of the general Japanese population; identify effects of radiation on adult health, including the delayed effects of disease morbidity or physiological change; determine histological pathologies not identifiable by clinical examination, such as delayed effects of ionizing radiation on cells; determine the effects on offspring of parental radiation exposure. Reassesses radiation dosimetry to provide accurate information on the radiation dose produced by the atomic bombs detonated during World War II. Also conducts studies in ophthalmology, radiobiology, immunology, cancer, cardiovascular disease, growth and development, metabolic disorders, and aging. Operates laboratories in Hiroshima and Nagasaki. **Publications:** Bibliographies, periodic. Contains information on technical reports and articles. • Reports, periodic. Contains research information. • *RERF Annual Report*, annual. • *RERF Commentary and Review Series.* • *RERF Newsletter*, monthly. • *RERF Report Series*, periodic. • *RERF Update*, quarterly. • *U.S.-Japan Joint Reassessment of Atomic Bomb Radiation Dosimetry in Hiroshima and Nagasaki*. **Formerly:** Atomic Bomb Casualty Commission.

★11068★ **Radiation Research Society (RRS)**
2021 Spring Rd., Ste. 600
Oak Brook, IL 60521
Phone: (708)571-2881
Fax: (708)571-7837
Mark G. Watson, Exec.Sec.

Founded: 1952. **Members:** 2,150. **Description:** Professional society of biologists, physicists, chemists, and physicians contributing to knowledge of radiation and its effects. Promotes original research in the natural sciences relating to radiation; facilitates integration of different disciplines in the study of radiation effects. Maintains placement service. **Publications:** Membership Directory, annual. • *Radiation Research*, monthly. Journal. Reports original research in the natural sciences relating to radiation. *Price:* $68 for members; $1000 for institutions.

★11069★ **Ukrainian Foundation for the Victims of Chernobyl**
Gefta St. 1
Odessa, Ukraine
Phone: 048 2933487
Fax: 048 2936975
Nikolai Malyenko, Chm.

★11070★ **Union Chernobyl**
Tchicherina St. 93
270045 Odessa, Ukraine
Phone: 048 265463
Fax: 048 445065
Peter Fedoseev, Pres.

Description: Offers assistance to victims of the Chernobyl accident.

Research Centers

★11071★ **Canadian Institute for Radiation Safety (CAIRS)**
Saskatoon, SK, Canada S7N 3R3
Phone: (306)975-0566
Fax: (306)975-0494
Dr. R. Moridi, Act.Dir.

Research Activities and Fields: Radiation, radiation safety, radon, radiation and health, radioactive waste, nuclear power, training, early lung cancer detection, and mediation.

★11072★ **Colorado State University Center for Environmental Toxicology**
Fort Collins, CO 80521
Phone: (303)491-8522
Fax: (303)491-8304
Dr. Stephen A. Benjamin, Codir.

Research Activities and Fields: Hazards associated with environmental exposure to chemical and physical agents, focusing on complex chemical mixtures and chemical-radiation interaction. Also studies growth, reproduction, immune function, physiologically based pharmacokinetics, genetic and molecular markers of disease, and ecotoxicology and bioremediation, focusing on hazardous waste mixtures. **Formerly:** Collaborative Radiological Health Laboratory (1991).

★11073★ **Laboratory of Radiobiology and Environmental Health**
Univ. of California, San Francisco
Box 0750
San Francisco, CA 94143-0750
Phone: (415)476-1636
Fax: (415)476-0721
Dr. Sheldon Wolff, Dir.

Research Activities and Fields: Radiobiology, cytogenetics, biophysics, DNA synthesis and repair, cell biology, and developmental biology.

★ 11074 ★   San Jose State University
Institute for Biopsychological Studies of
   Color, Light, Radiation, Health
Dept. of Psychology
San Jose, CA 95192-0120
Phone: (408)277-2786
Fax: (408)924-5605
Dr. Robert J. Pellegrini, Dir.

Research Activities and Fields: Organismic effects of electromagnetic energy, particularly studies of physical health and behavior as affected by environmental color and lighting in institutional settings and toxic radiation exposure. **Publications:** Newsletter; Journal.

U.S. Department of Defense
Armed Forces Institute of Pathology
Center for Advanced Pathology
Radiologic Pathology Department
See: Entry 10163

★ 11075 ★   U.S. Department of Defense
Armed Forces Radiobiology Research
   Institute
Bethesda, MD 20889-5603
Phone: (301)295-1210
Fax: (301)295-4967
Capt. Robert L. Bumgarner, MC, USN,
Director

Research Activities and Fields: AFRRI's mission is to conduct research in the field of radiobiology and related matters that are essential to the operational and medical support of the Department of Defense (DOD) and the U.S. military services. To support this mission, AFRRI conducts a comprehensive in-house radiobiology research and training program on the biological effects of ionizing radiation. AFRRI research is organized around four major fields of study: casualty management, including developing innovative treatment strategies for persons injured by ionizing radiation; performance management, including developing strategies to model and mitigate against the performance degrading effects of ionizing radiation; molecular and cellular modulation, including investigating new methods to regulate biological processes to mitigate damage from ionizing radiation and other toxicants; and radiation hazards analysis, including assessing risks associated with acute and chronic exposure to internal and external sources of radiation and other hazardous materials. The Institute provides technical consultation to DOD and other federal agencies on a wide range of issues related to the biological effects of radiation.

★ 11076 ★   U.S. Department of Defense
Armed Forces Radiobiology Research
   Institute
Behavioral Sciences Department
Bethesda, MD 20814-5145
Phone: (301)295-1516
Dr. A.H. Harris, Department Head

Research Activities and Fields: The Behavioral Sciences Department conducts research on the effects of ionizing radiation, chemicals, and drugs on performance. Department comprises the Experimental Psychology Division and Physiological Psychology Division.

★ 11077 ★   U.S. Department of Defense
Armed Forces Radiobiology Research
   Institute
Experimental Hematology Department
8901 Wisconsin Ave.
Bethesda, MD 20889-5603
Phone: (301)295-1352
Fax: (301)295-6503
Dr. T.J. Macvittie, Department Head

Research Activities and Fields: Activities of the Experimental Hematology Department involve investigations of radiation injury of bone marrow; development of therapy for immunologic and hematologic damage from intermediate radiation doses; and determination and treatment of injuries caused by combined effects of radiation, blast, and burns. Department comprises the Hematology Division, Immunology Division, and Pathology Division.

★ 11078 ★   U.S. Department of Defense
Armed Forces Radiobiology Research
   Institute
Physiology Department
8901 Wisconsin Ave., Bldg. 42
Bethesda, MD 20889-5603
Phone: (301)295-1212
Fax: (301)295-0313
Dr. David R. Livengood, Department Chairman

Research Activities and Fields: The Physiology Department conducts research on cellular, tissue, and whole-animal models to determine physiological and biophysical changes associated with performance decrements and physiological failures resulting from radiation (either alone or in combination with drugs or other chemicals). Department comprises the Cellular Physiology Project, the Neurophysiology Project, and the Gastrointestinal Physiology Project.

★ 11079 ★   U.S. Department of Defense
Armed Forces Radiobiology Research
   Institute
Radiation Biochemistry Department
Bldg. 42
Bethesda, MD 20889-5145
Phone: (301)295-0309
Fax: (301)295-1032
Dr. E.P. Clark, Department Head

Research Activities and Fields: Department conducts research on the elucidation of mechanisms of injury, repair, and protection from ionizing radiation alone or in combination with other agents; and on the development of improved methods to detect and quantify the severity of radiation injury. Department comprises the Molecular Radiobiology Division, Physical Chemistry Division, and Physiological Division.

U.S. Department of Health and Human
   Services
Food and Drug Administration
Center for Devices and Radiological Health
See: Entry 10994

U.S. Department of Health and Human
   Services
National Cancer Institute
Chemical and Physical Carcinogenesis
   Program
Radiation Effects Branch
See: Entry 6127

U.S. Department of Health and Human
   Services
National Cancer Institute
Division of Cancer Treatment
Radiation Research Program
See: Entry 6164

U.S. Department of Health and Human
   Services
National Cancer Institute
Epidemiology and Biostatistics Program
Radiation Epidemiology Branch
See: Entry 6171

★ 11080 ★   University of Texas Health
   Science Center at San Antonio
Center for Environmental Radiation
   Toxicology
7703 Floyd Curl Dr.
San Antonio, TX 78284-7800
Phone: (210)567-5560
Fax: (210)567-3446
Martin Meltz, Ph.D., Dir.

Research Activities and Fields: Effects of individual and combined exposures to microwave radiation and X-rays on biological systems. Current investigations focus on in vitro cell lines representative of the human immune system, and peripheral blood lymphocytes, with the endpoints studied including signal transduction mechanisms, DNA binding, protein and protooncogene induction, and primary DNA damage and repair. Also conducts low dose rate and hyperthermia investigations. **E-mail Address:** meltz@uthscsa.edu. **Formerly:** Center for Basic Research in Radiation Bioeffects (1993).

★ 11081 ★   University of Utah
Radiobiology Division
Bldg. 586
Salt Lake City, UT 84112
Phone: (801)581-6600
Fax: (801)581-7008
Dr. Scott C. Miller, Dir.

Research Activities and Fields: Chemistry, physics, hematology, biochemistry, bone sciences, and veterinary aspects and pathology of long-term physiological and biochemical effects of internally deposited radioisotopes. **Publications:** *Research in Radiobiology* (annual report to sponsor). Holds annual symposia for interested scientists from the University and abroad and sponsors annual meeting on the morphological aspects of bone. **E-mail Address:** ufafric@nervm.nerdc.ufl.edu. **Formerly:** Radiobiology Laboratories.

Chapter 56
Radiology

National & International Organizations

★ 11082 ★ **American Academy of Thermology (AAT)**
138 Church St. NE
Vienna, VA 22180
Phone: (703)938-6140
Fax: (703)938-1482
Andrew Fischer, M.D., Pres.

Founded: 1968. **Members:** 400. **Description:** Physicians, physicists, and technicians interested in the field of thermography (infrared imaging of the human body). Objectives are to disseminate knowledge concerning the application of thermography to various medical specialties and to promote technical advancements in the field. Sponsors training programs. **Publications:** Membership Directory, annual. • Newsletter, quarterly. • *Thermology - The Official Journal of the American Academy of Thermology and the International College of Thermology*, semiannual. Journal. **Formerly:** (1983) American Thermographic Society.

★ 11083 ★ **American Association for Women Radiologists (AAWR)**
1891 Preston White Dr.
Reston, VA 22091
Phone: (703)648-8939
Fax: (703)391-0397
Ann Rosser Wieseneck, Exec.Dir.

Founded: 1981. **Members:** 2,000. **Local Groups:** 3. **Description:** Physicians involved in diagnostic or therapeutic radiology, nuclear medicine, or radiologic physics. Facilitates exchange of knowledge and information as it relates to women in radiology; encourages publication of materials on radiology and medicine by members; supports women who are training in the field and encourages women at all levels to participate in radiological societies. Maintains ad hoc committees on affirmative action, radiation therapists, and policy on pregnancy. **Publications:** *AAWR Focus*, quarterly. Newsletter. *Price:* Free, to members only. • *AAWR Membership Directory*, annual. Membership Directory. *Price:* Free, to members only.

★ 11084 ★ **American Board of Nuclear Medicine (ABNM)**
900 Veteran Ave.
Los Angeles, CA 90024-1786
Phone: (310)825-6787
Fax: (310)825-9433
Joseph F. Ross, M.D., Pres.

Founded: 1971. **Members:** 12. **Description:** A primary medical specialty board and member of the American Board of Medical Specialties. Provides educational standards and evaluates the competence of physicians in nuclear medicine; establishes requirements for certification. Conducts examinations and issues certification. Maintains registry of certificate holders. Aids in the assessment and accreditation of nuclear medicine programs in hospitals and institutions offering graduate training. **Publications:** *American Board of Nuclear Medicine Information, Policies and Procedures*, annual. Brochure. Provides information on the annual certifying examination. *Price:* Free. • *Tracers*, 1-2/year. Newsletter. Includes information on new members. *Price:* Free.

★ 11085 ★ **American Board of Radiology (ABR)**
5255 E. Williams Cir., Ste. 6800
Tucson, AZ 85711-7401
Phone: (602)790-2900
Fax: (602)790-3200
M. Paul Capp, M.D., Exec.Dir.

Founded: 1934. **Members:** 23. **Description:** Certification board to establish qualifications, conduct examinations, and certify physicians in the specialty of radiology and physicists in radiological physics and related branches (science dealing with X-rays or rays from radioactive substances for medical use). **Publications:** Booklets. On examinations in diagnostic radiology, radiological physics, radiation oncology, and special competence in nuclear radiology.

★ 11086 ★ **American Chiropractic Registry of Radiologic Technologists (ACRRT)**
2330 Gull Rd.
Kalamazoo, MI 49001
Phone: (616)343-6666
Dr. Edward Maurer, Exec.VP

Founded: 1982. **Members:** 2,000. **Description:** Chiropractic assistants and radiologic technologists employed in chiropractic offices. Educates the general public concerning the importance of having highly skilled radiologic technologists (those who administer X-rays) in chiropractic offices. Serves as a national certifying agency for individuals in the field; maintains registry of certified chiropractic radiologic technologists. **Publications:** *Wavelengths*, bimonthly. Newsletter.

American College of Medical Physics
See: Entry 2523

★ 11087 ★ **American College of Nuclear Medicine (ACNM)**
PO Box 175
Landisville, PA 17538
Phone: (717)898-6006
Fax: (717)898-0713
Thomas Johnson, Jr., Exec.Dir.

Founded: 1972. **Members:** 500. **Description:** Physicians and medical scientists in nuclear medicine united to: advance the science of nuclear medicine; improve its benefits to patients; study the socioeconomic aspects of the practice of nuclear medicine; encourage improved and continuing education for practitioners in this and allied fields. **Publications:** *ACNM Directory*, biennial. Directory. • *ACNM Report*, bimonthly. Newsletter.

★ 11088 ★ **American College of Nuclear Physicians (ACNP)**
1200 19th St. NW, No. 300
Washington, DC 20036
Phone: (202)857-1135
Fax: (202)223-4579
Carol A. Lively, Exec.Dir.

Founded: 1974. **Members:** 1,600. **Description:** Nuclear medicine physicians, scientists, and corporations. Objectives are: to foster the highest standards of nuclear medicine service and consultation to the public, hospitals, and referring physicians; to advance the science of nuclear medicine and improve nuclear medicine consultation and service through study, education, and improvement of the socioeconomic aspects of the practice of nuclear medicine; to promote the continuing competence of practitioners of nuclear medicine. Problem-solving areas include: unnecessary and costly regulations and restrictions; public fear, lack of understanding, and misinformation; complex state and federal legislation; transportation difficulties involving nuclear medicine supplies; previous lack of cohesive effort in attacking such problems. Conducts educational seminars and continuing education program; maintains speakers' bureau. **Publications:** Directory, annual. • *Scanner*, 10/year.

American College of Podiatric Radiologists (ACPR)
See: Entry 10761

★ 11089 ★ **American College of Radiation Oncology (ACRO)**
2021 Spring Rd., Ste. 600
Oak Brook, IL 60521
Phone: (708)368-3733
Fax: (708)571-7837
Del Stauffer

Founded: 1989. **Description:** Radiation oncologists, physicists, and administrators. Seeks to ensure that regulatory legislation is fair to radiation oncologists. Lobbies on behalf of radiation onocolgy physicians. Represents physicans in fee disputes with Medicare. **Publications:** Newsletter, every 6-8 weeks. *Price:* Included in membership dues.

American College of Veterinary Radiology (ACVR)
See: Entry 13050

American Healthcare Radiology Administrators (AHRA)
See: Entry 5550

★ 11090 ★ **American Institute of Ultrasound in Medicine (AIUM)**
14750 Sweetzer Ln., Ste. 100
Laurel, MD 20707-5906
Phone: (301)498-4100
Free: 800-638-5352
Fax: (301)498-4450
James S. Packer, Ph.D., Exec.Dir.

Founded: 1951. **Members:** 11,000. **Description:** Physicians, engineers, scientists, sonographers, and other professionals involved with diagnostic medical ultrasound. Promotes the application of ultrasound in clinical medicine, diagnostically, and in research; studies its effects on tissue and recommend standards for its applications. Promotes education in the use of ultrasonics for medical purposes. Administers educational programs and placement service. Maintains hall of fame; operates speakers' bureau. **Publications:** *AIUM Newsletter*, monthly. Newsletter. Covers institute activities and developments in diagnostic ultrasound. Includes listing of continuing education courses and employment opportunities. *Price:* Included in membership dues; $20/year nonmembers. • *Journal of Ultrasound in Medicine*, monthly. Journal. Contains research papers and case reports covering all aspects of diagnostic ultrasound, advances in instrumentation, and biological effects. *Price:* Included in membership dues; $110/year for nonmembers; $132/year for institutions. • Videos. • *AIUM Annual Convention Proceedings. Price:* $12/copy for members; $22/copy for nonmembers.

American Osteopathic College of Radiology (AOCR)
See: Entry 9992

★ 11091 ★ **American Radiological Nurses Association (ARNA)**
2021 Spring Rd., Ste. 600
Oak Brook, IL 60521
Phone: (708)571-9072
Fax: (708)571-7837
Betty Rohr, Exec.Sec.

Founded: 1981. **Members:** 1,238. **State Groups:** 16. **Description:** Radiological nurses. Seeks to provide, promote, and maintain continuity of quality patient care through education, standards of care, professional growth, and collaboration with other health care providers. **Publications:** *Images*, quarterly. Journal. Conveys news related to developments in practice, technology, and research. Prints timely papers. *Price:* Free to members; $15/copy; $50/year.

★ 11092 ★ **American Registry of Diagnostic Medical Sonographers (ARDMS)**
2368 Victory Pky., Ste. 510
Cincinnati, OH 45206-2810
Phone: (513)281-7111
Free: 800-541-9754
Fax: (513)281-7524
Mimi Wong, Exec.Dir.

Founded: 1975. **Members:** 25,000. **Description:** Administers examinations in the field of diagnostic medical sonography and vascular technology throughout the U.S. and Canada and registers candidates passing those exams in the specialties of their expertise. Maintains central office for administering examination plans and schedules and assisting registered candidates and those interested in becoming registered. **Publications:** *American Registry of Diagnostic Medical Sonographers Directory*, annual. Directory. *Price:* Free. • *Annual Examination Information and Application Booklet*. Booklet. • *Continuing Competency Requirements*. Brochure. • *Informational Brochure*, annual. Brochure. • *Mailing List Brochure*. Brochure.

★ 11093 ★ **American Registry of Radiologic Technologists (ARRT)**
1255 Northland Dr.
St. Paul, MN 55120
Phone: (612)687-0048
Jerry B. Reid, Exec.Dir.

Founded: 1922. **Members:** 201,500. **Description:** Radiologic certification boards that administer examinations, issues certificates of registration to radiographers, nuclear medicine technologists, and radiation therapists, and investigates the qualifications of practicing radiologic technologists. Governed by trustees appointed from American College of Radiology and American Society of Radiologic Technologists. **Publications:** Annual Report. • *Directory of Registered Technologists*, biennial. Directory. **Formerly:** American Registry of X-Ray Technicians; (1936) American Registry of Radiological Technicians.

★ 11094 ★ **American Roentgen Ray Society (ARRS)**
c/o Paul R. Fullagar
1891 Preston White Dr.
Reston, VA 22091
Phone: (703)648-8992
Free: 800-438-2777
Fax: (703)264-8863
Paul R. Fullagar, Exec.Dir.

Founded: 1900. **Members:** 10,420. **Description:** Specialists in diagnostic and/or therapeutic roentgenology. Conducts regional and educational programs. **Publications:** *American Journal of Roentgenology*, monthly, Peer reviewed. Journal. *Price:* $125/year. • *Categorical Course Syllabi*. • Membership Directory, biennial. • Newsletter, quarterly. **Formerly:** (1906) Roentgen Society of the U.S..

★ 11095 ★ **American Society of Echocardiography (ASE)**
4101 Lake Boone Trl., Ste. 201
Raleigh, NC 27607
Phone: (919)787-5181
Fax: (919)787-4916
Sharon Perry, Exec.Dir.

Founded: 1976. **Members:** 5,000. **Description:** Physicians and sonographers specializing in ultrasound heart imaging and diagnosis. Promotes excellence in the ultrasonic examination of the heart and assists in establishing standards for education of physicians and cardiac-sonographers in echocardiography. Sponsors educational activities including distribution of self-testing materials, continuing education calendar, and annual scientific sessions. Maintains liaison with governmental agencies and other professional groups. **Publications:** *American Society of Echocardiography Standards Documents*, periodic. • *ASE Member*, biennial. Membership Directory. • *Journal of the American Society of Echocardiography*, bimonthly. Journal. For physicians and sonographers covering echocardiography. Includes legislative and membership updates. Also publishes standards documents.

American Society for Laser Medicine and Surgery (ASLMS)
See: Entry 12240

★ 11096 ★ **American Society of Neuroimaging (ASN)**
2221 University Ave. SE, Ste. 340
Minneapolis, MN 55414
Phone: (612)378-7240
Fax: (612)623-3504
Carol Hamel, Mgr.

Founded: 1977. **Members:** 800. **Description:** Neurologists, neurosurgeons, neuroradiologists, and scientists. Promotes the development of computerized tomography (CT scanning), magnetic resonanace imaging (MRI), neurosonology, and other neurodiagnostic techniques for clinical service, teaching, and research. Encourages the collaboration of members to improve techniques through educational programs and scientific research. Holds annual certification exam in computerized tomography and neurosonology. **Publications:** *Journal of Neuroimaging*, quarterly. Journal. • Newsletter, semiannual. **Formerly:** (1980) Society for Computerized Tomography and Neuroimaging.

★ 11097 ★ **American Society of**
Neuroradiology (ASNR)
2210 Midwest Rd., Ste. 207
Oak Brook, IL 60521
Phone: (708)574-0220
Fax: (708)574-0661
James B. Gantenberg, Exec.Dir.

Founded: 1962. **Members:** 2,222. **Description:** Neuroradiologists who spend at least half of their time practicing neuroradiology. Fosters education, basic science research, and communication in neuroradiology. **Publications:** *American Journal of Neuroradiology*, 10/year. Journal. *Price:* Included in membership dues; $185/year for nonmembers; $240/year for nonmembers outside the U.S.; $90 in training. • *Membership Roll*, annual.

★ 11098 ★ **American Society of Radiologic**
Technologists (ASRT)
15000 Central Ave. SE
Albuquerque, NM 87123
Phone: (505)298-4500
Fax: (505)298-5063
Ward M. Keller, CEO

Founded: 1920. **Members:** 35,000. **Regional Groups:** 10. **State Groups:** 50. **Description:** Professional society of diagnostic radiography, radiation therapy, ultrasound, and nuclear medicine technologists. Advances the science of radiologic technology; establishes and maintains high standards of education; evaluates the quality of patient care; improves the welfare and socioeconomics of radiologic technologists. Operates ASRT Educational Foundation, which provides educational materials to radiologic technologist programs. **Publications:** *ASRT Scanner*, bimonthly. Newsletter. Includes calendar of events, member profiles, state affiliate news, educational opportunities, and research updates. *Price:* Included in membership dues. • *Radiologic Technology*, bimonthly. Journal. Includes advertisers and cumulative annual author and title indexes, book reviews, literature abstracts, and calendar of events. *Price:* Included in membership dues; $49/year for nonmembers; $55/year for nonmembers outside the U.S.; $29.50/year for students. **Formerly:** (1934) American Society of Radiographers; (1964) American Society of X-Ray Technicians.

★ 11099 ★ **American Society for**
Therapeutic Radiology and Oncology
(ASTRO)
1891 Preston White Dr.
Reston, VA 22091
Free: 800-962-7876
Fax: (703)648-9176
Gregg Robinson, COO

Founded: 1955. **Members:** 4,200. **Description:** Physicians who limit their practice to radiation therapy; associate members are scientists and health care personnel who have a major interest "in furthering the aims of the society"; junior members are residents who have completed one year of training in radiation therapy. Aim is "to extend the benefits of radiation therapy to patients with cancer or other disorders, to advance its scientific basis, and to provide for the education and professional fellowship of its members." **Publications:** *ASTRO Membership Directory*, annual. Membership Directory. *Price:*

Included in membership dues; $150 for nonmembers. • *ASTRO Newsletter*, 3/year. Newsletter. • *The International Journal of Radiation Oncology, Biology, and Physics*, 3/year. Journal. **Formerly:** (1983) American Society of Therapeutic Radiologists.

★ 11100 ★ **Association of Freestanding**
Radiation Oncology Centers (AFROC)
2755 Bristol St., Ste. 110
Costa Mesa, CA 92626
Phone: (714)545-2087
Sharon Urch, Exec.Dir.

Founded: 1986. **Members:** 300. **Description:** Freestanding radiation oncology center employees; radiologists; oncologists; physicists; radiation therapists; laboratory clinicians. Promotes the interests of freestanding radiation oncology centers to insure high quality care for patients. Upgrades management services offered. Represents members in legal matters and to other associations. **Publications:** Directory, annual. • *The Source*, quarterly.

★ 11101 ★ **Association of German**
Radiologists and Nuclear Physicians
(Berufsverband der Deutschen Radiologen
und Nuklearmediziner eV)
Sonnenstr. 3
80331 Munich, Germany
Phone: 89 592690
Fax: 89 553896
RA Dipl.-Urm. Udo H. Cramer, Contact

Members: 1,000. **Languages:** English. **Description:** Radiologists and nuclear physicians in Germany. Promotes and represents the interests of members. **Publications:** *Roubgeupraxis mit Migliedes-Info*, 10/year, monthly except January and July.

★ 11102 ★ **Association of University**
Radiologists (AUR)
1891 Preston White Dr.
Reston, VA 22091
Phone: (703)716-7597
Fax: (703)476-8167
Gregg Robinson, Exec.Dir.

Founded: 1953. **Members:** 1,600. **Description:** Physician and non-physician scientists who have been appointed to a university faculty. Seeks to: encourage excellence in laboratory and clinical investigation, teaching, and clinical practice; stimulate interest in academic radiology as a medical career; advance radiology as a medical science; provide a forum for university based radiologists to present and discuss results of research, teaching, and administrative issues. **Publications:** *Academic Radiology*, monthly. Journal. Also publishes award and scientific papers.

★ 11103 ★ **Australian Institute of**
Radiography (AIR)
PO Box 1169
Collingwood, VIC 3069, Australia
Phone: 3 4193336
Fax: 3 4160783
E.M. Hughes, Gen.Sec.

Founded: 1950. **Members:** 3,300. **Languages:** English. **Description:** Diagnostic radiographers, radiation therapists, and sonographers in Aus-

tralia. Fosters cooperation and exchange of information between members. Conducts educational and research projects; prepares guidelines and policies for the practice of radiography in Australia. Encourages high professional standards. Disseminates information; offers educational programs and seminars. **Publications:** *Radiographer*, quarterly. Journal. • *Spectrum*, monthly. **Formerly:** Australasian Institute of Radiography.

★ 11104 ★ **British Institute of Radiology**
(BIR)
36 Portland Pl.
London W1N 4AT, England
Phone: 171 5804085
Fax: 171 2553209
Mary-Anne Piggott, CEO

Founded: 1897. **Members:** 200. **Regional Groups:** 1. **Local Groups:** 4. **Languages:** English. **Description:** Medical radiologists, scientists, and allied professionals in 55 countries. Conducts seminars; bestows awards. **Publications:** *British Journal of Radiology*, monthly. Journal. Multidisciplinary research. • *Current Research in Osteoporosis and Bone Mineral Measurement*. Proceedings. • Membership Directory, periodic. • *Reccomendations for Brachytherapy Dosimetry*. Report. • Reports. **Formerly:** (1924) British Association for the Advancement of Radiology and Physiotherapy.

★ 11105 ★ **British Medical Ultrasound**
Society (BMUS)
36 Portland Pl.
London W1N 3DG, England
Phone: 171 6363714
Fax: 171 3232175
Ms. La Summers, Gen.Sec.

Founded: 1969. **Members:** 1,550. **Languages:** English. **Description:** Medical practitioners, physicists/scientists, radiographers, veterinarians, and manufacturers of sonographic equipment. Seeks to advance the science and technology of ultrasound and to improve education in the field. **Publications:** *BMUS Bulletin*, quarterly. Newsletter. • *BMUS Membership Register*, triennial. • *Proceedings of Annual Meeting*, annual. Published in the British Journal of Radiology. **Formerly:** (1984) British Medical Ultrasound Group.

★ 11106 ★ **Canadian Association of**
Medical Radiation Technologists
(CAMRT)
(Association Canadienne des
Technologues en Radiation Medicale —
ACTRM)
294 Albert St., Ste. 601
Ottawa, ON, Canada K1P 6E6
Phone: (613)234-0012
Fax: (613)234-1097
Richard Lauzon, Ph.D., Exec.Dir.

Founded: 1942. **Members:** 9,795. **Languages:** English, French. **Description:** Certified radiation technologists in the fields of radiography, radiation therapy, and nuclear medicine. Provides and enforces standards in the training and certification of members; promotes and maintains code of ethics. Participates in the accreditation of medical radiation technologist training programs; organizes continuing education programs. Advises private and governmental organizations involved in the fields of health and education. Provides placement assistance, professional liability insurance, car rental discounts, and network of reciprocity agreements allowing members to practice in foreign countries without having to be recertified. **Publications:** *CAMRT News*, 5/year. Newsletter. Contains activity information and education programmes. • *Canadian Journal of Medical Radiation Technology*, quarterly. Journal.

★ 11107 ★   **Computerized Medical Imaging Society (CMIS)**
c/o Natl. Biomedical Research Found.
Georgetown Univ. Med. Center
3900 Reservoir Rd. NW
Washington, DC 20007
Phone: (202)687-2121
Fax: (202)687-1662
Robert S. Ledley, Editor-in-Chief

Founded: 1976. **Members:** 350. **Description:** Physicians and other medical personnel concerned with computerized tomography (a diagnostic technique using X-ray photographs in which the shadows of structures before and behind the section under scrutiny do not show), and other radiological diagnostic procedures. Provides a forum for the exchange of information concerning the medical use of computerized tomography in radiological diagnosis. **Publications:** *Computerized Medical Imaging and Graphics*, bimonthly. **Formerly:** (1983) Computerized Tomography Society; (1988) Computerized Radiology Society.

★ 11108 ★   **Council on Diagnostic Imaging**
52 W. Colfax
Palatine, IL 60067
Phone: (708)705-1177
Fax: (708)705-1178
Dr. Lawrence Pyzik, Sec.-Treas.

Founded: 1936. **Members:** 2,000. **Description:** Professional society of chiropractic roentgenologists, educators, students, and chiropractors interested in roentgenology. **Formerly:** (1963) National Council of Chiropractic Roentgenologists; (1968) American Council on Chiropractic Roentgenology; (1970) American Chiropractic Council on Roentgenology; (1983) Council on Roentgeneology to the American Chiropractic Association.

★ 11109 ★   **Czech Radiological Society (SRT)**
(Ceska Radiologicka Spolecnost — CRS)
Budinova 2
CS-180 81 Prague 8, Czech Republic
Phone: 2 822431
Fax: 2 822431
Prof. Jaromir Kolar, M.D.

Founded: 1929. **Members:** 100. **Local Groups:** 2. **Languages:** Czech, Slovak. Does not correspond in English. **Description:** Diagnostic radiologists in the Czech Republic. Disseminates information on developments in diagnostic imaging. Bestows awards. Acts as a forum for discussion among professionals. **Publications:** *Ceska Radiologie*, bimonthly. Journal. **Formerly:** (1993) Czechoslovak Radiological Society.

★ 11110 ★   **European Association of Radiology (EAR)**
(Association Europeenne de Radiologie — AER)
University Hospitals
Department of Radiology
Herestraat 49
B-3000 Louvain, Belgium
Phone: 16 343770
Fax: 16 343769
Dr. M. Blery, Sec.Gen.

Founded: 1962. **Members:** 28. **Languages:** English, French, German. **Description:** National European societies of radiology representing 20,000 radiologists. Objectives are to: promote radiology as a unified scientific and clinical discipline; further and monitor the application of radiology in biology and medicine; investigate the theoretical and technical problems connected with different applications of radiation; coordinate study and examination programs in the field of radiology in member countries; standardize training for radiologists and nonmedical assistants; encourage a constructive rapport with scientific, professional, and industrial organizations; promote international exchange of medical and paramedical personnel. **Publications:** *European Radiology*, bimonthly. Newsletter.

★ 11111 ★   **European Federation of Societies of Ultrasound in Medicine and Biology (EFSUMB)**
36 Portland Pl.
London W1N 3DG, England
Phone: 1171 5807662
Fax: 1171 5807693
Mrs. Elaine Brown, Exec.Sec.

Founded: 1972. **Members:** 1,200. **National Groups:** 22. **Languages:** English, French, German. **Description:** Interdisciplinary national organizations and subgroups of bodies representing 19 countries. Members promote the application of ultrasound in biology and medicine or engage in research and development in the field. Proposes standards for ultrasound use and interpretation; arranges congresses and study and development meetings; promotes the exchange of information on ultrasound as applied to biology and medicine. Represents the European national societies in the World Federation of Societies for Ultrasound in Medicine and Biology. **Publications:** *European Journal of Ultrasound*, quarterly. Journal.

★ 11112 ★   **European Laser Association (ELA)**
(Association Europeenne du Laser — AEL)
Meibergdreef 9
NL-1105 AZ Amsterdam, Netherlands
Phone: 20 5669111
Fax: 3120 6919840
Prof. G. Titgat, Contact

Founded: 1981. **Members:** 680. **National Groups:** 8. **Languages:** English, French. **Description:** Physicians and surgeons in 15 countries concerned with laser medical instruments. Purpose is to advance the use of lasers in medicine. Conducts symposia and workshops. **Publications:** *Lasers in Medical Science*, periodic. Journal. • Newsletter, periodic.

★ 11113 ★   **European Society of Paediatric Radiology (ESPR)**
Hopital St. Vincent de Paul
7432, ave. Denfert-Rochereau
F-75674 Paris Cedex 14, France
Phone: 1 40488111
Fax: 1 4248836
Prof. Gabriel Kalifa, Gen.Sec.

Founded: 1963. **Members:** 471. **Languages:** English. **Description:** Radiologists involved or interested in pediatric radiology. Seeks to contribute to the advancement of the clinical and scientific aspects of pediatric radiology in European countries through educational activities. Conducts Annual postgraduate courses; sponsors research programs. Bestows awards. **Publications:** *Annales de Radiologie*, annual. Includes proceedings. • Bulletin, semiannual. • *Paediatric Radiology*, annual.

European Society for Therapeutic Radiology and Oncology (ESTRO)
See: Entry 5943

★ 11114 ★   **Foundation for Blood Irradiation (FFBI)**
1315 Apple Ave.
Silver Spring, MD 20910
Phone: (301)587-8686
Dr. Carl Schleicher, Exec. Officer

Founded: 1964. **Members:** 175. **Description:** Persons concerned with the research and development of ultraviolet blood irradiation therapy (intravenously applied ultraviolet energy administered to increase the body's natural ability to fight infection and resist disease). Conducts training programs. Compiles statistics and sponsors charitable programs. **Publications:** Bulletin, annual. • Monographs. • Proceedings, periodic.

★ 11115 ★   **International Association of Dento-Maxillo-Facial Radiology (IADMFR)**
c/o Prof. Robert Langlais
UTHSC Dental School
Dental Diagnostic Sciences
7703 Floyd Curl Dr.
San Antonio, TX 78284
Phone: (210)567-3347
Prof. Robert Langlais, Exec. Officer

Founded: 1968. **Members:** 500. **Regional Groups:** 8. **Description:** Dento-maxillo-facial radiologists and others professionally interested in radiology and allied diagnostic procedures. Promotes advancement in dento-maxillo-facial radiological research, teaching, and clinical service. **Publications:** *Journal of Dento-Maxillo-Facial Radiology*, 4/year. Journal. • Newsletter, triennial, 2/year. Includes triennial directory. • Proceedings, triennial. Abstracts. **Formerly:** (1974) International Association of Maxillo-Facial Radiology.

★ 11116 ★   **International Association for Radiation Research (IARR)**
Medical Research Council
Radiobiology Unit
Chilton, Oxon. OX11 0RD, England
Phone: 1235 834393
Fax: 1235 834776
Dr. E.M. Fielden, Sec.-Treas.

Founded: 1962. **Members:** 16. **Languages:** English. **Description:** National and regional societies, comprising 3315 individuals, that promote research in radiation physics, chemistry, medicine, and biology. To foster and maintain scientific cooperation and communication and to promote and facilitate international scientific conferences and symposia. Maintains liaison with the International Council of Scientific Unions. **Publications:** Newsletter, periodic. • *Proceedings of Congress*, quadrennial.

International Association of Radiopharmacology (IAR)
See: Entry 10411

★ 11117 ★ International Commission on Radiation Units and Measurements (ICRU)
7910 Woodmont Ave., Ste. 800
Bethesda, MD 20814
Phone: (301)657-2652
Free: 800-229-2652
Fax: (301)907-8768
W. Roger Ney, Exec.Sec.

Founded: 1925. **Members:** 101. **Description:** Commission members, senior advisors, consultants, and representatives of report committees in 12 countries. Develops internationally acceptable recommendations regarding: quantities and units of radiation and radionuclides; procedures suitable for the measurement and application of these quantities in clinical radiology and radiobiology; physical data needed in the application of these procedures, the use of which tends to assure uniformity in reporting. The commission has divided its field of interest into 15 technical areas. **Publications:** *ICRU Reports*, periodic. Report. **Formerly:** (1931) International X-Ray Unit Committee; (1950) International Committee for Radiological Units; (1956) International Commission on Radiological Units; (1965) International Commission on Radiological Units and Measurements.

★ 11118 ★ International Skeletal Society (ISS)
c/o Donald Resnick, M.D.
Veterans Administration Hospital
Department of Radiology
3350 La Jolla Village Dr.
San Diego, CA 92161
Phone: (619)552-8585
Fax: (619)552-7452
Donald Resnick, M.D., Contact

Founded: 1973. **Members:** 325. **Description:** Physicians and scientists interested in skeletal muscle disease. Seeks to advance the science of skeletal radiology; brings together radiologists and individuals in related disciplines; provides continuing education courses. **Publications:** Membership Directory, annual. • Newsletter, semiannual. • *Skeletal Radiology*, 8/year. Journal. Contains scientific articles and case reports. *Price:* Included in membership dues.

★ 11119 ★ International Society for Ophthalmic Ultrasound (SIDUO)
Josef-Schneiderstr. 11
97080 Wurzburg, Germany
Phone: 931 2012401
Fax: 931 2012245
Dr. G. Hasenfratz, Contact

Founded: 1963. **Members:** 550. **Regional Groups:** 5. **Languages:** English, French, German. **Description:** Ophthalmologists and physicists in 43 countries united for the study of the applications of ultrasonography in ophthalmic diagnosis, therapeutics, and biometrics. **Publications:** *Newsletter*, annual. Newsletter. • *Proceedings of the Congresses*, biennial.

International Society of Podiatric Laser Surgery (ISPLS)
See: Entry 10773

★ 11120 ★ International Society of Radiographers and Radiological Technicians Jamaica (Sociedad Internacional de Radiografos y Tecnicos de Radiologia - Jamaica)
PO Box 38
Kingston 6, Jamaica

Description: Organized to improve standards of education for radiographers and radiological technicians in Jamaica. Fosters communication and information exchange between members. **Publications:** *Newsletter*.

★ 11121 ★ International Society of Radiographers and Radiological Technologists (ISRRT) (Societe Internationale des Radiographes et Techniciens de Radiologie)
52 Addison Crescent
Don Mills, ON, Canada M3B 1K8
Phone: (416)445-7841
Fax: (416)445-4268
T.J.D. West, Sec.Gen.

Founded: 1959. **Members:** 60. **Languages:** English. **Description:** National radiographic societies and other organizations having radiographers as members. Objectives are to: advance the science and practice of radiography, radiotherapy, and allied subjects by promoting improved standards of training and research in technical aspects of radiation medicine and protection; make results of research and experience available to practitioners; raise funds to further these objectives. Compiles statistics and maintains museum. Has established educational trust fund. Conducts teachers' seminars. **Publications:** Newsletter, semiannual. • Proceedings, periodic. • *Teaching Guides*, periodic. **Formerly:** International Society of Radiographers and Radiological Technicians.

★ 11122 ★ International Society of Radiology (ISR) (Societe Internationale de Radiologie)
Department of Radiology
Helsinki University Central Hospital
Meilahti Clinics
SF-00290 Helsinki, Finland
Phone: 0 4712480
Fax: 0 4714404
C.G. Standertskjold-Nordenstam, Gen.Sec.

Founded: 1953. **Members:** 69. **Languages:** English, French, German. **Description:** National radiological associations. Seeks to promote medical radiology worldwide through the work of its sections and international commissions. Undertakes business referred to it by member societies. Provides financial support for the work of its commissions. **Publications:** Congress

Proceedings, biennial. • Newsletter, semiannual. • *Reports of Commissions of ISR*, periodic.

★ 11123 ★ Joint Review Committee on Education in Diagnostic Medical Sonography (JRCDMS)
7108-C S. Alton Way
Englewood, CO 80112
Phone: (303)741-3533
Fax: (303)741-3655
Annamarie Dubies-Appel, Exec.Dir.

Founded: 1979. **Members:** 8. **Description:** Participants are physicians and medical ultrasonographers. In collaboration with the Commission on Accreditation for Allied Health Education Programs, accredits post-secondary education programs in diagnostic medical sonography. (Sonography utilizes ultrasonic waves to take two-dimensional pictures of internal body structures.) **Publications:** *JRCDMS News*, semiannual. Newsletter.

★ 11124 ★ Joint Review Committee on Education in Radiologic Technology (JRCERT)
20 N. Wacker Dr., Ste. 900
Chicago, IL 60606
Phone: (312)704-5300
Fax: (312)704-5304
Marilyn Fay, Exec.Dir.

Founded: 1969. **Description:** Purpose is to evaluate and accredit educational programs in the fields of radiography and radiation therapy; participants are radiologists and radiation oncologists, radiographers, and radiation therapists. **Publications:** *JRCERT Handbook for Educational Programs. Price:* $75. • *JRCERT Review*, 3/year. Newsletter. Includes interpretations of educational standards. *Price:* $6/year.

★ 11125 ★ Malaysian Society of Radiographers (MSR) (Persatuan Juru X-Ray Malaysia — PJXM)
General Hospital
Department of Radiology
50586 Jalan Pahang
Kuala Lumpur, Malaysia
Phone: 3 2906674
Fax: 3 2989845
M.R.B. Hashim, Pres.

Founded: 1968. **Members:** 200. **Languages:** English, Malay. **Description:** Radiographers working in diagnostic and radiotherapeutic specialties. Represents the interests of radiographers and allied practitioners through professional and social activities. Works to foster interest in radiography and radiotherapeutic technique and to improve the standards of practice. Operates a research program in radiation protection. Sponsors weekend lectures, technical sessions, seminars, symposia, workshops, and conferences. **Publications:** *Journal*, annual. Journal. • *Newsletter*, quarterly. Newsletter.

★ 11126 ★ Medical Radiological Technicians Belgium (MRTB)
86-88, rue Neuve
B-1640 Rhode-Saint-Genese, Belgium
Phone: 2 3802161
Alain Hembise, Exec. Officer

Founded: 1974. **Members:** 500. **Local Groups:** 5. **Languages:** Dutch, English, French,

German. **Description:** Radiological technicians and nurses. Encourages recognition of radiological technicians in Belgium, who currently are not required to be certified. Coordinates research activities with groups with similar concerns. Sponsors educational and exchange programs; organizes quarterly scientific meetings. **Publications:** *Delta*, 3/year. Also publishes *Tomodensitometries Technics* (book).

★ 11127 ★ **National Foundation for Non-Invasive Diagnostics (NFNID)**
103 Carnegie Center, Ste. 311
Princeton, NJ 08540
Phone: (609)520-1300
Fax: (609)452-8544
Philip B. Papier, Jr., Trustee

Founded: 1977. **Description:** Provides continuing education program for physicians and technologists in the field of echocardiography (the use of ultrasound in examining the heart and diagnosing abnormalities). Bestows designation of Professional Ultrasound Technologist to seminar participants who meet certification standards.

★ 11128 ★ **Nuclear Medicine Technology Certification Board (NMTCB)**
2970 Clairmont Rd., Ste. 610
Atlanta, GA 30329
Phone: (404)315-1739
Fax: (404)315-6502
James E. Greene, Jr., P, Exec.Dir.

Founded: 1977. **Members:** 14,000. **Description:** Purposes are to provide for the certification of nuclear medical technologists and to develop, assess, and administer an examination relevant to nuclear medicine technology. Compiles statistics. **Publications:** Brochures. • *Certification Examination Validation Report*, annual. • Directory, annual. • *Examination Report*, annual. • *NMTCB News*, semiannual. *Price:* Free to members.

Radiation Therapy Oncology Group (RTOG)
See: Entry 5983

★ 11129 ★ **Radiological Society of North America (RSNA)**
2021 Spring Rd., Ste. 600
Oak Brook, IL 60521
Phone: (708)571-2670
Fax: (708)571-7837
Delmar J. Stauffer, Exec.Dir.

Founded: 1915. **Members:** 26,000. **Description:** Radiologists and scientists in fields closely related to radiology. Promotes study and practical application of radiology, radium, electricity, and other branches of physics related to medical science. **Publications:** Membership Directory, annual. • *Radiographics*, bimonthly. Features pictorial presentations of selected scientific exhibits from the society's annual meeting. Includes case studies. • *Radiology*, monthly. Journal. Covers diagnostic radiology, neuroradiology, nuclear medicine, pediatric radiology, therapeutic radiology, cardiovascular radiology, and ultrasound. • *RSNA Educational Materials*, annual. Catalog. Lists video/slide set series for CME credits. **Formerly:** (1918) Western Roentgen Society.

Radiology Business Management Association (RBMA)
See: Entry 5601

★ 11130 ★ **Royal College of Radiologists (RCR)**
38 Portland Pl.
London W1N 3DG, England
Phone: 171 6364432
Fax: 171 3233100
Anthony J. Cowles, Gen.Sec.

Founded: 1939. **Members:** 3,444. **Languages:** English. **Description:** Diagnostic and interventional radiologists, nuclear medicine specialists, oncologists, radiotherapists, and ultrasound specialists. Works to advance the science and practice of radiological technology. Offers courses to further the education of practitioners. Establishes qualifications and examinations for fellowships and diplomas. Bestows awards. Conducts scientific meetings. **Publications:** *Clinical Oncology*, bimonthly. Journal. • *Clinical Radiology*, monthly. Journal. • *Members' Handbook*, biennial. Handbook. • *Newsletter*, quarterly. Newsletter. **Formerly:** (1975) Faculty of Radiologists.

★ 11131 ★ **Slovak Society of Nuclear Medicine and Radiation Hygiene**
Rastislavova 43
SK-040 01 Kosice, Slovakia
Phone: 95 765968
Fax: 95 52662
Jozef Zimacek, M.D., Contact

Languages: English, Slovak. **Description:** Health care professional working in the fields of nuclear medicine and radiology. Seeks to advance the professional standing of members and improve the practice of nuclear medicine and radiology; represents members' interests.

★ 11132 ★ **Society of Cardiovascular and Interventional Radiology (SCVIR)**
10201 Lee Hwy., Ste. 160
Fairfax, VA 22030
Phone: (703)691-1805
Free: 800-488-7284
Fax: (703)691-1855

Founded: 1973. **Members:** 2,190. **Description:** Physicians who are leaders in the field of cardiovascular and interventional radiology. Facilitates exchange of new ideas and techniques and provides educational courses for all physicians working in the field. Conducts annual postgraduate course. Conducts Interventional Radiology Political Action. **Publications:** *Directory of Angiography and Interventional Radiology Fellowship Programs*. Directory. • *Journal of Vascular and Interventional Radiology*, bimonthly. Journal. • *SCVIR Membership Directory*, annual. Membership Directory. • *SCVIR Newsletter*, bimonthly. Newsletter. **Formerly:** (1983) Society of Cardiovascular Radiology.

★ 11133 ★ **Society of Computed Body Tomography and Magnetic Resonance (SCBT/MR)**
c/o Matrix Meetings
PO Box 1026
Rochester, MN 55903-1026
Phone: (507)288-5620
Fax: (507)288-0014
Barbara McLeod, Exec.Dir.

Founded: 1977. **Members:** 80. **Description:** Radiologists. Provides educational course on computed tomography and magnetic resonance imaging of the body. Sponsors case presentations. Course syllabus. **Formerly:** (1991) Society of Computed Body Tomography.

★ 11134 ★ **Society of Diagnostic Medical Sonographers (SDMS)**
12770 Coit Rd., Ste. 508
Dallas, TX 75251
Phone: (214)239-7367
Fax: (214)239-7378
Gwen Grim, Exec.Dir.

Founded: 1970. **Members:** 11,000. **Regional Groups:** 7. **State Groups:** 50. **Local Groups:** 40. **Description:** Sonographers, physician sonologists, and those in medical specialties utilizing high frequency sound for diagnostic purposes. Works to advance the science of diagnostic medical sonography to establish and maintain high standards of education, to provide an identity and sense of direction for members. Collects information concerning educational programs and informs schools of minimum standards currently being proposed. Has developed American Registry of Diagnostic Medical Sonographers, the first registering body for the field of diagnostic ultrasound. Maintains list of job openings. **Publications:** Books. • *Directory of Education*. Directory. • *Guidelines for Student Review*. • *Journal of Diagnostic Medical Sonography*, biennial. Journal. • *News Wave*, biennial. • *1995 Compensation Survey*. Survey. • Videos. **Formerly:** (1980) American Society of Ultrasound Technical Specialists.

★ 11135 ★ **Society of Magnetic Resonance**
22118 Milvia St., Ste. 201
Berkeley, CA 94704
Phone: (510)841-1899
Fax: (510)841-2340
Jane Tiemann, Dir.

Founded: 1981. **Members:** 4,151. **Description:** Devoted to furthering the development and application of MRI and its techniques in medicine and biology. Sponsors educational and research programs. **Publications:** Brochure. • Directory. • *Journal of Magnetic Resonance Imaging*, bimonthly. Journal. • *Magnetic Resonance in Medicine*, monthly. Newsletter.

★ 11136 ★ **Society for Magnetic Resonance Imaging (SMRI)**
2118 Milvia St., Ste. 201
Berkeley, CA 94704
Phone: (510)841-1899
Fax: (510)841-2340
Jane Tiemann, Exec.Dir.

Founded: 1982. **Members:** 2,269. **Description:** Physicians and basic scientists promoting the applications of magnetic resonance techniques to medicine and biology, with special emphasis on imaging. **Publications:** *Echoes*, quarterly. Newsletter. • *Journal of Magnetic Resonance Imaging*, bimonthly. Journal. *Price:* $100/year.

★11137★ Society of Nuclear Medicine (SNM)
1850 Samuel Morse Dr.
Reston, VA 22090
Phone: (703)708-9000
Fax: (703)708-9015
Torry Mark Sansone, Exec.Dir.

Founded: 1954. **Members:** 12,000. **Regional Groups:** 16. **Description:** Professional society of physicians, physicists, chemists, radiopharmacists, nuclear medicine technologists, and others interested in nuclear medicine, nuclear magnetic resonance, and the use of radioactive isotopes in clinical practice, research, and teaching. Disseminates information concerning the utilization of nuclear phenomena in the diagnosis and treatment of disease. Oversees the Technologist Section of the Society of Nuclear Medicine. **Publications:** *The Journal of Nuclear Medicine*, monthly. Journal. Includes advertisers' index, case reports, technical notes, book reviews, calendar of events and information on new products. *Price:* Included in membership dues; $120/year for nonmembers; $130/year for nonmembers in Canada and Mesico; $160/year for nonmembers outside North America. • *Journal of Nuclear Medicine Technology*, quarterly. Journal. Includes teaching editorials, commentaries, continuing education, and technologist news. Contains advertisers' index and calendar of events. *Price:* Included in membership dues; $60/year for nonmembers; $65/year for nonmembers in Canada and Mexico; $70/year for nonmembers outside North America. • *Society of Nuclear Medicine Membership Directory*, every 3 years. Directory. Arranged geographically and alphabetically. *Price:* Included in membership dues; $50/issue for nonmembers. Also publishes other books and patient pamphlets; produces audiovisual materials.

Society for Pediatric Radiology (SPR)
See: Entry 3295

Society for Radiation Oncology Administrators (SROA)
See: Entry 5603

★11138★ Society of Radiographers (SR)
14 Upper Wimpole St.
London W1M 8BN, England
Phone: 171 9355726
Fax: 171 4873483
Mr. S. Evans, Exec. Officer

Founded: 1920. **Members:** 12,500. **Regional Groups:** 14. **Languages:** English. **Description:** Represents the interests of radiographers in the United Kingdom. **Publications:** *Radiography Today*, monthly. Journal.

★11139★ Society of Radiographers of South Africa (SRSA) (Vereniging van Radiograwe van Suid-Afrika — VRSA)
PO Box 6014
Roggebaai 8012, Republic of South Africa
Phone: 21 4194857
Fax: 21 212566
Mrs. L. Munro, Natl.Sec.

Founded: 1951. **Members:** 1,500. **Local Groups:** 7. **Languages:** Afrikaans, English. **Description:** Radiographers in South Africa. Strives for the establishment and maintenance of professional standards in the training and practice of radiography. Cooperates with governmental bodies in order to improve working conditions, salaries, and benefits. Represents members' interests nationally and internationally. Communicates with relevant authorities on educational and employment matters. Maintains liaisons with similar national and international organizations. Sponsors seminars and workshops. **Publications:** Newsletter, quarterly. • *The South African Radiographer*, semiannual. Journal.

★11140★ Society of Thoracic Radiology (STR)
PO Box 1925
Roswell, GA 30077-1925
Phone: (404)641-9773
Fax: (404)552-9859
Dr. David Godwin, M.D., Pres.

Founded: 1983. **Members:** 200. **Description:** Radiologists. Provides for continuing medical education.

★11141★ Technologist Section of the Society of Nuclear Medicine (TSSNM)
136 Madison Ave.
New York, NY 10016
Phone: (703)708-9000
Fax: (703)708-9015
Virginia M. Pappas, Admin.

Founded: 1970. **Members:** 7,000. **Regional Groups:** 15. **Description:** Members of the Society of Nuclear Medicine who have received formal training in nuclear medicine technology. Purposes are to: promote the continued development and improvement of nuclear medicine technology; enhance the development of nuclear medicine technologists; stimulate continuing education; develop a forum for the exchange of ideas and information. Serves as the central source of information for those interested and involved in the field of nuclear medicine technology. Represents the field in areas of licensure, accreditation, and certification. Sponsors training sessions. Conducts surveys; compiles statistics. **Publications:** Books. • *Journal of Nuclear Medicine Technology*, quarterly. Journal. *Price:* Included in membership dues. • Membership Directory, biennial. • Videos.

Research Centers

★11142★ Baylor College of Medicine NMR Laboratories
9450 Grogan's Mill Rd.
The Woodlands, TX 77380
Phone: (713)298-1398
Fax: (713)363-0230

Research Activities and Fields: Nuclear magnetic resonance imaging and spectroscopy, including development of software and hardware and applications to biological and clinical conditions. Concentrates on in vivo spectroscopy. **Publications:** *Magnetic Resonance Update* (quarterly). **Formerly:** Formed after split of Magnetic Resonance Imaging Center.

Center for Imaging and Pharmaceutical Research
See: Entry 10428

Center for Radiation Therapy
See: Entry 6016

★11143★ Columbia University Center for Radiological Research
630 W. 168th St.
VC B9, Rm. 11-230
New York, NY 10032
Phone: (212)305-5660
Fax: (212)305-3229
Dr. Eric J. Hall, Dir.

Research Activities and Fields: Human and rodent cell transformation assay systems at the cellular and molecular levels.

★11144★ Harvard University Harvard Cyclotron Laboratory
44 Oxford St.
Cambridge, MA 02138
Phone: (617)495-2885
Fax: (617)495-8054
Miles S. Wagner, Dir.

Research Activities and Fields: Proton beam technology for medical applications in both experimental and routine treatment of benign and cancerous tumors, including associated technical developments and clinical trials of proton radiation therapy and radiobiology. Other interests include proton activation analysis and other uses of proton beams, accelerator design study, and occasional radiation damage studies for commercial uses from aerospace and similar industries. **Publications:** Annual Report.

Institute for Applied Laser Surgery
See: Entry 12321

★11145★ Joint Center for Radiation Therapy
50 Binney St.
Boston, MA 02115
Phone: (617)432-1889
C. Norman Coleman, Chm.

Research Activities and Fields: Tumor cell biology, focusing on microenvironments and molecular biology techniques and radiation induced processes.

★ 11146 ★ Kettering Medical Center
Nuclear Medicine Department
Wright State Univ. School of Medicine
Section of Nuclear Medicine
3535 Southern Blvd.
Kettering, OH 45429
Phone: (513)296-7211
Fax: (513)296-4265
Joseph C. Mantil, M.D., Dir.

Research Activities and Fields: Clinical studies of dementia, deep venous thrombosis, pulmonary response to radiation exposure, utility of thallium scans (SPECT), and In-111 labeled white cells in evaluation of microscopic changes in infectious disease and malignancy; positron emission tomography (PET) studie s of cardiac, neurologic, and oncologic cases; serotonin receptor studies; and PET studies of chemo- and radiation therapy responses. Clinical activities include serial lung scans of radiation therapy patients, retrospective reviews of radionuclide venograms, cisternograms, and thallium scans. Utilizes lung scans to assess canine response to oleic acid injection.

★ 11147 ★ **Kettering-Scott Magnetic Resonance Laboratory**
Wright State Univ. School of Medicine
Kettering Medical Center
3535 Southern Blvd.
Kettering, OH 45429
Phone: (513)296-7877
Fax: (513)296-4265
Joseph C. Mantil, M.D., Dir.

Research Activities and Fields: Magnetic resonance imaging of radiation injury to brain, brain abnormalities in chronic alcoholism and hyponatremia, and normal pressure hydrocephalus. Performs magnetic resonance spectroscopic evaluations of arthritic joints, cerebral and cardiac hypoxia, and glucose metabolism in the liver as a function of insulin and glucogen. Utilizes animal models for glucose and arthritic joint studies.

★ 11148 ★ **Laser Technology Center**
10521 Research Dr., Ste. 300
Knoxville, TN 37932
Phone: (615)675-9571
Dr. James E. Parks, Dir.

Research Activities and Fields: Lasers, including medical and biological applications and projects utilizing resonance ionization spectroscopy and surface-enhanced Raman scattering. Fosters commercialization of laser-related technologies. **Publications:** *Laser Technology Center Reflections Newsletter.*

★ 11149 ★ **Long Island Jewish Medical Center**
Nuclear Medicine Division
270-05 76th Ave.
New Hyde Park, NY 11042
Phone: (718)470-7080
Fax: (718)470-9247
Christopher Palestro, M.D., Dir.

Research Activities and Fields: Applications of radioisotopes to clinical medicine. The Division is especially concerned with research on new applications, including instrumentation, and in use of isotopes in study of metabolic processes and infection.

★ 11150 ★ **Massachusetts Institute of Technology**
Center for Magnetic Resonance
Francis Bitter National Magnet Laboratory
NW14-5113
170 Albany St.
Cambridge, MA 02139
Phone: (617)253-5597
Fax: (617)253-5405
Prof. Robert G. Griffin, Dir.

Research Activities and Fields: Nuclear magnetic resonance (NMR) imaging for the study of liquid- or solid-state biological molecules, viral particles, cells, or intact tissues, and small animals. Areas of expertise include natural and model membrane structure, dynamics, and function; phase diagrams; phase transitions; solid-state studies of amino acids, peptides, and bone; protein conformation and interactions; dynamics of energy metabolism in skeletal muscle, cells, animal brain, and human eye lens; repressor-DNA operator structure and dynamics; DNA structure and dynamics; NMR microimaging; human imaging; in vitro spectroscopy; and high frequency EPR and DNP/NMR DNP. **E-mail Address:** griffin@ccnmr.mit.edu. **Formerly:** National NMR Facility for Biomolecular Research; Comprehensive NMR Center for Biomedical Research.

★ 11151 ★ **Massachusetts Institute of Technology**
Laser Biomedical Research Center
77 Massachusetts Ave.
Cambridge, MA 02139
Phone: (617)253-7700
Fax: (617)253-4513
Dr. Michael S. Feld, Dir.

Research Activities and Fields: Lasers and medicine. Uses a tunable laser facility for measuring optical properties of tissue and studying tissue ablation mechanisms; develops new methods for real-time spectroscopic identification of tissue types and conditions; performs laser fluorescence studies in single cells; investigates UV Raman and resonance Raman applications in biology and medicine; and conducts time-resolved picosecond studies in tissue and other biological systems. Pursues collaborative research with researchers from outside institutions and provides facilities to outside scientists and physicians nationwide. **Publications:** Annual Summary Report; *The Spectrograph* (newsletter).

Mayo Biomedical Imaging Resource
See: Entry 2454

★ 11152 ★ **Medical College of Wisconsin**
Biophysics Research Institute
8701 Watertown Plank Rd.
Milwaukee, WI 53226
Phone: (414)456-4000
Fax: (414)456-8515
James S. Hyde, Ph.D., Dir.

Research Activities and Fields: Biophysics, with emphasis on functional magnetic resonance imaging and electron spin resonance.

New York University
Laboratory of Cancer and Radiobiological Research
See: Entry 6088

★ 11153 ★ **Pittsburgh NMR Institute**
3260 5th Ave.
Pittsburgh, PA 15213
Phone: (412)647-6679
Fax: (412)647-8520
Dr. Emanuel Kanal, M.D., Med.Dir.

Research Activities and Fields: Human disease studies using magnetic resonance imaging (MRI) and spectroscopy. Develops new contrast agents to enhance tissue specificity or measure organ function with magnetic resonance, as well as new techniques for studying animals and patients with magnetic resonance. Also uses MRI to evaluate therapeutic response of patients to new or old drugs. **Publications:** Newsletter.

★ 11154 ★ **Radiation Oncology Research & Development Center**
4201 St. Antoine
Detroit, MI 48201
Phone: (313)745-9207
Fax: (313)745-2314
Arthur T. Porter, M.D., Pres.

Research Activities and Fields: Radiation therapy, cancer research, medical information systems, three-dimensional imaging, neutron therapy, radiosurgery, brachytherapy, clinical protocols, and unsealed source therapy.

★ 11155 ★ **Rochester Institute of Technology**
Center for Imaging Science
54 Lomb Memorial Dr.
Rochester, NY 14623
Phone: (716)475-7294
Fax: (716)475-5988
Dr. Edwin P. Przybylowicz, Dir.

Research Activities and Fields: Imaging sciences, including remote sensing, digital image processing, color science, silver halide science, optics, holography, electrophotography, and medical diagnostic imaging.

★ 11156 ★ **UCI / AMI Magnetic Resonance Imaging Center**
101 The City Dr.
Orange, CA 92668
Phone: (714)634-4253
Fax: (714)634-4279
Rosalind Dietrich, M.D., Med.Dir.

Research Activities and Fields: Evaluates basic principles and clinical applications of magnetic resonance imaging and spectroscopy. **Formerly:** AMI Medical Center.

★ 11157 ★ **U.S. Department of Commerce**
National Institute of Standards and Technology
Physics Laboratory
Ionizing Radiation Division
Radiation Physics Bldg.
Gaithersburg, MD 20899
Phone: (301)975-5525
Fax: (301)869-7682
Dr. Randall S. Caswell, Chief

Research Activities and Fields: Division comprises four main research groups: 1) Office of Radiation Measurements; 2) Radiation Interactions and Dosimetry; 3) Neutron Interactions and Dosimetry; and 4) Radioactivity. Research and other Division activities support such areas of national concern as medicine (e.g., radioactivity standards for nuclear medicine and dosimetry standards for neutron radiation therapy); fission and fusion nuclear power (neutron cross sections, fission rate measurements in power reactors, environmental radioactivity standards); environment (radon standards and environmental radioactivity in natural matrices); occupational safety (neutron personnel monitoring); and science (radiation physics and chemistry, biochemistry, and interaction of radiation with matter).

★11158★ U.S. Department of Energy
Lawrence Berkeley Laboratory
Research Medicine and Radiation
   Biophysics Division
1 Cyclotron Rd.
Berkeley, CA 94720
Phone: (510)486-5435
Fax: (510)486-4786
T.F. Budinger, Division Director

Research Activities and Fields: Division is primarily concerned with modern approaches to human physiology, including experimental patient treatment, development of diagnostic imaging devices, and radiation biophysics. In addition, Division provides support for graduate and postdoctoral training in hemopoietic cellular proliferation and its regulation, cardiovascular flow and metabolism, and lipoprotein methodology, structure, and function.

★11159★ U.S. Department of Energy
Oak Ridge National Laboratory
Environmental, Life, and Social Sciences
   Directorate
Assessment Technology Section
PO Box 2008
Oak Ridge, TN 37831-6383
Phone: (615)576-2100
Fax: (615)574-1778
Dr. Paul S. Rohwer, Associate Director

Research Activities and Fields: Activities in this Section involve: 1) expert systems development using hazardous surveys and radiation dosimetry; 2) database development; 3) radiological dosimetry research; 4) research at the Health Physics Research Reactor; 5) biokinetic modeling; 6) evaluation of radiological impacts of energy production; 7) modeling of environmental transport of pollution; 8) radiological and chemical field survey activities; 9) survey instrumentation development; and 10) radiopharmaceutical research.

U.S. Department of Energy
Office of Health and Environmental
   Research
Medical Applications and Biophysical
   Research Division
See: Entry 5093

U.S. Department of Health and Human
   Services
National Cancer Institute
Division of Cancer Treatment
Diagnostic Imaging Research Branch
See: Entry 6158

U.S. Department of Health and Human
   Services
National Cancer Institute
Division of Cancer Treatment
Radiation Oncology Branch
See: Entry 6163

U.S. Department of Health and Human
   Services
National Cancer Institute
Division of Cancer Treatment
Radiotherapy Development Branch
See: Entry 6165

★11160★ University of California, Irvine
Beckman Laser Institute and Medical Clinic
1002 Health Sciences Rd. E.
Irvine, CA 92715
Phone: (714)856-6996
Fax: (714)856-8413
Michael Berns, Ph.D., Dir.

Research Activities and Fields: Basic research includes genetics, cell biology, spectroscopy, and biophysics. Conducts basic laser studies of cellular functions, including genetic expression, cell motility, and cell membrane behavior; and biophysical studies of thermal, fluorescence, acoustic/mechanical, photochemical, and ionization effects of radiation on biological material. Conducts applied research in cancer detection and treatment; ablation of plaque from blood vessels; reshaping of cornea with excimer laser, laser destruction of ureteral and biliary stones; laser-induced welding of severed nerves, blood vessels, and other ducts; diagnosis (imaging) and treatment of portwine stain birthmarks; and development of medical laser devices. **Publications:** *Beckman Laser Institute News* (quarterly newsletter). **E-mail Address:** mberns@nova.bli.uci.edu.

★11161★ University of California, Irvine
Brain Imaging Center
College of Medicine
164 Irvine Hall
Irvine, CA 92717-3960
Phone: (714)856-4244
Richard J. Haier, Ph.D., Mng.Dir.

Research Activities and Fields: PET scan analysis of brain functions focusing on mental illness, brain tumors, Alzheimer's disease, near drowing, and aberrant behavior.

★11162★ University of California, Irvine
Laser Microbeam Program (LAMP)
1002 Health Sciences Rd. E.
Irvine, CA 92715
Phone: (714)824-6291
Fax: (714)824-8413
Dr. Michael W. Berns, Dir.

Research Activities and Fields: Combines sophisticated methods of microscopy, computer image processing, and laser technology to investigate cellular, genetic, and developmental problems that are related to cancer, heart disease, neurobiology, and other health problems. Focuses on clinical and veterinary medicine, particularly in the areas of laser and computer application in photoradiation therapy of cancer, treatment of port wine hemangiomas, and laser angioplasty. Develops techniques for life-time imaging of cells. **E-mail Address:** mburns@nova.hi.uci.edu.

★11163★ University of California, Los
   Angeles
Leo G. Rigler Center for Radiological
   Research
UCLA Medical Center
Department of Radiology
Center for Health Sciences, Rm. BV-135
Los Angeles, CA 90024
Phone: (310)825-6561
John Robert, Research Assoc.

Research Activities and Fields: Radiological science and its application to diagnosis and treatment of catastrophic diseases, involving such techniques as magnetic resonance imaging (MRI), internal radiation management of carcinomatous lesions, vascular occlusion with ferrosilicone in tumor management, and cobalt source gamma irradiation of brain tumors.

University of California, Los Angeles
UCLA-DOE Laboratory of Structural
   Biology and Molecular Medicine
See: Entry 2663

★11164★ University of California, San
   Francisco
Radiation Oncology Research Laboratory
1855 Folsom, Rm. MCB 200
San Francisco, CA 94103
Phone: (415)476-9084
Fax: (415)476-9069
Dr. Michael Christman, Asst.Prof.

Research Activities and Fields: Molecular genetics and biochemistry, focusing on yeast DNA topoisomerases and their relationship to nuclear structure. **E-mail Address:** christman@radonc4.ucsf.edu.

★11165★ University of Chicago
Franklin McLean Memorial Research
   Institute
5841 S. Maryland Ave.
MC 1037
Chicago, IL 60637
Phone: (312)702-6271
Fax: (312)702-5986
Prof. Robert N. Beck, Dir.

Research Activities and Fields: Application of various forms of radiant energy in treatment of cancerous and other neoplastic growth, including the biological aspects of radioactive elements and penetrating radiations in normal and diseased human beings, use of radioisotopes both as therapeutic measures and as diagnostic tools for research on cancer and fundamental life processes, and related topics in biology, metabolism, and biochemistry in vivo and in vitro. **Formerly:** Argonne Cancer Research Hospital.

★11166★ University of Florida
Cardiovascular Laser Lab
1600 SW Archer Rd.
Gainesville, FL 32610
Phone: (904)395-0457
Dr. Richard Conti, Chief

Research Activities and Fields: Laser guidance systems for equipment used to clear blocked blood vessels.

University of Florida
NMR Imaging and Spectroscopy In Vivo
Resource
See: Entry 2485

★ 11167 ★ **University of Florida**
Radiation Oncology Clinic
Shands Cancer Center
PO Box 100385
Gainesville, FL 32610-0385
Phone: (904)395-0287
Fax: (904)395-0546
Dr. Nancy Mendenhall, Dept.Ch.

Research Activities and Fields: Cancer and radiation therapy and treatment.

★ 11168 ★ **University of Iowa**
Radiation Research Laboratory
14 Medical Laboratories
Iowa City, IA 52242
Phone: (319)335-8019
Fax: (319)335-8049

Research Activities and Fields: Radiation effects, tumor biology, and free radical biology.

★ 11169 ★ **University of Kentucky**
Radiation Therapy Oncology Center
Medical Center
800 Rose St.
Lexington, KY 40536
Phone: (606)323-6486
Fax: (606)257-4931
Mohammed Mohiuddin, M.D., Dir.

Research Activities and Fields: Radiation oncology research, participates in national cooperative group studies, RTOG, SWOG, NSABP, and GOG. Studies brain, bowel, head and neck cancer, and chemotherapy. Conducts research on radiation therapy, cancer treatment using radiation, hyperthermia, and chemotherapy.

★ 11170 ★ **University of Missouri—**
Columbia
Radiation Oncology Program
Alis Fifchel Cancer Center
115 Business Loop 70 W.
Columbia, MO 65203
Phone: (314)882-2100
Fax: (314)882-8817
Steven Westgate, Contact

Research Activities and Fields: Clinical protocols; national multi-institutional studies for cancer problems. **Formerly:** Cooperative Radiation Therapy Program.

★ 11171 ★ **University of New Mexico**
Center for Non-Invasive Diagnosis
1201 Yale Blvd. NE
Albuquerque, NM 87131
Phone: (505)377-6636
Fax: (505)277-9494
Dr. Nicholas A. Matwiyoff, Dir.

Research Activities and Fields: Nuclear magnetic resonance, cardiology, oncology, and neurology, especially as applied to cancer.

★ 11172 ★ **University of Pennsylvania**
Metabolic Magnetic Resonance Research
and Computing Center
Dept. of Radiology
Blockley Hall Basement
Philadelphia, PA 19104-6021
Phone: (215)898-2044
Fax: (215)573-2113
John S. Leigh, Ph.D., Dir.

Research Activities and Fields: Performs in vivo monitoring of specific metabolites in localized regions of tissues and organs in humans utilizing multinuclear magnetic resonance spectroscopy and metabolic imaging; develops targeted magnetite-based contrast agents for gene therapy and diagnosis; and develops techniques for near infrared optical imaging and spectroscopy in humans. **Publications:** Newsletter.

★ 11173 ★ **University of Pennsylvania**
Pendergrass Diagnostic Radiology
Laboratories
School of Medicine
Dept. of Radiology
Philadelphia, PA 19104
Phone: (215)662-6630
Fax: (215)349-5115
Harold L. Kundel, M.D., Dir.

Research Activities and Fields: Diagnostic imaging, emphasizing digital computers, computed tomography, ultrasound, radiography, and nuclear magnetic resononce (NMR). The Laboratories study the radiologic/physiologic correlation and the basic biology of NMR imaging.

★ 11174 ★ **University of Rochester**
Rochester Center for Biomedical
Ultrasound
309 Hopeman Engineering Bldg.
Rochester, NY 14627
Phone: (716)275-9542
Fax: (716)473-0486
Prof. Kevin J. Parker, Dir.

Research Activities and Fields: Ultrasonic diagnosis, including imaging and Doppler ultrasound; ultrasonic treatment, including diathermy and the treatment of glaucoma and kidney and gall stones ultrasonic biophysics, including acoustic cavitation, generation and detection of ultrasound, tissue characterization, attenuation and scattering, shock fields, and nonlinear sound propagation; and biological effects of ultrasound. Also conducts research to establish safety limits for the use of ultrasound and to discover new applications, including new contrast agents. **Publications:** Annual Report. **E-mail Address:** parker@ee.rochester.edu.

★ 11175 ★ **University of Texas**
Southwestern Medical Center at Dallas
Mary Nell and Ralph B. Rogers Magnetic
Resonance Center
5801 Forest Park Rd.
Dallas, TX 75235-9085
Phone: (214)648-5886
Fax: (214)648-5881
Craig Malloy, M.D., Dir.

Research Activities and Fields: Nuclear magnetic resonance (NMR) spectroscopy and imaging for the analysis of metabolism in various

small animal and tissue culture models, including high energy phosphate metabolism, intracellular cations, intermediary metabolism, and perfusion. **Formerly:** Biomedical Magnetic Resonance Center.

★ 11176 ★ **University of Utah**
Dixon Laser Institute
391 Chipeta Way, Ste. G
Salt Lake City, UT 84108
Phone: (801)581-8201
Fax: (801)585-3098
R. Kim Davis, M.D., Dir.

Research Activities and Fields: Basic and applied laser research, including applications of lasers in medicine, industry, and the military. Biomedical studies focus on gastroenterology, cardiology, otolaryngology, obstetrics-gynecology, urology, genetics, microsurgery, dentistry, and photodynamic therapy. In association with the Vanderbildt University Free Electron Laser Lab, the Institute is investigating the development and application of free electron laser technology in medicine and materials science. **Formerly:** Endoscopic and Laser Surgery Unit (1984); Laser Institute.

★ 11177 ★ **University of Washington**
Diagnostic Imaging Sciences Center
Dept. of Radiology
SB-05
Seattle, WA 98195
Phone: (206)543-0873
Fax: (206)543-3495
James Nelson, M.D., Dir.

Research Activities and Fields: Diagnostic imaging, including PET, NMR spectroscopy and imaging, nucle ar medicine imaging and therapy, x-ray physics, ultrasound imaging, physiology, including angio-intervention techniques, image processing, and contrast media testing. **Formerly:** Imaging Research Laboratory (1990).

★ 11178 ★ **Washington University**
Mallinckrodt Institute of Radiology
510 S. Kingshighway Blvd.
St. Louis, MO 63110
Phone: (314)362-2866
Fax: (314)362-1907
Ronald G. Evens, M.D., Dir.

Research Activities and Fields: Radiological diagnostic, treatment, research, and training center including nuclear medicine, radiation oncology, radiation sciences, and diagnostic radiology. The diagnostic radiology division is comprised of seven sections: abdominal, cardiac, chest, computer, musculoskeletal, pediatric, and neuroradiology. Maintains laboratories for research in digital image processing, computer sciences, nuclear medicine, radiation oncology, cancer biology, diagnostic radiology, and magnetic resonance imaging. **Publications:** *Focal Spot* (three per year).

★ 11179 ★ **Wayne State University**
MR Center
Harper Hospital
3990 John R Rd.
Detroit, MI 48201
Phone: (313)745-1395
Fax: (313)993-0233
Dr. Jeffrey L. Evelhoch, Res.Dir.

Research Activities and Fields: Evaluates the potential for NMR (nuclear magnetic resonance) spectroscopy and imaging to provide predictors of response to chemotherapeutic drugs. **E-mail Address:** evel-hoch@onegate.rol.wayne.edu.

Chapter 57
Reproduction & Family Planning

Foundations & Other Funding Organizations

Private Foundations

A. V. Hunter Trust
See: Entry 23

Aaron and Lillie Straus Foundation
See: Entry 25

★ 11180 ★ **Albert A. List Foundation**
998 Fifth Ave.
New York, NY 10028
Phone: (212)535-8002
Olga List Mack, President

Foundation Philosophy: The foundation has selected six focus areas and has already committed 95% of the total giving for the next three to five years. The focus areas are countering the religious right; energy and the environment; first amendment rights; censorship; reproductive health and rights; and governmental accountability in Israel. The remaining 5% of funds is already committed in honor of the founder, Albert A. List. **Giving Priorities:** In 1993, approximately 40% of funding went to civic and public affairs, primarily supporting civil rights causes. International funds received 33% of funding including the two highest grants of $175,000 each to the New Israel Fund; religious concerns, 8%; social services, 8%; and environmental organizations, 7%; The remaining support went to the arts, educational institutions, and health care. **Typical Health-Related Recipients:** Clinics/Medical Centers, Family Planning. **Geographic Distribution:** Principally to national organizations.

Blumenthal Foundation
See: Entry 70

★ 11181 ★ **Buffett Foundation**
222 Kiewit Plz.
Omaha, NE 68131
Phone: (402)451-6011
Allen Greenburg, Director

Foundation Philosophy: The Buffet Foundation makes most of its grants to social service organizations. Planned parenthood makes up the majority of the giving. The foundation also contributes to international relief organizations, including health care and development projects. Civic affairs is a secondary interest, with support to immigration reform and civic institutes. Other recipient areas also are considered for support. **Giving Priorities:** In fiscal 1993, the foundation awarded 34% of its total giving to social service organizations, including multiple grants to Planned Parenthood. Another 34% of support went to international organizations primarily in the area of population concerns. Civic groups received 14% of funds; educational institutions, 12%; and health care, 2%. The remainder went to religious organizations and the arts. **Typical Health-Related Recipients:** Clinics/Medical Centers, Family Planning, Medical Education, Public Health. **Geographic Distribution:** Only gives in Northeast United States.

★ 11182 ★ **Burdine Johnson Foundation**
760 Southpark One Bldg.
1701 Directors Blvd.
Austin, TX 78744-1066
Phone: (512)441-1588
Robert C. Giberson, Trustee

Foundation Philosophy: The Burdine Johnson Foundation primarily supports religious, private, and secondary education. Other interests include the performing arts, family planning, and civic affairs. **Giving Priorities:** In 1993, the foundation gave 74% of its funding to education. The foundation's largest grant totaled $438,200 and went to St. Stephen's Episcopal School in Texas. The arts received 21% of the giving. Social services accounted for 4% of the funding, supporting Planned Parenthood and centers for battered women, rape crisis, and senior citizens. The remaining 1% was divided between international affairs, health care and civic affairs. **Typical Health-Related Recipients:** Cancer, Domestic Violence, Family Planning, Medical Education, Medical Research, Sexual Abuse, Single-Disease Health Associations. **Geographic Distribution:** Focus on Texas.

★ 11183 ★ **Cameron Baird Foundation**
Box 564
Hamburg, NY 14075
Phone: (716)845-6000
Brian D. Baird, Trustee

Foundation Philosophy: The Cameron Baird Foundation makes most of its grants in the areas of the arts, civic affairs, and education. Arts funding favors musical performances in Buffalo, NY. Funding for civic affairs emphasizes the environment. Educational giving focuses on minority scholarships. The foundation funds a variety of other interests, such as family planning and youth organizations. **Giving Priorities:** In 1993, the foundation awarded 43% of funding to the arts. Educational institutions received 15%; civic affairs, 12%; and social services, 12%. Environmental concerns received 7%; international affairs, 7%; religion, 2%; and health care, 1%. **Typical Health-Related Recipients:** Family Planning, Hospices, People with Disabilities. **Geographic Distribution:** Emphasis on the Buffalo, NY, area.

Chichester duPont Foundation
See: Entry 98

Crestlea Foundation
See: Entry 120

David M. Whitney Fund
See: Entry 131

★ 11184 ★ **Erik E. and Edith H. Bergstrom Foundation**
PO Box 126
Palo Alto, CA 94302-0126
Phone: (415)323-0596
Erik E. Bergstrom, President

Foundation Philosophy: The foundation primarily supports projects focusing on family planning and reproductive health issues in Latin America. **Giving Priorities:** In fiscal 1992, the foundation contributed 98% of its total funding to international organizations. The remaining funds supported social service organizations and civic groups. **Typical Health-Related Recipients:** Family Planning. **Geographic Distribution:** U.S.-based organizations operating in Latin America.

★ 11185 ★ General Service Foundation
411 E Main St.
Ste. 205
Aspen, CO 81611
Phone: (303)920-6834
Fax: (303)920-4578
Robert W. Musser, President

Foundation Philosophy: The current interests of the foundation are international peace, reproductive health and rights, and resources. **Giving Priorities:** In 1994, the foundation gave approximately 59% of total contributions to international affairs. Civic concerns received about 17% of total contributions; environmental programs, 11%; social services, 7%; and educational institutions, 6%. **Typical Health-Related Recipients:** Family Planning. **Geographic Distribution:** Emphasis on national organizations; internationally to Mexico, Central and Latin America, and the Caribbean.

George Gund Foundation
See: Entry 217

Harry and Grace Steele Foundation
See: Entry 252

★ 11186 ★ Huber Foundation
PO Box 277
Rumson, NJ 07760
Phone: (908)872-2322
Lorraine Barnhart, Asst. Sec. and Exec. Dir.

Foundation Philosophy: The foundation focuses its grant making on "the issues of reproductive freedom, population education, and family planning." **Giving Priorities:** In 1993, the foundation gave approximately 40% of its contributions to social service organizations. Civic affairs organizations received 39% of giving. International organizations, exclusively groups concerned with population issues, received 10%. Health care received 5%; religious concerns, 3%; education, 1%; environmental causes, 1%; and the arts received the remainder. **Typical Health-Related Recipients:** Clinics/Medical Centers, Family Planning, Health Organizations, Hospitals. **Geographic Distribution:** Emphasis on national organizations and regional affiliates.

★ 11187 ★ Jessie Smith Noyes Foundation
16 E 34th St., 22nd Fl.
New York, NY 10016
Phone: (212)684-6577
Fax: (212)689-6549
Stephen Viederman, President

Foundation Philosophy: Currently, the foundation funds projects that promote environmentally sound approaches to development, and that address ground water and toxics, sustainable agriculture, and reproductive rights. The foundation favors programs that deal with the connections between these problems and their global implications, especially activities that have a potentially widespread impact. The population program seeks to promote quality reproductive health care as a human right. Priorities are to build local leadership and to illuminate the relationships between human fertility, the role of women, economic development, and the environment. Reproductive rights in North America are also a focus, especially programs assisting

women of color. **Giving Priorities:** In 1993, the foundation gave approximately 27% of its contributions to one of its four program areas, Reproductive Rights, which includes support for domestic and international groups concerned with women's affairs and civil rights. Another program area, Water and Toxics received 26% of funds. In the foundation's Related Interests program, it contributed 26% of total program grants. Sustainable Agriculture received 21%. In addition to its program grants, the foundation also makes annual contributions to preselected charities, discretionary grants, and membership contributions. **Typical Health-Related Recipients:** Family Planning. **Geographic Distribution:** National and Latin America.

John D. and Catherine T. MacArthur Foundation
See: Entry 7230

★ 11188 ★ Lynn R. and Karl E. Prickett Fund
PO Box 20124
Greensboro, NC 27420
Phone: (910)274-5471
Diana Davis, Account Administrator

Foundation Philosophy: The foundation generally supports civic affairs, social service groups, and education. Civic affairs funding favors civil rights, the environment, a municipalities. Funding for social services emphasizes community relations and planned parenthood. Educational funding favors funds, higher education, and political education. The arts and health care also are supported. **Giving Priorities:** In fiscal 1992, civic affairs received 56% of total funding, including grants of $70,000 each to the Foundation of Greater Greensboro, NC, and the American Civil Liberties Union Foundation of Northern California in San Francisco. Social service organizations received 23%, with major support to the Center for Individual Recovery Services in Fortuna, CA, and family planning services. Educational institutions received 14%; the arts, 4%; and health care services, 2%. **Typical Health-Related Recipients:** Family Planning, Single-Disease Health Associations, Substance Abuse. **Geographic Distribution:** National.

Offield Family Foundation
See: Entry 415

Prospect Hill Foundation
See: Entry 434

★ 11189 ★ Robert Sterling Clark Foundation
112 E 64th St.
New York, NY 10021
Phone: (212)308-0411
Fax: (212)755-2133
Margaret C. Ayers, Executive Director

Foundation Philosophy: The foundation concentrates its funding in three fields. Interest in improving the performance of public institutions is premised on the belief that a foundation can play an important role by working with government agencies, and by supporting organizations that monitor government actions. The foundation favors initiatives to monitor human services

delivery programs, to protect the environment in accordance with federal and state mandates, to promote affordable housing and encourage the development of New York's economic base, and to improve the effectiveness and accountability of local and state agencies. The foundation has expanded its arts program to include support for advocacy efforts at the national level with a focus on freedom of expression in the arts. The third area of foundation interest is reproductive rights. It primarily funds organizations working at the national level to ensure continued access to family planning services. The foundation has stated that it has begun to make grants to pro-choice organizations working in selected states in addition to its support for national pro-choice organizations. **Giving Priorities:** In fiscal 1993, civic affairs received approximately 35% of total contributions, most of which went to support reproductive rights analysis and litigation, womens issues, and other public policy concerns. Social service organizations, primarily family planning programs, received 22%. The arts received about 20%, including the foundation's highest grant of $100,000 for the National Cultural Alliance, New York, NY. Environmental causes received 7%, and education received 6% of giving. Religious groups and international affairs each received 4%. Health care received the remaining funds. **Typical Health-Related Recipients:** Family Planning, Long-Term Care. **Geographic Distribution:** Primarily New York City for the arts and civic causes and nationally for reproductive rights.

Rockefeller Foundation
See: Entry 460

★ 11190 ★ Scherman Foundation
16 E 52nd St., Ste. 601
New York, NY 10022-5306
Phone: (212)832-3086
Sandra Silverman, Executive Director

Foundation Philosophy: The foundation's main interests are conservation and the environment, disarmament and peace, family planning, human rights and liberties, social welfare, and the arts. **Giving Priorities:** In 1993, the foundation gave about 25% of its funding to civic and public affairs, with an emphasis on legal aid, national and international family planning policy, human rights, and disarmament and peace. International oganizations, primarily those that deal with population issues, received about 21%. Social services, particularly family planning programs, received 12%. The arts and humanities also received 12% of foundation giving. Environmental causes, including resource conservation programs, received 11%. Educational programs received 9% of total funding. Religion received about 7%, including the foundation's highest grant of $130,000 for the United Jewish Appeal -- Federation of Jewish Philanthropies, New York, NY. Health concerns (2%) and scientific interests (1%) received the remaining funds. **Typical Health-Related Recipients:** AIDS/HIV, Domestic Violence, Family Planning, Health Organizations. **Geographic Distribution:** National, with emphasis on metropolitan New York City for the arts and social welfare programs.

Shelby Cullom Davis Foundation
See: Entry 487

★ 11191 ★ **Sunnen Foundation**
7910 Manchester Ave.
St. Louis, MO 63143
Phone: (314)781-2100
Fax: (314)781-1533
Helen S. Sly, President and Director

Foundation Philosophy: Available funds are confined to programs or projects with national scope and impact to protect First Amendment rights and reproductive freedom. Grant giving in St. Louis focuses on local social service agencies and programs. **Giving Priorities:** In 1993, the foundation gave approximately 60% of funds to social service organizations. Health services and civic affairs were each awarded 14% of total giving. Educational programs and schools received 7%; religious organizations, 4%, and the arts, 1%. **Typical Health-Related Recipients:** Children's Health/Hospitals, Domestic Violence, Emergency/Ambulance Services, Family Planning, Health Organizations, Health Policy/Cost Containment, Medical Education, People with Disabilities, Single-Disease Health Associations, Speech & Hearing, Substance Abuse. **Geographic Distribution:** Principally to national organizations.

Victoria Foundation
See: Entry 3144

Wallace Alexander Gerbode Foundation
See: Entry 533

William and Flora Hewlett Foundation
See: Entry 545

William Penn Foundation
See: Entry 551

Corporate Foundations

H & R Block Foundation
See: Entry 718

Lotus Development Foundation
See: Entry 6606

Reily Foundation
See: Entry 833

Other Funding Organizations

★ 11192 ★ **AVSC International**
79 Madison Ave., 7th Fl.
New York, NY 10016-7802
Phone: (212)561-8093
Fax: (212)779-9349

Description: Sponsors research studies on medical, public health, legal, psychological, ethical, and socioeconomic aspects of voluntary sterilization and other contraceptive methods.

★ 11193 ★ **Family Planning International Assistance**
810 7th Ave.
New York, NY 10019
Phone: (212)261-4762
Fax: (212)247-6274
Dr. Daniel R. Weintraub, VP

Description: Provides financial, technical, and commodity assistance to organizations in developing countries interested in family planning programs.

★ 11194 ★ **Population Council**
1 Dag Hammarskjold Plaza
New York, NY 10017
Phone: (212)339-0500
Fax: (212)755-6052
Margaret Catley Carlson, Pres.

Description: Sponsors postdoctoral training in biomedical research relating to human reproductive physiology and grants fellowships for advanced degree training in population-related studies.

National & International Organizations

★ 11195 ★ **Advocates for Youth**
1025 Vermont Ave. NW, Ste. 200
Washington, DC 20005
Phone: (202)347-5700
Fax: (202)347-2263
Margaret Pruitt Clark, Exec.Dir. & Pres.

Founded: 1980. **Description:** Objectives are to: reduce the incidence of unintended teenage pregnancy and childbearing and promote adolescent health through education; to prevent the proliferation of the human immunodeficiency virus (HIV) among adolescents; motivate teens to think and act responsibly about birth control and parenting; conduct programs and advocacy campaigns to assure minors' access to family planning information and services. Provides technical assistance on program planning, implementation, and evaluation of sexuality education in the U.S. and, through International Center on Adolescent Fertility, to health, education, and social service workers worldwide. Operates Support Center for School-Based Health Care and media project. Monitors legislative activities for various organizations concerned with youth issues. Conducts research to evaluate promising prevention strategies. Compiles statistics; maintains speakers' bureau. **Publications:** *Linkx*, quarterly. Newsletter. Details school-based health care. • *Options*, quarterly. Newsletter. • *Passages*, quarterly. • Reports. Also publishes fact sheets, resource guides, and life planning education curricula. **Formerly:** Center for Population Options.

★ 11196 ★ **Advocates for Youth's Media Project**
3733 Motor Ave., Ste. 204
Los Angeles, CA 90034
Phone: (310)559-5700
Fax: (310)599-5784
Jennifer Daves, Dir.

Founded: 1983. **Description:** A project of Advocates for Youth. Serves as an advisory and information resource for the entertainment industry to encourage positive and relevant messages about family planning, sexuality, and reproductive health, especially in programming directed toward adolescents. Conducts research and charitable programs. Operates speakers' bureau. **Formerly:** Center for Population Options' Media Project.

★ 11197 ★ **Alan Guttmacher Institute (AGI)**
120 Wall St., 21st Fl.
New York, NY 10005
Phone: (212)248-1111
Fax: (212)248-1951
Jeannie I. Rosoff, Pres.

Founded: 1968. **Description:** Fosters sound public policies on voluntary fertility control and population issues and encourages responsive reproductive health programs through policy analysis, public education, and research in the U.S. and internationally. Compiles statistics and conducts policy-relevant research on the provision of services relating to reproductive health care. **Publications:** Annual Report. • *Family Planning Perspectives*, bimonthly. Journal. Focuses on reproductive health issues. *Price:* $32/year for individuals; $42/year for institutions. • *International Family Planning Perspectives*, quarterly. Journal. Highlights population and reproductive health research and program achievements in developing countries. *Price:* $26/year for individuals; $36/year for institutions. • *Preventing Pregnancy, Protecting Health: A New Look at Birth Control in the U.S.*. • *Sex and America's Teenagers*. Book. Discusses teenage secual and reproductive behavior. • *Testing Positive: Sexually Transmitted Disease and the Public Health Response*. • *Washington Memo*, 20/year. Newsletter. Covers legislative developments. Monitors federal appropriations for family planning and contraceptive research. *Price:* $50/year for individuals; $60/year for institutions. **Formerly:** (1975) Center for Family Planning Program Development; (1977) Research and Development Division of Planned Parenthood Federation of America.

★ 11198 ★ **American Academy of Natural Family Planning (AANFP)**
615 S. New Ballas Rd.
St. Louis, MO 63141
Phone: (314)279-2048
Donna Vondrak, Pres.

Founded: 1982. **Members:** 300. **Description:** Individuals who participate in natural family planning instruction. (Natural family planning refers to methods that do not employ contraceptive devices of any kind, using instead the natural phases of fertility.) Seeks to improve the quality of natural family planning services by establishing specific certification and accreditation requirements for teachers and educational programs. Conducts training programs throughout the U.S. Promotes public recognition and acceptance of natural family planning; disseminates information. **Publications:** *Academy Activity*, quarterly. Newsletter. • *Certification Directory*, annual. Directory. • Membership Directory, annual.

★ 11199 ★ **American Association of Pro Life Obstetricians and Gynecologists (AAPLOG)**
850 Elm Grove Rd.
Elm Grove, WI 53122
Phone: (414)789-7984
Fax: (414)782-8788
Dan Martin, M.D., Contact

Founded: 1973. **Members:** 800. **Regional Groups:** 9. **Description:** Obstetricians and gynecologists who oppose abortions, perform no abortions, and take no part in arranging abortions. Seeks "to draw attention to the value of all human life from the moment of conception." Supports programs that assist unwed mothers who choose to have their babies. Conducts research on complications experienced by women who have had legal abortions and compiles statistics on illnesses and deaths; studies the long-range effects of abortion on fertility and reproductive capability. Offers postgraduate course on the subject of care and concern for women experiencing mental and physical trauma after abortions. **Publications:** Directory, triennial. • Newsletter, quarterly.

★ 11200 ★ **American Association of Pro-Life Pediatricians (AAPLP)**
11055 S. St. Louis Ave.
Chicago, IL 60655
Phone: (312)233-8000
E. F. Diamond, M.D., Sec.

Founded: 1978. **Members:** 620. **State Groups:** 50. **Description:** Members of the American Academy of Pediatrics interested in issues such as abortion, infanticide, and definition of death. Coordinates member activities; publicizes political trends; educates members. **Publications:** *Monograph on Fetal Pain.* Monograph. • Newsletter, quarterly. • *This Curette For Hire.* Book.

★ 11201 ★ **American Society for Reproductive Medicine (ASRM)**
1209 Montgomery Hwy.
Birmingham, AL 35216-2809
Phone: (205)978-5000
Fax: (205)978-5005
Nancy C. Hayley, Adm.Dir.

Founded: 1944. **Members:** 11,000. **Description:** Gynecologists, obstetricians, urologists, reproductive endocrinologists, veterinarians, research workers, and others interested in reproductive health in humans and animals. Seeks to extend knowledge of all aspects of fertility and problems of infertility and mammalian reproduction; provides a rostrum for the presentation of scientific studies dealing with these subjects. Offers patient resource information and placement service. **Publications:** *American Fertility Society--Membership Directory*, biennial. Membership Directory. Arranged alphabetically and geographically. *Price:* Included in membership dues. • *Fertility and Sterility*, monthly. Journal. Includes book reviews and announcements of meetings, courses, services, and employment opportunities. *Price:* Included in membership dues; $150/year nonmembers; $140/year institutions. • *Fertility News*, quarterly. Newsletter. Includes new member and regional postgraduate course listings. *Price:* Included in membership dues. Also publishes syllabi used for postgraduate courses. **Formerly:** American Fertility Society; (1966) American Society for the Study of Sterility.

★ 11202 ★ **Association for Improvements in the Maternity Services (AIMS)**
40 Kingswood Ave.
London NW6 6LS, England
Phone: 181 9605585
Sandar Warshal, Contact

Founded: 1960. **Members:** 1,000. **Local Groups:** 10. **Languages:** English. **Description:** Parents and health care professionals. Campaigns to improve maternity services. **Publications:** *AIMS Journal*, quarterly. Journal. • Pamphlets, periodic.

★ 11203 ★ **Association Ivoirienne de Bien-Etre Familial (AIBEF)**
Treichville
Bd. Giscard d'Estaing
BP 5315
Abidjan 01, Cote d'Ivoire
Phone: 251811
Fax: 251868
Paul Agodio, Exec.Dir.

Founded: 1979. **Members:** 650. **Languages:** French. **Description:** Promotes advances in women's health care and family planning programs.

★ 11204 ★ **Association of Reproductive Health Professionals (ARHP)**
2401 Pennsylvania Ave. NW, Ste. 350
Washington, DC 20037-1718
Phone: (202)466-3825
Fax: (202)466-3826
Dennis J. Barbour, J.D., Pres.

Founded: 1963. **Members:** 1,800. **Description:** Professionals in reproductive health, including obstetricians, gynecologists, family practitioners, pediatricians, nurse clinicians, researchers, educators, and administrators. Interested in abortion, AIDS, contraception, cancer, family planning, genitourinary diseases, infertility, obstetrics and gynecology, reproductive medicine, sexual health, and sexually transmitted diseases. Maintains speakers' bureau; conducts educational programs. **Publications:** *American Journal of Gynecologic Health*, bimonthly. Journal. • *Health and Sexuality*, quarterly. Newsletter. • Journals. • Proceedings. • Videos. **Formerly:** (1973) American Association of Parenthood Physicians; (1982) Association of Planned Parenthood Physicians; (1987) Association of Planned Parenthood Professionals.

Association Rwandaise pour le Bien-Etre Familial (ARBEF)
See: Entry 9635

Association of Teachers of Maternal and Child Health (ATMCH)
See: Entry 3191

★ 11205 ★ **AVSC International (AVSC)**
79 Madison Ave., 7th Fl.
New York, NY 10016-7802
Phone: (212)561-8093
Fax: (212)779-9349
Hugo Hoogenboom, Pres.

Founded: 1975. **Members:** 7,000. **Description:** Seeks to provide women and men with access to voluntary and safe contraception. Helps countries and institutions develop, improve, and expand systems for the provision of clinic-based contraception services. **Publications:** *AVSC News*, quarterly. Newsletter. *Price:* Free, for members only. • Brochures. Also publishes clinical guides and resources for family planning counseling for professionals. **Formerly:** (1985) Association for Voluntary Sterilization; (1993) World Federation of Health Agencies for the Advancement of Voluntary Surgical Contraception; (1994) Association for Voluntary Surgical Contraception.

★ 11206 ★ **Canadian Fertility and Andrology Society**
2065 Alexandre-de-Seve, Ste. 409
Montreal, PQ, Canada H2L 2W5
Phone: (514)524-9009
Fax: (514)524-2163
Susan Orr-Mongeau, Exec. Officer

Founded: 1954. **Members:** 400. **Description:** Medical professionals, scientists, and others with an interest in human fertility and andrology. Serves as a forum for exchange of information.

★ 11207 ★ **Caribbean Family Planning Affiliation (CFPA)**
PO Box 419
Factory and Airport Rds.
St. Johns, Antigua-Barbuda
Phone: (809)462-4170
Fax: (809)462-4171
Dr. Tirbani P. Jagdeo

Founded: 1971. **Members:** 21. **Languages:** English. **Description:** Family planning associations in Caribbean countries. Works to increase awareness and acceptance of family planning in the region. Advocates family planning as a basic human right and assists member governments in incorporating family planning into maternal and child health care services. Develops training programs for adolescents and young mothers. Studies demographic, sociological, and health issues. Offers training to teachers, family planning workers, and clinicians. Produces and distributes audiovisual educational materials. Compiles statistics. Offers research programs; sponsors competitive. Operates Documentation Centre for students, teachers, and researchers. Offers educational programs. **Publications:** *Annual Report.* • *Current Awareness Bulletin*, semiannual. Lists current data on population and health issues in the Caribbean. • *Selected Bibliographies*, annual. Also produces pamphlets, videos, booklets, and posters.

★ 11208 ★ **Center for Study of Multiple Birth (CSMB)**
333 E. Superior St., Ste. 464
Chicago, IL 60611
Phone: (312)266-9093
Louis Keith, M.D., Pres.

Founded: 1977. **Description:** Medical research foundation concerned with the study of multiple birth and the care of multiple birth children. Disseminates information on the medical risks of multiple birth. Encourages funding for the support of medical and social research. Serves as resource center for the media and the public. **Formerly:** (1981) Center for Study of Multiple Gestation.

★ 11209 ★ **Chinese Association for Birth Planning and Childhood Health Improvement Sciences**
Bldg. 12, Block 2
Anhua Xili
Chaoyang District
Beijing 100011, People's Republic of China
Phone: 1 4213546
Xinzhong Qian

Founded: 1979. **Members:** 12. **Languages:** Chinese. **Description:** Family planning and child health care consulting service to departments of central and local governments. Provides counseling and information. Conducts research; compiles data.

★ 11210 ★ **CHOICE**
1233 Locust St., Fl. 3
Philadelphia, PA 19107
Phone: (215)985-3355
Fax: (215)985-3369
Lisa Shulock, Exec.Dir.

Founded: 1971. **Members:** 1,500. **Description:** Concerned with reproductive health care, child care, and HIV/AIDS. Goal of CHOICE, which began as an outgrowth of the Clergy Consultation Service, is to make available, with dignity and concern, high-quality medical and social services to all people at every economic level. Operates resource information hotlines; provides training and consulting services. Conducts training programs. **Publications:** *The Choice is Yours*, periodic. Directory. Directory of HIV testing services. • *Where to Find*, periodic. Directory. Lists family planning services. *Price:* Free. **Also Known As:** Concern for Health Options - Information, Care and Education.

★ 11211 ★ **Coalition for the Medical Rights of Women (CMRW)**
558 Lapp St.
San Francisco, CA 94110
Phone: (415)647-2694

Founded: 1977. **Members:** 1,200. **Description:** Individuals interested in reproductive rights; health organizations. Conducts community education and activism concerning reproductive rights including abortion, sterilization, and prenatal care. Provides speakers for high schools, community colleges, and universities. Maintains speakers' bureau. **Publications:** *CDRR News*, quarterly. *Price:* $25/year. Also publishes fact sheets. **Formerly:** (1994) Committee to Defend Reproductive Rights.

★ 11212 ★ **Couple to Couple League (CCL)**
PO Box 111184
Cincinnati, OH 45211
Phone: (513)471-2000
John F. Kippley, Pres.

Founded: 1971. **Local Groups:** 450. **Description:** Assists married and engaged couples interested in natural family planning (a method of spacing pregnancies through reliance on the woman's natural fertility cycle). Believes natural birth control strengthens family bonds and is healthier and more morally acceptable than artificial birth control devices. Sponsors local teaching groups where couples are taught basic natural family planning techniques. Provides special training program for those who wish to become CCL teaching couples. Promotes premarital chastity through speakers and materials. **Publications:** *The Art of Natural Family Planning, Breastfeeding and Natural Child Spacing.* • *CCL Family Foundations*, bimonthly. Newsletter. • *Fertility, Cycles and Nutrition.* • Manual. • *Sex and the Marriage Covenant.* Also publishes workbooks.

★ 11213 ★ **Danish Family Planning Association (DFPA)**
(Foreningen for Familieplanlaegning — FF)
Aurehojvej 2
Sex 09 Samfund
DK-2900 Hellerup, Denmark
Phone: 31625688
Fax: 31620282
Nell Rasmussen, Exec.Dir.

Founded: 1956. **Members:** 17. **Languages:** Danish. **Description:** Health, social, and educational societies and institutions in Denmark. Promotes improved education and research in family planning. Provides contraceptives and contraceptive information to individuals and family planning professionals in an effort to increase family planning practices and lessen the need for abortions. Operates 2 family planning clinics; offers counseling services. Conducts sex education classes for young students in connection with compulsory integrated sex education in Danish schools. Distributes materials on contraception, abortion, sexually transmitted diseases, and AIDS; holds demonstrations, seminars, and workshops. **Publications:** *Annual Report.* • Brochures, periodic. • *Information and Debate*, quarterly. • Pamphlets, periodic. • *Sex and Health*, semiannual. **Also Known As:** Association for Family Planning.

★ 11214 ★ **DES Action Canada**
PO Box 233, Snowdon
Montreal, PQ, Canada H3X 3T4
Phone: (514)482-3204
Fax: (514)482-1445
Dawn Kiddell, Exec.Dir.

Founded: 1982. **Members:** 1,000. **Regional Groups:** 11. **Languages:** English, French. **Description:** Persons who have been exposed to the drug DES (diethylstilbestrol) and/or concerned individuals. Seeks to detect, instruct, support, and defend the rights of people endangered by DES. Seeks to prevent health problems caused by DES and similar health concerns, especially in the field of reproductive health care. Provides informative written material as well as audio-visual aids. Offer physician referrals and peer counseling. **Publications:** *Breast Cancer: Risk, Protection, Detection, and Treatment*, periodic. Pamphlet. • *Bulletin DES*, quarterly. Bulletin. • *DES Action Canada Newsletter*, quarterly. Newsletter. • *Fertility and Pregnancy Guide for DES Daughters and Sons*, periodic. Pamphlet. • *Nursing Curriculum*, periodic. Pamphlet.

★ 11215 ★ **Family of the Americas Foundation (FAF)**
PO Box 1170
Dunkirk, MD 20754-1170
Phone: (301)627-3346
Free: 800-443-3395
Fax: (301)627-0847
Mercedes Wilson, Pres.

Founded: 1977. **Members:** 270. **Description:** Promotes teaching of the Ovulation Method of birth regulation in which a woman is taught to recognize the fertile phase of her menstrual cycle by analyzing the appearance of mucus secreted from the cervix. Maintains permanent teacher training centers; certifies instructors of the method. Conducts regional, national, and international workshops to present new scientific information concerning the method and to train new and existing teachers; assists in the planning and implementation of local workshops. Sponsors teacher training and preparation of instructional materials for developing countries. Holds conferences to educate the public about the use of natural family planning in developed and developing countries. Participates in conferences with medical, religious, government, and educational personnel. Assists parents in providing effective sex education for their children; teaches adolescents about fertility and the importance of accepting responsibility for their sexual behavior. Provides referral services and technical assistance; maintains library of natural family planning reference materials. Offers standard teacher certification programs for Master Teachers and Master Trainers. **Publications:** *Love and Fertility.* • *OM Teaching Posters and Client Charting Kit.* • *The Ovulation Method.* Film. **Formerly:** (1982) World Organization of the Ovulation Method-Billings, U.S.A..

★ 11216 ★ **Family Health International (FHI)**
PO Box 13950
Durham, NC 27709
Phone: (919)544-7040
Fax: (919)544-7261
Dr. Theodore King

Founded: 1971. **Members:** 300. **Description:** Biomedical researchers and technical assistants. Promotes increased availability, safety, effectiveness, acceptability, and ease of using family planning methods. Works to improve the delivery of voluntary fertility planning and primary health care services, and reduce the spread of sexually transmitted diseases, especially HIV infection. Conducts, analyzes, and disseminates research on contraception and distribution of family planning services. Supports a program of contraceptive safety and health records. Maintains library of 6000 monographs, journals, and reports. Operates computerized services. **Publications:** *Biennial Report. Price:* Free. • *Family Health International--Network*, quarterly. Journal. Covers reproductive health and family planning for health care personnel and policymakers in developing countries. *Price:* Free. • *Publications Catalog*, annual. **Formerly:** (1982) International Fertility Research Program; (1983) Family Health International/International Fertility Research Program.

★11217★ Family Planning Association of Kenya (FPAK)
PO Box 30581
Nairobi, Kenya
Phone: 2 215676
Fax: 2 213757

Founded: 1961. **Languages:** English. **Description:** Encourages the use of more effective methods of birth control and family planning. Establishes family planning clinics; provides educational services for rural citizens. Conducts seminars and film presentations.

★11218★ Family Planning Association of Liberia (FPAL)
PO Box 938
Monrovia, Liberia
Phone: 224649
Philip S.K. Suakweli, Exec.Dir.

Founded: 1956. **Local Groups:** 2. **Languages:** English. **Description:** Promotes enhanced awareness of family planning services. Believes that planned parenthood is a basic human right. Sponsors educational programs. Conducts research. **Publications:** *Directory*, periodic. Directory. • *FPAL Informer Magazine*, annual. Magazine.

★11219★ Family Planning International Assistance (FPIA)
810 7th Ave.
New York, NY 10019
Phone: (212)261-4762
Fax: (212)247-6274
Dr. Daniel R. Weintraub, VP

Founded: 1973. **Description:** Provides financial, technical, and commodity assistance to organizations in developing countries interested in family planning programs. **Publications:** Annual Report.

★11220★ Fertility Research Foundation (FRF)
877 Park Ave.
New York, NY 10021
Phone: (212)744-5500
Fax: (212)744-6536
Masood A. Khatamee, M.D., Exec.Dir.

Founded: 1962. **Description:** Specializes in human reproduction. Provides therapeutic, diagnostic, and consultation service for childless couples. Conducts comprehensive infertility surveys which include: endoscopy, sperm antibodies determination, bacteriological assessment, endocrine studies, laboratory facilities for complete hormone assays, surgical correction of genital diseases, artificial donor insemination, and ovulation induction. Maintains research projects in human reproduction pertaining to: the study of influence of mycoplasma on infertility; the relationship of prostaglandins and infertility; the study of genetic defects and dermatoglyphics; immunology research; sperm physiology and migration; ovum transplantation. Conducts educational programs for practicing physicians, residents, and medical students in infertility and education of the public about the human reproductive processes. **Formerly:** (1967) New York Fertility Institute; (1981) New York Fertility Research Foundation.

Gabriela Commission on Women's Health and Reproductive Rights (GCWHRR)
See: Entry 9650

★11221★ Infertility Awareness Association of Canada (IAAC) (Association Canadienne de Sensibilisation a l'Infertilite)
774 Echo Dr., Ste. 523
Ottawa, ON, Canada K7S 5N8
Phone: (613)730-1322
Fax: (613)730-1323
Trish Maynard, Coord.

Founded: 1990. **Members:** 600. **Regional Groups:** 5. **Languages:** English, French. **Description:** Individuals and organizations working to increase the awareness and understanding of the causes, treatments, and the emotional impact of infertility. Represents the interests of those with infertility concerns. Collaborates with infertility support groups to advance the organization's agenda. Disseminates information through media interviews, seminars, and educational materials. Maintains resource center and speakers' bureau. **Publications:** *Infertility Awareness*, bimonthly. Newsletter.

★11222★ Institute for Reproductive Health (IRH)
433 S. Beverly Dr.
Beverly Hills, CA 90212
Phone: (310)553-5821
Free: 800-953-5821
Fax: (310)553-5725
Vicki Hufnagel, M.D., Med.Dir.

Description: Persons supporting informed, responsible health care for women and working toward the passage of regulatory legislation for informed consent. Conducts research and disseminates information on women's health issues including: technological advances, education, social and behavioral sciences, and belief systems; uterine endocrinology, female reconstructive surgery, sexually-transmitted diseases and their effect on female fertility; substance abuse and obstetrical problems; analysis of risks and losses due to hysterectomy and surgical abuses against women. **Publications:** *Women's Health quarterly*, quarterly.

★11223★ International Dalkon Shield Victims Education Association (IDEA)
212 Pioneer Bldg.
Seattle, WA 98104
Phone: (206)329-1371
Fax: (206)623-4251
Constance Miller, Treas.

Founded: 1986. **Members:** 2,000. **State Groups:** 2. **Description:** Women who have contracted illnesses and/or been disabled through use of the Dalkon Shield intrauterine contraceptive device; their supporters. Promotes public education about the dangers of using the Dalkon Shield. Disseminates information regarding Dalkon Shield injuries, claim resolution, and related topics. Offers seminars. Maintains speakers' bureau.

★11224★ International Federation of Fertility Societies (IFFS)
Rotunda Hospital, RCSI Dept. OB/GYN
Dublin 1, Ireland
Phone: 1 727599
Fax: 431 5972149
Prof. Robert F. Harrison, Sec.Gen.

Founded: 1953. **Languages:** English. **Description:** National fertility and sterility societies. Conducts congresses to study human reproduction and problems relating to fertility and sterility in humans and animals. **Publications:** *International Journal of Fertility*, quarterly. Journal.

★11225★ International Planned Parenthood Federation (IPPF) (Federation Internationale pour la Planification Familiale — IPPF)
Regent's College
Inner Circle
Regent's Park
London NW1 4NS, England
Phone: 171 4860741
Fax: 171 4877950
Dr. Halfdan Mahler, Sec.Gen.

Founded: 1952. **Members:** 107. **National Groups:** 134. **Regional Groups:** 6. **Languages:** Arabic, English, French, Spanish. **Description:** National, independent, and nongovernmental family planning associations. Works to: initiate and support family planning services throughout the world; heighten governmental and public awareness of the population problems of local communities and the world. Promotes effective family planning services in order to preserve and protect the mental and physical health of parents and their children; concerns itself with the efficacy and safety of various methods of contraception. Seeks to: create strong volunteer participation; promote family planning as a basic human right; extend and improve family planning services; meet the needs of young people; improve the status of women; increase male involvement in family planning; develop human financial and material resources; stimulate research on subjects related to human fertility and disseminate the findings of such research; encourage and coordinate training of the federation's professional workers. Offers programs that concentrate on family life, population, and sex education. Sponsors workshops and seminars. **Publications:** *Family Planning Handbook for Doctors*. Handbook. • *IPPF Annual Report*. Annual Report. • *IPPF Directory of Contraceptives*, periodic. Booklet. • *IPPF Medical Bulletin*, bimonthly. Bulletin. • *Open File*, monthly. Newsletter. • *People and the Planet*, quarterly. Magazine. • *Planned Parenthood Challenges*, semiannual. Magazine.

★11226★ International Planned Parenthood Federation, Western Hemisphere Region (IPPF/WHR)
902 Broadway, 10th Fl.
New York, NY 10010
Phone: (212)995-8800
Fax: (212)995-8853
Hernan Sanhueza, Regional Dir.

Founded: 1952. **Members:** 46. **Description:** A division of the International Planned Parenthood Federation. Independent family planning organizations in Canada, Latin America, Caribbean Islands, and the United States. Views family planning as "the expression of the human right of couples to have only the children they want and to have them when they want them." Works to extend the practice of voluntary family planning by providing information, education, and services to couples. Seeks to persuade governments to establish national family planning programs. Conducts research programs; maintains speakers' bureau; sponsors specialized education programs. **Publications:** Annual Report. • *Forum*, quarterly. Magazine. Includes calendar of events. Distributed primarily to affiliated family planning programs. Also publishes occasional monographs, studies, and position papers.

★ 11227 ★ **International Society for Immunology of Reproduction (ISIR)**
c/o University of Liverpool
Dept. of Immunology
PO Box 147
Liverpool, Merseyside L89 3BX, England
Phone: 51 7064353
Fax: 51 7065814
Peter M. Johnson, Sec.Gen.

Founded: 1976. **Members:** 250. **Regional Groups:** 12. **Description:** Scientists and physicians interested in the immunological processes involved in all aspects of reproduction. Seeks to encourage and develop research on immunological processes through scientific publications, workshops, and colloquia. **Publications:** *American Journal of Reproductive Immunology*. Journal. • *ISIR Newsletter*, semiannual. Newsletter. Provides minutes of meetings, notices of upcoming meetings, and general news updates. *Price:* Included in membership dues. • *Journal of Reproductive Immunology*. Journal.

★ 11228 ★ **International Society of Reproductive Medicine (ISRM)**
c/o Donald C. McEwen, M.D.
11 Furman Ct.
Rancho Mirage, CA 92270
Phone: (619)340-5080
Fax: (619)340-6920
Donald C. McEwen, M.D., Sec.

Founded: 1968. **Members:** 300. **Description:** Research specialists in reproductive medicine, obstetrics/gynecology, and endocrinology; associate members are laypersons interested in world population problems. Encourages basic and clinical research on the physiology of reproduction with special emphasis on the normal reproductive process, methods for enhancement of fertility, conception control, the pharmacology of steroids and polypeptides, and the immunology of reproduction. Fosters discussion and evaluation of new concepts, controversies in management of patients with reproductive disorders, and clinical relevance of advances in reproductive biology. Disseminates information and promotes continuing education for physicians and scientists. **Publications:** *Annual Proceedings*. **Formerly:** (1970) Family Planning Association of the Americas; (1980) International Family Planning Research Association.

★ 11229 ★ **International Women's Health Coalition (IWHC)**
24 E. 21st St., 5th Fl.
New York, NY 10010
Phone: (212)979-8500
Fax: (212)979-9009
Joan B. Dunlop, Pres.

Founded: 1980. **Description:** Seeks to promote and provide high quality reproductive health care for women in the Third World. Provides technical assistance, supports innovative health care projects and policy-oriented field research in Africa, Asia and Latin America. Produces public education materials. **Publications:** Reports. • *The Sexuality Connection in Reproductive Health*. Report. Explores the importance of the study of sexuality and gender-based power relations to reproductive health policies and programs. • *Special Challenges in Third World Women's Health: Reproductive Tract Infections, Cervical Cancer, and Contraceptive Safety*. Report. • *Women's Political Action and Population Policy in Three Developing Countries*. Report. **Formerly:** (1980) National Women's Health Coalition.

★ 11230 ★ **International Women's Health Coalition**
24 E. 21st St.
New York, NY 10010
Joan B. Dunlop, Pres.

Languages: English. **Description:** Works with women and men in Asia, Africa, and Latin America to secure reproductive and sexual health and rights in these regions. Supports innovative reproductive health and population control strategies stressing education; conducts lobbying activities at the national and international levels. **Publications:** *Population Policies Reconsidered: Health, Empowerment, and Rights*. Book.

★ 11231 ★ **Issue Ltd.**
509 Aldridge Rd.
Great Barr
Birmingham, W. Midlands B44 8NA, England
Phone: 121 3444414
Fax: 121 3444336
John R. Dickson, Dir.

Founded: 1976. **Members:** 6,000. **Languages:** English. **Description:** Infertile women and men. Disseminates information and provides support and counseling to infertile individuals regarding: treatment; adoption; inter-country adoption; and coping with infertility. Finances research into infertility. **Publications:** *ISSUE*, quarterly. Magazine. **Also Known As:** National Fertility Association.

★ 11232 ★ **IUD Claims Information Source (ICIS)**
PO Box 84151
Seattle, WA 98104
Phone: (206)329-1371
Fax: (206)623-4251
Constance Miller, Mng.Dir.

Founded: 1989. **Description:** Provides information and referrals to women filing lawsuits because of injuries sustained through use of an intrauterine contraceptive device (IUD). Offers professional seminars in claims filing and resolution. Maintains speakers' bureau. **Publications:** *Dalkon Shield Claims Guidebook*. • *Dalkon Shield Legal Guide*.

★ 11233 ★ **Jordanian Association for Family Planning and Protection (JAFPP)**
Abdali-Amman Commercial Center Bldg., 6th Fl.
PO Box 8066
Amman, Jordan
Phone: 6 678083
Fax: 6 674534
Mr. Basem Abu raad, Exec.Dir.

Founded: 1964. **Members:** 300. **Local Groups:** 3. **Languages:** Arabic, English. **Description:** Social workers and health care professionals in Jordan. Advocates responsible parenthood and family planning in Jordan. Operates family planning clinics and mobile units for rural areas. Offers advice to parents on issues such as child spacing, marital problems, and child rearing; encourages couples to plan children according to financial means. Provides medical assistance to couples with infertility problems and helps them to overcome the social stigma attached to infertility through counseling services. Conducts annual family planning week. Organizes family planning courses for social workers and volunteers. **Publications:** Brochures, periodic. • *Selected Lectures in Family Planning*.

★ 11234 ★ **Miscarriage Association**
Clayton Hospital
Northgate
Wakefield, W. Yorkshire WF1 3JS, England
Phone: 1924 200799
Fax: 1924 298834
Mrs. Ruth Bender Atik, Dir.

Founded: 1982. **Members:** 1,300. **Languages:** English. **Description:** Women who have had a miscarriage. Provides support and information to members and their families, professionals, students, media, and the general public. **Publications:** Booklet. Information on miscarriages. • Newsletter, quarterly.

★ 11235 ★ **Miscarriage Infant Death Stillbirth Support Group (MIDS)**
c/o Janet Tischler
16 Crescent Dr.
Parsippany, NJ 07054-1605
Phone: (201)263-6730
Janet Tischler, Founder/Pres.

Founded: 1982. **Members:** 700. **State Groups:** 2. **Local Groups:** 4. **Description:** Offers friendship and support to parents who have experienced miscarriage, infant death, or stillbirth. Provides monthly meetings, friendships, in-hospital visits, workshops, and speakers. **Publications:** Brochure. • *MIDS Newsletter*, 5/year. Newsletter. *Price:* $18/year.

★ 11236 ★ **National Abortion Federation (NAF)**
1436 U St. NW, Ste. 103
Washington, DC 20009
Phone: (202)667-5881
Fax: (202)667-5890
Sylvia Stengle, Exec.Dir.

Founded: 1977. **Members:** 300. **Description:** National professional forum for abortion service providers (physician offices, clinics, feminist health centers, Planned Parenthood affiliates) and others committed to making safe, legal abortions accessible to all women. Unites abortion service providers into a professional community dedicated to health care; upgrades abortion services by providing standards and guidelines; serves as clearinghouse of information on variety and quality of services offered; keeps abreast of educational, legislative, and public policy developments in reproductive health care. Provides consultations. **Publications:** *Annual Meeting Workbook*, annual. • Books. • Bulletins. • *Consumer's Guide to Abortion Services*. • *Government Relations Report*, periodic. Report. • *Meeting Notes*, periodic. • Membership Directory, annual. • *Membership News*, periodic. Newsletter. • *Risk Management Workbook*, semiannual. • *Unsure About Your Pregnancy? A Guide to Making the Right Decision for You*. Also publishes fact sheets, bulletins, and position papers on abortion.

National Association of Nurse Practitioners in Reproductive Health (NANPRH)
See: Entry 9105

★ 11237 ★ National Commission on Human Life, Reproduction and Rhythm (NCHLRR)
PO Box 508
Oak Park, IL 60303
Phone: (708)383-8766
Herbert Ratner, M.D., Sec.-Treas.

Founded: 1967. **Members:** 25. **Description:** Physicians united to strengthen the family unit and support what the commission views as traditional concepts of marriage, sex, and life. Encourages physicians to place more emphasis on personal attention to patients and less emphasis on the prescribing of medication; promotes pro-life values. Conducts scientific meetings dealing with subjects including: the role of the mother, particularly during her child's first three years; sex education; natural family planning; obstetric delivery; breastfeeding; abortion. Sponsors public meetings. **Publications:** *Child and Family*, quarterly. Journal. Contains scientific and philosophical articles in support of the traditional family. Consists primarily of reprinted material. *Price:* $12/year; $16/year outside U.S. Also publishes reprint booklets.

★ 11238 ★ National Family Planning and Reproductive Health Association (NFPRHA)
122 C St. NW, Ste. 380
Washington, DC 20001
Phone: (202)628-3535
Fax: (202)737-2690
Judith M. DeSarno, Pres.

Founded: 1971. **Members:** 1,000. **Description:** Hospitals, state and city departments of health, health care providers, private nonprofit clinics, and consumers concerned with the maintenance and improvement of family planning and reproductive health services. Serves as a national communications network and advocacy organization. Maintains contact with Congress and government agencies in order to monitor government policy and regulations. **Publications:** *NFPRHA Alert*, periodic. • *NF-PRHA News*, bimonthly. • *NFPRHA Report*, bimonthly. Report. Also publishes professional papers and educational materials. **Formerly:** (1979) National Family Planning Forum.

★ 11239 ★ National Organization of Adolescent Pregnancy, Parenting and Prevention (NOAPP)
4421A East-West Hwy.
Bethesda, MD 20814
Phone: (301)913-0378
Fax: (301)913-0380
Kathleen Sheeran, Exec.Dir.

Founded: 1979. **Members:** 2,000. **Description:** Professionals, policymakers, community and state leaders, and other concerned individuals and organizations. Promotes comprehensive and coordinated services designed for the prevention and resolution of problems associated with adolescent pregnancy, parenthood and prevention. Supports families in expanding their capability of nurturing children and setting standards that encourage their healthy development through loving, stable relationships. Programs include: providing advocacy services at local, state, and national levels for adolescent pregnancy issues; sharing information and promoting public awareness; conducting conferences, training institutes and workshops to encourage the establishment of effective programs; coalition building assistance. **Publications:** *NOAPP Network Newsletter*, quarterly. Newsletter. Contains resource and research reviews, state highlights, legislative focus, and successful program models. **Formerly:** (1993) National Organization of Adolescent Pregnancy and Parenting.

National Women's Coalition
See: Entry 9684

★ 11240 ★ Ovulation Method Research and Reference Centre of Australia
27 Alexandra Parade
North Fitzroy, VIC 3068, Australia
Phone: 3 481 1722
Fax: 3 4824208
Dr. J.J. Billings, Dir.

Description: Works to research, study, and evaluate the female ovulation cycle and its direct relation to reproductive medicine. Disseminates information. **Publications:** Bulletin.

★ 11241 ★ Ovulation Method Teachers Association (OMTA)
PO Box 101780
Anchorage, AK 99510-1780
Frances Butzke, Sec.

Description: Certifies teachers of the ovulation method of birth control. (The ovulation method is a means by which women can determine the fertile days of their menstrual cycle by analyzing the appearance of cervical mucus and charting the results.) Promotes the ovulation method as a safe and effective contraceptive. Upgrades the quality of ovulation method instruction through the evaluation and certification of teachers. Compiles and disseminates information for the continuing education of health professionals and the public. Provides a national teachers referral service to pair interested persons with teachers in their geographic area. **Publications:** *Ovulation Method Newsletter*, quarterly. Newsletter. Includes calendar of events, notices of the availability of educational materials, and news of the association's educational programs. *Price:* Included in membership dues.

★ 11242 ★ Pathfinder International (PI)
9 Galen St., Ste. 217
Watertown, MA 02172
Phone: (617)924-7200
Fax: (617)924-3833
Daniel E. Pellegrom, Pres.

Founded: 1957. **Description:** Established to find, demonstrate, and promote new and more efficient family planning programs in developing countries. Objectives are to introduce and expand the availability of effective family planning services; improve the welfare of families in developing countries; assist developing countries in implementing population policies favorable to national development. Conducts activities with a concern for upholding human rights, enhancing the status and role of women, and respecting the views of family planning clients. **Publications:** Annual Report, annual. • *Pathways*, quarterly. Newsletter. Provides information on programs and updates on services. **Also Known As:** PF.

★ 11243 ★ Pharmacists for Life International (PFLI)
PO Box 1281
Powell, OH 43065-1281
Phone: (614)881-5520
Free: 800-227-8359
Fax: (614)881-5520
Bogomir M. Kuhar, Pharm., Exec.Dir.

Founded: 1984. **Members:** 1,000. **Regional Groups:** 15. **Description:** Pharmacists and interested groups and individuals. Seeks to educate pharmacists, other medical professionals, and the public about the "abortion holocaust." Defends the right to life from conception to natural death, regardless of biological stage, dependency, or residence. Provides medical supplies and vitamins to women and crisis pregnancy centers. Provides children's services; sponsors charitable, educational, and research programs. Maintains speakers' bureau; compiles statistics. **Publications:** *Beginnings*, bimonthly. Newsletter. Contains book and literature reviews, guest analyses and editorials, and news on current events. *Price:* $35/year. • *Can Cancer Pain be Relieved?*. • *Evidence Which Demands a Conclusion: Norplant*. • *Gambling with Life: the Birth Control Game*. • *Infant Homicides through Contraceptives*. • *Is Your Pharmacy Prolife?*. • *IUD: Device of Death*. • *Model Pharmacists Conscience Clause*. • *The New Abortionists II: An Update on Chemical and Mechanical Killing*. • *Norplant: A New Abortifacient*. • *Norplant Fact Sheet*. • *The personality of the Pill*. • *Pharmaceutical Companies: the New Abortionists*. • *Pharmacists Code of Ethics*. • *The Pill Fact Sheet*. • *RU 486 Fact Sheet*. **Formerly:** (1993) Pharmacists for Life.

★ 11244 ★ Physicians for Choice (PFC)
c/o Planned Parenthood Federation of America
810 7th Ave.
New York, NY 10019
Phone: (212)541-7800
Fax: (212)261-4352
Caren Spruch, Coord.

Founded: 1981. **Members:** 3,000. **Description:** Physicians who believe in preserving the right of all women to decide when or whether to bear a child. Conducts a variety of activities to educate legislators and the public on the health benefits of reproductive freedom. Testifies at congressional hearings; circulates petitions; lobbies legislators. Maintains speakers' bureau.

★11245★ **Planned Parenthood Association of South Africa (PPASA) (Gesinsbeplanningsvereniging van Suid-Afrika — GSA)**
Institute for Social and Economic Research
University of Durban-Westville
Private Bag X54001
Durban 4000, Republic of South Africa
Phone: 31 8202298
J. Butler-Adam

Founded: 1930. **Members:** 180. **Regional Groups:** 5. **Languages:** Afrikaans, English, Sotho, Tswana, Xhosa, Zulu. **Description:** Encourages family planning activities in South Africa and promotes family planning as a basic human right. Works to: improve maternal and child health; reduce the incidence of unwanted pregnancy and abortion; address issues related to adolescent sexuality and teen pregnancy; increase public knowledge of the prevention of AIDS and other sexually transmitted diseases; increase societal awareness of the relationship between population growth, natural resource consumption, and the conservation of the environment. Coordinates information, education, and training programs on sexual responsibility and reproductive health. Conducts research. **Publications:** *Aids Scan*, quarterly. Also publishes *Responsible Teenage Sexuality* (book).

★11246★ **Planned Parenthood Federation of America (PPFA)**
810 7th Ave.
New York, NY 10019
Phone: (212)541-7800
Fax: (212)245-1845
Pamela J. Maraldo, Pres.

Founded: 1916. **Regional Groups:** 169. **Description:** Organizations providing leadership in making effective means of voluntary fertility regulation, including contraception, abortion, sterilization, and infertility services, available and fully accessible to all as a central element of reproductive health; stimulating and sponsoring relevant biomedical, socioeconomic, and demographic research; developing appropriate information, education, and training programs to increase knowledge about human reproduction and sexuality. Supports and assists efforts to achieve similar goals worldwide. Operates 900 centers that provide medically supervised reproductive health services and educational programs. **Publications:** Annual Report. • Books. • Pamphlets. **Also Known As:** Planned Parenthood; Planned Parenthood/World Population. **Formerly:** (1939) American Birth Control League.

★11247★ **Population Council (PC)**
1 Dag Hammarskjold Plz.
New York, NY 10017
Phone: (212)339-0500
Fax: (212)755-6052
Margaret Catley-Carlson, Pres.

Founded: 1952. **Regional Groups:** 6. **Description:** Conducts health and social science programs and research relevant to developing countries; conducts biomedical research to develop and improve contraceptive technology; provides advice and technical assistance to governments, international agencies, and organizations; disseminates information on population issues. Areas of study include: contraceptive development and reproductive physiology; family planning and fertility; reproductive health and child survival; women's roles and status; contraceptive introduction; development of human and institutional resources. Sponsors postdoctoral training in biomedical research related to human reproductive physiology. **Publications:** Brochures. • Monographs. • Newsletters. • Pamphlets. • Papers. • *Population and Development Review*, quarterly. Journal. Covers the interrelationships between population and socioeconomic change and related public policy issues. *Price:* Free to qualified individuals; $24/year for nonmembers. • *Population Council Annual Report*. Annual Report. *Price:* Free. • *Studies in Family Planning*, bimonthly. Journal. Covers family planning and related health and development issues; including such aspects as fertility regulation and contraceptive technology. *Price:* Free to qualified individuals; $18/year for nonmembers.

★11248★ **Pregnancy Advisory Service**
11-13 Charlotte St.
London W1P 1HD, England
Phone: 171 6378962
Fax: 171 3234215
Jonathan Tuppeny, Mkt.Mgr.

Founded: 1968. **Languages:** English, French, German, Spanish. **Description:** Promotes improved sexual education programs in England. Disseminates information and advice on topics such as: abortion; pregnancy testing; morning after birth control; cervical smears; donor insemination; and male and female sterilization.

★11249★ **Resolve, Inc.**
1310 Broadway
Somerville, MA 02144-1731
Phone: (617)623-1156
Fax: (617)623-0252
Diane D. Aronson, Exec.Dir.

Founded: 1973. **Members:** 25,000. **Local Groups:** 60. **Description:** Persons with problems of infertility and associated professionals who work with infertile couples such as adoption workers, physicians, and counselors. Offers information, referral, and support to persons with problems of infertility. **Publications:** Bibliography. • Brochure. • *Resolve National Newsletter*, quarterly. Newsletter. Provides information on medical, emotional, and legislative issues, and upcoming conferences. Includes book reviews, research reports, and letters. *Price:* Included in membership dues; $4/issue for nonmembers. Also publishes fact sheets and briefs.

Safe Motherhood Initiative
See: Entry 9693

★11250★ **SIDELINES National Support Network**
PO Box 1808
Laguna Beach, CA 92652
Phone: (714)497-2265
Fax: (714)497-5722
Candace Hurley, Exec.Dir.

Founded: 1992. **Regional Groups:** 30. **State Groups:** 3. **Local Groups:** 1. **Description:** Parents and friends dedicated to supporting women and their families experiencing a complicated or high-risk pregnancy. A pregnancy is termed "complicated" when the life or health of the mother and/or baby may be at risk. Committed to helping women overcome the risks of preterm birth, low birthweight, and other serious consequences of high risk pregnancies. Operates the One-On-One program where a mother and her family are paired with a trained "Phone Friend" who has previously been through a complicated pregnancy. Offers prenatal care information and grief and loss counseling. Provides the families with resources and referrals to local businesses, agencies, and services that can assist them. **Publications:** *Left Side Lines*. Magazine. *Price:* $3.50.

★11251★ **Society for Assisted Reproductive Technology (SART)**
c/o American Fertility Society
1209 Montgomery Hwy.
Birmingham, AL 35216-2809
Phone: (205)978-5000
Fax: (205)978-5005
Mary Fasshauer, Contact

Members: 140. **Description:** Institutions conducting assisted reproductive procudures. Works to extend knowledge of human in vitro fertilization techniques. Conducts educational programs; gathers and disseminates information.

★11252★ **Society for Prevention of Infertility (SPI)**
877 Park Ave.
New York, NY 10021
Phone: (212)774-5500
Fax: (212)744-6536
Masood A. Khatamee, Exec.Dir.

Founded: 1990. **Members:** 500. **Description:** Physicians specializing in obstetrics and gynecology; scientists representing public and private teaching hospitals, medical school faculties, and university research departments; practitioners who work with infertile men and women. Objectives are to: study sexually transmitted infectious diseases (STDs) and their effects on human fertility; reduce the incidence of infection and the possibility of resulting infertility. Coordinates and encourages research that can lead to successful forms of treatment and control of STDs, thus enhancing the opportunities for childless couples to achieve intrauterine pregnancies and bear healthy children. Encourages the exchange of information among those involved in research on and treatment of STDs. Designs educational and informational strategies intended for the prevention of infertility. **Formerly:** (1991) International Society of Infectious Diseases and Human Infertility.

★ 11253 ★ Society of Reproductive Endocrinologists (SRE)
c/o American Fertility Society
1209 Montgomery Hwy.
Birmingham, AL 35216-2809
Phone: (205)978-5000
Fax: (205)978-5005
Mary Fasshauer, Contact

Members: 420. **Description:** Medical doctors with American Board of Obstetrics and Gynecology certification as reproductive endocrinologists. Works to extend knowledge of human reproduction and endocrinology; makes available to members continuing education programs. Conducts seminars.

Society for Reproductive Surgeons (SRE)
See: Entry 12308

★ 11254 ★ Society for the Study of Reproduction (SSR)
1506 Jefferson
Madison, WI 53711-2106
Phone: (608)256-2777
Fax: (217)256-4610
Judith Janson, Exec.Sec.

Founded: 1967. **Members:** 2,400. **Description:** Researchers in obstetrics and gynecology, urology, zoology, animal husbandry, and physiology; clinicians in human and veterinary medicine. Purposes are to promote the study of reproduction by fostering interdisciplinary communication within the science. **Publications:** *Biology of Reproduction*, monthly. Journal. Includes peer-reviewed scientific research in the field of reproductive biology.

★ 11255 ★ Women of Color Partnership Program (WOCPP)
100 Maryland Ave. NE, Ste. 307
Washington, DC 20002
Phone: (202)543-7032
Fax: (202)543-7820
Elizabeth Castro, Dir.

Founded: 1985. **Description:** A division of the Religious Coalition for Abortion Rights. Educates women about reproductive health issues such as accessibility and cost of health care, role of the church, male responsibility, sterilization, and medical abuse of women. Conducts forums and workshops. Maintains speakers' bureau. **Publications:** *Common Ground - Different Planes*, semiannual. Newsletter.

★ 11256 ★ Women's Global Network for Reproductive Rights (WGNRR)
N.Z. Voorburgwal 32
NL-1012 RZ Amsterdam, Netherlands
Phone: 20 6209672
Fax: 20 6222450
Conchita de Roba Cortada, Editor

Founded: 1978. **Members:** 2,000. **Languages:** Dutch, English, French, German, Spanish. **Description:** International network of women's health groups, reproductive rights campaigns, clinics, health workers, and interested individuals. Supports the woman's right to decide if and when to have children; defends the right to safe, effective contraceptives and legal abortion and freedom from sterilization abuse. Campaigns on issues including what the group considers the

"dumping of dangerous contraceptives in the Third World," the lack of complete information that would provide women with the opportunity to make informed decisions on spacing and controlling births, and the lack of availability of safe contraceptive methods to women who want them. Seeks to raise public awareness of issues surrounding maternal mortality and illness. Serves as information clearinghouse for abortion, sterilization and the research, testing, and distribution of contraceptives and other reproductive health and services issues. **Publications:** *Conference Reports*, annual. • Newsletter, quarterly. • Pamphlets. • *Seminar Reports*. **Formerly:** (1980) International Campaign for Abortion Rights; (1985) International Contraception, Abortion and Sterilization Campaign.

Women's Health
See: Entry 1535

★ 11257 ★ Zimbabwe Invitro Fertilization Association
PO Box 5665
Harare, Zimbabwe
Phone: 4 731443
Fax: 4 706431
Mr. A. Robertson, Chmn.

Members: 200. **Description:** Seeks to enable infertile couples to have children by funding laboratory costs. Raises money for medical equipment subsidies for needy patients. Disseminates information. **Publications:** Brochures. Medical information.

Research Centers

★ 11258 ★ Advocates for Youth
1025 Vermont Ave. NW, Ste. 200
Washington, DC 20005
Phone: (202)347-5700
Fax: (202)347-2263
Marge Pruitt Clark, Dir.

Research Activities and Fields: Sex education, life planning for adolescents, impact of television sex on adolescents, AIDS education, and evaluation of school-based comprehensive health care clinics that provide family planning services. **Publications:** *Make a Life for Yourself* (English, Spanish); *Transitions* (quarterly publication on public policy); *Passages* (quarterly publication on international issues); *Linkx* (quarterly publication on school-based clinics and related issues); *School-based Clinics Update* (annually); Fact Sheets. **Formerly:** Center for Population Options (1994).

★ 11259 ★ Alan Guttmacher Institute
120 Wall St.
21st Fl.
New York, NY 10005
Phone: (212)248-1111
Fax: (212)248-1952
Jeannie Rosoff, Pres.

Research Activities and Fields: Societal and political issues related to human reproduction, especially concerning the economically and socially disadvantaged, including family planning,

sex education, abortion, teenage pregnancy, maternal and prenatal health care, contraceptive development and use, sexually transmitted diseases, and reproductive health services. The Institute submits its research program to a scientific advisory panel whose members are drawn from academic research centers throughout the U.S. **Publications:** *Family Planning Perspectives* (bimonthly); *International Family Planning Perspectives* (quarterly); *Washington Memo* (ten per year); *State Reproductive Health Monitor: Legislative Proposals and Action* (quarterly); Annual Report. **Formerly:** Center for Family Planning Program Development, at the time a division of the Planned Parenthood Federation of America (1977).

★ 11260 ★ AVSC International
79 Madison Ave.
New York, NY 10016
Phone: (212)561-8000
Fax: (212)779-9439
Hugo Hoogenboom, Pres.

Research Activities and Fields: Conducts surveys on incidence, prevalence, and trends of voluntary sterilization in the U.S. Also studies legal aspects of voluntary sterilization and trends in surgical practices. Conducts studies throughout the world on medical practices, voluntary choice, informed consent, and decision making for sterilization and other family planning methods. Also conducts research regarding contraceptive implants, intrauterine devices, and injectables. **Publications:** *AVSC News* (quarterly); also publishes patient education pamphlets. **E-mail Address:** avsc@delphi.com. **Formerly:** Association for Voluntary Surgical Contraception (1994); Association for Voluntary Sterilization (1986).

★ 11261 ★ Baylor College of Medicine Center for Population Research and Studies in Reproduction
Dept. of Cell Biology
Houston, TX 77030
Phone: (713)798-6200
Fax: (713)790-1275
Dr. Bert W. O'Malley, Chm.

Research Activities and Fields: Human reproduction, including studies on mechanism of hormone action, male reproduction, steroid regulation and protein synthesis, spermatogenesis, reproductive endocrinology, nucleic acid chemistry and genetic expression, steroid hormonal receptors, physical chemistry, cell proliferation and regulation, biochemistry of chromatin, ribonucleic acid, deoxyribonucleic acid, and cell biology.

★ 11262 ★ Center for Biomedical Research
Population Council
1230 York Ave.
New York, NY 10021
Phone: (212)327-8717
Fax: (212)327-7678
Dr. C. Wayne Bardin, Dir.

Research Activities and Fields: Physiology of human reproduction, especially the male reproductive system, including studies on gametogenesis, sperm ultrastructure, steroid receptors, hormone action, and testicular function. Contraceptive development includes studies on subdermal implants, the contraceptive ring, the levonorgestrel-releasing intrauterine device, an LHRH analog for ovulation inhibition in women and for spermatogenic inhibition in men, and pregnancy vaccines. Health issues research relates to current and potential contraceptive methods, hormone replacement therapy, and microbicides that prevent sexually transmitted diseases.

★ 11263 ★ Center for Population Research
Univ. of California, San Diego
Dept. of Reproductive Medicine, 0802
9500 Gilman Dr.
La Jolla, CA 92093
Phone: (619)543-3718
Fax: (619)543-5447
Prof. Samuel S. Yen, Dir.

Research Activities and Fields: Hypothalamic control of the pituitary and gonadal function in human and animal models, focusing on issues related to neuroendicrine metabolic dysfunction in the aging population.

**Center for Reproduction and
   Transplantation Immunology**
See: Entry 2097

**★ 11264 ★ Columbia University
Center for Population and Family Health**
Level B-3
60 Haven Ave.
New York, NY 10032
Phone: (212)314-5201
Fax: (212)305-7024
Dr. James McCarthy, Dir.

Research Activities and Fields: Adolescent health, especially adolescent reproductive health; maternal and child health in the U.S. Conducts social science research on fertility and contraceptive decision making, adoption, and the consequences of adolescent childbearing; and applied research on family planning, AIDS, maternal mortality, and primary health care in developing countries. Studies legal and policy issues related to reproductive rights and the status of women. **E-mail Address:** jm25@columbia.edu. **Formerly:** Absorbed the former International Institute for Human Reproduction.

**★ 11265 ★ Contraceptive and Population
   Research Center**
Walter P. Martin Research Ctr.
1124 W. Carson St.
Torrance, CA 90502
Phone: (310)212-1887
Dr. Ronald Swerdloff, Dir.

Research Activities and Fields: Male contraceptives and infertility and heat as a male contraceptive. Activities include a study of couples testing the use of a synthetic version of the male sex hormone as a male contraceptive. Also tests the effects of GNRH agonists, antagonists, and progestogens compounded with androgens for the effect on suppression of sperm counts. **Formerly:** Male Reproductive Research Center.

**★ 11266 ★ Contraceptive Research and
   Development Program (CONRAD)**
1611 N. Kent St., Ste. 806
Arlington, VA 22209
Phone: (703)524-4744
Fax: (703)524-4770
Henry L. Gabelnick, Ph.D., Dir.

Research Activities and Fields: Improvement of contraception methods, especially for use in developing countries. Studies include new barrier methods and spermicides; long-acting injectable and implantable contraceptives for women and men; nonsurgical and/or reversible sterilization techniques for women and men; contraceptive vaccines directed against sperm, ova, or hormones; nonsteroidal gonadal proteins that regulate pituitary and/or gonadal functions; methods that are suitable for lactating women; and vaginal and transdermal delivery systems. Studies also include heterosexual transmission of HIV and other sexually transmitted disease pathogens. **Publications:** Monograph Series. **E-mail Address:** dcolvard@conrad.org.

★ 11267 ★ Family Health International
PO Box 13950
Research Triangle Park, NC 27709
Phone: (919)544-7040
Fax: (919)544-7261
Dr. Theodore M. King, Pres.

Research Activities and Fields: New contraceptive technology, contraceptive acceptability, contraceptive effectiveness and safety, breastfeeding practices, maternal/child health, demography, interventions to reduce the transmission of sexually transmitted diseases and AIDS, technology transfer, institutional development, economics of family planning and financing of AIDS programming. Operates the AIDS Control and Prevention Project (AIDSCAP), which seeks to support the local capacity of developing countries to prevent and control HIV. **Publications:** *Network* (quarterly newsletter), plus editions in French and Spanish (semiannually). **Formerly:** International Fertility Research Program.

★ 11268 ★ Fertility Research Foundation
877 Park Ave.
New York, NY 10021
Phone: (212)744-5500
Fax: (212)744-6536
Masood Khatamee, M.D., Exec.Dir.

Research Activities and Fields: Fertility and human reproduction, including studies on microsurgery, fertilization, fallopian tube transplant, artificial embryonation, education and prevention of human infertility, in vitro fertilization gender selection, therapeutic donor insemination, and counselling. **Publications:** *Infertility Journal.*

**★ 11269 ★ Fertility and Women's Health
   Care Center**
130 Maple St.
Springfield, MA 01103
Phone: (413)781-8220
Fax: (413)732-9088
Ronald K. Burke, M.D., Head

Research Activities and Fields: Conducts basic and clinical studies of male and female in-

fertility, with special emphasis on sperm motility and velocity, reproductive endocrinology, gender preselection, ovulation induction, vaginal ultrasonography, and gamete intrafallopian tube transfer. **E-mail Address:** rk-burke@umassmed.ummed.edu. **Formerly:** Fertility Institute of Western Massachusetts (1991).

**★ 11270 ★ Harvard University
Center for Population and Development
   Studies**
9 Bow St.
Cambridge, MA 02138
Phone: (617)495-2021
Fax: (617)495-5418
Lincoln Chen, Dir.

Research Activities and Fields: Demography, human ecology, and economic, social, and environmental determinants and consequences of population changes in America and other developed and developing countries, including studies of public health aspects of fertility and the balance between populations and their resources, theories of population dynamics and their implications for public policy, political and ethical aspects of population, and the effect of nutrition and exercise on female reproduction. Conducts laboratory and clinical research programs in human reproductive biology. **Formerly:** Center for Population Studies (1991).

**★ 11271 ★ Howard and Georgeanna Jones
   Institute for Reproductive Medicine**
601 Colley Ave.
Norfolk, VA 23507
Phone: (804)446-5266
Fax: (804)446-5905
Dr. Gary Hodgen, Pres.

Research Activities and Fields: Human reproduction, including studies of reproductive physiology during the hours and days surrounding fertilization, fertilization process, gametogenesis, neuroendocrinology, ovarian follicular development, gene expression, reproductive toxicology, endocrine control of menstrual cycle, andrology, reproductive immunology, and cancer.

**★ 11272 ★ Johns Hopkins University
Hopkins Population Center**
615 N. Wolfe St.
Baltimore, MD 21205
Phone: (410)955-7803
Fax: (410)955-0792
Constance A. Nathanson, Ph.D., Dir.

Research Activities and Fields: Demography, family planning, reproductive biology, contraceptive development, reproductive health, adolescent fertility, and international migration. **Publications:** Working Papers; Reprint Series. **E-mail Address:** can@hpcsun01.sph.jhu.edu.

**Kinsey Institute for Research in Sex,
   Gender, and Reproduction, Inc.**
See: Entry 11721

**★ 11273 ★ Laval University
Medical Research Centre
Ontogeny and Reproduction Research
   Group**

2705, boulevard Laurier
Ste. Foy, PQ, Canada G1V 4G2
Phone: (418)656-4141
Fax: (418)654-2714
Michel A. Fortier, Dir.

Research Activities and Fields: Characterization of cell types that make up the uterus; mechanisms responsible for follicular growth control and selection in bovines; immune response suppressing factors involving maternal tolerance to embryo; regulation of gene expression and production of transgenic animals; embryo-maternal interactions, and male fertility and contraception. **E-mail Address:** mafortier@crchul.ulaval.ca.

★ 11274 ★ **Laval University**
Saint-Francois-d'Assise Hospital Research
  Centre
10, rue de l'Espinay
Quebec, PQ, Canada G1L 3L5
Phone: (418)525-4461
Fax: (418)525-4481
Jean-Claude Forest, M.D., Dir.

Research Activities and Fields: Centre conducts studies in reproductive endocrinology, perinology, human genetics, and biomaterials.

★ 11275 ★ **Laval University**
Saint-Francois-d'Assise Hospital Research
  Centre
Reproductive Endocrinology Unit
10, rue de l'Espinay
Quebec, PQ, Canada G1L 3L5
Phone: (418)525-4307
Fax: (418)525-4481
Andre Lemay, M.D., Dir.

Research Activities and Fields: Treatment and diagnosis of endometriosis, new diagnosis methods, new medical and surgical methods, new modalities of hormonal replacement therapy for menopause, and basic research on growth and immune factors implicated in endometriosis and breast cancer. **E-mail Address:** alemay@vmi.ulaval.ca.

Massachusetts General Hospital
Reproductive Endocrine Unit
See: Entry 4895

Medical Research Institute of Worcester,
  Inc.
See: Entry 4896

★ 11276 ★ **Meharry Medical College**
I Have a Future Program
1005 D.B. Todd Blvd.
Campus Box A-90
Nashville, TN 37208
Phone: (615)327-6100
Fax: (615)327-6992
Lorraine W. Greene, Dir.

Research Activities and Fields: Develops models to prevent teen pregnancy, substance abuse, homicide and violence and unemployment. Conducts annual assessments of youth between the ages of 10- and 17-years-old to measure knowledge, attitudes, and behaviors related to sexuality, contraception, pregnancy, self-concept, delinquency activity, social support, family environment, and psychosocial maturity. **E-mail Address:** fosterh63@ccvax.mmc.edu.

★ 11277 ★ **Northwestern University**
Center for Reproductive Sciences
2-120 Hogan Hall
Evanston, IL 60208

Research Activities and Fields: Reproductive biology, focusing on the regulation of ovarian synthesis and secretion of steroid and peptide hormones on the metabolic pathways and messengers within ovarian structures; regulation of testicular development, secretion of spermatogenesis, and the regulation of synthesis and secretion of the pituitary gonadotropic hormones and prolactin, as well as their actions on the brain, gonads, and breast tissue; and interactions of neural tissue in the brain and spinal cord with the pituitary-gonadal axis.

★ 11278 ★ **Northwestern University**
Program for Applied Research on Fertility
  Regulation
680 N. Lakeshore Dr., Ste. 1000
Chicago, IL 60611
Phone: (312)908-6558
Fax: (312)908-0014
Gerald I. Zatuchni, M.D., Dir.

Research Activities and Fields: Provides scientific and technical assistance to U.S. institutions for applied research in the field of fertility regulation. Research includes animal or human investigations leading to the development of contraceptive methods. Specific projects include development of biodegradable contraceptive steroidal-release systems for female and male contraception, intravaginal chemical and barrier methods, pharmacological methods for male contraception, and female contraception, reversible occlusive devices for male and female sterilization, and pharmacological, mechanical, and surgical methods of male and female sterilization. **Publications:** *Research Frontiers in Fertility Regulation.*

★ 11279 ★ **Population Action International**
1120 19th St. NW, Ste. 550
Washington, DC 20036
Phone: (202)659-1833
Fax: (202)293-1795
Dr. J. Joseph Speidel, Pres.

Research Activities and Fields: Conducts studies to enhance family planning in developing nations. Analyzes the relationships between world population growth and socio-economic development, political stability, health, the environment, and the status of women. Also studies the impact of public and private sector funding of population/family planning programs on human welfare and U.S. foreign policy interests. **Formerly:** Population Crisis Committee (1993).

★ 11280 ★ **Population Council**
1 Dag Hammarskjold Plaza
New York, NY 10017
Phone: (212)339-0500
Fax: (212)755-6052
Margaret Catley-Carlson, Pres.

Research Activities and Fields: Social and health science programs and research relevant to developing countries, emphasizing population policy, family planning and fertility, reproductive health and child survival, roles and status of women, development of human and insti-

tutional resources, and expanding contraceptive choice; and biomedical research to develop and improve contraceptive technology. **Publications:** Annual Report; *Studies in Family Planning* (bimonthly); *Population and Development Review* (quarterly); Fact Books; Newsletter.

★ 11281 ★ **Population Resource Center**
1725 K St. NW, Ste. 1102
Washington, DC 20006
Phone: (202)467-5030
Fax: (202)467-5034
Jane DeLung, Pres.

Research Activities and Fields: Demographics, population and international development, contraception, and family planning, and public policy, including studies on international labor migration, demographic trends, residential segregation, reproductive health care, demographic and economic trends in rural America, marriage and divorce statistics, population programs in undeveloped nations, international family planning funding, effects of demographic change on U.S. and foreign policy.

Reproductive Toxicology Center
See: Entry 10451

★ 11282 ★ **Transnational Family Research**
  Institute
8307 Whitman Dr.
Bethesda, MD 20817
Phone: (301)469-6313
Fax: (301)469-0461
Dr. Henry P. David, Ph.D., Dir.

Research Activities and Fields: Develops cooperative transnational research on couple communication, fertility regulation, and choice behavior. Seeks to increase understanding of psychosocial, demographic, epidemiological, and public health aspects of fertility-regulating behavior and of the abortion/contraception relationship. Also encourages cooperative studies in consumer acceptance of fertility-regulating methods, effects of changes in sex roles, delivery of services, and prevention of unwanted pregnancy, especially in adolescents.

★ 11283 ★ **United Nations Population Fund**
220 E. 42nd St.
New York, NY 10017
Phone: (212)297-5111
Fax: (212)557-6416
Nafis Sadik, Exec.Dir.

Research Activities and Fields: Supports demographic data collection and research, and population studies, family planning activities, role and status of women in development research, and sustainable development programmes and research. Funds family planning and related activities in all regions of the world. **Publications:** *Policy Development Studies*; *Global Population Assistance Report*; *Inventory of Population Projects in Developing Countries Around the World* (annually); *Guide to Sources of International Population Assistance* (triennially); *Population* (monthly newsletter); *Populi* (quarterly).

U.S. Department of Health and Human
  Services
National Institute of Child Health and
  Human Development
See: Entry 3354

★ 11284 ★ U.S. Department of Health and
  Human Services
National Institute of Child Health and
  Human Development
Center for Population Research
6100 Executive Blvd., Rm. 8B07
Bethesda, MD 20892
Phone: (301)496-1101
Fax: (301)496-0962
Dr. Florence P. Haseltine, Director

Research Activities and Fields: As the agency
of the federal government with primary responsibility for population research, Center provides
support through grants and contracts for projects in the reproductive sciences, contraceptive
development, contraceptive evaluation, and the
demographic and behavioral sciences (population aspects). Center also awards grants to
leading U.S. institutions for the establishment of
program projects and research centers in reproductive sciences research and in demographic
and behavioral aspects of population research;
supports population research manpower development programs; coordinates federal population research programs; and provides for the
communication of biomedical and behavioral research information in the population sciences.
Center comprises branches for Contraceptive
Development, Contraceptive and Reproductive
Evaluation, Demographic and Behavioral Sciences, and Reproductive Sciences. **Publications:** Progress Report (annually).

★ 11285 ★ U.S. Department of Health and
  Human Services
National Institute of Child Health and
  Human Development
Center for Population Research
Contraceptive Development Branch
6100 Executive Blvd., Rm. 8B13
Bethesda, MD 20892
Phone: (301)496-1661
Nancy J. Alexander, Ph.D., Chief

Research Activities and Fields: Branch administers grants and contracts to support projects aimed at developing safe and effective
methods for regulating fertility in both men and
women. Research activities include: 1) synthesis and biological evaluation of promising new
compounds that may affect reproductive processes in the male or female; 2) technology development for improved administration of contraceptive drugs; 3) development of improved
vaginal and uterine contraceptives based on
chemical or physical methods; 4) clinical trials of
barriers, sex steroids, and peptides for assessment of their potential as male or female contraceptives; 5) clinical and toxicological evaluation
of long-acting progestin as a female contraceptive; 6) laboratory studies and clinical trials to
develop and evaluate antifertility methods
based on periodic abstinence; and 7) studies required to clarify mechanisms of action of specific contraceptive drugs.

★ 11286 ★ U.S. Department of Health and
  Human Services
National Institute of Child Health and
  Human Development
Center for Population Research
Contraceptive Evaluation Branch
Executive Plaza North, Rm. 607
6100 Executive Blvd.
Bethesda, MD 20892
Phone: (301)496-4924
Robert Spirtas, Chief

Research Activities and Fields: Branch supports activities that assess the safety and efficacy of short- and long-term contraceptive methods. Research activities include: 1) studies of
the medical effects (risks and benefits) of steroid contraceptives, including the association
between contraceptive use and neoplasia, cardiovascular diseases, and other common disorders; 2) studies of the medical effects and the
mechanisms of action of intrauterine devices
(IUDs), including their effects on the occurrence
of undesired infertility; 3) studies of the immediate and long term medical effects of sterilization
in men and women involving the relative risks
and benefits of vasectomy and tubal sterilization; and 4) studies to assess the use-
effectiveness of barrier methods of contraception, including the adverse and beneficial effects
of spermicides.

★ 11287 ★ U.S. Department of Health and
  Human Services
National Institute of Child Health and
  Human Development
Center for Population Research
Demographic and Behavioral Sciences
  Branch
6100 Executive Blvd. Rm. 8B13
Bethesda, MD 20892
Phone: (301)496-1174
Fax: (301)496-0962
Dr. Christine Bachrach, Chief

Research Activities and Fields: Branch supports studies on the social, psychological, economic, and environmental factors governing
population growth; the impact of population
changes on individuals, families, and society;
and research related to AIDS. Research activities include: 1) studies of the determinants, correlates, and consequences of fertility and fertili-
ty-related behavior; 2) studies of the differences
in mortality between various social and economic groups and the socioeconomic factors affecting trends in mortality; and 3) studies of the determinants and consequences of movements of
a population within a country.

★ 11288 ★ U.S. Department of Health and
  Human Services
National Institute of Child Health and
  Human Development
Center for Population Research
Reproductive Sciences Branch
Bldg. 61E, Rm. 8B01
6100 Executive Blvd.
Bethesda, MD 20892
Phone: (301)496-6515
Fax: (301)496-0962
Dr. Michael E. McClure, Chief

Research Activities and Fields: Branch supports fundamental biomedical research and re-

search training in reproductive biology and medicine, involving the development of new or improved methods of human fertility regulation,
the alleviation of human infertility, and the amelioration or cure of human reproductive diseases
and disorders. Research is carried out in five
areas: 1) reproductive biology, including gamete
development and transport, ovulation, sperm
maturation, fertilization, and embryo transport
and implantation; 2) reproductive genetics and
immunology, such as gene activation by reproductive hormones, recombinant DNA applications in reproduction, and immune response influences on reproduction; 3) reproductive endocrinology, including the secretion and assay of
reproductive hormones and their releasing or inhibiting substances, cellular mechanisms of reproductive hormone action, and neural regulation of reproductive hormone secretion; 4) reproductive medicine, involving studies on the alleviation of infertility and the amelioration or
cure of reproductive diseases or disorders; and
5) periimplantation developmental biology
studies, involving early embryo formation and
function.

U.S. Department of Health and Human
  Services
National Institute of Child Health and
  Human Development
Epidemiology, Statistics and Prevention
  Research Division
See: Entry 5190

U.S. Department of Health and Human
  Services
National Institute of Environmental Health
  Sciences
Laboratory of Reproductive and
  Developmental Toxicology
See: Entry 5111

★ 11289 ★ U.S. Department of Health and
  Human Services
Public Health Service
Office of Adolescent Pregnancy Programs
U.S. Dept. of Health and Human Services
North Bldg., East-West Hwy.
5600 Fishers Ln.
Rockville, MD 20857
Phone: (301)594-4004
Fax: (301)492-2017
Patrick J. Sheeran, Acting Director

Research Activities and Fields: Supports care
demonstration projects to help pregnant teenagers, their children and families; and prevention demonstration projects to reach teenagers
before they become sexually active. Programs
include the award of research and evaluation
grants and contracts for studies on the causes
and consequences of adolescent sexual behavior, contraceptive use, and early childbearing;
and evaluation of service delivery.

★ 11290 ★ U.S. Department of Health and
  Human Services
Public Health Service
Office of Family Planning
Family Planning Program (Service Delivery
  Improvement Research)

U.S. Dept. of Health and Human Services
Office of Population Affairs
North Bldg., East-West Hwy.
5600 Fisher Ln.
Rockville, MD 20857
Phone: (301)245-1181
Fax: (301)245-6498
Eugenia Eckard, Program Director

Research Activities and Fields: Through the award of SDI grants, the Office of Family Planning supports applied research on the improvement of family planning services delivery for low-income women and others in need of such services. Two types of grants are awarded: individual research project grants and New Investigator Research Awards. Proposals are encouraged from a variety of social and behavioral science disciplines, with preference given to proposals in priority areas announced by the Office of Family Planning. Priorities include: family planning client behavior; adolescent family planning clients; male family planning clients; targeting of family planning services to subgroups with special needs (i.e., low-income families, minorities, and handicapped); clinic personnel behavior; organization and management of family planning services; the role of private physicians; natural family planning; infertility services; and counseling services (evaluation of role and effectiveness).

★11291★ **University of California, Los Angeles**
Population Research Center
Harbor-UCLA Medical Center
Walter Martin Research Bldg., RB-1
1124 W. Carson St.
Torrance, CA 90509
Phone: (310)222-1867
Fax: (310)533-0627
Dr. Ronald S. Swerdloff, Dir.

Research Activities and Fields: Clinical investigations of overpopulation and infertility through analysis of endocrinology, physiology, pathology, and molecular biology of the reproductive system.

University of California, San Francisco
Reproductive Endocrinology Center
See: Entry 4931

★11292★ **University of Connecticut**
Contraceptive Development Center
Dept. of Physiology
MC-3505
Farmington, CT 06030
Phone: (203)679-2239
Dr. Paul Primakoff, Contact

Research Activities and Fields: Conducting research on the development of a birth control vaccine using sperm adhesion proteins. Also analyzing molecular mechanisms in mammalian fertilization.

★11293★ **University of Kentucky**
Center for Reproductive Medicine
Coll. of Med.
Dept. of OB/GYN
800 Rose St.
Lexington, KY 40536
Phone: (606)323-6166
Fax: (606)323-1931
Prof. Thomas Curry, Dir.

Research Activities and Fields: Reproductive medicine, including artificial insemination; in-vitro fertilization; interfallopian tube transfer; ovulation; and follicular development.

★11294★ **University of Maryland at Baltimore**
Center for Studies in Reproduction
Bressler Research Lab., Rm. 11-019
655 W. Baltimore St.
Baltimore, MD 21201
Phone: (410)706-3391
Fax: (410)706-5747
Dr. Eugene D. Albrecht, Dir.

Research Activities and Fields: Reproductive biology, including reproductive neuroendocrinology and cellular reproductive endocrinology, cellular endocrinology, perinatal endocrinology, fetal-placental development, uterine and ovarian physiology and biochemistry, steroid regulation of cancer, embryology and physiology, neuroendocrine regulation of peptidergic neurons, neuroendocrinology of prolactin secretion, neuroendocrinology of aging, and cancer research.

★11295★ **University of Michigan**
Reproductive Sciences Program
300 N. Ingalls Bldg., Rm. 1123 NW
Ann Arbor, MI 48109-0404
Phone: (313)763-0248
Fax: (313)936-8620
A. Rees Midgley, Dir.

Research Activities and Fields: Biological and behavioral aspects of reproduction, including clinical medicine relating to endocrinological disorders; neuroendocrine regulation of reproduction; morphological and functional studies on the hypothalmic-pituitary-gonadal axis; development of novel, nonradioactive analytical techniques; biosensors and on-line feedback control systems; biological signalling and chronobiology; neuroendocrine physiology and psychology; biochemical endrocrinology relevant to steroidogenesis and hormone action; molecular biology and gene expression; reproductive pharmacology; neurophysiological and sensory regulation of behavior; growth regulation; physical activity and its relationship to neuroendocrine function; biochemical, biological, and behavioral correlates of pregnancy; chemistry and immunology of hormones; synthesis, processing, and secretion of cellular products, including gonadotropins and extracellular matrix; calcium/calmodulin actions; and infertility research. **E-mail Address:** rmidgey@umich.edu. **Formerly:** Reproductive Endocrinology Program (1968); Consortium for Research in Developmental and Reproductive Biology.

★11296★ **University of Montreal**
Research Group on Quebec Demography
C.P. 6128, Succ. Centre-ville
Montreal, PQ, Canada H3C 3J7
Phone: (514)343-5870
Fax: (514)343-2309
Robert Bourbeau, Dir.

Research Activities and Fields: Quebec population, including past and recent evolution, historical demography, fertility and the family, sterilization, cost of child rearing, population aging, small populations and subpopulations, and health indicators and mortality. **E-mail Address:** bourbrob@ere.umontreal.ca.

★11297★ **University of Montreal**
Sainte-Justine Hospital Research Centre
3175, chemin de la Cote-Sainte-Catherine
Montreal, PQ, Canada H3T 1C5
Phone: (514)345-4692
Fax: (514)345-4801
Robert Collu, Dir.

Research Activities and Fields: Basic and clinical research in the field of diseases of the mother and child, including cardiology and pulmonary medicine, endocrinology, biology of reproduction and development, experimental cardiovascular surgery, and gastroenterology and nutrition. Studies also include hematology-oncology, immunology, microbiology, virology, medical genetics, nephrology, and obstetrics.

★11298★ **University of Pennsylvania**
Population Studies Center
3718 Locust Walk
Philadelphia, PA 19104-6298
Phone: (215)898-6441
Fax: (215)898-2124
Dr. Jane Menken, Dir.

Research Activities and Fields: Demography, particularly interrelations of economic and social factors, fertility, mortality, and migration. Interests include health and population, aging, historical demography, population and development, international and internal migration, adolescent fertility, population policy, research methods, education, AIDS, health communication, design and evaluation of family planning programs, and racial and ethnic differentials. Demography of Africa and South Asia is emphasized. **Publications:** African Demography Working Paper Series. **E-mail Address:** hneff@pop.upenn.edu.

University of Pittsburgh
Center for Research in Reproductive Physiology
See: Entry 13231

University of Tennessee
Division of Reproductive Endocrinology
See: Entry 4943

University of Texas at Austin
Institute of Reproductive Biology
See: Entry 11724

★ 11299 ★ **University of Texas**
  Southwestern Medical Center at Dallas
Cecil H. and Ida Green Center for
  Reproductive Biology Sciences
5323 Harry Hines Blvd.
Dallas, TX 75235-9051
Phone: (214)648-3260
Fax: (214)648-8683
Dr. Paul MacDonald, Dir.

Research Activities and Fields: Reproductive
biology and immunology, including immigration
of lymphoid cells into the uterus during the ovarian cycle and pregnancy, as well as the influences of lymphoid cell populations on placental
growth and pregnancy success in rodent model
systems.

★ 11300 ★ **Vanderbilt University**
Center for Fertility and Reproductive
  Research (C-FARR)
Division of Reproductive Endocrinology
Dept. of Obstetrics & Gynecology
C-1100 MCN
Nashville, TN 37232-2515
Phone: (615)322-6576
Fax: (615)343-4902
Esther Eisenberg, M.D., Codir.

Research Activities and Fields: Reproductive
biology, focusing on infertile males and females.
Activities emphasize the disciplines of cell biology, physiology, endocrinology, gamete biology,
molecular biology, and metabolism.

Worcester Foundation for Experimental
  Biology
Male Fertility Program
See: Entry 2711

Chapter 58
Respiratory Diseases

Federal Government Agencies

U.S. Department of Health and Human Services
National Heart, Lung, and Blood Institute
See: Entry 2781

Foundations & Other Funding Organizations

Private Foundations

Francis Families Foundation
See: Entry 197

Other Funding Organizations

★ 11301 ★ **American Lung Association**
1740 Broadway
New York, NY 10019-4374
Phone: (212)315-8700
Fax: (212)265-5642
John R. Garrison, Mng. Dir.

Description: Provides grants and fellowships to support research and research training relating to lung diseases.

Cystic Fibrosis Foundation
See: Entry 5258

Medical & Allied Health Schools

Respiratory Therapy

Listed below are respiratory therapist educational programs accredited by the Commission on Accreditation of Allied Health Education Programs, 515 N. State St., Ste. 7530, Chicago, IL 60610, (312) 464-4636, in collaboration with the Joint Review Committee for Respiratory Therapy Education. Information on accredited respiratory therapy technician programs may be obtained by contacting the Joint Review Committee for Respiratory Therapy Education, 1701 W. Euless Blvd., Ste. 300, Euless, TX 76040, (817) 283-2835.

Alabama

★ 11302 ★ **George C. Wallace Community College**
Respiratory Therapist Program
Dothan, AL 36303
Phone: (205)983-3521

★ 11303 ★ **University of Alabama at Birmingham**
School of Health Related Professions
Respiratory Therapist Program
1714 9th Ave. S.
Birmingham, AL 35294-1270
Phone: (205)934-3783

★ 11304 ★ **University of South Alabama**
College of Allied Health Professions
Respiratory Therapy Program
1504 Springfield Ave., Rm. 2545
Mobile, AL 36604
Phone: (205)434-3405

★ 11305 ★ **Wallace State College**
Respiratory Therapist Program
PO Box 2000
Hanceville, AL 35077-2000
Phone: (205)352-2090

Arizona

★ 11306 ★ **Apollo College at Mesa**
Respiratory Therapist Program
630 W. Southern Ave.
Mesa, AZ 85210
Phone: (602)831-6585

★ 11307 ★ **Apollo College at Phoenix**
Respiratory Therapist Program
8503 N. 27th Ave.
Phoenix, AZ 85051
Phone: (602)864-1571

★ 11308 ★ **Gateway Community College**
Respiratory Therapist Program
108 N. 40th St.
Phoenix, AZ 85034
Phone: (602)392-5062

★ 11309 ★ **Pima Community College**
Respiratory Therapy Program
2202 W. Anklam Rd.
Tucson, AZ 85709
Phone: (602)884-6910

★ 11310 ★ **Pima Medical Institute**
Respiratory Therapist Program
3350 E. Grant Rd., Ste. 200
Tucson, AZ 85716
Phone: (602)326-1600

★ 11311 ★ **Pima Medical Institute**
Respiratory Therapist Program
2300 E. Broadway Rd.
Tempe, AZ 85282
Phone: (602)345-7777

Arkansas

★ 11312 ★ **University of Arkansas for Medical Sciences**
Area Health Education Center
Respiratory Therapy Program
600 Walnut St.
Texarkana, AR 75502
Phone: (501)774-5608

★ 11313 ★ **University of Arkansas for Medical Sciences**
College of Health Related Professions
Respiratory Therapist Program
4301 W. Markham, Mail Slot 704
Little Rock, AR 72205-7199
Phone: (501)661-1202

California

★ 11314 ★ **American River College**
Respiratory Therapist Program
4700 College Oak Dr.
Sacramento, CA 95841
Phone: (916)484-8876

★11315★ **Butte Community College**
Respiratory Therapist Program
3536 Butte Campus Dr.
Oroville, CA 95965
Phone: (916)895-2423

★11316★ **California College for Health Sciences**
Respiratory Therapist Program
222 W. 24th St.
National City, CA 91950
Phone: (619)477-4800

★11317★ **California Paramedical and Technical College**
Respiratory Therapy Program
4550 La Sierra Ave.
Riverside, CA 92505-2907
Phone: (909)687-9006

★11318★ **College of the Desert**
Respiratory Therapist Program
43-500 Monterey Ave.
Palm Desert, CA 92260
Phone: (619)773-2578

★11319★ **Crafton Hills College**
Respiratory Therapist Program
11711 Sand Canyon Rd.
Yucaipa, CA 92399
Phone: (909)794-2161

★11320★ **East Los Angeles College**
Respiratory Therapist Program
1301 Avienda Cesar Chavez
Monterey Park, CA 91754
Phone: (213)265-8612

★11321★ **El Camino College**
Respiratory Therapist Program
16007 Crenshaw Blvd.
Torrance, CA 90506
Phone: (310)715-3248

★11322★ **Foothill DeAnza Community College District**
Respiratory Therapist Program
12345 El Monte Rd.
Los Altos Hills, CA 94022
Phone: (415)949-7292

★11323★ **Fresno City College**
Respiratory Therapist Program
1101 E. University
Fresno, CA 93741
Phone: (209)442-4600

★11324★ **Grossmont College**
Respiratory Therapist Program
8800 Grossmont College Dr.
El Cajon, CA 92020
Phone: (619)465-1700

★11325★ **Loma Linda University School of Allied Health Professions**
Respiratory Therapy Program
Nichol Hall, Rm. 1926
Loma Linda, CA 92350
Phone: (909)824-4932

★11326★ **Los Angeles Valley College**
Respiratory Therapist Program
5800 Fulton Ave.
Van Nuys, CA 91401
Phone: (818)781-1200

★11327★ **Modesto Junior College**
Respiratory Therapist Program
435 College Ave.
Modesto, CA 95350
Phone: (209)575-6381

★11328★ **Mt. San Antonio College**
Respiratory Therapist Program
1100 N. Grand Ave.
Walnut, CA 91789
Phone: (714)594-5611

★11329★ **Napa Valley College**
Respiratory Therapist Program
2277 Napa-Vallejo Hwy.
Napa, CA 94558
Phone: (707)253-3147

★11330★ **Ohlone College**
Respiratory Therapist Program
43600 Mission Blvd.
Fremont, CA 94539-0390
Phone: (510)659-6029

★11331★ **Orange Coast College**
Respiratory Therapist Program
2701 Fairview Rd.
PO Box 5005
Costa Mesa, CA 92628-5005
Phone: (714)432-5541

★11332★ **San Joaquin Valley College**
Respiratory Therapist Program
8400 W. Mineral King
Visalia, CA 93291
Phone: (209)651-2500

★11333★ **Skyline College**
Respiratory Therapist Program
3300 College Dr.
San Bruno, CA 94066
Phone: (415)738-4382

★11334★ **University of California, Los Angeles Medical Center / Santa Monica College**
Respiratory Therapist Program
10833 LeConte Ave.,Rm. 47-155 CHS
Los Angeles, CA 90024-1658
Phone: (310)825-7222

★11335★ **Victor Valley College**
Respiratory Therapist Program
18422 Bear Valley Rd.
Victorville, CA 92392
Phone: (619)245-4275

Colorado

★11336★ **Front Range Community College**
Respiratory Therapist Program
North Campus
3645 W. 112th Ave.
Westminster, CO 80030
Phone: (303)466-8811

★11337★ **Pima Medical Institute**
Respiratory Therapist Program
701 W. 72nd Ave.
Denver, CO 80221
Phone: (303)426-1800

★11338★ **Pueblo Community College**
Respiratory Therapist Program
900 W. Orman Ave.
Pueblo, CO 81004
Phone: (719)549-3266

Connecticut

★11339★ **Manchester Community-Technical College**
Respiratory Therapist Program
60 Bidwell St.
Manchester, CT 06040
Phone: (203)647-6191

★11340★ **Norwalk Hospital**
Respiratory Therapy Program
24 Maple St.
Norwalk, CT 06856
Phone: (203)852-2479

★11341★ **Quinnipiac College**
Respiratory Therapy Program
Mt. Carmel Ave.
Hamden, CT 06518
Phone: (203)281-8682

★11342★ **Sacred Heart University / St. Vincent's Medical Center**
Respiratory Therapist Program
5151 Park Ave.
Fairfield, CT 06432-1000
Phone: (203)576-5329

★11343★ **University of Hartford**
Respiratory Therapist Program
200 Bloomfield Ave.
West Hartford, CT 06117
Phone: (203)768-4823

Delaware

★11344★ **Delaware Technical and Community College**
Respiratory Therapist Program
Health Education Cluster, Southern Campus
PO Box 610, Rte. 18
Georgetown, DE 19947
Phone: (302)856-5400

★11345★ **Delaware Technical and Community College**
Respiratory Therapist Program
Wilmington Campus
333 Shipley St.
Wilmington, DE 19801
Phone: (302)571-5355

District of Columbia

★11346★ **University of the District of Columbia**
Respiratory Therapist Program
4200 Connecticut Ave., NW
Washington, DC 20008
Phone: (202)282-7527

Florida

★ 11347 ★ ATI Health Education Centers
Respiratory Therapist Program
1395 NW 167 St., Ste. 200
Miami, FL 33169
Phone: (305)628-1000

★ 11348 ★ Brevard Community College
Respiratory Therapist Program
1519 Clearlake Rd.
Cocoa, FL 32922
Phone: (407)632-1111

★ 11349 ★ Broward Community College
Respiratory Therapist Program
3501 SW Davie Rd.
Fort Lauderdale, FL 33314
Phone: (305)475-6784

★ 11350 ★ Daytona Beach Community
College
Respiratory Therapist Program
1200 W. International Speedway Blvd.
PO Box 2811
Daytona Beach, FL 32120-2811
Phone: (904)255-8131

★ 11351 ★ Edison Community College
Respiratory Therapist Program
8099 College Pkwy., SW.
Fort Myers, FL 33906
Phone: (813)489-9239

★ 11352 ★ Flagler Career Institute
Respiratory Therapist Program
3225 University Blvd. S.
Jacksonville, FL 32216
Phone: (904)721-1622

★ 11353 ★ Florida A&M University
School of Allied Health Sciences
Respiratory Therapy Program
Ware-Rhaney Bldg., Rm. 223
Tallahassee, FL 32307
Phone: (904)561-2186

★ 11354 ★ Florida Community College at
Jacksonville
Respiratory Therapist Program
North Campus
4501 Capper Rd., Rm. C-102
Jacksonville, FL 32218
Phone: (904)766-6513

★ 11355 ★ Indian River Community College
Respiratory Therapist Program
3209 Virginia Ave.
Fort Pierce, FL 34981-5599
Phone: (407)462-4358

★ 11356 ★ Manatee Community College
Respiratory Therapist Program
5840 26th St. W.
PO Box 1849
Bradenton, FL 34206
Phone: (813)755-1511

★ 11357 ★ Miami-Dade Community College
Respiratory Therapist Program
Medical Center Campus
950 NW 20th St.
Miami, FL 33127
Phone: (305)237-4031

★ 11358 ★ Palm Beach Community College,
Eissey Campus
Respiratory Therapist Program
3160 PGA Blvd.
Palm Beach Gardens, FL 33410
Phone: (407)625-2587

★ 11359 ★ Pensacola Junior College
Respiratory Therapist Program
Warrington Campus
5555 W. Hwy. 98
Pensacola, FL 32507
Phone: (904)484-2210

★ 11360 ★ St. Petersburg Junior College
Respiratory Therapist Program
PO Box 13489
St. Petersburg, FL 33733
Phone: (813)341-3629

★ 11361 ★ Santa Fe Community College
Respiratory Therapist Program
3000 NW 83rd St.
Gainesville, FL 32606-6200
Phone: (904)395-5651

★ 11362 ★ Seminole Community College
Respiratory Therapist Program
100 Weldon Blvd.
Sanford, FL 32773
Phone: (407)323-2293

★ 11363 ★ Tallahassee Community College
Respiratory Therapist Program
444 Appleyard Dr.
Tallahassee, FL 32304
Phone: (904)922-8103

★ 11364 ★ University of Central Florida
Cardiopulmonary Sciences Program
PO Box 25000
Orlando, FL 32816-0125
Phone: (407)823-2214

★ 11365 ★ Valencia Community College
Respiratory Therapist Program
PO Box 3028
Orlando, FL 32802
Phone: (407)299-5000

Georgia

★ 11366 ★ Armstrong State College
Respiratory Therapist Program
11935 Abercorn St.
Savannah, GA 31419
Phone: (912)927-5204

★ 11367 ★ Athens Area Technical Institute
Respiratory Therapist Program
U.S. Hwy. 29 N.
Athens, GA 30610-0399
Phone: (706)542-8050

★ 11368 ★ Columbus College
Respiratory Therapist Program
4225 University Ave.
Columbus, GA 31907-5645
Phone: (706)568-2130

★ 11369 ★ Georgia State University
School of Allied Health Professions
Department of Cardiopulmonary Care
Sciences
Respiratory Therapy Program
University Plaza
Atlanta, GA 30303
Phone: (404)651-3037

★ 11370 ★ Medical College of Georgia
Respiratory Therapy Program
815 St. Sebastian Way, Rm. HM-143
Augusta, GA 30912-0850
Phone: (706)721-3554

Hawaii

★ 11371 ★ Kapiolani Community College /
University of Hawaii
Respiratory Therapist Program
4303 Diamond Head Rd.
Honolulu, HI 96816
Phone: (808)734-9243

Idaho

★ 11372 ★ Boise State University
College of Technology
Respiratory Therapy Program
1910 University Dr., G-108
Boise, ID 83725
Phone: (208)385-3383

Illinois

★ 11373 ★ Black Hawk College
Respiratory Therapist Program
6600 34th Ave.
Moline, IL 61265
Phone: (309)796-1311

★ 11374 ★ College of DuPage
Respiratory Therapist Program
22nd St. and Lambert Rd.
Glen Ellyn, IL 60137
Phone: (708)858-2800

★ 11375 ★ Illinois Central College
Respiratory Therapist Program
201 S.W. Adams
Peoria, IL 61603
Phone: (309)999-4663

★ 11376 ★ Lincoln Land Community
College
Respiratory Therapist Program
Shepherd Rd.
Springfield, IL 62794-9256
Phone: (217)788-3380

★ 11377 ★ Malcolm X College
Respiratory Therapist Program
1900 W. Van Buren St.
Chicago, IL 60612
Phone: (312)850-7381

★ 11378 ★ **Moraine Valley Community College**
Respiratory Therapist Program
10900 S. 88th Ave.
Palos Hills, IL 60465
Phone: (708)974-2110

★ 11379 ★ **National-Louis University / University of Chicago Medical Center**
Respiratory Therapist Program
2840 Sheridan Rd.
Evanston, IL 60201
Phone: (708)256-5150

★ 11380 ★ **Parkland College**
Respiratory Therapist Program
2400 W. Bradley
Champaign, IL 61821-1899
Phone: (217)351-2296

★ 11381 ★ **Rock Valley College**
Respiratory Therapist Program
3301 N. Mulford
Rockford, IL 61114
Phone: (815)654-4413

★ 11382 ★ **Southern Illinois University at Carbondale**
Department of Health Care Professions
Respiratory Therapy Program
Carbondale, IL 62901-6615
Phone: (618)453-7221

★ 11383 ★ **Triton College**
Respiratory Therapist Program
2000 N. 5th Ave.
River Grove, IL 60171
Phone: (708)456-0300

Indiana

★ 11384 ★ **Ball State University / Methodist Hospital of Indiana**
Respiratory Therapist Program
1701 N. Senate Blvd.
Indianapolis, IN 46202
Phone: (317)929-8475

★ 11385 ★ **Indiana University**
School of Medicine
Respiratory Therapist Program
CF 224
1140 W. Michigan St.
Indianapolis, IN 46202
Phone: (317)274-7381

★ 11386 ★ **Indiana University Northwest**
Respiratory Therapist Program
Allied Health-Hawthorne Hall
3400 Broadway
Gary, IN 46408
Phone: (219)980-6548

★ 11387 ★ **Indiana Vocational Technical College**
Respiratory Therapist Program
3800 N. Anthony Blvd.
Fort Wayne, IN 46805
Phone: (219)482-9171

★ 11388 ★ **Indiana Vocational Technical College**
Respiratory Therapist Program
1 W. 26th St.
PO Box 1763
Indianapolis, IN 46206
Phone: (317)921-4402

★ 11389 ★ **University of Southern Indiana**
Respiratory Therapist Program
8600 University Blvd.
Evansville, IN 47712
Phone: (812)464-1702

★ 11390 ★ **Vincennes University**
Respiratory Therapist Program
1002 N. 1st St.
Vincennes, IN 47591
Phone: (812)888-4421

Iowa

★ 11391 ★ **Des Moines Area Community College**
Respiratory Therapist Program
Bldg. 9
2006 S. Ankeny Blvd.
Ankeny, IA 50021
Phone: (515)964-6298

★ 11392 ★ **Kirkwood Community College**
Respiratory Therapist Program
6301 Kirkwood Blvd. SW
PO Box 2068
Cedar Rapids, IA 52406
Phone: (319)398-4987

Kansas

★ 11393 ★ **Johnson County Community College**
Respiratory Therapist Program
12345 College Blvd.
Overland Park, KS 66210-1299
Phone: (913)469-8500

★ 11394 ★ **Labette Community College**
Respiratory Therapist Program
200 S. 14th St.
Parsons, KS 67357
Phone: (316)421-6700

★ 11395 ★ **Seward County Community College**
Respiratory Therapist Program
Box 1137
Liberal, KS 67901
Phone: (316)624-3080

★ 11396 ★ **University of Kansas**
School of Allied Health
Respiratory Therapy Program
Medical Center
3901 Rainbow Blvd.
Kansas City, KS 66160-7606
Phone: (913)588-4630

★ 11397 ★ **Washburn University of Topeka**
School of Applied and Continuing Education
Respiratory Therapist Program
1700 College Blvd.
Topeka, KS 66621
Phone: (913)231-1010

★ 11398 ★ **Wichita State University**
College of Health Professions
Respiratory Therapist Program
Box 43
1845 Fairmount
Wichita, KS 67260-0043
Phone: (316)689-3619

Kentucky

★ 11399 ★ **Jefferson Community College**
Respiratory Therapist Program
109 E. Broadway
Louisville, KY 40202
Phone: (502)584-0181

★ 11400 ★ **Lexington Community College**
Respiratory Care Program
Oswald Bldg., Rm. 330
Cooper Dr.
Lexington, KY 40506-0235
Phone: (606)257-6154

★ 11401 ★ **Madisonville Community College**
Consortium for Respiratory Care Education
200 College Dr.
Madisonville, KY 42431
Phone: (502)821-2250

★ 11402 ★ **Northern Kentucky University**
College of Professional Studies
Department of Allied Health, Human Services, and Social Work
Respiratory Therapy Program
Highland Heights, KY 41099
Phone: (606)572-5557

★ 11403 ★ **University of Louisville**
School of Medicine
Division of Allied Health
Respiratory Therapist Program
Carmichael Bldg.
Louisville, KY 40292
Phone: (502)852-7815

Louisiana

★ 11404 ★ **Alton Ochsner Medical Foundation**
School of Allied Health Sciences
Respiratory Therapist Program
880 Commerce Rd., W.
New Orleans, LA 70123-3335
Phone: (504)842-3266

★ 11405 ★ **Bossier Parish Community College**
Respiratory Therapist Program
2719 Airline Dr. N.
Bossier City, LA 71111
Phone: (318)746-9851

★ 11406 ★ **Delgado Community College**
Respiratory Therapist Program
615 City Park Ave.
New Orleans, LA 70119
Phone: (504)483-4007

★ 11407 ★ **Louisiana State University**
Department of Cardiopulmonary Science
Respiratory Therapy Program
1900 Gravier St.
New Orleans, LA 70112-2262
Phone: (504)568-4229

★ 11408 ★ **Southern University at**
Shreveport
Respiratory Therapist Program
3050 Martin Luther King Jr. Dr.
Shreveport, LA 71107
Phone: (318)674-3329

Maine

★ 11409 ★ **Southern Maine Technical**
College
Respiratory Therapist Program
Fort Rd.
South Portland, ME 04106
Phone: (207)767-9592

Maryland

★ 11410 ★ **Allegany Community College**
Respiratory Therapist Program
Willow Brook Rd.
PO Box 1695
Cumberland, MD 21501
Phone: (301)724-7700

★ 11411 ★ **Baltimore City Community**
College
Respiratory Therapist Program
2901 Liberty Heights Ave.
Baltimore, MD 21215-7893
Phone: (410)333-5922

★ 11412 ★ **Columbia Union College**
Respiratory Therapist Program
7600 Flower Ave.
Takoma Park, MD 20912
Phone: (301)891-4187

★ 11413 ★ **Frederick Community College**
Respiratory Therapy Program
7932 Oppossumtown Pike
Frederick, MD 21702
Phone: (301)846-2528

★ 11414 ★ **Prince George's Community**
College
Respiratory Therapist Program
301 Largo Rd.
Largo, MD 20772-2199
Phone: (301)322-0733

★ 11415 ★ **Salisbury State College**
Respiratory Therapy Program
College and Camden Aves.
Salisbury, MD 21801
Phone: (410)543-6418

Massachusetts

★ 11416 ★ **Berkshire Community College**
Respiratory Therapist Program
1350 West St.
Pittsfield, MA 01201
Phone: (413)499-4660

★ 11417 ★ **Massasoit Community College**
Respiratory Therapist Program
1 Massasoit Blvd.
Brockton, MA 02402
Phone: (508)588-9100

★ 11418 ★ **Newbury College**
Respiratory Therapist Program
129 Fisher Ave.
Brookline, MA 02146
Phone: (617)730-7061

★ 11419 ★ **North Shore Community College**
Respiratory Therapist Program
Box 3340
1 Ferncroft Rd.
Danvers, MA 01923
Phone: (508)762-4000

★ 11420 ★ **Northeastern University**
College of Pharmacy and Allied Health
Professions
Respiratory Therapy Program
100 Dockser Hall
360 Huntington Ave.
Boston, MA 02115
Phone: (617)373-3671

★ 11421 ★ **Northern Essex Community**
College
Respiratory Therapist Program
100 Elliott Way
Haverhill, MA 01830
Phone: (508)374-3900

★ 11422 ★ **Quinsigamond Community**
College
Respiratory Therapist Program
670 W. Boylston St.
Worcester, MA 01606
Phone: (508)853-2300

★ 11423 ★ **Springfield Technical**
Community College
Respiratory Therapist Program
1 Armory Sq.
Springfield, MA 01105
Phone: (413)781-7822

Michigan

★ 11424 ★ **Charles Stewart Mott**
Community College
Respiratory Therapist Program
1401 E. Court St.
Flint, MI 48503
Phone: (810)762-0317

★ 11425 ★ **Delta College**
Respiratory Therapist Program
University Center, MI 48710
Phone: (517)686-9489

★ 11426 ★ **Ferris State University**
College of Allied Health Sciences
Respiratory Therapist Program
901 S. State St.
Big Rapids, MI 49307
Phone: (616)592-2312

★ 11427 ★ **Henry Ford Community College**
Respiratory Therapist Program
22586 Ann Arbor Trail
Dearborn Heights, MI 48127
Phone: (313)730-5970

★ 11428 ★ **Kalamazoo Valley Community**
College
Respiratory Therapist Program
6767 W. O Ave.
Kalamazoo, MI 49009
Phone: (616)372-5356

★ 11429 ★ **Lansing Community College**
Respiratory Therapist Program
PO Box 40010
Lansing, MI 48901
Phone: (517)483-1411

★ 11430 ★ **Macomb Community College**
Respiratory Therapist Program
E Bldg., Rm. 219
44575 Garfield Rd.
Clinton Township, MI 48038-1139
Phone: (810)286-2033

★ 11431 ★ **Marygrove College**
Respiratory Therapist Program
8425 W. McNichols Rd.
Detroit, MI 48221-2599
Phone: (313)862-8000

★ 11432 ★ **Monroe County Community**
College
Respiratory Therapist Program
1555 S. Raisinville Rd.
Monroe, MI 48161
Phone: (313)242-7300

★ 11433 ★ **Muskegon Community College**
Respiratory Therapist Program
221 S. Quarterline Rd.
Muskegon, MI 49442
Phone: (616)777-0370

★ 11434 ★ **Oakland Community College**
Respiratory Therapist Program
George Bee Administrative Center
2480 Opdyke Rd.
Bloomfield Hills, MI 48304-2266
Phone: (810)552-2673

★ 11435 ★ **Washtenaw Community College**
Respiratory Therapist Program
4800 E. Huron River Dr.
PO Box D-1
Ann Arbor, MI 48106
Phone: (313)973-3331

Minnesota

★ 11436 ★ **College of St. Catherine**
St. Mary's Campus
Respiratory Therapist Program
601 25th Ave. S.
Minneapolis, MN 55454
Phone: (612)690-7819

★ 11437 ★ Duluth Technical College /
Range Technical College
Respiratory Therapist Program
2101 Trinity Rd.
Duluth, MN 55811
Phone: (218)722-2801

★ 11438 ★ Northwest Technical College
Respiratory Therapist Program
Box 111
Hwy. 220 N.
East Grand Forks, MN 56721
Phone: (218)773-3441

★ 11439 ★ Rochester Community College /
Mayo Foundation
Respiratory Therapist Program
Box 24
851 30th Ave., SE
Rochester, MN 55904-4999
Phone: (507)285-7210

★ 11440 ★ St. Paul Technical College
Respiratory Therapist Program
235 Marshall Ave.
St. Paul, MN 55102
Phone: (612)221-1300

Mississippi

★ 11441 ★ Hinds Community College
Respiratory Therapist Program
Nursing Allied Health Center
1750 Chadwick Dr.
Jackson, MS 39204-3402
Phone: (601)372-3517

★ 11442 ★ Itawamba Community College
Respiratory Therapist Program
602 W. Hill St.
Fulton, MS 38843-1099
Phone: (601)862-3101

★ 11443 ★ Northwest Mississippi
Community College
Respiratory Therapist Program
8700 Northwest Dr.
Southaven, MS 38671
Phone: (601)342-1570

★ 11444 ★ University of Mississippi
School of Health Related Professions
Respiratory Therapy Program
Medical Center
2500 n. State St.
Jackson, MS 39216-4505
Phone: (601)984-6306

Missouri

★ 11445 ★ Heart of the Ozarks Technical
Community College
Respiratory Therapist Program
1417 N. Jefferson
Springfield, MO 65802
Phone: (417)895-7127

★ 11446 ★ St. Louis Community College at
Forest Park
Respiratory Therapist Program
5600 Oakland
St. Louis, MO 63110
Phone: (314)644-9079

★ 11447 ★ University of Missouri—
Columbia
School of Health Related Professions
Respiratory Therapy Program
504 Lewis Hall
Columbia, MO 65211
Phone: (314)882-8011

Montana

★ 11448 ★ Great Falls Vocational Technical
Center
Respiratory Therapist Program
2100 16th Ave. S.
Great Falls, MT 59405
Phone: (406)771-1310

Nebraska

★ 11449 ★ Metropolitan Community
College
Respiratory Therapist Program
PO Box 3777
Omaha, NE 68103-0777
Phone: (402)449-8510

★ 11450 ★ Midland Lutheran College /
Immanuel Medical Center
Respiratory Therapist Program
6901 N. 72nd St.
Omaha, NE 68122
Phone: (402)572-2312

★ 11451 ★ Nebraska Methodist College of
Nursing and Allied Health
Respiratory Therapist Program
8501 W. Dodge Rd.
Omaha, NE 68144
Phone: (402)390-4913

★ 11452 ★ Southeast Community College
Respiratory Therapist Program
8800 O St.
Lincoln, NE 68520
Phone: (402)437-2780

New Hampshire

★ 11453 ★ New Hampshire Technical
College
Respiratory Therapist Program
1 College Dr.
Claremont, NH 03743
Phone: (603)542-7744

New Jersey

★ 11454 ★ Bergen Community College
Respiratory Therapist Program
400 Paramus Rd.
Paramus, NJ 07652
Phone: (201)447-7178

★ 11455 ★ Brookdale Community College
Respiratory Therapist Program
765 Newman Springs Rd.
Lincroft, NJ 07738
Phone: (908)224-2854

★ 11456 ★ Fairleigh Dickinson University
Respiratory Therapist Program
Florham Madison Campus
285 Madison Ave.
Madison, NJ 07940
Phone: (201)625-6723

★ 11457 ★ Union County College
Respiratory Therapist Program
1033 Springfield Ave.
Cranford, NJ 07016
Phone: (908)412-3562

★ 11458 ★ University of Medicine and
Dentistry of New Jersey
School of Health Related Professions
Respiratory Therapist Program
Box 200, Jefferson Hall
Blackwood, NJ 08012
Phone: (609)227-7200

★ 11459 ★ University of Medicine and
Dentistry of New Jersey
School of Health Related Professions
Respiratory Therapist Program
65 Bergen St.
Newark, NJ 07107-3001
Phone: (201)982-5503

New Mexico

★ 11460 ★ Albuquerque Technical
Vocational Institute
Respiratory Therapist Program
525 Buena Vista SE
Albuquerque, NM 87106
Phone: (505)224-4111

New York

★ 11461 ★ Borough of Manhattan
Community College of City University of
New York
Respiratory Therapist Program
199 Chambers St.
New York, NY 10007
Phone: (212)346-8731

★ 11462 ★ Erie Community College
Respiratory Therapist Program
6205 Main St.
Williamsville, NY 14221-7095
Phone: (716)851-1530

★ 11463 ★ Hudson Valley Community
College
Respiratory Care Program
80 Vandenburg Ave.
Troy, NY 12180
Phone: (518)270-7454

★ 11464 ★ Long Island University
Respiratory Therapist Program
Brooklyn Campus
University Plaza
Brooklyn, NY 11201
Phone: (718)488-1492

★ 11465 ★ Molloy College
Respiratory Therapist Program
1000 Hempstead Ave.
Rockville Centre, NY 11570-1199
Phone: (516)678-5000

★ 11466 ★ **Nassau Community College**
Respiratory Therapist Program
1 Education Dr.
Garden City, NY 11530
Phone: (516)572-7550

★ 11467 ★ **New York City Health and**
    Hospitals Corporation / Empire State
    College
Respiratory Therapist Program
C&D Bldg.,4th Fl. E.
Bellevue Hospital Center
27th St. and 1st Ave.
New York, NY 10016
Phone: (212)561-4151

★ 11468 ★ **New York University Medical**
    Center
Center for Allied Health Education
Respiratory Therapist Program
342 E. 26th St.
New York, NY 10010
Phone: (212)263-6644

★ 11469 ★ **Onondaga Community College**
Respiratory Therapist Program
Syracuse, NY 13215
Phone: (315)469-7741

★ 11470 ★ **Rockland Community College**
Respiratory Therapist Program
145 College Rd.
Suffern, NY 10901
Phone: (914)574-4532

★ 11471 ★ **State University of New York**
    Health Science Center at Syracuse
Respiratory Therapy Program
750 E. Adams St.
Syracuse, NY 13210
Phone: (315)464-5580

★ 11472 ★ **State University of New York at**
    Stony Brook
School of Health Technology and
    Management
Respiratory Therapy Program
Health Sciences Center, Level 2, Rm. 052
Stony Brook, NY 11794-8203
Phone: (516)444-3180

★ 11473 ★ **Westchester Community**
    College
Respiratory Therapist Program
75 Grasslands Rd.
Valhalla, NY 10595-1698
Phone: (914)285-6883

North Carolina

★ 11474 ★ **Carteret Community College**
Respiratory Therapist Program
3505 Arendell St.
Morehead City, NC 28557
Phone: (919)247-6000

★ 11475 ★ **Central Piedmont Community**
    College
Respiratory Therapist Program
PO Box 35009
Charlotte, NC 28235
Phone: (704)342-6274

★ 11476 ★ **Durham Technical Community**
    College
Respiratory Therapist Program
1637 Lawson St.
PO Box 11307
Durham, NC 27703
Phone: (919)598-9243

★ 11477 ★ **Edgecombe Community College**
Respiratory Therapist Program
225 Tarboro St.
Rocky Mount, NC 27801
Phone: (919)446-0436

★ 11478 ★ **Fayetteville Technical**
    Community College
Respiratory Care Technology
2201 Hull Rd.
Fayetteville, NC 28303-0236
Phone: (910)678-8316

★ 11479 ★ **Forsyth Technical Community**
    College
Respiratory Therapist Program
2100 Silas Creek Pkwy.
Winston-Salem, NC 27103
Phone: (919)723-0371

★ 11480 ★ **Pitt Community College**
Respiratory Therapist Program
PO Drawer 7007
Greenville, NC 27835-7007
Phone: (919)321-4378

★ 11481 ★ **Sandhills Community College**
Respiratory Therapist Program
2200 Airport Rd.
Pinehurst, NC 28374
Phone: (910)695-3835

★ 11482 ★ **Southwestern Community**
    College
Respiratory Therapist Program
275 Webster Rd.
Sylva, NC 28779
Phone: (704)586-4091

★ 11483 ★ **Stanly Community College**
Respiratory Therapist Program
141 College Dr.
Albemarle, NC 28001
Phone: (704)982-0121

North Dakota

★ 11484 ★ **North Dakota State University /**
    St. Luke's Hospital MeritCare
Respiratory Therapist Program
720 4th St. N., Rte. 25
Fargo, ND 58102
Phone: (701)234-6147

★ 11485 ★ **University of Mary / St. Alexius**
    Medical Center
North Dakota School of Respiratory Care
900 East Broadway
Bismarck, ND 58506
Phone: (701)224-7524

Ohio

★ 11486 ★ **Bowling Green State University**
Respiratory Therapist Program
901 Rye Beach Rd.
Huron, OH 44839-9791
Phone: (419)433-5560

★ 11487 ★ **Cincinnati State Technical and**
    Community College
Respiratory Therapist Program
3520 Central Pkwy.
Cincinnati, OH 45223
Phone: (513)569-1690

★ 11488 ★ **Columbus State Community**
    College
Respiratory Therapist Program
550 E. Spring St.
Columbus, OH 43215-1609
Phone: (614)227-5151

★ 11489 ★ **Cuyahoga Community College**
Respiratory Therapist Program
11000 Pleasant Valley Rd.
Parma, OH 44130
Phone: (216)987-5267

★ 11490 ★ **Jefferson Technical College**
Respiratory Therapist Program
4000 Sunset Blvd.
Steubenville, OH 43952
Phone: (614)264-5591

★ 11491 ★ **Kettering College of Medical**
    Arts
Respiratory Therapist Program
3737 Southern Blvd.
Kettering, OH 45429
Phone: (513)296-7201

★ 11492 ★ **Lakeland Community College**
Respiratory Therapist Program
7700 Clocktower Dr.
Kirtland, OH 44094-5198
Phone: (216)953-7343

★ 11493 ★ **Lima Technical College**
Respiratory Therapist Program
4240 Campus Dr.
Lima, OH 45804
Phone: (419)221-1112

★ 11494 ★ **North Central Technical College**
Respiratory Therapist Program
2441 Kenwood Circle
PO Box 698
Mansfield, OH 44901-0698
Phone: (419)755-4800

★ 11495 ★ **Ohio State University**
Respiratory Therapy Division
1583 Perry St.
Columbus, OH 43210-1234
Phone: (614)292-8445

★ 11496 ★ **Shawnee State University**
Respiratory Therapist Program
940 2nd St.
Portsmouth, OH 45662
Phone: (614)355-2235

★11497★ Sinclair Community College
Respiratory Therapist Program
444 W. 3rd St.
Dayton, OH 45402
Phone: (513)226-2849

★11498★ Stark Technical College
Respiratory Therapist Program
6200 Frank Ave. NW
Canton, OH 44720
Phone: (216)494-6170

★11499★ University of Akron
Respiratory Therapist Program
325 E. Buchtel Ave.
Akron, OH 44325
Phone: (216)972-7906

★11500★ University of Toledo
Community and Technical College
Respiratory Therapist Program
2801 W. Bancroft St.
Toledo, OH 43606-3390
Phone: (419)537-3372

★11501★ Youngstown State University
Respiratory Therapist Program
410 Wick Ave.
Youngstown, OH 44555
Phone: (216)742-3327

Oklahoma

★11502★ Rose State College
Respiratory Therapist Program
6420 SE 15th St.
Midwest City, OK 73110
Phone: (405)733-7571

★11503★ Tulsa Junior College
Respiratory Therapist Program
909 S. Boston Ave., Rm. MP458
Tulsa, OK 74119
Phone: (918)631-7016

Oregon

★11504★ Apollo College at Portland
Respiratory Therapist Program
2600 SE 98th St.
Portland, OR 97216
Phone: (503)761-6100

★11505★ Lane Community College
Respiratory Therapist Program
4000 E. 30th Ave.
Eugene, OR 97405
Phone: (503)747-4501

★11506★ Mt. Hood Community College
Respiratory Therapist Program
26000 SE Stark St.
Gresham, OR 97030
Phone: (503)669-6904

★11507★ Rogue Community College
Respiratory Therapist Program
3345 Redwood Hwy.
Grants Pass, OR 97527
Phone: (503)471-3500

Pennsylvania

★11508★ Community College of Allegheny County
Respiratory Therapist Program
Allegheny Campus
808 Ridge Ave.
Pittsburgh, PA 15212
Phone: (412)237-2607

★11509★ Community College of Philadelphia
Respiratory Therapist Program
1700 Spring Garden St.
Philadelphia, PA 19130
Phone: (215)751-8423

★11510★ Delaware County Community College / Crozer-Chester Medical Center
Respiratory Therapist Program
1 Medical Center Blvd.
Upland, PA 19013-3995
Phone: (610)447-2435

★11511★ Gannon University
Respiratory Therapist Program
University Sq.
Erie, PA 16541
Phone: (814)871-5637

★11512★ Gwynedd Mercy College
Respiratory Therapist Program
Sumneytown Pike
Gwynedd Valley, PA 19437
Phone: (215)641-5536

★11513★ Harrisburg Area Community College
Respiratory Therapist Program
1 HACC Dr.
Harrisburg, PA 17110-2999
Phone: (717)780-2315

★11514★ Indiana University of Pennsylvania
Respiratory Therapy Program
Western Pennsylvania Hospital
4800 Friendship Ave.
Pittsburgh, PA 15224
Phone: (412)578-7000

★11515★ Lehigh Carbon Community College
Respiratory Therapist Program
4525 Eduation Park Dr.
Schnecksville, PA 18078-2598
Phone: (610)799-1504

★11516★ Mansfield University
Department of Health Sciences
Respiratory Therapist Program
Mansfield, PA 16933
Phone: (717)882-4513

★11517★ Millersville University
Respiratory Therapist Program
Millersville, PA 17551
Phone: (717)291-8208

★11518★ Reading Area Community College
Respiratory Therapist Program
Box 1706
10 S. 2nd St.
Reading, PA 19602
Phone: (215)372-4721

★11519★ University of Pittsburgh at Johnstown
Respiratory Therapist Program
224 Krebs Hall
Johnstown, PA 15904
Phone: (814)269-2960

★11520★ West Chester University / Bryn Mawr Hospital
Respiratory Therapist Program
130 Bryn Mawr Ave.
Bryn Mawr, PA 19010
Phone: (610)526-3347

★11521★ Western School of Health and Business Careers
Respiratory Therapist Program
327 5th Ave.
Pittsburgh, PA 15222
Phone: (412)281-7083

★11522★ York College of Pennsylvania
Respiratory Therapy Program
1001 S. George St.
York, PA 17405
Phone: (717)771-2464

Puerto Rico

★11523★ Adventista de las Antillas University
Respiratory Therapy Program
PO Box 118
Mayaguez, PR 00681-0118
Phone: (809)834-9595

★11524★ Universidad Metropolitana
Respiratory Therapist Program
PO Box 21150
Rio Piedras, PR 00928
Phone: (809)766-1717

★11525★ University of Puerto Rico
College of Health Related Professions
Respiratory Therapist Program
Medical Sciences Campus
PO Box 365067
San Juan, PR 00936-5067
Phone: (809)758-2525

Rhode Island

★11526★ Community College of Rhode Island
Respiratory Therapist Program
Flanagan Campus
1762 Louisquisset Pike
Lincoln, RI 02865
Phone: (401)333-7252

South Carolina

★11527★ Florence-Darlington Technical College
Respiratory Therapist Program
PO Box 100548
Florence, SC 29501-0548
Phone: (803)661-8148

★ 11528 ★ **Greenville Technical College**
Respiratory Therapist Program
PO Box 5616
Greenville, SC 29606-5616
Phone: (803)250-8373

★ 11529 ★ **Midlands Technical College**
Respiratory Therapist Program
PO Box 2408
Columbia, SC 29202
Phone: (803)822-3433

★ 11530 ★ **Piedmont Technical College**
Respiratory Therapy Program
PO Drawer 1467
Greenwood, SC 29646
Phone: (803)223-8357

★ 11531 ★ **Spartanburg Technical College**
Respiratory Therapist Program
PO Box 4386
Spartanburg, SC 29305-4386
Phone: (803)591-3869

★ 11532 ★ **Trident Technical College**
Respiratory Therapist Program
PO Box 118067, AH-M
Charleston, SC 29423-8067
Phone: (803)569-6460

South Dakota

★ 11533 ★ **Dakota State University**
College of Natural Sciences
Respiratory Therapist Program
Madison, SD 57042-1799
Phone: (605)256-5194

Tennessee

★ 11534 ★ **Chattanooga State Technical**
Community College
Respiratory Therapist Program
4501 Amnicola Hwy.
Chattanooga, TN 37406-1097
Phone: (615)697-4450

★ 11535 ★ **Columbia State Community**
College
Respiratory Therapist Program
PO Box 1315
Columbia, TN 38402-1315
Phone: (615)540-2663

★ 11536 ★ **East Tennessee State University**
Department of Health Related Professions
Respiratory Therapy Program
1000 W. E St.
Elizabethton, TN 37643
Phone: (615)543-2230

★ 11537 ★ **Jackson State Community**
College
Respiratory Therapist Program
2046 N. Pkwy. St.
Jackson, TN 38301-3797
Phone: (901)424-3520

★ 11538 ★ **Roane State Community College**
Respiratory Therapist Program
Patton Lane
Rte. 8, Box 69
Harriman, TN 37748
Phone: (615)354-3000

★ 11539 ★ **Tennessee State University**
Respiratory Therapy Program
3500 John A. Merritt Blvd.
Nashville, TN 37209-1561
Phone: (615)320-3145

Texas

★ 11540 ★ **Alvin Community College**
Respiratory Therapist Program
3110 Mustang Rd.
Alvin, TX 77511-4898
Phone: (713)388-4695

★ 11541 ★ **Amarillo College**
Respiratory Therapist Program
PO Box 447
Amarillo, TX 79178
Phone: (806)354-6058

★ 11542 ★ **Collin County Community**
College District
Respiratory Therapist Program
2200 W. University Dr.
McKinney, TX 75069
Phone: (214)548-6870

★ 11543 ★ **Del Mar College**
Respiratory Therapist Program
101 Baldwin
Corpus Christi, TX 78404
Phone: (512)886-1101

★ 11544 ★ **El Centro College**
Respiratory Therapist Program
Main and Lamar Sts.
Dallas, TX 75202-3604
Phone: (214)746-2279

★ 11545 ★ **El Paso Community College**
Respiratory Therapist Program
PO Box 20500
El Paso, TX 79998
Phone: (915)534-4072

★ 11546 ★ **Houston Community College**
System
Eastwood Center for Health Careers
Respiratory Therapist Program
3100 Shenandoah
Houston, TX 77021
Phone: (713)746-5353

★ 11547 ★ **Kingwood College-NHMCCD**
Respiratory Therapist Program
East Campus
20000 Kingwood Dr.
Kingwood, TX 77339
Phone: (713)359-1683

★ 11548 ★ **Lamar University**
Institute of Technology
Respiratory Therapist Program
PO Box 10061
Beaumont, TX 77710
Phone: (409)880-8845

★ 11549 ★ **Midland College**
Respiratory Therapist Program
3600 N. Garfield
Midland, TX 79705
Phone: (915)685-4601

★ 11550 ★ **Odessa College**
Respiratory Therapist Program
201 W. University
Odessa, TX 79764
Phone: (915)335-6456

★ 11551 ★ **San Jacinto College, Central**
Campus
Respiratory Therapist Program
8060 Spencer Hwy.
Pasadena, TX 77501-2007
Phone: (713)476-1864

★ 11552 ★ **South Plains College**
Respiratory Therapist Program
1302 Main St.
Lubbock, TX 79401
Phone: (806)747-0576

★ 11553 ★ **Southeast College of the**
Houston Community College System
Eastwood Center for Health Careers
Respiratory Therapy Program
3100 Shenendoah
Houston, TX 77201
Phone: (713)746-5356

★ 11554 ★ **Southwest Texas State**
University
Respiratory Therapist Program
601 University Dr.
San Marcos, TX 78666
Phone: (512)245-8243

★ 11555 ★ **Tarrant County Junior College**
Respiratory Therapist Program
Northeast Campus
828 Harwood Rd.
Hurst, TX 76054
Phone: (817)788-6574

★ 11556 ★ **Temple Junior College**
Respiratory Therapist Program
2600 S. 1st St.
Temple, TX 76504-7435
Phone: (817)778-4811

★ 11557 ★ **Texas Southern University**
Respiratory Therapist Program
3100 Cleburne
Houston, TX 77004
Phone: (713)527-7265

★ 11558 ★ **Texas Southmost College /**
University of Texas Brownsville
Respiratory Therapist Program
80 Fort Brown
Brownsville, TX 78520
Phone: (210)544-8262

★ 11559 ★ **Tyler Junior College**
Respiratory Therapist Program
PO Box 9020
Tyler, TX 75711
Phone: (903)510-2472

★ 11560 ★ **University of Texas Medical**
Branch at Galveston
Respiratory Therapist Program
4015 Ave. Q
Galveston, TX 77550
Phone: (409)763-6551

★ 11561 ★ **Victoria College**
Respiratory Therapist Program
2200 E. Red River
Victoria, TX 77901
Phone: (512)573-3291

★ 11562 ★ **Wichita General Hospital**
Midwestern State University Consortium
Respiratory Therapy Program
1600 8th St.
Wichita Falls, TX 76301
Phone: (817)723-8970

Utah

★ 11563 ★ **Weber State University**
College of Allied Health Sciences
Respiratory Therapy Program
3750 Harrison Blvd.
Ogden, UT 84408-3904
Phone: (801)626-7071

Vermont

★ 11564 ★ **Champlain College**
Respiratory Therapy Program
163 S. Willard St.
Burlington, VT 05402
Phone: (802)658-0800

Virginia

★ 11565 ★ **Community Hospital of Roanoke Valley**
College of Health Sciences
Respiratory Therapist Program
PO Box 13186
Roanoke, VA 24031
Phone: (703)985-8487

★ 11566 ★ **J. Sargeant Reynolds Community College**
Respiratory Therapy Tech Program
PO Box 85622
Richmond, VA 23285-5622
Phone: (804)786-1375

★ 11567 ★ **Northern Virginia Community College**
Respiratory Therapist Program
8333 Little River Tpke.
Annandale, VA 22003
Phone: (703)323-3280

★ 11568 ★ **Shenandoah University / Winchester Medical Center**
Respiratory Therapist Program
203 S. Cameron St.
Winchester, VA 22601
Phone: (703)665-5517

★ 11569 ★ **Southwest Virginia Community College**
Respiratory Therapist Program
Box SVCC
Richlands, VA 24641-1510
Phone: (703)964-7306

★ 11570 ★ **Tidewater Community College**
Respiratory Therapist Program
1700 College Crescent
Virginia Beach, VA 23456
Phone: (804)427-7257

Washington

★ 11571 ★ **Highline Community College**
Respiratory Therapist Program
2400 S. 240th St.
PO Box 98000
Des Moines, WA 98198-9800
Phone: (206)878-3710

★ 11572 ★ **Pima Medical Institute**
Respiratory Therapist Program
1627 Eastlake Ave. E., Ste. 100
Seattle, WA 98102
Phone: (206)322-6100

★ 11573 ★ **Seattle Central Community College**
Respiratory Therapist Program
1701 Broadway
Seattle, WA 98122
Phone: (206)587-4056

★ 11574 ★ **Spokane Community College**
Respiratory Therapist Program
N. 1810 Greene St., MS 2090
Spokane, WA 99207
Phone: (509)533-7307

★ 11575 ★ **Tacoma Community College**
Respiratory Therapist Program
Allied Health Bldg.
5900 S. 12th St.
Tacoma, WA 98465
Phone: (206)566-5163

★ 11576 ★ **Walla Walla Community College**
Respiratory Therapist Program
500 Tausick Way
Walla Walla, WA 99362
Phone: (509)527-4354

West Virginia

★ 11577 ★ **College of West Virginia**
Respiratory Therapist Program
609 S. Kanawha St.
Beckley, WV 25801-2830
Phone: (304)253-7351

★ 11578 ★ **University of Charleston**
College of Health Sciences
Respiratory Therapist Program
2300 MacCorkle Ave. SE
Charleston, WV 25304
Phone: (304)357-4837

★ 11579 ★ **West Virginia Northern Community College**
Respiratory Therapist Program
College Sq.
Wheeling, WV 26003
Phone: (304)233-5900

★ 11580 ★ **Wheeling Jesuit College**
Respiratory Therapy Program
316 Washington Ave.
Wheeling, WV 26003-6295
Phone: (304)243-2372

Wisconsin

★ 11581 ★ **Madison Area Technical College**
Respiratory Therapist Program
3550 Anderson St.
Madison, WI 53704
Phone: (608)246-6686

★ 11582 ★ **Mid-State Technical College**
Respiratory Therapist Program
2600 W. 5th St.
Marshfield, WI 54449
Phone: (715)387-2538

★ 11583 ★ **Milwaukee Area Technical College**
Respiratory Therapist Program
700 W. State St.
Milwaukee, WI 53233
Phone: (414)297-7130

★ 11584 ★ **Northeast Wisconsin Technical College**
Respiratory Therapist Program
2740 W. Mason St.
PO Box 19042
Green Bay, WI 54307-9042
Phone: (414)498-5432

★ 11585 ★ **Western Wisconsin Technical College**
Respiratory Therapist Program
304 N. 6th St.
La Crosse, WI 54602-0908
Phone: (608)785-9186

Wyoming

★ 11586 ★ **Western Wyoming Community College**
Respiratory Therapist Program
2500 College Dr.
PO Box 428
Rock Springs, WY 82902
Phone: (307)382-1600

National & International Organizations

★ 11587 ★ **Alpha 1 National Association**
1829 Portland Ave.
Minneapolis, MN 55404
Phone: (612)871-7332
Fax: (612)871-9441
Sandra Brandley, Exec. Officer

Founded: 1989. **Members:** 1,000. **Local Groups:** 26. **Description:** Individuals with Alpha 1 Antitrypsin deficiency emphysema. Provides advocacy and educational programs. **Publications:** *Alpha 1 News*, quarterly. Newsletter. **Formerly:** (1991) Alpha 1 Antitrypsin Support Group.

★11588★ **American Association for Respiratory Care (AARC)**
11030 Ables Ln.
Dallas, TX 75229
Phone: (214)243-2272
Fax: (214)484-2720
Sam P. Giordano, Exec.Dir.

Founded: 1947. **Members:** 37,000. **State Groups:** 50. **Description:** Allied health society of respiratory care technicians and therapists employed by hospitals, skilled nursing facilities, home care companies, group practices, educational institutions, and municipal organizations. To encourage, develop, and provide educational programs for persons interested in the profession of respiratory care; and to advance the science of respiratory care. **Publications:** *AARC Times: The Magazine for the Respiratory Care Professional*, monthly. Magazine. Includes advertisers' index, calendar of events, employment opportunities, and legislative update. *Price:* Included in membership dues; $60/year for nonmembers. • *Respiratory Care*, monthly. Provides original studies, case reports, and method/device evaluations in cardiopulmonary clinical medicine. *Price:* Included in membership dues; $60/year for nonmembers; $5/copy. **Formerly:** (1954) Inhalation Therapy Association; (1967) American Association of Inhalation Therapists; (1973) American Association for Inhalation Therapy; (1986) American Association for Respiratory Therapy.

★11589★ **American Broncho-Esophagological Association (ABEA)**
c/o Rodney P. Lusk, M.D.
1 Children's Place, Rm. 3S35
St. Louis, MO 63110
Phone: (314)454-2138
Fax: (314)454-2174
Rodney P. Lusk, M.D., Sec.

Founded: 1917. **Members:** 300. **Description:** Professional society of otolaryngologists, chest specialists, thoracic surgeons, and gastroenterologists engaged in the practice of broncho-esophagology (diseases and injuries of the respiratory system and upper digestive tract). Conducts program on study of foreign bodies. **Publications:** *Annals of Otology, Rhinology and Laryngology*. Proceedings. • *Transactions*, annual. **Formerly:** (1928) American Bronchoscopic Society.

American College of Chest Physicians (ACCP)
See: Entry 2826

★11590★ **American Lung Association (ALA)**
1740 Broadway
New York, NY 10019-4374
Phone: (212)315-8700
Fax: (212)265-5642
John R. Garrison, Mng.Dir.

Founded: 1904. **Members:** 9,500. **State Groups:** 59. **Local Groups:** 72. **Description:** Federation of state and local associations of physicians, nurses, and laymen interested in the prevention and control of lung disease. Works with other organizations in planning and conducting programs in community services, public, professional and patient education, and re-

search. Maintains the American Thoracic Society as its medical section. Makes policy recommendations regarding medical care of lung disease, occupational health, hazards of smoking, and air conservation. ALA is financed by annual Christmas Seal Campaign and other fundraising activities. **Publications:** Annual Report. • Brochures. • Pamphlets. • Videos. **Formerly:** (1918) National Association for the Study and Prevention of Tuberculosis; (1968) National Tuberculosis Association; (1973) National Tuberculosis and Respiratory Disease Association.

★11591★ **American Thoracic Society (ATS)**
1740 Broadway
New York, NY 10019-4374
Phone: (212)315-8700
Fax: (212)315-6498
Marilyn Hansen, Exec.Dir.

Founded: 1905. **Members:** 11,000. **State Groups:** 43. **Description:** The medical section of the American Lung Association. Specialists in pulmonary diseases, physicians in the public health field concerned with tuberculosis control, thoracic surgeons, and research workers in lung diseases. Acts as adviser in scientific matters. **Publications:** *American Journal of Respiratory Cell and Molecular Biology*, monthly. Journal. • *American Review of Respiratory Disease*, monthly. Journal. Includes society news, book reviews, and case reports. *Price:* Included in membership dues. • *ATS News*, monthly. Newsletter. Includes summary of health legislation and annual index. *Price:* Included in membership dues. • Membership Directory, biennial. **Formerly:** (1939) American Sanatorium Association; (1960) American Trudeau Society.

Asbestos Litigation Group (ALG)
See: Entry 7174

Asbestos Victims of America (AVA)
See: Entry 9791

★11592★ **Black Lung Association (BLA)**
c/o Bill Bailey
Box 872
Crab Orchard, WV 25827
Phone: (304)252-9654
Bill Bailey, Exec. Officer

Founded: 1968. **Members:** 73,000. **Regional Groups:** 14. **State Groups:** 7. **Local Groups:** 2. **Description:** Working miners, disabled miners, and friends. Objectives are to promote safer working conditions for coal miners and just compensation for disabled miners. Strives for increases in: mine health and safety standards; state and federal benefits for victims of black lung (pneumoconiosis), and other chronic respiratory and pulmonary diseases caused by coal dust; Social Security disability insurance benefits; workmen's compensation; hospitalization and pension benefits for disabled miners and the widows and orphans of miners who have died as a result of their occupation. Attempts to secure better political representation for miners. Maintains training program for members to assist others in obtaining black lung benefits through Social Security and the Department of Labor. Maintains speakers' bureau; compiles statistics; conducts research programs. **Publi-**

cations: *Black Bulletin*, biweekly. Bulletin. • Directory, biennial. • *Federal Black Lung Journal*, bimonthly. Journal. • Newsletter, monthly. • *United Mine Workers Journal*, periodic. Journal.

★11593★ **Christina Lazar Foundation for Laryngeal Papillomatosis**
84D Broadway, Ste. 174
Denville, NJ 07834
Phone: (201)627-1243
Fax: (201)627-9465
William Lazar, Pres.

Founded: 1991. **Members:** 50. **Regional Groups:** 5. **Description:** Individuals and families affected by laryngeal papillomatosis (LP), a rare disease in which tumors grow inside the trachea or larynx preventing normal breathing. Also known as recurrent respiratory papillomatosis. Promotes the health and welfare of victims. Seeks to increase public awareness, solicit donations, and support research efforts. Conducts a vitamin program; maintains national register of those afflicted with the disease. Provides children's services and educational programs; compiles statistics. **Publications:** Brochure, annual. *Price:* Free. • *CLF National Newsletter*, semiannual. Newsletter. *Price:* Free. **Formerly:** (1992) Christina Lazar Foundation for Juvenile Papillomatosis.

★11594★ **Congress of Lung Association Staff (CLAS)**
1726 M St. NW, Ste. 902
Washington, DC 20036-4502
Phone: (202)785-3355
Fax: (202)452-1805
Janet Widmer, Exec.Dir.

Founded: 1912. **Members:** 800. **Description:** Professional society of executives and staff members of the American Lung Association. Sponsors network opportunities and staff development and training programs. Offers specialized education courses. **Publications:** Booklets. • *CLAS Action Report*, quarterly. • Membership Directory, annual. **Formerly:** National Conference of Tuberculosis Secretaries; (1968) National Conference of Tuberculosis Workers; (1973) National Respiratory Disease Conference.

Cystic Fibrosis Foundation (CFF)
See: Entry 5275

★11595★ **Emphysema Anonymous, Inc. (EAI)**
726 N. Highland Ave.
Clearwater, FL 34615-5463
Phone: (813)391-9977
William E. Jaeckle, Exec.Dir.

Founded: 1965. **Members:** 3,000. **Description:** Interested individuals and persons who suffer from emphysema (a condition affecting breathing capacity). Aims to help victims of emphysema through education, encouragement, and mutual assistance. National office provides nonmedical counseling service for patients and their families. **Publications:** *Batting the Breeze*, bimonthly. Newsletter. *Price:* $15/year.

French-Language Infant Pneumology and Phthisiology Group (FLIPPG)
(Groupe de Pneumologie et Phtisiologie Infantile de Langue Francaise)
See: Entry 3229

★ 11596 ★   International Association of Asthmology (INTERASMA)
(Asociacion Internacional de Asmologia — INTERASMA)
Hopital Arnaud de Villeneuve
Maladies Respiratoires
F-34295 Montpellier Cedex 5, France
Phone: 67336117
Fax: 67521848
P. Godard, M.D., Sec.Gen.

Founded: 1954. **Members:** 1,200. **Regional Groups:** 12. **Languages:** English, French, German, Russian, Spanish. **Description:** Doctors and other individuals interested in asthmology. Promotes a broadening of knowledge of bronchial asthma and related diseases, especially with regard to their etiology, pathological mechanisms, patho-physiology, therapy, epidemiology, rehabilitation, and prevention. Sponsors specialized training in allergology. Holds biennial symposium. **Publications:** *Allergologia et Immunopathologia*, bimonthly. • *INTERASMA Membership Directory*, triennial. Directory.

International Association for the Study of Lung Cancer (IASLC)
See: Entry 5952

★ 11597 ★   International Bronchoesophagological Society (IBES)
c/o David R. Sanderson, M.D.
Mayo Clinic Scottsdale
13400 E. Shea Blvd.
Scottsdale, AZ 85259
Phone: (602)301-8000
Fax: (602)301-8610
David R. Sanderson, M.D., Exec.Sec.-Treas.

Founded: 1951. **Members:** 400. **Description:** Endoscopists from varying disciplines. Fosters advances in laryngology, bronchoscopy, upper gastrointestinal endoscopy, diagnostic techniques, and endoscopic therapy. Encourages exchange of ideas; conducts original investigations and research.

International Cystic Fibrosis (Mucoviscidosis) Association (ICFMA)
See: Entry 5279

★ 11598 ★   International Society for Respiratory Protection (ISRP)
PO Box 158
Jonesborough, TN 37659
Phone: (615)753-1388
Fax: (615)753-8645
Bradley Squibb, Sec.-Treas.

Founded: 1982. **Members:** 400. **Languages:** English. **Description:** Technical and professional people involved with all aspects of nonmedical occupational respiratory protection. Seeks to advance knowledge of respiratory protection for firefighters, commercial divers, persons working in and around foundries, coke ovens, and mines, and other individuals exposed to airborne particles and other unsuitable

breathing conditions. **Publications:** *ISRP Journal*, quarterly. Journal. Includes scientific articles. • Membership Directory, annual. • *Special Conference Proceedings*, biennial. Proceedings. Also publishes technical papers.

★ 11599 ★   International Union Against Tuberculosis and Lung Disease (IUATLD)
(Union Internationale Contre la Tuberculose et les Maladies Respiratoires — UICTMR)
68, blvd. St. Michel
F-75006 Paris, France
Phone: 1 46330830
Fax: 1 43299087
Dr. Nils Billo, Exec. Dir.

Founded: 1920. **Members:** 4,500. **Languages:** English, French, Spanish. **Description:** National associations, physicians, and other individuals in 124 countries dedicated to the fight against tuberculosis and other respiratory diseases. Promotes community health and, within its framework, the delivery of preventive, diagnostic, and therapeutic measures against tuberculosis. Aids governmental efforts to improve health services; helps countries formulate, prepare, and execute national tuberculosis control programs. Provides training, advice, antitubercular drugs and vaccines, medical equipment, and transportation. Encourages community participation. Activities include: dissemination of scientific knowledge; exchange of experience and conferences; operational and applied research; field projects under the Mutual Assistance Programme. Acts as liaison with the World Health Organization and other organizations. **Publications:** Newsletter, 3/year. • *Tubercle and Lung Disease*, bimonthly. Includes Summaries in English and Spanish. **Formerly:** (1986) International Union Against Tuberculosis.

★ 11600 ★   Joint Review Committee for Respiratory Therapy Education (JRCRTE)
1701 W. Euless Blvd., Ste. 300
Euless, TX 76040
Phone: (817)283-2835
Free: 800-874-5615
Fax: (817)354-8519
Philip A. VonDerHeydt, Exec.Dir.

Founded: 1963. **Members:** 13. **Description:** Physicians (6); respiratory therapists (6); public representative (1). Purposes are to develop standards and requirements for accredited educational programs of respiratory therapy for recommendation to the American Medical Association (see separate entry); to conduct evaluations of educational programs that have applied for accreditation of the AMA and to make recommendations to the AMA's Committee on Allied Health Education and Accreditation ; to maintain a working liaison with other organizations interested in respiratory therapy education and evaluation. Publishes lists of programs. **Formerly:** (1970) Board of Schools of Inhalation Therapy.

★ 11601 ★   Latin American Union of Societies of Phthisiology
(Union Latinoamericana de Sociedades de Tisiologia)
San Lucar 1554
Montevideo, Uruguay
Prof. Fernando D. Gomez, Sec.Gen.

Description: Promotes scientific progress and studies in all aspects of tuberculosis and its eradication. **Publications:** *ULAST Boletin - Comision Honoraia para Lucha Antituberculosa*, quarterly.

★ 11602 ★   National Association of Pneumologists
(Bundesverband der Pneumologen)
Schlossstr. 22
45468 Muhlheim, Germany
Phone: 208 445267
Dr. Dietrich Rohde, Contact

Description: Represents the interests of physicians in the lung and bronchial medical fields.

★ 11603 ★   National Board for Respiratory Care (NBRC)
8310 Nieman Rd.
Lenexa, KS 66214
Phone: (913)599-4200
Steven K. Bryant, Exec.Dir.

Founded: 1960. **Members:** 90,000. **Description:** Offers credentialing examinations for respiratory therapists, respiratory therapy technicians, pulmonary technologists, and perinatal/pediatric respiratory care specialists. **Publications:** Directory, annual. • Newsletter, bimonthly. **Formerly:** (1974) American Registry of Inhalation Therapists; (1982) National Board for Respiratory Therapy.

★ 11604 ★   National Coalition of Black Lung and Respiratory Disease Clinics (NCBLRDC)
PO Box 209
Jacksboro, TN 37757
Phone: (615)562-1156
David Haden, Chair

Founded: 1981. **Members:** 200. **Description:** Clinics receiving federal aid for research or clinic operations; allied health organizations working in conjunction with black lung clinics; interested individuals. Works to develop a pulmonary rehabilitation program; to provide a forum for continuing education, training, facilitation of meetings, and technical assistance. Strives to unite and promote the networking of federally funded projects that treat miners who have been diagnosed as suffering from black lung disease; encourages victims of respiratory diseases to participate in the coalition. Seeks improved billing and reimbursement for clinics through the U.S. Department of Labor. Compiles statistics. **Publications:** *Membership List*, annual. Membership Directory. • Newsletter, quarterly.

★ 11605 ★   National Jewish Center for Immunology and Respiratory Medicine
1400 Jackson St.
Denver, CO 80206
Phone: (303)388-4461
Fax: (303)270-2165
Lynn Taussig, Pres.

Founded: 1978. **Description:** Devoted to treatment, research, and education in chronic respiratory diseases and immunological disorders such as asthma, tuberculosis, cystic fibrosis, chronic bronchitis, emphysema, interstitial lung disease, and systemic lupus erythematosus. Accepts non-sectarian patients of all ages. Disseminates information to the public. Maintains research library of 15,000 volumes. **Publications:** *Lung Line Letter*, quarterly. Newsletter. *Price:* Free. • *National Jewish Center for Immunology and Respiratory Medicine--Medical Scientific Update*, monthly. Newsletter. *Price:* Free. • *National Jewish Center for Immunology and Respiratory Medicine--Annual Report. Price:* Free. • *New Directions*, quarterly. Newsletter. Updates the center's research programs. *Price:* Free. **Formerly:** (1984) National Jewish Hospital/National Asthma Center.

Nordic Federation of Heart and Lung Associations (NHL)
See: Entry 2868

Norwegian Cystic Fibrosis Association (NCFA)
(Norsk Forening for Cystisk Fibrose — NFCF)
See: Entry 5296

Pan-American Society for Chemotherapy of Tuberculosis (PASCT)
(Sociedad Panamericana de Quimioterapia de la Tuberculosis — SAQT)
See: Entry 10419

Respiratory Nursing Society (RNS)
See: Entry 9133

★ 11606★ **Slovak Society of Physiology and Pathology of Respiration**
Mickiewiczowa 13
SK-813 69 Bratislava, Slovakia
Phone: 7 321527
Fax: 7 321527

Languages: English, Slovak. **Description:** Health care professionals treating respiratory ailments. Promotes professional advancement of members; represents members' interests.

Society of Thoracic Radiology (STR)
See: Entry 11140

Society of Thoracic Surgeons (STS)
See: Entry 12309

United Patients Association for Pulmonary Hypertension (UPAPH)
See: Entry 2880

★ 11607★ **White Lung Association (WLA)**
PO Box 1483
Baltimore, MD 21203-1483
Phone: (410)243-5864
Fax: (410)243-5234
James Fite, Exec.Dir.

Founded: 1979. **Members:** 45,000. **Description:** A selfhelp organization for those with conditions associated with exposure to asbestos. Serves as a clearinghouse providing information on legal and medical assistance to asbestos victims and interested persons. Conducts investigations of suspected contamination; monitors

the removal of asbestos in workplaces. Maintains speakers' bureau; conducts charitable programs. Conducts training for those working in areas where asbestos is present. Offers classes in the Asbestos Hazard Emergency Response Act. Sponsors Technical Information Center. **Publications:** *Asbestos Watch*, quarterly.

Research Centers

Baylor College of Medicine
Acute Viral Respiratory Disease Unit
See: Entry 6762

★ 11608★ **Boston University**
Pulmonary Center
School of Medicine
80 E. Concord, K-603
Boston, MA 02118
Phone: (617)638-4860
Fax: (617)638-8093
Mary C. Williams, Ph.D., Assoc.Dir.

Research Activities and Fields: Clinical research efforts aim at developing an integrated approach to the cell and molecular biology of lung cells.

★ 11609★ **Carl Stough Institute of Breathing Coordination, Inc.**
200 E. 66th St.
New York, NY 10021
Phone: (212)308-7138
L. H. Raglan, Mgr.

Research Activities and Fields: Respiratory science, especially relief of dyspnea (breathlessness) and prophylaxis. Emphasizes the Stough Method of Breathing Coordination (SIM-BIC), a physiological discovery made by Carl Stough in the early 1960s during his work with emphysema patients.

Case Western Reserve University
Cystic Fibrosis and Pediatric Pulmonary Center
See: Entry 5317

★ 11610★ **Cornell University**
Will Rogers Pulmonary Research Laboratory
785 Mamaroneck Ave.
White Plains, NY 10605
Phone: (914)948-0050
Fax: (914)421-0796
Henry M. Thomas, III, M.D., Dir.

Research Activities and Fields: Control of pulmonary circulation as it relates to gas exchange in disease and pulmonary hypoxic vasoconstriction.

Cystic Fibrosis Center
See: Entry 5324

Cystic Fibrosis Foundation
See: Entry 5326

Cystic Fibrosis Research Center
See: Entry 5327

Duke University
Cystic Fibrosis Research Center
See: Entry 5328

Emory University
Cystic Fibrosis Care, Teaching and Research Center
See: Entry 5329

Indiana University-Purdue University at Indianapolis
Cystic Fibrosis and Pediatric Pulmonary Clinic
See: Entry 5331

Johns Hopkins University
Cystic Fibrosis Research Center
See: Entry 5335

Laval University
Laval Hospital Research Centre
See: Entry 2911

★ 11611★ **McGill University**
Montreal Chest Hospital Research Centre
3650 St. Urbain St.
Montreal, PQ, Canada H2X 2P4
Phone: (514)982-6686
Fax: (514)982-6840
Seymour Heisler, Dir.

Research Activities and Fields: Respiratory medicine, focusing on chronic obstructive pulmonary diseases (COPD). Research also includes structure-function, physiology, pharmacology, rehabilitation, environment, body surface motion, asthma, cystic fibrosis, and airway hyperresponsiveness.

Medical College of Pennsylvania and Hahnemann University
Hahnemann Cystic Fibrosis Research Center
See: Entry 5339

Medical College of Wisconsin
Cystic Fibrosis Research Center
See: Entry 5340

National Jewish Center for Immunology and Respiratory Medicine
See: Entry 2109

Ohio State University
Pulmonary Laboratories
See: Entry 2111

★ 11612★ **Pediatric Pulmonary Unit**
Massachusetts General Hospital
Vincent Burnham Bldg.
Boston, MA 02114
Phone: (617)726-2906
Fax: (617)726-1036
Daniel Shannon, M.D., Assoc.Dir.

Research Activities and Fields: Sudden infant death, control of autonomic functions, cystic fibrosis, and pediatric pulmonary and pediatric gastrointestinal diseases, including isoelectric focusing in cystic fibrosis detection and use of beta-2 stimulants in childhood asthma. **Formerly:** Pediatric Pulmonary Research Center.

Sleep Disorders Center for Children
See: Entry 3349

State University of New York Health Science Center at Syracuse
Robert C. Schwartz Cystic Fibrosis Center
See: Entry 5353

Tulane University
Cystic Fibrosis Research Center and Pediatric Pulmonary Disease Center
See: Entry 5357

U.S. Department of Defense
Armed Forces Institute of Pathology
Center for Advanced Pathology
Pulmonary and Mediastinal Pathology Department
See: Entry 10162

U.S. Department of Health and Human Services
National Center for Infectious Diseases
Division of Bacterial and Mycotic Diseases
Childhood and Respiratory Diseases Branch
See: Entry 6796

U.S. Department of Health and Human Services
National Center for Infectious Diseases
Division of Viral and Rickettsial Diseases
Respiratory and Enteric Virus Branch
See: Entry 6810

U.S. Department of Health and Human Services
National Center for Prevention Services
Tuberculosis Elimination Division
Surveillance and Epidemiologic Investigations Branch
See: Entry 10880

U.S. Department of Health and Human Services
National Heart, Lung, and Blood Institute
See: Entry 2929

U.S. Department of Health and Human Services
National Heart, Lung, and Blood Institute
Division of Epidemiology and Clinical Applications
See: Entry 2930

U.S. Department of Health and Human Services
National Heart, Lung, and Blood Institute
Division of Epidemiology and Clinical Applications
Clinical Applications and Prevention Program
See: Entry 2931

U.S. Department of Health and Human Services
National Heart, Lung, and Blood Institute
Division of Epidemiology and Clinical Applications
Epidemiology and Biometry Program
See: Entry 2932

U.S. Department of Health and Human Services
National Heart, Lung, and Blood Institute
Division of Intramural Research
See: Entry 2939

U.S. Department of Health and Human Services
National Heart, Lung, and Blood Institute
Division of Intramural Research
Pathology Branch
See: Entry 2943

★11613★ U.S. Department of Health and Human Services
National Heart, Lung, and Blood Institute
Division of Intramural Research
Pulmonary Branch
NIH Bldg. 10, Rm. 6D03
9000 Rockville Pike
Bethesda, MD 20892
Phone: (301)496-1597
Joel Moss, Acting Chief

Research Activities and Fields: Research investigates the structure and function of the lung in health and disease through cellular and biochemical methods. Both laboratory and clinical investigations are conducted and techniques of protein chemistry, molecular biology, tissue culture, and immunology are used. Emphasis is on the regulation of the inflammatory and immune processes in the normal and diseased lung. Clinical research is directed toward correlating physiologic, biochemical, immunologic, and morphologic observations in patients with interstitial lung disease, destructive lung disease, hereditary disorders of connective tissue, hypersensitivity lung disease, and other lung disorders with an immunologic basis.

★11614★ U.S. Department of Health and Human Services
National Heart, Lung, and Blood Institute
Division of Lung Diseases
Westwood Blvd., Rm. 6A16
5333 Westbard Ave.
Bethesda, MD 20892
Phone: (301)594-7408
Fax: (301)594-7408
Dr. Suzanne S. Hurd, Director

Research Activities and Fields: Division serves as a focal point for planning and coordinating research and research training programs for all diseases of the respiratory system, including: 1) chronic obstructive pulmonary diseases; 2) pediatric pulmonary diseases; 3) occupational and immunologic lung diseases; 4) pulmonary vascular diseases; 5) acute lung injury; 6) asthma; 7) critical care; 8) cystic fibrosis; 9) lung cell biology; 10) respiratory neurobiology and sleep; and 11) pulmonary complications of AIDS.

★11615★ U.S. Department of Health and Human Services
National Heart, Lung, and Blood Institute
Division of Lung Diseases
Airways Diseases Branch
5333 Westbard Ave., Rm. 6A15
Bethesda, MD 20892
Phone: (301)594-7443
Fax: (301)594-7487
Dr. James Kiley, Chief

Research Activities and Fields: Branch provides support for basic and clinical research related to the cause and prevention of airways diseases, with particular interest in: 1) the delay or reversal of the progression of airways diseases through greater knowledge of their pathogenesis; and 2) the amelioration of their effects through improved early diagnosis and more effective management. Principal areas of research interest include: chronic obstructive lung diseases, asthma, cystic fibrosis, respiratory neurobiology, and sleep.

★11616★ U.S. Department of Health and Human Services
National Heart, Lung, and Blood Institute
Division of Lung Diseases
Cell and Developmental Biology Branch
5333 Westbard Ave., Rm. 6A07
Bethesda, MD 20892
Phone: (301)594-7428
Dr. Dorothy Gail, Chief

Research Activities and Fields: Branch supports research on pediatric pulmonary diseases, lung cell biology, acute lung injury, and critical care.

★11617★ U.S. Department of Health and Human Services
National Heart, Lung, and Blood Institute
Division of Lung Diseases
Interstitial Lung Diseases Branch
5333 Westbard Ave., Rm. 6A09
Bethesda, MD 20892
Phone: (301)594-7425
Fax: (301)594-7487
Anthony R. Kalica, Chief

Research Activities and Fields: Branch supports research in: 1) occupational and immunologic lung diseases; 2) pulmonary vascular diseases; and 3) pulmonary complications of AIDS.

★11618★ U.S. Department of Health and Human Services
National Heart, Lung, and Blood Institute
Division of Lung Diseases
Prevention, Education, and Research Training Branch
5333 Westbard Ave., Rm. 640
Bethesda, MD 20892
Phone: (301)594-7466
Fax: (301)594-7487
Dr. Sydney R. Parker, Branch Chief

Research Activities and Fields: Branch supports programs in research training development and programs in prevention, control, and education in lung diseases.

U.S. Department of Health and Human Services
National Heart, Lung, and Blood Institute
Laboratory of Biochemical Genetics
See: Entry 2944

U.S. Department of Health and Human Services
National Heart, Lung, and Blood Institute
Laboratory of Biochemistry
See: Entry 2945

U.S. Department of Health and Human Services
National Heart, Lung, and Blood Institute
Laboratory of Biophysical Chemistry
See: Entry 2946

U.S. Department of Health and Human Services
National Heart, Lung, and Blood Institute
Laboratory of Cell Biology
See: Entry 2948

U.S. Department of Health and Human Services
National Heart, Lung, and Blood Institute
Laboratory of Cellular Metabolism
See: Entry 2949

U.S. Department of Health and Human Services
National Heart, Lung, and Blood Institute
Laboratory of Chemical Pharmacology
See: Entry 2950

U.S. Department of Health and Human Services
National Institute of Allergy and Infectious Diseases
Division of Microbiology and Infectious Diseases
Respiratory Diseases Branch
See: Entry 6830

U.S. Department of Health and Human Services
National Institute of Diabetes and Digestive and Kidney Diseases
Division of Diabetes, Endocrinology, and Metabolic Diseases
Diabetes Programs Branch
See: Entry 5363

U.S. Department of Health and Human Services
National Institute of Environmental Health Sciences
Laboratory of Pulmonary Pathobiology
See: Entry 5110

U.S. Department of Health and Human Services
National Institute for Occupational Safety and Health
Appalachian Laboratory for Occupational Safety and Health
See: Entry 9825

U.S. Department of Health and Human Services
National Institute for Occupational Safety and Health
Respiratory Disease Studies Division
See: Entry 9835

U.S. Department of Health and Human Services
National Institute for Occupational Safety and Health
Respiratory Disease Studies Division
Clinical Investigations Branch
See: Entry 9836

U.S. Department of Health and Human Services
National Institute for Occupational Safety and Health
Respiratory Disease Studies Division
Environmental Investigations Branch
See: Entry 9837

University of Alabama at Birmingham
Gregory Fleming James Cystic Fibrosis Research Center
See: Entry 5366

University of Arkansas at Little Rock
Arkansas Children's Hospital Cystic Fibrosis Center
See: Entry 5368

★ 11619 ★ University of California, Los Angeles
Will Rogers Institute Pulmonary Research Laboratory
Los Angeles, CA 90024
Phone: (310)825-6112
Fax: (310)206-8766
Tomas Ganz, Ph.D., Dir.

Research Activities and Fields: Lung injury and inflammation and host defense mechanisms. **E-mail Address:** tganz@medicine.medsch.ucla.edu.

★ 11620 ★ University of California, San Diego
Division of Pulmonary and Critical Care Medicine
200 W. Arbor Dr.
San Diego, CA 92103-8372
Phone: (619)543-5970
Kenneth M. Moser, M.D., Dir.

Research Activities and Fields: Acute respiratory failure, including its pathogenesis and management. **Formerly:** Specialized Center of Research in Acute Respiratory Failure.

★ 11621 ★ University of California, San Diego
Pediatric Pulmonary and Cystic Fibrosis Center
200 W. Arbor
MC 8448
San Diego, CA 92103
Phone: (619)294-6125
Fax: (619)296-3758
Dr. Michael J. Light, M.D., Dir.

Research Activities and Fields: Neonatal and pediatric pulmonary medicine, including cystic fibrosis, chronic illness, neonatal pulmonary mechanics and control of breathing, and pulmonary surfactant.

University of Colorado
Cystic Fibrosis Center
See: Entry 5370

University of Illinois at Chicago
Institute for Tuberculosis Research
See: Entry 2143

University of Miami
Cystic Fibrosis Research Center
See: Entry 5373

★ 11622 ★ University of Michigan
Pulmonary and Critical Care Medicine Division
Univ. Hospital
3916 Taubman Center
Ann Arbor, MI 48109-0360
Phone: (313)936-5010
Fax: (313)936-5048
Dr. Galen B. Toews, Dir.

Research Activities and Fields: Pulmonary diseases and critical care, including cell biology, immunology, and biochemistry of lung and heart. **Formerly:** Pulmonary Medicine Division (1982).

University of Minnesota
Cystic Fibrosis Center
See: Entry 5374

University of Missouri—Columbia
Cystic Fibrosis Research Center
See: Entry 5376

University of Nebraska at Omaha
Pediatric Pulmonary and Cystic Fibrosis Research Center
See: Entry 5378

University of Oklahoma
Pulmonary and Cystic Fibrosis Center
See: Entry 5379

University of Pittsburgh
Cystic Fibrosis Research Center
See: Entry 5380

University of Utah
Intermountain Cystic Fibrosis Center
See: Entry 5385

University of Washington
Cystic Fibrosis Research Center
See: Entry 5388

University of Wisconsin—Madison
Pediatric Pulmonary Center
See: Entry 5390

★ 11623 ★ University of Wisconsin—Madison
Pulmonary and Critical Care Medicine Section
Dept. of Medicine
600 Highland Ave., H6/380
Madison, WI 53792-3240
Phone: (608)263-3035
Fax: (608)263-3104
Dr. James Skatrud, Section Head

Research Activities and Fields: Pulmonary physiology, occupational lung disease, and mechanisms of acute lung injury.

★ 11624 ★ University of Wisconsin— Madison
Respiratory Virus Research Laboratory
517 Stovall Bldg.
465 Henry Mall
Madison, WI 53706-1578
Phone: (608)262-2638
Fax: (608)262-3257
Elliot C. Dick, Ph.D., Prof. of Preventive Medicine
Research Activities and Fields: Etiology, pathogenesis, interruption, and epidemiology of respiratory infections in man and animals. **E-mail Address:** ecdick@slh.wisc.edu.

Washington University
Cystic Fibrosis Research Center
See: Entry 5391

★ 11625 ★ Washington University
Hyperthermia Service
Radiation Oncology Center
4939 Children's Pl., Ste. 5500
Box 8224
St. Louis, MO 63110
Phone: (314)362-8503
Fax: (314)362-8521
Robert J. Myerson, M.D., Chief
Research Activities and Fields: Hyperthermia treatment of cancer, simultaneous thermoradiotherapy, and bioassay of predictors of hyperthermic response. **E-mail Address:** moros@zelda.wustl.edu.

Wayne State University
Cystic Fibrosis Care, Teaching and Resource Center
See: Entry 5393

West Virginia University
Cystic Fibrosis Center
See: Entry 5395

Yale University
Cystic Fibrosis Research Center
See: Entry 5396

State & Regional Organizations

Respiratory Diseases

The associations listed below are constituents of the American Lung Association, 1740 Broadway, New York, NY 10019-4374, (212) 315-8700.

Alabama

★ 11626 ★ American Lung Association of Alabama
900 S. 18th St.
PO Box 55209
Birmingham, AL 35255
Phone: (205)933-8821
Fax: (205)930-1717

Alaska

★ 11627 ★ American Lung Association of Alaska
1057 W. Fireweed Ln., Ste. 201
Anchorage, AK 99503-1736
Phone: (907)276-5864
Fax: (907)263-2090

Arizona

★ 11628 ★ American Lung Association of Arizona
102 W. McDowell Rd.
Phoenix, AZ 85003-1299
Phone: (602)258-7505
Fax: (602)258-7507

Arkansas

★ 11629 ★ American Lung Association of Arkansas
211 Natural Resources Dr.
Little Rock, AR 72205-1539
Phone: (501)224-5864
Fax: (501)224-5645

California

★ 11630 ★ American Lung Association of California
424 Pendleton Way
Oakland, CA 94621-2189
Phone: (510)638-5864
Fax: (510)638-8984

Colorado

★ 11631 ★ American Lung Association of Colorado
1600 Race St.
Denver, CO 80206-1198
Phone: (303)388-4327
Fax: (303)377-1102

Connecticut

★ 11632 ★ American Lung Association of Connecticut
45 Ash St.
East Hartford, CT 06108-3272
Phone: (203)289-5401
Free: 800-992-2263
Fax: (203)289-5405

Delaware

★ 11633 ★ American Lung Association of Delaware
1021 Gilpin Ave., Ste. 202
Wilmington, DE 19806-3280
Phone: (302)655-7258
Fax: (302)655-8546

District of Columbia

★ 11634 ★ American Lung Association of the District of Columbia
475 H St. NW
Washington, DC 20001-2617
Phone: (202)682-5864
Fax: (202)682-5874

Florida

★ 11635 ★ American Lung Association of Florida
5526 Arlington Rd.
PO Box 8127
Jacksonville, FL 32239-0127
Phone: (904)743-2933
Free: 800-940-2933
Fax: (904)743-2916

Georgia

★ 11636 ★ American Lung Association of Georgia
2452 Spring Rd.
Smyrna, GA 30080-3862
Phone: (404)434-5864
Fax: (404)319-0349

Hawaii

★ 11637 ★ American Lung Association of Hawaii
245 N. Kukui St., Ste. 100
Honolulu, HI 96817
Phone: (808)537-5966
Fax: (808)537-5971

Idaho

★ 11638 ★ American Lung Association of Idaho
1111 S. Orchard, Ste. 245
Boise, ID 83705-1966
Phone: (208)344-6567
Fax: (208)345-5896

Illinois

★ 11639 ★ American Lung Association of Illinois
PO Box 2576
Springfield, IL 62708-2576
Phone: (217)528-3441
Fax: (217)528-9192

★ 11640 ★ American Lung Association of Metropolitan Chicago
1440 W. Washington Blvd.
Chicago, IL 60607-1878
Phone: (312)243-2000
Fax: (312)243-3954

Indiana

★11641★ American Lung Association of
Indiana
9410 Priority Way W. Dr.
Indianapolis, IN 46240-1470
Phone: (317)573-3900
Fax: (317)573-3909

Iowa

★11642★ American Lung Association of
Iowa
1025 Ashworth Rd., Ste. 410
West Des Moines, IA 50265-6600
Phone: (515)224-0800
Free: 800-362-1643
Fax: (515)224-0540

Kansas

★11643★ American Lung Association of
Kansas
4300 Drury Ln.
Topeka, KS 66604-2419
Phone: (913)272-9290
Fax: (913)272-9297

Kentucky

★11644★ American Lung Association of
Kentucky
4100 Churchman Ave.
Louisville, KY 40209-0067
Phone: (502)363-2652
Fax: (502)363-0222

Louisiana

★11645★ American Lung Association of
Louisiana
333 St. Charles Ave., Ste. 500
New Orleans, LA 70130-3180
Phone: (504)523-5864
Fax: (504)523-5867

Maine

★11646★ American Lung Association of
Maine
128 Sewall St.
Augusta, ME 04330
Phone: (207)622-6394
Free: 800-499-5864
Fax: (207)626-2919

Maryland

★11647★ American Lung Association of
Maryland
1840 York Rd., Ste. K-M
Timonium, MD 21093-5156
Phone: (410)560-2120
Fax: (410)560-0829

Massachusetts

★11648★ American Lung Association of
Massachusetts
1505 Commonwealth Ave.
Brighton, MA 02135-3605
Phone: (617)787-5864
Fax: (617)787-2446

Michigan

★11649★ American Lung Association of
Michigan
18860 W. 10 Mile Rd.
Southfield, MI 48075-2689
Phone: (810)559-5100
Fax: (810)559-7434

Minnesota

★11650★ American Lung Association of
Minnesota
490 Concordia Ave.
St. Paul, MN 55103-2441
Phone: (612)227-8014
Fax: (612)227-5459

Mississippi

★11651★ American Lung Association of
Mississippi
353 N. Mart Plaza
PO Box 9865
Jackson, MS 39286-0865
Phone: (601)362-5453
Free: 800-737-5453
Fax: (601)362-5456

Missouri

★11652★ American Lung Association of
Eastern Missouri
1118 Hampton Ave.
St. Louis, MO 63139-3196
Phone: (314)645-5505
Fax: (314)645-7128

★11653★ American Lung Association of
Western Missouri
2007 Broadway
Kansas City, MO 64108-2080
Phone: (816)842-5242
Fax: (816)842-5470

Montana

★11654★ American Lung Association of
Montana
825 Helena Ave.
Helena, MT 59601-3459
Phone: (406)442-6556
Fax: (406)442-2346

Nebraska

★11655★ American Lung Association of
Nebraska
7101 Newport Ave., Ste. 303
Omaha, NE 68152
Phone: (402)572-3030
Fax: (402)572-3028

Nevada

★11656★ American Lung Association of
Nevada
6119 Ridgeview Ct., Ste. 100
PO Box 7056
Reno, NV 89510-7056
Phone: (702)829-5864
Fax: (702)829-5850

New Hampshire

★11657★ American Lung Association of
New Hampshire
456 Beech St.
PO Box 1014
Manchester, NH 03105-1014
Phone: (603)669-2411
Fax: (603)627-9833

New Jersey

★11658★ American Lung Association of
New Jersey
1600 Rte. 22 E.
Union, NJ 07083-3407
Phone: (201)687-9340
Fax: (908)851-2625

New Mexico

★11659★ American Lung Association of
New Mexico
216 Truman Ave. NE
Albuquerque, NM 87108
Phone: (505)265-0732
Free: 800-221-5864
Fax: (505)260-1739

New York

★11660★ American Lung Association of
Brooklyn
165 Cadman Plaza E., Rm. 300B
Brooklyn, NY 11201-1484
Phone: (718)624-8531
Fax: (718)624-8534

★11661★ American Lung Association of
New York
432 Park Ave. S., 8th Fl.
New York, NY 10016
Phone: (212)889-3370
Fax: (212)889-3375

★11662★ American Lung Association of
New York State
8 Mountain View Ave.
Albany, NY 12205-2899
Phone: (518)459-4197
Fax: (518)489-5864

★ 11663 ★ American Lung Association of Queens
112-25 Queens Blvd.
Forest Hills, NY 11375
Phone: (718)263-5656
Fax: (718)263-6471

North Carolina

★ 11664 ★ American Lung Association of North Carolina
916 W. Morgan St.
PO Box 27985
Raleigh, NC 27611-7985
Phone: (919)832-8326
Free: 800-892-5650
Fax: (919)856-8530

North Dakota

★ 11665 ★ American Lung Association of North Dakota
212 N. 2nd St.
PO Box 5004
Bismarck, ND 58502-5004
Phone: (701)223-5613
Free: 800-252-6325
Fax: (701)223-5727

Ohio

★ 11666 ★ American Lung Association of Ohio
1700 Arlingate Ln.
Columbus, OH 43228-4102
Phone: (614)279-1700
Fax: (614)279-4940

Oklahoma

★ 11667 ★ American Lung Association of Oklahoma
2442 N. Walnut
PO Box 53303
Oklahoma City, OK 73152-3303
Phone: (405)524-8471
Free: 800-522-8577
Fax: (405)525-6979

Oregon

★ 11668 ★ American Lung Association of Oregon
Capitol Plaza Bldg.
9320 SW Barbur Blvd., Ste. 140
Portland, OR 97219-5430
Phone: (503)246-1997
Fax: (503)246-1924

Pennsylvania

★ 11669 ★ American Lung Association of Pennsylvania
6041 Linglestown Rd.
Harrisburg, PA 17112-1208
Phone: (717)541-5864
Fax: (717)541-8828

Puerto Rico

★ 11670 ★ Asociacion Puertorriquena del Pulmon
PO Box 195247
San Juan, PR 00919-5247
Phone: (809)765-5664
Fax: (809)765-5964

Rhode Island

★ 11671 ★ American Lung Association of Rhode Island
10 Abbott Park Pl.
Providence, RI 02903-3700
Phone: (401)421-6487
Fax: (401)331-5266

South Carolina

★ 11672 ★ American Lung Association of South Carolina
1817 Gadsden St.
Columbia, SC 29201-2392
Phone: (803)779-5864
Free: 800-849-5864
Fax: (803)254-2711

South Dakota

★ 11673 ★ American Lung Association of South Dakota
208 E. 13th St.
Sioux Falls, SD 57102-1099
Phone: (605)336-7222
Free: 800-873-5864
Fax: (605)336-7227

Tennessee

★ 11674 ★ American Lung Association of Tennessee
1808 West End Ave., Ste. 514
Nashville, TN 37203
Phone: (615)329-1151
Fax: (615)329-1723

Texas

★ 11675 ★ American Lung Association of Texas
3520 Executive Center Dr., Ste. G-100
PO Box 26460
Austin, TX 78755-0460
Phone: (512)343-0502
Fax: (512)343-0598

Utah

★ 11676 ★ American Lung Association of Utah
1930 South 1100 East
Salt Lake City, UT 84106-2317
Phone: (801)484-4456
Fax: (801)484-5461

Vermont

★ 11677 ★ American Lung Association of Vermont
30 Farrell St.
South Burlington, VT 05403
Phone: (802)863-6817
Fax: (802)863-6818

Virgin Islands

★ 11678 ★ American Lung Association of the Virgin Islands
PO Box 974
St. Thomas, VI 00804
Phone: (809)774-8620
Fax: (809)776-2320

Virginia

★ 11679 ★ American Lung Association of Virginia
311 South Blvd.
PO Box 7065
Richmond, VA 23221-0065
Phone: (804)355-3295
Fax: (804)342-1063

Washington

★ 11680 ★ American Lung Association of Washington
2625 3rd Ave.
Seattle, WA 98121-1213
Phone: (206)441-5100
Fax: (206)441-3277

West Virginia

★ 11681 ★ American Lung Association of West Virginia
415 Dickinson St.
PO Box 3980
Charleston, WV 25339-3980
Phone: (304)342-6600
Fax: (304)342-6096

Wisconsin

★ 11682 ★ American Lung Association of Wisconsin
150 S. Sunny Slope Rd., Ste. 105
Brookfield, WI 53005-6461
Phone: (414)782-7833
Fax: (414)782-7834

Wyoming

★ 11683 ★ American Lung Association of Wyoming
c/o American Lung Association
Field Services, Planning & Marketing
1740 Broadway
New York, NY 10019-4374
Phone: (212)315-8716
Free: 800-586-4872
Fax: (307)772-6599

Chapter 59
Sexuality

National & International Organizations

★ 11684 ★ **American Association of Physicians for Human Rights (AAPHR)**
273 Church St.
San Francisco, CA 94114
Phone: (415)255-4547
Benjamin Schatz, Exec.Dir.

Founded: 1979. **Members:** 1,500. **State Groups:** 13. **Local Groups:** 21. **Description:** Physicians and medical students. Seeks elimination of discrimination on the basis of sexual orientation in the health professions; promotes unprejudiced medical care for gay and lesbian patients. Maintains a referral and support program for HIV infected physicians. Sponsors annual symposium on lesbian and gay health issues. Offers support to homosexual physicians; encourages research into the health needs of gays and lesbians. Maintains liaison with medical schools and other organizations concerning needs of gay patients and professionals; fosters communication and cooperation among members and other groups and individuals supportive of gay and lesbian physicians. Offers referral service. **Publications:** *AAPHR Reporter*, quarterly. Newsletter. Covers the activities of the association, the medical community, and the public regarding lesbian and gay health issues. *Price:* Included in membership dues.

★ 11685 ★ **American Association of Sex Educators, Counselors and Therapists (AASECT)**
435 N. Michigan Ave., Ste. 1717
Chicago, IL 60611
Phone: (312)644-0828
Fax: (312)644-8557
Kenneth R. Mulcrone, Exec.Dir.

Founded: 1967. **Members:** 2,450. **Regional Groups:** 7. **Description:** Professionals concerned with sex education, counseling, and therapy; students pursuing degrees in the field. Certifies sex educators, counselors, and therapists. Provides educational services. Acts as a referral service for the general public. **Publications:** *Contemporary Sexuality*, monthly. Newsletter. *Price:* $65. • *Journal of Sex Education and Therapy*, quarterly. Journal. *Price:* $30 U.S.;

$45 outside U.S.. • *National Register of Certified Sex Educators and Sex Therapists*, annual. Directory. *Price:* $15. **Formerly:** (1976) American Association of Sex Educators and Counselors.

★ 11686 ★ **Association for the Treatment of Sexual Abusers (ABTSA)**
PO Box 866
Lake Oswego, OR 97034
Phone: (503)233-2312
Fax: (503)494-6152
Dianne Price, Exec.Sec.

Founded: 1985. **Members:** 400. **Description:** Professionals working with sex offenders or victims of sexual assault. Provides training to professionals on the treatment of sex offenders; offers instruction in the operation of the penile plethysmograph, a device used to determine and record variations in the size of the penis due to the amount of blood present or passing through it. Maintains speakers' bureau. Offers consultation on program development and treatment of sex offenders; grants certification of behavioral therapists. **Formerly:** (1986) Association for the Behavioral Treatment of Sexual Aggression; (1992) Association for the Behavioral Treatment of Sexual Abusers.

★ 11687 ★ **Bay Area Physicians for Human Rights (BAPHR)**
PO Box 14128
San Francisco, CA 94114-0128
Phone: (415)558-9353

Founded: 1977. **Members:** 350. **Description:** Graduates of and students in approved schools of medicine and osteopathy; dentist and podiatrists. Objectives are: to improve the quality of medical care for gay and lesbian patients; to educate physicians, both gay and nongay, in the special problems of gay and lesbian patients; to educate the public about health care needs of the homosexual; to maintain liaison with public officials about gay and lesbian health concerns; to offer the gay and lesbian physician support through social functions and consciousness-raising groups. Sponsors research into medical problems and issues which are of special interest to homosexual patients. Provides medical and physician referral service and monthly educational programs; operates speakers' bureau; compiles statistics. Membership is concentrat-

ed in the San Francisco, CA Bay Area. **Publications:** *BAPHRON*, bimonthly. Newsletter. Concerned with medical-related human rights issues, especially gay and lesbian rights and public policy on AIDS. Includes statistics. *Price:* Included in membership dues. • *Medical Evaluation of Persons at Risk of HIV Infection*. Monograph.

★ 11688 ★ **Coalition on Sexuality and Disability (CSD)**
122 E. 23rd St.
New York, NY 10010
Phone: (212)242-3900
Fax: (516)737-5547
Lou Markowitz, Pres.

Founded: 1978. **Members:** 300. **Description:** Promotes sexual health care services through education, training, and advocacy for people with disabilities. Seeks to educate and heighten the awareness of health professionals and disabled people; also promotes research in the area of sexuality and disability, development of resources, and exchange of information. Sponsors educational-training programs, seminars, and symposia. Offers speakers' bureau. **Publications:** *Coalition Newsletter*, quarterly. Newsletter. • *The Sexual Rights of Persons with Developmental Disabilities: Guidelines for Programming with Severely Impaired Persons.* **Formerly:** Northeast Coalition on Sexuality and Disability.

★ 11689 ★ **COSA**
PO Box 14537
Minneapolis, MN 55414
Phone: (612)537-6904
CONVERSION 930122 COSA

Description: Selfhelp program for those involved in relationships with people who have compulsive sexual behavior. Makes use of the Twelve Steps of Alcoholics Anonymous World Services, adapted for sexual behavior. **Also Known As:** Co-Dependents of Sex Addicts.

★ 11690 ★ **Council for Sex Information and Education (CSIE)**
2272 Colorado Blvd., No. 1228
Los Angeles, CA 90041
Joel Adams, Dir.

Founded: 1977. **Description:** A national clearinghouse for information on sexuality and related topics. Premise is that adequate knowledge and understanding of sexuality contributes not only to sexual well-being but to physical and emotional well-being and that helpful information should be readily available. Is compiling lists of books, pamphlets, cassette recordings, and other materials on sexuality and health. **Formerly:** Sex Information Council of America.

★ 11691 ★ **Exodus Trust (ET)**
1523 Franklin St.
San Francisco, CA 94109
Phone: (415)928-1133
Ted McIlvenna, Pres.

Founded: 1968. **Description:** Established to: educate and train professionals interested in sex counseling, therapy, education, or research; provide sex education, counseling, and therapy for adults; research human sexuality; produce films, slides, and literature for use in sex counseling, therapy, and education. Works with the Institute for Advanced Study of Human Sexuality, a professional graduate school accredited by the state of California to grant masters and doctoral degrees in human sexuality. Conducts continuing education programs for physicians and nurses, and workshops and counseling programs for professional and laypeople in San Francisco, CA and other cities. **Formerly:** (1989) National Sex Forum.

★ 11692 ★ **Gay AA (GAA)**
84 Broadway
New Haven, CT 06511
Phone: (203)865-6354

Founded: 1976. **Members:** 37. **Description:** Provides a support system for gay and lesbian alcoholics.

★ 11693 ★ **German Society for Sex Research (GSSR)**
(Deutsche Gesellschaft fur Sexualforschung — DGSF)
Niemannsweg 147
24105 Kiel, Germany
Phone: 431 5972655
Fax: 431 5972651

Founded: 1952. **Members:** 250. **Description:** Conducts research in sexology. **Publications:** *Beitrage zur Sexualforschung*, periodic. • *Zeitschrift fur Sexualforschung*, quarterly. Journal. Also publishes research findings.

★ 11694 ★ **Giarretto Institute (AMACU)**
232 E. Gish Rd., 1st Fl.
San Jose, CA 95112
Phone: (408)453-7616
Fax: (408)453-9064
Brian Abbott, Ph.D., Exec.Dir.

Founded: 1971. **Description:** A sponsoring agency for Parents United. Purpose is to offer therapy and guided self-help support to sexually abused children and their families, and to men and women unable to cope with the trauma of having been sexually abused as children. Offers group, family, and individual therapy designed to help victims alleviate their guilt by giving responsibility for the abuse back to the abuser. Uses the Giarretto approach (named after group's founder), a program for the humanistic treatment of sexual abuse victims. Also trains profes-

sionals in developing comprehensive, multidisciplinary systems of intervention that reduce trauma to the victim. Experienced volunteers act as sponsors for one-on-one encouragement and advice; psychology students serve a s volunteer interns in the second year of their master's degree programs. Currently treats child and adult victim, offenders, and non-offending parents. Maintains speakers' bureau; conducts professional training programs. **Publications:** Audiotapes. • Book. • *Chapter Contact List*, quarterly. Directory. • *Parents United Newsletter*, monthly. Newsletter. • *Trainning Update*, quarterly. Newsletter. Information on training opportunities and serveral information on child sexual abuse. *Price:* Free. • Videos. Also publishes fact sheets related to child sexual abuse. **Formerly:** (1991) Adults Molested as Children United.

★ 11695 ★ **I-ANON**
119 S. Ruth St.
Maryville, TN 37801
Phone: (615)983-6064
Eileen V. MacKenzie, Founder and Conslt.

Founded: 1982. **State Groups:** 100. **Local Groups:** 3. **Description:** Concerned partners of impotent males. Seeks to provide information and group support to members. Refers members to doctors who treat impotence. Supplies patients with information on prosthetic implants, and other forms of treatment. **Publications:** *Answers to the Most Often Asked Questions About Impotence.*

★ 11696 ★ **Impotence Institute of America (IIA)**
119 S. Ruth St.
Maryville, TN 37801
Phone: (615)983-6064
Bruce MacKenzie, Founder & Chm.

Founded: 1983. **Description:** Urologists, psychiatrists, psychologists, sex therapists and counselors, and plastic surgeons; manufacturers of penile implant devices and other products used in the treatment of impotence; impotent men and their partners; hospitals and other institutions that offer assistance and meeting facilities for Impotents Anonymous and I-ANON. Informs and educates the public on the subject of impotency and its causes and treatments. Provides information on various programs and organizations that can assist individuals concerned about impotence. Aids other charitable, educational, and social welfare organizations. Compiles statistics.

★ 11697 ★ **Impotents Anonymous (IA)**
119 S. Ruth St.
Maryville, TN 37801
Phone: (615)983-6064
Bruce MacKenzie, Founder

Founded: 1982. **National Groups:** 100. **Description:** Serves as an educational organization providing concerned individuals with information regarding impotence. Provides information on medical and psychiatric counseling resources available to impotent males; offers group support during pre-treatment and post-treatment.

★ 11698 ★ **International Professional Surrogates Association (IPSA)**
PO Box 74156
Los Angeles, CA 90004
Phone: (213)469-4720
Valri Jean Swift, Pres.

Founded: 1973. **Members:** 50. **Description:** Provides referrals for therapists and clients to professional surrogates who serve as intimate partners to people wishing to improve sexual functioning and relational skills. Surrogates and clients work in conjunction with licensed therapists. Sponsors 12-week training program for potential surrogates and for therapists who want to learn to work with surrogates. Maintains screening committee in order to maintain high ethical standards. Provides information and referral to therapists, educators, and community members; operates speaker's bureau and information/referral phone-line. **Publications:** Newsletter, monthly. Also publishes brochures.

★ 11699 ★ **John Augustus Foundation (JAF)**
PO Box 82085
Portland, OR 97282-0085
Phone: (503)790-0847
Jude Patton, Pres.

Founded: 1969. **Description:** Purpose is to conduct research and disseminate information about gender dysphoria (sexual identity conflict, or unhappiness with one's gender). Conducts medical, psychological, and legal research on sexual identity conflict. Provides lectures for universities, professional groups, and public agencies. Conducts seminars and develops brochures and books for professionals. Offers medical and psychological counseling referral service. Offers charitable program. Compiles statistics. **Publications:** Annual Report. • *Update*, quarterly.

★ 11700 ★ **Lesbian, Gay and Bisexual People in Medicine (LGBPM)**
c/o American Medical Student Association
1902 Association Dr.
Reston, VA 22091
Phone: (703)620-6600
Fax: (703)620-5873

Founded: 1976. **Members:** 350. **Local Groups:** 35. **Description:** Standing committee of the American Medical Student Association Physicians and physicians in training; others interested in gay/lesbian issues. Purposes are to improve the quality of health care for gay patients; to improve working conditions and professional status of gay health professionals and students. Administers educational workshops for health professionals; designs training materials; conducts research on the health problems of gay people and surveys on admissions, hiring, and promotion policies of medical schools and hospitals; provides referrals; sponsors support groups for gay professionals to meet, socialize, and organize; presses for legislative and political action to end discrimination against gay people. Maintains speakers' bureau. **Publications:** *LGBPM Newsletter*, semiannual. Newsletter. **Formerly:** (1980) Gay People in Medicine; (1985) Lesbian and Gay People in Medicine.

Lesbian and Gay Caucus of Public Health Workers (LGCPHW)
See: Entry 10956

★ **11701** ★ **Molesters Anonymous (M.AN)**
c/o Batterers Anonymous
8485 Tamarind, Ste. D
Fontana, CA 92335
Phone: (909)355-1100
Jerry M. Goffman, Ph.D., Coord.

Founded: 1986. **Members:** 1,000. **Regional Groups:** 10. **Description:** Selfhelp group for child molesters. **Publications:** *M.AN Program.* Book. • *Self Help Counseling for Men Who Molest Children. Price:* $12.95.

Montgomery Medical and Psychological Institute (MMPI)
See: Entry 7447

★ **11702** ★ **National Association of Lesbian / Gay Alcoholism Professionals (NALGAP)**
1147 S. Alvarado St.
Los Angeles, CA 90006
Phone: (213)381-8524
Fax: (213)381-8525
Sandi Armstrong, M.S.W., Pres.

Founded: 1979. **Members:** 600. **Description:** Doctors, nurses, social workers, psychologists, certified counselors, and other professionals who work with gay, lesbian, and bisexual alcoholics and addicts; drug, alcohol, and gay agencies, organizations, and institutes. Provides a network for support and communication among professionals working with chemically dependent gay, lesbian, and bisexual people. Seeks to educate members of organizations and agencies about gay, lesbian, and bisexual people and addiction; assure that workshops, seminars, conferences, and publications that deal with addiction address the special needs and problems of gay, lesbian, and bisexual people and their families; coordinates services provided by educators and training personnel who are available to help others in the addiction field to better serve gay and lesbian clients. Acts as a clearinghouse for resource and research information in the field of addiction as it pertains to homosexuality; provides referral information about gay, lesbian, and bisexual groups of Alcoholics Anonymous World Services; develops and distributes a list of resource facilities for gay, lesbian, and bisexual alcoholics, addicts and their family and friends. Maintains a training and speakers' bureau. **Publications:** Monographs. • *The NALGAP Annotated Bibliography: Alcoholism, Subtance Abuse, and Lesbians/Gay Men.* Book. • *NALGAP Newsletter,* periodic. Newsletter. *Price:* For members only. • *NALGAP Reporter,* semiannual. Newsletter. Includes book reviews. • *National Directory of Facilities and Services for Lesbian and Gay Alcoholics,* periodic. Directory. **Formerly:** (1984) National Association of Gay Alcoholism Professionals.

★ **11703** ★ **National Clearinghouse on Marital and Date Rape (NCOMDR)**
2325 Oak St.
Berkeley, CA 94708
Phone: (510)524-1582
Laura X, Dir.

Founded: 1980. **Members:** 500. **Description:** Students, attorneys, legislators, faculty members, rape crisis centers, shelters, and other social service groups. Operates as speaking/consulting firm. Is presently launching a nationwide call for members to help marital, cohabitant, and date rape victims and to stop the rape of potential victims by vigorously educating the public and by providing resources to battered women's shelters, crisis centers, district attorneys and legislators through media appearances and lectures at college campuses and conferences. Ultimate goal is to "make intimate relationships truly egalitarian". Holds training sessions and workshops. Provides fee-based phone consultation and fee-based document search and delivery services for the media, prosecutors, expert witnesses, victim/witness advocates, legislators, police, rape crisis workers, and others. Offers sociological and legal research on court cases and legislation; year round interhip program for credit. Compiles statistics. Maintains speakers' bureau. **Publications:** *Date Rape.* • *Marital Rape Victims Fight Back. Price:* $3. • *Prosecution Statistics on Marital Rape. Price:* $3. • *Rideout Trial Pamphlet. Pamphlet. Price:* $3. • *State Law Chart on Marital Rape. Pamphlet. Price:* $3. **Formerly:** (1969) Women's History Research Center.

★ **11704** ★ **National Coalition Against Sexual Assault (NCASA)**
912 N. 2nd St.
Harrisburg, PA 17102
Phone: (202)483-7165
Fax: (717)232-6771
Kate Issari, Pres.

Founded: 1978. **Members:** 500. **Regional Groups:** 6. **Description:** Works to build a network through which individuals and organizations working against sexual assault can share expertise, experience, and information. Acts as an advocate for and on behalf of rape victims. Disseminates information on sexual assault. Sponsors Sexual Assault Awareness Month in April. **Publications:** *NCASA News,* quarterly. Newsletter.

★ **11705** ★ **National Lesbian and Gay Health Association (NLGHA)**
1407 S St., NW
Washington, DC 20009
Phone: (202)797-3536
Fax: (202)797-3504
Christopher J. Portelli, Exec.Dir.

Founded: 1994. **Description:** Lesbian, gay, and nongay health professionals providing care to lesbians and gay men; individuals concerned with the accessibility and quality of health care for lesbians and gay men. Purpose is to develop and coordinate interdisciplinary health programs and activities. Seeks to develop a healthier environment for all lesbians and gay men and to further the delivery of appropriate health care to them. Promotes research on issues of lesbian and gay health care. Serves as liaison among members, health agencies, and other private and governmental bodies. Facilitates networking among national lesbian and gay health organizations. Provides educational and consultative service to associations, hospitals, institutions, and schools regarding lesbian and gay health issues. Conducts training programs on gay health issues and assists in local conferences. **Publications:** *Check-up,* quarterly. Newsletter. **Formerly:** (1984) National Gay Health Education Foundation.

★ **11706** ★ **National Organization of Restoring Men (NORM)**
c/o R. Wayne Griffiths
3205 Northwood Dr., Ste. 209
Concord, CA 94520
Phone: (510)827-4077
Fax: (510)827-4119
R. Wayne Griffiths, Exec.Dir.

Founded: 1989. **Members:** 2,500. **National Groups:** 4. **Local Groups:** 12. **Description:** Provides support for men who desire to restore their foreskin after circumcision. Acts as a forum for exchange of information on methods and techniques of foreskin restoration. Helps men to "regain a sense of wholeness and self-directedness". Promotes the idea that infant circumcision is a form of "mutilation" and that men should have a choice whether or not to be circumcised. Maintains speakers' bureau. Compiles statistics. Conducts educational programs. **Formerly:** RECAP (Recover a Penis).

★ **11707** ★ **National Sex Information Network**
216 Willow Rd.
Menlo Park, CA 94025
Phone: (415)326-1155
Kara S. Ellynn, Contact

Founded: 1993. **Description:** Provides free and low-cost information on sexual health to organizations, government agencies, corporations, political groups, professional associations, support groups, and individuals. Strives to feature diverse topics on sexual education. Offers referrals, educational programs, and a speakers' bureau. **Publications:** *A Research Guide to Human Sexuality: Locating Print, Media, and Organizational Resources.* Book. • *Network News,* quarterly. Newsletter. • *Sex and Reproduction in Library of Congress Subject Headings: A Thesaurus.* Book. • *Sexperts U.S.A.: A Directory,* annual. Directory.

★ **11708** ★ **Potency Restored**
8630 Fenton St., Ste. 218
Silver Spring, MD 20910
Phone: (301)588-5777
Fax: (301)588-6220
Giulio I. Scarzella, M.D., Exec.Dir.

Founded: 1981. **Members:** 90. **Description:** Impotent men who have undergone inflatable penile implant (prosthetic) surgery or are considering the operation; partners of impotent men. Provides mutual help, understanding, and emotional support. Encourages members to become informed spokepersons in the field of impotence; presents scientific programs. Plans to start other groups around the country. **Publications:** Newsletter, monthly. **Formerly:** (1982) Impotence Anonymous.

★ 11709 ★ Recovery of Male Potency (ROMP)
27211 Lahser Rd., No. 208
Southfield, MI 48034
Phone: (810)357-1314
Fax: (810)357-2814
Nancy Petts, R.N., Nurse Mgr.
Founded: 1983. **Local Groups:** 1. **Description:** Hospital-based educational and selfhelp group for impotent men and their partners. Presents and exchanges information on subjects relating to the causes, testing, and emotional aspects of sexual impotence; disseminates medical literature related to impotency and reports on medical devices, treatments, and drugs used for restoring potency. **Publications:** *A Patient's Guide to Implant Surgery.*

Safe Motherhood Initiative
See: Entry 9693

★ 11710 ★ Sex Addicts Anonymous (SAA)
PO Box 70949
Houston, TX 77270
Phone: (713)869-4902
Jerry B., Office Mngr.
Founded: 1977. **Members:** 4,500. **State Groups:** 50. **Local Groups:** 450. **Description:** Purpose is to provide a support group for sex addicts that follows a program adapted from the 12-step program of Alcoholics Anonymous World Services in dealing with sexual behavior. (Sex addicts are described as people who compulsively repeat sexual behavior that is damaging to their lives.) **Publications:** *Abstinence and Boundaries.* • *The Bubble.* • *Exploring Healthy Sexuality.* • *First Step to Recovery.* • *Getting Started in SAA.* • *The Plain Brown Wrapper*, monthly. Newsletter. *Price:* $12/year. • *SAA Directory*, annual. Directory. *Price:* $2. • *Sex Addicts Anonymous 12 Questions.* Also publishes group guides.

★ 11711 ★ Sex Information and Education Council of the U.S. (SIECUS)
130 W. 42nd St., Ste. 350
New York, NY 10036
Phone: (212)819-9770
Fax: (212)819-9776
Debra Haffner, Exec.Dir.
Founded: 1964. **Members:** 3,600. **State Groups:** 1. **Description:** Educators, social workers, physicians, clergy, youth organizations and parents' groups, and others concerned about human sexuality education and sexual health care. Objective is to promote and affirm the concept of human sexuality as the integration of the emotional, intellectual, physical, and social aspects of sexual being in ways that are enriching, and that enhance health, personality, communication, human caring, and social justice. Goals are to: support and examine scientific research on human sexuality; disseminate data and provide education, training, and leadership programs in the field of human sexuality; identify, develop, and promote social policies that foster positive attitudes, values, and practices related to human sexuality. Supports the individual's right to acquire knowledge of sexuality and exercise nonexploitative sexual choices; encourages the development of responsible standards of sexual behavior. Issues

position statements on topics concerning human sexuality; serves as a clearinghouse of information for professionals and laypersons interested in helping people to understand sexuality. Conducts seminars and internship program; offers technical assistance; operates information service. Maintains speakers' bureau. **Publications:** Booklets. • *How to Talk to Your Children About AIDS.* Book. • Manuals. • *Oh NO! What Do I Do Now.* Book. • Pamphlets. • *SIECUS Report*, bimonthly. Journal. Covers sex education, human sexuality, and AIDS. Includes book and audiovisual reviews, and conference and seminar calendar. *Price:* Included in membership dues; $75/year for nonmembers (U.S., Canada, and Mexico); $85/year for nonmembers (overseas). Also publishes curricula and position statement.

★ 11712 ★ Sex and Love Addicts Anonymous (SLAA)
The Augustine Fellowship
PO Box 119, New Town Br.
Boston, MA 02258
Phone: (617)332-1845
Founded: 1976. **National Groups:** 1200. **Description:** Individuals recovering from a compulsive need for sex, a desperate attachment to one person, or other sexual or emotional obsessive-compulsive behavior. Functions as a support group to help members achieve comfortable, long-term sexual and emotional sobriety. Employs the 12 Steps of Alcoholics Anonymous World Services, adapted to sexual addiction. **Publications:** Audiotapes. • Books. *Price:* $13.50 for softcover; $23.50 for hardcover. • *The Journal*, monthly. Magazine. Covers upcoming conferences and current events. *Price:* $15/year. • Pamphlets. • *Sex and Love Addicts Anonymous.* • *SLAA Newsletter*, quarterly. Newsletter. **Also Known As:** Augustine Fellowship.

★ 11713 ★ Sexaholics Anonymous (SA)
PO Box 300
Simi Valley, CA 93062
Phone: (805)581-3343
Founded: 1979. **Members:** 8,000. **Regional Groups:** 700. **Description:** Individuals wishing to stop their sexually self-destructive thinking and behavior such as fantasy, pornography, adultery, masturbation, incest, or criminal sexual activity. Group believes that the sexaholic is addicted to lust and sex as others are to alcohol or drugs; this behavior is often followed by guilt, remorse, and depression, and may damage relationships with family and peers. Conducts programs based on the 12-step recovery program used in Alcoholics Anonymous to help members achieve "sexual sobriety." **Publications:** Brochure. • *Member Stories.* Book. • Newsletter, quarterly. • *Recovery Continues.* Book. • *Sexaholic Anonymous.* Book. Also publishes meeting guide.

★ 11714 ★ Society for the Psychological Study of Lesbian and Gay Issues (SPSLGI)
c/o American Psychological Association
750 1st St. NE
Washington, DC 20002-4242
Phone: (202)336-6041
Fax: (202)336-6040
Armand Cerbone, Ph.D., Pres.
Founded: 1984. **Members:** 1,600. **Regional Groups:** 1. **Description:** Psychologists, graduate students in psychology, and others interested in the psychological study of lesbian, gay, and bisexual issues and the delivery of affirmative mental health services to gay, lesbian, and bisexual individuals. Promotes scholarship in the study of psychology related to bisexual, gay, and lesbian issues; provides training for psychologists in the field. Cooperates with other groups sharing similar goals, including the American Psychological Association. Conducts scholarly programs. **Publications:** *Division 44 Newsletter*, 3/year. Newsletter. • *Psychological Perspectives on Lesbian and Gay Issues*, annual. *Price:* Included in membership dues.

★ 11715 ★ Society for the Scientific Study of Sex (SSSS)
c/o Howard J. Ruppel, Jr.
PO Box 208
Mount Vernon, IA 52314
Phone: (319)895-8407
Fax: (319)895-6203
Dr. Howard J. Ruppel, Jr., Exec.Dir.
Founded: 1957. **Members:** 1,200. **Regional Groups:** 3. **State Groups:** 4. **Description:** Professional society of psychiatrists, psychologists, physicians, sociologists, anthropologists, social workers, historians, demographers, criminologists, educators, attorneys and others conducting sexual research. Promotes educational programs. **Publications:** *Annual Review of Sex Research.* Contains review articles on selected topics in the field of sexology. *Price:* $50/volume. • *Journal of Sex Research*, quarterly. Journal. Contains book reviews and case studies. *Price:* Included in membership dues; $50/year for nonmembers; $85/year for libraries. • *Society for the Scientific Study of Sex-Membership Handbook/Directory.* Membership Directory. *Price:* Available to members only. • *Society for the Scientific Study of Sex-Newsletter*, quarterly. Newsletter. Includes calendar of events. *Price:* Included in membership dues; $20/year for nonmembers. Also publishes research and clinical material.

★ 11716 ★ Society for Sex Therapy and Research (SSTAR)
c/o Dr. P. Schreiner-Engel
Mt. Sinai Medical Ctr.
1176 Fifth Ave., Box 1170
New York, NY 10029
Phone: (212)241-6758
Fax: (212)360-6917
Dr. Patricia Schreiner-Engel, Ph.D., Pres.
Founded: 1974. **Members:** 200. **Description:** Professionals in social work, nursing, physiology, gynecology, urology, internal medicine, primate research, psychiatry, and psychology who have clinical or research interests in human sexual concerns. Seeks to facilitate communica-

tions among clinicians who treat problems of sexual identity, sexual function, and reproductive life. Provides a forum for exchange of ideas between researchers and patient care providers. **Publications:** Membership Directory, biennial. • Newsletter, 3-4/year. **Formerly:** (1979) Eastern Academy of Sexual Therapy.

★ 11717 ★ Women Against Rape (WAR)
Box 02084
Columbus, OH 43202
Phone: (614)291-9751

Founded: 1972. **Members:** 60. **Local Groups:** 1. **Description:** Works toward the prevention of rape. Sponsors crisis intervention services including rape survivor support groups. Also offers rape prevention training including self-defense classes for women. Maintains speakers' bureau. **Publications:** *W.A.R. Newsletter*, semiannual. Newsletter. Includes current information on rape issues and calendar of events. *Price:* Included in membership dues.

Research Centers

Baylor College of Medicine
Sleep Disorders and Research Center
See: Entry 8332

★ 11718 ★ California State University, Northridge
Center for Sex Research
Northridge, CA 91330
Phone: (818)986-5954
Fax: (818)990-5143
James Elias, Dir.

Research Activities and Fields: Human sexuality, focusing on social, cultural, biological, and psychological aspects.

★ 11719 ★ Institute for Advanced Study of Human Sexuality
Exodus Trust
1523 Franklin St.
San Francisco, CA 94109
Phone: (415)928-1133
Fax: (415)928-8284
Dr. Ted McIlvenna, Dir.

Research Activities and Fields: Erotology and human sexual behavior and attitudes.

★ 11720 ★ Johns Hopkins University
Johns Hopkins Hospital Sexual Disorders Clinic
Meyer Bldg., Rm. 101
600 N. Wolfe St.
Baltimore, MD 21205
Phone: (410)955-4150
Fax: (410)539-1664
Fred S. Berlin, M.D., Dir.

Research Activities and Fields: Biological correlates and treatment of sexual disorders, including pedophilia, sadism, transvestism, voyeurism, exhibitionism, compulsive rape, and other psychosexual disorders. Analyzes and evaluates antiandrogenic and counseling treatment of sex offenders, including the effects of the synthetic progestin, Depo-Provera. **Formerly:** Biosexual Psychohormonal Clinic.

Johns Hopkins University
Office of Psychohormonal Research
See: Entry 4890

★ 11721 ★ Kinsey Institute for Research in Sex, Gender, and Reproduction, Inc.
Morrison Hall, 3rd Fl.
Indiana Univ.
Bloomington, IN 47405
Phone: (812)855-7686
Fax: (812)855-8277
Dr. Stephanie Sanders, Interim Dir.

Research Activities and Fields: Effects of prenatal exposure to drugs and hormones, human sexual behavior, sexual orientation as it relates to sexually transmitted diseases, and sexual identity roles and attitudes, including studies of sexual and psychosexual development and biomedical and psychobiological approaches to sex, gender, and reproduction. **E-mail Address:** sanders@ucs.indiana.edu. **Formerly:** Institute for Sex Research (1981).

Ohio State University
Sleep Disorders Center
See: Entry 8413

★ 11722 ★ San Francisco State University
Center for Research and Education in Sexuality (CERES)
Psychology Bldg., Rm. 502
San Francisco, CA 94132
Phone: (415)338-1137
Fax: (415)824-5380
Dr. John P. De Cecco, Dir.

Research Activities and Fields: Seeks to integrate research from the humanities and the behavioral, social, and biological sciences in the study of human sexuality. **Publications:** *Journal of Homosexuality* (quarterly); Research Monograph Series; *Haworth's Gay and Lesbian Studies*.

★ 11723 ★ Society for the Scientific Study of Male Psychology and Physiology
321 Iuka
Montpelier, OH 43543
Phone: (419)485-3602
Dr. Jerry Bergman, Dir.

Research Activities and Fields: Male psychology and physiology, including sex roles, rape, sexism, and women's history. Examines male and female differences relating to suicide, homocide and other crimes, health, longevity, and developmental differences. **Formerly:** Society for the Study of Male Psychology and Physiology.

Thomas Jefferson University
Sleep Disorders Center
See: Entry 8436

★ 11724 ★ University of Texas at Austin
Institute of Reproductive Biology
Zoology Dept.
Patterson 28
Austin, TX 78712
Phone: (512)471-3807
Fax: (512)471-9651
Prof. Frank H. Bronson, Dir.

Research Activities and Fields: Studies domestic and wild animal stocks to develop fundamental principles on how environmental factors affect the nervous and endocrine systems and regulate reproduction and sexual behavior. **E-mail Address:** bronson@bongo.cc.utexas.edu.

Chapter 60
Smoking

National & International Organizations

★ **11725** ★ **Action on Smoking and Health (ASH)**
109 Gloucester Pl.
London W1H 4EJ, England
Phone: 171 9353519
Fax: 171 9353463
Pamela Furness, Chief Exec.

Founded: 1971. **Members:** 1,000. **Local Groups:** 10. **Languages:** English. **Description:** Publicizes the dangers of smoking. Campaigns for smoke-free public areas and aids those wishing to quit smoking; helps organize National No Smoking Day; liaises with medical charities, health promotion organizations, and private groups. Disseminates information; monitors media, scientific, and trade publications. **Publications:** *ASH Information Bulletin*, biweekly. Bulletin. Digest of news on smoking and health. • *ASH Supporter News*, quarterly. • *Fact Sheets*.

★ **11726** ★ **Action on Smoking and Health (ASH)**
2013 H St. NW
Washington, DC 20006
Phone: (202)659-4310
Fax: (202)833-3921
John F. Banzhaf, III, Exec.Dir.

Founded: 1967. **Description:** Works for the rights of nonsmokers against the problems of smoking. Provides scientific, educational, legal, and advocacy services. Accomplishments include: ban of tobacco ads from radio and television; establishment of no-smoking sections on airplanes, trains, and interstate buses; persuading the National Association of Insurance Commissioners to adopt a resolution urging insurance companies to force smokers to pay their fair share of health insurance costs by charging them higher rates than non smokers; sued the Occupational Safety and Health Administration (OSHA) to ban smoking in all workplaces. **Publications:** *ASH Smoking and Health Review*, bimonthly. Newsletter. Covers medical, legal, regulatory, commercial, institutional, and humorous news related to smoking. *Price:* $15/year. Also publishes informational handouts on addiction

to nicotine, effects of passive smoking, workplace smoking costs, workplace nonsmokers' rights, filing for workers' compensation, and other materials.

★ **11727** ★ **Action on Smoking and Health (ASH)**
Women and Smoking Group
109 Gloucester Pl.
London W1H 4EJ, England
Phone: 171 9353519
Fax: 171 9353463
Amanda Sandford, Development Officer

Founded: 1985. **Members:** 18. **Languages:** English. **Description:** Women's health specialists. Stimulates research pertaining to the health risks of smoking for women. Promotes public awareness of the dangers associated with smoking. Disseminates information. **Publications:** *Her Share of Misfortune*. Booklet. Contains information about smoking among poor women. • *Smoke Still Gets in Her Eyes*. Booklet. Contains information about tobacco advertising in women's magazines. • *Teenage Girls and Smoking*. Booklet. • *Women and Smoking*. Booklet.

★ **11728** ★ **Action on Smoking and Health—Northern Ireland (ASH-NI)**
Ulster Cancer Foundation
40-42 Eglantine Ave.
Belfast, Antrim BT9 6DX, Northern Ireland
Phone: 1232 663281
Fax: 1232 660081
Michael Wood, Dir.

Description: Northern Ireland division of Action on Smoking and Health. Individuals united to disseminate information on the dangers of smoking. Seeks to establish smoke-free public areas and help those addicted to smoking. Works with medical and health groups in support of its aims.

★ **11729** ★ **Action on Smoking and Health—Scotland (ASH-S)**
8 Frederick St.
Edinburgh EH2 2HB, Scotland
Phone: 131 2254725
Fax: 131 2206604
Alison Hillhouse, Dir.

Founded: 1973. **Local Groups:** 1. **Languages:** English. **Description:** Seeks to inform the public

about the dangers of smoking. Works in conjunction with health and medical groups; campaigns for smoke-free public areas; assists those wishing to stop smoking. Conducts smoking cessation courses. **Publications:** *ASH Scotland Supporter's Newsletter*, semiannual. Newsletter. • *The Essential Guide to Stopping Smoking*. • *The Smoking Epidemic: Counting the Cost in Scotland*. Book. • *Women and Smoking*. Brochure.

★ **11730** ★ **Action on Smoking and Health—Wales (ASHW)**
(Ashyng Nghymru)
372 Cowbridge Rd. E
Cardiff, S. Glam CF5 1HE, Wales
Phone: 1222 641101
Fax: 1222 641045
Naomi King, Sec.

Description: Welsh section of Action on Smoking and Health. Individuals united to publicize the health risks of smoking. Works with health and medical groups; disseminates information; attempts to provide smoke-free public areas; assists those wishing to quit smoking.

★ **11731** ★ **Americans for Nonsmokers' Rights (ANR)**
2530 San Pablo Ave., Ste. J
Berkeley, CA 94702
Phone: (510)841-3032
Fax: (510)841-7702
Julia Carol, Exec.Dir.

Founded: 1976. **Members:** 15,000. **Description:** Seeks to protect the rights of nonsmokers in the workplace and other public settings. Maintains American Nonsmokers' Rights Foundation, which promotes smoking prevention, nonsmokers' rights, and public education about passive smoking. **Publications:** *ANR Update*, quarterly. Newsletter. • *Legislative Approaches to a Smokefree Society*. • *Matrix of Major Local Smoking Ordinances in the U.S.*. **Formerly:** (1976) California Group Against Smoking Pollution; (1986) Californians for Nonsmokers' Rights.

★ 11732 ★ **Asia Pacific Association for the Control of Tobacco (APACT)**
12/F-3 No. 57 Fu Hsin N. Rd.
Taipei 10559, Taiwan
Phone: 2 7766133
Fax: 2 7522455
Dr. David D. Yen, Hon. Life Pres.

Founded: 1989. **Languages:** English, Mandarin. **Description:** Working to create a "smoke-free Taiwan." Monitors advertising and government policy on tobacco trade. Campaigns for prohibition of cigarette advertising in Taiwan. **Publications:** *Health for All*, monthly. Magazine.

★ 11733 ★ **Canadian Council on Smoking and Health (CCSH)**
170 Laurier Ave. W, Ste. 1000
Ottawa, ON, Canada K1P 5V5
Phone: (613)567-3050
Fax: (613)567-2730
Janice Forsythe, Exec.Dir.

Founded: 1974. **Languages:** English, French. **Description:** Seeks to raise public awareness regarding the dangers of smoking. Lobbies for reduced tobacco use in Canada; assists those wishing to quit smoking. Disseminates information.

★ 11734 ★ **Chinese Association on Smoking and Health**
Bldg. 12, District 1
Andingmenwai Anhuaxili
Beijing 100011, People's Republic of China
Phone: 1 4260978
Fax: 1 4260067
Yi-fang Zhang, Sec.Gen.

Founded: 1990. **Members:** 50,000. **National Groups:** 1. **Local Groups:** 300. **Languages:** Chinese. Does not correspond in English. **Description:** Organizations in the People's Republic of China representing 28,000 individuals and promoting smoking cessation. Conducts research and educational programs; compiles statistics. Offers consulting services. Maintains speakers' bureau. Sponsors competitions. **Publications:** *Newsletter of Chinese Smoking and Health*, quarterly. Newsletter.

★ 11735 ★ **Citizens for a Tobacco-Free Society (CATS)**
8660 Lynnehaven Dr.
Cincinnati, OH 45236
Phone: (513)677-6666
Ahron Leichtman, Exec.Dir.

Founded: 1985. **Regional Groups:** 5. **State Groups:** 9. **Local Groups:** 120. **Description:** Health and environmental organizations; individuals concerned with indoor air pollution caused by tobacco smoke. Seeks to create a tobacco-free society by the year 2000. Supports a total ban on smoking in enclosed public places, restaurants, and work places. Encourages young people not to smoke. Serves as a resource center for the news media on smoking and health issues. Sponsors Smokefree Skies Campaign, which supports a total ban on smoking on all domestic and international airline flights and in airports. Distributes information about the effects of second-hand smoke and how to lobby for clean indoor air laws. Maintains speakers' bureau. Compiles statistics; offers educational programs. **Publications:** *Affiliates Directory*, annual. Directory. *Price:* Available to news media only. • *CATS Affiliates Newsletter*, quarterly. Newsletter. • *CATS News Report*, 4/year. • *News Releases*, periodic. **Formerly:** (1991) Citizens Against Tobacco Smoke.

★ 11736 ★ **Coalition on Smoking OR Health (CSH)**
1150 Connecticut Ave. NW, Ste. 820
Washington, DC 20036
Phone: (202)452-1184
Fax: (202)452-1417
Scott Ballin, Chair

Founded: 1982. **Description:** Formed by the American Lung Association, the American Heart Association, and the American Cancer Society to more effectively bring tobacco use prevention and education issues to the attention of federal and state legislators and policymakers. Has supported an increase in cigarette excise tax, the replacement of current health warnings on cigarette packages and advertisements with more specific and effective warnings concerning tobacco use and its effects on health, the banning of smoking on all domestic and international passenger airline flights and in federal buildings, the restriction of U.S. exports of tobacco products, the elimination of federal support for the tobacco industry, the regulation by the Food and Drug Administration of tobacco and tobacco products, restrictions on smoking in public places, and measures to restrict youth access to tobacco products. **Publications:** *Framework for Public Policy*, annual. • *News from the Coalition*, quarterly. Newsletter. • *State Legislated Actions on Tobacco Issues*, annual. Compilation of state tobacco control laws. *Price:* $7.50.

★ 11737 ★ **Group Against Smokers' Pollution (GASP)**
PO Box 632
College Park, MD 20741-0632
Phone: (301)459-4791
Willard K. Morris, Sec.

Founded: 1971. **Members:** 10,000. **Local Groups:** 100. **Description:** Nonsmokers who are adversely affected by tobacco smoke united to promote the rights of nonsmokers, educate the public about the problems of second-hand smoke, and regulate smoking in places where nonsmokers are exposed. Supports the establishment and enforcement of laws and other public policy measures which reduce environmental tobacco smoke. Provides information and referral services; distributes educational literature, buttons, posters, and bumper stickers. Helps members find local GASP chapters or establish a chapter. **Publications:** Booklets. • *Nonsmokers' Bill of Rights*. • *The Nonsmokers' Liberation Guide*. Handbook. • Pamphlets. **Also Known As:** GASP of America.

★ 11738 ★ **SmokeFree Educational Services**
375 South End Ave., Ste. 32F
New York, NY 10280-1085
Phone: (212)912-0960
Fax: (212)488-8911
Joseph Cherner, Contact

Founded: 1990. **Description:** Mission statement is "to win the right to live and work in a smokefree environment, and to educate youth about the unhealthy and socially undesirable consequences of tobacco addiction." Works for: more education for young people on the consequences of tobacco addiction; tobacco-free schools; larger health warnings on cigarette ads and cigarette packs; health warnings on cigarettes sold to less developed countries; ending tobacco sponsorship of youth oriented events; eliminating cigarette vending machines; and 100% smokefree public places. **Publications:** Newsletter, quarterly. *Price:* Included in membership dues. **Also Known As:** Smokefree America. **Formerly:** National Association of Nonsmokers.

★ 11739 ★ **Stop Teen-Age Addiction to Tobacco (STAT)**
511 E Columbus Ave.
Springfield, MA 01105
Phone: (413)732-STAT
Fax: (413)732-4219
Joe Tye, Exec. Officer

Founded: 1985. **Members:** 6,000. **Description:** Works to raise public awareness of the role of tobacco advertisements and promotions in influencing children to smoke. Works in cooperation with merchants to prevent children from purchasing cigarettes. Conducts research; maintains library and speakers' bureau; bestows awards; compiles statistics. **Publications:** *60 Years of Deception: An Analysis and Compilation of Cigarette Advertising From 1925-1985*. • *Tobacco Free Youth Reporter*, semiannual. *Price:* Included in membership dues.

TARGET - Helping Students Cope with Tobacco, Alcohol and Other Drugs
See: Entry 12079

★ 11740 ★ **Tobacco Products Liability Project (TPLP)**
Northeastern University School of Law
400 Huntington Ave.
Boston, MA 02115
Phone: (617)373-2026
Fax: (617)373-3672
Prof. Richard Daynard, Chairperson

Founded: 1984. **Description:** An autonomous project of the Tobacco Control Resource Center comprising doctors, lawyers, public health officials, and academics. Encourages product liability suits against the tobacco products marketers in order to: compensate victims of tobacco-related diseases and injuries such as cancer or burns; discourage smoking among teenagers; publicize the effects of smoking on health. Works for an end to what TPLP describes as the "disinformation campaign" of the tobacco companies in their understanding of the dangers of tobacco. Acts as information clearinghouse. **Publications:** *Tobacco on Trial*, 8/year. Newsletter. Covers product liability cases against tobacco companies. *Price:* $35/year for individuals; $95/year for institutions.

Research Centers

★11741★ **Smoking Cessation Research Institute**
PO Box 60249
Palo Alto, CA 94306-0249
Phone: (415)424-8992
Fax: (415)424-8991
Dr. David P.L. Sachs, M.D., Dir.
Research Activities and Fields: Assesses optimal methods for smoking cessation and weight gain prevention treatment strategies.

★11742★ **Studies on Smoking, Inc. (SOS)**
125 High St.
Edinboro, PA 16412
Phone: (814)734-5538
Dr. G.H. Miller, Dir.
Research Activities and Fields: Studies the effect of smoking. Projects have focused on the longevity of both smoking and nonsmoking men and women, the incidence of lung cancer between Amish and non-Amish populations, smoking cessation, carbon monoxide studies, passive smoking, asbestos, smoking (active and passive) and its effect on lung cancer, breast cancer, and diabetes.

★11743★ **Tobacco and Health Research Institute**
Univ. of Kentucky
Cooper & Univ. Drs.
Lexington, KY 40546
Phone: (606)257-4600
Fax: (606)258-1077
Dr. John N. Diana, Dir.
Research Activities and Fields: Tobacco production, manufacture of tobacco products, chemistry and physics of tobacco products and smoke, response of nonhuman biological systems to tobacco products, human response to tobacco products, tobacco and cardiovascular and pulmonary diseases, and relationship between tobacco and health. Develops ways to identify and eliminate detrimental compounds.
Publications: Conference and Workshop Series.

★11744★ **University of California Tobacco-Related Disease Research Program**
300 Lakeside Dr., 12th Fl.
Oakland, CA 94612-3550
Phone: (510)987-9870
Fax: (510)835-4740
Charles L. Gruder, Ph.D., Dir.
Research Activities and Fields: Manages research grants to investigators at nonprofit research institutions in California for research on the causes, prevention, and treatment of tobacco-related diseases, including cancer and heart and lung diseases; and for research on sociobehavioral, epidemiological, public health, public policy, economic, and legal issues regarding tobacco-related diseases and tobacco control. Grant mechanisms include research project grants and career awards to postdoctoral fellows and new investigators.

Chapter 61
Social Work

Medical & Allied Health Schools

Social Work

The following institutions offer accredited master's degree programs in social work. For information on accredited baccalaureate degree programs, contact the Council on Social Work Education, 1600 Duke St., Ste. 300, Alexandria, VA 22314-3421, (703) 683-8080.

Alabama

★11745★ **University of Alabama**
School of Social Work
Box 870314
Tuscaloosa, AL 35487-0314
Phone: (205)348-7027
Fax: (205)348-9419

Arizona

★11746★ **Arizona State University**
School of Social Work
Tempe, AZ 85287-1802
Phone: (602)965-3304
Fax: (602)965-5986

Arkansas

★11747★ **University of Arkansas at Little Rock**
School of Social Work
2801 S. University
Little Rock, AR 72204
Phone: (501)569-3240
Fax: (501)569-3184

California

★11748★ **California State University, Fresno**
Department of Social Work Education
2325 E. San Ramon Ave.
Fresno, CA 93740-0102
Phone: (209)278-3992
Fax: (209)278-7179

★11749★ **California State University, Long Beach**
Department of Social Work
1250 Bellflower Blvd.
Long Beach, CA 90840-0902
Phone: (310)985-4616
Fax: (310)985-5514

★11750★ **California State University, Sacramento**
Division of Social Work
6000 J St.
Sacramento, CA 95819-6090
Phone: (916)278-6943
Fax: (916)278-7167

★11751★ **California State University, San Bernardino**
Department of Social Work
5500 University Pkwy.
San Bernardino, CA 92407-2397
Phone: (909)880-5501
Fax: (909)880-5985

★11752★ **San Diego State University**
School of Social Work
Hepper Hall, Rm. 119
San Diego, CA 92182-0369
Phone: (619)594-6247
Fax: (619)594-7103

★11753★ **San Francisco State University**
Department of Social Work Education
1600 Holloway Ave.
San Francisco, CA 94132
Phone: (415)338-1005
Fax: (415)338-0591

★11754★ **San Jose State University**
College of Social Work
1 Washington Sq.
San Jose, CA 95192-0124
Phone: (408)924-5800
Fax: (408)924-5892

★11755★ **University of California at Berkeley**
Master of Social Welfare Program
120 Haviland Hall
Berkeley, CA 94720
Phone: (510)642-4341
Fax: (510)643-6126

★11756★ **University of California, Los Angeles**
School of Social Welfare
405 Hilgard Ave.
Los Angeles, CA 90024-1452
Phone: (310)825-7822
Fax: (310)206-7564

★11757★ **University of Southern California**
School of Social Work
Montgomery Ross Fisher Bldg., Rm. 0411
University Park MC0411
Los Angeles, CA 90089-0411
Phone: (213)740-2711
Fax: (213)740-0789

Colorado

★11758★ **Colorado State University**
Department of Social Work
202 Eddy Bldg.
Ft. Collins, CO 80523
Phone: (303)491-6612
Fax: (303)491-7280

★11759★ **University of Denver**
Graduate School of Social Work
University Park
2148 South High St.
Denver, CO 80208-0274
Phone: (303)871-2886
Fax: (303)871-2845

★11760★ **University of Southern Colorado**
Social Work Department
2200 Bonforte Blvd.
Pueblo, CO 81001-4901
Phone: (719)549-2268
Fax: (719)459-2705

Connecticut

★11761★ **Southern Connecticut State University**
Graduate Social Work Program
Lang Social Work Center
501 Crescent St.
New Haven, CT 06515
Phone: (203)397-4331
Fax: (203)397-4309

★ 11762 ★ University of Connecticut
School of Social Work
1798 Asylum Ave.
West Hartford, CT 06117-2698
Phone: (203)241-4730
Fax: (203)241-4786

Delaware

★ 11763 ★ Delaware State University
Department of Social Work
1200 N. Dupont Hwy.
Dover, DE 19901-2277
Phone: (302)739-5175
Fax: (302)739-5035

District of Columbia

★ 11764 ★ Catholic University of America
National Catholic School of Social Service
Washington, DC 20064
Phone: (202)319-5454
Fax: (202)319-5093

★ 11765 ★ Howard University
School of Social Work
601 Howard Pl. NW
Washington, DC 20059
Phone: (202)806-7300
Fax: (202)387-4309

Florida

★ 11766 ★ Barry University
School of Social Work
11300 NE 2nd Ave.
Miami, FL 33161
Phone: (305)899-3904
Fax: (305)899-3934

★ 11767 ★ Florida International University
School of Social Work
ACI Rm. 234
300 NE 145 St.
North Miami, FL 33181-3600
Phone: (305)940-5880
Fax: (305)956-5313

★ 11768 ★ Florida State University
School of Social Work
Box 2024
Tallahassee, FL 32306-2024
Phone: (904)644-4752
Fax: (904)644-9750

★ 11769 ★ University of South Florida
Department of Social Work
4202 E. Fowler Ave.
Tampa, FL 33612
Phone: (813)974-2063
Fax: (813)974-2668

Georgia

★ 11770 ★ Clark Atlanta University
School of Social Work
2223 James P. Brawley Dr. SW
Atlanta, GA 30314-4391
Phone: (404)880-8551
Fax: (404)880-8222

★ 11771 ★ University of Georgia
School of Social Work
Tucker Hall
Athens, GA 30602-7016
Phone: (404)542-3282

Hawaii

★ 11772 ★ University of Hawaii at Manoa
School of Social Work
2500 Campus Rd.
Honolulu, HI 96822
Phone: (808)956-7180
Fax: (808)956-5964

Illinois

★ 11773 ★ Aurora University
George Williams College
School of Social Work
347 S. Gladstone
Aurora, IL 60506
Phone: (708)844-5419
Fax: (708)844-4923

★ 11774 ★ George Williams College at
Aurora University
School of Social Work
347 S. Gladstone
Aurora, IL 60506
Phone: (708)844-5419
Fax: (708)844-5463

★ 11775 ★ Loyola University of Chicago
School of Social Work
820 Michigan Ave.
Chicago, IL 60611
Phone: (312)915-7005
Fax: (312)915-7645

★ 11776 ★ Southern Illinois University at
Carbondale
School of Social Work
Quigley Hall, Rm. 4
Carbondale, IL 62901
Phone: (618)453-2243
Fax: (618)453-1219

★ 11777 ★ University of Chicago
School of Social Service Administration
969 E. 60th St.
Chicago, IL 60637-2460
Phone: (312)702-1144
Fax: (312)702-0874

★ 11778 ★ University of Illinois at Chicago
Jane Addams College of Social Work
1040 W. Harrison St.
Chicago, IL 60607-7134
Phone: (312)996-3219
Fax: (312)996-1802

★ 11779 ★ University of Illinois at Urbana-
Champaign
School of Social Work
1207 W. Oregon St.
Urbana, IL 61801
Phone: (217)333-2261
Fax: (217)244-5220

Indiana

★ 11780 ★ Indiana University
School of Social Work
Education/Social Work Bldg., Rm. 4188C
902 W. New York St.
Indianapolis, IN 46202-5156
Phone: (317)274-8362
Fax: (317)274-8630

Iowa

★ 11781 ★ University of Iowa
School of Social Work
308 N. Hall
Iowa City, IA 52242
Phone: (319)335-1269
Fax: (319)335-1711

Kansas

★ 11782 ★ University of Kansas
School of Social Welfare
Twente Hall
Lawrence, KS 66045-2510
Phone: (913)864-4720
Fax: (913)864-5277

Kentucky

★ 11783 ★ Southern Baptist Theological
Seminary
Carver School of Social Work
2825 Lexington Rd.
Louisville, KY 40280
Phone: (502)897-4605
Fax: (502)897-4880

★ 11784 ★ University of Kentucky
College of Social Work
619 Patterson Office Tower
Lexington, KY 40506-0027
Phone: (606)257-6654
Fax: (606)323-1030

★ 11785 ★ University of Louisville
Raymond A. Kent School of Social Work
Louisville, KY 40292
Phone: (502)588-6402
Fax: (502)852-0422

Louisiana

★ 11786 ★ Grambling State University
School of Social Work
PO Box 907
Grambling, LA 71245
Phone: (318)274-3305
Fax: (318)274-3254

★ 11787 ★ Louisiana State University
School of Social Work
Baton Rouge, LA 70803
Phone: (504)388-1351
Fax: (504)388-1357

★ 11788 ★ **Southern University at New Orleans**
School of Social Work
6400 Press Dr.
New Orleans, LA 70126-1009
Phone: (504)286-5376
Fax: (504)286-5131

★ 11789 ★ **Tulane University**
School of Social Work
New Orleans, LA 70118-5672
Phone: (504)865-5314
Fax: (504)862-8727

Maine

★ 11790 ★ **University of Maine**
School of Social Work
5770 Annex C
Orono, ME 04469-5770
Phone: (207)581-2387
Fax: (207)581-2396

★ 11791 ★ **University of New England**
School of Social Work
11 Hills Beach Rd.
Biddeford, ME 04005-9599
Phone: (207)283-0171
Fax: (207)284-7633

Maryland

★ 11792 ★ **University of Maryland at Baltimore**
School of Social Work
Louis L. Kaplan Hall
525 W. Redwood St.
Baltimore, MD 21201-1777
Phone: (410)706-7794
Fax: (410)706-6046

Massachusetts

★ 11793 ★ **Boston College**
Graduate School of Social Work
McGuinn Hall
Chestnut Hill, MA 02167
Phone: (617)552-4020
Fax: (617)552-4024

★ 11794 ★ **Boston University**
School of Social Work
264 Bay State Rd.
Boston, MA 02215
Phone: (617)353-3750
Fax: (617)353-5612

★ 11795 ★ **Salem State College**
School of Social Work
352 Lafayette St.
Salem, MA 01970
Phone: (508)741-6650
Fax: (508)741-6818

★ 11796 ★ **Simmons College**
School of Social Work
51 Commonwealth Ave.
Boston, MA 02116-2307
Phone: (617)738-2930
Fax: (617)738-2299

★ 11797 ★ **Smith College**
School of Social Work
Lilly Hall
Northampton, MA 01063
Phone: (413)585-7977
Fax: (413)585-7974

★ 11798 ★ **Springfield College**
Department of Social Work
263 Alden St.
Springfield, MA 01109-3797
Phone: (413)748-3773
Fax: (413)748-3291

Michigan

★ 11799 ★ **Grand Valley State University**
School of Social Work
25 Commerce St., SW
Grand Rapids, MI 49503-4100
Phone: (616)771-6550
Fax: (616)771-6570

★ 11800 ★ **Michigan State University**
School of Social Work
254 Baker Hall
East Lansing, MI 48824-1118
Phone: (517)353-8632
Fax: (517)363-3038

★ 11801 ★ **University of Michigan**
School of Social Work
1065 Frieze Bldg.
Ann Arbor, MI 48109-1285
Phone: (313)764-3309
Fax: (313)936-1961

★ 11802 ★ **Wayne State University**
School of Social Work
Thompson Home
4756 Cass Ave.
Detroit, MI 48202
Phone: (313)577-4400
Fax: (313)577-8770

★ 11803 ★ **Western Michigan University**
School of Social Work
Kalamazoo, MI 49008-5034
Phone: (616)387-3170
Fax: (616)387-3183

Minnesota

★ 11804 ★ **College of St. Catherine / University of St. Thomas**
Department of Social Work
2115 Summit Ave., Mail No. LOR 405
St. Paul, MN 55105
Phone: (612)962-5800
Fax: (612)962-6410

★ 11805 ★ **University of Minnesota**
School of Social Work
400 Ford Hall
224 Church St., SE
Minneapolis, MN 55455
Phone: (612)624-5888
Fax: (612)626-0395

★ 11806 ★ **University of Minnesota, Duluth**
Social Work Program
220 Bohannon Hall
10 University Dr.
Duluth, MN 55812-2496
Phone: (218)726-7245
Fax: (218)726-7073

Mississippi

★ 11807 ★ **University of Southern Mississippi**
School of Social Work
PO Box 5114
Hattiesburg, MS 39406-5114
Phone: (601)266-4163
Fax: (601)266-4165

Missouri

★ 11808 ★ **St. Louis University**
School of Social Service
3550 Lindell Blvd.
St. Louis, MO 63103
Phone: (314)658-2722
Fax: (314)658-2298

★ 11809 ★ **University of Missouri— Columbia**
School of Social Work
702 Clark Hall
Columbia, MO 65211
Phone: (314)882-4477
Fax: (314)882-8926

★ 11810 ★ **Washington University**
George Warren Brown School of Social Work
1 Brookings Dr.
PO Box 1196
St. Louis, MO 63130-4899
Phone: (314)935-6693
Fax: (314)935-8511

Nebraska

★ 11811 ★ **University of Nebraska at Omaha**
School of Social Work
50th and Dodge Sts.
Omaha, NE 68182-0293
Phone: (402)554-2793
Fax: (402)554-3788

Nevada

★ 11812 ★ **University of Nevada, Las Vegas**
School of Social Work
4505 Maryland Pkwy.
PO Box 455032
Las Vegas, NV 89154-5032
Phone: (702)895-3314
Fax: (702)895-4079

★ 11813 ★ **University of Nevada, Reno**
School of Social Work
Business Bldg., No. 525
Mail Stop No. 90
Reno, NV 89557-0068
Phone: (702)784-6542
Fax: (702)784-4573

New Jersey

★11814★ **Rutgers University**
School of Social Work
327 Cooper St.
Camden, NJ 08102
Phone: (609)757-6346
Fax: (609)757-6155

★11815★ **Rutgers University**
School of Social Work
707 Hill Hall
Newark, NJ 07102
Phone: (908)932-7583
Fax: (908)932-8181

★11816★ **Rutgers University**
School of Social Work
536 George St.
New Brunswick, NJ 08903
Phone: (908)932-7253
Fax: (908)932-8181

New Mexico

★11817★ **New Mexico Highlands**
University
Department of Social Work
Singer Hall, Rm. 205
Las Vegas, NM 87701
Phone: (505)454-3563

★11818★ **New Mexico State University**
Department of Social Work
Dept. 3SW, Academic Res. Unit A
Standley St. at Research Dr.
PO Box 3001
Las Cruces, NM 88003-8001
Phone: (505)646-2143

New York

★11819★ **Adelphi University**
School of Social Work
Garden City, NY 11530
Phone: (516)877-4341
Fax: (516)877-4392

★11820★ **Columbia University**
School of Social Work
McVicker Hall
622 W. 113th St.
New York, NY 10025-7982
Phone: (212)854-5189
Fax: (212)854-2975

★11821★ **Fordham University**
Graduate School of Social Service
113 W. 60th St.
New York, NY 10023-7479
Phone: (212)636-6616
Fax: (212)636-6613

★11822★ **Hunter College of City**
University of New York
School of Social Work
129 E. 79th St.
New York, NY 10021
Phone: (212)452-7085
Fax: (212)452-7150

★11823★ **New York University**
School of Social Work
3 Washington Sq., N.
New York, NY 10003
Phone: (212)998-5959
Fax: (212)995-4172

★11824★ **State University of New York at**
Albany
School of Social Welfare
135 Western Ave.
Richardson Hall
Albany, NY 12222
Phone: (518)442-5324
Fax: (518)442-5380

★11825★ **State University of New York at**
Buffalo
School of Social Work
360 Baldy Hall
Buffalo, NY 14260
Phone: (716)645-3381
Fax: (716)645-3883

★11826★ **State University of New York at**
Stony Brook
School of Social Welfare
Health Sciences Center, Level 2
Stony Brook, NY 11794-8230
Phone: (516)444-2138
Fax: (516)444-7565

★11827★ **Syracuse University**
School of Social Work
Brockway Hall
Syracuse, NY 13244-6350
Phone: (315)443-5582
Fax: (315)443-5576

★11828★ **Yeshiva University**
Wurzweiler School of Social Work
Belfer Hall
500 W. 185th St.
New York, NY 10033
Phone: (212)960-0820
Fax: (212)960-0822

North Carolina

★11829★ **East Carolina University**
School of Social Work
134 Ragsdale Bldg.
Greenville, NC 27858-4353
Phone: (919)757-4208
Fax: (919)757-4189

★11830★ **University of North Carolina at**
Chapel Hill
School of Social Work
CB 3550
223 E. Franklin St.
Chapel Hill, NC 27599-3550
Phone: (919)962-1225
Fax: (919)962-0890

North Dakota

★11831★ **University of North Dakota**
Social Work Department
PO Box 7135
Grand Forks, ND 58202-7135
Phone: (701)777-2669
Fax: (701)777-4257

Ohio

★11832★ **Case Western Reserve**
University
Mandel School of Applied Social Sciences
10900 Euclid Ave.
Cleveland, OH 44106-7164
Phone: (216)368-2270
Fax: (216)368-2850

★11833★ **Ohio State University**
College of Social Work
103 Stillman Hall
1947 College Rd.
Columbus, OH 43210
Phone: (614)292-2972
Fax: (614)292-6940

★11834★ **University of Cincinnati**
School of Social Work
PO Box 210108
Cincinnati, OH 45221-0108
Phone: (513)556-4615
Fax: (513)556-2077

Oklahoma

★11835★ **University of Oklahoma**
School of Social Work
Ryhne Hall
1005 Jenkins Ave.
Norman, OK 73019-0475
Phone: (405)325-2821
Fax: (405)325-5068

Oregon

★11836★ **Portland State University**
Graduate School of Social Work
PO Box 751
Portland, OR 97207-0751
Phone: (503)725-4712
Fax: (503)725-5545

Pennsylvania

★11837★ **Bryn Mawr College**
Graduate School of Social Work and Social
Research
300 Airdale Rd.
Bryn Mawr, PA 19010
Phone: (610)527-5403
Fax: (610)527-1910

★11838★ **Marywood College**
School of Social Work
2300 Adams Ave.
Scranton, PA 18509
Phone: (717)348-6282
Fax: (717)348-0459

★11839★ **Temple University**
School of Social Administration
Ritter Hall Annex, Rm. 555
13th & Cecil B. Moore Ave.
Philadelphia, PA 19122
Phone: (215)204-8623
Fax: (215)204-9606

★11840★ **University of Pennsylvania**
School of Social Work
3701 Locust Walk
Philadelphia, PA 19104
Phone: (215)898-5511
Fax: (215)573-2099

★11841★ **University of Pittsburgh**
School of Social Work
2117 Cathedral of Learning
Pittsburgh, PA 15260
Phone: (412)624-6300
Fax: (412)624-6323

Puerto Rico

★11842★ **University of Puerto Rico**
Beatriz Lassalle Graduate School of Social
Work
GPO Box 23345
San Juan, PR 00931-3345
Phone: (809)763-3725
Fax: (809)763-5599

Rhode Island

★11843★ **Rhode Island College**
School of Social Work
600 Mt. Pleasant Ave.
Providence, RI 02908
Phone: (401)456-8042
Fax: (401)456-8620

South Carolina

★11844★ **University of South Carolina**
College of Social Work
Columbia, SC 29208
Phone: (803)777-4886
Fax: (803)777-3498

Tennessee

★11845★ **University of Tennessee,**
Knoxville
College of Social Work
109 Hensen Hall
Knoxville, TN 37996-3333
Phone: (615)974-3176
Fax: (615)974-4803

★11846★ **University of Tennessee at**
Memphis
College of Social Work
822 Beale St., Rm. 220
Memphis, TN 38163
Phone: (901)448-4463
Fax: (901)448-4850

★11847★ **University of Tennessee at**
Nashville
College of Social Work
1720 W. End Ave., Rm. 230
Nashville, TN 37202
Phone: (615)329-1212
Fax: (615)329-1267

Texas

★11848★ **Our Lady of the Lake University**
Worden School of Social Service
411 SW 24th St.
San Antonio, TX 78207-4689
Phone: (210)434-6711
Fax: (210)436-0824

★11849★ **University of Houston**
Graduate School of Social Work
4800 Calhoun
Houston, TX 77204-4492
Phone: (713)743-8085
Fax: (713)743-3267

★11850★ **University of Texas at Arlington**
School of Social Work
UTA Box 19129
Arlington, TX 76019-0129
Phone: (817)273-3944
Fax: (817)273-2046

★11851★ **University of Texas at Austin**
School of Social Work
2609 University Ave.
Austin, TX 78712-1703
Phone: (512)471-1937
Fax: (512)471-9514

Utah

★11852★ **Brigham Young University**
School of Social Work
221 Knight-Mangum Bldg.
Provo, UT 84602
Phone: (801)378-3282
Fax: (801)378-4049

★11853★ **University of Utah**
Graduate School of Social Work
Salt Lake City, UT 84112
Phone: (801)581-6194
Fax: (801)585-3219

Vermont

★11854★ **University of Vermont**
Department of Social Work
499-B Waterman Bldg.
Burlington, VT 05405-0160
Phone: (802)656-8800
Fax: (802)656-8565

Virginia

★11855★ **Norfolk State University**
Ethelyn R. Strong School of Social Work
2401 Corprew Ave.
Norfolk, VA 23504
Phone: (804)683-8668
Fax: (804)683-2556

★11856★ **Virginia Commonwealth**
University
School of Social Work
Box 842027
1001 W. Franklin St.
Richmond, VA 23284-2027
Phone: (804)828-1030
Fax: (804)828-7016

Washington

★11857★ **Eastern Washington University**
Inland Empire School of Social Work and
Human Services
MS-19 Senior Hall
Cheney, WA 99004
Phone: (509)359-2324
Fax: (509)359-6475

★11858★ **University of Washington**
School of Social Work
JH-30
4101 15th Ave. NE
Seattle, WA 98195
Phone: (206)543-5676
Fax: (206)543-1228

★11859★ **Walla Walla College**
Graduate School of Social Work
204 S. College Ave.
College Place, WA 99324
Phone: (509)527-2590
Fax: (509)527-2253

West Virginia

★11860★ **West Virginia University**
School of Social Work
PO Box 6830
Morgantown, WV 26506
Phone: (304)293-3501
Fax: (304)293-5936

Wisconsin

★11861★ **University of Wisconsin—**
Madison
School of Social Work
1300 University Ave.
Madison, WI 53706-1510
Phone: (608)262-3660
Fax: (608)263-3836

★11862★ **University of Wisconsin—**
Milwaukee
School of Social Welfare
Enderis Hall
PO Box 786
Milwaukee, WI 53201
Phone: (414)229-4400
Fax: (414)229-5311

National & International Organizations

American Association of Spinal Cord Injury
 Psychologists and Social Workers
 (AASCIPSW)
See: Entry 7283

★11863★ American Association of State Social Work Boards (AASSWB)
400 S. Ridge Pky., Ste. B
Culpeper, VA 22701
Phone: (703)829-6880
Fax: (703)829-0142

Founded: 1979. **Members:** 50. **Description:** State boards and authorities empowered to regulate the practice of social work within their own jurisdictions. Seeks to protect the recipient of social work service and promote confidence in and accountability of the social work profession by establishing national regulatory standards for the practice of professional social work. Works to facilitate communication and the exchange of information concerning the regulation of social workers; promote the standardization of credential assessment by encouraging collaborative efforts by states to develop compatible standards and procedures for regulation; provide guidance and education on regulation of the practice of social work to legal bodies, regulatory agencies, and other groups concerned with the protection of the public; offer assistance in fulfilling statutory, public, and ethical obligations in legal regulation and enforcement. Provides uniform examinations to state boards and agencies to enable them to evaluate qualifications for social work credentials. Promotes research on matters regarding legal regulations; has established the American Foundation for Research and Consumer Education in Social Work Regulation to research the ramifications of licensing, explore ethical issues raised by professional regulation, and educate the public in what constitutes good social work practice. **Publications:** *AASSWB Newsletter*, bimonthly. Newsletter. Includes association and state legislative information; contains calendar of events. • *Reciprocity and Endorsement in Social Work Licensure*. Also publishes examination study guides.

Association for Applied Poetry (AAP)
See: Entry 7320

★11864★ Association of Oncology Social Work (AOSW)
1910 E. Jefferson St.
Baltimore, MD 21205
Phone: (410)614-3990
Fax: (410)614-3991
Kimberly Bell, Admin. Coord.

Founded: 1984. **Members:** 900. **Description:** Oncology social workers possessing a degree in social work; associate members are professionals functioning as social workers without the professional degree and students in an accredited social work degree program. Seeks to: enable professional social workers in oncology to better serve the needs of clients, practitioners, managers, educators, and researchers; advocate sound public policy and professional programs; promote high professional standards and ethics; foster communication and support among members and between members and other oncology and social work organizations; encourage continuing education and research on psychosocial issues in oncology. **Publications:** *AOSW News*, quarterly. Newsletter. Includes career opportunity listings and meeting announcements. *Price:* Included in membership dues. **Formerly:** (1993) National Association of Oncology Social Workers.

Association of Pediatric Oncology Social Workers (APOSW)
See: Entry 3187

Cancer Care (CC)
See: Entry 5930

★11865★ Council on Accreditation of Services for Families and Children (COA)
520 8th Ave., Ste. 2202B
New York, NY 10018
Phone: (212)714-9399
Fax: (212)976-8624
David P. Shover, Exec.Dir.

Founded: 1977. **Description:** Works to strengthen and actively promote the quality of social and mental health services that support and improve the lives of families and children and the well-being of society, by leading and cooperating in partnerships of social service and mental health agencies. Strives to develop standards of best practice; deliver a program of provider recognition and acredition; design and provide educational and technical assistance programs; advocate for effective services for families and children; build multicultural and multiracial insights and capacities and the respect for diversity; promote a focus on capacity-building, in individuals and families. The Council is a multinational accrediting organization sponsored by the USA, Child Welfare League of America, Family Service America, Lutheran Social Ministry System, National Association of Homes and Services for Children, National Council for Adoption, National Foundation for Consumer Credit, and National Network of Runaway and Youth Services. Participants are direct service agencies that provide any of 42 programs of social and mental health services for which the COA has developed standards. **Publications:** *A Voice for Quality*, quarterly. Newsletter. • *Directory of Accredited Agencies*, biennial. Directory. • *Guidelines for Accreditation*. • *Manual for Agency Accreditation*. • *Standards for Agency Management and Service Delivery*.

★11866★ Council on Social Work Education (CSWE)
1600 Duke St., Ste. 300
Alexandria, VA 22314
Phone: (703)683-8080
Fax: (703)683-8099
Donald W. Beless, Ph.D., Exec.Dir.

Founded: 1952. **Members:** 5,000. **Description:** Graduate and undergraduate programs of social work education; national, regional, and local social welfare agencies; libraries and individuals. Formulates criteria and standards for all levels of social work education; accredits graduate and undergraduate social work programs; provides consulting to social work educators on curriculum, faculty recruitment and development, students and admissions, and teaching methods and materials. Conducts research and compiles data on social work education. **Publications:** Books. • Catalog. • *Directory of Colleges and Universities With Accredited Social Work Degree Programs*, annual. Directory. • *Journal of Social Work Education*, 3/year. Journal. • Monographs. • Pamphlets. • Reports. • *Social Work Education Reporter*, 3/year. • *Statistics on Social Work Education*, annual. •

Summary Information on Masters of Social Work Programs, annual. Also publishes teaching materials.

★11867★ National Assembly of National Voluntary Health and Social Welfare Organizations
1319 F St. NW, Ste. 601
Washington, DC 20004
Phone: (202)347-2080
Fax: (202)393-4517
Gordon A. Raley, Exec. Officer

Founded: 1923. **Members:** 42. **Description:** Facilitates intercommunication and cooperation among national voluntary health and social welfare organizations in the interests of increasing the impact of the individual agencies and of voluntarism on human needs. **Publications:** *Assembly Line*, periodic. Newsletter. • *Community Collaborations Manual*. Book. • *Salary and Benefits Survey of National Voluntary Human Service Organizations*. Book. **Formerly:** (1945) National Social Work Council; (1967) National Social Welfare Assembly; (1973) National Assembly for Social Policy and Development.

★11868★ National Association of Social Workers (NASW)
750 First St. NE, Ste. 700
Washington, DC 20002-4241
Phone: (202)408-8600
Free: 800-638-8799
Fax: (202)336-8312
Sheldon Goldstein, Exec.Dir.

Founded: 1955. **Members:** 150,000. **State Groups:** 55. **Description:** Regular members are persons who hold a minimum of a baccalaureate degree in social work. Associate members are persons engaged in social work who have a baccalaureate degree in another field. Student members are persons enrolled in accredited (by the Council on Social Work Education) graduate or undergraduate social work programs. Purposes are to: create professional standards for social work practice; advocate sound public social policies through political and legislative action; provide a wide range of membership services, including continuing education opportunities and an extensive professional program. Operates National Center for Social Policy and Practice. Conducts research; compiles statistics. **Publications:** *Encyclopedia of Social Work*. Book. • *Health and Social Work*, quarterly. Journal. Gives information on improving social work practice for physical and mental health personnel. Includes legislation updates and innovative practices. *Price:* $43/year for members; $64/year for nonmembers; $28/year for students; $83/year for libraries and other institutions. • *NASW News*, 10/year. Reports on developments in the profession. Includes updates on social policy developments in such areas as child welfare, Medicaid, AIDS, and housing. *Price:* Included in membership dues; $25/year for nonmembers. • *Professional Writing for the Human Services*. • *Social Work*, bimonthly. Journal. Covers social work and social welfare. Examines current social problems such as child abuse, homelessness, working parents, and women's roles. *Price:* Included in membership dues; $93/year for libraries; $67/year for nonmembers. • *Social Work Abstracts*, quarterly.

Price: $45/year for members; $65/year for nonmembers; $30/year for students; $95/year for libraries and institutions. • *Social Work Almanac.* • *The Social Work Dictionary.* • *Social Work in Education: A Journal for Social Workers in Schools*, quarterly. Journal. Focuses on problems encountered by social workers and educators in schools. Includes information on new developments, practices, and programs. *Price:* $37/year for members; $58/year for nonmembers; $28/year for student members; $81/year for libraries and institutions. • *Social Work Research*, quarterly. Journal. Provides over 500 abstracts from 300 journals on social work and related fields. Includes original research articles and research methods. *Price:* $38/year for members; $60/year for nonmembers; $26/year for students; $84/year for libraries and institutions.

★11869★ **National Federation of Societies for Clinical Social Work (NFSCSW)**
PO Box 3740
Arlington, VA 22203
Phone: (703)522-3866
Fax: (703)522-9441
Linda B. O'Leary, Adm. Coord.

Founded: 1971. **Members:** 11,,500. **State Groups:** 31. **Description:** State societies of clinical social work united to provide a vehicle for states and/or regional societies to share concerns common to clinical social work, develop consensual solutions to problems beyond the jurisdiction of any single society, and carry out appropriate courses of action. **Publications:** *Clinical Social Work Journal*, quarterly. Journal. • *National News*, quarterly. • *Progress Report*, semiannual. Newsletter. Includes book reviews and legislative updates. *Price:* Included in membership dues; $25/year for nonmembers. **Formerly:** (1976) National Federation of Clinical Social Workers.

★11870★ **National Network for Social Work Managers**
Administrative Office
6501 N. Federal Hwy., Ste. 5
Boca Raton, FL 33487
Phone: (407)997-7560
Fax: (407)241-6746
Harold A. Benson, Jr., Exec.Dir.

Founded: 1985. **Members:** 800. **Description:** Individuals with degrees in social work who are engaged or interested in management within the human services field. Seeks to enhance social work managers' careers in such areas as administration, management, planning, budgeting, economics, and legislative work. Serves as a network to connect social work professionals in human service-related activities. Conducts National Management Institute, regional management development workshops, and other educational programs. Maintains speakers' bureau. **Publications:** *Administration in Social Work*, quarterly. Journal. *Price:* Included in membership dues. • *Annual Monograph of Papers*, annual. Monograph. • *Membership Directory*, annual. *Price:* Included in membership dues. • *Social Work Executive*, quarterly. Newsletter. Provides information on the national management of social policies; includes conference and member information. *Price:* Included in membership dues.

★11871★ **North American Association of Christians in Social Work (NACSW)**
Box 7090
St. Davids, PA 19087-7090
Phone: (610)687-5777
Fax: (610)687-5777
Edward G. Kuhlmann, Exec.Dir.

Founded: 1954. **Members:** 1,200. **Regional Groups:** 4. **State Groups:** 7. **Local Groups:** 18. **Description:** Professional social workers and related professionals; students; interested individuals. Purpose is to provide opportunities for Christian fellowship, growth, learning, outreach, and witness. Promotes a Christian world view in social work and social welfare and encourages awareness within the Christian community of human need and of social work as a means for ministering to this need. Holds regional seminars, evening meetings, one-day conferences, and small study and support group meetings. Compiles statistics; maintains employment service. Operates speakers' bureau. **Publications:** *A Christian Response to Domestic Violence: A Reconciliation Model for Social Workers*. Monograph. *Price:* $6. • *Catalyst*, bimonthly. Newsletter. Examines the relationship between churches and social work. Reports on association activities; includes calendar of events and chapter news. *Price:* Included in membership dues. • *Church Social Work.* • *Encounters with Children.* • *Giving and Taking Help. Price:* $15. • *Hearts Strangely Warmed: A Reflection on Biblical Passages Relevant to Social Work.* • *Integrating Faith and Practice: A History of the North American Association of Christians in Social Work.* • *The Poor You Have With You Always: Concepts of Aid to the Poor in the Western World from Biblical Times to the Present.* • *So You Want to Be a Social Worker: A Primer for the Christian Student.* Monograph. • *Social Work and Christianity*, semiannual. Journal. Concerned with contributing to the "growth of social workers in the Christian faith." Includes book reviews. *Price:* Included in membership dues; $10/year for institutions in U.S.; $12/year for institutions outside U.S.. • *Spirit-Led Helping: A Model for Evangelical Social Work Counseling.* Monograph. **Formerly:** Evangelical Social Work Conference; (1984) National Association of Christians in Social Work.

★11872★ **Society for Hospital Social Work Directors (SHSWD)**
c/o Amer. Hospital Assn.
840 N. Lake Shore Dr.
Chicago, IL 60611
Phone: (312)280-6414
Harry Bryan, Dir.

Founded: 1966. **Members:** 2,475. **Local Groups:** 60. **Description:** Directors of social work departments in health care institutions. Promotes the improvement and extension of adequate health services for all persons and advances the development of effective social work administration in health care institutions by: promoting educational programs and activities to strengthen and develop social work administration; strengthening relationships with hospital administration and cooperating with allied hospital associations and professional social work organizations in relation to social work in health care; providing a medium for the interchange of

ideas and dissemination of material relative to social work administration; promoting standards and ethics for the delivery of social work in health care sett ings. Sponsors a biennial 13-month course in social work management, and other national and regional programs. Compiles statistics. **Publications:** *Discharge Planning Update*, bimonthly. Contains articles on discharge planning evaluation; also includes Washington report and book reviews. *Price:* $37/year. • *Social Work Administration*, bimonthly.

Society for the Psychological Study of Social Issues (SPSSI)
See: Entry 7517

Research Centers

Oregon Social Learning Center, Inc.
See: Entry 3070

★11873★ **Portland State University**
Regional Research Institute for Human Services
PO Box 751
Portland, OR 97207
Phone: (503)725-4040
Fax: (503)725-4180
Dr. William Feyerherm, Dir.

Research Activities and Fields: Human services, including child welfare and family research, rehabilitation, child and adult mental health, youth services, aging services, child care, employment, criminal justice, substance abuse, and self-help and support groups. Aims to improve the manner in which social services are conceived, managed, and evaluated at local, regional, and national levels. Projects include surveys and evaluations of employee and employer-sponsored child care, development of methods to help three-generational families, surveys of dependent care needs, studies of child protective services in Oregon, study of prosecution of child sexual abuse offenders in Oregon, evaluation of teen mothers programs, national study of efficacy of family services as alternative to foster care placement of children, and survey of service needs of economically insecure. **Publications:** *Focal Point.* **E-mail Address:** whf@rri.pdx.edu.

★11874★ **Tulane University**
Elizabeth Wisner Social Welfare Research Center for Families and Children
School of Social Work
New Orleans, LA 70118-5672
Phone: (504)865-5314
Fax: (504)802-8727
Dr. Raymond Swan, Dir.

Research Activities and Fields: Community-based studies on the welfare of families and children. Projects focus on violence in families of the mentally ill and the development of research and training related to HIV-AIDS victims and their families. **Publications:** Monographs; *Tulane Studies in Social Welfare.* **Formerly:** Social Work Research Center.

★ 11875 ★ **University of California at Berkeley**
Berkeley Child Welfare Research Center
1950 Addison St., Ste. 104
Berkeley, CA 94704
Phone: (510)642-1899
Fax: (510)642-1895
Jill Duerr Berrick, Dir.

Research Activities and Fields: Child welfare, including child abuse and welfare, family preservation and maintenance, foster care and adoptions, drug and AIDS-affected children, and the organization, financing, and evaluation of child welfare services. Activities include the California Long Range Adoption Study, an investigation of 1,400 children and families at the onset of adoption, including prenatal drug exposure, sibling groups, open adoption, and after prior adoptions. **Publications:** *Child Welfare Research Review* (biennially).

★ 11876 ★ **University of Illinois at Chicago**
Jane Addams Center for Social Policy and Research
1040 W. Harrison St., Rm. 4010
MC-309
Chicago, IL 60607-7134
Phone: (312)996-8511
Fax: (312)996-2770
Dr. Creasie Finney Hairston, Dean

Research Activities and Fields: Research and demonstration projects in child welfare, mental health, and corrections. **Publications:** Jane Addams Occasional Papers on Social Policy and Research.

★ 11877 ★ **University of Pennsylvania**
Lazarus-Goldman Center for Study of Social Work Practice
3701 Locust Walk
Philadelphia, PA 19104-6214
Phone: (215)898-5541
Fax: (215)573-2099
Ira M. Schwartz, Dir.

Research Activities and Fields: Theory-guided, systematic studies on various forms of professional social work practice, including research on service effectiveness, aging, family/child welfare, education and training in social work, health/medical care, mental health, and employment/unemployment. Assists with research education of masters and doctoral students. **Publications:** *Journal of Social Work Process* (irregularly).

University of South Dakota
Social Science Research Institute
See: Entry 7687

★ 11878 ★ **University of Texas at Austin**
Center for Social Work Research
School of Social Work
1925 San Jacinto
Austin, TX 78712
Phone: (512)471-9832
Fax: (512)471-9514
Ruth G. McRoy, Ph.D., Dir.

Research Activities and Fields: Conducts research on the design and delivery of health and social services in the Southwest and Mexico. Also conducts survey and field research on family relationships and economic trends, child welfare and adoption, at-risk children, adolescent pregnancy, mental health, persistent poverty, substance abuse, computer applications for human services, and child care. **E-mail Address:** jtrapp@mail.utexas.edu. **Formerly:** School of Social Work Research Center.

★ 11879 ★ **University of Washington**
Center for Policy and Practice
4101 15th Ave. NE
JH-30
Seattle, WA 98195
Phone: (206)543-4175
Fax: (206)543-1228
Dr. Lewayne D. Gilchrist, Dir.

Research Activities and Fields: Design, implementation, and evaluation of human service programs and policies in the areas of adolescent health care, aging, drug abuse, juvenile delinquency, mental health, youth development, health promotion, family violence, child welfare, workplace issues, health care, ethnic minority issues, income maintenance, gerontological services to the elderly, physical and developmental disabilities, and women's issues. **Publications:** Monograph Series (periodically). **Formerly:** Center for Social Welfare Research.

State & Regional Organizations

Social Work

Listed below are chapters of the National Association of Social Workers, 750 1st St. NE, Washington, DC 20002, (202) 408-8600.

Alabama

★ 11880 ★ **National Association of Social Workers**
Alabama Chapter
Governors Park II
2921 Marti Ln., Ste. G
Montgomery, AL 36116
Phone: (205)288-2633
Fax: (205)288-1398

Alaska

★ 11881 ★ **National Association of Social Workers**
Alaska Chapter
1727 Wickersham Dr.
Anchorage, AK 99507
Phone: (907)563-4502
Fax: (907)563-4504

Arizona

★ 11882 ★ **National Association of Social Workers**
Arizona Chapter
610 W. Broadway, Ste. 218
Tempe, AZ 85281
Phone: (602)968-4595
Fax: (602)894-9726

Arkansas

★ 11883 ★ **National Association of Social Workers**
Arkansas Chapter
1123 S. University, Ste. 1010
Little Rock, AR 72204
Phone: (501)663-0658
Fax: (501)663-6406

California

★ 11884 ★ **National Association of Social Workers**
California Chapter
1016 23rd St.
Sacramento, CA 95816
Phone: (916)442-4565
Free: 800-538-2565
Fax: (916)442-2075

Colorado

★ 11885 ★ **National Association of Social Workers**
Colorado Chapter
Bldg. 1, Ste. 121
6000 E. Evans
Denver, CO 80222
Phone: (303)753-8890

Connecticut

★ 11886 ★ **National Association of Social Workers**
Connecticut Chapter
2139 Silas Deane Hwy., Ste. 205
Rocky Hill, CT 06067
Phone: (203)257-8066
Fax: (203)257-8074

Delaware

★ 11887 ★ **National Association of Social Workers**
Delaware Chapter
3301 Green St.
Claymont, DE 19703
Phone: (302)792-0646
Fax: (302)792-0678

District of Columbia

★ 11888 ★ **National Association of Social Workers**
Metro DC Chapter
2025 I St. NW, Ste. 106
Washington, DC 20006
Phone: (202)457-0492
Fax: (202)296-5106

Florida

★ 11889 ★ National Association of Social
   Workers
Florida Chapter
345 S. Magnolia Dr., Ste. 14-B
Tallahassee, FL 32301
Phone: (904)224-2400
Free: 800-352-6279
Fax: (904)561-6279

Georgia

★ 11890 ★ National Association of Social
   Workers
Georgia Chapter
Bldg. 1, Ste. 310
300 W. Wieuca Rd.
Atlanta, GA 30342
Phone: (404)255-6422
Fax: (404)255-5759

Hawaii

★ 11891 ★ National Association of Social
   Workers
Hawaii Chapter
245 N. Kukui St., Ste. 206
Honolulu, HI 96817
Phone: (808)521-1787
Fax: (808)531-1708

Idaho

★ 11892 ★ National Association of Social
   Workers
Idaho Chapter
200 N. 4th St.
Boise, ID 83702
Phone: (208)343-2752
Fax: (208)345-1163

Illinois

★ 11893 ★ National Association of Social
   Workers
Illinois Chapter
180 N. Michigan Ave., Ste. 400
Chicago, IL 60601
Phone: (312)236-8308
Fax: (312)236-6627

Indiana

★ 11894 ★ National Association of Social
   Workers
Indiana Chapter
1100 W. 42nd St., Ste. 316
Indianapolis, IN 46208
Phone: (317)923-9878
Fax: (317)925-9364

Iowa

★ 11895 ★ National Association of Social
   Workers
Iowa Chapter
4211 Grand Ave., Level 3
Des Moines, IA 50312
Phone: (515)277-1117

Kansas

★ 11896 ★ National Association of Social
   Workers
Kansas Chapter
Jayhawk Towers, Ste. 901
700 SW Jackson St.
Topeka, KS 66603-3740
Phone: (913)354-4804
Fax: (913)354-1456

Kentucky

★ 11897 ★ National Association of Social
   Workers
Kentucky Chapter
230 W. Main
Frankfort, KY 40601
Phone: (502)223-0245
Fax: (502)223-0525

Louisiana

★ 11898 ★ National Association of Social
   Workers
Louisiana Chapter
700 N. 10th St., Ste. 200
Baton Rouge, LA 70802
Phone: (504)346-1234
Fax: (504)346-5035

Maine

★ 11899 ★ National Association of Social
   Workers
Maine Chapter
181 State St.
PO Box 5065
Augusta, ME 04332
Phone: (207)622-7592
Fax: (207)623-4860

Maryland

★ 11900 ★ National Association of Social
   Workers
Maryland Chapter
5710 Executive Dr., Ste. 105
Baltimore, MD 21228
Phone: (410)788-1066
Fax: (410)747-0635

Massachusetts

★ 11901 ★ National Association of Social
   Workers
Massachusetts Chapter
14 Beacon St., Ste. 409
Boston, MA 02108
Phone: (617)227-9635
Fax: (617)227-9877

Michigan

★ 11902 ★ National Association of Social
   Workers
Michigan Chapter
230 N. Washington Sq., Ste. 212
Lansing, MI 48933
Phone: (517)487-1548
Fax: (517)487-0675

Minnesota

★ 11903 ★ National Association of Social
   Workers
Minnesota Chapter
480 Concordia Ave.
St. Paul, MN 55103
Phone: (612)293-1935
Fax: (612)293-0952

Mississippi

★ 11904 ★ National Association of Social
   Workers
Mississippi Chapter
PO Box 4228
Jackson, MS 39216
Phone: (601)981-8359
Fax: (601)981-6922

Missouri

★ 11905 ★ National Association of Social
   Workers
Missouri Chapter
Parkade Center, Ste. 138
601 Business Loop 70 W.
Columbia, MO 65203
Phone: (314)874-6140
Free: 800-333-6279
Fax: (314)874-8738

Montana

★ 11906 ★ National Association of Social
   Workers
Montana Chapter
555 Fuller Ave., Lower Level
Helena, MT 59601
Phone: (406)449-6208

Nebraska

★ 11907 ★ National Association of Social
Workers
Nebraska Chapter
PO Box 83732
Lincoln, NE 68501
Phone: (402)477-7344
Fax: (402)476-6547

Nevada

★ 11908 ★ National Association of Social
Workers
Nevada Chapter
1651 E. Flamingo Rd.
Las Vegas, NV 89119
Phone: (702)791-5872
Fax: (702)791-5873

New Hampshire

★ 11909 ★ National Association of Social
Workers
New Hampshire Chapter
c/o New Hampshire Association for the Blind
25 Walker St.
Concord, NH 03301
Phone: (603)226-7135
Fax: (603)226-7135

New Jersey

★ 11910 ★ National Association of Social
Workers
New Jersey Chapter
110 W. State St.
Trenton, NJ 08608
Phone: (609)394-1666
Fax: (609)394-0200

New Mexico

★ 11911 ★ National Association of Social
Workers
New Mexico Chapter
1503 University Blvd. NE
Albuquerque, NM 87102
Phone: (505)247-2336
Fax: (505)246-8761

New York

★ 11912 ★ National Association of Social
Workers
New York City Chapter
545 8th Ave., 6th Fl.
New York, NY 10018
Phone: (212)947-5000
Fax: (212)947-5311

★ 11913 ★ National Association of Social
Workers
New York State Chapter
225 Lark St.
Albany, NY 12210
Phone: (518)463-4741
Free: 800-724-6479
Fax: (518)463-6446

North Carolina

★ 11914 ★ National Association of Social
Workers
North Carolina Chapter
PO Box 27582
Raleigh, NC 27611-7582
Phone: (919)828-9650
Free: 800-280-6207
Fax: (919)828-1341

North Dakota

★ 11915 ★ National Association of Social
Workers
North Dakota Chapter
PO Box 1775
Bismarck, ND 58502-1775
Phone: (701)223-4161

Ohio

★ 11916 ★ National Association of Social
Workers
Ohio Chapter
42 E. Gay St., Ste. 700
Columbus, OH 43215
Phone: (614)461-4484
Fax: (614)461-9793

Oklahoma

★ 11917 ★ National Association of Social
Workers
Oklahoma Chapter
116 E. Sheridan, Ste. 210
Oklahoma City, OK 73104-2419
Phone: (405)239-7017
Fax: (405)236-3638

Oregon

★ 11918 ★ National Association of Social
Workers
Oregon Chapter
7688 SW Capitol Hwy.
Portland, OR 97219
Phone: (503)452-8420
Fax: (503)452-8506

Pennsylvania

★ 11919 ★ National Association of Social
Workers
Pennsylvania Chapter
1007 N. Front St., Ste. 2 N.
Harrisburg, PA 17102-3320
Phone: (717)232-4125
Fax: (717)232-4140

Puerto Rico

★ 11920 ★ National Association of Social
Workers
Puerto Rico Chapter
271 Ramon Ramos Casellas St.
Hato Rey, PR 00918
Phone: (809)758-3588
Fax: (809)281-8433

Rhode Island

★ 11921 ★ National Association of Social
Workers
Rhode Island Chapter
341A Broadway
Providence, RI 02909
Phone: (401)274-4940
Fax: (401)274-4941

South Carolina

★ 11922 ★ National Association of Social
Workers
South Carolina Chapter
PO Box 5008
Columbia, SC 29250
Phone: (803)256-8406
Fax: (803)254-4116

South Dakota

★ 11923 ★ National Association of Social
Workers
South Dakota Chapter
830 State St.
Spearfish, SD 57783
Phone: (605)642-0711
Fax: (605)642-0822

Tennessee

★ 11924 ★ National Association of Social
Workers
Tennessee Chapter
1720 West End Ave., Ste. 607
Nashville, TN 37203
Phone: (615)321-5095
Fax: (615)327-2676

Texas

★ 11925 ★ National Association of Social
Workers
Texas Chapter
810 W. 11th St.
Austin, TX 78701
Phone: (512)474-1454
Free: 800-888-6279
Fax: (512)474-1317

Utah

★ 11926 ★ National Association of Social
Workers
Utah Chapter
Graduate School of Social Work
University of Utah
Salt Lake City, UT 84112
Phone: (801)583-8855
Fax: (801)583-6218

Vermont

★ 11927 ★ National Association of Social
    Workers
Vermont Chapter
PO Box 147
Woodstock, VT 05091-0147
Phone: (802)457-3645
Fax: (802)457-4489

Virgin Islands

★ 11928 ★ National Association of Social
    Workers
Virgin Islands Chapter
Havensight Secretarial Services
2 Buccaneer Mall
St. Thomas, VI 00802
Phone: (809)776-3424
Fax: (809)777-8108

Virginia

★ 11929 ★ National Association of Social
    Workers
Virginia Chapter
Virginia Bldg., Ste. 410
1 N. 5th St.
Richmond, VA 23219
Phone: (804)643-1833
Fax: (804)643-1845

Washington

★ 11930 ★ National Association of Social
    Workers
Washington Chapter
2601 Elliott Ave., Ste. 4175
Seattle, WA 98121
Phone: (206)448-1660
Free: 800-864-2078
Fax: (206)448-1674

West Virginia

★ 11931 ★ National Association of Social
    Workers
West Virginia Chapter
1608 Virginia St. E.
Charleston, WV 25311
Phone: (304)343-6141
Fax: (304)343-3295

Wisconsin

★ 11932 ★ National Association of Social
    Workers
Wisconsin Chapter
14 Mifflin St., Ste. 104
Madison, WI 53703
Phone: (608)257-6334
Fax: (608)257-8233

Wyoming

★ 11933 ★ National Association of Social
    Workers
Wyoming Chapter
PO Box 701
Cheyenne, WY 82003
Phone: (307)634-2118
Fax: (307)634-7512

Chapter 62
Sports Medicine

National & International Organizations

Academy for Sports Dentistry (ASD)
See: Entry 3849

★11934★ American Academy of Podiatric Sports Medicine (AAPSM)
1729 Glastonberry Rd.
Potomac, MD 20854
Phone: (301)424-7440
Larry I. Shane, Exec.Dir.

Founded: 1970. **Members:** 800. **Description:** Podiatrists, medical doctors, and athletic trainers interested in promoting professional participation and research in sports medicine. Directs 12 committees that deal with individual sports. Compiles statistics. **Publications:** *AAPSM Newsletter*, quarterly. Newsletter. Features articles on the treatment of sports injuries in the field of podiatry. Includes calendar of events and research updates. *Price:* $25/year. • Directory, annual.

★11935★ American Academy of Sports Physicians (AASP)
17113 Gledhill St.
Northridge, CA 91325
Phone: (818)886-7891
Janie Zimmer, Coord.

Founded: 1979. **Members:** 150. **Description:** Clinical physicians engaged in the practice of sports medicine who have made contributions in research, academics, or related fields. Objectives are to educate and inform physicians whose practices comprise mainly sports medicine and to register and recognize physicians who have expertise in sports medicine. Operates referral service for amateur and professional athletes. Conducts research; compiles statistics; sponsors seminars. **Publications:** Newsletter, quarterly.

★11936★ American Board of Ringside Medicine and Surgery (ABRMS)
c/o Bartholomew A. Sinatra
522 Rossmore Dr.
Las Vegas, NV 89110-4123
Phone: (702)452-9538
Fax: (702)452-1031
Bartholomew A. Sinatra, M.D., Chm.

Founded: 1984. **Members:** 130. **Description:** Physicians who provide medical assistance and opinion at boxing matches. Works to further scientific knowledge and provide educational opportunities in the field. Conducts charitable activities.

American Canine Sports Medicine Association (ACSMA)
See: Entry 13044

★11937★ American College of Sports Medicine (ACSM)
PO Box 1440
Indianapolis, IN 46206-1440
Phone: (317)637-9200
Fax: (317)634-7817
James R. Whitehead, Exec.VP

Founded: 1954. **Members:** 14,500. **Regional Groups:** 12. **Description:** Promotes and integrates scientific research, education, and practical applications of sports medicine and exercise science to maintain and enhance physical performance, fitness, health, and quality of life. Certifies fitness leaders, fitness instructors, exercise specialists, exercise test technologists, health/fitness program directors, and U.S. military fitness personnel. Grants continuing medical education (CME) and continuing education credits (CEC). Operates more than 50 committees. **Publications:** *ACSM Fitness Book*. Book. • *ACSM's Health/Fitness Consumer Selection Guide*. • *ACSM's Health/Fitness Facility Standards and Guidelines*. • *American College of Sports Medicine Career Services Bulletin*, monthly. Newsletter. Lists career and fellowship opportunities in sports medicine in the United States and abroad. *Price:* $10/year for members; $20/year for nonmembers. • *American College of Sports Medicine Directory of Graduate Programs in Sports Medicine and Exercise Science*, annual. Directory. Lists graduate programs in fields related to exercise science and sports medicine at North American institutions.

Price: $12. • *American College of Sports Medicine Guidelines for the Team Physician*. • *American College of Sports Medicine Membership Directory*, annual. Membership Directory. Arranged alphabetically and geographically. Contains advertisers' index. *Price:* Included in membership dues. • *Exercise and Sport Sciences Reviews*, annual. Monographs. *Price:* Included in membership dues; $49.95/year for nonmembers. • *Guidelines for Exercise Testing and Prescription*. • *Medicine and Science in Sports and Exercise*, monthly. Journal. *Price:* Included in membership dues; $45/year for nonmembers. • *Medicine and Science in Sports and Exercise Cumulative Index*. • *Resource Manual for Guidelines for Exercise Testing and Prescription*. Manual. • *Sports Medicine Bulletin*, quarterly. Newsletter. Covers association activities and professional topics. Includes book reviews, calendar of events, and information on membership and fellowship. *Price:* Included in membership dues. Also publishes position statements.

★11938★ American Medical Equestrian Association (AMEA)
103 Surrey Rd.
Waynesville, NC 28786-5047
Phone: (704)456-3392
Fax: (704)456-3392
J. W. Thomas Byrd, M.D., Contact

Founded: 1990. **Members:** 100. **Description:** Physicians, health personnel, and individuals interested in equestrian safety. Seeks to decrease accidents related to horseback riding through education and awareness programs. Advocates use of headgear for riders. Offers recommendations, consultations, and leadership to equestrian organizations. Conducts studies and surveys. Compiles statistics. **Publications:** *AMEA News*, quarterly. Newsletter. Includes articles and statistics on horse-related human injuries. *Price:* Included in membership dues. • *Planning Event Coverage*. Booklet. • *When Can My Child Ride a Horse*. Brochure.

★ 11939 ★ American Sports Medicine Association Board of Certification (ASMA)
660 W. Duarte Rd.
Arcadia, CA 91007
Phone: (818)445-1978
Joe S. Borland, Bd.Chm.

Founded: 1994. **Description:** Verifies and qualifies the educational competency of active athletic trainers and sports medicine trainers for certification. Establishes minimum competency standards of education required for the prevention and care of athletic injuries and sports medicine. Maintains speakers' bureau. **Publications:** Brochure. • Newsletter, quarterly. *Price:* Included in membership dues. • *Special Bulletin*, periodic. Bulletin.

★ 11940 ★ Association for the Advancement of Sports Potential (AASP)
c/o Houyhnhnm Farm
Box 376, RDS
Coatesville, PA 19320
Phone: (610)383-5579
Patrice Miller, Deputy Dir.

Founded: 1976. **Members:** 50. **Description:** Supports projects on anti-violence. Conducts research; compiles statistics.

★ 11941 ★ Association of Chartered Physiotherapists in Sports Medicine (ACPSM)
Nottingham School of Physiotherapy
Hucknall Rd.
Nottingham NG5 1PG, England
Phone: 115 9627681
Fax: 115 9606993
Judy P. Wright, Sec.

Founded: 1975. **Members:** 850. **Languages:** English. **Description:** Chartered physiotherapists specializing in sports injuries. Seeks to improve techniques and facilities for the prevention and treatment of sports injuries. Offers sports physiotherapy courses in conjuction with Crewe & Alsager College of Higher Education leading to M.Sc., advanced certificate, and post graduate diploma. **Publications:** *Directory*, biennial. Directory. • *Physiotherapy in Sport*, 3/year. Newsletter.

★ 11942 ★ Association of Professional Baseball Physicians (APBP)
c/o Dr. Leonard J. Michienzi
6500 Barrie Rd., Ste. 150
Edina, MN 55435
Phone: (612)920-5663
Free: 800-747-3641
Fax: (612)924-1659

Founded: 1970. **Members:** 36. **Description:** Physicians and surgeons of the professional baseball teams in the U.S. Aim is to provide the best possible medical care to all players and associated personnel. Conducts drug abuse seminars on topics such as the use of amphetamines, steroids, and cocaine by athletes.

★ 11943 ★ Central American Federation of Sports Medicine (Confederacion Centroamericano de Medicina del Deporte)
Apartado Postal 172
Heredia 3000, Costa Rica
Phone: 2371835
Fax: 2378956
Dr. Rafeal Brenes Rojas, Pres.

Founded: 1986. **Members:** 6. **Description:** Promotes the advancement of sports medicine in Central America.

International Academy of Sports Vision (NASV)
See: Entry 13478

★ 11944 ★ International Association of Olympic Medical Officers (IAOMO) (Association Internationale des Cadres Medicaux Olympiques — IAOMO)
20 Devonshire Gardens
Chiswick
London W43 TN, England
Dr. M.S. Irani, Sec.

Founded: 1968. **Members:** 170. **Languages:** English, French. **Description:** Medical doctors who are or who have been nominated by their national Olympic committees as official doctors to their respective teams at Olympic games; representatives of national Olympic committees; individuals rendering distinguished service to the association. Promotes friendship among members. Works to facilitate the exchange of ideas and information regarding the medical care of Olympic competitors. Reviews and makes recommendations to appropriate authorities on matters regarding the medical well-being of Olympic teams.

★ 11945 ★ International Federation of Sports Medicine (FIMS)
Tres Figueiras
91330-250 Porto Alegre, Rio Grande do Sul, Brazil
Phone: 51 3348083
Fax: 51 2272295
Prof. Eduardo H. de Rose, Contact

Founded: 1928. **Languages:** English, French, Russian, Spanish. **Description:** National federations of physicians, physiologists, and individuals interested in maintaining and improving physical and mental health through sporting activities such as physical education, gymnastics, games, and other sports. Conducts scientific studies of the pathological and normal effects of sporting activities. Bestows awards. **Publications:** *FIMS Directory*, annual. Directory. • *The World of Sports Medicine*, quarterly.

★ 11946 ★ International Society for Ski Traumatology and Medicine of Winter Sports (Societe Internationale de Traumatologie de Ski et de Medecine d'Hiver)
Centre Medical
F-74110 Avoriaz, France
Phone: 50 740542
Fax: 50 740758
Dr. M. Binet, Sec.Gen.

Founded: 1956. **Languages:** English, French, German, Italian, Spanish. **Description:** Encour-

ages an international exchange of medical experiences and ideas on the treatment of injuries resulting from mountaineering and other winter sports. **Publications:** *Congress Reports*, biennial.

★ 11947 ★ International Society of Sports Psychology (ISSP)
c/o Prof. Glyn C. Roberts
University of Illinois at Urbana - Champaign
Department of Kinesiology
906 S. Goodwin Ave.
Urbana, IL 61801
Phone: (217)333-6563
Fax: (217)333-0404
Prof. Glyn C. Roberts, Gen.Sec.

Founded: 1965. **Members:** 3,000. **Description:** Professionally qualified individuals in 47 countries interested in sports psychology. Supports and promotes scientific research and professional relations between scholars in the field; participates in information and documentation services in sports psychology; advises and facilitates the establishment of other continental, regional, and national societies of sport psychology. Provides the International Olympic Committee and United States Olympic Committee with information on sport psychology services. Maintains speakers' bureau and bestows awards; operates children's services. **Publications:** *International Journal of Sport Psychology*, 3/year. Journal. • *ISSP Newsletter*, semiannual. Newsletter. Covers professional issues in sports psychology; includes conference reports, employment opportunities, and membership list. *Price:* Included in membership dues. • *The Sport Psychologist*, quarterly. Journal. For those who teach or provide psychological services to athletes; covers research, practice, and professionals in the field. *Price:* $24/year for members; $28/year for nonmembers. Also publishes proceedings.

★ 11948 ★ International Sports Massage Federation (ISMF)
2156 Newport Blvd.
Costa Mesa, CA 92627
Phone: (714)642-0735
Fax: (714)642-1729
M. K. Hungerford, Ph.D., Pres.

Founded: 1989. **Members:** 43. **Description:** National sports massage federations. Facilitates exchange of techniques and ideas among members; emphasizes improving relations between Socialist and non-Socialist countries. Conducts international exchange programs. Plans to publish newsletter and hold annual meeting. **Publications:** *Sports Massage Journal*, quarterly. Journal. *Price:* $35/year.

★ 11949 ★ Joint Commission on Sports Medicine and Science (JCSMS)
Oklahoma State University
Student Health Center
Stillwater, OK 74078
Phone: (405)744-7031
Donald L. Cooper, M.D., Co-Chm.

Founded: 1966. **Members:** 5. **Description:** Organizations of educational institutions or their faculty and staff. Members include: American College Health Association; National Association of Intercollegiate Athletics; National Athletic

Trainers Association; National Federation of State High School Associations; National Junior College Athletic Association. Promotes communication among organizations concerned with the health and safety of those engaged in athletics; disseminates information to the public. Establishes guidelines and standards for athletic programs; recommends rule and administration policies for athletic programs; stimulates research; compiles statistics. **Formerly:** (1988) Joint Commission on Competitive Safeguards and the Medical Aspects of Sports.

★ **11950 ★   Latin and Mediterranean Group for Sport Medicine (LMGSM) (Groupement Latin et Mediterraneen de Medecine du Sport — GLMMS)**
23, blvd. Carabacel
F-06000 Nice, France
Phone: 93 853377
Fax: 93 130762
Dr. Francisque Commandre, Sec.Gen.

Founded: 1956. **Members:** 2,000. **Languages:** French. **Description:** Physicians in 27 Mediterranean countries interested in the medical study of sports and exercise. Objectives are to further sports medicine and to conduct studies on medical problems related to amateur and professional sports and physical activity in general. Offers continuing education classes to members. Organizes competitions and periodic scientific meetings. Operates speakers' bureau. **Publications:** *Apunto*, periodic. • *Archivos de Medicina del Deporte*, quarterly. • *Cinesiologie*, bimonthly. • *Medecine du Sport*, bimonthly. • *Medecine du Sud-Est*, quarterly.

★ **11951 ★   South American Federation of Sports Medicine (Confederacion Sudamericana de Medicina del Deporte)**
PO Box 994
1000 Buenos Aires, Argentina
Dr. D'Angelo, Pres.

Description: Promotes the development of sports medicine throughout South America. Seeks advanced treatment and prevention methods.

★ **11952 ★   United States Sports Massage Federation (USMF)**
2156 Newport Blvd.
Costa Mesa, CA 92627
Phone: (714)642-0735
Fax: (714)642-1729
M. K. Hungerford, Ph.D., Pres.

Founded: 1989. **Members:** 17. **Description:** Sports massage therapists. Facilitates exchange of techniques and ideas among members. Promotes more widespread use of massage therapy by U.S. professional sports teams.

★ **11953 ★   World Sports Medicine Association of Registered Therapists (WORLD SMAR)**
206 Marine Ave.
PO Box 5642
Newport Beach, CA 92662
Phone: (818)574-1999

Founded: 1993. **Description:** Athletic trainers, fitness trainers, and individuals involved in sports medicine and certified by any nationally recognized athletic trainers association. Establishes standards of competency for trainers, therapists, and sports care providers that are recognized worldwide. **Publications:** Brochure. • Bulletin, periodic. • Newsletter, quarterly. *Price:* Included in membership dues.

Research Centers

★ **11954 ★   Adelphi University Human Performance Laboratory**
Woodruff Hall
Garden City, NJ 11530
Phone: (516)877-4270
Fax: (516)877-4258
Dr. Robert Otto, Dir.

Research Activities and Fields: Human performance as it relates to exercise.

★ **11955 ★   Arizona State University Exercise and Sport Research Institute**
Exercise Science & Physical Education Dept.
Tempe, AZ 85287-0404
Phone: (602)965-7473
Fax: (602)965-8108
Dr. James S. Skinner, Dir.

Research Activities and Fields: Exercise and sport, including exercise physiology, sports psychology, exercise biochemistry, biomechanics, and motor behavior of various populations (children, athletes, elderly, adults). Provides exercise testing and exercise programs for research purposes. **E-mail Address:** skinner@espea.la.asu.edu. **Formerly:** Human Performance Laboratory.

★ **11956 ★   Ball State University Human Performance Laboratory**
Muncie, IN 47306
Phone: (317)285-1156
Fax: (317)285-8596
Dr. David L. Costill, Dir.

Research Activities and Fields: Human performance, including studies on effects of physical training on skeletal muscular metabolism, nutritional demands during muscular activity, fluid replacement during and following acute dehydration, muscle glycogen utilization during prolonged exertion, and swimming research.

★ **11957 ★   Baylor / UTSW Sports Science Research Lab**
411 N. Washington, Ste. 3000
Dallas, TX 75245
Phone: (214)820-7848
Dr. James Stray-Gundersen, Dir.

Research Activities and Fields: Sports science, including exercise physiology and nutrition. Also studies neuroimmunomodulation and adult aging. **Formerly:** Human Performance Center (University of Texas Southwestern Medical Center at Dallas).

★ **11958 ★   Boston University Human Bioenergetics Laboratory**
635 Commonwealth Ave., 4th floor
Boston, MA 02215
Phone: (617)353-2719
Dr. Gary S. Skrinar, Dir.

Research Activities and Fields: Exercise physiology and fitness for disabled and non-disabled populations. **Formerly:** Applied Physiology Lab.

★ **11959 ★   Bridgewater State College Human Performance Lab**
Bridgewater, MA 02324
Phone: (508)697-1200
Dr. Robert Haslam, Dir.

Research Activities and Fields: Exercise physiology, including metabolic responses to exercise, blood flow responses to exercise, prediction of athlete success, and police and fire fighter fitness.

★ **11960 ★   Brigham Young University Human Performance Research Center**
Provo, UT 84601
Phone: (801)378-3981
A. Garth Fisher, Ph.D., Dir.

Research Activities and Fields: Exercise physiology, including studies of cardiovascular changes due to exercise, energy cost of various types of exercise, body composition changes due to exercise, and animal studies to determine the effects of cocaine on exercise.

★ **11961 ★   Center for Athletic Injury Research**
PO Box 104
Wascott, WI 54890-0104
Phone: (217)586-2118
Edward P. Grogg, M.D., Dir.

Research Activities and Fields: Athletic injury.

★ **11962 ★   Cincinnati Sports Medicine Research and Education Foundation**
Deaconess Hospital
311 Straight St.
Cincinnati, OH 45219
Phone: (513)559-2818
Fax: (513)475-5263
Frank R. Noyes, M.D., Dir.

Research Activities and Fields: Orthopedic and sports medicine with emphasis on clinical problems and surgical treatment. Areas of interest include rehabilitation protocols, use of allografts and autografts to replace knee ligaments, meniscal allografts, biomechanics of the knee and shoulder, and gait analysis.

★ **11963 ★   Colorado State University Human Performance Laboratory**
Dept. of Exercise & Sport Science
Fort Collins, CO 80523
Phone: (303)491-7436
Fax: (303)491-0445
Dr. Loren Cordain, Dir.

Research Activities and Fields: Human performance, body composition, metabolism, nutrition and sports performance, and exercise physiology.

★ 11964 ★ Delaware All-Sports Research
1601 Milltown Rd., Ste. 24
Wilmington, DE 19808
Phone: (302)998-0178
Dr. J.P. Contompasis, Dir.

Research Activities and Fields: Sports medicine, including clinical and biomechanics research and etiology, treatment, and prevention of sports injuries. Biomechanics research is primarily concerned with lower extremity functions and pathomechanics.

★ 11965 ★ Grand Valley State University
Human Performance Laboratory
132 Fieldhouse
Allendale, MI 49401
Phone: (616)895-3228
Fax: (616)895-3838
James R. Scott, Contact

Research Activities and Fields: Human performance studies, including elite athlete performance profiles (wrestlers), functional electro-stimulation exercise with quadriplegic participants, and faculty/staff fitness and lifestyle assessments.

★ 11966 ★ High Technology Fitness
Research Institute
2434 N. Greenview, Ste. 305
Chicago, IL 60614
Phone: (312)528-1000
Fax: (312)929-5733
Dr. Bob Goldman, Dir.

Research Activities and Fields: Effects of drugs and ergogenetics on human performance and analysis of health and fitness products and programs on the market, including fitness technology applications in the treatment and prevention of lifestyle-induced pathologies. Programs include training methods for athletes, the development of protocols and standards for fitness technology evaluation, drug dependency, longevity, and aids to conventional physical therapy for patients with chronic back pain. Acts as a forum for professionals interested in controversial topics such as the use of hormone drugs, dairy supplemental calcium and estrogen supplements for prevention or reversal of osteoporosis in women, fad diets, and high-impact versus nonballistic low-impact aerobics.

★ 11967 ★ Human Performance
International (HPI-MSRG)
Motor Sport Research Group
2570 International Speedway Blvd.
Daytona Beach, FL 32114
Phone: (904)239-6190
Fax: (904)239-6191
Dr. Dan Q. Marisi, Dir.

Research Activities and Fields: Biomechanical, physiological, and psychological and medical factors affecting human performance during competitive racing and other athletic activities, such as the influence of body heat on cardiovascular stress. Formerly: Motorsport Research Group at McGill University.

★ 11968 ★ Kent State University
Applied Physiology Research Laboratory
Kent, OH 44242
Phone: (216)672-2857
Fax: (216)672-4106
Dr. Wayne E. Sinning, Contact

Research Activities and Fields: Exercise physiology, body composition, and physical fitness, including studies of protein metabolism and exercise, cardiovascular/respiratory responses during exercise in heat and cold, an neuromuscular integration/biomechanics, and psychosocial reactivity to behavioral stressors.

Laban / Bartenieff Institute of Movement
Studies, Inc.
See: Entry 12736

★ 11969 ★ Laval University
Exercise Physiology Group
Laboratoire des sciences de l'activite
physique
Pavillon de l'education physique et des sports
Quebec, PQ, Canada G1K 7P4
Phone: (418)656-7003
Fax: (418)656-3020
Claude Bouchard, Dir.

Research Activities and Fields: Genetic and molecular basis of adaptation to exercise and nutritional stresses by obese individuals and highly active or sedentary individuals and their relatives. Research focuses on lipid and lipoprotein metabolism, adipose tissue and skeletal muscle metabolism, fat distribution, and the role of genetic polymorphism.

★ 11970 ★ Melpomene Institute for
Women's Health Research
1010 Univ. Ave.
St. Paul, MN 55104
Phone: (612)642-1951
Fax: (612)642-1871
Judy Mahle Lutter, Pres.

Research Activities and Fields: Physically active women and girls, including effects of exercise on menstruation, pregnancy, adolescent girls, self-esteem and physical activity, menopause, body image, osteoporosis, stress and aging, children's introduction to physical activity, and disabled women and exercise. Publications: Melpomene Journal (published three times per year); The Bodywise Woman; Reliable Information about Physical Activity and Health, A Guide for Physically Active Women; One in Nine; Breast Cancer: A Handbook.

★ 11971 ★ National Institute for Fitness
and Sport
250 N. University Blvd.
Indianapolis, IN 46202-5192
Phone: (317)274-3432
Fax: (317)274-7408
Jerry Taylor, Adm.

Research Activities and Fields: Exercise physiology, sports medicine, and health and fitness education.

★ 11972 ★ Nicholas Institute of Sports
Medicine and Athletic Trauma
130 E. 77th St.
New York, NY 10021
Phone: (212)434-2700
Fax: (212)434-2687
Dr. James Nicholas, Dir.

Research Activities and Fields: Sports medicine in the areas of orthopedics and trauma, fluid and electrolyte balance, nutrition, endocrinology and physical therapy, and cardiology.

★ 11973 ★ Ohio State University
Exercise Physiology Laboratory
129 Larkins Hall
337 W. 17th Ave.
Columbus, OH 43210
Phone: (614)292-6887
Fax: (614)292-7240
Dr. David R. Lamb, Dir.

Research Activities and Fields: Cardiovascular and metabolic effects of exercise, athletic nutrition, exercise in cardiac and musculoskeletal rehabilitation, exercise and carbohydrate metabolism, mechanisms of exercise-induced muscle hypertrophy, and aging. Formerly: Laboratory of Work Physiology.

★ 11974 ★ Pennsylvania State University
Biomechanics Laboratory
200 Biomechanics Laboratory
University Park, PA 16802
Phone: (814)865-3445
Fax: (814)865-2440
Dr. Richard C. Nelson, Dir.

Research Activities and Fields: Human movement, including scientific study and analysis of human motion as observed in sports, industry, and activities of daily living. Analyzes gymnastics, diving, cross-country skiing, swimming, and other sports through use of high-speed video, force measuring devices, and online computer techniques. Studies of elite athletes in Olympic and world championships are conducted with support of U.S. Olympic Committee and the Medical Commission of the International Olympic Committee. Testing, evaluation, and development of sports equipment and playground surface materials are also conducted. Special activities involve forensic biomechanics-personal injury and product liability. Publications: International Journal of Sport Biomechanics. E-mail Address: rcni@psuvm.psu.edu.

★ 11975 ★ Pennsylvania State University
Center for Sports Medicine
117 Ann Bldg.
University Park, PA 16802
Phone: (814)865-7107
Fax: (814)865-7077
Dr. Howard Knuttgen, Dir.

Research Activities and Fields: Physiology of human performance, sports conditioning, and the role of exercise in the prevention and rehabilitation of sports injuries. Areas of investigation include molecular biology, physiology, biomechanics, locomotion studies, nutrition, bioengineering, and epidemiology. Publications: Penn State Sports Medicine Newsletter (monthly).

★ 11976 ★ **Pennsylvania State University**
Laboratory for Human Performance
    Research
Noll Laboratory Bldg.
University Park, PA 16802
Phone: (814)865-3453
Fax: (814)865-4602
Dr. William J. Evans, Dir.

Research Activities and Fields: Nutrition sciences, metabolic adaptations to stress, biology of aging, and environmental and exercise physiology. Studies the effects of aging, physical activity, nutritional status, and heat, cold, and altitude stress on muscle metabolism and function, thermoregulation and cardiovascular control, immune function, and carbohydrate, insulin, and protein metabolism.

★ 11977 ★ **Temple University**
Biokinetics Research Laboratory
Pearson Hall
Philadelphia, PA 19122
Phone: (215)204-8753
Fax: (215)204-4662
Dr. Zebulon Kendricks, Dir.

Research Activities and Fields: Exercise physiology, biomechanics, and motor learning, including studies on biochemical adaptations to exercise, muscular strength and endurance, longitudinal effects of regular vigorous physical activity, environmental influences on physical work, metabolism, and perceptual motor behavior.

★ 11978 ★ **Temple University**
Center for Sports Medicine and Science
Health Science Center Campus
3400 N. Broad St.
Philadelphia, PA 19140
Phone: (215)787-6298
Fax: (215)221-2324
Dr. Ray A. Moyer, Dir.

Research Activities and Fields: Post-operative knee surgery follow-up, post-operative arthroscopic shoulder surgery follow-up, and development of instrument for arthroscopic knee reconstruction.

★ 11979 ★ **Texas A&M University**
Human Performance Laboratories
Dept. of Health & Kinesiology
College Station, TX 77843-4243
Phone: (409)845-4802
Fax: (409)847-8987
Dr. R.B. Armstrong, Hd.

Research Activities and Fields: Conducts studies in human performance, including exercise physiology, motor learning/control/development, and biomechanics.

★ 11980 ★ **United States Sports Academy**
    (USSA)
1 Academy Dr.
Daphne, AL 36526
Phone: (334)626-3303
Fax: (334)626-3874
Dr. A.G. Applin, Dean of Acad.

Research Activities and Fields: Sport and sport education in an effort to upgrade sports medicine, sport coaching, sport management, and fitness management, including studies of athletic injuries, body composition of adults, motor performance of youth, physical fitness of adults, ECG abnormalities and changes due to exercise, biomechanical analysis of gross motor skills and three-dimensional gait analysis, product and equipment evaluation and drug use/abuse in sports evaluation and analysis. Research is carried on with local high school athletes, members of the USSA student body, youth involved in the Academy's overseas projects, and selected off-campus program participants. **Publications:** *USSA News* (quarterly). E-mail Address: academy@ussa___sport.ussa.edu.

★ 11981 ★ **University of Central Florida**
Institute for Exercise Physiology and
    Health
College of Education
Dept. of Exceptional & Physical Education
Orlando, FL 32816
Phone: (407)823-2049
Fax: (407)823-5135
Dr. Frank D. Rohter, Dir.

Research Activities and Fields: The human body's responses and adaptations to exercise. Studies include coronary heart disease prevention, rehabilitation, and stress testing, aerobic and anerobic testing and training of elite athletes, development of elite women athletes, exercise and fitness of preschool children, exercise and aging, and obesity as it relates to exercise and nutrition. Also studies optimal cardiovascular and neuromuscular development programs for secondary schools, higher education, business, the U.S. armed forces, and the community; therapeutic effects of exercise and mental health, humoral, biochemical, and behavioral changes; and effects of heat and other environmental stresses on exercise.

★ 11982 ★ **University of Delaware**
Sports Science Laboratory
Carpenter Sports Blvd.
Newark, DE 19716
Phone: (302)451-2265
Fax: (302)831-3693
Michelle Provost-Craig, Ph.D., Codir.

Research Activities and Fields: Sports science, biomechanics, excercise physiology, bone density, and elite skaters.

★ 11983 ★ **University of Florida**
Center for Exercise Science
301 Florida Gym
Gainesville, FL 32611
Phone: (904)392-9575
Michael L. Pollock, Ph.D., Dir.

Research Activities and Fields: Fitness as it relates to athletic performance, as well as the general population, including research on biomechanics and skill acquisition; health risk factors; exercise and the lumbar and cervical spine, sports, aging, menopause, diabetes, and athletic performance. **Publications:** *Journal of Cardiopulmonary Rehabilitation.* **Formerly:** Center for Physical and Motor Fitness (1986).

★ 11984 ★ **University of Illinois at Urbana-**
    Champaign
Biomechanics Research Laboratory of
    Illinois
Dept. of Kinesiology
906 S. Goodwin
Freer Hall
Urbana, IL 61801
Phone: (217)333-2461
Fax: (217)244-7322

Research Activities and Fields: Sports biomechanics (tennis, fencing, athletics, volleyball, and rope jumping), biomechanics of sports safety and injury potential, force production, occupational biomechanics (firefighting tasks), movement patterns of the elderly, and strength training. **E-mail Address:** jchow@ux1.cso.uiuc.edu.

★ 11985 ★ **University of Illinois at Urbana-**
    Champaign
Sports Injuries / Therapeutic Exercise
    Research Unit
906 S. Goodwin
Urbana, IL 61801
Phone: (217)333-7699
Fax: (217)244-7322
Prof. Gerald W. Bell, Dir.

Research Activities and Fields: Therapeutic affects of exercise on musculoskeletal injuries, medical supervision of sports programs, response of wheelchair athletes to exercise and training programs, and epidemiological of sports injuries for high school participants, intramural sports participants, and dance students. **Publications:** *Journal of Athletic Training*; *Journal of Orthopedic Sports PT*; *Journal of Mosby-Times Mirror Texts.* **E-mail Address:** gwbell@vmd.cso.uiuc.edu.

★ 11986 ★ **University of Miami**
Human Performance Laboratory
PO Box 248065
Coral Gables, FL 33124
Phone: (305)284-3024
Fax: (305)284-3003
Dr. Perry, Dir.

Research Activities and Fields: Kinesiology, muscle cell and cardiovascular physiology, sports nutrition, obesity, electromyography, lipid physiology, exercise biochemistry, and athlete's evaluation. **Publications:** *International Journal of Sports Medicine*; *Journal of Applied Physiology*; *Medicine and Science in Sports and Exercise.*

★ 11987 ★ **University of Michigan**
Fitness Research Center
401 Washtenaw Ave., Rm. 103
Ann Arbor, MI 48109-2214
Phone: (313)763-2462
Fax: (313)763-2206
Dr. D.W. Edington, Dir.

Research Activities and Fields: Examines the relationships between lifestyle behaviors, quality of life, organizational productivity, and health care costs. **Publications:** *Healthlines* (monthly newsletter); *Targets* (fact sheets). **E-mail Address:** dwe@umich.edu.

★ 11988 ★ **University of Missouri—Columbia**
Exercise Physiology Laboratory
Dept. of Health & Physical Education
38 Rothwell Gymnasium
Columbia, MO 65211
Phone: (314)882-0062
Fax: (314)884-4855
Tom Thomas, Ph.D., Dir.

Research Activities and Fields: Exercise physiology, including calorie expenditure and different modes of exercise; sports performance, and lactate threshold.

★ 11989 ★ **University of Nevada, Las Vegas**
Exercise Physiology Laboratory
4505 Maryland Pkwy.
Las Vegas, NV 89154-3016
Phone: (702)895-3766
Fax: (702)895-4191
Dr. Lawrence A. Golding, Dir.

Research Activities and Fields: Primary function and research emphasis is the study of the biology of exercise. Studies include the physiological effect of both the immediate effect of exercise and the long range effect of physical training, the effect of the environment on physical performance (heat, humidity, cold, altitude, and pollution), the effect of aging on physical performance, and the impact of exercise on the older adult, the effects of drug use and diet supplement on physical performance, and a longitudinal study on the effect of regular exercise on coronary risk factors and aging.

★ 11990 ★ **University of North Carolina at Chapel Hill**
National Center for Catastrophic Sports Injury Research
311 Woollen Gymnasium
CB 8605
Chapel Hill, NC 27599-8605
Phone: (919)962-2021
Fax: (919)962-7060
Dr. Frederick O. Mueller, Dir.

Research Activities and Fields: Fatality and permanent injury in sports, especially football. **Publications:** Annual Report.

★ 11991 ★ **University of Oregon**
International Institute for Sport and Human Performance
Bowerman Bldg.
Eugene, OR 97403-1243
Phone: (503)346-4114
Fax: (503)345-0935
Henriette Heiny, Ph.D., Dir.

Research Activities and Fields: Sport and exercise sciences, health, general wellness, and sport issues in the humanities and arts. **Publications:** *Bulletin in Health, Physical Education, and Recreation* (also available in microform). **E-mail Address:** hheiny@oregon.uoregon.edu.

★ 11992 ★ **University of Pittsburgh**
Human Energy Research Laboratory
242 Trees Hall
Pittsburgh, PA 15261
Phone: (412)624-4387
Dr. Robert J. Robertson, Dir.

Research Activities and Fields: Physiology of exercise and work, perception of physical exertion, cardiac rehabilitation, and ergogenic aids, including studies conducted by full-time faculty members and graduate students of the University.

★ 11993 ★ **University of Rhode Island**
Human Performance Laboratory
Independence Square
Kingston, RI 02881
Phone: (401)792-2087
Thomas Manfred, Ph.D., Co-dir.

Research Activities and Fields: Physiological profiles of athletic populations. **Formerly:** Exercise Science Laboratories.

★ 11994 ★ **University of Utah**
Human Performance Research Laboratory
230e HPR-N
Salt Lake City, UT 84112
Phone: (801)581-8687
Dr. Stephen C. Johnson, Dir.

Research Activities and Fields: Effects of exercise and environment on muscular, cardiovascular, respiratory, nervous, and thermoregulatory systems of the mammalian body. Programs are conducted on exercise and pregnant women, female marathoners, blood reinfusion, fitness levels of men 35-50 years old, and effects of aerobic conditioning program on fitness levels and brain function of sedentary men 60-70 years of age.

University of Vermont
McClure Musculoskeletal Research Center
See: Entry 7962

★ 11995 ★ **University of Wisconsin—La Crosse**
Human Performance Laboratory
Mitchell Hall
1820 Pine St.
La Crosse, WI 54601
Phone: (608)785-8685
N.K. Butts, Dir.

Research Activities and Fields: Provides facilities for research fellows and graduate students to perform short-term and long-term medical and paramedical research in areas of exercise and cardiovascular diseases. Conducts body composition testing (hydrostatic weighing), cardiovascular and pulmonary testing, and blood chemistry testing for faculty, students, and members of the public. **E-mail Address:** nkbutts@uwlax.edu.

★ 11996 ★ **Vanderbilt University**
Energy Balance Laboratory
Clinical Research Center
21st Ave. S.
Nashville, TN 37232-2195
Phone: (615)343-8497
Fax: (615)343-8915
Dr. Ming Sun, Dir.

Research Activities and Fields: Use of indirect calorimetry to measure energy expenditure, and metabolic rate and physical activities under a variety of conditions, including exercise, dietary intake, and environmental changes. Emphasis is on the identification of determinants of energy expenditure and body weight regulation. Uses hydrostatic weighing, bioelectrical impedance, and other methods to measure body composition.

Chapter 63
Substance Abuse

Federal Government Agencies

★ 11997 ★ U.S. Department of Health and Human Services
National Institute on Alcohol Abuse and Alcoholism
6000 Executive Blvd.
Rockville, MD 20852
Phone: (301)443-3885

Description: The Institute conducts and supports biomedical and behavioral research, health services research, research training, and health information dissemination with respect to the prevention and treatment of alcohol abuse and alcoholism, and provides a national focus for the Federal effort to increase knowledge and promote effective strategies to deal with health problems and issues associated with alcohol abuse and alcoholism.

★ 11998 ★ U.S. Department of Health and Human Services
National Institute on Drug Abuse
5600 Fishers Lane
Rockville, MD 20857
Phone: (301)443-6480

Description: The Institute provides leadership, policies, and goals for the federal effort in the prevention, control, and treatment of narcotic addiction and drug abuse, and the rehabilitation of affected individuals. In carrying out these responsibilities the Institute conducts and supports research on the biological, psychological, sociological, and epidemiological aspects of narcotic addiction and drug abuse; supports the training of professional and paraprofessional personnel in the prevention, treatment, and control of drug abuse; conducts and supports research on the development and improvement of drug abuse services delivery, administration, and financing; and supports services, programs, and projects.

★ 11999 ★ U.S. Department of Health and Human Services
Substance Abuse and Mental Health Services Administration
5600 Fishers Ln.
Rockville, MD 20857
Phone: (301)443-4795

Description: Mission of SAMHSA is to ensure that knowledge, based on science and state-of-the-art practice is effectively used for the prevention and treatment of addictive and mental disorders. Major components include: Center for Substance Abuse, Center for Substance Abuse Treatment, Center for Mental Health Services, and Office of Management, Planning, and Communications.

Foundations & Other Funding Organizations

Private Foundations

Aaron Diamond Foundation
See: Entry 24

John G. and Marie Stella Kenedy Memorial Foundation
See: Entry 319

Corporate Foundations

Anheuser-Busch Foundation / Anheuser-Busch Charitable Trust
See: Entry 581

Emerson Charitable Trust
See: Entry 673

General Mills Foundation
See: Entry 700

Louisiana Land & Exploration Co. Foundation
·*See:* Entry 761

National & International Organizations

★ 12000 ★ **Al-Anon Family Group Headquarters (AFG)**
PO Box 862, Midtown Sta.
New York, NY 10018
Phone: (212)302-7240
Free: 800-356-9996
Fax: (212)869-3757
Carole Kuney, Contact

Founded: 1951. **Regional Groups:** 30000. **Description:** Relatives and friends of individuals with an alcohol problem. Operates Alateen for members 12-20 years of age whose lives have been adversely affected by someone else's drinking problem, usually a parent's. **Publications:** *Al-Anon Family Group Headquarters--The Forum: A Meeting in My Pocket*, monthly. Magazine. Written by Al-Anon members. Includes calendar of events. *Price:* $9/year. • *Al-Anon in Institutions*, 3/year. Newsletter. *Price:* $2/year. • *Al-Anon Speaks Out*, semiannual. For the professional community regarding alcohol abuse. *Price:* Free. • *Alateen Talk*, bimonthly. Newsletter. Contains written and artistic contributions from Alateen members. Includes articles written by adult Alateen sponsors and coordinators. *Price:* Included in Alateen Group Registration; $2.50/year for individuals; $.15/copy. • *Inside Al-Anon: World Service Office Highlights*, bimonthly. Newsletter. Presents news, policy, and commentary from Al-Anon volunteers, staff, and readers sharing experiences of individual and group growth. *Price:* $3/year; $.15/copy. • *Loner's Letter Box*, bimonthly. Newsletter. *Price:* Available to members only. Also publishes leaflets, pamphlets, and books.

★ 12001 ★ **Alcohol and Drug Problems Association of North America (ADPA)**
1555 Wilson Blvd., Ste. 300
Arlington, VA 22209
Phone: (703)875-8684
Fax: (703)528-7510

Founded: 1949. **Members:** 1,325. **Description:** Individuals (1100), official state or provincial alcoholism program members (75), and other alcoholism and/or drug agencies and institutions (150). Seeks to facilitate governmental and professional activities in the fields of alcoholism, alcohol-related problems, and drug abuse by exchange of information, promotion of legislation and standards which will contribute to the care and control of alcoholism, and research and cooperation. Maintains continuing education program and placement service. **Publications:** *ADPA Professional*, bimonthly. Newsletter. On public policy concerning drug and alcohol abuse. Includes book reviews; calendar of events; educational opportunities. *Price:* Included in membership dues. • *Special Reports*, periodic. **Formerly:** (1956) National States Conference on Alcoholism; (1972) North American Association of Alcoholism Programs.

★ 12002 ★ Alcohol Research Information Service (ARIS)
1106 E. Oakland
Lansing, MI 48906
Phone: (517)485-9900
Fax: (517)485-1928
Robert Hammond, Exec.Dir.

Founded: 1931. **Description:** Individual and corporate contributors. Collects, correlates, and disseminates information regarding alcohol and alcoholic products, their manufacture, sale, and use for beverage, industrial, or other purposes, and their relation to the health and well-being of the people of the United States. Operates clearinghouse for substance abuse information. Compiles statistics. **Publications:** *The Bottom Line on Alcohol and Society*, quarterly. Journal. *Price:* $20/year. • *Monday Morning Report*, semimonthly. Report. • Newsletter, semimonthly. *Price:* $30/year. Also provides teaching materials for elementary and secondary school levels, and adults. **Formerly:** (1984) American Business Men's Research Foundation.

★ 12003 ★ Alcoholics Anonymous World Services (AA)
475 Riverside Dr.
New York, NY 10163
Phone: (212)870-3400
Fax: (212)870-3003

Founded: 1935. **Description:** Individuals recovering from alcoholism. AA maintains that members can solve their common problem and help others achieve sobriety through a twelve step program that includes sharing their experience, strength, and hope with each other. Self-supported through members' contributions, AA is not allied with any sect, denomination, political organization, or institution and does not endorse nor oppose any cause. **Publications:** *AA Comes of Age.* • *Alcoholics Anonymous.* • *As Bill Sees It.* • *Dr. Bob and the Good Oldtimers.* • *Pass it On.* • *Twelve Steps and Twelve Traditions.*

★ 12004 ★ American Academy of Psychiatrists in Alcoholism and Addictions (aaPaa)
PO Box 376
Greenbelt, MD 20768
Phone: (301)220-0951
Fax: (301)474-0219
Alice Conde, Exec.Dir.

Founded: 1985. **Members:** 1,300. **Description:** Psychiatrists and residents in training. Purposes are to: provide a forum for discussion of issues related to substance abuse; further education, research, and clinical work in the field; assist in the development of appropriate standards of care for alcoholics and other drug-dependent persons. Facilitates worldwide communication among psychiatrists and others on issues and practices related to substance abuse and addiction. Maintains speakers' bureau; conducts placement service; compiles statistics. **Publications:** *aaPaa Newsletter*, periodic. Newsletter. *Price:* Included in membership dues. • *American Journal on Addictions*, quarterly. Journal. Covers the preclinical, clinical, and social aspects involved in the study and treatment of drug abuse and alcoholism. Contains annual indexes. *Price:* Included in membership dues. • *Membership Directory of the Academy of Psychiatrists in Alcoholism and Addictions*, annual. Membership Directory.

American College of Addiction Treatment Administrators (ACATA)
See: Entry 5543

★ 12005 ★ American Council on Alcohol Problems (ACAP)
3426 Bridgepath Dr.
Bridgeton, MO 63044
Phone: (314)739-5944
Fax: (314)739-0848
Dr. Curt Scarborough, Exec.Dir.

Founded: 1895. **Members:** 2000. **Local Groups:** 37. **Description:** Seeks long-range solutions to the problems posed by alcohol. Employs research, educational, and legislative approaches for the prevention of alcoholism and other alcohol-related problems. Coordinates the work of state affiliates who carry on their programs under provisions of the 21st Amendment, putting alcohol control largely at state level. Denominations channel their cooperative social concerns through elected directors who guide the program and activities of ACAP. **Publications:** *ACAP Alert*, periodic. • *ACAP Recap*, monthly. Newsletter. • *The American Issue*, monthly. • *Directory*, periodic. **Formerly:** (1948) Anti-Saloon League of America; (1950) Temperance League of America; (1964) National Temperance League, formed by merger of National Temperance Movement and Temperance League of America.

★ 12006 ★ American Council on Alcoholism (ACA)
2522 St. Paul St.
Baltimore, MD 21218
Phone: (410)889-0100
Free: 800-527-5344
Fax: (410)889-0100
Robert G. Kirk, Exec.Dir.

Founded: 1953. **Members:** 400. **Description:** Works to combat alcohol abuse and alcoholism. Initiates and advocates national, state, and local alcoholism programs that emphasize education, prevention, early diagnosis, and rehabilitation. Seeks to: educate the public on issues concerning alcoholism; promote employee assistance programs at the worksite; work closely with professionals in the alcoholism field to promote understanding of the alcoholic. Maintains 2,000 volume library on subjects related to the study of alcoholism and alcohol abuse. Conducts education seminars. Bestows annual Silver Chalice Award for singular contributions to reducing alcoholism. **Publications:** *ACA News*, monthly. Publicizes issues concerning alcoholism; promotes the understanding that alcoholism is a treatable disease; contains research results. *Price:* Included in membership dues. • *Annual Report.* • Also publishes *Alcoholism Questions and Answers*, *Teenage Drinking*, and other materials. **Formerly:** Maryland Society on Alcoholism; (1974) Baltimore Area Council on Alcoholism.

★ 12007 ★ American Council for Drug Education (ACDE)
136 E. 64th St.
New York, NY 10021
Phone: (212)758-8060
Free: 800-488-DRUG

Founded: 1977. **Members:** 1,500. **Description:** Doctors, mental health counselors, teachers, clergymen, school librarians, parent groups, industry leaders, and concerned individuals. Disseminates information and research on marijuana, cocaine, and other psychoactive drugs. Makes available resource information kits that include both written and audiovisual materials. Compiles statistics. Maintains speakers' bureau. **Publications:** Brochures. • Handbooks. • Monographs. Scientific. • Proceedings. • Videos. For parents, children, and schools. Also produces films and radio and television spots. **Formerly:** (1983) American Council on Marijuana and Other Psychoactive Drugs.

★ 12008 ★ American Osteopathic Academy of Addictionology
270 Tavistock
Cherry Hill, NJ 08034-4017
Phone: (609)795-0026
Fax: (609)354-8029
William Vilensky, D.O., Pres.

Founded: 1986. **Members:** 225. **Description:** Physicians. Conducts research into the diagnosis, intervention, and treatment of substance abuse problems. Seeks to educate society, and to influence the passage of legislation regarding drug abuse. Provides seminars and lectures to students, physicians, medical and dental societies, civic groups, religious organizations, bar associations, and law enforcement bodies.

★ 12009 ★ American Outreach Association (AOA)
PO Box 25042
Colorado Springs, CO 80936
Phone: (719)592-1134
Free: 800-489-HEAL
Fax: (719)592-1134
Charles Prusch, Dir.

Founded: 1989. **Regional Groups:** 5. **Description:** Collects and disseminates information on subjects such as alcoholism, drug abuse, inhalants, and smoking to the public. Organizes community awareness activities and presentations. Reviews drug policies, programs, and educational material. Assists business and industry in establishing drug-free work environments. Sponsors Project HOLD, a program that fosters a change of attitudes, values, and behaviors in the home away from drug abuse. Operates placement service; maintains speakers' bureau.

Publications: *Health Watch*, quarterly. Newsletter. • *Mommy, What Are Drugs?*. • *Mommy, What is Alcohol?*. • *Mommy, What is Smoking?*.

★ 12010 ★ **American Society of Addiction Medicine (ASAM)**
4601 N. Park Ave., Ste. 101
Chevy Chase, MD 20815
Phone: (301)656-3920
James F. Callahan, D.P.A.

Founded: 1954. **Members:** 3,000. **State Groups:** 23. **Description:** Physicians with special interest and experience in the field of alcoholism and other drug dependencies and who wish to share this experience with other professionals in order to extend their knowledge of addictive diseases; promote dissemination of that knowledge; enlighten the public regarding these problems; advance education and research in the field of addiction. Holds annual Ruth Fox Course for Physicians. **Publications:** *ASAM News*, quarterly. Newsletter. *Price:* $25. • *ASAM Patient Placement Criteria for the Treatment of Psychoactive Substance Use Disorders. Price:* $65. • *Guidelines for Facilities Treating Chemically Dependent Patients at Risk for AIDS.* • *Journal of Addictive Diseases*, quarterly. Journal. • *Principles of Addiction Medicine. Price:* $140. Also publishes abstracts, book notices, news events, and summaries of articles in leading journals. **Formerly:** (1967) New York City Medical Society on Alcoholism; (1989) American Medical Society on Alcoholism and Other Drug Dependencies.

★ 12011 ★ **Association of Halfway House Alcoholism Programs of North America (AHHAP)**
680 Stewart Ave.
St. Paul, MN 55102-4117
Phone: (612)227-7818
John H. Curtiss, Pres.

Founded: 1966. **Members:** 300. **Regional Groups:** 13. **State Groups:** 50. **Description:** Halfway house corporations, staff, board members, and individuals closely related to the halfway house movement. Charitable organization dedicated to educating and serving halfway house programs through technical assistance, consultant services, workshops, conferences, and related services. Operates placement service. Disseminates information and materials. **Publications:** *AHHAP Membership Directory*, annual. Membership Directory. • *Communications and Services Newsletter*, quarterly. Newsletter. • *Conference Proceedings*, annual. Proceedings.

★ 12012 ★ **Association of Medical Education and Research in Substance Abuse (AMERSA)**
Brown University
Center for Alcohol and Addiction Studies
Box G-BH
Providence, RI 02912
Phone: (401)863-7791
Fax: (401)863-3510
David C. Lewis, M.D., Exec.Dir.

Founded: 1976. **Members:** 500. **Description:** Medical school faculty members and others concerned with general medical education who are involved with providing information on alcohol and drug-related topics to medical professionals and students. **Publications:** Membership Directory, biennial. • *Substance Abuse*, quarterly. Journal. *Price:* Included in membership dues; $40/year for nonmembers.

★ 12013 ★ **Association of Recovering Motorcyclists (ARM)**
1503 Market St.
La Crosse, WI 54601
Phone: (608)784-8462
Mr. Leslie J. Jensen, Pres.

Founded: 1985. **Members:** 500. **State Groups:** 44. **Description:** Support group for motorcyclists who are recovering from alcohol or drug addiction. Helps members enjoy the hobby of motorcycling; tries to eliminate the notion of motorcycling as a negative lifestyle. Sponsors motorcycle runs, picnics, and dances. Operates speakers' bureau. **Publications:** *ARM Newsletter*, quarterly. Newsletter. *Price:* Free to inmates; Included in membership dues. • Directory, periodic.

★ 12014 ★ **BACCHUS and Gamma Peer Education Network**
National Headquarters
PO Box 100430
Denver, CO 80250
Phone: (303)871-3068
Fax: (303)871-2013
Drew Hunter, Exec.Dir.

Founded: 1980. **Members:** 23,000. **National Groups:** 3. **Regional Groups:** 13. **Local Groups:** 700. **Description:** Students, advisors, faculty, and staff of colleges and universities in the U.S., Canada, and Mexico. Primary mission is to deliver alcohol abuse prevention and health education to college students and their communities. Through positive peer pressure, promotes responsibile decisions and healthy lifestyles and discourages irresponsible or illegal use of alcohol. Encourages year-round prevention and education programs and activities. Operates: Project GAMMA (Greeks Advocating Mature Management of Alcohol), a cooperative effort between BACCHUS and national greek-letter organizations to increase undergraduate participation in alsohol education programs; area consultant program, through which campus-based professionals with an interest in alcohol education coordinate networking for three-to-five state areas; BACCHUS Designated Driver Program, which provides innovative approaches to the prevention of drinking/driving accidents; National Collegiate Alcohol Awareness Week; and Safe Spring Break. Offers the Certified Peer Educator Training Progam, a skill-based training curriculum for students. (Bacchus is the acronym for Boost Alcohol Consciousness Concerning the Health of University Students and the name of the Roman god of wine.) **Publications:** *The Bacchus Beat*, monthly. Newsletter. *Price:* Free for members. • Catalog. Lists educational materials. • Newsletter, 10/year. • Pamphlets. • Videos. **Formerly:** (1993) BACCHUS of the U.S..

★ 12015 ★ **Calix Society (CS)**
7601 Wayzata Blvd.
St. Louis Park, MN 55426
Phone: (612)546-0544
Free: 800-398-0524
Bill Fox, Officer

Founded: 1947. **Members:** 3,000. **Local Groups:** 42. **Description:** Catholic alcoholics who are maintaining sobriety through affiliation with and participation in Alcoholics Anonymous World Services. Non-Catholic alcoholics and interested individuals are welcome. Promotes total abstinence for Catholic alcoholics and encourages spiritual development. ("Calix" means "chalice" in Latin and refers to the society's belief in "substituting the cup that sactifies for the cup that stupefies.") **Publications:** *Calix and the Twelve Steps.* • *The Chalice*, bimonthly. Newsletter. Contains contributed stories regarding spiritual and physical recovery. Includes book reviews, obituaries, research reports, and statistics. *Price:* $15/year. • *Directory of Calix Units in the U.S. and Canada*, periodic. Directory. • *The Light of Faith*. Book. • *What and Why*. Brochure.

★ 12016 ★ **Children of Alcoholics Foundation (COAF)**
PO Box 4185, Grand Central Sta.
New York, NY 10163-4185
Phone: (212)754-0656
Free: 800-359-COAF
Fax: (212)754-0664
Migs Woodside, Pres.

Founded: 1982. **Description:** Seeks to educate the public and professionals about children of alcoholics and the effects of parental alcohol abuse, and stimulate interest in seeking solutions to their problems. Promotes research, educational and informational programs, and public discussion on alcoholism, alcohol abuse, and its effects on children; disseminates reports and research results; investigates the effectiveness of public policies, programs, and laws; encourages participation and assists government and community agencies in providing assistance to children of alcoholics and seeking solutions to the problems of these children. Facilitates research and educational and informational programs on other aspects of childhood, the parent-child relationship, physiological and psychological aspects of human development, child abuse and neglect, and substance abuse of other psychoactive substances. Maintains library, including more than 500 pieces of artwork, letters, and poetry by children of alcoholics. **Publications:** *Children of Alcoholics.* • *Children of Alcoholics: A Review of the Literature.* • *Children of Alcoholics on the Job.* • *Conference on Research Needs and Opportunities for Children of Alcoholics.* • *Directory of National Resources for Children of Alcoholics*, periodic. Directory. • *Images Within.* • *Kids Talking to Kids.* Video. • *Report of Conference on Prevention Research*, periodic. Report. • *Trying to Find Normal.* Video. • Videos.

**★ 12017 ★ Christian Addiction
     Rehabilitation Association (CARA)**
c/o Richard Barth
Pocahontas, MS 39072
Phone: (601)362-4295
Richard Barth, Contact

Founded: 1967. **Members:** 48. **Description:**
Provides support and serves as a clearinghouse
of information for individuals involved in ministry
to addicts. **Formerly:** Christian Alcoholic Rehabilitation Association.

**★ 12018 ★ Citizens for a Drug Free
     America (CDFA)**
3595 Bayside Walk
San Diego, CA 92109-7451
Phone: (619)207-9300
Roger Chapin, Pres.

Founded: 1984. **Description:** A coalition of individuals seeking to mobilize an effort to "win
the war on drugs" and achieve "a drug free
America" by the year 2000. Plans to develop:
Be Your Best, a project which will encourage a
positive, healthy lifestyle with emphasis on exercise, diet, and moral and self-worth values for
young people; Operation Open Door, a program
which will keep school doors open until six
o'clock in the evening. Fosters support for the
formation of a specially-appointed presidential
commission to recommend a long-term game
plan to restore "traditional American values and
ethics to society." Also plans to use mass mailings, media tours, press conferences, a speakers' bureau, and other media events to heighten
support. **Formerly:** (1988) Let's Beat Deficits
Committee.

**★ 12019 ★ Cocaine Anonymous World
     Services (CAWS)**
3740 Overland Ave., Ste. H
Los Angeles, CA 90034-6337
Phone: (310)559-5833
Free: 800-347-8998
Fax: (310)559-2554
K.D. McCann, Office Mgr.

Founded: 1982. **Members:** 15,000. **Regional
Groups:** 2000. **Description:** Fellowship of men
and women who share their experience,
strength, and hope with each other that they
may solve their common problem and help others to recover from addiction and remain free
from cocaine and all other mind-altering drugs.
Applies the Alcoholics Anonymous World Services' 12-step approach to persons addicted to
cocaine. **Publications:** *A Higher Power.* Pamphlet. *Price:* $.15. • *And All Other Mind Altering
Substances.* Pamphlet. *Price:* $.15. • *Choosing
Your Sponsor.* Pamphlet. *Price:* $.15. • *Crack.*
Pamphlet. *Price:* $.15. • *The First 30 Days.*
Pamphlet. *Price:* $.15. • *Hope, Faith, and Cour-
age.* Book. *Price:* $12.95. • *The Newsgram,*
quarterly. Newsletter. *Price:* Free. • *Self Test for
Cocaine Addiction.* Pamphlet. *Price:* $.15. •
*Suggestions for Relapse Prevention and Re-
covery.* Pamphlet. *Price:* $.15. • *Tips on Staying
Clean and Sober.* Pamphlet. *Price:* $.15. • *To
the Newcomer.* Pamphlet. *Price:* $.15. • *Tools
of Recovery.* Pamphlet. *Price:* $.15. • *What Is
C.A.?.* Pamphlet. *Price:* $.15.

**★ 12020 ★ Co-Dependents Anonymous
     (CoDA)**
PO Box 33577
Phoenix, AZ 85067-3577
Phone: (602)277-7991
Fax: (602)274-6111

Founded: 1986. **Members:** 50,000. **Description:** Selfhelp group based on an adaptation of
the 12-step program of Alcoholics Anonymous
World Services. Conducts recovery program for
co-dependents. **Publications:** Audiotapes. •
Co-NNECTIONS, quarterly. Newsletter. *Price:*
$8/year. • *Listening and Sharing at a Meeting.*
Pamphlet. • Pamphlets. • *Welcome to CoDA.*
Pamphlet. • *What is Co-Dependency.* Pamphlet.

**★ 12021 ★ Committees of Correspondence
     (COC)**
Drug Prevention Newsletter/Resources
24 Adams St.
Danvers, MA 01923-2718
Phone: (508)774-2641
Otto Moulton, Pres.

Founded: 1980. **Members:** 1,000. **Description:** Disseminates accurate and scientifically-
approved material on substance abuse. Seeks
to create a network linking citizens whose "active involvement will help combat the deadly epidemic of drug use in our country." **Publications:**
Committees of Correspondence--Newsletter,
quarterly. Newsletter. Covers drug abuse issues. *Price:* Included in membership dues. •
Drug Prevention Resource Manual, periodic.
Manual. Makes age-appropriate recommendations for anti-drug reading and audiovisual materials; includes special resources for parents and
teachers. *Price:* $21/issue. • Pamphlets. • *Par-
ent Portfolio Manual.* Manual.

**★ 12022 ★ Cottage Program International
     (CPI)**
57 W. South Temple, Ste. 420
Salt Lake City, UT 84101-1511
Phone: (801)532-6185
Free: 800-752-6100
Fax: (801)532-7769
Bernell Boswell, Pres.

Founded: 1972. **Members:** 8,211. **Description:** Organizations and volunteers seeking to
implement alcohol and drug abuse prevention
programs involving modification of behavior patterns that lead to alcohol and drug abuse while
providing positive reinforcement for behavior
patterns consistent with sobriety. Seeks to assist other organizations in developing alcohol
and drug abuse prevention and treatment programs. Provides services to families to prevent
family deterioration through examining the negative consequences of alcohol and drug abuse
and the family role in alcoholism prevention.
Provides trained volunteers who function as
group moderators working with families,
schools, civic groups, churches, and other organizations in community settings; seeks to alter
practices, attitudes, and norms of entire communities impacting the total environment. Operates Families in Focus Program, through which
volunteers work with families in their homes to
open lines of communication and facilitate responsible decisionmaking among family members, and Vietnam VetLink Program, which offers services to Vietnam veterans and their families, especially if there is a developmentally dis-
able child in the home. Maintains speakers'
bureau; compiles statistics. Holds workshops
and on-site training for affiliate members and
conducts research in the field for other organizations. Offers children's services. **Publications:** Brochures. • *Families in Focus Home
Learning Guide--Seven Secrets to a Successful
Family.* Video. • *Vietnam VetLink.* Brochure. •
*What Every Family Should Know About Alcohol-
ism. . .Our Common Problem.* Brochure. Also
distributes audiovisual prevention program
training materials.

★ 12023 ★ Do It Now Foundation (DINF)
PO Box 27568
Tempe, AZ 85285
Phone: (602)491-0393
Fax: (602)491-2849
James D. Parker, Exec.Dir.

Founded: 1968. **Members:** 40. **Description:**
Works to provide factual information to students
and adults about prescription drugs, over-the-
counter drugs, street drugs, alcohol, eating disorders, AIDS, and related health issues. Assists
organizations engaged in alcohol and drug
abuse education. **Publications:** *Newservice,* bimonthly. Newsletter. Contains articles on substance abuse, health, mental health, personal
growth, and sexuality. *Price:* $15/year. Also
publishes educational materials; offers pamphlets, posters, books, and radio public service
tapes.

**Drug and Alcohol Nursing Association
     (DANA)**
See: Entry 9085

★ 12024 ★ Drug-Anon Focus
PO Box 20806, Park West Sta.
New York, NY 10025
Phone: (212)484-9095

Founded: 1978. **Members:** 100. **Local
Groups:** 8. **Description:** A self-help support organization for the families and friends of persons addicted to mood altering drugs. Follows
the 12-step method originated by Alcoholics
Anonymous World Services and as adopted by
the Al-Anon Family Groups. **Formerly:** (1986)
Pil-Anon Family Program.

★ 12025 ★ Dual Disorders Anonymous
PO Box 4045
Des Plaines, IL 60016
Phone: (708)462-3380

Founded: 1982. **Members:** 500. **Regional
Groups:** 3. **State Groups:** 1. **Local Groups:** 21.
Description: Individuals with alcohol or drug addictions as well as mental or emotional disorders. Provides support group opportunities to
emotionally or mentally disordered alcoholics
and addicts; conducts volunteer programs for
dually diagnosed patients. Utilizes the 12-step
method of self-help. **Publications:** Booklet. •
Brochures.

★ **12026** ★ **Entertainment Industries Council (EIC)**
1760 Reston Pky., Ste. 415
Reston, VA 22090
Phone: (703)481-1414
Fax: (703)481-1414
Brian L. Dyak, Pres.

Founded: 1983. **Members:** 130. **Description:** Corporations and representatives of the entertainment industry including actors, agents, publicists, producers, directors, and writers. Goal is to utilize the power and influence of the entertainment industry in a national campaign to combat and deglamorize substance abuse, especially among young people. Seeks to identify and provide celebrity role models for young people. Hopes to increase youth awareness of drug abuse through television, radio, music, and motion pictures. Develops projects to aid in eliminating substance abuse problems within the entertainment industry. Conducts seminars and training sessions on drug abuse prevention; also conducts radio interview series, television specials, outreach programs, and employee assistance and fundraising programs. Collects and disseminates information on progress made by the entertainment industry in drug abuse prevention. In conjunction with IMMEDIA Foundation, coordinates network of 400 radio stations involved in public affairs projects designed to discourage substance abuse. Provides celebrity speakers' bureau on drug prevention, seat belt awareness, and intravenous drug use/AIDS. Bestows EIC Drug Prevention Award annually to a leader from entertainment industry contributing to drug awareness. **Publications:** Annual Report. • *Entertainment Industries Council Newsletter*, bimonthly. Newsletter. Includes policy updates and statistics. *Price:* $25/year. • *Research Paper*, 3/year.

★ **12027** ★ **Ethos Foundation (EF)**
5201 Leesburg Pike, Ste. 100
Falls Church, VA 22041
Phone: (703)671-5335
Philip I. Brennan, Pres.

Founded: 1978. **Regional Groups:** 1. **Description:** Provides counseling, education, and rehabilitation services and crisis intervention in the area of substance abuse. Aims to educate alcohol and drug abusers, their families, and the public on substance abuse. Conducts training programs for counselors, physicians, clergy, social workers, and employees; offers programs for hospitals, federal and local governments, and the private and public sectors. Cooperates with criminal justice departments. Conducts research. Sponsors workshops and seminars. Maintains speakers' bureau; compiles statistics. (Ethos is the Greek word for sentiment, values, and moral nature.)

★ **12028** ★ **Families Anonymous (FA)**
PO Box 3475
Culver City, CA 90231-3475
Phone: (310)313-5800
Free: 800-736-9805
Fax: (310)313-6841

Founded: 1971. **Members:** 540. **Description:** Local groups of parents, relatives, and friends concerned about drug abuse or related behavioral problems. Self-supported, self-help modeled after Al-Anon Family Group Headquarters and Alcoholics Anonymous World Services programs. Assists families in overcoming overprotectiveness of drug abusers and developing a better understanding of their problems, thereby improving interfamily relationships. Aids in establishing community meetings; makes referrals to other agencies. Maintains speakers' bureau. **Publications:** Catalog. • Directory, periodic. • Pamphlets. • *The Twelve Step Rag: For Relatives and Friends Concerned about the Use of Drugs or Related Behavioral Problems*, bimonthly. Newsletter. Contains information for friends and relatives of substance abusers. *Price:* Free for FA groups; $4.50/year for individuals.

★ **12029** ★ **Friendly Peersuasion (FP)**
c/o Janet Green Berg
30 E. 33rd St.
New York, NY 10016
Phone: (212)689-3700
Fax: (212)683-1253
Marilyn Russo, Project Dir.

Description: A project of Girls Incorporated. Seeks to prevent drug and alcohol abuse among girls 11 to 14 years old. Recognizes that girls are more socially apt to become users of substances such as tobacco and weight reduction stimulants containing amphetamines. Offers a peer leadership training course whereby older girls discourage younger ones from using addictive substances. Program consists of a flexible, 12-week course including instruction in managing stress, decision making, and techniques for alcohol and drug refusal.

Gay AA (GAA)
See: Entry 11692

★ **12030** ★ **Hazelden Foundation (HF)**
15245 Pleasant Valley Rd.
PO Box 11
Center City, MN 55012-0011
Phone: (612)257-4010
Free: 800-257-7800
Fax: (612)257-5101

Founded: 1949. **Description:** Provides rehabilitation, education, and professional services for chemical dependency and other addictive behaviors. Operates: Hazelden Rehabilitation Center, a treatment center; Fellowship Club in New York, St. Paul and West Palm Beach, Florida, a halfway house; Hazelden Pioneer House Program for adolescents and young adults; Hazelden Renewal Center for individuals recovering from addictive behaviors and their families; Hanley-Hazelden Center at St. Mary's in West Palm Beach, Florida, for inpatient and outpatient treatment; Also provides: aftercare therapy; counselor training; 5-7 day, live-in family program that acquaints relatives and other associates of chemically-dependent individuals with problems of chemical dependency; continuing education programs for professionals; and communities. **Publications:** Books. • *Educational Materials Catalog*, monthly. Catalog. • *Hazelden News and Professional Update*, quarterly. Newsletter. Provides information on health and recovery from addictive behavior. • *Hazelden Report*, weekly. • Pamphlets. Makes available educational and audiovisual materials.

★ **12031** ★ **Ibero-American Association for the Study of Alcohol and Drug Problems (Asociacion Iberoamericana de Estudio de los Problemas del Alcohol y la Droga)**
Casilla de Correo 164
5000 Cordoba, Argentina

Description: Supports the study of alcohol and drug abuses and the problems associated with addiction. Sponsors educational programs focusing on the effects of these abuses.

★ **12032** ★ **Impaired Physician Program (IPP)**
c/o Georgia Impaired Health Professionals Program
5448 Yorktown Dr.
College Park, GA 30349
Phone: (404)994-0185
Free: 800-445-4232
Fax: (404)994-2024
G. Douglas Talbott, M.D., Founder & Dir.

Founded: 1975. **Description:** Purpose is to provide assistance to physicians, other health professionals, and their spouses with problems such as alcoholism, substance abuse, or codependence; seeks to locate and identify persons in need of help and to provide assistance. Conducts in- and outpatient treatment programs. Offers counseling; maintains advocacy program to assist physicians and other health professionals in re-entering their profession. Maintains speakers' bureau.

★ **12033** ★ **Institute for a Drug-Free Workplace**
1301 K St. NW
East Tower, Ste. 1010
Washington, DC 20005
Phone: (202)842-7400
Fax: (202)842-0011
Mark A. de Bernardo, Exec.Dir.

Founded: 1989. **Members:** 120. **Description:** Businesses, organizations, and individuals united to preserve the rights of employers and employees involved in corporate drug abuse prevention programs. Seeks to influence public policy pertaining to drug abuse prevention in the workplace. Conducts surveys. **Publications:** *A Guide to State Drug Testing Laws and Legislation*, annual. *Price:* $95. • Brochures. • *Does Drug Testing Work?*. *Price:* $36. • *Drug and Alcohol Abuse Prevention and the ADA: An Employer's Guide*. *Price:* $32. • *The Drug-Free Workplace Report*, quarterly. *Price:* $45/year. • *The Employee Drug Education Bulletin*, semiannual. Bulletin. *Price:* $0.50/issue. • *Policy on Drug and Alcohol Abuse Prevention: An Employer's Development and Implementation Guide*. *Price:* $4.50/copy. • *What Every Employer Should Know About Drug Abuse-- Answers to 20 Good Questions*. *Price:* $1.80/copy.

★ **12034** ★ **Institute for Integral Development (IID)**
PO Box 2172
Colorado Springs, CO 80901
Phone: (719)634-7943
Dan Barmettler, Dir.

Founded: 1977. **Description:** Provides a forum for discussion of issues pertaining to alcoholism and other addictions; seeks to train educators, medical professionals, and mental health practitioners in understanding and assisting addicted individuals. Sponsors seminars and workshops; provides educational audiotapes; offers consulting services. Maintains speakers' bureau; operates small library.

★ 12035 ★ **Inter-Association Task Force (IATF)**
c/o Bacchus and Gamma Peer Education
 Network
PO Box 100430
Denver, CO 80250
Phone: (303)871-3068
Drew Hunter, Convener

Founded: 1983. **Members:** 19. **Description:** Associations of college professionals and student leaders. Purposes are to enhance the development and implementation of alcohol and other substance abuse education activities in institutions of higher education throughout the U.S. and to encourage collaboration among professionals and student associations. Sponsors National Collegiate Alcohol Awareness Week and National Collegiate Alcohol Health and Wellness Week. **Publications:** *First National Conference on Alcohol Policy Initiatives.* • *Guidelines for Marketing of Alcohol Beverage on Campus.* Pamphlet. • *National Collegiate Alcohol Awareness Week Mailing Handbook.* Handbook. **Formerly:** Inter-Association Task Force on Alcohol Issues; (1992) Inter-Association Task Force on Campus Alcohol and Other Substance Abuse Issues.

★ 12036 ★ **International Advisory Council for Homosexual Men and Women in Alcoholics Anonymous (IAC)**
PO Box 90
Washington, DC 20044-0090

Founded: 1980. **Members:** 1,000. **Description:** Regular groups of Alcoholics Anonymous World Services specifically composed of gays and lesbians. Purpose is to serve the gay and lesbian members of AA and to provide advice and support to other members of AA. Works for unity and service with AA for the betterment of the gay and lesbian members and AA; advocates freedom in communication as an important aid to recovery. Provides alcoholism professionals with information about gay and lesbian AA groups for use in counseling lesbian and gay alcoholics. Assists in the exchange of recorded tapes of lesbian and gay AA speakers. **Publications:** Newsletter, 4/year. • *World Directory of Gay/Lesbian Groups of Alcoholics Anonymous,* annual. Directory. Also publishes calendar of events and pamphlet.

★ 12037 ★ **International Commission for the Prevention of Alcoholism and Drug Dependency (ICPA)**
12501 Old Columbia Pike
Silver Spring, MD 20904
Phone: (301)680-6719
Fax: (301)680-6090
Thomas R. Neslund, Exec.Dir.

Founded: 1952. **Languages:** English. **Description:** Representatives of national public health committees and other individuals interested in the physical and social effects of alcoholism and

drug dependency. Fosters the scientific study of alcohol and drugs, their effects on the physical, mental, and moral powers of the individual, and their effects on social, economic, political, and religious life. Encourages preventive education; disseminates information on drug and alcohol abuse. Serves as a liaison with similar groups around the world. Sponsors exchange and research programs. Conducts film shows, forums, and radio and television events. **Publications:** *ICPA Alert.* • *ICPA Dispatch,* periodic. • *ICPA Reporter,* quarterly. **Formerly:** (1982) International Commission for the Prevention of Alcoholism.

★ 12038 ★ **International Council on Alcohol and Addictions (ICAA)**
(Conseil International sur les Problemes de l'Alcoolisme et des Toxicomanies — CIPAT)
Case Postale 189
CH-1001 Lausanne, Switzerland
Phone: 21 3209865
Fax: 21 3209817
Eva Tongue, LL.D., Dir.

Founded: 1907. **Members:** 520. **Languages:** English, French, German, Hungarian, Spanish. **Description:** Persons (400) and organizations (120) interested in or working with problems of alcoholism or drug addiction in 80 countries. Encourages interdisciplinary exchange of information and experience in research, prevention, treatment, and rehabilitation for alcoholism and drug addiction. Organizes training courses on the management of drug dependence. Sponsors competitions. **Publications:** *Alcoholism,* semiannual. • *Conference Proceedings,* triennial. • *ICAA News,* quarterly. **Formerly:** (1935) International Bureau Against Alcoholism; (1968) International Union Against Alcoholism.

★ 12039 ★ **International Doctors in Alcoholics Anonymous (IDAA)**
PO Box 199
Augusta, MO 63332
Phone: (314)482-4548
C. Richard McKinley, M.D., Sec.-Treas.

Founded: 1949. **Members:** 5,100. **Description:** Doctors who are alcoholics; doctors interested in Alcoholics Anonymous World Services. Seeks to exchange knowledge and experience in the recovery from and management of alcoholism for members and persons who fall within their sphere of influence. Supports AA-type group activities. **Publications:** *International Doctors in Alcoholics Anonymous--Newsletter,* quarterly. Newsletter. *Price:* Included in membership dues. • *Letter,* 3/year.

★ 12040 ★ **International Federation of the Blue Cross (IFBC)**
(Federation Internationale de la Croix-Bleue — FICB)
44, rue du Decarcadere
PO Box 658
CH-2501 Bienne, Switzerland
Phone: 32 227565
Fax: 32 227556
Eric Ziehli, Gen.Sec.

Founded: 1877. **Members:** 2,520. **Languages:** English, French, German, Portuguese. **Description:** National societies (20) and local groups

(2500) representing 125,000 individuals in 33 countries. Works to help alcoholics and drug addicts. Disseminates information concerning alcoholism. Operates cure homes and clinics. **Publications:** *INFO,* semiannual. • *Report,* quarterly. **Formerly:** (1983) International Federation of the Temperance Blue Cross Societies.

★ 12041 ★ **International Health and Temperance Association (IHTA)**
12501 Old Columbia Pike
Silver Spring, MD 20904
Phone: (301)680-6719
Fax: (301)680-6090
Thomas R. Neslund, Exec.Sec.

Founded: 1947. **Members:** 650,000. **National Groups:** 68. **Description:** Seeks to "enlighten the public concerning the harmful effects of alcohol, tobacco, and narcotics and to mount an educational campaign to solve these problems." Promotes principles of health and temperance. **Publications:** *Listen,* monthly. **Formerly:** (1982) International Temperance Association.

★ 12042 ★ **International Lawyers in Alcoholics Anonymous (ILAA)**
14643 Sylvan St.
Van Nuys, CA 91411
Phone: (808)785-6541
Eliseo Gauna, Sec.-Treas.

Founded: 1975. **Members:** 1,300. **Description:** Alcoholic lawyers who are seeking sobriety through their affiliation with Alcoholics Anonymous World Services. Seeks to: spread the message of AA to alcoholic attorneys; work to educate the judiciary and lawyers on the problem of alcoholism; support attorneys in their recovery. **Publications:** *ILAA,* 3-4/year. Newsletter.

★ 12043 ★ **International Nurses Anonymous (INA)**
c/o Pat Green
1020 Sunset Dr.
Lawrence, KS 66044
Phone: (913)749-2626
Pat Green, Sec.-Treas.

Founded: 1988. **Members:** 500. **Description:** Nurses, nursing students, and former nurses who are involved in a 12-step recovery program. Provides mutual support and networking; serves as a resource for newly recovering nurses. **Publications:** *INA Newsletter,* semiannual. Newsletter. *Price:* Free to members.

★ 12044 ★ **International Society for Biomedical Research on Alcoholism (ISBRA)**
Univ. of Toronto
Dept. of Pharmacology
Medical Sciences Bldg.
Toronto, ON, Canada M5S 1A8
Phone: (416)978-6374
Fax: (416)978-7437
Dr. Harold Kalant, Pres.

Founded: 1980. **Members:** 535. **Regional Groups:** 3. **Languages:** English. **Description:** Physicians, psychologists, biologists, and other scientists in over 20 countries who conduct research on biological factors in the etiology and treatment of alocholism and its medical complications. Official collaborating agency of the World Health Organization. Conducts international collaborative research projects and training courses. **Publications:** *Advances in Biomedical Alcohol Research*, biennial. Book. Contains proceedings of the biennial congresses. • *Alcoholism: Clinical and Experimental Research*, bimonthly. Journal.

★12045★   **"Just Say No" International**
2101 Webster St., Ste. 1300
Oakland, CA 94612
Phone: (510)451-6666
Free: 800-258-2766
Fax: (510)451-9360
Ivy Cohen, Pres.

Founded: 1985. **Members:** 13,000. **Regional Groups:** 10. **Description:** Local clubs comprised of children aged 5-18. Develops, promotes, and evaluates the work of member and affiliate clubs. Conducts research-based programs in youth development and primary prevention including tobacco, alcohol, and illegal substance abuse, dropouts, and teenage pregnancy programs. Sponsors "Just Say No" Awareness Week. **Publications:** Annual Reports. Also publishes fact sheets. **Formerly:** (1988) "Just Say No" Foundation.

★12046★   **Licensed Beverage Information Council (LBIC)**
1225 Eye St. NW, Ste. 500
Washington, DC 20005
Phone: (202)682-4776
Mindy K. Stein, Admin.

Founded: 1979. **Members:** 10. **Description:** National trade associations concerned with all aspects of alcohol abuse. Purpose is to fund multimedia public education programs on the health effects of drinking during pregnancy, alcoholism as an identifiable and treatable illness, underage drinking, and drunk driving. Encourages the communication of information on prevention of drinking to high school and college students. Cautions pregnant women against abusive consumption of alcohol to guard against fetal abnormalities; facilitates contact among alcohol intervention and treatment agencies and pregnant alcoholic women. Encourages medical professionals' continuing study of the effects of alcohol abuse and their periodic consultation with authoritative sources. **Publications:** Brochures. • *Licensed Beverage Information Council--News Bulletin*, periodic. Bulletin. • Reprints. **Formerly:** (1982) Beverage Alcohol Information Council.

★12047★   **NarAnon**
World Service Office
PO Box 2562
Palos Verdes, CA 90274
Phone: (213)547-5800

Description: Provides assistance to drug-dependent individuals and their families. Organizes discussion groups.

★12048★   **Narcotic Educational Foundation of America (NEFA)**
5055 Sunset Blvd.
Los Angeles, CA 90027
Phone: (213)663-5171
Henry B. Hall, Exec.Dir.

Founded: 1924. **Description:** Conducts an education program revealing the dangers that result from the illicit and abusive use of narcotics and dangerous drugs, so that youth and adults will be protected from both mental and physical drug dependency and harm. **Publications:** *Drugs and the Automotive Age.* • *Get the Answers - An Open Letter to Youth.* • *Glue Sniffing.* • Papers. Contains information about the dangers of drug use. *Price:* $.98/set. • *Some Things You Should Know About Prescription Drugs.* • *Student Reference Sheets.* Outlines the dangers associated with the use of various substances.

★12049★   **Narcotics Anonymous (NA)**
PO Box 9999
Van Nuys, CA 91409
Phone: (818)780-3951
Fax: (818)785-0923
George Hollahan, Contact

Founded: 1953. **Members:** 500,000. **Local Groups:** 26000. **Description:** Recovering addicts throughout the world meet to offer help to fellow addicts seeking recovery. Members meet regularly to facilitate and stabilize their recovery. Uses 12-step program adapted from Alcoholics Anonymous to aid in the recovery process. **Publications:** Audiotapes. • Books. • *NA Way Magazine: The International Journal of the Fellowship of Narcotics Anonymous*, monthly. Magazine. Recounts experiences of members during their recoveries. Includes calendar of events and annual index. *Price:* $15/year. • *Newsline*, quarterly. • Pamphlets. • *Narcotics Anonymous.* Book. Basic textbook of NA. • *It Works: How and Why.* Book. Guide to NA primary principles. • *Just For Today: Daily Meditations for Recovering Addicts.* Book.

★12050★   **National Association of Addiction Treatment Providers (NAATP)**
1 Massachusetts Ave. NW, Ste. 860
Washington, DC 20001
Phone: (202)371-6731
Fax: (202)682-0136
Sam Muszynski, Mng.Dir.

Founded: 1978. **Members:** 450. **State Groups:** 12. **Description:** Corporate and private institutional alcohol and/or drug dependency treatment facilities. Promotes awareness of chemical dependency as a treatable disease; advocates high standards of health care in substance abuse treatment facilities. Encourages member education. Maintains contact with U.S. Congress and state and local governments. Serves in an advisory capacity to the Joint Commission on Accreditation of Healthcare Organizations and to the Commission on Accreditation of Rehabilitation Facilities. Compiles statistics on chemical dependency treatment and recovery. **Publications:** *NAATP Update*, bimonthly. *Price:* free, for members only. **Formerly:** National Association of Alcoholism Treatment Programs.

★12051★   **National Association of Alcoholism and Drug Abuse Counselors (NAADAC)**
3717 Columbia Pike, Ste. 300
Arlington, VA 22204-4254
Phone: (703)920-4644
Free: 800-548-0497
Fax: (703)920-4672
Linda Kaplan, Exec.Dir.

Founded: 1972. **Members:** 18,000. **Regional Groups:** 8. **State Groups:** 47. **Local Groups:** 75. **Description:** Counselors in alcoholism and drug abuse treatment. Objective is to provide national representation for counselors as well as for their training and education. Works to gain public recognition of alcoholism as a disease. Seeks legislation establishing accreditation standards for counselors. Informs the public about chemical dependency and the availability of assistance. **Publications:** *Counseling Lesbian, Gay and Bisexual Persons with Alcohol and Drug Problems.* Papers. • *The Counselor*, bimonthly. Magazine. For counselors on alcohol and drug abuse. Includes book, pamphlet, and film list. Also contains notices of employment and educational opportunities. *Price:* Included in membership dues. • *The Counselor.* Reprint. • *NAADAC Ethical Standards.* • *NAADAC Newsletter*, bimonthly. Newsletter. *Price:* Included in membership. • *NAADAC Study Guide on Additional Counseling.* • *Register of NCAC Professionals.* Directory. • *Salary and Compensation Study.* Papers. Also publishes 1993 and 1994 conference papers. **Formerly:** (1982) National Association for Alcoholism Counselors.

★12052★   **National Association for Children of Alcoholics (NACoA)**
11426 Rockville Pike, St. 100
Rockville, MD 20852
Phone: (301)468-0985
Fax: (301)468-0987
Sis Wenger, Pres.

Founded: 1983. **Members:** 3,000. **State Groups:** 22. **Description:** Authors, educators, physicians, psychologists, therapists, and children of alcoholics. Supports and serves as a resource for individuals of all age groups who are COAs. Objectives are to increase public and professional awareness and recognition of the special needs of children of alcoholics; to provide leadership in public policy at the national, state, and local level; to act as an informational and educational resource to academic and other community systems; to create networks which facilitate the exchange of information and resources; to initiate and advance professional knowledge and understanding; to advocate for accessible programs and services. Compiles statistics; conducts educational programs. **Publications:** *Children of Alcoholics: Meeting the Needs of the Youth COA in the School Setting.* • *Children of Alcoholics: Selected Readings.* Book. • *It's Elementary: Meeting the Needs of High Risk Youth in the School Setting.* • *Network*, bimonthly. Newsletter. • *Poor Jennifer: She's Always Losing Her Hat.* Video. Also makes available posters.

★ 12053 ★ **National Association on Drug Abuse Problems (NADAP)**
355 Lexington Ave.
New York, NY 10017
Phone: (212)986-1170
Fax: (212)697-2939
Warren F. Pelton, Pres.

Founded: 1971. **Description:** Sponsored by business and labor organizations. Serves as an information clearinghouse and referral bureau for corporations and local communities interested in prevention of substance abuse and treatment of substance abusers. Provides: resources to local communities seeking to combat drug and alcohol abuse; corporate services for employers interested in creating a drug-free workplace. Community education and development services include: development of drug and alcohol awareness presentations for community organizations; identification of local substance abuse treatment resources; consultation on development of local prevention, treatment, and vocational programs. Corporate services include: provision of drug and alcohol information seminars in the workplace and through union organizations; assistance in formulation of company drug and alcohol policies; aid in the development and implementation of employee assistance programs; training of supervisors; assistance for companies and labor unions wishing to make full use of local treatment agency networks. Makes available vocational education services including training in job hunting, job interview workshops, training programs for substance abuse treatment professionals, and individual consultations for recovering substance abusers seeking to return to the job market. Provides placement services; has conducted surveys on the employability of rehabilitated drug users and found that former addicts perform comparably with others hired for similar jobs. Operates Neighborhood Prevention Network, through which local communities develop parent support groups and youth peer leadership groups dedicated to combatting drug and alcohol abuse. NPN provides substance abuse prevention and early intervention services for children and youth and ongoing training and materials dealing with specific issues in urban substance abuse. Maintains speakers' bureau. **Publications:** *Conference Proceedings*, biennial. Proceedings. • *NADAP News/Report*, quarterly. Newsletter. Covers current issues in the field of substance abuse. *Price:* Free. • Reports.

National Association of Lesbian / Gay Alcoholism Professionals (NALGAP)
See: Entry 11702

★ 12054 ★ **National Association for Perinatal Addiction Research and Educati on (NAPARE)**
200 N. Michigan Ave., Ste. 300
Chicago, IL 60601
Phone: (312)541-1272
Fax: (312)541-1271
Judith C. Burnison, Exec. Officer

Founded: 1987. **Members:** 750. **Regional Groups:** 3. **Description:** Conducts educational and research programs on substance abuse during pregnancy, and the effects of substance abuse on the fetus. Sponsors training forums

and charitable programs; operates cocaine baby helpline. Compiles statistics; maintains speakers' bureau. **Publications:** *Update*, quarterly. Newsletter. Contains information on model programs and research. *Price:* Included in membership dues.

National Association of State Alcohol and Drug Abuse Directors (NASADAD)
See: Entry 5588

★ 12055 ★ **National Association of Substance Abuse Trainers and Educators (NASATE)**
1521 Hillary St.
New Orleans, LA 70118
Phone: (504)861-4756
Dr. Tom Lief, Chairperson

Founded: 1982. **Members:** 100. **Regional Groups:** 2. **Description:** Accredited colleges and universities offering 12 or more continuing education credit hours in the field of substance abuse. Goal is to provide a network for exchange on courses, student population, degreed and nondegreed programs, and graduate study in chemical dependency training. Acts as a clearinghouse for students interested in substance abuse training programs; assists universities with the development of such programs. Provides for the exchange of information among universities concerning certificates, continuing education units, degrees, and opportunities for transfer and enrollment in undergraduate, graduate, and professional schools. Examines the educational and training needs of students and their career mobility as substance abuse practitioners. Maintains placement service. **Publications:** *Annual Directory*. Directory.

★ 12056 ★ **National Black Alcoholism Council (NBAC)**
1629 K St. NW, Ste. 802
Washington, DC 20006
Phone: (202)296-2696
Fax: (202)296-2707
Dr. Celia Willis, Exec.Dir.

Founded: 1978. **Members:** 1,050. **Description:** Individuals concerned about alcoholism among black Americans. Works to support and initiate activities that will improve alcoholism treatment services and lead to the prevention of alcoholism in the black community. Provides training on how to treat black alcoholics from a cultural perspective. Bestows political and service awards. Maintains biographical archives. Compiles statistics concerning alcoholism among blacks. **Publications:** *Model for Working With Children of Alcoholic and Drug Addicted Parents*. • *National News and Views*, semiannual. • *Treatment of Black Alcoholics*.

★ 12057 ★ **National Catholic Council on Alcoholism and Related Drug Problems (NCCA)**
1550 Hendrickson St.
Brooklyn, NY 11234-3514
Phone: (718)951-7177
Fax: (718)951-7233
Msgr. K. Martin, Contact

Founded: 1949. **Members:** 500. **Description:** Promotes adequate treatment for all clergy and religious men and women suffering from alco-

holism and drug dependency through consultation and supportive services. Cooperates with treatment programs for the spiritual, physical, and mental rehabilitation of alcoholics and drug dependent persons, especially with Alcoholics Anonymous World Services. Promotes pastoral ministry to alcoholics and their families. Educates Catholics, especially priests and religious men and women in pastoral ministries, on alcohol and alcohol problems as well as the use and abuse of alcohol and drugs. Sponsors workshops; conducts alcohol and drug abuse education programs in houses of formation and seminaries. Maintains speakers' bureau. **Publications:** *The Blue Book*, annual. Proceedings of annual symposium. *Price:* $15. • Newsletter, quarterly. • *Wine as Sacramental Matter and the Use of Mustum*. Book. **Formerly:** National Clergy Conference on Alcoholism; (1988) National Clergy Council on Alcoholism and Related Drug Problems.

★ 12058 ★ **National Committee for the Prevention of Alcoholism and Drug Dependency (NCPADD)**
c/o Thomas R. Neslund
12501 Old Columbia Pike
Silver Spring, MD 20904-6600
Phone: (301)680-6719
Fax: (301)680-6290
Thomas R. Neslund, Exec.Dir.

Founded: 1950. **Members:** 50. **Description:** Health officials, physicians, educators, social workers, youth leaders, clergymen, temperance leaders, businessmen, judges, and others. To further the study of the effects of alcohol and other drugs on the physical, mental and moral powers of the individual citizen and on the social, economic, political, and religious life of the nation. Fosters nationwide educational program through films, lectures, forums, radio, and television programs. **Publications:** *Quarterly ICPA*, quarterly. Bulletin. **Formerly:** National Committee for the Prevention of Alcoholism.

National Consortium of Chemical Dependency Nurses (NCCDN)
See: Entry 9115

★ 12059 ★ **National Council on Alcoholism and Drug Dependence (NCADD)**
12 W. 21st St.
New York, NY 10010
Phone: (212)206-6770
Free: 800-NCA-CALL
Fax: (212)645-1690
Paul Wood, Ph.D., Pres.

Founded: 1944. **Local Groups:** 170. **Description:** Works for the prevention and control of alcoholism through programs of public and professional education, medical and scientific information, and public policy advocacy. Sponsors National Alcohol Awareness Month each April. **Publications:** *Alcoholism Report*, monthly. Newsletter. • Annual Report. • *NCADD Amethyst*, quarterly. *Price:* $50. • Pamphlets. • *Resource and Referral Guide*, periodic. • *What are the Signs of Alcoholism?*. • *What Can You Do About Someone Else's Drinking?*. **Formerly:** (1949) National Committee for Education on Alcoholism; (1955) National Committee on Alcoholism; (1990) National Council on Alcoholism.

★ 12060 ★ **National Episcopal Coalition on Alcohol and Drugs (NECAD)**
876 Market Way
Clarkston, GA 30021
Phone: (404)292-2610
Virginia M. King, Exec.Dir.

Founded: 1982. **Members:** 600. **Description:** A network of individuals, parishes, and Episcopal church diocesan committees addressing the issue of alcohol and drug use and addiction. Seeks to involve the Episcopal church in alcohol and other drug addiction issues. Serves as a resource clearinghouse. Sponsors annual Alcohol-Drug Awareness Sunday to provide information to congregations. **Publications:** *Alcohol-Drug Awareness Sunday Information Packet*, annual. Educational material. *Price:* $6. • Brochures. • *The NECAD News*, quarterly. *Price:* Available to members only. • Newsletter.

★ 12061 ★ **National Families in Action (NFIA)**
2296 Henderson Mill Rd., Ste. 300
Atlanta, GA 30345
Phone: (404)934-6364
Fax: (404)934-7137
Sue Rusche, Exec.Dir.

Founded: 1977. **Description:** Parents and other adults concerned about preventing drug abuse. Seeks to: educate parents, children, and the community about the use of drugs; counteract social pressures that condone and promote drug use; stop drug use. Lobbied for passage of statewide drug paraphernalia statutes. Collects and disseminates information about the effects of drugs. Maintains Drug Information Center, which contains more than 500,000 documents, studies, books, brochures, and films and videos relating to drug abuse. Operates program for parents and youth in public housing. **Publications:** *Crack Update*. Brochure. Describes the effects of this highly addictive form of cocaine. *Price:* $35/100. • *Drug Abuse Update*, quarterly. Magazine. Contains abstracts from newspapers, medical journals, and other sources concerned with the use and effects of drugs. *Price:* $30/year. • *Drug Abuse Update for Kids*, quarterly. *Price:* $10/year. • *12 Reasons Not to Legalize Drugs*. *Price:* $15/100. • *12 Tips for Helping Your Children Stay Drug-Free*. *Price:* $15/100. • *You Have the Right to Know Curriculum Series*. Books. *Price:* $10/each. **Formerly:** (1982) DeKalb Families in Action; (1983) Families in Action; (1984) Families in Action Drug Information Center; (1990) Families in Action National Drug Information Center.

★ 12062 ★ **National Family Partnership (NFP)**
11159-B South Towne Square
St. Louis, MO 63123
Phone: (314)845-1933
Carol Reeves, Board Pres.

Founded: 1980. **Members:** 3,000. **Description:** Provides services, resources, and drug prevention programs for local parent and youth groups across the country. Sponsors Annual Red Ribbon Celebration in October, provides two-day drug prevention training to middle/junior and high school students, and serves as a clearinghouse for state and federal legislation. **Publications:** Books. • *Community Team Man-*

ual. Manual. • Manuals. • *NFP News*, quarterly. Newsletter. *Price:* $25/year for individuals; $100/year for groups. • *REACH and Lifers Manual*. Manual. **Formerly:** National Federation of Parents for Drug-Free Youth.

National Nurses Society on Addictions (NNSA)
See: Entry 9123

★ 12063 ★ **National Parents' Resource Institute for Drug Education (PRIDE)**
10 Park Place S, Ste. 540
Atlanta, GA 30303
Phone: (404)577-4500
Dr. Thomas J. Gleaton, Pres.

Founded: 1977. **Description:** Parents, youth groups, educators, law enforcement officials, community groups, and corporations. Promotes drug abuse prevention through education. Provides current research information on drug abuse and facilitates the organization of parent peer groups, parent-school teams, and community action groups to reduce adolescent drug abuse. Gathers and disseminates information on the latest medical and scientific findings on the effects of drugs on youth, current patterns of drug and alcohol use among youth, social and cultural pressures that encourage youth to use drugs, and institutional and legal efforts being made to prevent drug abuse, reduce drug supplies, and prosecute drug traffickers. Conducts the PRIDE Community Action Plan to assist communities in establishing an effective drug abuse program and the PRIDE's Parent Training Program to assist concerned parents. Offers America's PRIDE, ClubPRIDE, and PRIDE Junior youth programs. Develops workplace drug training programs for corporations. Sponsors the annual PRIDE World Drug Conference, which seeks to bring parents, youth, and the public into contact with scientists, physicians, and policymakers dealing with adolescent drug abuse; also sponsors a series of one-day conferences for local community teams who are trained to return to their neighborhoods to organize workshops. Operates speakers' bureau; conducts educatonal programs and children's services; compiles statistics. Maintains library. **Publications:** *PRIDE Quarterly*. Newsletter. Discusses the legal, pharmacological, psychological, social, cultural, and physiological effects of adolescent drug use. Includes overviews. *Price:* $25/year. Also publishes books and pamphlets. **Also Known As:** PRIDE (Parents' Resource Institute for Drug Education). **Formerly:** (1982) Parent Resources and Information on Drug Education.

★ 12064 ★ **National Prevention Network (NPN)**
444 N. Capitol St. NW, Ste. 642
Washington, DC 20001
Phone: (202)783-6868
Fax: (202)783-2704
Stephanie Kashangaki, Prevention Dir.

Founded: 1982. **Members:** 61. **Regional Groups:** 5. **Description:** Officials of state alcohol and drug agencies. Works to enhance national, state, and local programs for drug and alcohol abuse prevention; serves as a network among state agency personnel and other pre-

vention professionals to assist in the development of effective and innovative substance abuse prevention strategies; seeks to establish guidelines for quality service. Collects and disseminates information and statistics on prevention services, programs, trends, activities, and issues. Provides consultation on technical matters; conducts research. **Publications:** *Network News*, bimonthly. Newsletter. Includes association news and events and related legislation. *Price:* Included in membership dues; $60/year for nonmembers. • *NPN Membership List*, quarterly.

★ 12065 ★ **National Treatment Consortium for Alcohol and Other Drugs (NTC)**
c/o Jeffrey T. Kramer
444 N. Capitol St. NW, Ste. 642
Washington, DC 20001
Phone: (202)434-4780
Fax: (202)434-4783
Jeffrey T. Kramer, Exec.VP

Founded: 1990. **Members:** 400. **Description:** Professional organization of employers, benefits managers, insurance providers, employee assistance programs, and substance abuse treatment providers. Works to expand education efforts, and broaden the network of professionals concerned with the treatment of alcohol and drug addiction. Makes available current research and information on treatment; conducts educational programs; maintains speakers' bureau; offers placement service.

★ 12066 ★ **Nordic Council for Alcohol and Drug Research (ECADR)**
(Nordiska Namnden for Alkohol- och Drogforskning — NAD)
Annegatan 29 A 23
SF-00100 Helsinki 10, Finland
Phone: 0 6948082
Fax: 0 6949081
Pia Rosenqvist, Exec. Officer

Founded: 1978. **Members:** 15. **Languages:** Danish, Norwegian, Swedish. **Description:** Researchers from Denmark, Finland, Iceland, Norway, and Sweden. Coordinates alcohol and drug research within Scandinavia; initiates new research projects. Organizes seminars. Disseminates information. **Publications:** *Barns Socialisation och Alkohol*. Book. • *Reports From Seminars*, annual. • *Social Problems Around the Baltic Sea - Report from the Baltic Study*. Book. • *Women, Alcohol, and Drugs in the Nordic Countries*. Book.

★ 12067 ★ **North Conway Institute (NCI)**
14 Beacon St.
Boston, MA 02108
Phone: (617)742-0424
Rev. David A. Works, Pres.

Founded: 1951. **Members:** 110. **Description:** Interfaith organization that addresses the problems of alcoholism and drug abuse and aims to improve society's ability to treat and care for substance abusers and their families. Acts as a network among 16 major religious and secular organizations to disseminate information on alcohol use and misuse; refers interested parties to groups or individuals that offer training in counseling alcoholics and provide assistance to those affected by drugs. Promotes individual responsibility with regard to the drinking of alcohol, and unified action on alcohol and drug problems across professional, institutional, and cultural boundaries. Operates speakers' bureau; provides placement service. Compiles statistics. **Publications:** *College Drinking.* • *NCI Catalyst,* semiannual. Newsletter. *Price:* Free. • *Teen-Age Drinking.*

★ 12068 ★ Partnership for a Drug Free America (DFA)
405 Lexington Ave.
New York, NY 10174
Phone: (212)922-1560
Fax: (212)922-1570
Richard Bonnette, Pres.

Founded: 1986. **Members:** 2,500. **Description:** A coalition of individuals and organizations representing the advertising, production, and communications industries. Seeks to utilize the creative skills of members to change social attitudes towards illegal drugs. Believes that drug abuse is a major crisis affecting American families and work environments. Works to evoke a social revulsion to what the group views as current public acceptance and complacency toward illegal drugs. Focuses on advertising strategies that will "unsell" illegal drugs, "denormalize" drug usage in the U.S., and reinforce positive factors of life without drugs. Creates advertising campaigns targeted toward preteens, teenagers, young adults, and "influencers" (peers, parents, health care professionals, teachers, and opinion leaders). Is currently running media anti-drug advertisements, including an advertisement depicting an egg being fried as an analogy to the effects of drugs on the human brain. Conducts research evaluation program to assess attitudinal changes of targeted groups toward illegal drugs, monitor usage trends, and evaluate the effectiveness of these advertisments. **Publications:** Bulletin, periodic. • *Partnership for a Drug-Free America Newsletter,* quarterly. Newsletter. **Formerly:** (1990) Media-Advertising Partnership for a Drug-Free America.

People Against Rape (PAR)
See: Entry 3283

★ 12069 ★ Pharmacists Against Drug Abuse (PADA)
10 Park Pl. S, Ste. 540
Atlanta, GA 30303
Phone: (404)577-4500
Herbert W. Browne, Chm.

Founded: 1982. **Description:** Anti-drug abuse campaign that focuses on informing parents and children of the dangers of commonly abused drugs such as alcohol, marijuana, and cocaine. Urges pharmacists to establish their pharmacies as community clearinghouses for information on substance abuse programs and to display and distribute drug abuse information. Encourages pharmacists to speak on the subject of drugs and drug abuse problems before parent groups and civic, school, and community group meetings. Conducts public service campaigns that include radio and television broadcasts, distribution of literature, point-of-purchase displays, and posters that identify pharmacies as participants in the program.

Sponsors continuing education programs to assist pharmacists in their role in the fight against drug abuse. **Publications:** *Pharmacist's Guide to Drug Abuse.*

★ 12070 ★ Pills Anonymous (PA)
PO Box 772
Bronx, NY 10451
Phone: (212)874-0700

Founded: 1975. **Local Groups:** 3. **Description:** Persons addicted to drugs including tranquilizers, stimulants, analgesics, sedatives, cocaine, and marijuana. Purpose is to apply the Alcoholics Anonymous World Services' 12-step approach to persons dependent on addictive drugs. Provides emotional support to members, many of whom became addicted after using the drugs for legitimate reasons (for example, to alleviate the chronic pain of migraine headaches or arthritis) and teaches them methods of coping with pain that do not require drugs. **Formerly:** (1984) Pills Anonymous; (1992) Drugs Anonymous.

★ 12071 ★ Potsmokers Anonymous (PA)
208 W. 23rd St., Apt. 1414
New York, NY 10011-2139
Phone: (212)254-1777
Francis Duffy, Dir.

Founded: 1978. **Members:** 5,000. **Description:** Educational program consisting of a nine-week course for people who want to stop smoking marijuana. Offers intensive weekend courses for people from outside the greater New York City area. Holds public information meetings. **Publications:** Newsletter, periodic.

★ 12072 ★ Rational Recovery Systems (RRS)
PO Box 800
Lotus, CA 95651
Phone: (916)621-4374
Fax: (916)621-2667
Jack Trimpey, Exec.Dir.

Founded: 1986. **Local Groups:** 1000. **Description:** Assists in recovery from substance abuse and other addictive behavior. Conducts self-help groups teaching people how to become emotionally independent from alcohol, chemicals, or food. Promotes the belief that the individual has the power to overcome addiction, rather than relying on spiritualism. Uses the psychological techniques of addictive voice recognition technique (AVRT) rational emotive therapy to help people learn to reject irrational thoughts and beliefs which impede recovery. Operates RR-Residential, a live-in substance abuse recovery program. **Publications:** Audiotapes. • *Journal of Rational Recovery,* bimonthly. Journal. Contains articles by recovered addicts of alcohol, drugs, and eating disorders. *Price:* $17.50/year. • *The Small Book: A Revolutionary Alternative for Overcoming Alcohol and Drug Dependence. Price:* $19.95. • *Taming the Feast Beast. Price:* $19.95. • Videos.

★ 12073 ★ ReachOut—A Community Intervention
c/o Denise Bozich
14950 444th Ave. SE
North Bend, WA 98045
Phone: (206)888-3739
Denise Bozich, Exec. Officer

Founded: 1983. **Local Groups:** 1. **Description:** Seeks to give adolescents, families, schools, and other elements of the community a better understanding of the problem of adolescent substance abuse. Aids schools and communities in establishing substance abuse programs; sponsors support groups for adolescents and parents; works with schools and state juvenile facilities in programming after-care support groups. Maintains speakers' bureau.

★ 12074 ★ Recovered Alcoholic Clergy Association (RACA)
1515 Wilder Ave.
Honolulu, HI 96822
Phone: (808)395-0766
Fax: (808)944-9325
Rev. Stephen M. Winsett, Exec. Officer

Founded: 1968. **Members:** 400. **Local Groups:** 100. **Description:** Clergy in the Episcopal church orders and persons attending or teaching at Episcopal seminaries who have drinking problems. Recommends alcohol addiction treatment centers for members; trains individuals involved in confronting persons with drinking problems. Seeks to provide moral support to members; provides guidance to the families and/or colleagues of problem drinkers; maintains speakers' bureau. **Publications:** Pamphlets. • *RACA,* monthly. • *RACA Directory,* annual. Directory.

★ 12075 ★ Research Society on Alcoholism (RSA)
4314 Medical Pky., No. 300
Austin, TX 78756
Phone: (512)454-0022
Fax: (512)454-0022
Debra Sharp, Dir.

Founded: 1976. **Members:** 1,200. **Description:** Scientists who hold an M.D. or Ph.D. degree and others actively engaged in research on alcoholism and alcohol-related problems; doctoral students; professionals in related fields who are interested in supporting alcohol research. Purposes are to: serve as a forum for researchers working in the field; aid and further the application of research to problems related to alcoholism; disseminate scientific information; protect the rights of researchers and human research subjects; assess research priorities; enlighten the public about problems of alcoholism. Provides opportunities for communication and discussion among scientists, clinicians, and lay workers in alcoholism research, diagnosis, and treatment. Conducts lectures. **Publications:** *Alcoholism: Clinical and Experimental Research,* bimonthly. Journal. Includes book reviews and research reports. *Price:* Included in membership dues; $70/year for nonmembers; $95/year for institutions. • *Recent Developments in Alcoholism,* annual. Monograph. • *RSA Directory,* periodic. Directory. *Price:* available to members only.

★ 12076 ★ **Secular Organizations for Sobriety (SOS)**
National Clearinghouse
Box 5
Buffalo, NY 14215-0005
Phone: (716)834-2922
Fax: (716)834-0841
James R. Christopher, Founder

Founded: 1986. **Members:** 20,000. **Description:** Recovering alcoholics and drug addicts; families and friends of alcoholics or drug addicts. Serves as a support system free of any religious or spiritual undercurrent; believes sobriety is a process of personal responsibility. Espouses "a healthy skepticism" and encourages self-reliance and free thought. Maintains speakers' bureau. Compiles statistics. **Publications:** *Save Our Selves*, quarterly. Newsletter.

★ 12077 ★ **Society for the Study of Addiction to Alcohol and Other Drugs (SSA)**
c/o Prof. Ray Hodgson
Dept. of Psychology
Whitchurch Hospital
Whitchurch
Cardiff CF4 7XB, England
Phone: 1222 521118
Fax: 1222 522161
Prof. R. Hodgson, Pres.

Founded: 1884. **Members:** 528. **Regional Groups:** 1. **Languages:** English. **Description:** Medical and allied health professionals seeking to stimulate scientific study of alcohol and drug addiction. Conducts research and educational programs. **Publications:** *Addiction*, monthly. Journal. • Monographs.

★ 12078 ★ **Solvent Abuse Foundation for Education (SAFE)**
750 17th St. NW, Ste. 250
Washington, DC 20006
Phone: (202)332-7233
Fax: (202)429-0655
Hugh Young, Pres.

Founded: 1984. **Description:** Seeks to educate young people about the dangers of solvent abuse. Distributes comic book.

Substance Abuse Librarians and Information Specialists (SALIS)
See: Entry 7011

★ 12079 ★ **TARGET - Helping Students Cope with Tobacco, Alcohol and Other Drugs**
11724 NW Plaza Cir.
PO Box 20626
Kansas City, MO 64195
Phone: (816)464-5400
Free: 800-366-6667
Fax: (816)464-5571
Robert Kanaby, Exec.Dir.

Founded: 1984. **Description:** Provides healthy lifestyle education and prevention information for high school athletic activity participants, state high school athletic and activitiy associations, and secondary school personnel. Maintains National RADAR Network Specialty Center for resources on steriods and other performance-enhancing drugs. **Publications:** Catalog, annual. • *On Target: A Road Map to Healthy Lifestyles.* Two-volume publication furnished to public and private elementary schools in the United States. *Price:* $4/volume. • *On Target: Developing Chemically-Free Student Leadership.* Publication furnished to public and private secondary schools in the United States. *Price:* $4/volume. **Formerly:** (1991) Target - Helping Students Cope with Alcohol and Other Drugs.

★ 12080 ★ **TOVA—The Other Victims of Alcoholism (TOVA)**
PO Box 1528, Radio City Sta.
New York, NY 10101
Phone: (212)247-8087
Josie Balaban Couture, Pres.

Founded: 1976. **Description:** Provides and disseminates public information and education about the less visible victims of alcoholism, from family members to industry. Focuses on what the organization calls the domino effect of alcoholism and its impact on society. Serves as information clearinghouse; acts as an advocate. Maintains Friends of TOVA, a network of individuals and organizations that serves as the fundraising and networking arm. **Publications:** Brochures. • *The Domino Quarterly.* • Pamphlets. • Reports. • Reprints.

★ 12081 ★ **Unitarian Universalist Society for Alcohol and Drug Education (UUA)**
83 Sea St.
PO Box 38
North Weymouth, MA 02191
Phone: (617)335-8504
Fax: (617)367-3237
Rev. Thomas Martin, Dir.

Founded: 1886. **Members:** 2,000. **Description:** Individuals concerned with preventing the adverse effects that alcohol and drug abuse have on society. Disseminates literature pertaining to alcohol and drug education and examines problems associated with alcoholism and drug addiction. Conducts seminars and workshops. Bestows annual awards for best sermon and best essay written on alcohol and drug education. **Publications:** Newsletter, annual. Also publishes resource sheets on alcohol and drug education. **Formerly:** (1989) Unitarian Universalist Society for Alcohol Education.

Women in Crisis (WIC)
See: Entry 1534

★ 12082 ★ **Women for Sobriety (WFS)**
PO Box 618
Quakertown, PA 18951
Phone: (215)536-8026
Free: 800-333-1606
Fax: (215)536-8026
Dr. Jean Kirkpatrick, Exec.Dir.

Founded: 1975. **Members:** 5,000. **Local Groups:** 450. **Description:** Self-help groups of women alcoholics who use a program "based on abstinence, comprised of Thirteen Acceptance Statements that, when accepted and used, will provide each woman with a new way of life through a new way of thinking. Starts with coping first but then moves on to overcoming and a whole change in the approach to each day." Recognizes differences between male and female alcoholics in the method of successful recovery. Small groups organize and meet independently. Maintains speakers' bureau. **Publications:** Booklets. • Books. • Pamphlets. • *Sobering Thoughts*, monthly. Newsletter. Contains book reviews, calendar of events, and research updates. *Price:* $18/year.

Women in Transition (WIT)
See: Entry 7528

Research Centers

★ 12083 ★ **Addiction Research Foundation Social Evaluation and Research Department**
UWO Research Park
100 Collip Cir., Mogenson Bldg., Ste. 200
London, ON, Canada N6G 4X8
Phone: (519)858-5000
Fax: (519)858-5199
Dr. Louis Gliksman, Actg.Dir.

Research Activities and Fields: Health promotion and public education, development of treatment services, and employee assistance programs. Studies include elderly substance abusers, alcohol management policy, needs assessment for intensive addiction treatment services, and information systems for employee assistance programs. **Publications:** *The Journal.*

★ 12084 ★ **Addiction Research and Treatment Corporation**
22 Chapel St.
Brooklyn, NY 11201
Phone: (718)260-2917
Fax: (718)522-3186
Dr. Lawrence S. Brown, Jr., Sr.VP

Research Activities and Fields: Alcohol and drug addiction, including studies on alcoholism among those addicted to opiates, immunological parameters of drug abuse, stress among patients and staff, and the relationship of patterns of drug abuse and sexual practices to the frequency of human immunodeficiency virus (HIV) infection (exposure to AIDS virus). Conducts clinical trials of drugs for drug abuse and the treatment of HIV disease.

★ 12085 ★ **Alcohol and Drug Abuse Research Center**
McLean Hospital/Harvard Medical School
115 Mill St.
Belmont, MA 02178
Phone: (617)855-2000
Dr. Nancy K. Mello, Codirector

Research Activities and Fields: Alcohol and drug abuse, emphasizing behavioral pharmacology, neuroendocrinology, pharmacotherapy, and the effects of drug abuse on the brain as assessed by brain imaging techniques, including MRI, SPECT, and EEG.

★ 12086 ★ Alcohol Research Group
2000 Hearst Ave.
Berkeley, CA 94709
Phone: (510)642-5208
Fax: (510)642-7175
Dr. Raul Caetano, Dir.

Research Activities and Fields: Epidemiology of alcohol problems, including national studies of the general population, ethnic groups and women. Performs health services research on drinking practices and problems, attitudes concerning drinking, community responses to drinking, dimensions of alcohol dependence and alcohol's role in behaviors that carry a risk of contracting AIDS, homelessness and alcohol-related policies. Publications: *The Drinking and Drug Practices Surveyor* (annually).

★ 12087 ★ Alcohol Research Information
    Service (ARIS)
1106 E. Oakland Ave.
Lansing, MI 48906
Phone: (517)485-9900
Fax: (517)485-1928
Robert Hammond, Dir.

Research Activities and Fields: Health concerns and social and economic impact of alcohol and other drug use. **Publications:** *The Bottom Line on Alcohol in Society* (quarterly journal); *Monday Morning Report Newsletter* (two per month). **Formerly:** American Business Men's Research Foundation (1980).

★ 12088 ★ Andrews University
Institute of Alcoholism & Drug Dependency
School of Graduate Studies
Berrien Springs, MI 49104-0211
Phone: (616)471-3558
Fax: (616)471-6611
Dr. Patricia Mutch, Dir.

Research Activities and Fields: Conducts research and evaluation, project development, and educational services in prevention and rehabilitation of chemical dependencies, and examines religiosity and chemical dependency. Research also focuses on motivational factors promoting abstinence. **Publications:** Technical Reports (on Institute projects). **E-mail Address:** iadd@andrews.edu.

★ 12089 ★ Brown University
Center for Alcohol and Addiction Studies
Box G-BH
Providence, RI 02912
Phone: (401)863-1109
David C. Lewis, M.D., Dir.

Research Activities and Fields: Alcohol and addiction studies, including an individual's relationship to alcohol and the effectiveness of community reinforcement on treatment, the relationship between smoking and drinking among alcoholics, matching treatment focus to dysfunction, social skills treatment of cocaine abusers, cue exposure and social skills treatment for alcoholics, deterring preadolescent drug and AIDS-risky behavior, time dynamics of alcohol treatment outcome, treatment research validation and extension program, substance abuse prevention program for Native American youth, and hospital intervention services. **Publications:** *Digest of Addiction Theory and Application* (monthly). **E-mail Address:** david__lewis@brown.edu.

★ 12090 ★ Center for Addiction and
    Behavioral Health Research
Enderis Hall, Rm. 1049
2400 E. Hartford Ave.
Milwaukee, WI 53211
Phone: (414)229-5008
Fax: (414)229-5311
Dr. Allen Zweben, Dir.

Research Activities and Fields: Mental health and alcohol and drug abuse, including alcohol treatment matching, cost-offset of effective matching, economic analysis of managed care, alcohol-related injuries in the emergency setting, and adolescent moral reasoning and decisions to use or not use alcohol and other drugs. Recent research studies include controlled alcohol and substance abuse treatment outcomes, drug use prevention, early detection and intervention, econometric analysis, and substance evaluations. **E-mail Address:** rac@csd.uwm.edu. **Formerly:** Wisconsin Center for Addiction Studies (1993).

★ 12091 ★ Colorado State University
Tri-Ethnic Center for Study of Drug Abuse
    and Prevention
Department of Psychology
Fort Collins, CO 80523
Free: 800-835-6091
Fax: (303)491-0527
Dr. E.R. Oetting, Scientific Dir.

Research Activities and Fields: Drug abuse prevention research for Native-American, Mexican-American, and western White-American youths, serving as an access point for data on epidemiology and etiology. Studies school-based youths and high risk groups such as dropouts and delinquents, and examines the social, psychological, and cultural elements of drug abuse using both cross-sectional and longitudinal studies.

★ 12092 ★ Columbia University
Center on Addiction and Substance Abuse
    (CASA)
152 W. 57 St.
New York, NY 10019
Joseph A. Califano, Jr., Chm.

Research Activities and Fields: Substance abuse and addiction, with emphasis on the cost-effectiveness of treatment programs, reviewing various efforts in the public and private sectors, substance abuse and the American woman, the responsibility of teachers, and public awareness.

Emanuel Research Center
See: Entry 8365

★ 12093 ★ Friends Medical Science
    Research Center, Inc.
2330 W. Joppa Rd., Ste. 103
Lutherville, MD 21093
Phone: (410)823-5116
Fax: (410)823-5131
Patrick Bogan, Contact

Research Activities and Fields: Studies narcotic addiction to provide statistical documentation of its relation to crime, effectiveness of addiction treatment programs, and HIV as a result of lifestyle. Also conducts pharmaceutical and medical device research. **Publications:** Newsletter.

★ 12094 ★ Indiana University
Institute for Drug Abuse Prevention
Creative Arts Bldg., Rm. 10
840 State Rd. 46 Bypass
Bloomington, IN 47405
Phone: (812)855-2162
Fax: (812)855-4940
William J. Bailey, Codir.

Research Activities and Fields: Alcohol, tobacco, and drug prevention; incidence and prevalence of alcohol, tobacco, and other drug use; education research; evaluation of prevention strategies amd materials; health behavior related to alcohol, tobacco, and other drug use; and geodemographic research in needs assessment and community analysis. **Publications:** *Prevention Newsline* (quarterly); *Catalog of Prevention Resources* (annually); Ocassional Monographs; Project Reports. **E-mail Address:** bailey@ucs.indiana.edu.

★ 12095 ★ Johns Hopkins University
Behavioral Pharmacology Research Unit
Johns Hopkins/Bayview Campus
5510 Nathan Shock Dr.
Baltimore, MD 21224-6823
Phone: (410)550-0035
Fax: (410)550-0030
George E. Bigelow, Ph.D., Scientific Dir.

Research Activities and Fields: Human behavioral pharmacology of substance abuse and dependence, including clinical studies on abuse liability assessment, performance effects, and applied treatment interventions for opioids (analgesics) and narcotics, sedatives, anxiolytics, tobacco, nicotine, caffeine, and cocaine. **E-mail Address:** bigelow@bpru.uucp.jhu.edu.

Meharry Medical College
I Have a Future Program
See: Entry 11276

★ 12096 ★ National Development and
    Research Institutes, Inc.
11 Beach St.
New York, NY 10013
Phone: (212)966-8700
Fax: (212)334-8058
Fred Streit, Exec.Dir

Research Activities and Fields: Drug abuse, including evaluations of treatment and prevention programs; AIDS research as it relates to substance abuse; epidemiology of drug abuse; drugs and crime; drug abuse and the criminal justice system; street studies of drug sales, use, and prevention; evaluation and enhancement of AIDS outreach; and intervention services for high-risk adolescents. **Formerly:** Narcotic and Drug Research, Inc..

North Charles Mental Health Research and
    Training Foundation
See: Entry 7590

★ 12097 ★ Pacific Institute for Research
    and Evaluation (PIRE)
7315 Wisconsin Ave., Ste. 1300 W.
Bethesda, MD 20814
Phone: (301)951-4233
Fax: (301)907-8637
Allan Y. Cohen, Ph.D., Exec.Dir.

Research Activities and Fields: Drug and alcohol abuse prevention and juvenile delinquency prevention, especially among high-risk youth. Specializes in large-scale multi-site program evaluations.

★ 12098 ★ **Prevention Research Center**
2150 Shattuck Ave., Ste. 900
Berkeley, CA 94704
Phone: (510)486-1111
Fax: (510)644-0594
Harold D. Holder, Ph.D., Dir.

Research Activities and Fields: Environmental approaches to the prevention of alcohol-related problems. Projects include studies of individual and environmental factors within the worksite associated with alcohol problems, peer influences and the influences of prime time television on adolescent values and attitudes about drinking, risk factors associated with alcohol-impaired driving, beverage server training to reduce intoxication among customers, the structure and function of alcohol beverage control agencies, legal issues and legislation, drinking and alcohol problems among Mexican-Americans, computer simulation to determine regional alcohol use and abuse, and community trial prevention projects to seek innovative and effective strategies to reduce alcohol-involved injury and deaths, and postdoctoral and multidisciplinary health service research training programs. **E-mail Address:** server_@ucbcmsa.

★ 12099 ★ **Research Institute on Addictions**
1021 Main St.
Buffalo, NY 14203
Phone: (716)887-2566
Fax: (716)887-2252
Howard T. Blane, Ph.D., Dir.

Research Activities and Fields: Etiology, course, treatment, and prevention of alcoholism and substance abuse. Studies the following six aspects of substance abuse: 1) normative patterns; 2) biochemical, physiological, psychological, and social antecedents and consequences; 3) biopsychosocial aspects of consumption in early and middle adulthood; 4) family aspects; 5) alcohol-drug interactions, and 6) treatment and prevention strategies. **Publications:** *RIA Report* (quarterly); *RIA Publications* (annually). **E-mail Address:** htb%riavax@ubvms.cc.buffalo.edu. **Formerly:** Research Institute on Alcoholism (1992).

★ 12100 ★ **Rockefeller University**
Laboratory of Biology of Addictive Diseases
1230 York Ave.
New York, NY 10021-6399
Phone: (212)327-8247
Fax: (212)327-8574
Dr. Mary Jeanne Kreek, Dir.

Research Activities and Fields: Basic and clinical studies of the biological basis of opiate, alcohol, and cocaine addiction; the biological correlates of addictive disease, including the physiological and pharmacological effects of chronic drug use; and the medical complications of drug use, especially hepatitis B, hepatitis delta, and human immunodeficiency viral infections. Other areas include molecular neurobiology of the addictive diseases with special at-

tention on the role of the endogenous opioid system in these disorders, including cocaine dependency and alcoholism, as well as opiate addition; and the role of the endogenous opioids and the specific opioid receptors in the addictive diseases and in normal and abnormal physiology of the neuroendocrine and gastrointestinal systems.

★ 12101 ★ **Rutgers University**
Center of Alcohol Studies
Busch Campus
Smithers Hall
Piscataway, NJ 08855-0969
Phone: (908)445-2190
Fax: (908)445-3500
Robert J. Pandina, Ph.D., Dir.

Research Activities and Fields: Causes and treatment of alcoholism, diverse actions of alcohol on the body, means to prevent alcohol misuse, and the incidence and prevalence of normal and problem alcohol consumption in the U.S. and the world, including human enzyme systems important in alcohol metabolism, development of tolerance and physical dependence on alcohol, and hormonal changes. **Publications:** *Journal of Studies on Alcohol* (bimonthly); Monographs of the Rutgers Center of Alcohol Studies; *National Institute of Alcohol Abuse and Alcoholism-Rutgers University Center of Alcohol Studies (NIAAA-RUCAS) Treatment Series*.

★ 12102 ★ **Southern California Research Institute**
11914 W. Washington Blvd.
Los Angeles, CA 90066
Phone: (310)390-8481
Fax: (310)398-6651
Dr. Marcelline Burns, Dir.

Research Activities and Fields: Effects of alcohol and drugs on behavior, including effects of alcohol and drugs on driving.

State University of New York at Buffalo Research Center for Children and Youth
See: Entry 3071

★ 12103 ★ **U.S. Department of Health and Human Services**
National Institute on Alcohol Abuse and Alcoholism
5600 Fishers Ln.
Rockville, MD 20857
Phone: (301)443-3885
Fax: (301)443-7043
Enoch Gordis, Director

Research Activities and Fields: NIAAA oversees research focused on improving the prevention and treatment of alcohol-related problems and alcoholism. Seeks to develop new scientific knowledge that will reduce the incidence and prevalence of alcohol abuse and alcoholism and the associated morbidity and mortality. Conducts and supports research aimed at determining the causes of alcoholism, discovering how alcohol damages the organs of the body, and developing prevention and treatment strategies for application in the nation's health care system. Conducts policy studies with broad implications for alcohol prevention and treatment; and conducts epidemiological studies to assess

the risks for and problems among various population groups.

★ 12104 ★ **U.S. Department of Health and Human Services**
National Institute on Alcohol Abuse and Alcoholism
Basic Research Division
6000 Executive Rd.
Rockville, MD 20892-7003
Phone: (301)443-2530
Dr. William Lands, Director

Research Activities and Fields: Division provides support for basic and applied research programs on the multiple determinants and processes of alcoholism and other alcohol-related problems; on the prevention of alcohol abuse; and on the diagnosis, treatment, and rehabilitation of persons who abuse alcohol. Division administers the Institute's National Alcohol Research Centers Program as well as its research scientists development and training programs. In addition, it collaborates with other national and international agencies, universities, and scientific organizations and provides technical assistance to universities, federal agencies, state and local governments, and community and voluntary organizations. Principal Division components are: Biomedical Research Branch and Neurosciences Research Branch.

★ 12105 ★ **U.S. Department of Health and Human Services**
National Institute on Alcohol Abuse and Alcoholism
Basic Research Division
Biomedical Research Branch
6000 Executive Blvd., Ste. 402
Rockville, MD 20892
Phone: (301)443-4224
Dr. Sam Carkari, Chief

Research Activities and Fields: Branch supports and administers NIAAA extramural research grants and training programs on the effects of alcohol abuse and alcoholism as related to the central nervous system, the fetal alcohol syndrome, and neuroendocrine and pathological conditions. Research is aimed at reduction of morbidity and mortality associated with alcoholism and alcohol abuse and includes research in the areas of etiology, pathogenesis, identification, treatment, and prevention as well as in the development of basic research tools and methodologies.

★ 12106 ★ **U.S. Department of Health and Human Services**
National Institute on Alcohol Abuse and Alcoholism
Basic Research Division
National Centers and Special Programs
5600 Fishers Ln.
Rockville, MD 20857
Phone: (301)443-1273
Fax: (301)594-0673
Dr. Ernestine Vanderveen, Associate Director

Research Activities and Fields: NIAAA provides grant support for Alcohol Research Centers to conduct interdisciplinary research on alcoholism and problems related to alcohol abuse. These grants are typically for a five-year period and are intended to encourage research by providing stable, long term support of research on the nature, causes, diagnosis, treatment, control, prevention, and consequences of alcohol abuse and alcoholism.

★ 12107 ★ U.S. Department of Health and
Human Services
National Institute on Alcohol Abuse and
Alcoholism
Basic Research Division
Neurosciences and Behavioral Research
Branch
6000 Executive Blvd.
Rockville, MD 20892
Phone: (301)443-4225
Fax: (301)594-0673
Walter A. Hunt, Ph.D., Branch Chief

Research Activities and Fields: Studies the effect of alcohol on the brain and behavior.

★ 12108 ★ U.S. Department of Health and
Human Services
National Institute on Alcohol Abuse and
Alcoholism
Biometry and Epidemiology Division
6000 Executive Dr.
Rockville, MD 20892
Phone: (301)443-3306
Thomas Harford, Ph.D., Director

Research Activities and Fields: Division plans and conducts studies and surveys on the incidence and prevalence of alcohol abuse and alcoholism (both nationally and in specific population groups); conducts national surveillance activities to collect and analyze alcohol-related program data through various information systems; and develops and maintains information systems to collect and analyze alcohol-related data. Division also collaborates with other organizations engaged in alcohol data collection activities, such as state-based information systems, in order to exchange pertinent data and to utilize existing data systems where appropriate.

★ 12109 ★ U.S. Department of Health and
Human Services
National Institute on Alcohol Abuse and
Alcoholism
Clinical and Prevention Research Division
5600 Fishers Ln., Fl. 14C10
Rockville, MD 20857
Phone: (301)443-1206
Fax: (301)443-8774
Richard K. Fuller, M.D., Director

Research Activities and Fields: Supports alcohol abuse and alcoholism treatment and prevention research through grants and cooperative agreements. Principal Division components are the Prevention Research Branch and Treatment Research Branch.

★ 12110 ★ U.S. Department of Health and
Human Services
National Institute on Alcohol Abuse and
Alcoholism
Clinical Studies Laboratory
NIH Bldg. 10, Rm. 3B19
9000 Rockville Pike
Bethesda, MD 20892
Phone: (301)496-5353
Michael Eckhardt, Chief

Research Activities and Fields: Principal areas of research are neuroscience, clinical pharmacology, analytical biochemistry, internal medicine, and psychiatry, all as related to alcoholism.

★ 12111 ★ U.S. Department of Health and
Human Services
National Institute on Alcohol Abuse and
Alcoholism
Intramural Clinical and Biological Research
Division
NIH Bldg. 10, Rm. 3C103
9000 Rockville Pike
Bethesda, MD 20892
Phone: (301)496-8996
Fax: (301)402-0445
Dr. Markku Linnoila, Director

Research Activities and Fields: Division conducts basic and applied studies on the multiple determinants and processes of alcoholism and other alcohol-related problems and on prevention, diagnosis, treatment, and rehabilitation. It also provides in-house research scientist training in a variety of disciplines for work in alcohol-related research and collaborates with other agencies, universities, and scientific organizations. Division comprises laboratories of Clinical Studies; Metabolism; Membrane Biochemistry and Biophysics; Molecular and Cellular Neurobiology; and Neurogenetics.

★ 12112 ★ U.S. Department of Health and
Human Services
National Institute on Alcohol Abuse and
Alcoholism
Intramural Clinicaland Biological Research
Division
Metabolism Laboratory
12501 Washington Ave.
Rockville, MD 20852
Phone: (301)443-3063
Fax: (301)443-0930
Dr. Richard L. Veech, Chief

Research Activities and Fields: Laboratory conducts metabolic research on the consequences of alcoholism and on genetic factors related to alcoholism.

★ 12113 ★ U.S. Department of Health and
Human Services
National Institute on Alcohol Abuse and
Alcoholism
Physiologic and Pharmacologic Studies
Laboratory
NIH Bldg. 10
9000 Rockville Pike
Bethesda, MD 20892
Phone: (301)443-1234
Fax: (301)443-5894
George Kunos, Ph.D., Director

Research Activities and Fields: Studies focus on alcohol and alcoholism, physiology, and pharmacology.

★ 12114 ★ U.S. Department of Health and
Human Services
National Institute on Drug Abuse
5600 Fishers Ln.
Rockville, MD 20857
Phone: (301)443-6480
Fax: (301)443-9127
Richard Millstein, Acting Director

Research Activities and Fields: Institute's mission is to increase knowledge and promote effective strategies to deal with health problems and issues associated with drug abuse. In carrying out these responsibilities, the Institute conducts and supports research on: the neurobiological, behavioral, and social mechanisms underlying drug abuse and addiction; the specific biomedical and behavioral effects of abused drugs on the body and brain, including marijuana, heroin, and cocaine; effective prevention and treatment approaches, including a broad research program designed to develop new treatment medications and behavioral therapies for drug abuse; the causes and consequences of drug abuse, including the effect on society and the morbidity and mortality in selected populations such as ethnic minorities, youth, and women; the relationship of drug use to other problem behaviors such as psychopathology, unemployment, and violence; the biomedical, behavioral, and social factors associated with vulnerability and invulnerability to drug abuse and addiction; the role of drug abuse as a factor contributing to the spread of HIV/AIDS, tuberculosis, and other diseases and the development of effective prevention and intervention strategies; the mechanisms of pain and the search for a nonaddictive analgesic; and tobacco and nicotine dependence. Components include the Addiction Research Center and Divisions of Epidemiology and Prevention Research, Basic Research, Clinical Research, and Medications Development.

★ 12115 ★ U.S. Department of Health and
Human Services
National Institute on Drug Abuse
Addiction Research Center
4940 Eastern Ave., Bldg. C
PO Box 5180
Baltimore, MD 21224
Phone: (301)550-1538
Fax: (301)550-1645
Dr. Roy W. Pickens, Acting Director

Research Activities and Fields: The Addiction Research Center: 1) plans, develops, and conducts intramural preclinical and clinical research on the causes, hazards, treatment, and prevention of drug abuse and addiction, the nature of the addiction process, and the addiction liability of new drugs, drawing on the biomedical, neuroscience, psychological, and behavioral sciences; 2) provides in-house research to train scientists in a variety of disciplines for work in drug abuse-related research; and 3) develops preclinical and clinical research studies and procedures for protection of human subjects from research risks and monitors the provision of medical care to these subjects. The Center is organized in six main branches: Clinical Pharmacology Branch; Neuroscience Research Branch; Preclinical Pharmacology Research Branch; Etiology Branch; Research Support Branch; and Treatment Branch.

★ 12116 ★ U.S. Department of Health and Human Services
National Institute on Drug Abuse
Addiction Research Center
Clinical Pharmacology Branch
4940 Eastern Ave.
PO Box 5180
Baltimore, MD 21224
Phone: (301)550-1494
Fax: (301)550-1849
Jack E. Henningford, Ph.D., Director

Research Activities and Fields: Branch conducts studies to develop and evaluate new pharmacological treatment modalities for substance abuse. Research also involves assessing the abuse potential of new drugs, analyzing metabolic pathways of drugs of abuse, developing analytical procedures and methods, and measuring drugs in biological fluids. In addition, Branch conducts research on medical illnesses associated with drug abuse, such as Acquired Immunodeficiency Syndrome (AIDS).

★ 12117 ★ U.S. Department of Health and Human Services
National Institute on Drug Abuse
Addiction Research Center
Etiology Research Branch
4940 Eastern Ave.
PO Box 5180
Baltimore, MD 21224
Phone: (410)550-1538
Fax: (410)550-1645
Dr. Roy Pickens, Director

Research Activities and Fields: Branch conducts research on the psychological, biological, and family origins of drug dependence and on conduct and personality disorders that are frequently associated with drug dependence. It also investigates drug-produced alterations in cognition and performance, such as the deficits observed during drug withdrawal. In addition, Branch evaluates sensory and cognitive information processing abilities of those at risk for drug abuse and characterizes drug effects on brain electrical activity.

★ 12118 ★ U.S. Department of Health and Human Services
National Institute on Drug Abuse
Addiction Research Center
Neuroscience Research Branch
4940 Eastern Ave.
PO Box 5180
Baltimore, MD 21224
Phone: (301)550-1473
Fax: (301)550-1672
M. Kuhar, Chief

Research Activities and Fields: Interdisciplinary studies on the mechanism of action and the effects of drug abuse on biological systems. Identifies new treatment and prevention strategies and new medications for drug abusers.

★ 12119 ★ U.S. Department of Health and Human Services
National Institute on Drug Abuse
Addiction Research Center
Preclinical Pharmacology Research Laboratory
4940 Eastern Ave.
PO Box 5180
Baltimore, MD 21224
Phone: (301)550-1522
Fax: (301)550-1648
S. Goldberg, Chief

Research Activities and Fields: Laboratory conducts research on the reinforcing properties of drugs of abuse, their effects on learned operant behavior, and their discriminative stimulus properties, as well as studies on the role of genetic variables in these effects of drugs of abuse. Research involves studies on drug self-administration, operant behavior models, and correlation of behavioral and physiological effects of drugs. Laboratory also conducts evaluative screening of new drugs for abuse potential by comparing their behavioral and neuropharmacological profiles of activity with those of prototypic drugs of abuse.

★ 12120 ★ U.S. Department of Health and Human Services
National Institute on Drug Abuse
Addiction Research Center
Treatment Branch
4940 Eastern Ave.
PO Box 5180
Baltimore, MD 21224
Phone: (301)550-1478
Fax: (301)550-1438
Dr. David A. Gorelick, Chief

Research Activities and Fields: Branch develops and studies the safety and efficacy of psychopharmacologic and psychosocial treatments for drug abuse, using a variety of residential and outpatient research designs and techniques. Branch also identifies predictors of treatment response, optimizing matching of patients to treatment, and determining the extent to which biomedical and psychosocial consequences of drug abuse are affected by treatment. Long-term follow-up obtained to assess the persistence of any treatment effects.

★ 12121 ★ U.S. Department of Health and Human Services
National Institute on Drug Abuse
Basic Research Division
5600 Fishers Ln.
Rockville, MD 20857
Phone: (301)443-1887
Fax: (301)594-6043
Dr. Christine R. Hartel, Acting Director

Research Activities and Fields: Division is responsible for planning, developing, and administering an extramural program of biomedical research that seeks to develop new knowledge concerning the mechanisms underlying drug abuse and its etiology and hazards. The Division supports studies to develop new methodologies for testing the abuse potential of new compounds as well as studies designed to determine the neurological and biochemical effects of newly developed pharmacological agents. It also supports training of research investigators in biomedical and preclinical disciplines in the drug abuse field; develops and supports research into the quota levels for new substances, synthesis of new drugs and metabolites, new methods development, and pharmaceutical for-

mulations; and manages the distribution of controlled substances, research drugs, and chemicals. Division comprises the Biomedical, Neurosciences Research, and Research Technology branches.

★ 12122 ★ U.S. Department of Health and Human Services
National Institute on Drug Abuse
Basic Research Division
Behavioral Pharmacology Branch
5600 Fishers Ln.
Rockville, MD 20857
Phone: (301)443-1263
John J. Boren, Chief

Research Activities and Fields: Branch is responsible for administering an interdisciplinary national program of research in behavioral pharmacology of drug abuse that includes: 1) behavioral, physiological, and cognitive factors contributing to the development, maintenance, and elimination of drug abuse; 2) reinforcing effectiveness and abuse liability of individual drugs and drug combinations; 3) effects of drugs on diverse aspects of behavioral and cognitive performance changes; and 4) effects of drugs on complex performance and simple functional behaviors.

★ 12123 ★ U.S. Department of Health and Human Services
National Institute on Drug Abuse
Basic Research Division
Biomedical Research Branch
5600 Fishers Ln.
Rockville, MD 20857
Phone: (301)443-6300
Fax: (301)594-6043
Dr. Karen J. Skinner, Director

Research Activities and Fields: Branch administers a national program of research concerned with: 1) the mechanisms of actions of drugs of abuse, including tolerance and dependence and the metabolic processes of drug action; 2) the pharmacological and toxicological aspects of developing drugs for treating addiction; 3) the effects of drugs of abuse on pregnancy, offspring, and genetic effects; 4) short- and long-term effects of multiple drug use; 5) the cellular and molecular mechanisms associated with drug actions. Other activities involve conducting studies and making recommendations relative to scientific and medical considerations in drug scheduling; supporting research training; providing consultation; and developing, supporting, and monitoring the Institute's biomedical research center program.

★ 12124 ★ U.S. Department of Health and Human Services
National Institute on Drug Abuse
Basic Research Division
Clinical Medicine Branch
5600 Fishers Ln., Rm. 10A-38
Rockville, MD 20857
Phone: (301)443-6697
Fax: (301)443-2317
Harry W. Haverkos, M.D., Acting Director

Research Activities and Fields: Branch administers an interdisciplinary national program of research focusing on clinical and medical aspects of infectious diseases that occur among drug abusers.

★ 12125 ★ U.S. Department of Health and Human Services
National Institute on Drug Abuse
Basic Research Division
Neurosciences Research Branch
5600 Fishers Ln., Rm. 10A-19
Rockville, MD 20857
Phone: (301)443-6975
Dr. Roger Brown, Chief

Research Activities and Fields: Activities of the Neurosciences Research Branch involve planning, stimulating, developing, and supporting a national program of research concerned with: 1) the effects of acute and chronic administration of abused drugs on the structure and functions of the central nervous system; 2) the effects of abused drugs on the development of the nervous system; 3) the neurobiology of pain, dysphoria, and euphoria; 4) the neurobiology of the reinforcing properties of drugs; and 5) studies of the interaction between brain environment and drugs of abuse.

★ 12126 ★ U.S. Department of Health and Human Services
National Institute on Drug Abuse
Basic Research Division
Research Technology Branch
5600 Fishers Ln., Rm. 10A-19
Rockville, MD 20857
Phone: (301)443-5280
Dr. Dingell, Director

Research Activities and Fields: Branch administers a national program of research in the areas of: 1) synthesizing new drugs and metabolites useful in drug abuse research; 2) new analytical methods for the determination of abused drugs; 3) metabolism and pharmacokinetics of drugs of abuse; and 4) relationships between molecular structure and pharmacological activity of drugs of abuse. Activities include designing and developing pharmaceutical formulations and planning and managing distribution of controlled substances, research drugs and chemicals, and related compounds; and providing direct technical expertise to other agencies involved in drug abuse research technology issues.

★ 12127 ★ U.S. Department of Health and Human Services
National Institute on Drug Abuse
Clinical and Prevention Research Divsion
Treatment Research Branch
5600 Fishers Ln., Rm. 10A30
Rockville, MD 20857
Phone: (301)443-4060
Fax: (301)443-4317
Jack Blaine, M.D., Chief

Research Activities and Fields: Branch is responsible for administering a national program of drug abuse treatment research which involves studies on: 1) effectiveness of current and innovative pharmacologic and nonpharmacologic treatment/rehabilitation methods; 2) impact of traditional drug abuse treatment/rehabilitation methods such as outreach, vocational rehabilitation, self-help, and individual, group, and family therapy counseling; 3) diagnostic strategies for identifying sub-populations within drug abuse and for examining the impact of treatment/rehabilitation on sub-populations;

and 4) roles and functions of both clients and service providers.

★ 12128 ★ U.S. Department of Health and Human Services
National Institute on Drug Abuse
Clinical Research Division
5600 Fishers Ln.
Rockville, MD 20857
Phone: (301)443-6697
Fax: (301)443-2317
Dr. Harry W. Haverkos, Contact

Research Activities and Fields: Division plans, stimulates, develops, and supports a broad extramural program of basic and applied research focusing on drug abuse treatment; supports studies designed to describe and understand drug abusing behavior and to ascertain the effects of drugs on performance; supports clinical and other applied research designed to assess the efficacy of new and existing treatment intervention techniques to meet the needs of both active and prospective drug abuse treatment clients; and supports research training. Division comprises the Clinical-Behavioral Pharmacology, Clinical Medicine, Medical Affairs, and Treatment Research branches.

★ 12129 ★ U.S. Department of Health and Human Services
National Institute on Drug Abuse
Epidemiology and Prevention Research Division
5600 Fishers Ln., 9A53
Rockville, MD 20857
Phone: (301)443-6504
Fax: (301)443-2636
Zili Sloboda, Acting Director

Research Activities and Fields: Division plans, conducts, and supports epidemiological studies and surveys on the nature and extent of drug abuse and monitors emerging trends in drug abuse; plans, conducts, and supports prevention research; designs, develops, operates, and maintains the Institute's drug abuse information systems; conducts ongoing surveys and develops analytical methodologies where information gaps exist in understanding special population drug abuse problems; works cooperatively with states and private organizations to encourage sharing of drug abuse epidemiology and treatment information; and provides consultation and technical assistance, upon request, to states concerned with developing and refining drug abuse information systems. Division comprises branches for Epidemiologic Research, Systems Analysis, Epidemiology Studies and Surveillance, Statistics and Analysis, and Prevention Research.

★ 12130 ★ U.S. Department of Health and Human Services
National Institute on Drug Abuse
Epidemiology and Prevention Research Division
Epidemiology Studies and Surveillance Branch

5600 Fishers Ln., Rm. 9A-42
Rockville, MD 20857
Phone: (301)443-6543
Fax: (301)443-2636
Nicolas Kozel, Chief

Research Activities and Fields: Branch's activities involve: 1) planning and directing an intramural program of epidemiologic research and statistical analysis; 2) developing and recommending policies, guidelines, and procedures concerning epidemiologic research data utilization; 3) planning, directing, or conducting studies and analyzing data to address high risk drug use issues and factors; 4) monitoring drug use patterns and trends; 5) providing advice and consultation in research methodology and analysis to the drug abuse field; 6) developing and coordinating the Division's International Epidemiology Research Program; 7) reviewing and assessing documents for validity of data on drug abuse activities; 8) preparing responses to inquiries and providing specialized epidemiologic materials and publications for the Institute, general public, and federal, state, and local agencies.

★ 12131 ★ U.S. Department of Health and Human Services
National Institute on Drug Abuse
Epidemiology and Prevention Research Division
Prevention Research Branch
5600 Fishers Ln.
Rockville, MD 20857
Phone: (301)443-1514
William J. Bukoski, Chief

Research Activities and Fields: Branch administers a national program of prevention and early intervention research in drug abuse, including studies on: 1) drug use practices and problems; 2) motivations, opinions, and perceptions in drug users and abusers; 3) relationships between drug use and psychosocial functioning; 4) institutional and community responses to the drug abuse problem; 5) the psychological and economic correlations of drug abuse and dependence; 6) group processes associated with behavior and attitudinal change related to drug use; 7) effectiveness of current and innovative prevention models; 8) strategies for community drug abuse prevention efforts; and 9) impact of changes in law on the incidence and prevalence of drug use.

★ 12132 ★ University of Alaska Anchorage
Center for Alcohol and Addiction Studies
3211 Providence Dr.
Anchorage, AK 99508
Phone: (907)786-1805
Fax: (907)786-4866
Dennis Fisher, Ph.D., Dir.

Research Activities and Fields: Basic, applied, and evaluative research in alcohol and substance abuse and intervention strategies in Alaska. Conducts epidemiological studies of drug use in the state, social impact and public policy research pertaining to drug use/abuse, and survey and cross-cultural research to define personality and social antecedents and correlates of drug use/abuse. Also conducts a statewide survey of substance use/abuse in Alaska.

★12133★ **University of California, Los Angeles**
Alcohol Research Center
Neuropsychiatric Inst.
760 Westwood Plaza
Los Angeles, CA 90024
Phone: (310)825-1891
Fax: (310)206-7309
Dr. Ernest P. Noble, Dir.

Research Activities and Fields: Causes of alcoholism, including genetic predisposition.

University of California, San Francisco
Center for AIDS Prevention Studies (CAPS)
See: Entry 10884

★12134★ **University of California, San Francisco**
Ernest Gallo Clinic and Research Center
San Francisco General Hospital
Bldg. 1, Rm. 101
1001 Botrero Ave.
San Francisco, CA 94110
Phone: (415)648-7111
Fax: (415)648-7116
Dr. Ivan Diamond, Contact

Research Activities and Fields: Alcoholism, with special emphasis on cellular and molecular mechanisms of alcohol dependence and genetic differences between cells of alcoholics and cells of non-alcoholics.

University of Colorado
National Center for American Indian and Alaska Native Mental Health Research
See: Entry 7663

★12135★ **University of Colorado—Denver**
Alcohol Research Center
4200 E. 9th Ave.
Denver, CO 80262
Phone: (303)270-7076
Dr. Richard A. Deitrich, Scientific Dir.

Research Activities and Fields: Mechanism of the action of alcohol to determine the ways in which alcohol affects the brain during both acute and chronic periods of intake, including studies on alcohol as a stimulus, different responses elicited by alcohol, and the products of alcohol metabolism. Uses genetic manipulation in animal models to define the acute and chronic affects of alcohol in relation to heredity.

★12136★ **University of Colorado—Denver**
Rocky Mountain Taste and Smell Center
4200 E. 9th Ave.
Box B-205
Denver, CO 80262-0205
Phone: (303)270-6600
Fax: (303)270-8787
Bruce W. Jafek, M.D., Med.Dir.

Research Activities and Fields: Taste and smell dysfunction, using animal and human models, including ultrastructural change in the sense of smell during post viral states, head trauma, studies on the mammalian vomeronasal organ, and aging and taste dysfunction due to cancer, radiation, and drugs. **E-mail Address:** jafek__b@defiance.hsc.colorado.edu.

★12137★ **University of Connecticut**
Alcohol Research Center
263 Farmington Ave.
Farmington, CT 06030-1410
Phone: (203)679-3423
Fax: (203)679-1296
Thomas F. Babor, Ph.D., Scientific Dir.

Research Activities and Fields: Genetic, psychiatric, biological, behavioral, and cross-cultural aspects of alcoholism, including alcoholic typologies, treatment matching, familial alcoholism, alcohol dependence syndrome, and early intervention. Activities focus on clinical trials of new psychotherapies and pharmacotherapies, biological responses to alcohol-related stimuli, diagnosis of alcohol dependence, animal studies of neurobiological correlates of alcohol consumption, ASP and family history variables as risk factors in the development of alcohol dependence, and research on treatment services for alcoholics.

★12138★ **University of Kentucky**
Multidisciplinary Research Center on Drug and Alcohol Abuse
210 Medical Center, Annex 2
Lexington, KY 40536-0080
Phone: (606)257-2355
Fax: (606)323-1193
Dr. Carl G. Leukefeld, Dir.

Research Activities and Fields: Biological, social, and psychological aspects of alcohol and drug abuse; and HIV/AIDS. Conducts household and other surveys.

★12139★ **University of Maryland**
Center for Substance Abuse Research
4321 Hartwick Rd., Ste. 501
College Park, MD 20740
Phone: (301)403-8329
Fax: (301)403-8342
Dr. Eric Wish, Dir.

Research Activities and Fields: Substance abuse issues, focusing on monitoring alcohol and drug use indicators throughout Maryland and at the national level, and on the evaluation of treatment programs. **Publications:** *CESAR Reports* (newsletter); *CESAR Special Topics Series*; Research Reports. **E-mail Address:** cesar@cesar.umd.edu.

★12140★ **University of Michigan**
Alcohol Research Center
Bldg. 2, Ste. A
400 E. Eisenhower Pkwy.
Ann Arbor, MI 48108
Phone: (313)998-7952
Fax: (313)998-7994
Dr. Frederick Blow, Res.Dir.

Research Activities and Fields: Alcohol abuse among the elderly, including the relationship of alcohol and aging on the central nervous system. **E-mail Address:** frederic.blow@um.cc.umich.edu.

★12141★ **University of North Carolina at Chapel Hill**
Center for Alcohol Studies
Medical Research Bldg. A
CB 7175
Chapel Hill, NC 27599
Phone: (919)962-6576
Fax: (919)966-5679
David S. Janowsky, M.D., Dir.

Research Activities and Fields: Neurobehavioral analyses of alcohol effects in several species, including humans.

★12142★ **University of North Texas Health Science Center at Fort Worth**
Substance Abuse Institute of North Texas (SAINT)
3500 Camp Bowie Blvd.
Ft. Worth, TX 76107-2699
Phone: (817)735-2063
Fax: (817)735-2091
Harbans Lal, Ph.D., Exec. Dir.

Research Activities and Fields: Medication development against alcoholism, cocaine abuse, and sedative dependence, brain function deterioration resulting from substance abuse, and drug-induced reinforcing mechanisms.

★12143★ **University of Pennsylvania**
Substance Abuse Treatment Unit
VA Medical Center
Bldg. 7, 116-D
Univ. & Woodland Aves.
Philadelphia, PA 19143
Phone: (215)823-5809
Fax: (215)823-4248
George Woody, M.D., Dir.

Research Activities and Fields: Alcohol and drug dependence, including research on psychotherapy, endocrine system, alcoholism and schizophrenia, methadone-maintained cocaine abusers, and outpatient versus inpatient detoxification.

University of Texas—Houston Health Science Center
Mental Sciences Institute
See: Entry 7692

★12144★ **University of Washington**
Alcohol and Drug Abuse Institute
3937 15th Ave. NE, NL-15
Seattle, WA 98195
Phone: (206)543-0937
Fax: (206)543-5473
Dennis M. Donovan, Ph.D., Dir.

Research Activities and Fields: Social and biomedical aspects of alcohol and drug abuse. **Publications:** *ADAI News* **E-mail Address:** ddonovan@u.washington.edu.

★12145★ **Vermont Alcohol Research Center**
2000 Mountain View Dr.
Colchester, VT 05446-1910
Phone: (802)655-6000
Fax: (802)655-6565
M.W. Perrine, Ph.D., Dir.

Research Activities and Fields: Alcoholism, alcohol and drug abuse, drunken driving, injury risk, mental health, alcohol tolerance, effects of alcohol on performance, and drinking patterns. **E-mail Address:** vtadmin@varc.usa.com.

★ 12146 ★ Wayne State University Addiction Research Institute
4201 St. Antoine, 9A
Detroit, MI 48201
Phone: (313)577-1388
Fax: (313)577-6685
Eugene P. Schoener, Ph.D., Dir.

Research Activities and Fields: Prevention of alcohol and drug abuse, including the relationship between alcohol availability, consumption, and related damage; the effects of subjective, social, and physical availability on alcohol consumption; community-based prevention program evaluation; medical training in substance abuse; the relationship between physical abuse and substance abuse; alcohol use among older adults; substance abuse among the mentally ill; health promotion in the American Indian community; and substance abuse attitudes among college students.

Wayne State University Fetal Alcohol Research Center
See: Entry 9722

State Government Agencies

Substance Abuse

★ 12147 ★ Alabama Department of Mental Health and Mental Retardation
Substance Abuse Services Division
PO Box 3710
Montgomery, AL 36109-0710
Phone: (334)270-4650
Fax: (334)240-3195

★ 12148 ★ Alaska Department of Health and Social Services
Alcoholism and Drug Abuse Division
PO Box 110607
Juneau, AK 99811-0607
Phone: (907)465-2071
Fax: (907)465-2185

★ 12149 ★ Arizona Department of Health Services
Behaviorial Health Services Division
Substance Abuse Office
2122 E. Highland
Phoenix, AZ 85016
Phone: (602)381-8999
Fax: (602)553-9143

★ 12150 ★ Arkansas Department of Health
Alcohol and Drug Abuse Prevention Division
PO Box 3278
Little Rock, AR 72203-3278
Phone: (501)280-4505
Fax: (501)671-1450

★ 12151 ★ California Health and Welfare Agency
Alcohol and Drug Programs Department
1700 K St.
Sacramento, CA 95814
Phone: (916)445-0834
Fax: (916)323-5873

★ 12152 ★ Colorado Department of Human Services
Alcohol and Drug Abuse Division
4300 Cherry Creek Dr., S.
Denver, CO 80222-1530
Phone: (303)692-2932
Fax: (303)753-9775

★ 12153 ★ Connecticut Department of Public Health
Addictions and Community Health Bureau
150 Washington St.
Hartford, CT 06106
Phone: (203)566-2520
Fax: (203)566-3302

★ 12154 ★ Delaware Department of Health and Social Services
Alcoholism, Drug Abuse, and Mental Health Division
1901 N. Dupont Hwy.
New Castle, DE 19720
Phone: (302)577-4461
Fax: (302)577-4510

★ 12155 ★ District of Columbia Department of Human Services
Public Health Commission
Alcohol and Drug Abuse Administration
1300 1st St., NE
Washington, DC 20002
Phone: (202)727-0740
Fax: (202)727-0379

★ 12156 ★ Florida Department of Health and Rehabilitative Services
Human Services Program Office
Alcohol, Drug Abuse and Mental Health Office
1317 Winewood Blvd.
Tallahassee, FL 32399-0700
Phone: (904)488-8304
Fax: (904)922-2993

★ 12157 ★ Georgia Department of Human Resources
Mental Health, Mental Retardation and Substance Abuse Division
Alcohol and Drug Abuse Services Office
2 Peachtree St., NW
Atlanta, GA 30303
Phone: (404)657-6400
Fax: (404)657-2256

★ 12158 ★ Hawaii Department of Health
Behavioral Health Administration
Alcohol and Drug Abuse Division
1270 Queen Emma St., Rm. 706
Honolulu, HI 96813
Phone: (808)586-3962
Fax: (808)586-4444

★ 12159 ★ Idaho Department of Health and Welfare
Family and Community Services Division
Substance Abuse Bureau
PO Box 83720
Boise, ID 83720-0036
Phone: (208)334-5700
Fax: (208)334-6558

★ 12160 ★ Illinois Department of Alcoholism and Substance Abuse
100 W. Randolph, Ste. 5-600
Chicago, IL 60601
Phone: (312)814-3840
Fax: (312)814-2419

★ 12161 ★ Indiana Family and Social Services Administration
Addiction Services Division
402 W. Washington St., Rm. W341
Indianapolis, IN 46204
Phone: (317)232-7939
Fax: (317)233-4693

★ 12162 ★ Iowa Department of Public Health
Substance Abuse and Health Promotion Division
Lucas State Office Bldg.
321 E. 12th St.
Des Moines, IA 50319
Phone: (515)281-4417
Fax: (515)281-4958

★ 12163 ★ Kansas Department of Social and Rehabilitation Services
Alcohol and Drug Abuse Services
Biddle Bldg., 2nd Fl.
300 SW Oakley
Topeka, KS 66606
Phone: (913)296-3925
Fax: (913)296-0494

★ 12164 ★ Kentucky Human Resources Cabinet
Mental Health and Mental Retardation Department
Substance Abuse Division
275 E. Main St.
Frankfort, KY 40621
Phone: (502)564-2880
Fax: (502)564-3844

★ 12165 ★ Louisiana Department of Health and Hospitals
Alcohol and Drug Abuse Office
PO Box 2790
Baton Rouge, LA 70821
Phone: (504)342-6717
Fax: (504)342-3931

★ 12166 ★ Maine Office of the Governor
Substance Abuse Office
State House Sta. 159
Augusta, ME 04333
Phone: (207)287-2595
Fax: (207)287-4334

★ 12167 ★ Maryland Department of Health and Mental Hygiene
Alcohol and Drug Abuse Administration
201 W. Preston St., 5th Fl.
Baltimore, MD 21201
Phone: (410)225-6925
Fax: (410)225-6489

★ 12168 ★ Massachusetts Executive Office of Health and Human Services
Public Health Department
Substance Abuse Division
150 Tremont St.
Boston, MA 02111
Phone: (617)727-1960
Fax: (617)727-2559

★ 12169 ★ Michigan Department of Public
Health
Substance Abuse Services Office
3423 N. Logan St.
PO Box 30195
Lansing, MI 48909
Phone: (517)335-8809
Fax: (517)335-9476

★ 12170 ★ Minnesota Department of
Human Services
Social Services Administration
Chemical Dependency Division
444 Lafayette Rd.
St. Paul, MN 55155
Phone: (612)296-4610
Fax: (612)297-1949

★ 12171 ★ Mississippi Department of
Mental Health
Alcohol and Drug Abuse Division
1101 Robert E. Lee Bldg.
Jackson, MS 39201
Phone: (601)359-1288
Fax: (601)359-6295

★ 12172 ★ Missouri Department of Mental
Health
Alcohol and Drug Abuse Division
1706 E. Elm St.
PO Box 687
Jefferson City, MO 65102
Phone: (314)751-4942
Fax: (314)751-8224

★ 12173 ★ Montana Department of Health
Environmental Sciences
Alcohol and Drug Abuse Division
Cogswell Bldg.
PO Box 200901
Helena, MT 59620-0901
Phone: (406)444-4927

★ 12174 ★ Nebraska Department of Public
Institutions
Alcoholism and Drug Abuse Division
PO Box 94728
Lincoln, NE 68509-4728
Phone: (402)471-2851
Fax: (402)479-5145

★ 12175 ★ Nevada Department of
Employment Training and Rehabilitation
Rehabilitation Division
Alcohol and Drug Abuse Bureau
500 E. 3rd St
Carson City, NV 89710
Phone: (702)687-4790
Fax: (702)687-8351

★ 12176 ★ New Hampshire Department of
Health and Human Services
Alcohol and Drug Abuse Prevention Office
6 Hazen Dr.
Concord, NH 03301
Phone: (603)271-6100
Fax: (603)271-4232

★ 12177 ★ New Jersey Department of
Health
Alcholism and Addiction Services Division
129 E. Hanover St., CN 362
Trenton, NJ 08625-0362
Phone: (609)292-5760
Fax: (609)292-3816

★ 12178 ★ New Mexico Department of
Health
Behavioral Health Services Division
1190 St. Francis Dr.
PO Box 26110
Santa Fe, NM 87502-6110
Phone: (505)827-2601
Fax: (505)827-0097

★ 12179 ★ New York State Office of
Alcohol and Substance Abuse Services
1450 Western Ave.
Albany, NY 12203-8200
Phone: (518)457-2061
Fax: (518)457-5474

★ 12180 ★ North Carolina Department of
Human Resources
Mental Health, Developmental Disabilities
and Substance Abuse Services Division
PO Box 29526
Raleigh, NC 27626-0526
Phone: (919)733-7011
Fax: (919)715-4645

★ 12181 ★ North Dakota Department of
Human Services
Alcoholism and Drug Abuse Division
600 E. Boulevard Ave.
State Capitol
Bismarck, ND 58505
Phone: (701)328-2769
Fax: (701)328-2359

★ 12182 ★ Ohio Department of Alcohol and
Drug Addiction Services
280 N. High St.
Columbus, OH 43215-2537
Phone: (614)466-3445
Fax: (614)752-8645

★ 12183 ★ Oklahoma Department of Mental
Health
Substance Abuse Division
PO Box 53277
Oklahoma City, OK 73152-3277
Phone: (405)522-3908
Fax: (405)522-3650

★ 12184 ★ Oregon Department of Human
Resources
Alcohol and Drug Abuse Programs Office
500 Summer St. NE, 3rd Fl.
Salem, OR 97310-1016
Phone: (503)945-5763
Fax: (503)378-8467

★ 12185 ★ Pennsylvania Department of
Health
Drug and Alcohol Programs Office
Box 90
Harrisburg, PA 17108
Phone: (717)783-8200
Fax: (717)772-6959

★ 12186 ★ Rhode Island Department of
Substance Abuse
Access Rd.
PO Box 20363
Cranston, RI 02920
Phone: (401)464-2091
Fax: (401)464-2089

★ 12187 ★ South Carolina Department of
Alcohol and Other Drug Abuse Services
3700 Forest Dr., Ste. 300
Columbia, SC 29204
Phone: (803)734-9520
Fax: (803)734-9663

★ 12188 ★ South Dakota Department of
Human Services
Alcohol and Drug Abuse Division
E. Hwy. 344
Pierre, SD 57501
Phone: (605)773-4828
Fax: (605)773-5483

★ 12189 ★ Tennessee Department of
Health
Alcohol and Drug Abuse Services Bureau
312 8th Ave. N, 12th Fl.
Nashville, TN 37247-0101
Phone: (615)741-1921
Fax: (615)532-2286

★ 12190 ★ Texas Commission on Alcohol
and Drug Abuse
710 Brazos
Austin, TX 78701-2576
Phone: (512)867-8700
Fax: (512)867-8181

★ 12191 ★ Utah Department of Human
Services
Substance Abuse Division
PO Box 45500
Salt Lake City, UT 84145
Phone: (801)538-3938
Fax: (801)538-4016

★ 12192 ★ Vermont Agency of Human
Services
Alcohol and Drug Abuse Programs Office
State Complex
103 S. Main St.
Waterbury, VT 05671-0204
Phone: (802)241-2175
Fax: (802)241-2979

★ 12193 ★ Virginia Office of Health and
Human Resources
Mental Health, Retardation and Substance
Abuse Services Department
Substance Abuse Services Division
PO Box 1797
Richmond, VA 23214
Phone: (804)786-3906
Fax: (804)371-6638

★ 12194 ★ Washington Department of
Social and Health Services
Health and Rehabilitative Services Office
Alcohol and Substance Abuse Division
PO Box 45060
Olympia, WA 98504-5060
Phone: (360)438-8200
Fax: (360)586-5874

★ 12195 ★ West Virginia Department of
Health and Human Resources
Human Resources Bureau
Behavioral Health Services Office
Alcoholism and Drug Abuse Division
State Capitol Complex, Bldg. 6, Rm. 617
Charleston, WV 25305
Phone: (304)558-2276
Fax: (304)558-1008

★ 12196 ★   Wisconsin Department of Health and Social Services
Community Services Division
Substance Abuse Bureau
PO Box 7850
Madison, WI 53707-7850
Phone: (608)266-3719
Fax: (608)266-2579

★ 12197 ★   Wyoming Department of Health
Behavioral Health Division
Substance Abuse Program
446 Hathaway Bldg.
Cheyenne, WY 82002-0710
Phone: (307)777-7094
Fax: (307)777-5580

Chapter 64
Surgery

Foundations & Other Funding Organizations

Other Funding Organizations

American Association of Neurological Surgeons
See: Entry 8124

American Association of Oral and Maxillofacial Surgeons
See: Entry 3782

★ 12198 ★ **American Foundation for Surgery of the Hand**
6060 Greenwood Plaza Blvd., No. 100
Englewood, CO 80111-4801
Phone: (303)755-4588
Gail M. Gorman, Exec. Dir.

Description: Awards grants to medical, educational, research, and public education programs related to the field of hand surgery.

★ 12199 ★ **International College of Surgeons**
1516 N. Lake Shore Dr.
Chicago, IL 60610
Phone: (312)642-3555
Fax: (312)787-1624
Elisabeth Braam, Exec. Dir.

Description: Offers grants, scholarships, and loans for residencies and research, and to individuals for advanced study in surgery.

★ 12200 ★ **Plastic Surgery Educational Foundation**
444 E. Algonquin Rd.
Arlington Heights, IL 60005
Phone: (708)228-9900
Fax: (708)228-9131
Dave Fellers, Exec. Dir.

Description: Provides research grants to plastic surgeons and plastic surgery residents in training; and awards scholarships in basic science, clinical research, and senior categories.

National & International Organizations

Academy of Ambulatory Foot Surgery (AAFS)
See: Entry 10754

★ 12201 ★ **Accreditation Review Committee on Education in Surgical Technology (ARC-ST)**
c/o William J. Teutsch
7108-C S. Alton Way
Englewood, CO 80112-2106
Phone: (303)694-9262
Fax: (303)694-9169
William J. Teutsch, Exec.Dir.

Founded: 1974. **Description:** Reviews accreditation applications of surgical techology programs in hospitals, community colleges, technical schools, and universities and makes recommendations to the Commission on Accreditation of Allied Health Education Programs. Collaborates with American College of Surgeons, American Hospital Association, and the Association of Surgical Technologists. **Publications:** *Surgical Technology: A Growing Career*. Brochure. Contains information on careers in surgical technology, educational requirements, and a list of accredited programs. *Price:* Free (first copy); $1/each additional copy. **Formerly:** (1987) Joint Review Committee on Education for the Surgical Technologist; (1990) Accreditation Review Committee for Educational Programs in Surgical Technology.

★ 12202 ★ **American Academy of Cosmetic Surgery (AACS)**
401 N. Michigan Ave.
Chicago, IL 60611-4212
Phone: (312)527-6713
Fax: (312)644-1815
Jeffrey P. Knezovich, Exec.Dir.

Founded: 1985. **Members:** 1,250. **Description:** Licensed cosmetic surgeons. Seeks to encourage high-quality cosmetic medical and dental care; provides continuing education for cosmetic surgeons; promotes research. Compiles statistics. Operates American Board of Cosmetic Surgery. Maintains hall of fame and speakers'

bureau. **Publications:** *American Journal of Cosmetic Surgery*, quarterly. Journal. • *Membership Roster*, annual. Membership Directory. • Newsletter, quarterly.

★ 12203 ★ **American Academy of Facial Plastic and Reconstructive Surgery (AAFPRS)**
1110 Vermont Ave. NW, Ste. 220
Washington, DC 20005
Phone: (202)842-4500
Fax: (202)371-1514
Stephen C. Duffy, Exec. Officer

Founded: 1964. **Members:** 2,900. **Description:** Physicians specializing in facial plastic surgery. Promotes research and study in the field. Maintains speakers' bureau. Conducts educational and charitable programs; compiles statistics. **Publications:** Brochures. • *The Face Book: The Pros and Cons of Facial Plastic Surgery*. • *Face Facts*, quarterly. • *Facial Plastic Surgery Today*, quarterly. • *Facial Plastic Times*, monthly. Newsletter. Includes calendar of events and book reviews. *Price:* Available to members only. • *Membership Directory*, annual. Includes buyers' guide. *Price:* $35/copy for members; $75/copy for nonmember physicians; $300/copy for others. • Monographs. • *The Teen Face Book*. • Videos.

★ 12204 ★ **American Academy of Neurological and Orthopaedic Surgeons (FAANaOS)**
c/o Bartholomew A. Sinatra, M.D.
522 Rossmore Dr.
Las Vegas, NV 89110-4123
Phone: (702)452-9538
Fax: (702)452-1031
Bartholomew A. Sinatra, M.D., Chm.

Founded: 1977. **Members:** 1,100. **Description:** Neurological and orthopaedic surgeons, neurologists, physiatrists, and professionals in allied medical or surgical specialties. Provides and encourages information about and understanding of neurological and orthopaedic medicine and surgery, a branch of medicine that deals with diseases and injuries to the human neuromusculo-skeletal system; seeks to improve patient care. Maintains American Board of Neurological and Orthopaedic Medicine and Surgery and American Board for Medical-Legal Analysis in Medicine and Surgery. Sponsors charitable program. Maintains a complete collection of recordings of scientific meetings since 1977. Operates 40 colleges of experts in individual disciplines related to neurological and orthopaedic medicine and surgery. Acronym stands for Fellowship of the American Academy of Neurological and Orthopaedic Surgeons. **Publications:** *American Academy of Neurological and Orthopaedic Surgeons--Directory*, biennial. Directory. • *Journal of Neurological and Orthopaedic Surgery*, quarterly. Journal. *Price:* $30/year.

★ 12205 ★ **American Academy of**
Neurological Surgery
2128 Taubman
University Hospital
Ann Arbor, MI 48109
Phone: (313)936-5015
Fax: (313)936-9294
Dr. Julian Hoff, Sec.

Founded: 1938. **Members:** 168. **Description:** Leaders in the field of neurological surgery united for neurosurgical education.

★ 12206 ★ **American Academy of**
Orthopaedic Surgeons (AAOS)
6300 N. River Rd.
Rosemont, IL 60018-4226
Phone: (708)823-7186
Free: 800-346-AAOS
Fax: (708)823-8125
Dr. William Tipton, Exec.VP

Founded: 1933. **Members:** 15,100. **Description:** Professional society of orthopedic surgeons certified by the American Board of Orthopedic Surgery to practice orthopedic (bone and joint) surgery. **Publications:** Bulletin, quarterly.

★ 12207 ★ **American Academy of**
Otolaryngology - Head and Neck
Surgery (AAO-HNS)
1 Prince St.
Alexandria, VA 22314
Phone: (703)836-4444
Fax: (703)683-5100
Dr. Michael Maves, Exec.VP

Founded: 1982. **Members:** 10,000. **Description:** Professional society of medical doctors specializing in otolaryngology (diseases of the ear, nose, and throat) and head and neck surgery. Represents otolaryngology in governmental and socioeconomic areas and provides high-quality medical education for otolaryngologists. Coordinates Combined Otolaryngological Spring Meetings for nine national otolaryngological societies. Operates job information exchange service and museum. **Publications:** *American Academy of Otolaryngology-Head and Neck Surgery--Bulletin*, monthly. Magazine. Includes academy news, calendar of events, employment opportunity listings, legislative news, and research updates. *Price:* Included in membership dues; $55/year for nonmembers. • *Conjoint Directory of the American Academy of Otolaryngology - Head and Neck Surgery*, semiannual. Directory. • Monographs. • *Otolaryngology - Head and Neck Surgery*, monthly. Journal. *Price:* Included in membership dues; $93/year for domestic nonmembers; $158/year for domestic institutions. • Videos.

★ 12208 ★ **American Academy of Spinal**
Surgeons (AASS)
522 Rossmore Dr.
Las Vegas, NV 89110-4123
Phone: (702)452-9538
Fax: (702)452-1031
Bartholomew A. Sinatra, M.D., Chm.

Founded: 1982. **Members:** 600. **Description:** Physicians specializing in spinal surgery. Promotes scientific and educational advancement in the field. Conducts charitable activities.

★ 12209 ★ **American Association for**
Accreditation of Ambulatory Surgery
Facilities (AAAASF)
1202 Allanson Rd.
Mundelein, IL 60060
Phone: (708)949-6058
Fax: (708)566-4580
Gustavo A. Colon, M.D., Pres.

Founded: 1981. **Members:** 400. **Description:** Board-certified surgeon-operated ambulatory surgical facilities. To maintain high standards through adherence to a voluntary program of inspection and accreditation of ambulatory surgery facilities. **Publications:** Newsletter, semiannual. **Formerly:** (1994) American Association for Accreditation of Ambulatory Plastic Surgery Facilities.

★ 12210 ★ **American Association of**
Genito-Urinary Surgeons (AAGUS)
Baylor College of Medicine
6560 Fannin, Ste. 1002
Houston, TX 77030
Phone: (713)798-4001
C. Eugene Carlton, Jr., M, Sec.-Treas.

Founded: 1886. **Members:** 180. **Description:** Professional society of physicians specializing in genito-urinary surgery. Bestows Keyes and Barringer medals.

★ 12211 ★ **American Association for Hand**
Surgery (AAHS)
444 E. Algonquin Rd.
Arlington Heights, IL 60005
Phone: (708)228-9758
Fax: (708)228-8509
Laura D. Hornauer, Contact

Founded: 1970. **Members:** 1,060. **Description:** Plastic, orthopedic, and general surgeons having a specific interest in hand surgery; individuals in the medical profession, basic sciences, or allied services interested in the improvement of hand surgery. Purpose is to advance hand surgery. Conducts symposia; offers specialized education. **Publications:** *Annual Program*. • *Hand Surgery Newsletter*, quarterly. Newsletter. *Price:* Included in membership dues.

★ 12212 ★ **American Association of**
Neurological Surgeons (AANS)
22 S. Washington St., Ste. 100
Park Ridge, IL 60068
Phone: (708)692-9500
Fax: (708)692-2589
Carl H. Hauber, Exec.Dir.

Founded: 1931. **Members:** 3,904. **Description:** Neurological surgeons united to promote excellence in neurological surgery and its relat-

ed sciences. Provides funding to foster research in the neurosciences. Conducts specialized education. **Publications:** *American Association of Neurological Surgeons Bulletin*, quarterly. Bulletin. *Price:* Included in membership dues. • Books. • Catalog. Lists publications. • *Directory of Neurological Surgery*, annual. Directory. *Price:* $50 for members. • *Journal of Neurosurgery*, monthly. Journal. *Price:* $100/year for members; $110/year for nonmembers; $60/year for residents. • *Neurosurgical Topics*, quarterly. Books. *Price:* $80 for members; $90 for nonmembers; $70 for residents. • *Self-Assessment in Neurological Surgery*, triennial. Booklet. Contains multiple choice and patient management tests. *Price:* $175/copy for members; $225/copy for nonmembers; $145 for residents. **Formerly:** (1966) Harvey Cushing Society.

American Association of Oral and
Maxillofacial Surgeons (AAOMS)
See: Entry 3877

★ 12213 ★ **American Association of Plastic**
Surgeons (AAPS)
c/o Stephen H. Miller, M.D.
10666 N. Torrey Pines Rd.
La Jolla, CA 92037
Phone: (619)554-9940
Fax: (619)554-3209
Stephen H. Miller, M.D., Pres.

Founded: 1921. **Members:** 425. **Description:** Professional society of plastic surgeons. **Formerly:** (1942) American Association of Oral and Plastic Surgeons.

★ 12214 ★ **American Association of**
Surgeon Assistants (AASA)
1730 N. Lynn St., No. 502
Arlington, VA 22209
Phone: (703)525-1191
Fax: (703)276-8196
Richard A. Guggolz, Exec.Dir.

Founded: 1973. **Members:** 600. **Description:** Surgeon assistants, surgical physician assistants, students, and allied health professionals. Purposes are to promote academic and clinical excellence among members, to respond to the needs of surgical physician assistants and surgeon assistants, and to educate the medical community and the public about the role of surgical physician assistants and surgeon assistants in health care. **Publications:** *The Sutureline*, quarterly. Newsletter. *Price:* Included in membership dues. **Formerly:** (1990) American Association of Surgeon's Assistants.

★ 12215 ★ **American Association for**
Thoracic Surgery (AATS)
13 Elm St.
PO Box 1565
Manchester, MA 01944
Phone: (508)526-8330
Fax: (508)526-4018
William T. Maloney, Exec.Sec.

Founded: 1917. **Members:** 900. **Description:** Specialists in surgery of the chest region, including cardiovascular surgeons. Encourages investigation and study of intrathoracic physiology, pathology, and therapy. **Publications:** *Journal of Thoracic and Cardiovascular Surgery*, monthly. Journal. • Membership Directory, annual.

★12216★ **American Board of Abdominal Surgery (ABAS)**
675 Main St.
Melrose, MA 02176
Phone: (617)665-6101
Fax: (617)665-4127
Louis F. Alfano, M.D., Exec.Sec.

Founded: 1957. **Members:** 1,865. **Description:** Specialists in abdominal surgery. Improves the quality of graduate education for abdominal surgery. Establishes minimum educational and training standards for the specialty. Determines whether candidates have received adequate preparation as defined by the board. Provides comprehensive examinations to determine the ability and fitness of candidates. Certifies surgeons who have satisfied the requirements of the board as a protection to the public and the profession. Gives oral and written examinations in abdominal surgery.

★12217★ **American Board of Colon and Rectal Surgery (ABCRS)**
20600 Eureka Rd., Ste. 713
Taylor, MI 48180
Phone: (313)282-9400
Fax: (313)282-9402
Herand Abcarian, M.D., Exec.Dir.

Founded: 1934. **Description:** Certification board established to investigate qualifications, administer examinations, and provide certification as diplomates for medical doctors specializing in colon and rectal surgery. **Publications:** *American Board of Colon and Rectal Surgery--Newsletter to Diplomates*, annual. Newsletter. Includes research updates. *Price:* Included in membership dues. **Formerly:** American Board of Proctology.

American Board of Dental Medicine and Surgery (ABDMS)
See: Entry 3881

★12218★ **American Board of Hand Surgery (ABHS)**
522 Rossmore Dr.
Las Vegas, NV 89110-4123
Phone: (702)452-9538
Fax: (702)452-1031
Bartholomew A. Sinatra, M.D., Chm.

Members: 500. **Description:** Hand surgeons dedicated to advancing scientific knowledge and providing educational opportunities in the field. Conducts charitable activities.

★12219★ **American Board of Neurological Microsurgery (ABNM)**
522 Rossmore Dr.
Las Vegas, NV 89110-4123
Phone: (702)452-1031
Fax: (702)452-9538
Bartholomew A. Sinatra, M.D., Chm.

Members: 175. **Description:** Neurological microsurgery specialists. Promotes scientific advancement and provides educational courses in the field of neurological microsurgery. Conducts charitable activities.

★12220★ **American Board of Neurological / Orthopaedic Laser Surgery (ABNOLS)**
522 Rossmore Dr.
Las Vegas, NV 89110-4123
Phone: (702)452-9538
Fax: (702)452-1031
Bartholomew A. Sinatra, M.D., Chm.

Members: 150. **Description:** Laser surgeons united to advance scientific knowledge and provide educational opportunities in the field. Conducts charitable activities. **Formerly:** (1991) American Board of Laser Surgery.

★12221★ **American Board of Neurological and Orthopaedic Medicine and Surgery (ABNOMS)**
c/o Bartholomew A. Sinatra
522 Rossmore Dr.
Las Vegas, NV 89110-4123
Phone: (702)452-9538
Fax: (702)452-1031
Bartholomew A. Sinatra, M.D., Chm.

Founded: 1977. **Description:** Individuals proficient in neurological and orthopaedic medicine and surgery who have previous board certification and proper preceptorship and have made significant contributions to the field. Objective is to demonstrate expertise and capability in the field of neurological and orthopaedic medicine and surgery through written and oral certification examinations. Conducts research and educational programs on neuromusculoskeletal disorders of the limbs and spine. Maintains hall of fame. Operates charitable program and placement service. **Publications:** *American Board of Neurological and Orthopedic Medicine and Surgery Journal*, quarterly. Journal. Includes annual membership directory. *Price:* $30/year.

★12222★ **American Board of Neurological Surgery (ABNS)**
6550 Fannin St., No. 2139
Houston, TX 77030-2722
Phone: (713)790-6015
Dr. Howard M. Eisenberg, Sec.-Treas.

Founded: 1940. **Description:** Certification board to investigate qualifications of, administer examinations to, and certify as diplomates medical doctors specializing in neurological surgery. Works to stimulate development of adequate training facilities and aids in evaluating residencies under consideration by the Accreditation Council on Graduate Medical Education of the American Medical Association. **Publications:** *Newsletter to Diplomates*, annual. Newsletter.

★12223★ **American Board of Oral and Maxillofacial Surgery (ABOMS)**
625 N. Michigan Ave., Ste. 1820
Chicago, IL 60611
Phone: (312)642-0070
Sheryl Mouts, Sec.

Founded: 1946. **Members:** 3,580. **Description:** Certification board to establish qualifications, conduct examinations, and certify surgeons whom the board finds qualified to practice oral and maxillofacial medicine, including diagnostic, surgical, and adjunctive treatment of the diseases, injuries, and defects of the oral and maxillofacial regions. **Formerly:** (1978) American Board of Oral Surgery.

★12224★ **American Board of Orthopaedic Microneurosurgery (ABOM)**
522 Rossmore Dr.
Las Vegas, NV 89110-4123
Phone: (702)452-9538
Fax: (702)452-1031
Bartholomew A. Sinatra, M.D., Chm.

Founded: 1984. **Members:** 100. **Description:** Orthopaedic microneurosurgeons. Seeks to advance scientific knowledge and provide educational opportunities in the field of orthopaedic microneurosurgery. Conducts charitable activities.

★12225★ **American Board of Orthopaedic Surgery (ABOS)**
400 Silver Cedar Ct.
Chapel Hill, NC 27514
Phone: (919)929-7103
Fax: (919)942-8988
G. Paul DeRosa, M.D., Exec.Dir.

Founded: 1934. **Members:** 12. **Description:** Certification board to establish qualifications, conduct annual examinations, and certify as diplomates those whom the board finds qualified to practice orthopaedic surgery. **Publications:** *Directory of Diplomates*, annual. Directory. *Price:* $25, plus shipping and handling.

★12226★ **American Board of Plastic Surgery (ABPS)**
7 Penn Center, Ste. 400
1635 Market St.
Philadelphia, PA 19103
Phone: (215)587-9322
Gilbert P. Gradinger, M.D., Contact

Founded: 1937. **Description:** Certification board established to investigate the qualifications of, administer examinations to, and certify as diplomates medical doctors specializing in general plastic surgery.

American Board of Podiatric Surgery (ABPS)
See: Entry 10759

★12227★ **American Board of Spinal Surgery (ABSS)**
522 Rossmore Dr.
Las Vegas, NV 89110-4123
Phone: (702)452-9538
Fax: (702)452-1031
Bartholomew A. Sinatra, M.D., Chm.

Founded: 1977. **Members:** 450. **Description:** Spinal surgeons seeking to advance knowledge and provide education in the field of spinal surgery. Conducts charitable, education, and research programs; maintains hall of fame; offers placement service; compiles statistics; maintains speakers' bureau. **Publications:** *Journal of Neurological and Orthopaedic Surgery*, quarterly. Journal. *Price:* $99/year.

★12228★ **American Board of Surgery (ABS)**
1617 John F. Kennedy Blvd., Ste. 860
Philadelphia, PA 19103
Phone: (215)568-4000
Fax: (215)563-5718
Dr. Wallace P. Ritchie, Jr., Exec.Dir.

Founded: 1937. **Members:** 29. **Description:** Examining and certifying board in general surgery; also certifies Special Qualifications in Pediatric Surgery, General Vascular Surgery and Added Qualifications in General Vascular Surgery, Surgical Critical Care, and Hand Surgery. Membership is drawn from 21 national and regional surgical and specialty societies and organizations. Currently offers Recertification in General Surgery, Pediatric Surgery, General Vascular Surgery, and Surgical Critical Care. **Publications:** *ABMS Directories of Certified Specialists.* Directory. • *Directory of Medical Specialists.* • *Service Booklets of Information,* annual.

★ 12229 ★ American Board of Thoracic Neurological Orthopaedic Medicine and Surgery (ABTNOMS)
522 Rossmore Dr.
Las Vegas, NV 89110-4123
Phone: (702)452-9538
Fax: (702)452-1031
Bartholomew A. Sinatra, M.D., Chm.

Founded: 1984. **Members:** 80. **Description:** Physicians specializing in thoracic neurological orthopedic medicine and surgery. Works to advance scientific knowledge and provide educational opportunities in the field. Conducts charitable activities.

★ 12230 ★ American College of Cryosurgery (ACCRYO)
PO Box 4014
Schaumburg, IL 60168-4014
Fax: (708)350-0050
Bobby Limmer, M.D., Pres.

Founded: 1977. **Members:** 336. **Description:** Physicians, general surgeons, surgical specialists, scientists, and veterinarians involved in the clinical application of cryosurgery (surgery in which the tissue to be dissected is frozen). Promotes knowledge in clinical cryosurgery and the use of instrumentation for the destruction of unwanted tissue. Conducts specialized education and research programs; maintains biographical archives. Serves as a national faculty to educate members and teach at university training centers. Established the Foundation for the Advancement of Cryosurgery in 1979.

★ 12231 ★ American College of Foot and Ankle Surgeons (ACFAS)
444 N. Northwest Hwy., Ste. 150
Park Ridge, IL 60068
Phone: (708)292-2237
Fax: (708)292-2022
Cheryl Beversdorf, Exec.Dir.

Founded: 1940. **Members:** 4,000. **Description:** Objectives are to: promote and disseminate information on podiatric surgery among the public, podiatric surgeons, and other health professionals; encourage and publish research findings and related literature; provide intensive programs for clinical and experimental research to improve podiatric surgery. **Publications:** *American College of Foot and Ankle Surgeons--Newsletter,* quarterly. Newsletter. *Price:* Included in membership dues. • *Complications in Foot and Ankle Surgery.* • *Journal of Foot and Ankle Surgery,* bimonthly. Journal. Includes book reviews and journal abstracts. *Price:* Included in membership dues; $73/year for nonmember individuals; $97/year for nonmember institutions.

• *Membership Roster,* annual. Membership Directory. **Formerly:** (1993) American College of Foot Surgeons.

American College of MOHS Micrographic Surgery and Cutaneous Oncology (ACMMSCO)
See: Entry 5911

★ 12232 ★ American College of Oral and Maxillofacial Surgeons (ACOMS)
c/o James E. Bauerle, D.D.S., M.S.
1100 NW Loop 410, Ste. 520
San Antonio, TX 78213-2266
Phone: (210)344-5674
Free: 800-522-6676
Fax: (210)344-9754
James E. Bauerle, D.D.S., Sec.-Treas.

Founded: 1975. **Members:** 1,700. **Description:** Diplomates of the American Board of Oral and Maxillofacial Surgery who practice oral and maxillofacial surgery. To advance the integrity of the profession through continuing education, exchange of ideas, certification procedures, and cooperation with allied groups. **Publications:** *ACOMS Review,* quarterly. **Formerly:** (1975) Association of Diplomates of the American Board of Oral Surgery.

American College of Osteopathic Surgeons (ACOS)
See: Entry 9978

★ 12233 ★ American College of Surgeons (ACS)
55 E. Erie St.
Chicago, IL 60611
Phone: (312)664-4050
Fax: (312)440-7014
Paul A. Ebert, M.D., Dir.

Founded: 1913. **Members:** 54,000. **Local Groups:** 67. **Description:** Professional association of surgeons worldwide organized primarily to improve the quality of care for surgical patients by elevating the standards of surgical education and practice. Conducts nationwide programs to improve emergency medical services and hospital cancer programs. Sponsors continuing education and self-assessment courses for surgeons in practice. **Publications:** *ACS Publications and Services Catalog,* annual. Catalog. Lists ASC publications. *Price:* Free. • *American College of Surgeons Yearbook,* triennial. Yearbook. Lists ACS fellows. *Price:* Free, for members only. • *Bulletin of the American College of Surgeons,* monthly. Bulletin. Includes ACS and Washington news. *Price:* Included in membership dues. • *Journal of the American College of Surgeons,* monthly. Journal. Includes The Surgeon at Work Section, collective literature reviews, and book reviews. *Price:* $60/year for individuals; $70/year for institutions; $30/year for medical residents and students. • *Resources for Optimal Care of the Injured Patient. Price:* $12. • *Scientific American Surgery. Price:* $247.50. • *Socio-Economic Factbook for Surgery,* annual. Provides information on socioeconomic and legislative issues affecting the field. Lists statistics on charts and graphs. *Price:* $5/issue. • *Surgical Forum,* annual. Abstracts of research papers presented during clinical congress. *Price:* $20/issue.

American College of Veterinary Surgeons (ACVS)
See: Entry 13051

★ 12234 ★ American Shoulder and Elbow Surgeons (ASES)
6300 N. River Rd., Ste. 727
Rosemont, IL 60018-4226
Phone: (708)698-1629
Fax: (708)823-0536
Karen Jared, Mgr.

Founded: 1984. **Members:** 85. **Description:** Orthopedic surgeons. Purpose is to promote the exchange and dissemination of information on shoulder and elbow surgery and treatment. Sponsors educational courses.

★ 12235 ★ American Society of Abdominal Surgeons (ASAS)
675 Main St.
Melrose, MA 02176
Phone: (617)665-6102
Fax: (617)665-4127
Louis F. Alfano, M.D., Exec.Sec.

Founded: 1959. **Members:** 9,300. **Description:** Medical doctors specializing in abdominal surgery. Sponsors extensive program of surgical education including study courses, postgraduate programs, lectures, and demonstrations. **Publications:** *Abdominal Surgery,* monthly. Journal. *Price:* Available to members only. • Books. • *The Surgeon,* bimonthly. Newsletter. Includes calendar of events. *Price:* Available to members only.

★ 12236 ★ American Society for Aesthetic Plastic Surgery (ASAPS)
3922 Atlantic Ave.
Long Beach, CA 90807
Phone: (310)595-4275
Fax: (310)427-2234
Robert G. Stanton, Exec.Dir.

Founded: 1967. **Members:** 1,052. **Description:** Board-certified plastic surgeons. Provides continuing education to members in the area of aesthetic plastic surgery, through presentation of papers, study sessions, and scientific sessions. Operates grant program. Provides speakers; conducts research programs. **Publications:** *Aesthetic Surgery,* 3/year. Newsletter. Reviews developments in the field and research results; includes society news. *Price:* Included in membership dues.

★ 12237 ★ American Society of Colon and Rectal Surgeons (ASCRS)
85 W. Algonquin Rd., Ste. 550
Arlington Heights, IL 60005
Phone: (708)290-9184
Fax: (708)290-9203
James R. Slawny, Exec.Dir.

Founded: 1899. **Members:** 1,600. **Regional Groups:** 19. **Description:** Professional society of surgeons specializing in the diagnosis and treatment of diseases of the colon, rectum, and anus. Offers placement service; conducts research programs. **Publications:** *Diseases of the Colon and Rectum,* monthly. Journal. *Price:* $112 U.S. individual; $168 institution.

★ 12238 ★ **American Society for
Dermatologic Surgery (ASDS)**
PO Box 4014
Schaumburg, IL 60173
Phone: (708)330-0230
Fax: (708)330-0050
Bradford Calixton, Exec.Dir.

Founded: 1970. **Members:** 2,157. **Description:** Physicians specializing in dermatologic surgery. Purpose is to maintain the highest possible standards in medical education, clinical practice, and patient care. Seeks to promote high standards in allied health professions and services as they relate to dermatology. Maintains audiovisual library. **Publications:** *Journal of Dermatologic Surgery and Oncology*, monthly. Journal. • *Roster*, annual.

★ 12239 ★ **American Society for Head and
Neck Surgery (ASHNS)**
John Hopkins Hospital
Carnegie Bldg., Rm. 466
PO Box 41402
Baltimore, MD 21203
Phone: (410)955-3669
Fax: (410)955-0035
Dr. Charles Cummings, Sec.

Founded: 1959. **Members:** 600. **Description:** Otolaryngologists and others of the American College of Surgeons whose primary interest is head and neck surgery. To advance knowledge relevant to surgical treatment of diseases of the head and neck, including reconstruction and rehabilitation. Promotes development of programs of training in head and neck surgery. **Publications:** *Archives of Otolaryngology*, annual.

★ 12240 ★ **American Society for Laser
Medicine and Surgery (ASLMS)**
2404 Stewart Sq.
Wausau, WI 54401
Phone: (715)845-9283
Fax: (715)848-2493
Ellet H. Drake, Sec.

Founded: 1980. **Members:** 1,902. **Description:** Physicians, physicists, and other scientists; nurses, dentists, podiatrists, veterinarians, and other paramedical personnel; technicians and commercial representatives concerned with the medical applications of lasers. Facilitates exchange of information concerning lasers. **Publications:** *Lasers in Surgery and Medicine*, bimonthly. Journal. *Price:* Included in membership dues. • *Official ASLMS Newsletter*, periodic. Newsletter.

★ 12241 ★ **American Society of Lipo-
Suction Surgery (ASLSS)**
401 N. Michigan Ave.
Chicago, IL 60611-4212
Phone: (312)527-6713
Jeffery Knezozich, Exec.Dir.

Founded: 1982. **Members:** 650. **Description:** Surgeons specializing in dermatology, general surgery, gynecology, otolaryngology, plastic and reconstructive surgery, and cosmetic surgery. Trains surgeons in the art and methods of lipo-suction surgery. (Lipo-suction surgery is a procedure wherein fatty tissue is removed from the body by suction. It is not meant to reduce weight but to adjust body contours. Lipo-suction surgery is not currently part of the ordinary medical school curriculum.) Conducts workshops and seminars. **Publications:** *American Journal of Cosmetic Surgery*, quarterly. Journal. • *Membership Roster*, annual. Membership Directory. • Newsletter, quarterly.

★ 12242 ★ **American Society of
Maxillofacial Surgeons (ASMS)**
444 E. Algonquin Rd.
Arlington Heights, IL 60005
Phone: (708)228-9900
Fax: (708)228-6509
Douglas K. Ousterhout, DDS MD, Pres.

Founded: 1947. **Members:** 385. **Description:** Professional society of doctors of medicine and doctors of dental surgery who have at least five years of recognized graduate training and experience in maxillofacial surgery. Seeks to stimulate and advance knowledge of the science and art of maxillofacial surgery and improve and elevate the standard of practice.

★ 12243 ★ **American Society of Outpatient
Surgeons (ASOS)**
401 N. Michigan Ave.
Chicago, IL 60611-4267
Free: 800-237-3768
Pat Curl, Exec.Dir.

Founded: 1978. **Members:** 400. **Description:** Surgeons with various specialties who practice surgery in an office-based setting; anesthesiologists. Seeks to provide improved surgical care at lower costs and further education of surgeons. Makes patients and insurers aware of the benefits of office-based surgery. Conducts surveys and prepares statistical reports. Conducts seminars on office-based surgery. **Publications:** Membership Directory, annual. • *Monitor*, quarterly. Newsletter. **Formerly:** (1986) Society for Office-Based Surgery.

**American Society for Pediatric
Neurosurgery (ASPN)**
See: Entry 3174

★ 12244 ★ **American Society of Plastic and
Reconstructive Surgeons (ASPRS)**
444 E. Algonquin Rd.
Arlington Heights, IL 60005
Phone: (708)228-9900
Fax: (708)228-9131
Dave Fellers, Exec.Dir.

Founded: 1931. **Members:** 5,000. **Regional Groups:** 61. **Description:** Professional society of plastic surgeons. Works in cooperation with the Plastic Surgery Educational Foundation to promote optimal care for plastic surgery patients through research, service, and education activities. Sponsors public/patient education program, clinical symposia, and professional development workshops. Acts as a liaison between members and government and medical organizations. Conducts charitable activities; maintains speakers' bureau; compiles statistics. **Publications:** *American Society of Plastic and Reconstructive Surgeons Combined Roster*, annual. • *Journal of Plastic and Reconstructive Surgery*, monthly. Journal. Includes research reports and book reviews. *Price:* Free to members; $110 for nonmembers. • *Plastic Surgery News*, monthly. Tabloid including information on employment opportunities and current events. *Price:* Free to members; $75 for nonmembers.

**American Society of Plastic and
Reconstructive Surgical Nurses
(ASPRSN)**
See: Entry 9067

★ 12245 ★ **American Society for
Stereotactic and Functional
Neurosurgery (ASSFN)**
c/o Philip L. Gildenberg, M.D.
6560 Fannin, Ste. 1530
Houston, TX 77030
Phone: (713)790-0795
Fax: (713)669-0388
Philip L. Gildenberg, M.D., Sec.-Treas.

Founded: 1968. **Members:** 300. **Description:** Neurosurgeons practicing stereotactic surgery united to promote communication in the field. (Stereotactic surgery utilizes a technique for inserting delicate instruments in precise areas of the nervous system.) Compiles statistics. Plans to establish museum. **Publications:** *Stereotactic and Functional Neurosurgery*, bimonthly. Journal. **Formerly:** (1972) International Society for Research in Stereoencephalotomy, American Branch.

★ 12246 ★ **American Society for Surgery of
the Hand (ASSH)**
6060 Greenwood Plaza Blvd., No. 100
Englewood, CO 80111-4801
Phone: (303)771-9236
Fax: (303)771-9269
Gail M. Gorman, Exec.Dir.

Founded: 1946. **Members:** 1,350. **Description:** Surgeons specializing in surgery of the hand. Promotes contributions and funds research in the field of hand surgery. Sponsors educational programs. Maintains museum and practice opportunities exchange. **Publications:** *Ethical Billing Practices for Hand Surgery.* Booklet. • *Global Service Information for Hand Surgery.* Manual. • *The Hand--Examination and Diagnosis.* • *The Hand--Primary Care of Common Problems.* • *Hand Surgery Update.* Book. • *Journal of Hand Surgery*, bimonthly. Journal. • *Patient Education Brochures.* Brochures. Series of 12 brochures with information for patients. • *Self-Assessment Examinations in Hand Surgery*, biennial.

★ 12247 ★ **American Society of Transplant
Surgeons (ASTS)**
716 Lee St.
Des Plaines, IL 60016
Phone: (708)824-5700
Fax: (708)824-0394
Janet H. Wright, Administrator

Founded: 1975. **Members:** 672. **Description:** Surgeons specializing in transplantation. Promotes and encourages education and research, especially in transplantation surgery; collaborates with public and private organizations; participates and assists in developing programs and coordinates efforts on projects that will benefit organ recipients. **Publications:** *Chimera*, quarterly. • *Transplantation*, monthly.

★ 12248 ★   American Surgical Association (ASA)
c/o George F. Sheldon, M.D.
University of North Carolina at Chapel Hill
136 Burnett-Womack
Box CB 7245
Chapel Hill, NC 27599-7245
Phone: (919)966-6320
Fax: (919)966-6009
George F. Sheldon, M.D., Sec.

Founded: 1880. **Members:** 949. **Description:** Surgeons organized to promote the science and art of surgery. Bestows medallion for scientific achievement. **Publications:** *Annals of Surgery,* monthly. • *Transactions,* annual.

★ 12249 ★   Arthroscopy Association of North America (AANA)
6300 N. River Rd.
Rosemont, IL 60018
Phone: (708)292-2262
Fax: (708)292-2268
Donald F. Reid, Exec.Dir.

Founded: 1982. **Members:** 1,150. **Description:** Orthopedic surgeons. To advance arthroscopy, a diagnostic or surgical procedure in which a thin tool, an arthroscope, is inserted into a joint. The surgeon can either look directly into the arthroscope or observe on a screen the view projected by the arthroscope. In this way the surgeon can diagnose a condition using only a small incision for insertion of the arthroscope. A tool used with the arthroscope also allows certain surgical procedures to be performed within viewing range of the scope. Sponsors research and continuing education programs. **Publications:** *AANA Membership Directory,* annual. Membership Directory. *Price:* Included in membership dues. • *Arthroscopy: A Patient's Guide.* • *Arthroscopy: The Journal of Arthroscopic and Related Surgery,* quarterly. Journal. *Price:* $170/year for individuals; $220/year for institutions. • *Inside AANA,* quarterly. Newsletter.

★ 12250 ★   Asian-Australasian Society of Neurological Surgeons (AASNS)
201 Wickham Terr.
Brisbane, QLD 4000, Australia
Phone: 7 8393393
Fax: 7 8322005
Dr. Leigh Atkinson, Sec.

Founded: 1964. **Members:** 5,000. **National Groups:** 16. **Languages:** English. **Description:** Neurosurgeons seeking to advance neurosurgical studies and promote understanding between members from different countries. Conducts educational programs; bestows awards. **Publications:** Newsletter, annual.

★ 12251 ★   Asian-Pacific Section - IPRS (APS-IPRS)
Department of Plastic Surgery
Singapore General Hospital
Singapore 0316, Singapore
Phone: 3214686
Dr. S.T. Lee, Gen.Sec.

Members: 1,200. **National Groups:** 13. **Languages:** English. **Description:** Plastic and reconstructive surgeons who are members of national societies of the International Confederation for Plastic and Reconstructive Surgery. Pro-

motes high standards of practice and continuing education for members. **Publications:** *Newsletter of the Asian Pacific Section,* semiannual. Newsletter.

★ 12252 ★   Asian Surgical Association (ASA)
Dept. of Surgery
Queen Mary Hospital
University of Hong Kong
Pokfulam Rd.
Hong Kong, Hong Kong
Phone: 8180232
Fax: 8181186
Dr. John Wong, Sec.Gen.

Founded: 1976. **Members:** 750. **Languages:** English. **Description:** Surgeons in 30 Asian countries. Seeks to improve standards of surgical care in the region. Promotes cooperation and information exchange among members. Maintains Hong Kong Surgical Trust Fund, which finances lecturers' travel expenses and provides for training fellowships. **Publications:** *Asian Journal of Surgery,* semiannual. Journal. Also publishes pamphlets. **Formerly:** (1988) Association of Surgeons of South East Asia.

★ 12253 ★   Association for Academic Surgery (AAS)
Box 242 UMHC
420 Delaware St. SE
Minneapolis, MN 55455
Phone: (612)626-1999
Fax: (612)625-8496
Dr. David Dunn, Pres.

Founded: 1966. **Members:** 2,400. **Description:** Active (1100) and senior (1300) surgeons with backgrounds in all surgical specialties in academic surgical centers at chief resident level or above. Encourages young surgeons to pursue careers in academic surgery; supports them in establishing themselves as investigators and educators by providing a forum in which senior surgical residents and junior faculty members may present papers on subjects of clinical or laboratory investigations; promotes interchange of ideas between senior surgical residents, junior faculty, and established academic surgeons; facilitates communication among academic surgeons in all surgical fields. Maintains placement service. **Publications:** *Journal of Surgical Research,* monthly. Journal. *Price:* Included in membership dues.

Association of Operating Room Nurses (AORN)
See: Entry 9073

★ 12254 ★   Association of Physician Assistants in Cardiovascular Surgery (APACVS)
11250 Rodger Bacon Dr. Ste., 8
Reston, VA 22090
Phone: (703)707-0476
Fax: (703)435-4390
Richard A. Guggok, Exec.Dir.

Founded: 1981. **Members:** 675. **Description:** Physician assistants who work with cardiovascular surgeons. Objective is to assist in defining the role of physician assistants in the field of cardiovascular surgery through educational forums. **Publications:** *CardioVision,* quarterly.

Newsletter. • Membership Directory, annual. • *Salary and Benefits Survey,* annual. Survey.

★ 12255 ★   Association of Program Directors in Surgery
4900B 31st St.
Arlington, VA 22206
Phone: (703)820-7400
Fax: (703)931-4520
Thomas F. Fise, Contact

Founded: 1978. **Members:** 507. **Description:** Program directors in surgery. Conducts educational programs and scientific meetings. **Publications:** *Current Surgery,* 9/year. *Price:* $40 for members.

★ 12256 ★   Association for Research in Vascular Surgery (ARVS) (Association de Recherche en Chirurgie Vasculaire — ARCV)
Clinique de Franciscaines
9, impasse Jean-Bouin
F-30000 Nimes, France
Phone: 66 766048
Fax: 66 269812
Jean Marie Cardon, Exec. Officer

Founded: 1986. **Members:** 30. **Languages:** French. **Description:** Vascular and cardiac surgeons, vascular radiologists, and anesthesiologists. Conducts research in the field, particularly on the uses of the atherectomy laser. Members exchange information on technological advancement in the field.

★ 12257 ★   Association for Surgical Education (ASE)
c/o Merrill T. Dayton
University Medical Center
50 N. Medical Cr., Rm. 3B 312
Salt Lake City, UT 84132
Phone: (801)581-7124
Merrill T. Dayton, M.D., Pres.

Founded: 1980. **Members:** 700. **Description:** Surgeons and individuals involved or interested in undergraduate surgical education. Purpose is to develop and disseminate information on motivation, techniques, research, and applications for presenting curricula in undergraduate surgical education. Acts as forum for research in surgical education; serves as information clearinghouse. Compiles statistics; maintains speakers' bureau. Conducts educational programs. **Publications:** *Focus on Surgical Education,* quarterly. Journal. *Price:* Included in membership dues.

★ 12258 ★   Association of Surgical Technologists (AST)
7108-C S. Alton Way
Englewood, CO 80112
Phone: (303)694-9130
Fax: (303)694-9169
William J. Teutsch, Exec.Dir.

Founded: 1969. **Members:** 15,800. **Local Groups:** 151. **Description:** Individuals who have received specific education and training to deliver surgical patient care in the operating room. Membership categories are available for both certified and uncertified technologists. Emphasis is placed on encouraging members to participate actively in a continuing education program. Aims are: to study, discuss, and exchange knowledge, experience, and ideas in the field of surgical technology; to promote a high standard of surgical technology performance in the community for quality patient care; to stimulate interest in continuing education. Local groups sponsor workshops and institutes. Conducts research. **Publications:** *AST Core Curriculum for Surgical First Assisting.* Book. • *AST Core Curriculum for Surgical Technology.* Book. • *AST News*, bimonthly. Newsletter. *Price:* Included in membership dues. • *Study and Test Skills for Health Professionals.* Book. • *The Surgical Technologist*, monthly. Journal. Covers surgical procedures and equipment, aseptic techniques, medical law, and legislation. Also includes association news, and annual subject index. *Price:* Included in membership dues; $36/year for nonmembers. **Formerly:** (1978) Association of Operating Room Technicians.

★ 12259 ★ **Association of Women Surgeons (AWS)**
414 Plaza Dr., Ste. 209
Westmont, IL 60559
Phone: (708)655-0392
Fax: (708)655-0391
Stephanie Taylor, Mng.Dir.

Founded: 1981. **Members:** 1,200. **Description:** Women surgeons, interns, and residents; retired women surgeons; women in medical school interested in a career in surgery; interested individuals. Promotes the professional and personal goals of women surgeons and women involved and interested in the medical profession. Encourages interaction between women surgeons internationally. Serves as a network for the exchange of ideas and information. Helps women find employment opportunities. Conducts surveys. **Publications:** *AWS Newsletter*, quarterly. Newsletter. Includes notice of meetings, lists employment opportunities, profiles of outstanding women surgeons. • Membership Directory, annual. Serves as a networking device among members. • *Pocket Mentor*. Handbook. Features information for residents and interns.

AVSC International (AVSC)
See: Entry 11205

★ 12260 ★ **British Association of Aesthetic Plastic Surgeons (BAAPS)**
Royal College of Surgeons of England
35-43 Lincoln's Inn Fields
London WC2A 3PN, England
Phone: 171 4052234
Fax: 171 8314041
Mr. B.M. Jones, Pres.

Members: 140. **Languages:** English. **Description:** Fosters exchange of information among surgeons for the advancement of aesthetic plastic surgery. Encourages specialized training among plastic surgeons. Develops and advocates high standards of professional conduct; advises, promotes, and disseminates information on aesthetic plastic surgery. Provides educational programs for general practitioners and the press; conducts semiannual educational program for trainees and consultants. Holds competitions. **Publications:** *Directory*, annual. Membership Directory. **Formerly:** (1979) Association of Cosmetic Plastic Surgeons of Great Britain.

British Association of Paediatric Surgeons (BAPS)
See: Entry 3194

★ 12261 ★ **Canadian Implant Association (CIA)**
(Association Canadienne des Implantes Intraoculaires — ACII)
5591, rue Cote des Neiges
Montreal, PQ, Canada H3T 1Y8
Phone: (514)735-1133
Fax: (514)731-0651
Dr. Marvin L. Kwitko, M.D., Pres.

Founded: 1975. **Members:** 480. **Languages:** English, French. **Description:** Eye surgeons in Canada. Promotes advancement in the training and practice of ophthalmic implant surgery.

★ 12262 ★ **Canadian Society for Aesthetic (Cosmetic) Plastic Surgery (CSACPS)**
4650 Hwy., No. 7
Woodbridge, ON, Canada L4L 1S7
Phone: (905)831-7750
Free: 800-263-4429
Fax: (905)831-7248
Pat Hewitt, Exec.Sec.

Founded: 1972. **Members:** 101. **Languages:** English, French. **Description:** Educates plastic surgeons and residents, in the United States and Canada, on cosmetic surgery techniques. Conducts educational programs.

★ 12263 ★ **Canadian Society of Otolaryngology - Head and Neck Surgery (CSO-HNS)**
55 MacGregor Ave.
Toronto, ON, Canada M6S 2A1
Phone: (416)767-8190
Fax: (416)767-6782
Donna Humphrey, Exec.Sec.

Founded: 1947. **Members:** 650. **Languages:** English, French. **Description:** Professional society of practicing and retired otolaryngologists; otolaryngology residents join as associates. Provides for the discussion of professional issues. Arranges educational programs. Sponsors competitions, bestows awards. **Publications:** Brochure, annual. • *Canadian Journal of Otolaryngology*, bimonthly. • Membership Directory, periodic. • Newsletter, semiannual.

★ 12264 ★ **Cardiothoracic Research and Education Foundation (CREF)**
PO Box 23220
San Diego, CA 92193
Phone: (619)541-1444
Karen Morgan, Admin.Dir.

Founded: 1980. **Description:** Conducts research and education in the field of cardiothoracic surgery. Offers continuing medical education programs for surgeons, nurses, and perfusionists to improve their cardiothoracic surgical skills. (Perfusionists are involved with injecting blood or other fluids into arteries.) Conducts seminars on topics including pathophysiology and cardiopulmonary bypass techniques. **Publications:** *Monograph*, annual.

Children's Craniofacial Association (CCA)
See: Entry 2744

★ 12265 ★ **Clinical Orthopaedic Society (COS)**
2416 W. Washington St., Ste. D-3
Bloomington, IL 61704
Phone: (309)662-0545
Free: 800-843-9735
Barbara Dehority, Contact

Founded: 1912. **Members:** 700. **Description:** Orthopedic surgeons practicing in cities of the Midwest. **Publications:** Directory, annual.

Command Trust Network (CTN)
See: Entry 1248

★ 12266 ★ **Congress of Neurological Surgeons (CNS)**
c/o Daniel L. Barrow
The Emory Clinic
1365 Clifton Rd. NE
Atlanta, GA 30322
Phone: (404)248-4369
Fax: (404)248-3791
Daniel L. Barrow, M.D., Contact

Founded: 1951. **Members:** 3,500. **Description:** Professional society of neurological surgeons in the United States and 55 other countries who meet annually to express their views on various aspects of the principles and practice of neurological surgery; to exchange technical information and experience; to join study of the developments in scientific fields allied to neurological surgery. Promotes interest of neurological surgeons in their practice; provides placement service; honors a living leader in the field of neurological surgery annually. **Publications:** *Clinical Neurosurgery*, annual. • *Neurosurgery*, monthly. • Newsletter, quarterly. • *U.S. and Canada Directory*, annual. Directory. • *World Directory*, biennial. Directory.

★ 12267 ★ **European Academy of Facial Surgery (EAFS)**
The Royal College of Surgeons
35-43 Lincoln's Inn Fields
London WC2A 3PN, England
Phone: 171 4048373
Fax: 171 4044200
Prof. Jacques Soudant, Pres.

Founded: 1977. **Members:** 500. **Languages:** English. **Description:** Practicing and student facial and neck surgeons. Aims to further plastic and reconstructive surgery by stimulating research in neurosurgery, ophthalmology, otorhinolaryngology, and maxillofacial surgery; encourages cooperation among members, particularly between surgeons working in different specialties. Offers program on techniques in reconstructive surgery. **Publications:** *Facial Plastic Surgery*, quarterly. Monograph. • *Membership List*, periodic. **Formerly:** Joseph Society.

★ 12268 ★ **European Association for Cranio-Maxillo-Facial Surgery (EACMFS)**
Rijnstate Hospital
Gz. Dept. of Oral and Maxillo Facial Surgery
Wagnerlaan 55
NL-6815 AD Arnhem, Netherlands
Dr. P.W. Stoelinga, Contact

Founded: 1970. **Members:** 800. **National Groups:** 2. **Regional Groups:** 5. **Languages:** English, French, German. **Description:** Surgeons involved in oral and cranio-maxillofacial surgery. Encourages discussion and conducts medical courses on subjects such as orthognathic and temporomandibular joint surgery and plastic and aesthetic surgery. Maintains speakers' bureau; holds workshops, symposia, and seminars. **Publications:** *Journal of Cranio-maxillo-facial Surgery*, bimonthly. Journal.

European Rhinologic Society (ERS)
See: Entry 3522

★ 12269 ★ **European Society for Cardiovascular Surgery (ESCVS) (Societe Europeenne de Chirurgie Cardiovasculaire)**
Cliniques Universitaires U.C.L.
B-5530 Yvoir, Belgium
Phone: 81 422113
Fax: 81 422549
Dr. Jean-Claude Schoevaerdts, Gen.Sec.

Founded: 1952. **Members:** 1,000. **National Groups:** 30. **Languages:** English. **Description:** European Chapter of the International Society Cardiovascular Surgery. Members are cardiac and vascular surgeons. Promotes the study of cardiovascular diseases; facilitates exchange of information and ideas concerning cardiovascular diseases. Sponsors competitions. **Publications:** *Cardiovascular Surgery*, bimonthly. Journal.

European Society for Cataract and Refractive Surgeons (ESCRS) (Club International d'Implants Oculaires)
See: Entry 13448

★ 12270 ★ **European Society of Ophthalmic Plastic and Reconstructive Surgery (ESOPRS)**
Opthalmologie Service
CHU Dupuytren
F-87042 Limoges, France
Phone: 55 056234
Fax: 55 056211
Prof. J.P. Adenis, Hon.Sec.

Founded: 1981. **Members:** 152. **National Groups:** 12. **Languages:** English. **Description:** Coordinates activities in the field of plastic and reconstructive surgery of the eye. Disseminates information on the latest scientific advancements. **Publications:** *Orbit*, monthly. Journal.

★ 12271 ★ **European Union of Paediatric Surgical Associations (EUPSA)**
St. Gorans Hospital
Department of Pediatric Surgery
S-112 81 Stockholm, Sweden
Phone: 8 130500
Fax: 8 6187014
Bjorn Thomasson, M.D., Pres.

Founded: 1972. **Members:** 24. **Languages:** English. **Description:** National associations of pediatric surgeons. Promotes high standards of practice. Works to: standardize educational requirements in pediatric surgery; define the scope of pediatric surgery. Participates in the exchange of trainees among member associations. **Publications:** *Directory*, annual. Directory.

★ 12272 ★ **Federated Ambulatory Surgery Association (FASA)**
700 N. Fairfax St., No. 520
Alexandria, VA 22314
Phone: (703)836-8808
Gail D. Durant, Exec.Dir.

Founded: 1974. **Members:** 1,200. **Description:** Physicians, nurses, health administrators, and other individuals representing more than 400 outpatient surgery facilities. Promotes the concept of freestanding ambulatory (outpatient) surgical care. Facilitates exchange of knowledge and ideas regarding the care of ambulatory surgical patients. Represents members' interests at national level. Provides information to members, other organizations, and the public regarding government activities, legislation, statistical studies, group purchase programs, and the availability of malpractice insurance. Sponsors seminars, educational programs, and panel discussions; conducts studies and surveys in the field. **Publications:** *FASA Update*, bimonthly. Newsletter. • *Membership Directory*, annual.
Formerly: Society for the Advancement of Freestanding Ambulatory Surgical Care; (1986) Freestanding Ambulatory Surgery Association.

French Society of Pediatric Surgery (FSPS) (Societe Francaise de Chirurgie Pediatrique — SFCP)
See: Entry 3230

★ 12273 ★ **International Academy of Chest Physicians and Surgeons (IACPS)**
c/o American College of Chest Physicians
3300 Dundee Rd.
Northbrook, IL 60062
Phone: (708)498-1400
Fax: (708)698-1791
Alvin Lever, Exec.Dir.

Founded: 1941. **Members:** 15,000. **Description:** Aim is to further the continuing education of specialists in chest medicine and surgery. Offers teaching materials at nominal cost to help members stay informed of new developments in chest medicine. Sponsors postgraduate sessions and holds seminars. **Publications:** Books. • *Chest: For Pulmonologists, Cardiologists, Cardiothoracic Surgeons, Critical Care Physicians and Related Specialists*, monthly. Journal. Peer-reviewed journal. Includes index of advertisers; semiannual author, subject, and content indexes; book reviews; calendar of events. *Price:* Included in membership dues; $90/year for nonmembers; $126/year for institutions; $69/year for students, residents, and interns. • *Member Bulletin*, periodic. Bulletin. • *Membership Directory*, annual. • Monographs.

★ 12274 ★ **International Academy of Cosmetic Surgery (IACS)**
Via della Camilluccia 643
I-00135 Rome, Italy
Phone: 6 3270317
Giorgio Fischer, M.D., Pres.

Founded: 1970. **Members:** 410. **Description:** Cosmetic and reconstructive surgeons. Conducts training programs for doctors from underdeveloped countries. **Publications:** *Bulletin*, quarterly. Bulletin.

★ 12275 ★ **International Association of Ocular Surgeons (IAOS)**
4711 W. Golf Rd., Ste. 408
Skokie, IL 60076
Phone: (708)568-1500
Fax: (708)568-1527
Randall T. Bellows, M.D., Dir.

Founded: 1981. **Members:** 900. **Description:** A division of the American Society of Contemporary Ophthalmology. Seeks to develop a global community of ophthalmic surgeons who examine and deliberate on all aspects of ocular surgery; encourage information exchange among members; disseminate information about contemporary diagnostic and surgical procedures. **Publications:** *Annals of Ophthalmology*. Continuing medical education for ophthalmologists. *Price:* $120.

★ 12276 ★ **International Association of Oral and Maxillofacial Surgeons (IAOMS)**
Medical College of Virginia
Box 410, MCV
Richmond, VA 23298
Phone: (804)828-8515
Fax: (804)828-1753
Dr. Daniel M. Laskin, Sec.Gen.

Founded: 1962. **Members:** 1,650. **Description:** Oral and maxillofacial surgeons in 61 countries promoting the science of oral surgery. Sponsors educational programs. **Publications:** *I.A.O.M.S.*, semiannual. Newsletter. • *International Journal of Oral and Maxillofacial Surgery*, bimonthly. Journal. • *Registry of Fellows*. • *Rules and Regulations of the IAOMS*.

★ 12277 ★ **International College for Maxillo-Facial Surgery (ICMFS)**
Bayreuther Strasse 11
04207 Leipzig, Germany
Phone: 341 4772679
H.A. Gitt, DDS, Sec.

Founded: 1970. **Members:** 3,200. **Languages:** English, French, German. **Description:** Medical doctors from 49 countries working in the field of maxillo-facial, head and neck surgery. Organizes congresses, symposia, and workshops. **Publications:** *ICMFS Report*, annual. Newsletter.

★ 12278 ★ **International College of Surgeons (ICS)**
1516 N. Lake Shore Dr.
Chicago, IL 60610
Phone: (312)642-3555
Fax: (312)787-1624
J. Thomas Viall, Exec.Dir.

Founded: 1935. **Members:** 14,000. **National Groups:** 67. **Regional Groups:** 6. **Description:** General surgeons and surgical specialists in 111 countries maintaining official relations with the World Health Organization. Promotes the universal teaching and advancement of surgery and its allied sciences. Maintains International Museum of Surgical Sciences containing specialty rooms showing the growth and perfection of many surgical specialties and unique national exhibits tracing the development of surgery within each country. Maintains library open to researchers, individuals working in the profession, and the public. Organizes postgraduate clinics around the world; conducts lecture series and periodic congresses; offers grants, scholarships, and loans for residencies, research, and advanced study in surgery. Sends surgical teaching teams to developing countries. Bestows honorary fellowship. **Publications:** *International College of Surgeons Newsletter*, quarterly. Newsletter. Covers college news and business. • *International Surgery*, quarterly. Journal. Presents papers on clinical, experimental, cultural, and historical topics pertinent to surgery and related fields. Contains book reviews. *Price:* $25/year for members; $50/year for nonmembers.

★ 12279 ★ International Confederation for Plastic, Reconstructive and Aesthetic Surgery (IPRAS)
(Confederation Internationale pour la Chirurgie Plastic et Reconstructive — CICPR)
Clinica Mirasierra
Calle de la Maso, 83
E-28034 Madrid, Spain
Phone: 1 7388867
Fax: 1 7398083
Dr. Ulrich T. Hinderer, Gen.Sec.

Founded: 1955. **Members:** 70. **National Groups:** 70. **Regional Groups:** 3. **Languages:** English, French, German, Spanish. **Description:** National associations representing 9,500 plastic surgeons. Promotes plastic surgery both clinically and scientifically. Encourages closer relationships between international members and direct contact between national societies. Disseminates information on developments in other countries. Seeks to widen the scope of understanding and knowledge in the field and reinforce the worldwide fraternity of plastic surgeons. Maintains the International Plastic, Reconstructive and Aesthetic Foundation (IPRAF). **Publications:** *Newsletter of the IPRAS*, semiannual. Newsletter.

★ 12280 ★ International Federation of Surgical Colleges (IFSC)
Royal Australasian College of Surgeons
College of Surgeons' Gardens
Spring St.
Melbourne, VIC 3000, Australia
Phone: 3 6621033
Fax: 3 6634075
Mr. E. Durham Smith, Hon.Sec.

Founded: 1958. **Members:** 795. **National Groups:** 44. **Languages:** English. **Description:** National colleges, academies, and associations of surgery in 36 countries; interested individuals. Works to improve standards of surgery throughout the world. Promotes cooperation and exchange of medical and surgical information among surgical institutions. Encourages high standards of education, training, and research in surgery and its allied sciences. Supports clinical and scientific congresses in the surgical community. Fosters cooperation in developing the best possible standards of surgical facilities and treatment, and in providing appropriate surgical training in countries requesting aid. Collaborates with the World Health Organization in attempts to strengthen rural health services in developing countries; maintains distribution facility for journals to Third World nations. **Publications:** Newsletter, annual.

International Oculoplastic Society, Inc. (IOSI)
See: Entry 13492

International Society for Cardiovascular Surgery (ISCVS)
See: Entry 2859

★ 12281 ★ International Society for Dermatologic Surgery (ISDS)
PO Box 4014
Schaumburg, IL 60168-4014
Phone: (708)330-9830
Fax: (708)330-0050
Lawrence F. Rosenthal, Ph.D., Exec.Dir.

Founded: 1976. **Members:** 1,096. **Description:** Dermatologists, otolaryngologists, plastic surgeons, and skin surgery specialists. Goals are to: promote high standards of patient care; provide for continuing education and research in dermatologic surgery; encourage public interest in the field. Provides a forum for the exchange of ideas and methodology in dermatologic surgery and related basic sciences. **Publications:** Directory, annual. • *Journal of Dermatologic Surgery and Oncology*, monthly. Journal.

International Society for Pediatric Neurosurgery (ISPN)
See: Entry 3248

★ 12282 ★ International Society of Surgery (ISS)
(Societe Internationale de Chirurgie — SIC)
Netzibodenstr. 34
PO Box 1527
CH-4133 Pratteln, Switzerland
Phone: 61 8114770
Fax: 61 8114775
Dr. Thomas Ruedi, Sec.Gen.

Founded: 1902. **Members:** 3,700. **National Groups:** 80. **Languages:** English. **Description:** Surgeons from 80 countries wishing to contribute to the progress of science by researching and discussing surgical problems at congresses and general assemblies. **Publications:** *Membership Booklet*. Booklet. • Newsletter, 2-3/year. • *State of the Art of Surgery*, biennial, always even-numbered years. Booklet. Includes congress proceedings. • *World Journal of Surgery*, bimonthly. Journal. Scientific publication on general surgery.

★ 12283 ★ Interplast
2458 Embarcadero Way
Palo Alto, CA 94303
Phone: (415)424-0123
Fax: (415)424-8761
Carl L. Nale, Pres.

Founded: 1969. **Regional Groups:** 6. **State Groups:** 3. **Description:** Sends volunteer teams of medical professionals to developing countries to perform free reconstructive surgery on patients with birth defects, burns, and other crippling deformities. Plans include travel to foreign sites such as Ecuador, Peru, Honduras, Nepal, Mexico, Brazil, China, Thailand, Vietnam and the Philippines to perform an estimate of 2000 free surgeries. Conducts teaching programs during trips to developing countries. **Publications:** *Interplast News*, quarterly.

★ 12284 ★ Israel Society of Plastic and Cosmetic Surgery (IAPRS)
Dept. of Plastic Surgery
Rambam Medical Center
31096 Haifa, Israel
Phone: 3 6919793
Fax: 3 6966693
Dr. Haim Kaplon, Sec.

Founded: 1952. **Members:** 65. **Languages:** English, Hebrew. **Description:** Board certified plastic surgeons united to foster development in the field of plastic surgery. Bestows awards. **Formerly:** (1991) Israel Association of Plastic and Reconstructive Surgeons; (1994) Israel Association of Plastic Reconstructive and Aesthetic Surgery.

★ 12285 ★ Japan Society of Plastic and Reconstructive Surgery (JSPRS)
Kitasato University, School of Medicine
Department of Plastic and Reconstructive Surgery
1-15-1, Kitasato, Sagamihara
Kanagawa 228, Japan
Phone: 427 788111
Fax: 427 788441
Prof. Nobuyuki Shioya, Exec. Officer

Founded: 1958. **Members:** 598. **Languages:** English, Japanese. **Description:** Promotes practice of plastic and reconstructive surgery in Japan. Maintains high professional standards. Disseminates information among members. **Publications:** *Journal of JSPRS*. Journal.

★ 12286 ★ Korean Society of Plastic and Reconstructive Surgery (KSPRS)
(Dae Han Sung Hyung Owe Gua)
Yonsei Univ. College of Medicine
Severance Hospital
Seoul, Republic of Korea
Phone: 2 2632159
Fax: 2 2368531
Dr. Sei II Lee, Sec.Gen.

Founded: 1966. **Members:** 300. **Local Groups:** 3. **Languages:** Korean. **Description:** Aims to: increase scientific knowledge in the field of plastic and reconstructive surgery; promote friendship and communication between surgeons. Conducts continuing medical education, resident teaching program, courses, and symposia. Sponsors research. **Publications:** *Journal of the Korean Society of Plastic and Reconstructive Surgery*, periodic. • *List of Members KSPRS*, periodic. • *Newsletter KSPRS*, quarterly.

★ 12287 ★ Latin American Federation of Surgeons
Calle 97A, No. 10-67
Apartado 503
Bogota, Colombia

Description: Promotes the interests of surgeons throughout Latin America. Fosters the exchange of information between surgeons in order to advance the interests of the surgical community.

★ 12288 ★ **Michael E. DeBakey International Surgical Society (MEDISS)**
c/o Kenneth L. Mattox
1 Baylor Plz.
Department of Surgery
Houston, TX 77030
Phone: (713)798-4557
Kenneth L. Mattox, M.D., Sec.-Treas.

Founded: 1976. **Members:** 640. **Description:** Physicians organized to encourage, advance, and promote scientific research relating to the treatment of cardiac and cardiovascular defects and diseases through cardiovascular surgery. **Formerly:** (1983) Michael E. DeBakey International Cardiovascular Society.

★ 12289 ★ **Middle East Neurosurgical Society**
(Societe de Neurochirurgie du Moyen Orient)
American Univ. Medical Center
PO Box 113-6044
Beirut, Lebanon
Phone: 353486
Fax: 373 1450231
Dr. Fuad Sami Haddad, Pres.

Founded: 1958. **Members:** 545. **Languages:** English. **Description:** Individuals in 12 countries. Disseminates information to the medical profession and to the public on clinical advancements and scientific research in neurosurgery and similar disciplines.

★ 12290 ★ **National College of Foot Surgeons (NCFS)**
c/o Dr. Albert Apkarian
PO Box 264
Woodland Hills, CA 95776
Phone: (818)340-0616
Dr. Albert Apkarian, Sec.

Founded: 1960. **Description:** Doctors of surgical podiatry. Certifies foot surgeons as fellows and associates of the college. Holds seminars and courses; conducts research programs. Maintains speakers' bureau and hall of fame. **Publications:** Journal, annual.

★ 12291 ★ **National Foundation for Facial Reconstruction (NFFR)**
317 E. 34th St., Ste. 901
New York, NY 10016
Phone: (212)263-6656
Free: 800-422-FACE
Fax: (212)263-7534
Mary Hughes, PhD, Exec.Dir.

Founded: 1951. **Regional Groups:** 1. **Description:** Sponsors surgical and rehabilitation service programs for patients suffering facial disfigurements from accidents and severe burns, congenital malformations, and diseases such as cancer, as well as patients needing hand and microsurgical reconstruction. Supports the Institute of Reconstructive Plastic Surgery at the New York University Medical Center in its interdisciplinary programs of research, teaching, and patient care. Maintains patient referral service. Activities concentrated in New York City. Is beginning national program of public education about facial disfigurement. **Publications:** NFFR Newsletter, annual. Newsletter. Reports on the rehabilitation of individuals with facial disfigure-

ment. Includes case histories and research updates. *Price:* Free. • *Out of the Shadows. . .Into a Bright New Future.* Brochure. • Proceedings. **Formerly:** (1986) Society for the Rehabilitation of the Facially Disfigured.

★ 12292 ★ **Neurosurgical Society of America (NSA)**
c/o Dr. Russell W. Hardy
University Neurosurgeons of Clearing House
11100 Euclid Ave.
Cleveland, OH 44106-5042
Phone: (216)844-5949
Fax: (216)844-3014
Dr. Troy Tippett, Sec.

Founded: 1948. **Members:** 162. **Description:** Young specialists in neurological surgery.

★ 12293 ★ **Operation Smile International (OSI)**
717 Boush St.
Norfolk, VA 23510
Phone: (804)625-0375
Dr. William P. Magee, Jr., Founder

Founded: 1982. **Description:** Volunteers include plastic surgeons, anesthesiologists, nurses, nutritionists, physical therapists, child life specialists, geneticists, photographers, and psychologists. Provides reconstructive surgery and quality health care to individuals from Third World countries and in the United States. Sponsors the World Care Program, which allows children and adults with severe deformities to reside with an American host family while awaiting reconstructive surgery in the U.S. Also sponsors the Operation Happy Clubs, an organization run by students across the nation, that raises funds and holds special activities for needy children in the U.S. and abroad. Conducts annual medical mission in 11 countries: the Philippines, China, Nicaragua, Venezuela, Kenya, Panama, Russia, Romania, Colombia, Vietnam, and the Middle East. Maintains speakers' bureau; conducts research programs. **Publications:** *Operation Smile Newsletter*, quarterly. Newsletter. **Formerly:** (1993) Operation Smile.

★ 12294 ★ **Outpatient Ophthalmic Surgery Society (OOSS)**
PO Box 23220
San Diego, CA 92193
Phone: (619)692-4426
Fax: (619)692-3143
Karen Morgan, Admin.

Founded: 1981. **Description:** Ophthalmic surgeons. Purpose is to gather and share information about outpatient eye surgery in order to promote high-quality, low-cost patient care. **Publications:** *Dollars and Disease: The True Cost of Cataracts.* • Journal, annual. • Newsletter, quarterly. Also publishes books; produces videotapes.

★ 12295 ★ **Pan-Pacific Surgical Association (PPSA)**
1360 S Beretania St., Ste. 304
Honolulu, HI 96814-1520
Phone: (808)593-1180
Fax: (808)593-1176
Gayle Yoshida, Exec.Admin.

Founded: 1929. **Members:** 2,716. **Regional Groups:** 3. **Description:** Professional international association of surgeons. Coordinates exchange programs and educational projects. Conducts volunteer pogram in which surgeons go to Micronesia and the Pacific for two or more weeks. Sponsors educational programs; operates speakers' bureau. **Publications:** *Pan-Pacific Surgical Association Bulletin*, quarterly. Newsletter. Also publishes program.

★ 12296 ★ **Plastic Surgery Educational Foundation (PSEF)**
444 E. Algonquin Rd.
Arlington Heights, IL 60005
Phone: (708)228-9900
Fax: (708)228-9131
Dave Fellers, CAE, Exec.Dir.

Founded: 1948. **Members:** 4,500. **Description:** Plastic and reconstructive surgeons. Purpose is to identify and respond to the educational needs of members and their patients. Sponsors regional and national demonstrations, lectures, educational seminars, symposia, and workshops focusing on plastic surgery techniques and procedures. Conducts annual in-service and self-assessment examinations dealing with topics such as aesthetic and breast surgery, hand and extremities, integument, maxillofacial surgery, and pediatric plastic surgery. Administers Visiting Professors Program; compiles statistics; sponsors charitable programs. **Publications:** Booklets. • *Plastic and Reconstructive Surgery.* Journal. • *Plastic Surgery News.* **Formerly:** (1981) Education Foundation of American Society of Plastic and Reconstructive Surgeons.

★ 12297 ★ **Plastic Surgery Research Council (PSRC)**
c/o Peter Johnson
University of Pittsburgh
676 Scaife Hall
Pittsburgh, PA 15261
Phone: (412)648-8100
Peter Johnson, M.D., Contact

Founded: 1955. **Members:** 232. **Description:** To foster fundamental research in the fields of plastic and reconstructive surgery. **Publications:** *Meeting Abstracts*, annual.

Portuguese Society of Stomatology and Dental Medicine (PSSDM)
(Sociedade Portugesa de Estomatologia Emedicina Dentaria — SPEMD)
See: Entry 3986

★ 12298 ★ **Royal College of Surgeons of England (RCS Eng)**
35/43 Lincoln's Inn Fields
London WC2A 3PN, England
Phone: 171 4053474
Fax: 171 8319438
R.H.E. Duffett, Sec.

Founded: 1800. **Members:** 15,000. **Languages:** English. **Description:** Surgeons and dental surgeons in the United Kingdom. Aims to promote and encourage the study and practice of surgery as an art and a science. Maintains professional standards through examinations; establishes criteria for the qualification of consultant and dental surgeons in the National Health Service; advises government and other professional bodies on surgical matters; conducts research. Offers postgraduate courses in surgery and related subjects; sponsors seminars and workshops. Bestows awards. Operates the Hunterian Institute and Museum. **Publications:** *Annals of the Royal College of Surgeons of England*, bimonthly. Report.

★ 12299 ★ Scandinavian Association of Paediatric Surgeons (SCAPS) (Nordisk Barnkirurgisk Forening — NBF)
Dept. of Pediatric Surgery
Regionsykehuset
N-7006 Trondheim, Norway
Phone: 7 3998000
Fax: 7 3997428
Torbjorn Kufaas, Contact

Founded: 1964. **Members:** 146. **National Groups:** 5. **Languages:** Danish, English, Norwegian, Swedish. **Description:** Pediatric surgeons in 5 countries. Promotes the development of pediatric surgery and cooperation among members; represents members internationally. Encourages cooperative studies.

★ 12300 ★ Scandinavian Association of Plastic Surgeons (SAPS) (Nordisk Plastikkirurgisk Forening — NPF)
Bokbackgranden 4B
SF-20900 Turku, Finland
Phone: 21 2581560
Fax: 21 612229
Dr. Mikael Relander, Hon.Sec.

Founded: 1951. **Members:** 215. **Languages:** Danish, Finnish, Icelandic, Norwegian, Swedish. **Description:** Plastic surgeons in 5 countries. Promotes the advancement of plastic surgery. Keeps members informed of developments in plastic surgery. Sponsors courses. **Publications:** *List of Members*, periodic. • *Scandinavian Journal of Plastic and Reconstructive Surgery and Hand Surgery*, quarterly. Journal.

★ 12301 ★ Scandinavian Association for Thoracic Surgery (SATS) (Nordisk Thoraxkirurgisk Forening — NTF)
Department of Cardio-Thoracic Surgery
University Hospital
S-581 85 Linkoping, Sweden
Phone: 13 224800
Fax: 13 100246
Christian Olin, M.D., Sec.Gen.

Founded: 1949. **Members:** 250. **Languages:** English. **Description:** Scandinavian thoracic and cardiovascular surgeons. Conducts graduate lectures and presentations of scientific papers. **Formerly:** Scandinavian Association for Thoracic and Cardiovascular Surgery.

Scandinavian Neurosurgical Society (SNS) (Nordisk Neurokirurgisk Forening — NNF)
See: Entry 8303

★ 12302 ★ Scandinavian Surgical Society (SSS)
Department of Surgery
Buskerud Central Hospital
N-3004 Drammen, Norway
Phone: 32 803000
Fax: 32 803399
Jon Haffner, M.D., Sec.Gen.

Founded: 1893. **Members:** 4,321. **National Groups:** 5. **Languages:** Danish, English, Finn-

ish, Icelandic, Norwegian, Swedish. **Description:** Surgeons in Denmark, Finland, Iceland, Norway, and Sweden. Seeks to: promote clinical and research work and training in the field of surgery; encourage scientific and clinical communication between surgeons in the Scandinavian countries and elsewhere. Offers courses in surgical disciplines. **Formerly:** (1994) Nordic Surgical Society.

★ 12303 ★ Slovak Society of Plastic Surgery
Hospital
Lucna 57
SK-040 15 Kosice, Slovakia
Phone: 95 6842129
Jan Babik, M.D., Contact

Languages: English, Slovak. **Description:** Plastic surgeons. Promotes professional advancement of members and continued improvement in the practice of cosmetic surgery; represents members' interests.

Society of American Gastrointestinal Endoscopic Surgeons (SAGES)
See: Entry 5230

★ 12304 ★ Society For Surgery of the Alimentary Tract (SSAT)
c/o John H.C. Ranson M.D.
N.Y.U. Medical Center
Department. of Surgery
530 1st Ave., Ste. 6B
New York, NY 10016
Phone: (212)263-6387
Fax: (212)263-7606
John H.C. Ranson, M.D., Sec.

Founded: 1960. **Members:** 1,200. **Description:** Physicians specializing in alimentary tract surgery. Purposes are: to stimulate and foster the study of and research in the function and diseases of the alimentary tract; to provide a forum for presentation of such information; to edit, encourage, or sponsor publications. **Formerly:** Association of Colon Surgery.

★ 12305 ★ Society of Head and Neck Surgeons (SHNS)
4900 B S. 31st St.
Arlington, VA 22206
Phone: (703)820-7400
Fax: (703)931-4520
Ernst T. Bomar, Jr., Exec.Dir.

Founded: 1954. **Members:** 700. **Description:** Surgeons. Seeks to advance the art and science of surgery of diseases of the head and neck, particularly cancer.

★ 12306 ★ Society of Neurological Surgeons (SNS)
750 Washinton St.
Box 178
Boston, MA 02111
Phone: (617)636-5858
Fax: (617)636-7587
William Shucart, M.D., Sec.

Founded: 1920. **Members:** 215. **Description:** Neurological surgeons interested in and contributing to education.

Society of Neurosurgical Anesthesia and Critical Care (SNACC)
See: Entry 8309

★ 12307 ★ Society of Pelvic Surgeons (SPS)
c/o Dr. Carmel Cohen
Mt. Sinai School of Medicine
Department of OB-GYN
1176 5th Ave.
New York, NY 10029
Phone: (212)241-6554
Fax: (212)360-6917
Dr. Carmel Cohen, Sec.-Treas.

Founded: 1952. **Members:** 125. **Description:** Professional society of physicians specializing in surgery of the pelvis. Purpose is to hold meetings for the free and informal interchange of ideas pertaining to various phases of pelvic surgery and related fields and to exert influence for the betterment of the teaching and practice of pelvic surgery. Membership is by nomination. Maintains library and archives. Conducts educational programs.

★ 12308 ★ Society for Reproductive Surgeons (SRE)
c/o American Fertility Society
1209 Montgomery Hwy.
Birmingham, AL 35216-2809
Phone: (205)978-5000
Fax: (205)978-5005
Mary Fasshauer, Contact

Members: 450. **Description:** Reproductive surgeons. Gathers and disseminates information on reproductive surgery; conducts continuing education programs for members. Makes available referrals list.

Society of Surgical Oncology (SSO)
See: Entry 5989

★ 12309 ★ Society of Thoracic Surgeons (STS)
401 N. Michigan Ave.
Chicago, IL 60611-4267
Phone: (312)644-6610
Fax: (312)527-6635
Walter G. Purcell, Bus.Mgr.

Founded: 1964. **Members:** 3,535. **Description:** Surgeons who confine their practice to the field of thoracic-cardiovascular surgery. Objectives are: to improve the quality and practice of thoracic and cardiovascular surgery as a specialty; to strengthen and establish basic standards in training programs; to encourage clinical and basic research; to promote the professional development of those surgeons specializing in the field; to represent and sponsor those surgeons who have recently entered the field. Conducts annual postgraduate program and three-day scientific session. **Publications:** *Annals of Thoracic Surgery*, monthly.

Society of United States Air Force Flight Surgeons
See: Entry 7811

★ 12310 ★ **Society of University Otolaryngologists - Head and Neck Surgeons (SUO-HNS)**
c/o Marvin Fried
Joint Center for Otolarynology
333 Longwood Ave.
Boston, MA 02115
Phone: (617)732-7003
Fax: (617)277-1372
Marvin Fried, M.D., Contact

Founded: 1964. **Members:** 500. **Description:** Otolaryngologists affiliated with universities through an approved residency training program, faculty appointment, or teaching or research position. Promotes the advancement of the art and science of otolaryngology by the development and improvement of undergraduate and graduate teaching programs. Encourages basic research and clinical investigation as an integral part of university training programs. Sponsors annual course; maintains society records. **Publications:** Directory, annual. **Formerly:** (1983) Society of University Olodaryngologists.

★ 12311 ★ **Society of University Surgeons (SUS)**
c/o Keith D. Lillemoe
PO Box 7069
New Haven, CT 06519
Phone: (203)932-0541
Keith D. Lillemoe, M.D., Contact

Founded: 1938. **Members:** 1,280. **Description:** Professional society of surgeons connected with university teaching. Works to advance the art and science of surgery by encouraging original investigations both in the clinic and in the laboratory and by developing methods of graduate teaching of surgery with particular reference to the resident system. **Publications:** *Surgery.*

★ 12312 ★ **Society for Vascular Surgery (SVS)**
13 Elm St.
PO Box 1565
Manchester, MA 01944
Phone: (508)526-8330
Fax: (508)526-4018
William T. Maloney, Exec.Dir.

Founded: 1945. **Members:** 594. **Description:** Professional society of board-certified surgeons interested in promoting the study of and research in the circulatory system. **Publications:** *Journal of Vascular Surgery*, monthly.

South African Association of Paediatric Surgeons (SAAPS)
(Suid-Afrikaanse Vereniging van Kinderchirurge — SAVK)
See: Entry 3298

★ 12313 ★ **Surgical Infection Society (SIS)**
c/o David N. Herndon, M.D.
Shriners Burns Institute
815 Market St.
Galveston, TX 77550
Phone: (409)744-6049
David N. Herndon, M.D., Sec.

Founded: 1981. **Members:** 420. **Description:** Surgeons and surgical specialists engaged in laboratory or clinical research in the field of surgical infections; other specialists with an interest in surgical infections. Objective is to promote and encourage education and research in the nature, prevention, diagnosis, and treatment of surgical infections. Offers fellowship program for the study of surgical infectious diseases.

★ 12314 ★ **Surgical Research Society of Southern Africa (SRSSA)**
(Chirurgiese Navorsingsvereniging van Suidelike Afrika — CNSA)
Pretoria University
Department of Surgery
PO Box 667
Pretoria 0001, Republic of South Africa
Phone: 12 3291111
Fax: 12 3291343
Prof. C.J. Mieny, Pres.

Founded: 1972. **Members:** 270. **Local Groups:** 5. **Languages:** Afrikaans, English. **Description:** Surgeons and surgeons in training. Promotes research, particularly among younger members, in clinical and experimental surgery. Sets surgical research standards. Provides funding to surgery departments of South African universities; offers grants and scholarships; sponsors competitions. **Publications:** *Abstracts of Society Meeting*, annual. • *South Africa Journal of Surgery*, periodic.

Union of Middle Eastern and Mediterranean Pediatric Societies (UMEMPS)
(Union des Societes de Pediatrie du Moyen-Orient et de la Mediterranee — USPMOM)
See: Entry 3304

★ 12315 ★ **Western Surgical Association (WSA)**
Mayo Clinic
200 1st St. SW
Rochester, MN 55905
Phone: (507)284-3364
Jon A. Van Heerden, M.D., Sec.

Founded: 1891. **Members:** 600. **Description:** Surgeons who have contributed to surgical education and advancement. Objectives are: to cultivate, promote, and diffuse knowledge of the art and science of surgery; to sponsor and maintain the highest standards of practice; to deliver the best possible care to all people. **Publications:** *Western Surgical Association Newsletter*, quarterly. Newsletter. Includes information on new members. • *Western Surgical Association Program*, annual. Contains abstracts of papers to be presented at annual meeting. • *Western Surgical Association Transactions*, annual. Proceedings of annual meeting.

★ 12316 ★ **World Federation of Neurosurgical Societies (WFNS)**
c/o Dr. Edward Laws
University of Virginia Health Services
Box 212
Charlottesville, VA 22904
Fax: (804)924-5894
Dr. Edward Laws, Sec.

Founded: 1957. **Members:** 50. **Regional Groups:** 5. **Description:** National neurosurgical societies representing 12,000 neurosurgeons. Works for the advancement of neurological surgery. **Publications:** *Federation News*, 1-2/year. • *Proceedings of International Congress*, quadrennial. Proceedings. • *World Directory*, periodic. Directory.

★ 12317 ★ **World Society for Stereotactic and Functional Neurosurgery (WSSFN)**
c/o Philip L. Gildenberg, M.D.
6560 Fannin, Ste. 1530
Houston, TX 77030
Phone: (713)790-0795
Fax: (713)669-0388
Philip L. Gildenberg, M.D., Pres.

Founded: 1963. **Members:** 600. **Regional Groups:** 4. **Description:** Neurosurgeons and professors dedicated to the advancement of stereotactic studies and procedures. Original manuscripts submitted at meetings are published and used as reference books throughout the world. **Publications:** *Stereotactic and Functional Neurosurgery*, quarterly. Journal. • *Studies in Stereoencephalotomy*, quadrennial. **Also Known As:** World Stereotactic Society; WSSFN. **Formerly:** (1973) International Society for Research in Stereoencephalotomy.

Research Centers

★ 12318 ★ **Alamo Institute of Research**
8122 Datapoint, Ste. 1200
San Antonio, TX 78229
Phone: (210)696-8534
Fax: (210)614-7270
James W. Simmons, M.D., Dir.

Research Activities and Fields: Sports medicine and rehabilitation. Conducts cooperative research in the area of human performance measurement for therapy and rehabilitation, and clinical and surgical studies for the spine and musculoskeletal system.

★ 12319 ★ **Duke University**
Plastic Surgery Research Laboratories
Medical Center
Box 3906
Durham, NC 27710
Phone: (919)684-3929
Fax: (919)681-2670
Prof. Bruce Klitzman, Dir.

Research Activities and Fields: Microvascular physiology, plastic surgery, including wound healing, monitoring tissue viability, thrombolytic therapy, preservation of organs, and biocompatibility of synthetic vascular grafts (prostheses). Also conducts studies on microcirculation, skin cancer, and aging skin. **E-mail Address:** klitz@acpub.duke.edu.

★ 12320 ★ **Edward Dana Mitchell Surgical Research Laboratory**
Univ. of Tennessee Medical School
956 Court., E288
Memphis, TN 38163
Phone: (901)448-8370
Fax: (901)448-7306
Dr. Kenneth Kudsk, Dir.

Research Activities and Fields: Surgery, transplantation, sepsis, shock, nutrition, hepatic dysfunction, and gut immunology.

★ 12321 ★ Institute for Applied Laser Surgery
2 Bala Plaza, Ste. PL-13
Bala Cynwyd, PA 19004
Phone: (610)667-4080
Dr. Ronald A. Kirschner, Dir.

Research Activities and Fields: Surgical applications of lasers and laser-related accessory development. Activities include development of new procedures in cardiovascular, peripheral vascular, cutaneeur, plastic, urologic, gynocologic, and orthopedic surgery. **Publications:** Newsletter. **Formerly:** Medical Laser Technology Center.

Jane Forbes Clark Surgical Research Laboratories
See: Entry 2104

★ 12322 ★ New York University
Institute of Reconstructive Plastic Surgery
550 1st Ave.
New York, NY 10016
Phone: (212)263-5209
Fax: (212)263-5400
Joseph G. McCarthy, M.D., Dir.

Research Activities and Fields: Etiology and treatment of craniofacial anomalies, bone physiology, including distraction, computer graphics, microvascular surgery, and wound healing, including studies of cleft lip and cleft palate, jaw deformities, ear malformations, hand injuries, and allied problems.

★ 12323 ★ St. Louis University
Theodore Cooper Surgical Research Institute
3635 Vista Ave. at Grand Blvd.
PO Box 15250
St. Louis, MO 63110-0250
Phone: (314)577-8561
Fax: (314)771-1945
Dr. Albert P. Li, Ph.D, Dir.

Research Activities and Fields: Gastrointestinal and hepatic physiology, bioartificial liver, myocardial revascularization, drug metabolism, pharmacokinetics, toxicokinetics, organ transplantation and preservation, cardiac assist and replacement, myocardial preservation and pulmonary function, islet cell transplantation, immunology/nutrition, shock and multiple organ failure, neuropharmacology, transplantation immunogenetics, image guided surgery, and molecular biology. **Publications:** *SRI Insights* (quarterly); *Research Prospectus* (annually). **Formerly:** Vallee Willman Surgical Research Institute (1995); Institute of Experimental Surgery (1990).

U.S. Department of Defense
Army Medical Research and Development Command
Army Institute of Surgical Research
See: Entry 7819

U.S. Department of Defense
Army Medical Research and Development Command
Walter Reed Army Institute of Research
Surgery Division
See: Entry 7836

U.S. Department of Health and Human Services
National Cancer Institute
Division of Cancer Treatment
Surgery Branch
See: Entry 6166

U.S. Department of Health and Human Services
National Institute of Neurological Disorders and Stroke
Surgical Neurology Branch
See: Entry 8472

University of Alabama at Birmingham
Alabama Congenital Heart Disease Diagnosis and Treatment Center
See: Entry 2953

★ 12324 ★ University of Louisville
Department of Surgery
Ambulatory Care Building, 2nd Fl.
Louisville, KY 40292
Phone: (502)852-1700
Fax: (502)852-8915
Ms. Parnell Langston, Business Mgr.

Research Activities and Fields: Microsurgical procedures and materials, surgical infections, growth factors, microcirculation, and thoracic and cardiovascular research. **Formerly:** Price Institute of Surgical Research.

★ 12325 ★ University of Michigan
Pediatric Surgery Research Laboratories
F3970 Mott Children's Hospital
Ann Arbor, MI 48109-0245
Phone: (313)764-4151
Fax: (313)936-9784
Arnold G. Coran, M.D., Dir.

Research Activities and Fields: Pediatric surgery, including physiological and biochemical changes during septic and hemorrhagic shock in puppies, physiology and metabolism of patients receiving total parenteral nutrition, physiology of endorectal pull-through operations for Hirschprung's disease in dogs, determination of trace element levels in infants receiving oral feedings or total parenteral nutritional solutions, and bacterial translocation in newborn babies.

★ 12326 ★ University of Michigan
Thoracic Surgery Research Lab
B560 MSRB II, Box 0686
Univ. Medical Center
Ann Arbor, MI 48109
Phone: (313)763-1147
Dr. Mark Orringer, Dir.

Research Activities and Fields: Cardiovascular and pulmonary physiology and transplantations, cellular and molecular aspects of allograft rejection and tolerance, molecular genetics of human lung and esophageal cancer, regional ventricular function (using sonomicrometry measurements) in conditions of ischemia, infarction, and reperfusion, neonatal myocardial performance and protection of the neonatal heart during ischemia, and role of cytokines in cardiac and pulmonary injury.

University of Missouri—Columbia
Division of Cardiothoracic Surgery
See: Entry 2972

★ 12327 ★ University of Pennsylvania
Harrison Department of Surgical Research
313 Stemmler Hall
Margarett M. Clark Laboratories
Philadelphia, PA 19104-6070
Phone: (215)898-8081
Fax: (215)573-2001
Clyde F. Barker, M.D., Dir.

Research Activities and Fields: Cancer, cardiovascular disease, gastrointestinal physiology, shock and surgical bacteriology, nutrition of surgical patients, and surgical specialities, including studies of stomach and duodenum, pancreas, colon, liver, blood flow, hypertension, equilibrium tissue oxygen requirements, tissue oxygen, oxygen supply in shock and shock-like states, chemotherapy, patient antitumor agents, immunology, ultraviolet light in protection against wound infection, transplantation of tissues and organs, and role of electronics in surgical research. **Publications:** Annual Report.

University of Texas Medical Branch at Galveston
Cardiovascular Surgical Research Laboratory
See: Entry 2977

★ 12328 ★ Vanderbilt University
S.R. Light Laboratory for Surgical Research
MCN, Rm. A-2219
Nashville, TN 37232
Phone: (615)322-0940

Research Activities and Fields: All phases of medicine involving use of experimental animals. Specific research includes studies of metabolism, particularly mechanisms of stress-related changes in glucose and amino acids; cardiothoracic study of pathophysiology of ischemic myocardium; and renovascular physiology. Also develops new surgical instrumentation and techniques.

★ 12329 ★ Wayne State University
Laura S. Nye Surgical Research Fund for Desmoid Tumors
Dept. of Surgery
Harper Hosp.
3990 John R.
Detroit, MI 48201
Phone: (313)745-8778
Fax: (313)745-1873
David Fromm, M.D., Chairman

Research Activities and Fields: Desmoid tumor treatment, including photodynamic therapy after excision of tumor.

Chapter 65
Therapy & Rehabilitation

Foundations & Other Funding Organizations

Private Foundations

Clara Blackford Smith and W. Aubrey Smith Charitable Foundation
See: Entry 102

Dora Roberts Foundation
See: Entry 144

Mericos Foundation
See: Entry 400

Ordean Foundation
See: Entry 418

Perkins-Prothro Foundation
See: Entry 425

Swalm Foundation
See: Entry 510

Corporate Foundations

USX Foundation
See: Entry 894

Other Funding Organizations

★ 12330 ★ American Occupational Therapy Foundation
1383 Piccard Dr., Ste. 301
PO Box 1725
Rockville, MD 20849-1725
Phone: (301)652-2682
Free: 800-SAY-AOTA
Fax: (301)948-5529
Jeanette Bair, Exec. Dir.

Description: Awards scholarships, fellowships, and grants to support training and research in the field of occupational therapy.

★ 12331 ★ Foundation for Physical Therapy
1055 N. Fairfax St., Ste. 350
Alexandria, VA 22314
Phone: (703)684-5984
Fax: (703)684-3218
Fred A. de Gregorio, Exec. Dir.

Description: Promotes the use and development of physical therapy. Grants research and doctoral scholarships.

★ 12332 ★ Round Table International
30707 Butia Palm
Homeland, CA 92548
Phone: (909)926-4517
R. Bennett Crawford, Exec. Dir.

Description: Awards scholarships to student therapists training to work with the physically handicapped.

Medical & Allied Health Schools

Occupational Therapy

The following entry level programs (baccalaureate and graduate) for the occupational therapist are accredited by the Accreditation Council for Occupational Therapy Education of the American Occupational Therapy Association. For career information and for a listing of approved entry level programs (associate and certificate) for occupational therapy assistants, contact the American Occupational Therapy Association at 4720 Montgomery Lane, PO Box 301220, Bethesda, MD 20824-1220, (301) 652-2682.

Alabama

★ 12333 ★ Tuskegee University
School of Nursing and Allied Health
Division of Allied Health
Occupational Therapist Program
Tuskegee, AL 36088-1696
Phone: (205)727-8696

★ 12334 ★ University of Alabama at Birmingham
School of Health Related Professions
Division of Occupational Therapy
1714 9th Ave. S., Rm. 237
Birmingham, AL 35294-1270
Phone: (205)934-3568

★ 12335 ★ University of South Alabama
Occupational Therapy Program
Springhill Academic Campus
1504 Springhill Ave., Rm. 5112
Mobile, AL 36688
Phone: (205)460-6260

Arkansas

★ 12336 ★ University of Central Arkansas
Department of Occupational Therapy
PO Box 5001
Conway, AR 72035-0001
Phone: (501)450-3192

California

★ 12337 ★ Loma Linda University
School of Allied Health Professions
Department of Occupational Therapy
Nichol Hall, Rm. 903
Loma Linda, CA 92350-0001
Phone: (714)824-4628

★ 12338 ★ Samuel Merritt College
Occupational Therapy Program
370 Hawthorne Ave.
Oakland, CA 94609
Phone: (510)869-8923

★ 12339 ★ San Jose State University
College of Applied Arts and Sciences
Department of Occupational Therapy
1 Washington Sq.
San Jose, CA 95192-0059
Phone: (408)924-3070

★ 12340 ★ University of Southern California
Department of Occupational Therapy
1540 Alcazar, HSOB-130
Los Angeles, CA 90033-1091
Phone: (213)342-2850

Colorado

★ 12341 ★ Colorado State University
Department of Occupational Therapy
200 Occupational Therapy Bldg.
Ft. Collins, CO 80523
Phone: (303)491-6253

Connecticut

★ 12342 ★ Quinnipiac College
School of Allied Health and Natural
  Sciences
Department of Occupational Therapy
Hamden, CT 06518
Phone: (203)288-5251

★ 12343 ★ University of Hartford
College of Education, Nursing and Health
  Professions
Department of Occupational Therapy
Dana Hall 232
200 Bloomfield Ave.
West Hartford, CT 06117
Phone: (203)768-5303

District of Columbia

★ 12344 ★ Howard University
College of Allied Health Sciences
Department of Occupational Therapy
6th and Bryant Sts. NW
Washington, DC 20059
Phone: (202)806-7614

Florida

★ 12345 ★ Barry University
Division of Biological and Biomedical
  Sciences
Department of Occupational Therapy
Academic Health Science Center
11300 NE 2nd Ave.
Miami Shores, FL 33161-6695
Phone: (305)899-3213

★ 12346 ★ Florida A&M University
School of Allied Health Sciences
Department of Occupational Therapy
Tallahassee, FL 32307
Phone: (904)599-3879

★ 12347 ★ Florida International University
Department of Occupational Therapy
University Park Campus, CH102
Miami, FL 33199
Phone: (305)348-2263

★ 12348 ★ Nova Southeastern University
College of Allied Health
Health Professions Division
Occupational Therapy Program
1750 NE 167th St.
North Miami Beach, FL 33162-3017
Phone: (305)949-4000

★ 12349 ★ University of Florida
Department of Occupational Therapy
J. Hillis Miller Health Center, Box 100164
Gainesville, FL 32610-0164
Phone: (904)392-2617

Georgia

★ 12350 ★ Medical College of Georgia
School of Allied Health Sciences
Department of Occupational Therapy
Augusta, GA 30912
Phone: (706)721-2725

Illinois

★ 12351 ★ Chicago State University
College of Nursing and Allied Health
  Professions
Occupational Therapist Program
9501 S. King Dr.
Chicago, IL 60628-1598
Phone: (312)995-2366

★ 12352 ★ Midwestern University
College of Allied Health Professions
Occupational Therapy Program
555 31st St.
Downers Grove, IL 60515
Phone: (708)515-6388

★ 12353 ★ Rush University
Department of Occupational Therapy
Rush/Presbyterian/St.Luke's Medical Center
1653 W. Congress Pkwy.
Chicago, IL 60612-3833
Phone: (312)942-5099

★ 12354 ★ University of Illinois at Chicago
College of Associated Health Professions
Department of Occupational Therapy
1919 W. Taylor St., M/C 811
Chicago, IL 60612
Phone: (312)996-6901

Indiana

★ 12355 ★ Indiana University
School of Medicine
Division of Allied Health Sciences
Occupational Therapy Program
1140 W. Michigan St., CF311
Indianapolis, IN 46202-5119
Phone: (317)274-8006

★ 12356 ★ University of Indianapolis
Occupational Therapist Program
1400 E. Hanna Ave.
Indianapolis, IN 46227-3697
Phone: (317)788-3432

★ 12357 ★ University of Southern Indiana
School of Nursing and Health Professions
Occupational Therapy Program
8600 University Blvd.
Evansville, IN 47712
Phone: (812)428-7208

Iowa

★ 12358 ★ St. Ambrose University
Department of Occupational Therapy
518 W. Locust
Davenport, IA 52803
Phone: (319)383-8903

Kansas

★ 12359 ★ Kansas Newman College
Occupational Therapy Program
3100 McCormick Ave.
Wichita, KS 67213-2097
Phone: (316)942-4291

★ 12360 ★ University of Kansas
School of Allied Health
Department of Occupational Therapy
3303 Robinson
3901 Rainbow Blvd.
Kansas City, KS 66160-7602
Phone: (913)588-7195

Kentucky

★ 12361 ★ Eastern Kentucky University
Department of Occupational Therapy
Dizney 103
Richmond, KY 40475-3135
Phone: (606)622-3300

Louisiana

★ 12362 ★ Louisiana State University
School of Allied Health Professions
Department of Occupational Therapy
1900 Gravier St.
New Orleans, LA 70112-2223
Phone: (504)568-4301

★ 12363 ★ Northeast Louisiana University
School of Allied Health Sciences
Occupational Therapy Program
Monroe, LA 71209-0430
Phone: (318)342-1610

Maine

★ 12364 ★ Lewiston-Auburn College /
  University of Southern Maine
Occupational Therapy Program
51-55 Westminster St.
Lewiston, ME 04240-3534
Phone: (207)783-4860

★ 12365 ★ University of New England
College of Arts and Sciences
Division of Occupational Therapy
Biddeford, ME 04005-9599
Phone: (207)283-0171

Maryland

★ 12366 ★ Towson State University
Occupational Therapy Department
Towson, MD 21204-7097
Phone: (410)830-2640

Massachusetts

★ 12367 ★ Boston University
**Sargent College of Allied Health
  Professions**
Department of Occupational Therapy
635 Commonwealth Ave.
Boston, MA 02215
Phone: (617)353-2727

★ 12368 ★ Springfield College
Department of Occupational Therapy
263 Alden St.
Springfield, MA 01109-3797
Phone: (413)748-3762

★ 12369 ★ Tufts University
Boston School of Occupational Therapy
26 Winthrop St.
Medford, MA 02155
Phone: (617)627-3720

★ 12370 ★ Worcester State College
Department of Occupational Therapy
486 Chandler St.
Worcester, MA 01602-2597
Phone: (508)793-8624

Michigan

★ 12371 ★ Baker College of Flint
Occupational Therapy Program
G-1050 W. Bristol Rd.
Flint, MI 48507-5508
Phone: (810)766-4100

★ 12372 ★ Eastern Michigan University
**Department of Associated Health
  Professions**
Occupational Therapy Program
328 King Hall
Ypsilanti, MI 48197-2239
Phone: (313)487-4094

★ 12373 ★ Saginaw Valley State University
**College of Nursing and Allied Health
  Sciences**
Occupational Therapy Program
Ryder Center W., Rm. 105
7400 Bay Rd.
University Center, MI 48710-0001
Phone: (517)790-4153

★ 12374 ★ Wayne State University
**College of Pharmacy and Allied Health
  Professions**
Department of Occupational Therapy
Detroit, MI 48202-3489
Phone: (313)577-1435

★ 12375 ★ Western Michigan University
Department of Occupational Therapy
Kalamazoo, MI 49008-5051
Phone: (616)387-3850

Minnesota

★ 12376 ★ College of St. Catherine
Department of Occupational Therapy
2004 Randolph Ave.
St. Paul, MN 55105-1794
Phone: (612)690-6505

★ 12377 ★ College of St. Scholastica
Occupational Therapy Program
1200 Kenwood Ave.
Duluth, MN 55811
Phone: (218)723-6698

★ 12378 ★ University of Minnesota
Health Sciences Center
Program in Occupational Therapy
Box 388, UMHC
Minneapolis, MN 55455-0392
Phone: (612)626-5887

Mississippi

★ 12379 ★ University of Mississippi
School of Health Related Professions
Department of Occupational Therapy
2500 N. State St.
Jackson, MS 39216-4505
Phone: (601)984-6350

Missouri

★ 12380 ★ Kirksville College of
  Osteopathic Medicine
Occupational Therapy Program
800 W. Jefferson St.
Kirksville, MO 63501
Phone: (816)626-2237

★ 12381 ★ Rockhurst College
College of Arts and Sciences
Occupational Therapy Program
1100 Rockhurst Rd.
Kansas City, MO 64110-2508
Phone: (816)926-4635

★ 12382 ★ St. Louis University Medical
  Center
School of Allied Health Professions
Occupational Therapy Program
1504 S. Grand Blvd.
St. Louis, MO 63104-1395
Phone: (314)577-8514

★ 12383 ★ University of Missouri—
  Columbia
School of Health Related Professions
Occupational Therapy Curriculum
126 Lewis Hall
Columbia, MO 65211
Phone: (314)882-3988

★ 12384 ★ Washington University
School of Medicine
Program in Occupational Therapy
4567 Scott Ave.
St. Louis, MO 63110-1093
Phone: (314)362-6911

Nebraska

★ 12385 ★ Creighton University
**School of Pharmacy and Allied Health
  Professions**
Occupational Therapist Program
2500 California Plaza
Omaha, NE 68178-0259
Phone: (402)325-2830

New Hampshire

★ 12386 ★ University of New Hampshire
School of Health and Human Services
Occupational Therapy Department
Hewitt Hall
Durham, NH 03824-3563
Phone: (603)862-2167

New Jersey

★ 12387 ★ Kean College of New Jersey
Occupational Therapy Department
Willis 311, Morris Ave.
Union, NJ 07083-9982
Phone: (908)527-2590

New Mexico

★ 12388 ★ University of New Mexico
School of Medicine
Occupational Therapy Program
Health Sciences and Services Bldg., Rm. 217
Albuquerque, NM 87131-5641
Phone: (505)277-1966

New York

★ 12389 ★ Columbia University
College of Physicians and Surgeons
Programs in Occupational Therapy
630 W. 168th St.
New York, NY 10032
Phone: (212)305-3781

★ 12390 ★ Dominican College
Occupational Therapy Program
10 Western Hwy.
Orangeburg, NY 10962
Phone: (914)359-6449

★ 12391 ★ D'Youville College
Department of Occupational Therapy
One D'Youville Sq.
320 Porter Ave.
Buffalo, NY 14201-1084
Phone: (716)881-7626

★ 12392 ★ Ithaca College
Occupational Therapy Program
Ithaca, NY 14850
Phone: (607)274-3111

★ 12393 ★ Keuka College
Department of Occupational Therapy
Keuka Park, NY 14478-0098
Phone: (315)536-5254

★ 12394 ★ Mercy College
Occupational Therapy Program
555 Broadway
Dobbs Ferry, NY 10522
Phone: (914)674-9331

★ 12395 ★ New York University
**School of Education, Health, Nursing and
  Arts Professions**
Department of Occupational Therapy
35 W. 4th St., 11th Fl.
New York, NY 10012-1172
Phone: (212)998-5825

★ 12396 ★ Sage Colleges
Occupational Therapy Program
45 Ferry St.
Troy, NY 12180-4115
Phone: (518)270-2266

★ 12397 ★ State University of New York at Buffalo
Department of Occupational Therapy
515 Stockton Kimball Tower
3435 Main St.
Buffalo, NY 14214-3079
Phone: (716)831-3141

★ 12398 ★ State University of New York Health Science Center at Brooklyn
Occupational Therapy Program
450 Clarkson Ave., 81
Brooklyn, NY 11203-2098
Phone: (718)270-7730

★ 12399 ★ State University of New York at Stony Brook
School of Health Technology and Management
Division of Rehabilitation Sciences
Occupational Therapy Program
L2-031
Stony Brook, NY 11794-8201
Phone: (718)270-7730

★ 12400 ★ Syracuse University
Utica College
Division of Health Sciences
Curriculum in Occupational Therapy
1600 Burrstone Rd.
Utica, NY 13502-4892
Phone: (315)792-3006

★ 12401 ★ Touro College
Department of Occupational Therapy
135 Carman Rd., Bldg. 10
Dix Hills, NY 11746-5641
Phone: (516)673-3200

★ 12402 ★ York College of City University of New York
Occupational Therapy Program
94-20 Guy R. Brewer Blvd.
Jamaica, NY 11451-9902
Phone: (718)262-2720

North Carolina

★ 12403 ★ East Carolina University
School of Allied Health Sciences
Department of Occupational Therapy
Greenville, NC 27858-4353
Phone: (919)328-4441

★ 12404 ★ University of North Carolina at Chapel Hill
Division of Occupational Therapy
Medical School, Wing E CB7120
Chapel Hill, NC 27599-7120
Phone: (919)966-2451

North Dakota

★ 12405 ★ Casper College / University of North Dakota
Occupational Therapy Program
Box 7126
University Station
Grand Forks, ND 58202-7126
Phone: (701)777-2209

★ 12406 ★ University of North Dakota
Department of Occupational Therapy
PO Box 7126, University Station
Grand Forks, ND 58202-7126
Phone: (701)777-2209

Ohio

★ 12407 ★ Cleveland State University
Department of Health Sciences
Occupational Therapy Program
Fenn Tower 609
Euclid Ave. at E. 24th St.
Cleveland, OH 44115-2440
Phone: (216)687-3568

★ 12408 ★ Medical College of Ohio at Toledo
School of Allied Health
Occupational Therapy Program
PO Box 10008
Toledo, OH 43699-0008
Phone: (419)381-4117

★ 12409 ★ Ohio State University
School of Allied Medical Professions
Occupational Therapy Division
1583 Perry St.
Columbus, OH 43210-1234
Phone: (614)292-5824

★ 12410 ★ Shawnee State University
Occupational Therapy Program
940 2nd St.
Portsmouth, OH 45662
Phone: (614)355-2209

★ 12411 ★ Xavier University
College of Social Sciences
Occupational Therapy Program
3800 Victory Pkwy.
Cincinnati, OH 45207-7341
Phone: (513)745-3301

Oklahoma

★ 12412 ★ University of Oklahoma
College of Allied Health
Department of Occupational Therapy
Health Sciences Center
801 NE 13th St.
Oklahoma City, OK 73190-1090
Phone: (405)271-2411

Oregon

★ 12413 ★ Pacific University
Department of Occupational Therapy
2043 College Way
Forest Grove, OR 97116-1797
Phone: (503)359-2203

Pennsylvania

★ 12414 ★ College Misericordia
Division of Health Sciences
Occupational Therapy Program
Dallas, PA 18612
Phone: (717)674-6461

★ 12415 ★ Duquesne University
John G. Rangos School of Health Sciences
Occupational Therapy Program
227 Health Sciences Bldg.
Pittsburgh, PA 15282-0001
Phone: (412)396-6220

★ 12416 ★ Elizabethtown College
Department of Occupational Therapy
1 Alpha Dr.
Elizabethtown, PA 17022-2298
Phone: (717)361-1174

★ 12417 ★ Gannon University
Villa Maria College of Health Sciences
Occupational Therapy Program
University Square
Erie, PA 16541-0001
Phone: (814)871-7407

★ 12418 ★ Temple University
College of Allied Health Professions
Department of Occupational Therapy
Health Sciences Campus
3307 N. Broad St.
Philadelphia, PA 19140
Phone: (215)221-4813

★ 12419 ★ Thomas Jefferson University
College of Allied Health Sciences
Department of Occupational Therapy
Edison Bldg., Rm. 820
130 S. 9th St.
Philadelphia, PA 19107-5233
Phone: (215)955-8010

★ 12420 ★ University of Pittsburgh
School of Health and Rehabilitation Sciences
Program in Occupational Therapy
116 Pennsylvania Hall
Pittsburgh, PA 15261-1813
Phone: (412)624-8860

Puerto Rico

★ 12421 ★ University of Puerto Rico
College of Health Related Professions
Physical and Occupational Therapy Department
Medical Sciences Campus
PO Box 365067
San Juan, PR 00936-5067
Phone: (809)758-2525

South Carolina

★ 12422 ★ Medical University of South Carolina
College of Health Related Professions
Occupational Therapy Educational Department
171 Ashley Ave., Rm. 123-CHP
Charleston, SC 29425-2701
Phone: (803)792-2961

South Dakota

★ 12423 ★ **University of South Dakota**
Occupational Therapy Program
236 Julian Hall
414 E. Clark St.
Vermillion, SD 57069-2390
Phone: (605)677-5600

Tennessee

★ 12424 ★ **Tennessee State University**
School of Allied Health Professions
Occupational Therapy Program
3500 John Merritt Blvd.
Nashville, TN 37209-1561
Phone: (615)320-3161

★ 12425 ★ **University of Tennessee, Memphis**
College of Allied Health Sciences
Department of Rehabilitation Sciences
Health Science Center
822 Beale St., Ste. 345
Memphis, TN 38163
Phone: (901)448-8393

Texas

★ 12426 ★ **Texas Tech University**
Health Sciences Center
School of Allied Health
Department of Occupational Therapy
3601 4th St.
Lubbock, TX 79430-0001
Phone: (806)743-3240

★ 12427 ★ **Texas Woman's University**
School of Occupational Therapy
PO Box 23718, TWU Station
Denton, TX 76204-1718
Phone: (817)898-2802

★ 12428 ★ **University of Texas Health Science Center at San Antonio**
Occupational Therapy Program
7703 Floyd Curl Dr.
San Antonio, TX 78284-7770
Phone: (210)567-3111

★ 12429 ★ **University of Texas Medical Branch at Galveston**
School of Allied Health Sciences
Department of Occupational Therapy
Galveston, TX 77555-1028
Phone: (409)772-3060

Virginia

★ 12430 ★ **Shenandoah University**
Occupational Therapy Program
333 W. Cork St.
Winchester, VA 22601
Phone: (703)665-1630

★ 12431 ★ **Virginia Commonwealth University**
Medical College of Virginia
Department of Occupational Therapy
PO Box 980008
Richmond, VA 23298-0008
Phone: (804)828-2219

Washington

★ 12432 ★ **University of Puget Sound**
School of Occupational Therapy
1500 N. Warner St.
Tacoma, WA 98416-0510
Phone: (206)756-3211

★ 12433 ★ **University of Washington**
School of Medicine
Department of Rehabilitation Medicine
Division of Occupational Therapy
RJ-30 University Hospital
Seattle, WA 98195
Phone: (206)685-7411

Wisconsin

★ 12434 ★ **Concordia University, Wisconsin**
Occupational Therapy Program
12800 N. Lake Shore Dr.
Mequon, WI 53092-7699
Phone: (414)243-4300

★ 12435 ★ **Mt. Mary College**
Department of Occupational Therapy
2900 N. Menomonee River Pkwy.
Milwaukee, WI 53222-4597
Phone: (414)258-4810

★ 12436 ★ **University of Wisconsin—Madison**
Occupational Therapy Program
1300 University Ave. (2110/MSC)
Madison, WI 53706-1532
Phone: (608)262-4917

★ 12437 ★ **University of Wisconsin—Milwaukee**
School of Allied Health Professions
Occupational Therapy Program
PO Box 413
Milwaukee, WI 53201-0413
Phone: (414)229-5981

Physical Therapy

The following bachelor, certificate, and masters degree programs for physical therapists are accredited by the American Physical Therapy Association (APTA), 1111 N. Fairfax St., Alexandria, VA 22314, (703) 684-2782. APTA also accredits and maintains a listing of educational programs for physical therapy assistants.

Alabama

★ 12438 ★ **University of Alabama at Birmingham**
School of Health Related Professions
Division of Physical Therapy
SHRP Bldg., Rm. 116
UAB Station
Birmingham, AL 35294-1270
Phone: (205)934-3566

★ 12439 ★ **University of South Alabama**
College of Allied Health Professions
Department of Physical Therapy
1504 Spring Hill Ave.
Mobile, AL 36604
Phone: (205)434-3575

Arizona

★ 12440 ★ **Northern Arizona University**
Department of Physical Therapy
C.U. Box 15105
Flagstaff, AZ 86011
Phone: (602)523-4092

Arkansas

★ 12441 ★ **University of Central Arkansas**
Department of Physical Therapy
201 Donaghey, HSC 200
Conway, AR 72035-0001
Phone: (501)450-5548

California

★ 12442 ★ **California State University, Fresno**
Physical Therapy Department
2345 E. San Ramon
Fresno, CA 93740-0029
Phone: (209)278-2022

★ 12443 ★ **California State University, Long Beach**
College of Health and Human Services
Physical Therapy Department
1250 Bellflower Blvd.
Long Beach, CA 90840
Phone: (213)985-4072

★ 12444 ★ **California State University, Northridge**
Department of Health Science
Physical Therapy Program
Northridge, CA 91330
Phone: (818)885-3101

★ 12445 ★ **Chapman University**
School of Physical Therapy
333 N. Glassell
Orange, CA 92666
Phone: (714)744-6786

★ 12446 ★ **College of Osteopathic Medicine of the Pacific**
Department of Physical Therapy
352 Pomona Mall E.
Pomona, CA 91766-1889
Phone: (909)623-6116

★ 12447 ★ Loma Linda University
School of Allied Health Professions
Department of Physical Therapy
Loma Linda, CA 92350
Phone: (909)824-4632

★ 12448 ★ Mt. St. Mary's College
Department of Physical Therapy
12001 Chalon Rd.
Los Angeles, CA 90049
Phone: (310)471-9519

★ 12449 ★ University of California, San Francisco
School of Medicine
Graduate Program in Physical Therapy
Box 0736
San Francisco, CA 94143
Phone: (415)476-3146

★ 12450 ★ University of the Pacific
Physical Therapy Department
Stockton, CA 95211
Phone: (209)946-2886

★ 12451 ★ University of Southern California
Department of Physical Therapy
2025 Zonal Ave., CSA-208
Los Angeles, CA 90033
Phone: (213)342-2900

Colorado

★ 12452 ★ University of Colorado—Denver Health Science Center
Physical Therapy Program
4200 E. 9th Ave.
Box E-224
Denver, CO 80262
Phone: (303)372-9144

Connecticut

★ 12453 ★ Quinnipiac College
School of Allied Health and Natural Sciences
Department of Physical Therapy
Hamden, CT 06518
Phone: (203)281-8681

★ 12454 ★ University of Connecticut
School of Allied Health Professions
Program in Physical Therapy
358 Mansfield Rd.
Storrs Mansfield, CT 06269-2101
Phone: (203)486-0049

Delaware

★ 12455 ★ University of Delaware
School of Life and Health Sciences
Physical Therapy Program
319 McKinly Laboratory
Newark, DE 19716
Phone: (302)831-8910

District of Columbia

★ 12456 ★ Howard University
College of Allied Health Sciences
Department of Physical Therapy
6th and Bryant Sts. NW
Washington, DC 20059
Phone: (202)806-7613

Florida

★ 12457 ★ Barry University
Department of Physical Therapy
11300 NE 2nd Ave.
Miami Shores, FL 33161-6695
Phone: (305)899-3540

★ 12458 ★ Florida A&M University
School of Allied Health Sciences
Division of Physical Therapy
Ware-Rhaney Bldg., Rm. 223
Tallahassee, FL 32307
Phone: (904)599-3820

★ 12459 ★ Florida International University
College of Health Sciences
Department of Physical Therapy
Miami, FL 33199
Phone: (305)348-3831

★ 12460 ★ University of Central Florida
Department of Physical Therapy
PO Box 160000
Orlando, FL 32816-2200
Phone: (407)823-3470

★ 12461 ★ University of Florida
College of Health Related Professions
Department of Physical Therapy
J. Hillis Miller Health Center
PO Box 100154
Gainesville, FL 32610-0154
Phone: (904)395-0085

★ 12462 ★ University of Miami
School of Medicine
Department of Orthopaedics and Rehabilitation
Division of Physical Therapy
5915 Ponce de Leon Blvd., 5th Fl.
Coral Gables, FL 33146
Phone: (305)284-4535

★ 12463 ★ University of North Florida
College of Health
Physical Therapy Program
Founders Hall
4567 St. John's Bluff Rd. S.
Jacksonville, FL 32224
Phone: (904)646-2840

Georgia

★ 12464 ★ Emory University
Division of Physical Therapy
1441 Clifton Rd. NE
Atlanta, GA 30322
Phone: (404)727-6138

★ 12465 ★ Georgia State University
Department of Physical Therapy
University Plaza
Atlanta, GA 30303
Phone: (404)651-3091

★ 12466 ★ Medical College of Georgia
Department of Physical Therapy
Augusta, GA 30912-0800
Phone: (706)721-2141

Idaho

★ 12467 ★ Idaho State University
Department of Physical Therapy
Box 8002
Pocatello, ID 83209
Phone: (208)236-4095

Illinois

★ 12468 ★ Bradley University
Department of Physical Therapy
1501 W. Bradley Ave.
Peoria, IL 61625
Phone: (309)677-3489

★ 12469 ★ Finch University of Health Sciences / Chicago Medical School
School of Related Health Sciences
Physical Therapy Program
3333 Green Bay Rd.
North Chicago, IL 60064
Phone: (708)578-3307

★ 12470 ★ Northern Illinois University
School of Allied Health Professions
Physical Therapy Program
De Kalb, IL 60115
Phone: (815)753-1383

★ 12471 ★ Northwestern University Medical School
Programs in Physical Therapy
345 E. Superior St., Rm. 1323
Chicago, IL 60611
Phone: (312)908-8160

★ 12472 ★ University of Illinois at Chicago
Department of Physical Therapy
1919 W. Taylor St. M/C 898
Chicago, IL 60612
Phone: (312)996-7764

Indiana

★ 12473 ★ Indiana University
Division of Allied Health Sciences
Physical Therapy Program
NIFS Bldg., 2nd Fl.
250 N. University Blvd.
Indianapolis, IN 46202-5192
Phone: (317)274-3432

★ 12474 ★ University of Evansville
Department of Physical Therapy
1800 Lincoln Ave.
Evansville, IN 47722
Free: 800-423-8633

★ 12475 ★ University of Indianapolis
Krannert Graduate School of Physical
   Therapy
1400 E. Hanna Ave.
Indianapolis, IN 46227-3697
Phone: (317)788-3500

Iowa

★ 12476 ★ University of Iowa
College of Medicine
Physical Therapy Education Program
2600 Steindler Bldg.
Iowa City, IA 52242
Phone: (319)353-9791

★ 12477 ★ University of Osteopathic
   Medicine and Health Sciences
College of Biological Sciences
Physical Therapy Program
3200 Grand Ave.
Des Moines, IA 50312
Phone: (515)271-1634

Kansas

★ 12478 ★ University of Kansas
Department of Physical Therapy Education
3056 Robinson Hall
3901 Rainbow Blvd.
Kansas City, KS 66160-7601
Phone: (913)588-6799

★ 12479 ★ Wichita State University
College of Health Professions
Department of Physical Therapy
Wichita, KS 67260-0043
Phone: (316)689-3604

Kentucky

★ 12480 ★ University of Kentucky
Physical Therapy Division
Medical Center, Rm. 4, Annex 1
Lexington, KY 40536-0079
Phone: (606)233-5415

★ 12481 ★ University of Louisville
Division of Allied Health Science
Physical Therapy Program
525 E. Madison St.
Louisville, KY 40292
Phone: (502)852-7815

Louisiana

★ 12482 ★ Louisiana State University
School of Allied Health Professions
Department of Physical Therapy
PO Box 33932
Shreveport, LA 71130-3932
Phone: (318)674-6820

Maine

★ 12483 ★ University of New England
Department of Physical Therapy
11 Hills Beach Rd.
Biddeford, ME 04005
Phone: (207)283-0171

Maryland

★ 12484 ★ University of Maryland
School of Medicine
Department of Physical Therapy
100 Penn St., Rm. 115
Baltimore, MD 21201
Phone: (410)706-7720

★ 12485 ★ University of Maryland Eastern
   Shore
Department of Physical Therapy
PO Box 1061
Princess Anne, MD 21853
Phone: (410)651-6301

Massachusetts

★ 12486 ★ Boston University
Sargent College of Allied Health
   Professions
Department of Physical Therapy
635 Commonwealth Ave.
Boston, MA 02215
Phone: (617)353-2720

★ 12487 ★ Northeastern University
Department of Physical Therapy
360 Huntington Ave.
Boston, MA 02115
Phone: (617)373-3160

★ 12488 ★ Simmons College
Graduate School for Health Studies
Department of Physical Therapy
300 The Fenway
Boston, MA 02115
Phone: (617)521-2650

★ 12489 ★ Springfield College
Department of Physical Therapy
263 Alden St.
Springfield, MA 01109
Phone: (413)748-3369

★ 12490 ★ University of Massachusetts
   Lowell
Program in Physical Therapy
Weed Hall-South Campus
Lowell, MA 01854
Phone: (508)934-4515

Michigan

★ 12491 ★ Andrews University
Department of Physical Therapy
Berrien Springs, MI 49104
Phone: (616)471-2878

★ 12492 ★ Grand Valley State University
School of Health Sciences
Physical Therapy Program
Allendale, MI 49401
Phone: (616)895-3356

★ 12493 ★ Oakland University
School of Health Sciences
Program in Physical Therapy
Rochester, MI 48309-4401
Phone: (313)370-4041

★ 12494 ★ University of Michigan—Flint
School of Health Professions and Studies
Physical Therapy Department
Flint, MI 48502-2186
Phone: (810)762-3373

★ 12495 ★ Wayne State University
College of Pharmacy and Allied Health
   Professions
Department of Physical Therapy
Detroit, MI 48202
Phone: (313)577-1432

Minnesota

★ 12496 ★ College of St. Scholastica
Department of Physical Therapy
1200 Kenwood Ave.
Duluth, MN 55811
Phone: (218)723-6786

★ 12497 ★ Mayo Foundation
School of Health-Related Sciences
Physical Therapy Program
1104 Siebens Bldg.
Rochester, MN 55905
Phone: (507)284-2054

★ 12498 ★ University of Minnesota
Program in Physical Therapy
Box 388, UMHC
Minneapolis, MN 55455
Phone: (612)626-5887

Mississippi

★ 12499 ★ University of Mississippi
School of Health Related Professions
Department of Physical Therapy
2500 N. State St.
Jackson, MS 39216
Phone: (601)984-6330

Missouri

★ 12500 ★ Maryville University
Department of Physical Therapy
13550 Conway Rd.
St. Louis, MO 63141
Phone: (314)576-9523

★ 12501 ★ Rockhurst College
Physical Therapy Program
1100 Rockhurst Rd.
Kansas City, MO 64110
Phone: (816)926-4059

★ 12502 ★ St. Louis University
Department of Physical Therapy
St. Louis University Medical Center
1504 S. Grand Blvd., Rm. 306
St. Louis, MO 63104
Phone: (314)577-8505

★ 12503 ★ University of Missouri—
Columbia
School of Health Related Professions
Physical Therapy Program
121 Lewis Hall
Columbia, MO 65211
Phone: (314)882-7103

★ 12504 ★ Washington University
School of Medicine
Program in Physical Therapy
Campus Box 8502
4444 Forest Park Blvd.
St. Louis, MO 63108
Phone: (314)286-1400

Montana

★ 12505 ★ University of Montana
Physical Therapy Program
Missoula, MT 59812
Phone: (406)243-4753

Nebraska

★ 12506 ★ University of Nebraska at
Omaha
College of Medicine
Division of Physical Therapy Education
600 S. 42nd
Omaha, NE 68198-4420
Phone: (402)559-4259

New Jersey

★ 12507 ★ Richard Stockton College of
New Jersey
Physical Therapy Program
Jim Leeds Rd.
Pomona, NJ 08240
Phone: (609)652-4621

★ 12508 ★ Rutgers University / University
of Medicine and Dentistry of New Jersey
School of Health Related Professions
Physical Therapy Program
401 Haddon Ave.
Camden, NJ 08103-1506
Phone: (609)964-2690

★ 12509 ★ University of Medicine and
Dentistry of New Jersey / Kean College
of New Jersey / Seton Hall University
School of Allied Health Related
Professions
Physical Therapy Program
65 Bergen St.
Newark, NJ 07107-3001
Phone: (201)982-5272

New Mexico

★ 12510 ★ University of New Mexico
School of Medicine
Division of Physical Therapy
Albuquerque, NM 87131
Phone: (505)277-5755

New York

★ 12511 ★ Columbia University
Program in Physical Therapy
630 W. 168th St.
New York, NY 10032
Phone: (212)305-3781

★ 12512 ★ Daemen College
Physical Therapy Department
4380 Main St.
Amherst, NY 14226
Phone: (716)839-3600

★ 12513 ★ D'Youville College
Physical Therapy Program
1 D'Youville Square
320 Porter Ave.
Buffalo, NY 14201-1084
Phone: (716)881-7624

★ 12514 ★ Hunter College of City
University of New York
School of Health Sciences
Physical Therapy Program
425 E. 25th St.
New York, NY 10010
Phone: (212)481-4469

★ 12515 ★ Ithaca College
Division of Physical Therapy
953 Danby Rd.
Ithaca, NY 14850-7183
Phone: (607)274-3124

★ 12516 ★ Long Island University
Division of Physical Therapy
University Plaza
Brooklyn, NY 11201
Phone: (718)488-1063

★ 12517 ★ New York University
Department of Physical Therapy
345 E. 24th St.
Weissman Bldg., 2nd Fl.
New York, NY 10010-4086
Phone: (212)998-9400

★ 12518 ★ Russell Sage College
Department of Physical Therapy
Troy, NY 12180
Phone: (518)270-2266

★ 12519 ★ State University of New York at
Buffalo
Department of Physical Therapy and
Exercise Science
Physical Therapy Program
410 Kimball Tower, Main St. Campus
Buffalo, NY 14214
Phone: (716)829-2941

★ 12520 ★ State University of New York
Health Science Center at Brooklyn
Physical Therapy Program
Box 16
450 Clarkson Ave.
Brooklyn, NY 11203
Phone: (718)270-7720

★ 12521 ★ State University of New York
Health Science Center at Syracuse
College of Health Related Professions
Program in Physical Therapy
750 E. Adams St.
Syracuse, NY 13210
Phone: (315)464-6914

★ 12522 ★ State University of New York at
Stony Brook
School of Health Technology and
Management
Department of Physical Therapy
Health Sciences Center
Stony Brook, NY 11794
Phone: (516)444-3251

★ 12523 ★ Touro College
Barry Z. Levine School of Allied Health
Sciences
Physical Therapy Program
135 Carman Rd.
Dix Hills, NY 11746
Phone: (516)673-3200

North Carolina

★ 12524 ★ Duke University
Department of Physical Therapy
PO Box 3965
Durham, NC 27710
Phone: (919)684-3135

★ 12525 ★ East Carolina University
School of Allied Health Sciences
Department of Physical Therapy
Greenville, NC 27858-4353
Phone: (919)757-4450

★ 12526 ★ University of North Carolina at
Chapel Hill
Division of Physical Therapy
Medical School Wing E 222-H
Caller Box 7135
Chapel Hill, NC 27599-7135
Phone: (919)966-4708

North Dakota

★ 12527 ★ University of North Dakota
School of Medicine
Department of Physical Therapy
PO Box 9037
Grand Forks, ND 58202
Phone: (701)777-2831

Ohio

★ 12528 ★ Cleveland State University
Department of Health Sciences
Physical Therapy Department
1983 E. 24th St.
Cleveland, OH 44115
Phone: (216)687-3567

★ 12529 ★ Medical College of Ohio /
Bowling Green State University /
University of Toledo
Physical Therapy Program
2601 Ida Marie Dowling Hall
PO Box 10008
Toledo, OH 43699-0008
Phone: (419)381-3518

★ 12530 ★ Ohio State University
School of Allied Medical Professions
Division of Physical Therapy
1583 Perry St., 306
Columbus, OH 43210
Phone: (614)292-5921

★ 12531 ★ Ohio University
School of Physical Therapy
Convocation Center, Rm. 199
Athens, OH 45701
Phone: (614)593-1225

Oklahoma

★ 12532 ★ Langston University
Physical Therapy Program
Langston, OK 73050
Phone: (405)466-3411

★ 12533 ★ University of Oklahoma
College of Allied Health
Department of Physical Therapy
Health Sciences Center
PO Box 26901
Oklahoma City, OK 73190
Phone: (405)271-2131

Oregon

★ 12534 ★ Pacific University
School of Physical Therapy
2043 College Way
Forest Grove, OR 97116
Phone: (503)357-6151

Pennsylvania

★ 12535 ★ Beaver College
Department of Physical Therapy
450 S. Easton Rd.
Glenside, PA 19038
Phone: (215)572-2950

★ 12536 ★ Medical College of Pennsylvania
and Hahnemann University
Physical Therapy Program
201 N. 15th St., MS 502
Philadelphia, PA 19102
Phone: (215)762-1750

★ 12537 ★ Philadelphia College of
Pharmacy and Science
Physical Therapy Program
600 S. 43rd St.
Philadelphia, PA 19104
Phone: (215)596-8810

★ 12538 ★ Temple University
College of Allied Health Professions
Department of Physical Therapy
3307 N. Broad St.
Philadelphia, PA 19140
Phone: (215)707-4815

★ 12539 ★ Thomas Jefferson University
College of Allied Health Sciences
Department of Physical Therapy
130 S. 9th St., Rm. 830
Philadelphia, PA 19107
Phone: (215)955-8025

★ 12540 ★ University of Pittsburgh
School of Health Related Professions
Department of Physical Therapy
101 Pennsylvania Hall
Pittsburgh, PA 15261
Phone: (412)624-8990

★ 12541 ★ University of Scranton
Department of Physical Therapy
800 Linden St.
Scranton, PA 18510-4586
Phone: (717)941-7494

Puerto Rico

★ 12542 ★ University of Puerto Rico
College of Health Related Professions
Physical Therapy Program
Medical Science Campus
GPO Box 365067
San Juan, PR 00936
Phone: (809)758-2525

Rhode Island

★ 12543 ★ University of Rhode Island
Physical Therapy Program
Independence Square II
Kingston, RI 02881-0180
Phone: (401)792-5001

South Carolina

★ 12544 ★ Medical University of South
Carolina
Physical Therapy Program
171 Ashley Ave.
Charleston, SC 29425
Phone: (803)792-2961

South Dakota

★ 12545 ★ University of South Dakota
Department of Physical Therapy
414 E. Clark
Vermillion, SD 57069
Phone: (605)677-5915

Tennessee

★ 12546 ★ Tennessee State University
Physical Therapy Department
3500 John A. Meritt Blvd.
Nashville, TN 37209-1561
Phone: (615)320-3185

★ 12547 ★ University of Tennessee at
Chattanooga
Department of Physical Therapy
615 McCallie Ave.
Chattanooga, TN 37403-2598
Phone: (615)755-4747

★ 12548 ★ University of Tennessee,
Memphis
Department of Rehabilitation Sciences
Program in Physical Therapy
822 Beale St., 3rd Fl.
Memphis, TN 38163
Phone: (901)528-5888

Texas

★ 12549 ★ Southwest Texas State
University
Physical Therapy Program
Health Science Center
601 University Dr.
San Marcos, TX 78666
Phone: (512)245-3400

★ 12550 ★ Texas Tech University
Health Sciences Center
School of Allied Health
Department of Physical Therapy
Lubbock, TX 79430
Phone: (806)743-3226

★ 12551 ★ Texas Woman's University
School of Physical Therapy
Box 22487, TWU Station
Denton, TX 76204
Phone: (817)898-2460

★ 12552 ★ U.S. Army / Baylor University
Program in Physical Therapy
Academy of Health Sciences, U.S. Army
Ft. Sam Houston, TX 78234
Phone: (713)756-8139

★ 12553 ★ University of Texas Health
Science Center at San Antonio
Physical Therapy Program
7703 Floyd Curl Dr.
San Antonio, TX 78284
Phone: (210)567-3150

★ 12554 ★ University of Texas Medical
Branch at Galveston
School of Allied Health Sciences
Department of Physical Therapy
Galveston, TX 77550
Phone: (409)772-3068

★ 12555 ★ University of Texas
Southwestern Medical Center at Dallas
School of Allied Health Sciences
Department of Physical Therapy
5323 Harry Hines Blvd.
Dallas, TX 75235
Phone: (214)648-1550

Utah

★ 12556 ★ **University of Utah**
College of Health
Division of Physical Therapy
Annex Wing B, Rm. 1130
Salt Lake City, UT 84112
Phone: (801)581-8681

Vermont

★ 12557 ★ **University of Vermont**
School of Allied Health Sciences
Department of Physical Therapy
305 Rowell Bldg.
Burlington, VT 05405
Phone: (802)656-3252

Virginia

★ 12558 ★ **Old Dominion University**
College of Health Sciences
**School of Community Health Professions
and Physical Therapy**
Program in Physical Therapy
Norfolk, VA 23529-0288
Phone: (804)683-4409

★ 12559 ★ **Shenendoah University /
Winchester Medical Center**
Program in Physical Therapy
333 W. Cork St.
Winchester, VA 22601
Free: 800-432-2266

★ 12560 ★ **Virginia Commonwealth
University**
Medical College of Virginia
Department of Physical Therapy
PO Box 980224, MCV Station
Richmond, VA 23298
Phone: (804)786-0234

Washington

★ 12561 ★ **Eastern Washington University**
Department of Physical Therapy
Mail Stop 4
Cheney, WA 99004
Phone: (509)458-6435

★ 12562 ★ **University of Puget Sound**
School of Physical Therapy
1500 N. Warner
Tacoma, WA 98416
Phone: (206)756-3211

★ 12563 ★ **University of Washington**
School of Medicine
Department of Rehabilitation Medicine
Division of Physical Therapy
RJ-30
Seattle, WA 98195
Phone: (206)685-7408

West Virginia

★ 12564 ★ **West Virginia University**
School of Medicine
Division of Physical Therapy
Medical Center
1195 Health Sciences N.
Morgantown, WV 26506-9226
Phone: (304)293-3610

Wisconsin

★ 12565 ★ **Marquette University**
Program in Physical Therapy
Walter Schroeder Complex
Milwaukee, WI 53233
Phone: (414)288-7161

★ 12566 ★ **University of Wisconsin—La
Crosse**
Department of Physical Therapy
243 Cowley Hall
La Crosse, WI 54601
Phone: (608)785-8470

★ 12567 ★ **University of Wisconsin—
Madison**
Physical Therapy Program
1300 University Ave.
Madison, WI 53706
Phone: (608)263-5869

Rehabilitation

*The institutions listed below offer baccalaureate
and/or advanced degree programs in rehabilitation education. All are members of the National
Council on Rehabilitation Education, c/o Dept.
of Special Education and Rehabilitation, Utah
State University, Logan, UT 84322-2870, (801)
797-3241.*

Alabama

★ 12568 ★ **Auburn University**
**Department of Counseling and Counseling
Psychology**
Rehabilitation Counseling Program
2014 Haley Center
Auburn, AL 36849
Phone: (205)844-5160

Arizona

★ 12569 ★ **University of Arizona**
College of Education
**Department of Special Education and
Rehabilitation**
Rehabilitation Counseling Program
Tucson, AZ 85721
Phone: (520)621-7822

Arkansas

★ 12570 ★ **Arkansas Tech University**
Rehabilitation Counseling Program
Witherspoon Hall
Russellville, AR 72801
Phone: (501)968-0305

★ 12571 ★ **University of Arkansas**
**Department of Rehabilitation Education
and Research**
Rehabilitation Counseling Program
346 N. West Ave.
Fayetteville, AR 72701
Phone: (501)575-3656

California

★ 12572 ★ **California State University,
Fresno**
**School of Education and Human
Development**
Rehabilitation Counseling Program
Fresno, CA 93740-0003
Phone: (209)278-2105

★ 12573 ★ **California State University,
Sacramento**
School of Education
Rehabilitation Counseling Program
6000 J St.
Sacramento, CA 95819
Phone: (916)278-5568

★ 12574 ★ **California State University, San
Bernardino**
Rehabilitation Counselor Program
5500 University Pkwy.
San Bernardino, CA 92407
Phone: (909)880-5680

★ 12575 ★ **San Diego State University**
Rehabilitation Counselng Program
5850 Hardy Ave., No. 112
San Diego, CA 92182-0163
Phone: (619)594-7178

★ 12576 ★ **San Francisco State University**
Counseling Department
Rehabilitation Counselor Training Program
1600 Holloway Ave.
San Francisco, CA 94132
Phone: (415)338-1333

★ 12577 ★ **University of San Francisco**
**Department of Rehabilitation
Administration**
Rehabilitation Counseling Program
2130 Fulton St., CAM D-9
San Francisco, CA 94117-1080

Colorado

★ 12578 ★ **University of Northern Colorado**
Human Services Department
Rehabilitation Education Programs
McKee Hall, Rm. 41
Greeley, CO 80639
Phone: (303)351-1586

District of Columbia

★ 12579 ★ **Gallaudet University**
Department of Counseling
Rehabilitation Counseling Programs
Fowler Hall, Rm. 104
800 Florida Ave. NE
Washington, DC 20002
Phone: (202)651-5515

★12580★ George Washington University
Regional Rehabilitation Continuing
Education Programs
2011 I St. NW, Ste. 300
Washington, DC 20052
Phone: (202)676-5929

Florida

★12581★ Florida State University
Department of Human Services and
Studies
Rehabilitation Education Programs
215 Stone Bldg.
Tallahassee, FL 32306
Phone: (904)644-3854

★12582★ University of Florida
Department of Rehabilitation Counseling
J. Hillis Miller Health Center
PO Box 100175
Gainesville, FL 32610-0175
Phone: (904)392-6946

★12583★ University of South Florida
Department of Rehabilitation Counseling
4202 E. Fowler Ave.
Tampa, FL 33620-8100
Phone: (813)974-2855

Georgia

★12584★ Georgia State University
Department of Counseling and
Psychological Services
Rehabilitation Counseling Program
University Plaza
Atlanta, GA 30303-3083
Phone: (404)651-2550

★12585★ University of Georgia
Rehabilitation Counseling Program
413 Aderhold Hall
Athens, GA 30602-7142
Phone: (404)542-4134

Hawaii

★12586★ University of Hawaii at Manoa
Department of Counselor Education
Rehabilitation Counseling Program
1776 University Ave., Rm. WA2-222
Honolulu, HI 96822
Phone: (808)956-7501

Idaho

★12587★ University of Idaho
College of Education
Department of Counseling and Special
Education
Rehabilitation Counseling Program
Moscow, ID 83843
Phone: (208)885-6556

Illinois

★12588★ DePaul University
Rehabilitation Services Program
25 E. Jackson Blvd.
Chicago, IL 60604-2287
Phone: (312)341-8442

★12589★ Illinois Institute of Technology
Psychology Department
Rehabilitation Counseling Program
Life Sciences Bldg.
Chicago, IL 60616
Phone: (312)567-3514

★12590★ Northern Illinois University
Department of Communicative Disorders
Rehabilitation Counseling Program
De Kalb, IL 60115-2899
Phone: (815)753-6545

★12591★ Southern Illinois University at
Carbondale
Rehabilitation Institute
Rehabilitation Counseling Program
Rehn Hall 317
Carbondale, IL 62901-4609
Phone: (618)536-7704

★12592★ University of Illinois
Division of Rehabilitation Education
Services
1207 S. Oak St.
Champaign, IL 61820
Phone: (217)333-4622

Iowa

★12593★ Drake University
Rehabilitation Counseling Program
2507 University Ave.
Des Moines, IA 50311
Phone: (515)271-3061

★12594★ University of Iowa
Rehabilitation Counselor Training Program
N-356 Lindquist Center
Iowa City, IA 52242-1529
Phone: (319)335-5284

Kansas

★12595★ Emporia State University
Divisions of Counselor Education and
Rehabilitation Program
Campus Box 4036
1200 Commercial
Emporia, KS 66801
Phone: (316)343-5795

Kentucky

★12596★ University of Kentucky
Graduate Program in Rehabilitation
Counseling
124 Taylor Education Bldg.
Lexington, KY 40506
Phone: (606)257-3834

Louisiana

★12597★ Louisiana State University
School of Allied Health Professions
Rehabilitation Counseling Program
1900 Gravier St., Ste. 8C1
New Orleans, LA 70112-2262
Phone: (504)568-4315

★12598★ Southern University and
Agricultural and Mechanical College
Department of Psychology
Rehabilitation Counseling and Services
PO Box 9681
Baton Rouge, LA 70813
Phone: (504)771-2990

Maine

★12599★ University of Maine at
Farmington
Rehabilitation Counseling Program
88 Main St.
Farmington, ME 04938
Phone: (207)778-7097

Maryland

★12600★ Coppin State College
Rehabilitation Counseling Program
2500 W. North Ave.
Baltimore, MD 21216-3698
Phone: (410)383-5400

★12601★ University of Maryland Eastern
Shore
Rehabilitation Counseling Program
UMES Campus, Box 1027
Princess Anne, MD 21853-1299
Phone: (301)651-2200

Massachusetts

★12602★ Boston University
Sargent College of Allied Health
Professions
Department of Rehabilitation Counseling
635 Commonwealth Ave.
Boston, MA 02215
Phone: (617)353-2725

★12603★ Springfield College
Rehabilitation Services Department
Rehabilitation Counseling Program
Locklin Hall
210 Alden St.
Springfield, MA 01109
Phone: (413)788-3319

Michigan

★12604★ Michigan State University
Rehabilitation Counseling Program
335 Erickson Hall
East Lansing, MI 48824-1034
Phone: (517)355-1838

★ 12605 ★ **Wayne State University**
Rehabilitation Counseling Program
337 Education Bldg.
Detroit, MI 48202
Phone: (313)577-1743

Minnesota

★ 12606 ★ **Mankato State University**
Rehabilitation Counseling Program
MSU Box 52, PO Box 8400
Mankato, MN 56002-8400
Phone: (507)389-5438

★ 12607 ★ **St. Cloud State University**
Department of Applied Psychology
Rehabilitation Counseling Program
St. Cloud, MN 56301
Phone: (612)255-3131

Mississippi

★ 12608 ★ **Jackson State University**
Rehabilitation Counseling Program
PO Box 17501
Jackson, MS 39217-7501
Phone: (601)968-2380

★ 12609 ★ **Mississippi State University**
Department of Counselor Education and
Educational Psychology
Rehabilitation Counseling Program
PO Drawer GE
Mississippi State, MS 39762
Phone: (601)325-3331

Missouri

★ 12610 ★ **University of Missouri—**
Columbia
Department of Educational and Counseling
Psychology
Rehabilitation Education Programs
16 Hill Hall
Columbia, MO 65211
Phone: (314)882-7775

Montana

★ 12611 ★ **Montana State University**
Department of Counseling and
Psychological Services
Rehabilitation Counseling Program
1500 N. 30th St.
Billings, MT 59102-0298
Phone: (406)657-2011

★ 12612 ★ **Salish Kootenai College**
Rehabilitation Counseling Program
PO Box 117
Pablo, MT 59855
Phone: (406)675-4800

★ 12613 ★ **University of Montana**
Rural Institute on Disabilities
Rehabilitation Counseling Program
52 Corbin Hall
Missoula, MT 59812
Phone: (406)243-5467

New York

★ 12614 ★ **Hofstra University**
Department of Counseling, Research,
Special Education and Rehabilitation
Rehabilitation Counseling Program
111 Mason Hall
124 Hofstra University
Hempstead, NY 11550-1090
Phone: (516)560-5782

★ 12615 ★ **Hunter College of City**
University of New York
Rehabilitation Counselor Education
Program
695 Park Ave.
New York, NY 10021
Phone: (212)772-4755

★ 12616 ★ **New York University**
Rehabilitation Counseling Program
35 W. 4th St., Rm. 1200
New York, NY 10012-1172
Phone: (212)998-5293

★ 12617 ★ **State University of New York at**
Albany
Department of Counseling Psychology
Rehabilitation Counseling Program
1400 Washington Ave.
Albany, NY 12222
Phone: (518)442-5041

★ 12618 ★ **State University of New York at**
Buffalo
Department of Counseling and Educational
Psychology
Rehabilitation Counseling Program
409 Christopher Baldy Hall
Buffalo, NY 14260
Phone: (716)636-2476

★ 12619 ★ **Syracuse University**
Rehabilitation Counseling Program
259 Huntington Hall
Syracuse, NY 13244-2340
Phone: (315)443-9646

North Carolina

★ 12620 ★ **East Carolina University**
School of Allied Health Sciences
Department of Rehabilitation Studies
Rehabilitation Counseling Program
Greenville, NC 27858-4353
Phone: (919)757-4452

★ 12621 ★ **University of North Carolina at**
Chapel Hill
School of Medicine
Division of Rehabilitation Counseling
Campus Box 7205
118 Medical School Wing E
Chapel Hill, NC 27599-7205
Phone: (919)966-3351

Ohio

★ 12622 ★ **Bowling Green State University**
Department of Special Education
Rehabilitation Counseling Program
Bowling Green, OH 43403-0255
Phone: (419)372-7301

★ 12623 ★ **Kent State University**
Rehabilitation Counseling Program
White Hall, Rm. 310
Kent, OH 44242
Phone: (216)672-2662

★ 12624 ★ **Ohio State University**
Department of Educational Services and
Research
Rehabilitation Counseling Program
356 Arps Hall
1945 N. High St.
Columbus, OH 43210
Phone: (614)292-8787

★ 12625 ★ **Ohio University**
Rehabilitation Counseling Program
386 McCracken Hall
Athens, OH 45701
Phone: (614)593-0032

★ 12626 ★ **Wright State University**
Human Services Department
Rehabilitation Education Programs
MO52 Creative Arts Center
Dayton, OH 45435-0001
Phone: (513)873-2777

Oklahoma

★ 12627 ★ **East Central University**
Department of Human Resources
Rehabilitation Education Programs
Box Z-2
Ada, OK 74820
Phone: (405)332-8000

★ 12628 ★ **University of Oklahoma**
Center for Public Management and
Education Development
Rehabilitation Counseling Program
1700 Asp Ave., Bldg. 158
Norman, OK 73072-7820
Phone: (405)325-4913

Pennsylvania

★ 12629 ★ **Pennsylvania State University**
Division of Counseling and Rehabilitation
Education
327 CEDAR Bldg.
University Park, PA 16802-3110
Phone: (814)863-2416

★ 12630 ★ **University of Scranton**
College of Health, Education, and Human
Resources
Department of Counseling and Human
Resources
Rehabilitation Counseling Program
O'Hara Hall, Rm. 311
Scranton, PA 18510-4523
Phone: (717)941-4127

Puerto Rico

★ 12631 ★ University of Puerto Rico, Rio
Piedras
Faculty of Social Sciences
School of Rehabilitation Counseling
PO Box 23345
Rio Piedras, PR 00931
Phone: (809)751-8310

South Carolina

★ 12632 ★ South Carolina State College
Department of Human Services
Rehabilitation Counselor Training Program
300 College St. NE
PO Box 1532
Orangeburg, SC 29117-0001
Phone: (803)536-8600

★ 12633 ★ University of South Carolina
Rehabilitation Counseling Program
Wardlaw 252
Columbia, SC 29208
Phone: (803)777-3859

Tennessee

★ 12634 ★ University of Memphis
Counseling, Educational Psychology, and
Research
Rehabilitation Counseling Program
100 Ball Hall
Memphis, TN 38152
Phone: (901)678-2841

★ 12635 ★ University of Tennessee,
Knoxville
Department of Special Services Education
Rehabilitation Counseling Program
337 Claxton Addition
Knoxville, TN 37996-3400
Phone: (615)974-8111

Texas

★ 12636 ★ Stephen F. Austin State
University
Department of Counseling and Special
Education Programs
Rehabilitation Counseling Program
SFA Box 13019
Nacogdoches, TX 75962-3019
Phone: (409)568-1154

★ 12637 ★ University of North Texas
Center for Rehabilitation Studies
Rehabilitation Counseling Program
PO Box 13438, UNT Sta.
Denton, TX 76203-3438
Phone: (817)565-2488

★ 12638 ★ University of Texas—Pan
American
Division of Health Related Professions
Rehabilitative Services Program
1201 W. University Dr.
Edinburg, TX 78539-2999
Phone: (512)381-2295

★ 12639 ★ University of Texas
Southwestern Medical Center at Dallas
Department of Rehabilitation Science
Rehabilitation Counseling Program
5323 Harry Hines Blvd.
Dallas, TX 75235-9088
Phone: (214)648-2860

Utah

★ 12640 ★ Utah State University
Department of Special Education and
Rehabilitation
Rehabilitation Services Program
Logan, UT 84322-2865
Phone: (801)750-3241

Virginia

★ 12641 ★ Virginia Commonwealth
University
Department of Rehabilitation Counseling
921 W. Franklin St.
PO Box 842030
Richmond, VA 23284-2030
Phone: (804)367-1132

Washington

★ 12642 ★ Western Washington University
Rehabilitation Education Program
14110 NE 21st
Bellevue, WA 98007-3719
Phone: (206)957-4522

West Virginia

★ 12643 ★ West Virginia University
Department of Counseling, Rehabilitation
Counseling and Counseling Psychology
Rehabilitation Counseling Program
PO Box 6122
Morgantown, WV 26506
Phone: (304)293-3807

Wisconsin

★ 12644 ★ University of Wisconsin—
Madison
Department of Rehabilitation Psychology
and Special Education
Rehabilitation Counseling Program
432 N. Murray St.
Madison, WI 53706
Phone: (608)263-7917

★ 12645 ★ University of Wisconsin—
Milwaukee
Department of Educational Psychology
Rehabilitation Services Program
773 Enderis Hall
PO Box 413
Milwaukee, WI 53201
Phone: (414)229-5681

★ 12646 ★ University of Wisconsin—Stout
Department of Rehabilitation
Rehabilitation Counseling Program
Menomonie, WI 54751
Phone: (715)232-2499

National & International Organizations

★ 12647 ★ American Academy of Physical
Medicine and Rehabilitation (AAPM&R)
1 IBM Plz., 25th Fl.
Chicago, IL 60611-3604
Phone: (312)464-9700
Fax: (312)464-0227
Ronald A. Henrichs, Exec.Dir.

Founded: 1938. Members: 4,500. Description: National medical specialty society of physical medicine and rehabilitation physicians whose patients include people with physical disabilities and chronic, disabling illnesses. Mission is to maximize quality of life, minimize the incidence and prevalence of impairments, disability, and handicaps, promote societal health, and enhance the understanding and development of physiatry. Offers educational opportunities and advocacy support to members and provides information, referrals, and patient education materials. Publications: AAPM&R Membership Directory, annual. Membership Directory. Arranged alphabetically, geographically, and by special interest group. Price: Included in membership dues. • Archives of Physical Medicine and Rehabilitation, monthly. Journal. Provides original research and clinical reports to health professionals who work with the disabled, elderly, and handicapped. Price: Included in membership dues; $130/year for nonmembers; $156/year for institutions; $59/year for students. • Course Handouts. • Daily Calendar. • Official Program. • The Physiatrist, 10/year. Newsletter. Provides information on organizational activities, legislative and practice issues. Includes research updates, calendar, and quarterly inserts. Price: Included in membership dues. • Study Guide. Published part of Self-Directed Medical Knowledge Program. Formerly: (1956) American Society of Physical Medicine and Rehabilitation.

★ 12648 ★ American Board of Physical
Medicine and Rehabilitation (ABPMR)
Norwest Center, Ste. 674
21 1st St. SW
Rochester, MN 55902
Phone: (507)282-1776
Fax: (507)282-9242
Dr. Joachim L. Opitz, Exec.Dir.

Founded: 1947. Members: 4,642. Description: Certification board to establish qualifications, conduct examinations, and certify physicians who have completed the requirements in physical medicine and rehabilitation. Publications: Booklet, annual. Price: Free.

★ 12649 ★ American Center for the Alexander Technique (ACAT)
129 W. 67th St.
New York, NY 10023
Phone: (212)799-0468
Kathryn M. Miranda, Exec.Dir.

Founded: 1964. **Members:** 80. **Description:** Promotes the Alexander Technique, an educational technique that enables individuals to use their bodies with ease, grace, flexibility, and freedom from strain in any physical activity. Formed to assure further development of the technique in this country and to maintain its standards. Answers requests for information and refers interested people to certified teachers. Sponsors Teacher Certification Program consisting of 1600 hours over nine ten-week terms, the last a teaching apprenticeship, to certify students who have demonstrated, to the satisfaction of the faculty, a high standard both of teaching skills and of personal use. **Publications:** *ACAT News*, periodic. Newsletter. • *Annual Certified Member/Teacher List*.

★ 12650 ★ American Congress of Rehabilitation Medicine (ACRM)
5700 Old Orchard Rd., 1st Fl.
Skokie, IL 60077-1057
Phone: (708)966-0095
Fax: (708)966-9418
Richard G. Muir, Exec.Dir.

Founded: 1921. **Members:** 2,000. **Description:** Physicians, nurses, physical therapists, psychologists, occupational therapists, social workers, speech/language pathologists, and other allied health specialists active in and contributing to advancement in the field of medical rehabilitation. **Publications:** *Archives of Physical Medicine and Rehabilitation*, monthly. • Membership Directory, annual. • *Vital Connections*, quarterly. Newsletter. **Formerly:** American Congress of Physical Medicine; American Congress of Physical Medicine and Rehabilitation.

American Counseling Association (ACA)
See: Entry 7293

★ 12651 ★ American Horticultural Therapy Association (AHTA)
362A Christopher Ave.
Gaithersburg, MD 20879
Phone: (301)948-3010
Free: 800-634-1603
Fax: (301)869-2397
Steven Davis, Dir.

Founded: 1973. **Members:** 750. **Regional Groups:** 10. **Description:** Professional horticultural therapists and rehabilitation specialists; horticultural therapy students; institutions and commercial organizations. Promotes and encourages the development of horticulture and related activities as a therapeutic and rehabilitative medium. Horticultural therapy is considered particularly useful in the field of geriatrics and with regard to people who have mental disabilities. Coordinates efforts of professional and educational organizations and conducts professional consultations, regional workshops, and seminars. Operates placement service; provides resource information; conducts research in an effort to understand why horticultural ther-

apy works; offers papers at various conferences. Registers professional horticultural therapists. Maintains library of 400 publications including journal articles, books, theses, magazines, and newsletters. **Publications:** *Journal of Therapeutic Horticulture*, annual. Journal. • *Membership Directory*, annual. • *Organizing a Horticultural Therapy Workshop*. Booklet. • *People Plant Connection Newsletter*, monthly. Newsletter. Includes association news and lists of newly registered horticulture therapists. *Price:* $35/year.

★ 12652 ★ American Israeli Lighthouse (AIL)
30 E. 60th St., Ste. 309
New York, NY 10022
Phone: (212)838-5322
Mrs. Leonard F. Dank, Pres.

Founded: 1927. **Members:** 1,500. **State Groups:** 8. **Local Groups:** 7. **Description:** Works to raise funds for the maintenance of a rehabilitation center in Kiriat Haim, Israel for adult blind and physically handicapped persons. Promotes research in the development of techniques in education, vocational training, and rehabilitation. **Publications:** *The Tower*, annual.

★ 12653 ★ American Kinesiotherapy Association (AKTA)
PO Box 5188
Vancouver, WA 98668-5188
Phone: (360)696-2271
Free: 800-296-AKTA
Carol A. Holsman, Exec.Dir.

Founded: 1946. **Members:** 450. **Regional Groups:** 8. **State Groups:** 50. **Description:** Professional society of kinesiotherapists, and associate and student members with interest in physical and mental rehabilitation and adapted physical education. (Kinesiology is the study of human movement; kinesiotherapists use kinesiology to design and implement therapeutic exercise to meet the rehabilitative needs of persons with disease, injury, and/or physical disorders.) Goal is to promote the profession of kinseotheraphy by working toward public recognition of kinesiotherapy and to pursue and support legislative concerns of the profession. Works to maintain and advance the standard of care through educational opportunities. **Publications:** *Career in Kinesiology*. • *Cinical Kinesiology*, quarterly. Journal. Publishes manuscripts of professional and scientific nature in disciplines relates to kinesiotherapy. *Price:* $25 individuals; $45 library or institution. • *Mobility*, quarterly. Newsletter. Also publishes rehabilitation brochures. **Formerly:** (1968) Association for Physical and Mental Rehabilitation; (1987) American Corrective Therapy Association.

★ 12654 ★ American Massage Therapy Association (AMTA)
820 Davis St., Ste. 100
Evanston, IL 60201-4444
Phone: (708)864-0123
Fax: (708)864-1178
Mark C. Anderson, Dir.

Founded: 1943. **Members:** 18,000. **State Groups:** 52. **Description:** Massage therapists or technicians. Provides referrals to area therapists and certified schools. Conducts communi-

ty outreach programs and research and educational projects. Accredits massage training programs and offers a national certification program for massage therapists. Operates speakers' bureau; conducts charitable programs. **Publications:** *A Guide to Massage Therapy in America*. • *Applications of Therapeutic Massage*. Brochure. • *Hands On*, quarterly. Newsletter. • *Massage Therapy*. Brochure. • *Massage Therapy Journal*, quarterly. Journal. Contains scholarly articles on massage techniques and the therapeutic effect of massages. *Price:* $20/year in U.S.; $40/year outside U.S. • *Membership Registry*, annual. Membership Directory. • *Sports Massage*. Brochure. • *Stress*. Brochure. **Formerly:** American Association of Masseurs and Masseuses; (1983) American Massage and Therapy Association.

★ 12655 ★ American Occupational Therapy Association (AOTA)
4720 Montgomery Ln.
PO Box 31220
Bethesda, MD 20824-1220
Phone: (301)652-2682
Fax: (301)652-7711
Jeanette Bair, Exec.Dir.

Founded: 1917. **Members:** 48,000. **Description:** Registered occupational therapists and certified occupational therapy assistants who provide services to people whose lives have been disrupted by physical injury or illness, developmental problems, the aging process, or social or psychological difficulties. Occupational therapy focuses on the active involvement of the patient in specially designed therapeutic tasks and activities to improve function, performance capacity, and the ability to cope with demands of daily living. Conducts research and educational programs and compiles statistics. Supports the American Occupational Therapy Foundation, which administers a program of professional training and development in research and provides research information related to occupational therapy. **Publications:** *American Journal of Occupational Therapy*, monthly. Journal. • *Occupational Therapy Week*, weekly. • *Publications Catalog*. Catalog. Also publishes more than 100 single titles. **Formerly:** National Society for the Promotion of Occupational Therapy.

★ 12656 ★ American Occupational Therapy Certification Board (AOTCB)
4 Research Pl., Ste. 160
Rockville, MD 20850-3226
Phone: (301)990-7979
Fax: (301)869-8492
Roy Swift, Exec.Dir.

Founded: 1986. **Description:** Participants are occupational therapists and occupational therapy assistants. Administers certification program and maintains certification records of certificants; operates disciplinary mechanisms. **Publications:** Brochures. • Newsletters, quarterly. • Reports.

American Osteopathic College of Rehabilitation Medicine (AOCRM)
See: Entry 9993

★ 12657 ★ American Physical Therapy Association (APTA)
1111 N. Fairfax St.
Alexandria, VA 22314
Phone: (703)684-2782
Francis J. Mallon, Esq, CEO

Founded: 1921. **Members:** 62,000. **Regional Groups:** 52. **Description:** Professional organization of physical therapists and physical therapist assistants and students. Fosters the development and improvement of physical therapy service, education, and research; evaluates the organization and administration of curricula; directs the maintenance of standards and promotes scientific research. Acts as an accrediting body for educational programs in physical therapy and is responsible for establishing standards. Offers advisory and consultation services to schools of physical therapy and facilities offering physical therapy services; provides placement services at conference. **Publications:** Brochures. • Monographs. • *Physical Therapy*, monthly. Journal. Features peer-reviewed scientific and professional articles, continuing education course listings, abstracts of current literature, and book reviews. *Price:* Included in membership dues; $60/year for nonmembers. • *PT Bulletin*, weekly. Newsletter. Includes employment listings and information on upcoming seminars. *Price:* Included in membership dues; $80 for nonmembers. • *PT Magazine*, monthly. Journal. Features columns on risk management and reimbursement strategies. Contains advertisers' index and information on new products and literature. *Price:* Included in membership dues; $55/year for nonmembers; $7/copy. Also issues bulletins to chapters and publishes anthologies, handbooks, and educational resource guides. **Formerly:** (1921) American Women's Physical Therapeutic Association; (1948) American Physiotherapy Association.

★ 12658 ★ American Physical Therapy Association (PPS)
Private Practice Section
1101 17th St. NW, Ste. 1000
Washington, DC 20036
Phone: (202)457-1115
Fax: (202)457-9191
Carmine Valente, CEO

Founded: 1955. **Members:** 4,500. **Description:** Physical therapists who are members of the American Physical Therapy Association and who are in private practice. Purposes are: to provide physical therapists with information on establishing and managing a private practice; to promote high standards of private practice physical therapy; to represent private practitioners before governmental and professional agencies; to disseminate information relating to private practice. Monitors federal and state legislation. Holds forums and seminars. Bestows Robert G. Dicus Award to recognize individuals for achievement in and commitment to the private practice of physical therapy. **Publications:** *An Employers Guide to Obtaining Physical Therapy Services.* • *An Employers Guide to Obtaining PT Services.* • *How to Start a PT Private Practice.* • *Physical Therapy Today*, quarterly. Magazine. Covers practice management, marketing, clinical developments, legislative and regulatory news, and research and professional

issues. *Price:* Included in membership dues; $50/year for nonmembers. • *Private Practice Section Membership Directory*, annual. Membership Directory. Arranged alphabetically and geographically. Includes meeting schedule. *Price:* Included in membership dues; $300 for nonmembers. • *Private Practice Valuation Primer - How to Value a Practice for Sale or Purchase.* • *Twenty Questions About Private Practice.* Pamphlet. Also makes available blood borne pathogen kit.

★ 12659 ★ American Rehabilitation Association (NARF)
1910 Association Dr., Ste. 200
Reston, VA 22091
Phone: (703)648-9300
Fax: (703)648-0346
James Studzinski, Dir.

Founded: 1969. **Members:** 812. **State Groups:** 29. **Description:** Rehabilitation facilities in the U.S. and Canada; agencies operating established medical, residential and vocational rehabilitation facilities. Promotes expansion and improvement of rehabilitation services to disabled persons as provided in rehabilitation facilities. Represents the concerns of rehabilitation providers before Congress and government agencies. Is concerned with quality operation of rehabilitation centers and facilities. Conducts research and development programs in national rehabilitation policy. Sponsors seminars and provides specialized education programs. **Publications:** Books. • Monographs. • *Rehabilitation Insurance Report*, monthly. Newsletter. Analyzes insurance issues relevant to rehabilitation services. *Price:* $50/year to members; $65/year to nonmembers. • *Rehabilitation Review*, weekly. Newsletter. Monitors developments in the rehabilitation industry. Includes research updates and a calendar of events. *Price:* Included in membership dues; $125/year for nonmembers. • Videos. **Formerly:** (1975) International Association of Rehabilitation Facilities; (1980) Association of Rehabilitation Facilities; (1994) National Association of Rehabilitation Facilities.

★ 12660 ★ American Rehabilitation Counseling Association (ARCA)
c/o American Counseling Association
5999 Stevenson Ave.
Alexandria, VA 22304
Phone: (703)823-9800
Free: 800-347-6647
Fax: (703)823-0252
John L. Jaco, Exec.Dir.

Founded: 1958. **Members:** 2,329. **Description:** A division of the American Counseling Association. Rehabilitation counselors and interested professionals and students. Purpose is to improve the rehabilitation counseling profession and its services to individuals with disabilities. Promotes high standards in rehabilitation counseling, practice, research, and education. Encourages the exchange of information between rehabilitation professionals and consumer groups. Serves as liaison among members and public and private rehabilitation counselors across the country. Sponsors educational and training programs. **Publications:** *ARCA News*, quarterly. Newsletter. Provides information on the procedures and problems involved in reha-

bilitation counseling and special education for the disabled and the aged. *Price:* Included in membership dues. • *Rehabilitation Counseling Bulletin*, quarterly. Journal. *Price:* Included in membership dues; $18/year for nonmembers.

★ 12661 ★ American Society of Hand Therapists (ASHT)
401 N. Michigan Ave.
Chicago, IL 60611
Phone: (312)321-6866
Fax: (312)527-6636
Ruth Easterling, Exec.Dir.

Founded: 1977. **Members:** 1,950. **Description:** Registered and licensed occupational and physical therapists specializing in hand therapy and committed to excellence and professionalism in hand rehabilitation. Purposes are to promote research, publish information, improve treatment techniques, and standardize hand evaluation and care. Fosters education and communication between therapists in the U.S. and abroad. Compiles statistics; conducts research and education programs and continuing education seminars. **Publications:** *American Society of Hand Therapists--News*, monthly. Newsletter. *Price:* Included in membership dues. • *ASHT Membership Directory*, annual. Membership Directory. *Price:* Included in membership dues. • *ASHT News*, quarterly. Newsletter. *Price:* Included in membership dues. • *Journal of Hand Therapy*, quarterly. Journal. *Price:* Included in membership dues.

American Society of Neurorehabilitation
See: Entry 8177

★ 12662 ★ American Therapeutic Recreation Association (ATRA)
PO Box 15215
Hattiesburg, MS 39404-5215
Phone: (601)264-3413
Free: 800-553-0304
Fax: (601)264-3337
Lamar Evans, Adm.Dir.

Founded: 1984. **Members:** 3,500. **Regional Groups:** 14. **Description:** Therapeutic recreation professionals and students; interested others. (Therapeutic recreation involves the use of sports, handicrafts, and other recreational activities to improve the physical, mental, and emotional functions of persons with illnesses or disabling conditions.) Promotes the use of therapeutic recreation in hospitals, mental rehabilitation centers, physical rehabilitation centers, senior citizen treatment centers, and other public health facilities. Conducts discussions on certification and legislative and regulatory concerns that affect the industry. Sponsors seminars and workshops; conducts research. **Publications:** *Employment Update*, monthly. Features employment and internship opportunities for therapeutic recreation professionals. *Price:* Included in membership dues. • *Evaluation of Therapeutic Recreation Through Quality Assurance.* • Newsletter, bimonthly. *Price:* Included in membership dues. • *Risk Management in Therapeutic Recreation.* • *The Therapeutic Recreation Journal*, annual. Journal. Published in conjunction with American Association for Leisure and Recreation. *Price:* Included in membership dues. • *Third Party Reimbursements.*

★ 12663 ★ Association of Academic Physiatrists (AAP)
7100 Lakewood Bldg., Ste. 112
5987 E. 71st St.
Indianapolis, IN 46220
Phone: (317)845-4200
Fax: (317)845-4299
Carolyn L. Braddom, EdD, Exec.Dir.

Founded: 1967. **Members:** 1,000. **Description:** Academic physicians practicing physical medicine and rehabilitation and certified by the American Board of Physical Medicine and Rehabilitation. Objectives are: to advance teaching and research in physical medicine and rehabilitation within the area of academic medicine; to promote the dissemination of information to future physicians planning to work in this field; to become involved in the exchange of information from other areas of medicine both in basic sciences and in the clinical areas of teaching and research. **Publications:** *American Journal of Physical Medicine and Rehabilitation*, bimonthly. Journal. • Membership Directory, annual. • Newsletter, quarterly. • *Residency Program Directory*, annual. Directory.

★ 12664 ★ Association for Dance Movement Therapy—United Kingdom (ADMT)
Arts Therapies Dept.
Springfield Hospital
Glenburnie Rd.
Tooting Bec
London SW17 7DJ, England
Penny Best, Chair

Founded: 1982. **Members:** 100. **Languages:** English. **Description:** Individuals united to promote dance movement therapy. Monitors and promotes training. Offers professional services. Organizes summer schools. **Publications:** *ADMT Newsletter*, quarterly. Newsletter. • Articles, periodic. • Pamphlets, periodic.

★ 12665 ★ Association of Independent Physical Therapists (Interessenverband Freiberuflicher Krankengymnasten)
Konigsallee 178A
44799 Bochum, Germany
Phone: 234 72026
Fax: 234 72639
M. Schulte-Westenberg, Contact

Founded: 1981. **Members:** 1,400. **Description:** Physical therapists in Germany. Promotes the physical therapy industry. Represents the interests of free-lance physical therapists.

★ 12666 ★ Association for Past-Life Research and Therapies (APRT)
PO Box 20151
Riverside, CA 92516
Phone: (909)784-1570
Fax: (909)784-8440
Hazel M. Denning, Ph.D., Exec.Dir. Emeritus

Founded: 1980. **Members:** 950. **Description:** Psychiatrists, psychologists, counselors, and students; organizations and individuals interested in past-life regression therapy. Promotes past-life therapy as a means of helping individuals realize their capacity to change and improve their lives. Works for progressive application of the therapy and the establishment of clinical standards for training therapists. Acts as a communications network for the exchange of information and experiences. Disseminates information to the public about benefits of the therapy. Registers therapists. Offers training programs in past-life regression techniques. Promotes research in the field. Maintains speakers' bureau. **Publications:** *An Evening with Brian Weiss.* • Audiotapes. • Directory, periodic. • *Exploring Your Past Lives as a Pathway to Healing.* • *The Franklin Loehr Memorial Lecture.* • *Journal of Regression Therapy*, annual. Journal. • *Past Life Research and Therapies*, quarterly. Newsletter. Contains editorials, Open Forum, reviews, and calender of events. *Price:* $10/year. • Videos. • *The Wambach Method: A Manual for Past-Life Recall*. Manual. **Formerly:** (1991) Association for Past-Life Research and Therapy.

★ 12667 ★ Association for Play Therapy
c/o Kevin O'Connor
California School of Prof. Psychology
1350 M St.
Fresno, CA 93721
Phone: (209)486-0851
Fax: (209)486-0734
Kevin O'Connor, Exec.Dir.

Founded: 1982. **Members:** 2,900. **Description:** Professionals and students involved in play therapy. Promotes interests of members. Provides books and materials at a discount to members. **Publications:** *Association for Play Therapy Newsletter*, quarterly. Newsletter. *Price:* Included in membership dues. • *International Journal of Play Therapy*, semiannual. Journal. *Price:* Included in membership dues.

Association of Rehabilitation Nurses (ARN)
See: Entry 9074

★ 12668 ★ Associazione la Nostra Famiglia (LNF)
Via don Luigi Monza 1
I-22037 Ponte Lambro, Italy
Phone: 31 625111
Fax: 31 625275
Zaira Spreafico

Founded: 1947. **Members:** 150. **Languages:** English, Italian. **Description:** Association, based on evangelical principles, devoted to the social and physical rehabilitation of disabled children and young adults. Particular emphasis is placed on individuals with physical neuromotor and sensorial dysfunctions. Maintains more than 30 rehabilitation centers throughout Italy; also operates work centers and family homes providing social and educational training. Offers continuing education courses to specialists in the field. Sponsors seminars; maintains the Eugenio Medea Institute for hospitalization and treatment. Conducts research; compiles statistics. Maintains a clinic. **Publications:** *Notiziario d'Informazione*, quarterly. • *Saggi*, semiannual. Contains English summaries. Also publishes books and monographs.

★ 12669 ★ Australian Music Therapy Association (AMTA)
18 Collins St.
Box Hill, VIC 3128, Australia
Phone: 3 8981147
Helen Shoemark, Pres.

Founded: 1975. **Members:** 250. **State Groups:** 3. **Languages:** English. **Description:** Registered music therapists, students, and interested others. Promotes the theory and practice of music therapy. Offers registration accreditation of training program and in-service education for other professional groups; provides printed resources; conducts research. **Publications:** *Australian Journal of Music Therapy*, annual, always April. Journal. • *Bulletin*, semiannual. Newsletter. • *Network*, quarterly. Newsletter.

★ 12670 ★ Canadian Association of Physical Medicine and Rehabilitation (CAPM&R)
774 Promenade Echo Dr.
Ottawa, ON, Canada K1S 5N8
Phone: (613)730-6245
Fax: (613)730-1116
Dr. G.S. Tardif, Pres.

Founded: 1962. **Members:** 240. **Languages:** English, French. **Description:** Organizes scientific retreats. Bestows awards. **Publications:** *CAPM&R Newsletter*, 3/year. Newsletter.

★ 12671 ★ Canadian Rehabilitation Council for the Disabled (CRCD) (Conseil Canadien pour la Readaptation des Handicapes — CCRH)
45 Sheppard Ave. E, Ste. 801
Toronto, ON, Canada M2N 5W9
Phone: (416)250-7490
Fax: (416)229-1371
Henry Botchford, Exec.Dir.

Founded: 1962. **Members:** 74. **Languages:** English, French. **Description:** Organizations and individuals working with Canadians with disabilities, their families, and similar groups. Works to enhance the quality of life of the disabled. Operates awards program. **Publications:** *Access*, 6/year. Newsletter. • *Annual Report.* • *Directory of Canadian Rehabilitation Services*, periodic. • *Rehabilitation Digest*, quarterly.

★ 12672 ★ Certification Board for Music Therapists (CBMT)
1407 Huguenot Rd.
Midlothian, VA 23113
Phone: (804)379-9497
Free: 800-765-CBMT
Fax: (804)379-9354
Joy S. Schneck, Exec.Dir.

Founded: 1982. **Members:** 4,000. **Description:** Board-certified professional music therapists. Certifies and recertifies (every 5 years) professional music therapists through examination and continuing professional education. Monitors competence and professional growth of members. Offers training before and after certification. **Publications:** *BC-Status*, semiannual. Newsletter. Includes list of new members and updates on recertification process. *Price:* Free for members. • *Candidate Handbook.* Handbook. • *Recertification Manual.* Manual. • *Recertification, Self-Growth, and You.*

★ 12673 ★ **Commission on Accreditation of Rehabilitation Facilities (CARF)**
101 N. Wilmot Rd., Ste. 500
Tucson, AZ 85711
Phone: (602)748-1212
Donald E. Galvin, PhD, Pres./CEO

Founded: 1966. **Description:** Sponsored by 31 rehabilitation/habilitation organizations. The commission is the standard setting and accrediting authority for organizations providing services to people with disabilities. Encourages development and improvement of uniformly high standards of performance for all organizations serving individuals with developmental, physical, or emotional disabilities. Surveys and accredits rehabilitation/habilitation organizations; conducts research and educational activities related to standards for organizations offering programs in comprehensive inpatient rehabilitation, spinal cord injury, chronic pain management, brain injury, outpatient medical rehabilitation, work hardening, infant and early childhood development, vocational evaluation, work adjustment, occupational skill training, job placement, work services, supported employment, industry-based programs, community living, psychosocial programs, respite programs, alcoholism and other drug abuse rehabilitation programs, and community mental health programs. Accreditation Program is administered by a 38-member appointed board of trustees. **Publications:** *CARF Report*, semiannual. Covers commission activities; includes listing of accredited organizations. *Price:* Free. • *Standards Manual for Organizations Serving People with Disabilities*, annual. Describes accreditation standards for programs providing services to the disabled; includes glossary. *Price:* $35/year.

★ 12674 ★ **Council on Rehabilitation Education (CORE)**
1835 Rohlwing Rd., Ste. E
Rolling Meadows, IL 60008
Phone: (708)394-1785
Fax: (708)394-2108
Jeanne Boland Patterson, Dir.

Founded: 1972. **Members:** 29. **Description:** Sponsored by the American Rehabilitation Counseling Association, Council of State Administrators of Vocational Rehabilitation, National Association of Rehabilitation Facilities, National Council on Rehabilitation Education, and the National Rehabilitation Counseling Association. Promotes effective delivery of rehabilitation services to people with disabilities. Surveys, critiques, and works to improve rehabilitation educational programs at the postgraduate level; bestows recognition on programs judged effective. **Publications:** *CORE News*, annual. Lists recognized rehabilitation counselor education programs.

Council of Rehabilitation Specialists (CRS)
See: Entry 13445

★ 12675 ★ **Council of State Administrators of Vocational Rehabilitation (CSAVR)**
PO Box 3776
Washington, DC 20007
Phone: (202)638-4634
Joseph H. Owens, Exec.Dir.

Founded: 1940. **Members:** 82. **Regional Groups:** 10. **State Groups:** 83. **Description:** Administrators of state vocational rehabilitation agencies. Serves as an advisory body to federal agencies and the public in the development of policies affecting rehabilitation of handicapped persons; acts as a forum for discussion on the provision of quality rehabilitation services. Compiles statistics. **Publications:** *CSAVR Memorandum*, semimonthly. • Manuals. • *Proceedings of Conferences*, semiannual. • Reports. • *State Rehabilitation Directors*, periodic. Directory.

★ 12676 ★ **Danish Occupational Therapy Association**
Department of Rehabilitation
College of Health and Caring Sciences
PO Box 25109
S-400 31 Goteborg, Sweden
Phone: 31 413700
Fax: 31 412996

Languages: Danish. **Description:** Occupational therapists and other health care professionals engaged in occupational medicine in Denmark. Promotes scientific inquiry in the field of occupational therapy and serves as a forum for the dissemination of research results. Areas of inquiry include: physical disability; mental health and disabilities; therapeutic equipment, environments, and techniques; assessment and evaluation of disabilities; vocational and educational training.

★ 12677 ★ **Delta Society (DS)**
PO Box 1080
321 Burnett Ave. S., 3rd Fl.
Renton, WA 98057-9906
Phone: (206)226-7357
Free: 800-869-6898
Linda M. Hines, Exec.Dir.

Founded: 1977. **Members:** 5,000. **Description:** Doctors, nurses, veterinarians, therapists, nursing home personnel, animal trainers and breeders, pet owners, academicians, and students of gerontology, psychology, therapeutic recreation, and other health fields. Seeks to study human-animal interactions and examine the bond that exists between people and the living environment. Assesses the role of animal companions in society and studies the effect of human-animal interaction on the mental and physical well-being of people. Seeks to establish an interdisciplinary approach to studying human-animal interactions, and to increase awareness of these interactions among health and social care professionals. Serves as resource for persons seeking to establish and maintain programs that involve animals in animal-assisted activities/therapy. Operates national Service Dog Center in conjunction with the American Humane Association; and Pet Partners, a national registration for volunteers and animals involved in programs. Distributes information on research, programs, and legislation concerning human-animal relationships. Maintains collection of article reprints. **Publications:** *Alert*, quarterly. Newsletter. *Price:* $7.50/year; $10/year outside U.S. • *Anthrozoos: A Multidisciplinary Journal on the Interactions of People, Animals, and Nature*, quarterly. Journal. Includes book reviews and research reports. *Price:* $40/year; $50/year outside U.S.; $50/year for institutions. • *InterActions*, quarterly.

Magazine. *Price:* $15/year; $22/year outside U.S. • *Pet Partners Newsletter*, bimonthly. Newsletter. Includes practical information for volunteers in animal-assisted activities and therapy programs. *Price:* $6/year; $9/year outside U.S.

★ 12678 ★ **Finnish Occupational Therapy Association**
Department of Rehabilitation
College of Health and Caring Sciences
PO Box 25109
S-400 31 Goteborg, Sweden
Phone: 31 413700
Fax: 31 412996

Languages: Finnish. **Description:** Occupational therapists and other health care professionals engaged in occupational medicine in Finland. Promotes scientific inquiry in the field of occupational therapy and serves as a forum for the dissemination of research results. Areas of inquiry include: physical disability; mental health and disabilities; therapeutic equipment, environments, and techniques; assessment and evaluation of disabilities; vocational and educational training.

★ 12679 ★ **German Association for Physiotherapy (Deutscher Verband fur Physiotherapie Zentral Verband der Krankensgymnasten und Physiotherapeuten)**
Deutzer Freiheit 72-74
50679 Cologne, Germany
Phone: 221 884031
Fax: 221 885225
Heinz Christian Esser, Contact

Founded: 1949. **Members:** 26,000. **Description:** Promotes physical therapy education. Maintains contacts with medical and scientific associations. Represents the interests of physical therapists.

★ 12680 ★ **Hong Kong Society for Rehabilitation (HKSR)**
7 Sha Wan Dr.
Pokfulam, Hong Kong
Phone: 8176277
Fax: 8551947
Mabel Chau, Exec.Dir.

Founded: 1959. **Members:** 107. **Languages:** Chinese, English. **Description:** Works to restore victims of physical disability brought on by disease or injury to economic self-sufficiency. Promotes continued professional advancement by members. Conducts research, educational, and charitable programs. **Publications:** Pamphlet, periodic. • Report, periodic.

★ 12681 ★ **Icelandic Occupational Therapy Association**
Department of Rehabilitation
College of Health and Caring Sciences
PO Box 25109
S-400 31 Goteborg, Sweden
Phone: 31 413700
Fax: 31 412996

Languages: Icelandic. **Description:** Occupational therapists and other health care professionals engaged in occupational medicine in Iceland. Promotes scientific inquiry in the field of occupational therapy and serves as a forum for the dissemination of research results. Areas of inquiry include: physical disability; mental health and disabilities; therapeutic equipment, environments, and techniques; assessment and evaluation of disabilities; vocational and educational training.

International Association of Colon Therapy (ACTA)
See: Entry 5221

★**12682**★ **International Association of Human-Animal Interaction Organizations (IAHAIO)**
321 Burnett Ave. S, 3rd Fl.
PO Box 1080
Renton, WA 98057
Phone: (206)226-7357
Fax: (206)235-1076
Linda M. Hines, Sec.-Treas.

Founded: 1974. **Description:** Steering committee comprised of representatives from: Society for Companion Animal Studies; Human-Animal Contact Study Group in South Africa; Association Francaise d'Information et de Recherche sur l'Animal de Compagnie; Institute for Interdisciplinary Research on the Human-Pet Relationship; and Delta Society (see separate entry, Vol. 1). Provides a forum for exchange of ideas and information among organizations concerned with the study of the mutual welfare of people and animals. Encourages research and promotes educational and practical developments in the field of human-animal interactions. **Publications:** *Proceedings of International Conference*, periodic. Proceedings. Also contributes to and distributes *Anthrozoos: Journal of the Delta Society.* **Formerly:** (1990) International Society for the Study of the Human-Companion Animal Bond.

★**12683**★ **International Association of Laryngectomees (IAL)**
c/o American Cancer Society
1599 Clifton Rd. NE
Atlanta, GA 30329
Phone: (404)320-3333
Fax: (404)636-5567

Founded: 1952. **National Groups:** 295. **Description:** Persons who have had their larynx removed; physicians, surgeons, speech therapists, rehabilitation experts, nurses, and others interested in the rehabilitation of laryngectomees. Encourages exchange of ideas and methods for training and teaching of alaryngeal methods of communication. Fosters recognized standards for the rehabilitation of laryngectomees. Maintains the Voice Rehabilitation Institute for training teachers of alaryngeal voice and the Lost Chord Clubs. Organizes support groups for laryngectomees and their families. **Publications:** Directory, annual. • Films. On first aid and post-laryngectomy speech. • *IAL News*, 3/year. Newsletter. *Price:* Free. • Pamphlets. On laryngectomees, esophageal voice, and rehabilitation. • Reprints. On laryngectomees, esophageal voice, and rehabilitation.

★**12684**★ **International Association for Oxygen Therapy (IAOT)**
PO Box 1360
Priest River, ID 83856
Phone: (208)448-2504
Arlene A. Steiner, Contact

Founded: 1898. **Members:** 3,500. **Regional Groups:** 12. **State Groups:** 24. **Local Groups:** 150. **Description:** Oxidation therapists. Promotes the use of oxidation enhancing therapies to physicians and the general public. Compiles statistics. Conducts research, educational, and charitable programs. Maintains museum and speakers' bureau. **Publications:** *IAOT Newsletter (Oxidation News)*, quarterly. Newsletter.

★**12685**★ **International Federation of Physical Medicine and Rehabilitation (IFPMR)**
Department Rehabilitation Medicine
Mt. Sinai Hospital
600 University Ave.
Toronto, ON, Canada M5G 1X5
Phone: (416)586-5033
Fax: (416)586-8771
Jose Jimenez, M.D., Sec.

Founded: 1950. **Members:** 45. **Description:** National societies of physical medicine and rehabilitation controlled by and composed of qualified physicians and surgeons, and approved by the federation's International Committee of Physical Medicine and Rehabilitation. Seeks to link, on an international level, societies of physical medicine and rehabilitation. Collects and distributes data on rehabilitation. Promotes equivalent standards in education and training, the total rehabilitation process, the importance of physical medicine and rehabilitation, and the exchange of information between medical and nonmedical workers in the field of rehabilitation. **Publications:** *Regulations and List of Members*, quadrennial. • *White Book on Education and Training*, every eight years.

★**12686**★ **International French-Speaking Association of Paraplegic Therapy Groups (AFIGAP) (Association Francophone Internationale des Groupes d'Animation de la Paraplegie — AFIGAP)**
Centre de Reeducation Neurologique
Rte. de Liverdy
Coubert
F-77170 Brie-Comte-Robert, France
Phone: 1 64422081
Fax: 1 64422082
Dr. Jean-Francois Desert, Sec.Gen.

Founded: 1976. **Members:** 180. **Regional Groups:** 6. **Languages:** French. **Description:** Doctors, nurses, physical therapists, occupational therapists, social workers, and others who have an interest in the treatment and rehabilitation of paraplegics. Purpose is to study and develop all means of advancing the knowledge and treatment of paraplegia. Provides for the exchange of information, publications, and research. Organizes professional training for nurses, physiotherapists, and occupational therapists; conducts seminars, workshops, and meetings of paraplegics and specialists. **Publications:** *Annales de Medecine de Reeducation, Readaptation, et Medecin Physique*, peri-

odic. • Brochures, periodic. • *Congress Proceedings*, annual. • *Early Treatment of Paraplegia*. Book.

★**12687**★ **International Myomassethics Federation (IMF)**
17172 Bolsa Chica, No. 23
Huntington Beach, CA 92649
Phone: (801)484-1912
Free: 800-433-4463
Fax: (801)467-4792
Nancy E. Muro, Sec.

Founded: 1971. **Members:** 650. **State Groups:** 14. **Description:** Educates members about therapeutic massage techniques. Conducts continuous learning program consisting of lectures, video presentations, and demonstrations. Maintains speakers' bureau, research programs and educational fund. Also conducts charitable program and placement service. **Publications:** *Intramyomassethics Forum*, bimonthly. Journal. Provides information on massage techniques; includes book reviews, research reports, and employment opportunity listings. *Price:* Included in membership dues. • *Membership Roster*, annual.

★**12688**★ **International Rehabilitation Medicine Association (IRMA)**
Dept. of Physical Medicine
1333 Moursund Ave., Rm. A-221
Houston, TX 77030
Phone: (713)799-5086
Fax: (713)799-5058
Donna Jones, Exec.Dir.

Founded: 1966. **Members:** 2,000. **Description:** Physicians from all specialties of medicine and surgery interested in promoting improvement of health through understanding and utilization of rehabilitation medicine. Goal is to convince governments and society that rehabilitation medicine services should be provided to aged, chronically diseased, and disabled persons who need help in entering the vocational and social mainstream of their communities. Provides a forum for continuous graduate medical education; provides speakers on rehabilitation medicine. Maintains liaisons with the International Federation of Physical Medicine and Rehabilitation and the World Health Organization and is a member of the Council for International Organizations on Medical Sciences and Organizations on Medical Sciences. **Publications:** *Book of Abstracts*, quadrennial. Proceedings. • *IRMA*, biennial. Directory. • *News and Views*, quarterly. • *Scientific Monographs*, semiannual. Monographs.

★**12689**★ **International Union of Therapeutics (Union Therapeutique Internationale)**
Hopital Universitaire Louis Mourier
178, rue des Renouillers
F-92701 Colombes Cedex, France
Phone: 47 606705
Fax: 47 606072
Prof. Andre Pradalier, Pres.

Founded: 1934. **Members:** 350. **Languages:** English, French. **Description:** International organizations in 22 countries interested in the development of therapeutics. Conducts training, research, and exchange programs. **Publica-**

tions: *Abstracts or Communications' Book of the Congress*, biennial.

Intravenous Nurses Society (INS)
See: Entry 9099

★ 12690 ★ **Israel Rehabilitation Society (IRS)**
18 David Elazar St.
Hakiryah
61909 Tel Aviv, Israel
Phone: 3 6930333
Fax: 3 6919885
E. Chigier, M.D., Sec.

Members: 25. **Languages:** English, Hebrew. **Description:** Governmental, public, and voluntary rehabilitation agencies. Works to improve standards of rehabilitation services. Conducts seminars, workshops, and symposia.

Israeli Association of Creative-Expressive Therapy (ICET)
See: Entry 2220

Joint Review Committee for Respiratory Therapy Education (JRCRTE)
See: Entry 11600

★ 12691 ★ **Latin American Association of Therapeutic Communities**
Gradiva Therapeutic Community Center
Avenida Rivadavia 5830/5822
Buenos Aires, Argentina
Dr. Juan Alberto Yaria

Description: Promotes research into new forms of physical and mental therapy programs.

★ 12692 ★ **Laughter Therapy (LT)**
2359 Nichols Canyon Rd.
Los Angeles, CA 90046
Phone: (213)851-3394
Allen A. Funt, Pres.

Founded: 1981. **Description:** To supply tapes of Candid Camera to patients, nursing homes, doctors, hospices, and clinics. (Candid Camera was a regular weekly comedy series on CBS that ran from 1960-67 and was produced by Allen Funt. The program displayed people from all walks of life and their reactions to strange or unexpected occurrences or situations.) Because studies and experiences have shown that humor is one of the most useful forms of therapy, the tapes are being used in a variety of cases where terminal illness, depression, or other ailments are evident. Maintains library of 6 one-hour tapes.

★ 12693 ★ **National Association for Independent Living (NAIL)**
Independent Association
55 City Hall Plz.
Brockton, MA 02401
Phone: (508)559-9091
Fax: (508)580-4345
Eric Griffin, Chief Officer

Founded: 1980. **Members:** 400. **Regional Groups:** 11. **Description:** A division of the National Rehabilitation Association. Seeks to promote independent living, especially for persons with disabilities. Purpose is to encourage persons with and without disabilities to work togeth-

er to facilitate independent living. Works to remove barriers, create new options, and provide support services that will enable persons with disabilities to control their own lives. Supports civil rights of persons with disabilities. Promotes publication and presentation of innovative developments in independent living; legislation leading to removal of barriers and disincentives to independent living and the creation of opportunities and services which would facilitate independent living. **Publications:** *NAIL Newsletter*, quarterly. Newsletter. Includes legislative updates. *Price:* Included in membership dues.

National Association of Nurse Massage Therapists (NANMT)
See: Entry 9104

★ 12694 ★ **National Association of Rehabilitation Instructors (NARI)**
c/o Donna Rowe
4 Medical Office Park
Talladega, AL 35160
Free: 800-441-7592
Donna Rowe, Pres.

Members: 325. **State Groups:** 3. **Description:** Objective is to promote rehabilitation of all persons with disabilities. Acts as a medium through which rehabilitation instructors can coordinate their efforts with other instructors, facilities, workshops, individuals, and organizations serving the handicapped. Conducts training workshops at the state level. **Publications:** Bulletin, 3/year.

★ 12695 ★ **National Association of Rehabilitation Professionals in the Private Sector (NARPPS)**
313 Washington St., Ste. 302
Newton, MA 02158
Phone: (617)558-5333
Fax: (617)558-5440

Founded: 1977. **Members:** 3,000. **State Groups:** 30. **Description:** Private rehabilitation companies, insurance companies, rehabilitation nurses, and rehabilitation professionals in the private sector. Seeks to promote the field of private rehabilitation and to provide for information exchange on rehabilitation issues and techniques. **Publications:** *NARPPS Journal*, quarterly. Journal. Includes book reviews. *Price:* Included in membership dues; $60/year for non-members; $35/year for libraries and schools. • *NARPPS National Directory*, annual. Directory. Contains membership listings by state; includes member name and advertisers indexes. *Price:* Included in membership dues; $50/copy for nonmembers. • *Rehab Review*, bimonthly. Newsletter.

★ 12696 ★ **National Association of Rehabilitation Secretaries (NARS)**
PO Box 3781
Little Rock, AR 72203
Phone: (501)682-6703
Fax: (501)682-6484
Mary Linn, Pres.

Founded: 1971. **Members:** 1,349. **Regional Groups:** 7. **State Groups:** 48. **Local Groups:** 48. **Description:** A division of the National Rehabilitation Association (see separate entry). Initiates and encourages recruitment of qualified

persons for secretarial and clerical positions in the rehabilitation field. Determines and analyzes the skills and knowledge needed by secretaries, stenographers, clerical workers, and technical office professional staff in a rehabilitation setting and devises appropriate training. Seeks to increase public understanding of the social and economic gains to individuals and communities by providing opportunities for all persons with disabilities to become self-sufficient, self-supporting, and contributing members of society. Promotes highest ethical conduct and practices in respecting the rights of the individuals served and in maintaining confidentiality of records. Conducts in-service training programs. **Publications:** Newsletter, quarterly.

National Board for Respiratory Care (NBRC)
See: Entry 11603

★ 12697 ★ **National Council on Rehabilitation Education (NCRE)**
c/o Dr. Garth Eldredge
Utah State University
Department of Special Education
Logan, UT 84322-2870
Phone: (801)797-3241
Fax: (801)797-3572
Dr. Garth Eldredge, Admin.Sec.

Founded: 1961. **Members:** 540. **Description:** Academic institutions and organizations; professional educators, researchers, and students. Goals are to: assist in the documentation of the effect of education in improving services to persons with disability; determine the skills and training necessary for effective rehabilitation services; develop role models, standards, and uniform licensure and certification requirements for rehabilitation personnel; interact with consumers and public and private sector policy makers. Disseminates information and provides forum for discussion. Sponsors specialized education and placement service. Compiles statistics. Serves as an advisory body to the National Rehabilitation Association and the Rehabilitation Services Administration; works closely with other agencies and associations in the field. **Publications:** Membership Directory, annual. *Price:* $25. • Monographs. • *NCRE Newsletter*, quarterly. Newsletter. • *Rehabilitation Education*, quarterly. Journal. *Price:* $90/year for institutions. • Report, quarterly. **Formerly:** (1976) Council of Rehabilitation Counselor Educators.

★ 12698 ★ **National Council for Therapeutic Recreation Certification (NCTRC)**
479 Theills
Spring Valley, NY 10984
Phone: (914)947-4346
Peg Connolly, Ph.D., Exec.Dir.

Founded: 1981. **Members:** 12,000. **Description:** Objectives are to: establish national evaluative standards for certification and recertification of individuals who work in the therapeutic recreation field; grant recognition to individuals who voluntarily apply and meet established standards; monitor adherence to standards by certified personnel. **Publications:** *NCTRC Newsletter*, semiannual. Newsletter.

★ 12699 ★ **National Rehabilitation Association (NRA)**
633 S. Washington St.
Alexandria, VA 22314
Phone: (703)836-0850
Fax: (703)836-0848
Dr. Ann Tourigny, Exec.Dir.

Founded: 1925. **Members:** 15,000. **National Groups:** 9. **Regional Groups:** 7. **State Groups:** 59. **Description:** Administrators, instructors, placement specialists, secretaries, counselors, therapists, vocational evaluators, ADA specialists and others interested in rehabilitation of persons with disabilities. Conducts legislative activities; develops accessibility guidelines; offers specialized education. **Publications:** *Contemporary Rehabilitation*, 8/year. Magazine. Includes calendar of events, listing of employment opportunities, chapter news, human interest stories, and practice information. *Price:* Included in membership dues. • *Journal of Rehabilitation*, quarterly. Journal. Includes articles on rehabilitation research and new technology. Also includes book reviews and annual index. *Price:* Included in membership dues; $45/year for nonmembers. • *Report of the Annual Mary E. Switzer Memorial Seminar*. Monographs. *Price:* $15/monograph.

★ 12700 ★ **National Rehabilitation Counseling Association (NRCA)**
8807 Sudley Rd., Ste. 102
Manassas, VA 22110-4719
Phone: (703)361-2077
Fax: (703)361-2489
Jack Hackett, Pres.

Founded: 1958. **Members:** 4,000. **Description:** A division of the National Rehabilitation Association. Professional and student rehabilitation counselors. Works to expand the role of counselors in the rehabilitation process and seeks to advance members' professional development. Supports legislation favoring the profession. **Publications:** *Journal of Applied Rehabilitation Counseling*, quarterly. Journal. Includes research information and literature and book reviews. *Price:* Included in membership dues; $15 for nonmembers; $30 for institutions. • *Professional Report of the National Rehabilitation Counseling Association*. bimonthly. Membership activities newsletter; includes legislative news and listing of employment opportunities. *Price:* Included in membership dues.

★ 12701 ★ **National Rehabilitation Information Center (NARIC)**
8455 Colesville Rd., Ste. 935
Silver Spring, MD 20910-3319
Phone: (301)588-9284
Free: 800-346-2742
Fax: (301)587-1967
Mark Odum, Dir.

Founded: 1977. **Description:** Purpose is to improve delivery of information to the rehabilitation community. Maintains library of: research reports; conference proceedings; books; microfiche; audiovisual material; material on individuals with sensory, physical, mental, or psychiatric disabilities; reports on professional and administrative practices in the rehabilitation field; over 300 journals on the rehabilitation of persons with physical and mental disabilities. Dissemi-

nates the findings of programs funded by the National Institute on Disability and Rehabilitation Research; prepares custom bibliographies; helps locate answers to reference questions; searches for relevant materials in other commercially available databases. **Publications:** *Directory of Librarians and Information Specialists in Disability and Rehabilitation*, periodic. Directory. • *NARIC Guide to Disability and Rehabilitation Periodicals*. • *NARIC Quarterly*, quarterly. Newsletter. Available in braille and large print and on cassette and diskette. *Price:* Free. • *Rehabdata Thesaurus*.

★ 12702 ★ **National Therapeutic Recreation Society (NTRS)**
2775 S. Quincy St., Ste. 300
Arlington, VA 22206
Phone: (703)578-5548
Free: 800-626-6772
Fax: (703)671-6772
Rikki S. Epstein, Prog.Mgr.

Founded: 1966. **Members:** 2,700. **Description:** Professionals, educators, and students involved in the provision of therapeutic recreation services for persons with disabilities in clinical facilities and in the community. Offers technical assistance services to agencies, institutions, and individuals on matters related to the field. Encourages professional growth through research, training, and workshops. A branch of the National Recreation and Park Association. **Publications:** *Guidelines for the Administration of Therapeutic Recreation Services*. • *Management of Therapeutic Recreation Services*. • *NTRS Report*, quarterly. Newsletter. *Price:* Included in membership dues. • *Parks and Recreation*, monthly. Magazine. *Price:* Included in membership dues. • *Philosophy of Therapeutic Recreation: Ideas and Issues*. • *Preparing for a Career in Therapeutic Recreation*. • *Protocols in Therapeutic Recreation*. • *Standards of Practice for Therapeutic Recreation Service*. • *Therapeutic Recreation Journal*, quarterly. Journal. *Price:* Included in membership dues.

★ 12703 ★ **Neuro-developmental Treatment Association (NDTA)**
401 N. Michigan Ave.
Chicago, IL 60611-4267
Phone: (312)321-5151
Free: 800-869-9295
Fax: (312)321-5158
Ruth Easterling, Exec.Dir.

Founded: 1967. **Members:** 4,400. **Regional Groups:** 14. **Description:** Physical and occupational therapists, speech pathologists, special educators, physicians, parents, and others interested in neurodevelopmental treatment. (NDT is a form of therapy for individuals who suffer from central nervous system disorders resulting in abnormal movement. Treatment attempts to initiate or refine normal stages and processes in the development of movement.) Informs members of new developments in the field and with ideas that will eventually improve fundamental independence. Locates articles related to NDT. Regional groups maintain libraries. **Formerly:** International Bobath Alumni Association.

★ 12704 ★ **New Zealand Society for Music Therapy (NZSMT)**
47 The Crows Nest
Whitby
Wellington, New Zealand
Phone: 4 2347192
B. Lewis, Admin.

Founded: 1974. **Members:** 180. **Regional Groups:** 4. **Local Groups:** 4. **Languages:** English. **Description:** Music therapy professionals. Promotes the therapeutic use of music as an educational tool for the intellectually and physically disabled, rehabilitation patients, and special education students. Initiates discussions with government departments concerning professional training courses and job establishment for music therapists. Encourages hospitals and community groups to consider employment of music therapists. Offers training courses; local branches conduct workshops and provide speakers. **Publications:** *Journal*, annual. Journal. • *MusT*, periodic. Newsletter.

★ 12705 ★ **Nordic Association for Rehabilitation (NAR) (Nordisk Forening for Rehabilitering — NFR)**
Postboks 4375
Torshov
N-0402 Oslo, Norway
Phone: 22 222450
Fax: 22 223833
Finn Groenseth, Pres.

Founded: 1930. **Members:** 35. **Regional Groups:** 5. **Languages:** Danish, Norwegian, Swedish. **Description:** Organizations that represent disabled people and rehabilitation professionals. Works to improve and facilitate cooperation of organizations and institutions that deal with medical, educational, and social rehabilitation.

Nordic Committee on Disability (Nordiska Namnden for Handikappfragor — NNH)
See: Entry 4541

★ 12706 ★ **North American Society of Teachers of the Alexander Technique (NASTAT)**
PO Box 517
Urbana, IL 61801
Phone: (217)367-6956
Free: 800-473-0620
Missy Vineyard, Chair

Founded: 1987. **Members:** 450. **Description:** Individuals who have completed a three-year training course and have been certified by NASTAT; students currently enrolled in an approved NASTAT teacher training course. Promotes and trains teachers of the Alexander Technique. (Created by Australian actor F. M. Alexander (1863-1955), the technique employs reeducation of habitual movement patterns so the body is used efficiently with the least amount of "wear and tear.") Seeks to: promote proficiency, knowledge, and skill in the field of psycho-physical reeducation; encourage education and study in the Alexander Technique; approve the establishment and continuation of teacher training courses. Promotes communication and the interchange of skills and information between the society and other organizations of teachers in the Alexander Technique; works to achieve reciprocal memberships between such organizations. Promotes and conducts research. Compiles information regarding teacher members and members of affiliated societies and disseminates this information to the public. Maintains speakers' bureau. **Publications:** *List of Certified Training Courses*, semiannual. • *NASTAT News*, quarterly. *Price:* $20/year. • *Teaching Members List*, semiannual.

★ 12707 ★ **Norwegian Occupational Therapy Association**
PO Box 2959 Toyen
N-0608 Oslo, Norway
Phone: 22 575353

Description: Occupational therapists and other health care professionals engaged in occupational medicine in Norway. Promotes scientific inquiry in the field of occupational therapy and serves as a forum for the dissemination of research results. Areas of inquiry include: physical disability; mental health and disabilities; therapeutic equipment, environments, and techniques; assessment and evaluation of disabilities; vocational and educational training.

★ 12708 ★ **Orthopaedic Section, American Physical Therapy Association**
505 King St., Ste. 103
La Crosse, WI 54601
Phone: (608)784-0910
Free: 800-444-3982
Fax: (608)784-3350
Terri A. Pericak, Exec.Dir.

Founded: 1974. **Members:** 11,700. **Description:** Orthopaedic physical therapists and physical therapist assistants who belong to the American Physical Therapy Association; physical therapy educators and students. Supports the continued growth of the physical therapy profession through education and research; promotes development of a standard certification procedure for the field. Seeks to assure the quality of physical therapy curricula at both the undergraduate and postgraduate levels. Facilitates communication among orthopedic physical therapists and other health care professionals. Gathers and disseminates information on the care of musculoskeletal disorders. Provides access to a network of orthopaedic study groups. **Publications:** *Journal of Orthopaedic and Sports Physical Therapy*, monthly. Journal. • *Orthopaedic Physical Therapy Practice*, quarterly. • *Orthopaedic Section of the American Physical Therapy Association*. Brochure. Describes orthopaedic physical therapy and what the section is all about.

★ 12709 ★ **People-Animals-Love (PAL)**
c/o MacArthur Animal Hospital
4832 MacArthur Blvd. NW
Washington, DC 20007
Phone: (202)965-2601
Fax: (202)965-3438
Earl Strimple, D.V.M., Pres.

Founded: 1981. **Description:** Purpose is to improve the quality of life of the elderly, the widowed, and the institutionalized by providing them with an appropriate pet and a trained volunteer. (Volunteers are responsible for periodi-

cally monitoring the pet's health; PAL provides for all the pet's needs, including food and veterinary care.) Has initiated programs in nursing homes, prisons, hospices, and mental institutions. Compiles statistics; conducts research on the human/animal bond. Preliminary studies suggest that: pets may positively affect a person's blood pressure and general well-being; prisoners with pets often require less disciplinary action and medical attention; pets help lessen loneliness, hopelessness, and boredom; and that animals may be used effectively to reach at-risk children. **Publications:** Brochure. • *PAL Newsletter*, quarterly. Newsletter.

★ 12710 ★ **PRIDE Foundation - Promote Real Independence for the Disabled and Elderly**
Box 1293
391 Long Hill Rd.
Groton, CT 06340
Phone: (203)445-1448
Evelyn S. Kennedy, Exec.Dir.

Founded: 1978. **Description:** Provides rehabilitation assistance for the handicapped and elderly in the areas of home management, independent dressing, and personal grooming. Designs and develops special garments that will help the handicapped feel more comfortable and dress independently; designs assistive devices for use in the kitchen, bedroom, and bathroom. Provides discussion leaders for community outreach and assistance to health agencies, social service groups, and volunteer organizations. Conducts workshops and educational forums for rehabilitation centers, educational institutions, and community agencies. Sponsored Project Pride, an in-class training program providing physically and mentally handicapped individuals with entry-level occupational skills in the sewing field. Conducts public exhibitions and demonstrations of clothing and adaptive devices. **Publications:** *Clothing Accessibility*. • *Dressing With Pride*. Book. • *Resources and Clothing for Special Needs*.

★ 12711 ★ **Project Magic (PM)**
Kansas Rehabilitation Hospital
1504 SW 8 St.
Topeka, KS 66606
Phone: (913)235-6600
Julie DeJean, Dir.

Founded: 1982. **Description:** Provides information and facilitates communication between magicians, occupational therapists, and patients with physical, psychosocial, and developmental disabilities. Created by television magician David Copperfield, the project works to rehabilitate patients by teaching them magic tricks instead of, or in addition to, traditional therapy techniques. Seeks to motivate patients to develop new skills and improve their self-image by demonstrating magical tricks. Tricks such as sleight-of-hand teach physical dexterity and mental puzzles help people to improve memory, concentration, and the ability to think sequentially. PM provides interested magicians and occupational therapists with information and written material on the therapeutic value of magic for disabled persons. Sponsors educational seminars and workshops for rehabilitation facilities and health professionals. **Publications:**

David Copperfield's Project Magic Booklet, periodic.

★ 12712 ★ **Rehabilitation Information Round Table (RIRT)**
c/o Phyllis Quinn
American Physical Therapy Association
1111 N. Fairfax St.
Alexandria, VA 22314
Phone: (703)706-3210
Fax: (703)684-7343

Founded: 1979. **Members:** 60. **Description:** Individuals and organizations concerned with improving the dissemination of information relating to all types of disabilities. Seeks to foster the cooperative sharing of rehabilitation information by: conducting workshops; establishing informal linkages among information providers; promoting networks among the membership and other organizations. **Publications:** Newsletter, semiannual.

★ 12713 ★ **Rehabilitation International (RI)**
25 E. 21st St.
New York, NY 10010
Phone: (212)420-1500
Fax: (212)505-0871
Susan Parker, Sec.Gen.

Founded: 1922. **Members:** 150. **Description:** Organizations in 90 countries conducting programs for the rehabilitation of people with physical and mental disabilities. Disseminates information on every phase of disability prevention and rehabilitation. Assists experts in planning work or study programs outside their own countries; aids in practical development of national rehabilitation programs. **Publications:** Directory, annual. • *International Journal of Rehabilitation Research*, quarterly. Journal. • *International Rehabilitation Review*, triennial. Newsletter. Provides coverage of United Nations agencies, discusses the elimination of architectural and environmental barriers for the disabled. *Price:* $30/year. • *One-In-Ten*, quarterly. Newsletter. • *Proceedings of World Congress*, quadrennial. • *Rehabilitation*, semiannual. Also publishes booklets and papers. **Formerly:** (1939) International Society for Crippled Children; (1960) International Society for the Welfare of Cripples; (1976) International Society for Rehabilitation of the Disabled.

★ 12714 ★ **Rehabilitation International - Swaziland**
PO Box 1467
Mbabane, Swaziland
Phone: 46653

Description: Provides rehabilitative services to disabled people in Swaziland.

★ 12715 ★ **Rehabilitation and Resource Centre for Torture Victims (RCT) (Rehabiliterings-og Forskningscentret for Torturofre)**
Juliane Maries vej 34
DK-2100 Copenhagen O, Denmark
Phone: 31394694
Fax: 31395020
Dr. Inge Genefke, Medical Dir.

Founded: 1982. **Description:** Medical doctors, nurses, psychologists, social workers, physiotherapists, interpreters, and administrative staff. Studies and develops optimal treatment and rehabilitation programs for victims of torture. Provides, on outpatient basis, traditional medical treatment and personal and social counseling. Participates in information campaigns against torture. Sponsors seminars and symposia. Maintains documentation center. **Publications:** *Annual Report*, annual. • *Torture*, quarterly. Journal. Includes information on rehabilitation of torture victims and prevention of torture. Also publishes journal articles, research reports, and textbooks.

★ **12716** ★ **RESNA**
1700 N. Moore St., Ste. 1540
Arlington, VA 22209-1903
Phone: (703)524-6686
Fax: (703)524-6630
James R. Geletka, Exec.Dir.

Founded: 1980. **Members:** 1,800. **Description:** Rehabilitation professionals, providers, and consumers. An interdisciplinary association for the advancement of rehabilitation and assistive technologies. Objectives are to improve the quality of life for disabled persons through the application of science and technology; influence policy relating to delivery of technology to disabled persons. Is concerned with the design and development of rehabilitation devices and the modification of housing and transportation systems. **Publications:** *The Assessment: The Critical First Step.* Video. Contains information on assessing an individual's need for assistive technology for funding sources and case managers. *Price:* $60. • *Assistive Technology Funding Workbook. Price:* $25. • *Assistive Technology Journal*, semiannual. Journal. • *Assistive Technology Sourcebook. Price:* $60. • *Augmentative Communication: Finding a Voice.* Video. Contains information on augmentative and alternative communication systems for funding sources and case managers. *Price:* $60. • *Backs: Correction or Accommodation.* Video. Contains information about static and adjustable back supports for funding sources and case managers. *Price:* $60. • Brochures. • *Communication: The Key to Teamwork.* Video. Includes explanations of assistive technology by rehabilitation experts for funding sources and case managers. *Price:* $60. • *Independent Living Environments for Seniors and Persons with Disabilities. Price:* $35. • *Interactive Robotic Aids. Price:* $5. • *Managing a Rehabilitation Technology Practice. Price:* $15. • *Manual Mobility: Finding the Right Wheels.* Video. Contains information about rigid, folding, and lightweight wheelchairs for funding sources and case managers. *Price:* $60. • Manuals. • Membership Directory, annual. • Monographs. • *On-line Access to Disability-Related Information. Price:* $2. • *Powered Mobility: Moving toward Independence.* Video. Contains information on powered wheelchairs for funding sources and case managers. *Price:* $60. • Proceedings, annual. • Reports. • *RESNA News*, bimonthly. • *Seating and Mobility Needs of Severely Disabled and Elderly Persons. Price:* $5. • *Seats: The Bottom Line.* Video. Contains information about seating options for funding sources and case managers. *Price:* $60. • *Understanding the Technology When Selecting Wheelchairs. Price:* $16. Also publishes an education series. **Formerly:** Reha-

bilitation Engineering Society of North America; (1988) RESNA: Association for the Advancement of Rehabilitation Technology.

★ **12717** ★ **Rukariro Rehabilitation Organisation**
PO Box 1287
Mutare, Zimbabwe
Phone: 20 64212
Peter Philipo

Members: 30. **Description:** Rehabilitates mentally and physically ill persons in Zimbabwe. Aims to create and promote public and private rehabilitation services for disabled people.

Scandinavian Association of Zone Therapeutists (SFFF) (Skandinavisk Forening for (Fodreflexologer) Zoneterapeutes — SFFF)
See: Entry 2237

Section for Rehabilitation Hospitals and Programs (SRHP)
See: Entry 6469

★ **12718** ★ **Sister Kenny Institute (SKI)**
800 E. 28th St. at Chicago Ave.
Minneapolis, MN 55407
Phone: (612)863-4457
D. Brunn, Exec.Dir.

Founded: 1942. **Description:** To investigate, evaluate, promote, and support projects in rehabilitation and provide rehabilitative patient care. (Named for Elizabeth Kenny, 1886-1952, an Australian nurse who developed a method for treating poliomyelitis with thermal compresses and physical therapy.) Compiles statistics on research activities and patient care activities. Specializes in the treatment of acutely and chronically disabled patients. A large number of patients are stroke victims, spinal cord-injured, or brain-damaged. Rehabilitation services are also used by patients with arthritis, cerebral palsy, Parkinson's disease, polio residuals, or other neuromuscular disorders or muskuloskeletal injuries. Offers professional education programs to instruct medical and allied health professionals in the most recent and most relevant rehabilitation practices. Teaches rehabilitation personnel nursing skills needed to fill the special requirements of chronically ill and physically disabled people. **Formerly:** (1965) Sister Kenny Foundation; (1976) American Rehabilitation Foundation.

★ **12719** ★ **Society for Companion Animal Studies (SCAS)**
1A Hilton Rd.
Milngavie
Glasgow G62 7DN, Scotland
Phone: 141 9565950
Anne Docherty, Dir.

Founded: 1979. **Members:** 350. **Languages:** English. **Description:** Academics, physicians, psychologists, veterinarians, and lay persons in 13 countries interested in the study of the relationship between people and companion animals. Examines the effects animals have on the emotional and physical well-being of individuals. Studies and disseminates results on the bene-

fits companion animals bring to the clients of health and social care professionals. Conducts surveys and research projects. **Publications:** *Death of an Animal Friend.* Booklet. • *Guidelines for the Introduction of Pets in Nursing Homes and Other Institutions.* • *Issues in Research in Companion Animal Studies.* Report. • *Journal of Society for Companion Animal Studies*, quarterly. Journal. • *Pet Loss and Support for Bereaved Pet Owners.* Report. • *Pets, Health and Quality of Life for Older People.* **Formerly:** (1981) Group for the Study of the Human/Companion Animal Bond.

★ **12720** ★ **South African Association of Occupational Therapists (SAAOT) (Suid Afrikaanse Vereniging van Arbeidsterapeute — SAVAT)**
PO Box 11695
Arcadia 0082, Republic of South Africa
Phone: 12 3425400
Fax: 12 3425400
D. Van Der Reyden, Pres.

Founded: 1945. **Members:** 850. **Regional Groups:** 9. **Languages:** English. **Description:** Occupational therapists and assistants. Promotes and represents members' professional concerns. Works to ensure that adequate and up-to-date training is available for individuals entering the field; encourages members to continue professional education after they are qualified. Organizes workshops and lectures; conducts research. **Publications:** *Focus*, quarterly. Newsletter. • *South African Journal of Occupational Therapy*, semiannual. Journal.

★ **12721** ★ **Swedish Association for Dance Therapy (Svenska Foreningen for Dansterapi)**
Duvnas Udde 21
S-131 50 Saltsjo-Duvna, Sweden

Languages: English, Swedish. **Description:** Therapists and other health care professionals. Promotes dance as a means of physical therapy. Conducts educational and training programs.

★ **12722** ★ **Swedish Association of Occupational Therapists (SAOT) (Forbundet Sveriges Arbetsterapeuter — FSA)**
Planiavagen 13
Box 760
S-131 24 Nacka, Sweden
Phone: 8 4662440
Fax: 8 4662424
Mrs. Inga-Britt Lindstom, Pres.

Founded: 1979. **Members:** 7,000. **Regional Groups:** 30. **Languages:** English, Swedish. **Description:** Union of occupational therapists in Sweden. Compiles statistics; conducts research and educational programs; negotiates working conditions and wages. **Publications:** *Arbetsterapeuten*, 16/year. Journal. • *Arbetsterapeuten Publicerar Sig.* • *FOU-Rapporter*, bimonthly. • *Principprogram*, 8/year.

★ 12723 ★ **Swedish Occupational Therapy Association**
Department of Rehabilitation
College of Health and Caring Sciences
PO Box 25109
S-400 31 Goteborg, Sweden
Phone: 31 413700
Fax: 31 412996
Languages: Swedish. **Description:** Occupational therapists and other health care professionals engaged in occupational medicine in Sweden. Promotes scientific inquiry in the field of occupational therapy and serves as a forum for the dissemination of research results. Areas of inquiry include: physical disability; mental health and disabilities; therapeutic equipment, environments, and techniques; assessment and evaluation of disabilities; vocational and educational training.

★ 12724 ★ **Therapy Dogs International (TDI)**
c/o Ursula Kempe
6 Hilltop Rd.
Mendham, NJ 07945
Phone: (908)429-0670
Fax: (908)879-7893
Ursula Kempe, Treas.-Admin.
Founded: 1979. **Members:** 2,300. **Local Groups:** 32. **Description:** Owners of registered Therapy Dogs (dogs of various breeds who have had formal obedience training, are under total verbal control, and have a good temperament). Promotes the use of dogs as helpful in the rehabilitation of physical and mental illnesses of patients living in nursing homes, hospitals, and other institutions. Believes that dogs can enhance the quality of life for patients by providing companionship and a diversion from the institutional routine. Seeks to gain the same rights for therapy dogs as those granted to service and guide dogs. Is currently working on a program in which dogs will actually live in nursing homes. **Publications:** Brochures. • Newsletter, quarterly. • *Pets and the Elderly.*

★ 12725 ★ **U.S. Physical Therapy Association (USPTA)**
1803 Avon Ln.
Arlington Heights, IL 60004
James J. McCoy, Pres.
Founded: 1970. **Members:** 12,700. **Regional Groups:** 3. **State Groups:** 44. **Description:** Professional physical therapists and assistants. Maintains U.S. Physical Therapy Academy which: conducts continuing education programs for members; sponsors workshops to acquaint personnel from other medical fields with physical therapy; accredits hospital and nursing home physical therapy departments, universities, and colleges of physical therapy; certifies physical therapists through board examinations. Promotes ethical standards; maintains placement service and charitable program; compiles statistics; conducts children's services. **Publications:** Journal, periodic. Also publishes news updates.

★ 12726 ★ **Verband Deutscher Badearzte (VDB)**
Elisabethstrasse 7
32545 Bad Oeynhausen, Germany
Phone: 5731 21203
Fax: 5731 260880
Dr. Wolfram Enders, Pres.
Founded: 1947. **Members:** 1,300. **Regional Groups:** 16. **Languages:** English, German. **Description:** Physicians responsible for the rehabilitation of spa patients. Conducts courses in balneology (spa rehabilitation).

★ 12727 ★ **World Confederation for Physical Therapy (WCPT) (Confederation Mondiale pour la Therapie Physique)**
4A Abbots Pl.
London NW6 4NP, England
Phone: 171 3285448
Fax: 171 6247579
Ms. B.J. Myers, Contact
Founded: 1951. **Members:** 54. **National Groups:** 54. **Regional Groups:** 5. **Languages:** English, French, Spanish. **Description:** National physical therapy associations. Aims to improve and strengthen contacts among physical therapists, associations representing physical therapists, and others involved in the physical therapy and rehabilitation fields. Offers counseling and assistance on matters of concern to physical therapists. Sponsors educational programs. **Publications:** *Annual Report.* • Books, periodic. • Reports, periodic. • *WCPT Newsletter,* semiannual. Newsletter.

★ 12728 ★ **World Federation of Occupational Therapists (WFOT) (Federation Mondiale des Ergotherapeutes)**
Disability Services Commission
PO Box 441
West Perth, WA, Australia
Phone: 9 4269380
Fax: 9 4269325
Carolyn Webster, Contact
Founded: 1952. **Members:** 43. **Languages:** English. **Description:** Occupational therapists in 43 countries. Objectives are to: promote the occupational therapy profession; provide for exchange of information and publications; encourage international cooperation; establish standards of education for occupational therapists; maintain professional ethics; facilitate international exchange and placement of therapists and students. Promotes research; assists developing countries in formulating education programs for occupational therapists. **Publications:** Bibliographies, periodic. Contains information on standards and requirements. • *Conference Proceedings,* quadrennial. • Manuals, periodic. Contains information on study courses. • Pamphlets, periodic. Contains information on standards and requirements. • *WFOT Bulletin,* semiannual. Journal.

World Sports Medicine Association of Registered Therapists (WORLD SMAR)
See: Entry 11953

★ 12729 ★ **Wound, Ostomy and Continence Nurses Society: An Association of E.T. Nurses (WOCN)**
2755 Bristol St., Ste. 110
Costa Mesa, CA 92626
Phone: (714)476-0268
Free: 800-228-4238
Fred Droz, Exec.Dir.
Founded: 1969. **Members:** 3,200. **Regional Groups:** 11. **Description:** Enterostomal therapy (ET) nurses in 10 countries trained in WOCN approved schools; individuals interested in objectives of the association who hold a valid license in medicine or nursing; health-related firms. Seeks to support ET nurses by promoting educational, clinical, and research opportunities and to guide the delivery of expert health care to individuals with wounds, ostomies, and incontinence. **Publications:** *ET Nursing Brochure: A Specialty.* Brochure. *Price:* Included in membership dues. • *Journal of Wound, Ostomy and Continence Nursing,* bimonthly. Journal. • *Management of Urinary Incontinence.* Slides and handout. *Price:* $50 for members; $85 for nonmembers. • Membership Directory, annual. *Price:* $15 for members; $35 for nonmembers. • Newsletter, bimonthly. • *Professional Practice Manual.* Manual. *Price:* $52.50 for members; $77.50 for nonmembers. • *Standards of Care.* Booklets. *Price:* $10/each for members; $15/each for nonmembers. • *WOCN ET Nursing.* Video. *Price:* $7.50 for members; $20 for nonmembers. **Formerly:** Wound, Ostomy and Continence Nurses Society, An Association of E.T. Nurses; (1993) International Association for Enterostomal Therapy.

Research Centers

★ 12730 ★ **Auburn University Center for Special Services**
Library Tower, 9th Fl.
7300 University Dr.
Montgomery, AL 36117-3596
Phone: (334)244-3468
Fax: (334)244-3762
Nancy McDaniel, Ed.D., Dir.
Research Activities and Fields: Works with existing agencies and information sources in securing data and services to meet the needs of Alabama's citizens and students with disabilities. Activities include development and implementation of postsecondary intervention program related to disabilities, the Americans with Disabilities Act, and Section 504 of the Rehabilitation Act. **Formerly:** Facilities & Information Network Development (FIND); Center for Rehabilitation Resources (1992).

★ 12731 ★ **Dallas Rehabilitation Institute**
9713 Harry Hines Blvd.
Dallas, TX 75220-5441
Phone: (214)358-5441
Fax: (214)358-8453
Research Activities and Fields: Provides treatment and assesses physical disabilities, including those associated with spinal cord injury, head injury, stroke, arthritis, amputations, spinal

pain, and other orthopedic or neuromuscular problems. Conducts cooperative studies on a human performance measurement system designed to assess 500 aspects of human performance. **Publications:** *Spokes* (quarterly).

★ 12732 ★ Georgia Institute of Technology Center for Rehabilitation Technology
490 10th St.
Atlanta, GA 30332-0156
Phone: (404)894-4960
Fax: (404)853-9320
Carolyn Ann Whitescarver, Interim Dir.

Research Activities and Fields: Develops equipment and procedures to help persons with disabilities. Maintains design and development laboratories and a national information center for the collection and dissemination of information on all aspects of rehabilitation. Coordinates research and services related to rehabilitation technology within the University System of Georgia. **Publications:** Newsletter (quarterly). **E-mail Address:** zena.rubin@arch.gatech.edu.

★ 12733 ★ ICD-International Center for the Disabled
340 E. 24th St.
New York, NY 10010
Phone: (212)679-0100
Fax: (212)889-2440
Herbert H. Krauss, Ph.D., Dir. of Rehabilitation Research

Research Activities and Fields: The Institute conducts research on promising techniques designed to prevent, reduce, and control disabilities arising from persistent physical disorders. Studies focus on the control of deterioration and disability associated with recurring ear infections in children, symptom magnification in those with disabling conditions, and factors associated with gainful employment. Other projects examine the parameters of postlaryngectomy speech, nerve conduction patterns in overuse syndromes, relapse factors in alcoholism, and methods used in the management of individuals with Alzheimer's disease. Techniques that prove effective are transferred to ICD clinical programs and communicated to professionals nationally and internationally. **Publications:** *Education and Training Catalog*; Annual Report. **Formerly:** ICD Rehabilitation and Research Center (1980).

★ 12734 ★ Institute for Rehabilitation and Research (TIRR)
1333 Moursund Ave.
Houston, TX 77030
Phone: (713)799-5000
Fax: (713)797-5289
Charles C. Beall, Pres.

Research Activities and Fields: Clinical neurophysiologic, neuroendocrinologic, psychoecologic, and exercise tolerance studies of patients with severe spinal cord injuries; development and assessment of mechanical and electronic assistive devices for neurologically impaired individuals; research and technical developments concerned with the effects of pressure on human tissue; provision of personal assistance for persons with severe physical disabilities; and program evaluations to improve services for persons with head injury, amputa-

tion, or spinal cord injury. **Publications:** *TIRR Research Projects Guide*.

★ 12735 ★ Kennedy Krieger Institute
707 N. Broadway
Baltimore, MD 21205
Phone: (410)550-9483
Fax: (410)550-9344
Gary W. Goldstein, M.D., Pres.

Research Activities and Fields: Pediatric rehabilitation evaluation, treatment, and research, including interdisciplinary studies in genetics, biochemistry, toxicology, neurochemistry, metabolic diseases, speech and hearing, pharmacology, behavioral sciences, and special education. Major emphasis is placed on physical rehabilitation, effectiveness of drug support, behavior modification, evaluation of neurological disorders in children, and developing and testing training techniques. **Formerly:** Originally designated as Children's Rehabilitation Institute and John F. Kennedy Institute (1986); Kennedy Institute Inc.

★ 12736 ★ Laban / Bartenieff Institute of Movement Studies, Inc.
11 E. 4th St.
New York, NY 10001
Phone: (212)477-4299
Tom Borek, Exec.Dir.

Research Activities and Fields: Perception, description, and analysis of human movement for applications in dance and theater, physical therapy, psychotherapy, nonverbal communication, management consulting, anthropology, and fitness and sports training. The Institute's mission is to further the studies of the principles of movement formulated by Rudolf Laban (1879-1958), an Austro-Hungarian dancer, choreographer, and philosopher, and Irmgard Bartenieff (1900-1981), who applied her Laban training to physical therapy, dance therapy, anthropology, and dance. **Publications:** *Movement Studies* (journal); Member's Newsletter.

Massachusetts Institute of Technology Eric P. and Evelyn E. Newman Laboratory for Biomechanics and Human Rehabilitation
See: Entry 2453

National Institute for Rehabilitation Engineering
See: Entry 2457

★ 12737 ★ New York University Medical Center Head Trauma Program
345 E. 24th St., Rm. 818
New York, NY 10010
Phone: (212)263-6806
Fax: (212)263-6807
Dr. Yehuda Ben-Yishay, Dir.

Research Activities and Fields: Young adults suffering from head injuries. Conducts systematic remedial training in attention and concentration, various aspects of perception, perceptual-motor integration (eye-hand integration), and logical reasoning and interpersonal skills. Provides individual and family counseling and prevocational explorations. **Publications:** *Working Approaches to Remediation of Cognitive Deficits in Brain Damaged Persons* (annually).

★ 12738 ★ New York University Medical Rehabilitation Research and Training Center
400 E. 34th St.
New York, NY 10016
Phone: (212)340-6105
Dr. Mathew Lee, M.D., Actg.Chm.

Research Activities and Fields: Rehabilitation for brain trauma and stroke victims and comprehensive management of neuromuscular disease. Seeks to identify and validate specific treatment modalities applied to persons disabled by neuromuscular disorders, develop and improve new and existing treatment modalities, and quantify and standardize methods of evaluating disease activity and remission.

★ 12739 ★ New York University Rusk Institute of Rehabilitation Medicine
400 E. 34th St.
New York, NY 10016
Phone: (212)263-6150
Dr. Mathew Lee, Dir.

Research Activities and Fields: Conducts clinical and basic research on neuromuscular diseases, head trauma, stroke, and music therapy.

★ 12740 ★ Northern Arizona University American Indian Rehabilitation Research and Training Center
PO Box 5630
Flagstaff, AZ 86011-5630
Phone: (602)523-4791
Fax: (602)523-9127
Priscilla Lansing Sanderson, Dir.

Research Activities and Fields: Core areas include identifying and facilitating effective and culturally appropriate rehabilitation services for American Indians with disabilities, developing and implementing strategies to improve and maintain employment and independent living for American Indians with disabilities, increasing the awareness of high incidences and prevalence of disabilities among American Indians, and promoting the development of qualified American Indian researchers and service providers. **Publications:** *American Indian Rehabilitation* (newsletter); *Hotline* (newsletter). **E-mail Address:** prs@nauvax.ucc.nau.edu. **Formerly:** Native American Research and Training Center (1988).

★ 12741 ★ Packard Children's Hospital at Stanford Rehabilitation Engineering Center
725 Welch Rd.
Palo Alto, CA 94304
Phone: (415)497-8192
Fax: (415)497-8154
Maurice LeBlanc, Dir. of Research

Research Activities and Fields: Rehabilitation technology, emphasizing speech aids, prosthetics, orthotics, seating, mobility, and worksite accommodation for people with disabilities. **E-mail Address:** leblanc@roses.stanford.edu.

★ 12742 ★ Rancho Rehabilitation Engineering Program
Los Amigos Research & Education Institute, Inc.
Bonita Hall
7503 Bonita St.
Downey, CA 90242
Phone: (310)940-7994
Fax: (310)803-6117
Don McNeal, Ph.D., Dir.

Research Activities and Fields: Develops appropriate technology and assessment procedures in the field of orthopedic rehabilitation and assures their availability to children with physical disabilities. Projects are focused on identifying the changing needs for worksite accommodation as employees with disabilities grow older.

★ 12743 ★ Rehabilitation Institute of Chicago
345 E. Superior
Chicago, IL 60611
Phone: (312)908-3381
Fax: (312)908-2208
Dr. W. Zev Rymer, Dir. of Research

Research Activities and Fields: Rehabilitation medicine, brain trauma, stroke, atherosclerosis, neuromuscular diseases, applied neurophysiology, deep venous thrombosis, spinal cord injury, arthritis, prosthetics/orthotics, rehabilitation nursing, allied health, and communicative disorders.

★ 12744 ★ Rehabilitation Institute of Michigan
261 Mack Blvd.
Detroit, MI 48201
Phone: (313)745-9731
Fax: (313)745-9863
Dr. Marcel Dijkers, Dir. of Research

Research Activities and Fields: Physical medicine and rehabilitation medicine, including electromyography, rehabilitation robotics, rehabilitation engineering, neuropsychology, measures of rehabilitation outcome, and methods of evaluation and treatment of patients with closed head injuries, spinal cord injuries, cerebrovascular accidents, and other diagnoses. **Publications:** *Excellence* (quarterly newsletter). **Formerly:** Rehabilitation Institute (1990).

★ 12745 ★ Rehabilitation Research and Planning Center
Casa Colina Hospital for Rehabilitative Medicine
225 E. Bonita Ave.
Pomona, CA 91767
Phone: (909)593-7521
Fax: (909)593-0153
Dr. Robert Allen Keith, Dir.

Research Activities and Fields: Clinical research on physical medicine populations, organizational analysis of rehabilitation hospitals, program evaluation, and design research studies conducted with hospital staff on head injury, stroke, spinal cord injury, and other conditions.

★ 12746 ★ Research & Training Center in Vocational Rehabilitation
PO Box 1358
Hot Springs, AR 71902
Phone: (501)624-4411
Fax: (501)624-3515
Dr. Roy C. Farley, Dir.

Research Activities and Fields: Vocational rehabilitation for individuals with disabilities, including assessment, placement strategies, and skills for employment. **Publications:** Research Reports. **Formerly:** Arkansas Rehabilitation Research & Training Center (1985).

★ 12747 ★ Revici Foundation for Lipid Research
26 E. 36th St.
New York, NY 10016
Phone: (212)685-0111
Fax: (212)685-0112
Emanuel Revici, M.D., Scientific Dir.

Research Activities and Fields: Develops lipid therapy for various physiopathological conditions. Conducts studies on experimental theories in oncology, particulary the use of lipid therapy in physiopathological conditions. Investigates alternatives to the traditional treatments for cancer and other degenerative diseases, including AIDS. **Formerly:** Incorporated the activities of the former Institute of Applied Biology (1991).

★ 12748 ★ Roosevelt Warm Springs Institute for Rehabilitation
PO Box 1000
Warm Springs, GA 31830-0268
Phone: (706)655-5008
Fax: (706)655-5011
Carolyn McKinley, Adm.

Research Activities and Fields: Clinical aspects of rehabilitation, marketing, administration, and product development. **E-mail Address:** janettho@gomail.doas.state.ga.us.

★ 12749 ★ Sister Kenny Institute
800 E. 28th St. at Chicago Ave.
Minneapolis, MN 55407
Phone: (612)863-4367
Fax: (612)863-2833
Dr. Kent Canine, Dir.-Research and Education

Research Activities and Fields: Physical medicine and rehabilitation. Aims to improve the quality, effectiveness, and efficiency of rehabilitation patient care. Conducts research in spasticity management in post-polio and cardiovascular conditioning in spinal cord injuries, traumatic brain injuries, and cerebral vascular accidents.

Southern Illinois University at Carbondale Evaluation and Developmental Center
See: Entry 4584

★ 12750 ★ Southern Illinois University at Carbondale Rehabilitation Institute
Rehn Hall, Rm. 317
Carbondale, IL 62901
Phone: (618)536-7704
Fax: (618)453-1646
Dr. Gary Austin, Dir.

Research Activities and Fields: Rehabilitation, including studies on the blind, developmen-

tally and physically disabled, adult and juvenile offenders, and economically disadvantaged. Conducts counseling process and outcome studies, counseling of special populations, and behavior therapy with diverse populations, including programs in alcoholism, substance abuse, and aging. Involved in rehabilitation administration and supervision, vocational evaluation, employee assistance, transition, supported employment, ethics, adjustment services, job development, and placement.

Stanford University
Stanford Cardiac Rehabilitation Program
See: Entry 2923

★ 12751 ★ Syracuse University Special Education Programs
805 S. Crouse Ave.
Syracuse, NY 13244-2280
Phone: (315)443-9651
Fax: (315)443-3289

Research Activities and Fields: Applied studies focusing on special education and inclusive schooling. Projects include work on statewide educational systems change, facilitated communication, effect of special education program models, public policy affecting persons with disabilities, attitudes toward people with disabilities, qualitative analysis of human service settings, community integration and deinstitutionalization, aggression replacement training, effects of inclusive schooling, and social relationships of children and youth with severe disability. **E-mail Address:** lmeyer@suvm.syr.edu.

★ 12752 ★ Texas A&M University Hyperbaric Laboratories
College Station, TX 77843-1264
Phone: (409)845-5031
Fax: (409)845-8913
Dr. William P. Fife, Dir.

Research Activities and Fields: Hyperbaric medicine, diving medicine, and clinical medicine. Specific studies include migraine headaches, post-polio syndrome, cystoid macular edema, chronic fatigue syndrome, and closed head injuries.

★ 12753 ★ Thomas Jefferson University Regional Spinal Cord Injury Center of Delaware Valley
375 Main Bldg.
132 S. 10th St.
Philadelphia, PA 19107-5099
Phone: (215)955-6579
Fax: (215)955-5152
John F. Ditunno, Jr., M.D., Proj.Dir.

Research Activities and Fields: Acute care and rehabilitation for individuals disabled by spinal cord injury. Projects focus on evaluating therapeutic interventions such as surgery, traction, electrical stimulation, and biofeedback; validating techniques for monitoring neural recovery; and developing methods to accurately measure muscle strength, fatigue, psychological status, and functional capacity. Studies the use of electrical stimulation to prevent deep vein thrombosis, minimize muscle spasticity, and preserve fertility. **Publications:** Newsletter; *SCI Research Update* (quarterly).

★ 12754 ★ Tufts University
Medical Rehabilitation Research & Training Center in Childhood Trauma
750 Washington St., 75 K/R
Boston, MA 02111-4094
Phone: (617)956-5622
Fax: (617)956-5353
Marvin M. Brooke, M.D., Dir.

Research Activities and Fields: Impact of rehabilitation on children with traumatic injury. Projects include: 1) National Pediatric Trauma Registry; 2) outcome of injuries to children with preexisting medical conditions; 3) impact of medical insurance and local rehabilitation resources on injured children; 4) causes and costs of of severe injuries to children that occur at school; 5) study of head injuries to children while bicycling and during informal recreation; 6) natural history of injury recovery in children; 7) evaluation of early rehabilitation interventions to decrease complications in children; and 8) family-centered service coordination for educational and vocational needs. **Publications:** *Rehab Update* (biannually); Family Guides on effects of childhood injuries.

★ 12755 ★ University of Alabama at Birmingham
Medical Rehabilitation Research and Training Center in Secondary Complications in Spinal Cord Injury
UAB Sta.
Spain Rehab. Center
Birmingham, AL 35233-7330
Phone: (205)934-3334
Dr. J. Scott Richards, Research Dir.

Research Activities and Fields: Prevention and treatment of secondary complications of spinal cord injury (SCI), including urologic and pulmonary complications, obstetric/gynecologic concerns of women with SCI, spasticity, interventions for pressure ulcers, caregiver impact, coping and problem solving skills, and causes of repeat hospitalization. **Publications:** Research Update; *Pushin' On.* **E-mail Address:** key@sun.rehab.uab.edu. **Formerly:** Medical Rehabilitation Research and Training Center for Prevention and Treatment of Secondary Complications of Spinal Cord Injury.

★ 12756 ★ University of Alabama at Birmingham
Spinal Cord Injury Care System
Spain Rehab. Ctr.
UAB Sta.
Birmingham, AL 35233-7330
Phone: (205)934-3330
Dr. Amie Jackson, Project Dir.

Research Activities and Fields: Rehabilitation needs of those with spinal cord injury (SCI), including urological studies. System objectives include the following: 1) to deliver and improve comprehensive medical, vocational, and psychosocial rehabilitation services for individuals with SCI; 2) to evaluate both the effectiveness of services and their costs and benefits; 3) to produce new and useful information; 4) to demonstrate and evaluate the application of improved methods and equipment; and 5) to participate in national studies of the benefits of a spinal cord injury service system. **E-mail Address:** key@sun.rehab.uab.edu.

★ 12757 ★ University of Arizona
Rehabilitation Center
College of Education
Tucson, AZ 85721
Phone: (520)621-7822
Fax: (520)621-9271
Dr. Amos Sales, Dir.

Research Activities and Fields: Psychological, social, medical, and vocational problems of rehabilitation, including interdisciplinary studies on various aspects of disability (with particular emphasis on relation of disability to everyday life), community organization for rehabilitation, management of arthritis, emphysema, and stroke, the hard-core unemployed, aptitudes of educable high school age mental retardates, and disabled college students. **Publications:** Newsletter Reports.

★ 12758 ★ University of California, San Diego
Hyperbaric Medicine Center
Medical Center
200 W. Arbor Dr.
San Diego, CA 92103
Phone: (619)543-5222
Dr. Tom Neuman, Dir.

Research Activities and Fields: Hyperbaric oxygen therapy, including application in burns, infectious diseases, wound healing, and diving medicine.

★ 12759 ★ University of Hawaii at Manoa
Rehabilitation Research & Training Center
320 Ward., Ste. 107
Honolulu, HI 96814
Phone: (808)592-5900
Fax: (808)592-5909
Daniel D. Anderson, Ed.D., Dir.

Research Activities and Fields: Medical rehabilitation, vocational rehabilitation, and special education in the Pacific area, including the multicultural aspects of providing rehabilitation services in the developing Pacific areas, needs and follow-up training, referral systems and assessment methods, data systems and client tracking, prevalence of disabilities, transition study of community living, postsecondary handicapped, utilization of health services by the profoundly deaf in Hawaii, technology of assistive devices, satellite communications, post-polio muscular atrophy in Hawaii and the Marshall Islands, and the effectiveness of training ende avors. **Publications:** Newsletter (semiannually), and *Rehab Journal* (semiannually), available to agencies and individuals in the Pacific Area. **E-mail Address:** t056150@uhccmvs.uhcc.hawaii.edu.

★ 12760 ★ University of Miami
Touch Research Institute
Dept. of Pediatrics
Medical School
PO Box 016820
Miami, FL 33101
Phone: (305)547-6781
Tiffany M. Field, Ph.D., Dir.

Research Activities and Fields: Sense of touch, including the biology of touch in health and development, and the role of touch therapy in medicine and the treatment of disease. Specific research areas include the use of massage in enhancing immune function in AIDS and cancer patients, massage effects on growth in premature infants, underlying mechanism responsible for the relationship between touch and physical growth and emotional development in infants and children, the role of massage in sports medicine and wound healing, the effects of touch therapy on addictive personalities, pain reduction during invasive medical procedures, and alleviation of skin disorders such as eczema and psoriasis. Studies the effects of touch on persons of all ages. **Publications:** *Touchpoints* (newsletter); Touch Research Series.

University of Michigan
Center for Occupational Rehabilitation and Health
See: Entry 9857

★ 12761 ★ University of Montana
Research and Training Center on Rural Rehabilitation
52 Corbin Hall
Missoula, MT 59812
Phone: (406)243-5467
Fax: (406)243-2349
Dr. Tom Seekins, Dir.

Research Activities and Fields: Employment and vocational rehabilitation service needs of people with disabilities in rural areas; intervention development to improve employment outcomes; rural supported employment models; rural independent living; improvement of transportation, health care, housing, and accessibility; rural models for prevention of secondary disabilities; disability legislation and American Indian Tribes; and alternative models of delivery of rural rehabilitation services. **Publications:** Newsletter (quarterly). **Formerly:** Research and Training Center on Rural Disabilities.

★ 12762 ★ University of Montreal
Montreal Research Centre
Rehabilitation Institute
6300, ave. Darlington
Montreal, PQ, Canada H3S 2J4
Phone: (514)340-2078
Fax: (514)340-2154
Robert W. Dykes, Dir.

Research Activities and Fields: Biomedical research, focusing on rehabilitation of patients suffering from spinal cord injury, amputation, stroke, and traumatic head injuries; behaviorial research, including studies of the physical, psychological, and occupational obstacles that prevent brain-injured persons from being reintegrated into society; and rehabilitation engineering for upper and lower limb amputees. **E-mail Address:** dykes@ere.umontreal.ca.

★ 12763 ★ University of North Texas
Center for Rehabilitation Studies
School of Community Services
PO Box 13438
Denton, TX 76203-3438
Phone: (817)565-2488
Fax: (817)565-3960
Dr. Thomas L. Evenson, Dir.

Research Activities and Fields: Research programs based upon faculty interests, including biofeedback and self-regulation for physical and psychiatric disorders, supported employment and community integration, chemical dependence prevention and treatment, impact of vocational evaluation on rehabilitation outcomes, and vocational rehabilitation of the older client. The Institute for Addiction Studies conducts research on addictions. **Publications:** *CRS Rehabilitation Treatise* (irregularly).

★ 12764 ★ **University of Vermont**
Vermont Rehabilitation Engineering Center
for Low Back Pain
1 S. Prospect St.
Burlington, VT 05401
Phone: (802)656-4582
Free: 800-527-7320
Fax: (802)660-9243
Martin Krag, M.D., Dir.

Research Activities and Fields: Prevention, assessment, and rehabilitation of low back pain, injury, and disability. Past projects have focused on disability prediction and prevention; development and testing of tools and techniques for evaluating intervertebral motion; lifting capacity and effort; effects of exercise; orthotic devices; effects of posture, seating, and vibration; and work demands. Planned work includes improved employment opportunities and conditions for people with low back disorders through workplace design, worker education, and worker and job matching programs. **E-mail Address:** vtrec@salus.med.uvm.edu.

University of Waterloo
Centre for Habilitation Education and
Research (CHER)
See: Entry 4599

★ 12765 ★ **University of Wisconsin—**
Madison
Rehabilitation Research Institute
Dept. of Rehabilitation & Psychology
432 N. Murray St.
Madison, WI 53706
Phone: (608)263-5971
Fax: (608)262-8108
George N. Wright, Ph.D., Dir.

Research Activities and Fields: Rehabilitation, including the role and professional function of vocational rehabilitation counselors and improvement of their effectiveness in coping with problems of the physically and mentally handicapped. **Publications:** *Rehabilitation Professional Competencies.*

★ 12766 ★ **Virginia Commonwealth**
University
Rehabilitation Research and Training
Center on Severe Traumatic Brain Injury
Box 677, MCV Sta.
Richmond, VA 23298-0677
Phone: (804)828-4097
Fax: (804)828-5074
Dr. David X. Cifu, M.D., Dir.

Research Activities and Fields: Severe brain injury. Specific projects include studying changes in the circulation of brain fluid after an injury to develop treatments that minimize intellectual problems, investigating academic and emotional problems resulting from traumatic injury in children, studying brain activity during coma, comparing vocational rehabilitation strategies to improve employment rates of people

with severe traumatic brain injury, investigating the changes in a brain-injured patient's family, studying changes in various types of memory problems resulting from head trauma, analyzing nutritional needs of patients after injury, and using laboratory animals to test drugs that may improve recovery rates following injury.

★ 12767 ★ **Western Michigan University**
Center for Developmentally Disabled
Adults
Kalamazoo, MI 49008
Phone: (616)383-0045
Dr. Carol Sundberg, Dir.

Research Activities and Fields: Behavioral and other interventions with severely and profoundly developmentally disabled adults. Also conducts administrative studies. Provides training opportunities for developmentally disabled individuals from the community. **Publications:** Reports.

★ 12768 ★ **Western Michigan University**
Occupational Therapy Teaching Research
Clinic
Occupational Therapy Dept.
179 Wood Hall
Kalamazoo, MI 49008
Phone: (616)387-3850
Fax: (616)387-3845
Deborah Lindstrom-Hazel, Coord.

Research Activities and Fields: Occupational therapy and clinical research on developmental disabilities and learning disabilities.

★ 12769 ★ **Wichita State University**
National Rehabilitation Engineering Center
CB 44
Wichita, KS 67208
Phone: (316)689-3415
Fax: (316)689-3853
Roy H. Norris, Dir.

Research Activities and Fields: Employment for handicapped adults.

State Government Agencies

Rehabilitation

★ 12770 ★ **Alabama Department of**
Rehabilitation Services
2129 E. South Blvd.
PO Box 11586
Montgomery, AL 36111-0586
Phone: (334)242-4628
Fax: (334)281-1973

★ 12771 ★ **Alaska Department of Education**
Vocational Rehabilitation Division
801 W. 10th St., Ste. 200
Juneau, AK 99801-1894
Phone: (907)465-2814
Fax: (907)465-2856

★ 12772 ★ **Arizona Department of**
Economic Security
Employment and Rehabilitation Services
Division
Rehabilitation Services Administration
1789 W. Jefferson NW, 2nd Fl.
Phoenix, AZ 85007
Phone: (602)542-3332
Fax: (602)542-5339

★ 12773 ★ **Arkansas Department of**
Education
Rehabilitation Services Division
Donaghey Plaza North
PO Box 3781
Little Rock, AR 72203
Phone: (501)296-1616

★ 12774 ★ **California Health and Welfare**
Agency
Rehabilitation Department
830 K St. Mall
PO Box 944333
Sacramento, CA 94244
Phone: (916)445-3971
Fax: (916)327-4567

★ 12775 ★ **Colorado Department of Human**
Services
Rehabilitation Services Division
110 16th St.
Denver, CO 80202
Phone: (303)620-4156

★ 12776 ★ **Connecticut Department of**
Social Services
Rehabilitation Services Bureau
10 Griffin Rd. N.
Windsor, CT 06095
Phone: (203)298-2003

★ 12777 ★ **Delaware Department of Labor**
Vocational Rehabilitation Division
Elwyn Bldg.
321 E. 11th St.
Wilmington, DE 19801
Phone: (302)577-2850
Fax: (302)577-2735

★ 12778 ★ **District of Columbia Department**
of Human Services
Social Services Commission
Rehabilitation Services Administration
605 G St. NW, Rm. 1111
Washington, DC 20001
Phone: (202)727-3227
Fax: (202)727-1687

★ 12779 ★ **Florida Department of Labor**
and Employment Security
Vocational Rehabilitation Division
2002 Old St. Augustine Rd., Bldg. A
Tallahassee, FL 32399-0696
Phone: (904)488-6210
Fax: (904)488-8062

★ 12780 ★ **Georgia Department of Human**
Resources
Rehabilitation Services Division
2 Peachtree St. NW
Atlanta, GA 30303
Phone: (404)894-6670

★ 12781 ★ Hawaii Department of Human Services
Vocational Rehabilitation and Blind Services Division
Bishop Trust Bldg., Rm. 615
1000 Bishop St.
Honolulu, HI 96813
Phone: (808)586-5366
Fax: (808)586-4890

★ 12782 ★ Idaho Board of Education
Vocational Education Division
650 W. State St.
PO Box 83720
Boise, ID 83720
Phone: (208)334-3216
Fax: (208)334-2365

★ 12783 ★ Illinois Department of Rehabilitation Services
Rehabilitation Services Bureau
623 E. Adams St.
PO Box 19429
Springfield, IL 62794-9429
Phone: (217)782-2004

★ 12784 ★ Indiana Family and Social Services Administration
Disability, Aging and Rehabilitative Services Division
402 W. Washington St.
PO Box 7083
Indianapolis, IN 46207-7083
Phone: (317)232-1147
Fax: (317)233-4693

★ 12785 ★ Iowa Department of Education
Vocational Rehabilitation Division
510 E. 12th St.
Des Moines, IA 50319
Phone: (515)281-6731
Fax: (515)281-4122

★ 12786 ★ Kansas Department of Social and Rehabilitation Services
Rehabilitation Services Division
Biddle Bldg.
300 SW Oakley St.
Topeka, KS 66606
Phone: (913)296-3911
Fax: (913)296-0511

★ 12787 ★ Kentucky Education, Arts and Humanities Cabinet
Vocational Rehabilitation Department
500 Mero St.
Frankfort, KY 40601
Phone: (502)564-4566

★ 12788 ★ Louisiana Department of Social Services
Rehabilitation Services Division
8225 Florida St.
Baton Rouge, LA 70804-9371
Phone: (504)925-4168
Fax: (504)925-4184

★ 12789 ★ Maine Department of Education
Rehabilitation Services Office
35 Anthony Ave.
Augusta, ME 04333
Phone: (207)624-5300
Fax: (207)287-5802

★ 12790 ★ Maryland Department of Education
Vocational Rehabilitation Division
2301 Argonne Dr.
Baltimore, MD 21218
Phone: (410)554-9385
Fax: (410)554-9384

★ 12791 ★ Massachusetts Rehabilitation Commission
Fort Point Pl.
27-43 Wormwood St.
Boston, MA 02210-1606
Phone: (617)727-2172
Fax: (617)727-1354

★ 12792 ★ Michigan Department of Education
Rehabilitation Commission
PO Box 30010
Lansing, MI 48909
Phone: (517)373-3391

★ 12793 ★ Minnesota Economic Security Department
Rehabilitation Services Division
390 N. Robert St., 5th Fl.
St. Paul, MN 55101
Phone: (612)296-1822
Fax: (612)296-0994

★ 12794 ★ Mississippi Department of Rehabilitation Services
PO Box 1698
Jackson, MS 39215-1698
Phone: (601)853-5201
Fax: (601)853-5205

★ 12795 ★ Missouri Department of Elementary and Secondary Education
Vocational Rehabilitation Division
2401 E. McCarty St.
Jefferson City, MO 65101
Phone: (314)751-3251

★ 12796 ★ Montana Department of Social and Rehabilitation Services
Rehabilitative Services / Visual Services Division
PO Box 4210
Helena, MT 59604-4210
Phone: (406)444-2590

★ 12797 ★ Nebraska Department of Education
Rehabilitation Services Division
301 Centennial Mall S.
PO Box 94987
Lincoln, NE 68509
Phone: (402)471-3645
Fax: (402)471-0117

★ 12798 ★ Nevada Department of Employment Training and Rehabilitation
Rehabilitation Division
Vocational Rehabilitation Bureau
500 E. 3rd St.
Carson City, NV 89713
Phone: (702)687-4470
Fax: (702)687-8351

★ 12799 ★ New Hampshire Department of Education
Vocational Rehabilitation Bureau
78 Regional Dr.
Concord, NH 03301
Phone: (603)271-3471

★ 12800 ★ New Jersey Department of Labor
Vocational Rehabilitation Services Division
CN 052
Trenton, NJ 08625-0398
Phone: (609)292-7318
Fax: (609)984-4542

★ 12801 ★ New Mexico Department of Education
Vocational Rehabilitation Division
435 St. Michaels Dr., Bldg. D
Santa Fe, NM 87505
Phone: (505)827-3511

★ 12802 ★ New York State Department of Education
Vocational and Educational Services for Individuals with Disabilities Office
Albany, NY 12243
Phone: (518)474-2714
Fax: (518)473-6073

★ 12803 ★ North Carolina Department of Human Resources
Vocational Rehabilitation Services Division
PO Box 26053
Raleigh, NC 27611
Phone: (919)733-3364

★ 12804 ★ North Dakota Department of Human Services
Vocational Rehabilitation Division
600 E. Boulevard
Bismarck, ND 58505
Phone: (701)328-2907
Fax: (701)328-2359

★ 12805 ★ Ohio Rehabilitation Services Commission
Vocational Rehabilitation Bureau
400 E. Campus View Blvd.
Columbus, OH 43235-4604
Phone: (614)438-1250
Fax: (614)438-1257

★ 12806 ★ Oklahoma Department of Rehabilitation Services
Rehabilitative Services Bureau
2409 N. Kelley
PO Box 36659
Oklahoma City, OK 73136
Phone: (405)522-6377
Fax: (405)427-3027

★ 12807 ★ Oregon Department of Human Resources
Vocational Rehabilitation Division
500 Summer St., NE
Salem, OR 97310-1018
Phone: (503)945-5880
Fax: (503)378-3318

★12808★ **Pennsylvania Department of Labor and Industry**
Vocational Rehabilitation Office
1300 Labor and Industry Bldg.
7th and Forster Sts.
Harrisburg, PA 17120
Phone: (717)787-5244
Fax: (717)787-8826

★12809★ **Puerto Rico Department of Social Services**
Vocational Rehabilitation Division
PO Box 191118
San Juan, PR 00909-1118
Phone: (809)725-1792

★12810★ **Rhode Island Department of Human Services**
Vocational Rehabilitation Services
40 Fountain St.
Providence, RI 02903
Phone: (401)421-7005

★12811★ **South Carolina Department of Vocational Rehabilitation**
1410 Boston Ave.
PO Box 15
West Columbia, SC 29171-0015
Phone: (803)822-5303
Fax: (803)822-5386

★12812★ **South Dakota Department of Human Services**
Rehabilitation Services Division
E. Hwy. 34
c/o 500 E. Capitol
Pierre, SD 57501-5070
Phone: (605)773-3195
Fax: (605)773-5483

★12813★ **Tennessee Department of Human Services**
Rehabilitation Services Division
Citizen Plaza Bldg., 15th Fl.
400 Deaderick St.
Nashville, TN 37248
Phone: (615)741-2521

★12814★ **Texas Rehabilitation Commission**
4900 N. Lamar Blvd.
Austin, TX 78751-2399
Phone: (512)483-4001
Fax: (512)483-4012

★12815★ **Utah Rehabilitation Office**
Rehabilitation Services Division
250 East 500 South
Salt Lake City, UT 84111
Phone: (801)538-7538
Fax: (801)538-7522

★12816★ **Vermont Agency of Human Services**
Social and Rehabilitation Services Department
Vocational Rehabilitation Division
Osgood Bldg.
103 S. Main St.
Waterbury, VT 05676
Phone: (802)241-2186

★12817★ **Virgin Islands Department of Human Services**
Disabilities and Rehabilitation Services Division
1303 Hospital Ground
St. Thomas, VI 00802
Phone: (809)774-0930

★12818★ **Virginia Office of Health and Human Resources**
Rehabilitative Services Department
8004 Franklin Farms Dr.
PO Box K-300
Richmond, VA 23288
Phone: (804)662-7010

★12819★ **Washington Department of Social and Health Services**
Health and Rehabilitative Services Office
Vocational Rehabilitation Division
PO Box 45060
Olympia, WA 98504-5060
Phone: (360)753-2544
Fax: (360)586-5874

★12820★ **West Virginia State Board of Education and the Arts**
Rehabilitation Services Division
State Capitol Complex
PO Box 50890
Charleston, WV 25305
Phone: (304)766-4601

★12821★ **Wisconsin Department of Health and Social Services**
Vocational Rehabilitation Division
1 W. Wilson St., 8th Fl.
PO Box 7852
Madison, WI 53707-7852
Phone: (608)266-5466
Fax: (608)267-3657

★12822★ **Wyoming Department of Employment**
Vocational Rehabilitation Division
117 Hathaway Bldg.
Cheyenne, WY 82002
Phone: (307)777-7191
Fax: (307)777-5939

State & Regional Organizations

Physical Therapy

The following are state chapters of the American Physical Therapy Association, 1111 N. Fairfax St., Alexandria, VA 22314-1488, (703) 684-2782. Those states not listed have presidents that change regularly. Current contact information can be obtained from the national organization.

Alabama

★12823★ **American Physical Therapy Association**
Alabama Chapter
323 De la Mare Ave.
Fairhope, AL 36532-2319
Phone: (334)990-9666
Fax: (334)990-8019

Arizona

★12824★ **American Physical Therapy Association**
Arizona Chapter
3900 E. Camelback, Ste. 2000
Phoenix, AZ 85018-2614
Phone: (602)912-5310
Fax: (602)952-8230

Arkansas

★12825★ **American Physical Therapy Association**
Arkansas Chapter
PO Box 2068
Conway, AR 72033-2068
Phone: (501)336-8247
Fax: (501)329-0718

California

★12826★ **American Physical Therapy Association**
California Chapter
1107 9th St., Ste. 1050
Sacramento, CA 95814-3610
Phone: (916)446-0069
Fax: (916)448-2362

Colorado

★12827★ **American Physical Therapy Association**
Colorado Chapter
7853 E. Arapahoe Ct., Ste. 2100
Englewood, CO 80112-1361
Phone: (303)694-4728
Fax: (303)694-4869

Connecticut

★12828★ **American Physical Therapy Association**
Connecticut Chapter
55 Farmington Ave., Ste. 403
Hartford, CT 06105-3722
Phone: (203)246-4414
Fax: (203)493-7476

Florida

★12829★ **American Physical Therapy Association**
Florida Chapter
235 E. Virginia St.
Tallahassee, FL 32301-1263
Phone: (904)222-1243
Fax: (904)224-5281

Georgia

★ 12830 ★ American Physical Therapy Association
Georgia Chapter
2850 Faraday Ct.
Decatur, GA 30033-2409
Phone: (404)982-0776
Fax: (404)636-8165

Idaho

★ 12831 ★ American Physical Therapy Association
Idaho Chapter
PO Box 1273
Boise, ID 83701-1273
Phone: (208)345-4855
Fax: (208)342-6647

Illinois

★ 12832 ★ American Physical Therapy Association
Illinois Chapter
2720 River Rd., Ste. 131
Des Plaines, IL 60018
Phone: (708)296-8859
Fax: (708)296-8865

Indiana

★ 12833 ★ American Physical Therapy Association
Indiana Chapter
11953 Glen Cove Dr.
Indianapolis, IN 46236-9014
Phone: (317)823-3681
Fax: (317)823-3681

Iowa

★ 12834 ★ American Physical Therapy Association
Iowa Chapter
1228 8th St., Ste. 106
West Des Moines, IA 50265-2622
Phone: (515)222-9838
Fax: (515)222-9839

Kansas

★ 12835 ★ American Physical Therapy Association
Kansas Chapter
15761 Dearborn
Overland Park, KS 66223-3415
Phone: (913)897-7252
Fax: (913)897-6207

Kentucky

★ 12836 ★ American Physical Therapy Association
Kentucky Chapter
102 St. James Ct., Ste. B
Frankfort, KY 40601
Phone: (502)875-7529
Fax: (606)223-5479

Louisiana

★ 12837 ★ American Physical Therapy Association
Louisiana Chapter
8550 United Plaza Blvd., Ste. 1001A
Baton Rouge, LA 70809-2256
Phone: (504)922-4614
Fax: (504)922-4611

Maine

★ 12838 ★ American Physical Therapy Association
Maine Chapter
PO Box 1783
Portland, ME 04104-1783
Phone: (207)799-1584

Maryland

★ 12839 ★ American Physical Therapy Association
Maryland Chapter
PO Box 4236
Largo, MD 20775-0236
Phone: (301)808-9418
Fax: (301)808-5245

Massachusetts

★ 12840 ★ American Physical Therapy Association
Massachusetts Chapter
14 Beacon St., Ste. 719
Boston, MA 02108-2301
Phone: (617)523-4285
Fax: (617)523-1427

Michigan

★ 12841 ★ American Physical Therapy Association
Michigan Chapter
PO Box 21236
Lansing, MI 48909-1236
Free: 800-242-8131
Fax: (517)349-8928

Minnesota

★ 12842 ★ American Physical Therapy Association
Minnesota Chapter
1711 W. County Rd. B, Ste. 101S
Roseville, MN 55113
Phone: (612)635-0902
Fax: (612)635-0903

Mississippi

★ 12843 ★ American Physical Therapy Association
Mississippi Chapter
921 N. Congress St.
Jackson, MS 39202-2554
Phone: (601)354-3629
Fax: (601)355-1506

Missouri

★ 12844 ★ American Physical Therapy Association
Missouri Chapter
101 Corporate Lake Dr., B2
Columbia, MO 65203
Phone: (314)875-8595
Fax: (314)875-8158

Montana

★ 12845 ★ American Physical Therapy Association
Montana Chapter
1545 W. Sussex
PO Box 4553
Missoula, MT 59806-4553
Phone: (406)721-7334
Fax: (406)721-7016

Nebraska

★ 12846 ★ American Physical Therapy Association
Nebraska Chapter
PO Box 540427
Omaha, NE 68154-0427
Phone: (402)491-3660
Fax: (402)491-3660

Nevada

★ 12847 ★ American Physical Therapy Association
Nevada Chapter
PO Box 12190
Reno, NV 89510-2190
Phone: (702)323-6003
Fax: (702)853-2166

New Hampshire

★ 12848 ★ American Physical Therapy Association
New Hampshire Chapter
PO Box 978
Manchester, NH 03105
Phone: (603)627-7970
Fax: (603)432-1580

New Jersey

★ 12849 ★ American Physical Therapy Association
New Jersey Chapter
133 S. Main St.
PO Box 1259
Hightstown, NJ 08520-3338
Phone: (609)426-0216
Fax: (609)426-1584

New Mexico

★12850★ American Physical Therapy
Association
New Mexico Chapter
PO Box 91600
Albuquerque, NM 87199-1600
Phone: (505)891-5443
Fax: (505)260-1919

New York

★12851★ American Physical Therapy
Association
New York Chapter
4 Palisades Dr.
Albany, NY 12205-1438
Phone: (518)459-4499
Fax: (518)459-8953

North Carolina

★12852★ American Physical Therapy
Association
North Carolina Chapter
1418 Aversboro Rd.
Garner, NC 27529-4547
Phone: (919)772-6850
Fax: (919)779-5642

North Dakota

★12853★ American Physical Therapy
Association
North Dakota Chapter
Department of Physical Therapy
University of North Dakota School of Medicine
Grand Forks, ND 58201
Phone: (701)777-2831
Fax: (701)777-3894

Ohio

★12854★ American Physical Therapy
Association
Ohio Chapter
4355 N. High St., Ste. 201
Columbus, OH 43214-2612
Phone: (614)267-7000
Fax: (614)267-1186

Oklahoma

★12855★ American Physical Therapy
Association
Oklahoma Chapter
PO Box 18508
Oklahoma City, OK 73154-0508
Phone: (405)424-6782
Fax: (405)340-3884

Oregon

★12856★ American Physical Therapy
Association
Oregon Chapter
PO Box 342
Wilsonville, OR 97070-0342
Phone: (503)694-2121
Fax: (503)694-2404

Pennsylvania

★12857★ American Physical Therapy
Association
Pennsylvania Chapter
2090 Linglestown Rd., Ste. 101
Harrisburg, PA 17110-9428
Phone: (717)541-9169
Fax: (717)541-9182

Rhode Island

★12858★ American Physical Therapy
Association
Rhode Island Chapter
PO Box 1409
Kingston, RI 02881-0492
Phone: (401)792-5391
Fax: (401)792-5630

South Carolina

★12859★ American Physical Therapy
Association
South Carolina Chapter
826 Assembly St.
PO Box 11937
Columbia, SC 29211-1937
Phone: (803)771-4271
Fax: (803)771-4272

Tennessee

★12860★ American Physical Therapy
Association
Tennessee Chapter
175 Winding Way
Mt. Juliet, TN 37122-2098
Phone: (615)754-9013
Fax: (615)758-4228

Texas

★12861★ American Physical Therapy
Association
Texas Chapter
400 W. 15th St., Ste. 805
Austin, TX 78701-1647
Phone: (512)477-1818
Fax: (512)477-1434

Utah

★12862★ American Physical Therapy
Association
Utah Chapter
PO Box 453
Centerville, UT 84014
Phone: (801)532-7105
Fax: (801)973-8270

Virginia

★12863★ American Physical Therapy
Association
Virginia Chapter
1055 N. Fairfax St.
Alexandria, VA 22314-3492
Free: 800-999-2782
Fax: (703)706-8575

Washington

★12864★ American Physical Therapy
Association
Washington Chapter
208 NW Rogers
Olympia, WA 98502-4940
Phone: (206)352-7290
Fax: (206)352-7298

Wisconsin

★12865★ American Physical Therapy
Association
Wisconsin Chapter
2800 Royal Ave., Ste. 206C
Madison, WI 53713-1518
Phone: (608)221-9191
Fax: (608)221-9697

Chapter 66
Transplantation

National & International Organizations

★ 12866 ★ **American Association of Tissue Banks (AATB)**
1350 Beverly Rd., Ste. 220-A
Mc Lean, VA 22101
Phone: (703)827-9582
Jeanne Mowe, Exec.Dir.

Founded: 1976. **Members:** 800. **Description:** Goals are to encourage the development of regional tissue banks and the establishment of guidelines and standards for the retrieval, preservation, distribution, and use of tissues for transplantation. **Publications:** *AATB Membership Directory*, annual. Membership Directory. Lists individuals and institutions. *Price:* Included in membership dues. • *American Association of Tissue Banks--Technical Manual*, periodic. • *Standards for Tissue Banking*. • *Technical Manual for Tissue Banking*.

★ 12867 ★ **American Society of Transplant Physicians**
6900 Grove Rd.
Thorofare, NJ 08086
Phone: (609)848-1000
Fax: (609)853-5991
Susan Nelson, Exec.Dir.

Members: 644. **Description:** Promotes and encourages education and research with respect to transplantation medicine and immunology; provides a forum for exchange of scientific information related to transplantation. **Publications:** *Transplantation*, monthly. *Price:* Included in membership dues.

American Society of Transplant Surgeons (ASTS)
See: Entry 12247

Association for Nordic Transplant and Dialysis Personnel (NORDIATRAN)
See: Entry 12903

Association of Nurses Endorsing Transplantation (ANET)
See: Entry 9072

★ 12868 ★ **Center for Organ Recovery and Education (CORE)**
204 Silema Dr.
Pittsburgh, PA 15238
Free: 800-366-6777
Fax: (412)963-3563
Brian A. Broznick, Dir.

Founded: 1978. **Description:** Develops and executes educational and medical/surgical programs designed to increase the number of postmortem donations and the surgical retrieval of vital organs and tissues for transplantation at the transplant centers in Pittsburgh, PA, West Virginia, and other transplant centers in the U.S. and Canada. Teams are available around the clock for organ and tissue retrieval from hospitals in western Pennsylvania, West Virginia, eastern Ohio, and southern New York. Provides access to UNOS, a national computer system, for matching and distributing organs (hearts, livers, lungs, and kidneys) and tissue for transplantation. Seeks to educate the public regarding organ and tissue donation and brain death. Sponsors continuing education programs for health professionals in regional hospitals and associations. Also provides speakers for presentation to medical groups. Compiles statistics. **Publications:** Newsletter, quarterly. • Pamphlets. Also publishes protocols. **Formerly:** (1984) Transplant Coordinators Organization; (1992) Pittsburgh Transplant Foundation.

European Dialysis and Transplant Nurses Association / European Renal Care Association (EDTNA/ERCA)
See: Entry 9087

European Society for Cataract and Refractive Surgeons (ESCRS)
(Club International d'Implants Oculaires)
See: Entry 13448

★ 12869 ★ **Eurotransplant Foundation (EF)**
PO Box 2304
NL-2301 NL Leiden, Netherlands
Phone: 71 182838
Fax: 71 149480
Dr. Guido A. Persyn, Medical Dir.

Founded: 1966. **Languages:** English. **Description:** Sponsors human organ exchange program. **Publications:** *Annual Report*. • *Eurotransplant Manual*, periodic. • *Eurotransplant Newsletter*, monthly. Newsletter.

Eye Bank Association of America (EBAA)
See: Entry 13450

Eye-Bank for Sight Restoration (EBSR)
See: Entry 13451

★ 12870 ★ **International Society for Artificial Organs (ISAO)**
8937 Euclid Ave.
Cleveland, OH 44106
Phone: (216)421-0757
Fax: (216)421-1652
Dr. Yukihiko Nose, M.D., Dir.

Founded: 1977. **Members:** 1,000. **Regional Groups:** 4. **Languages:** English. **Description:** Medical doctors, technicians, bioengineers, and researchers. Publishes materials covering all aspects of artificial organs; conducts research. Maintains museum. **Publications:** *Artificial Organs*, bimonthly. Also publishes books.

★ 12871 ★ **International Society for Heart and Lung Transplantation (ISHLT)**
14673 Midway Rd., Ste. 108
Dallas, TX 75244
Phone: (214)490-9495
Amanda W. Rowe, Exec.Dir.

Founded: 1981. **Members:** 1,550. **Description:** Medical doctors, Ph.D.s, nurses, researchers, and others interested in artificial hearts and in heart and heart-lung preservation and transplantation. Provides a center for discussion, exchange of information, and activities that promote the interests of heart and lung transplantation. Seeks to heighten awareness of public and governmental agencies regarding developments in the field. Maintains the International Heart and Lung Transplantation Registry. **Publications:** *The Journal of Heart and Lung Transplantation*, bimonthly. Journal. **Formerly:** (1991) International Society for Heart Transplantation.

International Transplant Nurses Society (ITNS)
See: Entry 9098

★ 12872 ★ LifeBanc
20600 Chagrin Blvd., Ste. 350
Cleveland, OH 44122-5343
Phone: (216)752-5433
Free: 800-558-5433
Fax: (216)791-4204
Kristine Nelson, RN MN, Exec.Dir.

Founded: 1986. **Description:** Program "designed to increase the number of useful body organs and tissues available for transplant by encouraging individuals to consider the possibility of donating their body organs and tissues for use after death." Originally concerned with kidney donation, program has now expanded to include "all organs and tissues when circumstances are favorable and transplant is medically feasible." Organizes and implements public and professional education programs. Coordinates recovery teams on 24-hour call from participating hospitals and medical institutions. Conducts training programs for hospital staff on organ donation procedures and solicitation. **Publications:** Pamphlets.

★ 12873 ★ The Living Bank (TLB)
PO Box 6725
Houston, TX 77265
Phone: (713)961-9431
Free: 800-528-2971
Fax: (713)961-0979
Bruce B. Conway, Pres. & CEO

Founded: 1968. **Members:** 326,000. **Description:** National registry created to help those persons who, upon their deaths, wish to donate a part or parts of their bodies for the purposes of transplantation, therapy, or medical research. A primary objective is to encourage the general public to donate organs. Explains the procedure and provides a donor registration form and a uniform donor card. Enters information from the completed form into a central registry of potential donors for instant retrieval of data when needed. Anyone who is of legal age may register. Persons younger than 18 must have parent's or guardian's signature. Conducts educational programs; operates speakers' bureau; compiles statistics. **Publications:** *Bank Account*, quarterly. Newsletter. Includes news updates on advances in the fields of organ donation and transplantation. *Price:* Free. Also publishes educational and informational materials.

★ 12874 ★ National Marrow Donor Program (NMDP)
c/o Steve Beseke
3433 Broadway NE, Ste. 400
Minneapolis, MN 55413-1762
Phone: (612)627-5800
Free: 800-627-7692
Fax: (612)627-5899
Craig W.S. Howe, M.D., CEO

Founded: 1986. **Members:** 230. **Description:** Donor and bone marrow transplant centers. Acts as a central registry of U.S. bone marrow donors; works to develop a large pool of potential donors and facilitate searches and matching of donors and recipients; tests the effectiveness of unrelated donor transplants. NMDP works to make use of human leukocyte antigen typing to develop a list of potential volunteer donors for patients with leukemia and other potentially fatal blood diseases. Trains member centers in re-

cruiting donors. **Publications:** Brochures. • *Chance of a Lifetime*, annual. • *Hematologists/Oncologists Guide to Unrelated Marrow Transplantation*. • *Living Gift of Life*. Brochure. • *Search for Life-Savers*, quarterly. **Formerly:** National Bone Marrow Donor Registry.

★ 12875 ★ North American Society for Dialysis and Transplantation (NASDT)
c/o Dr. Wadi Suki
6550 Fannin, Ste. 1273
Houston, TX 77030
Phone: (713)790-3275
Fax: (713)790-5053
Dr. Wadi Suki, Sec.-Treas.

Founded: 1981. **Members:** 200. **Description:** Professionals active in the area of teaching, manufacturing, and administration in the fields of nephrology and transplantation including nephrologists, transplant surgeons and physicians, registered nurses, dialysis nurses, and transplant coordinators. Promotes education and research and disseminates current knowledge and technology in the field of kidney dialysis and transplantation.

★ 12876 ★ North American Transplant Coordinators Organization (NATCO)
PO Box 15384
Lenexa, KS 66285-5384
Phone: (913)492-3600
Fax: (913)541-0156
Deidre Panjada, Exec.Dir.

Founded: 1979. **Members:** 1,600. **Description:** Nurses and allied health professionals working with organ recipients and those working to obtain and distribute human organs and tissues to waiting victims of end-stage organ failure. Seeks to influence increased procurement and use of transplantable organs and tissues under the direction of individuals and institutions responsible for the employment of members. Disseminates information to members, medical personnel, technicians, and the public regarding the benefits of organ transplantation, new techniques in organ procurement, advancements in immunology and preservation, transplant surgery, and other aspects of organ transplantation. Promotes and supports training and development programs for new transplant coordinators. Sponsors seminars, workshops, and annual training course on procurement for transplant coordinators. Offers job referral information. **Publications:** *Journal of Transplant Coordination*, 3/year. Journal. Includes clinical articles addressing transplantation issues. *Price:* $65/year. • *NATCO--Newsletter*, quarterly. Newsletter. Includes calendar of events, employment opportunity listings, legislative updates, and conference reports. *Price:* Included in membership dues. • *North American Transplant Coordinators Organization--Membership Directory*, annual. Directory. *Price:* Included in membership dues.

★ 12877 ★ Organ Transplant Fund
1027 S. Yates Rd.
Memphis, TN 38119
Free: 800-489-3863
Fax: (901)684-1128
Suzanne D. Norman, Dir.

Founded: 1983. **Regional Groups:** 53. **Description:** Works to guide and assist fundraising

for transplant patients and their families. Provides transplant team necessities. Makes hospital social services recommendations. Provides financial, support, and charitable programs; compiles statistics.

★ 12878 ★ Tissue Banks International (TBI)
815 Park Ave.
Baltimore, MD 21201
Phone: (301)752-3800
Fax: (410)545-4457

Founded: 1962. **Description:** Medical eye and tissue banks. Provides eye tissue for sight-restoring corneal transplant surgery. Also distributes bone, skin, and other soft tissues. Assists members with operational areas. Provides grants for research into the causes and cures of blindness. Distributes information on eye, tissue, and organ donation. Conducts educational and charitable programs; maintains speakers' bureau. **Publications:** Brochure.

★ 12879 ★ Transplant Recipients International Organization (TRIO)
1735 I St. NW, Ste. 917
Washington, DC 20006
Phone: (202)293-0980
Free: 800-TRI-O386
Fax: (202)293-0973
Robert P. Casey, Pres.

Founded: 1987. **Members:** 7,000. **Description:** Transplant candidates, recipients, family members, donor families, and medical personnel. Provides support and medical information to patients and their families. Conducts educational programs. Provides fund-raising guidelines. **Publications:** *TRIO Lifelines*, bimonthly. Newsletter. Includes chapter activities and current transplantation news.

★ 12880 ★ Transplantation Society (TS)
c/o Eduardo A. Santiago-Delpin
PR Transplant Program
Auxilio Mutuo Hospital
Box 191227
Hato Rey, PR 00919
Phone: (809)765-7650
Fax: (809)766-4038
Eduardo A. Santiago-Delpin, M.D., Contact

Founded: 1966. **Members:** 1,400. **Description:** Physicians and scientists who have made significant contributions to the advancement of knowledge in transplantation biology and medicine. Purpose is to further information in the general area of transplantation biology and medicine, with related interests in cancer immunology and host responses to infectious microorganisms. **Publications:** *Transplantation Proceedings*, bimonthly. Proceedings.

★ 12881 ★ United Network for Organ Sharing (UNOS)
1100 Boulders Pky., Ste. 500
PO Box 13770
Richmond, VA 23225
Phone: (804)330-8500
Fax: (804)330-8517
Gene A. Pierce, Exec.Dir.

Founded: 1984. **Members:** 422. **Regional Groups:** 11. **Description:** Transplant and organ procurement centers, tissue-typing labs, and health care professionals engaged in organ transplant operations. Administers the National Organ Procurement and Transplantation Network and the U.S. Scientific Registry for Organ Transplantation, as mandated by law. Operates the Organ Center, which matches patients in need of transplants with donated organs. Formulates and implements national policies on equitable access and organ allocation and organ procurement standards. Conducts professional education courses for transplant personnel. Maintains and publicizes national statistics on organ donation and transplantation. **Publications:** *UNOS Update*, monthly. Newsletter. *Price:* Free to domestic subscribers. **Also Known As:** UNOS.

Research Centers

★ 12882 ★ **Baylor University**
Bone Marrow Transplantation Research
Center
3409 Worth St., Ste. 410
Dallas, TX 75246
Phone: (214)820-2619
Fax: (214)820-7346
Joseph W. Fay, M.D., Dir.

Research Activities and Fields: Bone marrow transplantation research in leukemia/lymphoma studies, including graft-vs-host disease, evaluation of immune recovery post transplant, evaluation of growth factors in transplantation, and applications of molecular biology/gene rearrangement in marrow transplantation.

★ 12883 ★ **Bone Marrow Transplant**
Laboratory
Children's Hospital of Orange County
455 S. Main St.
Orange, CA 92668
Phone: (714)532-8548
Fax: (714)532-8771
Mitchell Cairo, Dir.

Research Activities and Fields: Bone marrow immunology experiments, including tumor purging using chemotherapy and monoclonal antibodies, molecular detection of minimal residual diesase, purification of hematopoietic stem cells, and purging and cultivation of bone marrow. Also studies umbilical cord blood harvesting, storage, and expansion; and T-cell depletion for unrelated bone marrow transplantation.

Center for Reproduction and
Transplantation Immunology
See: Entry 2097

Connecticut Eye Bank & Visual Research
Foundation, Inc.
See: Entry 13587

Jane Forbes Clark Surgical Research
Laboratories
See: Entry 2104

★ 12884 ★ **Loyola University Chicago**
Cardiac Transplant Program
2160 S. 1st Ave.
Maywood, IL 60153
Phone: (708)216-4810
Fax: (708)216-5600
Dr. Maria Rosa Costanzo, Dir.

Research Activities and Fields: Cardiac transplantation and immunology, including allograft rejection, vascular diseases, and transplant tolerance.

★ 12885 ★ **Oregon Health Sciences**
University
Transplant and Immunogenetics
Laboratory
3181 SW Sam Jackson Park Rd.
Portland, OR 97201
Phone: (503)494-8311
Douglas Norman, M.D., Dir.

Research Activities and Fields: Human immunobiology of organ transplantation.

★ 12886 ★ **Stanford University**
Laboratory for Transplantation
Immunology
Stanford, CA 94305-5247
Phone: (415)723-5641
Fax: (415)725-3846
Dr. Randall E. Morris, Dir.

Research Activities and Fields: Develops compounds to reduce rejection of transplanted organs. Studies focus on molecules, monoclonal antibodies, and naturally occurring substances.

U.S. Department of Defense
Naval Medical Research and Development
Command
Naval Medical Research Institute
Immune Cell Biology Program
See: Entry 7849

U.S. Department of Health and Human
Services
National Institute of Allergy and Infectious
Diseases
Division of Allergy, Immunology, and
Transplantation
Genetics and Transplantation Branch
See: Entry 2128

★ 12887 ★ **University of California, Irvine**
Reconstructive Microsurgery and
Transplantation Laboratories
Medical Sciences I
Dept. of Surgery
Irvine, CA 92717
Phone: (714)856-5880
Kirby S. Black, Ph.D, Dir.

Research Activities and Fields: Composite tissue transplantation (including skin, muscle, nerve, bone, and joint), kidney transplantation, transplantation immunology, cell-mediated immunology, humoral-mediated immunology, immunosuppressive pharmacokinetics, burn research, and pathology of rejection.

★ 12888 ★ **University of California, Los**
Angeles
Bone Marrow Transplantation Program
Center for Health Sciences
Los Angeles, CA 90024-1678
Phone: (310)825-9677
Fax: (310)206-5511
Mary Territo, M.D., Dir.

Research Activities and Fields: Treatment of leukemia, lymphoma, myeloma, breast cancer, solid tumors, and aplastic anemia. Evaluates the use of bone marrow and stem cell transplantation as treatment for a number of hematologic and malignant diseases.

University of California, San Francisco
Immunogenetics and Transplantation
Laboratory
See: Entry 2141

★ 12889 ★ **University of California, San**
Francisco
Liver Transplant Division
Dept. of Surgery
PO Box 0780
San Francisco, CA 94143
Phone: (415)496-1236
Nancy Ascher, M.D., Director

Research Activities and Fields: Molecular and immunological mechanisms of allograft rejection, focusing on molecular approaches to monitoring transplant patients and experimental transplant models in SCID-Hu mice.

★ 12890 ★ **University of Florida**
Center for Transplantation Biology
College of Medicine
Box 100-275
Gainesville, FL 32610
Phone: (904)392-3790
Fax: (904)392-6249
Dr. Edward Wakelind, Dir.

Research Activities and Fields: Transplantation biology, including graft rejection, and immunological tolerance and disease.

★ 12891 ★ **University of Michigan**
Transplant and Health Policy Center
Medical Center
115 Zinapitcher Pl.
Box 0716
Ann Arbor, MI 48109-0716
Phone: (313)998-7271
Fax: (313)998-7981
Jeremiah G. Turcotte, M.D., Dir.

Research Activities and Fields: Public policy, social, ethical, patient, and educational issues related to organ transplantation. **Publications:** Periodic Activity Report.

Chapter 67
Urology

Federal Government Agencies

U.S. Department of Health and Human Services
National Institute of Diabetes and Digestive and Kidney Diseases
See: Entry 4820

Foundations & Other Funding Organizations

Other Funding Organizations

★ 12892 ★ **American Kidney Fund**
6110 Executive Blvd., Ste. 1010
Rockville, MD 20852
Phone: (301)881-3052
Free: 800-638-8299
Fax: (301)881-0898
Francis J. Soldovere, Exec. Dir.

Description: Provides direct financial assistance to needy kidney disease patients for costs related to their treatment. Also supports dialysis center emergency funds and clinical research fellowships.

★ 12893 ★ **National Kidney Foundation**
30 E. 33rd St., Ste. 1100
New York, NY 10016
Phone: (212)889-2210
Free: 800-622-9010
Fax: (212)689-9261
John Davis, Exec. Dir.

Description: Awards fellowships and Young Investigator grants to support research and training relating to kidney function and disease.

National & International Organizations

American Association of Genito-Urinary Surgeons (AAGUS)
See: Entry 12210

★ 12894 ★ **American Association of Kidney Patients (AAKP)**
100 S. Ashley Dr., Ste. 280
Tampa, FL 33602-5346
Phone: 800-749-2257
Fax: (813)254-3270
Kris Robinson, Exec.Dir.

Founded: 1969. **Members:** 6,000. **Local Groups:** 26. **Description:** Persons on hemodialysis, peritoneal dialysis, and with kidney transplants; their families and friends; professionals in the dialysis field. Educates the patient and the public regarding kidney disease; works for improved quality of care for all patients; promotes a donor program. **Publications:** *Americans with Disabilities Act.* • *Blood Chemistry Levels.* • *Bulletin,* quarterly. Newspaper. *Price:* $15. • *Na-K Counter.* • *Renalife,* semiannual. Magazine. *Price:* $15. Also publishes other informational materials. **Formerly:** National Association of Patients on Hemodialysis; National Association of Patients on Hemodialysis and Transplantation.

★ 12895 ★ **American Board of Urologic Allied Health Professionals (ABUAHP)**
407 Strawberry Hill Ave.
Stamford, CT 06902
Phone: (609)256-2351
Mikel Gray, Pres.

Founded: 1972. **Description:** Conducts annual certification exam for urological professionals.

★ 12896 ★ **American Board of Urology (ABU)**
31700 Telegraph Rd., Ste. 150
Bingham Farms, MI 48025
Phone: (810)646-9720
Alan D. Perlmutter, M.D., Exec.Sec.

Founded: 1935. **Description:** Conducts examinations and certifies physicians in the specialty of urology (branch of medicine that is concerned with the genito-urinary tract). **Publications:** *Information for Applicants and Candidates,* annual. Includes certification details and schedule of exams.

★ 12897 ★ **American Foundation for Urologic Disease (AFUD)**
300 W. Pratt St., Ste. 401
Baltimore, MD 21201
Phone: (410)727-2908
Free: 800-242-2383
Fax: (410)528-0550
Tom Bruckman, Assoc.Dir.

Founded: 1987. **Description:** Participants include urologists, patients, and medical and pharmaceutical manufacturers. Medical research and education organization working to broaden the base of urological research and enhance public awareness of urologic disease in the U.S. Conducts public educational programs on topics including childhood urological problems, prostate disease, and bladder disorders. Sponsors US TOO patient support groups for prostate cancer survivors. Makes available research fellowships and grants.

★ 12898 ★ **American Kidney Fund (AKF)**
6110 Executive Blvd., Ste. 1010
Rockville, MD 20852
Phone: (301)881-3052
Free: 800-638-8299
Fax: (301)881-0898
Francis J. Soldovere, Exec.Dir.

Founded: 1971. **Regional Groups:** 3. **Description:** Works to alleviate the financial burdens caused by kidney disease; improve the quality of life for kidney patients; promote kidney health care nationwide. Provides direct financial assistance to needy kidney disease victims with costs related to their treatment. Funds are raised through direct mail from the public. Supports dialysis center emergency funds. Programs include: American Kidney Fund Clinical Scientist in Nephrology program, which provides assistance to nephrology students pursuing scholarship in the provision of clinical care; patient and community services; public and professional education; kidney donor development; and research. **Publications:** *AKF Newsletter for Nephrology Professionals,* 2/year. Newsletter. *Price:* Free. • *American Kidney Fund--Annual Report,* annual. Annual Report. *Price:* Free. • Brochures.

American Nephrology Nurses' Association (ANNA)
See: Entry 9061

★ 12899 ★ American Society of Nephrology (ASN)
1200 19th St. NW, Ste. 300
Washington, DC 20036
Phone: (202)857-1190
Fax: (202)223-4579
Judith Thomas, Exec.Dir.

Founded: 1966. **Members:** 5,300. **Description:** Nephrologists united for the exchange of scientific information. Seeks to contribute to the education of members and to improve the quality of patient care. Conducts educational courses. Maintains placement service. **Publications:** *Abstracts and Program*, annual. • *ASN Highlights*, quarterly. Newsletter. • *Journal of the American Society of Nephrology*, monthly. Journal. • Membership Directory, periodic.

★ 12900 ★ American Urological Association (AUA)
1120 N. Charles St.
Baltimore, MD 21201
Phone: (410)727-1100
Fax: (410)625-2390
G. James Gallagher, Exec.Dir.

Founded: 1902. **Members:** 9,000. **Regional Groups:** 8. **Description:** Professional society of physicians specializing in urology. Provides placement service. Condusts educational programs; maintains museum. **Publications:** *AUA Today*, monthly. • *Journal of Urology*, monthly. Journal. • *Membership Roster*, biennial.

★ 12901 ★ American Urological Association Allied (AUAA)
11512 Allecingie Pky.
Richmond, VA 23235
Phone: (804)379-1306
Fax: (804)379-1386
Heather Renehan, Exec.Dir.

Founded: 1972. **Members:** 2,500. **Regional Groups:** 8. **Local Groups:** 37. **Description:** Registered and licensed practical nurses, technicians, physician assistants, those working in urology-related industries, and secretarial employees in urology offices. Provides continuing education; chapters and sections conduct regional and local seminars. Presents Chapter of the Year, Literary, and Research Poster awards. **Publications:** *AUAA Membership Directory*, annual. Membership Directory. • *Standards of Urological Nursing Practice*. Booklet. • *Urogram*, quarterly. Newsletter. Informing members on the association's continuing educational programs. *Price:* Included in membership dues. • *Urologic Nursing*, quarterly. Journal. *Price:* Included in membership dues; $30/year for nonmembers.

★ 12902 ★ Association of German Urologists
(Berufsverband der Deutschen Urologen)
Erdinger Str. 19
84404 Dorfen, Germany
Phone: 8081 41313
Fax: 8081 4468
Dr. Klaus Schalkhauser, Contact

Founded: 1956. **Members:** 2,550. **State Groups:** 19. **Description:** Urologists practicing in Germany. Promotes the advancement of the field of urology. **Publications:** *Urologeb*, bimonthly. Journal. • *Urotelegramm*, bimonthly. Newsletter.

★ 12903 ★ Association for Nordic Transplant and Dialysis Personnel (NORDIATRAN)
Dialyseavdelingen
Regionsykehuset
N-7006 Trondheim, Norway
Phone: 73 998530
Fax: 73 997546
Ingrid Lian, Pres.

Founded: 1972. **Members:** 550. **Languages:** Danish, Finnish, Icelandic, Norwegian, Swedish. **Description:** Professionals from 5 countries working in the field of dialysis and transplantation. Disseminates information on the latest medical transplantation practices. **Publications:** *Nordiatrans*, semiannual. Journal.

Board of Nephrology Examiners—Nursing and Technology (BONENT)
See: Entry 9077

★ 12904 ★ Continence Restored, Inc. (CRI)
785 Park Ave.
New York, NY 10021
Phone: (212)879-3131
Anne Smith-Young, Pres.

Founded: 1985. **State Groups:** 2. **Description:** Participants are people with bladder control problems and interested individuals. Organizes support groups. Provides information on incontinence devices and treatment; offers referrals. Compiles statistics.

European Dialysis and Transplant Nurses Association / European Renal Care Association (EDTNA/ERCA)
See: Entry 9087

European Society for Paediatric Nephrology (ESPN)
See: Entry 3225

★ 12905 ★ Help for Incontinent People (HIP)
PO Box 544
Union, SC 29379
Phone: (803)579-7900
Free: 800-BLA-DDER
Fax: (803)579-7902
Katherine F. Jeter, Dir.

Founded: 1982. **Members:** 75,000. **Description:** Works to help individuals who have bladder control problems. Acts as a clearinghouse of information and services involving incontinence and assistive devices for consumers and their families as well as medical, nursing, and social service organizations. Offers tips and advice on bladder control. **Publications:** *The Hip Report*, quarterly. Brochures. *Price:* $15/year. • *HIP Report*, periodic. Newsletter. Includes information on new resources. *Price:* $15/year. • *Resource Guide of Continence Products and Services*. **Also Known As:** HIP, Inc..

International Pediatric Nephrology (IPNA)
See: Entry 3245

International Society for Peritoneal Dialysis (ISPD)
See: Entry 2426

★ 12906 ★ International Society of Urological Endoscopy
Zabala 3280, 6A
1426 Buenos Aires, Argentina
Phone: 1 5524726
Dr. Edgardo A. Giorgini

Description: Works to improve the diagnosis of, and treatment associated with, endoscopic-urologic problems.

★ 12907 ★ International Society of Urology (ISU)
(Societe Internationale d'Urologie — SIU)
3, place de la Republique
F-59000 Lille, France
Phone: 20 576389
Fax: 20 782628
Etienne Mazeman, M.D., Sec.Gen.

Founded: 1907. **Members:** 3,623. **National Groups:** 86. **Languages:** English. **Description:** Surgeons and other specialists in the field of urology. Promotes research in urology; fosters communication among members. Sponsors meetings and programs in postgraduate education. **Publications:** *Membership List*, periodic. • Monograph, triennial. • *Newsletter*, periodic. Newsletter.

★ 12908 ★ Interstitial Cystitis Association (ICA)
PO Box 1553, Madison Square Sta.
New York, NY 10159
Phone: (212)979-6057
Dr. Vicki Ratner, Pres.

Founded: 1984. **Description:** Support network for patients suffering or suspected of suffering from interstitial cystitis, an inflammation of the bladder wall that primarily affects women; its cause and cure are unknown. Works to inform the public and especially the medical profession about the seriousness of IC. Raises funds for research into treatments and cures; maintains a medical advisory board. Is establishing a national registry to record facts about IC. **Publications:** *ICA Update*, quarterly. Newsletter. Covers IC research and political and educational activities of the ICA. *Price:* $35/year.

★ 12909 ★ National Kidney Foundation (NKF)
30 E. 33rd St., Ste. 1100
New York, NY 10016
Phone: (212)889-2210
Free: 800-622-9010
Fax: (212)689-9261
John Davis, Exec.Dir.

Founded: 1950. **Local Groups:** 200. **Description:** Supports research, patient services, professional and public education, organ donor program, and community service. Affiliates conduct community and patient services including: drug banks; transportation; early screening; patient seminars. Sponsors symposium for health care professionals. Maintains speakers' bureau and biographical archives; compiles statistics. **Publications:** *American Journal of Kidney Diseases*, monthly. Journal. Covers research in kidney and urinary tract diseases. Includes annual index and conference reports. *Price:* Included in membership dues. • *CNNT Action Update,* quarterly. Newsletter. Contains employment opportunity listings and regional news. *Price:* Included in membership dues. • *CNSW Newsletter,* quarterly. Newsletter. Includes calendar of events, information on current literature, employment opportunities, and legislative and regional reports. *Price:* Included in membership dues. • *Council of Nephrology Social Workers Bibliography.* • *Council on Renal Nutrition Bibliography Updates.* • *CRN Quarterly.* Newsletter. Contains employment opportunity listings, legislative news, and research reports. *Price:* Included in membership dues. • *Kidney '90,* bimonthly. Newsletter. Includes calendar of events, medical news, legislative update, and articles of interest to health care providers. *Price:* Free. • *National Kidney Foundation--Abstracts of Annual Scientific Meeting.* • *Perspectives: The Journal of the Council of Nephrology Social Workers,* annual. Journal. *Price:* Included in membership dues. Also publishes educational booklets, and resource manual; produces audiovisual materials including films and slide presentations on kidney disease and treatments. **Formerly:** (1958) National Nephrosis Foundation; (1964) National Kidney Disease Foundation.

★ 12910 ★ **National Kidney and Urologic Diseases Information Clearinghouse (NKUDIC)**
3 Information Way
Bethesda, MD 20892-3580
Phone: (301)654-4415
Fax: (301)907-8906
Kathy Kranzfelder

Founded: 1987. **Description:** A networking, referral, and resource service that disseminates educational information on kidney and urologic diseases and their causes and treatments. Collects, abstracts, and indexes informational materials supplied by professional health organizations; redistributes abstracted information to medical and allied health professionals, patients, and the public. Provides direct responses to written and telephone inquiries. Established by the National Institutes of Health. **Publications:** Booklets. • Directories. • *KU Notes,* semiannual. Newsletter. Also publishes a variety of patient education materials including fact sheets and literature searches from the Combined Health Information Database (CHID).

National Renal Administrators Association (NRAA)
See: Entry 5598

North American Society for Dialysis and Transplantation (NASDT)
See: Entry 12875

★ 12911 ★ **Renal Physicians Association (RPA)**
2011 Pennsylvania Ave. NW, Ste. 800
Washington, DC 20006-1808
Phone: (202)835-0436
Free: 800-RPA-7525
Fax: (202)835-0443
Carol Cooper Chadsey, Exec.Dir.

Founded: 1973. **Members:** 1,700. **Description:** Physicians specializing in the treatment of

renal (kidney) diseases. Promotes optimal care and high standards of treatment for patients. Serves as a national representative for physicians engaged in the study and management of patients with kidney and related disorders; specifically, expresses the concerns and needs of renal physicians to congressional and governmental agencies legislating, executing, and regulating the federal End Stage Renal Disease Program. Provides resources for the development of national policies concerning kidney disease such as ESRD legislative and network activities, federal funding for related research, and studies relative to treatment procedures and common practices. Conducts educational programs. **Publications:** *RPA News,* bimonthly. Newsletter. *Price:* Included in membership dues.

★ 12912 ★ **Scandinavian Association of Urology (SAU)**
(Nordisk Urologisk Forening — NUF)
Odense University Hospital
DK-5000 Odense C, Denmark
Phone: 65412229
Fax: 65412229
Prof. Steen Walter, M.D., Exec. Officer

Founded: 1957. **Members:** 750. **Languages:** Danish, English, Finnish, Icelandic, Norwegian, Swedish. **Description:** Scandinavian physicians specializing in urology or having an interest in the field. Maintains international working groups. **Publications:** *NUF-Bulletinen,* semiannual. • *Scandinavian Journal of Urology and Nephrology,* quarterly.

★ 12913 ★ **Simon Foundation for Continence (SFC)**
Box 815
Wilmette, IL 60091
Phone: (708)864-3913
Free: 800-23-SIMON
Fax: (708)864-9758
Cheryle B. Gartley, Pres.

Founded: 1983. **Members:** 140,000. **Description:** Persons with urinary and bowel incontinence; family members, doctors, medical personnel, and others concerned with the condition. Seeks to educate the public on urinary and bowel problems, to provide information to persons with incontinence, and to remove the stigma attached to the condition. Acts as support group. Organizes "I Will Manage" selfhelp groups. Conducts research on the manufacture and usability of incontinence products, the number of people who have the problems, and the types and causes of incontinence; compiles statistics. Maintains speakers' bureau. **Publications:** *A Time for Action.* Video. • *The Informer: Helping People with Incontinence,* quarterly. Newsletter. *Price:* Included in membership dues. • *Managing Incontinence: A Guide to Living with the Loss of Bladder Control.* Book. • *The Solution Starts with You.* Film. **Formerly:** Simon Foundation.

★ 12914 ★ **Society of Government Service Urologists**
7027 Weathered Post
San Antonio, TX 78238
Phone: (210)681-0587
Free: 800-531-3333
Fax: (210)680-7725
Preston Littrell, Admin.

Founded: 1952. **Members:** 731. **Description:** Urologists. Promotes exchange of information on advancements in urological research.

Society for Pediatric Urology (SPU)
See: Entry 3297

★ 12915 ★ **Society of University Urologists (SUU)**
600 S. 42nd St.
PO Box 850
Omaha, NE 68198-2360
Phone: (402)559-4292
Fax: (402)559-6529
Dr. Rod Taylor, Sec.-Treas.

Founded: 1967. **Members:** 400. **Description:** Urologists holding faculty or teaching positions in residency training programs. Seeks to promote high standards in the field by: acting as a forum for the interchange of ideas and materials relative to university urology educational programs; fostering a balance of all phases of academic work in urology. **Publications:** *Objectives for Urology Residency Education.*

★ 12916 ★ **Zimbabwe Kidney Fund Association**
Renal Unit
Parirenyatwa Hospital
Harare, Zimbabwe
Phone: 4 792588
Fax: 4 792588

Description: Supports research on kidney disease. Promotes appropriate care and treatment of kidney patients. Works to improve legislation regarding the welfare of kidney patients.

Research Centers

★ 12917 ★ **Columbia University Molecular Urology Laboratory**
Dept. of Urology
College of Physicians and Surgeons
630 W. 168th St.
New York, NY 10032
Phone: (212)305-1589
Fax: (212)305-7638
Dr. Ralph Buttyan, Dir.

Research Activities and Fields: Molecular biology, focusing on prostate cancer, bladder disease, renal disease, erectile dysfunction, and cell death research. **Formerly:** Urology Research Laboratory.

Pennsylvania State University E. Coli Reference Center
See: Entry 13165

★ 12918 ★ Polycystic Kidney Research Foundation
922 Walnut St., Ste. 411
Kansas City, MO 64106
Phone: (816)421-1869
Free: 800-PKD-CURE
Fax: (816)421-7208
Jared J. Grantham, M.D., Chm.
Research Activities and Fields: Conducts, promotes, and supports studies on the cause, treatment, and cure of polycystic kidney disease (PKD). Activities include identification of gene defect responsible for PKD, analysis of abnormal cell and cyst growth, and analysis of kidney function and progressive kidney failure. **Publications:** *PKR Progress* (newsletter); Symposium Proceedings.

U.S. Department of Defense
Armed Forces Institute of Pathology
Center for Advanced Pathology
Genitourinary Pathology Department
See: Entry 10151

U.S. Department of Defense
Armed Forces Institute of Pathology
Genitourinary Pathology Department
Medical Nephropathology Division
See: Entry 10166

U.S. Department of Defense
Armed Forces Institute of Pathology
Genitourinary Pathology Department
Urologic Pathology Division
See: Entry 10167

U.S. Department of Health and Human Services
National Heart, Lung, and Blood Institute
Laboratory of Kidney and Electrolyte Metabolism
See: Entry 2951

U.S. Department of Health and Human Services
National Institute of Diabetes and Digestive and Kidney Diseases
See: Entry 4906

U.S. Department of Health and Human Services
National Institute of Diabetes and Digestive and Kidney Diseases
Division of Intramural Research
See: Entry 4919

★ 12919 ★ U.S. Department of Health and Human Services
National Institute of Diabetes and Digestive and Kidney Diseases
Division of Kidney, Urologic, and Hematologic Diseases
NIH Bldg. 31, Room 9A17
9000 Rockville Pike
Bethesda, MD 20892
Phone: (301)496-6325
Fax: (301)496-2830
Gary E. Striker, M.D., Director
Research Activities and Fields: Division supports basic and clinical biomedical research in kidney, urinary, and hematologic disorders, including epidemiologic studies and clinical trials.

Offers investigator-initiated research grants and awards, program/project grants, center grants, and cooperative agreements. Also sponsors research fellowships, training grants, career development awards, and resource and research and development contracts. Scientific activities conducted through eleven major programs: 1) Renal Physiology/Cell Biology Program, which focuses on the underlying mechanisms of kidney disease; 2) Urology Program, which focuses on basic and clinical studies of normal and disease states of genitourinary system; 3) Centers Program, which focuses on clinical studies in nephrology and urology; 4) Manpower Program, which offers research training and career development awards; 5) Chronic Renal Diseases Program, which supports basic and clinical research on chronic kidney diseases; 6) End-Stage Renal Disease (ESRD) Program, which focuses on the mechanisms involved in ESRD; 7) MDRD Clinical Trial Program, which focuses on diet modification in renal disease patients; 8) Hematology Program, which focuses on normal and disease states of hematopoietic system; 9) Epidemiology Program, which supports development of epidemiologic data related to major kidney, urologic, and hematologic diseases; 10) HIV Program, which focuses on effects of HIV infection on renal, urinary, and hematopoietic function; and 11) Small Business Innovation Research Program, which promotes commercialization of and small business involvement in federally funded research.

★ 12920 ★ U.S. Department of Health and Human Services
National Institute of Diabetes and Digestive and Kidney Diseases
Division of Kidney, Urologic, and Hematologic Diseases
Chronic Renal Diseases Program
Westwood Bldg. 3A04
5333 Westbard Ave.
Bethesda, MD 20892
Phone: (301)594-7584
Fax: (301)594-7501
Gladys H. Hirschman, M.D., Program Director
Research Activities and Fields: Supports basic and clinical research on chronic kidney diseases and develops treatments to prevent their onset and progression. Focuses on pathophysiology (including immunopathogenic mechanisms) of chronic renal diseases such as lupus nephritis, polycystic kidney disease, interstitial nephritis, IgA nephropathy, and glomerulopathies/glomerulonephritis; progressive renal disease; kidney disease in children and in minority populations; role of nutrition in renal disease; kidney disease caused by diabetes mellitus, including studies on pathogenic mechanisms and morphologic and functional markers; and natural history of diabetic nephropathy.

★ 12921 ★ U.S. Department of Health and Human Services
National Institute of Diabetes and Digestive and Kidney Diseases
Division of Kidney, Urologic, and Hematologic Diseases
Renal Physiology/Cell Biology Program

5333 Westbard Ave., Rm. 3A-04
Bethesda, MD 20892
Phone: (301)594-7522
Fax: (301)594-7501
Dr. M. James Scherbenske, Director
Research Activities and Fields: Program supports molecular, structural, and functional renal physiology and cell biology studies, including the effects of various hormones and pharmacologic agents on metabolism, filtration, transport, and fluid-electrolyte dynamics of the kidney. Activities focus on examining the effects of nephrotoxins, environmental toxins on the kidney, and drugs, including diuretics and immunosuppressive agents, such as cyclosporine.

★ 12922 ★ U.S. Department of Health and Human Services
National Institute of Diabetes and Digestive and Kidney Diseases
Division of Kidney, Urologic, and Hematologic Diseases
Urology and Women's Urological Health Program
Westwood Bldg., Rm. 3A05
Bethesda, MD 20892
Phone: (301)594-7555
Fax: (301)594-7501
Leroy M. Nyberg, Jr., M.D., Director
Research Activities and Fields: Basic and clinical studies of normal and disease states of genitourinary system, including structure and function of the bladder, urethra, and prostate. Program interests include pyelonephritis, interstitial cystitis, urolithiasis, benign prostatic hyperplasia, prostatitis, impotence and sexual dysfunction, and urinary incontinence.

★ 12923 ★ University of Alabama at Birmingham
Nephrology Research and Training Center
Division of Nephrology
UAB Sta.
Birmingham, AL 35294-0007
Phone: (205)934-3585
Fax: (205)934-1879
David G. Warnock, M.D., Dir.
Research Activities and Fields: Membrane transport, renal tubular transport, acid base physiology, renal hypertension, renal ultrastructure, epithelial ion transport, electron microprobe, erythropoietin, and population studies of genetic factors in hypertension.

★ 12924 ★ University of Alabama at Birmingham
Urological Rehabilitation and Research Center
1717 6th Ave. S.
Birmingham, AL 35233
Phone: (205)934-5359
Fax: (205)934-5584
L. Keith Lloyd, M.D., Head
Research Activities and Fields: Urological dysfunctions.

★12925★ University of Kansas
Kidney and Urology Research Center
3901 Rainbow Blvd.
Kansas City, KS 66160-7382
Phone: (913)588-6076
Fax: (913)588-3867
Jared J. Grantham, M.D., Pres.

Research Activities and Fields: Laboratory and clinical investigations into kidney physiology, polycystic kidney disease, basement membrane structure and function, kidney stones, acute renal failure, and diuretics. Research methods include tubule microperfusion, amino acid analyses, peptide synthesis, and morphometrics.

★12926★ University of Louisville
Kidney Disease Program
615 S. Preston St.
Louisville, KY 40292
Phone: (502)852-5757
Fax: (502)852-7643
George R. Aronoff, M.D., Chief

Research Activities and Fields: Kidney disease, focusing on the following areas: cellular physiology, second messengers, biological transport, cellular immunology, transplantation, artificial membranes, dialysis, clinical pharmacology, pharmacokinetics, nephrotoxicity, drug metabolism, hypertension, and tissue typing.
Formerly: Bioengineering Laboratory.

★12927★ University of Medicine and
Dentistry of New Jersey
Urology Research Laboratory
185 S. Orange Ave., Rm. G539
Newark, NJ 07103-2757
Phone: (201)456-4300
Alan K. Hall, Ph.D., Dir.

Research Activities and Fields: Characterizing cloned retinoid-responsive genes in neuroblastoma cells and cloning gonadotropin-responsive genes/thymosins.

★12928★ University of Pennsylvania
Women's Center for Interstitial Cystitis
Hospital of the Univ. of Pennsylvania
Division of Urology
3400 Spruce St.
Philadelphia, PA 19104
Phone: (215)662-2891
Gregory A. Broderick, M.D., Dir.

Research Activities and Fields: Interstitial cystitis, including development of an animal model to study bladder pathophysiology for the purpose of finding causes, remedies, and cures for the disease. **Publications:** Lectures and presentations on request.

★12929★ University of Rochester
Nephrology Research Program
601 Elmwood Ave., Box 675
Rochester, NY 14642
Phone: (716)275-4517
Fax: (716)442-9201
Dr. David Bushinsky, Dir.

Research Activities and Fields: Physiological regulation of water and salt excretion, renal potassium handling in vivo and in the isolated perfused kidney, regulation of intrarenal blood flow, fluorescence videomicroscopy studies of inner medullary blood flow, role of nucleosides as regulators of kidney function and hemodynamics, renal microvascular endothelium and epithelial cell cultures, in vivo perfusion of capillaries from the renal microcirculation, pathogenesis of acute renal failure, modulators of renal ischemic injury, and studies of tubular functioning in humans. **E-mail Address:** dbushi@medicine.rochester.edu. **Formerly:** Regional Kidney Disease Program.

★12930★ University of Southern
California
Division of Nephrology
2025 Zonal Ave.
Los Angeles, CA 90033
Phone: (213)226-7307
Fax: (213)226-5390
Dr. Shaul G. Massry, Head

Research Activities and Fields: Calcium, phosphorus metabolism, vitamin D metabolism, sympathetic nervous system in hypertension, and parathyroid hormone toxicity in uremia. Kidney dialysis studies include improved dialysis, immunologic aspects of renal disease, hypertension, and control of salt and water balance.
Formerly: Kidney Dialysis Research Unit.

★12931★ Urodynamic Laboratory
375 Segvine Ave.
Staten Island, NY 10309
Phone: (718)226-2260
Fax: (718)226-2832
Dr. Adley Raboy, Dir.

Research Activities and Fields: Urology. Develops urodynamic equipment to diagnose bladder dysfunction.

★12932★ Washington University
Chromalloy American Kidney Center
1 Barnes Hospital Plaza, Box 8129
St. Louis, MO 63110
Phone: (314)362-7208
Fax: (314)362-7875
Dr. Eduardo Slatopolsky, Dir.

Research Activities and Fields: Basic and clinical research in lipid abnormalities in uremia, muscle protein metabolism in uremia, metabolic bone disease in uremia, parathyroid hormone, and vitamin D and aluminum metabolism.

State & Regional
Organizations

Kidney

The following organizations are affiliates of the National Kidney Foundation, 1150 Grand Ave., Ste. 300, Kansas City, MO 64106, (816) 221-9559; 800-522-9559.

Alabama

★12933★ National Kidney Foundation of
Alabama
746 Adams Ave.
PO Box 342
Montgomery, AL 36101
Phone: (334)265-1033
Fax: (334)264-6296

Arizona

★12934★ National Kidney Foundation of
Arizona
4019 N. 44th St., Ste. 201
Phoenix, AZ 85018
Phone: (602)840-1644
Fax: (602)840-2360

Arkansas

★12935★ National Kidney Foundation of
Arkansas
4942 W. Markham, Ste. 1
PO Box 453
Little Rock, AR 72203
Phone: (501)664-4343
Fax: (501)664-9485

California

★12936★ National Kidney Foundation of
Northern California
553 Pilgrim Dr., Ste. C
Foster City, CA 94404
Phone: (415)349-5111
Fax: (415)349-5115

★12937★ National Kidney Foundation of
Southern California
5777 W. Century Blvd., Ste. 1450
Los Angeles, CA 90045
Phone: (310)641-8152
Free: 800-747-5527
Fax: (310)641-5246

Colorado

★12938★ National Kidney Foundation of
Colorado
3801 E. Florida Ave., St. 503
Denver, CO 80210
Phone: (303)759-5151
Fax: (303)759-5162

Connecticut

★12939★ National Kidney Foundation of
Connecticut
920 Farmington Ave.
West Hartford, CT 06107
Phone: (203)232-6054
Free: 800-441-1280
Fax: (203)236-1367

Delaware

★ **12940 ★ National Kidney Foundation of the Delaware Valley**
Constitution Pl., No. 1016
325 Chestnut St.
Philadelphia, PA 19106
Phone: (215)923-8611
Fax: (215)923-2199

District of Columbia

★ **12941 ★ National Kidney Foundation of the National Capital Area**
5335 Wisconsin Ave. NW, Ste. 830
Washington, DC 20015
Phone: (202)244-7900
Fax: (202)244-7405

Florida

★ **12942 ★ National Kidney Foundation of Florida**
Palmetto Bldg., No. 119
1040 Woodcock Rd.
Orlando, FL 32803
Phone: (407)894-7325
Free: 800-927-9659
Fax: (407)895-0051

Georgia

★ **12943 ★ National Kidney Foundation of Georgia**
1655 Tullie Circle, No. 111
Atlanta, GA 30329
Phone: (404)248-1315
Free: 800-633-2339
Fax: (404)248-1320

Hawaii

★ **12944 ★ National Kidney Foundation of Hawaii**
1311 Kapiolani Blvd., No. 308
Honolulu, HI 96814
Phone: (808)593-1515
Fax: (808)593-1515

Illinois

★ **12945 ★ National Kidney Foundation of Illinois**
600 S. Federal, No. 201
Chicago, IL 60605
Phone: (312)663-3103
Fax: (312)663-5729

Indiana

★ **12946 ★ National Kidney Foundation of Indiana**
850 N. Meridian St., Ste. 203
Indianapolis, IN 46204-1108
Phone: (317)693-6534
Free: 800-382-9971
Fax: (317)693-6538

Iowa

★ **12947 ★ National Kidney Foundation of Iowa**
Executive Plaza, No. 201
4403 1st Ave., SE
Cedar Rapids, IA 52402
Phone: (319)393-8684
Free: 800-369-3619
Fax: (319)393-8791

Kansas

★ **12948 ★ National Kidney Foundation of Kansas and Western Missouri**
1900 W. 47th Pl., Ste. 107
Westwood, KS 66205
Phone: (913)262-1551
Fax: (913)722-4841

Kentucky

★ **12949 ★ National Kidney Foundation of Kentucky**
250 E. Liberty St., No. 710
Louisville, KY 40202
Phone: (502)585-5433
Fax: (502)585-1445

Louisiana

★ **12950 ★ National Kidney Foundation of Louisiana**
8200 Hampson, Ste. 425
New Orleans, LA 70118
Phone: (504)861-4500
Free: 800-462-3694
Fax: (504)861-1976

Maine

★ **12951 ★ National Kidney Foundation of Maine**
169 Lancaster St.
PO Boix 1134
Portland, ME 04104
Phone: (207)772-7270
Free: 800-639-7220
Fax: (207)772-4202

Maryland

★ **12952 ★ National Kidney Foundation of Maryland**
1107 Kenilworth Dr., No. 202
Baltimore, MD 21204
Phone: (410)494-8545
Fax: (410)494-8549

Massachusetts

★ **12953 ★ National Kidney Foundation of Massachusetts and Rhode Island**
105 Eastern Ave., No. 211
PO Box 9103
Dedham, MA 02027-9103
Phone: (617)326-7225
Free: 800-542-4001
Fax: (617)329-5074

Michigan

★ **12954 ★ National Kidney Foundation of Michigan**
2350 S. Huron Pkwy.
Ann Arbor, MI 48104
Phone: (313)971-2800
Free: 800-482-1455
Fax: (313)971-5655

Minnesota

★ **12955 ★ National Kidney Foundation of the Upper Midwest**
920 S. 7th St.
Minneapolis, MN 55415
Phone: (612)337-7300
Fax: (612)337-7308

Mississippi

★ **12956 ★ National Kidney Foundation of Mississippi**
2640 River Hills Dr., No.101
PO Box 55802
Jackson, MS 39296
Phone: (601)981-3611
Fax: (601)981-3612

Missouri

★ **12957 ★ National Kidney Foundation of Eastern Missouri and Metro-East**
3117 S. Big Bend Blvd., Ste. 200
PO Box 430007
St. Louis, MO 63143
Phone: (314)647-9585
Free: 800-489-9585
Fax: (314)647-2644

★ **12958 ★ National Kidney Foundation of Kansas and Western Missouri**
1900 W. 47th Pl., Ste. 107
Westwood, KS 66205
Phone: (913)262-1551
Fax: (913)722-4841

Nebraska

★ **12959 ★ National Kidney Foundation of Nebraska**
7101 Newport Ave., Ste. 301
Omaha, NE 68152-2116
Phone: (402)572-3180
Free: 800-642-1255
Fax: (402)572-3002

Nevada

★ **12960 ★ National Kidney Foundation of Nevada**
3050 E. Desert Inn Rd., No. 121
Las Vegas, NV 89121
Phone: (702)735-9222
Fax: (702)735-9224

New Hampshire

★ 12961 ★ National Kidney Foundation of
New Hampshire
1 Tremont St.
Concord, NH 03301
Phone: (603)224-6641
Free: 800-354-3639
Fax: (603)229-1724

New Jersey

★ 12962 ★ National Kidney Foundation of
New York / New Jersey
1250 Broadway, No. 2001
New York, NY 10001
Phone: (212)629-9770
Fax: (212)629-5652

New Mexico

★ 12963 ★ National Kidney Foundation of
New Mexico
1330 San Pedro NE, Ste. 103
Albuquerque, NM 87110
Phone: (505)266-4573
Fax: (505)266-9479

New York

★ 12964 ★ National Kidney Foundation of
Central New York
731 James St., No. 200
Syracuse, NY 13203
Phone: (315)476-0311
Fax: (315)476-3707

★ 12965 ★ National Kidney Foundation of
New York / New Jersey
1250 Broadway, No. 2001
New York, NY 10001
Phone: (212)629-9770
Fax: (212)629-5652

★ 12966 ★ National Kidney Foundation of
Northeast New York
23 Computer Dr. E.
Albany, NY 12205
Phone: (518)458-9697
Fax: (518)458-9690

★ 12967 ★ National Kidney Foundation of
Upstate New York
1 Grove St., Ste. 202A
Pittsford, NY 14534
Phone: (716)264-0420
Free: 800-724-9421
Fax: (716)264-0109

★ 12968 ★ National Kidney Foundation of
Western New York
165 Genessee St., No. 102
PO Box 651
Buffalo, NY 14209
Phone: (716)853-6675

North Carolina

★ 12969 ★ National Kidney Foundation of
North Carolina
3 Fairview Plaza, Ste. 408
5970 Fairview Rd.
Charlotte, NC 28210
Phone: (704)552-1351
Free: 800-356-5362
Fax: (704)552-7870

Ohio

★ 12970 ★ National Kidney Foundation of
Ohio
1373 Gerandview Ave., Ste. 200
Columbus, OH 43212-2804
Phone: (614)481-4030
Fax: (614)481-4038

Oklahoma

★ 12971 ★ National Kidney Foundation of
Oklahoma
3617 NW 58th, Ste. 317
Oklahoma City, OK 73112
Phone: (405)947-6405
Free: 800-946-6405
Fax: (405)947-6463

Oregon

★ 12972 ★ National Kidney Foundation of
Oregon
3330 NW Yeon Ave., No. 130
Portland, OR 97210
Phone: (503)228-1898
Fax: (503)228-2124

Pennsylvania

★ 12973 ★ National Kidney Foundation of
Western Pennsylvania
555 Grant St., No. 380
Pittsburgh, PA 15219
Phone: (412)261-4115
Fax: (412)261-1405

Rhode Island

★ 12974 ★ National Kidney Foundation of
Massachusetts and Rhode Island
105 Eastern Ave., No. 211
PO Box 9103
Dedham, MA 02027-9103
Phone: (617)326-7225
Free: 800-542-4001
Fax: (617)329-5074

South Carolina

★ 12975 ★ National Kidney Foundation of
South Carolina
100 Executive Center Dr., Ste. 224
PO Box 212634
Columbia, SC 29221-2634
Phone: (803)798-3805
Free: 800-822-3216
Fax: (803)798-3809

Tennessee

★ 12976 ★ National Kidney Foundation of
East Tennessee
4450 Walker Blvd., Ste. 2
Knoxville, TN 37917
Phone: (615)688-5481
Fax: (615)688-0196

★ 12977 ★ National Kidney Foundation of
Middle Tennessee
2120 Crestmoor Rd.
Nashville, TN 37215
Phone: (615)383-3887
Fax: (615)383-2647

★ 12978 ★ National Kidney Foundation of
West Tennessee
5545 Murray Rd., Ste. 206
Memphis, TN 38119
Phone: (901)683-6185
Free: 800-727-1039
Fax: (901)683-6189

Texas

★ 12979 ★ National Kidney Foundation of
South Texas
84 NE Loop 410, Ste. 171
San Antonio, TX 78216
Phone: (210)344-6325
Fax: (210)344-6327

★ 12980 ★ National Kidney Foundation of
Southeast Texas
2400 Augusta Dr., No. 252
Houston, TX 77057
Phone: (713)952-5499
Fax: (713)952-5497

★ 12981 ★ National Kidney Foundation of
Texas
13500 Midway Rd., Ste. 101
Dallas, TX 75244
Phone: (214)934-8057
Free: 800-441-1281
Fax: (214)934-9357

★ 12982 ★ National Kidney Foundation of
the Texas Coastal Bend
719 N. Upper Broadway
PO Box 9172
Corpus Christi, TX 78469
Phone: (512)884-5892
Fax: (512)884-2332

★ 12983 ★ National Kidney Foundation of
West Texas
3801 19th St., No. 402
Lubbock, TX 79410
Phone: (806)799-7753
Fax: (806)796-7529

Utah

★ 12984 ★ National Kidney Foundation of
Utah
Edgemont Professional Plaza, 1-D
3707 N. Canyon Rd.
Provo, UT 84604
Phone: (801)226-5111
Fax: (801)226-8278

Virginia

★ 12985 ★   **National Kidney Foundation of Virginia**
5001 W. Broad St., Ste. 217
Richmond, VA 23230
Phone: (804)288-8342
Fax: (804)282-7835

Washington

★ 12986 ★   **National Kidney Foundation of Washington**
400 S. Jefferson, No. 164
PO Box 30261
Spokane, WA 99223-3004
Phone: (509)455-6680
Free: 800-500-6680
Fax: (509)455-6681

Wisconsin

★ 12987 ★   **National Kidney Foundation of Wisconsin**
280 Regency Ct., Ste. 100
Brookfield, WI 53045-6165
Phone: (414)821-0705
Free: 800-543-6393
Fax: (414)821-5641

Chapter 68
Veterinary Medicine

Federal Government Agencies

★ 12988 ★ U.S. Department of Agriculture
Animal and Plant Health Inspection Service
Veterinary Services
14th St. and Independence Ave. SW
Washington, DC 20250
Phone: (202)720-5193
Fax: (202)690-4171

Description: Veterinary Services officials are responsible for determining the existence and extent of outbreaks of communicable diseases and pests affecting livestock and poultry. They organize and conduct control and eradication programs in cooperation with state officials, and cooperate with animal health officials in other countries in planning and conducting disease control efforts in those countries. Veterinary Services officials also maintain inspection and quarantine service at designated ports of entry for imported animals and birds. They are responsible for the health certification of livestock and poultry exported to other countries.

★ 12989 ★ U.S. Department of Agriculture
National Agricultural Library
National Agricultural Library Bldg.
Beltsville, MD 20705
Phone: (301)504-5755
Fax: (301)504-5472

Description: The National Agricultural Library provides information services over a broad range of agricultural interests to a wide cross-section of users, from research scientists to the general public. The Library assists users through a variety of specialized information centers. Subjects include agricultural trade and marketing, alternative farming systems, animal welfare, aquaculture, biotechnology, critical agricultural materials, family, fiber and textiles, food and nutrition, food irradiation, horticulture, rural development, technology transfer, water quality, and youth development.

★ 12990 ★ U.S. Department of Health and
** Human Services**
Food and Drug Administration
Center for Veterinary Medicine

7500 Standish Pl.
Rockville, MD 20855
Phone: (301)594-1740
Fax: (301)594-1830

Description: The Center develops and conducts programs with respect to the safety and efficacy of veterinary preparations and devices; evaluates proposed use of veterinary preparations for animal safety and efficacy; and evaluates FDA's surveillance and compliance programs relating to veterinary drugs and other veterinary medical matters.

Medical & Allied Health Schools

Veterinary Medicine

Colleges of veterinary medicine listed in this section are accredited by the American Veterinary Medical Association, 1931 N. Meacham Rd., Ste. 100, Schaumburg, IL 60173-4360, (708) 925-8070; (800)248-2862.

Alabama

★ 12991 ★ Auburn University
College of Veterinary Medicine
Auburn, AL 36849
Phone: (205)844-4546
Fax: (205)844-3697

★ 12992 ★ Tuskegee University
School of Veterinary Medicine
Tuskegee, AL 36088
Phone: (205)727-8174
Fax: (205)727-8177

California

★ 12993 ★ University of California, Davis
School of Veterinary Medicine
Davis, CA 95616
Phone: (916)752-1361
Fax: (916)752-2801

Colorado

★ 12994 ★ Colorado State University
College of Veterinary Medicine and
** Biomedical Sciences**
Ft. Collins, CO 80523
Phone: (303)491-7051
Fax: (303)491-2250

Florida

★ 12995 ★ University of Florida
College of Veterinary Medicine
J. Hillis Miller Health Science Center
Gainesville, FL 32610-0125
Phone: (904)392-4700
Fax: (904)392-8351

Georgia

★ 12996 ★ University of Georgia
College of Veterinary Medicine
Athens, GA 30602
Phone: (706)542-3461
Fax: (706)542-8254

Illinois

★ 12997 ★ University of Illinois
College of Veterinary Medicine
2001 S. Lincoln
Urbana, IL 61801
Phone: (217)333-2760
Fax: (217)333-4628

Indiana

★ 12998 ★ Purdue University
School of Veterinary Medicine
1240 Lynn Hall
West Lafayette, IN 47907
Phone: (317)494-7607
Fax: (317)496-1261

Iowa

★ 12999 ★ **Iowa State University**
College of Veterinary Medicine
Ames, IA 50011
Phone: (515)294-1242
Fax: (515)294-8341

Kansas

★ 13000 ★ **Kansas State University**
College of Veterinary Medicine
Manhattan, KS 66506
Phone: (913)532-5660
Fax: (913)532-5884

Louisiana

★ 13001 ★ **Louisiana State University**
School of Veterinary Medicine
Baton Rouge, LA 70803
Phone: (504)346-3100
Fax: (504)346-5702

Massachusetts

★ 13002 ★ **Tufts University**
School of Veterinary Medicine
200 Westboro Rd.
North Grafton, MA 01536
Phone: (508)839-5302
Fax: (508)839-2953

Michigan

★ 13003 ★ **Michigan State University**
College of Veterinary Medicine
East Lansing, MI 48824-1314
Phone: (517)355-6509
Fax: (517)336-1037

Minnesota

★ 13004 ★ **University of Minnesota**
College of Veterinary Medicine
St. Paul, MN 55108
Phone: (612)624-9227
Fax: (612)624-8753

Mississippi

★ 13005 ★ **Mississippi State University**
College of Veterinary Medicine
Mississippi State, MS 39762
Phone: (601)325-3432
Fax: (601)325-1498

Missouri

★ 13006 ★ **University of Missouri—**
Columbia
College of Veterinary Medicine
Columbia, MO 65211
Phone: (314)882-3877
Fax: (314)884-5044

New York

★ 13007 ★ **Cornell University**
College of Veterinary Medicine
Ithaca, NY 14853
Phone: (607)253-3000
Fax: (607)253-3708

North Carolina

★ 13008 ★ **North Carolina State University**
College of Veterinary Medicine
4700 Hillsborough St.
Raleigh, NC 27606
Phone: (919)829-4200
Fax: (919)829-4452

Ohio

★ 13009 ★ **Ohio State University**
College of Veterinary Medicine
Columbus, OH 43210
Phone: (614)292-1171
Fax: (614)292-7185

Oklahoma

★ 13010 ★ **Oklahoma State University**
College of Veterinary Medicine
Stillwater, OK 74078
Phone: (405)744-6648
Fax: (405)744-6633

Oregon

★ 13011 ★ **Oregon State University**
College of Veterinary Medicine
Corvallis, OR 97331
Phone: (503)737-2141
Fax: (503)737-4245

Pennsylvania

★ 13012 ★ **University of Pennsylvania**
School of Veterinary Medicine
3800 Spruce St.
Philadelphia, PA 19104-6044
Phone: (215)898-5438

Tennessee

★ 13013 ★ **University of Tennessee,**
Knoxville
College of Veterinary Medicine
Knoxville, TN 37901
Phone: (615)974-7262
Fax: (615)974-8222

Texas

★ 13014 ★ **Texas A&M University**
College of Veterinary Medicine
College Station, TX 77843-4461
Phone: (409)845-5051
Fax: (409)845-5088

Virginia

★ 13015 ★ **Virginia Polytechnic Institute**
and State University / University of
Maryland
Virginia/Maryland Regional College of
Veterinary Medicine
Blacksburg, VA 24061-0442
Phone: (703)231-7666
Fax: (703)231-7367

Washington

★ 13016 ★ **Washington State University**
College of Veterinary Medicine
Pullman, WA 99164-7010
Phone: (509)335-9515
Fax: (509)335-6094

Wisconsin

★ 13017 ★ **University of Wisconsin—**
Madison
School of Veterinary Medicine
Madison, WI 53706
Phone: (608)263-6716
Fax: (608)263-6573

National & International Organizations

★ 13018 ★ **Academy of Veterinary Allergy**
(AVA)
c/o Dr. Douglas DeBoer
University of Wisconsin
School of Veterinary Medicine
2015 Linden Dr. W.
Madison, WI 53706
Phone: (608)263-8399
Fax: (608)263-6573
Dr. Douglas DeBoer, Pres.

Founded: 1960. **Members:** 300. **Description:**
Veterinarians, research M.D.s, and allergy extract firms. Promotes education and research in
veterinary and comparative allergy and immunology. **Publications:** *Membership List*, periodic. • *Veterinary Allergist*, quarterly.

★ 13019 ★ **Academy of Veterinary**
Cardiology (AVC)
51 Alantic Ave.
PO Box 208
Floral Park, NY 11002
Phone: (516)358-4500
Larry Patrick Tilley, D.V.M., Exec.Sec.

Founded: 1967. **Members:** 600. **Description:**
Persons with an interest in veterinary or comparative cardiology. Purpose is to disseminate literature, reviews, and materials of interest to veterinary practitioners. Maintains specialized education program. **Publications:** Membership Directory, biennial. • Newsletter, periodic. Also
publishes abstracts and bibliography.

★ 13020 ★ All-Breeds Rescue Conservancy (ARC)
Rainbow Ridge RR, Box 100
Ferryville, WI 54628
Phone: (608)734-3605
Dr. J. E. Mueller, Exec.Sec.

Founded: 1985. **Members:** 45. **Description:** Animal breeders, veterinarians, animal science researchers, and others interested in controlling and eliminating fatal lentiviruses in sheep and goats. Disseminates information on lentiviruses. Encourages testing for Ovine Progressive Pneumonia and Caprine Arthritis Encephalitis. Certifies OPP- and CAE-negative sheep and goats, respectively. **Publications:** *The ARC Ark*, periodic.

★ 13021 ★ American Academy of Veterinary and Comparative Toxicology (AAVCT)
College of Veterinary Medicine
Dept of Rural Practic
CVM Box 1071
Univ. of Tennessee
Knoxville, TN 37901
Phone: (615)974-5701
Fax: (615)974-8222
Larry Kerr, Sec.-Treas.

Founded: 1957. **Members:** 178. **Description:** Veterinarians specializing in toxicology and others interested in veterinary comparative toxicology. Sponsors and encourages scientific and technical meetings and promotes discussion and interchange of information in the following fields of veterinary comparative toxicology: teaching, research and development, diagnosis, nomenclature, public health, and other problems of common interest. Reviews manuscripts and literature pertaining to toxicology and keeps a file of such literature for use by its members. Encourages the use of uniform toxicologic nomenclature. Facilitates and implements the exchange of proven methods among veterinary comparative toxicologists. **Publications:** *Veterinary and Human Toxicology*, bimonthly. Journal. Contains annual directory. **Formerly:** American College of Veterinary Toxicologists.

★ 13022 ★ American Academy of Veterinary Dermatology (AAVD)
c/o Dr. Nita Gulbas
Desert Sage Veterinary Clinic
2249 W. Bethany Home Rd.
Phoenix, AZ 85015
Phone: (602)433-0198
Fax: (602)336-0146
Dr. Nita Gulbas, Sec. & Pres.

Founded: 1964. **Members:** 348. **Description:** Veterinarians who devote a significant portion of their professional activities to research, teaching, or practice of veterinary dermatology. Seeks to: further scientific progress in veterinary and comparative dermatology; coordinate research of veterinary dermatology; encourage adequate dermatological training in veterinary colleges; provide by means of meetings and seminars the opportunity for graduate veterinarians to carry on advanced studies in dermatology; promote improved methods of diagnosis, treatment, and prevention of skin diseases in animals. Provides funding for research projects employing veterinary dermatology residents.

Maintains speakers' bureau. **Publications:** *Derm-Dialogue*, quarterly. • Membership Directory, annual. • Newsletter, semiannual.

★ 13023 ★ American Academy of Veterinary Nutrition (AAVN)
c/o David J. Mayberry
270 Spalding Cir.
Athens, GA 30605
Phone: (404)972-6941
David J. Mayberry, Sec.-Treas.

Founded: 1956. **Members:** 320. **Description:** Veterinarians and nutritional scientists interested in animal nutrition and health. Works to promote research and discussion in fields where health of animals may be influenced by nutrition. Sponsors programs on animal nutrition. Maintains speakers' bureau. **Publications:** Membership Directory, annual. • Newsletter, biennial. **Formerly:** (1978) American Association of Veterinary Nutritionists.

★ 13024 ★ American Academy of Veterinary Pharmacology and Therapeutics (AAVPT)
c/o Dr. Jean Powers
Department of Clinical Sciences
1935 Coffey Rd.
Columbus, OH 43210
Phone: (614)722-2729
Fax: (614)292-0895
Dr. Jean Powers, Sec.-Treas.

Founded: 1977. **Members:** 187. **Description:** Veterinary pharmacologists and clinicians interested in clinical therapeutics; representatives of academia, industry, and government; private practitioners. Supports and promotes education and research in comparative pharmacology, clinical veterinary pharmacology, and other aspects of pharmacology of interest to the veterinary profession; aims to enhance the exchange of educational materials and ideas among veterinary pharmacologists. Organizes committees of experts to research and make recommendations to the profession on current problems in veterinary therapeutics. Sponsors and conducts workshops and other scientific and educational meetings. **Publications:** Directory, periodic. • *Journal of Veterinary Pharmacology and Therapeutics*, 8/year. Journal. • Newsletter, quarterly.

★ 13025 ★ American Animal Hospital Association (AAHA)
PO Box 150899
Denver, CO 80215-0899
Phone: (303)986-2800
Free: 800-252-2242
Fax: (303)986-1700
John W. Albers, D.V.M., Exec.Dir.

Founded: 1933. **Members:** 14,000. **Description:** Veterinarians engaged in small animal practice who own or staff small animal hospitals. Works for the promotion of excellence in small animal medicine and improvement of hospital facilities. Maintains 20 committees; operates AAHA Foundation, which gives grants for small animal medical research. Maintains speakers' bureau. Compiles statistics. **Publications:** *American Animal Hospital Association Scientific Proceedings*, annual. Proceedings. Includes manuscripts of papers delivered at AAHA meet-

ing. Contains authors index. *Price:* Included in membership dues; $42 for nonmembers. • *American Animal Hospital Association--Trends*, bimonthly. Magazine. Covers management trends, social issues, and paraprofessional topics in veterinary medicine; includes association news, book reviews, and calendar. *Price:* Included in membership dues; $60/year for nonmembers. • *Journal of the American Animal Hospital Association*, bimonthly. Journal. Includes advertisers' index. *Price:* Included in membership dues; $97/year for nonmembers. • Membership Directory, annual. Has also published atlases for ophthalmology, dermatology, cytology, and cardiology and a manual of standards.

★ 13026 ★ American Association for Accreditation of Laboratory Animal Care (AAALAC)
11300 Rockville Pike, Ste. 1211
Rockville, MD 20852-3035
Phone: (301)231-5353
Free: 800-926-0066
Fax: (301)231-8282
Albert E. New, D.V.M., Exec.Dir.

Founded: 1965. **Members:** 39. **Description:** National education, health, and research organizations professionally concerned with the care, study, and use of laboratory animals in research, breeding, teaching, and testing programs. Operates accreditation program for laboratory animal care whereby organizations are site-visited, peer-reviewed, and evaluated. **Publications:** *Communique*. Newsletter.

★ 13027 ★ American Association of Avian Pathologists (AAAP)
University of Pennsylvania
New Bolton Center
Kennett Square, PA 19348
Phone: (610)444-4282
Fax: (610)444-5387
Dr. Robert J. Eckroade, Sec.-Treas.

Founded: 1957. **Members:** 1,016. **Description:** Membership limited to graduates of recognized veterinary colleges. Associate members are not veterinarians but are engaged in some form of avian medicine. Maintains 29 committees. **Publications:** *American Association of Avian Pathologists Proceedings*, periodic. Proceedings. • *Avian Diseases*, quarterly. Journal. Contains case reports. *Price:* Included in membership dues; $100/year for nonmembers in U.S.; $110/year for nonmembers outside U.S.. • Manuals. • Videos.

★ 13028 ★ American Association of Bovine Practitioners (AABP)
c/o Dr. James A. Jarrett
Box 1755
Rome, GA 30162
Phone: (706)232-2220
Fax: (706)232-2232
Dr. James A. Jarrett, Exec.VP

Founded: 1965. **Members:** 5,000. **Description:** Veterinarians who practice bovine medicine. Aims to elevate standards in the field; cooperates with veterinary and agricultural organizations and regulatory agencies. **Publications:** *AABP Newsletter*, monthly. Newsletter. Contains meetings calendar. *Price:* Included in membership dues. • *American Association of*

Bovine Practitioners Directory, triennial. Directory. Includes annual supplements. *Price:* Included in membership dues; $25/copy for select others. • *American Association of Bovine Practitioners Proceedings of Annual Meeting. Price:* Included in membership dues; $40/copy for nonmembers. • *Bovine Practitioner*, annual. Covers new developments in bovine practice. *Price:* Included in membership dues; $20/copy for nonmembers.

★ 13029 ★ American Association of Equine Practitioners (AAEP)
4075 Iron Works Pike
Lexington, KY 40511
Phone: (606)233-0147
Free: 800-443-0177
Fax: (606)233-1968
Gary L. Carpenter, Exec.Dir.

Founded: 1955. **Members:** 5,000. **Description:** Veterinarians who specialize in equine medicine and surgery. Disseminates the latest scientific information relative to the practice of equine medicine; promotes research on horses. Maintains 30 professional committees. **Publications:** Books. • Directory, annual. • Newsletter, bimonthly. • Proceedings, annual.

★ 13030 ★ American Association of Feline Practitioners (AAFP)
c/o Kristi Thomson
7007 Wyoming NE, Ste. E3
Albuquerque, NM 87109
Phone: (505)821-8910
Fax: (505)828-0621
Kristi Thomson, Exec.Dir.

Founded: 1970. **Members:** 1,400. **Description:** Doctors of veterinary medicine who specialize or have a general interest in the field of feline medicine and surgery. Works to promote the interests and improve the public stature of feline practice and to increase the knowledge of veterinarians in the field. Cooperates with other veterinary and cat fancier organizations. **Publications:** Newsletter, semiannual.

★ 13031 ★ American Association of Industrial Veterinarians (AAIV)
c/o Caroline & Co.
1015 E. Broadway
Columbia, MO 65201
Phone: (314)449-3109
Fax: (314)874-2451
Caroline Shuerman, Pres.

Founded: 1954. **Members:** 450. **Description:** Veterinarians, many of whom are members of the American Veterinary Medical Association and are employed in a professional capacity in industrial activities, for example, with drug and chemical firms, in livestock and poultry enterprises, or in independent research. Holds workshops. **Publications:** *AAIV Highlights*, semiannual. Newsletter. Membership activities newsletter. Includes member biographical sketches. *Price:* Included in membership dues. • Directory, annual. **Formerly:** Industrial Veterinarians Association.

★ 13032 ★ American Association for Laboratory Animal Science (AALAS)
70 Timber Creek, Ste. 5
Cordova, TN 38018
Phone: (901)754-8620
Fax: (901)753-0046
Michael R. Sondag, Exec.Dir.

Founded: 1949. **Members:** 7,000. **Local Groups:** 45. **Description:** Persons and institutions professionally concerned with the production, use, care, and study of laboratory animals. Serves as clearinghouse for collection and exchange of information on all phases of laboratory animal care and management and on the care, use, and procurement of laboratory animals used in biomedical research. Conducts examinations and certification through its Animal Technician Certification Program. **Publications:** *American Association for Laboratory Animal Science--Membership Directory*, annual. Membership Directory. Arranged alphabetically by name and geographically. *Price:* Included in membership dues. • *Contemporary Topics in Laboratory Animal Science*, bimonthly. Contains refereed papers covering topics in laboratory animal science; covers association activities. *Price:* Included in membership dues. • *Laboratory Animal Science*, bimonthly. Journal. Covers comparative and experimental medicine related to laboratory animal science. *Price:* $50/year for members; $90/year for nonmembers. Also publishes educational materials. **Formerly:** (1967) Animal Care Panel.

★ 13033 ★ American Association of Retired Veterinarians
PO Box 4826
Ithaca, NY 14852
Russell H. Anthony, Pres.

Founded: 1986. **Members:** 560. **Description:** Individuals with a degree in veterinary medicine who are retired or considering retiring, and their spouses. Seeks to advance the science and art of veterinary medicine. Encourages friendship among those in the profession. Promotes social and professional lives of retired veterinarians. Attempts to assist future retirees in achievement of their goals in retirement life. Organizes group trips and cruises. **Publications:** Membership Directory, periodic. • Newsletter.

★ 13034 ★ American Association of Small Ruminant Practitioners (AASRP)
1675 Ellis Hollow Rd.
Ithaca, NY 14850
Phone: (607)539-6181
Fax: (607)539-6181
Dr. Phyllis Larsen, Asst to Exec. Dir.

Founded: 1968. **Members:** 1,200. **Description:** Practicing veterinarians and veterinary students; associate members are producers, feeders, hobbyists, and others interested in sheep, goats, llamas, deer, and exotic small ruminants. Aims are to: elevate standards of practice in the field; further research programs that will assist in solving small ruminant health problems; foster communication between veterinarians, owners, and researchers in order to improve small ruminant health management programs. Sponsors specialized education programs. Offers placement service; conducts educational programs. Maintains speakers' bureau. **Publica-**

tions: Bibliographies. • *Proceedings of Symposium on Health and Disease of Small Ruminants*, annual. Proceedings. *Price:* Included in membership dues; $12 for nonmembers. • *Wool and Wattles*, quarterly. Newsletter. *Price:* Included in membership dues. Also publishes fact sheets and abstracts. **Formerly:** (1988) American Association of Sheep and Goat Practitioners.

★ 13035 ★ American Association of Swine Practitioners (AASP)
c/o Dr. Tomas A. Neuzil
5921 Fleur Dr.
Des Moines, IA 50321
Phone: (515)285-7808
Fax: (515)285-7809
Dr. Tomas A. Neuzil, Exec.Sec.

Founded: 1969. **Members:** 1,580. **Description:** Veterinarians concerned with swine health and nutrition. To improve public stature and increase the knowledge of veterinarians in the field of swine practice. **Publications:** Directory, annual. • Journal, bimonthly. • *Proceedings*, annual.

★ 13036 ★ American Association of Veterinary Anatomists (AAVA)
c/o Dr. Paul F. Rumph
Auburn University
College of Veterinary Medicine
Department of Anatomy and Histology
Auburn, AL 36849
Phone: (205)844-6743
Dr. Paul F. Rumph, Contact

Founded: 1949. **Members:** 250. **Description:** Veterinary anatomists actively engaged in teaching and research. Fosters research in the fields of veterinary gross anatomy, neurobiology, cytology, and cytochemistry. Conducts scientific and educational programs. **Publications:** Directory, biennial. • Newsletter, semiannual.

★ 13037 ★ American Association of Veterinary Laboratory Diagnosticians (AAVLD)
c/o Dr. Harvey Gosser
UMC Veterinary Med. Diagnostic Lab.
PO Box 6023
Columbia, MO 65205
Phone: (314)882-6811
Fax: (314)882-1411
Dr. Harvey Gosser, Sec.-Treas.

Founded: 1957. **Members:** 800. **Description:** Each state has an official delegate and alternate to the association's executive board. Individual membership is open to persons active in veterinary laboratory diagnostic medicine. Disseminates information on diagnosis of animal disease; coordinates diagnostic activities of regulatory, research, and service laboratories; establishes uniform diagnostic techniques; seeks to improve existing diagnostic techniques and facilitate the development of new ones; establishes guides for personnel qualifications and facilities; acts as consultant to the U.S. Animal Health Association on uniform diagnostic criteria. **Publications:** *AAVLD Newsletter*, semiannual. Newsletter. Contains association news and information on employment opportunities. *Price:* Included in membership dues. • *Journal* *of Veterinary Diagnostic Investigation*, quarterly. Journal. *Price:* Included in membership dues.

★ 13038 ★ American Association of Veterinary Parasitologists (AAVP)
c/o Mallinckrodt Veterinary
421 E. Howley
Mundelein, IL 60060
Phone: (708)970-4514
Fax: (708)970-4513
Dr. Tom Kennedy, Exec.Sec.-Treas.

Founded: 1956. **Members:** 450. **Description:** Persons actively engaged in teaching and researching parasitology. Encourages education and research in the field; provides for exchange of information. Compiles summaries of papers presented at annual scientific meeting. **Publications:** *AAVP Directory*, biennial. Directory. • *AAVP Newsletter*, quarterly. Newsletter. • *Annual Meeting Proceedings*.

★ 13039 ★ American Association of Veterinary State Boards (AAVSB)
PO Box 633
Jefferson City, MO 65102
Phone: (314)751-0031
Fax: (314)751-4176
G. T. Barrows, DVM, Contact

Founded: 1957. **Members:** 54. **Description:** State boards of examiners in veterinary medicine. Aids state boards of veterinary medicine in the protection of the public health and welfare. Acts as a clearing house for research, collects and disseminates information about legal regulation of the veterinary profession. Works to simplify and standardize licensing and certification processes for veterinarians and veterinary technicians. Interacts with other veterinary organizations; legislative, judicial, regulatory, and executive governmental bodies; and other associations whose areas of interest may coincide. Assists member boards in fulfilling statutory, public, and ethical obligations in legal regulation and enforcement. Cooperates with the National Board Examination Committee in the design and use of entry level, relicensure and disciplinary examinations regarding the practice of veterinary medicine and regulation. Collects and disseminates information regarding disciplinary actions taken by member boards. Provides veterinary medical educational programs. **Formerly:** (1968) Association of American Board of Examiners in Veterinary Medicine; (1974) American Association State Boards, Veterinary.

★ 13040 ★ American Association of Wildlife Veterinarians (AAWV)
c/o Dr. Mike Miller
Colorado Division of Wildlife
317 W. Prospect
Fort Collins, CO 80526-2097
Phone: (303)484-2836
Dr. Mike Miller, Exec. Officer

Founded: 1979. **Members:** 350. **Description:** Veterinarians in state and federal wildlife resource agencies, universities, private practice, public health service agencies, agricultural agencies, and diagnostic laboratories; veterinary students; and interested individuals. To deal with problems confronting veterinarians who work with free-ranging wildlife. Encourages colleges of veterinary medicine to increase em-

phasis on management of and preventive medicine for free-ranging species; educates governmental agencies and wildlife resource interest groups; promotes utilization of veterinarians in the field of wildlife resource management and research; encourages cooperation among resource management professionals and wildlife veterinarians; promotes continuing education programs for wildlife veterinari ans; emphasizes interrelationships of man, domestic animals, and wildlife with disease; encourages recognition of disease syndromes as potentially influenced by habitat succession, alteration, and pollution. **Publications:** Membership Directory, periodic. • Newsletter, quarterly.

★ 13041 ★ American Association of Zoo Veterinarians (AAZV)
c/o Dr. Wilbur Amand
3400 W. Girard Ave.
Philadelphia, PA 19104-1196
Phone: (215)387-9094
Fax: (215)387-2165
Dr. Wilbur Amand, Exec.Dir.

Founded: 1947. **Members:** 1,100. **Description:** Veterinarians actively engaged in the practice of zoo and wildlife medicine for at least four years; veterinarians who do not qualify for active membership; persons interested in diseases of wildlife; students of veterinary medicine in any accredited veterinary school. Purposes are to: advance programs for preventive medicine, husbandry, and scientific research dealing with captive and free-ranging wild animals; provide a forum for the presentation and discussion of problems related to the field; enhance and uphold the professional ethics of veterinary medicine. **Publications:** *Conference Proceedings*, annual. Proceedings. Contains papers presented at the annual conference. *Price:* $45. • *Journal of Zoo and Wildlife Medicine*, quarterly. Journal. Contains original manuscripts, book and paper reviews and research notes/case reports. *Price:* Included in membership dues. • Membership Directory, annual. • Newsletter, quarterly.

★ 13042 ★ American Board on Veterinary Specialties (ABVS)
1931 N. Meacham Rd., Ste. 100
Schaumburg, IL 60173-4360
Phone: (708)925-8070
Free: 800-248-2802
Fax: (708)925-1329
Edward R. Ames, D.V.M., Staff Admin.

Founded: 1959. **Members:** 21. **Description:** A board of the American Veterinary Medical Association (see separate entry). Organization of veterinarians with advanced training in one or more specialty areas of veterinary practice, research, or study whose purpose is to recognize and supervise organizations that provide certification to qualified specialists. Acts as mediator upon request in appeals submitted to the AVMA. Seeks to provide advanced veterinary services to the public. **Formerly:** Advisory Board on Veterinary Specialties.

★ 13043 ★ American Board of Veterinary Toxicology (ABVT)
University of Pennsylvania
School of Veterinary Medicine
382 W. State Rd.
Kennett Square, PA 19348
Phone: (610)444-5800
Dr. Robert Poppenga, Sec.-Treas.

Founded: 1967. **Members:** 80. **Description:** Seeks to: further education and scientific progress in veterinary toxicology; encourage research and training; establish and maintain the highest possible standards of training and experience for qualification in toxicology; recognize qualified specialists through certification. Conducts annual examination. **Publications:** *American Board of Veterinary Toxicology--Directory of Diplomates*, annual. Directory. Lists diplomates certified as veterinary toxicologists by the board.

★ 13044 ★ American Canine Sports Medicine Association (ACSMA)
12062 SW 117th Ct., Ste. 146
Miami, FL 33186
Phone: (305)633-2402
Fax: (305)252-7392
Dr. Ronald Stone, Contact

Founded: 1991. **Members:** 200. **Description:** Promotes interests of members. Conducts research and educational programs. **Publications:** *Newsletter of the ACSMA*, quarterly. Newsletter. *Price:* Included in membership dues.

★ 13045 ★ American College of Theriogenologists
Texas A&M University
Department of Large Animal Medicine and Surgery
Texas Veterinary Med. Center
College Station, TX 77843-4475
Phone: (409)845-9150
Fax: (409)847-8863
D.D. Varner, D.V.M., Sec.

Founded: 1970. **Members:** 285. **Description:** Veterinarians specializing in animal reproduction. Advances knowledge, education, and services in theriogenology. Acts as certifying agency for theriogenologists. Sponsors scientific programs. Conducts educational programs. **Publications:** Directory, annual. • *Newsletter of ACT*, bimonthly. Newsletter. *Price:* Free.

★ 13046 ★ American College of Veterinary Dermatology (ACVD)
c/o Dr. Kenneth W. Kwochka
Veterinary Clinical Sciences
College of Veterinary Medicine
Ohio State University
601 Vernon L. Tharp St.
Columbus, OH 43210
Phone: (614)292-3551
Fax: (614)292-0895
Dr. Kenneth W. Kwochka, Pres.

Founded: 1982. **Members:** 90. **Description:** Specialists in veterinary dermatology who have satisfied examination requirements; individuals with national reputation and standing are charter diplomates. Purposes are to promote veterinary dermatology and to enhance the competency of professionals in the field. Seeks to develop guidelines for postdoctoral education and to establish experience prerequisites for certification in veterinary dermatology. Administers examinations and certifies veterinarians as veterinary dermatology specialists. Encourages research and other contributions in areas of pathogenesis, diagnosis, therapy, prevention, and control of diseases affecting the skin of animals. Authorizes training programs in the field.

★ 13047 ★ American College of Veterinary
Internal Medicine (ACVIM)
7175 W. Jefferson Ave., Ste. 2125
Lakewood, CO 80235
Phone: (303)980-7136
Free: 800-245-9081
Fax: (303)980-7137
June Johnson, Exec.Dir.

Founded: 1972. Members: 678. Description:
Veterinarians certified in internal medicine and related specialties such as cardiology, neurology, and oncology. Works to advance the scope and ideals of veterinary internal medicine and to increase the competence of those practicing in the field. Issues certifying diplomas. Publications: Directory, annual. Provides membership activity information. • Journal of Veterinary Internal Medicine, bimonthly. Journal. • Proceedings of Annual Veterinary Medical Forum.

★ 13048 ★ American College of Veterinary
Ophthalmologists (ACVO)
c/o Dr. Mary B. Glaze
Louisiana State University
Veterinary Teaching Hospital
S. Stadium Dr.
Baton Rouge, LA 70803
Phone: (504)346-3333
Fax: (504)346-3295
Dr. Mary B. Glaze, Sec.-Treas.

Founded: 1969. Members: 155. Description:
Veterinarians certified by examination in veterinary ophthalmology. Purposes are: continuing education, research, and practice in veterinary ophthalmology; establishment of standards of training and experience; recognition of individuals who have fulfilled such standards; certification of qualified veterinarians. Publications: Directory of Diplomates, quinquennial. Directory. Price: $10.

★ 13049 ★ American College of Veterinary
Pathologists (ACVP)
875 King Hwy., Ste. 200
Woodbury, NJ 08096-3172
Phone: (609)848-7784
Fax: (609)853-0411
Dr. Margaret Miller, Sec.-Treas.

Founded: 1948. Members: 921. Description:
Professional society of specialists in veterinary pathology (origin, nature, and course of diseases in animals). Aims to further scientific progress in the specialty of veterinary pathology; to establish standards of training and experience for qualification of specialists in veterinary pathology; to further the recognition of such qualified specialists by suitable certification and other means. Recognized as the certifying agency for the specialty of veterinary pathology in the U.S. and Canada. Conducts specialized education programs and certifying exams. Publications:

American College of Veterinary Pathologists--Newsletter, bimonthly. Newsletter. Covers developments in veterinary pathology; also includes association news, calendar of events, obituaries, and listing of employment opportunities. Price: Included in membership dues. • Membership List, annual. Directory. • Proceedings, annual. • Veterinary Pathology: An International Journal of Natural and Experimental Disease in Animals, bimonthly. Includes book reviews and periodic special supplements on a scientific topic. Price: $75/year.

★ 13050 ★ American College of Veterinary
Radiology (ACVR)
c/o Dr. M. Bernstein
PO Box 87
Glencoe, IL 60022
Phone: (708)251-5517
Fax: (708)446-8618
Dr. M. Bernstein, Sec.

Founded: 1964. Members: 160. Description:
Diplomate members (160) are veterinarians certified by the college in veterinary radiology; associate members (6) are individuals distinguished in radiological science but who are not certified veterinary radiologists. Educational association working to advance the art and science of radiology. Certifies candidates who have demonstrated proficiency in veterinary radiology. Encourages the development of teaching personnel and training facilities in veterinary radiology. Aids in the evaluation of residencies and fellowships in veterinary radiology under consideration by the Council on Education of the American Veterinary Medical Association. Advises veterinarians who desire certification in veterinary radiology. Conducts continuing education seminars in conjunction with other veterinary organizations. Publications: Brochure. • Veterinary Radiology and Ultrasound, bimonthly. Journal. Covers diagnostic and therapeutic radiology, ultrasound, MR, CT, and scintigraphy. Price: Included in membership dues; $78/year for institutions. Formerly: (1969) American Board of Veterinary Radiology.

★ 13051 ★ American College of Veterinary
Surgeons (ACVS)
4330 East West Hwy., No. 1117
Bethesda, MD 20814-4408
Phone: (301)718-6504
Fax: (301)656-0989
Ann Loew, Exec.Dir.

Founded: 1965. Members: 593. Description:
Acts as certification board for veterinary surgeons. Publications: American College of Veterinary Surgeons--Directory of Diplomates, biennial. Membership Directory. Includes photographic and biographical information on each member; includes alphabetical name and geographic region indexes. Price: Included in membership dues. • Journal of Veterinary Surgery, bimonthly. Journal. Presents clinical and research papers on veterinary surgery; topics include surgical techniques and management of the surgical patient. Price: $69/year for individuals; $100/year for institutions.

★ 13052 ★ American Heartworm Society
(AHS)
PO Box 667
Batavia, IL 60510-0667
Phone: (708)844-9676
Fax: (708)892-2322
Eve Larocca, Contact

Founded: 1974. Members: 1,200. Description:
Veterinarians, physicians, parasitologists, and other scientists. Promotes scientific programs for the study of heartworm disease, an infestation of the filaria worm in the pulmonary arteries of dogs. Encourages standardization of procedures for diagnosis, treatment, and prevention of heartworm disease. Keeps members abreast of current research and recent developments concerning the disease. Publications: AHS Bulletin, quarterly. Bulletin. Price: Included in membership dues; $38/year for nonmembers. • Proceedings.

American Holistic Veterinary Medical
Association (AHVMA)
See: Entry 2168

★ 13053 ★ American Society of Veterinary
Ophthalmology (ASVO)
1528 Shalamar
Stillwater, OK 74074
Phone: (405)377-2134
A. J. Quinn, D.V.M., Sec.-Treas.

Founded: 1957. Members: 250. Description:
Veterinarians with a special interest in ophthalmology (the science of the eye and its diseases). Sponsors research proposal competition. Publications: Directory, annual. • Newsletter, periodic. • Proceedings, annual.

★ 13054 ★ American Veterinary Medical
Association (AVMA)
1931 N. Meacham Rd., Ste. 100
Schaumburg, IL 60173-4360
Phone: (708)925-8070
Free: 800-248-2862
Fax: (708)925-1329
A. Roland Dommert, D.V.M., Contact

Founded: 1863. Members: 52,000. Local
Groups: 433. Description: Professional society of veterinarians. Conducts educational and research programs. Provides placement service. Maintains the American Society of Laboratory Animal Practitioners. Sponsors American Veterinary Medical Association Foundation (also known as AVMA Foundation) and Educational Commission for Foreign Veterinary Graduates. Compiles statistics. Publications: American Journal of Veterinary Research, monthly. Journal. • Directory, annual. • Journal of the AVMA, semimonthly. Journal. Formerly: (1988) United States Veterinary Medical Association.

★ 13055 ★ American Veterinary Society of
Animal Behavior (AVSAB)
c/o Dr. Debra Horwitz
Veterinary Behavior Consultations
253 S. Graeser
St. Louis, MO 63141
Phone: (314)567-3864
Fax: (314)567-3864
Dr. Debra Horwitz, Sec.-Treas.

Founded: 1975. Members: 425. Description:
Veterinarians and veterinary students. Pro-

motes inquiry and research into animal behavior. Seeks to advance ethological knowledge regarding the care and utilization of captive, domesticated, and free-living animals. Promotes and facilitates the exchange of information among those concerned with animal behavior and well-being; encourages discussion on veterinary aspects of animal behavior and the publication of materials in the field. **Publications:** *American Veterinary Society of Animal Behavior*, quarterly. Newsletter. *Price:* Included in membership dues; $20/year for nonmembers. Also publishes speakers list and plans to publish a directory. **Formerly:** (1984) American Society of Veterinary Ethology.

★ **13056 ★ Animal Health Foundation (AHF)**
105 Carmel Woods
Ellisville, MO 63021
Phone: (314)451-4009
Donald M. Walsh, D.V.M., Pres.

Founded: 1984. **Members:** 1,000. **Description:** Individuals interested in finding the causes, treatments, and cure for the crippling equine disease laminitis/founder syndrome. (Laminitis is an inflammation of the laminae, the semi-rigid internal supporting structures of the horse's foot; founder is the crippling result of laminitis in which the coffin bone in the horse's foot puts pressure on the sole of the foot, and sometimes actually penetrates the sole.) These ailments affect horses of any age or breed, and are counted by the AHF as the second ranking disease leading to the need to euthanize horses. Supports extensive research and collects a range of related data. **Publications:** *AHF Newsletter*, periodic. Newsletter. • Brochure.

Animal Health Institute (AHI)
See: Entry 5823

★ **13057 ★ Animal Medical Center (AMC)**
510 E. 62nd St.
New York, NY 10021-8383
Phone: (212)838-8100
Fax: (212)832-9630
William J. Kay, Chief of Staff

Founded: 1910. **Description:** Provides quality medical and surgical care for small pets; conducts educational programs for veterinarians, students, and technicians; conducts clinical investigations in veterinary and comparative medicine. Sponsors charitable outreach programs including bereavement counseling, pet therapy, and subsidized care for elderly pet owners and guide dog owners; maintains library. **Publications:** *Annual Report.* • *The Center Scope*, 3/year. **Formerly:** (1959) New York Women's League for Animals.

★ **13058 ★ Association of American Veterinary Medical Colleges (AAVMC)**
1101 Vermont Ave., Ste. 710
Washington, DC 20005
Phone: (202)371-9195
Fax: (202)842-0773
Lester M. Crawford, DVM, Exec.Dir.

Founded: 1966. **Members:** 40. **Description:** Represents colleges of veterinary medicine in the United States and Canada; departments of veterinary science and departments of comparative medicine. **Publications:** *Journal of Veteri-*

nary Medical Education, semiannual. Journal. **Formerly:** (1962) Association of Deans of American Colleges of Veterinary Medicine.

★ **13059 ★ Association of Avian Veterinarians (AAV)**
PO Box 811720
Boca Raton, FL 33481
Phone: (407)393-8901
Fax: (407)393-8902
Adina Rae Freedman, CAE, Exec.Dir.

Founded: 1980. **Members:** 3,300. **Description:** Veterinarians; veterinary students; breeders and importers of captive birds. Works to further knowledge in the field of avian medicine; conducts educational programs. Organizes student chapters. Operates speakers' bureau. **Publications:** *AAV Membership Directory*, annual. Membership Directory. *Price:* Available to members only. • *Journal of the Association of Avian Veterinarians*, quarterly. Journal. Includes refereed articles and practice tips. *Price:* Included in membership dues; $70/year for nonmembers. • *Proceedings of Annual Seminars*. Proceedings. • *Technical Proceedings*, annual. Proceedings. Also publishes information packets.

★ **13060 ★ Association for Equine Sports Medicine (AESM)**
c/o Veterinary Practice Publishing Co.
PO Box 4457
Santa Barbara, CA 93160-4457
Phone: (805)965-1028
Fax: (805)965-0722
Nancy A. Bull, Exec.Dir.

Founded: 1982. **Members:** 400. **Description:** Veterinarians and students of veterinary medicine; horse owners and trainers; farriers; health professionals. Works to improve the health of horses competing in athletic events. Disseminates information on current research in equine medicine, physiology, and biomechanics. Offers wet lab training. **Publications:** *The Equine Athlete*, bimonthly. Magazine. Includes proceeding of annual meeting. *Price:* Included in membership dues. • *Membership List*, periodic. • *Proceedings of Annual Conference*.

★ **13061 ★ Association for Gnotobiotics (AG)**
65 Brooklea Dr.
East Aurora, NY 14052-1917
Phone: (716)655-1680
Fax: (716)655-1680
Dr. Patricia M. Bealmear, Exec.Sec.

Members: 415. **Description:** Veterinarians, doctors, animal husbandry personnel, and gnotobiologists. Stimulates research in the field of basic and applied gnotobiotics. (Gnotobiotics is the science of maintaining a microbiologically controlled environment.) Encourages production, maintenance, distribution, and use of gnotobiotes and seeks to establish standards for the microbiological testing and husbandry practice with gnotobiotes. Provides researchers with information about raising animals in germ-free and controlled environments so that such animals may be used for research, especially for studies on cancer and infectious diseases. Works to develop certification program and to establish acceptable nomenclature in the field.

Maintains office in Madison, WI. **Publications:** Membership Directory, annual. • Newsletter, annual. Also publishes papers from international meetings. **Formerly:** (1968) Association for Applied Gnotobiotics.

★ **13062 ★ Association for Women Veterinarians (AWV)**
c/o Chris Stone Payne, D.V.M.
32205 Allison Dr.
Union City, CA 94587
Phone: (510)471-8379
Fax: (510)471-8379
Chris Stone Payne, D.V.M., Sec.

Founded: 1947. **Members:** 625. **Description:** Women veterinarians; students of veterinary medicine. **Publications:** *AWV Bulletin*, quarterly. Bulletin. *Price:* Included in membership dues; $10/year for nonmembers. • *Roster of Women Veterinarians*, periodic. **Formerly:** (1981) Women's Veterinary Medical Association.

★ **13063 ★ Australian Veterinary Association (AVA)**
PO Box 371
Artarmon, NSW 2064, Australia
Phone: 2 4112733
Fax: 2 4115089
Dr. Philip Greenwood

Founded: 1921. **Members:** 4,000. **Local Groups:** 52. **Languages:** English. **Description:** Graduates of Australian veterinary schools; graduates of overseas veterinary schools qualified for registration in Australia; veterinary students; associate members are nonveterinarians with close ties to the veterinary profession. Promotes the professional practice of veterinary medicine; seeks improvements in the areas of animal health, productivity, and welfare. Represents members' interests; lobbies governmental bodies on matters related to animal welfare, quarantine, and agricultural problems. Maintains 16 special interest groups offering continuing education programs. Maintains museum. **Publications:** *Australian Veterinary Journal*, monthly. Journal. • *AVA News*, monthly. Newsletter. • *Members Directory and Policy Compendium*, every 2-3 years. Directory. • Report, annual.

★ **13064 ★ Belgian Veterinary Association (USVB)**
(Union Syndicat Veterinaire Belge — USVB)
41, ave. Fonsny
B-1060 Brussels, Belgium
Phone: 2 5381754
Fax: 2 5373254
Dr. H. Marion, Admin.

Languages: Dutch, English, French. **Description:** Representatives from all branches of veterinary science. Represents and protects the interests of veterinarians. **Publications:** *Veterinaria*, monthly. **Also Known As:** Belgische Syndicaat Dierenartsenvereniging.

★ 13065 ★ British Small Animal Veterinary Association (BSAVA)
Kingsley House
Church Ln.
Shurdington
Cheltenham, Glos. GL51 5TQ, England
Phone: 1242 862994
Fax: 1242 863009
Alison J. Hunt, Contact

Founded: 1957. **Members:** 3,500. **Local Groups:** 13. **Languages:** English. **Description:** Veterinarians in 20 countries. Operates speakers' bureau; sponsors educational programs. Compiles statistics. Sponsors competitions and bestows awards; conducts charitable activities. **Publications:** *BSAVA Handbook*, annual. Handbook. • *BSAVA News*, monthly. Newsletter. • *Journal of Small Animal Practice*, monthly. Journal.

★ 13066 ★ British Veterinary Association (BVA)
7 Mansfield St.
London W1M 0AT, England
Phone: 171 6366541
Fax: 171 4362970
J.H. Baird, Chief Exec.

Founded: 1882. **Members:** 8. **National Groups:** 20. **Local Groups:** 31. **Description:** Veterinarians and veterinary students. Promotes interests of members and the animals in their care. Monitors activities of, provides advice to, and develops and maintains contact with organizations interested in animal health including government agencies, local authorities, professional societies, animal rights groups, and universities. Disseminates information to the public and the media. Conducts charitable programs; operates speakers' bureau. Sponsors seminars and symposia. Maintains 20 specialist divisions. **Publications:** *Annual Report*. • *In Practice*, monthly. • *Research in Veterinary Science*, bimonthly. • *Veterinary Record*, weekly. **Formerly:** (1952) National Veterinary Medical Association.

★ 13067 ★ Canadian Animal Health Institute (CAHI)
27 Cork St. W.
Guelph, ON, Canada N1H 2W9
Phone: (519)763-7777
Fax: (519)763-7407
Jean Szkotnicki

Founded: 1968. **Languages:** English, French. **Description:** Developers, manufacturers, and distributors of animal health care products. Encourages development and research in veterinary science. Disseminates information among members. **Publications:** *Communique*, periodic. Newsletter.

★ 13068 ★ Canadian Veterinary Medical Association (CVMA)
(Association Candienne des Medecins Veterinaires — ACMV)
339 Booth St.
Ottawa, ON, Canada K1R 7K1
Phone: (613)236-1162
Fax: (613)236-9681
Claude Paul Boivin, Exec.Dir.

Founded: 1948. **Members:** 4,300. **Languages:** English, French. **Description:** Veterinarians in Canada. Encourages excellence in the field of veterinary medicine; seeks to increase awareness of the importance of animals; represents the interests of members. **Publications:** *Canadian Journal of Veterinary Research*, quarterly. • *Canadian Veterinary Journal*, monthly. • *Directory of Canadian Veterinarians*, annual.

★ 13069 ★ Chinese Association of Animal Science and Veterinary Medicine
33 Dongdaqiao
Nongfengli
Chao Yang District
Beijing 100020, People's Republic of China
Phone: 1 5005934
Fax: 1 5005670
Hanping Yan, Sec.Gen.

Founded: 1936. **Members:** 20,000. **Languages:** Chinese, English. **Description:** Veterinarians and interested individuals in the People's Republic of China. Promotes the study of veterinary science. Conducts research and educational programs. Disseminates information on animal husbandry. Fosters technical exchange among members. Offers consulting services. Maintains speakers' bureau. Compiles statistics. **Publications:** *Chinese Journal of Animal Science*, periodic. Journal. • *Chinese Journal of Veterinary Sciences Thesis*, bimonthly. Journal.

★ 13070 ★ Conference of Research Workers in Animal Diseases (CRWAD)
c/o Dr. Robert Ellis
Department of Microbiology
Colorado State University
Fort Collins, CO 80523
Phone: (303)491-5740
Fax: (303)491-1815
Dr. Robert Ellis, Exec.Dir.

Founded: 1919. **Members:** 700. **Description:** Research workers in animal diseases. **Publications:** *Abstracts of the Annual Meeting-- CRWAD*, annual. Journal. Contains abstracts presented at annual meeting. *Price:* $15/year.

★ 13071 ★ European Association of Veterinary Anatomists (EAVA)
(Europaische Vereinigung der Veterinaranatomen — EVVA)
Rijksuniversiteit Gent
Vakgroep Morfologie
Fakulteit Diergeneeskunde, Casinoplein 24
B-9000 Ghent, Belgium
Phone: 9 2333765
Fax: 9 2332234
Prof. P. Simoens, Sec.Gen.

Founded: 1963. **Members:** 236. **Languages:** English, French, German, Spanish. **Description:** European and international veterinarians from 34 countries interested in morphologic research on domestic animals.

★ 13072 ★ European Society of Veterinary Pathology (ESVP)
(Europaische Gesellschaft fur Veterinarpathologie)
Winterthurer Str. 280
CH-8057 Zurich, Switzerland
Phone: 1 3651204
Fax: 1 3130130
Dr. Andreas Pospischil, Contact

Founded: 1952. **Members:** 230. **Languages:** English, French, German. **Description:** Veteri-

nary pathologists in 20 countries. Promotes the exchange of information and research findings. **Publications:** *Seminar Reports*, annual.

★ 13073 ★ Federal Chamber of Veterinarians eV (Bundestierarzte Kammer eV)
Oxfordstrasse 10
53111 Bonn, Germany
Phone: 228 655760
Fax: 228 692767
E.W.H. Roesener, Mgr.

Founded: 1954. **Members:** 31. **Regional Groups:** 17. **State Groups:** 14. **Languages:** English, French, German. **Description:** Local chambers of veterinarians and special veterinary organizations. Cultivates group awareness among German veterinarians; encourages cooperation among German veterinary medical organizations. Represents members' interests before the West German government; provides information and expert evaluations to government agencies and public and private institutions interested in veterinary medicine. Fosters communication between national veterinary medical organizations worldwide. Operates Academy for Continuing Veterinary Education. **Publications:** *Deutsches Tierartzeblatt*, monthly. Journal. **Formerly:** German Veterinarian Association; Deutsche Tierarzteschaft.

★ 13074 ★ Federation of European Veterinarians in Industry and Research (FEVIR)
(Federation Europeenne des Veterinaires de l'Industrie et de la Recherche)
270-272, ave. de Tervuren
B-1115 Brussels, Belgium
Phone: 2 7764111
Fax: 2 7764040
Dr. W. Vandaele, Pres.

Founded: 1975. **National Groups:** 7. **Languages:** English, French. **Description:** Organizations representing 4000 veterinarians working in industry and research. Represents members before the Federation of Veterinarians in Europe and provides expert opinions to European Economic Community groups. Works to improve the status of salaried veterinarians. Maintains a file on positions available for veterinarians in Europe. Conducts seminars and symposia.

★ 13075 ★ Federation of Veterinarians of the EC (FVE)
41, ave. Fonsny
B-1060 Brussels, Belgium
Phone: 2 5382963
Fax: 2 5372828
Dr. Marcel Lux, Pres.

Founded: 1961. **Members:** 23. **Languages:** English, French, German. **Description:** Professional organizations of veterinarians and interested individuals in 18 countries. Serves as a liaison to the European Economic Community. Works toward the unification of veterinary programs in member countries of the EC and its observers. **Publications:** Brochure. • *FVE Newsletter*, monthly. Newsletter.

★13076★ Feline Advisory Bureau and Central Fund for Feline Studies (FABCFFS)
235 Upper Richmond Rd.
Putney
London SW15 6SN, England
Phone: 181 7899553
Betty Thomas, Gen.Sec.

Founded: 1958. **Members:** 2,200. **Languages:** English. **Description:** Veterinary surgeons, cat breeders, and pet owners. Promotes humane behavior toward cats and provides information on feline health and care. Raises funds for feline clinical research. Provides cat boarding service. **Publications:** *Fab Journal*, quarterly. Journal.

★13077★ Finnish Veterinary Association (Finlands Veterinarforbund)
Makelank 2C
SF-00520 Helsinki, Finland
Phone: 0 7011388
Fax: 0 7018397

Founded: 1892. **Members:** 1,250. **Languages:** English, Finnish, Swedish. **Description:** Practitioners of veterinary medicine in Finland. Seeks to develop veterinary medicine in Finland. Encourages exchange and cooperation among members; promotes and represents the professional, social, and economic welfare of members. Makes recommendations to authorities on policy matters affecting veterinary medicine; fosters international contacts. Holds Annual veterinary seminar and talks and lectures. Conducts research. Operates charitable program. **Publications:** *Suomen Elainlaarkarilehti*, monthly. Journal. with English summaries. Also publishes report of about 400 pages from lectures of the Finnish Veterinary Congress.

★13078★ Flying Veterinarians Association (FVA)
PO Box 1081
Columbia, MO 65205
Phone: (314)882-7228
Fax: (314)882-2950
Robert C. McClure, D.V.M., Sec.-Treas.

Founded: 1966. **Members:** 328. **Description:** Veterinarians holding valid private pilot certificates; individuals in the field who have an interest in flying; nonveterinarians who either teach in veterinary schools or who represent companies serving the veterinary industry. Promotes aviation safety through example and education; seeks to increase knowledge and proficiency in the operation of aircraft. Seeks to heighten awareness of and interest in aviation among young people. Emphasizes utilization of aircraft in veterinary practice. Sponsors two to four educational programs per year in conjunction with other professional veterinary medical meetings; organizes fly-ins. **Publications:** Directory, periodic. • Newsletter, periodic.

German-Speaking Mycological Society (Deutschsprachige Mykologische Gesellschaft)
See: Entry 6671

★13079★ Hong Kong Veterinary Association (HKVA)
Veterinary Dept.
Equine Hosp.
Sha Tin Race Course
New Territories, Hong Kong
Phone: 29666608
Fax: 26023305
Dr. K.L. Watkins, Hon.Pres.

Founded: 1982. **Members:** 65. **Languages:** Cantonese, Chinese, English. **Description:** Veterinary surgeons. Fosters advancement in the field of veterinary medicine. Sponsors clinical lectures. Seeks to influence veterinary legislation in Hong Kong.

★13080★ Indonesia Veterinary Drug Association (IVDA) (Asosiasi Obat Hewan Indonesia)
Jalan Raya Pasar Minggu, No. 97A
12510 Jakarta, Indonesia
Phone: 21 7982679
Fax: 21 7982678
A. Karim Mahanan, Gen.Chm.

Founded: 1979. **Members:** 1,344. **Languages:** English, Indonesian. **Description:** Organizes veterinary industry activities in Indonesia. Maintains regulations and policies for the production of veterinary medicines. Compiles statistics. **Publications:** *Directory of Veterinary Company*, biennial. Book. • *Infovet*, quarterly. Magazine. Includes information on veterinary medicine. • *Veterinary Drug Index of Indonesia*. Book.

★13081★ Institute of Laboratory Animal Resources (ILAR)
National Research Council
2101 Constitution Ave. NW
Washington, DC 20418
Phone: (202)334-2590
Fax: (202)334-1687
Thomas L. Wolfle, D.V.M., Dir.

Founded: 1952. **Description:** Organized under the auspices of the National Academy of Sciences (see separate entry). Acts in an advisory capacity to the federal government, upon request, and to other public and private agencies. Maintains information center and answers inquiries concerning animal models for biomedical research, location of unique animal colonies, availability of genetically defined animals from those colonies and from animal breeders, and nonanimal alternatives. Committees develop guidelines on breeding, conservation, and humane care and use of animals, including species-specific documents on cats, nonhuman primates, and rodents. Also prepares documents on guidelines and poicy issues of biotechnology and use of animals in precollege education, facilities, disease prevention, and other topics in laboratory animal science. Sources of financial support include government agencies and private organizations. Maintains advisory council and several committees comprising scientists from universities, research organizations, and medical schools. **Publications:** *Guide for the Care and Use of Laboratory Animals*. Book. • *ILAR News*, quarterly. • Proceedings. • Reports, Laboratory animal management documents.

★13082★ Inter-African Bureau for Animal Resources (IBAR)
PO Box 30786
Nairobi, Kenya
Phone: 2 338544
Fax: 2 332046
Dr. W.N. Masiga, Dir.

Founded: 1951. **Members:** 50. **Regional Groups:** 5. **Languages:** Arabic, English, French, Portuguese. **Description:** Countries belonging to the Organization of African Unity. Aims to control widespread animal diseases; seeks improvements in animal health and production in Africa. **Publications:** *Bulletin of Animal Health and Production in Africa*, quarterly. Bulletin. • *Information Leaflet*, weekly. • *Proceedings of ISCTRC Meeting*, biennial. **Formerly:** (1960) InterAfrican Bureau for Epizootic Diseases.

★13083★ International Association for Aquatic Animal Medicine (IAAAM)
c/o Beverly Dixon, Ph.D.
25800 Carlos Bee Blvd.
Hayward, CA 94542
Phone: (510)881-3422
Fax: (510)727-2035
Beverly Dixon, Ph.D., Sec.-Treas.

Founded: 1969. **Members:** 450. **Description:** Veterinarians, Ph.D.s, and marine biologists involved in aquatic animal medicine and husbandry. Objectives are: to advance the art of aquatic animal medicine; to promote the free exchange of knowledge in the interest of improving the health care and husbandry of domestic aquatic animals and the proper management of aquatic animal resources in the wild; to provide an organization in which interested and professionally qualified individuals can work together to achieve these objectives; to provide a setting in which the development of the practice of aquatic animal medicine may be facilitated and enhanced; to promote the application of veterinary medical principles to aquatic animal disease problems. **Publications:** *IAAAM Conference Proceedings*, annual. • *IAAAM Directory*, annual. Directory. • *IAAAM News*, quarterly. Newsletter. Includes association news, book reviews, calendar of events, and research updates. *Price:* Included in membership dues.

★13084★ International Association of Equine Dental Technicians (IAEDT)
PO Box 6095
Wilmington, DE 19804-6095
Phone: (302)892-9215
Free: 800-334-6095
Gail A. Emerson, Pres.

Founded: 1987. **Members:** 40. **Description:** Equine dental technicians, veterinarians, and others interested in equine dental maintenance. Promotes the health and welfares of horses, and high standards and recognition in the field of equine dentistry. Acts as a forum for the exchange of information and experiences in the field. Sponsors educational programs. Offers certification program and testing. Maintains hall of fame. **Publications:** *IAEDT Newsletter*, quarterly. Newsletter. *Price:* Included in membership dues.

★ 13085 ★ International Committee on Veterinary Anatomical Nomenclature (ICVAN)
(Commission Internationale de la Nomenclature Anatomique Veterinaire — CINAV)
Winterthurerstrasse 260
CH-8057 Zurich, Switzerland
Phone: 1 3651253
Fax: 1 3651323
Prof. Josef Frewein, Sec.

Founded: 1957. **Languages:** English. **Description:** An umbrella organization of the International Committee on Gross Veterinary Anatomical Nomenclature, the International Committee on Veterinary Histological Nomenclature, the International Committee on Veterinary Embryological Nomenclature, and the International Committee on Avian Anatomical Nomenclature. Primary aim is to promote anatomical nomenclature and to coordinate the activities of member committees. **Publications:** *Handbook of Avian Anatomy: Nomina Anatomica Avium.* Handbook. • *Nomina Anatomica Veterinaria.* • *Nomina Embryologica Veterinaria.* • *Nomina Histologica, 2nd rev. ed.*.

★ 13086 ★ International Embryo Transfer Society (IETS)
309 W. Clark St.
Champaign, IL 61820-4690
Phone: (217)356-3182
Fax: (217)398-4119
Carl D. Johnson, Mgr.

Founded: 1974. **Members:** 850. **Description:** Veterinarians; researchers in reproductive physiology, animal science, genetics, endocrinology, and immunology; representatives of regulatory agencies such as government agencies and breed associations; sales representatives of drugs or equipment; students. Works to disseminate scientific and educational information; to promote more effective research; to foster and maintain high standards of education and ethics. Conducts Code Numbers to Identify Units Freezing Embryos Program, through which containers of frozen embryos are labelled with a permanent, recognized identification number. Sponsors exhibits of drugs and equipment used in embryo transfer. Conducts student competition to promote excellence in research. Maintains speakers' bureau. **Publications:** Manuals, annual. Covers information on minimum sanitary standards for embryo transfer procedures. • Membership Directory, annual. • Newsletter, quarterly. • *Proceedings of Annual Symposium and Conference.*

★ 13087 ★ International Organization for Mycoplasmology (IOM)
c/o Dr. Mary B. Brown
Department of Infectious Diseases
University of Florida
Gainesville, FL 32611-0926
Phone: (904)392-5961
Fax: (904)392-7629
Dr. Mary B. Brown, Contact

Founded: 1974. **Members:** 450. **Description:** Medical, veterinary, plant pathology, and molecular biology scientists who study mycoplasmas; commercial companies that produce diagnostic reagents; animal suppliers; pharmaceutical and chemical companies. Works to support and encourage mycoplasmal research and dissemination of information. (Mycoplasmas are microrganisms that cause disease in humans, animals, and a wide variety of plants. These diseases include: corn stunt, asters yellows, and citrus stubborn in plants; urogenital, respiratory, and joint diseases are found in poultry, swine, sheep, goats, and cows; pneumonia and genitourinary tract disease in humans.) Sponsors educational programs including a training program in methodology and a biennial techniques course. Offers placement service. Maintains speakers' bureau. **Publications:** *Congress Abstracts*, biennial. • *Congress Proceedings*, biennial. Proceedings. • Membership Directory, periodic. • Newsletter, quarterly.

★ 13088 ★ International Regional Organization of Plant Protection and Animal Health (OIRSA)
(Organismo Internacional Regional de Sanidad Agropecuaria — OIRSA)
Apdo. (01)61
Calle Ramon Belloso y Fnal. Pje. Isolde
Col. Escalon
San Salvador, El Salvador
Phone: 2238923
Fax: 2982119
Jorge Anibal Escobedo, Exec.Dir.

Founded: 1953. **Members:** 8. **Languages:** Spanish. **Description:** Ministries of agriculture and livestock from the countries of Costa Rica, Dominican Republic, El Salvador, Guatemala, Honduras, Mexico, Nicaragua, and Panama. Objective is to prevent epidemics and exotic diseases among crops and farm animals in Central America. Informs and advises members and coordinates their activities. Special programs include: plant and animal quarantine; a regional effort to prevent Foot and Mouth Disease and a joint effort with Honduras and Guatemala to control Coffee Berry Borer; and a cooperative. Cooperative projects with the United States Department of Agriculture include identification and classification of fruit flies and the eradication of the Africanized bee. Presents national and international courses on the quarantining of cattle. **Publications:** *Newsletter*, quarterly. Newsletter.

★ 13089 ★ International Society for Applied Ethology (ISAE)
(Societe International d'Ethologie Applie)
Institute of Ecological Resource Management
Edinburgh School of Agriculture
Edinburgh EH9 3JG, Scotland
Phone: 131 6671041
Fax: 131 6672601
Dr. Michael Appleby, Sec.

Founded: 1966. **Members:** 400. **Languages:** English. **Description:** Veterinarians; scientists and individuals with special knowledge of ethology, the study of animal behavior. Purpose is to advance the study of ethology as it affects animal health and welfare. Seeks to: stimulate ethological teaching and research in the veterinary and related professions; encourage discussion among members and publication of original works; further ethological knowledge on domesticated, captive, and wild animals; acts as clearinghouse for veterinarians and other interested individuals. **Publications:** Newsletter, semiannual. • *Proceedings*, semiannual. Published in *Applied Animal Behavior Science.* **Formerly:** (1991) Society for Veterinary Ethology; (1993) Societe d'Ethologie Veterinaire.

★ 13090 ★ International Standing Committee of the International Congress on Animal Reproduction
Swedish University of Agricultural Sciences
Faculty of Veterinary Medicine
Department of Obstetrics and Gynaecology
Box 7039
S-750 07 Uppsala, Sweden
Phone: 18 671000
Fax: 18 673545
Prof. Stig Einarsson, Sec.Gen.

Founded: 1948. **Languages:** English. **Description:** Scientists from 50 countries. Primary activity is to conduct an international congress dealing with agricultural problems such as the fundamental study and practical application of reproduction in farm animals. Congresses concentrate on physiology, pathology, and biotechnology. Other discussion topics include: techniques of artificial insemination and embryo transfer; intensification of animal reproduction; and the control and prevention of animal diseases. Fosters information exchange among scientists on an international level. **Publications:** *Congress Proceedings*, quadrennial. • *Report Booklet*, periodic. Booklet. **Formerly:** International Standing Committee of the International Congress of Phsyiology and Pathology of Animal Reproduction; International Standing Committee of International Congress on Animal Reproduction and Artificial Insemination.

★ 13091 ★ International Veterinary Acupuncture Society (IVAS)
c/o Dr. Meredith L. Snader
2140 Conestoga Rd.
Chester Springs, PA 19425
Phone: (215)827-7245
Fax: (215)687-3605
Dr. Meredith L. Snader, Exec.Dir.

Founded: 1974. **Members:** 400. **Description:** Veterinarians and veterinary students. Encourages knowledge and research of the philosophy, technique, and practice of veterinary acupuncture. Fosters high standards in the field; promotes scientific investigation. Accumulates resources for scientific research and education; collects data concerning clinical and research cases where animals have been treated with acupuncture; disseminates information to veterinary students, practitioners, other scientific groups, and the public. Offers 120 contact hour basic veterinary acupuncture course; administers accreditation examination. **Publications:** *Computerized Membership Directory*, periodic. Directory. • Newsletter, quarterly. • *Proceeding*, annual.

★ 13092 ★ International Veterinary Students' Association (IVSA)
(Association Internationale des Etudiants Veterinaires)
Information Office, Rm. CO 15
Faculteit der Diergeneeskunde
Yalelaan 1, De Uithof
NL-3584 CL Utrecht, Netherlands
Phone: 30 534694
Fax: 30 531407

Founded: 1951. **Members:** 10,000. **Languages:** English. **Description:** Veterinary students from 30 countries. Promotes international exchanges for veterinary students; advances veterinary medicine by establishing and encouraging interesting and stimulating student programs. **Publications:** *The International Veterinary Student*, 3/year. Magazine. • *IVSA Address List*, periodic. • *IVSA Headlines*, periodic.

Laboratory Animal Management Association Lab Animal Program (LAMA)
See: Entry 5583

National Association for Biomedical Research (NABR)
See: Entry 2541

★ 13093 ★ National Association of Federal Veterinarians (NAFV)
1101 Vermont Ave. NW, Ste. 710
Washington, DC 20005-3521
Phone: (202)289-6334
Edward L. Menning, D.V.M., Exec.VP

Founded: 1918. **Members:** 1,600. **State Groups:** 30. **Description:** Professional society of veterinarians employed by the U.S. Government. Maintains speakers' bureau. **Publications:** *Federal Veterinarian*, monthly. Newsletter. Includes abstracts, obituaries, federal regulatory and legislative news, and association news. *Price:* Included in membership dues; $30/year for nonmembers. • *National Association of Federal Veterinarians--Directory*, annual. Directory. *Price:* $4 for members only. • *National Association of Federal Veterinarians--Proceedings of Symposia*, annual. Proceedings. Reprints papers presented at professional symposia. **Formerly:** Bureau of Animal Industry Veterinarians; (1943) National Association of Bureau of Animal Industry Veterinarians.

★ 13094 ★ National Association of General Practitioner Veterinarians
(Bundesverband Praktischer Tierarzte)
Lyonerstr. 16
60528 Frankfurt, Germany
Phone: 69 6698180
Fax: 69 6668170
Jurgen Neubrand, Contact

Founded: 1951. **Members:** 5,000. **Description:** Veterinarians in Germany. Represents the professional, economic, and social interests of members. Advocates for animal health and welfare.

National Association of State Public Health Veterinarians (NASPHV)
See: Entry 5592

★ 13095 ★ National Mastitis Council (NMC)
c/o Anne Saeman
1840 Wilson Blvd., Ste. 400
Arlington, VA 22201
Phone: (703)243-8268
Fax: (703)841-9328
Anne Saeman, Exec.Dir.

Founded: 1961. **Members:** 1,900. **Description:** Seeks to resolve the problem of bovine mastitis (inflammation of the udder) by developing and distributing factual information on mastitis control and encouraging mastitis research. Conducts research and education programs. Helps organize and coordinate the activities of state councils. **Publications:** *National Mastitis Council--Annual Meeting Proceedings*. Proceedings. Contains papers on topics related to the production of high quality milk and the prevention of mastitis. *Price:* Included in membership dues; $11 to nonmembers. • *Udder Topics*, bimonthly. Newsletter. For people working in the dairy industry concerned with milk production. Covers topics related to the production of high quality milk. *Price:* Included in membership dues. Also publishes books, brochures, flyers, and monographs.

★ 13096 ★ National Veterinary Association of Morocco (NVAM)
(Association Nationale des Veterinaires du Maroc — ANVM)
BP 572
Rabat 10000, Morocco
Phone: 7 770096
Fax: 7 775838
Dr. Sedrati, Exec. Officer

Members: 500. **Regional Groups:** 10. **Languages:** Arabic, French. **Description:** Veterinarians in Morocco. Promotes and protects members' interests. Organizes continuing education programs; conducts seminars. Participates in regional and international professional events. **Publications:** *Bulletin de Liaison*, bimonthly. Newsletter. • *Dictionaire des Medicaments Veterinaires*. • *Maghreb Veterinaire*, quarterly. Includes abstracts in Arabic and English.

★ 13097 ★ New Zealand Veterinary Association (NZVA)
PO Box 27499
Wellington, New Zealand
Phone: 4 4710484
Fax: 4 4710494
R.H. Duckworth, Exec.Dir.

Founded: 1923. **Members:** 1,150. **Local Groups:** 15. **Languages:** English. **Description:** Promotes and represents the professional interests of veterinarians in New Zealand. **Publications:** *New Zealand Veterinary Journal*, bimonthly. Journal. • *New Zealand Vetscript*, monthly.

★ 13098 ★ Norwegian Veterinary Association (DNV)
(Norske Veterinarforening — DNV)
Sognsveien 4
N-0451 Oslo 4, Norway
Phone: 22 567650
Fax: 22 690450
Eirik Morkholm, Contact

Founded: 1888. **Members:** 1,650. **National Groups:** 5. **Local Groups:** 15. **Languages:** English, Norwegian. **Description:** Promotes the advancement of veterinary science in Norway. Sponsors educational and research programs. Compiles statistics; conducts charitable projects. **Publications:** *Norsk Veterinartidsskrift*, monthly. Journal.

★ 13099 ★ Office International des Epizooties (OIE)
12, rue de Prony
F-75017 Paris, France
Phone: 1 44151888
Fax: 1 42670987
Dr. Jean Blancou, Dir.Gen.

Founded: 1924. **Members:** 140. **Regional Groups:** 5. **Languages:** English, French, Spanish. **Description:** Veterinary services of national ministries of agriculture. Promotes and coordinates activities and research involving the epidemiology and control of contagious diseases in livestock. Collects and presents to governmental agencies data pertaining to epizootic diseases. Examines governmental agreements regarding animal health measures and assists in the supervision of their enforcement. Conducts specialized conferences and disease reporting seminars for chief veterinary officers and epidemiologists of member countries. Compiles statistics. **Publications:** *International Zoo-Sanitary Code*, every 3-4 years. Includes recommendations for import/export of animals, animal products, diagnostic techniques, and vaccines. • *OIE Bulletin*, monthly. Bulletin. • Papers, periodic. Contains technical information. • *Proceedings of Regional Conferences*, periodic. • *Scientific and Technical Review*, quarterly. • *World Animal Health*, annual.

★ 13100 ★ Omega Tau Sigma
c/o Harriet Rodenberg
PO Box 90264
Indianapolis, IN 46290
Phone: (317)255-4379
Fax: (317)253-5067
Harriet Rodenberg, Exec. Officer

Founded: 1906. **Members:** 7,148. **Regional Groups:** 13. **State Groups:** 8. **Description:** Professional fraternity - veterinary medicine. Maintains charitable fund. **Publications:** *Inner Square*, semiannual. Newsletter. Contains chapter news. *Price:* Included in membership dues. • *OTS Directory*, periodic. Directory.

★ 13101 ★ Options for Animals Foundation (OAF)
12202 256th St. N
PO Box 249
Port Byron, IL 61275
Phone: (309)523-3995
Dr. Sharon Willoughby, Dir.

Founded: 1983. **Members:** 120. **Description:** Individuals promoting chiropractic health care for animals. Encourages interaction and communication with health care professionals and pet owners regarding current developments in noninvasive animal health care. Disseminates information; conducts and promotes research. Operates speakers' bureau. **Publications:** *Options Newsletter*, bimonthly. Newsletter.

★ 13102 ★ Orthopedic Foundation for Animals (OFA)
2300 Nifong Blvd.
Columbia, MO 65201
Phone: (314)442-0418
Dr. E. A. Corley, Project Dir.

Founded: 1967. **Description:** National and local dog clubs and individual breeders. Acts as a clearinghouse for information on orthopedic diseases of animals, particularly hip dysplasia in dogs (a hereditary condition resulting in abnormal development of the hip joints). Is attempting to develop a national control program through monitoring animals and conducting selective breeding and research. Conducts educational seminars; compiles statistics; sponsors a national referral service for animal breeders. Maintains library of all breed canine pelvic radiographs. **Publications:** *Proceedings of Canine Hip Dysplasia Symposium and Workshop.*

★ 13103 ★ Pan American Association of Veterinary Sciences
(Asociacion Panamericana de Sciencas Veterinarias)
Apartado 55
Cornado
San Jose, Costa Rica
Phone: 2290222
Fax: 2294741
Dr. Hector Campos, Exec.Dir.

Description: Promotes the study of veterinary science in Central America. Interested in developing advanced research programs.

★ 13104 ★ Phi Zeta
c/o Dr. Robert McClure
University of Missouri
Department of Veterinary Biomedical Sciences
W150 Veterinary Medicine Bldg.
Columbia, MO 65211
Phone: (314)882-7228
Fax: (314)882-2950
Robert McClure, Sec.-Treas.

Founded: 1925. **Local Groups:** 27. **Description:** Honor society for veterinary medicine.

★ 13105 ★ Polish Society of Veterinary Science (PSVS)
(Polskie Towarzystwo Nauk Weterynaryjnych)
ulica Grochowska 272
PL-03-849 Warsaw, Poland
Phone: 22 103397
Fax: 22 107889
Prof. Edmund Prost, Pres.

Founded: 1952. **Members:** 2,400. **National Groups:** 12. **Regional Groups:** 17. **Languages:** English, Polish. **Description:** Veterinarians in Poland. Promotes excellence in veterinary medicine. Maintains museum. **Publications:** *Medycyna Weterynaryjna*, monthly. Journal. Also publishes periodic congress and conference materials of divisions.

Registry of Comparative Pathology (RCP)
See: Entry 10137

★ 13106 ★ Royal Netherlands Veterinary Association (RNVA)
(Koninklijke Nederlandse Maatschappij voor Diergeneeskunde — KNMD)
Julianalaan 8-10
Postbus 14031
NL-3508 SB Utrecht, Netherlands
Phone: 30 510111
Fax: 30 511787
Dr. T. Jorna, Sec.Gen.

Founded: 1862. **Members:** 4,500. **National Groups:** 10. **Regional Groups:** 10. **Local Groups:** 27. **Languages:** Dutch, English. **Description:** Veterinary surgeons in the Netherlands. Promotes veterinary science; protects the interests of members. Compiles statistics. **Publications:** *Annual Yearbook.* • *Tijdschrift voor Diergeneeskunde*, semimonthly. • *Veehouder en Dierenarts*, quarterly. • *Veterinary Quarterly.* Journal. Includes veterinary research results and studies and case reports.

★ 13107 ★ Society of Laboratory Animal Science (GV-SOLAS)
(Gesellschaft fur Versuchstierkunde — GV-SOLAS)
BRL Ltd.
Wolferstrasse 4
CH-4414 Fullinsdorf, Switzerland
Phone: 61 9014242
Fax: 61 9017604
Dr. U. Marki, Exec. Officer

Founded: 1964. **Members:** 500. **Languages:** English, German. **Description:** Biologists, physicians, veterinarians, zoologists, and other laboratory animal scientists. Purposes are to promote education in laboratory animal science and to foster improvements in the care of laboratory animals. Commissions research projects and organizes lectures. Awards the title of Expert for Laboratory Animal Science. Sponsors competitions and bestows awards for publications on laboratory animal themes. **Publications:** *Laboratory Animals*, quarterly. • *Membership List*, periodic. Also publishes handbooks, guidelines, and recommendations.

★ 13108 ★ Society for Theriogenology (ST)
PO Box 2118
Hastings, NE 68902
Phone: (402)463-0392
Fax: (402)463-5683
Don Ellerbee, Exec.Dir.

Founded: 1954. **Members:** 2,508. **Description:** Veterinarians united to promote the practice of qualified veterinarians examining animals for breeding soundness; to facilitate these procedures by standardization of the criteria used by veterinarians; to assemble and evaluate the measurements of breeding soundness from literature and from unbiased records accumulated from all sources and distribute this information to all members. (Theriogenology is a branch of veterinary medicine that deals with reproduction, veterinary obstetrics, gynecology, and seminology.) Distributes morphology stain for use in making breeding soundness evaluations and standard forms for use in recording such evaluations. Maintains speakers' bureau. **Publications:** Newsletter, bimonthly. • *Proceedings of Annual Meeting.* **Formerly:** (1975) American Veterinary Society for the Study of Breeding Soundness.

★ 13109 ★ South American Commission for the Control of Foot-and-Mouth Disease (COSALFA)
(Centro Panamericano de Fiebre Aftosa)
Caixa Postal 589
20001-970 Rio de Janeiro, RJ, Brazil
Phone: 21 7713128
Fax: 21 7712387
Dr. Vicente Astudillo, Exec. Officer

Founded: 1973. **Members:** 11. **Languages:** English, Portuguese, Spanish. **Description:** Heads of animal health services in South American countries. Aims to eradicate foot-and-mouth disease in South America; encourages South American countries to form national commissions for the eradication foot-and-mouth disease. Coordinates and evaluates national programs to control foot-and-mouth disease. Operates Epidemiological Surveillance Systems of Animal Vesicular Diseases in the Americas; maintains liaison with the Pan-American Foot-and-Mouth Disease Center. Provides assistance and guidance to research projects; disseminates research information; encourages South American states to form national commissions for the eradication of foot-and-mouth disease; formulates and recommends protective strategies for the international cattle trade; cooperates with and represents members before similar organizations outside the region. Compiles statistics. **Publications:** *Final Report of Meeting*, annual. Proceedings. • *Special Reports*, periodic.

★ 13110 ★ Swedish Veterinary Association (Sveriges Veterinarforbund — SVF)
Box 12709
S-112 94 Stockholm, Sweden
Phone: 8 6542480
Fax: 8 6517082
Herbert Lundstrom, Pres.

Founded: 1860. **Members:** 2,100. **Languages:** English, Swedish. **Description:** Swedish veterinarians. Functions as a trade union and professional organization. Conducts continuing education courses for members. **Publications:** *Svensk Veterinartidning - SVT*, 15/year. Journal.

★ 13111 ★ United States Animal Health Association (USAHA)
PO Box K227
8100 Three Chopt Rd., Ste. 203
Richmond, VA 23288
Phone: (804)285-3210
Fax: (804)285-3367

Founded: 1897. **Members:** 1,350. **Regional Groups:** 4. **Description:** Veterinarians, livestock producers, and transportation and livestock companies concerned with the improvement of the health of livestock and poultry through disease control and eradication. Maintains 28 committees including: Animal Disease Surveillance; Animal Welfare; Environmental Residue; Epizootic Attack Plans; Food Safety; Foreign Animal Diseases; Infectious Diseases of Cattle; Infectious Diseases of Horses; Livestock Identification; Parasitic Diseases; Pharmaceutical and Toxicology; Public Health and Environmental Quality; Transmissible Diseases of Poultry; Transmissible Diseases of Swine; Wild and Marine Life Diseases; Zoological Animals. **Publications:** *Foreign Animal Diseases*

Diagnosis and Control. • *Proceedings*, annual. *Price:* $30. **Formerly:** Association of State Sanitary Boards; United States Livestock Sanitary Association.

★ 13112 ★ **Veterinary Cancer Society (VCS)**
c/o Dr. Robert Rosenthal
2816 Monroe Ave.
Rochester, NY 14618
Phone: (716)271-5454
Fax: (716)271-7815
Dr. Robert Rosenthal, Corr.Sec.

Founded: 1974. **Members:** 500. **Description:** Veterinarians and others who have an interest in cancer in animals. Goals are to: achieve and maintain high standards of diagnosis, treatment, and prevention of animal cancers; advance interdisciplinary research in neoplastic diseases of animals; collect and disseminate information about animal tumors; conduct and evaluate studies, including cooperative clinical trials, of animal neoplasms. **Publications:** Directory, periodic. • Newsletter, quarterly.

★ 13113 ★ **Veterinary Orthopaedic Society (VOS)**
PO Box 9491
Salt Lake City, UT 84109-0491
Phone: (801)484-8912
Nancy Bunker, Exec.Sec.

Founded: 1972. **Members:** 600. **Description:** Veterinarians interested in orthopedic surgery. Promotes education and research in veterinary orthopedic surgery. Provides a forum for the exchange of ideas among veterinarians in academia, research, and practice. **Publications:** *Membership List*, periodic. • *VOS Newsletter*, annual. Newsletter. *Price:* Included in membership dues.

★ 13114 ★ **Western Veterinary Conference (WVC)**
2425 E. Oquendo Rd.
Las Vegas, NV 89120
Phone: (702)739-6698
Kenneth Weide, D.V.M., Exec.Dir.

Founded: 1928. **Members:** 4,100. **Description:** International veterinarians attending annual conference. Provides practical continuing education for veterinarians and technicians. Topics of study at conference include small and large animal medicine and surgery, general medicine, emergency clinic operation, radiographic and clinical pathologic methods, and current research. Autotutorial programs are available. **Formerly:** (1986) Intermountain Veterinary Medical Association.

★ 13115 ★ **World Association for the Advancement of Veterinary Parasitology (WAAVP)**
c/o Dr. S. D. Folz
Dept. 9690-190-40
700 Portage Rd.
Kalamazoo, MI 49001
Phone: (616)385-6523
Free: 800-647-4547
Fax: (616)384-2295
Dr. S. D. Folz, Sec.-Treas.

Founded: 1963. **Members:** 560. **Description:** Veterinarians and other scientists in 60 coun-

tries interested in veterinary parasitology. Objectives are to encourage research in veterinary parasitology, to promote the exchange of information and material between organizations and individuals, and to organize meetings for the study of parasites of veterinary importance. Maintains scientific committees; bestows award. **Publications:** Membership Directory, annual. • Newsletter, annual. • *Proceedings of Scientific Conferences*, biennial. • *Statutes - List of Members*, biennial. **Also Known As:** Association Mondiale pour l'Advancement de Parasitologie Veterinaire.

★ 13116 ★ **World Association for Buiatrics (WAB)**
(Welt-Gesellschaft fur Buiatrik)
Saint Tilman, bte. B42
B-4000 Liege, Belgium
Phone: 41 564030
Fax: 41 562935
Prof. P. Lekeux, Sec.Gen.

Founded: 1962. **Members:** 10,000. **Languages:** English, French, German, Spanish. **Description:** Veterinarians, practitioners, and scientists working with cattle in 48 countries. Seeks to study the diseases of cattle, including diagnosis, treatment, and prevention, and factors influencing cattle production. **Publications:** *Congress Reports*, biennial. • Newsletter, quarterly.

★ 13117 ★ **World Association of Veterinary Anatomists (WAVA)**
Department of Veterinary Anatomy
Purdue University
West Lafayette, IN 47907
Phone: (317)494-7882
Melvin W. Stromberg, D.V.M., Sec.Gen.

Founded: 1957. **Members:** 350. **Regional Groups:** 8. **Description:** Veterinarians and other professionals teaching and researching at veterinary institutions. Promotes the study and teaching of domestic animal anatomy. Seeks to establish a uniform nomenclature. Maintains International Committee on Veterinary Anatomical Nomenclature. **Publications:** *Anatomia, Histologia, Embryologia (Zentralblatt for Veterinarmedizin, Section C)*, quarterly. Journal. • *Nomina Anatomica Veterinaria - Nomina Histologica*. Book. • *WAVA-News*, annual.

★ 13118 ★ **World Association of Veterinary Food Hygienists (WAVFH)**
(Asociacion Mundial de Veterinarios Higienistas de los Alimentos — AMVHA)
Diedersdorferweg 1
12277 Berlin, Germany
Phone: 30 72362101
Fax: 30 72362951
Dr. P. Teufel, Sec.-Treas.

Founded: 1956. **Languages:** English, French, German. **Description:** National veterinary societies in 37 countries. Facilitates international exchange of research results that involve food microbiology, food hygiene, food-related zoonotic diseases, and environmental pollution affecting either animal or human food. Organizes roundtables and meetings. **Publications:** *Symposia Proceedings*, quadrennial. Proceedings of the 11th International Symposium of the WAVFA, Bangkok 1993. Also publishes conference reports.

★ 13119 ★ **World Association of Veterinary Laboratory Diagnosticians (WAVLD)**
Texas Veterinary Medical Diagnosticians Laboratory
PO Drawer 3040
College Station, TX 77841
Phone: (409)845-9000
Fax: (409)845-1794
A. K. Eugster, Sec.Treas.

Founded: 1977. **Members:** 650. **National Groups:** 5. **Description:** Individuals in 30 countries engaged in laboratory diagnosis of animal diseases. Coordinates activities of regulatory, research, and service laboratories. Maintains guidelines for personnel qualifications and facility standards. Establishes uniform laboratory methods and seeks to improve and develop existing diagnostic techniques. Disseminates information; maintains speakers' bureau. **Publications:** *Symposium Proceedings*, triennial. Proceedings.

★ 13120 ★ **World Association of Veterinary Microbiologists, Immunologists, and Specialists in Infectious Diseases (WAVMI)**
(Association Mondiale des Veterinaires Microbiologistes, Immunologistes et Specialistes des Maladies Infectieuses — AMVMI)
7, ave. du General de Gaulle
F-94704 Maisons-Alfort Cedex, France
Phone: 1 43689882
Fax: 1 48931920
Charles Pilet, Pres.

Founded: 1968. **Languages:** English, French. **Description:** Facilitates international exchange among veterinary microbiologists, immunologists, and specialists in infectious diseases. Sponsors international course in animal immunology; conducts symposia. **Publications:** *Comparative Immunology, Microbiology and Infectious Diseases*, quarterly.

★ 13121 ★ **World Veterinary Association (WVA)**
(Welt-Tierarztegesellschaft)
Rosenlunds Alle 8
DK-2720 Vanlose, Denmark
Phone: 38710888
Fax: 38710322
Dr. Lars Holsaae, Contact

Founded: 1959. **Members:** 96. **Languages:** English, French, German, Spanish. **Description:** Association of national (70), international (20), and commercial (4) organizations. Purposes are to: unify and promote the veterinary profession; encourages high standards of health and welfare in all species of animals; improve veterinary science through the exchange of information and education; establish uniform nomenclature. Sends volunteers to developing countries to assist in food production, processing and distribution, to teach basic techniques in disease control and eradication and to develop national veterinary services. **Publications:** Bulletin, semiannual. • Membership Directory, annual. • *Report on Resolutions*, periodic. • *World Veterinary Directory*, periodic. Directory.

★13122★ World Veterinary Poultry Association (WVPA)
(Asociacion Mundial Veterinaria de Avicola — AMVA)
Justus-Liebig-Universitat Giessen
Frankfurter Str. 87
35392 Giessen, Germany
Phone: 641 7024865
Fax: 641 201548
Prof. E.F. Kaleta, Sec.-Treas.

Founded: 1959. **Members:** 1,350. **National Groups:** 24. **Languages:** English, French, German. **Description:** Veterinarians and other scientists in 47 countries engaged in practice, research, or education connected with avian pathology. Objectives are to: organize meetings for studying diseases and conditions; encourage research; promote the exchange of information and material for study between individuals and organizations; establish and maintain liaisons with other groups. Organizes avian medicine sections of the World Veterinary Congresses. **Publications:** *Aerosols*, annual. Newsletter. • *Avian Pathology*, quarterly. Journal.

★13123★ Zimbabwe Veterinary Association (ZVA)
PO Box CY 168
Causeway
Harare, Zimbabwe
Dr. J. Nyika, Pres.

Founded: 1920. **Members:** 180. **Local Groups:** 1. **Languages:** English. **Description:** Veterinarians practicing in Zimbabwe. Encourages contact and information exchange among members. Conducts clinical meetings and seminars. **Publications:** *Zimbabwe Veterinary Journal*, quarterly. Journal. • *ZVA Newsletter*, quarterly. Newsletter. **Formerly:** (1980) Rhodesian Veterinary Association.

Research Centers

★13124★ Agriculture and Agri-Food Canada
Animal Diseases Research Institute
3851 Fallowfield Rd.
Box 11300, Sta. H
Nepean, ON, Canada K2H 8P9
Phone: (613)998-9320
Fax: (613)941-0891
Dr. Peter Ide, Dir.

Research Activities and Fields: Diseases of livestock, poultry, and wildlife. Develops antibody and organism detection procedures for certain foreign animal diseases (bluetongue, foot and mouth disease, pseudorabies) and indigenous diseases (bovine viral diarrhea, transmissible gastroenteritis of pigs, bovine immunodeficiency-like virus, avian leukosis, avian reticuloendotheliosis, Marek's disease, brucellosis, bovine tuberculosis, and rabies); disease transmission potential of in vitro fertilized embryos; detection and control of pathogens in semen; procedures to prevent carrier states/rapid tests for food-borne pathogens; and vaccination to control wildlife rabies. Provides diag-

nostic and consultative services, evaluates commercial veterinary biologics and produces biological reagents for Canada's Animal Health and Food Safety Programs. **E-mail Address:** idep@em.agr.ca.

★13125★ Agriculture and Agri-Food Canada
Health of Animals Laboratory
4 College St.
Sackville, NB, Canada E0A 3C0
Phone: (506)536-0135
Fax: (506)536-1801
Dr. R.G. Stevenson, Dir.

Research Activities and Fields: In vitro systems for the study of the pathogenic mechanisms of Listeria monocytogenes; comparison of clinical, environmental, and food isolates of Listeria monocytogenes; development of serological tests for the diagnosis of maedi-visna in sheep and caprine arthritis-encephalitis; prevalence of aeromonas in meat; and virulence attributes of aeromonas. **Formerly:** Animal Pathology Laboratory (Sackville).

★13126★ Agriculture and Agri-Food Canada
Health of Animals Laboratory
110 Stone Rd. W.
Guelph, ON, Canada N1G 3W4
Phone: (519)822-3300
Fax: (519)822-2280
Dr. R.C. Clarke, Dir.

Research Activities and Fields: Nature, diagnosis, and prevention of animal diseases and food safety, including meat bacteriology and diseases transmitted in food. Conducts bacteriological examinations of fresh and processed food products and uses immunological methods to verify species of origin. Tests and develops methods to reduce time needed to determine the presence of significant bacteria and adulterated substances in foods and investigates the mechanisms by which intestinal infections establish themselves, including the pathogenic mechanisms that play a role in bovine and avian salmonellosis. Studies focus on reducing the incidence of diseases, developing new methods to detect them, and epidemiological investigations. **E-mail Address:** clarker@em.agr.ca. **Formerly:** Animal Pathology Laboratory (Guelph).

★13127★ Auburn University
Scott-Ritchey Research Center
College of Veterinary Medicine
Auburn, AL 36849
Phone: (334)844-5573
Fax: (334)844-5850
Dr. Henry Baker, Dir.

Research Activities and Fields: Molecular medicine, companion animal nutrition, cardiopulmonary diseases, neuromuscular diseases, and surgical research. **Publications:** Annual Progress Report. **E-mail Address:** bakerhj@vetmed.auburn.edu.

★13128★ Colorado State University
Animal Reproduction and Biotechnology Laboratory
College of Veterinary Medicine
Fort Collins, CO 80523
Phone: (303)491-5621
Fax: (303)491-7569
G.D. Niswender, Dir.

Research Activities and Fields: Applications of biotechnology, genetic engineering, molecular biology, and reproductive biology to improvement of reproductive efficiency in cattle, horses, sheep, and other domestic animals. Specific areas include clinical andrology, cryopreservation of bovine and equine embryos, microsurgical procedures with embryos, in vitro fertilization, embryo sexing, microinjection of sperm or genetic information into oocytes, production of transgenic animals, hastening puberty in bull calves, neuroendocrine control of puberty in bulls, mechanisms controlling the function and secretions of epididymal cells, improved procedures for evaluating spermatozoal quality, procedures for cryopreservation of stallion semen, neuroendocrine control of ovulation in mares, role of nutrition in horse reproduction, nonsurgical transfer of equine embryos, viral diseases of embryos, integrated reproductive management of cattle, reducing the problem of postpartum anestrus, control of corpus lutem function, mechanisms regulating secretion of GnRH and LH, cyclic changes in the oviductal epithelium, and mechanism of action of peptide, protein, and steroid hormones. **Formerly:** Animal Reproduction Laboratory.

★13129★ Cornell University
Bovine Research Center
Ithaca, NY 14853
Phone: (607)253-3081
Fax: (607)253-3055
Robert O. Gilbert, M. Med. Vet., Dir.

Research Activities and Fields: Diseases of the bovine species, including diseases of the respiratory and digestive systems, mastitis, and metabolic and reproductive disorders. Also conducts studies on management and husbandry practices to maximize efficiency of production of beef and dairy cattle. **E-mail Address:** rog1@cornell.edu. **Formerly:** Bovine Health Research Center.

★13130★ Cornell University
Cornell Feline Health Center
College of Veterinary Medicine
Ithaca, NY 14853
Phone: (607)253-3414
Fax: (607)253-3419
Dr. Fred W. Scott, Dir.

Research Activities and Fields: Basic and clinical research on diseases of domestic and non-domestic cats, designed to help prevent or cure cat diseases and to aid veterinarians when new or unknown diseases occur. Performs multidisciplinary studies on antiviral substances (including interferon); cardiovascular, respiratory, urinary tract, reproductive, nutritional, neurological, fungal, and hormonal diseases; infectious peritonitis; leukemia; panleukopenia (enteritis); feline immunodeficiency virus; and vaccines. **Publications:** *Feline Information Bulletin* (periodically); *Feline Health Topics* (quarterly, for veterinarians); *Perspectives on Cats* (quarterly, for cat fanciers and breeders). **Formerly:** Cornell Feline Research Laboratory (1980).

★ 13131 ★ **Cornell University**
Diagnostic Laboratory
College of Veterinary Medicine
PO Box 5786
Ithaca, NY 14852-5786
Phone: (607)253-3900
Fax: (607)253-3943
Dr. Donald Lein, Dir.

Research Activities and Fields: Animal health, including virology, toxicology, serology, parasitology, pathology, clinical pathology, bacteriology, epidemiology, and endocrinology. Special facilities and programs include mastitis service and research program, equine and porcine extension program, surveillance research and evaluation programs for blue tongue, bovine leukosis and Johne's disease.

★ 13132 ★ **Cornell University**
Equine Research Park
1 Blue Grass Ln.
Ithaca, NY 14850
Phone: (607)255-7753
Fax: (607)253-3055
Carol Collyr, Dir.

Research Activities and Fields: Horse research, including studies on bone and joint diseases, drug trials, growth trials, reproduction studies, and experiments on surgical procedures.

★ 13133 ★ **Cornell University**
J.A. Baker Institute for Animal Health
Ithaca, NY 14853
Phone: (607)256-5600
Fax: (607)256-5608
Dr. Douglas F. Antczak, Dir.

Research Activities and Fields: Host-response, designed to prevent loss from infectious diseases in animals, especially dogs and horses, including basic studies on organisms which cause disease, osteoarthritis, basic studies of the immune response to viruses, and bacteria parasites. Seeks to increase knowledge concerning the nature of infectious animal diseases and the means and control of their spread. **Publications:** Annual Report. **Formerly:** Veterinary Virus Research Institute (1975).

★ 13134 ★ **Cornell University**
P. Philip Levine Laboratory
College of Veterinary Medicine
Dept. of Avian & Aquatic Animal Medicine
Schurman Hall
Ithaca, NY 14850
Phone: (607)253-3365
Fax: (607)253-3369
Dr. B.W. Calnek, Chm.

Research Activities and Fields: Chickens, including studies on Marek's disease and infectious bronchitis, other avian species, and fish. Holds patents for two vaccines for Marek's disease.

★ 13135 ★ **Equine Research Centre**
Univ. of Guelph
Guelph, ON, Canada N1G 2W1
Phone: (519)837-0061
Fax: (519)767-1081
Dr. Andrew F. Clarke, Dir.

Research Activities and Fields: Equine respiratory problems affecting exercise, racing performance, and quality of life; early embryonic losses and equine infertility; nutritional, growth, and developmental disorders affecting young horses; exercise physiology and equine biomechanics; and specific preliminary field studies to identify new and emerging equine problems. Emphasis is on naturally occurring equine problems and minimally invasive research techniques. **Publications:** Newsletter (three per year). **E-mail Address:** kcounsel@uoguelph.ca. **Formerly:** Guelph Centre for Equine Research.

★ 13136 ★ **Harvard University**
New England Regional Primate Research Center
1 Pine Hill Dr.
PO Box 9102
Southborough, MA 01772-9102
Phone: (508)624-8002
Fax: (508)460-0612
Dr. Ronald D. Hunt, Dir.

Research Activities and Fields: Conducts biomedical research using simian primates as test animals and also conducts individual studies of diseases of simian primates, including clinical and comparative pathology, behavioral biology, immunology, molecular virology, microbiology, viral oncology, nutrition, cardiovascular physiology, and primatology.

★ 13137 ★ **Iowa State University of Science and Technology**
Center for Immunity Enhancement in Domestic Animals (CIEDA)
College of Veterinary Medicine
MIPM Dept.
Ames, IA 50011-1250
Phone: (515)294-8459
Fax: (515)294-8500
Dr. James A. Roth, Professor in Charge

Research Activities and Fields: Infectious diseases of domestic animals and immunity enhancement. Seeks to increase communication and collaboration among animal health specialists, industry, and the U.S. Department of Agriculture. **Publications:** *CIEDA Science Review* (semiannually). **E-mail Address:** jgalyon@iastate.edu.

★ 13138 ★ **Iowa State University of Science and Technology**
Veterinary Diagnostic Laboratory
Ames, IA 50011
Phone: (515)294-1950
Dr. John J.A. Andrews, Int.Hd.

Research Activities and Fields: Infectious diseases of animals, veterinary chemistry, and toxicology. Characterizes infectious diseases as well as chemical toxicants by means of pathology, bacteriology, virology, seriology, chemistry, and toxicology studies. Serves as a reference laboratory for veterinary diagnostic procedures. **Formerly:** Veterinary Medical Diagnostic Laboratory.

★ 13139 ★ **Iowa State University of Science and Technology**
Veterinary Medical Research Institute
Ames, IA 50011
Phone: (515)294-7644
Fax: (515)294-1401
Prem S. Paul, Assoc.Dir.

Research Activities and Fields: Infectious and selected zoonotic diseases of importance to the livestock industry, emphasizing etiology, pathogenesis, disease control, molecular pathogenesis, and endocrine and reproductive physiology of domesticated animals.

★ 13140 ★ **Iowa State University of Science and Technology**
Veterinary Medicine Clinical Microbiology Laboratory
1471 Veterinary Medicine Bldg.
Ames, IA 50011
Phone: (515)294-9411
Fax: (515)294-4990
Joanne Kinyon, Codirector

Research Activities and Fields: Enteric diseases of animals.

★ 13141 ★ **Johns Hopkins University**
Center for Alternatives to Animal Testing
School of Public Health
111 Marketplace, Ste. 840
Baltimore, MD 21202-6709
Phone: (410)223-1693
Fax: (410)223-1603
Dr. Alan M. Goldberg, Dir.

Research Activities and Fields: Fosters development of scientifically acceptable in vitro and other alternatives to animal testing for use in development and safety evaluation of commercial and therapeutic products. Catalyzes validation of alternative methods. **Publications:** Newsletter (a national and international resource for alternative test methodology and development); *Alternative Methods in Toxicology* (book series); Technical Report Series. **E-mail Address:** caat@jhuhyg.sph.jhu.edu.

★ 13142 ★ **Kansas State University**
Veterinary Diagnostic Laboratory
College of Veterinary Medicine
Veterinary Clinical Science Bldg.
1800 Denison
Manhattan, KS 66506
Phone: (913)532-5650
Fax: (913)532-4481
Dr. M.W. Vorhies, Dir.

Research Activities and Fields: Infectious diseases.

★ 13143 ★ **Louisiana Animal Breeders Cooperative**
Louisiana State Univ.
2288 Gourrier
Baton Rouge, LA 70820
Phone: (504)388-3293
Fax: (504)388-3235
Dr. Arnold Baham, Mgr.

Research Activities and Fields: Animal health, especially bovine semen physiology.

★ 13144 ★ Louisiana State University
Mastitis Research Laboratory
Rte. 1, Box 10
Homer, LA 71040
Phone: (318)927-9654
Fax: (318)927-4139
Stephen C. Nickerson, Dir.

Research Activities and Fields: Bovine mastitis, focusing on pathology and epidemiology studies. Develops control measures based on vaccine formulations and management techniques.

★ 13145 ★ Mannheimer Foundation, Inc.
20255 SW 360th St.
Homestead, FL 33034
Phone: (305)245-1551
Fax: (305)245-7650
Dr. Joseph L. Wagner, Contact

Research Activities and Fields: Produces non-human primates for behavioral, reproductive, and developmental experiments. Studies animal models for their applications to both animal and human health and disease, especially in the areas of pharmacokinetics, spinal surgery, diabetes, bone and renal physiology, and reproductive physiology and biology. Performs contract testing of biological products for industry.

★ 13146 ★ The Marine Mammal Center
Marin Headlands
Golden Gate National Recreation Area
Sausalito, CA 94965
Phone: (415)289-7325
Peigin Barrett, Exec.Dir.

Research Activities and Fields: Rescues, rehabilitates (and eventually returns to the oceans) sick, injured, or distressed marine mammals (seals, sea otters, sea lions, dolphins, porpoises, and whales) that strand along the northern California coastline. Data from the Center's treatment files serves as a basis for investigations of marine mammal diseases, medicine, immunology, and aspects of population biology that relate to marine mammal rehabilitation, surgery. **Publications:** *The Release* (quarterly newsletter). **E-mail Address:** tmmc@aol.com. **Formerly:** California Marine Mammal Center (1991).

★ 13147 ★ Michigan State University
Animal Health Diagnostic Laboratory
PO Box 30076
Lansing, MI 48909-7576
Phone: (517)353-1683
Fax: (517)353-5096
Dr. Willie M. Reed, Dir.

Research Activities and Fields: Applied research and problem solving in etiology and pathogenesis of infectious and toxicologic animal diseases. The following sections make up the Laboratory: endocrinology, epidemiology, microbiology, nutrition, parasitology, pathology, and toxicology. **E-mail Address:** reed@ahdlnw.cvm.msu.edu. **Formerly:** Pathology Diagnostic Laboratory.

★ 13148 ★ Montana State University-
Bozeman
Veterinary Molecular Biology Laboratory
Bozeman, MT 59717
Phone: (406)994-4705
Fax: (406)994-4303
Dr. C. A. Speer, Professor and Head

Research Activities and Fields: Animal diseases, including studies in parasitology, clinical pathology, molecular virology, genetic engineering, recombinant DNA, immunology, electron microscopy, bacteriology, and biochemistry, with emphasis on diseases of cattle. **Formerly:** Veterinary Research Laboratory (1990).

★ 13149 ★ New Hampshire Veterinary
Diagnostic Laboratory
Univ. of New Hampshire
Kendall Hall
129 Main St.
Durham, NH 03824
Phone: (603)862-2726
Fax: (603)862-0179
Dr. Joseph J. Moore, Dir.

Research Activities and Fields: Provides support for investigations in gross and histologic pathology, microbiology, and parasitology. Also studies avian diseases, particularly infectious diseases of poultry and captive waterfowl.

★ 13150 ★ New Mexico State University
Clayton Livestock Research Center
Rte. 1, Box 109
Clayton, NM 88415
Phone: (505)374-2566
Fax: (505)374-2568
Dr. Michael Galyean, Supt.

Research Activities and Fields: Studies of stocker and feeder cattle, including problems and diseases associated with the stress of weaning, gathering, and marketing livestock, especially bovine respiratory disease complex, sometimes known as shipping fever. Associated programs study management and nutritional requirements of cattle and cattle grazing on wheat pastures.

★ 13151 ★ New York University
Laboratory for Experimental Medicine and
Surgery in Primates
550 1st Ave.
New York, NY 10016
Phone: (212)263-6626
Fax: (212)213-2654
J. Moor-Jankowski, M.D., Dir.

Research Activities and Fields: Medical primatology, including drug testing, hepatitis, and AIDS and other infectious disease studies in chimpanzees and other primates. Provides research, educational facilities, and collaboration for academic investigators and industry. Serves as World Health Organization Collaborating Centre for Hematology of Primate Animals. Trains professionals. **Publications:** *Primates in Medicine* Monograph Series; *Journal of Medical Primatology.*

★ 13152 ★ North Dakota State University
North Dakota Agricultural Experiment
Station
Box 5435, State Univ. Sta.
Fargo, ND 58105
Phone: (701)237-7654
Fax: (701)237-8520
Dr. Robert L. Todd, Dir.

Research Activities and Fields: Plant sciences, animal and range sciences, biochemistry, biotechnology of plants and animals, botany, cereal science, food science, entomology, microbiology, plant pathology, soil science, veterinary medicine, and agricultural economics, education, and engineering. **Publications:** *North Dakota Farm Research* (bimonthly). **E-mail Address:** r.todd@badlands.nodak.edu.

★ 13153 ★ North Dakota State University
Veterinary Diagnostic Laboratory
Dept. of Veterinary and Microbiological
Sciences
Van Es Hall
Fargo, ND 58105
Phone: (701)231-8307
Fax: (701)231-7514
Dr. Smith, Dir.

Research Activities and Fields: Immunology, virology, toxicology, microbiology, pathogenic mechanisms, and parasitology. **Publications:** Annual Report. **E-mail Address:** hsmith@plains.nodak.edu.

★ 13154 ★ Ohio State University
Analytical Toxicology Laboratory
OSU Veterinary Hospital
601 Vernon Tharp St.
Columbus, OH 43210
Phone: (614)292-5970
Fax: (614)292-4299
Dr. Richard Sams, Dir.

Research Activities and Fields: Concentrates on developing methodology for detection of drugs and quantitation of drug concentrations in biological samples, pharmacokinetics, and drug metabolism. Analyzes samples from race horses to detect illegally administered drugs. **Formerly:** Ohio Racing Commission Laboratory (1991).

★ 13155 ★ Ohio State University
Animal Genetics Laboratory
144 Plumb Hall
2027 Coffey Rd.
Columbus, OH 43210
Phone: (614)292-6659
Fax: (614)292-7116
Dr. H.C. Hines, Dir.

Research Activities and Fields: Bovine lymphocyte antigens, bovine blood group antigens, and molecular genetics. **E-mail Address:** hhines@magnus.acs.ohio-state.edu. **Formerly:** Immunogenetics Laboratory.

★ 13156 ★ Ohio State University
Herd Milk Quality Laboratory
239 Sisson Hall
1900 Coffey Rd.
Columbus, OH 43210
Phone: (614)292-9453
Fax: (614)292-4142
Dr. Kent Hoblet, Dir.

Research Activities and Fields: Bacteriologic identification and susceptibility testing of pathogens in individual cow or bulk tank samples. Staff projects include identification of pathogens, evaluation of new mastitis prophylactic and therapeutic agents, evaluation of environmental mastitis control procedures, and mastitis epidemiologic research in cattle and sheep. **Formerly:** Bovine Mastitis Control Laboratory.

Ohio University
Edison Biotechnology Institute (EBI)
See: Entry 2724

★ 13157 ★ Oklahoma State University
Oklahoma Agricultural Experiment Station
Stillwater, OK 74078-0500
Phone: (405)744-5398
Fax: (405)744-5339
Dr. Charles B. Browning, Dir.

Research Activities and Fields: Agriculture and related industry, including agricultural economics, biosystems and agricultural engineering, agronomy, animal science, biochemistry, molecular biology, soil science, dairy science, entomology, forestry, horticulture, plant pathology, poultry science, veterinary medicine, and biotechnology. **E-mail Address:** okdivag@osucc.bitnet.

★ 13158 ★ Oklahoma State University
Oklahoma Animal Disease Diagnostic
   Laboratory
Stillwater, OK 74078
Phone: (405)744-6623
Fax: (405)744-8612
Dr. W.C. Edwards, Dir.

Research Activities and Fields: Test procedures for common animal diseases and emerging diseases with the potential for catastrophic losses, including malignant catarrhal fever, parvovirus disease, and toxicoses related to oilfield wastes and agricultural chemicals.

★ 13159 ★ Oklahoma State University
Oklahoma Center for Equine Research
308 Veterinary Medicine
Stillwater, OK 74078
Phone: (405)744-6728
Fax: (405)744-6633
Dr. Richard Eberle, Assoc. Dean, Research

Research Activities and Fields: Veterinary medicine, including studies of orthopedic surgery, electrophysiology of bone growth, cartilage metabolism and healing, degenerative joint disease pathophysiology, diagnostic nuclear medical imaging in equine musculoskeletal disorders, physical therapy modalities and rehabilitation in equine sports medicine, and equine exercise physiology. Also conducts research on bovine pneumonic pasteurellosis, anaplasmosis, reproductive biology, interval training of equine athletes, heart rate monitors, and instrumentation techniques.

★ 13160 ★ Oklahoma State University
Veterinary Research
308 College of Veterinary Medicine
Stillwater, OK 74078
Phone: (405)744-6663
Fax: (405)744-6633
Richard W. Eberle, Assoc. Dean

Research Activities and Fields: Diseases of domestic animals and biomedical sciences. Conducts studies on ostriches and broilers.

★ 13161 ★ Oregon Regional Primate
   Research Center
505 NW 185th Ave.
Beaverton, OR 97006
Phone: (503)645-1141
Fax: (503)690-5532
Dr. Vaughn Critchlow, Dir.

Research Activities and Fields: Seeks to advance biomedical knowledge through basic research with nonhuman primates, including studies on reproductive biology, neuroscience, and experimental pathology. Specific projects include studies on the events that control fertility in primates, causes and control of premature labor, mechanisms of steroid action, and factors affecting neural differentiation, function and plasticity. Other projects seek to understand physiological mechanisms involved in atherosclerosis and immune deficiency diseases. Provides research facilities for staff and collaborative scientists.

★ 13162 ★ Oregon State University
Eastern Oregon Agricultural Research
   Center
PO Box E
Union, OR 97883
Phone: (503)562-5129
Fax: (503)562-5348
Tim DelCurdo, Contact

Research Activities and Fields: Agricultural chemistry, agricultural and resource economics, agricultural engineering, agronomic crop science, animal science, botany and plant pathology, entomology, fisheries and wildlife, food science and technology, home economics, horticulture, microbiology, poultry science, soil science, and veterinary medicine. **Publications:** *Progress Reports: Research in Rangeland Management* (annually); *Beef Cattle and Range Resources* (annually); Special Reports (as research is completed).

★ 13163 ★ Pennsylvania State University
Animal Diagnostic Laboratory
Animal Disease Bldg.
Orchard Rd.
University Park, PA 16802
Phone: (814)863-0837
Fax: (814)865-3907
Dr. Anthony Castro, Assoc.Dir.

Research Activities and Fields: Performs diagnostic services for farm animals fish, and wildlife, supplemented by use of research laboratories, other facilities, personnel, and techniques of the Department of Veterinary Science. **Formerly:** Animal Disease Diagnostic Laboratory; Veterinary Diagnostic/Investigation Center.

★ 13164 ★ Pennsylvania State University
Center for Mastitis Research
Dept. of Veterinary Science
101 Henning Bldg.
University Park, PA 16802
Phone: (814)863-2165
Fax: (814)863-6140
Lorraine Sordillo, Dir.

Research Activities and Fields: Research on the microbiology, immunology, and physiology of mastitis in cows. Also tests veterinary pharmaceuticl products used in the prevention and treatment of mastitis. **Publications:** *Center for Mastitis Research Newsletter.* **E-mail Address:** lsordill@psupen.psu.edu.

★ 13165 ★ Pennsylvania State University
E. Coli Reference Center
Dept. of Veterinary Science
105 Henning Bldg.
University Park, PA 16802
Phone: (814)863-2167
Fax: (814)863-6140
Richard A. Wilson, Ph.D., Dir.

Research Activities and Fields: Research and diagnostic services on Escherichia coli (E. coli), and production of O, H, and fimbriae antisera. Research projects include studies on urinary tract infections of humans and animals caused by E. coli, regulation of expression of fimbrial antigens (adherence factors causing pathogens to attach to the gastrointestinal tract), plasmid identification and characterization of E. coli strains, upgrading of K antigen identification techniques, examination of the antibody response to fimbrial vaccines, and analysis of E. coli clonal structure based on electrophoretic types using multilocus enzyme electrophoresis. **E-mail Address:** raw14@psuvm.psu.edu.

★ 13166 ★ Pennsylvania State University
Poultry Disease Research Laboratory
Dept. of Veterinary Science
Wiley Laboratory
University Park, PA 16802
Phone: (814)863-0839
Fax: (814)865-4717
Dr. C. Channa Reddy, Head

Research Activities and Fields: Avian influenza, ascites, immunopathology, leg weakness in chickens, and urolithiasis in layers. **Formerly:** Poultry Disease Diagnostic Laboratory.

★ 13167 ★ Pennsylvania State University
Wiley Laboratory
College of Agric. Sci.
Dept. of Veterinary Science
University Park, PA 16802
Phone: (814)863-4369
Fax: (814)865-4710
Dr. Barrett S. Cowen, Coord.

Research Activities and Fields: Identifies the etiologies of new and emerging avian diseases and develops control measures. Specific projects include AC-ELISA studies of avian influenza, avian ascites syndrome, avian urolithiasis, and comparative IBV pathogenicity and pathogenesis studies.

**★ 13168 ★ Purdue University
Center for Paralysis Research**
Sch. of Veterinary Medicine
1244 VCPR
West Lafayette, IN 47907-1244
Phone: (317)494-7600
Fax: (317)494-7605
Dr. Richard Borgens, Dir.

Research Activities and Fields: Experimental treatments for spinal cord injury, focusing on recruitment of spared pathways in the spinal cord through the use of 4-Aminopyridine (4-AP), reconnection and regeneration of severely damaged nerve pathways through the use of oscillating electrical fields, and replacement of spinal cord using enteric neuron transplantation. **E-mail Address:** hae@vet.vet.purdue.edu.

**★ 13169 ★ Regional Primate Research
Center**
Univ. of Washington
Health Sciences Center, SJ-50
Seattle, WA 98195
Phone: (206)543-1430
Fax: (206)685-0305
William R. Morton, V.M.D., Actg.Dir.

Research Activities and Fields: Central nervous and cardiovascular systems, immunobiology, virology, behavior, reproduction and perinatal studies, development and application of advanced electronic and mechanical instruments, and data acquisition systems for use in primate research. **Publications:** *Current Primate References*; *Primate Supply Information Clearinghouse*. **E-mail Address:** rprc@bart.rprc.washington.edu.

**★ 13170 ★ Rockefeller University
Laboratory Animal Research Center**
1230 York Ave.
Box 2
New York, NY 10021
Phone: (212)327-8535
Fax: (212)327-8536
M.D. Hayre, Dir.

Research Activities and Fields: Disease problems of laboratory animals and in vitro toxicology assessment. **Publications:** *Journal of Experimental Medicine*. **Formerly:** Animal Facility.

**★ 13171 ★ Scientists Center for Animal
Welfare**
7833 Walker Dr., Ste. 340
Greenbelt, MD 20770
Phone: (301)345-3500
Fax: (301)345-3503
Lee Krulisch, Exec.Dir.

Research Activities and Fields: Compiles information and encourages discussion on public accountability, public policy, and the scientist's responsibilities regarding proper standards of animal care and use, particularly in biomedical research, testing, and education. Other areas of interest include agricultural animals and acceptable standards for wildlife research. **Publications:** Newsletter (quarterly); *Field Research Guidelines*; *Laboratory Animal Welfare Bibliography*.

**★ 13172 ★ South Dakota State University
Animal Disease Research and Diagnostic
Laboratory**
Veterinary Science Dept.
Box 2175
Brookings, SD 57007-1396
Phone: (605)688-5171
Fax: (605)688-6003
John U. Thomson, Head Dir.

Research Activities and Fields: Animal diseases, including studies on E. coli and viral enteritis in young calves and pigs, abortion and infertility of cattle and swine, mycotic problems in livestock production, and laboratory assistance in disease diagnosis for practitioners of veterinary medicine. Laboratory procedures encompass three areas: pathology, including necropsy, clinical pathology, electron microscopy, and histopathology; microbiology, including bacteriology, mycology, mycoplasma, ureaplasma, serology, and virology; and toxicology/analytical chemistry, including state meat inspection and diagnostic work with feed, water, and animal specimens. **Publications:** Annual Report; *DVM News* (extension veterinary medicine newsletter). **E-mail Address:** thomsonj@mg.sdstate.edu. **Formerly:** Veterinary Research Laboratory.

**★ 13173 ★ State University of New York
Health Science Center at Brooklyn
Primate Behavior Laboratory**
450 Clarkson Ave., Box 120
Brooklyn, NY 11203
Phone: (718)270-1447
Fax: (718)270-3887
Dr. Leonard A. Rosenblum, Dir.

Research Activities and Fields: Normative and experimental studies of the development of bonnet and pigtail macaques and squirrel monkeys, including the development of mother-infant relations and infant social development, environmental factors and social development, psychosocial factors, nonhuman primate sexual behavior, primate models of psychopathology, and experimental studies of environmental enrichment, learning, and perception with computer-mediated video tasks in individual and group settings.

**★ 13174 ★ Texas A&M University
Center for Tropical Animal Health**
College Station, TX 77843-4467
Phone: (409)845-4275
Fax: (409)862-2344
Dr. G. Gale Wagner, Dir.

Research Activities and Fields: Tropical diseases and conditons of poultry, fish, small ruminants, cattle, and agriculturally important draft animals such as mules and burros. Collaborates with various laboratories and universities in Mexico and Latin America. Studies selected animal and plant health problems important for free trade between the U.S. and Mexico as part of the USAID University Development Linkage Program Agreement. **E-mail Address:** gwagner@vetmed.tamu.edu. **Formerly:** Institute of Tropical Veterinary Medicine (1979).

**★ 13175 ★ Texas A&M University
Poultry Disease Laboratory at Center**
635 Malone Dr.
Center, TX 75935
Phone: (409)598-4451
Dr. T.B. Blount, Jr., In Charge

Research Activities and Fields: Poultry pathology, including identification, treatment, and control of poultry diseases, especially those prevalent in east Texas. **Formerly:** East Texas Poultry Disease Field Laboratory.

**★ 13176 ★ Texas A&M University
Schubot Exotic Bird Health Center**
Dept. of Veterinary Pathobiology
College Station, TX 77843-4467
Phone: (409)845-4177
Fax: (409)845-9231
Dr. David L. Graham, Dir.

Research Activities and Fields: Avian health, with emphasis on pet, exotic, and wild birds, including infectious and noninfectious diseases, avian reproduction, and captive breeding. **Formerly:** Schubot Center for Avian Health.

**Texas A&M University
Texas Agricultural Experiment Station**
See: Entry 9529

**★ 13177 ★ Texas Veterinary Medical
Diagnostic Laboratory at Amarillo**
PO Box 3200
Amarillo, TX 79116
Phone: (806)353-7478
Fax: (806)359-0636
Dr. Robert W. Sprowls, Resident Dir.

Research Activities and Fields: Laboratory diagnoses of animal diseases, including tests in pathology, virology, bacteriology, serology, and toxicology. Seeks to develop better diagnostic techniques.

**★ 13178 ★ Texas Veterinary Medical
Diagnostic Laboratory at College Station**
PO Drawer 3040
College Station, TX 77841-3040
Phone: (409)845-3414
Fax: (409)845-1794
Dr. A. Konrad Eugster, Exec.Dir.

Research Activities and Fields: Laboratory diagnoses of animal diseases, including tests in pathology, virology, bacteriology, serology, and toxicology, in an effort to develop better diagnostic techniques.

**★ 13179 ★ Tufts University
Center for Animals & Public Policy**
School of Veterinary Medicine
200 Westboro Rd.
North Grafton, MA 01536
Phone: (508)839-7991
Fax: (508)839-2953
Andrew Rowan, Contact

Research Activities and Fields: Use of animals in research and testing. Seeks new techniques to reduce animal distress, replace animal use, or reduce the number of animals required for experimentation, and other aspects of animal-assisted therapy and animals in society. **Publications:** *Animal Policy Report* (newsletter); *The Alternatives Report*.

★ 13180 ★ Tulane University
Tulane Regional Primate Research Center
Covington, LA 70433
Phone: (504)892-2040
Fax: (504)893-1352
Dr. Peter J. Gerone, Dir.

Research Activities and Fields: Use of nonhuman primates in biomedical research projects in fields of cancer, immunology, infectious diseases, primate medicine, parasitology, primatology, pathology, reproductive physiology, urology, and veterinary science. **Formerly:** Delta Regional Primate Research Center.

Tuskegee University
George Washington Carver Agricultural Experiment Station
See: Entry 9530

★ 13181 ★ TVMDL Poultry Diagnostic Laboratory
PO Box 84
Gonzales, TX 78629
Phone: (210)672-2834
Dr. S.E. Glass, Dir.

Research Activities and Fields: Poultry pathology. Maintains a diagnostic laboratory for autopsy, culture, and serological testing of poultry. Contributes to poultry disease incidence reports for Texas and for southern states as published by Southern Conference on Avian Diseases. **Formerly:** South Texas Poultry Disease Laboratory; Texas A&M University Poultry Disease Laboratory.

★ 13182 ★ U.S. Department of Agriculture
Agricultural Research Service
Animal Disease Research Unit
Washington State University
Bustad Hall, Rm. 337
Pullman, WA 99164-7030
Phone: (509)335-6029
Fax: (509)335-8328
Dr. John R. Gorham, Research Leader

Research Activities and Fields: Unit conducts basic and applied research on hemoparasitic diseases of domestic animals; the molecular biology of animal herpes viruses; and caprine arthritis encephalitis virus and scrapie. Research involves: 1) molecular biology studies of *Anaplasma* and *Babesia* species; 2) studies of the epidemiology of these hemoparasitic diseases; 3) determination of the nature of the scrapie agent and development of a diagnostic procedure; and 4) studies of the genome of infectious bovine rhinotracheitis and bovine herpes type four to determine genes controlling virulence and persistence in the host.

★ 13183 ★ U.S. Department of Agriculture
Agricultural Research Service
Arthropod-Borne Animal Diseases Research Laboratory
PO Box 3965, University Station
Laramie, WY 82071-3965
Phone: (307)766-3600
Fax: (307)766-3500
Dr. Walter J. Tabachnick, Research Leader

Research Activities and Fields: Laboratory conducts research on arthropod-borne virus diseases of domestic animals, including studies on bluetongue disease in cattle and sheep, with attention given to natural reservoirs of this disease in wild animals such as deer and antelope. Principal disciplines involved in Laboratory's research programs are virology, immunology, entomology, ecology, molecular biology, and serology. **Additional Contact Information:** Laboratory is located in the Agriculture Bldg., 5th Fl., University of Wyoming, Laramie, WY.

★ 13184 ★ U.S. Department of Agriculture
Agricultural Research Service
Avian Disease and Oncology Laboratory
3606 E. Mount Hope Rd.
East Lansing, MI 48823
Phone: (517)337-6828
Fax: (517)337-6776
Dr. Richard L. Witter, Laboratory Director

Research Activities and Fields: Avian viral and neoplastic diseases, including genetics of disease resistance, viral-vectored vaccines, and mapping of the avian genome. Principal fields of study include virology, immunology, genetics, pathology, and biochemistry.

★ 13185 ★ U.S. Department of Agriculture
Agricultural Research Service
Food Animal Protection Research Laboratory
F and B Rd.
Route 5, Box 810
College Station, TX 77845
Phone: (409)260-9372
Fax: (409)260-9377
Dr. G. Wayne Ivie, Director

Research Activities and Fields: Laboratory's mission is to conduct research that leads to improved methods of protecting livestock and poultry from natural and synthetic poisons, from debilitating arthropod pests, and from the *Salmonella* disease organism that can lead to foodborne toxicosis in man. Research efforts are targeted at minimizing the adverse toxicological and economic impact of mycotoxins, pesticides, and other poisons on livestock and poultry production; developing new and/or improved methods for the management of arthropod pests that attack livestock and poultry; and reducing the incidence of *Salmonella* occurrence in live poultry.

★ 13186 ★ U.S. Department of Agriculture
Agricultural Research Service
Food Animal Protection Research Laboratory
Veterinary Entomology Research Unit
F and B Rd.
Rte. 5, Box 810
College Station, TX 77845
Phone: (409)260-9401
Fax: (409)260-9377
Don L. Bull, Research Leader

Research Activities and Fields: Primary mission is to develop improved methods of controlling arthropods that attack livestock. Principal fields of research are: 1) biological control; 2) insect toxicology; and 3) insect physiology.

★ 13187 ★ U.S. Department of Agriculture
Agricultural Research Service
Knipling-Bushland U.S. Livestock Insects Laboratory
PO Box 232
Kerrville, TX 78029-0232
Phone: (512)257-3566
Fax: (512)792-3637
Dr. Sidney E. Kunz, Director

Research Activities and Fields: Laboratory conducts basic and applied research on the biology and control of arthropods affecting livestock. Research on the formulation and use of pesticides for livestock is included. Specific areas of interest include the behavior, biology, and ecology of arthropod livestock pests; cytology and genetics of ticks and insects; host parasite interactions; genetic engineering; immunology; radiation biology; sterile insect control; genetic control; entomopathogens; controlled-release pesticides; population modeling; and pesticide resistance management.

★ 13188 ★ U.S. Department of Agriculture
Agricultural Research Service
Knipling-Bushland U.S. Livestock Insects Laboratory
Cattle Fever Tick Research Laboratory
PO Box 969
Mission, TX 78572
Phone: (512)580-7268
Fax: (512)580-7261
Dr. Ronald B. Davey, Research Entomologist

Research Activities and Fields: Laboratory conducts both field and laboratory research. Principal fields of study include basic tick biology; chemical control of cattle ticks; and tick ecology and behavior.

★ 13189 ★ U.S. Department of Agriculture
Agricultural Research Service
Livestock and Poultry Sciences Institute
Biosystematic Parasitology Laboratory
BARC—East
Bldg. 1180
Beltsville, MD 20705
Phone: (301)504-8444
Fax: (301)504-8279
J.R. Lichtenfels, Research Leader

Research Activities and Fields: Primary mission is to develop new information on the classification, distribution, and identification of parasites of animals, especially those of medical and veterinary importance, by utilizing classical morphology and molecular genetic techniques.

★ 13190 ★ U.S. Department of Agriculture
Agricultural Research Service
Livestock and Poultry Sciences Institute
Helminthic Diseases Laboratory
BARC—East
Bldg. 1040
Beltsville, MD 20705
Phone: (301)504-8195
Fax: (301)504-5306
Dr. Joseph F. Urban, Jr., Research Leader

Research Activities and Fields: Laboratory develops control procedures to reduce or eliminate economic loss and human health risks resulting from parasitic helminthic infections of ruminants, primarily cattle and sheep, and nonruminants, primarily swine. Both basic and applied studies are carried out in parasite biology and host-parasite relationships, with special emphasis on immunological, molecular biological, and biochemical investigations. Results of these studies will guide the development of both biological- and chemical-control strategies, including vaccines, for the integrated control of parasitic helminths.

★ 13191 ★ **U.S. Department of Agriculture**
Agricultural Research Service
Livestock and Poultry Sciences Institute
Livestock Insects Laboratory
BARC—East
Bldg. 307, Rm. 120
Beltsville, MD 20705
Phone: (301)504-8474
Fax: (301)504-9062
Dora K. Hayes, Ph.D., Research Leader

Research Activities and Fields: Primary function is to investigate integrative pest management strategies for the control of muscoid flies that affect livestock, poultry, and humans; of the northern fowl mite; and of the vector of Lyme disease, the deer tick. Basic approaches include insect dormancy and chronobiology, which focuses on rhythms of insect metabolism; and studies of the structure, function, and analogies of fly neurohormones. Applied research is aimed at improving chemical release formulations. For example, studies on the ecology and survival of larval muscoid flies in calf pens lead to new management methodologies for reducing these pest species on farms. Studies on fly vision, attractants, and repellents have resulted in new trap designs that give promise in integrated pest management systems for management of muscoid flies on farms and in other locations such as waste dumps.

★ 13192 ★ **U.S. Department of Agriculture**
Agricultural Research Service
Livestock and Poultry Sciences Institute
Protozoan Diseases Laboratory
BARC—East
Bldg. 1040
Beltsville, MD 20705
Phone: (301)344-2300
Fax: (301)344-4306
Michael D. Ruff, Research Leader

Research Activities and Fields: Primary mission is to develop methods to prevent or reduce losses from protozoan parasites of livestock and poultry, primarily chickens and turkeys. Basic and applied research is carried out on the biology of the parasites, including their life cycle, development, and nutrient requirements; the pathophysiological mechanisms by which these parasites affect the host; and chemical and immunological methods to control parasites, including vaccines.

★ 13193 ★ **U.S. Department of Agriculture**
Agricultural Research Service
Medical and Veterinary Entomology
 Research Laboratory
1600 S W 23rd Dr.
PO Box 14565
Gainesville, FL 32604
Phone: (904)374-5900
Fax: (904)374-5834
Dr. Gary A. Mount, Director

Research Activities and Fields: Laboratory conducts basic and applied research on the biology and control of medical and veterinary in-

sects, ticks, and mites. Major research thrusts include chemical and biological control, bioecology, genetic engineering, and modeling and computer simulation.

★ 13194 ★ **U.S. Department of Agriculture**
Agricultural Research Service
National Animal Disease Center
2300 Dayton Rd.
PO Box 70
Ames, IA 50010
Phone: (515)239-8201
Fax: (515)239-8677
Dr. Harley Moon, Director

Research Activities and Fields: Primary mission is to conduct basic and applied research on the diseases of livestock and poultry of major economic importance to agriculture. This includes studies of approximately 30 diseases or disease complexes affecting cattle, swine, poultry, sheep, and other animals. Research activities are carried out in eight research units: Leptospirosis/Mycobacteriosis Research Unit, Brucellosis Research Unit, Cattle Virology Research Unit, Metabolic Diseases and Immunology Research Unit, Avian Diseases Research Unit, Physiopathology Research Unit, Respiratory Disease Research Unit, and Swine Virology Research Unit. Collaborates with researchers at U.S. universities and with veterinarians in Egypt, India, Pakistan, Spain, Yugoslavia, and Israel.

★ 13195 ★ **U.S. Department of Agriculture**
Agricultural Research Service
National Animal Disease Center
Brucellosis Research Unit
2300 Dayton Ave.
PO Box 70
Ames, IA 50010
Phone: (515)239-8204
Fax: (515)239-8458
Dr. Norman F. Cheville, Research Leader

Research Activities and Fields: Brucellosis and other infectious diseases of domestic animals, including fowl cholera, chlamydial infections, and septicemic infections of birds.

★ 13196 ★ **U.S. Department of Agriculture**
Agricultural Research Service
National Animal Disease Center
Cattle Virology Research Unit
2300 Dayton Ave.
PO Box 70
Ames, IA 50010
Phone: (515)239-8349
Fax: (515)239-8458
Janice M. Miller, D.V.M., Vet. Med. Officer

Research Activities and Fields: Unit is responsible for conducting research on viral diseases of cattle. Principal fields of research are virology, immunology, pathology, and molecular biology.

★ 13197 ★ **U.S. Department of Agriculture**
Agricultural Research Service
National Animal Disease Center
Metabolic Diseases and Immunology
 Research Unit

2300 Dayton Ave.
PO Box 70
Ames, IA 50010
Phone: (515)239-8312
Fax: (515)239-8458
Dr. Ronald L. Horst, Research Leader

Research Activities and Fields: Unit is responsible for conducting basic research on diseases of domestic farm animals. Areas of current interest involve studies of vitamin D, vitamin A, calcium, mastitis, and immunology.

★ 13198 ★ **U.S. Department of Agriculture**
Agricultural Research Service
National Animal Disease Center
Physiopathology Research Unit
2300 Dayton Ave.
PO Box 70
Ames, IA 50010
Phone: (515)239-8200
Fax: (515)239-8458
Dr. Shannon C. Whipp, Research Leader

Research Activities and Fields: Research is directed toward defining pathogenic mechanisms of infectious diseases of domestic animals, the carrier state of food-borne pathogens in domestic animals, and the metabolism of toxic forages by rumen anaerobes. Particular areas of expertise are: 1) anaerobic microbiology; 2) virulence attributes of gastrointestinal pathogens; 3) diarrheagenic mechanisms; and 4) molecular biology.

★ 13199 ★ **U.S. Department of Agriculture**
Agricultural Research Service
National Animal Disease Center
Respiratory Disease Research Unit
2300 Dayton Ave.
PO Box 70
Ames, IA 50010
Phone: (515)239-8000
Fax: (515)239-8458
Dr. Randall C. Cutlip, Research Leader

Research Activities and Fields: Unit conducts research on the cause, pathogenesis, and control of infectious diseases of the respiratory tract of cattle, sheep, and goats. Also conducts research on the transmission and diagnosis of scrapie.

★ 13200 ★ **U.S. Department of Agriculture**
Agricultural Research Service
National Animal Disease Center
Swine Virology Research Unit
2300 Dayton Ave.
PO Box 70
Ames, IA 50010
Phone: (515)239-8254
Fax: (515)239-8458
Dr. William L. Mengeling, Research Leader

Research Activities and Fields: Research is conducted on economically significant diseases of swine caused by viral agents. Studies involve various immunological, biochemical, and biophysical techniques; cell culture systems; and animal inoculations. Basic studies are conducted on virus-cell interactions and host responses using ultracentrifugation, ultrafiltration, molecular biology, monoclonal antibody, fluorescent, and electron microscopy, and radiochemical techniques.

★ 13201 ★ **U.S. Department of Agriculture**
Agricultural Research Service
Plum Island Animal Disease Center
PO Box 848
Greenport, NY 11944-0848
Phone: (516)323-2500
Fax: (516)323-2507
Dr. R.G. Breeze, Director

Research Activities and Fields: Center is a USDA research and diagnostic laboratory for studies in the prevention of animal diseases exotic to the United States. Principal fields of research are: structural biology, virology, microbiology, immunology, pathology, and veterinary medicine as related to animal diseases foreign to the United States.

★ 13202 ★ **U.S. Department of Agriculture**
Agricultural Research Service
Plum Island Animal Disease Center
Microbiology Laboratory
PO Box 848
Greenport, NY 11944-0848
Phone: (516)323-2500
Fax: (516)323-2507
Dr. Dan Rock, Dir.

Research Activities and Fields: African swine fever and foot-and-mouth disease virus, emphasizing control of these diseases and mechanisms of heritable resistance.

★ 13203 ★ **U.S. Department of Agriculture**
Agricultural Research Service
Plum Island Animal Disease Center
Molecular Pathology Laboratory
PO Box 848
Greenport, NY 11944-0848
Phone: (516)323-2500
Fax: (516)323-2507
Dr. W. Laegreid, Contact

Research Activities and Fields: Laboratory provides pathology support to other research units at the Center (including histopathology; light, electron, and immunomicroscopy; and gross necropsy diagnosis); and conducts basic research in: 1) the molecular pathogenesis of the various immuno-inflammatory and agent-specific mechanisms involved in transmission and establishment of disease agents and 2) the development of biochemical, ultrastructural, histological, and morphological lesions of foreign animal diseases.

U.S. Department of Agriculture
Agricultural Research Service
Richard B. Russell Agricultural Research
Center
Toxicology and Mycotoxin Research Unit
See: Entry 10463

★ 13204 ★ **U.S. Department of Agriculture**
Agricultural Research Service
Screwworm Research Laboratory
PO Box 3149
Laredo, TX 78041
Phone: (409)260-9343
Chandler Whitten, Project Leader

Research Activities and Fields: Laboratory's research program includes both field and laboratory activities. Principal fields of research in the laboratory have included genetics, physiolo-

gy, and biochemistry; field studies have been conducted in the areas of ecology and biology. All research is related to screwworms. **Additional Contact Information:** Laboratory is located in Tuxtla Gutierrez, Chiapas, Mexico (phone: 9-011-529-61-33-550). Unit also has a worksite in San Jose, Costa Rica. (The Texas address is for U.S. mailings; location serves only as a support unit for the Mexico and Costa Rica locations.)

★ 13205 ★ **U.S. Department of Agriculture**
Agricultural Research Service
South Central Poultry Research Laboratory
PO Box 5367
Mississippi State, MS 39762
Phone: (601)323-2230
Dr. James D. May, Director

Research Activities and Fields: Laboratory conducts research in poultry husbandry, physiology, chemistry, pathology, bacteriology, blood analysis, and agricultural engineering, with emphasis on the relationship of management and environment to disease. Program includes basic and applied studies on the effects of management and environment on growth, quality, feed utilization, and mortality as well as development and evaluation of methods of growth feed conversion and livability.

★ 13206 ★ **U.S. Department of Agriculture**
Agricultural Research Service
Southeast Poultry Research Laboratory
Poultry Disease Research Unit
934 College Station Rd.
Athens, GA 30605
Phone: (404)546-3432
Fax: (404)546-3161
Dr. Max Brugh, Actg. Lab. Dir.

Research Activities and Fields: Unit conducts research on poultry diseases, including avian influenza, Newcastle disease, and Salmonella. This includes research on: environmental influences on disease responses in chickens; immunology of chickens; and the mechanisms by which genetic selection affects changes.

★ 13207 ★ **U.S. Department of Agriculture**
Animal and Plant Health Inspection Service
National Veterinary Services Laboratories
PO Box 844
Ames, IA 50010
Phone: (515)239-8266
Fax: (515)239-8397
Dr. Joan M. Arnoldi, Dir.

Research Activities and Fields: Comprises seven laboratory units that evaluate veterinary biologics and diagnose animal diseases: 1) Biologics Bacteriology Laboratory; 2) Biologics Virology Laboratory; 3) Diagnostic Bacteriology Laboratory; 4) Diagnostic Virology Laboratory; 5) Foreign Animal Disease Diagnostic Laboratory; 6) Pathobiology Laboratory; and 7) Scientific Services Laboratory.

★ 13208 ★ **U.S. Department of Agriculture**
Conservation and Production Research
Laboratory
Bovine Respiratory Disease Unit

PO Drawer 10
Bushland, TX 79012
Phone: (806)356-5748
Fax: (806)356-5750
Dr. N.A. Cole, Research Leader

Research Activities and Fields: Unit conducts basic and applied research on stress, nutrition, and microbial factors associated with bovine respiratory disease. Principal fields of research interest are microbiology, immunology, stress physiology, and nutrition.

U.S. Department of Defense
Armed Forces Institute of Pathology
Veterinary Pathology Department
Laboratory Animal Medicine Division
See: Entry 10178

U.S. Department of Defense
Armed Forces Institute of Pathology
Veterinary Pathology Department
Veterinary Pathology Division
See: Entry 10179

U.S. Department of Defense
Army Medical Research and Development
  Command
Walter Reed Army Institute of Research
Veterinary Medicine Division
See: Entry 7837

★ 13209 ★ **U.S. Department of Health and**
  Human Services
Food and Drug Administration
Center for Veterinary Medicine
5600 Fishers Ln., Metro Park North 2
Rockville, MD 20857
Phone: (301)295-8740
Fax: (301)295-8830
Gerald B. Guest, DVM, Director

Research Activities and Fields: Center develops and conducts programs on the safety and efficacy of veterinary preparations and devices; evaluates proposed use of veterinary preparations for animal safety and efficacy; and evaluates FDA's surveillance and compliance programs relating to veterinary drugs and other veterinary medical matters.

University of Arizona
Arizona Agricultural Experiment Station
See: Entry 9547

★ 13210 ★ **University of California, Davis**
California Regional Primate Research
  Center
Davis, CA 95616
Phone: (916)752-0447
Fax: (916)752-8201
Dr. Andrew G. Hendrickx, Dir.

Research Activities and Fields: Developmental and reproductive biology, behavioral biology, genetics, neurosciences, virology and immunology, infectious diseases, pulmonary and respiratory diseases, primate medicine, and primate pathology. Focuses onpreventive medicine for humans through the use of nonhuman primates as animal models in such studies as the effects of toxic compounds, developmental toxicology, metabolic diseases, infectious agents, altered environments, and pharmacokinetics of various drugs. **Publications:** Annual Progress Report. **E-mail Address:** aghendrickx@vcdavis.edu. **Formerly:** National Center for Primate Biology; California Primate Research Center.

★ 13211 ★ University of California, Davis Center for Companion Animal Health
School of Veterinary Medicine
Davis, CA 95616
Phone: (916)752-7295
Fax: (916)752-6042
Niels C. Pedersen, Dir.

Research Activities and Fields: Health problems in companion animals, including studies on cancer, infectious diseases, congenital diseases, eye diseases, skin diseases, kidney diseases, animal population control, behavior problems, nutrition, medicine, and surgery (including laser surgery and therapies). **Formerly:** Comparative Cancer Center; Companion Animal Program (1992).

★ 13212 ★ University of California, Davis Dairy Goat Research Facility
Animal Science Dept.
Davis, CA 95616
Phone: (916)752-6792
Fax: (916)752-0175
LaDonna G. Foley, Supv.

Research Activities and Fields: Goats, including studies on diseases, reproduction, nutrition, toxicity, and behavior. Activities focus on studies of caprine arthritis-encephalitis, body protein turnover, fat mobilization and by-product feeding during lactation, comparison of nutritional quality of goat milk and kid replacer, milk protein analyses-caserns, heat synchronization for does, crucial time and type of human contact needed to keep dairy goats tame, climatic effects of heat on health, in vitro tests of sperm fertility, and embryo transfer/chimera formation. Also investigates milk withholding time for drugs and metabolism of feed. **Publications:** Newsletter (quarterly). **E-mail Address:** lgfoley@ucd.edu.

★ 13213 ★ University of California, Davis Equine Research Laboratory
School of Veterinary Medicine
Mail ID 1415
Davis, CA 95616-8589
Phone: (916)752-6433
Fax: (916)752-9379
John P. Hughes, D.V.M., Dir.

Research Activities and Fields: Basic and clinical studies related to health and behavioral problems in horses. The Laboratory's programs cover many areas of infectious and noninfectious disease research, including reproduction, genetics, musculoskeletal system, performance testing, medical and surgical diseases, respiratory conditions, nutrition, and parasites. **Publications:** *The Horse Report* (quarterly); *ERL Updates* (monthly); *ERL News Briefs;* Annual Report. **Formerly:** Equine Disease Research Laboratory.

★ 13214 ★ University of California, Davis Veterinary Genetics Laboratory
School of Veterinary Medicine
Davis, CA 95616
Phone: (916)752-8124
Fax: (916)752-3556
Dr. John P. Hughes, Dir.

Research Activities and Fields: Domestic animals, including cattle, sheep, dogs, pigs, and camelids, with emphasis on horses. Activities include chromosome studies, infertility research, and blood typing for animal identification, parentage verification, and the study of breed relationships through gene frequency analysis. Projects include research on evaluation of the mode of inheritance of suspected hereditary diseases; the genetic structure of wild populations; investigation and development of DNA technology for animal genetics; gene mapping; development of image scanning computer systems for biomedical data capture, analysis, and reporting using Fourier spectral vectors and neural networks; development of bar code assisted data entry and sample logging; and implementation of electronic data inte rchange for accurate and timely reporting of laboratory results. **Formerly:** Serology Laboratory (1992).

★ 13215 ★ University of California, Davis Veterinary Medicine Teaching and Research Center
18830 Rd. 112
Tulare, CA 93274
Phone: (209)688-1731
Fax: (209)686-4231
Dr. Leon D. Weaver, Dir.

Research Activities and Fields: Livestock health, medicine, food safety, and production.

★ 13216 ★ University of Connecticut Storrs Agricultural Experiment Station
1376 Storrs Rd.
Storrs, CT 06269-4010
Phone: (203)486-2917
Fax: (203)486-4128
Dr. Kirklyn M. Kerr, Dir.

Research Activities and Fields: Conducts basic and applied research in diverse agricultural disciplines and areas, including agricultural economics, natural resource management, forest micrometeorology, controlled environment crop production systems, agronomy, environmental horticulture, animal and human nutrition, animal and avian virology, veterinary microbiology, developmental genetics and toxicology, microchemistry, livestock management, reproductive physiology, wildlife diseases, and rural sociology and demography. Performs diagnostic testing on wildlife, farm, and companion animals. Conducts soil and environmental analytical chemical tests. **E-mail Address:** ns7net.kkerr@canr1.cag.uconn.edu.

★ 13217 ★ University of Georgia Southeastern Cooperative Wildlife Disease Study
College of Veterinary Medicine
Athens, GA 30602
Phone: (706)542-1741
Fax: (706)542-5865
Dr. Victor S. Nettles, Dir.

Research Activities and Fields: Wildlife diseases and parasites for application to wildlife

management, domestic livestock and poultry production, and human health policy. Sample projects have included studies on hemorrhagic disease of white-tailed deer, brucellosis and leptospirosis in cattle, toxoplasmosis, deer management, game birds, wild swine, and interstate translocation of racoons. Performs diagnostic investigations of various species of mammals, birds, reptiles, and amphibians. **Publications:** *SCWDS Briefs* (newsletter); *Field Manual of Wildlife Diseases in the Southeastern United States* (handbook). **Formerly:** Southeastern Cooperative Deer Disease Study (1960).

★ 13218 ★ University of Georgia Veterinary Medical Experiment Station
Athens, GA 30602-7371
Phone: (706)542-5734
Fax: (706)542-8254
Dr. John M. Bowen, Dir.

Research Activities and Fields: Biomedical studies, including various aspects of animal health and disease research. **Publications:** Annual Report. **Formerly:** Institute of Comparative Medicine (1973).

University of Hawaii at Manoa Kewalo Marine Laboratory
See: Entry 2668

University of Idaho Idaho Agricultural Experiment Station
See: Entry 9554

★ 13219 ★ University of Illinois Dixon Springs Agricultural Center
Rte. 1, Box 256
Simpson, IL 62985
Phone: (618)695-2441
Fax: (618)695-2492
Frank Ireland, Comm. Chair.

Research Activities and Fields: Agronomy, animal science, veterinary medicine, forestry, and horticulture, including studies on cattle and swine production, control of cattle parasites, corn culture, crop rotation, fertilizers, vegetable and small fruit production, livestock waste management, land utilization, pasture production, short leaf and loblolly pines, soil management problems, and supplementary winter feeding of cattle.

★ 13220 ★ University of Kentucky Maxwell H. Gluck Equine Research Center
Limestone St.
Lexington, KY 40546-0099
Phone: (606)257-4757
Fax: (606)257-8542
Peter Timoney, Dir.

Research Activities and Fields: Provides facilities and equipment for research on various equine health problems, including infectious diseases, reproductive physiology, pharmacology, immunogenetics, parasitology, biomechanics, growth and development, pathology, and anatomy.

★ 13221 ★ **University of Massachusetts**
Eastern Massachusetts Extension Center
240 Beaver St.
Waltham, MA 02154
Phone: (617)891-0650
Fax: (617)899-6054
Dr. Gurber, Dir.

Research Activities and Fields: Environmental biology in areas of agronomy, entomology, horticulture, plant pathology, and veterinary science, including studies on diseases and parasites of animals, flowers, fruit, plants, trees, and vegetable crops. Also conducts varietal and performance testing and weed and insect control studies under New England soil and climatic conditions. **Formerly:** Waltham Field Station; Suburban Experiment Station-Waltham (1991).

★ 13222 ★ **University of Michigan**
Unit for Laboratory Animal Medicine
Animal Research Facility
Ann Arbor, MI 48109-0614
Phone: (313)764-0277
Fax: (313)936-3235
Dr. D.H. Ringler, Dir.

Research Activities and Fields: Biomedical sciences including comparative medicine, laboratory animal medicine, animal models for biomedical research, and proper use and care of laboratory animals. Provides veterinary care for all vertebrate animals used in research and education at the University.

★ 13223 ★ **University of Minnesota**
Gabbert Raptor Center
1920 Fitch Ave.
St. Paul, MN 55108
Phone: (612)624-4745
Fax: (612)624-8740
Dr. Pat Redig, Contact

Research Activities and Fields: Avian diseases, avian toxicology, endangered species management, avian migration, and avian parasitology. **Publications:** *Raptor Release* (quarterly newsletter).

★ 13224 ★ **University of Minnesota**
Minnesota Agricultural Experiment Station
220 Coffey Hall
1420 Eckles Ave.
St. Paul, MN 55108
Phone: (612)625-4211
Fax: (612)625-0286
Dr. C. Eugene Allen, Dir.

Research Activities and Fields: All major areas of agriculture, forestry, home economics, veterinary medicine, economics, rhetoric, and rural sociology. **Publications:** *Minnesota Science* (quarterly); Station Bulletins.

University of Missouri—Columbia
Missouri Agricultural Experiment Station
See: Entry 9558

★ 13225 ★ **University of Missouri—**
Columbia
Research Animal Diagnostic &
Investigative Laboratory
College of Veterinary Medicine
1600 E. Rollins
Columbia, MO 65211
Phone: (314)882-6628
Fax: (314)882-2950
Dr. Joseph E. Wagner, Dir.

Research Activities and Fields: Human health research through the use of animals.

★ 13226 ★ **University of Missouri—Kansas**
City
Laboratory Animal Center
1015 E. 50th St.
Kansas City, MO 64110
Phone: (816)235-1681
Fax: (816)235-5275
David K. Peters, D.V.M., Dir.

Research Activities and Fields: Physiology, exploratory surgery, and immunology.

★ 13227 ★ **University of Montreal**
Research Group on Swine Infectious
Diseases
College of Veterinary Medicine
3200 Sicotte
Case Postale 5000
St. Hyacinthe, PQ, Canada J2S 7C6
Phone: (514)773-8521
Fax: (514)773-5633
Dr. John M. Fairbrother, Dir.

Research Activities and Fields: Infectious diseases of swine. Develops microbiological methods for the diagnosis of infectious diseases, identifies risk factors to improve control of infectious diseases on farms, conducts epidemiological studies of diseases on farms, and studies host reactions to bacterial aggresion. Projects on virulent strains include characterizing virulence factors produced by bacterial pathogens of pigs, identifying new virulence factors by comparisons of virulent and avirulent strains, purifying virulence factors, manipulating bacterial cells to determine role of virulence factors, and developing gene probes and serological assays for diagnosis. **E-mail Address:** fairbro@ere.umontreal.ca.

★ 13228 ★ **University of Nebraska—Lincoln**
Institute of Agriculture & Natural
Resources
Dept. of Veterinary and Biochemical Sciences
Basic Science Bldg.
Fair St. at E. Campus Loop
Lincoln, NE 68583-0905
Phone: (402)472-2952
Fax: (402)472-9690
Dr. John A. Schmitz, Head

Research Activities and Fields: Food animal disease, including molecular biologic, microbiologic, pathologic, virologic and immunologic studies of the respiratory, enteric, and reproductive systems. **E-mail Address:** vets001@unlvm.unl.edu.

University of Nevada, Reno
Nevada Agricultural Experiment Station-
221
See: Entry 9559

University of New Hampshire
New Hampshire Agricultural Experiment
Station
See: Entry 9561

★ 13229 ★ **University of Oklahoma**
Animal Resources
Health Sciences Center, BMSB 203
PO Box 26901
Oklahoma City, OK 73190
Phone: (405)271-5185
Gary L. White, D.V.M., Dir.

Research Activities and Fields: Biomedical studies in general areas of physiology, pathology, microbiology, surgery, and internal medicine. **Formerly:** Laboratory Animal Facility; Division of Comparative Medicine; Animal Resources and Facilities (1984).

★ 13230 ★ **University of Pennsylvania**
Referral Center for Animal Models of
Human Genetic Disease
Veterinary Hospital
3850 Spruce St.
Philadelphia, PA 19104-6010
Phone: (215)898-8880
Fax: (215)898-9923
Dr. Donald F. Patterson, Prin. Investigator

Research Activities and Fields: Identification, characterization, evaluation, and dissemination of animal models of human genetic disease, particularly models that occur in domestic animals, with emphasis on hereditary metabolic diseases, hereditary defects in sexual development, congenital malformations, and hereditary diseases of blood. Activities include characterization of mutant genes at the molecular level.

★ 13231 ★ **University of Pittsburgh**
Center for Research in Reproductive
Physiology
W. 1451 Biomedical Science Tower
Pittsburgh, PA 15261
Phone: (412)648-9281
Fax: (412)648-8330
Tony M. Plant, Ph.D., Dir.

Research Activities and Fields: Neuroendocrine control of reproduction in rhesus monkeys. **Formerly:** Center for Research in Primate Reproduction (1984).

★ 13232 ★ **University of Puerto Rico**
Caribbean Primate Research Center
Medical Science Campus
PO Box 1053
Sabana Seca, PR 00952-1053
Phone: (809)784-0322
Fax: (809)795-6700
Dr. Matthew J. Kessler, Dir.

Research Activities and Fields: General primate behavior and biology with emphasis on spontaneous and sociobiology diseases of nonhuman primates. The nonhuman primate populations and associated genealogical records make possible an evaluation of genetic, ecological, and social influences on the incidence and progress of disorders of adaptation and enable research to be conducted on control of population growth, evolution of social interaction by family selection, inbreeding potential of confined populations, reproductive behavior, positional behaviors and the development of degenerative joint disease, diabetes, obesity, and macular degenerations. The Center has been active as a site for dissertation research and for long-term, follow-up studies on a collaborative basis with research investigators. **Formerly:** Santiago Island Primate Colony (1956); Section on Primate Ecology, Laboratory of Perinatal Physiology (1970).

★ 13233 ★ **University of Saskatchewan Veterinary Infectious Diseases Organization**
124 Veterinary Rd.
Saskatoon, SK, Canada S7N 0W0
Phone: (306)966-7465
Fax: (306)966-7478
Dr. Lorne Babiuk, Dir.

Research Activities and Fields: Genetically engineered novel live and bacterial vaccines, development of performance enhancement vaccines for growth and reproduction, development of subunit vaccines against bovine herpevirus-1 and actino bacillus pleuropneumonlae suis in swine, prevention of colisepticemin in turkeys, viral vaccines for bovine respiratory disease complex, use of cytokines for disease protection, and immunological control of endocrine.

★ 13234 ★ **University of South Alabama Primate Research Laboratory**
College of Medicine
Dept. of Comparative Medicine, MSB 992
Mobile, AL 36688
Phone: (205)460-6293
Fax: (205)460-6286
Bob Ricker, Lab Supv.

Research Activities and Fields: Primates, especially as animal models of human diseases.

University of Southwestern Louisiana New Iberia Research Center
See: Entry 1723

★ 13235 ★ **University of Tennessee, Knoxville**
Center of Excellence in Livestock Diseases and Human Health
College of Veterinary Medicine
Institute of Agriculture
PO Box 1071
Knoxville, TN 37901
Phone: (615)974-7262
Fax: (615)974-4773
Dr. Michael Shires, Dir.

Research Activities and Fields: Livestock diseases and animal models of human diseases, with five targeted research areas: 1) inflammation and host defense; 2) carcinogenesis and experimental therapeutics; 3) in vitro toxicology and toxicokinetics; 4) infectious disease and population medicine; and 5) growth factors. **Publications:** Annual Report. **E-mail Address:** shires.michael@hospital.vet.utk.edu.

★ 13236 ★ **University of Texas Southwestern Medical Center at Dallas Animal Resources Diagnostic and Investigative Laboratory**
5232 Harry Hines Blvd.
Dallas, TX 75235
Phone: (214)648-3340
Fax: (214)648-2656
Steven P. Pakes, D.V.M., Dir.

Research Activities and Fields: Pathogenesis, control, and prevention of murine mycoplasmosis, genetic susceptibility and resistance to infectious agents, feline immunodeficiency virus infection as a model for HIV infection, and animal models for Lyme disease.

University of Utah Radiobiology Division
See: Entry 11081

★ 13237 ★ **University of Wisconsin—Madison**
Gnotobiotic Laboratory
706 Williamson St.
Madison, WI 53703
Phone: (608)262-0456
Fax: (608)262-6042
Dr. Edward Balish, Dir.

Research Activities and Fields: Host/parasite interactions, implicating immunology, kidney and thymus transplants, caries, bladder cancer, and toxicology; provides investigators with the technology and equipment necessary to carry out their research on animals that are either completely free of viable microorganisms or have a known microbial flora (flora-defined or gnotobiotic); improves methods used in the care of gnotobiotes, the units housing them, and equipment maintaining them; offers germfree foster mothers, rats, and mice, athymic and euthymic, to qualified researchers; performs caesarian derivations for affiliated organizations and commercial suppliers to upgrade the quality of research animals. **Publications:** *Investigator's Manual* (every three years).

★ 13238 ★ **University of Wisconsin—Madison**
Harlow Primate Laboratory
22 N. Charter St.
Madison, WI 53715
Phone: (608)263-3550
Fax: (608)262-6020
Christopher L. Coe, Dir.

Research Activities and Fields: Psychology and psychophysiology, with emphasis on psychological stress and immune responsiveness, cause and cure of depression, behavioral toxicology, social behavior, and development of affectional systems in monkeys. **E-mail Address:** prilab@macc.wisc.edu. **Formerly:** Primate Laboratory.

★ 13239 ★ **University of Wisconsin—Madison**
International Agricultural Programs
240 Agriculture Hall
1450 Linden Dr.
Madison, WI 53706-1562
Phone: (608)262-1271
Fax: (608)262-8852
Dr. Kenneth Shapiro, Dir.

Research Activities and Fields: Animal nutrition, animal diseases, plant diseases, soils, cereal and forage crops, agricultural engineering, horticulture, agricultural education, agricultural economics, data systems, extension, and rural sociology, with special reference to developing countries. **E-mail Address:** inter.ag@mail.admin.wisc.edu.

★ 13240 ★ **University of Wisconsin—Madison**
Research Animal Resources Center
127 Biotron
2115 Observatory Dr.
Madison, WI 53706
Phone: (608)262-1238
Fax: (608)262-7871
Christine M. Parks, Dir.

Research Activities and Fields: Laboratory animal diseases. **Publications:** *Animals* (Newsletter).

University of Wisconsin—Madison Wisconsin Agricultural Experiment Station
See: Entry 9570

★ 13241 ★ **University of Wisconsin—Madison**
Wisconsin Regional Primate Research Center
1223 Capitol Ct.
Madison, WI 53715-1299
Phone: (608)263-3500
Fax: (608)263-4031
Dr. John Hearn, Dir.

Research Activities and Fields: Reproduction and development, neurobiology, physiological ethology, psychobiology, aging and metabolic diseases, and immunology and virology. Emphasizes biomedical research and studies on captive and wild primate conservation; rhesus colonies for research in aging, AIDS, and developmental biology; and stumptail macaques, common marmosets, and cotton top tamarins. **Publications:** *Centerline Newsletter* (3 per year); *International Directory of Primatology* (biennially); *Audio Visual Catalog* (biennially). **E-mail Address:** hearn@primate.wisc.edu.

University of Wyoming Wyoming Agricultural Experiment Station
See: Entry 9571

★ 13242 ★ **University of Wyoming Wyoming State Veterinary Laboratory**
1174 Snowy Range Rd.
Laramie, WY 82070
Phone: (307)742-6638
Fax: (307)742-2051
Dr. Lynn Woodard, Dir.

Research Activities and Fields: Animal disease problems, including experimental control measures of animal diseases, etiology of animal diseases, and diseases of food-providing animals. **Publications:** Annual Report.

★ 13243 ★ **Utah State University**
Biotechnology Center
Logan, UT 84322-4700
Phone: (801)750-2753
Fax: (801)750-2766
William H. Scouten, Ph.D., Dir.

Research Activities and Fields: Promotes bio-technology in research and education at the University and in the region. Supports several programs, including three biotechnology service laboratories and facility operations. Also houses individual research programs, which conduct studies in bioremediation, affinity chromatography, bioseparations, molecular genetics of animals, vaccine production, embryo transfer, and immunodiagnostic methods for disease control and food safety. Consortia are set up as needed to develop technologies and to provide for inter-disciplinary research. **Publications:** *Utah Biotechnology* (newsletter); *Techtalk* (laboratory notes series). **E-mail Address:** johnlo-hr@cc.usu.edu. **Formerly:** Center of Excellence in Biotechnology.

Utah State University
Utah Agricultural Experiment Station
See: Entry 9572

★ 13244 ★ **Utah State University**
Veterinary Diagnostic Laboratory, Provo
   Branch
2031 S. State
Provo, UT 84606
Phone: (801)373-6383
Fax: (801)375-6870
Dr. E. Kelley, Dir.

Research Activities and Fields: Animal diseases and parasites. Conducts field experiments in support of studies conducted by members of the staff at the Experiment Station. **Formerly:** Branch Veterinary Laboratory.

★ 13245 ★ **Utah State University**
Veterinary Science Research Center
Logan, UT 84322-4815
Phone: (801)797-2162
Fax: (801)797-2118
Dr. R.C. Lamb, Department Head

Research Activities and Fields: Animal diseases and parasites. **E-mail Address:** bob@agx.usu.edu.

★ 13246 ★ **Veterinary Infectious Disease**
   Organization (VIDO)
124 Veterinary Rd.
Saskatoon, SK, Canada S7N 0W0
Phone: (306)966-7465
Fax: (306)966-7478
Dr. L. Babiuk, Dir.

Research Activities and Fields: Livestock and poultry disease research, including neonatal diarrhea in cattle, bovine and swine respiratory diseases, mastitis, colisepticemia in poultry, and performance enhancement through hormone immunoneutralization. **Publications:** Annual Report; *VIDO Reports* (newsletter); *VIDO Views* (factsheets).

★ 13247 ★ **Virginia Polytechnic Institute**
   and State University
Marion Du Pont Scott Equine Medical
   Center
PO Box 1938
Leesburg, VA 22075
Phone: (703)771-6800
Pamela Woolley, Contact

Research Activities and Fields: Equine research, including colic, gastric ulcers, and lameness.

Virginia Polytechnic Institute and State
   University
Virginia Agricultural Experiment Station
See: Entry 9575

★ 13248 ★ **Washington State University**
College of Agriculture and Home
   Economics Research Center
Agricultural Research Center
Pullman, WA 99164-6240
Phone: (509)335-4563
Fax: (509)335-6751
Dr. James R. Carlson, Dir.

Research Activities and Fields: Agriculture and rural life, including agricultural economics; agricultural engineering; agronomy and soils; animal sciences; child, consumer, and family studies; food science and human nutrition; apparel; merchandising; interior design; rural sociology; entomology; natural resource management; horticulture and landscape architecture; plant pathology; veterinary science; plant and animal biotechnology; and low-input sustainable agriculture. Performs forage and seed testing. **Publications:** Research Bulletins; Annual Reports; *Washington's Land and People*. **E-mail Address:** carlson@wsuvm1.csc.wsu.edu. **Formerly:** Washington Agricultural Experiment Station, Agricultural Research Center (1988).

★ 13249 ★ **Yale University**
Resource for the Study of Laboratory
   Animal Diseases
333 Cedar St.
New Haven, CT 06510
Phone: (203)785-2525
Dr. Robert O. Jacoby, Chm.

Research Activities and Fields: Diagnostic and laboratory animal medicine, including research on animal diseases, research on diseases of laboratory animals, and preliminary studies to determine if a disease is suitable as a model for human disease. Studies include Sendai virus, rodent parvoviruses, rodent corona virus, animal models of papillomatosis, and animal models of pneumocystosis.

State Government Agencies

Veterinarians

★ 13250 ★ **Alabama Department of**
   Agriculture and Industries
State Veterinarian
1445 Federal Dr., Rm. 220
PO Box 3336
Montgomery, AL 36109-0336
Phone: (205)242-2647
Fax: (205)240-3135

★ 13251 ★ **Alaska Department of**
   Environmental Conservation
Environmental Health Division
State Veterinarian
500 S. Alaska St., Ste. A
Palmer, AK 99645
Phone: (907)745-3236
Fax: (907)745-8125

★ 13252 ★ **Arizona Department of**
   Agriculture
Animal Services Division
State Veterinarian
1601 N. 7th St.
Phoenix, AZ 85006
Phone: (602)542-4293
Fax: (602)542-3244

★ 13253 ★ **Arkansas Livestock and Poultry**
   Commission
State Veterinarian
1 Natural Resources Dr.
PO Box 5497
Little Rock, AR 72215
Phone: (501)225-5138
Fax: (501)225-9727

★ 13254 ★ **California Department of Food**
   and Agriculture
Animal Industry Division
Animal Health Bureau
1220 N St.
PO Box 942871
Sacramento, CA 94271-0001
Phone: (916)654-0881
Fax: (916)653-2215

★ 13255 ★ **Colorado Department of**
   Agriculture
Animal Industry Division
State Veterinarian
700 Kipling St., Ste. 4000
Lakewood, CO 80215
Phone: (303)239-4161
Fax: (303)239-4073

★ 13256 ★ **Connecticut Department of**
   Agriculture
State Veterinarian
State Office Bldg., Rm. 283
165 Capitol Ave.
Hartford, CT 06106
Phone: (203)566-5894
Fax: (203)566-6094

★ 13257 ★ **Delaware Department of Agriculture**
Poultry and Animal Health Section
2320 S. DuPont Hwy.
Dover, DE 19901
Phone: (302)739-4811
Fax: (302)697-4463

★ 13258 ★ **Florida Department of Agriculture and Consumer Services**
Animal Industry Division
State Veterinarian
Mayo Bldg., Rm. 335
Tallahassee, FL 32399-0800
Phone: (904)488-7747
Fax: (904)487-3641

★ 13259 ★ **Georgia Department of Agriculture**
Animal Industry Division
State Veterinarian
Agriculture Bldg.
Capitol Sq.
Atlanta, GA 30334
Phone: (404)656-3671
Fax: (404)651-8206

★ 13260 ★ **Hawaii Department of Agriculture**
Animal Industry Division
State Veterinarian
99-941 Halawa Valley St.
Aiea, HI 96701-5699
Phone: (808)483-7111
Fax: (808)483-7110

★ 13261 ★ **Idaho Department of Agriculture**
Animal Industries Division
Animal Health Bureau
2270 Old Penitentiary Rd.
PO Box 790
Boise, ID 83701
Phone: (208)334-3256
Fax: (208)334-2170

★ 13262 ★ **Illinois Department of Agriculture**
Animal Health Bureau
State Fairgrounds
PO Box 19281
Springfield, IL 62794-9281
Phone: (217)782-4944
Fax: (217)785-4505

★ 13263 ★ **Indiana State Board of Animal Health**
805 N. Beachway Dr., Ste. 50
Indianapolis, IN 46224
Phone: (317)232-1344
Fax: (317)248-4063

★ 13264 ★ **Iowa Department of Agriculture**
Regulatory Division
Animal Health Bureau
Wallace Bldg.
Des Moines, IA 50319
Phone: (515)281-5305
Fax: (515)281-6236

★ 13265 ★ **Kansas Department of Animal Health**
Anchor Savings Bldg., Ste. 4B
712 Kansas Ave.
Topeka, KS 66603
Phone: (913)296-2326
Fax: (913)296-1765

★ 13266 ★ **Kentucky Department of Agriculture**
State Veterinarian
100 Fair Oaks Ln.
Frankfort, KY 40601
Phone: (502)564-3956
Fax: (502)564-7852

★ 13267 ★ **Louisiana Livestock Sanitary Board**
State Veterinarian
PO Box 1951
Baton Rouge, LA 70821
Phone: (504)925-3980
Fax: (504)925-6012

★ 13268 ★ **Maine Department of Agriculture, Food and Rural Resources**
Veterinary Services Division
State House, Station 28
Augusta, ME 04333
Phone: (207)287-3701
Fax: (207)287-7548

★ 13269 ★ **Maryland Department of Agriculture**
Food Safety Consumer Services Office
Animal Health Division
50 Harry S. Truman Pkwy.
Annapolis, MD 21401
Phone: (410)841-5810
Fax: (410)841-5914

★ 13270 ★ **Massachusetts Executive Office of Environmental Affairs**
Food and Agriculture Department
Animal Health Division
Leverett Saltonstall Bldg.
100 Cambridge St.
Boston, MA 02202
Phone: (617)727-3000
Fax: (617)727-7235

★ 13271 ★ **Michigan Department of Agriculture**
Animal Industry Division
State Veterinarian
PO Box 30017
Lansing, MI 48909
Phone: (517)373-1077
Fax: (517)335-6015

★ 13272 ★ **Minnesota Board of Animal Health**
Agriculture Bldg.
90 W. Plato Blvd.
St. Paul, MN 55107
Phone: (612)296-2942
Fax: (612)296-7417

★ 13273 ★ **Mississippi Department of Agriculture and Commerce**
Animal Health Board
PO Box 4389
Jackson, MS 39216
Phone: (601)354-6089
Fax: (601)354-6097

★ 13274 ★ **Missouri Department of Agriculture**
Animal Health Division and State Veterinarian
1616 Missouri Blvd.
PO Box 630
Jefferson City, MO 65102-0630
Phone: (314)751-3377
Fax: (314)751-6919

★ 13275 ★ **Montana Department of Livestock**
Animal Health Division
PO Box 202001
Helena, MT 59620-2001
Phone: (406)444-2043
Fax: (406)444-1929

★ 13276 ★ **Nebraska Department of Agriculture**
Animal Industry Bureau
State Veterinarian
301 Centennial Mall, S.
PO Box 94947
Lincoln, NE 68509
Phone: (402)471-2351
Fax: (402)471-2759

★ 13277 ★ **Nevada Department of Business and Industry**
Agriculture Division
Animal Industry Bureau
State Veterinarian
350 Capitol Hill Ave.
PO Box 11100
Reno, NV 89510
Phone: (702)688-1180
Fax: (702)688-1178

★ 13278 ★ **New Hampshire Department of Agriculture**
Animal Industry Division
State Veterinarian
10 Ferry St., 4th Fl.
PO Box 2042
Concord, NH 03302-2042
Phone: (603)271-2404
Fax: (603)271-1109

★ 13279 ★ **New Jersey Department of Agriculture**
Animal Health Division
John Fitch Plaza
CN 330
Trenton, NJ 08625
Phone: (609)292-3965
Fax: (609)292-3978

★ 13280 ★ **New Mexico Livestock Board**
State Veterinarian
7013 Central NE
Albuquerque, NM 87108-2049
Phone: (505)841-4000
Fax: (505)841-4012

★ 13281 ★ **New York Department of Agriculture and Markets**
Animal Industry Division
State Veterinarian
1 Winners Circle
Albany, NY 12235
Phone: (518)457-3502
Fax: (518)485-7773

★ 13282 ★ **North Carolina Department of Agriculture**
Veterinary Division
PO Box 26026
Raleigh, NC 27611
Phone: (919)733-7601
Fax: (919)733-2277

★ 13283 ★ **North Dakota Board of Animal Health**
600 E. Blvd.
Bismarck, ND 58505-0390
Phone: (701)328-2655
Fax: (701)328-3000

★ 13284 ★ **Ohio Department of Agriculture**
Animal Industry Division
State Veterinarian
8995 E. Main St.
Reynoldsburg, OH 43068
Phone: (614)866-6361
Fax: (614)575-2068

★ 13285 ★ **Oklahoma Department of Agriculture**
Animal Industry Division
State Veterinarian
2800 N. Lincoln
Oklahoma City, OK 73105
Phone: (405)521-3864
Fax: (405)521-4912

★ 13286 ★ **Oregon Department of Agriculture**
State Veterinarian
635 Capitol St. NE
Salem, OR 97310-0110
Phone: (503)986-4680
Fax: (503)986-4147

★ 13287 ★ **Pennsylvania Department of Agriculture**
Animal Industry Bureau
State Veterinarian
2301 N. Cameron St.
Harrisburg, PA 17110
Phone: (717)783-5301
Fax: (717)787-2387

★ 13288 ★ **Puerto Rico Department of Agriculture**
Veterinary Services
PO Box 10163
Santurce, PR 00908
Phone: (809)723-0922

★ 13289 ★ **Rhode Island Department of Environmental Management**
Agriculture Division
Animal Health Section
Roger Williams Bldg.
22 Hayes St.
Providence, RI 02908
Phone: (401)277-2781

★ 13290 ★ **South Carolina State Veterinarian**
c/o Livestock/Poultry Health Division
Clemson University
Elgin, SC 29224-2406
Phone: (803)788-2260
Fax: (803)788-8058

★ 13291 ★ **South Dakota Animal Industry Board**
State Veterinarian
411 S. Fort St.
Pierre, SD 57501-4503
Phone: (605)773-3321
Fax: (605)773-5459

★ 13292 ★ **Tennessee Department of Agriculture**
Animal Industries Division
State Veterinarian
PO Box 40627
Nashville, TN 37204
Phone: (615)360-0120
Fax: (615)360-0194

★ 13293 ★ **Texas Animal Health Commission**
2105 Kramer Lane
PO Box 12966
Austin, TX 78711-2966
Phone: (512)719-0700
Fax: (512)719-0719

★ 13294 ★ **Utah Department of Agriculture**
Animal Health Division
350 N. Redwood Rd.
Salt Lake City, UT 84116
Phone: (801)538-7160
Fax: (801)538-7126

★ 13295 ★ **Vermont Department of Agriculture**
State Veterinarian
116 State St.
Drawer 20
Montpelier, VT 05620-2901
Phone: (802)828-2421
Fax: (802)828-2361

★ 13296 ★ **Virgin Islands Department of Economic Development and Agriculture**
Veterinary Services Division
Estate Lower Love, Kingshill
St. Croix, VI 00850
Phone: (809)778-0997
Fax: (809)778-3101

★ 13297 ★ **Virginia Office of Commerce and Trade**
Agriculture and Consumer Services Department
Animal Health Division
1100 Bank St.
PO Box 1163
Richmond, VA 23209
Phone: (804)786-2481
Fax: (804)371-2945

★ 13298 ★ **Washington Department of Agriculture**
Food Safety and Animal Health Division
Animal Health Section
1111 Washington St.
PO Box 42560
Olympia, WA 98504-2560
Phone: (206)902-1878
Fax: (206)902-2087

★ 13299 ★ **West Virginia Department of Agriculture**
Animal Health Division
1900 Kanawhoo Blvd. E.
Charleston, WV 25305-0170
Phone: (304)558-2214
Fax: (304)558-0451

★ 13300 ★ **Wisconsin Department of Agriculture, Trade and Consumer Protection**
Animal Health Division
PO Box 8911
Madison, WI 53708
Phone: (608)224-4873
Fax: (608)224-4871

★ 13301 ★ **Wyoming Livestock Board**
State Veterinarian
2020 Carey Ave., 4th Fl.
Cheyenne, WY 82002
Phone: (307)777-7515
Fax: (307)777-6561

State & Regional Organizations

Veterinary Medicine

The following are state groups of the American Veterinary Medical Association, 1931 N. Meacham Rd., Ste. 100, Schaumburg, IL 60173-4360, 800-248-2862.

Alabama

★ 13302 ★ **Alabama Veterinary Medical Association**
PO Box 2370
Auburn, AL 36831-2370
Phone: (334)844-2687
Fax: (334)844-2652

Alaska

★ 13303 ★ **Alaska State Veterinary Medical Association**
Box 112269
Anchorage, AK 99511-2269
Phone: (907)344-7913
Fax: (907)349-1255

Arizona

★ 13304 ★ **Arizona Veterinary Medical Association**
5502 N. 19th Ave.
Phoenix, AZ 85015
Phone: (602)242-7936
Fax: (602)249-3828

Arkansas

★ 13305 ★ Arkansas Veterinary Medical Association
PO Box 21061
Little Rock, AR 72221
Phone: (501)221-1477

California

★ 13306 ★ California Veterinary Medical Association
5231 Madison Ave.
Sacramento, CA 95841
Phone: (916)344-4985
Fax: (916)344-6147

Colorado

★ 13307 ★ Colorado Veterinary Medical Association
1780 S. Bellaire, Ste. 701
Denver, CO 80222
Phone: (303)759-1251
Fax: (303)759-1477

Connecticut

★ 13308 ★ Connecticut Veterinary Medical Association
PO Box 270623
West Hartford, CT 06127-0623
Phone: (203)232-5000
Fax: (203)521-4932

Delaware

★ 13309 ★ Delaware Veterinary Medical Association
126 E. Cleveland Ave.
Newark, DE 19711
Phone: (302)737-1098
Fax: (302)737-3367

District of Columbia

★ 13310 ★ District of Columbia Veterinary Medical Association
8302 Frontwell Cir.
Gaithersburg, MD 20879-4922
Phone: (703)759-7880
Fax: (703)847-6958

Florida

★ 13311 ★ Florida Veterinary Medical Association
7131 Lake Ellenor Dr.
Orlando, FL 32809-5738
Phone: (407)851-3862
Fax: (407)240-3710

Georgia

★ 13312 ★ Georgia Veterinary Medical Association
3050 Holcomb Bridge Rd.
Norcross, GA 30071-1362
Phone: (404)416-1633
Fax: (404)416-9095

Hawaii

★ 13313 ★ Hawaii Veterinary Medical Association
PO Box 61309
Honolulu, HI 96839-1309
Phone: (808)733-8828

Idaho

★ 13314 ★ Idaho Veterinary Medical Association
PO Box 6573
Boise, ID 83707
Phone: (208)375-1551
Fax: (208)334-1502

Illinois

★ 13315 ★ Illinois State Veterinary Medical Association
161 S. Lincolnway, Ste. 302
North Aurora, IL 60542
Phone: (708)892-2321
Fax: (708)892-0818

Indiana

★ 13316 ★ Indiana Veterinary Medical Association
4901 Seville Ct.
Indianapolis, IN 46208
Phone: (317)293-1317
Fax: (317)293-1317

Iowa

★ 13317 ★ Iowa Veterinary Medical Association
5921 Fleur Dr.
Des Moines, IA 50321
Phone: (515)285-6701
Fax: (515)285-7809

Kansas

★ 13318 ★ Kansas Veterinary Medical Association
816 SW Tyler, Ste. 200
Topeka, KS 66612-1635
Phone: (913)233-4141
Fax: (913)233-2534

Kentucky

★ 13319 ★ Kentucky Veterinary Medical Association
PO Box 12737
Lexington, KY 40583-2737
Phone: (606)233-0062
Fax: (606)233-4998

Louisiana

★ 13320 ★ Louisiana Veterinary Medical Association
263 3rd St., Ste. 703
Baton Rouge, LA 70801
Phone: (504)381-9707
Free: 800-524-2996
Fax: (504)344-4699

Maine

★ 13321 ★ Maine Veterinary Medical Association
PO Box 8
Rumford Center, ME 04278
Phone: (207)364-8660

Maryland

★ 13322 ★ Maryland Veterinary Medical Association
PO Box 439
Fallston, MD 21047-0439
Phone: (301)879-9108
Fax: (301)893-2541

Massachusetts

★ 13323 ★ Massachusetts Veterinary Medical Association
200 Westboro Rd.
North Grafton, MA 01536
Phone: (508)839-6155
Fax: (508)839-7002

Michigan

★ 13324 ★ Michigan Veterinary Medical Association
2356 Science Pkwy., Ste. 100
Okemos, MI 48864
Phone: (517)347-4710
Fax: (517)347-4666

Minnesota

★ 13325 ★ Minnesota Veterinary Medical Association
2469 University Ave.
St. Paul, MN 55114
Phone: (612)645-7533
Fax: (612)645-7539

Mississippi

★ 13326 ★ **Mississippi Veterinary Medical Association**
209 S. Lafayette St.
Starkville, MS 39759
Phone: (601)324-0235
Fax: (601)324-9380

Missouri

★ 13327 ★ **Missouri Veterinary Medical Association**
1221 Jefferson St.
Jefferson City, MO 65109
Phone: (314)636-8612
Fax: (314)659-7175

Montana

★ 13328 ★ **Montana Veterinary Medical Association**
PO Box 209
Roy, MT 59471
Phone: (406)464-7577

Nebraska

★ 13329 ★ **Nebraska Veterinary Medical Association**
2727 W. 2nd
PO Box 2118
Hastings, NE 68902-2118
Phone: (402)463-4704
Fax: (402)463-5683

Nevada

★ 13330 ★ **Nevada Veterinary Medical Association**
50 Washington St., Ste. 101
Reno, NV 89503
Phone: (702)324-5344
Fax: (702)322-1039

New Hampshire

★ 13331 ★ **New Hampshire Veterinary Medical Association**
169 Rt. 27
Raymond, NH 03077
Phone: (603)895-3163

New Jersey

★ 13332 ★ **New Jersey Veterinary Medical Association**
66 Morris Ave.
Springfield, NJ 07081
Phone: (201)379-1100
Fax: (201)379-6507

New Mexico

★ 13333 ★ **New Mexico Veterinary Medical Association**
3736 Eubank, N.E., Ste. A-1
Albuquerque, NM 87111
Phone: (505)294-1351
Fax: (505)294-9958

New York

★ 13334 ★ **New York State Veterinary Medical Society**
1735 Central Ave., Ste. 203
Albany, NY 12205
Phone: (518)464-9669
Fax: (518)464-9548

North Carolina

★ 13335 ★ **North Carolina State Veterinary Medical Association**
4020 Westchase Blvd., Ste. 230
Raleigh, NC 27607
Phone: (919)828-8872
Fax: (919)828-8856

North Dakota

★ 13336 ★ **North Dakota Veterinary Medical Association**
c/o Veterinary Science Dept.
North Dakota State University
Vanes Hall
Fargo, ND 58105
Phone: (701)231-8307
Fax: (701)231-7514

Ohio

★ 13337 ★ **Ohio Veterinary Medical Association**
3168 Riverside Dr.
Columbus, OH 43212
Phone: (614)486-7253
Fax: (614)486-1325

Oklahoma

★ 13338 ★ **Oklahoma Veterinary Medical Association**
1 Benham Pl.
9400 N. Broadway, Ste. 504
Oklahoma City, OK 73114
Phone: (405)478-1002
Fax: (405)478-3631

Oregon

★ 13339 ★ **Oregon Veterinary Medical Association**
1880 Lancaster Dr. NE, Ste. 118
Salem, OR 97305
Phone: (503)399-0311
Fax: (503)363-4218

Pennsylvania

★ 13340 ★ **Pennsylvania Veterinary Medical Association**
PO Box 403
Harrisburg, PA 17108-0403
Phone: (717)233-7720
Fax: (410)893-2541

Puerto Rico

★ 13341 ★ **Colegio de Medicos Veterinarios de Puerto Rico**
GPO Box 360545
San Juan, PR 00936-0545
Phone: (809)754-1670
Fax: (809)754-1670

Rhode Island

★ 13342 ★ **Rhode Island Veterinary Medical Association**
PO Box 154
Barrington, RI 02806
Phone: (401)521-0101
Fax: (508)643-0141

South Carolina

★ 13343 ★ **South Carolina Association of Veterinarians**
225-A N. Greene St.
PO Box 218
Snow Hill, NC 28580
Phone: (919)747-8180
Fax: (919)747-4100

South Dakota

★ 13344 ★ **South Dakota Veterinary Medical Association**
Rte. 2, Box 42
Elkton, SD 57026
Phone: (605)693-4445
Fax: (605)688-6003

Tennessee

★ 13345 ★ **Tennessee Veterinary Medical Association**
530 Church St., Ste. 300
Nashville, TN 37219
Phone: (615)254-3687
Fax: (615)254-7047

Texas

★ 13346 ★ **Texas Veterinary Medical Association**
6633 Hwy. 290 E., Ste. 201
Austin, TX 78723
Phone: (512)452-4224
Fax: (512)452-6633

Utah

★ 13347 ★ Utah Veterinary Medical Association
PO Box 26
Kaysville, UT 84037
Phone: (801)546-4974

Vermont

★ 13348 ★ Vermont Veterinary Medical Association
1693 Williston Rd.
South Burlington, VT 05403
Phone: (802)862-7021
Fax: (802)879-7460

Virginia

★ 13349 ★ Virginia Veterinary Medical Association
3108 Parham Rd., Ste. 200
Richmond, VA 23229
Phone: (804)270-9013
Fax: (804)270-2160

Washington

★ 13350 ★ Washington State Veterinary Medical Association
PO Box 962
Bellevue, WA 98009
Phone: (206)454-8381
Fax: (206)454-8382

West Virginia

★ 13351 ★ West Virginia Veterinary Medical Association
PO Box 711
Oak Hill, WV 25901-0711
Phone: (304)465-8267
Fax: (304)469-9745

Wisconsin

★ 13352 ★ Wisconsin Veterinary Medical Association
301 N. Broom St.
Madison, WI 53703
Phone: (608)257-3665
Fax: (608)257-8989

Wyoming

★ 13353 ★ Wyoming Veterinary Medical Association
PO Box 6573
Boise, ID 83707
Phone: (208)375-1551
Fax: (208)376-4430

Chapter 69
Vision

Federal Government Agencies

★ 13354 ★ **U.S. Department of Health and Human Services**
National Eye Institute
9000 Rockville Pike
Bethesda, MD 20892
Phone: (301)496-2234
Fax: (301)496-9970

Description: The Institute conducts and supports fundamental studies on the eye and visual system, and on the causes, prevention, diagnosis, and treatment of visual disorders.

U.S. Library of Congress
National Library Service for the Blind and
Physically Handicapped
See: Entry 6909

Foundations & Other Funding Organizations

Private Foundations

Margaret W. and Herbert Hoover, Jr.
Foundation
See: Entry 377

Solon E. Summerfield Foundation
See: Entry 495

Wayne and Gladys Valley Foundation
See: Entry 538

Corporate Foundations

★ 13355 ★ **Alcon Foundation**
6201 S Fwy.
Ft. Worth, TX 76134
Phone: (817)293-0450
Fax: (817)568-7128
Mary Dulle, Director, Professional Relations

Giving Priorities: *Health:* 35% to 40% of total giving. About two-thirds of gifts for health go to eye-related health funds, medical research, and health associations for vision. *Education:* 30% to 35%. Over one-half of support goes to colleges and universities, and education associations for ophthalmologic or optometric research. *Social Services:* About 15% of contributions. About one-third of contributions fund child welfare and youth organizations. Other priorities include the blind and disabled, community centers, food distribution, homes, shelters, and religious welfare. *Arts & Humanities:* 5% to 10%. *Civic & Public Affairs:* Less than 5%. **Typical Health-Related Recipients:** Children's Health/Hospitals, Clinics/Medical Centers, Eyes/Blindness, Health Funds, Hospitals, Medical Education, Medical Research, People with Disabilities. **Geographic Distribution:** Nationally, with emphasis on Ft. Worth, TX.

D.B. Reinhart Family Foundation
See: Entry 657

Ladish Co. Foundation
See: Entry 6404

Other Funding Organizations

★ 13356 ★ **American Foundation for the Blind**
11 Penn Plz., Ste. 30
New York, NY 10001
Phone: (212)502-7600
Free: 800-AFB-LIND
Fax: (212)502-7777
Carl Augusto, Exec. Dir. & Pres.

Description: Awards various scholarships to legally blind graduate and undergraduate students. Also supports doctoral social research on blindness.

★ 13357 ★ **American Foundation for Vision Awareness**
243 N. Lindbergh Blvd.
St. Louis, MO 63141
Phone: (314)991-4100
Free: 800-927-2382
Fax: (314)991-4101
Huck Roberts, Exec. Dir.

Description: Offers grants for postgraduate study and research.

★ 13358 ★ **American Optometric Foundation**
4330 East West Hwy., Ste. 1117
Bethesda, MD 20814-4408
Phone: (301)718-6514
Fax: (301)656-0989
Dale Lervick, O.D., Pres.

Description: Offers research and scholarship grants to colleges and institutions, and supports fellowships in graduate research.

★ 13359 ★ **Fight for Sight**
500 E. Rennington Rd.
Schaumburg, IL 60173-4557
Phone: (708)843-2020
Fax: (708)843-8458
Robert S. Bolan, Exec. Dir.

Supports research in vision and opthalmology to restore and preserve sight through detection, prevention, treatment, and cure. Awards postdoctoral fellowships for basic or clinical research in vision or opthalmology and funds studies of priority interest through grants.

★ 13360 ★ **The Foundation Fighting Blindness**
1401 Mt. Royal Ave., 4th Fl.
Baltimore, MD 21217-4245
Phone: (410)225-9400
Free: 800-638-5555
Fax: (410)225-3936
Robert M. Gray, Exec. Dir.

Description: Conducts fundraising to support research on retinal degenerative diseases.

★ 13361 ★ **Glaucoma Research Foundation**
490 Post St., Ste. 830
San Francisco, CA 94102
Phone: (415)986-3162
Free: 800-826-6693
Fax: (415)986-3763
Tara L. Steele, Exec. Dir.

Description: Sponsors clinical and basic research programs to improve glaucoma patient care and increase knowledge of the eye disease. Awards annual research grants.

National Children's Eye Care Foundation
See: Entry 3151

★ 13362 ★ Research to Prevent Blindness
598 Madison Ave.
New York, NY 10022
Phone: (212)752-4333
Free: 800-621-0026
Fax: (212)688-6231
David F. Weeks, Pres.
Description: Provides annual unrestricted grants for eye research to departments of ophthalmology at university medical schools; funds for equipment; eye research professorships with five-year salary support; assistance in financing construction of eye research laboratory facilities; and travel expenses for international scholars for short-term collaborative research in the U.S. Presents Special Scholars Awards to assist unusually talented young scientists, and an award for outstanding ophthalmic achievement.

★ 13363 ★ Welfare of the Blind
1730 N. Lynn St., Ste. 500
Arlington, VA 22209
Phone: (703)528-3046
Fax: (703)243-1681
James A. Cudney, Pres.
Description: Supports church-related projects and programs for the blind and visually impaired in developing countries.

Medical & Allied Health Schools

Optometry

Schools and colleges listed below are accredited by the Council on Optometric Education of the American Optometric Association (AOA), 243 N. Lindbergh Blvd., St. Louis, MO 63141-7881, (314) 991-4100. For general information about the profession, contact the AOA or the Association of Schools and Colleges of Optometry, 6110 Executive Blvd., Ste. 690, Rockville, MD 20852, (301) 231-5944.

Alabama

★ 13364 ★ University of Alabama at Birmingham
School of Optometry
UAB Station
Birmingham, AL 35294
Phone: (205)934-6150

California

★ 13365 ★ Southern California College of Optometry
2575 Yorba Linda Blvd.
Fullerton, CA 92631-1699
Phone: (714)449-7444
Free: 800-829-9949

★ 13366 ★ University of California at Berkeley
School of Optometry
381 Minor Hall
Berkeley, CA 94720
Phone: (510)642-9537

Florida

★ 13367 ★ Nova Southeastern University
Health Professions Division
College of Optometry
1750 NE 167th St.
North Miami Beach, FL 33162-3097
Phone: (305)949-4000

Illinois

★ 13368 ★ Illinois College of Optometry
3241 S. Michigan Ave.
Chicago, IL 60616
Phone: (312)225-1700
Free: 800-397-2424

Indiana

★ 13369 ★ Indiana University
School of Optometry
800 E. Atwater Ave.
Bloomington, IN 47405
Phone: (812)855-1917

Massachusetts

★ 13370 ★ New England College of Optometry
424 Beacon St.
Boston, MA 02115
Phone: (617)236-2030

Michigan

★ 13371 ★ Ferris State University
College of Optometry
901 South State St.
Big Rapids, MI 49307
Phone: (616)592-2100

Missouri

★ 13372 ★ University of Missouri—St. Louis
School of Optometry
8001 Natural Bridge Rd.
St. Louis, MO 63121
Phone: (314)553-6263

New York

★ 13373 ★ State University of New York
College of Optometry
100 E. 24th St.
New York, NY 10010
Phone: (212)780-5100

Ohio

★ 13374 ★ Ohio State University
College of Optometry
338 W. 10th Ave.
Columbus, OH 43210-1240
Phone: (614)292-2647

Oklahoma

★ 13375 ★ Northeastern State University
College of Optometry
600 N. Grand Ave.
Tahlequah, OK 74464
Phone: (918)456-5511

Oregon

★ 13376 ★ Pacific University
College of Optometry
2043 College Way
Forest Grove, OR 97116
Phone: (503)359-2900
Free: 800-933-9308

Pennsylvania

★ 13377 ★ Pennsylvania College of Optometry
1200 W. Godfrey Ave.
Philadelphia, PA 19141
Phone: (215)276-6262
Free: 800-824-6262

Puerto Rico

★ 13378 ★ Inter-American University of Puerto Rico
School of Optometry
118 Eleanor Roosevelt
GPO Box 1293
Hato Rey, PR 00919
Phone: (809)765-1915

Tennessee

★ 13379 ★ Southern College of Optometry
1245 Madison Ave.
Memphis, TN 38104
Phone: (901)722-3225
Free: 800-238-0180

Texas

★ 13380 ★ University of Houston
College of Optometry
4800 Calhoun Rd.
Houston, TX 77204-6052
Phone: (713)743-2040

National & International Organizations

★ 13381 ★ Academia Ophthalmologica Internationalis (AOI)
Centre Medical Ophtalmologique
6, rue Saint Clair
F-81000 Albi, France
Phone: 63 541509
Fax: 63 471466
Pierre Almaric, M.D., Sec.Gen.
Founded: 1975. **Members:** 50. **Languages:** English, French, German, Spanish. **Description:** Ophthalmologists in 31 countries who have been practicing or teaching ophthalmology for at least 20 years and have published at least 100 papers or 1 book. Promotes ethics and high standards in the field of ophthalmology. Addresses problems of medicine, surgery, and ophthalmology. Provides consulting services.

★ 13382 ★ ACB Radio Amateurs (ACBRA)
c/o American Council of the Blind
1155 15th St., Ste. 720
Washington, DC 20005
Phone: (202)467-5081
Free: 800-424-8666
Fax: (202)467-5085
Jeff Hawkinson, Pres.
Members: 50. **Description:** Blind and visually impaired individuals interested in ham radio operation. Provides call sign directories, manual exchange programs, and new operator assistance. **Publications:** Newsletter, periodic.

★ 13383 ★ Affiliated Leadership League of and for the Blind of America (ALL)
1101 17th St. NW, Ste. 803
Washington, DC 20036
Phone: (202)298-8151
Fax: (202)298-8151
Robert R. Humphreys, Natl.Admin. & Counsel
Founded: 1985. **Members:** 100. **Description:** Coalition of public and private organizations of and for the blind. Advocates improvement of the social and economic conditions of the blind and visually impaired. Aims to protect the rights of blind consumers. Testifies before congressional committees and advises federal agencies and national and private organizations on the needs and rights of blind persons. Reports on pending legislation, current hearings, and regulatory issues.

Air National Guard Optometric Society (ANGOS)
See: Entry 7796

★ 13384 ★ All Russian Federation of the Blind (Vserossiiskoe Obschestvo Slepykn)
Novaya ploschad' 14
103672 Moscow, Russia
Phone: 95 9281374
Fax: 95 9237600
Aleksandr Yakovlevich Neumyvakin, Contact
Members: 150,000. **Languages:** Russian. **Description:** People with visual impairments, health care professionals, and others with an interest in the situation of people with visual impairments. Promotes the rights of people with visual impairments; represents members' interests.

★ 13385 ★ American Academy of Ophthalmology (AAO)
655 Beach St.
San Francisco, CA 94109
Phone: (415)561-8500
Fax: (415)561-8533
H. Dunbar Hoskins, M.D., Exec.VP
Founded: 1896. **Members:** 20,000. **Description:** Ophthalmologists concerned with high-quality eye care and the continuing education of members. Sponsors Basic and Clinical Science Course for practitioners and residents to maintain current status (includes annual self-assessment); offers information on new techniques. Operates museum of ophthalmological instruments and artifacts. Operates American Academy of Ophthalmology Government Affairs Office which serves as a liaison between the AAO and the federal government, monitors pending legislation affecting ophthalmology, and prepares statements and testimonies to be presented to congressional committees and regulatory agencies. Also operates Foundation of the American Academy of Ophthalmology, which functions as the charitable arm of the academy. Current activities of the foundation include National Eye Care Project ; Oral Histories Program; Centennial Program. **Publications:** Argus, monthly. Newspaper. • Basic and Clinical Science Course. • Directory, biennial. • Manuals. • Ophthalmology, monthly. Journal. • Videos. Also publishes slide script packages and study guides.

★ 13386 ★ American Academy of Optometry (AAO)
4330 East West Hwy., Ste. 1117
Bethesda, MD 20814-4408
Phone: (301)718-6500
Fax: (301)656-0989
David Lewis, Exec.Dir.
Founded: 1921. **Members:** 4,500. **Local Groups:** 20. **Description:** Professional society of optometrists, educators, and scientists interested in clinical practice standards, optometric education, and experimental research in visual problems. Conducts postgraduate education for optometrists and physicians. Sponsors annual two-day postgraduate courses and three-day research and clinical papers program. Confers Diplomate status in five fields of optometric practice. **Publications:** Geographic Directory of Members, biennial. Membership Directory. Complete geographical/alphabetical listing of academy fellows. Price: $15. • Newsletter, bimonthly. • Optometry and Vision Science, monthly. Includes academy news, book reviews, and periodic index. Price: Included in membership dues; $55/year for nonmembers; $70/year for institutions; $30/year for students.

★ 13387 ★ American Association of Certified Orthoptists (AACO)
Texas Children's Hospital
MC 3-2700
6621 Fannin
Houston, TX 77030-2399
Phone: (713)770-3225
Fax: (713)796-8110
Cynthia W. Avilla, C.O., Pres.
Founded: 1940. **Members:** 350. **Description:** Orthoptists certified by the American Orthoptic Council, after completing a minimum of 24 months' special training, to treat defects in binocular function. Treatment entails reeducation at the cortical level of abnormal visual usage to bring about normal single binocular vision. Assists in postgraduate instruction courses; conducts programs and courses at international, national, and regional meetings; helps individual orthoptists with special or unusual problem cases; trains new orthoptists. Operates a placement listing. **Publications:** American Association of Certified Orthoptists--Directory, annual. Directory. Price: Included in membership dues. • American Orthoptic Journal, annual. Journal. Presents new material in the fields of amblyopia and strabismus. Includes book reviews and abstracts of current English and French literature. Price: $22/copy for individuals; $56/copy for institutions. • The Prism, 3/year. **Formerly:** (1963) American Association of Orthopic Technicians.

★ 13388 ★ American Association of the Deaf-Blind (AADB)
814 Thayer Ave., Ste. 302
Silver Spring, MD 20910
Fax: (301)588-8705
Joy Larson, Contact
Founded: 1937. **Members:** 600. **State Groups:** 3. **Description:** Deaf-blind persons and individuals directly concerned with their well-being, including spouses, children, friends, and health care professionals. Seeks to encourage independent living for deaf-blind individuals. Conducts service programs; advocates interests of members before public policy bodies; acts as a referral service. Compiles statistics. **Publications:** Deaf-Blind American, quarterly. In large print and braille. Price: $15. **Formerly:** (1950) American League for Deaf-Blind.

American Association for Pediatric Ophthalmology and Strabismus
See: Entry 3161

★ 13389 ★ American Blind Bowling Association (ABBA)
c/o Alice Hoover
411 Sheriff
Mercer, PA 16137
Phone: (412)662-5748
Alice Hoover, Sec.-Treas.
Founded: 1951. **Members:** 2,900. **Regional Groups:** 3. **Local Groups:** 140. **Description:** Legally blind men and women, 18 years of age and older, competing in organized tenpin bowling. Promotes bowling as a recreational activity for adult blind persons. Sanctions member leagues; sponsors annual mail-o-graphic. Presents awards. **Publications:** The Blind Bowler, 3/year.

★ 13390 ★ **American Blind Skiing Foundation (ABSF)**
610 S. William St.
Mount Prospect, IL 60056
Phone: (708)255-1739
Sam Skobel, Exec.Dir.

Founded: 1972. **Members:** 175. **Description:** Volunteers who teach downhill and cross-country recreational and competitive skiing to the blind and visually handicapped. Holds giant slalom, downhill, and cross-country races; awards trophies. Travels with blind skiers to skiing areas in Colorado, Wisconsin, and Michigan. Sponsors international races in Canada, World Cup for Disabled in Switzerland, and Olympics for Disabled in Austria.

★ 13391 ★ **American Board of Ophthalmology (ABO)**
111 Presidential Blvd., Ste. 241
Bala Cynwyd, PA 19004
Phone: (215)664-1175
William H. Spencer, M.D., Exec.Dir.

Founded: 1916. **Members:** 17. **Description:** Medical specialty board to determine the adequacy of training, the professional preparation, and ophthalmic knowledge of ophthalmologists who wish to be certified. Works to improve the standards of graduate medical education and the facilities for special ophthalmic training. **Publications:** *Qualifications Brochure*, annual. Brochure. **Formerly:** (1933) American Board for Ophthalmic Examinations.

★ 13392 ★ **American Board of Opticianry (ABO)**
10341 Democracy Ln.
Fairfax, VA 22030
Phone: (703)691-8356
Fax: (703)691-3929
Nancy Roylance, Exec.Dir.

Founded: 1947. **Members:** 24,750. **Description:** Provides uniform standards for dispensing opticians by administering the National Opticianry Competency Examination and by issuing the Certified Optician Certificate to those passing the exam. Also administers the Master in Ophthalmic Optics Examination and issues certificates to opticians at the advanced level passing the exam. Maintains records of persons certified for competency in eyeglass dispensing. Adopts and enforces continuing education requirements; assists and encourages state licensing boards in the use of the National Opticianry Competency Examination for licensure purposes. **Publications:** *Bulletin of Information for Candidates*, periodic. Bulletin.

American College of Veterinary Ophthalmologists (ACVO)
See: Entry 13048

★ 13393 ★ **American Council of the Blind (ACB)**
1155 15th St. NW, Ste. 720
Washington, DC 20005
Phone: (202)467-5081
Free: 800-424-8666
Fax: (202)467-5085
Oral O. Miller, Natl. Rep.

Founded: 1961. **Members:** 20,000. **State Groups:** 51. **Description:** Blind and visually impaired persons. Serves as a national information clearinghouse on blindness for individuals, organizations, and institutions. Provides information and advisory service on federal legislation, administrative action, and rule-making on the national and state levels. Is active in such areas as administrative and service delivery issues, standards for accrediting quality service delivery programs, visually impaired citizen-consumer participation in service programs, civil rights for people, education of students, a federal comprehensive health care system, doubling job opportunities in vending facility programs, liberalizing Social Security and supplemental security income programs, radio reading services, special library services, eye research, and low vision technology. Offers group insurance plans, professional assistance in public interest, class action litigation, and public education about blindness and the abilities of visually impaired people. **Publications:** *Braille Forum*, monthly. Newsletter. Concerned with legislative developments, new products and services, medical and technological advances, and human interest stories for the blind. *Price:* Free.

★ 13394 ★ **American Council of the Blind Enterprises and Services (ACBES)**
120 S. 6th St., Ste. 1005
Minneapolis, MN 55402-1839
Phone: (612)332-3242
James R. Olsen, Exec.Dir.

Founded: 1978. **Members:** 15. **Description:** Board of directors of the American Council of the Blind. Owns and operates 13 ACB thrift stores, directed by blind persons, which help finance ACB and its programs and aid the blind and visually impaired in leading productive and independent lives.

★ 13395 ★ **American Council of Blind Government Employees (ACBGE)**
c/o America Council of the Blind
1155 15th St. NW, Ste. 720
Washington, DC 20005
Phone: (202)467-5081
Free: 800-424-8666
Fax: (202)467-5085
Mitch Pomerantz, Pres.

Founded: 1978. **Members:** 50. **Description:** Government employees, retirees from government employment who are blind or visually handicapped, and other interested persons. Strives to improve opportunities in government employment for the blind and visually handicapped; provides career development material; works with personnel policymakers. Members participate as speakers and panelists in workshops and other meetings. Offers technical assistance through specialized education program. **Publications:** Newsletter, periodic. Available in large print or cassette. **Formerly:** (1991) American Council of Blind Federal Employees.

★ 13396 ★ **American Council of Blind Lions (ACBL)**
c/o American Council of the Blind
1155 15th St. NW, Ste. 720
Washington, DC 20005
Phone: (202)467-5081
Free: 800-424-8666
Fax: (202)467-5081
Nelson Malbone, Pres.

Founded: 1970. **Members:** 141. **Description:** Legally blind members of Lions Clubs International. Informs the public of the needs and capabilities of blind persons; exchanges information on club activities benefiting work for the blind; encourages blind people to join Lions Clubs and other civic organizations. Supports speakers' bureau. **Publications:** Newsletter, quarterly. **Formerly:** (1985) World Council of Blind Lions; (1986) Council of Blind Lions.

★ 13397 ★ **American Diopter and Decibel Society (ADDS)**
3518 5th Ave.
Pittsburgh, PA 15213
Phone: (412)682-6300
Fax: (412)682-8137
Albert W. Biglan, M.D., Exec.Dir.

Founded: 1960. **Members:** 200. **Description:** Physicians who specialize in ophthalmology (the eye and its diseases), otolaryngology (the ear and throat and their diseases), rhinology (the nose and its diseases), or allied sciences. Devotes any available income in excess of cost of operation or other resources to research and educational projects. **Publications:** Directory, annual. • *Seminar Transactions of Meetings*, biennial.

★ 13398 ★ **American Foundation for the Blind (AFB)**
11 Penn Plz., Ste. 300
New York, NY 10001
Phone: (212)502-7600
Free: 800-AFB-LINE
Fax: (212)502-7777
Carl R. Augusto, Pres.

Founded: 1921. **Description:** Dedicated to helping those who cannot see live like those who do. Develops, collects, and disseminates information that benefits people who are blind or visually impaired, their families and friends, professionals in the blindness field, and the general public. Takes a leadership role in identifying issues critical to people who are blind or visually impaired; conducts research, and acts as a catalyst for change. Educates the public and policymakers as to the needs and capabilities of people who are blind or visually impaired; records and duplicates Talking Books for the Library of Congress and other audio materials for various corporations and organizations. develop public education programs. Records and manufactures Talking Book titles in conjunction with the Library of Congress. Adapts, evaluates, manufactures, and sells special devices and consumer products to help blind and visually impaired people live and work independently. **Publications:** *AFB Directory of Services for Blind and Visually Impaired Persons in the U.S. and Canada*, periodic. Directory. Lists over 2000 local, state, regional, and national services, including educational, informational, rehabilitative, low-vision, and aging services. *Price:* $75/copy. • *AFB News*, semiannual. Newsletter. Covers programs and activities of the AFB. *Price:* Free. • *Journal of Visual Impairment and Blindness*, bimonthly. Journal. Contains articles on research and practice in the areas of rehabilitation, psychology, education, legislation, medicine, and sensory devices. *Price:* $54/year for individuals in the U.S. and Canada; $79/year for individuals outside the U.S. and Canada; $79/year for institutions in the U.S. and Canada; $104/year for institutions outside the U.S. and Canada. Also publishes textbooks, training manuals, and resource guides and educational materials for teachers.

★ 13399 ★ **American Foundation for Vision Awareness (AFVA)**
243 N. Lindbergh Blvd.
St. Louis, MO 63141
Free: 800-927-2382
Fax: (314)991-4101
Huck Roberts, Exec.Dir.

Founded: 1927. **Members:** 5,000. **Description:** Seeks to present educational information to the public pertaining to vision. **Publications:** *In Focus*, quarterly. **Formerly:** (1970) Women's Auxiliary to the American Optometric Association; (1989) Auxiliary to the American Optometric Association.

★ 13400 ★ **American Ophthalmological Society (AOS)**
c/o W. Banks Anderson, M.D.
Duke University Eye Center
Durham, NC 27710
Phone: (919)684-5365
Fax: (919)684-2230
W. Banks Anderson, M.D., Exec. Officer

Founded: 1864. **Members:** 225. **Description:** Professional honorary society of physicians specializing in the functions and treatment of the eye. **Publications:** *Transactions of the American Ophthalmological Society*, annual.

★ 13401 ★ **American Optometric Association (AOA)**
243 N. Lindbergh Blvd.
St. Louis, MO 63141
Phone: (314)991-4100
Fax: (314)991-4101
Earle L. Hunter, O.D., Exec.Dir.

Founded: 1898. **Members:** 30,000. **State Groups:** 53. **Local Groups:** 500. **Description:** Professional society of optometrists, students of optometry, and paraoptometric assistants and technicians. Purposes are: to improve the quality, availability, and accessibility of eye and vision care; to represent the optometric profession; to help members conduct their practices; to promote the highest standards of patient care. Monitors and promotes legislation concerning the scope of optometric practice, alternate health care delivery systems, health care cost containment, Medicare, and other issues relevant to eye/vision care. Supports the International Library, Archives and Museum of Optometry which includes references on ophthalmic and related sciences with emphasis on the history and socieconomic aspects of optometry. Operates Vision U.S.A. program, which provides free eye care to the working poor. Conducts

specialized education program and charitable programs; operates placement service; compiles statistics. Maintains museum. Conducts Seal of Certification and Acceptance Program. **Publications:** *American Optometric Association--News*, semimonthly. Newspaper. Includes employment listings, classified ads, promotional news, and obituaries. *Price:* $42/year for nonmembers; $48 in Canada; $54 outside U.S. and Canada. • *Journal of the American Optometric Association*, monthly. Journal. Includes research articles, book reviews, calendar of events, legislative news, new products information, and advertisers' index. *Price:* $50/year for nonmembers; $65/year in Canada; $75/year outside U.S. and Canada. • *Optometric Economics*, monthly. Covers topics in optometric practice management. *Price:* $30/year for nonmembers; $33/year in Canada; $55/year outside U.S. and Canada. **Formerly:** (1903) American Optical Association.

★ 13402 ★ **American Optometric Foundation (AOF)**
4330 East West Hwy., Ste. 1117
Bethesda, MD 20814-4408
Phone: (301)718-6514
Fax: (301)656-0989
James S. Vrac, Admin.

Founded: 1947. **Members:** 1,000. **Description:** Optometrists, optometric organizations, corporations, and the public. Promotes research, education, literature, and professional advancement in the visual sciences. Supports fellowships in graduate research. **Publications:** *The Torch*, quarterly. Newsletter. Updates on foundation's activities. *Price:* Free.

★ 13403 ★ **American Optometric Student Association (AOSA)**
243 N. Lindbergh
St. Louis, MO 63141
Phone: (314)991-4100
Fax: (314)991-4101
Carol Freihaut, Exec.Dir.

Founded: 1972. **Members:** 5,200. **Local Groups:** 19. **Description:** Optometric students, state optometric associations, optical corporations, and family members of optometric students. Collects updated information on progress in the optometry field. Provides members with opportunities to work in areas of health care need such as local community health projects, school curriculum changes, and health manpower legislation. Works to improve optometric education and health care for the general population. Maintains active liaison with other optometric associations. Conducts communications program. Maintains speakers' bureau. **Publications:** *AOSA Foresight: Optometry Looking Forward*, semiannual. Reports information concerning scholarships, grants, internships, and other educational issues related to the study of optometry. *Price:* Included in membership dues. • *Communicator*, 9/year. Newsletter.

★ 13404 ★ **American Orthoptic Council (AOC)**
c/o Leslie France
3914 Nakoma Rd.
Madison, WI 53711
Phone: (608)233-5383
Fax: (608)263-7694
Leslie France, Adm.Asst.

Founded: 1935. **Members:** 20. **Description:** Ophthalmologists and orthoptists. Directs practice of orthoptists; determines qualifications of candidates; regulates training and certification of orthoptists; supervises the practice of orthoptists after certification. **Publications:** *A Career in Orthoptics*, annual. Pamphlet. • *American Orthoptic Journal*, annual. Journal. Covers ocular motility and visual physiology. Contains abstracts of ophthalmic literature. *Price:* Included in membership dues; $20/year for nonmembers; $35/year for institutions. • *Orthoptic Training Centers*, annual. Pamphlet.

American Printing House for the Blind (APH)
See: Entry 6972

★ 13405 ★ **American Society of Cataract and Refractive Surgery (ASCRS)**
4000 Legato Rd. No., 850
Fairfax, VA 22033
Phone: (703)591-2220
Fax: (703)591-0614
David A. Karcher, Exec.Dir.

Founded: 1974. **Members:** 6,000. **Description:** Ophthalmologists interested in anterior segment surgery and refractive corneal surgery. Offers continuing medical education to ophthalmologists on cataract and refractive surgery techniques, intraocular lens designs, and related research areas; assists allied health care professionals in ophthalmology on medical and surgical care of pseudophakic (lens implant) patients. Works to improve public education in the field of eye care. Conducts research in ocular pathology in cataract and refractive surgery. Compiles statistics. **Publications:** *Administrative Ophthalmology*, quarterly. *Price:* Included in membership dues; $45/year for nonmembers. • *ASCRS Roster*, biennial. Membership Directory. *Price:* Free for members. • *Journal of Cataract and Refractive Surgery*, bimonthly. Journal. *Price:* Included in membership dues; $60/year for nonmembers. • Newsletter, monthly. **Formerly:** (1986) American Intra-Ocular Implant Society.

★ 13406 ★ **American Society of Contemporary Ophthalmology (ASCO)**
4711 W. Golf Rd., Ste. 408
Skokie, IL 60076
Phone: (708)568-1527
Free: 800-621-4002
Randall T. Bellows, M.D., Dir.

Founded: 1966. **Members:** 6,000. **Description:** Ophthalmologists interested in promoting clinical investigative advances in ophthalmology. Offers continuing education courses approved by the American Council for Continuing Medical Education (ACCME) on new opthalmic developments in medical, therapeutic, diagnostic, and surgical procedures. **Publications:** *Annals of Ophthalmology/Glaucoma*, bimonthly.

Journal. Includes book reviews and information on educational activities and new products. A continuing medical education publication for ophthalmologist. *Price:* $120. **Formerly:** (1970) Society for Cryo-Opthamology.

American Society of Ophthalmic Administrators (ASOA)
See: Entry 5556

American Society of Ophthalmic Registered Nurses (ASORN)
See: Entry 9066

American Society of Veterinary Ophthalmology (ASVO)
See: Entry 13053

★ 13407 ★ Asia-Pacific Academy of Ophthalmology (APAO)
Mount Elizabeth Medical Centre
3 Mount Elizabeth, 06-05/08
Singapore 0922, Singapore
Phone: 22 77255
Fax: 22 77290
Prof. Arthur S.M. Lim, Contact

Founded: 1958. **Description:** National ophthalmological societies, ophthalmologists, and scientists in 21 countries. Promotes research, exchange, and dissemination of scientific information on diseases of the eye including blinding diseases. Encourages closer relations among members to improve the teaching and practice of ophthalmology. Maintains liaison with International Agency for the Prevention of Blindness and the International Federation of Ophthalmological Societies. Encourages support of the World Health Organization Programme for Prevention of Blindness. Sponsors Holmes Lecture on Preventative Ophthalmology and Ocampo Lecture on Clinical Research; organizes workshops and instructional courses on advances in ophthalmology.

★ 13408 ★ Assistance Dogs International (ADI)
c/o Robin Dickson
10175 Wheeler Rd.
Central Point, OR 97502
Phone: (503)826-9220
Fax: (503)826-6696
Robin Dickson, Pres.

Founded: 1986. **Members:** 31. **Description:** Centers for training hearing ear dogs, seeing eye dogs, and service dogs. Encourages cooperation among training centers and establish standards of excellence.

★ 13409 ★ The Associated Blind (TAB)
135 W. 23rd St.
New York, NY 10011
Phone: (212)255-1122
Michael Helmers, Exec.Dir.

Founded: 1938. **Regional Groups:** 1. **Local Groups:** 1. **Description:** Persons concerned with improving the economic and social conditions of the blind and the physically disabled. Social service department conducts a program of rehabilitation referral and follow-up; offers counseling and guidance for blind people and their families. Sponsors an apartment complex

designed to facilitate independent living for the blind and the physically disabled; provides recreation, arts and crafts, and other activities. Has adapted the American flag so that the stars and stripes can be recognized by touch. Is actively interested in all quality of life enterprises affecting the blind on local, state, and federal levels. Social, cultural, recreational, and educational activities are designed to enable blind individuals to live independently in a metropolitan community environment. Conducts programming and engineering for internal radio station. **Publications:** *Closeups*, quarterly. • *TAB News*, weekly.

★ 13410 ★ Associated Services for the Blind (ASB)
919 Walnut St.
Philadelphia, PA 19107
Phone: (215)627-0600
Fax: (215)922-0692
Patricia C. Johnson, Chief Exec.Dir.

Founded: 1984. **Description:** Multiservice agency that provides services to blind and visually impaired people. Objective is to help blind and visually impaired people live independently. Activities include: operating retail store that sells items of special interest to blind and visually impaired people; operating a braille printing house that transcribes print materials into braille; radio reading service that reads newspapers and magazines over closed-circuit radio. Offers rehabilitation program, social services, and recorded periodicals. **Publications:** Annual Report, annual. Report on services, board, financials • Brochure. • *Perspective*, semiannual. Newsletter. • *Sense-Sations*, annual. Catalog. Mail order catalog of products for the blind. *Price:* Free.

Association for Advancement of Blind and Retarded (AABR)
See: Entry 4280

★ 13411 ★ Association Burkinabe pour la Promotion des Aveugles et Malvoyants (ABPAM)
BP 5588
Ouagadougou 01, Burkina Faso
Phone: 303354
Dr. Diarra Siaka

Languages: French. **Description:** Promotes the interests of the blind. Works to raise public awareness of issues of concern for the blind. Provides educational programs.

★ 13412 ★ Association for Education and Rehabilitation of the Blind and Visually Impaired (AER)
206 N. Washington St., Ste. 320
Alexandria, VA 22314
Phone: (703)548-1884
Kathleen Megivern, Exec.Dir.

Founded: 1984. **Members:** 5,500. **Regional Groups:** 7. **State Groups:** 44. **Description:** Educators, rehabilitators, administrators, parents, agencies, schools, and others interested in the education, guidance, vocational rehabilitation, or occupational placement of the blind and partially sighted. To expand the opportunities for the visually handicapped to take a contributory place in society. Cooperates with colleges and

universities in conferences and workshops. Conducts certification programs; maintains job exchange services and speakers' bureau. **Publications:** *AER Report*, bimonthly. Newsletter. For professionals in the field of service to blind and visually impaired persons; includes legislative and membership news. *Price:* Included in membership dues. • *Association for Education and Rehabilitation of the Blind and Visually Impaired--Job Exchange*, monthly. Bulletin. Lists job openings in the field of services to blind and visually impaired children and and adults. *Price:* Free to members for first 6 months. • *Careers Video*. Videos. • *Don't Settle for Just a Job: Choose a Career*. Brochures. • *Re:View*, quarterly. Journal.

★ 13413 ★ Association for Macular Diseases (AMD)
210 E. 64th St.
New York, NY 10021
Phone: (212)605-3719
Nikolai Stevenson, Pres.

Founded: 1977. **Members:** 4,500. **Description:** Individuals afflicted with macular diseases, and their families. (The macula of the eye is the posterior middle portion of the retina responsible for central vision. Disorders involving the macula include inflammations, tumors, retinal growths, and degenerative problems.) Purposes are to: disseminate information on available resources such as recorded material and low vision aids; promote public awareness of macular diseases; encourage growth of research into the causes, treatment, and possible prevention of macular diseases; inform the public of the need for postmortem donation of eyes having a history of macular disease and advise on procedures for making such a donation. Provides counseling programs and group sharing for afflicted persons and their families. **Publications:** Newsletter, quarterly.

Association of Nurses Endorsing Transplantation (ANET)
See: Entry 9072

★ 13414 ★ Association of Optometric Educators (AOE)
c/o Dr. Debra Bezan
NSU College of Optometry
Tahlequah, OK 74464-7017
Phone: (918)456-5511
Dr. Debra Bezan, Pres.

Founded: 1972. **Members:** 100. **Description:** Teachers in schools and colleges of optometry. Works to enhance the professional and academic status and conditions of service of optometric educators and to promote communication among members. Concerned with faculty welfare, faculty-administration relations, faculty-student relations, and faculty-professional relations.

★ 13415 ★ Association of Radio Reading Services (ARRS)
2100 Wharton St., Ste. 140
Pittsburgh, PA 15203
Phone: (412)488-3944
Fax: (412)488-3953
William Pasco, Pres.

Founded: 1976. **Members:** 85. **Description:** Radio reading services that provide independently operated closed-circuit radio broadcasts of daily newspapers and additional printed materials for the blind and others incapable of reading for themselves. Broadcasts are delivered by trained volunteers to selected listeners who are provided with special closed-circuit equipment designed to receive these programs. Seeks to provide for the development and exchange of technological advances. Promotes solidarity in the pursuit of supportive legislation. Works to foster public understanding of and involvement in radio reading services. Facilitates networking among major services in order to supply broadcasts to listeners in areas with smaller populations. Maintains library and speakers' bureau. Conducts educational programs; compiles statistics. **Publications:** *Directory of Radio Reading Services*, annual. Directory. *Price:* $25. • *HEARRSAY*, quarterly. Newsletter. Also publishes brochure.

★ 13416 ★ **Association for Research in Vision and Ophthalmology (ARVO)**
9650 Rockville Pke.
Bethesda, MD 20814-3998
Phone: (301)571-1844
Fax: (301)571-8311
Joanne G. Angle, Exec.Dir.

Founded: 1928. **Members:** 7,600. **Description:** Professional society of researchers in vision and ophthalmology. To encourage ophthalmic research in the field of blinding eye disease. Administers Scientific Review Fight for Sight/Prevent Blindness research grant program. Operates placement service. Maintains 13 scientific sections. **Publications:** *Abstract Program Book Supplement.* • *ARVO Membership Directory*, periodic. Directory. *Price:* $20. • *ARVO Newsletter*, periodic. Newsletter. *Price:* Free. • *Guidebook to Finding Sources in Eye and Vision Research*, biennial. *Price:* $20. • *Handbook For the Use of Animals in Biomedical Research.* • *Investigative Ophthalmology and Visual Science*, 13/year. Includes announcements and information for authors. *Price:* Included in membership dues; $109/year for nonmembers; $142/year for institutions; $15/copy. Also publishes membership brochure; makes available posters. **Formerly:** (1970) Association for Research in Ophthalmology.

★ 13417 ★ **Association of Schools and Colleges of Optometry (ASCO)**
6110 Executive Blvd., Ste. 690
Rockville, MD 20852
Phone: (301)231-5944
Fax: (301)770-1828
Martin A. Wall, CAE, Exec.Dir.

Founded: 1941. **Members:** 37. **Description:** Institutional members of 17 schools and colleges of optometry in the U.S. and two in Canada. Promotes academic optometry. **Publications:** *Admissions to Schools and Colleges of Optometry*, annual. • *Annual Survey of Optometric Education*, annual. Survey. • *Eye on Education*, quarterly. Newsletter. Reports on association and member news. • *Faculty Directory*, semiannual. Directory. • *Journal of Optometric Education*, quarterly. Journal. Includes reports, book and other media reviews, and annual index. *Price:*

Included in membership dues; $20/year for nonmembers; $25/year outside of United States. • *Optometric Education*, quarterly. Journal. Presents reports, research findings, book reviews, and sustaining members' news. • Proceedings, annual. • *Residency and Graduate Program Directory*, annual. Directory.

★ 13418 ★ **Association of Technical Personnel in Ophthalmology (ATPO)**
c/o Peggy Yamada
306 Humboldt Rd.
Brisbane, CA 94005
Phone: (415)467-6304
Peggy Yamada, Contact

Founded: 1969. **Members:** 1,000. **Local Groups:** 41. **Description:** Certified and noncertified allied health personnel in ophthalmology. Objectives are to: advance and preserve the vision and health of all persons through the improvement of medical eye care; support programs and activities leading to the promotion of allied health personnel in ophthalmology. Cosponsors, with the Joint Commission on Allied Health Personnel in Ophthalmology (see separate entry), a continuing education program for ophthalmic medical personnel. Provides placement services; compiles statistics. Operates speakers' bureau; conducts educational programs. **Publications:** *Placement*, monthly. • *Viewpoints*, bimonthly. Newsletter. **Formerly:** (1989) American Association of Certified Allied Health Personnel in Ophthalmology.

★ 13419 ★ **Association of University Professors of Ophthalmology (AUPO)**
PO Box 420369
San Francisco, CA 94142-0369
Phone: (415)561-8548
Fax: (415)561-8575
George W. Weinstein, M.D., Exec.VP

Founded: 1966. **Members:** 218. **Description:** Heads of departments or divisions of ophthalmology in accredited medical schools throughout the U.S.; directors of ophthamology residency programs in institutions not connected to medical schools. Promotes medical education, research, and patient care relating to ophthalmology. Operates Ophthalmology Matching Program and faculty placement service, which aids ophthalmologists interested in being associated with university ophthalmology programs to locate such programs. **Publications:** Bulletin, quarterly. • Membership Directory, annual.

★ 13420 ★ **Beta Sigma Kappa**
c/o Linda McCrary
4500 Beechwood Rd.
College Park, MD 20740
Phone: (301)927-0508
Linda McCrary, Adm.Dir.

Founded: 1925. **Members:** 1,800. **Local Groups:** 17. **Description:** Honorary fraternity - ocular science. **Publications:** *Ocularum*, semiannual. *Price:* Available to members only.

★ 13421 ★ **Better Vision Institute (BVI)**
1800 N. Kent St., Ste. 904
Rosslyn, VA 22209
Phone: (703)243-1508
Free: 800-424-VICA
Fax: (703)243-1537
Susan Burton, Exec.Dir.

Founded: 1929. **Description:** Advisory council of the Vision Council of America. Carried out in consultation with a board of eye care professionals who inform the public of the need for more adequate vision care. **Publications:** Booklets. • *BVI News Bureau*, periodic. • Pamphlets. Also publishes charts and posters; produces school kits and counter displays for vision care practitioners, schools, and the public.

★ 13422 ★ **Blind Children's Fund (BCF)**
2875 Northwind Dr., 211
East Lansing, MI 48823
Phone: (517)333-1725
Fax: (517)333-1730
Sherry Raynor, Pres.

Founded: 1978. **Members:** 1,300. **Regional Groups:** 1. **Description:** A subcommittee of the International Council for Education of the Visually Handicapped. Parents and teachers of visually handicapped children from birth to seven years old. Promotes the health, education, and welfare of preschool blind and visually impaired infants and young children. Encourages development of activities and programs pertaining to growth, development, and education of visually handicapped children. Maintains speakers' bureau; conducts educational programs. **Publications:** Books. • *Get A Wiggle On*. Booklet. For parents of blind or visually impaired infants with suggestions for assisting development form birth to the walking stage. *Price:* $5. • *Get Ready...Get Set...Go!*. Teaches techniques for the parent or educator of the blind child, focusing on self-help skills. *Price:* $7. • *Learning to Look*. Book. For parents of severely visually impaired children. Contains specific suggestions on how to help your child use what vision she/ he has or may have. *Price:* $9. • *Make It*. Booklet. Contains toys and furniture you can make at home for multiply handicapped preschool children. *Price:* $3. • *Move It*. Booklet. Contains suggestions for the development of a preschool blind or visully impaired child from walking to school entrance age. *Price:* $5. • *Movement Education*. A movement curriculum for preschoolers. *Price:* $13. • *Parent Packet #1*. Booklet. Includes activities to teach skills at home, toys to make, how to stimulate language, and readings on blindness for parents and children. *Price:* $7. • *Our Kids Are Great!*. Parents of visually impaired children share short stories about what their children can do because of their help, love, and attention. *Price:* $3. • Pamphlets. • Proceedings. • Videos. • *VIP Newsletter*, quarterly. Newsletter. Contains information and articles for parents of blind or visually impaired children. *Price:* $10/year. • *Watch Me Grow*. Book. Contains month by month suggestions for assisting the development of a blind or visually impaired infant from birth to age three. *Price:* $12. **Formerly:** (1987) International Institute for Visually Impaired.

★ 13423 ★ Blind Outdoor Leisure Development (BOLD)

PO Box 5266
Snowmass Village, CO 81615-5266
Phone: (303)923-3811
Fax: (303)923-3811
Amanda Boxtel, Prog.Dir.

Founded: 1969. **Members:** 120. **Description:** Local BOLD clubs. Assists blind people in appreciating outdoor recreation. Operates on the "can-do" theory for blind people. Aids in the establishment of local clubs that help the blind enjoy the outdoors by skiing, skating, hiking, fishing, horseback riding, swimming, and biking. Designs and conducts training courses for activity leaders in downhill skiing; has designed distinctive bibs to identify participants as blind or as guides.

★ 13424 ★ Blind Service Association (BSA)

22 W. Monroe, 11th Fl.
Chicago, IL 60603
Phone: (312)236-0808
Anna N. Perlberg, Exec.Dir.

Founded: 1924. **Members:** 550. **Description:** Individuals who promote the welfare of blind and partially blind persons through voluntary service or financial support. Through its service program, the association maintains reading rooms for daily oral readings of textbooks and work-related material primarily to blind students, senior citizens, and business and professional people; records textbooks on cassette tapes for blind people's home, study, work and leisure needs; supplies visual aids, field trips, and other assistance to blind and visually handicapped children in Chicago, IL schools; helps maintain eye clinics in hospitals; helps support recreational programs for visually impaired minors and workshop program for the blind retarded; sponsors cultural activities for blind adults and provides tickets for some events; provides emergency relief for blind in need of assistance and cooperates with other charitable agencies in referral cases.

★ 13425 ★ Blinded American Veterans Foundation (BAVF)

PO Box 65900
Washington, DC 20035-5900
Phone: (202)462-4430
Free: 800-284-2283
Fax: (301)622-3330
John Fales, Pres.

Founded: 1985. **Description:** Assists blinded and sensory-disabled veterans in attaining their full potential through research, rehabilitation, and re-employment. Offers employment networking and rehabilitation and resource counseling; provides funding for rehabilitation centers. Operates speakers' bureau and placement service; compiles statistics. Conducts research, educational, and charitable programs. **Publications:** *Raising Cane*, quarterly. Newspaper. Large-print. Covers veteran legislation and programs. *Price:* Free.

★ 13426 ★ Blinded Veterans Association (BVA)

477 H St. NW
Washington, DC 20001
Phone: (202)371-8880
Free: 800-669-7079
Fax: (202)371-8258
Ronald L. Miller, Ph.D., Exec.Dir.

Founded: 1945. **Members:** 7,434. **Regional Groups:** 41. **Description:** Veterans who lost their sight as a result of military service in the armed forces of the U.S.; associate members are veterans whose loss of sight was not connected with military service. Assists blinded veterans in attaining benefits and employment and with reestablishing themselves as adjusted, active, and productive citizens in their communities. Offers placement service; supports research programs; compiles statistics. **Publications:** *BVA Bulletin*, bimonthly. Newsletter. Reports on legislation, benefits, and Department of Veterans Affairs programs affecting blind veterans; also includes association news. *Price:* Free to blind veterans.

★ 13427 ★ Braille Authority of North America (BANA)

1939 Frankfurt
Louisville, KY 40206-0085
Phone: (502)899-2322
Free: 800-223-1839
Fax: (502)899-2363
Hilda Caton, Chm.

Founded: 1976. **Members:** 12. **Description:** Braille publishers, producers, and transcribers; representatives of consumer groups; educators of the visually handicapped; professional organizations. To promote and facilitate the use, teaching, and production of braille texts and other braille items. Promulgates rules, makes interpretations, and renders opinions concerning literary and technical braille codes and related forms and formats of embossed materials for the blind. **Publications:** *Braille Textbook Code Formats and Techniques.* Book. • *Directory,* annual. • *English Braille, American Edition.* • *Learning the Nemeth Code.* • *Nemeth Code of Braille Mathematics and Scientific Notation.*

★ 13428 ★ Braille Revival League (BRL)

6521 Oleatha Ave.
St. Louis, MO 63139-2142
Phone: (314)771-2338
Free: 800-424-8666
Alma Murphey, Pres.

Founded: 1981. **Members:** 1,000. **State Groups:** 6. **Description:** Blind and visually impaired persons; professionals interested in promoting the use, production, and teaching of braille. Encourages blind people to read and write in braille; advocates the mandatory use of braille instruction in educational facilities for the blind; promotes use of braille material available through libraries and printing houses. Lends support to the Braille Authority of North America. Conducts research into braille efficiency. **Publications:** *BRL Memorandum,* quarterly. Volumes are in braille and large print.

★ 13429 ★ Canadian Council of the Blind (CCB) (Conseil Canadien des Aveugles — CCA)

405-396 Cooper St.
Ottawa, ON, Canada K2P 2H7
Phone: (613)567-0311
Fax: (613)567-2728
Mary Lee Moran, Exec.Dir.

Founded: 1945. **Members:** 4,000. **Local Groups:** 95. **Languages:** English, French. **Description:** Blind and visually impaired individuals in Canada. Acts as an advocate for the visually impaired in educational, employment, and social and recreational spheres. **Publications:** *CCB Newsletter*, monthly. Newsletter.

Canadian Implant Association (CIA) (Association Canadienne des Implantes Intraoculaires — ACII)

See: Entry 12261

★ 13430 ★ Carroll Center for the Blind (CCB)

770 Centre St.
Newton, MA 02158
Phone: (617)969-6200
Free: 800-852-3131
Fax: (617)969-6204
Rachel Ethier Rosenbaum, Pres.

Founded: 1936. **Description:** Rehabilitation center that specializes in services for adults ages 16 and up who have become blind. Provides programs for resident and commuter clients. Offers diagnostic evaluation, personal adjustment training, low vision, and children's services. Trains professionals in work with the blind through supervision of student internships and seminars for workers in the field. Maintains information and referral service. Offers computer training in specialized access devices for blind and job training. Operates charitable program. **Publications:** *Blindess: What It Is, What It Does, and How to Live With It. Price:* $15. • *Carroll Center for the Blind--Focus*, semiannual. Newsletter. Covers membership activities. Includes information for donors and new program information. *Price:* Free. • *Computer Access, Resource Manual. Price:* $20. • *Educational Software, Compiled Listing. Price:* $5. • *Facing the Wind. Price:* $25. • *Mapping. Price:* $15. • *Medical Transcription Training Manual. Price:* 125. • *Resource Manual for Teaching Blind Persons to Use Computers*, annual. *Price:* $20/ year; $10 for tape. • *Selected Exercises in Sensory Training. Price:* $15. • *Sensory Training, Principles of. Price:* $15. • *Videation and Spatial Orientation, Vols. I & II. Price:* $50. **Formerly:** (1972) Catholic Guild for All the Blind; (1974) Carroll Rehabilitation Center for the Visually Impaired.

★ 13431 ★ Catholic Association of Persons With Visual Impairment (CAPVI)

1018 Centre Ave.
Pittsburgh, PA 15219-3502
Phone: (412)471-6209
Msgr. Paul Lackner, Pres.

Founded: 1984. **Members:** 50. **Description:** To aid, support, and further the vocational, spiritual, and social integration of blind and visually impaired persons in local parishes and communities; to involve the visually handicapped as active members in the ministry of the Catholic church. Seeks to raise awareness of the ability and spiritual needs of blind and visually handicapped persons to participate in the spiritual and social life of the church; promotes the acceptance of the visually impaired within the community; exchanges ideas and resource information. Works to establish diocesan offices to serve the needs of the blind. Provides transportation for blind persons to Mass and other activities; instructs volunteers to act as guides. Assists in obtaining audiotapes and religious materials printed in braille and large type. **Publications:** *CAPVI Newsletter*, quarterly. Newsletter.

★ **13432** ★ **Christian Blind Mission**
           International (CBMI)
450 E. Park Ave.
Greenville, SC 29601
Phone: (803)239-0065
Free: 800-YES-CBMI
Fax: (803)239-0069
Art Brooker, Dir.

Founded: 1908. **National Groups:** 12. **Description:** Interdenominational Christian organization dedicated to service of the blind, visually impaired, and physically handicapped in more than 100 countries. Supports national activities of missions, churches, and voluntary organizations in developing countries with financial aid to cover operational expenses and the provision of equipment, drugs, medicines, and instruments. Fosters prevention of visually disabling ailments such as glaucoma, trachoma, and blinding cataracts. Assists in education and rehabilitation of all disabled indiviudals through establishment of vocational training centers and a corps of community volunteers to coordinate and stimulate project participation. Contributes to international efforts in the battle against blindness; conducts research on onchocerciasis, xerophthalmia, and glaucoma. Has established the International Agency for the Prevention of Blindness in conjuction with the Royal Commonwealth Society for the Blind. Sponsors rural education programs on personal and environmental hygiene and nutrition. **Publications:** *CBMI Report*, annual. Report. • *Human Interest Stories*, monthly. • *Light*, quarterly. Newsletter.

★ **13433** ★ **Christian Record Services (CRS)**
4444 S. 52nd St.
Lincoln, NE 68516
Phone: (402)488-0981
Fax: (402)488-7582
Clarence E. Hodges, Pres.

Founded: 1899. **Description:** Assists blind, visually impaired, and hearing impaired individuals. Sponsors Bible correspondence courses. Representatives visit about 40,000 blind people annually. Conducts glaucoma screening clinics in cooperation with local physicians and organizations; provides home visitation program. Sponsors camps for deaf youth and National Camps for Blind Children; maintains speakers' bureau. **Publications:** *Campfire Light*, semiannual. Schedule and description of camps for the blind. *Price:* Free. • *Children's Friend*, quarterly. In braille; for children through age 12. • *Christian Record*, quarterly. In braille; for adults. • *Christian Record Talking Magazine*, quarterly.

Magazine. On flexible disc; for adults. • *Deaflight*, quarterly. • *Encounter*, bimonthly. On flexible disc; for late teens and adults. • *Lifeglow*, quarterly. In large print; for adults. • *New Dawn*, quarterly. Newsletter. • *Review*, quarterly. In braille. • *The Student*, monthly. In braille and on flexible disc. • *Vider Radiante*, quarterly. Large print. • *Young and Alive*, quarterly. In braille and large print; for teenages/young adults. Also publishes braille and sign language cards. **Formerly:** Christian Record Benevolent Association; (1989) Christian Record Braille Foundation.

★ **13434** ★ **Christian Services for the Blind**
1124 Fair Oaks
PO Box 26
South Pasadena, CA 91031
Phone: (818)799-3935
Frank Tucker, Contact

Founded: 1949. **Description:** Makes available books on cassette for blind and physically disabled individuals. **Publications:** *Bartimaeus Review*, 3/year. Newsletter. *Price:* Free. **Formerly:** Christian Fellowship for the Blind.

★ **13435** ★ **Christian Tapes for the Disabled**
PO Box 455
Buffalo, NY 14209-0455
Phone: (716)885-0307
Fax: (716)839-0218
Red Bainbridge, Contact

Founded: 1980. **Members:** 300. **Description:** Volunteers united to make Christian literature available to visually and physically disabled people. Provides Christian books on cassette tapes via free mail lending library. **Publications:** Catalog, annual. Lists books by title with brief review. Also lists resources for blind/disabled persons.

★ **13436** ★ **Christoffel Blindenmission**
           (CBM)
Nibelungenstr. 124
64625 Bensheim, Germany
Phone: 6251 1310
Fax: 6251 131165
C. Garms, Dir.

Founded: 1908. **Languages:** English, French, German, Spanish. **Description:** Seeks to prevent and cure blindness and improve the quality of life for blind and partially sighted people. Represents the interests of visually impaired people; works to combat discrimination. Seeks to educate and rehabilitate blind and other handicapped persons. **Publications:** *Fam.-Album*, bimonthly. Newsletter. • *Light*, bimonthly. Newsletter. • Report, periodic.

★ **13437** ★ **College of Optometrists in**
           Vision Development (COVD)
PO Box 285
Chula Vista, CA 91912
Phone: (619)425-6191
Fax: (619)425-0733
Robert M. Wold, O.D., Sec.

Founded: 1970. **Members:** 1,600. **Regional Groups:** 5. **State Groups:** 40. **Description:** Optometrists involved in orthoptics and optometric vision therapy with emphasis on visual information processing in visually related learning problems; optometrists interested in such therapy;

students. Seeks to establish a body of practitioners who are knowledgeable in functional and developmental concepts of vision, to insure that the public will receive continually improving vision care; to promote, foster, and engage in interdisciplinary cooperation; to enable members to maintain the highest standards of professional knowledge and competency; to educate and encourage optometrists to qualify for membership and fellowship in the college; to certify optometrists skilled in this specialty. Conducts national educational programs and public information programs. **Publications:** Brochures. • *College of Optometrists in Vision Development-- Fellow Directory*, annual. *Price:* Included in membership dues; $1/copy for nonmembers. • *College of Optometrists in Vision Development--Newsletter*, quarterly. *Price:* Included in membership dues. • *Journal of Optometric Vision Development*, quarterly. *Price:* $45/year. • Monographs. Also publishes research reviews.

★ **13438** ★ **Commission on Opticianry**
           Accreditation (COA)
10111 Martin Luther King, Jr. Hwy., No. 100
Bowie, MD 20720
Phone: (301)459-8075
Fax: (301)577-3880
Floyd H. Holmgrain, Jr., Exec.Dir.

Founded: 1979. **Members:** 26. **Description:** Accrediting agency for ophthalmic dispensing and ophthalmic laboratory technology programs in postsecondary institutions. Conducts an evaluator's workshop to train on-site evaluators. **Publications:** *Accreditation Guide for Ophthalmic Dispensing Programs*. Manual. *Price:* $10. • *COA News*, semiannual. • *Evaluator's Checklist for Ophthalmic Laboratory Technology Programs*. Manual. • *Evaluator's Handbook for Ophthalmic Dispensing Programs*. Handbook. • *Evaluator's Handbook for Ophthalmic Laboratory Technology Programs*. Handbook. • *Self-Study Report Format for Ophthalmic Dispensing Programs*. Manual.

★ **13439** ★ **Contact Lens Association of**
           Ophthalmologists (CLAO)
c/o John S. Massare
523 Decatur St., Ste. 1
New Orleans, LA 70130-1027
Phone: (504)581-4000
Fax: (504)581-5884
John S. Massare, Exec.Dir.

Founded: 1962. **Members:** 2,000. **Description:** Active and resident ophthalmologists and doctors of osteopathy specializing in ophthalmology. Objective is to disseminate scientific information on ophthalmology. Provides for the sharing of techniques and expertise; makes available statistics and information on related courses, seminars, meetings, and special events. Sponsors exhibits and scientific posters. **Publications:** *CLAO Directory*, biennial. Directory. • *CLAO Journal*, quarterly. Journal. • *CLAOgram*, monthly. Bulletin. • Report.

★ 13440 ★ **Contact Lens Manufacturers Association (CLMA)**
4400 East-West Hwy., Ste. 33
Bethesda, MD 20814
Phone: (301)654-2229
Fax: (301)654-1611
Janis Marshall, Mng.Dir.
Founded: 1962. **Members:** 130. **Description:** Individuals, firms, or corporations engaged in fabricating finished contact lenses from raw materials; individuals, firms, or corporations engaged in the business of manufacturing parts for or producing material used with contact lenses or in any way changing, altering, or completing the structure of a finished contact lens made from raw materials. **Publications:** *Contact Lens Manufacturers Association--Membership Directory*, annual. Membership Directory. *Price:* Included in membership dues. • *Contact Lenses and You*, periodic. Magazine. • *The Contact Report*, bimonthly. Newsletter. *Price:* Included in membership dues. • Videos.

Contact Lens Society of America (CLSA)
See: Entry 5832

★ 13441 ★ **Council for the Blind**
131 Fort St.
Bulawayo, Zimbabwe
Phone: 4 791933
Description: Supports research focusing on the prevention of blindness. Offers educational programs and rehabilitation services to visually impaired people.

★ 13442 ★ **Council of Citizens With Low Vision (CCLV)**
1400 N. Drake Rd., No. 218
Kalamazoo, MI 49006
Phone: (616)381-9566
Free: 800-733-2258
Elizabeth Lennon, Pres.
Founded: 1978. **Members:** 2,000. **State Groups:** 11. **Description:** Partially sighted and low-vision individuals, their families, and professional workers. Provides a vehicle through which partially sighted people may voice their needs, preferences, and interests. Promotes the concept that partially sighted and low-vision individuals are not blind and that they have the right to maximize the use of residual vision through the use of any visual aid, service, or technology. Keeps abreast of all developments benefiting partially sighted persons. Promotes educational, engineering, medical, rehabilitative, scientific, and social research that facilitates the lives of individuals with residual vision. Supports the development of preservice professional training programs for the establishment and expansion of multidisciplinary low-vision services. Strives to educate the public about the existence, capabilities, and needs of such individuals. Establishes outreach programs to insure access to available services for partially sighted persons. Maintains speakers' bureau. **Publications:** *Vision Access*, quarterly. Newsletter. Reports on research and resources. Available on audiocassete and large print. *Price:* Included in membership dues.

Council for Exceptional Children (DVH) Division for Visual Handicaps
See: Entry 3218

★ 13443 ★ **Council of Families with Visual Impairment (CFVI)**
26616 Rouge River Dr.
Dearborn Heights, MI 48127
Free: 800-424-8666
Bonnie Weaver, Pres.
Founded: 1979. **Members:** 400. **Description:** Sighted parents of blind and visually impaired children; blind and visually impaired parents, professionals, and interested individuals. Offers forum for support and outreach, sharing of experiences in parent-child relationships, and educational and cultural information about child development. Monitors developments in technical and legislative arenas. **Publications:** *Reflections*, 3/year. Newsletter. Published in large print. *Price:* $6; $8 for tape. **Formerly:** (1990) American Council of the Blind Parents.

★ 13444 ★ **Council on Optometric Education (COE)**
243 N. Lindbergh Blvd.
St. Louis, MO 63141
Phone: (314)991-4100
Fax: (314)991-4101
Joyce L. Urbeck, Admin.Dir.
Founded: 1930. **Members:** 11. **Description:** Accrediting body for professional optometric degree (O.D.) programs (examination, diagnosis, and treatment of the conditions or impairments of the vision system), paraoptometric educational programs, and optometric residency programs. Members are appointed by the president of the American Optometric Association. Works to ensure the quality of optometric education, announces list of accredited programs, and compiles statistics on optometric education, schools and colleges of optometry, and their student bodies.

★ 13445 ★ **Council of Rehabilitation Specialists (CRS)**
c/o American Council of the Blind
1155 15th St. NW, Ste. 720
Washington, DC 20005
Phone: (202)467-5081
Free: 800-424-8666
Fax: (202)467-5085
Charles Leroy, Pres.
Founded: 1979. **Members:** 100. **Description:** Rehabilitation and social service professionals, students pursuing careers in these fields, and interested individuals. Promotes the establishment of academic and professional standards; advocates adequate rehabilitation services for all blind and visually impaired persons. **Publications:** *Synergist Newsletter*, 3/year. Newsletter. Informs members of new resources and techniques used to help blind adults. *Price:* Included in membership dues.

★ 13446 ★ **European Association of Schools and Colleges of Optometry (EASCO)**
(Association Europeene des Ecoles et Colleges d'Optometre — AESCO)
134, rte. de Chartres
F-91440 Bures-sur-Yvette, France
Phone: 1 69076737
Fax: 1 69284999
Jean-Paul Roosen, Sec.
Founded: 1979. **Members:** 50. **Languages:** English, French. **Description:** Schools in 17 countries providing education for optometrists and opticians. Promotes the development of optometry in Europe; seeks the standardization of optometric instruction and qualifications on a European level. Encourages cooperation and information exchange among teaching institutions. Compiles scientific and pedagogic documentation concerning optometric education in Europe. **Publications:** *Communication*, 5/year. Newsletter. **Also Known As:** EUROPTOM.

★ 13447 ★ **European Blind Union (EBU) (Union Europeenne des Aveugles — UEA)**
Norwegian Association for the Blind
Box 5900
Sporveis Gata 10
N-0308 Oslo, Norway
Phone: 22466990
Fax: 22607054
Mr. Arne Husweg, Sec.Gen.
Founded: 1984. **Languages:** English, French, German. **Description:** European national associations for the blind. Works to enhance the quality of life of blind and visually impaired persons. Fosters equality and full participation of such individuals in society; promotes the prevention of blindness and visual impairment in Europe. Serves as a forum for the exchange of information concerning blindness. Provides social rights advocacy, seminars, and technical aids. **Publications:** *Europa-Cassette: EEC Informations*, 5/year. • *Proceedings*, triennial. • *Review of the European Blind Union*, quarterly.

★ 13448 ★ **European Society for Cataract and Refractive Surgeons (ESCRS) (Club International d'Implants Oculaires)**
10 Hagan Court
Lad Lane
Dublin 2, Ireland
Phone: 1 6760928
Fax: 1 6785047
P. Sourdille, Pres.
Founded: 1958. **Members:** 3,000. **Languages:** English. **Description:** Strives to advance scientific knowledge in the field of intraocular lens implantation and in the art and practice of such surgery. **Publications:** *Membership List*, annual. • Newsletter, semiannual. **Formerly:** European Intraocular Implant Council.

European Society of Ophthalmic Plastic and Reconstructive Surgery (ESOPRS)
See: Entry 12270

★ 13449 ★ **European Strabismological Association (ESA)**
Clinica Oculistica
Via del Pozzo 71
I-41100 Modena, Italy
Phone: 59 360309
Fax: 59 371532
Dr. E. Campos, Sec.-Treas.
Founded: 1960. **Members:** 250. **Languages:** English, French, German. **Description:** Physicians in 21 countries interested in strabismology and neuro-ophthalmology. (Strabismology is the study of the condition known as strabismus, in which an individual is unable to fix both eyes on a single point due to muscular imbalance. Neuro-ophthalmology refers to visual representation in the central nervous system.) **Publications:** *Proceedings*, annual.

★ 13450 ★   Eye Bank Association of America (EBAA)
1001 Connecticut Ave. NW, Ste. 601
Washington, DC 20036
Phone: (202)775-4999
Fax: (202)429-6036
Patricia O'Neill, CEO & Pres.

Founded: 1961. **Members:** 109. **Description:** Eye banks working to restore sight through the promotion and advancement of eye banking. Makes possible over 43,000 corneal transplants annually. Establishes standards for the procurement and distribution of eyes and corneal tissue. Offers training and certification programs for eye banking personnel. Compiles statistics; maintains speakers' bureau. Conducts research and educational programs. **Publications:** *Eye Bank Association of America--Eye Bank Statistics Report*, annual. Annual Report. Includes statistics on eye donations and corneal transplants. • *Eye Bank Association of America--Insight*, periodic. Newsletter. Contains association and industry news. • *Eye Bank Association of America--Membership Directory*, annual. Membership Directory. Lists member eye banks; listed geographically by state. • *Guidelines and Resources for Successful Public and Professional Relations and Development*.

★ 13451 ★   Eye-Bank for Sight Restoration (EBSR)
210 E. 64th St.
New York, NY 10021
Phone: (212)980-6700
Fax: (212)319-6211
Mary Jane O'Neill, Exec.Dir.

Founded: 1944. **Description:** Collects and distributes healthy corneal tissue obtained from individuals who have arranged to donate their eyes, or whose relatives have authorized such donation, at the time of death. Provides speakers to explain the eye-bank program to hospital, professional, and clinic groups. **Publications:** *Eye-Bank for Sight Restoration--Eye to Eye*, quarterly. Newsletter. Includes annual report. *Price:* Free.

★ 13452 ★   Eye Care (EC)
1412 28th NW
Washington, DC 20007
Phone: (202)628-3816
Fax: (703)904-3945
Donna A. Fujiwara, Dir.

Founded: 1978. **Description:** Serves the visually neglected by bringing up-to-date ophthalmic care to people who would otherwise have little or no access to professional help for eye injuries or eye diseases. Maintains seven clinics, a paraprofessional ophthalmic assistants training program, three ophthalmic operating suites, and a rehabilitation program in Haiti. Sponsors an educational exhibit about eyes in the Children's Museum in Washington, DC. Shares information on unique cases discovered in areas served. **Publications:** Brochure.

★ 13453 ★   Fidelco Guide Dog Foundation (FGDF)
PO Box 142
Bloomfield, CT 06002
Phone: (203)243-5200
Fax: (203)243-7215
Roberta C. Kaman, Exec.VP

Founded: 1960. **Members:** 25,000. **Description:** Purpose is to breed, train, and place Fidelco German shepherd guide dogs with blind persons (the Fidelco shepherd is a special breed ideally suited for guide work because of its intelligence, strength, health, and stability). Provides "In-Community" training services to blind persons; reviews performance of the guide dog teams (dog and blind individual) to see that satisfactory level of achievement is maintained; utilizes genetic processes and clinical methods to improve and refine the breed; maintains an ongoing program for development and improvement of training methods. Fidelco puppies are raised in a volunteer family for the first 12-14 months, then trained by FGDF staff for six months before final introduction to and training in the workplace and home environment of the blind recipient with a trainer's help. Maintains speakers' bureau. FGDF activities, training, and placement of guide dogs is concentrated in New England and metropolitan New York. **Publications:** Annual Report, annual. • *Between Friends*, 3/year. Newsletter. • *FAN*, 3/year. Published in conjunction with *Between Friends*. **Formerly:** Fidelco Foundation; (1981) Fidelco Breeder's Foundation.

★ 13454 ★   Fight for Sight (FFS)
500 E. Remington Rd.
Schaumburg, IL 60173-4557
Phone: (708)843-2020
Fax: (708)843-8458
Mildred Weisenfeld, Founder&Exec.Dir.

Founded: 1946. **Description:** A research division of Prevent Blindness America. Supports research in vision and ophthalmology to restore and preserve sight through advances in detection, prevention, treatment, and curing of visual disorders and diseases.

★ 13455 ★   Focus
Department of Ophthalmology
Loyola University Med. Center
2160 S. 1st Ave.
Maywood, IL 60153
Phone: (708)216-3408
Fax: (708)216-3557
James E. McDonald, M.D., Pres.

Founded: 1961. **Members:** 400. **Description:** Volunteer eye surgeons. Allows American ophthalmologists the opportunity to represent their profession and country by working overseas in an area of desperate need. Doctors pay their own transportation and expenses, and contribute two working weeks of their vacation time to treating patients in Nigeria, where eye care would otherwise not be available. Medical equipment and drugs have been donated by U.S. drug and medical supply firms to the clinics operated by Focus in these countries. Group is unrelated to association of same name. **Publications:** Newsletter, 4-6/month.

★ 13456 ★   The Foundation Fighting Blindness (RPFFB)
1401 Mt. Royal Ave., 4th Fl.
Baltimore, MD 21217-4245
Phone: (410)225-9400
Free: 800-638-5555
Fax: (410)225-3936
Robert M. Gray, Exec.Dir.

Founded: 1971. **Members:** 65,000. **Local Groups:** 55. **Description:** Conducts fundraising to support research on retinal degenerative diseases including retinitis pigmentosa, macular degeneration, and Usher syndrome. Coordinates: retina donor and registry program for persons with RP and their blood relatives; self-help networks for persons with Usher syndrome and Bardet-Biedl-Syndrome and young people 16-35 years old. Produces and supplies information and materials; provides referral service. **Publications:** Annual Report. • Audiotapes. • *Fighting Blindness News*, 3-4/year. Newsletter. Contains scientific research updates and feature articles on persons with retinitis pigmentosa and allied retinal degenerations. *Price:* Free. • *Information About RP and Other Retinal Degenerative Diseases*. • *Information About Usher's Syndrome (RP with Hearing Loss)*. • *Keeping the Future in Sight*. • Videos. **Formerly:** RP Foundation Fighting Blindness; (1984) National Retinitis Pigmentosa Foundation.

★ 13457 ★   Glaucoma Research Foundation (ARF)
490 Post St., Ste. 830
San Francisco, CA 94102
Phone: (415)986-3162
Free: 800-826-6693
Fax: (415)986-3763
Tara L. Steele, Exec.Dir.

Founded: 1978. **Description:** Seeks to protect the sight of people who have glaucoma through research and education. Sponsors clinical and basic research programs to improve glaucoma patient care and increase public knowledge of the disease. Sponsors the Glaucoma Support Network, a national, telephone-based peer support network for glaucoma patients and their families. **Publications:** *Gleams*, quarterly. Newsletter. Includes research updates, foundation news, and medical column. *Price:* Free. • *Keeping an Eye on Glaucoma*. Brochure. *Price:* Free. • *Understanding and Living with Glaucoma*. *Price:* Free. **Formerly:** (1993) Foundation for Glaucoma Research.

★ 13458 ★   Glaucoma Society of the International Congress of Ophthalmology (GSICO)
c/o Y. Kitazawa, M.D.
Gifu University
Tsukasa-Machi 40
Gifu 500, Japan
Phone: 11 81651241
Fax: 11 81659012
Y. Kitazawa, M.D., Sec.

Founded: 1978. **Members:** 100. **Languages:** English. **Description:** Ophthalmologists with a special interest in glaucoma. Provides a forum for the exchange of information on new treatments of eye disease. **Publications:** *Glaucoma Updates I-IV*, quadrennial. • *Transaction*, quadrennial.

★ 13459 ★ Gospel Association for the Blind (GAB)
PO Box 62
Delray Beach, FL 33447
Phone: (407)274-9700
Fax: (407)274-4288
Beatrice Montanus, Pres.

Founded: 1947. **Description:** Religious corporation supported by contributions "to evangelize the physically blind by presenting the Gospel of the Lord Jesus Christ." Provides counseling; sponsors radio programs and summer camp. **Publications:** *Gospel Messenger*, monthly. Newsletter. Carries the message of the Gospel to the blind. Contains religious stories, poems, and articles. Available on cassette. *Price:* Free to the blind. • *Jottings*, monthly. Newsletter. Christian-oriented; includes profiles of blind people. *Price:* Free.

★ 13460 ★ Guide Dog Foundation for the Blind (GDFB)
371 E. Jericho Tpke.
Smithtown, NY 11787
Phone: (516)265-2121
Free: 800-548-4337
Fax: (516)361-5192
Wells B. Jones, CAE, Exec.Dir.

Founded: 1946. **Members:** 60,000. **Description:** Works to provide independence and mobility for qualified blind applicants by presenting them with trained guide dogs, free of charge. Dogs are raised in volunteer homes for the first year, then trained for four to six months. Conducts 26-day residential training program for blind persons and their dogs at Smithtown, NY. Guarantees continuing free services for life. Maintains speakers' bureau. **Publications:** Annual Report, annual. • *Guideways*, 3-5/year. Newsletter. Updates the foundation's activities. *Price:* Free. **Also Known As:** Second Sight; Guiding Eyes; Guide Dog Foundation.

★ 13461 ★ Guide Dog Users, Inc. (GDUI)
57 Grandview Ave.
Watertown, MA 02172
Phone: (617)926-9198
Kim Charlson, Contact

Founded: 1969. **Members:** 600. **State Groups:** 17. **Description:** Persons who are visually handicapped or blind and who use guide dogs; other interested individuals. Conducts seminars, workshops, and public relations programs. Encourages promotion of aids for mobility skills and employment of the blind; promotes selfhelp concept for blind persons. Operates speakers' bureau. **Publications:** Brochures. • *Pawtracks*, quarterly. Newsletter. Provides medical, legal, and financial information on canine maintenance on audiocassette, with specific emphasis on the needs of guide dog users. *Price:* Included in membership dues; $10/year for nonmembers.

★ 13462 ★ Guide Dogs of America (GDA)
13445 Glenoaks Blvd.
Sylmar, CA 91342
Phone: (818)362-5834
Fax: (818)362-6870
John B. Pettitt, Pres.

Founded: 1948. **Description:** Works to specially train labrador retrievers, golden retrievers, and German shepherds guide dogs for blind persons. Blind students live at the GDA school during an intensive four-week training period during which a guide dog is "matched" to each student. Training and dogs are provided without charge to the blind; GDA is supported by donations from individuals, companies, and various organizations and service clubs. Maintains speakers' bureau. **Publications:** *Partners*, 3/year. Newsletter.

★ 13463 ★ Guide Dogs for the Blind (GDB)
PO Box 151200
San Rafael, CA 94915-1200
Phone: (415)499-4000
Fax: (415)499-4035
Bruce C. Benzler, Exec.Dir.

Founded: 1942. **Description:** Supported by individuals, firms, foundations, clubs, and bequests. Provides guide dogs and in-residence training on their use to qualified blind persons, free of charge. **Publications:** *Guide Dog News*, quarterly. Newsletter.

★ 13464 ★ Guide Dogs for the Blind Association (GDBA)
Hillfields
Burghfield
Reading, Berks. RG7 3YG, England
Phone: 1734 835555
Fax: 1734 835433
J.C. Oxley, Dir.Gen.

Founded: 1934. **Members:** 2,000. **Local Groups:** 450. **Languages:** English. **Description:** Breeds and trains guide dogs for the visually impaired; provides instruction for the use and care of the dogs. Offers ancillary services and facilities for the visually impaired. **Publications:** *FORWARD*, quarterly. Magazine. Also available in Braille and on audiotape.

★ 13465 ★ Guiding Eyes for the Blind (GEB)
611 Granite Springs Rd.
Yorktown Heights, NY 10598
Phone: (914)245-4024
Free: 800-942-0149
Fax: (914)245-1609
William D. Badger, Pres.

Founded: 1954. **Description:** Provides fully trained guide dogs and instruction in their use to visually impaired and blind individuals including special needs students wish additional challenges. Conducts 3-year course for instructors and 4-week training programs for blind persons in proper use and care of guide dogs at Yorktown Heights, NY. Provides in-service education for staff and seminars for orientation and mobility instructors and other rehabilitation professionals. Maintains speakers' bureau of program graduates. **Publications:** *Guide Lines*, quarterly. Newsletter. • *Insight*, biennial. Magazine. • *Lions Connection*, quarterly.

★ 13466 ★ Helen Keller International (HKI)
90 Washington St., 15th Fl.
New York, NY 10006
Phone: (212)943-0890
Fax: (212)943-1220
John M. Palmer, Exec.Dir.

Founded: 1915. **Description:** Assists governments and voluntary agencies throughout Asia, Africa, and the Americas (including the United States) to establish and integrate, into their national health and welfare systems, services to prevent or cure eye diseases and blindness and to rehabilitate and educate visually disabled persons. Focuses on programs in the prevention and treatment of blindness caused by malnutrition, trachoma, onchocerciasis and cataracts. Trains health workers at all levels in the use of specially developed materials to diagnose and treat eye problems and to refer patients to hospitals. Conducts courses for teachers of blind children and for vocational and mobility instructors of blind adults; offers training for indigenous field workers who instruct the rural blind in daily living skills and provide vocational education. Provides information on programs and services on the problem of blindness throughout the world. Compiles statistics. **Publications:** *Helen Keller International--Annual Report*. *Price:* Free. • *Insight*, 3/year. Newsletter. *Price:* Free. Also publishes fact sheets, technical reports, training materials on nutritional blindness detection and treatment, and educational materials. **Formerly:** (1925) Permanent Blind Relief War Fund; (1946) American Braille Press for War and Civilian Blind; (1977) American Foundation for Overseas Blind.

★ 13467 ★ Helen Keller International
2139 Fidel Reyes St.
Malata
Manila, Philippines
Phone: 2 595421
Rolf D. W. Klemm, Dir.

Languages: English, Tagalog. **Description:** Fosters community-based blindness prevention and rehabilitation programs and services. Provides technical assistance and materials for the design and implementation of eye care within the existing primary health care system. Conducts projects and disseminates information on: preventing nutritional blindness; reducing cataract blindness; combatting onchocerciasis ("river blindness"); and improving the quality of life of the visually impaired. Distributes medicines; offers educational services.

★ 13468 ★ Helen Keller International
17 Rajawatte Terrace
Sieble Ave.
Colombo 5, Sri Lanka
Phone: 1 552411
Dr. Tilak Munasinghe, Dir.

Languages: English. **Description:** Fosters community-based blindness prevention and rehabilitation programs and services. Provides technical assistance and materials for the design and implementation of eye care within the existing primary health care system. Conducts projects and disseminates information on: preventing nutritional blindness; reducing cataract blindness; combatting onchocerciasis ("river blindness"); and improving the quality of life of the visually impaired. Distributes medicines; offers educational services.

★ 13469 ★ **Helen Keller International (HKIN)**
PO Box 3255
Kathmandu, Nepal
Phone: 1 410992
Dale Davis, Liaison

Description: Works to prevent blindness; provides rehabilitative services to the blind. Cooperates with government agencies to devise and implement vision care initiatives. Programs focus on preventing nutritional and other preventable forms of blindness. Makes available routine eye care services; distributes medicine for treatment of diseases causing blindness.

★ 13470 ★ **Helen Keller International (HKII)**
Bina Mulia Bldg., 9th Fl.
Jalan H.R. Resuna Said
10 Kunigan, Kav
12950 Jakarta, Indonesia
Phone: 21 5207297
Steven E. Wilbur, Dir.

Description: National branch of the international organization. Fosters community-based blindness prevention and rehabilitation programs and services. Provides technical assistance and materials for the design and implementation of eye care within the existing primary health care system. Conducts projects and disseminates information on: preventing nutritional blindness; reducing cataract blindness; combatting onchocerciasis ("river blindness"); and improving the quality of life of the blind. Distributes medicine for eye disease treatment. Offers educational services.

★ 13471 ★ **Helen Keller International (HKI)**
PO Box 76
Dodoma, United Republic of Tanzania
Phone: 61 24514
Fax: 61 24514
Dr. B.B.O. Mmbaga, Director

Languages: English. **Description:** Fosters community-based blindness prevention and rehabilitation programs and services. Provides technical assistance and materials for the design and implementation of eye care within the existing primary health care system. Conducts projects and disseminates information on: preventing nutritional blindness; reducing cataract blindness; combatting onchocerciasis ("river blindness"); and improving the quality of life of the blind. Distributes medicine for eye disease treatment. Offers educational services. **Publications:** *Prevention of Blindness on Trauchoma, Vitamin Deficiency, Cataract and Others.*

★ 13472 ★ **Helen Keller International (HKI)**
BP 11728
Niamey, Niger
Phone: 735026
Fax: 732963
Else Sanogo-Glenthoj, Country Dir.

Founded: 1987. **Languages:** French. **Description:** Fosters community-based blindness prevention and rehabilitation programs and services. Provides technical assistance and materials for the design and implementation of eye care within the existing primary health care system. Conducts projects and disseminates information on: preventing nutritional blindness; re-

ducing cataract blindness; combatting onchocerciasis ("river blindness"); and improving the quality of life of the blind. Distributes medicine for eye disease treatment. Offers educational services.

★ 13473 ★ **Helen Keller International (HKI)**
3, rue Sekkoura
Rabat, Morocco
Phone: 7 756636
Fatima-Zohra Akalay

Founded: 1915. **Languages:** Arabic, French. **Description:** Fosters community-based blindness prevention and rehabilitation programs and services. Provides technical assistance and materials for the design and implementation of eye care within the existing primary health care system. Conducts projects and disseminates information on: preventing nutritional blindness; reducing cataract blindness; combatting onchocerciasis ("river blindness"); and improving the quality of life of the blind. Distributes medicine for eye disease treatment. Offers educational services.

★ 13474 ★ **Helen Keller International (HKI)**
c/o Dr. Siaka Diarra
ABPA 01
BP 5588
Ouagadougou, Burkina Faso
Phone: 303354
Dr. Tetevi D. Logovi

Languages: French. **Description:** Provides blindness prevention and rehabilitation services in developing countries. Works primarily with ministries of health in developing nations enabling indigenous personnel to design, implement, and evaluate preventative eye care and rehabilitation projects. Provides training, equipment, and technical assistance towards integrating eye care services within the existing health care system. Project activities include: preventing nutritional blindness and death through the promotion of vitamin A-rich foods, supplements, and food fortification; reducing the occurrence of cataract blindness using innovative approaches; combatting onchocerciasis, "river blindness," through surveillance and education; strengthening primary eye care services; improving the quality of life of the blind through the establishment of community-based rehabilitation and integrated education.

★ 13475 ★ **Helen Keller International**
Universidade de Campinas
Nucleus of Blindness Prevention
Caixa Postal 1170
13100 Campinas, SP, Brazil
Phone: 19 2397766
Dra Alzira Delgado, Contact

Description: Works to prevent blindness; provides rehabilitative services to the blind. Cooperates with government agencies to devise and implement vision care initiatives. Programs focus on preventing nutritional and other preventable forms of blindness. Makes available routine eye care services; distributes medicine for treatment of diseases causing blindness.

★ 13476 ★ **Helen Keller National Center for Deaf-Blind Youths and Adults (HKNC)**
111 Middle Neck Rd.
Sands Point, NY 11050
Phone: (516)944-8900
Fax: (516)944-7302
Joseph J. McNulty, Dir.

Founded: 1969. **Regional Groups:** 10. **Description:** Established to provide and develop maximum support and training to deaf-blind individuals. Objectives are to: evaluate the degree of physical and psychosocial functioning of deaf-blind individuals; determine rehabilitation needs, interests, and potential; design and improve rehabilitation techniques. Provides: rehabilitation to achieve meaningful contact with the environment, effective means of communication, and constructive participation in the home and community; community education programs; job placement for people who are deaf-blind; placement in residential settings. Acts as a resource center. Conducts research on the implications of deaf-blindness and the impact of the disability. Is operated by Helen Keller Services for the Blind. Sponsors annual National Helen Keller Deaf-Blind Awareness Week. **Publications:** *Directory of Agencies and Organizations Serving Deaf-Blind Individuals*, periodic. Directory. Lists federally, publically, and privately funded programs that aid deaf-blind individuals. Includes director's name and geographical service area. • *Facts About Deaf-Blindness.* Brochure. • *Guidelines for Helping Deaf-Blind Persons.* Brochure. • *Nat-Cent News*, 3/year. Magazine. Covers resources, new technology, and issues of interest to professionals, families, and deaf-blind persons. Available in large print and braille. *Price:* Free to deaf-blind readers and libraries; $10/year for others. **Formerly:** National Rehabilitation of Deaf-Blind Adults.

HIKE Fund
See: Entry 3528

In Touch Networks (ITN)
See: Entry 7000

★ 13477 ★ **Independent Visually Impaired Enterprisers (IVIE)**
c/o American Council of the Blind
1155 15th St. NW, Ste. 720
Washington, DC 20005
Phone: (202)467-5081
Free: 800-424-8666
Fax: (202)467-5085
Arnold Austin, Pres.

Founded: 1980. **Members:** 50. **Description:** Blind and visually impaired people who own or operate small businesses. Seeks to: broaden vocational opportunities in business for the blind and visually impaired; improve rehabilitational facilities for all types of business enterprises; publicize capabilities of the blind and visually impaired. Maintains speakers' bureau.

★ 13478 ★ **International Academy of Sports Vision (NASV)**
200 S. Progress Ave.
Harrisburg, PA 17109
Phone: (717)652-8080
Fax: (717)652-8878
Dr. A. I. Garner, Exec.Dir.

Founded: 1984. **Members:** 1,000. **Description:** Optometrists and opthalmologists; athletic trainers, team physicians, coaches, and students; educational institutions and eyewear manufacturers. Purpose is to: provide comprehensive vision care for individuals active in sports and fitness programs; foster the promotion and advancement of research, development, and education in the field; facilitate the design, development, and fitting of both protective and corrective contact lenses and eyewear for athletes; advance and enhance the role of the sports specialist to the public through a public relations program. Acts as a forum for the discussion and exchange of information in the areas of developmental vision, vision training, and therapy. Offers referral services. Bestows the Blanton Collier Award; maintains speakers' bureau; compiles statistics. **Publications:** Audiotapes. • *Journal of the International Academy of Sports Vision.* Journal. • Membership Directory, annual. • *SportsVision*, quarterly. Magazine. • *Update*, quarterly. • Videos. **Formerly:** (1991) National Academy of Sports Vision.

★ 13479 ★ **International Agency for the Prevention of Blindness (IAPB)**
Grosvenor Hall
Bolnore Rd.
Haywards Heath, W. Sussex RH16 4BX, England
Phone: 1444 458810
Fax: 1444 458810
Alan W. Johns, Sec.Gen.

Founded: 1975. **Members:** 65. **Languages:** English. **Description:** Ophthalmic societies and societies for the prevention of blindness whose members include ophthalmologists, public health officers, nutritionists, geneticists, and other health workers. Coordinates international research into the causes of impaired vision or blindness; promotes measures calculated to eliminate such causes; disseminates knowledge worldwide on preventing blindness and on matters pertaining to care of the eyes. Cooperates with the World Health Organization, United Nations Children's Fund, and other international agencies. Bestows awards. **Publications:** *IAPB News*, semiannual. Newsletter. • *World Blindness and Its Prevention*, quadrennial. Proceedings.

★ 13480 ★ **International Association of Boards of Examiners in Optometry (IAB)**
4330 East West Hwy., Ste. 1117
Bethesda, MD 20814
Phone: (301)718-6506
Fax: (301)656-0989
James S. Vrac, Exec.Dir.

Founded: 1919. **Members:** 54. **National Groups:** 4. **State Groups:** 50. **Description:** State, territorial, and provincial boards of optometry. Purposes are to: exchange information and engage in programs and joint activities relating to the licensing and education of optometrists, including accreditation of schools and colleges; classify continuing education programs; develop examinations in clinical skills and use of pharmaceutical agents. Seeks to: improve reciprocal relations between licensing jurisdictions; cooperate in solving the mutual problems of member boards; improve the standards of the

profession, the delivery of health services, and the services of regulatory licensing agencies for the welfare and protection of the public. **Publications:** *Directory of Boards of Optometry*, annual. Directory. Lists members of state boards with addresses and phone/fax. *Price:* $20. • *IAB Greensheet*, quarterly. Newsletter.

International Association of Ocular Surgeons (IAOS)
See: Entry 12275

★ 13481 ★ **International Association of Optometric Executives (IAOE)**
100 S. University Ave., Ste. 311
Little Rock, AR 72205-5216
Phone: (501)661-7675
Fax: (501)661-1039
Betty Valachovic, CAE, Dir.

Members: 75. **Description:** Executives of optometric associations in 10 countries. Promotes continuing education in optometric association management. **Formerly:** Society of Association Optometric Executives.

★ 13482 ★ **International Blind Sports Association (IBSA)**
(Association Internationale pour le Sport des Aveugles)
Quevedo 1
E-28014 Madrid, Spain
Phone: 1 5894533
Fax: 1 5894537
Mr. Enrique Sanz, Pres.

Founded: 1981. **Members:** 90. **Regional Groups:** 7. **Languages:** English, French, German, Italian, Russian, Spanish. **Description:** National organizations, institutions, and committees involved in sports for the blind. Objectives are to: involve and inspire blind persons in regular sports activities; encourage friendship among blind athletes; promote and disseminate the ideas of competitive sport and recreational sport for the blind; uphold the Olympic ideal and act in accordance with its principles. Plans, promotes, and coordinates international sports events for the blind; registers records and best performances. Sponsors competitions. **Publications:** *Blind Sports International*, quarterly. Magazine.

★ 13483 ★ **International Council for Education of the Visually Handicapped (ICEVH)**
(Conseil International pour l'Education des Handicapes de la Vue — CIEHV)
37 Jesselton Crescent
10450 Penang, Malaysia
Phone: 4 369933
Fax: 4 369357
William G. Brohier, Pres.

Founded: 1952. **Regional Groups:** 8. **Languages:** English, Spanish. **Description:** Teachers and educators of the visually handicapped and other interested persons. Advocates education of the visually handicapped worldwide; works to improve existing facilities through training programs for teachers, refresher courses, and provision of teaching materials. Offers assistance for professional training. Conducts teacher training courses in developing countries. **Publications:** *The Educator*, semiannual.

Journal. • *International Resource Directory.* Book. **Formerly:** (1972) International Conference of Educators of Blind Youth.

★ 13484 ★ **International Ergophthalmological Society (Societas Ergophthalmologica Internationalis — SEI)**
55 Front St.
Nanaimo, BC, Canada V9R 5H9
Phone: (604)753-1612
Fax: (604)753-2767
Dr. Paul de Jong, Pres.

Founded: 1966. **Members:** 150. **National Groups:** 15. **Languages:** English, French, German, Spanish. **Description:** National ergophthalmological associations in 47 countries; interested individuals. Promotes scientific research in the area of industrial ophthalmology (ergophthalmology) and the establishment and development of professional contacts. Conducts periodic symposia. **Publications:** Handbook, periodic. • *Problems of Industrial Medicine in Ophthalmology*, periodic.

★ 13485 ★ **International Eye Foundation (IEF)**
7801 Norfolk Ave., Ste. 200
Bethesda, MD 20814
Phone: (301)986-1830
Fax: (301)986-1876
Victoria M. Sheffield, Exec.Dir.

Founded: 1961. **Description:** Qualified ophthalmologists who are members of the Society of Eye Surgeons. Promotes the prevention of blindness worldwide. Disseminates information to ophthalmologists on recent advances in eye surgery and trains physicians, nurses, paramedical personnel, and technicians in the care and treatment of eye patients. Aids in the establishment of eye care delivery systems and eye banks; provides eye tissues for operations. Collaborates with governments and international health agencies. **Publications:** Annual Report. • *International Eye Foundation--Eye to Eye*, semiannual. Newsletter. Concerned with the prevention of blindness in the developing countries; includes information on foundation programs. *Price:* Free. Also publishes fact sheets.

★ 13486 ★ **International Eye Foundation - Malawi**
PO Box 2273
Blantyre, Malawi
Phone: 630237
Fax: 631527
Mr. Joe Canner, Country Dir.

Members: 35. **Description:** Works to guarantee eye care and treatments for eye diseases to citizens of Malawi. Collaborates with governments and NGOs. Disseminates information.

★ 13487 ★ **International Federation of Asian and Pacific Associations of Optometrists (IFAPAO)**
7 Cookson St.
Camberwell, VIC 3124, Australia
Phone: 3 8829122
Fax: 3 8826203
Dr. Damien P. Smith, Sec.Gen.

Founded: 1978. **Members:** 26. **Languages:** English. **Description:** National associations of optometrists in 20 countries. Purpose is to improve the delivery of eye care and standards of visual welfare to people in the the Asian-Pacific region. **Publications:** *Vision Asia-Pacific*, quarterly. Journal. **Formerly:** International Federation of Asian and Pacific Associations of Optometry.

★ 13488 ★ **International Federation of Ophthalmological Societies (IFOS) (Federation Internationale des Societes d'Ophtalmologie — IFOS)**
Institute of Ophthalmology
Philips van Leydenlaan 15
NL-6526 EX Nijmegen, Netherlands
Phone: 80 613138
Fax: 80 540522
Dr. August F. Deutman, Sec.Gen.

Founded: 1933. **Members:** 60. **Languages:** English, French, German, Spanish. **Description:** National ophthalmological societies. Works to promote the science of ophthalmology and to ensure permanent cooperation between ophthalmological societies. **Publications:** *Proceedings*, quadrennial. Also publishes periodic abstracts.

★ 13489 ★ **International Friendly Circle of the Blind (IFCB)**
PO Box 222
Berkeley, CA 94704
Phone: (415)338-6436
Don Brown, Pres.

Founded: 1987. **Description:** Individuals who collect braille writers, braille paper, pens, pencils, and other writing materials and send this material to blind or visually impaired students in developing countries.

★ 13490 ★ **International Glaucoma Congress (IGC)**
4711 W. Golf Rd., Ste. 408
Skokie, IL 60076
Phone: (312)951-1400
Fax: (312)951-1410
John G. Bellows, M.D., Dir.

Founded: 1977. **Members:** 6,000. **Languages:** English. **Description:** Licensed physicians from 10 countries dedicated to disseminating information pertinent to glaucoma and its treatment. Educational activities include review courses; tutorials and workshops designed to improve skills and teach new procedures; clinical seminars on recent advances in opthalmology. Is seeking to adopt modern communicative technologies to convey glaucoma information to ophthalmologists worldwide. **Publications:** *Glaucoma*, bimonthly. Journal. Includes information on educational opportunities.

★ 13491 ★ **International Myopia Prevention Association (IMPA)**
RD 5, Box 171
Ligonier, PA 15658
Phone: (412)238-2101
Donald S. Rehm, Pres.

Founded: 1974. **Members:** 100. **Description:** Concerned individuals and organizations united to: work for the widespread acceptance of the concept, now supported by studies and research, that acquired myopia is caused by excessive close work and is not an inherited condition; inform the public in an impartial manner about the methods available for preventing and controlling myopia; promote the periodic testing of the vision of children so that the potential and beginning myopes can be found early when treatment is most effective; promote the use of proper reading habits and adequate lighting in schools, homes, and offices; maintain a register of eye care practitioners who are interested in myopia prevention and skilled in its techniques; assist the public in coming into contact with these practition ers; maintain an advisory board of scientists, researchers, educators, optometrists, and ophthalmologists who are involved with the myopia problem and can advise on the activities of the association; solicit contributions to carry on educational and scientific activities related to myopia prevention. **Publications:** *Myopia--A Preventable Tragedy*. Film. • *The Myopia Myth: The Truth About Nearsightedness and How to Prevent It*. • *The Prevention of Acquired Myopia*. Booklet.

★ 13492 ★ **International Oculoplastic Society, Inc. (IOSI)**
c/o Pierre Guibor, M.D.
630 Park Ave.
New York, NY 10021
Phone: (212)734-1010
Fax: (201)871-8474
Pierre Guibor, M.D., Dir.

Founded: 1978. **Members:** 3,000. **Regional Groups:** 4. **Local Groups:** 2. **Description:** Surgeons specializing in ophthalmology, otolaryngology, dermatology, and plastic surgery. Sponsors professional education and clinically applied research in the prevention, diagnosis, and treatment of disorders of the eye, orbit, adnexa, face, and skin. Seeks to promote and establish successful forms of patient care and treatment through open discussions, seminars, and instructional courses on clinical research, surgery, and medical advances. Conducts educational and charitable programs. Maintains speakers' bureau and placement servic. Compiles statistics. **Publications:** *Oculoplastic Newsletter*, semiannual. Newsletter. *Price:* Free.

★ 13493 ★ **International Opticians Association**
113 Eastbourne Mews
Paddington
London W2 6LQ, England
Phone: 171 2580240
Fax: 171 7241175
A.P.D. Westhead, Gen.Sec.

Founded: 1955. **Members:** 5. **Languages:** English. **Description:** National associations of opticians. Promotes the science of optics by fostering cooperation among members. Seeks to maintain the highest possible educational, ethical, and professional standards in the field. **Formerly:** International Guild of Opticians.

★ 13494 ★ **International Optometric and Optical League (IOOL) (Ligue Internationale d'Optometrie et d'Optique)**
10 Knaresborough Pl.
London SW5 0TG, England
Phone: 171 3704765
Fax: 171 3731143
Dorothy Leason, Sec.

Founded: 1927. **Members:** 65. **National Groups:** 60. **Regional Groups:** 3. **Languages:** English. **Description:** National optical and optometric organizations in 50 countries. Promotes optometry and vision care worldwide. Works to develop optometry through education, legal and legislative advice, discussion with authorities, and support of similar associations. Is concerned with protecting optometry from what the league sees as proposed restrictive legislation, and apathy toward the profession. Establishes educational standards; offers evaluation program for schools and colleges of optometry; provides consulting services. **Publications:** Brochure, periodic. • *International Country Contact Register*, periodic. • *Interoptics*, quarterly. Newsletter. • *Members Journals*, periodic. • *Optometric Mailing Directory*, periodic. Directory. Lists information on optometric organizations. • *Publications List*, periodic. • *Register of Schools and Colleges of Optometry*, periodic.

★ 13495 ★ **International Organization Against Trachoma (IOAT) (Organisation Internationale pour la Lutte Contre le Trachome)**
Universite de Paris-Val-de-Marne
Centre Hospitalier Intercommunal
Clinique Ophtalmologique de Creteil
40, ave. de Verdun
F-94010 Creteil, France
Phone: 1 45175220
Fax: 1 45175227
Gabriel Coscas, Pres.

Founded: 1923. **Members:** 1,200. **Languages:** English, French. **Description:** Circulates information in 20 countries on current trachoma research (trachoma is a chronic, contagious eye disease) and supplies the latest information on etiology, diagnosis, epidemiology, prevention, and treatment, thus providing a scientific basis for the fight against the disease. Promotes research on trachoma; facilitates the adoption of sanitary and other regulations aimed at implementing the fight against trachoma. Maintains close contact with the World Health Organization and other institutions engaged in the fight against trachoma. **Publications:** *Revue Internationale du Trachome*, 3/year. Journal.

★ 13496 ★ **International Orthokeratology Society (IOS)**
1575 W. Big Beaver, Ste. C-11
Troy, MI 48084
Phone: (810)649-6490
Free: 800-626-7846
Anthony Vincent Potts, O.D., Chm.

Founded: 1985. **Members:** 125. **Description:** Orthokeratologists (contact lens specialists) who are doctors of optometry or doctors of ophthalmology. Purpose is to increase public awareness of orthokeratology and support contact lens research. Sponsors clinical and university research. Maintains speakers' bureau. **Pub-lications:** *International Orthokeratology Soci-ety*, quarterly. Newsletter. • *Membership Direc-tory of the International Orthokeratology Society*, annual. Membership Directory.

★ 13497 ★ International Orthoptic Association (IOA)
Moorfields Eye Hospital
City Rd.
London EC1V 2PD, England
Phone: 171 2533411
Joyce Pinnick, Sec.-Treas.

Founded: 1967. **Members:** 4,000. **Languages:** English. **Description:** Orthoptists in 22 coun-tries certified to treat defects in binocular vision, faulty visual habits, and low visual acuity. Orga-nizes and conducts an international congress of orthoptists; shares information through newslet-ters. **Publications:** *Abstracts of Congress*, qua-drennial. Journal. • *Newsletter*, annual. News-letter.

★ 13498 ★ International Perimetric Society (IPS)
Department of Neurology
200 Hawkins Dr., No. 2007 RCP
Iowa City, IA 52242
Phone: (319)356-8758
Fax: (319)356-4505
Michael Wall, M.D., Sec.

Founded: 1974. **Members:** 300. **Languages:** English. **Description:** Opthalmologists, scien-tists, and technicians in 20 countries working in the field of perimetry (visual field testing) and re-lated areas. Promotes the study of normal and abnormal visual function and encourages world-wide cooperation and friendship among those working in the field. **Publications:** Proceedings, biennial.

★ 13499 ★ International Research Group on Colour Vision Deficiencies (IRGCVD)
Dept. of Communication and Neuroscience
Keele University
Stafford ST5 5BG, England
Phone: 1782 583060
Fax: 1782 583055
Prof. J.D. Moreland, Contact

Founded: 1971. **Members:** 280. **Languages:** English. **Description:** Ophthalmologists, op-tometrists, physicists, physiologists, psycholo-gists, and zoologists. Seeks to collaborate on the study of congenital and acquired color vision deficiencies. **Publications:** *Daltoniana*, quarter-ly. Newsletter. • *Proceedings of the IRGCVD Symposia*, biennial.

★ 13500 ★ International Society of Geographic Ophthalmology (ISGO) (Societe Internationale d'Ophtalmologie Geographique — SIOG)
5591, rue Cote des Neiges
Montreal, PQ, Canada H3T 1Y8
Phone: (514)735-1133
Fax: (514)731-0651
Dr. Marvin L. Kwitko, M.D., Exec.Sec.

Founded: 1970. **Members:** 250. **Languages:** English, French, German, Spanish. **Descrip-tion:** Ophthalmologists and others with an inter-est and expertise in the geographic distribution

of ocular disease, epidemiology, and pathology. Encourages international research on the geo-graphic distribution of ocular diseases; con-ducts related studies. Sends lecturers, ophthal-mic technicians, ophthalmologists, and other experts to developing countries to estimate the needs of programs for the prevention and cure of ocular diseases. Offers funding to students in ophthalmology from developing countries. Gathers statistics and compiles bibliography.

★ 13501 ★ International Society on Metabolic Eye Disease (ISMED)
1125 Park Ave.
New York, NY 10128
Phone: (212)427-1246
Fax: (212)360-7009
Heskel M. Haddad, M.D., Sec.-Treas.

Founded: 1971. **Members:** 600. **Description:** Ophthalmologists, pediatricians, endocrinolog-ists, internists, and paramedical personnel in 20 countries. Promotes the study of metabolic eye problems and biochemical and genetic aspects of such problems. **Publications:** Book. • *Meta-bolic, Pediatric, and Systemic Ophthalmology*, quarterly. Journal. *Price:* $160/year.

★ 13502 ★ International Society for Ocular Fluorophotometry (ISOF)
Hopital de Creteil
Eye University Clinic
40, ave. Verdun
F-94000 Creteil, France
Phone: 1 48987781
Fax: 1 48987787
Prof. C. Coscas, Exec.Sec.

Founded: 1982. **Members:** 500. **Regional Groups:** 3. **Languages:** English, French. **De-scription:** Persons from 20 countries interested in ocular fluorophotometry, the diagnosis of eye disease by observing the levels of fluorescein diffusion emitted from the eye. **Publications:** *ISOF Newsletter*, quarterly. Newsletter.

International Society for Ophthalmic Ultrasound (SIDUO)
See: Entry 11119

★ 13503 ★ International Society for Orbital Disorders (ISOD)
Academic Med. Center
Dept. of Ophthalmology
Orbital Center
Meibergdreef 9
NL-1105 AZ Amsterdam, Netherlands
Phone: 20 5669111
P. Mourits, Sec.

Founded: 1977. **Members:** 200. **Regional Groups:** 32. **Languages:** English. **Description:** Individuals in 43 countries engaged in the treat-ment of disorders of the human orbit and re-search on the orbit. (The orbit is the bony socket surrounding the eyeball.) **Publications:** *Orbit*, quarterly. Journal.

★ 13504 ★ International Strabismological Association (ISA)
c/o Dr. Eugene Helveston
702 Rotary Cir.
Indianapolis, IN 46202
Phone: (317)274-1214
Fax: (317)274-1111
Eugene Helveston, Sec.

Description: Ophthalmologists specializing in strabismus (eye movement disorders). Encour-ages research and education among members. Bestows quadrennial Linksz Medal and Award to outstanding strabismologists. **Publications:** Membership Directory, periodic. • *Proceedings Volume*, quadrennial. **Also Known As:** Associa-tion Internationale de Strabisme.

★ 13505 ★ Interprofessional Fostering of Opthalmic Care for Underserved Sectors (InFOCUS)
4444 Cullen Blvd., No. 1304
Houston, TX 77004
Phone: (713)748-2453
Fax: (713)743-2053
Dr. Ian B. Berger, Exec. Officer

Founded: 1988. **Members:** 40. **Description:** Eye care specialists, public health care profes-sionals, and international health care profes-sionals. Works to develop eye care systems for underserved populations; encourages self-reliance. Conducts educational and charitable programs; maintains speakers' bureau; spon-sors research on appropriate technology for pri-mary eye care.

★ 13506 ★ Jewish Braille Institute of America (JBI)
110 E. 30th St.
New York, NY 10016
Phone: (212)889-2525
Fax: (212)689-3692
Gerald M. Kass, Exec.VP

Founded: 1931. **Description:** Serves the reli-gious, cultural, educational, and communal needs of the Jewish blind, visually impaired, and reading disabled, and provides information on Judaism to the blind in general. Distributes ma-terials in braille, audio cassette, and large print Provides services in over 40 countries, including the U.S., Isreal, and the former Soviet Union. Is accredited as a non-governmental organization of the United Nations. **Publications:** Audi-otapes. • *English Braille*. • *Hebrew Braille Bible*. • *Hebrew Self-Taught*. Braille primer. • *JBI Voice*, 10/year. Magazine. Cassette format for non-braille reading blind and visually impaired. Includes articles on Jewish-related topics, poli-tics, stories, and poetry. *Price:* Free to blind and visually impaired persons. • *Jewish Braille Insti-tute of America--Directory of Services*, annual. Directory. Describes institute services and pro-grams. *Price:* Free. • *Jewish Braille Review*, 10/year. Magazine. In braille with articles, stories, and poetry culled from other sources of Judaic content for blind readers interested in Judaica. *Price:* Free to braille-reading blind. • *Jewish Reference Calendar*, annual. • *Likutim*, semian-nual. Magazine. Cassette and inkprint formats; contains articles on blindness, employment, parenting, and computer technology for the blind. *Price:* Free to blind and visually impaired. Also publishes prayerbooks and religious texts in Hebrew.

★ 13507 ★ **Jewish Guild for the Blind (JGB)**
15 W. 65th St.
New York, NY 10023
Phone: (212)769-6200
Fax: (212)595-4907
John F. Heimerdinger, Pres. & CEO

Founded: 1914. **Description:** Volunteer service agency for blind, visually handicapped, and multihandicapped people of all ages, races, and creeds. Provides social work, counseling, and AIDS case management; job development, placement, and training; support group services; rehabilitation, including vocational, high school equivalency training in orientation and mobility, activities of daily living, and transcription typing; adapted physical education; communication skills; medical services; adult day healthcare program called GuildCare in New York City, Yonkers, Bronx, Buffalo, and Albany, New York. Operates Early Intervention Program and preschool program for infants (up to age 5); school for multihandicapped children; state licensed psychiatric clinic for emotionally disturbed blind persons and their families; day treatment programs for multihandicapped blind adults; Joselow House, an intermediate care facility for blind developmentally disabled adults; Low Vision Services; Comprehensive Outpatient Rehabilitation Facility (C.O.R.F.), J.G.B. Facilities Corporation, the residential health care affiliate, operates Home for Aged Blind (a nursing home), the Newman Center for Alzheimer's Care, and Center for AIDS Care, a specialized facility for visually impaired persons with AIDS, in Yonkers, NY. Cosponsors health fairs/screenings for the community. Operates In Touch Network, a 24-hour reading service for blind and visually impaired persons. **Publications:** Newsletter, quarterly. Contains guild programs and events involving professional and volunteer supporters of guild services. *Price:* Included in membership dues. **Formerly:** (1960) New York Guild for the Jewish Blind.

★ 13508 ★ **John Milton Society for the Blind (JMS)**
475 Riverside Dr., Rm. 455
New York, NY 10115
Phone: (212)870-3336
Fax: (212)870-3229
Rev. Richard Randall Preston, Exec.Dir.

Founded: 1928. **Description:** Nondenominational Christian worldwide service to persons who cannot see to read regular print. Works to make Christian religious materials available to blind and visually impaired persons worldwide. Operates referral service. Provides materials for displays and exhibits. **Publications:** *A Faith More Precious Than Gold.* • *Directory of Resources for the Blind and Visually Impaired.* Directory. • *Discovery*, monthly. Religious digest for young people 8-18, in braille. *Price:* Free to blind persons. • *James: An Integrity of Faith.* • *John Milton Adult Lesson Quarterly.* Contains Bible studies and texts, in braille. *Price:* Free to blind persons. • *John Milton Magazine*, monthly. Magazine. Reprints, in braille, of reading material offered in over 50 religious periodicals for the sighted. Available in large print. *Price:* Free to blind persons. • *John Milton Talking Book Magazine*, bimonthly. Magazine. Cassette containing sacred music, poetry, stories,

historical and biographical information, and devotional and informative articles. • *May Fellowship Service*, annual. Transcript of the May service prepared by Church Women United. Available in large print and braille. • *Motto Calendar*, annual. Braille reproduction of the ink-print Motto Calendar published by a Quaker family in Pennsylvania. • *Prayers of the Bible for a Faithful Journey.* • *Special Bible Study*, annual. Available in braille. • *We Decide Together - A Guide to Making Ethical Decisions.* • *World Community Day Service*, annual. Transcript of the November service prepared by Church Women United. Available in large print and braille. • *World Day of Prayer Service*, annual. Transcript of the March service prepared by Church Women United. Available in large print and braille. Also publishes publications brochure. **Formerly:** John Milton Society.

★ 13509 ★ **Joint Commission on Allied Health Personnel in Ophthalmology (JCAHPO)**
2025 Woodlane Dr.
St. Paul, MN 55125-2995
Phone: (612)731-2944
Free: 800-284-3937
Fax: (612)731-0410
Maynard Wheeler, M.D., Pres.

Founded: 1969. **Description:** A certifying agency for allied health personnel. Objectives are: to encourage the establishment of medically oriented programs for training allied health personnel in ophthalmology; to develop standards of education and training in the field; to examine, certify, and recertify ophthalmic medical personnel, and encourage their continued occupational development. Conducts annual national certifying examinations and continuing education programs. **Publications:** Annual Report. *Price:* Free. • *Directory of Certified Ophthalmic Medical Personnel*, annual. Directory. Arranged alphabetically and geographically. *Price:* Free to certified ophthalmic allied health staff. • *JCAHPO Outlook*, bimonthly. Newspaper. Includes continuing education course listings. *Price:* Free to certified ophthalmic medical personnel; $20/year.

★ 13510 ★ **Joint Review Committee for Ophthalmic Medical Personnel (JRCOMP)**
2025 Woodlane Dr.
St. Paul, MN 55125-2995
Phone: (612)731-2944
Free: 800-284-3937
Lisa P. Rovick, Pres.

Members: 4. **Description:** Individuals from collaborating health organizations including the Association of Technical Personnel in Ophthalmology and Joint Commission on Allied Health Personnel in Ophthalmology. Evaluates ophthalmic educational programs applying for accreditation from the Commission on Accreditation of Allied Health Education Programs. Reviews and revises guidelines, maintains policies, and approves processes that comply with standards established for national accrediting agencies. Analyzes self-study reports; provides teams of representatives to conduct site visits of programs. Compiles statistics. **Publications:** *Educational Programs for Ophthalmic Medical Personnel*, 3/year. Brochure. *Price:* Free. **Former-**

ly: (1988) Joint Review Committee for the Ophthalmic Medical Assistant; (1989) Joint Review Commission for the Ophthalmic Medical Personnel.

★ 13511 ★ **Kamerata Inter-Regional Association (Mezregionalnaya Assotsiaisiya "Kamerata")**
ulitsa E. Pugacheva 11
603003 Nizhny-Novgorod, Russia
Phone: 8312 294488
Andrey Vladimirovich Temnov, Contact

Members: 10. **Languages:** Russian. **Description:** Promotes the social and professional development of the visually impaired.

★ 13512 ★ **Kerato-Refractive Society (KRS)**
PO Box 796728
Dallas, TX 75379
Phone: (214)601-5750
Fax: (214)713-9722
Ronald A. Schachar, M.D., Exec.Sec.

Founded: 1979. **Members:** 2,000. **Description:** Ophthalmologists and scientists interested in the latest advances in keratorefractive and laser techniques. (Keratorefraction is a surgical procedure in which the shape of the cornea and iris is changed in order to correct nearsightedness and astigmatism. The procedure is now performed with a diamond knife; use of lasers is still in the investigational stage.) Purpose is to keep professionals and others informed of the most recent advances and developments in ophthalmologic care. Conducts research and raises funds. Sponsors training programs. **Publications:** *Keratorefraction.* Book. • Newsletter, biennial. • *Radical Keratotomy.* Book. • *Refractive Keratoplasty.* Book. • *Refractive Modulation of the Cornea.* Book.

Keren-Or, Inc. (K-OI)
See: Entry 3253

★ 13513 ★ **Latin American Blind Union (Union Latinoamericano de Ciegos)**
Lavalle 3758, Ap. 1
1190 Buenos Aires, Argentina
Elina T. de Walsh, Sec.Gen.

Description: Blind and visually impaired individuals throughout Latin America. Acts as an advocate for the visually impaired. **Publications:** *America Latina.*

★ 13514 ★ **Latin American Blind Union (LABU) (Union Latinoamericana de Ciegos — ULAC)**
Durazno 1772
11200 Montevideo, Uruguay
Phone: 2 480618
Fax: 2 400789
Enrique Elissalde, Contact

Founded: 1985. **Members:** 155. **Languages:** Spanish. **Description:** Organizations for the blind in Latin American countries. Works for the prevention of blindness. Promotes the welfare of the blind and seeks to put them in control of their lives through the abolition of laws that discriminate against the visually handicapped. Sponsors educational programs in coordination with the International Agency for the Prevention of Blindness and the International Council for the Education of the Visually Handicapped. **Publications:** *America Latina*, quarterly. Newsletter.

★ **13515** ★ **Leader Dogs for the Blind (LDB)**
1039 S. Rochester Rd.
Rochester, MI 48307
Phone: (810)651-9011
Fax: (810)651-5812
William C. Hansen, Pres.

Founded: 1939. **Description:** Trains dogs to serve as guides for blind persons and conducts a supervised course of training to coordinate blind persons and their Leader Dogs as operating units; there is no charge for the service. Conducts research to determine the most satisfactory breed of dog for leader dog purposes. Facilities include a dormitory, kennel, veterinary hospital, and training center. **Publications:** Newsletter, quarterly. Available in large print, braille, and tape. • *Orientation of Dog Guide Users to New Environments.* **Formerly:** Path-Finder Guide Dogs; (1952) Leader Dog League for the Blind.

★ **13516** ★ **Lutheran Braille Evangelism Association (LBEA)**
1740 Eugene St.
White Bear Lake, MN 55110
Phone: (612)426-0469
Rev. Dennis Hawkinson, Exec.Dir.

Founded: 1952. **Members:** 2,000. **Description:** Supported by contributions of members. **Publications:** *Braille Evangelism Bulletin*, quarterly. Newsletter. Contains membership activities. *Price:* Free. • *Christian Magnifier: A Christian Magazine in Magnified Print*, monthly. Magazine. Contains large-print Christian inspirational readings. *Price:* $6/year. • *Tract Messenger*, monthly. Braille publication of Christian devotional readings and LBEA news. *Price:* Free. Also provides religious material in braille.

★ **13517** ★ **Lutheran Braille Workers (LBW)**
Box 5000
Yucaipa, CA 92399
Phone: (909)795-8977
Fax: (909)795-8970
LeRoy Delafosse, Exec.Dir.

Founded: 1943. **Members:** 7,000. **Description:** Volunteers staffing 201 work centers worldwide, through which they seek to bring the Bible to the blind and visually impaired. Teaches sighted volunteers to transcribe printed material into braille and large print. Produces and distributes free biblical and devotional material in braille and large print in 40 languages. Works to constantly upgrade the systems necessary for the production of braille materials. **Publications:** *Lutheran Braille Workers--Newsletter*, quarterly. Newsletter. Covers association activities. *Price:* Free. • *Work Center Directory*, annual. Directory. • *Work Center Memo*, monthly. Newsletter. Provides information to LBW work centers.

★ **13518** ★ **Middle East Committee for the Affairs of the Blind (MECAB)**
PO Box 3465
Riyadh 11471, Saudi Arabia
Phone: 1 4882200
Fax: 1 4888260
Sheikh Abdullah M. Al-Ghanim, Pres.

Founded: 1971. **Members:** 14. **Languages:** Arabic, English. **Description:** Repesentatives of Middle Eastern countries. Works to assist the blind, especially with respect to education and vocational training. Offers training courses and programs on prevention of blindness and rehabilitation of the blind. Operates a braille printing press. Funds charitable programs; provides placement service. Maintains talking book library. Sponsors Al-Noor Institute for the Blind and Regional Vocational Centre for Rehabilitation and Training of the Blind Girls. Maintains Permanent Regional Bureau of the Middle East Committee for the Affairs of the Blind. **Publications:** *Al-Fajr Magazine*, periodic. Magazine. • *Conference Proceeding*, quadrennial. • *Directory*, periodic. Directory.

★ **13519** ★ **Myopia International Research Foundation (MIRF)**
1265 Broadway, Rm. 608
New York, NY 10001
Phone: (212)684-2777
Joel Weintraub, M.D., Pres.

Founded: 1963. **Description:** Physicians and other professionals, myopes and their families, and other interested persons. Promotes interdisciplinary research in the causes, prevention, and treatment of myopia (condition of nearsightedness that may be progressive and result in blindness). Sponsors National Registries of Myopia Pathology, which receive bequests of eyes by myopes for study and research. Sponsors Myopia International Research Network to promote worldwide cooperative research on myopia. **Publications:** *Myopia Research Reports*. Reports. • *Proceedings of Myopia Conferences of MIRF*, periodic. Proceedings. **Formerly:** Myopia Research Foundation.

★ **13520** ★ **National Academy of Opticianry (NAO)**
10111 Martin Luther King, Jr. Hwy., Ste. 112
Bowie, MD 20720
Phone: (301)577-4828
Fax: (301)577-3880
Floyd H. Holmgrain, Jr., Exec.Dir.

Founded: 1973. **Members:** 6,000. **Description:** Offers review courses for national certification and state licensure examinations to members. Maintains speakers' bureau and Career Progression Program. **Publications:** *Academy Newsletter*, quarterly. Newsletter. • Brochure. • *Exam Review for Ophthalmic Dispensing*. • *Ophthalmic Dispensing Review Book*. Book. • *Optical Math Review*. • Videos.

★ **13521** ★ **National Accreditation Council for Agencies Serving the Blind and Visually Handicapped (NAC)**
15 E. 40th St., Ste. 1004
New York, NY 10016
Phone: (212)683-5068
Fax: (212)683-4475
Ruth Westman, Exec.Dir.

Founded: 1966. **Description:** Develops standards and administers a voluntary system of accreditation for local, state, and national agencies providing direct services to blind and visually handicapped persons. Sponsors training seminars for members and chairpersons of onsite review teams that visit organizations applying for accreditation and reaccreditation. **Publications:** Annual Report. • *The Standard-Bearer*, 3/year. Also publishes self-study and evaluation guides, incorporating standards for management and services of agencies and schools for people who are blind and visually handicapped; publications are available in print, braille, and recorded editions.

★ **13522** ★ **National Alliance of Blind Students (NABS)**
c/o American Council of the Blind
1155 15th St. NW, Ste. 720
Washington, DC 20005
Phone: (202)467-5081
Free: 800-424-8666
Monty Cassellius, Pres.

Founded: 1974. **Members:** 125. **State Groups:** 1. **Description:** Postsecondary students in academic, vocational, trade, and professional programs as well as disabled student service personnel. Aims to educate agencies, governments, institutions, and the public dealing with blind students as to their needs and educational pursuits in accredited postsecondary educational programs. Acts to protect rights and interests of blind students. Participates in annual National Student Seminar at the national convention of the American Council of the Blind. **Publications:** *Student Advocate*, quarterly.

★ **13523** ★ **National Association of Blind Teachers (NABT)**
c/o American Council of the Blind
1155 15th St. NW, Ste. 720
Washington, DC 20005
Phone: (202)467-5081
Free: 800-424-8666
Fax: (202)476-5085
John Buckley, Pres.

Founded: 1971. **Members:** 81. **State Groups:** 1. **Description:** Public school teachers, college and university professors, and teachers in residential schools for the blind. Purpose is to promote employment and professional goals of blind persons entering the teaching profession or those established in their respective teaching fields. Serves as a vehicle for the dissemination of information and the exchange of ideas addressing special problems of members. Compiles statistics. **Publications:** *The Blind Teacher*, quarterly. Newsletter. • *National Directory of Blind Teachers*, periodic. Directory.

National Association of Manufacturing Opticians (NAMO)
See: Entry 5866

★ **13524** ★ **National Association of Optometrists and Opticians (NAOO)**
18903 S. Miles Rd.
Cleveland, OH 44128
Phone: (216)475-8925
Fax: (216)475-8862
Franklin D. Rozak, VP

Founded: 1960. **Members:** 13,225. **Description:** Licensed optometrists, opticians, and corporations. Conducts public affairs programs of mutual importance to members; serves as an organizational center for special purpose programs; acts as a clearinghouse for information affecting the retail optical industry. **Formerly:** National Optical Association.

★13525★ **National Association for Parents of the Visually Impaired (NAPVI)**
PO Box 317
Watertown, MA 02272-0317
Phone: (617)972-7441
Free: 800-562-6265
Fax: (617)972-7444
Eileen Hudson, Pres.

Founded: 1980. **Members:** 2,000. **Regional Groups:** 7. **State Groups:** 15. **Description:** Parents and families of visually impaired children; community groups and agencies; interested individuals. Goals are to provide support for members and to promote public understanding of the needs and rights of the visually impaired child. Seeks to address parental needs for: emotional support; information about care, education, and treatment for their children; aid in establishing local, state, and regional groups; quality services for blind and impaired children; communication of their expertise and expectations with other parents and federal, state, and local service agencies; assurance that their children are accepted by society. Conducts workshops for parents. Conducts research programs. **Publications:** Audiotapes. • *Awareness*, quarterly. Newsletter. *Price:* Included in membership dues. • Brochures. • *How to Pack 'Em In: A Guide to Planning Workshops.* • *Mainstreaming Your Visually Impaired Child: Legislative Handbook for Parents.* Handbook. • *Parents to the Rescue.* Book. • *Preschool Learning Activities for the Visually Impaired Child: A Guide for Parents.* Book. • Reprints. • *Take Charge!: A Resource Guide for Parents of the Visually Impaired.* • Videos. • *Your Child's Information Journal.*

★13526★ **National Association of Vision Professionals (NAVP)**
c/o Prevention of Blindness Soc.
1775 Church St. NW
Washington, DC 20036
Phone: (202)234-1010
Fax: (202)234-1020
Arnold Simonse, Exec.Sec.

Founded: 1976. **Members:** 200. **Description:** Individuals responsible for or connected with vision conservation and eye health programs in public or private agencies and institutions. Serves as a forum for ideas and programs, cooperates with other agencies, and promotes professional standards. Certifies vision screening personnel. **Publications:** *National Association of Vision Professionals--Newsletter*, quarterly. Newsletter. *Price:* Included in membership dues. **Formerly:** (1986) National Association of Vision Program Consultants.

★13527★ **National Association for Visually Handicapped (NAVH)**
22 W. 21st St.
New York, NY 10010
Phone: (212)889-3141
Fax: (212)727-2931
Lorraine Marchi, Exec.Dir.

Founded: 1954. **Members:** 2,750. **Regional Groups:** 2. **Description:** Individuals, clubs, organizations, and foundations supporting NAVH's work in publishing and distributing large-print informational literature for the partially seeing. Acts as information clearinghouse regarding all public and private services available to the partially seeing. Offers guidance and counseling to parents of partially seeing children and to partially seeing adults. Educates the public and the professional community about the needs of the partially seeing. **Publications:** *About Children's Eyes.* • Catalog. Features visual aids. • *It's All Right to Be Angry.* • Knitting Instructions. • *Large Print Loan Library Catalog*, biennial. Catalog. Lists books in large print available from NAVH; also lists some commercial publishers' titles. • *National Association for Visually Handicapped--Bulletin: Annual Program Report*, periodic. Newsletter. Reports on association activities and programs. Includes obituaries. • *National Association for Visually Handicapped--In Focus*, 1-2/year. Newsletter. Provides visually handicapped children with stories, poems, and drawings contributed by young readers; large-print format. *Price:* Free. • *Seeing Clearly*, annual. Newsletter. Provides news, stories, and poems of interest to visually handicapped adults; large-print format. *Price:* Free. Also publishes guides, booklets, and manuals on eye diseases and services for visually impaired. **Formerly:** (1972) National Aid to Visually Handicapped.

★13528★ **National Beep Baseball Association (NBBA)**
2231 W. 1st Ave.
Topeka, KS 66606-1304
Phone: (913)234-2156
Michael Garrett, Pres.

Founded: 1975. **Members:** 500. **Local Groups:** 20. **Description:** Blind and visually impaired athletes, sighted volunteers, and others interested in participating in beep baseball. (Beep baseball uses a ball and two bases which emit sounds. Once the batter hits the ball, he or she must get to whichever base buzzes before one of the six other players fields the ball. The pitcher and catcher are sighted volunteers.) Promotes the development of amateur beep baseball and other recreational and competitive programs for the blind and physically handicapped; holds tournaments. Sponsors speakers' bureau; conducts research programs. **Publications:** *NBBA Guide*, annual. Includes a list of World Series champions, a history of beep baseball, and a description of the game. *Price:* Free. • Newsletter, quarterly. Includes score statistics, tournament information and rule changes. *Price:* Included in membership dues.

★13529★ **National Board of Examiners in Optometry**
4340 E. West Hwy., Ste. 1010
Bethesda, MD 20814
Phone: (301)652-5192
Fax: (301)907-0013
Dr. Norman E. Wallis, Exec.Dir.

Founded: 1951. **Description:** Administers entry-level criterion-referenced credentialing examinations to students and graduates of accredited schools and colleges of optometry for use by individual state licensing boards. Provides other evaluation, assessment, and survey services to the profession. **Publications:** Annual Report. • *Candidates Guide*, annual. • Manuals. • *Test Points*, 3/year. Newsletter.

★13530★ **National Braille Association (NBA)**
3 Townline Cir.
Rochester, NY 14623-2513
Phone: (716)427-8260
Fax: (716)427-0263
Angela Coffaro, Exec.Dir.

Founded: 1945. **Members:** 2,000. **Description:** Volunteers and professionals who produce materials in braille and large type, and on tape; teachers, educators, librarians, publishers, and other professional workers for the blind; visually impaired persons who use braille materials. Assists transcribers and narrators in the development and improvement of skills and techniques required for the production of reading materials for visually impaired individuals. Prepares vocational materials for blind professional persons. Operates transcription service which accepts requests for transcriptions of college textbooks, technical and nontechnical materials, and information helpful in work, recreation, and daily living. Cooperates with other organizations in developing and expanding use of advanced baille codes; offers training workshops for transcribers. NBA Braille Book Bank maintains over 2000 titles and 500 standard technical tables for immediate thermoform duplication. **Publications:** *Braille Technical Table Catalog*, periodic. Catalog. Contains technical tables in the NBA collection. Covers the fields of mathematics, statistics, chemistry, physics, computer science, and business. *Price:* Free. • Manuals. Covers tape recording, tactile graphics, mathematics and science braille, textbook format braille, computer-assisted transcription, and large type. • *National Braille Association--Bulletin*, quarterly. Newsletter. Features articles of interest to members and persons working in the field of services to the visually impaired. Contains calendar of events. *Price:* Included in membership dues; $30/year for nonmembers. • *National Braille Association--General Interest Catalog*, periodic. Directory. Topics include work, recreation, and daily living. Directory of titles available in braille from NBA collection. Available on audio tape. *Price:* Free. • *National Braille Association--Music Catalog*, periodic. Directory. Directory of music titles available in braille from NBA collection. Available on audio tape. *Price:* Free. • *National Braille Association--Textbook Catalog*, periodic. Directory. Directory of titles of braille books from NBA collection of college-level and technical materials. Available on audio cassette. *Price:* Free. **Formerly:** (1964) National Braille Club.

★ 13531 ★ National Braille Press (NBP)
88 St. Stephen St.
Boston, MA 02115
Phone: (617)266-6160
Fax: (617)437-0456
William M. Raeder, Mng.Dir.

Founded: 1927. **Description:** Publishes books and magazines in braille, including booklets on cooking and handicrafts and children's books (also in print). Supported by private gifts and legacies. Sponsors Children's Braille Book Club, offering monthly selections of print-braille books. **Publications:** *National Braille Press Release*, semiannual. Newsletter. • *Our Special*, monthly. • *Solutions*. • *Syndicated Columnists Weekly*. • *Take Charge*.

National Children's Eye Care Foundation (NCECF)
See: Entry 3266

★ 13532 ★ National Contact Lens Examiners (NCLE)
10341 Democracy Ln.
Fairfax, VA 22030
Phone: (703)691-1061
Fax: (703)691-3929
Nancy Roylance, Exec.Dir.

Founded: 1976. **Members:** 7,500. **Description:** National certifying agency promoting continued development of opticians and technicians as contact lens fitters by formulating standards and procedures for determination of entry-level competency. Assists in the continuation, development, administration, and monitoring of a national Contact Lens Registry Examination (CLRE), which verifies entry-level competency of contact lens fitters. Issues certificates. Activities include: maintaining records of those certified in contact lens fitting; encouraging state occupational licensing and credentialing agencies to use the CLRE for licensure purposes; identifying contact lens dispensing education needs as a result of findings of examination programs; disseminating information to sponsors of contact lens continuing education programs.

★ 13533 ★ National Council of State Agencies for the Blind (NCSAB)
1213 29th St. NW
Washington, DC 20007
Phone: (202)298-8468
Fax: (202)333-5881
Jack Duncan, Contact

Members: 54. **Description:** State agencies (and counterparts in District of Columbia, Puerto Rico, and U.S. territorial possessions) involved in prevention of blindness and extension of direct services to individuals with severe visual disability.

National Deaf-Blind League (NDBL)
See: Entry 3554

★ 13534 ★ National Eye Care Project (NECP)
PO Box 429098
San Francisco, CA 94142
Phone: (415)561-8520
Free: 800-222-EYES
B. Thomas Hutchinson, M.D., Chm.

Founded: 1986. **Description:** Ophthalmologists dedicated to ensuring eye care for the elderly, particularly those who are economically disadvantaged. Provides medical and surgical eye care to individuals 65 and over who normally would not have access or the means to consult an ophthalmologist. Disseminates information on participating physicians and eye diseases of the aging. Offers referral services. A project of the Foundation of the American Academy of Ophthalmology. Publishes a fact sheet and information packet.

★ 13535 ★ National Eye Research Foundation (NERF)
c/o Pamela Baker
910 Skokie Blvd., No. 207A
Northbrook, IL 60062
Phone: (708)564-4652
Free: 800-621-2258
Andrew Kim, VP, Corporate Planning

Founded: 1955. **Members:** 500. **Description:** Persons with graduate degrees in the eye professions; persons without graduate degrees but employed in the field of eye care; others participating in the work of the foundation for charitable or public welfare purposes. Works to sponsor research and education relating to the eye and contact lenses and to promote interprofessional relations for better eye care. Serves as public information center for questions on eye care. Supports Vision Foundation for Blind Youth. Conducts research and certification program. **Publications:** *Contacto*, quarterly. Journal. *Price:* Included in membership dues; $85/year for nonmembers. • *The Pinnacle*, monthly. Newsletter.

★ 13536 ★ National Federation of the Blind (NFB)
1800 Johnson St.
Baltimore, MD 21230
Phone: (410)659-9314
Free: 800-638-7518
Fax: (410)685-5653
Marc Maurer, Pres.

Founded: 1940. **Members:** 50,000. **Description:** Federation of state (50 plus Washington, DC and Puerto Rico) and local (600) organizations representing 50,000 blind people. Seeks the complete equality and integration of the blind into society. Monitors all legislation affecting the blind; evaluates present programs for the blind; stimulates and assists in promoting needed services. Supports and conducts scholarly research and publication of results. Works to improve policies toward the blind in such places as the U.S. Office of Personnel Management. Sponsors National White Cane Week annually for fundraising and educational purposes. Distributes information. Maintains National Blindness Information Center. **Publications:** *Braille Monitor*, monthly. Reports on action by the NFB on current legislative issues, legal cases, and social concerns affecting the blind;

gives news of aids and appliances. *Price:* Included in membership dues; Available to nonmembers by donation. • Brochures. • *Future Reflections*, quarterly. Magazine. Offers guidance in the day-to-day aspects of raising a blind child. Includes literature reviews, calendar of events, and new product list. *Price:* Included in membership dues; $15/year for nonmembers. • Pamphlets. • *Voice of the Diabetic*, quarterly. Personal stories and practical guidance from blind diabetics and medical professionals; medical news; resource column; recipe corner. *Price:* Included in membership dues.

★ 13537 ★ National Industries for the Blind (NIB)
524 Hamburg Tpke., CN 969
Wayne, NJ 07474-0969
Phone: (201)595-9200
Fax: (201)595-9122
Judith D. Peters, Contact

Founded: 1938. **Members:** 112. **Description:** Association of agencies employing blind persons who undertake the production of certain goods and services for the federal government under the Javits-Wagner-O'Day Act. Offers gainful employment in these workshops, located in 37 states, Puerto Rico, and the District of Columbia for those blind or multidisabled blind persons who are able and willing to work. Researches and recommends new products, prices, and price revisions to the Committee for Purchase From People Who Are Blind or Severely Handicapped; allocates federal work orders among these agencies. Devises quality control systems; provides management and engineering services to increase plant efficiency and broaden opportunities for blind persons; assists the workshops in procurement of raw materials. Marketing Division offers marketing, subcontracting, and industrial engineering expertise; Division of Rehabilitation Services works to establish evaluation and training programs to make possible the greater employment of multidisabled blind persons; Government Business Division deals with federal government contract administration, quality control, and pricing. Compiles statistics. **Publications:** Annual Report, annual. • *Choices*. • *Guiding Futures Toward Tomorrow*. • *National Industries for the Blind—Opportunity*, quarterly. Magazine. Covers news and feature articles on agencies for the blind; describes industries, agencies, and projects that employ blind workers. • *Products and Services Catalog*. Catalog.

★ 13538 ★ National League of the Blind of Ireland (NLBI)
Hillstreet
Dublin 1, Ireland
Phone: 1 8742792
Larry Carroll, Gen.Sec.

Founded: 1898. **Languages:** English. **Description:** A self-administered organization of blind individuals in the Republic of Ireland. Conducts advocacy activities, negotiating with local authorities and utility companies for better services for blind people. Offers income support programs to provide financial assistance with optical, medical, dental, clothing, and educational expenses. Advises members on their rights regarding entitlement programs; offers free legal aid. Organizes hospital visitations and sporting and social events including debates and lectures.

★ 13539 ★ **National Optometric Association (NOA)**
4426 Cambridge Ct.
Bloomington, IN 47401
Phone: (812)855-4475
Fax: (812)855-7045
Dr. Edwin Marshall, Exec.Dir.
Founded: 1969. **Members:** 350. **Regional Groups:** 5. **Description:** Optometrists dedicated to increasing minority optometric manpower. Conducts research programs and national recruiting program. Maintains speakers' bureau. Offers specialized education program. **Publications:** *NOA Newsletter*, quarterly. Newsletter.

★ 13540 ★ **New Eyes for the Needy (NEN)**
PO Box 332
549 Millburn Ave.
Short Hills, NJ 07078
Phone: (201)376-4903
Susannah Likins, Dir.
Founded: 1932. **Members:** 200. **Description:** Provides new prescription eyeglasses for individuals in the United States to whom no other funds, public or private, are available. Tests, grades, and distributes reusable plastic framed glasses to overseas missions and hospital clinics upon request. Funds are derived from the melt of precious metals found in jewelry and eyeglass frames donated to the organization and through contributions from individuals and grants.

★ 13541 ★ **Omega Delta**
Southern Coll. of Optometry
1245 Madison Ave.
Memphis, TN 38104
Phone: (901)278-7567
Robin Bennett, Pres.
Founded: 1917. **Members:** 90. **Description:** Professional fraternity - optometry. **Publications:** *Omega Delta Fraternity Directory*, periodic. Directory.

★ 13542 ★ **Omega Epsilon Phi**
960 Hamilton Mall
Allentown, PA 18101-1199
Phone: (215)437-3507
Alvin H. Freedman, O.D., Pres.
Founded: 1919. **Members:** 4,120. **Regional Groups:** 7. **Description:** Professional fraternity - men and women, optometry. Conducts educational programs. Maintains speakers' bureau. **Publications:** *Optist*, quarterly.

★ 13543 ★ **Operation Eyesight Universal (OEU)**
PO Box 123, Sta. M
Calgary, AB, Canada T2P 2H6
Phone: (403)283-6323
Fax: (403)270-1899
D.P. O'Dwyer, Exec.Dir.
Founded: 1963. **Members:** 30,000. **Regional Groups:** 3. **Languages:** English. **Description:** Individuals, firms, churches, schools, service clubs, and other organizations united to promote sight restoration and blindness prevention

through programs in Third World countries. Provides medical, educational, and financial assistance to needy individuals. Assists in the establishment of: special programs to combat blindness due to malnutrition; eye care hospitals; eye care departments in health care institutions; rural mobile eye programs. Conducts examinations in order to determine eye care needs of citizens of Third World countries. Works with local blindness prevention societies. Operates training programs. **Publications:** *Gift of Sight*, quarterly. Newsletter.

★ 13544 ★ **Ophthalmic Photographers' Society (OPS)**
c/o Patrick J. Saine
Davis Dueher Eye Associates
1025 Regent St.
462 Grider St.
Madison, WI 53715
Patrick J. Saine, M.ED., CRA
Founded: 1969. **Members:** 1,200. **Regional Groups:** 9. **Description:** Ophthalmologists, pathologists, medical and ophthalmic photographers, nurses, ophthalmic assistants, technicians, technologists, researchers, and engineers; organizations and individuals who are actively involved with ophthalmology or ophthalmic photography. Objective is to encourage the highest quality of ophthalmic photography and to promote development of new and improved techniques and equipment. (Ophthalmic photography involves photography of the eye for documentation and diagnostic purposes.) Provides continuing education and technical information. Serves as a forum for the discussion of ophthalmic photography. Provides testing, and subsequent certification as Certified Retinal Angiographer and Certified Ophthalmic Photographer Retinal Angiographer, in performance of ophthalmic photography. **Publications:** *Journal of Ophthalmic Photography*, semiannual. Journal. • *OPS Directory*, annual. Directory. • *OPS Newsletter*, bimonthly. Newsletter.

★ 13545 ★ **Ophthalmic Research Institute (ORI)**
4330 East West Hwy., Ste. 1117
Bethesda, MD 20814-4408
Phone: (301)718-6524
Fax: (301)656-0989
James S. Vrac, Admin.
Founded: 1972. **Description:** Conducts coordinated vision research, and instrumentation and procedure evaluation; offers continuing education program. Coordinates research needed by ophthalmic industry; research programs include new examination and treatment methods. **Formerly:** (1988) Optometric Research Institute.

Optical Industry Association (OMA)
See: Entry 5876

Optical Laboratories Association (OLA)
See: Entry 5877

★ 13546 ★ **Opticians Association of America (OAA)**
10341 Democracy Ln.
Fairfax, VA 22030
Phone: (703)691-8355
Fax: (703)691-3929
Paul Houghland, Jr., CAE, Exec.Dir.
Founded: 1926. **Members:** 10,000. **State Groups:** 48. **Description:** Retail dispensing opticians who fill prescriptions for glasses or contact lenses written by a vision care specialist. Works to advance the science of ophthalmic optics. Conducts research and educational programs. Maintains museum and speakers' bureau. Compiles statistics. **Publications:** *American Optician*, bimonthly. Magazine. Contains calendar of events and research reports. *Price:* Included in membership dues. **Formerly:** (1972) Guild of Prescription Opticians of America.

★ 13547 ★ **Optometric Extension Program Foundation (OEPF)**
2912 S. Daimler St.
Santa Ana, CA 92705
Phone: (714)250-8070
Fax: (714)250-8157
Robert A. Williams, Exec.Dir.
Founded: 1928. **Members:** 4,000. **Description:** Registered optometrists (3100) and optometric assistants (900) enrolled for continuing education courses. Maintains speakers' bureau. Sponsors educational programs. **Publications:** *Journal of Behavioral Optometry*, bimonthly. Journal. Includes professional articles, calendar of events, and current affairs. *Price:* $65/year. • *Optometric Extension Program Foundation--Curriculum II*, annual. Text of 6-8 courses covering various optometry subjects. Includes literature and research reviews and annual index. *Price:* $275/year. Available to members only. • *Reference Directory*, biennial. Directory.

★ 13548 ★ **Optometric Historical Society (OHS)**
243 N. Lindbergh Blvd.
St. Louis, MO 63141
Phone: (314)991-4100
Fax: (314)991-4101
Founded: 1969. **Description:** Optometrists and other individuals or groups interested in optometry, optics, and related disciplines. Purposes are to encourage the collection and preservation of materials relating to the history of optometry and to assist in the care of archives of optometric interest. **Publications:** Newsletter, quarterly.

★ 13549 ★ **ORBIS International**
330 W. 42nd St., Ste. 1900
New York, NY 10036
Phone: (212)244-2525
Free: 800-ORBIS-US
Fax: (212)244-2744
Oliver I. Foot, Pres. and Exec.Dir.
Founded: 1973. **Description:** Dedicated to fighting blindness worldwide through medical education and hands-on training for ophthalmologists, nurses, anesthesiologists, biomedical technicians, and community health care workers. Conducts programs in local hospitals and in ORBIS, a DC-10 jet converted into a fully

equipped eye surgery hospital and teaching facility. (Visiting faculty members join ORBIS's 25-member team of healthcare professionals to demonstrate their subspecialties and share their skills with their host-country colleagues.) Offers programs without the plane in surgery, nursing, technical services, and community health. **Publications:** *Eye on Houston.* • *ORBIS Observer*, quarterly. Newsletter. *Price:* Free. • *ORBIS Observer - Hong Kong.* Newsletter. • *ORBIS Observer - U.K..* Newsletter. **Formerly:** Project Orbis.

Outpatient Ophthalmic Surgery Society (OOSS)
See: Entry 12294

★ 13550 ★ **Pan-American Association of Ophthalmology (PAAO)**
1301 S. Bowen Rd., Ste. 365
Arlington, TX 76013
Phone: (817)265-2831
Fax: (817)275-3961
Teresa J. Bradshaw, Exec. Officer

Founded: 1939. **Members:** 10,000. **Languages:** English, Portuguese, Spanish. **Description:** Ophthalmologists throughout the Western Hemisphere. Seeks to improve the treatment of eye diseases and prevention of blindness in the Americas through the exchange of ideas and treatments. **Publications:** *Noticiero*, quarterly. • *Pan-American Association of Ophthalmology--OJO-EYE-OLHO*, semiannual. Newsletter. Includes obituaries and conference calendar.

★ 13551 ★ **Parents Active for Vision Education (PAVE)**
9620 Chesapeake Dr., Ste. 105
San Diego, CA 92123
Phone: (619)467-9620
Free: 800-PAVE-988
Fax: (619)467-9624
Marjie Thompson, Pres.

Founded: 1988. **Regional Groups:** 24. **State Groups:** 13. **Description:** Parents and teachers with children in their homes and classrooms who suffer or have suffered from the effects of undiagnosed vision problems. Works to raise public awareness of learning related vision problems. Supports the development of comprehensive learning related vision screenings, vision education, and vision hygiene programs in schools and communities. Maintains speakers' bureau **Publications:** Pamphlet. • *Pavestones*, semiannual. Newsletter. *Price:* Free.

★ 13552 ★ **Partially Sighted Society (PSS)**
Queen's Rd.
Doncaster, S. Yorkshire DN1 2NX, England
Phone: 1302 323132

Founded: 1973. **Description:** Strives to improve social, medical, and domestic services available to the visually impaired in the United Kingdom and to increase educational and employment opportunities. Represents the interests of visibly impaired individuals before government bodies and other organizations. Offers information and advice; provides visual aids and special printing and enlargement services. Operates 2 sight centers that offer vision assessment and training services. Arranges confer-

ences, exhibitions, and displays. **Publications:** Brochures, periodic. • Catalog, periodic. • *Oculus*, bimonthly. Newsletter. In large print.

Pharmacists in Ophthalmic Practice (P1OP)
See: Entry 10618

★ 13553 ★ **Physicians Education Network (P.E.N.)**
3944 Shore Acres Blvd. NE
St. Petersburg, FL 33703
George P. Russell, Exec.Dir.

Founded: 1977. **Description:** Ophthalmologists, other physicians, and concerned individuals whose current focus is on eye health care. Encourages high standards of health care. Sponsors National Eye Health Care Month. Promotes consumer safety legislation; opposes legislation that could allow lower medical standards. Seeks requirement of an M.D. or D.O. degree as the minimum standard for persons delivering health care. Promotes required referral legislation in each state, requiring optometrists to refer patients to ophthalmologists for any medical treatment or prescription. Campaigns against optometric drug use legislation; assesses and addresses laws, policies, and practices that may adversely affect eye health care and develops plans and programs to achieve necessary reform. Prepares speeches, position papers, and news releases; sponsors workshops on promotion of needed reforms; offers advice and counsel to members; provides speakers. Compiles statistics. **Publications:** *The Lantern*, bimonthly. Newsletter. • *The PEN*, bimonthly. Newspaper. *Price:* Free. • *PENpoints*, bimonthly. Newsletter.

★ 13554 ★ **Pilot Dogs (PD)**
625 W. Town St.
Columbus, OH 43215
Phone: (614)221-6367
Fax: (614)221-1577
J. Jay Gray, Exec.Dir.

Founded: 1950. **Members:** 20,841. **Description:** Provides guide dogs and training for the blind. **Publications:** *Pilot Light*, quarterly.

★ 13555 ★ **Pilot Guide Dog Foundation (PGDF)**
625 W. Town St.
Columbus, OH 43215
Phone: (614)221-6367
Fax: (614)221-6368
John J. Gray, Exec.Dir.

Founded: 1945. **Description:** Provides Pilot Guide Dogs to blind persons regardless of race, creed, age, or sex. Supported by individual contributors, clubs, business organizations, and philanthropic groups, which either make regular donations or set up scholarship funds. **Formerly:** (1951) Master Eye Foundation.

★ 13556 ★ **Prevent Blindness America (NSPB)**
500 E. Remington Rd.
Schaumburg, IL 60173
Phone: (708)843-2020
Free: 800-331-2020
Fax: (708)843-8458
Richard Hellner, Exec.Dir.

Founded: 1908. **Members:** 150,000. **Description:** Professional and laypersons interested in

preventing blindness and conserving sight through nationwide comprehensive programs of public and professional education, research, industrial, and community services. Services include promotion and support of local glaucoma screening programs, preschool vision testing, industrial eye safety, and collection of statistical and other data on nature and extent of causes of blindness and defective vision. Operates NSPB Center for Sight, an information line dealing with eye health and safety topics. Through the NSPB Fight for Sight Research Division, the organization awards student fellowships, postdoctoral awards and grants in aid for medical research. Sponsors Wise Owl Program to promote widespread use of safety eyewear for various activities and occupations. Compiles statistics. **Publications:** *Member New/Wise Owl News*, 4/year. • *Member News*, quarterly. Newsletter on eye health and safety. *Price:* $25/year. • *National Society to Prevent Blindness-- Annual Report.* Covers highlights and accomplishments of the previous fiscal year. Includes financial statements. *Price:* Free. **Formerly:** (1927) National Committee for the Prevention of Blindness; (1979) National Society for the Prevention of Blindness; (1994) National Society to Prevent Blindness.

★ 13557 ★ **Protestant Guild for Human Services**
411 Waverley Oaks Rd.
Waltham, MA 02154
Phone: (617)893-6000
Fax: (617)893-1171
Edmund T. Hagerty, Exec.Dir.

Founded: 1945. **Local Groups:** 2. **Description:** Individuals who wish to contribute to the welfare of persons who are blind or visually handicapped, deaf or hearing impaired, mentally impaired, or multihandicapped. Sponsors a chaplaincy program that provides support and advocacy to blind and visually handicapped persons. Provides information and referral by acting as liaison between blind individuals and appropriate community service organizations. Operates Learning Center for the Multiply Handicapped, an approved private school providing a year-round day and residential program to multihandicapped adolescents and young adults. Day program curriculum includes prevocational and work skill training (for both sheltered and competitive workshops), functional academics and personal-social survival skill training, and community survival skills/behaviors. Students live in 6 community-based homes. Provides speakers' bureau. **Publications:** *Projections*, annual. Newsletter. **Formerly:** Protestant Guild for the Blind.

★ 13558 ★ **Recording for the Blind (RFB)**
20 Roszel Rd.
Princeton, NJ 08540
Phone: (609)452-0606
Fax: (609)987-8116
Ritchie L. Geisel, Pres.

Founded: 1948. **Members:** 30,000. **Regional Groups:** 31. **Description:** Provides library services, computerized books, books on audiotape, and other educational materials free of charge to individuals who are unable to read standard print because of a visual, physical, or perceptual disability. Materials are produced by 4800 volunteers at 31 recording studios throughout the U.S. Titles recorded supplement, but do not duplicate, those of the Library of Congress Talking Book program. **Publications:** *Catalog (QDC).* • *Disk Catalog,* quarterly. *Price:* $16/year. • *Recorded Catalog,* quarterly. *Price:* $16/year. • *Recording for the Blind--Annual Report,* annual. Annual Report. Includes financial statements for the fiscal year as well as highlights from the previous year. *Price:* Free. • *Recording for the Blind--Catalog of Recorded Books,* periodic. Lists title, author, subject, and complete bibliographic information for approximately 77,000 recorded books in RFB's Master Tape Library. *Price:* $20. • *Recording for the Blind--Catalog Supplement,* periodic. • *RFB News,* quarterly. Newsletter. For donors, agencies, and schools serving the blind and print-disabled. *Price:* Free. **Formerly:** (1951) National Committee for Recording for the Blind.

★ 13559 ★ **Royal National Institute for the Blind Northern Ireland Service Bureau**
40 Linenhall St.
Belfast BT2 8BG, Northern Ireland
Phone: 1232 329373

Languages: English. **Description:** Seeks to prevent blindness and improve the quality of life for people with visual impairment in Northern Ireland. Conducts public education and lobbying campaigns. Maintains training facilities.

★ 13560 ★ **Royal National Institute for the Blind Scotland**
10 Magdala Crescent
Edinburgh EH12 5BE, Scotland
Phone: 131 3131498

Languages: English. **Description:** Seeks to prevent blindness and improve the quality of life for people with visual impairment in Scotland. Conducts public education and lobbying campaigns. Maintains training facilities.

★ 13561 ★ **Sight Savers—Royal Commonwealth Society for the Blind**
Grosvenor Hall
Bolnore Rd.
PO Box 191
Haywards Heath, W. Sussex RH16 4YF, England
Phone: 14 412424
Fax: 14 415866
Alan Johns, Exec.Dir.

Languages: English. **Description:** Volunteers working to prevent and cure blindness in economically developing countries. Cooperates with indigenous government agencies and local leadership to develop and implement vision care programs. Conducts leadership development and educational programs to make projects sustainable using local resources and expertise. Makes available technical assistance and medications to local vision care programs.

★ 13562 ★ **Sight Savers—Royal Commonwealth Society for the Blind**
Langata Rd.
PO Box 34690
Nairobi, Kenya
Phone: 2 503835
Fax: 2 505548
Alan Johns, Exec.Dir

Description: Promotes programs for the blind in Kenya. Offers assistance and educational programs. Fosters public awareness. **Publications:** *Horizens.* • *Xerophthaimia Bulletin,* periodic. Bulletin.

★ 13563 ★ **Slovak Society of Ophthalmology**
Derer Hospital
Limbova 5
SK-845 45 Bratislava, Slovakia
Phone: 7 376103
Fax: 7 376243
A. Gerinec, M.D., Contact

Languages: English, Slovak. **Description:** Ophthalmologists. Promotes advancement of ophthalmology; represents members' interests.

Society of Geriatric Ophthalmology (SGO)
See: Entry 1920

★ 13564 ★ **Surgical Eye Expeditions International (SEE Int'l)**
27C-2 E. de la Guerra St.
Santa Barbara, CA 93101
Phone: (805)963-3303
Fax: (805)965-3564
Baillie R. Brown, Exec.Dir.

Founded: 1974. **Members:** 300. **Regional Groups:** 30. **State Groups:** 33. **Description:** Provides free sight-restoring surgery to indigent and disadvantaged blind individuals in the United States and throughout the developing world. Recruits volunteer opthalmologists, nurses, and technicians. Maintains speakers' bureau. Conducts charitable and educational programs. Provides children's services. Compiles statistics. Organizes symposia. **Publications:** *Affiliate Action,* bimonthly. Newsletter. Provides recap of current and future programs for professional members. • Annual Report. • *SEE Scan,* quarterly. Newsletter. Includes news on surgical expeditions, vision care programs, and group activities.

★ 13565 ★ **Tanzania Society for the Blind**
PO Box 2254
Dar es Salaam, United Republic of Tanzania
Phone: 51 26139

Description: Seeks to meet the special needs of the visually-impaired in Tanzania. Offers educational, training, and rehabilitation programs.

★ 13566 ★ **Taping for the Blind (TFTB)**
3935 Essex Ln.
Houston, TX 77027
Phone: (713)622-2767
Fax: (713)622-2772
Beth O'Callaghan, Exec.VP

Founded: 1967. **Members:** 250. **Local Groups:** 1. **Description:** Provides audio versions of written materials for persons whose reading ability is impaired, in order to expand

their access to printed information. Promotes increased interest in, and use of, free audio materials. Daily newspapers, books, magazines, and special interest publications are broadcast 24 hours per day via FM frequency to specially tuned radio sets or by secondary audio program channel on stereo television to private homes, nursing homes, and hospitals. Maintains fully equipped recording studio and broadcast radio station; trains volunteers in use of recording and broadcast equipment; operates speakers' bureau. Provides audio description, live and recorded, for theater, films, movies, and museum exhibits, turning what is seen into what is heard. **Publications:** Annual Report. • Brochure. • *The Open Mike,* quarterly. Newsletter. *Price:* Free. • *Roster/Schedule,* quarterly. Also publishes radio program schedule.

★ 13567 ★ **Union Nationale des Syndicats d'Opticien de France (UNSOF)**
45, rue de Lancry
F-75010 Paris, France
Phone: 1 42034097
Fax: 1 42000060

Formerly: Association of Opticians of the European Common Market.

★ 13568 ★ **U.S. Association for Blind Athletes (USABA)**
33 N. Institute St.
Colorado Springs, CO 80903
Phone: (719)630-0422
Fax: (719)630-0610
Dr. Charly Hueber, Exec.Dir.

Founded: 1976. **Members:** 1,900. **Regional Groups:** 4. **State Groups:** 49. **Description:** Visually impaired athletes; fully sighted physical educators, coaches, and special education teachers; interested volunteers. Aims to develop individual independence through athletic competition. Promotes sports for the legally blind and visually impaired, organizes regional, national, and international competitions; works with other international organizations to promote goodwill and independence through friendly competition. Sports contested include alpine skiing, goalball, gymnastics, judo, nordic skiing, powerlifting, speed skating, swimming, tandem cycling, track and field and wrestling. Has sponsored 14 National Championships and 4 North American Games for the Blind between Canada and the U.S. Competed in the Paralympics in Seoul, Korea in 1988. Sent paralympic teams to Barcelona, Spain and Albertville, France in 1992. Sponsors coaches' training seminars, panel discussions, and training groups. Bestows awards; offers children's services; compiles statistics. **Publications:** *Directory of Organization Representatives,* quarterly. Directory. • *USABA Agenda,* monthly. Includes information on upcoming events. • *Vision,* quarterly. Magazine. Includes results of competitions and calender of events. *Price:* Included in membership dues. Also publishes programs and grant proposals.

★ 13569 ★ United States Blind Golfers' Association (USBGA)
3094 Shamrock St. N
Tallahassee, FL 32308
Phone: (904)893-4511
Fax: (904)893-4511
Bob Andrews, Pres.

Founded: 1953. **Members:** 25. **Description:** Blind golfers who compete for a national championship and whose tournaments raise funds for various blind charities. **Publications:** *The Midnight Golfer*, quarterly. Newsletter. *Price:* Free. • Video. Instructional. Also provides learning packets and information on blind golf.

★ 13570 ★ Vision Council of America (VICA)
1800 N. Kent St., Ste. 904
Arlington, VA 22209
Phone: (703)243-1508
Fax: (703)243-1537
Susan Burton, Exec.Dir.

Founded: 1985. **Members:** 450. **Description:** Trade association of optical industry companies that sponsor exhibits at industry trade shows. Works to serve the collective interests of the ophthalmic community; encourages the public to visit eye care practitioners regularly. Seeks to produce top quality trade shows. Conducts public educational programs. **Formerly:** (1990) Vision Industry Council of America.

★ 13571 ★ Vision Educational Foundation (VEF)
PO Box 472305
Tulsa, OK 74147-2305
Phone: (918)762-3947
Fax: (918)451-9207
Mack Smith, O.D., Pres.

Founded: 1972. **Description:** Optometric doctors, ophthalmic laboratories, manufacturers, related technicians, and other professionals in the field. Objectives are to promote a long-range program of support to optometric educational institutions; to allow practicing optometrists opportunities to update and expand their clinical skills and keep abreast of new technology; to expose students to pathology cases; to provide access to the most advanced diagnostic equipment available. Provides referral services. Maintains VEF Educational and Diagnostic Center, which provides practicing optometrists and senior professional students of optometric colleges with clinical education of a diagnostic and therapeutic nature. The clinic provides patie nts with secondary and tertiary care on a referral basis only and treats such conditions as cataracts, retinal detachments, and diabetic retinopathy as well as rare or unusual ocular pathology. Maintains Ocular Pathology residency program. Maintains speakers' bureau. **Publications:** *Focus*, quarterly. Newsletter.

★ 13572 ★ Vision Foundation (VF)
818 Mt. Auburn St.
Watertown, MA 02172
Phone: (617)926-4232
Free: 800-852-3029
Fax: (617)926-1412
Barbara R. Kibler, Exec.Dir.

Founded: 1970. **Members:** 500. **Description:** Selfhelp organization serving individuals who are newly blind or partially sighted, and those with progressive eye disease. Provides information and referral services, individualized advocacy, a "buddy" telephone network to share information, and selfhelp support groups for persons recently blinded or becoming blind. Operates the Visually Impaired Elders Project. Distributes materials in large print, braille, and cassette. **Publications:** *Vision Resource List*, annual. Catalog. In large print. Lists print, large print, cassette, disc, and braille brochures, pamphlets, fact sheets, and catalogs. Also available on cassette. *Price:* Free. • *Vision Resource Update*, bimonthly. Newsletter. In large print. Describes services and adaptive equipment for visually impaired individuals. Also available on cassette. *Price:* Included in membership. **Formerly:** Vision Foundation of Massachusetts, Inc..

★ 13573 ★ Visually Impaired Data Processors International (VIDPI)
c/o American Council of the Blind
1155 15th St. NW, Ste. 720
Washington, DC 20005
Phone: (202)467-5081
Free: 800-424-8666
Fax: (202)467-5085
Michael Mady, Exec. Officer

Founded: 1970. **Members:** 75. **Description:** Visually impaired electronic data processing employees; those seeking employment; employers, instructors, manufacturers, and students in the electronic data processing field. Advocates high standards in training visually impaired students. Seeks to increase employment opportunities; encourages the exchange of work technique ideas and the development of new equipment. Works with agencies to increase the availability of braille and recorded materials. Supports a speakers' bureau. **Publications:** *Views*, quarterly.

★ 13574 ★ Visually Impaired Empowering Women (VIEW)
National Office, RNZABPB
PO Box 37-414
Parnell
Auckland, New Zealand
Phone: 9 3779215
Fax: 9 3022140
Rosemary C. Wilkinson

Languages: English. **Description:** Strives to improve social and medical services available to visually impaired women. Conducts advocacy activities; offers information and advice.

★ 13575 ★ Visually Impaired Information Specialists (VIISI)
5707 Brockton Dr., Ste. 302
Indianapolis, IN 46220-5481
Phone: (317)254-1185
Fax: (317)251-6588
Patricia Price, Contact

Founded: 1972. **Members:** 50. **State Groups:** 1. **Description:** Blind and visually impaired secretaries, information specialists, and transcribers; other interested persons. Seeks to protect and improve the training, employment, and related interests of visually impaired persons in these fields. Provides vocational counseling. Maintains speakers' bureau. **Publications:** *VIIS Newsletter*, quarterly. Newsletter. Contains general information of interest to secretaries and office employees. *Price:* Included in membership dues. **Formerly:** Visually Impaired Secretarial Transcribers Association.

★ 13576 ★ Visually Impaired Veterans of America (VIVA)
c/o American Council of the Blind
1155 15th St. NW, Ste. 720
Washington, DC 20005
Phone: (202)467-5081
Free: 800-424-8666
Fax: (202)467-5085
Tom Stout, Pres.

Founded: 1975. **Members:** 117. **Description:** Veterans of the armed forces of the U.S. who have suffered blindness or visual impairment. Purposes are: to maintain and foster the wellbeing and rehabilitation of all visually impaired veterans; to preserve the legal rights of all visually impaired veterans on the local, state, and national levels; to maintain, promote, and foster the social, economic, and cultural level of these veterans and to promote opportunities to increase their knowledge of educational, professional, and rehabilitation standards and methods. Seeks to acquire, preserve, and disseminate information relative to the functions and accomplishments of visually impaired veterans. Encourages research and development of new products for the blind. Maintains speakers' bureau; offers specialized education program. **Publications:** *VIVA Membership List*, annual. Membership Directory. • *VIVA Viewpoints*, quarterly. Newsletter. For blind veterans. *Price:* Included in membership dues.

★ 13577 ★ Volunteer Optometric Services to Humanity, International (VOSH)
505 S. Clay
Taylorville, IL 62568
Free: 800-395-8674
Phil Freitag, O.D., Pres.

Founded: 1973. **Members:** 900. **State Groups:** 22. **Description:** Optometrists, optometric students, opticians, and other interested individuals. Conducts missions to disadvantaged countries, mostly in the Caribbean, Central and South America, Africa, Asia, and Eastern Europe to provide free visual care to the needy. Members pay their own travel, food, and lodging expenses, establish temporary clinics, and examine and distribute eyeglasses to an average of 2500 patients during each one-week mission. (Glasses are donated by civic clubs, churches, private citizens, and optical companies.) **Publications:** Brochure. • Newsletter, quarterly.

★ 13578 ★ Welfare of the Blind (WOTB)
1730 N. Lynn St., Ste. 500
Arlington, VA 22209
Fax: (703)243-1681
James A. Cudney, Pres.

Founded: 1956. **Description:** Supports church-related programs and projects for the sightless and visually impaired in developing countries. **Publications:** *A Modern Miracle*. Brochure.

**★13579★ World Blind Union (WBU)
(Union Mondiale des Aveugles — UMA)**
La Coruna, 18
E-28020 Madrid, Spain
Phone: 1 5713685
Fax: 1 5715777
Pedro Zurita, Sec.Gen.

Founded: 1984. **Members:** 162. **Regional Groups:** 7. **Languages:** English, French, Spanish. **Description:** National associations of the blind and international agencies for the blind. Fosters international cooperation among organizations working for the welfare of the blind and the prevention of blindness in 139 countries. Encourages creation and development of national organizations of and for the blind; seeks to provide necessary technical and material aid to such groups. Provides guidance in fields of education, rehabilitation, vocational training, and employment. Works toward the introduction and improvement of minimum standards for the welfare of the blind worldwide. Encourages and conducts studies in the field of service to the blind and the prevention of blindness. Collects and disseminates information on the conditions of the blind in different countries; informs members of social and legislative matters relating to blindness and its prevention. Maintains relations with numerous United Nations agencies including the World Health Organization, the International Council on Disability, and the International Agency for the Prevention of Blindness; sponsors the International Council for the Education of the Visually Impaired. **Publications:** *General Assembly Proceedings*, periodic. • *Review of the European Blind*, quarterly. • *The World Blind*, quarterly. Magazine.

**★13580★ Xavier Society for the Blind
(XSB)**
154 E. 23rd St.
New York, NY 10010
Phone: (212)473-7800
Free: 800-637-9193
Fax: (212)473-7801
Thomas R. Fitzpatrick, Dir.

Founded: 1900. **Description:** A center for publications, primarily Catholic, for the blind and visually handicapped, supported by charitable contributions. Transcribes numerous titles, including religious textbooks. Maintains a circulating library of books and other materials in braille, large type, and on tape. Items are loaned by mail from mini-catalogs of titles in each of 3 forms. Tapes are also circulated to the physically handicapped. **Publications:** *Catholic Review*, monthly.

Research Centers

**★13581★ Baylor College of Medicine
Cullen Eye Institute**
6550 Fannin, Ste. 1501
Houston, TX 77030
Phone: (713)798-5942
Fax: (713)798-4364
Dan B. Jones, M.D., Chm.

Research Activities and Fields: Restoring vision and preventing blindness through a better understanding of the structure, function, and diseases of the eye. Current areas of study include retina research, retinitis pigmentosa, amblyopia, ocular infections, corneal transplantation, genetic diseases of the eye, ocular trauma, cataract, glaucoma, ocular tumors, optic neuritis, and laser treatment. Special Resources: Lions of Texas Eye Bank.

**★13582★ Baylor College of Medicine
Vision Research Center**
Cullen Eye Institute
6501 Fannin, NC200
Houston, TX 77030
Phone: (713)798-5942
Fax: (713)798-4364
Dr. Dan B. Jones, Head

Research Activities and Fields: Diseases of the retina and choroid, the cornea, and the sensory motor visual system, including studies of the anatomy, biochemistry, physiology, and pathology of the neural retina, retinal pigment epithelium and choroid, retinal organization and information processing, the role of herpes virus in corneal disease, endogenous fungal endophthalmitis, and visual dysfunction of strabismus and amblyopia.

**★13583★ Columbia University
Biochemistry and Molecular Biology
    Laboratory**
Dept. of Ophthalmology
630 W. 168th St.
New York, NY 10032
Phone: (212)305-6716
Fax: (212)305-6205
Dr. Abraham Spector, Dir.

Research Activities and Fields: Phosphorylation of lens proteins and their biological implications, oxidation of lens materials, and the development of cataract.

**★13584★ Columbia University
Edward S. Harkness Eye Institute**
Columbia-Presbyterian Medical Center
635 W. 165th St., Rm. 218
New York, NY 10032-3784
Phone: (212)305-2724
Anthony Donn, M.D., Dir.

Research Activities and Fields: Ophthalmology, including excimer lasers, new pulsed infrared lasers, patholophysiology and surgical management of orbitopathy, topical and depot corticosteriods in the treatment of post-cataract cystoid macular edema, glaucoma, endothelial growth factors for wound healing in animal models, and effects of diabetes mellitus upon the retinal microvasculature.

**Columbia University
Eye Radiation and Environmental Research
    Laboratory**
See: Entry 2388

**★13585★ Columbia University
Retina Research Laboratory**
Columbia-Presbyterian Medical Center
635 W. 165th St.
New York, NY 10032-3784
Phone: (212)305-5688
Fax: (212)305-9087
Peter Gouras, Ph.D., Dir.

Research Activities and Fields: Retinal transplantation, biochemical markers for vitamin A metabolism in cultured human retinal epithelial cells, and gene insertion technology.

**★13586★ Columbia University
Tear Film Laboratory**
Columbia-Presbyterian Medical Center
635 W. 165th St., Rm. 218
New York, NY 10032-3784
Phone: (212)305-2724
Fax: (212)305-8073
Anthony Donn, Dir.

Research Activities and Fields: Tear film composition and its alterations in keratoconjunctivitis sicca (KCS), and the formation of contact lens deposits in relation to tear film composition.

**★13587★ Connecticut Eye Bank & Visual
    Research Foundation, Inc.**
100 Grand St.
New Britain, CT 06052
Phone: (203)224-5550
Michael J. Rinehart, Pres. & C.E.O.

Research Activities and Fields: Production of eye material for use in corneal transplantation surgery, surgical study, and for research on blindness. Projects include the Vision Immunology Program, a study of how the eye defends against disease.

★13588★ Dean A. McGee Eye Institute
608 Stanton L. Young Blvd.
Oklahoma City, OK 73104
Phone: (405)271-6363
Fax: (405)271-3013
David W. Parke, II, M.D., Pres.

Research Activities and Fields: Basic and clinical investigation in visual sciences; studies also include retinal biochemistry, molecular biology, and ocular microbiology.

★13589★ Doheny Eye Institute
1450 San Pablo St.
Los Angeles, CA 90033
Phone: (213)342-6690
Fax: (213)342-7114
Stephen J. Ryan, M.D., Pres.

Research Activities and Fields: Restoration, preservation, and conservation of eyesight, including studies on ophthalmic pathology, infectious ocular diseases, simplex viruses, and tissue cultures. **Publications:** *Update* (quarterly newsletter); *Postscript* (biennial alumni newsletter); Annual Report. **Formerly:** Estelle Doheny Eye Foundation (1987).

★ 13590 ★ Dry Eye and Tear Research
    Center
St. Paul-Ramsay Medical Center
Dept. of Ophthalmology
640 Jackson St.
St. Paul, MN 55101
Phone: (612)221-8745
Fax: (612)292-4040
J. Daniel Nelson, M.D., Dir.

Research Activities and Fields: Basic and clinical studies of dry eye and tearing disorders, focusing on ocular surface diseases, the effects of chemicals and nutrients on corneal epithelium, and the role of hormones in the development of dry eye states. **E-mail Address:** nels009@tc.umn.edu.

★ 13591 ★ Duke University
Eye Center
PO Box 3802
Durham, NC 27710
Phone: (919)684-5365
Fax: (919)684-2230

Research Activities and Fields: Eye disorders, with special focus on retinal detachment, corneal diseases, and proliferative diabetic retinopathy.

★ 13592 ★ Ellen Gregg Ingalls Eye
    Research Institute
700 S. 18th St., Ste. 300
Birmingham, AL 35233
Phone: (205)325-8507
Harold W. Skalka, M.D., Chm.

Research Activities and Fields: Ophthalmic research, including laboratory and clinical research into causes and treatment of cataract formation, ocular metabolism, corneal diseases, and systemic diseases involving the eye.

★ 13593 ★ Emory University
Laboratory for Ophthalmic Research
1327 Clifton Rd. NE, Rm. 3704S
Atlanta, GA 30322
Phone: (404)248-4100
Fax: (404)248-4143
Henry F. Edelhauser, Dir.

Research Activities and Fields: Various biochemical, pathobiochemical, physiological, and pathophysiological aspects of fundamental causes of blindness-producing diseases, especially cataract, glaucoma, retinal detachment, diabetes, and diabetic vasculopathy. Maintains strong clinical liaison in research programming.

★ 13594 ★ Eye Institute of New Jersey
New Jersey Medical School
90 Bergen St.
Newark, NJ 07103
Phone: (201)982-2050
Fax: (201)982-2069
Marshall S. Klein, Dir.

Research Activities and Fields: Ophthalmology, including cornea, retina, uveitis, glaucoma, pediatric ophthalmolgy, and neuro-ophthalmology.

★ 13595 ★ Florida Ophthalmic Institute
7106 NW 11th Pl.
Gainesville, FL 32605-3192
Phone: (904)331-2020
Fax: (904)331-2019
Norman S. Levy, M.D., Dir.

Research Activities and Fields: Understanding and treatment of human ocular diseases, including glaucoma and external ocular pathology.

★ 13596 ★ Francis I. Proctor Foundation
    for Research in Ophthalmology
Univ. of California, San Francisco
San Francisco, CA 94143-0412
Phone: (415)476-1441
Fax: (415)476-6085
Chandler R. Dawson, M.D., Dir.

Research Activities and Fields: Infectious and inflammatory diseases of the eye with particular emphasis on chlamydial infections, trachoma, herpetic eye infections, dry eye conditions, and uveitis.

★ 13597 ★ Georgetown University
Worthen Center for Eye Research
Medical Center
3800 Reservoir Rd. NW
Washington, DC 20007
Phone: (202)687-4359
Fax: (202)687-5064
Jonathan C. Javitt, M.D.,,, Dir.

Research Activities and Fields: Effectiveness, outcomes, and utilization of eye care; epidemiology of eye care delivery; functional status and utility assessment. Research includes outcomes of cataract, glaucoma, diabetic eye disease, and barrier reduction related to eye care use.

★ 13598 ★ Glaucoma Laser
    Trabeculoplasty Study
Sinai Hospital of Detroit
Franklin Eye Consultants
29275 Northwestern Hwy.
Southfield, MI 48034
Phone: (810)493-5157
Hugh Beckman, M.D., Chm.

Research Activities and Fields: Examines the effectiveness and safety of argon laser trabeculoplasty as compared to traditional topical therapy in the treatment of newly diagnosed open-angle glaucoma.

★ 13599 ★ Glaucoma Research Foundation
490 Post St., 830
San Francisco, CA 94102
Phone: (415)986-3162
Fax: (415)986-3763
Tara Steele, Exec.Dir.

Research Activities and Fields: Clininical and laboratory studies of glaucoma. Sponsors the Normal Tension Glaucoma Study, a collaborative 25 center study; the Glaucoma Research Catalyst Program; and the Glaucoma Research Eye Donor Network, which provides laboratory scientists access to glaucomatous eye tissue. **Publications:** *Gleams* (quarterly newsletter); *Understanding and Living with Glaucoma*; *Eye News.* **E-mail Address:** glaucoma@ucsfvm.ucsf.edu. **Formerly:** Foundation for Glaucoma Research.

★ 13600 ★ Harvard University
Berman-Gund Laboratory for the Study of
    Retinal Degenerations
Massachusetts Eye & Ear Infirmary
243 Charles St.
Boston, MA 02114
Phone: (617)573-3600
Fax: (617)573-3216
Eliot Berson, M.D., Dir.

Research Activities and Fields: Effects of nutrition and light on the retina. Also studies causes of retinitis pigmentosa and animal models of hereditary retinal degenerations.

★ 13601 ★ Harvard University
Howe Laboratory of Ophthalmology
Massachusetts Eye & Ear Infirmary
243 Charles St.
Boston, MA 02114
Phone: (617)573-3963
Fax: (617)573-3364
Elio Raviola, M.D., Dir.

Research Activities and Fields: Developmental ophthalmology and eye research, including glaucoma, cataracts, retina, cornea, ocular tumors, laser studies, neuro-ophthalmology, immunology and uveitis, diabetes, and molecular biology.

★ 13602 ★ Helen Keller International (HKI)
90 Washington St., 15th Fl.
New York, NY 10006
Phone: (212)943-0890
Fax: (212)943-1220
John M. Palmer, Exec.Dir.

Research Activities and Fields: Etiology, prevalence, incidence, and treatment of xerophthalmia (nutritional blindness), trachoma, cataract, onchocerciasis (river blindness), and other eye diseases in developing nations. Research and technical assistance conducted in Bangladesh, Bolivia, Brazil, Burkina Faso, Cameroon, the Caribbean, Chile, China, Columbia, Ecuador, Ethiopia, Fiji, Haiti, India, Indonesia, Kenya, Malawi, Mali, Mauritania, Mexico, Morocco, Nepal, Niger, Nigeria, Papua New Guinea, Peru, Philippines, Senegal, Solomon Islands, Sri Lanka, Sudan, Tanzania, Thailand, Uruguay, Western Samoa, and Zambia. **Publications:** *Insight* (three times per year); Annual Report. **Formerly:** American Foundation for the Overseas Blind (1977).

★ 13603 ★ Institute for Visual Sciences,
    Inc.
1 E. 71st St.
New York, NY 10021
Phone: (212)305-2919
Melissa Mount, Exec.Dir.

Research Activities and Fields: Ophthalmology, with emphasis on the development of diagnostic and therapeutic techniques for the care of the eye using existing physical sciences technology such as optical imagery (cameras, lasers, video scanning, holography) and ultrasonography. Studies focus on the applications of liquid dye, carbon dioxide, and neodymium-YAG lasers to the treatment of eye diseases and conditions that threaten sight, including glaucoma, macular degeneration, cataract, and diabetic retinopathy. Also develops instruments to aid individuals with defective vision, such as spectacles to provide focusing and wide-field capabilities and improve depth perception.

**★ 13604 ★ Johns Hopkins University
Center for Hereditary Eye Diseases**
Wilmer Ophthalmological Institute
Maumenee Bldg., Rm. 517
600 N. Wolfe St.
Baltimore, MD 21287-9237
Phone: (410)955-5214
Fax: (410)614-4363
Dr. Irene Hussels Maumenee, Dir.

Research Activities and Fields: Studies of molecular mechanisms underlying genetic eye diseases. Emphasis on diagnosis and management of common as well as rare genetic eye diseases, and the prevention of vision loss through early medical or surgical intervention. **E-mail Address:** tnm@ishtar.med.jhu.edu.

**★ 13605 ★ Johns Hopkins University
Dana Center for Preventive Ophthalmology**
Wilmer Ophthalmological Institute
Wilmer, Rm. 120
601 N. Broadway
Baltimore, MD 21205
Phone: (410)955-2770
Fax: (410)955-2542
Harry A. Quigley, Dir.

Research Activities and Fields: Aims to identify eye disorders amenable to intervention and to develop intervention strategies. Studies concentrate on cataract and glaucoma, including the role of ultraviolet light in the development of cataract, evaluation of new techniques for diagnosing glaucoma at its earlier stages, and why black Americans develop glaucoma nine times more frequently than white Americans. Other studies focus on diet and measles and other infections as causes of blindness in Asia and Africa, including the effectiveness of periodic, massive dosing with vitamin A, vitamin A fortification of commonly consumed foods, nutritional education to reduce eye disorders caused by vitamin A deficiency in c hildren, and vitamin A in relation to childhood morbidity and mortality; infrequent washing of the face as a cause of trachoma in such water-poor nations as Mexico; and evaluation of the safety and efficacy of drugs used to combat river blindness or onchocerciasis.

**★ 13606 ★ Johns Hopkins University
Lions Vision Research and Rehabilitation
  Center**
Wilmer Low Vision Consultation Service
550 N. Broadway, 6th Fl.
Baltimore, MD 21205
Phone: (410)955-0580
Fax: (410)955-1829
Dr. Robert Massof, Dir.

Research Activities and Fields: Development and refinement of devices and procedures for rehabilitating visual function using psychophysics, optics, computer-assisted video enhancement, and electrophysiology; mechanisms and progression of diseases of the retina, optic nerve, and visual pathways in the brain; glaucoma, optic ne uritis, and other neurologic disorders; and diseases primarily limited to the retina such as retinitis pigmentosa, diabetic retino-

pathy, and age-related macular degeneration. **Formerly:** Laboratory of Physiological Optics.

**★ 13607 ★ Johns Hopkins University
Ocular Immunology Laboratory**
Wilmer Ophthalmological Institute
Woods Research, Rm. 457
600 N. Wolfe St.
Baltimore, MD 21287-9142
Phone: (410)955-3524
Fax: (410)614-1114
Dr. Robert A. Prendergast, Dir.

Research Activities and Fields: Cause, detection, treatment, and prevention of immunogenic and other inflammatory diseases of the eye, and rejection of corneal grafts.

**★ 13608 ★ Johns Hopkins University
Retinal Degenerations Research Center**
Wilmer Ophthalmological Institute
Maumenee Research Bldg., Rm. 519
600 N. Wolfe St.
Baltimore, MD 21205
Phone: (410)955-7589
Fax: (410)955-0749
Dr. Ruben Adler, Dir.

Research Activities and Fields: Biochemistry of essential constituents of the retina and its adjacent tissues and potential interactions among them as related to retinitis pigmentosa and other retinal degenerations. **E-mail Address:** radler@ishtar.med.jhu.edu. **Formerly:** Michael M. Wynn Center for the Study of Retinal Degenerations.

**★ 13609 ★ Johns Hopkins University
Retinal Vascular Center**
Wilmer Ophthalmological Institute
Maumenee Bldg., Rm. 205
600 N. Wolfe St.
Baltimore, MD 21287-9275
Phone: (410)955-3518
Fax: (410)955-0675
Dr. Andrew Schachat, Dir.

Research Activities and Fields: Focuses on halting the progression of a variety of retinal-damaging disorders, including macular degeneration, diabetic retinopathy, and eye tumors. Studies the use of lasers in treating retinal, vascular, and macular disorders and explores the underlying causes of retinal, blood vessel, pigment epithelial, and photoreceptor diseases.

**★ 13610 ★ Johns Hopkins University
Wilmer Ophthalmological Institute**
600 N. Wolfe St.
Baltimore, MD 21287-9278
Phone: (410)955-6846
Fax: (410)955-0675
Morton F. Goldberg, M.D., Chm.

Research Activities and Fields: Ophthalmology, including studies of cataracts and the cornea, ocular immunology, uveitis (inflammatory eye diseases), retinal-damaging disorders, retinal degenerations, glaucoma, preventive ophthalmology, strabismus (misaligned or crossed eyes), double vision, amblyopia (reduced vision in one eye), hereditary eye diseases, neuroophthalmology, oculomotor functions, correlation of changes in the structure and form of eye tissue with symptoms of illness, development of new

technology and techniques to study visual function disorders, development of new optical aids for the visually handicapped, immunohistochemical analysis of the blood retina barrier, retinal gene expression, genetics of eye diseases, molecular biology of eye development, molecular biology of glaucoma, and retinal pigment epithelium (RPE). **E-mail Address:** ISHTAR 128.220.55.44.

**★ 13611 ★ Laval University
Medical Research Centre
Ophthalmology Research Group**
2705, boulevard Laurier
Ste. Foy, PQ, Canada G1V 4G2
Phone: (418)654-2105
Fax: (418)654-2131
Dr. Alain Rousseau, Dir.

Research Activities and Fields: Viscoelastics, laser corneal surgery, ocular melanoma, corneal wound healing and corneal transplantation.

★ 13612 ★ Lighthouse Research Institute
800 2nd Ave.
New York, NY 10017
Phone: (212)808-0077
Fax: (212)808-0110
Aries Arditi, Ph.D., Dir., Vision Research

Research Activities and Fields: Physical, functional, and psychological consequences of vision impairment. Vision research areas include helping individuals with low vision maximize their remaining vision, understanding how best to assess visual function, and devising ways of modifying environments for the safety and comfort of people who are visually impaired. Social research areas include the effects of visual impairment on the ability of people of all ages to function, the processes of adaption to a vision loss, and the social and psychological characteristics that influence adaptive and rehabilitation outcomes. **Publications:** Lighthouse Research *Monograph and Technical Series*. **E-mail Address:** aries@cns.nyu.edu.

**★ 13613 ★ Louisiana State University
Eye Center**
2020 Gravier St., Ste. B
New Orleans, LA 70112
Phone: (504)568-6700
Fax: (504)568-4210
Dr. Herbert Kaufman, Dir.

Research Activities and Fields: Ophthalmology, including a study linking hazy peripheral vision with colored contact lenses, lasers in ophthalmology, ocular surgery techniques, biomaterials and drug delivery, graft rejection, neurobiology and neurochemisty, and viral infection, latency, and treatment.

★ 13614 ★ Macula Foundation, Inc.
210 E. 64th St.
New York, NY 10021
Phone: (212)605-3777
Lawrence A. Yannuzzi, M.D., Dir.

Research Activities and Fields: Clinical and basic research and teaching on the basis of macular diseases, including epidemiologic, immunologic, biochemical, and clinical therapeutic studies. **Formerly:** Retinal Research Fund (1983).

★13615★ Medical College of Wisconsin
Eye Institute
8700 W. Wisconsin Ave.
Milwaukee, WI 53226
Phone: (414)257-6505
Richard Schultz, M.D., Dir.

Research Activities and Fields: Ophthalmology, including pediatric ophthalmology, neuro-ophthalmology, orbital and ophthalmic reconstructive surgery, anterior segment studies, corneal diseases, cataracts, retinal detachment, diabetic retinopathy, glaucoma, and laser treatment.

★13616★ Medical University of South Carolina
Storm Eye Institute
171 Ashley Ave.
Charleston, SC 29425-2236
Phone: (803)792-3206
Fax: (803)792-4854
David J. Apple, Chm.

Research Activities and Fields: Metabolism of vitamin A in the eye, toxicity of oxygen in lens and cornea, ocular parasites, and photoreceptor electrophysiology.

★13617★ Mississippi State University
Rehabilitation Research and Training Center on Blindness and Low Vision
PO Drawer 6189
Mississippi State, MS 39762
Phone: (601)325-2001
Fax: (601)325-8989
Dr. J. Elton Moore, Dir.

Research Activities and Fields: Career development intervention strategies for people who are blind or severely visually impaired; employment aspects of blindness and low vision. **Publications:** Monographs. **E-mail Address:** rrtc@ra.msstate.edu.

★13618★ Missouri Lions Eye Research Foundation
404 Portland St.
Columbia, MO 65201
Phone: (314)443-1471
Fax: (314)443-1657
Dr. Ronald J. Walkenbach, Dir.

Research Activities and Fields: Cell biology, biochemistry, and pharmacology involving research on cornea, cataract, and retina. **Formerly:** Eye Research Foundation of Bethesda, Maryland.

★13619★ Mount Sinai School of Medicine of City University of New York
Vision Research Center in Ophthalmology
1 Gustave Levy Pl.
PO Box 1183
New York, NY 10029
Phone: (212)241-6249
Fax: (212)289-5945
Dr. Oscar A. Candia, Dir.

Research Activities and Fields: Basic and clinical research in various areas of ophthalmology.

★13620★ Oakland University
Eye Research Institute
422 Dodge Hall
Rochester, MI 48309-4401
Phone: (810)370-2391
Fax: (810)370-2006
Dr. Venkat N. Reddy, Dir.

Research Activities and Fields: Biochemistry, biophysics, cell biology, physiology, pharmacology, and photobiology. Research focuses on ocular tissues and includes the following topics of interest: molecular genetics of lens proteins, ion transport and radiation damage of the cornea, light damage of the retina, signal transduction in photoreceptors, ocular drug metabolism and detoxification, and experimental models of proliferative vitreoretinopathy, uveoretinitis, cataracts (radiation and oxidation and calcium), and diabetic complications of the eye. **E-mail Address:** reddy@vela.acs.oakland.edu. **Formerly:** Institute of Biological Sciences (1986).

★13621★ Ohio Wesleyan University
Eye Research Projects
Delaware, OH 43015
Phone: (614)368-3801
Fax: (614)368-3299
David O. Robbins, Ph.D., Dir.

Research Activities and Fields: Visual psychophysics and electrophysiology, color vision, and effects of laser irradiation on retinal morphology and function.

★13622★ Ophthalmic Research Laboratory and Eye Institute
Swedish Medical Center-Seattle
747 Broadway Ave.
Seattle, WA 98104-0999
Phone: (206)386-6000
Fax: (206)386-2625
Dr. Richard Peterson, Dir.

Research Activities and Fields: Color vision physiology; demyelinating disease, especially vision loss from multiple sclerosis; and laser surgery technology.

★13623★ Oregon Health Sciences University
Elks' Children's Eye Clinic
Casey Eye Institute
3375 SW Terwilliger Blvd.
Portland, OR 97201-4197
Phone: (503)494-7675
Fax: (503)494-5347
Earl A. Palmer, M.D., Dir.

Research Activities and Fields: Pediatric ophthalmology with particular reference to abnormalities of binocular vision. Studies in strabismus, infantile and congenital glaucoma, retinopathy in premature infants, toxicology, congenital cataract, and genetic diseases. Programs are clinically oriented, including retrospective and prospective studies of patients. Develops instruments and techniques to advance pediatric ophthalmology.

★13624★ Pennsylvania College of Optometry
Eye Institute
1201 W. Spencer St.
Philadelphia, PA 19141-3399
Phone: (215)276-6000
Fax: (215)276-1329
Eugene C. Wayne, Exec.Dir.

Research Activities and Fields: Eye care research and services are provided through the Institute and its secondary units: the Learning Center, which studies visual dysfunctions as they relate to audiology, proper nutrition, and psycho-educational problems; the Infant Vision Center, which examines how infants see, how eyes work together, and how vision is used in learning and motion; the Feinbloom Vision Rehabilitation Center, which studies and rehabilitates persons with macular degeneration, albinism, nystagmus, cataracts, retinitis pigmentosa, diabetic retinopathy, glaucoma, and other partial conditions of sight; the Glaucoma Service which is a participating site in the NSI Ocular Hypertension Treatment Study (OHTS); and the Center for Molecular and Regulatory Biology, Genetics and Genetic Eye Diseases. **Publications:** PLO Alumni World.

★13625★ Retina Institute of Maryland
O'Dea Medical Arts Bldg., Ste. 103
7505 Osler Dr.
Baltimore, MD 21204
Phone: (410)337-4500
Fax: (410)337-3975
Dr. Bert Glaser, Dir.

Research Activities and Fields: Abnormal events in the retina and vitreous that result from diabetes, sickle cell anemia, injury, and retinal detachment. **Formerly:** Retinal Research Center at St. Joseph's Hospital (1993).

★13626★ Schepens Eye Research Institute
20 Staniford St.
Boston, MA 02114
Phone: (617)742-3140
Fax: (617)720-1069
Dr. J. Wayne Streilen, Research Dir.

Research Activities and Fields: Retina, vitreous, cornea, glaucoma, immunology, neuroscience, transplantation, physiological optics, biomedical physics, oculartumors, and pharmacology with strong collaboration between clinic and laboratory studies on diseases of the retina and cornea, and on glaucoma. Develops ophthalmic instruments and devices for diagnosis and treatment of eye disease, and for low vision aids. **Publications:** Sundial (semiannually). **E-mail Address:** seri@vision.eri.harvard.edu. **Formerly:** Retina Foundation; Eye Research Institute of Retina Foundation (1991).

★13627★ Sensory Electrophysiology Research Unit
Touro Infirmary
1401 Foucher St.
New Orleans, LA 70115
Phone: (504)897-8179
Fax: (504)897-7637
David A. Newsome, M.D., Dir.

Research Activities and Fields: Mechanisms, causes, and treatment of retinal dystrophies and diseases, including transplantation of retinal cells. Multidisciplinary studies focus on cell biology, molecular biology, biochemistry, immunohistology, and clinical trials. **Formerly:** Outgrowth of the Retinitis Pigmentosa and Retinal Degenerations Clinical Research Center at Louisiana State University (1988); Sensory Eye Research Center.

Sherbrooke University
Fundamental Electrophysiology Research
Group
See: Entry 2621

★ 13628 ★ **Smith-Kettlewell Eye Research**
Institute
2232 Webster St.
San Francisco, CA 94115
Phone: (415)561-1620
Fax: (415)561-1610
Alan B. Scott, M.D., Dir.

Research Activities and Fields: Visual sciences, oculomotor functioning, and rehabilitation engineering, including long-term study of the surgical and pharmacological treatment of strabismus; development of diagnostic tests for glaucoma, retinitis pigmentosa, diabetic retinopathy, and senile macular degeneration; research on the physiological basis of eye movements and retinal development; studies in motion detection, pattern perception, and stereopsis; and development and evaluation of sensory aids and devices for the deaf, blind, deaf/blind, and sensory-impaired individuals. **Publications:** *Rehabilitation Engineering Center Annual Report.* **Formerly:** Smith-Kettlewell Institute of Visual Sciences.

Smith-Kettlewell Eye Research Institute
Rehabilitation Engineering Center
See: Entry 2471

Texas A&M University
Institute of Ocular Pharmacology
See: Entry 10460

U.S. Department of Defense
Armed Forces Institute of Pathology
Center for Advanced Pathology
Ophthalmic Pathology Department
See: Entry 10158

★ 13629 ★ **U.S. Department of Health and**
Human Services
National Eye Institute
NIH Bldg. 31, Rm. 6A03
9000 Rockville Pike
Bethesda, MD 20892
Phone: (301)496-2234
Fax: (301)496-9970
Dr. Carl Kupfer, Director

Research Activities and Fields: NEI has primary responsibility within the federal government for supporting and conducting research aimed at improving prevention, diagnosis, and treatment of visual disorders. Specifically, the Institute: 1) supports research and research training through grants, fellowships, and contracts to medical schools and research institutions; 2) conducts laboratory and clinical research in its own facilities and fosters statistical and epidemiological studies of visual disorders

in human populations; 3) fosters research on rehabilitation of the visually handicapped; 4) encourages the application of research findings to clinical practice; 5) heightens public awareness of vision problems; and 6) cooperates with voluntary organizations that engage in related activities. The NEI organization includes a Biometry and Epidemiology Program, Extramural and Collaborative Programs, and an Intramural Research Program. **Publications:** Planning Report (every five years).

★ 13630 ★ **U.S. Department of Health and**
Human Services
National Eye Institute
Biometry and Epidemiology Program
Clinical Trials Branch
NIH Bldg. 31, Rm. 6A52
9000 Rockville Pike
Bethesda, MD 20892
Phone: (301)496-6583
Fax: (301)496-2297
Frederick L. Ferris, Chief

Research Activities and Fields: Branch is responsible for three national multiclinic trials involving vitrectomy, drugs, and photocoagulation as treatments to prevent disease progression in patients with diabetic retinopathy. These studies include hundreds or thousands of patients and combine the skills of ophthalmologists and biostatisticians. Data generated in these studies not only provide a base for treatment strategies, but permit investigation of factors other than treatment related to disease progression.

★ 13631 ★ **U.S. Department of Health and**
Human Services
National Eye Institute
Biometry and Epidemiology Program
Epidemiology Branch
NIH Bldg. 31, Rm. 6A52
9000 Rockville Pike
Bethesda, MD 20892
Phone: (301)496-6583
Dr. Roy Milton, Acting Dir.

Research Activities and Fields: Branch conducts studies of the prevalence and incidence of diseases of the eye in the general population and of personal, environmental, genetic, and biologic factors in the population that may be related. Data from these studies are used to generate and evaluate hypotheses about the causes of such diseases. Data from the Framingham Eye Study and the Health and Nutrition Examination Study are currently being analyzed to explicate the risk factors for changes in the lens and retina. Other activities include a national case-control study to investigate factors related to the development of several eye diseases and a survey of the Framingham population for factors related to the incidence and natural history of cataract and age-related maculopathy.

★ 13632 ★ **U.S. Department of Health and**
Human Services
National Eye Institute
Division of Biometry and Epidemiology

NIH Bldg. 31, Rm. 6A52
9000 Rockville Pike
Bethesda, MD 20892
Phone: (301)496-1331
Fax: (301)496-2297
Roy C. Milton, Ph.D., Acting Director

Research Activities and Fields: Program conducts studies in the areas of clinical trials, natural history, and epidemiology. Activities are carried out in the Clinical Trials Branch and Epidemiology Branch.

★ 13633 ★ **U.S. Department of Health and**
Human Services
National Eye Institute
Extramural and Collaborative Programs
Strabismus, Amblyopia, and Visual
Processing Branch
NIH Bldg. 31
9000 Rockville Pike
Bethesda, MD 20892
Phone: (301)496-5301
Fax: (301)402-0528
Constance Atwell, Chief

Research Activities and Fields: Branch supports basic and clinical research on the structure, function, and development of the extraocular muscles and those portions of the brain that make vision possible. Research focuses on studies of normal vision and the causes of visual deficits and blindness that do not appear to result from specific dysfunction of the eye. Areas of research include: preventing or treating strabismus (misalignment of the eyes); amblyopia (commonly known as "lazy eye"); myopia (nearsightedness); and neuro-ophthalmological disorders.

★ 13634 ★ **U.S. Department of Health and**
Human Services
National Eye Institute
Extramural Research
NIH EPS, Ste. 350
6120 Executive Blvd
Bethesda, MD 20892
Phone: (301)496-9110
Dr. Jack McLaughlin, Associate Director

Research Activities and Fields: Unit administers NEI programs that support research aimed at improving the prevention, diagnosis, and treatment of visual disorders. This support includes the award of grants, cooperation agreements, fellowships, and contracts for research in retinal and choroidal diseases, corneal diseases, cataract, glaucoma, strabismus, amblyopia, and visual processing. Program offices include: 1) Anterior Segment Diseases Branch; 2) Collaborative Clinical Research Branch; 3) Retinal Diseases Branch; 4) Strabismus, Amblyopia, and Visual Processing Branch; and 5) Extramural Services Branch.

★ 13635 ★ **U.S. Department of Health and**
Human Services
National Eye Institute
Extramural Research
Anterior Segment Diseases Branch

NIH Bldg. EPS, Rm. 350
6120 Executive Blvd.
Rockville, MD 20892
Phone: (301)496-5301
Fax: (301)402-0528
Lore Anne McNicol, Ph.D., Chief

Research Activities and Fields: Branch supports basic and applied ophthalmic research relating to corneal diseases, cataract, and glaucoma. Principal areas of research are: diseases of the cornea and the external ocular structures, including the conjunctiva and eyelids; corneal transplantation and wound healing; contact lenses and surgical correction of refractive problems; prevention and nonsurgical treatment of cataract; structures and mechanisms of glaucoma; and prevention, diagnosis, and treatment of glaucoma.

**★ 13636 ★ U.S. Department of Health and
      Human Services
National Eye Institute
Extramural Research
Collaborative Clinical Research Branch**
NIH EPS, Ste. 350
6120 Executive Blvd.
Rockville, MD 20892
Phone: (301)496-5983
Fax: (301)402-0528
Richard L. Mowery, Ph.D., Director

Research Activities and Fields: Conducts clinical trials in opthalmology and epidemiology studies on vision.

**★ 13637 ★ U.S. Department of Health and
      Human Services
National Eye Institute
Extramural Research
Retinal and Choroidal Diseases Branch**
NIH Bldg. 31, Rm. 6A51
9000 Rockville Pike
Bethesda, MD 20892
Phone: (301)496-0484
Fax: (301)402-0528
Peter A. Dudley, Ph.D., Chief

Research Activities and Fields: Branch supports basic and applied studies on the structure and function of the retina and choroid in health and disease. NEI-fostered investigations include studies of the structure and metabolism of photoreceptor cells and their relationship to the underlying pigment epithelium; the retina's response to light and the initial processing of visual information transmitted to the visual centers of the brain; inflammation of the uveal tract (the iris, choroid, and ciliary body); and of the vitreous humor, the clear gel that fills the center of the eye and which assumes importance in a number of ocular disorders. NEI also supports studies aimed at understanding causes of blindness such as developmental and hereditary retinal disorders; diabetic retinopathy and other vascular and circulatory abnormalities; myopia; ocular tumors; diseases of the macula, the small area of the retina responsible for the central vision used in reading; retinal detachment; and inflammatory disorders, including uveitis. Also conducts clinical trials of the effects of treatment in certain retinal diseases, most notably diabetic retinopathy.

**★ 13638 ★ U.S. Department of Health and
      Human Services
National Eye Institute
Intramural Research**
NIH Bldg. 10, Rm. 10N202
9000 Rockville Pike
Bethesda, MD 20892
Phone: (301)496-3123
Dr. Robert B. Nussenblatt, Acting Director

Research Activities and Fields: Program involves in-house research aimed at improving the prevention, diagnosis, and treatment of visual disorders. Major subject of research include retinal and choroidal diseases, corneal diseases, cataract, glaucoma, and sensory and motor disorders of vision. Program comprises a Clinical Branch and laboratories of Mechanisms of Ocular Diseases, Molecular and Developmental Biology, Ophthalmic Pathology, Retinal Cell and Molecular Biology, and Sensorimotor Research.
Publications: NEI's Annual Report.

**★ 13639 ★ U.S. Department of Health and
      Human Services
National Eye Institute
Intramural Research
Laboratory of Immunology**
NIH Bldg. 10, Rm. 10N202
9000 Rockville Pike
Bethesda, MD 20892
Phone: (301)496-3123
Fax: (301)402-0485
Dr. Robert B. Nussenblatt, Scientific Director

Research Activities and Fields: Branch plans and conducts clinical research into the causes, preventions, diagnosis, and treatment of visual system disorders. It translates laboratory research results into clinical application, directs and administers the Institute's clinical care program, and assures functioning of the eye ward and clinic in the NIH Clinical Center. Principal Branch components are: the Cataract Section, Neuro-Ophthalmology Section, Ocular Immunology Section, Ophthalmic Genetics and Pediatric Ophthalmology Section, and Retinal and Ocular Connective Tissue Diseases Section.

**★ 13640 ★ U.S. Department of Health and
      Human Services
National Eye Institute
Laboratory on Mechanisms of Ocular
      Diseases**
NIH Bldg. 6, Rm. 237
9000 Rockville Pike
Bethesda, MD 20892
Phone: (301)496-6669
Fax: (301)496-1759
J. Samuel Zigler, Acting Chief

Research Activities and Fields: Laboratory plans, conducts, and directs basic and applied research on mechanisms involved in cataract formation, pharmacologic and pathophysiologic aspects of aldose reductase in diabetic complications, molecular biology of a retinal dystrophy, and cataract caused by an enzyme deficiency. Laboratory also provides training opportunities in related diabetes and cataract research.

**★ 13641 ★ U.S. Department of Health and
      Human Services
National Eye Institute
Laboratory of Molecular and
      Developmental Biology**
NIH Bldg. 6
9000 Rockville Pike
Bethesda, MD 20892
Phone: (301)496-2764
Fax: (301)496-1759
Dr. Joram Piatigorsky, Chief

Research Activities and Fields: Laboratory conducts basic research in cellular and molecular biology, with emphasis on molecular and developmental genetics. The research is designed to elucidate both normal and disease processes, and particular attention is given to hereditary diseases that can be studied at the gene level. Much (but not all) of the work uses eye tissue as models for general problems concerning cellular differentiation and gene expression. In addition, normal and pathogenic visual processes are related to the structure and function of genes; and phospholipid metabolism-- particularly at the cell membrane--is investigated in order to advance knowledge of cellular differentiation and differential gene expression.

**★ 13642 ★ U.S. Department of Health and
      Human Services
National Eye Institute
Laboratory of Retinal Cell and Molecular
      Biology**
NIH Bldg. 6, Rm. 310
9000 Rockville Pike
Bethesda, MD 20892
Phone: (301)496-3447
Fax: (301)402-1883
Dr. Gerald J. Chader, Chief

Research Activities and Fields: Laboratory conducts basic and clinical vision research in biochemistry, pathology, and neurobiology of the retina.

**★ 13643 ★ U.S. Department of Health and
      Human Services
National Eye Institute
Laboratory of Sensorimotor Research**
NIH Bldg. 10, Room 10C101
9000 Rockville Pike
Bethesda, MD 20892
Phone: (301)496-9375
Fax: (301)402-0511
Dr. Robert H. Wurtz, Chief

Research Activities and Fields: Laboratory conducts research on the sensorimotor organization of the primate visual and oculomotor systems using a multidisciplinary approach that includes physiological, behavioral, psychophysical, and anatomical methods. Principal areas of research interest are: vision and oculomotor research, visuomotor integration, neuro-ophthalmologic mechanisms, and oculomotor control. A primary focus of research concerns the visuomotor control of eye movements, encompassing studies of rapid or saccadic eye movements that move the eye rapidly from one part of the visual field to another; pursuit eye movements that allow the eye to follow a moving target; vergence eye movements that allow the eyes to fixate on objects at different distances with concomitant adjustment of accommodation to maintain a clear image; and the vestibulo-ocular reflex that steadies the eye in spite of head and body movements.

★ 13644 ★ U.S. Department of Health and Human Services
National Eye Institute
Office of International Program Activities
NIH Bldg. 31, Rm. 6A-17
9000 Rockville Pike
Bethesda, MD 20892
Phone: (301)496-4876
Fax: (301)480-3246
Barbara A. Underwood, Ph.D., Assistant Director

Research Activities and Fields: Programs involve research and data collection and analysis, including activities in vitamin A metabolism, maternal and child nutrition, and nutritional diseases.

★ 13645 ★ University of California, Los Angeles
Jules Stein Eye Institute
Los Angeles, CA 90024-7000
Phone: (310)825-5053
Fax: (310)206-7488
Bartly J. Mondino, M.D., Dir.

Research Activities and Fields: Research and study in sciences related to vision, care of patients with eye disease, and education in ophthalmology.

★ 13646 ★ University of California, San Francisco
Ocular Oncology Research Unit
Beckman Vision Center
10 Kirkham St.
San Francisco, CA 94143
Phone: (415)476-3204
Fax: (415)476-8727
Devron H. Char, M.D., Dir.

Research Activities and Fields: Ocular immunology, tumor immunology, immunology of intraocular inflammation, and eye tumor immunology.

★ 13647 ★ University of Chicago
Visual Sciences Center
939 E. 57th St.
Chicago, IL 60637
Phone: (312)702-8888
Fax: (312)702-4442
J. Terry Ernest, M.D., Dir.

Research Activities and Fields: Ophthalmology, visual physiology and function of the retina, color vision, evoked occipital response, laser and xenon photocoagulation for retinal disease, and pharmacology of the retinal pigment epithelium. Also conducts electron microscopy and visual molecular biology studies. **Formerly:** Eye Research Laboratories (1990).

★ 13648 ★ University of Florida
Center for Low Vision Study, Care and Rehabilitation
JHMHC, Box 100284
Gainesville, FL 32610
Phone: (904)392-3451
Fax: (904)392-8554
Dr. G.M. Hope, Dir.

Research Activities and Fields: Low vision and basic visual science, patient care, and rehabilitation.

★ 13649 ★ University of Florida
Vision Research Center
JHMHC, Box J-284
Gainesville, FL 32610
Phone: (904)392-3451
Fax: (904)392-8554
Melvin L. Rubin, M.D., Chm.

Research Activities and Fields: Electrophysiology of the retina and biochemistry, immunology, molecular genetics, and oncology of ocular diseases.

★ 13650 ★ University of Illinois at Chicago
Laboratory for the Assessment of Functional Vision
Dept. of Ophthalmology
1855 W. Taylor St.
Chicago, IL 60612
Phone: (312)996-7179
Fax: (312)996-7770
Janet Szylk, Dir.

Research Activities and Fields: Physiology of normal and pathologic retinas utilizing computer analyzed digitized images. **Formerly:** Television Retinal Imaging Laboratory; Image Processing Laboratory.

★ 13651 ★ University of Illinois at Chicago
Lions of Illinois Eye Research Institute
UIC Eye Center
1905 W. Taylor St.
Chicago, IL 60612
Phone: (312)996-6590
Fax: (312)996-7770
Prof. John W. Chandler, M.D., Head

Research Activities and Fields: Diabetic retinopathy, glaucoma, cataracts, macular degeneration, herpes keratitis, retinitis pigmentosa, corneal biochemistry, molecular biology, and retinal photoreceptors. Houses the clinical trials of the UIC Department of Ophthalmology and Visual Sciences, including the Advanced Glaucoma Intervention Study, Collaborative Ocular Melanoma Study, Glaucoma Laser Trabeculoplasty Trial, Herpetic Eye Disease Study, 5-Fluorouracil Filtering Surgery Study, Home Tonometer Study, and Galardin Infectious Keratitis Study; research studies of the Applied Physics Laboratory, Lens Biochemistry Laboratory, Ophthalmic Pathology Laboratory, Ocular Immunology Laboratory, Ocular Molecular Biology Laboratories, Ocular Biochemistry Laboratory, Photoreceptor Research Laboratory, Laboratory of Retinal Physiology and Neurobiology, and Retinal Cell Biology Laboratory. **Publications:** *Eyewitness News*; *Eye Facts*; Annual Report.

★ 13652 ★ University of Illinois at Chicago
UIC Eye Center
1855 W. Taylor
Chicago, IL 60612
Phone: (312)996-6590
Fax: (312)996-7770
Dr. J. Chandler, Head

Research Activities and Fields: Various diseases affecting the eye, including diabetic retinopathy, retinitis pigmentosa, branch vein oc-clusion, sickle cell eye disease, ocular trauma, ocular and corneal immunology, genetic eye diseases, glaucoma, vitreous fluorophotometry, external eye diseases, retinopathy of prematurity, optic neuritis, ocular melanoma, herpes simplex virus, macular degeneration, and uveitis. **Publications:** *Eyewitness News*; *Eye Facts*, Annual Report.

★ 13653 ★ University of Louisville
Kentucky Lions Eye Research Institute
301 E. Muhammad Ali Blvd.
Louisville, KY 40202
Phone: (502)852-5460
Fax: (502)852-7446
Christopher A. Paterson, Ph.D., Dir. of Research

Research Activities and Fields: Visual sciences and eye diseases. **Publications:** *Current Eye Research Journal*.

★ 13654 ★ University of Miami
Bascom Palmer Eye Institute
Dept. of Ophthalmology
1638 NW 10th Ave.
Miami, FL 33136
Phone: (305)326-6031
Fax: (305)326-6306
Dr. John G. Clarkson, M.D., Chair

Research Activities and Fields: Clinical and basic research in the areas of glaucoma, infectious and external corneal diseases, molecular biology and genetics, neurophysiology, ocular virology, ocular immunology, hereditary retinal diseases with special emphasis on Retinitis Pigmentosa, and ophthalmic applications of lasers and polymers. Also conducts studies to improve the techniques and technology related to patient care and the prevention of blindness.

★ 13655 ★ University of Michigan
W.K. Kellogg Eye Center
Dept. of Ophthalmology
1000 Wall St.
Ann Arbor, MI 48105-1994
Phone: (313)763-1415
Fax: (313)936-2340
Prof. Paul R. Lichter, Chm.

Research Activities and Fields: Basic and clinical eye research, focusing on medical and molecular genetics and molecular biology of ophthalmic disease, retinal physiology, corneal wound healing, psychophysics of color vision, diabetic retinopathy, and eye diseases in children and adults.

★ 13656 ★ University of Missouri—St. Louis
Center for Corneal and Contact Lens Research
School of Optometry
8001 Natural Bridge
St. Louis, MO 63121
Phone: (314)516-5606
Fax: (314)516-5150
Gary Bachman, O.D., Interim Dir.

Research Activities and Fields: Clinical research in contact lens design, materials, and applications; and basic ocular studies relating to the effects of contact lens. Conducts research on excimer laser corneal reshaping and biomedical materials.

★ 13657 ★ University of North Texas
Health Science Center at Fort Worth
North Texas Eye Research Institute (NTERI)
3500 Camp Bowie Blvd.
Ft. Worth, TX 76107-2699
Phone: (817)735-2048
Fax: (817)735-2610
James F. Turner, Ph.D., Dir.

Research Activities and Fields: Eye diseases, including studies on the retina, RPE cells, trophic factors, ocular diabetes, autoimmune diseases, optic nerve regeneration, glaucoma, corneal wound healing, cell death, and aging.

★ 13658 ★ University of Pennsylvania
Vision Research Center
School of Medicine, 143 Anatomy Chemistry
36th & Hamilton Walk
Philadelphia, PA 19104
Phone: (215)898-6917
Dr. Paul Liebman, Prin. Investigator

Research Activities and Fields: Serves as a branch of the National Eye Institute of the National Institutes of Health to fund eye research projects at the University. Studies concentrate on mechanisms of normal and defective vision, including their molecular, genetic, developmental, electrophysiological, neural, and cognitive aspects.

★ 13659 ★ University of Rochester
Center for Visual Science
Rochester, NY 14627
Phone: (716)275-2459
Fax: (716)271-3043
Dr. David Williams, Dir.

Research Activities and Fields: Optical, physiological, perceptual, and computational aspects of visual science. Encourages research in vision in Departments of Optics, Psychology, Neurology, Neurobiology and Anatomy, Ophthalmology, Physiology, and Computer Science. **E-mail Address:** david@cvs.rochester.edu.

★ 13660 ★ University of Texas—Houston
Health Science Center
Hermann Eye Center
Dept. of Ophthalmology
6431 Fannin St., Ste. 7024
Houston, TX 77030
Phone: (713)704-1777
Fax: (713)794-4583
Richard S. Ruiz, M.D., Chm.

Research Activities and Fields: Cataracts, corneal disease, glaucoma, neuroophthalmology, ophthalmic surgery, pediatric ophthalmology, strabismus, and retinal disease. Additional studies include ocular melanoma, retinitis pigmentosa, diabetes, retinal pigment epithelial transplantation, ischemic optic neuropathy decompression, and pattern electrogram in Alzheimer's disease.

★ 13661 ★ University of Waterloo
Centre for Contact Lens Research
School of Optometry
200 University Ave. W
Waterloo, ON, Canada N2L 3G1
Phone: (519)888-4742
Fax: (519)725-0784
Dr. Desmond Fonn, Contact

Research Activities and Fields: Conducts basic and applied research in all areas related to contact lenses in order to monitor and understand the effects of contact lenses on the eye, to assist in the development of methods for evaluating and measuring the reactions to contact lens wear, and to evaluate the safety and efficacy of pre and post market release of new lens materials and related products. **E-mail Address:** cclra@sc.borg.uwaterloo.ca.

★ 13662 ★ Wayne State University
Kresge Eye Institute
4717 St. Antoine
Detroit, MI 48201
Phone: (313)577-1320
Fax: (313)577-5482
Dr. Abrams, Dir.

Research Activities and Fields: Cellular and molecular biology, electron microscopy, electrophysiology, neuro-ophthalmology, ophthalmic pathology, orthoptics, biochemistry of phototransduction in the vertebrate retina, cornea, glaucoma, vitreoretinal, and biochemistry and immunology of the eye.

★ 13663 ★ Wills Eye Hospital
Research Division
900 Walnut St.
Philadelphia, PA 19107
Phone: (215)928-3274
Fax: (215)591-4628
Larry A. Donoso, M.D., Codir.

Research Activities and Fields: Vitreoretinal surgery, and vitreoretinal disease management and research. Develops new instrumentation and surgical techniques and ocular application of various laser wavelengths in the various ophthalmic subspecialties in addition to vitreoretinal diseases. **Formerly:** Wills Eye Hospital Research Institute (1980).

★ 13664 ★ Yale University
Vision Research Center
Boardman Bldg., Box 208061
330 Cedar St.
New Haven, CT 06520-8061
Phone: (203)785-2713
Fax: (203)737-4227
Marvin L. Sears, Prin. Investigator

Research Activities and Fields: Vision including studies on transduction, transport, myopia, neurobiology of growth and development, glaucoma, and diabetic retinopathy. **E-mail Address:** searsml@maspo1.mas.yale.edu.

State Government Agencies

Blind

★ 13665 ★ Alabama Department of Rehabilitation Services
2129 E. South Blvd.
PO Box 11586
Montgomery, AL 36111-0586
Phone: (334)242-4628
Fax: (334)281-1973

★ 13666 ★ Alaska Department of Education
Vocational Rehabilitation Division
801 W. 10th St., Ste. 200
Juneau, AK 99801-1894
Phone: (907)465-2814
Fax: (907)465-2856

★ 13667 ★ Arizona Department of Economic Security
Employment and Rehabilitation Services Division
Rehabilitation Services Administration
1789 W. Jefferson NW, 2nd Fl.
Phoenix, AZ 85007
Phone: (602)542-3332
Fax: (602)542-5339

★ 13668 ★ Arkansas Department of Human Services
Blind Services Division
411 Victory St.
PO Box 3237
Little Rock, AR 72203
Phone: (501)324-9270
Fax: (501)686-6836

★ 13669 ★ California Health and Welfare Agency
Rehabilitation Department
830 K St. Mall
PO Box 944333
Sacramento, CA 94244
Phone: (916)445-3971
Fax: (916)327-4567

★ 13670 ★ Colorado Department of Human Services
Rehabilitation Services Division
110 16th St.
Denver, CO 80202
Phone: (303)620-4156

★ 13671 ★ Connecticut Board of Education and Services for the Blind
170 Ridge Rd.
Wethersfield, CT 06109
Phone: (203)566-5800
Fax: (203)278-6920

★ 13672 ★ Delaware Department of Health and Social Services
Visually Impaired Division
1901 N. DuPont Hwy.
New Castle, DE 19720
Phone: (302)577-4731
Fax: (302)577-4758

★ 13673 ★ **District of Columbia Department**
   of Human Services
Social Services Commission
Rehabilitation Services Administration
605 G St. NW, Ste. 1111
Washington, DC 20001
Phone: (202)727-3227
Fax: (202)727-1687

★ 13674 ★ **Florida Department of**
   Education
Blind Services Division
Douglas Bldg.
2540 Executive Center Circle W.
Tallahassee, FL 32301
Phone: (904)488-1330

★ 13675 ★ **Georgia Department of Human**
   Resources
Rehabilitation Services Division
2 Peachtree St. NW
Atlanta, GA 30303
Phone: (404)894-6670

★ 13676 ★ **Hawaii Department of Human**
   Services
Vocational Rehabilitation and Blind
   Services Division
Bishop Trust Bldg., Rm. 615
1000 Bishop St.
Honolulu, HI 96813
Phone: (808)586-5366
Fax: (808)586-4890

★ 13677 ★ **Idaho Commission for the Blind**
   and Visually Impaired
341 W. Washington St.
Boise, ID 83702
Phone: (208)334-3220
Fax: (208)334-2963

★ 13678 ★ **Illinois Department of**
   Rehabilitation Services
Blind Services Bureau
623 E. Adams St.
PO Box 19429
Springfield, IL 62794-9429
Phone: (217)785-3887

★ 13679 ★ **Indiana Family and Social**
   Services Administration
Aging and Rehabilitative Services Division
402 W. Washington St.
PO Box 7083
Indianapolis, IN 46207-7083
Phone: (317)232-1147
Fax: (317)233-4693

★ 13680 ★ **Iowa Department for the Blind**
524 4th St.
Des Moines, IA 50309
Phone: (515)281-1334
Fax: (515)281-1263

★ 13681 ★ **Kansas Department of Social**
   and Rehabilitation Services
Rehabilitation Services Division
Biddle Bldg.
300 SW Oakley St.
Topeka, KS 66606
Phone: (913)296-3911
Fax: (913)296-0511

★ 13682 ★ **Kentucky Education, Arts and**
   Humanities Cabinet
Blind Department
427 Versailles Rd.
Frankfort, KY 40601
Phone: (502)573-4754

★ 13683 ★ **Louisiana Department of Social**
   Services
Rehabilitation Services Division
8225 Florida Blvd.
PO Box 94371
Baton Rouge, LA 70804-9371
Phone: (504)925-4168
Fax: (504)925-4184

★ 13684 ★ **Maine Department of Education**
Rehabilitation Services Office
Blind and Visually Impaired Division
35 Anthony Ave.
Augusta, ME 04333
Phone: (207)624-5323
Fax: (207)287-5802

★ 13685 ★ **Maryland Department of**
   Education
Vocational Rehabilitation Division
Blind Services Office
2301 Argonne Dr.
Baltimore, MD 21218
Phone: (410)554-9401
Fax: (410)554-9384

★ 13686 ★ **Massachusetts Commission for**
   the Blind
88 Kingston St.
Boston, MA 02111-2227
Phone: (617)727-5550
Fax: (617)727-5960

★ 13687 ★ **Michigan Department of Labor**
Blind Commission
201 N. Washington Sq.
PO Box 30015
Lansing, MI 48909
Phone: (517)373-2062

★ 13688 ★ **Minnesota Economic Security**
   Department
Blind Services Office
2200 University Ave., Ste. 240
St. Paul, MN 55104
Phone: (612)642-0508
Fax: (612)649-5927

★ 13689 ★ **Mississippi Department of**
   Rehabilitation Services
PO Box 1698
Jackson, MS 39215-1698
Phone: (601)853-5201
Fax: (601)853-5205

★ 13690 ★ **Missouri Department of Social**
   Services
Family Services Division
Rehabilitation Services for the Blind
0619 Howerton Ct.
PO Box 88
Jefferson City, MO 65109
Phone: (314)751-4249

★ 13691 ★ **Montana Department of Social**
   and Rehabilitation Services
Rehabilitative Services / Visual Services
   Division
PO Box 4210
Helena, MT 59604
Phone: (406)444-2590

★ 13692 ★ **Nebraska Department of Public**
   Institutions
Rehabilitation Services for the Visually
   Impaired Division
4600 Valley Rd.
Lincoln, NE 68510
Phone: (402)471-2891
Fax: (402)483-4184

★ 13693 ★ **Nevada Department of**
   Employment Training and Rehabilitation
Rehabilitation Division
Blind Services Bureau
500 E. 3rd St.
Carson City, NV 89713
Phone: (702)687-4444
Fax: (702)687-8351

★ 13694 ★ **New Hampshire Department of**
   Education
Vocational Rehabilitation Bureau
78 Regional Dr.
Concord, NH 03301
Phone: (603)271-3471

★ 13695 ★ **New Jersey Department of**
   Human Services
Blind Commission
153 Halsey St., 6th Fl.
PO Box 47017
Newark, NJ 07101
Phone: (201)648-2324
Fax: (201)648-7364

★ 13696 ★ **New Mexico Commission for**
   the Blind
PERA Bldg., Rm. 553
Santa Fe, NM 87503
Phone: (505)827-3511

★ 13697 ★ **New York State Department of**
   Social Services
Blind and Visually Handicapped
   Commission
1 Commerce Plaza, 16th Fl.
Albany, NY 12243
Phone: (518)473-1801

★ 13698 ★ **North Carolina Department of**
   Human Resources
Blind Services Division
309 Ashe Ave.
Raleigh, NC 27606
Phone: (919)733-9822
Fax: (919)733-9769

★ 13699 ★ **North Dakota Department of**
   Human Services
Vocational Rehabilitation Division
600 E. Boulevard
Bismarck, ND 58505
Phone: (701)328-2907
Fax: (701)328-2359

★ 13700 ★ **Ohio Rehabilitation Services Commission**
Services for the Visually Impaired Bureau
400 E. Campus View Blvd.
Columbus, OH 43235-4604
Phone: (614)438-1255
Fax: (614)438-1257

★ 13701 ★ **Oklahoma Department of Rehabilitation Services**
Visual Services Bureau
2409 N. Kelley
PO Box 36659
Oklahoma City, OK 73136
Phone: (405)522-6377
Fax: (405)427-3027

★ 13702 ★ **Oregon Commission for the Blind**
535 SE 12th Ave.
Portland, OR 97214
Phone: (503)731-3221
Fax: (503)731-3230

★ 13703 ★ **Pennsylvania Department of Public Welfare**
Blindness and Visual Services Bureau
Bertolino Bldg., 1st Fl.
1401 N. 7th St.
PO Box 2675
Harrisburg, PA 17120
Phone: (717)787-6176

★ 13704 ★ **Puerto Rico Department of Social Services**
Vocational Rehabilitation Division
PO Box 191118
San Juan, PR 00909-1118
Phone: (809)725-1792

★ 13705 ★ **Rhode Island Department of Human Services**
Blind Services
275 Westminster St.
Providence, RI 02903
Phone: (401)277-2300

★ 13706 ★ **South Carolina Commission for the Blind**
1430 Confederate Ave.
Columbia, SC 29202
Phone: (803)734-7522
Fax: (803)734-7885

★ 13707 ★ **South Dakota Department of Human Services**
Services to the Blind and Visually Impaired Division
E. Hwy. 34
c/o 500 E. Capitol
Pierre, SD 57501-5070
Phone: (605)773-4644
Fax: (605)773-5483

★ 13708 ★ **Tennessee Department of Human Services**
Rehabilitation Services Division
Citizen Plaza Bldg., 15th Fl.
400 Deaderick St.
Nashville, TN 37248
Phone: (615)741-2521

★ 13709 ★ **Texas Commission for the Blind**
4800 N. Lamar Blvd..
PO Box 12866
Austin, TX 78711-2866
Phone: (512)459-2600
Fax: (512)459-2685

★ 13710 ★ **Utah Rehabilitation Office**
Visually Handicapped Services Division
309 East 100 South
Salt Lake City, UT 84111
Phone: (801)533-9393

★ 13711 ★ **Vermont Agency of Human Services**
Social and Rehabilitation Services Department
Blind and Visually Impaired Division
Osgood Bldg.
103 S. Main St.
Waterbury, VT 05676
Phone: (802)241-2211

★ 13712 ★ **Virgin Islands Department of Human Services**
Disabilities and Rehabilitation Services Division
1303 Hospital Ground
St. Thomas, VI 00802
Phone: (809)774-0930

★ 13713 ★ **Virginia Office of Health and Human Resources**
Visually Handicapped Department
397 Azalea Ave.
Richmond, VA 23227
Phone: (804)371-3145
Fax: (804)371-3157

★ 13714 ★ **Washington Department of Services for the Blind**
South 1400 Evergreen Park Dr. SW
PO Box 40933
Olympia, WA 98504-0933
Phone: (360)586-1224

★ 13715 ★ **West Virginia State Board of Education and the Arts**
Rehabilitation Services Division
State Capitol Complex
PO Box 50890
Charleston, WV 25305
Phone: (304)766-4601

★ 13716 ★ **Wisconsin Department of Health and Social Services**
Vocational Rehabilitation Division
1 W. Wilson St., 8th Fl.
PO Box 7852
Madison, WI 53707-7852
Phone: (608)266-5466
Fax: (608)267-3657

★ 13717 ★ **Wyoming Department of Employment**
Vocational Rehabilitation Division
117 Hathaway Bldg.
Cheyenne, WY 82002
Phone: (307)777-7191
Fax: (307)777-5939

Optometry Boards

★ 13718 ★ **Alabama State Board of Optometry**
PO Box 448
Attalla, AL 35954
Phone: (205)538-9903

★ 13719 ★ **Alaska Board of Examiners in Optometry**
PO Box 110806
Juneau, AK 99811-0806
Phone: (907)465-2580

★ 13720 ★ **Arizona State Board of Optometry**
1645 W. Jefferson, Rm. 410
Phoenix, AZ 85007
Phone: (602)542-3095

★ 13721 ★ **Arkansas Board of Examiners in Optometry**
PO Box 512
Searcy, AR 72145
Phone: (501)268-4351

★ 13722 ★ **California Board of Optometry**
400 R. St., Ste. 3130
Sacramento, CA 95814
Phone: (916)323-8720

★ 13723 ★ **Colorado Board of Examiners in Optometry**
1560 Broadway, Rm. 1310
Denver, CO 80224
Phone: (303)894-7755

★ 13724 ★ **Connecticut Board of Examiners in Optometry**
150 Washington St.
Hartford, CT 06106
Phone: (203)566-6259

★ 13725 ★ **Delaware Board of Examiners in Optometry**
Cannon Bldg., Ste. 203
Dover, DE 19903
Phone: (302)739-4522

★ 13726 ★ **District of Columbia Board of Optometry**
614 H St. NW, Rm. 904
Washington, DC 20001
Phone: (202)727-7856

★ 13727 ★ **Florida Board of Optometry**
1940 Monroe St.
Tallahassee, FL 32399-0776
Phone: (904)488-7484

★ 13728 ★ **Georgia State Board of Examiners in Optometry**
166 Pryor St. SW, Rm. 506-B
Atlanta, GA 30303
Phone: (404)656-3912

★ 13729 ★ **Hawaii Board of Examiners in Optometry**
1010 Richards St.
PO Box 3469
Honolulu, HI 96801
Phone: (808)586-2694

★ 13730 ★ Idaho State Optometry Board
1109 Main St., Ste. 220
Boise, ID 83702
Phone: (208)334-3233

★ 13731 ★ Illinois Optometry Examining Committee
320 W. Washington, 3rd. Fl.
Springfield, IL 62786
Phone: (217)782-1663

★ 13732 ★ Indiana Optometry Board
402 Washington St., Rm. 041
Indianapolis, IN 46204
Phone: (317)233-4407

★ 13733 ★ Iowa Board of Optometry Examiners
Lucas State Office Bldg.
Des Moines, IA 50319-0075
Phone: (515)242-5936

★ 13734 ★ Kansas Board of Optometry Examiners
1001 SW Mulvanc St.
Topeka, KS 66604
Phone: (913)296-0824

★ 13735 ★ Kentucky Board of Optometric Examiners
1000 W. Main St.
Georgetown, KY 40324
Phone: (502)863-5816

★ 13736 ★ Louisiana State Board of Optometric Examiners
414 E. 7th Ave.
Oakdale, LA 71463
Phone: (318)335-3276

★ 13737 ★ Maine Board of Registration and Examination in Optometry
24 Stone St.
State House Station No. 713
Augusta, ME 04333
Phone: (207)287-2535

★ 13738 ★ Maryland Board of Examiners in Optometry
4201 Patterson Ave.
Baltimore, MD 21215-2299
Phone: (410)764-4725

★ 13739 ★ Massachusetts Board of Registration in Optometry
Leverett Saltonstall Bldg.
100 Cambridge St.
Boston, MA 02202
Phone: (617)727-1817

★ 13740 ★ Michigan State Board of Optometry Examiners
PO Box 30018
Lansing, MI 48909
Phone: (517)335-0930

★ 13741 ★ Minnesota State Board of Optometry
2700 University Ave. W., Rm. 103
St. Paul, MN 55114
Phone: (612)642-0594

★ 13742 ★ Mississippi State Board of Optometry
PO Box 737
Louisville, MS 39339
Phone: (601)773-5027

★ 13743 ★ Missouri State Board of Optometry
PO Box 423
Jefferson City, MO 65102
Phone: (314)751-0814

★ 13744 ★ Montana Board of Optometry
111 N. Jackson
Helena, MT 59620-0513
Phone: (406)444-1698

★ 13745 ★ Nebraska Board of Examiners in Optometry
PO Box 95007
Lincoln, NE 68509
Phone: (402)471-2115

★ 13746 ★ Nevada Board of Optometry
PO Box 1824
Carson City, NV 89702
Phone: (702)883-8367

★ 13747 ★ New Hampshire Board of Registration in Optometry
2 Industrial Park Dr.
Concord, NH 03301
Phone: (603)271-2428

★ 13748 ★ New Jersey Board of Optometrists
124 Halsey St.
PO Box 45012
Newark, NJ 07101
Phone: (201)504-6440

★ 13749 ★ New Mexico Board of Examiners in Optometry
PO Box 25101
Santa Fe, NM 87504
Phone: (505)827-7170

★ 13750 ★ New York State Board of Examiners in Optometry
Cultural Education Center, Rm. 3043
Empire State Plaza
Albany, NY 12230
Phone: (518)474-3867

★ 13751 ★ North Carolina State Board of Examiners in Optometry
109 N. Graham St.
Wallace, NC 28466
Phone: (910)285-3160

★ 13752 ★ North Dakota State Board of Optometry
45 W. 8th St.
Dickinson, ND 58601
Phone: (701)225-0460

★ 13753 ★ Ohio State Board of Optometry
77 S. High St., 16th Fl.
Columbus, OH 43266-0318
Phone: (614)466-5115

★ 13754 ★ Oklahoma State Board of Examiners in Optometry
PO Box 719
Bristow, OK 74010
Phone: (918)367-6780

★ 13755 ★ Oregon Board of Optometry
3218 Pringle Rd., SE
Salem, OR 97302
Phone: (503)373-7721

★ 13756 ★ Pennsylvania State Board of Optometry
PO Box 2649
Harrisburg, PA 17105-2649
Phone: (717)783-7134

★ 13757 ★ Puerto Rico Board of Examiners in Optometry
Call Box 10200
Santurce, PR 00908
Phone: (809)725-8161

★ 13758 ★ Rhode Island State Board of Optometry
3 Capitol Hill, Rm. 104
Providence, RI 02908
Phone: (401)277-2827

★ 13759 ★ South Carolina Board of Examiners in Optometry
PO Box 11329
Columbia, SC 29211-1329
Phone: (803)734-4217

★ 13760 ★ South Dakota Board of Optometry
PO Box 370
Sturgis, SD 57785
Phone: (605)347-2136

★ 13761 ★ Tennessee State Board of Optometry
287 Plus Park Blvd.
Nashville, TN 37217
Phone: (615)367-6425

★ 13762 ★ Texas Optometry Board
9101 Burnet Rd., Ste. 214
Austin, TX 78758
Phone: (512)835-1938

★ 13763 ★ Utah Optometry Board
160 East 300 South, 4th Fl.
Salt Lake City, UT 84145
Phone: (801)530-6767

★ 13764 ★ Vermont Board of Optometry
109 State St.
Montpelier, VT 05609-1106
Phone: (802)828-2191

★ 13765 ★ Virgin Islands Board of Optometrical Examiners
St. Thomas Hospital
48 Sugar Estate
St. Thomas, VI 00802
Phone: (809)774-0117

★ 13766 ★ Virginia Board of Optometry
6606 W. Broad St., 4th Fl.
Richmond, VA 23230
Phone: (804)662-9910

★ 13767 ★ Washington State Optometry
Board
1300 SE Quince
PO Box 47863
Lynnwood, WA 98504
Phone: (206)753-4614

★ 13768 ★ West Virginia Board of
Optometry
101 Michael St.
Clarksburg, WV 26301-3937
Phone: (304)627-2106

★ 13769 ★ Wisconsin Optometry
Examining Board
PO Box 8935
Madison, WI 53708
Phone: (608)267-7222

★ 13770 ★ Wyoming State Board of
Optometric Examiners
Barrett Bldg.
2301 Central Ave.
Cheyenne, WY 82002
Phone: (307)777-6313

State & Regional
Organizations

Blind

The following are state affiliates of Prevent Blindness America, 500 E. Remington Rd., Schaumburg, IL 60173-4557, (708) 843-2020. For states that do not have affiliates listed, contact the national organization for help with inquiries.

California

★ 13771 ★ Prevent Blindness America
Northern California Affiliate
4200 California St., Ste. 101
San Francisco, CA 94118
Phone: (415)387-0934
Free: 800-338-3041
Fax: (415)387-1689

★ 13772 ★ Prevent Blindness America
Southern California Division
3702 Ruffin Rd., Ste. 201
San Diego, CA 92123-2122
Phone: (619)576-2122
Fax: (619)576-2122

Connecticut

★ 13773 ★ Prevent Blindness America
Connecticut Affiliate
1275 Washington St.
Middletown, CT 06457
Phone: (203)347-2020
Free: 800-850-2020
Fax: (203)347-0613

Florida

★ 13774 ★ Prevent Blindness America
Florida Affiliate
711 E. Kennedy Blvd.
PO Box 172418
Tampa, FL 33672
Phone: (813)874-2020
Free: 800-226-6772
Fax: (813)225-2048

Georgia

★ 13775 ★ Prevent Blindness America
Georgia Affiliate
455 E. Paces Ferry Rd., No. 222
Atlanta, GA 30305
Phone: (404)266-0071
Fax: (404)266-0860

Indiana

★ 13776 ★ Prevent Blindness America
Indiana Affiliate
911 E. 86th St.
Indianapolis, IN 46240
Phone: (317)259-8163
Fax: (317)259-8175

Iowa

★ 13777 ★ Prevent Blindness America
Iowa Affiliate
1111 9th St., Ste. 250
Des Moines, IA 50314
Phone: (515)244-4341
Fax: (515)244-4718

Kentucky

★ 13778 ★ Prevent Blindness America
Kentucky Affiliate
101 W. Chestnut St.
Louisville, KY 40202
Phone: (502)584-6127
Free: 800-828-1179
Fax: (502)584-0828

Massachusetts

★ 13779 ★ Prevent Blindness America
Massachusetts Affiliate
375 Concord Ave.
Belmont, MA 02178
Phone: (617)489-0007

Nebraska

★ 13780 ★ Prevent Blindness America
Nebraska Affiliate
7101 Newport Ave., Ste. 308
Omaha, NE 68152-2172
Phone: (402)572-3520
Fax: (402)572-3522

New Jersey

★ 13781 ★ Prevent Blindness America
New Jersey Affiliate
200 Centennial Ave., Ste. 203
Piscataway, NJ 08854-3910
Phone: (908)844-2020
Fax: (908)980-0011

New York

★ 13782 ★ Prevent Blindness America
New York Division
160 E. 56th St., 8th Fl.
New York, NY 10022
Phone: (212)980-2020
Fax: (212)688-9641

North Carolina

★ 13783 ★ Prevent Blindness America
North Carolina Affiliate
3801 Lake Boone Trail, No. 410
Raleigh, NC 27607
Phone: (919)832-2020
Fax: (919)571-1502

Ohio

★ 13784 ★ Prevent Blindnes America
Ohio Affiliate
1500 W. 3rd Ave., Ste. 200
Columbus, OH 43212-2874
Phone: (614)464-2020
Fax: (614)481-9670

Oklahoma

★ 13785 ★ Prevent Blindness America
Oklahoma Affiliate
6 NE 63rd St., Ste. 150
Oklahoma City, OK 73105
Phone: (405)848-7123
Fax: (405)848-6935

Puerto Rico

★ 13786 ★ Prevent Blindness America
Puerto Rico Affiliate
PO Box 3232
San Juan, PR 00904
Phone: (809)722-3531
Fax: (809)725-0809

Rhode Island

★ 13787 ★ Prevent Blindness America
Rhode Island Affiliate
1800 17th Post Rd.
Warwick, RI 02886
Phone: (401)738-1150

Tennessee

★ 13788 ★ **Prevent Blindness America**
Tennessee Affiliate
95 White Bridge Rd., Ste. 513
Nashville, TN 37205
Phone: (615)352-0450
Fax: (615)352-5750

Texas

★ 13789 ★ **Prevent Blindness America**
Texas Affiliate
3211 W. Dallas
Houston, TX 77019
Phone: (713)526-2559
Fax: (713)529-8310

Utah

★ 13790 ★ **Prevent Blindness America**
Utah Affiliate
661 South 200 East
Salt Lake City, UT 84111
Phone: (801)524-2020
Free: 800-675-5665
Fax: (801)322-3647

Virginia

★ 13791 ★ **Prevent Blindness America**
Virginia Affiliate
3820 Augusta Ave.
Richmond, VA 23230
Phone: (804)355-0773
Fax: (804)355-3142

Wisconsin

★ 13792 ★ **Prevent Blindness America**
Wisconsin Affiliate
759 N. Milwaukee St.
Milwaukee, WI 53202
Phone: (414)765-0505
Fax: (414)765-0377

Optometry

The state optometric organizations listed below are affiliated with the American Optometric Association, 243 N. Lindbergh Blvd., St. Louis, MO 63141-7881, (314) 991-4100.

Alabama

★ 13793 ★ **Alabama Optometric Association**
400 S. Union St., Ste. 435
Montgomery, AL 36104
Phone: (334)834-1057

Alaska

★ 13794 ★ **Alaska Optometric Association**
2211 E. Northern Lights, No. 202
Anchorage, AK 99508
Phone: (907)276-2080

Arizona

★ 13795 ★ **Arizona Optometric Association**
3625 N. 16th St., Ste. 119
Phoenix, AZ 85016
Phone: (602)279-0055

Arkansas

★ 13796 ★ **Arkansas Optometric Association**
100 S. University, Ste. 311
Little Rock, AR 72205-5216
Phone: (501)661-7675

California

★ 13797 ★ **California Optometric Association**
801 12th St., Ste. 2020
Sacramento, CA 95814
Phone: (916)441-3990

Colorado

★ 13798 ★ **Colorado Optometric Association**
410 17th St., Ste. 2060
Denver, CO 80202-4433
Phone: (303)892-8898

Connecticut

★ 13799 ★ **Connecticut Association of Optometrists**
638 Prospect Ave.
Hartford, CT 06105-4298
Phone: (203)586-7508

Delaware

★ 13800 ★ **Delaware Optometric Association**
419 Market St.
Wilmington, DE 19801
Phone: (302)654-6490

District of Columbia

★ 13801 ★ **Optometric Society of the District of Columbia**
7705 Cayuga Ave.
Bethesda, MD 20817
Phone: (301)229-4990

Florida

★ 13802 ★ **Florida Optometric Association**
PO Box 13429
Tallahassee, FL 32317
Phone: (904)877-4697

Georgia

★ 13803 ★ **Georgia Optometric Association**
2175 Northlake Pkwy., Ste. 128
Tucker, GA 30084
Phone: (404)908-0208

Hawaii

★ 13804 ★ **Hawaii Optometric Association**
1580 Makaloa St., Ste. 590
Honolulu, HI 96814
Phone: (808)947-0111

Idaho

★ 13805 ★ **Idaho Optometric Association**
9077 Maple Hill Dr.
Boise, ID 83709
Phone: (208)378-7700

Illinois

★ 13806 ★ **Illinois Optometric Association**
304 W. Washington St.
Springfield, IL 62701
Phone: (217)525-8012

Indiana

★ 13807 ★ **Indiana Optometric Association**
201 N. Illinois St., Ste. 1920
Indianapolis, IN 46204-4236
Phone: (317)237-3560

Iowa

★ 13808 ★ **Iowa Optometric Association**
1454 30th St., Ste. 304
West Des Moines, IA 50266-1312
Phone: (515)222-5679

Kansas

★ 13809 ★ **Kansas Optometric Association**
1266 SW Topeka Blvd.
Topeka, KS 66612
Phone: (913)232-0225

Kentucky

★ 13810 ★ **Kentucky Optometric Association**
PO Box 572
Frankfort, KY 40602
Phone: (502)875-3516

Louisiana

★ 13811 ★ **Louisiana State Association of Optometrists**
PO Box 13451
Alexandria, LA 71315-3451
Phone: (318)449-9467

Maine

★ 13812 ★ Maine Optometric Association
RR1, Box 2675
Gardiner, ME 04345
Phone: (207)582-9910

Maryland

★ 13813 ★ Maryland Optometric Association
720 Light St.
Baltimore, MD 21230
Phone: (410)727-7800

Massachusetts

★ 13814 ★ Massachusetts Society of Optometrists
101 Tremont St., Rm. 600
Boston, MA 02108
Phone: (617)542-9200

Michigan

★ 13815 ★ Michigan Optometric Association
530 W. Ionia St., Ste. A
Lansing, MI 48933
Phone: (517)482-0616

Minnesota

★ 13816 ★ Minnesota Optometric Association
1821 University Ave., Ste. 492N
St. Paul, MN 55104
Phone: (612)646-2883

Mississippi

★ 13817 ★ Mississippi Optometric Association
5420 I-55 N., Ste. D
PO Box 16441
Jackson, MS 39236-6441
Phone: (601)956-7412

Missouri

★ 13818 ★ Missouri Optometric Association
417 E. High St.
Jefferson City, MO 65101-3274
Phone: (314)635-6151

Montana

★ 13819 ★ Montana Optometric Association
36 S. Last Chance Gulch, Ste. A
Helena, MT 59601
Phone: (406)443-1160

Nebraska

★ 13820 ★ Nebraska Optometric Association
PO Box 81706
Lincoln, NE 68501-1706
Phone: (402)474-7716

Nevada

★ 13821 ★ Nevada Optometric Association
9230 W. Sahara
Las Vegas, NV 89117
Phone: (702)228-8644

New Hampshire

★ 13822 ★ New Hampshire Optometric Association
195 Hanover St.
Portsmouth, NH 03801
Phone: (603)431-6814

New Jersey

★ 13823 ★ New Jersey Optometric Association
652 Whitehead Rd.
Trenton, NJ 08648
Phone: (609)695-3456

New Mexico

★ 13824 ★ New Mexico Optometric Association
10131 Coors Rd. NW, No. 227
Albuquerque, NM 87114
Phone: (505)898-6885

New York

★ 13825 ★ New York State Optometric Association
90 S. Swan St.
Albany, NY 12210
Phone: (518)449-7300

North Carolina

★ 13826 ★ North Carolina State Optometric Society
PO Box 1206
Wilson, NC 27894-1206
Phone: (919)237-6197

North Dakota

★ 13827 ★ North Dakota Optometric Association
204 W. Thayer Ave., No. 302
Bismarck, ND 58501-3772
Phone: (701)258-6766

Ohio

★ 13828 ★ Ohio Optometric Association
169 E. Livingston Ave.
Columbus, OH 43215
Phone: (614)224-2600

Oklahoma

★ 13829 ★ Oklahoma Optometric Association
4545 N. Lincoln Blvd., Ste. 105
Oklahoma City, OK 73105
Phone: (405)524-1075

Oregon

★ 13830 ★ Oregon Optometric Association
6901 SE Lake Rd., Ste. 26
Milwaukie, OR 97267-2195
Phone: (503)654-5036

Pennsylvania

★ 13831 ★ Pennsylvania Optometric Association
PO Box 3312
Harrisburg, PA 17105
Phone: (717)233-6455

Rhode Island

★ 13832 ★ Rhode Island Optometric Association
PO Box 8400
Warwick, RI 02888-0400
Phone: (401)461-7550

South Carolina

★ 13833 ★ South Carolina Optometric Association
2730 Devine St.
Columbia, SC 29205
Phone: (803)799-6721

South Dakota

★ 13834 ★ South Dakota Optometric Society
PO Box 1173
Pierre, SD 57501
Phone: (605)224-8199

Tennessee

★ 13835 ★ Tennessee Optometric Association
3200 West End Ave., Ste. 402
Nashville, TN 37203
Phone: (615)269-9092

Texas

★ 13836 ★ **Texas Optometric Association**
1503 S. IH35
Austin, TX 78741
Phone: (512)707-2020

Utah

★ 13837 ★ **Utah Optometric Association**
230 West 200 South, Ste. 2110
Salt Lake City, UT 84101-3409
Phone: (801)364-9103

Vermont

★ 13838 ★ **Vermont Optometric
Association**
26 State St.
PO Box 1531
Montpelier, VT 05601
Phone: (802)233-1197

Virginia

★ 13839 ★ **Virginia Optometric Association**
118 N. 8th St.
Richmond, VA 23219-2305
Phone: (804)643-0309

Washington

★ 13840 ★ **Washington Association of
Optometric Physician**
555 116th NE, Ste. 166
Bellevue, WA 98004-5274
Phone: (206)455-0874

West Virginia

★ 13841 ★ **West Virginia Optometric
Association**
815 Quarrier St., Ste. 215
Charleston, WV 25301-2616
Phone: (304)345-4710

Wisconsin

★ 13842 ★ **Wisconsin Optometric
Association**
5721 Odana Rd.
Madison, WI 53719
Phone: (608)274-4322

Wyoming

★ 13843 ★ **Wyoming Optometric
Association**
520 Randall St.
Cheyenne, WY 82001
Phone: (307)632-8819

Alphabetical Name and Keyword Index

*This index is an alphabetical listing of all organizations, agencies, and institutions included in EMOA, as well as former or alternate names that appear within the text of entries. Index references are to book **entry numbers** rather than to page numbers. Entry numbers appear in boldface type if the reference is to the unit for which information is provided in EMOA and in lightface type if the reference is to a former or alternate name included within the text of the cited entry. Consult the "User's Guide" at the front of this directory for more detailed information about the index.*

A

A. C. Buehler Foundation **1869**
A. E. Finley Foundation **21**
A. L. Mailman Family Foundation **22**
A.O. Smith Foundation **561**
A.T. Still Osteopathic Library and Research Center **10011**
A. V. Hunter Trust **23**
AA; Gay **11692**
AAMR - National Association on Intellectual Disability 4297
Aansteeklike Siektesvereniging van Suider Afrika 6677
Aaron Diamond Aids Research Center **6760**
Aaron Diamond Foundation **24**
Aaron and Lillie Straus Foundation **25**
AARP Andrus Foundation **1874**
Abbot and Dorothy H. Stevens Foundation **26**
Abbott Laboratories Fund **562**
Abbott-Northwestern Hospital • School of Anesthesia **2289**
Abdominal Surgeons; American Society of **12235**
Abdominal Surgery; American Board of **12216**
Abell-Hanger Foundation **27**
Abercrombie Foundation **28**
Abilene Christian University • Abilene Intercollegiate School of Nursing **8979**
Abney Foundation **6328**
Abortion Federation; National **11236**
Abortion Rights; International Campaign for 11256
Abortion and Sterilization Campaign; International Contraception, 11256
AboutFace **7256**
Abuse; Center on Addiction and Substance • Columbia University **12092**
Abuse Counselors; National Association of Alcoholism and Drug **12051**
Abuse by Counselors; Stop **7523**
Abuse Directors; National Association of State Alcohol and Drug 5588
Abuse and Family Violence; National Council on Child **3061**
Abuse Finally Ends; SAFE - Self **7502**
Abuse Foundation for Education; Solvent **12078**
Abuse Institute; Alcohol and Drug • University of Washington **12144**
Abuse Institute of North Texas; Substance • University of North Texas Health Science Center at Fort Worth **12142**
Abuse Institute of Research; Child **3047**
Abuse Listening and Mediation; Child **3048**
Abuse; Multidisciplinary Research Center on Drug and Alcohol • University of Kentucky **12138**
Abuse; National Committee for Prevention of Child **3060**
Abuse and Neglect; C. Henry Kempe National Center for the Prevention and Treatment of Child • University of Colorado **3073**
Abuse and Neglect Information; Clearinghouse on Child 3058
Abuse and Neglect Information; National Clearinghouse on Child **3058**
Abuse and Neglect; International Society for Prevention of Child **3056**
Abuse and Neglect; National Center on Child • Administration for Children and Families • U.S. Department of Health and Human Services **3045, 3072**
Abuse Prevention; Institute for Drug • Indiana University **12094**
Abuse and Prevention; Tri-Ethnic Center for Study of Drug • Colorado State University **12091**

Abuse Problems; National Association on Drug **12053**
Abuse Program Coordinators; National Association of State Drug 5588
Abuse Project; Domestic • Evaluation and Research Unit **3068**
Abuse; Psychiatrists Against Psychiatric **7488**
Abuse Research; Center for Substance • University of Maryland **12139**
Abuse Services; Special Constituency Section for Psychiatric and Substance **6473**
Abuse Trainers and Educators; National Association of Substance **12055**
Abuse Treatment Unit; Substance • University of Pennsylvania **12143**
Abused Women's Services; North Dakota Council on **3110**
Abusers; Association for the Behavioral Treatment of Sexual 11686
Abusers; Association for the Treatment of Sexual **11686**
Abusive Men Exploring New Directions **7264**
Academia Espanola de Dermatologia 4259
Academia Mexicana de Dermatologia 4247
Academia Ophthalmologica Internationalis **13381**
Academic Associations of General Practitioners / Family Physicians; World Organization of National Colleges, Academies and **1550**
Academic Emergency Medicine; Society for **4757**
Academic Health Centers; Association of **1194**
Academic Health Sciences Library Directors; Association of **6975**
Academic Medicine Club 1215
Academic Orthopaedic Society **9916**
Academic Physiatrists; Association of **12663**
Academic Standards Association; Straight Chiropractic **3461**
Academic Surgery; Association for **12253**
Academie Canadienne d'Endodontie 3912
Academie Europeenne d'Allergologie et d'Immunologie Clinique 2072
Academie Internationale de Medecine Legal et de Medecine Sociale 7178
Academies and Academic Associations of General Practitioners / Family Physicians; World Organization of National Colleges, **1550**
Academies et Associations Academiques des Generalistes et des Medecins de Famille; Organisation Mondiale des Colleges Nationaux, 1550
Academies of Medicine; Latin American Association of National **1370**
Academies des Generalistes et des Medecins de Famille; Organisation Mondiale des Colleges Nationaux, Academies et Associations 1550
Academy of Ambulatory Foot Surgery **10754**
Academy of Aphasia **3473**
Academy of Applied Osteopathy 9969
Academy of Behaviorial Medicine Research **7257**
Academy of Dental Materials **3841**
Academy of Dentistry for the Handicapped 3843
Academy of Dentistry International **3842**
Academy of Dentistry for Persons with Disabilities **3843**
Academy of Dispensing Audiologists **3474**
Academy of General Dentistry **3844**
Academy of General Practice of Pharmacy 10575
Academy for Implants and Transplants **3845**
Academy of Laser Dentistry **3846**
Academy of Operative Dentistry **3847**
Academy of Oral Diagnosis, Radiology, and Medicine 3879
Academy of Oral Dynamics **3848**
Academy of Osteopathic Directors of Medical Education 9968
Academy of Pharmaceutical Research and Science **10574**
Academy of Pharmaceutical Sciences 10574

Advisors for the Health Professions; National Association of **1394**
Advisory Board on Veterinary Specialties 13042
Advisory Center; Breast Cancer **5924**
Advisory and Research Council; Nursing Home **9270**
Advocacy Systems; National Association of Protection and **4517**
Advocacy; Vietnam Veterans Institute for Research and 7815
Advocate Health Care **2150**
Advocates for Advanced Cancer Treatment; Patient **5980**
Advocates for Child Psychiatric Nursing 3178
Advocates for Youth **11195, 11258**
Advocates for Youth's Media Project **11196**
Aero Medical Association 2381
Aerobics Association; American 10839
Aerobics and Fitness Foundation of America **10834**
Aerobics International Research Society **10835**
Aerobics Research; Cooper Institute for **10864**
Aerobics Research; Institute for **10852**
Aeromedical Institute; Civil • Federal Aviation Administration • U.S.
    Department of Transportation **2404**
Aeromedical Research Division • Civil Aeromedical Institute • Federal
    Aviation Administration • U.S. Department of Transportation **2405**
Aeromedical Research Laboratory; Army • Army Medical Research and
    Development Command • U.S. Department of Defense **2402**
Aeromedical Transport Association; Professional **4753**
Aeronautics and Space Administration; National
        Ames Research Center • Space Human Factors Office **2389**
        Lyndon B. Johnson Space Center
                Medical Sciences Division **2390**
                Space Biomedical Research Institute **2391**
Aerospace Medical Association **2381**
Aerospace Medical Research Laboratory; Naval • Naval Medical Research
    and Development Command • U.S. Department of Defense **2403**
Aerospace Medicine; Air Force School of • Air Force Materiel Command •
    U.S. Department of Defense **2393**
Aerospace Pathology Division; Forensic and • Office of the Armed Forces
    Medical Examiner • Armed Forces Institute of Pathology • U.S.
    Department of Defense **10171**
Aesculapius 1124
Aesculapius International Medicine **1124**
Aesthetic (Cosmetic) Plastic Surgery; Canadian Society for **12262**
Aesthetic Plastic Surgeons; British Association of **12260**
Aesthetic Plastic Surgery; American Society for **12236**
Aesthetic Surgery; International Confederation for Plastic, Reconstructive
    and **12279**
Aesthetic Surgery; Israel Association of Plastic Reconstructive and 12284
Aesthetics; American Society for Dental **3899**
Aetna Foundation **564**
AFASIC - Overcoming Speech Impairments **3477**
Affective Disorders Association; Depression and Related **7365**
Affective Disorders Research Unit • University of Iowa **7666**
Affiliated/Associated Drug Stores 5830
Affiliated Leadership League of and for the Blind of America **13383**
Africa; Anatomical Society of Southern **2526**
Africa; Church World Service Aids for the Horn of **1243**
Africa; Infectious Diseases Society of Southern **6677**
Africa; Inter church Response for the Horn of 1243
Africa; Leprosy Mission - Southern **6692**
Africa; Regional Office for • World Health Organization **1541**
Africa; Research Organization for Food and Nutrition in 9485
Africa; Surgical Research Society of Southern **12314**
Africa; Traditional Healers Organisation for **2243**
Africaine des Sciences Neurologiques; Association Pan- 8296
Africaines; Organisme de Recherches sur l' Alimentation et la Nutrition
    9485
African AIDS Project **6614**
African Alimentation and Nutrition; Research Organization on **9485**
African-American Natural Foods Association **9437**
African Bureau for Animal Resources; Inter- **13082**
African Bureau for Epizootic Diseases; Inter 13082
African Committee Against Harmful Traditional Practices; British Support
    Group - Inter- **1223**
African Division; European • International Society of Hematology **5959**
African Health Community; West **1531**
African Medical and Research Foundation 1131
African Medical and Research Foundation [Dar es Salaam, United Republic
    of Tanzania] **1125**
African Medical and Research Foundation [Kampala, Uganda] **10933**
African Medical and Research Foundation [Munich, Germany] **1129**
African Medical and Research Foundation [Nairobi, Kenya] **1130**
African Medical and Research Foundation [Rome, Italy] **1128**
African Medical and Research Foundation [Stockholm, Sweden] **1127**

African Medical and Research Foundation [Voorschoten, Netherlands]
    1126
African Medical and Research Foundation, U.S.A. **1131**
African Research Foundation 1131
Africana per la Medicina e la Ricerca; Fondzione 1128
Afrika; Aansteeklike Siektesvereniging van Suider **6677**
Afrika; Anatomiese Vereniging van Suider- 2526
Afrika; Chirurgiese Navorsingsvereniging van Suidelike 12314
Afrika; Gesellschaft fur Medizin und Forschung in 1129
Afrique Centrale; Organisation de Coordination pour la Lutte Contre les
    Endemies en 6741
Aftosa; Centro Panamericano de Fiebre 13109
Aga Khan Cetral Health Board for Pakistan; His Royal Highness Prince
    1132
Aga Khan Health Service Pakistan **1132**
Aged; Central Bureau for the Jewish 1905
Aged; Jewish Association for Services for the [New York, NY] **1904**
Aged; Jewish Association for Services for the [Rego Park, NY] **1905**
Aged; National Association of Jewish Homes for the 1916
Aged; National Caucus and Center on Black **1910**
Ageing; British Society for Research on **1893**
Agencies for the Blind; National Council of State **13533**
Agencies Serving the Blind and Visually Handicapped; National
    Accreditation Council for **13521**
Agency for Health Care Policy and Research
        Center for General Health Services Extramural Research • U.S.
            Department of Health and Human Services **5643**
        Center of General Health Services Intramural Research • U.S.
            Department of Health and Human Services **5644**
        Office of Health Technology Assessment • U.S. Department of Health
            and Human Services **5645**
        U.S. Department of Health and Human Services **5642**
Agency for Toxic Substances and Disease Registry
        Division of Health Studies • U.S. Department of Health and Human
            Services **5095**
        Division of Toxicology • U.S. Department of Health and Human
            Services **5096**
        U.S. Department of Health and Human Services **5005, 5094**
Agent Orange Victims International 7814
Agent Orange Victims; Vietnam Veterans **7814**
Aggression; Association for the Behavioral Treatment of Sexual **11686**
Aging; Administration on • Office of the Secretary • U.S. Department of
    Health and Human Services **1865**
Aging and Adult Services Division
        Arkansas Department of Human Services **2006**
        Colorado Department of Human Services **2008**
        Mississippi Department of Human Services **2026**
        Utah Department of Human Services **2046**
Aging and Adult Services Office
        Florida Department of Health and Rehabilitative Services **2012**
        Washington Department of Social and Health Services **2049**
Aging and Adult Services Program Division • Social Services Administration
    • Minnesota Department of Human Services **2025**
Aging; Alabama Commission on **2003**
Aging in America **1878**
Aging; American Association of Homes for the 1882
Aging; American Association of Homes and Services for the **1882**
Aging; American Society on **1887**
Aging; Arizona Center on • University of Arizona **1970**
Aging Association; American **1880**
Aging Bureau • Community Services Division • Wisconsin Department of
    Health and Social Services **2051**
Aging; Center on
        Auburn University **1921**
        University of Alabama at Birmingham **1968**
        University of Kansas **1979**
        University of Maryland **1982**
        University of West Florida **1997**
Aging; Center on Adult Development and • University of Miami **1984**
Aging; Center for the Neurobiology of • University of Florida **8498**
Aging; Center for Studies in • University of North Texas **1991**
Aging; Center for the Study of
        University of Alabama **1967**
        University of Bridgeport **1971**
        University of Missouri—Columbia **1986**
Aging; Center for Understanding **1896**
Aging; Centre on • University of Manitoba **1981**
Aging; Centre for Studies of • University of Toronto **1995**
Aging; Claude D. Pepper Center for Research on Oral Health in • University
    of Florida **1977**
Aging Commission • West Virginia Department of Health and Human
    Resources **2050**

Aging and Community Services Division • Arizona Department of Economic Security **2005**
Aging Department
    California Health and Welfare Agency **2007**
    Virginia Department of Health and Human Resources **2048**
Aging and Disability Department • Vermont Agency of Human Services **2047**
Aging Division
    Delaware Department of Health and Social Services **2010**
    Missouri Department of Social Services **2027**
    New Jersey Department of Community Affairs **2032**
    North Carolina Department of Human Resources **2035**
    South Carolina Office of the Governor **2042**
    Wyoming Department of Health **2052**
Aging; Federal Council on the • Office of the Secretary • U.S. Department of Health and Human Services **1866**
Aging; Georgia Consortium on the Psychology of **1935**
Aging and Health; University Center on • Case Western Reserve University **1928**
Aging and Human Development; Center for Study of • Duke University **1933**
Aging; Human Nutrition Research Center on • Agricultural Research Service • U.S. Department of Agriculture **9538**
Aging; Idaho Office on **2015**
Aging; Illinois Department on **2016**
Aging, Inc.; Center for the Study of **1930**
Aging; Institute on
    Portland State University **1945**
    Temple University **1947**
    University of Pennsylvania **1993**
    University of Wisconsin—Madison **1998**
Aging; Institute for Health & • University of California, San Francisco **1974**
Aging Institute; Neuroscience and • Loyola University Chicago **8388**
Aging; Kansas Department on **2019**
Aging and Long Term Care Services; Special Constituency Section for **6472**
Aging and Long Term Care; Special Constituency Section on **6472**
Aging; Maryland Office on **2022**
Aging; Michigan Office on **2024**
Aging; Multidisciplinary Center for the Study of **1942**
Aging; National Asian Pacific Center on **1906**
Aging; National Association of State Units on **1909**
Aging; National Center for Health Promotion and **1901**
Aging; National Council on the **1877, 1911**
Aging; National Institute on
    Behavioral and Social Research Program • U.S. Department of Health and Human Services **1949**
    Biology of Aging Program
        Biology Branch • U.S. Department of Health and Human Services **1951**
        Geriatrics Branch • U.S. Department of Health and Human Services **1952**
        U.S. Department of Health and Human Services **1950**
    Epidemiology, Demography, and Biometry Program • U.S. Department of Health and Human Services **1953**
    Intramural Research Program • Longitudinal Studies Branch • U.S. Department of Health and Human Services **1955**
    Laboratory of Behavioral Sciences • U.S. Department of Health and Human Services **1956**
    Laboratory of Cardiovascular Science
        Membrane Biology Section • U.S. Department of Health and Human Services **1958**
        U.S. Department of Health and Human Services **1957**
    Laboratory of Cellular and Molecular Biology • U.S. Department of Health and Human Services **1959**
    Laboratory of Clinical Physiology • U.S. Department of Health and Human Services **1960**
    Laboratory of Molecular Genetics • U.S. Department of Health and Human Services **1961**
    Laboratory of Neurosciences • U.S. Department of Health and Human Services **1962**
    Laboratory of Personality and Cognition • U.S. Department of Health and Human Services **1963**
    Neuroscience and Neuropsychology of Aging Program • U.S. Department of Health and Human Services **1964**
    Office of Extramural Affairs • U.S. Department of Health and Human Services **1965**
    U.S. Department of Health and Human Services **1864, 1948**
Aging; National Pacific/ Asian Resource Center on **1906**
Aging of National Social Welfare Assembly; National Committee on **1911**
Aging; National Voluntary Organizations for Independent Living for the **1915**
Aging; Nebraska Department on **2029**

Aging; New Mexico State Agency on **2033**
Aging; New York State Office on **2034**
Aging; North American Association of Jewish Homes and Housing for the **1916**
Aging Office
    District of Columbia Diversity and Special Services Office **2011**
    Hawaii Office of the Governor **2014**
Aging Office; Adult Services on • Program Management Division • South Dakota Department of Social Services **2043**
Aging; Ohio Department on **2037**
Aging Parents; Children of **1897**
Aging; Pennsylvania Department on **2040**
Aging; Policy Center on • Brandeis University **5612**
Aging Program; Biology of • National Institute on Aging • U.S. Department of Health and Human Services **1950**
Aging Program; Neuroscience and Neuropsychology of • National Institute on Aging • U.S. Department of Health and Human Services **1964**
Aging Project; Center for Research on • University of California, Los Angeles **7655**
Aging and Rehabilitation; J. Paul Sticht Center on **1937**
Aging and Rehabilitative Services Division • Indiana Family and Social Services Administration **13679**
Aging and Rehabilitative Services Division; Disability, • Indiana Family and Social Services Administration **2017**
Aging Research; Alliance for **1879**
Aging Research; American Federation for **1875, 1884**
Aging Research; American Foundation for **1876, 1885**
Aging Research Branch; Mental Disorders of the • Clinical Research Division • National Institute of Mental Health • U.S. Department of Health and Human Services **7621**
Aging Research; Institute for Health, Health Care Policy, and • Rutgers University **1659**
Aging; Roy M. and Phyllis Gough Huffington Center on • Baylor College of Medicine **1923**
Aging; Sam and Rose Stein Institute for Research on • University of California, San Diego **1972**
Aging; Sanders-Brown Center on • University of Kentucky **1980**
Aging Services Bureau • Montana Family Services Department **2028**
Aging Services Division
    Nevada Department of Human Resources **2030**
    North Dakota Department of Human Services **2036**
    Oklahoma Department of Human Services **2038**
    Social Services Department • Kentucky Human Resources Cabinet **2020**
Aging Services Office • Georgia Department of Human Resources **2013**
Aging Services Programs; National Association of Nutrition and **1907**
Aging Services Research; Center for Clinical and • University of California, San Francisco **1973**
Aging Skin Clinic • University of Pennsylvania **4270**
Aging; Special Committee on • U.S. Senate **1868**
Aging Studies; Center for
    University of Missouri—Kansas City **1987**
    University of Missouri—Rolla **1988**
Aging Studies; Laboratory for Health and • Maharishi International University **1622**
Aging; Subcommittee on • Committee on Labor and Human Resources • U.S. Senate **1867**
Aging; Tennessee Commission on **2044**
Aging; Texas Department on **2045**
Aging; Texas Institute for Research and Education on • University of North Texas Health Science Center at Fort Worth **1992**
Aging; Travelers Center on • University of Connecticut **1975**
Aging; Understanding **1896**
Aging; Virginia Center on • Virginia Commonwealth University **1999**
Agnes M. Lindsay Trust **33**
Agoraphobics Anonymous **7260**
Agoraphobics In Motion **7261**
Agricole et de Sante Rurale; Association Internationale de Medecine **9797**
Agricultural Center; Dixon Springs • University of Illinois **13219**
Agricultural Disease and Injury Research, Education, and Prevention; Center for • University of Iowa **9852**
Agricultural Experiment Station
    Cornell University **9500**
    New Mexico State University **9515**
    University of California, Davis **9549**
Agricultural Experiment Station; Arizona • University of Arizona **9547**
Agricultural Experiment Station; George Washington Carver • Tuskegee University **9530**
Agricultural Experiment Station; Idaho • University of Idaho **9554**
Agricultural Experiment Station; Minnesota • University of Minnesota **13224**
Agricultural Experiment Station; Missouri • University of Missouri— Columbia **9558**

University of Michigan **6848**
University of Texas Medical Branch at Galveston **6855**
AIDS; National Council on **6734**
AIDS; National Leadership Coalition on **6736**
AIDS; National Mobilization Against **6696**
AIDS; National Policy Director for • Domestic Policy Council • Executive Office of the President **6601**
AIDS; National Resource Center on Women and **6738**
AIDS Network; National Catholic **6731**
AIDS Office
    Health Services Department • California Health and Welfare Agency **6861**
    Public Health Department • Massachusetts Executive Office of Health and Human Services **6877**
AIDS Office; HIV /
    Community and Family Health Division • Washington Department of Health **6903**
    Disease Prevention Services Division • Arizona Department of Health Services **6859**
AIDS Pathology Division • Infectious and Parasitic Disease Pathology Department • Armed Forces Institute of Pathology • U.S. Department of Defense **10168**
AIDS Policy; Americans for a Sound **6637**
AIDS Prevention and Control; National Committee for **6733**
AIDS Prevention and Control Program; National [Manila, Philippines] **6727**
AIDS Prevention and Intervention Section; HIV / • Infectious Disease Control Bureau • Michigan Department of Public Health **6878**
AIDS Prevention League **2151**
AIDS Prevention Program • Preventive Medicine Division • Wyoming Department of Health **6906**
AIDS Prevention Services Bureau; STD / • Health Resources Adminstration • Hawaii Department of Health **6867**
AIDS Prevention Studies; Center for • University of California, San Francisco **10884**
AIDS Prevention; Teens Teaching **6751**
AIDS Program
    Canadian Public Health Association **6647**
    Disease Control Division • Preventive Health Section • North Dakota Department of Health **6890**
    Disease Control Office • Preventive Health Bureau • Mississippi Department of Health **6880**
    Preventive Health Services Bureau • Health Services Division • Montana Department of Health and Environmental Sciences **6882**
    Tennessee Department of Health **6898**
AIDS Program; HIV / **6674**
    Communicable Disease Section • Health Promotion and Disease Prevention Bureau • Nebraska Department of Health **6883**
    Public Health Bureau • West Virginia Department of Health and Human Resources **6904**
AIDS Program; STD / • Clinical and Preventive Services Bureau • Idaho Department of Health and Welfare **6868**
AIDS Project; African **6614**
AIDS Project; CAVDA- Citizens **6648**
AIDS Research; American Foundation for **6607, 6629**
AIDS Research; Center for
    Purdue University **6783**
    Stanford University **6790**
Aids Research Center; Aaron Diamond **6760**
AIDS Research and Education / AIDS Clinical Trials Unit; UCLA Center for Clinical • University of California, Los Angeles **6840**
AIDS Research Group • Rutgers University **6786**
AIDS Resource Foundation for Children **6622**
AIDS Section
    Connecticut Department Public Health **6863**
    Disease Control Bureau • Health Division • Kansas Department of Health and Environment **6872**
    Health Protection Division • Iowa Department of Public Health **6871**
AIDS Section; STD / • Disease Control and Environmental Epidemiology Division • Health Office • Colorado Public Health and Environment Department **6862**
AIDS Service Organisations; Namibia Network of **6698**
AIDS Society; Canadian **6646**
AIDS Society; International **6678**
AIDS Specialist • South Dakota Department of Health **6897**
AIDS / STD Administrative Office • Arkansas Department of Health **6860**
AIDS / STD Prevention Services • Minnesota Department of Health **6879**
AIDS / STD Program • Disease Control Division • Family Health Office • Rhode Island Department of Health **6895**
AIDS Task Force for the American College Health Association **6623**
AIDS Task Force; National **6728**
AIDS Treatment and Development Center; SUNY Stony Brook • State University of New York Health Science Center at Stony Brook **6792**
AIDS Trust; National **6729**

AIDS Unit **6624**
    Health Protection and Promotion Bureau • Communicable Disease Control Division • Louisiana Department of Health and Hospitals **6874**
AIDS Virus Diagnostic Laboratory • University of California, Davis **6839**
Air Force Anesthesiologists; Society of **2362**
Air Force Flight Surgeons; Society of United States **7811**
Air Force Physicians; Society of **7807**
Air Force School of Aerospace Medicine • Air Force Materiel Command • U.S. Department of Defense **2393**
Air Force Surgeon General • Vice Chief of Staff of the Air Force • Department of the Air Force • U.S. Department of Defense **7783**
Air Medical Services; American Society of Hospital-Based Emergency **4737**
Air Medical Services; Association of **4737**
Air National Guard Health Technicians; National Association of **7802**
Air National Guard Optometric Society **7796**
Air Pollution, and General Pathobiology Unit; Lung Disease, Cancer, Lymphocytes, • University of Southern California **10181**
Air Pollution Health Effects Laboratory • University of California, Irvine **5115**
Air Pollution Research Laboratory • University of Florida **9851**
Air Products Foundation **565**
Air Research; Center for Indoor **5065**
AirLifeLine **4731**
Airlift; Mercy Medical **1391**
Airline Medical Directors Association **2382**
Airline Medical Examiners Association **2383**
Airways Diseases Branch • Division of Lung Diseases • National Heart, Lung, and Blood Institute • U.S. Department of Health and Human Services **11615**
Aitken Neurosurgery Laboratory • Cornell University **8358**
Akron Area Chapter • Lupus Foundation of America **8094**
Akupunktur; Norsk Forening for Klassisk **2229**
Akupunktur; Osterreichische Gesellschaft fur **2180**
Akupunktur; Schweizerische Arztegesellschaft fur **2240**
Alabama Affiliate
    American Diabetes Association **4950**
    American Heart Association **2989**
Alabama; American Lung Association of **11626**
Alabama; Arc of **4394**
Alabama Board of Funeral Service **3728**
Alabama Board of Nursing **9152**
Alabama Chapter
    American Physical Therapy Association **12823**
    Arthritis Foundation **7963**
    Cystic Fibrosis Foundation **5397**
    National Association of Social Workers **11880**
Alabama Coalition Against Domestic Violence **3076**
Alabama Commission on Aging **2003**
Alabama Congenital Heart Disease Diagnosis and Treatment Center • University of Alabama at Birmingham **2953**
Alabama Dental Association **4155**
Alabama Department of Agriculture and Industries • State Veterinarian **13250**
Alabama Department of Labor • Occupational Injury Statistics and Fatality Data Division **9865**
Alabama Department of Mental Health and Mental Retardation **4343, 7708**
    Substance Abuse Services Division **12147**
Alabama Department of Public Health **11005**
    Dental Health Division **4102**
    Disease Control Bureau • HIV / AIDS Division **6857**
    Environmental Services Bureau **5128**
    Family Health Services Bureau **3378, 9724**
    Health Care Standards Bureau
        Emergency Medical Services Division **4767**
        Licensure and Certification Division **6476**
    Health Statistics Center • Vital Records Division **7040**
Alabama Department of Rehabilitation Services **12770, 13665**
Alabama Division • American Cancer Society **6271**
Alabama Easter Seal Society **4605**
Alabama Health Planning and Development Agency **5664**
Alabama Hospital Association **6527**
Alabama; Learning Disabilities Association of **4684**
Alabama Medicaid Agency **5768**
Alabama; Medical Association of the State of **1810**
Alabama; National Kidney Foundation of **12933**
Alabama Nursing Home Association **9326**
Alabama Optometric Association **13793**
Alabama Osteopathic Medical Association **10066**
Alabama Pharmacy Association **10694**

Index

Alcohol and Drug Programs Department • California Health and Welfare Agency **12151**
Alcohol and Drug Research; Nordic Council for **12066**
Alcohol and Drugs; National Episcopal Coalition on **12060**
Alcohol Education; Unitarian Universalist Society for **12081**
Alcohol Information Council; Beverage **12046**
Alcohol Issues; Inter-Association Task Force on **12035**
Alcohol and Other Drug Abuse Services; South Carolina Department of **12187**
Alcohol and Other Drugs; National Treatment Consortium for **12065**
Alcohol and Other Drugs; Society for the Study of Addiction to **12077**
Alcohol and Other Drugs; Target - Helping Students Cope with **12079**
Alcohol and Other Drugs; TARGET - Helping Students Cope with Tobacco, **12079**
Alcohol and Other Substance Abuse Issues; Inter-Association Task Force on Campus **12035**
Alcohol Problems; American Council on **12005**
Alcohol Programs Office; Drug and • Pennsylvania Department of Health **12185**
Alcohol Research Center
    University of California, Los Angeles **12133**
    University of Colorado—Denver **12135**
    University of Connecticut **12137**
    University of Michigan **12140**
Alcohol Research Center; Fetal • Wayne State University **9722**
Alcohol Research Center; Vermont **12145**
Alcohol Research Group **12086**
Alcohol Research Information Service **12002, 12087**
Alcohol Studies; Center of
    Rutgers University **12101**
    University of North Carolina at Chapel Hill **12141**
Alcohol and Substance Abuse Services; New York State Office of **12179**
Alcoholic Clergy Association; Recovered **12074**
Alcoholic Rehabilitation Association; Christian **12017**
Alcoholics Anonymous; International Advisory Council for Homosexual Men and Women in **12036**
Alcoholics Anonymous; International Doctors in **12039**
Alcoholics Anonymous; International Lawyers in **12042**
Alcoholics Anonymous World Services **12003**
Alcoholics Foundation; Children of **12016**
Alcoholics; National Association for Children of **12052**
Alcoholism and Addictions; American Academy of Psychiatrists in **12004**
Alcoholism; American Council on **12006**
Alcoholism; Baltimore Area Council on **12006**
Alcoholism Council; National Black **12056**
Alcoholism Counselors; National Association for **12051**
Alcoholism and Drug Abuse Counselors; National Association of **12051**
Alcoholism and Drug Abuse Division
    Alaska Department of Health and Social Services **12148**
    Behavioral Health Services Office • Human Resources Bureau • West Virginia Department of Health and Human Resources **12195**
    Nebraska Department of Public Institutions **12174**
    North Dakota Department of Human Services **12181**
Alcoholism, Drug Abuse, and Mental Health Division • Delaware Department of Health and Social Services **7715, 12154**
Alcoholism and Drug Dependence; National Council on **12059**
Alcoholism & Drug Dependency; Institute of • Andrews University **12088**
Alcoholism and Drug Dependency; International Commission for the Prevention of **12037**
Alcoholism and Drug Dependency; National Committee for the Prevention of **12058**
Alcoholism; International Bureau Against **12038**
Alcoholism; International Society for Biomedical Research on **12044**
Alcoholism; International Union Against **12038**
Alcoholism; Maryland Society on **12006**
Alcoholism; National Clergy Conference on **12057**
Alcoholism; National Committee on **12059**
Alcoholism; National Committee for Education on **12059**
Alcoholism; National Committee for the Prevention of **12058**
Alcoholism; National Council on **12059**
Alcoholism; National Nurses Society on **9123**
Alcoholism; National States Conference on **12001**
Alcoholism; New York City Medical Society on **12010**
Alcoholism and Other Drug Dependencies; American Medical Society on **12010**
Alcoholism Professionals; National Association of Gay **11702**
Alcoholism Professionals; National Association of Lesbian / Gay **11702**
Alcoholism Programs of North America; Association of Halfway House **12011**
Alcoholism Programs; North American Association of **12001**

Alcoholism and Related Drug Problems; National Catholic Council on **12057**
Alcoholism and Related Drug Problems; National Clergy Council on **12057**
Alcoholism; Research Institute on **12099**
Alcoholism; Research Society on **12075**
Alcoholism and Substance Abuse; Illinois Department of **12160**
Alcoholism; TOVA—The Other Victims of **12080**
Alcoholism Treatment Programs; National Association of **12050**
Alcon Foundation **13355**
Alcoolisme et des Toxicomanies; Conseil International sur les Problemes de l' **12038**
Alcor Foundation **3704**
Alcor Life Extension Foundation **3704**
Alcorn State University • Division of Nursing **8780**
Alden Trust; George I. **219**
Alderian Psychology; American Society of **7477**
Alderson-Broaddus College
    Department of Nursing **9024**
    Physician Assistant Program **1117**
Alex. Brown and Sons Charitable Foundation Inc. **568**
Alex Hillman Family Foundation **37**
Alexander & Baldwin Foundation **569**
Alexander Foundation; Joseph **329**
Alexander Graham Bell Association for the Deaf **3466, 3478**
Alexander Graham Bell Association for the Deaf; Parents' Section of the **3571**
Alexander and Margaret Stewart Trust u/w/o Helen S. Devore **3132**
Alexander and Margaret Stewart Trust u/w/o Mary E. Stewart **5890**
Alexander Technique; American Center for the **12649**
Alexander Technique; North American Society of Teachers of the **12706**
Alfred Adler Institute **7243, 7262**
Alfred Adler Institute for Individual Psychology **7262**
Alfred I. duPont Foundation **38**
Alfred I. duPont Institute of the Nemours Foundation **1643**
Algology; American Academy of **8154**
Alhambra; Order of **4275**
Alimentary Tract; Society For Surgery of the **12304**
Alimentation et du Developpement de l'Enfant; Association Europeenne pour l'Etude de l' **9455**
Alimentation et la Nutrition Africaines; Organisme de Recherches sur l' **9485**
Alimentation and Nutrition; Research Organization on African **9485**
Alimentos; Asociacion Mundial de Veterinarios Higienistas de los **13118**
Alkohol- och Drogforskning; Nordiska Namnden for **12066**
All-Breeds Rescue Conservancy **13020**
All India Nature Cure Federation **2152**
All Russian Federation of the Blind **13384**
All-Russian Federation of the Deaf **3479**
All-Russian Society of the Deaf **3479**
All-Union Society of the Deaf **3479**
Allegany Community College • Respiratory Therapist Program **11410**
Allegheny Ludlum Foundation **570**
Allegheny-Singer Research Institute **1553**
Allegheny Valley Hospital / La Roche College • School of Anesthesia • Nurse Anesthesia Program **2312**
Allen College of Nursing **8690**
Allendale Insurance Foundation **571**
Allentown College of St. Francis de Sales • Department of Nursing and Health • Baccalaureate Nursing Program **8909**
Allergic Disease Center • Creighton University **2098**
Allergic Disease Center; Asthma and • Duke University **2100**
Allergic Disease Center; Ernest S. Bazley Asthma and • Northwestern University **2110**
Allergic Disease Cooperative Research Center; Asthma & • Brigham and Women's Hospital **2094**
Allergic Diseases; American Foundation for **2068**
Allergic Diseases Center; Asthma and • State University of New York Health Science Center at Stony Brook **2119**
Allergic Diseases Research Laboratory • Mayo Clinic and Foundation **2108**
Allergists; American Association of Certified **2061**
Allergists; International Correspondence Society of **2075**
Allergologie et d'Immunologie Clinique; Academie Europeenne d' **2072**
Allergologie; Nederlandse Vereniging voor **2085**
Allergologistes et Immunologistes de Langues Latines; Groupement des **2067**
Allergologists and Immunologists; Association of Latin Languages **2067**
Allergology and Clinical Immunology; European Academy of **2072**
Allergology and Clinical Immunology; International Association of **2074**
Allergology; Netherlands Society of **2085**
Allergy; Academy of Veterinary **13018**
Allergy; Action Against **2056**

Index

American Academy of Insurance Medicine **5719**
American Academy of Legal and Industrial Medicine 7172
American Academy of Maxillofacial Prosthetics **3863**
American Academy McAllister Institute of Funeral Service, Inc. **3686**
American Academy of Medical Acupuncture **2155**
American Academy of Medical Administrators **5537**
American Academy of Medical Administrators Research and Educational Foundation **5538**
American Academy of Medical Hypnoanalysts **6581**
American Academy of Medical-Legal Analysis **7160**
American Academy of Medical Preventics **10837**
American Academy on Mental Retardation **4276**
American Academy of Microbiology **6626**
American Academy of Natural Family Planning **11198**
American Academy of Neurological and Orthopaedic Surgeons **12204**
American Academy of Neurological Surgery **12205**
American Academy of Neurology **8153**
American Academy of Nurse Practitioners **9048**
American Academy of Obstetrics and Gynecology 9626
American Academy of Ophthalmology **13385**
American Academy of Optometry **13386**
American Academy Oral and Maxillofacial Pathology **10117**
American Academy of Oral and Maxillofacial Radiology **3864**
American Academy of Oral Medicine **3865**
American Academy Oral Pathology **10117**
American Academy of Oral Roentgenology **3864**
American Academy of Orofacial Pain **3866**
American Academy of Orthodontics for the General Practitioner **3867**
American Academy of Orthopaedic Surgeons **12206**
American Academy of Orthotists and Prosthetists **4457**
American Academy of Osteopathic Surgeons 9972
American Academy of Osteopathy **9969**
American Academy of Otolaryngic Allergy **2054, 2059**
American Academy of Otolaryngology - Head and Neck Surgery **12207**
American Academy of Pain Medicine **8154**
American Academy of Pediatric Dentistry **3159**
American Academy of Pediatrics **3149, 3160**
  Department of Research **5606**
American Academy of Pedodontics 3159
American Academy of Periodontology **3868**
American Academy of Physical Medicine and Rehabilitation **12647**
American Academy of Physician Assistants **1137**
American Academy for Plastics Research in Dentistry 3841
American Academy of Podiatric Administration **5539**
American Academy of Podiatric Management 5539
American Academy of Podiatric Sports Medicine **11934**
American Academy of Practice Management in Podiatry 5539
American Academy of Psychiatrists in Alcoholism and Addictions **12004**
American Academy of Psychiatry and the Law **7161**
American Academy of Psychoanalysis **7267**
American Academy of Psychotherapists **7268**
American Academy of Restorative Dentistry, D.D.S. **3869**
American Academy of Sanitarians **5032**
American Academy of Sclerotherapy 9980
American Academy of Somnology **8155**
American Academy of Speech Correction 3492
American Academy of Spinal Surgeons **12208**
American Academy of Sports Physicians **11935**
American Academy of Thermology **11082**
American Academy of Tropical Medicine **6627**
American Academy of Tropical Medicine and Surgery **6761**
American Academy of Veterinary and Comparative Toxicology **13021**
American Academy of Veterinary Dermatology **13022**
American Academy of Veterinary Nutrition **13023**
American Academy of Veterinary Pharmacology and Therapeutics **13024**
American Acupuncture Association **2156**
American Aerobics Association **10839**
American Affiliation of Visiting Nurses Associations and Services 9138
American Aging Association **1880**
American Allergy Association **2060**
American Alliance for Health, Physical Education and Recreation 1138
American Alliance for Health, Physical Education, Recreation and Dance **1138**
American Ambulance Association **4732**
American Ambulatory Fracture Association 9919
American Amputee Foundation **4450, 4458**
American Animal Hospital Association **13025**
American Anorexia / Bulimia Association **7269**
American Anorexia Nervosa Association 7269
American Apitherapy Society **2157**

American Art Therapy Association **7270**
American Assembly for Men in Nursing **9049**
American Association for Accreditation of Ambulatory Plastic Surgery Facilities 12209
American Association for Accreditation of Ambulatory Surgery Facilities **12209**
American Association for Accreditation of Laboratory Animal Care **13026**
American Association for Acupuncture and Oriental Medicine **2158**
American Association for Advancement of Physical Education 1138
American Association for the Advancement of Tension Control 7428
American Association of Anatomists **1139**
American Association for Automotive Medicine 10842
American Association of Avian Pathologists **13027**
American Association of Ayurvedic Medicine **2159**
American Association of Behavioral Therapists **7271**
American Association of Bioanalysts **7114**
American Association of Blood Banks **7115**
American Association of Bovine Practitioners **13028**
American Association for Cancer Education **5908**
American Association for Cancer Research **5909**
American Association of Cardiovascular Nurses 9051
American Association of Cardiovascular and Pulmonary Rehabilitation **2822**
American Association of Certified Allergists **2061**
American Association of Certified Allied Health Personnel in Ophthalmology 13418
American Association of Certified Orthoptists **13387**
American Association of Chairmen of Departments of Psychiatry **7272**
American Association of Chairmen of Medical School Departments of Pathology 10126
American Association for Child Psychoanalysis 3179
American Association of Children's Residential Centers **7273**
American Association for Cleft Palate Rehabilitation 2740
American Association for Clinical Chemistry **7116**
American Association of Clinical Chemists 7116
American Association of Clinical Endocrinologists **4827**
American Association for Clinical Histocompatibility Testing 2066
American Association of Clinical Laboratory Supervisors and Administrators 7129
American Association of Colleges of Chiropody 10755
American Association of Colleges of Nursing **9050**
American Association of Colleges of Osteopathic Medicine **9970**
American Association of Colleges of Pharmacy **10578**
American Association of Colleges of Podiatric Medicine **10755**
American Association of Colleges of Podiatry 10755
American Association of Community Psychiatrists **7274**
American Association for Comprehensive Health Planning 5551
American Association for Continuity of Care **5540**
American Association for Counseling and Development 7293
American Association of Critical-Care Nurses **9051**
American Association of the Deaf-Blind **13388**
American Association of Dental Consultants **3870**
American Association of Dental Editors **6966**
American Association of Dental Examiners **3871**
American Association for Dental Research **3781, 3872**
American Association of Dental Schools **3873**
American Association of Dental Victims **3874**
American Association of Diabetes Educators **4828**
American Association of Directors of Psychiatric Residency Training **7275**
American Association of Electrodiagnostic Medicine **2415**
American Association of Electromyography and Electrodiagnosis 2415
American Association of Endodontists **3875**
American Association of Equine Practitioners **13029**
American Association of Eye and Ear Hospitals **6423**
American Association of Feline Practitioners **13030**
American Association of First Responders 4748
American Association of Fitness Directors in Business and Industry 10844
American Association of Foundations for Medical Care 5722
American Association of Genito-Urinary Surgeons **12210**
American Association for Geriatric Psychiatry **1881**
American Association of Gynecological Laparoscopists **9622**
American Association for Hand Surgery **12211**
American Association for the Hard of Hearing 3546
American Association of Healthcare Consultants **5820**
American Association for Health, Physical Education and Recreation 1138
American Association for the History of Medicine **1140**
American Association for the History of Nursing **9052**
American Association of Homes for the Aging 1882
American Association of Homes and Services for the Aging **1882**
American Association of Hospital Accountants 5728
American Association of Hospital Consultants 5820

American Association of Hospital Dental Chiefs   3876
American Association of Hospital Dentists   **3876**
American Association of Hospital Podiatrists   **10756**
American Association for Humanistic Psychology   7327
American Association of Immunologists   **2062**
American Association of Industrial Nurses   9055
American Association of Industrial Veterinarians   **13031**
American Association of Inhalation Therapists   11588
American Association for Inhalation Therapy   11588
American Association of Kidney Patients   **12894**
American Association for Laboratory Animal Science   **13032**
American Association of Legal Nurse Consultants   **7162**
American Association of Managed Care Nurses   **9053**
American Association of Marriage Counselors   7276
American Association of Marriage and Family Counselors   7276
American Association for Marriage and Family Therapy   **7276**
American Association of Masseurs and Masseuses   12654
American Association of Medical Assistants   **1141**
American Association of Medical Clinics   1163
American Association of Medical Milk Commissions   **10934**
American Association of Medical Record Librarians   6968
American Association of Medical Society Executives   **1142**
American Association for Medical Transcription   **6967**
American Association of Medico-Legal Consultants   **7163**
American Association on Mental Deficiency   4277
American Association of Mental Health Professionals in Corrections   **7277**
American Association on Mental Retardation   **4277, 4307**
American Association for Music Therapy   **7278**
American Association of Nephrology Nurses and Technicians   9061
American Association of Neurological Surgeons   **8124, 12212**
American Association of Neuropathologists   **10118**
American Association of Neuroscience Nurses   **9054**
American Association of Nurse Anesthetists   **2348**
The American Association of Nurse Attorneys   **7164**
American Association of Nutritional Consultants   **9438**
American Association of Occupational Health Nurses   **9055**
American Association of Office Nurses   **9056**
American Association of Oral and Maxillofacial Surgeons   **3782, 3877**
American Association of Oral and Plastic Surgeons   12213
American Association of Oriental Healing Arts   2173
American Association of Orthodontists   **3878**
American Association of Orthopedic Medicine   **9917**
American Association of Orthopic Technicians   13387
American Association of Osteopathic Colleges   9970
American Association of Osteopathic Examiners   **9971**
American Association of Osteopathic Specialists   **9972**
American Association of Parenthood Physicians   11204
American Association for Partial Hospitalization   **7279**
American Association of Pathologists   10125
American Association of Pathologists' Assistants   **10119**
American Association of Pediatric Ophthalmology   3161
American Association for Pediatric Ophthalmology and Strabismus   **3161**
American Association of Pharmaceutical Scientists   **10579**
American Association of Physician-Hospital Organizations   **5541**
American Association of Physicians for Human Rights   **11684**
American Association of Physicians Practicing the Transcendental Meditation Program   2159
American Association of Physicians Practicing the Transcendental Meditation and TM-Sidhi Programs   2159
American Association of Physicists in Medicine   **2521**
American Association of Plastic Surgeons   **12213**
American Association of Podiatric Physicians and Surgeons   **10757**
American Association of Poison Control Centers   **10391**
American Association of Preferred Provider Organizations   **5720**
American Association of Professional Hypnotherapists   **6582**
American Association of Professional Standards Review Organizations   1170
American Association of Pro Life Obstetricians and Gynecologists   **11199**
American Association of Pro-Life Pediatricians   **11200**
American Association to Promote the Teaching of Speech to the Deaf   3478
American Association of Psychiatric Administrators   **5542**
American Association of Psychiatric Clinics for Children   3162
American Association of Psychiatric Services for Children   **3162**
American Association of Psychiatric Technicians   **7280**
American Association on Psychiatrists   7281
American Association of Psychiatrists from India   **7281**
American Association of Public Health Dentistry   **10935**
American Association of Public Health Dentists   10935
American Association of Public Health Physicians   **10936**
American Association of the Red Cross   1177

American Association of Registration Executives   6979
American Association for Respiratory Care   **11588**
American Association for Respiratory Therapy   11588
American Association of Retired Veterinarians   **13033**
American Association of School Physicians   1181
American Association of Sex Educators and Counselors   11685
American Association of Sex Educators, Counselors and Therapists   **11685**
American Association of Sheep and Goat Practitioners   13034
American Association of Sleep Disorders Centers   8173
American Association of Small Ruminant Practitioners   **13034**
American Association for Social Psychiatry   **7282**
American Association of Spinal Cord Injury Nurses   **9057**
American Association of Spinal Cord Injury Psychologists and Social Workers   **7283**
American Association State Boards, Veterinary   13039
American Association of State Social Work Boards   **11863**
American Association of Stomatologists   **3879**
American Association for the Study of the Feebleminded   4277
American Association for the Study of Headache   **8156**
American Association for the Study of Liver Diseases   **5201**
American Association of Suicidology   **7284**
American Association of Surgeon Assistants   **12214**
American Association of Surgeon's Assistants   12214
American Association of Swine Practitioners   **13035**
American Association for Therapeutic Humor   **7285**
American Association for Thoracic Surgery   **12215**
American Association of Tissue Banks   **12866**
American Association of University Affiliated Programs for the Developmentally Disabled   4459
American Association of University Affiliated Programs for Persons With Developmental Disabilities   **4459**
American Association of Veterinary Anatomists   **13036**
American Association of Veterinary Laboratory Diagnosticians   **13037**
American Association of Veterinary Nutritionists   13023
American Association of Veterinary Parasitologists   **13038**
American Association of Veterinary State Boards   **13039**
American Association for Vital Records and Public Health Statistics   6979
American Association of Wildlife Veterinarians   **13040**
American Association of Women Dentists   **3783, 3880**
American Association for Women Radiologists   **11083**
American Association for World Health   **1143**
American Association of Zoo Veterinarians   **13041**
American Athletic Association for the Deaf   **3480**
American Audiology Society   3481
American Auditory Society   **3481**
American Auto Immune Related Diseases Association   **7859**
American Baptist Homes and Hospitals Association   **1144**
American Behcet's Association   **7860**
American Birth Control League   11246
American Black Chiropractors Association   **3447**
American Blind Bowling Association   **13389**
American Blind Skiing Foundation   **13390**
American Blood Resources Association   **7117**
American Board of Abdominal Surgery   **12216**
American Board for Accreditation in Psychoanalysis; National Association for the Advancement of Psychoanalysis and the   **7450**
American Board of Allergy and Immunology   **2063**
American Board of Anesthesiology   **2349**
American Board of Bionic Rehabilitative Psychology   **7286**
American Board of Cardiovascular Perfusion   **2823**
American Board for Certification in Orthotics and Prosthetics   **4460**
American Board of Chelation Therapy   **2160**
American Board of Chiropodical Dermatology   10765
American Board of Colon and Rectal Surgery   **12217**
American Board of Dental Medicine and Surgery   **3881**
American Board of Dental Public Health   **10937**
American Board of Dermatology   **4214**
American Board of Emergency Medicine   **4733**
American Board of Endodontics   **3882**
American Board of Environmental Medicine   **5033**
American Board of Examiners in Professional Psychology   **7289**
American Board of Examiners of Psychodrama, Sociometry, and Group Psychotherapy   **7287**
American Board of Examiners in Psychological Hypnosis   **6583**
American Board of Family Practice   **1145**
American Board of Forensic Anthropology   **7165**
American Board of Funeral Service Education   **3705**
American Board of Hand Surgery   **12218**
American Board of Health Physics   **2522**
American Board of Industrial Hygiene   **9784**
American Board of Industrial Medicine and Surgery   **9785**

American Board of Internal Medicine 1146
American Board of Laser Surgery 12220
American Board of Medical Genetics 5268
American Board of Medical-Legal Analysis in Medicine and Surgery 7166
American Board of Medical Psychotherapists 7288
American Board of Medical Specialties 1147
American Board of Medical Toxicology 10392
American Board of Medical Toxicology of the American Academy of Clinical Toxicology 10392
American Board of Neurological Microsurgery 12219
American Board of Neurological / Orthopaedic Laser Surgery 12220
American Board of Neurological and Orthopaedic Medicine and Surgery 12221
American Board of Neurological Surgery 12222
American Board of Neuroscience Nursing 9058
American Board of Nuclear Medicine 11084
American Board of Nutrition 9439
American Board of Obstetrics and Gynecology 9623
American Board for Occupational Health Nurses 9059
American Board for Ophthalmic Examinations 13391
American Board of Ophthalmology 13391
American Board of Opticianry 13392
American Board of Oral and Maxillofacial Surgery 12223
American Board of Oral Pathology 10120
American Board of Oral Surgery 12223
American Board of Orthodontia 3883
American Board of Orthodontics 3883
American Board of Orthodontics; College of Diplomates of the 3916
American Board of Orthopaedic Microneurosurgery 12224
American Board of Orthopaedic Surgery 12225
American Board of Otolaryngology 3482
American Board of Pathology 10121
American Board of Pediatric Dentistry 3163
American Board of Pediatrics 3164
American Board of Pedodontics 3163
American Board of Periodontology 3884
American Board of Physical Medicine and Rehabilitation 12648
American Board of Plastic Surgery 12226
American Board of Podiatric Orthopedics 10758
American Board of Podiatric Orthopedics and Primary Medicine 10758
American Board of Podiatric Surgery 10759
American Board of Post Anesthesia Nursing Certification 2350
American Board of Preventive Medicine 10836
American Board of Preventive Medicine and Public Health 10836
American Board of Proctology 12217
American Board of Professional Psychology 7289
American Board of Professional Psychology in Hypnosis 6583
American Board of Prosthodontics 3885
American Board of Psychiatry and Neurology 7290
American Board of Psychological Hypnosis 6583
American Board of Quality Assurance and Utilization Review Physicians 1148
American Board of Radiology 11085
American Board of Registration of EEG and EP Technologists 8157
American Board of Registration of EEG Technologists 8157
American Board of Ringside Medicine and Surgery 11936
American Board of Sleep Medicine 8158
American Board of Spinal Surgery 12227
American Board of Surgery 12228
American Board of Thoracic Neurological Orthopaedic Medicine and Surgery 12229
American Board of Toxicology 10393
American Board of Tropical Medicine 6628
American Board of Urologic Allied Health Professionals 12895
American Board of Urology 12896
American Board of Veterinary Radiology 13050
American Board on Veterinary Specialties 13042
American Board of Veterinary Toxicology 13043
American Boards of Examiners in Speech Pathology and Audiology 3511
American Braille Press for War and Civilian Blind 13466
American Brain Tumor Association 8125, 8159
American Broncho-Esophagological Association 11589
American Bronchoscopic Society 11589
American Bureau for Medical Advancement in China 1149
American Bureau for Medical Aid to China 1149
American Burn Association 2766, 2767
American Burn Research Corporation 2773
American Business Men's Research Foundation 12002, 12087
American Campaign for Prevention of Child Abuse and Family Violence 3061
American Cancer Institutes; Association of 5919

American Cancer Society 5897, 5910
　Alabama Division 6271
　Alaska Division 6272
　Arizona Division 6273
　Arkansas Division 6274
　California Division 6275
　Colorado Division 6276
　Connecticut Division 6277
　Delaware Division 6278
　District of Columbia Division 6279
　Florida Division 6280
　Georgia Division 6281
　Hawaii Pacific Division 6282
　Idaho Division 6283
　Illinois Division 6284
　Indiana Division 6285
　Iowa Division 6286
　Kansas Division 6287
　Kentucky Division 6288
　Long Island Division 6303
　Louisiana Division 6289
　Maine Division 6290
　Maryland Division 6291
　Massachusetts Division 6292
　Michigan Division 6293
　Minnesota Division 6294
　Mississippi Division 6295
　Missouri Division 6296
　Montana Division 6297
　Nebraska Division 6298
　Nevada Division 6299
　New Hampshire Division 6300
　New Jersey Division 6301
　New Mexico Division 6302
　New York City Division 6304
　New York State Division 6305
　North Carolina Division 6308
　North Dakota Division 6309
　Ohio Division 6310
　Oklahoma Division 6311
　Oregon Division 6312
　Pennsylvania Division 6313
　Philadelphia Division 6314
　Puerto Rico Division 6315
　Queens Division 6306
　Rhode Island Division 6316
　South Carolina Division 6317
　South Dakota Division 6318
　Tennessee Division 6319
　Texas Division 6320
　Utah Division 6321
　Vermont Division 6322
　Virginia Division 6323
　Washington Division 6324
　West Virginia Division 6325
　Westchester Division 6307
　Wisconsin Division 6326
　Wyoming Division 6327
American Canine Sports Medicine Association 13044
American Cardiology Technologists Association 2828
American and Caribbean Women's Health Network; Latin 1371
American Catholic Psychological Association 7490
American Celiac Society / Dietary Support Coalition 5202
American Center for the Alexander Technique 12649
American Center for Chinese Medical Sciences 1150
American Center for Chinese Medicine 1150
American Central European Dental Institute 3886
American Chinese Medical Society 1237
American Chiropractic Association 3448
American Chiropractic Council on Roentgenology 11108
American Chiropractic Registry of Radiologic Technologists 11086
American Chronic Pain Association 8160
American Cleft Palate Association 2740
American Cleft Palate-Craniofacial Association 2740
American Clinical and Climatological Association 1151
American Clinical Laboratory Association 7118
American College of Addiction Treatment Administrators 5543
American College for Advancement in Medicine 10837
American College of Allergy and Immunology 2064
American College of Angiology 2824

American College of Apothecaries **10580**
American College of Apothecaries Research and Education Foundation **10626**
American College of Cardiology **2825**
American College of Cardiovascular Administrators **5544**
American College of Chemosurgery 5911
American College of Chest Physicians **2784, 2826**
American College of Chiropodial Roentgenologists 10761
American College of Chiropractic Orthopedists **9918**
American College of Clinic Managers 5547
American College of Clinical Pharmacology **10394**
American College of Clinical Pharmacy **10581**
American College of Cryosurgery **12230**
American College of Dentists **3887**
American College of Emergency Physicians **4734**
American College of Epidemiology **5179**
American College of Foot and Ankle Orthopedics and Medicine **10760**
American College of Foot and Ankle Pediatrics **3165**
American College of Foot and Ankle Surgeons **12231**
American College of Foot Orthopedists 10760
American College of Foot Roentgenologists 10761
American College of Foot Surgeons **12231**
American College of Forensic Psychiatry **7167**
American College of Gastroenterology **5203**
American College of General Practice 1155
American College of General Practitioners in Osteopathic Medicine and Surgery 9975
American College Health Association **1152**
American College Health Association; AIDS Task Force for the **6623**
American College of Health Care Administrators **5545**
American College of Health Care Administrators; Foundation of **5576**
American College of Healthcare Executives **5546**
American College of Home Obstetrics **9624**
American College of Hospital Administrators 5546
American College of International Physicians **1153**
American College of Legal Medicine **7168**
American College of Medical Group Administrators 5547
American College of Medical Physics **2523**
American College of Medical Practice Executives 5547
American College of Medical Quality **1154**
American College of Medicine **1155**
American College of Mental Health Administration **5548**
American College of MOHS Micrographic Surgery and Cutaneous Oncology 5911
American College of Neuropsychiatrists **9973**
American College of Neuropsychopharmacology **10395**
American College of Nuclear Medicine **11087**
American College of Nuclear Physicians **11088**
American College of Nurse-Midwifery 9625
American College of Nurse-Midwives **9625**
American College of Nursing Home Administrators 5545
American College of Nutrition **9440**
American College of Obstetricians and Gynecologists **9576, 9626**
American College of Occupational and Environmental Medicine **9786**
American College of Occupational Medicine 9786
American College of Oral and Maxillofacial Surgeons **12232**
American College of Orgonomy **2161**
American College of Osteopathic Emergency Physicians **9974**
American College of Osteopathic Family Physicians **9975**
American College of Osteopathic Hospital Administrators 5570
American College of Osteopathic Internists **9976**
American College of Osteopathic Obstetricians and Gynecologists **9977**
American College of Osteopathic Pediatricians **3166**
American College of Osteopathic Surgeons **9978**
American College of Pain Medicine **8161**
American College of Physician Executives **5549**
American College of Physicians **914, 1156**
American College of Podiatric Radiologists **10761**
American College of Podopediatrics **3165**
American College of Preventive Medicine **10838**
American College of Prosthodontists **3888**
American College of Psychiatrists **7291**
American College of Psychoanalysts **7292**
American College of Radiation Oncology **11089**
American College of Rheumatology **7861**
American College of Sports Medicine **11937**
American College of Surgeons **12233**
American College of Theriogenologists **13045**
American College of Toxicology **10396**
American College of Tropical Medicine **6628**
American College of Veterinary Dermatology **13046**

American College of Veterinary Internal Medicine **13047**
American College of Veterinary Ophthalmologists **13048**
American College of Veterinary Pathologists **13049**
American College of Veterinary Radiology **13050**
American College of Veterinary Surgeons **13051**
American College of Veterinary Toxicologists **13021**
American Colon Therapy Association **5221**
American Committee for Shaare Zedek Hospital in Jerusalem **6424**
American Conference of Governmental Industrial Hygienists **9787**
American Conference of Pharmaceutical Faculties 10578
American Congress of Physical Medicine **12650**
American Congress of Physical Medicine and Rehabilitation 12650
American Congress of Rehabilitation Medicine **12650**
American Correctional Health Services Association **1157**
American Corrective Therapy Association **12653**
American Council on Alcohol Problems **12005**
American Council on Alcoholism **12006**
American Council of Applied Clinical Nutrition **9441**
American Council of the Blind **13393**
American Council of the Blind Enterprises and Services **13394**
American Council of Blind Federal Employees 13395
American Council of Blind Government Employees **13395**
American Council of Blind Lions **13396**
American Council of the Blind Parents 13443
American Council on Chiropractic Physiotherapy **3453**
American Council on Chiropractic Roentgenology **11108**
American Council for Drug Education **12007**
American Council for Headache Education **8162**
American Council for Health Care Reform **1158**
American Council of Hypnotist Examiners **6584**
American Council on Marijuana and Other Psychoactive Drugs **12007**
American Council on Pharmaceutical Education **10582**
American Council on Science and Health **1555, 10938**
American Counseling Association **7293**
American Cryonics Society **3706**
American Dance Therapy Association **7294**
American Deaf Volleyball Association **3483**
American Deafness and Rehabilitation Association **3484**
American Dental Assistants Association **3784, 3889**
American Dental Assistants Association; Certifying Board of the 3923
American Dental Association **3890**
American Dental Association; Alliance of the **3850**
American Dental Association; Auxiliary to the 3850
American Dental Association; Women's Auxiliary to the 3850
American Dental Hygienists' Association **3785, 3891**
American Dental Institute **3892**
American Dental Interfraternity Council **3893**
American Dental Society of Anesthesiology **2351**
American Dental Trade Association **5821**
American Dermatologic Society of Allergy and Immunology **4215**
American Dermatological Association **4216**
American Diabetes Association **4821, 4829**
    Alabama Affiliate **4950**
    Alaska Affiliate **4951**
    Arizona Affiliate **4952**
    Arkansas Affiliate **4953**
    California Affiliate **4954**
    Colorado Affiliate **4955**
    Connecticut Affiliate **4956**
    Delaware Affiliate **4957**
    Downstate Illinois Affiliate **4963**
    Florida Affiliate **4959**
    Georgia Affiliate **4960**
    Hawaii Affiliate **4961**
    Idaho Affiliate **4962**
    Indiana Affiliate **4965**
    Iowa Affiliate **4966**
    Kansas Affiliate **4967**
    Kentucky Affiliate **4968**
    Louisiana Affiliate **4969**
    Maine Affiliate **4970**
    Maryland Affiliate **4971**
    Massachusetts Affiliate **4972**
    Michigan Affiliate **4973**
    Minnesota Affiliate **4974**
    Mississippi Affiliate **4975**
    Missouri Affiliate **4976**
    Montana Affiliate **4977**
    Nebraska Affiliate **4978**
    Nevada Affiliate **4979**

Index

American Neurotology Society **3489**
American Nurses Association **9062**
American Nurses in Business Association **9063**
American Nurses' Foundation **8541**
American Nursing Care Foundation 9064, **9064**
American Nursing Home Association **9264**
American Occupational Therapy Association **12655**
American Occupational Therapy Certification Board **12656**
American Occupational Therapy Foundation **12330**
American Ophthalmological Society **13400**
American Optical Association 13401
American Optometric Association **13401**
American Optometric Foundation 13358, **13402**
American Optometric Student Association **13403**
American Organization for the Education of the Hearing Impaired 3539
American Organization of Nurse Executives **5552**
American Oriental Bodywork Therapy Association 2173
American Orthodontic Society **3897**
American Orthopaedic Association **9921**
American Orthopaedic Foot and Ankle Society **9922**
American Orthopaedic Foot Society 9922
American Orthopaedic Society 9916
American Orthopaedic Society for Sports Medicine **9923**
American Orthopsychiatric Association **7300**
American Orthoptic Council 13404
American Orthotic and Prosthetic Association **5822**
American Osler Society **1173**
American Osteopathic Academy of Addictionology **12008**
American Osteopathic Academy of Orthopedics **9979**
American Osteopathic Academy of Physical Medicine and Rehabilitation 9993
American Osteopathic Academy of Sclerotherapy 9980, **9980**
American Osteopathic Academy of Sports Medicine **9981**
American Osteopathic Association 9949, **9982**
American Osteopathic Association; Auxiliary to the **9950, 9995**
American Osteopathic Association; Bureau of Professional Education of the **9997**
American Osteopathic Board of Emergency Medicine **9983**
American Osteopathic Board of Family Physicians **9984**
American Osteopathic Board of General Practice 9984
American Osteopathic Board of Pediatrics **9985**
American Osteopathic College of Allergy and Immunology **9986**
American Osteopathic College of Anesthesiologists **9987**
American Osteopathic College of Dermatology **9988**
American Osteopathic College of Pathologists **9989**
American Osteopathic College of Physical Medicine and Rehabilitation 9993
American Osteopathic College of Preventive Medicine **9990**
American Osteopathic College of Proctology **9991**
American Osteopathic College of Radiology **9992**
American Osteopathic College of Rehabilitation Medicine **9993**
American Osteopathic Healthcare Association **6426**
American Osteopathic Hospital Association 6426
American Osteopathic Society of Anesthesiologists 9987
American Otological Society 3468, **3490**
American Outreach Association **12009**
American Pain Society **8168**
American Pancreatic Association **5207**
American Pancreatic Study Group 5207
American Paralysis Association 8126, **8169**
American Paraplegia Society **8170**
American Parkinson Disease Association 8127, **8171**
American Pathologists; College of 7131
American Pathology Foundation **10122**
American Pediatric Gastroesophageal Reflux Association 3168
American Pediatric Society **3169**
American Personnel and Guidance Association 7293
American Pharmaceutical Association **10585**
American Pharmaceutical Association; Auxiliary to the **10591**
American Pharmaceutical Association Student Section 10576
American Pharmaceutical Association; Women's Auxiliary of the 10591
American Physical Education Association 1138
American Physical Therapy Association **12657**
   Alabama Chapter **12823**
   Arizona Chapter **12824**
   Arkansas Chapter **12825**
   California Chapter **12826**
   Colorado Chapter **12827**
   Connecticut Chapter **12828**
   Florida Chapter **12829**
   Georgia Chapter **12830**

   Idaho Chapter **12831**
   Illinois Chapter **12832**
   Indiana Chapter **12833**
   Iowa Chapter **12834**
   Kansas Chapter **12835**
   Kentucky Chapter **12836**
   Louisiana Chapter **12837**
   Maine Chapter **12838**
   Maryland Chapter **12839**
   Massachusetts Chapter **12840**
   Michigan Chapter **12841**
   Minnesota Chapter **12842**
   Mississippi Chapter **12843**
   Missouri Chapter **12844**
   Montana Chapter **12845**
   Nebraska Chapter **12846**
   Nevada Chapter **12847**
   New Hampshire Chapter **12848**
   New Jersey Chapter **12849**
   New Mexico Chapter **12850**
   New York Chapter **12851**
   North Carolina Chapter **12852**
   North Dakota Chapter **12853**
   Ohio Chapter **12854**
   Oklahoma Chapter **12855**
   Oregon Chapter **12856**
   Pennsylvania Chapter **12857**
   Private Practice Section **12658**
   Rhode Island Chapter **12858**
   South Carolina Chapter **12859**
   Tennessee Chapter **12860**
   Texas Chapter **12861**
   Utah Chapter **12862**
   Virginia Chapter **12863**
   Washington Chapter **12864**
   Wisconsin Chapter **12865**
American Physical Therapy Association; Orthopaedic Section, **12708**
American Physicians; Association of **1198**
American Physicians Association of Computer Medicine **1174**
American Physicians and Dentists; Union of **1524**
American Physicians Fellowship for the Israel Medical Association 1175
American Physicians Fellowship for Medicine in Israel **1175**
American Physicians and Surgeons; Association of **1199**
American Physiological and Natural Hygiene Society 2171
American Physiotherapy Association 12657
American Phyto Aromatherapy Association **2174**
American Podiatric Circulatory Society **2175**
American Podiatric Medical Association 10746, **10762**
American Podiatric Medical Association Auxiliary **10763**
American Podiatric Medical Students Association **10764**
American Podiatric Medical Writers Association **6971**
American Podiatric Students Association 10764
American Podiatry Association 10762
American Podiatry Association Auxiliary 10763
American Podiatry Association; Women's Auxiliary, 10763
American Porphyria Foundation 4822, **4830**
American Printing House for the Blind **6972**
American Professional Practice Association **1176**
American Prostate Society **4831**
American Prosthodontic Society **3898**
American Pseudo-Obstruction and Hirschsprung's Disease Society **3170**
American Psychiatric Association **7301**
American Psychiatric Association; Caucus of Gay, Lesbian, and Bisexual Members of the 7325
American Psychiatric Association; Gay Caucus of Members of the 7325
American Psychiatric Association; Gay, Lesbian, and Bisexual Caucus of the 7325
American Psychiatric Nurses Association **9065**
American Psychoanalytic Association **7302**
American Psychological Association **7303**
   Division of Applied Experimental and Engineering Psychologists **7304**
   Division of Family Psychology **7305**
   Division of Psychotherapy **7306**
American Psychology-Law Society **7169**
American Psychopathological Association **7307**
American Psychosomatic Society **7308**
American Public Health Association **10939**
American Public Health AssociatioN; New Professionals Section of the **1437**
American Public Welfare Association **10940**

American Society for Parenteral and Enteral Nutrition **9445**
American Society of Pediatric Hematology / Oncology **3173**
American Society for Pediatric Neurosurgery **3174**
American Society of Pharmacognosy **10398**
American Society for Pharmacology and Experimental Therapeutics **10183, 10399**
American Society for Pharmacy Law **7173**
American Society of Physical Medicine and Rehabilitation 12647
American Society of Plastic and Reconstructive Surgeons **12244**
American Society of Plastic and Reconstructive Surgical Nurses **9067**
American Society of Podiatric Dermatology **10765**
American Society of Podiatric Medical Assistants **10766**
American Society of Podiatric Medicine **10767**
American Society of Post Anesthesia Nurses **9068**
American Society of Preventive Oncology **10841**
American Society of Psychoanalytic Physicians **7310**
American Society of Psychopathology of Expression **7311**
American Society for Psychoprophylaxis in Obstetrics **9630**
American Society of Radiographers 11098
American Society of Radiologic Technologists **11098**
American Society of Regional Anesthesia **2354**
American Society for Reproductive Medicine **11201**
American Society for Research in Psychosomatic Problems 7308
American Society for Stereotactic and Functional Neurosurgery **12245**
American Society for the Study of Arteriosclerosis 2842
American Society for the Study of Disorders of Speech 3492
American Society for the Study of Sterility 11201
American Society for Surgery of the Hand **12246**
American Society of Therapeutic Radiologists 11099
American Society for Therapeutic Radiology and Oncology **11099**
American Society of Transplant Physicians **12867**
American Society of Transplant Surgeons **12247**
American Society of Tropical Medicine and Hygiene **6636**
American Society of Ultrasound Technical Specialists 11134
American Society of Veterinary Ethology 13055
American Society of Veterinary Ophthalmology **13053**
American Society of X-Ray Technicians 11098
American Speech Correction Association 3492
American Speech and Hearing Association 3492
American Speech-Language-Hearing Association **3492**
American Spinal Injury Association **8178**
American Sports Medicine Association Board of Certification **11939**
American Student Dental Association **3901**
American Student Health Association 1152
American Subacute Care Association **1186**
American Sudden Infant Death Syndrome Institute **3175, 3309**
American Surgical Association **12248**
American Surgical Trade Association 5853
American Syringomyelia Alliance Project **8179**
American Therapeutic Recreation Association **12662**
American Thermographic Society 11082
American Thoracic Society **11591**
American Tinnitus Association **3469, 3493**
American Trauma Society **4735**
American Trudeau Society 11591
American Ukrainian Medical Society 1522
American University • National Center for Health Fitness **10863**
American Urological Association **12900**
American Urological Association Allied **12901**
American Veterans; Disabled **4483**
American Veterans Foundation; Blinded **13425**
American Veterinary Holistic Medical Association 2168
American Veterinary Medical Association **13054**
American Veterinary Medical Colleges; Association of **13058**
American Veterinary Society of Animal Behavior **13055**
American Veterinary Society for the Study of Breeding Soundness 13108
American Wheelchair Bowling Association **4463**
American Women's Hospitals 6433
American Women's Hospitals Service 6433
American Women's Hospitals Service Committee of AMWA **6422, 6433**
American Women's Physical Therapeutic Association 12657
Americans for Medical Progress Educational Foundation **1187**
Americans for Nonsmokers' Rights **11731**
Americans for a Sound AIDS / HIV Policy **6637**
Americans for a Sound AIDS Policy 6637
Americares Foundation **1188**
Americas; Amigos de las **1189**
Americas; Medical Mycological Society of the **6694**
Ameritech-Ohio Foundation **575**
Ames Charitable Trust; Harriett **246**

Ames Research Center • Space Human Factors Office • Space Administration; National Aeronautics and **2389**
AMETEK Foundation **576**
AMHS Institute **6434**
AMHS Institute; Association 6434
AMI Medical Center **11156**
Amigos de las Americas **1189**
Amiotrofia; Associazione Sclerosis Lateral **8191**
Amiotrofia Lateral Esclerosis in Uruguay; Motor Neurone Disease and **8252**
Amis de Moulin a Poudre **6638**
Amoco Foundation **577**
Amon G. Carter Foundation **42**
Amon G. Carter Star Telegram Employees Fund **578**
AMP Foundation **579**
Amputation Foundation; National **4511**
Amputee Foundation; American **4450, 4458**
Amputee Golf Association; National **4512**
Amputee Shoe and Glove Exchange **4464**
Amputee Skiers Association; National 4528
Amputees in Motion **4465**
AMR / American Airlines Foundation **580**
AMREF - Nederland; Stichting 1126
AMWA; American Women's Hospitals Service Committee of **6422, 6433**
Amyotrophic Lateral Sclerosis Association **8128, 8180**
Amyotrophic Lateral Sclerosis Clinical Research Center **8326**
Amyotrophique; Association pour la Recherche sur la Sclerose Laterale **8190**
ANAD - National Association of Anorexia Nervosa and Associated Disorders **7312**
Anaesthesia; European Society of Regional **2365**
Anaesthesia Intensive Care; Romanian Society for **2371**
Anaesthesia Section of the Canadian Medical Association 2359
Anaesthesiologists; European Association of Cardiothoracic **2364**
Anaesthesiologists; World Federation of Societies of **2376**
Anaesthesiology; European Academy of **2363**
Anaesthesiology and Intensive Medicine; German Society of **2366**
Anaesthetic Research Society **2355**
Anaesthetists; Canadian Society of 2359
Anaesthetists of Great Britain and Ireland; Association of Paediatric **2356**
Anaesthetists' Society; Canadian 2359
Anaesthetists of West Africa; Society of **2374**
Analisis Transaccional; Asociacion Latinoamericana de 7437
Analitica; Sociedade Internacional de Trilogia 7418
Analysis Association; International Transactional 7429
Analysis Association; Latin American Transactional 7437
Analysis; Center for Expressive 7391
Analysis Center; Statistical Data and • Harvard University **7013**
Analysis; Institute for Expressive 7391
Analysis; International Institute for Bioenergetic **2216**
Analysis; Office of Surveillance and • National Center for Chronic Disease Prevention and Health Promotion • U.S. Department of Health and Human Services **10877**
Analytical Chemistry Center • University of Texas Health Science Center at Houston **2693**
Analytical Chemistry; Laboratory of • National Institute of Diabetes and Digestive and Kidney Diseases • U.S. Department of Health and Human Services **4924**
Analytical Psychology; C. G. Jung Foundation for **7348**
Analytical Toxicology Laboratory • Ohio State University **13154**
Analytical Trilogy; Finnish Society of **7377**
Analytical Trilogy; International Society of **7418**
Analytical Trilogy; Swedish Society of **7526**
Analytisk Trilogi; Svenska Sallskapet for 7526
Analyttinen Trilogia Yhdistys; Suomen 7377
Anasthesiologie und Intensivmedizin; Deutsche Gesellschaft fur 2366
Anatoma Jugoslavije; Drustvo 2549
Anatomia; Societa Italiana di 1363
Anatomic and Clinical; World Association of Societies of Pathology— **10141**
Anatomical Nomenclature Committee; International **7002**
Anatomical Nomenclature; International Committee on Veterinary **13085**
Anatomical Society **2524**
Anatomical Society of Great Britain and Ireland **2525**
Anatomical Society; Polish **2542**
Anatomical Society of Southern Africa **2526**
Anatomical and Zoological Society; Polish 2542
Anatomiczne; Polskie Towarzystwo 2542
Anatomiese Vereniging van Suider-Afrika 2526
Anatomique et Clinique; Association Mondiale des Societes de Pathologie - 10141

Animal Health Section
　　Agriculture Division • Rhode Island Department of Environmental Management **13289**
　　Food Safety and Animal Health Division • Washington Department of Agriculture **13298**
Animal Health Section; Poultry and • Delaware Department of Agriculture **13257**
Animal Hospital Association; American **13025**
Animal Industry Veterinarians; Bureau of **13093**
Animal Industry Veterinarians; National Association of Bureau of **13093**
Animal Interaction Organizations; International Association of Human- **12682**
Animal Management Association Lab Animal Program; Laboratory **5583**
Animal Managers Association; Laboratory **5583**
Animal Medical Center **13057**
Animal Medicine Division; Laboratory • Veterinary Pathology Department • Armed Forces Institute of Pathology • U.S. Department of Defense **10178**
Animal Medicine; International Association for Aquatic **13083**
Animal Medicine; Unit for Laboratory • University of Michigan **13222**
Animal Models of Human Genetic Disease; Referral Center for • University of Pennsylvania **13230**
Animal Protection Research Laboratory; Food • Agricultural Research Service • U.S. Department of Agriculture **13185**
Animal Psychophysics Laboratory; Auditory Prosthesis • Kresge Hearing Research Institute • University of Michigan **3642**
Animal Relationships and Environments; Center to Study Human- • University of Minnesota **1705**
Animal Reproduction and Artificial Insemination; International Standing Committee of International Congress on **13090**
Animal Reproduction and Biotechnology Laboratory • Colorado State University **13128**
Animal Reproduction; International Standing Committee of the International Congress on **13090**
Animal Reproduction; International Standing Committee of the International Congress of Phsyiology and Pathology of **13090**
Animal Research Center; Laboratory • Rockefeller University **13170**
Animal Research; Incurably Ill for **1323**
Animal Resources • University of Oklahoma **13229**
Animal Resources Center; Research • University of Wisconsin—Madison **13240**
Animal Resources Diagnostic and Investigative Laboratory • University of Texas Southwestern Medical Center at Dallas **13236**
Animal Resources; Institute of Laboratory **13081**
Animal Resources; Inter- African Bureau for **13082**
Animal Resources and Research Facility; Laboratory • Texas A&M University **2630**
Animal Science; American Association for Laboratory **13032**
Animal Science; Society of Laboratory **13107**
Animal Science and Veterinary Medicine; Chinese Association of **13069**
Animal Studies; Society for Companion **12719**
Animal Testing; Center for Alternatives to • Johns Hopkins University **13141**
Animal Veterinary Association; British Small **13065**
Animal Welfare; Scientists Center for **13171**
Animals; Center for Immunity Enhancement in Domestic • Iowa State University of Science and Technology **13137**
Animals Foundation; Options for **13101**
Animals Laboratory; Health of [Guelph, ON, Canada] • Agriculture and Agri-Food Canada **13126**
Animals Laboratory; Health of [Sackville, NB, Canada] • Agriculture and Agri-Food Canada **13125**
Animals-Love; People- **12709**
Animals; New York Women's League for **13057**
Animals; Orthopedic Foundation for **13102**
Animals & Public Policy; Center for • Tufts University **13179**
Animation de la Paraplegie; Association Francophone Internationale des Groupes d' **12686**
Ankle Orthopedics and Medicine; American College of Foot and **10760**
Ankle Pediatrics; American College of Foot and **3165**
Ankle Society; American Orthopaedic Foot and **9922**
Ankle Surgeons; American College of Foot and **12231**
Ankylosing Spondylitis Association **7911**
Ann Jackson Family Foundation **4445**
Anne Burnett and Charles Tandy Foundation **79**
Annenberg Foundation **44**
Annie E. Casey Foundation **3133**
Anomalies and Communicative Disorders; H.K. Cooper Institute for Oral-Facial **2758**
Anomalies Research Center; Craniofacial **2757**
Anomaly Clinic; Craniofacial • University of Pennsylvania **2763**
Anorexia / Bulimia Association; American **7269**
Anorexia and Bulimia; Center for the Study of **7551**

Anorexia Nervosa Aid Society **7269**
Anorexia Nervosa and Associated Disorders **7312**
Anorexia Nervosa and Associated Disorders; ANAD - National Association of **7312**
Anorexia Nervosa; Center for the Research and Treatment of **7550**
Anorexia Nervosa and Related Eating Disorders **7313**
Anorexic Aid Society **7463**
Anorexic Aid Society; National **7463**
ANR Foundation **582**
Anschutz Family Foundation **45**
Anterior Segment Diseases Branch • Extramural Research • National Eye Institute • U.S. Department of Health and Human Services **13635**
Anthropology; American Board of Forensic **7165**
Anthropology; Laboratory of Biological • University of Kansas **2674**
Anthroposophical Medicine; Physicians Association for **2233**
Anthroposophical Nurses Association of America **9069**
Anti-AIDS Association; Romanian **6747**
Antibiotics; Alliance for the Prudent Use of **10389**
Anticancereuse; Groupe Europeen de Chimiotherapie **5941**
Anti-Fraud Association; National Health Care **5742**
Antigen Immunochemistry; Laboratory of Tumor **6064**
Anti-Inflammatory Research; Center for • Florida A&M University **10431**
Anti-Leprosy Associations; International Federation of **6680**
Antillian Adventista University • School of Nursing **8939**
Antimicrobial Chemotherapy; British Society for **2531**
Anti-Saloon League of America **12005**
Anti-Sickle Cell Anemia League **5916**
Antitrypsin Support Group; Alpha 1 **11587**
Antiviral Laboratory • University of Michigan **10478**
Antiviral Research Branch • Division of Microbiology and Infectious Diseases • National Institute of Allergy and Infectious Diseases • U.S. Department of Health and Human Services **6825**
Antrophy International Association; Charcot-Marie-Tooth Disease/ Peroral Muscular **8199**
Anxiety Disorders Association of America **7314**
Anxiety Disorders; Center for Stress and • University at Albany, State University of New York **7654**
Anxiety Disorders; Council on **7362**
Anxiety Disorders; Special Interest Group on Phobias and Related **7521**
Anxiety, and Personality Disorders Research Branch; Mood, • Clinical Research Division • National Institute of Mental Health • U.S. Department of Health and Human Services **7622**
Anxiety Research; Society for Stress and **7520**
Anxiety Research; Society for Test **7520**
Anxiety and Traumatic Stress Program • Duke University **7558**
AON Foundation **583**
Aphasia; Academy of **3473**
Aphasia Research Center • Boston University **8333**
Apheresis; American Society for **7121**
Apio-Therapy Society; North American **2157**
Apitherapy Society; American **2157**
Aplastic Anemia Foundation of America **5917**
Apnea Association; American Sleep **8172**
Apnea Professionals; National Association of **8266**
Apollo College at Mesa • Respiratory Therapist Program **11306**
Apollo College at Phoenix • Respiratory Therapist Program **11307**
Apollo College at Portland • Respiratory Therapist Program **11504**
Apothecaries; American College of **10580**
Apothecaries Research and Education Foundation; American College of **10626**
Apotheker; Bundesverband Deutscher **10609**
Appalachian Laboratory for Occupational Safety and Health • National Institute for Occupational Safety and Health • U.S. Department of Health and Human Services **9825**
Applebaum Foundation **46**
Appliance and Limb Manufacturers Association; Orthopedic **5822**
Applications of Psychological Type; Center for **7352**
Applied Behavioral Sciences; Center for the • St. Louis University **7597**
Applied Bioengineering Center • Worcester Polytechnic Institute **2508**
Applied Bioinformatics; Welch Laboratory for • Johns Hopkins University **7016**
Applied Biology Branch • Biomedical and Behavioral Science Division • National Institute for Occupational Safety and Health • U.S. Department of Health and Human Services **9827**
Applied Biology; Institute of **12747**
Applied Clinical Nutrition; American Council of **9441**
Applied Ethics; Center for
　　Santa Clara University **7215**
　　University of British Columbia **7217**
Applied Ethology; International Society for **13089**
Applied Experimental and Engineering Psychologists; Division of • American Psychological Association **7304**

Applied Gerontological Research; Center on • Cleveland State University 1931

Applied Gnotobiotics; Association for 13061

Applied Hypnosis; Association for 6590

Applied Kinesiology; International College of 2211

Applied Mathematics; Program in • University of Arizona 7036

Applied Microcirculatory Research; Center for • University of Louisville 2969

Applied Neural Control Laboratory • Case Western Reserve University 8346

Applied Nutrition; Center for Food Safety and • Food and Drug Administration • U.S. Department of Health and Human Services 10900, 10996

Applied Osteopathy; Academy of 9969

Applied Pharmacokinetics; Laboratory of • University of Southern California 10484

Applied Physiology and Medicine; Institute of 1607

Applied Physiology Research Laboratory • Kent State University 11968

Applied Poetry; Association for 7320

Applied Psychoanalysis; Association for 7321

Applied Psychology and Ergonomics Branch • Biomedical and Behavioral Science Division • National Institute for Occupational Safety and Health • U.S. Department of Health and Human Services 9828

Applied Psychology; International Association of 7397

Applied Psychometrics and Clinical Assessment; Inquiry Group on • Texas A&M University 7609

Applied Psychophysiology and Biofeedback; Association for 2419

Applied Research Center • California State University, Bakersfield 1565

Applied Research Division • Department of Health Administration and Policy • Medical University of South Carolina 5633

Applied Research on Fertility Regulation; Program for • Northwestern University 11278

Applied Research; Herman Schneider Laboratory of Basic and • University of Cincinnati 2480

Applied Science; Center for Biotechnology and • Northwestern University 2722

Applied Studies Laboratory • Division of Computer Research and Technology • National Institutes of Health • U.S. Department of Health and Human Services 2656

Appropriate Health Resources and Technologies Action Group 1190

Appropriate Technology in Healthcare; Brazilian Association for the Promotion of 10945

Appropriate Technology in Health; Program for 1481

Apraxia and Dyspraxia; National Organization for 8279

Aquatic Animal Medicine; International Association for 13083

Arab American Medical Association 1191

Arbeidsterapeute; Suid Afrikaanse Vereniging van 12720

Arbetsterapeuter; Forbundet Sveriges 12722

Arbovirus Diseases Branch • Division of Vector-Borne Infectious Diseases • National Center for Infectious Diseases • U.S. Department of Health and Human Services 6803

Arbovirus Research Unit; Yale • Yale University 6856

The ARC 4279

Arc of Alabama 4394

Arc of Alaska 4395

Arc of Arizona 4396

Arc of Arkansas 4397

Arc of California 4398

Arc of Connecticut 4400

Arc of Delaware 4401

Arc; District of Columbia 4402

Arc of Florida 4403

Arc of Georgia 4404

Arc of Hawaii 4405

Arc of Illinois 4406

Arc of Indiana 4407

Arc of Iowa 4408

Arc of Kansas 4409

Arc of Kentucky 4410

Arc of Louisiana 4411

Arc of Maryland 4412

Arc of Massachusetts 4413

Arc of Michigan 4414

Arc of Minnesota 4415

Arc of Mississippi 4416

Arc of Montana 4417

Arc of Nebraska 4418

Arc of New Hampshire 4419

Arc of New Jersey 4420

Arc of New Mexico 4421

Arc of North Carolina 4423

Arc of North Dakota 4424

Arc of Ohio 4425

Arc of Oregon 4426

Arc of Pennsylvania 4427

Arc; Rhode Island 4428

Arc of South Carolina 4429

Arc of South Dakota 4430

Arc of Tennessee 4431

Arc of Texas 4432

Arc of Utah 4433

Arc of Virginia 4434

Arc of Washington State 4435

Arc of Wisconsin 4436

Arc of Wyoming 4437

Arcadia Foundation 47

Arcana Foundation 48

ARCEPs 7315

Archaeus Project 2176

Archbold Charitable Trust; Adrian and Jessie 32

Architectes et Hygienistes Municipaux de France, Algerie, Tunisie, Belgique, Suisse et Luxembourg; Association Generale des Ingenieurs, 10954

Architectural and Transportation Barriers Compliance Board 4438

Archivists and Librarians in the Health Sciences 6973

Arctic Biology; Institute of • University of Alaska Fairbanks 1682

Arctic Investigations Program • National Center for Infectious Diseases • U.S. Department of Health and Human Services 6795

Arctic Medical Research; Nordic Council for 1440

Arecibo Technical College; University of Puerto Rico / • School of Nursing 8948

Argentine Association for the Study of Pain 8181

Argentinian Association of Dermatology 4219

Argonne National Laboratory • U.S. Department of Energy 2633

Arie and Ida Crown Memorial 49

Arise 1192

Aristolochite Society 10620

Arizona Affiliate
     American Diabetes Association 4952
     American Heart Association 2991

Arizona Agricultural Experiment Station • University of Arizona 9547

Arizona; American Lung Association of 11628

Arizona; Arc of 4396

Arizona Board of Examiners for Nursing Care Institution Administrators 9277

Arizona Board of Osteopathic Examiners in Medicine and Surgery 10014

Arizona Cancer Center • University of Arizona 6209

Arizona Center on Aging • University of Arizona 1970

Arizona Chapter
     American Physical Therapy Association 12824
     Cystic Fibrosis Foundation 5398
     National Association of Social Workers 11882

Arizona Chapter; Central • Arthritis Foundation 7964

Arizona Chapter; Greater • Lupus Foundation of America 8031

Arizona Chapter; Southern
     Arthritis Foundation 7965
     Lupus Foundation of America 8032

Arizona Coalition Against Domestic Violence 3078

Arizona Department of Agriculture • Animal Services Division • State Veterinarian 13252

Arizona Department of Economic Security
     Aging and Community Services Division 2005
     Developmental Disabilities Division 4345
     Employment and Rehabilitation Services Division • Rehabilitation Services Administration 12772, 13667

Arizona Department of Environmental Quality • Disease Prevention Services Division • Risk Assessment and Environmental Investigation Office 5130

Arizona Department of Health Services 11007
     Behavioral Health Services Division 7710
     Behaviorial Health Services Division • Substance Abuse Office 12149
     Disease Prevention Services Division • HIV and AIDS Office 6859
     Emergency Medical Services Division 4769
     Family Health and Community Services Division
          Oral Health Office 4104
               Women and Children's Health Office 3380, 9726
     Health Care Licensure Office 6478
     Planning Office 5665
     Vital Records Office 7042

Arizona Division • American Cancer Society 6273

Arizona; Easter Seal Society of 4607

Arizona Health Care Association 9328

Arizona Health Care Cost Containment System • Medicaid Program 5770

Arizona Heart Institute 2881

Arizona Hospital Association 6529
Arizona Industrial Commission • Occupational Safety Division 9867
Arizona; Learning Disabilities Association of 4686
Arizona Medical Association 1812
Arizona; National Kidney Foundation of 12934
Arizona Nurses Association 9213
Arizona Optometric Association 13795
Arizona Osteopathic Medical Association 10068
Arizona Pharmacy Association 10696
Arizona Poison and Drug Information Center • University of Arizona 10468
Arizona State Board of Dental Examiners 4051
Arizona State Board of Funeral Directors and Embalmers 3730
Arizona State Board of Medical Examiners 1758
Arizona State Board of Nursing 9154
Arizona State Board of Optometry 13720
Arizona State Board of Pharmacy 10643
Arizona State Board of Podiatry Examiners 10781
Arizona State Dental Association 4157
Arizona State University
    Biomedical Engineering Laboratories 2434
    Cancer Research Institute 5999
    College of Business • School of Health Administration and Policy •
      Graduate Program in Health Services Adminstration 5473
    College of Nursing 8558
    Exercise and Sport Research Institute 11955
    School of Health Administration and Policy 5608
    School of Social Work 11746
Arizona Veterinary Medical Association 13304
Arkansas Affiliate
    American Diabetes Association 4953
    American Heart Association 2992
Arkansas; American Lung Association of 11629
Arkansas; Arc of 4397
Arkansas Board of Examiners in Optometry 13721
Arkansas Cancer Research Center • University of Arkansas at Little Rock 6210
Arkansas Chapter
    American Physical Therapy Association 12825
    Arthritis Foundation 7966
    Cystic Fibrosis Foundation 5399
    Lupus Foundation of America 8033
    National Association of Social Workers 11883
Arkansas Children's Hospital Cystic Fibrosis Center • University of Arkansas at Little Rock 5368
Arkansas Coalition Against Domestic Violence 3079
Arkansas Department of Education • Rehabilitation Services Division 12773
Arkansas Department of Health 11008
    AIDS / STD Administrative Office 6860
    Alcohol and Drug Abuse Prevention Division 12150
    Dental Health Office 4105
    Emergency Medical Services Division 4770
    Environmental Health Services Bureau 5131
    Health Resources Bureau
        Health Facility Services and Systems Division 6479
        Vital Records Division 7043
    Planning Bureau 5666
    Public Health Programs Bureau • Maternal and Child Health Division 3381, 9727
Arkansas Department of Human Services
    Aging and Adult Services Division 2006
    Blind Services Division 13668
    Developmental Disabilities Services Division 4346
    Medical Services Division 5771
        Long Term Care Office • Nursing Home Certification and
          Licensure Section 9278
    Mental Health Services Division 7711
Arkansas Department of Labor • Safety Division 9868
Arkansas Division • American Cancer Society 6274
Arkansas Easter Seal Society 4608
Arkansas Health Care Association 9329
Arkansas Hospital Association 6530
Arkansas; Learning Disabilities Association of 4687
Arkansas Livestock and Poultry Commission • State Veterinarian 13253
Arkansas Medical Society 1813
Arkansas; National Kidney Foundation of 12935
Arkansas Nurses Association 9214
Arkansas Optometric Association 13796
Arkansas Osteopathic Medical Association 10069
Arkansas Pharmacists Association 10697
Arkansas Rehabilitation Research & Training Center 12746

Arkansas State Board of Dental Examiners 4052
Arkansas State Board of Embalmers and Funeral Directors 3731
Arkansas State Board of Nursing 9155
Arkansas State Board of Pharmacy 10644
Arkansas State Dental Association 4158
Arkansas State Medical Board 1759, 10015
Arkansas State Podiatry Examining Board 10782
Arkansas State University • College of Nursing and Health Professions •
  Department of Nursing 8562
Arkansas Tech University
    Department of Nursing 8563
    Health Information Administration Program 6916
    Rehabilitation Counseling Program 12570
Arkansas Veterinary Medical Association 13305
Arkell Hall Foundation 50
Arktisk Medicinsk Forskning; Nordiska Samarbetskommitten for 1440
The Arlin J. Brown Information Center 6974
Armand-Frappier Institute • Immunology Research Center 2092
Armand Hammer Center for Cancer Biology 6000
Armco Foundation 584
Armed Forces Institute of Pathology
    Cellular Pathology Department
        Cytopathology Division • U.S. Department of Defense 10146
        Molecular Pathology Division • U.S. Department of Defense 10147
        U.S. Department of Defense 10145
    Center for Advanced Pathology
        Cardiovascular Pathology Department • U.S. Department of Defense 10148
        Dermatopathology Department • U.S. Department of Defense 10149
        Environmental and Drug-Induced Pathology Department • U.S. Department of Defense 10150
        Genitourinary Pathology Department • U.S. Department of Defense 10151
        Gynecologic and Breast Pathology Department • U.S. Department of Defense 10152
        Hematologic and Lymphatic Pathology Department • U.S. Department of Defense 10153
        Hepatic and Gastrointestinal Pathology Department • U.S. Department of Defense 10154
        Infectious and Parasitic Disease Pathology Department • U.S. Department of Defense 10155
        Legal Medicine, Quality Assurance, and Risk Management Department • U.S. Department of Defense 10156
        Neuropathology Department • U.S. Department of Defense 10157
        Ophthalmic Pathology Department • U.S. Department of Defense 10158
        Oral Pathology Department • U.S. Department of Defense 10159
        Orthopedic Pathology Department • U.S. Department of Defense 10160
        Pediatric Pathology Department • U.S. Department of Defense 10161
        Pulmonary and Mediastinal Pathology Department • U.S. Department of Defense 10162
        Radiologic Pathology Department • U.S. Department of Defense 10163
        Soft Tissue Pathology Department • U.S. Department of Defense 10164
    Center for Medical Illustration • U.S. Department of Defense 7025
    Environmental Pathology Department • Biochemistry Division • U.S. Department of Defense 10165
    Genitourinary Pathology Department
        Medical Nephropathology Division • U.S. Department of Defense 10166
        Urologic Pathology Division • U.S. Department of Defense 10167
    Infectious and Parasitic Disease Pathology Department
        AIDS Pathology Division • U.S. Department of Defense 10168
        Geographic Pathology Division • U.S. Department of Defense 10169
        Microbiology Division • U.S. Department of Defense 10170
    National Museum of Health and Medicine • U.S. Department of Defense 7026
    Office of the Armed Forces Medical Examiner
        Forensic and Aerospace Pathology Division • U.S. Department of Defense 10171
        Toxicology Division • U.S. Department of Defense 10172
    Oral Pathology Department • Forensic Dentistry Division • U.S. Department of Defense 10173

University of Alabama at Birmingham **7944**
Arthritis and Musculoskeletal Diseases Center; Robert B. Brigham Multipurpose • Brigham and Women's Hospital **7915**
Arthritis and Musculoskeletal and Skin Diseases Information Clearinghouse; National **7891**
Arthritis and Musculoskeletal and Skin Diseases; National Institute of Extramural Activities Program
    Centers Program • U.S. Department of Health and Human Services **7937**
    Muscle Biology Program • U.S. Department of Health and Human Services **7938**
    Musculoskeletal Diseases Branch • U.S. Department of Health and Human Services **7939**
    Rheumatic Diseases Branch • U.S. Department of Health and Human Services **7940**
    Skin Diseases Branch • U.S. Department of Health and Human Services **4268**
  Intramural Research Program • Arthritis and Rheumatism Branch • U.S. Department of Health and Human Services **7941**
  Laboratory of Physical Biology • U.S. Department of Health and Human Services **7942**
  U.S. Department of Health and Human Services **7854, 7936**
Arthritis Organization; American Juvenile **7862**
Arthritis Pediatric Research Center **3345**
Arthritis Research Center; Harold C. Simmons • University of Texas Southwestern Medical Center at Dallas **7961**
Arthritis Research Center; Harrington **7919**
Arthritis Research Center; Scleroderma and • Thomas Jefferson University **7935**
Arthritis Research Center; Thurston • University of North Carolina at Chapel Hill **7958**
Arthritis Research; Kuzell Institute for **7921**
Arthritis Research Unit • University of Puerto Rico **7960**
Arthritis Research Unit; Rackham • University of Michigan **7955**
Arthritis and Rheumatism Branch • Intramural Research Program • National Institute of Arthritis and Musculoskeletal and Skin Diseases • U.S. Department of Health and Human Services **7941**
Arthritis and Rheumatism Foundation **7866**
Arthritis; Rosalind Russell Medical Research Center for • University of California, San Francisco **7946**
Arthritis; Specialized Center of Research in Rheumatoid • University of Michigan **7956**
Arthrogryposis Multiplex Congenita; Avenues—National Support Group for **2742**
Arthropod-Borne Animal Diseases Research Laboratory • Agricultural Research Service • U.S. Department of Agriculture **13183**
Arthropod-Pathogen Studies; Center for Host- • Oklahoma State University **6782**
Arthroscopy Association; International **9927**
Arthroscopy Association of North America **12249**
Arthur D. Little Foundation **586**
Arthur M. Fishberg Research Center in Neurobiology **8327**
Arthur Vining Davis Foundations **52**
Artificial Heart Research Laboratory • University of Utah **2979**
Artificial Heart Research Project • Pennsylvania State University **2919**
Artificial Insemination; International Standing Committee of International Congress on Animal Reproduction and **13090**
Artificial Language Laboratory • Michigan State University **3613**
Artificial Organs; International Society for **12870**
Artists Confronting AIDS **6639**
Artists; Doctors for **1268**
Arts; Alliance for the **6625**
Arts; Center for Safety in the **9794, 9804**
Arts for the Handicapped; National Committee, **4566**
Arts Therapy Associations; National Coalition of **7459**
Arts; Very Special **4566**
Arvin Foundation **587**
Arzneimittel-Hersteller; Europaischer Fachverband der **5846**
Arzneipflanzenforschung; Gesellschaft fur **10420**
Arztebund; Okologischer **1272**
Arztegesellschaft fur Akupunktur; Schweizerische **2240**
Arzteverband Deutschland; Unabhangiger **1325**
Asbestos Litigation Group **7174**
Asbestos Victims of America **9791**
Ashbee Research Laboratories; Barry • Medical College of Pennsylvania and Hahnemann University **6071**
Ashland Oil Foundation **588**
Ashton Graybiel Spatial Orientation Lab • Brandeis University **2387**
Ashyng Nghymru **11730**
Asia; Association of Surgeons of South East **12252**
Asia-Pacific Academy of Ophthalmology **13407**
Asia Pacific Association for the Control of Tobacco **11732**
Asia; Regional Office for South-East • World Health Organization **1544**

Asian-Australasian Society of Neurological Surgeons **12250**
Asian Chapter; International Academy of Myodontics, **3951**
Asian Health Institute **10941**
Asian / International Bioethics Program • Center for Bioethics • Georgetown University **7201**
Asian and Pacific Associations of Optometrists; International Federation of **13487**
Asian and Pacific Associations of Optometry; International Federation of **13487**
Asian Pacific Center on Aging; National **1906**
Asian / Pacific Community Health Organizations; Association of **1200**
Asian Pacific Dental Federation / Asian Pacific Regional Organization **3902**
Asian Pacific Regional Organisation of the International Dental Federation **3902**
Asian Pacific Regional Organization; Asian Pacific Dental Federation / **3902**
Asian-Pacific Section - IPRS **12251**
Asian Parasite Control Organization **6640**
Asian Region; Association of Pediatric Societies of the Southeast **3188**
Asian Resource Center on Aging; National Pacific/ **1906**
Asian Science and Medicine; Institute for Advanced Research in **918, 2204**
Asian Surgical Association **12252**
Asmologia; Asociacion Internacional de **11596**
Asociacion Apostol de la Salud **1193**
Asociacion Argentina de Dermatologia **4219**
Asociacion Argentina para el Estudio del Dolor **8181**
Asociacion Ayuda a Madres de Minusvalidos **9631**
Asociacion Distrofia Muscular **8182**
Asociacion de Enfermedades Motoneuronales y Esclerosis Lateral Amiotrofica del Uruguay (MON DELA) **8252**
Asociacion Espanola de Dietistas/Nutricion **9488**
Asociacion Iberoamericana de Estudio de los Problemas del Alcohol y la Droga **12031**
Asociacion Inter-Americana de Gastroenterologia **5220**
Asociacion Internacional de Asmologia **11596**
Asociacion Latinoamericana de Analisis Transaccional **7437**
Asociacion Latinoamericana de Facultades y Escuelas de Medicina de America Latina **1369**
Asociacion Latinoamericana de Fisica Medica **2539**
Asociacion Latinoamericana de Medecina de Aviacion y del Espacio **2386**
Asociacion Latinoamericana de Psicologia Social **7435**
Asociacion Latinoamericana de Psiquiatria **7436**
Asociacion Mundial Veterinaria de Avicola **13122**
Asociacion Mundial de Veterinarios Higienistas de los Alimentos **13118**
Asociacion Nacional Contra el Cancer **5918**
Asociacion Panamericana de Otorrinolaringologia y Broncoesofagologia **3570**
Asociacion Panamericana de Sciencas Veterinarias **13103**
Asociacion Puertorriquena del Pulmon **11670**
Asociatia Handicapatilor Neuromotori din Romania **8183**
Asosiasi Obat Hewan Indonesia **13080**
Aspirin Foundation of America **5824**
Assault; National Coalition Against Sexual **11704**
Assault Prevention Center; National **3057**
Assault Prevention; National Center for **3057**
Assembly of Hospital Schools of Nursing **9093**
Assembly of Nursing Care and Related Institutions **6472**
Assembly of Skilled Nursing and Related Long Term Care Services **6472**
Assessment & Demographic Studies; Center for • Gallaudet University **3600**
Assessment and Disease Prevention; Center for Health Risk • University of Alabama at Birmingham **10881**
Assessment Technology Section • Environmental, Life, and Social Sciences Directorate • Oak Ridge National Laboratory • U.S. Department of Energy **11159**
Assistance Dog Services; National Education for **3557**
Assistance Dogs of America **4466**
Assistance Dogs International **13408**
Assistance to Travellers; International Association for Medical **1336**
Assistant Programs; Association of Physician **1214**
Assistant Secretary of Defense for Health Affairs; Office of • U.S. Department of Defense **7790**
Assistant Secretary for Environment, Safety, and Health • U.S. Department of Energy **5004**
Assistant Secretary for Health; Office of the • Public Health Service • U.S. Department of Health and Human Services **10902**
Assistants; Accreditation Review Committee on Education for Physician **1122**
Assistants; American Academy of Physician **1137**
Assistants; American Association of Medical **1141**

Assistants; American Association of Pathologists' **10119**
Assistants; American Association of Surgeon **12214**
Assistants of American Medical Technologists; Registered Medical **1490**
Assistants; American Registry of Medical **1180**
Assistants; American Society of Podiatric Medical **10766**
Assistants Association; American Dental **3784, 3889**
Assistants Association; National Dental **3972**
Assistants in Cardiovascular Surgery; Association of Physician **12254**
Assistants; National Association of Childbirth **9681**
Assistants; National Association of Dental **3966**
Assistants; National Commission on Certification of Physician **1411**
Assistants; Registered Medical **1490**
Assisted Reproductive Technology; Society for **11251**
Assisting National Board; Dental **3923**
Assistive Device Center • California State University, Sacramento **2436**
Associacao Brasileira de Distrofia Muscular **8184**
Associacao Brasileira de Tecnologia Alternativa na Promocao da Saude **10945**
Associacao Portuguesa Dietistas **9482**
Associacao Portuguesa de Miastenia Gravis e Doencas Neuromusculares **8185**
Associacio de Musicoterapia do Rio de Janeiro **7448**
Associacion Latinoamericana de Imunologia **2082**
Associacion Medica Pan Americana **1462**
Associate Degree Nursing; National Organization for **9125**
The Associated Blind **13409**
Associated Bodywork and Massage Professionals **2177**
Associated Professional Massage Therapists and Allied Health Practitioners International **2177**
Associated Professional Massage Therapists and Bodyworkers **2177**
Associated Professional Sleep Societies **8186**
Associated Services for the Blind **13410**
Associates of Clinical Pharmacology **10400**
Associates and Practitioners; National Association of Pediatric Nurse **9107**
Associates; Society of Gastroenterology Nurses and **5231**
Association of Academic Health Centers **1194**
Association of Academic Health Sciences Library Directors **6975**
Association of Academic Physiatrists **12663**
Association for Academic Surgery **12253**
Association to Advance Ethical Hypnosis **6589**
Association for the Advancement of Automotive Medicine **10842**
Association for Advancement of Behavior Therapy **7316**
Association for Advancement of the Behavioral Therapies **7316**
Association for Advancement of Blind Children **4280**
Association for Advancement of Blind and Retarded **4280**
Association for the Advancement of Health Education **1195**
Association for the Advancement of Medical Instrumentation **2418**
Association for Advancement of Psychoanalysis (of the Karen Horney Psychoanalytic Institute and Center) **7317**
Association for Advancement of Psychology **7318**
Association for the Advancement of Psychotherapy **7319**
Association for Advancement of Research on Multiple Sclerosis **8278**
Association for the Advancement of Sports Potential **11940**
Association of Air Medical Services **4737**
Association for Ambulatory Pediatric Services **3157**
Association of American Board of Examiners in Veterinary Medicine **13039**
Association of American Cancer Institutes **5919**
Association of American Indian Physicians **1196**
Association of American Medical Colleges **1197**
Association of American Physicians **1198**
Association of American Physicians and Surgeons **1199**
Association of American Veterinary Medical Colleges **13058**
Association of American Women Dentists **3880**
Association AMHS Institute **6434**
Association for Applied Gnotobiotics **13061**
Association for Applied Hypnosis **6590**
Association for Applied Poetry **7320**
Association for Applied Psychoanalysis **7321**
Association for Applied Psychophysiology and Biofeedback **2419**
Association of Areawide Health Planning Agencies **5551**
Association of Asian / Pacific Community Health Organizations **1200**
Association of Avian Veterinarians **13059**
Association of Baptist Homes and Hospitals **1144**
Association for the Behavioral Sciences and Medical Education **7322**
Association for the Behavioral Treatment of Sexual Abusers **11686**
Association for the Behavioral Treatment of Sexual Aggression **11686**
Association of Benedictin Children **2741**
Association des Bibliotheques de la Sante du Canada **6984**
Association of Biomedical Communication Directors **6976**
Association of Birth Defect Children **2741**
Association for Birth Psychology **7323**

Association of Black Cardiologists **2831**
Association of Black Chiropractors **3447**
Association of Black Nursing Faculty **9070**
Association of Black Psychologists **7324**
Association of Bone and Joint Surgeons **9924**
Association for Brain Tumor Research **8159**
Association of Brethren Caregivers **1889**
Association of British Dental Surgery Assistants **3903**
Association of British Paediatric Nurses **3176**
Association Burkinabe pour la Promotion des Aveugles et Malvoyants **13411**
Association Canadienne des Implantes Intraoculaires **12261**
Association Canadienne de l'Ataxie de Friedreich **7871**
Association Canadienne pour la Sante Mentale **7350**
Association Canadienne de Sensibilisation a l'Infertilite **11221**
Association Canadienne des Technologues en Radiation Medicale **11106**
Association of Cancer Institute Directors **5919**
Association Candienne des Medecins Veterinaires **13068**
Association for the Care of Children in Hospitals **3177**
Association for the Care of Children's Health **3177**
Association of Chartered Physiotherapists in Sports Medicine **11941**
Association for Chemoreception Sciences **8187**
Association of Child and Adolescent Psychiatric Nurses **3178**
Association for Child Psychoanalysis **3179**
Association for Child Psychology and Psychiatry **3180**
Association of Child Psychotherapists **3181**
Association for Childbirth at Home **9632**
Association for Childbirth at Home, International **9632**
Association for Children and Adults with Learning Disabilities **4504**
Association for Children with Down Syndrome **5270**
Association for Children with Learning Disabilities **4504**
Association for Children with Retarded Mental Development **4281**
Association for Children with Russell-Silver Syndrome **3182**
Association of Children's Prosthetic-Orthotic Clinics **3183**
Association of Chiropractic College Presidents **3449**
Association of Chiropractic Colleges **3449**
Association of Clinic Managers **5584**
Association of Clinical Scientists **7126**
Association of Colon Surgery **12304**
Association to Combat Huntington's Disease **8227**
Association of Community Cancer Centers **5920**
Association de Conjoints de Medecins **1201**
Association of Cosmetic Plastic Surgeons of Great Britain **12260**
Association for Dance Movement Therapy—United Kingdom **12664**
Association of the Deaf in Israel **3494**
Association of Deans of American Colleges of Veterinary Medicine **13058**
Association for Death Education and Counseling **3708**
Association of Delaware Hospitals **6534**
Association of Democratic Pharmacists **10589**
Association Dentaire Francaise **3904**
Association for Dental Education in Europe **3905**
Association for Denture Prosthesis **3915**
Association de Dieteticiens de Lange Francaise **9446**
Association of Diplomates of the American Board of Oral Surgery **12232**
Association of Driver Educators for the Disabled **4467**
Association des Ecoles de Sante Publique de la Regional Europeenne **10943**
Association for Education and Rehabilitation of the Blind and Visually Impaired **13412**
Association of Educators for Homebound and Hospitalized Children **4479**
Association for the Electrically Oversensitive **5035**
Association des Epidemiologistes de Langue Francaise **5180**
Association for Equine Sports Medicine **13060**
Association Espanola de ELA **8310**
Association of Estonian Cardiologists **2832**
Association Europeene des Ecoles et Colleges d'Optometre **13446**
Association Europeenne des Centres Anti-Poisons et de Toxicologie Clinique **10407**
Association Europeenne des Centres d'Audiophonologie **3521**
Association Europeenne du Laser **11112**
Association Europeenne pour l'Etude du Diabete **4839**
Association Europeenne pour l'Etude de l'Alimentation et du Developpement de l'Enfant **9455**
Association Europeenne de Psychologie Sociale **7371**
Association Europeenne de Radiologie **11110**
Association Europeenne Thyroide **4842**
Association Executives; National Council of State Pharmacy **5597**
Association for Faculty in the Medical Humanities **1202**
Association for Family Planning **11213**
Association of Family Practice Residency Directors **5557**
Association for Fitness in Business **10844**

Association for Fitness Professionals; IDEA: The   10850
Association Francaise des Diabetiques   4843
Association Francophone Internationale des Groupes d'Animation de la Paraplegie   12686
Association of Freestanding Radiation Oncology Centers   **11100**
Association of French Language Epidemiologists   **5180**
Association of French-Language Leprologists   **6641**
Association of French-Speaking Dietitians   **9446**
Association of Gay and Lesbian Psychiatrists   **7325**
Association Generale des Hygienistes et Techniciens Municipaux   10954
Association Generale des Ingenieurs, Architectes et Hygienistes Municipaux de France, Algerie, Tunisie, Belgique, Suisse et Luxembourg   10954
Association of German Dietitians   **9447**
Association of German Radiologists and Nuclear Physicians   **11101**
Association of German Urologists   **12902**
Association for Gerontology in Higher Education   **1890**
Association for Glycogen Storage Disease   **4832**
Association for Gnotobiotics   **13061**
Association for Group Psychoanalysis and Process   **7326**
Association of Haitian Physicians Abroad   **1203**
Association of Halfway House Alcoholism Programs of North America   **12011**
Association of Health Care Information & Medical Records Officers   7001
Association for Health-Care Institutions   **1204**
Association of Healthcare Internal Auditors   **5558**
Association for Healthcare Philanthropy   **6435**
Association of Health Facility Licensure and Certification Directors   5559
Association of Health Facility Survey Agencies   **5559**
Association of Health Occupations Teacher Educators   **1205**
Association for Health Services Research   **1206**
Association for Health Without Vaccination   **2178**
Association for the Help of Retarded Children   **4282**
Association of High Medicare Hospitals   **6436**
Association on Higher Education and Disability   **4468**
Association for Hispanic Handicapped of New Jersey   **4469**
Association of Hospital Directors of Medical Education   6437
Association for Hospital Medical Education   **6437**
Association of Hospital Superintendents of U.S. and Canada   6425
Association for Humanistic Psychology   **7327**
Association of Humanistic Psychology Practitioners   **7328**
Association for Improvements in the Maternity Services   **11202**
Association of Independent Physical Therapists   **12665**
Association of Independent Research Institutes   **2527**
Association des Infirmieres et Infirmiers du Canada   9079
Association for International Cancer Research   **5921**
Association of International Health Researchers   **1207**
Association Internationale des Cadres Medicaux Olympiques   11944
Association Internationale des Etudiants Dentaires   3955
Association Internationale des Etudiants Veterinaires   13092
Association Internationale pour l'Etude du Foie   5222
Association Internationale de Logopedie et Phoniatrie   3530
Association Internationale de Medecine des Accidents et du Trafic   1335
Association Internationale de Medecine Agricole et de Sante Rurale   9797
Association Internationale de Medecine et de Biologie de l'Environnement   5041
Association Internationale de Pediatrie   3244
Association Internationale de Psychiatrie de l'Enfant et de l'Adolescent et des Professions Associees   3240
Association Internationale de Psychologie Appliquee   7397
Association Internationale de Psychologie du Travail de Langue Francaise   **7329**
Association Internationale pour la Recherche Medicale et les Echanges Culturels   1337
Association Internationale des Registres du Cancer   7003
Association Internationale pour le Sport des Aveugles   13482
Association Internationale de Standardisation Biologique   5860
Association Internationale de Strabisme   13504
Association Internationale des Technologistes de Laboratoire Medical   7137
Association Ivoirienne de Bien-Etre Familial   **11203**
Association for Jewish Retarded   **4292**
Association of Late-Deafened Adults   **3495**
Association of Latin Languages Allergologists and Immunologists   **2067**
Association des Leprologues de Langue Francaise   6641
Association of Librarians in the History of the Health Sciences   6973
Association of Life Insurance Medical Directors of America   5719
Association of Limb Manufacturers of America   5822
Association Luxembourgeoise du Diabete   4836
Association for Macular Diseases   **13413**
Association of Managerial Hospital Doctors of Germany   **5560**
Association of Maternal and Child Health Programs   **3184**

Association of Medical Deans in Europe   1209
Association of Medical Education and Research in Substance Abuse   **12012**
Association of Medical Illustrators   **6977**
Association of Medical Laboratory Technologists of Zimbabwe   **7127**
Association of Medical Officers of American Institutions of Idiotic and Feebleminded Children   4277
Association of Medical Research Charities   **1208**
Association of Medical School Pediatric Department Chairmen   **3185**
Association of Medical Schools in Europe   **1209**
Association of Medical Superintendents of American Institutions for Insane   7301
Association of Medical Superintendents of Mental Hospitals   5542
Association Medicale Mondiale   1546
Association Medico-Sociale Protestante de Langue Francaise   1388
Association of Mental Health Administrators   **5561**
Association of Mental Health Chaplains   7330
Association of Mental Health Clergy   **7330**
Association of Mental Health Librarians   **6978**
Association of Mental Hospital Chaplains   7330
Association of Microbiological Diagnostic Manufacturers   **5825**
Association for Microbiological Media Manufacturers   5825
Association of Military Surgeons of the U.S.   **7797**
Association of Minority Health Professions Schools   **1210**
Association Mondiale pour l'Advancement de Parasitologie Veterinaire   13115
Association Mondiale des Medecins Francophones   **1211**
Association Mondiale des Societes de Pathologie - Anatomique et Clinique   10141
Association Mondiale des Veterinaires Microbiologistes, Immunologistes et Specialistes des Maladies Infectieuses   13120
Association of Muscle Disorders   **7868**
Association de Musicotherapie du Canada   7349
Association of National, European and Mediterranean Societies of Gastroenterology   **5210**
Association Nationale des Veterinaires du Maroc   13096
Association Nationales des Dieteticiens du Luxembourg   9472
Association des Neurologues Liberaux de Langue Francaise   **8188**
Association of Neuro-Metabolic Disorders   **5271**
Association for Nordic Transplant and Dialysis Personnel   **12903**
Association of Nurses in AIDS Care   **9071**
Association of Nurses Endorsing Transplantation   **9072**
Association of Oncology Social Work   **11864**
Association of Operating Room Nurses   **9073**
Association of Operating Room Technicians   12258
Association of Opticians of the European Common Market   13567
Association of Optometric Educators   **13414**
Association of Orthopaedic Chairmen   9916
Association of Osteopathic State Executive Directors   **9994**
Association of Otolaryngology Administrators   **5562**
Association of Paediatric Anaesthetists of Great Britain and Ireland   **2356**
Association of Pakistani Physicians   **1212**
Association Pan-Africaine des Sciences Neurologiques   8296
Association for Past-Life Research and Therapies   **12666**
Association for Past-Life Research and Therapy   12666
Association of Pathology Chairmen   10126
Association of Pathology Chairs   **10126**
Association of Pediatric Oncology Nurses   **3186**
Association of Pediatric Oncology Social Workers   **3187**
Association of Pediatric Societies of the Southeast Asian Region   **3188**
Association for Persons With Severe Handicaps; TASH: The   **4563**
Association Pharmaceutique Canadienne   10592
Association of Pharmacy Proprietors   **10590**
Association of Philippine Physicians in America   **1213**
Association of Philippine Practicing Physicians in America   1213
Association for Physical and Mental Rehabilitation   12653
Association of Physician Assistant Programs   **1214**
Association of Physician Assistants in Cardiovascular Surgery   **12254**
Association of Planned Parenthood Physicians   11204
Association of Planned Parenthood Professionals   11204
Association for Play Therapy   **12667**
Association for Poetry Therapy   7453
Association of Polysomnographic Technologists   **8189**
Association for Practitioners in Infection Control   **6642**
Association of Professional Baseball Physicians   **11942**
Association of Professional Sleep Societies   8186
Association of Professors of Cardiology   **2833**
Association of Professors of Gynecology and Obstetrics   **9633**
Association of Professors of Medicine   **1215**
Association of Program Directors in Internal Medicine   **1216**
Association of Program Directors in Surgery   **12255**

Bell Association for the Deaf; Alexander Graham **3466, 3478**
Bell Association for the Deaf; Parents' Section of the Alexander Graham **3571**
Bell Research Centre; Jack • University of British Columbia **1684**
Bellamah Foundation; Dale J. **124**
Bellarmine College • Lansing School of Nursing **8710**
Bellefaire **7541**
Bellin College of Nursing **9034**
Belmont University • School of Nursing **8967**
Beltsville Human Nutrition Research Center
    Agricultural Research Service • U.S. Department of Agriculture **9531**
    Carbohydrate Nutrition Laboratory • U.S. Department of Agriculture • Agricultural Research Service **9532**
    Diet and Human Performance • U.S. Department of Agriculture • Agricultural Research Service **9533**
    Food Composition Laboratory • U.S. Department of Agriculture • Agricultural Research Service **9534**
    Lipid Nutrition Laboratory • U.S. Department of Agriculture • Agricultural Research Service **9535**
Bemis Company Foundation **603**
Ben B. Cheney Foundation **64**
Ben B. and Joyce E. Eisenberg Foundation **65**
Ben May Institute • University of Chicago **6218**
Benedictin Children; Association of **2741**
Benedum Foundation; Claude Worthington **104**
Beneficiary Studies Division • Office of Research and Demonstrations • Health Care Financing Administration • U.S. Department of Health and Human Services **5759**
Benelux Phlebology Society **2834**
Beneluxienne de Phlebologie; Societe **2834**
Benenson Foundation; Frances and Benjamin **194**
Benevolent Association of the Christian Church (Disciples of Christ); National **7457**
Benevolent Institutions; Commission on **1258**
Benign Essential Blepharospasm Research Foundation **7913, 8195**
Benjamin Franklin Literary and Medical Society **6980**
Benjamin Jacobson & Sons Foundation **604**
Benjamin and Mary Siddons Measey Foundation **66**
Benjamin and Roberta Russell Educational Foundation **6332**
Benson Agriculture and Food Institute; Ezra Taft • Brigham Young University **1562**
Benson and Edith Ford Fund **6333**
Benwood Foundation **67**
Berea College • Department of Nursing **8711**
Bereavement; SEASONS: Suicide **7505**
Bergen Community College • Respiratory Therapist Program **11454**
Berger Foundation; H. N. and Frances C. **239**
Bergstrom Foundation; Erik E. and Edith H. **11184**
Berkeley Child Welfare Research Center • University of California at Berkeley **11875**
Berkeley Laboratory; Lawrence
    Cholesterol Research Center • U.S. Department of Energy **4902**
    Environment, Health and Safety Division • U.S. Department of Energy **9821**
    Life Science Division • U.S. Department of Energy **6124**
    Research Medicine and Radiation Biophysics Division • U.S. Department of Energy **11158**
Berkshire Community College • Respiratory Therapist Program **11416**
Berkshire Medical Center • School of Anesthesia **2282**
Berman-Gund Laboratory for the Study of Retinal Degenerations • Harvard University **13600**
Bermuda Dental Association **3910**
Bernard Baruch College / Mt. Sinai School of Medicine of City University of New York • Graduate Program in Health Care Administration **5507**
Bernsen Foundation; Grace and Franklin **229**
Bernstein and Co. Foundation; Sanford C. **841**
Berry Foundation; Loren M. **360**
Berufsverband der Arzte fur Orthopadie **9934**
Berufsverband der Deutschen Radiologen und Nuklearmedizinier eV **11101**
Berufsverband der Deutschen Urologen **12902**
Berufsverband Deutscher Internisten **1480**
Berufsverband Padagogischer Psychotherapeuten **7483**
Berufsverband fur den Rettungsdienst **4742**
Besartan Beyisrael; Haagudah Lemilchama **5965**
Bessin Liver Research Center; Marion • Yeshiva University **5256**
Beta Sigma Kappa **13420**
Beth El College of Nursing **8594**
Beth Israel Hospital; General Clinical Research Center at **1590**
Bethel College [Mishawaka, IN] • Division of Nursing **8671**
Bethel College [North Newton, KS] • Department of Nursing **8701**
Bethel College [St. Paul, MN] • Department of Nursing **8772**
Bethesda Lutheran Homes and Services **4285**

Bethesda National Foundation of Massachusetts **5976**
Bethune-Cookman College • School of Nursing **8614**
Better Hearing Australia **3497**
Better Hearing Institute **3498**
Better Sleep Council **5828**
Better Sleep Council (of the International Sleep Products Association) **5828**
Better Sleep Council (of the National Association of Bedding Manufacturers) **5828**
Better Vision Institute **13421**
Bettingen Corporation; Burton G. **81**
Betz Foundation **605**
Beverage Alcohol Information Council **12046**
Beverage Information Council; Licensed **12046**
Beveridge Foundation; Frank Stanley **200**
Beverly Foundation **1891**
Beyisrael; Haagudah Lemilchama Besartan **5965**
Beyisrael; Haagudah LeSukereth Neurim **3252**
BFGoodrich Foundation **606**
BHP Petroleum Americas (HI) Foundation **607**
Biblio-Poetry Therapy; National Federation for **7464**
Bibliotheques de la Sante du Canada; Association des **6984**
Bien-Etre Familial; Association Ivoirienne de **11203**
Bien-Etre Familial; Association Rwandaise pour le **9635**
Bigelow Foundation; F. R. **176**
Biliary Association; International **5223**
Biliary Diseases Program; Liver and • Division of Digestive Diseases and Nutrition • National Institute of Diabetes and Digestive and Kidney Diseases • U.S. Department of Health and Human Services **5245**
Bill Wilkerson Center **3589**
Billy Barty Foundation **7869**
Billy Barty Foundation for Little People **7869**
Bingham Second Betterment Fund; William **543**
Bio Center; Princeton **4898**
Bioacoustics and Biocommunications Branch • Crew Systems Directorate • Air Force Materiel Command • U.S. Department of Defense **2394**
Bioanalysts; American Association of **7114**
Biochemical Genetics; Department of • City of Hope Beckman Research Institute **5320**
Biochemical Genetics Laboratory
    Baylor College of Medicine **4880**
    National Heart, Lung, and Blood Institute • U.S. Department of Health and Human Services **2944**
    National Institute of Mental Health • U.S. Department of Health and Human Services **7617**
Biochemical Genetics and Metabolism; Laboratory of • Rockefeller University **5346**
Biochemical Institute • University of Texas at Austin **2689**
Biochemical Parasitology; Laboratory for • University of Colorado **6844**
Biochemical Pharmacology; Laboratory of • National Institute of Diabetes and Digestive and Kidney Diseases • U.S. Department of Health and Human Services **2642**
Biochemical Physiology; Laboratory of • National Cancer Institute • U.S. Department of Health and Human Services **6174**
Biochemical Risk Analysis Laboratory • National Institute of Environmental Health Sciences • U.S. Department of Health and Human Services **5102**
Biochemical Society **2528**
Biochemistry Branch; Genetics and • Division of Intramural Research • National Institute of Diabetes and Digestive and Kidney Diseases • U.S. Department of Health and Human Services **5364**
Biochemistry Department; Radiation • Armed Forces Radiobiology Research Institute • U.S. Department of Defense **11079**
Biochemistry Division
    Environmental Pathology Department • Armed Forces Institute of Pathology • U.S. Department of Defense **10165**
    Walter Reed Army Institute of Research • Army Medical Research and Development Command • U.S. Department of Defense **7829**
Biochemistry Facility; University • Kansas State University **2584**
Biochemistry Laboratory
    Kresge Hearing Research Institute • University of Michigan **3643**
    National Cancer Institute • U.S. Department of Health and Human Services **6175**
    National Heart, Lung, and Blood Institute • U.S. Department of Health and Human Services **2945**
    University of Michigan **4032**
Biochemistry; Laboratory for Comparative **2585**
Biochemistry Laboratory; General and Comparative • National Institute of Mental Health • U.S. Department of Health and Human Services **7633**
Biochemistry Laboratory; Nutrition • University of Pittsburgh **5196**
Biochemistry; Latin American Confederation of Clinical **2540**
Biochemistry and Metabolism; Laboratory of • National Institute of Diabetes and Digestive and Kidney Diseases • U.S. Department of Health and Human Services **2643**

Biochemistry and Molecular Biology Laboratory
  Columbia University **13583**
  Texas Southern University **5356**
Biochemistry and Molecular Biophysics Program • Columbia University **2566**
Biochemistry Program • State University of New York College at Plattsburgh **2625**
Biochemistry Research Unit • Western Human Nutrition Research Center • Agricultural Research Service • U.S. Department of Agriculture **9541**
BioChemists; International Association of Clinical **7140**
Biocognitive Studies; Center for • Yale University **7703**
Biocommunication Research Laboratory • University of Alabama at Birmingham **3632**
Biocommunications Branch; Bioacoustics and • Crew Systems Directorate • Air Force Materiel Command • U.S. Department of Defense **2394**
Biocommunications Division; Biodynamics and • Crew Systems Directorate • Air Force Materiel Command • U.S. Department of Defense **2395**
Biocommunications Societies; Federation of **6987**
Biodynamics and Biocommunications Division • Crew Systems Directorate • Air Force Materiel Command • U.S. Department of Defense **2395**
Biodynamics Laboratory • University of Wisconsin—Madison **2983**
Biodynamics Laboratory; Naval • Naval Medical Research and Development Command • U.S. Department of Defense **7838**
Bioelectrical Repair and Growth Society **2547**
Bioelectrical Sciences Laboratory • University of Michigan **2489**
Bio-Electro-Magnetics Institute **2529**
Bioenergetic Analysis; International Institute for **2216**
Bioenergetics Laboratory; Human • Boston University **11958**
Bioenergetics Research Unit • Western Human Nutrition Research Center • Agricultural Research Service • U.S. Department of Agriculture **9542**
Bioengineering and Aiding Persons with Disabilities Program • Division of Bioengineering and Environmental Systems • Directorate for Engineering • National Science Foundation **2458**
Bioengineering Center
  Georgia Institute of Technology **2445**
  University of Washington **2501**
  Wayne State University **2506**
Bioengineering Center; Applied • Worcester Polytechnic Institute **2508**
Bioengineering; Department of • Orthopaedic Institute **9944**
Bioengineering Laboratory • University of Michigan **2490**
Bioengineering Research Institute • Rice University **2468**
Bioenvironmental Research; Center for **5063**
Bioethics; Center for **7196**
Bioethics; Center for the Study of • Medical College of Wisconsin **7209**
Bioethics Education Laboratory; Human Genetics and • Ball State University **5309**
Bioethics Program; Asian / International • Center for Bioethics • Georgetown University **7201**
Biofeedback; Association for Applied Psychophysiology and **2419**
Biofeedback Research Society **2419**
Biofeedback Society of America **2419**
Biogenic Institutes of America **2166**
Biogerontology Research; Institute for **1946**
Bioglass Research Center • University of Florida **2482**
Bioinformatics; Welch Laboratory for Applied • Johns Hopkins University **7016**
Biokinetics Research Laboratory • Temple University **11977**
Biola University • Department of Baccalaureate Nursing **8571**
Biologic Research Center; Schizophrenic • Mount Sinai School of Medicine of City University of New York **7585**
Biological Anthropology; Laboratory of • University of Kansas **2674**
Biological Carcinogenesis Program • Division of Cancer Etiology • National Cancer Institute • U.S. Department of Health and Human Services **6138**
Biological Chemistry; Laboratory of • National Cancer Institute • U.S. Department of Health and Human Services **6176**
Biological and Computational Learning; Center for • Massachusetts Institute of Technology **8390**
Biological Engineering; American Institute for Medical and **2416**
Biological Imaging; Crump Institute for • University of California, Los Angeles **2477**
Biological Interactions Between Environment and Health; Centre for Study of • University of Quebec at Montreal **9861**
Biological Macromolecules; Center for • University at Albany, State University of New York **2659**
Biological and Medical Sciences; Institute of **2555**
Biological Photographic Association **6981**
Biological Psychiatry Branch • Intramural Research Programs Division (Clinical Research) • National Institute of Mental Health • U.S. Department of Health and Human Services **7635**
Biological Psychiatry; Society of **7511**
Biological Psychiatry; World Federation of the Societies of **2548**
Biological Research; Bureau of • Rutgers University **2613**

Biological Research; California Institute of **5315**
Biological Research Division; Intramural Clinical and • National Institute on Alcohol Abuse and Alcoholism • U.S. Department of Health and Human Services **12111**
Biological Research; EM Core Facility for • University of Chicago **2667**
Biological Resources Branch • Division of Cancer Treatment • National Cancer Institute • U.S. Department of Health and Human Services **6150**
Biological Response Modifiers Program • Division of Cancer Treatment • National Cancer Institute • U.S. Department of Health and Human Services **6151**
Biological Stain Commission **2530**
Biological Stains; Commission on Standardization of **2530**
Biological Standardization; International Association of **5860**
Biological Studies; Salk Institute for **2618**
Biological Timing; Center for • University of Virginia **4944**
Biologics Evaluation and Research; Center for • Food and Drug Administration • U.S. Department of Health and Human Services **10898, 10993**
Biologie de l'Environnement; Association Internationale de Medecine et de **5041**
Biologique; Association Internationale de Standardisation **5860**
Biology of Addictive Diseases; Laboratory of • Rockefeller University **12100**
Biology of Aging Program • National Institute on Aging • U.S. Department of Health and Human Services **1950**
Biology; American Institute of Oral **3896**
Biology; Armand Hammer Center for Cancer **6000**
Biology / Biomaterials Interface; Center for the Enhancement of the • University of Texas Health Science Center at San Antonio **2694**
Biology Branch • Biology of Aging Program • National Institute on Aging • U.S. Department of Health and Human Services **1951**
Biology Branch; Applied • Biomedical and Behavioral Science Division • National Institute for Occupational Safety and Health • U.S. Department of Health and Human Services **9827**
Biology Branch; Cancer • Division of Cancer Biology, Diagnosis, and Centers Extramural Research Program • National Cancer Institute • U.S. Department of Health and Human Services **6136**
Biology Branch; Cell and Developmental • Division of Lung Diseases • National Heart, Lung, and Blood Institute • U.S. Department of Health and Human Services **11616**
Biology; Brookdale Center for Molecular • Mount Sinai School of Medicine of City University of New York **2594**
Biology; Center for Advanced Training in Cell and Molecular • Catholic University of America **2560**
Biology; Center for Cancer • Texas A&M University **6120**
Biology; Center for Craniofacial Molecular • University of Southern California **4046**
Biology Center; Developmental
  Case Western Reserve University **2559**
  University of California, Irvine **2661**
Biology; Center for Environmental Medicine and Lung • University of North Carolina at Chapel Hill **5126**
Biology; Center for Extracellular Matrix • Texas A&M University **2627**
Biology; Center for Transplantation • University of Florida **12890**
Biology Council; Human **1322**
Biology; Department of Molecular • Princeton University **2609**
Biology, Diagnosis, and Centers; Division of Cancer • National Cancer Institute • U.S. Department of Health and Human Services **6128**
Biology; Division of
  City of Hope Beckman Research Institute **2564**
  Environmental, Life, and Social Sciences Directorate • Oak Ridge National Laboratory • U.S. Department of Energy **2635**
Biology; Division of Human • Fels Research Institute • Wright State University **1753**
Biology of Environment; International Association of Medicine and **5041**
Biology; European Federation of Societies of Ultrasound in Medicine and **11111**
Biology; Federation of American Societies for Experimental • Life Sciences Research Office **2574**
Biology; Fels Institute for Cancer Research and Molecular • Temple University **6119**
Biology and Genetics; Laboratory of Cell • National Institute of Diabetes and Digestive and Kidney Diseases • U.S. Department of Health and Human Services **4925**
Biology, Genetics and Teratology Branch; Developmental • Center for Research for Mothers and Children • National Institute of Child Health and Human Development • U.S. Department of Health and Human Services **5358**
Biology Group of the International Association for Dental Research; Craniofacial **3919**
Biology and Immunology; Center for Advanced Molecular • State University of New York at Buffalo **2726**
Biology; Institute of Applied **12747**
Biology; Institute of Arctic • University of Alaska Fairbanks **1682**

Biology Institute; Medical **2591**

Biology; Institute of Reproductive • University of Texas at Austin **11724**

Biology; International Conference on Mechanics in Medicine and **2423**

Biology; International Society of Cranio-Facial **3919**

Biology; Laboratory of • National Cancer Institute • U.S. Department of Health and Human Services **6177**

Biology Laboratory; Biochemistry and Molecular
 Columbia University **13583**
 Texas Southern University **5356**

Biology; Laboratory of Cancer • New England Deaconess Hospital **6083**

Biology; Laboratory of Cell
 National Heart, Lung, and Blood Institute • U.S. Department of Health and Human Services **2948**
 National Institute of Mental Health • U.S. Department of Health and Human Services **7618**

Biology; Laboratory for Cell and Molecular • Harvard University **2579**

Biology; Laboratory of Cellular and Developmental • National Institute of Diabetes and Digestive and Kidney Diseases • U.S. Department of Health and Human Services **2645**

Biology; Laboratory of Cellular and Molecular
 National Cancer Institute • U.S. Department of Health and Human Services **6180**
 National Institute on Aging • U.S. Department of Health and Human Services **1959**

Biology; Laboratory of Chemical • National Institute of Diabetes and Digestive and Kidney Diseases • U.S. Department of Health and Human Services **2646**

Biology; Laboratory of Developmental
 National Institute of Dental Research • U.S. Department of Health and Human Services **2641**
 University of Southern California **2686**

Biology Laboratory; Diagnostic Molecular • Brigham and Women's Hospital **2556**

Biology; Laboratory of GI Tumor • Memorial Sloan-Kettering Cancer Center **6075**

Biology; Laboratory of Mathematical • National Cancer Institute • U.S. Department of Health and Human Services **6190**

Biology; Laboratory of Molecular
 Division of Intramural Research • National Institute on Deafness and Other Communication Disorders • U.S. Department of Health and Human Services **3628**
 National Cancer Institute • U.S. Department of Health and Human Services **6192**
 National Institute of Diabetes and Digestive and Kidney Diseases • U.S. Department of Health and Human Services **2648**
 National Institute of Mental Health • U.S. Department of Health and Human Services **7643**
 National Institute of Neurological Disorders and Stroke • U.S. Department of Health and Human Services **8460**
 University of Illinois at Chicago **2671**
 University of Michigan **2677**

Biology; Laboratory of Molecular and Cellular • National Institute of Diabetes and Digestive and Kidney Diseases • U.S. Department of Health and Human Services **2649**

Biology; Laboratory of Molecular and Developmental • National Eye Institute • U.S. Department of Health and Human Services **13641**

Biology; Laboratory of Physical • National Institute of Arthritis and Musculoskeletal and Skin Diseases • U.S. Department of Health and Human Services **7942**

Biology; Laboratory of Retinal Cell and Molecular • National Eye Institute • U.S. Department of Health and Human Services **13642**

Biology; Laboratory of Theoretical and Physical • National Institute of Child Health and Human Development • U.S. Department of Health and Human Services **2639**

Biology; Laboratory of Tumor Cell • National Cancer Institute • U.S. Department of Health and Human Services **6199**

Biology; Laboratory of Tumor Immunology and • National Cancer Institute • U.S. Department of Health and Human Services **6200**

Biology; Laboratory of Tumor Virus • National Cancer Institute • U.S. Department of Health and Human Services **6201**

Biology Laboratory; Veterinary Molecular • Montana State University-Bozeman **13148**

Biology of Leukocytes; Laboratory of Cell and Molecular • Duke University **2569**

Biology and Medicine; Society for Experimental **2545**

Biology and Medicine; Society for Physical Regulation in **2547**

Biology and Metabolism Branch; Cell • Intramural Research Program • National Institute of Child Health and Human Development • U.S. Department of Health and Human Services **2637**

Biology and Molecular Medicine; UCLA-DOE Laboratory of Structural • University of California, Los Angeles **2663**

Biology of Natural Systems; Center for the • Queens College of City University of New York **5084**

Biology of Oral Diseases; Center for Molecular • University of Illinois at Chicago **4027**

Biology Organization; European Cell **2532**

Biology Program; Genetics and Developmental • West Virginia University **2706**

Biology Program; Immune Cell • Naval Medical Research Institute • Naval Medical Research and Development Command • U.S. Department of Defense **7849**

Biology Program; Molecular and Cell • University of Texas at Dallas **2692**

Biology Program; Muscle • Extramural Activities Program • National Institute of Arthritis and Musculoskeletal and Skin Diseases • U.S. Department of Health and Human Services **7938**

Biology; Research Center of Excellence in Cell and Molecular • Meharry Medical College **2593**

Biology Research Center; Harvard Cutaneous • Massachusetts General Hospital **4265**

Biology; Research Center in Oral
 University of Alabama at Birmingham **4024**
 University of Pennsylvania **4043**
 University of Washington **4047**

Biology Research Centre; Molecular • Sherbrooke University **5348**

Biology Research Group; Actinomycete • Sherbrooke University **6788**

Biology Research Laboratory; Cancer • Stanford University **6113**

Biology Research Program; Cardiovascular • Oklahoma Medical Research Foundation **2917**

Biology (A Reticuloendothelial Society); Society for Leukocyte **2090**

Biology Sciences; Cecil H. and Ida Green Center for Reproductive • University of Texas Southwestern Medical Center at Dallas **11299**

Biology Section; Viruses and Cellular • Intramural Research Program • National Institute of Child Health and Human Development • U.S. Department of Health and Human Services **2638**

Biology Society; IEEE Engineering in Medicine and **2421**

Biology; Society for InVitro **2546**

Biology; W.M. Keck Center for Computational **2703**

Biology; Wistar Institute of Anatomy and **2708**

Biology; Worcester Foundation for Experimental **2709**
 Cancer Center **2710**
 Male Fertility Program **2711**

Biomaterials Interface; Center for the Enhancement of the Biology / • University of Texas Health Science Center at San Antonio **2694**

Biomaterials Laboratory • Tulane University **2473**

Biomaterials; Organizing Committee of the World Congress on Implantology and **3982**

Biomaterials Research Center • University of Michigan **4033**

Biomaterials; Research Group in Biomechanics and • Polytechnical School of Montreal **2463**

Biomaterials; Society for **2432**

Biomateriaux; Comite d'Organisation du Congress Mondial d' Implantologie des **3982**

Biomathematics Branch; Statistics and • National Institute of Environmental Health Sciences • U.S. Department of Health and Human Services **5112**

Biomechanics and Biomaterials; Research Group in • Polytechnical School of Montreal **2463**

Biomechanics; European Society of **2533**

Biomechanics and Human Rehabilitation; Eric P. and Evelyn E. Newman Laboratory for • Massachusetts Institute of Technology **2453**

Biomechanics Institute, Inc. **2552**

Biomechanics Laboratory
 Georgia Institute of Technology **2446**
 Pennsylvania State University **11974**

Biomechanics Laboratory; Gurdjian-Lissner • Wayne State University **2507**

Biomechanics Laboratory; Orthopaedic **9943**

Biomechanics Research Laboratory of Illinois • University of Illinois at Urbana-Champaign **11984**

Biomechanics Research Unit **9946**

Biomechanics Studies and Research; Center for • University of Cincinnati **2729**

Biomedical and Behavioral Science Division • National Institute for Occupational Safety and Health • U.S. Department of Health and Human Services **9826**

Biomedical and Behavioral Sciences Branch • Medical Specialties Division • Federal Aviation Administration • U.S. Department of Transportation **2411**

Biomedical Center; Marine • Duke University **2570**

Biomedical Climatology; American Institute of **5034**

Biomedical Communication Directors; Association of **6976**

Biomedical Communications Associations; Council for **6987**

Biomedical Communications; Lister Hill National Center for
 Audiovisual Program Development Branch • U.S. Department of Health and Human Services • National Institutes of Health **7030**
 Communications Engineering Branch • U.S. Department of Health and Human Services • National Institutes of Health **7031**

Computer Science Branch • U.S. Department of Health and Human Services • National Institutes of Health **7032**

Educational Technology Branch • U.S. Department of Health and Human Services • National Institutes of Health **7033**

Information Technology Branch • U.S. Department of Health and Human Services • National Institutes of Health **7034**

National Institutes of Health • U.S. Department of Health and Human Services **7029**

Biomedical Computer Laboratory • Washington University **2504**

Biomedical Computing; Institute for • Washington University **2505**

Biomedical Computing; Special Interest Group on **2433**

Biomedical Engineering; Center for

New Jersey Institute of Technology **2460**

Ohio State University **2462**

University of Florida **2483**

University of New Hampshire **2494**

Biomedical Engineering; Center for Rehabilitation Science and • Louisiana Tech University **2452**

Biomedical Engineering Center; William A. Hillenbrand • Purdue University **2466**

Biomedical Engineering; Clinical / • University of Arizona **2476**

Biomedical Engineering; Department of • University of Virginia **2500**

Biomedical Engineering; Graduate Center for • University of Kentucky **2487**

Biomedical Engineering; Institute for

University of California, San Diego **2479**

University of Montreal **2493**

University of Utah **2499**

Biomedical Engineering; Joint Program in • University of Texas Southwestern Medical Center at Dallas **2496**

Biomedical Engineering Laboratories • Arizona State University **2434**

Biomedical Engineering Program

Carnegie Mellon University **2437**

Iowa State University of Science and Technology **2450**

University of Texas at Austin **2495**

Biomedical Engineering Research; Institute for • University of Akron **2474**

Biomedical Engineering and Science Institute • Drexel University **2441**

Biomedical Engineering Society **2420**

Biomedical and Environmental Sciences; Laboratory of • University of California, Los Angeles **1687**

Biomedical and Environmental Sciences; Marine • Medical University of South Carolina **2592**

Biomedical Equipment Technicians; National Society of **2543**

Biomedical Equipment Technicians; Society of **2543, 2543**

Biomedical Ethics; Center for

Case Western Reserve University **7194**

Stanford University **7216**

University of Minnesota **5654**

Biomedical Imaging Computer Resource; Mayo **2454**

Biomedical Imaging Resource; Mayo **2454**

Bionic Informatics Association **6982**

Biomedical Information Communication Center • Oregon Health Sciences University **7019**

Biomedical Institute; Marine • University of Texas Medical Branch at Galveston **2695**

Biomedical Modeling Research Group • University of Montreal **2492**

Biomedical Problems; National ESCA and Surface Analysis Center for • University of Washington **2502**

Biomedical Research on Alcoholism; International Society for **12044**

Biomedical Research Branch

Basic Research Division

National Institute on Alcohol Abuse and Alcoholism • U.S. Department of Health and Human Services **12105**

National Institute on Drug Abuse • U.S. Department of Health and Human Services **12123**

Biomedical Research; Center for **11262**

University of Kansas **2673**

Biomedical Research Center; Laser • Massachusetts Institute of Technology **11151**

Biomedical Research Center; Pacific • University of Hawaii at Manoa **2669**

Biomedical Research; Foundation for **2535**

Biomedical Research Foundation; National **2596**

Biomedical Research Foundation of Northwest Louisiana **2553**

Biomedical Research Group; Marine • University of New Hampshire **2681**

Biomedical Research Institute **6763**

Milwaukee School of Engineering **2456**

University of Texas at Austin **2691**

Biomedical Research; Institute for Biophysical and **2582**

Biomedical Research Institute; Boston **2555**

Biomedical Research Institute; Pearlman **2606**

Biomedical Research Institute; Philadelphia **2607**

Biomedical Research Institute; Seattle **6787**

Biomedical Research Institute; Southwest **5349**

Biomedical Research Institute; Space • Lyndon B. Johnson Space Center • National Aeronautics and Space Administration **2391**

Biomedical Research Laboratories; U.S.-Japan • Tulane University **4901**

Biomedical Research; National Association for **2541**

Biomedical Research; Southwest Foundation for **2624**

Biomedical Research Support Program; Minority • National Institute of General Medical Sciences • U.S. Department of Health and Human Services **2654**

Biomedical Research; Vollum Institute for Advanced • Oregon Health Sciences University **2602**

Biomedical Research; Webb-Waring Institute for **2705**

Biomedical Research; Whitehead Institute for **2707**

Biomedical Sciences Center; Marine / Freshwater

Oregon State University **10450**

University of Miami **10477**

University of Wisconsin—Milwaukee **2700**

Biomedical Sciences; McLaughlin Research Institute for **2590**

Biomedical Sensor Technology; Resource for • Case Western Reserve University **2440**

Biomedical Technology Center **2716**

Biomedical Technology Research Center; Emory- Georgia Tech **2444**

Biomedical Toxicological Research and Hazardous Waste Management; Center for • Florida State University **10432**

Biomedical Ultrasound; Rochester Center for • University of Rochester **11174**

Biomedical Visualization Laboratory • University of Illinois at Chicago **2670**

Biomembrane Institute • University of Washington **2699**

Biometric Research Branch • Division of Cancer Treatment • National Cancer Institute • U.S. Department of Health and Human Services **6152**

Biometric Research; Coordinating Centers for • University of Minnesota **7038**

Biometrics Unit • Division of Viral and Rickettsial Diseases • National Center for Infectious Diseases • U.S. Department of Health and Human Services **6807**

Biometry Branch; Epidemiology and • Division of Microbiology and Infectious Diseases • National Institute of Allergy and Infectious Diseases • U.S. Department of Health and Human Services **6828**

Biometry and Epidemiology Division • National Institute on Alcohol Abuse and Alcoholism • U.S. Department of Health and Human Services **12108**

Biometry Facility; Medical Biostatistics/ • University of Vermont **7039**

Biometry and Field Studies Branch • National Institute of Neurological Disorders and Stroke • U.S. Department of Health and Human Services **8442**

Biometry Program; Epidemiology and • Division of Epidemiology and Clinical Applications • National Heart, Lung, and Blood Institute • U.S. Department of Health and Human Services **2932**

Biometry Program; Epidemiology, Demography, and • National Institute on Aging • U.S. Department of Health and Human Services **1953**

Biomolecular Nuclear Magnetic Resonance, Structure, and Design; Center for • Purdue University **2465**

Bionic Rehabilitative Psychology; American Board of **7286**

Bioorganic Chemistry; Laboratory of • National Institute of Diabetes and Digestive and Kidney Diseases • U.S. Department of Health and Human Services **2644**

Biophysical and Biomedical Research; Institute for **2582**

Biophysical Chemistry; Laboratory of • National Heart, Lung, and Blood Institute • U.S. Department of Health and Human Services **2946**

Biophysical Research Division; Medical Applications and • Office of Health and Environmental Research • U.S. Department of Energy **5093**

Biophysics Division; Research Medicine and Radiation • Lawrence Berkeley Laboratory • U.S. Department of Energy **11158**

Biophysics; Laboratory of Molecular

National Institute of Environmental Health Sciences • U.S. Department of Health and Human Services **5107**

University of Alabama at Birmingham **2658**

Biophysics Laboratory; Neurophysiology and • Kresge Hearing Research Institute • University of Michigan **3647**

Biophysics and Physiological Sciences Program • National Institute of General Medical Sciences • U.S. Department of Health and Human Services **2650**

Biophysics Program; Biochemistry and Molecular • Columbia University **2566**

Biophysics Research Institute • Medical College of Wisconsin **11152**

Biophysics Section • National Institute of Neurological Disorders and Stroke • U.S. Department of Health and Human Services **8443**

Biopolymers at Interfaces; Center for • University of Utah **2497**

Biopsychological Studies of Color, Light, Radiation, and Health; Institute for • San Jose State University **11074**

Bioquimica Clinica; Confederacion Latinoamericana de **2540**

Bioregulation Research Group; Hormonal • Medical Research Centre • Laval University **4893**

Biosciences Center; Higuchi • University of Kansas **10473**

Biosciences & Technology; Institute of • Texas A&M University **2629**

Blind and Physically Handicapped; National Library Service for the • U.S. Library of Congress **6909**
Blind; Protestant Guild for the 13557
Blind; Recording for the **13558**
Blind; Rehabilitation Services for the • Family Services Division • Missouri Department of Social Services **13690**
Blind Relief War Fund; Permanent 13466
Blind and Retarded; Association for Advancement of **4280**
Blind Scotland; Royal National Institute for the **13560**
Blind Service Association **13424**
Blind Services • Rhode Island Department of Human Services **13705**
Blind Services Bureau
    Illinois Department of Rehabilitation Services **13678**
    Rehabilitation Division • Nevada Department of Employment Training and Rehabilitation **13693**
Blind Services Division
    Arkansas Department of Human Services **13668**
    Florida Department of Education **13674**
    North Carolina Department of Human Resources **13698**
Blind Services Division; Vocational Rehabilitation and • Hawaii Department of Human Services **12781, 13676**
Blind Services Office • Vocational Rehabilitation Division • Maryland Department of Education **13685**
Blind; Sight Savers— Royal Commonwealth Society for the [Haywards Heath, England] **13561**
Blind; Sight Savers— Royal Commonwealth Society for the [Nairobi, Kenya] **13562**
Blind Skiing Foundation; American **13390**
Blind; South Carolina Commission for the **13706**
Blind Sports Association; International **13482**
Blind Students; National Alliance of **13522**
Blind; Tanzania Society for the **13565**
Blind; Taping for the **13566**
Blind Teachers; National Association of **13523**
Blind; Texas Commission for the **13709**
Blind Union; European **13447**
Blind Union; Latin American [Buenos Aires, Argentina] **13513**
Blind Union; Latin American [Montevideo, Uruguay] **13514**
Blind Union; World **13579**
Blind and Visually Handicapped Commission • New York State Department of Social Services **13697**
Blind and Visually Handicapped; National Accreditation Council for Agencies Serving the **13521**
Blind and Visually Impaired; Association for Education and Rehabilitation of the **13412**
Blind and Visually Impaired Division
    Rehabilitation Services Office • Maine Department of Education **13684**
    Social and Rehabilitation Services Department • Vermont Agency of Human Services **13711**
Blind and Visually Impaired Division; Services to the • South Dakota Department of Human Services **13707**
Blind and Visually Impaired; Idaho Commission for the **13677**
Blind; Washington Department of Services for the **13714**
Blind; Welfare of the **13363, 13578**
Blind; Xavier Society for the **13580**
Blind Youth; International Conference of Educators of 13483
Blind Youths and Adults; Helen Keller National Center for Deaf- **13476**
Blinded American Veterans Foundation **13425**
Blinded Veterans Association **13426**
Blindenmission; Christoffel **13436**
Blindnes America; Prevent • Ohio Affiliate **13784**
Blindness America; Prevent **13556**
    Connecticut Affiliate **13773**
    Florida Affiliate **13774**
    Georgia Affiliate **13775**
    Indiana Affiliate **13776**
    Iowa Affiliate **13777**
    Kentucky Affiliate **13778**
    Massachusetts Affiliate **13779**
    Nebraska Affiliate **13780**
    New Jersey Affiliate **13781**
    New York Division **13782**
    North Carolina Affiliate **13783**
    Northern California Affiliate **13771**
    Oklahoma Affiliate **13785**
    Puerto Rico Affiliate **13786**
    Rhode Island Affiliate **13787**
    Southern California Division **13772**
    Tennessee Affiliate **13788**
    Texas Affiliate **13789**
    Utah Affiliate **13790**

    Virginia Affiliate **13791**
    Wisconsin Affiliate **13792**
Blindness; The Foundation Fighting **13360, 13456**
Blindness; International Agency for the Prevention of **13479**
Blindness and Low Vision; Rehabilitation Research and Training Center on • Mississippi State University **13617**
Blindness; National Committee for the Prevention of 13556
Blindness; National Society to Prevent 13556
Blindness; National Society for the Prevention of 13556
Blindness; Research to Prevent **13362**
Blindness; RP Foundation Fighting 13456
Blindness and Visual Services Bureau • Pennsylvania Department of Public Welfare **13703**
Bloch Cancer Foundation; R. A. **5982**
Block Foundation; H & R **718**
Blood Banks; American Association of **7115**
Blood-Brain Barrier Laboratory • Johns Hopkins University **8381**
Blood CARE **2554**
Blood Center of Southeastern Wisconsin **6002, 7112**
Blood Centers; Council of Community **7132**
Blood Club; National Rare **7148**
Blood Diseases; Herbert L. Orlowitz Institute for Cancer and 6053
Blood Diseases; Institute for Cancer and **6053**
Blood Diseases and Resources; Division of • National Heart, Lung, and Blood Institute • U.S. Department of Health and Human Services **6203**
Blood Disorders; Center for Cancer and • Albany Medical College **5996**
Blood Disorders; Children's Center for Cancer and **6021**
Blood Donor Organizations; International Federation of **7139**
Blood Flow Laboratories; Cerebral **8350**
Blood Foundation; Children's **3204**
Blood Institute; National Heart, Lung, and
    Division of Blood Diseases and Resources • U.S. Department of Health and Human Services **6203**
    Division of Epidemiology and Clinical Applications
        Clinical Applications and Prevention Program • U.S. Department of Health and Human Services **2931**
        Epidemiology and Biometry Program • U.S. Department of Health and Human Services **2932**
        U.S. Department of Health and Human Services **2930**
    Division of Heart and Vascular Diseases
        Arteriosclerosis, Hypertension, and Lipid Metabolism Program • U.S. Department of Health and Human Services **2934**
        Cardiac Functions Branch • U.S. Department of Health and Human Services **2935**
        Cardiology Program • U.S. Department of Health and Human Services **2936**
        Devices and Technology Branch • U.S. Department of Health and Human Services **2937**
        Research Training and Development Branch • U.S. Department of Health and Human Services **2938**
        U.S. Department of Health and Human Services **2933**
    Division of Intramural Research
        Cardiology Branch • U.S. Department of Health and Human Services **2940**
        Hematology Branch • U.S. Department of Health and Human Services **6204**
        Hypertension-Endocrine Branch • U.S. Department of Health and Human Services **2941**
        Laboratory of Molecular Hematology • U.S. Department of Health and Human Services **6205**
        Molecular Disease Branch • U.S. Department of Health and Human Services **2942**
        Pathology Branch • U.S. Department of Health and Human Services **2943**
        Pulmonary Branch • U.S. Department of Health and Human Services **11613**
        U.S. Department of Health and Human Services **2939**
    Division of Lung Diseases
        Cell and Developmental Biology Branch • U.S. Department of Health and Human Services **11616**
        Interstitial Lung Diseases Branch • U.S. Department of Health and Human Services **11617**
        Prevention, Education, and Research Training Branch • U.S. Department of Health and Human Services **11618**
        U.S. Department of Health and Human Services **11614**
    Laboratory of Biochemical Genetics • U.S. Department of Health and Human Services **2944**
    Laboratory of Biochemistry • U.S. Department of Health and Human Services **2945**
    Laboratory of Biophysical Chemistry • U.S. Department of Health and Human Services **2946**
    Laboratory of Cardiac Energetics • U.S. Department of Health and Human Services **2947**

Brown University
    Center for Alcohol and Addiction Studies **12089**
    Center for Gerontology and Health Care Research **1926**
    Center for Neural Sciences **8345**
    Child Study Center **3313**
    Division of Biology and Medicine • Molecular and Biochemical Pharmacology Section **10348**
    International Health Institute **2557**
    School of Medicine **1029**
Broyhill Family Foundation **77**
Broyhill Foundation **77**
Bruce McMillan, Jr. Foundation **5891**
Brucellosis Research Unit • National Animal Disease Center • Agricultural Research Service • U.S. Department of Agriculture **13195**
Bruening Foundation; Eva L. and Joseph M. **174**
Brunswick Foundation **616**
Brush Cancer Research Institute; Geraldine **6042**
Bryan Family Foundation; Kathleen Price and Joseph M. **341**
Bryan Memorial Hospital / University of Kansas • School of Anesthesia **2295**
Bryant Cancer Center; Natalie Warren **6081**
Bryn Mawr College
    Child Study Institute **3314**
    Graduate School of Social Work and Social Research **11837**
Bryn Mawr Hospital; West Chester University / • Respiratory Therapist Program **11520**
BT Foundation **6393**
Buchanan Family Foundation **6334**
Bucknell University • Immunobiology Research Laboratory **2095**
Bucks, Chester, Delaware and Montgomery Counties; Easter Seal Society of Philadelphia, **4666**
Bucyrus-Erie Foundation **617**
Buehler Foundation; A. C. **1869**
Buell Foundation; Temple Hoyne **513**
Buffett Foundation **11181**
Bugher Foundation **2782**
Buiatrics; World Association for **13116**
Buiatrik; Welt-Gesellschaft fur **13116**
Bulgarian Dermatological Society **4222**
Bulgarian Society of Immunology **2069**
Bulimia Association; American Anorexia / **7269**
Bulimia; Center for the Study of Anorexia and **7551**
Bunbury Company **78**
Bund Freiberuflicher Hebammen Deutschlands eV **9690**
Bundestierarzte Kammer eV **13073**
Bundesverband der Deutschen Zahnarzte **3941**
Bundesverband Deutscher Apotheker **10609**
Bundesverband der Pneumologen **11602**
Bundesverband Praktischer Tierarzte **13094**
Bundesverband der Zahnarzte des Offentlichen Gesundheitsdienstes **3968**
Bundesvereinigung Lebenshilfe fur Geistig Behinderte **4296**
Bundeszahnarziekammer **3941**
Bundle Branch Block Association; International **2856**
Burden Foundation; Florence V. **184**
Burdine Johnson Foundation **11182**
Bureau of Animal Industry Veterinarians **13093**
Bureau of Biological Research • Rutgers University **2613**
Bureau Central pour le SIDA **6624**
Bureau of Child Research • University of Kansas **4329**
Bureau des Formations Medicales Agrees au Rwanda **1295**
Bureau of Health Professions • Health Resources and Services Administration • Public Health Service • U.S. Department of Health and Human Services **9**
Bureau of Health Standards and Quality • Health Care Financing Administration • U.S. Department of Health and Human Services **5711**
Bureau International pour l'Epilepsie **8236**
Bureau for the Jewish Aged; Central **1905**
Bureau of Maternal and Child Health • Health Resources and Services Administration • Public Health Service • U.S. Department of Health and Human Services **3131**
Bureau of Medicine and Surgery • Chief of Naval Operations • Department of the Navy • U.S. Department of Defense **7787**
Bureau of Professional Education of the American Osteopathic Association **9997**
Bureau of Program Operations • Health Care Financing Administration • U.S. Department of Health and Human Services **5712**
Burger King Cancer Caring Center **5929**
Burke Medical Research Institute; Winifred Masterson • Dementia Research Service • Cornell University **8359**
Burlington Industries Foundation **6394**
Burn Association; American **2766, 2767**
Burn Association; Israeli **2771**

Burn Center • University of Michigan **2780**
Burn Injuries; International Society for **2770**
Burn Medicine; Institute for **2773**
Burn Medicine; National Institute for **2773, 2776**
Burn Research Corporation; American **2773**
Burn and Shock Trauma Institute • Loyola University Chicago **4763**
Burn Survivors; Phoenix Society for **2774**
Burn Trauma Center **2775**
Burn Victim Foundation; National **2772**
Burnett Co. Charitable Foundation; Leo **757**
Burnett-Tandy Foundation **79**
Burns Foundation; Fritz B. **6351**
Burns Institute; Shriners [Galveston, TX] **2777**
Burns Institute; Shriners • University of Cincinnati **2779**
Burns Institutes; Shriners [Boston, MA] **2778**
Burns School of Medicine; John A.
    Department of Pharmacology • University of Hawaii at Manoa **10224**
    University of Hawaii at Manoa **948**
Burns United Support Groups **2768**
Burton D. Morgan Foundation **80**
Burton G. Bettingen Corporation **81**
Burzynski Research Institute **6007**
Bush Charitable Foundation; Edyth **161**
Bush Foundation **82**
Bushland U.S. Livestock Insects Laboratory; Knipling-
    Agricultural Research Service • U.S. Department of Agriculture **13187**
    Cattle Fever Tick Research Laboratory • U.S. Department of Agriculture • Agricultural Research Service **13188**
Business Administrators; American Society of Mental Health **5561**
Business; Association for Fitness in **10844**
Business Communications Council; Health Industry **5852**
Business Consultants; Institute of Certified Professional **5859**
Business and Industry; American Association of Fitness Directors in **10844**
Business Innovation Research Program; Small • National Institute of Neurological Disorders and Stroke • U.S. Department of Health and Human Services **8471**
Business Management Association; Radiology **5601**
Business Managers Association; Radiologists **5601**
Business Men's Research Foundation; American **12002, 12087**
Business Regulation Administration • District of Columbia Department of Consumer and Regulatory Affairs **5136**
Butler Foundation; J.E. and Z.B. **296**
Butler University
    College of Pharmacy **10517**
    Graduate Pharmacology Program **10235**
Butte Community College • Respiratory Therapist Program **11315**

C

C. G. Jung Foundation for Analytical Psychology **7348**
C.G. Jung Institute of Chicago **7240**
C.G. Jung Institute of Los Angeles **7237**
C.G. Jung Institute of New York **7244**
C. Henry Kempe National Center for the Prevention and Treatment of Child Abuse and Neglect • University of Colorado **3073**
C.M. Hincks Institute **3315**
C. R. Bard Foundation **618**
C.S. Mott Center for Human Growth and Development • Wayne State University **2765**
C/SEC **9636**
C/SEC (Cesarean Sections: Education and Concern) **9636**
Cabell Foundation; Robert G. Cabell III and Maude Morgan **452**
CACH Network **2837**
Cafritz Foundation; Morris and Gwendolyn **408**
Cain Foundation; Effie and Wofford **162**
Cain Foundation; Gordon and Mary **226**
Cajal Club **8197**
Calcified Tissue Society; European **1276**
Calcutta Medical Association of America; University of **1528**
Calder Foundation; Louis **361**
Caleb C. and Julia W. Dula Educational and Charitable Foundation **6335**
Calgary WHO Centre for Research and Training in Mental Health **7543**
California Affiliate
    American Diabetes Association **4954**
    American Heart Association **2993**
California Alliance Against Domestic Violence **3080**
California; American Lung Association of **11630**
California; Arc of **4398**
California Association of Health Facilities **9330**

Canadian Health Association   6439
Canadian Health Libraries Association   6984
Canadian Heart Association   2838
Canadian Hospital Association   6439
Canadian Implant Association   12261
Canadian Injury Prevention Foundation   10845
Canadian Institute for Radiation Safety   11071
Canadian Intravenous Nurses Association   9078
Canadian Medical Association   1224
Canadian Mental Health Association   7350
Canadian Nurses Association   9079
Canadian Organization for Advancement of Computers in Health   6985
Canadian Paediatric Society   3195
Canadian Pelvic Inflammatory Disease Society   9637
Canadian Pharmaceutical Association   10592
Canadian Psychiatric Association   7351
Canadian Public Health Association   10946
    AIDS Program   6647
Canadian Rehabilitation Council for the Disabled   12671
Canadian Society for Aesthetic (Cosmetic) Plastic Surgery   12262
Canadian Society of Anaesthetists   2359
Canadian Society of Hospital Pharmacists   10593
Canadian Society of Laboratory Technologists   7128
Canadian Society of Orthopaedic Technologists   9925
Canadian Society of Otolaryngology - Head and Neck Surgery   12263
Canadian Society for the Study of Diseases of Children   3195
Canadian Veterinary Medical Association   13068
Canadien des Aveugles; Conseil   13429
Canadien pour la Readaptation des Handicapes; Conseil   12671
Canadienne des Anesthesistes; Societe   2359
Canadienne; Association Pharmaceutique   10592
Canadienne de Cardiologie; Societe   2838
Canadienne d'Endodontie; Academie   3912
Canadienne des Implantes Intraoculaires; Association   12261
Canadienne de l'Ataxie de Friedreich; Association   7871
Canadienne de Pediatrie; Societe   3195
Canadienne des Pharmaciens d'Hopitaux; Societe   10593
Canadienne de Sensibilisation a l'Infertilite; Association   11221
Canadienne des Technologistes de Laboratoire; Societe   7128
Canadienne des Technologistes en Orthopedie; Societe   9925
Canadienne des Technologues en Radiation Medicale; Association   11106
Canadienne; Troubles d'Apprentissage - Association   4505
Canberra Women's Health Centre   1225
Cancer; Action   5907
Cancer Advisory Center; Breast   5924
Cancer and Allied Diseases; Eppley Institute for Research in • University of Nebraska at Omaha   6233
Cancer; American Joint Committee on   5912
Cancer; Asociacion Nacional Contra el   5918
Cancer Association; Israel   5965
Cancer; Association for Research of Childhood   3189, 5898
Cancer Biology; Armand Hammer Center for   6000
Cancer Biology Branch • Division of Cancer Biology, Diagnosis, and Centers Extramural Research Program • National Cancer Institute • U.S. Department of Health and Human Services   6136
Cancer Biology; Center for • Texas A&M University   6120
Cancer Biology, Diagnosis, and Centers; Division of • National Cancer Institute • U.S. Department of Health and Human Services   6128
Cancer Biology; Laboratory of • New England Deaconess Hospital   6083
Cancer Biology Research Laboratory • Stanford University   6113
Cancer and Blood Diseases; Herbert L. Orlowitz Institute for   6053
Cancer and Blood Diseases; Institute for   6053
Cancer and Blood Disorders; Center for • Albany Medical College   5996
Cancer and Blood Disorders; Children's Center for   6021
Cancer and Blood Research; Institute for   6054
Cancer Care   5930
Cancer Care; Breast   5925
Cancer Care Center; Evanston   6057
Cancer Care Center; J.L. and Helen Kellogg   6057
Cancer Care Foundation; National   5930
Cancer Care; International School for   5956
Cancer Care Research; Mary Margaret Walther Program for   6066
Cancer Caring Center; Burger King   5929
Cancer Center
    Howard University   6048
    Medical College of Wisconsin   6072
    Purdue University   6104
    University of California, San Diego   6214
    University of Illinois at Chicago   6222
    University of Iowa   6223
    University of Kansas   6224

    University of Pennsylvania   6240
    University of Rochester   6244
    University of Texas Medical Branch at Galveston   6254
    Worcester Foundation for Experimental Biology   2710
Cancer Center; Arizona • University of Arizona   6209
Cancer Center; Center for Molecular Medicine and Immunology / Garden State   2096
Cancer Center; Columbia-Presbyterian • Columbia University   6024
Cancer Center; Comprehensive
    Ohio State University   6095
    University of Alabama at Birmingham   6208
    University of Wisconsin   6258
    Wake Forest University   6263
Cancer Center; Drew / Meharry / Morehouse Consortium   6029
Cancer Center; Duke Comprehensive • Duke University   6031
Cancer Center; Fox Chase   6038
Cancer Center; Kaplan Comprehensive • New York University   6087
Cancer Center; Lincoln   6065
Cancer Center; Lucille Parker Markey • University of Kentucky   6226
Cancer Center; Mary Babb Randolph • West Virginia University   6268
Cancer Center; Masonic • University of Minnesota   6232
Cancer Center; Mayo   6068
Cancer Center of the Medical College of Virginia; Massey • Virginia Commonwealth University   6262
Cancer Center; Memorial Sloan-Kettering   6074
    Laboratory of GI Tumor Biology   6075
Cancer Center; Memphis • University of Tennessee   6250
Cancer Center of Metropolitan Detroit; Meyer L. Prentis Comprehensive   6077
Cancer Center; Natalie Warren Bryant   6081
Cancer Center; National   5971
Cancer Center; Norris Comprehensive • University of Southern California   6249
Cancer Center; Norris Cotton   6089
Cancer Center; Northern California   6092
Cancer Center; Puerto Rico • University of Puerto Rico   6243
Cancer Center and Research Institute; H. Lee Moffitt   6044
Cancer Center; Robert H. Lurie • Northwestern University   6094
Cancer Center; Roger Williams   6106
Cancer Center; Rush   6108
Cancer Center; Sylvester Comprehensive • University of Miami   6229
Cancer Center; UCLA Jonsson Comprehensive • University of California, Los Angeles   6213
Cancer Center; UNC Lineberger Comprehensive • University of North Carolina at Chapel Hill   6238
Cancer Center; University of Maryland • University of Maryland at Baltimore   6228
Cancer Center; University of Texas M.D. Anderson • University of Texas   6253
Cancer Center; Vermont • University of Vermont   6257
Cancer Center; Winship • Emory University   6035
Cancer Center; Yale Comprehensive • Yale University   6270
Cancer Centers; Association of Community   5920
Cancer Centers Branch • Division of Cancer Biology, Diagnosis, and Centers • National Cancer Institute • U.S. Department of Health and Human Services   6129
Cancer Clinical Research Center; Tulane   6018
Cancer Connection   5982
Cancer Control Campaign; Women's Nationwide   5993
Cancer Control Science Program • Division of Cancer Prevention and Control • National Cancer Institute • U.S. Department of Health and Human Services   6141
Cancer Control Society   5931
Cancer Cytology Center; National   5971
Cancer Cytology Foundation of America   5971
Cancer Data System; Rocky Mountain • University of Utah   6256
Cancer Diagnosis Branch • Division of Cancer Biology, Diagnosis, and Centers • National Cancer Institute • U.S. Department of Health and Human Services   6130
Cancer Drug Center; Grace • Roswell Park Cancer Institute   10454
Cancer Education; American Association for   5908
Cancer Etiology; Division of • National Cancer Institute • U.S. Department of Health and Human Services   6137
Cancer; European Organization for Research and Treatment of   5941
Cancer Federation, Inc.   5932
Cancer Foundation; Candlelighters Childhood   3196
Cancer Foundation; Eugene L. Garey   5971
Cancer Foundation; Michigan   6078
Cancer Foundation; National   5930
Cancer Foundation; R. A. Bloch   5982
Cancer Foundation; Skin   5906, 5986
Cancer Foundation; Susan G. Komen Breast   5990

Index

Laboratory of Tumor Immunology and Biology • U.S. Department of Health and Human Services **6200**

Laboratory of Tumor Virus Biology • U.S. Department of Health and Human Services **6201**

Laboratory of Viral Carcinogenesis • U.S. Department of Health and Human Services **6202**

U.S. Department of Health and Human Services **5889, 6125**

Cancer Institute; Pittsburgh **6102**

Cancer Institute; Roswell Park **6107**

Grace Cancer Drug Center **10454**

Cancer Institute; Rush **6108**

Cancer Institute; Santa Barbara Breast **6110**

Cancer Institute; Sidney Farber **6027**

Cancer Institute; Walt Disney Memorial • Cancer Research Division **6264**

Cancer Institutes; Association of American **5919**

Cancer; International Agency for Research on **5949**

Cancer; International Association for the Study of Lung **5952**

Cancer; International Society Against Breast **5957**

Cancer; International Society for Environmental Toxicology and **5045**

Cancer; International Union Against **5963**

Cancer and Leukemia Group B **6009**

Cancer, Lymphocytes, Air Pollution, and General Pathobiology Unit; Lung Disease, • University of Southern California **10181**

Cancer Management and Control; Institute for Familial **6046**

Cancer Network; McDowell **6061**

Cancer Organization; Y-ME National Breast **5995**

Cancer Organizations; National Alliance of Breast **5969**

Cancer; People Against **5981**

Cancer Prevention Center; Strang **6117**

Cancer Prevention and Control; Division of • National Cancer Institute • U.S. Department of Health and Human Services **6140**

Cancer Prevention and Early Detection Foundation; Ovarian **5979**

Cancer Prevention Organization; European **5939**

Cancer Prevention Research Institute **6010**

Cancer Prevention Research Program • Division of Cancer Prevention and Control • National Cancer Institute • U.S. Department of Health and Human Services **6142**

Cancer Prevention Studies Branch • Division of Cancer Prevention and Control • National Cancer Institute • U.S. Department of Health and Human Services **6143**

Cancer Program; Human Immunology and • University of Tennessee, Knoxville **6252**

Cancer Program; Kentucky **6061**

Cancer and Radiobiological Research; Laboratory of • New York University **6088**

Cancer Registrars Association; National **5973**

Cancer Registries; International Association of **7003**

Cancer Research; American Association for **5909**

Cancer Research; Association for International **5921**

Cancer Research; Bob Hipple Laboratory for **6047**

Cancer Research; British Association for **5928**

Cancer Research Center

Boston University **6005**

Brigham Young University **6006**

Massachusetts Institute of Technology **6067**

Northeast Louisiana University **6091**

University of Chicago **6219**

Cancer Research Center [Bronx, NY] **6012**

Cancer Research Center [Columbia, MO] **6011**

Cancer Research Center; AMC **5997**

Cancer Research Center; Arkansas • University of Arkansas at Little Rock **6210**

Cancer Research; Center for Basic • Kansas State University **6060**

Cancer Research Center; City of Hope **6022**

Cancer Research Center; Fred Hutchinson **6039**

Cancer Research Center; Frederick **6040**

Cancer Research Center of Hawaii • University of Hawaii **6221**

Cancer Research Center; Hipple **6047**

Cancer Research Center; Roger Williams Clinical **6106**

Cancer Research Center; Vincent T. Lombardi • Georgetown University **6041**

Cancer Research Data Bank; International • National Cancer Institute • U.S. Department of Health and Human Services **6173**

Cancer Research; Detroit Institute for **6078**

Cancer Research and Development Center; Frederick • National Cancer Institute • U.S. Department of Health and Human Services **6172**

Cancer Research Division

Medical College of Ohio **6070**

Walt Disney Memorial Cancer Institute **6264**

Cancer Research; European Association for **5938**

Cancer Research Foundation **5899**

Cancer Research Foundation; Children's **6027**

Cancer Research Foundation; La Jolla **6062**

Cancer Research Foundation; National Immunotherapy **5978**

Cancer Research Fund of the Damon Runyon-Walter Winchell Foundation **5900**

Cancer Research; Goodwin Institute for **6043**

Cancer Research Institute **5901, 6055**

Arizona State University **5999**

University of California, Irvine **6212**

University of California, San Francisco **6216**

Cancer Research Institute; Children's **6020**

Cancer Research Institute; Geraldine Brush **6042**

Cancer Research Institute; Henry Vogt • University of Louisville **6227**

Cancer Research Institute; Syracuse **6118**

Cancer Research; International Medical Sports Federation for Aid to **5954**

Cancer Research Laboratories; H.M. Bligh • Chicago Medical School **6019**

Cancer Research Laboratory

Mercy Cancer Institute **6076**

Rutgers University **6109**

University of California at Berkeley **6211**

Cancer Research Laboratory; Allie M. Lee • University of Nevada, Reno **6234**

Cancer Research Laboratory, Inc.; Pohl **6103**

Cancer Research Laboratory; Pediatric **6100**

Cancer Research; McArdle Laboratory for • University of Wisconsin—Madison **6261**

Cancer Research and Molecular Biology; Fels Institute for • Temple University **6119**

Cancer Research; National Coalition for **5974**

Cancer Research; National Foundation for **5976, 6082**

Cancer Research Program; Colorado **6023**

Cancer Research Program; Immunology and • Oklahoma Medical Research Foundation **6098**

Cancer Research Project • Carson-Newman College **6014**

Cancer Research; Stehlin Foundation for **6116**

Cancer Research; Susan G. Komen Foundation for the Advancement of **5990**

Cancer Research and Treatment Center • University of New Mexico **6235**

Cancer Research Unit • Saskatoon Cancer Centre **6111**

Cancer Societies; Federation of Latin American **5945**

Cancer Society; American **5897, 5910**

Alabama Division **6271**

Alaska Division **6272**

Arizona Division **6273**

Arkansas Division **6274**

California Division **6275**

Colorado Division **6276**

Connecticut Division **6277**

Delaware Division **6278**

District of Columbia Division **6279**

Florida Division **6280**

Georgia Division **6281**

Hawaii Pacific Division **6282**

Idaho Division **6283**

Illinois Division **6284**

Indiana Division **6285**

Iowa Division **6286**

Kansas Division **6287**

Kentucky Division **6288**

Long Island Division **6303**

Louisiana Division **6289**

Maine Division **6290**

Maryland Division **6291**

Massachusetts Division **6292**

Michigan Division **6293**

Minnesota Division **6294**

Mississippi Division **6295**

Missouri Division **6296**

Montana Division **6297**

Nebraska Division **6298**

Nevada Division **6299**

New Hampshire Division **6300**

New Jersey Division **6301**

New Mexico Division **6302**

New York City Division **6304**

New York State Division **6305**

North Carolina Division **6308**

North Dakota Division **6309**

Ohio Division **6310**

Oklahoma Division **6311**

Oregon Division **6312**

Pennsylvania Division **6313**

Philadelphia Division **6314**
Puerto Rico Division **6315**
Queens Division **6306**
Rhode Island Division **6316**
South Carolina Division **6317**
South Dakota Division **6318**
Tennessee Division **6319**
Texas Division **6320**
Utah Division **6321**
Vermont Division **6322**
Virginia Division **6323**
Washington Division **6324**
West Virginia Division **6325**
Westchester Division **6307**
Wisconsin Division **6326**
Wyoming Division **6327**
Cancer Society; Barbados **5922**
Cancer Society; Veterinary **13112**
Cancer Staging and End Results Reporting; American Joint Committee for **5912**
Cancer Statistics; Georgia Center for • Emory University **6034**
Cancer Study Group; Children's
University of Kentucky **6225**
University of Wisconsin—Madison **6259**
Cancer Support Service; Breast **5926**
Cancer Support; Y-Me Breast **5995**
Cancer Survival Center; Thompson **6122**
Cancer Survivorship; National Coalition for **5975**
Cancer Therapies; Foundation for Alternative **2194**
Cancer Therapy; Committee for Freedom of Choice in **2188**
Cancer Therapy Evaluation Program • Division of Cancer Treatment • National Cancer Institute • U.S. Department of Health and Human Services **6153**
Cancer Therapy; Foundation for Advancement in **2194**
Cancer Therapy and Research Center **6013**
Cancer Therapy; Technology Extension Center for Investigational **6058**
Cancer Treatment; Division of • National Cancer Institute • U.S. Department of Health and Human Services **6149**
Cancer Treatment Group; North Central **6090**
Cancer Treatment; John P. Caufield Technology Extension Center for Investigational **6058**
Cancer Treatment; Patient Advocates for Advanced **5980**
Cancer Victims and Friends; International Association of **5950**
Cancer Victors and Friends; International Association of **5950**
Cancerologia; Federacion Latinoamericana de Sociedades de **5945**
Cancerologique; Federation Internationale du Sport Medical pour l'Aide a la Recherche **5954**
Candienne des Medecins Veterinaires; Association **13068**
Candlelighters Childhood Cancer Foundation **3196**
Candlelighters Foundation **3196**
Canine Companions for Independence **4470**
Canine Sports Medicine Association; American **13044**
Cannabis Therapeutics; Alliance for **2154**
Cannon Foundation **6337**
CAPCOM **3501**
Capital Affiliate; Nation's • American Heart Association **2998**
Capital Area Easter Seal Society **4673**
Capital Area; National Kidney Foundation of the National **12941**
Capital Cities / ABC Foundation **620**
Capital Communications Service for the Hearing-Impaired **3501**
Capital University • School of Nursing **8872**
Capstone College of Nursing • University of Alabama **8551**
Captioned Film Center; Judaica **3541**
Captioning Institute; National **3548**
Carbohydrate Nutrition Laboratory • Beltsville Human Nutrition Research Center • Agricultural Research Service • U.S. Department of Agriculture **9532**
Carcinogenesis Branch; Chemical and Physical • Chemical and Physical Carcinogenesis Program • National Cancer Institute • U.S. Department of Health and Human Services **6126**
Carcinogenesis Laboratory • Michigan State University **6079**
Carcinogenesis; Laboratory of Comparative • National Cancer Institute • U.S. Department of Health and Human Services **6183**
Carcinogenesis; Laboratory of Experimental • National Cancer Institute • U.S. Department of Health and Human Services **6184**
Carcinogenesis; Laboratory of Human • National Cancer Institute • U.S. Department of Health and Human Services **6188**
Carcinogenesis; Laboratory of Molecular • National Cancer Institute • U.S. Department of Health and Human Services **6193**
Carcinogenesis; Laboratory of Viral • National Cancer Institute • U.S. Department of Health and Human Services **6202**

Carcinogenesis Program; Biological • Division of Cancer Etiology • National Cancer Institute • U.S. Department of Health and Human Services **6138**
Carcinogenesis and Tumor Promotion; Laboratory of Cellular • National Cancer Institute • U.S. Department of Health and Human Services **6179**
Carcinogens; International Commission for Protection Against Environmental Mutagens and **5043**
Carcinogens, and Teratogens Societies; Latin American Association of Environmental Mutagens, **5047**
Cardeza Foundation for Hematologic Research • Thomas Jefferson University **6121**
Cardiac Angiography and Interventions; Society for **2877**
Cardiac Catheterization Laboratory • Emory University **2893**
Cardiac Catheterization Laboratory; Pediatric • Duke University **3333**
Cardiac Center • Creighton University **2890**
Cardiac Energetics; Laboratory of • National Heart, Lung, and Blood Institute • U.S. Department of Health and Human Services **2947**
Cardiac Functions Branch • Division of Heart and Vascular Diseases • National Heart, Lung, and Blood Institute • U.S. Department of Health and Human Services **2935**
Cardiac Rehabilitation Program; Stanford • Stanford University **2923**
Cardiac Rehabilitation Research Group • Laval University **2910**
Cardiac Society; Finnish **2847**
Cardiac Society; Icelandic **2853**
Cardiac Transplant Program • Loyola University Chicago **12884**
Cardiaques; Societe Internationale de Recherches **2858**
Cardinal Stritch College • Department of Nursing **9035**
Cardiographic and Cardiovascular Dynamics; European Society for Ballisto **2846**
Cardiographic Research; European Society for Ballisto **2846**
Cardiologia; Sociedad Interamericana de **2854**
Cardiologie; Nederlandse Vereniging voor **2843**
Cardiologie; Societatea de **2873**
Cardiologie; Societe Canadienne de **2838**
Cardiologie; Societe et Federation Internationale de **2860**
Cardiologisk Sekskap; Norsk **2870**
Cardiologists; Association of Black **2831**
Cardiologists; Association of Estonian **2832**
Cardiologists; Moscow Association of **2863**
Cardiology; Academy of Veterinary **13019**
Cardiology; American College of **2825**
Cardiology; Association of Professors of **2833**
Cardiology Branch • Division of Intramural Research • National Heart, Lung, and Blood Institute • U.S. Department of Health and Human Services **2940**
Cardiology; Division of
University of Michigan **2970**
University of Texas Southwestern Medical Center at Dallas **2978**
Cardiology; Dutch Society of **2843**
Cardiology Foundation; International **2787**
Cardiology and Health Services Research Unit; Multicenter **2885**
Cardiology; Hungarian Society of **2852**
Cardiology Institute • Montreal Research Centre • University of Montreal **2973**
Cardiology; Inter-American Society of **2854**
Cardiology; International Society and Federation of **2860**
Cardiology; Krannert Institute of **2909**
Cardiology; Laboratory of Molecular • National Heart, Lung, and Blood Institute • U.S. Department of Health and Human Services **2952**
Cardiology; Norwegian Society of **2870**
Cardiology Program • Division of Heart and Vascular Diseases • National Heart, Lung, and Blood Institute • U.S. Department of Health and Human Services **2936**
Cardiology; Romanian Society of **2873**
Cardiology Technologists Association; American **2828**
Cardiology; Turkish Society of **2879**
Cardiology Unit; Vascular Medicine and Preventive • University of Virginia **2982**
Cardiopulmonary Credentialing; National Board for **2839**
Cardiopulmonary Technologists; National Society of **2828**
Cardiopulmonary Technology; National Society for **2828**
Cardiothoracic Anaesthesiologists; European Association of **2364**
Cardiothoracic Research and Education Foundation **12264**
Cardiothoracic Surgery; Division of • University of Missouri—Columbia **2972**
Cardiovasculaire; Societe Europeenne de Chirurgie **12269**
Cardiovascular Administrators; American College of **5544**
Cardiovascular Anesthesiologists; Society of **2375**
Cardiovascular Biology Research Program • Oklahoma Medical Research Foundation **2917**
Cardiovascular Center; Hypertension and • Cornell University **2889**
Cardiovascular Center; Iowa • University of Iowa **2965**
Cardiovascular Credentialing International **2839**

Cardiovascular Credentialing International/Board of Cardiovascular Technology 2839

Cardiovascular Disease; Gladstone Foundation Laboratories for 2896

Cardiovascular Disease; Gladstone Institute of **2896**

Cardiovascular Diseases; Division of • University of Tennessee **2976**

Cardiovascular Dynamics; European Society for Ballisto Cardiographic and 2846

Cardiovascular Dynamics; European Society for Noninvasive **2846**

Cardiovascular Genetic Research Clinic • University of Utah **2980**

Cardiovascular Health Services Research; Center for **2885**

Cardiovascular Health; Tulane Center for • Tulane University **2928**

Cardiovascular Institute; Likoff • Medical College of Pennsylvania and Hahnemann University **2915**

Cardiovascular Institute; Whitaker • Boston University **2884**

Cardiovascular and Interventional Radiology; Society of **11132**

Cardio-Vascular Laboratory • University of Cincinnati **2962**

Cardiovascular Laser Lab • University of Florida **11166**

Cardiovascular Nurses; American Association of 9051

Cardiovascular Pathology Department • Center for Advanced Pathology • Armed Forces Institute of Pathology • U.S. Department of Defense **10148**

Cardiovascular Perfusion; American Board of **2823**

Cardiovascular Professionals; American Society of **2828**

Cardiovascular and Pulmonary Credentialing; National Board for 2839

Cardiovascular and Pulmonary Rehabilitation; American Association of **2822**

Cardiovascular Radiology; Society of 11132

Cardiovascular Research Center; John M. Dalton • University of Missouri—Columbia **1707**

Cardiovascular Research Institute • University of California, San Francisco **2665**

Cardiovascular Research; Institute for Nutrition and • Oregon Health Sciences University **9521**

Cardiovascular Research; International Society for **2858**

Cardiovascular Research Laboratory • University of California, Los Angeles **2958**

Cardiovascular Research and Training Center • University of Alabama at Birmingham **2954**

Cardiovascular Research and Training Institute; Nora Eccles Harrison • University of Utah **2981**

Cardiovascular Science; Laboratory of • National Institute on Aging • U.S. Department of Health and Human Services **1957**

Cardiovascular Society; Canadian **2838**

Cardiovascular Society; International 2859

Cardiovascular Society; Michael E. DeBakey International 12288

Cardiovascular Studies; Institute for • University of Houston **2964**

Cardiovascular Surgery; Association of Physician Assistants in **12254**

Cardiovascular Surgery; European Society for **12269**

Cardiovascular Surgery; International Society for **2859**

Cardiovascular Surgery; Scandinavian Association for Thoracic and 12301

Cardiovascular Surgical Research Laboratory • University of Texas Medical Branch at Galveston **2977**

Cardiovascular Technologies; Engineering Research Center for Emerging • Duke University **2443**

Cardiovascular Technologists; National Alliance of 2828

Cardiovascular Technology; Cardiovascular Credentialing International/Board of 2839

Care of Children in Hospitals; Association for the 3177

Care Foundation; Child 3242

Care Needs; La Rabida Research and Policy Center for the Study of Children and Families with Special Health • University of Chicago **3358**

Care Panel; Animal 13032

Care Providers of Minnesota **9349**

Care for the Severely Mentally Ill; Center on the Organization and Financing of **5614**

Career Development of the Council for Exceptional Children; Division on 3216

Career Development and Transition; Division on • Council for Exceptional Children **3216**

Career Schools; National Association of Health **1399**

Careers Program; Minority Access to Research • National Institute of General Medical Sciences • U.S. Department of Health and Human Services **2653**

Caregivers; Association of Brethren **1889**

Cargill Foundation **621**

Caribbean Association on Mental Retardation and Other Development Disabilities **4286**

Caribbean Family Planning Affiliation **11207**

Caribbean Primate Research Center • University of Puerto Rico **13232**

Caribbean Women's Health Network; Latin American and **1371**

Caribean University College • School of Nursing **8940**

Carie; Organisme Europeen de Recherche sur la 3930

Caries Research Center; Rochester • University of Rochester **4045**

Caries Research Center; Specialized [Boston, MA] **4006**

Caries Research; European Organization for **3930**

Caries, Restorative Materials and Salivary Research Branch • Extramural Program • National Institute of Dental Research • U.S. Department of Health and Human Services **4014**

Caring Foundation **622**

Carl B. and Florence E. King Foundation **6338**

Carl J. Herzog Foundation **84**

Carl and Lily Pforzheimer Foundation **85**

Carl Stough Institute of Breathing Coordination, Inc. **11609**

Carleton Washburne Early Childhood Center • Brooklyn College of City University of New York **3591**

Carlow College • Division of Nursing **8911**

Carmen Torres de Tiburcio School of Nursing • Inter-American University of Puerto Rico **8941**

Carnation Company Foundation **793**

Carnegie Corporation of New York **3134**

Carnegie Council on Adolescent Development **3197**

Carnegie Institution of Washington • Carnegie Laboratories of Embryology, Davis Division **2558**

Carnegie Laboratories of Embryology, Davis Division • Carnegie Institution of Washington **2558**

Carnegie Mellon University
    Biomedical Engineering Program **2437**
    Science and Technology Center **2438**

Carolinas Chapter
    Arthritis Foundation **8004, 8017**
    Cystic Fibrosis Foundation **5446, 5458**

Carolinas Medical Center / University of North Carolina at Charlotte • Nurse Anesthesia Program **2302**

Carolyn Foundation **86**

Carpenter Technology Corp. Foundation **623**

Carreras International Leukemia Foundation; Friends of the Jose **5946**

Carrie Estelle Doheny Foundation **87**

Carrier Foundation • Division of Research **7545**

Carroll Center for the Blind **13430**

Carroll College
    Department of Nursing **8800**
    Health Information Management Program **6938**

Carroll Rehabilitation Center for the Visually Impaired 13430

Carson-Newman College
    Cancer Research Project **6014**
    Department of Nursing **8968**

Carter Center for Immunology Research; Beirne • University of Virginia **2147**

Carter Foundation; Amon G. **42**

Carter Star Telegram Employees Fund; Amon G. **578**

Carter-Wallace Foundation **624**

Carteret Community College • Respiratory Therapist Program **11474**

Carvel Foundation; Thomas and Agnes **516**

Carver Agricultural Experiment Station; George Washington • Tuskegee University **9530**

Carver Charitable Trust; Roy J. **470**

Carver School of Social Work • Southern Baptist Theological Seminary **11783**

Case Western Reserve University
    Applied Neural Control Laboratory **8346**
    Bolton-Brush Growth Study Center **3998**
    Center for Biomedical Ethics **7194**
    Center for Human Genetics **5316**
    Center for Inherited Disorders of Energy Metabolism **4881**
    Center for Practice Innovations **1566**
    Clinical Research Center **1567**
    Cystic Fibrosis and Pediatric Pulmonary Center **5317**
    Developmental Biology Center **2559**
    Elderly Care Research Center **1927**
    Frances Payne Bolton School of Nursing **8873**
        Graduate Program in Nurse-Midwifery **9608**
    Health Systems Management Center **5613**
    Institute of Pathology **10142**
    Law-Medicine Center **7195**
    Mandel School of Applied Social Sciences **11832**
    Mental Development Center **4309**
    Northeast Ohio Multipurpose Arthritis Center **7916**
    Rehabilitation Engineering Center **2439**
    Resource for Biomedical Sensor Technology **2440**
    School of Dentistry **3823**
    School of Medicine **1011**
        Department of Pharmacology **10315**
    Skeletal Research Center **7917**
    University Center on Aging and Health **1928**

Cellular, and Nutritional Endocrinology Branch; Molecular, • Division of Intramural Research • National Institute of Diabetes and Digestive and Kidney Diseases • U.S. Department of Health and Human Services **4923**

Cellular Oncology; Laboratory of • National Cancer Institute • U.S. Department of Health and Human Services **6181**

Cellular Pathology Department • Armed Forces Institute of Pathology • U.S. Department of Defense **10145**

Cellular Physiology and Immunology; Laboratory of • Rockefeller University **2114**

Cemetery Services; Indiana State Board of Funeral and **3742**

Cenla Chapter • Lupus Foundation of America **8058**

Center for Addiction and Behavioral Health Research **12090**

Center on Addiction and Substance Abuse • Columbia University **12092**

Center on Adult Development and Aging • University of Miami **1984**

Center for Advanced Biotechnology • Cornell University **2719**

Center for Advanced Biotechnology and Medicine **2717**

Center for Advanced Medical Technology • San Francisco State University **2619**

Center for Advanced Molecular Biology and Immunology • State University of New York at Buffalo **2726**

Center for Advanced Study in Behavioral Sciences **7546**

Center for Advanced Study in Health Care Fiscal Management, Organization and Control • University of Wisconsin—Madison **5766**

Center for Advanced Training in Cell and Molecular Biology • Catholic University of America **2560**

Center on Aging
  Auburn University **1921**
  University of Alabama at Birmingham **1968**
  University of Kansas **1979**
  University of Maryland **1982**
  University of West Florida **1997**

Center for Aging Studies
  University of Missouri—Kansas City **1987**
  University of Missouri—Rolla **1988**

Center for Agricultural Disease and Injury Research, Education, and Prevention • University of Iowa **9852**

Center for AIDS Prevention Studies • University of California, San Francisco **10884**

Center for AIDS Research
  Purdue University **6783**
  Stanford University **6790**

Center for Alcohol and Addiction Studies
  Brown University **12089**
  University of Alaska Anchorage **12132**

Center of Alcohol Studies
  Rutgers University **12101**
  University of North Carolina at Chapel Hill **12141**

Center for Allergy and Immunological Disorders • Baylor College of Medicine **2093**

Center for Alternatives to Animal Testing • Johns Hopkins University **13141**

Center for Ambulatory Studies • University of Florida **2484**

Center for Animals & Public Policy • Tufts University **13179**

Center for Anti-Inflammatory Research • Florida A&M University **10431**

Center for Applications of Psychological Type **7352**

Center for the Applied Behavioral Sciences • St. Louis University **7597**

Center for Applied Ethics
  Santa Clara University **7215**
  University of British Columbia **7217**

Center on Applied Gerontological Research • Cleveland State University **1931**

Center for Applied Microcirculatory Research • University of Louisville **2969**

Center for Assessment & Demographic Studies • Gallaudet University **3600**

Center for Athletic Injury Research **11961**

Center for Attitudinal Healing **2182**

Center for Auditory and Speech Sciences • Gallaudet University **3601**

Center for Basic Cancer Research • Kansas State University **6060**

Center for Basic Research in Digestive Diseases **7918**

Center for Biocognitive Studies • Yale University **7703**

Center for Bioengineering • University of Washington **2501**

Center for Bioenvironmental Research **5063**

Center for Bioethics **7196**

Center for Biological and Computational Learning • Massachusetts Institute of Technology **8390**

Center for Biological Macromolecules • University at Albany, State University of New York **2659**

Center for Biological Timing • University of Virginia **4944**

Center for Biologics Evaluation and Research • Food and Drug Administration • U.S. Department of Health and Human Services **10898, 10993**

Center for the Biology of Natural Systems • Queens College of City University of New York **5084**

Center for Biomechanics Studies and Research • University of Cincinnati **2729**

Center for Biomedical Engineering • New Jersey Institute of Technology **2460**

Center for Biomedical Ethics
  Case Western Reserve University **7194**
  Stanford University **7216**
  University of Minnesota **5654**

Center for Biomedical Research **11262**
  University of Kansas **2673**

Center for Biomedical Toxicological Research and Hazardous Waste Management • Florida State University **10432**

Center for Biomolecular Nuclear Magnetic Resonance, Structure, and Design • Purdue University **2465**

Center for Biopolymers at Interfaces • University of Utah **2497**

Center for Biostatistics and Epidemiology • Pennsylvania State University **7020**

Center for Biotechnology **2718**
  Baylor College of Medicine **2715**
  University of Texas at Austin **2736**

Center for Biotechnology and Applied Science • Northwestern University **2722**

Center for Blood Research **6015**

Center for Cancer Biology • Texas A&M University **6120**

Center for Cancer and Blood Disorders • Albany Medical College **5996**

Center for Cancer Research • Massachusetts Institute of Technology **6067**

Center for Cardiovascular Health Services Research **2885**

Center for Cell Research • Pennsylvania State University **2392**

Center for Cellular and Molecular Nutrition • Texas A&M University **9527**

Center for Child and Family Studies • University of California, San Diego **3356**

Center for Children with Chronic Illness and Disability **3317**

Center on Children and the Law **7197**

Center for Clinical and Aging Services Research • University of California, San Francisco **1973**

Center for Clinical Epidemiology and Biostatistics • University of Pennsylvania **5195**

Center for Clinical Medical Ethics • University of Chicago **7219**

Center for Clinical Pharmacology • Vanderbilt University **10491**

Center for Clinical Research—Pediatric Unit • Columbia University **3331**

Center for Clinical Studies
  Northwestern College of Chiropractic **3463**
  University of Iowa **4028**

Center for Cognitive Therapy • University of Pennsylvania **7681**

Center for Communication Programs **6986**
  Johns Hopkins University **7015**

Center for Communicative Development, Inc. **3593**

Center for Community Inclusion • University of Maine **4333**

Center for Community Study • University of Rochester **7685**

Center for Companion Animal Health • University of California, Davis **13211**

Center for Complex Systems
  Florida Atlantic University **8368**
  University of Arizona **8478**

Center for Controlled Chemical Delivery • University of Utah **10487**

Center for Corneal and Contact Lens Research • University of Missouri—St. Louis **13656**

Center for Cost-Effective Care • Harvard University **5750**

Center for Craniofacial Molecular Biology • University of Southern California **4046**

Center for Crystallographic Research **2561**

Center for Dance Medicine **10846**

Center on Deafness • University of California, San Francisco **3634**

Center for Death Education and Research • University of Minnesota **3727**

Center for Designing Foods to Improve Nutrition • Iowa State University of Science and Technology **9505**

Center for Developmental and Health Genetics • Pennsylvania State University **5345**

Center for Developmental Neuroscience and Developmental Disabilities • College of Staten Island of City University of New York **8353**

Center for Developmentally Disabled Adults • Western Michigan University **12767**

Center for Devices and Radiological Health • Food and Drug Administration • U.S. Department of Health and Human Services **10994, 11058**

Center for Dream Drama **7359**

Center for Drug Delivery Research • University of Kansas **10472**

Center for Drug Discovery • University of Florida **10632**

Center for Drug Evaluation and Research • Food and Drug Administration • U.S. Department of Health and Human Services **10899, 10995**

Center on Drugs and Public Policy • University of Maryland 10635
Center for Emergency Medicine of Western Pennsylvania 4761
Center for Employment Relations and Law • Florida State University 7198
Center for Endocrinology, Metabolism and Molecular Medicine 4882
Center for Endocrinology Metabolism and Nutrition 4882
Center for Engineering Design • University of Utah 2498
Center for the Enhancement of the Biology / Biomaterials Interface • University of Texas Health Science Center at San Antonio 2694
Center for Environment and Health Policy • University of Minnesota 5125
Center for Environmental Health • University of Connecticut 5118
Center for Environmental Health Sciences • Massachusetts Institute of Technology 5079
Center for Environmental and Human Toxicology • University of Florida 5119
Center for Environmental Management • Tufts University 5087
Center for Environmental Medicine and Lung Biology • University of North Carolina at Chapel Hill 5126
Center for Environmental Radiation Toxicology • University of Texas Health Science Center at San Antonio 11080
Center for Environmental Sciences • University of Colorado—Denver 5117
Center for Environmental Toxicology • Colorado State University 11072
Center for Epidemiologic Research 9802
Center for Ergonomics • University of Michigan 9856
Center for Ethics, Medicine, and Public Issues • Baylor College of Medicine 5609
Center for Ethics and Social Policy • Graduate Theological Union 7203
Center for Evaluative Clincial Sciences • Dartmouth College 5622
Center of Excellence in Livestock Diseases and Human Health • University of Tennessee, Knoxville 13235
Center of Excellence in Otolaryncology 6045
Center of Excellence in Pediatric Pharmacokinetics and Therapeutics • University of Tennessee 10485
Center for Exercise Science • University of Florida 11983
Center for Experimental Therapeutics • Baylor College of Medicine 10427
Center for Expressive Analysis 7391
Center for Expressive Psychotherapy 7391
Center for Extracellular Matrix Biology • Texas A&M University 2627
Center for Family Learning 7547
Center for Family Planning Program Development 11197, 11259
Center for Family Research in Rural Mental Health • Iowa State University of Science and Technology 7577
Center for Family Support 4287
Center for Fast Kinetics Research • University of Texas at Austin 2690
Center for Fertility and Reproductive Research • Vanderbilt University 11300
Center for Food Safety and Applied Nutrition • Food and Drug Administration • U.S. Department of Health and Human Services 10900, 10996
Center for Food Safety & Quality Enhancement • University of Georgia 9553
Center for Gene Research and Biotechnology • Oregon State University 2725
Center for General Health Services Extramural Research • Agency for Health Care Policy and Research • U.S. Department of Health and Human Services 5643
Center for General Health Services Intramural Research • Agency for Health Care Policy and Research • U.S. Department of Health and Human Services 5644
Center for Genome Research • Texas A&M University 5354
Center for Geriatrics, Gerontology • Columbia University 1932
Center for Gerontological Research • Medical College of Pennsylvania and Hahnemann University 1939
Center for Gerontological Studies • University of Florida 1976
Center for Gerontology
    Ball State University 1922
    Old Dominion University 1943
Center for Gerontology and Health Care Research • Brown University 1926
Center for Handicapped Children • University of Illinois at Chicago 4588
Center for Hazardous Materials Research 5064
Center for Health Action 1230
Center for Health Administration Studies • University of Chicago 5647
Center for Health and Advanced Policy Studies • Boston University 5610
Center for Health Care Ethics • St. Louis University 7214
Center for Health Care Research and Evaluation • University of Texas at Austin 9150
Center for Health Economics Research 5747
Center for Health Effects of Environmental Contamination • University of Iowa 5121
Center for Health Ethics and Policy • University of Colorado—Denver 5648
Center for Health Management Studies • Rush University 5638
Center for Health Policy and Ethics • Creighton University 5621
Center for Health Policy Research • American Medical Association 5607

Center for Health Policy Research and Education • Duke University 5623
Center for Health Promotion and Disease Prevention • University of North Carolina at Chapel Hill 10887
Center for Health Promotion Research & Development • University of Texas—Houston Health Science Center 10890
Center for Health Research 1568
    Wayne State University 1749
Center for Health Risk Assessment and Disease Prevention • University of Alabama at Birmingham 10881
Center for Health and Safety Studies • Indiana University Bloomington 1603, 10866
Center for Health Services • Vanderbilt University 1736
Center for Health Services and Policy Research • Northwestern University 5635
Center for Health Services Research
    University of Colorado 5764
    University of Illinois at Chicago 9718
    University of Iowa 5650
    University of Memphis 5652
Center for Health and Social Systems Research 1571, 5618
Center for Health Systems Research and Analysis • University of Wisconsin—Madison 5661
Center for Health Systems & Technology • Texas A&M University 5640
Center for Hereditary Eye Diseases • Johns Hopkins University 13604
Center for Hip and Knee Surgery 9940
Center for the History of Foot Care and Footwear • Pennsylvania College of Podiatric Medicine 10777
Center for Hospital Finance and Management • Johns Hopkins University 5752
Center for Host-Arthropod-Pathogen Studies • Oklahoma State University 6782
Center on Human Development • University of Oregon 4337
Center for Human Genetics 5318
    Boston University 5314
    Case Western Reserve University 5316
Center for Human Growth and Development • University of Michigan 1701
Center for Human Nutrition • University of Texas Southwestern Medical Center at Dallas 9565
Center on Human Policy 4471
Center for Human Toxicology • University of Utah 10488
Center for Humane Options in Childbirth Experiences 9638
Center for Imaging and Pharmaceutical Research 10428
Center for Imaging Science • Rochester Institute of Technology 11155
Center for Immunity Enhancement in Domestic Animals • Iowa State University of Science and Technology 13137
Center for Immunization Research • Johns Hopkins University 6774
Center for the Improvement of Human Functioning International, Inc. • Research Division 5319
Center for Indoor Air Research 5065
Center for Industrial Ergonomics • University of Louisville 2733
Center for Infectious Diseases • University of Texas—Houston Health Science Center 6853
Center for Inherited Disorders of Energy Metabolism • Case Western Reserve University 4881
Center for Injury Research and Policy • Johns Hopkins University 10867
Center for Interdisciplinary Research on Immunological Diseases • Washington University 2148
Center for International Community Health Studies • University of Connecticut 10997
Center for International Resource Development • Tulane University 5641
Center for International Rural and Environmental Health • University of Iowa 1699
Center for Locomotion Studies • Pennsylvania State University 9947
Center for Low Vision Study, Care and Rehabilitation • University of Florida 13648
Center for Macromolecular Design • Texas A&M University 2628
Center for Magnetic Resonance • Massachusetts Institute of Technology 11150
Center for Mastitis Research • Pennsylvania State University 13164
Center for Medical Consumers and Health Care Information 1231
Center for Medical Consumers and Health Information 1569
Center for Medical Economics Studies • Northeastern University 1646
Center for Medical Ethics • University of Pittsburgh 7222
Center for Medical Illustration • Armed Forces Institute of Pathology • U.S. Department of Defense 7025
Center for Medicinal Chemistry Research • University of Texas at Arlington 2688
Center for Modern Psychoanalytic Studies 7548
Center for Molecular and Behavioral Neuroscience • Rutgers University 8423
Center for Molecular Biology of Oral Diseases • University of Illinois at Chicago 4027
Center for Molecular Genetics • University of California, San Diego 2664

Center for the Study of Bioethics · Medical College of Wisconsin **7209**

Center for the Study of the Cellular and Molecular Basis of Development · City College of City University of New York **2562**

Center for the Study of Cerebrovascular Disease and Stroke · University of Maryland **8506**

Center for the Study of Communication and Deafness · Boston University **3590**

Center for the Study of Drug Development **10628**

Center for the Study of Ethics and Contemporary Moral Problems; HUC-UC **7204**

Center to Study Human-Animal Relationships and Environments · University of Minnesota **1705**

Center for the Study of Human Performance in Dentistry · University of Maryland **9855**

Center for the Study of Inflammatory Bowel Disease · University of California, Los Angeles **5248**

Center for Study of Multiple Birth **9705, 11208**

Center for Study of Multiple Gestation **9705, 11208**

Center for the Study of Pharmacy and Therapeutics for the Elderly **1895** University of Maryland **10475**

Center for the Study of Psychiatry **7354**

Center for the Study of Social Development and Education · University of Massachusetts Boston **4594**

Center for the Study of Social Policy **5617**

Center for the Study of Society and Medicine · Columbia University **5619**

Center for the Study of Suicide · University of South Carolina at Columbia **7686**

Center for Study of Trauma · University of California, San Francisco **7660**

Center for the Study of Women · University of California, Los Angeles **1685**

Center for Substance Abuse Research · University of Maryland **12139**

Center for Thanatology Research **3724**

Center for Thrombosis and Hemostasis · University of North Carolina at Chapel Hill **6237**

Center for Transplantation Biology · University of Florida **12890**

Center for Tropical Animal Health · Texas A&M University **13174**

Center on Tropical Diseases · Meharry Medical College **6778**

Center for Tropical and Parasitic Diseases · University of Miami **6847**

Center for Ulcer Research and Education · University of California, Los Angeles **5249**

Center for Understanding Aging **1896**

Center for Urban and Public Health Entomology · Texas A&M University **10985**

Center for Values and Social Policy · University of Colorado at Boulder **7220**

Center for VDT and Health Research · Johns Hopkins University **9811**

Center for Veterinary Medicine · Food and Drug Administration · U.S. Department of Health and Human Services **12990, 13209**

Center for Virology, Immunology and Infectious Disease Research · George Washington University **6770**

Center for Visual Science · University of Rochester **13659**

Center for Vulnerable Populations **4575**

Center for the Well-Being of Health Professionals **7353, 9803**

Center for Women's Health · Medical College of Pennsylvania and Hahnemann University **9710**

Center for Worksite Health Enhancement · Pennsylvania State University **9817**

Centerior Energy Foundation **627**

Centers for Disease Control and Prevention · U.S. Department of Health and Human Services **10896, 10990**

Centers for Health, Education and Social Systems Studies **1571, 5618**

Centers Program · Extramural Activities Program · National Institute of Arthritis and Musculoskeletal and Skin Diseases · U.S. Department of Health and Human Services **7937**

Central Africa; Organization for Co-Ordination in Control of Endemic Diseases in **6741**

Central America Health Rights Network; National **1409**

Central America and Panama; Institute of Nutrition of **9464**

Central America and Panama; Odontological Federation of **3979**

Central American Federation of Sports Medicine **11943**

Central American Society of Pharmacology **10403**

Central Arizona Chapter · Arthritis Foundation **7964**

Central Association of Medical Chiropodists of Germany **10769**

Central Bureau for the Jewish Aged **1905**

Central California Easter Seal Society **4609**

Central European Dental Institute; American **3886**

Central Fidelity Banks Foundation **628**

Central Florida Blood Bank, Inc. · Specialist in Blood Bank Technology Program **7094**

Central Indiana Easter Seal Society **4635**

Central Institute for the Deaf **3594**

Central Missouri State University · Department of Nursing **8788**

Central Nervous System Studies; Laboratory of · National Institute of Neurological Disorders and Stroke · U.S. Department of Health and Human Services **8458**

Central New York Chapter
    Arthritis Foundation **7998**
    Cystic Fibrosis Foundation **5440**
    Lupus Foundation of America **8081**

Central Ohio Chapter
    Arthritis Foundation **8006**
    Cystic Fibrosis Foundation **5448**

Central Ohio; Fibromyalgia Association of **7876**

Central Ohio Fibrositis Association **7876**

Central Pennsylvania Chapter
    Arthritis Foundation **8013**
    Cystic Fibrosis Foundation **5453**

Central Piedmont Community College · Respiratory Therapist Program **11475**

Central Service Material Management; International Association of Healthcare **6449**

Central Service Personnel; American Society for Healthcare **6427**

Central Society for Clinical Research **1232**

Central Soya Foundation **629**

Central Virginia Chapter · Lupus Foundation of America **8116**

Centre on Aging · University of Manitoba **1981**

Centre for Contact Lens Research · University of Waterloo **13661**

Centre hospitalier Cote-des-Neiges Research Centre · University of Montreal **1989**

Centre for Gerontology · University of Alberta **1969**

Centre for Habilitation Education and Research · University of Waterloo **4599**

Centre International de Recherche sur le Cancer **5949**

Centre for Nonlinear Dynamics in Physiology and Medicine · McGill University **1630**

Centre for Occupational Stress and Health · University of Montreal **9859**

Centre for Research in Neurodegenerative Diseases · University of Toronto **8530**

Centre for Studies of Aging · University of Toronto **1995**

Centre for Study of Biological Interactions Between Environment and Health · University of Quebec at Montreal **9861**

Centre for the Study of Host Resistance · McGill University **6776**

Centro America y Panama; Instituto de Nutricion de **9464**

Centro-Americana de Farmacologia; Sociedad **10403**

Centro Internazionale di Ipnosi Medica e Psicologica **6592**

Centro Panamericano de Fiebre Aftosa **13109**

Centroamerica; Cides- **6653**

Centroamericano de Medicina del Deporte; Confederacion **11943**

Ceramics; American Society of Dental **3869**

Cerebral Blood Flow Laboratories **8350**

Cerebral Metabolism Laboratory · National Institute of Mental Health · U.S. Department of Health and Human Services **7619**

Cerebral Palsy; American Academy for **8151**

Cerebral Palsy Associations; United **8320**

Cerebral Palsy Athletic Association; United States **8323**

Cerebral Palsy and Developmental Medicine; American Academy for **8151**

Cerebral Palsy International Sports and Recreation Association **4472**

Cerebral Palsy Ireland **4473**

Cerebral Palsy; National Foundation for **8320**

Cerebral Palsy Research and Educational Foundation; United **8140**

Cerebral Palsy Society; International **8237**

Cerebral Vascular Disease Research Center · University of Miami **8510**

Cerebrovascular Disease and Stroke; Center for the Study of · University of Maryland **8506**

Cerebrovascular Research; Baylor Center for **8350**

Cerebrovascular Research Center
    University of Pennsylvania **8519**
    Wake Forest University **8534**

CertainTeed Corp. Foundation **630**

Certification of Acupuncturists; National Commission for the **2227**

Certification Agency for Medical Lab Personnel; National **7146**

Certification; American Board of Post Anesthesia Nursing **2350**

Certification; American Sports Medicine Association Board of **11939**

Certification Board; American Occupational Therapy **12656**

Certification Board; International Healthcare Safety Professional **9798**

Certification Board for Music Therapists **12672**

Certification Board; Nuclear Medicine Technology **11128**

Certification Corporation for the Obstetric, Gynecologic and Neonatal Nursing Specialties; National **9114**

Certification of Dental Laboratories; National Board for **3970**

Certification in Dental Technology; National Board for **3971**

Certification Directors; Association of Health Facility Licensure and **5559**

Certification; National Commission for Electrologist **1413**

Certification; National Council for Therapeutic Recreation **12698**

Chest Hospital Research Centre; Montreal • McGill University **11611**

Chest Physicians; American College of **2784, 2826**

Chest Physicians and Surgeons; International Academy of **12273**

Chester, Delaware and Montgomery Counties; Easter Seal Society of Philadelphia, Bucks, **4666**

Chestnut Lodge Research Institute **7552**

Chi Delta Mu **1234**

Chi Eta Phi Sorority **9080**

Chicago Affiliate; Metropolitan • American Heart Association **3004**

Chicago; American Lung Association of Metropolitan **11640**

Chicago Chapter; Greater • Arthritis Foundation **7978**

Chicago College of Osteopathic Medicine • Department of Pharmacology **10226**

Chicago Institute of Neurosurgery and Neuroresearch **8351**

Chicago Medical School • H.M. Bligh Cancer Research Laboratories **6019**

Chicago Medical School; Finch University of Health Sciences / **949**

    Department of Pharmacology **10227**

    Physician Assistant Program **1073**

    School of Related Health Sciences • Physical Therapy Program **12469**

Chicago State University

    College of Nursing **8644**

    College of Nursing and Allied Health Professions • Occupational Therapist Program **12351**

    Health Information Administration Program **6924**

Chichester duPont Foundation **98**

Child Abuse and Family Violence; National Council on **3061**

Child Abuse Institute of Research **3047**

Child Abuse Listening and Mediation **3048**

Child Abuse; National Committee for Prevention of **3060**

Child Abuse and Neglect; C. Henry Kempe National Center for the Prevention and Treatment of • University of Colorado **3073**

Child Abuse and Neglect Information; Clearinghouse on **3058**

Child Abuse and Neglect Information; National Clearinghouse on **3058**

Child Abuse and Neglect; International Society for Prevention of **3056**

Child Abuse and Neglect; National Center on • Administration for Children and Families • U.S. Department of Health and Human Services **3045, 3072**

Child and Adolescent Disorders Research Branch • Clinical Research Division • National Institute of Mental Health • U.S. Department of Health and Human Services **7620**

Child Adolescent Health Division • Community Health Bureau • Connecticut Department of Public Health **3384, 9730**

Child and Adolescent Psychiatric Nurses; Association of **3178**

Child and Adolescent Psychiatry and Allied Professions; International Association for **3240**

Child and Adolescent Psychiatry; American Academy of **3158**

Child and Adolescent Psychiatry; European Society of **3222**

Child and Adolescent Psychiatry; Society of Professors of **7516**

Child Behavior Laboratory; Infant and • State University of New York Health Science Center at Brooklyn **3352**

Child Behavior Research; Institute for **7540**

Child Behavior Research Unit • State University of New York Health Science Center at Brooklyn **3350**

Child Brain Development; International Academy for **3238**

Child Care Foundation **3242**

Child Care (U.S.A.); International **3242**

Child Development Center **3319**

    Howard University **3338**

Child Development Center; Frank Porter Graham • University of North Carolina at Chapel Hill **3368**

Child Development; European Association for Studies on Nutrition and **9455**

Child Development; Foundation for **192**

Child Development Institute • University of North Carolina at Chapel Hill **3367**

Child Development; Mailman Center for • University of Miami **3364**

Child Development and Mental Retardation Center • University of Washington **4338**

Child Development Research and Evaluation Center **4315**

Child Evaluation Center • University of Louisville **4592**

Child and Family Health Center • Health Division • Oregon Department of Human Resources **3415, 9761**

Child Family Health Section; Maternal and • Public Health Division • Alaska Department of Health and Social Services **3379, 9725**

Child and Family Services Bureau • Michigan Department of Public Health **3400, 9746**

Child and Family Studies; Center for • University of California, San Diego **3356**

Child and Family Studies; Division of • University of Connecticut **4587**

Child and Family; University Center for the • University of Michigan **3365**

Child Growth and Development; Philadelphia Center for Research in **3373**

Child Growth and Development; W.M. Krogman Center for Research in **3373**

Child Health; American Foundation for Maternal and **3167**

Child Health Association of the Philippines; Maternal and **3257**

Child Health; Association of Teachers of Maternal and **3191**

Child Health Branch; Maternal and

    Family Health Services Division • Health Resources Administration • Hawaii Department of Health **3389, 9735**

    Health Services Department • California Health and Welfare Agency **3382, 9728**

Child Health Bureau; Family, Maternal and • Health Services Division • Montana Department of Health and Environmental Sciences **3404, 9750**

Child Health Bureau; Maternal and

    Family Health Services Division • Utah Department of Health **3422, 9768**

    Health Division • Idaho Department of Health and Welfare **3390, 9736**

    Health Resources and Services Administration • Public Health Service • U.S. Department of Health and Human Services **3131**

    Health Services Office • South Carolina Department of Health and Environmental Control **3418, 9764**

    Maternal and Child Health Division • Ohio Department of Health **3413, 9759**

    Public Health Division • New Mexico Department of Health **3409, 9755**

    Public Health Services Division • New Hampshire Department of Health and Human Services **3407, 9753**

Child Health Clearinghouse; National Maternal and **3269**

Child Health and Crippled Children's Directors; Association of State and Territorial Maternal and **3184**

Child Health Division; Maternal and

    Georgia Department of Medical Assistance **3388, 9734**

    Health Bureau • Maine Department of Human Services **3397, 9743**

    Health Director's Office • North Carolina Department of Environment, Health, and Natural Resources **3411, 9757**

    Maternal and Child Health Bureau • Pennsylvania Department of Health **3416, 9762**

    Preventive Health Section • North Dakota Department of Health and Consolidated Laboratories **3412, 9758**

    Public Health Programs Bureau • Arkansas Department of Health **3381, 9727**

Child Health Foundation **3198**

Child Health Foundation; International **3198**

Child Health; Gurson Foundation for **3233**

Child Health and Human Development; National Institute of

    Center for Population Research

        Contraceptive Development Branch • U.S. Department of Health and Human Services **11285**

        Contraceptive Evaluation Branch • U.S. Department of Health and Human Services **11286**

        Demographic and Behavioral Sciences Branch • U.S. Department of Health and Human Services **11287**

        Reproductive Sciences Branch • U.S. Department of Health and Human Services **11288**

        U.S. Department of Health and Human Services **11284**

    Center for Research for Mothers and Children

        Developmental Biology, Genetics and Teratology Branch • U.S. Department of Health and Human Services **5358**

        Endocrinology, Nutrition, and Growth Branch • U.S. Department of Health and Human Services **4903**

        Human Learning and Behavior Branch • U.S. Department of Health and Human Services **7613**

        Mental Retardation and Developmental Disabilities Branch • U.S. Department of Health and Human Services **4320**

        Perinatal Emphasis Research Centers Program • U.S. Department of Health and Human Services **9713**

        Pregnancy and Perinatology Branch • U.S. Department of Health and Human Services **9714**

        U.S. Department of Health and Human Services **9712**

    Epidemiology, Statistics and Prevention Research Division • U.S. Department of Health and Human Services **5190**

    Human Genetics Branch • Drug Biotransformation Section • U.S. Department of Health and Human Services **5359**

    Intramural Research Division • U.S. Department of Health and Human Services **1675**

    Intramural Research Program

        Cell Biology and Metabolism Branch • U.S. Department of Health and Human Services **2637**

        Developmental Endocrinology Branch • U.S. Department of Health and Human Services **4904**

        Endocrinology and Reproduction Research Branch • U.S. Department of Health and Human Services **4905**

        Growth Factors Section • U.S. Department of Health and Human Services **8437**

Department of Health Sciences
  Occupational Therapy Program **12407**
  Physical Therapy Department **12528**
Department of Nursing **8875**
James J. Nance College of Business Administration • Graduate Study in Health Care Administration **5513**
Climatism; Latin American Federation of Thermalism and **5048**
Climatological Association; American Clinical and **1151**
Climatologie Medicale; Societe Internationale d' Hydrologie et de **5046**
Climatology; American Institute of Biomedical **5034**
Climatology; American Institute of Medical **5034**
Climatology; International Society of Medical Hydrology and **5046**
Climatotherapie; Federation Europeenne de **5039**
Climatotherapy; European Society of **5039**
Clincal Medicine and Science; Foundation for Advances in **1294**
Clicial Radioassay Society **7130**
Clincial Sciences; Center for Evaluative • Dartmouth College **5622**
Clinic; Karen Horney **7433**
Clinic; Karen Horney Psychoanalytic **7433**
Clinic Managers; American College of **5547**
Clinic Managers; Association of **5584**
Clinica; Confederacion Latinoamericana de Bioquimica **2540**
Clinica; Societatea Romana de Neurofiziologie **8301**
Clinical and Aging Services Research; Center for • University of California, San Francisco **1973**
Clinical AIDS Research and Education / AIDS Clinical Trials Unit; UCLA Center for • University of California, Los Angeles **6840**
Clinical Applications; Division of Epidemiology and • National Heart, Lung, and Blood Institute • U.S. Department of Health and Human Services **2930**
Clinical Applications and Prevention Program • Division of Epidemiology and Clinical Applications • National Heart, Lung, and Blood Institute • U.S. Department of Health and Human Services **2931**
Clinical Assessment; Inquiry Group on Applied Psychometrics and • Texas A&M University **7609**
Clinical and Basic Research; Alzheimer's Research Center for • Medical College of Georgia **8392**
Clinical and Behavioral Studies; Human Immunodeficiency Virus Center for **6772**
Clinical Biochemistry; Latin American Confederation of **2540**
Clinical and Biological Research Division; Intramural • National Institute on Alcohol Abuse and Alcoholism • U.S. Department of Health and Human Services **12111**
Clinical / Biomedical Engineering • University of Arizona **2476**
Clinical Biostatistics; International Society for **7005**
Clinical Brain Disorders Branch • Intramural Research Programs Division (Research at St. Elizabeth's Hospital) • National Institute of Mental Health • U.S. Department of Health and Human Services **7641**
Clinical Cancer Research Center; Roger Williams **6106**
Clinical Center; Multiple Sclerosis • University of Maryland **8507**
Clinical Center for Research in Parkinson's and Allied Disorders • Mount Sinai School of Medicine of City University of New York **8399**
Clinical Center; Warren Grant Magnuson
  National Institutes of Health • U.S. Department of Health and Human Services **1679**
  U.S. Department of Health and Human Services **2515**
Clinical Chemistry; American Association for **7116**
Clinical Chemistry; International Federation of **7140**
Clinical Chemistry; National Registry in **7149**
Clinical Chemists; American Association of **7116**
Clinical and Climatological Association; American **1151**
Clinical Dental Technicians Association **3915**
Clinical Dermatologic Society; North American **4252**
Clinical Ecology; Society for **5031**
Clinical Endocrinologists; American Association of **4827**
Clinical Enzymology; International Society for **7142**
Clinical Epidemiology and Biostatistics; Center for • University of Pennsylvania **5195**
Clinical Epidemiology Branch • Epidemiology and Biostatistics Program • National Cancer Institute • U.S. Department of Health and Human Services **6168**
Clinical Evoked Potentials; American Society for **8174**
Clinical and Experimental Hypnosis; Society for **6598**
Clinical Hematology Branch • Division of Intramural Research • National Institute of Diabetes and Digestive and Kidney Diseases • U.S. Department of Health and Human Services **6206**
Clinical Hypnosis; American Society of **6587**
  Education and Research Foundation **6588**
Clinical Immunology Branch • Division of Allergy, Immunology, and Transplantation • National Institute of Allergy and Infectious Diseases • U.S. Department of Health and Human Services **2127**
Clinical Immunology; European Academy of Allergology and **2072**
Clinical Immunology; International Association of Allergology and **2074**

Clinical Immunology; Max Samter Institute of Allergy and **2091**
Clinical Immunology Program; Allergy- • University of California, Davis **2140**
Clinical Immunology and Rheumatology; Division of • University of Alabama at Birmingham **7943**
Clinical Immunology Section • School of Medicine • Tulane University **2122**
Clinical Immunology Society **2070**
Clinical Infant Programs; National Center for **3308**
Clinical Investigation; American Society for **1183**
Clinical Investigation; Department of • Dwight David Eisenhower Army Medical Center **1584**
Clinical Investigation Facility • Wilford Hall USAF Medical Center • U.S. Department of Defense **1673**
Clinical Investigation; Laboratory of • National Institute of Allergy and Infectious Diseases • U.S. Department of Health and Human Services **2133**
Clinical Investigations Branch
  Division of Cancer Treatment • National Cancer Institute • U.S. Department of Health and Human Services **6154**
  Respiratory Disease Studies Division • National Institute for Occupational Safety and Health • U.S. Department of Health and Human Services **9836**
Clinical Investigations and Patient Care Branch • Intramural Research Program • National Institute of Dental Research • U.S. Department of Health and Human Services **4019**
Clinical Laboratory Association; American **7118**
Clinical Laboratory Management Association **7129**
Clinical Laboratory Science; American Society for **7122**
Clinical Laboratory Sciences; National Accrediting Agency for **7144**
Clinical Laboratory Standardization; European Committee for **7135**
Clinical Laboratory Standards; European Committee for **7135**
Clinical Laboratory Standards; National Committee for **7151**
Clinical Laboratory Standards Organization; NCCLS—The **7151**
Clinical Laboratory Supervisors and Administrators; American Association of **7129**
Clinical Laboratory Technicians; American Society of **7122**
Clinical Laboratory Technologists; International Society of **7143**
Clinical Laboratory Technology; International Society for **7143**
Clinical Ligand Assay Society **7130**
Clinical Managers; National Association of **5584**
Clinical Mass Spectrometry Research Resource • University of Colorado **2481**
Clinical and Medical Electrologists; Society of **1506**
Clinical Medical Ethics; Center for • University of Chicago **7219**
Clinical Medicine Branch • Basic Research Division • National Institute on Drug Abuse • U.S. Department of Health and Human Services **12124**
Clinical Microbiology Laboratories • University of Texas Medical Branch at Galveston **6854**
Clinical Microbiology Laboratory; Veterinary Medicine and • Iowa State University of Science and Technology **13140**
Clinical Microbiology Research Group; Southeastern New England • University of Massachusetts Dartmouth **2675**
Clinical Neuroendocrinology Branch • Intramural Research Programs Division (Clinical Research) • National Institute of Mental Health • U.S. Department of Health and Human Services **7637**
Clinical Neurogenetics Branch • Intramural Research Programs Division (Clinical Research) • National Institute of Mental Health • U.S. Department of Health and Human Services **7638**
Clinical Neurophysiology; American Academy of **8152**
Clinical Neurophysiology; Finnish Society of **8219**
Clinical Neurophysiology; French-Language Society for **8220**
Clinical Neurophysiology; International Federation of **8238**
Clinical Neurophysiology; International Federation of Societies for Electroencephalography and **8238**
Clinical Neurophysiology; Romanian Society of **8301, 8301**
Clinical Neuroscience Branch • National Institute of Neurological Disorders and Stroke • U.S. Department of Health and Human Services **8444**
Clinical Nursing Education; Institute for Hospital **9093**
Clinical Nutrition; American Council of Applied **9441**
Clinical Nutrition; American Society for **9444**
Clinical Nutrition Center • University of Wisconsin—Madison **9568**
Clinical Nutrition Research Unit
  University of California, Davis **9550**
  University of Chicago **9551**
  University of Washington **9566**
  Vanderbilt University **9573**
Clinical Nutrition Research Unit; Cooperative Core Laboratories and **9499**
Clinical Nutrition Research Units Program • National Institute of Diabetes and Digestive and Kidney Diseases • U.S. Department of Health and Human Services **4907**
Clinical Occupational Medicine / Environmental Health Evaluation Center; Southeastern • Emory University **9806**

Clinical Toxicology; American Academy of **10390**

Clinical Toxicology Centers and Poison Control Centers; World Federation of Associations of **10425**

Clinical Trials Branch • Biometry and Epidemiology Program • National Eye Institute • U.S. Department of Health and Human Services **13630**

Clinical Trials Program • Division of Digestive Diseases and Nutrition • National Institute of Diabetes and Digestive and Kidney Diseases • U.S. Department of Health and Human Services **5239**

Clinical Trials Program; Diabetes • Division of Diabetes, Endocrinology, and Metabolic Diseases • National Institute of Diabetes and Digestive and Kidney Diseases • U.S. Department of Health and Human Services **4910**

Clinical Trials; Society for **1507**

Clinical Trials Unit; UCLA Center for Clinical AIDS Research and Education / AIDS • University of California, Los Angeles **6840**

Clinical; World Association of Societies of Pathology— Anatomic and **10141**

Clinics; American Association of Medical **1163**

Clinique; Academie Europeenne d' Allergologie et d' Immunologie **2072**

Clinique; Association Europeenne des Centres Anti- Poisons et de Toxicologie **10407**

Clinique; Association Mondiale des Societes de Pathologie - Anatomique et **10141**

Clinique de Langue Francaise; Societe de Neurophysiologie **8220**

Clipper Ship Foundation **107**

Clisby Charitable Trust **181**

Clorox Company Foundation **639**

Clowes Fund **108**

Club International d'Implants Oculaires **13448**

Club of Neuropathologists **10118**

CMT International **8202**

CNS Injury and Edema Research Center • University of California, San Francisco **8488**

Coagulation Laboratory; Thrombosis & • University of Oklahoma **6239**

Coagulation Research Laboratory—Clinical • University of Michigan **6230**

Coalition of Digestive Disease Organizations **5217**

Coalition for the Medical Rights of Women **11211**

Coalition on Sexuality and Disability **11688**

Coalition on Smoking OR Health **11736**

Coalition of Spanish Speaking Mental Health Organizations **1410**

Co-Arts Association; Haitian and **1312**

Cocaine Anonymous World Services **12019**

Cochlear Implant Club International **3503**

Cochran Research Center • Temple University **5639**

Cockrell Foundation **109**

Cocuk Sagligi Vakfi; Gurson **3233**

Co-Dependents Anonymous **12020**

Co-Dependents of Sex Addicts **11689**

Coe College • Department of Nursing Education **8693**

Coeliac Society of the United Kingdom **5214**

Coffin-Lowry Syndrome Foundation **5273**

Cognition; Laboratory of Personality and • National Institute on Aging • U.S. Department of Health and Human Services **1963**

Cognitive Neuroscience Laboratory • University of Quebec at Montreal **3653**

Cognitive Sciences; Federation of Behavioral, Psychological and **7375**

Cognitive Therapy; Center for • University of Pennsylvania **7681**

Colby-Sawyer College • Department of Nursing **8810**

Colectivo Mujer y Salud **1246**

Colegio de Cirujanos Dentistas de Puerto Rico **4194**

Colegio de Farmaceuticos de Puerto Rico **10733**

Colegio Ibero-Latino-Americano de Dermatologia **4240**

Colegio de Medicos Veterinarios de Puerto Rico **13341**

Coleman Foundation **110**

Colitis Foundation of America; Crohn's and **5199, 5215**

Colitis; Foundation for Ileitis and **5215**

Colitis; National Foundation for Ileitis and **5215**

Collaborative Clinical Research Branch • Extramural Research • National Eye Institute • U.S. Department of Health and Human Services **13636**

Collaborative Nurse-Midwifery Graduate Program • University of Texas at El Paso / Texas Tech University **9615**

College of Agriculture and Home Economics Research Center • Washington State University **13248**

College of American Pathologists **7131**

College of Clinic Managers; American **5547**

College Council; Tri- **1261**

College of the Desert • Respiratory Therapist Program **11318**

College of Diplomates of the American Board of Orthodontics **3916**

College of DuPage • Respiratory Therapist Program **11374**

College of Family Physicians of Canada **1247**

College Health Association; AIDS Task Force for the American **6623**

College Health Association; American **1152**

College International de Recherches Implantaires et Lariboisiere **3917**

College des Medecins de Famille du Canada **1247**

College of Medical Group Administrators; American **5547**

College Misericordia

Division of Health Sciences • Occupational Therapy Program **12414**

Nursing Program **8913**

College of Mt. St. Joseph • Department of Nursing **8876**

College of Mt. St. Vincent • Department of Nursing **8824**

College of New Rochelle • School of Nursing **8825**

College of Occupational Medicine; American **9786**

College of Optometrists in Vision Development **13437**

College of Optometry; State University of New York **13373**

College of Osteopathic Healthcare Executives **5570**

College of Osteopathic Hospital Administrators; American **5570**

College of Osteopathic Medicine of the Pacific **9952**

Department of Pharmacology **10192**

Department of Physical Therapy **12446**

Physician Assistant Program **1059**

College of Physicians of Philadelphia • Francis Clark Wood Institute for the History of Medicine **1575**

College of St. Benedict

Department of Nursing **8773**

Nutrition Department • Dietetics Program **9404**

College of St. Catherine

Department of Nursing **8774**

Department of Occupational Therapy **12376**

St. Mary's Campus • Respiratory Therapist Program **11436**

College of St. Catherine / University of St. Thomas • Department of Social Work **11804**

College of St. Mary • Health Information Management Program **6939**

College of St. Scholastica

Department of Health Information Administration **6934**

Department of Nursing **8775**

Department of Physical Therapy **12496**

Occupational Therapy Program **12377**

College of Staten Island of City University of New York • Center for Developmental Neuroscience and Developmental Disabilities **8353**

College of Technology at Canton; State University of New York • Mortuary Science Program **3690**

College of Veterinary Medicine • Cornell University **13007**

College of West Virginia

Respiratory Therapist Program **11577**

School of Nursing **9025**

Colleges, Academies and Academic Associations of General Practitioners / Family Physicians; World Organization of National **1550**

Colleges of Acupuncture and Oriental Medicine; Council of **2189**

Colleges of Acupuncture and Oriental Medicine; National Accreditation Commission for Schools and **2223**

Colleges; American Association of Osteopathic **9970**

Colleges; Association of American Medical **1197**

Colleges; Association of American Veterinary Medical **13058**

Colleges; Association of Chiropractic **3449**

Colleges d'Optometre; Association Europeene des Ecoles et **13446**

Colleges; International Federation of Surgical **12280**

Colleges; National Council of Acupuncture Schools and **2189**

Colleges Nationaux, Academies et Associations Academiques des Generalistes et des Medecins de Famille; Organisation Mondiale des **1550**

Colleges of Nursing; American Association of **9050**

Colleges of Optometry; Association of Schools and **13417**

Colleges of Optometry; European Association of Schools and **13446**

Colleges of Osteopathic Medicine; American Association of **9970**

Colleges of Pharmacy; American Association of **10578**

Colleges of Podiatric Medicine; American Association of **10755**

Colleges of Podiatry; American Association of **10755**

Colleges of Veterinary Medicine; Association of Deans of American **13058**

Collegium Internationale Activitatis Nervosae Superioris **8203**

Collegium Internationale Neuro-Psychopharmacologicum **8204**

Collin County Community College District • Respiratory Therapist Program **11542**

Collins & Aikman Holdings Foundation **640**

Collins Foundation **111**

Collins Foundation; Treacher **5303**

Colombian Pediatric Society **3212**

Colombian Society of Dermatology **4225**

Colombiana de Dermatologia; Sociedad **4225**

Colombiana de Pediatria; Sociedad **3212**

Colon and Rectal Surgeons; American Society of **12237**

Colon and Rectal Surgery; American Board of **12217**

Colon Surgery; Association of **12304**

Colon Therapy Association; American **5221**

Community Mental Health Center; Sound View-Throgs Neck • Yeshiva University   7706
Community Mental Health Centers; National Council of   7460
Community Mental Health Centers; National Council of Comprehensive   7460
Community Mental Health Division • Nebraska Department of Public Institutions   7735
Community Nutrition Institute   9451
Community Oncology Program; Early Detection and • Division of Cancer Prevention and Control • National Cancer Institute • U.S. Department of Health and Human Services   6145
Community Options and Resources; American Network of   4278
Community Projects; World   4571
Community Psychiatrists; American Association of   7274
Community Psychiatry; Institute on Hospital and   7392
Community Referenced Behavior Management; Research and Training Center for   7594
Community Study; Center for • University of Rochester   7685
Community Systems Foundation   1255
Companion Animal Bond; Group for the Study of the Human/   12719
Companion Animal Health; Center for • University of California, Davis   13211
Companion Animal Studies; Society for   12719
Compaq Computer Foundation   643
Comparative Biochemistry; Laboratory for   2585
Comparative Biochemistry Laboratory; General and • National Institute of Mental Health • U.S. Department of Health and Human Services   7633
Comparative Carcinogenesis; Laboratory of • National Cancer Institute • U.S. Department of Health and Human Services   6183
Comparative Ethology; Laboratory of • National Institute of Child Health and Human Development • U.S. Department of Health and Human Services   7614
Comparative Immunology; International Society of Developmental and   2077
Comparative Leukemia Unit • University of Pennsylvania   6241
Comparative Medicine Clinical Research Center • Wake Forest University   1746
Comparative Medicine; Division of • Johns Hopkins University   1611
Comparative Pathology; Registry of   10137
Comparative Physiology Lab • Southern Illinois University at Carbondale   2622
Comparative Psychology; International Society for   7420
Comparative Research on Leukemia and Related Diseases; International Association for   5951
Comparative Toxicology; American Academy of Veterinary and   13021
Compass Bank Foundation   644
Compensation Medicine; American Academy of   7172
Competency Assurance; National Organization for   1428
Complementary Medicine; Institute for   2205
Complex Systems; Center for
    Florida Atlantic University   8368
    University of Arizona   8478
Complications in Spinal Cord Injury; Medical Rehabilitation Research and Training Center in Secondary • University of Alabama at Birmingham   12755
Comprehensive AIDS Center   6767
Comprehensive Cancer Center
    Ohio State University   6095
    University of Alabama at Birmingham   6208
    University of Wisconsin   6258
    Wake Forest University   6263
Comprehensive Cancer Center; Kaplan • New York University   6087
Comprehensive Cancer Center of Metropolitan Detroit; Meyer L. Prentis   6077
Comprehensive Cancer Center; Norris • University of Southern California   6249
Comprehensive Cancer Center; Sylvester • University of Miami   6229
Comprehensive Cancer Center; UCLA Jonsson • University of California, Los Angeles   6213
Comprehensive Cancer Center; UNC Lineberger • University of North Carolina at Chapel Hill   6238
Comprehensive Cancer Center; Yale • Yale University   6270
Comprehensive Epilepsy Program • Wake Forest University   8535
Comprehensive Health Education Foundation   1256
Comprehensive Sickle Cell Center
    Duke University   6030
    Meharry Medical College   6073
    University of Southern California   6245
    Wayne State University   6267
Comprehensive Sickle Cell Center [Cincinnati, OH]   6026
Comprehensive Sickle Cell Center [New York, NY]   6025
Comprehensive Sickle Cell Center; Northern California • University of California, San Francisco   6217

Compulsive Anonymous; Obsessive-   7480
Compulsive Disorder Foundation; Obsessive   7481
Compulsive Foundation; Obsessive   7481
Compulsive Stutterers Anonymous   3505
Computational Biology; W.M. Keck Center for   2703
Computational Learning; Center for Biological and • Massachusetts Institute of Technology   8390
Computed Body Tomography and Magnetic Resonance; Society of   11133
Computed Body Tomography; Society of   11133
Computer Graphics Laboratory • University of California, San Francisco   10470
Computer Laboratory; Biomedical • Washington University   2504
Computer Medicine; American Physicians Association of   1174
Computer Research and Technology; Division of • National Institutes of Health • U.S. Department of Health and Human Services   2512, 2655
Computer Resource; Mayo Biomedical Imaging   2454
Computer Science Branch • Lister Hill National Center for Biomedical Communications • National Institutes of Health • U.S. Department of Health and Human Services   7032
Computer Users in Speech and Hearing   3506
Computerized Medical Imaging Society   11107
Computerized Radiology Society   11107
Computerized Tomography and Neuroimaging; Society for   11096
Computerized Tomography Society   11107
Computers in Health; Canadian Organization for Advancement of   6985
Computers and the Physically Handicapped; Special Interest Committee for   4559
Computers and the Physically Handicapped; Special Interest Group for   4559
Computing Center; Metabolic Magnetic Resonance Research and • University of Pennsylvania   11172
Computing; Institute for Biomedical • Washington University   2505
Computing; Special Interest Group on Biomedical   2433
Comstock Foundation   114
Concern for Health Options - Information, Care and Education   11210
Concern for Public Health; International Institute of   5077
Concerned Citizens for Stronger Legislation Against Molesters   3065
Concerned Relatives of Nursing Home Patients   9266
Concordia College • West Suburban College of Nursing   8645
Concordia University Wisconsin
    Nursing Division   9037
    Occupational Therapy Program   12434
Confederacion Centroamericano de Medicina del Deporte   11943
Confederacion Latinoamericana de Bioquimica Clinica   2540
Confederacion Latinoamericana de Sociedades de Anestesia   2370
Confederacion Sudamericana de Medicina del Deporte   11951
Confederation of European Specialists in Pediatrics   3213
Confederation Internationale pour la Chirurgie Plastic et Reconstructive   12279
Confederation Internationale des Sages-Femmes   9662
Confederation Mondiale pour la Therapie Physique   12727
Conference of Educational Administrators Serving the Deaf   3507
Conference of Executives of American Schools for the Deaf   3507
Conference of Funeral Service Examining Boards of the United States   3711
Conference of Local Environmental Health Administrators   5594
Conference of Local Health Officers; United States   5605
Conference of Municipal Public Health Engineers   5594
Conference of Podiatry Executives   10770
Conference of Presidents and Officers of State Medical Associations   1293
Conference of Professors of Preventive Medicine   10843
Conference of Radiation Control Program Directors   11061
Conference of Research Workers in Animal Diseases   13070
Conference of State and Territorial Directors of Public Health Education   5565
Conference of State and Territorial Epidemiologists   5181
Conference of World Organizations Interested in the Handicapped   4495
Congele de Groupes Rares; Banque Europeenne de Sange   7134
Congenital Heart Disease Diagnosis and Treatment Center; Alabama • University of Alabama at Birmingham   2953
Congential Heart Network; Canadian Adult   2837
Congres des Psychanalystes de Langue Francaise   7361
Congress of Lung Association Staff   11594
Congress of Neurological Surgeons   12266
Congress of Organizations of the Physically Handicapped   4478
Congress of Romance Language Psychoanalysts   7361
Conjoints de Medecins; Association de   1201
Conley Speech and Hearing Center • University of Maine   3637
Conn Memorial Foundation   4446
Connecticut Affiliate
    American Diabetes Association   4956
    American Heart Association   2996

Counseling; Association for Death Education and **3708**
Counseling Association; National Rehabilitation **12700**
Counseling and Development; American Association for 7293
Counseling and Education to Stop Male Violence; Emerge: **7368**
Counseling; Forum for Death Education and 3708
Counseling and Psychotherapy; International Academy of Behavioral Medicine, **7395**
Counseling; Rabbinic Center for Research and **7494**
Counseling Service on Domestic Violence; Emerge: A Men's 7368
Counselor Educators; Council of Rehabilitation 12697
Counselors; American Association of Marriage 7276
Counselors; American Association of Marriage and Family 7276
Counselors; American Association of Sex Educators and 11685
Counselors Association; American Mental Health **7298**
Counselors; National Association for Alcoholism 12051
Counselors; National Association of Alcoholism and Drug Abuse **12051**
Counselors; National Society of Genetic **5294**
Counselors; Stop Abuse by **7523**
Counselors and Therapists; American Association of Sex Educators, **11685**
Counselors and Therapists; International Association of **7398**
CounterStroke Fiji **8206**
County and City Health Officials; National Association of **10961**
County Health Officers; National Association of 10961
County Health Officials; National Association of 10961
Couple to Couple League **11212**
Cowell Foundation; S. H. **472**
Cowles Charitable Trust **119**
Cowley Shock Trauma Center; R.A. **4764**
Cox Charitable Trust; Jessie B. **313**
COX Foundation 4833
Cox Foundation of Georgia; James M. **6403**
Cox Institute • Wright State University **1752**
Cox, Jr. Foundation; James M. **308**
CP & L Foundation **6395**
CPK Mothers' Union **1262**
Crafton Hills College • Respiratory Therapist Program **11319**
Crane and Co. Fund **650**
Cranial Academy **9998**
Cranial Association; Osteopathic 9998
Craniofacial Anomalies Development and Disorders Program • Extramural Program • National Institute of Dental Research • U.S. Department of Health and Human Services **4015**
Craniofacial Anomalies Research Center **2757**
Craniofacial Anomaly Clinic • University of Pennsylvania **2763**
Craniofacial Association; American Cleft Palate- **2740**
Craniofacial Association; Children's **2744**
Craniofacial Biology Group of the International Association for Dental Research **3919**
Cranio-Facial Biology; International Society of 3919
Craniofacial Center **3999**
    University of Florida **2760**
    University of Illinois at Chicago **2761**
Craniofacial Center; Cleft Palate- • University of Pittsburgh **2764**
Cranio-Facial Deformities; Debbie Fox Foundation for Treatment of 4514
Craniofacial Foundations; International 2744
Craniofacial Molecular Biology; Center for • University of Southern California **4046**
Craniofacially Handicapped; National Association for the **2739, 4514**
Craniomandibular Disorders; American Academy of 3866
Craniomandibular Orthopedics; American Academy of 3866
Cranio-Maxillo-Facial Surgery; European Association for **12268**
Cranston Foundation **651**
Creative-Expressive Therapy; Israeli Association of **2220**
Creative Non-Violence; Community for **1254**
Credentialing Commission **7133**
Credentialing International/Board of Cardiovascular Technology; Cardiovascular 2839
Credentialing International; Cardiovascular **2839**
Credentialing; National Board for Cardiopulmonary 2839
Credentialing; National Board for Cardiovascular and Pulmonary 2839
Creighton University
    Allergic Disease Center **2098**
    Cardiac Center **2890**
    Center for Health Policy and Ethics **5621**
    Midwest Hypertension Research Center **2891**
    School of Dentistry **3815**
    School of Medicine **986**
        Department of Pharmacology **10282**
    School of Nursing **8803**

    School of Pharmacy and Allied Health Professions **10536**
        Occupational Therapist Program **12385**
Crestar Foundation **652**
Crestlea Foundation **120**
Crime Research Group; Mental Disorders and • University of Montreal **7676**
Crime Victims Research and Treatment Center • Medical University of South Carolina **7210**
Crippled Children; International Society for 12713
Crippled Children; Shriners Hospital for [St. Louis, MO] • Metabolic Research Unit **7930**
Crippled Children; Shriners Hospitals for [Portland, OR] • Research Unit **7931**
Crippled Children; Shriners Hospitals for **6470**
Crippled Children's Directors; Association of State and Territorial Maternal and Child Health and 3184
Crippled; New York Society for the Relief of the Ruptured and **7925**
Cripples; International Society for the Welfare of 12713
Crisis Interveners; American Academy of **7266**
Crisis; Women in **1534**
Criss Memorial Foundation; Dr. C.C. and Mabel L. **6345**
Cristina Foundation; National **4524**
Critical Care; Laboratory of Pediatric • Cornell University **10430**
Critical Care Medicine; Division of Pulmonary and
    University of California, San Diego **11620**
    University of Michigan **11622**
Critical Care Medicine; Institute of **4762**
Critical Care Medicine Section; Pulmonary and • University of Wisconsin— Madison **11623**
Critical Care Medicine; Society of **4758**
Critical Care Medicine; World Federation of Societies of Intensive and **4760**
Critical-Care Nurses; American Association of **9051**
Critical Care Society; International Trauma Anesthesia and **2369**
Critical Care; Society of Neurosurgical Anesthesia and **8309**
Crohn's and Colitis Foundation of America **5199, 5215**
Croix-Bleue; Federation Internationale de la 12040
Crown and Bridge Prosthodontics; American Academy of 3856
Crown Central Petroleum Foundation **653**
Crown Memorial; Arie and Ida **49**
Crozer-Chester Medical Center; Delaware County Community College / • Respiratory Therapist Program **11510**
Crump Institute for Biological Imaging • University of California, Los Angeles **2477**
Cryo-Opthamology; Society for 13406
Cryobiology; Society for **2544**
Cryonics Society; American **3706**
Cryonics Society; Bay Area 3706
Cryosurgery; American College of **12230**
Crystal Trust **121**
Crystallographic Research; Center for **2561**
CS First Boston Foundation Trust **654**
CTC World Federation 10425
Cued Speech Association; National **3553**
Cued Speech Center **3512**
Cullen Eye Institute • Baylor College of Medicine **13581**
Cullen Foundation **122**
Cultural Exchange; International Association for Medical Research and **1337**
Culture Collections; World Federation for **6758**
Culture and Nursing; Institute for the Study of • University of Miami **9148**
Culturels; Association Internationale pour la Recherche Medicale et les Echanges 1337
Culver-Stockton / Blessing-Rieman College • School of Nursing **8646**
Cumberland University • School of Nursing **8969**
Cummings Foundation; James H. **306**
Cummings Foundation; Nathan **409**
Cummings Memorial Fund; Frances L. & Edwin L. **195**
Cummins School of Nurse Anesthesia; Manley L. **2258**
Cumulative Trauma Disorders; Physical Therapy Laboratory for • University of Michigan—Flint **9858**
CUNA Mutual Charitable Foundation **655**
Cunningham Foundation; Laura Moore **6370**
Cure Federation; All India Nature **2152**
CURE Formaldehyde Poisoning Association **10406**
Cure Foundation **5200, 5216**
Curry College • Division of Nursing Studies **8748**
Curtice-Burns / Pro-Fac Foundation **656**
Curtis Blake Center • American International College **4573**
Cushing Society; Harvey **12212**
Cutaneous Biology Research Center; Harvard • Massachusetts General Hospital **4265**

D

Dental Federation; International 3935
Dental Fraternity; Alpha Omega International 3851
Dental Gold Institute 5837
Dental Group Management Association 5573
Dental Group Practice; American Academy of 3853
Dental Health; American Fund for 3786
Dental Health Bureau
    Ambulatory Health Care Administration Division • Public Health
      Commission • District of Columbia Department of Human Services
      4110
    Family and Community Health Division • Iowa Department of Public
      Health 4117
    Family Health Services Division • Utah Department of Health 4147
    Health Division • Nevada Department of Human Resources 4130
    Maternal, Child, and Family Health Division • Missouri Department of
      Health 4127
    Maternal and Child Health • Ohio Department of Health 4137
    New York State Department of Health 4134
    Public Health Services Division • New Hampshire Department of
      Health and Human Services 4131
    Texas Department of Health 4146
Dental Health Care Boards; Washington 4098
Dental Health Division
    Alabama Department of Public Health 4102
    Community Health Office • Illinois Department of Public Health 4115
    Health Bureau • Maine Department of Human Services 4121
    Health Department
      Vermont Agency of Human Services 4148
      Virginia Office of Health and Human Resources 4150
    Health Director's Office • North Carolina Department of Environment,
      Health, and Natural Resources 4135
    Health Promotion and Disease Prevention • Nebraska Department of
      Health 4129
    Health Resources Administration • Hawaii Department of Health
      4113
    Maternal and Child Health Office • Public Health Bureau • West
      Virginia Department of Health and Human Resources 4152
    Public Health Department • Massachusetts Executive Office of Health
      and Human Services 4123
    Rhode Island Department of Health 4142
Dental Health Foundation; International 3959
Dental Health International 3928
Dental Health Office • Arkansas Department of Health 4105
Dental Health Program
    Community Health Care Access Section • Public Health Division •
      Delaware Department of Health and Social Services 4109
    Maternal and Child Health Division • Preventive Health Section •
      North Dakota Department of Health and Consolidated
      Laboratories 4136
    Maternal and Child Health Services Division • Health Service
      Department • Kentucky Human Resources Cabinet 4119
    Public Health Division • New Mexico Department of Health 4133
    Women and Children's Services Division • South Carolina Department
      of Health and Environmental Control 4143
Dental Health Section
    Health Division • Oregon Department of Human Resources 4139
    Maternal and Child Health Division • Public Health Services Office •
      Louisiana Department of Health and Hospitals 4120
Dental Health Services
    Health Services Bureau • Mississippi Department of Health 4126
    Oklahoma Department of Health 4138
    Public Health Division • Wyoming Department of Health 4154
    Virgin Islands Department of Health 4149
Dental-Hospital Bureaus of America; Medical- 5862
Dental Hygienists' Association; American 3785, 3891
Dental Hygienists' Association; National 3974
Dental-Industrie; Verband der Deutschen 5886
Dental Industry; Federation of the European 5849
Dental Infirmary for Children; Forsyth 4001
Dental Information 3892
Dental Institute; American 3892
Dental Institute; American Central European 3886
Dental Interfraternity Council; American 3893
Dental Laboratories; National Association of 3967
Dental Laboratories; National Association of Certified 3967
Dental Laboratories; National Board for Certification of 3970
Dental Management Consultants; Society of Medical- 5882
Dental Manufacturers of America 5838
Dental Manufacturers; Danish 5834
Dental Materials; Academy of 3841
Dental Medicine; Portuguese Society of Stomatology and 3986
Dental Medicine Practitioners; European Union of 3933

Dental Medicine and Surgery; American Board of 3881
Dental Plans Association; Delta 3921
Dental Practice Administration; American Academy of 3854
Dental Program
    Administrative Services Division • Alaska Department of Health and
      Social Services 4103
    Chronic Disease and Injury Control Branch • Health Services
      Department • California Health and Welfare Agency 4106
    Health and Medical Services Division • South Dakota Department of
      Health 4144
    Local and Family Health Administration • Maryland Department of
      Health and Mental Hygiene 4122
    Local and Rural Health Systems Bureau • Health Division • Kansas
      Department of Health and Environment 4118
    Preventive Health Services Bureau • Health Services Division •
      Montana Department of Public Health and Human Services 4128
    Special Child Health Services • Family Health Services Division • New
      Jersey Department of Health 4132
Dental Program; Public Health • Family Health Services Office • Florida
    Department of Health and Rehabilitative Services 4111
Dental Public Health; American Board of 10937
Dental Radiology; American Academy of 3864
Dental Research; American Association for 3781, 3872
Dental Research Center
    University of Medicine and Dentistry of New Jersey 4030
    University of North Carolina at Chapel Hill 4041
Dental Research; Craniofacial Biology Group of the International
    Association for 3919
Dental Research; Dows Institute for • University of Iowa 4029
Dental Research Institute
    University of California, Los Angeles 4025
    University of Minnesota 4039
Dental Research Institute; Naval • Naval Medical Research and
    Development Command • U.S. Department of Defense 7839
Dental Research; International Association for 3954
Dental Research Laboratory; George C. Paffenbarger • Ohio State
    University 4005
Dental Research; National Institute of
    Epidemiology and Oral Disease Prevention Program
      Disease Prevention and Health Promotion Branch • U.S.
        Department of Health and Human Services 4010
        Epidemiology Branch • U.S. Department of Health and Human
          Services 4011
        Sampling, Statistics, and Data Management • U.S. Department
          of Health and Human Services 4012
        U.S. Department of Health and Human Services 4009
    Extramural Program
      Caries, Restorative Materials and Salivary Research Branch •
        U.S. Department of Health and Human Services 4014
      Craniofacial Anomalies Development and Disorders Program •
        U.S. Department of Health and Human Services 4015
      Periodontal and Soft Tissue Diseases Research Program • U.S.
        Department of Health and Human Services 4016
      U.S. Department of Health and Human Services 4013
    Intramural Research Program
      Bone Research Branch • U.S. Department of Health and Human
        Services 4018
      Clinical Investigations and Patient Care Branch • U.S.
        Department of Health and Human Services 4019
      Neurobiology and Anesthesiology Branch • U.S. Department of
        Health and Human Services 4020
      Pain Research Clinic • U.S. Department of Health and Human
        Services 8439
      U.S. Department of Health and Human Services 4017
    Laboratory of Cellular Development and Oncology • U.S. Department
      of Health and Human Services 2640
    Laboratory of Developmental Biology • U.S. Department of Health and
      Human Services 2641
    Laboratory of Immunology • U.S. Department of Health and Human
      Services 4021
    Laboratory of Microbial Ecology • U.S. Department of Health and
      Human Services 4022
    Laboratory of Oral Medicine • U.S. Department of Health and Human
      Services 4023
    U.S. Department of Health and Human Services 3779, 4008
Dental Research Program • University of Missouri—Kansas City 4040
Dental Schools; American Association of 3873
Dental Service Plans; National Association of 3921
Dental Society; Alaska 4156
Dental Society of Anesthesiology; American 2351
Dental Society; Bangladesh 3908
Dental Society; Cayman Islands Medical and 1229
Dental Society; Christian 3914

Dental Society; Christian Medical and **1241**
Dental Society; Delaware State **4162**
Dental Society; District of Columbia **4163**
Dental Society; Finnish **3939**
Dental Society; Illinois State **4168**
Dental Society; Massachusetts **4176**
Dental Society; Medical Group Missions of the Christian Medical and **1381**
Dental Society; New Hampshire **4184**
Dental Society; North Carolina **4188**
Dental Society of the State of New York **4187**
Dental Society; Vermont State **4201**
Dental Students; International Association of **3955**
Dental Surgery Assistants; Association of British **3903**
Dental Technicians Association; Clinical **3915**
Dental Technicians; International Association of Equine **13084**
Dental Technologists; American Society of Master **3900**
Dental Technology; National Board for Certification in **3971**
Dental Therapists Association; New Zealand **3978**
Dental Trade Association; American **5821**
Dental Trade Association; British **5829**
Dental Trade Association; Swedish **5883**
Dental Victims; American Association of **3874**
Dentalbranchforeningen Producentsektion **5834**
Dentaria; Sociedade Portugesa de Estomatologia Emedicina **3986**
Dentarie Italiane; Unione Nazionale Industrie **5885**
Dentistry; Academy of General **3844**
Dentistry; Academy of Laser **3846**
Dentistry; Academy of Operative **3847**
Dentistry; Academy for Sports **3849**
Dentistry; American Academy of Esthetic **3855**
Dentistry; American Academy of the History of **3860**
Dentistry; American Academy of Implant **3780, 3861**
Dentistry; American Academy of Pediatric **3159**
Dentistry; American Academy for Plastics Research in **3841**
Dentistry; American Association of Public Health **10935**
Dentistry; American Board of Pediatric **3163**
Dentistry; American Society for Advancement of Anesthesia in **2352, 2377**
Dentistry; American Society for Geriatric **1888**
Dentistry; Center for the Study of Human Performance in • University of Maryland **9855**
Dentistry for Children; American Society of **3172**
Dentistry, D.D.S.; American Academy of Restorative **3869**
Dentistry; District of Columbia Board of **4057**
Dentistry Division; Forensic • Oral Pathology Department • Armed Forces Institute of Pathology • U.S. Department of Defense **10173**
Dentistry Examining Board; Wisconsin **4100**
Dentistry; Federation of Special Care Organizations and **3938**
Dentistry; Florida Board of **4058**
Dentistry; Georgia Board of **4059**
Dentistry for the Handicapped; Academy of **3843**
Dentistry for the Handicapped; National Foundation of **4526**
Dentistry; Idaho State Board of **4061**
Dentistry; Illinois State Board of **4062**
Dentistry International; Academy of **3842**
Dentistry; International Association of Paediatric **3241**
Dentistry; Kentucky Board of **4066**
Dentistry; Louisiana State Board of **4067**
Dentistry; Massachusetts Board of Registration in **4070**
Dentistry; Michigan Board of **4071**
Dentistry; Minnesota Board of **4072**
Dentistry; Montana Board of **4075**
Dentistry; New Jersey State Board of **4079**
Dentistry; New Mexico Board of **4080**
Dentistry; New York State Board of **4081**
Dentistry; North Dakota Board of **4083**
Dentistry; Oregon Board of **4086**
Dentistry; Pennsylvania State Board of **4087**
Dentistry for Persons with Disabilities; Academy of **3843**
Dentistry; Rhode Island State Board of Examiners in **4089**
Dentistry; South Carolina State Board of **4090**
Dentistry; South Dakota State Board of **4091**
Dentistry; Tennessee Board of **4092**
Dentistry; Virginia Board of **4097**
Dentistry; Women in **3996**
Dentists; American Association of Hospital **3876**
Dentists; American Association of Public Health **10935**
Dentists; American Association of Women **3783, 3880**
Dentists; American College of **3887**
Dentists; Association of American Women **3880**
Dentists Association; Flying **3940**

Dentists' Associations; Group of Francophone **3942**
Dentists and Dental Hygienists; Utah Board of **4094**
Dentists; European Union of **3934**
Dentists; Independent Association of German **3946**
Dentists; International College of **3957**
Dentists; Missionary **3964**
Dentists; National Association of Public Health Service **3968**
Dentists; National Association of Seventh-Day Adventist **3969**
Dentists; National Association of VA Physicians and **7804**
Dentists; Oklahoma Board of Governors of Registered **4085**
Dentists Society; Diving **3929**
Dentists; Union of American Physicians and **1524**
Dento-Maxillo-Facial Radiology; International Association of **11115**
Denture Prosthesis; Association for **3915**
Dentures; American Academy of Implant **3861**
Denturist Association; National **3975**
Denver Research Center • Bureau of Mines • U.S. Department of the Interior **9844**
Department of Biochemical Genetics • City of Hope Beckman Research Institute **5320**
Department of Bioengineering • Orthopaedic Institute **9944**
Department of Biomedical Engineering • University of Virginia **2500**
Department Chairmen; Association of Medical School Pediatric **3185**
Department of Clinical Investigation • Dwight David Eisenhower Army Medical Center **1584**
Department of Food Science and Technology • Oregon State University **9522**
Department of Gerontology • University of Nebraska at Omaha **1990**
Department of Health Sciences and Epidemiology • Naval Health Research Center • Naval Medical Research and Development Command • U.S. Department of Defense **7841**
Department of Medical Education • University of Illinois at Chicago **1698**
Department of Medical Research • Methodist Hospital **1634**
Department of Microbiology and Immunology • University of Rochester **6850**
Department of Molecular Biology • Princeton University **2609**
Department of Molecular and Cellular Engineering • University of Pennsylvania **6849**
Department of Neuropharmacology • Scripps Research Institute **8424**
Department of Nursing Research and Education • City of Hope National Medical Center **9140**
Department of Nutrition Sciences • University of Alabama at Birmingham **9546**
Department of Perfusion Technology • John G. Rangos School of Health Sciences • Duquesne University **2813**
Department of Psychiatry
    University of Michigan **7672**
    University of Minnesota **7674**
Department of Research
    American Academy of Pediatrics **5606**
    Menninger Clinic **7582**
    St. Francis Hospital and Medical Center **2616**
Department of Research and Graduate Studies • College of Pharmacy • University of Georgia **10633**
Department of School Nurses/NEA **9111**
Department of Social Work • College of St. Catherine / University of St. Thomas **11804**
Department of Speech and Hearing Sciences • University of Washington **3658**
Department of Surgery • University of Louisville **12324**
Departments of Psychiatry; American Association of Chairmen of **7272**
DePaul Community Health Center • DePaul University **7557**
DePaul Medical Center • School of Anesthesia **2341**
DePaul University
    Department of Nursing **8647**
    DePaul Community Health Center **7557**
    Rehabilitation Services Program **12588**
DePaul University; Ravenswood Hospital Medical Center / • School of Nurse Anesthesia **2270**
DePauw University • School of Nursing **8672**
Dependence; National Council on Alcoholism and Drug **12059**
Dependency; International Commission for the Prevention of Alcoholism and Drug **12037**
Dependency; National Committee for the Prevention of Alcoholism and Drug **12058**
Dependency Nurses; National Consortium of Chemical **9115**
Dependent and Disabled; National Legal Center for the Medically **7189**
Deporte; Confederacion Centroamericano de Medicina del **11943**
Deporte; Confederacion Sudamericana de Medicina del **11951**
Depression; Dave Garroway Laboratory for the Study of **7556**
Depression; Depressives Anonymous: Recovery From **7366**
Depression and Manic Depression; Foundation for **7378**

Development; Center for Human Growth and • University of Michigan **1701**

Development Center; Mental Retardation Research and Human **4315**

Development; Center for Psychological Services and • Virginia Commonwealth University **7699**

Development Center; South Texas Vaccine • University of Texas Health Science Center at San Antonio **6852**

Development; Center for Studies in Education and Human • Gallaudet University **3602**

Development; Center for Study of Aging and Human • Duke University **1933**

Development; Center for the Study of the Cellular and Molecular Basis of • City College of City University of New York **2562**

Development Center; SUNY Stony Brook AIDS Treatment and • State University of New York Health Science Center at Stony Brook **6792**

Development Center; Trace Research and • University of Wisconsin—Madison **4600**

Development; College of Optometrists in Vision **13437**

Development Disabilities Bureau • Family and Community Services Division • Idaho Department of Health and Welfare **4355**

Development Disabilities; Caribbean Association on Mental Retardation and Other **4286**

Development Division; Health Planning and Resource • Health Resources and Lab Services Bureau • Mississippi Department of Health **5686**

Development and Education; Center for the Study of Social • University of Massachusetts Boston **4594**

Development; Eugene McDermott Center for Human Growth and • University of Texas Southwestern Medical Center at Dallas **5384**

Development; European Association for Studies on Nutrition and Child **9455**

Development and Family Studies; Institute of Human • University of Texas at Austin **3075**

Development; Foundation for Women's Health Research and **1303**

Development Institute; Child • University of North Carolina at Chapel Hill **3367**

Development; Institute on Disability and Human • University of Illinois at Chicago **4328**

Development; Institute for Drug **10439**

Development; Institute for Human
> Northern Arizona University **4583**
> University of Kentucky **4591**

Development; Institute for Integral **12034**

Development Institute; Self-Help **7010**

Development; International Academy for Child Brain **3238**

Development; Jean Piaget Society: Society for the Study of Knowledge and **7432**

Development; John F. Kennedy Center for Research on Human • Vanderbilt University **4339**

Development Laboratory; Motor • Temple University **3353**

Development; Mailman Center for Child • University of Miami **3364**

Development and Mental Retardation Center; Child • University of Washington **4338**

Development; Multidisciplinary Institute for Neuropsychological **8259, 8400**

Development; National Assembly for Social Policy and **11867**

Development; National Association for Human **1401**

Development Office; Epidemiology and Health Systems • Illinois Department of Public Health **5676**

Development Office; Planning, Research and • Washington Department of Social and Health Services **5707**

Development Office; Statewide Health Planning and • California Health and Welfare Agency **5667**

Development Research Center; Brain and • University of North Carolina at Chapel Hill **4336**

Development Research Center; R.L. Smith Mental Retardation and Human • University of Kansas **4331**

Development Research and Evaluation Center; Child **4315**

Development and Research Institutes, Inc.; National **12096**

Development; Rose F. Kennedy Center for Research in Mental Retardation and Human • Yeshiva University **4342**

Development Services Bureau; Health • Planning and Administration Division • Iowa Department of Public Health **5678**

Development Studies; Center for Population and • Harvard University **11270**

Development; Task Force for Child Survival and **3302**

Development of Traditional Chinese Medicine and Pharmacy; China Association of Research and **2183**

Development; W.M. Krogman Center for Research in Child Growth and **3373**

Developmental Analysis; Heinz Werner Institute for • Clark University **7554**

Developmental Biology Branch; Cell and • Division of Lung Diseases • National Heart, Lung, and Blood Institute • U.S. Department of Health and Human Services **11616**

Developmental Biology Center
> Case Western Reserve University **2559**

University of California, Irvine **2661**

Developmental Biology, Genetics and Teratology Branch • Center for Research for Mothers and Children • National Institute of Child Health and Human Development • U.S. Department of Health and Human Services **5358**

Developmental Biology; Laboratory of
> National Institute of Dental Research • U.S. Department of Health and Human Services **2641**
> University of Southern California **2686**

Developmental Biology; Laboratory of Cellular and • National Institute of Diabetes and Digestive and Kidney Diseases • U.S. Department of Health and Human Services **2645**

Developmental Biology; Laboratory of Molecular and • National Eye Institute • U.S. Department of Health and Human Services **13641**

Developmental Biology Program; Genetics and • West Virginia University **2706**

Developmental Center; Evaluation and • Southern Illinois University at Carbondale **4584**

Developmental and Comparative Immunology; International Society of **2077**

Developmental Disabilities; Administration on
> Administration for Children and Families • U.S. Department of Health and Human Services **4442**
> Maryland Department of Health and Mental Hygiene **4363**

Developmental Disabilities Administration; Mental Retardation and • Social Services Commission • District of Columbia Department of Human Services **4351**

Developmental Disabilities; American Association of University Affiliated Programs for Persons With **4459**

Developmental Disabilities Branch; Mental Retardation and • Center for Research for Mothers and Children • National Institute of Child Health and Human Development • U.S. Department of Health and Human Services **4320**

Developmental Disabilities Bureau • Community Services Division • Wisconsin Department of Health and Social Services **4392**

Developmental Disabilities Center • Columbia University **6766**

Developmental Disabilities; Center for Developmental Neuroscience and • College of Staten Island of City University of New York **8353**

Developmental Disabilities Center; Douglass • Rutgers University **7596**

Developmental Disabilities Centre • University of Alberta **4322**

Developmental Disabilities; Commonwealth Association for Mental Handicap and **4477**

Developmental Disabilities Council
> Hawaii Department of Health **4354**
> Michigan Department of Mental Health **4365**

Developmental Disabilities Councils; National Association of **4515**

Developmental Disabilities Division
> Arizona Department of Economic Security **4345**
> Colorado Department of Human Services **4348**
> Health and Rehabilitative Services Office • Washington Department of Social and Health Services **4390**
> Human Resources Bureau • West Virginia Department of Health and Human Resources **4391**
> Montana Department of Social and Rehabilitation Services **4369**
> Nebraska Department of Public Institutions **4370**
> New Jersey Department of Human Services **4373**
> New Mexico Department of Health **4374**
> North Dakota Department of Human Services **4377**
> Rhode Island Department of Mental Health, Retardation and Hospitals **4382**
> Social Services Administration • Minnesota Department of Human Services **4366**
> South Dakota Department of Human Services **4384**
> Wyoming Department of Health **4393**

Developmental Disabilities Division; Birth Defects and • National Center for Environmental Health • U.S. Department of Health and Human Services **2759**

Developmental Disabilities Division; Mental Health and • Alaska Department of Health and Social Services **4344**

Developmental Disabilities Division; Mental Health, Mental Retardation and • Iowa Department of Human Services **4358**

Developmental Disabilities; Division on Mental Retardation and • Council for Exceptional Children **4288**

Developmental Disabilities; Illinois Department of Mental Health and **4356**

Developmental Disabilities; Institute for the Study of • Indiana University Bloomington **4578**

Developmental Disabilities; John F. Kennedy Center for • University of Colorado **4326**

Developmental Disabilities; National Conference on **4515**

Developmental Disabilities; New York State Agency of Mental Retardation and **4375**

Developmental Disabilities; New York State Institute for Basic Research in **4582**

Developmental Disabilities; Nisonger Center for Mental Retardation and • Ohio State University **4317**

Developmental Disabilities; Ohio Department of Mental Retardation and **4378**

Developmental Disabilities Services Division • Arkansas Department of Human Services **4346**

Developmental Disabilities Services Office • Mental Health and Developmental Disabilities Services Division • Oregon Department of Human Resources **4380**

Developmental Disabilities and Substance Abuse Services Division; Mental Health, • North Carolina Department of Human Resources **4376**

Developmental Disabilities; University Affiliated Center for • West Virginia University **4341**

Developmental Disabilities; University Affiliated Program for • University of Missouri—Kansas City **4335**

Developmental Disabilities; Vince Moseley Center for Children with • Medical University of South Carolina **4579**

Developmental Disability Division; Mental Retardation and • Missouri Department of Mental Health **4368**

Developmental Disability Services Division • Oklahoma Department of Human Services **4379**

Developmental Disorders; University Affiliated Cincinnati Center for **4321**

Developmental Endocrinology Branch • Intramural Research Program • National Institute of Child Health and Human Development • U.S. Department of Health and Human Services **4904**

Developmental Handicap; National Society for Persons with **4298**

Developmental and Health Genetics; Center for • Pennsylvania State University **5345**

Developmental Medicine; American Academy for Cerebral Palsy and **8151**

Developmental and Metabolic Neurology Branch • National Institute of Neurological Disorders and Stroke • U.S. Department of Health and Human Services **8445**

Developmental and Molecular Immunity; Laboratory of • National Institute of Child Health and Human Development • U.S. Department of Health and Human Services **2139**

Developmental Neurology Branch • Division of Convulsive, Developmental, and Neuromuscular Disorders • National Institute of Neurological Disorders and Stroke • U.S. Department of Health and Human Services **8447**

Developmental, and Neuromuscular Disorders; Division of Convulsive, • National Institute of Neurological Disorders and Stroke • U.S. Department of Health and Human Services **8446**

Developmental Neuroscience and Developmental Disabilities; Center for • College of Staten Island of City University of New York **8353**

Developmental Neuroscience; International Society for **8243**

Developmental Pediatrics; Meyer Center for • Baylor College of Medicine **3311**

Developmental Psychobiology; International Society for **7421**

Developmental Psychobiology; Laboratory of • Stanford University **7602**

Developmental Psychology Laboratory • National Institute of Mental Health • U.S. Department of Health and Human Services **7625**

Developmental Services Bureau; Community • Mental Health Division • New Hampshire Department of Health and Human Services **4372**

Developmental Services Department • California Health and Welfare Agency **4347**

Developmental Services Office • Florida Department of Health and Rehabilitative Services **4352**

Developmental Services and Studies; Stone Center for • Wellesley College **7702**

Developmental Therapeutics; Laboratories for **10441**

Developmental Therapeutics Program • Division of Cancer Treatment • National Cancer Institute • U.S. Department of Health and Human Services **6157**

Developmental Toxicology; Laboratory of Reproductive and • National Institute of Environmental Health Sciences • U.S. Department of Health and Human Services **5111**

Developmentally Disabled Adults; Center for • Western Michigan University **12767**

Developmentally Disabled; American Association of University Affiliated Programs for the **4459**

Deviance and Behavioral Health; Center for Research on • University of Georgia **7664**

Deviance; Laboratory for the Study of Social • Texas A&M University **7610**

Device Development Center; Drug and • Johns Hopkins University **5888**

Devices and Radiological Health; Center for • Food and Drug Administration • U.S. Department of Health and Human Services **10994, 11058**

Devices and Technology Branch • Division of Heart and Vascular Diseases • National Heart, Lung, and Blood Institute • U.S. Department of Health and Human Services **2937**

DeVos Foundation; Richard and Helen **446**

Diabetes Association; American **4821, 4829**

    Alabama Affiliate **4950**

    Alaska Affiliate **4951**

    Arizona Affiliate **4952**

    Arkansas Affiliate **4953**

    California Affiliate **4954**

    Colorado Affiliate **4955**

    Connecticut Affiliate **4956**

    Delaware Affiliate **4957**

    Downstate Illinois Affiliate **4963**

    Florida Affiliate **4959**

    Georgia Affiliate **4960**

    Hawaii Affiliate **4961**

    Idaho Affiliate **4962**

    Indiana Affiliate **4965**

    Iowa Affiliate **4966**

    Kansas Affiliate **4967**

    Kentucky Affiliate **4968**

    Louisiana Affiliate **4969**

    Maine Affiliate **4970**

    Maryland Affiliate **4971**

    Massachusetts Affiliate **4972**

    Michigan Affiliate **4973**

    Minnesota Affiliate **4974**

    Mississippi Affiliate **4975**

    Missouri Affiliate **4976**

    Montana Affiliate **4977**

    Nebraska Affiliate **4978**

    Nevada Affiliate **4979**

    New Hampshire Affiliate **4980**

    New Jersey Affiliate **4981**

    New Mexico Affiliate **4982**

    New York Downstate Affiliate **4983**

    New York Upstate Affiliate **4984**

    North Carolina Affiliate **4985**

    North Dakota Affiliate **4986**

    Northern Illinois Affiliate **4964**

    Ohio Affiliate **4987**

    Oklahoma Affiliate **4988**

    Oregon Affiliate **4989**

    Pennsylvania Affiliate **4990**

    Rhode Island Affiliate **4991**

    South Carolina Affiliate **4992**

    South Dakota Affiliate **4993**

    Tennessee Affiliate **4994**

    Texas Affiliate **4995**

    Utah Affiliate **4996**

    Vermont Affiliate **4997**

    Virginia Affiliate **4998**

    Washington Affiliate **4999**

    Washington, DC Area Affiliate **4958**

    West Virginia Affiliate **5000**

    Wisconsin Affiliate **5001**

    Wyoming Affiliate **5002**

Diabetes Association; French **4843**

Diabetes Association; Latin American **4854**

Diabetes Association; Maltese **4855**

Diabetes Association; Norwegian **4866**

Diabetes Association; South African **4874**

Diabetes; Barbara Davis Center for Childhood **4879**

Diabetes Branch • Division of Intramural Research • National Institute of Diabetes and Digestive and Kidney Diseases • U.S. Department of Health and Human Services **4920**

Diabetes Center; Cosmopolitan International • University of Missouri—Columbia **4940**

Diabetes Center; Joslin **4853, 4891**

Diabetes Centers Program • Division of Diabetes, Endocrinology, and Metabolic Diseases • National Institute of Diabetes and Digestive and Kidney Diseases • U.S. Department of Health and Human Services **4909**

Diabetes Clinical Trials Program • Division of Diabetes, Endocrinology, and Metabolic Diseases • National Institute of Diabetes and Digestive and Kidney Diseases • U.S. Department of Health and Human Services **4910**

Diabetes Data Group; National • Division of Diabetes, Endocrinology, and Metabolic Diseases • National Institute of Diabetes and Digestive and Kidney Diseases • U.S. Department of Health and Human Services **4915**

Diabetes and Digestive and Kidney Diseases; National Institute of

    Clinical Nutrition Research Units Program • U.S. Department of Health and Human Services **4907**

    Division of Diabetes, Endocrinology, and Metabolic Diseases

        Cystic Fibrosis Research Program • U.S. Department of Health and Human Services **5362**

        Diabetes Centers Program • U.S. Department of Health and Human Services **4909**

        Diabetes Clinical Trials Program • U.S. Department of Health and Human Services **4910**

        Diabetes Programs Branch • U.S. Department of Health and Human Services **5363**

Urology and Women's Urological Health Program • U.S. Department of Health and Human Services **12922**

Laboratory of Analytical Chemistry • U.S. Department of Health and Human Services **4924**

Laboratory of Biochemical Pharmacology • U.S. Department of Health and Human Services **2642**

Laboratory of Biochemistry and Metabolism • U.S. Department of Health and Human Services **2643**

Laboratory of Bioorganic Chemistry • U.S. Department of Health and Human Services **2644**

Laboratory of Cell Biology and Genetics • U.S. Department of Health and Human Services **4925**

Laboratory of Cellular and Developmental Biology • U.S. Department of Health and Human Services **2645**

Laboratory of Chemical Biology • U.S. Department of Health and Human Services **2646**

Laboratory of Chemical Physics • U.S. Department of Health and Human Services **2647**

Laboratory of Molecular Biology • U.S. Department of Health and Human Services **2648**

Laboratory of Molecular and Cellular Biology • U.S. Department of Health and Human Services **2649**

Laboratory of Neuroscience • U.S. Department of Health and Human Services **8440**

U.S. Department of Health and Human Services **4820, 4906**

U.S.-Japan Malnutrition Panel • U.S. Department of Health and Human Services **9545**

Dijabete; Ghaqda Kontra d- **4855**

Dillard University

Division of Nursing **8720**

School of Nursing **8721**

Dinshah Health Society **2190**

Diopter and Decibel Society; American **13397**

Diplom Dietician Association Austria **9454**

Diplomates of the American Board of Orthodontics; College of **3916**

Diplomierten Diatassistentinnen Osterreichs; Verband der **9454**

Direct Relief Foundation **1265**

Direct Relief International **1265**

Directors and Administrators; National Association of **1396**

Directors; Association of Academic Health Sciences Library **6975**

Directors Association; Airline Medical **2382**

Directors Association; American Medical **9265**

Directors; Association of Biomedical Communication **6976**

Directors; Association of Family Practice Residency **5557**

Directors Association; National Funeral **3719**

Directors Association; State Medicaid **5745**

Directors; Conference of Radiation Control Program **11061**

Directors of Health, Physical Education and Recreation; Society of State **5604**

Directors of Medical Education; Academy of Osteopathic **9968**

Directors of Medical Education; Association of Hospital **6437**

Directors and Morticians Association; National Funeral **3720**

Directors; National Association of State Alcohol and Drug Abuse **5588**

Directors; National Association of State EMS **5589**

Directors; National Association of State Mental Health Program **5590**

Directors; National Association of State Mental Retardation Program **5591**

Directors of Nursing Administration in Long Term Care; National Association of **5585**

Directors of Nursing; Association of State and Territorial **5564**

Director's Office • Missouri Department of Health **5687**

Directors of Psychiatric Residency Training; American Association of **7275**

Directors of Public Health Education; Association of State and Territorial **5565**

Directors; Society for Hospital Social Work **11872**

Directors of Volunteer Services; American Society of **1184**

Disabilities; Academy of Dentistry for Persons with **3843**

Disabilities; Accreditation Council on Services for People with **4453**

Disabilities; Administration on Developmental

Administration for Children and Families • U.S. Department of Health and Human Services **4442**

Maryland Department of Health and Mental Hygiene **4363**

Disabilities Administration; Mental Retardation and Developmental • Social Services Commission • District of Columbia Department of Human Services **4351**

Disabilities; American Association of University Affiliated Programs for Persons With Developmental **4459**

Disabilities Association of America; Learning **4504**

Disabilities Association of Canada; Learning **4505**

Disabilities; Association for Children and Adults with Learning **4504**

Disabilities; Association for Children with Learning **4504**

Disabilities Branch; Mental Retardation and Developmental • Center for Research for Mothers and Children • National Institute of Child Health and Human Development • U.S. Department of Health and Human Services **4320**

Disabilities Bureau; Development • Family and Community Services Division • Idaho Department of Health and Welfare **4355**

Disabilities Bureau; Developmental • Community Services Division • Wisconsin Department of Health and Social Services **4392**

Disabilities; Canadian Association for Children and Adults with Learning **4505**

Disabilities; Caribbean Association on Mental Retardation and Other Development **4286**

Disabilities Center; Developmental • Columbia University **6766**

Disabilities; Center for Developmental Neuroscience and Developmental • College of Staten Island of City University of New York **8353**

Disabilities Center; Douglass Developmental • Rutgers University **7596**

Disabilities; Center for Persons with • Utah State University **4601**

Disabilities Centre; Developmental • University of Alberta **4322**

Disabilities; Commonwealth Association for Mental Handicap and Developmental **4477**

Disabilities Council; Developmental

Hawaii Department of Health **4354**

Michigan Department of Mental Health **4365**

Disabilities; Council for Learning **4480**

Disabilities Councils; National Association of Developmental **4515**

Disabilities Division; Birth Defects and Developmental • National Center for Environmental Health • U.S. Department of Health and Human Services **2759**

Disabilities; Division for Children with Learning **4480**

Disabilities Division; Developmental

Arizona Department of Economic Security **4345**

Colorado Department of Human Services **4348**

Health and Rehabilitative Services Office • Washington Department of Social and Health Services **4390**

Human Resources Bureau • West Virginia Department of Health and Human Resources **4391**

Montana Department of Social and Rehabilitation Services **4369**

Nebraska Department of Public Institutions **4370**

New Jersey Department of Human Services **4373**

New Mexico Department of Health **4374**

North Dakota Department of Human Services **4377**

Rhode Island Department of Mental Health, Retardation and Hospitals **4382**

Social Services Administration • Minnesota Department of Human Services **4366**

South Dakota Department of Human Services **4384**

Wyoming Department of Health **4393**

Disabilities Division; Mental Health and Developmental • Alaska Department of Health and Social Services **4344**

Disabilities Division; Mental Health, Mental Retardation and Developmental • Iowa Department of Human Services **4358**

Disabilities; Division on Mental Retardation and Developmental • Council for Exceptional Children **4288**

Disabilities; Division for Physical and Health • Council for Exceptional Children **4479**

Disabilities Division; Services for People with • Utah Department of Human Services **4387**

Disabilities; Foundation for Children with Learning **4521**

Disabilities; Illinois Department of Mental Health and Developmental **4356**

Disabilities; Institute on • Temple University **4319**

Disabilities; Institute for Research in Learning • University of Kansas **4589**

Disabilities; Institute for the Study of Developmental • Indiana University Bloomington **4578**

Disabilities; Interdisciplinary Center for • University of South Dakota **4597**

Disabilities; John F. Kennedy Center for Developmental • University of Colorado **4326**

Disabilities; National Center for Learning **4521**

Disabilities; National Center for Youth with **4522**

Disabilities; National Conference on Developmental **4515**

Disabilities; National Information Center for Children and Youth with **4529**

Disabilities; Networking Project for Young Adults with **4539**

Disabilities; New York State Agency of Mental Retardation and Developmental **4375**

Disabilities; New York State Institute for Basic Research in Developmental **4582**

Disabilities; Nisonger Center for Mental Retardation and Developmental • Ohio State University **4317**

Disabilities Office; Vocational and Educational Services for Individuals with • New York State Department of Education **12802**

Disabilities; Ohio Department of Mental Retardation and Developmental **4378**

Disabilities; President's Committee on Employment of People With **4440**

Disease Support Group; Motor Neurone **8258**

Disease Support and Research Association; Batten's **8194**

Diseases Association of Romania; Neuromuscular **8288**

Diseases of Children; Canadian Society for the Study of 3195

Diseases Clearinghouse; Digestive 5227

Diseases Education and Information Clearinghouse; National Digestive 5227

Diseases of the Esophagus; International Organization for Statistical Studies on **5224**

Diseases of the Esophagus; International Society for **5225**

Diseases and Human Infertility; International Society of Infectious 11252

Diseases Information Clearinghouse; National Arthritis and Musculoskeletal and Skin **7891**

Diseases; International Association for Comparative Research on Leukemia and Related **5951**

Diseases Laboratory; Helminthic • Livestock and Poultry Sciences Institute • Agricultural Research Service • U.S. Department of Agriculture **13190**

Diseases Laboratory; Protozoan • Livestock and Poultry Sciences Institute • Agricultural Research Service • U.S. Department of Agriculture **13192**

Diseases; Ma Ayesha Memorial Center for Care and Control of Neuromuscular **8250**

Diseases; Medical Society for the Study of Venereal **6695**

Diseases; National Clearinghouse for Human Genetic 3265

Diseases; Organization for Co-Ordination and Co-Operation in the Control of Endemic **5183**

Diseases and the Treponematoses, Regional Office for North America; International Union Against the Venereal **6684**

Disinfected Mail Study Circle **6665**

Disney Co. Foundation; Walt **897**

Disney Memorial Cancer Institute; Walt • Cancer Research Division **6264**

Disorders; American Academy of Craniomandibular 3866

Disorders Association; American Sleep **8173**

Disorders Association; Dizziness and Balance 3585

Disorders Centers; American Association of Sleep **8173**

Disorders Centers; Association of Sleep **8173**

Disorders; Children with Attention-Deficit **8201**

Disorders; Council for Children with Behavioral 3214

Disorders; National Organization for Rare **921, 1429**

Dispensing Audiologists; Academy of 3474

Disposable Hypodermic and Allied Equipment Manufacturers Association of Europe **5839**

Dissatisfied Parents Together 3273

Dissociation; International Society for the Study of **7426**

Dissociation; International Society for the Study of Multiple Personalities and 7426

Distribution Committee; Joint 1167

Distributors Association; Health Industry **5853**

Distributors Association; Independent Medical **5858**

District of Columbia; American Lung Association of the **11634**

District of Columbia Arc **4402**

District of Columbia Board of Dentistry **4057**

District of Columbia Board of Funeral Directors and Embalmers **3736**

District of Columbia Board of Medicine **1764, 10020**

District of Columbia Board of Nursing **9161**

District of Columbia Board of Nursing Home Administration **9283**

District of Columbia Board of Optometry **13726**

District of Columbia Board of Pharmacy **10649**

District of Columbia Board of Podiatry Examiners **10787**

District of Columbia Dental Society **4163**

District of Columbia Department of Consumer and Regulatory Affairs
    Business Regulation Administration **5136**
    Service Facility Regulations Administration • Health Facility Division **6484**

District of Columbia Department of Employment Services • Labor Standards Office • Occupational Safety and Health Office **9873**

District of Columbia Department of Human Services
    Health Systems Development Agency **5671**
    Mental Health Commission **7716**
    Public Health Commission **11013**
        Alcohol and Drug Abuse Administration **12155**
        Ambulatory Health Care Administration Division • Dental Health Bureau **4110**
        Emergency Health and Medical Services **4775**
        Maternal and Child Health Services Office **3386, 9732**
    Research and Statistics Division • Vital Records Branch **7048**
    Social Services Commission
        Income Maintenance Administration • Medicaid Unit **5776**
        Mental Retardation and Developmental Disabilities Administration **4351**
        Rehabilitation Services Administration **12778, 13673**

District of Columbia Diversity and Special Services Office • Aging Office **2011**

District of Columbia Division • American Cancer Society **6279**

District of Columbia Easter Seal Society for Disabled Children and Adults **4621**

District of Columbia Health Care Association **9334**

District of Columbia Hospital Association **6535**

District of Columbia; Learning Disabilities Association of the **4691**

District of Columbia; Medical Society of the **1818**

District of Columbia Nurses Association **9219**

District of Columbia; Optometric Society of the **13801**

District of Columbia; Osteopathic Association of the **10074**

District of Columbia Veterinary Medical Association **13310**

Distrofia Muscular; Asociacion **8182**

Distrofia Muscular; Associacao Brasileira de **8184**

Diving Dentists Society **3929**

Diving Medicine Department • Naval Medical Research Institute • Naval Medical Research and Development Command • U.S. Department of Defense **7848**

Division of Acquired Immunodeficiency Syndrome (AIDS) • National Institute of Allergy and Infectious Diseases • U.S. Department of Health and Human Services **6816**

Division of Allergy, Immunology, and Transplantation • National Institute of Allergy and Infectious Diseases • U.S. Department of Health and Human Services **2124**

Division of Applied Experimental and Engineering Psychologists • American Psychological Association **7304**

Division of Biology • City of Hope Beckman Research Institute **2564**

Division of Biometry and Epidemiology • National Eye Institute • U.S. Department of Health and Human Services **13632**

Division of Biostatistics • Dana-Farber Cancer Institute **6028**

Division of Blood Diseases and Resources • National Heart, Lung, and Blood Institute • U.S. Department of Health and Human Services **6203**

Division of Cancer Biology, Diagnosis, and Centers • National Cancer Institute • U.S. Department of Health and Human Services **6128**

Division of Cancer Etiology • National Cancer Institute • U.S. Department of Health and Human Services **6137**

Division of Cancer Prevention and Control • National Cancer Institute • U.S. Department of Health and Human Services **6140**

Division of Cancer Treatment • National Cancer Institute • U.S. Department of Health and Human Services **6149**

Division of Cardiology • University of Michigan **2970**

Division of Cardiothoracic Surgery • University of Missouri—Columbia **2972**

Division of Cardiovascular Diseases • University of Tennessee **2976**

Division on Career Development of the Council for Exceptional Children **3216**

Division on Career Development and Transition • Council for Exceptional Children **3216**

Division of Child and Family Studies • University of Connecticut **4587**

Division for Children with Learning Disabilities **4480**

Division of Clinical Immunology and Rheumatology • University of Alabama at Birmingham **7943**

Division of Communication and Sciences Disorders • National Institute on Deafness and Other Communication Disorders • U.S. Department of Health and Human Services **3626**

Division of Comparative Medicine • Johns Hopkins University **1611**

Division of Computer Research and Technology • National Institutes of Health • U.S. Department of Health and Human Services **2512, 2655**

Division of Convulsive, Developmental, and Neuromuscular Disorders • National Institute of Neurological Disorders and Stroke • U.S. Department of Health and Human Services **8446**

Division of Demyelinating, Atrophic, and Dementing Disorders • National Institute of Neurological Disorders and Stroke • U.S. Department of Health and Human Services **8449**

Division of Diabetes, Endocrinology, and Metabolic Diseases • National Institute of Diabetes and Digestive and Kidney Diseases • U.S. Department of Health and Human Services **4908**

Division of Digestive Diseases and Nutrition • National Institute of Diabetes and Digestive and Kidney Diseases • U.S. Department of Health and Human Services **5238**

Division for Early Childhood • Council for Exceptional Children **3217**

Division of Epidemiology • University of Minnesota **5194**

Division of Epidemiology and Biostatistics • University of Cincinnati **5192**

Division of Epidemiology and Clinical Applications • National Heart, Lung, and Blood Institute • U.S. Department of Health and Human Services **2930**

Division of Extramural Activities • National Institute of Allergy and Infectious Diseases • U.S. Department of Health and Human Services **2129**

Division of Extramural Programs • National Institute for Nursing Research • U.S. Department of Health and Human Services **9146**

Division of Extramural Research and Training • National Institute of Environmental Health Sciences • U.S. Department of Health and Human Services **5103**

Division of Family Psychology • American Psychological Association **7305**

Domestic Violence Coalition; Colorado **3081**
Domestic Violence; Connecticut Coalition Against **3082**
Domestic Violence; DC Coalition Against **3084**
Domestic Violence; Delaware Coalition Against **3083**
Domestic Violence; Emerge: A Men's Counseling Service on **7368**
Domestic Violence; Florida Coalition Against **3085**
Domestic Violence; Idaho Coalition Against Sexual and **3088**
Domestic Violence; Illinois Coalition Against **3089**
Domestic Violence; Indiana Coalition Against **3090**
Domestic Violence; Iowa Coalition Against **3091**
Domestic Violence; Kansas Coalition Against Sexual and **3092**
Domestic Violence; Louisiana Coalition Against **3094**
Domestic Violence; Maryland Network Against **3096**
Domestic Violence; Michigan Coalition Against **3098**
Domestic Violence; Mississippi Coalition Against **3100**
Domestic Violence; Missouri Coalition Against **3101**
Domestic Violence; Montana Coalition Against **3102**
Domestic Violence; National Coalition Against **3059**
Domestic Violence Network; Ohio **3111**
Domestic Violence; Nevada Network Against **3104**
Domestic Violence; New Mexico State Coalition Against **3107**
Domestic Violence; New York State Coalition Against **3108**
Domestic Violence; North Carolina Coalition Against **3109**
Domestic Violence; Pennsylvania Coalition Against **3114**
Domestic Violence; Rhode Island Council on **3116**
Domestic Violence and Sexual Assault; Alaska Network on **3077**
Domestic Violence and Sexual Assault Coalition; Nebraska **3103**
Domestic Violence and Sexual Assault; Oklahoma Coalition on **3112**
Domestic Violence and Sexual Assault; South Carolina Coalition Against **3117**
Domestic Violence and Sexual Assault; South Dakota Coalition Against **3118**
Domestic Violence and Sexual Assault; Vermont Network Against **3122**
Domestic Violence and Sexual Assault; Wyoming Coalition Against **3129**
Domestic Violence; Virginians Against **3125**
Domestic Violence; Washington State Coalition Against **3126**
Domestic Violence; West Virginia Coalition Against **3127**
Domestic Violence; Wisconsin Coalition Against **3128**
Domicile; Union Nationale des Associations de Soins et Service a **1525**
Dominica de Pediatria; Sociedad **3220**
Dominican College
    Occupational Therapy Program **12390**
    School of Nursing **8580**
Dominican College of Blauvelt • Division of Nursing **8827**
Dominican Society of Pediatrics **3220**
Don and Sybil Harrington Foundation **141**
Donacion Voluntaria de Sangre; Federacion Panamericana pro **7152**
Donald E. and Delia B. Baxter Foundation **142**
Donald Guthrie Foundation for Education and Research **2099**
Donald Guthrie Foundation for Medical Research **2099**
Donald W. Reynolds Foundation **143**
Donaldson Charitable Trust; Oliver S. and Jennie R. **5894**
Donaldson Foundation **665**
Donatori di Sangue; Federazione Internazionale delle Organizzazioni dei **7139**
Donner Foundation; William H. **549**
Donor Organizations; International Federation of Blood **7139**
Donor Program; National Marrow **12874**
Donor Registry; National Bone Marrow **12874**
Dooley Foundation; Dr. Thomas A. **1270**
Dooley Foundation / INTERMED **1270**
Dooley Foundation/INTERMED - U.S.A. **1270**
Dooley Foundation/INTERMED U.S.A.; Thomas A. **1270**
Dooley Foundation; Thomas A. **1270**
Dora Roberts Foundation **144**
Dorothea Dix Hospital • Clinical Research Unit **1581**
Dorothy U. Dalton Foundation **145**
Doss Foundation; M. S. **372**
Douglass Developmental Disabilities Center • Rutgers University **7596**
Dovas Nordiske Rad **3564**
Dove Hunt Association; One-Arm **4544**
Dove Kinderen; Nederlandse Federatie van Organisaties van Ouders van **3563**
Doveforbund; Norges **3565**
Dovenraad; Stichting Nederlandse **3518**
Dover Foundation **146**
Dow Neurological Sciences Institute; R.S. **8417**
Down Syndrome; Association for Children with **5270**
Down Syndrome Association; Zimbabwe **5307**
Down Syndrome Children; Parents of **5300**
Down Syndrome Congress; National **5288**

Down Syndrome; National Association for **5287**
Down Syndrome; Parents of Children with **5300**
Down Syndrome Society; National **4274, 5289**
Down's Syndrome Association **4289**
Down's Syndrome Association; National **5290**
Down's Syndrome Congress **5288**
Down's Syndrome Congress; National **5288**
Downstate Illinois Affiliate • American Diabetes Association **4963**
Dows Institute for Dental Research • University of Iowa **4029**
Drake University
    College of Pharmacy and Health Sciences • Pharmacy Programs **10519**
    Department of Nursing • Clinical Specialization in Nurse Anesthesia **2273**
    Rehabilitation Counseling Program **12593**
Drama Therapy; National Association for **7451**
Dream Drama; Center for **7359**
Dream Factory **3221**
Dreams; Association for the Study of **7336**
Dreamsharing Grassroots Network **7359**
Dreamsharing Network; Community **7359**
Dreamsharing Network; New York/ New Jersey **7359**
Dresser Foundation **666**
Drew / Meharry / Morehouse Consortium Cancer Center **6029**
Drew University of Medicine and Science; Charles R.
    College of Allied Health
        Dietetics Program **9386**
        Physician Assistant Program **1058**
    College of Allied Health Sciences • Nurse-Midwifery Certificate Education Program **9579**
    Hypertension Research Center **2886**
Drexel University
    Biomedical Engineering and Science Institute **2441**
    Environmental Studies Institute **5070**
    Fibrous Materials Research Center **2442**
Dreyfus Foundation; Jean and Louis **312**
Dreyfus Foundation; Max and Victoria **389**
Drinking Water Administrators; Association of State **10944**
Driver Educators for the Disabled; Association of **4467**
Droga; Asociacion Iberoamericana de Estudio de los Problemas del Alcohol y la **12031**
Drogforskning; Nordiska Namnden for Alkohol- och **12066**
Drogisten; Verband Deutscher **10600**
Drown Foundation; Joseph **331**
Drug Abuse Administration; Alcohol and • Public Health Commission • District of Columbia Department of Human Services **12155**
Drug Abuse Bureau; Alcohol and • Rehabilitation Division • Nevada Department of Employment Training and Rehabilitation **12175**
Drug Abuse Counselors; National Association of Alcoholism and **12051**
Drug Abuse Directors; National Association of State Alcohol and **5588**
Drug Abuse Division; Alcohol and
    Behavioral Health Administration • Hawaii Department of Health **12158**
    Colorado Department of Human Services **12152**
    Missouri Department of Mental Health **12172**
    Montana Department of Health Environmental Sciences **12173**
    South Dakota Department of Human Services **12188**
Drug Abuse Division; Alcoholism and
    Alaska Department of Health and Social Services **12148**
    Behavioral Health Services Office • Human Resources Bureau • West Virginia Department of Health and Human Resources **12195**
    North Dakota Department of Human Services **12181**
Drug Abuse Institute; Alcohol and • University of Washington **12144**
Drug Abuse, and Mental Health Division; Alcoholism, • Delaware Department of Health and Social Services **12154**
Drug Abuse and Mental Health Office; Alcohol, • Human Services Program Office • Florida Department of Health and Rehabilitative Services **12156**
Drug Abuse; National Institute on
    Addiction Research Center
        Clinical Pharmacology Branch • U.S. Department of Health and Human Services **12116**
        Etiology Research Branch • U.S. Department of Health and Human Services **12117**
        Neuroscience Research Branch • U.S. Department of Health and Human Services **12118**
        Preclinical Pharmacology Research Laboratory • U.S. Department of Health and Human Services **12119**
        Treatment Branch • U.S. Department of Health and Human Services **12120**
        U.S. Department of Health and Human Services **12115**

Department of Physical Therapy **12524**
Duke Center for the Advanced Study of Epilepsy **8361**
Duke Comprehensive Cancer Center **6031**
Engineering Research Center for Emerging Cardiovascular
  Technologies **2443**
Epilepsy Research Center **8362**
Eye Center **13591**
F.G. Hall Hyper-Hypo-Baric Center **1582**
Fuqua School of Businesss • Program in Health Services
  Management **5511**
General Clinical Research Center **1583**
Laboratory of Cell and Molecular Biology of Leukocytes **2569**
Marine Biomedical Center **2570**
Occupational Mental Health Programs **9805**
Pediatric Cardiac Catheterization Laboratory **3333**
Pediatric Oncology Consortium **3334**
Plastic Surgery Research Laboratories **12319**
Preuss Laboratory for Brain Tumor Research **8363**
School of Medicine **1006**
        Department of Pharmacology **10309**
        Physician Assistant Program **1097**
Southeastern Regional Trophoblastic Disease Center **6032**
Specialized Center of Research in Ischemic Heart Disease **2892**
Dula Educational and Charitable Foundation; Caleb C. and Julia W. **6335**
Duluth Technical College / Range Technical College • Respiratory
  Therapist Program **11437**
Dun & Bradstreet Corp. Foundation **668**
Dunn Research Foundation; John S. **324**
Dunspaugh-Dalton Foundation **148**
duPont Foundation; Alfred I. **38**
duPont Foundation; Chichester **98**
duPont Fund; Jessie Ball **314**
duPont Institute of the Nemours Foundation; Alfred I. **1643**
duPont Religious, Charitable and Educational Fund; Jessie Ball **314**
Duquesne University
        John G. Rangos School of Health Sciences
                Department of Perfusion Technology **2813**
                Occupational Therapy Program **12415**
        John G. Rangos Sr. School of Health Sciences • Physician Assistant
          Program **1103**
        School of Nursing **8914**
        School of Pharmacy **10554**
                Department of Pharmacology and Toxicology **10334**
Durham Regional Hospital • School of Anesthesia for Nurses **2303**
Durham Technical Community College • Respiratory Therapist Program
  11476
Dutch Association for Dermatology and Venereology **4231**
Dutch Deaf Association **3518**
Dutch Parents Organization of Hearing and Speech Impaired Children
  3519
Dutch Society for Advancement of Pharmacy; Royal **10621**
Dutch Society of Cardiology **2843**
Dutch Society of Immunology **2071**
Dutton Society; Damien- **6661**
Dutton Society for Leprosy Aid; Damien **6661**
Dwight David Eisenhower Army Medical Center • Department of Clinical
  Investigation **1584**
Dying Project; Living / **3718**
Dying—The National Council for the Right to Die; Choice in **3710**
Dynamet Foundation **669**
Dynamic Psychiatry; World Association for **7529**
Dynamics; Academy of Oral **3848**
Dynamics Institute; Drug • University of Texas at Austin **10639**
Dynamics in Physiology and Medicine; Centre for Nonlinear • McGill
  University **1630**
D'Youville College
        Department of Occupational Therapy **12391**
        Dietetics Program **9408**
        Division of Nursing **8828**
        Physical Therapy Program **12513**
        Physician Assistant Program **1090**
Dysautonomia Association **8208**
Dysautonomia Foundation **5259, 8208**
Dysfunction Center; Autonomic • Vanderbilt University **2984**
Dysfunction Syndrome Activation Network; Chronic Fatigue Immune **6652**
Dysleksiforbund; Norsk **4543**
Dyslexia Association; Norwegian **4543**
Dyslexia Research Institute **4576**
Dyslexia Society; Orton **3569**
Dyson Foundation **149**
Dysphagia Foundation **1598**

Dysphoric Association; Montgomery Foundation for Gender **7447**
Dysplasia; International Center for Skeletal **5333**
Dysplasias; National Foundation for Ectodermal **5291**
Dyspraxia; National Organization for Apraxia and **8279**
Dystonia Clinical Research Center • Columbia University **8357**
Dystonia Medical Research Foundation **5260, 8209, 8364**
Dystonia National Association; Tardive Dyskinesia / Tardive **8316**
Dystrophic Epidermolysis Bullosa Research Association of America **5261,
  5277**
Dystrophy Association; Biruduma Muscular **8196**
Dystrophy Association; Indian Muscular **8230**
Dystrophy Association; Reflex Sympathetic **8300**

E

E. Coli Reference Center • Pennsylvania State University **13165**
E. J. Grassmann Trust **6346**
E. K. and Lillian F. Bishop Foundation **3137**
E. L. Wiegand Foundation **150**
E. M. Lynn Foundation **151**
Ear Dog Program; Hearing **3557**
Ear Foundation **3520**
Ear Hospitals; American Association of Eye and **6423**
Ear Institute; House **3529, 3606**
Ear, Nose, and Throat Advances in Children; Society for **3291**
Ear Research Foundation; Houston **3607**
Ear Research Institute **3529, 3606**
Ear Research; Temporal Bone Laboratory for • University of Chicago **3635**
Earl C. Sams Foundation **152**
Early Childhood Center; Carleton Washburne • Brooklyn College of City
  University of New York **3591**
Early Childhood; Division for • Council for Exceptional Children **3217**
Early Detection and Community Oncology Program • Division of Cancer
  Prevention and Control • National Cancer Institute • U.S. Department of
  Health and Human Services **6145**
Early Detection Foundation; Ovarian Cancer Prevention and **5979**
Early Intervention Research Institute • Utah State University **4602**
East Carolina University
        School of Allied Health Sciences
                Department of Environmental Health **5019**
                Department of Health Information Management **6946**
                Department of Occupational Therapy **12403**
                Department of Physical Therapy **12525**
                Department of Rehabilitation Studies • Rehabilitation Counseling
                  Program **12620**
        School of Medicine **1007**
                Department of Pharmacology **10310**
        School of Nursing **8855**
                Nurse-Midwifery Graduate Program **9607**
        School of Social Work **11829**
East Central University
        Department of Health Information Management **6949**
        Department of Human Resources • Rehabilitation Education
          Programs **12627**
        Department of Nursing **8891**
        School of Mathematics and Sciences • Department of Environmental
          Science **5024**
East Coast Migrant Health Project Inc. **1271**
East Los Angeles College • Respiratory Therapist Program **11320**
East Mississippi Community College • Funeral Service Technology
  Program **3682**
East Stroudsburg University of Pennsylvania • Department of Nursing
  8915
East Tennessee Chapter • Lupus Foundation of America **8106**
East Tennessee State University
        College of Nursing **8970**
        Department of Environmental Health **5026**
        Department of Health Related Professions • Respiratory Therapy
          Program **11536**
        James H. Quillen College of Medicine **1033**
                Department of Pharmacology **10354**
East Texas Baptist University **8983**
East West Academy of Healing Arts **2191**
Easter Seal Society; Alabama **4605**
Easter Seal Society of Alaska **4606**
Easter Seal Society of Arizona **4607**
Easter Seal Society; Arkansas **4608**
Easter Seal Society of the Bay Area **4610**
Easter Seal Society of Broward County **4622**
Easter Seal Society; Capital Area **4673**
Easter Seal Society; Central California **4609**

Economic Opportunity; Research and Training Center for Access to Rehabilitation and • Howard University **4577**

Economic Studies Division; Reimbursement and • Office of Research and Demonstrations • Health Care Financing Administration • U.S. Department of Health and Human Services **5762**

Economics; Center for Pharmaceutical • University of Arizona **10631**

Economics; Institute for Medical Record **7008**

Economics; Leonard Davis Institute of Health • University of Pennsylvania **5657**

Economics and Management Institute; International Health **5734**

Economics Research; Center for Health **5747**

Economics Studies; Center for Medical • Northeastern University **1646**

ECRI **1585, 5841**

Ectodermal Dysplasias; National Foundation for **5291**

Eczema Association for Science and Education **4232**

Edema Research Center; CNS Injury and • University of California, San Francisco **8488**

Eden Hall Foundation **153**

Edgecombe Community College • Respiratory Therapist Program **11477**

Edgewood College • Nursing Department **9038**

Edinboro University of Pennsylvania

    Department of Biology and Health Services • Dietetics Program **9419**

    Department of Nursing **8916**

Edison Biotechnology Institute • Ohio University **2724**

Edison Community College • Respiratory Therapist Program **11351**

Edison Fund; Charles **92**

Edith L. Trees Charitable Trust **4271**

Editors; American Association of Dental **6966**

Edmund S. Muskie Institute of Public Affairs • University of Southern Maine **5659**

Edna McConnell Clark Foundation **154**

Edna Sproull Williams Foundation **8121**

Educacion Comunitaria para la Salud **10948**

Educati on; National Association for Perinatal Addiction Research and **12054**

Education; Academy of Osteopathic Directors of Medical **9968**

Education and Accreditation; Committee on Allied Health **1249**

Education; Accreditation Council for Continuing Medical **1120**

Education; Accreditation Council for Graduate Medical **1121**

Education and Action Project; Pesticide **5056**

Education on Aging; Texas Institute for Research and • University of North Texas Health Science Center at Fort Worth **1992**

Education / AIDS Clinical Trials Unit; UCLA Center for Clinical AIDS Research and • University of California, Los Angeles **6840**

Education on Alcoholism; National Committee for **12059**

Education; Alliance for Environmental **5030**

Education; American Association for Advancement of Physical **1138**

Education; American Association for Cancer **5908**

Education; American Board of Funeral Service **3705**

Education; American Council for Drug **12007**

Education; American Council for Headache **8162**

Education; American Council on Pharmaceutical **10582**

Education; American Foundation for Pharmaceutical **10497, 10583**

Education of the American Medical Association; Council on Medical **1260**

Education of the American Osteopathic Association; Bureau of Professional **9997**

Education; Association for the Advancement of Health **1195**

Education Association; American Physical **1138**

Education; Association for the Behavioral Sciences and Medical **7322**

Education Association; Childbirth Without Pain **9641**

Education; Association for Gerontology in Higher **1890**

Education; Association for Hospital Medical **6437**

Education Association; International Dalkon Shield Victims **11223**

Education Association; Nutrition **9477**

Education; Association of State and Territorial Directors of Public Health **5565**

Education; Association for Surgical **12257**

Education and Awareness for Rockers; Hearing **3527**

Education; Blumenthal Foundation for Charity, Religion and **70**

Education; Center for Health Policy Research and • Duke University **5623**

Education; Center for Organ Recovery and **12868**

Education Center; Pope John XXIII Medical- Moral Research and **7213**

Education; Center for the Study of Social Development and • University of Massachusetts Boston **4594**

Education; Center for Ulcer Research and • University of California, Los Angeles **5249**

Education Centre; Suicide Information and **7524**

Education and Clinical center; Geriatric Research, • Veterans Affairs Medical Center [Gainesville, FL] **10493**

Education; Community Health **10948**

Education; Concern for Health Options - Information, Care and **11210**

Education; Council of Administrators of Special **5572**

Education; Council on Chiropractic **3451**

Education; Council on Electrolysis **1257**

Education; Council on Health Information and **6988**

Education Council; International Patient **1355**

Education; Council on Optometric **13444**

Education; Council on Podiatric Medical **10771**

Education; Council on Rehabilitation **12674**

Education; Council for Sex Information and **11690**

Education; Council on Social Work **11866**

Education Council of the U.S.; Sex Information and **11711**

Education and Counseling; Association for Death **3708**

Education and Counseling; Forum for Death **3708**

Education of the Deaf; Council on **3510**

Education and Defense Fund; Disability Rights **4482**

Education; Department of Medical • University of Illinois at Chicago **1698**

Education in Diagnostic Medical Sonography; Joint Review Committee on **11123**

Education and Disability; Association on Higher **4468**

Education; Division of Health Policy Research and • Harvard University **5625**

Education; Eczema Association for Science and **4232**

Education in Europe; Association for Dental **3905**

Education; Foundation for Accredited Chiropractic **3458**

Education Foundation of American Society of Plastic and Reconstructive Surgeons **12296**

Education Foundation; Bay Medical Research and **2550**

Education Foundation; Cardiothoracic Research and **12264**

Education Foundation; Childbirth **9639**

Education Foundation; Comprehensive Health **1256**

Education; Foundation for Hand Research and **7878**

Education Foundation; Hawaii Heptachlor Research and **10433**

Education Foundation; Health **10955**

Education Foundation; Marshfield Medical Research and **1625**

Education Foundation; National Gay Health **11705**

Education Foundation; Pan American Health and **1453**

Education; Foundation of Pharmacists and Corporate America for AIDS **6669**

Education des Handicapes de la Vue; Conseil International pour l' **13483**

Education and Health Care; Center for Research in Medical • Thomas Jefferson University **1670**

Education; Health Media **6996**

Education for Health Services Administration; Accrediting Commission on **5535**

Education of the Hearing Impaired; American Organization for the **3539**

Education of the Hearing Impaired; International Organization for the **3539**

Education; Homeopathic Council for Research and **2201**

Education for Hospital Administration; Accrediting Commission on Graduate **5535**

Education and Human Development; Center for Studies in • Gallaudet University **3602**

Education Information Center; National Special **4529**

Education and Information Clearinghouse; National Digestive Diseases **5227**

Education Institute; Hospice **3715**

Education; Institute for Hospital Clinical Nursing **9093**

Education Institute, Inc; Research and **1596**

Education; International Academy of Pediatric Transdisciplinary **3239**

Education; International Society for AIDS **6682**

Education; International Union for Health Promotion and **1360**

Education; Jackson Foundation for Medical Research & **1610**

Education; Joint Review Committee for Respiratory Therapy **11600**

Education; Liaison Committee on Continuing Medical **1120**

Education and Licensure; Federation for Accessible Nursing **9088**

Education; Marshfield Clinic Foundation for Medical Research and **1625**

Education in Maternal and Child Health; National Center for **3265**

Education; National Association for State Administrators of Health Occupations **5593**

Education; National Association of State Directors of Special **4519**

Education; National Association of Supervisors and Administrators of Health Occupations **5593**

Education; National Center for Health **1408**

Education; National Council on Patient Information and **10612**

Education; National Council on Rehabilitation **12697**

Education; National Parents' Resource Institute for Drug **12063**

Education Network; BACCHUS and Gamma Peer **12014**

Education Network; Physicians **13553**

Education; Nordic Federation for Medical **1442**

Education; Northwest Center for Medical • Indiana University Northwest **1604**

Education; Oak Ridge Institute for Science and **2597**

Education in Obstetrics and Gynecology; Council on Resident **9644**

El Salvador; Committee for Health Rights in   1353
El Salvador; Medical Aid for   1378
Elbow Surgeons; American Shoulder and   12234
Elder and Adult Services Bureau • Maine Department of Human Services
    2021
Elder Affairs; Iowa Department of   2018
Elder Affairs; Massachusetts Department of   2023
Elderly and Adult Services Division • New Hampshire Department of Health
    and Human Services   2031
Elderly Affairs; Rhode Island Department of   2041
Elderly Bridging the Unknown Together; Daughters of the   1898
Elderly Care Research Center • Case Western Reserve University   1927
Elderly; Center for the Study of Pharmacy and Therapeutics for the   1895
    University of Maryland   10475
Elderly; PRIDE Foundation - Promote Real Independence for the Disabled
    and   12710
Elderly Services Division • Connecticut Department of Social Services
    2009
Eleanor and Edsel Ford Fund   6347
Eleanor Naylor Dana Charitable Trust   2517
Eleanor Roosevelt Institute   2571
Electrical Stimulation Laboratory • Boston University   8334
Electrically Oversensitive; Association for the   5035
Electrically Sensitive; Self-Help Association for the   5058
Electrically and VDT Injured in Denmark   5037
Electrically and VDT Injured; Swedish Association for the   5061
Electrocardiology; International Society of   2424
Electrodiagnosis; American Association of Electromyography and   2415
Electrodiagnostic and Electromyographic Laboratory • University of
    Michigan   4035
Electrodiagnostic Medicine; American Association of   2415
Electroencephalographic Association; American Medical   8165
Electroencephalographic Society; American   8163
Electroencephalographic Technologists; American Society of   8175
Electroencephalography and Clinical Neurophysiology; International
    Federation of Societies for   8238
Electroencephalography Laboratory • University of Illinois at Chicago   8500
Electrologist Certification; National Commission for   1413
Electrologists; International Guild of Professional   1347
Electrologists; Society of Clinical and Medical   1506
Electrology Association; American   1159
Electrology Educators; Institute of   1342
Electrology Educators; International   1342
Electrology Educators; National   1342
Electrolysis Association; American   1159
Electrolysis Education; Council on   1257
Electrolyte Metabolism; Laboratory of Kidney and • National Heart, Lung,
    and Blood Institute • U.S. Department of Health and Human Services
    2951
Electromedical Information; National Institute of   2430
Electromyographic Laboratory; Electrodiagnostic and • University of
    Michigan   4035
Electromyography and Electrodiagnosis; American Association of   2415
Electromyography Laboratory • New England Medical Center   8405
Electron Microscope Laboratory • University of Michigan   7157
Electroneurodiagnostic Technologists; American Society of   8175
Electronics; Laboratory of • Rockefeller University   2469
Electrophysiological Kinesiology; International Society of   2425
Electrophysiologique; Societe Internationale de Kinesiologie   2425
Electrophysiology Laboratory
    Boston University   8335
    Kresge Hearing Research Institute • University of Michigan   3644
Electrophysiology; North American Society of Pacing and   2789, 2869
Electrophysiology Research Group; Fundamental • Sherbrooke University
    2621
Electrophysiology Research Unit; Sensory   13627
Electrosurgery; American Academy of Dental   3852
Eli Lilly and Co. Foundation   672
Eliot Division of Child Psychiatry; William Greenleaf • Washington
    University   7701
Elis Olsson Memorial Foundation   164
Elisabeth Severance Prentiss Foundation   165
Elizabeth Wisner Social Welfare Research Center for Families and Children
    • Tulane University   11874
Elizabethtown College • Department of Occupational Therapy   12416
Elks' Children's Eye Clinic • Oregon Health Sciences University   13623
Ellen Browning Scripps Foundation   166
Ellen Gregg Ingalls Eye Research Institute   13592
Ellison Foundation   167
Ellwood Foundation   168
Elmer and Mamdouha Bobst Foundation   169

Elmhurst College • Deicke Center for Nursing Education   8648
Elmira College • Nursing Education Program   8829
Elms College • Department of Nursing   8749
Elsa U. Pardee Foundation   5892
EM Core Facility for Biological Research • University of Chicago   2667
Emanuel Research Center   8365
Embalmers; Arizona State Board of Funeral Directors and   3730
Embalmers; California Board of Funeral Directors and   3732
Embalmers; District of Columbia Board of Funeral Directors and   3736
Embalmers; Florida Board of Funeral Directors and   3737
Embalmers and Funeral Directors; Arkansas State Board of   3731
Embalmers and Funeral Directors; Connecticut Board of Examiners of
    3734
Embalmers and Funeral Directors; Kentucky State Board of   3745
Embalmers and Funeral Directors; Louisiana State Board of   3746
Embalmers and Funeral Directors; Ohio Board of   3763
Embalmers and Funeral Directors; Oklahoma State Board of   3764
Embalmers Licensing and Discipline Boards; Funeral Directors and • Illinois
    Department of Professional Regulation   3741
Embalmers; Missouri State Board of Funeral Directors and   3753
Embalmers; New Hampshire Board of Registration of Funeral Directors
    and   3757
Embalmers, and Operators of Cemeterics and Crematoriums; Nevada State
    Board of Funeral Directors,   3756
Embalmers; Tennessee Board of Funeral Directors and   3770
Embalmers; Virginia Board of Funeral Directors and   3774
Embalmers; West Virginia Board of Funeral Directors and   3776
Embalming Chemical Manufacturers Association   5842
Embalming and Funeral Directing; Rhode Island Board of Examiners in
    3767
Embalming and Funeral Service; Massachusetts Board of Registration in
    3749
Embalming; Wyoming State Board of   3778
Embryo Transfer Society; International   13086
Embryology, Davis Division; Carnegie Laboratories of • Carnegie Institution
    of Washington   2558
Emedicina Dentaria; Sociedade Portugesa de Estomatologia   3986
Emerge: A Men's Counseling Service on Domestic Violence   7368
Emerge: Counseling and Education to Stop Male Violence   7368
Emergency Air Medical Services; American Society of Hospital-Based
    4737
Emergency Care Research Institute   5841
Emergency Centers; National Association of Freestanding   1395
Emergency Department Nurses Association   9086
Emergency Department Nurses Association; National   9086
Emergency Fund; United Nations International Children's   3305
Emergency Health and Medical Services • Public Health Commission •
    District of Columbia Department of Human Services   4775
Emergency Health Services Division • Health Resources Section • North
    Dakota Department of Health and Consolidated Laboratories   4801
Emergency Medical Service Physicians; National Association of   4746
Emergency Medical Services
    Hawaii Department of Health   4778
    Health Division • Wisconsin Department of Health and Social
        Services   4818
    Health Facilities Evaluation and Licensing Division • New Jersey
        Department of Health   4797
    Health Program Office • Florida Department of Health and
        Rehabilitative Services   4776
    Iowa Department of Public Health   4782
    Maine Department of Public Safety   4786
    Ohio Department of Public Safety   4802
    Oklahoma Department of Health   4803
    Public Health Division • Georgia Department of Human Resources
        4777
    Virgin Islands Department of Health   4814
Emergency Medical Services Authority • California Health and Welfare
    Agency   4771
Emergency Medical Services Branch • Health Services Department •
    Kentucky Human Resources Cabinet   4784
Emergency Medical Services Bureau
    Health Division • Idaho Department of Health and Welfare   4779
    Health Resources Division • Missouri Department of Health   4792
    Health Services Division • Montana Department of Health and
        Environmental Sciences   4793
    Health Systems Improvement Division • Utah Department of Health
        4812
    Public Health Services Division • New Hampshire Department of
        Health and Human Services   4796
    Public Health Services Office • Louisiana Department of Health and
        Hospitals   4785
Emergency Medical Services Commission • Indiana State Emergency
    Management Agency   4781

Environmental Medicine; Army Research Institute of
Army Medical Research and Development Command • U.S. Department of Defense **7822**
Environmental Pathophysiology Directorate • U.S. Department of Defense • Army Medical Research and Development Command **7823**
Environmental Physiology and Medicine Directorate • U.S. Department of Defense • Army Medical Research and Development Command **7824**
Occupational Health and Performance Directorate • U.S. Department of Defense • Army Medical Research and Development Command **7825**
Environmental Medicine and Epidemiology; Division of Occupational/ • University of California, Davis **9849**
Environmental Medicine; Institute of
New York University **5080**
University of Pennsylvania **5127**
Environmental Medicine; International Board of **5042**
Environmental Medicine and Lung Biology; Center for • University of North Carolina at Chapel Hill **5126**
Environmental Medicine and Toxicology Division • Thomas Jefferson University **10461**
Environmental Mutagens and Carcinogens; International Commission for Protection Against **5043**
Environmental Mutagens, Carcinogens, and Teratogens Societies; Latin American Association of **5047**
Environmental and Occupational Health Bureau • Michigan Department of Public Health **5150, 9887**
Environmental and Occupational Health Sciences Institute **5072**
Environmental Pathophysiology Directorate • Army Research Institute of Environmental Medicine • Army Medical Research and Development Command • U.S. Department of Defense **7823**
Environmental Physiology and Medicine Directorate • Army Research Institute of Environmental Medicine • Army Medical Research and Development Command • U.S. Department of Defense **7824**
Environmental Planning and Applied Studies; WHO Western Pacific Regional Centre for the Promotion of **5062**
Environmental Protection Agency **5003**
Office of Research and Development
Office of Health and Environmental Assessment **5073**
Office of Health Research **5074**
Environmental Radiation Toxicology; Center for • University of Texas Health Science Center at San Antonio **11080**
Environmental Repercussions; Save Us From Formaldehyde **10406**
Environmental Research Laboratory; Eye Radiation and • Columbia University **2388**
Environmental Research; Office of Health and • Office of Energy Research • U.S. Department of Energy **5092**
Environmental Resource Center International; Safety, Health, and **5057**
Environmental Sciences; Center for • University of Colorado—Denver **5117**
Environmental Sciences; Laboratory of Biomedical and • University of California, Los Angeles **1687**
Environmental Sciences; Marine Biomedical and • Medical University of South Carolina **2592**
Environmental Services of the American Hospital Association; American Society for Healthcare **6430**
Environmental Services Bureau
Alabama Department of Public Health **5128**
Community Health Services Division • Utah Department of Health **5172**
Environmental Simulation Laboratory • University of California, Irvine **9850**
Environmental Studies Institute
Drexel University **5070**
University of Illinois at Urbana-Champaign **5120**
Environmental Studies Laboratory; Socio- • National Institute of Mental Health • U.S. Department of Health and Human Services **7652**
Environmental Toxicology and Cancer; International Society for **5045**
Environmental Toxicology; Center for
Colorado State University **11072**
University of Wisconsin—Madison **10489**
Environmental Toxicology; Center for Research on Occupational and • Oregon Health Sciences University **9816**
Environmental Toxicology; Institute for • Michigan State University **10446**
Environmental Toxicology Research Group; Occupational and • University of Montreal **9860**
Environments; Center to Study Human- Animal Relationships and • University of Minnesota **1705**
Environments Research Center; Work **9864**
Environnement; Association Internationale de Medecine et de Biologie de l' **5041**
Environnement; WHO Centre Regional du Pacifique Occidental pour la Promotion de la Planification et des Etudes Appliquees en Matiere d' **5062**

Enzymology; International Society for Clinical **7142**
Enzymology Research Laboratory **2573**
EP Technologists; American Board of Registration of EEG and **8157**
Epidemiologic Investigations Branch; Surveillance and • Tuberculosis Elimination Division • National Center for Prevention Services • U.S. Department of Health and Human Services **10880**
Epidemiologic Research; Center for **9802**
Epidemiologic Research; Society for **5184**
Epidemiologic and Services Research Division • National Institute of Mental Health • U.S. Department of Health and Human Services **7627**
Epidemiological Association; International **5182**
Epidemiologistes de Langue Francaise; Association des **5180**
Epidemiologists of America; Society of Hospital **5185**
Epidemiologists; Association of French Language **5180**
Epidemiologists; Conference of State and Territorial **5181**
Epidemiologists; Council of State and Territorial **5181**
Epidemiology; American College of **5179**
Epidemiology and Biometry Branch • Division of Microbiology and Infectious Diseases • National Institute of Allergy and Infectious Diseases • U.S. Department of Health and Human Services **6828**
Epidemiology and Biometry Program • Division of Epidemiology and Clinical Applications • National Heart, Lung, and Blood Institute • U.S. Department of Health and Human Services **2932**
Epidemiology and Biostatistics; Center for Clinical • University of Pennsylvania **5195**
Epidemiology and Biostatistics; Division of • University of Cincinnati **5192**
Epidemiology and Biostatistics Program • Division of Cancer Etiology • National Cancer Institute • U.S. Department of Health and Human Services **6139**
Epidemiology Branch
Biometry and Epidemiology Program • National Eye Institute • U.S. Department of Health and Human Services **13631**
Epidemiology and Oral Disease Prevention Program • National Institute of Dental Research • U.S. Department of Health and Human Services **4011**
National Institute of Environmental Health Sciences • U.S. Department of Health and Human Services **5105**
Epidemiology Branch; Clinical • Epidemiology and Biostatistics Program • National Cancer Institute • U.S. Department of Health and Human Services **6168**
Epidemiology Branch; Environmental • Epidemiology and Biostatistics Program • National Cancer Institute • U.S. Department of Health and Human Services **6169**
Epidemiology Branch; Radiation • Epidemiology and Biostatistics Program • National Cancer Institute • U.S. Department of Health and Human Services **6171**
Epidemiology; Center for Biostatistics and • Pennsylvania State University **7020**
Epidemiology and Clinical Applications; Division of • National Heart, Lung, and Blood Institute • U.S. Department of Health and Human Services **2930**
Epidemiology and Clinical Research Branch; Phoenix • Division of Intramural Research • National Institute of Diabetes and Digestive and Kidney Diseases • U.S. Department of Health and Human Services **5191**
Epidemiology, Demography, and Biometry Program • National Institute on Aging • U.S. Department of Health and Human Services **1953**
Epidemiology; Department of Health Sciences and • Naval Health Research Center • Naval Medical Research and Development Command • U.S. Department of Defense **7841**
Epidemiology Directorate • Consumer Product Safety Commission **10975**
Epidemiology; Division of • University of Minnesota **5194**
Epidemiology; Division of Biometry and
National Eye Institute • U.S. Department of Health and Human Services **13632**
National Institute on Alcohol Abuse and Alcoholism • U.S. Department of Health and Human Services **12108**
Epidemiology; Division of Occupational/ Environmental Medicine and • University of California, Davis **9849**
Epidemiology Division; Surveillance and • Epidemiology Program Office • Centers for Disease Control and Prevention • U.S. Department of Health and Human Services **5189**
Epidemiology and Health Systems Development Office • Illinois Department of Public Health **5676**
Epidemiology Laboratory • University of Michigan **4036**
Epidemiology Office • Public Health Division • Georgia Department of Human Resources **6866**
Epidemiology and Oral Disease Prevention Program • National Institute of Dental Research • U.S. Department of Health and Human Services **4009**
Epidemiology and Prevention Research Division • National Institute on Drug Abuse • U.S. Department of Health and Human Services **12129**
Epidemiology Program Office • Centers for Disease Control and Prevention • U.S. Department of Health and Human Services **5188**
Epidemiology and Psychopathology Research Branch • Epidemiology and Services Research Division • National Institute of Mental Health • U.S. Department of Health and Human Services **7629**

Europeenne d'Allergologie et d'Immunologie Clinique; Academie   2072
Europeenne d'Anesthesie Loco-Regionale; Societe   2365
Europeenne du Laser; Association   11112
Europeenne pour l'Etude du Diabete; Association   4839
Europeenne pour l'Etude de l'Alimentation et du Developpement de l'Enfant; Association   9455
Europeenne de Pharmacopee; Commission   10598
Europeenne des Practiciens en Medecine Dentaire; Union   3933
Europeenne de Psychanalyse; Federation   7372
Europeenne de Psychologie Sociale; Association   7371
Europeenne de Radiologie; Association   11110
Europeenne pour la Recherche et le Traitement du Cancer; Organisation   5941
Europeenne de Sange Congele de Groupes Rares; Banque   7134
Europeenne Thyroide; Association   4842
Europeenne des Veterinaires de l'Industrie et de la Recherche; Federation   13074
Europeennes et Mediterraneennes de Gastroenterologie; Association des Societes Nationales,   5210
Europese Vereniging voor Pediatrische Hematologie en Immunologie   3224
EUROPTOM   13446
EUROTOX   10409
Eurotransplant Foundation   12869
Ev. Lutheran Good Samaritan Society   1281
Eva L. and Joseph M. Bruening Foundation   174
Evaluating Professionals; National Association of Disability   7183
Evaluation Association; International Health   5861
Evaluation Center; Child • University of Louisville   4592
Evaluation Center; Child Development Research and   4315
Evaluation and Developmental Center • Southern Illinois University at Carbondale   4584
Evaluation; Foundation for Health Care   1297
Evaluation and Research Center; Psychological • Hofstra University   7566
Evaluation and Research Group • Northwestern Woodhaven Center   4316
Evaluation Research Group, Inc.   3070
Evaluation and Research Unit • Domestic Abuse Project   3068
Evaluations; Office of Demonstrations and • Office of Research and Demonstrations • Health Care Financing Administration • U.S. Department of Health and Human Services   5760
Evaluative Clincial Sciences; Center for • Dartmouth College   5622
Evan and Marion Helfaer Foundation   6349
Evangelical Social Work Conference   11871
Evans Memorial Department of Clinical Research; Robert Dawson • Boston University   1560
Evans Syndrome Research and Support Group   7875
Evanston Cancer Care Center   6057
Evnesvages Vel; Landsforeningen   4298
Evoked Potentials; American Society for Clinical   8174
Ewing Society; James   5989
Examination Commission; Foreign Pharmacy Graduate   10599
Examination Committee; Foreign Pharmacy Graduate   10599
Examiners; American Association of Dental   3871
Examiners; American Association of Osteopathic   9971
Examiners; American Council of Hypnotist   6584
Examiners Association; Airline Medical   2383
Examiners; International Association of Coroners and Medical   7179
Examiners; National Association of Disability   5737
Examiners; National Association of Medical   7184
Examiners; National Board of Medical   1406
Examiners; National Board of Naturopathic   2225
Examiners; National Board of Osteopathic Medical   10003
Examiners; National Board of Podiatric Medical   10774
Examiners; National Board of Podiatry   10774
Examiners; National Contact Lens   13532
Examiners for Nursing Home Administrators; National Association of Boards of   9268
Examiners—Nursing and Technology; Board of Nephrology   9077
Examiners in Optometry; International Association of Boards of   13480
Examiners in Optometry; National Board of   13529
Examiners for Osteopathic Physicians and Surgeons; National Board of   10003
Examiners in Professional Psychology; American Board of   7289
Examiners of Psychodrama, Sociometry, and Group Psychotherapy; American Board of   7287
Examining Boards; Nebraska Bureau of   10806
Examining Boards of the United States; Conference of Funeral Service   3711
Exanthems and Herpesvirus Branch; Viral • Division of Viral and Rickettsial Diseases • National Center for Infectious Diseases • U.S. Department of Health and Human Services   6812
Exceptional Children; Council for   3215
    Division on Career Development and Transition   3216

Division for Early Childhood   3217
    Division on Mental Retardation and Developmental Disabilities   4288
    Division for Physical and Health Disabilities   4479
    Division for Visual Handicaps   3218
Exceptional Children; Foundation for   3150, 3228
Exceptional Children; National Association of Private Schools for   3263
Exceptional Children and Youth; Institute for Study of • University of Maryland   4593
Executive Directors; Association of Osteopathic State   9994
Executive Office of the President
    Domestic Policy Council • National Policy Director for AIDS   6601
    Office of Management and Budget • Health Division • Health Programs and Social Services Bureau   1
Executive Program in Health Administration • Graduate School of Business Administration • University of Colorado—Denver / Western Network for Education in Health Administration   5480
Executives; American Association of Medical Society   1142
Executives; American College of Healthcare   5546
Executives; American College of Medical Practice   5547
Executives; American College of Physician   5549
Executives; American Organization of Nurse   5552
Executives of American Schools for the Deaf; Conference of   3507
Executives Association; Medical Society   1142
Executives; College of Osteopathic Healthcare   5570
Executives; Conference of Podiatry   10770
Executives; International Association of Optometric   13481
Executives; National Association of Health Services   5586
Executives; National Council of State Pharmacy Association   5597
Executives; Society of Association Optometric   13481
Exercise Association; IDEA: International Dance   10850
Exercise; International Dance   10850
Exercise Physiology Group • Laval University   11969
Exercise Physiology and Health; Institute for • University of Central Florida   11981
Exercise Physiology Laboratory
    Ohio State University   11973
    University of Missouri—Columbia   11988
    University of Nevada, Las Vegas   11989
Exercise Research Laboratory • University of Connecticut   7949
Exercise Research Unit; Sports Injuries / Therapeutic • University of Illinois at Urbana-Champaign   11985
Exercise Science; Center for • University of Florida   11983
Exercise and Sport Research Institute • Arizona State University   11955
Exer-Safety Association   10848
Exer-Safety Association; International   10848
Exocrine Physiology; Laboratory of • University of Alabama at Birmingham   4927
Exodontists; American Society of   3877
Exodus Trust   11691
Exotic Bird Health Center; Schubot • Texas A&M University   13176
Exotic Pathology Society   6667
Exotique; Societe de Pathologie   6667
Experimental Biology; Federation of American Societies for • Life Sciences Research Office   2574
Experimental Biology and Medicine; Society for   2545
Experimental Biology; Worcester Foundation for   2709
    Cancer Center   2710
    Male Fertility Program   2711
Experimental Carcinogenesis; Laboratory of • National Cancer Institute • U.S. Department of Health and Human Services   6184
Experimental Cytology; Laboratory of • University of Michigan   2676
Experimental and Engineering Psychologists; Division of Applied • American Psychological Association   7304
Experimental Hematology Department • Armed Forces Radiobiology Research Institute • U.S. Department of Defense   11077
Experimental Hypnosis; Society for Clinical and   6598
Experimental Immunology Laboratories   2104
Experimental Immunology; Laboratory of • National Cancer Institute • U.S. Department of Health and Human Services   6185
Experimental Inhalation Research Group • University of Montreal   10480
Experimental Medicine and Surgery in Primates; Laboratory for • New York University   13151
Experimental Neuropathology; Laboratory of • National Institute of Neurological Disorders and Stroke • U.S. Department of Health and Human Services   8459
Experimental Oncology; Laboratory for
    Indiana University-Purdue University at Indianapolis   6052
    University of Tennessee, Knoxville   6251
Experimental Pathology; Laboratory of
    National Cancer Institute • U.S. Department of Health and Human Services   6186
    University of Michigan   2491

Experimental Pathology Section • Laboratory of Immunology • National Institute of Allergy and Infectious Diseases • U.S. Department of Health and Human Services **2136**

Experimental Psychologists; Society of **7512**

Experimental Psychology; Society of Multivariate **7514**

Experimental Social Psychology; European Association of **7371**

Experimental Therapeutics; American Society for Pharmacology and **10183, 10399**

Experimental Therapeutics Branch

    Intramural Research Programs Division (Clinical Research) • National Institute of Mental Health • U.S. Department of Health and Human Services **7640**

    National Institute of Neurological Disorders and Stroke • U.S. Department of Health and Human Services **8457**

Experimental Therapeutics; Center for • Baylor College of Medicine **10427**

Experimental Therapeutics Division • Walter Reed Army Institute of Research • Army Medical Research and Development Command • U.S. Department of Defense **7831**

Experimental Therapeutics; Interdisciplinary Program in Cell and Molecular Pharmacology and • Medical University of South Carolina **10445**

Experimental Toxicology Branch • Biomedical and Behavioral Science Division • National Institute for Occupational Safety and Health • U.S. Department of Health and Human Services **9829**

Experimentation Division; Hospital • Office of Demonstrations and Evaluations • Health Care Financing Administration • U.S. Department of Health and Human Services **5756**

Experimentation Division; Long-Term Care • Office of Demonstrations and Evaluations • Health Care Financing Administration • U.S. Department of Health and Human Services **5757**

Exploration of Human Potential; National Center for the **2198**

Exploration of Psychotherapy Integration; Society for the **7513**

Expression; American Society of Psychopathology of **7311**

Expressive Analysis; Center for **7391**

Expressive Analysis; Institute for **7391**

Expressive Psychotherapy; Center for **7391**

Extension Program Foundation; Optometric **13547**

Extracellular Matrix Biology; Center for • Texas A&M University **2627**

Extracorporeal Circulation Technicians; American Society of **2829**

Extra-Corporeal Technology; American Society of **2829**

Extramural Activities; Division of

    National Institute of Allergy and Infectious Diseases • U.S. Department of Health and Human Services **2129**

    National Institute on Deafness and Other Communication Disorders • U.S. Department of Health and Human Services **3630**

Extramural Affairs; Office of • National Institute on Aging • U.S. Department of Health and Human Services **1965**

Extramural Program • National Institute of Dental Research • U.S. Department of Health and Human Services **4013**

Extramural Programs Branch • Epidemiology and Biostatistics Program • National Cancer Institute • U.S. Department of Health and Human Services **6170**

Extramural Programs; Division of

    National Institute for Nursing Research • U.S. Department of Health and Human Services **9146**

    National Library of Medicine • National Institutes of Health • U.S. Department of Health and Human Services **7035**

Extramural Research • National Eye Institute • U.S. Department of Health and Human Services **13634**

Extramural Research; Center for General Health Services • Agency for Health Care Policy and Research • U.S. Department of Health and Human Services **5643**

Extramural Research Program • Division of Cancer Biology, Diagnosis, and Centers • National Cancer Institute • U.S. Department of Health and Human Services **6133**

Extramural Research and Training; Division of • National Institute of Environmental Health Sciences • U.S. Department of Health and Human Services **5103**

Exxon Education Foundation **678**

Eye Acquisition; Consortium of Registered Nurses for **9072**

Eye Bank Association of America **13450**

Eye-Bank for Sight Restoration **13451**

Eye Bank & Visual Research Foundation, Inc.; Connecticut **13587**

Eye Care **13452**

Eye Care Foundation; Children's **3266**

Eye Care Foundation; National Children's **3151, 3266**

Eye Care Project; National **13534**

Eye Center

    Duke University **13591**

    Louisiana State University **13613**

Eye Center; Hermann • University of Texas—Houston Health Science Center **13660**

Eye Center; UIC • University of Illinois at Chicago **13652**

Eye Center; W.K. Kellogg • University of Michigan **13655**

Eye Clinic; Elks' Children's • Oregon Health Sciences University **13623**

Eye Disease; International Society on Metabolic **13501**

Eye Diseases; Center for Hereditary • Johns Hopkins University **13604**

Eye and Ear Hospitals; American Association of **6423**

Eye Expeditions International; Surgical **13564**

Eye Foundation; Estelle Doheny **13589**

Eye Foundation; International **13485**

Eye Foundation - Malawi; International **13486**

Eye Foundation; Master **13555**

Eye Hospital Research Institute; Wills **13663**

Eye Hospital; Wills • Research Division **13663**

Eye Institute

    Medical College of Wisconsin **13615**

    Pennsylvania College of Optometry **13624**

Eye Institute; Bascom Palmer • University of Miami **13654**

Eye Institute; Cullen • Baylor College of Medicine **13581**

Eye Institute; Dean A. McGee **13588**

Eye Institute; Doheny **13589**

Eye Institute; Edward S. Harkness • Columbia University **13584**

Eye Institute; Jules Stein • University of California, Los Angeles **13645**

Eye Institute; Kresge • Wayne State University **13662**

Eye Institute; National

    Biometry and Epidemiology Program

        Clinical Trials Branch • U.S. Department of Health and Human Services **13630**

        Epidemiology Branch • U.S. Department of Health and Human Services **13631**

    Division of Biometry and Epidemiology • U.S. Department of Health and Human Services **13632**

    Extramural and Collaborative Programs • Strabismus, Amblyopia, and Visual Processing Branch • U.S. Department of Health and Human Services **13633**

    Extramural Research

        Anterior Segment Diseases Branch • U.S. Department of Health and Human Services **13635**

        Collaborative Clinical Research Branch • U.S. Department of Health and Human Services **13636**

        Retinal and Choroidal Diseases Branch • U.S. Department of Health and Human Services **13637**

        U.S. Department of Health and Human Services **13634**

    Intramural Research

        Laboratory of Immunology • U.S. Department of Health and Human Services **13639**

        U.S. Department of Health and Human Services **13638**

    Laboratory on Mechanisms of Ocular Diseases • U.S. Department of Health and Human Services **13640**

    Laboratory of Molecular and Developmental Biology • U.S. Department of Health and Human Services **13641**

    Laboratory of Retinal Cell and Molecular Biology • U.S. Department of Health and Human Services **13642**

    Laboratory of Sensorimotor Research • U.S. Department of Health and Human Services **13643**

    Office of International Program Activities • U.S. Department of Health and Human Services **13644**

    U.S. Department of Health and Human Services **13354, 13629**

Eye Institute of New Jersey **13594**

Eye Institute; Ophthalmic Research Laboratory and **13622**

Eye Institute; Storm • Medical University of South Carolina **13616**

Eye Radiation and Environmental Research Laboratory • Columbia University **2388**

Eye Research Center; Sensory **13627**

Eye Research Foundation of Bethesda, Maryland **13618**

Eye Research Foundation; Missouri Lions **13618**

Eye Research Foundation; National **13535**

Eye Research Institute • Oakland University **13620**

Eye Research Institute; Ellen Gregg Ingalls **13592**

Eye Research Institute; Kentucky Lions • University of Louisville **13653**

Eye Research Institute; Lions of Illinois • University of Illinois at Chicago **13651**

Eye Research Institute; North Texas • University of North Texas Health Science Center at Fort Worth **13657**

Eye Research Institute of Retina Foundation **13626**

Eye Research Institute; Schepens **13626**

Eye Research Institute; Smith-Kettlewell **13628**

    Rehabilitation Engineering Center **2471**

Eye Research Projects • Ohio Wesleyan University **13621**

Eye Research; Worthen Center for • Georgetown University **13597**

Eye and Tear Research Center; Dry **13590**

Eyes for the Blind; Guiding **13465**

Eyes for the Needy; New **13540**

Eyesight Universal; Operation **13543**

Ezer Metzion **1282**

Ezra Taft Benson Agriculture and Food Institute • Brigham Young University   **1562**

F

F. Edward Hebert School of Medicine
    Pharmacology Department • Uniformed Services University of the Health Sciences   **10256**
    Uniformed Services University of the Health Sciences   **969**
F.G. Hall Hyper-Hypo-Baric Center • Duke University   **1582**
F. M. Kirby Foundation   **175**
F. R. Bigelow Foundation   **176**
Face; Forward   **2746**
Fachverband der Eisen- und Metallwarenindustrie Osterreichs   **5847**
facial Foundations; International Cranio   2744
Facial and Neck Pain and TMJ Orthopedics; American Academy of Head, **3859**
Facial Plastic and Reconstructive Surgery; American Academy of   **12203**
Facial Reconstruction; National Foundation for   **12291**
Facial Surgery; European Academy of   **12267**
Facilities Administration Bureau; Health • Public Health Services Division • New Hampshire Department of Health and Human Services   **6505**
Facilities; American Association for Accreditation of Ambulatory Surgery **12209**
Facilities; Commission on Accreditation of Rehabilitation   **12673**
Facilities; Consultant Dietitians in Health Care   **9452**
Facilities Division; Health
    Health Office • Colorado Public and Environment Department   **6481**
    Health Resources Section • North Dakota Department of Health and Consolidated Laboratories   **6510**
    Iowa Department of Inspections and Appeals   **6491**
    Montana Department of Health and Environmental Sciences   **6502**
Facilities Division; Health Care • Manpower and Facilities Bureau • Tennessee Department of Health   **6518**
Facilities, Licensing, and Certification; Health • Health Systems Bureau • Michigan Department of Public Health   **6498**
Facilities Licensing and Certification Office; Health
    Medical Assistance Division • Alaska Department of Health and Social Services   **6477**
    Public Health Division • Delaware Department of Health and Social Services   **6483**
Facilities Licensure Division; Health • Environmental Health Bureau • Nebraska Department of Health   **6503**
Facilities Licensure Section • Preventive Medicine Division • Wyoming Department of Health   **6526**
Facilities Regulation Bureau; Health • Health Regulation Division • South Carolina Department of Health and Environmental Control   **6516**
Facilities Regulation Division; Health • Ohio Department of Health   **6511**
Facilities Regulation Office; Health • Health Department • Virginia Office of Health and Human Resources   **6522**
Facilities Regulations Division • Health Services Regulations Office • Rhode Island Department of Health   **6515**
Facilities Services; Medical • Oklahoma Department of Health   **6512**
Facility Administrators; Board of Registration and Education for Health • Indiana Health Professions Bureau   **9289**
Facility Division; Health • Service Facility Regulations Administration • District of Columbia Department of Consumer and Regulatory Affairs **6484**
Facility Licensure Bureau • Health Systems Improvement Division • Utah Department of Health   **6520**
Facility Licensure and Certification Bureau; Health • Texas Department of Health   **6519**
Facility Licensure and Certification Directors; Association of Health   **5559**
Facility Licensure and Certification Office; Health • Public Health Bureau • West Virginia Department of Health and Human Resources   **6524**
Facility and Provider Compliance Division • Health Quality Assurance Bureau • Minnesota Department of Health   **6499**
Facility Services Division • North Carolina Department of Human Resources   **6509**
Facility Services and Systems Division; Health • Health Resources Bureau • Arkansas Department of Health   **6479**
Facility Standards Bureau • Medicaid Division • Idaho Department of Health and Welfare   **6488**
Facility Survey Agencies; Association of Health   **5559**
Factor Family Foundation; Max   **1871**
Facultades y Escuelas de Medicina; Federacion Panamericana de Asociaciones de   1452
Faculties; Latin American Association of Medical Schools and   **1369**
Faculty; Association of Black Nursing   **9070**
Faculty in the Medical Humanities; Association for   **1202**
Faculty of Radiologists   11130
Fairchild Foundation; Sherman   **488**

Fairfield University • School of Nursing   **8600**
Fairleigh Dickinson University
    Department of Nursing   **8815**
    Psychological Research Center   **7562**
    Respiratory Therapist Program   **11456**
Faith and Ethics; Park Ridge Center for the Study of Health,   **7212**
Falciforme; Ligue Anti- Anemie   5916
Famiglia; Associazione la Nostra   **12668**
Familia para el Desarrollo; Oficina de la Mujer y la • Instituto Costarricense de Acueductors y Alcantarrillados   **1329**
Familial; Association Ivoirienne de Bien-Etre   **11203**
Familial; Association Rwandaise pour le Bien-Etre   **9635**
Familial Cancer Management and Control; Institute for   6046
Familiale; Conseil International des Services d'Aide   1340
Familiale; Federation Internationale pour la Planification   11225
Familiares y Amigos de Enfermos de la Neurona Motora   **8217**
Familieplanlaegning; Foreningen for   11213
Families in Action   12061
Families in Action Drug Information Center   12061
Families in Action; National   **12061**
Families in Action National Drug Information Center   12061
Families; Administration on Children, Youth and • Administration for Children and Families • U.S. Department of Health and Human Services **6**
Families Anonymous   **12028**
Families and Children; Council on Accreditation of Services for   **11865**
Families and Children; Elizabeth Wisner Social Welfare Research Center for • Tulane University   **11874**
Families and Children; Institute for   **7570**
Families with Maple Syrup Urine Disease   3261
Families of S.M.A.   **8218**
Families with Visual Impairment; Council of   **13443**
Famille du Canada; College des Medecins de   1247
Famille; Organisation Mondiale des Colleges Nationaux, Academies et Associations Academiques des Generalistes et des Medecins de   1550
Family Alliance; VHL   **5306**
Family of the Americas Foundation   **11215**
Family and Child Studies Center • Miami University   **3069**
Family and Community Health Services Division • Health Office • Colorado Public and Environment Depratment   **3383, 9729**
Family and Consumer Sciences Research Institute • Iowa State University of Science and Technology   **9506**
Family Counselors; American Association of Marriage and   7276
Family Crisis Services; Maine Coalition for   **3095**
Family Group Headquarters; Al-Anon   **12000**
Family and Health   **1283**
Family Health Administration; Local and • Public Health Services Office • Maryland Department of Health and Mental Hygiene   **3398, 9744**
Family Health Association; Kiribati   **1367**
Family Health Bureau • Health Division • Kansas Department of Health and Environment   **3394, 9740**
Family Health; Center for Population and • Columbia University   **11264**
Family Health; Council on   **5833**
Family Health Division
    Community Health Center • New York State Department of Health   **3410, 9756**
    Community Health Office • Illinois Department of Public Health   **3391, 9737**
    Minnesota Department of Health   **3401, 9747**
Family Health International   **11216, 11267**
Family Health International/International Fertility Research Program   11216
Family Health Office • Rhode Island Department of Health   **3417, 9763**
Family and Health Section   **1284**
Family Health Section; Maternal and Child • Public Health Division • Alaska Department of Health and Social Services   **3379, 9725**
Family and Health Section of the National Council on Family Relations **1284**
Family Health Service • Health Division • Nevada Department of Human Resources   **3406, 9752**
Family Health Services Bureau • Alabama Department of Public Health **3378, 9724**
Family Health Services Division • Public Health Department • Massachusetts Executive Office of Health and Human Services   **3399, 9745**
Family Health Services Division; Community and • Washington Department of Health   **3425, 9771**
Family Institute   7259, **7563**
Family Institute; Nathan W. Ackerman   7259
Family Learning; Center for   **7547**
Family Life Achievement Center   3060
Family, Maternal and Child Health Bureau • Health Services Division • Montana Department of Health and Environmental Sciences   **3404, 9750**

Family Medicine Research Group • Medical Research Centre • Laval University **1616**
Family Medicine; Society of Teachers of **1512**
Family Network; Treacher Collins **5303**
Family Partnership; National **12062**
Family Physicians; American Academy of **913, 1136**
Family Physicians; American College of Osteopathic **9975**
Family Physicians; American Osteopathic Board of **9984**
Family Physicians of Canada; College of **1247**
Family Physicians; Uniformed Services Academy of **7812**
Family Physicians; World Organization of National Colleges, Academies and Academic Associations of General Practitioners / **1550**
Family Planning Affiliation; Caribbean **11207**
Family Planning; American Academy of Natural **11198**
Family Planning Association of the Americas **11228**
Family Planning Association; Danish **11213**
Family Planning Association of Kenya **11217**
Family Planning Association of Liberia **11218**
Family Planning Forum; National **11238**
Family Planning International Assistance **11193, 11219**
Family Planning Program Development; Center for **11197, 11259**
Family Planning Program (Service Delivery Improvement Research) • Office of Family Planning • Public Health Service • U.S. Department of Health and Human Services **11290**
Family Planning and Protection; Jordanian Association for **11233**
Family Planning and Reproductive Health Association; National **11238**
Family Planning Research Association; International **11228**
Family Practice; American Board of **1145**
Family Practice Residency Directors; Association of **5557**
Family Program; Pil-Anon **12024**
Family Psychology; Division of • American Psychological Association **7305**
Family Relations; Family and Health Section of the National Council on **1284**
Family Relations Family Therapy Section; National Council on **7374, 7374**
Family Research Institute **1285**
Family Research Institute; Transnational **11282**
Family Research Laboratory • University of New Hampshire **3074**
Family Research in Rural Mental Health; Center for • Iowa State University of Science and Technology **7577**
Family Studies; Center for Child and • University of California, San Diego **3356**
Family Studies; Division of Child and • University of Connecticut **4587**
Family Studies; Institute of Human Development and • University of Texas at Austin **3075**
Family Support; Center for **4287**
Family Support and Children's Mental Health; Research and Training Center on • Portland State University **7593**
Family Support Group; MSUD **3261**
Family Therapy; Ackerman Institute for **7259, 7536**
Family Therapy; American Association for Marriage and **7276**
Family Therapy Network **3052**
Family Therapy Section of the National Council on Family Relations **7374**
Family; University Center for the Child and • University of Michigan **3365**
Family Violence; Hawaii State Committee on **3087**
Family Violence; National Council on Child Abuse and **3061**
Family Violence; Texas Council on **3120**
Famous Fone Friends **3226**
Fan Fox and Leslie R. Samuels Foundation **177**
Fanconi's Anemia Research Fund **5278**
Fanconi's Anemia Support Group **5278**
Fannie E. Rippel Foundation **178**
Farber Cancer Institute; Sidney **6027**
Farish Fund; William Stamps **554**
Farm Medicine Center; National **9813**
Farmaceuticos de Puerto Rico; Colegio de **10733**
Farmacologia; Sociedad Centro-Americana de **10403**
Farmakologie Vereniging; Suid Afrikaanse **10422**
Farmers Group Safety Foundation **679**
Fast Kinetics Research; Center for • University of Texas at Austin **2690**
Fatigue Syndrome Association; National Chronic **6732**
Fatigue Syndrome and Fibromyalgia Association; National Chronic **6732**
Fauchard Academy; Pierre **3985**
Faye McBeath Foundation **179**
Fayetteville Technical Community College
    Funeral Service Education Department **3691**
    Respiratory Care Technology **11478**
FDI - World Dental Federation **3935**
Federacion Internacional de Asociaciones de Estudiantes de Medicina **1345**
Federacion Internacional de Hospitales **6452**
Federacion Internacional de Patologia Cervical y Colposcopia **9664**

Federacion Latinoamericana de Hospitales **6454**
Federacion Latinoamericana de Sociedades de Cancerologia **5945**
Federacion Latinoamericana de Termalismo **5048**
Federacion Mundial de Medicos que Respectan la Vida Humana **1538**
Federacion Nacional de Empresas de Instrumentacion Cientifica, Medica, Tecnica y Dental **5848**
Federacion Panamericana de Asociaciones de Facultades y Escuelas de Medicina **1452**
Federacion Panamericana pro Donacion Voluntaria de Sangre **7152**
Federal Aviation Administration
    Civil Aeromedical Institute
        Aeromedical Research Division • U.S. Department of Transportation **2405**
        Data Analysis Staff • U.S. Department of Transportation **2406**
        Human Resources Research Division • U.S. Department of Transportation **2407**
        Protection and Survival Laboratory • U.S. Department of Transportation **2408**
        Toxicology and Accident Research Laboratory • U.S. Department of Transportation **2409**
        U.S. Department of Transportation **2404**
    Medical Specialties Division
        Biomedical and Behavioral Sciences Branch • U.S. Department of Transportation **2411**
        U.S. Department of Transportation **2410**
Federal Chamber of Veterinarians eV **13073**
Federal Council on the Aging • Office of the Secretary • U.S. Department of Health and Human Services **1866**
Federal Mine Safety and Health Review Commission **9775**
Federal-Mogul Corp. Charitable Trust Fund **680**
Federal Physicians Association **1286**
Federal Service Campaign for National Health Agencies; National Committee of the **1433**
Federal Trade Commission **5819**
Federal Veterinarians; National Association of **13093**
Federated Ambulatory Surgery Association **12272**
Federaties van Ouders van Slechthorende- en Spraakgestoorde **3519**
Federation for Accessible Nursing Education and Licensure **9088**
Federation of American Health Systems **6442**
Federation of American Hospitals **6442**
Federation of American Societies for Experimental Biology • Life Sciences Research Office **2574**
Federation of Associations of Health Regulatory Boards **1287**
Federation of Associations of Regulatory Boards **1287**
Federation of Behavioral, Psychological and Cognitive Sciences **7375**
Federation of Biocommunications Societies **6987**
Federation for Children with Special Needs **4485**
Federation of the European Dental Industry **5849**
Federation of European Veterinarians in Industry and Research **13074**
Federation Europeenne des Associations de Dieteticiens **9456**
Federation Europeenne de Climatotherapie **5039**
Federation Europeenne de Psychanalyse **7372**
Federation Europeenne des Veterinaires de l'Industrie et de la Recherche **13074**
Federation of Feminist Women's Health Centers **1288**
Federation of French-Language Gynecologists and Obstetricians **9648**
Federation des Gynecologues et Obstetriciens de Langue Francaise **9648**
Federation of Hungarian Medical Societies **1289**
Federation Internationale des Associations Contre la Lepre **6680**
Federation Internationale des Associations Medicales Catholiques **1343**
Federation Internationale des Associations de Psoriasis **4243**
Federation Internationale Balint **7404**
Federation Internationale de Chimie Clinique **7140**
Federation Internationale de la Croix-Bleue **12040**
Federation Internationale du Diabete **4848**
Federation Internationale des Etudiants en Pharmacie **10605**
Federation Internationale de Gynecologie Infantile et Juvenile **3243**
Federation Internationale de Gynecologie et d'Obstetrique **9665**
Federation Internationale de Medicine Manuelle **10000**
Federation Internationale des Mutiles, des Invalides du Travail et des Invalides Civils **4496**
Federation Internationale des Organismes de Psychologie Medicale **7409**
Federation Internationale Pharmaceutique **10604**
Federation Internationale des Pharmaciens Catholiques **10603**
Federation Internationale pour la Planification Familiale **11225**
Federation Internationale pour la Sante **2213**
Federation Internationale des Societes d'Histochimie et de Cytochimie **2537**
Federation Internationale des Societes d'Ophtalmologie **13488**
Federation Internationale des Societes Oto-Rhino-Laryngologiques **3535**
Federation Internationale de Sport pour Handicapes **4499**

Fiscal Management, Organization and Control; Center for Advanced Study in Health Care • University of Wisconsin—Madison **5766**
Fish Foundation; Ray C. **439**
Fishbein Center for the History of Science and Medicine; Morris • University of Chicago **1692**
Fishberg Research Center in Neurobiology; Arthur M. **8327**
Fisher Brothers Foundation **690**
Fisica Medica; Asociacion Latinoamericana de 2539
Fitchburg State College • Department of Nursing **8750**
Fitness Association; American **10839**
Fitness in Business; Association for 10844
Fitness Directors in Business and Industry; American Association of 10844
Fitness Foundation of America; Aerobics and **10834**
Fitness Fund; Children's Health and **3207**
Fitness Motivation Institute of America Association **10849**
Fitness; National Center for Health • American University **10863**
Fitness Professionals; IDEA: International Association of **10850**
Fitness Professionals; IDEA: The Association for 10850
Fitness Research Center • University of Michigan **11987**
Fitness Research Institute; High Technology **11966**
Fitness Research; International Committee on Physical 10853
Fitness Research; International Council for Physical 10853
Fitness Research; International Council for Physical Activity and **10853**
Fitness and Sport; National Institute for **11971**
Fitness and Sports; National Association of Governor's Councils on Physical **10855**
Fitzpatrick Oncology Center **6036**
Fixed Prosthodontics; American Academy of **3856**
Flagler Career Institute • Respiratory Therapist Program **11352**
Flagler Counties; Easter Seal Society of Volusia and **4627**
Flagler Foundation **181**
Fleet Bank of Upstate New York Foundation Trust **691**
Fleet Charitable Trust **692**
Fleet/Norstar Charitable Trust 692
Fletcher Jones Foundation **182**
Flight Nurses Association; National **9120**
Flight Paramedics Association; National **4751**
Flight Surgeons; Society of United States Air Force **7811**
Flinn Foundation **183**
Floatation Tank Association **2192**
Floating Hospital **6443**
Floating Hospital; St. John's Guild - The 6443
Florence-Darlington Technical College • Respiratory Therapist Program **11527**
Florence V. Burden Foundation **184**
Florida A&M University
  Center for Anti-Inflammatory Research **10431**
  College of Pharmacy and Pharmaceutical Sciences **10509**
    Pharmacology and Toxicology Program **10213**
  Health Information Management Division **6919**
  School of Allied Health Sciences
    Department of Occupational Therapy **12346**
    Division of Physical Therapy **12458**
    Respiratory Therapy Program **11353**
  School of Nursing **8615**
Florida Affiliate
  American Diabetes Association **4959**
  American Heart Association **2999**
Florida Agency Health Care Administration **5672**
  Medicaid Office **5777**
Florida; American Lung Association of **11635**
Florida; Arc of **4403**
Florida Atlantic University
  Center for Complex Systems **8368**
  College of Nursing **8616**
Florida Blood Services • Transfusion Medicine Academic Center • Specialist in Blood Bank Technology Program **7095**
Florida Board of Dentistry **4058**
Florida Board of Funeral Directors and Embalmers **3737**
Florida Board of Medicine **1765**
Florida Board of Nursing **9162**
Florida Board of Nursing Home Administrators **9284**
Florida Board of Optometry **13727**
Florida Board of Osteopathic Medicine **10021**
Florida Board of Pharmacy **10650**
Florida Board of Podiatric Medicine **10788**
Florida Chapter
  American Physical Therapy Association **12829**
  Arthritis Foundation **7975**
  Cystic Fibrosis Foundation **5410**
  Lupus Foundation of America **8040**

  National Association of Social Workers **11889**
Florida Chapter; Northeast • Lupus Foundation of America **8041**
Florida Chapter; Northwest • Lupus Foundation of America **8042**
Florida Chapter; Southeast • Lupus Foundation of America **8043**
Florida Coalition Against Domestic Violence **3085**
Florida Community College at Jacksonville • Respiratory Therapist Program **11354**
Florida Dental Association **4164**
Florida Department of Agriculture and Consumer Services • Animal Industry Division • State Veterinarian **13258**
Florida Department of Education • Blind Services Division **13674**
Florida Department of Health and Rehabilitative Services
  Aging and Adult Services Office **2012**
  Developmental Services Office **4352**
  Family Health Services Office **3387, 9733**
    Public Health Dental Program **4111**
  Health Program Office **11014**
    Disease Control and AIDS Prevention Office **6865**
    Emergency Medical Services **4776**
    Environmental Health Services Office **5137**
  Human Services Program Office • Alcohol, Drug Abuse and Mental Health Office **7717, 12156**
  Licensure and Certification Office **6485**
  Vital Statistics Office **7049**
Florida Department of Labor and Employment Security
  Safety Division **9874**
  Vocational Rehabilitation Division **12779**
Florida Division • American Cancer Society **6280**
Florida Easter Seal Society **4628**
Florida; Easter Seal Society of East Central **4624**
Florida; Easter Seal Society of North **4625**
Florida; Easter Seal Society of Southwest **4626**
Florida Health Care Association **9335**
Florida Hospital Association **6536**
Florida Institute of Technology
  Life Science Research Complex **1587**
  Medical Genetics Laboratory **5330**
Florida International University
  College of Health Sciences • Department of Physical Therapy **12459**
  Department of Dietetics and Nutrition **9392**
  Department of Health Services Administration • Program in Health Services Administration **5484**
  Department of Occupational Therapy **12347**
  Health Information Management Program **6920**
  School of Nursing **8617**
  School of Social Work **11767**
Florida; Learning Disabilities Association of **4692**
Florida Medical Association **1819**
Florida Medical Entomology Laboratory • University of Florida **10998**
Florida Mental Health Institute • University of South Florida **7688**
Florida; National Kidney Foundation of **12942**
Florida Nurses Association **9220**
Florida Ophthalmic Institute **13595**
Florida Optometric Association **13802**
Florida Osteopathic Medical Association **10075**
Florida Pharmacy Association **10703**
Florida State University
  Center for Biomedical Toxicological Research and Hazardous Waste Management **10432**
  Center for Employment Relations and Law **7198**
  Center for Prevention and Early Intervention **3335**
  Communication Science Laboratory **3599**
  Department of Human Services and Studies • Rehabilitation Education Programs **12581**
  Institute for Health and Human Services Research **5624**
  School of Nursing **8618**
  School of Social Work **11768**
Florida Veterinary Medical Association **13311**
Flotation Health Care Foundation; National **1417**
Flow Cytometry Facility • University of Iowa **2672**
Flow Cytometry; Laboratory of • Roswell Park Cancer Institute **2612**
Flower Essence Society **2193**
Fluency; Foundation for **3524**
Fluorophotometry; International Society for Ocular **13502**
Flying Chiropractors Association **3456**
Flying Dentists Association **3940**
Flying Doctors of Mercy **1372**
Flying Doctors Service **1130**
Flying Physicians Association **1292**
Flying Veterinarians Association **13078**
FMC Foundation **6397**

Fry Foundation; Lloyd A.   357
F.S.H. Society   **7879**
Fuld Health Trust; Helene   **8538**
Fuld School of Nursing; Helene • Coppin State College   **8740**
Fuller E. Callaway Foundation   **206**
Fuller Foundation; George F. and Sybil H.   **214**
Fullerton Foundation   **207**
Fulton Skin Institute   **4263**
Functional Neurosurgery; American Society for Stereotactic and   **12245**
Functional Neurosurgery; World Society for Stereotactic and   **12317**
Functional Studies; Institute for Structural and   2582
Functional Vision; Laboratory for the Assessment of • University of Illinois at Chicago   **13650**
Fundacao Instituto Integrado de Saude   **1305**
Fundacio Sandoz para Investigacion en Gerontologia Regional para Latin America   1919
Fundacion Omega   **8223**
Fundacion Salvadorena para el Desarrollo de la Mujer y el Nino   **1306**
Fundacja Akcja dla Zdrowia   1314
Fundacja Rytm Serca   2850
Fundamental Electrophysiology Research Group • Sherbrooke University   **2621**
Fundamental Neurosciences; Division of • National Institute of Neurological Disorders and Stroke • U.S. Department of Health and Human Services   **8451**
Funding; Ad Hoc Group for Medical Research   **1123**
Funeral and Cemetery Boards; Washington   **3775**
Funeral and Cemetery Services; Indiana State Board of   **3742**
Funeral Directing; New York Bureau of   **3760**
Funeral Directing; Rhode Island Board of Examiners in Embalming and   **3767**
Funeral Directors; Arkansas State Board of Embalmers and   **3731**
Funeral Directors Association; National   **3719**
Funeral Directors; Connecticut Board of Examiners of Embalmers and   **3734**
Funeral Directors and Embalmers; Arizona State Board of   **3730**
Funeral Directors and Embalmers; California Board of   **3732**
Funeral Directors and Embalmers; District of Columbia Board of   **3736**
Funeral Directors and Embalmers; Florida Board of   **3737**
Funeral Directors and Embalmers Licensing and Discipline Boards • Illinois Department of Professional Regulation   **3741**
Funeral Directors and Embalmers; Missouri State Board of   **3753**
Funeral Directors and Embalmers; New Hampshire Board of Registration of   **3757**
Funeral Directors, Embalmers, and Operators of Cemeterics and Crematoriums; Nevada State Board of   **3756**
Funeral Directors and Embalmers; Tennessee Board of   **3770**
Funeral Directors and Embalmers; Virginia Board of   **3774**
Funeral Directors and Embalmers; West Virginia Board of   **3776**
Funeral Directors Examining Board; Wisconsin   **3777**
Funeral Directors; Kentucky State Board of Embalmers and   **3745**
Funeral Directors; Louisiana State Board of Embalmers and   **3746**
Funeral Directors and Morticians Association; National   **3720**
Funeral Directors; Ohio Board of Embalmers and   **3763**
Funeral Directors; Oklahoma State Board of Embalmers and   **3764**
Funeral Directors; Pennsylvania State Board of   **3766**
Funeral Service; Alabama Board of   **3728**
Funeral Service Board; Colorado   **3733**
Funeral Service Board; Georgia State   **3738**
Funeral Service Board; Utah   **3772**
Funeral Service Commission; Texas   **3771**
Funeral Service Education; American Board of   **3705**
Funeral Service Examining Board; Hawaii   **3739**
Funeral Service Examining Boards of the United States; Conference of   **3711**
Funeral Service; Maine Board of   **3747**
Funeral Service; Massachusetts Board of Registration in Embalming and   **3749**
Funeral Service; Mississippi State Board of   **3752**
Funeral Service; Montana Board of   **3754**
Funeral Service; National Foundation of • National Research and Information Center   **3726**
Funeral Service; Nebraska Board of   **3755**
Funeral Service; North Dakota State Board of   **3762**
Funeral Service; South Carolina State Board of   **3768**
Funeral Service; South Dakota State Board of   **3769**
Funeral Service; Vermont Board of   **3773**
Funeral Services; Delaware State Board of   **3735**
Fusspfleger Deutschlands; Zentralverband der Medizinischen   10769
Future; Program on Psychosocial Adaptation and the • University of California, Los Angeles   **7657**
Futures; Institute for Alternative   **1606**

G

G. Harold and Leila Y. Mathers Charitable Foundation   **208**
G-Jo Institute   **2195**
Gabbert Raptor Center • University of Minnesota   **13223**
Gabriela Commission on Women's Health and Reproductive Rights   **9650**
Gaisman Foundation; Catherine and Henry J.   **88**
Gait Analysis Laboratory   9943
Gait Study Center • Pennsylvania College of Podiatric Medicine   **10778**
Galactosemic Children; Parents of   **4869**
Gallaudet Research Institute • Gallaudet University   **3603**
Gallaudet University
    Center for Assessment & Demographic Studies   **3600**
    Center for Auditory and Speech Sciences   **3601**
    Center for Studies in Education and Human Development   **3602**
    Department of Counseling • Rehabilitation Counseling Programs   **12579**
    Gallaudet Research Institute   **3603**
Gallo Clinic and Research Center; Ernest • University of California, San Francisco   **12134**
Gallo Foundation   **697**
Gamble Institute of Medical Research; James N.   **6773**
Gamma; Lambda Omicron   10002
Gamma Peer Education Network; BACCHUS and   **12014**
Gannon University
    Department of Nursing   **8917**
    Physician Assistant Program   **1104**
    Respiratory Therapist Program   **11511**
    Villa Maria College of Health Sciences
        Department of Science and Mathematics • Dietetics Program   **9420**
        Occupational Therapy Program   **12417**
Gannon University; Hamot Medical Center / • School of Anesthesia   **2315**
Gap Foundation   **6605**
GAR Foundation   **209**
Garden Club; Sup Sup   **9489**
Garden State Cancer Center; Center for Molecular Medicine and Immunology /   **2096**
Garey Cancer Foundation; Eugene L.   5971
Garroway Laboratory for the Study of Depression; Dave   **7556**
GASP of America   11737
Gastroenterologia; Asociacion Inter-Americana de   5220
Gastroenterological Association; American   **5204**
Gastroenterological Association; National   5203
Gastroenterologie; Association des Societes Nationales, Europeennes et Mediterraneennes de   5210
Gastroenterologie; Organisation Mondiale de   5233
Gastroenterology; American College of   **5203**
Gastroenterology; Association of National, European and Mediterranean Societies of   **5210**
Gastroenterology; Bockus International Society of   **5211**
Gastroenterology Clinic • Stanford University   **5236**
Gastroenterology; Inter-American Association of   **5220**
Gastroenterology; Motility Laboratory/ • Temple University   **5237**
Gastroenterology; North American Society for Pediatric   **3277**
Gastroenterology Nurses and Associates; Society of   **5231**
Gastroenterology and Nutrition Center • University of California, Davis   **5247**
Gastroenterology and Nutrition; North American Society for Pediatric   **3277**
Gastroenterology; Society for the Advancement of   5203
Gastroenterology; World Organization of   **5233**
Gastroesophageal Reflux Association; American Pediatric   **3168**
Gastrointestinal Assistants; Society of   5231
Gastrointestinal Digestion Program • Division of Digestive Diseases and Nutrition • National Institute of Diabetes and Digestive and Kidney Diseases • U.S. Department of Health and Human Services   **5241**
Gastrointestinal Endoscopic Surgeons; Society of American   **5230**
Gastrointestinal Endoscopy; American Society for   **5209**
Gastrointestinal Endoscopy; Indonesian Society of   **5219**
Gastrointestinal Immunology Program • Division of Digestive Diseases and Nutrition • National Institute of Diabetes and Digestive and Kidney Diseases • U.S. Department of Health and Human Services   **5242**
Gastrointestinal Indonesia; Perhimpunan Endoskopi   5219
Gastrointestinal Motility Program • Division of Digestive Diseases and Nutrition • National Institute of Diabetes and Digestive and Kidney Diseases • U.S. Department of Health and Human Services   **5243**
Gastrointestinal Neuroendocrinology Program • Division of Digestive Diseases and Nutrition • National Institute of Diabetes and Digestive and Kidney Diseases • U.S. Department of Health and Human Services   **5244**
Gastrointestinal Pathology Club   10130

Genetics Center • University of Texas—Houston Health Science Center **5383**

Genetics; Center for Developmental and Health • Pennsylvania State University **5345**

Genetics; Center for Human **5318**

    Boston University **5314**

    Case Western Reserve University **5316**

    Indiana University-Purdue University at Indianapolis **5332**

Genetics; Center for Molecular • University of California, San Diego **2664**

Genetics; Center for Molecular Medicine and • Wayne State University **5392**

Genetics; Committee for Responsible **2713**

Genetics; Council for Responsible **2713**

Genetics; Department of Biochemical • City of Hope Beckman Research Institute **5320**

Genetics and Developmental Biology Program • West Virginia University **2706**

Genetics; Division of Human • University of California, Irvine **5369**

Genetics Group; New England Regional **5343**

Genetics; Hattie B. Munroe Center for Human • University of Nebraska Medical Center **5377**

Genetics; Institute for Behavioral • University of Colorado at Boulder **5371**

Genetics; Institute of Human • University of Minnesota **5375**

Genetics; Institute for Molecular • Baylor College of Medicine **5311**

Genetics; Laboratory of

    National Cancer Institute • U.S. Department of Health and Human Services **6187**

    University of Vermont **5387**

    University of Wisconsin—Madison **5389**

Genetics Laboratory; Animal • Ohio State University **13155**

Genetics Laboratory; Biochemical

    Baylor College of Medicine **4880**

    National Heart, Lung, and Blood Institute • U.S. Department of Health and Human Services **2944**

    National Institute of Mental Health • U.S. Department of Health and Human Services **7617**

Genetics; Laboratory of Cell Biology and • National Institute of Diabetes and Digestive and Kidney Diseases • U.S. Department of Health and Human Services **4925**

Genetics Laboratory; Medical

    Florida Institute of Technology **5330**

    University of Alabama at Birmingham **5367**

Genetics Laboratory; Molecular

    Columbia University **5322**

    National Institute on Aging • U.S. Department of Health and Human Services **1961**

    National Institute of Child Health and Human Development • U.S. Department of Health and Human Services **5361**

    National Institute of Environmental Health Sciences • U.S. Department of Health and Human Services **5108**

    Southwest Foundation for Biomedical Research **5350**

Genetics Laboratory; Perinatal • University of Utah **5386**

Genetics Laboratory; Veterinary • University of California, Davis **13214**

Genetics and Metabolism; Laboratory of Biochemical • Rockefeller University **5346**

Genetics / Oncology Laboratory; Molecular **5342**

Genetics Program • National Institute of General Medical Sciences • U.S. Department of Health and Human Services **5365**

Genetics Program; Interdepartmental Medical • Stanford University **5352**

Genetics Research Group; Ontogenesis and Molecular • Medical Research Centre • Laval University **5336**

Genetics Section of Pediatrics • Louisiana State University **5338**

Genetics and Transplantation Branch • Division of Allergy, Immunology, and Transplantation • National Institute of Allergy and Infectious Diseases • U.S. Department of Health and Human Services **2128**

Genitourinary Pathology Department • Center for Advanced Pathology • Armed Forces Institute of Pathology • U.S. Department of Defense **10151**

Genito-Urinary Surgeons; American Association of **12210**

Genome Center; Human • Baylor College of Medicine **5310**

Genome Informatics; W.M. Keck Center for • Texas A&M University **5355**

Genome Project; Malaria • University of Florida **6845**

Genome Research; Center for • Texas A&M University **5354**

Genome Research; National Center for Human • U.S. Department of Health and Human Services **5257**

Geochemistry and Health; Society for Environmental **5059**

Geographic, and Ecologic; International Society of Dermatology: Tropical, [Rochester, MN] **4244**

Geographic, and Ecological; International Society of Dermatology: Tropical, [Bogota, Colombia] **4245**

Geographic Ophthalmology; International Society of **13500**

Geographic Pathology Division • Infectious and Parasitic Disease Pathology Department • Armed Forces Institute of Pathology • U.S. Department of Defense **10169**

Geographical Pathology; International Society of **10134**

Geographique; Societe Internationale d' Ophtalmologie **13500**

George B. Storer Foundation **211**

George C. Paffenbarger Dental Research Laboratory • Ohio State University **4005**

George C. Wallace Community College • Respiratory Therapist Program **11302**

George D. Smith Fund **212**

George F. Baker Trust **213**

George F. and Sybil H. Fuller Foundation **214**

George Foundation **215**

George Frederick Jewett Foundation **216**

George Gund Foundation **217**

George H. Deuble Foundation **218**

George Hoag Family Foundation **6352**

George I. Alden Trust **219**

George Link, Jr. Foundation **220**

George and Mary Josephine Hamman Foundation **221**

George Mason University • College of Nursing and Health • Baccalaureate Nursing Program **9009**

George S. and Dolores Dore Eccles Foundation **222**

George W. Brackenridge Foundation **223**

George Warren Brown School of Social Work • Washington University **11810**

George Washington Carver Agricultural Experiment Station • Tuskegee University **9530**

George Washington University

    Center for Virology, Immunology and Infectious Disease Research **6770**

    Intergovernmental Health Policy Project **7200**

    Lipid Research Clinic **2895**

    National Cooperative Drug Discovery Group for the Treatment of AIDS **6771**

    Regional Rehabilitation Continuing Education Programs **12580**

    School of Business and Public Management • Department of Health Services Administration • Graduate Program in Health Services Management and Policy **5482**

    School of Medicine and Health Sciences **938**

        Department of Pharmacology **10210**

        Physician Assistant Program **1067**

George Williams College • School of Social Work • Aurora University **11773**

George Williams College at Aurora University • School of Social Work **11774**

George Williams Hooper Foundation • University of California, San Francisco **6842**

Georgetown Institute for the Neurosciences; Fidia- • Georgetown University **8369**

Georgetown University

    Center for Bioethics • Asian / International Bioethics Program **7201**

    Fidia-Georgetown Institute for the Neurosciences **8369**

    Institute for Health Care Research and Policy **5749**

    International Center for Interdisciplinary Studies of Immunology at Georgetown **2101**

    Kennedy Institute of Ethics **7202**

    Research Resources Facility **1593**

    School of Medicine **939**

        Department of Pharmacology **10211**

    School of Nursing **8610**

        Graduate Program in Nurse-Midwifery **9590**

    Sleep Disorders Center **8370**

    Vincent T. Lombardi Cancer Research Center **6041**

    Worthen Center for Eye Research **13597**

Georgia Advocates for Battered Women and Children **3086**

Georgia Affiliate

    American Diabetes Association **4960**

    American Heart Association **3000**

Georgia; American Lung Association of **11636**

Georgia; Arc of **4404**

Georgia Baptist College of Nursing **8631**

Georgia Board of Dentistry **4059**

Georgia Board of Nursing **9163**

Georgia Center for Cancer Statistics • Emory University **6034**

Georgia Chapter

    American Physical Therapy Association **12830**

    Arthritis Foundation **7976**

    Cystic Fibrosis Foundation **5413**

    National Association of Social Workers **11890**

Georgia College • School of Nursing **8632**

Georgia Composite State Board of Medical Examiners **1766, 10022**
Georgia Consortium on the Psychology of Aging **1935**
Georgia Dental Association **4165**
Georgia Department of Agriculture • Animal Industry Division • State Veterinarian **13259**
Georgia Department of Human Resources
    Aging Services Office **2013**
    Mental Health, Mental Retardation and Substance Abuse Division **4353, 7718**
        Alcohol and Drug Abuse Services Office **12157**
    Public Health Division **11015**
        Emergency Medical Services **4777**
        Environmental Health Section **5138**
        Epidemiology Office **6866**
        Oral Health Section **4112**
        Vital Statistics Office **7050**
    Regulatory Services Office • Health Care Section **6486**
    Rehabilitation Services Division **12780, 13675**
Georgia Department of Labor • Occupational Safety and Health Division **9875**
Georgia Department of Medical Assistance **5778**
    Maternal and Child Health Division **3388, 9734**
Georgia Division • American Cancer Society **6281**
Georgia; Easter Seal Society of East **4629**
Georgia Easter Seal Society; Middle **4631**
Georgia; Easter Seal Society of North **4630**
Georgia Easter Seal Society; Southwest **4632**
Georgia Hospital Association **6537**
Georgia Institute of Human Nutrition • Medical College of Georgia **9511**
Georgia Institute of Technology
    Bioengineering Center **2445**
    Biomechanics Laboratory **2446**
    Center for Rehabilitation Technology **12732**
    Georgia Tech Research Institute **2447**
Georgia; Learning Disabilities Association of **4693**
Georgia; Medical Association of **1820**
Georgia; Mental Health Association of **7762**
Georgia; National Kidney Foundation of **12943**
Georgia Nurses Association **9221**
Georgia Nursing Home Association **9336**
Georgia Optometric Association **13803**
Georgia Osteopathic Medical Association **10076**
Georgia Pharmacy Association **10704**
Georgia Power Foundation **702**
Georgia Southern University • Department of Nursing **8633**
Georgia State Board of Examiners for Nursing Home Administrators **9285**
Georgia State Board of Examiners in Optometry **13728**
Georgia State Board of Licensed Practical Nurses **9164**
Georgia State Board of Pharmacy **10651**
Georgia State Board of Podiatry **10789**
Georgia State Funeral Service Board **3738**
Georgia State Health Planning Agency **5673**
Georgia State University
    College of Business Administration • Institute of Health Administration • Master of Health Administration Program **5487**
    Department of Counseling and Psychological Services • Rehabilitation Counseling Program **12584**
    Department of Nutrition and Dietetics **9393**
    Department of Physical Therapy **12465**
    School of Allied Health Professions • Department of Cardiopulmonary Care Sciences • Respiratory Therapy Program **11369**
    School of Nursing **8634**
Georgia Tech Biomedical Technology Research Center; Emory- **2444**
Georgia Tech Research Institute • Georgia Institute of Technology **2447**
Georgia University Affiliated Program • University of Georgia **4327**
Georgia Veterinary Medical Association **13312**
Geraldine Brush Cancer Research Institute **6042**
Gerber Cos. Foundation **3146**
Gerbode Foundation; Wallace Alexander **533**
Geriatric Care Managers; National Association of Professional **1908**
Geriatric Dentistry; American Society for **1888**
Geriatric Ophthalmology; Society of **1920**
Geriatric Psychiatry; American Association for **1881**
Geriatric Research, Education and Clinical center • Veterans Affairs Medical Center [Gainesville, FL] **10493**
Geriatric Research Institute; Dallas **9272**
Geriatrics Branch • Biology of Aging Program • National Institute on Aging • U.S. Department of Health and Human Services **1952**
Geriatrics and Gerontology; Brazilian Society of **1892**
Geriatrics, Gerontology; Center for • Columbia University **1932**
Geriatrics Society; American **1886**

Geriatrics Society; Hispanic American **1902**
German Academy for Psychoanalysis **7380**
German Association of Non-Medical Practitioners **2196**
German Association for Physiotherapy **12679**
German Association of Suicide Prevention **7381**
German Dental Association **3941**
German Dentists; Independent Association of **3946**
German Dermatological Society **4235**
German Dietitians; Association of **9447**
German Druggists Association **10600**
German Hospital Association **6445**
German Internists; Professional Association of **1480**
German Pharmacists; National Association of **10609**
German Radiologists and Nuclear Physicians; Association of **11101**
German Society of Anaesthesiology and Intensive Medicine **2366**
German Society for Aviation and Space Medicine **2385**
German Society for Medicinal Plant Research **10420**
German Society for Sex Research **11693**
German-Speaking Mycological Society **6671**
German Urologists; Association of **12902**
German Veterinarian Association **13073**
German Women Physicians Association **1307**
Germany; National Association for Persons with Mental Handicap of **4296**
Germfree Life Research Center **6043**
Gerontological Research; Center for • Medical College of Pennsylvania and Hahnemann University **1939**
Gerontological Research; Center on Applied • Cleveland State University **1931**
Gerontological Research Institute **1934**
Gerontological Research in Latin America; Sandoz Foundation for Regional **1919**
Gerontological Society **1900**
Gerontological Society of America **1900**
Gerontological Society; Western **1887**
Gerontological Studies; Center for • University of Florida **1976**
Gerontological Studies; Institute for • Baylor University **1924**
Gerontology; Center for
    Ball State University **1922**
    Boston University **1925**
    Kent State University **1938**
    Old Dominion University **1943**
    Pennsylvania State University **1944**
    University of Georgia **1978**
Gerontology Center; Ethel Percy Andrus • University of Southern California **1994**
Gerontology; Center for Geriatrics, • Columbia University **1932**
Gerontology Center; Oxford **9273**
Gerontology Center; Resnick • Yeshiva University **2002**
Gerontology; The Center for Social **1894**
Gerontology Center; University • University of Utah **1996**
Gerontology Centre
    Memorial University of Newfoundland **1940**
    University of Alberta **1969**
Gerontology; Department of • University of Nebraska at Omaha **1990**
Gerontology and Health Care Research; Center for • Brown University **1926**
Gerontology in Higher Education; Association for **1890**
Gerontology; Institute of
    University of Michigan **1985**
    Wayne State University **2000**
Gerontology Institute and Center • University of Massachusetts Boston **1983**
Gerontology; Institute for Life-Span Development and • University of Akron **1966**
Gerontology; International Center for Social **1894**
Gerontology Program • Western Kentucky University **2001**
Gerontology Research Center **1936**
Gerontology Research Institute **1936**
Gerson Institute **2197**
Gerstacker Foundation; Rollin M. **462**
Gesellschaft fur Arzneipflanzenforschung **10420**
Gesellschaft fur Medizin und Forschung in Afrika **1129**
Gesellschaft fur Versuchstierkunde **13107**
Gesinsbeplanningsvereniging van Suid-Afrika **11245**
Gestation; Center for Study of Multiple **9705, 11208**
Gestosis - Society for the Study of Pathophysiology of Pregnancy; Organisation **9688**
Gesundheitsdienstes; Bundesverband der Zahnarzte des Offentlichen **3968**
Gezondheidsraad **6719**
Ghaqda Kontra d-Dijabete **4855**

Groundwater Research Center • University of Cincinnati **5116**
Group for the Advancement of Psychiatry **7383**
Group Against Smokers' Pollution **11737**
Group B Strep Association **9651**
Group for Community Guidance Centers 7360
Group of Francophone Dentists' Associations **3942**
Group Health Association of America **5727**
Group Management Association; Dental **5573**
Group Management Association; Medical **5584**
Group Missions of the Christian Medical and Dental Society; Medical **1381**
Group Outreach Program; Midwest Cooperative **6080**
Group Practice; American Academy of Dental **3853**
Group Practice Association; American **1163**
Group Psychoanalysis and Process; Association for **7326**
Group Psychotherapy; American Board of Examiners of Psychodrama,
   Sociometry, and **7287**
Group Psychotherapy Association; American **7296**
Group Psychotherapy; International Association of **7400**
Group Psychotherapy and Psychodrama; American Society of **7309**
Group for the Study of the Human/Companion Animal Bond 12719
Groupe Europeen de Chimiotherapie Anticancereuse 5941
Groupe de Pneumologie et Phtisiologie Infantile de Langue Francaise
   3229
Groupement des Allergologistes et Immunologistes de Langues Latines
   2067
Groupement des Associations Dentaires Francophones 3942
Groupement Europeen de Lymphologie 5940
Groupement International pour la Recherche Scientifique en Stomatologie
   et Odontologie 3961
Groupement Latin et Mediterraneen de Medecine du Sport 11950
Grover Hermann Foundation **234**
Groves Foundation **712**
Growth Branch; Endocrinology, Nutrition, and • Center for Research for
   Mothers and Children • National Institute of Child Health and Human
   Development • U.S. Department of Health and Human Services **4903**
Growth and Development; C.S. Mott Center for Human • Wayne State
   University **2765**
Growth and Development; Center for Human • University of Michigan
   1701
Growth and Development; Eugene McDermott Center for Human •
   University of Texas Southwestern Medical Center at Dallas **5384**
Growth and Development; W.M. Krogman Center for Research in Child
   3373
Growth Factors Section • Intramural Research Program • National Institute
   of Child Health and Human Development • U.S. Department of Health
   and Human Services **8437**
Growth Foundation; Human **3237, 4823´**
Growth Society; Bioelectrical Repair and 2547
Growth Study Center; Bolton-Brush • Case Western Reserve University
   3998
Grundy Foundation **235**
Grupo Nacional Mujer, Salud y Desarrollo **1309**
GTE Foundation **6400**
Guam Board of Medical Examiners **1767, 10023**
Guam Board of Nurse Examiners **9165**
Guam Lytico and Bodig Association **1310**
Guam Medical Society **1821**
Guam Nurses Association **9222**
Guardians of Hydrocephalus Research Foundation **8224**
Gudelsky Family Foundation; Homer and Martha **280**
Guelph Centre for Equine Research 13135
Guggenheim Foundation; Harry Frank **251**
Guidance Association; American Personnel and 7293
Guidance Centers; Group for Community 7360
Guidance Service; Community **7360**
Guide Dog Foundation 13460
Guide Dog Foundation for the Blind **13460**
Guide Dog Foundation; Fidelco **13453**
Guide Dog Foundation; Pilot **13555**
Guide Dog Users, Inc. **13461**
Guide Dogs of America **13462**
Guide Dogs for the Blind **13463**
Guide Dogs for the Blind Association **13464**
Guide Dogs for the Handicapped 4466
Guide Dogs; Path-Finder 13515
Guiding Eyes 13460
Guiding Eyes for the Blind **13465**
Guild of Catholic Psychiatrists 7466
Guild for Infant Survival 3268
Guild of Prescription Opticians of America 13546
Guilds for Infant Survival; National Council of **3268**
Guilds; National Federation of Catholic Physicians **1416**

Guillain-Barre Syndrome Foundation International **8225**
Guillian-Barre Syndrome Support Group 8225
Guillian-Barre Syndrome Support Group International 8225
Gulf Coast Allergy Study Group 2087
Gulf Coast; Easter Seal Society of the **4676**
Gulf Coast School of Blood Bank Technology **7108**
Gund Foundation; George **217**
Gund Laboratory for the Study of Retinal Degenerations; Berman- • Harvard
   University **13600**
Gupton College; John A. • Funeral Service Education Program **3697**
Gupton-Jones College of Funeral Service **3670**
Gurdjian-Lissner Biomechanics Laboratory • Wayne State University **2507**
Gurson Cocuk Sagligi Vakfi 3233
Gurson Foundation for Child Health 3233
Guthrie Foundation for Education and Research; Donald **2099**
Guthrie Foundation for Medical Research; Donald 2099
Guttmacher Institute; Alan **11197, 11259**
Guttman Foundation; Stella and Charles **502**
Gwen Knapp Center for Lupus and Immunology Research • University of
   Chicago **7947**
Gwynedd Mercy College
   Health Information Administration Program **6951**
   Respiratory Therapist Program **11512**
Gynakologie FMH; Geburtshilfe und 9688
Gynecologic and Breast Pathology Department • Center for Advanced
   Pathology • Armed Forces Institute of Pathology • U.S. Department of
   Defense **10152**
Gynecologic Investigation; Society for **9694**
Gynecologic, and Neonatal Nurses; NAACOG: The Organization of
   Obstetric, 9075
Gynecologic and Neonatal Nursing Specialties; National Certification
   Corporation for the Obstetric, **9114**
Gynecologic Oncologists; Society of **5987**
Gynecologic Oncology Group **5947**
   New England Medical Center **6084**
Gynecological Laparoscopists; American Association of **9622**
Gynecological and Obstetrical Society; American **9627**
Gynecologie Infantile et Juvenile; Federation Internationale de 3243
Gynecologie et d'Obstetrique; Federation Internationale de 9665
Gynecologists; American Association of Pro Life Obstetricians and **11199**
Gynecologists; American College of Obstetricians and **9576, 9626**
Gynecologists; American College of Osteopathic Obstetricians and **9977**
Gynecologists; International Correspondence Society of Obstetricians and
   9663
Gynecologists; Nurses Association of the American College of Obstetricians
   and 9075
Gynecologists and Obstetricians; Federation of French-Language **9648**
Gynecologues et Obstetriciens de Langue Francaise; Federation des 9648
Gynecology; American Academy of Obstetrics and 9626
Gynecology; American Board of Obstetrics and **9623**
Gynecology; Council on Resident Education in Obstetrics and **9644**
Gynecology; Federation of Scandinavian Societies of Obstetrics and **9649**
Gynecology; International Federation of Infantile and Juvenile 3243
Gynecology; International Society for the Advancement of Humanistic
   Studies in **9669**
Gynecology and Obstetrics; Association of Professors of **9633**
Gynecology and Obstetrics; International Federation of **9665**
Gynekologi; Nordisk Forening for Obstetrikk og 9649

H

H. A. and Mary K. Chapman Charitable Trust **236**
H.C.S. Foundation **237**
H. J. Heinz Co. Foundation **713**
H.K. Cooper Clinic 2758
H.K. Cooper Institute for Oral-Facial Anomalies and Communicative
   Disorders 2758
H.L. Snyder Memorial Research Foundation 2576
H. Lee Moffitt Cancer Center and Research Institute **6044**
H. Leslie Hoffman and Elaine S. Hoffman Foundation **238**
H.M. Bligh Cancer Research Laboratories • Chicago Medical School **6019**
H. N. and Frances C. Berger Foundation **239**
H & R Block Foundation **718**
Haagudah Lemilchama Besartan Beyisrael 5965
Haagudah LeSukereth Neurim Beyisrael 3252
Haas Fund; Walter and Elise **535**
Habig Foundation **714**
Habilitation Education and Research; Centre for • University of Waterloo
   4599
Hachershim Beisrael; Agudat 3494

Hacienda Heights Office • Southern California / Southern Nevada Chapter • Cystic Fibrosis Foundation **5403**
Hadassah, The Women's Zionist Organization of America **1311**
Haematology and Immunology; European Society for Paediatric **3224**
Haematology; International Council for Standardization in **5953**
Hagedorn Fund **240**
Haggar Foundation **241**
Hahnemann Cystic Fibrosis Research Center • Medical College of Pennsylvania and Hahnemann University **5339**
Hahnemann University Hospital • Program in Cardiovascular Perfusion Technology **2815**
Hahnemann University; Medical College of Pennsylvania and
    Barry Ashbee Research Laboratories **6071**
    Center for Gerontological Research **1939**
    Center for the Study of Atherosclerosis **2914**
    Center for Women's Health **9710**
    Clinical Research Unit **10443**
    Eastern Pennsylvania Psychiatric Institute **7581**
    Graduate Program of Nurse Anesthesia **2317**
    Hahnemann Cystic Fibrosis Research Center **5339**
    Huntington's Disease Diagnostic and Referral Center **8393**
    Krancer Center for Inflammatory Bowel Disease Research **5235**
    Laboratory of Human Pharmacology **10444**
    Likoff Cardiovascular Institute **2915**
    Malignant Hyperthermia Research Center **2378**
    Mid Atlantic Regional Epilepsy Center **8394**
    Neuroscience Program **8395**
    Orthopedic and Arthritis Center **7922**
    Physical Therapy Program **12536**
    School of Health Sciences and Humanities • Physician Assistant Program **1106**
    School of Medicine **1020**
        Department of Pharmacology **10335**
Hahnemannian Research Center, Inc. **2248**
Hair Loss Council; American **4217**
Hair Research and Treatment Center; Baylor • Baylor University **4262**
Haiti Voluntary Central Committee **1312**
Haitian Coalition on AIDS **6673**
Haitian and Co-Arts Association **1312**
Haitian Medical Association Abroad **1203**
Haitian Physicians Abroad; Association of **1203**
Halfway House Alcoholism Programs of North America; Association of **12011**
Hall Family Foundations **3139**
Hall Foundation **242**
Hall Hyper-Hypo-Baric Center; F.G. • Duke University **1582**
Hallmark Corporate Foundation **715**
Halsa i Finland; Suomen Mielenterveysseura-Foreningen for Mental **7376**
Hamilton Bank Foundation **716**
Hamman Foundation; George and Mary Josephine **221**
Hammaslaakariseura; Suomen **3939**
Hamot Medical Center • Research Department **1595**
Hamot Medical Center / Gannon University • School of Anesthesia **2315**
Hampton Roads Office • Virginia Chapter • Cystic Fibrosis Foundation **5467**
Hampton University • School of Nursing **9010**
Hancock Foundation; Luke B. **367**
Hand; American Foundation for Surgery of the **12198**
Hand; American Society for Surgery of the **12246**
Hand Research and Education; Foundation for **7878**
Hand Research; Foundation for **917, 7877**
Hand Surgery; American Association for **12211**
Hand Surgery; American Board of **12218**
Hand Surgical Research; Indiana Foundation for **7878**
Hand Therapists; American Society of **12661**
Handicap and Developmental Disabilities; Commonwealth Association for Mental **4477**
Handicap of Germany; National Association for Persons with Mental **4296**
Handicap International **4490**
Handicap; International League of Societies for Persons With Mental **7411**
Handicap Internationale; Operation **4490**
Handicap Introductions **4481**
Handicap; National Society for Persons with Developmental **4298**
Handicapatilor Neuromotori din Romania; Asociatia **8183**
Handicapes; Conseil Canadien pour la Readaptation des **12671**
Handicapes; Federation Internationale de Sport pour **4499**
Handicapes de la Vue; Conseil International pour l' Education des **13483**
Handicapped; Academy of Dentistry for the **3843**
Handicapped; Adventures in Movement for the **4455**
Handicapped Association; North American Riding for the **4542**
Handicapped; The Association for the Severely **4563**

Handicapped Children; Center for • University of Illinois at Chicago **4588**
Handicapped Children and Young Persons, Ltd.; The Hong Kong Association for Mentally **4290**
Handicapped Children and Youth; National Information Center for **4529**
Handicapped Children and Youth; Parents Campaign for **4529**
Handicapped; Clearinghouse on the **4475**
Handicapped Commission; Blind and Visually • New York State Department of Social Services **13697**
Handicapped; Conference of World Organizations Interested in the **4495**
Handicapped; Congress of Organizations of the Physically **4478**
Handicapped; Council of World Organizations Interested in the **4495**
Handicapped Department; Visually • Virginia Office of Health and Human Resources **13713**
Handicapped; Division for Physically **4479**
Handicapped; Division for the Visually **3218**
Handicapped; 52 Association for the **4486**
Handicapped; Foundation for Science and the **4487**
Handicapped; Guide Dogs for the **4466**
Handicapped; Homebound and Hospitalized; Division on Physically **4479**
Handicapped; Hong Kong Association for the Mentally **4290**
Handicapped; International Council for Education of the Visually **13483**
Handicapped; International Federation of Disabled Workers and Civilian **4496**
Handicapped; National Accreditation Council for Agencies Serving the Blind and Visually **13521**
Handicapped; National Aid to Visually **13527**
Handicapped; National Association for the Craniofacially **2739, 4514**
Handicapped; National Association of the Physically **4516**
Handicapped; National Association for Visually **13527**
Handicapped; National Committee, Arts for the **4566**
Handicapped; National Congress of Organizations of the Physically **4478**
Handicapped; National Foundation of Dentistry for the **4526**
Handicapped; National Industries for the Severely **4540**
Handicapped; National Information Center for the **4529**
Handicapped; National Legislative Council for the **4530**
Handicapped; National Library Service for the Blind and Physically • U.S. Library of Congress **6909**
Handicapped of New Jersey; Association for Hispanic **4469**
Handicapped.; Nordic Association for the **4562**
Handicapped Organized Women **4506**
Handicapped; People-to-People Committee for the **4549**
Handicapped Physicians; American Society of **4462**
Handicapped; Research and Training Center for the • University of Mississippi **4595**
Handicapped Scuba Association **4491**
Handicapped Services Division; Visually • Utah Rehabilitation Office **13710**
Handicapped; Society for the Advancement of Travel for the **4556**
Handicapped; Society of Homes for the **4558**
Handicapped; Special Interest Committee for Computers and the Physically **4559**
Handicapped; Special Interest Group for Computers and the Physically **4559**
Handicapped Sports; National **4528**
Handicapped Sports and Recreation Association; National **4528**
Handicapped; Support Dogs for the **4561**
Handicaps; National Information Center for Children and Youth with **4529**
Handicaps; TASH: The Association for Persons With Severe **4563**
Handikappforbundet; Nordiska **4562**
Handikappfragor; Nordiska Namnden for **4541**
Handleman Charitable Foundation **717**
Handwriting; International Society of Psychology of **7425**
Handwriting Psychology; European Society of **7373**
Hansen Foundation; Dane G. **126**
Hansen's Disease Center; Gillis W. Long • Health Resources and Services Administration • U.S. Department of Health and Human Services **6793**
Harbor Branch Oceanographic Institution, Inc. **2577**
Harbor-UCLA Medical Center • University of California, Los Angeles **2728**
Harbor-UCLA Medical Center; General Clinical Research Center at **1591**
Harbor-UCLA Research and Education Institute **1596**
Harborview Injury Prevention and Research Center • University of Washington **10892**
Harcourt General Charitable Foundation **719**
Hard of Hearing; British Association of the **3499**
    Hearing Concern **3499**
Hard of Hearing; Cleveland Association for the **3596**
Hard of Hearing; International Federation of the **3533**
Hard of Hearing; National Council for the **3552**
Hard of Hearing People; International Federation of **3533**
Hard of Hearing People; Norwegian Association of **3566**
Hard of Hearing People; Self Help for **3576**

Health Services Department
   California Health and Welfare Agency **11009**
   Kentucky Human Resources Cabinet **11022**
Health Services Division
   Federal Bureau of Prisons • Office of the Deputy Attorney General • U.S. Department of Justice **11**
   Montana Department of Health and Environmental Sciences **11031**
Health Services Executives; National Association of **5586**
Health Services Extramural Research; Center for General • Agency for Health Care Policy and Research • U.S. Department of Health and Human Services **5643**
Health Services Financing Bureau • Louisiana Department of Health and Hospitals **5786**
Health Services Intramural Research; Center of General • Agency for Health Care Policy and Research • U.S. Department of Health and Human Services **5644**
Health Services Management and Policy • University of Michigan **5653**
Health Services Office • South Carolina Department of Health and Environmental Control **11046**
Health Services Planning and Review Bureau • Public Health Services Division • New Hampshire Department of Health and Human Services **5691**
Health Services and Policy Research; Center for • Northwestern University **5635**
Health Services Research; Association for **1206**
Health Services Research; Cecil G. Sheps Center for • University of North Carolina at Chapel Hill **5656**
Health Services Research Center 1568
   University of Colorado **5764**
   University of Illinois at Chicago **9718**
   University of Iowa **5650**
   University of Memphis **5652**
Health Services Research Department • Naval Health Research Center • Naval Medical Research and Development Command • U.S. Department of Defense **7842**
Health Services Research and Development Center • Johns Hopkins University **5631**
Health Services Research; Foundation for **1298**
Health Services Research; Institute for • University of Minnesota **5655**
Health Services Research; Office of • West Virginia University **5663**
Health Services Studies; European Association of Programmes in **5575**
Health Services Studies; Wisconsin International Center for • University of Wisconsin—Madison **5662**
Health and Social Policy Corporation **1319**
Health and Social Systems Research; Center for 1571
Health; Society of Medical Officers of 10968
Health; Society for Occupational and Environmental **9801**
Health Statistics; American Association for Vital Records and Public 6979
Health Statistics Center
   Health Care Planning, Financing, and Information Services Development Division • New Jersey Department of Health **7070**
   Washington Department of Health **7087**
Health Statistics Division • Epidemiology and Health Promotion Office • Public Health Bureau • West Virginia Department of Health and Human Resources **7088**
Health Statistics and Vital Records Bureau • Utah Department of Health **7084**
Health Statistics and Vital Records Division • Administration and Support Office • Colorado Public and Environment Department **7045**
Health Studies Branch • Environmental Hazards and Health Effects Division • National Center for Environmental Health • U.S. Department of Health and Human Services **5099**
Health Studies; Division of • Agency for Toxic Substances and Disease Registry • U.S. Department of Health and Human Services **5095**
Health Studies; Institute for Circumpolar • University of Alaska Anchorage **1681**
Health Studies Section • Environmental, Life, and Social Sciences Directorate • Oak Ridge National Laboratory • U.S. Department of Energy **5090**
Health Surveillance and Planning Division • Connecticut Department of Public Health **5669**
Health; Swiss Institute for Public **10970**
Health Systems Association; Illinois Hospital and **6540**
Health Systems Association; New Mexico Hospital and **6558**
Health Systems; California Association of Hospitals and **6531**
Health Systems Development Agency • District of Columbia Department of Human Services **5671**
Health Systems Management Center • Case Western Reserve University **5613**
Health Systems; Nebraska Association of Hospitals and **6554**
Health Systems Protection Branch • Public Health Division • Delaware Department of Health and Social Services **5135**
Health Systems Research • University of Illinois **1697**

Health Systems and Special Studies Division • Office of Demonstrations and Evaluations • Health Care Financing Administration • U.S. Department of Health and Human Services **5755**
Health Underwriters; International Association of 5738
Health Underwriters; International Association of Accident and 5738
Health Underwriters; National Association of Accident and 5738
Health Unit Clerks-Coordinators; National Association of 6459
Health Veterinarians; Association of State Public 5592
Health Veterinarians; Association of State and Territorial Public 5592
Health Veterinarians; National Association of State and Territorial Public 5592
Health Visitors' Association **9091**
Health Volunteers Overseas **1320**
The Health and Welfare of All Women Partnership 9699
Health and Welfare Association; National Presbyterian 1479
Health and Welfare Services, United Church of Christ; Council for 1258
Health for Women; Integral **9657**
Health Workers Association; Mental 7280
Health Workers Caucus; Gay Public 10956
Health Workers; National New Professional 1437
Health, and Working Conditions; Office of Safety, • Office of Compensation and Working Conditions • Bureau of Labor Statistics • U.S. Department of Labor **9847**
Health Working Group; Behavioral Research Aspects of Safety and • University of Kentucky **9854**
Health; World Medical Association for Perfect 2159
Healthcare Association of Hawaii **6538**
Healthcare Association of New York State **6559**
HEALTHsports, Inc. 4555
Healthy Mothers, Healthy Babies **3235**
Hear Center **3525**
Hear Now **3471**
Hearing Aid Audiologists; Society of 3538
Hearing Aid Industry Conference 5856
Hearing Aid Society; National 3538
Hearing Aided Young Adults **3526**
Hearing; American Association for the Hard of 3546
Hearing; American Federation of Organizations for the Hard of 3546
Hearing; American Society for the Hard of 3546
Hearing Association; American Speech and 3492
Hearing Association; American Speech- Language- **3492**
Hearing Association; National Student Speech and 3560
Hearing Association; National Student Speech Language **3560**
Hearing Australia; Better **3497**
Hearing; British Association of the Hard of 3499
   Hearing Concern **3499**
Hearing Center; Conley Speech and • University of Maine **3637**
Hearing Center; Keys Speech and • University of Oklahoma **3652**
Hearing Center; Speech and
   Brooklyn College of City University of New York **3592**
   University of Alabama **3631**
Hearing; Cleveland Association for the Hard of 3596
Hearing Clinic; Speech and • Kent State University **3609**
Hearing Clinic; Speech- Language and • State University of New York at Buffalo **3621**
Hearing; Computer Users in Speech and **3506**
Hearing Concern • British Association of the Hard of Hearing **3499**
Hearing Conservation Association; National **3558**
Hearing Conservation; Council for Accreditation in Occupational **9795**
Hearing Dog, Inc.; International **3537**
Hearing Dog Information; National Center for 3577
Hearing Dog Program 3577
Hearing Dog Project 3577
Hearing Dog Resource Center 3577
Hearing Dogs 3537
Hearing Ear Dog Program 3557
Hearing Education and Awareness for Rockers **3527**
Hearing Education Through Auditory Research Foundation 3525
Hearing Impaired; American Organization for the Education of the 3539
Hearing-Impaired; Capital Communications Service for the 3501
Hearing Impaired Hockey Association; American **3485**
Hearing Impaired; International Organization for the Education of the **3539**
Hearing Impaired Kids Endowment Fund 3528
Hearing-Impaired Section; Oral **3568**
Hearing Industries Association **5856**
Hearing Institute; Better **3498**
Hearing Institute; Parmly • Loyola University Chicago **3612**
Hearing; International Federation of the Hard of 3533
Hearing; National Black Association for Speech, Language and **3547**
Hearing; National Council for the Hard of **3552**
Hearing People; Self Help for Hard of **3576**

Index

I

Illinois State Veterinary Medical Association **13315**

Illinois Wesleyan University • School of Nursing **8649**

Illness Branch; Acute and Chronic • Division of Extramural Programs • National Center for Nursing Research • U.S. Department of Health and Human Services **9142**

Illness and Disability; Center for Children with Chronic **3317**

Illness and Loss; American Institute of Life Threatening **3707**

Illness; National Foundation for Depressive **7465**

Illness; National Resource Center on Homelessness and Mental **7472**

Illusion Theater **3053**

Illustration; Center for Medical • Armed Forces Institute of Pathology • U.S. Department of Defense **7025**

Illustrators; Association of Medical **6977**

Image Analysis Laboratory • New England Medical Center **2459**

Imagerie Mentale; Societa Internazionale per le Techniche d' **7422**

Imagery Techniques; International Society for Mental **7422**

Imaging Center; Brain • University of California, Irvine **11161**

Imaging Computer Resource; Mayo Biomedical **2454**

Imaging; Council on Diagnostic **11108**

Imaging; Crump Institute for Biological • University of California, Los Angeles **2477**

Imaging and Pharmaceutical Research; Center for **10428**

Imaging Research Branch; Diagnostic • Division of Cancer Treatment • National Cancer Institute • U.S. Department of Health and Human Services **6158**

Imaging Resource; Mayo Biomedical **2454**

Imaging Science; Center for • Rochester Institute of Technology **11155**

Imaging Sciences Center; Diagnostic • University of Washington **11177**

Imaging Society; Computerized Medical **11107**

Imaging; Society for Magnetic Resonance **11136**

Imaging and Spectroscopy In Vivo Resource; NMR • University of Florida **2485**

Immanuel Medical Center; Midland Lutheran College / • Respiratory Therapist Program **11450**

Immortality; International Institute for the Study of Death and **3717**

Immune Cell Biology Program • Naval Medical Research Institute • Naval Medical Research and Development Command • U.S. Department of Defense **7849**

Immune Deficiency Foundation **2073**

Immune Deficiency Foundation; Norwegian **2086**

Immune Dysfunction Syndrome Activation Network; Chronic Fatigue **6652**

Immunity Enhancement in Domestic Animals; Center for • Iowa State University of Science and Technology **13137**

Immunity; Laboratory of Developmental and Molecular • National Institute of Child Health and Human Development • U.S. Department of Health and Human Services **2139**

Immunization Research; Center for • Johns Hopkins University **6774**

Immunobiology; Laboratory of • National Cancer Institute • U.S. Department of Health and Human Services **6189**

Immunobiology; Laboratory of Molecular **2586**

Immunobiology Research Laboratory • Bucknell University **2095**

Immunobiology Research Unit • Sherbrooke University **2117**

Immunochemistry; Laboratory of Tumor Antigen **6064**

Immunodeficiency Virus Center for Clinical and Behavioral Studies; Human **6772**

Immunogenetics; American Society for Histocompatibility and **2066**

Immunogenetics; Laboratory of • National Institute of Allergy and Infectious Diseases • U.S. Department of Health and Human Services **2134**

Immunogenetics Laboratory; Transplant and • Oregon Health Sciences University **12885**

Immunogenetics and Transplantation Laboratory • University of California, San Francisco **2141**

Immunologic Disease Cooperative Research Center • Johns Hopkins University **2106**

Immunological Diseases; Center for Interdisciplinary Research on • Washington University **2148**

Immunological Disorders; Center for Allergy and • Baylor College of Medicine **2093**

Immunological Societies; International Union of **2079**

Immunologiczne; Polskie Towarzystwo **2088**

Immunologie Clinique; Academie Europeenne d' Allergologie et d' **2072**

Immunologie; Europese Vereniging voor Pediatrische Hematologie en **3224**

Immunologie; Societe Hollandaise d' **2071**

Immunologistes de Langues Latines; Groupement des Allergologistes et **2067**

Immunologistes et Specialistes des Maladies Infectieuses; Association Mondiale des Veterinaires Microbiologistes, **13120**

Immunologists; American Association of **2062**

Immunologists; Association of Latin Languages Allergologists and **2067**

Immunologists, and Specialists in Infectious Diseases; World Association of Veterinary Microbiologists, **13120**

Immunology; American Academy of Allergy and **2058**

Immunology; American Board of Allergy and **2063**

Immunology; American College of Allergy and **2064**

Immunology; American Dermatologic Society of Allergy and **4215**

Immunology; American Osteopathic College of Allergy and **9986**

Immunology and Biology; Laboratory of Tumor • National Cancer Institute • U.S. Department of Health and Human Services **6200**

Immunology Branch • Division of HIV / AIDS • National Center for Infectious Diseases • U.S. Department of Health and Human Services **6798**

Immunology Branch; Basic • Division of Allergy, Immunology, and Transplantation • National Institute of Allergy and Infectious Diseases • U.S. Department of Health and Human Services **2126**

Immunology Branch; Cancer • Division of Cancer Biology, Diagnosis, and Centers • National Cancer Institute • U.S. Department of Health and Human Services **6131**

Immunology Branch; Clinical • Division of Allergy, Immunology, and Transplantation • National Institute of Allergy and Infectious Diseases • U.S. Department of Health and Human Services **2127**

Immunology; Bulgarian Society of **2069**

Immunology and Cancer Program; Human • University of Tennessee, Knoxville **6252**

Immunology and Cancer Research Program • Oklahoma Medical Research Foundation **6098**

Immunology; Center for Advanced Molecular Biology and • State University of New York at Buffalo **2726**

Immunology Center; Allergy & • University of Colorado **2142**

Immunology; Center for Reproduction and Transplantation **2097**

Immunology Clinic; Allergy and • University of Kansas **2144**

Immunology; Department of Microbiology and • University of Rochester **6850**

Immunology; Division of • City of Hope Beckman Research Institute **2565**

Immunology Division; Communicable Diseases and • Walter Reed Army Institute of Research • Army Medical Research and Development Command • U.S. Department of Defense **7830**

Immunology; Division of Rheumatology and • University of Southern California **2146**

Immunology; Dutch Society of **2071**

Immunology; Ernest Witebsky Center for • State University of New York at Buffalo **2118**

Immunology; European Academy of Allergology and Clinical **2072**

Immunology; European Society for Paediatric Haematology and **3224**

Immunology / Garden State Cancer Center; Center for Molecular Medicine and **2096**

Immunology at Georgetown; International Center for Interdisciplinary Studies of • Georgetown University **2101**

Immunology Group; International Nutritional **2076**

Immunology and Infectious Disease Research; Center for Virology, • George Washington University **6770**

Immunology; International Association of Allergology and Clinical **2074**

Immunology; International Society of Developmental and Comparative **2077**

Immunology; Joint Council of Allergy and **2081**

Immunology Laboratories; Experimental **2104**

Immunology Laboratories; Therapeutic • Ohio State University **2112**

Immunology Laboratory **4002**

   Harvard University **2102**

   Intramural Research • National Eye Institute • U.S. Department of Health and Human Services **13639**

   National Institute of Allergy and Infectious Diseases • U.S. Department of Health and Human Services **2135**

   National Institute of Dental Research • U.S. Department of Health and Human Services **4021**

   Rockefeller University **2115**

   University of Michigan **4037**

Immunology; Laboratory of Bacterial Pathogenesis and • Rockefeller University **2113**

Immunology; Laboratory of Bacteriology and • Rockefeller University **6784**

Immunology; Laboratory of Cellular and Molecular • National Institute of Allergy and Infectious Diseases • U.S. Department of Health and Human Services **2132**

Immunology; Laboratory of Cellular Physiology and • Rockefeller University **2114**

Immunology; Laboratory of Experimental • National Cancer Institute • U.S. Department of Health and Human Services **6185**

Immunology; Laboratory of Human Cancer **6064**

Immunology Laboratory; Ocular • Johns Hopkins University **13607**

Immunology; Laboratory for Transplantation • Stanford University **12886**

Immunology; Max Samter Institute of Allergy and Clinical **2091**

Immunology; Polish Society for **2088**

Immunology Program; Allergy- Clinical • University of California, Davis **2140**

Immunology Program; Gastrointestinal • Division of Digestive Diseases and Nutrition • National Institute of Diabetes and Digestive and Kidney Diseases • U.S. Department of Health and Human Services **5242**

Immunology of Reproduction; International Society for **11227**

Immunology Research; Beirne Carter Center for • University of Virginia **2147**

Immunology Research Center • Armand-Frappier Institute **2092**

Immunology Research; Center for Neurobiology and • University of Kansas **8502**

Immunology Research; Gwen Knapp Center for Lupus and • University of Chicago **7947**

Immunology Research Laboratory; Surgical **2120**

Immunology Research Program; Arthritis / • Oklahoma Medical Research Foundation **7927**

Immunology Research; Specialized Center for **6022**

Immunology Research Unit; Metabolic Diseases and • National Animal Disease Center • Agricultural Research Service • U.S. Department of Agriculture **13197**

Immunology and Respiratory Medicine; National Jewish Center for **2109, 11605**

Immunology and Rheumatology; Division of Clinical • University of Alabama at Birmingham **7943**

Immunology, and Rheumatology Research Group; Inflammation, • Medical Research Centre • Laval University **2107**

Immunology Section; Clinical • School of Medicine • Tulane University **2122**

Immunology Service; Allergy / **2091**

Immunology Society; American In-Vitro Allergy / **2065**

Immunology Society; Clinical **2070**

Immunology, and Transplantation; Division of Allergy, • National Institute of Allergy and Infectious Diseases • U.S. Department of Health and Human Services **2124**

Immunopathology Division • Scientific Laboratory Department • Armed Forces Institute of Pathology • U.S. Department of Defense **10177**

Immunopathology; Laboratory of • National Institute of Allergy and Infectious Diseases • U.S. Department of Health and Human Services **2137**

Immunoregulation; Laboratory of • National Institute of Allergy and Infectious Diseases • U.S. Department of Health and Human Services **2138**

Immunoregulation; Laboratory of Molecular • National Cancer Institute • U.S. Department of Health and Human Services **6194**

Immunotherapy Cancer Research Foundation; National **5978**

Immunotherapy; International Society for Thymology and **2078**

Immunsviktforening; Norsk **2086**

Immuntherapie; Internationale Gesellschaft fur Thymologie und **2078**

Impact Protection Branch; Escape and • Crew Systems Directorate • Air Force Materiel Command • U.S. Department of Defense **2397**

Impaired; Association for Education and Rehabilitation of the Blind and Visually **13412**

Impaired Bureau; Services for the Visually • Ohio Rehabilitation Services Commission **13700**

Impaired; Center for Research Initiatives and Strategies for the Communicatively • University of Memphis **3638**

Impaired Data Processors International; Visually **13573**

Impaired Division; Blind and Visually
  Rehabilitation Services Office • Maine Department of Education **13684**
  Social and Rehabilitation Services Department • Vermont Agency of Human Services **13711**

Impaired Division; Rehabilitation Services for the Visually • Nebraska Department of Public Institutions **13692**

Impaired Division; Services to the Blind and Visually • South Dakota Department of Human Services **13707**

Impaired Enterprisers; Independent Visually **13477**

Impaired; Idaho Commission for the Blind and Visually **13677**

Impaired Information Specialists; Visually **13575**

Impaired; International Organization for the Education of the Hearing **3539**

Impaired; National Association for Parents of the Visually **13525**

Impaired Physician Program **12032**

Impaired Secretarial Transcribers Association; Visually **13575**

Impaired Veterans of America; Visually **13576**

Impairment; Catholic Association of Persons With Visual **13431**

Impairment; Council of Families with Visual **13443**

Implant Association; Canadian **12261**

Implant Club International; Cochlear **3503**

Implant Dentistry; American Academy of **3780, 3861**

Implant Dentures; American Academy of **3861**

Implant Prosthodontics; American Academy of **3862**

Implant Society; American Intra- Ocular **13405**

Implantaires et Lariboisiere; College International de Recherches **3917**

Implantes Intraoculaires; Association Canadienne des **12261**

Implantologie des Biomateriaux; Comite d'Organisation du Congress Mondial d' **3982**

Implantologists; International College of Oral **3958**

Implantologists; International Congress of Oral **3958**

Implantology and Biomaterials; Organizing Committee of the World Congress on **3982**

Implants Oculaires; Club International d' **13448**

Implants and Transplants; Academy for **3845**

Impotence Anonymous **11708**

Impotence Institute of America **11696**

Impotents Anonymous **11697**

Improvements in the Maternity Services; Association for **11202**

Imunologia; Associacion Latinoamericana de **2082**

In Touch Networks **7000**

Inborn Errors of Metabolism; Society for the Study of **4873**

Incarnate Word College • Division of Nursing **8985**

Incest Anonymous; Survivors of **3066**

Incest Concerned Effort; Victims of **3067**

Incest Survivors Anonymous **3054**

Incest Survivors Resource Network, International **3055**

Inclusion; Center for Community • University of Maine **4333**

Income Maintenance Office • Human Resources Bureau • West Virginia Department of Health and Human Resources **5816**

Incontinent People; Help for **12905**

Inconvenienced Sportsmen's Association; National **4528**

Incurably Ill for Animal Research **1323**

INDENT **5857**

Independence for the Disabled and Elderly; PRIDE Foundation - Promote Real **12710**

Independence Dogs, Inc. **4493**

Independence Foundation **8539**

Independent Association of German Dentists' **3946**

Independent Citizens Research Foundation for the Study of Degenerative Diseases **1324, 1602, 6611**

Independent Hospital Workers Union **6447**

Independent Living for the Aging; National Voluntary Organizations for **1915**

Independent Living; National Association for **12693**

Independent Living; National Council on **4523**

Independent Living; Research and Training Center on **4551**
  University of Kansas **4590**

Independent Medical Distributors Association **5858**

Independent Physicians Association of Germany **1325**

Independent Research Institutes; Association of **2527**

Independent Visually Impaired Enterprisers **13477**

India; American Association of Psychiatrists from **7281**

India; Protein Foods and Nutrition Development Association of **9484**

Indian Affairs; Committee on • U.S. Senate **20**

Indian and Alaska Native Mental Health Research; National Center for American **7458**
  University of Colorado **7663**

Indian Dental Association **3947**

Indian Dental Association (U.S.A.) **3948**

Indian Health Board; National **1422**

Indian Health Care Association; American **1166**

Indian Health Service • Public Health Service • U.S. Department of Health and Human Services **10**

Indian Hospital Association **6448**

Indian Muscular Dystrophy Association **8230**

Indian Physicians; Association of American **1196**

Indian Rehabilitation Research and Training Center; American • Northern Arizona University **12740**

Indian River Community College • Respiratory Therapist Program **11355**

Indiana Affiliate
  American Diabetes Association **4965**
  American Heart Association **3005**

Indiana; American Lung Association of **11641**

Indiana; Arc of **4407**

Indiana Association of Osteopathic Physicians and Surgeons **10080**

Indiana Chapter
  American Physical Therapy Association **12833**
  Arthritis Foundation **7980**
  Cystic Fibrosis Foundation **5417**
  Lupus Foundation of America **8052**
  National Association of Social Workers **11894**

Indiana Chapter; Northeast • Lupus Foundation of America **8053**

Indiana Chapter; Northwest • Lupus Foundation of America **8054**

Indiana Coalition Against Domestic Violence **3090**

Indiana Dental Association **4169**

Indiana Department of Health **11019**
  Acute Care Division **6490**
  Consumer Health Services Division **5142**
  Health Planning Division **5677**
  HIV / STD Program **6870**
  Maternal and Child Health Services Division **3392, 9738**

Institute for Molecular Virology • St. Louis University **2617**
Institute of Neurobiology • University of Puerto Rico **8523**
Institute for Neuroscience
    Northwestern University **8410**
    University of Oregon **8516**
Institute of Noetic Sciences **2251**
Institute of Nutrition • University of North Carolina **9562**
Institute for Nutrition and Cardiovascular Research • Oregon Health
   Sciences University **9521**
Institute of Nutrition of Central America and Panama **9464**
Institute of Occupational and Environmental Health • West Virginia
   University **9863**
Institute of Ocular Pharmacology • Texas A&M University **10460**
Institute for Pain Management **7928**
Institute of Pathology • Case Western Reserve University **10142**
Institute for Policy Research and Evaluation • Pennsylvania State
   University **5636**
Institute of Psychiatric Research • Indiana University-Purdue University at
   Indianapolis **7569**
Institute of Psychiatry and Human Behavior • University of Maryland **7669**
Institute for Psychoanalysis **7572**
Institute for Psychoanalytic Psychotherapy **7254**
Institute for Psychosomatic and Psychiatric Research and Training **7573**
Institute of Public Law • University of New Mexico **1712**
Institute for Rational-Emotive Therapy **7393, 7574**
Institute for Rational Living **7574**
Institute for Reality Therapy **7389**
Institute for Reconstructive Plastic Surgery • New York University **12322**
Institute for Rehabilitation and Research **12734**
Institute of Reproductive Biology • University of Texas at Austin **11724**
Institute for Reproductive Health **11222**
Institute for Research in Behavioral Neuroscience **8376**
Institute for Research in Hypnosis **6591**
Institute for Research in Hypnosis and Psychotherapy **6579, 6591, 6599**
Institute for Research in Learning Disabilities • University of Kansas **4589**
Institute for Research in Psychotherapy **7484**
Institute of Rural Environmental Health • Colorado State University **5068**
Institute for Scientific Research, Inc. **1608**
Institute for Sensory Research • Syracuse University **8432**
Institute for Sex Research **11721**
Institute for Social Studies and Action **1328**
Institute of Society, Ethics and the Life Sciences **2580, 7176**
Institute for Structural and Functional Studies **2582**
Institute for the Study of Culture and Nursing • University of Miami **9148**
Institute for the Study of Developmental Disabilities • Indiana University
   Bloomington **4578**
Institute for Study of Exceptional Children and Youth • University of
   Maryland **4593**
Institute of Technology at Utica / Rome; State University of New York •
   Health Information Administration Program **6944**
Institute for Toxicology
    University of California, Los Angeles **10469**
    University of Southern California **10483**
Institute of Toxicology; Chemical Industry **10404**
Institute of Toxicology and Environmental Health • University of California,
   Davis **5114**
Institute of Trichologists **4241**
Institute for Tuberculosis Research • University of Illinois at Chicago **2143**
Institute for Victims of Terrorism **7394**
Institute for Victims of Trauma **7394**
Institute for Visual Sciences, Inc. **13603**
Institutes for the Achievement of Human Potential **8231, 8377**
Institutes for Behavior Resources, Inc. **7575**
Institutes of Medical Sciences **1564**
Institutes of Religion and Health **1609**
Institutions; Association for Health-Care **1204**
Institutions; Commission on Benevolent **1258**
Institutions; National Association of Children's Hospitals and Related **3262**
Instituto Costarricense de Acueductors y Alcantarrillados • Oficina de la
   Mujer y la Familia para el Desarrollo **1329**
Instituto de Nutricion de Centro America y Panama **9464**
Instructors of the Deaf; Convention of American **3508**
Instructors; National Association of Rehabilitation **12694**
Instrumentacion Cientifica, Medica, Tecnica y Dental; Federacion Nacional
   de Empresas de **5848**
Instrumentation; Association for the Advancement of Medical **2418**
Instrumentation Laboratory; Medical • University of Wisconsin—Madison
   2503
Insurance Association of America; Health **5730**
Insurance; Committee for National Health **5725**
Insurance Medical Directors of America; Association of Life **5719**

Insurance Medicine; American Academy of **5719**
Insurance Services; Alternative Health **2153**
Insurance Training Council; Disability **5726**
Insurers Association of America; Physician **5743**
Insurers' Conference; Industrial **5735**
Insurers Conference; Life **5735**
Insurers' Conference; Southern Industrial **5735**
INTACT of Pennsylvania **3274**
Integrado de Saude; Fundacao Instituto **1305**
Integral Development; Institute for **12034**
Integral Health for Women **9657**
Integral Human Sciences; International Institute of **2252**
Integral Psychoanalysis; Society of **7418**
Integration; Institute on Community • University of Minnesota **4334**
Integration; Rolf Institute of Structural **2256**
Integration; Society for the Exploration of Psychotherapy **7513**
Integrative Neurosciences; Keck Center for • University of California, San
   Francisco **8489**
Integrative Neurosciences; Laboratory of Molecular and • National Institute
   of Environmental Health Sciences • U.S. Department of Health and
   Human Services **5109**
Intellectual Disability; AAMR - National Association on **4297**
Intellectual Disability; Australian Society for the Study of **4283**
Intellectual Disability; International Association for the Scientific Study of
   4291
Intellectual Disability; National Council on **4297**
Intelligent Electronics Foundation **3148**
Intensifs et de Reanimation; Federation Mondiale des Societes de Soins
   4760
Intensiva; Societatea Romana de Anestezie Terapie **2371**
Intensive Care Medicine; Slovak Society of Anesthesiology and **2372**
Intensive Care; Romanian Society for Anaesthesia **2371**
Intensive Care Society **1330**
Intensive and Critical Care Medicine; World Federation of Societies of
   4760
Intensive Medicine; German Society of Anaesthesiology and **2366**
Intensivmedizin; Deutsche Gesellschaft fur Anasthesiologie und 2366
Inter-African Bureau for Animal Resources **13082**
Inter-African Committee Against Harmful Traditional Practices; British
   Support Group - **1223**
Inter-American Association of Gastroenterology **5220**
Inter-Americana de Gastroenterologia; Asociacion 5220
Inter-Association Task Force on Alcohol Issues **12035**
Inter-Association Task Force on Campus Alcohol and Other Substance
   Abuse Issues **12035**
Interactions Between Environment and Health; Centre for Study of
   Biological • University of Quebec at Montreal **9861**
InterAfrican Bureau for Epizootic Diseases 13082
Interagency Planning, Research and Coordination Bureau • South Carolina
   Health and Human Services Finance Commission **5701**
Interamerican College of Physicians and Surgeons **1331**
Interamerican Medical and Health Association **1332**
Inter-American Society of Cardiology **2854**
Inter-American University of Puerto Rico
    Carmen Torres de Tiburcio School of Nursing **8941**
    School of Nursing **8942, 8943**
    School of Optometry **13378**
Interamericana de Cardiologia; Sociedad 2854
Inter-Association Task Force **12035**
Intercare **9267**
Interchurch Medical Assistance **1333**
Interchurch Response for the Horn of Africa 1243
Interco Inc. Charitable Trust **735**
Interdepartmental Medical Genetics Program • Stanford University **5352**
Interdisciplinary Center for Biotechnology Research • University of Florida
   2730, 2731
Interdisciplinary Center for Disabilities • University of South Dakota **4597**
Interdisciplinary Program in Cell and Molecular Pharmacology and
   Experimental Therapeutics • Medical University of South Carolina **10445**
Interdisciplinary Research Group on Work Organization and Occupational
   Health and Safety • Laval University **9812**
Interdisciplinary Research on Immunological Diseases; Center for •
   Washington University **2148**
Interdisciplinary Studies of Immunology at Georgetown; International Center
   for • Georgetown University **2101**
Interesseforeningen fur LMBB i Norge **5297**
Interessenverband Freiberuflicher Krankengymnasten 12665
Interface; Center for the Enhancement of the Biology / Biomaterials •
   University of Texas Health Science Center at San Antonio **2694**
Interfaces; Center for Biopolymers at • University of Utah **2497**
Interfraternity Council; American Dental **3893**

Index

International Stoke Mandeville Games Federation 4500
International Stoke Mandeville Wheelchair Sports Federation **4500**
International Strabismological Association **13504**
International Stress Management Association **7428**
International Stress and Tension Control Association 7428
International; Stroke Clubs, **8314**
International Study Committee of Catholic Nursing Associations 9094
International Study Group for Steroid Hormones **4851**
International Surgical Society; Michael E. DeBakey **12288**
International Tanking Association 2192
International Temperance Association 12041
International; Therapy Dogs **12724**
International; Tissue Banks **12878**
International Transactional Analysis Association **7429**
International Transplant Nurses Society **9098**
International Trauma Anesthesia and Critical Care Society **2369**
International Travelers Health Institute **1359**
International Tremor Foundation **8245**
International Twin Study • University of Southern California **5197**
International U.S.A.; Mobility **4510**
International Union Against Alcoholism 12038
International Union Against Cancer **5963**
International Union Against Tuberculosis 11599
International Union Against Tuberculosis and Lung Disease **11599**
International Union Against Venereal Diseases and Treponematoses **6683**
International Union Against the Venereal Diseases and the
    Treponematoses, Regional Office for North America **6684**
International Union for Health Promotion and Education **1360**
International Union of Immunological Societies **2079**
International Union of Microbiological Societies **6685**
International Union of Nutritional Sciences **9466**
International Union of Pharmacology **10415**
International Union of Phlebology **5964**
International Union for Physical and Engineering Sciences in Medicine
    2428
International Union of Psychological Science **7430**
International Union of Railway Medical Services **9799**
International Union of Reticuloendothelial Societies **2080**
International Union of Societies for the Aid of Mental Health **7431**
International Union of Therapeutics **12689**
International Veterinary Acupuncture Society **13091**
International Veterinary Students' Association **13092**
International; Visually Impaired Data Processors **13573**
International Vitamin A Consultative Group **9467**
International; Volunteer Optometric Services to Humanity, **13577**
International Wheelchair Road Racers Club **4501**
International Women's Health Coalition **11229, 11230**
International X-Ray Unit Committee 11117
Internationale Activitatis Nervosae Superioris; Collegium **8203**
Internationale Gesellschaft fur Musik in der Medizin 7423
Internationale Gesellschaft fur Thymologie und Immuntherapie 2078
Internationale Neuro-Psychopharmacologicum; Collegium **8204**
Internationale de Psychologie du Travail de Langue Francaise;
    Association **7329**
Internationalis; Academia Ophthalmologica **13381**
Interne; Societe Internationale de Medecine 1358
Internisten; Berufsverband Deutscher 1480
Internists; American College of Osteopathic **9976**
Internists; Professional Association of German **1480**
Interns; National Association of Residents and **1404**
Interns and Residents; Committee of **1250**
Interns and Residents in New York City; Committee of 1250
Internship Centers; Association of Psychology 7334
Internship Centers; Association of Psychology Postdoctoral and **7334**
Internships; National InterAssociation Committee on 1430
Interplast **12283**
Interpreters for the Deaf; Registry of **3574**
Interpreters and Translators for the Deaf; National Registry of
    Professional 3574
Interprofessional Fostering of Opthalmic Care for Underserved Sectors
    13505
Interscience Research Institute **7496**
Intersociety Committee on Pathology Information **10136**
Inter-Society Cytology Council 7124
Interstate Dental Association 3973
Interstate Postgraduate Medical Association of North America **1361**
Interstitial Cystitis Association **12908**
Interstitial Cystitis; Women's Center for • University of Pennsylvania **12928**
Interstitial Lung Diseases Branch • Division of Lung Diseases • National
    Heart, Lung, and Blood Institute • U.S. Department of Health and Human
    Services **11617**

InterStudy 5627
Inter-University Centre for Toxicology **10440**
Interveners; American Academy of Crisis **7266**
Intervention; Center for Prevention and Early • Florida State University
    3335
Intervention; ReachOut—A Community **12073**
Intervention Research Institute; Early • Utah State University **4602**
Interventional Radiology; Society of Cardiovascular and **11132**
Interventions; Society for Cardiac Angiography and **2877**
Intractable Pain Foundation; American 8273
Intractable Pain; National Committee on the Treatment of **8273**
Intramural Clinical and Biological Research Division • National Institute on
    Alcohol Abuse and Alcoholism • U.S. Department of Health and Human
    Services **12111**
Intramural Research • National Eye Institute • U.S. Department of Health
    and Human Services **13638**
Intramural Research; Center of General Health Services • Agency for
    Health Care Policy and Research • U.S. Department of Health and
    Human Services **5644**
Intramural Research; Division of
        National Heart, Lung, and Blood Institute • U.S. Department of Health
            and Human Services **2939**
        National Institute of Child Health and Human Development • U.S.
            Department of Health and Human Services **1675**
        National Institute of Diabetes and Digestive and Kidney Diseases •
            U.S. Department of Health and Human Services **4919**
        National Institute of Environmental Health Sciences • U.S. Department
            of Health and Human Services **5104**
        National Institute of Neurological Disorders and Stroke • U.S.
            Department of Health and Human Services **8453**
Intramural Research Program
        Division of Cancer Biology, Diagnosis, and Centers • National Cancer
            Institute • U.S. Department of Health and Human Services **6134**
        National Institute on Aging • U.S. Department of Health and Human
            Services **1954**
        National Institute of Dental Research • U.S. Department of Health and
            Human Services **4017**
Intramural Research Programs Division • National Institute of Mental Health
    • U.S. Department of Health and Human Services **7634**
Intraoculaires; Association Canadienne des Implantes 12261
Intravenous Nurses Association; Canadian **9078**
Intravenous Nurses Society **9099**
Invalides du Travail et des Invalides Civils; Federation Internationale des
    Mutiles, des 4496
Investigation; American Society for Clinical **1183**
Investigation and Prevention of Torture; Canadian Center for the 7544
Investigation; Society for Gynecologic **9694**
Investigational Cancer Therapy; Technology Extension Center for 6058
Investigational Cancer Treatment; John P. Caufield Technology Extension
    Center for **6058**
Investigational Drug Branch • Division of Cancer Treatment • National
    Cancer Institute • U.S. Department of Health and Human Services **6159**
Investigations, and Research Branch; Surveillance, • Immunization Division
    • National Center for Prevention Services • U.S. Department of Health
    and Human Services **10878**
Investigative Dermatology; Laboratory for • Rockefeller University **4267**
Investigative Dermatology; Society for **4258**
Investigative Pathology; American Society for **10125**
Investigators Society; International REST **7416**
In-Vitro Allergy / Immunology Society; American **2065**
Invitro Fertilization Association; Zimbabwe **11257**
Ionizing Radiation Division • Physics Laboratory • National Institute of
    Standards and Technology • U.S. Department of Commerce **11157**
Iota Tau Sigma **10001**
Iowa Affiliate
        American Diabetes Association **4966**
        American Heart Association **3006**
Iowa; American Lung Association of **11642**
Iowa; Arc of **4408**
Iowa Board of Dental Examiners **4064**
Iowa Board of Mortuary Science Examiners **3743**
Iowa Board of Nursing **9170**
Iowa Board of Optometry Examiners **13733**
Iowa Board of Pharmacy Examiners **10656**
Iowa Board of Podiatric Medicine **10794**
Iowa Cardiovascular Center • University of Iowa **2965**
Iowa Center for Agricultural Safety and Health **9809**
Iowa Chapter
        American Physical Therapy Association **12834**
        Arthritis Foundation **7981**
        Cystic Fibrosis Foundation **5418**
        Lupus Foundation of America **8055**

Index

Johns Hopkins University
    Alzheimer's Disease Research Center **8379**
    Asthma and Allergy Center **2105**
    Baltimore Huntington's Disease Project **8380**
    Behavioral Pharmacology Research Unit **12095**
    Blood-Brain Barrier Laboratory **8381**
    Center for Alternatives to Animal Testing **13141**
    Center for Communication Programs **7015**
    Center for Hereditary Eye Diseases **13604**
    Center for Hospital Finance and Management **5752**
    Center for Immunization Research **6774**
    Center for Injury Research and Policy **10867**
    Center for VDT and Health Research **9811**
    Child Health Research Center **3340**
    Cystic Fibrosis Research Center **5335**
    Dana Center for Preventive Ophthalmology **13605**
    Division of Comparative Medicine **1611**
    Drug and Device Development Center **5888**
    Health Services Research and Development Center **5631**
    Hopkins Population Center **11272**
    Immunologic Disease Cooperative Research Center **2106**
    Ischemic Heart Disease Specialized Center of Research **2907**
    Johns Hopkins Hospital Sexual Disorders Clinic **11720**
    Lions Vision Research and Rehabilitation Center **13606**
    Lipid Research Atherosclerosis Unit **2908**
    Middle Atlantic Mass Spectrometry Laboratory **2451**
    Neuropathology Laboratory **8382**
    Ocular Immunology Laboratory **13607**
    Office of Psychohormonal Research **4890**
    Oncology Center **6059**
    Orthopaedic Research Laboratories **9942**
    Outpatient General Clinical Research Center **1612**
    Pediatric Clinical Research Unit **3341**
    Retinal Degenerations Research Center **13608**
    Retinal Vascular Center **13609**
    School of Hygiene and Public Health **10917**
        Department of Health Policy and Management • MHS Program
        in Health Finance and Management **5497**
    School of Medicine **968**
        Department of Art as Applied to Medicine • Medical Illustrator
        Program **6912**
        Department of Pharmacology and Molecular Sciences **10255**
    School of Nursing **8741**
    Sleep Disorders Center **8383**
    Welch Laboratory for Applied Bioinformatics **7016**
    Wilmer Ophthalmological Institute **13610**
Johnson Controls Foundation **747**
Johnson County Community College • Respiratory Therapist Program
11393
Johnson Foundation; Burdine **11182**
Johnson Foundation; Helen K. and Arthur E. **261**
Johnson Foundation; Robert Wood **459**
Johnson Foundation; Willard T. C. **542**
Johnson Fund; Edward C. **156**
Johnson & Johnson Family of Cos. Contribution Fund **748**
Johnson Medical School at Camden; Robert Wood • University of Medicine
and Dentistry of New Jersey **992**
Johnson Medical School; Robert Wood
    Physician Assistant Program • Rutgers University; University of
    Medicine and Dentistry of New Jersey / **1086**
    University of Medicine and Dentistry of New Jersey **991**
Johnson Medical School; Rutgers University / Robert Wood
    Graduate Program in Pharmacology **10286**
        Rutgers College of Pharmacy • Graduate Program in Pharmacology
        10287
Johnson Space Center; Lyndon B.
    Medical Sciences Division • Space Administration; National
    Aeronautics and **2390**
    Space Biomedical Research Institute • Space Administration; National
    Aeronautics and **2391**
Johnson's Wax Fund **749**
Johnston Trust for Charitable and Educational Purposes; James M. **309**
Joint Center for Radiation Therapy **11145**
Joint Commission on Accreditation of Healthcare Organizations **1366**
Joint Commission on Accreditation of Hospitals **1366**
Joint Commission on Allied Health Personnel in Ophthalmology **13509**
Joint Commission on Competitive Safeguards and the Medical Aspects of
Sports **11949**
Joint Commission on Sports Medicine and Science **11949**
Joint Committee on Mortuary Education **3705**
Joint Council of Allergy and Immunology **2081**

Joint Council of Socio-Economics of Allergy **2081**
Joint Distribution Committee **1167**
Joint Distribution Committee for Relief of Jewish War Sufferers **1167**
Joint Division of Newborn Medicine **9709**
Joint Program in Biomedical Engineering • University of Texas
Southwestern Medical Center at Dallas **2496**
Joint Review Commission for the Ophthalmic Medical Personnel **13510**
Joint Review Committee on Education in Diagnostic Medical Sonography
11123
Joint Review Committee on Education in Radiologic Technology **11124**
Joint Review Committee on Education for the Surgical Technologist **12201**
Joint Review Committee on Educational Programs for the EMT-
Paramedic **4745**
Joint Review Committee on Educational Programs for Physician's
Assistants **1122**
Joint Review Committee for the Ophthalmic Medical Assistant **13510**
Joint Review Committee for Ophthalmic Medical Personnel **13510**
Joint Review Committee for Respiratory Therapy Education **11600**
Joint Review on Educational Programs for Physician Assistants **1122**
Joint Surgeons; Association of Bone and **9924**
Joints Allied Musculo-Skeletal Disorders Foundation; Jaw **7883**
Jones Cell Science Center, Inc.; W. Alton **2702**
Jones Charitable Trust; Harvey and Bernice **6356**
Jones Foundation; Daisy Marquis **123**
Jones Foundation; Fletcher **182**
Jones Institute for Reproductive Medicine; Howard and Georgeanna
11271
Jonsson Comprehensive Cancer Center; UCLA • University of California,
Los Angeles **6213**
Jordan Charitable Foundation; Mary Ranken Jordan and Ettie A. **383**
Jordanian Association for Family Planning and Protection **11233**
Jose Carreras International Leukemia Foundation; Friends of the **5946**
Joseph Alexander Foundation **329**
Joseph B. Kirsner Center for the Study of Digestive Diseases • University of
Chicago **5250**
Joseph B. Whitehead Foundation **330**
Joseph Diseases Foundation; International **8240**
Joseph Drown Foundation **331**
Joseph P. Kennedy, Jr. Foundation **4272**
Joseph P. Kennedy, Jr. Mental Retardation Research Center • University of
Chicago **4324**
Joseph-Rheaume Laboratory • Laval University **9509**
Joseph Society **12267**
Josiah Macy, Jr. Foundation **332**
Josiah W. and Bessie H. Kline Foundation **333**
Joslin Diabetes Center **4853, 4891**
Joslin Diabetes Foundation **4853, 4891**
Joubert Syndrome Parents in Touch Network **5282**
Joukowsky Family Foundation **334**
Journal Gazette Foundation **750**
Judaica Captioned Film Center **3541**
Jude Express; St. **1499**
Judge David L. Bazelon Center for Mental Health Law **7207**
Jugoslavije; Drustvo Anatoma **2549**
Jules and Doris Stein Foundation **335**
Jules Stein Eye Institute • University of California, Los Angeles **13645**
Julia R. and Estelle L. Foundation **336**
Julius and Ray Charlestein Foundation **751**
June Rockwell Levy Foundation **337**
Jung Foundation for Analytical Psychology; C. G. **7348**
Jung Institute of Chicago; C.G. **7240**
Jung Institute of Los Angeles; C.G. **7237**
Jung Institute of New York; C.G. **7244**
Jurisprudence; Society of Medical **7193**
Jurisprudence and State Medicine; Society of Medical **7193**
Jurodin Fund **338**
Just One Break **4503**
"Just Say No" Foundation **12045**
"Just Say No" International **12045**
Justin and Valere Potter Foundation **339**
Juvenile Arthritis Organization; American **7862**
Juvenile Diabetes Foundation **3251**
Juvenile Diabetes Foundation International **3251, 4824**
Juvenile Diabetes Foundation in Israel **3252**
Juvenile; Federation Internationale de Gynecologie Infantile et **3243**
Juvenile Gynecology; International Federation of Infantile and **3243**
Juvenile Papillomatosis; Christina Lazar Foundation for **11593**

K

K. H. Hofmann Foundation   3147
K-T Support Group   7884
Kade Foundation; Max   388
Kaiser Family Foundation; Henry J.   265
Kaiser Permanente / California State University, Long Beach • School of Anesthesia for Nurses   2260
Kaiser Permanente Center for Health Research   5632
Kaiser Permanente Medical Care Program • Division of Research   5186
Kalamazoo Valley Community College • Respiratory Therapist Program   11428
Kamerata Inter-Regional Association   13511
Kanawha Valley Chapter • Lupus Foundation of America   8118
Kansas Affiliate
      American Diabetes Association   4967
      American Heart Association   3007
Kansas; American Lung Association of   11643
Kansas; Arc of   4409
Kansas Association of Osteopathic Medicine   10082
Kansas Board of Adult Care Home Administrators   9291
Kansas Board of Emergency Medical Services   4783
Kansas Board of Healing Arts   10795
Kansas Board of Optometry Examiners   13734
Kansas Center for Research in Mental Retardation • University of Kansas   4330
Kansas Chapter
      American Physical Therapy Association   12835
      Arthritis Foundation   7982
      National Association of Social Workers   11896
Kansas City Chapter • Lupus Foundation of America   8068
Kansas City Chapter; Western Missouri / Greater • Arthritis Foundation   7992
Kansas City, Kansas Community College • Mortuary Science Department   3676
Kansas Coalition Against Sexual and Domestic Violence   3092
Kansas Dental Association   4171
Kansas Dental Board   4065
Kansas Department on Aging   2019
Kansas Department of Animal Health   13265
Kansas Department of Health and Environment
      Health Division   5679, 11021
            Adult and Child Care Facilities Bureau • Hospital Program   6492
            Disease Control Bureau • AIDS Section   6872
            Environmental Health Services Bureau   5144
            Family Health Bureau   3394, 9740
            Local and Rural Health Systems Bureau • Dental Program   4118
      Health and Environment Statistics Division • Vital Statistics Office   7056
Kansas Department of Human Resources • Labor-Management Relations and Employment Standards Division • Industrial Safety and Health Section   9881
Kansas Department of Social and Rehabilitation Services
      Adult Medical Services Commission   5784
      Alcohol and Drug Abuse Services   12163
      Mental Health and Retardation Services Division   4359, 7724
      Rehabilitation Services Division   12786, 13681
Kansas Division • American Cancer Society   6287
Kansas; Goodwill Industries / Easter Seal Society of   4639
Kansas Health Care Association   9342
Kansas Hospital Association   6543
Kansas; Learning Disabilities Association of   4699
Kansas Medical Society   1827
Kansas Newman College
      Occupational Therapy Program   12359
      School of Nursing   8703
Kansas Newman College; St. Joseph Medical Center / • Perfusion Technology Program   2798
Kansas Optometric Association   13809
Kansas Pharmacists Association   10710
Kansas State Board of Healing Arts   1773, 10029
Kansas State Board of Mortuary Arts   3744
Kansas State Board of Nursing   9171
Kansas State Board of Pharmacy   10657
Kansas State Nurses Association   9228
Kansas State University
      Center for Basic Cancer Research   6060
      College of Veterinary Medicine   13000
            Department of Anatomy and Physiology • Graduate Veterinary Pharmacology Programs   10243

      Department of Hotel, Restaurant, Institution Management and Dietetics   9399
      University Biochemistry Facility   2584
      Veterinary Diagnostic Laboratory   13142
Kansas Veterinary Medical Association   13318
Kansas and Western Missouri; National Kidney Foundation of   12948, 12958
Kapiolani Community College / University of Hawaii • Respiratory Therapist Program   11371
Kaplan Comprehensive Cancer Center • New York University   6087
Kaplan Fund; J. M.   298
Kappa Psi   10606
Kardiologinen Seura; Suomen   2847
Kardiologov; Moskovskaya Assotsiatsiya   2863
Kardiologusok Tarsasaga; Magyar   2852
Kardiyoloji Dernegi; Turk   2879
Karen; Friends of   3231
Karen Horney Clinic   7433
Karen Horney Psychoanalytic Clinic   7433
Kate B. Reynolds Charitable Trust   340
Katherine Mabis McKenna Foundation   6369
Kathleen Price and Joseph M. Bryan Family Foundation   341
Kean College of New Jersey
      Health Information Administration Program   6940
      Occupational Therapy Department   12387
Kean College of New Jersey / Seton Hall University; University of Medicine and Dentistry of New Jersey • School of Allied Health Related Professions • Physical Therapy Program   12509
Keck Center for Computational Biology; W.M.   2703
Keck Center for Genome Informatics; W.M. • Texas A&M University   5355
Keck Center for Integrative Neurosciences • University of California, San Francisco   8489
Keck Foundation; W. M.   531
Keller Child Psychiatry Research Center • University of Louisville   3362
Keller International; Helen [Campinas, Brazil]   13475
Keller International; Helen [Colombo, Sri Lanka]   13468
Keller International; Helen [Dodoma, United Republic of Tanzania]   13471
Keller International; Helen [Jakarta, Indonesia]   13470
Keller International; Helen [Kathmandu, Nepal]   13469
Keller International; Helen [Manila, Philippines]   13467
Keller International; Helen [New York, NY]   13466
Keller International; Helen [Niamey, Niger]   13472
Keller International; Helen [Ouagadougou, Burkina Faso]   13474
Keller International; Helen [Rabat, Morocco]   13473
Keller National Center for Deaf-Blind Youths and Adults; Helen   13476
Kellogg Cancer Care Center; J.L. and Helen   6057
Kellogg Eye Center; W.K. • University of Michigan   13655
Kellogg Foundation; W. K.   530
Kempe National Center for the Prevention and Treatment of Child Abuse and Neglect; C. Henry • University of Colorado   3073
Kemper Foundation; William T.   555
Kemper Research Foundation   5078
Kempner Fund; Harris and Eliza   247
Kenedy Memorial Foundation; John G. and Marie Stella   319
Kenkyu-sho; Hoshasen Eikyo   11067
Kennametal Foundation   752
Kennedy Center for Developmental Disabilities; John F. • University of Colorado   4326
Kennedy Center for Research on Human Development; John F. • Vanderbilt University   4339
Kennedy Center for Research in Mental Retardation and Human Development; Rose F. • Yeshiva University   4342
Kennedy Institute of Ethics • Georgetown University   7202
Kennedy Institute Inc.   12735
Kennedy Institute; John F.   12735
Kennedy, Jr. Foundation; Joseph P.   4272
Kennedy, Jr. Mental Retardation Research Center; Joseph P. • University of Chicago   4324
Kennedy Krieger Institute   12735
Kennedy Shriver Center for Mental Retardation; Eunice   4310
Kennesaw State University • School of Nursing   8635
Kenneth T. and Eileen L. Norris Foundation   342
Kenneth W. Ford Foundation   694
Kenny Foundation; Sister   12718
Kenny Institute; Sister   12718, 12749
Kent School of Social Work; Raymond A. • University of Louisville   11785
Kent State University
      Applied Physiology Research Laboratory   11968
      Gerontology Center   1938
      Rehabilitation Counseling Program   12623
      School of Nursing   8878

Speech and Hearing Clinic **3609**
Kent Waldrep International Spinal Cord Research Foundation 8169
Kentland Foundation **343**
Kentuckiana Chapter • Lupus Foundation of America **8057**
Kentucky Affiliate
    American Diabetes Association **4968**
    American Heart Association **3008**
Kentucky; American Lung Association of **11644**
Kentucky; Arc of **4410**
Kentucky Association of Health Care Facilities **9343**
Kentucky Board of Dentistry **4066**
Kentucky Board of Licensure for Nursing Home Administrators **9292**
Kentucky Board of Medical Licensure **1774, 10030**
Kentucky Board of Nursing **9172**
Kentucky Board of Optometric Examiners **13735**
Kentucky Board of Pharmacy **10658**
Kentucky Board of Podiatry **10796**
Kentucky Cancer Program **6061**
Kentucky Chapter
    American Physical Therapy Association **12836**
    Arthritis Foundation **7983**
    National Association of Social Workers **11897**
Kentucky Dental Association **4172**
Kentucky Department of Agriculture • State Veterinarian **13266**
Kentucky Division • American Cancer Society **6288**
Kentucky Domestic Violence Association **3093**
Kentucky Easter Seal Society **4640**
Kentucky Education, Arts and Humanities Cabinet
    Blind Department **13682**
    Vocational Rehabilitation Department **12787**
Kentucky Hospital Association **6544**
Kentucky Human Resources Cabinet
    Health Planning and Certification Office **5680**
    Health Service Department • Maternal and Child Health Services
        Division • Dental Health Program **4119**
    Health Services Department **11022**
        Emergency Medical Services Branch **4784**
        Environmental Health and Community Safety Division **5145**
        Epidemiology and Disease Control Division • AIDS Education
            Program **6873**
        Maternal and Child Health Services Division **3395, 9741**
        Vital Statistics Division **7057**
    Inspector General Office • Licensing and Regulation Division **6493**
    Medicaid Services Department **5785**
    Mental Health and Mental Retardation Department
        Mental Health Division **7725**
        Mental Retardation Division **4360**
        Substance Abuse Division **12164**
    Social Services Department • Aging Services Division **2020**
Kentucky Labor Cabinet • Occupational Safety and Health Review
    Commission **9882**
Kentucky; Learning Disabilities Association of **4700**
Kentucky Lions Eye Research Institute • University of Louisville **13653**
Kentucky Medical Association **1828**
Kentucky; Mental Health Association of **7766**
Kentucky; National Kidney Foundation of **12949**
Kentucky Nurses Association **9229**
Kentucky Optometric Association **13810**
Kentucky Osteopathic Medical Association **10083**
Kentucky Pharmacists Association **10711**
Kentucky State Board of Embalmers and Funeral Directors **3745**
Kentucky Veterinary Medical Association **13319**
Kentucky / West Virginia Chapter • Cystic Fibrosis Foundation **5420, 5469**
Kenya; Family Planning Association of **11217**
Kenya Food and Nutrition Action Network **9470**
Kenya National AIDS Control Program **6688**
Kenya; National Nurses Association of **9122**
Kerato-Refractive Society **13512**
Keren-Or, Inc. **3253**
Kerr Fund; Grayce B. **230**
Kettering College of Medical Arts
    Physician Assistant Program **1101**
    Respiratory Therapist Program **11491**
Kettering Fund **344**
Kettering Medical Center • Nuclear Medicine Department **11146**
Kettering-Scott Magnetic Resonance Laboratory **11147**
Keuka College
    Department of Occupational Therapy **12393**
    Nursing Division **8833**
Kewalo Marine Laboratory • University of Hawaii at Manoa **2668**
Keys Speech and Hearing Center • University of Oklahoma **3652**

Khan Cetral Health Board for Pakistan; His Royal Highness Prince Aga
  1132
Khan Health Service Pakistan; Aga **1132**
Kidney Center; Chromalloy American • Washington University **12932**
Kidney Disease Foundation; National 12909
Kidney Disease Program • University of Louisville **12926**
Kidney Diseases; National Institute of Diabetes and Digestive and
    Clinical Nutrition Research Units Program • U.S. Department of Health
      and Human Services **4907**
    Division of Diabetes, Endocrinology, and Metabolic Diseases
        Cystic Fibrosis Research Program • U.S. Department of Health
          and Human Services **5362**
        Diabetes Centers Program • U.S. Department of Health and
          Human Services **4909**
        Diabetes Clinical Trials Program • U.S. Department of Health
          and Human Services **4910**
        Diabetes Programs Branch • U.S. Department of Health and
          Human Services **5363**
        Diabetes Research Program • U.S. Department of Health and
          Human Services **4911**
        Endocrine and Metabolic Diseases Research Programs Branch
          • U.S. Department of Health and Human Services **4912**
        Endocrinology Research Program • U.S. Department of Health
          and Human Services **4913**
        Metabolic Diseases and Gene Therapy Research Program •
          U.S. Department of Health and Human Services **4914**
        National Diabetes Data Group • U.S. Department of Health and
          Human Services **4915**
        Research Career Development Program • U.S. Department of
          Health and Human Services **4916**
        Special Programs Branch • U.S. Department of Health and
          Human Services **4917**
        U.S. Department of Health and Human Services **4908**
    Division of Digestive Diseases and Nutrition
        Clinical Trials Program • U.S. Department of Health and Human
          Services **5239**
        Digestive Diseases Branch • U.S. Department of Health and
          Human Services **5240**
        Gastrointestinal Digestion Program • U.S. Department of Health
          and Human Services **5241**
        Gastrointestinal Immunology Program • U.S. Department of
          Health and Human Services **5242**
        Gastrointestinal Motility Program • U.S. Department of Health
          and Human Services **5243**
        Gastrointestinal Neuroendocrinology Program • U.S. Department
          of Health and Human Services **5244**
        Liver and Biliary Diseases Program • U.S. Department of Health
          and Human Services **5245**
        Nutrient Metabolism Program • U.S. Department of Health and
          Human Services **9544**
        Obesity, Eating Disorders, and Energy Regulation Program •
          U.S. Department of Health and Human Services **7615**
        Pancreas Program • U.S. Department of Health and Human
          Services **4918**
        U.S. Department of Health and Human Services **5238**
    Division of Intramural Research
        Clinical Hematology Branch • U.S. Department of Health and
          Human Services **6206**
        Diabetes Branch • U.S. Department of Health and Human
          Services **4920**
        Digestive Diseases Branch • U.S. Department of Health and
          Human Services **5246**
        Endocrinology Section • U.S. Department of Health and Human
          Services **4921**
        Genetics and Biochemistry Branch • U.S. Department of Health
          and Human Services **5364**
        Mathematical Research Branch • U.S. Department of Health and
          Human Services **7028**
        Metabolic Diseases Branch • U.S. Department of Health and
          Human Services **4922**
        Molecular, Cellular, and Nutritional Endocrinology Branch • U.S.
          Department of Health and Human Services **4923**
        Phoenix Epidemiology and Clinical Research Branch • U.S.
          Department of Health and Human Services **5191**
        U.S. Department of Health and Human Services **4919**
    Division of Kidney, Urologic, and Hematologic Diseases
        Chronic Renal Diseases Program • U.S. Department of Health
          and Human Services **12920**
        Hematology Program • U.S. Department of Health and Human
          Services **6207**
        Renal Physiology/Cell Biology Program • U.S. Department of
          Health and Human Services **12921**
        U.S. Department of Health and Human Services **12919**

Koninklijke Nederlandse Maatschappij voor Diergeneeskunde   13106
Kontaktgruppen for ALS **8249**
Korean Academy of Psychotherapists **7434**
Korean Hospital Association **6453**
Korean Medical Association of America **1368**
Korean Society of Pharmacology **10416**
Korean Society of Plastic and Reconstructive Surgery **12286**
Korhazszovetseg; Magyar 6446
Krancer Center for Inflammatory Bowel Disease Research • Medical College of Pennsylvania and Hahnemann University **5235**
Krankengymnasten; Interessenverband Freiberuflicher 12665
Krankenhaeuser; Vereinigung Schweizerischer 6474
Krankenhaus Direktoren; Europaische Vereinigung der 5574
Krankenhausarzte Deutschlands; Verband der Leitenden 5560
Krankenhausdirektoren Deutschlands; Verband der 5579
Krankenhausgesellschaft; Deutsche 6445
Krannert Graduate School of Physical Therapy • University of Indianapolis **12475**
Krannert Institute of Cardiology **2909**
Kresge Center for Environmental Health • Harvard University **5075**
Kresge Eye Institute • Wayne State University **13662**
Kresge Foundation **346**
Kresge Hearing Research Institute
    Auditory Anatomy Laboratory • University of Michigan **3641**
    Auditory Prosthesis Animal Psychophysics Laboratory • University of Michigan **3642**
    Biochemistry Laboratory • University of Michigan **3643**
    Electrophysiology Laboratory • University of Michigan **3644**
    Microcirculation Laboratory • University of Michigan **3645**
    Neuropharmacology Laboratory • University of Michigan **3646**
    Neurophysiology and Biophysics Laboratory • University of Michigan **3647**
    University of Michigan **3640**
Kresge Hearing Research Laboratory of the South • Louisiana State University **3611**
Krieger Institute; Kennedy **12735**
Kriser Dental Center; David B. • New York University **4004**
Kroch Center for Twin Studies; Jeanette Kennelly **9708**
Krogman Center for Research in Child Growth and Development; W.M. **3373**
KS and Associates **5283**
Kuzell Institute for Arthritis and Infectious Diseases **7921**
Kuzell Institute for Arthritis Research 7921
Kyokai; Nippon Igaku Toshokan 7006

L

L. E. Support Club **7885**
L. K. Whittier Foundation **347**
L. and S. Milken Foundation **348**
La Jolla Cancer Research Foundation **6062**
La Leche League International **9670**
La Rabida Research and Policy Center for the Study of Children and Families with Special Health Care Needs • University of Chicago **3358**
La Roche College; Allegheny Valley Hospital / • School of Anesthesia • Nurse Anesthesia Program **2312**
La Roche College; St. Elizabeth Hospital Medical Center / • School for Nurse Anesthetists **2309**
La Roche College; St. Francis Medical Center / • School of Anesthesia **2321**
La Roche College; United Hospital Center / • Nurse Anesthesia Program **2346**
La Roche College; Westmoreland-Latrobe Hospitals / • School of Anesthesia for Nurses **2324**
Lab Personnel; National Certification Agency for Medical **7146**
Laban / Bartenieff Institute of Movement Studies, Inc. **12736**
Labette Community College • Respiratory Therapist Program **11394**
Labor & Mental Health; Institute for **7571, 9796**
Laboratoire Medical; Association Internationale des Technologistes de 7137
Laboratoire; Societe Canadienne des Technologistes de 7128
Laboratories Association; Optical **5877**
Laboratories for Connective Tissue Research • University of Michigan **7953**
Laboratories for Developmental Therapeutics **10441**
Laboratories for Molecular Neuroscience • Harvard University **8371**
Laboratories; National Association of Dental 3967
Laboratories; National Board for Certification of Dental 3970
Laboratorium Tegnoloe van Suid-Afrika; Vereniging van Geneeskundige 7153

Laboratory of Analytical Chemistry • National Institute of Diabetes and Digestive and Kidney Diseases • U.S. Department of Health and Human Services **4924**
Laboratory Animal Care; American Association for Accreditation of 13026
Laboratory Animal Center • University of Missouri—Kansas City **13226**
Laboratory Animal Diseases; Resource for the Study of • Yale University **13249**
Laboratory Animal Management Association Lab Animal Program **5583**
Laboratory Animal Managers Association 5583
Laboratory Animal Medicine Division • Veterinary Pathology Department • Armed Forces Institute of Pathology • U.S. Department of Defense **10178**
Laboratory Animal Medicine; Unit for • University of Michigan **13222**
Laboratory Animal Research Center • Rockefeller University **13170**
Laboratory Animal Resources; Institute of **13081**
Laboratory Animal Resources and Research Facility • Texas A&M University **2630**
Laboratory Animal Science; American Association for 13032
Laboratory Animal Science; Society of **13107**
Laboratory of Applied Pharmacokinetics • University of Southern California **10484**
Laboratory for the Assessment of Functional Vision • University of Illinois at Chicago **13650**
Laboratory Association; American Clinical **7118**
Laboratory of Bacterial Pathogenesis and Immunology • Rockefeller University **2113**
Laboratory of Bacteriology and Immunology • Rockefeller University **6784**
Laboratory of Behavioral Sciences • National Institute on Aging • U.S. Department of Health and Human Services **1956**
Laboratory of Biochemical Genetics • National Heart, Lung, and Blood Institute • U.S. Department of Health and Human Services **2944**
Laboratory of Biochemical Genetics and Metabolism • Rockefeller University **5346**
Laboratory for Biochemical Parasitology • University of Colorado **6844**
Laboratory of Biochemical Pharmacology • National Institute of Diabetes and Digestive and Kidney Diseases • U.S. Department of Health and Human Services **2642**
Laboratory of Biochemical Physiology • National Cancer Institute • U.S. Department of Health and Human Services **6174**
Laboratory of Biochemistry
    National Cancer Institute • U.S. Department of Health and Human Services **6175**
    National Heart, Lung, and Blood Institute • U.S. Department of Health and Human Services **2945**
Laboratory of Biochemistry and Metabolism • National Institute of Diabetes and Digestive and Kidney Diseases • U.S. Department of Health and Human Services **2643**
Laboratory of Biological Anthropology • University of Kansas **2674**
Laboratory of Biological Chemistry • National Cancer Institute • U.S. Department of Health and Human Services **6176**
Laboratory of Biology • National Cancer Institute • U.S. Department of Health and Human Services **6177**
Laboratory of Biology of Addictive Diseases • Rockefeller University **12100**
Laboratory of Biomedical and Environmental Sciences • University of California, Los Angeles **1687**
Laboratory of Bioorganic Chemistry • National Institute of Diabetes and Digestive and Kidney Diseases • U.S. Department of Health and Human Services **2644**
Laboratory of Biophysical Chemistry • National Heart, Lung, and Blood Institute • U.S. Department of Health and Human Services **2946**
Laboratory of Cancer Biology • New England Deaconess Hospital **6083**
Laboratory of Cancer and Radiobiological Research • New York University **6088**
Laboratory for Cancer Research • Rutgers University **6109**
Laboratory of Cardiac Energetics • National Heart, Lung, and Blood Institute • U.S. Department of Health and Human Services **2947**
Laboratory of Cardiovascular Science • National Institute on Aging • U.S. Department of Health and Human Services **1957**
Laboratory of Cell Biology
    National Cancer Institute • U.S. Department of Health and Human Services **6178**
    National Heart, Lung, and Blood Institute • U.S. Department of Health and Human Services **2948**
Laboratory of Cell Biology and Genetics • National Institute of Diabetes and Digestive and Kidney Diseases • U.S. Department of Health and Human Services **4925**
Laboratory for Cell and Molecular Biology • Harvard University **2579**
Laboratory of Cell and Molecular Biology of Leukocytes • Duke University **2569**
Laboratory of Cell Physiology and Virology • Rockefeller University **6785**
Laboratory of Cellular Carcinogenesis and Tumor Promotion • National Cancer Institute • U.S. Department of Health and Human Services **6179**
Laboratory of Cellular Development and Oncology • National Institute of Dental Research • U.S. Department of Health and Human Services **2640**

Laboratory of Cellular and Developmental Biology • National Institute of Diabetes and Digestive and Kidney Diseases • U.S. Department of Health and Human Services **2645**

Laboratory of Cellular Metabolism • National Heart, Lung, and Blood Institute • U.S. Department of Health and Human Services **2949**

Laboratory of Cellular and Molecular Biology

> National Cancer Institute • U.S. Department of Health and Human Services **6180**

> National Institute on Aging • U.S. Department of Health and Human Services **1959**

Laboratory of Cellular and Molecular Immunology • National Institute of Allergy and Infectious Diseases • U.S. Department of Health and Human Services **2132**

Laboratory of Cellular and Molecular Pharmacology • National Institute of Environmental Health Sciences • U.S. Department of Health and Human Services **5106**

Laboratory of Cellular Oncology • National Cancer Institute • U.S. Department of Health and Human Services **6181**

Laboratory of Cellular Physiology and Immunology • Rockefeller University **2114**

Laboratory of Central Nervous System Studies • National Institute of Neurological Disorders and Stroke • U.S. Department of Health and Human Services **8458**

Laboratory of Chemical Biology • National Institute of Diabetes and Digestive and Kidney Diseases • U.S. Department of Health and Human Services **2646**

Laboratory of Chemical Pharmacology • National Heart, Lung, and Blood Institute • U.S. Department of Health and Human Services **2950**

Laboratory of Chemical Physics • National Institute of Diabetes and Digestive and Kidney Diseases • U.S. Department of Health and Human Services **2647**

Laboratory of Chemoprevention • National Cancer Institute • U.S. Department of Health and Human Services **6182**

Laboratory for Circadian and Sleep Disorders Medicine **8384**

Laboratory of Clinical Investigation • National Institute of Allergy and Infectious Diseases • U.S. Department of Health and Human Services **2133**

Laboratory of Clinical Physiology • National Institute on Aging • U.S. Department of Health and Human Services **1960**

Laboratory for Comparative Biochemistry **2585**

Laboratory of Comparative Carcinogenesis • National Cancer Institute • U.S. Department of Health and Human Services **6183**

Laboratory of Comparative Ethology • National Institute of Child Health and Human Development • U.S. Department of Health and Human Services **7614**

Laboratory of Dermatology Research **4264**

Laboratory of Developmental Biology

> National Institute of Dental Research • U.S. Department of Health and Human Services **2641**

> University of Southern California **2686**

Laboratory of Developmental and Molecular Immunity • National Institute of Child Health and Human Development • U.S. Department of Health and Human Services **2139**

Laboratory of Developmental Neurobiology • National Institute of Child Health and Human Development • U.S. Department of Health and Human Services **8438**

Laboratory of Developmental Psychobiology • Stanford University **7602**

Laboratory Diagnosticians; American Association of Veterinary **13037**

Laboratory Diagnosticians; World Association of Veterinary **13119**

Laboratory of Electronics • Rockefeller University **2469**

Laboratory of Exocrine Physiology • University of Alabama at Birmingham **4927**

Laboratory of Experimental Carcinogenesis • National Cancer Institute • U.S. Department of Health and Human Services **6184**

Laboratory of Experimental Cytology • University of Michigan **2676**

Laboratory of Experimental Immunology • National Cancer Institute • U.S. Department of Health and Human Services **6185**

Laboratory for Experimental Medicine and Surgery in Primates • New York University **13151**

Laboratory of Experimental Neuropathology • National Institute of Neurological Disorders and Stroke • U.S. Department of Health and Human Services **8459**

Laboratory for Experimental Oncology • Indiana University-Purdue University at Indianapolis **6052**

Laboratory of Experimental Pathology • National Cancer Institute • U.S. Department of Health and Human Services **6186**

Laboratory of Flow Cytometry • Roswell Park Cancer Institute **2612**

Laboratory of Genetics

> National Cancer Institute • U.S. Department of Health and Human Services **6187**

> University of Wisconsin—Madison **5389**

Laboratory of GI Tumor Biology • Memorial Sloan-Kettering Cancer Center **6075**

Laboratory for Health and Aging Studies • Maharishi International University **1622**

Laboratory of History of Medicine and Science • Rockefeller University **7021**

Laboratory of Human Behavior and Metabolism • Rockefeller University **4899**

Laboratory of Human Cancer Immunology **6064**

Laboratory of Human Carcinogenesis • National Cancer Institute • U.S. Department of Health and Human Services **6188**

Laboratory for Human Performance Research • Pennsylvania State University **11976**

Laboratory of Human Pharmacology • Medical College of Pennsylvania and Hahnemann University **10444**

Laboratory of Immunobiology • National Cancer Institute • U.S. Department of Health and Human Services **6189**

Laboratory of Immunogenetics • National Institute of Allergy and Infectious Diseases • U.S. Department of Health and Human Services **2134**

Laboratory of Immunology

> Harvard University **2102**

> Intramural Research • National Eye Institute • U.S. Department of Health and Human Services **13639**

> National Institute of Allergy and Infectious Diseases • U.S. Department of Health and Human Services **2135**

> National Institute of Dental Research • U.S. Department of Health and Human Services **4021**

> Rockefeller University **2115**

Laboratory of Immunopathology • National Institute of Allergy and Infectious Diseases • U.S. Department of Health and Human Services **2137**

Laboratory of Immunoregulation • National Institute of Allergy and Infectious Diseases • U.S. Department of Health and Human Services **2138**

Laboratory of Infectious Diseases • National Institute of Allergy and Infectious Diseases • U.S. Department of Health and Human Services **6832**

Laboratory for Investigative Dermatology • Rockefeller University **4267**

Laboratory of Kidney and Electrolyte Metabolism • National Heart, Lung, and Blood Institute • U.S. Department of Health and Human Services **2951**

Laboratory Management Association; Clinical **7129**

Laboratory of Mathematical Biology • National Cancer Institute • U.S. Department of Health and Human Services **6190**

Laboratory on Mechanisms of Ocular Diseases • National Eye Institute • U.S. Department of Health and Human Services **13640**

Laboratory of Medical Genetics • University of Alabama at Birmingham **5367**

Laboratory of Medicinal Chemistry • National Cancer Institute • U.S. Department of Health and Human Services **6191**

Laboratory Medicine; Division of • University of Wisconsin—Madison **7158**

Laboratory of Metabolism-Pharmacology • Rockefeller University **10453**

Laboratory of Microbial Ecology

> National Institute of Dental Research • U.S. Department of Health and Human Services **4022**

> New York University **5081**

Laboratory of Microbial Structure and Function • National Institute of Allergy and Infectious Diseases • U.S. Department of Health and Human Services **6833**

Laboratory of Molecular Biology

> Division of Intramural Research • National Institute on Deafness and Other Communication Disorders • U.S. Department of Health and Human Services **3628**

> National Cancer Institute • U.S. Department of Health and Human Services **6192**

> National Institute of Diabetes and Digestive and Kidney Diseases • U.S. Department of Health and Human Services **2648**

> National Institute of Neurological Disorders and Stroke • U.S. Department of Health and Human Services **8460**

> University of Illinois at Chicago **2671**

Laboratory of Molecular Biophysics

> National Institute of Environmental Health Sciences • U.S. Department of Health and Human Services **5107**

> University of Alabama at Birmingham **2658**

Laboratory of Molecular Carcinogenesis • National Cancer Institute • U.S. Department of Health and Human Services **6193**

Laboratory of Molecular Cardiology • National Heart, Lung, and Blood Institute • U.S. Department of Health and Human Services **2952**

Laboratory of Molecular and Cellular Biology • National Institute of Diabetes and Digestive and Kidney Diseases • U.S. Department of Health and Human Services **2649**

Laboratory of Molecular and Cellular Neurobiology • National Institute of Neurological Disorders and Stroke • U.S. Department of Health and Human Services **8461**

Laboratory of Molecular and Developmental Biology • National Eye Institute • U.S. Department of Health and Human Services **13641**

Laboratory of Molecular Genetics

> National Institute on Aging • U.S. Department of Health and Human Services **1961**

> National Institute of Child Health and Human Development • U.S. Department of Health and Human Services **5361**

National Institute of Environmental Health Sciences • U.S. Department of Health and Human Services **5108**

Laboratory of Molecular Hematology • Division of Intramural Research • National Heart, Lung, and Blood Institute • U.S. Department of Health and Human Services **6205**

Laboratory of Molecular Immunobiology **2586**

Laboratory of Molecular Immunoregulation • National Cancer Institute • U.S. Department of Health and Human Services **6194**

Laboratory of Molecular and Integrative Neurosciences • National Institute of Environmental Health Sciences • U.S. Department of Health and Human Services **5109**

Laboratory of Molecular Microbiology • National Institute of Allergy and Infectious Diseases • U.S. Department of Health and Human Services **6834**

Laboratory of Molecular Oncology
>National Cancer Institute • U.S. Department of Health and Human Services **6195**
>Rockefeller University **6105**

Laboratory of Molecular Pharmacology • National Cancer Institute • U.S. Department of Health and Human Services **6196**

Laboratory of Molecular Structure • Division of Intramural Research • National Institute of Allergy and Infectious Diseases • U.S. Department of Health and Human Services **2131**

Laboratory of Molecular Virology • National Cancer Institute • U.S. Department of Health and Human Services **6197**

Laboratory of Motor Physiology • Rockefeller University **8418**

Laboratory of Neural Control • National Institute of Neurological Disorders and Stroke • U.S. Department of Health and Human Services **8462**

Laboratory of Neurobiology • National Institute of Neurological Disorders and Stroke • U.S. Department of Health and Human Services **8463**

Laboratory of Neurochemistry • National Institute of Neurological Disorders and Stroke • U.S. Department of Health and Human Services **8464**

Laboratory of Neuroendocrine Regulation • Massachusetts Institute of Technology **8391**

Laboratory of Neuroendocrinology
>Rockefeller University **8419**
>University of Texas—Houston Health Science Center **8526**

Laboratory of Neurophysiology • National Institute of Neurological Disorders and Stroke • U.S. Department of Health and Human Services **8465**

Laboratory of Neuropsychology • Boston University **8336**

Laboratory of Neuroscience • National Institute of Diabetes and Digestive and Kidney Diseases • U.S. Department of Health and Human Services **8440**

Laboratory of Neurosciences • National Institute on Aging • U.S. Department of Health and Human Services **1962**

Laboratory for Neurotrauma • University of California, San Francisco **8490**

Laboratory for Ophthalmic Research • Emory University **13593**

Laboratory of Oral Medicine • National Institute of Dental Research • U.S. Department of Health and Human Services **4023**

Laboratory of Parasitic Diseases • National Institute of Allergy and Infectious Diseases • U.S. Department of Health and Human Services **6835**

Laboratory of Pathology • National Cancer Institute • U.S. Department of Health and Human Services **6198**

Laboratory of Pediatric Critical Care • Cornell University **10430**

Laboratory of Persistent Viral Diseases • National Institute of Allergy and Infectious Diseases • U.S. Department of Health and Human Services **6836**

Laboratory of Personality and Cognition • National Institute on Aging • U.S. Department of Health and Human Services **1963**

Laboratory of Physical Biology • National Institute of Arthritis and Musculoskeletal and Skin Diseases • U.S. Department of Health and Human Services **7942**

Laboratory of Psychobiology • Ohio State University **7591**

Laboratory of Pulmonary Pathobiology • National Institute of Environmental Health Sciences • U.S. Department of Health and Human Services **5110**

Laboratory of Radiobiology and Environmental Health **11073**

Laboratory of Reproductive and Developmental Toxicology • National Institute of Environmental Health Sciences • U.S. Department of Health and Human Services **5111**

Laboratory of Research in Human and Social Ecology • University of Quebec at Montreal **11001**

Laboratory of Retinal Cell and Molecular Biology • National Eye Institute • U.S. Department of Health and Human Services **13642**

Laboratory Schools; Accrediting Bureau of Medical **7113**

Laboratory Science; American Society for Clinical **7122**

Laboratory Sciences; National Accrediting Agency for Clinical **7144**

Laboratory of Sensorimotor Research • National Eye Institute • U.S. Department of Health and Human Services **13643**

Laboratory of Signal Transduction **6063**

Laboratory Standardization; European Committee for Clinical **7135**

Laboratory Standards; European Committee for Clinical **7135**

Laboratory Standards; National Committee for Clinical **7151**

Laboratory Standards Organization; NCCLS—The Clinical **7151**

Laboratory for the Study of Social Deviance • Texas A&M University **7610**

Laboratory Technicians; American Society of Clinical **7122**

Laboratory Technologists; Canadian Society of **7128**

Laboratory Technologists; International Association of Medical **7137**

Laboratory Technologists; International Society of Clinical **7143**

Laboratory Technologists of South Africa; Society of Medical **7153**

Laboratory Technologists of Zimbabwe; Association of Medical **7127**

Laboratory Technology in the EEC; Standing Representative Committee for Medical **7154**

Laboratory Technology; International Society for Clinical **7143**

Laboratory of Theoretical and Physical Biology • National Institute of Child Health and Human Development • U.S. Department of Health and Human Services **2639**

Laboratory for Transplantation Immunology • Stanford University **12886**

Laboratory of Tumor Antigen Immunochemistry **6064**

Laboratory of Tumor Cell Biology • National Cancer Institute • U.S. Department of Health and Human Services **6199**

Laboratory of Tumor Immunology and Biology • National Cancer Institute • U.S. Department of Health and Human Services **6200**

Laboratory of Tumor Virus Biology • National Cancer Institute • U.S. Department of Health and Human Services **6201**

Laboratory of Vectors and Pathogens • National Institute of Allergy and Infectious Diseases • U.S. Department of Health and Human Services **6837**

Laboratory of Viral Carcinogenesis • National Cancer Institute • U.S. Department of Health and Human Services **6202**

Laboratory of Viral Diseases • National Institute of Allergy and Infectious Diseases • U.S. Department of Health and Human Services **6838**

Laboratory of Viral and Molecular Pathogenesis • National Institute of Neurological Disorders and Stroke • U.S. Department of Health and Human Services **8466**

Laboratory of Viral Pathogenesis • Harvard Medical School **2578**

Lactation Center; Human **9653, 9707**

Lactation Consultant Association; International **9666**

Ladies Auxiliary to the National Dental Association **3907**

Ladish Co. Foundation **6404**

Laekarfoerbund; Sveriges **1518**

Laffey-McHugh Foundation **349**

Lahey Clinic Foundation **1613**

Lake Erie College of Osteopathic Medicine **9964**

Lake Superior State University • Department of Nursing **8763**

Lakeland Community College • Respiratory Therapist Program **11492**

Lakemedelsnamnden; Nordiska **1441**

Lakeview College • School of Nursing **8650**

Lamar University • Institute of Technology • Respiratory Therapist Program **11548**

Lamar University—Beaumont • Department of Nursing **8986**

Lamaze Birth Without Pain Education Association **9641**

Lambda Kappa Sigma **10607**

Lambda Omicron Gamma **10002**

Lambda Omicron Gamma Medical Society **10002**

Lancaster Cleft Palate Clinic **2758**

Lance Foundation **756**

Lander College • School of Nursing **8957**

Landsforbund; Horselshemmedes **3566**

Landsforening for Huntingtons Sykdom **8292**

Landsforeningen for Autister **7478**

Landsforeningen Evnesvages Vel **4298**

Lane Community College • Respiratory Therapist Program **11505**

Langeloth Foundation; Jacob and Valeria **6364**

Langley Porter Psychiatric Institute • University of California, San Francisco **7661**

Langston University
>Physical Therapy Program **12532**
>School of Nursing **8892**

Language-Hearing Association; American Speech- **3492**

Language Hearing Association; National Student Speech **3560**

Language and Hearing Clinic; Speech- • State University of New York at Buffalo **3621**

Language and Hearing; National Black Association for Speech, **3547**

Language Laboratory; Artificial • Michigan State University **3613**

Language Pathology and Audiology; Council on Professional Standards in Speech- **3511**

Language Pathology and Audiology Department; Speech and • University of Nevada, Reno **3650**

Lankenau Hospital • School of Nurse Anesthesia **2316**

Lankenau Medical Research Center **1614**

Lansing Community College • Respiratory Therapist Program **11429**

Lansing School of Nursing • Bellarmine College **8710**

Laparoscopists; American Association of Gynecological **9622**

Lariboisiere; College International de Recherches Implantaires et **3917**

Laryngeal Papillomatosis; Christina Lazar Foundation for **11593**

Laryngectomees; International Association of **12683**
Laryngological Association; American **3487**
Laryngological, Rhinological and Otological Society; American **3488**
Laryngologiques; Federation Internationale des Societes Oto- Rhino- 3535
Las Vegas Chapter • Lupus Foundation of America **8074**
Laser Acupuncture Society; International **2217**
Laser Association; European **11112**
Laser; Association Europeenne du **11112**
Laser Biomedical Research Center • Massachusetts Institute of Technology **11151**
Laser Dentistry; Academy of **3846**
Laser Institute; Dixon • University of Utah **11176**
Laser Institute and Medical Clinic; Beckman • University of California, Irvine **11160**
Laser Lab; Cardiovascular • University of Florida **11166**
Laser Medicine and Surgery; American Society for **12240**
Laser Microbeam Program • University of California, Irvine **11162**
Laser Surgery; American Board of 12220
Laser Surgery; American Board of Neurological / Orthopaedic **12220**
Laser Surgery; Institute for Applied **12321**
Laser Surgery; International College of Podiatric 10773
Laser Surgery; International Society of Podiatric 10773, **10773**
Laser Technology Center **11148**
Laser Technology Center; Medical **12321**
Laser Trabeculoplasty Study; Glaucoma **13598**
Lassalle Graduate School of Social Work; Beatriz • University of Puerto Rico **11842**
Late-Deafened Adults; Association of **3495**
Latin American Association of Aviation and Space Medicine **2386**
Latin American Association of Environmental Mutagens, Carcinogens, and Teratogens Societies **5047**
Latin American Association of Immunology **2082**
Latin American Association for Medical Physics **2539**
Latin American Association of Medical Schools and Faculties **1369**
Latin American Association of National Academies of Medicine **1370**
Latin American Association for Social Psychology **7435**
Latin American Association for the Study of the Liver **5226**
Latin American Association of Therapeutic Communities **12691**
Latin American Blind Union [Buenos Aires, Argentina] **13513**
Latin American Blind Union [Montevideo, Uruguay] **13514**
Latin American Cancer Societies; Federation of **5945**
Latin American and Caribbean Women's Health Network **1371**
Latin American Confederation of Clinical Biochemistry **2540**
Latin American Confederation of Societies of Anesthesia **2370**
Latin American Diabetes Association **4854**
Latin American Federation of Surgeons **12287**
Latin American Federation of Thermalism and Climatism **5048**
Latin American Hospital Federation **6454**
Latin American Psychiatric Association **7436**
Latin American Transactional Analysis Association **7437**
Latin American Union of Societies of Phthisiology **11601**
Latin Languages Allergologists and Immunologists; Association of **2067**
Latin and Mediterranean Group for Sport Medicine **11950**
Latin et Mediterraneen de Medecine du Sport; Groupement 11950
Latina; Asociacion Latinoamericana de Facultades y Escuelas de Medicina de America 1369
Latina Health Organization; National **10962**
Latines; Groupement des Allergologistes et Immunologistes de Langues 2067
Latinoamericana de Analisis Transaccional; Asociacion 7437
Latinoamericana de Bioquimica Clinica; Confederacion 2540
Latinoamericana de Ciegos; Union 13514
Latinoamericana de Facultades y Escuelas de Medicina de America Latina; Asociacion 1369
Latinoamericana de Fisica Medica; Asociacion 2539
Latinoamericana de Hospitales; Federacion 6454
Latinoamericana de Imunologia; Asociacion 2082
Latinoamericana de Medecina de Aviacion y del Espacio; Asociacion 2386
Latinoamericana de Psicologia Social; Asociacion 7435
Latinoamericana de Psiquiatria; Asociacion 7436
Latinoamericana de Sociedades de Anestesia; Confederacion 2370
Latinoamericana de Sociedades de Cancerologia; Federacion 5945
Latinoamericana de Sociedades de Tisiologia; Union 11601
Latinoamericana de Termalismo; Federacion 5048
Latinoamericana de Ciegos; Union 13513
Lattner Foundation; Forrest C. **190**
Laughter Therapy **12692**
Laura Moore Cunningham Foundation **6370**
Laura S. Nye Surgical Research Fund for Desmoid Tumors • Wayne State University **12329**
Laurence-Moon-Bardet-Biedl Syndrome Network **5284**

Laurence-Moon-Biedl Syndrome Network **5284**
Laval Hospital Research Centre • Laval University **2911**
Laval University
    Cardiac Rehabilitation Research Group **2910**
    Exercise Physiology Group **11969**
    Human Nutrition Research Group **9508**
    Interdisciplinary Research Group on Work Organization and Occupational Health and Safety **9812**
    Joseph-Rheaume Laboratory **9509**
    Laval Hospital Research Centre **2911**
    Medical Research Centre **1615**
        Diabetes Research Group **4892**
        Family Medicine Research Group **1616**
        Hormonal Bioregulation Research Group **4893**
        Hypertension Research Group **2912**
        Infection Research Group **6775**
        Inflammation, Immunology, and Rheumatology Research Group **2107**
        Mental Health Research Group **7578**
        Molecular Endocrinology Research Group **4894**
        Ontogenesis and Molecular Genetics Research Group **5336**
        Ontogeny and Reproduction Research Group **11273**
        Ophthalmology Research Group **13611**
        Public Health Research Group **10981**
        Research Centre on Lipid Disorders **2913**
    Molecular Microbiology and Protein Engineering Group **5337**
    Robert-Giffard Research Centre **7579**
    Saint-Francois-d'Assise Hospital Research Centre **11274**
        Reproductive Endocrinology Unit **11275**
    Saint-Sacrement Hospital Research Centre **1617**
        Epidemiology Research Group **5187**
Law; American Academy of Psychiatry and the **7161**
Law; American Society for Pharmacy **7173**
Law; Center on Children and the **7197**
Law; Center for Employment Relations and • Florida State University **7198**
Law; Commission on Mental and Physical Disability **4476**
Law and Deafness; National Center for **3549**
Law and Disability; Pike Institute on • Boston University **4574**
Law, and Human Sexuality; Program in Psychiatry, • University of California, Los Angeles **7218**
Law; Institute for Health • Loyola University Chicago **7208**
Law; Institute on Mental Disability and the **7206**
Law; Institute of Public • University of New Mexico **1712**
Law; International Center for Medicine and **7180**
Law; Judge David L. Bazelon Center for Mental Health **7207**
Law and Medicine; American Society of 7171
Law-Medicine Center • Case Western Reserve University **7195**
Law, Medicine and Ethics; American Society of 7171
Law and Medicine; Massachusetts Society of 7171
Law Program; National Health **7187**
Law Society; American Psychology- **7169**
Lawrence Berkeley Laboratory
    Cholesterol Research Center • U.S. Department of Energy **4902**
    Environment, Health and Safety Division • U.S. Department of Energy **9821**
    Life Science Division • U.S. Department of Energy **6124**
    Research Medicine and Radiation Biophysics Division • U.S. Department of Energy **11158**
Lawrence Livermore National Laboratory
    Hazards Control Department • Special Projects Division • U.S. Department of Energy **9822**
    U.S. Department of Energy **2634**
Lawson Research Institute • University of Western Ontario **9720**
Lawyers in Alcoholics Anonymous; International **12042**
Lawyers Association; National Health **7188**
Lawyers; National Alliance of Victims of Minamata Disease and **5049**
Lazar Foundation for Juvenile Papillomatosis; Christina **11593**
Lazar Foundation for Laryngeal Papillomatosis; Christina **11593**
Lazarus-Goldman Center for Study of Social Work Practice • University of Pennsylvania **11877**
La-Z-Boy Foundation **755**
LCF Foundation, Inc 1613
Lead Poisoning; Alliance to End Childhood **3155**
Leader Dog League for the Blind **13515**
Leader Dogs for the Blind **13515**
Leadership Center on Longevity and Society; International • Mount Sinai School of Medicine of City University of New York **1941**
Leadership Coalition on AIDS; National **6736**
Lean Line **9471**

Learning and Behavior Branch; Human • Center for Research for Mothers and Children • National Institute of Child Health and Human Development • U.S. Department of Health and Human Services **7613**
Learning; Center for Family **7547**
Learning Center, Inc.; Oregon Social **3070**
Learning Disabilities Association of Alabama **4684**
Learning Disabilities Association of Alaska **4685**
Learning Disabilities Association of America **4504**
Learning Disabilities Association of Arizona **4686**
Learning Disabilities Association of Arkansas **4687**
Learning Disabilities Association of California **4688**
Learning Disabilities Association of Canada **4505**
Learning Disabilities; Association for Children with 4504
Learning Disabilities; Association for Children and Adults with 4504
Learning Disabilities Association of Colorado **4689**
Learning Disabilities Association of Connecticut **4690**
Learning Disabilities Association of the District of Columbia **4691**
Learning Disabilities Association of Florida **4692**
Learning Disabilities Association of Georgia **4693**
Learning Disabilities Association of Hawaii **4694**
Learning Disabilities Association of Idaho **4695**
Learning Disabilities Association of Illinois **4696**
Learning Disabilities Association of Indiana **4697**
Learning Disabilities Association of Iowa **4698**
Learning Disabilities Association of Kansas **4699**
Learning Disabilities Association of Kentucky **4700**
Learning Disabilities Association of Louisiana **4701**
Learning Disabilities Association of Maine **4702**
Learning Disabilities Association of Maryland **4703**
Learning Disabilities Association of Massachusetts **4704**
Learning Disabilities Association of Michigan **4705**
Learning Disabilities Association of Minnesota **4706**
Learning Disabilities Association of Mississippi **4707**
Learning Disabilities Association of Missouri **4708**
Learning Disabilities Association of Montana **4709**
Learning Disabilities Association of Nebraska **4710**
Learning Disabilities Association of New Hampshire **4711**
Learning Disabilities Association of New Jersey **4712**
Learning Disabilities Association of New Mexico **4713**
Learning Disabilities Association of New York **4714**
Learning Disabilities Association of North Carolina **4715**
Learning Disabilities Association of North Dakota **4716**
Learning Disabilities Association of Ohio **4717**
Learning Disabilities Association of Oklahoma **4718**
Learning Disabilities Association of Pennsylvania **4719**
Learning Disabilities Association of Puerto Rico **4720**
Learning Disabilities Association of Rhode Island **4721**
Learning Disabilities Association of South Carolina **4722**
Learning Disabilities Association of Tennessee **4723**
Learning Disabilities Association of Texas **4724**
Learning Disabilities Association of Utah **4725**
Learning Disabilities Association of Vermont **4726**
Learning Disabilities Association of Virginia **4727**
Learning Disabilities Association of Washington **4728**
Learning Disabilities Association of West Virginia **4729**
Learning Disabilities Association of Wisconsin **4730**
Learning Disabilities; Canadian Association for Children and Adults with 4505
Learning Disabilities; Council for **4480**
Learning Disabilities; Division for Children with 4480
Learning Disabilities; Foundation for Children with 4521
Learning Disabilities; Institute for Research in • University of Kansas **4589**
Learning Disabilities; National Center for 4521
Learning Disabilities Special Interest Group **4293**
Learning Disabled Adults; National Network of 4531
Learning Disabled Student Sig 4293
Learning How **4506**
Learning and Memory; Center for the Neurobiology of • University of California, Irvine **8481**
Leavey Foundation; Thomas and Dorothy **518**
Lebanon; Save **1502**
Lebenshilfe **4296**
Lebenshilfe fur Geistig Behinderte; Bundesvereinigung 4296
Ledarska Spolocnost; Slovenska 1504
Lee Cancer Research Laboratory; Allie M. • University of Nevada, Reno **6234**
Legal Analysis; American Academy of Medical- **7160**
Legal Analysis in Medicine and Surgery; American Board of Medical- **7166**
Legal Center for the Medically Dependent and Disabled; National **7189**
Legal Duty; Children's Healthcare is a **3206**
Legal and Industrial Medicine; American Academy of 7172

Legal and Industrial Medicine; American Society of **7172**
Legal et de Medecine Sociale; Academie Internationale de Medecine **7178**
Legal Medicine; American College of **7168**
Legal Medicine, Quality Assurance, and Risk Management Department • Center for Advanced Pathology • Armed Forces Institute of Pathology • U.S. Department of Defense **10156**
Legal Medicine and Social Medicine; International Academy of **7178**
Legal Nurse Consultants; American Association of **7162**
Legal Nurse Consultants; National Association of Medical 7162
Legal Nurse Consultants; San Diego Association of Medical 7162
Legal Research Services and Databases; Mental and Physical Disability **4476**
Legal Resource Center; Mental Disability 4476
Legislation Against Molesters; Concerned Citizens for Stronger 3065
Legislative Council for the Handicapped; National **4530**
Lehigh Carbon Community College • Respiratory Therapist Program **11515**
Lehigh University
    Center for Social Research **1618**
    Institute for Health Sciences **2587**
Lehman College of the City University of New York; Harlem Hospital Center / Herbert H. • Nurse Anesthesia Program **2299**
Lehman College of the City University of New York; Herbert H. • Department of Nursing **8831**
Leighton-Oare Foundation **350**
Leisure Development; Blind Outdoor **13423**
Leland Fikes Foundation **351**
Lemilchama Besartan Beyisrael; Haagudah **5965**
Lenoir Rhyne College • Department of Nursing **8856**
Lens Research; Centre for Contact • University of Waterloo **13661**
Leo Burnett Co. Charitable Foundation **757**
Leo G. Rigler Center for Radiological Research • University of California, Los Angeles **11163**
Leon Lowenstein Foundation **352**
Leonard Cheshire Foundation International **4507**
Leonard Davis Institute of Health Economics • University of Pennsylvania **5657**
Leonard Wood Memorial (American Leprosy Foundation) **6689**
Leonard Wood Memorial for the Eradication of Leprosy 6689
LEPRA [Blantyre, Malawi] **6691**
LEPRA [Colchester, England] **6690**
Lepre; Federation Internationale des Associations Contre la 6680
Leprologists; Association of French-Language 6641
Leprologues de Langue Francaise; Association des 6641
Leprosy Aid; Damien Dutton Society for **6661**
Leprosy Association; China **6651**
Leprosy Foundation; American 6689
Leprosy; Leonard Wood Memorial for the Eradication of 6689
Leprosy Mission; International Christian **6679**
Leprosy Mission - Southern Africa **6692**
Leprosy Missions; American **6608, 6631**
Leprosy Relief Association; British 6690
Lesbian, and Bisexual Caucus of the American Psychiatric Association; Gay, 7325
Lesbian, and Bisexual Members of the American Psychiatric Association; Caucus of Gay, 7325
Lesbian / Gay Alcoholism Professionals; National Association of **11702**
Lesbian, Gay and Bisexual People in Medicine **11700**
Lesbian and Gay Caucus of Public Health Workers **10956**
Lesbian and Gay Health Association; National **11705**
Lesbian and Gay Issues; Society for the Psychological Study of **11714**
Lesbian and Gay People in Medicine 11700
Lesbian Psychiatrists; Association of Gay and 7325
Lester T. Sunderland Foundation **6371**
LeSukereth Neurim Beyisrael; Haagudah 3252
Let's Beat Deficits Committee 12018
Lettie Pate Whitehead Foundation **353**
Leukemia Association; National 5933
Leukemia Foundation; Friends of the Jose Carreras International **5946**
Leukemia Group B; Acute **6009**
Leukemia Group B; Cancer and **6009**
Leukemia and Related Diseases; International Association for Comparative Research on **5951**
Leukemia Research Association; Children's **5902, 5933**
Leukemia Society of America **5904, 5966**
Leukemia Stricken American Children; Aiding 3156
Leukemia Unit; Comparative • University of Pennsylvania 6241
Leukocyte Biology (A Reticuloendothelial Society); Society for **2090**
Leukocytes; Laboratory of Cell and Molecular Biology of • Duke University **2569**
Leukodystrophy Foundation; United **8321**
Levi Strauss Foundation **758**

Lions; American Council of Blind **13396**
Lions Eye Research Foundation; Missouri **13618**
Lions of Illinois Eye Research Institute • University of Illinois at Chicago **13651**
Lions Vision Research and Rehabilitation Center • Johns Hopkins University **13606**
Lipid Disorders; Research Centre on • Medical Research Centre • Laval University **2913**
Lipid Institute; Sequoia Hospital • University of California at Berkeley **2957**
Lipid Laboratory • University of Kansas **2967**
Lipid and Lipoprotein Laboratory • Oklahoma Medical Research Foundation **2918**
Lipid Metabolism Program; Arteriosclerosis, Hypertension, and • Division of Heart and Vascular Diseases • National Heart, Lung, and Blood Institute • U.S. Department of Health and Human Services **2934**
Lipid Nutrition Laboratory • Beltsville Human Nutrition Research Center • Agricultural Research Service • U.S. Department of Agriculture **9535**
Lipid Research Atherosclerosis Unit • Johns Hopkins University **2908**
Lipid Research Clinic
    George Washington University **2895**
    University of Iowa **2966**
Lipid Research Division; Atherosclerosis, Nutrition, and • Washington University **2988**
Lipid Research Laboratory • Texas A&M University **9528**
Lipid Research; Revici Foundation for **12747**
Lipoprotein Laboratory; Lipid and • Oklahoma Medical Research Foundation **2918**
Lipo-Suction Surgery; American Society of **12241**
Lipton Foundation; Thomas J. **877**
Lisa Foundation; Paul and **3064**
Lisa Madonia Memorial Fund **5967**
Lisa; Paul and **3064**
List Foundation; Albert A. **11180**
Listening and Mediation; Child Abuse **3048**
Lister Hill National Center for Biomedical Communications
    Audiovisual Program Development Branch • U.S. Department of Health and Human Services • National Institutes of Health **7030**
    Communications Engineering Branch • U.S. Department of Health and Human Services • National Institutes of Health **7031**
    Computer Science Branch • U.S. Department of Health and Human Services • National Institutes of Health **7032**
    Educational Technology Branch • U.S. Department of Health and Human Services • National Institutes of Health **7033**
    Information Technology Branch • U.S. Department of Health and Human Services • National Institutes of Health **7034**
    National Institutes of Health • U.S. Department of Health and Human Services **7029**
Literary and Medical Society; Benjamin Franklin **6980**
Lithotripsy Society; American **2417**
Litigation Group; Asbestos **7174**
Little City Foundation **4294**
Little Foundation; Arthur D. **586**
Little People of America **7886**
Liver and Biliary Diseases Program • Division of Digestive Diseases and Nutrition • National Institute of Diabetes and Digestive and Kidney Diseases • U.S. Department of Health and Human Services **5245**
Liver Center; Yale • Yale University **5255**
Liver Diseases; American Association for the Study of **5201**
Liver Foundation; American **5198, 5205**
Liver; International Association for the Study of the **5222**
Liver; Latin American Association for the Study of the **5226**
Liver Program Project • Virginia Commonwealth University **5254**
Liver Research Center; Marion Bessin • Yeshiva University **5256**
Liver Research Unit • University of Southern California **5253**
Liver Study Unit • University of Chicago **5251**
Liver Transplant Division • University of California, San Francisco **12889**
Livermore National Laboratory; Lawrence
    Hazards Control Department • Special Projects Division • U.S. Department of Energy **9822**
    U.S. Department of Energy **2634**
Livestock Diseases and Human Health; Center of Excellence in • University of Tennessee, Knoxville **13235**
Livestock Insects Laboratory • Livestock and Poultry Sciences Institute • Agricultural Research Service • U.S. Department of Agriculture **13191**
Livestock Insects Laboratory; Knipling- Bushland U.S.
    Agricultural Research Service • U.S. Department of Agriculture **13187**
    Cattle Fever Tick Research Laboratory • U.S. Department of Agriculture • Agricultural Research Service **13188**
Livestock Research Center; Clayton • New Mexico State University **13150**
Livestock Sanitary Association; United States **13111**
The Living Bank **12873**
Living / Dying Project **3718**

The Living Room **7507**
Liz Claiborne Foundation **759**
Lloyd A. Fry Foundation **357**
LMBB i Norge; Interesseforeningen fur **5297**
LMBB's Syndrome Association; Norwegian **5297**
LMBS Network **5284**
Lobund Laboratory • University of Notre Dame **2683**
Local Boards of Health; National Association of **1402**
Local Environmental Health Administrators; Conference of **5594**
Local Environmental Health Administrators; National Conference of **5594**
Local and Family Health Administration • Public Health Services Office • Maryland Department of Health and Mental Hygiene **3398, 9744**
Local Health Officers; United States Conference of **5605**
Locomotion Studies; Center for • Pennsylvania State University **9947**
Loews Foundation **760**
Logan College of Chiropractic **3441**
Logopedics and Phoniatrics; International Association of **3530**
Logopedie et Phoniatrie; Association Internationale de **3530**
Lok Swasthya Parampara Samuardhan Samithi **2222**
Lok Swasthya Parampara Samvardhan **2222**
Loma Linda University
    Health Information Administration Program **6917**
    School of Allied Health Professions
        Department of Nutrition and Dietetics **9387**
        Department of Occupational Therapy **12337**
        Department of Physical Therapy **12447**
        Respiratory Therapy Program **11325**
    School of Dentistry **3788**
    School of Medicine **927**
        Department of Physiology and Pharmacology **10193**
    School of Nursing **8582**
    School of Public Health **10907**
    Sleep Disorders Center **8385**
Lombardi Cancer Research Center; Vincent T. • Georgetown University **6041**
Lon V. Smith Foundation **358**
Lone Star Chapter • Cystic Fibrosis Foundation **5461**
Long Hansen's Disease Center; Gillis W. • Health Resources and Services Administration • U.S. Department of Health and Human Services **6793**
Long Island Chapter • Arthritis Foundation **8000**
Long Island Division • American Cancer Society **6303**
Long Island Jewish Medical Center • Nuclear Medicine Division **11149**
Long Island Office • Greater New York Chapter • Cystic Fibrosis Foundation **5442**
Long Island Society of Anesthetists **2353**
Long Island University
    Arnold and Marie Schwartz College of Pharmacy and Health Sciences **10540**
    Division of Physical Therapy **12516**
    Health Information Administration Program **6942**
    Pharmaceutical Study Center **10629**
    Respiratory Therapist Program **11464**
    School of Health Professions • Division of Nursing **8834**
Long Island University / Brooklyn Hospital Center • Physician Assistant Program **1091**
Long Term Care Association; North Dakota **9360**
Long Term Care Campaign **5736**
Long-Term Care Experimentation Division • Office of Demonstrations and Evaluations • Health Care Financing Administration • U.S. Department of Health and Human Services **5757**
Long-Term Care, and Health Insurance; Subcommittee on Medicare, • Committee on Finance • U.S. Senate **5717**
Long Term Care; National Association of Directors of Nursing Administration in **5585**
Long-Term Care; National Institute on Community-Based **1914**
Long Term Care Services; Assembly of Skilled Nursing and Related **6472**
Long Term Care Services; Skilled Nursing and Related **6472**
Long Term Care Services; Special Constituency Section for Aging and **6472**
Long Term Care; Special Constituency Section on Aging and **6472**
Long Term Health Care Administrators; South Carolina Board of **9315**
Longevity and Society; International Leadership Center on • Mount Sinai School of Medicine of City University of New York **1941**
Longitudinal Studies Branch • Intramural Research Program • National Institute on Aging • U.S. Department of Health and Human Services **1955**
Longwood Foundation **359**
Loren M. Berry Foundation **360**
Los Alamos National Laboratory • Quality, Environment, Safety, and Health Assurance Division • U.S. Department of Energy **9823**
Los Amigos Research and Education Institute, Inc. **1619**
Los Angeles Affiliate; Greater • American Heart Association **2994**

Lung Association of Indiana; American **11641**
Lung Association of Iowa; American **11642**
Lung Association of Kansas; American **11643**
Lung Association of Kentucky; American **11644**
Lung Association of Louisiana; American **11645**
Lung Association of Maine; American **11646**
Lung Association of Maryland; American **11647**
Lung Association of Massachusetts; American **11648**
Lung Association of Metropolitan Chicago; American **11640**
Lung Association of Michigan; American **11649**
Lung Association of Minnesota; American **11650**
Lung Association of Mississippi; American **11651**
Lung Association of Montana; American **11654**
Lung Association of Nebraska; American **11655**
Lung Association of Nevada; American **11656**
Lung Association of New Hampshire; American **11657**
Lung Association of New Jersey; American **11658**
Lung Association of New Mexico; American **11659**
Lung Association of New York; American **11661**
Lung Association of New York State; American **11662**
Lung Association of North Carolina; American **11664**
Lung Association of North Dakota; American **11665**
Lung Association of Ohio; American **11666**
Lung Association of Oklahoma; American **11667**
Lung Association of Oregon; American **11668**
Lung Association of Pennsylvania; American **11669**
Lung Association of Queens; American **11663**
Lung Association of Rhode Island; American **11671**
Lung Association of South Carolina; American **11672**
Lung Association of South Dakota; American **11673**
Lung Association Staff; Congress of **11594**
Lung Association of Tennessee; American **11674**
Lung Association of Texas; American **11675**
Lung Association of Utah; American **11676**
Lung Association of Vermont; American **11677**
Lung Association of the Virgin Islands; American **11678**
Lung Association of Virginia; American **11679**
Lung Association of Washington; American **11680**
Lung Association of West Virginia; American **11681**
Lung Association of Western Missouri; American **11653**
Lung Association; White **11607**
Lung Association of Wisconsin; American **11682**
Lung Association of Wyoming; American **11683**
Lung Associations; Nordic Federation of Heart and **2868**
Lung Biology; Center for Environmental Medicine and • University of North Carolina at Chapel Hill **5126**
Lung, and Blood Institute; National Heart,
    Division of Blood Diseases and Resources • U.S. Department of Health and Human Services **6203**
    Division of Epidemiology and Clinical Applications
        Clinical Applications and Prevention Program • U.S. Department of Health and Human Services **2931**
        Epidemiology and Biometry Program • U.S. Department of Health and Human Services **2932**
        U.S. Department of Health and Human Services **2930**
    Division of Heart and Vascular Diseases
        Arteriosclerosis, Hypertension, and Lipid Metabolism Program • U.S. Department of Health and Human Services **2934**
        Cardiac Functions Branch • U.S. Department of Health and Human Services **2935**
        Cardiology Program • U.S. Department of Health and Human Services **2936**
        Devices and Technology Branch • U.S. Department of Health and Human Services **2937**
        Research Training and Development Branch • U.S. Department of Health and Human Services **2938**
        U.S. Department of Health and Human Services **2933**
    Division of Intramural Research
        Cardiology Branch • U.S. Department of Health and Human Services **2940**
        Hematology Branch • U.S. Department of Health and Human Services **6204**
        Hypertension-Endocrine Branch • U.S. Department of Health and Human Services **2941**
        Laboratory of Molecular Hematology • U.S. Department of Health and Human Services **6205**
        Molecular Disease Branch • U.S. Department of Health and Human Services **2942**
        Pathology Branch • U.S. Department of Health and Human Services **2943**
        Pulmonary Branch • U.S. Department of Health and Human Services **11613**

        U.S. Department of Health and Human Services **2939**
    Division of Lung Diseases
        Airways Diseases Branch • U.S. Department of Health and Human Services **11615**
        Cell and Developmental Biology Branch • U.S. Department of Health and Human Services **11616**
        Interstitial Lung Diseases Branch • U.S. Department of Health and Human Services **11617**
        Prevention, Education, and Research Training Branch • U.S. Department of Health and Human Services **11618**
        U.S. Department of Health and Human Services **11614**
    Laboratory of Biochemical Genetics • U.S. Department of Health and Human Services **2944**
    Laboratory of Biochemistry • U.S. Department of Health and Human Services **2945**
    Laboratory of Biophysical Chemistry • U.S. Department of Health and Human Services **2946**
    Laboratory of Cardiac Energetics • U.S. Department of Health and Human Services **2947**
    Laboratory of Cell Biology • U.S. Department of Health and Human Services **2948**
    Laboratory of Cellular Metabolism • U.S. Department of Health and Human Services **2949**
    Laboratory of Chemical Pharmacology • U.S. Department of Health and Human Services **2950**
    Laboratory of Kidney and Electrolyte Metabolism • U.S. Department of Health and Human Services **2951**
    Laboratory of Molecular Cardiology • U.S. Department of Health and Human Services **2952**
    U.S. Department of Health and Human Services **2781, 2929**
Lung Cancer; International Association for the Study of **5952**
Lung Disease, Cancer, Lymphocytes, Air Pollution, and General Pathobiology Unit • University of Southern California **10181**
Lung Disease; International Union Against Tuberculosis and **11599**
Lung Diseases Branch; Interstitial • Division of Lung Diseases • National Heart, Lung, and Blood Institute • U.S. Department of Health and Human Services **11617**
Lung Diseases; Division of • National Heart, Lung, and Blood Institute • U.S. Department of Health and Human Services **11614**
Lung Institute; Webb-Waring **2705**
Lung and Respiratory Disease Clinics; National Coalition of Black **11604**
Lung Transplantation; International Society for Heart and **12871**
Lupus Foundation of America **7857, 7887**
    Akron Area Chapter **8094**
    Alaska Chapter **8030**
    Arkansas Chapter **8033**
    Bay Area Chapter **8034**
    Birmingham Chapter **8028**
    Bronx Chapter **8080**
    Cenla Chapter **8058**
    Central New York Chapter **8081**
    Central Virginia Chapter **8116**
    Charlotte Chapter **8091**
    Colorado Chapter **8036**
    Columbus Chapter **8046**
    Columbus, Marcy Zitron Chapter **8095**
    Connecticut Chapter **8037**
    Danville Chapter **8050**
    Delaware Chapter **8038**
    Delaware Valley Chapter **8099**
    East Tennessee Chapter **8106**
    Eastern Virginia Chapter **8117**
    El Paso Chapter **8109**
    Florida Chapter **8040**
    Genesee Valley Chapter **8082**
    Greater Arizona Chapter **8031**
    Greater Atlanta Chapter **8047**
    Greater Cleveland Chapter **8096**
    Greater Washington, DC Chapter **8039**
    Hawaii Chapter **8048**
    Idaho Chapter **8049**
    Illinois Chapter **8051**
    Indiana Chapter **8052**
    Iowa Chapter **8055**
    Kanawha Valley Chapter **8118**
    Kansas City Chapter **8068**
    Kentuckiana Chapter **8057**
    Las Vegas Chapter **8074**
    Long Island/Queens Chapter **8083**
    Louisiana Chapter **8059**
    Lubbock Area Chapter **8110**
    Maine Chapter **8062**

Marguerite Curri Chapter **8084**
Maryland Chapter **8063**
Massachusetts Chapter **8064**
Memphis Area Chapter **8107**
Michigan Chapter **8065**
Minnesota Chapter **8066**
Mississippi Chapter **8067**
Missouri Chapter **8069**
Montana Chapter **8071**
Montgomery Chapter **8029**
Nashville Area Chapter **8108**
New Hampshire Chapter **8076**
New Jersey Chapter **8077**
New Mexico Chapter **8079**
New York Southern Tier Chapter **8085**
North Texas Chapter **8111**
Northeast Florida Chapter **8041**
Northeast Indiana Chapter **8053**
Northeast Louisiana Chapter **8060**
Northeast Pennsylvania Chapter **8100**
Northeastern New York Chapter **8086**
Northern Nevada Chapter **8075**
Northwest Florida Chapter **8042**
Northwest Indiana Chapter **8054**
Northwest Ohio Lupus Chapter **8097**
Northwestern Pennsylvania Chapter **8101**
Oklahoma Chapter **8098**
Omaha Chapter **8072**
Ozarks Chapter **8070**
Philadelphia Chapter **8102**
Raleigh Chapter **8092**
Rhode Island Chapter **8104**
Rockland/Orange County Chapter **8087**
Shreveport Chapter **8061**
South Carolina Chapter **8105**
South Central Texas Chapter **8112**
South Jersey Chapter **8078**
Southeast Florida Chapter **8043**
Southern Arizona Chapter **8032**
Southern California Chapter **8035**
Suncoast Chapter **8044**
Tampa Area Chapter **8045**
Texas Gulf Coast Chapter **8113**
Utah Chapter **8114**
Vermont Chapter **8115**
Westchester Chapter **8088**
Western Nebraska Chapter **8073**
Western New York Chapter **8089**
Western Pennsylvania Chapter **8103**
Wichita Chapter **8056**
Winston-Triad Chapter **8093**
Wisconsin Chapter **8119**
Lupus and Immunology Research; Gwen Knapp Center for • University of Chicago **7947**
Lupus Network **7888**
Lupus Research Institute; Terri Gotthelf **7933**
Lupus Society; American **7855, 7863**
Lupus Study Center • Thomas Jefferson University **7934**
Lurie Cancer Center; Robert H. • Northwestern University **6094**
Lurie Foundation; Louis R. **364**
Lurleen B. Wallace College of Nursing • Jacksonville State University **8547**
Luther College • Department of Nursing **8696**
Lutheran Braille Evangelism Association **13516**
Lutheran Braille Workers **13517**
Lutheran Good Samaritan Society; Ev. **1281**
Lutheran Homes and Services; Bethesda **4285**
Lutheran Hospital Association of America **6455**
Lutheran Hospitals and Homes Society **6456**
Lutheran Liaison/National Christian Resource Center **4285**
Luxembourg; Diabetic Association of **4836**
Luxembourg Dietetic Association **9472**
Luxembourgeoise du Diabete; Association **4836**
Lycoming College • Department of Nursing **8920**
Lyme Borreliosis Foundation **7889**
Lyme Disease Center • University of Medicine and Dentistry of New Jersey **7952**
Lyme Disease Foundation **7889**
Lymphatic Pathology Department; Hematologic and • Center for Advanced Pathology • Armed Forces Institute of Pathology • U.S. Department of Defense **10153**
Lymphedema Network; National **4862**

Lymphocytes, Air Pollution, and General Pathobiology Unit; Lung Disease, Cancer, • University of Southern California **10181**
Lymphokine Research Laboratory • Ohio State University **6097**
Lymphologie; Groupement Europeen de **5940**
Lymphology; European Group of **5940**
Lymphology; International Society of **5960**
Lynchburg College • Department of Nursing **9013**
Lyndon B. Johnson Space Center
    Medical Sciences Division • Space Administration; National Aeronautics and **2390**
    Space Biomedical Research Institute • Space Administration; National Aeronautics and **2391**
Lyndon C. Whitaker Charitable Foundation **6372**
Lynn Foundation; E. M. **151**
Lynn R. and Karl E. Prickett Fund **11188**
Lynn University • Institute for Funeral Service Education **3667**
Lysosomal Diseases; European Study Group on **4841**
Lytico and Bodig Association; Guam **1310**

M

M.D. Anderson Cancer Center; University of Texas • University of Texas **6253**
M. D. Anderson Foundation **368**
M. G. and Lillie A. Johnson Foundation **369**
M. J. Murdock Charitable Trust **370**
M. R. Bauer Foundation **371**
M. S. Doss Foundation **372**
Ma Ayesha Memorial Center for Care and Control of Neuromuscular Diseases **8250**
Mabee Foundation; J. E. and L. E. **295**
MacArthur Foundation; John D. and Catherine T. **7230**
Machine-Environment Systems Laboratory; Man- • University of California, Los Angeles **2478**
Machne Israel **1373**
MacMurray College • Nursing Department **8653**
Macomb Community College • Respiratory Therapist Program **11430**
Macromolecular Design; Center for • Texas A&M University **2628**
Macromolecules; Center for Biological • University at Albany, State University of New York **2659**
Macula Foundation, Inc. **13614**
Macular Diseases; Association for **13413**
Macy, Jr. Foundation; Josiah **332**
Madagascar Pediatrics Society **3254**
Madison Area Technical College • Respiratory Therapist Program **11581**
Madison University; James • Department of Nursing **9011**
Madisonville Community College • Consortium for Respiratory Care Education **11401**
Madonia Memorial Fund; Lisa **5967**
Madonna University • College of Nursing • Baccalaureate Nursing Program **8764**
MADRE **1374**
Madres de Minusvalidos; Asociacion Ayuda a **9631**
Magic; Project **12711**
Magnetic Resonance; Center for • Massachusetts Institute of Technology **11150**
Magnetic Resonance Center; Mary Nell and Ralph B. Rogers • University of Texas Southwestern Medical Center at Dallas **11175**
Magnetic Resonance Imaging Center; UCI / AMI **11156**
Magnetic Resonance Imaging; Society for **11136**
Magnetic Resonance Laboratory; Kettering-Scott **11147**
Magnetic Resonance Research and Computing Center; Metabolic • University of Pennsylvania **11172**
Magnetic Resonance; Society of **11135**
Magnetic Resonance; Society of Computed Body Tomography and **11133**
Magnuson Clinical Center; Warren Grant
    National Institutes of Health • U.S. Department of Health and Human Services **1679**
    U.S. Department of Health and Human Services **2515**
Magyar Dermatologiai Tarsulat **4239**
Magyar Kardiologusok Tarsasaga **2852**
Magyar Korhazszovetseg **6446**
Magyar Orvostudomanyi Tarsasagok es Egyesuletek Szovetsege **1289**
Magyar Taplalkozastudomanyi Tarsasag **9462**
Mahadh Foundation **373**
Maharishi International University • Laboratory for Health and Aging Studies **1622**
Mahoney Institute of Neurological Sciences; David • University of Pennsylvania **8520**
Mahoning, Trumbull and Columbiana Counties; Easter Seal Society of **4659**

American Heart Association   **3011**
Maryland; American Lung Association of   **11647**
Maryland; Arc of   **4412**
Maryland Board of Examiners for Nursing Home Administrators   **9295**
Maryland Board of Examiners in Optometry   **13738**
Maryland Board of Nursing   **9176**
Maryland Board of Pharmacy   **10661**
Maryland Board of Physician Quality Assurance   **1777, 10033**
Maryland Board of Podiatric Medicine   **10799**
Maryland Chapter
    American Physical Therapy Association   **12839**
    Arthritis Foundation   **7986**
    Cystic Fibrosis Foundation   **5424**
    Lupus Foundation of America   **8063**
    National Association of Social Workers   **11900**
Maryland Department of Agriculture • Food Safety Consumer Services Office • Animal Health Division   **13269**
Maryland Department of Education
    Vocational Rehabilitation Division   **12790**
        Blind Services Office   **13685**
Maryland Department of the Environment • Environmental Health Coordinator   **5148**
Maryland Department of Health and Mental Hygiene
    Alcohol and Drug Abuse Administration   **12167**
    Developmental Disabilities Administration   **4363**
    Health Resources Planning Commission   **5683**
    Licensing and Certification Administration   **6496**
    Local and Family Health Administration • Dental Program   **4122**
    Medical Care Policy Administration • Medical Care Finance and Compliance Division   **5788**
    Mental Hygiene Administration   **7728**
    Policy and Health Statistics Division   **7060**
    Public Health Services Office   **11025**
        AIDS Administration   **6876**
        Local and Family Health Administration   **3398, 9744**
Maryland Department of Licensing and Regulation • Labor and Industry Division • Occupational Safety and Health Section   **9885**
Maryland Division • American Cancer Society   **6291**
Maryland; Health Facilities Association of   **9346**
Maryland Hospital Association   **6547**
Maryland Institute for Emergency Medical Services Systems   **4787**
Maryland; Learning Disabilities Association of   **4703**
Maryland; Medical and Chirurgical Faculty of the State of   **1831**
Maryland Medical Research Institute   **7017**
Maryland; Mental Health Association of   **7768**
Maryland; National Kidney Foundation of   **12952**
Maryland Network Against Domestic Violence   **3096**
Maryland Nurses Association   **9232**
Maryland Office on Aging   **2022**
Maryland Optometric Association   **13813**
Maryland Osteopathic Association   **10086**
Maryland Pharmacists Association   **10714**
Maryland Psychiatric Research Center   **7580**
Maryland Society on Alcoholism   **12006**
Maryland State Board of Dental Examiners   **4069**
Maryland State Board of Morticians   **3748**
Maryland State Dental Association   **4175**
Maryland Veterinary Medical Association   **13322**
Maryville University
    Department of Nursing   **8791**
    Department of Physical Therapy   **12500**
Marywood College
    Department of Human Ecology • Dietetics Program   **9421**
    Department of Nursing   **8922**
    School of Social Work   **11838**
Masco Corp. Charitable Trust   **767**
Mason Research Center; Virginia   **1745**
Mason University; George • College of Nursing and Health • Baccalaureate Nursing Program   **9009**
Masonic Cancer Center • University of Minnesota   **6232**
Masonic Medical Research Laboratory   **1627**
Mass Spectrometry Facility • University of California, San Francisco   **2666**
Mass Spectrometry Laboratory; Middle Atlantic • Johns Hopkins University   **2451**
Mass Spectrometry Research Resource; Clinical • University of Colorado   **2481**
Massachusetts Affiliate
    American Diabetes Association   **4972**
    American Heart Association   **3012**
Massachusetts Alzheimer's Disease Research Center   **8389**
Massachusetts; American Lung Association of   **11648**

Massachusetts Board of Examiners in Podiatry   **10800**
Massachusetts Board of Pharmacy   **10662**
Massachusetts Board of Registration in Dentistry   **4070**
Massachusetts Board of Registration in Embalming and Funeral Service   **3749**
Massachusetts Board of Registration in Medicine   **1778, 10034**
Massachusetts Board of Registration in Nursing   **9177**
Massachusetts Board of Registration for Nursing Home Administrators   **9296**
Massachusetts Board of Registration in Optometry   **13739**
Massachusetts Chapter
    American Physical Therapy Association   **12840**
    Arthritis Foundation   **7987**
    Cystic Fibrosis Foundation   **5425**
    Lupus Foundation of America   **8064**
    National Association of Social Workers   **11901**
Massachusetts Coalition of Battered Women Service Groups   **3097**
Massachusetts College of Pharmacy and Allied Health Sciences
    Department of Pharmacology   **10261**
    Pharmacy Programs   **10526**
Massachusetts Commission for the Blind   **13686**
Massachusetts Dental Society   **4176**
Massachusetts Department of Elder Affairs   **2023**
Massachusetts Division • American Cancer Society   **6292**
Massachusetts Easter Seal Society   **4643**
Massachusetts Executive Office of Environmental Affairs • Food and Agriculture Department • Animal Health Division   **13270**
Massachusetts Executive Office of Health and Human Services
    Medical Assistance Division   **5789**
    Mental Health Department   **7729**
    Mental Retardation Services Department   **4364**
    Public Health Department   **11026**
        AIDS Office   **6877**
        Dental Health Division   **4123**
        Emergency Medical Services Division   **4788**
        Environmental Assessment Division   **5149**
        Family Health Services Division   **3399, 9745**
        Health Care Quality Division   **6497**
        Policy and Planning Office   **5684**
        Substance Abuse Division   **12168**
        Vital Records and Statistics Division   **7061**
Massachusetts Executive Office of Labor • Labor and Industries Department • OSHA Consultation Division   **9886**
Massachusetts Federation of Nursing Homes   **9347**
Massachusetts General Hospital
    Harvard Cutaneous Biology Research Center   **4265**
    Reproductive Endocrine Unit   **4895**
Massachusetts Health Data Consortium   **7018**
Massachusetts Health Research Institute, Inc.   **1628**
Massachusetts Hospital Association   **6548**
Massachusetts Institute of Technology
    Center for Biological and Computational Learning   **8390**
    Center for Cancer Research   **6067**
    Center for Environmental Health Sciences   **5079**
    Center for Magnetic Resonance   **11150**
    Clinical Research Center   **1629**
    Eric P. and Evelyn E. Newman Laboratory for Biomechanics and Human Rehabilitation   **2453**
    Laboratory of Neuroendocrine Regulation   **8391**
    Laser Biomedical Research Center   **11151**
Massachusetts; Learning Disabilities Association of   **4704**
Massachusetts Medical Society   **1832**
Massachusetts Nurses Association   **9233**
Massachusetts Osteopathic Society   **10087**
Massachusetts Pharmacists Association   **10715**
Massachusetts Rehabilitation Commission   **12791**
Massachusetts and Rhode Island; National Kidney Foundation of   **12953, 12974**
Massachusetts Society of Law and Medicine   **7171**
Massachusetts Society of Optometrists   **13814**
Massachusetts Veterinary Medical Association   **13323**
Massage Federation; International Sports   **11948**
Massage Federation; United States Sports   **11952**
Massage Professionals; Associated Bodywork and   **2177**
Massage Therapists and Allied Health Practitioners International; Associated Professional   **2177**
Massage Therapists and Bodyworkers; Associated Professional   **2177**
Massage Therapists; National Association of Nurse   **9104**
Massage Therapy Association; American   **12654**
Massasoit Community College • Respiratory Therapist Program   **11417**
Masseurs and Masseuses; American Association of   **12654**

Medical and Dental Society; Cayman Islands **1229**

Medical Department • Brookhaven National Laboratory • U.S. Department of Energy **1674**

Medical Directors of America; Association of Life Insurance 5719

Medical Editors' Association; Mississippi Valley 6970

Medical Education of the American Medical Association; Council on **1260**

Medical Education; Liaison Committee on Continuing 1120

Medical Education; Liaison Committee on Graduate 1121

Medical Education; Northwest Center for • Indiana University Northwest **1604**

Medical Engineering; Pritzker Institute of • Illinois Institute of Technology **2448**

Medical Equipment Suppliers; National Association of 5867

Medical Ethics; European Association of Centres of **7175**

Medical Examiners; Alabama State Board of **1756, 10012**

Medical Examiners; Arizona State Board of **1758**

Medical Examiners Association; Airline 2383

Medical Examiners; Colorado State Board of **1761, 10017**

Medical Examiners; Georgia Composite State Board of **1766, 10022**

Medical Examiners; Guam Board of **1767, 10023**

Medical Examiners; Hawaii Board of **1768, 10024**

Medical Examiners; Iowa State Board of **1772, 10028**

Medical Examiners; Louisiana Board of **10797**

Medical Examiners; Louisiana State Board of **1775, 10031**

Medical Examiners; Montana Board of **1783, 10039**

Medical Examiners; Nevada State Board of **1785**

Medical Examiners; New Jersey Board of **10809**

Medical Examiners; New Jersey State Board of **1787, 10043**

Medical Examiners; New Mexico State Board of **1788**

Medical Examiners; North Carolina Board of **1790, 10046**

Medical Examiners; North Dakota State Board of **1791, 10047**

Medical Examiners; Oregon Board of **1794, 10050, 10816**

Medical Examiners; Puerto Rico Board of **1796, 10052**

Medical Examiners; South Carolina Board of **1798, 10054**

Medical Examiners; Tennessee State Board of **1800**

Medical Examiners; Texas State Board of **1801, 10057**

Medical Examiners; Virgin Islands Board of **1804, 10060**

Medical Examining Board; Wisconsin **1808, 10064**

Medical Facilities Services • Oklahoma Department of Health **6512**

Medical; Federation Mondiale pour l' Enseignement 1539

Medical Foundation of Buffalo, Inc. 4886

Medical Genetics Laboratory • Florida Institute of Technology 5330

Medical Graduates; Educational Commission for Foreign **1273**

Medical Graduates; Educational Council for Foreign 1273

Medical Group Administrators; American College of 5547

Medical Group Management Association **5584**

Medical Group Missions of the Christian Medical and Dental Society **1381**

Medical and Health Association; Interamerican **1332**

Medical Heritage Center; Cincinnati • University of Cincinnati **1693**

Medical Hydrology; International Society of 5046

Medical Illustration; Center for • Armed Forces Institute of Pathology • U.S. Department of Defense **7025**

Medical Institute; American Holistic 2166

Medical Institute; Howard Hughes **1600**

Medical Instrumentation Laboratory • University of Wisconsin—Madison **2503**

Medical Jurisprudence and State Medicine; Society of 7193

Medical Laboratory / Omegatech; King James **9507**

Medical Laboratory Schools; Accrediting Bureau of 7113

Medical Laboratory Technologists of Zimbabwe; Association of **7127**

Medical pour l'Aide a la Recherche Cancerologique; Federation Internationale du Sport 5954

Medical Laser Technology Center 12321

Medical Legal Nurse Consultants; National Association of 7162

Medical Legal Nurse Consultants; San Diego Association of 7162

Medical Letter **10417**

Medical Library Association **7007**

Medical Licensing Board • Indiana Health Professions Bureau **1771**

Medical Licensure and Discipline; Rhode Island Board of **1797, 10053**

Medical Licensure; Kentucky Board of **1774, 10030**

Medical Licensure; Mississippi State Board of **1781, 10037, 10803**

Medical Licensure and Supervision; Oklahoma State Board of **1793**

Medical Mission Sisters **1382**

Medical Museums; International Association of 10131

Medical Mycological Society of the Americas **6694**

Medical Nephropathology Division • Genitourinary Pathology Department • Armed Forces Institute of Pathology • U.S. Department of Defense **10166**

Medical Network for Missing Children **3258**

Medical Neurology Branch • National Institute of Neurological Disorders and Stroke • U.S. Department of Health and Human Services **8467**

Medical Officers of American Institutions of Idiotic and Feebleminded Children; Association of 4277

Medical Officers of Health; Society of 10968

Medical Oncology Research Program • University of Southern California **6248**

Medical and Osteopathic Examiners; South Dakota State Board of **1799**

Medical Outreach for Armenians **1383**

Medical Physics; Latin American Association for **2539**

Medical Practice; Delaware Board of **1763, 10019**

Medical Practice; Minnesota Board of **1780, 10036**

Medical Practice; Vermont Board of **1803, 10059**

Medical Practice; Vermont State Board of **10825**

Medical Practitioners; German Association of Non- **2196**

Medical Preventics; American Academy of 10837

Medical Programs Division • Illinois Department of Public Aid **5781**

Medical Psycho-theatrerapy; International Federation of 7410

Medical Quality Assurance; Connecticut State Board of **1762, 10018**

Medical QUEST Division • Hawaii Department of Human Services **5779**

Medical Radiological Technicians Belgium **11126**

Medical Record Economics; Institute for 7008

Medical Record Librarians; American Association of 6968

Medical Records Association; American 6968

Medical Records Institute **7008**

Medical Records Officers; Association of Health Care Information & 7001

Medical Rehabilitation Research and Training Center • New York University **12738**

Medical Rehabilitation Research & Training Center in Childhood Trauma • Tufts University **12754**

Medical Rehabilitation Research and Training Center for Multiple Sclerosis • New York Medical College **8406**

Medical Rehabilitation Research and Training Center in Secondary Complications in Spinal Cord Injury • University of Alabama at Birmingham **12755**

Medical Research; California Institute for **1563**

Medical Research Centre • Laval University **1615**

Medical Research; Coriell Institute for **2568**

Medical Research Council of New Zealand 1318

Medical and Research Foundation; African 1131

Medical and Research Foundation; International 1131

Medical Research Foundation; Santa Barbara 9483

Medical Research; Heineman **2901**

Medical Research; Hektoen Institute for **1599**

Medical Research Institute Detachment (Toxicology); Naval • Naval Medical Research and Development Command • U.S. Department of Defense **7851**

Medical Research Institute; Naval

    Casualty Care Research Department • U.S. Department of Defense • Naval Medical Research and Development Command **7847**

    Diving Medicine Department • U.S. Department of Defense • Naval Medical Research and Development Command **7848**

    Immune Cell Biology Program • U.S. Department of Defense • Naval Medical Research and Development Command **7849**

    Infectious Diseases Department • U.S. Department of Defense • Naval Medical Research and Development Command **7850**

    Naval Medical Research and Development Command • U.S. Department of Defense **7846**

Medical Research Institute of San Francisco 1564

Medical Research Institute of Worcester, Inc. **4896**

Medical Research Institutes; Huntington **8372**

Medical Research Institutes; Wesley **1751**

Medical Research Modernization Committee **1384**

Medical Research, San Jose; Institute for 1563

Medical School Departments of Pathology; American Association of Chairmen of 10126

Medical Schools in Europe; Association of **1209**

Medical Sciences Division • Lyndon B. Johnson Space Center • National Aeronautics and Space Administration **2390**

Medical Sciences; Institutes of 1564

Medical Scientist Training Program • National Institute of General Medical Sciences • U.S. Department of Health and Human Services **2652**

Medical Service Association of America; Ambulance and 4732

Medical Services; American Society of Hospital-Based Emergency Air 4737

Medical Services Bureau • Human Services Division • New Hampshire Department of Health and Human Services **5797**

Medical Services Division

    Arkansas Department of Human Services **5771**

    Nebraska Department of Social Services **5795**

    North Dakota Department of Human Services **5802**

    Rhode Island Department of Human Services **5807**

Medical Services Office • Program Management Division • South Dakota Department of Social Services **5809**

Medical Society of Acupuncture; Swiss   2240
Medical Society on Alcoholism; New York City   12010
Medical Society on Alcoholism and Other Drug Dependencies; American   12010
Medical Society; Alpha Omega Alpha Honor   **1134**
Medical Society; American Chinese   **1237**
Medical Society; American Ukrainian   **1522**
Medical Society; Christian   **1241**
Medical Society of Delaware   **1817**
Medical Society of the District of Columbia   **1818**
Medical Society Executives; American Association of   **1142**
Medical Society Executives Association   1142
Medical Society of New Jersey   **1841**
Medical Society; People's   **1467**
Medical Society of the State of New York   **1843**
Medical Society for the Study of Venereal Diseases   **6695**
Medical Society of the United States and Mexico [Los Angeles, CA]   **1385**
Medical Society of the United States and Mexico [Phoenix, AZ]   **1386**
Medical Society of Virginia   **1859**
Medical Specialties Division • Federal Aviation Administration • U.S. Department of Transportation   **2410**
Medical Specialty Societies; Council of   **1261**
Medical Staff Services; National Association   **5587**
Medical Superintendents of American Institutions for Insane; Association of   **7301**
Medical Superintendents Club   5602
Medical Superintendents of Mental Hospitals; Association of   5542
Medical Technicians - Ambulance; Registry of Emergency   4752
Medical Technologists; American Society of   7122
Medical Technologists; Registered Medical Assistants of American   **1490**
Medical Technology; American Society for   7122
Medical Technology; Center for Advanced • San Francisco State University   **2619**
Medical Technology and Practice Patterns Institute, Inc.   **2720**
Medical Toxicology of the American Academy of Clinical Toxicology; American Board of   10392
Medical Ultrasound Group; British   11105
Medical University of South Carolina
    Arthritis Clinical and Research Center   **7923**
    College of Dental Medicine   **3831**
    College of Health Professions
        Department of Health Administration and Policy • Master of Health Administration Program   **5522**
        ECT Educational Program   **2818**
    College of Health Related Professions
        Anesthesia for Nurses Program   **2329**
        Department of Health Information Administration   **6956**
        Occupational Therapy Educational Department   **12422**
    College of Medicine   **1030**
        Department of Pharmacology   **10350**
    College of Nursing   **8958**
        Graduate Program in Nurse-Midwifery   **9612**
    College of Pharmacy   **10560**
    Crime Victims Research and Treatment Center   **7210**
    Department of Health Administration and Policy • Applied Research Division   **5633**
    General Clinical Research Center   **1632**
    Interdisciplinary Program in Cell and Molecular Pharmacology and Experimental Therapeutics   **10445**
    Marine Biomedical and Environmental Sciences   **2592**
    Physical Therapy Program   **12544**
    Storm Eye Institute   **13616**
    Vince Moseley Center for Children with Developmental Disabilities   **4579**
Medical and Veterinary Entomology Research Laboratory • Agricultural Research Service • U.S. Department of Agriculture   **13193**
Medical Women's International Association   **1387**
Medical Women's Organisation; New Zealand   **1438**
Medicale; Association Canadienne des Technologues en Radiation   11106
Medicale et les Echanges Culturels; Association Internationale pour la Recherche   1337
Medicale; Federation Internationale des Organismes de Psychologie   7409
Medicale Mondiale; Association   1546
Medicale; Societe Internationale d' Hydrologie et de Climatologie   5046
Medicales Agrees au Rwanda; Bureau des Formations   1295
Medicales Catholiques; Federation Internationale des Associations   1343
Medicales; Conseil des Organisations Internationales des Sciences   1259
Medicare Hospitals; Association of High   **6436**
Medicare, Long-Term Care, and Health Insurance; Subcommittee on • Committee on Finance • U.S. Senate   **5717**
Medicare; National Committee to Preserve Social Security and   **5740**
Medicaux des Chemins de Fer; Union Internationale des Services   9799

Medicaux Olympiques; Association Internationale des Cadres   11944
Medicaux Penitentiaires; Conseil International des Services   1341
Medicina de America Latina; Asociacion Latinoamericana de Facultades y Escuelas de   1369
Medicina del Deporte; Confederacion Centroamericano de   11943
Medicina del Deporte; Confederacion Sudamericana de   11951
Medicina; Federacion Internacional de Asociaciones de Estudiantes de   1345
Medicina; Federacion Panamericana de Asociaciones de Facultades y Escuelas de   1452
Medicina e la Ricerca; Fondzione Africana per la   1128
Medicina Sociale; Unione Europea di   10953
Medicinae Generalis; Societas Internationalis   1357
Medicinal Chemistry Group • University of Wisconsin—Milwaukee   **10490**
Medicinal Chemistry; Laboratory of • National Cancer Institute • U.S. Department of Health and Human Services   **6191**
Medicinal Chemistry Research; Center for • University of Texas at Arlington   **2688**
Medicinal Plant Research; German Society for   10420
Medicine; Academy of Oral Diagnosis, Radiology, and   3879
Medicine; American Academy of Compensation   7172
Medicine; American Academy of Legal and Industrial   7172
Medicine; American Association for Automotive   10842
Medicine; American Center for Chinese   1150
Medicine; American College of   **1155**
Medicine; American College for Advancement in   **10837**
Medicine; American College of Occupational   9786
Medicine; American Congress of Physical   12650
Medicine; American Foundation of Traditional Chinese   **2163**
Medicine; American Society of Law and   7171
Medicine; Association of Deans of American Colleges of Veterinary   13058
Medicine Association; Pacific Women's Traditional   **2232**
Medicine; Association of Professors of   **1215**
Medicine; Association for Psychoanalytic and Psychosomatic   7331
Medicine; Board of • Illinois Department of Professional Regulation   **1770**
Medicine Branch • Division of Cancer Treatment • National Cancer Institute • U.S. Department of Health and Human Services   **6160**
Medicine; Conference of Professors of Preventive   10843
Medicine Department; Diving • Naval Medical Research Institute • Naval Medical Research and Development Command • U.S. Department of Defense   **7848**
Medicine; District of Columbia Board of   **1764, 10020**
Medicine Division • Walter Reed Army Institute of Research • Army Medical Research and Development Command • U.S. Department of Defense   **7832**
Medicine; Florida Board of   **1765**
Medicine; Francis Clark Wood Institute for the History of • College of Physicians of Philadelphia   **1575**
Medicine; Gay People in   11700
Medicine; Idaho State Board of   **1769, 10025**
Medicine; Institute of Applied Physiology and   **1607**
Medicine; Institute for Burn   2773
Medicine; Institute of Forensic   7182
Medicine; International Association for Accident and Traffic   **1335**
Medicine; Latin American Association of Aviation and Space   **2386**
Medicine; Lesbian and Gay People in   11700
Medicine; Maine Board of Licensure in   **1776**
Medicine Manuelle; Federation Internationale de   10000
Medicine; Massachusetts Board of Registration in   **1778, 10034**
Medicine; Massachusetts Society of Law and   7171
Medicine; Michigan Board of   **1779**
Medicine; New Frontiers of   **1436**
Medicine; New Hampshire Board of Registration in   **1786, 10042**
Medicine; New York State Board for   **1789, 10045**
Medicine; Pennsylvania State Board of   **1795**
Medicine and Pharmacy; International Committee of Military   7800
Medicine and Public Health; American Board of Preventive   10836
Medicine in the Public Interest   **10959**
Medicine and Rehabilitation; American Congress of Physical   12650
Medicine and Rehabilitation; American Osteopathic Academy of Physical   9993
Medicine and Rehabilitation; American Osteopathic College of Physical   9993
Medicine and Rehabilitation; American Society of Physical   12647
Medicine and Science; Foundation for Advances in Clincal   1294
Medicine; Slovak Society of Anesthesiology and Intensive Care   **2372**
Medicine; Society of Community   10968
Medicine; Society of Medical Jurisprudence and State   7193
Medicine; Society of Research and Education in Primary Care Internal   1508
Medicine and Surgery; American College of General Practitioners in Osteopathic   9975

Medicine and Surgery; Arizona Board of Osteopathic Examiners in **10014**
Medicine and Surgery; Nebraska State Board of Examiners in **1784, 10040**
Medicine and Surgery; Washington Board of Osteopathic **10062**
Medicine; Virginia Board of **1805, 10061**
Medicine; West Virginia Board of **1807**
Medicine; West Virginia State Board of **10828**
Medicine; Wyoming Board of **1809, 10065**
Medicines; Nordic Council on **1441**
Medicinsk Forskning; Nordiska Samarbetskommitten for Arktisk **1440**
Medicinsk Undervisning; Nordisk Federation for 1442
Medico-Legal Consultants; American Association of **7163**
Medico-Legal Society **7193**
Medico Psychological Association; American 7301
Medicos que Respectan la Vida Humana; Federacion Mundial de 1538
Medico-Social Assistants; International Committee of Catholic Nurses and **9094**
Medico-Sociale Association of French-Speaking Protestants **1388**
Medico-Sociale Protestante de Langue Francaise; Association 1388
Medico Sociales; Comite International Catholique des Infirmieres et Assistantes 9094
Medicus Mundi **1389**
Medicus Mundi Belgium 1389
Medicus Mundi Internationalis 1354
Medische Dienst; Wetenschappelijke Vereniging van de Militaire 7806
Meditation Program; American Association of Physicians Practicing the Transcendental 2159
Meditation and TM-Sidhi Programs; American Association of Physicians Practicing the Transcendental 2159
Mediterranean Group for Sport Medicine; Latin and **11950**
Mediterranean Pediatric Societies; Union of Middle Eastern and **3304**
Mediterranean; Regional Office for the Eastern • World Health Organization **1542**
Mediterranean Societies of Gastroenterology; Association of National, European and **5210**
Mediterranean Society of Chemotherapy **10418**
Mediterranee; Union des Societes de Pediatrie du Moyen-Orient et de la 3304
Mediterraneen de Medecine du Sport; Groupement Latin et 11950
Mediterraneenne de Chimiotherapie; Societe 10418
Mediterraneennes de Gastroenterologie; Association des Societes Nationales, Europeennes et 5210
Medizin und Forschung in Afrika; Gesellschaft fur 1129
Medizin; Internationale Gesellschaft fur Musik in der 7423
Medizin; Schweizerische Aerztegesellschaft fur Holistische 2239
Medizinischen Fusspfleger Deutschlands; Zentralverband der 10769
Medtronic Foundation **10832**
Meharry Medical College
    Center on Tropical Diseases **6778**
    Clinical Research Center **1633**
    Comprehensive Sickle Cell Center **6073**
    Division of Community Health Sciences • Health Services Administration Program **5524**
    I Have a Future Program **11276**
    Institute on Health Care for the Poor and Underserved **5634**
    Research Center of Excellence in Cell and Molecular Biology **2593**
    School of Dentistry **3832**
    School of Medicine **1034**
        Department of Pharmacology **10355**
Meharry / Morehouse Consortium Cancer Center; Drew / **6029**
Melanoma Group; WHO International 5992
Melanoma; International Group for the Clinical Study of 5992
Melanoma Programme; WHO **5992**
Melanoma; WHO Collaborating Centres for Evaluation of Methods of Diagnosis and Treatment of 5992
Melanoma; WHO International Reference Centres for the Evaluation of Methods of Diagnosis and Treatment of 5992
Melanomi; WHO Gruppo 5992
Mellon Bank Foundation **775**
Mellon Foundation; Richard King **447**
Melpomene Institute for Women's Health Research **1390, 11970**
Membership Section for Health Care Systems **6457**
Membership Section for Multihospital Systems 6457
Membrane Biology Section • Laboratory of Cardiovascular Science • National Institute on Aging • U.S. Department of Health and Human Services **1958**
Membrane Biotechnology; Research Group in • University of Quebec at Trois-Rivieres **2735**
Memorial Blood Center of Minneapolis • Specialist in Blood Bank Technology Program **7103**
Memorial Foundation; Weston A. Price 9483
Memorial Hospital of Rhode Island • School of Nurse Anesthesia **2327**

Memorial Research Center • University of Tennessee **2687**
Memorial Sloan-Kettering Cancer Center **6074**
    Laboratory of GI Tumor Biology **6075**
Memorial University of Newfoundland • Gerontology Centre **1940**
Memory; Center for the Neurobiology of Learning and • University of California, Irvine **8481**
Memory Disorders Clinic • University of California, Irvine **8482**
Memphis Area Chapter • Lupus Foundation of America **8107**
Memphis Cancer Center • University of Tennessee **6250**
Memphis State University • School of Nursing **8971**
Men Exploring New Directions; Abusive 7264
Men; National Organization of Restoring **11706**
Men in Nursing; American Assembly for **9049**
Men and Women in Alcoholics Anonymous; International Advisory Council for Homosexual **12036**
Menasha Corporation Foundation **6411**
Mended Hearts **2861**
Mended Hearts Club 2861
Meniere's Network **3542**
Menke's Disease; Corporation for **5274**
Menninger Clinic • Department of Research **7582**
Mennonite College of Nursing **8654**
Menopause Society; International **9667**
Menopause Society; North American **9687**
Menopauze: Probleemopvang **9675**
Men's Counseling Service on Domestic Violence; Emerge: A 7368
Men's Health Crisis; Gay **6670**
Menstrual Cycle Research; Society for **9695**
Menstruation; Museum of **9679**
Mental After Care Association **7441**
Mental Deficiency; American Association on 4277
Mental Deficiency; International Association for the Scientific Study of 4291
Mental Deficiency; New Zealand Association for the Scientific Study of **4299**
Mental Development; Association for Children with Retarded **4281**
Mental Development Center • Case Western Reserve University **4309**
Mental Development; Parents Association for Children with Retarded 4281
Mental Disability and the Law; Institute on **7206**
Mental Disability Legal Resource Center 4476
Mental Disease; Association for Research in Nervous and **7335**
Mental Disorders of the Aging Research Branch • Clinical Research Division • National Institute of Mental Health • U.S. Department of Health and Human Services **7621**
Mental Disorders and Crime Research Group • University of Montreal **7676**
Mental Halsa i Finland; Suomen Mielenterveysseura-Foreningen for 7376
Mental Handicap and Developmental Disabilities; Commonwealth Association for **4477**
Mental Handicap of Germany; National Association for Persons with **4296**
Mental Handicap; International League of Societies for Persons With **7411**
Mental Health Administration; American College of **5548**
Mental Health Administration; Community • Minnesota Department of Human Services **7731**
Mental Health Administration Office • Missouri Department of Mental Health **7733**
Mental Health Administrators; Association of **5561**
Mental Health Alliance; Black **7343**
Mental Health Association 7467
Mental Health Association; Alaska **7759**
Mental Health Association in California **7760**
Mental Health Association in Delaware **7761**
Mental Health Association of Georgia **7762**
Mental Health Association in Hawaii **7763**
Mental Health Association in Illinois **7764**
Mental Health Association in Indiana **7765**
Mental Health Association of Kentucky **7766**
Mental Health Association in Louisiana **7767**
Mental Health Association of Maryland **7768**
Mental Health Association in Michigan **7769**
Mental Health Association of Montana **7770**
Mental Health Association; National **7235, 7467**
Mental Health Association in New Jersey **7771**
Mental Health Association in New York State **7772**
Mental Health Association in North Carolina **7773**
Mental Health Association of North Dakota **7774**
Mental Health Association in Ohio **7775**
Mental Health Association of Rhode Island **7776**
Mental Health Association in South Carolina **7777**
Mental Health Association in Texas **7778**
Mental Health Association in Utah **7779**

U.S. Department of Health and Human Services   **7223, 7616**
Mental Health; New York State Office of   **7740**
Mental Health Office
   Louisiana Department of Health and Hospitals   **7726**
   Pennsylvania Department of Public Welfare   **7746**
Mental Health Office; Alcohol, Drug Abuse and • Human Services Program
Office • Florida Department of Health and Rehabilitative Services   **7717**
Mental Health; Ohio Department of   **7743**
Mental Health; Oklahoma Department of   **7744**
Mental Health Organizations; Coalition of Spanish Speaking   **1410**
Mental Health Policy Resource Center   **7443**
Mental Health; Postgraduate Center for   **7484**
Mental Health Professionals in Corrections; American Association of   **7277**
Mental Health Program • Behavioral Health Division • Wyoming Department
of Health   **7758**
Mental Health Program Directors; National Association of State   **5590**
Mental Health Programs; Occupational • Duke University   **9805**
Mental Health and Psychiatric Services; Special Constituency Section for
6473
Mental Health Research Group • Medical Research Centre • Laval
University   **7578**
Mental Health Research; Institute for
   State University of New York at Stony Brook   **7608**
   University of Michigan   **7673**
Mental Health Research Institute; Aurora   **7539**
Mental Health Research; National Center for American Indian and Alaska
Native   **7458**
   University of Colorado   **7663**
Mental Health; Research and Training Center for Children's • University of
South Florida   **7689**
Mental Health; Research and Training Center on Family Support and
Children's • Portland State University   **7593**
Mental Health Research and Training Foundation; North Charles   **7590**
Mental Health and Retardation Services Division • Kansas Department of
Social and Rehabilitation Services   **4359, 7724**
Mental Health Services Administration; Substance Abuse and • U.S.
Department of Health and Human Services   **11999**
Mental Health Services Division
   Arkansas Department of Human Services   **7711**
   New Jersey Department of Human Services   **7738**
   Tennessee Department of Mental Health and Mental Retardation
   7750
Mental Health Services; National Consortium for Child   **3267**
Mental Health Services Office • Mental Health and Developmental
Disabilities Services Division • Oregon Department of Human
Resources   **7745**
Mental Health; South Carolina Department of   **7748**
Mental Health Workers Association   **7280**
Mental Health; World Association for Infant   **3306**
Mental Health; World Federation for   **7532**
Mental Hospital Chaplains; Association of   **7330**
Mental Hospitals; Association of Medical Superintendents of   **5542**
Mental Hygiene Administration • Maryland Department of Health and Mental
Hygiene   **7728**
Mental Hygiene; International Committee for   **7532**
Mental Hygiene and Mental Retardation Division • Nevada Department of
Human Resources   **4371, 7736**
Mental Illness Foundation   **7444**
Mental Illness; International Committee Against   **7405**
Mental Illness; National Resource Center on Homelessness and   **7472**
Mental Illness Research and Education Institute   **7700**
Mental Illness Research and Training; Washington Institute for   **7700**
Mental Illness; Rockland Research Center for   **7586**
Mental Imagery Techniques; International Society for   **7422**
Mental Patients; Recovery, Inc., The Association of Nervous and Former
7499
Mental and Physical Disability Law; Commission on   **4476**
Mental and Physical Disability Legal Research Services and Databases
4476
Mental Rehabilitation; Association for Physical and   **12653**
Mental Research Institute   **7445**
Mental Retardation; Alabama Department of Mental Health and   **4343**
Mental Retardation; American Academy on   **4276**
Mental Retardation; American Association on   **4277, 4307**
Mental Retardation Association of America   **4295**
Mental Retardation Center; Child Development and • University of
Washington   **4338**
Mental Retardation; Connecticut Department of   **4349**
Mental Retardation of the Council for Execptional Children; Division on
4288
Mental Retardation and Developmental Disabilities Administration • Social
Services Commission • District of Columbia Department of Human
Services   **4351**

Mental Retardation and Developmental Disabilities Branch • Center for
Research for Mothers and Children • National Institute of Child Health
and Human Development • U.S. Department of Health and Human
Services   **4320**
Mental Retardation and Developmental Disabilities; Division on • Council for
Exceptional Children   **4288**
Mental Retardation and Developmental Disabilities Division; Mental Health,
• Iowa Department of Human Services   **4358**
Mental Retardation and Developmental Disabilities; New York State Agency
of   **4375**
Mental Retardation and Developmental Disabilities; Nisonger Center for •
Ohio State University   **4317**
Mental Retardation and Developmental Disabilities; Ohio Department of
4378
Mental Retardation and Developmental Disability Division • Missouri
Department of Mental Health   **4368**
Mental Retardation Division
   Delaware Department of Health and Social Services   **4350**
   Maine Department of Mental Health and Mental Retardation   **4362**
   Mental Health, Retardation and Substance Abuse Services
   Department • Virginia Office of Health and Human Resources   **4389**
   Texas Department of Mental Health and Mental Retardation   **4386**
Mental Retardation Division; Mental Hygiene and • Nevada Department of
Human Resources   **4371**
Mental Retardation; Eunice Kennedy Shriver Center for   **4310**
Mental Retardation and Human Development Research Center; R.L. Smith
• University of Kansas   **4331**
Mental Retardation and Human Development; Rose F. Kennedy Center for
Research in • Yeshiva University   **4342**
Mental Retardation; Kansas Center for Research in • University of
Kansas   **4330**
Mental Retardation; New York State Institute for Basic Research in   **4582**
Mental Retardation Office • Pennsylvania Department of Public Welfare
4381
Mental Retardation and Other Development Disabilities; Caribbean
Association on   **4286**
Mental Retardation Program Directors; National Association of State   **5591**
Mental Retardation Programs Division • Mental Health Department •
Vermont Agency of Human Services   **4388**
Mental Retardation Research Center
   Baylor College of Medicine   **4308**
   University of California, Los Angeles   **4323**
Mental Retardation Research Center; Joseph P. Kennedy, Jr. • University of
Chicago   **4324**
Mental Retardation Research and Human Development Center   **4315**
Mental Retardation Services Department • Massachusetts Executive Office
of Health and Human Services   **4364**
Mental Retardation Services Division • Tennessee Department of Mental
Health and Mental Retardation   **4385**
Mental Retardation and Substance Abuse Division; Mental Health, •
Georgia Department of Human Resources   **4353**
Mental Sciences Institute • University of Texas—Houston Health Science
Center   **7692**
Mentale; Societa Internazionale per le Techniche d' Imagerie   **7422**
Mentale; Union Internationale des Societes d'Aide a la Sante   **7431**
Mentally Disabled; Commission on the   **4476**
Mentally Handicapped Children and Young Persons, Ltd.; The Hong Kong
Association for   **4290**
Mentally Handicapped; Hong Kong Association for the   **4290**
Mentally Ill; Alliance for the   **7263**
Mentally Ill; Center on the Organization and Financing of Care for the
Severely   **5614**
Mentally Ill; Center for Research on the Organization and Financing of Care
for the Severely • Rutgers University   **7595**
Mentally Ill; National Alliance for the   **7449**
Mentally Retarded; Accreditation Council for Facilities for the   **4453**
Mentally Retarded; Australian Association for the   **4297**
Mentally Retarded; Australian Council for the   **4297**
Mentally Retarded Children; National Association of Parents and Friends
of   **4279**
Mentally Retarded; National Association of Coordinators of State Programs
for the   **5591**
Mentally Retarded; National Association of Private Residential Facilities for
the   **4278**
Mentally Retarded and Other Developmentally Disabled Persons;
Accreditation Council for Services for   **4453**
Mentally Retarded Persons in Finland; Organization for Swedish Speaking
4301
Mercer County Community College • Funeral Service Curriculum   **3685**
Mercer University
   School of Medicine   **946**
   Southern School of Pharmacy   **10512**
Merck Co. Foundation   **776**

Merck Fund; John 4449
Mercy Cancer Institute • Cancer Research Laboratory 6076
Mercy College • Occupational Therapy Program 12394
Mercy Fund; World 1549
Mercy Medical Airlift 1391
Mercyhurst College • Department of Human Ecology • Dietetics Program 9422
Meres et Enfants d'Haiti 3259
Mericos Foundation 400
Merrill Lynch & Co. Foundation 777
Mervin Bovaird Foundation 401
Mesa State College • Department of Nursing and Allied Health • Baccalaureate Nursing Program 8595
Messiah College • Department of Nursing 8923
Metabolic Diseases Branch • Division of Intramural Research • National Institute of Diabetes and Digestive and Kidney Diseases • U.S. Department of Health and Human Services 4922
Metabolic Diseases; Division of Diabetes, Endocrinology, and • National Institute of Diabetes and Digestive and Kidney Diseases • U.S. Department of Health and Human Services 4908
Metabolic Diseases and Gene Therapy Research Program • Division of Diabetes, Endocrinology, and Metabolic Diseases • National Institute of Diabetes and Digestive and Kidney Diseases • U.S. Department of Health and Human Services 4914
Metabolic Diseases and Immunology Research Unit • National Animal Disease Center • Agricultural Research Service • U.S. Department of Agriculture 13197
Metabolic Diseases Research Programs Branch; Endocrine and • Division of Diabetes, Endocrinology, and Metabolic Diseases • National Institute of Diabetes and Digestive and Kidney Diseases • U.S. Department of Health and Human Services 4912
Metabolic Eye Disease; International Society on 13501
Metabolic Laboratory; Pediatric • Oregon Health Sciences University 5344
Metabolic Magnetic Resonance Research and Computing Center • University of Pennsylvania 11172
Metabolic Neurology Branch; Developmental and • National Institute of Neurological Disorders and Stroke • U.S. Department of Health and Human Services 8445
Metabolic Research; Institute for 4889
Metabolic Research Society of the Hypoglycemia Foundation; Adrenal 4825
Metabolic Research Unit
    Shriners Hospital for Crippled Children [St. Louis, MO] 7930
    University of California, San Francisco 4930
Metabolism Branch • Division of Cancer Biology, Diagnosis, and Centers • National Cancer Institute • U.S. Department of Health and Human Services 6135
Metabolism Branch; Cell Biology and • Intramural Research Program • National Institute of Child Health and Human Development • U.S. Department of Health and Human Services 2637
Metabolism; Center for Inherited Disorders of Energy • Case Western Reserve University 4881
Metabolism Laboratory • Intramural Clinicaland Biological Research Division • National Institute on Alcohol Abuse and Alcoholism • U.S. Department of Health and Human Services 12112
Metabolism; Laboratory of Biochemical Genetics and • Rockefeller University 5346
Metabolism; Laboratory of Biochemistry and • National Institute of Diabetes and Digestive and Kidney Diseases • U.S. Department of Health and Human Services 2643
Metabolism; Laboratory of Cellular • National Heart, Lung, and Blood Institute • U.S. Department of Health and Human Services 2949
Metabolism Laboratory; Cerebral • National Institute of Mental Health • U.S. Department of Health and Human Services 7619
Metabolism; Laboratory of Human Behavior and • Rockefeller University 4899
Metabolism; Laboratory of Kidney and Electrolyte • National Heart, Lung, and Blood Institute • U.S. Department of Health and Human Services 2951
Metabolism and Molecular Medicine; Center for Endocrinology, 4882
Metabolism and Nutrition; Center for Endocrinology 4882
Metabolism-Pharmacology; Laboratory of • Rockefeller University 10453
Metabolism Program; Arteriosclerosis, Hypertension, and Lipid • Division of Heart and Vascular Diseases • National Heart, Lung, and Blood Institute • U.S. Department of Health and Human Services 2934
Metabolism Program; Nutrient • Division of Digestive Diseases and Nutrition • National Institute of Diabetes and Digestive and Kidney Diseases • U.S. Department of Health and Human Services 9544
Metabolism; Society for the Study of Inborn Errors of 4873
Metal Occupational Health Institute; Sheet 9800
Metallwarenindustrie Osterreichs; Fachverband der Eisen- und 5847
Methodist Association of Health and Welfare Ministries; United 1527
Methodist Church; Board of Hospitals and Homes of the 1527
Methodist Church; Division of Health and Welfare Ministries of the United 1527

Methodist Church; National Association of Health and Welfare Ministries of the United 1527
Methodist Hospital • Department of Medical Research 1634
Methodist Hospital of Indiana; Ball State University / • Respiratory Therapist Program 11384
Methodist Hospital; Sid W. Richardson Institute for Preventive Medicine of the 10871
Methods Research Branch • Physical Sciences and Engineering Division • National Institute for Occupational Safety and Health • U.S. Department of Health and Human Services 9834
Metro DC Chapter • National Association of Social Workers 11888
Metro Detroit Chapter • Cystic Fibrosis Foundation 5428
Metro-East; National Kidney Foundation of Eastern Missouri and 12957
Metro Washington, DC Chapter • Arthritis Foundation 7974
Metropolitan Chicago Affiliate • American Heart Association 3004
Metropolitan Community College • Respiratory Therapist Program 11449
Metropolitan Hospitals; Section for 6468
Metropolitan Life Foundation 778
Metropolitan Washington, DC Chapter • Cystic Fibrosis Foundation 5409
Mexican Academy of Dermatology 4247
Mexicana de Dermatologia; Academia 4247
Mexico Border Health Association; United States- 10971
Mexico Border Public Health Association; United States- 10971
Mexico; Medical Society of the United States and [Los Angeles, CA] 1385
Mexico; Medical Society of the United States and [Phoenix, AZ] 1386
Meyer Center for Developmental Pediatrics • Baylor College of Medicine 3311
Meyer Foundation; Eugene and Agnes E. 171
Meyer Foundation; Robert R. 455
Meyer L. Prentis Comprehensive Cancer Center of Metropolitan Detroit 6077
Meyer Memorial Trust 402
Meyer Rehabilitation Institute • University of Nebraska at Omaha 3366
Mezregionalnaya Assotsiaisiya "Kamerata" 13511
Miami Children's Hospital Research Institute 3343
Miami-Dade Community College
    Respiratory Therapist Program 11357
    W.L. Philbrick School of Funeral Sciences 3668
Miami Heart Research Institute 2916
Miami Project to Cure Paralysis • University of Miami 8511
Miami University • Family and Child Studies Center 3069
Miastenia Gravis e Doencas Neuromusculares; Associacao Portuguesa de 8185
Michael E. DeBakey International Cardiovascular Society 12288
Michael E. DeBakey International Surgical Society 12288
Michigan Affiliate
    American Diabetes Association 4973
    American Heart Association 3013
Michigan Alzheimer's Disease Research Center • University of Michigan 8512
Michigan; American Lung Association of 11649
Michigan; Arc of 4414
Michigan Association of Osteopathic Physicians and Surgeons 10088
Michigan Board of Dentistry 4071
Michigan Board of Examiners in Mortuary Science 3750
Michigan Board of Medicine 1779
Michigan Board of Nursing 9178
Michigan Board of Nursing Home Administrators 9297
Michigan Board of Osteopathic Medicine and Surgery 10035
Michigan Board of Pharmacy 10663
Michigan Board of Podiatric Medicine and Surgery 10801
Michigan Cancer Foundation 6078
Michigan Chapter
    American Physical Therapy Association 12841
    Arthritis Foundation 7988
    Lupus Foundation of America 8065
    National Association of Social Workers 11902
Michigan Chapter—Eastern Region; Greater • Cystic Fibrosis Foundation 5426
Michigan Chapter—Western Region; Greater • Cystic Fibrosis Foundation 5427
Michigan Coalition Against Domestic Violence 3098
Michigan Consortium for Enabling Technology 2455
Michigan Dental Association 4177
Michigan Department of Agriculture • Animal Industry Division • State Veterinarian 13271
Michigan Department of Education • Rehabilitation Commission 12792
Michigan Department of Labor • Blind Commission 13687
Michigan Department of Mental Health 7730
    Developmental Disabilities Council 4365

Montana Chapter; Oregon / Idaho / • Cystic Fibrosis Foundation **5415, 5434, 5452**

Montana Coalition Against Domestic Violence **3102**

Montana Dental Association **4181**

Montana Department of Health Environmental Sciences
　Alcohol and Drug Abuse Division **12173**
　Health Facilities Division **6502**
　Health Services Division **11031**
　　Emergency Medical Services Bureau **4793**
　　Family, Maternal and Child Health Bureau **3404, 9750**
　　Food and Consumer Safety Bureau **5154**
　　Health Planning Bureau **5688**
　　Preventive Health Services Bureau • AIDS Program **6882**
　　Vital Records and Statistics Bureau **7066**
　Mental Health Division **7734**

Montana Department of Labor and Industry • Employment Relations Division • Safety Bureau **9891**

Montana Department of Livestock • Animal Health Division **13275**

Montana Department of Public Health and Human Services • Health Services Division • Preventive Health Services Bureau • Dental Program **4128**

Montana Department of Social and Rehabilitation Services
　Developmental Disabilities Division **4369**
　Medicaid Services Division **5794**
　Rehabilitative Services / Visual Services Division **12796, 13691**

Montana Division • American Cancer Society **6297**

Montana Family Services Department • Aging Services Bureau **2028**

Montana Health Care Association **9352**

Montana Hospital Association **6553**

Montana; Learning Disabilities Association of **4709**

Montana Medical Association **1837**

Montana; Mental Health Association of **7770**

Montana Nurses Association **9238**

Montana Optometric Association **13819**

Montana Osteopathic Association **10092**

Montana Professional and Occupational Licensing Bureau **10805**

Montana State Board of Nursing **9182**

Montana State Pharmaceutical Association **10720**

Montana State University
　College of Nursing **8801**
　Department of Counseling and Psychological Services • Rehabilitation Counseling Program **12611**
　Department of Microbiology • Environmental Health Option in Microbiology **5018**

Montana State University-Bozeman
　Home Economics Research Program **9512**
　Veterinary Molecular Biology Laboratory **13148**

Montana University Affiliated Rural Institute on Disability • University of Montana **4596**

Montana Veterinary Medical Association **13328**

Montefiore Medical Center • Jack D. Weiler Hospital of the Albert Einstein College of Medicine • School of Perfusion Technology **2806**

Monterey Bay Region; Easter Seal Society of the **4613**

Monterey Bay Scleroderma Foundation **7912**

Montgomery Allergy Research Laboratory • University of Michigan **2145**

Montgomery Chapter • Lupus Foundation of America **8029**

Montgomery Counties; Easter Seal Society of Philadelphia, Bucks, Chester, Delaware and **4666**

Montgomery Foundation for Gender Dysphoric Association **7447**

Montgomery Hospital • Frank J. Tornetta School of Anesthesia **2318**

Montgomery Medical and Psychological Institute **7447**

Montgomery Street Foundation **406**

Montreal Chest Hospital Research Centre • McGill University **11611**

Montreal Children's Hospital Research Institute • McGill University **3342**

Montreal Research Centre, Hotel-Dieu • University of Montreal **1709**

Montreal Research Centre; Philippe Pinel Institute of • University of Montreal **7677**

Mood, Anxiety, and Personality Disorders Research Branch • Clinical Research Division • National Institute of Mental Health • U.S. Department of Health and Human Services **7622**

Moody Foundation **407**

Moore Foundation; Edward S. **160**

Moores Foundation; Harry C. **249**

Moraine Valley Community College • Respiratory Therapist Program **11378**

Moral Drug Policy; Religious Coalition for a **1491**

Moral Problems; HUC-UC Center for the Study of Ethics and Contemporary **7204**

Moral Research and Education Center; Pope John XXIII Medical- **7213**

Morehead State University • Department of Nursing and Allied Health Sciences • Baccalaureate Nursing Program **8713**

Morehouse Consortium Cancer Center; Drew / Meharry / **6029**

Morehouse School of Medicine **947**
　Department of Graduate Education in the Biomedical Sciences **10221**

Morgan Foundation; Burton D. **80**

Morgan Memorial and Cooperative Industries and Stores **4489**

Morgan Stanley Foundation **6412**

Morningside College • Department of Nursing Education **8697**

Morningside House **1878**

Moroccan Paediatric Society **3260**

Morocco; National Veterinary Association of **13096**

Morris Fishbein Center for the History of Science and Medicine • University of Chicago **1692**

Morris Foundation; Margaret T. **376**

Morris Foundation; William T. **556**

Morris and Gwendolyn Cafritz Foundation **408**

Morris Stulsaft Foundation **3141**

Morrison Knudsen Corp. Foundation Inc. **784**

Morticians Association; National Funeral Directors and **3720**

Morticians; Idaho State Board of **3740**

Morticians; Maryland State Board of **3748**

Mortuary Arts; Kansas State Board of **3744**

Mortuary and Cemetery Board; Oregon State **3765**

Mortuary Education; Joint Committee on 3705

Mortuary Science; Alaska Board of **3729**

Mortuary Science Examiners; Iowa Board of **3743**

Mortuary Science; Michigan Board of Examiners in **3750**

Mortuary Science; New Jersey State Board of **3758**

Mortuary Science; North Carolina Board of **3761**

Mortuary Science Unit; Minnesota **3751**

Moscow Association of Cardiologists **2863**

Moseley Center for Children with Developmental Disabilities; Vince • Medical University of South Carolina **4579**

Moses Fund; Henry and Lucy **267**

Moskovskaya Assotsiatsiya Kardiologov 2863

Mother and Child International **9659**

Motherhood and Childhood; Society for Protection of **9698**

Motherhood Initiative; Safe **9693**

Mothers Anonymous 3062

Mothers of Asthmatics 3154

Mothers of Asthmatics; Allergy and Asthma Network / **3154**

Mothers and Children; Center for Research for • National Institute of Child Health and Human Development • U.S. Department of Health and Human Services **9712**

Mothers, Healthy Babies; Healthy **3235**

Mothers' Union; CPK **1262**

Mothers of Young Mongoloids **5300**

Motility Laboratory/Gastroenterology • Temple University **5237**

Motility Program; Gastrointestinal • Division of Digestive Diseases and Nutrition • National Institute of Diabetes and Digestive and Kidney Diseases • U.S. Department of Health and Human Services **5243**

Motility Society; American **5206**

Motion Analysis Laboratory • Boston University **8337**

Motion Institute; Repetitive **9819**

Motivation Institute of America Association; Fitness **10849**

Motor Control Laboratory; Stuttering Center and Speech • Baylor College of Medicine **3588**

Motor Development Laboratory • Temple University **3353**

Motor Neurone Disease and Amiotrofia Lateral Esclerosis in Uruguay **8252**

Motor Neurone Disease Association **8253**

Motor Neurone Disease Association of Australia **8254**

Motor Neurone Disease Association; Irish **8246**

Motor Neurone Disease Association; Scottish **8304**

Motor Neurone Disease Association of South Africa **8255**

Motor Neurone Disease Research Institute; ALS - **8145**

Motor Neurone Disease Society in Iceland **8256**

Motor Neurone Disease Society of New Zealand **8257**

Motor Neurone Disease Support Group **8258**

Motor Physiology; Laboratory of • Rockefeller University **8418**

Motor Sport Research Group • Human Performance International **11967**

Motor Unit Laboratory • Boston University **8338**

Motorcycle Association; Wheelchair **4567**

Motorcyclists; Association of Recovering **12013**

Motorola Foundation **785**

Motorsport Research Group at McGill University **11967**

Mott Center for Human Growth and Development; C.S. • Wayne State University **2765**

Mott Community College; Charles Stewart • Respiratory Therapist Program **11424**

Moulin a Poudre; Amis de **6638**

Mount Carmel College of Nursing **8882**

Mt. Hood Community College
    Department of Funeral Service Education **3694**
    Respiratory Therapist Program **11506**
Mount Ida College • New England Institute of Applied Arts and Sciences •
  Funeral Service Education Program **3679**
Mt. Marty College
    Graduate Program in Nurse Anesthesiology **2332**
    Nursing Program **8963**
Mt. Mary College
    Department of Dietetics **9434**
    Department of Occupational Therapy **12435**
Mt. Mercy College • Department of Nursing **8698**
Mt. St. Mary College • Division of Nursing **8836**
Mt. St. Mary's College
    Department of Nursing **8583**
    Department of Physical Therapy **12448**
Mt. San Antonio College • Respiratory Therapist Program **11328**
Mt. Sinai Medical Center; Barry University / • Master of Science in
  Anesthesiology Program **2267**
Mt. Sinai Medical Center / Case Western Reserve University • Frances
  Payne Bolton School of Nursing • School of Nurse Anesthesia **2308**
Mt. Sinai School of Medicine of City University of New York **996**
    Alzheimer's Disease Research Center **8398**
    Brookdale Center for Molecular Biology **2594**
    Clinical Center for Research in Parkinson's and Allied Disorders
      8399
    Department of Pharmacology **10296**
    General Clinical Research Center **1640**
    International Leadership Center on Longevity and Society **1941**
    Physician Assistant Program at Harlem Hospital Center **1092**
    Schizophrenic Biologic Research Center **7585**
    Vision Research Center in Ophthalmology **13619**
Mt. Sinai School of Medicine of City University of New York; Bernard
  Baruch College / • Graduate Program in Health Care Administration
  5507
Mouse Mutant Gene Resource 2595
Mouse Mutant Resource **2595**
Mouse Mutant Stock Center 2595
Movement for the Handicapped; Adventures in **4455**
Movement Studies, Inc.; Laban / Bartenieff Institute of **12736**
Moxibustion Societies; World Federation of Acupuncture- **2244**
Moyen-Orient et de la Mediterranee; Union des Societes de Pediatrie du
  3304
Moyen Orient; Societe de Neurochirurgie du 12289
MPCo/Entech Foundation **786**
MPS; Parents for 4863
MPS Society 4863
MPS Society; National **4863**
MR Center • Wayne State University **11179**
MSUD Family Support Group **3261**
Mucopolysaccharide Diseases; Society for **4872**
Mujer y la Familia para el Desarrollo; Oficina de la • Instituto Costarricense
  de Acueductors y Alcantarrillados **1329**
Mujer y el Nino; Fundacion Salvadorena para el Desarrollo de la **1306**
Mujer y del Nino; Red de Grupos por la Salud de la **1488**
Mujer y Salud; Colectivo **1246**
Mujer, Salud y Desarrollo; Grupo Nacional **1309**
Mujer, Salud y Desarrollo; Organizacion Panamericana de la Salud -
  Programa **1450**
Mulher; SOS Corpo - Grupo de Saude da **1513**
Multicenter Cardiology and Health Services Research Unit 2885
Multidisciplinary Center for the Study of Aging **1942**
Multidisciplinary Institute for Neuropsychological Development **8259, 8400**
Multidisciplinary Research Center on Drug and Alcohol Abuse • University
  of Kentucky **12138**
Multihospital Systems; Membership Section for 6457
Multi-Institutional Arrangements; Center for 6457
Multipel Sklerose Forbundet i Norge 8291
Multiple Birth; Center for Study of **9705, 11208**
Multiple Gestation; Center for Study of 9705, 11208
Multiple Personalities and Dissociation; International Society for the Study
  of 7426
Multiple Sclerosis; Association for Advancement of Research on 8278
Multiple Sclerosis Center • Rush University **8422**
Multiple Sclerosis Center; Rocky Mountain **8420**
Multiple Sclerosis Clinical Center • University of Maryland **8507**
Multiple Sclerosis Foundation **8260**
Multiple Sclerosis; Medical Rehabilitation Research and Training Center for
  • New York Medical College **8406**
Multiple Sclerosis Societies; International Federation of **8239**
Multiple Sclerosis Society; National **8134, 8278**

Multiple Sclerosis Society; Norway **8291**
Multiple Sclerosis Society of Zimbabwe **8261**
Multipurpose Arthritis Center
    University of Connecticut **7950**
    University of Michigan **7954**
Multipurpose Arthritis Center; Northeast Ohio • Case Western Reserve
  University **7916**
Multipurpose Arthritis and Musculoskeletal Diseases Center **7924**
    Indiana University-Purdue University at Indianapolis **7920**
    Northwestern University **7926**
    University of Alabama at Birmingham **7944**
Multipurpose Arthritis and Musculoskeletal Diseases Center; Robert B.
  Brigham • Brigham and Women's Hospital **7915**
Multivariate Experimental Psychology; Society of **7514**
Mundi Internationalis; Medicus **1354**
Municipal Health and Technical Experts; General Association of **10954**
Municipal Public Health Engineers; Conference of 5594
Municipaux; Association Generale des Hygienistes et Techniciens 10954
Municipaux de France, Algerie, Tunisie, Belgique, Suisse et Luxembourg;
  Association Generale des Ingenieurs, Architectes et Hygienistes 10954
Munroe Center for Human Genetics; Hattie B. • University of Nebraska
  Medical Center **5377**
Murdock Charitable Trust; M. J. **370**
Murphy Foundation; Dan **125**
Murphy Foundation; John P. **323**
Murray State University • Department of Nursing **8714**
Murray State University; Trover Clinic Foundation / • Nurse Anesthesia
  Program **2276**
Muscle Biology Program • Extramural Activities Program • National Institute
  of Arthritis and Musculoskeletal and Skin Diseases • U.S. Department of
  Health and Human Services **7938**
Muscle Disorders; Association of **7868**
Muscle Fatigue Laboratory • Boston University **8339**
Muscle Institute; Pennsylvania • University of Pennsylvania **2974**
Muscular Antrophy International Association; Charcot-Marie-Tooth Disease/
  Peroral **8199**
Muscular; Asociacion Distrofia **8182**
Muscular; Associacao Brasileira de Distrofia **8184**
Muscular Atrophy; National Foundation for Peroneal 8198
Muscular Dystrophy Association **8132**
Muscular Dystrophy Association; Biruduma **8196**
Muscular Dystrophy Association; Indian **8230**
Muscular Dystrophy; Clinical Research Center for • Columbia University
  8356
Muscular Dystrophy Societies of Croatia; Union of **8319**
Musculoskeletal Diseases Branch • Extramural Activities Program • National
  Institute of Arthritis and Musculoskeletal and Skin Diseases • U.S.
  Department of Health and Human Services **7939**
Musculoskeletal Diseases Center; Multipurpose Arthritis and **7924**
    Indiana University-Purdue University at Indianapolis **7920**
    Northwestern University **7926**
    University of Alabama at Birmingham **7944**
Musculoskeletal Diseases Center; Robert B. Brigham Multipurpose Arthritis
  and • Brigham and Women's Hospital **7915**
Musculo-Skeletal Disorders Foundation; Jaw Joints Allied **7883**
Musculoskeletal Research Center; McClure • University of Vermont **7962**
Musculoskeletal and Skin Diseases Information Clearinghouse; National
  Arthritis and **7891**
Musculoskeletal and Skin Diseases; National Institute of Arthritis and
    Extramural Activities Program
        Centers Program • U.S. Department of Health and Human
          Services **7937**
          Muscle Biology Program • U.S. Department of Health and
            Human Services **7938**
          Musculoskeletal Diseases Branch • U.S. Department of Health
            and Human Services **7939**
          Rheumatic Diseases Branch • U.S. Department of Health and
            Human Services **7940**
          Skin Diseases Branch • U.S. Department of Health and Human
            Services **4268**
        Intramural Research Program • Arthritis and Rheumatism Branch •
          U.S. Department of Health and Human Services **7941**
        Laboratory of Physical Biology • U.S. Department of Health and
          Human Services **7942**
        U.S. Department of Health and Human Services **7854, 7936**
Museum of Health and Medicine; National • Armed Forces Institute of
  Pathology • U.S. Department of Defense **7026**
Museum of Menstruation **9679**
Museums; International Association of Medical 10131
Music in Medicine; International Society for **7423**
Music Therapists; Certification Board for **12672**
Music Therapists; Urban Federation for 7278
Music Therapy; American Association for **7278**

Music Therapy Association; Australian **12669**
Music Therapy Association of Rio de Janeiro **7448**
Music Therapy; Canadian Association for **7349**
Music Therapy; National Association for **7452**
Music Therapy; New Zealand Society for **12704**
Musicoterapia do Rio de Janeiro; Associacio de **7448**
Musicotherapie du Canada; Association de **7349**
Musik in der Medizin; Internationale Gesellschaft fur **7423**
Muskegon Community College • Respiratory Therapist Program **11433**
Muskelsvindfonden **7890**
Muskie Institute of Public Affairs; Edmund S. • University of Southern Maine **5659**
Musu Lako **1393**
Mutagens, Carcinogens, and Teratogens Societies; Latin American Association of Environmental **5047**
Mutant Gene Resource; Mouse **2595**
Mutant Resource; Mouse **2595**
Mutant Stock Center; Mouse **2595**
Mutiles, des Invalides du Travail et des Invalides Civils; Federation Internationale des **4496**
Mutism; Foundation for Elective **3575**
Mutism Foundation; Selective **3575**
Mutual Help Centers; International Network for **7412**
Myanmar Dental Association **3965**
Myasthenia Gravis Foundation **8133, 8262**
Mycobacteriology; European Society for **6666**
Mycological Society of the Americas; Medical **6694**
Mycological Society; German-Speaking **6671**
Mycology Branch; Bacteriology and • Division of Microbiology and Infectious Diseases • National Institute of Allergy and Infectious Diseases • U.S. Department of Health and Human Services **6826**
Mycoplasmology; International Organization for **13087**
Mycotoxin Research Unit; Toxicology and • Richard B. Russell Agricultural Research Center • Agricultural Research Service • U.S. Department of Agriculture **10463**
Myeloma Foundation; International **5955**
Mykologische Gesellschaft; Deutschsprachige **6671**
Myoclonus Families United **8263**
Myodontics, Asian Chapter; International Academy of **3951**
Myodontics; International Academy of **3950**
Myodontics, Oceanic Chapter; International Academy of **3952**
Myomassethics Federation; International **12687**
Myopia International Research Foundation **13519**
Myopia Prevention Association; International **13491**
Myopia Research Foundation **13519**
Myositis; National Support Group for **7895**

N

NAACOG Certification Corporation **9114**
NAACOG: The Organization of Obstetric, Gynecologic, and Neonatal Nurses **9075**
Nabisco Foundation Trust **787**
Naeringarradgjafafelag Islands **9463**
Nager and Miller Syndromes; Foundation for **2747**
Nalco Foundation **788**
Names Project **6697**
Names Project Foundation **6697**
Namibia Network of AIDS Service Organisations **6698**
Nance College of Business Administration; James J. • Graduate Study in Health Care Administration • Cleveland State University **5513**
Napa Valley College • Respiratory Therapist Program **11329**
Naprapathic Association; American **2170**
NarAnon **12047**
Narcolepsy Association; American **8166**
Narcolepsy Network **8264**
Narcotic and Drug Research, Inc. **12096**
Narcotic Educational Foundation of America **12048**
Narcotics Anonymous **12049**
NARD **5863**
Narodowy Fundusz Ochrony Zdrowia **1466**
Nashville Area Chapter • Lupus Foundation of America **8108**
Nasionale Genootskap van Onkologiese Verpleging van Suid Afrika **9124**
Nassau Community College
　　Mortuary Science Department **3688**
　　Respiratory Therapist Program **11466**
Natalie Warren Bryant Cancer Center **6081**
Nathan Cummings Foundation **409**
Nathan S. Kline Institute for Psychiatric Research **7586**
Nathan W. Ackerman Family Institute **7259**

Nationaal Ziekenhuisinstituut **6466**
National Abortion Federation **11236**
National Academies of Medicine; Latin American Association of **1370**
National Academy of Neuropsychology **8265**
National Academy of Opticianry **13520**
National Academy of Sports Vision **13478**
National Accreditation Commission for Schools and Colleges of Acupuncture and Oriental Medicine **2223**
National Accreditation Council for Agencies Serving the Blind and Visually Handicapped **13521**
National Accreditation Council for Environmental Health Curricula **5053**
National Accreditation Council for Environmental Health Science and Protection **5053**
National Accrediting Agency for Clinical Laboratory Sciences **7144**
National Addison's Disease Foundation **4856**
National Adrenal Diseases Foundation **4856**
National Advisory Committee on AIDS [St. Michael, Barbados] **6700**
National Advisory Committee on AIDS [Suva, Fiji] **6699**
National Aeronautics and Space Administration
　　Ames Research Center • Space Human Factors Office **2389**
　　Lyndon B. Johnson Space Center
　　　　Medical Sciences Division **2390**
　　　　　　Space Biomedical Research Institute **2391**
National Agricultural Library • U.S. Department of Agriculture **12989**
National Aid to Visually Handicapped **13527**
National AIDS Clearinghouse **6649**
National AIDS Clearinghouse; CDC **6649**
National AIDS Committee **6688**
National AIDS Committee [Bangkok, Thailand] **6714**
National AIDS Committee [Beijing, People's Republic of China] **6706**
National AIDS Committee [Bonn, Germany] **6704**
National AIDS Committee [Castries, St. Lucia] **6716**
National AIDS Committee [Dublin, Ireland] **6701**
National AIDS Committee [The Hague, Netherlands] **6719**
National AIDS Committee [Kingston, Jamaica] **6702**
National AIDS Committee [Kingstown, St. Vincent] **6717**
National AIDS Committee [La Paz, Bolivia] **6707**
National AIDS Committee [Lusaka, Zambia] **6711**
National AIDS Committee [Managua, Nicaragua] **6721**
National AIDS Committee [Manama, Bahrain] **6708**
National AIDS Committee [Mexico City, Mexico] **6723**
National AIDS Committee [Mogadishu, Somalia] **6712**
National AIDS Committee [Oslo, Norway] **6722**
National AIDS Committee [Paramaribo, Suriname] **6713**
National AIDS Committee [Port of Spain, Trinidad and Tobago] **6715**
National AIDS Committee [Riyadh, Saudi Arabia] **6718**
National AIDS Committee [St. Johns, Antigua-Barbuda] **6710**
National AIDS Committee [San Jose, Costa Rica] **6705**
National AIDS Committee [Tegucigalpa, Honduras] **6724**
National AIDS Committee [Tokyo, Japan] **6703**
National AIDS Committee [Victoria, Seychelles] **6720**
National AIDS Committee [Vienna, Austria] **6709**
National AIDS Control Programme [Dar es Salaam, United Republic of Tanzania] **6725**
National AIDS Control Programme [Harare, Zimbabwe] **6726**
National AIDS Information Clearinghouse **6649**
National AIDS Prevention and Control Program [Manila, Philippines] **6727**
National AIDS-STD Prevention and Control Program **6727**
National AIDS Task Force **6728**
National AIDS Trust **6729**
National Allergy and Asthma Network **3154**
National Alliance of Blind Students **13522**
National Alliance of Breast Cancer Organizations **5969**
National Alliance of Cardiovascular Technologists **2828**
National Alliance for Infusion Therapy **9473**
National Alliance for the Mentally Ill **7449**
National Alliance of Nurse Practitioners **9101**
National Alliance for Research on Schizophrenia and Depression **7234**
National Alliance of Victims of Minamata Disease and Lawyers **5049**
National Alopecia Areata Foundation **4209, 4248**
National Amputation Foundation **4511**
National Amputee Golf Association **4512**
National Amputee Skiers Association **4528**
National Animal Disease Center
　　Agricultural Research Service • U.S. Department of Agriculture **13194**
　　Brucellosis Research Unit • U.S. Department of Agriculture • Agricultural Research Service **13195**
　　Cattle Virology Research Unit • U.S. Department of Agriculture • Agricultural Research Service **13196**

National Association of Psychiatric Treatment Centers for Children **3264**
National Association of Public Health Service Dentists **3968**
National Association of Public Hospitals **6462**
National Association of Quality Assurance Professionals 1398
National Association of Registered Nurses **9110**
National Association of Rehabilitation Facilities 12659
National Association of Rehabilitation Instructors **12694**
National Association of Rehabilitation Professionals in the Private Sector **12695**
National Association of Rehabilitation Secretaries **12696**
National Association of Residents and Interns **1404**
National Association of Retail Druggists 5863
National Association of Retail Druggists; Woman's Organization of the **5887**
National Association for Retarded Children 4279
National Association for Retarded Citizens 4279
National Association for Rural Mental Health **7454**
National Association of Sanitarians 5052
National Association of School Nurses **9111**
National Association of School Psychologists **7455**
National Association of Seventh-Day Adventist Dentists **3969**
National Association for Sickle Cell Disease 5984
National Association of Social Workers **11868**
   Alabama Chapter **11880**
   Alaska Chapter **11881**
   Arizona Chapter **11882**
   Arkansas Chapter **11883**
   California Chapter **11884**
   Colorado Chapter **11885**
   Connecticut Chapter **11886**
   Delaware Chapter **11887**
   Florida Chapter **11889**
   Georgia Chapter **11890**
   Hawaii Chapter **11891**
   Idaho Chapter **11892**
   Illinois Chapter **11893**
   Indiana Chapter **11894**
   Iowa Chapter **11895**
   Kansas Chapter **11896**
   Kentucky Chapter **11897**
   Louisiana Chapter **11898**
   Maine Chapter **11899**
   Maryland Chapter **11900**
   Massachusetts Chapter **11901**
   Metro DC Chapter **11888**
   Michigan Chapter **11902**
   Minnesota Chapter **11903**
   Mississippi Chapter **11904**
   Missouri Chapter **11905**
   Montana Chapter **11906**
   Nebraska Chapter **11907**
   Nevada Chapter **11908**
   New Hampshire Chapter **11909**
   New Jersey Chapter **11910**
   New Mexico Chapter **11911**
   New York City Chapter **11912**
   New York State Chapter **11913**
   North Carolina Chapter **11914**
   North Dakota Chapter **11915**
   Ohio Chapter **11916**
   Oklahoma Chapter **11917**
   Oregon Chapter **11918**
   Pennsylvania Chapter **11919**
   Puerto Rico Chapter **11920**
   Rhode Island Chapter **11921**
   South Carolina Chapter **11922**
   South Dakota Chapter **11923**
   Tennessee Chapter **11924**
   Texas Chapter **11925**
   Utah Chapter **11926**
   Vermont Chapter **11927**
   Virgin Islands Chapter **11928**
   Virginia Chapter **11929**
   Washington Chapter **11930**
   West Virginia Chapter **11931**
   Wisconsin Chapter **11932**
   Wyoming Chapter **11933**
National Association of Spanish Speaking-Spanish Surnamed Nurses 9102
National Association of Special Needs State Administrators **4518**

National Association for State Administrators of Health Occupations Education 5593
National Association of State Alcohol and Drug Abuse Directors **5588**
National Association of State Directors of Special Education **4519**
National Association of State Drug Abuse Program Coordinators 5588
National Association of State EMS Directors **5589**
National Association of State Mental Health Program Directors **5590**
National Association of State Mental Retardation Program Directors **5591**
National Association of State Public Health Veterinarians **5592**
National Association of State and Territorial Public Health Veterinarians 5592
National Association of State Units on Aging **1909**
National Association of State Veterans Homes **7803**
National Association for the Study and Prevention of Tuberculosis 11590
National Association of Substance Abuse Trainers and Educators **12055**
National Association of Supervisors and Administrators of Health Occupations Education **5593**
National Association; Tardive Dyskinesia / Tardive Dystonia **8316**
National Association of Title Seven Directors 1907
National Association of Traveling Nurses **9112**
National Association of Utilization Review Coordinators 1398
National Association of VA Physicians and Dentists **7804**
National Association of Vision Professionals 13526
National Association of Vision Program Consultants 13526
National Association for Visually Handicapped **13527**
National Association of Women Pharmacists **10610**
National Asthma Center; National Jewish Hospital/ 11605
National Asthma Center; National Jewish Hospital and Research Center/ 2109
National Ataxia Foundation **8267**
National Attention-Deficit Disorder Association **8268**
National Autism Hotline 7339
National Autistic Society **7456**
National Back Pain Association **8269**
National Beep Baseball Association **13528**
National Benevolent Association of the Christian Church (Disciples of Christ) **7457**
National Biomedical Research Foundation **2596**
National Biotherapy Study Group **5970**
National Black Alcoholism Council **12056**
National Black Association for Speech, Language and Hearing **3547**
National Black Nurses Association **9113**
National Black Women's Health Project **1405**
National Blood Transfusion Service **7145**
National Board for Cardiopulmonary Credentialing 2839
National Board for Cardiovascular and Pulmonary Credentialing 2839
National Board for Certification of Dental Laboratories **3970**
National Board for Certification in Dental Technology **3971**
National Board for Certification of Orthopaedic Technologists **9931**
National Board; Dental Assisting **3923**
National Board of Examiners in Optometry **13529**
National Board of Examiners for Osteopathic Physicians and Surgeons 10003
National Board of Medical Examiners **1406**
National Board of Naturopathic Examiners **2225**
National Board of Osteopathic Medical Examiners **10003**
National Board of Podiatric Medical Examiners **10774**
National Board of Podiatry Examiners 10774
National Board for Respiratory Care **11603**
National Board for Respiratory Therapy 11603
National Bone Marrow Donor Registry 12874
National Braille Association **13530**
National Braille Club 13530
National Braille Press **13531**
National Brain Injury Research Foundation **8270**
National Burn Victim Foundation **2772**
National Cancer Care Foundation 5930
National Cancer Center **5971**
National Cancer Cytology Center 5971
National Cancer Foundation 5930
National Cancer Institute
   Chemical and Physical Carcinogenesis Program
      Chemical and Physical Carcinogenesis Branch • U.S. Department of Health and Human Services **6126**
      Radiation Effects Branch • U.S. Department of Health and Human Services **6127**
   Division of Cancer Biology, Diagnosis, and Centers
      Cancer Centers Branch • U.S. Department of Health and Human Services **6129**
      Cancer Diagnosis Branch • U.S. Department of Health and Human Services **6130**

Index

National Center for Biomedical Communications; Lister Hill
　　Audiovisual Program Development Branch • U.S. Department of
　　　Health and Human Services • National Institutes of Health　**7030**
　　Communications Engineering Branch • U.S. Department of Health and
　　　Human Services • National Institutes of Health　**7031**
　　Computer Science Branch • U.S. Department of Health and Human
　　　Services • National Institutes of Health　**7032**
　　Educational Technology Branch • U.S. Department of Health and
　　　Human Services • National Institutes of Health　**7033**
　　Information Technology Branch • U.S. Department of Health and
　　　Human Services • National Institutes of Health　**7034**
　　National Institutes of Health • U.S. Department of Health and Human
　　　Services　**7029**
National Center for Biotechnology Information • U.S. Department of Health
　and Human Services　**2727**
National Center for Catastrophic Sports Injury Research • University of
　North Carolina at Chapel Hill　**11990**
National Center on Child Abuse and Neglect • Administration for Children
　and Families • U.S. Department of Health and Human Services　**3045,
3072**
National Center for Children in Poverty • Columbia University　**3332**
National Center for Chronic Disease Prevention and Health Promotion
　　Chronic Disease Control and Community Intervention Division • U.S.
　　　Department of Health and Human Services　**10875**
　　Diabetes Translation Division • Epidemiology and Statistics Branch •
　　　U.S. Department of Health and Human Services　**10876**
　　Office of Surveillance and Analysis • U.S. Department of Health and
　　　Human Services　**10877**
　　U.S. Department of Health and Human Services　**10831, 10874**
National Center for Clinical Infant Programs　**3308**
National Center for Deaf-Blind Youths and Adults; Helen Keller　**13476**
National Center for Disability Services　**4520**
　　Research and Training Institute　**4580**
National Center for Education in Maternal and Child Health　**3265**
National Center for Environmental Health
　　Birth Defects and Developmental Disabilities Division • U.S.
　　　Department of Health and Human Services　**2759**
　　Environmental Hazards and Health Effects Division
　　　　Health Studies Branch • U.S. Department of Health and Human
　　　　　Services　**5099**
　　　　U.S. Department of Health and Human Services　**5098**
　　Environmental Health Laboratory Sciences Division • U.S. Department
　　　of Health and Human Services　**5100**
　　U.S. Department of Health and Human Services　**5006, 5097**
National Center for Environmental Health Strategies　**5050**
National Center for the Exploration of Human Potential　**2198**
National Center for Food and Agricultural Policy　**9513**
National Center for Health Education　**1408**
National Center for Health Fitness • American University　**10863**
National Center for Health Promotion and Aging　**1901**
National Center for Health Statistics • U.S. Department of Health and
　Human Services　**6907, 7027**
National Center for Hearing Dog Information　**3577**
National Center for Homeopathy　**2226**
National Center for Human Genome Research • U.S. Department of Health
　and Human Services　**5257**
National Center for Infectious Diseases
　　Arctic Investigations Program • U.S. Department of Health and Human
　　　Services　**6795**
　　Division of Bacterial and Mycotic Diseases • Childhood and
　　　Respiratory Diseases Branch • U.S. Department of Health and
　　　Human Services　**6796**
　　Division of HIV / AIDS
　　　　Immunology Branch • U.S. Department of Health and Human
　　　　　Services　**6798**
　　　　U.S. Department of Health and Human Services　**6797**
　　Division of Parasitic Diseases
　　　　Malaria Branch • U.S. Department of Health and Human
　　　　　Services　**6800**
　　　　Parasitic Diseases Branch • U.S. Department of Health and
　　　　　Human Services　**6801**
　　　　U.S. Department of Health and Human Services　**6799**
　　Division of Vector-Borne Infectious Diseases
　　　　Arbovirus Diseases Branch • U.S. Department of Health and
　　　　　Human Services　**6803**
　　　　Dengue Branch • U.S. Department of Health and Human
　　　　　Services　**6804**
　　　　Plague Section • U.S. Department of Health and Human
　　　　　Services　**6805**
　　　　U.S. Department of Health and Human Services　**6802**
　　Division of Viral and Rickettsial Diseases
　　　　Biometrics Unit • U.S. Department of Health and Human
　　　　　Services　**6807**

　　　　Hepatitis Branch • U.S. Department of Health and Human
　　　　　Services　**6808**
　　　　Influenza Branch • U.S. Department of Health and Human
　　　　　Services　**6809**
　　　　Respiratory and Enteric Virus Branch • U.S. Department of
　　　　　Health and Human Services　**6810**
　　　　Retrovirus Diseases Branch • U.S. Department of Health and
　　　　　Human Services　**6811**
　　　　U.S. Department of Health and Human Services　**6806**
　　　　Viral Exanthems and Herpesvirus Branch • U.S. Department of
　　　　　Health and Human Services　**6812**
　　　　Viral and Rickettsial Zoonoses Branch • U.S. Department of
　　　　　Health and Human Services　**6813**
　　Hospital Infections Program
　　　　Hospital Environment Laboratory Branch • U.S. Department of
　　　　　Health and Human Services　**6815**
　　　　U.S. Department of Health and Human Services　**6814**
　　U.S. Department of Health and Human Services　**6602, 6794**
National Center for Law and the Deaf　**3549**
National Center for Law and Deafness　**3549**
National Center for Learning Disabilities　**4521**
National Center for Nursing Research
　　Division of Extramural Programs
　　　　Acute and Chronic Illness Branch • U.S. Department of Health
　　　　　and Human Services　**9142**
　　　　Health Promotion and Disease Prevention Branch • U.S.
　　　　　Department of Health and Human Services　**9143**
　　　　Nursing Systems Branch • U.S. Department of Health and
　　　　　Human Services　**9144**
National Center for Prevention Services
　　Immunization Division • Surveillance, Investigations, and Research
　　　Branch • U.S. Department of Health and Human Services　**10878**
　　Sexually Transmitted Disease/HIV Prevention Division • Behavioral
　　　and Prevention Research Branch • U.S. Department of Health and
　　　Human Services　**10879**
　　Tuberculosis Elimination Division • Surveillance and Epidemiologic
　　　Investigations Branch • U.S. Department of Health and Human
　　　Services　**10880**
National Center for Research Resources • U.S. Department of Health and
　Human Services　**2509, 2636**
National Center for the Study of Wilson's Disease　**4857, 5263**
National Center for Stuttering　**3550**
National Center for Toxicological Research • Food and Drug Administration
　• U.S. Department of Health and Human Services　**10182, 10464**
National Center for Youth with Disabilities　**4522**
National Centers and Special Programs • Basic Research Division •
　National Institute on Alcohol Abuse and Alcoholism • U.S. Department of
　Health and Human Services　**12106**
National Central America Health Rights Network　**1409**
National Certification Agency for Medical Lab Personnel　**7146**
National Certification Corporation for the Obstetric, Gynecologic and
　Neonatal Nursing Specialties　**9114**
National Challenge Committee on Disability　**4474**
National Challenge Committee of the Disabled　**4474**
National Children's Eye Care Foundation　**3151, 3266**
National Chiropractic Association　**3448**
National Chronic Epstein-Barr Virus Association　**6732**
National Chronic Fatigue Syndrome Association　**6732**
National Chronic Fatigue Syndrome and Fibromyalgia Association　**6732**
National Chronic Pain Outreach Association　**8271**
National Citizens Coalition for Nursing Home Reform　**9269**
National Citizens Committee for the World Health Organization　**1143**
National Citizens Hearings for Radiation Victims　**11065**
National City Corporation Charitable Foundation Trust　**789**
National Clearinghouse on Child Abuse and Neglect Information　**3058**
National Clearinghouse for Human Genetic Diseases　**3265**
National Clearinghouse on Marital and Date Rape　**11703**
National Clergy Conference on Alcoholism　**12057**
National Clergy Council on Alcoholism and Related Drug Problems　**12057**
National Coalition Against Domestic Violence　**3059**
National Coalition Against the Misuse of Pesticides　**5051**
National Coalition Against Sexual Assault　**11704**
National Coalition of Arts Therapy Associations　**7459**
National Coalition of Black Lung and Respiratory Disease Clinics　**11604**
National Coalition for Cancer Research　**5974**
National Coalition for Cancer Survivorship　**5975**
National Coalition of Hispanic Health and Human Services Organizations
　1410
National Coalition of Independent Living Programs　**4523**
National Coalition for Research in Neurological and Communicative
　Disorders　**8272**
National Coalition for Research in Neurological Disorders　**8272**
National College of Chiropractic　**3437**

Intramural Research Programs Division (Clinical Research)
  Biological Psychiatry Branch • U.S. Department of Health and Human Services **7635**
  Child Psychiatry Branch • U.S. Department of Health and Human Services **7636**
  Clinical Neuroendocrinology Branch • U.S. Department of Health and Human Services **7637**
  Clinical Neurogenetics Branch • U.S. Department of Health and Human Services **7638**
  Clinical Psychobiology Branch • U.S. Department of Health and Human Services **7639**
  Experimental Therapeutics Branch • U.S. Department of Health and Human Services **7640**
Intramural Research Programs Division (Research at St. Elizabeth's Hospital)
  Clinical Brain Disorders Branch • U.S. Department of Health and Human Services **7641**
  Neuropsychiatry Branch • U.S. Department of Health and Human Services **7642**
Molecular Biology Laboratory • U.S. Department of Health and Human Services **7643**
Neurochemistry Laboratory • U.S. Department of Health and Human Services **7644**
Neurophysiology Laboratory • U.S. Department of Health and Human Services **7645**
Neuropsychology Laboratory • U.S. Department of Health and Human Services **7646**
Neuroscience and Behavioral Science Division
  Behavioral, Cognitive, and Social Science Research Branch • U.S. Department of Health and Human Services **7648**
  Behavioral and Integrative Neuroscience Research Branch • U.S. Department of Health and Human Services **7649**
  Molecular and Cellular Neuroscience Research Branch • U.S. Department of Health and Human Services **7650**
  U.S. Department of Health and Human Services **7647**
Psychology and Psychopathology Laboratory • U.S. Department of Health and Human Services **7651**
Socio-Environmental Studies Laboratory • U.S. Department of Health and Human Services **7652**
U.S. Department of Health and Human Services **7223, 7616**
National Institute of Neurological Disorders and Stroke
Biometry and Field Studies Branch • U.S. Department of Health and Human Services **8442**
Biophysics Section • U.S. Department of Health and Human Services **8443**
Clinical Neuroscience Branch • U.S. Department of Health and Human Services **8444**
Developmental and Metabolic Neurology Branch • U.S. Department of Health and Human Services **8445**
Division of Convulsive, Developmental, and Neuromuscular Disorders
  Developmental Neurology Branch • U.S. Department of Health and Human Services **8447**
  Epilepsy Branch • U.S. Department of Health and Human Services **8448**
  U.S. Department of Health and Human Services **8446**
Division of Demyelinating, Atrophic, and Dementing Disorders
  Huntington's Disease Research Roster • U.S. Department of Health and Human Services **8450**
  U.S. Department of Health and Human Services **8449**
Division of Fundamental Neurosciences
  Neural Prosthesis Program • U.S. Department of Health and Human Services **8452**
  U.S. Department of Health and Human Services **8451**
Division of Intramural Research • U.S. Department of Health and Human Services **8453**
Division of Intramural Research (Basic Neurosciences Program) • U.S. Department of Health and Human Services **8454**
Division of Intramural Research (Clinical Neurosciences Program) • U.S. Department of Health and Human Services **8455**
Division of Stroke and Trauma • U.S. Department of Health and Human Services **8456**
Experimental Therapeutics Branch • U.S. Department of Health and Human Services **8457**
Laboratory of Central Nervous System Studies • U.S. Department of Health and Human Services **8458**
Laboratory of Experimental Neuropathology • U.S. Department of Health and Human Services **8459**
Laboratory of Molecular Biology • U.S. Department of Health and Human Services **8460**
Laboratory of Molecular and Cellular Neurobiology • U.S. Department of Health and Human Services **8461**
Laboratory of Neural Control • U.S. Department of Health and Human Services **8462**

Laboratory of Neurobiology • U.S. Department of Health and Human Services **8463**
Laboratory of Neurochemistry • U.S. Department of Health and Human Services **8464**
Laboratory of Neurophysiology • U.S. Department of Health and Human Services **8465**
Medical Neurology Branch • U.S. Department of Health and Human Services **8467**
Molecular Medicine and Neurological Science Laboratory • U.S. Department of Health and Human Services **8468**
Neuroepidemiology Branch • U.S. Department of Health and Human Services **8469**
Neuroimmunology Branch • U.S. Department of Health and Human Services **8470**
Small Business Innovation Research Program • U.S. Department of Health and Human Services **8471**
Surgical Neurology Branch • U.S. Department of Health and Human Services **8472**
U.S. Department of Health and Human Services **8120, 8441**
National Institute for Nursing Research
Division of Extramural Programs • U.S. Department of Health and Human Services **9146**
U.S. Department of Health and Human Services **9145**
National Institute of Nutrition **9514**
National Institute for Occupational Safety and Health
Appalachian Laboratory for Occupational Safety and Health • U.S. Department of Health and Human Services **9825**
Biomedical and Behavioral Science Division
  Applied Biology Branch • U.S. Department of Health and Human Services **9827**
  Applied Psychology and Ergonomics Branch • U.S. Department of Health and Human Services **9828**
  Experimental Toxicology Branch • U.S. Department of Health and Human Services **9829**
  Physical Agents Effects Branch • U.S. Department of Health and Human Services **9830**
  U.S. Department of Health and Human Services **9826**
Physical Sciences and Engineering Division
  Engineering Control Technology Branch • U.S. Department of Health and Human Services **9832**
  Measurements Research Support Branch • U.S. Department of Health and Human Services **9833**
  Methods Research Branch • U.S. Department of Health and Human Services **9834**
  U.S. Department of Health and Human Services **9831**
Respiratory Disease Studies Division
  Clinical Investigations Branch • U.S. Department of Health and Human Services **9836**
  Environmental Investigations Branch • U.S. Department of Health and Human Services **9837**
  U.S. Department of Health and Human Services **9835**
Robert A. Taft Laboratories • U.S. Department of Health and Human Services **9838**
Safety Research Division • U.S. Department of Health and Human Services **9839**
Surveillance, Hazard Evaluations, and Field Studies Division
  Hazard Evaluations and Technical Assistance Branch • U.S. Department of Health and Human Services **9841**
  Industrywide Studies Branch • U.S. Department of Health and Human Services **9842**
  Surveillance Branch • U.S. Department of Health and Human Services **9843**
  U.S. Department of Health and Human Services **9840**
U.S. Department of Health and Human Services **9779, 9824**
National Institute for Rehabilitation Engineering **2431, 2457**
National Institutes of Health
Division of Computer Research and Technology • U.S. Department of Health and Human Services **2512**
Research Grants Division • U.S. Department of Health and Human Services **2514**
U.S. Department of Health and Human Services **1677, 2511**
National InterAssociation Committee on Internships **1430**
National Intern Matching Program **1430**
National Intern and Resident Matching Program **1430**
National Iridology Research Association **2228**
National Jewish Center for Immunology and Respiratory Medicine **2109, 11605**
National Jewish Hospital/National Asthma Center **11605**
National Jewish Hospital and Research Center/National Asthma Center **2109**
National Kidney Disease Foundation **12909**
National Kidney Foundation **12893, 12909**
National Kidney Foundation of Alabama **12933**
National Kidney Foundation of Arizona **12934**

National Kidney Foundation of Arkansas **12935**
National Kidney Foundation of Central New York **12964**
National Kidney Foundation of Colorado **12938**
National Kidney Foundation of Connecticut **12939**
National Kidney Foundation of the Delaware Valley **12940**
National Kidney Foundation of East Tennessee **12976**
National Kidney Foundation of Eastern Missouri and Metro-East **12957**
National Kidney Foundation of Florida **12942**
National Kidney Foundation of Georgia **12943**
National Kidney Foundation of Hawaii **12944**
National Kidney Foundation of Illinois **12945**
National Kidney Foundation of Indiana **12946**
National Kidney Foundation of Iowa **12947**
National Kidney Foundation of Kansas and Western Missouri **12948, 12958**
National Kidney Foundation of Kentucky **12949**
National Kidney Foundation of Louisiana **12950**
National Kidney Foundation of Maine **12951**
National Kidney Foundation of Maryland **12952**
National Kidney Foundation of Massachusetts and Rhode Island **12953, 12974**
National Kidney Foundation of Michigan **12954**
National Kidney Foundation of Middle Tennessee **12977**
National Kidney Foundation of Mississippi **12956**
National Kidney Foundation of the National Capital Area **12941**
National Kidney Foundation of Nebraska **12959**
National Kidney Foundation of Nevada **12960**
National Kidney Foundation of New Hampshire **12961**
National Kidney Foundation of New Mexico **12963**
National Kidney Foundation of New York / New Jersey **12962, 12965**
National Kidney Foundation of North Carolina **12969**
National Kidney Foundation of Northeast New York **12966**
National Kidney Foundation of Northern California **12936**
National Kidney Foundation of Ohio **12970**
National Kidney Foundation of Oklahoma **12971**
National Kidney Foundation of Oregon **12972**
National Kidney Foundation of South Carolina **12975**
National Kidney Foundation of South Texas **12979**
National Kidney Foundation of Southeast Texas **12980**
National Kidney Foundation of Southern California **12937**
National Kidney Foundation of Texas **12981**
National Kidney Foundation of the Texas Coastal Bend **12982**
National Kidney Foundation of the Upper Midwest **12955**
National Kidney Foundation of Upstate New York **12967**
National Kidney Foundation of Utah **12984**
National Kidney Foundation of Virginia **12985**
National Kidney Foundation of Washington **12986**
National Kidney Foundation of West Tennessee **12978**
National Kidney Foundation of West Texas **12983**
National Kidney Foundation of Western New York **12968**
National Kidney Foundation of Western Pennsylvania **12973**
National Kidney Foundation of Wisconsin **12987**
National Kidney and Urologic Diseases Information Clearinghouse **12910**
National Latina Health Organization **10962**
National Leadership Coalition on AIDS **6736**
National League of the Blind of Ireland **13538**
National League for Nursing **9121**
National Legal Center for the Medically Dependent and Disabled **7189**
National Legislative Council for the Handicapped **4530**
National Lesbian and Gay Health Association **11705**
National Leukemia Association **5933**
National Library of Medicine
  Extramural Programs Division • U.S. Department of Health and Human Services • National Institutes of Health **7035**
  National Institutes of Health • U.S. Department of Health and Human Services **6908**
National Library Service for the Blind and Physically Handicapped • U.S. Library of Congress **6909**
National Live Stock and Meat Board **9383**
National-Louis University / University of Chicago Medical Center • Respiratory Therapist Program **11379**
National Lymphedema Network **4862**
National Machinery Foundation **790**
National Male Nurse Association **9049**
National Marfan Foundation **5265, 7892**
National Marrow Donor Program **12874**
National Mastitis Council **13095**
National Maternal and Child Health Clearinghouse **3269**
National Medical Association **1423**
National Medical Association; Auxiliary to the **1218**
National Medical Association; Student **1515**

National Medical Association; Women's Auxiliary to the **1218**
National Medical and Dental Association **3976**
National Medical Fellowships **920, 1424**
National Mental Health Association **7235, 7467**
National Mental Health Consumer Self-Help Clearinghouse **7468**
National Migraine Foundation **8276**
National Migrant Referral Project **1425**
National Migrant Resource Program **1425**
National Migrant Workers Council **1426, 1426**
National Minority AIDS Council **6737**
National Minority Health Association **1427**
National Mobilization Against AIDS **6696**
National MPS Society **4863**
National Multiple Sclerosis Society **8134, 8278**
National Museum of Health and Medicine • Armed Forces Institute of Pathology • U.S. Department of Defense **7026**
National Nephrosis Foundation **12909**
National Network of Learning Disabled Adults **4531**
National Network for Social Work Managers **11870**
National Networker **4531**
National New Professional Health Workers **1437**
National Nurses Association of Kenya **9122**
National Nurses Society on Addictions **9123**
National Nurses Society on Alcoholism **9123**
National Ocean Access Project **4532**
National Odd Shoe Exchange **4533**
National Odd Shoe Foundation **4533**
National Office on Disability **4534**
National Oncology Nursing Society of South Africa **9124**
National Optical Association **13524**
National Optometric Association **13539**
National Organisation for Home Care **1525**
National Organization of Adolescent Pregnancy and Parenting **11239**
National Organization of Adolescent Pregnancy, Parenting and Prevention **11239**
National Organization for Advancement of Associate Degree Nursing **9125**
National Organization for Albinism and Hypopigmentation **4864**
National Organization for Apraxia and Dyspraxia **8279**
National Organization for Associate Degree Nursing **9125**
National Organization of Circumcision Information Resource Centers **3270**
National Organization for Competency Assurance **1428**
National Organization on Disability **4534**
National Organization of Physicians Who Care **1477**
National Organization for Rare Disorders **921, 1429**
National Organization of Restoring Men **11706**
National Organization for Seasonal Affective Disorder **7469**
National Organization of World War Nurses **9126**
National Orthotic and Prosthetic Research Institute **4535**
National Osteopathic Foundation **9951, 10004**
National Osteopathic Guild Association **10005**
National Osteopathic Women Physician's Association **10006**
National Osteoporosis Foundation **7858, 7893**
National Pacific/Asian Resource Center on Aging **1906**
National Paraplegia Foundation **8284**
National Parents' Resource Institute for Drug Education **12063**
National Parkinson Foundation **8135, 8280**
National Pediculosis Association **10963**
National Perinatal Association **9683**
National Pesticide Information Clearinghouse **5054**
National Pesticide Telecommunication Network **5054**
National Pharmaceutical Association **10613**
National Pharmaceutical Council **5873**
National Phlebotomy Association **7147**
National Pituitary Agency **4860**
National Podiatric Medical Association **10775**
National Podiatric Medical Association; Student **10776**
National Podiatry Association **10775**
National Policy Director for AIDS • Domestic Policy Council • Executive Office of the President **6601**
National Presbyterian Health and Welfare Association **1479**
National Prevention Network **12064**
National Psoriasis Foundation **4210, 4249**
National Psychological Association for Psychoanalysis **7470**
National Public Services Research Institute **1641**
National Rare Blood Club **7148**
National Register of Health Service Providers in Psychology; Council for the **7363**
National Registry in Clinical Chemistry **7149**
National Registry of Emergency Medical Technicians **4752**
National Registry of Professional Interpreters and Translators for the Deaf **3574**

National Rehabilitation Association **12699**
National Rehabilitation Counseling Association **12700**
National Rehabilitation of Deaf-Blind Adults 13476
National Rehabilitation Engineering Center • Wichita State University **12769**
National Rehabilitation Information Center **12701**
National Remotivation Technique Organization 7471
National Remotivation Therapy Organization **7471**
National Renal Administrators Association **5598**
National Research and Information Center • National Foundation of Funeral Service **3726**
National Resident Matching Program **1430**
National Resource Center on Homelessness and Mental Illness **7472**
National Resource Center for Paraprofessionals in Education and Related Services 4536, **4536**
National Resource Center for Paraprofessionals in Special Education and Related Human Services 4536
National Resource Center on Women and AIDS **6738**
National Respiratory Disease Conference 11594
National Retinitis Pigmentosa Foundation 13456
National Reye's Syndrome Foundation **3152, 3271**
National Runaway Switchboard **7473**
National Rural Health Association **1431**
National Safe Workplace Institute **9814**
National Sanitation Foundation 5055
National Science Foundation • Directorate for Engineering • Division of Bioengineering and Environmental Systems • Bioengineering and Aiding Persons with Disabilities Program **2458**
National Scleroderma Club 7904
National Scoliosis Foundation **7894**
National Self-Help Clearinghouse **7474**
National Sex Forum 11691
National Sex Information Network **11707**
National Shut-In Day Society 1432
National SIDS Resource Center **3272**
National Sjogren's Syndrome Association **2084**
National Skin Cancer Foundation 5986
National Sleep Foundation **8281**
National Social Welfare Assembly 11867
National Social Work Council 11867
National Society for Autistic Children 7340
National Society of Biomedical Equipment Technicians 2543
National Society of Cardiopulmonary Technologists 2828
National Society for Cardiopulmonary Technology 2828
National Society of Genetic Counselors **5294**
National Society for Histotechnology **7150**
National Society of Hypnotherapists **6597**
National Society for Persons with Developmental Handicap **4298**
National Society to Prevent Blindness 13556
National Society for the Prevention of Blindness 13556
National Society for the Promotion of Occupational Therapy 12655
National Society for Shut-Ins **1432**
National Spasmodic Dysphonia Association **8282**
National Spasmodic Torticollis Association **8283**
National Special Education Information Center 4529
National Spinal Cord Injury Association **8284**
National Spinal Cord Injury Foundation 8284
National Spinal Cord Injury Statistical Center • University of Alabama at Birmingham **8474**
National Starch & Chemical Foundation **791**
National States Conference on Alcoholism 12001
National STD / AIDS Control Programme **6739**
National Stroke Association **8285**
National Student Nurses' Association 8542, 9127
National Student Speech and Hearing Association 3560
National Student Speech Language Hearing Association 3560
National Stuttering Project **3561**
National Sudden Infant Death Syndrome Clearinghouse 3272
National Support Group for Dermatomyositis 7896
National Support Group for Myositis **7895**
National Support Group for PM/DM **7896**
National Tay-Sachs and Allied Diseases Association **4865**
National Tay-Sachs Association 4865
National Technical Institute for the Deaf • Rochester Institute of Technology **3618**
National Teen Education Program; Ryan White **3285**
National Temperance League 12005
National Temperance Movement 12005
National Temporal Bone Banks Program of The DRF 3562
National Temporal Bone Registry **3562**
National Therapeutic Recreation Society **12702**

National Toxicology Program • Public Health Service • U.S. Department of Health and Human Services **10467**
National Treatment Consortium for Alcohol and Other Drugs **12065**
National Tuberculosis Association 11590
National Tuberculosis and Respiratory Disease Association 11590
National Tuberous Sclerosis Association **5295**
National Tumor Registrars Association 5973
National Ulcer Foundation **5228**
National Vaccine Information Center **3273**
National Vascular Malformations Foundation **8286**
National Veterinary Association of Morocco **13096**
National Veterinary Medical Association 13066
National Veterinary Services Laboratories • Animal and Plant Health Inspection Service • U.S. Department of Agriculture **13207**
National; VietNow **7816**
National Vitiligo Foundation **4250**
National Voluntary Health Agencies **1433**
National Voluntary Health and Social Welfare Organizations; National Assembly of **11867**
National Voluntary Organizations for Independent Living for the Aging **1915**
National Well Spouse Foundation 7527
National Wellness Association **10856**
National Wellness Institute **10857**
National Wheelchair Athletic Association 4568
National Wheelchair Basketball Association **4537**
National Wheelchair Softball Association **4538**
National Wholesale Druggists' Association **5874**
National Women's Coalition **9684**
National Women's Health Coalition 11229
National Women's Health Network **1434**
National Women's Health Resource Center **1435**
Nationale Ziekenhuisraad 6465
Nationaler AIDS-Beirat 6704
Nation's Capital Affiliate • American Heart Association **2998**
Nationwide Insurance Enterprise Foundation **792**
Native American Research and Training Center • University of Arizona **1683**
Native Americans; Administration for • Administration for Children and Families • U.S. Department of Health and Human Services **7**
Native Mental Health Research; National Center for American Indian and Alaska **7458**
      University of Colorado **7663**
Natural Childbirth Foundation; Read **9691**
Natural Family Planning; American Academy of **11198**
Natural Food Associates **9474**
Natural Foods Association; African-American **9437**
Natural Hygiene Society; American **2171**
Natural Hygiene Society; American Physiological and 2171
Natural Hygiene Society; Australian **2179**
Natural Hygienists; International Association of Professional **2210**
Natural Marketing Association 2153
Natural Products Lab • University of Nevada, Reno **2680**
Natural Resources; Institute of Agriculture & • University of Nebraska—Lincoln **13228**
Natural Systems; Center for the Biology of • Queens College of City University of New York **5084**
Nature Cure Federation; All India **2152**
Naturopathic Association; American **2172**
Naturopathic Association; International 2209
Naturopathic Examiners; National Board of **2225**
Naturopathy Institute **2254**
Naval Aerospace Medical Research Laboratory • Naval Medical Research and Development Command • U.S. Department of Defense **2403**
Naval Biodynamics Laboratory • Naval Medical Research and Development Command • U.S. Department of Defense **7838**
Naval Dental Research Institute • Naval Medical Research and Development Command • U.S. Department of Defense **7839**
Naval Health Research Center
    Department of Health Sciences and Epidemiology • U.S. Department of Defense • Naval Medical Research and Development Command **7841**
    Health Services Research Department • U.S. Department of Defense • Naval Medical Research and Development Command **7842**
    Naval Medical Research and Development Command • U.S. Department of Defense **7840**
    Operational Performance Department • U.S. Department of Defense • Naval Medical Research and Development Command **7843**
    Physiological Performance and Operational Department • U.S. Department of Defense • Naval Medical Research and Development Command **7844**

Network for Organ Sharing; United   **12881**

Networking Institute; Gazette International   **4488**

Networking Project for Young Adults with Disabilities   **4539**

Neumann College • Division of Nursing and Health Sciences • Baccalaureate Nursing Program   **8924**

Neural Control; Laboratory of • National Institute of Neurological Disorders and Stroke • U.S. Department of Health and Human Services   **8462**

Neural Control Laboratory; Applied • Case Western Reserve University   **8346**

Neural Network Society; International   **9096**

Neural Prosthesis Program • Division of Fundamental Neurosciences • National Institute of Neurological Disorders and Stroke • U.S. Department of Health and Human Services   **8452**

Neural Science; Center for • New York University   **8407**

Neural Science; Program in • Indiana University Bloomington   **8375**

Neural Sciences; Center for • Brown University   **8345**

Neurobiological Sciences; Center for • University of Florida   **8497**

Neurobiology of Aging; Center for the • University of Florida   **8498**

Neurobiology and Anesthesiology Branch • Intramural Research Program • National Institute of Dental Research • U.S. Department of Health and Human Services   **4020**

Neurobiology; Arthur M. Fishberg Research Center in   **8327**

Neurobiology and Immunology Research; Center for • University of Kansas   **8502**

Neurobiology; Institute of • University of Puerto Rico   **8523**

Neurobiology; Laboratory of
National Institute of Neurological Disorders and Stroke • U.S. Department of Health and Human Services   **8463**
University of Michigan   **8513**

Neurobiology; Laboratory of Developmental • National Institute of Child Health and Human Development • U.S. Department of Health and Human Services   **8438**

Neurobiology; Laboratory of Molecular and Cellular • National Institute of Neurological Disorders and Stroke • U.S. Department of Health and Human Services   **8461**

Neurobiology of Learning and Memory; Center for the • University of California, Irvine   **8481**

Neurobiology Research Center • University of Alabama at Birmingham   **8475**

Neurobiology Research Laboratory • University of Kansas   **8503**

Neuroblastoma Screening Research Group; Quebec • Sherbrooke University   **6112**

Neurochemistry; American Society for   **8176**

Neurochemistry; Center for   **8347**

Neurochemistry & Drug Addiction; New York State Research Institute for   8347

Neurochemistry; European Society for   **8215**

Neurochemistry; Ibero-American Society for   **8229**

Neurochemistry; International Society for   **8244**

Neurochemistry Laboratory
National Institute of Mental Health • U.S. Department of Health and Human Services   **7644**
National Institute of Neurological Disorders and Stroke • U.S. Department of Health and Human Services   **8464**

Neurochimie; Societe Internationale de   8244

Neurochirurgie du Moyen Orient; Societe de   12289

Neurodegenerative Diseases; Centre for Research in • University of Toronto   **8530**

Neurodevelopmental Studies, Inc.; Center for   **8348**

Neurodevelopmental Treatment Association   **8136, 12703**

Neurodynamic Laboratory • State University of New York Health Science Center at Brooklyn   **7604**

Neuroendocrine Regulation; Laboratory of • Massachusetts Institute of Technology   **8391**

Neuroendocrinology Branch; Clinical • Intramural Research Programs Division (Clinical Research) • National Institute of Mental Health • U.S. Department of Health and Human Services   **7637**

Neuroendocrinology; Laboratory of
Rockefeller University   **8419**
University of Texas—Houston Health Science Center   **8526**

Neuroendocrinology Program; Gastrointestinal • Division of Digestive Diseases and Nutrition • National Institute of Diabetes and Digestive and Kidney Diseases • U.S. Department of Health and Human Services   **5244**

Neuroepidemiology Branch • National Institute of Neurological Disorders and Stroke • U.S. Department of Health and Human Services   **8469**

Neurofibromatosis, Inc.   **8287**

Neurofiziologie Clinica; Societatea Romana de   8301

Neurofysiologian Yhdistys; Suomen Kliinisen   8219

Neurogenetics Branch; Clinical • Intramural Research Programs Division (Clinical Research) • National Institute of Mental Health • U.S. Department of Health and Human Services   **7638**

Neuroimaging; American Society of   **11096**

Neuroimaging; Society for Computerized Tomography and   11096

Neuroimmunology Branch • National Institute of Neurological Disorders and Stroke • U.S. Department of Health and Human Services   **8470**

Neuroimmunology; Center for • University of Alabama at Birmingham   **8473**

Neurokirurgisk Forening; Nordisk   8303

Neuro-Linguistic Programming; International Association of   **8233**

Neurologic Diseases; Center for • Brigham and Women's Hospital   **8344**

Neurologic Study; Center for   **8349**

Neurological Association; American   **8167**

Neurological Association; Scandinavian   **8302**

Neurological and Communicative Disorders; National Coalition for Research in   8272

Neurological Diseases; Center for • University of Miami   **8509**

Neurological Disorders; National Coalition for Research in   **8272**

Neurological Disorders; National Committee for Research in   8272

Neurological Disorders and Stroke; National Institute of
Biometry and Field Studies Branch • U.S. Department of Health and Human Services   **8442**
Biophysics Section • U.S. Department of Health and Human Services   **8443**
Clinical Neuroscience Branch • U.S. Department of Health and Human Services   **8444**
Developmental and Metabolic Neurology Branch • U.S. Department of Health and Human Services   **8445**
Division of Convulsive, Developmental, and Neuromuscular Disorders
Developmental Neurology Branch • U.S. Department of Health and Human Services   **8447**
Epilepsy Branch • U.S. Department of Health and Human Services   **8448**
U.S. Department of Health and Human Services   **8446**
Division of Demyelinating, Atrophic, and Dementing Disorders
Huntington's Disease Research Roster • U.S. Department of Health and Human Services   **8450**
U.S. Department of Health and Human Services   **8449**
Division of Fundamental Neurosciences
Neural Prosthesis Program • U.S. Department of Health and Human Services   **8452**
U.S. Department of Health and Human Services   **8451**
Division of Intramural Research • U.S. Department of Health and Human Services   **8453**
Division of Intramural Research (Basic Neurosciences Program) • U.S. Department of Health and Human Services   **8454**
Division of Intramural Research (Clinical Neurosciences Program) • U.S. Department of Health and Human Services   **8455**
Division of Stroke and Trauma • U.S. Department of Health and Human Services   **8456**
Experimental Therapeutics Branch • U.S. Department of Health and Human Services   **8457**
Laboratory of Central Nervous System Studies • U.S. Department of Health and Human Services   **8458**
Laboratory of Experimental Neuropathology • U.S. Department of Health and Human Services   **8459**
Laboratory of Molecular Biology • U.S. Department of Health and Human Services   **8460**
Laboratory of Molecular and Cellular Neurobiology • U.S. Department of Health and Human Services   **8461**
Laboratory of Neural Control • U.S. Department of Health and Human Services   **8462**
Laboratory of Neurobiology • U.S. Department of Health and Human Services   **8463**
Laboratory of Neurochemistry • U.S. Department of Health and Human Services   **8464**
Laboratory of Neurophysiology • U.S. Department of Health and Human Services   **8465**
Medical Neurology Branch • U.S. Department of Health and Human Services   **8467**
Molecular Medicine and Neurological Science Laboratory • U.S. Department of Health and Human Services   **8468**
Neuroepidemiology Branch • U.S. Department of Health and Human Services   **8469**
Neuroimmunology Branch • U.S. Department of Health and Human Services   **8470**
Small Business Innovation Research Program • U.S. Department of Health and Human Services   **8471**
Surgical Neurology Branch • U.S. Department of Health and Human Services   **8472**
U.S. Department of Health and Human Services   **8120, 8441**

Neurological Institute   **8401**

Neurological Institute; Barrow   **8329**

Neurological Microsurgery; American Board of   **12219**

Neurological / Orthopaedic Laser Surgery; American Board of   **12220**

Neurological and Orthopaedic Medicine and Surgery; American Board of   **12221**

Neurological Orthopaedic Medicine and Surgery; American Board of Thoracic   **12229**

Index

Neuroscience Nursing; American Board of **9058**
Neuroscience Program
  Medical College of Pennsylvania and Hahnemann University **8395**
  Ohio State University **8412**
  University of Texas Southwestern Medical Center at Dallas **2697**
Neuroscience and Regeneration Research of Yale University; PVA/EPVA Center for **8416**
Neuroscience Research Branch • Addiction Research Center • National Institute on Drug Abuse • U.S. Department of Health and Human Services **12118**
Neuroscience Research Branch; Behavioral and Integrative • Neuroscience and Behavioral Science Division • National Institute of Mental Health • U.S. Department of Health and Human Services **7649**
Neuroscience Research Branch; Molecular and Cellular • Neuroscience and Behavioral Science Division • National Institute of Mental Health • U.S. Department of Health and Human Services **7650**
Neuroscience Research Institute • University of California, Santa Barbara **8491**
Neuroscience; Society for **8308**
Neurosciences and Behavioral Research Branch • Basic Research Division • National Institute on Alcohol Abuse and Alcoholism • U.S. Department of Health and Human Services **12107**
Neurosciences; Division of • City of Hope Beckman Research Institute **8352**
Neurosciences; Division of Fundamental • National Institute of Neurological Disorders and Stroke • U.S. Department of Health and Human Services **8451**
Neurosciences; Fidia- Georgetown Institute for the • Georgetown University **8369**
Neurosciences Institute **8404**
Neurosciences; Keck Center for Integrative • University of California, San Francisco **8489**
Neurosciences; Laboratory of • National Institute on Aging • U.S. Department of Health and Human Services **1962**
Neurosciences; Laboratory of Molecular and Integrative • National Institute of Environmental Health Sciences • U.S. Department of Health and Human Services **5109**
Neurosciences Research Branch • Basic Research Division • National Institute on Drug Abuse • U.S. Department of Health and Human Services **12125**
Neurosciences Research Institute • University of Ottawa **8517**
Neurosurgery; American Society for Pediatric **3174**
Neurosurgery; American Society for Stereotactic and Functional **12245**
Neurosurgery; International Society for Pediatric **3248**
Neurosurgery Laboratory • University of Michigan **8514**
Neurosurgery Laboratory; Aitken • Cornell University **8358**
Neurosurgery and Neuroresearch; Chicago Institute of **8351**
Neurosurgery Research Laboratories • Thomas Jefferson University **8435**
Neurosurgery; World Society for Stereotactic and Functional **12317**
Neurosurgical Anesthesia and Critical Care; Society of **8309**
Neurosurgical Nurses **9058**
Neurosurgical Societies; European Association of **8213**
Neurosurgical Societies; World Federation of **12316**
Neurosurgical Society of America **12292**
Neurosurgical Society; Middle East **12289**
Neurosurgical Society; Scandinavian **8303**
Neurotics Anonymous International Liaison **7475**
Neurotology Society; American **3489**
Neurotrauma; Laboratory for • University of California, San Francisco **8490**
Nevada Affiliate
  American Diabetes Association **4979**
  American Heart Association **3019**
Nevada Agricultural Experiment Station-221 • University of Nevada, Reno **9559**
Nevada; American Lung Association of **11656**
Nevada Board of Optometry **13746**
Nevada Chapter
  American Physical Therapy Association **12847**
  Arthritis Foundation **7994**
  National Association of Social Workers **11908**
Nevada Chapter; Northern • Lupus Foundation of America **8075**
Nevada Chapter; Southern California / Southern • Cystic Fibrosis Foundation **5402, 5436**
Nevada Dental Association **4183**
Nevada Department of Business and Industry
  Agriculture Division • Animal Industry Bureau • State Veterinarian **13277**
  Industrial Relations Division • Occupational Safety and Health Enforcement Section **9893**
Nevada Department of Employment Training and Rehabilitation
  Rehabilitation Division
    Alcohol and Drug Abuse Bureau **12175**
    Blind Services Bureau **13693**

  Vocational Rehabilitation Bureau **12798**
Nevada Department of Human Resources
  Aging Services Division **2030**
  Health Division **11033**
    Communicable Disease Section **6884**
    Dental Health Bureau **4130**
    Emergency Medical Services Office **4795**
    Family Health Service **3406, 9752**
    Health Planning Bureau **5690**
    Health Protection Services Bureau **5156**
    Licensure and Certification Bureau **6504**
    Vital Records Bureau **7068**
  Mental Hygiene and Mental Retardation Division **4371, 7736**
  Welfare Division • Medicaid Program **5796**
Nevada Division • American Cancer Society **6299**
Nevada Easter Seal Society **4651**
Nevada Health Care Association **9354**
Nevada Hospital Association **6555**
Nevada; National Kidney Foundation of **12960**
Nevada Network Against Domestic Violence **3104**
Nevada Nurses Association **9240**
Nevada Optometric Association **13821**
Nevada Osteopathic Medical Association **10094**
Nevada Pharmacists Association **10722**
Nevada State Board of Dental Examiners **4077**
Nevada State Board of Examiners for Nursing Home Administrators **9303**
Nevada State Board of Funeral Directors, Embalmers, and Operators of Cemeterics and Crematoriums **3756**
Nevada State Board of Medical Examiners **1785**
Nevada State Board of Nursing **9184**
Nevada State Board of Osteopathic Medicine **10041**
Nevada State Board of Pharmacy **10669**
Nevada State Board of Podiatric Medicine **10807**
Nevada State Medical Association **1839**
Nevada Veterinary Medical Association **13330**
New Britain School of Nurse Anesthesia **2265**
New England Assistance Dog Program **3557**
New England Assistance Dog Service **3557**
New England Chapter; Northern • Cystic Fibrosis Foundation **5423, 5437, 5465**
New England College of Optometry **13370**
New England Deaconess Hospital • Laboratory of Cancer Biology **6083**
New England Institute of Applied Arts and Sciences • Funeral Service Education Program • Mount Ida College **3679**
New England Medical Center
  Electromyography Laboratory **8405**
  General Clinical Research Center **1644**
  Gynecologic Oncology Group **6084**
  Image Analysis Laboratory **2459**
New England Regional Genetics Group **5343**
New England Regional Primate Research Center • Harvard University **13136**
New Eyes for the Needy **13540**
New Frontiers of Medicine **1436**
New Hampshire Affiliate
  American Diabetes Association **4980**
  American Heart Association **3020**
New Hampshire Agricultural Experiment Station • University of New Hampshire **9561**
New Hampshire; American Lung Association of **11657**
New Hampshire; Arc of **4419**
New Hampshire Board of Dental Examiners **4078**
New Hampshire Board of Examiners of Nursing Home Administrators **9304**
New Hampshire Board of Nursing **9185**
New Hampshire Board of Pharmacy **10670**
New Hampshire Board of Registration of Funeral Directors and Embalmers **3757**
New Hampshire Board of Registration in Medicine **1786, 10042**
New Hampshire Board of Registration in Optometry **13747**
New Hampshire Board of Registration in Podiatry **10808**
New Hampshire Chapter
  American Physical Therapy Association **12848**
  Arthritis Foundation **7995**
  Lupus Foundation of America **8076**
  National Association of Social Workers **11909**
New Hampshire Coalition Against Domestic and Sexual Violence **3105**
New Hampshire Dental Society **4184**
New Hampshire Department of Agriculture • Animal Industry Division • State Veterinarian **13278**

New Mexico State Board of Medical Examiners **1788**
New Mexico State Board of Thanatopractice **3759**
New Mexico State Coalition Against Domestic Violence **3107**
New Mexico State University
    Agricultural Experiment Station **9515**
    Clayton Livestock Research Center **13150**
    Department of Social Work **11818**
New Mexico Tumor Registry • University of New Mexico **6236**
New Mexico Veterinary Medical Association **13333**
New Professionals Section of the American Public Health AssociatioN
  1437
New World Foundation **10903**
New York Alliance for the Eradication of Venereal Disease **6630**
New York; American Lung Association of **11661**
New York Board of Examiners of Nursing Home Administrators **9307**
New York Bureau of Funeral Directing **3760**
New York Center for Agricultural Medicine and Health **9815**
New York Chapter
    American Physical Therapy Association **12851**
    Arthritis Foundation **8001**
New York Chapter; Central
    Arthritis Foundation **7998**
    Cystic Fibrosis Foundation **5440**
    Lupus Foundation of America **8081**
New York Chapter; Greater • Cystic Fibrosis Foundation **5441**
New York Chapter; Northeastern
    Arthritis Foundation **8002**
    Cystic Fibrosis Foundation **5443**
    Lupus Foundation of America **8086**
New York Chapter; Vermont and Northern • Arthritis Foundation **8024**
New York Chapter; Western
    Arthritis Foundation **8003**
    Cystic Fibrosis Foundation **5445**
    Lupus Foundation of America **8089**
New York Chiropractic College **3442**
New York City Affiliate • American Heart Association **3023**
New York City Chapter • National Association of Social Workers **11912**
New York City Division • American Cancer Society **6304**
New York City Health and Hospitals Corporation / Empire State College •
  Respiratory Therapist Program **11467**
New York City Medical Society on Alcoholism **12010**
New York College of Osteopathic Medicine
    Department of Pharmacology, Toxicology, and Experimental
      Therapeutics **10297**
    New York Institute of Technology **9961**
New York College of Podiatric Medicine **10751**
New York; Dental Society of the State of **4187**
New York Department of Agriculture and Markets • Animal Industry Division
  • State Veterinarian **13281**
New York Downstate Affiliate • American Diabetes Association **4983**
New York Easter Seal Society **4655**
New York Fertility Institute **11220**
New York Fertility Research Foundation **11220**
New York Foundation **411**
New York Foundation for Otologic Research **3614**
New York Guild for the Jewish Blind **13507**
New York Institute for Medical Research, Inc. **7587**
New York Institute of Technology
    New York College of Osteopathic Medicine **9961**
    Science and Technology Research Center **2461**
New York; Learning Disabilities Association of **4714**
New York Life Foundation **794**
New York Medical College **997**
    Department of Pharmacology **10298**
    Diabetes Research Center **4897**
    Division of Neoplastic Diseases **6085**
    Institute of Breast Diseases **6086**
    Medical Rehabilitation Research and Training Center for Multiple
      Sclerosis **8406**
    School of Pharmacy • Department of Pharmacology **10299**
New York; Medical Society of the State of **1843**
New York; National Kidney Foundation of Central **12964**
New York; National Kidney Foundation of Northeast **12966**
New York; National Kidney Foundation of Upstate **12967**
New York; National Kidney Foundation of Western **12968**
New York/New Jersey Dreamsharing Network **7359**
New York / New Jersey; National Kidney Foundation of **12962, 12965**
New York Obesity Research Center • Columbia University **1578**
New York; Pharmaceutical Society of the State of **10726**
New York; Sickle Cell Disease Foundation of Greater **5985**
New York Society of Anesthetists **2353**

New York Society for the Relief of the Ruptured and Crippled **7925**
New York Southern Tier Chapter • Lupus Foundation of America **8085**
New York State Affiliate • American Heart Association **3024**
New York State Agency of Mental Retardation and Developmental
  Disabilities **4375**
New York State; American Lung Association of **11662**
New York State Board of Dentistry **4081**
New York State Board of Examiners in Optometry **13750**
New York State Board for Medicine **1789, 10045**
New York State Board of Nursing **9188**
New York State Board of Pharmacy **10673**
New York State Board of Podiatry **10811**
New York State Chapter • National Association of Social Workers **11913**
New York State Coalition Against Domestic Violence **3108**
New York State College of Veterinary Medicine • Department of
  Pharmacology • Cornell University **10295**
New York State Department of Education • Vocational and Educational
  Services for Individuals with Disabilities Office **12802**
New York State Department of Health **11037**
    Administration Office • Planning, Policy, and Resource Group **5694**
    AIDS Institute **6888**
    Community Health Center • Family Health Division **3410, 9756**
    Dental Health Bureau **4134**
    Emergency Medical Services Program **4799**
    Environmental Health Center **5160**
    Health Systems Management Office • Hospital Services Bureau
      6508
    Vital Statistics Section **7072**
New York State Department of Labor • Occupational Safety and Health
  Division **9897**
New York State Department of Social Services
    Blind and Visually Handicapped Commission **13697**
    Health and Long term Care Division **5800**
New York State Division • American Cancer Society **6305**
New York State Health Facilities Association **9358**
New York State; Healthcare Association of **6559**
New York State Institute for Basic Research in Developmental Disabilities
  4582
New York State Institute for Basic Research in Mental Retardation **4582**
New York State; Mental Health Association in **7772**
New York State Nurses Association **9244**
New York State Office on Aging **2034**
New York State Office of Alcohol and Substance Abuse Services **12179**
New York State Office of Mental Health **7740**
New York State Optometric Association **13825**
New York State Osteopathic Medical Society **10098**
New York State Psychiatric Institute **7588**
New York State Research Institute for Neurochemistry & Drug Addiction
  8347
New York State Veterinary Medical Society **13334**
New York Stock Exchange Foundation **6413**
New York; United Jewish Appeal - Federation of Jewish Philanthropies of
  1526
New York University
    Center for Neural Science **8407**
    College of Dentistry **3819**
    David B. Kriser Dental Center **4004**
    Department of Physical Therapy **12517**
    Division of Nursing **8837**
    General Clinical Research Center **1645**
    Institute of Environmental Medicine **5080**
    Institute of Reconstructive Plastic Surgery **12322**
    Jerry Lewis Neuromuscular Disease Center **8408**
    Kaplan Comprehensive Cancer Center **6087**
    Laboratory of Cancer and Radiobiological Research **6088**
    Laboratory for Experimental Medicine and Surgery in Primates
      13151
    Laboratory of Microbial Ecology **5081**
    Medical Center Head Trauma Program **12737**
    Medical Rehabilitation Research and Training Center **12738**
    Mental Health Clinical Research Center **7589**
    Millhauser Laboratories **8409**
    Nurse-Midwifery Education Program **9604**
    Rehabilitation Counseling Program **12616**
    Robert F. Wagner Graduate School of Public Service • Health Policy
      and Management Program **5509**
    Rusk Institute of Rehabilitation Medicine **12739**
    School of Education, Health, Nursing and Arts Professions •
      Department of Occupational Therapy **12395**
    School of Medicine **998**
      Department of Pharmacology **10300**

Index

School of Social Work **11823**
New York University Medical Center • Center for Allied Health Education • Respiratory Therapist Program **11468**
New York Upstate Affiliate • American Diabetes Association **4984**
New York Women's League for Animals 13057
New Zealand Association for the Scientific Study of Mental Deficiency **4299**
New Zealand; Childbirth Educators— **9640**
New Zealand College of Midwives **9685**
New Zealand Dental Association **3977**
New Zealand Dental Therapists Association **3978**
New Zealand Endometriosis Foundation **9686**
New Zealand; Federation of Women's Health Councils— **1291**
New Zealand; Health Research Council of **1318**
New Zealand Medical Women's Organisation **1438**
New Zealand Nurses Association **9128**
New Zealand Pain Society **8289**
New Zealand Perinatal Society 9689, **9689**
New Zealand Psychological Society **7476**
New Zealand Society for Music Therapy **12704**
New Zealand Veterinary Association **13097**
Newborn Medicine; Joint Division of **9709**
Newborn Rights Society **3274**
Newbury College • Respiratory Therapist Program **11418**
Newhouse Foundation; Samuel I. **475**
Newman Laboratory for Biomechanics and Human Rehabilitation; Eric P. and Evelyn E. • Massachusetts Institute of Technology **2453**
Newman's Own Foundation **795**
Niagara University • College of Nursing **8838**
Nias Foundation; Henry **269**
Nicaragua Medical Aid **1439**
Nicholas H. Noyes, Jr. Memorial Foundation **8540**
Nicholas Institute of Sports Medicine and Athletic Trauma **11972**
Nicholls State University • Baccalaureate Nursing Program **8726**
NIDRR Research & Training Center for Rehabilitation in Neuromuscular Diseases • University of California, Davis **8480**
Niehoff School of Nursing; Marcella • Loyola University of Chicago **8652**
Nigeria; Women's Health Research Network in **1537**
Nihon Joi Kai 1364
Nihon Kango Kyokai 9100
Nihon Kiseichu Yobokai 6687
NIMH Mental Health Clinical Research Center • Veterans Affairs Medical Center [Palo Alto, CA] **7698**
Nino; Fundacion Salvadorena para el Desarrollo de la Mujer y el **1306**
Nino; Red de Grupos por la Salud de la Mujer y del **1488**
Nippon Igaku Toshokan Kyokai 7006
NISH **4540**
Nisonger Center for Mental Retardation and Developmental Disabilities • Ohio State University **4317**
NMR Imaging and Spectroscopy In Vivo Resource • University of Florida **2485**
NMR Institute; Pittsburgh **11153**
NMR Laboratories • Baylor College of Medicine **11142**
Noah Worcester Dermatological Society **4251**
Noble Foundation; Samuel Roberts **476**
Noetic Sciences; Institute of **2251**
Noise Effects Branch • Occupational and Environmental Health Directorate • Air Force Materiel Command • U.S. Department of Defense **2400**
Noise Technical Assistance Center • Rutgers University **5085**
Nomenclature Anatomique Veterinaire; Commission Internationale de la 13085
Nomenclature Committee; International Anatomical **7002**
Nomenclature; International Committee on Veterinary Anatomical **13085**
Non-Circumcision Educational Foundation **3275**
Non-Circumcision Information Foundation **3276**
Noninvasive Cardiovascular Dynamics; European Society for **2846**
Non-Invasive Diagnosis; Center for • University of New Mexico **11171**
Non-Invasive Diagnostics; National Foundation for **11127**
Nonlinear Dynamics in Physiology and Medicine; Centre for • McGill University **1630**
Nonprescription Drug Manufacturers Association **5875**
Nonsmokers; National Association of 11738
Nonsmokers' Rights; Americans for **11731**
Nonsmokers' Rights; Californians for 11731
Non-Violence; Community for Creative **1254**
Nora Eccles Harrison Cardiovascular Research and Training Institute • University of Utah **2981**
Nora Eccles Treadwell Foundation **2783**
Nordic Association for the Handicapped. 4562
Nordic Association for Rehabilitation **12705**
Nordic Committee on Disability **4541**

Nordic Council for Alcohol and Drug Research **12066**
Nordic Council for Arctic Medical Research **1440**
Nordic Council for the Deaf **3564**
Nordic Council on Medicines **1441**
Nordic Federation of Heart and Lung Associations **2868**
Nordic Federation for Medical Education **1442**
Nordic Hospital Administrators Associations; Committee for **5571**
Nordic Society of Forensic Odonto-Stomatology **7190**
Nordic Surgical Society 12302
Nordic Transplant and Dialysis Personnel; Association for **12903**
Nordisk Barnkirurgisk Forening 12299
Nordisk Federation for Medicinsk Undervisning 1442
Nordisk Forening for Obstetrikk og Gynekologi 9649
Nordisk Forening for Obstetrik Och Gynekologi 9649
Nordisk Forening for Rehabilitering 12705
Nordisk Neurokirurgisk Forening 8303
Nordisk Neurologisk Forening 8302
Nordisk Plastikkirurgisk Forening 12300
Nordisk Rattsmedicinsk Forening 7192
Nordisk Thoraxkirurgisk Forening 12301
Nordisk Urologisk Forening 12912
Nordiska Handikappforbundet 4562
Nordiska Lakemedelsnamnden 1441
Nordiska Namnden for Alkohol- och Drogforskning 12066
Nordiska Namnden for Handikappfragor 4541
Nordiska Samarbetskommitten for Arktisk Medicinsk Forskning 1440
Norfolk Southern Foundation **796**
Norfolk State University
    Department of Nursing **9014**
    Ethelyn R. Strong School of Social Work **11855**
    School of Health Related Professions and Natural Sciences • Health Information Administration Program **6963**
Norge; Interesseforeningen fur LMBB i 5297
Norges Diabetesforbund 4866
Norges Doveforbund 3565
Norges Fibromialge Forbund 7897
Norges Parkinsonforbund 8294
Norman Foundation **412**
Norman and Rosita Winston Foundation **413**
Norris Comprehensive Cancer Center • University of Southern California **6249**
Norris Cotton Cancer Center **6089**
Norris Foundation; Dellora A. and Lester J. **135**
Norris Foundation; Kenneth T. and Eileen L. **342**
Norris Research Center; ALS Forbes **8144**
Norsk Cardiologisk Sekskap 2870
Norsk Dermatologisk Selskap 4253
Norsk Dysleksiforbund 4543
Norsk Epilepsiforbund 8293
Norsk Fibrositt Forbund 7897
Norsk Forening for Cystisk Fibrose 5296
Norsk Forening for Ernaering og Dietetikk 9476
Norsk Forening for Klassisk Akupunktur 2229
Norsk Forening for Osteogenesis Imperfecta 5298
Norsk Forening for Stomiopererte 5229
Norsk Immunsviktforening 2086
Norsk Interesse Forening for Stamme 3567
Norske Veterinarforening 13098
North America; Alcohol and Drug Problems Association of **12001**
North America; Arthroscopy Association of **12249**
North America; Association of Halfway House Alcoholism Programs of **12011**
North America; Association of Record Librarians of 6968
North America; Bangladesh Medical Association of **1220**
North America; Braille Authority of **13427**
North America; Employee Assistance Society of **7370**
North America; Gluten Intolerance Group of **5218**
North America; International Life Sciences Institute— **10412**
North America; International Union Against the Venereal Diseases and the Treponematoses, Regional Office for **6684**
North America; Interstate Postgraduate Medical Association of **1361**
North America; Midwives Alliance of **9677**
North America; Pediatric Orthopaedic Society of **3281**
North America; Radiological Society of **11129**
North America Regional Center; Pesticide Action Network **5056**
North America; Tall Cedars of Lebanon of **8138**
North America; Ukrainian Medical Association of **1522**
North American Apio-Therapy Society **2157**
North American Association of Alcoholism Programs 12001
North American Association of Christians in Social Work **11871**

Nuclear Medicine Technology Certification Board **11128**
Nuclear Physicians; American College of **11088**
Nuclear Physicians; Association of German Radiologists and **11101**
Nuclear Regulatory Commission **10894**
Nuclear War; International Physicians for the Prevention of **1356**
Nuklearmediziner eV; Berufsverband der Deutschen Radiologen und **11101**
Nurse Anesthesia Educational Programs / Schools; Council on Accreditation of **2360**
Nurse Anesthesia Program • Bowman Gray School of Medicine • North Carolina Baptist Hospital / University of North Carolina at Greensboro **2304**
Nurse Anesthetists; American Association of **2348**
Nurse Anesthetists; Council on Certification of **2361**
Nurse Associates and Practitioners; National Association of Pediatric **9107**
Nurse Associations; National Male **9049**
Nurse Associations of America; Visiting **9138**
Nurse Attorneys; The American Association of **7164**
Nurse Consultants; American Association of Legal **7162**
Nurse Consultants; National Association of Medical Legal **7162**
Nurse Consultants; San Diego Association of Medical Legal **7162**
Nurse Corps Association; Retired Army **7805**
Nurse Education and Service; National Association for Practical **9109**
Nurse Examiners; Guam Board of **9165**
Nurse Examiners; Louisiana State Board of Practical **9174**
Nurse Examiners; Puerto Rico Board of **9195**
Nurse Examiners; Texas Board of **9200**
Nurse Examiners; Texas Board of Vocational **9201**
Nurse Executives; American Organization of **5552**
Nurse Healers—Professional Association **2230**
Nurse Licensure; Virgin Islands Board of **9204**
Nurse Massage Therapists; National Association of **9104**
Nurse-Midwifery; American College of **9625**
Nurse-Midwifery Certificate Program • Parkland School of Nurse-Midwifery **9614**
Nurse-Midwives; American College of **9625**
Nurse Practitioners; American Academy of **9048**
Nurse Practitioners; National Alliance of **9101**
Nurse Practitioners in Reproductive Health; National Association of **9105**
Nurse Recruiters; National Association of **5865**
Nurse Registration and Nursing Education; Rhode Island Board of **9196**
Nursery Nursing Administrators; Society of **3292**
Nurses in AIDS Care; Association of **9071**
Nurses; American Association of Cardiovascular **9051**
Nurses; American Association of Critical-Care **9051**
Nurses; American Association of Industrial **9055**
Nurses; American Association of Managed Care **9053**
Nurses; American Association of Neuroscience **9054**
Nurses; American Association of Occupational Health **9055**
Nurses; American Association of Office **9056**
Nurses; American Association of Spinal Cord Injury **9057**
Nurses; American Board for Occupational Health **9059**
Nurses; American Society of Ophthalmic Registered **9066**
Nurses; American Society of Plastic and Reconstructive Surgical **9067**
Nurses; American Society of Post Anesthesia **9068**
Nurses Anonymous; International **12043**
Nurses Associated Alumnae of United States and Canada **9062**
Nurses and Associates; Society of Gastroenterology **5231**
Nurses Association; Alabama State **9211**
Nurses Association; Alaska **9212**
Nurses Association of America; Anthroposophical **9069**
Nurses Association; American **9062**
Nurses Association of the American College of Obstetricians and Gynecologists **9075**
Nurses Association; American Holistic **2167**
Nurses Association; American Licensed Practical **9060**
Nurses' Association; American Nephrology **9061**
Nurses Association; American Psychiatric **9065**
Nurses Association; American Radiological **11091**
Nurses Association; Arizona **9213**
Nurses Association; Arkansas **9214**
Nurses Association; Baromedical **9076**
Nurses; Association of British Paediatric **3176**
Nurses Association; California **9215**
Nurses Association; Canadian **9079**
Nurses; Canadian Intravenous **9078**
Nurses; Association of Child and Adolescent Psychiatric **3178**
Nurses Association; Colorado **9216**
Nurses Association; Connecticut **9217**
Nurses Association; Delaware **9218**
Nurses' Association; Dermatology **9084**

Nurses Association; District of Columbia **9219**
Nurses Association; Emergency **9086**
Nurses Association; Emergency Department 9086
Nurses Association / European Renal Care Association; European Dialysis and Transplant **9087**
Nurses Association; Federation of Specialty Nursing Organizations and the American **9119**
Nurses Association; Florida **9220**
Nurses Association; Georgia **9221**
Nurses Association; Guam **9222**
Nurses Association; Hawaii **9223**
Nurses Association; Hospice **9092**
Nurses Association; Idaho **9224**
Nurses Association; Illinois **9225**
Nurses Association; Indiana State **9226**
Nurses Association; Iowa **9227**
Nurses Association; Kansas State **9228**
Nurses Association; Kentucky **9229**
Nurses Association of Kenya; National **9122**
Nurses Association; Louisiana State **9230**
Nurses Association; Maine State **9231**
Nurses Association; Maryland **9232**
Nurses Association; Massachusetts **9233**
Nurses Association; Michigan **9234**
Nurses Association; Minnesota **9235**
Nurses Association; Mississippi **9236**
Nurses Association; Missouri **9237**
Nurses Association; Montana **9238**
Nurses Association; National Black **9113**
Nurses Association; National Emergency Department 9086
Nurses Association; National Flight **9120**
Nurses' Association; National Student **8542, 9127**
Nurses Association; Nebraska **9239**
Nurses Association; Nevada **9240**
Nurses Association; New Hampshire **9241**
Nurses Association; New Jersey State **9242**
Nurses Association; New Mexico **9243**
Nurses Association; New York State **9244**
Nurses Association; New Zealand **9128**
Nurses Association; North Carolina **9245**
Nurses Association; North Dakota **9246**
Nurses Association; Ohio **9247**
Nurses Association; Oklahoma **9248**
Nurses; Association of Operating Room **9073**
Nurses Association; Oregon **9249**
Nurses; Association of Pediatric Oncology **3186**
Nurses Association; Pennsylvania **9250**
Nurses; Association of Rehabilitation **9074**
Nurses Association; Rhode Island State **9251**
Nurses Association; South Carolina **9252**
Nurses Association; South Dakota **9253**
Nurses Association; Tennessee **9254**
Nurses Association; Texas **9255**
Nurses Association; Utah **9256**
Nurses Association; Vermont State **9257**
Nurses Association; Virgin Islands State **9258**
Nurses Association; Virginia **9259**
Nurses Association; Washington State **9260**
Nurses Association; West Virginia **9261**
Nurses Association; Wisconsin **9262**
Nurses; Association of Women's Health, Obstetric, and Neonatal **9075**
Nurses Association; Wyoming **9263**
Nurses Associations and Services; American Affiliation of Visiting 9138
Nurses in Business Association; American **9063**
Nurses Educational Funds **8543**
Nurses Endorsing Transplantation; Association of **9072**
Nurses for Eye Acquisition; Consortium of Registered 9072
Nurses Federation; Commonwealth **9083**
Nurses' Foundation; American **8541**
Nurses; Georgia State Board of Licensed Practical **9164**
Nurses and Health Professionals; Federation of **9089**
Nurses' House **9130**
Nurses; International Council of **9095**
Nurses and Medico-Social Assistants; International Committee of Catholic **9094**
Nurses; NAACOG: The Organization of Obstetric, Gynecologic, and Neonatal 9075
Nurses; National Association of Hispanic **9102**
Nurses; National Association of Neonatal **9103**
Nurses; National Association of Orthopaedic **9106**
Nurses; National Association of Physician **9108**

O

Occupational Safety Division
  Arizona Industrial Commission **9867**
  Rhode Island Department of Labor **9904**
Occupational Safety and Health Administation • U.S. Department of Labor **9782**
Occupational Safety and Health Administration • Industrial Affairs Division • Delaware Department of Labor **9872**
Occupational Safety and Health; Appalachian Laboratory for • National Institute for Occupational Safety and Health • U.S. Department of Health and Human Services **9825**
Occupational Safety and Health Branch • Hawaii Department of Labor and Industrial Relations **9876**
Occupational Safety and Health Bureau • Iowa Department of Employment Services **9880**
Occupational Safety and Health Division
  California Department of Industrial Relations **9869**
  Connecticut Department of Labor **9871**
  Environmental Health Bureau • Mississippi Department of Health **9889**
  Georgia Department of Labor **9875**
  New York State Department of Labor **9897**
  Oregon Consumer and Business Services Department **9902**
  South Carolina Department of Labor, Licensing, and Regulation **9905**
  Tennessee Department of Labor **9907**
  Vermont Department of Labor and Industry **9910**
Occupational Safety and Health Enforcement Section • Industrial Relations Division • Nevada Department of Business and Industry **9893**
Occupational Safety and Health; National Institute for
  Appalachian Laboratory for Occupational Safety and Health • U.S. Department of Health and Human Services **9825**
  Biomedical and Behavioral Science Division
    Applied Biology Branch • U.S. Department of Health and Human Services **9827**
    Applied Psychology and Ergonomics Branch • U.S. Department of Health and Human Services **9828**
    Experimental Toxicology Branch • U.S. Department of Health and Human Services **9829**
    Physical Agents Effects Branch • U.S. Department of Health and Human Services **9830**
    U.S. Department of Health and Human Services **9826**
  Physical Sciences and Engineering Division
    Engineering Control Technology Branch • U.S. Department of Health and Human Services **9832**
    Measurements Research Support Branch • U.S. Department of Health and Human Services **9833**
    Methods Research Branch • U.S. Department of Health and Human Services **9834**
    U.S. Department of Health and Human Services **9831**
  Respiratory Disease Studies Division
    Clinical Investigations Branch • U.S. Department of Health and Human Services **9836**
    Environmental Investigations Branch • U.S. Department of Health and Human Services **9837**
    U.S. Department of Health and Human Services **9835**
  Robert A. Taft Laboratories • U.S. Department of Health and Human Services **9838**
  Safety Research Division • U.S. Department of Health and Human Services **9839**
  Surveillance, Hazard Evaluations, and Field Studies Division
    Hazard Evaluations and Technical Assistance Branch • U.S. Department of Health and Human Services **9841**
    Industrywide Studies Branch • U.S. Department of Health and Human Services **9842**
    Surveillance Branch • U.S. Department of Health and Human Services **9843**
    U.S. Department of Health and Human Services **9840**
  U.S. Department of Health and Human Services **9779, 9824**
Occupational Safety and Health Office • Labor Standards Office • District of Columbia Department of Employment Services **9873**
Occupational Safety and Health Review Board • North Carolina Department of Labor **9898**
Occupational Safety and Health Review Commission **9776**
  Kentucky Labor Cabinet **9882**
Occupational Safety and Health Section
  Labor and Industry Division • Maryland Department of Licensing and Regulation **9885**
  Labor Standards and Safety Division • Alaska Department of Labor **9866**
Occupational Stress and Health; Centre for • University of Montreal **9859**
Occupational and Systems Compliance Section • Health Quality Assurance Bureau • Minnesota Department of Health **4790**
Occupational Therapists; South African Association of **12720**

Occupational Therapists; Swedish Association of **12722**
Occupational Therapists; World Federation of **12728**
Occupational Therapy Association; American **12655**
Occupational Therapy Association; Danish **12676**
Occupational Therapy Association; Finnish **12678**
Occupational Therapy Association; Icelandic **12681**
Occupational Therapy Association; Norwegian **12707**
Occupational Therapy Association; Swedish **12723**
Occupational Therapy Certification Board; American **12656**
Occupational Therapy Foundation; American **12330**
Occupational Therapy; National Society for the Promotion of **12655**
Occupational Therapy Program • John G. Rangos School of Health Sciences • Duquesne University **12415**
Occupational Therapy Teaching Research Clinic • Western Michigan University **12768**
Occupational and Traffic Safety Education Research Laboratory • Iowa State University of Science and Technology **9810**
Occupations Education; National Association of Supervisors and Administrators of Health **5593**
Occupations Teacher Educators; Association of Health **1205**
Ocean Access Project; National **4532**
Oceanic Chapter; International Academy of Myodontics, **3952**
Oceanographic Institution, Inc.; Harbor Branch **2577**
Ochsner Medical Foundation; Alton **1554**
  Extracorporeal Technology Program **2799**
  School of Allied Health Sciences • Respiratory Therapist Program **11404**
  Specialist in Blood Bank Technology Program **7098**
Oculaires; Club International d' Implants **13448**
Ocular Diseases; Laboratory on Mechanisms of • National Eye Institute • U.S. Department of Health and Human Services **13640**
Ocular Fluorophotometry; International Society for **13502**
Ocular Immunology Laboratory • Johns Hopkins University **13607**
Ocular Implant Society; American Intra- **13405**
Ocular Oncology Research Unit • University of California, San Francisco **13646**
Ocular Pharmacology; Institute of • Texas A&M University **10460**
Ocular Surgeons; International Association of **12275**
Oculoplastic Society, Inc.; International **13492**
Odd Shoe Exchange; National **4533**
Odd Shoe Exchange; Ruth Rubin Feldman National **4533**
Odd Shoe Foundation; National **4533**
Odell Fund; Robert Stewart Odell and Helen Pfeiffer **457**
Odessa College • Respiratory Therapist Program **11550**
O'Donnell Foundation **6376**
Odonto-Stomatologica; Associazione Italiana di Anestesia **2358**
Odonto-Stomatology; Scandinavian Society of Forensic **7190**
Odontological Federation of Central America and Panama **3979**
Odontologie; Groupement International pour la Recherche Scientifique en Stomatologie et **3961**
Odontology; American Society of Forensic **7170**
Odontology; International Group for Scientific Research in Stomatology and **3961**
Odonto-Stomatology; International Organization for Forensic **3963**
Odonto-Stomatology; Nordic Society of Forensic **7190**
ODPHP Health Information Center **1446**
ODPHP National Health Information Center **1446**
Odyssey Institute Corp. of Connecticut **7211**
Oesophage; Organisation Internationale d'Etudes Statistiques pour les Maladies de l' **5224**
Office of Adolescent Pregnancy Programs • Public Health Service • U.S. Department of Health and Human Services **11289**
Office of Assistant Secretary of Defense for Health Affairs • U.S. Department of Defense **7790**
Office of the Assistant Secretary for Health • Public Health Service • U.S. Department of Health and Human Services **10902**
Office of Aviation Medicine • Associate Administrator for Regulation and Certification • Federal Aviation Administration • U.S. Department of Transportation **2380**
Office-Based Surgery; Society for **12243**
Office of Civilian Health and Medical Program of the Uniformed Services • Office of Assistant Secretary of Defense for Health Affairs • U.S. Department of Defense **7791**
Office of Demonstrations and Evaluations • Office of Research and Demonstrations • Health Care Financing Administration • U.S. Department of Health and Human Services **5760**
Office of Educational Resources and Research • University of Michigan **1704**
Office of Extramural Affairs • National Institute on Aging • U.S. Department of Health and Human Services **1965**
Office of Health and Environmental Assessment • Office of Research and Development • Environmental Protection Agency **5073**

Ohio State University Hospitals / American Red Cross Blood Services, Central Ohio Region • Specialist in Blood Bank Technology Program 7107
Ohio University
    College of Osteopathic Medicine 9962
    Department of Zoological and Biomedical Sciences 10321
    Edison Biotechnology Institute 2724
    Health Promotion and Research Division 1648
    Rehabilitation Counseling Program 12625
    School of Health and Sport Sciences • Environmental Health Science Program 5022
    School of Hearing and Speech Sciences 3616
    School of Physical Therapy 12531
Ohio Veterinary Medical Association 13337
Ohio Wesleyan University
    Eye Research Projects 13621
    Riverside School of Nursing 8884
Ohlone College • Respiratory Therapist Program 11330
Ohrstrom Foundation 416
Oklahoma Affiliate
    American Diabetes Association 4988
    American Heart Association 3029
Oklahoma Agricultural Experiment Station • Oklahoma State University 13157
Oklahoma; American Lung Association of 11667
Oklahoma Animal Disease Diagnostic Laboratory • Oklahoma State University 13158
Oklahoma Baptist University • School of Nursing 8894
Oklahoma Board of Governors of Registered Dentists 4085
Oklahoma Board of Nursing 9192
Oklahoma Board of Osteopathic Examiners 10049
Oklahoma Center for Equine Research • Oklahoma State University 13159
Oklahoma Center for Molecular Medicine 2598
Oklahoma Chapter
    American Physical Therapy Association 12855
    Arthritis Foundation 8011
    Lupus Foundation of America 8098
    National Association of Social Workers 11917
Oklahoma Chapter; Eastern • Arthritis Foundation 8010
Oklahoma City University • School of Nursing 8895
Oklahoma Coalition on Domestic Violence and Sexual Assault 3112
Oklahoma Dental Association 4191
Oklahoma Department of Agriculture • Animal Industry Division • State Veterinarian 13285
Oklahoma Department of Health 11041
    Dental Health Services 4138
    Emergency Medical Services 4803
    Environmental Health Services 5164
    Health Promotion and Policy Analysis Office 5698
    HIV and STD Services 6892
    Maternal and Child Health Services 3414, 9760
    Medical Facilities Services 6512
    Vital Records Division 7076
Oklahoma Department of Human Services
    Aging Services Division 2038
    Developmental Disability Services Division 4379
Oklahoma Department of Labor • OSHA Consultation Division 9901
Oklahoma Department of Mental Health 7744
    Substance Abuse Division 12183
Oklahoma Department of Rehabilitation Services
    Rehabilitative Services Bureau 12806
    Visual Services Bureau 13701
Oklahoma Division • American Cancer Society 6311
Oklahoma Easter Seal Society 4664
Oklahoma Gas & Electric Co. Foundation 802
Oklahoma Health Care Association 9362
Oklahoma Health Care Authority 5804
Oklahoma Hospital Association 6563
Oklahoma; Learning Disabilities Association of 4718
Oklahoma Medical Research Foundation 2599
    Arthritis / Immunology Research Program 7927
    Cardiovascular Biology Research Program 2917
    Immunology and Cancer Research Program 6098
    Lipid and Lipoprotein Laboratory 2918
    Molecular Toxicology Research Group 2600
    Protein Studies Program 2601
Oklahoma; National Kidney Foundation of 12971
Oklahoma Nurses Association 9248
Oklahoma Optometric Association 13829
Oklahoma Osteopathic Association 10101
Oklahoma Pharmaceutical Association 10730

Oklahoma State Board of Embalmers and Funeral Directors 3764
Oklahoma State Board of Examiners for Nursing Home Administrators 9311
Oklahoma State Board of Examiners in Optometry 13754
Oklahoma State Board of Medical Licensure and Supervision 1793
Oklahoma State Board of Pharmacy 10677
Oklahoma State Board of Podiatry 10815
Oklahoma State Medical Association 1847
Oklahoma State University
    Center for Host-Arthropod-Pathogen Studies 6782
    College of Osteopathic Medicine 9963
        Department of Physiology and Pharmacology 10326
    College of Veterinary Medicine 13010
        Department of Physiological Sciences • Graduate Pharmacology Programs 10327
    Oklahoma Agricultural Experiment Station 13157
    Oklahoma Animal Disease Diagnostic Laboratory 13158
    Oklahoma Center for Equine Research 13159
    Veterinary Research 13160
Oklahoma Veterinary Medical Association 13338
Okologischer Arztebund 1272
Old Dominion University
    Center for Gerontology 1943
    College of Health Sciences
        School of Community Health • Environmental Health Program 5027
        School of Community Health Professions and Physical Therapy • Program in Physical Therapy 12558
    School of Nursing 9015
Oley Foundation for Home Parenteral and Enteral Nutrition 9481
Olin Corp. Charitable Trust 803
Olive View Medical Center; University of California, Los Angeles / • Nurse Anesthesia Program 2262
Oliver S. and Jennie R. Donaldson Charitable Trust 5894
Olivet Nazarene University • Division of Nursing 8658
Ollier's Disease Self-Help Group 7898
Olodaryngologists; Society of University 12310
Olsson Memorial Foundation; Elis 164
Olympics International; Special 4304
Olympiques; Association Internationale des Cadres Medicaux 11944
Omaha Chapter • Lupus Foundation of America 8072
Omaha Department of Veteran Affairs Medical Center • Research and Development Service 1649
Omaha National Bank Charitable Trust 689
Omega Delta 13541
Omega Epsilon Phi 13542
Omega Tau Sigma 13100
Omegatech; King James Medical Laboratory / 9507
Omicron Gamma; Lambda 10002
Omicron Kappa Upsilon 3980
On-site Safety and Health Consultation Program • Labor Standards Division • Missouri Department of Labor and Industrial Relations 9890
Oncologie Pediatrique; Societe Internationale d' 3249
Oncologists; Society of Gynecologic 5987
Oncology Administrators; Radiation 5603
Oncology Administrators; Society for Radiation 5603
Oncology; American College of MOHS Micrographic Surgery and Cutaneous 5911
Oncology; American College of Radiation 11089
Oncology; American Society of Clinical 5914
Oncology; American Society of Pediatric Hematology / 3173
Oncology; American Society of Preventive 10841
Oncology; American Society for Therapeutic Radiology and 11099
Oncology Branch; NCI- Navy Medical • Division of Cancer Treatment • National Cancer Institute • U.S. Department of Health and Human Services 6161
Oncology Branch; Radiation • Division of Cancer Treatment • National Cancer Institute • U.S. Department of Health and Human Services 6163
Oncology Center • Johns Hopkins University 6059
Oncology Center; Fitzpatrick 6036
Oncology Center; Radiation Therapy • University of Kentucky 11169
Oncology Center; Walther 6266
Oncology Centers; Association of Freestanding Radiation 11100
Oncology Clinic; Radiation • University of Florida 11167
Oncology Consortium; Pediatric • Duke University 3334
Oncology Day Care Clinic • Stanford University 6114
Oncology; Division of Hematology and
    Ohio State University 6096
    University of Michigan 6231
Oncology; European Society for Medical 5942
Oncology; European Society for Therapeutic Radiology and 5943

Public Health Bureau • Health Division • Wisconsin Department of Health and Social Services **4153**
Oral Health Research Institute • Indiana University-Purdue University at Indianapolis **4003**
Oral Health Section
  Minnesota Department of Health **4125**
  Public Health Division • Georgia Department of Human Resources **4112**
Oral Health Services Division
  Indiana Department of Health **4116**
  Tennessee Department of Health **4145**
Oral Health Services Program • Washington Department of Health **4151**
Oral Hearing-Impaired Section **3568**
Oral Implantologists; International College of **3958**
Oral Implantologists; International Congress of **3958**
Oral and Maxillofacial Pathology; American Academy **10117**
Oral and Maxillofacial Radiology; American Academy of **3864**
Oral and Maxillofacial Surgeons; American Association of **3782, 3877**
Oral and Maxillofacial Surgeons; American College of **12232**
Oral and Maxillofacial Surgeons; International Association of **12276**
Oral and Maxillofacial Surgery; American Board of **12223**
Oral Medicine; American Academy of **3865**
Oral Medicine; Laboratory of • National Institute of Dental Research • U.S. Department of Health and Human Services **4023**
Oral Medicine and Toxicology; International Academy of **3953**
Oral Pathologists; International Association of **10132**
Oral Pathology; American Academy **10117**
Oral Pathology; American Board of **10120**
Oral Pathology Department • Center for Advanced Pathology • Armed Forces Institute of Pathology • U.S. Department of Defense **10159**
Oral and Plastic Surgeons; American Association of **12213**
Oral Roberts University • Anna Vaughn School of Nursing **8896**
Oral Roentgenology; American Academy of **3864**
Oral Surgeons; American Society of **3877**
Oral Surgery; American Board of **12223**
Oral Surgery; Association of Diplomates of the American Board of **12232**
Orange Coast College • Respiratory Therapist Program **11331**
Orange Counties; Easter Seal Society of Los Angeles and **4612**
Orange County Chapter; Rockland/ • Lupus Foundation of America **8087**
ORBIS International **13549**
Orbis; Project **13549**
Orbital Disorders; International Society for **13503**
Ordean Foundation **418**
Order of Alhambra **4275**
Oregon Affiliate
  American Diabetes Association **4989**
  American Heart Association **3030**
Oregon Agricultural Experiment Station • Oregon State University **9523**
Oregon; American Lung Association of **11668**
Oregon; Arc of **4426**
Oregon Association of Hospitals and Health Systems **6564**
Oregon Board of Dentistry **4086**
Oregon Board of Examiners of Nursing Home Administrators **9312**
Oregon Board of Medical Examiners **1794, 10050, 10816**
Oregon Board of Optometry **13755**
Oregon Chapter
  American Physical Therapy Association **12856**
  Arthritis Foundation **8012**
  National Association of Social Workers **11918**
Oregon Coalition Against Domestic and Sexual Violence **3113**
Oregon Commission for the Blind **13702**
Oregon Consumer and Business Services Department • Occupational Safety and Health Division **9902**
Oregon Dental Association **4192**
Oregon Department of Agriculture • State Veterinarian **13286**
Oregon Department of Human Resources
  Alcohol and Drug Abuse Programs Office **12184**
  Health Diivision • Environment and Health Systems Offic **5165**
  Health Division **11042**
    Child and Family Health Center **3415, 9761**
    Dental Health Section **4139**
    Emergency Medical Services and Systems **4804**
    Health Care Licensure and Certification Section **6513**
    Sexually Transmitted Diseases Program **6893**
    Vital Statistics Section **7077**
  Health Policy Office **5699**
  Medical Assistance Program Office **5805**
  Mental Health and Developmental Disabilities Services Division
    Developmental Disabilities Services Office **4380**
    Mental Health Services Office **7745**
  Senior and Disabled Services Division **2039**

Vocational Rehabilitation Division **12807**
Oregon Division • American Cancer Society **6312**
Oregon; Easter Seal Society of **4665**
Oregon Health Care Association **9363**
Oregon Health Sciences University
  Biomedical Information Communication Center **7019**
  Center for Research on Occupational and Environmental Toxicology **9816**
  DMSO Research Laboratory and Clinic **10449**
  Elks' Children's Eye Clinic **13623**
  General Clinical Research Center **1650**
  Hormone Receptor Laboratory **6099**
  Institute for Nutrition and Cardiovascular Research **9521**
  Oregon Hearing Research Center **3617**
  Pediatric Metabolic Laboratory **5344**
  School of Dentistry **3826**
  School of Medicine **1019**
    Department of Pharmacology **10330**
  School of Nursing **8903**
    Graduate Program in Nurse-Midwifery **9609**
  Transplant and Immunogenetics Laboratory **12885**
  Vollum Institute for Advanced Biomedical Research **2602**
Oregon Hearing Research Center • Oregon Health Sciences University **3617**
Oregon / Idaho / Montana Chapter • Cystic Fibrosis Foundation **5415, 5434, 5452**
Oregon Institute of Technology • School of Nursing **8904**
Oregon Medical Association **1848**
Oregon; National Kidney Foundation of **12972**
Oregon Nurses Association **9249**
Oregon Optometric Association **13830**
Oregon; Osteopathic Physicians and Surgeons of **10102**
Oregon Regional Primate Research Center **13161**
Oregon Research Institute **7592**
Oregon Social Learning Center, Inc. **3070**
Oregon State Board of Nursing **9193**
Oregon State Board of Pharmacy **10678**
Oregon State Mortuary and Cemetery Board **3765**
Oregon State Pharmacists Association **10731**
Oregon State University
  Center for Gene Research and Biotechnology **2725**
  College of Pharmacy **10553**
    Department of Pharmacology **10331**
  College of Veterinary Medicine **13011**
  Department of Food Science and Technology **9522**
  Eastern Oregon Agricultural Research Center **13162**
  Environmental Health Sciences Center **5083**
  Marine / Freshwater Biomedical Sciences Center **10450**
  Mark O. Hatfield Marine Science Center • Graduate Pharmacology Programs **10332**
  Oregon Agricultural Experiment Station **9523**
  Rehabilitation Counseling Program **5025**
  School of Medicine **10333**
Oregon Veterinary Medical Association **13339**
Orentreich Foundation for the Advancement of Science, Inc. **2603**
Organ Recovery and Education; Center for **12868**
Organ Sharing; United Network for **12881**
Organ Transplant Fund **12877**
Organic Acidemia Association **4867**
Organisation de Coordination et de Cooperation pour la Lutte Contre Grandes Endemies **5183**
Organisation de Coordination pour la Lutte Contre les Endemies en Afrique Centrale **6741**
Organisation Europeenne pour la Recherche et le Traitement du Cancer **5941**
Organisation Gestosis - Society for the Study of Pathophysiology of Pregnancy **9688**
Organisation Internationale d'Etudes Statistiques pour les Maladies de l'Oesophage **5224**
Organisation Internationale pour la Lutte Contre le Trachome **13495**
Organisation Internationale de Psychophysiologie **7413**
Organisation Internationale de Recherche sur le Cerveau **8235**
Organisation Mondiale des Colleges Nationaux, Academies et Associations Academiques des Generalistes et des Medecins de Famille **1550**
Organisation Mondiale de Gastroenterologie **5233**
Organisation Mondiale de la Sante **1540**
Organisation Mondiale de la Sante - Congo **1449**
Organisme Europeen de Recherche sur la Carie **3930**
Organisme de Recherches sur l'Alimentation et la Nutrition Africaines **9485**
Organismo Internacional Regional de Sanidad Agropecuaria **13088**

Organizacion Panamericana de la Salud - Costa Rica 1459
Organizacion Panamericana de la Salud - Programa Mujer, Salud y
Desarrollo 1450
Organization and Control; Center for Advanced Study in Health Care Fiscal
Management, • University of Wisconsin—Madison 5766
Organization for Co-Ordination in Control of Endemic Diseases in Central
Africa 6741
Organization for Co-Ordination and Co-Operation in the Control of Endemic
Diseases 5183
Organization and Financing of Care for the Severely Mentally Ill; Center on
the 5614
Organization and Financing of Care for the Severely Mentally Ill; Center for
Research on the • Rutgers University 7595
Organization Internationale de Cooperation pour la Sante 1451
Organization and Occupational Health and Safety; Interdisciplinary
Research Group on Work • Laval University 9812
Organization for Swedish Speaking Mentally Retarded Persons in Finland
4301
Organization of Teachers of Oral Diagnosis 3981
Organization of University Health Center Administrators 1194
Organizations and Dentistry; Federation of Special Care 3938
Organizations; Federation of Prosthodontic 3937
Organizations; Federation of Straight Chiropractors and 3455
Organizations for Independent Living for the Aging; National Voluntary
1915
Organizations; Joint Commission on Accreditation of Healthcare 1366
Organizations; National Alliance of Breast Cancer 5969
Organizations; National Assembly of National Voluntary Health and Social
Welfare 11867
Organizations; National Association of Health Data 7009
Organizations; National Coalition of Hispanic Health and Human Services
1410
Organizations; National Federation of Housestaff 6464
Organizations; National Federation for Specialty Nursing 9119
Organizations of the Physically Handicapped; Congress of 4478
Organizations of the Physically Handicapped; National Congress of 4478
Organizations for Sobriety; Secular 12076
Organizations; United Federation of CFS / CFIDS / CEBV 6755
Organizicion Panamerican de la Salud - Chile 1461
Organizing Committee of the World Congress on Implantology and
Biomaterials 3982
Organs; International Society for Artificial 12870
Orgonomy; American College of 2161
Oriental Bodywork Therapy Association; American 2173
Oriental Healing Arts; American Association of 2173
Oriental Medicine; American Association for Acupuncture and 2158
Oriental Medicine; Council of Colleges of Acupuncture and 2189
Oriental Medicine; International Foundation of 2215
Oriental Medicine; National Accreditation Commission for Schools and
Colleges of Acupuncture and 2223
Orlowitz Institute for Cancer and Blood Diseases; Herbert L. 6053
Orofacial Pain; American Academy of 3866
Orphan Products Development; Office of • Food and Drug Administration •
U.S. Department of Health and Human Services 10630
Orphans; International 3050
Orscheln Industries Foundation 804
Orthese; Societe Internationale de Prothese et 4498
Orthodontia; American Board of 3883
Orthodontia Society; European 3931
Orthodontic Associations; Federation of 3936
Orthodontic Education and Research Foundation 3983
Orthodontic Society; American 3897
Orthodontic Society; European 3931
Orthodontics; American Board of 3883
Orthodontics; College of Diplomates of the American Board of 3916
Orthodontics for the General Practitioner; American Academy of 3867
Orthodontics; International Academy of 3956
Orthodontics; International Association of 3956
Orthodontists; American Association of 3878
Orthodontists; American Society of 3878
Orthogenic School; Sonia Shankman 7601
Orthokeratology Society; International 13496
Orthopadie; Berufsverband der Arzte fur 9934
Orthopaedic Association; American 9921
Orthopaedic Association; Scandinavian 9936
Orthopaedic Association; South African 9937
Orthopaedic Association; Western Pacific 9939
Orthopaedic Biomechanics Laboratory 9943
Orthopaedic Chairmen; Association of 9916
Orthopaedic Foot and Ankle Society; American 9922
Orthopaedic Institute • Department of Bioengineering 9944
Orthopaedic Laser Surgery; American Board of Neurological / 12220

Orthopaedic Medicine and Surgery; American Board of Neurological and
12221
Orthopaedic Medicine and Surgery; American Board of Thoracic
Neurological 12229
Orthopaedic Microneurosurgery; American Board of 12224
Orthopaedic Nurses; National Association of 9106
Orthopaedic Research Institute 9945
Orthopaedic Research Laboratories
Johns Hopkins University 9942
University of Michigan 9948
Orthopaedic Section, American Physical Therapy Association 12708
Orthopaedic Society; Academic 9916
Orthopaedic Society; American 9916
Orthopaedic Society; American- Israeli 9920
Orthopaedic Society; Clinical 12265
Orthopaedic Society of North America; Pediatric 3281
Orthopaedic Society; Ruth Jackson 9935
Orthopaedic Society for Sports Medicine; American 9923
Orthopaedic Society; Veterinary 13113
Orthopaedic Surgeons; American Academy of 12206
Orthopaedic Surgeons; American Academy of Neurological and 12204
Orthopaedic Surgeons; Society of Military 7809
Orthopaedic Surgery; American Board of 12225
Orthopaedic Surgery and Traumatology; International Society of 9929
Orthopaedic Technologists; Canadian Society of 9925
Orthopaedic Technologists; National Association of 9930
Orthopaedic Technologists; National Board for Certification of 9931
Orthopaedics Overseas 9932
Orthopaedics and Traumatology; Turkish Association of 9938
Orthopedic Appliance and Limb Manufacturers Association 5822
Orthopedic and Arthritis Center • Medical College of Pennsylvania and
Hahnemann University 7922
Orthopedic Engineering and Research Center 9946
Orthopedic Foundation for Animals 13102
Orthopedic Medicine; American Association of 9917
Orthopedic Pathology Department • Center for Advanced Pathology •
Armed Forces Institute of Pathology • U.S. Department of Defense
10160
Orthopedic Research Society 9933
Orthopedic Surgical Manufacturers Association 5878
Orthopedics; American Academy of Craniomandibular 3866
Orthopedics; American Academy of Gnathologic 3857
Orthopedics; American Academy of Head, Facial and Neck Pain and TMJ
3859
Orthopedics; American Board of Podiatric 10758
Orthopedics; American Osteopathic Academy of 9979
Orthopedics; Council on Chiropractic 3452
Orthopedics International Association; Conservative 9926
Orthopedics and Medicine; American College of Foot and Ankle 10760
Orthopedics; Physicians Association for 9934
Orthopedics and Primary Medicine; American Board of Podiatric 10758
Orthopedie; Societe Canadienne des Technologistes en 9925
Orthopedique et de Traumatologie; Societe Internationale de Chirurgie
9929
Orthopedistes; Union Internationale des Techniciens 2422
Orthopedists; American College of Chiropractic 9918
Orthopedists; American College of Foot 10760
Orthopic Technicians; American Association of 13387
Orthopsychiatric Association; American 7300
Orthoptic Association; International 13497
Orthoptic Council; American 13404
Orthoptists; American Association of Certified 13387
Orthotic Clinics; Association of Children's Prosthetic- 3183
Orthotic and Prosthetic Association; American 5822
Orthotic and Prosthetic Research Institute; National 4535
Orthotics; International Society for Prosthetics and 4498
Orthotics and Prosthetics; American Board for Certification in 4460
Orthotists and Prosthetists; American Academy of 4457
Orthotists and Prosthetists; International Association of 2422
Orton Dyslexia Society 3569
Orton Society 3569
Ortopedi ve Travmatoloji Dernegi; Turk 9938
Ortopediese Vereniging; Suid-Afrikaanse 9937
Orvis School of Nursing • University of Nevada, Reno 8809
OSG Foundation 805
OSHA Consultation Division
Labor and Industries Department • Massachusetts Executive Office of
Labor 9886
Oklahoma Department of Labor 9901
OSHA Consultation Unit • Work Place Services Division • Minnesota
Department of Labor and Industry 9888

Index

Otolaryngologists - Head and Neck Surgeons; Society of University   **12310**
Otolaryngologists; Society of Military   **7810**
Otolaryngology Administrators; Association of   **5562**
Otolaryngology; American Board of   **3482**
Otolaryngology - Head and Neck Surgery; American Academy of   **12207**
Otolaryngology - Head and Neck Surgery; Canadian Society of   **12263**
Otologic Research; New York Foundation for   **3614**
Otological Research Laboratories • Ohio State University   **3615**
Otological Society; American   **3468, 3490**
Otological Society; American Laryngological, Rhinological and   **3488**
O'Toole Foundation; Theresa and Edward   **6382**
Oto-Rhino-Laryngological Societies; International Federation of   **3535**
Oto-Rhino-Laryngology and Broncho-Esophagology; Pan American Association of   **3570**
Otorhinolaryngology; Osteopathic College of Ophthalmology and   **10007**
Otorrinolaringologia y Broncoesofagologia; Asociacion Panamericana de 3570
Ottawa; AIDS Committee of   **6616**
Otterbein College • Nursing Program   **8885**
Otto Bremer Foundation   **420**
Ouders van Dove Kinderen; Nederlandse Federatie van Organisaties van **3563**
Ouders van Slechthorende- en Spraakgestoorde; Federaties van   3519
Our Lady of Holy Cross College • Division of Nursing   **8729**
Our Lady of the Lake University • Worden School of Social Service   **11848**
Our Lady of Lourdes Medical Center • Nurse Anesthesia Program   **2296**
Outdoor Leisure Development; Blind   **13423**
Outpatient General Clinical Research Center • Johns Hopkins University **1612**
Outpatient Ophthalmic Surgery Society   **12294**
Outpatient Surgeons; American Society of   **12243**
Outpatient Unit for Clinical Research • University of Puerto Rico   **1719**
Outreach Association; American   **12009**
Outreach Program; Midwest Cooperative Group   **6080**
Ovarian Cancer Prevention and Early Detection Foundation   **5979**
Overbrook Foundation   **421**
Overcome; Project   **7486**
Overcoming Speech Impairments; AFASIC -   **3477**
Overeaters Anonymous   **7482**
Overseas Blind; American Foundation for   13466, 13602
Overseas; Health Volunteers   **1320**
Overseas Research Center • Wake Forest University   **1747**
Ovulation Method-Billings, U.S.A.; World Organization of the   11215
Ovulation Method Research and Reference Centre of Australia   **11240**
Ovulation Method Teachers Association   **11241**
Owen Trust; B. B.   **6331**
Owens-Corning Fiberglas Foundation   **806**
Oxalosis and Hyperoxaluria Foundation   **4868**
Oxford Foundation   **422**
Oxford Gerontology Center   **9273**
Oxy USA Charitable Foundation   **807**
Oxygen Therapy; International Association for   **12684**
Ozarks Chapter • Lupus Foundation of America   **8070**

P

P. Philip Levine Laboratory • Cornell University   **13134**
PACCAR Foundation   **6414**
Pace University • Lienhard School of Nursing   **8839**
Pacific Academy of Ophthalmology; Asia-   **13407**
Pacific/Asian Resource Center on Aging; National   1906
Pacific Association for the Control of Tobacco; Asia   **11732**
Pacific Associations of Optometrists; International Federation of Asian and   **13487**
Pacific Associations of Optometry; International Federation of Asian and 13487
Pacific Biomedical Research Center • University of Hawaii at Manoa   **2669**
Pacific Center on Aging; National Asian   **1906**
Pacific Community Health Organizations; Association of Asian /   **1200**
Pacific Dental Federation / Asian Pacific Regional Organization; Asian **3902**
Pacific Dermatologic Association   **4254**
Pacific Health Research Institute   **1651**
Pacific Institute for Research and Evaluation   **12097**
Pacific Lutheran University • School of Nursing   **9020**
Pacific Mutual Charitable Foundation   **808**
Pacific Northwest Research Foundation   **2604**
Pacific Orthopaedic Association; Western   **9939**
Pacific Regional Environmental Health Centre; WHO Western   **5062**
Pacific; Regional Office for the Western • World Health Organization   **1545**

Pacific Regional Organisation of the International Dental Federation; Asian   3902
Pacific Section - IPRS; Asian-   **12251**
Pacific Underwater Medicine Society; South   **1514**
Pacific University
    College of Optometry   **13376**
    Department of Occupational Therapy   **12413**
    School of Physical Therapy   **12534**
Pacific Women's Traditional Medicine Association   **2232**
Pacing and Electrophysiology; North American Society of   **2789, 2869**
Packaging Council; Health Care Compliance   **5851**
Packard Children's Hospital at Stanford • Rehabilitation Engineering Center   **12741**
Packard Foundation; David and Lucile   **3136**
Paediatric Anaesthetists of Great Britain and Ireland; Association of   **2356**
Paediatric Association; Malaysian   **3256**
Paediatric Dentistry; International Association of   **3241**
Paediatric Endocrinology; European Society for   **3223**
Paediatric Haematology and Immunology; European Society for   **3224**
Paediatric Nephrology; European Society for   **3225**
Paediatric Radiology; European Society of   **11113**
Paediatric Society; Canadian   **3195**
Paediatric Society; Moroccan   **3260**
Paediatric Society; Papua New Guinea   **3278**
Paediatric Society; Singapore   **3287**
Paediatric Surgeons; British Association of   **3194**
Paediatric Surgeons; Scandinavian Association of   **12299**
Paediatric Surgeons; South African Association of   **3298**
Paediatric Surgical Associations; European Union of   **12271**
Paffenbarger Dental Research Laboratory; George C. • Ohio State University   **4005**
Paget Foundation for Paget's Disease of Bone and Related Disorders **7900**
Paget's Disease of Bone and Related Disorders; Paget Foundation for **7900**
Paget's Disease Foundation   7900
Pain; American Academy of Orofacial   **3866**
Pain; Argentine Association for the Study of   **8181**
Pain Association; American Chronic   **8160**
Pain Association; National Back   **8269**
Pain Center • University of Alabama at Birmingham   **8476**
Pain Concern—U.K.   **8295**
Pain Education Association; Lamaze Birth Without   9641
Pain Foundation; American Intractable   8273
Pain Foundation; Vulvar   **9702**
Pain Institute   **7928**
Pain; International Association for the Study of   **8234**
Pain Management; Institute for   7928
Pain Management Service; Stanford • Stanford University   **8431**
Pain Medicine; American Academy of   **8154**
Pain Medicine; American College of   **8161**
Pain; National Committee on the Treatment of Intractable   **8273**
Pain Outreach Association; National Chronic   **8271**
Pain Research Clinic • Intramural Research Program • National Institute of Dental Research • U.S. Department of Health and Human Services   **8439**
Pain Research and Control Institute   7928
Pain Society; American   **8168**
Pain Society; New Zealand   **8289**
Pain and TMJ Orthopedics; American Academy of Head, Facial and Neck **3859**
Pain; Vermont Rehabilitation Engineering Center for Low Back • University of Vermont   **12764**
Pakistan; Aga Khan Health Service   **1132**
Pakistan; His Royal Highness Prince Aga Khan Cetral Health Board for 1132
Pakistan Voluntary Health and Nutrition Association   **10964**
Pakistani Physicians; Association of   **1212**
Palate Association; American Cleft   2740
Palate-Craniofacial Association; American Cleft   **2740**
Palate Prosthesis; American Academy of Cleft   2740
Palate Rehabilitation; American Association for Cleft   2740
Palestine Endowment Funds   1464
Palm Beach Community College, Eissey Campus • Respiratory Therapist Program   **11358**
Palm Beach Regional Office • Florida Chapter • Cystic Fibrosis Foundation   **5411**
Palmer College of Chiropractic   **3438**
Palmer College of Chiropractic, West   **3434**
Palmer Eye Institute; Bascom • University of Miami   **13654**
Palmer Fund; Frank Loomis   **199**
Palo Alto Institute of Molecular Medicine   **2605**

Parsons Foundation; Ralph M.   437
Parsons Research Center   **4318**
Parsons - W.D. Charities; Vera Davis   6385
Partial Hospitalization; American Association for   **7279**
Partial Hospitalization Study Group   7279
Partially Sighted Society   **13552**
Participaction   **1463**
Partnership for a Drug Free America   **12068**
Partnership for a Drug-Free America; Media- Advertising   12068
Partnership Program; Women of Color   **11255**
Past-Life Research and Therapies; Association for   **12666**
Path-Finder Guide Dogs   13515
Pathfinder International   **11242**
Pathobiology; Laboratory of Pulmonary • National Institute of Environmental Health Sciences • U.S. Department of Health and Human Services   5110
Pathobiology Unit; Lung Disease, Cancer, Lymphocytes, Air Pollution, and General • University of Southern California   **10181**
Pathogen Studies; Center for Host- Arthropod- • Oklahoma State University   **6782**
Pathogenesis Branch • Division of Acquired Immunodeficiency Syndrome (AIDS) • National Institute of Allergy and Infectious Diseases • U.S. Department of Health and Human Services   **6819**
Pathogenesis and Immunology; Laboratory of Bacterial • Rockefeller University   **2113**
Pathogenesis; Laboratory of Viral • Harvard Medical School   **2578**
Pathogenesis; Laboratory of Viral and Molecular • National Institute of Neurological Disorders and Stroke • U.S. Department of Health and Human Services   **8466**
Pathogens; Laboratory of Vectors and • National Institute of Allergy and Infectious Diseases • U.S. Department of Health and Human Services   **6837**
Pathologie - Anatomique et Clinique; Association Mondiale des Societes de   10141
Pathologie Exotique; Societe de   6667
Pathologie Geographique; Societe Internationale de   10134
Pathologists; American Association of   10125
Pathologists; American Association of Avian   **13027**
Pathologists; American College of Veterinary   **13049**
Pathologists; American Osteopathic College of   **9989**
Pathologists; American Society of Clinical   **7123**
Pathologists' Assistants; American Association of   **10119**
Pathologists; College of American   **7131**
Pathologists; International Association of Oral   **10132**
Pathologists; Society of Toxicologic   **10138**
Pathology; American Academy Oral   10117
Pathology; American Academy Oral and Maxillofacial   **10117**
Pathology; American Association of Chairmen of Medical School Departments of   10126
Pathology; American Board of   **10121**
Pathology; American Board of Oral   **10120**
Pathology; American Registry of   **10123**
Pathology; American Society for Colposcopy and Cervical   **9629**
Pathology; American Society for Investigative   **10125**
Pathology—Anatomic and Clinical; World Association of Societies of   **10141**
Pathology; Armed Forces Institute of
  Cellular Pathology Department
    Cytopathology Division • U.S. Department of Defense   **10146**
    Molecular Pathology Division • U.S. Department of Defense   **10147**
    U.S. Department of Defense   **10145**
  Center for Advanced Pathology
    Cardiovascular Pathology Department • U.S. Department of Defense   **10148**
    Dermatopathology Department • U.S. Department of Defense   **10149**
    Environmental and Drug-Induced Pathology Department • U.S. Department of Defense   **10150**
    Genitourinary Pathology Department • U.S. Department of Defense   **10151**
    Gynecologic and Breast Pathology Department • U.S. Department of Defense   **10152**
    Hematologic and Lymphatic Pathology Department • U.S. Department of Defense   **10153**
    Hepatic and Gastrointestinal Pathology Department • U.S. Department of Defense   **10154**
    Infectious and Parasitic Disease Pathology Department • U.S. Department of Defense   **10155**
    Legal Medicine, Quality Assurance, and Risk Management Department • U.S. Department of Defense   **10156**
    Neuropathology Department • U.S. Department of Defense   **10157**

    Ophthalmic Pathology Department • U.S. Department of Defense   **10158**
    Oral Pathology Department • U.S. Department of Defense   **10159**
    Orthopedic Pathology Department • U.S. Department of Defense   **10160**
    Pediatric Pathology Department • U.S. Department of Defense   **10161**
    Pulmonary and Mediastinal Pathology Department • U.S. Department of Defense   **10162**
    Radiologic Pathology Department • U.S. Department of Defense   **10163**
    Soft Tissue Pathology Department • U.S. Department of Defense   **10164**
  Center for Medical Illustration • U.S. Department of Defense   **7025**
  Environmental Pathology Department • Biochemistry Division • U.S. Department of Defense   **10165**
  Genitourinary Pathology Department
    Medical Nephropathology Division • U.S. Department of Defense   **10166**
    Urologic Pathology Division • U.S. Department of Defense   **10167**
  Infectious and Parasitic Disease Pathology Department
    AIDS Pathology Division • U.S. Department of Defense   **10168**
    Geographic Pathology Division • U.S. Department of Defense   **10169**
    Microbiology Division • U.S. Department of Defense   **10170**
  National Museum of Health and Medicine • U.S. Department of Defense   **7026**
  Office of the Armed Forces Medical Examiner
    Forensic and Aerospace Pathology Division • U.S. Department of Defense   **10171**
    Toxicology Division • U.S. Department of Defense   **10172**
  Oral Pathology Department • Forensic Dentistry Division • U.S. Department of Defense   **10173**
  Otolaryngic and Endocrine Pathology Department
    Endocrine Pathology Division • U.S. Department of Defense   **10174**
    Otolaryngic Pathology Division • U.S. Department of Defense   **10175**
  Scientific Laboratories Department • Altitude and Hyperbaric Physiology Division • U.S. Department of Defense   **10176**
  Scientific Laboratory Department • Immunopathology Division • U.S. Department of Defense   **10177**
  U.S. Department of Defense   **10116**
  Veterinary Pathology Department
    Laboratory Animal Medicine Division • U.S. Department of Defense   **10178**
    Veterinary Pathology Division • U.S. Department of Defense   **10179**
Pathology and Audiology; American Boards of Examiners in Speech   3511
Pathology and Audiology; Council on Professional Standards in Speech-Language   **3511**
Pathology and Audiology Department; Speech and Language • University of Nevada, Reno   **3650**
Pathology Branch • Division of Intramural Research • National Heart, Lung, and Blood Institute • U.S. Department of Health and Human Services   **2943**
Pathology Chairmen; Association of   10126
Pathology Chairs; Association of   **10126**
Pathology Club; Gastrointestinal   10130
Pathology and Colposcopy; International Federation of Cervical   **9664**
Pathology Department; Cardiovascular • Center for Advanced Pathology • Armed Forces Institute of Pathology • U.S. Department of Defense   **10148**
Pathology Department; Cellular • Armed Forces Institute of Pathology • U.S. Department of Defense   **10145**
Pathology Department; Environmental and Drug-Induced • Center for Advanced Pathology • Armed Forces Institute of Pathology • U.S. Department of Defense   **10150**
Pathology Department; Genitourinary • Center for Advanced Pathology • Armed Forces Institute of Pathology • U.S. Department of Defense   **10151**
Pathology Department; Gynecologic and Breast • Center for Advanced Pathology • Armed Forces Institute of Pathology • U.S. Department of Defense   **10152**
Pathology Department; Hematologic and Lymphatic • Center for Advanced Pathology • Armed Forces Institute of Pathology • U.S. Department of Defense   **10153**
Pathology Department; Hepatic and Gastrointestinal • Center for Advanced Pathology • Armed Forces Institute of Pathology • U.S. Department of Defense   **10154**
Pathology Department; Infectious and Parasitic Disease • Center for Advanced Pathology • Armed Forces Institute of Pathology • U.S. Department of Defense   **10155**

Pathology Department; Ophthalmic • Center for Advanced Pathology • Armed Forces Institute of Pathology • U.S. Department of Defense **10158**

Pathology Department; Oral • Center for Advanced Pathology • Armed Forces Institute of Pathology • U.S. Department of Defense **10159**

Pathology Department; Orthopedic • Center for Advanced Pathology • Armed Forces Institute of Pathology • U.S. Department of Defense **10160**

Pathology Department; Pediatric • Center for Advanced Pathology • Armed Forces Institute of Pathology • U.S. Department of Defense **10161**

Pathology Department; Pulmonary and Mediastinal • Center for Advanced Pathology • Armed Forces Institute of Pathology • U.S. Department of Defense **10162**

Pathology Department; Radiologic • Center for Advanced Pathology • Armed Forces Institute of Pathology • U.S. Department of Defense **10163**

Pathology Department; Soft Tissue • Center for Advanced Pathology • Armed Forces Institute of Pathology • U.S. Department of Defense **10164**

Pathology Division • Walter Reed Army Institute of Research • Army Medical Research and Development Command • U.S. Department of Defense **7834**

Pathology Division; AIDS • Infectious and Parasitic Disease Pathology Department • Armed Forces Institute of Pathology • U.S. Department of Defense **10168**

Pathology Division; Endocrine • Otolaryngic and Endocrine Pathology Department • Armed Forces Institute of Pathology • U.S. Department of Defense **10174**

Pathology Division; Forensic and Aerospace • Office of the Armed Forces Medical Examiner • Armed Forces Institute of Pathology • U.S. Department of Defense **10171**

Pathology Division; Geographic • Infectious and Parasitic Disease Pathology Department • Armed Forces Institute of Pathology • U.S. Department of Defense **10169**

Pathology Division; Molecular • Cellular Pathology Department • Armed Forces Institute of Pathology • U.S. Department of Defense **10147**

Pathology Division; Otolaryngic • Otolaryngic and Endocrine Pathology Department • Armed Forces Institute of Pathology • U.S. Department of Defense **10175**

Pathology Division; Urologic • Genitourinary Pathology Department • Armed Forces Institute of Pathology • U.S. Department of Defense **10167**

Pathology Division; Veterinary • Veterinary Pathology Department • Armed Forces Institute of Pathology • U.S. Department of Defense **10179**

Pathology; European Society of **10128**

Pathology; European Society of Veterinary **13072**

Pathology Foundation; American **10122**

Pathology Foundation; Mallory Institute of **10144**

Pathology Foundation; Private Practitioners of **10122**

Pathology, Inc.; Universities Associated for Research and Education in **10180**

Pathology Information; Intersociety Committee on **10136**

Pathology; Institute of • Case Western Reserve University **10142**

Pathology; Institute for Gravitational Strain **2206, 2250**

Pathology; International Academy of **10131**

Pathology; International Council of Societies of **10133**

Pathology; International Society of Geographical **10134**

Pathology; Laboratory of • National Cancer Institute • U.S. Department of Health and Human Services **6198**

Pathology; Laboratory of Experimental
    National Cancer Institute • U.S. Department of Health and Human Services **6186**
    University of Michigan **2491**

Pathology Laboratory; Molecular • Plum Island Animal Disease Center • Agricultural Research Service • U.S. Department of Agriculture **13203**

Pathology; Registry of Comparative **10137**

Pathology of Respiration; Slovak Society of Physiology and **11606**

Pathology Section; Experimental • Laboratory of Immunology • National Institute of Allergy and Infectious Diseases • U.S. Department of Health and Human Services **2136**

Pathology Society; Exotic **6667**

Pathology Society; Gastrointestinal **10130**

Pathology; United States and Canadian Academy of **10139**

Pathology; Universities Associated for Research and Education in **10140**

Pathophysiology Directorate; Environmental • Army Research Institute of Environmental Medicine • Army Medical Research and Development Command • U.S. Department of Defense **7823**

Pathophysiology of Pregnancy; Organisation Gestosis - Society for the Study of **9688**

Pathophysiology of Pregnancy; Society for the Study of **9688**

Patient Advocates for Advanced Cancer Treatment **5980**

Patient Care Branch; Clinical Investigations and • Intramural Research Program • National Institute of Dental Research • U.S. Department of Health and Human Services **4019**

Patient Education Council; International **1355**

Patient Information and Education; National Council on **10612**

Patients; American Association of Kidney **12894**

Patients' Association; Norwegian Fibrositis **7897**

Patients Association for Pulmonary Hypertension; United **2880**

Patients; Concerned Relatives of Nursing Home **9266**

Patients on Hemodialysis; National Association of **12894**

Patients on Hemodialysis and Transplantation; National Association of **12894**

Patients; The Information Exchange on Young Adult Chronic **7387**

Patients; Recovery, Inc., The Association of Nervous and Former Mental **7499**

Patologia Cervical y Colposcopia; Federacion Internacional de **9664**

Paul and Lisa **3064**

Paul and Lisa Foundation **3064**

Pauline Allen Gill Foundation **423**

Pauling Institute of Science and Medicine; Linus **2588**

Paws With a Cause **4548**

Payne Foundation; Frank E. and Seba B. **198**

Peabody Charitable Fund; Amelia **6329**

Peabody Foundation; Amelia **41**

Peace of Mind; Operation: **7501**

Peaceful Beginnings **3279**

Pearlman Biomedical Research Institute **2606**

Pedagogical Psychotherapists Association **7483**

Pediatria; Sociedad Colombiana de **3212**

Pediatria; Sociedad Dominica de **3220**

Pediatric AIDS Foundation **3280**

Pediatric Association; Ambulatory **3157**

Pediatric Association; Bahrain **3192**

Pediatric Association; Chinese Taipei **3211**

Pediatric Association; International **3244**

Pediatric Association of Republic of China **3211**

Pediatric Branch • Division of Cancer Treatment • National Cancer Institute • U.S. Department of Health and Human Services **6162**

Pediatric Cancer Research Laboratory **6100**

Pediatric Cardiac Catheterization Laboratory • Duke University **3333**

Pediatric Clinical Research Center **3323**
    University of California, San Francisco **3357**

Pediatric Clinical Research Unit • Johns Hopkins University **3341**

Pediatric Critical Care; Laboratory of • Cornell University **10430**

Pediatric Dentistry; American Academy of **3159**

Pediatric Dentistry; American Board of **3163**

Pediatric Department Chairmen; Association of Medical School **3185**

Pediatric Dermatology; Society for **3293**

Pediatric Endocrine Department • University of Kansas **4934**

Pediatric Gastroenterology; North American Society for **3277**

Pediatric Gastroenterology and Nutrition; North American Society for **3277**

Pediatric Gastroesophageal Reflux Association; American **3168**

Pediatric Hematology / Oncology; American Society of **3173**

Pediatric Metabolic Laboratory • Oregon Health Sciences University **5344**

Pediatric Nephrology; International **3245**

Pediatric Neurosurgery; American Society for **3174**

Pediatric Neurosurgery; International Society for **3248**

Pediatric Nurse Associates and Practitioners; National Association of **9107**

Pediatric Oncology Consortium • Duke University **3334**

Pediatric Oncology Group **6101**

Pediatric Oncology; International Society of **3249**

Pediatric Oncology Nurses; Association of **3186**

Pediatric Oncology Social Workers; Association of **3187**

Pediatric Ophthalmology; American Association of **3161**

Pediatric Ophthalmology and Strabismus; American Association for **3161**

Pediatric Orthopaedic Society of North America **3281**

Pediatric Pathology Department • Center for Advanced Pathology • Armed Forces Institute of Pathology • U.S. Department of Defense **10161**

Pediatric Pharmacokinetics and Therapeutics; Center of Excellence in • University of Tennessee **10485**

Pediatric Projects **3282**

Pediatric Psychology; Society for **3294**

Pediatric Pulmonary Center • University of Wisconsin—Madison **5390**

Pediatric Pulmonary Center; Cystic Fibrosis and • Case Western Reserve University **5317**

Pediatric Pulmonary Clinic; Cystic Fibrosis and • Indiana University-Purdue University at Indianapolis **5331**

Pediatric Pulmonary and Cystic Fibrosis Care, Research & Teaching Center • Albany Medical College **5308**

Pediatric Pulmonary and Cystic Fibrosis Center • University of California, San Diego **11621**

Pediatric Pulmonary and Cystic Fibrosis Research Center • University of Nebraska at Omaha **5378**

Pediatric Pulmonary Disease Center; Cystic Fibrosis Research Center and • Tulane University **5357**

Pediatric Pulmonary Research Center **11612**

Pediatric Pulmonary Unit **11612**
Pediatric Radiology; Society for **3295**
Pediatric Research Center; Arthritis **3345**
Pediatric Research; Eastern Society for **3296**
Pediatric Research; Herman B. Wells Center for • Indiana University **6051**
Pediatric Research Institute **3344**
Pediatric Research; Society for **3296**
Pediatric Rheumatoid Clinic **3345**
Pediatric Services; Association for Ambulatory **3157**
Pediatric Societies of the Southeast Asian Region; Association of **3188**
Pediatric Societies; Union of Middle Eastern and Mediterranean **3304**
Pediatric Society; American **3169**
Pediatric Surgery; French Society of **3230**
Pediatric Surgery Research Laboratories • University of Michigan **12325**
Pediatric Transdisciplinary Education; International Academy of **3239**
Pediatric Urology; Society for **3297**
Pediatricians; American Association of Pro-Life **11200**
Pediatricians; American College of Osteopathic **3166**
Pediatrics; American Academy of **3149, 3160**
       Department of Research **5606**
Pediatrics; American Board of **3164**
Pediatrics; American College of Foot and Ankle **3165**
pediatrics; American College of Podo **3165**
Pediatrics; American Osteopathic Board of **9985**
Pediatrics; Confederation of European Specialists in **3213**
Pediatrics; Dominican Society of **3220**
Pediatrics; Genetics Section of • Louisiana State University **5338**
Pediatrics; International Society of Tropical **3250**
Pediatrics; Meyer Center for Developmental • Baylor College of Medicine **3311**
Pediatrics; Society for Behavioral **3290**
Pediatrics Society; Madagascar **3254**
Pediatrie; Association Internationale de **3244**
Pediatrie du Moyen-Orient et de la Mediterranee; Union des Societes de **3304**
Pediatrie; Societe Canadienne de **3195**
Pediatrie; Societe Malgache de **3254**
Pediatrie; Societe Marocaine de **3260**
Pediatrique; Societe Francaise de Chirurgie **3230**
Pediatrique; Societe Internationale d' Oncologie **3249**
Pediatrische Hematologie en Immunologie; Europese Vereniging voor **3224**
Pediculosis Association; National **10963**
Pedodontics; American Academy of **3159**
Pedodontics; American Board of **3163**
Pedorthics; Board of Certification in **10768**
Pedriatric Society; Colombian **3212**
Peer Education Network; BACCHUS and Gamma **12014**
Peer Review Association; American Medical **1170**
Peersuasion; Friendly **12029**
PEF Israel Endowment Funds **1464**
Pelvic Inflammatory Disease Society; Canadian **9637**
Pelvic Surgeons; Society of **12307**
PemCo. Foundation **810**
Pendergrass Diagnostic Radiology Laboratories • University of Pennsylvania **11173**
Penitentiaires; Conseil International des Services Medicaux **1341**
Penn Foundation; William **551**
Pennington Foundation; Irene W. and C. B. **292**
Pennsylvania Affiliate
       American Diabetes Association **4990**
       American Heart Association **3031**
Pennsylvania Affiliate; Southeastern • American Heart Association **3032**
Pennsylvania; American Lung Association of **11669**
Pennsylvania; Arc of **4427**
Pennsylvania; Center for Emergency Medicine of Western **4761**
Pennsylvania Chapter
       American Physical Therapy Association **12857**
       National Association of Social Workers **11919**
Pennsylvania Chapter; Central
       Arthritis Foundation **8013**
       Cystic Fibrosis Foundation **5453**
Pennsylvania Chapter; Eastern • Arthritis Foundation **8014**
Pennsylvania Chapter; Northeast • Lupus Foundation of America **8100**
Pennsylvania Chapter; Northeastern • Cystic Fibrosis Foundation **5455**
Pennsylvania Chapter; Northwestern • Lupus Foundation of America **8101**
Pennsylvania Chapter; Western
       Arthritis Foundation **8015**
       Cystic Fibrosis Foundation **5456**
       Lupus Foundation of America **8103**
Pennsylvania Coalition Against Domestic Violence **3114**

Pennsylvania College of Optometry **13377**
       Eye Institute **13624**
Pennsylvania College of Podiatric Medicine **10753**
       Center for the History of Foot Care and Footwear **10777**
       Gait Study Center **10778**
Pennsylvania Dental Association **4193**
Pennsylvania Department on Aging **2040**
Pennsylvania Department of Agriculture • Animal Industry Bureau • State Veterinarian **13287**
Pennsylvania Department of Health **11043**
       Drug and Alcohol Programs Office **12185**
       Emergency Medical Services Division **4805**
       Environmental Health Division **5166**
       Health Planning Bureau **5700**
       HIV and AIDS Bureau **6894**
       Maternal and Child Health Bureau • Maternal and Child Health Division **3416, 9762**
       Preventive Health Programs Bureau • Oral Health Program **4140**
       Quality Assurance Bureau • Hospitals Division **6514**
       Vital Records Division **7078**
Pennsylvania Department of Labor and Industry
       Occupational and Industrial Safety Bureau **9903**
       Vocational Rehabilitation Office **12808**
Pennsylvania Department of Public Welfare
       Blindness and Visual Services Bureau **13703**
       Medical Assistance Office **5806**
       Mental Health Office **7746**
       Mental Retardation Office **4381**
Pennsylvania Division • American Cancer Society **6313**
Pennsylvania Easter Seal Society **4667**
Pennsylvania Health Care Association **9364**
Pennsylvania Hospital • School of Nurse Anesthesia **2320**
Pennsylvania; Hospital Association of **6565**
Pennsylvania; Learning Disabilities Association of **4719**
Pennsylvania Medical Society **1849**
Pennsylvania Muscle Institute • University of Pennsylvania **2974**
Pennsylvania; National Kidney Foundation of Western **12973**
Pennsylvania Nurses Association **9250**
Pennsylvania Optometric Association **13831**
Pennsylvania Osteopathic Medical Association **10103**
Pennsylvania Pharmacists Association **10732**
Pennsylvania State Board of Dentistry **4087**
Pennsylvania State Board of Examiners of Nursing Home Administrators **9313**
Pennsylvania State Board of Funeral Directors **3766**
Pennsylvania State Board of Medicine **1795**
Pennsylvania State Board of Nursing **9194**
Pennsylvania State Board of Optometry **13756**
Pennsylvania State Board of Osteopathic Medicine **10051**
Pennsylvania State Board of Pharmacy **10679**
Pennsylvania State Board of Podiatry **10817**
Pennsylvania State University
       Animal Diagnostic Laboratory **13163**
       Artificial Heart Research Project **2919**
       Biomechanics Laboratory **11974**
       Center for Biostatistics and Epidemiology **7020**
       Center for Cell Research **2392**
       Center for Developmental and Health Genetics **5345**
       Center for Locomotion Studies **9947**
       Center for Mastitis Research **13164**
       Center for Special Populations and Health **1652**
       Center for Sports Medicine **11975**
       Center for Worksite Health Enhancement **9817**
       College of Health and Human Development • Graduate Studies in Health Policy and Administration **5516**
       College of Medicine **1021**
          Department of Pharmacology **10336**
       Division of Counseling and Rehabilitation Education **12629**
       Doctors Kienle Center for Humanistic Medicine **1653**
       E. Coli Reference Center **13165**
       Gerontology Center **1944**
       Institute for Policy Research and Evaluation **5636**
       Laboratory for Human Performance Research **11976**
       Milton S. Hershey Medical Center • CV Perfusion Technology Training Program **2816**
       Poultry Disease Research Laboratory **13166**
       School of Nursing **8925**
       Wiley Laboratory **13167**
Pennsylvania Veterinary Medical Association **13340**
Pensacola Christian College • School of Nursing **8620**
Pensacola Junior College • Respiratory Therapist Program **11359**

Penzance Foundation **424**
People Against Cancer **5981**
People Against Rape **3283**
People-Animals-Love **12709**
People with Disabilities; Accreditation Council on Services for **4453**
People First International **4302**
People; International Committee of Hard of Hearing Young **3534**
People-to-People Committee on Disability **4549**
People-to-People Committee for the Handicapped **4549**
People-to-People Health Foundation **1465**
People With AIDS; National Association of **6730**
People's Center for Housing Change **4550**
Peoples Health Care Foundation **1466**
People's Medical Society **1467**
Pepper Center for Research on Oral Health in Aging; Claude D. • University of Florida **1977**
Pepper Laboratory; William • University of Pennsylvania **2685**
Peptide Research Center; Michigan Gastrointestinal • University of Michigan **5252**
Performance Department; Operational • Naval Health Research Center • Naval Medical Research and Development Command • U.S. Department of Defense **7843**
Performance; Diet and Human • Beltsville Human Nutrition Research Center • Agricultural Research Service • U.S. Department of Agriculture **9533**
Performance Directorate; Occupational Health and • Army Research Institute of Environmental Medicine • Army Medical Research and Development Command • U.S. Department of Defense **7825**
Performance Institute; Human • University of Texas at Arlington **1725**
Performance; International Institute for Sport and Human • University of Oregon **11991**
Performance Laboratory; Human
 University of Rhode Island **11993**
 University of Wisconsin—La Crosse **11995**
Performance Research; Laboratory for Human
 Pennsylvania State University **11976**
 University of Utah **11994**
Perfusion; American Board of Cardiovascular **2823**
Perfusion Training Program • State University of New York Health Science Center at Brooklyn **2807**
Perhimpunan Endocrinology Indonesia **4847**
Perhimpunan Endoskopi Gastrointestinal Indonesia **5219**
Perimetric Society; International **13498**
Perinatal Addiction Research and Educati on; National Association for **12054**
Perinatal Association; National **9683**
Perinatal Center • University of Chicago **9717**
Perinatal Doppler Society; International **9668**
Perinatal Emphasis Research Centers Program • Center for Research for Mothers and Children • National Institute of Child Health and Human Development • U.S. Department of Health and Human Services **9713**
Perinatal Genetics Laboratory • University of Utah **5386**
Perinatal Obstetricians; Society of **9697**
Perinatal Research Institute **9711**
Perinatal Society of New Zealand **9689**, 9689
Perinatologi Indonesia; Perkumpulan **9655**
Perinatology Branch; Pregnancy and • Center for Research for Mothers and Children • National Institute of Child Health and Human Development • U.S. Department of Health and Human Services **9714**
Perinatology; Indonesian Society for **9655**
Perinatology; Society for Obstetric Anesthesia and **9696**
Periodontal Disease Research Center
 State University of New York at Buffalo **4007**
 University of Florida **4026**
Periodontal Diseases; Clinical Research Center for • Virginia Commonwealth University **4048**
Periodontal Diseases Research Center • University of Pennsylvania **4042**
Periodontal and Soft Tissue Diseases Research Program • Extramural Program • National Institute of Dental Research • U.S. Department of Health and Human Services **4016**
Periodontology; American Academy of **3868**
Periodontology; American Board of **3884**
Peripheral Vascular Nursing; Society for **9137**
Peritoneal Dialysis; International Society for **2426**
Perkins-Prothro Foundation **425**
Perkumpulan Perinatologi Indonesia **9655**
Permanent Blind Relief War Fund **13466**
Permian Basin; Easter Seal Society of the **4677**
Peroneal Muscular Atrophy International Association; Charcot-Marie- Tooth Disease/ **8202**
Peroneal Muscular Atrophy; National Foundation for **8198**
Peroral Muscular Antrophy International Association; Charcot-Marie-Tooth Disease/ **8199**

Perot Foundation **426**
Persatuan Dermatologi Malaysia **4228**
Persatuan Juru X-Ray Malaysia **11125**
Persatuan Pediatric Malaysia **3256**
Persis Hawaii Foundation **811**
Persistent Viral Diseases; Laboratory of • National Institute of Allergy and Infectious Diseases • U.S. Department of Health and Human Services **6836**
Personality Assessment; Society for **7515**
Personality and Cognition; Laboratory of • National Institute on Aging • U.S. Department of Health and Human Services **1963**
Personality Disorders Research Branch; Mood, Anxiety, and • Clinical Research Division • National Institute of Mental Health • U.S. Department of Health and Human Services **7622**
Personnel; American Society for Healthcare Central Service **6427**
Personnel and Guidance Association; American **7293**
Personnel; Joint Review Committee for Ophthalmic Medical **13510**
Personnel; National Certification Agency for Medical Lab **7146**
Personnel in Ophthalmology; Association of Technical **13418**
Personnel in Ophthalmology; Joint Commission on Allied Health **13509**
Persons with Disabilities; Academy of Dentistry for **3843**
Persons with Disabilities; Center for • Utah State University **4601**
Persons With Visual Impairment; Catholic Association of **13431**
Peruvian Heart Association **2871**
Pesticide Action Network North America Regional Center **5056**
Pesticide Education and Action Project **5056**
Pesticide Hazard Assessment Program; Iowa • University of Iowa **5122**
Pesticide Information Clearinghouse; National **5054**
Pesticide Residue, Toxic Waste and Basic Research Analytical Laboratory • University of Miami **5123**
Pesticide Telecommunication Network; National **5054**
Pesticides; National Coalition Against the Misuse of **5051**
Peter Kiewit Foundation **427**
Pew Charitable Trusts **428**
PF **11242**
Pfizer Foundation **812**
Pforzheimer Foundation; Carl and Lily **85**
Pharmaceutical Association **10615**
Pharmaceutical Association; Alaska **10695**
Pharmaceutical Association; American **10585**
Pharmaceutical Association; Auxiliary to the American **10591**
Pharmaceutical Association; Canadian **10592**
Pharmaceutical Association; Chinese **10594**
Pharmaceutical Association; Commonwealth **10596**
Pharmaceutical Association; Hawaii **10705**
Pharmaceutical Association; Idaho State **10706**
Pharmaceutical Association; Montana State **10720**
Pharmaceutical Association; National **10613**
Pharmaceutical Association; National Council of State **5597**
Pharmaceutical Association; New Mexico **10725**
Pharmaceutical Association; North Carolina **10727**
Pharmaceutical Association; North Dakota **10728**
Pharmaceutical Association; Oklahoma **10730**
Pharmaceutical Association; Rhode Island **10734**
Pharmaceutical Association Secretaries; National Conference of State **5597**
Pharmaceutical Association; South Dakota **10736**
Pharmaceutical Association; Student American **10576**
Pharmaceutical Association Student Section; American **10576**
Pharmaceutical Association; Utah **10739**
Pharmaceutical Association; Washington, DC **10702**
Pharmaceutical Association; Women's Auxiliary of the American **10591**
Pharmaceutical Biotechnology; Center for • University of Illinois at Chicago **10471**
Pharmaceutical Council; National **5873**
Pharmaceutical Economics; Center for • University of Arizona **10631**
Pharmaceutical Education; American Council on **10582**
Pharmaceutical Education; American Foundation for **10497**, **10583**
Pharmaceutical Engineering; International Society for **2427**
Pharmaceutical Engineers; International Society of **2427**
Pharmaceutical Faculties; American Conference of **10578**
Pharmaceutical Federation; International **10604**
Pharmaceutical Group of the European Community **10616**
Pharmaceutical Industry Association; Generic **5850**
Pharmaceutical Manufacturers Association **5880**, **10184**
Pharmaceutical Manufacturers; National Association of **5868**
Pharmaceutical Marketing and Management Research Program • University of Mississippi **10636**
Pharmaceutical Physicians; International Federation of Associations of **10602**
Pharmaceutical Research; Center for Imaging and **10428**

Pharmaceutical Research and Science; Academy of **10574**

Pharmaceutical Science and Technology Center • University of Kentucky **10634**

Pharmaceutical Sciences; Academy of 10574

Pharmaceutical Sciences; Research Institute of • University of Mississippi **10637**

Pharmaceutical Scientists; American Association of **10579**

Pharmaceutical Society; Delaware **10701**

Pharmaceutical Society of Great Britain; Royal **10623**

Pharmaceutical Society of Singapore **10617**

Pharmaceutical Society of the State of New York **10726**

Pharmaceutical Students' Federation; International **10605**

Pharmaceutical Study Center • Long Island University **10629**

Pharmaceutique Canadienne; Association 10592

Pharmaceutique; Federation Internationale 10604

Pharmacie; Federation Internationale des Etudiants en 10605

Pharmacie; Koninklijke Nederlandse Maatschappij ter Bevordering der 10621

Pharmaciens Catholiques; Federation Internationale des 10603

Pharmaciens d'Hopitaux; Societe Canadienne des 10593

Pharmaciens Homeopathiques; Comite International des 2212

Pharmacies; National Association of Mail Service 5721

Pharmacists Against Drug Abuse **12069**

Pharmacists; American Society of Consultant **10587**

Pharmacists; American Society of Hospital **10588**

Pharmacists Association; Arkansas **10697**

Pharmacists Association; California **10698**

Pharmacists Association; Colorado **10699**

Pharmacists Association; Connecticut **10700**

Pharmacists; Association of Democratic **10589**

Pharmacists Association; Illinois **10707**

Pharmacists Association; Indiana **10708**

Pharmacists Association; Iowa **10709**

Pharmacists Association; Kansas **10710**

Pharmacists Association; Kentucky **10711**

Pharmacists Association; Louisiana **10712**

Pharmacists Association; Maryland **10714**

Pharmacists Association; Massachusetts **10715**

Pharmacists Association; Michigan **10716**

Pharmacists Association; Minnesota **10717**

Pharmacists Association; Mississippi **10718**

Pharmacists Association; Nebraska **10721**

Pharmacists Association; Nevada **10722**

Pharmacists Association; New Hampshire **10723**

Pharmacists Association; New Jersey **10724**

Pharmacists Association; Ohio **10729**

Pharmacists Association; Oregon State **10731**

Pharmacists Association; Pennsylvania **10732**

Pharmacists Association; Tennessee **10737**

Pharmacists Association; Vermont **10740**

Pharmacists Association; Virginia **10741**

Pharmacists Association; Washington State **10742**

Pharmacists Association; West Virginia **10743**

Pharmacists Association; Wisconsin **10744**

Pharmacists Association; Wyoming **10745**

Pharmacists; Canadian Society of Hospital **10593**

Pharmacists and Corporate America for AIDS Education; Foundation of **6669**

Pharmacists; European Association of Hospital **10597**

Pharmacists Fellowship International; Christian **10595**

Pharmacists Guild of the United States; National Catholic **10611**

Pharmacists; International Committee of Homeopathic **2212**

Pharmacists; International Federation of Catholic **10603**

Pharmacists for Life 11243

Pharmacists for Life International **11243**

Pharmacists; National Association of German **10609**

Pharmacists; National Association of Women **10610**

Pharmacists in Ophthalmic Practice **10618**

Pharmacists; Panhellenic Association of **10614**

Pharmacists Research and Education Foundation; American Society of Hospital **10498**

Pharmacoepidemiology Research; Center for • State University of New York at Buffalo **10457**

Pharmacognosy; American Society of **10398**

Pharmacokinetics; Laboratory of Applied • University of Southern California **10484**

Pharmacokinetics Laboratory; Clinical • State University of New York at Buffalo **10458**

Pharmacokinetics and Therapeutics; Center of Excellence in Pediatric • University of Tennessee **10485**

Pharmacologic Studies Laboratory; Physiologic and • National Institute on Alcohol Abuse and Alcoholism • U.S. Department of Health and Human Services **12113**

Pharmacological Society; British **10402**

Pharmacological Society; Chinese **10405**

Pharmacological Society; South African **10422**

Pharmacology; American College of Clinical **10394**

Pharmacology; Associates of Clinical **10400**

Pharmacology and Biorelated Chemistry Program • National Institute of General Medical Sciences • U.S. Department of Health and Human Services **10465**

Pharmacology Branch; Behavioral • Basic Research Division • National Institute on Drug Abuse • U.S. Department of Health and Human Services **12122**

Pharmacology Branch; Clinical • Addiction Research Center • National Institute on Drug Abuse • U.S. Department of Health and Human Services **12116**

Pharmacology; Center for Clinical • Vanderbilt University **10491**

Pharmacology; Central American Society of **10403**

Pharmacology; China Association of Traditional Chinese Medicine and **2184**

Pharmacology Division; Clinical • Ohio State University **10448**

Pharmacology and Experimental Therapeutics; American Society for **10183, 10399**

Pharmacology and Experimental Therapeutics; Interdisciplinary Program in Cell and Molecular • Medical University of South Carolina **10445**

Pharmacology; Institute of Ocular • Texas A&M University **10460**

Pharmacology; International Union of **10415**

Pharmacology; Korean Society of **10416**

Pharmacology; Laboratory of Biochemical • National Institute of Diabetes and Digestive and Kidney Diseases • U.S. Department of Health and Human Services **2642**

Pharmacology; Laboratory of Cellular and Molecular • National Institute of Environmental Health Sciences • U.S. Department of Health and Human Services **5106**

Pharmacology; Laboratory of Chemical • National Heart, Lung, and Blood Institute • U.S. Department of Health and Human Services **2950**

Pharmacology; Laboratory of Human • Medical College of Pennsylvania and Hahnemann University **10444**

Pharmacology; Laboratory of Metabolism- • Rockefeller University **10453**

Pharmacology; Laboratory of Molecular • National Cancer Institute • U.S. Department of Health and Human Services **6196**

Pharmacology Research Associate Program • National Institute of General Medical Sciences • U.S. Department of Health and Human Services **10466**

Pharmacology Research Laboratory • Indiana University-Purdue University at Indianapolis **10437**

Pharmacology Research Laboratory; Preclinical • Addiction Research Center • National Institute on Drug Abuse • U.S. Department of Health and Human Services **12119**

Pharmacology Research Unit; Behavioral • Johns Hopkins University **12095**

Pharmacology Society; Behavioral **7342**

Pharmacologic and Therapeutics; American Academy of Veterinary **13024**

Pharmacology and Therapeutics; American Society for Clinical **10397**

Pharmacology; Upjohn Center for Clinical • University of Michigan **10479**

Pharmacopee; Commission Europeenne de 10598

Pharmacopeial Convention; United States **10625**

Pharmacopoeia Commission; European 10598

Pharmacopoeia; Academy of General Practice of 10575

Pharmacy; Academy of Students of **10576**

Pharmacy; Alabama State Board of **10641**

Pharmacy; Alaska Board of **10642**

Pharmacy; American Association of Colleges of **10578**

Pharmacy; American College of Clinical **10581**

Pharmacy; American Institute of the History of **10584, 10627**

Pharmacy; American Society for Automation in **10586**

Pharmacy; Arizona State Board of **10643**

Pharmacy; Arkansas State Board of **10644**

Pharmacy Association; Alabama **10694**

Pharmacy Association; American Managed Care **5721**

Pharmacy Association; Arizona **10696**

Pharmacy Association Executives; National Council of State **5597**

Pharmacy Association; Florida **10703**

Pharmacy Association; Georgia **10704**

Pharmacy Association; Maine **10713**

Pharmacy Association; Missouri **10719**

Pharmacy Association; South Carolina **10735**

Pharmacy Association; Texas **10738**

Pharmacy; Board of
    Illinois Department of Professional Regulation **10654**
    Indiana Health Professions Bureau **10655**

Physical Fitness and Sports; National Association of Governor's Councils on **10855**

Physical and Health Disabilities; Division for • Council for Exceptional Children **4479**

Physical and Health Education; Society of State Directors of **5604**

Physical Medicine and Rehabilitation; American Academy of **12647**

Physical Medicine and Rehabilitation; American Board of **12648**

Physical Medicine and Rehabilitation; American Osteopathic Academy of 9993

Physical Medicine and Rehabilitation; American Osteopathic College of 9993

Physical Medicine and Rehabilitation; American Society of **12647**

Physical Medicine and Rehabilitation; Canadian Association of **12670**

Physical Medicine and Rehabilitation; International Federation of **12685**

Physical and Mental Rehabilitation; Association for **12653**

Physical Regulation in Biology and Medicine; Society for **2547**

Physical Sciences and Engineering Division • National Institute for Occupational Safety and Health • U.S. Department of Health and Human Services **9831**

Physical Sciences Laboratory • Division of Computer Research and Technology • National Institutes of Health • U.S. Department of Health and Human Services **2657**

Physical Therapeutic Association; American Women's **12657**

Physical Therapists; Association of Independent **12665**

Physical Therapy Association; American **12657**

    Alabama Chapter **12823**

    Arizona Chapter **12824**

    Arkansas Chapter **12825**

    California Chapter **12826**

    Colorado Chapter **12827**

    Connecticut Chapter **12828**

    Florida Chapter **12829**

    Georgia Chapter **12830**

    Idaho Chapter **12831**

    Illinois Chapter **12832**

    Indiana Chapter **12833**

    Iowa Chapter **12834**

    Kansas Chapter **12835**

    Kentucky Chapter **12836**

    Louisiana Chapter **12837**

    Maine Chapter **12838**

    Maryland Chapter **12839**

    Massachusetts Chapter **12840**

    Michigan Chapter **12841**

    Minnesota Chapter **12842**

    Mississippi Chapter **12843**

    Missouri Chapter **12844**

    Montana Chapter **12845**

    Nebraska Chapter **12846**

    Nevada Chapter **12847**

    New Hampshire Chapter **12848**

    New Jersey Chapter **12849**

    New Mexico Chapter **12850**

    New York Chapter **12851**

    North Carolina Chapter **12852**

    North Dakota Chapter **12853**

    Ohio Chapter **12854**

    Oklahoma Chapter **12855**

    Oregon Chapter **12856**

    Pennsylvania Chapter **12857**

    Private Practice Section **12658**

    Rhode Island Chapter **12858**

    South Carolina Chapter **12859**

    Tennessee Chapter **12860**

    Texas Chapter **12861**

    Utah Chapter **12862**

    Virginia Chapter **12863**

    Washington Chapter **12864**

    Wisconsin Chapter **12865**

Physical Therapy Association; Orthopaedic Section, American **12708**

Physical Therapy Association; U.S. **12725**

Physical Therapy; Foundation for **12331**

Physical Therapy Laboratory for Cumulative Trauma Disorders • University of Michigan—Flint **9858**

Physical Therapy; World Confederation for **12727**

Physically Handicapped; Congress of Organizations of the **4478**

Physically Handicapped; Division for **4479**

Physically Handicapped, Homebound and Hospitalized; Division on **4479**

Physically Handicapped; National Association of the **4516**

Physically Handicapped; National Congress of Organizations of the **4478**

Physically Handicapped; Special Interest Committee for Computers and the 4559

Physically Handicapped; Special Interest Group for Computers and the **4559**

Physician Assistant Program

    Finch University of Health Sciences / Chicago Medical School **1073**

    State University of New York Health Science Center at Brooklyn **1094**

Physician Assistant Programs; Association of **1214**

Physician Assistants; Accreditation Review Committee on Education for **1122**

Physician Assistants; American Academy of **1137**

Physician Assistants in Cardiovascular Surgery; Association of **12254**

Physician Assistants; Joint Review on Educational Programs for **1122**

Physician Assistants; National Commission on Certification of **1411**

Physician Executives; American College of **5549**

Physician-Hospital Organizations; American Association of **5541**

Physician Insurers Association of America **5743**

Physician Nurses; National Association of **9108**

Physician Program; Impaired **12032**

Physician Quality Assurance; Maryland Board of **1777, 10033**

Physician Recruiters; National Association of **5869**

Physicians Abroad; Association of Haitian **1203**

Physicians in America; Association of Philippine **1213**

Physicians in America; Association of Philippine Practicing 1213

Physicians; American Academy of Disability Evaluating **4456**

Physicians; American Academy of Family **913, 1136**

Physicians; American Academy of Sports **11935**

Physicians; American Association of Parenthood **11204**

Physicians; American Association of Public Health **10936**

Physicians; American Association of School **1181**

Physicians; American Board of Quality Assurance and Utilization Review **1148**

Physicians; American College of **914, 1156**

Physicians; American College of Chest **2784, 2826**

Physicians; American College of Emergency **4734**

Physicians; American College of International **1153**

Physicians; American College of Nuclear **11088**

Physicians; American College of Osteopathic Emergency **9974**

Physicians; American College of Osteopathic Family **9975**

Physicians; American Osteopathic Board of Family **9984**

Physicians; American Society of Bariatric **1182**

Physicians; American Society of Handicapped **4462**

Physicians; American Society of Psychoanalytic **7310**

Physicians; American Society of Transplant **12867**

Physicians Assistants; Accreditation Committee on Education for 1122

Physician's Assistants; Joint Review Committee on Educational Programs for 1122

Physician's Assistants; National Commission on Certification of 1411

Physicians; Association of American **1198**

Physicians; Association of American Indian **1196**

Physicians Association for Anthroposophical Medicine **2233**

Physicians Association of Computer Medicine; American **1174**

Physicians Association; Federal **1286**

Physicians Association; Flying **1292**

Physicians; Association of German Radiologists and Nuclear **11101**

Physician's Association; National Osteopathic Women **10006**

Physicians Association for Orthopedics **9934**

Physicians; Association of Pakistani **1212**

Physicians; Association of Planned Parenthood **11204**

Physicians; Association of Professional Baseball **11942**

Physicians Association; Renal **12911**

Physicians Association; Turkish American **1521**

Physicians in Audiology; International Association of **3531**

Physicians of Canada; College of Family **1247**

Physicians for Choice **11244**

Physicians Committee for Responsible Medicine **1475**

Physicians and Dentists; National Association of VA **7804**

Physicians and Dentists; Union of American **1524**

Physicians Education Network **13553**

Physicians Fellowship for the Israel Medical Association; American **1175**

Physicians Fellowship for Medicine in Israel; American **1175**

Physicians Forum **5744**

Physicians Guilds; National Federation of Catholic **1416**

Physicians' Health Study Research Group • Harvard University **1597**

Physicians for Human Rights; American Association of **11684**

Physicians for Human Rights; Bay Area **11687**

Physicians; International Federation of Associations of Pharmaceutical **10602**

Physicians Licensing Board; Utah **1802, 10058**

Physicians; Louisiana Association of Osteopathic **10084**

Physicians; National Association of Emergency Medical Service **4746**
Physicians; National Association of EMS 4746
Physicians; National Association of Managed Care **5739**
Physicians Practicing the Transcendental Meditation Program; American Association of 2159
Physicians Practicing the Transcendental Meditation and TM-Sidhi Programs; American Association of 2159
Physicians for the Prevention of Nuclear War; International **1356**
Physicians; Royal College of **1495**
Physicians for Social Responsibility **1476**
Physicians; Society of Air Force **7807**
Physicians and Surgeons; American Association of Podiatric **10757**
Physicians and Surgeons; Association of American **1199**
Physicians and Surgeons of California; Osteopathic **10070**
Physicians and Surgeons of Canada; Royal College of **1496**
Physicians and Surgeons; Hawaii Association of Osteopathic **10077**
Physicians and Surgeons; Illinois Association of Osteopathic **10079**
Physicians and Surgeons; Indiana Association of Osteopathic **10080**
Physicians and Surgeons; Interamerican College of **1331**
Physicians and Surgeons; International Academy of Chest **12273**
Physicians and Surgeons; Michigan Association of Osteopathic **10088**
Physicians and Surgeons; Missouri Association of Osteopathic **10091**
Physicians and Surgeons; National Board of Examiners for Osteopathic 10003
Physicians and Surgeons; Nebraska Association of Osteopathic **10093**
Physicians and Surgeons; New Jersey Association of Osteopathic **10096**
Physicians and Surgeons; North Dakota Association of Osteopathic **10099**
Physicians and Surgeons (of United States of America); Royal College of **1497**
Physicians and Surgeons of Oregon; Osteopathic **10102**
Physicians and Surgeons; Rhode Island Society of Osteopathic **10104**
Physicians and Surgeons; Vermont State Association of Osteopathic **10110**
Physicians and Surgeons; Wisconsin Association of Osteopathic **10114**
Physicians and Surgeons; Wyoming Association of Osteopathic **10115**
Physicians; Uniformed Services Academy of Family **7812**
Physicians; United States Association of 2159
Physicians Who Care **1477**
Physicians; World Organization of National Colleges, Academies and Academic Associations of General Practitioners / Family **1550**
Physicists in Medicine; American Association of **2521**
Physics; American Board of Health **2522**
Physics; American College of Medical **2523**
Physics; International Organization for Medical **2538**
Physics; Laboratory of Chemical • National Institute of Diabetes and Digestive and Kidney Diseases • U.S. Department of Health and Human Services **2647**
Physics; Latin American Association for Medical **2539**
Physics Society; Health **11062**
Physiologic and Pharmacologic Studies Laboratory • National Institute on Alcohol Abuse and Alcoholism • U.S. Department of Health and Human Services **12113**
Physiological and Natural Hygiene Society; American **2171**
Physiological Performance and Operational Department • Naval Health Research Center • Naval Medical Research and Development Command • U.S. Department of Defense **7844**
Physiological Sciences Program; Biophysics and • National Institute of General Medical Sciences • U.S. Department of Health and Human Services **2650**
physiological Study of Sleep; Association for the Psycho **8305**
Physiological Therapeutics; Council on Chiropractic **3453**
Physiology/Cell Biology Program; Renal • Division of Kidney, Urologic, and Hematologic Diseases • National Institute of Diabetes and Digestive and Kidney Diseases • U.S. Department of Health and Human Services **12921**
Physiology Center; Auditory • University of Wisconsin **3659**
Physiology; Center for Research in Reproductive • University of Pittsburgh **13231**
Physiology Department • Armed Forces Radiobiology Research Institute • U.S. Department of Defense **11078**
Physiology Division; Altitude and Hyperbaric • Scientific Laboratories Department • Armed Forces Institute of Pathology • U.S. Department of Defense **10176**
Physiology; Eaton-Peabody Laboratory of Auditory **3598**
Physiology Group; Exercise • Laval University **11969**
Physiology and Health; Institute for Exercise • University of Central Florida **11981**
Physiology and Immunology; Laboratory of Cellular • Rockefeller University **2114**
physiology; International Federation of Societies for Electroencephalography and Clinical Neuro 8238
Physiology Lab; Comparative • Southern Illinois University at Carbondale **2622**

Physiology Laboratory; Behavioral • University of Kentucky **7668**
Physiology; Laboratory of Biochemical • National Cancer Institute • U.S. Department of Health and Human Services **6174**
Physiology; Laboratory of Clinical • National Institute on Aging • U.S. Department of Health and Human Services **1960**
Physiology Laboratory; Exercise
  Ohio State University **11973**
  University of Missouri—Columbia **11988**
  University of Nevada, Las Vegas **11989**
Physiology; Laboratory of Exocrine • University of Alabama at Birmingham **4927**
Physiology; Laboratory of Motor • Rockefeller University **8418**
Physiology Laboratory; Stomatognathic • University of Michigan **8515**
Physiology and Medicine; Center for Space • Vanderbilt University **2413**
Physiology and Medicine; Centre for Nonlinear Dynamics in • McGill University **1630**
Physiology and Medicine Directorate; Environmental • Army Research Institute of Environmental Medicine • Army Medical Research and Development Command • U.S. Department of Defense **7824**
Physiology and Medicine Division; Altitude • Environmental Physiology and Medicine Directorate • Army Medical Research and Development Command • U.S. Department of Defense **7826**
Physiology and Medicine; Institute of Applied **1607**
Physiology and Pathology of Respiration; Slovak Society of **11606**
Physiology Program; Endocrinology- Reproductive • University of Wisconsin—Madison **9721**
Physiology Research Laboratory; Applied • Kent State University **11968**
Physiology; Society for the Scientific Study of Male Psychology and **11723**
Physiology; Society for the Study of Male Psychology and 11723
Physiology and Virology; Laboratory of Cell • Rockefeller University **6785**
Physiopathology Research Unit • National Animal Disease Center • Agricultural Research Service • U.S. Department of Agriculture **13198**
Physiotherapie Zentral Verband der Krankensgymnasten und Physiotherapeuten; Deutscher Verband fur 12679
Physiotherapists within the EC; Standing Liaison Committee of **7522**
Physiotherapists in Sports Medicine; Association of Chartered **11941**
Physiotherapy; American Council on Chiropractic 3453
Physiotherapy Association; American **12657**
Physiotherapy; British Association for the Advancement of Radiology and 11104
Physiotherapy; German Association for **12679**
Physique; Confederation Mondiale pour la Therapie 12727
Phyto Aromatherapy Association; American **2174**
Piaget Society; Jean 7432
Piaget Society: Society for the Study of Knowledge and Development; Jean **7432**
Pick, Jr. Fund; Albert **36**
Picower Institute for Medical Research **2608**
Piedmont Technical College • Respiratory Therapy Program **11530**
Pierre Fauchard Academy **3985**
Pigmentosa Foundation; National Retinitis 13456
Pike Institute on Law and Disability • Boston University **4574**
Pikes Peak Office • Colorado Chapter • Cystic Fibrosis Foundation **5406**
Pil-Anon Family Program 12024
Pills Anonymous 12070, **12070**
Pilot Dogs **13554**
Pilot Guide Dog Foundation **13555**
Pilot Parents **4303**
Pima Community College • Respiratory Therapy Program **11309**
Pima Medical Institute [Denver, CO] • Respiratory Therapist Program **11337**
Pima Medical Institute [Seattle, WA] • Respiratory Therapist Program **11572**
Pima Medical Institute [Tempe, AZ] • Respiratory Therapist Program **11311**
Pima Medical Institute [Tucson, AZ] • Respiratory Therapist Program **11310**
Pineal Society; European **4840**
Pinel Institute of Montreal Research Centre; Philippe • University of Montreal **7677**
Pinewood Foundation **431**
Piper Jaffray Cos. Foundation **817**
Pitt Community College • Respiratory Therapist Program **11480**
Pittsburg State University • Department of Nursing **8705**
Pittsburgh Cancer Institute **6102**
Pittsburgh; General Clinical Research Center at Children's Hospital of **3337**
Pittsburgh Institute of Mortuary Science **3696**
Pittsburgh National Bank Foundation **818**
Pittsburgh NMR Institute **11153**
Pittsburgh Research Center • Bureau of Mines • U.S. Department of the Interior **9845**
Pittsburgh Research Institute **5754**

Pittsburgh Transplant Foundation 12868
Pittway Corp. Charitable Foundation **819**
Pituitary Agency; National 4860
Pituitary Program; National Hormone and **4860**
PKU Parents **4870**
Plague Section • Division of Vector-Borne Infectious Diseases • National Center for Infectious Diseases • U.S. Department of Health and Human Services **6805**
Planes; The Angel **4736**
Planification Familiale; Federation Internationale pour la 11225
Planned Parenthood 11246
Planned Parenthood Association of South Africa **11245**
Planned Parenthood Federation of America **11246**
Planned Parenthood Federation of America; Research and Development Division of 11197
Planned Parenthood Federation; International **11225**
Planned Parenthood Federation, Western Hemisphere Reg ion; International **11226**
Planned Parenthood/World Population 11246
Planning Agency; Georgia State Health **5673**
Planning Association; American Health **5551**
Planning Bureau • Arkansas Department of Health **5666**
Planning Bureau; Health
   Health Division • Nevada Department of Human Resources **5690**
   Health Services Division • Montana Department of Health and Environmental Sciences **5688**
   Pennsylvania Department of Health **5700**
Planning; Center for Population • University of Michigan **1702**
Planning and Certification Office; Health • Kentucky Human Resources Cabinet **5680**
Planning Commission; Health Resources • Maryland Department of Health and Mental Hygiene **5683**
Planning and Development Agency; Alabama Health **5664**
Planning and Development Agency; Health • Hawaii Department of Health **5674**
Planning and Development Office; Statewide Health • California Health and Welfare Agency **5667**
Planning Division; Health
   Indiana Department of Health **5677**
   Maine Department of Human Services **5682**
Planning Division; Health Surveillance and • Connecticut Department of Public Health **5669**
Planning Evaluation Bureau; Systems • Nebraska Department of Health **5689**
Planning and Evaluation Division • Social and Rehabilitation Services Department • Vermont Agency of Human Services **5705**
Planning, and Evaluation Office; Policy, • Michigan Department of Public Health **5685**
Planning, Financing and Information Services Development Division; Health Care • New Jersey Department of Health **5692**
Planning and Marketing of the American Hospital Association; Society for Healthcare **6471**
Planning Office • Arizona Department of Health Services **5665**
Planning Office; Policy and • Public Health Department • Massachusetts Executive Office of Health and Human Services **5684**
Planning, Policy, and Resource Group • Administration Office • New York State Department of Health **5694**
Planning Program Development; Center for Family 11197
Planning, Research and Coordination Bureau; Interagency • South Carolina Health and Human Services Finance Commission **5701**
Planning, Research and Development Office • Washington Department of Social and Health Services **5707**
Planning and Resource Development Division; Health • Health Resources and Lab Services Bureau • Mississippi Department of Health **5686**
Planning and Review Bureau; Health Services • Public Health Services Division • New Hampshire Department of Health and Human Services **5691**
Planning Section; State Medical Facilities • Facility Services Division • North Carolina Department of Human Resources **5695**
Plans and Medical Services; Health • Health Care Policy and Financing Division • Colorado Department of Human Services **5668**
Plant Protection and Animal Health; International Regional Organization of **13088**
Plant Research; German Society for Medicinal 10420
Plant Research; Society for Medicinal **10420**
Plastic and Cosmetic Surgery; Israel Society of **12284**
Plastic, Reconstructive and Aesthetic Surgery; International Confederation for **12279**
Plastic Reconstructive and Aesthetic Surgery; Israel Association of 12284
Plastic et Reconstructive; Confederation Internationale pour la Chirurgie 12279
Plastic and Reconstructive Surgeons; American Society of **12244**

Plastic and Reconstructive Surgeons; Education Foundation of American Society of 12296
Plastic and Reconstructive Surgeons; Israel Association of 12284
Plastic and Reconstructive Surgery; American Academy of Facial **12203**
Plastic and Reconstructive Surgery; European Society of Ophthalmic **12270**
Plastic and Reconstructive Surgery; Japan Society of **12285**
Plastic and Reconstructive Surgery; Korean Society of **12286**
Plastic and Reconstructive Surgical Nurses; American Society of **9067**
Plastic Surgeons; American Association of **12213**
Plastic Surgeons; American Association of Oral and 12213
Plastic Surgeons; British Association of Aesthetic **12260**
Plastic Surgeons of Great Britain; Association of Cosmetic 12260
Plastic Surgeons; Scandinavian Association of **12300**
Plastic Surgery; American Board of **12226**
Plastic Surgery; American Society for Aesthetic **12236**
Plastic Surgery; Canadian Society for Aesthetic (Cosmetic) **12262**
Plastic Surgery Educational Foundation **12200, 12296**
Plastic Surgery Facilities; American Association for Accreditation of Ambulatory 12209
Plastic Surgery; Institute of Reconstructive • New York University **12322**
Plastic Surgery Research Council **12297**
Plastic Surgery Research Laboratories • Duke University **12319**
Plastic Surgery; Slovak Society of **12303**
Plastics Research in Dentistry; American Academy for 3841
Plastikkirurgisk Forening; Nordisk 12300
Plastination; International Society for **2714**
Play Therapy; Association for **12667**
Plough Foundation **432**
Plum Island Animal Disease Center
   Agricultural Research Service • U.S. Department of Agriculture **13201**
   Microbiology Laboratory • U.S. Department of Agriculture • Agricultural Research Service **13202**
   Molecular Pathology Laboratory • U.S. Department of Agriculture • Agricultural Research Service **13203**
PM/DM; National Support Group for **7896**
Pneumologen; Bundesverband der 11602
Pneumologie et Phtisiologie Infantile de Langue Francaise; Groupe de 3229
Pneumologists; National Association of **11602**
Pneumology and Phthisiology Group; French-Language Infant 3229
Podiatric Administration; American Academy of **5539**
Podiatric Circulatory Society; American **2175**
Podiatric Dermatology; American Society of **10765**
Podiatric Examiners; Maine Board of **10798**
Podiatric Laser Surgery; International College of 10773
Podiatric Laser Surgery; International Society of 10773, **10773**
Podiatric Management; American Academy of 5539
Podiatric Medical Assistants; American Society of **10766**
Podiatric Medical Association; American **10746, 10762**
Podiatric Medical Association Auxiliary; American **10763**
Podiatric Medical Association; National **10775**
Podiatric Medical Association; Student National **10776**
Podiatric Medical Boards; Federation of **10772**
Podiatric Medical Education; Council on **10771**
Podiatric Medical Examiners; National Board of **10774**
Podiatric Medical Students Association; American **10764**
Podiatric Medical Writers Association; American **6971**
Podiatric Medicine; Alabama State Board of **10779**
Podiatric Medicine; American Association of Colleges of **10755**
Podiatric Medicine; American Society of **10767**
Podiatric Medicine; California Board of **10783**
Podiatric Medicine; Committee of • Indiana Health Professions Bureau **10793**
Podiatric Medicine; Florida Board of **10788**
Podiatric Medicine; Hawaii Board of **10790**
Podiatric Medicine; Iowa Board of **10794**
Podiatric Medicine; Maryland Board of **10799**
Podiatric Medicine; Minnesota Board of **10802**
Podiatric Medicine; Nevada State Board of **10807**
Podiatric Medicine; New Mexico Board of **10810**
Podiatric Medicine; Pennsylvania College of
   Center for the History of Foot Care and Footwear **10777**
   Gait Study Center **10778**
Podiatric Medicine; South Carolina Board of **10820**
Podiatric Medicine and Surgery; Michigan Board of **10801**
Podiatric Medicine; Texas State Board of **10823**
Podiatric Orthopedics; American Board of 10758
Podiatric Orthopedics and Primary Medicine; American Board of **10758**
Podiatric Physicians and Surgeons; American Association of **10757**

Podiatric Radiologists; American College of   10761
Podiatric Sports Medicine; American Academy of   11934
Podiatric Students Association; American   10764
Podiatric Surgery; American Board of   10759
Podiatrists; American Association of Hospital   10756
Podiatry; American Academy of Practice Management in   5539
Podiatry; American Association of Colleges of   10755
Podiatry Association; American   10762
Podiatry Association Auxiliary; American   10763
Podiatry Association; National   10775
Podiatry Association; Women's Auxiliary, American   10763
Podiatry Board; Colorado   10784
Podiatry Board; Rhode Island   10819
Podiatry Boards; Federation of   10772
Podiatry Council; Wisconsin   10829
Podiatry; Delaware Board of Examiners in   10786
Podiatry Education; Council on   10771
Podiatry Examiners; Arizona State Board of   10781
Podiatry Examiners; District of Columbia Board of   10787
Podiatry Examiners; National Board of   10774
Podiatry Examiners; North Carolina Board of   10812
Podiatry Examiners; Puerto Rico Board of   10818
Podiatry Examining Board; Arkansas State   10782
Podiatry Examining Board; Utah   10824
Podiatry Examining Committee • Illinois Department of Professional
    Regulation   10792
Podiatry Executives; Conference of   10770
Podiatry; Georgia State Board of   10789
Podiatry; Idaho State Board of   10791
Podiatry; Kentucky Board of   10796
Podiatry Licensing Committee; Virginia   10826
Podiatry Licensure; Connecticut Board of   10785
Podiatry; Massachusetts Board of Examiners in   10800
Podiatry Medical Boards; Federation of   10772
Podiatry; Missouri State Board of   10804
Podiatry; New Hampshire Board of Registration in   10808
Podiatry; New York State Board of   10811
Podiatry; North Dakota Board of Registry in   10813
Podiatry; Oklahoma State Board of   10815
Podiatry; Pennsylvania State Board of   10817
Podiatry; South Dakota Board of   10821
Podiatry; Tennessee State Board of Registration in   10822
Podiatry; Washington State Board of   10827
Podiatry; Wyoming Board of Registration in   10830
Podopediatrics; American College of   3165
Poetry; Association for Applied   7320
Poetry Therapy; Association for   7453
Poetry Therapy Association; World   7453
Poetry Therapy; National Association for   7453
Pohl Cancer Research Laboratory, Inc.   6103
Point Loma Nazarene College • Department of Nursing   8584
Poison Center; West Virginia • West Virginia University   10495
Poison Control Center of the Childrens Hospital of Alabama   10456
Poison Control Centers; American Association of   10391
Poison Control Centers; World Federation of Associations of Clinical
    Toxicology Centers and   10425
Poison Control Centres; European Association of   10407
Poison and Drug Information Center; Arizona • University of Arizona   10468
Poisoning; Alliance to End Childhood Lead   3155
Poisons Centres and Clinical Toxicologists; European Association of
    10407
Poisons; Federation Mondiale des Associations des Centres de
    Toxicologies Clinique et des Centres Anti-   10425
Poisons et de Toxicologie Clinique; Association Europeenne des Centres
    Anti-   10407
Polaroid Foundation   820
Policy, and Aging Research; Institute for Health, Health Care • Rutgers
    University   1659
Policy Center on Aging • Brandeis University   5612
Policy; Center on Drugs and Public • University of Maryland   10635
Policy; Center for Environment and Health • University of Minnesota   5125
Policy; Center for Ethics and Social • Graduate Theological Union   7203
Policy Center; Health • Vanderbilt University   5767
Policy; Center for Health Ethics and • University of Colorado—Denver
    5648
Policy; Center on Human   4471
Policy; Center for Injury Research and • Johns Hopkins University   10867
Policy Center for the Study of Children and Families with Special Health
    Care Needs; La Rabida Research and • University of Chicago   3358
Policy; Center for the Study of Social   5617
Policy Center; Transplant and Health • University of Michigan   12891

Policy; Center for Values and Social • University of Colorado at Boulder
    7220
Policy Center; Vital Statistics and Health • Idaho Department of Health and
    Welfare   5675
Policy Commission; New Mexico Health   5693
Policy and Ethics; Center for Health • Creighton University   5621
Policy and External Affairs Office • South Dakota Department of Health
    5702
Policy Forum; National Health   1421
Policy; Health Services Management and • University of Michigan   5653
Policy and Health Statistics Division • Maryland Department of Health and
    Mental Hygiene   7060
Policy; Institute for Child Health • University of Florida   3360
Policy; Institute for Health
    Brandeis University   5611
    University of Pittsburgh   5658
    University of Texas—Houston Health Science Center   5660
Policy; Institute for Health Care Research and • Georgetown University
    5749
Policy; Malcolm Wiener Center for Social • Harvard University   5626
Policy and Management Institute; International Health   5734
Policy; National Council on Alternative Health Care   1414
Policy Office; Health • Oregon Department of Human Resources   5699
Policy Office; Management and • Health Division • Wisconsin Department of
    Health and Social Services   5708
Policy, Planning, and Evaluation Office • Michigan Department of Public
    Health   5685
Policy and Planning Office • Public Health Department • Massachusetts
    Executive Office of Health and Human Services   5684
Policy and Practice; Center for • University of Washington   11879
Policy Project; Intergovernmental Health   5582
    George Washington University   7200
Policy and Promotion; Center for Nutrition • U.S. Department of
    Agriculture   9378
Policy; Religious Coalition for a Moral Drug   1491
Policy and Research; Agency for Health Care
    Center for General Health Services Extramural Research • U.S.
        Department of Health and Human Services   5643
    Center of General Health Services Intramural Research • U.S.
        Department of Health and Human Services   5644
    Office of Health Technology Assessment • U.S. Department of Health
        and Human Services   5645
    U.S. Department of Health and Human Services   5642
Policy Research; Center for Health • American Medical Association   5607
Policy Research; Center for Health Services and • Northwestern
    University   5635
Policy Research and Education; Center for Health • Duke University   5623
Policy Research and Education; Division of Health • Harvard University
    5625
Policy Research and Evaluation; Institute for • Pennsylvania State
    University   5636
Policy Research; Institute for Health • University of Florida   5649
Policy and Research; Jane Addams Center for Social • University of Illinois
    at Chicago   11876
Policy Resource Center; Mental Health   7443
Policy; School of Health Administration and • Arizona State University
    5608
Policy Studies; Center for   5615
Policy Studies; Center for Health and Advanced • Boston University   5610
Policy Studies; Institute for Health • University of California, San
    Francisco   5646
Policy Unit; Health • Policy and Planning Office • Ohio Department of
    Health   5697
Polio League for Information and Outreach; Post-   6742
Polio; Malawi Against   6693
Polio Network; International   6681
Polio Society   6742
Polish Anatomical Society   2542
Polish Anatomical and Zoological Society   2542
Polish Deaf Union   3573
Polish Medical Association   1478
Polish Society for Immunology   2088
Polish Society of Veterinary Science   13105
Polisher Research Institute; Edward and Esther   1934
Political Psychology; International Society of   7424
Politique de Sante; Forum Europeen de   1277
Pollution, and General Pathobiology Unit; Lung Disease, Cancer,
    Lymphocytes, Air • University of Southern California   10181
Pollution; Group Against Smokers'   11737
Pollution Health Effects Laboratory; Air • University of California, Irvine
    5115
Pollution Research Laboratory; Air • University of Florida   9851
Polski Towarzystwo Lekarskie   1478

Polski Zwiazek Gluchych 3573
Polskie Towarzystwo Anatomiczne 2542
Polskie Towarzystwo Immunologiczne 2088
Polskie Towarzystwo Nauk Weterynaryjnych 13105
Polycystic Kidney Research Foundation 12918
Polysomnographic Technologists; Association of 8189
Polytechnical School of Montreal • Research Group in Biomechanics and
    Biomaterials 2463
Ponce School of Medicine 1026
        Department of Pharmacology and Toxicology 10345
Pontifical Catholic University of Puerto Rico • Department of Nursing 8944
Poor; Sisters Concerned for the Rural 1426
Poor and Underserved; Institute on Health Care for the • Meharry Medical
    College 5634
Pope Foundation 6377
Pope John XXIII Medical-Moral Research and Education Center 7213
Population Action International 11279
Population Center; Hopkins • Johns Hopkins University 11272
Population Council 11194, 11247, 11280
Population Crisis Committee 11279
Population and Development Studies; Center for • Harvard University
    11270
Population and Family Health; Center for • Columbia University 11264
Population Fund; United Nations 11283
Population Information Program 6986
Population Options; Center for 11195, 11258
Population Options' Media Project; Center for 11196
Population; Planned Parenthood/World 11246
Population Planning; Center for • University of Michigan 1702
Population Research; Center for 11263
        National Institute of Child Health and Human Development • U.S.
            Department of Health and Human Services 11284
        University of California, Los Angeles 11291
Population Research Center; Contraceptive and 11265
Population Research and Studies in Reproduction; Center for • Baylor
    College of Medicine 11261
Population Resource Center 11281
Population Studies Branch; Special • Division of Cancer Prevention and
    Control • National Cancer Institute • U.S. Department of Health and
    Human Services 6147
Population Studies Center • University of Pennsylvania 11298
Populations; Center for Vulnerable 4575
Populations and Health; Center for Special • Pennsylvania State
    University 1652
Porphyria Foundation; American 4822, 4830
Porter Psychiatric Institute; Langley • University of California, San
    Francisco 7661
Portland State University
        Center for Public Health Studies 10983
        Graduate School of Social Work 11836
        Institute on Aging 1945
        Regional Research Institute for Human Services 11873
        Research and Training Center on Family Support and Children's
            Mental Health 7593
Portsmouth Hospital Foundation 3138
Portugesa de Estomatologia Emedicina Dentaria; Sociedade 3986
Portuguesa de Miastenia Gravis e Doencas Neuromusculares;
    Associacao 8185
Portuguese Association of Dietitians 9482
Portuguese Society of Stomatology and Dental Medicine 3986
Positive Behavior Support; Research and Training Center for 7594
Positively Women 6743
Post Anesthesia Nurses; American Society of 9068
Post Anesthesia Nursing Certification; American Board of 2350
Post-Polio League for Information and Outreach 6742
Postdoctoral and Internship Centers; Association of Psychology 7334
Postgraduate Center for Mental Health 7484
Postgraduate Center for Psychotherapy 7484
Postgraduate Medical Association of North America; Interstate 1361
Postpartum Support, International 7485
Potency; Recovery of Male 11709
Potency Restored 11708
Potential; Association for the Advancement of Sports 11940
Potential; Institutes for the Achievement of Human 8231, 8377
Potsmokers Anonymous 12071
Pott Foundation; Herman T. and Phenie R. 272
Pottenger Foundation; Price- 9483
Potter Foundation; Justin and Valere 339
Poudre; Amis de Moulin a 6638
Poultry and Animal Health Section • Delaware Department of Agriculture
    13257
Poultry Association; World Veterinary 13122

Poultry Diagnostic Laboratory; TVMDL 13181
Poultry Disease Laboratory at Center • Texas A&M University 13175
Poultry Disease Laboratory; South Texas 13181
Poultry Disease Laboratory; Texas A&M University 13181
Poultry Disease Research Laboratory • Pennsylvania State University
    13166
Poultry Disease Research Unit • Southeast Poultry Research Laboratory •
    Agricultural Research Service • U.S. Department of Agriculture 13206
Poultry Processing and Meat Quality and Safety Research Unit • Richard B.
    Russell Agricultural Research Center • Agricultural Research Service •
    U.S. Department of Agriculture 10988
Poultry Research Laboratory; South Central • Agricultural Research Service
    • U.S. Department of Agriculture 13205
Poultry Research Laboratory; Southeast • Poultry Disease Research Unit •
    U.S. Department of Agriculture • Agricultural Research Service 13206
Pounds Sensibly; Take Off 1520
Poverty; National Center for Children in • Columbia University 3332
PPG Industries Foundation 821
Practical Allergy Research Foundation 2089
Practical Nurse Education and Service; National Association for 9109
Practical Nurse Examiners; Louisiana State Board of 9174
Practical Nurses Association; American Licensed 9060
Practical Nurses; Georgia State Board of Licensed 9164
Practical Nurses; National Federation of Licensed 9118
Practical Nurses; West Virginia Board of Examiners for 9207
Practice; Academy of Pharmacy 10575
Practice Administration; American Academy of Dental 3854
Practice; American Academy of Dental Group 3853
Practice; American Board of Family 1145
Practice; American College of General 1155
Practice Association; American Group 1163
Practice Association; American Professional 1176
Practice; Center for Policy and • University of Washington 11879
Practice Executives; American College of Medical 5547
Practice Innovations; Center for • Case Western Reserve University 1566
Practice and Management; Academy of Pharmacy 10575
Practice Management in Podiatry; American Academy of 5539
Practice Patterns Institute, Inc.; Medical Technology and 2720
Practice; Pharmacists in Ophthalmic 10618
Practice of Pharmacy; Academy of General 10575
Practice Section of APhA; General 10575
Practitioner; American Academy of Orthodontics for the General 3867
Practitioners; American Academy of Nurse 9048
Practitioners; American Association of Bovine 13028
Practitioners; American Association of Equine 13029
Practitioners; American Association of Feline 13030
Practitioners; American Association of Small Ruminant 13034
Practitioners; American Association of Swine 13035
Practitioners; Association of Humanistic Psychology 7328
Practitioners; European Union of Dental Medicine 3933
Practitioners; European Union of General 1279
Practitioners / Family Physicians; World Organization of National Colleges,
    Academies and Academic Associations of General 1550
Practitioners in Infection Control; Association for 6642
Practitioners; International Association of Holistic Health 2209
Practitioners; National Alliance of Nurse 9101
Practitioners; National Association of Pediatric Nurse Associates and 9107
Practitioners in Osteopathic Medicine and Surgery; American College of
    General 9975
Practitioners in Reproductive Health; National Association of Nurse 9105
Prader-Willi Foundation 2750
Prader-Willi Syndrome Association 2751
Prader-Willi Syndrome Association U.S.A. 2751
Prader-Willi Syndrome International Information Forum 2752
Prader-Willi Syndrome Parents and Friends 2751
Prairie View A&M University • College of Nursing 8988
Precision Chiropractic Research Society 3460, 3464
Preclinical Pharmacology Research Laboratory • Addiction Research Center
    • National Institute on Drug Abuse • U.S. Department of Health and
    Human Services 12119
Preferred Provider Organizations; American Association of 5720
Pregnancy Advisory Service 11248
Pregnancy; Organisation Gestosis - Society for the Study of
    Pathophysiology of 9688
Pregnancy and Parenting; National Organization of Adolescent 11239
Pregnancy, Parenting and Prevention; National Organization of
    Adolescent 11239
Pregnancy and Perinatology Branch • Center for Research for Mothers and
    Children • National Institute of Child Health and Human Development •
    U.S. Department of Health and Human Services 9714
Pregnancy Programs; Office of Adolescent • Public Health Service • U.S.
    Department of Health and Human Services 11289

Preventive Medicine; American Board of   **10836**
Preventive Medicine; American College of   **10838**
Preventive Medicine; American Osteopathic College of   **9990**
Preventive Medicine; Association of Teachers of   **10843**
Preventive Medicine; Conference of Professors of   10843
Preventive Medicine Division • Walter Reed Army Institute of Research • Army Medical Research and Development Command • U.S. Department of Defense   **7835**
Preventive Medicine; International Academy of Nutrition and   **9465**
Preventive Medicine of the Methodist Hospital; Sid W. Richardson Institute for   **10871**
Preventive Medicine and Public Health; American Board of   10836
Preventive Medicine Research Center of Cleveland   9507
Preventive Medicine Research Institute   **10869**
Preventive Oncology; American Society of   **10841**
Preventive Oncology; International Society for   **5961**
Preventive Ophthalmology; Dana Center for • Johns Hopkins University   **13605**
PRI Foundation   607
Price Associates Foundation; T. Rowe   **868**
Price Foundation; Louis and Harold   **363**
Price Memorial Foundation; Weston A.   9483
Price-Pottenger Foundation   9483
Price-Pottenger Nutrition Foundation   **9483**
Prickett Fund; Lynn R. and Karl E.   **11188**
PRIDE Foundation - Promote Real Independence for the Disabled and Elderly   **12710**
PRIDE (Parents' Resource Institute for Drug Education)   12063
Primary Care Internal Medicine; Society of Research and Education in   1508
Primary Care Research Group; North American   **1444**
Primary Medicine; American Board of Podiatric Orthopedics and   **10758**
Primate Behavior Laboratory • State University of New York Health Science Center at Brooklyn   **13173**
Primate Laboratory; Harlow • University of Wisconsin—Madison   **13238**
Primate Research Center; California Regional • University of California, Davis   **13210**
Primate Research Center; Caribbean • University of Puerto Rico   **13232**
Primate Research Center; New England Regional • Harvard University   **13136**
Primate Research Center; Oregon Regional   **13161**
Primate Research Center; Regional   **13169**
Primate Research Center; Tulane Regional • Tulane University   **13180**
Primate Research Center; Wisconsin Regional • University of Wisconsin—Madison   **13241**
Primate Research Center; Yerkes Regional • Emory University   **2572**
Primate Research Laboratory • University of South Alabama   **13234**
Primates; Laboratory for Experimental Medicine and Surgery in • New York University   **13151**
Primerica Foundation   882
Prince George's Community College • Respiratory Therapist Program   **11414**
Princeton Bio Center   **4898**
Princeton University
    Cutaneous Communication Laboratory   **8415**
    Department of Molecular Biology   **2609**
Principal Financial Group Foundation   **823**
Principals of American Schools for the Deaf; Association of Superintendents and   3507
Printing House for the Blind; American   **6972**
Prison Medical Services; International Council of   **1341**
Pritzker Foundation   433
Pritzker Institute of Medical Engineering • Illinois Institute of Technology   **2448**
Pritzker School of Medicine
    Department of Pharmacological and Physiological Sciences • University of Chicago   **10231**
    University of Chicago   **954**
Private Hospitals Association of Malawi   **6467**
Private Practice Research Group • University of Pennsylvania   **7683**
Private Practice Section • American Physical Therapy Association   **12658**
Private Practitioners of Pathology Foundation   10122
Private Psychiatric Hospitals; National Association of   6461
Private Schools for Exceptional Children; National Association of   **3263**
Private Sector; National Association of Rehabilitation Professionals in the   **12695**
Pro-Fac Foundation; Curtice-Burns /   **656**
Procter & Gamble Cosmetic & Fragrance Foundation   **824**
Procter & Gamble Fund   **825**
Proctology; American Board of   12217
Proctology; American Osteopathic College of   **9991**
Proctor Foundation for Research in Ophthalmology; Francis I.   **13596**

Productive Rehabilitation Institute of Dallas for Ergonomics   **9818**
Products Liability Project; Tobacco   **11740**
Professional Aeromedical Transport Association   **4753**
Professional Association of German Internists   **1480**
Professional Association of Health Care Office Managers   **5599**
Professional Baseball Physicians; Association of   **11942**
Professional Board for Radiography   **11066**
Professional Business Consultants; Institute of Certified   **5859**
Professional Certification Board; International Healthcare Safety   **9798**
Professional Education of the American Osteopathic Association; Bureau of   **9997**
Professional Electrologists; International Guild of   **1347**
Professional Geriatric Care Managers; National Association of   **1908**
Professional Health Workers; National New   1437
Professional and Hospital Activities; Commission on   **6440**
Professional Hypnosis; International Society for   **6594**
Professional Hypnotherapists; American Association of   **6582**
Professional Managers; Institute of Certified   **5581**
Professional Midwives Association of Germany   **9690**
Professional Natural Hygienists; International Association of   **2210**
Professional and Occupational Licensing Bureau; Montana   **10805**
Professional Practice Association; American   **1176**
Professional Psychology; American Board of   **7289**
Professional Psychology; American Board of Examiners in   7289
Professional Sleep Societies; Associated   **8186**
Professional Sleep Societies; Association of   8186
Professional Standards Review Council of America   **5600**
Professional Standards in Speech-Language Pathology and Audiology; Council on   **3511**
Professional Surrogates Association; International   **11698**
Professional Well Being; Center for   **9803**
Professional Well-Being; Center for   **7353**
Professionals; American Society of Cardiovascular   **2828**
Professionals; Associated Bodywork and Massage   **2177**
Professionals; Association of Reproductive Health   **11204**
Professionals; Association of SIDS Program   **3190**
Professionals; Center for the Well-Being of Health   7353, 9803
Professionals; Federation of Nurses and Health   **9089**
Professionals; IDEA: International Association of Fitness   **10850**
Professionals; IDEA: The Association for Fitness   10850
Professionals; International Academy of Health Care   **1334**
Professionals; International Association of Eating Disorders   **7399**
Professionals; National Association of Activity   **4513**
Professionals; National Association of Apnea   **8266**
Professionals; National Association of Disability Evaluating   **7183**
Professionals; National Association of Vision   **13526**
Professionals in the Private Sector; National Association of Rehabilitation   **12695**
Professionals for Safe Alternatives in Childbirth; International Association of Parents and   **9660**
Professionals Section of the American Public Health AssociatioN; New   **1437**
Professionals; Society for Ambulatory Care   **1505**
Professionals Society; Regulatory Affairs   **5881**
Professions; Bureau of Health • Health Resources and Services Administration • Public Health Service • U.S. Department of Health and Human Services   **9**
Professions; International Association for Child and Adolescent Psychiatry and Allied   **3240**
Professions; National Association of Advisors for the Health   **1394**
Professors of Cardiology; Association of   **2833**
Professors of Child and Adolescent Psychiatry; Society of   **7516**
Professors of Child Psychiatry; Society of   7516
Professors of Gynecology and Obstetrics; Association of   **9633**
Professors of Medicine; Association of   **1215**
Professors of Ophthalmology; Association of University   **13419**
Professors of Preventive Medicine; Conference of   10843
Program in Applied Mathematics • University of Arizona   **7036**
Program for Applied Research on Fertility Regulation • Northwestern University   **11278**
Program for Appropriate Technology in Health   **1481**
Program Directors in Internal Medicine; Association of   **1216**
Program Directors in Surgery; Association of   **12255**
Program in International Nutrition • Cornell University   **9502**
Program in Neural Science • Indiana University Bloomington   **8375**
Program in Neuronal Growth and Development • Colorado State University   **8354**
Program Operations; Bureau of • Health Care Financing Administration • U.S. Department of Health and Human Services   **5712**
Program in Psychiatry, Law, and Human Sexuality • University of California, Los Angeles   **7218**

Psychiatrie de l'Enfant et de l'Adolescent et des Professions Associees; Association Internationale de   3240

Psychiatrie de l'Enfant et de l'Adolescent; Societe Europeene de   3222

Psychiatrie; Weltverband fur   7533

Psychiatrists Against Psychiatric Abuse   **7488**

Psychiatrists in Alcoholism and Addictions; American Academy of   **12004**

Psychiatrists of America; Black   **7344**

Psychiatrists; American Academy of Clinical   **7265**

Psychiatrists; American Association of   7281

Psychiatrists; American Association of Community   **7274**

Psychiatrists; American College of   **7291**

Psychiatrists; Association of Gay and Lesbian   **7325**

Psychiatrists; Guild of Catholic   7466

Psychiatrists from India; American Association of   **7281**

Psychiatrists; National Guild of Catholic   **7466**

Psychiatry and Allied Professions; International Association for Child   3240

Psychiatry and Allied Professions; International Association for Child and Adolescent   **3240**

Psychiatry; American Academy of Child and Adolescent   **3158**

Psychiatry; American Association of Chairmen of Departments of   **7272**

Psychiatry; American Association for Geriatric   **1881**

Psychiatry; American Association for Social   **7282**

Psychiatry; American College of Forensic   **7167**

Psychiatry; American Society for Adolescent   **3171**

Psychiatry; Association for Child Psychology and   **3180**

Psychiatry Branch; Biological • Intramural Research Programs Division (Clinical Research) • National Institute of Mental Health • U.S. Department of Health and Human Services   **7635**

Psychiatry Branch; Child • Intramural Research Programs Division (Clinical Research) • National Institute of Mental Health • U.S. Department of Health and Human Services   **7636**

Psychiatry; Center for the Study of   **7354**

Psychiatry Clinic; Riley Child • Indiana University-Purdue University at Indianapolis   **3339**

Psychiatry; Committee for Truth in   **7357**

Psychiatry; Department of
    University of Michigan   **7672**
    University of Minnesota   **7674**

Psychiatry; European Society of Child and Adolescent   **3222**

Psychiatry; Group for the Advancement of   **7383**

Psychiatry and Human Behavior; Institute of • University of Maryland   **7669**

Psychiatry; Institute on Hospital and Community   **7392**

Psychiatry; International Association for Social   7531

Psychiatry; International Society for Adolescent   **3247**

Psychiatry and the Law; American Academy of   **7161**

Psychiatry, Law, and Human Sexuality; Program in • University of California, Los Angeles   **7218**

Psychiatry and Neurology; American Board of   **7290**

Psychiatry; Radical Caucus in   **7495**

Psychiatry Research Center; Keller Child • University of Louisville   **3362**

Psychiatry Research Institute; Social   **7506, 7600**

Psychiatry Research Program; Child • State University of New York Health Science Center at Brooklyn   **3351**

Psychiatry Seminar; San Francisco Social   7429

Psychiatry; Society of Biological   **7511**

Psychiatry; Society of Professors of Child   7516

Psychiatry; Society of Professors of Child and Adolescent   **7516**

Psychiatry; William Greenleaf Eliot Division of Child • Washington University   **7701**

Psychiatry; World Association for Dynamic   **7529**

Psychiatry; World Association for Social   **7531**

Psychiatry; World Federation of the Societies of Biological   **2548**

Psycho-theatrerapy; International Federation of Medical   7410

Psychoactive Drugs; American Council on Marijuana and Other   **12007**

Psychoanalyse; Deutsche Akademie fur   7380

Psychoanalysis; Academy of   7267

Psychoanalysis; American Academy of   **7267**

Psychoanalysis; American Association for Child   3179

Psychoanalysis and the American Board for Accreditation in Psychoanalysis; National Association for the Advancement of   **7450**

Psychoanalysis; Association for Applied   **7321**

Psychoanalysis; Association for Child   **3179**

Psychoanalysis; German Academy for   **7380**

Psychoanalysis; Institute for   **7572**

Psychoanalysis; Institute for Modern   **7246**

Psychoanalysis; National Psychological Association for   **7470**

Psychoanalysis (of the Karen Horney Psychoanalytic Institute and Center); Association for Advancement of   **7317**

Psychoanalysis and Process; Association for Group   **7326**

Psychoanalysis and Psychoanalysis in Groups; American Foundation for   **7295**

Psychoanalysis; Seattle Institute for   **7599**

Psychoanalysis; Society of Integral   **7418**

Psychoanalysts; American College of   **7292**

Psychoanalysts; Congress of Romance Language   **7361**

Psychoanalytic Association; American   **7302**

Psychoanalytic Center of Northern New Jersey   **7242**

Psychoanalytic Clinic; Karen Horney   7433

Psychoanalytic Medicine; Association for   **7331**

Psychoanalytic Physicians; American Society of   **7310**

Psychoanalytic and Psychosomatic Medicine; Association for   7331

Psychoanalytic Psychotherapy Study Center   **7248**

Psychoanalytic Societies; International Federation of   **7408**

Psychoanalytic Studies; Center for Modern   **7548**

Psychoanalytic Studies; Colorado Center for Modern   **7239**

Psychoanalytic Studies; Manhattan Center for Advanced   7548

Psychoanalytic Study; Center for   **7549**

Psychoanalytic Training and Research; Center for • Columbia University   **7555**

Psychoanalytical Association Trust; International   **7415**

Psycho-Analytical Federation; European   **7372**

Psychoanalytical Society; British   **7346**

Psychobiology Branch; Clinical • Intramural Research Programs Division (Clinical Research) • National Institute of Mental Health • U.S. Department of Health and Human Services   **7639**

Psychobiology of Ethnicity; Research Center on the • University of California, Los Angeles   **7658**

Psychobiology; International Society for Developmental   **7421**

Psychobiology; Laboratory of • Ohio State University   **7591**

Psychobiology; Laboratory of Developmental • Stanford University   **7602**

Psychodrama; American Society of Group Psychotherapy and   **7309**

Psychodrama, Sociometry, and Group Psychotherapy; American Board of Examiners of   **7287**

Psychogeriatric Association; International   **1903**

Psychohistory Forum   **7489**

Psychohormonal Research; Office of • Johns Hopkins University   **4890**

Psychological Association; American   **7303**
    Division of Applied Experimental and Engineering Psychologists   **7304**
    Division of Family Psychology   **7305**
    Division of Psychotherapy   **7306**

Psychological Association; American Catholic   7490

Psychological Association for Psychoanalysis; National   **7470**

Psychological Clinic • University of Tennessee, Knoxville   **7690**

Psychological and Cognitive Sciences; Federation of Behavioral,   **7375**

Psychological Evaluation and Research Center • Hofstra University   **7566**

Psychological Hypnosis; American Board of   **6583**

Psychological Hypnosis; American Board of Examiners in   6583

Psychological Hypnosis; International Center of Medical and   **6592**

Psychological Hypnosis, U.S.A. Office; International Society for Medical and   **6593**

Psychological Institute; Montgomery Medical and   **7447**

Psychological-Medical Organizations; International Federation of the   **7409**

Psychological Research Center • Fairleigh Dickinson University   **7562**

Psychological Research in Developing Countries; International Committee on Social   **7406**

Psychological Science; International Union of   **7430**

Psychological Services and Development; Center for • Virginia Commonwealth University   **7699**

Psychological Society; British   **7347**

Psychological Society; Chinese   **7355**

Psychological Society; Hong Kong   **7384**

Psychological Society; New Zealand   **7476**

Psychological Studies; Christian Association for   **7356**

Psychological Study of Lesbian and Gay Issues; Society for the   **11714**

Psychological Study of Social Issues; Society for the   **7517**

Psychological Type; Association for   **7332**

Psychological Type; Center for Applications of   **7352**

Psychologie Appliquee; Association Internationale de   7397

Psychologie; Europaische Gesellschaft fur Luftfahrt   2384

Psychologie Medicale; Federation Internationale des Organismes de   7409

Psychologie Scientifique de Langue Francaise; Association de   7379

Psychologie Sociale; Association Europeenne de   7371

Psychologie du Travail de Langue Francaise; Association de   7329

Psychologie du Travail de Langue Francaise; Association Internationale de   **7329**

Psychologists; Association of Black   **7324**

Psychologists; Association for Women   7337

Psychologists; Division of Applied Experimental and Engineering • American Psychological Association   **7304**

Psychologists Interested in Religious Issues   7490

Psychologists; International Council of   **7407**

Psychologists; International Council of Women   7407

Office of Vital Statistics • Delaware Department of Health and Social Services **7047**

Wyoming Department of Health **11057**

Public Health Education; Association of State and Territorial Directors of **5565**

Public Health Education; Society for **10969**

Public Health Educators; Society of 10969

Public Health Engineers; Conference of Municipal 5594

Public Health Entomology; Center for Urban and • Texas A&M University **10985**

Public Health Entomology Laboratory • Ball State University **10973**

Public Health in the European Regional; Association of Schools of **10943**

Public Health Foundation; California **10974**

Public Health and Hygiene; Royal Institute of **10622**

Public Health; Illinois Department of **11018**

Public Health; International Institute of Concern for **5077**

Public Health; Iowa Department of **11020**

Public Health; Michigan Department of **11027**

Public Health; Ministry of Concern for **10960**

Public Health Office • Louisiana Department of Health and Hospitals **5146**

Public Health Physicians; American Association of **10936**

Public Health Research Group • Medical Research Centre • Laval University **10981**

Public Health Research Institute **2610**

Public Health Research; International Center for • University of South Carolina **11002**

Public Health Service • U.S. Department of Health and Human Services **10901**

Public Health Service; Commissioned Officers Association of the United States **10947**

Public Health Service Dentists; National Association of **3968**

Public Health Services Division • New Hampshire Department of Health and Human Services **11034**

Public Health Services Office

Louisiana Department of Health and Hospitals **11023**

Maryland Department of Health and Mental Hygiene **11025**

Public Health Statistics; American Association for Vital Records and 6979

Public Health Statistics Division • Indiana Department of Health **7054**

Public Health Studies; Center for • Portland State University **10983**

Public Health Veterinarians; Association of State 5592

Public Health Veterinarians; Association of State and Territorial 5592

Public Health Veterinarians; National Association of State **5592**

Public Health Veterinarians; National Association of State and Territorial 5592

Public Health Workers Caucus; Gay 10956

Public Health Workers; Lesbian and Gay Caucus of **10956**

Public Hospitals; National Association of **6462**

Public Interest; Medicine in the **10959**

Public Interest Research Group; Minnesota **1639**

Public Law; Institute of • University of New Mexico **1712**

Public Policy; Center for Animals & • Tufts University **13179**

Public Policy; Center on Drugs and • University of Maryland **10635**

Public Relations; American Society for Health Care Marketing and **6431**

Public Relations; American Society for Hospital 6431

Public Relations; American Society for Hospital Marketing and 6431

Public Representation, Inc.; Center for **1570**

Public Responsibility in Medicine and Research **1486**

Public Safety Division • Illinois Department of Labor **9878**

Public Services Research Institute; National **1641**

Public Transit; American Disabled for Accessible 1883

Public Welfare Administrators; National Council of State 5596

Public Welfare Association; American **10940**

Public Welfare Foundation **10904**

Publique de la Regional Europeenne; Association des Ecoles de Sante 10943

Pueblo Community College • Respiratory Therapist Program **11338**

Puerto Rico Board of Dental Examiners **4088**

Puerto Rico Board of Examiners in Optometry **13757**

Puerto Rico Board of Medical Examiners **1796, 10052**

Puerto Rico Board of Nurse Examiners **9195**

Puerto Rico Board of Podiatry Examiners **10818**

Puerto Rico Cancer Center • University of Puerto Rico **6243**

Puerto Rico Chapter • National Association of Social Workers **11920**

Puerto Rico; Colegio de Cirujanos Dentistas de **4194**

Puerto Rico; Colegio de Farmaceuticos de **10733**

Puerto Rico; Colegio de Medicos Veterinarios de **13341**

Puerto Rico Department of Agriculture • Veterinary Services **13288**

Puerto Rico Department of Health **11044**

Emergency Medical System **4806**

Oral Health Division **4141**

Puerto Rico Department of Social Services • Vocational Rehabilitation Division **12809, 13704**

Puerto Rico Division • American Cancer Society **6315**

Puerto Rico Division of Examining Boards • Regulations and Certification of Health Professionals Office • Board of Pharmacy **10680**

Puerto Rico; Easter Seal Society of **4668**

Puerto Rico Heart Association **3033**

Puerto Rico Hospital Association **6566**

Puerto Rico; Learning Disabilities Association of **4720**

Puerto Rico Medical Association **1850**

Puertorriquena del Pulmon; Asociacion **11670**

Pulmonary Branch • Division of Intramural Research • National Heart, Lung, and Blood Institute • U.S. Department of Health and Human Services **11613**

Pulmonary Center • Boston University **11608**

Pulmonary Center; Cystic Fibrosis and Pediatric • Case Western Reserve University **5317**

Pulmonary Center; Pediatric • University of Wisconsin—Madison **5390**

Pulmonary Clinic; Cystic Fibrosis and Pediatric • Indiana University-Purdue University at Indianapolis **5331**

Pulmonary Credentialing; National Board for Cardiovascular and 2839

Pulmonary and Critical Care Medicine; Division of

University of California, San Diego **11620**

University of Michigan **11622**

Pulmonary and Critical Care Medicine Section • University of Wisconsin—Madison **11623**

Pulmonary and Cystic Fibrosis Care, Research & Teaching Center; Pediatric • Albany Medical College **5308**

Pulmonary and Cystic Fibrosis Center • University of Oklahoma **5379**

Pulmonary and Cystic Fibrosis Center; Pediatric • University of California, San Diego **11621**

Pulmonary and Cystic Fibrosis Research Center; Pediatric • University of Nebraska at Omaha **5378**

Pulmonary Disease Center; Cystic Fibrosis Research Center and Pediatric • Tulane University **5357**

Pulmonary Hypertension; United Patients Association for **2880**

Pulmonary Laboratories • Ohio State University **2111**

Pulmonary and Mediastinal Pathology Department • Center for Advanced Pathology • Armed Forces Institute of Pathology • U.S. Department of Defense **10162**

Pulmonary Pathobiology; Laboratory of • National Institute of Environmental Health Sciences • U.S. Department of Health and Human Services **5110**

Pulmonary Rehabilitation; American Association of Cardiovascular and **2822**

Pulmonary Research Center; Pediatric **11612**

Pulmonary Research Laboratory; Will Rogers • Cornell University **11610**

Pulmonary Research Laboratory; Will Rogers Institute • University of California, Los Angeles **11619**

pulmonary Technologists; National Society of Cardio 2828

pulmonary Technology; National Society for Cardio 2828

Pulmonary Unit; Pediatric **11612**

Purchasing Agents; American Society for Hospital 6432

Purchasing and Materials Management; American Society for Hospital 6432

Purdue University

Cancer Center **6104**

Center for AIDS Research **6783**

Center for Biomolecular Nuclear Magnetic Resonance, Structure, and Design **2465**

Center for Paralysis Research **13168**

Department of Foods and Nutrition • Dietetics Program **9397**

School of Nursing **8683**

School of Pharmacy and Pharmacal Sciences **10518**

Pharmacology and Toxicology Department **10238**

School of Veterinary Medicine **12998**

Department of Veterinary Physiology and Pharmacology **10239**

William A. Hillenbrand Biomedical Engineering Center **2466**

Purdue University at Indianapolis; Indiana University-

Cystic Fibrosis and Pediatric Pulmonary Clinic **5331**

Diabetes Research and Training Center **4887**

Endocrinology Research Laboratories **4888**

General Clinical Research Center **1605**

Human Genetics Center **5332**

Hypertension Research Center **2906**

Institute of Psychiatric Research **7569**

Laboratory for Experimental Oncology **6052**

Multipurpose Arthritis and Musculoskeletal Diseases Center **7920**

Oral Health Research Institute **4003**

Pharmacology Research Laboratory **10437**

Riley Child Psychiatry Clinic **3339**

PVA/EPVA Center for Neuroscience and Regeneration Research of Yale University **8416**

Q

Qigong; World Society of Medical **2245**
Quaker Chemical Foundation **830**
Quaker Oats Foundation **831**
Quality; American College of Medical **1154**
Quality Assurance; National Committee for **5741**
Quality Assurance Professionals; National Association of **1398**
Quality Assurance, and Risk Management Department; Legal Medicine, • Center for Advanced Pathology • Armed Forces Institute of Pathology • U.S. Department of Defense **10156**
Quality Assurance and Utilization Review Physicians; American Board of **1148**
Quality; Bureau of Health Standards and • Health Care Financing Administration • U.S. Department of Health and Human Services **5711**
Quality Compliance Bureau • Health Division • Wisconsin Department of Health and Social Services **6525**
Quality Enhancement; Center for Food Safety & • University of Georgia **9553**
Quality, Environment, Safety, and Health Assurance Division • Los Alamos National Laboratory • U.S. Department of Energy **9823**
Quality Health Care; National Committee for **5870**
Quality Management; Institute for Control Theory, Reality Therapy, and **7389**
Quality; National Association for Healthcare **1398**
Quebec Demography; Research Group on • University of Montreal **11296**
Quebec Neuroblastoma Screening Research Group • Sherbrooke University **6112**
Queens; American Lung Association of **11663**
Queens College • Division of Nursing **8859**
Queens College of City University of New York • Center for the Biology of Natural Systems **5084**
Queens Division • American Cancer Society **6306**
Queen's University at Kingston • Social Program Evaluation Group **1654**
Quillen College of Medicine; James H.
    Department of Pharmacology • East Tennessee State University **10354**
    East Tennessee State University **1033**
Quimioterapia de la Tuberculosis; Sociedad Panamericana de **10419**
Quinnipiac College
    Cardiovascular Perfusion Program **2791**
    Respiratory Therapy Program **11341**
    School of Allied Health and Natural Sciences
        Department of Occupational Therapy **12342**
        Department of Physical Therapy **12453**
    School of Nursing **8601**
Quinsigamond Community College • Respiratory Therapist Program **11422**

R

R. A. Bloch Cancer Foundation **5982**
R.A. Cowley Shock Trauma Center **4764**
R. C. Baker Foundation **435**
R. Dee and Joan Dale Hubbard Foundation **436**
R.L. Smith Mental Retardation and Human Development Research Center • University of Kansas **4331**
R.S. Dow Neurological Sciences Institute **8417**
Rabbinic Center for Research and Counseling **7494**
Racers Club; International Wheelchair Road **4501**
Rackham Arthritis Research Unit • University of Michigan **7955**
Radford University • School of Nursing **9016**
The Radiance Technique Association International **2234**
Radiation Biochemistry Department • Armed Forces Radiobiology Research Institute • U.S. Department of Defense **11079**
Radiation Biophysics Division; Research Medicine and • Lawrence Berkeley Laboratory • U.S. Department of Energy **11158**
Radiation Control Program Directors; Conference of **11061**
Radiation Division; Ionizing • Physics Laboratory • National Institute of Standards and Technology • U.S. Department of Commerce **11157**
Radiation Effects Branch • Chemical and Physical Carcinogenesis Program • National Cancer Institute • U.S. Department of Health and Human Services **6127**
Radiation Effects Research Foundation **11067**
Radiation and Environmental Research Laboratory; Eye • Columbia University **2388**
Radiation Epidemiology Branch • Epidemiology and Biostatistics Program • National Cancer Institute • U.S. Department of Health and Human Services **6171**
Radiation, and Health; Institute for Biopsychological Studies of Color, Light, • San Jose State University **11074**
Radiation Hygiene; Slovak Society of Nuclear Medicine and **11131**

Radiation Medicale; Association Canadienne des Technologues en **11106**
Radiation Oncology Administrators **5603**
Radiation Oncology Administrators; Society for **5603**
Radiation Oncology; American College of **11089**
Radiation Oncology Branch • Division of Cancer Treatment • National Cancer Institute • U.S. Department of Health and Human Services **6163**
Radiation Oncology Centers; Association of Freestanding **11100**
Radiation Oncology Clinic • University of Florida **11167**
Radiation Oncology Program • University of Missouri—Columbia **11170**
Radiation Oncology Research & Development Center **11154**
Radiation Oncology Research Laboratory • University of California, San Francisco **11164**
Radiation Protection Association; International **11063**
Radiation Research; International Association for **11116**
Radiation Research Laboratory • University of Iowa **11168**
Radiation Research Program • Division of Cancer Treatment • National Cancer Institute • U.S. Department of Health and Human Services **6164**
Radiation Research Society **11068**
Radiation Safety; Canadian Institute for **11071**
Radiation Technologists; Canadian Association of Medical **11106**
Radiation Therapy; Center for **6016**
Radiation Therapy; Joint Center for **11145**
Radiation Therapy Oncology Center • University of Kentucky **11169**
Radiation Therapy Oncology Group **5983**
Radiation, Toxic, and Indoor Air Quality Division • Environmental Health Office • Public Health Bureau • West Virginia Department of Health and Human Resources **9913**
Radiation Toxicology; Center for Environmental • University of Texas Health Science Center at San Antonio **11080**
Radiation Units and Measurements; International Commission on **11117**
Radiation Victims; National Citizens Hearings for **11065**
Radiation Victims; National Committee for **11065**
Radical Caucus in Psychiatry **7495**
Radical Midwives; Association of **9634**
Radio Amateurs; ACB **13382**
Radio Reading Services; Association of **13415**
Radio and Television Guild; Veterans Hospital **7813**
Radio and Television; International Medical Association for **1351**
Radioassay Society; Clincial **7130**
Radiobiological Research; Laboratory of Cancer and • New York University **6088**
Radiobiology Division • University of Utah **11081**
Radiobiology and Environmental Health; Laboratory of **11073**
Radiobiology Research Institute; Armed Forces
    Behavioral Sciences Department • U.S. Department of Defense **11076**
    Experimental Hematology Department • U.S. Department of Defense **11077**
    Physiology Department • U.S. Department of Defense **11078**
    Radiation Biochemistry Department • U.S. Department of Defense **11079**
    U.S. Department of Defense **11075**
Radiografos y Tecnicos de Radiologia - Jamaica; Sociedad Internacional de **11120**
Radiographers; American Society of **11098**
Radiographers; Malaysian Society of **11125**
Radiographers and Radiological Technicians Jamaica; International Society of **11120**
Radiographers and Radiological Technologists; International Society of **11121**
Radiographers; Society of **11138**
Radiographers of South Africa; Society of **11139**
Radiographes et Techniciens de Radiologie; Societe Internationale des **11121**
Radiography; Australasian Institute of **11103**
Radiography; Australian Institute of **11103**
Radiography; Professional Board for **11066**
Radiograwe van Suid-Afrika; Vereniging van **11139**
Radiologen und Nuklearmediziner eV; Berufsverband der Deutschen **11101**
Radiologia - Jamaica; Sociedad Internacional de Radiografos y Tecnicos de **11120**
Radiologic Pathology Department • Center for Advanced Pathology • Armed Forces Institute of Pathology • U.S. Department of Defense **10163**
Radiologic Technologists; American Chiropractic Registry of **11086**
Radiologic Technologists; American Registry of **11093**
Radiologic Technologists; American Society of **11098**
Radiologic Technology; Joint Review Committee on Education in **11124**
Radiological Health; Center for Devices and • Food and Drug Administration • U.S. Department of Health and Human Services **10994, 11058**
Radiological Nurses Association; American **11091**
Radiological Research; Center for • Columbia University **11143**

Radiological Research; Leo G. Rigler Center for • University of California, Los Angeles **11163**
Radiological Society; Czech **11109**
Radiological Society; Czechoslovak 11109
Radiological Society of North America **11129**
Radiological Technicians; American Registry of 11093
Radiological Technicians Belgium; Medical **11126**
Radiological Technicians Jamaica; International Society of Radiographers and **11120**
Radiological Technologists; International Society of Radiographers and **11121**
Radiological Units; International Commission on 11117
Radiological Units; International Committee for 11117
Radiological Units and Measurements; International Commission on 11117
Radiologicka Spolecnost; Ceska 11109
Radiologie; Association Europeenne de 11110
Radiologie; Societe Internationale de 11122
Radiologie; Societe Internationale des Radiographes et Techniciens de 11121
Radiologists; American Association for Women **11083**
Radiologists; American College of Podiatric **10761**
Radiologists; American Society of Therapeutic 11099
Radiologists; Association of University **11102**
Radiologists Business Managers Association 5601
Radiologists; Faculty of 11130
Radiologists and Nuclear Physicians; Association of German **11101**
Radiologists; Royal College of **11130**
Radiology Administrators; American Healthcare **5550**
Radiology Administrators; American Hospital 5550
Radiology; American Academy of Dental 3864
Radiology; American Academy of Oral and Maxillofacial **3864**
Radiology; American Board of **11085**
Radiology; American Board of Veterinary 13050
Radiology; American College of Veterinary **13050**
Radiology; American Osteopathic College of **9992**
Radiology; British Institute of **11104**
Radiology Business Management Association 5601
Radiology; European Association of **11110**
Radiology; European Society of Paediatric **11113**
Radiology; International Association of Dento-Maxillo-Facial **11115**
Radiology; International Association of Maxillo-Facial 11115
Radiology; International Society of **11122**
Radiology Laboratories; Pendergrass Diagnostic • University of Pennsylvania **11173**
Radiology; Mallinckrodt Institute of • Washington University **11178**
Radiology, and Medicine; Academy of Oral Diagnosis, 3879
Radiology and Oncology; American Society for Therapeutic **11099**
Radiology and Oncology; European Society for Therapeutic **5943**
Radiology and Physiotherapy; British Association for the Advancement of 11104
Radiology; Society of Cardiovascular 11132
Radiology; Society of Cardiovascular and Interventional **11132**
Radiology Society; Computerized 11107
Radiology; Society for Pediatric 3295
Radiology; Society of Thoracic **11140**
Radionic Association 2235
Radiopharmacology; International Association of 10411
Radiotherapy Development Branch • Division of Cancer Treatment • National Cancer Institute • U.S. Department of Health and Human Services 6165
Radium Society; American **5913**
Radix Institute 7496
Radix Teachers Association 7497
Raigarh Ambikapur Health Association 1487
Railroad Retirement Board 5709
Railway Medical Services; International Union of 9799
Rainbow Chapter • Cystic Fibrosis Foundation 5450
Raleigh Chapter • Lupus Foundation of America 8092
Raleigh School of Nurse Anesthesia • University of North Carolina at Greensboro 2305
Ralph M. Parsons Foundation 437
Ramapo Trust 1872
Rancho Los Amigos Medical Center 1619
Rancho Rehabilitation Engineering Program 12742
Randolph Cancer Center; Mary Babb • West Virginia University 6268
Range Technical College; Duluth Technical College / • Respiratory Therapist Program 11437
Rangos School of Health Sciences; John G.
    Department of Perfusion Technology • Duquesne University 2813
    Occupational Therapy Program • Duquesne University 12415
Rape; National Clearinghouse on Marital and Date **11703**

Rape; People Against **3283**
Rape; Women Against **11717**
Raptor Center; Gabbert • University of Minnesota **13223**
Rare Blood Club; National **7148**
Rare Disorders; National Organization for **921, 1429**
Raskob Foundation for Catholic Activities **438**
Rational-Emotive Therapy; Institute for **7393, 7574**
Rational Recovery Systems **12072**
Rattsmedicinsk Forening; Nordisk 7192
Raumfahrtmedizin; Deutsche Gesellschaft fur Luft- und 2385
Ravenswood Hospital Medical Center / DePaul University • School of Nurse Anesthesia **2270**
Ray C. Fish Foundation **439**
Raymond A. Kent School of Social Work • University of Louisville **11785**
Raymond John Wean Foundation **440**
Raynaud's Association Trust 2872
Raynaud's and Scleroderma Association **2872**
ReachOut—A Community Intervention **12073**
Read Natural Childbirth Foundation **9691**
Reading Area Community College • Respiratory Therapist Program **11518**
Reading Services; Association of Radio **13415**
Reality Therapy; Institute for 7389
Reality Therapy, and Quality Management; Institute for Control Theory, **7389**
Reanimation; Federation Mondiale des Societes de Soins Intensifs et de 4760
Reanimation; French-Language Society for **1304**
Reanimation de Langue Francaise; Societe de 1304
Reanimation; Societe Francaise d'Anesthesie et de **2373**
RECAP (Recover a Penis) **11706**
Receptor Laboratory; Hormone • Oregon Health Sciences University **6099**
Reclamation, Inc. **7498**
Reconstruction; National Foundation for Facial **12291**
Reconstructive and Aesthetic Surgery; International Confederation for Plastic, **12279**
Reconstructive and Aesthetic Surgery; Israel Association of Plastic 12284
Reconstructive; Confederation Internationale pour la Chirurgie Plastic et 12279
Reconstructive Microsurgery and Transplantation Laboratories • University of California, Irvine **12887**
Reconstructive Plastic Surgery; Institute of • New York University **12322**
Reconstructive Surgeons; American Society of Plastic and **12244**
Reconstructive Surgeons; Education Foundation of American Society of Plastic and 12296
Reconstructive Surgeons; Israel Association of Plastic and 12284
Reconstructive Surgery; American Academy of Facial Plastic and **12203**
Reconstructive Surgery; European Society of Ophthalmic Plastic and **12270**
Reconstructive Surgery; Japan Society of Plastic and **12285**
Reconstructive Surgery; Korean Society of Plastic and **12286**
Reconstructive Surgical Nurses; American Society of Plastic and **9067**
Record Benevolent Association; Christian 13433
Record Braille Foundation; Christian 13433
Record Division; Vital • Rhode Island Department of Health **7079**
Record Librarians; American Association of Medical 6968
Record Librarians of North America; Association of 6968
Record Services; Christian 13433
Recording for the Blind **13558**
Recording for the Blind; National Committee for 13558
Records Branch; Vital
    Health Services Department • California Health and Welfare Agency **7044**
    Research and Statistics Division • District of Columbia Department of Human Services **7048**
Records Bureau; Health Statistics and Vital • Utah Department of Health **7084**
Records Bureau; Vital
    Health Division • Nevada Department of Human Resources **7068**
    Health Resources Division • Missouri Department of Health **7065**
    Planning and Administration Division • Iowa Department of Public Health **7055**
Records Division; Health Statistics and Vital • Administration and Support Office • Colorado Public and Environment Department **7045**
Records Division; Vital
    Administrative Services Section • North Dakota Department of Health and Consolidated Laboratories **7074**
    Connecticut Department of Public Health **7046**
    Finance and Administration Office • Illinois Department of Public Health **7053**
    Health Resources Bureau • Arkansas Department of Health **7043**
    Oklahoma Department of Health **7076**
    Pennsylvania Department of Health **7078**

Rehabilitation; American Academy of Physical Medicine and   **12647**
Rehabilitation; American Association of Cardiovascular and Pulmonary   **2822**
Rehabilitation; American Association for Cleft Palate   2740
Rehabilitation; American Board of Physical Medicine and   **12648**
Rehabilitation; American Congress of Physical Medicine and   12650
Rehabilitation; American Middle East   1135
Rehabilitation; American Osteopathic Academy of Physical Medicine and   9993
Rehabilitation; American Osteopathic College of Physical Medicine and   9993
Rehabilitation; American Society of Physical Medicine and   12647
Rehabilitation Association; American   **12659**
Rehabilitation Association; American Deafness and   **3484**
Rehabilitation Association; Christian Addiction   **12017**
Rehabilitation Association; National   **12699**
Rehabilitation Association; Association for Physical and Mental   12653
Rehabilitation and Blind Services Division; Vocational • Hawaii Department of Human Services   **12781, 13676**
Rehabilitation of the Blind and Visually Impaired; Association for Education and   **13412**
Rehabilitation Bureau; Vocational
   New Hampshire Department of Education   **12799, 13694**
   Ohio Rehabilitation Services Commission   **12805**
   Rehabilitation Division • Nevada Department of Employment Training and Rehabilitation   **12798**
Rehabilitation; Canadian Association of Physical Medicine and   **12670**
Rehabilitation Center • University of Arizona   **12757**
Rehabilitation Center; Lions Vision Research and • Johns Hopkins University   **13606**
Rehabilitation; Center for Low Vision Study, Care and • University of Florida   **13648**
Rehabilitation Center of Philadelphia   8377
Rehabilitation; Center for Psychiatric • Boston University   **7542**
Rehabilitation Center and Research Institute; Kluge Children's • University of Virginia   **4598**
Rehabilitation Center for the Visually Impaired; Carroll   13430
Rehabilitation Clinic; Social   7507
Rehabilitation Clinic; Social / Vocational   **7507**
Rehabilitation Commission • Michigan Department of Education   **12792**
Rehabilitation Commission; Massachusetts   **12791**
Rehabilitation Commission; Texas   **12814**
Rehabilitation Council for the Disabled; Canadian   **12671**
Rehabilitation; Council of State Administrators of Vocational   **12675**
Rehabilitation Counseling Association; American   **12660**
Rehabilitation Counseling Association; National   **12700**
Rehabilitation Counselor Educators; Council of   12697
Rehabilitation of Deaf-Blind Adults; National   13476
Rehabilitation Department • California Health and Welfare Agency   **12774, 13669**
Rehabilitation Department; Vocational • Kentucky Education, Arts and Humanities Cabinet   **12787**
Rehabilitation of the Disabled; International Society for   12713
Rehabilitation Division; Vocational
   Alaska Department of Education   **12771, 13666**
   Delaware Department of Labor   **12777**
   Florida Department of Labor and Employment Security   **12779**
   Health and Rehabilitative Services Office • Washington Department of Social and Health Services   **12819**
   Iowa Department of Education   **12785**
   Maryland Department of Education   **12790**
   Missouri Department of Elementary and Secondary Education   **12795**
   New Mexico Department of Education   **12801**
   North Dakota Department of Human Services   **12804, 13699**
   Oregon Department of Human Resources   **12807**
   Puerto Rico Department of Social Services   **12809, 13704**
   Social and Rehabilitation Services Department • Vermont Agency of Human Services   **12816**
   Wisconsin Department of Health and Social Services   **12821, 13716**
   Wyoming Department of Employment   **12822, 13717**
Rehabilitation and Economic Opportunity; Research and Training Center for Access to • Howard University   **4577**
Rehabilitation Education; Council on   **12674**
Rehabilitation Education; National Council on   **12697**
Rehabilitation Engineering Center
   Case Western Reserve University   **2439**
   Packard Children's Hospital at Stanford   **12741**
   Smith-Kettlewell Eye Research Institute   **2471**
Rehabilitation Engineering Center for Low Back Pain; Vermont • University of Vermont   **12764**
Rehabilitation Engineering Center; National • Wichita State University   **12769**

Rehabilitation Engineering Institute   2457
Rehabilitation Engineering; National Institute for   **2431, 2457**
Rehabilitation Engineering Program; Rancho   **12742**
Rehabilitation Engineering Society of North America   12716
Rehabilitation; Eric P. and Evelyn E. Newman Laboratory for Biomechanics and Human • Massachusetts Institute of Technology   **2453**
Rehabilitation of the Facially Disfigured; Society for the   12291
Rehabilitation Facilities; Association of   12659
Rehabilitation Facilities; Commission on Accreditation of   **12673**
Rehabilitation Facilities; International Association of   12659
Rehabilitation Facilities; National Association of   12659
Rehabilitation Foundation; American   12718
Rehabilitation Gazette   4488
Rehabilitation and Health; Center for Occupational • University of Michigan   **9857**
Rehabilitation Hospitals and Programs; Section for   **6469**
Rehabilitation Information Center; National   **12701**
Rehabilitation Information Round Table   **12712**
Rehabilitation Institute   12744
      Montreal Research Centre • University of Montreal   **12762**
      Southern Illinois University at Carbondale   **12750**
Rehabilitation Institute of Chicago   **12743**
Rehabilitation Institute; Children's   12735
Rehabilitation Institute; Dallas   **12731**
Rehabilitation Institute of Dallas for Ergonomics; Productive   **9818**
Rehabilitation Institute; Meyer • University of Nebraska at Omaha   **3366**
Rehabilitation Institute of Michigan   **12744**
Rehabilitation Instructors; National Association of   **12694**
Rehabilitation International   **12713**
Rehabilitation; International Federation of Physical Medicine and   **12685**
Rehabilitation International - Swaziland   **12714**
Rehabilitation; J. Paul Sticht Center on Aging and   **1937**
Rehabilitation Medicine; American Congress of   12650
Rehabilitation Medicine; American Osteopathic College of   **9993**
Rehabilitation Medicine Association; International   **12688**
Rehabilitation Medicine; Rusk Institute of • New York University   **12739**
Rehabilitation; Mental Health Clinical Research Center for Schizophrenia and Psychiatric   **7583**
Rehabilitation in Neuromuscular Diseases; NIDRR Research & Training Center for • University of California, Davis   **8480**
Rehabilitation; Nordic Association for   **12705**
Rehabilitation Nurses; Association of   **9074**
Rehabilitation Office; Vocational • Pennsylvania Department of Labor and Industry   **12808**
Rehabilitation Professionals in the Private Sector; National Association of   **12695**
Rehabilitation Program; Stanford Cardiac • Stanford University   **2923**
Rehabilitation and Research Center; ICD   12733
Rehabilitation and Research Center; Urological • University of Alabama at Birmingham   **12924**
Rehabilitation Research and Development Center   **7818**
Rehabilitation Research Group; Cardiac • Laval University   **2910**
Rehabilitation and Research; Institute for   **12734**
      University of Wisconsin—Madison   **12765**
Rehabilitation Research Institute; Vocational and   **4340**
Rehabilitation Research; National Institute on Disability and • U.S. Department of Education   **4585**
Rehabilitation Research and Planning Center   **12745**
Rehabilitation Research & Training Center • University of Hawaii at Manoa   **12759**
Rehabilitation Research and Training Center; American Indian • Northern Arizona University   **12740**
Rehabilitation Research & Training Center; Arkansas   **12746**
Rehabilitation Research and Training Center on Blindness and Low Vision • Mississippi State University   **13617**
Rehabilitation Research & Training Center in Childhood Trauma; Medical • Tufts University   **12754**
Rehabilitation Research and Training Center; Medical • New York University   **12738**
Rehabilitation Research and Training Center for Multiple Sclerosis; Medical • New York Medical College   **8406**
Rehabilitation Research and Training Center for Persons Who Are Deaf or Hard of Hearing • University of Arkansas at Little Rock   **3633**
Rehabilitation; Research and Training Center on Rural • University of Montana   **12761**
Rehabilitation Research and Training Center in Secondary Complications in Spinal Cord Injury; Medical • University of Alabama at Birmingham   **12755**
Rehabilitation Research and Training Center on Severe Traumatic Brain Injury • Virginia Commonwealth University   **12766**
Rehabilitation; Research & Training Center in Vocational   **12746**
Rehabilitation and Resource Centre for Torture Victims   **12715**

Reproductive Physiology Program; Endocrinology- • University of Wisconsin—Madison **9721**

Reproductive Research; Center for Fertility and • Vanderbilt University **11300**

Reproductive Research Center; Male **11265**

Reproductive Rights; Committee to Defend **11211**

Reproductive Rights; Gabriela Commission on Women's Health and **9650**

Reproductive Rights; Women's Global Network for **11256**

Reproductive Sciences Branch • Center for Population Research • National Institute of Child Health and Human Development • U.S. Department of Health and Human Services **11288**

Reproductive Sciences; Center for
Columbia University **5321**
Northwestern University **11277**

Reproductive Sciences Program • University of Michigan **11295**

Reproductive Surgeons; Society for **12308**

Reproductive Technology; Society for Assisted **11251**

Reproductive Toxicology Center **10451**

Rescue Conservancy; All- Breeds **13020**

Research; Academy of Behavioral Medicine **7257**

Research Administration Office • Veterans Affairs Medical Center [Martinez, CA] **2701**

Research and Advancement of Traditional Chinese Medicine; Chinese Association for **2186**

Research and Advocacy; Vietnam Veterans Institute for **7815**

Research on Ageing; British Society for **1893**

Research on Alcoholism; International Society for Biomedical **12044**

Research in Ambulatory Health Care Administration; Center for **5569**

Research! America **1493**

Research; American Association for Cancer **5909**

Research; American Association for Dental **3872**

Research; American Federation for Aging **1875, 1884**

Research; American Federation for Clinical **7119**

Research; American Foundation for Aging **1876, 1885**

Research; American Foundation for AIDS **6607, 6629**

Research; American Society for Bone and Mineral **7864**

Research Animal Diagnostic & Investigative Laboratory • University of Missouri—Columbia **13225**

Research Animal Resources Center • University of Wisconsin—Madison **13240**

Research in Asian Science and Medicine; Institute for Advanced **918, 2204**

Research Association of America; Dystrophic Epidermolysis Bullosa **5261, 5277**

Research Association; Batten's Disease Support and **8194**

Research Association; Children's Leukemia **5902, 5933**

Research; Association for Health Services **1206**

Research; Association for International Cancer **5921**

Research Association; International Family Planning **11228**

Research Association; National Iridology **2228**

Research Association; Osteopathic Manipulative Therapeutic and Clinical **9969**

Research Association; Psoriasis **4211, 4255**

Research; British Association for Cancer **5928**

Research on Cancer; International Agency for **5949**

Research Career Development Program • Division of Diabetes, Endocrinology, and Metabolic Diseases • National Institute of Diabetes and Digestive and Kidney Diseases • U.S. Department of Health and Human Services **4916**

Research Careers Program; Minority Access to • National Institute of General Medical Sciences • U.S. Department of Health and Human Services **2653**

Research Center for Children and Youth • State University of New York at Buffalo **3071**

Research Center of Excellence in Cell and Molecular Biology • Meharry Medical College **2593**

Research; Center for Health **1568**

Research Center; Lankenau Medical **1614**

Research Center in Oral Biology
University of Alabama at Birmingham **4024**
University of Pennsylvania **4043**
University of Washington **4047**

Research Center on the Psychobiology of Ethnicity • University of California, Los Angeles **7658**

Research; Central Society for Clinical **1232**

Research Centre on Lipid Disorders • Medical Research Centre • Laval University **2913**

Research Charities; Association of Medical **1208**

Research; Child Abuse Institute of **3047**

Research of Childhood Cancer; Association for **3189, 5898**

Research; Committee for the Promotion of Medical **1251**

Research Corporation; American Burn **2773**

Research Council; National Health and Medical **1420**

Research Council of Neuromuscular Disorders; International **8242**

Research Council of New Zealand; Health **1318**

Research Council; Nursing Home Advisory and **9270**

Research Council; Plastic Surgery **12297**

Research Councils; European Medical **1278**

Research and Counseling; Rabbinic Center for **7494**

Research; Craniofacial Biology Group of the International Association for Dental **3919**

Research and Cultural Exchange; International Association for Medical **1337**

Research and Demonstrations; Office of • Health Care Financing Administration • U.S. Department of Health and Human Services **5758**

Research Department
Hamot Medical Center **1595**
St. Francis Hospital and Medical Center **2616**
Texas Scottish Rite Hospital for Children **8433**

Research; Department of Medical • Methodist Hospital **1634**

Research in Developing Countries; International Committee on Social Psychological **7406**

Research and Development; American Foundation for Alternative Health Care, **2162**

Research and Development Division of Planned Parenthood Federation of America **11197**

Research and Development; Foundation for Women's Health **1303**

Research and Development; Office of • Veterans Health Administration • U.S. Department of Veterans Affairs **7853**

Research and Development Program; Basic • Division of Acquired Immunodeficiency Syndrome (AIDS) • National Institute of Allergy and Infectious Diseases • U.S. Department of Health and Human Services **6817**

Research and Development Service
Omaha Department of Veteran Affairs Medical Center **1649**
Veterans Affairs Medical Center [Birmingham, AL] **1739**
Veterans Affairs Medical Center [Danville, IL] **1738**

Research and Development of Traditional Chinese Medicine and Pharmacy; China Association of **2183**

Research Division
Center for the Improvement of Human Functioning International, Inc. **5319**
Hospital for Special Surgery **9941**
The Lexington Center, Inc. **3610**
Wills Eye Hospital **13663**

Research and Educati on; National Association for Perinatal Addiction **12054**

Research and Education Foundation; Cardiothoracic **12264**

Research and Education; Foundation for Hand **7878**

Research and Education; Homeopathic Council for **2201**

Research and Education Institute, Inc **1596**

Research and Education in Pathology; Universities Associated for **10140**

Research and Educational Foundation; American Academy of Medical Administrators **5538**

Research and Educational Trust; Hospital **5580**

Research; European Organization for Caries **3930**

Research; European Society for Ballisto Cardiographic **2846**

Research and Evaluation Division • Central Psychiatric Clinic • University of Cincinnati **7662**

Research and Evaluation Staff • Child Welfare League of America **3322**

Research Facility of the Rockland State Hospital **7586**

Research; Federation of European Veterinarians in Industry and **13074**

Research Foundation; African **1131**

Research Foundation; African Medical and [Dar es Salaam, United Republic of Tanzania] **1125**

Research Foundation; African Medical and [Kampala, Uganda] **10933**

Research Foundation; African Medical and [Munich, Germany] **1129**

Research Foundation; African Medical and [Nairobi, Kenya] **1130**

Research Foundation; African Medical and [Rome, Italy] **1128**

Research Foundation; African Medical and [Stockholm, Sweden] **1127**

Research Foundation; African Medical and [Voorschoten, Netherlands] **1126**

Research Foundation; American Business Men's **12002**

Research Foundation; American Hearing **3467, 3486**

Research Foundation; American Medical Association Education and **916**

Research Foundation; AVKO Educational **4284**

Research Foundation; Benign Essential Blepharospasm **8195**

Research Foundation; Brain **8129**

Research Foundation; Cancer **5899**

Research Foundation for Children; Cooley's Anemia Blood and **5936**

Research Foundation; Chiropractic **3458**

Research; Foundation for Chiropractic Education and **3430, 3458**

Research Foundation; Deafness **3470, 3515**

Research Foundation; Dystonia Medical **5260, 8209**

Research Training Branch; Prevention, Education, and • Division of Lung Diseases • National Heart, Lung, and Blood Institute • U.S. Department of Health and Human Services **11618**

Research and Training Center for Access to Rehabilitation and Economic Opportunity • Howard University **4577**

Research and Training Center for Children's Mental Health • University of South Florida **7689**

Research and Training Center for Community Referenced Behavior Management **7594**

Research and Training Center on Family Support and Children's Mental Health • Portland State University **7593**

Research and Training Center for the Handicapped • University of Mississippi **4595**

Research and Training Center on Independent Living **4551** University of Kansas **4590**

Research and Training Center for Positive Behavior Support **7594**

Research and Training Center on Rural Rehabilitation • University of Montana **12761**

Research & Training Center in Vocational Rehabilitation **12746**

Research Training and Development Branch • Division of Heart and Vascular Diseases • National Heart, Lung, and Blood Institute • U.S. Department of Health and Human Services **2938**

Research and Training Institute • National Center for Disability Services **4580**

Research and Treatment of Cancer; European Organization for **5941**

Research Triangle Institute **1657**

Research Trust; AIDS Education and **6618**

Research Unit • Shriners Hospitals for Crippled Children [Portland, OR] **7931**

Research Unit on Children's Psychosocial Maladjustment **3347**

Research Unit on Communicative Processes • State University of New York Health Science Center at Brooklyn **7607**

Research in Vascular Surgery; Association for **12256**

Research and Vital Statistics Division • Maine Department of Human Services **7059**

Research Workers in Animal Diseases; Conference of **13070**

Researchers; Association of International Health **1207**

Residency Directors; Association of Family Practice **5557**

Residency Review Committee for Emergency Medicine **4754**

Residency Training; American Association of Directors of Psychiatric **7275**

Resident Education in Obstetrics and Gynecology; Council on **9644**

Resident Matching Program; National **1430**

Resident Matching Program; National Intern and **1430**

Residential Centers; American Association of Children's **7273**

Residential Facilities for the Mentally Retarded; National Association of Private **4278**

Residential Resources; National Association of Private **4278**

Residents' Association; Emergency Medicine **4741**

Residents; Committee of Interns and **1250**

Residents and Interns; National Association of **1404**

Residents in New York City; Committee of Interns and **1250**

Resistance; Centre for the Study of Host • McGill University **6776**

RESNA **12716**

RESNA: Association for the Advancement of Rehabilitation Technology **12716**

Resnick Gerontology Center • Yeshiva University **2002**

Resolve, Inc. **11249**

Resource for Biomedical Sensor Technology • Case Western Reserve University **2440**

Resource Center for Paraprofessionals in Education and Related Services; National **4536**

Resource Institute for Drug Education; National Parents' **12063**

Resource for the Study of Laboratory Animal Diseases • Yale University **13249**

Resources and Information on Drug Education; Parent **12063**

Resources; Institute of Laboratory Animal **13081**

Resources Management Bureau; Health • Public Health Office • Louisiana Department of Health and Hospitals **5681**

Resources and Services Administration; Health • Public Health Service • U.S. Department of Health and Human Services **8**

Resources and Technologies Action Group; Appropriate Health **1190**

Respiration; Slovak Society of Physiology and Pathology of **11606**

Respiratoires; Union Internationale Contre la Tuberculose et les Maladies **11599**

Respiratory Care; American Association for **11588**

Respiratory Care; National Board for **11603**

Respiratory Disease Association; National Tuberculosis and **11590**

Respiratory Disease Clinics; National Coalition of Black Lung and **11604**

Respiratory Disease Conference; National **11594**

Respiratory Disease Research Unit • National Animal Disease Center • Agricultural Research Service • U.S. Department of Agriculture **13199**

Respiratory Disease Studies Division • National Institute for Occupational Safety and Health • U.S. Department of Health and Human Services **9835**

Respiratory Disease Unit; Acute Viral • Baylor College of Medicine **6762**

Respiratory Disease Unit; Bovine • Conservation and Production Research Laboratory • U.S. Department of Agriculture **13208**

Respiratory Diseases Branch • Division of Microbiology and Infectious Diseases • National Institute of Allergy and Infectious Diseases • U.S. Department of Health and Human Services **6830**

Respiratory Diseases Branch; Childhood and • Division of Bacterial and Mycotic Diseases • National Center for Infectious Diseases • U.S. Department of Health and Human Services **6796**

Respiratory and Enteric Virus Branch • Division of Viral and Rickettsial Diseases • National Center for Infectious Diseases • U.S. Department of Health and Human Services **6810**

Respiratory Medicine; National Jewish Center for Immunology and **2109, 11605**

Respiratory Nursing Society **9133**

Respiratory Protection; International Society for **11598**

Respiratory Therapist Program

Delaware County Community College / Crozer-Chester Medical Center **11510**

Duluth Technical College / Range Technical College **11437**

Midland Lutheran College / Immanuel Medical Center **11450**

New York City Health and Hospitals Corporation / Empire State College **11467**

North Dakota State University / St. Luke's Hospital MeritCare **11484**

Rochester Community College / Mayo Foundation **11439**

Sacred Heart University / St. Vincent's Medical Center **11342**

St. Mary's Campus • College of St. Catherine **11436**

Shenandoah University / Winchester Medical Center **11568**

Texas Southmost College / University of Texas Brownsville **11558**

University of California, Los Angeles Medical Center / Santa Monica College **11334**

West Chester University / Bryn Mawr Hospital **11520**

Respiratory Therapy; American Association for **11588**

Respiratory Therapy Education; Joint Review Committee for **11600**

Respiratory Therapy; National Board for **11603**

Respiratory Virus Research Laboratory • University of Wisconsin—Madison **11624**

Responders; American Association of First **4748**

Responders; National Association of First **4748**

Responsibility in Medicine and Research; Public **1486**

Responsibility; Physicians for Social **1476**

Responsible Genetics; Council for **2713**

Responsible Medicine; Physicians Committee for **1475**

REST Investigators Society; International **7416**

Restorative Dentistry, D.D.S.; American Academy of **3869**

Restorative Materials and Salivary Research Branch; Caries, • Extramural Program • National Institute of Dental Research • U.S. Department of Health and Human Services **4014**

Restoring Hope Through Educational and Medical Aid **1494**

Restoring Men; National Organization of **11706**

Resuscitation Research; Safar Center for • University of Pittsburgh **4766**

Retail Druggists; National Association of **5863**

Retail Druggists; Woman's Organization of the National Association of **5887**

Retailers; American Society of Dermatological **4218**

Retardation; Alabama Department of Mental Health and Mental **4343**

Retardation; American Academy on Mental **4276**

Retardation; American Association on Mental **4277, 4307**

Retardation Association of America; Mental **4295**

Retardation Center; Child Development and Mental • University of Washington **4338**

Retardation; Connecticut Department of Mental **4349**

Retardation of the Council for Execptional Children; Division on Mental **4288**

Retardation and Developmental Disabilities Administration; Mental • Social Services Commission • District of Columbia Department of Human Services **4351**

Retardation and Developmental Disabilities Branch; Mental • Center for Research for Mothers and Children • National Institute of Child Health and Human Development • U.S. Department of Health and Human Services **4320**

Retardation and Developmental Disabilities; Division on Mental • Council for Exceptional Children **4288**

Retardation and Developmental Disabilities Division; Mental Health, Mental • Iowa Department of Human Services **4358**

Retardation and Developmental Disabilities; New York State Agency of Mental **4375**

Retardation and Developmental Disabilities; Nisonger Center for Mental • Ohio State University **4317**

Rhode Island Council on Domestic Violence **3116**
Rhode Island Dental Association **4195**
Rhode Island Department of Elderly Affairs **2041**
Rhode Island Department of Environmental Management • Agriculture Division • Animal Health Section **13289**
Rhode Island Department of Health **11045**
    Dental Health Division **4142**
    Environmental Health Services Office **5167**
    Family Health Office **3417, 9763**
        Disease Control Division • AIDS / STD Program **6895**
    Health Services Regulations Office
        Emergency Medical Services Division **4807**
        Facilities Regulations Division **6515**
    Vital Record Division **7079**
Rhode Island Department of Human Services
    Blind Services **13705**
    Medical Services Division **5807**
    Vocational Rehabilitation Services **12810**
Rhode Island Department of Labor • Occupational Safety Division **9904**
Rhode Island Department of Mental Health, Retardation and Hospitals
    Developmental Disabilities Division **4382**
    Mental Health and Management Services Division **7747**
Rhode Island Department of Substance Abuse **12186**
Rhode Island Division • American Cancer Society **6316**
Rhode Island; Easter Seal Society of **4669**
Rhode Island Health Care Association **9365**
Rhode Island; Hospital Association of **6567**
Rhode Island; Learning Disabilities Association of **4721**
Rhode Island Medical Society **1851**
Rhode Island; Mental Health Association of **7776**
Rhode Island; National Kidney Foundation of Massachusetts and **12953, 12974**
Rhode Island Optometric Association **13832**
Rhode Island Pharmaceutical Association **10734**
Rhode Island Podiatry Board **10819**
Rhode Island Society of Osteopathic Physicians and Surgeons **10104**
Rhode Island State Board of Examiners in Dentistry **4089**
Rhode Island State Board of Optometry **13758**
Rhode Island State Nurses Association **9251**
Rhode Island Veterinary Medical Association **13342**
Rhodebeck Charitable Trust **443**
Rhodesian Veterinary Association **13123**
Rhumatisme; Ligue Europeenne Contre le **7873**
Rhythm; National Commission on Human Life, Reproduction and **11237**
Ribicoff Research Facilities of the Connecticut Mental Health Center • Yale University **7704**
Rice Foundation **444**
Rice University • Bioengineering Research Institute **2468**
Rich Foundation **445**
Richard B. Russell Agricultural Research Center
    Poultry Processing and Meat Quality and Safety Research Unit • U.S. Department of Agriculture • Agricultural Research Service **10988**
    Toxicology and Mycotoxin Research Unit • U.S. Department of Agriculture • Agricultural Research Service **10463**
Richard and Helen DeVos Foundation **446**
Richard King Mellon Foundation **447**
Richard Lounsbery Foundation **448**
Richard and Rhoda Goldman Fund **449**
Richard S. Reynolds Foundation **450**
Richard Stockton College of New Jersey • Physical Therapy Program **12507**
Richardson Foundation; Sid W. **489**
Richardson Foundation; Smith **494**
Richardson Institute for Preventive Medicine of the Methodist Hospital; Sid W. **10871**
Richland Memorial Hospital / University of South Carolina • Graduate Program in Nurse Anesthesia **2330**
Richmond Fellowship International **7500**
Rickettsial Diseases; Division of Viral and • National Center for Infectious Diseases • U.S. Department of Health and Human Services **6806**
Rickettsial Zoonoses Branch; Viral and • Division of Viral and Rickettsial Diseases • National Center for Infectious Diseases • U.S. Department of Health and Human Services **6813**
Riding for the Disabled Association **4552**
Riding for the Handicapped Association; North American **4542**
Right to Die; Choice in Dying—The National Council for the **3710**
Rights; American Association of Physicians for Human **11684**
Rights; Bay Area Physicians for Human **11687**
Rights; International Association— Hopecenter for the Defense of Women's and Children's **9658**
Rights Network; National Central America Health **1409**
Rights Society; Newborn **3274**

Rights of the Terminally Ill; Center for the **3709**
Rights of Women; Coalition for the Medical **11211**
Rigler Center for Radiological Research; Leo G. • University of California, Los Angeles **11163**
Riley Child Psychiatry Clinic • Indiana University-Purdue University at Indianapolis **3339**
Ringside Medicine and Surgery; American Board of **11936**
Rio Grande Valley; Easter Seal Society of the **4678**
Rio de Janeiro; Music Therapy Association of **7448**
Rippel Foundation; Fannie E. **178**
Risk Analysis Laboratory; Biochemical • National Institute of Environmental Health Sciences • U.S. Department of Health and Human Services **5102**
Risk Assessment and Disease Prevention; Center for Health • University of Alabama at Birmingham **10881**
Risk Assessment and Environmental Investigation Office • Disease Prevention Services Division • Arizona Department of Environmental Quality **5130**
Risk Management; American Society for Healthcare **5554**
Risk Management; Center for **5066**
Risk Management Department; Legal Medicine, Quality Assurance, and • Center for Advanced Pathology • Armed Forces Institute of Pathology • U.S. Department of Defense **10156**
Risk Management Division • Colorado Department of Labor and Employment **9870**
Risk Science Research Center **10452**
Riverside School of Nursing • Ohio Wesleyan University **8884**
Riviere-des-Prairies Hospital Research Centre • University of Montreal **7679**
Road Racers Club; International Wheelchair **4501**
Roane State Community College • Respiratory Therapist Program **11538**
Robert A. Taft Laboratories • National Institute for Occupational Safety and Health • U.S. Department of Health and Human Services **9838**
Robert B. Brigham Multipurpose Arthritis and Musculoskeletal Diseases Center • Brigham and Women's Hospital **7915**
Robert C. Schwartz Cystic Fibrosis Center • State University of New York Health Science Center at Syracuse **5353**
Robert Dawson Evans Memorial Department of Clinical Research • Boston University **1560**
Robert E. Brennan Foundation **451**
Robert F. Wagner Graduate School of Public Service • Health Policy and Management Program • New York University **5509**
Robert G. Cabell III and Maude Morgan Cabell Foundation **452**
Robert-Giffard Research Centre • Laval University **7579**
Robert H. Lurie Cancer Center • Northwestern University **6094**
Robert I. Wishnick Foundation **6415**
Robert J. Kleberg, Jr. and Helen C. Kleberg Foundation **453**
Robert R. McCormick Charitable Trust **454**
Robert R. McCormick Tribune Foundation **454**
Robert R. Meyer Foundation **455**
Robert R. Young Foundation **456**
Robert Roesler de Villiers Foundation **5966**
Robert Sterling Clark Foundation **11189**
Robert Stewart Odell and Helen Pfeiffer Odell Fund **457**
Robert W. Woodruff Foundation **458**
Robert Wood Johnson Foundation **459**
Robert Wood Johnson Medical School
    Physician Assistant Program • Rutgers University; University of Medicine and Dentistry of New Jersey / **1086**
    University of Medicine and Dentistry of New Jersey **991**
Robert Wood Johnson Medical School at Camden • University of Medicine and Dentistry of New Jersey **992**
Robert Wood Johnson Medical School; Rutgers University /
    Graduate Program in Pharmacology **10286**
    Rutgers College of Pharmacy • Graduate Program in Pharmacology **10287**
Roberts Foundation; Dora **144**
Roberts Wesleyan College • Division of Nursing **8841**
Rochester Caries Research Center • University of Rochester **4045**
Rochester Center for Biomedical Ultrasound • University of Rochester **11174**
Rochester Chapter • Cystic Fibrosis Foundation **5444**
Rochester Community College / Mayo Foundation • Respiratory Therapist Program **11439**
Rochester Institute of Technology
    Center for Imaging Science **11155**
    Department of Allied Health • Physician Assistant Program **1093**
    National Technical Institute for the Deaf **3618**
    School of Food, Hotel, and Travel Management • Dietetics Program **9409**
Rock Valley College • Respiratory Therapist Program **11381**
Rockburn Institute **5637**
Rockefeller Brothers Fund **6604**
Rockefeller Family Fund **10905**

Rockefeller Foundation **460**
Rockefeller University
    Clinical Research Center **1658**
    Laboratory Animal Research Center **13170**
    Laboratory of Bacterial Pathogenesis and Immunology **2113**
    Laboratory of Bacteriology and Immunology **6784**
    Laboratory of Biochemical Genetics and Metabolism **5346**
    Laboratory of Biology of Addictive Diseases **12100**
    Laboratory of Cell Physiology and Virology **6785**
    Laboratory of Cellular Physiology and Immunology **2114**
    Laboratory of Electronics **2469**
    Laboratory of History of Medicine and Science **7021**
    Laboratory of Human Behavior and Metabolism **4899**
    Laboratory of Immunology **2115**
    Laboratory for Investigative Dermatology **4267**
    Laboratory of Metabolism-Pharmacology **10453**
    Laboratory of Molecular Oncology **6105**
    Laboratory of Motor Physiology **8418**
    Laboratory of Neuroendocrinology **8419**
Rockers; Hearing Education and Awareness for **3527**
Rockford College • School of Nursing **8659**
Rockhurst College
    College of Arts and Sciences • Occupational Therapy Program **12381**
    Physical Therapy Program **12501**
    Research College of Nursing **8794**
Rockland Community College • Respiratory Therapist Program **11470**
Rockland Institute for Psychotherapy **7249**
Rockland/Orange County Chapter • Lupus Foundation of America **8087**
Rockland Research Center for Mental Illness **7586**
Rockland Research Institute **7586**
Rockland State Hospital; Research Facility of the **7586**
Rockwell Fund **461**
Rockwell International Corp. Trust **837**
Rocky Mountain Cancer Data System • University of Utah **6256**
Rocky Mountain Center for Occupational and Environmental Health • University of Utah **9862**
Rocky Mountain Chapter • Arthritis Foundation **7971**
Rocky Mountain Easter Seal Society; Northern **4649**
Rocky Mountain Heart Consortium **2921**
Rocky Mountain Heart Research Institute **2921**
Rocky Mountain Multiple Sclerosis Center **8420**
Rocky Mountain Operations Branch • Division of Intramural Research • National Institute of Allergy and Infectious Diseases • U.S. Department of Health and Human Services **6823**
Rocky Mountain Taste and Smell Center • University of Colorado—Denver **12136**
Roentgen Ray Society; American **11094**
Roentgen Society of the U.S. **11094**
Roentgen Society; Western **11129**
Roentgeneology to the American Chiropractic Association; Council on **11108**
Roentgenologists; American College of Chiropodial **10761**
Roentgenologists; American College of Foot **10761**
Roentgenologists; National Council of Chiropractic **11108**
Roentgenology; American Academy of Oral **3864**
Roentgenology; American Chiropractic Council on **11108**
Roentgenology; American Council on Chiropractic **11108**
Roesler de Villiers Foundation; Robert **5966**
Roger Williams Cancer Center **6106**
Roger Williams Clinical Cancer Research Center **6106**
Roger Wyburn-Mason and Jack M. Blount Foundation for the Eradication of Rheumatoid Disease **7902**
Rogers Magnetic Resonance Center; Mary Nell and Ralph B. • University of Texas Southwestern Medical Center at Dallas **11175**
Rogue Community College • Respiratory Therapist Program **11507**
Rolf Foundation for Structural Integration; Ida P. **2236**
The Rolf Institute **2236**
Rolf Institute of Structural Integration **2256**
Rollin M. Gerstacker Foundation **462**
Romana de Anestezie Terapie Intensiva; Societatea **2371**
Romana de Neurofiziologie Clinica; Societatea **8301**
Romance Language Psychoanalysts; Congress of **7361**
Romanian Anti-AIDS Association **6747**
Romanian Society for Anaesthesia Intensive Care **2371**
Romanian Society of Cardiology **2873**
Romanian Society of Clinical Neurophysiology **8301, 8301**
Romision para los Asuntos de la Mujer **3115**
Roosevelt Institute; Eleanor **2571**
Roosevelt Warm Springs Institute for Rehabilitation **12748**
Rorschach Internationale; Societe **7417**

Rorschach Research Exchange **7515**
Rorschach Society; International **7417**
Rosalind Russell Medical Research Center for Arthritis • University of California, San Francisco **7946**
RosaMary Foundation **463**
Rosamond Gifford Charitable Corporation **464**
Roscoe B. Jackson Memorial Laboratory **5334**
Rose F. Kennedy Center for Research in Mental Retardation and Human Development • Yeshiva University **4342**
Rose M. Badgeley Residuary Charitable Trust **465**
Rose State College • Respiratory Therapist Program **11502**
Rosenstiel Basic Medical Sciences Research Center **2611**
Rosenstiel Foundation **466**
Rosenwald Family Fund; William **553**
Ross Foundation **467**
Roswell Park Cancer Institute **6107**
    Grace Cancer Drug Center **10454**
    Laboratory of Flow Cytometry **2612**
Round Table International **12332**
Rowland Foundation **6379**
Roy A. Hunt Foundation **468**
Roy and Christine Sturgis Charitable and Educational Trust **469**
Roy J. Carver Charitable Trust **470**
Roy M. and Phyllis Gough Huffington Center on Aging • Baylor College of Medicine **1923**
Royal College of Midwives **9692**
Royal College of Physicians **1495**
Royal College of Physicians and Surgeons of Canada **1496**
Royal College of Physicians and Surgeons (of United States of America) **1497**
Royal College of Radiologists **11130**
Royal College of Surgeons of England **12298**
Royal Commonwealth Society for the Blind; Sight Savers— [Haywards Heath, England] **13561**
Royal Commonwealth Society for the Blind; Sight Savers— [Nairobi, Kenya] **13562**
Royal Dutch Society for Advancement of Pharmacy **10621**
Royal Institute of Public Health and Hygiene **10622**
Royal National Institute for the Blind Northern Ireland Service Bureau **13559**
Royal National Institute for the Blind Scotland **13560**
Royal Netherlands Veterinary Association **13106**
Royal Pharmaceutical Society of Great Britain **10623**
Royal Society of Medicine Foundation **1498**
Royal Society of Tropical Medicine and Hygiene **6748**
RP Foundation Fighting Blindness **13456**
Rubbermaid Foundation **838**
Rubin Feldman National Odd Shoe Exchange; Ruth **4533**
Rubinstein Foundation; Helena **262**
Rubinstein-Taybi Parent Group **2753**
Rudin Foundation; Louis and Rachel **365**
Rukariro Rehabilitation Organisation **12717**
Ruminant Practitioners; American Association of Small **13034**
Runaway Hotline **7501**
Runaway Switchboard; National **7473**
Ruptured and Crippled; New York Society for the Relief of the **7925**
Rural and Environmental Health; Center for International • University of Iowa **1699**
Rural Environmental Health; Institute of • Colorado State University **5068**
Rural Health Association; China **1235**
Rural Health Association; National **1431**
Rural Health; Center for • University of Kentucky **5651**
Rural Health; International Association of Agricultural Medicine and **9797**
Rural Health Research; Center for • Marshall University **10982**
Rural Health; UND Center for • University of North Dakota **1714**
Rural Hospitals; General Constituency Section for Small or **6444**
Rural Institute on Disability; Montana University Affiliated • University of Montana **4596**
Rural Mental Health; Center for Family Research in • Iowa State University of Science and Technology **7577**
Rural Mental Health; National Association for **7454**
Rural Rehabilitation; Research and Training Center on • University of Montana **12761**
Rural Women Health Association **1536**
Rurale; Association Internationale de Medecine Agricole et de Sante **9797**
Rush Alzheimer's Disease Center **8421**
Rush Cancer Center **6108**
Rush Cancer Institute **6108**
Rush Medical College • Rush University **952**
Rush University
    Center for Health Management Studies **5638**

College of Health Science • School of Perfusion Technology   **2796**
College of Health Sciences • Graduate Program in Health Systems Management   **5490**
College of Nursing   **8660**
    Nurse Anesthesia Program   **2271**
Department of Occupational Therapy   **12353**
Multiple Sclerosis Center   **8422**
Rush Medical College   **952**
Steroid Research Laboratory   **4900**
Rusk Institute of Rehabilitation Medicine • New York University   **12739**
Russell Agricultural Research Center; Richard B.
    Poultry Processing and Meat Quality and Safety Research Unit • U.S. Department of Agriculture • Agricultural Research Service   **10988**
    Toxicology and Mycotoxin Research Unit • U.S. Department of Agriculture • Agricultural Research Service   **10463**
Russell Educational Foundation; Benjamin and Roberta   **6332**
Russell Medical Research Center for Arthritis; Rosalind • University of California, San Francisco   **7946**
Russell Sage College
    Department of Nursing   **8842**
    Department of Physical Therapy   **12518**
Russell-Silver Syndrome; Association for Children with   **3182**
Russian Federation of the Deaf; All-   **3479**
Rutgers College of Pharmacy • Graduate Program in Pharmacology • Johnson Medical School; Rutgers University / Robert Wood   **10287**
Rutgers University
    AIDS Research Group   **6786**
    Bureau of Biological Research   **2613**
    Camden College of Arts and Sciences • Department of Nursing   **8816**
    Cell and Cell Products Fermentation Facility   **2614**
    Center of Alcohol Studies   **12101**
    Center for Molecular and Behavioral Neuroscience   **8423**
    Center for Research on the Organization and Financing of Care for the Severely Mentally Ill   **7595**
    College of Nursing   **8817**
    College of Pharmacy   **10538**
    Controlled Drug-Delivery Research Center   **10455**
    Douglass Developmental Disabilities Center   **7596**
    Institute for Health, Health Care Policy, and Aging Research   **1659**
    Laboratory for Cancer Research   **6109**
    New Jersey Agricultural Experiment Station   **9524**
    Noise Technical Assistance Center   **5085**
    School of Social Work   **11816**
    School of Social Work [Camden, NJ]   **11814**
    School of Social Work [Newark, NJ]   **11815**
    Waksman Institute   **2615**
Rutgers University / Robert Wood Johnson Medical School
    Graduate Program in Pharmacology   **10286**
    Rutgers College of Pharmacy • Graduate Program in Pharmacology   **10287**
Rutgers University; University of Medicine and Dentistry of New Jersey / Robert Wood Johnson Medical School • Physician Assistant Program   **1086**
    School of Health Related Professions • Physical Therapy Program   **12508**
Ruth Jackson Orthopaedic Society   **9935**
Ruth Jackson Society   **9935**
Ruth Rubin Feldman National Odd Shoe Exchange   **4533**
Ruth and Vernon Taylor Foundation   **471**
Rwandaise pour le Bien-Etre Familial; Association   **9635**
Ryan White National Teen Education Program   **3285**
Ryder System Charitable Foundation   **839**

S

S.E. Child Safety Institute of the Childrens Hospital of Alabama   **10456**
S. H. Cowell Foundation   **472**
S.R. Light Laboratory for Surgical Research • Vanderbilt University   **12328**
Sackett Research Laboratory; Samuel Jefferson • Northwestern University   **6780**
Sacramento; Heart Research Foundation of   **2899**
Sacramento Medical Foundation Blood Bank • Specialist in Blood Bank Technology Program   **7092**
Sacred Heart Medical Center / Gonzaga University • Master of Anesthesiology Education Program   **2344**
Sacred Heart University / St. Vincent's Medical Center • Respiratory Therapist Program   **11342**
Safar Center for Resuscitation Research • University of Pittsburgh   **4766**
Safe Alternatives in Childbirth; International Association of Parents and Professionals for   **9660**
Safe Motherhood Initiative   **9693**

SAFE - Self Abuse Finally Ends   **7502**
Safe Water Coalition   **10966**
Safe Water Foundation   **1230**
Safe Workplace Institute; National   **9814**
Safety and Applied Nutrition; Center for Food • Food and Drug Administration • U.S. Department of Health and Human Services   **10900, 10996**
Safety in the Arts; Center for   **9794, 9804**
Safety and Buildings Division • Wisconsin Department of Industry, Labor and Human Relations   **9914**
Safety Bureau • Employment Relations Division • Montana Department of Labor and Industry   **9891**
Safety Commission; Consumer Product   **10893**
Safety Division
    Arkansas Department of Labor   **9868**
    Florida Department of Labor and Employment Security   **9874**
    Idaho Department of Labor and Industrial Services   **9877**
    Labor Standards Bureau • Maine Department of Labor   **9884**
    Nebraska Department of Labor   **9892**
Safety Division; Environment, Health and • Lawrence Berkeley Laboratory • U.S. Department of Energy   **9821**
Safety Division; Health and • Worker's Compensation Office • Louisiana Department of Labor   **9883**
Safety Education Research Laboratory; Occupational and Traffic • Iowa State University of Science and Technology   **9810**
Safety, Education and Training Bureau • Indiana Department of Labor   **9879**
Safety and Health; Appalachian Laboratory for Occupational • National Institute for Occupational Safety and Health • U.S. Department of Health and Human Services   **9825**
Safety, and Health Assurance Division; Quality, Environment, • Los Alamos National Laboratory • U.S. Department of Energy   **9823**
Safety and Health Consultation Program; On-site • Labor Standards Division • Missouri Department of Labor and Industrial Relations   **9890**
Safety, Health, and Environmental Resource Center International   **5057**
Safety and Health; Iowa Center for Agricultural   **9809**
Safety and Health; National Institute for Occupational
    Appalachian Laboratory for Occupational Safety and Health • U.S. Department of Health and Human Services   **9825**
    Biomedical and Behavioral Science Division
        Applied Biology Branch • U.S. Department of Health and Human Services   **9827**
        Applied Psychology and Ergonomics Branch • U.S. Department of Health and Human Services   **9828**
        Experimental Toxicology Branch • U.S. Department of Health and Human Services   **9829**
        Physical Agents Effects Branch • U.S. Department of Health and Human Services   **9830**
        U.S. Department of Health and Human Services   **9826**
    Physical Sciences and Engineering Division
        Engineering Control Technology Branch • U.S. Department of Health and Human Services   **9832**
        Measurements Research Support Branch • U.S. Department of Health and Human Services   **9833**
        Methods Research Branch • U.S. Department of Health and Human Services   **9834**
        U.S. Department of Health and Human Services   **9831**
    Respiratory Disease Studies Division
        Clinical Investigations Branch • U.S. Department of Health and Human Services   **9836**
        Environmental Investigations Branch • U.S. Department of Health and Human Services   **9837**
        U.S. Department of Health and Human Services   **9835**
    Robert A. Taft Laboratories • U.S. Department of Health and Human Services   **9838**
    Safety Research Division • U.S. Department of Health and Human Services   **9839**
    Surveillance, Hazard Evaluations, and Field Studies Division
        Hazard Evaluations and Technical Assistance Branch • U.S. Department of Health and Human Services   **9841**
        Industrywide Studies Branch • U.S. Department of Health and Human Services   **9842**
        Surveillance Branch • U.S. Department of Health and Human Services   **9843**
        U.S. Department of Health and Human Services   **9840**
    U.S. Department of Health and Human Services   **9779, 9824**
Safety, Health, and Working Conditions; Office of • Office of Compensation and Working Conditions • Bureau of Labor Statistics • U.S. Department of Labor   **9780, 9847**
Safety and Health Working Group; Behavioral Research Aspects of • University of Kentucky   **9854**
Safety and Inspection Service; Food • U.S. Department of Agriculture   **10895**
Safety Institute of the Childrens Hospital of Alabama; S.E. Child   **10456**

Samter Institute of Allergy and Clinical Immunology; Max 2091
Samuel Freeman Charitable Trust 5895
Samuel Goldwyn Foundation 474
Samuel I. Newhouse Foundation 475
Samuel Jefferson Sackett Research Laboratory • Northwestern University 6780
Samuel Merritt College
     Graduate Program of Nurse Anesthesia 2261
     Occupational Therapy Program 12338
Samuel Merritt College / St. Mary College • Intercollegiate Nursing Program 8585
Samuel Roberts Noble Foundation 476
Samuel S. Fels Fund 477
Samuels Foundation; Fan Fox and Leslie R. 177
San Antonio College • Mortuary Science Program 3700
San Diego Association of Medical Legal Nurse Consultants 7162
San Diego Chapter • Arthritis Foundation 7969
San Diego County; Easter Seal Society of 4615
San Diego State University
     Graduate School of Public Health 10908
       Graduate Program in Health Services Administration 5475
     Rehabilitation Counselng Program 12575
     School of Nursing 8586
     School of Social Work 11752
San Francisco AIDS Foundation 6749
San Francisco College of Mortuary Science 3664
San Francisco Heart Institute 2922
San Francisco Injury Center for Research and Prevention 10870
San Francisco Injury Prevention Center 10870
San Francisco; Medical Research Institute of 1564
San Francisco Social Psychiatry Seminar 7429
San Francisco State University
     Center for Advanced Medical Technology 2619
     Center for Research and Education in Sexuality 11722
     Counseling Department • Rehabilitation Counselor Training Program 12576
     Department of Nursing 8587
     Department of Social Work Education 11753
San Jacinto College, Central Campus • Respiratory Therapist Program 11551
San Joaquin Valley College • Respiratory Therapist Program 11332
San Jose State University
     College of Applied Arts and Sciences • Department of Occupational Therapy 12339
     College of Social Work 11754
     Department of Nursing 8588
     Institute for Biopsychological Studies of Color, Light, Radiation, and Health 11074
     School of Nursing 8589
Sanatorium Association; American 11591
Sanders-Brown Center on Aging • University of Kentucky 1980
Sandhills Community College • Respiratory Therapist Program 11481
Sandoz Foundation for Regional Gerontological Research in Latin America 1919
Sandra Atlas Bass and Edythe and Sol G. Atlas Fund 478
Sanford C. Bernstein and Co. Foundation 841
Sange Congele de Groupes Rares; Banque Europeenne de 7134
Sangre; Federacion Panamericana pro Donacion Voluntaria de 7152
Sangue; Federazione Internazionale delle Organizzazioni dei Donatori di 7139
Sanguine; Societe Internationale de Transfusion 7141
Sanidad Agropecuaria; Organismo Internacional Regional de 13088
Sanitarians; American Academy of 5032
Sanitarians; California Association of 5052
Sanitarians; National Association of 5052
Sanitary Association; United States Livestock 13111
Sanitary Boards; Association of State 13111
Sanitation Foundation; National 5055
Sansum Clinic Research Foundation 1661
Sansum Medical Research Foundation 1661
Santa Barbara Breast Cancer Institute 6110
Santa Barbara Medical Research Foundation 9483
Santa Clara University • Center for Applied Ethics 7215
Santa Fe Community College • Respiratory Therapist Program 11361
Santa Fe Pacific Foundation 842
Santa Monica College; University of California, Los Angeles Medical Center / • Respiratory Therapist Program 11334
Sante; L'Action des Eglises pour la 1244
Sante du Canada; Association des Bibliotheques de la 6984
Sante Canada par la Strategie Nationale sur la Sida 6647
Sante - Congo; Organisation Mondiale de la 1449

Sante et d'Education pour la Sante; Union Internationale de Promotion de la 1360
Sante Ethique et Libertes 7177
Sante; Federation Internationale pour la 2213
Sante; Forum Europeen de Politique de 1277
Sante Mentale; Union Internationale des Societes d'Aide a la 7431
Sante; Organisation Mondiale de la 1540
Sante; Organization Internationale de Cooperation pour la 1451
Sante Publique de la Regional Europeenne; Association des Ecoles de 10943
Sante Rurale; Association Internationale de Medecine Agricole et de 9797
Sante; Union Internationale de Promotion de la Sante et d' Education pour la 1360
Sante sans Vaccination; Association pour la 2178
Santos Ambulance Fund; Todos 4759
Sarcoidosis; International Committee of 6757
Sarcoidosis and Other Granulomatous Disorders; World Association on 6757
Sarcoma Research and Education Foundation; AIDS/Kaposi's 6749
Sargent College of Allied Health Professions
     Department of Occupational Therapy • Boston University 12367
     Department of Physical Therapy • Boston University 12486
     Department of Rehabilitation Counseling • Boston University 12602
Sarkeys Foundation 479
Saskatoon Cancer Centre • Cancer Research Unit 6111
Saude; Associacao Brasileira de Tecnologia Alternativa na Promocao da 10945
Saude; Fundacao Instituto Integrado de 1305
Saude da Mulher; SOS Corpo - Grupo de 1513
Save Lebanon 1502
Save Us From Formaldehyde Environmental Repercussions 10406
Scaife Family Foundation 480
Scandinavian Association of Obstetrics and Gynecology 9649
Scandinavian Association of Paediatric Surgeons 12299
Scandinavian Association of Plastic Surgeons 12300
Scandinavian Association for Thoracic and Cardiovascular Surgery 12301
Scandinavian Association for Thoracic Surgery 12301
Scandinavian Association of Urology 12912
Scandinavian Association of Zone Therapeutists 2237
Scandinavian Endodontic Association 3988
Scandinavian Neurological Association 8302
Scandinavian Neurosurgical Society 8303
Scandinavian Orthopaedic Association 9936
Scandinavian Societies of Obstetrics and Gynecology; Federation of 9649
Scandinavian Society of Forensic Medicine 7192
Scandinavian Society of Forensic Odonto-Stomatology 7190
Scandinavian Surgical Society 12302
Schepens Eye Research Institute 13626
Schering-Plough Foundation 843
Scherman Foundation 11190
Schiefelbusch Institute for Life Span Studies • University of Kansas 4332
Schizophrenia and Depression; National Alliance for Research on 7234
Schizophrenia; Mental Health Clinical Research Center for the Study of 7583
Schizophrenia; Neuroscience Center for Research in • University of Maryland 7670
Schizophrenia and Psychiatric Rehabilitation; Mental Health Clinical Research Center for 7583
Schizophrenia Research Branch • Clinical Research Division • National Institute of Mental Health • U.S. Department of Health and Human Services 7623
Schizophrenic Biologic Research Center • Mount Sinai School of Medicine of City University of New York 7585
Schizophrenics Anonymous 7504
Schlieder Educational Foundation; Edward G. 158
Schlumberger Foundation 844
Schmidlapp Trust No. 1; Jacob G. 304
Schneider Laboratory of Basic and Applied Research; Herman • University of Cincinnati 2480
Scholl College of Podiatric Medicine; Dr. William M. 10749
Scholl Foundation; Dr. 137
School for Cancer Care; International 5956
School for the Deaf; Model Secondary 3543
School of Health Administration and Policy • Arizona State University 5608
School Health Association; American 1181
School Health Division of American Association for Health, Physical Education and Recreation 1195
School of Hearing and Speech Sciences • Ohio University 3616
School of Nurse Anesthesia
     Frances Payne Bolton School of Nursing • Mt. Sinai Medical Center / Case Western Reserve University 2308

Northeastern University Graduate School of Nursing at New England Medical Center **2283**

School Nurses; National Association of **9111**

School Nurses/NEA; Department of **9111**

School of Nursing • College of Health and Human Services • Wright State University **8889**

School Pediatric Department Chairmen; Association of Medical **3185**

School Physicians; American Association of **1181**

School Psychologists; National Association of **7455**

School of Public Health Demography Program • University of Puerto Rico **11000**

Schools; Accrediting Bureau of Health Education **7113**

Schools; Accrediting Bureau of Medical Laboratory **7113**

Schools; American Association of Dental **3873**

Schools of the ASCP; Board of **7144**

Schools; Association of Minority Health Professions **1210**

Schools and Colleges of Acupuncture and Oriental Medicine; National Accreditation Commission for **2223**

Schools and Colleges of Optometry; Association of **13417**

Schools and Colleges of Optometry; European Association of **13446**

Schools; Council on Accreditation of Nurse Anesthesia Educational Programs / **2360**

Schools for the Deaf; Association of Superintendents and Principals of American **3507**

Schools for the Deaf; Conference of Executives of American **3507**

Schools in Europe; Association of Medical **1209**

Schools for Exceptional Children; National Association of Private **3263**

Schools and Faculties; Latin American Association of Medical **1369**

Schools; National Association of Health Career **1399**

Schools of Nursing; Assembly of Hospital **9093**

Schools; PanAmerican Federation of Associations of Medical **1452**

Schools of Public Health; Association of **10942**

Schools of Public Health in the European Regional; Association of **10943**

Schriftexpertise; Europaische Gesellschaft fur Schriftpsychologie und **7373**

Schriftpsychologie und Schriftexpertise; Europaische Gesellschaft fur **7373**

Schubot Exotic Bird Health Center • Texas A&M University **13176**

Schultz Foundation **481**

Schwab Corp. Foundation; Charles **633**

Schwartz College of Pharmacy and Health Sciences; Arnold and Marie • Long Island University **10540**

Schwartz Cystic Fibrosis Center; Robert C. • State University of New York Health Science Center at Syracuse **5353**

Schweiz Homoopathie Gesellschaft **2240**

Schweizerische Aerztegesellschaft fur Holistische Medizin **2239**

Schweizerische Arztegesellschaft fur Akupunktur **2240**

Schweizerischer Krankenhaeuser; Vereinigung **6474**

Schweizerischer Verband Diplomierter **9492**

Sciencas Veterinarias; Asociacion Panamericana de **13103**

Science; Academy of Pharmaceutical Research and **10574**

Science; American Association for Laboratory Animal **13032**

Science; American Society for Clinical Laboratory **7122**

Science; Center for Biotechnology and Applied • Northwestern University **2722**

Science; Center for Sports Medicine and • Temple University **11978**

Science Club; Clinical **7126**

Science and Disability; Foundation for **4451, 4487**

Science and Education; Eczema Association for **4232**

Science and Education; Oak Ridge Institute for **2597**

Science; Foundation for the Advancement of Chiropractic Tenets and **3429, 3457**

Science; Foundation for Advances in Clincal Medicine and **1294**

Science; Foundation for Advances in Medicine and **1294**

Science Foundation; National • Directorate for Engineering • Division of Bioengineering and Environmental Systems • Bioengineering and Aiding Persons with Disabilities Program **2458**

Science and the Handicapped; Foundation for **4487**

Science and Health; American Council on **1555, 10938**

Science, Inc.; Orentreich Foundation for the Advancement of **2603**

Science Institute; Biomedical Engineering and • Drexel University **2441**

Science; International Union of Psychological **7430**

Science; Joint Commission on Sports Medicine and **11949**

Science; Laboratory of History of Medicine and • Rockefeller University **7021**

Science and Medicine; Institute for Advanced Research in Asian **918, 2204**

Science and Medicine; Linus Pauling Institute of **2588**

Science and Medicine; Morris Fishbein Center for the History of • University of Chicago **1692**

Science, Medicine, and Society Division • Department of the History of Science and Technology • National Museum of American History • Smithsonian Institution **2**

Science and Philosophy of the U.S.A.; Himalayan International Institute of Yoga **2199**

Science; Polish Society of Veterinary **13105**

Science and Protection Accreditation Council; National Environmental Health **5053**

Science in the Public Interest; Center for **9496**

science Research Institute; Inter **7496**

Science and Technology Center • Carnegie Mellon University **2438**

Science and Technology; Iowa State University of

Biomedical Engineering Program **2450**

Center for Designing Foods to Improve Nutrition **9505**

Center for Family Research in Rural Mental Health **7577**

Center for Immunity Enhancement in Domestic Animals **13137**

Family and Consumer Sciences Research Institute **9506**

Food Safety Research Center **10980**

Occupational and Traffic Safety Education Research Laboratory **9810**

Veterinary Diagnostic Laboratory **13138**

Veterinary Medical Research Institute **13139**

Veterinary Medicine and Clinical Microbiology Laboratory **13140**

Science and Technology Research Center • New York Institute of Technology **2461**

Science and Veterinary Medicine; Chinese Association of Animal **13069**

Sciences; Academy of Pharmaceutical **10574**

Sciences; Archivists and Librarians in the Health **6973**

Sciences; Association for Chemoreception **8187**

Sciences Communications Association; Health **6997**

Sciences Consortium; Health **6998**

Sciences; Council for International Organizations of Medical **1259**

Sciences; Federation of Behavioral, Psychological and Cognitive **7375**

Sciences; Hungarian Society of Nutritional **9462**

Sciences Institute - Nutrition Foundation; International Life **10412**

Sciences; Institute of Society, Ethics, and the Life **7176**

Sciences; International Reference Organization in Forensic Medicine and **7181**

Sciences; International Union of Nutritional **9466**

Sciences and Medical Education; Association for the Behavioral **7322**

Sciences Medicales; Conseil des Organisations Internationales des **1259**

Sciences in Medicine; International Union for Physical and Engineering **2428**

Sciences; National Accrediting Agency for Clinical Laboratory **7144**

Sciences Neurologiques; Association Pan- Africaine des **8296**

Sciences de la Nutrition; Union Internationale des **9466**

Sciences; Pan-African Association of Neurological **8296**

Sciences; Pan American Association of Veterinary **13103**

Scientific Hypnotherapy; Academy of **6580**

Scientific Psychology; French-Language Association of **7379**

Scientific Research, Inc.; Institute for **1608**

Scientific Research in Stomatology and Odontology; International Group for **3961**

Scientific Study of Intellectual Disability; International Association for the **4291**

Scientific Study of Male Psychology and Physiology; Society for the **11723**

Scientific Study of Mental Deficiency; International Association for the **4291**

Scientific Study of Mental Deficiency; New Zealand Association for the **4299**

Scientific Study of Sex; Society for the **11715**

Scientifique de Langue Francaise; Association de Psychologie **7379**

Scientifique en Stomatologie et Odontologie; Groupement International pour la Recherche **3961**

Scientists; American Association of Pharmaceutical **10579**

Scientists; Association of Clinical **7126**

Scientists Center for Animal Welfare **13171**

Scleroderma and Arthritis Research Center • Thomas Jefferson University **7935**

Scleroderma Association; Raynaud's and **2872**

Scleroderma Club; National **7904**

Scleroderma Federation **7903**

Scleroderma Foundation; Monterey Bay **7912**

Scleroderma Foundation; United **4212, 7912**

Scleroderma International Foundation **7904**

Scleroderma Research Foundation **7905**

Scleroderma Support Group **7906**

Sclerose Laterale Amyotrophique; Association pour la Recherche sur la **8190**

Sclerosis Lateral Amiotrofia; Associazione **8191**

Sclerotherapy; American Academy of **9980**

Sclerotherapy; American Osteopathic Academy of **9980, 9980**

Scoliosis Association [Boca Raton, FL] **7907**

Scoliosis Association [London, England] **7908**

Scoliosis Associations; International Federation of **7880**

Scoliosis Foundation; National **7894**
Scoliosis Research Society **7909**
Scotland; Action on Smoking and Health— **11729**
Scott-Ritchey Research Center • Auburn University **13127**
Scott and White School of Nursing • University of Mary Hardin-Baylor
   8993
Scottish Motor Neurone Disease Association **8304**
Screwworm Research Laboratory • Agricultural Research Service • U.S.
   Department of Agriculture **13204**
Scripps Clinic; Research Institute of 1662
Scripps Foundation; Ellen Browning 166
Scripps Research Institute **1662**
      Autoimmune Disease Center **2116**
      Department of Neuropharmacology **8424**
Scrittura; Societa Internazionale di Psicologia della 7425
Scuba Association; Handicapped **4491**
Seabury Foundation **482**
Sealy Center for Molecular Science • University of Texas Medical Branch at
   Galveston **2696**
Searle Charitable Trust **845**
Seasonal Affective Disorder; National Organization for **7469**
SEASONS: Suicide Bereavement **7505**
Seattle Biomedical Research Institute **6787**
Seattle Central Community College • Respiratory Therapist Program
   11573
Seattle Institute for Psychoanalysis **7599**
Seattle Pacific University • School of Health Sciences • Department of
   Nursing **9021**
Seattle University • School of Nursing **9022**
Second Sight 13460
Secondary Complications in Spinal Cord Injury; Medical Rehabilitation
   Research and Training Center in • University of Alabama at Birmingham
   12755
Secondary School for the Deaf; Model **3543**
Secretarial Transcribers Association; Visually Impaired 13575
Secretaries; National Association of Rehabilitation **12696**
Secretaries; National Conference of Tuberculosis 11594
Secretions; Association for Study of Internal 4838
Section of Audiology and Auditory Research • Temple University **3623**
Section for Metropolitan Hospitals **6468**
Section for Rehabilitation Hospitals and Programs **6469**
Secular Organizations for Sobriety **12076**
Securite des Substances Chimiques; Programme International sur la 5044
Security Action Council; Health **5731**
Security Benefit Life Insurance Co. Charitable Trust **846**
Security; International Association for Hospital 6450
Security and Safety; International Association for Healthcare **6450**
Seeing; Council for the Education of the Partially 3218
Sein; Societe Internationale pour la Lutte Contre le Cancer du 5957
Sela, Inc. **2470**
Selbhilfen fur Elektrosensible 5058
Selby Foundation; William G. Selby and Marie **548**
Selective Mutism Foundation **3575**
Self Foundation **483**
Self-Help Association for the Electrically Sensitive 5058
Self-Help Center **7010**
Self-Help Clearinghouse; National **7474**
Self-Help Clearinghouse; National Mental Health Consumer **7468**
Self Help for Hard of Hearing People **3576**
Self-Help Network; Usher Syndrome **5305**
Self-Help Research and Knowledge Dissemination; Center for • University
   of Michigan **7671**
Self-Mutilators Support Group 7502
Self-Help Development Institute 7010
Seminars on Hypnosis Foundation 6588
Seminole Community College • Respiratory Therapist Program **11362**
Senility Studies: Alzheimer's Disease Treatment Research; Center for
   1929
Senility Studies; Center for 1929
Senior Citizens for Health Care Through Social Security; National Council
   of 1912
Senior Citizens; National Council of **1912**
Senior and Disabled Services Division • Oregon Department of Human
   Resources **2039**
Senior Services Division • Alaska Department of Administration **2004**
Senses Center; Monell Chemical **8396**
Senses; Center for Research in the Special • University of Louisville **8505**
Sensor Technology; Resource for Biomedical • Case Western Reserve
   University **2440**
Sensorimotor Research; Laboratory of • National Eye Institute • U.S.
   Department of Health and Human Services **13643**
Sensory Electrophysiology Research Unit **13627**

Sensory Eye Research Center 13627
Sensory Research; Institute for • Syracuse University **8432**
Sensory Sciences Center • University of Texas—Houston Health Science
   Center **8527**
Sentara-Norfolk General Hospital • Graduate Program of Nurse
   Anesthesia **2342**
Sequin Research Centre; Fernand • University of Montreal **10481**
Sequoia Hospital Lipid Institute • University of California at Berkeley **2957**
Serendipity Association 2238
Serendipity Association for Research and Implementation of Holistic Health
   and World Peace **2238**
Service Association for Health; INSA, The International 1308
Service Dog Center **3577**
Services for the Aged; Jewish Association for [New York, NY] **1904**
Services for the Aged; Jewish Association for [Rego Park, NY] **1905**
Services for the Aging; American Association of Homes and **1882**
Services to the Blind and Visually Impaired Division • South Dakota
   Department of Human Services **13707**
Services for Families and Children; Council on Accreditation of **11865**
Services for People with Disabilities Division • Utah Department of Human
   Services **4387**
Services Research Branch • Epidemiology and Services Research Division
   • National Institute of Mental Health • U.S. Department of Health and
   Human Services **7631**
Services Research Division; Epidemiologic and • National Institute of Mental
   Health • U.S. Department of Health and Human Services **7627**
Services for the Visually Impaired Bureau • Ohio Rehabilitation Services
   Commission **13700**
Servizio di Neuroradiologia 8216
Seth Sprague Educational and Charitable Foundation **484**
Seton Hall University • College of Nursing **8818**
Seton Hall University; University of Medicine and Dentistry of New Jersey /
   Kean College of New Jersey / • School of Allied Health Related
   Professions • Physical Therapy Program **12509**
Seton Hill College • Department of Human Ecology • Dietetics Program
   9423
Seva Foundation **1503**
Seven Directors; National Association of Title 1907
Seventh-Day Adventist Dentists; National Association of **3969**
Seventh-Day Adventist Dietetic Association **9486**
Severe Handicaps; TASH: The Association for Persons With **4563**
Severe Traumatic Brain Injury; Rehabilitation Research and Training Center
   on • Virginia Commonwealth University **12766**
Severely Mentally Ill; Center on the Organization and Financing of Care for
   the **5614**
Severely Mentally Ill; Center for Research on the Organization and
   Financing of Care for the • Rutgers University **7595**
Seward County Community College • Respiratory Therapist Program
   11395
Sex Addicts Anonymous **11710**
Sex Addicts; Co-Dependents of 11689
Sex Educators and Counselors; American Association of 11685
Sex Educators, Counselors and Therapists; American Association of
   11685
Sex Forum; National 11691
Sex, Gender, and Reproduction, Inc.; Kinsey Institute for Research in
   11721
Sex Information Council of America 11690
Sex Information and Education; Council for **11690**
Sex Information and Education Council of the U.S. **11711**
Sex Information Network; National **11707**
Sex and Love Addicts Anonymous **11712**
Sex Research; Center for • California State University, Northridge **11718**
Sex Research; German Society for **11693**
Sex Research; Institute for 11721
Sex; Society for the Scientific Study of **11715**
Sex Therapy and Research; Society for **11716**
Sexaholics Anonymous **11713**
Sexual Abusers; Association for the Behavioral Treatment of 11686
Sexual Abusers; Association for the Treatment of **11686**
Sexual Aggression; Association for the Behavioral Treatment of 11686
Sexual Assault; Alaska Network on Domestic Violence and 3077
Sexual Assault Coalition; Nebraska Domestic Violence and 3103
Sexual Assault; National Coalition Against **11704**
Sexual Assault; Oklahoma Coalition on Domestic Violence and 3112
Sexual Assault; South Carolina Coalition Against Domestic Violence and
   3117
Sexual Assault; South Dakota Coalition Against Domestic Violence and
   3118
Sexual Assault; Vermont Network Against Domestic Violence and 3122
Sexual Assault; Wyoming Coalition Against Domestic Violence and 3129

Simon Foundation 12913
Simon Foundation for Continence **12913**
Simon Foundation; William E. and Carol G. **544**
Sinclair Community College • Respiratory Therapist Program **11497**
Singapore; Dermatological Society of **4229**
Singapore Medical Association **10967**
Singapore Paediatric Society **3287**
Singapore; Pharmaceutical Society of **10617**
Sioux Falls Medical Research Center • University of South Dakota **1721**
Sister Kenny Foundation 12718
Sister Kenny Institute **12718**, **12749**
Sisters Concerned for the Rural Poor 1426
Sisters; Medical Mission **1382**
Sjogren's Syndrome Association; National **2084**
Sjogren's Syndrome Foundation **7910**
Skandinavisk Forening for (Fodreflexologer) Zoneterapeutes 2237
Skeletal Dysplasia; International Center for **5333**
Skeletal Research Center • Case Western Reserve University **7917**
Skeletal Society; International **11118**
Ski for Light 4555, **4555**
Ski et de Medecine d'Hiver; Societe Internationale de Traumatologie de 11946
Ski Traumatology and Medicine of Winter Sports; International Society for **11946**
Skiers Association; National Amputee 4528
Skiers Association; United States Deaf **3584**
Skiing Foundation; American Blind **13390**
Skilled Nursing and Related Long Term Care Services 6472
Skillman Foundation **492**
Skin Cancer Foundation **5906**, **5986**
Skin Clinic; Aging • University of Pennsylvania **4270**
Skin Diseases Branch • Extramural Activities Program • National Institute of Arthritis and Musculoskeletal and Skin Diseases • U.S. Department of Health and Human Services **4268**
Skin Diseases Information Clearinghouse; National Arthritis and Musculoskeletal and **7891**
Skin Diseases; National Institute of Arthritis and Musculoskeletal and
    Extramural Activities Program
        Centers Program • U.S. Department of Health and Human Services **7937**
        Muscle Biology Program • U.S. Department of Health and Human Services **7938**
        Musculoskeletal Diseases Branch • U.S. Department of Health and Human Services **7939**
        Rheumatic Diseases Branch • U.S. Department of Health and Human Services **7940**
        Skin Diseases Branch • U.S. Department of Health and Human Services **4268**
    Intramural Research Program • Arthritis and Rheumatism Branch • U.S. Department of Health and Human Services **7941**
    Laboratory of Physical Biology • U.S. Department of Health and Human Services **7942**
    U.S. Department of Health and Human Services **7854**, **7936**
Skin Institute; Fulton **4263**
Skin Types; FIRST - Foundation for Ichthyosis and Related **4234**
Skirball Foundation **6381**
Sklerose Forbundet i Norge; Multipel 8291
Skyline College • Respiratory Therapist Program **11333**
Slant/Fin Foundation **852**
SLE Foundation **8090**
Slechthorende- en Spraakgestoorde; Federaties van Ouders van 3519
Sleep Apnea Association; American **8172**
Sleep; Association for the Psycho physiological Study of 8305
Sleep and Circadian Rhythm; Center for Research on • Stanford University **8429**
Sleep Council; Better **5828**
Sleep Council (of the International Sleep Products Association); Better 5828
Sleep Council (of the National Association of Bedding Manufacturers); Better 5828
Sleep Disorders Association; American **8173**
Sleep Disorders Center
    Dartmouth College **8360**
    Georgetown University **8370**
    Johns Hopkins University **8383**
    Loma Linda University **8385**
    Ohio State University **8413**
    Thomas Jefferson University **8436**
    University of Arizona **8479**
Sleep Disorders Center for Children **3349**
Sleep Disorders Center of Henry Ford Hospital **8425**
Sleep Disorders Centers; American Association of 8173

Sleep Disorders Centers; Association of 8173
Sleep Disorders Medicine; Laboratory for Circadian and **8384**
Sleep Disorders and Research Center
    Baylor College of Medicine **8332**
    Stanford University **8430**
Sleep Foundation; National **8281**
Sleep Medicine; American Board of **8158**
Sleep Optimization Research Laboratory • Naval Health Research Center • Naval Medical Research and Development Command • U.S. Department of Defense **7845**
Sleep Research Foundation **8426**
Sleep Research Laboratory • Emory University **8366**
Sleep Research Society **8305**
Sleep Societies; Associated Professional **8186**
Sleep Societies; Association of Professional 8186
Sleep Study Unit • University of Texas **8525**
Sloan-Kettering Cancer Center; Memorial **6074**
    Laboratory of GI Tumor Biology **6075**
Slovak Medical Society **1504**
Slovak Society of Anesthesiology and Intensive Care Medicine **2372**
Slovak Society of Angiology **2874**
Slovak Society of Cardiology **2875**
Slovak Society of Clinical Neurophysiology **8306**
Slovak Society of Diabetes **4871**
Slovak Society of Neurology **8307**
Slovak Society of Nuclear Medicine and Radiation Hygiene **11131**
Slovak Society of Ophthalmology **13563**
Slovak Society of Pediatrics **3288**
Slovak Society of Physiology and Pathology of Respiration **11606**
Slovak Society of Plastic Surgery **12303**
Slovenian Dental Association **3990**
Slovenska Ledarska Spolocnost 1504
S.M.A.; Families of **8218**
Small Animal Veterinary Association; British **13065**
Small Business Innovation Research Program • National Institute of Neurological Disorders and Stroke • U.S. Department of Health and Human Services **8471**
Small Ruminant Practitioners; American Association of **13034**
Small or Rural Hospitals; General Constituency Section for **6444**
Smart Family Foundation **493**
Smell Center; Rocky Mountain Taste and • University of Colorado—Denver **12136**
Smell and Taste Center • University of Pennsylvania **8521**
Smile International; Operation **12293**
Smile; Operation 12293
Smith Charitable Foundation; Clara Blackford Smith and W. Aubrey **102**
Smith Charitable Trust; W. W. **532**
Smith College • School of Social Work **11797**
Smith Foundation; A.O. **561**
Smith Foundation; Lon V. **358**
Smith Fund; George D. **212**
Smith-Kettlewell Eye Research Institute **13628**
    Rehabilitation Engineering Center **2471**
Smith-Kettlewell Institute of Visual Sciences 13628
Smith Richardson Foundation **494**
SmithKline Beecham Foundation **853**
Smithsonian Institution • National Museum of American History • Department of the History of Science and Technology • Science, Medicine, and Society Division **2**
Smokefree America 11738
SmokeFree Educational Services **11738**
Smokers' Pollution; Group Against **11737**
Smoking Cessation Research Institute **11741**
Smoking and Health; Action on **11725**, **11726**
    Women and Smoking Group **11727**
Smoking and Health; Canadian Council on **11733**
Smoking and Health; Chinese Association on **11734**
Smoking and Health—Northern Ireland; Action on **11728**
Smoking and Health—Scotland; Action on **11729**
Smoking and Health—Wales; Action on **11730**
Smoking, Inc.; Studies on **11742**
Smoking OR Health; Coalition on **11736**
Smoking Pollution; California Group Against 11731
Snyder Memorial Research Foundation; H.L. **2576**
Sobriety; Secular Organizations for **12076**
Sobriety; Women for **12082**
Social; Asociacion Latinoamericana de Psicologia 7435
Social and Behavioral Sciences; Center for • University of California, San Francisco **7659**
Social Development and Education; Center for the Study of • University of Massachusetts Boston **4594**

Societatea de Cardiologie 2873
Societatea Romana de Anestezie Terapie Intensiva 2371
Societatea Romana de Neurofiziologie Clinica 8301
Societe Beneluxienne de Phlebologie 2834
Societe Canadienne des Anesthesistes 2359
Societe Canadienne de Cardiologie 2838
Societe Canadienne de Pediatrie 3195
Societe Canadienne des Pharmaciens d'Hopitaux 10593
Societe Canadienne des Technologistes de Laboratoire 7128
Societe Canadienne des Technologistes en Orthopedie 9925
Societe d'Ethologie Veterinaire 13089
Societe Europeenne de Psychiatrie de l'Enfant et de l'Adolescent 3222
Societe Europeenne de Chirurgie Cardiovasculaire 12269
Societe Europeenne d'Anesthesie Loco-Regionale 2365
Societe et Federation Internationale de Cardiologie 2860
Societe Francaise d'Anesthesie et de Reanimation **2373**
Societe Francaise d'Angeiologie **2876**
Societe Francaise de Chirurgie Infantile 3230
Societe Francaise de Chirurgie Pediatrique 3230
Societe Hollandaise d'Immunologie 2071
Societe International d'Ethologie Applie 13089
Societe Internationale de Chimiotherapie 10413
Societe Internationale de Chirurgie 12282
Societe Internationale de Chirurgie Orthopedique et de Traumatologie 9929
Societe Internationale d'Hydrologie et de Climatologie Medicale 5046
Societe Internationale d'Oncologie Pediatrique 3249
Societe Internationale d'Ophtalmologie Geographique 13500
Societe Internationale d'Urologie 12907
Societe Internationale de Kinesiologie Electrophysiologique 2425
Societe Internationale pour la Lutte Contre le Cancer du Sein 5957
Societe Internationale de Medecine de Catastrophe 4743
Societe Internationale de Medecine Interne 1358
Societe Internationale de Neurochimie 8244
Societe Internationale de Neuropathologie 10135
Societe Internationale de Pathologie Geographique 10134
Societe Internationale de Prothese et Orthese 4498
Societe Internationale de Psychopathologie de l'Expression 7419
Societe Internationale des Radiographes et Techniciens de Radiologie 11121
Societe Internationale de Radiologie 11122
Societe Internationale de Recherches Cardiaques 2858
Societe Internationale de Transfusion Sanguine 7141
Societe Internationale de Traumatologie de Ski et de Medecine d'Hiver 11946
Societe de l'Osteoporose du Canada 7899
Societe Malgache de Pediatrie 3254
Societe Marocaine de Pediatrie 3260
Societe Mediterraneenne de Chimiotherapie 10418
Societe de Neurochirurgie du Moyen Orient 12289
Societe de Neurophysiologie Clinique de Langue Francaise 8220
Societe de Neuropsychologie de Langue Francaise 8221
Societe de Pathologie Exotique 6667
Societe de Reanimation de Langue Francaise 1304
Societe Rorschach Internationale 7417
Societe Royale Belge de Dermatologie et de Venereologie 4220
Societe Scientifique du Service Medical Militaire 7806
Societies for Clinical Social Work; National Federation of **11869**
Societies; International Federation of Teratology **5280**
Societies of Pathology; International Council of **10133**
Society for Academic Emergency Medicine 4757
Society for Adolescent Medicine **3289**
Society for the Advancement of the Field Theory 7508
Society for the Advancement of Freestanding Ambulatory Surgical Care 12272
Society for the Advancement of Gastroenterology 5203
Society for the Advancement of Social Psychology 7509
Society for the Advancement of Travel for the Handicapped **4556**
Society of Air Force Anesthesiologists 2362
Society of Air Force Physicians **7807**
Society for Ambulatory Care Professionals **1505**
Society of American Bacteriologists 6635
Society of American Gastrointestinal Endoscopic Surgeons **5230**
Society of Anaesthetists of West Africa **2374**
Society for Assisted Reproductive Technology **11251**
Society of Association Optometric Executives 13481
Society of Behavioral Medicine **7510**
Society for Behavioral Pediatrics **3290**
Society of Biological Psychiatry **7511**
Society for Biomaterials **2432**
Society of Biomedical Equipment Technicians 2543, **2543**

Society for Cardiac Angiography and Interventions **2877**
Society of Cardiology 2873
Society of Cardiovascular Anesthesiologists **2375**
Society of Cardiovascular and Interventional Radiology **11132**
Society of Cardiovascular Radiology 11132
Society for Clinical Ecology 5031
Society for Clinical and Experimental Hypnosis **6598**
Society of Clinical and Medical Electrologists **1506**
Society for Clinical Trials **1507**
Society of Community Medicine 10968
Society for Companion Animal Studies **12719**
Society of Computed Body Tomography 11133
Society of Computed Body Tomography and Magnetic Resonance **11133**
Society for Computerized Tomography and Neuroimaging 11096
Society of Critical Care Medicine **4758**
Society for Cryo-Opthamology 13406
Society for Cryobiology **2544**
Society of Dermatology of Uruguay **4257**
Society of Diagnostic Medical Sonographers **11134**
Society for Disability Studies **4557**
Society for Drug Research 10624
Society for Ear, Nose, and Throat Advances in Children **3291**
Society of Engineering Psychologists 7304
Society for Environmental Geochemistry and Health **5059**
Society for Epidemiologic Research **5184**
Society, Ethics and the Life Sciences; Institute of 2580, 7176
Society for Experimental Biology and Medicine **2545**
Society of Experimental Psychologists **7512**
Society for the Exploration of Psychotherapy Integration **7513**
Society of Extracorporeal Circulation Technicians; American 2829
Society For Surgery of the Alimentary Tract **12304**
Society of Gastroenterology Nurses and Associates **5231**
Society of Gastrointestinal Assistants 5231
Society of General Internal Medicine **1508**
Society of Geriatric Ophthalmology **1920**
Society of Government Service Urologists **12914**
Society for Gynecologic Investigation **9694**
Society of Gynecologic Oncologists **5987**
Society of Head and Neck Surgeons **12305**
Society for Healthcare Planning and Marketing of the American Hospital Association **6471**
Society for Health and Human Values **1509**
Society of Hearing Aid Audiologists 3538
Society for Hematopathology **5988**
Society of Homes for the Handicapped **4558**
Society of Hospital Attorneys 7159
Society of Hospital Epidemiologists of America **5185**
Society for Hospital Planning of the American Hospital Association 6471
Society for Hospital Planning and Marketing of the American Hospital Association 6471
Society for Hospital Social Work Directors **11872**
Society for Human Ecology **5060**
Society of Integral Psychoanalysis 7418
Society; International Leadership Center on Longevity and • Mount Sinai School of Medicine of City University of New York **1941**
Society for Investigative Dermatology **4258**
Society for InVitro Biology **2546**
Society of Laboratory Animal Science **13107**
Society for Leukocyte Biology (A Reticuloendothelial Society) **2090**
Society for Life History Research **1510**
Society for Life History Research in Psychopathology 1510
Society of Magnetic Resonance **11135**
Society for Magnetic Resonance Imaging **11136**
Society of Medical Administrators **5602**
Society of Medical Consultants to the Armed Forces **7808**
Society of Medical-Dental Management Consultants **5882**
Society of Medical Jurisprudence **7193**
Society of Medical Jurisprudence and State Medicine 7193
Society of Medical Laboratory Technologists of South Africa **7153**
Society of Medical Officers of Health 10968
Society for Medicinal Plant Research **10420**
Society and Medicine; Center for the Study of • Columbia University **5619**
Society for Medicines Research **10624**
Society for Menstrual Cycle Research **9695**
Society of Mental Health Librarians 6978
Society of Military Orthopaedic Surgeons **7809**
Society of Military Otolaryngologists 7810
Society of Military Otolaryngologists - Head and Neck Surgeons **7810**
Society for Mucopolysaccharide Diseases **4872**
Society of Multivariate Experimental Psychology **7514**
Society of Neurological Surgeons **12306**

Health Services Office **11046**
   Environmental Health Bureau **5168**
   Maternal and Child Health Bureau **3418, 9764**
   Preventive Health Services Bureau • STD / HIV Division **6896**
  Vital Records and Public Health Statistics Office **7080**
  Women and Children's Services Division • Dental Health Program **4143**
South Carolina Department of Labor, Licensing, and Regulation • Occupational Safety and Health Division **9905**
South Carolina Department of Mental Health **7748**
South Carolina Department of Vocational Rehabilitation **12811**
South Carolina Division • American Cancer Society **6317**
South Carolina Health Care Association **9366**
South Carolina Health and Human Services Department • Health Services Bureau • Medicaid Program **5808**
South Carolina Health and Human Services Finance Commission • Interagency Planning, Research and Coordination Bureau **5701**
South Carolina Hospital Association **6568**
South Carolina; Learning Disabilities Association of **4722**
South Carolina; Life Abilities— Easter Seal Society of **4670**
South Carolina Medical Association **1852**
South Carolina; Mental Health Association in **7777**
South Carolina; National Kidney Foundation of **12975**
South Carolina Nurses Association **9252**
South Carolina Office of the Governor • Aging Division **2042**
South Carolina Optometric Association **13833**
South Carolina Osteopathic Medical Association **10105**
South Carolina Pharmacy Association **10735**
South Carolina State Board of Dentistry **4090**
South Carolina State Board of Funeral Service **3768**
South Carolina State Board of Nursing **9197**
South Carolina State College
  Department of Human Services • Rehabilitation Counselor Training Program **12632**
  School of Nursing **8959**
South Carolina State Veterinarian **13290**
South Central Poultry Research Laboratory • Agricultural Research Service • U.S. Department of Agriculture **13205**
South Central Texas Chapter
  Arthritis Foundation **8021**
  Lupus Foundation of America **8112**
South Dakota Affiliate • American Diabetes Association **4993**
South Dakota; American Lung Association of **11673**
South Dakota Animal Industry Board • State Veterinarian **13291**
South Dakota; Arc of **4430**
South Dakota Board of Examiners for Nursing Home Administrators **9316**
South Dakota Board of Nursing **9198**
South Dakota Board of Optometry **13760**
South Dakota Board of Podiatry **10821**
South Dakota Chapter • National Association of Social Workers **11923**
South Dakota Coalition Against Domestic Violence and Sexual Assault **3118**
South Dakota Dental Association **4197**
South Dakota Department of Health **11047**
  AIDS Specialist **6897**
  Division of Public Health • Regulation and Quality Assurance Division **5169**
  Emergency Medical Services Program **4809**
  Health and Medical Services Division • Dental Program **4144**
  Licensure and Certification Program **6517**
  Maternal and Child Health Program **3419, 9765**
  Policy and External Affairs Office **5702**
  Systems Development and Regulation Division **9906**
  Vital Records Program **7081**
South Dakota Department of Human Services
  Alcohol and Drug Abuse Division **12188**
  Developmental Disabilities Division **4384**
  Mental Health Division **7749**
  Rehabilitation Services Division **12812**
  Services to the Blind and Visually Impaired Division **13707**
South Dakota Department of Social Services
  Program Management Division
    Adult Services on Aging Office **2043**
    Medical Services Office **5809**
South Dakota Division • American Cancer Society **6318**
South Dakota; Easter Seal Society of **4671**
South Dakota Health Care Association **9367**
South Dakota Hospital Association **6569**
South Dakota Nurses Association **9253**
South Dakota Optometric Society **13834**
South Dakota Osteopathic Association **10106**

South Dakota Pharmaceutical Association **10736**
South Dakota State Board of Dentistry **4091**
South Dakota State Board of Funeral Service **3769**
South Dakota State Board of Medical and Osteopathic Examiners **1799, 10055**
South Dakota State Board of Pharmacy **10683**
South Dakota State Medical Association **1853**
South Dakota State University
  Animal Disease Research and Diagnostic Laboratory **13172**
  College of Nursing **8965**
  College of Pharmacy **10562**
South Dakota Veterinary Medical Association **13344**
South Jersey Chapter • Lupus Foundation of America **8078**
South Jersey Medical Research Foundation **2568**
South Pacific Underwater Medicine Society **1514**
South Plains College • Respiratory Therapist Program **11552**
South Texas Charitable Foundation **497**
South Texas Poultry Disease Laboratory **13181**
South Texas Vaccine Development Center • University of Texas Health Science Center at San Antonio **6852**
South East Asia; Association of Surgeons of **12252**
South-East Asia; Regional Office for • World Health Organization **1544**
Southeast Asian Region; Association of Pediatric Societies of the **3188**
Southeast College of the Houston Community College System • Eastwood Center for Health Careers • Respiratory Therapy Program **11553**
Southeast Community College • Respiratory Therapist Program **11452**
Southeast Florida Chapter • Lupus Foundation of America **8043**
Southeast Missouri State University • Department of Nursing **8797**
Southeast Poultry Research Laboratory • Poultry Disease Research Unit • U.S. Department of Agriculture • Agricultural Research Service **13206**
Southeastern Clinical Occupational Medicine / Environmental Health Evaluation Center • Emory University **9806**
Southeastern College of Osteopathic Medicine **10214**
Southeastern Cooperative Wildlife Disease Study • University of Georgia **13217**
Southeastern Louisiana University • School of Nursing **8730**
Southeastern New England Clinical Microbiology Research Group • University of Massachusetts Dartmouth **2675**
Southeastern Pennsylvania Affiliate • American Heart Association **3032**
Southeastern Regional Trophoblastic Disease Center • Duke University **6032**
Southern Africa; Anatomical Society of **2526**
Southern Africa; Infectious Diseases Society of **6677**
Southern Africa; Leprosy Mission - **6692**
Southern Africa; Surgical Research Society of **12314**
Southern Arizona Chapter
  Arthritis Foundation **7965**
  Lupus Foundation of America **8032**
Southern Baptist Theological Seminary • Carver School of Social Work **11783**
Southern California Chapter
  Arthritis Foundation **7970**
  Cystic Fibrosis Foundation **5401, 5414**
  Lupus Foundation of America **8035**
Southern California College of Optometry **13365**
Southern California Injury Prevention Research Center • University of California, Los Angeles **10883**
Southern California Neuropsychiatric Institute **8428**
Southern California Research Institute **12102**
Southern California / Southern Nevada Chapter • Cystic Fibrosis Foundation **5402, 5436**
Southern Casualty and Surety Conference **5735**
Southern College of Optometry **13379**
Southern Connecticut State University
  Graduate Social Work Program **11761**
  School of Nursing **8603**
Southern Connecticut State University / Bridgeport Hospital • Nurse Anesthesia Program **2266**
Southern Illinois University at Alton • School of Dental Medicine **3799**
Southern Illinois University at Carbondale
  Comparative Physiology Lab **2622**
  Department of Health Care Professions • Respiratory Therapy Program **11382**
  Evaluation and Developmental Center **4584**
  Mortuary Science and Funeral Service Program **3672**
  Rehabilitation Institute **12750**
    Rehabilitation Counseling Program **12591**
  School of Social Work **11776**
Southern Illinois University at Edwardsville
  School of Nursing **8666**
    Nurse Anesthesia Specialization **2272**

Toxicology Research Center **10459**

State University of New York College at Brockport • Nursing Department **8846**

State University of New York College of Optometry **13373**

State University of New York College at Plattsburgh
Auditory Research Laboratory **3622**
Biochemistry Program **2625**
Department of Nursing **8847**

State University of New York College of Technology at Canton • Mortuary Science Program **3690**

State University of New York Health Science Center at Brooklyn
Child Behavior Research Unit **3350**
Child Psychiatry Research Program **3351**
College of Health Related Professions
Health Information Administration Program **6943**
Nurse-Midwifery Certificate Program **9605**
College of Medicine **1000**
Department of Pharmacology **10304**
College of Nursing **8848**
General Clinical Research Center **1667**
Infant and Child Behavior Laboratory **3352**
Neurodynamic Laboratory **7604**
Occupational Therapy Program **12398**
Perfusion Training Program **2807**
Physical Therapy Program **12520**
Physician Assistant Program **1094**
Primate Behavior Laboratory **13173**
Psychophysiological Laboratory **7605**
Psychosomatic Research Program **7606**
Research Unit on Communicative Processes **7607**
Sickle Cell Center **6115**

State University of New York Health Science Center at Stony Brook
Asthma and Allergic Diseases Center **2119**
SUNY Stony Brook AIDS Treatment and Development Center **6792**

State University of New York Health Science Center at Syracuse
Cardiovascular Perfusion Program **2808**
Clinical Research Center **1668**
College of Health Related Professions • Program in Physical Therapy **12521**
College of Medicine **1001**
Department of Pharmacology **10305**
Respiratory Therapy Program **11471**
Robert C. Schwartz Cystic Fibrosis Center **5353**

State University of New York Institute of Technology at Utica / Rome • Health Information Administration Program **6944**

State University of New York at Stony Brook
Institute for Mental Health Research **7608**
School of Dental Medicine **3821**
School of Health Technology and Management
Department of Physical Therapy **12522**
Division of Rehabilitation Sciences • Occupational Therapy Program **12399**
Physician Assistant Program **1095**
Respiratory Therapy Program **11472**
School of Medicine **1002**
Department of Pharmacological Sciences **10306**
School of Nursing **8849**
School of Social Welfare **11826**

State Veterans Homes; National Association of **7803**

State Veterinarian
Alabama Department of Agriculture and Industries **13250**
Animal Industries Division • Tennessee Department of Agriculture **13292**
Animal Industry Bureau
Agriculture Division • Nevada Department of Business and Industry **13277**
Nebraska Department of Agriculture **13276**
Pennsylvania Department of Agriculture **13287**
Animal Industry Division
Colorado Department of Agriculture **13255**
Florida Department of Agriculture and Consumer Services **13258**
Georgia Department of Agriculture **13259**
Hawaii Department of Agriculture **13260**
Michigan Department of Agriculture **13271**
New Hampshire Department of Agriculture **13278**
New York Department of Agriculture and Markets **13281**
Ohio Department of Agriculture **13284**
Oklahoma Department of Agriculture **13285**
Animal Services Division • Arizona Department of Agriculture **13252**
Arkansas Livestock and Poultry Commission **13253**

Connecticut Department of Agriculture **13256**
Environmental Health Division • Alaska Department of Environmental Conservation **13251**
Kentucky Department of Agriculture **13266**
Louisiana Livestock Sanitary Board **13267**
New Mexico Livestock Board **13280**
Oregon Department of Agriculture **13286**
South Dakota Animal Industry Board **13291**
Vermont Department of Agriculture **13295**
Wyoming Livestock Board **13301**

Statewide Health Planning and Development Office • California Health and Welfare Agency **5667**

Statistical Center; National Spinal Cord Injury • University of Alabama at Birmingham **8474**

Statistical Consulting and Research; Center for • Southern Methodist University **7023**

Statistical Data and Analysis Center • Harvard University **7013**

Statistical Laboratory • University of California at Berkeley **7037**

Statistical Studies on Diseases of the Esophagus; International Organization for **5224**

Statistics; American Association for Vital Records and Public Health **6979**

Statistics; Association for Vital Records and Health **6979**

Statistics and Biomathematics Branch • National Institute of Environmental Health Sciences • U.S. Department of Health and Human Services **5112**

Statistics Branch; Epidemiology and • Diabetes Translation Division • National Center for Chronic Disease Prevention and Health Promotion • U.S. Department of Health and Human Services **10876**

Statistics Bureau; Vital
Ohio Department of Health **7075**
Texas Department of Health **7083**

Statistics Bureau; Vital Records and • Health Services Division • Montana Department of Health and Environmental Sciences **7066**

Statistics Bureau; Vital Records and Health • Public Health Services Division • New Hampshire Department of Health and Human Services **7069**

Statistics Center; Health
Health Care Planning, Financing, and Information Services Development Division • New Jersey Department of Health **7070**
Washington Department of Health **7087**

Statistics Center; State Registrar and Health • Michigan Department of Public Health **7062**

Statistics, and Data Management; Sampling, • Epidemiology and Oral Disease Prevention Program • National Institute of Dental Research • U.S. Department of Health and Human Services **4012**

Statistics Division; Health • Epidemiology and Health Promotion Office • Public Health Bureau • West Virginia Department of Health and Human Resources **7088**

Statistics Division; Policy and Health • Maryland Department of Health and Mental Hygiene **7060**

Statistics Division; Public Health • Indiana Department of Health **7054**

Statistics Division; Research and Vital • Maine Department of Human Services **7059**

Statistics Division; Vital
Health Services Department • Kentucky Human Resources Cabinet **7057**
Information Resources Bureau • Mississippi Department of Health **7064**

Statistics Division; Vital Records and • Public Health Department • Massachusetts Executive Office of Health and Human Services **7061**

Statistics; Georgia Center for Cancer • Emory University **6034**

Statistics; National Center for Health • U.S. Department of Health and Human Services **6907, 7027**

Statistics Office; Vital
Florida Department of Health and Rehabilitative Services **7049**
Health Division • Wisconsin Department of Health and Social Services **7089**
Health and Environment Statistics Division • Kansas Department of Health and Environment **7056**

Statistics Office; Vital Records and Health • Health Department • Virginia Office of Health and Human Resources **7086**

Statistics Office; Vital Records and Public Health • South Carolina Department of Health and Environmental Control **7080**

Statistics and Prevention Research Division; Epidemiology, • National Institute of Child Health and Human Development • U.S. Department of Health and Human Services **5190**

Statistics Section; Vital
Health Division • Oregon Department of Human Resources **7077**
Health Information Division • Louisiana Department of Health and Hospitals **7058**
New York State Department of Health **7072**
Public Health Division
Alaska Department of Health and Social Services **7041**
New Mexico Department of Health **7071**

Substance Abuse Issues; Inter-Association Task Force on Campus Alcohol and Other **12035**
Substance Abuse Librarians and Information Specialists **7011**
Substance Abuse and Mental Health Services Administration • U.S. Department of Health and Human Services **11999**
Substance Abuse Office
    Behaviorial Health Services Division • Arizona Department of Health Services **12149**
    Maine Office of the Governor **12166**
Substance Abuse Program • Behavioral Health Division • Wyoming Department of Health **12197**
Substance Abuse Research; Center for • University of Maryland **12139**
Substance Abuse; Rhode Island Department of **12186**
Substance Abuse Services Division
    Alabama Department of Mental Health and Mental Retardation **12147**
    Mental Health, Retardation and Substance Abuse Services Department • Virginia Office of Health and Human Resources **12193**
Substance Abuse Services Division; Mental Health, Developmental Disabilities and • North Carolina Department of Human Resources **12180**
Substance Abuse Services; New York State Office of Alcohol and **12179**
Substance Abuse Services Office • Michigan Department of Public Health **12169**
Substance Abuse Services; Special Constituency Section for Psychiatric and **6473**
Substance Abuse Trainers and Educators; National Association of **12055**
Substance Abuse Treatment Unit • University of Pennsylvania **12143**
Subtle Energies and Energy Medicine; International Society for the Study of **2218**
Sudamericana de Medicina del Deporte; Confederacion **11951**
Sudan; Friends of **1436**
Sudan Medical Students Association **1516**
Sudden Infant Death Syndrome Clearinghouse; National **3272**
Sudden Infant Death Syndrome Institute • University of Maryland **3363**
Sudden Infant Death Syndrome Institute; American **3175, 3309**
SUFFER **10406**
Suffering; International Community for the Relief of Starvation and **1338**
Suicide Bereavement; SEASONS: **7505**
Suicide; Center for the Study of • University of South Carolina at Columbia **7686**
Suicide Information and Education Centre **7524**
Suicide Prevention; German Association of **7381**
Suicide Prevention; International Association for **7403**
Suicide Prevention; National Committee on Youth **7534**
Suicide Prevention; Youth **7534**
Suicidology; American Association of **7284**
Suid-Afrika; Gesinsbeplanningsvereniging van **11245**
Suid-Afrika; Vereniging van Radiograwe van **11139**
Suid-Afrikaanse Diabetesberniging **4874**
Suid Afrikaanse Farmakologie Vereniging **10422**
Suid-Afrikaanse Ortopediese Vereniging **9937**
Suid Afrikaanse Vereniging van Arbeidsterapeute **12720**
Suid-Afrikaanse Vereniging van Kinderchirurge **3298**
Suidelike Afrika; Chirurgiese Navorsingsvereniging van **12314**
Suider Afrika; Aansteeklike Siektesvereniging van **6677**
Suider-Afrika; Anatomiese Vereniging van **2526**
Suizidpraevention; Deutsche Gesellschaft fur **7381**
Sulzberger Foundation **509**
Summerfield Foundation; Solon E. **495**
Sun Health Research Institute **1946**
Suncoast Chapter • Lupus Foundation of America **8044**
Sunderland Foundation; Lester T. **6371**
Sundstrand Corp. Foundation **865**
Sunnen Foundation **11191**
Sunshine Foundation **3301**
SUNY Stony Brook AIDS Treatment and Development Center • State University of New York Health Science Center at Stony Brook **6792**
Suomen Analyyttinen Trilogia Yhdistys **7377**
Suomen Dermatopatologiyhdistys **10129**
Suomen Hammaslaakariseura **3939**
Suomen Ihotautilaakariyhuistys Ry **4233**
Suomen Kardiologinen Seura **2847**
Suomen Kliinisen Neurofysiologian Yhdistys **8219**
Suomen Mielenterveysseura-Foreningen for Mental Halsa i Finland **7376**
Sup Sup Garden Club **9489**
Superintendents of American Institutions for Insane; Association of Medical **7301**
Superintendents Club; Medical **5602**
Superintendents of Mental Hospitals; Association of Medical **5542**

Superintendents and Principals of American Schools for the Deaf; Association of **3507**
Superintendents of U.S. and Canada; Association of Hospital **6425**
Superior-Pacific Fund **866**
Supervisors and Administrators; American Association of Clinical Laboratory **7129**
Supervisors and Administrators of Health Occupations Education; National Association of **5593**
Suppliers Associations; European Confederation of Medical **5844**
Support; Center for Family **4287**
Support Club; L. E. **7885**
Support Dogs for the Handicapped **4561**
Support Dogs, Inc. **4561**
Support Foundation; Cytochrome C Oxidase Deficiency Parental Research and **4833**
Support Group; Evans Syndrome Research and **7875**
Support Group; Freeman- Sheldon Parent **2748**
Support Group; HIV Information Exchange and **6675**
Support Group; Klippel- Trenaunay **7884**
Support Group for Monosomy 9P **5301**
Support Group; MSUD Family **3261**
Support Group for Myositis; National **7895**
Support Group for PM/DM; National **7896**
Support Group; Scleroderma **7906**
Support Groups; Alliance of Genetic **5267**
Support Groups of America; Parkinson **8297**
Support Groups; Burns United **2768**
Support Network; Beckwith- Wiedemann **2743**
Support Network; SIDELINES National **11250**
Support Organization for Trisomy 18/13 **5302**
Support; Y-Me National Organization for Breast Cancer Information and **5995**
Supreme Council, Ancient Accepted Scottish Rite of Free-Masonry **7236**
Surety Conference; Southern Casualty and **5735**
Surface Analysis Center for Biomedical Problems; National ESCA and • University of Washington **2502**
Surgeon Assistants; American Association of **12214**
Surgeon General; Air Force • Vice Chief of Staff of the Air Force • Department of the Air Force • U.S. Department of Defense **7783**
Surgeon General; Army • Chief of Staff of the Army • Department of the Army • U.S. Department of Defense **7786**
Surgeons; American Academy of Neurological and Orthopaedic **12204**
Surgeons; American Academy of Orthopaedic **12206**
Surgeons; American Academy of Osteopathic **9972**
Surgeons; American Academy of Spinal **12208**
Surgeons; American Association of Genito-Urinary **12210**
Surgeons; American Association of Neurological **8124, 12212**
Surgeons; American Association of Oral and Maxillofacial **3782, 3877**
Surgeons; American Association of Oral and Plastic **12213**
Surgeons; American Association of Plastic **12213**
Surgeons; American Association of Podiatric Physicians and **10757**
Surgeons; American College of **12233**
Surgeons; American College of Foot **12231**
Surgeons; American College of Foot and Ankle **12231**
Surgeons; American College of Oral and Maxillofacial **12232**
Surgeons; American College of Osteopathic **9978**
Surgeons; American College of Veterinary **13051**
Surgeons; American Shoulder and Elbow **12234**
Surgeons; American Society of Abdominal **12235**
Surgeons; American Society of Colon and Rectal **12237**
Surgeons; American Society of Maxillofacial **12242**
Surgeons; American Society of Oral **3877**
Surgeons; American Society of Outpatient **12243**
Surgeons; American Society of Plastic and Reconstructive **12244**
Surgeons; American Society of Transplant **12247**
Surgeons; Asian- Australasian Society of Neurological **12250**
Surgeon's Assistants; American Association of **12214**
Surgeons; Association of American Physicians and **1199**
Surgeons; Association of Bone and Joint **9924**
Surgeons; Association of Women **12259**
Surgeons; British Association of Aesthetic Plastic **12260**
Surgeons; British Association of Paediatric **3194**
Surgeons of California; Osteopathic Physicians and **10070**
Surgeons of Canada; Royal College of Physicians and **1496**
Surgeons; Congress of Neurological **12266**
Surgeons; Education Foundation of American Society of Plastic and Reconstructive **12296**
Surgeons of England; Royal College of **12298**
Surgeons; European Society for Cataract and Refractive **13448**
Surgeons of Great Britain; Association of Cosmetic Plastic **12260**
Surgeons; Hawaii Association of Osteopathic Physicians and **10077**

Surgeons; Illinois Association of Osteopathic Physicians and   **10079**
Surgeons; Indiana Association of Osteopathic Physicians and   **10080**
Surgeons; Interamerican College of Physicians and   **1331**
Surgeons; International Academy of Chest Physicians and   **12273**
Surgeons; International Association of Ocular   **12275**
Surgeons; International Association of Oral and Maxillofacial   **12276**
Surgeons; International College of   **12199, 12278**
Surgeons; Israel Association of Plastic and Reconstructive   **12284**
Surgeons; Latin American Federation of   **12287**
Surgeons; Michigan Association of Osteopathic Physicians and   **10088**
Surgeons; Missouri Association of Osteopathic Physicians and   **10091**
Surgeons; National Board of Examiners for Osteopathic Physicians and   **10003**
Surgeons; National College of Foot   **12290**
Surgeons; Nebraska Association of Osteopathic Physicians and   **10093**
Surgeons; New Jersey Association of Osteopathic Physicians and   **10096**
Surgeons; North Dakota Association of Osteopathic Physicians and   **10099**
Surgeons (of United States of America); Royal College of Physicians and   **1497**
Surgeons of Oregon; Osteopathic Physicians and   **10102**
Surgeons; Rhode Island Society of Osteopathic Physicians and   **10104**
Surgeons; Scandinavian Association of Paediatric   **12299**
Surgeons; Scandinavian Association of Plastic   **12300**
Surgeons; Society of American Gastrointestinal Endoscopic   **5230**
Surgeons; Society of Head and Neck   **12305**
Surgeons; Society of Military Orthopaedic   **7809**
Surgeons; Society of Military Otolaryngologists - Head and Neck   **7810**
Surgeons; Society of Neurological   **12306**
Surgeons; Society of Pelvic   **12307**
Surgeons; Society for Reproductive   **12308**
Surgeons; Society of Thoracic   **12309**
Surgeons; Society of United States Air Force Flight   **7811**
Surgeons; Society of University   **12311**
Surgeons; Society of University Otolaryngologists - Head and Neck   **12310**
Surgeons; South African Association of Paediatric   **3298**
Surgeons of South East Asia; Association of   **12252**
Surgeons of the U.S.; Association of Military   **7797**
Surgeons; Vermont State Association of Osteopathic Physicians and   **10110**
Surgeons; Wisconsin Association of Osteopathic Physicians and   **10114**
Surgeons; Wyoming Association of Osteopathic Physicians and   **10115**
Surgery; Academy of Ambulatory Foot   **10754**
Surgery of the Alimentary Tract; Society For   **12304**
Surgery; American Academy of Cosmetic   **12202**
Surgery; American Academy of Facial Plastic and Reconstructive   **12203**
Surgery; American Academy of Neurological - **12205**
Surgery; American Academy of Otolaryngology - Head and Neck   **12207**
Surgery; American Academy of Tropical Medicine and   **6761**
Surgery; American Association for Hand   **12211**
Surgery; American Association for Thoracic   **12215**
Surgery; American Board of   **12228**
Surgery; American Board of Abdominal   **12216**
Surgery; American Board of Colon and Rectal   **12217**
Surgery; American Board of Dental Medicine and   **3881**
Surgery; American Board of Hand   **12218**
Surgery; American Board of Industrial Medicine and   **9785**
Surgery; American Board of Laser   **12220**
Surgery; American Board of Medical- Legal Analysis in Medicine and   **7166**
Surgery; American Board of Neurological   **12222**
Surgery; American Board of Neurological / Orthopaedic Laser   **12220**
Surgery; American Board of Neurological and Orthopaedic Medicine and   **12221**
surgery; American Board of Neurological Micro   **12219**
Surgery; American Board of Oral   **12223**
Surgery; American Board of Oral and Maxillofacial   **12223**
Surgery; American Board of Orthopaedic   **12225**
Surgery; American Board of Plastic   **12226**
Surgery; American Board of Podiatric   **10759**
Surgery; American Board of Ringside Medicine and   **11936**
Surgery; American Board of Spinal   **12227**
Surgery; American Board of Thoracic Neurological Orthopaedic Medicine and   **12229**
Surgery; American College of General Practitioners in Osteopathic Medicine and   **9975**
surgery; American College of Chemo   **5911**
Surgery; American Society for Aesthetic Plastic   **12236**
Surgery; American Society of Cataract and Refractive   **13405**
Surgery; American Society for Dermatologic   **12238**
Surgery; American Society for Head and Neck   **12239**
Surgery; American Society for Laser Medicine and   **12240**
Surgery; American Society of Lipo-Suction   **12241**

Surgery; Arizona Board of Osteopathic Examiners in Medicine and   **10014**
Surgery Assistants; Association of British Dental   **3903**
Surgery; Association for Academic   **12253**
Surgery; Association of Colon   **12304**
Surgery; Association of Diplomates of the American Board of Oral   **12232**
Surgery Association; Federated Ambulatory   **12272**
Surgery Association; Freestanding Ambulatory   **12272**
Surgery; Association of Physician Assistants in Cardiovascular   **12254**
Surgery; Association of Program Directors in   **12255**
Surgery; Association for Research in Vascular   **12256**
Surgery Branch • Division of Cancer Treatment • National Cancer Institute • U.S. Department of Health and Human Services   **6166**
Surgery; Bureau of Medicine and • Chief of Naval Operations • Department of the Navy • U.S. Department of Defense   **7787**
Surgery; Canadian Society for Aesthetic (Cosmetic) Plastic   **12262**
Surgery; Canadian Society of Otolaryngology - Head and Neck   **12263**
Surgery; Center for Hip and Knee   **9940**
Surgery and Cutaneous Oncology; American College of MOHS Micrographic   **5911**
Surgery; Department of • University of Louisville   **12324**
Surgery Division • Walter Reed Army Institute of Research • Army Medical Research and Development Command • U.S. Department of Defense   **7836**
Surgery; Division of Cardiothoracic • University of Missouri—Columbia   **2972**
Surgery Educational Foundation; Plastic   **12200, 12296**
Surgery; European Academy of Facial   **12267**
Surgery; European Association for Cranio-Maxillo-Facial   **12268**
Surgery; European Society for Cardiovascular   **12269**
Surgery; European Society of Ophthalmic Plastic and Reconstructive   **12270**
Surgery Facilities; American Association for Accreditation of Ambulatory   **12209**
Surgery Facilities; American Association for Accreditation of Ambulatory Plastic   **12209**
Surgery; French Society of Pediatric   **3230**
Surgery of the Hand; American Foundation for   **12198**
Surgery of the Hand; American Society for   **12246**
Surgery; Hospital for Special • Research Division   **9941**
Surgery; Institute for Applied Laser   **12321**
Surgery; Institute of Reconstructive Plastic • New York University   **12322**
Surgery; International Academy of Cosmetic   **12274**
Surgery; International College for Maxillo-Facial   **12277**
Surgery; International College of Podiatric Laser   **10773**
Surgery; International Confederation for Plastic, Reconstructive and Aesthetic   **12279**
Surgery; International Society of   **12282**
Surgery; International Society for Cardio vascular   **2859**
Surgery; International Society for Dermatologic   **12281**
Surgery; International Society of Podiatric Laser   **10773, 10773**
Surgery; Israel Association of Plastic Reconstructive and Aesthetic   **12284**
Surgery; Japan Society of Plastic and Reconstructive   **12285**
Surgery; Korean Society of Plastic and Reconstructive   **12286**
Surgery; Michigan Board of Osteopathic Medicine and   **10035**
Surgery; Nebraska State Board of Examiners in Medicine and   **1784, 10040**
Surgery in Primates; Laboratory for Experimental Medicine and • New York University   **13151**
Surgery Research Council; Plastic   **12297**
Surgery Research Lab; Thoracic • University of Michigan   **12326**
Surgery Research Laboratories; Pediatric • University of Michigan   **12325**
Surgery Research Laboratories; Plastic • Duke University   **12319**
Surgery; Scandinavian Association for Thoracic   **12301**
Surgery; Scandinavian Association for Thoracic and Cardiovascular   **12301**
Surgery; Society for Office-Based   **12243**
Surgery Society; Outpatient Ophthalmic   **12294**
Surgery; Society for Vascular   **12312**
Surgery and Traumatology; International Society of Orthopaedic   **9929**
Surgery; Washington Board of Osteopathic Medicine and   **10062**
Surgical Association; American   **12248**
Surgical Association; Asian   **12252**
Surgical Association; Pan-Pacific   **12295**
Surgical Association; Western   **12315**
Surgical Associations; European Union of Paediatric   **12271**
Surgical Care; Society for the Advancement of Freestanding Ambulatory   **12272**
Surgical Colleges; International Federation of   **12280**
Surgical Contraception; Association for Voluntary   **11205, 11260**
Surgical Contraception; World Federation of Health Agencies for the Advancement of Voluntary   **11205**
Surgical Education; Association for   **12257**
Surgical Eye Expeditions International   **13564**

T

TARGET - Helping Students Cope with Tobacco, Alcohol and Other Drugs **12079**

Tarrant County; Easter Seal Society for Children and Adults of **4675**

Tarrant County Junior College • Respiratory Therapist Program **11555**

Tarsasag; Magyar Taplalkozastudomanyi 9462

Tarsasagok es Egyesuletek Szovetsege; Magyar Orvostudomanyi 1289

TASH: The Association for Persons With Severe Handicaps **4563**

Task Force for Child Survival and Development **3302**

Taste Center; Smell and • University of Pennsylvania **8521**

Taste and Smell Center; Rocky Mountain • University of Colorado—Denver **12136**

Taub Foundation; Henry and Marilyn **268**

Tay-Sachs and Allied Diseases Association; National **4865**

Tay-Sachs Association; National 4865

Taylor Foundation; Ruth and Vernon **471**

Te Kaunihera O Nga Neehi Maori O Aotearoa 9116

Teacher Educators; Association of Health Occupations **1205**

Teachers of the Alexander Technique; North American Society of **12706**

Teachers Association; Ovulation Method **11241**

Teachers Association; Radix **7497**

Teachers of Family Medicine; Society of **1512**

Teachers of Maternal and Child Health; Association of **3191**

Teachers; National Association of Blind **13523**

Teachers of Oral Diagnosis; Organization of **3981**

Teachers of Preventive Medicine; Association of **10843**

Teaching Hospitals; Council of **6441**

Teaching and Research Center; Veterinary Medicine • University of California, Davis **13215**

Teaching of Speech to the Deaf; American Association to Promote the 3478

Tear Film Laboratory • Columbia University **13586**

Tear Research Center; Dry Eye and **13590**

Technical Experts; General Association of Municipal Health and **10954**

Technical Institute for the Deaf; National • Rochester Institute of Technology **3618**

Technical Personnel in Ophthalmology; Association of **13418**

Technician examiners; California Board of Vocational Nurses and Psychiatric **9157**

Technicians; American Association of Nephrology Nurses and 9061

Technicians; American Association of Orthopic 13387

Technicians; American Association of Psychiatric **7280**

Technicians; American Registry of Radiological 11093

Technicians; American Registry of X-Ray 11093

Technicians; American Society of Clinical Laboratory 7122

Technicians; American Society of Extracorporeal Circulation 2829

Technicians; American Society of X-Ray 11098

Technicians Association; Clinical Dental **3915**

Technicians; Association of Operating Room 12258

Technicians Belgium; Medical Radiological **11126**

Technicians; International Association of Equine Dental **13084**

Technicians; National Association of Air National Guard Health **7802**

Technicians; National Association of Emergency Medical **4747**

Technicians; National Registry of Emergency Medical **4752**

Technicians; Society of Biomedical Equipment **2543**

Techniciens de Radiologie; Societe Internationale des Radiographes et 11121

Technologies Action Group; Appropriate Health Resources and **1190**

Technologies; Engineering Research Center for Emerging Cardiovascular • Duke University **2443**

Technologist; Joint Review Committee on Education for the Surgical 12201

Technologist Section of the Society of Nuclear Medicine **11141**

Technologistes de Laboratoire Medical; Association Internationale des 7137

Technologistes de Laboratoire; Societe Canadienne des 7128

Technologists; American Board of Registration of EEG 8157

Technologists; American Board of Registration of EEG and EP **8157**

Technologists; American Chiropractic Registry of Radiologic **11086**

Technologists; American Medical **7120**

Technologists; American Registry of Radiologic **11093**

Technologists; American Society of Electroencephalographic 8175

Technologists; American Society of Electroneurodiagnostic 8175

Technologists; American Society of Master Dental **3900**

Technologists; American Society of Medical 7122

Technologists; American Society of Radiologic **11098**

Technologists Association; American Cardiology 2828

Technologists; Association of Polysomnographic **8189**

Technologists; Association of Surgical **12258**

Technologists; Canadian Association of Medical Radiation **11106**

Technologists; Canadian Society of Laboratory **7128**

Technologists; Canadian Society of Orthopaedic **9925**

Technologists; International Association of Medical Laboratory **7137**

Technologists; International Society of Clinical Laboratory 7143

Technologists; International Society of Radiographers and Radiological **11121**

Technologists; National Alliance of Cardio vascular 2828

Technologists; National Association of Orthopaedic **9930**

Technologists; National Board for Certification of Orthopaedic **9931**

Technologists; National Society of Cardio pulmonary 2828

Technologists; Registered Medical Assistants of American Medical **1490**

Technologists of South Africa; Society of Medical Laboratory **7153**

Technologues en Radiation Medicale; Association Canadienne des 11106

Technology; Accreditation Review Committee on Education in Surgical **12201**

Technology; American Society of Extra-Corporeal **2829**

Technology; American Society for Medical 7122

Technology Assessment; Office of Health • Agency for Health Care Policy and Research • U.S. Department of Health and Human Services **5645**

Technology; Board of Nephrology Examiners— Nursing and **9077**

Technology Branch; Devices and • Division of Heart and Vascular Diseases • National Heart, Lung, and Blood Institute • U.S. Department of Health and Human Services **2937**

Technology Branch; Engineering Control • Physical Sciences and Engineering Division • National Institute for Occupational Safety and Health • U.S. Department of Health and Human Services **9832**

Technology Branch; Research • Basic Research Division • National Institute on Drug Abuse • U.S. Department of Health and Human Services **12126**

Technology at Canton; State University of New York College of • Mortuary Science Program **3690**

Technology; Center for Advanced Medical • San Francisco State University **2619**

Technology Center; Biomedical **2716**

Technology Center; Enabling • Western Michigan University **4603**

Technology; Center for Health Systems & • Texas A&M University **5640**

Technology Center; Laser **11148**

Technology Center; Medical Laser 12321

Technology Center; Pharmaceutical Science and • University of Kentucky **10634**

Technology; Center for Rehabilitation • Georgia Institute of Technology **12732**

Technology Center; Science and • Carnegie Mellon University **2438**

Technology Certification Board; Nuclear Medicine **11128**

Technology; Department of Food Science and • Oregon State University **9522**

Technology; Division of Computer Research and • National Institutes of Health • U.S. Department of Health and Human Services **2512, 2655**

Technology in the EEC; Standing Representative Committee for Medical Laboratory **7154**

Technology Extension Center for Investigational Cancer Therapy 6058

Technology Extension Center for Investigational Cancer Treatment; John P. Caufield **6058**

Technology Fitness Research Institute; High **11966**

Technology; Florida Institute of
    Life Science Research Complex **1587**
    Medical Genetics Laboratory **5330**

Technology; Georgia Institute of
    Bioengineering Center **2445**
    Biomechanics Laboratory **2446**
    Center for Rehabilitation Technology **12732**
    Georgia Tech Research Institute **2447**

Technology in Healthcare; Brazilian Association for the Promotion of Appropriate **10945**

Technology in Health; Program for Appropriate **1481**

Technology; Illinois Institute of • Pritzker Institute of Medical Engineering **2448**

Technology; Institute of Biosciences & • Texas A&M University **2629**

Technology; International Institute of Dental Ergonomics and **3962**

Technology; International Society for Clinical Laboratory **7143**

Technology; Iowa State University of Science and
    Biomedical Engineering Program **2450**
    Center for Designing Foods to Improve Nutrition **9505**
    Center for Family Research in Rural Mental Health **7577**
    Center for Immunity Enhancement in Domestic Animals **13137**
    Family and Consumer Sciences Research Institute **9506**
    Food Safety Research Center **10980**
    Occupational and Traffic Safety Education Research Laboratory **9810**
    Veterinary Diagnostic Laboratory **13138**
    Veterinary Medical Research Institute **13139**
    Veterinary Medicine and Clinical Microbiology Laboratory **13140**

Technology; Joint Review Committee on Education in Radiologic **11124**

Technology; Massachusetts Institute of
    Center for Biological and Computational Learning **8390**

Center for Cancer Research **6067**
Center for Environmental Health Sciences **5079**
Center for Magnetic Resonance **11150**
Clinical Research Center **1629**
Eric P. and Evelyn E. Newman Laboratory for Biomechanics and Human Rehabilitation **2453**
Laboratory of Neuroendocrine Regulation **8391**
Laser Biomedical Research Center **11151**
Technology; Michigan Consortium for Enabling **2455**
Technology; National Board for Certification in Dental **3971**
Technology; National Society for Cardio pulmonary **2828**
Technology; New Jersey Institute of • Center for Biomedical Engineering **2460**
Technology and Practice Patterns Institute, Inc.; Medical **2720**
Technology Research Center; Emory- Georgia Tech Biomedical **2444**
Technology Research Center; Science and • New York Institute of Technology **2461**
Technology Research Foundation; Frontier Science and **1588**
Technology; Resource for Biomedical Sensor • Case Western Reserve University **2440**
Technology; Rochester Institute of
    Center for Imaging Science **11155**
    National Technical Institute for the Deaf **3618**
    School of Food, Hotel, and Travel Management • Dietetics Program **9409**
Technology; Society for Assisted Reproductive **11251**
Technology at Utica / Rome; State University of New York Institute of • Health Information Administration Program **6944**
Tecnica y Dental; Federacion Nacional de Empresas de Instrumentacion Cientifica, Medica, **5848**
Tecumseh Community Health Study • University of Michigan **5193**
Ted Mann Foundation **512**
Teen Education Program; Ryan White National **3285**
Teen-Age Addiction to Tobacco; Stop **11739**
Teens Teaching AIDS Prevention **6751**
Tegnoloe van Suid-Afrika; Vereniging van Geneeskundige Laboratorium **7153**
Teikyo Marycrest University • Division of Nursing **8699**
Telecommunication Network; National Pesticide **5054**
Telecommunications for the Deaf, Inc. **3581**
Teletypewriters for the Deaf **3581**
Television Guild; Veterans Hospital Radio and **7813**
Television; International Medical Association for Radio and **1351**
Tel-Med, Inc. **7012**
Temas Atuais na Promocao da Saude **10945**
Temperance Association; International Health and **12041**
Temperance Blue Cross Societies; International Federation of the **12040**
Temperance League of America **12005**
Temperance League; National **12005**
Temperance Movement; National **12005**
Temple Foundation; T. L. L. **511**
Temple Hoyne Buell Foundation **513**
Temple-Inland Foundation **870**
Temple Junior College • Respiratory Therapist Program **11556**
Temple University
    Biokinetics Research Laboratory **11977**
    Center for Sports Medicine and Science **11978**
    Cochran Research Center **5639**
    College of Allied Health Professions
        Department of Health Information Management **6952**
        Department of Nursing **8927**
        Department of Occupational Therapy **12418**
        Department of Physical Therapy **12538**
    Fels Institute for Cancer Research and Molecular Biology **6119**
    General Clinical Research Center **1669**
    Institute on Aging **1947**
    Institute on Disabilities **4319**
    Motility Laboratory/Gastroenterology **5237**
    Motor Development Laboratory **3353**
    School of Business and Management • Graduate Program in Health Administration **5517**
    School of Dentistry **3827**
    School of Medicine **1022**
        Department of Pharmacology **10339**
    School of Pharmacy **10556**
        Department of Pharmacology **10340**
    School of Social Administration **11839**
    Section of Audiology and Auditory Research **3623**
    Sol Sherry Thrombosis Research Center **2924**
    Speech and Hearing Science Laboratories **3624**
Temporal Bone Banks Program of The DRF; National **3562**

Temporal Bone Laboratory for Ear Research • University of Chicago **3635**
Temporal Bone Registry; National **3562**
Tenets and Science; Foundation for the Advancement of Chiropractic **3429, 3457**
TennCare • Tennessee Department of Health **5703**
Tenncare Division • Tennessee Department of Finance and Administration **5810**
Tennessee Affiliate
    American Diabetes Association **4994**
    American Heart Association **3036**
Tennessee; American Lung Association of **11674**
Tennessee; Arc of **4431**
Tennessee Board of Dentistry **4092**
Tennessee Board of Examiners for Nursing Home Administrators **9317**
Tennessee Board of Funeral Directors and Embalmers **3770**
Tennessee Board of Pharmacy **10684**
Tennessee Chapter
    American Physical Therapy Association **12860**
    Arthritis Foundation **8018**
    Cystic Fibrosis Foundation **5460**
    National Association of Social Workers **11924**
Tennessee Chapter; East • Lupus Foundation of America **8106**
Tennessee Commission on Aging **2044**
Tennessee Dental Association **4198**
Tennessee Department of Agriculture • Animal Industries Division • State Veterinarian **13292**
Tennessee Department of Finance and Administration • Tenncare Division **5810**
Tennessee Department of Health
    Administrative Services Bureau • Health Statistics Division • Vital Records Section **7082**
    AIDS Program **6898**
    Alcohol and Drug Abuse Services Bureau **12189**
    Health Services Bureau **11048**
        Environmental Epidemiologist **5170**
        Maternal and Children's Health Section **3420, 9766**
    Manpower and Facilities Bureau
        Emergency Medical Services Division **4810**
        Health Care Facilities Division **6518**
    Oral Health Services Division **4145**
    TennCare **5703**
Tennessee Department of Human Services • Rehabilitation Services Division **12813, 13708**
Tennessee Department of Labor • Occupational Safety and Health Division **9907**
Tennessee Department of Mental Health and Mental Retardation
    Mental Health Services Division **7750**
    Mental Retardation Services Division **4385**
Tennessee Division • American Cancer Society **6319**
Tennessee; Easter Seal Society of **4672**
Tennessee Health Care Association **9368**
Tennessee Hospital Association **6570**
Tennessee; Learning Disabilities Association of **4723**
Tennessee Medical Association **1854**
Tennessee; National Kidney Foundation of East **12976**
Tennessee; National Kidney Foundation of Middle **12977**
Tennessee; National Kidney Foundation of West **12978**
Tennessee Nurses Association **9254**
Tennessee Optometric Association **13835**
Tennessee Osteopathic Medical Association **10107**
Tennessee Pharmacists Association **10737**
Tennessee State Board of Medical Examiners **1800**
Tennessee State Board of Nursing **9199**
Tennessee State Board of Optometry **13761**
Tennessee State Board of Osteopathic Examination **10056**
Tennessee State Board of Registration in Podiatry **10822**
Tennessee State University
    Department of Medical Record Administration **6958**
    Physical Therapy Department **12546**
    Respiratory Therapy Program **11539**
    School of Allied Health Professions • Occupational Therapy Program **12424**
    School of Nursing **8973**
Tennessee Task Force Against Domestic Violence **3119**
Tennessee Technological University • School of Nursing **8974**
Tennessee Valley Authority
    Vice President of Human Resources
        Health Services **3**
        Occupational Health and Safety Division **9777**
Tennessee Veterinary Medical Association **13345**
Tennis; National Foundation of Wheelchair **4527**

Thermalism and Climatism; Latin American Federation of   **5048**
Thermographic Society; American   11082
Thermology; American Academy of   **11082**
Theta Psi   **10010**
Thiel College • Nursing Department   **8928**
Thomas A. Dooley Foundation   1270
Thomas A. Dooley Foundation/INTERMED U.S.A.   1270
Thomas and Agnes Carvel Foundation   **516**
Thomas Anthony Pappas Charitable Foundation   **517**
Thomas & Betts Charitable Trust   **876**
Thomas and Dorothy Leavey Foundation   **518**
Thomas F. and Kate Miller Jeffress Memorial Trust   **519**
Thomas J. Emery Memorial   **520**
Thomas J. Lipton Foundation   **877**
Thomas Jefferson University
     Cardeza Foundation for Hematologic Research   **6121**
     Center for Research in Medical Education and Health Care   **1670**
     College of Allied Health Sciences
         Department of Nursing   **8929**
         Department of Occupational Therapy   **12419**
         Department of Physical Therapy   **12539**
     Daniel Baugh Institute   **2631**
     Environmental Medicine and Toxicology Division   **10461**
     Ischemia-Shock Research Center   **2927**
     Jefferson Institute of Molecular Medicine   **2632**
     Jefferson Medical College   **1023**
         Department of Pharmacology   **10341**
     Lupus Study Center   **7934**
     Neurosurgery Research Laboratories   **8435**
     Regional Spinal Cord Injury Center of Delaware Valley   **12753**
     Scleroderma and Arthritis Research Center   **7935**
     Sleep Disorders Center   **8436**
Thomas M. and Irene B. Kirbo Charitable Trust   **6383**
Thomas More College • Department of Nursing   **8716**
Thompson Cancer Survival Center   **6122**
Thompson Charitable Foundation   **521**
Thoracic and Cardiovascular Surgery; Scandinavian Association for   12301
Thoracic Neurological Orthopaedic Medicine and Surgery; American Board of   **12229**
Thoracic Radiology; Society of   **11140**
Thoracic Society; American   **11591**
Thoracic Surgeons; Society of   **12309**
Thoracic Surgery; American Association for   **12215**
Thoracic Surgery Research Lab • University of Michigan   **12326**
Thoracic Surgery; Scandinavian Association for   **12301**
Thoraxkirurgisk Forening; Nordisk   12301
Thorndike Laboratory; Harvard   **2897**
Throat Advances in Children; Society for Ear, Nose, and   **3291**
Thrombolysis; Center for Research in   **6017**
Thrombosis & Coagulation Laboratory • University of Oklahoma   **6239**
Thrombosis and Hemostasis; Center for • University of North Carolina at Chapel Hill   **6237**
Thrombosis and Hemostasis; International Society on   **5962**
Thrombosis Research Center; Sol Sherry • Temple University   **2924**
Thurston Arthritis Research Center • University of North Carolina at Chapel Hill   **7958**
Thymologie und Immuntherapie; Internationale Gesellschaft fur   2078
Thymology and Immunotherapy; International Society for   **2078**
Thyroid Association; European   **4842**
Thyroid Foundation of America   **4876**
Thyroide; Association Europeenne   4842
Tick Research Laboratory; Cattle Fever • Knipling-Bushland U.S. Livestock Insects Laboratory • Agricultural Research Service • U.S. Department of Agriculture   **13188**
Tidewater Community College • Respiratory Therapist Program   **11570**
Tierarzte; Bundesverband Praktischer   13094
Tierarztegesellschaft; Welt-   13121
Timberlawn Psychiatric Research Foundation   **7612**
Time Out to Enjoy   **4564**
Times Mirror Foundation   **878**
Timken Foundation of Canton   **6384**
Tinnitus Association; American   **3469, 3493**
Tinnitus International Service Association   **3582**
Tintera Memorial / Hypoglycemia Lay Group; Dr. John W.   **4837**
Tisch Foundation   **522**
Tisiologia; Union Latinoamericana de Sociedades de   11601
Tissue Banks; American Association of   **12866**
Tissue Banks International   **12878**
Tissue Culture Association   2546
Tissue Culture Commission   2546

Tissue Diseases Research Program; Periodontal and Soft • Extramural Program • National Institute of Dental Research • U.S. Department of Health and Human Services   **4016**
Tissue Pathology Department; Soft • Center for Advanced Pathology • Armed Forces Institute of Pathology • U.S. Department of Defense   **10164**
Tissue Research Institute; Connective   **2567**
Tissue Research; Laboratories for Connective • University of Michigan   **7953**
Tissue Resource Center; Brain   **8343**
Tissue Society; European Calcified   **1276**
Title Seven Directors; National Association of   1907
TJX Foundation   **879**
TM-Sidhi Programs; American Association of Physicians Practicing the Transcendental Meditation and   2159
TMJ Orthopedics; American Academy of Head, Facial and Neck Pain and   **3859**
Tobacco, Alcohol and Other Drugs; TARGET - Helping Students Cope with   **12079**
Tobacco; Asia Pacific Association for the Control of   **11732**
Tobacco-Free Society; Citizens for a   **11735**
Tobacco and Health Research Institute   **11743**
Tobacco Products Liability Project   **11740**
Tobacco-Related Disease Research Program • University of California   **11744**
Tobacco Smoke; Citizens Against   **11735**
Tobacco; Stop Teen-Age Addiction to   **11739**
Tobago Association in Aid of the Deaf; Trinidad and   **3583**
Tobago; Dental Association of Trinidad and   **3926**
Todos Santos Ambulance Fund   **4759**
Tomkins Industries Foundation   **880**
Tomography and Magnetic Resonance; Society of Computed Body   **11133**
Tomography and Neuroimaging; Society for Computerized   11096
Tomography; Society of Computed Body   11133
Tomography Society; Computerized   11107
Tongue Depressors; Association of   **5827**
Tooth Disease/Peroneal Muscular Atrophy International Association; Charcot-Marie-   8202
TOPS   1520
TOPS Club   **1520**
Tornetta School of Anesthesia; Frank J. • Montgomery Hospital   **2318**
Torture; Canadian Center for the Investigation and Prevention of   7544
Torture Victims; Canadian Center for   **7544**
Torture Victims; Rehabilitation and Resource Centre for   **12715**
Torturofre; Rehabiliterings-og Forskningscentret for   12715
Toshokan Kyokai; Nippon Igaku   7006
Totts Gap Medical Research Laboratories, Inc.   **1671**
Touch for Health Foundation   **2241**
Touch Research Institute • University of Miami   **12760**
Tourette Syndrome Association   **8139, 8317**
Tourette Syndrome Association; Gilles de la   8317
Touro College
     Barry Z. Levine School of Allied Health Sciences • Physical Therapy Program   **12523**
     Barry Z. Levine School of Health Sciences • Physician Assistant Program   **1096**
     Department of Occupational Therapy   **12401**
     Health Information Administration Program   **6945**
TOVA—The Other Victims of Alcoholism   **12080**
Towsley Foundation; Harry A. and Margaret D.   **248**
Towson State University
     Department of Nursing   **8743**
     Occupational Therapy Department   **12366**
Toxic Substance Research and Management Center; Hazardous Waste and • Clarkson University   **5067**
Toxic Substances and Disease Registry; Agency for
     Division of Health Studies • U.S. Department of Health and Human Services   **5095**
     Division of Toxicology • U.S. Department of Health and Human Services   **5096**
     U.S. Department of Health and Human Services   **5005, 5094**
Toxic Substances; Industry/University Cooperative Center for Research in Hazardous and   10434
Toxic Waste and Basic Research Analytical Laboratory; Pesticide Residue, • University of Miami   5123
Toxicologic Pathologists; Society of   **10138**
Toxicological History Society   **10423**
Toxicological Research and Hazardous Waste Management; Center for Biomedical • Florida State University   **10432**
Toxicological Research; National Center for • Food and Drug Administration • U.S. Department of Health and Human Services   **10182, 10464**

Training and Development Branch; Research • Division of Heart and Vascular Diseases • National Heart, Lung, and Blood Institute • U.S. Department of Health and Human Services **2938**

Training Foundation; North Charles Mental Health Research and **7590**

Training; Foundation for the Support of International Medical **1302**

Training Institute of the National Psychological Association for Psychoanalysis **7250**

Training Institute; Nora Eccles Harrison Cardiovascular Research and • University of Utah **2981**

Training; Institute for Psychosomatic and Psychiatric Research and **7573**

Training Institute; Research and • National Center for Disability Services **4580**

Training in Mental Health; Calgary WHO Centre for Research and **7543**

Training and Research; Center for Psychoanalytic • Columbia University **7555**

Training and Research Institute for Self Psychology **7251**

Training; Washington Institute for Mental Illness Research and **7700**

Transaccional; Asociacion Latinoamericana de Analisis 7437

Transactional Analysis Association; International **7429**

Transactional Analysis Association; Latin American **7437**

Transamerica Foundation **881**

Transcendental Meditation Program; American Association of Physicians Practicing the 2159

Transcendental Meditation and TM-Sidhi Programs; American Association of Physicians Practicing the 2159

Transcribers Association; Visually Impaired Secretarial 13575

Transcription; American Association for Medical **6967**

Transdisciplinary Education; International Academy of Pediatric **3239**

Transduction; Laboratory of Signal **6063**

Transfer Society; International Embryo **13086**

Transfusion; International Society of Blood **7141**

Transfusion Sanguine; Societe Internationale de 7141

Transfusion Service; National Blood **7145**

Transit; American Disabled for Accessible Public 1883

Transition; Women in **7528**

Translators for the Deaf; National Registry of Professional Interpreters and 3574

Transnational Family Research Institute **11282**

Transplant Coordinators Organization 12868

Transplant Coordinators Organization; North American **12876**

Transplant and Dialysis Personnel; Association for Nordic **12903**

Transplant Division; Liver • University of California, San Francisco **12889**

Transplant Foundation; Pittsburgh 12868

Transplant Fund; Organ **12877**

Transplant and Health Policy Center • University of Michigan **12891**

Transplant and Immunogenetics Laboratory • Oregon Health Sciences University **12885**

Transplant Laboratory; Bone Marrow **12883**

Transplant Nurses Association / European Renal Care Association; European Dialysis and **9087**

Transplant Nurses Society; International **9098**

Transplant Physicians; American Society of **12867**

Transplant Program; Cardiac • Loyola University Chicago **12884**

Transplant Recipients International Organization **12879**

Transplant Surgeons; American Society of **12247**

Transplantation; Association of Nurses Endorsing **9072**

Transplantation Biology; Center for • University of Florida **12890**

Transplantation Branch; Genetics and • Division of Allergy, Immunology, and Transplantation • National Institute of Allergy and Infectious Diseases • U.S. Department of Health and Human Services **2128**

Transplantation; Division of Allergy, Immunology, and • National Institute of Allergy and Infectious Diseases • U.S. Department of Health and Human Services **2124**

Transplantation Immunology; Center for Reproduction and **2097**

Transplantation Immunology; Laboratory for • Stanford University **12886**

Transplantation; International Society for Heart 12871

Transplantation; International Society for Heart and Lung **12871**

Transplantation Laboratories; Reconstructive Microsurgery and • University of California, Irvine **12887**

Transplantation Laboratory; Immunogenetics and • University of California, San Francisco **2141**

Transplantation; National Association of Patients on Hemodialysis and 12894

Transplantation; North American Society for Dialysis and **12875**

Transplantation Program; Bone Marrow • University of California, Los Angeles **12888**

Transplantation Research Center; Bone Marrow • Baylor University **12882**

Transplantation Society **12880**

Transplants; Academy for Implants and **3845**

Transport Association; Professional Aeromedical **4753**

Transportation Barriers Compliance Board; Architectural and **4438**

Trauma Anesthesia and Critical Care Society; International **2369**

Trauma Center; Burn **2775**

Trauma Center Foundation 10873

Trauma Center; R.A. Cowley Shock **4764**

Trauma; Center for Study of • University of California, San Francisco **7660**

Trauma Disorders; Physical Therapy Laboratory for Cumulative • University of Michigan—Flint **9858**

Trauma; Division of Stroke and • National Institute of Neurological Disorders and Stroke • U.S. Department of Health and Human Services **8456**

Trauma Foundation **10873**

Trauma Institute; Burn and Shock • Loyola University Chicago **4763**

Trauma; Institute for Victims of **7394**

Trauma; Medical Rehabilitation Research & Training Center in Childhood • Tufts University **12754**

Trauma; Nicholas Institute of Sports Medicine and Athletic **11972**

Trauma Nurses; Society of **9136**

Trauma Program; Medical Center Head • New York University **12737**

Trauma Society; American **4735**

Traumatic Brain Injury; Rehabilitation Research and Training Center on Severe • Virginia Commonwealth University **12766**

Traumatic Stress Program; Anxiety and • Duke University **7558**

Traumatic Stress Research Branch; Violence and • Epidemiology and Services Research Division • National Institute of Mental Health • U.S. Department of Health and Human Services **7632**

Traumatic Stress Studies; International Society for **7427**

Traumatic Stress Studies; Society for 7427

Traumatologie de Ski et de Medecine d'Hiver; Societe Internationale de 11946

Traumatologie; Societe Internationale de Chirurgie Orthopedique et de 9929

Traumatology; International Society of Orthopaedic Surgery and **9929**

Traumatology and Medicine of Winter Sports; International Society for Ski **11946**

Traumatology; Turkish Association of Orthopaedics and 9938

Travail de Langue Francaise; Association Internationale de Psychologie du **7329**

Travail de Langue Francaise; Association de Psychologie du 7329

Travel for the Handicapped; Society for the Advancement of **4556**

Travel Industry and Disabled Exchange **4565**

Travelers Center on Aging • University of Connecticut **1975**

Travelers Foundation **882**

Travelers Health Institute 1359

Travelers Health Institute; International **1359**

Traveling Nurses; National Association of **9112**

Travellers; International Association for Medical Assistance to **1336**

Travmatoloji Dernegi; Turk Ortopedi ve 9938

Treacher Collins Family Network 5303

Treacher Collins Foundation 5303

Treadwell Foundation; Nora Eccles **2783**

Treatment Action Group **6752**

Treatment Administrators; American College of Addiction **5543**

Treatment of AIDS; National Cooperative Drug Discovery Group for the **6779**

    Dana-Farber Cancer Institute **6768**

    George Washington University **6771**

    State University of New York at Buffalo **6791**

    University of Michigan **6848**

    University of Texas Medical Branch at Galveston **6855**

Treatment Association; Neurodevelopmental **8136, 12703**

Treatment Branch • Addiction Research Center • National Institute on Drug Abuse • U.S. Department of Health and Human Services **12120**

Treatment of Cancer; European Organization for Research and **5941**

Treatment Center; Alabama Congenital Heart Disease Diagnosis and • University of Alabama at Birmingham **2953**

Treatment Center; Cancer Research and • University of New Mexico **6235**

Treatment; Center for Osteoporosis Prevention and • University of North Texas Health Science Center at Fort Worth **7959**

Treatment Centers for Children; National Association of Psychiatric **3264**

Treatment of Child Abuse and Neglect; C. Henry Kempe National Center for the Prevention and • University of Colorado **3073**

Treatment Consortium for Alcohol and Other Drugs; National **12065**

Treatment; Division of Cancer • National Cancer Institute • U.S. Department of Health and Human Services **6149**

Treatment of High Blood Pressure; Citizens for the **2840**

Treatment of Intractable Pain; National Committee on the **8273**

Treatment; Patient Advocates for Advanced Cancer **5980**

Treatment Program; Eating Disorders Research & **7561**

Treatment Providers; National Association of Addiction **12050**

Treatment Research Branch • Clinical and Prevention Research Divsion • National Institute on Drug Abuse • U.S. Department of Health and Human Services **12127**

Treatment and Research Center; Diabetes **4885**

Turrell Fund **3143**
Tuskegee University
    George Washington Carver Agricultural Experiment Station **9530**
    School of Nursing and Allied Health
        Baccalaureate Nursing Program **8550**
        Division of Allied Health • Occupational Therapist Program
        12333
    School of Veterinary Medicine **12992**
        Department of Physiology, Pharmacology and Toxicology
        10187
Tuvalu National AIDS Committee **6753**
TVMDL Poultry Diagnostic Laboratory **13181**
21 International Holdings Foundation **885**
Twin Cities Research Center • Occupational Health Division • U.S.
  Department of the Interior • Bureau of Mines **9846**
Twin Studies; Jeanette Kennelly Kroch Center for **9708**
Twin Study; International • University of Southern California **5197**
Twin Study; Louisville • University of Louisville **5372**
Tyler Community College; John • Funeral Service Program **3701**
Tyler Junior College • Respiratory Therapist Program **11559**

U

U.S.A.; Operation **1447**
U.S.A.; Parkinson's Educational Program— **8299**
UCI / AMI Magnetic Resonance Imaging Center **11156**
UCI Diabetes Research Program • University of California, Irvine **4928**
UCLA Center for Clinical AIDS Research and Education / AIDS Clinical
  Trials Unit • University of California, Los Angeles **6840**
UCLA-DOE Laboratory of Structural Biology and Molecular Medicine •
  University of California, Los Angeles **2663**
UCLA Jonsson Comprehensive Cancer Center • University of California, Los
  Angeles **6213**
UCLA Research and Education Institute; Harbor- **1596**
Uganda Traditional Birth Attendants Association **9701**
Ugandan AIDS Project **6754**
UIC Eye Center • University of Illinois at Chicago **13652**
Ukrainian Foundation for the Victims of Chernobyl **11069**
Ukrainian Medical Association of North America **1522**
Ukrainian Medical Society; American **1522**
Ulcer Foundation; National **5228**
Ulcer Research and Education; Center for • University of California, Los
  Angeles **5249**
Ulster Cancer Foundation **5991**
Ultrasound Group; British Medical **11105**
Ultrasound; International Society for Ophthalmic **11119**
Ultrasound in Medicine; American Institute of **11090**
Ultrasound in Medicine and Biology; European Federation of Societies of
  11111
Ultrasound; Rochester Center for Biomedical • University of Rochester
  11174
Ultrasound Society; British Medical **11105**
Ultrasound Technical Specialists; American Society of **11134**
Unabhangiger Arzteverband Deutschland **1325**
UNC Lineberger Comprehensive Cancer Center • University of North
  Carolina at Chapel Hill **6238**
UND Center for Rural Health • University of North Dakota **1714**
Undersea and Hyperbaric Medical Society **1523**
Underserved; Institute on Health Care for the Poor and • Meharry Medical
  College **5634**
Understanding Aging **1896**
Undervisning; Nordisk Federation for Medicinsk **1442**
Underwater and Baromedical Society; European **2534**
Underwater Medicine Society; South Pacific **1514**
Underwriters Confederation; Women Life **5746**
Underwriters; International Association of Accident and Health **5738**
Underwriters; International Association of Health **5738**
Underwriters; National Association of Accident and Health **5738**
Underwriters; National Association of Health **5738**
Ungahonselskadade; Horselframjandets Riksforbund **3545**
Uniformed Services Academy of Family Physicians **7812**
Uniformed Services; Office of Civilian Health and Medical Program of the •
  Office of Assistant Secretary of Defense for Health Affairs • U.S.
  Department of Defense **7791**
Uniformed Services University of the Health Sciences
    F. Edward Hebert School of Medicine **969**
        Pharmacology Department **10256**
    Graduate School of Nursing • Nurse Anesthesia Program **2280**
    Office of Assistant Secretary of Defense for Health Affairs • U.S.
      Department of Defense **7792**
Union of American Physicians **1524**

Union of American Physicians and Dentists **1524**
Union Bank Foundation **886**
Union Camp Charitable Trust **887**
Union Carbide Foundation **888**
Union Chernobyl **11070**
Union College
    Division of Nursing **8806**
    Graduate Management Institute • Program in Health Systems
      Administration **5510**
Union County College • Respiratory Therapist Program **11457**
Union Europeenne des Aveugles **13447**
Union Europeenne des Practiciens en Medecine Dentaire **3933**
Union Internationale Contre le Cancer **5963**
Union Internationale Contre les Maladies Veneriennes et les
  Treponematoses **6683**
Union Internationale Contre la Tuberculose et les Maladies Respiratoires
  11599
Union Internationale de Phlebologie **5964**
Union Internationale de Promotion de la Sante et d'Education pour la
  Sante **1360**
Union Internationale des Sciences de la Nutrition **9466**
Union Internationale des Services Medicaux des Chemins de Fer **9799**
Union Internationale des Societes d'Aide a la Sante Mentale **7431**
Union Internationale des Societes de Microbiologie **6685**
Union Internationale des Techniciens Orthopedistes **2422**
Union Latinoamericana de Ciegos **13514**
Union Latinoamericana de Sociedades de Tisiologia **11601**
Union Latinoamericano de Ciegos **13513**
Union Memorial Hospital; Villa Julie College / • School of Nursing **8745**
Union of Middle Eastern and Mediterranean Pediatric Societies **3304**
Union Mondiale des Aveugles **13579**
Union of Muscular Dystrophy Societies of Croatia **8319**
Union Nationale des Associations de Soins et Service a Domicile **1525**
Union Nationale des Syndicats d'Opticien de France **13567**
Union Pacific Foundation **889**
Union des Societes de Pediatrie du Moyen-Orient et de la Mediterranee
  3304
Union Syndicat Veterinaire Belge **13064**
Union Therapeutique Internationale **12689**
Union University
    Albany College of Pharmacy **10543**
    Albany Medical College **1003**
    School of Nursing **8975**
Union of the Yugoslav Association of Anatomists **2549**
Unione Europea di Medicina Sociale **10953**
Unione Nazionale Industrie Dentarie Italiane **5885**
Unit Coordinators; National Association of Health **6459**
Unit for Laboratory Animal Medicine • University of Michigan **13222**
Unitarian Universalist Society for Alcohol and Drug Education **12081**
Unitarian Universalist Society for Alcohol Education **12081**
United Airlines Foundation **6417**
United Cerebral Palsy Associations **8320**
United Cerebral Palsy Research and Educational Foundation **8140**
United CFS/CFIDS/CEBV Federation **6755**
United Church of Christ; Council for Health and Human Services
  Ministries, **1258**
United Federation of CFS / CFIDS / CEBV Organizations **6755**
United Hospital Center / La Roche College • Nurse Anesthesia Program
  2346
United Jewish Appeal - Federation of Jewish Philanthropies of New York
  1526
United Kingdom; Association for Dance Movement Therapy— **12664**
United Kingdom; Coeliac Society of the **5214**
United Leukodystrophy Foundation **8321**
United Methodist Association of Health and Welfare Ministries **1527**
United Nations Children's Fund **3305**
United Nations Decade of Disabled Persons; World Committee for the
  4570
United Nations International Children's Emergency Fund **3305**
United Nations Population Fund **11283**
United Network for Organ Sharing **12881**
United Ostomy Association **5232**
United Parkinson Foundation **8141, 8322**
United Patients Association for Pulmonary Hypertension **2880**
United Presbyterian Health, Education and Welfare Association **1479**
United Scleroderma Foundation **4212, 7912**
U.S. Air Force • Physician Assistant Program **1111**
United States Air Force Flight Surgeons; Society of **7811**
U.S. Air Force / University of Texas Health Science Center at San Antonio
  • School of Nursing • Nurse Anesthesia Program **2338**
United States Animal Health Association **13111**

Army Medical Research Institute of Chemical Defense **7820**
Army Medical Research Institute of Infectious Diseases **7821**
Army Research Institute of Environmental Medicine **7822**
   Environmental Pathophysiology Directorate **7823**
   Environmental Physiology and Medicine Directorate **7824**
   Occupational Health and Performance Directorate **7825**
Environmental Physiology and Medicine Directorate • Altitude Physiology and Medicine Division **7826**
Occupational Health and Performance Directorate • Military Nutrition Division **7827**
Walter Reed Army Institute of Research **7828**
   Biochemistry Division **7829**
   Communicable Diseases and Immunology Division **7830**
   Experimental Therapeutics Division **7831**
   Medicine Division **7832**
   Neuropsychiatry Division **7833**
   Pathology Division **7834**
   Preventive Medicine Division **7835**
   Surgery Division **7836**
   Veterinary Medicine Division **7837**
Department of the Air Force
   Air Force Material Command • Human Systems Center **7782**
   Vice Chief of Staff of the Air Force • Air Force Surgeon General **7783**
Department of the Army
   Army Health Services Command **7784**
   Army Surgeon General • Army Medical Research and Material Command **7785**
   Chief of Staff of the Army • Army Surgeon General **7786**
Department of the Navy
   Chief of Naval Operations • Bureau of Medicine and Surgery **7787**
   Marine Corps • Office of Health Services **7788**
   Naval Medical Research and Development Command **7789**
Naval Medical Research and Development Command
   Naval Aerospace Medical Research Laboratory **2403**
   Naval Biodynamics Laboratory **7838**
   Naval Dental Research Institute **7839**
   Naval Health Research Center **7840**
      Department of Health Sciences and Epidemiology **7841**
      Health Services Research Department **7842**
      Operational Performance Department **7843**
      Physiological Performance and Operational Department **7844**
      Sleep Optimization Research Laboratory **7845**
   Naval Medical Research Institute **7846**
      Casualty Care Research Department **7847**
      Diving Medicine Department **7848**
      Immune Cell Biology Program **7849**
      Infectious Diseases Department **7850**
   Naval Medical Research Institute Detachment (Toxicology) **7851**
   Naval Submarine Medical Research Laboratory **7852**
Office of Assistant Secretary of Defense for Health Affairs **7790**
   Office of Civilian Health and Medical Program of the Uniformed Services **7791**
   Uniformed Services University of the Health Sciences **7792**
Wilford Hall USAF Medical Center • Clinical Investigation Facility **1673**
U.S. Department of Education
   National Institute on Disability and Rehabilitation Research **4585**
   Office of Special Education and Rehabilitative Services **4441**
U.S. Department of Energy
   Argonne National Laboratory **2633**
   Assistant Secretary for Environment, Safety, and Health **5004**
   Brookhaven National Laboratory • Medical Department **1674**
   Inhalation Toxicology Research Institute **5089**
   Lawrence Berkeley Laboratory
      Cholesterol Research Center **4902**
      Environment, Health and Safety Division **9821**
      Life Science Division **6124**
      Research Medicine and Radiation Biophysics Division **11158**
   Lawrence Livermore National Laboratory **2634**
      Hazards Control Department • Special Projects Division **9822**
   Los Alamos National Laboratory • Quality, Environment, Safety, and Health Assurance Division **9823**
   Oak Ridge National Laboratory
      Environmental, Life, and Social Sciences Directorate
         Assessment Technology Section **11159**
         Biology Division **2635**
         Health Studies Section **5090**

Office of Energy Research
   Health Effects and Life Sciences Research Division **5091**
   Office of Health and Environmental Research **5092**
Office of Health and Environmental Research • Medical Applications and Biophysical Research Division **5093**
U.S. Department of Health and Human Services **4**
Administration for Children and Families **5**
   Administration on Children, Youth and Families **6**
   Administration on Developmental Disabilities **4442**
   Administration for Native Americans **7**
   National Center on Child Abuse and Neglect **3045, 3072**
Agency for Health Care Policy and Research **5642**
   Center for General Health Services Extramural Research **5643**
   Center of General Health Services Intramural Research **5644**
   Office of Health Technology Assessment **5645**
Agency for Toxic Substances and Disease Registry **5005, 5094**
   Division of Health Studies **5095**
   Division of Toxicology **5096**
Centers for Disease Control and Prevention **10896, 10990**
   Epidemiology Program Office **5188**
      Surveillance and Epidemiology Division **5189**
   International Health Program Office **10991**
Food and Drug Administration **10897, 10992**
   Center for Biologics Evaluation and Research **10898, 10993**
   Center for Devices and Radiological Health **10994, 11058**
   Center for Drug Evaluation and Research **10899, 10995**
   Center for Food Safety and Applied Nutrition **10900, 10996**
   Center for Veterinary Medicine **12990, 13209**
   National Center for Toxicological Research **10182, 10464**
   Office of Orphan Products Development **10630**
Health Care Financing Administration **5710**
   Bureau of Health Standards and Quality **5711**
   Bureau of Program Operations **5712**
   Medicaid Bureau **5713**
   Office of Demonstrations and Evaluations
      Health Systems and Special Studies Division **5755**
      Hospital Experimentation Division **5756**
      Long-Term Care Experimentation Division **5757**
   Office of Research and Demonstrations **5758**
      Beneficiary Studies Division **5759**
      Office of Demonstrations and Evaluations **5760**
      Program Studies Division **5761**
      Reimbursement and Economic Studies Division **5762**
Health Resources and Services Administration • Gillis W. Long Hansen's Disease Center **6793**
National Cancer Institute **5889, 6125**
   Chemical and Physical Carcinogenesis Program
      Chemical and Physical Carcinogenesis Branch **6126**
      Radiation Effects Branch **6127**
   Division of Cancer Biology, Diagnosis, and Centers **6128**
      Cancer Centers Branch **6129**
      Cancer Diagnosis Branch **6130**
      Cancer Immunology Branch **6131**
      Dermatology Branch **6132**
      Extramural Research Program **6133**
      Intramural Research Program **6134**
      Metabolism Branch **6135**
   Division of Cancer Biology, Diagnosis, and Centers Extramural Research Program • Cancer Biology Branch **6136**
   Division of Cancer Etiology **6137**
      Biological Carcinogenesis Program **6138**
      Epidemiology and Biostatistics Program **6139**
   Division of Cancer Prevention and Control **6140**
      Cancer Control Science Program **6141**
      Cancer Prevention Research Program **6142**
      Cancer Prevention Studies Branch **6143**
      Chemoprevention Branch **6144**
      Early Detection and Community Oncology Program **6145**
      Health Education Section **6146**
      Special Population Studies Branch **6147**
      Surveillance Program **6148**
   Division of Cancer Treatment **6149**
      Biological Resources Branch **6150**
      Biological Response Modifiers Program **6151**
      Biometric Research Branch **6152**
      Cancer Therapy Evaluation Program **6153**
      Clinical Investigations Branch **6154**
      Clinical Oncology Program **6155**
      Clinical Research Branch **6156**
      Developmental Therapeutics Program **6157**
      Diagnostic Imaging Research Branch **6158**

Index

University Affiliated Program for Developmental Disabilities • University of Missouri—Kansas City **4335**

University Affiliated Programs for the Developmentally Disabled; American Association of **4459**

University Affiliated Programs for Persons With Developmental Disabilities; American Association of **4459**

University of Akron

    Center for Nursing **9147**

    College of Nursing **8886**

        Nurse Anesthesia Program **2310**

    Institute for Biomedical Engineering Research **2474**

    Institute for Life-Span Development and Gerontology **1966**

    Respiratory Therapist Program **11499**

    School of Home Economics and Family Ecology • Dietetics Program **9416**

University of Alabama

    Brewer-Porch Children's Center **3355**

    Capstone College of Nursing **8551**

    Center for the Study of Aging **1967**

    Department of Human Nutrition and Hospitality • Dietetics Program **9384**

    Psychology Clinic **7653**

    School of Social Work **11745**

    Speech and Hearing Center **3631**

University of Alabama at Birmingham

    Alabama Congenital Heart Disease Diagnosis and Treatment Center **2953**

    Biocommunication Research Laboratory **3632**

    Cardiovascular Research and Training Center **2954**

    Center for Aging **1968**

    Center for Health Risk Assessment and Disease Prevention **10881**

    Center for Neuroimmunology **8473**

    Civitan International Research Center/Alabama UAP **4586**

    Comprehensive Cancer Center **6208**

    Department of Nutrition Sciences **9546**

    Diabetes Research and Training Center **4926**

    Division of Clinical Immunology and Rheumatology **7943**

    General Clinical Research Center **1680**

    Gregory Fleming James Cystic Fibrosis Research Center **5366**

    Health Information Management Division **6915**

    Injury Control Research Center **10882**

    Laboratory of Exocrine Physiology **4927**

    Laboratory of Medical Genetics **5367**

    Laboratory of Molecular Biophysics **2658**

    Medical Rehabilitation Research and Training Center in Secondary Complications in Spinal Cord Injury **12755**

    Multipurpose Arthritis and Musculoskeletal Diseases Center **7944**

    National Spinal Cord Injury Statistical Center **8474**

    Nephrology Research and Training Center **12923**

    Neurobiology Research Center **8475**

    Ob/Gyn Infectious Disease Research Laboratory **9715**

    Pain Center **8476**

    Parkinson's Disease Center **8477**

    Regional Maxillofacial Prosthetics Treatment and Training Center **2475**

    Research Center in Oral Biology **4024**

    School of Dentistry **3787**

    School of Health Related Professions

        Department of Health Services Administration • Master of Science in Health Administration Program **5472**

        Division of Occupational Therapy **12334**

        Division of Physical Therapy **12438**

        Nurse Anesthetist Program **2259**

        Respiratory Therapist Program **11303**

        Surgeon's Assistant Program **1057**

    School of Medicine **923**

        Pharmacology Department **10188**

    School of Nursing **8552**

        Graduate Program in Nurse-Midwifery **9578**

    School of Optometry **13364**

    School of Public Health **10906**

    Specialized Center of Research in Ischemic Heart Disease **2955**

    Spinal Cord Injury Care System **12756**

    Urological Rehabilitation and Research Center **12924**

University of Alabama at Birmingham / American Red Cross Blood Services, Alabama Region • Specialist in Blood Bank Technology Program **7091**

University of Alabama in Huntsville • School of Nursing **8553**

University of Alaska Anchorage

    Center for Alcohol and Addiction Studies **12132**

    Denali Medical Research **4765**

    Institute for Circumpolar Health Studies **1681**

    School of Nursing and Health Sciences • Baccalaureate Nursing Program **8557**

University of Alaska Fairbanks • Institute of Arctic Biology **1682**

University at Albany, State University of New York

    Center for Biological Macromolecules **2659**

    Center for Stress and Anxiety Disorders **7654**

University of Alberta

    Centre for Gerontology **1969**

    Developmental Disabilities Centre **4322**

University Anesthesiologists; Association of **2357**

University Anesthetists; Association of **2357**

University of Arizona

    Advanced Biotechnology Laboratory **2379**

    Arizona Agricultural Experiment Station **9547**

    Arizona Cancer Center **6209**

    Arizona Center on Aging **1970**

    Arizona Poison and Drug Information Center **10468**

    Center for Complex Systems **8478**

    Center for Pharmaceutical Economics **10631**

    Clinical / Biomedical Engineering **2476**

    College of Education • Department of Special Education and Rehabilitation • Rehabilitation Counseling Program **12569**

    College of Medicine **925**

        Perfusion Sciences **2790**

    College of Medicine and College of Pharmacy • Department of Pharmacology **10190**

    College of Nursing **8561**

    College of Pharmacy **10501**

    Native American Research and Training Center **1683**

    Program in Applied Mathematics **7036**

    Rehabilitation Center **12757**

    Sleep Disorders Center **8479**

    Southwest Institute for Research on Women **9716**

    University Heart Center **2956**

University of Arkansas

    Department of Rehabilitation Education and Research • Rehabilitation Counseling Program **12571**

    School of Nursing **8566**

University of Arkansas at Little Rock

    Arkansas Cancer Research Center **6210**

    Arkansas Children's Hospital Cystic Fibrosis Center **5368**

    College of Medicine **926**

    Department of Health Services Administration • Graduate Program in Health Services Administration **5474**

    Rehabilitation Research and Training Center for Persons Who Are Deaf or Hard of Hearing **3633**

    School of Medicine • Department of Pharmacology and Toxicology **10191**

    School of Social Work **11747**

University of Arkansas for Medical Sciences

    Area Health Education Center • Respiratory Therapy Program **11312**

    College of Health Related Professions • Respiratory Therapist Program **11313**

    College of Nursing **8567**

    College of Pharmacy **10502**

University of Arkansas at Pine Bluff • Department of Nursing **8568**

University Biochemistry Facility • Kansas State University **2584**

University of Bridgeport

    Center for the Study of Aging **1971**

    College of Chiropractic **3435**

University of British Columbia

    Center for Applied Ethics **7217**

    Jack Bell Research Centre **1684**

University of Calcutta Medical Association of America **1528**

University of Calgary • Cell Regulation Group **2660**

University of California

    Center for Occupational and Environmental Health **9848**

    Cooperative Extension **9548**

    Tobacco-Related Disease Research Program **11744**

University of California at Berkeley

    Berkeley Child Welfare Research Center **11875**

    Cancer Research Laboratory **6211**

    Environmental Engineering and Health Sciences Laboratory **5113**

    Graduate School of Business Administration • Graduate Program in Health Services Management **5476**

    Master of Social Welfare Program **11755**

    School of Optometry **13366**

    School of Public Health **10909**

    Sequoia Hospital Lipid Institute **2957**

    Statistical Laboratory **7037**

University of California, Davis
  Agricultural Experiment Station **9549**
  AIDS Virus Diagnostic Laboratory **6839**
  Allergy-Clinical Immunology Program **2140**
  California Regional Primate Research Center **13210**
  Center for Companion Animal Health **13211**
  Clinical Nutrition Research Unit **9550**
  Dairy Goat Research Facility **13212**
  Division of Occupational/Environmental Medicine and Epidemiology **9849**
  Equine Research Laboratory **13213**
  Gastroenterology and Nutrition Center **5247**
  Institute of Toxicology and Environmental Health **5114**
  NIDRR Research & Training Center for Rehabilitation in Neuromuscular Diseases **8480**
  School of Medicine **929**
    Department of Family Practice • Physician Assistant Program **1063**
    Department of Medical Pharmacology and Toxicology **10195**
  School of Veterinary Medicine **12993**
    Department of Veterinary Pharmacology and Toxicology **10196**
  Veterinary Genetics Laboratory **13214**
  Veterinary Medicine Teaching and Research Center **13215**
University of California, Irvine
  Air Pollution Health Effects Laboratory **5115**
  Beckman Laser Institute and Medical Clinic **11160**
  Brain Imaging Center **11161**
  Cancer Research Institute **6212**
  Center for the Neurobiology of Learning and Memory **8481**
  College of Medicine **930**
    Department of Pharmacology **10197**
  Developmental Biology Center **2661**
  Division of Human Genetics **5369**
  Environmental Simulation Laboratory **9850**
  Hitachi Chemical Research Center **2662**
  Laser Microbeam Program **11162**
  Memory Disorders Clinic **8482**
  Reconstructive Microsurgery and Transplantation Laboratories **12887**
  UCI Birthing Center • Nurse-Midwifery Education Program **9581**
  UCI Diabetes Research Program **4928**
University of California, Los Angeles
  Alcohol Research Center **12133**
  Bone Marrow Transplantation Program **12888**
  Bone Research Laboratory **7945**
  Brain Research Institute **8483**
  Cardiovascular Research Laboratory **2958**
  Center for Research on Aging Project **7655**
  Center for the Study of Inflammatory Bowel Disease **5248**
  Center for the Study of Women **1685**
  Center for Ulcer Research and Education **5249**
  Crump Institute for Biological Imaging **2477**
  Dental Research Institute **4025**
  General Clinical Research Center **1686**
  Harbor-UCLA Medical Center **2728**
  Institute for Toxicology **10469**
  Jerry Lewis Neuromuscular Research Center **8484**
  Jules Stein Eye Institute **13645**
  Laboratory of Biomedical and Environmental Sciences **1687**
  Leo G. Rigler Center for Radiological Research **11163**
  Man-Machine-Environment Systems Laboratory **2478**
  Mental Retardation Research Center **4323**
  Neuropsychiatric Institute **7656**
  Population Research Center **11291**
  Program in Psychiatry, Law, and Human Sexuality **7218**
  Program on Psychosocial Adaptation and the Future **7657**
  Reed Neurological Research Center **8485**
  Research Center on the Psychobiology of Ethnicity **7658**
  School of Dentistry **3789**
  School of Medicine • Department of Molecular and Medical Pharmacology **10198**
  School of Nursing **8590**
    Graduate Nurse-Midwifery Education Program **9582**
  School of Public Health **10910**
    Program in Health Services Management **5477**
  School of Social Welfare **11756**
  Southern California Injury Prevention Research Center **10883**
  UCLA Center for Clinical AIDS Research and Education / AIDS Clinical Trials Unit **6840**
  UCLA-DOE Laboratory of Structural Biology and Molecular Medicine **2663**

  UCLA Jonsson Comprehensive Cancer Center **6213**
  UCLA School of Medicine **931**
  Will Rogers Institute Pulmonary Research Laboratory **11619**
University of California, Los Angeles Medical Center / Santa Monica College • Respiratory Therapist Program **11334**
University of California, Los Angeles / Olive View Medical Center • Nurse Anesthesia Program **2262**
University of California, San Diego
  Alzheimer's Disease Research Center **8486**
  Cancer Center **6214**
  Center for Child and Family Studies **3356**
  Center for Molecular Genetics **2664**
  Division of Pulmonary and Critical Care Medicine **11620**
  General Clinical Research Center **1688**
  Hyperbaric Medicine Center **12758**
  Institute for Biomedical Engineering **2479**
  Pediatric Pulmonary and Cystic Fibrosis Center **11621**
  Sam and Rose Stein Institute for Research on Aging **1972**
  School of Medicine **932**
    Department of Pharmacology **10199**
  Specialized Center of Research in Arteriosclerosis **2959**
  Specialized Center of Research in Heart Failure **2960**
  USCD School of Medicine • Department of Community and Family Medicine • Nurse-Midwifery Certificate Education Program **9583**
University of California, San Francisco
  AIDS Clinical Research Center **6841**
  Brain-Behavior Research Center **8487**
  Brain Tumor Research Center **6215**
  Cancer Research Institute **6216**
  Cardiovascular Research Institute **2665**
  Center for AIDS Prevention Studies **10884**
  Center for Clinical and Aging Services Research **1973**
  Center on Deafness **3634**
  Center for Social and Behavioral Sciences **7659**
  Center for Study of Trauma **7660**
  CNS Injury and Edema Research Center **8488**
  Computer Graphics Laboratory **10470**
  Dermatology Drug Research Unit **4269**
  Ernest Gallo Clinic and Research Center **12134**
  General Clinical Research Center **1689**
  General Clinical Research Center—Adults **1690**
  George Williams Hooper Foundation **6842**
  Hormone Research Institute **4929**
  Immunogenetics and Transplantation Laboratory **2141**
  Institute for Health & Aging **1974**
  Institute for Health Policy Studies **5646**
  Keck Center for Integrative Neurosciences **8489**
  Laboratory for Neurotrauma **8490**
  Langley Porter Psychiatric Institute **7661**
  Liver Transplant Division **12889**
  Mass Spectrometry Facility **2666**
  Metabolic Research Unit **4930**
  Northern California Comprehensive Sickle Cell Center **6217**
  Ocular Oncology Research Unit **13646**
  Pediatric Clinical Research Center **3357**
  Radiation Oncology Research Laboratory **11164**
  Reproductive Endocrinology Center **4931**
  Rosalind Russell Medical Research Center for Arthritis **7946**
  School of Dentistry **3790**
  School of Medicine **933**
    Department of Pharmacology **10200**
    Graduate Program in Physical Therapy **12449**
  School of Nursing **8591**
    Department of Physiological Nursing • Program in Nurse Anesthesia **2263**
  School of Pharmacy **10503**
    Graduate Pharmacology Program **10201**
University of California, San Francisco / San Francisco General Hospital
  Interdepartmental Nurse-Midwifery Certificate Education Program **9584**
  Interdepartmental Nurse-Midwifery Graduate Education Program **9585**
University of California, San Francisco / University of California, San Diego • UCSD School of Medicine • Department of Community and Family Medicine • Intercampus Nurse-Midwifery Graduate Education Program **9586**
University of California, Santa Barbara • Neuroscience Research Institute **8491**
University Center on Aging and Health • Case Western Reserve University **1928**
University Center for the Child and Family • University of Michigan **3365**

Natural Products Lab   2680
Nevada Agricultural Experiment Station-221   9559
Nutritional Education & Research Program   9560
Orvis School of Nursing   8809
School of Medicine   988
Department of Pharmacology   10284
School of Social Work   11813
Speech and Language Pathology and Audiology Department   3650
University of New England
College of Arts and Sciences • Division of Occupational Therapy
12365
College of Osteopathic Medicine   9956
Department of Pharmacology   10254
Department of Physical Therapy   12483
School of Nurse Anesthesia   2279
School of Social Work   11791
University of New Hampshire
Biomedical Engineering Center   2494
Department of Nursing   8812
Family Research Laboratory   3074
Marine Biomedical Research Group   2681
New Hampshire Agricultural Experiment Station   9561
School of Health and Human Services
Department of Health Management and Policy • Master of
Health Administration Program   5506
Occupational Therapy Department   12386
University of New Mexico
Cancer Research and Treatment Center   6235
Center for Non-Invasive Diagnosis   11171
College of Nursing   8821
Nurse-Midwifery Graduate Program   9602
College of Pharmacy   10539
General Clinical Research Center   1711
Institute of Public Law   1712
New Mexico Tumor Registry   6236
School of Medicine   993
Department of Pharmacology   10290
Division of Physical Therapy   12510
Occupational Therapy Program   12388
University of North Alabama • School of Nursing   8555
University of North Carolina • Institute of Nutrition   9562
University of North Carolina at Chapel Hill
Brain and Development Research Center   4336
Cecil G. Sheps Center for Health Services Research   5656
Center for Alcohol Studies   12141
Center for Environmental Medicine and Lung Biology   5126
Center for Health Promotion and Disease Prevention   10887
Center for Thrombosis and Hemostasis   6237
Child Development Institute   3367
Dental Research Center   4041
Department of Nutrition • Dietetics Program   9412
Division of Occupational Therapy   12404
Division of Physical Therapy   12526
Division of Speech and Hearing Sciences   3651
Frank Porter Graham Child Development Center   3368
General Clinical Research Center   1713
Injury Prevention Research Center   10888
National Center for Catastrophic Sports Injury Research   11990
School of Dentistry   3822
School of Medicine   1008
Department of Pharmacology   10311
Division of Rehabilitation Counseling   12621
School of Nursing   8860
School of Pharmacy   10545
School of Public Health   10926
Department of Health Policy and Administration • Master's
Program in Health Policy Administration   5512
School of Social Work   11830
Thurston Arthritis Research Center   7958
UNC Lineberger Comprehensive Cancer Center   6238
University of North Carolina at Charlotte
College of Nursing   8861
Social Science Working Group   7680
University of North Carolina at Charlotte; Carolinas Medical Center / •
Nurse Anesthesia Program   2302
University of North Carolina at Greensboro
Raleigh School of Nurse Anesthesia   2305
School of Nursing   8862
University of North Carolina at Greensboro; North Carolina Baptist Hospital
/ • Bowman Gray School of Medicine • Nurse Anesthesia Program   2304
University of North Carolina at Wilmington • School of Nursing   8863

University of North Dakota
College of Nursing   8871
Nurse Anesthesiology Program   2306
Department of Community Medicine and Rural Health • Physician
Assistant Program   1099
Department of Home Economics and Nutrition • Dietetics Program
9414
Department of Occupational Therapy   12406
Ireland Research Laboratory   2682
School of Medicine   1010
Department of Pharmacology and Toxicology   10314
Department of Physical Therapy   12527
Social Work Department   11831
UND Center for Rural Health   1714
University of North Dakota; Casper College / • Occupational Therapy
Program   12405
University of North Florida
College of Health
Department of Nursing   8624
Physical Therapy Program   12463
University of North Texas
Center for Rehabilitation Studies   12763
Rehabilitation Counseling Program   12637
Center for Studies in Aging   1991
University of North Texas Health Science Center at Fort Worth
Center for Osteoporosis Prevention and Treatment   7959
Graduate Program in Pharmacology   10365
Institute of Forensic Medicine   7221
North Texas Eye Research Institute   13657
Substance Abuse Institute of North Texas   12142
Texas College of Osteopathic Medicine   9966
Texas Institute for Research and Education on Aging   1992
Wound Healing Research Institute   1715
University of Northern Colorado
Human Services Department • Rehabilitation Education Programs
12578
School of Nursing   8598
University of Northern Iowa • Center for the Study of Adolescence   3369
University of Notre Dame • Lobund Laboratory   2683
University of Oklahoma
Animal Resources   13229
Center for Public Management and Education Development •
Rehabilitation Counseling Program   12628
College of Allied Health
Department of Nutritional Sciences • Dietetics Program   9418
Department of Occupational Therapy   12412
Department of Physical Therapy   12533
College of Dentistry   3825
College of Medicine   1017
Department of Pharmacology   10328
College of Nursing   8900
College of Pharmacy   10552
Department of Pharmacodynamics and Toxicology   10329
College of Public Health   10927
Keys Speech and Hearing Center   3652
Physician Associate Program   1102
Pulmonary and Cystic Fibrosis Center   5379
School of Social Work   11835
Thrombosis & Coagulation Laboratory   6239
Tulsa Medical College   1018
University of Oregon
Center on Human Development   4337
Institute of Neuroscience   8516
International Institute for Sport and Human Performance   11991
University of Osteopathic Medicine and Health Sciences
College of Biological Sciences • Physical Therapy Program   12477
College of Osteopathic Medicine and Surgery   9955
College of Podiatric Medicine and Surgery   10750
Department of Physiology and Pharmacology   10242
Physician Assistant.Program   1077
University Otolaryngologists - Head and Neck Surgeons; Society of   12310
University of Ottawa • Neurosciences Research Institute   8517
University of the Pacific
Physical Therapy Department   12450
School of Dentistry   3791
School of Pharmacy   10504
Department of Physiology and Pharmacology   10202
University of Pennsylvania
Aging Skin Clinic   4270
Brain Behavior Laboratory   8518
Cancer Center   6240

Index

College of Medicine   **924**
    Pharmacology Department   **10189**
College of Nursing   **8556**
Occupational Therapy Program   **12335**
Primate Research Laboratory   **13234**
University of South Carolina
    College of Pharmacy   **10561**
        Department of Basic Pharmaceutical Sciences • Division of
        Pharmacology   **10351**
    College of Social Work   **11844**
    International Center for Public Health Research   **11002**
    Rehabilitation Counseling Program   **12633**
    School of Medicine   **1031**
        Department of Pharmacology   **10352**
    School of Public Health   **10930**
        Department of Health Administration • Master of Health
        Administration Program   **5523**
University of South Carolina at Columbia
    Center for the Study of Suicide   **7686**
    College of Nursing   **8960**
University of South Carolina; Richland Memorial Hospital / • Graduate
Program in Nurse Anesthesia   **2330**
University of South Carolina at Spartanburg • Mary Black School of
Nursing   **8961**
University of South Dakota
    Department of Physical Therapy   **12545**
    Interdisciplinary Center for Disabilities   **4597**
    Occupational Therapy Program   **12423**
    School of Medicine   **1032**
        Department of Physiology and Pharmacology   **10353**
        Physician Assistant Program   **1108**
    Sioux Falls Medical Research Center   **1721**
    Social Science Research Institute   **7687**
University of South Dakota; McKennan Hospital / • School of
Anesthesiology for Registered Nurses   **2331**
University of South Florida
    College of Medicine   **943**
        Department of Pharmacology and Therapeutics   **10218**
    College of Nursing   **8625**
    College of Public Health   **10912**
    Department of Rehabilitation Counseling   **12583**
    Department of Social Work   **11769**
    Florida Mental Health Institute   **7688**
    Research and Training Center for Children's Mental Health   **7689**
University of Southern California
    Center for Craniofacial Molecular Biology   **4046**
    Clinical Research Center   **1722**
    Comprehensive Sickle Cell Center   **6245**
    Coronary Care Research   **2975**
    Department of Nursing   **8593**
    Department of Occupational Therapy   **12340**
    Department of Physical Therapy   **12451**
    Division of Nephrology   **12930**
    Division of Rheumatology and Immunology   **2146**
    Ethel Percy Andrus Gerontology Center   **1994**
    Hastings Foundation Infectious Disease Research Laboratories   **6851**
    Hematology Research Laboratory   **6246**
    Hematopathology Unit   **6247**
    Institute for Health Promotion and Disease Prevention Research
    10889
    Institute for Toxicology   **10483**
    International Twin Study   **5197**
    Laboratory of Applied Pharmacokinetics   **10484**
    Laboratory for Developmental Biology   **2686**
    Liver Research Unit   **5253**
    Lung Disease, Cancer, Lymphocytes, Air Pollution, and General
    Pathobiology Unit   **10181**
    Medical Oncology Research Program   **6248**
    Neonatology Research Units   **9719**
    Norris Comprehensive Cancer Center   **6249**
    Nurse-Midwifery Certificate Education Program   **9587**
    School of Dentistry   **3792**
    School of Medicine   **934**
        Department of Pharmacology and Nutrition   **10203**
        Primary Care Physician Assistant Program   **1064**
    School of Pharmacy   **10505**
        Department of Molecular Pharmacology and Toxicology   **10204**
    School of Public Administration • Health Services Administration
    Program   **5478**
    School of Social Work   **11757**

University of Southern California School of Medicine; Shock Research Unit
at   **4762**
University of Southern Colorado
    Department of Nursing   **8599**
    Social Work Department   **11760**
University of Southern Indiana
    Respiratory Therapist Program   **11389**
    School of Nursing   **8688**
    School of Nursing and Health Professions • Occupational Therapy
    Program   **12357**
University of Southern Maine
    Edmund S. Muskie Institute of Public Affairs   **5659**
    School of Nursing   **8737**
University of Southern Maine; Lewiston-Auburn College / • Occupational
Therapy Program   **12364**
University of Southern Mississippi
    College of Health and Human Sciences • Dietetics Program   **9406**
    School of Nursing   **8785**
    School of Social Work   **11807**
University of Southwestern Louisiana
    College of Nursing   **8732**
    Department of Health Information Management   **6931**
    New Iberia Research Center   **1723**
University Surgeons; Society of   **12311**
University of Tennessee
    Center of Excellence in Pediatric Pharmacokinetics and
    Therapeutics   **10485**
    Clinical Research Center   **1724**
    Division of Cardiovascular Diseases   **2976**
    Division of Reproductive Endocrinology   **4943**
    Drug Information Center   **10486**
    Memorial Research Center   **2687**
    Memphis Cancer Center   **6250**
    Molecular Resource Center   **5381**
University of Tennessee at Chattanooga
    Department of Physical Therapy   **12547**
    School of Nursing   **8976**
University of Tennessee at Chattanooga; Erlanger Medical Center / • Nurse
Anesthesia Program   **2333**
University of Tennessee, Knoxville
    Center of Excellence in Livestock Diseases and Human Health
    13235
    College of Nursing   **8977**
    College of Social Work   **11845**
    College of Veterinary Medicine   **13013**
        Department of Environmental Practice • Graduate Pharmacology
        Programs   **10356**
    Department of Special Services Education • Rehabilitation Counseling
    Program   **12635**
    Experimental Oncology Laboratory   **6251**
    Human Immunology and Cancer Program   **6252**
    Psychological Clinic   **7690**
    School of Nurse Anesthesia   **2335**
University of Tennessee at Memphis
    Center for Neuroscience   **8524**
    College of Allied Health Sciences
        Department of Health Information Management   **6959**
        Department of Rehabilitation Sciences   **12425**
    College of Dentistry   **3833**
    College of Medicine   **1035**
        Department of Pharmacology   **10357**
    College of Nursing   **8978**
    College of Pharmacy   **10563**
    College of Social Work   **11846**
    Department of Rehabilitation Sciences • Program in Physical
    Therapy   **12548**
University of Tennessee at Nashville • College of Social Work   **11847**
University of Texas
    Hogg Foundation for Mental Health   **7691**
    Sleep Study Unit   **8525**
    University of Texas M.D. Anderson Cancer Center   **6253**
University of Texas at Arlington
    Center for Medicinal Chemistry Research   **2688**
    Center for Nursing Research   **9149**
    Human Performance Institute   **1725**
    School of Nursing   **8994**
    School of Social Work   **11850**
University of Texas at Austin
    Biochemical Institute   **2689**
    Biomedical Engineering Program   **2495**
    Center for Biotechnology   **2736**

Center for Space Physiology and Medicine **2413**
Center for the Study of At-Risk Populations and Public Assistance Policy **3372**
Clinical Nutrition Research Unit **9573**
Clinical Research Center **1737**
Department of Cardiothoracic Surgery • Perfusion Training Program **2819**
Diabetes Research and Training Center **4946**
Energy Balance Laboratory **11996**
Health Policy Center **5767**
John F. Kennedy Center for Research on Human Development **4339**
Nutrition Center **9574**
S.R. Light Laboratory for Surgical Research **12328**
School of Medicine **1036**
 Department of Biochemistry • Center in Molecular Toxicology **10358**
 Department of Pharmacology **10359**
Specialized Center of Research in Hypertension **2985**
Vasculaire; Association de Recherche en Chirurgie 12256
Vascular Center; Retinal • Johns Hopkins University **13609**
Vascular Diseases; Division of Heart and • National Heart, Lung, and Blood Institute • U.S. Department of Health and Human Services **2933**
vascular Dynamics; European Society for Ballisto Cardiographic and Cardio 2846
Vascular Institute; Heart and **2900**
Vascular Malformations Foundation; National **8286**
Vascular Medicine and Preventive Cardiology Unit • University of Virginia **2982**
Vascular Nursing; Society for **9137**
Vascular Nursing; Society for Peripheral 9137
Vascular Research Division; Hypertension and • Henry Ford Hospital **2902**
Vascular Research Laboratory **2986**
vascular Society; International Cardio 2859
vascular Society; Michael E. DeBakey International Cardio 12288
Vascular Surgery; Association for Research in **12256**
vascular Surgery; International Society for Cardio 2859
Vascular Surgery; Society for **12312**
vascular Technologists; National Alliance of Cardio 2828
Vascular Technology; Society of **2878**
Vascular Technology; Society of Non-Invasive 2878
VD Awareness; Citizens Alliance for **6654**
VDT and Health Research; Center for • Johns Hopkins University **9811**
VDT Injured in Denmark; Electrically and **5037**
VDT Injured; Swedish Association for the Electrically and **5061**
Vector-Borne Infectious Diseases; Division of • National Center for Infectious Diseases • U.S. Department of Health and Human Services **6802**
Vectors and Pathogens; Laboratory of • National Institute of Allergy and Infectious Diseases • U.S. Department of Health and Human Services **6837**
Vegetarian Dietitians and Nutrition Educators; Association of **9448**
Venereal Disease; American Foundation for the Prevention of **6630**
Venereal Diseases; Medical Society for the Study of **6695**
Venereal Diseases and Treponematoses; International Union Against **6683**
Venereal Diseases and the Treponematoses, Regional Office for North America; International Union Against the **6684**
Venereologia; Sociedad Chilena de Dermatologia y 4224
Venereologie; Nederlandse Vereniging voor Dermatologie en 4231
Venereologie; Societe Royale Belge de Dermatologie et de 4220
Venereology; Belgian Royal Society of Dermatology and **4220**
Venereology; Chilean Society of Dermatology and **4224**
Venereology; Dutch Association for Dermatology and **4231**
Venereology; Hellenic Society of Dermatology and **4236**
Venereology; Hong Kong Society of Dermatology and **4238**
Venereology; Swedish Society for Dermatology and **4260**
Veneriennes et les Treponematoses; Union Internationale Contre les Maladies 6683
Vera Davis Parsons - W.D. Charities 6385
Vera Davis - W.D. Charities **6385**
Verband der Deutschen Dental-Industrie **5886**
Verband Deutscher Badearzte **12726**
Verband Deutscher Diatassistenten 9447
Verband Deutscher Drogisten 10600
Verband Deutscher Heilpraktiker 2196
Verband der Diplomierten Diatassistentinnen Osterreichs 9454
Verband der Krankenhausdirektoren Deutschlands 5579
Verband der Leitenden Krankenhausarzte Deutschlands 5560
Verbond der Verzorgingsinstellingen 1204
Verein Demokratischer Pharmazeutinnen und Pharmazeuten 10589
Vereinigung der Europaischen Dental-Industrie 5849
Vereinigung Schweizerischer Krankenhaeuser 6474

Vereniging van Geneeskundige Laboratorium Tegnoloe van Suid-Afrika 7153
Vereniging van Radiograwe van Suid-Afrika 11139
Vereniging Spierziekten Nederland 8324
Vermont Affiliate
 American Diabetes Association **4997**
 American Heart Association **3039**
Vermont Agency of Human Services
 Aging and Disability Department **2047**
 Alcohol and Drug Abuse Programs Office **12192**
 Health Department **11051**
  Dental Health Division **4148**
  Emergency Medical Services Division **4813**
  Environmental Health Division **5173**
  Maternal and Child Health Bureau **3423, 9769**
  Medical Care Regulation Division **6521**
  Public Health, Analysis and Policy Division • Vital Records Unit **7085**
  STD Program **6901**
 Mental Health Department
  Mental Health Division **7753**
  Mental Retardation Programs Division **4388**
 Social and Rehabilitation Services Department
  Blind and Visually Impaired Division **13711**
  Planning and Evaluation Division **5705**
  Vocational Rehabilitation Division **12816**
 Social Welfare Department • Medicaid Division **5813**
Vermont Alcohol Research Center **12145**
Vermont; American Lung Association of **11677**
Vermont Board of Examiners of Nursing Home Administrators **9320**
Vermont Board of Funeral Service **3773**
Vermont Board of Medical Practice **1803, 10059**
Vermont Board of Optometry **13764**
Vermont Board of Pharmacy **10687**
Vermont Cancer Center • University of Vermont **6257**
Vermont Chapter
 Lupus Foundation of America **8115**
 National Association of Social Workers **11927**
Vermont Department of Agriculture • State Veterinarian **13295**
Vermont Department of Labor and Industry • Occupational Safety and Health Division **9910**
Vermont Division • American Cancer Society **6322**
Vermont Health Care Association **9371**
Vermont Hospital Association **6573**
Vermont; Learning Disabilities Association of **4726**
Vermont Network Against Domestic Violence and Sexual Assault **3122**
Vermont and Northern New York Chapter • Arthritis Foundation **8024**
Vermont Optometric Association **13838**
Vermont Pharmacists Association **10740**
Vermont Rehabilitation Engineering Center for Low Back Pain • University of Vermont **12764**
Vermont State Association of Osteopathic Physicians and Surgeons **10110**
Vermont State Board of Dental Examiners **4095**
Vermont State Board of Medical Practice **10825**
Vermont State Board of Nursing **9203**
Vermont State Dental Society **4201**
Vermont State Medical Society **1857**
Vermont State Nurses Association **9257**
Vermont Veterinary Medical Association **13348**
Verpleging van Suid Afrika; Nasionale Genootskap van Onkologiese 9124
Versuchstierkunde; Gesellschaft fur 13107
Very Special Arts **4566**
Verzorgingsinstellingen; Verbond der 1204
Vestibular Disorder Laboratory; Communicative and • University of Texas Southwestern Medical Center at Dallas **3655**
Vestibular Disorders Association **3585**
Veteran Affairs Medical Center; Omaha Department of • Research and Development Service **1649**
Veterans Administration; Nurses Organization of the 9131
Veterans' Affairs; Committee on • U.S. Senate **7795**
Veterans Affairs Medical Center [Birmingham, AL] • Research and Development Service **1739**
Veterans Affairs Medical Center [Danville, IL] • Research and Development Service **1738**
Veterans Affairs Medical Center [Gainesville, FL] • Geriatric Research, Education and Clinical center **10493**
Veterans Affairs Medical Center [Martinez, CA] • Research Administration Office **2701**
Veterans Affairs Medical Center [Palo Alto, CA] • NIMH Mental Health Clinical Research Center **7698**
Veterans Affairs Medical Center [Pittsburgh, PA] • Research Service **1743**

Veterinary Medical Association; Connecticut **13308**
Veterinary Medical Association; Delaware **13309**
Veterinary Medical Association; District of Columbia **13310**
Veterinary Medical Association; Florida **13311**
Veterinary Medical Association; Georgia **13312**
Veterinary Medical Association; Hawaii **13313**
Veterinary Medical Association; Idaho **13314**
Veterinary Medical Association; Illinois State **13315**
Veterinary Medical Association; Indiana **13316**
Veterinary Medical Association; Intermountain 13114
Veterinary Medical Association; Iowa **13317**
Veterinary Medical Association; Kansas **13318**
Veterinary Medical Association; Kentucky **13319**
Veterinary Medical Association; Louisiana **13320**
Veterinary Medical Association; Maine **13321**
Veterinary Medical Association; Maryland **13322**
Veterinary Medical Association; Massachusetts **13323**
Veterinary Medical Association; Michigan **13324**
Veterinary Medical Association; Minnesota **13325**
Veterinary Medical Association; Mississippi **13326**
Veterinary Medical Association; Missouri **13327**
Veterinary Medical Association; Montana **13328**
Veterinary Medical Association; National 13066
Veterinary Medical Association; Nebraska **13329**
Veterinary Medical Association; Nevada **13330**
Veterinary Medical Association; New Hampshire **13331**
Veterinary Medical Association; New Jersey **13332**
Veterinary Medical Association; New Mexico **13333**
Veterinary Medical Association; North Carolina State **13335**
Veterinary Medical Association; North Dakota **13336**
Veterinary Medical Association; Ohio **13337**
Veterinary Medical Association; Oklahoma **13338**
Veterinary Medical Association; Oregon **13339**
Veterinary Medical Association; Pennsylvania **13340**
Veterinary Medical Association; Rhode Island **13342**
Veterinary Medical Association; South Dakota **13344**
Veterinary Medical Association; Tennessee **13345**
Veterinary Medical Association; Texas **13346**
Veterinary Medical Association; United States 13054
Veterinary Medical Association; Utah **13347**
Veterinary Medical Association; Vermont **13348**
Veterinary Medical Association; Virginia **13349**
Veterinary Medical Association; Washington State **13350**
Veterinary Medical Association; West Virginia **13351**
Veterinary Medical Association; Wisconsin **13352**
Veterinary Medical Association; Women's 13062
Veterinary Medical Association; Wyoming **13353**
Veterinary Medical Colleges; Association of American **13058**
Veterinary Medical Diagnostic Laboratory at Amarillo; Texas **13177**
Veterinary Medical Diagnostic Laboratory at College Station; Texas **13178**
Veterinary Medical Experiment Station • University of Georgia **13218**
Veterinary Medical Research Institute • Iowa State University of Science and Technology **13139**
Veterinary Medical Society; New York State **13334**
Veterinary Medicine; Association of American Board of Examiners in 13039
Veterinary Medicine; Association of Deans of American Colleges of 13058
Veterinary Medicine; Center for • Food and Drug Administration • U.S. Department of Health and Human Services **12990, 13209**
Veterinary Medicine; Chinese Association of Animal Science and **13069**
Veterinary Medicine and Clinical Microbiology Laboratory • Iowa State University of Science and Technology **13140**
Veterinary Medicine Division • Walter Reed Army Institute of Research • Army Medical Research and Development Command • U.S. Department of Defense **7837**
Veterinary Medicine Teaching and Research Center • University of California, Davis **13215**
Veterinary Microbiologists, Immunologists, and Specialists in Infectious Diseases; World Association of **13120**
Veterinary Molecular Biology Laboratory • Montana State University-Bozeman **13148**
Veterinary Nutrition; American Academy of **13023**
Veterinary Nutritionists; American Association of 13023
Veterinary Ophthalmologists; American College of **13048**
Veterinary Ophthalmology; American Society of **13053**
Veterinary Orthopaedic Society **13113**
Veterinary Parasitologists; American Association of **13038**
Veterinary Parasitology; World Association for the Advancement of **13115**
Veterinary Pathologists; American College of **13049**
Veterinary Pathology Division • Veterinary Pathology Department • Armed Forces Institute of Pathology • U.S. Department of Defense **10179**

Veterinary Pathology; European Society of **13072**
Veterinary Pharmacology and Therapeutics; American Academy of **13024**
Veterinary Poultry Association; World **13122**
Veterinary Radiology; American Board of 13050
Veterinary Radiology; American College of **13050**
Veterinary Research • Oklahoma State University **13160**
Veterinary Science; Polish Society of **13105**
Veterinary Science Research Center • Utah State University **13245**
Veterinary Sciences; Pan American Association of **13103**
Veterinary Services
    Animal and Plant Health Inspection Service • U.S. Department of Agriculture **12988**
    Puerto Rico Department of Agriculture **13288**
Veterinary Services Division
    Maine Department of Agriculture, Food and Rural Resources **13268**
    Virgin Islands Department of Economic Development and Agriculture **13296**
Veterinary Services Laboratories; National • Animal and Plant Health Inspection Service • U.S. Department of Agriculture **13207**
Veterinary Society of Animal Behavior; American **13055**
Veterinary Society for the Study of Breeding Soundness; American 13108
Veterinary Specialties; Advisory Board on 13042
Veterinary Specialties; American Board on **13042**
Veterinary State Boards; American Association of **13039**
Veterinary Students' Association; International **13092**
Veterinary Surgeons; American College of **13051**
Veterinary Toxicologists; American College of 13021
Veterinary Toxicology; American Board of **13043**
VHL Family Alliance **5306**
Vibration; Center for Sound and • North Carolina State University **5082**
Vibroacoustics; International Society for **2219**
Victim Foundation; National Burn **2772**
Victims of Alcoholism; TOVA—The Other **12080**
Victims; American Association of Dental **3874**
Victims; Canadian Center for Torture **7544**
Victims Education Association; International Dalkon Shield **11223**
Victims of Incest Can Emerge 3067
Victims of Incest Can Emerge Survivors 3067
Victims of Incest Concerned Effort 3067
Victims International; Agent Orange 7814
Victims; National Committee for Radiation **11065**
Victims; Rehabilitation and Resource Centre for Torture **12715**
Victims Research and Treatment Center; Crime • Medical University of South Carolina **7210**
Victims of Trauma; Institute for **7394**
Victims; Vietnam Veterans Agent Orange **7814**
Victor E. Speas Foundation **528**
Victor Valley College • Respiratory Therapist Program **11335**
Victoria College • Respiratory Therapist Program **11561**
Victoria Foundation **3144**
Vida Humana; Federacion Mundial de Medicos que Respectan la 1538
Vie; Comite International de Medecine d' Assurances sur la 5733
Vietnam Veterans Agent Orange Victims 7814
Vietnam Veterans Club 7816
Vietnam Veterans Institute **7815**
Vietnam Veterans Institute for Research and Advocacy 7815
VietNow 7816
VietNow National **7816**
Villa Banfi Foundation 596
Villa Julie College / Union Memorial Hospital • School of Nursing **8745**
Villa Maria College of Health Sciences • Department of Science and Mathematics • Dietetics Program • Gannon University **9420**
Village Education Programme **1529**
Villanova University • College of Nursing **8933**
Villiers Foundation; Robert Roesler de 5966
Vince Moseley Center for Children with Developmental Disabilities • Medical University of South Carolina **4579**
Vincennes University
    Funeral Service Education Program **3675**
    Respiratory Therapist Program **11390**
Vincent T. Lombardi Cancer Research Center • Georgetown University **6041**
Violence; Emerge: A Men's Counseling Service on Domestic 7368
Violence; Emerge: Counseling and Education to Stop Male 7368
Violence; National Coalition Against Domestic **3059**
Violence; National Council on Child Abuse and Family **3061**
Violence and Traumatic Stress Research Branch • Epidemiology and Services Research Division • National Institute of Mental Health • U.S. Department of Health and Human Services **7632**
Vira I. Heinz Endowment **529**

Vision Awareness; American Foundation for **13357**, **13399**
Vision Council of America **13570**
Vision; Council of Citizens With Low **13442**
Vision Deficiencies; International Research Group on Colour **13499**
Vision Development; College of Optometrists in **13437**
Vision Education; Parents Active for **13551**
Vision Educational Foundation **13571**
Vision Foundation **13572**
Vision Foundation of Massachusetts, Inc. **13572**
Vision Industry Council of America **13570**
Vision Institute; Better **13421**
Vision; International Academy of Sports **13478**
Vision; Laboratory for the Assessment of Functional • University of Illinois at Chicago **13650**
Vision; National Academy of Sports **13478**
Vision and Ophthalmology; Association for Research in **13416**
Vision Professionals; National Association of **13526**
Vision Program Consultants; National Association of **13526**
Vision; Rehabilitation Research and Training Center on Blindness and Low • Mississippi State University **13617**
Vision Research Center
    Baylor College of Medicine **13582**
    University of Florida **13649**
    University of Pennsylvania **13658**
    Yale University **13664**
Vision Research Center in Ophthalmology • Mount Sinai School of Medicine of City University of New York **13619**
Vision Research and Rehabilitation Center; Lions • Johns Hopkins University **13606**
Vision Study, Care and Rehabilitation; Center for Low • University of Florida **13648**
Visiting Nurse Associations of America **9138**
Visiting Nurses Associations and Services; American Affiliation of **9138**
Visitors' Association; Health **9091**
Visual Handicaps; Division for • Council for Exceptional Children **3218**
Visual Impairment; Catholic Association of Persons With **13431**
Visual Impairment; Council of Families with **13443**
Visual Processing Branch; Strabismus, Amblyopia, and • Extramural and Collaborative Programs • National Eye Institute • U.S. Department of Health and Human Services **13633**
Visual Research Foundation, Inc.; Connecticut Eye Bank & **13587**
Visual Science; Center for • University of Rochester **13659**
Visual Sciences Center • University of Chicago **13647**
Visual Sciences, Inc.; Institute for **13603**
Visual Sciences; Smith-Kettlewell Institute of **13628**
Visual Services Bureau • Oklahoma Department of Rehabilitation Services **13701**
Visual Services Bureau; Blindness and • Pennsylvania Department of Public Welfare **13703**
Visual Services Division; Rehabilitative Services / • Montana Department of Social and Rehabilitation Services **12796, 13691**
Visualization Laboratory; Biomedical • University of Illinois at Chicago **2670**
Visually Handicapped Commission; Blind and • New York State Department of Social Services **13697**
Visually Handicapped Department • Virginia Office of Health and Human Resources **13713**
Visually Handicapped; Division for the **3218**
Visually Handicapped; International Council for Education of the **13483**
Visually Handicapped; National Accreditation Council for Agencies Serving the Blind and **13521**
Visually Handicapped; National Aid to **13527**
Visually Handicapped; National Association for **13527**
Visually Handicapped Services Division • Utah Rehabilitation Office **13710**
Visually Impaired; Association for Education and Rehabilitation of the Blind and **13412**
Visually Impaired Bureau; Services for the • Ohio Rehabilitation Services Commission **13700**
Visually Impaired; Carroll Rehabilitation Center for the **13430**
Visually Impaired Data Processors International **13573**
Visually Impaired Division • Delaware Department of Health and Social Services **13672**
Visually Impaired Division; Blind and
    Rehabilitation Services Office • Maine Department of Education **13684**
    Social and Rehabilitation Services Department • Vermont Agency of Human Services **13711**
Visually Impaired Division; Rehabilitation Services for the • Nebraska Department of Public Institutions **13692**
Visually Impaired Division; Services to the Blind and • South Dakota Department of Human Services **13707**
Visually Impaired Empowering Women **13574**
Visually Impaired Enterprisers; Independent **13477**

Visually Impaired; Idaho Commission for the Blind and **13677**
Visually Impaired Information Specialists **13575**
Visually Impaired; International Institute for **13422**
Visually Impaired; National Association for Parents of the **13525**
Visually Impaired Secretarial Transcribers Association **13575**
Visually Impaired Veterans of America **13576**
Vital Record Division • Rhode Island Department of Health **7079**
Vital Records Branch
    Health Services Department • California Health and Welfare Agency **7044**
    Research and Statistics Division • District of Columbia Department of Human Services **7048**
Vital Records Bureau
    Health Division • Nevada Department of Human Resources **7068**
    Health Resources Division • Missouri Department of Health **7065**
    Planning and Administration Division • Iowa Department of Public Health **7055**
Vital Records Bureau; Health Statistics and • Utah Department of Health **7084**
Vital Records Division
    Administrative Services Section • North Dakota Department of Health and Consolidated Laboratories **7074**
    Connecticut Department of Public Health **7046**
    Finance and Administration Office • Illinois Department of Public Health **7053**
    Health Resources Bureau • Arkansas Department of Health **7043**
    Oklahoma Department of Health **7076**
    Pennsylvania Department of Health **7078**
Vital Records Division; Health Statistics and • Administration and Support Office • Colorado Public and Environment Department **7045**
Vital Records and Health Statistics; Association for **6979**
Vital Records and Health Statistics Bureau • Public Health Services Division • New Hampshire Department of Health and Human Services **7069**
Vital Records and Health Statistics Office • Health Department • Virginia Office of Health and Human Resources **7086**
Vital Records Office • Arizona Department of Health Services **7042**
Vital Records Program • South Dakota Department of Health **7081**
Vital Records and Public Health Statistics; American Association for **6979**
Vital Records and Public Health Statistics Office • South Carolina Department of Health and Environmental Control **7080**
Vital Records Section
    Health Director's Office • North Carolina Department of Environment, Health, and Natural Resources **7073**
    Health Statistics Division • Administrative Services Bureau • Tennessee Department of Health **7082**
    Health Status Monitoring Office • Hawaii Department of Health **7051**
    Preventive Medicine Division • Wyoming Department of Health **7090**
Vital Records and Statistics Bureau • Health Services Division • Montana Department of Health and Environmental Sciences **7066**
Vital Records and Statistics Division • Public Health Department • Massachusetts Executive Office of Health and Human Services **7061**
Vital Records Unit • Public Health, Analysis and Policy Division • Health Department • Vermont Agency of Human Services **7085**
Vital Statistics Bureau
    Ohio Department of Health **7075**
    Texas Department of Health **7083**
Vital Statistics Division
    Health Services Department • Kentucky Human Resources Cabinet **7057**
    Information Resources Bureau • Mississippi Department of Health **7064**
Vital Statistics Division; Research and • Maine Department of Human Services **7059**
Vital Statistics and Health Policy Center • Idaho Department of Health and Welfare **5675**
Vital Statistics Office
    Florida Department of Health and Rehabilitative Services **7049**
    Health Division • Wisconsin Department of Health and Social Services **7089**
    Health and Environment Statistics Division • Kansas Department of Health and Environment **7056**
Vital Statistics Section
    Health Division • Oregon Department of Human Resources **7077**
    Health Information Division • Louisiana Department of Health and Hospitals **7058**
    New York State Department of Health **7072**
    Public Health Division
        Alaska Department of Health and Social Services **7041**
        New Mexico Department of Health **7071**
Vitamin A Consultative Group; International **9467**
Vitamin E Research and Information Service **9494**
Viterbo College
    Dietetics Program **9436**

W

War and Civilian Blind; American Braille Press for   13466
War Fund; Permanent Blind Relief   13466
War; International Physicians for the Prevention of Nuclear   1356
War Nurses; National Organization of World   9126
War Sufferers; Joint Distribution Committee for Relief of Jewish   1167
Ware Foundation   6386
Warm Springs Institute for Rehabilitation; Roosevelt   12748
Warner-Lambert Charitable Foundation   898
Warren Clinical Research Center; W. Dean • Emory University   1586
Warren Foundation; William K.   550
Warren Grant Magnuson Clinical Center
    National Institutes of Health • U.S. Department of Health and Human
      Services   1679
    U.S. Department of Health and Human Services   2515
Washburn University of Topeka
    School of Applied and Continuing Education • Respiratory Therapist
      Program   11397
    School of Nursing   8708
Washburne Early Childhood Center; Carleton • Brooklyn College of City
  University of New York   3591
Washington Affiliate
    American Diabetes Association   4999
    American Heart Association   3041
Washington; American Lung Association of   11680
Washington Association of Optometric Physician   13840
Washington Board for Nursing Home Administrators   9322
Washington Board of Osteopathic Medicine and Surgery   10062
Washington Chapter
    American Physical Therapy Association   12864
    National Association of Social Workers   11930
Washington, DC Area Affiliate • American Diabetes Association   4958
Washington, DC Chapter; Greater • Lupus Foundation of America   8039
Washington, DC Chapter; Metro • Arthritis Foundation   7974
Washington, DC Chapter; Metropolitan • Cystic Fibrosis Foundation   5409
Washington, DC Pharmaceutical Association   10702
Washington Dental Health Care Boards   4098
Washington Department of Agriculture • Food Safety and Animal Health
  Division • Animal Health Section   13298
Washington Department of Health   11054
    Community and Family Health Division • HIV / AIDS Office   6903
    Community and Family Health Services Division   3425, 9771
    Emergency Medical Services and Trauma Systems   4816
    Environmental Health Office   5175
    Facility and Services Licensing Division • Field Services Office • Acute
      Care and Construction Review Section   6523
    Health Statistics Center   7087
    Oral Health Services Program   4151
Washington Department of Labor and Industries • Consultation and
  Compliance Services Division   9912
Washington Department of Services for the Blind   13714
Washington Department of Social and Health Services
    Aging and Adult Services Office   2049
    Health and Rehabilitative Services Office
      Alcohol and Substance Abuse Division   12194
      Developmental Disabilities Division   4390
      Mental Health Division   7755
      Vocational Rehabilitation Division   12819
    Medical Assistance Services   5815
    Planning, Research and Development Office   5707
Washington Division • American Cancer Society   6324
Washington; Easter Seal Society of   4682
Washington Funeral and Cemetery Boards   3775
Washington Health Care Association   9373
Washington Hospital • School of Anesthesia   2323
Washington Institute for Mental Illness Research and Training   7700
Washington; Learning Disabilities Association of   4728
Washington; National Kidney Foundation of   12986
Washington Osteopathic Medical Association   10112
Washington Quality Medical Assurance Commission   1806
Washington Research Project; Children's Defense Fund of the   3205
Washington Square Health Foundation   536
Washington Square Institute for Psychotherapy and Mental Health   7252
Washington State; Arc of   4435
Washington State Board of Nursing Care Quality Assurance Commission
  9206
Washington State Board of Pharmacy   10690
Washington State Board of Podiatry   10827
Washington State Chapter
    Arthritis Foundation   8026
    Cystic Fibrosis Foundation   5468
Washington State Coalition Against Domestic Violence   3126

Washington State Dental Association   4204
Washington State Hospital Association   6575
Washington State Medical Association   1860
Washington State Nurses Association   9260
Washington State Optometry Board   13767
Washington State Pharmacists Association   10742
Washington State University
    College of Agriculture and Home Economics Research Center
      13248
    College of Pharmacy   10570
      Graduate Program in Pharmacology and Toxicology   10380
    College of Veterinary Medicine   13016
      Department of Veterinary and Comparative Anatomy,
        Pharmacology and Physiology   10381
    Dietetics Program   9433
Washington State University / Whitworth College; Eastern Washington
  University / • Intercollegiate Center for Nursing Education   9019
Washington State Veterinary Medical Association   13350
Washington Trust Bank Foundation   899
Washington University
    Alzheimer's Disease Research Center   8536
    Atherosclerosis, Nutrition, and Lipid Research Division   2988
    Biomedical Computer Laboratory   2504
    Center for Interdisciplinary Research on Immunological Diseases
      2148
    Chromalloy American Kidney Center   12932
    Clinical Research Center   1748
    Cystic Fibrosis Research Center   5391
    Diabetes Research and Training Center   4947
    George Warren Brown School of Social Work   11810
    Hyperthermia Service   11625
    Institute for Biomedical Computing   2505
    Mallinckrodt Institute of Radiology   11178
    School of Medicine   985
      Department of Molecular Biology and Pharmacology   10280
      Health Administration Program   5505
      Program in Occupational Therapy   12384
      Program in Physical Therapy   12504
    William Greenleaf Eliot Division of Child Psychiatry   7701
Washtenaw Community College • Respiratory Therapist Program   11435
Washtenaw County Chapter • Cystic Fibrosis Foundation   5429
Wasie Foundation   7233
Wasserman Foundation   537
Waste and Basic Research Analytical Laboratory; Pesticide Residue, Toxic
  • University of Miami   5123
Waste Management; Center for Biomedical Toxicological Research and
  Hazardous • Florida State University   10432
Waste and Toxic Substance Research and Management Center; Hazardous
  • Clarkson University   5067
Water Administrators; Association of State Drinking   10944
Water Coalition; Safe   10966
Water Foundation; Safe   1230
Watson Foundation; Hyde and   289
Wayne and Gladys Valley Foundation   538
Wayne State University
    Addiction Research Institute   12146
    Bioengineering Center   2506
    C.S. Mott Center for Human Growth and Development   2765
    Center for Health Research   1749
    Center for Molecular Medicine and Genetics   5392
    College of Nursing   8771
    College of Pharmacy and Allied Health Professions
      Department of Nurse Anesthesia   2288
      Department of Occupational Therapy   12374
      Department of Pharmaceutical Sciences   10269
      Department of Physical Therapy   12495
      Pharmacy Programs   10530
    Comprehensive Sickle Cell Center   6267
    Cystic Fibrosis Care, Teaching and Resource Center   5393
    Cytogenetics Laboratory   5394
    Department of Mortuary Science   3680
    Department of Nutrition and Food Science • Dietetics Program   9403
    Fetal Alcohol Research Center   9722
    Gurdjian-Lissner Biomechanics Laboratory   2507
    Institute of Chemical Toxicology   10494
    Institute of Gerontology   2000
    Kresge Eye Institute   13662
    Laura S. Nye Surgical Research Fund for Desmoid Tumors   12329
    MR Center   11179
    Rehabilitation Counseling Program   12605

Western Hemisphere Reg ion; International Planned Parenthood Federation, **11226**

Western Hospitals; Association of **5577**

Western Human Nutrition Research Center
    Agricultural Research Service • U.S. Department of Agriculture **9540**
    Biochemistry Research Unit • U.S. Department of Agriculture • Agricultural Research Service **9541**
    Bioenergetics Research Unit • U.S. Department of Agriculture • Agricultural Research Service **9542**
    Micronutrients Research Unit • U.S. Department of Agriculture • Agricultural Research Service **9543**

Western Kentucky University
    Department of Nursing **8719**
    Gerontology Program **2001**

Western Medicines; Chinese Association for the Integration of Traditional Chinese and **2185**

Western Michigan University
    Center for Developmentally Disabled Adults **12767**
    Department of Occupational Therapy **12375**
    Enabling Technology Center **4603**
    Occupational Therapy Teaching Research Clinic **12768**
    Physician Assistant Program **1083**
    School of Social Work **11803**

Western Missouri / Greater Kansas City Chapter • Arthritis Foundation **7992**

Western Nebraska Chapter • Lupus Foundation of America **8073**

Western Network for Education in Health Administration; University of Colorado—Denver / • Graduate School of Business Administration • Executive Program in Health Administration **5480**

Western New York Chapter
    Arthritis Foundation **8003**
    Cystic Fibrosis Foundation **5445**
    Lupus Foundation of America **8089**

Western Pacific Orthopaedic Association **9939**

Western Pacific Regional Environmental Health Centre; WHO **5062**

Western Pacific; Regional Office for the • World Health Organization **1545**

Western Pennsylvania Chapter
    Arthritis Foundation **8015**
    Cystic Fibrosis Foundation **5456**
    Lupus Foundation of America **8103**

Western Psychiatric Institute and Clinic of Presbyterian University Hospital • University of Pittsburgh **7684**

Western Roentgen Society **11129**

Western Samoa Registered Nurses Association **9139**

Western School of Health and Business Careers • Respiratory Therapist Program **11521**

Western States Chiropractic College **3443**

Western Surgical Association **12315**

Western Veterinary Conference **13114**

Western Washington University • Rehabilitation Education Program **12642**

Western Wholesale Druggists **5874**

Western Wisconsin Technical College • Respiratory Therapist Program **11585**

Western Wyoming Community College • Respiratory Therapist Program **11586**

Westinghouse Foundation **900**

Westminster College • St. Mark's Westminster School of Nursing **9005**

Westmoreland-Latrobe Hospitals / La Roche College • School of Anesthesia for Nurses **2324**

Weston A. Price Memorial Foundation **9483**

Westvaco Foundation Trust **901**

Wetenschappelijke Vereniging van de Militaire Medische Dienst **7806**

Weterynaryjnych; Polskie Towarzystwo Nauk **13105**

Weyerhaeuser Co. Foundation **10833**

Wheat, First Securities/Butcher and Singer Foundation **902**

Wheat Foundation **902**

Wheelchair Athletic Association; National **4568**

Wheelchair Basketball Association; National **4537**

Wheelchair Bowling Association; American **4463**

Wheelchair Motorcycle Association **4567**

Wheelchair Road Racers Club; International **4501**

Wheelchair Softball Association; National **4538**

Wheelchair Sports Federation; International Stoke Mandeville **4500**

Wheelchair Sports, USA **4568**

Wheelchair Tennis; National Foundation of **4527**

Wheelchair Tennis Players Association **4569**

Wheeling Jesuit College
    Department of Nursing **9032**
    Respiratory Therapy Program **11580**

Whitaker Cardiovascular Institute • Boston University **2884**

Whitaker Charitable Foundation; Lyndon C. **6372**

Whitaker Foundation **2414**

White Consolidated Industries Foundation **903**

White Lung Association **11607**

White National Teen Education Program; Ryan **3285**

Whitehead Foundation; Joseph B. **330**

Whitehead Foundation; Lettie Pate **353**

Whitehead Institute for Biomedical Research **2707**

Whitman Corp. Foundation **904**

Whitney Foundation; Helen Hay **2518**

Whitney Fund; David M. **131**

Whittier Foundation; L. K. **347**

Whittier Institute for Diabetes and Endocrinology **4948**

Whitworth College; Eastern Washington University / Washington State University / • Intercollegiate Center for Nursing Education **9019**

WHO Centre Regional du Pacifique Occidental pour la Promotion de la Planification et des Etudes Appliquees en Matiere d'Environnement **5062**

WHO Collaborating Centres for Evaluation of Methods of Diagnosis and Treatment of Melanoma **5992**

WHO Gruppo Melanomi **5992**

WHO International Melanoma Group **5992**

WHO International Reference Centres for the Evaluation of Methods of Diagnosis and Treatment of Melanoma **5992**

WHO Melanoma Programme **5992**

WHO Western Pacific Regional Centre for the Promotion of Environmental Planning and Applied Studies **5062**

WHO Western Pacific Regional Environmental Health Centre **5062**

Wholesale Druggists' Association; National **5874**

Wholesale Druggists; Western **5874**

Wholesalers Association; Optical **5877**

WIC Services • Health Services Bureau • Mississippi Department of Health **3402, 9748**

Wichita Chapter • Lupus Foundation of America **8056**

Wichita General Hospital • Midwestern State University Consortium • Respiratory Therapy Program **11562**

Wichita State University
    College of Health Professions
        Department of Physical Therapy **12479**
        Physician Assistant Program **1078**
        Respiratory Therapist Program **11398**
    National Rehabilitation Engineering Center **12769**
    School of Nursing **8709**

Wickes Foundation **640**

Wickes Foundation; Harvey Randall **256**

WICOR Foundation **905**

Widener University
    School of Management • Graduate Program in Health and Medical Services Administration **5520**
    School of Nursing **8936**

Wiedemann Support Network; Beckwith- **2743**

Wiegand Foundation; E. L. **150**

Wiener Center for Social Policy; Malcolm • Harvard University **5626**

Wilbur May Foundation **6388**

Wilderness Medical Society **1532**

Wildlife Disease Study; Southeastern Cooperative • University of Georgia **13217**

Wildlife Veterinarians; American Association of **13040**

Wiley Laboratory • Pennsylvania State University **13167**

Wilford Hall USAF Medical Center • Clinical Investigation Facility • U.S. Department of Defense **1673**

Wilkerson Center; Bill **3589**

Wilkes Barre General Hospital / Wyoming Valley Health Care System Hospital • School of Anesthesia **2325**

Wilkes College • Department of Nursing **8937**

Will Rogers Institute Pulmonary Research Laboratory • University of California, Los Angeles **11619**

Will Rogers Pulmonary Research Laboratory • Cornell University **11610**

Willard L. Eccles Charitable Foundation **541**

Willard T. C. Johnson Foundation **542**

William A. Hillenbrand Biomedical Engineering Center • Purdue University **2466**

William Bingham Second Betterment Fund **543**

William Carey College • School of Nursing **8786**

William E. and Carol G. Simon Foundation **544**

William and Flora Hewlett Foundation **545**

William G. Baker, Jr. Memorial Fund **546**

William G. Irwin Charity Foundation **547**

William G. Selby and Marie Selby Foundation **548**

William Greenleaf Eliot Division of Child Psychiatry • Washington University **7701**

William H. Donner Foundation **549**

William Jewell College • Department of Nursing **8799**

William K. Warren Foundation **550**